The Europa World Year Book 1998

VOLUME I

PART ONE: INTERNATIONAL ORGANIZATIONS
PART TWO: AFGHANISTAN–JORDAN

EUROPA PUBLICATIONS LIMITED

First published 1926

18 Bedford Square, London, WC1B 3JN, United Kingdom

Australia and New Zealand
James Bennett Library Services, 3 Narabang Way,
Belrose, NSW 2085, Australia

Japan
Maruzen Co Ltd, POB 5050, Tokyo International 100-31

ISBN 1-85743-041-7 (The Set)
1-85743-042-5 (Vol. I)
ISSN 0956-2273
Library of Congress Catalog Card Number 59-2942

Typeset by UBL International and printed by Unwin Brothers Limited
The Gresham Press
Old Woking, Surrey

(Members of the MPG Information Division)

Bound by MPG Books Limited
Bodmin, Cornwall

(All members of the Martins Printing Group)

FOREWORD

THE EUROPA WORLD YEAR BOOK (formerly THE EUROPA YEAR BOOK: A WORLD SURVEY) was first published in 1926. Since 1960 it has appeared in annual two-volume editions, and has become established as an authoritative reference work, providing a wealth of detailed information on the political, economic and commercial institutions of the world.

Volume I contains a comprehensive listing of more than 1,650 international organizations and the first part of the alphabetical survey of countries of the world, from Afghanistan to Jordan. The Democratic Republic of the Congo, as Zaire was renamed in May 1997, is now included in Volume I. Volume II contains countries from Kazakhstan to Zimbabwe.

The International Organizations section gives extensive coverage to the United Nations and its related agencies and bodies. There are also detailed articles concerning more than 50 major international and regional organizations (including the World Trade Organization, the European Union, and, expanded for this edition, the Common Market for Eastern and Southern Africa and the European Space Agency); entries for many affiliated organizations appear within these articles. In addition, briefer details of more than 1,000 other international organizations appear in a separate section which starts on page 249. A comprehensive Index of International Organizations can be found at the end of Volume I.

Each country is covered by an individual chapter, containing: an introductory survey including recent history, economic affairs, government, defence, social welfare, education, and public holidays; an economic and demographic survey using the latest available statistics on area and population, agriculture, forestry, fishing, industry, finance, trade, transport, tourism, the media, and education; and a directory section containing names, addresses and other useful facts about government, political parties, diplomatic representation, judiciary, religious groups, the media, telecommunications, banks, insurance, trade and industry, development organizations, chambers of commerce, trade associations, utilities, trade unions, transport and tourism.

Readers are referred to our seven regional books, AFRICA SOUTH OF THE SAHARA, EASTERN EUROPE AND THE COMMONWEALTH OF INDEPENDENT STATES, THE FAR EAST AND AUSTRALASIA, THE MIDDLE EAST AND NORTH AFRICA, SOUTH AMERICA, CENTRAL AMERICA AND THE CARIBBEAN, THE USA AND CANADA and WESTERN EUROPE, for additional information on the geography, history and economy of these areas.

The information is extensively revised and updated annually by a variety of methods, including direct mailing to all the institutions listed. Many other sources are used, such as national statistical offices, government departments and diplomatic missions. The editors thank the innumerable individuals and organizations throughout the world whose generous co-operation in providing current information for this edition is invaluable in presenting the most accurate and up-to-date material available.

March 1998.

ACKNOWLEDGEMENTS

The editors gratefully acknowledge particular indebtedness for permission to reproduce material from the following publications: the United Nations' *Demographic Yearbook, Statistical Yearbook* and *Industrial Commodity Statistics Yearbook*; the United Nations Educational, Scientific and Cultural Organization's *Statistical Yearbook*; the Food and Agriculture Organization of the United Nations' *Production Yearbook, Yearbook of Fishery Statistics* and *Yearbook of Forest Products*; the International Labour Office's *Yearbook of Labour Statistics*; the World Bank's *Trends in Developing Economies, World Bank Atlas, Global Development Finance, World Development Report* and *World Development Indicators*; the International Monetary Fund's *International Financial Statistics* and *Government Finance Statistics Yearbook*; and *The Military Balance 1997–98*, a publication of the International Institute for Strategic Studies, 23 Tavistock Street, London, WC2E 7NQ.

CONTENTS

* A complete Index of International Organizations is to be found on p. 1919.

CONTENTS

PART TWO

Afghanistan–Jordan

CONTENTS

An Index of Territories is to be found at the end of Volume II.

ABBREVIATIONS

AB	Aktiebolag (Joint Stock Company)
Abog.	Abogado (Lawyer)
Acad.	Academician; Academy
ACP	African, Caribbean and Pacific (countries)
ACT	Australian Capital Territory
ADB	African Development Bank; Asian Development Bank
Adm.	Admiral
admin.	administration
AG	Aktiengesellschaft (Joint Stock Company)
a.i.	ad interim
AID	(US) Agency for International Development
AIDS	Acquired Immunodeficiency Syndrome
AK	Alaska
Al.	Aleja (Alley, Avenue)
AL	Alabama
ALADI	Asociación Latino-Americana de Integración
Alt.	Alternate
Alta	Alberta
AM	Amplitude Modulation
amalg.	amalgamated
Apdo	Apartado (Post Box)
APEC	Asia-Pacific Economic Co-operation
approx.	approximately
Apt	Apartment
AR	Arkansas
A/S	Aktieselskab (Joint Stock Company)
ASEAN	Association of South East Asian Nations
asscn	association
assoc.	associate
asst	assistant
Aug.	August
auth.	authorized
Ave	Avenue
Avda	Avenida (Avenue)
Avv.	Avvocato (Lawyer)
AZ	Arizona
BC	British Columbia
Bd	Board
Bd, Bld, Blv., Blvd	Boulevard
b/d	barrels per day
Bhd	Berhad (Public Limited Company)
Bldg	Building
BP	Boîte postale (Post Box)
br.(s)	branch(es)
Brig.	Brigadier
bte	boîte (box)
BTN	Brussels Tariff Nomenclature
bul.	bulvar (boulevard)
C	Centigrade
c.	circa; cuadra(s) (block(s))
CA	California
CACM	Central American Common Market
Cad.	Caddesi (Street)
cap.	capital
Capt.	Captain
CARICOM	Caribbean Community and Common Market
CCL	Caribbean Congress of Labour
Cdre	Commodore
Cen.	Central
CEO	Chief Executive Officer
CFA	Communauté Financière Africaine; Co-opération Financière en Afrique centrale
CFP	Communauté française du Pacifique; Comptoirs français du Pacifique
Chair.	Chairman/woman
CI	Channel Islands
Cia	Companhia
Cía	Compañía
Cie	Compagnie
c.i.f.	cost, insurance and freight
C-in-C	Commander-in-Chief
circ.	circulation
CIS	Commonwealth of Independent States
cm	centimetre(s)
CMEA	Council for Mutual Economic Assistance
Cnr	Corner
Co	Company; County
CO	Colorado
Col	Colonel
Col.	Colonia
COMESA	Common Market for Eastern and Southern Africa
Comm.	Commission; Commendatore
Commdr	Commander
Commdt	Commandant
Commr	Commissioner
Confed.	Confederation
Cont.	Contador (Accountant)
Corpn	Corporation
CP	Case Postale; Caixa Postal; Casella Postale (Post Box)
Cres.	Crescent
CSTAL	Confederación Sindical de los Trabajadores de América Latina
CT	Connecticut
CTCA	Confederación de Trabajadores Centro-americanos
Cttee	Committee
cu	cubic
cwt	hundredweight
DC	District of Columbia; Distrito Central
DE	Departamento Estatal; Delaware
Dec.	December
Del.	Delegación
Dem.	Democratic; Democrat
Dep.	Deputy
dep.	deposits
Dept	Department
devt	development
DF	Distrito Federal
Diag.	Diagonal
Dir	Director
Div.	Division(al)
DM	Deutsche Mark
DN	Distrito Nacional
Doc.	Docent
Dott.	Dottore
Dr	Doctor
Dr.	Drive
Dra	Doctora
dr.(e)	drachma(e)
Drs	Doctorandus
dwt	dead weight tons
E	East; Eastern
EBRD	European Bank for Reconstruction and Development
EC	European Community
ECA	(United Nations) Economic Commission for Africa
ECE	(United Nations) Economic Commission for Europe
ECLAC	(United Nations) Economic Commission for Latin America and the Caribbean
Econ.	Economist; Economics
ECOSOC	(United Nations) Economic and Social Council
ECOWAS	Economic Community of West African States
ECU	European Currency Unit
Edif.	Edificio (Building)
edn	edition
EEC	European Economic Community
EFTA	European Free Trade Association
e.g.	exempli gratia (for example)
EIB	European Investment Bank
eKv	electron kilovolt
EMS	European Monetary System
EMU	economic and monetary union
eMv	electron megavolt
Eng.	Engineer; Engineering
ERM	exchange rate mechanism
Esc.	Escuela; Escudos; Escritorio
ESCAP	(United Nations) Economic and Social Commission for Asia and the Pacific
ESCWA	(United Nations) Economic and Social Commission for Western Asia

ABBREVIATIONS

esq.	esquina (corner)
est.	established; estimate; estimated
etc.	et cetera
EU	European Union
eV	eingetragener Verein
excl.	excluding
exec.	executive
Ext.	Extension
F	Fahrenheit
f.	founded
FAO	Food and Agriculture Organization
Feb.	February
Fed.	Federation; Federal
FL	Florida
FM	frequency modulation
fmrly	formerly
f.o.b.	free on board
Fr	Father
Fr.	Franc
FRG	Federal Republic of Germany
Fri.	Friday
ft	foot (feet)
g	gram(s)
GA	Georgia
GATT	General Agreement on Tariffs and Trade
GCC	Gulf Co-operation Council
GDP	gross domestic product
Gen.	General
GeV	giga electron volts
GmbH	Gesellschaft mit beschränkter Haftung (Limited Liability Company)
GNP	gross national product
Gov.	Governor
Govt	Government
grt	gross registered tons
GWh	gigawatt hours
ha	hectares
HE	His (or Her) Eminence; His (or Her) Excellency
hf	hlutafelag (Company Limited)
HI	Hawaii
HIV	human immunodeficiency virus
hl	hectolitre(s)
HM	His (or Her) Majesty
Hon.	Honorary (or Honourable)
hp	horsepower
HQ	Headquarters
HRH	His (or Her) Royal Highness
IA	Iowa
IBRD	International Bank for Reconstruction and Development (World Bank)
ICC	International Chamber of Commerce
ICFTU	International Confederation of Free Trade Unions
ICRC	International Committee of the Red Cross
ID	Idaho
IDA	International Development Association
IDB	Inter-American Development Bank
i.e.	id est (that is to say)
IFC	International Finance Corporation
IL	Illinois
ILO	International Labour Organization/Office
IMF	International Monetary Fund
in (ins)	inch (inches)
IN	Indiana
Inc, Incorp., Incd	Incorporated
incl.	including
Ind.	Independent
INF	Intermediate-Range Nuclear Forces
Ing.	Engineer
Insp.	Inspector
Int.	International
Inzå.	Engineer
IRF	International Road Federation
irreg.	irregular
Is	Islands
ISIC	International Standard Industrial Classification
ITU	International Telecommunication Union
Jan.	January
Jnr	Junior
Jr	Jonkheer (Netherlands); Junior
Jt	Joint
kg	kilogram(s)
KG	Kommandit Gesellschaft (Limited Partnership)
kHz	kilohertz
KK	Kaien Kaisha (Limited Company)
km	kilometre(s)
kor.	korpus (block)
KS	Kansas
kv.	kvartal (apartment block); kvartira (apartment)
kW	kilowatt(s)
kWh	kilowatt hours
KY	Kentucky
LA	Louisiana
lb	pound(s)
Lic.	Licenciado
Licda	Licenciada
LNG	liquefied natural gas
LPG	liquefied petroleum gas
Lt, Lieut	Lieutenant
Ltd	Limited
m	metre(s)
m.	million
MA	Massachusetts
Maj.	Major
Man	Manitoba
Man.	Manager; managing
mbH	mit beschränkter Haftung (with limited liability)
Mc/s	megacycles per second
MD	Maryland
ME	Maine
mem.	member
MEP	Member of the European Parliament
MEV	mega electron volts
mfrs	manufacturers
Mgr	Monseigneur; Monsignor
MHz	megahertz
MI	Michigan
MIGA	Multilateral Investment Guarantee Agency
Mil.	Military
Mlle	Mademoiselle
mm	millimetre(s)
Mme	Madame
MN	Minnesota
MO	Missouri
Mon.	Monday
MP	Member of Parliament
MS	Mississippi
MSS	Manuscripts
MT	Montana
MW	megawatt(s); medium wave
MWh	megawatt hour(s)
N	North; Northern
n.a.	not available
nab.	naberezhnaya (embankment, quai)
NAFTA	North American Free Trade Agreement
nám.	náměští (square)
Nat.	National
NATO	North Atlantic Treaty Organization
NB	New Brunswick
NC	North Carolina
NCO	Non-Commissioned Officer
ND	North Dakota
NE	Nebraska
Nfld	Newfoundland
NGO	non-governmental organization
NH	New Hampshire
NJ	New Jersey
NM	New Mexico
NMP	net material product
no	número (number)
no.	number
Nov.	November
nr	near
nrt	net registered tons
NS	Nova Scotia
NSW	New South Wales
NV	Naamloze Vennootschap (Limited Company); Nevada
NY	New York
NZ	New Zealand
OAPEC	Organization of Arab Petroleum Exporting Countries
OAS	Organization of American States
OAU	Organization of African Unity
Oct.	October

ABBREVIATIONS

OECD	Organisation for Economic Co-operation and Development
OECS	Organization of East Caribbean States
Of.	Oficina (Office)
OH	Ohio
OIC	Organization of the Islamic Conference
OK	Oklahoma
Ont	Ontario
OPEC	Organization of the Petroleum Exporting Countries
opp.	opposite
OR	Oregon
Org.	Organization
ORIT	Organización Regional Interamericana de Trabajadores
OSCE	Organization for Security and Co-operation in Europe
p.	page
p.a.	per annum
PA	Pennsylvania
Parl.	Parliament(ary)
pas.	passazh (passage)
per.	pereulok (lane, alley)
Perm. Rep.	Permanent Representative
PF	Postfach (Post Box)
PK	Post Box (Turkish)
pl.	platz; place; ploshchad (square)
PLC	Public Limited Company
PLO	Palestine Liberation Organization
PMB	Private Mail Bag
POB	Post Office Box
PR	Puerto Rico
pr.	prospekt (avenue)
Pres.	President
Prin.	Principal
Prof.	Professor
Propr	Proprietor
Prov.	Province; Provincial; Provinciale (Dutch)
PT	Perseroan Terbatas (Limited Company)
Pte	Private
Pty	Proprietary
p.u.	paid up
publ.	publication; published
Publr	Publisher
Pvt.	Private
Qld	Queensland
Qué	Québec
q.v.	quod vide (to which refer)
Rag.	Ragioniere (Accountant)
Rd	Road
R(s)	rupee(s)
reg., regd	register; registered
reorg.	reorganized
Rep.	Republic; Republican; Representative
Repub.	Republic
res	reserve(s)
retd	retired
Rev.	Reverend
RI	Rhode Island
RJ	Rio de Janeiro
Rm	Room
ro-ro	roll-on roll-off
RP	Recette principale
Rp.(s)	rupiah(s)
Rt	Right
S	South; Southern; San
SA	Société Anonyme, Sociedad Anónima (Limited Company); South Australia
SADC	Southern African Development Community
SAR	Special Administrative Region
SARL	Sociedade Anônima de Responsabilidade Limitada (Joint Stock Company of Limited Liability)
Sask	Saskatchewan
Sat.	Saturday
SC	South Carolina
SD	South Dakota
Sdn Bhd	Sendirian Berhad (Private Limited Company)
SDR(s)	Special Drawing Right(s)
Sec.	Secretary
Secr.	Secretariat
Sen.	Senior; Senator
Sept.	September
SER	Sua Eccellenza Reverendissima (His Eminence)
SITC	Standard International Trade Classification
SJ	Society of Jesus
SMEs	small and medium-sized enterprises
Soc.	Society
Sok.	Sokak (Street)
SP	São Paulo
SpA	Società per Azioni (Joint Stock Company)
Sq.	Square
sq	square (in measurements)
Sr	Senior; Señor
Sra	Señora
Srl	Società a Responsabilità Limitata (Limited Company)
St	Saint; Street
Sta	Santa
Ste	Sainte
subs.	subscriptions; subscribed
Sun.	Sunday
Supt	Superintendent
Tas	Tasmania
TD	Teachta Dála (Member of Parliament)
tech., techn.	technical
tel.	telephone
Thur.	Thursday
TN	Tennessee
Treas.	Treasurer
Tue.	Tuesday
TV	television
TX	Texas
u.	utca (street)
u/a	unit of account
UAE	United Arab Emirates
UDEAC	Union Douanière et Economique de l'Afrique Centrale
UEE	Unidade Económica Estatal
UEMOA	Union économique et mońetaire ouest-africaine
UK	United Kingdom
ul.	ulitsa (street)
UN	United Nations
UNCTAD	United Nations Conference on Trade and Development
UNDCP	United Nations International Drug Control Programme
UNDP	United Nations Development Programme
UNEP	United Nations Environment Programme
UNESCO	United Nations Educational, Scientific and Cultural Organization
UNHCR	United Nations High Commissioner for Refugees
UNICEF	United Nations Children's Fund
Univ.	University
UNRWA	United Nations Relief and Works Agency for Palestine Refugees in the Near East
USA	United States of America
USAID	United States Agency for International Development
USSR	Union of Soviet Socialist Republics
UT	Utah
VA	Virginia
VAT	Value-added Tax
VEB	Volkseigener Betrieb (Public Company)
Ven.	Venerable
VHF	Very High Frequency
VI	(US) Virgin Islands
Vic	Victoria
viz.	videlicet (namely)
Vn	Veien (Street)
vol.(s)	volume(s)
VT	Vermont
vul.	vulitsa (street)
W	West; Western
WA	Western Australia; Washington (State)
WCL	World Confederation of Labour
Wed.	Wednesday
WEU	Western European Union
WFP	World Food Programme
WFTU	World Federation of Trade Unions
WHO	World Health Organization
WI	Wisconsin
WTO	World Trade Organization
WV	West Virginia
WY	Wyoming
yr	year

LATE INFORMATION

EUROPEAN UNION
(March 1998)

Court of Justice of the European Communities (p. 161)

Advocate-General: A. Saggio.

Court of First Instance of the European Communities (p. 162)

President: B. Vesterdorf.

AFGHANISTAN (p. 330)

Taliban Government Change
(March 1998)

Minister of Communications: Mawlawi Ahmadollah Nanai.

ARMENIA (p. 443)

Government Changes
(February 1998)

Minister of Foreign Affairs: Vartan Oskanian (acting).

(March 1998)

Following the resignation of Levon Ter-Petrossian in early February 1998, a presidential election was held on 16 March. Preliminary results indicated that the acting President and incumbent Prime Minister, Robert Kocharian, achieved the greatest number of votes, but had not gained an overall majority, thereby necessitating a second ballot (to be held on 30 March).

AZERBAIJAN (p. 509)

Government Changes
(January 1998)

Sudaba D. Hasanova, hitherto acting Minister of Justice, was confirmed in the post.

(March 1998)

Minister of Foreign Affairs: Tofig Zulfugarov.

BELARUS (p. 571)

Government Change
(February 1998)

Deputy Chairman of the Cabinet of Ministers: Leanid Kozik.

BRAZIL (p. 693)

On 20 March 1998 it was reported that the Minister of Health, Carlos César de Albuquerque, had resigned. José Serra was invited to replace him. On 24 March José Botafogo Goncalves was nominated to replace Francisco Oswaldo Neves Dornelles as Minister of Industry, Trade and Tourism.

CHILE (p. 876)

Government Change
(March 1998)

In early March 1998 Roberto Pizarro Hofer resigned as Minister of Planning and Co-operation.

THE PEOPLE'S REPUBLIC OF CHINA (pp. 909–910)

NATIONAL PEOPLE'S CONGRESS
(March 1998)

The first session of the Ninth National People's Congress (NPC) was convened in Beijing, and was attended by 2,979 deputies. The first session of the Ninth National Committee of the Chinese People's Political Consultative Conference took place simultaneously.

Jiang Zemin was re-elected President of the People's Republic of China and Hu Jintao was elected Vice-President. 134 members were elected to the Standing Committee of the Ninth NPC, in addition to the following:

Chairman: Li Peng.

Vice-Chairmen: Tian Jiyun, Xie Fei, Jiang Chunyun, Zou Jiahua, Pagbalha Geleg Namgyai, Wang Guangying, Cheng Siyuan, Buhe, Tomur Dawamat, Wu Jieping, Peng Peiyun, He Luli, Zhou Guangzhao, Cheng Kejie, Cao Zhi, Ding Shisun, Cheng Siwei, Xu Jialu, Jiang Zitenghua.

Secretary-General: He Chunlun.

STATE COUNCIL
(March 1998)

According to a resolution adopted by the Ninth NPC, the State Council was restructured, to comprise 29 Ministries and State Commissions.

Premier: Zhu Rongji.

Vice-Premiers: Li Lanqing, Qian Qichen, Wu Bangguo, Wen Jiabao.

State Councillors: Gen. Chi Haotian, Luo Gan, Wu Yi, Ismail Amat, Wang Zhongyu.

Minister of Foreign Affairs: Tang Jiaxuan.

Minister of National Defence: Gen. Chi Haotian.

Minister of State Development Planning Commission: Zeng Peiyan.

Minister of State Economic and Trade Commission: Sheng Huaren.

Minister of Education: Chen Zhili.

Minister of Science and Technology: Zhu Lilan.

Minister of Commission of Science, Technology and Industry for National Defence: Liu Jibin.

Minister of State Ethnic Affairs Commission: Li Dezhu.

Minister of Public Security: Jia Chunwang.

Minister of State Security: Xu Yongyue.

Minister of Supervision: He Yong.

Minister of Civil Affairs: Doje Cering.

Minister of Justice: Gao Changli.

Minister of Finance: Xiang Huaicheng.

Minister of Personnel: Song Defu.

Minister of Labour and Social Security: Zhang Zuoji.

Minister of Land and Natural Resources: Zhou Yongkang.

Minister of Construction: Yu Zhengsheng.

Minister of Railways: Fu Zhihuan.

Minister of Communications: Huang Zhendong.

Minister of Information Industry: Wu Jichuan.

Minister of Water Resources: Niu Maosheng.

Minister of Agriculture: Chen Yaobang.

Minister of Foreign Trade and Economic Co-operation: Shi Guangsheng.

Minister of Culture: Sun Jiazheng.

Minister of Health: Zhang Wenkang.

Minister of State Family Planning Commission: Zhang Weiqing.

Governor of the People's Bank of China: Dai Xianglong.

Auditor-General of Auditing Administration: Li Jinhua.

Provincial Government Changes
(February 1998)

Chen Huanyou was elected Chairman of the Standing Committee of Jiangsu People's Congress.

Wang Xiaofeng was elected acting Governor of Hainan Province.

COLOMBIA (p. 974)

Congressional Elections
(March 1998)

Congressional elections took place on 8 March 1998. According to preliminary results, the Partido Liberal won 54 seats in the Senate and 87 in the House of Representatives, while the Partido Social Conservador Colombiano secured 27 and 28 seats in each chamber respectively.

COSTA RICA (p. 1032)

In March 1998 President-elect Miguel Angel Rodríguez appointed his Cabinet, which was to take office on 8 May:

First Vice-President and Minister of Culture: ASTRID FISCHEL.
Second Vice-President and Minister of the Environment: ELIZABETH ODIO.
Minister of Foreign Affairs: ROBERTO ROJAS.
Minister of the Presidency and of Planning: ROBERTO TOVAR.
Minister of Finance: LEONEL BARUCH.
Minister of the Economy and Foreign Trade: SAMUEL GUZOWSKI.
Minister of Public Education: CLAUDIO GUTIÉRREZ.
Minister of Health: ROGELIO PARDO.
Minister of Labour and Social Security: VÍCTOR MORALES.
Minister of Housing: JOSÉ RAFAEL LIZANO.
Minister of Justice: MONICA NAGEL.
Minister of Public Works and Transport: RODOLFO MÉNDEZ.
Minister of Agriculture and Livestock: ESTEBAN BRENES.
Minister of Women's Affairs: YOLANDA INGIANNA.

CÔTE D'IVOIRE (p. 1049)

Government Changes
(March 1998)

Minister of Transport: ADAMA COULIBALY.
Minister of Energy: SAFIATOU BA NDAW.

CROATIA (p. 1069)

Government Changes
(March 1998)

Deputy Prime Minister responsible for Domestic Policy and Public Services and Minister for European Integration: Dr LJERKA MINTAS HODAK.
Minister of Education and Sports: BOZIDAR PUGELNIK.
Minister of Administration: MARIJAN RAMUŠČAK.

CYPRUS (p. 1102)

Government Changes
(February 1998)

Minister of Defence: YIANNAKIS OMIROU.
Minister of the Interior: DINOS MICHAELIDES.
Minister of Commerce, Industry and Tourism: NIKOS ROLANDIS.
Minister of Education and Culture: LIKOURGHOS KAPPAS.
Minister of Labour and Social Insurance: ANDREAS MOUSHOTTAS.
Minister of Agriculture, Natural Resources and the Environment: KOSTAS THEMISTOKLEOUS.

THE CZECH REPUBLIC (p. 1123)

Government Change
(February 1998)

Minister of the Environment: MARTIN BURSÍK (Ind.).

DENMARK (p. 1138)

General Election
(March 1998)

General Election, 11 March 1998

	% of votes	Seats
Social Democratic Party	36.0	63
Liberal Party	24.0	42
Conservative People's Party	8.9	16
Socialist People's Party	7.5	13
Danish People's Party	7.4	13
Centre Democrats	4.3	8
Social Liberals	3.9	7
Red-Green Alliance	2.7	5
Christian People's Party	2.4	4
Progress Party	2.4	4
Social Democratic Party (Faroe Is)*	n.a.	1
Union Party (Faroe Is)*	n.a.	1
Forward (Greenland)*	n.a.	1
Solidarity (Greenland)*	n.a.	1
Total (incl. others)	100.0	179

* Results for the Faroe Islands and Greenland are provisional.

Government Changes (p. 1138)
(March 1998)

A coalition of the Social Democratic Party (SD) and the Social Liberals (SL).

Minister of the Interior: THORKILD SIMONSEN (SD).
Minister of Housing and Urban Affairs: JYETTE ANDERSEN (SD).
Minister of Research and Information Technology: JAN TRØJBORG (SD).
Minister of Health: CARSTEN KOCH (SD).
Minister of Taxation: OLE STAVAD (SD).
Minister of Business and of Industry: PIA GJELLERUP (SD).
Minister of Transport: SONJA MIKKELSEN (SD).
Minister of Culture: ELSEBETH GERNER NIELSEN (SL).
Minister of Education and of Ecclesiastical Affairs: MARGRETHE VESTAGER (SL).
Minister of Labour: OVE HYGUM (SD).

ECUADOR (p. 1198)

Government Changes
(January 1998)

Minister of Government and Justice (Interior): EDGAR RIVADENEIRA.
Minister of Energy and Mines: ALVARO BERMEO.
Minister of Labour and Human Resources: SEBASTIÁN VALDIVIESO.

FRENCH OVERSEAS POSSESSIONS

FRENCH GUIANA (p. 1373)

Regional Council

President: ANTOINE KARAM (PSG).

Election, 15 March 1998

	Seats
Parti Socialiste Guyanais (PSG)	11
Rassemblement pour la République (RPR)	6
Walawari	2
Various left-wing candidates	9
Independents	3
Total	31

GUADELOUPE (p. 1378)

Regional Council

President: LUCETTE MICHAUX-CHEVRY (RPR).

Election, 15 March 1998

	Seats
Rassemblement pour la République (RPR)	25
Parti Socialiste (PS)	12
Parti Communiste Guadeloupéen (PCG)	2
Various right-wing candidates	2
Total	41

MARTINIQUE (p. 1383)

Regional Council

President: ALFRED MARIE-JEANNE (MIM).

Election, 15 March 1998

	Seats
Mouvement Indépendantiste Martiniquais (MIM)	13
Parti Progressiste Martiniquais (PPM)	7
Rassemblement pour la République (RPR)	6
Union pour la Démocratie Française (UDF)	5
Parti Martiniquais Socialiste (PMS)	3
Various right-wing candidates	3
Others	4
Total	41

RÉUNION (p. 1389)

Regional Council

President: PAUL VERGÈS (PCR).

Election, 15 March 1998

	Seats
Union pour la Démocratie Française (UDF)	8
Parti Communiste Réunionnais (PCR)	7
Parti Socialiste (PS)	6
Rassemblement pour la République (RPR)	4
Various right-wing candidates	15
Various left-wing candidates	5
Total	45

THE GAMBIA (p. 1436)

Government Changes

(March 1998)

Secretary of State for Trade, Industry and Employment: DOMINIC MENDY.

Secretary of State for Youth, Sports and Religious Affairs: Capt. (retd) YANKUBA TOURAY.

Secretary of State for Local Government and Lands: Capt. (retd) LAMIN BAJO.

Secretary of State for Finance and Economic Affairs: FAMARA JATTA.

INDIA (p. 1663)

Council of Ministers

(March 1998)

A coalition of the Bharatiya Janata Party (BJP), the All-India Anna Dravida Munnetra Kazhagam (AIADMK), the Samata Party (SAP), the Biju Janata Dal (BJD), the Shiromani Akali Dal (SAD), the Trinamul Congress, the Shiv Sena (SS), the Pattali Makkal Katchi (PMK), the Lok Shakti (LS), the MDMK, the Haryana Vikas Party, the Janata Dal, the Haryana Lok Dal, the Tamil Rajiv Congress (TRC) and Independents (Ind.).

Prime Minister and Minister of External Affairs and of Agriculture: ATAL BIHARI VAJPAYEE (BJP).

Minister of Home Affairs: LAL KRISHNA ADVANI (BJP).

Minister of Civil Aviation: H. N. ANANTA KUMAR (BJP).

Minister of Industry: SIKANDER BAKHT (BJP).

Minister of Chemicals and Fertilizers and of Food: SURJIT SINGH BARNALA (SAD).

Minister of Defence: GEORGE FERNANDES (SAP).

Minister of Commerce: RAM KRISHNA HEGDE (LS).

Minister of Labour: SATYANARAIN JATIYA (BJP).

Minister of Urban Development: RAM JETHMALANI (Ind.).

Minister of Human Resource Development and of Science and Technology: Dr MURLI MANOHAR JOSHI (BJP).

Minister of Petroleum and Natural Gas: K. RAMAMURTHY (TRC).

Minister of Parliamentary Affairs and of Tourism: MADAN LAL KHURANA (BJP).

Minister of Power: P. RANGARAJAN KUMARAMANGALAM (BJP).

Minister of Law, Justice and Company Affairs: M. THAMBI DURAI (AIADMK).

Minister of Railways: NITISH KUMAR (SAP).

Minister of Steel and of Mines: NAVEEN PATNAIK (BJD).

Minister of Environment and Forests: SURESH PRABHAKAR PRABHU (SS).

Minister of Textiles: KASHIRAM RANA (BJP).

Minister of Surface Transport: SEDAPATTI R. MUTHIAH (AIADMK).

Minister of Finance: YASHWANT SINHA (BJP).

Minister of Communications: BUTA SINGH (Ind.).

Minister of Information and Broadcasting: SUSHMA SWARAJ (BJP).

Ministers of State with Independent Charge

Minister of State for Coal: DILIP RAY (BJD).

Minister of State for Health and Family Welfare: DALIT EZHILMALAI (PMK).

Minister of State for Rural Development: BABAGOUDA R. PATIL (BJP).

Minister of State for Welfare: MANEKA GANDHI (Ind.).

There are, in addition, 17 Ministers of State without independent charge.

INDONESIA (p. 1706)

New Cabinet

(March 1998)

Co-ordinating Minister for Defence and Security: Gen. FEISAL TANJUNG.

Co-ordinating Minister for Economy, Finance and Industry, Chairman of the National Development Planning Board (Bappenas): Prof. Drs Ir GINANDJAR KARTASASMITA.

Co-ordinating Minister for Development Supervision and State Administrative Reform: Ir HARTARTO SASTROSUNARTO.

Co-ordinating Minister for People's Welfare and Poverty Eradication, Chairman of the National Family Planning Co-ordinating Board: Prof. Dr Haji HARYONO SUYONO.

Minister of Home Affairs: Gen. RADEN HARTONO.

Minister of Foreign Affairs: ALI ALATAS.

Minister of Defence and Security: Gen. WIRANTO.

Minister of Justice: Prof. Dr Haji MULADI.

Minister of Information: Prof. Dr MUHAMMAD ALWI DAHLAN.

Minister of Finance: Dr FUAD BAWAZIER.

Minister of Industry and Trade: MOHAMMAD (BOB) HASAN.

Minister of Agriculture: Prof. Dr Ir Hajjah YUSTIKA SYARIFUDIN BAHARSJAH.

Minister of Mining and Energy: Dr Ir KUNTORO MANGKUSUBROTO.

Minister of Forestry and Plantation: Ir SUMOHADI.

Minister of Public Works: Ir RACHMADI BAMBANG SUMADHIJO.

Minister of Communications: Ir GIRI SUSENO HADIHARDJONO.

Minister of Tourism, Arts and Culture: ABDUL LATIEF.

Minister of Co-operatives and Development of Small-scale Businesses: SUBIAKTO TJAKRAWERDAJA.

Minister of Manpower: Drs THEO SAMBUAGA.

Minister of Transmigration and Resettlement of Forest Dwellers: Drs ABDULLAH MAKHMUD HENDROPRIYONO.

Minister of Education and Culture: Prof. Dr Ir WIRANTO ARISMUNANDAR.

Minister of Health: Prof. Dr Haji FARID ANFASA MULUK.

Minister of Religious Affairs: Prof. Dr QURAISH SHIHAB.

Minister of Social Affairs: SITI HARDIYANTI RUKMANA.

Minister and State Secretary: Drs SAADILAH MURSJID.

Minister of State for Research and Technology, Chairman of the Agency for the Assessment and Application of Technology: Prof. Dr Ir RAHADI RAMELAN.

Minister of State for Investment, Chairman of the Investment Co-ordinating Board: Ir SANYOTO SASTROWARDOYO.

Minister of State for Agrarian Affairs, Chairman of the National Land Agency: ARY MARDJONO.

Minister of State for Housing and Settlements: Ir AKBAR TANDJUNG.

Minister of State for Environment, Chairman of the Environmental Control Agency: Prof. Dr JUWONO SUDARSONO.

Minister of State for Food Affairs, Drugs and Horticulture: Dr HARYANTO DHANUTIRTO.

Minister of State for Empowerment of State Enterprises: TANRI ABENG.

Minister of State for Women's Affairs: Dra Hajjah TUTY ALAWIYAH.

Minister of State for Youth Affairs and Sports: H.R. AGUNG LAKSONO.

Officials with the rank of Minister of State:

Attorney-General: SUJONO HANAFIAH ATMONEGORO.

Governor of Bank Indonesia: Dr SJAHRIL SABIRIN.

ISRAEL (p. 1798)

Head of State

On 4 March 1998 EZER WEIZMAN was re-elected as President by the Knesset for a five-year term.

PART ONE
International Organizations

THE UNITED NATIONS

Address: United Nations Plaza, New York, NY 10017, USA.

Telephone: (212) 963-1234; **fax:** (212) 963-4879; **internet:** http://www.un.org.

The United Nations was founded in 1945 to maintain international peace and security and to develop international co-operation in economic, social, cultural and humanitarian problems.

The United Nations was a name devised by President Franklin D. Roosevelt of the USA. It was first used in the Declaration by United Nations of 1 January 1942, when representatives of 26 nations pledged their governments to continue fighting together against the Axis powers.

The United Nations Charter (see p. 10) was drawn up by the representatives of 50 countries at the United Nations Conference on International Organization, which met at San Francisco from 25 April to 26 June 1945. The representatives deliberated on the basis of proposals put forward by representatives of China, the USSR, the United Kingdom and the USA at Dumbarton Oaks in August–October 1944. The Charter was signed on 26 June 1945. Poland, not represented at the Conference, signed it later but nevertheless became one of the original 51 members.

The United Nations officially came into existence on 24 October 1945, when the Charter had been ratified by China, France, the USSR, the United Kingdom and the USA, and by a majority of other signatories. United Nations Day is now celebrated annually on 24 October.

Membership

MEMBERS OF THE UNITED NATIONS

(with assessments for percentage contributions to the UN budget for 1996, and year of admission)

Afghanistan	0.01	1946
Albania	0.01	1955
Algeria	0.16	1962
Andorra	0.01	1993
Angola	0.01	1976
Antigua and Barbuda	0.01	1981
Argentina	0.48	1945
Armenia	0.05	1992
Australia	1.48	1945
Austria	0.86	1955
Azerbaijan	0.11	1992
Bahamas	0.02	1973
Bahrain	0.02	1971
Bangladesh	0.01	1974
Barbados	0.01	1966
Belarus[1]	0.29	1945
Belgium	1.00	1945
Belize	0.01	1981
Benin	0.01	1960
Bhutan	0.01	1971
Bolivia	0.01	1945
Bosnia and Herzegovina[2]	0.01	1992
Botswana	0.01	1966
Brazil	1.62	1945
Brunei	0.02	1984
Bulgaria	0.08	1955
Burkina Faso	0.01	1960
Burundi	0.01	1962
Cambodia	0.01	1955
Cameroon	0.01	1960
Canada	3.10	1945
Cape Verde	0.01	1975
Central African Republic	0.01	1960
Chad	0.01	1960
Chile	0.08	1945
China, People's Republic[3]	0.73	1945
Colombia	0.10	1945
Comoros	0.01	1975
Congo, Democratic Republic (formerly Zaire)	0.01	1960
Congo, Republic	0.01	1960
Costa Rica	0.01	1945
Côte d'Ivoire	0.01	1960
Croatia[2]	0.09	1992
Cuba	0.05	1945
Cyprus	0.03	1960
Czech Republic[4]	0.26	1993
Denmark	0.72	1945
Djibouti	0.01	1977
Dominica	0.01	1978
Dominican Republic	0.01	1945
Ecuador	0.02	1945
Egypt	0.07	1945
El Salvador	0.01	1945
Equatorial Guinea	0.01	1968
Eritrea	0.01	1993
Estonia	0.04	1991
Ethiopia	0.01	1945
Fiji	0.01	1970
Finland	0.61	1955
France	6.40	1945
Gabon	0.01	1960
The Gambia	0.01	1965
Georgia	0.11	1992
Germany	9.04	1973
Ghana	0.01	1957
Greece	0.38	1945
Grenada	0.01	1974
Guatemala	0.02	1945
Guinea	0.01	1958
Guinea-Bissau	0.01	1974
Guyana	0.01	1966
Haiti	0.01	1945
Honduras	0.01	1945
Hungary	0.14	1955
Iceland	0.03	1946
India	0.31	1945
Indonesia	0.14	1950
Iran	0.46	1945
Iraq	0.14	1945
Ireland	0.21	1955
Israel	0.26	1949
Italy	5.19	1955
Jamaica	0.01	1962
Japan	15.43	1956
Jordan	0.01	1955
Kazakhstan	0.20	1992
Kenya	0.01	1963
Korea, Democratic People's Republic	0.05	1991
Korea, Republic	0.82	1991
Kuwait	0.19	1963
Kyrgyzstan	0.03	1992
Laos	0.01	1955
Latvia	0.08	1991
Lebanon	0.01	1945
Lesotho	0.01	1966
Liberia	0.01	1945
Libya	0.20	1955
Liechtenstein	0.01	1990
Lithuania	0.08	1991
Luxembourg	0.07	1945
Macedonia, former Yugoslav republic[2]	0.01	1993
Madagascar	0.01	1960
Malawi	0.01	1964
Malaysia	0.14	1957
Maldives	0.01	1965
Mali	0.01	1960
Malta	0.01	1964
Marshall Islands	0.01	1991
Mauritania	0.01	1961
Mauritius	0.01	1968
Mexico	0.79	1945
Micronesia, Federated States	0.01	1991
Moldova	0.08	1992
Monaco	0.01	1993
Mongolia	0.01	1961
Morocco	0.03	1956
Mozambique	0.01	1975
Myanmar	0.01	1948
Namibia	0.01	1990
Nepal	0.01	1955
Netherlands	1.59	1945
New Zealand	0.24	1945

Nicaragua	0.01	1945
Niger	0.01	1960
Nigeria	0.11	1960
Norway	0.56	1945
Oman	0.04	1971
Pakistan	0.06	1947
Palau	0.01	1994
Panama	0.01	1945
Papua New Guinea	0.01	1975
Paraguay	0.01	1945
Peru	0.06	1945
Philippines	0.06	1945
Poland	0.34	1945
Portugal	0.27	1955
Qatar	0.04	1971
Romania	0.15	1955
Russia[5]	4.45	1945
Rwanda	0.01	1962
Saint Christopher and Nevis	0.01	1983
Saint Lucia	0.01	1979
Saint Vincent and the Grenadines	0.01	1980
Samoa (formerly Western Samoa)	0.01	1976
San Marino	0.01	1992
São Tomé and Príncipe	0.01	1975
Saudi Arabia	0.72	1945
Senegal	0.01	1960
Seychelles	0.01	1976
Sierra Leone	0.01	1961
Singapore	0.14	1965
Slovakia[4]	0.08	1993
Slovenia[2]	0.07	1992
Solomon Islands	0.01	1978
Somalia	0.01	1960
South Africa	0.32	1945
Spain	2.36	1955
Sri Lanka	0.01	1955
Sudan	0.01	1956
Suriname	0.01	1975
Swaziland	0.01	1968
Sweden	1.23	1946
Syria	0.05	1945
Tajikistan	0.02	1992
Tanzania[6]	0.01	1961
Thailand	0.13	1946
Togo	0.01	1960
Trinidad and Tobago	0.03	1962
Tunisia	0.03	1956
Turkey	0.37	1945
Turkmenistan	0.03	1992
Uganda	0.01	1962
Ukraine[1]	1.14	1945
United Arab Emirates	0.19	1971
United Kingdom	5.31	1945
USA	25.00	1945
Uruguay	0.04	1945
Uzbekistan	0.14	1992
Vanuatu	0.01	1981
Venezuela	0.34	1945
Viet Nam	0.01	1977
Yemen[7]	0.01	1947/67
Yugoslavia[2]	0.10	1945
Zambia	0.01	1964
Zimbabwe	0.01	1980

Total Membership: 185 (November 1997)

[1] Until December 1991 both Belarus and Ukraine were integral parts of the USSR and not independent countries, but had separate UN membership.

[2] Bosnia and Herzegovina, Croatia and Slovenia, previously republics within the Socialist Federal Republic of Yugoslavia, were each granted full UN membership in May 1992. Yugoslavia continued to exist (changing its official title to the Federal Republic of Yugoslavia in April 1992) but comprised only the two republics of Serbia and Montenegro. The remaining republic, Macedonia, declared itself a sovereign state in November 1991, and was admitted to the UN in April 1993 under the name of the former Yugoslav republic of Macedonia. In September 1992 the UN General Assembly (see p. 19) voted to suspend Yugoslavia from participation in its proceedings until the new Yugoslav state had applied and been accepted to fill the seat in the UN occupied by the former Yugoslavia. Yugoslavia was still permitted, however, to participate in the work of UN organs other than Assembly bodies.

[3] From 1945 until 1971 the Chinese seat was occupied by the Republic of China (confined to Taiwan since 1949).

[4] Czechoslovakia, which had been a member of the UN since 1945, ceased to exist as a single state on 31 December 1992. In January 1993, as Czechoslovakia's legal successors, the Czech Republic and Slovakia were granted UN membership, and seats on subsidiary bodies that had previously been held by Czechoslovakia were divided between the two successor states.

[5] Russia assumed the USSR's seat in the General Assembly and its permanent seat on the Security Council (see p. 20) in December 1991, following the USSR's dissolution.

[6] Tanganyika was a member of the United Nations from December 1961 and Zanzibar was a member from December 1963. From April 1964 the United Republic of Tanganyika and Zanzibar continued as a single member, changing its name to United Republic of Tanzania in November 1964.

[7] The Yemen Arab Republic (admitted to the UN as Yemen in 1947) and the People's Democratic Republic of Yemen (admitted as Southern Yemen in 1967) merged to form the Republic of Yemen in May 1990.

SOVEREIGN COUNTRIES NOT IN THE UNITED NATIONS
(November 1997)

China (Taiwan)
Kiribati
Nauru
Switzerland
Tonga
Tuvalu
Vatican City (Holy See)

Diplomatic Representation

MEMBER STATES' PERMANENT MISSIONS TO THE UNITED NATIONS
(with Permanent Representatives—November 1997)

Afghanistan: 360 Lexington Ave, 11th Floor, New York, NY 10017; tel. (212) 249-2059; fax (212) 535-2917; e-mail afgun@undp.org; Dr RAVAN A. G. FARHÂDI.

Albania: 320 East 79th St, New York, NY 10021; tel. (212) 249-2059; fax (212) 535-2917; e-mail albun@undp.org; Chargé d'affaires a.i. SOKOL KONDI.

Algeria: 326 East 48th St, New York, NY 10017; tel. (212) 750-1960; fax (212) 759-9538; e-mail dzaun@undp.org; ABDALLAH BAALI.

Andorra: 2 United Nations Plaza, 25th Floor, New York, NY 10017; tel. (212) 750-8064; fax (212) 750-6630; JULI MINOVES-TRIQUEIL.

Angola: 125 East 73rd St, New York, NY 10021; tel. (212) 861-5656; fax (212) 861-9295; AFONSO VAN-DÚNEM 'MBINDA'.

Antigua and Barbuda: 610 Fifth Ave, Suite 311, New York, NY 10020; tel. (212) 541-4117; fax (212) 757-1607; e-mail atgun@undp.org; Dr PATRICK ALBERT LEWIS.

Argentina: 1 United Nations Plaza, 25th Floor, New York, NY 10017; tel. (212) 688-6300; fax (212) 980-8395; e-mail argun@undp.org; FERNANDO ENRIQUE PETRELLA.

Armenia: 119 East 36th St, New York, NY 10016; tel. (212) 686-9079; fax (212) 686-3934; e-mail armun@undp.org; Chargé d'affaires a.i. Dr MOVSES ABELIAN.

Australia: 1 Dag Hammarskjöld Plaza, 885 Second Ave, 16th Floor, New York, NY 10017; tel. (212) 836-4100; fax (212) 836-4104; PENELOPE ANNE WENSLEY.

Austria: 823 United Nations Plaza, 8th Floor, New York, NY 10017; tel. (212) 949-1840; fax (212) 953-1302; e-mail autun@undp.org; Dr ERNST SUCHARIPA.

Azerbaijan: 747 Third Avenue, 17th Floor, New York, NY 10017; tel. (212) 371-2672; fax (212) 371-2784; e-mail azeun@undp.org; ELDAR G. KOULIEV.

Bahamas: 231 East 46th St, New York, NY 10017; tel. (212) 421-6925; fax (212) 759-2135; MAURICE MOORE.

Bahrain: 2 United Nations Plaza, 25th Floor, New York, NY 10017; tel. (212) 223-6200; fax (212) 319-0687; e-mail bhrun@undp.org; JASSIM MOHAMMED BUALLAY.

Bangladesh: 821 United Nations Plaza, 8th Floor, New York, NY 10017; tel. (212) 867-3434; fax (212) 972-4038; e-mail bgdun@undp.org; ANWARUL KARIM CHOWDHURY.

Barbados: 800 Second Ave, 2nd Floor, New York, NY 10017; tel. (212) 867-8431; fax (212) 986-1030; e-mail brbun@undp.org; CARLSTON B. BOUCHER.

Belarus: 136 East 67th St, New York, NY 10021; tel. (212) 535-3420; fax (212) 734-4810; e-mail blrun@undp.org; ALYAKSANDR N. SYCHOU.

Belgium: 823 United Nations Plaza, 4th Floor, New York, NY 10017; tel. (212) 599-5250; fax (212) 599-6843; e-mail belun@undp.org; ALEX REYN.

Belize: 820 Second Ave, Suite 922, New York, NY 10017; tel. (212) 599-0233; fax (212) 599-3391; Chargé d'affaires a.i. LAWRENCE A. SYLVESTER.

Benin: 4 East 73rd St, New York, NY 10021; tel. (212) 249-6014; fax (212) 734-4735; FASSASSI ADAM YACOUBOU.

Bhutan: 2 United Nations Plaza, 27th Floor, New York, NY 10017; tel. (212) 826-1919; fax (212) 826-2998; e-mail btnun@undp.org; UGYEN TSHERING.

Bolivia: 211 East 43rd St, 8th Floor (Room 802), New York, NY 10017; tel. (212) 682-8132; fax (212) 687-4642; e-mail bolun@undp.org; Chargé d'affaires a.i. MARCO ANTONIO VIDAURRE.

Bosnia and Herzegovina: 866 United Nations Plaza, Suite 580, New York, NY 10017; tel. (212) 751-9015; fax (212) 751-9019; MUHAMED SACIRBEY.

Botswana: 103 East 37th St, New York, NY 10016; tel. (212) 889-2277; fax (212) 725-5061; e-mail bwaun@undp.org; LEGWAILA JOSEPH LEGWAILA.

Brazil: 747 Third Ave, 9th Floor, New York, NY 10017; tel. (212) 832-6868; fax (212) 371-5716; e-mail braun@undp.org; CELSO LUIZ NUNES AMORIM.

Brunei: 866 United Nations Plaza, Room 248, New York, NY 10017; tel. (212) 838-1600; fax (212) 980-6478; e-mail brun@undp.org; Pengiran MAIDIN Pengiran HASHIM.

Bulgaria: 11 East 84th St, New York, NY 10028; tel. (212) 737-4790; fax (212) 472-9865; e-mail bgrun@undp.org; PHILIP DIMITROV.

Burkina Faso: 115 East 73rd St, New York, NY 10021; tel. (212) 288-7515; e-mail bfaun@undp.org; GAËTAN RIMWANGUIYA OUÉDRAOGO.

Burundi: 336 East 45th St, 12th Floor, New York, NY 10017; tel. (212) 499-0001; fax (212) 499-0006; GAMALIEL NDARUZANIYE.

Cambodia: 866 United Nations Plaza, Room 420, New York, NY 10017; tel. (212) 421-7627; fax (212) 421-7743; Prince SIRIRATH SISOWATH.

Cameroon: 22 East 73rd St, New York, NY 10021; tel. (212) 794-2295; fax (212) 249-0533; Chargé d'affaires a.i. JEAN-MARC MPAY.

Canada: 1 Dag Hammarskjöld Plaza, 885 Second Ave, 14th Floor, New York, NY 10017; tel. (212) 848-1100; fax (212) 848-1195; e-mail canun@undp.org; ROBERT R. FOWLER.

Cape Verde: 27 East 69th St, New York, NY 10021; tel. (212) 472-0333; fax (212) 794-1398; e-mail cpvun@undp.org; JOSÉ LUIS BARBOSA LEÃO MONTEIRO.

Central African Republic: 386 Park Ave South, Suite 1114, New York, NY 10016; tel. (212) 689-6195; Chargé d'affaires a.i. AMBROISINE KPONGO.

Chad: 211 East 43rd St, Suite 1703, New York, NY 10017; tel. (212) 986-0980; fax (212) 760-1691; AHMAT MAHAMAT SALEH.

Chile: 3 Dag Hammarskjöld Plaza, 305 East 47th St, 10th/11th Floor, New York, NY 10017; tel. (212) 832-3323; fax (212) 832-8714; e-mail chiun@undp.org; JUAN O. SOMAVÍA.

China, People's Republic: 155 West 66th St, New York, NY 10023; tel. (212) 870-0300; fax (212) 870-0333; QIN HUASUN.

Colombia: 140 East 57th St, 5th Floor, New York, NY 10022; tel. (212) 355-7776; fax (212) 371-2813; e-mail colun@undp.org; JULIO LONDOÑO-PAREDES.

Comoros: 336 East 45th St, New York, NY 10017; tel. (212) 972-8010; fax (212) 983-4712; e-mail comun@undp.org; Chargé d'affaires a.i. MOHAMED ABOUD MAHMOUD.

Congo, Democratic Republic: 116 205th St, St Albans, NY 11412; ANDRÉ MWAMBA KAPANGA.

Congo, Republic: 14 East 65th St, New York, NY 10021; tel. (212) 744-7840; fax (212) 744-7975; DANIEL ABIBI.

Costa Rica: 211 East 43rd St, Room 903, New York, NY 10017; tel. (212) 986-6373; fax (212) 986-6842; e-mail cosun@undp.org; FERNANDO BERROCAL SOTO.

Côte d'Ivoire: 46 East 74th St, New York, NY 10021; tel. (212) 717-5555; fax (212) 717-4492; e-mail civun@undp.org; YOUSSOUFOU BAMBA.

Croatia: 820 Second Ave, 19th Floor, New York, NY 10017; tel. (212) 986-1585; fax (212) 986-2011; Dr IVAN ŠIMONOVIĆ.

Cuba: 315 Lexington Ave and 38th St, New York, NY 10016; tel. (212) 689-7215; fax (212) 779-1697; e-mail cubun@undp.org; BRUNO RODRÍGUEZ PARRILLA.

Cyprus: 13 East 40th St, New York, NY 10016; tel. (212) 481-6023; fax (212) 685-7316; e-mail cypun@undp.org; SOTOS ZACKHEOS.

Czech Republic: 1109–1111 Madison Ave, New York, NY 10028; tel. (212) 535-8814; fax (212) 772-0586; e-mail czeun@undp.org; VLADIMÍR GALUŠKA.

Denmark: 1 Dag Hammarskjöld Plaza, 885 Second Ave, 18th Floor, New York, NY 10017; tel. (212) 308-7009; fax (212) 308-3384; e-mail dnkun@undp.org; JØRGEN BØJER.

Djibouti: 866 United Nations Plaza, Suite 4011, New York, NY 10017; tel. (212) 753-3163; fax (212) 223-1276; ROBLE OLHAYE.

Dominica: 820 Second Ave, 9th Floor, New York, NY 10017; tel. (212) 949-0853; fax (212) 808-4975; SIMON PAUL RICHARDS.

Dominican Republic: 144 East 44th St, 4th Floor, New York, NY 10017; tel. (212) 867-0833; fax (212) 986-4694; CHRISTINA AGUIAR.

Ecuador: 866 United Nations Plaza, Room 516, New York, NY 10017; tel. (212) 935-1680; fax (212) 935-1835; e-mail ecuun@undp.org; LUIS VALENCIA RODRÍGUEZ.

Egypt: 36 East 67th St, New York, NY 10021; tel. (212) 879-6300; fax (212) 794-3874; e-mail egyun@undp.org; Dr NABIL A. ELARABY.

El Salvador: 46 Park Ave, New York, NY 10016; tel. (212) 679-1616; fax (212) 725-7831; e-mail salun@undp.org; Dr RICARDO G. CASTAÑEDA-CORNEJO.

Equatorial Guinea: 10 East 39th St, Rm 1124, New York, NY 10016; tel. (212) 683-5295; fax (212) 683-5791; Pastor MICHA ONDO BILE.

Eritrea: 211 East 43rd St, Suite 2203, New York, NY 10017; tel. (212) 687-3390; fax (212) 687-3138; e-mail eriun@undp.org; HAILE MENKERIOS.

Estonia: 630 Fifth Ave, Suite 2415, New York, NY 10111; tel. (212) 247-0499; fax (212) 262-0893; e-mail estun@undp.org; TRIVIMI VELLISTE.

Ethiopia: 866 United Nations Plaza, Room 560, New York, NY 10017; tel. (212) 421-1830; fax (212) 754-0360; Dr DURI MOHAMMED.

Fiji: 630 Third Ave, 7th Floor, New York, NY 10017; tel. (212) 687-4130; fax (212) 687-3963; e-mail fjiun@undp.org; POSECI W. BUNE.

Finland: 866 United Nations Plaza, 2nd Floor, New York, NY 10017; tel. (212) 355-2100; fax (212) 759-6156; WILHELM BREITENSTEIN.

France: 1 Dag Hammarskjöld Plaza, 245 East 47th St, 44th Floor, New York, NY 10017; tel. (212) 308-5700; fax (212) 421-6889; e-mail fraun@undp.org; ALAIN DEJAMMET.

Gabon: 18 East 41st St, 9th Floor, New York, NY 10017; tel. (212) 686-9720; fax (212) 689-5769; DENIS DANGUE RÉWAKA.

The Gambia: 820 Second Ave, 9th Floor, New York, NY 10017; tel. (212) 949-6640; fax (212) 808-4975; MOMODOU KEBBA JALLOW.

Georgia: 1 United Nations Plaza, 26th Floor, New York, NY 10021; tel. (212) 715-1949; fax (212) 759-1832; e-mail geoun@undp.org; Dr PETER P. CHKHEIDZE.

Germany: 600 Third Ave, 41st Floor, New York, NY 10016; tel. (212) 856-6200; fax (212) 856-6280; e-mail deuun@undp.org; Prof. TONO EITEL.

Ghana: 19 East 47th St, New York, NY 10017; tel. (212) 832-1300; fax (212) 751-6743; e-mail ghaun@undp.org; JACOB BOTWE WILMOT.

Greece: 733 Third Ave, 23rd Floor, New York, NY 10017; tel. (212) 490-6060; fax (212) 490-5894; e-mail greun@undp.org; CHRISTOS ZACHARAKIS.

Grenada: 820 Second Ave, Suite 900D, New York, NY 10017; tel. (212) 599-0301; fax (212) 599-1540; ROBERT E. MILLETTE.

Guatemala: 57 Park Ave, New York, NY 10016; tel. (212) 679-4760; fax (212) 685-8741; e-mail gtmun@undp.org; JULIO ARMANDO MARTINI HERRERA.

Guinea: 140 East 39th St, New York, NY 10016; tel. (212) 687-8115; fax (212) 687-8248; MAHAWA BANGOURA CAMARA.

Guinea-Bissau: 211 East 43rd St, Room 604, New York, NY 10017; tel. (212) 338-9394; fax (212) 293-0264; e-mail gbnun@undp.org; ALFREDO LOPES CABRAL.

Guyana: 866 United Nations Plaza, Suite 555, New York, NY 10017; tel. (212) 527-3232; fax (212) 935-7548; e-mail guyun@undp.org; SAMUEL R. INSANALLY.

Haiti: 801 Second Ave, Room 300, New York, NY 10017; tel. (212) 370-4840; fax (212) 661-8698; PIERRE LELONG.

Honduras: 866 United Nations Plaza, Suite 417, New York, NY 10017; tel. (212) 752-3370; fax (212) 223-0498; GERARDO MARTÍNEZ BLANCO.

Hungary: 227 East 52nd St, New York, NY 10022; tel. (212) 752-0209; fax (212) 755-5395; e-mail hunun@undp.org; ANDRÉ ERDÖS.

Iceland: 800 Third Ave, 36th Floor, New York, NY 10017; tel. (212) 593-2700; fax (212) 593-6269; GUNNAR PÁLSSON.

India: 235 East 43rd St, New York, NY 10017; tel. (212) 490-9660; fax (212) 490-9656; e-mail indun@undp.org; KAMALESH SHARMA.

Indonesia: 325 East 38th St, New York, NY 10016; tel. (212) 972-8333; fax (212) 972-9780; e-mail idnun@undp.org; Dr MAKARIM WIBISONO.

Iran: 622 Third Ave, 34th Floor, New York, NY 10017; tel. (212) 687-2020; fax (212) 867-7086; e-mail irnun@undp.org; Chargé d'affaires a.i. MAJID TAKHT-RAVANCHI.

Iraq: 14 East 79th St, New York, NY 10021; tel. (212) 737-4434; fax (212) 772-1794; e-mail irqun@undp.org; NIZAR HAMDOON.

Ireland: 1 Dag Hammarskjöld Plaza, 885 Second Ave, 19th Floor, New York, NY 10017; tel. (212) 421-6934; fax (212) 223-0926; e-mail irlun@undp.org; JOHN H. F. CAMPBELL.

Israel: 800 Second Ave, New York, NY 10017; tel. (212) 499-5510; fax (212) 499-5515; e-mail isrun@undp.org; DORE GOLD.

Italy: 2 United Nations Plaza, 24th Floor, New York, NY 10017; tel. (212) 486-9191; fax (212) 486-1036; e-mail itaun@undp.org; FRANCESCO PAOLO FULCI.

Jamaica: 767 Third Ave, 9th Floor, New York, NY 10017; tel. (212) 935-7509; fax (212) 935-7607; e-mail jamun@undp.org; PATRICIA DURRANT.

Japan: 866 United Nations Plaza, 2nd Floor, New York, NY 10017; tel. (212) 223-4300; fax (212) 751-1966; HISASHI OWADA.

Jordan: 866 United Nations Plaza, Room 550–552, New York, NY 10017; tel. (212) 752-0135; fax (212) 826-0830; HASAN ABU-NIMAH.

Kazakhstan: 866 United Nations Plaza, Suite 586, New York, NY 10017; tel. (212) 230-1900; fax (212) 230-1172; e-mail kazun@undp.org; AKMARAL KH. ARYSTANBEKOVA.

Kenya: 866 United Nations Plaza, Room 486, New York, NY 10017; tel. (212) 421-4740; fax (212) 486-1985; e-mail kenun@undp.org; NJUGUNA M. MAHUGU.

Korea, Democratic People's Republic: 820 Second Ave, 13th Floor, New York, NY 10017; tel. (212) 972-3105; fax (212) 972-3154; YI HYONG-CHOL (acting).

Korea, Republic: 866 United Nations Plaza, Suite 300, New York, NY 10017; tel. (212) 371-1280; fax (212) 371-8873; e-mail korun@undp.org; PARK SOO GIL.

Kuwait: 321 East 44th St, New York, NY 10017; tel. (212) 973-4300; fax (212) 370-1733; e-mail kwtun@undp.org; MOHAMMAD A. ABULHASAN.

Kyrgyzstan: 866 United Nations Plaza, Suite 477, New York, NY 10017; tel. (212) 486-4214; fax (212) 486-5259; e-mail kgzun@undp.org; ZAMIRA ESHMAMBETOVA.

Laos: 317 East 51st St, New York, NY 10022; tel. (212) 832-2734; fax (212) 750-0039; e-mail laoun@undp.org; ALOUNKÈO KITTIKHOUN.

Latvia: 333 East 50h St, New York, NY 10022; tel. (212) 838-8877; fax (212) 838-8920; e-mail latun@undp.org; AIVARS BAUMANIS.

Lebanon: 866 United Nations Plaza, Room 531–533, New York, NY 10017; tel. (212) 355-5460; fax (212) 838-2819; e-mail lbnun@undp.org; SAMIR MOUBARAK.

Lesotho: 204 East 39th St, New York, NY 10016; tel. (212) 661-1690; fax (212) 682-4388; e-mail lesothoun@aol.com; PERCY METSING MANGOAELA.

Liberia: 820 Second Ave, 13th Floor, New York, NY 10017; tel. (212) 687-1033; fax (212) 687-1035; WILLIAM BULL.

Libya: 309-315 East 48th St, New York, NY 10017; tel. (212) 752-5775; fax (212) 593-4787; ABUZED O. DORDA.

Liechtenstein: 405 Lexington Ave, 43rd Floor, New York, NY 10174; tel. (212) 599-0220; fax (212) 599-0064; e-mail lieun@undp.org; CLAUDIA FRITSCHE.

Lithuania: 420 Fifth Ave, 3rd Floor, New York, NY 10018; tel. (212) 354-7820; fax (212) 354-7833; e-mail ltuun@undp.org; Dr OSKARAS JUSYS.

Luxembourg: 17 Beekman Pl., New York, NY 10022; tel. (212) 935-3589; fax (212) 935-5896; e-mail luxun@undp.org; JEAN-LOUIS WOLZFELD.

Macedonia, former Yugoslav republic: 866 United Nations Plaza, Suite 517, New York, NY 10017; tel. (212) 308-3504; fax (212) 308-8724; e-mail mkdun@undp.org; NASTE CALOVSKI.

Madagascar: 801 Second Ave, Suite 404, New York, NY 10017; tel. (212) 986-9491; fax (212) 986-6271; e-mail mdgun@undp.org; Chargé d'affaires a.i. JOCELYNE LINGAYA.

Malawi: 600 Third Ave, 30th Floor, New York, NY 10016; tel. (212) 949-0180; fax (212) 599-5021; e-mail mwiun@undp.org; Prof. DAVID RUBADIRI.

Malaysia: 313 East 43rd St, New York, NY 10017; tel. (212) 986-6310; fax (212) 490-8576; e-mail mysun@undp.org; RAZALI ISMAIL.

Maldives: 820 Second Ave, Suite 800C, New York, NY 10017; tel. (212) 599-6195; fax (212) 661-6405; e-mail mdvan@undp.org; Chargé d'affaires a.i. AHMED KHALEEL.

Mali: 111 East 69th St, New York, NY 10021; tel. (212) 737-4150; fax (212) 472-3778; MOCTAR OUANE.

Malta: 249 East 35th St, New York, NY 10016; tel. (212) 725-2345; fax (212) 779-7097; e-mail mltun@undp.org; GEORGE SALIBA.

Marshall Islands: 220 East 42nd St, 31st Floor, New York, NY 10017; tel. (212) 983-3040; fax (212) 983-3202; e-mail mhlun@undp.org; LAURENCE N. EDWARDS.

Mauritania: 211 East 43rd St, Suite 2000, New York, NY 10017; tel. (212) 986-7963; fax (212) 986-8419; MAHFOUDH OULD DEDDACH.

Mauritius: 211 East 43rd St, 15th Floor, New York, NY 10017; tel. (212) 949-0190; fax (212) 697-3829; e-mail twwan@undp.org; TAYE WAH MICHEL WAN CHAT KWONG.

Mexico: 2 United Nations Plaza, 28th Floor, New York, NY 10017; tel. (212) 752-0220; fax (212) 688-8533; e-mail mexun@undp.org; MANUEL TELLO.

Micronesia, Federated States: 820 Second Ave, Suite 204, New York, NY 10017; tel. (212) 697-8370; fax (212) 697-8295; Chargé d'affaires a.i. TADAO P. SIGRAH.

Moldova: 573-577 Third Ave, New York, NY 10016; tel. (212) 682-3523; fax (212) 682-6274; Chargé d'affaires a.i. IGOR CIOBANU.

Monaco: 866 United Nations Plaza, Suite 520, New York, NY 10017; tel. (212) 832-0721; fax (212) 832-5358; JACQUES LOUIS BOISSON.

Mongolia: 6 East 77th St, New York, NY 10021; tel. (212) 861-9460; fax (212) 861-9464; e-mail enkhee@undp.org; JARGALSAIKHANY ENKHSAIKHAN.

Morocco: 767 Third Ave, 30th Floor, New York, NY 10017; tel. (212) 421-1580; fax (212) 980-1512; e-mail marun@undp.org; AHMED SNOUSSI.

Mozambique: 420 East 50th St, New York, NY 10022; tel. (212) 644-5965; fax (212) 734-3083; CARLOS DOS SANTOS.

Myanmar: 10 East 77th St, New York, NY 10021; tel. (212) 535-1310; fax (212) 737-2421; e-mail mmrun@undp.org; WIN MRA.

Namibia: 135 East 36th St, New York, NY 10016; tel. (212) 685-2003; fax (212) 685-1561; e-mail namibia@mail.idt.net; MARTIN ANDJABA.

Nepal: 820 Second Ave, Suite 202, New York, NY 10017; tel. (212) 370-4188; fax (212) 953-2038; e-mail nplun@undp.org; NARENDRA BIKRAM SHAH.

Netherlands: 235 East 45th St, 16th Floor, New York, NY 10017; tel. (212) 697-5547; fax (212) 370-1954; e-mail nldun@undp.org; JAAP RAMAKER.

New Zealand: 1 United Nations Plaza, 25th Floor, New York, NY 10017; tel. (212) 826-1960; fax (212) 758-0827; e-mail nzlun@undp.org; MICHAEL JOHN POWLES.

Nicaragua: 820 Second Ave, 8th Floor, New York, NY 10017; tel. (212) 490-7997; fax (212) 286-0815; e-mail nicun@undp.org; ENRIQUE PAGUAGA FERNÁNDEZ.

Niger: 417 East 50th St, New York, NY 10022; tel. (212) 421-3260; fax (212) 753-6931; JOSEPH DIATTA.

Nigeria: 828 Second Ave, New York, NY 10017; tel. (212) 953-9130; fax (212) 697-1970; Prof. IBRAHIM A. GAMBARI.

Norway: 825 Third Ave, 39th Floor, New York, NY 10022; tel. (212) 421-0280; fax (212) 688-0554; e-mail norun@undp.org; HANS JACOB BIØRN LIAN.

Oman: 866 United Nations Plaza, Suite 540, New York, NY 10017; tel. (212) 355-3505; fax (212) 644-0070; e-mail omnun@undp.org; SALIM BIN MUHAMMAD AL-KHUSSAIBY.

Pakistan: 8 East 65th St, New York, NY 10021; tel. (212) 879-8600; fax (212) 744-7348; e-mail pakun@undp.org; AHMAD KAMAL.

Palau: New York.

Panama: 866 United Nations Plaza, Suite 4030, New York, NY 10017; tel. (212) 421-5420; fax (212) 421-2694; e-mail panun@undp.org; AQUILINO O. BOYD DE LA GUARDIA.

Papua New Guinea: 201 East 42nd St, Suite 405, New York, NY 10017; tel. (212) 832-0043; fax (212) 832-0918; e-mail pngun@undp.org; (vacant).

Paraguay: 211 East 43rd St, Suite 400, New York, NY 10017; tel. (212) 687-3490; fax (212) 818-1282; e-mail parun@undp.org; HUGO SAGUIER CABALLERO.

Peru: 820 Second Ave, Suite 1600, New York, NY 10017; tel. (212) 687-3336; fax (212) 972-6975; e-mail perun@undp.org; FERNANDO GUILLÉN.

Philippines: 556 Fifth Ave, 5th Floor, New York, NY 10036; tel. (212) 764-1300; fax (212) 840-8602; e-mail phlun@undp.org; FELIPE H. MABILANGAN.

Poland: 9 East 66th St, New York, NY 10021; tel. (212) 744-2506; fax (212) 517-6771; e-mail polun@undp.org; Dr ZBIGNIEW MARIA WLOSOWICZ.

Portugal: 866 Second Ave, 9th Floor, New York, NY 10017; tel. (212) 759-9444; fax (212) 355-1124; e-mail prtun@undp.org; ANTÓNIO MONTEIRO.

Qatar: 747 Third Ave, 22nd Floor, New York, NY 10017; tel. (212) 486-9335; fax (212) 758-4952; e-mail qatun@undp.org; NASSER BIN HAMAD AL-KHALIFA.

Romania: 573–577 Third Ave, New York, NY 10016; tel. (212) 682-3273; fax (212) 682-9746; e-mail romun@undp.org; ION GORITA.

Russia: 136 East 67th St, New York, NY 10021; tel. (212) 861-4900; fax (212) 628-0252; e-mail rusun@undp.org; SERGEI V. LAVROV.

Rwanda: 336 East 45th St, 3rd Floor, New York, NY 10017; tel. (212) 808-9149; fax (212) 808-0975; GIDÉON KAYINAMURA.

Saint Christopher and Nevis: 414 East 75th St, 5th Floor, New York, NY 10021; tel. (212) 535-1234; fax (212) 734-6511; e-mail knaun@undp.org; LEE MOORE.

Saint Lucia: 820 Second Ave, Suite 900, New York, NY 10017; tel. (212) 697-9360; fax (212) 370-7867; Chargé d'affaires a.i. SONIA LEONCE.

Saint Vincent and the Grenadines: 801 Second Ave, 21st Floor, New York, NY 10017; tel. (212) 687-4490; fax (212) 949-5946; e-mail vctun@undp.org; HERBERT G. V. YOUNG.

Samoa: 820 Second Ave, Suite 800D, New York, NY 10017; tel. (212) 599-6196; fax (212) 972-3970; TUILOMA NERONI SLADE.

San Marino: 327 East 50th St, New York, NY 10022; tel. (212) 751-1234; fax (212) 751-1436; e-mail smrun@undp.org; GIAN NICOLA FILIPPI BALESTRA.

São Tomé and Príncipe: 122 East 42nd St, Suite 1604, New York, NY 10168; tel. (212) 697-4211; fax (212) 687-8389; Chargé d'affaires a.i. DOMINGOS AUGUSTO FERREIRA.

Saudi Arabia: 405 Lexington Ave, 56th Floor, New York, NY 10017; tel. (212) 697-4830; fax (212) 983-4895; e-mail sauun@undp.org; GAAFAR M. ALLAGANY (acting).

Senegal: 238 East 68th St, New York, NY 10021; tel. (212) 517-9030; fax (212) 517-7628; IBRA DEGUÈNE KA.

Seychelles: 820 Second Ave, Room 900F, New York, NY 10017; tel. (212) 972-1785; fax (212) 972-1786; Chargé d'affaires a.i. CLAUDE MOREL.

Sierra Leone: 245 East 49th St, New York, NY 10017; tel. (212) 688-1656; fax (212) 688-4924; e-mail sleun@undp.org; JAMES O. JONAH.

Singapore: 231 East 51st St, New York, NY 10022; tel. (212) 826-0840; fax (212) 826-2964; e-mail sgpun@undp.org; BILAHARI KAUSIKAN.

Slovakia: 866 United Nations Plaza, Suite 585, New York, NY 10017; tel. (212) 980-1558; fax (212) 980-3295; e-mail svkun@undp.org; Chargé d'affaires a.i. JÁN VARSO.

Slovenia: 600 Third Ave, 24th Floor, New York, NY 10016; tel. (212) 370-3007; fax (212) 370-1824; e-mail svnun@undp.org; Dr DANILO TÜRK.

Solomon Islands: 820 Second Ave, Suite 800B, New York, NY 10017; tel. (212) 599-6193; fax (212) 661-8925; e-mail slbun@undp.org; REX STEPHEN HOROI.

Somalia: 425 East 61st St, Suite 702, New York, NY 10021; tel. (212) 688-9410; fax (212) 759-0651; Chargé d'affaires a.i. FATUN MUHAMMAD HASSAN.

South Africa: 333 East 38th St, 9th Floor, New York, NY 10016; tel. (212) 213-5583; fax (212) 692-2498; e-mail zafun@undp.org; KHIPHUSIZI J. JELE.

Spain: 809 United Nations Plaza, 6th Floor, New York, NY 10017; tel. (212) 661-1050; fax (212) 949-7247; e-mail espun@undp.org; INOCENCIO F. ARIAS.

Sri Lanka: 630 Third Ave, 20th Floor, New York, NY 10017; tel. (212) 986-7040; fax (212) 986-1838; H. L. DE SILVA.

Sudan: 655 Third Ave, Suite 500-510, New York, NY 10017; tel. (212) 573-6033; fax (212) 573-6160; e-mail sdnun@undp.org; ELFATIH MOHAMED AHMED ERWA.

Suriname: 866 United Nations Plaza, Suite 320, New York, NY 10017; tel. (212) 826-0660; fax (212) 980-7029; e-mail surun@undp.org; SUBHAS CHANDRA MUNGRA.

Swaziland: 408 East 50th St, New York, NY 10022; tel. (212) 371-8910; fax (212) 754-2755; e-mail swzun@undp.org; MOSES MATHENDELE DLAMINI.

Sweden: 1 Dag Hammarskjöld Plaza, 885 Second Ave, 46th Floor, New York, NY 10017; tel. (212) 583-2500; fax (212) 832-0389; e-mail sweun@undp.org; HANS DAHLGREN.

Syria: 820 Second Ave, 15th Floor, New York, NY 10017; tel. (212) 661-1313; fax (212) 983-4439; e-mail syrun@undp.org; Dr MIKHAIL WEHBE.

Tajikistan: 136 East 67th St, New York, NY 10021; tel. (212) 744-2196; fax (212) 472-7645; e-mail tjkun@undp.org; RASHID ALIMOV.

Tanzania: 205 East 42nd St, 13th Floor, New York, NY 10017; tel. (212) 972-9160; fax (212) 682-5232; DAUDI NGELAUTWA MWAKAWAGO.

Thailand: 351 East 52nd St, New York, NY 10022; tel. (212) 754-2230; fax (212) 754-2535; e-mail thaun@undp.org; ASDA JAYANAMA.

Togo: 112 East 40th St, New York, NY 10016; tel. (212) 490-3455; fax (212) 983-6684; ROLAND YAO KPOTSRA.

Trinidad and Tobago: 820 Second Ave, 5th Floor, New York, NY 10017; tel. (212) 697-7620; fax (212) 682-3580; e-mail ttoun@undp.org; Chargé d'affaires a.i. YVONNE GITTENS-JOSEPH.

Tunisia: 31 Beekman Place, New York, NY 10022; tel. (212) 751-7503; fax (212) 751-0569; e-mail tunun@undp.org; ALI HACHANI.

Turkey: 821 United Nations Plaza, 11th Floor, New York, NY 10017; tel. (212) 949-0150; fax (212) 949-0086; HUSEYIN E. ÇELEM.

Turkmenistan: 866 United Nations Plaza, Suite 424, New York, NY 10021; tel. (212) 472-5921; fax (212) 772-2589; AKSOLTAN T. ATAEVA.

Uganda: 336 East 45th St, New York, NY 10017; tel. (212) 949-0110; fax (212) 687-4517; e-mail ugaun@undp.org; Prof. MATIA SEMAKULA KIWANUKA.

Ukraine: 220 East 51st St, New York, NY 10022; tel. (212) 759-7003; fax (212) 355-9455; e-mail ukrun@undp.org; ANATOLI M. ZLENKO.

United Arab Emirates: 747 Third Ave, 36th Floor, New York, NY 10017; tel. (212) 371-0480; fax (212) 371-4923; MUHAMMAD JASIM SAMHAN.

United Kingdom: 1 Dag Hammarskjöld Plaza, 885 2nd Ave, New York, NY 10017; tel. (212) 745-9200; fax (212) 745-9316; e-mail gbrun@undp.org; Sir JOHN WESTON.

USA: 799 United Nations Plaza, New York, NY 10017; tel. (212) 415-4000; fax (212) 415-4443; e-mail usaun@undp.org; WILLIAM B. RICHARDSON.

Uruguay: 747 Third Ave, 21st Floor, New York, NY 10017; tel. (212) 752-8240; fax (212) 593-0935; e-mail uruun@undp.org; JORGE PÉREZ-OTERMIN.

Uzbekistan: 866 United Nations Plaza, Suite 326, New York, NY 10017; tel. (212) 486-4242; fax (212) 486-7998; e-mail uzbun@undp.org; ALISHER VOHIDOV.

Vanuatu: 866 United Nations Plaza, 3rd Floor, New York, NY 10017; tel. (212) 593-0144; fax (212) 593-0219; JEAN RAVOU-AKII.

Venezuela: 335 East 46th St, New York, NY 10017; tel. (212) 557-2055; fax (212) 557-3528; e-mail venun@undp.org; RAMÓN ESCOVAR SALOM.

Viet Nam: 866 United Nations Plaza, Suite 435, New York, NY 10017; tel. (212) 679-3779; fax (212) 686-8534; e-mail vnmun@undp.org; NGO QUANG XUAN.

Yemen: 413 East 51st St, New York, NY 10022; tel. (212) 355-1730; fax (212) 750-9613; e-mail yemun@undp.org; ABDALLA SALEH AL-ASHTAL.

Yugoslavia: 854 Fifth Ave, New York, NY 10021; tel. (212) 879-8700; fax (212) 879-8705; e-mail yugun@undp.org; Chargé d'affaires a.i. VLADISLAV JOVANOVIĆ.

Zambia: 800 Second Ave, 9th Floor, New York, NY 10017; tel. (212) 758-1110; fax (212) 758-1319; e-mail zmbun@undp.org; PETER LESA KASANDA.

Zimbabwe: 128 East 56th St, New York, NY 10022; tel. (212) 980-9511; fax (212) 755-4188; MACHIVENYIKA TOBIAS MAPURANGA.

OBSERVERS

Non-member states, inter-governmental organizations, etc., which have received an invitation to participate in the sessions and the work of the General Assembly as Observers, maintaining permanent offices at the UN.

Non-member states

Holy See: 25 East 39th St, New York, NY 10016; tel. (212) 370-7885; fax (212) 370-9622; e-mail hsmission@holyseemission.org; Most Rev. RENATO RAFFAELE MARTINO, Titular Archbishop of Segermes.

Switzerland: 757 Third Ave, 21st Floor, New York, NY 10017; tel. (212) 421-1480; fax (212) 751-2104; e-mail 106335-3140@compuserve.com; JENÖ C. A. STAEHELIN.

Inter-governmental organizations*

Agency for Cultural and Technical Co-operation: 801 Second Ave, Suite 605, New York, NY 10017; tel. (212) 867-6771; fax (212) 867-3840; e-mail ny_acct@digex.net; RIDHA BOUABID.

Asian-African Legal Consultative Committee: 404 East 66th St, Apt 12C, New York, NY 10021; tel. (212) 734-7608; K. BHAGWAT-SINGH.

Caribbean Community: 97–40 62nd Drive, ISK, Rego Park, NY 11374–1336; tel. and fax (718) 896-1179.

Commonwealth Secretariat: 820 Second Ave, Suite 800A, New York, NY 10017; tel. (212) 599-6190; fax (212) 972-3970.

European Union: Delegation of the European Commission, 3 Dag Hammarskjöld Plaza, 12th Floor, 305 East 47th St, New York, NY 10017; tel. (212) 371-3804; fax (212) 758-2718; Dr ANGEL VIÑAS; Liaison Office of the General Secretariat of the Council of Ministers of the European Union, 345 East 46th St, 6th Floor, New York, NY 10017; tel. (212) 292-8600; fax (212) 681-6266; the Observer is the Permanent Representative to the UN of the country currently exercising the Presidency of the Council of Ministers of the European Union.

International Criminal Police Organization (INTERPOL): New York.

International Organization for Migration: 122 East 42nd St, Suite 1610, New York, NY 10168; tel. (212) 681-7000; fax (212) 867-5887; ANDREW R. BRUCE.

International Seabed Authority: New York.

Latin American Economic System: 820 Second Ave, Suite 1601, New York, NY 10017; tel. and fax (3212) 758-7545; OSCAR DE ROJAS.

League of Arab States: 747 Third Ave, 35th Floor, New York, NY 10017; tel. (212) 838-8700; fax (212) 355-3909; MAHMOUD ABOUL-NASR.

Organization of African Unity: 346 East 50th St, New York, NY 10022; tel. (212) 319-5490; fax (212) 319-7135; IBRAHIMA SY.

Organization of the Islamic Conference: 130 East 40th St, 5th Floor, New York, NY 10016; tel. (212) 883-0140; fax (212) 883-0143.

* The following inter-governmental organizations have a standing invitation to participate as Observers, but do not maintain permanent offices at the United Nations:
African, Caribbean and Pacific Group of States.
African Development Bank.
Agency for the Prohibition of Nuclear Weapons in Latin America and the Caribbean.
Commonwealth of Independent States.
Council of Europe.
Economic Co-operation Organization.
Latin American Parliament.
Organization for Security and Co-operation in Europe.
Organization of American States.
Permanent Court of Arbitration.
South Pacific Forum.

Other observers

International Committee of the Red Cross: 801 Second Ave, 18th Floor, New York, NY 10017; tel. (212) 599-6021; fax (212) 599-6009; PETER KÜNG.

International Federation of Red Cross and Red Crescent Societies: 630 Third Ave, Suite 2104, New York, NY 10017; tel. (212) 338-0161; fax (212) 338-9832; e-mail ifrcny@undp.org; EIGIL PEDERSEN.

Palestine: 115 East 65th St, New York, NY 10021; tel. (212) 288-8500; fax (212) 517-2377; Dr NASSER AL-KIDWA.

Sovereign Military Order of Malta: 416 East 47th St, 8th Floor, New York, NY 10017; tel. (212) 355-6213; fax (212) 355-4014; e-mail malta@tiac.com; PIERRE ELIAS AWAD.

United Nations Information Centres/Services

Afghanistan: (temporarily inactive).

Algeria: 9A rue Emile Payen, Hydra, Algiers.

Argentina: Junín 1940, 1°, 1113 Buenos Aires (also covers Uruguay).

Australia: POB 4045, 46-48 York St, 5th Floor, Sydney, NSW 2000 (also covers Fiji, Kiribati, Nauru, New Zealand, Samoa, Tonga, Tuvalu and Vanuatu).

Austria: POB 500, Vienna International Centre, Wagramerstrasse 5, 1220 Vienna (also covers Hungary).

Bahrain: Villa 131, Rd 2803, Segaya, Manama (also covers Qatar and the United Arab Emirates).

Bangladesh: POB 3658, House 60, Rd 11A, Dhanmandi, Dhaka 1209.

Belgium: 40 ave de Broqueville, 1200 Brussels (also covers Luxembourg and the Netherlands).

Bolivia: Apdo 9072, Avda Mariscal, Santa Cruz No. 1350, La Paz.

Brazil: Palacio Itamaraty, Avda Marechal Floriano 196, 20080-002 Rio de Janeiro.

Burkina Faso: PB 135, ave Georges Konseiga, Secteur no 4, Ouagadougou (also covers Chad, Mali and Niger).

Burundi: PB 2160, ave de la Révolution 117, Bujumbura.

Cameroon: PB 836, Immeuble Kamdem, rue Joseph Clère, Yaoundé (also covers the Central African Republic and Gabon).

Chile: Edif. Naciones Unidas, Avda Dag Hammarskjöld, Casilla 179-D, Santiago.

Colombia: Apdo Aéreo 058964; Calle 100, No. 8A–55, Of. 815, Santafé de Bogotá 2, DC (also covers Ecuador and Venezuela).

Congo, Democratic Republic: PB 7248, Batîment Deuxième République, blvd du 30 juin, Kinshasa.

Congo, Republic: POB 13210, ave Foch, Case Ortf 15, Brazzaville.

Czech Republic: Panská 5, 110 00 Prague 1 (also covers Slovakia).

Denmark: Midtermolen 3, 2100 Copenhagen Ø (also covers Finland, Iceland, Norway and Sweden).

Egypt: 1 Osiris St, Garden City, Cairo (also covers Saudi Arabia).

El Salvador: CP 1114, San Salvador.

Ethiopia: POB 3001, Africa Hall, Addis Ababa.

France: 1 rue Miollis, 75732 Paris Cédex 15.

Germany: 53175 Bonn, Haus Cartanjen, Martin-Luther-King-Str. 8; 53153 Bonn, Postfach 260111.

Ghana: POB 2339, Gamel Abdul Nassar/Liberia Roads, Accra (also covers Sierra Leone).

Greece: 36 Amalia Ave, 105 58 Athens (also covers Cyprus and Israel).

India: 55 Lodi Estate, New Delhi 110 003 (also covers Bhutan).

Indonesia: Gedung Dewan Pers, 5th Floor, 32–34 Jalan Kebon Sirih, Jakarta.

Iran: POB 15875-4557; 185 Ghaem Magham Farahani Ave, Teheran 15868.

Italy: Palazzetto Venezia, Piazza San Marco 50, 00186 Rome (also covers the Holy See and Malta).

Japan: UNU Bldg, 8th Floor, 53-70 Jingumae S-chome, Shibuya-ku, Tokyo 150 (also covers Palau).

Kenya: POB 30552, United Nations Office, Gigiri, Nairobi (also covers Seychelles and Uganda).

Lebanon: Riad es-Solh Sq., POB 4656, Chouran, Beirut (also covers Jordan, Kuwait and Syria).

Lesotho: POB 301; Letsie Rd, Food Aid Compound, behind Hotel Victoria, Maseru.

Libya: POB 286, Shara Muzzafar al-Aftas, Hay al-Andalous, Tripoli.

Madagascar: PB 1348, 22 rue Rainitovo, Antasahavola, Antananarivo.

Mexico: Presidente Masaryk 29, 6°, México 11570, DF (also covers Cuba and the Dominican Republic).

Morocco: PB 601, zankat Tarik Ibnou Zind (Angle rue Roudana) 6, Rabat.

Myanmar: POB 230, 6 Natmauk Rd, Yangon.

Namibia: Private Bag 13351, Paratus Bldg, 372 Independence Ave, Windhoek.

Nepal: POB 107, Pulchowk, Kathmandu.

Nicaragua: Apdo 3260, Del Portón del Hospital Militar, 1c. al lago y 1c. abajo, Managua.

Nigeria: POB 1068, 17 Kingsway Rd, Ikoyi, Lagos.

Pakistan: POB 1107, House No. 26, 88th St, G-6/3, Islamabad.

Panama: POB 6-9083, El Dorado; Banco Central Hispano Edif., Calle Gerardo Ortega y Av. Samuel Lewis, Panama City.

Paraguay: Casilla de Correo 1107, Edif. City, 3°, Asunción.

Peru: POB 14-0199, Lord Cochrane 130, San Isidro, Lima 27.

Philippines: NEDA Bldg, Ground Floor, 106 Amorsolo St, Legaspi Village, Makati City, Manila (also covers Papua New Guinea and Solomon Islands).

Poland: 00-608 Warsaw, Al. Niepodległości 186; 02-514 Warsaw, POB 1.

Portugal: Rua Latino Coelho No. 1, Edif. Aviz, Bloco A1, 10°, 1000 Lisbon.

Romania: POB 1-701, 16 Aurel Vlaic St, Bucharest.

Russia: 4/16 Glazovsky Per., Moscow.

Senegal: PB 154, 12 ave Roume, Dakar (also covers Cape Verde, Côte d'Ivoire, The Gambia, Guinea, Guinea-Bissau and Mauritania).

South Africa: Metro Park Bldg, 351 Schoeman St, POB 12677, Pretoria 0126.

Spain: Avda General Perón 32-1°, 28020 Madrid.

Sri Lanka: POB 1505, 202–204 Bauddhaloka Mawatha, Colombo 7.

Sudan: POB 913, UN Compound, Gamma'a Ave, Khartoum (also covers Somalia).

Switzerland: Palais des Nations, 1211 Geneva 10 (also covers Bulgaria).

Tanzania: POB 9224, Old Boma Bldg, Marogoro Rd/Sokoine Drive, Dar es Salaam.

Thailand: ESCAP, United Nations Bldg, Rajadamnern Ave, Bangkok 10200 (also covers Cambodia, Hong Kong, Laos, Malaysia, Singapore and Viet Nam).

Togo: PB 911, 107 blvd du 13 janvier, Lomé (also covers Benin).

Trinidad and Tobago: POB 130, Bretton Hall, 16 Victoria Ave, Port of Spain (also covers Antigua and Barbuda, the Bahamas, Barbados, Belize, Dominica, Grenada, Guyana, Jamaica, the Netherlands Antilles, Saint Christopher and Nevis, Saint Lucia, Saint Vincent and the Grenadines and Suriname).

Tunisia: PB 863, 61 blvd Bab-Benat, Tunis.

Turkey: PK 407, 197 Atatürk Bulvarı, Ankara.

United Kingdom: Millbank Tower, 21st Floor, 21-24 Millbank, London, SW1P 4QH (also covers Ireland).

USA: 1775 K St, NW, Washington, DC 20006.

Yemen: POB 237, Handhal St, 4 Al-Boniya Arca, San'a.

Zambia: POB 32905, Lusaka 10101 (also covers Botswana, Malawi and Swaziland).

Zimbabwe: POB 4408, Harare Zimre Centre, 3rd Floor, Leopold Takawira St/Union Ave, Harare.

OTHER UNITED NATIONS OFFICES

Armenia: 375001 Yerevan, 14 Karl Libknekht St, 1st Floor.

Azerbaijan: Baku, 3 Isteglialiyat St.

Belarus: 220050 Minsk, 17 Kirov St, 6th Floor.

Eritrea: POB 5366, Andinet St, Zone 4 Admin. 07, Airport Rd, Asmara.

Georgia: 380079 Tbilisi, Eristavi St 9.

Kazakhstan: 480100 Almaty, c/o KIMEP, 4 Abai Ave.

Ukraine: 252020 Kiev, 6 Klovsky Uzviz, 1.

Uzbekistan: 700029 Tashkent, 4 Taras Shevchenko St.

United Nations Publications

Annual Report of the Secretary-General on the Work of the Organization.

Basic Facts About the United Nations.

Bulletin on Narcotics (quarterly).

Demographic Yearbook.

Energy Statistics Yearbook.

Index to Proceedings (of the General Assembly; the Security Council; the Economic and Social Council; the Trusteeship Council).

Law of the Sea Bulletin (3 a year).

Monthly Bulletin of Statistics.

Population and Vital Statistics Report (quarterly).

Statistical Yearbook.

Transnational Corporations (3 a year).

The UN Chronicle (quarterly).

United Nations Disarmament Yearbook.

United Nations Juridical Yearbook.

Yearbook of the International Law Commission.

Yearbook of the United Nations.

Other UN publications are listed in the chapters dealing with the agencies concerned.

Finance

The majority of the UN's peace-keeping operations (q.v.) are financed separately from the UN's regular budget by assessed contributions from member states.

In recent years the UN has suffered financial difficulties, owing to an expansion of the UN's political and humanitarian activities and delay on the part of member states in paying their contributions. In 1993 the UN Secretary-General formulated a series of economy measures to be applied throughout the organization, in order to avert a financial crisis. However, the fragility of the organization's financial situation persisted, partly owing to delays in the process between approval of a peace-keeping operation and receipt of contributions for that budget. At 1 July 1997 members owed the UN some US $2,400m., of which $700m. was for the regular budget and $1,700m. for peace-keeping operations and international tribunals. More than one-half of the unpaid contributions was owed by the USA, which at that time advocated a reduction in its quota from 25% to 20% of the regular budget. In September a US business executive announced a donation of $1,000m., to be paid in regular instalments over a 10-year period, to finance humanitarian and environmental programmes.

In 1997 the UN Secretary-General pledged to implement administrative reforms of the UN and to reduce the organization's budget. The provisional budget for the two-year period 1998–99 amounted to US $2,583m., compared with the 1996–97 total of $2,712m. (later revised to $2,603m.). The Secretary-General's reform programme included a proposal to establish a Revolving Credit Fund of up to $1,000m. in voluntary contributions, which would ensure the solvency of the UN pending a permanent solution to the organization's financial situation. The proposal was approved by the General Assembly in November 1997.

TWO-YEAR BUDGET OF THE UNITED NATIONS (US $'000)

	1996–97*	1998–99†
Overall policy-making, direction and co-ordination	39,349.2	38,622.8
Political affairs	198,618.1	164,873.2
International justice and law	50,240.4	55,555.8
International co-operation for development	294,297.3	302,338.1
Regional co-operation for development	351,834.5	399,362.6
Human rights and humanitarian affairs	134,400.1	138,646.4
Public information	132,390.8	140,327.6
Common support services	916,081.5	904,192.9
Jointly-financed administrative activities and special expenses	68,834.2	59,949.6
Office of Internal Oversight Services	15,011.5	18,637.3
Capital expenditures	49,949.0	35,893.4
Staff assessment	348,280.6	324,600.1
International Seabed Authority	3,993.7	—
Total	2,603,280.9	2,582,999.9

* Revised figures. † Provisional figures.

Charter of the United Nations

We the peoples of the United Nations determined

to save succeeding generations from the scourge of war, which twice in our lifetime has brought untold sorrow to mankind, and

to reaffirm faith in fundamental human rights, in the dignity and worth of the human person, in the equal rights of men and women and of nations large and small, and

to establish conditions under which justice and respect for the obligations arising from treaties and other sources of international law can be maintained, and

to promote social progress and better standards of life in larger freedom,

And for these ends

to practise tolerance and live together in peace with one another as good neighbours, and

to unite our strength to maintain international peace and security, and

to ensure, by the acceptance of principles and the institution of methods, that armed force shall not be used, save in the common interest, and

to employ international machinery for the promotion of the economic and social advancement of all peoples,

Have resolved to combine our efforts to accomplish these aims.

Accordingly, our respective Governments, through representatives assembled in the city of San Francisco, who have exhibited their full powers found to be in good and due form, have agreed to the present Charter of the United Nations and do hereby establish an international organization to be known as the United Nations.

I. PURPOSES AND PRINCIPLES

Article 1

The Purposes of the United Nations are:

1. To maintain international peace and security, and to that end: to take effective collective measures for the prevention and removal of threats to the peace, and for the suppression of acts of aggression or other breaches of the peace, and to bring about by peaceful means, and in conformity with the principles of justice and international law, adjustment or settlement of international disputes or situations which might lead to a breach of the peace:

2. To develop friendly relations among nations based on respect for the principle of equal rights and self-determination of peoples, and to take other appropriate measures to strengthen universal peace;

3. To achieve international co-operation in solving international problems of an economic, social, cultural, or humanitarian character, and in promoting and encouraging respect for human rights and for fundamental freedoms for all without distinction as to race, sex, language, or religion; and

4. To be a centre for harmonizing the accusations of nations in the attainment of these common ends.

Article 2

The Organization and its Members, in pursuit of the Purposes stated in Article 1, shall act in accordance with the following Principles.

1. The Organization is based on the principle of the sovereign equality of all its Members.

2. All Members, in order to ensure to all of them the rights and benefits resulting from membership, shall fulfil in good faith the obligations assumed by them in accordance with the present Charter.

3. All Members shall settle their international disputes by peaceful means in such a manner that international peace and security, and justice, are not endangered.

4. All Members shall refrain in their international relations from the threat or use of force against the territorial integrity or political independence of any state, or in any manner inconsistent with the Purposes of the United Nations.

5. All Members shall give the United Nations every assistance in any action it takes in accordance with the present Charter, and shall refrain from giving assistance to any state against which the United Nations is taking preventive or enforcement action.

6. The Organization shall ensure that states which are not Members of the United Nations act in accordance with these Principles so far as may be necessary for the maintenance of international peace and security.

7. Nothing contained in the present Charter shall authorize the United Nations to intervene in matters which are essentially within the domestic jurisdiction of any state or shall require the Members to submit such matters to settlement under the present Charter; but this principle shall not prejudice the application of enforcement measures under Chapter VII.

II. MEMBERSHIP

Article 3

The original Members of the United Nations shall be the states which, having participated in the United Nations Conference on International Organization at San Francisco, or having previously signed the Declaration by United Nations of January 1, 1942, sign the present Charter and ratify it in accordance with Article 110.

Article 4

1. Membership in the United Nations is open to all other peace-loving states which accept the obligations contained in the present Charter and, in the judgement of the Organization, are able and willing to carry out these obligations.

2. The admission of any such state to membership in the United Nations will be effected by a decision of the General Assembly upon the recommendation of the Security Council.

Article 5

A member of the United Nations against which preventive or enforcement action has been taken by the Security Council may be suspended from the exercise of the rights and privileges of membership by the General Assembly upon the recommendation of the Security Council. The exercise of these rights and privileges may be restored by the Security Council.

Article 6

A Member of the United Nations which has persistently violated the Principles contained in the present Charter may be expelled from the Organization by the General Assembly upon the recommendation of the Security Council.

III. ORGANS

Article 7

1. There are established as the principal organs of the United Nations: a General Assembly, a Security Council, an Economic and Social Council, a Trusteeship Council, an International Court of Justice, and a Secretariat.

2. Such subsidiary organs as may be found necessary may be established in accordance with the present Charter.

Article 8

The United Nations shall place no restrictions on the eligibility of men and women to participate in any capacity and under conditions of equality in its principal and subsidiary organs.

IV. THE GENERAL ASSEMBLY

Composition

Article 9

1. The General Assembly shall consist of all the Members of the United Nations.

2. Each Member shall have not more than five representatives in the General Assembly.

Functions and Powers

Article 10

The General Assembly may discuss any questions or any matters within the scope of the present Charter or relating to the powers and functions of any organs provided for in the present Charter, and, except as provided in Article 12, may make recommendations to the Members of the United Nations or to the Security Council or to both on any such questions or matters.

Article 11

1. The General Assembly may consider the general principles of co-operation in the maintenance of international peace and security, including the principles governing disarmament and the regulation of armaments, and may make recommendations with regard to such principles to the Members or to the Security Council or to both.

2. The General Assembly may discuss any questions relating to the maintenance of international peace and security brought before it by any Member of the United Nations, or by the Security Council,

or by a state which is not a Member of the United Nations in accordance with Article 35, paragraph 2, and, except as provided in Article 12, may make recommendations with regard to any such question to the state or states concerned or to the Security Council or both. Any such question on which action is necessary shall be referred to the Security Council by the General Assembly either before or after discussion.

3. The General Assembly may call the attention of the Security Council to situations which are likely to endanger international peace and security.

4. The powers of the General Assembly set forth in this Article shall not limit the general scope of Article 10.

Article 12

1. While the Security Council is exercising in respect of any dispute or situation the functions assigned to it in the present Charter, the General Assembly shall not make any recommendations with regard to that dispute or situation unless the Security Council so requests.

2. The Secretary-General, with the consent of the Security Council, shall notify the General Assembly at each session of any matters relative to the maintenance of international peace and security which are being dealt with by the Security Council and shall similarly notify the General Assembly, or the Members of the United Nations if the General Assembly is not in session, immediately the Security Council ceases to deal with such matters.

Article 13

1. The General Assembly shall initiate studies and make recommendations for the purpose of:

(a) promoting international co-operation in the political field and encouraging the progressive development of international law and its codification;

(b) promoting international co-operation in the economic, social, cultural, educational, and health fields, and assisting in the realization of human rights and fundamental freedoms for all without distinction as to race, sex, language, or religion.

2. The further responsibilities, functions and powers of the General Assembly with respect to matters mentioned in paragraph 1(b) above are set forth in Chapters IX and X.

Article 14

Subject to the provision of Article 12, the General Assembly may recommend measures for the peaceful adjustment of any situation, regardless of origin, which it deems likely to impair the general welfare or friendly relations among nations, including situations resulting from a violation of the provisions of the present Charter setting forth the Purposes and Principles of the United Nations.

Article 15

1. The General Assembly shall receive and consider annual and special reports from the Security Council; these reports shall include an account of the measures that the Security Council has decided upon or taken to maintain international peace and security.

2. The General Assembly shall receive and consider reports from the other organs of the United Nations.

Article 16

The General Assembly shall perform such functions with respect to the international trusteeship system as are assigned to it under Chapters XII and XIII, including the approval of the trusteeship agreements for areas not designated as strategic.

Article 17

1. The General Assembly shall consider and approve the budget of the Organization.

2. The expenses of the Organization shall be borne by the Members as apportioned by the General Assembly.

3. The General Assembly shall consider and approve any financial and budgetary arrangements with specialized agencies referred to in Article 57 and shall examine the administrative budgets of such specialized agencies with a view to making recommendations to the agencies concerned.

Voting

Article 18

1. Each Member of the General Assembly shall have one vote.

2. Decisions of the General Assembly on important questions shall be made by a two-thirds majority of the members present and voting. These questions shall include: recommendations with respect to the maintenance of international peace and security, the election of the non-permanent Members of the Security Council, the election of the Members of the Economic and Social Council, the election of Members of the Trusteeship Council in accordance with paragraph 1(c) of Article 86, the admission of new Members to the United Nations, the suspension of the rights and privileges of membership, the expulsion of Members, questions relating to the operation of the trusteeship system, and budgetary questions.

3. Decisions on other questions, including the determination of additional categories of questions to be decided by a two-thirds majority, shall be made by a majority of the members present and voting.

Article 19

A Member of the United Nations which is in arrears in the payment of its financial contributions to the Organization shall have no vote in the General Assembly if the amount of its arrears equals or exceeds the amount of the contributions due from it for the preceding two full years. The General Assembly may, nevertheless, permit such a Member to vote if it is satisfied that the failure to pay is due to conditions beyond the control of the Member.

Procedure

Article 20

The General Assembly shall meet in regular annual sessions and in such special sessions as occasion may require. Special sessions shall be convoked by the Secretary-General at the request of the Security Council or of a majority of the members of the United Nations.

Article 21

The General Assembly shall adopt its own rules of procedure. It shall elect its President for each session.

Article 22

The General Assembly may establish such subsidiary organs as it deems necessary for the performance of its functions.

V. THE SECURITY COUNCIL

Composition

Article 23

1. The Security Council shall consist of 11 Members of the United Nations. The Republic of China*, France, the Union of Soviet Socialist Republics†, the United Kingdom of Great Britain and Northern Ireland, and the United States of America shall be permanent members of the Security Council. The General Assembly shall elect six other Members of the United Nations to be non-permanent members of the Security Council, due regard being specially paid, in the first instance to the contribution of Members of the United Nations to the maintenance of international peace and security and to the other purposes of the Organization, and also to equitable geographical distribution.

2. The non-permanent members of the Security Council shall be elected for a term of two years. In the first election of the non-permanent members, however, three shall be chosen for a term of one year. A retiring member shall not be eligible for immediate re-election.

3. Each member of the Security Council shall have one representative.

* From 1971 the Chinese seat in the UN General Assembly and its permanent seat in the Security Council were occupied by the People's Republic of China.

† In December 1991 Russia assumed the former USSR's seat in the UN General Assembly and its permanent seat in the Security Council.

Functions and Powers

Article 24

1. In order to ensure prompt and effective action by the United Nations, its Members confer on the Security Council primary responsibility for the maintenance of international peace and security, and agree that in carrying out its duties under this responsibility the Security Council acts on their behalf.

2. In discharging these duties the Security Council shall act in accordance with the Purposes and Principles of the United Nations. The specific powers granted to the Security Council for the discharge of these duties are laid down in Chapters VI, VII, VIII and XII.

3. The Security Council shall submit annual and, when necessary, special reports to the General Assembly for its consideration.

Article 25

The Members of the United Nations agree to accept and carry out the decisions of the Security Council in accordance with the present Charter.

Article 26

In order to promote the establishment and maintenance of international peace and security with the least diversion for armaments of the world's human and economic resources, the Security Council shall be responsible for formulating, with the assistance of the Military Staff Committee referred to in Article 47, plans to be submitted to the Members of the United Nations for the establishment of a system for the regulation of armaments.

Voting

Article 27

1. Each member of the Security Council shall have one vote.

2. Decisions of the Security Council on procedural matters shall be made by an affirmative vote of seven members.

3. Decisions of the Security Council on all other matters shall be made by an affirmative vote of seven members including the concurring votes of the permanent members; provided that, in decisions under Chapter VI, and under paragraph 3 of Article 52, a party to a dispute shall abstain from voting.

Procedure

Article 28

1. The Security Council shall be so organized as to be able to function continuously. Each member of the Security Council shall for this purpose be represented at all times at the seat of the Organization.

2. The Security Council shall hold periodic meetings at which each of its members may, if it so desires, be represented by a member of the government or by some other specially designated representative.

3. The Security Council may hold meetings at such places other than the seat of the Organization as in its judgment will best facilitate its work.

Article 29

The Security Council may establish such subsidiary organs as it deems necessary for the performance of its functions.

Article 30

The Security Council shall adopt its own rules of procedure, including the method of selecting its President.

Article 31

Any Member of the United Nations which is not a member of the Security Council may participate, without vote, in the discussion of any question brought before the Security Council whenever the latter considers that the interests of that Member are specially affected.

Article 32

Any Member of the United Nations which is not a member of the Security Council or any state which is not a Member of the United Nations, if it is a party to a dispute under consideration by the Security Council, shall be invited to participate, without vote, in the discussion relating to the dispute. The Security Council shall lay down such conditions as it deems just for the participation of a state which is not a Member of the United Nations.

VI. PACIFIC SETTLEMENT OF DISPUTES

Article 33

1. The parties to any dispute, the continuance of which is likely to endanger the maintenance of international peace and security, shall, first of all, seek a solution by negotiation, enquiry, mediation, conciliation, arbitration, judicial settlement, resort to regional agencies or arrangements, or other peaceful means of their own choice.

2. The Security Council shall, when it deems necessary, call upon the parties to settle their disputes by such means.

Article 34

The Security Council may investigate any dispute, or any situation which might lead to international friction or give rise to a dispute, in order to determine whether the continuance of the dispute or situation is likely to endanger the maintenance of international peace and security.

Article 35

1. Any Member of the United Nations may bring any dispute, or any situation of the nature referred to in Article 34, to the attention of the Security Council or of the General Assembly.

2. A state which is not a Member of the United Nations may bring to the attention of the Security Council or of the General Assembly any dispute to which it is a party if it accepts in advance, for the purposes of the dispute, the obligations of pacific settlement provided in the present Charter.

3. The proceedings of the General Assembly in respect of matters brought to its attention under this Article will be subject to the provisions of Articles 11 and 12.

Article 36

1. The Security Council may, at any stage of a dispute of the nature referred to in Article 33 or of a situation of like nature, recommend appropriate procedures or methods of adjustment.

2. The Security Council should take into consideration any procedures for the settlement of the dispute which have already been adopted by the parties.

3. In making recommendations under this Article the Security Council should also take into consideration that legal disputes should as a general rule be referred by the parties to the International Court of Justice in accordance with the provisions of the statute of the Court.

Article 37

1. Should the parties to a dispute of the nature referred to in Article 33, fail to settle it by the means indicated in that Article, they shall refer it to the Security Council.

2. If the Security Council deems that the continuance of the dispute is in fact likely to endanger the maintenance of international peace and security, it shall decide whether to take action under Article 36 or to recommend such terms of settlement as it may consider appropriate.

Article 38

Without prejudice to the provisions of Articles 33 to 37, the Security Council may, if all the parties to any dispute so request, make recommendations to the parties with a view to a pacific settlement of the dispute.

VII. ACTION WITH RESPECT TO THREATS TO THE PEACE, BREACHES OF THE PEACE, AND ACTS OF AGGRESSION

Article 39

The Security Council shall determine the existence of any threat to the peace, breach of the peace, or act of aggression and shall make recommendations, or decide what measures shall be taken in accordance with Articles 41 and 42, to maintain or restore international peace and security.

Article 40

In order to prevent an aggravation of the situation, the Security Council may, before making the recommendations or deciding upon the measures provided for in Article 39, call upon the parties concerned to comply with such provisional measures as it deems necessary or desirable. Such provisional measures shall be without prejudice to the rights, claims, or position of the parties concerned. The Security Council shall duly take account of failure to comply with such provisional measures.

Article 41

The Security Council may decide what measures not involving the use of armed force are to be employed to give effect to its decisions, and it may call upon the Members of the United Nations to apply such measures. These may include complete or partial interruption of economic relations and of rail, sea, air, postal, telegraphic, radio, and other means of communication, and the severance of diplomatic relations.

Article 42

Should the Security Council consider that measures provided for in Article 41 would be inadequate or have proved to be inadequate, it may take such action by air, sea, or land forces as may be necessary to maintain or restore international peace and security. Such action may include demonstrations, blockade, and other operations by air, sea, or land forces of Members of the United Nations.

Article 43

1. All Members of the United Nations, in order to contribute to the maintenance of international peace and security, undertake to make available to the Security Council, on its call and in accordance with a special agreement or agreements, armed forces, assistance, and facilities, including rights of passage, necessary for the purpose of maintaining international peace and security.

2. Such agreement or agreements shall govern the numbers and types of forces, their degree of readiness and general location, and the nature of the facilities and assistance to be provided.

3. The agreement or agreements shall be negotiated as soon as possible on the initiative of the Security Council. They shall be concluded between the Security Council and Members or between the Security Council and groups of Members and shall be subject to ratification by the signatory states in accordance with their respective constitutional processes.

Article 44

When the Security Council has decided to use force it shall, before calling upon a Member not represented on it to provide armed forces in fulfilment of the obligations assumed under Article 43, invite that Member, if the Member so desires, to participate in the decisions of the Security Council concerning the employment of contingents of that Member's armed forces.

Article 45

In order to enable the United Nations to take urgent military measures, Members shall hold immediately available national air-force contingents for combined international enforcement action. The strength and degree of readiness of these contingents and plans for their combined action shall be determined, within the limits laid down in the special agreement and agreements referred to in Article 43, by the Security Council with the assistance of the Military Staff Committee.

Article 46

Plans for the application of armed force shall be made by the Security Council with the assistance of the Military Staff Committee.

Article 47

1. There shall be established a Military Staff Committee to advise and assist the Security Council on all questions relating to the Security Council's military requirements for the maintenance of international peace and security, the employment and command of forces placed at its disposal, the regulation of armaments, and possible disarmament.

2. The Military Staff Committee shall consist of the Chiefs of Staff of the permanent members of the Security Council or their representatives. Any Member of the United Nations not permanently represented on the Committee shall be invited by the Committee to be associated with it when the efficient discharge of the Committee's responsibilities requires the participation of that Member in its work.

3. The Military Staff Committee shall be responsible under the Security Council for the strategic direction of any armed forces placed at the disposal of the Security Council. Questions relating to the command of such forces shall be worked out subsequently.

4. The Military Staff Committee, with the authorization of the Security Council and after consultation with appropriate regional agencies, may establish regional sub-committees.

Article 48

1. The action required to carry out the decisions of the Security Council for the maintenance of international peace and security shall be taken by all the Members of the United Nations or by some of them, as the Security Council may determine.

2. Such decisions shall be carried out by the Members of the United Nations directly and through their action in the appropriate international agencies of which they are members.

Article 49

The Members of the United Nations shall join in affording mutual assistance in carrying out the measures decided upon by the Security Council.

Article 50

If preventive or enforcement measures against any state are taken by the Security Council, any other state, whether a Member of the United Nations or not, which finds itself confronted with special economic problems arising from the carrying out of those measures shall have the right to consult the Security Council with regard to a solution of those problems.

Article 51

Nothing in the present Charter shall impair the inherent right of individual or collective self-defence if an armed attack occurs against a Member of the United Nations, until the Security Council has taken measures necessary to maintain international peace and security. Measures taken by Members in the exercise of this right of self-defence shall be immediately reported to the Security Council and shall not in any way affect the authority and responsibility of the Security Council under the present Charter to take at any time such action as it deems necessary in order to maintain or restore international peace and security.

VIII. REGIONAL ARRANGEMENTS

Article 52

1. Nothing in the present Charter precludes the existence of regional arrangements or agencies for dealing with such matters relating to the maintenance of international peace and security as are appropriate for regional action, provided that such arrangements or agencies and their activities are consistent with the Purposes and Principles of the United Nations.

2. The Members of the United Nations entering into such arrangements or constituting such agencies shall make every effort to achieve pacific settlement of local disputes through such regional agencies before referring them to the Security Council.

3. The Security Council shall encourage the development of pacific settlement of local disputes through such regional arrangements or by such regional agencies either on the initiative of the states concerned or by reference from the Security Council.

4. This Article in no way impairs the application of Articles 34 and 35.

Article 53

1. The Security Council shall, where appropriate, utilize such regional arrangements or agencies for enforcement action under its authority. But no enforcement action shall be taken under regional arrangements or by regional agencies without the authorization of the Security Council, with the exception of measures against any enemy state, as defined in paragraph 2 of this Article, provided for pursuant to Article 107 or in regional arrangements directed against renewal of aggressive policy on the part of any such state, until such time as the Organization may, on request of the Governments concerned, be charged with the responsibility for preventing further aggression by such a state.

2. The term enemy state as used in paragraph 1 of this Article applies to any state which during the Second World War has been an enemy of any signatory of the present Charter.

Article 54

The Security Council shall at all times be kept fully informed of activities undertaken or in contemplation under regional arrangements or by regional agencies for the maintenance of international peace and security.

IX. INTERNATIONAL ECONOMIC AND SOCIAL CO-OPERATION

Article 55

With a view to the creation of conditions of stability and well-being which are necessary for peaceful and friendly relations among nations based on respect for the principle of equal rights and self-determination of peoples, the United Nations shall promote:

(a) higher standards of living, full employment, and conditions of economic and social progress and development;

(b) solutions of international economic, social, health, and related problems; and international cultural and educational co-operation; and

(c) universal respect for, and observance of, human rights and fundamental freedoms for all without distinction as to race, sex, language, or religion.

Article 56

All Members pledge themselves to take joint and separate action in co-operation with the Organization for the achievement of the purposes set forth in Article 55.

Article 57

1. The various specialized agencies, established by intergovernmental agreement and having wide international responsibilities, as defined in their basic instruments, in economic, social, cultural, educational, health, and related fields, shall be brought into relationship with the United Nations in accordance with the provisions of Article 63.

2. Such agencies thus brought into relationship with the United Nations are hereinafter referred to as specialized agencies.

Article 58

The Organization shall make recommendations for the co-ordination of the policies and activities of the specialized agencies.

Article 59

The Organization shall, where appropriate, initiate negotiations among the states concerned for the creation of any new specialized agencies required for the accomplishment of the purposes set forth in Article 55.

Article 60

Responsibility for the discharge of the functions of the Organization set forth in this Chapter shall be vested in the General Assembly and, under the authority of the General Assembly, in the Economic and Social Council, which shall have for this purpose the powers set forth in Chapter X.

X. THE ECONOMIC AND SOCIAL COUNCIL

Composition

Article 61

1. The Economic and Social Council shall consist of 18 Members of the United Nations elected by the General Assembly.

2. Subject to the provisions of paragraph 3, six members of the Economic and Social Council shall be elected each year for a term of three years. A retiring member shall be eligible for immediate re-election.

3. At the first election, 18 members of the Economic and Social Council shall be chosen. The term of office of six members so chosen shall expire at the end of one year, and of six other members at the end of two years, in accordance with arrangements made by the General Assembly.

4. Each member of the Economic and Social Council shall have one representative.

Functions and Powers

Article 62

1. The Economic and Social Council may make or initiate studies and reports with respect to international economic, social, cultural, educational, health, and related matters and may make recommendations with respect to any such matters to the General Assembly, to the Members of the United Nations, and to the specialized agencies concerned.

2. It may make recommendations for the purpose of promoting respect for, and observance of, human rights and fundamental freedoms for all.

3. It may prepare draft conventions for submission to the General Assembly, with respect to matters falling within its competence.

4. It may call, in accordance with the rules prescribed by the United Nations, international conferences on matters falling within its competence.

Article 63

1. The Economic and Social Council may enter into agreements with any of the agencies referred to in Article 57, defining the terms on which the agency concerned shall be brought into relationship with the United Nations. Such agreements shall be subject to approval by the General Assembly.

2. It may co-ordinate the activities of the specialized agencies through consultation with and recommendations to such agencies and through recommendations to the General Assembly and to the Members of the United Nations.

Article 64

1. The Economic and Social Council may take appropriate steps to obtain regular reports from the specialized agencies. It may make arrangements with the Members of the United Nations and with specialized agencies to obtain reports on the steps taken to give effect to its own recommendations and to recommendations on matters falling within its competence made by the General Assembly.

2. It may communicate its observations on these reports to the General Assembly.

Article 65

The Economic and Social Council may furnish information to the Security Council and shall assist the Security Council upon its request.

Article 66

1. The Economic and Social Council shall perform such functions as fall within its competence in connection with the carrying out of the recommendations of the General Assembly.

2. It may, with the approval of the General Assembly, perform services at the request of Members of the United Nations and at the request of specialized agencies.

3. It shall perform such other functions as are specified elsewhere in the present Charter or as may be assigned to it by the General Assembly.

Voting

Article 67

1. Each member of the Economic and Social Council shall have one vote.

2. Decisions of the Economic and Social Council shall be made by a majority of the members present and voting.

Procedure

Article 68

The Economic and Social Council shall set up commissions in economic and social fields and for the promotion of human rights, and such other commissions as may be required for the performance of its functions.

Article 69

The Economic and Social Council shall invite any Member of the United Nations to participate, without vote, in its deliberations on any matter of particular concern to that Member.

Article 70

The Economic and Social Council may make arrangements for representatives of the specialized agencies to participate, without vote, in its deliberations and in those of the commissions established by it, and for its representatives to participate in the deliberations of the specialized agencies.

Article 71

The Economic and Social Council may make suitable arrangements for consultation with non-governmental organizations which are concerned with matters within its competence. Such arrangements may be made with international organizations and, where appropriate, with national organizations after consultation with the Member of the United Nations concerned.

Article 72

1. The Economic and Social Council shall adopt its own rules of procedure, including the method of selecting its President.

2. The Economic and Social Council shall meet as required in accordance with its rules, which shall include provision for the convening of meetings on the request of a majority of its members.

XI. NON-SELF-GOVERNING TERRITORIES

Article 73

Members of the United Nations which have or assume responsibilities for the administration of territories whose peoples have not yet attained a full measure of self-government recognize the principle that the interests of the inhabitants of these territories are paramount, and accept as a sacred trust the obligation to promote to the utmost, within the system of international peace and security established by the present Charter, the well-being of the inhabitants of these territories, and, to this end:

(a) to ensure, with due respect for the culture of the peoples concerned, their political, economic, social, and educational advancement, their just treatment, and their protection against abuses;

(b) to develop self-government, to take due account of the political aspirations of the peoples, and to assist them in the progressive development of their free political institutions, according to the particular circumstances of each territory and its peoples and their varying stages of advancement;

(c) to further international peace and security;

(d) to promote constructive measures of development, to encourage research, and to co-operate with one another and, when and where appropriate, with specialized international bodies with a view to the practical achievement of the social, economic, and scientific purposes set forth in this Article; and

(e) to transmit regularly to the Secretary-General for information purposes, subject to such limitations as security and constitutional considerations may require, statistical and other information, of a technical nature relating to economic, social, and educational conditions in the territories for which they are respectively responsible other than those territories to which Chapters XII and XIII apply.

Article 74

Members of the United Nations also agree that their policy in respect of the territories to which this Chapter applies, no less than in respect of their metropolitan areas, must be based on the general principles of good-neighbourliness, due account being taken of the interests and well-being of the rest of the world, in social, economic, and commercial matters.

XII. INTERNATIONAL TRUSTEESHIP SYSTEM*

Article 75

The United Nations shall establish under its authority an international trusteeship system for the administration and supervision of such territories as may be placed thereunder by subsequent individual agreements. These territories are hereinafter referred to as trust territories.

Article 76

The basic objectives of the trusteeship system, in accordance with the Purposes of the United Nations laid down in Article 1 of the present Charter, shall be:

(a) to further international peace and security;

(b) to promote the political, economic, social, and educational advancement of the inhabitants of the trust territories, and their progressive development towards self-government or independence as may be appropriate to the particular circumstances of each territory and its peoples and the freely expressed wishes of the peoples concerned, and as may be provided by the terms of each trusteeship agreement;

(c) to encourage respect for human rights and for fundamental freedoms for all without distinction as to race, sex, language, or religion, and to encourage recognition of the interdependence of the peoples of the world; and

(d) to ensure equal treatment in social, economic, and commercial matters for all Members of the United Nations and their nationals, and also equal treatment for the latter in the administration of justice, without prejudice to the attainment of the foregoing objectives and subject to the provisions of Article 80.

Article 77

1. The trusteeship system shall apply to such territories in the following categories as may be placed thereunder by means of trusteeship agreements.

(a) territories now held under mandate;

(b) territories which may be detached from enemy states as a result of the Second World War; and

(c) territories voluntarily placed under the system by states responsible for their administration.

2. It will be a matter for subsequent agreement as to which territories in the foregoing categories will be brought under the trusteeship system and upon what terms.

Article 78

The trusteeship system shall not apply to territories which have become Members of the United Nations, relationship among which shall be based on respect for the principle of sovereign equality.

Article 79

The terms of trusteeship for each territory to be placed under the trusteeship system, including any alteration or amendment, shall be agreed upon by the states directly concerned, including the mandatory power in the case of territories held under mandate by a Member of the United Nations, and shall be approved as provided for in Articles 83 and 85.

Article 80

1. Except as may be agreed upon in individual trusteeship agreements, made under Articles 77, 79, and 81, placing each territory under the trusteeship system, and until such agreements have been concluded, nothing in this Chapter shall be construed in or of itself to alter in any manner the rights whatsoever of any states or any peoples or the terms of existing international instruments to which Members of the United Nations may respectively be parties.

2. Paragraph 1 of this Article shall not be interpreted as giving grounds for delay or postponement of the negotiation and conclusion of agreements for placing mandated and other territories under the trusteeship system as provided for in Article 77.

Article 81

The trusteeship agreement shall in each case include the terms under which the trust territory will be administered and designate the authority which will exercise the administration of the trust territory. Such authority, hereinafter called the administering authority, may be one or more states or the Organization itself.

Article 82

There may be designated, in any trusteeship agreement, a strategic area or areas which may include part or all of the trust territory to which the agreement applies, without prejudice to any special agreement or agreements made under Article 43.

Article 83

1. All functions of the United Nations relating to strategic areas, including the approval of the terms of the trusteeship agreements and of their alteration or amendment, shall be exercised by the Security Council.

2. The basic objectives set forth in Article 76 shall be applicable to the people of each strategic area.

3. The Security Council shall, subject to the provisions of the trusteeship agreements and without prejudice to security considerations, avail itself of the assistance of the Trusteeship Council to perform those functions of the United Nations under the trusteeship system relating to political, economic, social, and educational matters in the strategic areas.

Article 84

It shall be the duty of the administering authority to ensure that the trust territory shall play its part in the maintenance of international peace and security. To this end the administering authority may make use of volunteer forces, facilities, and assistance from the trust territory in carrying out the obligations towards the Security Council undertaken in this regard by the administering authority, as well as for local defence and the maintenance of law and order within the trust territory.

Article 85

1. The functions of the United Nations with regard to trusteeship agreements for all areas not designated as strategic, including the approval of the terms of the trusteeship agreements and of their alteration or amendment, shall be exercised by the General Assembly.

2. The Trusteeship Council, operating under the authority of the General Assembly, shall assist the General Assembly in carrying out these functions.

XIII. THE TRUSTEESHIP COUNCIL*

Composition

Article 86

1. The Trusteeship Council shall consist of the following Members of the United Nations:

(a) those Members administering trust territories:

(b) such of those Members mentioned by name in Article 23 as are not administering trust territories; and

(c) as many other Members elected for three-year terms by the General Assembly as may be necessary to ensure that the total number of members of the Trusteeship Council is equally divided between those Members of the United Nations which administer trust territories and those which do not.

2. Each member of the Trusteeship Council shall designate one specially qualified person to represent it therein.

Functions and Powers

Article 87

The General Assembly and, under its authority, the Trusteeship Council, in carrying out their functions, may:

(a) consider reports submitted by the administering authority;

(b) accept petitions and examine them in consultation with the administering authority;

(c) provide for periodic visits to the respective trust territories at times agreed upon with the administering authority; and

(d) take these and other actions in conformity with the terms of the trusteeship agreements.

Article 88

The Trusteeship Council shall formulate a questionnaire on the political, economic, social, and educational advancement of the inhabitants of each trust territory, and the administering authority for each trust territory within the competence of the General Assembly shall make an annual report to the General Assembly upon the basis of such questionnaire.

Voting

Article 89

1. Each member of the Trusteeship Council shall have one vote.

2. Decisions of the Trusteeship Council shall be made by a majority of the members present and voting.

Procedure

Article 90

1. The Trusteeship Council shall adopt its own rules of procedure, including the method of selecting its President.

2. The Trusteeship Council shall meet as required in accordance with its rules, which shall include provision for the convening of meetings on the request of a majority of its members.

Article 91

The Trusteeship Council shall, when appropriate, avail itself of the assistance of the Economic and Social Council and of the specialized agencies in regard to matters with which they are respectively concerned.

---

* On 1 October 1994 the Republic of Palau, the last remaining territory under UN trusteeship, became independent. The Trusteeship Council formally suspended operations on 1 November; subsequently it was to be convened, as required, on an extraordinary basis.

XIV. THE INTERNATIONAL COURT OF JUSTICE

Article 92

The International Court of Justice shall be the principal judicial organ of the United Nations. It shall function in accordance with the annexed Statute, which is based upon the Statute of the Permanent Court of International Justice and forms an integral part of the present Charter.

Article 93

1. All Members of the United Nations are *ipso facto* parties to the Statute of the International Court of Justice.

2. A state which is not a Member of the United Nations may become a party to the Statute of the International Court of Justice on condition to be determined in each case by the General Assembly upon the recommendation of the Security Council.

Article 94

1. Each Member of the United Nations undertakes to comply with the decision of the International Court of Justice in any case to which it is a party.

2. If any party to a case fails to perform the obligations incumbent upon it under a judgment rendered by the Court, the other party may have recourse to the Security Council, which may, if it deems necessary, make recommendations or decide upon measures to be taken to give effect to the judgment.

Article 95

Nothing in the present Charter shall prevent Members of the United Nations from entrusting the solution of their differences to other tribunals by virtue of agreements already in existence or which may be concluded in the future.

Article 96

1. The General Assembly or the Security Council may request the International Court of Justice to give an advisory opinion on any legal question.

2. Other organs of the United Nations and specialized agencies, which may at any time be so authorized by the General Assembly, may also request advisory opinions of the Court on legal questions arising within the scope of their activities.

XV. THE SECRETARIAT

Article 97

The Secretariat shall comprise a Secretary-General and such staff as the Organization may require. The Secretary-General shall be appointed by the General Assembly upon the recommendation of the Security Council. He shall be the chief administrative officer of the Organization.

Article 98

The Secretary-General shall act in that capacity in all meetings of the General Assembly, of the Security Council, of the Economic and Social Council, and of the Trusteeship Council, and shall perform such other functions as are entrusted to him by these organs. The Secretary-General shall make an annual report to the General Assembly on the work of the Organization.

Article 99

The Secretary-General may bring to the attention of the Security Council any matter which in his opinion may threaten the maintenance of international peace and security.

Article 100

1. In the performance of their duties the Secretary-General and the staff shall not seek or receive instructions from any government or from any other authority external to the Organization. They shall refrain from any action which might reflect on their position as international officials responsible only to the Organization.

2. Each Member of the United Nations undertakes to respect the exclusively international character of the responsibilities of the Secretary-General and the staff and not to seek to influence them in the discharge of their responsibilities.

Article 101

1. The staff shall be appointed by the Secretary-General under regulations established by the General Assembly.

2. Appropriate staffs shall be permanently assigned to the Economic and Social Council, the Trusteeship Council, and, as required, to other organs of the United Nations. These staffs shall form a part of the Secretariat.

3. The paramount consideration in the employment of the staff and in the determination of the conditions of service shall be the necessity of securing the highest standards of efficiency, competence, and integrity. Due regard shall be paid to the importance of recruiting the staff on as wide a geographical basis as possible.

XVI. MISCELLANEOUS PROVISIONS

Article 102

1. Every treaty and every international agreement entered into by any Member of the United Nations after the present Charter comes into force shall as soon as possible be registered with the Secretariat and published by it.

2. No party to any such treaty or international agreement which has not been registered in accordance with the provisions of paragraph 1 of this Article may invoke that treaty or agreement before any organ of the United Nations.

Article 103

In the event of a conflict between the obligations of the Members of the United Nations under the present Charter and their obligations under any other international agreement, their obligations under the present Charter shall prevail.

Article 104

The Organization shall enjoy in the territory of each of its Members such legal capacity as may be necessary for the exercise of its functions and the fulfilment of its purposes.

Article 105

1. The Organization shall enjoy in the territory of each of its Members such privileges and immunities as are necessary for the fulfilment of its purposes.

2. Representatives of the Members of the United Nations and officials of the Organization shall similarly enjoy such privileges and immunities as are necessary for the independent exercise of their functions in connection with the Organization.

3. The General Assembly may make recommendations with a view to determining the details of the application of paragraphs 1 and 2 of this Article or may propose conventions to the Members of the United Nations for this purpose.

XVII. TRANSITIONAL SECURITY ARRANGEMENTS

Article 106

Pending the coming into force of such special agreements referred to in Article 43 as in the opinion of the Security Council enable it to begin the exercise of its responsibilities under Article 42, the parties to the Four-Nation Declaration signed at Moscow, October 30, 1943, and France, shall, in accordance with the provisions of paragraph 5 of that Declaration, consult with one another and as occasion requires with other Members of the United Nations with a view to such joint action on behalf of the Organization as may be necessary for the purpose of maintaining international peace and security.

Article 107

Nothing in the present Charter shall invalidate or preclude action, in relation to any state which during the Second World War has been an enemy of any signatory to the present Charter, taken or authorized as a result of that war by the Governments having responsibility for such action.

XVIII. AMENDMENTS

Article 108

Amendments to the present Charter shall come into force for all Members of the United Nations when they have been adopted by a vote of two-thirds of the members of the General Assembly and ratified in accordance with their respective constitutional processes by two-thirds of the Members of the United Nations, including all the permanent members of the Security Council.

Article 109

1. A General Conference of the Members of the United Nations for the purpose of reviewing the present Charter may be held at a date and place to be fixed by a two-thirds vote of the members of the General Assembly and by a vote of any seven members of the Security Council. Each Member of the United Nations shall have one vote in the conference.

2. Any alteration of the present Charter recommended by a two-thirds vote of the conference shall take effect when ratified in accordance with their respective constitutional processes by two-thirds of the Members of the United Nations including all the permanent members of the Security Council.

3. If such a conference has not been held before the tenth annual session of the General Assembly following the coming into force of the present Charter, the proposal to call such a conference shall be placed on the agenda of that session of the General Assembly, and

the conference shall be held if so decided by a majority vote of the members of the General Assembly and by a vote of any seven members of the Security Council.

XIX. RATIFICATION AND SIGNATURE

Article 110

1. The present Charter shall be ratified by the signatory states in accordance with their respective constitutional processes.

2. The ratifications shall be deposited with the Government of the United States of America, which shall notify all the signatory states of each deposit as well as the Secretary-General of the Organization when he has been appointed.

3. The present Charter shall come into force upon the deposit of ratifications by the Republic of China, France, the Union of Soviet Socialist Republics, the United Kingdom of Great Britain and Northern Ireland, and the United States of America, and by a majority of the other signatory states. A protocol of the ratifications deposited shall thereupon be drawn up by the Government of the United States of America which shall communicate copies thereof to all the signatory states.

4. The states signatory to the present Charter which ratify it after it has come into force will become original Members of the United Nations on the date of the deposit of their respective ratifications.

Article 111

The present Charter, of which the Chinese, French, Russian, English, and Spanish texts are equally authentic, shall remain deposited in the archives of the Government of the United States of America. Duly certified copies thereof shall be transmitted by that Government to the Governments of the other signatory states.

IN FAITH WHEREOF the representatives of the Governments of the United Nations have signed the present Charter.

DONE at the city of San Francisco the twenty-sixth day of June, one thousand nine hundred and forty-five.

Amendments

The following amendments to Articles 23 and 27 of the Charter came into force in August 1965.

Article 23

1. The Security Council shall consist of 15 Members of the United Nations. The Republic of China, France, the Union of Soviet Socialist Republics, the United Kingdom of Great Britain and Northern Ireland, and the United States of America shall be permanent members of the Security Council. The General Assembly shall elect 10 other Members of the United Nations to be non-permanent members of the Security Council, due regard being specially paid, in the first instance to the contribution of Members of the United Nations to the maintenance of international peace and security and to the other purposes of the Organization, and also to equitable geographical distribution.

2. The non-permanent members of the Security Council shall be elected for a term of two years. In the first election of the non-permanent members after the increase of the membership of the Security Council from 11 to 15, two of the four additional members shall be chosen for a term of one year. A retiring member shall not be eligible for immediate re-election.

3. Each member of the Security Council shall have one representative.

Article 27

1. Each member of the Security Council shall have one vote.

2. Decisions of the Security Council on procedural matters shall be made by an affirmative vote of nine members.

3. Decisions of the Security Council on all other matters shall be made by an affirmative vote of nine members including the concurring votes of the permanent members; provided that, in decisions under Chapter VI and under paragraph 3 of Article 52, a party to a dispute shall abstain from voting.

The following amendments to Article 61 of the Charter came into force in September 1973.

Article 61

1. The Economic and Social Council shall consist of 54 Members of the United Nations elected by the General Assembly.

2. Subject to the provisions of paragraph 3, 18 members of the Economic and Social Council shall be elected each year for a term of three years. A retiring member shall be eligible for immediate re-election.

3. At the first election after the increase in the membership of the Economic and Social Council from 27 to 54 members, in addition to the members elected in place of the nine members whose term of office expires at the end of that year, 27 additional members shall be elected. Of these 27 additional members, the term of office of nine members so elected shall expire at the end of one year, and of nine other members at the end of two years, in accordance with arrangements made by the General Assembly.

4. Each member of the Economic and Social Council shall have one representative.

The following amendment to Paragraph 1 of Article 109 of the Charter came into force in June 1968.

Article 109

1. A General Conference of the Members of the United Nations for the purpose of reviewing the present Charter may be held at a date and place to be fixed by a two-thirds vote of the members of the General Assembly and by a vote of any nine members of the Security Council. Each Member of the United Nations shall have one vote in the conference.

Secretariat

SECRETARY-GENERAL

The Secretary-General is the UN's chief administrative officer, elected for a five-year term by the General Assembly on the recommendation of the Security Council. He acts in that capacity at all meetings of the General Assembly, the Security Council, the Economic and Social Council, and the Trusteeship Council, and performs such other functions as are entrusted to him by those organs. He is required to submit an annual report to the General Assembly and may bring to the attention of the Security Council any matter which, in his opinion, may threaten international peace. (See Charter, p. 10.)

Secretary-General (1997–2001): KOFI ANNAN (Ghana).

The chief administrative staff of the UN Regional Commissions and of all the subsidiary organs of the UN are also members of the Secretariat staff and are listed in the appropriate chapters. The Secretariat staff also includes a number of special missions and special appointments, including some of senior rank.

In June 1997 the total number of staff of the Secretariat holding appointments continuing for a year or more was approximately 14,136, including those serving away from the headquarters, but excluding staff working for the UN specialized agencies and subsidiary organs.

In July 1997 the Secretary-General initiated a comprehensive reform of the administration of the UN and abolished some 1,000 Secretariat posts. A Senior Management Group was established as part of a new Secretariat leadership and management structure, to enhance day-to-day efficiency and accountability. The reforms aimed to restructure the Secretariat's substantive work programme around the UN's five core missions, i.e. peace and security, economic and social affairs, development co-operation, humanitarian affairs and human rights. Accordingly, the reforms provided for the consolidation of the Departments for Policy Co-ordination and Sustainable Development, for Economic and Social Information and Policy Analysis, and for Development Support and Management Services into a single Department of Economic and Social Affairs, and the replacement of the Department of Humanitarian Affairs by an Office of the Emergency Relief Co-ordinator. A Department for Disarmament and Arms Regulation was to be established; however, by November 1997 this proposal had yet to be implemented. During 1997 the Centre for Human Rights and the Office of the High Commissioner for Human Rights were consolidated into a single office under the reform process, while the UN Office in Vienna became the focus of integrated efforts to combat crime, drug abuse and terrorism, as the Office for Drug Control and Crime Prevention. In December the General Assembly endorsed a recommendation of the Secretary-General to create the position of Deputy Secretary-General, who was to assist in the management of Secretariat operations and represent the Secretary-General as required. The Deputy Secretary-General was to be responsible for overseeing the continuing reform process and the establishment of an Office of Development Financing. In January 1998 the Secretary-General appointed Louise Fréchette of Canada as the first Deputy Secretary-General. She was expected to assume the position at the end of February.

SECRETARIAT STAFF

(November 1997)

Executive Office of the Secretary-General

Under-Secretary-General, Chief of Staff: S. IQBAL RIZA (Pakistan).

Assistant Secretary-General, External Relations: GILLIAN SORENSEN (USA).

Department of Economic and Social Affairs

Under-Secretary-General: NITIN DESAI (India).

Assistant Secretary-General, Special Adviser on Gender Issues and the Advancement of Women: ANGELA KING (Jamaica).

Department for General Assembly Affairs and Conference Services

Under-Secretary-General: JIN YONGJIAN (China).

Department of Management

Under-Secretary-General: JOSEPH E. CONNOR (USA).

Assistant Secretary-General: JEAN-PIERRE HALBWACHS (Mauritius).

Assistant Secretary-General: RAFIAH SALIM (Malaysia).

Assistant Secretary-General: BENON SEVAN (Cyprus).

Department of Peace-keeping Operations

Under-Secretary-General: BERNARD MIYET (France).

Assistant Secretary-General: HÉDI ANNABI (Tunisia).

Assistant Secretary-General: MANFRED EISELE (Germany).

Department of Political Affairs

Under-Secretary-General: Sir KIERAN PRENDERGAST (United Kingdom).

Assistant Secretary-General: ALVARO DE SOTO (Peru).

Assistant Secretary-General: IBRAHIMA FALL (Senegal).

Office of Communications and Public Information

Assistant Secretary-General: SAMIR SANBAR (Lebanon).

Office for Drug Control and Crime Prevention

Address: Vienna International Centre, POB 500, 1400 Vienna, Austria.

Telephone: (1) 21345; **telex:** 135612; **fax:** (1) 21345-5819.

Under-Secretary-General: PINO ARLACCHI (Italy).

Office of the Emergency Relief Co-ordinator

Under-Secretary-General, Emergency Relief Co-ordinator: (from 1 January 1998) SERGIO VIEIRA DE MELLO (Brazil).

Office of the United Nations High Commissioner for Human Rights

Address: Palais des Nations, 1211 Geneva 10, Switzerland.

Telephone: (22) 9171873; **fax:** (22) 9170245; **internet:** http://www.unhchr.ch.

High Commissioner: MARY ROBINSON (Ireland).

Office of Internal Oversight Services

Under-Secretary-General: KARL PASCHKE (Germany).

Office of Legal Affairs

Under-Secretary-General, The Legal Counsel: HANS CORELL (Sweden).

Conference on Disarmament

Secretary-General: VLADIMIR PETROVSKY (Russia).

GENEVA OFFICE

Address: Palais des Nations, 1211 Geneva 10, Switzerland.

Telephone: (22) 9172300; **telex:** 412962; **fax:** (22) 9170123.

Director-General: VLADIMIR PETROVSKY (Russia).

UN CONFERENCES, 1998–2000

Third UN Conference on the Exploration and Peaceful Uses of Outer Space (UNISPACE III): Vienna, Austria, 1999 or 2000.

Review Conference of the States Parties to the Treaty on the Non-proliferation of Nuclear Weapons: 2000.

Second World Conference on Natural Disaster Reduction: 2000.

General Assembly

The General Assembly was established as a principal organ of the United Nations under the UN Charter (see p. 10). It first met on 10 January 1946. It is the main deliberative organ of the United Nations, and the only one composed of representatives of all the UN member states. Each delegation consists of not more than five representatives and five alternates, with as many advisers as may be required. The Assembly meets regularly for three months each year, and special sessions may also be held. It has specific responsibility for electing the Secretary-General and members of other UN councils and organs, and for approving the UN budget and the assessments for financial contributions by member states. It is also empowered to make recommendations (but not binding decisions) on questions of international security and co-operation.

After the election of its President and other officers, the Assembly opens its general debate, a three-week period during which the head of each delegation makes a formal statement of his or her government's views on major world issues. The Assembly then begins examination of the principal items on its agenda: it acts directly on a few agenda items, but most business is handled by the six Main Committees (listed below), which study and debate each item and present draft resolutions to the Assembly. After a review of the report of each Main Committee, the Assembly formally approves or rejects the Committee's recommendations. On designated 'important questions', such as recommendations on international peace and security, the admission of new members to the United Nations, or budgetary questions, a two-thirds majority is needed for adoption of a resolution. Other questions may be decided by a simple majority. In the Assembly, each member has one vote. Voting in the Assembly is sometimes replaced by an effort to find consensus among member states, in order to strengthen support for the Assembly's decisions: the President consults delegations in private to find out whether they are willing to agree to adoption of a resolution without a vote; if they are, the President can declare that a resolution has been so adopted.

Special sessions of the Assembly may be held to discuss issues which require particular attention (e.g. illicit drugs) and 'emergency special sessions' may also be convened to discuss situations on which the UN Security Council has been unable to reach a decision (for example, Israel's construction of new settlements in east Jerusalem in 1997). In June 1997 a special session was held to review the state of the environment and to renew commitment to the objectives of the UN Conference on Environment and Development, held five years previously in Rio de Janeiro, Brazil.

In September 1992 the Federal Republic of Yugoslavia (which in April had formally replaced the Socialist Federal Republic of Yugoslavia, although comprising only two of the six former Yugoslav republics) was suspended from the proceedings of the General Assembly. The Assembly required the new Yugoslav state to apply to occupy the former Yugoslavia's seat in the UN. Following the successful conclusion of democratic elections, South Africa was readmitted to the General Assembly in June 1994. In September 1997 the Credentials Committee (see below) ruled that Cambodia's seat in the General Assembly remain vacant, owing to internal conflict in that country.

President of 52nd Session (from September 1997): HENNADIY UDOVENKO (Ukraine).

MAIN COMMITTEES

There are six Main Committees, on which all members have a right to be represented. Each Committee includes an elected Chairperson and two Vice-Chairs.

First Committee: Disarmament and International Security.

Second Committee: Economic and Financial.

Third Committee: Social, Humanitarian and Cultural.

Fourth Committee: Special Political and Decolonization.

Fifth Committee: Administrative and Budgetary.

Sixth Committee: Legal.

OTHER SESSIONAL COMMITTEES

General Committee: f. 1946; composed of 28 members, including the Assembly President, the 21 Vice-Presidents of the Assembly and the Chairs of the six Main Committees.

Credentials Committee: f. 1946; composed of nine members elected at each Assembly session.

POLITICAL AND SECURITY MATTERS

Special Committee on Peace-keeping Operations: f. 1965; 34 appointed members.

Disarmament Commission: f. 1978 (replacing body f. 1952); 61 members.

UN Scientific Committee on the Effects of Atomic Radiation: f. 1955; 21 members.

Committee on the Peaceful Uses of Outer Space: f. 1959; 61 members; has a Legal Sub-Committee and a Scientific and Technical Sub-Committee.

Ad Hoc Committee on the Indian Ocean: f. 1972; 44 members.

Committee on the Exercise of the Inalienable Rights of the Palestinian People: f. 1975; 23 members.

Special Committee on the Implementation of the Declaration on Decolonization: f. 1961; 23 members.

Advisory Committee on the UN Educational and Training Programme for Southern Africa: f. 1967; 13 members.

DEVELOPMENT

Commission on Science and Technology for Development: f. 1992.

Committee on New and Renewable Sources of Energy and on Energy for Development: f. 1992.

United Nations Environment Programme (UNEP) Governing Council: f. 1972; 58 members (see p. 41).

LEGAL QUESTIONS

International Law Commission: f. 1947; 34 members elected for a five-year term; originally established in 1946 as the Committee on the Progressive Development of International Law and its Codification.

Advisory Committee on the UN Programme of Assistance in Teaching, Study, Dissemination and Wider Appreciation of International Law: f. 1965; 25 members.

UN Commission on International Trade Law: f. 1966; 36 members.

Special Committee on the Charter of the United Nations and on the Strengthening of the Role of the Organization: f. 1975; composed of all UN members.

Special Committee on Enhancing the Effectiveness of the Principle of Non-Use of Force in International Relations: f. 1977; 35 members.

There is also a UN Administrative Tribunal and a Committee on Applications for Review of Administrative Tribunal Judgments.

ADMINISTRATIVE AND FINANCIAL QUESTIONS

Advisory Committee on Administrative and Budgetary Questions: f. 1946; 16 members appointed for three-year terms.

Committee on Contributions: f. 1946; 18 members appointed for three-year terms.

International Civil Service Commission: f. 1972; 15 members appointed for four-year terms.

Committee on Information: f. 1978, formerly the Committee to review UN Policies and Activities; 89 members.

There is also a Board of Auditors, Investments Committee, UN Joint Staff Pension Board, Joint Inspection Unit, UN Staff Pension Committee, Committee on Conferences, and Committee for Programme and Co-ordination.

TRUSTEESHIP COUNCIL

The Trusteeship Council (comprising the People's Republic of China—a non-active member until May 1989—France, Russia, the United Kingdom and the USA) has supervised United Nations Trust Territories through the administering authorities to promote the political, economic, social and educational advancement of the inhabitants towards self-government or independence. (See Charter, p. 10.) On 1 October 1994 the last territory remaining under UN trusteeship, the Republic of Palau (part of the archipelago of the Caroline Islands), declared its independence under a compact of free association with the USA, its administering authority. The Security Council terminated the Trusteeship Agreement on 10 November, having determined that the objectives of the agreement had been fully attained. On 1 November the Trusteeship Council formally suspended its operations; in the future it was to be convened on an extraordinary basis as required.

Security Council

The Security Council was established as a principal organ under the United Nations Charter; its first meeting was held on 17 January 1946. Its task is to promote international peace and security in all parts of the world. (See Charter, p. 11 and p. 17.)

MEMBERS

Permanent members:

People's Republic of China, France, Russia*, United Kingdom, USA.

The remaining 10 members are normally elected (five each year) by the General Assembly for two-year periods (five countries from Africa and Asia, two from Latin America, one from eastern Europe, and two from western Europe and others). Non-permanent members from 1 January 1998: Bahrain, Brazil, Costa Rica, Gabon, The Gambia, Japan, Kenya, Portugal, Slovenia, Sweden.

* Russia assumed the USSR's permanent seat on the Council in December 1991, following the dissolution of the USSR in that month.

ORGANIZATION

The Security Council has the right to investigate any dispute or situation which might lead to friction between two or more countries, and such disputes or situations may be brought to the Council's attention either by one of its members, by any member state, by the General Assembly, by the Secretary-General or even, under certain conditions, by a state which is not a member of the United Nations.

The Council has the right to recommend ways and means of peaceful settlement and, in certain circumstances, the actual terms of settlement. In the event of a threat to or breach of international peace or an act of aggression, the Council has powers to take 'enforcement' measures in order to restore international peace and security. These include severance of communications and of economic and diplomatic relations and, if required, action by air, land and sea forces.

All members of the United Nations are pledged by the Charter to make available to the Security Council, on its call and in accordance with special agreements, the armed forces, assistance and facilities necessary to maintain international peace and security. These agreements, however, have not yet been concluded.

The Council is organized to be able to function continuously. The Presidency of the Council is held monthly in turn by the member states in English alphabetical order. Each member of the Council has one vote. On procedural matters decisions are made by the affirmative vote of any nine members. For decisions on other matters the required nine affirmative votes must include the votes of the five permanent members. This is the rule of 'great power unanimity' popularly known as the 'veto' privilege. In practice, an abstention by one of the permanent members is not regarded as a veto. Any member, whether permanent or non-permanent, must abstain from voting in any decision concerning the pacific settlement of a dispute to which it is a party. Any member of the UN that is party to a dispute under consideration by the Council may participate in the Council's discussions without a vote.

ACTIVITIES

In late January 1992 the first ever summit meeting of the Security Council was convened, and was attended by the heads of state or government of 13 of its 15 members, and by the ministers of foreign affairs of the remaining two. The subject of the summit meeting, which was presented in a report drafted by the Secretary-General (entitled 'An Agenda for Peace') was the UN's role in preventive diplomacy, peace-keeping and peace-making.

Consideration of reform of the Security Council commenced in 1993 at the 48th Session of the General Assembly, which established a Working Group to assess the issue. In October 1994 a general debate of the General Assembly revealed widespread support for expanding the Security Council to 20 seats and awarding permanent membership to Japan and Germany. The issue continued to be under consideration by an open-ended working group of the General Assembly in 1997. In March the President of the General Assembly formally introduced a proposal for reform, which envisaged a Council consisting of 24 members, including five new permanent members and four new non-permanent members.

In the early 1990s the number of Security Council meetings, resolutions and presidential statements escalated sharply, reflecting an expansion in the UN's political and humanitarian activities. This trend was gradually reversed as several large peace-keeping operations were terminated and, in particular, following the conclusion of a peace agreement in the former Yugoslavia in late 1995. During 1997 the Security Council continued to monitor closely all existing peace-keeping missions and the situations in countries where missions were being undertaken, and to authorize extensions of their mandates accordingly. In January the Council voted to reinforce the existing UN Verification Mission in Guatemala (MINUGUA), authorized by the General Assembly, by sending some 155 military observers to help to verify the implementation of a cease-fire agreement signed in the previous month. The military observer mission was concluded on the authorization of the Council in May. In March the Council supported the establishment of a multinational protection force to facilitate humanitarian relief efforts in Albania, which was to be organized and led by the Italian Government. The Council also adopted a resolution to strengthen the UN Mission in Bosnia and Herzegovina in order to support the International Police Task Force in that region. In June the Council approved a new Observer Mission in Angola (MONUA), with an initial seven-month mandate effective from the conclusion of the UN Angola Verification Mission on 1 July. In August the mandate of the UN Support Mission in Haiti was terminated, and the Council authorized a successor operation—the UN Transition Mission in Haiti—to further efforts towards creating a secure environment in that country and strengthening the national police force. The UN Observer Mission in Liberia was concluded in September. (For details of current UN observer missions and peace-keeping operations, see pp. 51–56)

In December 1996 the President of the Council determined that the Council would take a more comprehensive and integrated approach to the situation in the Great Lakes region of Central Africa, which had been a major preoccupation of the Council throughout that year. In February 1997 the Council endorsed a five-point plan to resolve the crisis in eastern Zaire (now the Democratic Republic of the Congo), which included an immediate cessation of hostilities, the withdrawal of all external forces, a reaffirmation of respect for national sovereignty and the territorial integrity of all the countries in the region, the protection of all refugees and displaced persons, and a rapid and peaceful settlement of the crisis through dialogue and the electoral process. Earlier in February representatives of several non-governmental organizations reported to the Council on aspects of humanitarian relief work and requirements in the Great Lakes region in the first briefing session ever held by the Council. The Council monitored the subsequent escalation of hostilities in Zaire and the ensuing humanitarian crisis involving refugees remaining in that country, and in August denounced efforts by the new authorities to obstruct a UN mission to investigate alleged abuses of human rights committed earlier in the year. In August the Council considered the internal conflict in the Republic of the Congo, but decided not to dispatch a UN peace-keeping mission, stating that any deployment would require a cease-fire agreement between the conflicting forces in that country, as well as a framework for political dialogue and secure conditions at the international airport. Plans for a force to monitor a buffer-zone in the Republic of the Congo were again under consideration by the Council in October. In early 1997 the Council resolved not to implement proposals for a UN mission to be deployed in Sierra Leone. The Council condemned the establishment of a military government in that country in May, and advocated an immediate restoration of constitutional order. In October the Council imposed punitive measures against Sierra Leone, demanding that the authorities relinquish power and prepare for a democratically-elected government. The Council authorized the Economic Community of West African States (ECOWAS) to enforce the measures, which included the prohibition of the sale or supply of armaments or related materials to Sierra Leone, and diplomatic sanctions against the members and relatives of the military Government. At the end of October the Council adopted a resolution implementing an earlier decision to apply diplomatic sanctions against the UNITA authorities in Angola, owing to their failure to comply with the obligations of a peace agreement. In March the USA used its veto, on two separate occasions, to prevent the Council from adopting a resolution advocating that the Israeli Government halt all settlement activities in east Jerusalem, in order to prevent further disruption to the Middle East peace process. During 1997 the Council also continued to monitor and support efforts to secure peace in Afghanistan, Cyprus, Georgia, Somalia, Tajikistan, Western Sahara and the former Yugoslavia.

In December 1996 the Council approved the implementation of resolution 986, which was adopted in April 1995, to provide for the limited sale of Iraqi petroleum to enable the purchase of humanitarian supplies and the provision of contributions to the UN Compensation Committee (which had been established to settle claims against Iraq resulting from the Gulf War). Exports of petroleum up to a value of US $1,000m. every 90 days were to be permitted under the agreement; the Council was responsible for renewing the mandate of the agreement and for approving contracts for the sale of petroleum and the purchase of food and medical goods. The Council monitored the situation in Iraq throughout 1997 and received regular reports from the UN Special Commission (UNSCOM), which had been established in 1991 to monitor the disposal of weapons. Accordingly, the Council determined not to reschedule the sanctions still in place against Iraq, and in mid-1997 criticized Iraqi interference and non-compliance with UNSCOM activities. In October UNSCOM proposed that further punitive measures be imposed on Iraq to force the Government to disclose its weapons programme. The Council adopted a resolution to threaten the imposition of new sanctions; however, the People's Republic of China, France and Russia abstained from the vote. A few days later Iraq announced that all US members of UNSCOM were obliged to leave the country, and rejected the use of US surveillance aircraft in the inspection programme. The Council issued a condemnation of the expulsion order, but was divided on the means of retaliation. Despite subsequent diplomatic negotiations, in mid-November the Council voted unanimously to impose a travel ban on all Iraqi officials deemed to be responsible for disrupting UNSCOM's operations. Iraq responded by implementing the expulsion of the US element of UNSCOM (having postponed the order pending negotiations), prompting the UN to withdraw almost all of the 97-member inspection team from the country in protest. UNSCOM resumed its activities in late November, following intense diplomatic efforts. However, by early 1998 the contentious issues regarding the composition of UNSCOM, and Iraq's refusal to grant unrestricted access to a substantial number of sensitive sites throughout the country, remained unresolved, and in mid-January a UNSCOM mission, led by a US citizen (whom Iraq accused of undertaking espionage activities), was barred entry to an inspection site. A few days later the Iraqi Government requested a suspension of UNSCOM activities, pending a technical evaluation of Iraq's weaponry by a multinational team of experts. The US and United Kingdom Governments attempted to generate support among Security Council members and other Governments in the Gulf region for the use of force, in the event of Iraq's continued refusal to co-operate with the inspection process, in order to destroy any Iraqi facilities for the manufacture of chemical, biological and nuclear weapons. In mid-February the Security Council authorized the UN Secretary-General to visit Iraq, in an attempt to resolve the escalating diplomatic crisis without resort to military confrontation.

COMMITTEES

At November 1997 there were two **Standing Committees**, each composed of representatives of all Council member states:

Committee of Experts on Rules of Procedure (studies and advises on rule of procedure and other technical matters);

Committee on the Admission of New Members.

***Ad hoc* Committees**, which are established as needed, comprise all Council members and meet in closed session:

Security Council Committee on Council Meetings away from Headquarters;

Security Council Committee established pursuant to resolution 985 (1995) concerning Liberia;

Security Council Committee established pursuant to resolution 918 (1994) concerning Rwanda;

Security Council Committee established pursuant to resolution 864 (1993) concerning Angola;

Security Council Committee established pursuant to resolution 751 (1992) concerning Somalia;

Security Council Committee established pursuant to resolution 748 (1992) concerning Libya;

Governing Council of the UN Compensation Commission established by Security Council resolution 692 (1991);

Security Council Committee established pursuant to resolution 661 (1990) concerning the situation between Iraq and Kuwait.

INTERNATIONAL TRIBUNALS

In May 1993 the Security Council, acting under Article VII of the UN Charter, adopted resolution 827, which established an *ad hoc* 'war crimes' tribunal. The so-called International Tribunal for the Prosecution of Persons Responsible for Serious Violations of International Humanitarian Law Committed in the Territory of the Former Yugoslavia (also referred to as the International Criminal Tribunal for the former Yugoslavia—ICTY) was inaugurated in The Hague, Netherlands, in November, comprising a prosecutor and 11 judges sitting in two trial chambers and one appeals chamber. Public hearings were initiated in November 1994. In July and November 1995 the Tribunal formally charged the Bosnian Serb political and military leaders Radovan Karadžić and Gen. Ratko Mladić, on two separate indictments, with genocide and crimes against humanity, and in July 1996 issued international warrants for their arrest. The enforcement of arrests has become one of the principal difficulties confronting the ICTY. The first trial proceedings commenced in May 1996, and the first sentence was imposed by the Tribunal in November. By November 1997 75 people had been indicted by the Tribunal, of whom 20 were being held in custody (including one man seized in an operation by multinational forces in July).

In November 1994 the Security Council adopted resolution 955, establishing an International Criminal Tribunal for Rwanda (ICTR) to prosecute persons responsible for genocide and other serious violations of humanitarian law that had been committed in Rwanda and by Rwandans in neighbouring states. The Tribunal was to consist of two three-member trial chambers and one appeals chamber with five additional judges, and was to be served by the same Prosecutor as that of the ICTY. Its temporal jurisdiction was limited to the period 1 January to 31 December 1994. The first plenary session of the Tribunal was held in The Hague in June 1995; formal proceedings at its permanent headquarters in Arusha, Tanzania, were initiated in November. The first trial of persons charged by the Tribunal commenced in January 1997, and sentences were imposed in July. At November 24 people had been charged by the Tribunal and were being held in custody. During the year the proceedings of the ICTR were undermined by reports of mismanagement and the need for administrative reforms.

Both Tribunals are supported by teams of investigators and human rights experts working in the field to collect forensic and other evidence in order to uphold indictments. Evidence of mass graves resulting from large-scale unlawful killings has been uncovered in both regions.

President of the ICTY: GABRIELLE KIRK MCDONALD (USA).
President of the ICTR: LAITY KAMA (Senegal).
Chief Prosecutor: LOUISE ARBOUR (Canada).

Economic and Social Council—ECOSOC

ECOSOC promotes world co-operation on economic, social, cultural and humanitarian problems. (See Charter, p. 13 and p. 17.)

MEMBERS

Fifty-four members are elected by the General Assembly for three-year terms: 18 are elected each year. Membership is allotted by regions as follows: Africa 14 members, western Europe and others 13, Asia 11, Latin America 10, eastern Europe 6.

President: JUAN O. SOMAVÍA (Chile).

ORGANIZATION

The Council, which meets annually for four to five weeks between May and July, alternately in New York and Geneva, is mainly a central policy-making and co-ordinating organ. It has a co-ordinating function between the UN and the specialized agencies, and also makes consultative arrangements with approved voluntary or non-governmental organizations which work within the sphere of its activities. The Council has functional and regional commissions to carry out much of its detailed work.

In November 1997 the General Assembly endorsed a series of recommendations of the Secretary-General to reform the management of the UN, which included plans to consolidate and strengthen the work of ECOSOC. Under the reforms, the Committees on New and Renewable Sources of Energy and Energy for Development and on Natural Resources were to be consolidated into the Commission on Sustainable Development, while the Commissions on Crime Prevention and Criminal Justice and on Narcotic Drugs were to be combined, the Commission on Science and Technology for Development was to become a subsidiary body of the Trade and Development Board of UNCTAD, and the Committee on Economic, Social and Cultural Rights was to report to the Council through the Commission on Human Rights.

SESSIONAL COMMITTEES

Each sessional committee comprises the 54 members of the Council: there is a First (Economic) Committee, a Second (Social) Committee and a Third (Programme and Co-ordination) Committee.

FUNCTIONAL COMMISSIONS

Commission on Crime Prevention and Criminal Justice: f. 1992; aims to formulate an international convention on crime prevention and criminal justice; 40 members.

Commission on Human Rights: f. 1946; seeks greater respect for the basic rights of man, the prevention of discrimination and the protection of minorities; reviews specific instances of human rights violation and dispatches rapporteurs to investigate allegations of abuses in particular countries; provides policy guidance; works on declarations, conventions and other instruments of international law; meets annually for six weeks; 53 members. There is a Sub-Commission on Prevention of Discrimination and Protection of Minorities, comprising working groups on issues such as slavery, indigenous populations, detention and communications.

Commission on Narcotic Drugs: f. 1946; mainly concerned in combating illicit traffic; 53 members. There is a Sub-Commission on Illicit Drug Traffic and Related Matters in the Near and Middle East.

Commission on Population and Development: f. 1946; advises the Council on population matters and their relation to socio-economic conditions; 47 members.

Commission on Science and Technology for Development: f. 1992; works on the restructuring of the UN in the economic, social and related fields; 53 members.

Commission for Social Development: f. 1946 as the Social Commission; advises ECOSOC on issues of social and community development; 46 members.

Commission on the Status of Women: f. 1946; aims at equality of political, economic and social rights for women, and supports the right of women to live free of violence; 45 members.

Commission on Sustainable Development: f. 1993 to oversee integration into the UN's work of the objectives set out in 'Agenda 21', the programme of action agreed by the UN Conference on Environment and Development in June 1992; 53 members.

Statistical Commission: Standardizes terminology and procedure in statistics and promotes the development of national statistics; 24 members.

COMMITTEES AND SUBSIDIARY BODIES

Committee for Development Planning: f. 1965.

Committee on Economic, Social and Cultural Rights: f. 1976.

Committee of Experts on the Transport of Dangerous Goods: f. 1953.

Commission on Human Settlements: f. 1977.

Committee on Natural Resources: f. 1992.

Committee on Negotiations with Intergovernmental Agencies: f. 1946.

Committee on New and Renewable Sources of Energy and Energy for Development: f. 1992.

Committee on Non-Governmental Organizations: f. 1946.

Committee for Programme and Co-ordination: f. 1962.

REGIONAL COMMISSIONS

(see pp. 26–33)

Economic Commission for Africa—ECA.

Economic Commission for Europe—ECE.

Economic Commission for Latin America and the Caribbean—ECLAC.

Economic and Social Commission for Asia and the Pacific—ESCAP.

Economic and Social Commission for Western Asia—ESCWA.

RELATED BODIES

Board of Trustees of the International Research and Training Institute for Women (INSTRAW): 11 members (see p. 24).

International Narcotics Control Board: f. 1964; 13 members.

UNDP Executive Board: 48 members, elected by ECOSOC (see p. 38).

UNHCR Executive Committee: 43 members, elected by ECOSOC (see p. 44).

UNICEF Executive Board: 41 members, elected by ECOSOC (see p. 35).

WFP Executive Board: one-half of the 36 members are elected by ECOSOC, one-half by the FAO; governing body of the World Food Programme (see p. 59).

International Court of Justice

Address: Peace Palace, Carnegieplein 2, 2517 KJ The Hague, Netherlands.

Telephone: (70) 302-23-23; **telex:** 32323; **fax:** (70) 364-99-28; **e-mail:** icj@pi.net; **internet:** http://www.icj–cij.org.

Established in 1945, the Court is the principal judicial organ of the UN. All members of the UN, and also Switzerland and Nauru, are parties to the Statute of the Court. (See Charter, p. 10.)

THE JUDGES

(November 1997; in order of precedence)

	Term Ends*
President: STEPHEN M. SCHWEBEL (USA)	2006
Vice-President: CHRISTOPHER G. WEERAMANTRY (Sri Lanka)	2006
Judges:	
SHIGERU ODA (Japan)	2003
MOHAMMED BEDJAOUI (Algeria)	2006

GILBERT GUILLAUME (France) 2000
RAYMOND RANJEVA (Madagascar) 2000
GÉZA HERCZEGH (Hungary) 2003
SHI JIUYONG (People's Republic of China) 2003
CARL-AUGUST FLEISCHHAUER (Germany) 2003
ABDUL G. KOROMA (Sierra Leone) 2003
VLADLEN S. VERESHCHETIN (Russia) 2006
ROSALYN HIGGINS (United Kingdom) 2000
GONZALO PARRA-ARANGUREN (Venezuela) 2000
PIETER H. KOOIJMANS (Netherlands) 2006
JOSÉ FRANCISCO REZEK (Brazil) 2006
Registrar: EDUARDO VALENCIA-OSPINA (Colombia)
* Each term ends on 5 February of the year indicated.

The Court is composed of 15 judges, each of a different nationality, elected with an absolute majority by both the General Assembly and the Security Council. Representation of the main forms of civilization and the different legal systems of the world are borne in mind in their election. Candidates are nominated by national panels of jurists.

The judges are elected for nine years and may be re-elected; elections for five seats are held every three years. The Court elects its President and Vice-President for each three-year period. Members may not have any political, administrative, or other professional occupation, and may not sit in any case with which they have been otherwise connected than as a judge of the Court. For the purposes of a case, each side—consisting of one or more States—may, unless the Bench already includes a judge with a corresponding nationality, choose a person from outside the Court to sit as a judge on terms of equality with the Members. Judicial decisions are taken by a majority of the judges present, subject to a quorum of nine Members. The President has a casting vote.

FUNCTIONS

The International Court of Justice operates in accordance with a Statute which is an integral part of the UN Charter. Only States may be parties in cases before the Court; those not parties to the Statute may have access in certain circumstances and under conditions laid down by the Security Council.

The Jurisdiction of the Court comprises:

1. All cases which the parties refer to it jointly by special agreement (indicated in the list below by a stroke between the names of the parties).

2. All matters concerning which a treaty or convention in force provides for reference to the Court. About 700 bilateral or multilateral agreements make such provision. Among the more noteworthy: Treaty of Peace with Japan (1951), European Convention for Peaceful Settlement of Disputes (1957), Single Convention on Narcotic Drugs (1961), Protocol relating to the Status of Refugees (1967), Hague Convention on the Suppression of the Unlawful Seizure of Aircraft (1970).

3. Legal disputes between States which have recognized the jurisdiction of the Court as compulsory for specified classes of dispute. Declarations by the following 58 States accepting the compulsory jurisdiction of the Court are in force: Australia, Austria, Barbados, Belgium, Botswana, Bulgaria, Cambodia (Kampuchea), Cameroon, Canada, Colombia, the Democratic Republic of the Congo, Costa Rica, Cyprus, Denmark, the Dominican Republic, Egypt, Estonia, Finland, The Gambia, Greece, Guinea-Bissau, Haiti, Honduras, Hungary, India, Japan, Kenya, Liberia, Liechtenstein, Luxembourg, Madagascar, Malawi, Malta, Mauritius, Mexico, Nauru, the Netherlands, New Zealand, Nicaragua, Nigeria, Norway, Pakistan, Panama, the Philippines, Poland, Portugal, Senegal, Somalia, Spain, Sudan, Suriname, Swaziland, Sweden, Switzerland, Togo, Uganda, the United Kingdom and Uruguay.

Disputes as to whether the Court has jurisdiction are settled by the Court.

Judgments are without appeal, but are binding only for the particular case and between the parties. States appearing before the Court undertake to comply with its Judgment. If a party to a case fails to do so, the other party may apply to the Security Council, which may make recommendations or decide upon measures to give effect to the Judgment.

Advisory opinions on legal questions may be requested by the General Assembly, the Security Council or, if so authorized by the Assembly, other United Nations organs or specialized agencies.

Rules of Court governing procedure are made by the Court under a power conferred by the Statute.

In July 1993 the Court established a seven-member Chamber for Environmental Matters, in view of the world-wide expansion of environmental law and protection.

CONSIDERED CASES

Judgments

Since 1946 more than 70 cases have been referred to the Court by States. Some were removed from the list as a result of settlement or discontinuance, or on the grounds of a lack of basis for jurisdiction. Cases which have been the subject of a Judgment by the Court include: Monetary Gold Removed from Rome in 1943 (Italy *v.* France, United Kingdom and USA); Sovereignty over Certain Frontier Land (Belgium/Netherlands); Arbitral Award made by the King of Spain on 23 December 1906 (Honduras *v.* Nicaragua); Temple of Preah Vihear (Cambodia *v.* Thailand); South West Africa (Ethiopia and Liberia *v.* South Africa); Northern Cameroons (Cameroon *v.* United Kingdom); North Sea Continental Shelf (Federal Republic of Germany/Denmark and Netherlands); Appeal relating to the Jurisdiction of the ICAO Council (India *v.* Pakistan); Fisheries Jurisdiction (United Kingdom *v.* Iceland; Federal Republic of Germany *v.* Iceland); Nuclear Tests (Australia *v.* France; New Zealand *v.* France); Aegean Sea Continental Shelf (Greece *v.* Turkey); United States of America Diplomatic and Consular Staff in Teheran (USA *v.* Iran); Continental Shelf (Tunisia/Libya); Delimitation of the Maritime Boundary in the Gulf of Maine Area (Canada/USA); Continental Shelf (Libya/Malta); Application for revision and interpretation of the Judgment of 24 February 1982 in the case concerning the Continental Shelf (Tunisia *v.* Libya); Military and Paramilitary Activities in and against Nicaragua (Nicaragua *v.* USA); Frontier Dispute (Burkina Faso/Mali); Delimitation of Maritime Boundary (Denmark *v.* Norway); Maritime Boundaries (Guinea-Bissau *v.* Senegal); Elettronica Sicula SpA (USA *v.* Italy); Land, Island and Maritime Frontier Dispute (El Salvador/Honduras) (in one aspect of which Nicaragua was permitted to intervene); Delimitation of Maritime Boundary in the area between Greenland and Jan Mayen island (Denmark *v.* Norway); Maritime Delimitation and Territorial Questions between Qatar and Bahrain (Qatar *v.* Bahrain); Territorial Dispute (Libya/Chad); East Timor (Portugal *v.* Australia); the Gabčíkovo-Nagymaros Hydroelectric Project (Hungary *v.* Slovakia).

The cases remaining under consideration at November 1997 were: cases brought by Libya against the United Kingdom and the USA concerning questions of interpretation and application of the 1971 Montreal Convention arising from the aerial incident at Lockerbie, United Kingdom, in 1988; a case brought by Iran against the USA concerning the destruction of oil platforms; a case brought by Bosnia and Herzegovina against the Federal Republic of Yugoslavia concerning the application of the Convention on the Prevention and Punishment of the Crime of Genocide; a case brought by Cameroon against Nigeria concerning the land and maritime boundary between those two states; a case brought by Spain against Canada concerning Fisheries Jurisdiction; and a case concerning the boundary around Kasikili/Sedudu Island brought by Botswana and Namibia.

Advisory Opinions

Matters on which the Court has delivered an Advisory Opinion at the request of the United Nations General Assembly, or an organ thereof, include the following: Condition of Admission of a State to Membership in the United Nations; Competence of the General Assembly for the Admission of a State to the United Nations; Interpretation of the Peace Treaties with Bulgaria, Hungary and Romania; International Status of South West Africa; Reservations to the Convention on the Prevention and Punishment of the Crime of Genocide; Effect of Awards of Compensation Made by the United Nations Administrative Tribunal (UNAT); Western Sahara; Application for Review of UNAT Judgment No. 333; Applicability of the Obligation to Arbitrate under Section 21 of the United Nations Headquarters Agreement of 26 June 1947 (relating to the closure of the Observer Mission to the United Nations maintained by the Palestine Liberation Organization).

An Advisory Opinion has been given at the request of the Security Council: Legal Consequences for States of the continued presence of South Africa in Namibia (South West Africa) notwithstanding Security Council resolution 276 (1970). In 1989 (at the request of the UN Economic and Social Council) the Court gave an Advisory Opinion on the Applicability of Article 6, Section 22, of the Convention on the Privileges and Immunities of the United Nations.

The Court has also, at the request of UNESCO, given an Advisory Opinion on Judgments of the Administrative Tribunal of the ILO upon Complaints made against UNESCO, and on the Constitution of the Maritime Safety Committee of the Inter-Governmental Maritime Consultative Organization, at the request of IMCO. In July 1996 the Court delivered Advisory Opinions on the Legality of the Use by a State of Nuclear Weapons in Armed Conflict, requested by WHO, and on the Legality of the Use or Threat of Nuclear Weapons, requested by the UN General Assembly.

FINANCE

The annual budget for the Court amounts to approximately US $11m. financed entirely by the United Nations.

PUBLICATIONS

Acts and Documents, No. 5 (contains Statute and Rules of the Court, the Resolution concerning its internal judicial practice and other documents).

Bibliography (annually).

Pleadings (Written Pleadings and Statements, Oral Proceedings, Correspondence): series.

Reports (Judgments, Opinions and Orders): series.

Yearbook (published in 3rd quarter each year).

United Nations Training and Research Institutes

UNITED NATIONS INSTITUTE FOR DISARMAMENT RESEARCH—UNIDIR

Address: Palais des Nations, 1211 Geneva 10, Switzerland.

Telephone: (22) 9173186; **telex:** 412962; **fax:** (22) 9170176; **e-mail:** newsletter@unog.ch.

UNIDIR is an autonomous institution within the United Nations. It was established by the General Assembly in 1980 for the purpose of undertaking independent research on disarmament and related problems, particularly international security issues. UNIDIR's statute became effective on 1 January 1985.

The work of the Institute is based on the following objectives: to provide the international community with more diversified and complete data on problems relating to international security, the armaments race and disarmament in all fields, so as to facilitate progress towards greater global security and towards economic and social development for all peoples; to promote informed participation by all states in disarmament efforts; to assist ongoing negotiations on disarmament, and continuing efforts to ensure greater international security at a progressively lower level of armaments, in particular nuclear weapons, by means of objective studies and analyses; and to conduct long-term research on disarmament in order to provide a general insight into the problems involved and to stimulate new initiatives for negotiations.

The work programme of UNIDIR is reviewed annually and is subject to approval by its Board of Trustees. In 1995 UNIDIR was to focus on three main areas of research: the non-proliferation of weapons of mass destruction; disarmament and conflict resolution processes, in particular the disarmament of warring parties as an integral part of peace-keeping operations; and regional security issues, notably in Latin America, West Africa and Asia. Research projects are conducted within the Institute, or commissioned to individual experts or research organizations. For some major studies, multinational groups of experts are established. The Institute offers internships, in connection with its research programme.

The Institute's budget for 1997 amounted to US $900,000. It is financed mainly by voluntary contributions from governments and public or private organizations. A contribution to the costs of the Director and staff may be provided from the UN regular budget.

The Director of UNIDIR reports annually to the General Assembly on the activities of the Institute. The UN Secretary-General's Advisory Board on Disarmament Studies functions as UNIDIR's Board of Trustees.

Director: Patricia Lewis (United Kingdom).

Publications: *UNIDIR Newsletter* (quarterly); research reports (6 a year); research papers (irregular).

UNITED NATIONS INSTITUTE FOR TRAINING AND RESEARCH—UNITAR

Address: Palais des Nations, 1211 Geneva 10, Switzerland.

Telephone: (22) 7985850; **telex:** 412962; **fax:** (22) 7331383; **e-mail:** unitar@.unicc.bitnet.

UNITAR was established in 1963, as an autonomous body within the United Nations, in order to enhance the effectiveness of the latter body in achieving its major objectives. In recent years the main focus of the Institute has shifted to training, with basic research being conducted only if extra-budgetary funds are made available. Training is provided at various levels for personnel on assignments under the United Nations and its specialized agencies or under organizations operating in related fields. Training programmes comprise courses on multilateral diplomacy and international co-operation. Other programmes, which are funded by special-purpose grants, are offered in environmental and natural resource management, environmental negotiations and dispute resolution, debt management (with special emphasis on the legal aspects) and training in energy and in disaster control. Most training programmes are designed and conducted in Geneva.

UNITAR offers a fellowship programme in peace-making and preventive diplomacy to provide advanced training for international and national civil servants in conflict analysis and mediation. It also organizes, jointly with the UN Office for Legal Affairs, an annual fellowship programme in international law.

By the end of September 1995 more than 24,000 participants from 180 countries had attended courses, seminars or workshops organized by UNITAR. Each year approximately 3,000 people participate in UNITAR training programmes.

UNITAR is financed by voluntary contributions from UN member states, by donations from foundations and other non-governmental sources, and by income generated by its Reserve Fund.

Executive Director: Marcel A. Boisard (Switzerland).

UNITED NATIONS INTERNATIONAL RESEARCH AND TRAINING INSTITUTE FOR THE ADVANCEMENT OF WOMEN—INSTRAW

Address: POB 21747, Santo Domingo, Dominican Republic.

Telephone: 685-2111; **telex:** 326-4280; **fax:** 685-2117; **e-mail:** instraw.hq.sd@codetel.net.do.

The Institute was established by ECOSOC, and endorsed by the General Assembly, in 1976, following a recommendation of the World Conference on the International Women's Year (1975). INSTRAW provides training, conducts research and collects and disseminates relevant information in order to stimulate and to assist the advancement of women and their integration in the development process, both as participants and beneficiaries.

INSTRAW is an autonomous body of the UN, funded by voluntary contributions from UN member states, inter- and non-governmental organizations, foundations and other private sources. An 11-member Board of Trustees meets annually to formulate the principles and guidelines for the activities of INSTRAW and to consider the current work progamme and budget proposals, and reports to ECOSOC. INSTRAW maintains a liaison office at the UN Secretariat in New York.

Director: Yakin Ertürk.

Publications: *INSTRAW News* (2 a year); training materials, research studies.

UNITED NATIONS RESEARCH INSTITUTE FOR SOCIAL DEVELOPMENT—UNRISD

Address: Palais des Nations, 1211 Geneva 10, Switzerland.

Telephone: (22) 7988400; **telex:** 412962; **fax:** (22) 7400791; **e-mail:** info@unrisd.org.

UNRISD was established in 1963 as an autonomous body within the United Nations, to conduct multi-disciplinary research into the social dimensions of contemporary problems affecting development.

The Institute aims to provide governments, development agencies, grass-roots organizations and scholars with a better understanding of how development policies and processes of economic, social and environmental change affect different social groups.

UNRISD's medium-term programme in 1993 included the following research themes: Environment, Sustainable Development and Social Change; Ethnic Diversity and Public Policies; Rebuilding War-torn Societies; Economic Restructuring and Social Policy; Political Violence and Social Movements; Socio-economic and Political Consequences of the International Trade in Illicit Drugs; Participation and Changes in Property Relations in Communist and Post-communist Societies; and Integrating Gender into Development Policy.

UNRISD research is undertaken in collaboration with a network of national research teams drawn from local universities and research institutions. UNRISD aims to promote and strengthen research capacities in developing countries.

The Institute is supported by voluntary grants from governments, and also receives financing from other UN organizations, and from various other national and international agencies.

Director: DHARAM GHAI (Kenya).

Publications: *UNRISD Social Development News* (quarterly), discussion papers and monographs.

UNITED NATIONS UNIVERSITY—UNU

Address: 53–70, Jingumae 5-chome, Shibuya-ku, Tokyo 150-8925, Japan.

Telephone: (3) 3499-2811; **fax:** (3) 3499-2828; **e-mail:** mbox@hq.unu.edu; **internet:** http://www.unu.edu.

The University is sponsored jointly by the United Nations and UNESCO. It is an autonomous institution within the United Nations, guaranteed academic freedom by a charter approved by the General Assembly in 1973. It is governed by a 28-member University Council of scholars and scientists, of whom 24 are appointed by the Secretary-General of the UN and the Director-General of UNESCO (who, together with the Executive Director of UNITAR, are ex-officio members of the Council; the Rector is also on the Council). The University is not traditional in the sense of having students or awarding degrees, but works through networks of collaborating institutions and individuals. These include Associated Institutions (universities and research institutes linked with the UNU under general agreements of co-operation). The UNU undertakes multi-disciplinary research on problems of human survival, development and welfare that are the concern of the United Nations and its agencies, and works to strengthen research and training capabilities in developing countries. It provides post-graduate fellowships for scientists and scholars from developing countries, and conducts various training activities in association with its programme.

The UNU's research and training centres and programmes include the World Institute of Development Economics Research (UNU/WIDER) in Helsinki, Finland, the Institute for New Technologies (UNU/INTECH) in Maastricht, the Netherlands, the International Institute for Software Technology (UNU/IIST) in Macau, the UNU Institute for Natural Resources in Africa in Accra, Ghana (UNU/INRA—with a mineral resources unit in Lusaka, Zambia), the UNU Programme for Biotechnology in Latin America and the Caribbean (UNU/BIOLAC), based in Caracas, Venezuela, the UNU International Leadership Academy (UNU/ILA) in Amman, Jordan, the Institute of Advanced Studies (UNU/IAS), based in Tokyo, Japan, and the UNU International Network on Water, Environment and Health (UNU/INWEH) in Ontario, Canada.

The UNU is financed by voluntary contributions from UN member states. By November 1997 US $342m. had been pledged, of which $312m. had been disbursed.

Rector: Prof. HANS J. A. VAN GINKEL (Netherlands).

Chairman of Council: Prof. JOSÉ JOAQUÍN BRUNNER RIED (Chile).

UNIVERSITY FOR PEACE

Address: POB 138, Ciudad Colón, Costa Rica.

Telephone: 249-1072; **fax:** 249-1929.

The University for Peace was established by the United Nations in 1980 to conduct research on, *inter alia*, disarmament, mediation, the resolution of conflicts, the preservation of the environment, international relations, peace education and human rights. In October 1991 there were 48 students from many different countries at the University, and 20 permanent and 25 visiting professors.

Rector: Dr JAIME MONTALVO CORREA (Spain).

Publications: *Dialogue*, *Infopaz*.

UNITED NATIONS REGIONAL COMMISSIONS

Economic Commission for Europe—ECE

Address: Palais des Nations, 1211 Geneva 10, Switzerland.

Telephone: (22) 9174444; **telex:** 412962; **fax:** (22) 9170505; **e-mail:** info.ece@unece.org; **internet:** http://www.unece.org.

The UN Economic Commission for Europe was established in 1947. Representatives of all European countries, the USA, Canada, Israel and central Asian republics study the economic, environmental and technological problems of the region and recommend courses of action. ECE is also active in the formulation of international legal instruments and the setting of international standards.

MEMBERS

Albania	Liechtenstein
Andorra	Lithuania
Armenia	Luxembourg
Austria	Macedonia, former Yugoslav republic
Azerbaijan	Malta
Belarus	Moldova
Belgium	Monaco
Bosnia and Herzegovina	Netherlands
Bulgaria	Norway
Canada	Poland
Croatia	Portugal
Cyprus	Romania
Czech Republic	Russia
Denmark	San Marino
Estonia	Slovakia
Finland	Slovenia
France	Spain
Georgia	Sweden
Germany	Switzerland
Greece	Tajikistan
Hungary	Turkey
Iceland	Turkmenistan
Ireland	Ukraine
Israel	United Kingdom
Italy	USA
Kazakhstan	Uzbekistan
Kyrgyzstan	Yugoslavia
Latvia	

Organization

(December 1997)

COMMISSION

ECE, with ECAFE (now ESCAP), was the earliest of the five regional economic commissions set up by the UN Economic and Social Council. The Commission holds an annual plenary session and several informal sessions, and meetings of subsidiary bodies are convened throughout the year.

President: Péter Náray (Hungary).

SECRETARIAT

The Secretariat services the meetings of the Commission and its subsidiary bodies and publishes periodic surveys and reviews, including a number of specialized statistical bulletins on coal, timber, steel, chemicals, housing and building, electric power, gas, general energy and transport (see list of publications below). It maintains close and regular liaison with the United Nations Secretariat in New York, with the secretariats of the other UN regional commissions and of other UN organizations, including the UN Specialized Agencies, and with other intergovernmental organizations. The Executive Secretary also carries out secretarial functions for the executive body of the 1979 Convention on Long-range Transboundary Air Pollution and its protocols. The ECE and UN Secretariats also service the ECOSOC Committee of Experts on the Transport of Dangerous Goods.

Executive Secretary: Yves Berthelot (France).

Activities

The guiding principle of ECE activities is the promotion of sustainable development. Within this framework, ECE's main objectives are to provide assistance to countries of central and eastern Europe in their transition from centrally-planned to market economies and to achieve the integration of all members into the European and global economies. Environmental protection, transport, statistics, trade facilitation and economic analysis are all principal topics in the ECE work programme, which also includes activities in the fields of timber, energy, trade, industry, science and technology, and human settlements. A programme of workshops was initiated in the early 1990s; by October 1995 more than 175 workshops had been held, mostly in the countries in transition.

The 50th annual session of the ECE, held in April 1997, introduced a programme of reform, reducing the number of principal subsidiary bodies from 14 to seven in order to concentrate resources on the core areas of work listed below, assisted by sub-committees and groups of experts.

Committee on Environmental Policy: Provides policy direction for the ECE region and promotes co-operation among member governments in developing and implementing policies for environmental protection, rational use of natural resources, and sustainable development; seeks solutions to environmental problems, particularly those of a transboundary nature; assists in strengthening environmental management capabilities, particularly in countries in transition; prepares ministerial conferences (normally held every three years—1998: Denmark); develops and promotes the implementation of international agreements on the environment; and assesses national policies and legislation.

Committee on Human Settlements: Reviews trends and policies in the field of human settlements. Undertakes studies and organizes seminars on these issues. Promotes international co-operation in the field of urban and regional research. Assists the countries of central and eastern Europe, which are currently in the process of economic transition, in reformulating their policies relating to housing, land management, sustainable human settlements, and planning and development.

Committee on Sustainable Energy: Exchanges information on general energy problems; work programme comprises energy policies and prospects; demand and supply; trade and co-operation; conservation; statistics; the project 'Energy Efficiency 2000'; the technical co-operation programme 'Promotion and Development of a Market-based Gas Industry in Economies in Transition'; and the Implementing Programme on Accelerating Clean Coal Technology (IMPACCT).

Committee for Trade, Industry and Enterprise Development: A forum for studying means of expanding and diversifying trade among European countries, as well as with countries in other regions, and for drawing up recommendations on how to achieve these ends. Analyses trends, problems and prospects in intra-European trade; explores means of encouraging the flow of international direct investment, including joint ventures, into the newly opening economies of central and eastern Europe; promotes new or improved methods of trading by means of marketing, industrial co-operation, contractual guides, and the facilitation of international trade procedures (notably by developing and diffusing electronic data interchange standards and messages for administration, commerce and transport—EDIFACT).

Conference of European Statisticians: Promotes improvement of national statistics and their international comparability in economic, social, demographic and environmental fields; promotes co-ordination of statistical activities of European international organizations; and responds to the increasing need for international statistical co-operation both within the ECE region and between the region and other regions. Works very closely with the OECD and the EU.

Inland Transport Committee: Prepares, updates and supplements international agreements, conventions and other instruments covering a wide range of questions relating to road, rail, inland water and combined transport, including infrastructure, border-crossing facilitation and international harmonization of regulations, particularly in the fields of transport of dangerous goods and perishable foodstuffs, road traffic safety and requirements for the construction of road vehicles. Also considers transport trends and economics and compiles transport statistics. Assists central and eastern European countries in developing their transport systems and infrastructures.

Timber Committee: Regularly reviews markets for forest products; analyses long-term trends and prospects for forestry and timber; keeps under review developments in the forest industries, including environmental and energy-related aspects. Subsidiary bodies run jointly with the FAO deal with forest technology, management and training and with forest economics and statistics.

ECE also co-ordinates the following advisory groups:

Senior Economic Advisers to ECE Governments: Brings together high-level governmental experts for an exchange of views on current, medium- and long-term economic development; organizes groups of experts, workshops and seminars. The current focus is on the analysis of selected structural issues, including the relationship between structural change, employment and unemployment in the market and transition economies, the inter-relationship between economics and the environment, and the integration of central and eastern European countries into the European and world economies.

Senior Advisers to ECE Governments on Science and Technology: Forum for exchange of experience in formulation and implementation of policies on science and technology. Major activities include: review of changes in national science and technology policies; compilation of science and technology statistics for economies in transition; promotion of innovation; and safety aspects in biotechnology.

BUDGET

ECE's provisional budget for the two years 1998-99 was estimated at US $49.3m.

PUBLICATIONS

ECE Annual Report.
Annual Bulletin of Housing and Building Statistics for Europe.
Annual Bulletin of Steel Statistics for Europe.
Annual Bulletin of Trade in Chemical Products.
Annual Bulletin of Transport Statistics for Europe.
Directory of Chemical Producers and Products.
Discussion Papers (quarterly).
Economic Bulletin for Europe.
Economic Survey of Europe.
Statistics of Road Traffic Accidents in Europe.
Statistics of World Trade in Steel.
The Steel Market.
Timber Bulletin for Europe.
Transport Information.
Trends in Europe and North America: Statistical Yearbook of the ECE (annually).
UN Manual of Tests and Criteria of Dangerous Goods.
UN Recommendations on the Transport of Dangerous Goods.
Series of studies on air pollution, the environment, forestry and timber, water, trade facilitation, industrial co-operation, energy, joint ventures, and economic reforms in eastern Europe.
Reports, proceedings of meetings, technical documents, codes of conduct, codes of practice, guidelines to governments, etc.

Economic and Social Commission for Asia and the Pacific—ESCAP

Address: United Nations Bldg, Rajdamnern Ave, Bangkok 10200, Thailand.

Telephone: (2) 288-1866; **telex:** 82392; **fax:** (2) 288-1052; **e-mail:** unisbkk.unescap@un.org; **internet:** http://www.un.org/depts/escap.

The Commission was founded in 1947 to encourage the economic and social development of Asia and the Far East; it was originally known as the Economic Commission for Asia and the Far East (ECAFE). The title ESCAP, which replaced ECAFE, was adopted after a reorganization in 1974.

MEMBERS

Afghanistan	Korea, Democratic People's Republic	Papua New Guinea
Armenia		Philippines
Australia	Korea, Republic	Russia
Azerbaijan	Kyrgyzstan	Samoa
Bangladesh	Laos	Singapore
Bhutan	Malaysia	Solomon Islands
Brunei	Maldives	Sri Lanka
Cambodia	Marshall Islands	Tajikistan
China, People's Republic	Micronesia, Federated States	Thailand
		Tonga
Fiji	Mongolia	Turkey
France	Myanmar	Turkmenistan
India	Nauru	Tuvalu
Indonesia	Nepal	United Kingdom
Iran	Netherlands	USA
Japan	New Zealand	Uzbekistan
Kazakhstan	Pakistan	Vanuatu
Kiribati	Palau	Viet Nam

ASSOCIATE MEMBERS

American Samoa	Hong Kong	Northern Mariana Islands
Cook Islands	Macau	
French Polynesia	New Caledonia	
Guam	Niue	

Organization

(December 1997)

COMMISSION

The Commission meets annually at ministerial level to examine the region's problems, to review progress, to establish priorities and to launch new projects.

Ministerial and inter-governmental conferences on specific issues may be held on an *ad hoc* basis with the approval of the Commission.

COMMITTEES AND SPECIAL BODIES

The following advise the Commission and help to oversee the work of the Secretariat:

Committee on the Environment and Natural Resources Development: meets annually.

Committee on Regional Economic-Co-operation: meets annually, prior to the session of the Commission, with a steering group, which meets twice a year, or as often as required.

Committee on Socio-economic Measures to Alleviate Poverty in Rural and Urban Areas: meets annually.

Committee on Statistics: meets annually.

Committee on Transport, Communications, Tourism and Infrastructure Development: meets annually.

Special Body on Least-Developed and Land-locked Developing Countries: meets every two years.

Special Body on Pacific Island Developing Countries: meets every two years.

In addition, an Advisory Committee of permanent representatives and other representatives designated by members of the Commission functions as an advisory body.

SECRETARIAT

Executive Secretary: Dr Adrianus Mooy (Indonesia).

The Secretariat operates under the guidance of the Commission and its subsidiary bodies. It consists of two servicing divisions, covering administration and programme management, in addition to the following substantive divisions: international trade and economic co-operation; industry and technology; environment and natural resources management; social development; population; rural and urban development; transport, communications and tourism; statistics; and development research and policy analysis.

The Secretariat also includes the ESCAP/UNCTAD Joint Unit on Transnational Corporations and the UN information services. In 1995/96 work continued on the establishment of an ESCAP Statistical Information System (ESIS) within the Secretariat.

SUB-REGIONAL OFFICE

ESCAP Pacific Operations Centre (ESCAP/POC): Port Vila, Vanuatu; f. 1984, to provide effective advisory and technical assistance at a sub-regional level and to identify the needs of island countries. Dir Savenaca Siwatibau.

Activities

ESCAP acts as a UN regional centre, providing the only intergovernmental forum for the whole of Asia and the Pacific, and executing a wide range of development programmes through technical assistance, advisory services to governments, research, training and information.

In 1992 ESCAP began to reorganize its programme activities and conference structures in order to reflect and serve the region's evolving development needs. The approach that was adopted focused on regional economic co-operation, poverty alleviation through economic growth and social development, and environmental and sustainable development. Accordingly, the following structure of sub-programmes came into effect in 1994:

Sub-programme on regional economic co-operation: in April 1992, meeting in Beijing for its annual session, ESCAP adopted a Declaration on Regional Economic Co-operation in which it advocated 'concrete measures for enhancing regional co-operation', specifically intra-regional trade and investment, science and technology and infrastructure. The sub-programme provides a framework for co-operation and the exchange of information between ESCAP countries.

In September 1992 ESCAP sponsored a conference on regional trade promotion, attended by representatives from Bangladesh, the People's Republic of China, India, the Republic of Korea, Malaysia, the Philippines, Sri Lanka, Thailand and Viet Nam. It was agreed at the conference to establish a regional chamber of commerce and industry.

Sub-programme on environment and sustainable development: aims to alleviate environmental problems and encourage sustainable development by integrating environmental considerations into the economic planning and other development processes. ESCAP publishes studies on specific development issues and on the environmental impact of activities such as human settlement or forestry and mineral exploitation. In November 1995 ESCAP organized a Ministerial Conference on Environment and Development in Asia and the Pacific, which reviewed a comprehensive assessment of the state of the environment in the region and adopted an Action Programme for Environmentally Sound and Sustainable Development for the period 1996–2000.

Sub-programme on poverty alleviation through economic growth and social development: is concerned with increasing the understanding of social problems and improving the quality and availability of data and analyses of social plans, issues and problems relating to the entrenched nature of poverty and its eradication. ESCAP aims to encourage the participation in development by disadvantaged groups, namely the disabled, women, the young and the elderly. In June 1994 the second Asian and Pacific Ministerial Conference on women in development was convened in Jakarta, Indonesia. In October a Ministerial Conference was held in Manila, the Philippines, as a preparatory meeting for the UN world summit for social development, which took place in Copenhagen, Denmark, in March 1995.

Sub-programme on transport and communications: aims to identify the problems of transport, communications and tourism in the region and to develop feasible solutions for strengthened infrastructure. Intergovernmental meetings of road experts are regularly held by ESCAP to discuss road transport. The Asian Highway Network Project comprises a network of 65,000 km of roads in 15 countries; ESCAP publishes maps of the network and reports on its development. ESCAP also publishes manuals on labour-intensive rural road construction and maintenace, and conducts training courses for officials in charge of road-works. ESCAP aims to help developing maritime members to adopt up-to-date technology in shipping, ports and inland waterways, and gives technical assistance to member countries for modernizing railways. An Asia-Pacific Railway Co-operation Group was established by transport ministers in 1983. ESCAP also assists member countries in matters relating to integrated transport planning, urban transport, the environmental impact of transport planning, and the facilitation of international traffic.

Sub-programme on statistics: undertakes to develop and improve the national capabilities of member countries to identify, collect, process, analyse and utilize the data needed for the formulation, monitoring and evaluation of development programmes. ESCAP also collects and publishes a wide range of statistical information on the Asia-Pacific region. The Statistical Institute for Asia and the Pacific (see below) operates under the auspices of ESCAP.

Sub-programme on least-developed, land-locked and island developing countries: assists these groups of countries to enhance their institutional capabilities for implementing macro-economic policies. The sub-programme also assists in the formulation and implementation of development plans and policies aimed at accelerating and sustaining development in these countries, while recognizing specific difficulties they may encounter.

CO-OPERATION WITH THE ASIAN DEVELOPMENT BANK

In July 1993 a memorandum of understanding was signed by ESCAP and the Asian Development Bank (ADB—q.v.), outlining priority areas of co-operation between the two organizations. These were: regional and sub-regional co-operation; issues concerning the least-developed, land-locked and island developing member countries; poverty alleviation; women in development; population; human resource development; the environment and natural resource management; statistics and data bases; economic analysis; transport and communications; and industrial restructuring and privatization. The two organizations were to co-operate in organizing workshops, seminars and conferences, in implementing joint projects, and in exchanging information and data on a regular basis.

ASSOCIATED BODIES

Asian and Pacific Centre for Transfer of Technology: Off New Mehrauli Rd, POB 4575, New Delhi 110 016, India; tel. (11) 6856276; fax (11) 6856274; e-mail postmaster@apctt.org; f. 1977 to assist countries of the ESCAP region by strengthening their capacity to develop, transfer and adopt technologies relevant to the region, and to identify and to promote regional technology development and transfer. Dir Dr Jürgen Bischoff. Publs *Asia Pacific Tech Monitor* (every 2 months), *VATIS Update on Biotechnology, Food Processing, Ozone Layer Protection* (every 2 months), *Non-Conventional Energy, Waste Technology* (every 2 months).

ESCAP/WMO Typhoon Committee: c/o UNDP, POB 7285, ADC, Pasay City, Metro Manila, Philippines; tel. (2) 9228055; telex 66682; fax (2) 9228413; e-mail tcs@cyber.cyb-live.com; f. 1968; an intergovernmental body sponsored by ESCAP and WMO for mitigation of typhoon damage. It aims at establishing efficient typhoon and flood warning systems through improved meteorological and telecommunication facilities. Other activities include promotion of disaster preparedness, training of personnel and co-ordination of research. The committee's programme is supported from national resources and also by UNDP and other international and bilateral assistance. Mems: Cambodia, People's Republic of China, Hong Kong, Japan, Democratic People's Republic of Korea, Republic of Korea, Laos, Macau, Malaysia, the Philippines, Thailand, Viet Nam. Co-ordinator of Secretariat: Dr Roman L. Kintanar.

Regional Co-ordination Centre for Research and Development of Coarse Grains, Pulses, Roots and Tuber Crops in the Tropics of Asia and the Pacific (CGPRT Centre): Jalan Merdeka 145, Bogor 16111, Indonesia; tel. (251) 343277; fax (251) 336290; e-mail cgprt@server.indo.net.id; internet http://www.cgprt.org.sg; f. 1981; initiates and promotes research, training and publications on the production, marketing and use of these crops. Dir Haruo Inagaki. Publs *Palawija News* (quarterly), working paper series and monograph series.

Statistical Institute for Asia and the Pacific: Akasaka POB 13, Tokyo 107–91, Japan; tel. (3) 3357-8351; telex 32217; fax (3) 3356-8305; f. 1970; trains government statisticians; prepares teaching materials, provides facilities for special studies and research of a statistical nature, assists in the development of statistical education and training at all levels in national and sub-regional centres. Dir Lau Kak En.

WMO/ESCAP Panel on Tropical Cyclones: Technical Support Unit, Abhawa Bhaban, Agargon, Dhaka 1207, Bangladesh; f. 1973 to mitigate damage caused by tropical cyclones in the Bay of Bengal and the Arabian Sea; mems: Bangladesh, India, Maldives, Myanmar, Pakistan, Sri Lanka, Thailand.

FINANCE

For the two-year period 1996–97 ESCAP's regular budget, an appropriation from the UN budget, was US $67.5m., compared with $59.8m. for 1994–95. The regular budget is supplemented annually by funds from various sources for technical assistance.

PUBLICATIONS

Economic and Social Survey of Asia and the Pacific (annually).

Agricultural Information Development Bulletin (quarterly).

Agro-chemicals News in Brief (quarterly).

Asia-Pacific Population Journal.

Atlas of Mineral Resources of the ESCAP Region.

Atlas of Stratigraphy.

Confluence (water resources newsletter).

Development Papers (occasional).

Economic Bulletin (2 a year).

Electric Power in Asia and the Pacific (2 a year).

ESCAP Energy News.

Fertilizer Trade Information (monthly).

Guidebook to Water Resources, Use and Management in Asia and the Pacific.

Industry and Technology Development News for Asia and the Pacific.

Quarterly Bulletin of Statistics for Asia and the Pacific.

Review of Developments in Shipping, Ports and Inland Waterways.
Sample Surveys in the ESCAP Region (annually).
Small Industry Bulletin for Asia and the Pacific.
Statistical Yearbook for Asia and the Pacific.
Transport and Communications Bulletin for Asia and the Pacific.
Water Resources Journal.
Bibliographies; trade profiles; commodity prices; statistics.

Economic Commission for Latin America and the Caribbean—ECLAC

Address: Edif. Naciones Unidas, Avda Dag Hammarskjöld, Casilla 179D, Santiago, Chile.

Telephone: (2) 2102000; **telex:** 340295; **fax:** (2) 2080252; **e-mail:** webmaster@eclac.cl; **internet:** http://www.eclac.org.

The UN Economic Commission for Latin America was founded in 1948 to co-ordinate policies for the promotion of economic development in the Latin American region. In 1984 the title 'Economic Commission for Latin America and the Caribbean' was adopted.

MEMBERS

Antigua and Barbuda	El Salvador	Portugal
Argentina	France	Saint Christopher and Nevis
Bahamas	Grenada	Saint Lucia
Barbados	Guatemala	Saint Vincent and the Grenadines
Belize	Guyana	Spain
Bolivia	Haiti	Suriname
Brazil	Honduras	Trinidad and Tobago
Canada	Italy	United Kingdom
Chile	Jamaica	USA
Colombia	Mexico	Uruguay
Costa Rica	Netherlands	Venezuela
Cuba	Nicaragua	
Dominica	Panama	
Dominican Republic	Paraguay	
Ecuador	Peru	

ASSOCIATE MEMBERS

Anguilla	Montserrat	Puerto Rico
Aruba	Netherlands Antilles	United States Virgin Islands
British Virgin Islands		

Organization

(January 1998)

COMMISSION

The Commission normally meets every two years in one of the Latin American capitals. The 27th session of the Commission was to take place in Aruba in May 1998; the chief topic of debate was to be fiscal management. The Commission has established the following permanent bodies:

Caribbean Development and Co-operation Committee.

Central American Development and Co-operation Committee.

Committee of High-Level Government Experts.

Committee of the Whole.

Regional Conference on the Integration of Women into the Economic and Social Development of Latin America and the Caribbean.

Regional Council for Planning.

SECRETARIAT

The Executive Secretariat employs some 555 staff and comprises the Office of the Executive Secretary; the Programme Planning and Operations Division; the Office of the Secretary of the Commission, which includes the Women and Development Unit and the Conference Service Unit; and the UN Information Services in Santiago, Chile.

Work in specific fields is carried out by divisions of the Secretariat as indicated below under 'Activities'. The work of the Secretariat is supported by a library, a computer centre, a documents and publications division and an Economic and Social Documentation Centre (CLADES).

ECLAC has two sub-regional headquarters: one in Mexico, covering Central America and the Spanish-speaking Caribbean; and the other in Port of Spain, Trinidad and Tobago, covering the remainder of the Caribbean. There are also offices in Bogotá, Brasília, Buenos Aires, Montevideo and Washington.

Executive Secretary: JOSÉ ANTONIO OCAMPO (Colombia).

Activities

ECLAC collaborates with regional governments in the investigation and analysis of regional and national economic problems, and provides guidance in the formulation of development plans. Many of its activities are undertaken in co-operation with other UN agencies. Under the programme headings listed below, ECLAC conducts: research; analysis; publication of information; provision of technical assistance; participation in seminars and conferences; training courses; and co-operation with national, regional and international organizations.

Economic and Institutional Policy and Reform
Environmental and Land Resource Sustainability
Integration, Open Regionalism and Regional Co-operation
Links with Global Economic Competitiveness and Production Specialization
Population and Development
Productive, Technological and Entrepreneurial Development
Social Foundations of Economic Development
Statistics and Economic Projections
Strategic Administration and State Reform
Subregional Activities in the Caribbean
Subregional Activities in Mexico and Central America

In April 1992 the Secretariat prepared a proposal for the consideration of member states on how to promote economic growth by changing production patterns, while simultaneously dealing with the grave social inequality existing in Latin America and the Caribbean. A second proposal considered the vital role of human resources training, and suggested changes which need to be introduced in the educational systems of the region. The Commission presented three further proposals regarding the region's development in April 1994. The first was concerned with 'open regionalism' and explored policies and instruments that might assist countries in making further progress in implementing existing integration agreements. The second proposal was concerned with policies to improve the region's integration into the world economy; and the third offered guidelines for preparations in the region for the World Summit on Social Development, held in Copenhagen in 1995.

Latin American and Caribbean Institute for Economic and Social Planning—ILPES: Edif. Naciones Unidas, Avda Dag Hammarskjöld, Casilla 1567, Santiago, Chile; tel. (2) 2102506; fax (2) 2066104; e-mail pdekock@eclac.cl; f. 1962; supports regional governments through the provision of training, advisory services and research in the field of public planning policy and co-ordination. Dir ARTURO NÚÑEZ DEL PRADO.

Latin American Demographic Centre—CELADE: Edif. Naciones Unidas, Avda Dag Hammarskjöld, Casilla 91, Santiago, Chile; tel. (2) 2102023; telex 340295; fax (2) 2080252; f. 1957, became an integral part of the Commission in 1975; provides technical assistance to governments, universities and research centres in demographic analysis, population policies, integration of population factors in development planning, and data processing; conducts three-month courses on demographic analysis for development and various national and regional seminars; provides demographic estimates and projections, documentation, data processing, computer packages and training. Dir REYNALDO F. BAJRAJ.

BUDGET

ECLAC's share of the UN budget for the two years 1996–97 was US $90.6m. In addition, voluntary extra-budgetary contributions are received, which were estimated to total $17.7m. for the same period.

PUBLICATIONS

Boletín del Banco de Datos del CELADE (annually).
Boletín demográfico (2 a year).
Boletín de Facilitación del Comercio y el Transporte (every 2 months).
CEPAL Review (Spanish and English, 3 a year).
CEPALINDEX (annually).
Co-operation and Development (Spanish and English, quarterly).
DOCPAL Resúmenes (population studies, 2 a year).
ECLAC Chronicle (monthly).
Economic Panorama of Latin America (annually).
Economic Survey of Latin America and the Caribbean (Spanish and English, annually).
Notas de Población (2 a year).
Notas sobre la Economía y el Desarrollo (monthly).
PLANINDEX (2 a year).
Preliminary Overview of the Economy of Latin America and the Caribbean (annually).
Social Panorama of Latin America (annually).
Statistical Yearbook for Latin America and the Caribbean (Spanish and English, annually).
Studies, reports, bibliographical bulletins.

Economic Commission for Africa—ECA

Address: Africa Hall, POB 3005, Addis Ababa, Ethiopia.
Telephone: (1) 517200; **telex:** 21029; **fax:** (1) 512233; **e-mail:** ecainfo@un.org; **internet:** http://www.un.org/depts/eca.

The UN Economic Commission for Africa was founded in 1958 by a resolution of ECOSOC to initiate and take part in measures for facilitating Africa's economic development.

MEMBERS

Algeria	Eritrea	Niger
Angola	Ethiopia	Nigeria
Benin	Gabon	Rwanda
Botswana	The Gambia	São Tomé and Príncipe
Burkina Faso	Ghana	Senegal
Burundi	Guinea	Seychelles
Cameroon	Guinea-Bissau	Sierra Leone
Cape Verde	Kenya	Somalia
Central African Republic	Lesotho	South Africa
Chad	Liberia	Sudan
Comoros	Libya	Swaziland
Congo, Democratic Republic	Madagascar	Tanzania
Congo, Republic	Malawi	Togo
Côte d'Ivoire	Mali	Tunisia
Djibouti	Mauritania	Uganda
Egypt	Mauritius	Zambia
Equatorial Guinea	Morocco	Zimbabwe
	Mozambique	
	Namibia	

Organization

(November 1997)

COMMISSION

The Commission may only act with the agreement of the government of the country concerned. It is also empowered to make recommendations on any matter within its competence directly to the government of the member or associate member concerned, to governments admitted in a consultative capacity, and to the UN Specialized Agencies. The Commission is required to submit for prior consideration by ECOSOC any of its proposals for actions that would be likely to have important effects on the international economy.

CONFERENCE OF MINISTERS

The Conference, which meets every two years, is attended by ministers responsible for economic or financial affairs, planning and development of governments of member states, and is the main deliberative body of the Commission.

The Commission's responsibility to promote concerted action for the economic and social development of Africa is vested primarily in the Conference, which considers matters of general policy and the priorities to be assigned to the Commission's programmes, considers inter-African and international economic policy, and makes recommendations to member states in connection with such matters.

OTHER POLICY-MAKING BODIES

A Conference of Ministers of Finance and a Conference of Ministers responsible for economic and social development and planning meet in alternate years to formulate policy recommendations. Each is served by a committee of experts. Five intergovernmental committees of experts attached to the Subregional Development Centres (see below) meet annually and report to the Commission through a Technical Preparatory Committee of the Whole, which was established in 1979 to deal with matters submitted for the consideration of the Conference.

Seven other committees meet regularly to consider issues relating to the following policy areas: women and development; development information; sustainable development; human development and civil society; industry and private sector development; natural resources and science and technology; and regional co-operation and integration.

SECRETARIAT

The Secretariat provides the services necessary for the meeting of the Conference of Ministers and the meetings of the Commission's subsidiary bodies, carries out the resolutions and implements the programmes adopted there. It comprises an Office of the Executive Secretary and the following eight divisions: Food Security and Sustainable Development; Development Management; Development Information Services; Regional Co-operation and Integration; Programme Planning, Finance and Evaluation; Economic and Social Policy; Human Resources and System Management; Conference and General Services.

Executive Secretary: KINGSLEY Y. AMOAKO (Ghana).

SUBREGIONAL DEVELOPMENT CENTRES

Multinational Programming and Operational Centres (MULPOC) were established to implement regional development programmes, being located in Yaoundé, Cameroon (serving central Africa), Gisenyi, Rwanda (Great Lakes Community), Lusaka, Zambia (east and southern Africa), Niamey, Niger (west Africa) and Tangier, Morocco (north Africa). In May 1997 the Commission decided to transform the MULPOCs into Subregional Development Centres (SRDCs) in order to enable member states to play a more effective role in the process of African integration and to facilitate the integration efforts of the other UN agencies active in the subregions. In addition, the SRDCs were to act as the operational arms of ECA at national and subregional levels: to ensure harmony between the objectives of subregional and regional programmes and those defined by the Commission; to provide advisory services; to facilitate subregional economic co-operation, integration and development; to collect and disseminate information; to stimulate policy dialogue; and to promote gender issues. In July 1997 it was reported that ECA intended to deploy 25% of its professional personnel in the SRDCs (up from 9%) and to allocate approximately 40% of its budget to the Centres.

Activities

The Commission's activities are designed to encourage sustainable socio-economic development in Africa and to increase economic co-operation among African countries and between Africa and other parts of the world. The Secretariat is guided in its efforts by major regional strategies including the Abuja Treaty establishing the African Economic Community signed under the aegis of the Organization of African Unity and the UN New Agenda for the Development of Africa covering the period 1991–2000. ECA's main programme areas for the period 1996–2001 were based on an Agenda for Action, which was announced by the OAU Council of Ministers in March 1995 and adopted by African heads of state in June, with the stated aim of 'relaunching Africa's economic and social development'. The five overall objectives were to facilitate economic and social policy analysis and implementation; to ensure food security and sustainable development; to strengthen development management; to harness information for development; and to promote regional co-operation and integration.

DEVELOPMENT INFORMATION SERVICES

The Pan-African Documentation and Information Service (PADIS) was established in 1980. The main objectives of PADIS are: to provide access to numerical and other information on African social, economic, scientific and technological development issues; to assist African countries in their efforts to develop national information handling capabilities through advisory services and training; to establish a data communication network to facilitate the timely use of information on development; and to design sound technical specifications, norms and standards to minimize technical barriers in the exchange of information. ECA is promoting the use of electronic systems to disseminate information throughout the region, under its commitment for the period 1996–2001 to harness information for development purposes. ECA aims to co-ordinate the implementation of the African Information Society Initiative (AISI), a framework for creating an information and communications infrastructure. In addition, ECA encourages member governments to liberalize the telecommunications sector and stimulate imports of computers in order to enable the expansion of information technology throughout Africa.

ECA also promotes the development and co-ordination of national statistical services in the region and undertakes the collection, evaluation and dissemination of statistical information. ECA's work in the field of statistics has been concentrated in five main areas: the African Household Survey Capability Programme, which aims to assist in the collection and analysis of demographic, social and economic data on households; the Statistical Training Programme for Africa, which aims to make the region self-sufficient in statistical personnel at all levels; the Technical Support Services, which provide technical advisory services for population censuses, demographic surveys and civil registration; the National Accounts Capability Programme, which aims at improving economic statistics generally by building up a capability in each country for the collection, processing and analysis of economic data; and the ECA-Regional Statistical Data Base, part of PADIS, which provides on-line statistical information to users. In 1997 ECA planned to upgrade its statistical database in order to provide a data services centre for the region.

ECA assists its member states in (i) population data collection and data processing; (ii) analysis of demographic data obtained from censuses or surveys; (iii) training demographers at the Regional Institute for Population Studies (RIPS) in Accra, Ghana, and at the Institut de formation et de recherche démographiques (IFORD) in Yaoundé, Cameroon; (iv) formulation of population policies and integrating population variables in development planning, through advisory missions and through the organization of national seminars on population and development; and (v) dissemination of information through its *Newsletter, Demographic Handbook for Africa,* the *African Population Studies* series and other publications. The strengthening of national population policies was an important element of ECA's objective of ensuring food security in African countries. The Ninth Joint Conference of African Planners, Statisticians and Demographers was held in March 1996, in Addis Ababa, Ethiopia.

DEVELOPMENT MANAGEMENT AND HUMAN RESOURCES

ECA aims to assist governments, public corporations, universities and the private sector in improving their financial management; strengthening policy-making and analytical capacities; adopting measures to redress skill shortages; enhancing human resources development and utilization; and promoting social development through programmes focusing on youth, people with disabilities and the elderly. The Secretariat organizes training workshops, seminars and conferences at national, subregional and regional levels for ministers, public administrators and senior policy-makers, as well as for private and non-governmental organizations. In 1997 ECA was planning to establish a resource centre for private and non-governmental organizations in order to enhance further its technical assistance and training capabilities. ECA aims to increase the participation of women in economic development and incorporates this objective into its administrative activities and work programmes.

ECONOMIC AND SOCIAL POLICY

The Economic and Social Policy division concentrates on the following three areas: economic policy analysis and research, social policy and development, and special issues. Monitoring economic and social trends in the African region and studying the development problems concerning it are among the fundamental tasks of the Commission, while the special issues programme updates legislative bodies regarding the progress made in the implementation of initiatives affecting the continent. Every year the Commission publishes the *Survey of Economic and Social Conditions in Africa* and the *Economic Report on Africa*.

The Commission gives assistance to governments in general economic analysis, fiscal, financial and monetary management, trade liberalization, regional integration and planning. The ECA's work on economic planning has been broadened in recent years, in order to give more emphasis to macro-economic management in a mixed economy approach: a project is being undertaken to develop short-term forecasting and policy models to support economic management. The Commission has also undertaken a major study of the informal sector in African countries. Special assistance is given to least-developed, land-locked and island countries which have a much lower income level than other countries and which are faced with heavier constraints. Studies are also undertaken to assist longer-term planning.

In 1989 ECA published a report which argued that programmes of strict economic reform, as imposed by the International Monetary Fund and the World Bank, had not resulted in sustained economic growth in Africa over the preceding decade. In July 1991 ECA proposed a series of measures advocating a more flexible approach to long-term development. These proposals were subsequently published under the title *Selected Policy Instruments* and included multiple exchange rates (as opposed to generalized currency devaluation), differential interest rates and subsidies to agricultural producers.

In May 1994 ECA ministers of economic and social development and of planning, meeting in Addis Ababa, adopted a *Framework Agenda for Building and Utilizing Critical Capacities in Africa.* The agenda aimed to identify new priority areas to stimulate development by, for example, strengthening management structures, a more efficient use of a country's physical infrastructure and by expanding processing or manufacturing facilities.

In 1997, with regard to social policy, ECA was focusing upon improving the socio-economic prospects of women through the promotion of social and legal equality, increasing opportunities for entering higher education and monitoring the prevalence of poverty.

FOOD SECURITY AND SUSTAINABLE DEVELOPMENT

During 1991–92 reports were compiled on the development, implementation and sound management of environmental programmes at national, subregional and regional levels. ECA members adopted a common African position for the UN Conference on Environment and Development, held in June 1992. In 1995 ECA published its first comprehensive report and statistical survey of human development issues in African countries. The *Human Development in Africa Report*, which was to be published every two years, aimed to demonstrate levels of development attained, particularly in the education and child health sectors, to identify areas of concern and to encourage further action by policy-makers and development experts. In 1997 ECA was actively involved in the promotion of food security in African countries and the study of the relationship between population, food security, the environment and sustainable development.

INDUSTRY AND PRIVATE-SECTOR DEVELOPMENT

Following the failure to implement many of the proposals under the UN Industrial Development Decade for Africa (IDDA, 1980–90) and the UN Programme of Action for African Economic Recovery and Development (1986–90), a second IDDA was adopted by the Conference of African Ministers of Industry in July 1991. The main objectives of the second IDDA include the consolidation and rehabilitation of existing industries, the expansion of new investments, and the promotion of small-scale industries and technological capabilities. Various technical publications were to be produced, including a directory of project profiles in the field of entrepreneurship in small-scale industries.

In June 1996 a conference, organized by ECA, was held in Accra, Ghana, with the aim of reviving private investment in Africa in order to stimulate the private sector and promote future economic development. The conference established a forum for African political leaders and business executives to discuss the development of capital markets in the region and to co-ordinate efforts in sectoral training and research.

ECA assists African countries in expanding trade among themselves and with other regions of the world and in promoting financial and monetary co-operation. ECA attempts to ensure that African countries participate effectively in international negotiations. To this end, assistance has been provided to member states in negotiations under UNCTAD and GATT; in the annual conferences of the IMF and the World Bank; in negotiations with the EU; and in meetings related to economic co-operation among developing countries. Studies have been prepared on problems and prospects likely to arise for the African region from the implementation of the Common Fund for Commodities and the Generalized System of Trade Preferences (both supervised by UNCTAD); the impacts of exchange-rate fluctuations on the economies of African countries; and on the long-term implications of different debt arrangements for African economies. ECA assists individual member states by undertaking studies on domestic trade, expansion of inter-African trade, transnational corporations, integration of women in trade and development, and strengthening the capacities of state-trading organizations. ECA aims to assist countries to manage effectively trade issues arising from the conclusion of the Uruguay Round of GATT negotiations and its implementation under the World Trade Organization.

The expansion of trade within Africa is constrained by the low level of industrial production, and by the strong emphasis on commodity trade. ECA encourages the diversification of production, the liberalization of cross-border trade and the expansion of domestic trade structures, within regional economic groupings. ECA helps to organize regional and 'All-Africa' trade fairs.

In March/April 1997 the Conference of African Ministers of Finance, meeting in Addis Ababa, reviewed a new initiative of the World Bank and IMF to assist the world's 41 most heavily-indebted poor countries, of which 33 were identified as being in sub-Saharan Africa. While the Conference recognized the importance of the involvement of multilateral institutions in assisting African economies to achieve a sustainable level of development, it criticized aspects of the structural adjustment programmes imposed by the institutions and advocated more flexible criteria to determine eligibility for the new initiative.

NATURAL RESOURCES AND SCIENCE AND TECHNOLOGY

ECA assists member states in the assessment and use of water resources and the development of river and lake basins common to more than one country. The annual information bulletin on water resources in Africa, *Maji*, disseminates technical information to African governments, and intergovernmental and non-governmental organizations. In the field of marine affairs, ECA extends advisory services to member states on the opportunities and challenges provided by the UN Convention on the Law of the Sea.

The Commission's activities in the field of science and technology focus on three areas: the development of policies and institutions; the training and effective utilization of the work-force; and the promotion of regional and inter-regional co-operation. ECA provides technical support to the African Regional Centre for Technology and the African Regional Organization for Standardization.

PROGRAMME PLANNING, FINANCE AND EVALUATION

Programme planning, finance and evaluation is one of the tasks of the Executive Direction and Management office. The office provides guidance in the formulation of policies towards the achievement of Africa's development objectives to the policy-making organs of the UN and OAU. It contributes to the work of the General Assembly and other specialized agencies by providing an African perspective in the preparation of development strategies. In March 1996 the UN announced a system-wide Special Initiative on Africa to mobilize resources and to implement a series of political and economic development objectives over a 10-year period. ECA's Executive Secretary is the Co-Chair, with the Administrator of the UNDP, of the Steering Committee for the Initiative.

REGIONAL CO-OPERATION AND INTEGRATION

The Regional Co-operation and Integration Division administers the transport and communications, mineral and energy sectors in addition to its activities concerning the Subregional Development Centres (SRDCs—see above).

The ECA was appointed lead agency for the second United Nations Transport and Communications Decade in Africa (UNTACDA II), comprising the period 1991–2000. The principal aim of UNTACDA II is the establishment of an efficient, integrated transport and communications system in Africa. The specific objectives of the programme include: (i) the removal of physical and non-physical barriers to intra-African trade and travel, and improvement in the road transport sector; (ii) improvement in the efficiency and financial viability of railways; (iii) development of Africa's shipping capacity and improvement in the performance of Africa's ports; (iv) development of integrated transport systems for each lake and river basin; (v) improvement of integration of all modes of transport in order to carry cargo in one chain of transport smoothly; (vi) integration of African airlines, and restructuring of civil aviation and airport management authorities; (vii) improvement in the quality and availability of transport in urban areas; (viii) development of integrated regional telecommunications networks; (ix) development of broadcasting services, with the aim of supporting socio-economic development; and (x) expansion of Africa's postal network.

ECA is the co-ordinator, with the World Bank, of a regional Road Maintenance Initiative, which was launched in 1988. By early 1996 13 African countries were receiving assistance under the initiative, which sought to encourage a partnership between the public and private sectors to manage and maintain road infrastructure more efficiently and thus to improve country-wide communications and transportation activities.

The Fourth Regional Conference on the Development and Utilization of Mineral Resources in Africa, held in March 1991, adopted an action plan that included the formulation of national mineral exploitation policies; and the promotion of the gemstone industry, small-scale mining and the iron and steel industry. ECA supports the Southern African Mineral Resources Development Centre in Dar-es-Salaam, Tanzania, and the Central African Mineral Development Centre in Brazzaville, Republic of the Congo, which provide advisory and laboratory services to their respective member states.

ECA sponsors the two leading institutions in the field of cartograpy and remote-sensing. The Regional Centre for Services in Surveying, Mapping and Remote-Sensing is based in Nairobi, Kenya; it is establishing a satellite receiving station for processing remotely-sensed data for use by member states. The Regional Centre for Training in Aerospace Surveys, based in Ile Ife, Nigeria, provides training in cartography and remote-sensing

ECA's Energy Programme provides assistance to member states in the development of indigenous energy resources and the formulation of energy policies to extricate member states from continued energy crises. The ECA Secretariat supports the African Regional Centre for Solar Energy, based at Bujumbura, Burundi.

BUDGET

For the two-year period 1996–97 ECA's regular budget, an appropriation from the UN budget, was US $78.4m.

PUBLICATIONS

Annual Report of the ECA.
Africa Index (3 a year).
African Compendium on Environmental Statistics (irregular).
African Directory of Demographers (irregular).
African Population Newsletter (2 a year).
African Population Studies series (irregular).
African Socio-Economic Indicators (annually).
African Statistical Yearbook.
African Trade Bulletin (2 a year).
Demographic Handbook for Africa (irregular).
Devindex Africa (quarterly).
Directory of African Statisticians (every 2 years).
ECA Environment Newsletter (3 a year).
Flash on Trade Opportunities (quarterly).
Focus on African Industry (2 a year).
Foreign Trade Statistics for Africa series.
  Direction of Trade (quarterly).
  Summary Table (annually).
Human Development in Africa Report (every two years).
Maji Water Resources Bulletin (annually).
PADIS Newsletter (quarterly).
Report of the Executive Secretary (every 2 years).
Rural Progress (2 a year).
Statistical Newsletter (2 a year).
Survey of Economic and Social Conditions in Africa (annually).

Economic and Social Commission for Western Asia—ESCWA

Address: Riad el-Solh Sq., POB 11-8575, Beirut, Lebanon.

Telephone (1) 981301; **telex:** 216917; **fax:** (1) 981510.

The UN Economic Commission for Western Asia was established in 1974 by a resolution of the UN Economic and Social Council (ECOSOC), to provide facilities of a wider scope for those countries previously served by the UN Economic and Social Office in Beirut (UNESOB). The name 'Economic and Social Commission for Western Asia' (ESCWA) was adopted in 1985.

MEMBERS

Bahrain	Palestine
Egypt	Qatar
Iraq	Saudi Arabia
Jordan	Syria
Kuwait	United Arab Emirates
Lebanon	Yemen
Oman	

Organization

(November 1997)

COMMISSION

The sessions of the Commission (held every two years) are attended by representatives of member states, of UN bodies and specialized agencies, of regional and intergovernmental organizations, and of other UN member states attending as observers.

SECRETARIAT

The Secretariat comprises an Executive Secretary, a Deputy Executive Secretary, a Senior Advisor and Secretary of the Commission, an Information Services Unit and a Programme Planning and Co-ordination Unit. ESCWA's technical and substantive activities are undertaken by the following divisions: energy, natural resources and environment; social development issues and policies; economic development issues and policies; sectoral issues and policies; statistics; and technical co-operation.

Executive Secretary: Dr HAZEM ABD EL-AZIZ EL-BEBLAWI (Egypt).

Activities

ESCWA is responsible for proposing policies and actions to support development and to further economic co-operation and integration in western Asia. ESCWA undertakes or sponsors studies of economic social and development issues of the region, collects and disseminates information, and provides advisory services to member states in various fields of economic and social development. It also organizes conferences and intergovernmental and export group meetings and sponsors training workshops and seminars. An ESCWA Statistics Committee held its first meeting in November 1995.

Much of ESCWA's work is carried out in co-operation with other UN bodies, as well as with other international and regional organizations, for example the League of Arab States (q.v.) the Co-operation Council for the Arab States of the Gulf (q.v.) and the Organization of the Islamic Conference (OIC, q.v.).

ESCWA works within the framework of medium-term plans, the latest of which covers the period 1992–97, which are divided into two-year programmes of action and priorities. The biennium 1994–95 was considered to be a transitional period during which the Commission restructured its work programme. This restructuring focused ESCWA activities from 15 to the following five sub-programmes:

Management of Natural Resources and the Environment: covers energy, water and environment activities; agricultural activities relating to the management of land and the environment; human settlements activities and industry activities relating to energy and the environment; statistics on energy and the environment.

Improvement of the Quality of Life: covers social development, population, women and human settlements activities; agricultural activities relating to rural development; small-scale industries, the participation of women in manufacturing industries and employment opportunities through small-scale industries; statistics on population, labour, women, human development and social development.

Economic Development and Co-operation: development issues, trade, public administration, finance and transnational corporations activities; most other activities relating to industry, technology, transport and agriculture not mentioned above; statistics on national accounts, finance and industry.

Regional Development and Global Change: the impact of the single European market, accords concluded under the General Agreement on Tariffs and Trade, privatizations and other relevant events; the social consequences of economic structural adjustment programmes.

Special Programmes and Issues: activities concerned with Palestine, the impact of the Middle East peace settlement on the region, the effects of war on specific countries, Yemen as a least-developed country, and other relevant concerns. In May 1996 ESCWA was designated the UN agency responsible for conducting a technical assessment of the human and material losses resulting from renewed hostilities in southern Lebanon.

During the biennium 1998–99 ESCWA's activities were to be aligned according to the following revised sub-programmes: Management of Natural Resources and the Environment; Improvement of the Quality of Life; Economic Development and Global Changes; Co-ordination of Policies and Harmonization of Norms and Regulations for Sectoral Development; and Development, Co-ordination and Harmonization of Statistics and Information.

BUDGET

ESCWA's share of the UN budget for the two years 1998–99 was US $49.5m., compared with $33.2m. for the 1996–97 biennium.

PUBLICATIONS

All publications are annual, unless otherwise indicated.

Agriculture and Development in Western Asia.

External Trade Bulletin.

National Accounts Studies.

Population Bulletin.

Prices and Financial Statistics in the ESCWA Region.

Socio-economic Data Sheet (every 2 years).

Statistical Abstract.

Survey of Economic and Social Developments in the ESCWA Region.

Transport Bulletin.

OTHER UNITED NATIONS BODIES

United Nations Centre for Human Settlements—UNCHS (Habitat)

Address: POB 30030, Nairobi, Kenya.

Telephone: (2) 621234; **telex:** 22996; **fax:** (2) 624266.

UNCHS (Habitat) was established in October 1978 to service the intergovernmental Commission on Human Settlements, and to serve as a focus for human settlements activities in the UN system.

Organization

(November 1997)

UN COMMISSION ON HUMAN SETTLEMENTS

The Commission (see ECOSOC, p. 22) is the governing body of UNCHS (Habitat). It meets every two years and has 58 members, serving for four years. Sixteen members are from Africa, 13 from Asia, six from eastern European countries, 10 from Latin America and 13 from western Europe and other countries.

CENTRE FOR HUMAN SETTLEMENTS

The Centre services the Commission on Human Settlements, implements its resolutions and ensures the integration and co-ordination of technical co-operation, research and policy advice. Its Work Programme incorporates the following priority areas, as defined by the Commission: Shelter and social services; Urban management; Environment and infrastructure; and Assessment, information and monitoring.

In 1992 the UN General Assembly designated UNCHS (Habitat) as the *ad hoc* secretariat for the Second UN Conference on Human Settlements, Habitat II, which was held in Istanbul, Turkey, in June 1996. As a result, most of the Centre's activities in recent years have been concerned with servicing and stimulating participation in the preparatory process for the Conference at global, regional, national and local levels.

Executive Director: Darshan Johal (Canada) (acting).

Activities

UNCHS (Habitat) supports and conducts capacity-building and operational research, provides technical co-operation and policy advice, and disseminates information with the aim of strengthening the development and management of human settlements.

In June 1996 representatives of 171 national governments and of more than 500 municipal authorities attending Habitat II adopted a Global Plan of Action (the 'Habitat Agenda'), which incorporated detailed programmes of action to realize economic and social development and environmental sustainability, and endorsed the Conference's objectives of ensuring 'adequate shelter for all' and 'sustainable human settlements development in an urbanizing world'. UNCHS (Habitat) was expected to provide the leadership and serve as a focal point for the implementation of the Agenda. It has consequently undertaken a process of restructuring its working methods and organization, which was still ongoing in late 1997. Following the Conference, UNCHS (Habitat) established a Global Urban Observatory to monitor implementation of the Habitat Agenda and to report on local and national plans of action, international and regional support programmes and ongoing research and development. The Observatory, which incorporated the existing monitoring facilities of the Best Practices Programme and the Urban Indicators Programme, operates through an international network of regional and national institutions, all of which provide local training in appropriate data collection methods and in the development, adoption and maintenance of reliable information systems.

UNCHS (Habitat) is the co-ordinating agency for the implementation of the Global Strategy for Shelter to the Year 2000 (GSS), adopted by the General Assembly in 1988. The Strategy aims to facilitate the construction and improvement of housing for all, in particular by and for the poorest in society, and promotes the use of legal and other incentives to encourage non-governmental parties to become engaged in housing and urban development.

Through its Women in Human Settlements Development Programme, which was established in 1990, UNCHS (Habitat) ensured that the issue of human settlements was included in the agenda ofthe UN Fourth World Conference on Women, which was held in Beijing, People's Republic of China, in September 1995, and successfully incorporated the right of women to ownership of land and property into the Global Platform for Action which resulted from the Conference. An advisory board, the Huairou Commission, comprising women from 'grass-roots' groups, non-governmental organizations (NGOs), the UN and research and political institutions, has since been established to ensure a link between the Beijing and Habitat Agendas and the inclusion of gender issues in the follow-up to Habitat II.

The Centre participates in implementing the human settlements component of Agenda 21, which was adopted at the UN Conference on Environment and Development in June 1992, and is also responsible for the chapter of Agenda 21 that refers to solid waste management and sewage related issues. UNCHS (Habitat) implements a programme entitled 'Localizing Agenda 21', to assist local authorities in developing countries to address local environmental and infrastructure-related problems. It also collaborates with national governments, private-sector and non-governmental institutions and UN bodies to achieve the objectives of Agenda 21. The Settlement Infrastructure and Environment Programme was initiated in 1992 to support developing countries in improving the environment of human settlements through policy advice and planning, infrastructure management and enhancing awareness of environmental and health concerns in areas such as water, sanitation, waste management and transport. An Urban Management Programme aims to strengthen the contribution of cities and towns in developing countries towards human development, including economic growth, social advancements, the reduction of poverty and the improvement of the environment. The Programme is an international technical co-operation project, of which UNCHS (Habitat) is the executing agency, the World Bank is an associated agency, while UNDP provides core funding and monitoring. The Programme is operated through regional offices, in collaboration with bilateral and multilateral support agencies, and brings together national and local authorities, community leaders and representatives of the private sector to consider specific issues and solutions to urban problems. A Sustainable Cities Programme, operated jointly with UNEP, is concerned with incorporating environmental issues into urban planning and management, in order to ensure sustainable and equitable development. Some 95% of the Programme's resources are spent at city level to strengthen the capacities of municipal authorities and their public-, private- and community-sector partners in the field of environmental planning and management, with the objective that the concepts and approaches of the Programme are replicated throughout the region. In addition, UNCHS (Habitat) supports training and other activities designed to strengthen management development (in particular in the provision and maintenance of services and facilities) at local and community level.

At mid-1997 UNCHS (Habitat) was undertaking 235 operational programmes and projects in 80 countries. Its principal collaborating partners within the UN system were UNDP, UNICEF, WHO and the Department of Humanitarian Affairs. Increasingly UNCHS (Habitat) is being called upon to contribute to the relief, rehabilitation and development activities undertaken by the UN in areas affected by regional and civil conflict. UNCHS (Habitat) has been actively involved in the reconstruction of human settlements and other development activities in Afghanistan, and in 1997 was also contributing to reconstruction programmes in Angola, Iraq, Rwanda and Somalia.

FINANCE

The Centre's work programme is financed from the UN regular budget, the Habitat and Human Settlements Foundation and from extra-budgetary resources. The total budget for the two-year period 1996–97 amounted to approximately US $46m.

PUBLICATIONS

Global Report on Human Settlements.

Habitat Debate (quarterly).

Technical reports and studies, occasional papers, bibliographies, directories.

United Nations Children's Fund—UNICEF

Address: 3 United Nations Plaza, New York, NY 10017, USA.

Telephone: (212) 326-7000; **telex:** 49620199; **fax:** (212) 888-7465; **e-mail:** webmaster@unicef.org; **internet:** http://www.unicef.org.

UNICEF was established in 1946 by the UN General Assembly as the UN International Children's Emergency Fund, to meet the emergency needs of children in post-war Europe and China. In 1950 its mandate was changed to respond to the needs of children in developing countries. In 1953 the General Assembly decided that UNICEF should continue its work, as a permanent arm of the UN system, with an emphasis on programmes giving long-term benefits to children everywhere, particularly those in developing countries who are in the greatest need. In 1965 UNICEF was awarded the Nobel Peace Prize.

Organization

(November 1997)

EXECUTIVE BOARD

The Executive Board, which is the governing body of UNICEF, meets once a year to establish policy, to review programmes and to approve expenditure. Membership comprises 36 governments from all regions, elected in rotation for a three-year term by ECOSOC.

SECRETARIAT

The Executive Director of UNICEF is appointed by the UN Secretary-General in consultation with the Executive Board. The administration of UNICEF and the appointment and direction of staff are the responsibility of the Executive Director, under policy directives laid down by the Executive Board, and under a broad authority delegated to the Executive Director by the Secretary-General. UNICEF has a network of country and regional offices serving more than 161 countries and territories.

Executive Director: Carol Bellamy (USA).

Deputy Executive Directors: Karin Sham Poo (Norway), Stephen Lewis (Canada).

MAJOR UNICEF OFFICES

The Americas and the Caribbean: Apdo 7555, Santafé de Bogotá, Colombia.

Central and Eastern Europe, Commonwealth of Independent States and Baltic States: 5–7 ave de la Paix, 1202 Geneva, Switzerland.

East Asia and the Pacific: POB 2-154, Bangkok 10200, Thailand.

Eastern and Southern Africa: POB 44145, Nairobi, Kenya.

Europe: Palais des Nations, 1211 Geneva 10, Switzerland.

Japan: UN Bldg, 8th Floor, 53-70, Jingumae 5-chome, Shibuya-ku, Tokyo 150, Japan.

Middle East and North Africa: POB 811721, 11181 Amman, Jordan.

South Asia: POB 5815, Leknath Marg, Kathmandu, Nepal.

West and Central Africa: BP 443, Abidjan 04, Côte d'Ivoire.

NATIONAL COMMITTEES

UNICEF is supported by 37 National Committees, mostly in industrialized countries, whose volunteer members raise money through various activities, including the sale of greetings cards. The Committees also undertake advocacy efforts and information activities within their own societies.

Activities

Through its extensive field network in developing countries, UNICEF undertakes, in co-ordination with governments, local communities and other aid organizations, programmes in health, nutrition, education, water and sanitation, the environment, women in development, and other fields of importance to children. Emphasis is placed on community-based programmes in which people actively participate and are trained in such skills as health care, midwifery and teaching. At mid-September 1997 UNICEF employed a total staff of 7,053 people serving in 257 locations (at their headquarters and at regional, country and sub-offices) around the world. UNICEF facilitates the exchange of programming experience among developing countries, and encourages governments to undertake a regular review of the situation of their children and to incorporate a national policy for children in their comprehensive development plans. UNICEF provides assistance on the basis of mutually agreed priorities for children in collaboration with the governments concerned. Priority is given to the world's most vulnerable children: almost all its resources are invested in the world's poorest developing countries, with the greatest share going to children in the high-risk early years, up to the age of five.

As the only UN agency devoted exclusively to the needs of children, UNICEF speaks on their behalf and promotes the implementation of the Convention on the Rights of the Child, which came into force in September 1990 addressing the individual rights of children and establishing universally accepted standards for their protection. By September 1997 the Convention had been ratified by 191 countries.

UNICEF was instrumental in organizing the World Summit for Children, held in September 1990 and attended by representatives from more than 150 countries, including 71 heads of state or government. The Summit produced a Plan of Action which recognized the rights of the young to 'first call' on their countries' resources and formulated objectives for the year 2000, including: (i) a reduction of the 1990 mortality rates for infants and children under five years by one-third, or to 50–70 per 1,000 live births, whichever is lower; (ii) a reduction of the 1990 maternal mortality rate by one-half; (iii) a reduction by one-half of the 1990 rate for severe malnutrition among children under the age of five; (iv) universal access to safe drinking water and to sanitary means of excreta disposal; and (v) universal access to basic education and completion of primary education by at least 80% of children. By October 1997 more than 160 countries had formulated national programmes of action to implement the Summit's objectives.

UNICEF co-sponsored (with UNESCO, UNDP and the World Bank) the World Conference on Education for All, which was held in Thailand in March 1990, and has made efforts to achieve the objectives formulated by the conference, which include the elimination of disparities in education between boys and girls. In December 1993 an Education for All Summit was convened in New Delhi, India, co-sponsored by UNICEF (with UNESCO and UNFPA), involving nine of the world's most populous countries—Bangladesh, Brazil, the People's Republic of China, Egypt, India, Indonesia, Mexico, Nigeria and Pakistan. In 1994 UNICEF, with UNDP, UNESCO, UNFPA, the World Bank and African education ministers, initiated 'A Focus on Education for All in Africa', which aimed to ensure the availability of adequate resources for the implementation of national education programmes.

Through UNICEF's efforts, the needs and interests of children were incorporated into Agenda 21, which was adopted as a plan of action for environment and development at the UN Conference on Environment and Development, held in June 1992. At the International Conference on Population and Development, which was held in Cairo, Egypt, in September 1994, UNICEF played a significant role in emphasizing the link between poverty, population growth and environmental deterioration, and the need for family planning, education and basic maternal and child health care to ensure child survival and development. With UNDP and UNFPA, UNICEF supported the 20/20 initiative, which urged governments of developing countries and donor countries to allocate at least 20% of their domestic and overseas aid budgets to these basic social services. UNICEF strongly promoted measures for child survival and development, through health care and female education, at the World Summit for Social Development, which took place in Copenhagen, Denmark, in March 1995. At the Fourth World Conference on Women, held in Beijing, People's Republic of China, in September 1995, UNICEF promoted the human rights of children, especially girls. The Beijing Declaration and Platform of Action, which were adopted by the Conference, emphasized eliminating gender discrimination and giving priority to girls' education as essential elements of development. Following each of these last three conferences UNICEF served as an active participant in *ad hoc* inter-agency task forces that were established to co-ordinate action on the priority objectives identified at each meeting. During 1996 UNICEF participated in preparations for the second UN Conference on Human Settlements, held in Istanbul, Turkey, in June, and for the World Food Summit, held in Rome, Italy, in November, at which the reduction of child malnutrition was emphasized as one of UNICEF's key concerns. In addition, in August 1996 UNICEF assisted the Swedish Government to organize the first World Congress against the Commercial Sexual Exploitation of Children, which was convened in Stockholm.

In October 1997 UNICEF, together with the International Labour Organization and the Norwegian Government, hosted an International Conference on Child Labour, in order to focus attention on the situation of the estimated 250m. children between the ages of five and 14 years working in developing countries, many of whom were thought to be engaged in hazardous or exploitative labour. Delegates attending the Conference in Oslo, Norway, adopted an Agenda for Action, which incorporated measures to prevent and eliminate all forms of child labour and urged governments to give priority to ending the most extreme forms of child labour and forced employment and work that denied children their right to education. The document incorporated recommendations to ensure that all children have access to free, basic education, to assist the families of child workers by providing employment and income opportunities, to formulate national programmes to eliminate child labour and ensure that all legislation conforms with international standards, and to improve means of obtaining information on child labour.

In co-operation with WHO, UNICEF supports the Expanded Programme on Immunization, which each year prevents more than 3m. child deaths from the following six diseases: measles, poliomyelitis, tuberculosis, diphtheria, whooping cough and tetanus. By 1996 129 countries had achieved the objective of immunizing 80% of children against these diseases before their first birthday (compared with less than 5% in 1975, when the programme was launched). The goal of immunizing 90% of children under one year by 2000 had been attained by 89 of these countries, including 59 developing nations. The two agencies also work in conjunction to control diarrhoeal dehydration, one of the largest causes of death among children under five years of age in the developing world. UNICEF-assisted programmes for the control of diarrhoeal diseases promote the low-cost manufacture and distribution of pre-packaged salts or home-made solutions. The use of 'oral rehydration therapy' rose from 17% in 1985 to more than 80% in 1996, and is believed to prevent more than 2m. deaths each year. Also in co-ordination with WHO, UNICEF announced, in June 1991, a 'baby-friendly hospital initiative' which aims to promote breast-feeding. By September 1997 more than 12,700 hospitals had implemented the recommendations of UNICEF and WHO, entitled '10 steps to successful breast-feeding', to become 'baby-friendly'. According to UNICEF estimates, 183m. children throughout the world are underweight, while each year malnutrition contributes to the deaths of almost 6m. children under five years of age in developing countries (or some 50% of total deaths in that age-group). UNICEF supports community-based efforts to reduce malnutrition, involving the promotion of household food security, disease control and prevention, and sound child-care and feeding. In 1996 UNICEF expressed its concern at the impact of international economic embargoes on child health, citing as an example the extensive levels of child malnutrition recorded in Iraq (which by May 1997 was estimated at 25% of all Iraqi children under five years of age). UNICEF's strategy on women's health focuses on the need to reduce the numbers of women who die during pregnancy and childbirth, estimated at 585,000 each year. UNICEF aims to strengthen access to quality pre-natal, delivery and post-natal care and to develop appropriate health promotion campaigns.

In emergency relief and rehabilitation, UNICEF works closely with other UN agencies and many non-governmental organizations. In 1996 it provided emergency assistance totalling US $145m., or 21% of total programme expenditure, to 58 countries affected by disasters and civil strife. In that year UNICEF responded to emergencies by providing support in the following four main areas: the monitoring and evaluation of fragile situations; local capacity-building to cope with emergencies; child survival, protection and development; and the physical and psychological rehabilitation of child victims. UNICEF has undertaken to enhance its emergency responsiveness capacity, for example, by establishing 'rapid response' teams, improving training in emergency management and developing memoranda of understanding with other UN partners, including UNHCR and WFP.

UNICEF campaigns for the demobilization of child soldiers and increasing the minimum legal age for combatants from 15 to 18 years. It also supports the establishment of an international criminal court mandated to prosecute war crimes committed against children. UNICEF was an active participant in the so-called 'Ottawa' process (supported by the Canadian Government) to negotiate an international ban on the production, sale and use of anti-personnel land-mines (see also International Committee of the Red Cross, q.v.).

In 1996 an estimated 2.6m. children were living with the human immunodeficiency virus (HIV) and AIDS, the majority of whom lived in sub-Saharan Africa. It has been estimated that by the end of the decade AIDS will have orphaned 5m. children. UNICEF supports AIDS education programmes and assists AIDS-affected communities in sub-Saharan Africa, Asia and Latin America. It works closely in this field with governments and co-operates with other UN agencies in the Joint UN Programme on HIV/AIDS (UNAIDS), which became operational on 1 January 1996.

FINANCE

UNICEF's work is accomplished with voluntary contributions from both governments and non-governmental sources. Total income in 1996 amounted to US $944m., of which 64% was from governments.

UNICEF's income is divided between contributions for general resources, for supplementary funds and for emergencies. General resources are the funds available to fulfil commitments for co-operation in country programmes approved by the Executive Board, and to meet administrative and programme support expenditures. They include contributions from governments, the net income from greetings cards sales, funds contributed by the public (mainly through National Committees) and other income. These funds amounted to US $551m. in 1996. Contributions for supplementary funds are those sought by UNICEF from governments and intergovernmental organizations to support projects for which general resources are insufficient, or for relief and rehabilitation programmes in emergency situations. Supplementary funding in 1996 amounted to $287m. Funding for emergencies in 1996 amounted to $106m.

UNICEF PROGRAMME EXPENDITURE BY SECTOR (1996)

	Cost (US $ million)
Child health	184
Emergency relief	145
Planning, advocacy and programme support	125
Education and early childhood development	68
Water supply and sanitation	67
Community development and programmes for women and children in especially difficult circumstances (CEDCs)	66
Child nutrition	29
Total	684

PUBLICATIONS

Facts and Figures (annually, in English, French and Spanish).

The Progress of Nations (annually, in English, French and Spanish and about 20 other national languages).

The State of the World's Children (annually, in English, French, Spanish, Arabic and about 30 other national languages).

UNICEF Annual Report (summarizes UNICEF policies and programmes; in English, French and Spanish).

UNICEF at a Glance (annually, in English, French and Spanish).

United Nations Conference on Trade and Development—UNCTAD

Address: Palais des Nations, 1211 Geneva 10, Switzerland.

Telephone: (22) 9071234; **telex:** 412962; **fax:** (22) 9070057; **internet:** http://www.unicc.org/unctad.

UNCTAD was established by the UN General Assembly as one of its permanent organs in December 1964. Its role is to promote the acceleration of economic growth and development, particularly in developing countries, in order to allow all the people of the world to enjoy economic and social well-being.

Organization

(November 1997)

CONFERENCE

The Conference is the organization's highest policy-making body and normally meets every four years at ministerial level in order to formulate major policy guidelines and to decide on UNCTAD's forthcoming programme of work. Ninth session: Midrand, South Africa, April/May 1996. UNCTAD has 188 members, including all the UN member states, and many intergovernmental and non-governmental organizations participate in its work as observers.

SECRETARIAT

As well as servicing the Conference, the UNCTAD secretariat undertakes policy analysis; monitoring, implementation and follow-up of decisions of intergovernmental bodies; technical co-operation in support of UNCTAD's policy objectives; and information exchanges and consultations of various types. In October 1996 some 450 staff were employed at the Secretariat.

Secretary-General: RUBENS RICUPERO (Brazil).

TRADE AND DEVELOPMENT BOARD

The Trade and Development Board is the executive body of UNCTAD. It comprises elected representatives from 141 UNCTAD member states and is responsible for ensuring the overall consistency of UNCTAD's activities, as well as those of its subsidiary bodies. The Board meets for a regular annual session lasting about 10 days, at which it examines global economic issues. It also reviews the implementation of the Programme of Action for the Least-Developed Countries and the UN New Agenda for the Development of Africa in the 1990s, with particular attention given to lessons that may be drawn from successful development experiences. The Board may also meet a further three times a year in order to address management or institutional matters.

COMMISSIONS

The 1996 Conference approved the establishment of three Commissions to replace existing committees and working groups: the Commission on Trade in Goods and Services and Commodities; the Commission on Investment, Technology and Related Financial Issues; and the Commission on Enterprise, Business Facilitation and Development. UNCTAD also services the ECOSOC Commission on Science and Technology for Development (see below).

Activities

During the 1980s one of UNCTAD's major roles was providing a forum for the negotiation of international agreements on commodities. These agreements were designed to ensure the stabilization of conditions in the trade of the commodities concerned. Agreements were negotiated on tin (1981), jute (1982), cocoa (1986), olive oil (1986) and rubber (1987). The establishment of the Common Fund for Commodities was agreed by UNCTAD in 1980, and the Fund came into operation in September 1989 (see p. 256). In January 1994 the contracting parties to the International Tropical Timber Agreement, meeting under UNCTAD auspices, decided to extend the existing agreement pending the entry into force of a replacement agreement. The new agreement entered into force in September 1996.

By the early 1990s most of the commodity agreements had lapsed and the conclusion of the GATT Uruguay Round of trade talks in December 1993 and the changes in international trading structures that had already taken place were deemed to necessitate a substantial reorientation of UNCTAD's role. Following restructuring agreed at the eighth session of the Conference in Cartagena, Colombia, in February 1992, further changes to UNCTAD's focus and organization were approved at the ninth Conference that was held in Midrand, South Africa, in April/May 1996. In particular, UNCTAD was to give special attention to assisting developing countries in taking advantage of the increased liberalization of world trade under the GATT and World Trade Organization agreements (see p. 244). Concern was expressed that the world's poorest countries would be even further marginalized if they were not given additional support to enable them to begin to compete with more successful economies. During 1996 a Trust Fund for the Least Developed Countries was established, with an initial target figure of US $5m., with the aim of assisting those countries to become integrated into the world economy. In UNCTAD's revised approach, encouragement of foreign direct investment and of domestic private enterprise in developing countries and countries in transition have become central to the agency's work. UNCTAD is also increasingly seeking the input and participation of non-governmental groups, such as the private sector, trade unions, academics and non-governmental organizations. UNCTAD has been mandated as the organ within the UN system responsible for negotiating a multilateral framework governing direct foreign investment that would protect the interests of the poorest countries, taking account of the work already undertaken by OECD in this area.

The Commission on Trade in Goods and Services and Commodities examines ways of maximizing the positive impact of globalization and liberalization on sustainable development by assisting in the effective integration of developing countries into the international trading system. In the field of services, where developing countries suffer from deficiencies in the customs, financial and communications sectors, the Commission recommends ways for countries to overcome problems in these areas. In the field of commodities, the Commission promotes diversification, to reduce dependence on single commodities, transparency in commodity markets and the sustainable management of commodity resources.

The Commission on Investment, Technology and Related Financial Issues provides a forum to help general understanding of trends in the flow of foreign direct investment, which is considered one of the principal instruments for the integration of developing economies into the global system; and assists developing countries in improving their overall investment climate. The Commission examines issues related to competition law and assists developing countries in formulating competition policies. The Commission also undertakes the functions of the former ECOSOC Commission on International Investment and Transnational Corporations, which aimed to provide an understanding of the nature of foreign direct investment and transnational corporations, to secure effective international agreements and to strengthen the capacity of developing countries in their dealings with transnational corporations through an integrated approach, including research, information and technical assistance. A subsidiary body—the Intergovernmental Group of Experts on International Standards of Accounting and Reporting—aimed to improve the availability of information disclosed by transnational corporations. In November 1997 the UN General Assembly endorsed a proposal of the UN Secretary-General that the Group report directly through the UNCTAD Commission on Investment, Technology and Related Financial Issues.

The Commission on Enterprise, Business Facilitation and Development advises countries on policy-related issues and training activities concerning the development of entrepreneurship. It facilitates the exchange of experiences on the formulation and implementation of enterprise development strategies, including privatization, public-sector co-operation and the special problems relating to enterprise development in countries in economic transition.

UNCTAD is responsible for the Generalized System of Preferences (GSP), initiated in 1971, whereby a proportion of both agricultural and manufactured goods that are exported by developing countries receive preferential tariff treatment by certain developed countries, Russia and several central European countries. UNCTAD monitors changes in and amendments to national GSP schemes and reviews the use of these schemes by beneficiary developing countries. In addition, the Commission on Trade in Goods and Services and Commodities (see above) is responsible for providing a forum to examine the operation of schemes, the benefits they offer and the future role of the GSP. At November 1997 15 national GSP schemes were in operation, offered by 29 countries (including the 15 member countries of the European Union). Following the signing of the GATT Uruguay Round trade agreement in April 1994, UNCTAD estimated that the value of trade preferences for developing countries would be substantially reduced, owing to a general reduction of tariffs. It advocated maintaining preferential margins for developing countries and extending GSP benefits to agricultural products and textiles from those countries after import quotas were eliminated, in accordance with the trade agreement.

Trade efficiency was discussed for the first time at the 1992 Conference, with computer-based technologies capable of substantially reducing the cost of transactions providing the focus. In 1994 a Global Trade Point Network (GTPNet), comprising an electronic network of trade-related information, was launched. The scheme, in which 114 countries were participating at November 1997, is monitored by the Commission on Enterprise, Business Facilitation and Development. An international symposium on trade efficiency was held in Columbus, Ohio (USA), in October 1994.

UNCTAD's work in the field of shipping and maritime activity resulted in the adoption of the UN Convention on a Code of Conduct for Liner Conferences (effective from 1983), which provides for the national shipping lines of developing countries to participate on an equal basis with the shipping lines of developed countries. Other UNCTAD initiatives have resulted in the adoption of the UN Convention on the Carriage of Goods by Sea (Hamburg Rules—1978), the UN Convention on International Multimodal Transport (1980), the UN Convention on Conditions for Registration of Ships (1986), and the International Convention on Maritime Liens and Mortgages. This last Convention was adopted in May 1993 in Geneva by a UN International Maritime Organization Conference of Plenipotentiaries, and its objectives were to encourage international uniformity in the field of maritime liens and mortgages and to improve conditions for ship financing. Technical co-operation and training projects, financed by UNDP and additional funds from bilateral donors, constitute an important component of UNCTAD's work in the fields of ports and multimodal transport and have resulted in the development of specialized courses. The soft-ware package entitled the Advance Cargo Information System (ACIS) enables shipping lines and railway companies to track the movement of cargo. Through the use of ACIS and the Automated System for Customs Data (ASYCUDA), operational in some 70 countries, UNCTAD aims to enhance the effective exchange of information in order to counter customs fraud.

UNCTAD aims to give particular attention to the needs of the world's 48 least developed countries (LDCs—as defined by the UN). The eighth session of the Conference requested that detailed analyses of the socio-economic situations and domestic policies of the LDCs, their resource needs, and external factors affecting their economies be undertaken as part of UNCTAD's work programme. The ninth session determined that particular attention be given to the problems of the LDCs in all areas of UNCTAD's work.

UNCTAD provides assistance to developing countries in the area of debt-management, and in seeking debt relief from their creditors. UNCTAD and the World Bank have begun a joint programme to extend technical co-operation to developing countries in the field of debt management, where UNCTAD is responsible for the soft-ware component of the project. The assistance is based on the development and distribution of soft-ware (the Debt Management and Financial Analysis System—DMFAS) designed to enable debtor countries to analyze data, make projections, and to plan strategies for debt repayment and reorganization. UNCTAD provides training for operators in the use of the soft-ware, and for senior officials, to increase their awareness of institutional reforms which might be necessary for effective debt management.

The Secretariat provided technical assistance to developing countries in connection with the Uruguay Round of multilateral trade negotiations (see WTO). The International Trade Centre in Geneva is operated jointly by WTO (q.v.) and UNCTAD.

Since May 1993 UNCTAD has serviced the ECOSOC Commission on Science and Technology for Development, which provides a forum for discussion of the following issues relating to science and technology for development: technology for small-scale economic activities to address the basic needs of low-income countries; gender implications of science and technology for developing countries; science and technology and the environment; the contribution of technologies to industrialization in developing countries; and the role of information technologies, in particular in relation to developing countries. The Commission meets every two years. In November 1997 the UN General Assembly approved a series of reform measures, proposed by the Secretary-General, according to which the Commission was to become a subsidiary body of the Trade and Development Board.

FINANCE

The operational expenses of UNCTAD are borne by the regular budget of the UN, and amount to approximately US $55m. annually. Technical co-operation activities, financed from extra-budgetary resources, amount to some $22m. annually.

PUBLICATIONS

Advanced Technology Assessment System Bulletin (occasional).
Guide to UNCTAD Publications (annually).
Handbook of International Trade and Development Statistics (annually).
The Least Developed Countries Report (annually).
Monthly Commodity Price Bulletin.
Review of Maritime Transport (annually).
Trade and Development Report (annually).
Transnational Corporations (3 a year).
UNCTAD Commodity Yearbook.
World Investment Report (annually).

United Nations Development Programme—UNDP

Address: One United Nations Plaza, New York, NY 10017, USA.

Telephone: (212) 906-5000; **fax:** (212) 826-2057; **internet:** http://www.undp.org.

The Programme was established in 1965 by the UN General Assembly. Its central mission is to help countries to eradicate poverty and achieve a sustainable level of human development.

Organization

(November 1997)

UNDP is responsible to the UN General Assembly, to which it reports through ECOSOC.

EXECUTIVE BOARD

The Executive Board is responsible for providing intergovernmental support to, and supervision of, the activities of UNDP and the UN Population Fund (UNFPA). It comprises 36 members: eight from Africa, seven from Asia, four from eastern Europe, five from Latin America and the Caribbean and 12 from western Europe and other countries.

SECRETARIAT

Administrator: JAMES GUSTAVE SPETH (USA).

Associate Administrator: RAFEEUDDIN AHMED (Pakistan).

REGIONAL OFFICES

Headed by assistant administrators, the regional offices share the responsibility for implementing the programme with the Administrator's office. Within certain limitations, large-scale projects may be approved, and funding allocated, by the Administrator, and smaller-scale projects by the Resident Representatives, based in 137 country and liaison offices world-wide.

Five regional bureaux, all at the Secretariat in New York, cover: Africa; Asia and the Pacific; the Arab states; Latin America and the Caribbean; and Europe and the Commonwealth of Independent States. There is also a Division for Global and Interregional Programmes.

FIELD OFFICES

In almost every country receiving UNDP assistance there is an office, headed by the UNDP Resident Representative, who co-ordinates all UN technical assistance, advises the Government on formulating the country programme, ensures that field activities are undertaken, and acts as the leader of the UN team of experts working in the country. Resident Representatives are normally designated as co-ordinators for all UN operational development activities; the field offices function as the primary presence of the UN in most developing countries.

Activities

As the world's largest source of grant technical assistance in developing countries, UNDP works with more than 150 governments and 40 international agencies in efforts to achieve faster economic growth and better standards of living throughout the developing world. Most of the work is undertaken in the field by the various United Nations agencies, or by the government of the country concerned. UNDP is committed to allocating some 87% of its core resources to low-income countries with an annual income per caput of less than US $750. Assistance is mostly non-monetary, comprising the provision of experts' services, consultancies, equipment, and fellowships for advanced study abroad. In 1996 35% of spending on projects was for the services of personnel, 25% for subcontracts, 18% for equipment, 16% for training, and the remainder was for other costs, such as maintenance of equipment. Most UNDP projects incorporate training for local workers. Developing countries themselves provide 50% or more of the total project costs in terms of personnel, facilities, equipment and supplies. At December 1996 there were 3,240 UN volunteer specialists and field workers, as well as 4,501 international experts and 5,703 national experts serving under UNDP. In that year UNDP awarded 13,393 fellowships for nationals of developing countries to study abroad.

In 1993 UNDP began to examine its role and effectiveness in promoting sustainable human development, an approach to economic growth that encompasses individual well-being and choice, equitable distribution of the benefits of development and conservation of the environment. In June 1994 the Executive Board endorsed a proposal of the UNDP Administrator to make sustainable human development the guiding principle of the organization. Within this framework there were to be four priority objectives: poverty elimination; the expansion of employment opportunities; environmental protection and regeneration; and the advancement and empowerment of women. A new Office of Evaluation and Strategic Planning was established to facilitate the restructuring required by these changes, while an Office of UN System Support and Services was created to assist in unifying various UN agencies around the new framework for sustainable human development. The allocation of programming resources since 1994 has reflected UNDP's new agenda, with 39% of core funding directed towards poverty eradication and livelihoods for the poor, 32% to capacity-building and governance, and 21% to projects concerned with the environmental and natural resources. Some 20% of total resources are allocated to promoting gender equality in all UNDP activities.

UNDP aims to help governments to reassess their development priorities and to design initiatives for sustainable development. UNDP country officers support the formulation of national human development reports (NHDRs), which aim to facilitate activities such as policy-making, the allocation of resources and monitoring progress towards poverty eradiction and sustainable development. In addition, the preparation of Advisory Notes and Country Co-operation Frameworks by UNDP officials help to highlight country-specific aspects of poverty eradiction and national strategic priorities. Since 1990 UNDP has published an annual *Human Development Report,* incorporating a Human Development Index, which ranks countries in terms of human development, using three key indicators: life expectancy, adult literacy and basic income required for a decent standard of living. In 1997 a Human Poverty Index and a Gender-related Development Index, which assesses gender equality on the basis of life expectancy, education and income, were introduced into the Report for the first time.

UNDP's activities to facilitate poverty eradiction include support for capacity-building programmes and initiatives to generate sustainable livelihoods, for example by improving access to credit, land and technologies. In March 1996 UNDP launched the Poverty Strategies Initiative (PSI) to strengthen national capacities to assess and monitor the extent of poverty and to combat the problem. By May 1997 80 projects had been approved for funding under the PSI. All PSI projects were intended to involve government representatives, the private sector, social organizations and research institutions in policy debate and formulation. In early 1997 a UNDP scheme to support private-sector and community-based initiatives to generate employment opportunities, MicroStart, became operational with some US $41m. in initial funds. UNDP supports the Caribbean Project Development Facility and the Africa Project Development Facility, which are administered by the International Finance Corporation (q.v.) and which aim to develop the private sector in these regions in order to generate jobs and sustainable livelihoods.

Approximately one-third of all UNDP programme resources support national efforts to ensure efficient governance and to build effective relations between the state, the private sector and civil society, which are essential to achieving sustainable development. UNDP undertakes assessment missions to help ensure free and fair elections and works to promote human rights, an accountable and competent public sector, a competent judicial system and decentralized government and decision-making. Since 1993, for example, UNDP has assisted more than 30 African countries to conduct elections, supported the Vietnamese Government in institutional reform and the formulation of a new legal framework and undertaken a programme of voter education in Bangladesh. In July 1997 UNDP organized an International Conference on Governance for Sustainable Growth and Equity, which was held in New York, USA, and attended by more than 1,000 representatives of national and local authorities and the business and non-governmental sectors. At the Conference UNDP initiated a four-year programme to promote activities and to encourage new approaches in support of good governance. UNDP's Local Initiative Facility for Urban Environment (LIFE) undertakes small-scale environmental projects in low-income communities, in collaboration with local authorities and community-based groups. Recent initiatives include canal and river improvement projects in Thailand, improvement of the urban environment in a suburb of Cairo, Egypt, and public-health improvements and the environmental rehabilitation of precipitous housing areas in Brazil. LIFE was initiated at the UN Conference on Environment and Development, which was held in June 1992. UNDP supports the development of national programmes that emphasize the sustainable management of natural resources, for example through its Sustainable Energy Initiative, which promotes more efficient use of energy resouces and the introduction of renewable alternatives to conventional fuels. UNDP is also concerned with forest management, the aquatic environment and sustainable agriculture and food security.

In the mid-1990s UNDP expanded its role in countries in crisis and with special circumstances, working in collaboration with other UN agencies to promote relief and development efforts. In particular, UNDP was concerned to achieve reconcilation, reintegration and reconstruction in affected countries, as well as to support emergency interventions and manage and delivery of programme aid. In 1995 the Executive Board decided that 5% of total UNDP core resources be allocated to countries in 'special development situations'. During 1996–97 special development initiatives to promote peace and national recovery were undertaken in more than 32 countries. Activities included strengthening democratic institutions in Guatemala, the clearance of anti-personnel land-mines in Cambodia and Laos, socio-economic rehabilitation in Lebanon and the rehabilitation of communities for returning populations in some 20 countries. In December 1996 UNDP launched the Civilian Reconstruction Teams programme, creating some 5,000 jobs for former combatants in Liberia to work on the rehabilitation of the country's infrastructure. UNDP has extended its Disaster Management Training Programme, in order, partly, to help countries to attain the objectives of the International Decade for Natural Disaster Reduction (announced in 1990).

In 1994 the Executive Board determined that UNDP should assume a more active and integrative role within the UN development system. This approach has been implemented by UNDP Resident Representatives, who aim to co-ordinate UN policies to achieve sustainable human development, in consultation with other agencies, in particular UNEP, FAO and UNHCR. In 1997 UNDP planned to allocate more resources to training and skill-sharing programmes in order to promote this co-ordinating role. UNDP is a co-sponsor, jointly with WHO, the World Bank, UNICEF, UNESCO and UNFPA, of a Joint UN Programme on HIV and AIDS, which became operational on 1 January 1996. UNDP was also to develop its role in co-ordinating activities following global UN conferences. In March 1995 government representatives attending the World Summit for Social Development, which was held in Copenhagen, Denmark, adopted the Copenhagen Declaration and a Programme of Action, which included initiatives to promote the eradication of poverty, to increase and reallocate official development assistance to basic social programmes and to promote equal access to education. With particular reference to UNDP, the Programme of Action advocated that UNDP support the implementation of social development programmes, co-ordinate these efforts through its field offices and organize efforts on the part of the UN system to stimulate capacity-building at local, national and regional levels. Following the UN Fourth World Conference on Women, held in Beijing, People's Republic of China, in September 1995, UNDP led inter-agency efforts to ensure the full participation of women in all economic, political and professional activities, and assisted with further situation analysis and training activities. (UNDP also created a Gender in Development Office to ensure that women participate more fully in UNDP-sponsored activities.) UNDP played an important role, at both national and international levels, in preparing for the second UN Conference on Human Settlements (Habitat II), which was held in Istanbul, Turkey, in June 1996 (see the UN Centre for Human Settlements, p. 34). At the conference UNDP announced the establishment of a new facility, which was designed to promote private-sector investment in urban infrastructure. The facility was to be allocated initial resources of US $10m., with the aim of generating a total of $1,000m. from private sources for this sector.

In 1996 UNDP implemented its first corporate communications and advocacy strategy, which aimed to generate public awareness of the activities of the UN system, to promote debate on development issues and to mobilize resources by increasing public and donor appreciation of UNDP. A series of national and regional workshops was held, while media activities focused on the publication of the annual *Human Development Report* and the International Day for the Eradication of Poverty, held on 17 October. UNDP aims to use the developments in information technology to advance its communications strategy and to disseminate guidelines and technical support throughout its country office network.

FINANCE

UNDP is financed by the voluntary contributions of members of the United Nations and the Programme's participating agencies. Contributions from recipient governments, or third-party sources, to share the cost of projects constitute an increasingly significant portion of UNDP's total income. In 1996 total voluntary contributions amounted to US $2,186m., compared with some $1,842m. in 1995. Contributions to UNDP's core resources amounted to US $844m. in 1996, compared with $927m. in 1995, while contributions to non-core funds, including cost-sharing arrangements, amounted to $1,342m. In 1996 estimated field programme expenditure under UNDP's core programme totalled $1,211m., of which $544m. was from general resources and $667m. cost-sharing contributions.

UNDP FIELD PROGRAMME EXPENDITURE BY REGION
(1996, UNDP core programme, US $ million)

Africa	248
Asia and the Pacific	196
Latin America and the Caribbean	613
Arab states	61
Europe and the CIS	43
Global and interregional	50
Total	1,211*

* Including government cash counterpart contributions.

PUBLICATIONS

Annual Report.

Choices (quarterly).

Co-operation South (twice a year).

Human Development Report (annually).

Associated Funds and Programmes

UNDP is the central funding, planning and co-ordinating body for technical co-operation within the UN system. A number of associated funds and programmes, financed separately by means of voluntary contributions, provide specific services through the UNDP network. In April 1996 the UNDP Administrator signed an agreement on the establishment of a new trust fund to promote economic and technical co-operation among developing countries.

Total expenditure of funds and programmes administered by UNDP amounted to an estimated US $263.3m. in 1996. The principal funds and programmes are listed below.

CAPACITY 21

UNDP initiated Capacity 21 at the UN Conference on Environment and Development, which was held in June 1992, to support developing countries in preparing and implementing policies for sustainable development (i.e. the objectives of Agenda 21, which was adopted by the Conference). Capacity 21 promotes new approaches to development, through national development strategies, community-based management and training programmes. During 1995 programmes under Capacity 21 were under way in 44 countries. By the end of that year the Capacity 21 fund had received pledges totalling US $51.7m. In 1996 expenditure under Capacity 21 totalled $7.4m.

GLOBAL ENVIRONMENT FACILITY—GEF

The GEF, which is managed jointly by UNDP, the World Bank and UNEP, began operations in 1991, with funding of US $1,500m. over a three-year period. Its aim is to support projects for the prevention of climate change, conserving biological diversity, protecting international waters, and reducing the depletion of the ozone layer in the atmosphere. UNDP is responsible for capacity-building, targeted research, pre-investment activities and technical assistance. UNDP also administers the Small Grants Programme of the GEF, which supports community-based activities by local non-governmental organizations. During the pilot phase of the GEF, in the period 1991–94, $242.5m. in funding was approved for 55 UNDP projects; by mid-1996 53 of these projects were being implemented. In March 1994 representatives of 87 countries agreed to provide $2,000m. to replenish GEF funds for a further three-year period from July of that year. Programme expenditure in 1996 amounted to $50.4m.

MONTREAL PROTOCOL

UNDP assists countries to eliminate the use of ozone-depleting substances (ODS), in accordance with the Montreal Protocol to the Vienna Convention for the Protection of the Ozone Layer (see p. 42), through the design, monitoring and evaluation of ODS phase-out projects and programmes. In particular, UNDP provides technical assistance and training, national capacity-building and demonstration projects and technology transfer investment projects. The latter accounted for more than 75% of UNDP's activities in this area in 1994. In 1996, through the Executive Committee of the Montreal Protocol, UNDP provided US $27.0m. to assist 28 countries in eliminating ozone-depleting substances.

OFFICE TO COMBAT DESERTIFICATION AND DROUGHT—UNSO

The Office was established following the conclusion, in October 1994, of the UN Convention to Combat Desertification in Those Countries Experiencing Serious Drought and/or Desertification, Particularly in Africa. It replaced the former UN Sudano–Sahelian Office (UNSO), while retaining the same acronym. UNSO is responsible for UNDP's role in desertification control and dryland management. Special emphasis is given to strengthening the environmental planning and management capacities of national institutions. During 1996 UNSO, in collaboration with other international partners, supported the implementation of the UN Convention in 43 designated countries. Programme expenditure in that year totalled US $6.1m.

Headquarters: BP 366, ave de la Résistance du 17 mai, Immeuble de la Caisse Générale de Péréquation, Ouagadougou, Burkina Faso; tel. 30-63-35; telex 5262; fax 31-05-81.

Director: Samuel Nyambi.

PROGRAMME OF ASSISTANCE TO THE PALESTINIAN PEOPLE—PAPP

PAPP is committed to strengthening newly-created institutions in the Israeli-occupied Territories and emerging Palestinian autonomous areas, to creating employment opportunities and to stimulating private and public investment in the area to enhance trade and export potential. Examples of PAPP activities include the following: construction of sewage collection networks and systems in the northern Gaza Strip; provision of water to 500,000 people in rural and urban areas of the West Bank and Gaza; construction of schools, youth and health centres; support to vegetable and fish traders through the construction of cold storage and packing facilities; and provision of loans to strengthen industry and commerce. Field programme expenditure in 1996 totalled US $47.1m.

UNITED NATIONS CAPITAL DEVELOPMENT FUND—UNCDF

The Fund was established in 1966 and became fully operational in 1974. It invests in poor communities in least-developed countries by providing economic and social infrastructure, credit for both agricultural and small-scale entrepreneurial activities, and local development funds which encourage people's participation as well as that of local governments in the planning and implementation of projects. UNCDF aims to promote the interests of women in community projects and to enhance their earning capacities. In May 1996 stable funding for the Fund was pledged by eight donors for a three-year period. During 1996 income from voluntary contributions amounted to US $34.8m., while programme expenditure totalled $41.1m.

Executive Secretary: Poul Grosen.

UNITED NATIONS DEVELOPMENT FUND FOR WOMEN—UNIFEM

UNIFEM is the UN's lead agency in addressing the issues relating to women in development and promoting the rights of women worldwide. The Fund provides direct financial and technical support to enable low-income women in developing countries to increase earnings, gain access to labour-saving technologies and otherwise improve the quality of their lives. It also funds activities that include women in decision-making related to mainstream development projects. UNIFEM has supported the preparation of national reports in 30 countries and used the priorities identified in these reports and in other regional initiatives to formulate a Women's Development Agenda for the 21st century. Through these efforts, UNIFEM played an active role in the preparation for the UN Fourth World Conference on Women, which was held in Beijing, People's Republic of China, in September 1995. Programme expenditure in 1996 totalled US $11m.

Headquarters: 304 East 45th St, New York, NY 10017, USA; tel. (212) 906-6400; fax (212) 906-6705.

Director: Noeleen Heyzer (Singapore).

UNITED NATIONS REVOLVING FUND FOR NATURAL RESOURCES EXPLORATION—UNRFNRE

The UNRFNRE was established in 1974 to provide risk capital to finance exploration for natural resources (particularly minerals) in developing countries and, when discoveries are made, to help to attract investment. The revolving character of the Fund lies in the undertaking of contributing governments to make replenishment contributions to the Fund when the projects it finances lead to commercial production. UNRFNRE publishes *Environmental Guidelines for the Mineral Sector* to encourage the sustainable development of resources. In 1996 voluntary contributions to the Fund amounted to US $1.3m.

Director: Shigeaki Tomita (Japan).

UNITED NATIONS VOLUNTEERS—UNV

The United Nations Volunteers is an important source of middle-level skills for the UN development system supplied at modest cost, particularly in the least-developed countries. Volunteers expand the scope of UNDP project activities by supplementing the work of international and host-country experts and by extending the influence of projects to local community levels. UNV also supports technical co-operation within and among the developing countries by encouraging volunteers from the countries themselves and by forming regional exchange teams comprising such volunteers. UNV is involved in areas such as peace-building, elections, human rights, humanitarian relief and community-based environmental programmes, in addition to development activities.

The UN Short-term Advisory Programme, which is the private-sector development arm of UNV, has increasingly focused its attention on countries in the process of economic transition. It completed 124 assignments in 18 countries in 1995.

In 1995 a total of 3,263 UNV specialists and field workers from 134 countries served in 139 countries. Total expenditure in 1996 amounted to US $14.9m.; in that year 3,240 UNVs served under the initiative.

Headquarters: Haus Carstanje, Bonn, Germany.

Executive Co-ordinator: BRENDA MCSWEENEY.

United Nations Environment Programme—UNEP

Address: POB 30552, Nairobi, Kenya.

Telephone: (2) 621234; **telex:** 22068; **fax:** (2) 226890; **internet:** http://www.unep.org.

The United Nations Environment Programme was established in 1972 by the UN General Assembly, following recommendations of the 1972 UN Conference on the Human Environment, in Stockholm, Sweden, to encourage international co-operation in matters relating to the human environment.

Organization

(December 1997)

GOVERNING COUNCIL

The main function of the Governing Council, which meets every two years, is to provide general policy guidelines for the direction and co-ordination of environmental programmes within the UN system. It comprises representatives of 58 states, elected by the UN General Assembly on a rotating basis.

HIGH-LEVEL COMMITTEE OF MINISTERS AND OFFICIALS IN CHARGE OF THE ENVIRONMENT

The Committee was established by the Governing Council in April 1997, with a mandate to consider the international environmental agenda and to make recommendations to the Council on reform and policy issues. In addition, the Committee, comprising 36 elected members, was to provide guidance and advice to the Executive Director, to enhance UNEP's collaboration and co-operation with other multilateral bodies and to help to mobilize financial resources for UNEP.

SECRETARIAT

The Secretariat serves as a focal point for environmental action within the UN system. At September 1997 UNEP had 616 members of staff, of whom 329 were based at the organization's headquarters and 287 at regional and other offices.

Executive Director: (from 1 February 1998) Dr KLAUS TÖPFER (Germany).

REGIONAL OFFICES

Africa: POB 30552, Nairobi, Kenya; tel. (2) 624283; fax (2) 623928.

Asia and the Pacific: UN Bldg, 10th Floor, Rajadamnern Ave, Bangkok 10200, Thailand; tel. (2) 288-1234; telex 82392; fax (2) 280-2829.

Europe: CP 356, 15 chemin des Anémones, 1219 Châtelaine, Geneva, Switzerland; tel. (22) 9799111; telex 415465; fax (22) 7973420.

Latin America and the Caribbean: Blvd de los Virreyes 155, Lomas Virreyes, 11000 México, DF, Mexico; tel. (5) 2024841; telex 177055; fax (5) 2020950.

North America: DC-2 Bldg, Room 0803, 2 United Nations Plaza, New York, NY 10017, USA; tel. (212) 963-8138; telex 422311; fax (212) 963-7341.

West Asia: 1083 Road No 425, Jufair 342, Manama, Bahrain; tel. 276072; telex 7457; fax 276075.

OTHER OFFICES

Convention on International Trade in Endangered Species of Wild Fauna and Flora (CITES): 15 chemin des Anémones, 1219 Châtelaine, Geneva, Switzerland; tel. (22) 9799139; telex 415391; fax (22) 7973417; e-mail cites@unep.ch; Sec.-Gen. IZGREV TOPKOV.

International Register of Potentially Toxic Chemicals (IRPTC): CP 356, 15 chemin des Anémones, 1219 Châtelaine, Geneva, Switzerland; tel. (22) 9799111; fax (22) 7973460; e-mail irptc@unep.ch; internet http://www.irptc.unep.ch/irptc/; Dir JAMES B. WILLIS.

Regional Co-ordinating Unit for East Asian Seas: UN Bldg, 10th Floor, Rajadamnern Ave, Bangkok 10200, Thailand; tel. (2) 281-2428; telex 82392; fax (2) 267-8008.

Regional Co-ordinating Unit for the Caribbean Environment Programme: 14-20 Port Royal St, Kingston, Jamaica; tel. (809) 9229267; fax (809) 9229292.

Secretariat of the Convention on Biological Diversity: World Trade Centre, 393 St Jacques St, Suite 300, Montréal, Québec, Canada H2Y 1N9; tel. (514) 288-2220; fax (514) 288-6588; e-mail chm@biodiv.org; internet http://www.biodiv.org; Exec. Sec. CALESTOUS JUMA.

Secretariat for the Multilateral Fund for the Implementation of the Montreal Protocol: 1800 McGill College Ave, 27th Floor, Montréal, Québec, Canada H3A 3J6; tel. (514) 282-1122; fax (514) 282-0068; Chief OMAR EL-ARINI.

UNEP Arab League Liaison Office: 24 Iraq St, Mohandessin, Cairo, Egypt; tel. (2) 3361349; fax (2) 3370658.

UNEP/CMS (Convention on the Conservation of Migratory Species of Wild Animals) **Secretariat:** Martin-Luther-King-Str 8, 53175 Bonn, Germany; tel. (228) 8152401; fax (228) 8152449; e-mail cms@unep.de; Exec. Sec. ARNULF MÜLLER-HELMBRECHT.

UNEP Co-ordinating Unit for the Mediterranean Action Plan (MEDU): Leoforos Vassileos Konstantinou 48, POB 18019, 11610 Athens, Greece; tel. (1) 7253190; fax (1) 7253196; e-mail unepmedu-@compulink.gr.

UNEP Industry and Environment: Tour Mirabeau, 39–43, Quai André Citroen, 75739 Paris Cédex 15, France; tel. 1-44-37-14-50; fax 1-44-37-14-74; e-mail unepie@unep.fr; Dir JACQUELINE ALOISI DE LARDEREL.

UNEP International Environmental Technology Centre: 2-110 Ryokuchi koen, Tsurmi-ku, Osaka 538, Japan; tel. (6) 915-4581; fax (6) 915-0304; e-mail ietc@unep.or.jp; Dir JOHN WHITELAW.

UNEP Ozone Secretariat: POB 30552, Nairobi, Kenya; tel. (2) 623885; telex 22068; fax (2) 623913; e-mail ozoneinfo@unep.org; internet http://www.unep.ch/ozone/; Exec. Sec. K. MADHAVA SARMA.

UNEP Secretariat of the Basel Convention: CP 356, 15 chemin des Anémones, 1219 Châtelaine, Geneva, Switzerland; tel. (22) 9799111; telex 415465; fax (22) 7973454; e-mail bulska@unep.ch; Exec. Sec. Dr I. RUMMEL-BULSKA.

UNEP Secretariat for the UN Scientific Committee on the Effects of Atomic Radiation: Vienna International Centre, Wagramerstrasse 5, POB 500, 1400 Vienna, Austria; tel. (1) 21345-4330; telex 135612; fax (1) 21345-5902; e-mail bbennett@unov.un.at; Sec. BURTON G. BENNET.

Activities

UNEP aims to maintain a constant watch on the changing state of the environment; to analyse the trends; to assess the problems using a wide range of data and techniques; and to promote projects leading to environmentally sound development. It plays a catalytic and co-ordinating role within and beyond the UN system. Many UNEP projects are implemented in co-operation with other UN agencies, particularly UNDP, the World Bank group, FAO, UNESCO and WHO. About 45 intergovernmental organizations outside the UN system and 60 international non-governmental organizations have official observer status on UNEP's Governing Council, and, through the Environment Liaison Centre in Nairobi, UNEP is linked to more than 6,000 non-governmental bodies concerned with the environment. UNEP also sponsors international conferences, programmes, plans and agreements regarding all aspects of the environment.

UNEP played a significant role in preparing for and conducting the UN Conference on Environment and Development (UNCED, or the 'Earth Summit'), which was held in Rio de Janeiro, Brazil, in June 1992. Agenda 21, a programme of activities to promote sustainable development, which was adopted at UNCED, reaffirmed UNEP's mandate and gave its Governing Council an enhanced role in the areas of policy guidance and development. The two-year 1994–95 programme was considered to be a transitional period for UNEP, during which its role and effectiveness as the UN's agency for environmental issues was re-evaluated. In May 1995 the Governing Council, at its 18th session, adopted a new programme of activities for the two-year period 1996–97, which aimed to incorporate the demands of Agenda 21 and achieve a more integrated approach to addressing environmental issues. UNEP's 12 previous sectoral subprogrammes were redesigned into the five main interdisciplinary areas of work listed below. Approaches to assessment and monitoring, formulation and evaluation of environment policy and management of environmental intitiatives (defined as priority actions by Agenda 21) were to be applied in all programme activities, in order to increase the efficacy of UNEP's work. The Governing Council resolved that UNEP should strengthen its co-operation partnerships with other UN agencies and regional, national and local institutions in order to benefit from their expertise and to address varying regional environmental concerns.

In February 1997 the Governing Council, at its 19th session, adopted a ministerial declaration on UNEP's future role and mandate, which recognized the organization as the principal UN body working in the field of the environment and as the leading global environmental authority, setting and overseeing the international environmental agenda. In June a Special Session of the UN General Assembly, referred to as the 'Earth Summit + 5', was convened to review the state of the environment and progress achieved in implementing UNCED's objectives. The meeting adopted a Programme for Further Implementation of Agenda 21 to intensify efforts in areas such as energy, freshwater resources and technology transfer. The meeting confirmed UNEP's essential role in advancing the Programme and as a global authority promoting a coherent legal and political approach to the environmental challenges of sustainable development.

SUSTAINABLE MANAGEMENT AND USE OF NATURAL RESOURCES

UNEP aims to promote the sustainable use of natural resources, in order to prevent degradation of the environment and natural ecosystems that results from intensified demands on land, water, marine and coastal resources.

UNEP estimates that one-third of the world's population will suffer chronic water shortages by 2025, owing to rising demand for drinking water as a result of growing populations, decreasing quality of water because of pollution, and increasing requirements of industries and agriculture. Efforts to address these problems include conducting a range of studies and assessments of river basins and regional seas, including the Nile River, the Caspian Sea and the Erhai Lake. In addition, UNEP provides scientific, technical and administrative support to facilitate the implementation and co-ordination of regional seas conventions and plans of action. UNEP promotes greater international co-operation in the management of river basins and coastal areas and for the development of tools and guidelines to achieve the sustainable management of freshwater and coastal resources. In particular, UNEP aims to control land-based activities, principally pollution, which affect freshwater resources, marine biodiversity and the coastal ecosystems of small-island developing states. In November 1995 110 governments adopted a Global Programme of Action for the Protection of the Marine Environment from Land-based Activities. UNEP provides the secretariat to the Programme and promotes its implementation.

UNEP supports the sound management and conservation of biological resources, in order to maintain biological diversity and to achieve sustainable development. UNEP was instrumental in the drafting of a Convention on Biological Diversity (CBD), which was adopted by UNCED in order to preserve the immense variety of plant and animal species, in particular those threatened with extinction. The Convention entered into force at the end of 1993; by mid-1997 166 countries were parties to the CBD. UNEP supports co-operation for biodiversity assessment and management in selected developing regions and for the development of strategies for the conservation and sustainable exploitation of individual threatened species (e.g. the Global Tiger Action Plan). UNEP also provides assistance for the preparation of individual country studies and strategies to strengthen national biodiversity management and research. In November 1995 UNEP published a Global Diversity Assessment, which was presented as the first comprehensive study on biodiversity throughout the world. UNEP provides administrative and technical support to other regional and international conventions, including the Convention on the Conservation of Migratory Species and the Convention on International Trade in Endangered Species of Wild Fauna and Flora (CITES). In December 1996 the Lusaka Agreement on Co-operative Enforcement Operations Directed at Illegal Trade in Wild Flora and Fauna entered into force, having been concluded under UNEP auspices in order to strengthen the implementation of the CBD and CITES agreements in Eastern and Central Africa. The first meeting of the Governing Council of Parties to the Agreement, held in March 1997, agreed to establish a Task Force to facilitate its implementation.

In October 1994 87 countries, meeting under UN auspices, signed a Convention to Combat Desertification (see UNSO, p. 40), which aimed to provide a legal framework to counter the degradation of drylands. An estimated 75% of all drylands has suffered some land degradation, affecting approximately 1,000m. people in 110 countries. UNEP continues to support the implementation of the Convention, as part of its efforts to protect land resources. UNEP also aims to improve the assessment of dryland degradation and desertification in co-operation with governments and other international bodies, as well as identifying the causes of degradation and measures to overcome these.

SUSTAINABLE PRODUCTION AND CONSUMPTION

The use of inappropriate industrial technologies and the widespread adoption of unsustainable production and consumption patterns have been identified as being inefficient in the use of renewable resources and wasteful, in particular, in the use of energy. UNEP, mainly through its office for industry and environment, aims to develop new policy and management tools for governments and industry and to encourage the use of environmentally-sound technologies, in order to reduce pollution and the unsustainable use of natural resources. UNEP organizes conferences and training workshops to promote sustainable production practices and disseminates relevant information through the International Cleaner Production Information Clearing House. UNEP, together with UNIDO, has established eight National Cleaner Production Centres to promote a preventive approach to industrial pollution control.

UNEP provides institutional servicing to the Basel Convention on the Control of Transboundary Movements of Hazardous Wastes and their Disposal, which was adopted in 1989 with the aim of preventing the disposal of wastes from industrialized countries in countries that have no processing facilities. (In March 1994 the second meeting of parties to the Convention agreed to ban exportation of hazardous wastes between OECD and non-OECD countries by the end of 1997.) Similar support is given to the Vienna Convention for the Protection of the Ozone Layer (1985) and its 1987 Montreal Protocol on Substances that Deplete the Ozone Layer, which provided for a 50% reduction in the production of chlorofluorocarbons (CFCs) by 2000. (An amendment to the Protocol was adopted in 1990, which required complete cessation of the production of CFCs by 2000 in industrialized countries and by 2010 in developing countries; these deadlines were advanced to 1996 and 2006 respectively, in November 1992.) A Multilateral Fund for the Implementation of the Montreal Protocol was established in June 1990, initially on an interim basis, to promote the use of suitable technologies and the transfer of technologies to developing countries. UNEP, UNDP, the World Bank and UNIDO are the sponsors of the Fund, which by early 1997 had financed 1,800 projects in 106 developing countries at a cost of US $565m. In November 1996 the Fund was replenished, with commitments totalling $540m. for the three-year period 1997–99. The OzonAction Programme of UNEP's industry and environment office works under the Fund to promote information exchange, training and technological awareness. Its objective is to strengthen the capacity of governments and industry in developing countries to undertake measures towards the cost-effective phasing-out of ozone-depleting substances.

UNEP encourages the development of alternative and renewable sources of energy. To achieve this, UNEP is supporting the establishment of a network of centres to research and exchange information of environmentally-sound energy technology resources. UNEP undertakes technical activities to support the implementation of the Framework Convention on Climate Change (FCCC), which was adopted at UNCED and entered into force in March 1994. The FCCC commits countries to submitting reports on measures being taken to reduce the emission of 'greenhouse gases' (i.e. carbon dioxide and other gases that have a warming effect on the atmosphere). The Convention recommends stabilizing these emissions at 1990 levels by 2000; however, this is not legally binding. In July 1996, at the second session of the Conference of the Parties (COP) to the Convention, representatives of developed countries declared their willingness to commit to legally-binding objectives for emission limitations in a specified timetable. Multilateral negotiations ensued to formulate a mandatory treaty on greenhouse gas emissions, which was expected to be concluded at a third session of the COP to be held in Kyoto, Japan, in December 1997. At the end of September the FCCC had received 169 instruments of ratification. At the Kyoto Conference, 38 industrial nations endorsed mandatory reductions of emissions of the six most harmful gases by an average of 5.2% from 1990 levels, between 2008 and 2012. The agreement was to enter into force on being ratified by countries representing 55% of the world's carbon dioxide emissions in 1990.

The realignment of UNEP activities, undertaken for the work programme 1996–97, addressed the concerns that unsustainable patterns of consumption and production, in particular in industrialized countries, were major contributing factors to the deterioration of the global environment. UNEP aims to adjust this situation by stimulating understanding and awareness of the relationship between production and consumption, and promoting dialogue among developed countries to attain an agreement on more sustainable forms of production.

A BETTER ENVIRONMENT FOR HUMAN HEALTH AND WELL-BEING

A guiding principle of Agenda 21 was that human beings were at the centre of concerns for sustainable development and that they were entitled to a healthy and productive life. The new UNEP sub-programme integrated its previous activities relating to health, human settlement and welfare with those concerned with toxic wastes and chemicals. UNEP continues to maintain the International Register of Potentially Toxic Chemicals (IRPTC). UNEP aims to facilitate access to data on chemicals and hazardous wastes, in order to assess and control health and environmental risks, by using the IRPTC as a clearing house facility of relevant information and by publishing information and technical reports on the impact of the use of chemicals. In 1996 UNEP, in collaboration with FAO, began to work towards promoting and formulating an international convention on prior informed consent (PIC) for hazardous chemicals in international trade, extending a voluntary PIC procedure of information exchange undertaken by more than 100 governments since 1991. UNEP is also working towards a multilateral agreement to reduce and ultimately eliminate the manufacture and use of Persistent Organic Pollutants, which are considered to be a major global environmental hazard.

In conjunction with UNCHS (Habitat), UNDP, the World Bank and other regional organizations and institutions, UNEP promotes environmental concerns in urban planning and management through the Sustainable Cities Programme, as well as regional workshops on urban pollution and the impact of transportation systems. In January 1994 UNEP inaugurated an International Environmental Technology Centre (IETC), with offices in Osaka and Shiga, Japan, in order to strengthen the capabilities of developing countries and countries with economies in transition to promote environmentally-sound management of cities and fresh water reservoirs through technology co-operation and partnerships.

UNEP aims to reduce the risk to human populations of environmental change and emergencies and works with the UN's Department of Humanitarian Affairs to provide immediate assistance to countries confronted with an environmental emergency, such as a chemical spill, forest fire or industrial accident. UNEP also aims to enhance accident prevention and emergency preparedness capabilities in all developing countries, for example through its APELL programme (Awareness and Preparedness for Emergencies at the Local Level). As part of its efforts to develop mechanisms to avoid and settle environmental disputes, UNEP participates in working groups in the Israeli-occupied Territories, under the Middle East peace process, and supports regional co-operation in the management of shared natural resources in the Nile river basin, the Arctic and Antarctica.

GLOBALIZATION AND THE ENVIRONMENT

With the globalization of the world's economy UNEP has identified a need to enhance the assessment of the environmental impact of trade patterns and policies, at country and regional level, and to undertake legal analyses of the relationship between environmental laws and international trade regimes. UNCED recommended the need to integrate environmental issues into economic priorities as a prerequisite of sustainable development. UNEP operates a system of environmental valuation and environmental impact assessment, which it aims to promote through national guidelines and technical workshops. Other so-called environmental economic tools may be developed through environmental and natural resource accounting and the eco-labelling of country export products (i.e. identifying products with a high environmental quality profile). UNEP aims to promote the exchange of information relevant to this sector and to assist countries to develop additional sources of finance for environmentally sustainable development. UNEP, together with UNDP and the World Bank, is an implementing agency of the Global Environment Facility (GEF), which was established in 1991 as a mechanism for international co-operation in projects concerned with biological diversity, climate change, international waters and depletion of the ozone layer. UNEP provides the secretariat for the Scientific and Technical Advisory Panel, which was established to provide expert advice on GEF programmes and operational strategies.

In order to complement the globalization process and the expanded environment agenda, UNEP supports the formulation and implementation of international and national legislation as environmental management tools. While it supports and helps co-ordinate the activities of the secretariats of international and regional conventions, UNEP is undertaking preliminary efforts to formulate a definitive international legal framework for sustainable development. At a national level UNEP assists governments to prepare environmental legislation and guidelines and to implement existing international conventions. Training workshops in various aspects of environmental law and its application are conducted.

UNEP aims to promote coherent decision-making, in the environment field, through its support for research and information exchange. It promotes the scientific research and review of key environmental issues and conducts workshops to develop policy recommendations. In 1996–97 UNEP aimed to integrate environmental concerns in the activities of international financial institutions and to encourage collaboration among these bodies.

GLOBAL AND REGIONAL SERVICING AND SUPPORT

UNEP has a major responsibility to identify and assess environmental issues of common concern, to alert the world community to these issues, to precipitate their resolution through international co-operation and to provide policy guidance for the direction and co-ordination of environmental programmes within the UN system. Under this sub-programme UNEP aims to fulfil its role and to deliver its programme of work through the basic institutional functions of environmental assessment, advisory services, public awareness and provision of information.

Through regional consultations and specialized centres world-wide, UNEP aims to develop and enhance frameworks, methodologies and indicators to achieve integrated environmental assessment and reporting. In particular, UNEP aims to strengthen early-warning mechanisms and region-specific assessment. UNEP is participating in the design of a Global Terrestrial Observing System, which was to be implemented by the GEF.

UNEP promotes and supports regional co-operation initiatives for environmental action by co-operation with regional banks, economic commissions and other organizations. In addition, UNEP provides policy and technical advice to governments in developing countries and countries with economies in transition for the integration of environmental considerations into national development plans.

UNEP's public education campaigns and outreach programmes promote community involvement in environmental issues. Further communication of environmental concerns is undertaken through the media, an information centre service and special promotional events, including World Environment Day, photograph competitions and the awarding of the Sasakawa Prize to recognize distinguished service to the environment by individuals and groups. In 1996 UNEP initiated a Global Environment Citizenship Programme to promote acknowledgment of the environmental responsibilities of all sectors of society.

UNEP's data and information services include a Global Resource Information Data-base (GRID), which converts data collected into information usable by decision-makers, and the INFOTERRA programme, which facilitates the exchange of environmental information through an extensive network of national 'focal points' (totalling 174 in early 1997), and the Environment and Natural Resource Information Networks (ENRIN), which UNEP aims to establish in every developing region. In 1996–97 UNEP aimed to integrate all its information resources in order to improve access to information and international environment information exchange. This was to be achieved through the design and implementation of UNEPNET, which was to operate throughout the UN system and be fully accessible through the world-wide information networks.

FINANCE

UNEP derives its finances from the regular budget of the United Nations and from voluntary contributions to the Environment Fund. UNEP's estimated budget for 1996–97 amounted to $9.9m. from the UN regular budget and $90m. (with an additional supplementary appropriation of $15m. if or when funds become available) from the Environment Fund. A budget of $75m. has been approved for the 1998–99 work programme.

APPROPRIATION FOR FUND PROGRAMME ACTIVITIES, 1996–97

	(US $'000)
Sustainable management and use of natural resources	
Freshwater, coastal, marine resources	13,500
Biological resources	7,200
Land resources	8,100
ENRIN	6,300
Sustainable production and consumption	
Sustainable production	7,200
Energy utilization	1,800
Production and consumption patterns	900
A better environment for human health and well-being	
Toxic chemicals and wastes	5,400
Urban areas	4,500
Environmental change and emergencies	900
Globalization and the environment	
Trade and the environment	900
Environment economics	900
Policy-relevant research	1,800
Global and regional servicing and support	
Environment assessment	6,300
Regional and subregional co-operation	8,550
Public awareness, education, major groups	7,650
UNEPNET	4,500
Total	90,000

PUBLICATIONS

Report of the Executive Director (every 2 years).
APELL Newsletter (2 a year).
Cleaner Production Newsletter (2 a year).
Climate Change Bulletin (quarterly).
Connect (UNESCO-UNEP newsletter on environmental degradation, quarterly).
Desertification Control Bulletin (2 a year).
EarthViews (quarterly).
Environment Forum (quarterly).
Environmental Law Bulletin (2 a year).
Financial Services Initiative (2 a year).
GEF News (quarterly).
Global Environment Outlook (annually).
Global Biodiversity Assessment.
IETC Insight (3 a year).
Industry and Environment Review (quarterly).
Leave it to Us (children's magazine, 2 a year).
Managing Hazardous Waste (2 a year).
Nature et Faune/Wildlife and Nature (quarterly, with FAO).
Our Planet (6 a year).
OzonAction Newsletter (quarterly).
Tiger Paper (quarterly, with FAO).
Tourism Focus (2 a year).
UNEP Update (monthly).
World Atlas of Desertification.
Studies, reports, legal texts, technical guidelines, etc.

United Nations High Commissioner for Refugees—UNHCR

Address: CP 2500, 1211 Geneva 2 dépôt, Switzerland.
Telephone: (22) 7398111; **telex:** 415740; **fax:** (22) 7319546; **internet:** http://www.unhcr.ch.

The Office of the High Commissioner was established in 1951 to provide international protection for refugees and to seek durable solutions to their problems.

Organization

(November 1997)

HIGH COMMISSIONER

The High Commissioner is elected by the United Nations General Assembly on the nomination of the Secretary-General, and is responsible to the General Assembly and to the UN Economic and Social Council (ECOSOC).

High Commissioner: SADAKO OGATA (Japan).

Deputy High Commissioner: GERALD WALZER (Austria).

EXECUTIVE COMMITTEE

The Executive Committee of the High Commissioner's Programme, established by ECOSOC, gives the High Commissioner policy directives in respect of material assistance programmes and advice in the field of international protection. In addition, it oversees UNHCR's general policies and use of funds. The Committee, which comprises representatives of 53 states, both members and non-members of the UN, meets once a year.

ADMINISTRATION

Headquarters includes the Executive Office, comprising the offices of the High Commissioner, the Deputy High Commissioner and the Assistant High Commissioner. The offices of Internal Oversight and of International Protection report directly to the Executive Office, as do the Secretariat, the Centre for Documentation and Research and the Department of Public Information. Refugee support services are undertaken by the divisions of Operations Support, Financial and Information Services and Human Resource Management. Operations are administered by regional bureaux covering Central, East and West Africa, Asia and the Pacific, Europe, the Americas, and Central Asia, South-West Asia, North Africa and the Middle East. Separate operational divisions—for the Great Lakes region of Africa, Southern Africa and the former Yugoslavia—are headed by field-based Directors. At February 1997 there were 239 UNHCR field offices in 119 countries. At that time UNHCR employed 5,411 people, including short-term staff, of whom 4,427 (or 82%) were working in the field.

Activities

The competence of the High Commissioner extends to any person who, owing to well-founded fear of being persecuted for reasons of race, religion, nationality or political opinion, is outside the country of his or her nationality and is unable or, owing to such fear or for reasons other than personal convenience, remains unwilling to accept the protection of that country; or who, not having a nationality and being outside the country of his or her former habitual residence, is unable or, owing to such fear or for reasons other than personal convenience, is unwilling to return to it. Refugees who are assisted by other United Nations agencies, or who have the same rights or obligations as nationals of their country of residence, are outside the mandate of UNHCR.

In the early 1990s there was a significant shift in UNHCR's focus of activities. Increasingly UNHCR is called upon to support people who have been displaced within their own country (i.e. with similar needs to those of refugees but who have not crossed an international border) or those threatened with displacement as a result of armed conflict. In addition, it is providing greater support to refugees who have returned to their country of origin, to assist their reintegration, and is working to enable the local community to support the returnees. At the start of 1997 the refugee population world-wide totalled 13.2m. and UNHCR was concerned with a further 4.9m. internally displaced persons, 3.3m. returnees and 1.4m. others.

INTERNATIONAL PROTECTION

As laid down in the Statute of the Office, one of the two primary functions of UNHCR is to extend international protection to refugees. In the exercise of this function, UNHCR seeks to ensure that refugees and asylum-seekers are protected against *refoulement* (forcible return), that they receive asylum, and that they are treated according to internationally recognized standards. UNHCR pursues these objectives by a variety of means which include promoting the conclusion and ratification by states of international conventions for the protection of refugees. UNHCR promotes the adoption of liberal practices of asylum by states, so that refugees and asylum-seekers are granted admission, at least on a temporary basis.

The most comprehensive instrument concerning refugees that has been elaborated at the international level is the 1951 United Nations Convention relating to the Status of Refugees. This Convention, the scope of which was extended by a Protocol adopted in 1967, defines the rights and duties of refugees and contains provisions dealing with a variety of matters which affect the day-to-day lives of refugees. The application of the 1951 United Nations Refugee Convention and the 1967 Protocol is supervised by UNHCR. Important provisions for the treatment of refugees are also contained in a number of instruments adopted at the regional level. These include the OAU Convention of 1969 Governing the Specific Aspects of Refugee Problems, the European Agreement on the Abolition of Visas for Refugees, and the 1969 American Convention on Human Rights.

UNHCR has actively encouraged states to accede to the 1951 United Nations Refugee Convention and the 1967 Protocol: 134 states had acceded to either or both of these basic refugee instruments by 1 November 1997. An increasing number of states have also adopted domestic legislation and/or administrative measures to implement the international instruments, particularly in the field of procedures for the determination of refugee status. Such measures provide an important guarantee that refugees will be accorded the standards of treatment which have been internationally established for their benefit. In recent years UNHCR has formulated a strategy designed to address the fundamental causes of refugee flows.

UNHCR has attempted to deal with the problem of military attacks on refugee camps, by formulating and encouraging the acceptance of a set of principles to ensure the safety of refugees. It also seeks to address the specific needs of refugee women and children.

ASSISTANCE ACTIVITIES

UNHCR assistance activities are divided into General Programmes (which include a Programme Reserve, a General Allocation for Voluntary Repatriation and an Emergency Fund) and Special Programmes. The latter are undertaken at the request of the UN General Assembly, the Secretary-General of the UN or member states, in response to a particular crisis.

The first phase of an assistance operation uses UNHCR's capacity of emergency preparedness and response. This enables UNHCR to address the immediate needs of refugees at short notice, for example, by employing specially-trained emergency teams and maintaining stockpiles of basic equipment, medical aid and materials. A significant proportion of UNHCR expenditure is allocated to the next phase of an operation, providing 'care and maintenance' in stable refugee circumstances. This assistance can take various forms, including the provision of food, shelter, medical care and essential supplies. Also covered in many instances are basic services, including education and counselling.

POPULATIONS OF CONCERN TO UNHCR BY REGION*

('000 persons, at 1 January 1997)

	Refugees	Returnees	Internally displaced	Others of concern†	Total
Africa	4,341	1,692	2,058	—	8,091
Asia	4,809	1,241	1,719	156	7,925
Europe	3,166	308	1,066	1,209	5,749
Latin America	88	70	11	—	169
North America	720	—	—	—	720
Oceania	75	—	—	—	75
Total	13,200	3,311	4,854	1,365	22,729

* In accordance with the regional classification of the UN's Department for Economic and Social Information and Policy Analysis, under which Africa includes countries of North Africa and Asia incorporates Turkey and all countries of the Middle East not located on the African continent; Latin America covers Central and South America and the Caribbean.

† Mainly persons who are in a refugee-like situation, that is, who are outside their country, but who have not been formally recognized as refugees. Also includes war-affected populations in the former Yugoslavia who have received UNHCR humanitarian assistance.

POPULATIONS OF CONCERN TO UNHCR BY COUNTRY*

('000 persons, at 31 December 1996)

	Refugees	Returnees	Internally displaced	Others of concern†
Africa				
Burundi	1.0‡	71.0	882.9	—
Côte d'Ivoire	327.7	—	—	—
Ethiopia	390.5	27.9	—	—
Guinea	663.9	—	—	—
Kenya	223.6	—	—	—
Liberia	120.1	11.1	320.0	—
Rwanda	25.3	1,300.6	—	—
Sierra Leone	13.5	0.2	654.6	—
Somalia	0.7	14.4	200.0	—
Sudan	393.9	0.6	—	—
Tanzania	498.7	—	—	—
Uganda	264.3	0.2	—	—
Zaire§	676.0	0.7	—	—
Zambia	131.1	—	—	—
Asia and the Pacific				
People's Republic of China	290.1	—	—	—
India	233.4	—	—	—
Myanmar	—	219.3	—	—
Nepal	126.8	—	—	—
Sri Lanka	0.0	54.0	200.0	—
Thailand	108.0	—	—	—
Viet Nam	34.4	105.6	—	—
Central Asia, South-West Asia, North Africa and the Middle East				
Afghanistan	18.8	613.4	273.8	—
Algeria	190.3	—	—	—
Cyprus	0.0	—	265.0	—
Iran	2,030.4	—	—	—
Iraq	113.0	115.3	32.0	—
Kuwait	3.8	—	—	120.0
Pakistan	1,202.7	—	—	—
Europe				
Armenia	219.0	—	72.0	—
Azerbaijan	233.0	60.4	549.0	—
Belarus	30.5	—	—	160.0‖
Bosnia and Herzegovina	—	252.3	760.1	200.0[1]
Croatia	165.4	55.7	144.1	—
France	151.3	—	—	—
Georgia	0.1	—	272.4	—
Germany	1,266.0	—	—	—
Netherlands	103.4	—	—	—
Russia	205.5	—	161.3	847.1[2]
Sweden	191.2	—	—	—
Yugoslavia	563.2	—	0.5	—
The Americas				
Canada	123.2[3]	—	—	—
USA	596.9[3]	—	—	—

* The list includes only those countries having 100,000 or more persons of concern to UNHCR.

† Mainly persons who are in a refugee-like situation, that is, who are outside their country but who have not been formally recognized as refugees.

‡ Excluding refugees from Zaire (figure not known).

§ Renamed the Democratic Republic of the Congo in May 1997. Figures are estimates; at the end of 1996 there were some 423,000 Rwandan refugees accounted for.

‖ Ethnic Belarusians returning from other countries in the Commonwealth of Independent States (CIS).

1 Including war-affected populations receiving UNHCR humanitarian assistance.

2 Mainly 'involuntarily relocating persons' from the Baltic states and other countries in the CIS.

3 Estimated figure.

As far as possible, assistance is geared towards the identification and implementation of durable solutions to refugee problems—this being the second statutory responsibility of UNHCR. Such solutions generally take one of three forms: voluntary repatriation, local integration or resettlement in another country. Voluntary repatriation is increasingly the preferred solution, given the easing of political tension in many regions from which refugees have fled. Where voluntary repatriation is feasible, the Office assists refugees to overcome obstacles preventing their return to their country of origin. This may be done through negotiations with governments involved, or by providing funds either for the physical movement of refugees or for the rehabilitation of returnees once back in their own country.

When voluntary repatriation is not an option, efforts are made to assist refugees to integrate locally and to become self-supporting in their countries of asylum. This may be done either by granting loans to refugees, or by assisting them, through vocational training or in other ways, to learn a skill and to establish themselves in gainful occupations. One major form of assistance to help refugees re-establish themselves outside camps is the provision of housing. In cases where resettlement through emigration is the only viable solution to a refugee problem, UNHCR negotiates with governments in an endeavour to obtain suitable resettlement opportunities, to encourage liberalization of admission criteria and to draw up special immigration schemes.

ORIGIN OF MAJOR REFUGEE POPULATIONS AND PERSONS IN REFUGEE-LIKE SITUATIONS*
('000 persons, estimated at July 1997)

Origin	Refugees
Afghanistan	2,673
Liberia	778
Bosnia and Herzegovina	673
Iraq	672
Somalia	572
Rwanda	467
Sudan	464
Burundi	427
Sierra Leone	374
Eritrea	331

* Excluding some 3.2m. Palestinian refugees who come under the mandate of UNRWA (q.v.). Palestinians who are outside the UNRWA area of operation, for example those in Iraq and Libya, are considered to be of concern to UNHCR.

In the early 1990s UNHCR aimed to consolidate efforts to integrate certain priorities into its programme planning and implementation, as a standard discipline in all phases of assistance. The considerations include awareness of specific problems confronting refugee women, the needs of refugee children, the environmental impact of refugee programmes and long-term development objectives. In an effort to improve the effectiveness of its programmes, UNHCR has initiated a process of delegating authority, as well as responsibility for operational budgets, to its regional and field representatives, increasing flexibility and accountability.

ASIA AND THE PACIFIC

In June 1989 an international conference was convened by UNHCR in Geneva to discuss the ongoing problem of refugees and displaced persons in and from the Indo-Chinese peninsula. The participants (representing 58 states, including Viet Nam) adopted the Comprehensive Plan of Action (CPA) for Indo-Chinese Refugees, which provided for the 'screening' of all Vietnamese arrivals in the region to determine their refugee status, the resettlement of 'genuine' refugees and the repatriation (described as voluntary 'in the first instance') of those deemed to be economic migrants. A steering committee of the international conference, representing 15 nations, met regularly to supervise the plan. In March 1996 UNHCR confirmed that it was to terminate funding for the refugee camps (except those in Hong Kong) on 30 June to coincide with the formal conclusion of the CPA; however, it pledged to support transitional arrangements regarding the completion of the repatriation process and maintenance of the remaining Vietnamese 'non-refugees' during the post-CPA phase-out period, as well as to continue its support for the reintegration and monitoring of returning nationals in Viet Nam and Laos. The prospect of forcible repatriation provoked rioting and violent protests in many camps throughout the region. By early July 16,800 Vietnamese remained in camps in Hong Kong, 4,000 in Indonesia, 3,700 in Thailand and 1,900 in the Philippines, with Malaysia and Singapore having completed the repatriation process. (At that time more than 88,000 Vietnamese and 22,000 Laotians had returned to their countries of origin under the framework of the CPA.) In late July the Philippines Government agreed to permit the remaining camp residents to settle permanently in that country. In September the remaining Vietnamese refugees detained on the island of Galang, in Indonesia, were repatriated, and in February 1997 the last camp for Vietnamese refugees in Thailand was formally closed. In mid-June of that year the main Vietnamese detention camp in Hong Kong was closed. However, the scheduled repatriation of all remaining Vietnamese (estimated at some 1,600 people qualifying as refugees and 700 non-refugees) before the transfer of sovereignty of the territory to the People's Republic of China on 30 June failed to be achieved.

At 31 December 1996 the People's Republic of China was hosting 288,805 Vietnamese refugees. In 1995, in accordance with an agreement concluded with the Chinese Government, UNHCR initiated a programme to redirect its local assistance to promote long-term self-sufficiency in the poorest settlements, including support for revolving-fund rural credit schemes.

Under a programme agreed by Thailand, Laos and UNHCR in 1991 all Laotian refugees, numbering an estimated 60,000, were to be resettled or repatriated by the end of 1994. Despite continuing UNHCR efforts to facilitate the repatriation process, some 3,293 Laotians remained in camps in Thailand at the end of 1996.

The conclusion of a political settlement of the conflict in Cambodia in October 1991 made possible the eventual repatriation of some 370,000 Cambodian refugees and displaced persons. Registration of the refugees began almost immediately, and reception centres were established in six areas in Cambodia. A land-mine survey was undertaken in order to identify the risk to returnees posed by unexploded mines (mine clearance was subsequently undertaken under UN auspices). The actual repatriation operation began in March 1992 and was completed in April 1993. At the same time, however, thousands of ethnic Vietnamese (of whom there were estimated to be 200,000 in Cambodia) were fleeing to Viet Nam, as a result of violence perpetrated against them by Cambodian armed groups. In March 1994 25,000 supporters of the Khmers Rouges in Cambodia fled across the border into Thailand, following advances by government forces. The refugees were immediately repatriated by the Thai armed forces into Khmer Rouge territory, which was inaccessible to aid agencies. At 31 December 1996 there were an estimated 34,400 Cambodians in Viet Nam, while a further 29,406 Cambodians displaced within their country were of concern to UNHCR. In mid-1997 some 31,000 Cambodians were displaced following clashes between government and loyalist FUNCINPEC forces in the north-east of the country. The Thai authorities closed the country's border with Cambodia in order to prevent an influx of refugees, although in early August 3,300 of the most vulnerable refugees were granted temporary refuge from heavy fighting, which threatened their border settlements.

A temporary cessation of hostilities between the Sri Lankan Government and Tamil separatists in early 1995 greatly facilitated UNHCR's ongoing efforts to repatriate Sri Lankan Tamils who had fled to India. By December 1995 54,000 Tamil refugees had been repatriated since 1992. UNHCR verifies the voluntary nature of the repatriations, while in Sri Lanka itself UNHCR operates two 'Open Relief Centres' (established in 1990) to provide food, water and medical assistance and secure shelter for people unable to return to their home area. In late 1995 an offensive by Sri Lankan government troops against the northern Jaffna peninsula caused a massive displacement of the local Tamil population. During 1996 more than 7,000 Sri Lankans sought refuge in India, bringing the total Sri Lankan refugee population in that country to 62,226 at the end of 1996. At that time there were 200,000 Sri Lankan internally displaced persons of concern to UNHCR. India's total refugee population, of some 233,370 at December 1996, also included 98,000 refugees from Tibet, 53,500 Bangladeshis and more than 18,000 Afghans.

From April 1991 increasing numbers of Rohingya Muslims in Myanmar fled into Bangladesh to escape the brutality and killings perpetrated by the Myanma armed forces. UNHCR launched an international appeal for financial aid for the refugees, at the request of Bangladesh, and collaborated with other UN agencies in giving them humanitarian assistance. By July 1992 there were about 270,000 Myanma refugees in Bangladesh. In May 1993 UNHCR and Bangladesh signed a memorandum of understanding, whereby UNHCR would be able to monitor the repatriation process and ensure that people were returning of their own free will. In November a memorandum of understanding, signed with the Myanma Government, secured UNHCR access to the returnees. The first refugees returned to Myanmar with UNHCR assistance at the end of April 1994. They were provided with a small amount of cash, housing grants and two months' food rations, and were supported by several small-scale reintegration projects. Despite disruption to the repatriation process owing to cyclone damage to repatriation facilities and attempts to prevent the spread of disease, by the end of December 1996 the Myanma refugee population in Bangladesh had declined to 30,578. UNHCR continued to monitor the estimated 219,282 returnees in Myanmar and to support their reintegration, for example through literacy and other education programmes. In January 1997 the Bangladesh and Myanma Governments agreed to conclude the repatriation of all refugees by 31 March, later extended to mid-August. In July, in advance of the revised deadline, Rohingya activists initiated a hunger-strike in protest at alleged efforts by the Bangladesh authorities to repatriate forcibly the remaining refugees.

In the early 1990s members of ethnic minorities in Myanmar attempted to flee attacks by government troops into Thailand; however, the Thai Government refused to recognize them as refugees or to offer them humanitarian assistance. By February 1997 there were 101,175 people in camps along the Myanma–Thai border, the majority of whom were Karen (Kayin) refugees.

In 1991–92 thousands of people of Nepalese ethnic origin living in Bhutan sought refuge from alleged persecution by fleeing to Nepal. By the end of 1996 their number totalled 106,801, of whom 91,801 were receiving UNHCR assistance in the form of food, shelter, medical care, water and camp assistance. UNHCR has agreed to maintain its funding of the refugee camps, provided that negotiations between the two Governments, under the auspices of a high-level joint committee (established in 1993), continue. UNHCR has also made known its willingness to provide technical support for the verification of citizenship of the refugees, which was the principal issue precluding a resolution of the situation.

CENTRAL ASIA, SOUTH-WEST ASIA, NORTH AFRICA AND THE MIDDLE EAST

From 1979, as a result of civil strife in Afghanistan, there was a massive movement of refugees from that country into Pakistan and Iran, creating the world's largest refugee population, which reached a peak of almost 6.3m. people in 1992. In 1988 UNHCR agreed to provide assistance for the voluntary repatriation of refugees, both in ensuring the rights of the returning population and in providing material assistance such as transport, immunization, and supplies of food and other essentials. In April 1992, following the establishment of a new Government in Afghanistan, refugees began to return in substantial numbers (hitherto only a small number had returned), although large numbers of people continued to flee into Pakistan as a result of the fighting that persisted. UNHCR efforts to facilitate the process of voluntary repatriation and to provide emergency assistance to camps within Afghanistan were disrupted in early 1994 by a renewal of serious hostilities, which also resulted in a further 76,000 Afghans fleeing to Pakistan during that year. However, repatriation of refugees to areas unaffected by the conflict continued. In Afghanistan UNHCR, with other UN agencies, has attempted to meet the immediate needs of the returnees and of the estimated 273,840 internally displaced persons (as at 31 December 1996), for example, by increasing rural water supply, initiating income-generation projects and providing food and tools. In Iran UNHCR has worked to ensure the voluntary nature of repatriation, while in Pakistan it has focused activities on strengthening refugees' capacity for self-sufficiency. By July 1996 an estimated 3.9m. refugees had returned to Afghanistan since the repatriation programme was initiated. From October 1996 renewed hostilities in northern and western regions of Afghanistan resulted in further massive population displacement (amounting to an estimated 300,000 people by July 1997), and in November 1996 UNHCR suspended its relief activities in the Afghan capital, Kabul, owing to mounting security concerns. Relief operations continued in other parts of the country. At July 1997 some 2.67m. Afghans remained in camps in Iran, Pakistan, India and countries of the former USSR.

In late 1992 people began to flee civil conflict in Tajikistan and to seek refuge in Afghanistan. In 1993 an emergency UNHCR operation established a reception camp to provide the 60,000 Tajik refugees with basic assistance, and began to move them away from the border area to safety. The UN issued an appeal for US $3m. to help the refugees, who were competing with Afghan returnees for bare essentials. In December 1993 a tripartite agreement was signed by UNHCR and the Tajik and Afghan Governments regarding the safety of refugees returning to Tajikistan. UNHCR monitored the repatriation process and provided materials for the construction of almost 20,000 homes. At 31 December 1996 an estimated 18,769 Tajik refugees remained in Afghanistan and were receiving assistance to facilitate their local integration. At that time there were some 25,285 internally displaced persons in Tajikistan, owing to continuing civil unrest. During 1996 UNHCR undertook activities in Kazakhstan, Kyrgyzstan, Turkmenistan and Uzbekistan to assist the Governments of those countries with institution- and capacity-building and training in migration and refugee issues.

In March–May 1991, following the war against Iraq by a multinational force, and the subsequent Iraqi suppression of resistance in Kurdish areas in the north of the country, there was a massive movement of some 1.5m., mainly Kurdish, refugees, into Iran and Turkey. UNHCR was designated the principal UN agency to seek to alleviate the crisis. In May the refugees began to return to Iraq in huge numbers, and UNHCR assisted in their repatriation, establishing relief stations along their routes from Iran and Turkey. By the end of the year, however, negotiations between the Kurds and the Iraqi Government had broken down and refugees were once again entering Iran in large numbers, following the resumption of the violent suppression of Kurdish activists. During 1994 some 8,000 Iraqi Kurds returned to their homeland under a UNHCR assistance project which covered transportation, food, shelter and measures to facilitate their reintegration. In April 1994 UNHCR initiated a programme to provide food and relief assistance to Turkish Kurds who had fled into northern Iraq. In September 1996 fighting escalated among the Kurdish factions in northern Iraq. By the time a cease-fire agreement was concluded in November some 65,000 Iraqi Kurds had fled across the border into Iran. UNHCR, together with the Iranian Government, provided these new refugees with basic humanitarian supplies. By the end of the year, however, the majority of refugees had returned to Iraq, owing to poor conditions in the temporary settlements, security concerns at being located in the border region and pressure from the Iranian authorities. During 1996 UNHCR activities in northern Iraq focused on assisting the repatriation and reintegration of Iraqi refugees from Iran and on the protection and provision of humanitarian requirements to the Kurdish refugee populations in that region. Nevertheless, at the end of December, UNHCR announced its intention to withdraw from the Atroush camp, which housed an estimated 15,000 Turkish Kurds, following several breaches of security in the camp, and expressed its concern at the political vacuum in the region resulting from the factional conflict. At that time Iraq was hosting some 113,000 refugees, approximately one-half of whom were from Palestine. By July 1997 the Iraqi refugee population in Iran, Pakistan, Saudi Arabia and other Middle Eastern countries still numbered an estimated 672,000.

At February 1997 Iran was the principal country of asylum in the world, hosting some 2m. refugees, mainly from Afghanistan and Iraq. In May UNHCR technical staff estimated that more than 100,000 people had been made homeless following an earthquake in eastern Iran.

In June 1992 people fleeing the civil war and famine in Somalia began arriving in Yemen in large numbers. UNHCR set up camps to accommodate some 50,000 refugees, providing them with shelter, food, water and sanitation. As a result of civil conflict in Yemen in mid-1994 a large camp in the south of the country was demolished and other refugees had to be relocated, while the Yemeni authorities initiated a campaign of forcible repatriation. At the end of 1996 Yemen was hosting 53,546 refugees (including 43,871 Somalis), of whom 6,395 were receiving UNHCR assistance.

AFRICA

During the early 1990s UNHCR provided assistance to refugee populations in many parts of the continent, where civil conflict, drought, extreme poverty, violations of human rights or environmental degradation had forced people to flee their countries. The majority of African refugees and returnees are located in countries that are themselves suffering major economic problems and are thus unable to provide the basic requirements of the uprooted people. Furthermore, UNHCR has often failed to receive adequate international financial support to implement effective relief programmes.

The Horn of Africa, afflicted in recent years by famine, separatist violence and ethnic conflict, has experienced large-scale population movements. In 1992 UNHCR initiated a repatriation programme for the estimated 500,000 Somali and Ethiopian refugees in Kenya, which included assistance with reconstruction projects and the provision of food to returnees and displaced persons. The implementation by UNHCR of community-based projects, for example seed distribution, the establishment of a women's bakery co-operative and support for a brick production initiative, served as important instruments of assistance and of bringing stability to areas of returnee settlements. By mid-1996 an estimated 150,000 Somalis had returned from Kenya with UNHCR assistance, bringing the total returnees to more than 400,000. However, the continuing instability in north-western Somalia prevented a completion of the repatriation process, and resulted in further population displacement. By July 1997 there were 572,000 Somali refugees in neighbouring countries, the majority of whom were in camps in eastern Ethiopia, and a further 200,000 were receiving UNHCR assistance, having been displaced within Somalia. At December 1996 Ethiopia was sheltering a total of 390,528 refugees (including some 287,761 Somalis and 75,743 Sudanese). Almost all the Ethiopians who had fled the country during the 1980s had returned by the end of 1996, including 36,000 from Djibouti by means of a UNHCR programme of assistance undertaken between September 1994 and April 1996. Throughout 1996 UNHCR continued to provide assistance to 27,900 Ethiopian returnees.

From 1992 some 500,000 Eritreans took refuge in Sudan as a result of separatist conflicts; however, by 1995 an estimated 125,000 had returned spontaneously, in particular following Eritrea's accession to independence in May 1993. A UNHCR repatriation programme to assist the remaining refugees, which had been delayed for various political, security and funding considerations, was initiated in November 1994. However, its implementation was hindered by a shortfall in donor funding and by disputes between the Eritrean and Sudanese Governments. At the end of 1996 Sudan still hosted a total of 393,874 refugees (including about 328,307 from Eritrea and 51,467 from Ethiopia). At July 1997 464,000 Sudanese refugees remained in the Democratic Republic of the Congo, Ethiopia, Kenya and Uganda, owing to continuing civil unrest. The Ugandan Government, hosting an estimated 230,000 of these refugees, has provided new resettlement sites and has supported refugee efforts to construct homes and cultivate crops in order to achieve some degree of self-sufficiency.

In West Africa the refugee population increased by one-third during 1992 and the first half of 1993, with the addition of new refugees fleeing Togo, Liberia and Senegal. In accordance with a peace agreement, signed in July 1993, UNHCR was responsible for the repatriation of 700,000 Liberian refugees who had fled to Guinea, Côte d'Ivoire and Sierra Leone during the civil conflict. The voluntary repatriation programme was to include substantial assistance to rebuild Liberia's infrastructure; UNHCR also began to provide emergency relief to displaced persons within the country. Persisting political insecurity prevented large-scale repatriation of Liberian refugees, and in mid-1996 UNHCR suspended its preparatory activities for a repatriation and reintegration operation, owing to an escalation in hostilities. At February 1997 the Liberian refugee population in West Africa totalled 758,000 (of whom some 415,000 were in Guinea); however, the prospect of a peaceful settlement in Liberia, with preparations under way for a general election to be conducted in July, prompted a movement of refugees returning home, and in April UNHCR initiated an organized repatriation of Liberian refugees from Ghana. Meanwhile, an escalation of civil violence in Sierra Leone in early 1995 displaced some 900,000 people, of whom an estimated 185,000 fled to Guinea and 90,000 to Liberia. By December 1996 there were 120,000 Sierra Leonean refugees in Liberia and 248,827 in Guinea, while a further 654,600 internally displaced Sierra Leoneans were of concern to UNHCR. The repatriation of Sierra Leonean refugees from Liberia was initiated in February 1997; however, the programme was suspended in May, owing to renewed political violence. By early June a further 14,000 refugees from Sierra Leone had registered at camps in Guinea.

Between February and August 1993 more than 300,000 people fled abuses of human rights in Togo, crossing the borders into Benin and Ghana. With the majority of Togolese being accommodated by individuals in the host countries, UNHCR aimed to strengthen these countries' infrastructures. Political developments in Togo in 1994 were considered to have accounted for a large-scale spontaneous repatriation movement of Togolese refugees. In August 1995 UNHCR and Togo signed an accord providing for the voluntary repatriation for some 168,000 Togolese refugees remaining in Ghana and Benin. Under the programme, which commenced in May 1996, returnees received a small financial grant and a three-month supply of food. By December there were 20,258 Togolese refugees in Ghana and 4,690 in Benin. In early 1994 UNHCR initiated an emergency relief effort to assist some 180,000 Ghanaians displaced within the north of that country as a result of ethnic violence. Also at that time some 40,000 Tuareg nomads, who had fled from northern Mali into Burkina Faso, received protection and material assistance from two newly-established UNHCR field offices. During 1995 large numbers of the Malian refugee population (totalling some 175,000) returned spontaneously from camps in Mauritania, Burkina Faso and Algeria, owing to political developments in Mali. An organized repatriation of the remaining refugees was initiated in 1996, although at the end of that year some 55,000 Malians were still in camps in neighbouring countries. In November UNHCR signed an agreement with the Malian and Nigerien Governments establishing the conditions of repatriation of 25,000 Tuareg refugees living in Niger. In May 1997 UNHCR appealed for US $17m. to finance the continuing repatriation and reintegration of Malian refugees, as well as some 20,000 refugees returning to Niger.

Since 1993 the Great Lakes region of central Africa has again experienced massive population displacement, causing immense operational challenges and demands on the resources of international humanitarian and relief agencies. In October of that year a military coup in Burundi prompted some 580,000 people to flee into Rwanda and Tanzania, although many had returned by early 1994. By May, however, an estimated 860,000 people from Burundi and Rwanda had fled to neighbouring states (following a resurgence of ethnic violence in both countries), including 250,000 mainly Rwandan Tutsi refugees who entered Tanzania over a 24-hour period in late April. In May UNHCR began an immediate operation to airlift emergency supplies to the refugees. Despite overcrowding in camps and a high incidence of cholera and dysentery (particularly in camps in eastern Zaire, where many thousands of Rwandan Hutus had sought refuge following the establishment of a new Rwandan Government in July) large numbers of refugees refused to accept UNHCR-assisted repatriation, owing to fears of reprisal ethnic killings. In late August the Zairean camps were further overburdened by an influx of Rwandan Hutu refugees, following the withdrawal of French troops from a 'safe haven' in south-west Rwanda. In September reports of mass ethnic violence, which were disputed by some UN agencies, continued to disrupt UNHCR's policy of repatriation and to prompt returnees to cross the border back into Zaire. Security in the refugee camps, which was undermined by the presence of military and political elements of the former Rwandan Government, remained an outstanding concern of UNHCR. A resurgence of violence in Burundi, in February 1995, provoked further mass population movements. However, in March the Tanzanian authorities, reportedly frustrated at the lack of international assistance for the refugees and the environmental degradation resulting from the camps, closed Tanzania's border with Burundi, thus preventing the admission into the country of some 100,000 Rwandan Hutu refugees who were fleeing camps in Burundi. While persisting disturbances in Rwanda disrupted UNHCR's repatriation programme, in April Rwandan government troops employed intimidation tactics to force some 90,000 internally displaced Hutus to leave a heavily-populated camp in the south-west of the country; other small camps were closed. Preparations for the resettlement of the population were undertaken by UNHCR, mainly in the form of community rehabilitation projects. In August the Zairean Government initiated a programme of forcible repatriation of the estimated 1m. Rwandan and 70,000 Burundian Hutu refugees remaining in the country, which prompted as many as 100,000 refugees to flee the camps into the surrounding countryside. Following widespread international condemnation of the forcible repatriation and expressions of concern for the welfare of the remaining refugees, the Zairean Government suspended the programme, having first received an assurance that UNHCR would assume responsibility for the repatriation of all the refugees by the end of 1995 (although in December the Government accepted that its deadline could not be achieved). In September Rwanda agreed to strengthen its reception facilities and to provide greater security and protection for returnees, in collaboration with UNHCR, in order to prepare for any large-scale repatriation. UNHCR, meanwhile, expanded its information campaign, to promote the return of refugees, and enhanced its facilities at official border entry points. In December UNHCR negotiated an agreement between the Rwandan and Tanzanian authorities concerning the repatriation of the estimated 500,000 Rwandans remaining in camps in Tanzania. UNHCR agreed to establish a separate camp in north-west Tanzania in order to accommodate elements of the refugee population that might disrupt the repatriation programme. The repatriation of Rwandan refugees from all host countries was affected by reports of reprisals against Hutu returnees by the Tutsi-dominated Government in Rwanda. In February 1996 the Zairean Government renewed its efforts to accelerate the repatriation process, owing to concerns that the camps were becoming permanent settlements and that they were being used to train and rearm a Hutu militia. In July the Burundian Government forcibly repatriated 15,000 Rwandan refugees, having announced the closure of all remaining refugee camps. The repatriation programme, which was condemned by UNHCR, was suspended by the country's new authorities, which were installed after a military coup later in that month. By 31 December the refugee population in Burundi had declined to less than 1,000 (although this estimate excluded Zairean refugees, the number of whom was unknown to UNHCR). At that time some 882,900 internally displaced Burundians and 71,031 returnees from Tanzania were of concern to UNHCR in Burundi.

In October 1996 an escalation of hostilities between Zairean government forces, accused by Rwanda of arming the Hutu *Interahamwe* militia, and Zairean (Banyamulenge) Tutsis, who had been the focus of increasingly violent assaults, resulted in an extreme humanitarian crisis. Some 250,000 refugees fled 12 camps in the east of the country, while an estimated 500,000 were left in Muganga camp, west of Goma, with insufficient relief assistance, following the evacuation of international aid workers. UNHCR appealed to all Rwandan Hutu refugees to return home, and issued assurances of the presence of human rights observers in Rwanda to enhance their security. In mid-November, with the apparent withdrawal of *Interahamwe* forces, more than 500,000 refugees unexpectedly returned to Rwanda; however, concern remained on the part of the international community for the substantial number of Rwandan Hutu refugees at large in eastern Zaire. In December several thousand Rwandan refugees returned from Tanzania following a threat of forcible repatriation by the Tanzanian Government.

In February 1997 violence in Zaire escalated, prompting some 56,000 Zaireans to flee into Tanzania and disrupting the distribution of essential humanitarian supplies to refugees remaining in Zaire. An estimated 170,000 refugees abandoned their temporary encampment at Tingi-Tingi, fearing attacks by the advancing rebel forces of the Tutsi-dominated Alliance des forces démocratiques pour la libération du Congo–Zaïre (AFDL). About 75,000 reassembled at Ubundu, south of Kisangani, while the fate of the other refugees remained uncertain. In March and April reports of attacks on refugee camps, by AFDL forces and local Zaireans, resulted in large numbers of people fleeing into the surrounding countryside, with the consequent deaths of many of the most vulnerable members of the refugee population from disease and starvation. At the end of April the leader of the AFDL, Laurent-Désiré Kabila, ordered the repatriation of all Rwandan Hutu refugees by the UN within 60 days. An operation to airlift some 85,000 refugees who had regrouped into temporary settlements was initiated a few days later, at an estimated cost of US $50m. The repatriation process, however, was hindered by administrative and logistical difficulties and lack of co-operation on the part of the AFDL forces. By the end of May some 40,000 Rwandans had been repatriated under the operation; at that time an estimated 300,000 Rwandans were still missing or dispersed throughout the former Zaire (renamed the Democratic Republic of the Congo by the AFDL in May). In the following months relations between the Kabila Government and UNHCR deteriorated as a result of several incidences of forcible repatriations of refugees to Rwanda and reports that the authorities were hindering a UN investigation into alleged abuses of human rights, committed against the Rwandan Hutu refugees by AFDL forces. In September UNHCR temporarily suspended its activities in the Democratic Republic of the Congo, and in the following month UNHCR and other aid workers were expelled from the Goma region in the east of the country. In August an agreement was concluded to provide for the voluntary repatriation of some 75,000 Congolese refugees remaining in Tanzania, under UNHCR supervision.

In the early 1990s UNHCR was the principal agency responsible for the channelling of food aid to the large population of Mozambican refugees dispersed throughout southern Africa. The subsequent repatriation programme, which followed the signing of a peace agreement in October 1992, was at that time UNHCR's largest-ever undertaking in Africa. UNHCR distributed food, provided seed rations and agricultural tools, to promote returnee self-sufficiency, and repaired local infrastructure. A reintegration strategy was formulated in 1994, which identified some 1,386 quick impact projects required in the four priority areas of water, education, health and roads. The voluntary repatriation operation was formally concluded on 31 December 1996, having registered 1,734,174 Mozambican returnees. During 1994 continuing civil conflict in Angola caused some 303,800 people to leave their home areas. Prior to the signing of a peace settlement in November, UNHCR provided assistance to 112,000 internally displaced Angolans and returnees, although military activities, which hindered accessibility, undermined the effectiveness of the assistance programme. In mid-1995, following a consolidation of the peace process in Angola, UNHCR appealed for US $44m. to support the voluntary repatriation of some 300,000 Angolan refugees over a two-and-a-half-year operation. Implementation of the repatriation programme was delayed, however, reportedly owing to poor accommodation and other facilities for returnees, limited progress in confining and disarming opposition troops and the continued hazard of land-mines throughout the country. By December 1996 more than 244,000 Angolans remained in camps throughout the region (including 108,284 in Zaire and 109,623 in Zambia).

THE AMERICAS

The International Conference on Central American Refugees (CIREFCA), held in Guatemala in May 1989, adopted a plan of action for the voluntary repatriation of refugees in the region, and established national co-ordinating committees to assist in this process. At that time there were some 150,000 refugees receiving UNHCR assistance, and a further estimated 1.8m. other refugees and displaced persons. The repatriation process initiated by CIREFCA was formally concluded in June 1994. In December a meeting was held, in San José, Costa Rica, to commemorate the 10th anniversary of the Cartagena Declaration, which had provided a comprehensive framework for refugee protection in the region. The meeting adopted the San José Declaration on Refugees and Displaced Persons, which aimed to harmonize legal criteria and procedures to consolidate actions for durable solutions of voluntary repatriation and local integration in the region. UNHCR's efforts in the region emphasized legal issues and refugee protection, while assisting governments to formulate national legislation on asylum and refugees. At the end of 1996 the outstanding populations of concern to UNHCR in Central America were the 32,593 Guatemalan refugees remaining in Mexico and the 37,791 Guatemalans and 30,887 Salvadoreans who had returned to their home areas. At that time Costa Rica was hosting a refugee population of some 23,176, the majority of whom were from Nicaragua.

Canada and the USA are major countries of resettlement for refugees. UNHCR provides counselling and legal services for asylum-seekers in these countries.

EUROPE

The political changes in eastern and central Europe during the early 1990s resulted in a dramatic increase in the number of asylum-seekers and displaced people in the region. UNHCR was the agency designated by the UN Secretary-General to lead the UN relief operation to assist those affected by the conflict in the former Yugoslavia. It was responsible for the supply of food and other humanitarian aid to the besieged capital of Bosnia and Herzegovina, Sarajevo, and to Muslim and Croatian enclaves in the country, under the armed escort of the UN Protection Force. In terms of its scale and the hazards involved in being active in a war zone, the operation in the former Yugoslavia was one of UNHCR's most challenging to date. Assistance was provided not only to Bosnian refugees in Croatia and displaced people within Bosnia and Herzegovina's borders, but also, in order to forestall further movements of people, to civilians whose survival was threatened. The operation was often seriously hampered by armed attacks (resulting, in some cases, in fatalities), distribution difficulties, in particular obstruction by Bosnian Serbs (attempting to prevent aid supplies from reaching the Muslim enclaves), and underfunding from international donors. From mid-1995 an escalation of tensions resulted in several further mass movements of local populations, including, in July, some 36,000 Muslims fleeing the enclaves of Srebrenica and Žepa (including several thousand under forced migration by Bosnian Serbs), in August, an estimated 180,000 Croatian Serbs (many of whom were troops) fleeing into northern Bosnia and Herzegovina from a Croat advance on Krajina, and in September, some 50,000 Serbs displaced by fighting in north-west Bosnia and Herzegovina following a Muslim-Croat offensive. The Dayton peace agreement, which was signed in December bringing an end to the conflict, secured the right for all refugees and displaced persons freely to choose their place of residence within the new territorial arrangements of Bosnia and Herzegovina. Thus, the immediate effect of the peace accord was further population displacement, including a mass exodus of almost the entire Serb population of Sarajevo. In addition, there was a significant increase in the numbers of Bosnians attempting to reach Germany before 31 March 1996, when the conditions for attaining refugee status were to be amended. Under the peace accord, UNHCR was responsible for planning and implementing the repatriation of all Bosnian refugees and displaced persons, estimated at 2m.; however, there were still immense obstacles to freedom of movement, in particular for minorities wishing to return to an area dominated by a different politico-ethnic faction. At July 1997 the Bosnian refugee population totalled 673,000, the majority of whom remained in Germany and the Federal Republic of Yugoslavia.

In December 1992 UNHCR dispatched teams to establish offices in both Armenia and Azerbaijan to assist people displaced as a result of the war between the two countries and to provide immediate relief. Despite a cease-fire, signed between the two sides in May 1994, at the end of 1996 the region was still supporting a massive displaced population: there were 200,000 Azerbaijani refugees in Armenia, 72,000 internally displaced persons of concern to UNHCR in Armenia, 549,030 in Azerbaijan (of whom 356,000 were receiving UNHCR assistance) and 60,402 returnees in Azerbaijan. UNHCR's humanitarian activities have focused on improving shelter, in particular for the most vulnerable among the refugee population, and promoting economic self-sufficiency and stability. In Georgia, where almost 300,000 people have left their homes as a result of civil conflict since 1991, UNHCR has attempted to encourage income-generating activities among the displaced population, to increase the Georgian Government's capacity to support those people and to assist the rehabilitation of people returning to their areas of origin. In March 1995 UNHCR initiated an assistance programme for people displaced as a result of conflict in the separatist republic of Chechnya (Russian Federation), as part of a UN inter-agency relief effort, in collaboration with the International Committee of the Red Cross (ICRC, q.v.). UNHCR continued its activities in 1996, at the request of the Russian Government, at which time the displaced population within Chechnya and in the surrounding republics totalled 490,000. During 1995 UNHCR pursued a process, initiated in the previous year, to establish a comprehensive approach to the problems of refugees, returnees, displaced persons and migrants in the Commonwealth of Independent States. A regional conference to consider the issue was convened in Geneva, Switzerland, in May 1996. The meeting endorsed a framework of activities aimed at managing migratory flows and at developing institutional capacities to prevent mass population displacements. At that time it was estimated that more than 9m. former citizens of the USSR had relocated since its disintegration as a result of conflict, economic pressures and ecological disasters.

CO-OPERATION WITH OTHER ORGANIZATIONS

UNHCR works closely with other UN agencies, intergovernmental organizations and non-governmental organizations to increase the scope and effectiveness of its emergency operations. Within the UN system UNHCR co-operates, principally, with the World Food Programme in the distribution of food aid and UNICEF and the World Health Organization in the provision of family welfare and child immunization programmes. UNHCR co-operates with the UN Development Programme in development-related activities and has participated in the preparation of guidelines for the continuum of emergency assistance to development programmes. In 1993 UNHCR and the International Council of Voluntary Agencies initiated a programme of Partnership in Action (PARinAC) to broaden dialogue and improve the effectiveness of the collaboration. Following regional consultations, this effort culminated in a world conference of UNHCR and 450 non-governmental organizations, held in Oslo, Norway, in June 1994, at which a Declaration to consolidate the relationship was adopted.

TRAINING

UNHCR organizes training programmes and workshops to enhance the capabilities of field workers and non-UNHCR staff, in the following areas: the identification and registration of refugees; people-orientated planning; resettlement procedures and policies; emergency response and management; security awareness; stress management; and the dissemination of information through the electronic media.

Finance

UNHCR's administrative expenditure is mostly financed as part of the United Nations' regular budget. General Programmes of material assistance are financed from voluntary contributions made by governments and also from non-governmental sources. In addition, UNHCR undertakes a number of Special Programmes, as requested by the UN General Assembly, the Secretary-General of the UN or a member state, to assist returnees and, in some cases, displaced persons. In 1995 expenditure from voluntary funds amounted to US $1,292m., of which $428m. was allocated to finance General Programmes and $864m. to Special Programmes.

PUBLICATIONS

Refugees (quarterly, in English, French, German, Italian, Japanese and Spanish).

Refugee Survey Quarterly.

The State of the World's Refugees.

UNHCR Handbook for Emergencies.

Press releases, reports.

United Nations International Drug Control Programme—UNDCP

Address: Vienna International Centre, POB 500, 1400 Vienna, Austria.

Telephone: (1) 213450; **telex:** 135612; **fax:** (1) 21345-5866; **e-mail:** undcp-hq@undcp.un.or.at; **internet:** http://www.undcp.org.

UNDCP was established in 1991, following a decision by the UN General Assembly, in order to enhance the effectiveness of the UN system for drug control and to provide leadership in the international control of drugs.

Organization

(November 1997)

The principal offices of UNDCP headquarters are those serving the Executive Director, the Division for Treaty Implementation and Support Services, which includes legal affairs and the secretariat of the International Narcotics Control Board, and the Division for Operational Activities and Technical Services. Four regional bureaux cover the following areas: Africa; Asia and the Pacific; Europe and the Middle East; and Latin America and the Caribbean. UNDCP maintains some 22 field offices to administer major country and regional programmes.

Executive Director: PINO ARLACCHI (Italy).

Activities

UNDCP was established to co-ordinate the activities of all UN specialized agencies and programmes in matters of international drug control. The structures of the former Division of Narcotic Drugs, the UN Fund for Drug Abuse Control and the secretariat of the International Narcotics Control Body (see below) were integrated into the new body. Accordingly, UNDCP became the focal point for promoting the UN Decade Against Drug Abuse (1991–2000) and for assisting member states to implement the Global Programme of Action that was adopted by the General Assembly in 1990 with the objective of achieving an international society free of illicit drugs and drug abuse.

UNDCP serves as an international centre of expertise and information on drug abuse control, with the capacity to provide legal and technical assistance in relevant concerns. The Programme supports governments in efforts to strengthen their institutional capacities for drug control (for example, drug identification and drug law enforcement training) and to prepare and implement national drug control 'master plans'. Efforts to enhance regional co-operation in the control of narcotics are also supported. Through these national and regional strategies, UNDCP aims to reduce the demand for illicit drugs, to suppress trafficking in these substances and to reduce the production of drugs, for example by creating alternative sources of income for farmers economically dependent on the production of illicit narcotic crops. This latter approach has been successfully applied in Laos, reducing the levels of opium cultivation, and in the coca-growing regions of Peru, Bolivia and Colombia.

UNDCP sponsors activities to generate public awareness of the harmful effects of drug abuse, as part of its efforts to reduce the demand for illicit drugs. In 1995 preventive education programmes, reaching some 650,000 schoolchildren, were undertaken in 13 Latin American and Caribbean countries and territories. UNDCP also works with governments, as well as non-governmental and private organizations, in the treatment, rehabilitation and social reintegration of drug addicts. UNDCP undertakes research to monitor the drugs problem: for example, assessing the characteristics of drug-users and the substances being used, to help identify people at risk of becoming drug abusers and to enhance the effectiveness of national programmes to address the issue. More recent specific concerns of UNDCP include the damaging environmental effects of the illicit cultivation of drugs, in particular in the Andean region of Latin America and in South and East Asia, and the abuse of drugs in sport. In February 1995 a memorandum of understanding was signed by the Programme and the International Olympic Committee, initiating a joint campaign entitled 'Sport against drugs'.

UNDCP promotes implementation of the following major treaties which govern the international drug control system: the Single Convention on Narcotic Drugs (1961) and a Protocol amending the Convention (1972); the Convention on Psychotropic Substances (1971); and the UN Convention against Illicit Traffic in Narcotic Drugs and Psychotropic Substances (1988). Among other important provisions, these treaties aim to restrict severely the production of narcotic drugs, while ensuring an adequate supply for medical and scientific purposes, to prevent profits obtained from the illegal sale of drugs being diverted into legal usage and to secure the extradition of drug-traffickers and the transfer of proceedings for criminal prosecution. UNDCP assists countries to adapt their national legislation and drug policies to facilitate their compliance with these conventions and to enhance co-ordinated efforts with other governments to control the movement of drugs. UNDCP services meetings of the International Narcotics Control Board, an independent body responsible for promoting and monitoring government compliance with the provisions of the drug control treaties, and of the Commission on Narcotic Drugs, which, as a functional committee of ECOSOC (q.v.), is the main policy-making organ within the UN system on issues relating to international drug abuse control.

BUDGET

The UNDCP Fund receives an allocation from the regular budget of the UN, although voluntary contributions from member states and private organizations represent the majority of its resources (some 90% in 1995). In 1995 UNDCP's budget for operational activities amounted to US $61m. for 274 projects in 54 countries. In December 1995 the Commission on Narcotic Drugs approved budget proposals for the UNDCP Fund for the biennium 1996–97 amounting to $152.5m.

PUBLICATIONS

Bulletin on Narcotics (quarterly).

Technical Series.

World Drug Report.

United Nations Peace-keeping Operations

Address: Department of Peace-keeping Operations, Room S-3727-B, United Nations, New York, NY 10017, USA.

Telephone: (212) 963-5055; **telex:** 420544; **fax:** (212) 963-4879; **internet:** http://www.un.org/Depts/dpko/.

United Nations peace-keeping operations have been conceived as instruments of conflict control. The UN has used these operations in various conflicts, with the consent of the parties involved, to maintain international peace and security, without prejudice to the positions or claims of parties, in order to facilitate the search for political settlements through peaceful means such as mediation and the good offices of the Secretary-General. Each operation has been established with a specific mandate, which requires periodic review by the Security Council. United Nations peace-keeping operations fall into two categories: peace-keeping forces and observer missions.

Peace-keeping forces are composed of contingents of military and civilian personnel, made available by member states. These forces assist in preventing the recurrence of fighting, restoring and maintaining peace, and promoting a return to normal conditions. To this end, peace-keeping forces are authorized as necessary to undertake negotiations, persuasion, observation and fact-finding. They conduct patrols and interpose physically between the opposing parties. Peace-keeping forces are permitted to use their weapons only in self-defence.

Military observer missions are composed of officers (usually unarmed), who are made available, on the Secretary-General's request, by member states. A mission's function is to observe and report to the Secretary-General (who, in turn, informs the UN Security Council) on the maintenance of a cease-fire, to investigate violations and to do what it can to improve the situation.

Peace-keeping forces and observer missions must at all times maintain complete impartiality and avoid any action that might affect the claims or positions of the parties. In January 1995 the UN Secretary-General presented a report to the Security Council, reassessing the UN's role in peace-keeping. The document stipulated that UN forces in conflict areas should not be responsible for peace-enforcement duties, and included a proposal for the establishment of a 'rapid reaction' force which would be ready for deployment within a month of being authorized by the Security Council. In September 1997 the UN Secretary-General established a staff to plan and organize the establishment of the so-called UN Stand-by Force High Readiness Brigade. At that time, however, only seven countries—Austria, Canada, Denmark, the Netherlands, Norway, Poland and Sweden—had formally committed troops to the force, which was expected to be fully operational in 1999.

By early 1997 the UN had undertaken a total of 43 peace-keeping operations, of which 15 were authorized in the period 1948–89 and 28 since 1989. In January 1997 the Security Council authorized the dispatch of some 155 military personnel to verify the implementation of a cease-fire in Guatemala, signed between the Government and opposition forces at the end of 1996. The observer mission was attached to the UN Mission for the Verification of Human Rights in Guatemala (MINUGUA), authorized by the UN General Assembly, and its mandate was concluded in May. In June the Security Council authorized the establishment of a new UN mission in Angola (MONUA), which was to succeed the third UN Angola Verification Mission (UNAVEM III) on its expiry at the end of that month. At the end of July the Security Council endorsed the establishment of the UN Transition Mission in Haiti (UNIMIH), to succeed the existing UN Support Mission (UNSMIH) with effect from 1 August. In September the mandate of the UN Observer Mission in Liberia (UNOMIL), which had been established in September 1993, was concluded, following the inauguration of a new national government in that country.

The UN's peace-keeping operations are financed by assessed contributions from member states (with the exception of two operations that are ongoing and financed through the regular budget of the UN). A significant expansion in the UN's peace-keeping activities during the early 1990s (see above) was accompanied by a perpetual financial crisis within the organization, as a result of the increased financial burden and the failure of member states to pay outstanding contributions. By May 1997 unpaid contributions to the peace-keeping accounts amounted to US $1,600m.

UNITED NATIONS DISENGAGEMENT OBSERVER FORCE—UNDOF

Headquarters: Damascus, Syria.

Commander: Maj.-Gen. David Stapleton (Ireland).

UNDOF was established for an initial period of six months by a UN Security Council resolution in May 1974, following the signature in Geneva of a disengagement agreement between Syrian and Israeli forces. The mandate has since been extended by successive resolutions. The initial task of the Force was to take over territory evacuated in stages by the Israeli troops, in accordance with the disengagement agreement, to hand over territory to Syrian troops, and to establish an area of separation on the Golan Heights.

UNDOF continues to monitor the area of separation; it carries out inspections of the areas of limited armaments and forces; uses its best efforts to maintain the cease-fire; and undertakes activities of a humanitarian nature, such as arranging the transfer of prisoners and war-dead between Syria and Israel. The Force operates exclusively on Syrian territory.

At 30 September 1997 the Force comprised 1,051 troops from Austria, Canada, Japan and Poland, assisted by approximately 80 military observers of UNTSO's Observer Group Golan. Further UNTSO military observers help UNDOF in the performance of its tasks, as required. The annual cost to the United Nations of the operation is approximately US $32.4m.

UNITED NATIONS INTERIM FORCE IN LEBANON—UNIFIL

Headquarters: Naqoura, Lebanon.

Commander: Maj.-Gen. Jioje Konousi Konrote (Fiji).

UNIFIL was established by a UN Security Council resolution in March 1978, following an invasion of Lebanon by Israeli forces. The mandate of the force is to confirm the withdrawal of Israeli forces, to restore international peace and security, and to assist the Government of Lebanon in ensuring the return of its effective authority in southern Lebanon. UNIFIL has also extended humanitarian assistance to the population of the area, particularly since the second Israeli invasion of Lebanon in 1982. By late 1997 Security Council resolution 425, requiring the unconditional withdrawal of Israeli troops from southern Lebanon, had yet to be implemented. In April 1992, however, in accordance with its mandate, UNIFIL completed the transfer of part of its zone of operations to the control of the Lebanese army. UNIFIL's monitoring activities are confined to the staffing of checkpoints and observation posts, which are designed to deter hostilities. UNIFIL provides civilians with food, water, medical supplies, fuel and escorts to farmers. UNIFIL medical centres and mobile teams provide care to an average 3,000 civilian patients each month, and a field dental programme has been established.

In April 1996 Israel initiated a large-scale offensive against suspected targets pertaining to the Hezbollah militia in southern Lebanon. During the offensive Israeli artillery shells struck a UNIFIL base at Qana, which was temporarily being used to shelter civilians displaced by the hostilities, resulting in the deaths of some 100 people. The UN Security Council condemned the attack and demanded the respect by all sides for UNIFIL's mandate and for the safety and freedom of movement of its troops. In May a UN inquiry concluded that the UN site had been deliberately targeted during the offensive, owing to the presence of Hezbollah activists in the camp. In June 1997 the UN General Assembly resolved that Israel should contribute US $1.8m. towards UNIFIL's operational costs, as compensation for the Qana incident.

At 30 September 1997 the Force comprised 4,454 troops from nine countries, assisted by some 60 military observers of UNTSO's Observer Group Lebanon, and other international and local civilian staff. The annual cost to the United Nations of the operation is estimated at US $122.2m.

UNITED NATIONS IRAQ-KUWAIT OBSERVATION MISSION—UNIKOM

Headquarters: Umm Qasr, Kuwait.

Commander: Maj.-Gen. Esa Kalervo Tarvainen (Finland).

UNIKOM was established by a UN Security Council resolution (initially for a six-month period) in April 1991, to monitor a 200-km demilitarized zone along the border between Iraq and Kuwait. The task of the mission was to deter violations of the border, to monitor the Khawr 'Abd Allah waterway between Iraq and Kuwait, and to prevent military activity within the zone. In February 1993 the Security Council adopted a resolution to strengthen UNIKOM, following incursions into Kuwaiti territory by Iraqi personnel. The resolution also expanded the mission's mandate to include the capacity to take physical action to prevent violations of the demilitarized zone and of the newly-defined boundary between Iraq and

Kuwait. UNIKOM provides technical support to other UN operations in the area, particularly the Iraq–Kuwait Boundary Demarcation Commission, and has assisted with the relocation of Iraqi citizens from Kuwait, which was completed in February 1994.

At 30 September 1997 UNIKOM comprised 891 troops and 202 military observers. The annual cost to the United Nations of the mission is approximately US $50.7m. Two-thirds of UNIKOM's total costs are met by the Government of Kuwait.

UNITED NATIONS MILITARY OBSERVER GROUP IN INDIA AND PAKISTAN—UNMOGIP

Headquarters: Rawalpindi, Pakistan (November–April), Srinagar, India (May–October).

Chief Military Observer: Maj.-Gen. AHN CHOUNG-JUN (Republic of Korea).

The Group was established in 1948 by UN Security Council resolutions aiming to restore peace in the region of Jammu and Kashmir, the status of which had become a matter of dispute between the Governments of India and Pakistan. Following a cease-fire which came into effect in January 1949, the military observers of UNMOGIP were deployed to assist in its observance. There is no periodic review of UNMOGIP's mandate. In 1971, following the signature of a new cease-fire agreement, India claimed that UNMOGIP's mandate had lapsed, since it was originally intended to monitor the agreement reached in 1949. Pakistan, however, regarded UNMOGIP's mission as unchanged, and the Group's activities have continued, although they have been somewhat restricted on the Indian side of the 'line of control', which was agreed by India and Pakistan in 1972.

At 30 September 1997 there were 44 observers from eight countries, deployed on both sides of the 'line of control'. The cost of the operation in 1997 was estimated to amount to US $6.4m., which was to be covered by the regular budget of the UN.

UNITED NATIONS MISSION IN BOSNIA AND HERZEGOVINA—UNMIBH

Headquarters: Sarajevo, Bosnia and Herzegovina.

Special Representative of the Secretary-General and Co-ordinator of UN Operations in Bosnia and Herzegovina: ELISABETH REHN (Finland).

Commissioner of the UN International Police Task Force: MANFRED SEITNER (Denmark).

In February 1992 the UN established a Protection Force (UNPROFOR), in response to the escalating conflict in the former Yugoslavia, which became one of the largest operations ever mounted by the UN. UNPROFOR assumed responsibility for monitoring the withdrawal of anti-aircraft and heavy weapons by both Bosnian Muslims and Serbs to agreed locations within Bosnia and Herzegovina, the delivery of humanitarian assistance and monitoring compliance with the prohibition on military flights in Bosnian airspace. In December 1995 leaders of the warring parties in the former Yugoslavia signed a peace accord, which had been concluded in the previous month in Dayton, USA. UNPROFOR's mandate was terminated a few days later, when a new multinational force under NATO command (the Implementation Force—IFOR) assumed authority for implementation of the peace accord, for a determined 12-month period, on 20 December.

On 21 December 1995 the Security Council agreed on the establishment of the UN International Police Task Force (IPTF) and a UN civilian office, in accordance with the Dayton peace agreement. The operation subsequently became known as the UN Mission in Bosnia and Herzegovina (UNMIBH). The IPTF's tasks included: monitoring, observing and inspecting law enforcement activities in Bosnia and Herzegovina; the training of police officers and personnel; assessing threats to public order and advising on the capability of law enforcement agencies to deal with such threats; and accompanying the Bosnian police forces in the execution of their duties. The UN Co-ordinator was to exercise authority over the IPTF Commissioner and to co-ordinate other UN activities in Bosnia and Herzegovina relating to humanitarian relief and refugees, demining, elections and economic reconstruction. UNMIBH was to co-operate closely with IFOR and, later, with its successor operation, the Stabilization Force (SFOR), which became operational in December 1996. In early 1996 the UN was criticized for slow deployment of the IPTF: at the start of February fewer than 300 out of a total authorized strength of 1,721 police officers had arrived in the country. The Force was charged with maintaining an observer presence in Serb-dominated suburbs of Sarajevo that were due to come under the administration of the Bosnian Federation in March, a presence that was intended to provide encouragement to Serbs to stay in these areas. However, the vast majority of the Serbs took flight into the Republika Srpska prior to the transition of authority. In March the Security Council authorized the deployment of five military liaison officers, in order to strengthen liaison arrangements with IFOR. In mid-August the mission reported failure on the part of Bosnian Federation police to protect political opponents of the Muslim nationalist Party of Democratic Action (PDA) from attacks by PDA loyalists in advance of the forthcoming all-Bosnia legislative elections. Prior to and during the elections, which were held on 14 September, the IPTF assisted IFOR in providing protection to refugees and displaced people returning to vote in their towns of origin. At the international conference to review implementation of the Dayton agreement, which was held in mid-November, it was agreed that the IPTF's mandate was to be strengthened, granting it enhanced powers to investigate the Bosnian police in both sectors of the country. In late 1996 the IPTF was attempting to effect the rational integration of Muslim and Croat police forces in the divided city of Mostar. In mid-December the Security Council extended UNMIBH's mandate until 21 December 1997. In February 1997 the IPTF criticized police officers for using excessive force against civilians during recent unrest between the Muslim and Croat populations in Mostar. In the following month the Security Council demanded that the Mostar authorities suspend and prosecute those officers responsible for the attacks. Also in March the Council authorized the strengthening of the IPTF by an additional 186 police officers and 11 civilian monitors in order to monitor, restructure and train the local police force in the contested north-eastern city of Brčko, which was temporarily under international supervision. In August UNMIBH criticized the forcible evacuation of some 500 Bosniaks from the Muslim Croat Federation and initiated an investigation into the role of the local police in the incident. An investigation was also initiated by the IPTF following the discovery of a large supply of unauthorized weapons at police facilities near the city of Banja Luka. The investigation uncovered similar stores of weapons at locations throughout the Republika Srpska. In Brčko, in August, 58 IPTF monitors had to be evacuated by SFOR troops after coming under attack by Bosnian Serbs demanding control of the local police station. In September UNMIBH co-operated with SFOR and an election monitoring group to assist safe and democratic voting in municipal elections in the Bosnian Federation, and monitored the movement of voters within the region and across boundary lines.

At 30 September 1997 UNMIBH comprised 1,952 civilian police officers and three army personnel. The annual cost to the UN of UNMIBH was estimated at US $165.6m.

UNITED NATIONS MISSION OF OBSERVERS IN PREVLAKA—UNMOP

Headquarters: Prevlaka peninsula, Croatia.

Chief Military Observer: Col HAROLD MWAKIO TANGAI (Kenya).

UNMOP was authorized by the Security Council in January 1996, following the termination of the mandate of the UN Confidence Restoration Operation, to assume responsibility for monitoring the demilitarization of the Prevlaka peninsula in Croatia, which had been occupied by the Serbian-dominated Yugoslav People's Army. UNMOP became operational on 1 February. While political tensions persisted throughout 1996, the UN Secretary-General reported that UNMOP's presence in the region had facilitated the process of bilateral negotiations between Croatia and the Federal Republic of Yugoslavia. In authorizing extensions of UNMOP's mandate in January and April 1997, the Security Council urged both parties to refrain from provocative actions in Prevlaka, to cease any violations of the demilitarized zone and to co-operate fully with UNMOP. The Council also reiterated the urgency of removing anti-personnel landmines from areas patrolled by UNMOP in order to improve the safety and security of the region and ensure freedom of movement to enable UNMOP to implement its mandate. In January 1998 UNMOP's mandate was extended to 15 July.

At 30 September 1997 UNMOP comprised 26 military observers. The cost of UNMOP is included in the budget of the UN Mission in Bosnia and Herzegovina (see above).

UNITED NATIONS MISSION OF OBSERVERS IN TAJIKISTAN—UNMOT

Headquarters: Dushanbe, Tajikistan.

Special Envoy of the UN Secretary-General: GERD MERREM (Germany).

Chief Military Observer: Brig.-Gen. BOLESŁAW IZYDORCZYK (Poland).

In December 1994 the UN Security Council authorized the establishment of UNMOT to monitor a cease-fire that had been agreed by the Tajik Government and opposition forces in September. The mission had an initial mandate of six months, which was conditional on an extension of the cease-fire agreement beyond February 1995. UNMOT's mandate was to assist a Tajik Joint Commission to monitor the cease-fire; to investigate and report on violations of the cease-fire; to provide good offices, as stipulated in the cease-fire agreement; to maintain close contact with the parties to the conflict, as well as close liaison with the mission of the OSCE and with the peace-keeping forces of the Commonwealth of Independent States; to provide political liaisons and co-ordination to facilitate humanitarian assistance by the international community; and to support the efforts of the Secretary-General's Special Envoy. In April 1995 there was an escalation of military activities on the Tajik-Afghan border, which threatened the conditions necessary for the continued deployment of the UN observers. In June the mission's mandate was extended for a further six months. However, the Security Council demanded that substantive progress be made by all sides on institutional and political issues and that they demonstrate commitment to the promotion of democracy and national reconciliation. In November 1996 UNMOT expressed concern at the outbreak of renewed hostilities in central Tajikistan and urged both sides to observe the agreed cease-fire. In early December UNHCR and UNMOT protested to the leadership of the Tajik opposition in exile over the alleged brutal treatment of Tajik refugees in northern Afghanistan. In mid-December a new cease-fire agreement was concluded by the Government and the opposition (which was violated almost immediately), and later in the month two new peace accords were signed in the presence of the UN Special Envoy. Also in December four UNMOT military observers were subjected to a 'mock execution', while seven others were taken hostage by Tajik guerrillas. Inter-Tajik peace talks continued in early 1997 in Teheran, Iran, with the Special Envoy's participation. However, in February the UN Secretary-General authorized the suspension of all UN activities in the country, with the exception of a small UNMOT team to be retained in Dushanbe, as a result of a deterioration in the security situation and, in particular, following an incident in which five UNMOT observers were taken hostage, along with seven other international personnel, by Tajik rebel Islamic forces. In March the two sides concluded an agreement on the integration of the country's armed forces and other confidence-building measures. In mid-March the Security Council authorized a six-month extension of UNMOT's mandate. In May the Tajik Government and opposition forces signed a protocol ending hostilities and guaranteeing implementation of the December 1996 peace accord. At the end of June 1997 the leaders of the two sides, with the UN Special Envoy, signed a Peace and National Reconciliation Accord formally ending the country's civil war. UNMOT's mandate was extended in June and again in September. It was to encourage co-operation within the country in implementing the peace accords and to supervise the return of Tajik refugees from Afghanistan and the reintegration of rebel soldiers. In November the Security Council agreed to strengthen the operation by 40 observers to monitor the implementation of the military aspects of the June accord, including the demobilization of opposition troops, and to investigate any reported violations of the cease-fire agreement. UNMOT was to continue to provide good offices and expert advice and to co-operate with the Commissions on National Reconciliation and on Elections and Holding of a Referendum.

At 30 September 1997 UNMOT comprised 44 military observers from nine countries. The annual cost of the mission to the UN is approximately US $8m.

UNITED NATIONS MISSION FOR THE REFERENDUM IN WESTERN SAHARA—MINURSO

Headquarters: el-Aaiún, Western Sahara.

Personal Envoy of the UN Secretary-General: JAMES A. BAKER, III (USA).

Commander: Brig.-Gen. BERND LUBENIK (Austria).

In April 1991 the UN Security Council endorsed the establishment of MINURSO to verify a cease-fire in the disputed territory of Western Sahara (claimed by Morocco), which came into effect in September 1991, to implement a programme of repatriation of Western Saharan refugees (in co-ordination with UNHCR), to secure the release of all Sahrawi political prisoners, and to organize a referendum on the future of the territory. The referendum, originally envisaged for January 1992, was, however, postponed indefinitely. In 1992 and 1993 the Secretary-General's Special Representative organized negotiations between the Frente Popular para la Liberación de Saguia el Hamra y Río de Oro (Frente Polisario) and the Moroccan Government, who were in serious disagreement regarding criteria for eligibility to vote in the referendum (in particular, the Moroccan Government insisted that more than 100,000 members of ethnic groups who had been forced to leave the territory under Spanish rule prior to the last official census in 1974, the results of which were to be used as a basis for voter registration, should be allowed to participate in a referendum). Nevertheless, in March 1993 the Security Council advocated that further efforts should be made to compile a satisfactory electoral list and to resolve the outstanding differences on procedural issues. An Identification Commission was consequently established to begin the process of voter registration, although this was obstructed by the failure of the Moroccan Government and the Frente Polisario to pursue political dialogue. In March 1994 the Security Council decided that the Commission should proceed with its work and the UN continue its efforts to obtain the co-operation of the two parties. Application forms were distributed to registration centres (located within the territory and in other areas inhabited by Sahrawis) from December 1993, and the identification and registration operation was formally initiated in late August 1994. The process was complicated by the dispersed nature of the Western Saharan population. In December the Secretary-General expressed his intention to commence the transitional period of the settlement plan, during which time MINURSO was to oversee a reduction of Moroccan government troops in the region, a confinement of Frente Polisario troops, the release of political prisoners and the exchange of other prisoners and refugees, with effect from 1 June 1995. While this date was later reviewed, in June 1995 a Security Council mission visited the region to assess the referendum process. The mission recognized legitimate difficulties in conducting the identification process; however, it urged all parties to co-operate with MINURSO and suggested that the operation's future would be reconsidered in the event of further delays. In December the UN Secretary-General reported that the identification of voters had stalled, owing to persistent obstruction of the process on the part of the Moroccan and Frente Polisario authorities. By May 1996 all efforts to resume the identification process had failed, as a result of the ongoing dispute regarding the number of potentially eligible voters, as well as the Frente Polisario's insistence on reviewing those already identified (a demand rejected by Morocco). Three registration offices in Western Sahara and one in Mauritania were closed. At the end of that month the Security Council endorsed a recommendation of the Secretary-General to suspend the identification process until all sides demonstrate their willingness to co-operate with the mission. The Security Council decided that MINURSO's operational capacity should be reduced by 20%, with sufficient troops retained to monitor and verify the cease-fire. The Secretary-General's acting Special Representative pursued efforts to maintain political dialogue in the region; however, no significant progress was achieved in furthering the identification process.

In early 1997 the new Secretary-General of the UN, Kofi Annan, attempted to revive the possibility of an imminent resolution of the dispute, amid increasing concerns that the opposing authorities were preparing for a resumption of hostilities in the event of a collapse of the existing cease-fire, and appointed James Baker, a former US Secretary of State, as his Personal Envoy to the region. Baker undertook his first official visit to Western Sahara in April, in order to review the prospects for the UN-sponsored referendum. In early June Baker obtained the support of Morocco and the Frente Polisario, as well as Algeria and Mauritania (which border the disputed territory), to conduct further negotiations in order to advance the referendum process. Direct talks between senior representatives of the Moroccan Government and the Frente Polisario authorities were initiated later in that month, in Lisbon, Portugal, under the auspices of the UN, and attended by Algeria and Mauritania in an observer capacity. In September the two sides concluded an agreement which aimed to resolve the outstanding issues of contention and enable the referendum to be conducted in late 1998. The agreement included a commitment by both parties to identify eligible Sahrawi voters on an individual basis, in accordance with the results of the 1974 census, and a code of conduct to ensure the impartiality of the poll. In October 1997 the Security Council extended MINURSO's mandate to 20 April 1998. The Council also endorsed a recommendation of the Secretary-General to increase the strength of the mission, initially by 32 identification staff and 36 civilian police officers to work at four identification centres. The proposal envisaged a maximum of nine administered identification centres. The process of voter identification resumed in December 1997. According to a report of the UN Secretary-General, the referendum was scheduled to be conducted on 7 December 1998.

The mission has headquarters in the north and south of the disputed territory, and there is a liaison office in Tindouf, Algeria, which was established in order to maintain contact with the Frente Polisario (which is based in Algeria) and the Algerian Government.

At 30 September 1997 MINURSO comprised 21 troops and 200 military observers. The annual cost to the United Nations of the mission is approximately US $29.1m.

UNITED NATIONS OBSERVER MISSION IN ANGOLA—MONUA

Headquarters: Luanda, Angola.

Commander: Maj.-Gen. PHILLIP VALERIO SIBANDA (Zimbabwe).

Special Representative of the UN Secretary-General: ALIOUNE BLONDIN BEYE (Mali).

The Security Council authorized the establishment of MONUA in June 1997, in order to maintain a UN security presence in Angola to facilitate the process of national reconciliation. MONUA succeeded the UN Angola Verification Mission (UNAVEM), which had been established in December 1988, at the request of the Governments of Angola and Cuba, to oversee the withdrawal of Cuban troops from the country, and subsequently extended to monitor accords to end the conflict between the Angolan Government and the opposition União nacional para la Independência Total de Angola (UNITA) and the process of reconstruction and reintegration, including the observation of general elections. The third mandated UNAVEM operation (UNAVEM III) undertook the administration of centres for the registration and disarmament of opposition UNITA soldiers and to assist the formation of a unified Angolan army. By December 1996 UNITA declared that its entire military contingent had been lodged and demobilized, and that all its weapons had been surrendered to the UN. At that time, however, UNAVEM III expressed concern that a sizeable number of the total 70,336 UNITA troops registered at confinement sites had deserted. MONUA continued to verify the demobilization of UNITA forces; however, in mid-1997 there were reports from Angola of large-scale troop movements. In October the Special Representative of the Secretary-General estimated that UNITA still had a residual force of between 6,000 and 35,000 troops. At the end of October the UN Security Council agreed to implement an earlier decision to impose diplomatic sanctions against UNITA officials, owing to the opposition's failure to adhere to certain conditions of the 1994 Lusaka Protocol, including the full disarmament of its army and the return of UNITA-controlled areas to the Government. The Council also endorsed a recommendation of the Secretary-General to postpone the withdrawal of the remaining UNAVEM III forces until the end of November, while MONUA's mandate was extended to 30 January 1998.

MONUA has an authorized strength of 83 military officers and 345 civilian police. At 30 September 1997 the withdrawal of UNAVEM III personnel had not been completed, and there were 313 civilian police, 2,479 UN troops and 238 military observers serving in Angola.

UNITED NATIONS OBSERVER MISSION IN GEORGIA—UNOMIG

Headquarters: Sukhumi, Georgia.

Special Representative of the UN Secretary-General: LIVIU BOTA (Romania).

Chief Military Observer: Maj.-Gen. HARUN AR-RASHID (Bangladesh).

UNOMIG was established in August 1993 to verify compliance with a cease-fire agreement, signed in July between the Government of Georgia and Abkhazian forces. The mission, which constituted the UN's first undertaking in the former USSR, was to consist of 88 military observers and a small number of support staff. In October the UN Secretary-General stated that a breakdown in the cease-fire agreement had invalidated UNOMIG's mandate. He proposed, however, to maintain, for information purposes, the eight-strong UNOMIG team in the city of Sukhumi, which had been seized by Abkhazian separatist forces in late September. In late December the Security Council authorized the deployment of additional military observers in response to the signing of a memorandum of understanding by the conflicting parties earlier that month. Further peace negotiations, which were conducted in January–March 1994 under the authority of the UN Secretary-General's Special Envoy, achieved no political consensus. While the Security Council approved new resolutions to prolong the existence of UNOMIG, the full deployment of a peace-keeping force remained dependent on progress in the peace process. In July the Security Council endorsed the establishment of a peace-keeping force, consisting of 3,000 troops from the Commonwealth of Independent States (CIS, q.v.), to verify a cease-fire agreement that had been signed in May. At the same time the Security Council increased the authorized strength of the mission to 136 military observers and expanded UNOMIG's mandate to incorporate the following tasks: to monitor and verify the implementation of the agreement and to investigate reported violations; to observe the CIS forces; to verify that troops and heavy military equipment remain outside the security zone and the restricted weapons zone; to monitor the storage of the military equipment withdrawn from the restricted zones; to monitor the withdrawal of Georgian troops from the Kodori Gorge region to locations beyond the Abkhazian frontiers; and to patrol regularly the Kodori Gorge. Peace negotiations were pursued in 1995, despite periodic outbreaks of violence in Abkhazia. In July 1996 the Security Council, extending UNOMIG's mandate, expressed its concern at the lack of progress being made towards a comprehensive political settlement in the region. The Council also urged the Abkhazian side to accelerate significantly the process of voluntary return of Georgian refugees and displaced persons to Abkhazia. In October the Council decided to establish a human rights office as part of UNOMIG. In January 1997 UNOMIG's mandate was extended to 31 July. In May the Security Council issued a Presidential Statement urging greater efforts towards achieving a peaceful solution to the dispute. The Statement endorsed a proposal of the UN Secretary-General to strengthen the political element of UNOMIG to enable the mission to assume a more active role in furthering a negotiated settlement. In July direct discussions between representatives of the Georgian and Abkhazian authorities, the first in more than two years, were held under UN auspices. In the same month the Security Council extended UNOMIG's mandate to 31 January 1998.

At 30 September 1997 UNOMIG comprised 110 military observers. The estimated annual cost to the United Nations of the mission in 1997 was US $19.9m.

UNITED NATIONS PEACE-KEEPING FORCE IN CYPRUS—UNFICYP

Headquarters: Nicosia, Cyprus.

Special Adviser to the Secretary-General: DIEGO CÓRDOVEZ (Ecuador).

Commander: Maj.-Gen. EVERGISTO ARTURO DE VERGARA (Argentina).

UNFICYP was established in March 1964 by a UN Security Council resolution (for a three-month period, subsequently extended) to prevent a recurrence of fighting between the Greek and Turkish Cypriot communities, and to contribute to the maintenance of law and order and a return to normal conditions. The Force controls a 180-km buffer zone, established (following the Turkish intervention in 1974) between the cease-fire lines of the Turkish forces and the Cyprus National Guard. The Force also performs humanitarian functions, such as facilitating the supply of electricity and water across the cease-fire lines, and offering emergency medical services. In August 1996 serious hostilities between elements of the two communities in the UN-controlled buffer zone resulted in the deaths of two people and injuries to many others, including 12 UN personnel. Following further intercommunal violence, UNFICYP advocated the prohibition of all weapons and military posts along the length of the buffer zone. The Force also proposed additional humanitarian measures to improve the conditions of minority groups living in the two parts of the island.

In September 1992 the troop-providing countries announced that they were going to reduce substantially the number of troops in UNFICYP, as a result of the lack of financing, as well as a more pressing need for military personnel in other peace-keeping operations.

At 30 September 1997 UNFICYP had an operational strength of 1,231 troops and 35 police officers, from nine countries. The estimated annual cost of the force is US $50.3m., of which about one-half is met by assessed contributions from UN member states; the Government of Cyprus pays one-third of the total amount, while Greece contributes an estimated $6.5m. annually.

UNITED NATIONS PREVENTIVE DEPLOYMENT FORCE—UNPREDEP

Headquarters: Skopje, former Yugoslav republic of Macedonia.

Special Representative of the Secretary-General and Chief of Mission: HENRYK SOKALSKI (Poland).

Commander: Brig.-Gen. BENT SOHNEMANN (Denmark).

In December 1992, in response to a request from the President of the former Yugoslav republic of Macedonia (FYRM), the Security Council approved the deployment of an UNPROFOR contingent on the FYRM's borders with the Federal Republic of Yugoslavia and Albania, in order to monitor any developments that might affect the FYRM's stability and threaten its territory. The mission's preventive role has been enhanced by close co-operation with monitors from the Organization for Security and Co-operation in Europe (OSCE, q.v.). On 31 March 1995 the UN operation in the FYRM was renamed UNPREDEP, and in February 1996, following the termination of the mandates of the UN Peace Forces and UNPROFOR (see above), UNPREDEP became an independent mission reporting directly to UN headquarters in New York. The Security Council also agreed to an additional 50 military personnel for UNPREDEP, to assist in projects to improve the FYRM's infrastructure. In December 1996 the Security Council decided to reduce the military component of the Force by 300 troops by 30 April 1997; however, the initiative was suspended by the Council in April, owing to an escalation of civil unrest in Albania, which threatened the security of the region. In September the UN Secretary-General recommended that the reduction in UNPREDEP's strength proceed over a two-month period, prior to the expiry of the Force's current mandate on 30 November. The Security Council subsequently extended UNPREDEP's mandate until 31 August 1998.

At 30 September 1997 UNPREDEP had an operational strength of 1,031 military personnel, 33 military observers and 26 civilian police. The mission is estimated to incur an annual cost of US $44.3m.

UNITED NATIONS TRANSITION MISSION IN HAITI—UNTMIH

Headquarters: Port-au-Prince, Haiti.

Special Representative of the UN Secretary-General and Chief of Mission: ENRIQUE TER HORST (Venezuela).

Commander: Brig.-Gen. J. J. (ROBIN) GAGNON.

The establishment and deployment of the original UN Mission in Haiti (UNMIH) was authorized by the Security Council in September 1993, with a mandate to maintain peace and respect for human rights during the transition of power from the military junta to the exiled President, Fr Jean-Bertrand Aristide, in accordance with an agreement reached by both sides at Governor's Island, USA, in July of that year. However, the military authorities repeatedly obstructed deployment of UNMIH troops and the transition of power failed to be achieved. Meanwhile, the security situation in the country continued to deteriorate. In July 1994 the Security Council authorized the establishment of a multinational force, under US command, to assume responsibility for ensuring the removal of Haiti's military leadership. The multinational troops were to be replaced by an enlarged UN mission when a 'secure and safe environment' had been established. Negotiations between US representatives and Haitian military leaders concluded with the agreement of the latter to retire from power by 15 October. On that day President Aristide returned to the country. UNMIH, with an authorized strength of 6,000 troops and 567 civilian police, assumed authority from the multinational force, at the end of March 1995. UNMIH troops and observers provided technical and security support for legislative and municipal elections in June and a presidential election in December. Following a request from the new President for an extension to UNMIH's mandate, which was to have ended in February 1996, the Security Council agreed to extend the mission until 30 June. However, the strength of the force was to be greatly reduced, to a total of 1,200 troops and 300 civilian police. In late June the Security Council decided to reduce further the size of the mission to 600; however, Canada resolved to finance a 700-strong contingent of its own troops, which was to be an integral part of the force. The name of the mission, which became operational on 1 July, was changed to the UN Support Mission in Haiti (UNSMIH) and had a mandate to assist the Government in the professionalization of Haiti's police force and in maintaining a secure and stable environment. In early December the Security Council agreed to extend UNSMIH's mandate for a final period, until 31 July 1997. In that month the UN Secretary-General recommended that the international community maintain support for the efforts of Haiti's national police force to consolidate a safe and secure environment in the country, at least until 30 November 1997. UNTMIH was consequently authorized by the Security Council on 30 July, with a four-month mandate to undertake specialist police training, to continue preparation, with UNDP, of an assistance programme to provide the national police with law enforcement expertise and to ensure the safety and freedom of movement of UN personnel working in the country. The Special Representative of the Secretary-General was to co-ordinate all UN activities in order to promote institution-building, national reconciliation and economic rehabilitation. At the end of November the Security Council authorized the establishment of a new operation, the UN Civilian Police Mission in Haiti (MIPONUH), comprising 300 police officers who were to remain in Haiti for a further year to complete UNTMIH's mandate.

UNTMIH's authorized strength consisted of 250 civilian police personnel and 50 military personnel. However, a number of additional troops, provided on the basis of voluntary funding by the Governments of Canada and Pakistan, were attached to UNTMIH's military contingent. At 30 September 1997 UNTMIH comprised 1,136 troops and 241 civilian police. The estimated budget of UNTMIH for the four-month period 1 August to 30 November 1997 was US $10.1m.

UNITED NATIONS TRANSITIONAL ADMINISTRATION FOR EASTERN SLAVONIA, BARANJA AND WESTERN SIRMIUM—UNTAES

Headquarters: Vukovar, Croatia.

Transitional Administrator: WILLIAM WALKER (USA).

Commander: Maj.-Gen. WILLY HANSET (Belgium).

In February 1992, following a cease-fire agreement in Croatia between the Croatian National Guard and the Yugoslav People's Army (JNA), the Security Council authorized the establishment of UNPROFOR to ensure the withdrawal of the JNA from Croatia and the complete demilitarization of three Serb-held enclaves within Croatia, designated UN Protected Areas (UNPAs). It was also to supervise the functioning of the local authorities and police in Croatia. UNPROFOR's mandate in Croatia was enlarged in June, to include monitoring Serb-dominated areas outside the UNPA boundaries, known as 'pink zones'; in August, to enable the force to control the entry of civilians into the UNPAs, and to perform immigration and customs functions at the UNPA borders coinciding with international frontiers; and in October, to include monitoring the withdrawal of the JNA from the Prevlaka peninsula (completed in mid-October), and to ensure control of the Peruca dam. Lack of co-operation by Serb local authorities, however, prevented UNPROFOR from achieving demilitarization within the UNPAs, while tension was renewed by an offensive begun by the Croatian armed forces against the UNPAs and 'pink zones' in January 1993. Hostilities continued in 1993 until a temporary truce, mediated by UNPROFOR, took effect in December. In March 1994 representatives of the Croatian Government and the Serb authorities in the UNPAs concluded a cease-fire agreement, whereby UNPROFOR was to supervise separation zones between the two sides and monitor the withdrawal of weapons. In January 1995 Croatia's President Tudjman demanded the withdrawal of the 14,000 UN troops, stating that their presence was substantiating the Serb position and preventing the negotiation of a peaceful solution to the conflict. In mid-March Tudjman, responding to international pressure, agreed to permit a reduced UN force to remain in the country with a revised mandate. The mandate that was authorized by the Security Council, on 31 March, established the UN Confidence Restoration Operation (UNCRO) to facilitate the implementation of the March 1994 cease-fire and other UN resolutions on security and freedom of movement, to ensure the demilitarization of the Prevlaka peninsula and to monitor the deployment of troops and weapons and their movement across Croatia's borders with Bosnia and Herzegovina and with the Federal Republic of Yugoslavia. In early May Croatian troops initiated a hostile offensive to reclaim a separatist enclave in Western Slavonia. The Security Council demanded the withdrawal of all Croatian and Serb troops from the zone of separation dividing the two forces, after which UNCRO was to be fully deployed. The attack marked the start of a period of escalating tensions and hostilities, during which the Security Council expressed its concern at the alleged intimidation of UNCRO troops and at reported violations of international humanitarian law by Croatian forces. UNCRO monitors and civilian police oversaw the mass movement of Serb refugees which resulted from a Croatian offensive on the separatist-held Krajina region in early August. Many of UNCRO's observation posts were captured or destroyed during the fighting. In October representatives of the Croatian Government and Serb separatists agreed a set of principles regarding the future of the disputed Eastern Slavonia region. The agreement was secured in mid-November, as part of the peace negotiations being conducted by leaders of all warring sides in the former Yugoslavia in Dayton, USA. In accordance with the agreement, the Serbs were to relinquish authority for Eastern Slavonia, Baranja and Western Srem (Sirmium) to Croatia. There was to be a transitional period of one year, with a possible extension of a year at the request of either side, during which that region was to be under international administration. An international force was to ensure the implementation of the agreement and oversee the demilitarization of the region. On 30 November the Security Council extended UNCRO's mandate for a final period until 15 January 1996. On that date the Security Council authorized the establishment of UNTAES to oversee the implementation of the provisions of the peace agreement, with an initial mandate of 12 months and an authorized military strength of 5,000 troops. At the end of January the Security Council authorized the deployment of 100 military observers for a six-month period as part of UNTAES, in order to supervise and facilitate the demilitarization of the region. The military component of UNTAES was also charged with contributing to the maintenance of peace and stability; monitoring the voluntary and safe return of refugees and displaced persons, in co-operation with UNHCR; and otherwise assisting in the implementation of the peace agreement. UNTAES also had a civilian component, comprising an authorized strength of 600 civilian police, with provision for 480 international staff, 720 locally-recruited staff and 100 UN Volunteers. The civilian component was charged with establishing a temporary police force and instituting a police training programme; monitoring treatment of offenders and the prison system; undertaking tasks relating to civil administration and the functioning of public services; organizing and overseeing elections in the region; assisting in the co-ordination of plans for the reconstruction and development of the region; monitoring parties' observance of human rights; promoting an atmosphere of confidence among the different ethnic communities; and supervising demining. UNTAES was also mandated to co-operate with the International Criminal Tribunal for the Former Yugoslavia (see p. 21). In May UNTAES oversaw the rehabilitation and reintegration of important communications and infrastructure systems in Eastern Slavonia, Baranja and Western Sirmium into those of Croatia as a whole. The demilitarization of the region was completed in a 30-day period from mid-May to mid-June, with heavy artillery removed from the region and soldiers and officers of the Serb army in Eastern Slavonia, Baranja and Western Sirmium demobilized. In the latter half of 1996 the Croatian Government threatened to obstruct the deployment of UNTAES beyond early 1997. However, in January of that year the Security Council extended UNTAES's mandate until 15 July with Croatia's consent. In early 1997 UNTAES assisted with preparations for, and the administration of, elections in the region, held on 13 April (having been postponed from the previous month), which aimed to facilitate the reintegration of the enclave into Croatia. The Transitional Administrator certified the results of the election and estimated that more than 126,000 people had cast votes, including 56,000 displaced Serbs through absentee ballots elsewhere in Croatia. In July the Security Council decided to extend UNTAES's mandate for a further six-month period, despite objections from the Croatian Government, but authorized a phased withdrawal of the military component of the mission. In the same month UNTAES undertook to co-operate with the efforts of UNHCR and the Croatian Government to identify the property of displaced persons and refugees and to assess war damage, in order to accelerate the process of reconstruction and national reconciliation. In October the Security Council expressed its concern at the outstanding areas of contention and non-compliance with the peace agreements on the part of the Croatian Government, and emphasized its support for the continued presence of UN civilian police and observers in the region.

At 30 September 1997 UNTAES comprised 2,346 troops, 97 military observers and 404 police officers. The annual cost of UNTAES to the UN was estimated at US $266.6m.

UNITED NATIONS TRUCE SUPERVISION ORGANIZATION—UNTSO

Headquarters: Government House, Jerusalem.

Chief-of-Staff: Maj.-Gen. RUFUS MODUPE KUPOLATI (Nigeria).

UNTSO was established initially to supervise the truce called by the UN Security Council in Palestine in May 1948 and has assisted in the application of the 1949 Armistice Agreements. Its activities have evolved over the years, in response to developments in the Middle East and in accordance with the relevant resolutions of the Security Council. There is no periodic renewal procedure for UNTSO's mandate.

UNTSO observers assist the UN peace-keeping forces in the Middle East (see above), UNIFIL and UNDOF. In addition, UNTSO operates six outposts in the Sinai region of Egypt to maintain a UN presence there, and one at Ismailia, Egypt, in the area of the Suez canal. There is also a small detachment of observers in Beirut, Lebanon and liaison offices in Amman, Jordan, and Gaza. UNTSO observers have been available at short notice to form the nucleus of other peace-keeping operations.

The operational strength of UNTSO at 30 September 1997 comprised 155 military observers, supported by international and local civilian staff. UNTSO expenditures are covered by the regular budget of the United Nations. The annual cost of the operation in 1997 was estimated to be US $23.7m.

United Nations Population Fund—UNFPA

Address: 220 East 42nd St, New York, NY 10017, USA.

Telephone: (212) 297-5020; **fax:** (212) 557-6416; **internet:** http://www.unfpa.org.

Created in 1967 as the Trust Fund for Population Activities, the UN Fund for Population Activities (UNFPA) was established as a Fund of the UN General Assembly in 1972 and was made a subsidiary organ of the UN General Assembly in 1979, with the UNDP Governing Council (now the Executive Board) designated as its governing body. In 1987 UNFPA's name was changed to the United Nations Population Fund (retaining the same acronym).

Organization

(November 1997)

EXECUTIVE DIRECTOR

The Executive Director, who has the rank of Under-Secretary-General of the UN, is responsible for the overall direction of the Fund, working closely with governments, other United Nations bodies and agencies, and non-governmental and international organizations to ensure the most effective programming and use of resources in population activities.

Executive Director: Dr NAFIS SADIK (Pakistan).

EXECUTING AGENCIES

UNFPA provides financial and technical assistance to developing countries at their request. In many projects assistance is extended through member organizations of the UN system (in particular, FAO, ILO, UNESCO, WHO), although projects are executed increasingly by national governments themselves. The Fund may also call on the services of international, regional and national non-governmental and training organizations, as well as research institutions. In addition, eight UNFPA regional technical support teams, composed of experts from the UN, its specialized agencies and non-governmental organizations, assist countries at all stages of project/programme development and implementation.

FIELD ORGANIZATION

UNFPA operates field offices, each headed by an UNFPA Representative, in 66 countries. In other countries UNFPA uses UNDP's field structure of Resident Representatives as the main mechanism for performing out its work. The field offices assist governments in formulating requests for aid and co-ordinate the work of the executing agencies in any given country or area. UNFPA has eight regional technical support teams (see above); at mid-1995 there were 593 UNFPA staff members in the field, of a world-wide total of 837.

Activities

During 1996 UNFPA provided assistance in 168 countries, of which 46 were in Africa, 44 in Asia and the Pacific, 37 in Latin America and the Caribbean, and 41 in the Arab states and Europe. Since it became fully operational in 1969 UNFPA has provided assistance totalling US $3,700m. to developing countries.

The major functions of UNFPA, according to its mandate, are: to build up the capacity to respond to needs in population and family planning; to promote awareness of population problems in developed and developing countries and possible strategies to deal with them; to assist countries, at their request, in dealing with their population problems, in the forms and means best suited to the individual countries' needs; and to play a leading role in the UN system in promoting population programmes, and to co-ordinate projects supported by the Fund.

In co-operation with the UN Population Division, UNFPA played an important role in preparing for and conducting the International Conference on Population and Development (ICPD), held in Cairo, Egypt, in September 1994. UNFPA's Executive Director, Dr Nafis Sadik, acted as Secretary-General of the Conference, which was attended by representatives of 182 countries. The ICPD adopted a Programme of Action, establishing the objectives to be pursued for the next 20 years (despite reservations recorded by the representatives of some predominantly Roman Catholic and Islamic countries, concerning sections which they regarded as endorsing abortion and sexual promiscuity). The Programme's objectives envisaged universal access to reproductive health and family planning services, a reduction in infant, child and maternal mortality, a life expectancy at birth of 75 years or more, and universal access to primary education for all children by 2015. The Programme emphasized the necessity of empowering and educating women, in order to achieve successful sustainable human development. Annual expenditure required for the implementation of the objectives was estimated to amount to US $17,000m. for the year 2000, increasing to $21,700m. in 2015: of these amounts, the international community or donor countries would need to contribute about one-third. During 1995 UNFPA undertook to redefine its programme directions, resource allocations and policy guidelines in order to implement effectively the recommendations of the Cairo Conference Programme of Action. The Executive Board subsequently endorsed the following as core programme areas: Reproductive Health, including Family Planning and Sexual Health; Population and Development Strategies; and Advocacy (for example, human rights, education, basic health services and the empowerment of women). All UNFPA's activities promote the autonomy and equality of women.

UNFPA recognizes that improving reproductive health is an essential requirement for improving the general welfare of the population and the basis for empowering women and achieving sustainable social and economic development. The ICPD succeeded in raising the political prominence of reproductive health issues and stimulating consideration by governments of measures to strengthen and restructure their health services and policies. During 1995 almost 50% of UNFPA assistance was allocated to reproductive health programmes. UNFPA encourages the integration of family planning into all maternal, child and other reproductive health care. Its efforts to improve the quality of these services include support for the training of health-care personnel and promoting greater accessibility. Many reproductive health projects focus on the reduction of maternal mortality, which was included as a central objective of the ICPD Programme and recognized as a legitimate element of international human rights instruments as the right to life/survival. The ICPD reported that the leading cause of maternal deaths (i.e. those related to pregnancy, which amount to some 585,000 each year) was unsafe abortions, and urged governments to confront the issue as a major public health concern. UNFPA is also concerned with reducing the use of abortion (i.e. its use as a means of family planning), and with preventing infertility, reproductive tract infections and sexually-transmitted diseases, including HIV and AIDS. Special attention is given to the specific needs of adolescents, for example through education and counselling initiatives, and to women in emergency situations. UNFPA also supports research into contraceptives and training in contraceptive technology. During the early 1990s UNFPA's Global Initiative on Contraceptive Requirements and Logisitics Management Needs in Developing Countries organized in-depth studies on contraceptive requirements in certain developing countries (including Brazil, Bangladesh and Egypt).

UNFPA helps countries to formulate and implement comprehensive population policies as a central part of any strategies to achieve sustainable development. The Fund aims to ensure that the needs and concerns of women are incorporated into development and population policies. Under this programme area UNFPA provides assistance and training for national statistical offices in undertaking basic data collection, for example censuses and demographic surveys. UNFPA also provides assistance for analysis of demographic and socio-economic data, for research on population trends and for the formulation of government policies. It supports a programme of fellowships in demographic analysis, data processing and cartography.

UNFPA's advocacy role is incorporated into all its programming activities in support of the objectives of the ICPD. Consequently, the Fund aims to encourage the participation of women at all levels of decision- and policy-making and supports programmes that improve the access of all girls and women to education and grant women equal access to land, credit and employment opportunities. UNFPA's 1997 *State of World Population Report* defined the improved welfare of women as an issue of basic human rights, which included the eradication of all forms of gender discrimination, reproductive choice and the protection of women from sexual and domestic violence. UNFPA helps to promote awareness of these objectives and to incorporate them into national programmes. In 1997 UNFPA appointed a special ambassador to generate international awareness of the dangers of female genital mutilation. UNFPA also has special programmes on youth, on ageing, and on AIDS, and is currently increasing educational and research activities in the area of population and the environment. UNFPA attempts to increase awareness of the issue of population through regional and national seminars, publications (see below) and audio-visual aids, participation in conferences, and through a pro-active relationship with the mass media.

In 1995 UNFPA actively participated in the World Summit for Social Development, an international conference held in Copenhagen, Denmark, in March, and the UN Fourth World Conference on Women, held in Beijing, People's Republic of China, in September, at which the key concepts of the ICPD Programme were emphasized and reinforced. In 1996 UNFPA contributed to the second UN Conference on Human Settlements (Habitat II), which was held in Istanbul, Turkey, in June, by reporting on current trends in urbanization and population distribution and their link to human settlements. UNFPA is participating in the Special Initiative on Africa that was initiated by the UN Secretary-General in March 1996. UNFPA's principal involvement is to assist countries to implement efforts for reproductive health and to promote the integration of population considerations into development planning. UNFPA's Executive Director chairs the inter-agency Task Force on Basic Social Services for All, which was initially established to strengthen collaboration on implementing the ICPD Programme of Action through the UN Resident Co-ordinator System. In 1996 the Task Force assumed its current name with an expanded mandate to co-ordinate the follow-up to other global conferences. UNFPA also collaborates with other UN agencies and international experts to develop a reliable, multidisciplinary set of indicators to measure progress towards achieving the objectives of different conferences and to help formulate reproductive health programmes and monitor their success.

FINANCE

UNFPA is supported entirely by voluntary contributions from donor countries. In 1996 UNFPA's income totalled US $305m. Total project expenditure from regular resources in 1995 amounted to $230.9m., of which more than 70% was allocated to some 59 priority countries.

PUBLICATIONS

Annual Report.

AIDS Update (annually).

Guide to Sources of International Population Assistance.

Inventory of Population Projects in Developing Countries around the World (annually in English and French).

Populi (10 a year, in English, French and Spanish).

State of World Population Report (annually).

Reports and reference works; videotapes and radio programmes.

United Nations Relief and Works Agency for Palestine Refugees in the Near East—UNRWA

Addresses: Al Azhar Rd, POB 61, Gaza;
Bayader Wadi Seer, POB 140157, Amman, Jordan.
Telephone (Gaza): (7) 861196; **fax:** (7) 822552.
Telephone (Amman): (6) 826171; **telex:** 21170; **fax:** (6) 864151.

UNRWA began operations in 1950 to provide relief, health, education and welfare services for Palestine refugees in the Near East.

Organization

(November 1997)

UNRWA employs an international staff of about 180 and more than 20,000 local staff, mainly Palestine refugees. In mid-1996 the agency's headquarters were relocated, from Vienna, Austria, to Gaza. The Commissioner-General is appointed by the UN General Assembly, is the head of all UNRWA operations and is assisted by an Advisory Commission consisting of representatives of the governments of:

Belgium	Jordan	Turkey
Egypt	Lebanon	United Kingdom
France	Syria	USA
Japan		

Commissioner-General: Peter Hansen (Denmark).

FIELD OFFICES

Each field office is headed by a director and has departments responsible for education, health and relief and social services programmes, finance, administration, supply and transport, legal affairs and public information.

Jordan: Al Zubeidi Bldg, Tla'a Al-Air, POB 484, Amman; tel. (6) 607194; telex 23402; fax (6) 685476.

Lebanon: POB 947, Beirut; tel. (1) 603437; fax (1) 603443.

Syria: POB 4313, Damascus; tel. (11) 6133035; fax (11) 6133047.

West Bank: Sheik Jarrah Qtr, POB 19149, Jerusalem; tel. (2) 890400; telex 26194; fax (2) 322714.

LIAISON OFFICES

Egypt: 2 Dar-el-Shifa St, Garden City, POB 277, Cairo; tel. (2) 354-8502; telex 94035; fax (2) 354-8504.

USA: Room DC 2-0550, United Nations, New York, NY 10017; tel. (212) 963-2255; telex 422311; fax (212) 935-7899.

Activities

SERVICES FOR PALESTINE REFUGEES

Since 1950 UNRWA has provided relief, health, education and social services for Palestine refugees in Lebanon, Syria, Jordan, the West Bank and the Gaza Strip. For UNRWA's purposes, a Palestine refugee is one whose normal residence was in Palestine for a minimum of two years before the 1948 conflict and who, as a result of the Arab–Israeli hostilities, lost his or her home and means of livelihood. To be eligible for assistance, a refugee must reside in one of the five areas in which UNRWA operates and be in need. A refugee's descendants who fulfil certain criteria are also eligible for UNRWA assistance. At 30 June 1996 UNRWA was providing essential services to 3,308,133 registered refugees (see table). Of these, an estimated 1,095,375 (approximately one-third) were living in 59 camps serviced by the Agency, while the remaining refugees had settled in the towns and villages already existing.

UNRWA's three principal areas of activity are education; health services; and relief and social services. More than 78% of the Agency's 1996 regular budget was devoted to these three operational programmes.

Education (under the technical supervision of UNESCO) accounted for 49% of UNRWA's 1996 budget. In the 1995/96 school year there were 421,854 pupils enrolled in 637 UNRWA schools (74 schools in Lebanon, 110 in Syria, 198 in Jordan, 100 on the West Bank and 155 in the Gaza Strip), and 13,140 educational staff. UNRWA also operated eight vocational and teacher-training centres, which provided a total of 4,624 training places. UNRWA awarded 943 scholarships for study at Arab universities in 1995/96. Technical co-operation for the Agency's education programme is provided by UNESCO.

Health services accounted for 18% of UNRWA's 1996 regular budget. At June 1996 there were 121 health units, of which 78 offered dental care, 120 offered family planning services and 108 offered special care. At that time annual patient visits to UNRWA medical units numbered 6.6m. UNRWA also operates a supplementary feeding programme, mainly for children, to combat malnutrition. Technical assistance for the health programme is provided by WHO.

Relief and social services accounted for 11% of UNRWA's regular budget for 1996. These services comprise the distribution of food rations, the provision of emergency shelter and the organization of welfare programmes for the poorest refugees (at June 1996 179,178 refugees, or 5.4% of the total registered refugee population, were eligible to receive special hardship assistance). In 1995/96 UNRWA's social services programme operated 68 women's centres and 30 community-based rehabilitation centres.

In order to encourage Palestinian self-reliance the Agency issues grants to ailing businesses and loans to families who qualify as special hardship cases. Between 1983 and early 1993 608 such grants and loans were made. In 1991 UNRWA launched an income generation programme, which was designed to combat rising unemployment, particularly in the Occupied Territories. By 30 June 1996 1,970 loans, with a total estimated value of US $9.8m., had been issued to new and existing Palestinian-owned enterprises.

AID TO DISPLACED PERSONS

After the renewal of Arab–Israeli hostilities in the Middle East in June 1967, hundreds of thousands of people fled from the fighting and from Israeli-occupied areas to east Jordan, Syria and Egypt. UNRWA provided emergency relief for displaced refugees and was additionally empowered by a UN General Assembly resolution to provide 'humanitarian assistance, as far as practicable, on an emergency basis and as a temporary measure' for those persons other than Palestine refugees who were newly displaced and in urgent need. In practice, UNRWA lacked the funds to aid the other displaced persons and the main burden of supporting them devolved on the Arab governments concerned. The Agency, as requested by the Government of Jordan in 1967 and on that Government's behalf, distributes rations to displaced persons in Jordan who are not registered refugees of 1948.

RECENT EMERGENCIES

Since 1982 UNRWA has managed a specially-funded operation in Lebanon, aimed at assisting refugees displaced by the continued civil conflict. In late 1986 and early 1987 fighting caused much destruction to Palestinian housing and UNRWA facilities in Lebanon, and an emergency relief operation was undertaken. In April 1996 UNRWA dispatched emergency supplies to assist some of the estimated 500,000 people displaced by renewed military activities in southern Lebanon.

Following the start of the Palestinian *intifada* (uprising) in December 1987 in the Israeli-occupied territories of the West Bank and the Gaza Strip, UNRWA provided expanded medical aid and relief to Palestinian residents in these areas.

In January 1991 (following the outbreak of war between Iraq and a multinational force whose aim was to enforce the withdrawal of Iraqi forces from Kuwait) the Israeli authorities imposed a curfew on Palestinians in the Israeli-occupied territories, and in February UNRWA began an emergency programme of food distribution to Palestinians who had thereby been prevented from earning a living. Following the conflict, Jordan absorbed more than 300,000 people fleeing Kuwait and other Gulf countries. Many of these people are eligible for UNRWA services.

In September 1992 an UNRWA mission was sent to Kuwait, following allegations of abuses of human rights perpetrated by the Kuwaiti authorities against Palestinian refugees living there. The mission was, however, limited to assessing the number of Palestinians from the Gaza Strip in Kuwait, who had been unable to obtain asylum in Jordan, since Jordan did not recognize Gazan identity documents.

Following the signing of the Declaration of Principles by the Palestine Liberation Organization and the Israeli Government in September 1993, UNRWA initiated a Peace Implementation Programme (PIP) to improve services and infrastructure for Palestinian refugees. In September 1994 the first phase of the programme (PIP I) was concluded after the receipt of US $93.2m. in pledged donations. PIP I projects included the construction of 33 schools and 24 classrooms and specialized education rooms, the rehabilitation of 4,700 shelters, the upgrading of solid waste disposal facilities throughout the Gaza Strip and feasibility studies for two sewerage systems. It was estimated that these projects created more than 5,500 jobs in the Gaza Strip for an average period of four months each. By mid-1996 the total number of PIP projects, including those under the second phase of the programme (PIP II), amounted to 276, while funds received or pledged to the Programme totalled $192.6m.

FINANCE

For the most part, UNRWA's income is composed of voluntary contributions, almost entirely from governments and the European Union, the remainder being provided by non-governmental organizations, business corporations and private sources.

As of January 1992 UNRWA adopted a biennial budgetary cycle. The general fund budget for 1994–95 amounted to US $632.3m., of which $552.8m. was to be in cash and $79.5m. in kind. The regular budget for 1996 amounted to $327.5m.

STATISTICS

Refugees Registered with UNRWA (30 June 1996)

Country	Number	% of total
Jordan	1,358,706	41.1
Gaza Strip	716,930	21.7
West Bank	532,438	16.1
Lebanon	352,668	10.7
Syria	347,391	10.5
Total	3,308,133	100.0

PUBLICATIONS

Annual Report of the Commissioner-General of UNRWA.

Palestine Refugees Today—the UNRWA Newsletter (2 a year).

UNRWA Accounts Summary (annually).

UNRWA—An Investment in People (every 2 years).

UNRWA News (monthly).

Catalogues of publications and audio-visual materials.

World Food Programme—WFP

Address: Via Cristoforo Colombo 426, 00145 Rome, Italy.

Telephone: (6) 522821; **telex:** 626675; **fax:** (6) 59602348; **e-mail:** wfpinfo@wfp.org; **internet:** http://www.wfp.org.

WFP, the food aid organization of the United Nations, became operational in 1963. It provides relief assistance to victims of natural and man-made disasters, and supplies food aid to people in developing countries with the aim of stimulating self-reliant communities.

Organization

(January 1998)

EXECUTIVE BOARD

At the end of 1995 the governing body of WFP, the 42-member Committee on Food Aid Policies and Programmes (CFA), was transformed into the WFP Executive Board, in accordance with a resolution of the UN General Assembly. The Board, comprising 36 members, held its first session in January 1996. It was to meet in three regular sessions each year.

SECRETARIAT

WFP's Executive Director is appointed jointly by the UN Secretary-General and the Director-General of FAO and is responsible for the management and administration of the Programme. At 31 December 1995 there were 1,969 long-term WFP staff members, of whom 1,460 (or 74%) were assigned to country offices.

Executive Director: CATHERINE A. BERTINI (USA).

Activities

WFP is the only multilateral organization with a mandate to use food aid as a resource. It is the second largest source of assistance in the UN, after the World Bank group, in terms of actual transfers of resources, and the largest source of grant aid in the UN system. WFP handles more than one-quarter of the world's food aid. WFP is also the largest contributor to South-South trade within the UN system, through the purchase of food and services from developing countries. WFP's mission is to provide food aid to save lives in refugee and other emergency situations, to improve the nutrition and quality of life of vulnerable groups and to help to develop assets and promote the self-reliance of poor families and communities. At the UN Fourth World Conference on Women, held in Beijing, People's Republic of China, in September 1995 WFP announced specific commitments to address the nutritional needs of women and to increase their access to food and development resources. In accordance with a decision of the CFA, WFP aimed to focus its efforts on the world's poorest countries and to provide at least 90% of its total assistance to those designated as 'low-income food-deficit' countries by 1997. At the World Food Summit, held in November 1996, WFP endorsed the commitment to reduce by 50% the number of undernourished people, no later than 2015. In 1996 WFP delivered some 2.2m. metric tons of food assistance, reaching an estimated 45.3m. people in 84 countries.

In the early 1990s there was a substantial shift in the balance between emergency relief and development assistance provided by WFP, owing to the growing needs of victims of drought and other natural disasters, refugees and displaced persons. By 1994 two-thirds of all food aid was for relief assistance and one-third for development, representing a direct reversal of the allocations five years previously. In addition, there was a noticeable increase in aid given to those in need as a result of civil war, compared with commitments for victims of natural disasters. By 1996, there was a decline in the numbers requiring relief assistance: 24.6m. people (compared with 24.8m. in 1995 and 32.5m. in 1994), of whom 4.5m. were refugees, 16m. internally displaced persons and 4.1m. victims of drought and other natural disasters. In 1996 WFP pursued its efforts to be prepared for emergency situations and to improve its capacity for responding effectively to situations as they arise. WFP established new field units to undertake vulnerability analysis and mapping (VAM) in Tanzania and Senegal, in addition to those already operational in Cambodia, Ethiopia, Malawi, Pakistan, Sudan and Zambia. These enable WFP to identify potentially vulnerable groups by providing information on food security and the capacity of different groups for coping with shortages, and to enhance emergency contingency-planning and long-term assistance objectives. The key elements of WFP's emergency response capacity are its strategic stores of food and logistics equipment (maintained in Nairobi, Kenya, and Pisa, Italy), stand-by arrangements to enable the rapid deployment of personnel, communications and other essential equipment, and the Augmented Logistics Intervention Teams, which undertake capacity assessments and contingency-planning. A Crisis Support Facility was established at WFP Headquarters during the year in order to process information and assist co-ordination between WFP and other UN agencies working in Liberia. The Facility was reactivated in November to ensure an effective response to the humanitarian crisis in the former Zaire.

More than one-half of WFP's relief activities in 1996 were in sub-Saharan Africa, and in particular in the Great Lakes region where civil conflict had resulted in massive population displacement. Throughout the year WFP distributed essential food rations to the most vulnerable groups in the region. It also maintained strategic food stocks and developed a logistics infrastructure to ensure that the relief operations could continue in extreme circumstances. WFP led international humanitarian relief efforts in Liberia, following an escalation of violence in that country in April, and provided assistance to more than 1.4m. refugees and displaced persons. During 1996 the former Yugoslavia received 16% of WFP's relief food assistance, which reached some 2.6m. refugees, returnees, displaced persons and other vulnerable groups, mainly in Bosnia and Herzegovina. In Iraq WFP provided emergency food rations to 2.2m. people during 1996. In accordance with a Security Council resolution providing for the limited sale of petroleum by the Iraqi Government in exchange for the purchase of essential humanitarian supplies, which came into effect in December 1996, WFP was to establish an observation system to ensure the fair and efficient distribution of food throughout the country. WFP was also required to transport and distribute the food supplies to local populations in the north of Iraq. In November 1995 WFP established an office in the Democratic People's Republic of Korea (DPRK), in order to monitor food deliveries and assess the food security situation in that country following widespread flooding which destroyed cereal and grain harvests. WFP aimed to provide food to more than 1.5m. victims of flooding and children under five years of age during 1996, at a total cost of US $25.9m. WFP remained actively concerned with the situation in the DPRK throughout 1997 and issued several appeals for international emergency assistance. In January 1998 WFP prepared to undertake its largest-ever relief operation, to assist more than 7m. people suffering severe food shortages in the DPRK, and appealed for emergency assistance totalling US $328m. for the year commencing 1 April. WFP estimated that some 660,000 metric tons of food would be distributed under the operation and resolved to strengthen the operational structure of its activities in the DPRK. In late 1997 WFP distributed emergency food supplies to more than 200,000 Somalis who had been displaced by severe flooding in the south of the country. Earlier in the year WFP appealed for assistance to enable the distribution of emergency food in the same region following crop failure.

Through its development activities, WFP aims to alleviate poverty in developing countries by promoting self-reliant families and communities. Food is supplied, for example, as an incentive in development self-help schemes and as part-wages in labour-intensive projects of many kinds. In all its projects WFP aims to assist the most vulnerable groups and to ensure that beneficiaries have an adequate and balanced diet. Activities supported by the Programme include the settlement and resettlement of groups and communities; land reclamation and improvement; irrigation; forestry; dairy development; road construction; training of hospital staff; community development; and human resources development such as feeding expectant or nursing mothers and schoolchildren, and support for education, training and health programmes. At the end of 1996 WFP was supporting 174 development projects, with total commitments valued at US $1,944m. The largest development operation approved in 1996 was for a rural development programme in Bangladesh, which was expected to benefit 2.25m. people at a cost to WFP of $59.3m. Other approved projects included forestry development in north-eastern Viet Nam, integrated agricultural development in Sichuan Province, People's Republic of China, and community-based rural development and food security in The Gambia.

Following a comprehensive evaluation of its activities, WFP is increasingly focused on linking its relief and development activities to provide a continuum between short-term relief and longer-term rehabilitation and development. In order to achieve this objective, WFP aims to integrate elements that strengthen disaster mitigation into development projects, including soil conservation, reforestation, irrigation infrastructure and transport construction and rehabilitation and to promote capacity-building elements within relief operations, e.g. training, income-generating activities and environmental protection measures. In 1996 WFP approved 14 new 'protracted refugee and displaced persons operations', where the emphasis is on fostering stability, rehabilitation and long-term development after an emergency. In all these operations, which are undertaken in collaboration with UNHCR and other international agencies, WFP is responsible for mobilizing basic food commodities and for related transport, handling and storage costs. The single largest protracted operations in 1996 were approved for Cambodia, to assist some 1.7m. people, for Liberia, where WFP committed US $77.8m. to assist some 1.5m. refugees and displaced persons, and for Afghanistan, where 1.5m. people were beneficiaries of an operation costing $80.0m.

OPERATIONAL EXPENDITURE IN 1996, BY REGION AND TYPE* (US $ '000, provisional figures)

Region	Development	Relief	Extra-budgetary†	Total
Sub-Saharan Africa .	89,896	408,491	55,288	553,675
South and East Asia .	100,273	46,511	10,259	157,043
Latin America and the Caribbean . . .	57,170	1,184	2,776	61,130
North Africa and the Middle East . . .	31,478	92,617	5,733	129,828
Europe and Newly-Independent States .	—	152,213	12,958	165,171
Total	278,817	701,015	87,014	1,066,847

* Excludes programme support, administrative and other non-operational costs. Also excludes operational expenditure, such as insurance premiums, warehouse facilities, etc., that can not be apportioned by operation, totalling some US $120m. in 1996.

† Non-programmable expenditures.

FINANCE

The Programme is funded by voluntary contributions from donor countries and intergovernmental bodies such as the European Union. Contributions are made in the form of commodities, finance and services (particularly shipping). Commitments to the International Emergency Food Reserve (IEFR), from which WFP provides the majority of its food supplies, and to the Immediate Response Account of the IEFR (IRA) are also made on a voluntary basis by donors. At the end of 1996 the total pledges and contributions announced by donors for that year amounted to US $1,445.2m.WFP's total expenditure in 1996 (including non-operational costs) amounted to $1,186.8m.

PUBLICATION

Annual Report.

SPECIALIZED AGENCIES WITHIN THE UN SYSTEM

Food and Agriculture Organization of the United Nations—FAO

Address: Viale delle Terme di Caracalla, 00100 Rome, Italy.

Telephone: (6) 57051; **telex:** 625852; **fax:** (6) 5705-3152; **e-mail:** telex-room@fao.org; **internet:** http://www.fao.org.

FAO, the first specialized agency of the UN to be founded after the Second World War, was established in Québec, Canada, in October 1945. The Organization aims to alleviate malnutrition and hunger, and serves as a co-ordinating agency for development programmes in the whole range of food and agriculture, including forestry and fisheries. It helps developing countries to promote educational and training facilities and the creation of appropriate institutions.

MEMBERS

176 members (including the European Union as a member organization) and one associate member: see Table on pp. 101–103.

Organization

(December 1997)

CONFERENCE

The governing body is the FAO Conference of member nations. It meets every two years, formulates policy, determines the Organization's programme and budget on a biennial basis, and elects new members. It also elects the Director-General of the Secretariat and the Independent Chairman of the Council. Every other year, FAO also holds conferences in each of its five regions (the Near East, Asia and the Pacific, Africa, Latin America and the Caribbean, and Europe).

COUNCIL

The FAO Council is composed of representatives of 49 member nations, elected by the Conference for staggered three-year terms. It is the interim governing body of FAO between sessions of the Conference. The most important standing Committees of the Council are: the Finance and Programme Committees, the Committee on Commodity Problems, the Committee on Fisheries, the Committee on Agriculture and the Committee on Forestry.

SECRETARIAT

The total number of staff at FAO headquarters in September 1997 was 2,465, of whom 67 were associate experts, while staff in field, regional and country offices numbered 1,967, including 133 associate experts. Work is supervised by the following Departments: Administration and Finance; General Affairs and Information; Economic and Social Policy; Agriculture; Forestry; Fisheries; Sustainable Development; and Technical Co-operation.

Director-General: JACQUES DIOUF (Senegal).

REGIONAL OFFICES

Africa: UN Agency Bldg, North Maxwell Rd, POB 1628, Accra, Ghana; tel. 666851; telex 2139; fax 233999; Regional Rep. B. F. DADA.

Asia and the Pacific: Maliwan Mansion, Phra Atit Rd, Bangkok 10200, Thailand; tel. (2) 281-7844; telex 82815; fax (2) 280-0445; Regional Rep. A. Z. M. OBAIDULLAH KHAN.

Europe: Viale delle Terme di Caracalla, 00100 Rome, Italy; tel. (6) 52251; telex 610181; fax (6) 5225-3152; Regional Rep. M. LINDAU.

Latin America and the Caribbean: Avda Dag Hammarskjold 3241, Casilla 10095, Vitacura, Santiago, Chile; tel. (2) 337-2100; fax (2) 337-2101; e-mail fao-rlc-registry@field.fao.org; Regional Rep. GUSTAVO GORDILLO.

Near East: 11 El-Eslah el-Zerai St, POB 2223, Dokki, Cairo, Egypt; tel. (2) 3372229; telex 21055; fax (2) 3495981; Regional Rep. ATIF YEHYA BUKHARI.

In addition, the following Sub-regional Offices are operational: in Harare, Zimbabwe (for Southern and Eastern Africa); in Bridgetown, Barbados (for the Caribbean); in Tunis, Tunisia (for North Africa); in Budapest, Hungary (for Central and Eastern Europe); and in Apia, Samoa (for the Pacific Islands).

JOINT DIVISIONS AND LIAISON OFFICES

Joint ECA/FAO Agriculture Division: Africa Hall, POB 3001, Addis Ababa, Ethiopia; tel. (1) 510406; telex 21029; fax (1) 514416.

Joint ECE/FAO Timber Section: Palais des Nations, 1211 Geneva 10, Switzerland; tel. (22) 917-2874; telex 412962; fax (22) 917-0041.

Joint ESCWA/FAO Agriculture Division: POB 927115, Amman, Jordan; tel. (6) 606847; telex 21691; fax (6) 674261.

Joint IAEA/FAO Division of Nuclear Techniques in Food and Agriculture: Wagramerstrasse 5, 1400 Vienna, Austria; tel. (1) 2060-21610; telex 1-12645; fax (1) 2060-29946.

European Union: 21 ave du Boulevard, 1210 Brussels, Belgium; tel. (2) 203-8852; e-mail fao-lobr@field.fao.org; Dir M. R. DE MONTALEMBERT.

Japan: 1-1-1 Yokohama International Organizations Centre, Minato Mirai, Nishi-ku, Yokohama, Japan; tel. (45) 222-1101; fax (45) 222-1103.

North America: Suite 300, 2175 K St, NW, Washington, DC 20437, USA; tel. (202) 653-2400; telex 64255; fax (202) 653-5760; e-mail fao-lowa@field.fao.org; Dir C. H. RIEMENSCHNEIDER.

United Nations: Suite DC1-1125, 1 United Nations Plaza, New York, NY 10017, USA; tel. (212) 963-6036; telex 236350; fax (212) 888-6188; Dir B. TOURÉ.

Activities

FAO aims to raise levels of nutrition and standards of living, by improving the production and distribution of food and other commodities derived from farms, fisheries and forests. FAO provides technical information, advice and assistance by disseminating information; acting as a neutral forum for discussion of food and agricultural issues; advising governments on policy and planning; and developing capacity directly in the field.

The most recent session of the FAO Conference, held in Rome in November 1997, identified the following areas of activity as FAO priorities for 1998–99: the Special Programme for Food Security; transboundary animal and plant pests and diseases; forest conservation; promotion of the Codex Alimentarius code on food standards; strengthening the technical co-operation programme (which funds 15% of FAO's field programme expenditure); and the implementation of a Programme Against Trypanosomiasis, following a serious outbreak. The Conference adopted guidelines on surveillance and on the introduction of export certification measures for the standardization of plant quarantine regulations, and strengthened the International Plant Protection Convention. The Conference also endorsed FAO's 'Telefood' initiative, a televised fund-raising event, broadcast to an estimated 500m. viewers in some 70 countries in October 1997. The initiative contributed approximately US $2m. towards projects aimed at helping small-scale farmers to increase crop production, and was expected to take place on an annual basis in order to raise public awareness of the problems of hunger and malnutrition.

In November 1996 FAO hosted the World Food Summit, which was held in Rome and was attended by heads of state and senior government representatives of 186 countries. Participants approved the Rome Declaration on World Food Security and the World Food Summit Plan of Action, with the aim of halving the number of people afflicted by undernutrition, at that time estimated to total 840m. world-wide, no later than 2015.

FAO's total field programme expenditure for 1996 was US $244m., compared with $264m. in 1995. An estimated 32% of field projects were in Africa, 23% in Asia and the Pacific, 11% in the Near East, 11% in Latin America and the Caribbean, 4% in Europe, and 19% were inter-regional or global.

AGRICULTURE

FAO's most important area of activity is crop production which annually accounts for about 24% of FAO's Field Programme expenditure. FAO assists developing countries in increasing agricultural production, by means of a number of methods, including improved seeds and fertilizer use, soil conservation and reforestation, better water resource management techniques, upgrading storage facilities, and improvements in processing and marketing. FAO places special emphasis on the cultivation of under-exploited traditional food crops, such as cassava, sweet potato and plantains. In 1994 FAO initiated a Special Programme for Food Security, which was designed to assist low-income countries with a food deficit to increase food production and productivity as rapidly as possible, primarily through the widespread adoption by farmers of improved production technologies, with emphasis on areas of high potential. At October 1997 86 countries were categorized as 'low-income food-deficit', of which 43 were in Africa. During 1997 the Special Programme was engaged in projects in 25 countries, while preparations were being made for projects to be carried out in a further 40.

In 1985 the FAO Conference approved an International Code of Conduct on the Distribution and Use of Pesticides, and in 1989 the Conference adopted an additional clause concerning 'Prior Informed Consent' (PIC), whereby international shipments of newly banned or restricted pesticides should not proceed without the agreement of importing countries. Under the clause, FAO aims to inform governments about the hazards of toxic chemicals and to urge them to take proper measures to curb trade in highly toxic agrochemicals while keeping the pesticides industry informed of control actions. In mid-1996 FAO publicized a new initiative which aimed to increase awareness of, and to promote international action on, obsolete and hazardous stocks of pesticides remaining throughout the world. By September 1997 22 pesticides and five industrial chemicals were subject to the PIC clause, and more than 150 countries were participating in the scheme. As part of its continued efforts to reduce the environmental risks posed by over-reliance on pesticides, FAO is extending to other regions its Integrated Pest Management (IPM) programme in Asia and the Pacific on the adoption of safer and more effective methods of pest control. IPM reduces the need for pesticides by introducing biological control methods and natural predators, such as spiders and wasps, to avert pests. Under this programme, which began in 1988, FAO helped to train chemists and pesticide control officers from 27 Asian and Pacific countries in pesticide regulation, quality control, testing protocols and risk-benefit analysis.

FAO's Joint Division with the International Atomic Energy Agency (IAEA) tests controlled-release formulas of pesticides and herbicides that gradually free their substances and can limit the amount of agrochemicals needed to protect crops. The Joint FAO-IAEA Division is engaged in exploring biotechnologies and in developing non-toxic fertilizers (especially those that are locally available) and improved strains of food crops (especially from indigenous varieties). In the area of animal production and health, the Joint Division has developed progesterone-measuring and disease diagnostic kits, of which thousands have been delivered to developing countries. FAO's Plant Nutrition Programme aims to promote activities for nutrient management based on the recycling of nutrients through crop production and the efficient use of mineral fertilizers.

The conservation and sustainable use of plant and animal genetic resources are promoted by FAO's Global System for Plant Genetic Resources, which includes five databases, and the Global Programme for Animal Genetic Resources. An FAO programme supports the establishment of gene banks, designed to maintain the world's biological diversity by preserving animal and plant species threatened with extinction. FAO, jointly with the UN Environment Programme (UNEP), has published a document listing the current state of global livestock genetic diversity. In June 1996 representatives of more than 150 governments convened in Leipzig, Germany, at a meeting organized by FAO (and hosted by the German Government) to consider the use and conservation of plant genetic resources as an essential means of enhancing food security. The meeting adopted a Global Plan of Action, which included measures to strengthen the development of plant varieties and to promote the use and availability of local varieties and locally-adapted crops to farmers, in particular following a natural disaster, war or civil conflict.

An Emergency Prevention System for Transboundary Animal and Plant Pests and Diseases (EMPRES) was established in 1994 to strengthen FAO's activities in the prevention, control and, where possible, eradication of highly contagious diseases and pests. EMPRES's initial priorities were locusts and rinderpest. During 1994 EMPRES published guidelines on all aspects of desert locust monitoring, commissioned an evaluation of recent control efforts and prepared a concept paper on desert locust management. FAO has assumed responsibility for technical leadership and co-ordination of the Global Rinderpest Eradication Campaign, which has the objective of eliminating the disease by 2010. In 1996/97 EMPRES helped to combat rinderpest outbreaks in five countries and desert locust outbreaks in North Africa, the Sahel and Red Sea basin.

ENVIRONMENT

In April 1991 a Conference on Agriculture and the Environment was held in the Netherlands, organized jointly by FAO and the Netherlands Government. The Conference's declaration indicated the measures necessary to ensure sustainable production in agriculture. At the UN Conference on Environment and Development (UNCED), held in Rio de Janeiro in June 1992, FAO participated in several working parties and supported the adoption of Agenda 21, a programme of activities to promote sustainable development. FAO is responsible for the chapters of Agenda 21 concerning water resources, forests, fragile mountain ecosystems and sustainable agriculture and rural development.

FISHERIES

FAO's Fisheries Department consists of a multi-disciplinary body of experts who are involved in every aspect of fisheries development from coastal surveys, improvement of production, processing and storage, to the compilation of statistics, development of computer databases, improvement of fishing gear, institution-building and training. In November 1993 the FAO Conference adopted an agreement to improve the monitoring and control of fishing vessels operating on the high seas that are registered under 'flags of convenience'. These ships, amounting to an estimated 20% of all fishing vessels, are often able to avoid compliance with internationally accepted marine conservation and management measures. In March 1995 a ministerial meeting of fisheries adopted a Rome Consensus on World Fisheries, which identified a need for immediate action to eliminate overfishing and to rebuild and enhance depleting fish stocks. In November the FAO Conference adopted a Code of Conduct for Responsible Fishing, which incorporated many global fisheries and aquaculture issues (including fisheries resource conservation and development, fish catches, seafood and fish processing, commercialization, trade and research) to promote the sustainable development of the sector. FAO promotes aquaculture as a valuable source of animal protein, and as an income-generating activity for rural communities. In 1996/97 FAO took part in 21 technical consultations on the management of marine resources. In addition, work on aquatic genetic resources was strengthened and studies were undertaken to monitor the impact of 'El Niño', a periodic warming of the tropical Pacific Ocean, on aquaculture in Latin America and Africa.

FORESTRY

FAO focuses on the contribution of forestry to food security, on effective and responsible forest management and on maintaining a balance between the economic, ecological and social benefits of forest resources. The Organization has helped to develop national forestry programmes and to promote the sustainable development of all types of forest. FAO's Forests, Trees and People Programme promotes the sustainable management of tree and forest resources, based on local knowledge and management practices, in order to improve the livelihoods of rural people in developing countries. In 1996–97 FAO chaired an Inter-Agency Task Force on Forests, which was to implement the decisions of an Intergovernmental Panel, while in October 1997 FAO supported the Eleventh World Forestry Congress, held in Antalya, Turkey.

NUTRITION

The International Conference on Nutrition, sponsored by FAO and WHO, took place in Rome in December 1992. It approved a World Declaration on Nutrition and a Plan of Action, aimed at promoting efforts to combat malnutrition as a development priority. Since the conference, more than 100 countries have formulated national plans of action for nutrition, many of which were based on existing development plans such as comprehensive food security initiatives, national poverty alleviation programmes and action plans to attain the targets set by the World Summit for Children in September 1990. By October 1995 several projects based on the national plans of action had been implemented in areas such as nutrition education, food quality and safety, micronutrient deficiency alleviation and nutrition surveillance. In October 1996 FAO jointly organized the first World Congress on Calcium and Vitamin D in Human Life, held in Rome. The Congress discussed methods to increase the intake of calcium and vitamin D by all members of the population in order to promote growth during childhood and adolescence and to reduce the prevalence of diseases such as osteoporosis, cancer and hypertension.

PROCESSING AND MARKETING

An estimated 20% of all food harvested is lost before it can be consumed, and in some developing countries the proportion is much higher. FAO helps reduce immediate post-harvest losses, with the introduction of improved processing methods and storage systems. It also advises on the distribution and marketing of agricultural produce and on the selection and preparation of foods for optimum nutrition. Many of these activities form part of wider rural development projects. Many developing countries rely on agricultural products as their main source of foreign earnings, but the terms under which they are traded are usually more favourable to the industrialized countries. FAO continues to favour the elimination of export subsidies and related discriminatory practices, such as protectionist measures that hamper international trade in agricultural commodities. FAO is assisting countries that were expected to be adversely affected by trade agreements concluded under the GATT Uruguay Round (see World Trade Organization, p. 244), in particular least-developed countries and those dependent on food imports. FAO evaluates new market trends and helps to develop improved plant and animal quarantine procedures. The Organization has also increased its support to member states concerning implementation of the Final Act of the Uruguay Round, signed in Marrakesh, Morocco, in April 1994. Assistance is provided by 18 regional workshops and 44 national projects, and has focused on agricultural policy, intellectual property rights, sanitary and phytosanitary measures, technical barriers to trade and the international standards of the Codex Alimentarius.

FOOD SECURITY

FAO's policy on food security aims to encourage the production of adequate food supplies, to maximize stability in the flow of supplies, and to ensure access on the part of those who need them. FAO's Global Information and Early Warning System (GIEWS), which become operational in 1975, monitors the crop and food outlook at global and national levels in order to detect emerging food supply difficulties and disasters and to ensure rapid intervention in countries experiencing food supply shortages. In 1996 the GIEWS conducted 30 missions to assess crops and food supply, and participated in a number of inter-agency surveillance programmes. The GIEWS intensified its efforts in monitoring the food situation in the former USSR and, in co-operation with the WFP, assessed crops and food supplies in the Democratic People's Republic of Korea. As a result of the GIEWS/WFP surveillance, an emergency fund amounting to some US $25.9m. was approved for food relief in that country. In the same year the GIEWS continued to monitor the food situation in the Great Lakes region of Africa, as well as in Angola, Liberia, Mozambique and Sierra Leone. By the end of 1996 FAO had identified 27 countries, of which 13 were in sub-Saharan Africa, that were confronting acute food shortages and required exceptional and/or emergency food assistance. In 1996 FAO was actively involved in the formulation of a Plan of Action on food security, adopted at the World Food Summit in November, and was to be responsible for monitoring and promoting its implementation.

FAO INVESTMENT CENTRE

The Investment Centre was established in 1964 to help countries to prepare viable investment projects that will attract external financing. The Centre focuses its evaluation of projects on two fundamental concerns: the promotion of sustainable activities for land management, forestry development and environmental protection, and the alleviation of rural poverty. In 1996 41 projects were approved, representing a total investment of some US $2,500m.

EMERGENCY RELIEF

FAO works to rehabilitate agricultural production following natural and man-made disasters by providing emergency seed, tools, and technical and other assistance. Jointly with the United Nations, FAO is responsible for the World Food Programme (q.v.), which provides emergency food supplies and food aid in support of development projects. In 1996 FAO's Special Relief Operations Service undertook 58 new projects in 31 countries, at a cost of US $26.3m. (44% of the projects were in Europe, 26% in Africa, 18% in the Near East, 7% in Asia and the Pacific, and 5% in Latin America and the Caribbean). The Service's operational activities focused on the supply of basic agricultural inputs in Bosnia and Herzegovina; the provision of vegetable seeds, veterinary vaccines, goats and animal feed to Iraq; and support for the rehabilitation of the agricultural sector in Burundi and Rwanda through the provision of agricultural inputs and the co-ordination of emergency assistance.

INFORMATION

FAO functions as an information centre, collecting, analysing, interpreting and disseminating information through various media. It issues regular statistical reports, commodity studies, and technical manuals in local languages (see list of publications below). Other materials produced by the FAO include information booklets, reference papers, reports of meetings, training manuals and audiovisuals.

FAO compiles and co-ordinates an extensive range of international databases on agriculture, fisheries, forestry, food and statistics, the most important of these being AGRIS (the International Information System for the Agricultural Sciences and Technology) and CARIS (the Current Agricultural Research Information System). Statistical databases include the GLOBEFISH databank and electronic library, FISHDAB (the Fisheries Statistical Database), FORIS (Forest Resources Information System), and GIS (the Geographic Information System). In addition, AGROSTAT PC has been designed to provide access to updated figures in six agriculture-related topics via personal computer. In 1996 FAO established a World Agricultural Information Centre (WAICENT), which offers wide access to agricultural data through the electronic media.

FAO Councils and Commissions

(Based at the Rome headquarters unless otherwise indicated.)

African Commission on Agricultural Statistics: c/o FAO Regional Office for Africa, POB 1628, Accra, Ghana: f. 1961 to advise member countries on the development and standardization of food and agricultural statistics; 37 member states.

African Forestry and Wildlife Commission: f. 1959 to advise on the formulation of forest policy and to review and co-ordinate its implementation on a regional level; to exchange information and advise on technical problems; 42 member states.

Asia and Pacific Commission on Agricultural Statistics: c/o FAO Regional Office, Maliwan Mansion, Phra Atit Rd, Bangkok 10200, Thailand; f. 1962 to review the state of food and agricultural statistics in the region and to advise member countries on the development and standardization of agricultural statistics; 24 member states.

Asia and Pacific Plant Protection Commission: c/o FAO Regional Office, Maliwan Mansion, Phra Atit Rd, Bangkok 10200, Thailand; f. 1956 (new title 1983) to strengthen international co-operation in plant protection to prevent the introduction and spread of destructive plant diseases and pests; 24 member states.

Asia-Pacific Fishery Commission: c/o FAO Regional Office, Maliwan Mansion, Phra Atit Rd, Bangkok 10200, Thailand; f. 1948 to develop fisheries, encourage and co-ordinate research, disseminate information, recommend projects to governments, propose standards in technique and management measures; 20 member states.

Asia-Pacific Forestry Commission: f. 1949 to advise on the formulation of forest policy, and review and co-ordinate its implementation throughout the region; to exchange information and advise on technical problems; 27 member states.

Caribbean Plant Protection Commission: f. 1967 to preserve the existing plant resources of the area.

Commission on African Animal Trypanosomiasis: f. 1979 to develop and implement programmes to combat this disease; 39 member states.

Commission for Controlling the Desert Locust in the Eastern Region of its Distribution Area in South West Asia: f. 1964 to carry out all possible measures to control plagues of the desert locust in Afghanistan, India, Iran and Pakistan.

Commission for Controlling the Desert Locust in the Near East: c/o FAO Regional Office for the Near East, POB 2223, Cairo, Egypt; f. 1967 to promote national and international research and action with respect to the control of the desert locust in the Near East.

Commission for Controlling the Desert Locust in North-West Africa: f. 1971 to promote research on control of the desert locust in NW Africa.

Commission on Fertilizers: f. 1973 to provide guidance on the effective distribution and use of fertilizers.

Commission for Inland Fisheries of Latin America: f. 1976 to promote, co-ordinate and assist national and regional fishery and limnological surveys and programmes of research and development leading to the rational utilization of inland fishery resources.

Commission on Plant Genetic Resources: f. 1983 to provide advice on programmes dealing with crop improvement through plant genetic resources.

European Commission on Agriculture: f. 1949 to encourage and facilitate action and co-operation in technological agricultural problems among member states and between international organizations concerned with agricultural technology in Europe.

European Commission for the Control of Foot-and-Mouth Disease: f. 1953 to promote national and international action for the control of the disease in Europe and its final eradication.

European Forestry Commission: f. 1947 to advise on the formulation of forest policy and to review and co-ordinate its implementation on a regional level; to exchange information and to make recommendations; 27 member states.

European Inland Fisheries Advisory Commission: f. 1957 to promote improvements in inland fisheries and to advise member governments and FAO on inland fishery matters.

FAO Regional Commission on Farm Management for Asia and the Far East: c/o FAO Regional Office, Maliwan Mansion, Phra Atit Rd, Bangkok 10200, Thailand; f. 1959 to stimulate and co-ordinate farm management research and extension activities and to serve as a clearing-house for the exchange of information and experience among the member countries in the region.

FAO/WHO Codex Alimentarius Commission: f. 1962 to make proposals for the co-ordination of all international food standards work and to publish a code of international food standards; 158 member states.

General Fisheries Council for the Mediterranean—GFCM: f. 1952 to develop aquatic resources, to encourage and co-ordinate research in the fishing and allied industries, to assemble and publish information, and to recommend the standardization of equipment, techniques and nomenclature.

Indian Ocean Fishery Commission: f. 1967 to promote national programmes, research and development activities, and to examine management problems; 41 member states.

International Poplar Commission: f. 1947 to study scientific, technical, social and economic aspects of poplar and willow cultivation; to promote the exchange of ideas and material between research workers, producers and users; to arrange joint research programmes, congresses, study tours; to make recommendations to the FAO Conference and to National Poplar Commissions.

International Rice Commission: f. 1948 to promote national and international action on production, conservation, distribution and consumption of rice, except matters relating to international trade; 61 member states.

Joint FAO/WHO/OAU Regional Food and Nutrition Commission for Africa: c/o FAO Regional Office for Africa, POB 1628, Accra, Ghana; f. 1962 to provide liaison in matters concerning food and nutrition, and to review food and nutritional problems in Africa; 43 member states.

Latin American and Caribbean Forestry Commission: f. 1948 to advise on formulation of forest policy and review and co-ordinate its implementation throughout the region; to exchange information and advise on technical problems; 31 member states.

Near East Forestry Commission: f. 1953 to advise on formulation of forest policy and review and co-ordinate its implementation throughout the region; to exchange information and advise on technical problems; 20 member states.

Near East Regional Commission on Agriculture: c/o FAO Regional Office, POB 2223, Cairo, Egypt; f. 1983 to conduct periodic reviews of agricultural problems in the region; to promote the formulation and implementation of regional and national policies and programmes for improving production of crops and livestock; to strengthen the management of crops, livestock and supporting services and research; to promote the transfer of technology and regional technical co-operation; and to provide guidance on training and human resources development.

Near East Regional Economic and Social Policy Commission: c/o FAO Regional Office, POB 2223, Cairo, Egypt; f. 1983 to review developments relating to food, agriculture and food security; to recommend policies on agrarian reform and rural development; and to review and exchange information on food and nutrition policies and on agricultural planning.

North American Forestry Commission: f. 1959 to advise on the formulation and co-ordination of national forest policies in Canada, Mexico and the USA; to exchange information and to advise on technical problems; three member states.

Regional Animal Production and Health Commission for Asia and the Pacific: c/o FAO Regional Office, Maliwan Mansion, Phra Atit Rd, Bangkok 10200, Thailand; f. 1973 to promote livestock development in general, and national and international research and action with respect to animal health and husbandry problems in the region; 14 member states.

Regional Commission on Food Security for Asia and the Pacific: c/o FAO Regional Office, Maliwan Mansion, Phra Atit Rd, Bangkok 10200, Thailand; f. 1982 to review regional food security; to assist member states in preparing programmes for strengthening food security and for dealing with acute food shortages; and to encourage technical co-operation; 17 member states.

Regional Commission on Land and Water Use in the Near East: f. 1967 to review the current situation with regard to land and water use in the region; to identify the main problems concerning the development of land and water resources which require research and study and to consider other related matters.

Regional Fisheries Advisory Commission for the Southwest Atlantic: f. 1961 to advise FAO on fisheries in the South-west Atlantic area, to advise member countries (Argentina, Brazil and Uruguay) on the administration and rational exploitation of marine and inland resources; to assist in the collection and dissemination of data, in training, and to promote liaison and co-operation.

Western Central Atlantic Fishery Commission: f. 1973 to assist international co-operation for the conservation, development and utilization of the living resources, especially shrimps, of the Western Central Atlantic.

FINANCE

FAO's Regular Programme, which is financed by contributions from member governments, covers the cost of the FAO's Secretariat, its Technical Co-operation Programme (TCP) and part of the cost of several special action programmes. The budget for the two years 1998–99 was maintained at US $650m., the same amount as was approved for the previous biennium. Much of FAO's technical assistance programme is funded from extra-budgetary sources. The single largest contributor is the United Nations Development Programme (UNDP), which in 1996 accounted for $47m., or 19% of field project expenditures. More important are the trust funds that come mainly from donor countries and international financing institutions. They totalled $158m., or 65% of field project expenditures in 1996. FAO's contribution under the TCP (FAO's regular budgetary funds for the Field Programme) was $36m., or 15% of field project expenditures, while the Organization's contribution under the Special Programme for Food Security was $2.8m., or some 1% of the total $244m.

PUBLICATIONS

Animal Health Yearbook.
Commodity Review and Outlook (annually).
Environment and Energy Bulletin.
Fertilizer Yearbook.
Food Outlook (quarterly).
Plant Protection Bulletin (quarterly).
Production Yearbook.
Quarterly Bulletin of Statistics.
The State of Food and Agriculture (annually).
The State of World Fisheries and Aquaculture (annually).
The State of the World's Forests.
Trade Yearbook.
Unasylva (quarterly).
Yearbook of Fishery Statistics.
Yearbook of Forest Products.
World Watch List for Domestic Animal Diversity.
Commodity reviews; studies; manuals.

International Atomic Energy Agency—IAEA

Address: POB 100, Wagramerstrasse 5, 1400 Vienna, Austria.

Telephone: (1) 20600; **telex:** 1-12645; **fax:** (1) 20607; **internet:** http://www.iaea.or.at.

The International Atomic Energy Agency (IAEA) is an intergovernmental organization, established in 1957 in accordance with a decision of the General Assembly of the United Nations. Although it is autonomous, the IAEA is administratively a member of the United Nations, and reports on its activities once a year to the UN General Assembly. Its main objectives are to enlarge the contribution of atomic energy to peace, health and prosperity throughout the world and to ensure, so far as it is able, that assistance provided by it or at its request or under its supervision or control is not used in such a way as to further any military purpose.

MEMBERS

127 members: see Table on pp. 101–103.

Organization

(December 1997)

GENERAL CONFERENCE

The Conference, comprising representatives of all member states, convenes each year for general debate on the Agency's policy, budget and programme. It elects members to the Board of Governors, and approves the appointment of the Director-General; it admits new member states.

BOARD OF GOVERNORS

The Board of Governors consists of 35 member states: 22 elected by the General Conference for two-year periods and 13 designated by the Board from among member states which are advanced in nuclear technology. It is the principal policy-making body of the Agency and is responsible to the General Conference. Under its own authority, the Board approves all safeguards agreements, important projects and safety standards.

SECRETARIAT

The Secretariat, comprising about 2,300 staff, is headed by the Director-General, who is assisted by six Deputy Directors-General. The Secretariat is divided into six departments: Technical Co-operation; Nuclear Energy; Nuclear Safety; Research and Isotopes; Safeguards; Administration. A Standing Advisory Group on Safeguards Implementation advises the Director-General on technical aspects of safeguards.

Director-General: Dr MOHAMMAD EL-BARADEI (Egypt).

Activities

The IAEA's functions can be divided into two main categories: technical co-operation (assisting research on and practical application of atomic energy for peaceful uses); and safeguards (ensuring that special fissionable and other materials, services, equipment and information made available by the Agency or at its request or under its supervision are not used for any military purpose).

TECHNICAL CO-OPERATION AND TRAINING

During 1995 1,049 technical co-operation projects and applications were being undertaken world-wide, with IAEA assistance in the form of experts, training and equipment, at a total cost of US $63m. The IAEA provided training to 1,355 scientists and assigned 3,857 experts and lecturers to provide specialized help on specific nuclear applications. Emphasis continued to be placed on radiation protection and safety-related activities, which accounted for 21.2% of the technical co-operation programme.

FOOD AND AGRICULTURE

In co-operation with FAO (q.v.), the Agency conducts programmes of applied research on the use of radiation and isotopes in six main fields: efficiency in the use of water and fertilizers; improvement of food crops by induced mutations; eradication or control of destructive insects by the introduction of sterilized insects; improvement of livestock nutrition and health; studies on improving efficacy and reducing residues of pesticides, and increasing utilization of agricultural wastes; and food preservation by irradiation. The programmes are implemented by the Joint FAO/IAEA Division of Nuclear Techniques in Food and Agriculture and by the FAO/IAEA Agriculture Biotechnology Laboratory, based at Seibersdorf, Austria.

LIFE SCIENCES

In co-operation with the World Health Organization (WHO, q.v.), IAEA promotes the use of nuclear techniques in medicine, biology and health-related environmental research, provides training, and conducts research on techniques for improving the accuracy of radiation dosimetry.

The IAEA/WHO Network of Secondary Standard Dosimetry Laboratories (SSDLs) comprises 73 laboratories in 58 member states. The Agency's Dosimetry Laboratory performs dose intercomparisons for both SSDLs and radiotherapy centres. The IAEA undertakes maintenance plans for nuclear laboratories; national programmes of quality control for nuclear medicine instruments; quality control of radioimmunoassay techniques; radiation sterilization of medical supplies; and improvement of cancer therapy.

PHYSICAL SCIENCES AND LABORATORIES

The Agency's programme in physical sciences includes industrial applications of isotopes and radiation technology; application of nuclear techniques to mineral exploration and exploitation; radiopharmaceuticals; and hydrology, involving the use of isotope techniques for assessment of water resources. Nuclear data services are provided, and training is given for nuclear scientists from developing countries. The IAEA Laboratory at Seibersdorf, Austria, supports the Agency's research, radio-isotope and agriculture programmes, while the Safeguards Analytical Laboratory analyses nuclear fuel-cycle samples collected by IAEA safeguards inspectors. The IAEA Marine Environment Laboratory, in Monaco, studies radionuclides and other ocean pollutants. In July 1992 the EC, Japan, Russia and the USA signed an agreement to co-operate in the engineering design of an International Thermonuclear Experimental Reactor (ITER). The project aimed to demonstrate the scientific and technological feasibility of fusion energy.

NUCLEAR POWER

At the end of 1996 there were 442 nuclear power plants in operation in 32 countries throughout the world, with a total generating capacity of 350,139 MW, providing about 17% of total electrical energy generated during the year. There were also 36 reactors under construction, in 14 countries. The Agency helps developing member states to introduce nuclear-powered electricity-generating plants through assistance with planning, feasibility studies, surveys of manpower and infrastructure, and safety measures. It publishes books on numerous aspects of nuclear power, and provides training courses on safety in nuclear power plants and other topics. An energy data bank collects and disseminates information on nuclear technology, and a power-reactor information system monitors the technical performance of nuclear power plants. There is increasing interest in the use of nuclear reactors for seawater desalination and radiation hydrology techniques to provide potable water.

RADIOACTIVE WASTE MANAGEMENT

The Agency provides practical help to member states in the management of radioactive waste. The Waste Management Advisory Programme (WAMAP) was established in 1987, and undertakes advisory missions in member states. A code of practice to prevent the illegal dumping of radioactive waste was drafted in 1989, and another on the international trans-boundary movement of waste was drafted in 1990. A ban on the dumping of radioactive waste at sea came into effect in February 1994, under the Convention on the Prevention of Marine Pollution by Dumping of Wastes and Other Matters (see IMO, p. 79). The IAEA was to determine radioactive levels, for purposes of the Convention, and provide assistance to countries for the safe disposal of radioactive wastes. In February 1993 the International Arctic Seas Assessment Project (IASAP) was inaugurated, with the objective of assessing risks to human health and the environment associated with radioactive waste in the Kara and Barents Seas, to the north of Russia.

In September 1997 a Joint Convention on the Safety of Spent Fuel Management and on the Safety of Radioactive Waste Management was opened for signature. The first internationally-binding legal device to address such issues, the Convention was to ensure the safe storage and disposal of nuclear and radioactive waste, during both the construction and operation of a nuclear power plant, as well as following its closure. The Convention was to come into force 90 days after being ratified by 25 member states, 15 of which were to be in possession of an operational nuclear reactor. By early October 1997 23 states had signed the Joint Convention.

NUCLEAR SAFETY

The IAEA's nuclear safety programme encourages international co-operation in the exchange of information, promoting implementation of its safety standards and providing advisory safety services. It includes the IAEA International Nuclear Event Scale; the Incident Reporting System; an emergency preparedness programme; operational safety review teams; the International Nuclear Safety Advisory Group (INSAG); the Radiation Protection Advisory Team; and a safety research co-ordination programme.

The revised edition of the Basic Safety Standards for Radiation Protection (IAEA Safety Series No. 9) was approved in 1994. The Nuclear Safety Standards programme, initiated in 1974 with five codes of practice and more than 60 safety guides, was revised in 1987 and again in 1995.

In 1982, to provide member states with advice on achieving and maintaining a high level of safety in the operation of nuclear power plants, the Agency established operational safety review teams, which, by the end of 1995, had conducted reviews of operational safety at 86 plants. At that time some 58 member states had agreed to report all nuclear events, incidents and accidents according to the International Nuclear Event Scale. Co-ordinated research programmes establish risk criteria for the nuclear fuel cycle and identify cost-effective means to reduce risks in energy systems. INSAG comprises 15 experts from nuclear safety licensing authorities, nuclear industry and research, and aims to provide a forum for exchange of information and to identify important current safety issues.

During 1995 there were 249 technical co-operation projects under way in the field of nuclear safety and radiation protection. Missions visited about 50 countries to assist with radiation protection.

Following a serious accident at the Chornobyl (Chernobyl) nuclear power plant in Ukraine (then part of the USSR) in April 1986, two conventions were formulated by the IAEA and entered into force in October. The first commits parties to provide early notification and information about nuclear accidents with possible trans-boundary effects (it had 76 parties by October 1996); and the second commits parties to endeavour to provide assistance in the event of a nuclear accident or radiological emergency (it had 72 parties by October 1996). During 1990 the IAEA organized an assessment of the consequences of the Chernobyl accident, undertaken by an international team of experts, who reported to an international conference on the effects of the accident, convened at the IAEA headquarters in Vienna in May 1991. In February 1993 INSAG published an updated report on the Chernobyl incident, which emphasized the role of design factors in the accident, and the need to implement safety measures in the RBMK-type reactor. In March 1994 an IAEA expert mission visited Chernobyl and reported continuing serious deficiencies in safety at the defunct reactor and the units remaining in operation. An international conference reviewing the radiological consequences of the accident, 10 years after the event, was held in April 1996, co-sponsored by the IAEA, WHO and the European Commission.

An International Convention on Nuclear Safety was adopted at an IAEA conference in June 1994. The Convention applies to land-based civil nuclear power plants: adherents commit themselves to fundamental principles of safety, and maintain legislative frameworks governing nuclear safety. The Convention entered into force in October 1996, after having been signed by 65 states and ratified or otherwise approved by 26 states. By August 1997 the Convention had been approved by 39 member states.

In September 1997 more than 80 member states adopted a protocol to revise the 1963 Vienna Convention on Civil Liability for Nuclear Damage, fixing the minimum limit of liability for the operator of a nuclear reactor at 300m. Special Drawing Rights (SDRs, the accounting units of the IMF) in the event of an accident. The amended protocol also extended the length of time during which claims may be brought for loss of life or injury. A Convention on Supplementary Funding established a further compensatory fund to provide for the payment of damages following an accident. Contributions to the Fund were to be calculated on the basis of the nuclear capacity of each member state.

DISSEMINATION OF INFORMATION

The International Nuclear Information System (INIS), which was established in 1970, provides a computerized indexing and abstracting service. Information on the peaceful uses of atomic energy is collected by member states and international organizations and sent to the IAEA for processing and dissemination (see list of publications below). The IAEA also co-operates with the FAO in an information system for agriculture (AGRIS). The IAEA Nuclear Data Section provides cost-free data centre services and co-operates with other national and regional nuclear and atomic data centres in the systematic worldwide collection, compilation, dissemination and exchange of nuclear reaction data, nuclear structure and decay data, and atomic and molecular data for fusion.

SAFEGUARDS

The Treaty on the Non-Proliferation of Nuclear Weapons (known also as the Non-Proliferation Treaty or NPT), which entered into force in 1970, requires each non-nuclear-weapon state (one which had not manufactured and exploded a nuclear weapon or other nuclear explosive device prior to 1 January 1967) which is a party to the Treaty to conclude a safeguards agreement with the IAEA. Under such an agreement, the state undertakes to accept IAEA safeguards on all nuclear material in all its peaceful nuclear activities for the purpose of verifying that such material is not diverted to nuclear weapons or other nuclear explosive devices. By October 1996 176 non-nuclear-weapon states and the five nuclear-weapon states (see below) had ratified and acceded to the Treaty, but 67 non-nuclear-weapon states had not complied, within the prescribed time-limit, with their obligations under the Treaty regarding the conclusion of the relevant safeguards agreement with the Agency. During 1993–95 four preparatory meetings were held prior to the Review and Extension Conference of parties to the NPT, which opened in April 1995, in New York, USA. In May the Conference agreed to extend the NPT indefinitely, and reaffirmed support for the IAEA's role in verification and the transfer of peaceful nuclear technologies. In November 1996 IAEA organized a meeting of representatives of 14 newly-independent states of the former USSR, attended by other international donors, to review the implementation of plans designed to ensure that these countries fulfil their nuclear non-proliferation commitments.

Five nuclear-weapon states, the People's Republic of China, France, Russia, the United Kingdom and the USA, have concluded safeguards agreements with the Agency that permit the application of IAEA safeguards to all their nuclear activities, excluding those with 'direct national significance'. A Comprehensive Test Ban Treaty (CTBT) was opened for signature in September 1996, having been adopted by the UN General Assembly. The Treaty was to enter into international law upon the receipt of signatures on behalf of all 44 nations with known nuclear capabilities. A separate verification organization was to be established, based in Vienna.

The IAEA administers full applications of safeguards in relation to the Treaty for the prohibition of Nuclear Weapons in Latin America (Tlatelolco Treaty). By the end of 1995 22 of the 30 states party to the Tlatelolco Treaty had concluded safeguards agreements with the IAEA, as had all 11 signatories of the South Pacific Nuclear-Free Zone Treaty (Rarotonga Treaty). In addition, the IAEA applies safeguards in eight states under agreements other than those in connection with the NPT, the Tlatelolco Treaty or the Rarotonga Treaty. In April 1996 an African Nuclear-Weapon Free Zone Treaty (the Pelindaba Treaty) was signed by 43 states at a ceremony in Cairo, Egypt. The IAEA provided technical and legal advice during the negotiations on the Treaty, which committed countries to renouncing the development, acquisition, testing or stationing of nuclear arms on their territories and prohibited all dumping of imported radioactive waste. The Treaty, as with the NPT and the other regional treaties, required and relied upon the IAEA safeguards systems.

In April 1992 the Democratic People's Republic of Korea (DPRK) ratified a safeguards agreement with the IAEA. In late 1992 and early 1993, however, the IAEA unsuccessfully requested access to two non-declared sites in the DPRK, where it was suspected that material capable of being used for the manufacture of nuclear weapons was stored. In March 1993 the DPRK announced its intention of withdrawing from the NPT: it suspended its withdrawal in June, but continued to refuse full access to its nuclear facilities for IAEA inspectors. In May 1994 the DPRK began to refuel an experimental nuclear power reactor at Yongbyon, but refused to allow the IAEA to analyse the spent fuel rods in order to ascertain whether plutonium had been obtained from the reactor for possible military use. In June the IAEA Board of Governors halted IAEA technical assistance to the DPRK (except medical assistance) because of continuous violation of the NPT safeguards agreements. In the same month the DPRK withdrew from the IAEA (though not from the NPT): however, it allowed IAEA inspectors to remain at the Yongbyon site to conduct safeguards activites. In October the Governments of the DPRK and the USA concluded an agreement whereby the former agreed to halt construction of two new nuclear reactors, on condition that it received international aid for the construction of two 'light water' reactors (which could not produce materials for the manufacture of nuclear weapons). The DPRK also agreed to allow IAEA inspections of all its nuclear sites, but only after the installation of one of the 'light water' reactors had been completed, a time lapse of at least five years. In November IAEA inspectors visited the DPRK to initiate verification of the suspension of the country's nuclear programme, in accordance with the agreement concluded in the previous month. During 1995 and 1996 the IAEA pursued technical discussions with the DPRK authorities as part of the Agency's efforts to achieve the full compliance of the DPRK with the IAEA safeguards agreement. By the end of 1996 some progress had been made in the removal of spent fuel rods from the Yongbyon nuclear power reactor, with some 50% of the rods having been recovered for analysis. Technical talks continued in 1997.

South Africa concluded a comprehensive safeguards agreement with the IAEA in September 1991. Numerous inspection missions subsequently verified the termination of a nuclear weapons programme and placed related nuclear material under IAEA safeguards.

In April 1991 the UN Security Council requested the IAEA to conduct investigations into Iraq's capacity to produce nuclear weapons, following the end of the war between Iraq and the UN-authorized, US-led multinational force. The IAEA was to work closely with a UN Special Commission of experts (UNSCOM), established by the Security Council, whose task was to inspect and dismantle Iraq's weapons of mass destruction (including chemical and biological weapons). In July the IAEA declared that Iraq had violated its safeguards agreement with the IAEA by not submitting nuclear material and relevant facilities in its uranium-enrichment programme to the Agency's inspection. This was the first time that a state party to the NPT had been condemned for concealing a programme of this nature. In October the sixth inspection team, composed of UNSCOM and representatives of the IAEA, was reported to have obtained conclusive documentary evidence that Iraq had a programme for developing nuclear weapons. By February 1994 all declared stocks of nuclear-weapons-grade material had been removed from Iraq. Subsequently, the IAEA has pursued a programme of long-term surveillance of nuclear activity in Iraq, under a mandate issued by the UN Security Council. Between August 1994 and September 1996 more than 600 inspections were conducted in Iraq, both by the IAEA team alone and jointly with UNSCOM. In September 1996 Iraq submitted to the IAEA a 'full, final and complete' declaration of its nuclear activities. However, in September–October 1997 the IAEA recommended that Iraq disclose further equipment, materials and information relating to its nuclear programme. In December, following the temporary expulsion of UNSCOM weapons inspectors by the Iraqi authorities in October–November, the IAEA announced that Iraq was not believed to have engaged in any illegal nuclear activities during that period.

In 1996 2,476 inspections were conducted under safeguards agreements at 574 nuclear installations in 68 non-nuclear-weapon states and five nuclear-weapon states. In 1995 some 500 automatic photographic and television surveillance systems operated in the field, and 23,877 seals that had been applied to nuclear material were detached and subsequently verified. In the same year, 3,805 samples of uranium and plutonium were analysed. Expenditure on safeguards operations amounted to US $87m. in 1996, while extrabudgetary contributions provided a further $8.5m.

In June 1995 the Board of Governors approved measures to strengthen the safeguards system, including allowing inspection teams greater access to suspected nuclear sites and to information on nuclear activities in member states, reducing the notice time for inspections by removing visa requirements for inspectors and using environmental monitoring (i.e. soil, water and air samples) to test for signs of radioactivity. In April 1996 the IAEA initiated a programme to prevent and combat illicit trafficking of nuclear weapons, and in April 1997 Namibia became the 50th nation to join the programme. In May 1997 the Board of Governors adopted a protocol approving measures to strengthen safeguards further, in order to ensure the compliance of non-nuclear-weapon states with IAEA commitments. The new protocol compelled member states to provide inspection teams with improved access to information concerning existing and planned nuclear activities, and to allow access to locations other than known nuclear sites within that country's territory. The protocol was opened for signature in September 1997.

NUCLEAR FUEL CYCLE

The Agency promotes the exchange of information between member states on technical, safety, environmental, and economic aspects of nuclear fuel cycle technology, including uranium prospecting and the treatment and disposal of radioactive waste; it provides assistance to member states in the planning, implementation and operation of nuclear fuel cycle facilities and assists in the development of advanced nuclear fuel cycle technology. Every two years, in collaboration with the OECD, the Agency prepares estimates of world uranium resources, demand and production.

BUDGET

The Agency is financed by regular and voluntary contributions from member states. Expenditure approved under the regular budget for 1998 amounted to some US $221.4m., and the target for voluntary contributions to finance the IAEA technical assistance and co-operation programme in 1998 was $71.5m.

PUBLICATIONS

Annual Report.
IAEA Bulletin (quarterly).
IAEA Newsbriefs (every 2 months).
IAEA Yearbook.
INIS Atomindex (bibliography, 2 a month).
INIS Reference Series.
INSAG Series.
Legal Series.
Meetings on Atomic Energy (quarterly).
The Nuclear Fuel Cycle Information System: A Directory of Nuclear Fuel Cycle Facilities.
Nuclear Fusion (monthly).
Nuclear Safety Review (annually).
Panel Proceedings Series.
Publications Catalogue (annually).
Safety Series.
Technical Directories.
Technical Reports Series.

International Bank for Reconstruction and Development—IBRD (World Bank)

Address: 1818 H St, NW, Washington, DC 20433, USA.
Telephone: (202) 477-1234; **telex:** 248423; **fax:** (202) 477-6391; **e-mail:** books@worldbank.org; **internet:** http://www.worldbank.org.

The IBRD was established in December 1945. Initially it was concerned with post-war reconstruction in Europe; since then its aim has been to assist the economic development of member nations by making loans where private capital is not available on reasonable terms to finance productive investments. Loans are made either direct to governments, or to private enterprises with the guarantee of their governments. The World Bank, as it is commonly known, comprises the IBRD and the International Development Association (IDA, q.v.). The affiliated group of institutions, comprising the IBRD, the IDA, the International Finance Corporation (IFC, q.v.), the Multilateral Investment Guarantee Agency (MIGA, q.v.) and the International Centre for Settlement of Investment Disputes (ICSID, see below), is now referred to as the World Bank Group.

MEMBERS

There are 181 members: see Table on pp. 101–103. Only members of the International Monetary Fund (IMF, q.v.) may be considered for membership in the World Bank. Subscriptions to the capital stock of the Bank are based on each member's quota in the IMF, which is designed to reflect the country's relative economic strength. Voting rights are related to shareholdings.

Organization

(December 1997)

Officers and staff of the IBRD serve concurrently as officers and staff in the IDA. The World Bank has offices in Brussels, New York, Paris, London and Tokyo; regional missions in Nairobi (for eastern Africa), Abidjan (for western Africa), Riga (in Latvia) and Bangkok (in Thailand); and resident missions in 75 countries.

BOARD OF GOVERNORS

The Board of Governors consists of one Governor appointed by each member nation. Typically, a Governor is the country's finance minister, central bank governor, or a minister or an official of comparable rank. The Board normally meets once a year.

EXECUTIVE DIRECTORS

With the exception of certain powers specifically reserved to them by the Articles of Agreement, the Governors of the Bank have delegated their powers for the conduct of the general operations of the World Bank to a Board of Executive Directors which performs its duties on a full-time basis at the Bank's headquarters. There are 24 Executive Directors (see table below); each Director selects an Alternate. Five Directors are appointed by the five members having the largest number of shares of capital stock, and the rest are elected by the Governors representing the other members. The President of the Bank is Chairman of the Board.

The Executive Directors fulfil dual responsibilities. First, they represent the interests of their country or groups of countries. Second, they exercise their authority as delegated by the Governors in overseeing the policies of the Bank and evaluating completed projects. Since the Bank operates on the basis of consensus (formal votes are rare), this dual role involves frequent communication and consultations with governments so as to reflect accurately their views in Board discussions.

The Directors consider and decide on Bank policy and on all loan and credit proposals. They are also responsible for presentation to the Board of Governors at its Annual Meetings of an audit of accounts, an administrative budget, the *Annual Report* on the operations and policies of the World Bank, and any other matter that, in their judgement, requires submission to the Board of Governors. Matters may be submitted to the Governors at the Annual Meetings or at any time between Annual Meetings.

OFFICE OF THE PRESIDENT

President and Chairman of Executive Directors: JAMES D. WOLFENSOHN (USA).

Managing Directors: SVEN SANDSTRÖM (Sweden), SHENGMAN ZHANG (People's Republic of China), CAIO KOCH-WESER (Brazil), JESSICA EINHORN (USA).

OFFICES

New York Office and World Bank Mission to the United Nations: 809 United Nations Plaza, Suite 900, New York, NY 10017, USA; Special Rep. to UN CARLSTON B. BOUCHER.

European Office: 66 ave d'Iéna, 75116 Paris, France; Dir HANS WYSS.

Brussels Office: 10 rue Montoyer, 1000 Brussels, Belgium.

London Office: New Zealand House, 15th Floor, Haymarket, London, SW1Y 4TE, United Kingdom; Resident Rep. GEOFFREY LAMB.

Regional Mission in Eastern Africa: POB 30577; Hill Park Bldg, Upper Hill, Nairobi, Kenya; Chief HAROLD E. WACKMAN.

Regional Mission in Latvia: Kaļķu iela 15, 4th Floor, Riga, LV 1162, Latvia; Chief LARS JUERLING.

Regional Mission in Thailand: Diethelm Towers, Tower A, 14th Floor, 93/1 Wireless Rd, Pathumwan, Bangkok 10330, Thailand; Chief ARNOUD GUINARD.

Regional Mission in Western Africa: angle rues Booker Washington/Jacques Aka, Cocody, BP 1850, Abidjan 01, Côte d'Ivoire; Chief SHIGEO KATSU.

Tokyo Office: 10th Floor, Fukoku Seimei Bldg, 2-2-2 Uchisaiwaicho, Chiyoda-ku, Tokyo 100, Japan; Dir SATORU MIYAMURA.

Activities

FINANCIAL OPERATIONS

IBRD capital is derived from members' subscriptions to capital shares, the calculation of which is based on their quotas in the International Monetary Fund (q.v.). At 30 June 1997 the total subscribed capital of the IBRD was $182,426m., of which the paid-in portion was $11,048m. (6.1%); the remainder is subject to call if required. Most of the IBRD's lendable funds come from its borrowing, on commercial terms, in world capital markets, and also from its retained earnings and the flow of repayments on its loans. IBRD loans carry a variable interest rate, rather than a rate fixed at the time of borrowing.

IBRD loans usually have a 'grace period' of five years and are repayable over 15 years or fewer. Loans are made to governments, or must be guaranteed by the government concerned, and are normally made for projects likely to offer a commercially viable rate of return. In 1980 the World Bank introduced structural adjustment lending, which (instead of financing specific projects) supports programmes and changes necessary to modify the structure of an economy so that it can restore or maintain its growth and viability in its balance of payments over the medium term.

The IBRD and IDA together made 241 new lending and investment commitments totalling US $19,146.6m. during the year ending 30 June 1997, compared with 256 (amounting to $21,352.2m.) in the previous year. During 1996/97 the IBRD alone approved commitments totalling $14,524.9m. (compared with $14,488.1m. in the previous year), of which $4,560.9m. was allocated to Europe and Central Asia and $4,437.5m. to Latin America and the Caribbean (see table). The largest single borrower of IBRD funds was the People's Republic of China ($2,490m. for nine projects), followed by Russia ($1,715.6m. for eight projects) and Argentina ($1,479.5m. for 10 projects). Disbursements by the IBRD in the year ending 30 June 1997 amounted to $13,998m., compared with $13,372m. in the previous year. (For details of IDA operations, see separate chapter on IDA.)

IBRD operations are supported by borrowings in international capital markets. New medium- and long-term borrowings totalled US $15,139m. in the year ending 30 June 1997. During the year the IBRD's net income amounted to $1,285m.

The World Bank's primary objectives are the achievement of sustainable economic growth and the reduction of poverty in developing countries. In the context of stimulating economic growth the Bank promotes both private-sector development and human resource development and has attempted to respond to the growing demands by developing countries for assistance in these areas. In mid-1994 the World Bank Group published a review of its role and activities, and identified the following five major development issues on which it intended to focus in the future: the pursuit of economic reforms; investment in people, in particular through education, health, nutrition and family-planning programmes; the protection of the environment; stimulation of the private sector; and reorientation of government, in order to enhance the private sector by reforming and strengthening the public sector.

In April 1997 the 'Strategic Compact', a programme which aimed to increase the proportion of projects regarded as satisfactory from 66% to 75% over a period of 30 months, was approved. It was hoped that this would be achieved through greater investment in front-line operations, the relocation of 21 country directors from Washington to field offices, and the creation of a knowledge management system to provide staff with greater access to information, comprising four thematic networks: the Human Development Network; the Environmentally and Socially Sustainable Development Network; the Finance, Private Sector and Infrastructure Development Network; and the Poverty Reduction and Economic Management Network. In July the World Bank initiated a review to assess the economic and social impact of its work in developing countries.

The Bank's efforts to reduce poverty comprise two main elements: the compiling of country-specific assessments and the formulation of country-specific strategies to ensure that the Bank's own projects support and complement the programmes of the country concerned. In 1996/97 the Bank established a Poverty Sector Board, within the Poverty Reduction and Economic Management Network, to direct the implementation of its poverty reduction efforts. A Committee on Development Effectiveness addresses issues relating to the relevance and effectiveness of operations and monitors implementation of decisions taken by the Board of Governors on these matters. During 1996/97 some 29% of lending was used for poverty reduction projects, compared with 32% in the previous year.

In June 1995 the World Bank joined other international donors (including regional development banks, other UN bodies, Canada, France, the Netherlands and the USA) in establishing a Consultative Group to Assist the Poorest (CGAP), which was to channel funds to the most needy through grass-roots agencies. An initial credit of approximately US $200m. was committed by the donors. The Bank manages the CGAP Secretariat, which is responsible for the administration of external funding and for the evaluation and approval of project financing. In addition, the CGAP was to provide training and information services on microfinance for policy-makers and practitioners.

In September 1996 the World Bank/IMF Development Committee endorsed a joint initiative to assist heavily indebted poor countries (HIPCs) to reduce their debt burden to a sustainable level, in order to make more resources available for poverty reduction and economic growth. A new Trust Fund was established by the World Bank in November to finance the initiative. The Fund, consisting of an initial allocation of US $500m. from the IBRD surplus and other contributions from multilateral creditors, was to be administered by IDA. Of the 41 HIPCs identified by the Bank, 33 were in sub-Saharan Africa. In the majority of cases a sustainable level of debt was targeted at 200%–250% of the net present value of the debt in relation to total annual exports. Other countries with a lower debt-to-export ratio were to be eligible for assistance under the initiative, providing that their export earnings were more than 40% of GDP and government revenue at least 20% of GDP. In April 1997 the World Bank and the IMF announced that Uganda was to be the first beneficiary of the initiative, enabling the Ugandan Government to reduce its external debt by some 20%, or an estimated US $338m. The Bank's approved loan of $160m. was to be disbursed in April 1998, conditional on the contribution by other official creditors and multinational institutions of their share of the debt relief and on Uganda's pursuing its programme of economic and social develop-

EXECUTIVE DIRECTORS AND THEIR VOTING POWER (30 June 1997)

Executive Director	Casting Votes of	IBRD Total votes	IBRD % of total	IDA Total votes	IDA % of total
Appointed:					
JAN PIERCY	USA	265,219	17.04	1,650,557	15.31
ATSUO NISHIHARA	Japan	94,020	6.04	1,154,286	10.70
HELMUT SCHAFFER	Germany	72,649	4.67	747,221	6.93
MARC-ANTOINE AUTHEMAN	France	69,647	4.47	451,054	4.18
AUGUSTINE (GUS) O'DONNELL	United Kingdom	69,647	4.47	540,211	5.01
Elected:					
LUC HUBLOUE (Belgium)	Austria, Belarus*, Belgium, Czech Republic, Hungary, Kazakhstan, Luxembourg, Slovakia, Slovenia, Turkey	76,720	4.93	457,116	4.24
PIETER STEK (Netherlands)	Armenia, Bosnia and Herzegovina, Bulgaria*, Croatia, Cyprus, Georgia, Israel, the former Yugoslav republic of Macedonia, Moldova, Netherlands, Romania*, Ukraine*	72,208	4.64	385,177	3.57
ENZO DEL BUFALO (Venezuela)	Costa Rica, El Salvador, Guatemala, Honduras, Mexico, Nicaragua, Panama, Spain, Venezuela*	69,110	4.44	233,470	2.19
LEONARD GOOD (Canada)	Antigua and Barbuda*, The Bahamas*, Barbados*, Belize, Canada, Dominica, Grenada, Guyana, Ireland, Jamaica*, Saint Christopher and Nevis, Saint Lucia, Saint Vincent and the Grenadines	62,217	4.00	437,950	4.06
JOAQUIM R. CARVALHO (Mozambique)	Angola, Botswana, Burundi, Eritrea, Ethiopia, The Gambia, Kenya, Lesotho, Liberia, Malawi, Mozambique, Namibia*, Nigeria, Seychelles*, Sierra Leone, South Africa, Sudan, Swaziland, Tanzania, Uganda, Zambia, Zimbabwe	55,190	3.55	442,655	4.11
FRANCO PASSACANTANDO (Italy)	Albania, Greece, Italy, Malta*, Portugal	55,093	3.54	389,870	3.62
SURENDRA SINGH (India)	Bangladesh, Bhutan, India, Sri Lanka	54,945	3.53	457,908	4.25
KACIM BRACHEMI (Algeria)	Afghanistan, Algeria, Ghana, Iran, Iraq, Morocco, Pakistan, Tunisia	54,602	3.51	237,006	2.20
ILKKA NIEMI (Finland)†	Denmark, Estonia*, Finland, Iceland, Latvia, Lithuania*, Norway, Sweden	50,839	3.27	516,892	4.79
JUANITA D. AMATONG (Philippines)	Brazil, Colombia, Dominican Republic, Ecuador, Haiti, Philippines, Suriname*, Trinidad and Tobago	49,148	3.16	303,203	2.81
YOUNG-HOI LEE (Republic of Korea)	Australia, Cambodia, Kiribati, Korea (Republic), Marshall Islands, Micronesia (Federated States), Mongolia, New Zealand, Papua New Guinea, Samoa, Solomon Islands, Vanuatu	49,089	3.15	316,906	2.94
JEAN-DANIEL GERBER (Switzerland)	Azerbaijan, Kyrgyzstan, Poland, Switzerland, Tajikistan, Turkmenistan*, Uzbekistan	46,096	2.96	367,389	3.41
LI YONG (China)	People's Republic of China	45,049	2.89	217,996	2.02
KHALID H. ALYAHYA (Saudi Arabia)	Saudi Arabia	45,045	2.89	377,100	3.50
ANDREI BUGROV (Russia)	Russia	45,045	2.89	28,202	0.26
KHALID AL-SAAD (Kuwait)	Bahrain*, Egypt, Jordan, Kuwait, Lebanon, Libya, Maldives, Oman, Qatar*, Syria, United Arab Emirates, Yemen	43,984	2.83	250,660	2.32
JANNES HUTAGALUNG (Indonesia)	Brunei*, Fiji, Indonesia, Laos, Malaysia, Myanmar, Nepal, Singapore*, Thailand, Tonga, Viet Nam	41,096	2.64	292,376	2.71
JUAN CARIAGA (Bolivia)	Argentina, Bolivia, Chile, Paraguay, Peru, Uruguay*	37,499	2.41	200,001	1.85
ALI BOURHANE (Comoros)	Benin, Burkina Faso, Cameroon, Cape Verde, Central African Republic, Chad, Comoros, Congo (Democratic Republic), Congo (Republic), Côte d'Ivoire, Djibouti, Equatorial Guinea, Gabon, Guinea, Guinea-Bissau, Madagascar, Mali, Mauritania, Mauritius, Niger, Rwanda, São Tomé and Príncipe, Senegal, Togo	32,252	2.07	327,811	3.04

Note: Somalia (802 votes in IBRD and 10,506 in IDA) did not participate in the 1996 regular election of Executive Directors.
* Members of IBRD only (not IDA). † From 5 August 1997.

ment reforms. A grant of $75m. was to be made available to the Ugandan authorities in the interim year. In September 1997 assistance was approved for Bolivia and Burkina Faso. Assistance was approved for Guyana in December, while Côte d'Ivoire and Mozambique underwent preliminary consideration in 1997.

In April 1997 the World Bank signed a co-operation agreement with the World Trade Organization, in order to co-ordinate efforts to integrate developing countries into the gloral economy.

TECHNICAL ASSISTANCE

The provision of technical assistance to member countries has become a major component of World Bank activities. The economic, sector and project analysis undertaken by the Bank in the normal course of its operations is the vehicle for considerable technical assistance. In addition, project loans and credits may include funds earmarked specifically for feasibility studies, resource surveys, management or planning advice, and training. During the calendar year 1995 US $1,300m., or 68% of the total of loan-financed technical assistance, funded components of projects, while $610m. was accounted for by 24 free-standing technical assistance projects.

The Bank serves as an executing agency for projects financed by the UN Development Programme. It also administers projects financed by various trust funds.

Technical assistance (usually reimbursable) is also extended to countries that do not need Bank financial support, e.g. for training and transfer of technology. The Bank encourages the use of local consultants to assist with projects and stimulate institutional capability.

In 1992 the Bank established an Institutional Development Fund (IDF), which became operational on 1 July; the purpose of the Fund was to provide rapid, small-scale financial assistance, to a maximum value of US $500,000, for capacity-building proposals. During 1995 105 IDF grants were approved, amounting to $24.2m., to 61 countries. By the end of 1996 the IDF had approved a cumulative total of 345 grants to 108 countries.

The Project Preparation Facility (PPF) was established in 1975 to provide cash advances to prepare projects that may be financed by the Bank. During 1995 122 PPF grants, with a total value of US $96m., were approved, the majority of which were to countries in sub-Saharan Africa. In December 1994 the PPF's commitment authority was increased from $220m. to $250m.

In 1993 a task force was established to consider measures to reduce poverty in sub-Saharan Africa, in consultation with local and national experts, non-governmental organizations and government officials. The task force published its assessment of the situation in December 1996 and recommended that the Bank revise its lending strategy to emphasize poverty-reduction objectives and strengthen systematic monitoring of the poverty situation in all sub-Saharan African countries receiving World Bank assistance.

In March 1996 a new programme to co-ordinate development efforts in Africa was announced by the UN Secretary-General. The World Bank was to facilitate the mobilization of the estimated US $25,000m. required to achieve the objectives of the Special Initiative over a 10-year period. In addition, the Bank was to provide technical assistance to enable countries to devise economic plans (in particular following a period of civil conflict), agricultural development programmes and a common strategy for African countries to strengthen the management capacities of the public sector.

ECONOMIC RESEARCH AND STUDIES

In the 1990s the World Bank's research, conducted by its own research staff, was increasingly concerned with providing information to reinforce the Bank's expanding advisory role to developing countries. Subsequently the principal areas of current research focus on issues such as maintaining sustainable growth while protecting the environment and the poorest sectors of society, encouraging the development of the private sector, and reducing and decentralizing government activities.

Consultative Group on International Agricultural Research—CGIAR: founded in 1971 under the sponsorship of the World Bank, FAO and UNDP. The Bank is chairman of the group (which includes governments, private foundations and multilateral development agencies) and provides its secretariat. In February 1995 UNEP was invited to become the fourth sponsoring member. The group was formed to raise financial support for international agricultural research work for improving crops and animal production in the developing countries. In 1996/97 the CGIAR supported 16 research centres. Donations to the group's core research agenda was estimated to amount to US $325m. in 1997. Exec. Sec. ALEXANDER VON DER OSTEN.

CO-OPERATION WITH OTHER ORGANIZATIONS

The World Bank co-operates closely with other UN bodies, at the project level, particularly in the design of social funds and social action programmes. It collaborates with the IMF in implementing economic adjustment programmes in developing countries. The Bank holds regular consultations with the European Union and OECD on development issues, and the Bank-NGO Committee provides an annual forum for discussion with non-governmental organizations (NGOs). In 1993/94 the Bank undertook the following activities to formulate a policy framework on co-financing: a Co-financing Task Force study, which reported in March 1994 on the importance of co-financing as a means of achieving joint objectives with other donors and mobilizing development resources; the initiation of a study on the use of guarantees to secure private capital for Bank operations; the establishment of Accelerated Co-financing Facilities with the Export-Import Bank of Japan to facilitate the arrangement of co-financing projects.

In September 1995 the Bank initiated the Information for Development Programme (InfoDev) with the aim of fostering partnerships between governments, multilateral institutions and private-sector experts in order to promote reform and investment in developing countries through improved access to information technology. The Programme was to be managed by the Bank's Industry and Energy Department.

The Bank conducts co-financing and aid co-ordination projects with official aid agencies, export credit institutions, and commercial banks. During the year ending 30 June 1997 a total of 119 IBRD and IDA projects involved co-financers' contributions amounting to US $7,221m.

Global Environment Facility—GEF: founded in 1990 by the World Bank, UNDP and the UN Environment Programme, as a three-year pilot programme designed to provide grants for investment projects and technical assistance. The aim of the GEF is to assist developing countries in implementing projects that benefit the global (not just the local) environment. At the UN Conference on Environment and Development in June 1992, the GEF was recognized, in Agenda 21, as a source of funds to assist with activities benefiting the global environment, and was designated as the operator of the financial mechanism serving the conventions on climate change and biological diversity. In March 1994 87 industrialized and developing countries agreed to restructure and replenish the GEF for a further three-year period from July of that year. Funds amounting to US $2,000m. were to be made available by 26 donor countries. At 30 June 1997 the GEF portfolio comprised 69 projects, with financing of $675m., covering the following areas: biodiversity; climate change; the phase-out of ozone-depleting substances; and international waters. CEO and Chair. MOHAMMED EL-ASHRY.

EVALUATION

The World Bank's Operations Evaluation Department studies and publishes the results of projects after a loan has been fully disbursed, so as to identify problems and possible improvements in future activities. Internal auditing is also carried out, to monitor the effectiveness of the Bank's operations and management.

In September 1993 the Bank's Board of Executive Directors agreed to establish an independent Inspection Panel, consistent with the Bank's objective of improving project implementation and accountability. The panel, which became operational in September 1994, was to conduct independent investigations and report on complaints concerning the design, appraisal and implementation of development projects supported by the Bank. The first project considered by the panel was that of the Arun III hydroelectric facilities in Nepal, which the panel ruled to be a violation of IDA social and environmental policies. In June 1995 the panel reported the findings of its investigations into the main areas of concern regarding the project, namely environmental assessment, involuntary resettlement and treatment of indigenous peoples. In August the Bank decided not to finance the project. By 30 June 1997 the panel had received 10 formal requests for inspection, eight of which were considered to be viable.

IBRD INSTITUTIONS

Economic Development Institute—EDI: founded in 1955. Training is provided for government officials at the middle and upper levels of responsibility who are concerned with development programmes and projects. The majority of courses are in economic and sector management and 'training of trainers', which aim to build up local capability to conduct projects courses in future. The Institute also produces training materials, and administers a fellowships scheme and the World Bank graduate scholarship programme (funded by the Government of Japan). In the year ending 30 June 1996 EDI conducted 358 conferences, seminars and workshops. During 1995/96 the EDI curriculum covered the following four broad areas: macroeconomic management and policy; environment and natural resources, in particular the management and valuation of natural assets; human resources and poverty, with an emphasis on the education of girls and on reproductive health; and regulatory reform of private and public sectors. In 1996/97 EDI conducted a programme of 'grass-roots' management training to provide women in sub-Saharan Africa with relevant management skills, supported the creation of a Centre for International Competitiveness in Slovenia to help businesses to forge a position for themselves in the European market, and held a conference on pensions in Washington, DC, USA, in November. Dir AMNON GOLAN.

International Centre for Settlement of Investment Disputes—ICSID: founded in 1966 under the Convention of the Settlement of Investment Disputes between States and Nationals of Other States. The Convention was designed to encourage the growth of private foreign investment for economic development, by creating the possibility, always subject to the consent of both parties, for a Contracting State and a foreign investor who is a national of another Contracting State to settle any legal dispute that might arise out of such an investment by conciliation and/or arbitration before an impartial, international forum. The governing body of the Centre is its Administrative Council, composed of one representative of each Contracting State, all of whom have equal voting power. The President of the World Bank is (ex officio) the non-voting Chairman of the Administrative Council.

At mid-1997 127 states had ratified the Convention to become ICSID member countries, with a further 14 states having signed the Convention. At that time 15 cases were pending before the Centre. Sec.-Gen. IBRAHIM F. I. SHIHATA.

PUBLICATIONS

Abstracts of Current Studies: The World Bank Research Program (annually).

Annual Report on Portfolio Performance.

EDI Annual Report.

Global Development Finance (annually).

Global Economic Prospects and Developing Countries (annually).

ICSID Annual Report.

ICSID Review—Foreign Investment Law Journal (2 a year).

Research News (quarterly).

Staff Working Papers.

Transition (every two months).

World Bank Annual Report.

World Bank Atlas (annually).

World Bank Catalog of Publications.

World Bank Economic Review (3 a year).

The World Bank and the Environment (annually).

World Bank News (fortnightly).

World Bank Research Observer.
World Development Indicators (annually).
World Development Report (annually).
World Tables (annually).

World Bank Statistics

LENDING OPERATIONS, BY PURPOSE
(projects approved, year ending 30 June 1997; US $ million)

	IBRD	IDA	Total
Agriculture	2,810.6	735.9	3,546.5
Education	762.3	255.1	1,017.4
Energy	1,613.4	275.8	1,889.2
Environment	22.5	224.2	246.7
Financial sector	993.7	201.1	1,194.8
Health, population and nutrition	245.8	694.1	939.9
Industry	145.0	50.5	195.5
Mining and other extractive activities	300.0	21.4	321.4
Multisector	1,373.0	813.6	2,186.6
Petroleum and gas	114.0	21.6	135.6
Public-sector management	729.7	190.2	919.9
Social sector	1,303.7	66.5	1,370.2
Transportation	3,084.7	607.0	3,691.7
Urban development	646.1	162.3	808.3
Water supply and sanitation	380.4	302.4	682.8
Total	14,524.9	4,621.7	19,146.6

IBRD INCOME AND EXPENDITURE
(US $ million, year ending 30 June)

Revenue	1996	1997
Income from loans:		
Interest	7,804	7,122
Commitment charges	118	113
Income from investments and securities	787	878
Other income	11	12
Total income	8,720	8,125

Expenditure	1996	1997
Interest on borrowings	6,455	5,827
Amortization of issuance and prepayment costs	115	125
Interest on payable-for-cash collateral received	67	44
Administrative expenses	733	651
Provision for loan losses	42	63
Other financial expenses	8	10
Total	7,420	6,720
Operating income	1,300	1,405
Contributions to special programmes	113	120
Net income	1,187	1,285

IBRD LOANS AND IDA CREDITS APPROVED, BY SECTOR AND REGION (1 July 1996–30 June 1997; US $million)

Sector	Africa	East Asia and Pacific	South Asia	Europe and Central Asia	Latin America and the Caribbean	Middle East and North Africa	Total
Agriculture	193.7	1,265.0	409.0	771.7	730.6	176.5	3,546.5
Energy							
Petroleum and gas	—	—	—	135.6	—	—	135.6
Power	163.7	1,131.4	24.2	504.9	—	65.0	1,889.2
Environment	95.4	—	64.8	—	86.5	—	246.7
Human resources							
Education	75.1	645.0	—	137.8	61.5	98.0	1,017.4
Health, population and nutrition	54.9	58.9	593.8	95.5	136.8	—	939.9
Social sector	—	—	—	935.2	405.0	30.0	1,370.2
Industry and finance							
Industry	23.8	60.0	—	111.8	—	—	195.5
Financial	65.9	28.4	105.0	290.3	630.2	75.0	1,194.8
Infrastructure and urban development							
Transportation	52.9	1,103.6	684.5	312.7	1,496.0	42.0	3,691.7
Urban development	147.3	405.1	—	56.0	100.0	100.0	808.3
Water supply and sanitation	25.0	168.6	98.6	67.3	200.0	123.3	682.8
Mining	21.4	—	—	300.0	—	—	321.4
Multisector	707.5	—	—	1,227.0	132.1	120.0	2,186.6
Public-sector management	110.1	—	31.7	109.1	584.0	85.0	919.9
Total	1,736.7	4,866.0	2,011.6	5,054.8	4,562.7	914.8	19,146.6
of which: IBRD	56.0	4,074.4	626.5	4,560.9	4,437.5	769.6	14,524.9
IDA	1,680.7	791.6	1,385.1	493.9	125.2	145.2	4,621.7
Number of operations	49	37	19	67	52	17	241

IBRD OPERATIONS AND RESOURCES, 1993–97 (US $ million, years ending 30 June)

	1992/93	1993/94	1994/95	1995/96	1996/97
Loans approved	16,945	14,244	16,853	14,656*	14,525
Gross disbursements	12,942	10,447	12,672	13,372*	13,998
Net disbursements†	2,331	–731	897	1,213	2,094
New medium- to long-term borrowings	12,676	8,908	9,026	10,883	15,139
Net income	1,130	1,051	1,354	1,187	1,285
Subscribed capital	165,589	170,003	176,438	180,630	182,426
Statutory lending limit	179,787	185,865	195,248	197,785	198,705
Loans and callable guarantees outstanding	104,606	109,468	123,676	110,369	105,954

* Including refinanced/rescheduled overdue charges of US $167.8m. for Bosnia and Herzegovina.

† Including disbursements, repayments and prepayments to/from all members, including third-party repayments.

Source: *World Bank Annual Report 1997.*

International Development Association—IDA

Address: 1818 H Street, NW, Washington, DC 20433, USA.

Telephone: (202) 477-1234; **telex:** 248423; **fax:** (202) 477-6391.

The International Development Association began operations in November 1960. Affiliated to the IBRD (see above), IDA advances capital to the poorer developing member countries on more flexible terms than those offered by the IBRD.

MEMBERS

160 members: see Table on pp. 101–103.

Organization

Officers and staff of the IBRD serve concurrently as officers and staff of IDA.

President and Chairman of Executive Directors: James D. Wolfensohn (ex officio).

Activities

IDA assistance is aimed at the poorer developing countries, (i.e. those with an annual GNP per head of less than US $785 in 1996 dollars). Under IDA lending conditions, credits can be extended to countries whose balance of payments could not sustain the burden of repayment required for IBRD loans. Terms are more favourable than those provided by the IBRD; credits are for a period of 35 or 40 years, with a 'grace period' of 10 years, and carry no interest charges. During 1994–1996 the number of countries eligible for IDA assistance increased from 70 to 79.

IDA's total development resources, consisting of members' subscriptions and supplementary resources (additional subscriptions and contributions), are replenished periodically by contributions from the more affluent member countries. In March 1996 representives of more than 30 donor countries concluded negotiations for the 11th replenishment of IDA funds (and for a one-year interim fund), to finance the period July 1996–June 1999. New contributions over the three-year period were to amount to US $11,000m., while total funds available for lending, including past donor contributions, repayments of IDA credits and the World Bank's contributions, were to amount to $22,000m.

During the year ending 30 June 1997 IDA credits totalling US $4,621.7m. were approved. Of total IDA assistance during that year, $1,680.7m. (36.4%) was for Africa, and $1,385.1m. (30.0%) for South Asia (see table on p. 71). The four largest borrowers of IDA credits were India ($903.0m. for six projects), Viet Nam ($349.2m. for three projects), the People's Republic of China ($325.0m. for two projects) and Bangladesh ($321.2m. for three projects). IDA gives priority to the funding for education sector, an AIDS programme in Africa, the reduction of poverty, economic adjustment and growth, and the protection of the environment. IDA administers a Trust Fund, which was established in November 1996 as part of a World Bank/IMF initiative to assist heavily indebted poor countries (see IBRD).

PUBLICATION

Annual Report.

IDA OPERATIONS AND RESOURCES, 1992–97 (US $ million, years ending 30 June)

	1991/92	1992/93	1993/94	1994/95	1995/96	1996/97
Commitments	6,550	6,752	6,592	5,669	6,861	4,622
Disbursements	4,765	4,947	5,532	5,703	5,884	5,979

Source: *World Bank Annual Report 1997.*

International Finance Corporation—IFC

Address: 2121 Pennsylvania Ave, NW, Washington, DC 20433, USA.

Telephone: (202) 473-1234; **telex:** 248423; **fax:** (202) 477-6391; **internet:** http://www.ifc.org.

IFC was founded in 1956 as a member of the World Bank Group to stimulate economic growth in developing countries by promoting private enterprise in those countries.

MEMBERS

173 members: see Table on pp. 101–103.

Organization

(December 1997)

IFC is a separate legal entity in the World Bank Group. Executive Directors of the World Bank also serve as Directors of IFC. The President of the World Bank is *ex-officio* Chairman of the IFC Board of Directors, which has appointed him President of IFC. Subject to his overall supervision, the day-to-day operations of IFC are conducted by its staff under the direction of the Executive Vice-President.

PRINCIPAL OFFICERS

President: JAMES D. WOLFENSOHN (USA).

Executive Vice-President: JANNIK LINDBAEK (Norway).

REGIONAL AND SPECIALIST DEPARTMENTS

The five Regional Departments cover: Asia; Central Asia, the Middle East and North Africa; Europe; Latin America and the Caribbean; and sub-Saharan Africa. Eight Specialist Departments cover agribusiness; central capital markets; chemicals, petrochemicals and fertilizers; corporate finance services; financial sector issues; power; telecommunications; transportation and utilities; and petroleum, gas and mining.

REGIONAL AND RESIDENT MISSIONS

There are Regional Missions in Côte d'Ivoire (for Central and West Africa), Egypt (for the Middle East), India (for South Asia), Indonesia, Kenya (for East Africa), Morocco (for North Africa), Pakistan, the Philippines, Russia, Thailand, and Zimbabwe (for Southern Africa). There are also four Special Representatives, seven Resident Missions and two IFC Advisers—based in Australia (for Australasia) and in Norway (for Scandinavia). The Africa Project Development Facility is based in Abidjan, Côte d'Ivoire; the African Management Services Company is based in Amsterdam, the Netherlands; the Caribbean and Central American Business Advisory Service is based at IFC's Washington headquarters; the South Pacific Project Facility is based in Sydney, Australia; and the Mekong Project Development Authority is based in Hanoi, Viet Nam.

Activities

IFC provides financial support and advice for private-sector ventures and projects, and assists governments in creating conditions that stimulate the flow of domestic and foreign private savings and investment. Increasingly, IFC has worked to mobilize additional capital from other financial institutions. In all its activities IFC is guided by three major principles:

(i) The catalytic principle. IFC should seek above all to be a catalyst in helping private investors and markets to make good investments.

(ii) The business principle. IFC should function like a business in partnership with the private sector and take the same commercial risks, so that its funds, although backed by public sources, are transferred under market disciplines.

(iii) The principle of the special contribution. IFC should participate in an investment only when it makes a special contribution that supplements or complements the role of market operators.

IFC's authorized capital is US $2,450m. At 30 June 1997 paid-in capital was $2,228.9m. The World Bank was originally the principal source of borrowed funds, but IFC also borrows from private capital markets. IFC's net income amounted to $431.9m. in 1996/97, compared with $345.8m. in the previous year.

To be eligible for financing, projects must be profitable for investors, must benefit the economy of the country concerned, and must comply with IFC's environmental guide-lines. IFC may provide finance for a project that is partly state-owned, provided that there is participation by the private sector and that the project is operated on a commercial basis.

In the year ending 30 June 1997 project financing approved by IFC amounted to US $6,722m. for 276 projects (compared with $8,118m. for 264 projects in the previous year). Of the total approved, $3,317m. was for IFC's own account, while $3,405m. was in the form of loan syndications and underwriting of securities issues and investment funds. IFC mobilizes participation by other investors for the projects that it supports: generally, the IFC limits its financing to no more than 25% of the total cost of a project. Disbursements for IFC's account amounted to $2,003m. (compared with $2,053m. in the previous year).

Projects approved during the year were located in 84 countries; IFC also approved a number of projects that were regional or world-wide in scope. The largest proportion of total financing by IFC was allocated to Latin America and the Caribbean (41%); Asia received 24%, Europe 17%, Central Asia, the Middle East and North Africa 9% and sub-Saharan Africa 6%, while world-wide projects were allocated 3% of funds. The Corporation invested in a wide variety of business and financial institutions in a broad range of sectors, particularly financial services (which accounted for 23% of total financing approved in that year), infrastructure (20%), food and agribusiness (12%), mining and the extraction of metals and other ores (11%), manufacturing (10%) and chemicals and petrochemicals (10%). During 1996/97 IFC inaugurated a new programme, 'Extending IFC's Reach', which aimed to encourage private investment in those countries where adverse political conditions had previously limited IFC intervention. As a result of the programme, IFC financed several projects in Cambodia and the former Yugoslav republic of Macedonia in 1996/97. Under the same initiative, IFC established a Small Enterprise Fund (SEF) of US $40m., which approved project financing of $17.6m. for 16 projects in that financial year.

IFC offers risk-management services, assisting institutions in avoiding financial risks that arise from changes in interest rates, in exchange rates or in commodity prices. In 1996/97 IFC approved seven risk-management projects for companies and banks, bringing the total number of projects approved since the introduction of the service in 1990 to 64.

IFC provides advisory services, particularly in connection with privatization and corporate restructuring, private infrastructure, and the development of capital markets. Under the Technical Assistance Trust Funds Program (TATF), established in 1988, IFC manages resources contributed by various governments and agencies to provide finance for feasibility studies, project identification studies and other types of technical assistance relating to project preparation. By 30 June 1997 the TATF had mobilized US $46m. through 26 trust funds, financing some 400 technical assistance projects. In 1996/97 approved technical assistance project financing amounted to $12.8m. for 93 projects (compared with $11m. for 83 technical assistance assignments in 1995/96). The Foreign Investment Advisory Service (FIAS), established in 1986, is operated jointly by IFC and the IBRD: it provides advice to governments on attracting foreign investment. During 1996/97 FIAS completed 31 new advisory projects in 27 countries. In that year FIAS conducted regional conferences on foreign direct investment (FDI) policy, including meetings on FDI promotion in the Asia-Pacific Region and in Association of South East Asian Nations (ASEAN) countries.

IFC's operations are complemented by the following facilities, which help small-scale entrepreneurs to develop business proposals and to raise financing for projects: the Africa Project Development Facility (based in Abidjan, Côte d'Ivoire, and with branches in Ghana, Zimbabwe and Kenya), which, since its establishment in 1986, had undertaken 281 projects in three countries, at an estimated cost of US $406m., by the end of 1996; the Business Advisory Service for the Caribbean and Central America (based in Washington, DC, and with branches in Costa Rica and Trinidad and Tobago); the Mekong Project Development Authority (based in Hanoi, Viet Nam); and the South Pacific Project Facility (based in Sydney, Australia). IFC helped to establish these facilities and is the executing agency for all of them.

In 1989 IFC (with UNDP, the African Development Bank and other agencies and governments) began operating a new facility, the African Management Services Company (AMSCO), which helps to find qualified senior executives from around the world to work with African companies, assist in the training of local managers, and provide supporting services. By 31 December 1995 AMSCO had management contracts with 33 companies in 16 countries. IFC's Africa Enterprise Fund (AEF) provides financial assistance to small and medium-sized enterprises. In 1995 a new facility, the Enterprise Support Service for Africa (ESSA), was established, to provide technical assistance to businesses after they have secured financing. ESSA commenced operations in February 1996 for an initial three-year period.

The dissolution of the USSR in 1991, and the transition to market economies there and in other central and eastern European countries, led to an increase in IFC activities in the region during the 1990s. In order to facilitate privatization process in that region, the IFC has conducted several single-enterprise advisory assignments and has undertaken work to formulate models that can be easily replicated, notably for small-scale privatization and the privatization of agricultural land in Russia, Ukraine and Belarus.

PUBLICATIONS

Annual Report.

Emerging Stock Markets Factbook (annually).

Global Agribusiness (series of industry reports).

Impact (quarterly).

Lessons of Experience (series).

Results on the Ground (series).

Discussion papers and technical documents.

IFC OPERATIONS AND RESOURCES, 1988–97 (fiscal years ending 30 June)

	1988	1989	1990	1991	1992	1993	1994	1995	1996	1997
Approved investments										
Number of new projects	95	92	122	152	167	185	231	213	264	276
Total financing (US $ million)	1,270	1,710	2,201	2,846	3,226	3,936	4,287	5,467	8,118	6,722
Total project costs* (US $ million)	5,010	9,698	9,490	10,683	12,000	17,422	15,839	19,352	19,633	17,945
Disbursements (IFC's own account, US $ million)	762	870	1,001	1,249	1,114	1,106	1,537	1,808	2,053	2,003
Resources and income (US $ million)										
Borrowings	2,047	2,255	3,580	4,130	5,114	5,565	6,531	7,993	8,956	10,123
Paid-in capital	850	948	1,072	1,145	1,251	1,423	1,658	1,875	2,076	2,229
Retained earnings	438	635	792	957	1,138	1,280	1,538	1,726	2,071	2,503
Net income	100.6	196.5	157.0	165.9	180.2	141.7	258.2	188.0	345.8	431.9

* Including investment mobilized from other sources.

Source: *IFC Annual Report 1997*.

Multilateral Investment Guarantee Agency—MIGA

Address: 1818 H Street, NW, Washington, DC 20433, USA.

Telephone: (202) 477-1234; **telex:** 248423; **fax:** (202) 477-6391; **internet:** http://www.ipanet.com.

MIGA was founded in 1988 as an affiliate of the World Bank. Its mandate is to encourage the flow of foreign direct investment to, and among, developing member countries, through the mitigation of political risk in the form of investment insurance.

MEMBERS

At 16 December 1997 MIGA had 142 member countries. Membership is open to all countries that are members of the World Bank.

Organization

(December 1997)

MIGA is legally and financially separate from the World Bank. It is supervised by a Board of Directors.

President: James D. Wolfensohn (USA).

Executive Vice-President: Akira Iida (Japan).

Activities

The convention establishing MIGA took effect in April 1988. Authorized capital was US $1,082m.

MIGA's purpose is to guarantee eligible investments against losses resulting from non-commercial risks, under four main categories:

(i) transfer risk resulting from host government restrictions on currency conversion and transfer;

(ii) risk of loss resulting from legislative or administrative actions of the host government;

(iii) repudiation by the host government of contracts with investors in cases in which the investor has no access to a competent forum;

(iv) the risk of armed conflict and civil unrest.

Before guaranteeing any investment, MIGA must ensure that it is commercially viable, contributes to the development process and is not harmful to the environment.

During the year ending 30 June 1997 MIGA issued 70 investment insurance contracts, compared with 68 contracts in 1995/96. The amount of direct investment associated with the contracts totalled approximately US $4,700m. (compared with $6,600m. in the previous year), and created an estimated 4,000 jobs in 25 developing member states.

MIGA also provides policy and advisory services to promote foreign investment in developing countries and in transitional economies, and to disseminate information on investment opportunities. In October 1995 MIGA established a new network on investment opportunities, which connected investment promotion agencies (IPAs) throughout the world on an electronic information network. The so-called IPA*net* aimed to encourage further investments among developing countries, to provide access to comprehensive information on investment laws and conditions and to strengthen links between governmental, business and financial associations and investors.

PUBLICATION

Annual Report.

International Civil Aviation Organization—ICAO

Address: 999 University St, Montreal, PQ H3C 5H7, Canada.

Telephone: (514) 954-8219; **telex:** 05-24513; **fax:** (514) 954-6077; **e-mail:** icaohq@icao.org; **internet:** http://www.cam.org/icao.

The Convention on International Civil Aviation was signed in Chicago in 1944. As a result, ICAO was founded in 1947 to develop the techniques of international air navigation and to help in the planning and improvement of international air transport.

MEMBERS

185 members: see Table on pp. 101–103.

Organization

(November 1997)

ASSEMBLY

Composed of representatives of all member states, the Assembly is the organization's legislative body and meets at least once in three years. It reviews the work of the organization, sets out the work programme for the next three years, approves the budget and determines members' contributions.

COUNCIL

Composed of representatives of 33 member states, elected by the Assembly. It is the executive body, and establishes and supervises subsidiary technical committees and makes recommendations to member governments; meets in virtually continuous session; elects the President, appoints the Secretary-General, and administers the finances of the organization. The functions of the Council are:

- (i) to adopt international standards and recommended practices and incorporate them as annexes to the Convention on International Civil Aviation;
- (ii) to arbitrate between member states on matters concerning aviation and implementation of the Convention;
- (iii) to investigate any situation which presents avoidable obstacles to development of international air navigation;
- (iv) to take whatever steps are necessary to maintain safety and regularity of operation of international air transport;
- (v) to provide technical assistance to the developing countries under the UN Development Programme and other assistance programmes.

President of the Council: Dr Assad Kotaite (Lebanon).

Secretary-General: Renato Claudio Costa Pereira (Brazil).

AIR NAVIGATION COMMISSION

The Commission comprises 15 members.

President: V. M. Aguado.

STANDING COMMITTEES

These include the Air Transport Committee, the Committee on Joint Support of Air Navigation Services, the Finance Committee, the Legal Committee, the Technical Co-operation Committee, the Committee on Unlawful Interference, the Personnel Committee, and the Edward Warner Award Committee.

REGIONAL OFFICES

Asia and Pacific: POB 11, Samyaek Ladprao, Bangkok 10901, Thailand.

Eastern and Southern Africa: POB 46294, Nairobi, Kenya.

Europe: 3 bis, Villa Emile-Bergerat, 92522 Neuilly-sur-Seine Cédex, France.

Middle East: Egyptian Civil Aviation Complex, Cairo Airport Rd, Cairo, Egypt.

North America, Central America and the Caribbean: Apdo Postal 5-377, CP 11590, México 5, DF, Mexico.

South America: Apdo 4127, Lima 100, Peru.

Western and Central Africa: BP 2356, Dakar, Senegal.

Activities

ICAO aims to ensure the safe and orderly growth of civil aviation; to encourage skills in aircraft design and operation; to improve airways, airports and air navigation; to prevent the waste of resources in unreasonable competition; to safeguard the rights of each contracting party to operate international air transport; and to prevent discriminatory practices.

ICAO SPECIFICATIONS

These are contained in annexes to the Chicago Convention, and in three sets of Procedures for Air Navigation Services (PANS Documents). The specifications are periodically revised in keeping with developments in technology and changing requirements. The 18 annexes to the Convention include personnel licensing, rules relating to the conduct of flights, meteorological services, aeronautical charts, air–ground communications, safety specifications, identification, air-traffic control, rescue services, environmental protection, security and the transporting of dangerous goods. Technical Manuals and Circulars are issued to facilitate implementation.

ICAO REGIONAL PLANS

These set out the technical requirements for air navigation facilities in the nine ICAO regions; Regional Offices offer assistance (see addresses above). Because of growth in air traffic and changes in the pattern of air routes, the Plans are periodically amended.

EUROPEAN AIR NAVIGATION PLANNING GROUP

Reviews current problems and the need for changes in the air navigation facilities in the European region.

ICAO PROJECTS

Studies of current problems aiming to apply new technology, including: airworthiness of aircraft, all-weather navigation, aircraft separation, obstacle clearances, noise abatement, operation of aircraft and carriage by air of dangerous goods, automated data interchange systems, aviation security and use of space technology in air navigation.

ENVIRONMENT

International standards and guide-lines for noise certification of aircraft and international provisions for the regulation of aircraft engine emissions have been adopted and published in Annex 16 to the Chicago Convention.

AIR TRANSPORT

Continuing functions include preparation of regional air transport development studies; studies of regulatory policy regarding international air transport; studies on international air transport fares and rates; review of the economic situation of airports and route facilities; development of guidance material on civil aviation forecasting and planning; collection and publication of statistics; facilitation of international air transport across international boundaries; and multilateral financing of certain air navigation facilities.

TECHNICAL CO-OPERATION BUREAU

The Bureau assists developing countries in the execution of various projects, financed by UNDP and other sources (see under Finance, below).

LEGAL COMMITTEE

The general work programme of the Committee, approved in November 1992, consisted of the following subjects: consideration, with regard to Global Navigation Satellite Systems (GNSS), of the establishment of a legal framework; action to expedite the ratification of the Montreal Protocols 3 and 4 of the 'Warsaw System'; study of the instruments of the 'Warsaw System'; consideration of liability rules that might be applicable to air traffic services (ATS) providers as well as other potentially liable parties; the UN Convention on the Law of the Sea and its implications, if any, for the application of the Chicago Convention, its annexes and other international law instruments; and the study of the liability of air-traffic control agencies.

FINANCE

ICAO is financed mainly by contributions from member states; the 31st Session of the Assembly, held in September 1995, approved budgets of US $50.3m. for 1996, $52.2m. for 1997 and $54.6m. for 1998. The administrative and operational costs of ICAO's technical co-operation programmes amounted to $59.3m. in 1996.

PUBLICATIONS

Aircraft Accident Digest.

The 18 Annexes to the Convention.

Digest of Statistics.
ICAO Journal (10 a year, in English, French and Spanish; quarterly digest in Russian).
ICAO Publications and Audio/Visual Training Aids Catalogue.
ICAO Training Manual.
Lexicon of Terms.
Minutes and Documents of the Legal Committee.
Procedures for Air Navigation Services.
Regional Air Navigation Plans.

International Fund for Agricultural Development—IFAD

Address: Via del Serafico 107, 00142 Rome, Italy.

Telephone: (6) 54591; **telex:** 620330; **fax:** (6) 5043463; **e-mail:** ifad@ifad.org; **internet:** http://www.unic.org/ifad.

Following a decision by the 1974 UN World Food Conference, IFAD was established in 1977 to fund rural development programmes specifically aimed at the poorest of the world's people. Funding operations began in January 1978.

MEMBERS

160 members: see Table on pp. 101–103.

Organization

(November 1997)

GOVERNING COUNCIL

Each member state is represented in the Governing Council (the Fund's highest authority) by a Governor and an Alternate. Sessions are held annually with special sessions as required. The Governing Council elects the President of the Fund (who also chairs the Executive Board) by a two-thirds majority for a four-year term. The President is eligible for re-election.

In January 1995 the Governing Council approved the report and recommendations of a Special Committee, which had been established to review IFAD's resource requirements and governance issues. Accordingly, the existing three-category system of membership (which ensured equal voting rights for industrialized countries, i.e. OECD members, petroleum-exporting developing countries, i.e. OPEC members, both of which contributed to the Fund's resources, and to recipient developing countries) was to be abolished, with effect from completion of the fourth replenishment of the Fund. Agreement on the replenishment was concluded in February 1997. Under the new voting system the 1,800 votes in the Governing Council and the Executive Board were to be distributed to reflect the size of the financial contribution of each donor country.

EXECUTIVE BOARD

Consists of 18 members and 17 alternates, elected by the Governing Council, who serve for three years. The Executive Board is responsible for the conduct and general operation of IFAD and approves loans and grants for projects; it holds three regular sessions each year.

President and Chairman of Executive Board: Fawzi Hamad al-Sultan (Kuwait).

Vice-President: Jim Moody (USA).

DEPARTMENTS

IFAD has three main administrative departments: the Economic Policy and Resource Strategy Department, the Programme Management Department (with five regional Divisions and a Technical Advisory Division); and the Management and Personnel Services Department (including Office of the Secretary, Management Information Systems, Personnel Division, and Administrative Services). At 30 September 1995 IFAD had 264 regular staff.

Activities

The Fund's objective is to mobilize additional resources to be made available on concessionary terms for agricultural development in developing member states. IFAD provides financing primarily for projects designed to improve food production systems and to strengthen related policies, services and institutions. In allocating resources IFAD is guided by: the need to increase food production in the poorest food-deficit countries; the potential for increasing food production in other developing countries; and the importance of improving the nutritional level of the poorest people in developing countries and the conditions of their lives. All projects focus on those who often do not benefit from other development programmes: small-scale farmers, artisanal fishermen, nomadic pastoralists, women, and the rural landless. IFAD is a leading repository in the world of knowledge, resources and expertise in the field of rural hunger and poverty alleviation. During 1995 a team established to review IFAD's activities focused on IFAD's role as an innovator, emphasizing the importance of pioneering practices and strategies that can be replicated, and of making its knowledge available to relevant agencies and governments.

IFAD is empowered to make both grants and loans. Under its Agreement, grants are limited to 5% of the resources committed in any one financial year. Loans are available on highly concessionary, intermediate and ordinary terms. Highly concessionary loans carry no interest but have an annual service charge of 0.75% and a repayment period of 40 years. Intermediate term loans are subject to a variable interest charge, equivalent to 50% of the interest rate charged on World Bank loans, and are repaid over 20 years. Ordinary loans carry a variable interest charge equal to that charged by the World Bank, and are repaid over 15–18 years. Highly concessionary loans form about two-thirds of the total lent annually by IFAD. To avoid duplication of work, the administration of loans, for the purposes of disbursements and supervision of project implementation, is entrusted to competent international financial institutions, with the Fund retaining an active interest. In order to increase the impact of its lending resources on food production, the Fund seeks as much as possible to attract other external donors and beneficiary governments as co-financiers of its projects.

In 1986 IFAD inaugurated a Special Programme for Sub-Saharan African countries affected by drought and desertification (SPA), aiming to improve food production (with emphasis on traditional food crops and biological pest control), water conservation, and other measures for environmental preservation in Africa. In the second phase of the Programme, which began in 1992, the SPA extended its lending criteria to cover off-farm activities and to promote economic diversification. At the same time the number of countries eligible for assistance increased from 22 to 27. By the end of 1995 IFAD had approved a cumulative total of 47 projects, amounting to SDR 283.4m., since 1986. During 1997, IFAD was funding 42 projects in 24 countries, with a total value of some US $750m.

Between 1978 and September 1995 the Fund approved 601 research and technical assistance grants, at a cost of US $227.4m., and loans totalling $4,548.3m. for 429 projects. IFAD's investment represented some 30% of total project costs, while the remainder was provided by other external donors and recipient governments.

In 1995 IFAD approved total loans (including those under the SPA) amounting to SDR 261.4m., or about US $391.7m. (The average value of the SDR—Special Drawing Right—in 1995 was $1.51695.) Of this total, 31.8% was for projects in sub-Saharan Africa, 31.2% for Asia and the Pacific, 18.6% for Latin America and the Caribbean, and 18.5% for the Near East and North Africa. Additionally, 58 technical assistance grants, amounting to SDR 14.6m. (for research, training and project preparation), were awarded, bringing the total financial assistance approved to SDR 276.0m. (about US $413.8m.).

IFAD's programme of work for 1996 envisaged loans and grants totalling SDR 304.3m., while the budget for administrative expenses amounted to US $52.5m.

IFAD's development projects usually include a number of components, such as infrastructure (e.g. improvement of water supplies, small-scale irrigation and road construction); input supply (e.g. improved seeds, fertilizers and pesticides); institutional support (e.g. research, training and extension services); and producer incentives (e.g. pricing and marketing improvements). IFAD also attempts to enable the landless to acquire income-generating assets: by increasing the provision of credit for the rural poor, it seeks to free them from dependence on the unorganized and exploitative capital market and to generate productive activities.

The Fund supports projects that are concerned with environmental conservation, in an effort to alleviate poverty that results from the deterioration of natural resources.

In addition to its regular efforts to identify projects and programmes, IFAD organizes special programming missions to certain selected countries to undertake a comprehensive review of the constraints affecting the rural poor, and to help countries to design strategies for the removal of these constraints. In general, projects based on the recommendations of these missions tend to focus on institutional improvements at the national and local level to direct inputs and services to small farmers and the landless rural poor. Monitoring and evaluation missions are also sent to check the progress of projects.

In November 1995 IFAD organized a Conference on Hunger and Poverty, which was held in Brussels, Belgium, together with the World Bank, the European Commission, FAO, WFP and several European governments. The conference was attended by representatives from some 300 non-governmental organizations, and approved a programme of action to combat hunger and poverty.

FINANCE

In accordance with the Articles of Agreement establishing IFAD, the Governing Council periodically undertakes a review of the adequacy of resources available to the Fund and may request members to make additional contributions. In January 1994 a Special Committee was established to review IFAD's financial requirements, in particular in view of the increasing assistance needs of developing country members. In February 1997 the Governing Council concluded an agreement on the fourth replenishment of the Fund's resources, amounting to US $485m. over a three-year period.

PUBLICATIONS

Annual Report.

IFAD Update (3 a year).

Staff Working Papers (series).

The State of World Rural Poverty.

PROJECTS APPROVED BY IFAD IN 1995

Country	Purpose	Loan Amount (SDR million)
Africa (excl. North Africa)		82.80
Angola	Foodcrops development	9.00‡
Benin	Income-generating	8.05
The Gambia	Agricultural development	3.40
Ghana	Agricultural development	6.75
Guinea	Small-holder development project	10.20
Madagascar	Upper Mandrare Basin development	4.65§
Niger	Special country programme	9.55*
Senegal	Rural micro-enterprise	5.00†
Togo	Village organization and development	5.10
Tanzania	Farmers' initiative project	9.65
Zambia	Irrigation and water use	4.30
Zimbabwe	Dry areas project	7.15
Asia and the Pacific		80.90
Bangladesh	Employment generation	9.95
Bangladesh	Water resources development	7.00
China	Jiangxi/Ganzhou agricultural development	15.95
India	Mewat Area development	9.65
Indonesia	Farming systems and livestock development	12.05
Democratic People's Republic of Korea	Sericulture development	10.45
Kyrgyzstan	Sheep development	2.35
Maldives	Southern atolls development	1.90
Philippines	Highland resources management	6.15
Sri Lanka	Rural development	5.45
Latin America and the Caribbean		48.95
Brazil	Community development	13.50
Mexico	Mayan rural development	6.95
Nicaragua	Dry region development	8.25
Panama	Sustainable development	5.35
Paraguay	Peasant credit fund	6.65
Peru	Natural resources management	8.25
Near East and North Africa		48.70
Armenia	Irrigation rehabilitation	5.40
Jordan	Agricultural resource management	8.70
Syria	Coastal/midlands agricultural development	13.65
Tunisia	Siliana agricultural development	7.55
Turkey	Ordu-Giresun rural development	13.40
Total loans		61.35
Technical assistance grants		14.60
Total operations		275.95

* Includes SDR 1.60m. from the SPA.
† Includes SDR 2.50m. from the SPA.
‡ Includes SDR 2.30m. from the SPA.
§ Includes SDR 1.10m. from the SPA.

International Labour Organization—ILO

Address: 4 route des Morillons, 1211 Geneva 22, Switzerland.

Telephone: (22) 7996111; **telex:** 415647; **fax:** (22) 7988685; **internet:** http://www.ilo.org.

ILO was founded in 1919 to work for social justice as a basis for lasting peace. It carries out this mandate by promoting decent living standards, satisfactory conditions of work and pay and adequate employment opportunities. Methods of action include the creation of international labour standards; the provision of technical co-operation services; and research and publications on social and labour matters. In 1946 ILO became a specialized agency associated with the UN. It was awarded the Nobel Peace Prize in 1969.

MEMBERS

174 members: see Table on pp. 101–103.

Organization

(November 1997)

INTERNATIONAL LABOUR CONFERENCE

The supreme deliberative body of ILO, the Conference meets annually in Geneva, with a session devoted to maritime questions when necessary; it is attended by about 2,000 delegates, advisers and observers. National delegations are composed of two government delegates, one employers' delegate and one workers' delegate. Non-governmental delegates can speak and vote independently of the views of their national government. Conference elects the Governing Body and adopts the Budget and International Labour Conventions and Recommendations.

The President and Vice-Presidents hold office for the term of the Conference only.

GOVERNING BODY

ILO's executive council meets three times a year in Geneva to decide policy and programmes. It is composed of 28 government members, 14 employers' members and 14 workers' members. Ten seats are reserved for 'states of chief industrial importance': Brazil, the People's Republic of China, France, Germany, India, Italy, Japan, Russia, the United Kingdom and the USA. The remaining 18 are elected from other countries every three years. Employers' and workers' members are elected as individuals, not as national candidates.

Chairman (1997–98): AHMED AHMED EL-AMAWI (Egypt).

Employers' Vice-Chairman: JEAN-JACQUES OECHSLIN (France).

Workers' Vice-Chairman: WILLIAM BRETT (United Kingdom).

INTERNATIONAL LABOUR OFFICE

The International Labour Office is ILO's secretariat, operational headquarters and publishing house. It is staffed in Geneva and in the field by about 1,700 people of some 115 nationalities. Operations are decentralized to regional, area and branch offices in nearly 40 countries.

Director-General: MICHEL HANSENNE (Belgium).

REGIONAL OFFICES

Regional Office for Africa: 01 BP 3960, Abidjan 01, Côte d'Ivoire.

Regional Office for the Americas: Apdo Postal 3638, Lima 1, Peru.

Regional Office for Arab States: POB 11-4088, Beirut, Lebanon.

Regional Office for Asia and the Pacific: POB 2-349, Bangkok 10200, Thailand.

Activities

INTERNATIONAL LABOUR CONFERENCE

83rd Session: June 1996. Adopted a convention and recommendation on the rights of homeworkers. Held general discussions on employment policies in a global context and on tripartite consultation at the national level on economic and social policy. The plenary debate focused on ILO activities in 1994–95.

84th (Maritime) Session: October 1996. Adopted a convention and recommendation on the inspection of seafarers' working and living conditions. Adopted a convention and recommendation on the recruitment and placing of seafarers. Adopted a convention and recommendation on seafarers' hours of work and the manning of ships. Adopted an optional protocol to the convention (no. 147) on merchant shipping.

85th Session: June 1997. Discussed a proposal aiming to ensure a universal respect for fundamental workers' rights in the global economy through the acceptance of freedom of association and collective bargaining and the prohibition of forced or child labour and discrimination against workers. The proposal was expected to be adopted through a 1998 declaration, to be annexed to the constitution. Amended article 19 of the constitution to enable international labour standards to be updated. Adopted a convention amending convention no. 96 on fee-charging employment agencies, in order to increase the efficiency of labour markets and protect those job-seekers using their services. Held a first discussion on contract labour, and a general discussion on the promotion of job creation in small and medium-sized enterprises.

INTERNATIONAL LABOUR STANDARDS

One of ILO's primary functions is the adoption by the International Labour Conference of Conventions and Recommendations setting minimum labour standards. Through ratification by member states, Conventions create binding obligations to put their provisions into effect. Recommendations provide guidance as to policy and practice. At December 1997 a total of 181 Conventions and 188 Recommendations had been adopted, ranging over a wide field of social and labour matters, including basic human rights such as freedom of association, abolition of forced labour and elimination of discrimination in employment. Together they form the International Labour Code. By December 1997 more than 6,400 ratifications of the Conventions had been registered by member states.

During 1996 ILO resolved to strengthen its efforts, working closely with UNICEF, to encourage member states to ratify and to implement relevant international standards on child labour. By April 1997 23 countries were taking part in ILO's International Programme for the Elimination of Child Labour.

TECHNICAL CO-OPERATION

Technical co-operation continues to be a major ILO activity, closely linked to the Active Partnership Policy. In 1996 some US $98.2m., from all sources, was spent on operational activities (compared with $112.9m. in the previous year) in particular for the promotion of employment and training, support for enterprise and co-operative development and development policy. Other commitments concerned working conditions and the environment, including the International Programme for the Elimination of Child Labour. Africa (excluding African Arab countries) accounted for some 37.4% of total expenditure, Asia and the Pacific for 25.5%, and Latin America and the Caribbean for some 10.2%. Expenditure in Europe decreased from 9.0% to 6.1% in 1996, while expenditure in the Arab countries remained at 2.6%.

EMPLOYMENT AND TRAINING

Through its Employment and Training Department, ILO aims to monitor, examine and report on the situation and trends in employment throughout the world, and considers the effects on employment and social justice of economic trade, investment and related phenomena. The Department is responsible for assisting and advising ILO constituents on the design and implementation of employment and training policies and programmes. It aims to generate greater awareness of specific related issues, for example poverty alleviation and the social dimensions of globalization, and ILO's work in the area.

The Department analyses and develops policies to promote the following objectives: full, productive and freely-chosen employment; a labour market that combines flexibility in the use of labour with employment security; enhanced employment opportunities for workers by adapting and improving their skills and competence through training; the protection and access to employment of specific groups, such as women, youths, migrant workers and disabled persons; and the rehabilitation of workers exposed to drug and alcohol abuse.

ILO maintains technical relations with the IMF, the World Bank, OECD, the WTO and other international organizations on global economic issues, international and national strategies for employment, structural adjustment, and labour market and training policies. A number of employment policy reviews have been carried out by the ILO within the framework of the UN Administrative Committee on Co-ordination Task Force on Full Employment and Sustainable Livelihoods.

MEETINGS

Among meetings held during 1997, in addition to the regular International Labour Conference, the Maritime session of the International Labour Conference and the Governing Body sessions, were the Tripartite Meeting of Experts on Future ILO Activities in the Field of Migration; the Tripartite Meeting on the Effects of New Technologies on Employment and Working Conditions in the Hotel, Catering and Tourism Sector; the Governing Body Committee on Freedom of Association; the Meeting of Experts on Workers' Health Surveillance; the Meeting of Experts on Safety and Health in Forest Work; the Meeting of Experts on Labour Statistics; the Tripartite Meeting on the Iron and Steel Workforce of the 21st Century; and the Tripartite Meeting on Breaking through the Glass Ceiling: Women in Management.

INTERNATIONAL INSTITUTE FOR LABOUR STUDIES

Established in 1960 and based at ILO's Geneva headquarters, the Institute promotes the study and discussion of policy issues of concern to ILO and its constituents, i.e. government, employers and workers. The core theme of the Institute's activities is the interaction between labour institutions, development and civil society in a global economy. It identifies emerging social and labour issues by developing new areas for research and action, and encourages dialogue on social policy between the tripartite constituency of the ILO and the international academic community and other experts. The Institute maintains research networks, conducts courses, seminars and social policy forums, and supports internships and visiting scholar and internship programmes.

INTERNATIONAL TRAINING CENTRE OF ILO

Address: Corso Unità d'Italia 125, 10127 Turin, Italy.

The Centre became operational in 1965. The ILO Director-General is Chairman of the Board of the Centre. It provides programmes for directors in charge of technical and vocational institutions, training officers, senior and middle-level managers in private and public enterprises, trade union leaders, and technicians, primarily from the developing regions of the world. Since 1991 the Centre has been increasingly used by UN agencies to provide training for improving the management of development and for building national capacities to sustain development programmes. In January 1996 a UN Staff College was established to improve staff training and to enhance collaboration among the various agencies and programmes of the UN.

FINANCE

The net expenditure budget for the two years 1998–99 was US $481m. (compared with $579m. for 1996–97).

PUBLICATIONS

(in English, French and Spanish unless otherwise indicated)

Bulletin of Labour Statistics (quarterly).

International Labour Review (quarterly).

International studies, surveys, works of practical guidance or reference on questions of social policy, manpower, industrial relations, working conditions, social security, training, management development, etc.

Labour Law Documents (selected labour and social security laws and regulations; 3 a year).

Official Bulletin (3 a year).

Reports for the annual sessions of the International Labour Conference, etc. (also in Arabic, Chinese and Russian).

World Employment (annually).

World Labour Report.

World of Work (magazine issued in several languages; quarterly).

Yearbook of Labour Statistics.

International Maritime Organization—IMO

Address: 4 Albert Embankment, London, SE1 7SR, England.

Telephone: (171) 735-7611; **telex:** 23588; **fax:** (171) 587-3210; **internet:** http://www.imo.org.

The Inter-Governmental Maritime Consultative Organization (IMCO) began operations in 1959, as a specialized agency of the UN to facilitate co-operation among governments on technical matters affecting international shipping. Its main functions are the achievement of safe and efficient navigation, and the control of pollution caused by ships and craft operating in the marine environment. IMCO became IMO in 1982.

MEMBERS

155 members and two associate members: see Table on pp. 101–103.

Organization

(November 1997)

ASSEMBLY

The Assembly consists of delegates from all member countries, who each have one vote. Associate members and observers from other governments and the international agencies are also present. Regular sessions are held every two years. The Assembly is responsible for the election of members to the Council. It considers reports from all subsidiary bodies and decides the action to be taken on them; it votes the agency's budget and determines the work programme and financial policy. The 19th regular session of the Assembly was held in London in November 1995.

The Assembly also recommends to members measures to promote maritime safety and to prevent and control maritime pollution from ships.

COUNCIL

The Council is the governing body of the Organization between the biennial sessions of the Assembly. Its members, representatives of 32 states, are elected by the Assembly for a term of two years. The Council appoints the Secretary-General; transmits reports by the subsidiary bodies, including the Maritime Safety Committee, to the Assembly, and reports on the work of the Organization generally; submits budget estimates and financial statements with comments and recommendations to the Assembly. The Council normally meets twice a year.

Chairman: G. A. DUBBELD (Netherlands).

Facilitation Committee: Constituted by the Council in May 1972 as a subsidiary body, this Committee deals with measures to facilitate maritime travel and transport and matters arising from the 1965 Facilitation Convention. Membership open to all IMO member states.

MARITIME SAFETY COMMITTEE

The Maritime Safety Committee is open to all IMO members. The Committee meets at least once a year and submits proposals to the Assembly on technical matters affecting shipping, including prevention of marine pollution.

Sub-Committees:

Bulk Liquids and Gases*.
Carriage of Dangerous Goods, Solid Cargoes and Containers.
Fire Protection.
Flag State Implementation*.
Radiocommunications and Search and Rescue.
Safety of Navigation.
Ship Design and Equipment.
Stability and Load Lines and Fishing Vessel Safety.
Standards of Training and Watchkeeping.

* Also sub-committees of the Marine Environment Protection Committee.

LEGAL COMMITTEE

Established by the Council in June 1967 to deal initially with problems connected with the loss of the tanker *Torrey Canyon,* and subsequently with any legal problems laid before IMO. Membership open to all IMO member states.

MARINE ENVIRONMENT PROTECTION COMMITTEE

Established by the eighth Assembly (1973) to co-ordinate IMO's work on the prevention and control of marine pollution from ships, and to assist IMO in its consultations with other UN bodies, and with international organizations and expert bodies in the field of marine pollution. Membership is open to all IMO members.

TECHNICAL CO-OPERATION COMMITTEE

Constituted by the Council in May 1972, this Committee evaluates the implementation of UN Development Programme projects for which IMO is the executing agency, and generally reviews IMO's technical assistance programmes. Its membership is open to all IMO member states.

SECRETARIAT

The Secretariat consists of the Secretary-General and a staff appointed by the Secretary-General and recruited on as wide a geographical basis as possible.

Secretary-General: WILLIAM A. O'NEIL (Canada).

Divisions of the Secretariat:

Administrative
Conference
Legal Affairs and External Relations
Marine Environment
Maritime Safety
Technical Co-operation

Activities

In addition to the work of its committees and sub-committees, the organization works in connection with the following Conventions, of which it is the depository:

International Convention for the Prevention of Pollution of the Sea by Oil, 1954. IMO has taken over administration from the United Kingdom.

Convention on Facilitation of International Maritime Traffic, 1965. Came into force in March 1967.

International Convention on Load Lines, 1966. Came into force in July 1968.

International Convention on Tonnage Measurement of Ships, 1969. Convention embodies a universal system for measuring ships' tonnage. Came into force in 1982.

International Convention relating to Intervention on the High Seas in Cases of Oil Pollution Casualties, 1969. Came into force in May 1975.

International Convention on Civil Liability for Oil Pollution Damage, 1969. Came into force in June 1975.

Intenational Convention on the Establishment of an International Fund for Compensation for Oil Pollution Damage, 1971. Came into force in October 1978.

Convention on the International Regulations for Preventing Collisions at Sea, 1972. Came into force in July 1977.

Convention on the Prevention of Marine Pollution by Dumping of Wastes and Other Matter, 1972. Came into force in August 1975. Extended to include a ban on low-level nuclear waste in November 1993; came into force in February 1994.

International Convention for Safe Containers, 1972. Came into force in September 1977.

International Convention for the Prevention of Pollution from Ships, 1973 (as modified by the Protocol of 1978). Came into force in October 1983. Extended to include a ban on air pollution in September 1997; amendments will come into force 12 months after 15 countries whose combined fishing fleets constitute 50% of the world's merchant fleet have become parties thereto.

International Convention for Safety of Life at Sea, 1974. Came into force in May 1980. A Protocol drawn up in 1978 came into force in May 1981. Extended to include an International Safety Management (ISM) Code in October 1997.

Athens Convention relating to the Carriage of Passengers and their Luggage by Sea, 1974. Came into force in April 1987.

Convention on the International Maritime Satellite Organization, 1976. Came into force in July 1979.

Convention on Limitation of Liability for Maritime Claims, 1976. Came into force in December 1986.

International Convention for the Safety of Fishing Vessels, Torremolinos, 1977. Will come into force 12 months after 15 countries whose combined fishing fleets constitute 50% of world fishing fleets of 24 metres in length and over have become parties thereto.

International Convention on Standards of Training, Certification and Watchkeeping for Seafarers, 1978. Came into force in April 1984; restructured in February 1997.

International Convention on Maritime Search and Rescue, 1979. Came into force in June 1985.

Paris Memorandum of Understanding on Port State Control, 1982.

International Convention for the Suppression of Unlawful Acts against the Safety of International Shipping, 1988. Came into force in March 1992.

International Convention on Salvage, 1989. Came into force in July 1996.

International Convention on Oil Pollution, Preparedness, Response and Co-operation, 1990. Came into force on 13 May 1995.

International Convention on Liability and Compensation for Damage in Connection with the Carriage of Hazardous and Noxious Substances by Sea, 1996.

WORLD MARITIME UNIVERSITY—WMU

Address: POB 500, Citadellsvägen 29, 201 24 Malmö, Sweden.

Telephone: (40) 356300; **telex:** 32132; **fax:** (40) 128442; **e-mail:** info@wmu.se.

The University was established by the IMO in 1983. It offers postgraduate courses in various maritime disciplines, mainly for students from developing countries. Rector K. LAUBSTEIN. Publs *WMU Newsletter*, *WMU Handbook*.

BUDGET

Contributions are received from the member states. The budget appropriation for the two years 1996–97 amounted to £36.6m.

PUBLICATIONS

IMO News (quarterly).

Numerous specialized publications, including international conventions of which IMO is depository.

International Monetary Fund—IMF

Address: 700 19th St, NW, Washington, DC 20431, USA.

Telephone: (202) 623-7430; **telex:** 64111; **fax:** (202) 623-6701; **internet:** http://www.imf.org.

The IMF was established at the same time as the World Bank in December 1945, to promote international monetary co-operation, to facilitate the expansion and balanced growth of international trade and to promote stability in foreign exchange.

MEMBERS

182 members: see Table on pp. 101–103.

Organization

(February 1998)

Managing Director: MICHEL CAMDESSUS (France).

First Deputy Managing Director: STANLEY FISCHER (USA).

Deputy Managing Directors: ALASSANE D. OUATTARA (Côte d'Ivoire); SHIGEMITSU SUGISAKI (Japan).

BOARD OF GOVERNORS

The highest authority of the Fund is exercised by the Board of Governors, on which each member country is represented by a Governor and an Alternate Governor. The Board of Governors meets once a year, but the Governors may take votes by mail or other means between annual meetings. The Board of Governors has delegated many of its powers to the Executive Directors. However, the conditions governing the admission of new members, adjustment of quotas and the election of Executive Directors, as well as certain other important powers, remain the sole responsibility of the Board of Governors. The voting power of each member on the Board of Governors is related to its quota in the Fund (see p. 84).

The Interim Committee of the Board of Governors, established in 1974, usually meets twice a year. It comprises 24 members, representing the same countries or groups of countries as those on the Board of Executive Directors (see below). It reviews the international monetary system and advises the Board of Governors, but has no decision-making authority.

The Development Committee (the Joint Ministerial Committee of the Boards of Governors of the World Bank and the IMF on the Transfer of Real Resources to Developing Countries) was also created in 1974, with a structure similar to that of the Interim Committee, to review development policy issues and financing requirements.

BOARD OF EXECUTIVE DIRECTORS

The 24-member Board of Executive Directors, responsible for the day-to-day operations of the Fund, is in continuous session in Washington, under the chairmanship of the Fund's Managing Director or Deputy Managing Directors. The USA, the United Kingdom, Germany, France and Japan each appoint one Executive Director, while the other 19 Executive Directors are elected by groups of the remaining countries. As in the Board of Governors, the voting power of each member is related to its quota in the Fund, but in practice the Executive Directors normally operate by consensus.

The Managing Director of the Fund serves as head of its staff, which is organized into departments by function and area. At 30 April 1997 the Fund staff comprised 1,999 people from 121 countries. In mid-1994 two new positions of Deputy Managing Director were created, bringing the total to three. This major structural development was approved by the Executive Board and reflected the increase in reponsibilities of that position, owing to the IMF's greatly enlarged membership.

Activities

The purposes of the IMF, as defined in the Articles of Agreement, are:

(i) To promote international monetary co-operation through a permanent institution which provides the machinery for consultation and collaboration on monetary problems.

(ii) To facilitate the expansion and balanced growth of international trade, and to contribute thereby to the promotion and maintenance of high levels of employment and real income and to the development of members' productive resources.

(iii) To promote exchange stability, to maintain orderly exchange arrangements among members, and to avoid competitive exchange depreciation.

(iv) To assist in the establishment of a multilateral system of payments in respect of current transactions between members and in the elimination of foreign exchange restrictions which hamper the growth of trade.

(v) To give confidence to members by making the general resources of the Fund temporarily available to them, under adequate safeguards, thus providing them with the opportunity to correct maladjustments in their balance of payments, without resorting to measures destructive of national or international prosperity.

(vi) In accordance with the above, to shorten the duration of and lessen the degree of disequilibrium in the international balances of payments of members.

In joining the Fund, each country agrees to co-operate with the above objectives. Under Article IV of the Articles of Agreement, the Fund monitors members' compliance by holding an annual consultation with each country, in order to survey the country's exchange rate policies and determine its need for assistance.

In accordance with its objective of facilitating the expansion of international trade, the IMF encourages its members to accept the obligations of Article VIII, Sections two, three and four, of the Articles of Agreement. Members that accept Article VIII undertake to refrain from imposing restrictions on the making of payments and transfers for current international transactions and from engaging in discriminatory currency arrangements or multiple currency practices without IMF approval. By October 1997 141 members had accepted Article VIII status.

In October 1995 the Interim Committee of the Board of Governors endorsed recent decisions of the Executive Board to strengthen IMF financial support to members requiring exceptional assistance. An emergency financing mechanism was to be introduced to enable the IMF to respond to potential or actual financial crises, while additional funds were to be available for short-term currency stabilization. Emergency assistance was to be available to countries in a post-conflict situation, to facilitate the rehabilitation of their economics and to improve their eligibility for further IMF concessionary arrangements.

In December 1996 the IMF and the World Trade Organization (q.v.) signed a co-operation agreement which provided for increased consultation and exchanges of information and data between the two organizations, and granted each organization observer status at certain of the other's decision-making bodies. In April 1997 the Interim Committee of the Board of Governors endorsed proposals to amend the Articles of Agreement to include the promotion of capital-account liberalization as a specific objective of the IMF and to extend the Fund's mandate to cover capital movements.

SURVEILLANCE

Under its Articles of Agreement, the Fund is mandated to oversee the effective functioning of the international monetary system and to review the policies of individual member countries to ensure the stability of the exchange rate system. The Fund's main tools of surveillance are regular consultations, conducted by IMF staff with officials from member countries, and World Economic Outlook discussions, held, normally twice a year, by the Executive Board to assess policy implications from a multilateral perspective and to monitor global developments. Following a rapid decline in the value of the Mexican peso in late 1994 and the ensuing financial crisis in that country, the IMF resolved to strengthen its surveillance activities. During 1995/96 these efforts focused on measures to ensure more continuous surveillance, to strengthen the focus of surveillance, in particular on countries or regions deemed to be at risk, and to encourage the full and timely provision of data by member countries. With respect to the latter objective, in April 1996 the IMF established the Special Data Dissemination Standard, which was intended to improve access to reliable economic statistical information for member countries that have, or are seeking, access to international capital markets. By 31 July 1997 42 countries had subscribed to the Standard. In March 1997 the Executive Board agreed to develop a General Data Dissemination System, to encourage all member countries to improve the production and dissemination of core economic data. In April 1997, in an effort to improve the value of surveillance by means of increased transparency, the Executive Board agreed to the voluntary issue of Press Information Notices, following each member's Article IV consultation with the Board, to those member countries wishing to make public the Fund's views.

SPECIAL DRAWING RIGHTS

The special drawing right (SDR) was introduced in 1970 as a substitute for gold in international payments. It was intended eventually to become the principal reserve asset in the international monetary system, although by 1997 this appeared unlikely to happen. SDRs are allocated to members in proportion to their quotas. The IMF has allocated a total of SDR 21,433m. since the SDR was created in 1970. At the end of April 1997 holdings of SDRs by member countries amounted to 1.7% of their cumulative allocations of SDRs and their total non-gold reserves. In October 1996 the Executive Board agreed to a new allocation of SDRs in order to achieve their equitable distribution among member states (i.e. all members would have an equal number of SDRs relative to the size of their quotas). In particular, this was deemed necessary since 38 countries that had joined the Fund since the last allocation of SDRs in 1981 had not yet received any of the units of account. In September 1997 at the annual meeting of the Executive Board, a resolution approving a special allocation of SDR 21,400m. was passed, in order to ensure an SDR to quota ratio of 29.32%, for all member countries. The resolution was to come into effect following its acceptance by 60% of member countries, having 85% of the total voting power.

From 1974 to 1980 the SDR was valued on the basis of the market exchange rate for a basket of 16 currencies, belonging to the members with the largest exports of goods and services; since 1981 it has been based on the currencies of the five largest exporters (France, Germany, Japan, the United Kingdom and the USA), although the list of currencies and the weight of each in the SDR valuation basket is revised every five years. A new valuation basket came into effect on 1 January 1996. The value of the SDR averaged US $1.45176 during 1996, and at 30 September 1997 stood at $1.36521.

The Second Amendment to the Articles of Agreement (1978) altered and expanded the possible uses of the SDR in transactions with other participants. These 'prescribed holders' of the SDRs have the same degree of freedom as Fund members to buy and sell SDRs and to receive or use them in loans, pledges, swaps, donations or settlement of financial obligations. In 1996/97 there were 15 'prescribed holders': the African Development Bank and the African Development Fund, the Arab Monetary Fund, the Asian Development Bank, the Bank of Central African States, the Bank for International Settlements, the Central Bank of West African States, the East African Development Bank, the Eastern Caribbean Central Bank, the International Bank for Reconstruction and Development and the International Development Association, the International Fund for Agricultural Development, the Islamic Development Bank, the Latin American Reserve Fund and the Nordic Investment Bank.

QUOTAS

Each member is assigned a quota related to its national income, monetary reserves, trade balance and other economic indicators. A member's subscription is equal to its quota and is payable partly in SDRs and partly in its own currency. The quota determines a member's voting power, which is based on one vote for each SDR 100,000 of its quota *plus* the 250 votes to which each member is entitled. A member's quota also determines its access to the financial resources of the IMF, and its allocation of SDRs.

Quotas are reviewed at intervals of not more than five years, to take into account the state of the world economy and members' different rates of development. General increases were made in 1959, 1966, 1970, 1978, 1980 and 1984, while special increases were made for the People's Republic of China in April 1980, for a group of 11 members in December 1980, and for Saudi Arabia in April 1981. In June 1990 the Board of Governors authorized proposals for a Ninth General Review of quotas. Total quotas were to be increased by roughly 50% (depending on various factors). At the same time the Board of Governors stipulated that the quota increase could occur only after the Third Amendment of the IMF's Articles of Agreement had come into effect. The amendment provides for the suspension of voting and other related rights of members that do not fulfil their obligations under the Articles. By September 1992 the necessary proportion of IMF members had accepted the amendment, and it entered into force on 11 November. The adoption of the Third Amendment permitted each member that had consented to its quota increase to make it effective by paying the necessary amount within 30 days. By 1 August 1997 total quotas in the Fund amounted to SDR 145,318.8m. (see table on pp. 84–85). The Tenth General Review of quotas was concluded in December 1994, with the Board recommending no further increase in quotas. However, the Board resolved to monitor closely the Fund's liquidity. In October 1995 the Interim Committee of the Board of Governors requested the Executive Board to proceed with the Eleventh General Review, which was to be completed by March 1998. In October 1996 the Fund's Managing Director advocated an increase in quotas under the latest review of at least two-thirds in the light of the IMF's reduced liquidity position. (The IMF had extended unprecedentedly large amounts in stand-by arrangements during the period 1995–96, notably to Mexico and Russia.) In February 1998 the Board of Governors adopted a resolution proposing an increase in quotas of 45%, subject to approval by member states constituting 85% of total quotas.

RESOURCES

Members' subscriptions form the basic resource of the IMF. They are supplemented by borrowing. Under the General Arrangements to Borrow (GAB), established in 1962, the 'Group of Ten' industrialized nations (G-10—Belgium, Canada, France, Germany, Italy, Japan, the Netherlands, Sweden, the United Kingdom and the USA) and Switzerland (which became a member of the IMF in May 1992 but which had been a full participant in the GAB from April 1984) undertake to lend the Fund as much as SDR 17,000m. in their own currencies, to assist in fulfilling the balance-of-payments requirements of any member of the group, or in response to requests to the Fund from countries with balance-of-payments problems that could threaten the stability of the international monetary system. In 1983 the Fund entered into an agreement with Saudi Arabia, in association with the GAB, making available SDR 1,500m., and other borrowing arrangements were completed in 1984 with the Bank for International Settlements, the Saudi Arabian Monetary Agency, Belgium and Japan, making available a further SDR 6,000m. In 1986 another borrowing arrangement with Japan made available SDR 3,000m. In May 1996 GAB participants concluded an agreement in principle to expand the resources available for borrowing to SDR 34,000m., by securing the support of 25 countries with the financial capacity to support the international monetary system. The so-called New Arrangements to Borrow (NAB) was approved by the Executive Board in January 1997. It was to enter into force, for an initial five-year period, as soon as the five largest potential creditors participating in NAB had approved the initiative and the total credit arrangement of participants endorsing the scheme had

BOARD OF EXECUTIVE DIRECTORS (October 1997)

Director	Casting Votes of	Total Votes	%
Appointed:			
KARIN LISSAKERS	USA	265,518	17.78
BERND ESDAR	Germany	82,665	5.54
YUKIO YOSHIMURA	Japan	82,665	5.54
MARC-ANTOINE AUTHEMAN	France	74,396	4.98
AUGUSTINE (GUS) O'DONNELL	United Kingdom	74,396	4.98
Elected:			
WILLY KIEKENS (Belgium)	Austria, Belarus, Belgium, Czech Republic, Hungary, Kazakhstan, Luxembourg, Slovakia, Slovenia, Turkey	75,983	5.09
J. DE BEAUFORT WIJNHOLDS (Netherlands)	Armenia, Bosnia and Herzegovina, Bulgaria, Croatia, Cyprus, Georgia, Israel, the former Yugoslav republic of Macedonia, Moldova, Netherlands, Romania, Ukraine	74,276	4.97
JUAN JOSÉ TORIBIO (Spain)	Costa Rica, El Salvador, Guatemala, Honduras, Mexico, Nicaragua, Spain, Venezuela	64,295	4.31
ENZO R. GRILLI (Italy)	Albania, Greece, Italy, Malta, Portugal, San Marino	59,987	4.02
THOMAS A. BERNES (Canada)	Antigua and Barbuda, Bahamas, Barbados, Belize, Canada, Dominica, Grenada, Ireland, Jamaica, Saint Christopher and Nevis, Saint Lucia, Saint Vincent and the Grenadines	55,500	3.72
EVA SREJBER (Sweden)	Denmark, Estonia, Finland, Iceland, Latvia, Lithuania, Norway, Sweden	51,771	3.47
ABDULRAHMAN A. AL-TUWAIJRI	Saudi Arabia	51,556	3.45
DINAH Z. GUTI (Zimbabwe)	Angola, Botswana, Burundi, Eritrea, Ethiopia, The Gambia, Kenya, Lesotho, Liberia, Malawi, Mozambique, Namibia, Nigeria, Sierra Leone, South Africa, Swaziland, Tanzania, Uganda, Zambia, Zimbabwe	51,292	3.43
GREGORY F. TAYLOR (Australia)	Australia, Kiribati, Republic of Korea, Marshall Islands, Federated States of Micronesia, Mongolia, New Zealand, Papua New Guinea, Philippines, Samoa, Seychelles, Solomon Islands, Vanuatu	49,182	3.29
A. SHAKOUR SHAALAN (Egypt)	Bahrain, Egypt, Iraq, Jordan, Kuwait, Lebanon, Libya, Maldives, Oman, Qatar, Syria, United Arab Emirates, Yemen	47,646	3.19
ZAMANI ABDUL GHANI (Malaysia)	Brunei, Cambodia, Fiji, Indonesia, Laos, Malaysia, Myanmar, Nepal, Singapore, Thailand, Tonga, Viet Nam	43,505	2.91
ALEKSEI V. MOZHIN	Russia	43,381	2.90
DANIEL KAESER (Switzerland)	Azerbaijan, Kyrgyzstan, Poland, Switzerland, Tajikistan, Turkmenistan, Uzbekistan	41,229	2.76
ABBAS MIRAKHOR (Iran)	Afghanistan, Algeria, Ghana, Iran, Morocco, Pakistan, Tunisia	39,542	2.65
ALEXANDRE KAFKA (Brazil)	Brazil, Colombia, Dominican Republic, Ecuador, Guyana, Haiti, Panama, Suriname, Trinidad and Tobago	39,270	2.63
M. R. SIVARAMAN (India)	Bangladesh, Bhutan, India, Sri Lanka	38,561	2.58
ZHANG ZHIXIANG	People's Republic of China	34,102	2.28
A. GUILLERMO ZOCCALI (Argentina)	Argentina, Bolivia, Chile, Paraguay, Peru, Uruguay	31,985	2.14
KOFFI YAO (Côte d'Ivoire)	Benin, Burkina Faso, Cameroon, Cape Verde, Central African Republic, Chad, Comoros, Congo, Côte d'Ivoire, Djibouti, Equatorial Guinea, Gabon, Guinea, Guinea-Bissau, Madagascar, Mali, Mauritania, Mauritius, Niger, Rwanda, São Tomé and Príncipe, Senegal, Togo	19,936	1.34

Note: At 1 August 1997 member countries' votes totalled 1,493,331, while votes in the Board of Executive Directors totalled 1,492,639. The latter total does not include the votes of Somalia, which did not participate in the 1996 election of Executive Directors; it also excludes the votes of the Democratic Republic of the Congo and Sudan, whose voting rights were suspended with effect from 2 June 1994 and 9 August 1993 respectively.

reached at least SDR 28,900m. While the GAB credit arrangement was to remain in effect, the NAB was expected to be the first facility to be activated in the event of the Fund's requiring supplementary resources.

DRAWING ARRANGEMENTS

Exchange transactions within the Fund take the form of members' purchases (i.e. drawings) from the Fund of the currencies of other members for the equivalent amounts of their own currencies. Fund resources are available to eligible members on an essentially short-term and revolving basis to provide members with temporary assistance to contribute to the solution of their payments problems. Before making a purchase, a member must show that its balance of payments or reserve position makes the purchase necessary. Apart from this requirement, reserve tranche purchases (i.e. purchases that do not bring the Fund's holdings of the member's currency to a level above its quota) are permitted unconditionally.

With further purchases, however, the Fund's policy of 'conditionality' means that a member requesting assistance must agree to adjust its economic policies, as stipulated by the IMF. All requests other than for use of the reserve tranche are examined by the Executive Board to determine whether the proposed use would be consistent with the Fund's policies, and a member must discuss its proposed adjustment programme (including fiscal, monetary, exchange and trade policies) with IMF staff. Purchases outside the reserve tranche are made in four credit tranches, each equivalent to 25% of the member's quota; a member must reverse the transaction by repurchasing its own currency (with SDRs or currencies specified by the Fund) within a specified time. A credit tranche purchase is usually made under a 'stand-by arrangement' with the Fund, or under the extended Fund facility. A stand-by arrangement is normally of one or two years' duration, and the amount is made available in instalments, subject to the member's observance of 'performance criteria'; repurchases must be made within three-and-a-quarter to five years. An extended arrangement is normally of three years' duration, and the member must submit detailed economic programmes and progress reports for each year; repurchases must be made within four-and-a-half to 10 years. A member whose payments imbalance is large in relation to its quota may make use of temporary facilities established by the Fund using borrowed resources, namely the 'enlarged access policy' established in 1981, which helps to finance stand-by and extended arrangements for such a member, up to a limit of between 90% and 110% of the member's quota annually. Repurchases are made within three-and-a-half to seven years. In October 1994 the Executive Board approved a temporary increase in members' access to IMF resources, on the basis of a recommendation by the Interim Committee. The annual access limit under IMF regular tranche drawings, stand-by arrangements and extended Fund facility credits was increased from 68% to 100% of a member's quota. In exceptional circumstances the access limit may be extended. This was the case in August 1997, when Thailand, following a financial crisis, purchased US $3,900m. under a stand-by arrangement, the second largest single purchase in the Fund's history, which amounted to more than 400% of that country's quota.

In addition, there are special-purpose arrangements, all of which are subject to the member's co-operation with the Fund to find an appropriate solution to its difficulties. The buffer stock financing facility (BSFF) was established in 1969 in order to enable members to pay their contributions to the buffer stocks which were intended to stabilize markets for primary commodities. The BSFF has not been used since 1984. In 1988 the Fund established the compensatory and contingency financing facility (CCFF), which replaced and expanded the former compensatory financing facility. The CCFF provides compensation to members whose export earnings are reduced as a result of circumstances beyond their control, or which are affected by excess costs of cereal imports. Contingency financing is provided to help members to maintain their efforts at economic adjustment even when affected by a sharp increase in interest rates or other externally-derived difficulties. Repurchases are made within three-and-a-quarter to five years.

In 1986 the Fund established a structural adjustment facility (SAF) to provide balance-of-payments assistance on concessionary terms to low-income developing countries. In November 1993 the Executive Board agreed that no new commitments would be made under the SAF. In 1987 the Fund established an enhanced structural adjustment facility (ESAF), which was to provide new resources of SDR 6,000m. (in addition to any amounts remaining undisbursed under the SAF), to assist the adjustment efforts of, in particular, heavily-indebted countries. Eligible members must develop a three-year adjustment programme (with assistance given jointly by staff of the Fund and of the World Bank) to strengthen the balance-of-payments situation and foster sustainable economic growth. Maximum access is set at 190% (255% in exceptional circumstances) of the member's quota. ESAF loans carry an interest rate of 0.5% per year and are repayable within 10 years, including a five-and-a-half-year grace period. In July 1992 the Executive Board decided to extend the deadline for commitments of resources under new ESAF arrangements by one year to the end of November 1993. In April 1993 the Board began examining the modalities and funding alternatives for a successor facility to the ESAF. In November 1993 the Executive Board determined to enlarge the ESAF Trust (the funding source for ESAF arrangements), as part of the process of extending the facility, by transferring the bulk of resources from the Special Disbursement Account (SDA) of the SAF. The enlarged ESAF came into effect on 23 February 1994, when the Executive Board accepted that sufficient contributions had been committed to the Loan and Subsidy Accounts of the ESAF Trust. The terms and conditions of the new Trust facility remained the same as those under the original ESAF, although the list of countries eligible for assistance was enlarged by six to 78. In January 1995 Eritrea became the 79th member eligible to receive assistance under the ESAF. The commitment period for lending from the ESAF Trust expired on 31 December 1996, with disbursements to be made through to the end of 1999. In September 1996 the Interim Committee of the Board of Governors endorsed measures to finance the ESAF for a further five-year (2000–2004) period, after which the facility was to become self-sustaining. The interim period of the ESAF was to be funded mainly from bilateral contributions, but drawing on the Fund's additional resources as necessary. The ESAF was to support, through long-maturity loans and grants, IMF participation in a joint initiative, with the World Bank, to provide exceptional assistance to heavily-indebted poor countries (HIPCs), in order to help them to achieve a sustainable level of debt management. The initiative was formally approved at the September 1996 meeting of the Interim Committee, having received the support of the 'Paris Club' of official creditors—which agreed to increase the relief on official debt from 67% to 80%. In February 1997 the Executive Board established an ESAF-HIPC Trust, through which the IMF was to channel resources for the HIPC initiative and interim ESAF operations. In all, 41 HIPCs were identified, 33 of which were in sub-Saharan Africa. In April 1997 Uganda was approved as the first beneficiary of the initiative (see World Bank, p. 67). The Fund was to provide assistance worth US $70m. in April 1998, on the condition that other official creditors contributed their agreed proportion of debt relief and that Uganda pursued a programme of economic and social policy reform. In September 1997 assistance was approved for Bolivia and Burkina Faso under the HIPC initiative. Assistance was approved for Guyana in December 1997, while Côte d'Ivoire and Mozambique underwent preliminary consideration in the same year. In June 1996 the management of the Fund had proposed that revenue for the debt-relief initiative could be raised by the sale of about 5% of the IMF's gold reserves (the proceeds from the sale would be reinvested and the interest arising from the new investment used for the initiative). However, some industrialized countries, notably Germany, Switzerland and Italy, threatened to obstruct such a sale, and a decision on the plan was postponed.

At 30 April 1997 35 ESAF arrangements were in effect, with commitments amounting to SDR 4,048m. In 1996/97 ESAF disbursements amounted to SDR 705m., while cumulative disbursements to the end of April 1997 totalled SDR 7,172m.

In April 1993 the Fund established the systemic transformation facility (STF) to assist countries of the former USSR and other economies in transition. The STF was intended to be a temporary facility to enable member countries to draw on financial assistance for balance-of-payments difficulties resulting from severe disruption of their normal trade and payments arrangements. Access to the facility was limited to not more than 50% of a member's quota, and repayment terms were equal to those for the extended Fund facility. The expiry date for access to resources under this facility was extended by one year from 31 December 1994, to the end of 1995. During the STF's period of operations purchases amounting to SDR 3,984m. were made by 20 countries, of which SDR 136m. was purchased in 1995/96.

During 1996/97 the IMF made total commitments of SDR 5,287m., which represented a significant reduction in demand for IMF resources when compared with the high levels of commitment that had characterized the previous two financial years. In 1995/96 commitments amounted to SDR 19,684m., the largest amount ever to be committed by the Fund in a single financial year, while commitments in 1994/95 totalled SDR 16,587m.; the Fund's substantial commitments resulted from the approval of exceptional arrangements, in particular for Mexico and Russia. In late 1997, however, the crisis affecting a number of east Asian economies led to the approval of large credit disbursements to countries including Thailand, Indonesia and South Korea, signalling a return to the unprecedented levels of commitment of previous years. Of the total amount in 1996/97, SDR 3,183m. was committed under 11 stand-by arrangements, SDR 1,193m. under five extended arrangements, and SDR 911m. under 12 ESAF arrangements. Overdue financial obligations to the Fund amounted to SDR 2,212m. at 30 April 1997. In December 1997 the Executive Board approved a Supplemental Reserve Facility to provide short-term assistance to countries experiencing balance-of-payments difficulties.

TECHNICAL ASSISTANCE

This is provided by special missions or resident representatives who advise members on every aspect of economic management. Specialized technical assistance is provided by the IMF's various departments, in particular the Fiscal Affairs Department (which in 1996/97 conducted expert assignments in 101 countries, including assistance in the West Bank and Gaza Strip and in Rwanda), the Monetary and Exchange Affairs Department (which undertook 120 advisory missions, 405 short-term expert assignments and 17 technical workshops) the Statistics Department (which conducted 140 technical assistance missions to 78 countries) and the Legal Department (which advised 44 member countries during 1995/96, particularly those with economies in transition seeking to establish a new legal framework). The IMF Institute, founded in 1964, trains officials from member countries in financial analysis and policy, balance-of-payments methodology and public finance: it also gives assistance to national and regional training centres. The IMF is co-sponsor of the Joint Vienna Institute, which was opened in the Austrian capital in October 1992 and which trains officials from former centrally-planned economies in various aspects of economic management and public administration. During 1996/97 a total of 1,182 people attended training courses or seminars at the IMF Institute or the Joint Vienna Institute, while some 1,110 senior officials participated in overseas training courses. In 1997 the IMF announced plans to establish a training institute in Singapore, in collaboration with the Singaporean Government, in order to provide training for officials from the Asia-Pacific region. The IMF-Singapore Training Institute was expected to open in May 1998.

PUBLICATIONS

Annual Report.

Balance of Payments Statistics Yearbook.

Direction of Trade Statistics (quarterly and annually).

Finance and Development (quarterly, published jointly with the World Bank).

Government Finance Statistics Yearbook.

IMF Survey (2 a month).

International Financial Statistics (monthly and annually).

Staff Papers (4 a year).

World Economic Outlook (2 a year).

Economic Issues.

Occasional papers, economic reviews, pamphlets, booklets.

Statistics

QUOTAS (SDR million)

	August 1997
Afghanistan	120.4
Albania	35.3
Algeria	914.4
Angola	207.3
Antigua and Barbuda	8.5
Argentina	1,537.1
Armenia	67.5
Australia	2,333.2
Austria	1,188.3
Azerbaijan	117.0
Bahamas	94.9
Bahrain	82.8
Bangladesh	392.5
Barbados	48.9
Belarus	280.4
Belgium	3,102.3
Belize	13.5
Benin	45.3
Bhutan	4.5
Bolivia	126.2
Bosnia and Herzegovina	121.2
Botswana	36.6
Brazil	2,170.8
Brunei	150.0
Bulgaria	464.9
Burkina Faso	44.2
Burundi	57.2
Cambodia*	65.0
Cameroon	135.1
Canada	4,320.3
Cape Verde	7.0
Central African Republic	41.2
Chad	41.3
Chile	621.7
China, People's Republic	3,385.2
Colombia	561.3
Comoros	6.5
Congo, Democratic Republic†	(394.8) 291.0
Congo, Republic	57.9
Costa Rica	119.0
Côte d'Ivoire	238.2
Croatia	261.6
Cyprus	100.0
Czech Republic	589.6
Denmark	1,069.9
Djibouti	11.5
Dominica	6.0
Dominican Republic	158.8
Ecuador	219.2
Egypt	678.4
El Salvador	125.6
Equatorial Guinea	24.3
Eritrea	11.5
Estonia	46.5
Ethiopia	98.3
Fiji	51.1
Finland	861.8
France	7,414.6
Gabon	110.3
The Gambia	22.9
Georgia	111.0
Germany	8,241.5
Ghana	274.0
Greece	587.6
Grenada	8.5
Guatemala	153.8
Guinea	78.7
Guinea-Bissau	10.5
Guyana	67.2
Haiti	60.7
Honduras	95.0
Hungary	754.8
Iceland	85.3
India	3,055.5
Indonesia	1,497.6
Iran	1,078.5
Iraq†	(864.8) 504.0
Ireland	525.0
Israel	666.2
Italy	4,590.7
Jamaica	200.9

— *continued*

	August 1997
Japan	8,241.5
Jordan	121.7
Kazakhstan	247.5
Kenya	199.4
Kiribati	4.0
Korea, Republic	799.6
Kuwait	995.2
Kyrgyzstan	64.5
Laos	39.1
Latvia	91.5
Lebanon	146.0
Lesotho	23.9
Liberia†	(96.2) 71.3
Libya	817.6
Lithuania	103.5
Luxembourg	135.5
Macedonia, former Yugoslav republic	49.6
Madagascar	90.4
Malawi	50.9
Malaysia	832.7
Maldives	5.5
Mali	68.9
Malta	67.5
Marshall Islands	2.5
Mauritania	47.5
Mauritius	73.3
Mexico	1,753.3
Micronesia, Federated States	3.5
Moldova	90.0
Mongolia	37.1
Morocco	427.7
Mozambique	84.0
Myanmar	184.9
Namibia	99.6
Nepal	52.0
Netherlands	3,444.2
New Zealand	650.1
Nicaragua	96.1
Niger	48.3
Nigeria	1,281.6
Norway	1,104.6
Oman	119.4
Pakistan	758.2
Panama	149.6
Papua New Guinea	95.3
Paraguay	72.1
Peru	466.1
Philippines	633.4
Poland	988.5
Portugal	557.6
Qatar	190.5
Romania	754.1
Russia	4,313.1
Rwanda	59.5
Saint Christopher and Nevis	6.5
Saint Lucia	11.0
Saint Vincent and the Grenadines	6.0
Samoa	8.5
San Marino	10.0
São Tomé and Príncipe	5.5
Saudi Arabia	5,130.6
Senegal	118.9
Seychelles	6.0
Sierra Leone	77.2
Singapore	357.6
Slovakia	257.4
Slovenia	150.5
Solomon Islands	7.5
Somalia†	(60.9) 44.2
South Africa	1,365.4
Spain	1,935.4
Sri Lanka	303.6
Sudan†	(233.1) 169.7
Suriname	67.6
Swaziland	36.5
Sweden	1,614.0
Switzerland	2,470.4
Syria	209.9
Tajikistan	60.0
Tanzania	146.9
Thailand	573.9
Togo	54.3
Tonga	5.0
Trinidad and Tobago	246.8

— *continued*	August 1997
Tunisia	206.0
Turkey	642.0
Turkmenistan	48.0
Uganda	133.9
Ukraine	997.3
United Arab Emirates	392.1
United Kingdom	7,414.6
USA	26,526.8
Uruguay	225.3
Uzbekistan	199.5
Vanuatu	12.5
Venezuela	1,951.3
Viet Nam	241.6
Yemen	176.5
Zambia	363.5
Zimbabwe	261.3

* Cambodia did not participate in the Ninth General Review of quotas. In March 1994 the Board of Governors approved an ad hoc increase in Cambodia's quota.
† As of 1 August 1997 these members had not yet paid for their quota increases under the Ninth General Review. The quotas listed are those determined under the Eighth General Review, and the figures in parentheses are the proposed Ninth Review quotas.

FINANCIAL ACTIVITIES (SDR million, year ending 30 April)

Type of Transaction	1992	1993	1994	1995	1996	1997
Total disbursements	5,903	5,877	5,903	11,178	12,303	5,644
Purchases by facility (General Resources Account)*	5,294	5,284	5,241	10,592	10,826	4,939
Stand-by and first credit tranche	2,343	2,940	1,052	7,587	9,127	1,836
Compensatory and contingency financing facility	1,381	90	718	287	9	282
Extended Fund facility	1,571	2,254	746	1,595	1,554	2,820
Systemic transformation facility	—	—	2,725	1,123	136	—
Loans under SAF/ESAF arrangements	608	593	662	587	1,477	705
Special Disbursement Account resources	138	49	68	19	185	—
ESAF Trust resources	470	544	594	568	1,292	705
By region: developing countries	5,903	5,877	5,903	11,178	12,303	5,644
Africa	740	377	1,185	1,022	2,304	992
Asia	1,476	1,806	690	383	367	181
Europe	1,516	1,343	3,258	2,896	5,156	3,381
Middle East	333	26	11	76	129	153
Western Hemisphere	1,838	2,325	758	6,801	4,427	937
Repurchases and repayments	4,770	4,117	4,509	4,231	7,100	7,196
Repurchases	4,768	4,081	4,343	3,984	6,698	6,668
Trust Fund and SAF/ESAF loan repayments	2	36	166	247	402	528
Total outstanding credit provided by Fund (end of year)	26,736	28,496	29,889	36,837	42,040	40,488
Of which:						
General Resources Account	23,432	24,635	25,533	32,140	36,268	34,539
Special Disbursement Account	1,865	1,879	1,835	1,651	1,545	1,220
Administered Accounts						
Trust Fund	158	158	105	102	95	90
ESAF Trust†	1,281	1,824	2,416	2,944	4,132	4,639

* Excluding reserve tranche purchases.
† Including Saudi Fund for Development associated loans.
Source: *International Monetary Fund Annual Report 1997.*

International Telecommunication Union—ITU

Address: Place des Nations, 1211 Geneva 20, Switzerland.
Telephone: (22) 7305111; **telex:** 421000; **fax:** (22) 7337256; **e-mail:** itumail@itu.int; **internet:** http://www.itu.int.

Founded in 1865, ITU became a specialized agency of the UN in 1947. It acts to encourage world co-operation in the use of telecommunication, to promote technical development and to harmonize national policies in the field.

MEMBERS

188 member states: see Table on pp. 101–103. A further 363 scientific and technical companies, public and private operators, broadcasters and other organizations are also ITU members.

Organization

(December 1997)

PLENIPOTENTIARY CONFERENCE

The supreme organ of ITU; normally meets every four years. The main tasks of the Conference are to establish policies, revise the Convention (see below) and approve limits on budgetary spending.

In December 1992 an Additional Plenipotentiary Conference was held in Geneva, Switzerland, which agreed on reforms to the structure and functioning of ITU. As a result, ITU comprised three sectors corresponding to its main functions: standardization; radiocommunication; and development. In October 1994 the ordinary Plenipotentiary Conference, held in Kyoto, Japan, adopted ITU's first strategic plan.

WORLD CONFERENCES ON INTERNATIONAL TELECOMMUNICATIONS

The World Conferences on International Telecommunications are held at the request of members and after approval by the Plenipotentiary Conference. The World Conferences are authorized to review and revise the regulations applying to the provision and operation of international telecommunications services. As part of the 1993 restructuring of ITU, separate Conferences were to be held by three sectors (see below): Radiocommunication Conferences (to be held every two years); Telecommunication Standardization Conferences (to be held every four years or at the request of one-quarter of ITU members); and Telecommunication Development Conferences (to be held every four years).

ITU COUNCIL

The Council (previously called the Administrative Council) meets annually in Geneva and is composed of 46 members elected by the Plenipotentiary Conference.

The Council ensures the efficient co-ordination and implementation of the work of the Union in all matters of policy, administration and finance, in the interval between Plenipotentiary Conferences, and approves the annual budget. It also co-ordinates the efforts of ITU to assist developing countries in the improvement of telecommunications equipment and networks.

GENERAL SECRETARIAT

The Secretary-General is elected by the Plenipotentiary Conference, and is responsible to it for the General Secretariat's work, and for the Union's administrative and financial services. The General Secretariat's staff totals about 712, representing 74 nationalities; the working languages are Arabic, Chinese, English, French, Russian and Spanish.

Secretary-General: Dr PEKKA TARJANNE (Finland).

Deputy Secretary-General: HENRY CHASIA (Kenya).

Convention

The International Telecommunication Convention is the definitive convention of the Union, member countries being those that signed it in 1932 or acceded to it later. Since 1932 it has been superseded by new versions adopted at successive Plenipotentiary Conferences. At the Additional Plenipotentiary Conference held in December 1992, in Geneva, Switzerland, a new constitution and convention were signed. They entered into force on 1 July 1994, but the provisions relating to the new structure and functioning of ITU became effective on 1 March 1993. The Constitution contains the fundamental provisions of ITU, whereas the Convention contains other provisions which complement those of the Constitution and which, by their nature, require periodic revision.

The Constitution and Convention establish the purposes and structure of the Union, contain the general provisions relating to telecommunications and special provisions for radio, and deal with relations with the UN and other organizations. Both instruments are further complemented by the administrative regulations listed below.

INTERNATIONAL TELECOMMUNICATIONS REGULATIONS

The International Telecommunications Regulations were adopted in 1988 and entered into force in 1990. They establish the general principles relating to the provision and operation of international telecommunication services offered to the public. They also establish rules applicable to administrations and recognized private operating agencies. Their provisions are applied to both wire and wireless telegraph and telephone communications in so far as the Radio Regulations do not provide otherwise.

RADIO REGULATIONS

The Radio Regulations, which first appeared in 1906, include general rules for the assignment and use of frequencies and the associated orbital positions for space stations. They include a Table of Frequency Allocations (governing the use of radio frequency bands between 9 kHz and 400 GHz) for the various radio services (*inter alia* radio broadcasting, television, radio astronomy, navigation aids, point-to-point service, maritime mobile, amateur).

The 1979 World Administrative Radio Conference undertook a complete revision of the radio spectrum allocation. Partial revisions were also made by subsequent world and regional administrative radio conferences, particularly with reference to space radiocommunications, using satellites.

Activities

On the basis of the structural changes adopted in 1992, and implemented on 1 March 1993, three sectors were created, into which functions that had previously been exercised by various ITU bodies were integrated.

RADIOCOMMUNICATION SECTOR

The role of the sector is to ensure an equitable and efficient use of the radio-frequency spectrum by all radiocommunication services. The Radio Regulations are reviewed and revised by the sector's conferences. The technical work on issues to be considered by conferences is conducted by Radiocommunication Assemblies, on the basis of recommendations made by Study Groups. These groups of experts study technical questions relating to radiocommunications, according to a study programme formulated by the Assemblies. The Assemblies may approve, modify or reject any recommendations of the Study Groups, and are authorized to establish new groups and to abolish others.

The procedural rules used in the application of the Radio Regulations were to be considered by a nine-member Radio Regulations Board, which may also perform duties relating to the allocation and use of frequencies and consider cases of interference.

The administrative work of the sector is the responsibility of the Radiocommunication Bureau, which is headed by an elected Director. The Bureau co-ordinates the work of Study Groups, provides administrative support for the Radio Regulations Board, and works alongside the General Secretariat to prepare conferences and to provide relevant assistance to developing countries. the Director is assisted by an Advisory Group.

Director: ROBERT JONES (Canada).

TELECOMMUNICATION STANDARDIZATION SECTOR

The sector was established to study technical, operational and tariff issues in order to standardize telecommunications throughout the world. The sector's conferences consider draft standards, referred to as Recommendations, which, if approved, establish ITU guidelines to guarantee the effective provision of telecommunication services. According to the priority given to different issues concerning draft standards, the conferences may maintain, establish or abolish Study Groups. Recommendations may be approved outside of the four-year interval between conferences if a Study Group concludes such action to be urgent.

In the period 1989–93 the ITU adopted 379 new telecommunication standards and amended a further 484, on the basis of work by its experts.

Preparations for conferences and other meetings of the sector are made by the Telecommunication Standardization Bureau (ITU-T). It administers the application of conference decisions, as well as relevant provisions of the International Telecommunications Regulations. The ITU-T is headed by an elected Director, who is assisted by an Advisory Group. The Director reports to conferences and to the ITU Council on the activities of the sector.

Director: THEODOR IRMER (Germany).

TELECOMMUNICATION DEVELOPMENT SECTOR

The sector's objectives are to promote the development of telecommunication networks and services in developing countries, to facilitate the transfer of appropriate technologies and the use of resources by preferential credit arrangements, and to provide advice on issues specific to telecommunications. The sector operates as an executing agency for projects under the UN development system or other funding arrangements. During 1988–93 the ITU implemented an average of 180 technical co-operation projects, administered 600 project-related expert missions, and granted some 1,200 study or training fellowships each year. In 1995 the ITU supported the establishment of an independent company, *World Tel*, which aimed to provide funding, technology and management assistance to telecommunications projects in low-income countries. The company's first large-scale project, finalized in 1997, aimed to provide local telephone services in Mexico.

The sector holds conferences regularly to encourage international co-operation in the development of telecommunications, and to determine strategies for development. Conferences consider the result of work undertaken by Study Groups on issues of benefit to developing countries, including development policy, finance, network planning and operation of services. The sector aims to hold one world conference and one regional conference each in Africa, Asia and the Pacific, the Americas, Europe, and the Arab States every four years. The first World Telecommunications Development Conference was held in Buenos Aires, Argentina, in 1994.

The administrative work of the sector is conducted by the Telecommunication Development Bureau, which may also study specific problems presented by a member state. The Director of the Bureau reports to conferences and the ITU Council, and is assisted by an Advisory Board.

Director: AHMED LAOUYANE (Tunisia).

INFORMATION

ITU issues numerous technical and statistical publications (see below) and maintains a library and archives. It also offers the use of an on-line computer-based Telecom information exchange service

(TIES), which provides access to ITU databases, document exchange, and other telecommunication information.

FINANCE

The total budget for the period 1998–99 amounted to 327.6m. Swiss francs.

PUBLICATIONS

List of Publications (2 a year).

Telecommunication Journal (monthly in English, French and Spanish).

World Telecommunication Development Report.

Conventions, statistics, regulations, technical documents and manuals, conference documents.

United Nations Educational, Scientific and Cultural Organization—UNESCO

Address: 7 place de Fontenoy, 75352 Paris, France.

Telephone: 1-45-68-10-00; **telex:** 204461; **fax:** 1-45-67-16-90; **internet:** http://www.unesco.org.

UNESCO was established in 1946 'for the purpose of advancing, through the educational, scientific and cultural relations of the peoples of the world, the objectives of international peace and the common welfare of mankind'.

MEMBERS

186 members, and four associate members: see Table on pp. 101–103.

Organization

(December 1997)

GENERAL CONFERENCE

The supreme governing body of the Organization, the Conference meets in ordinary session once in two years and is composed of representatives of the member states.

EXECUTIVE BOARD

The Board, comprising 58 members, prepares the programme to be submitted to the Conference and supervises its execution; it meets twice or sometimes three times a year.

SECRETARIAT

Director-General: FEDERICO MAYOR (Spain).

Director of the Executive Office: GEORGES MALEMPRÉ (Belgium).

CO-OPERATING BODIES

In accordance with UNESCO's constitution, national Commissions have been set up in most member states. These help to integrate work within the member states and the work of UNESCO.

PRINCIPAL REGIONAL OFFICES

Africa

Regional Office for Education in Africa: 12 ave Roume, BP 3311, Dakar, Senegal; tel. 23-50-82; telex 21735-51410; fax 23-83-93; e-mail uhdak@unesco.org; Dir PIUS A. J. OBANYA.

Regional Office for Science and Technology for Africa: POB 30592, Nairobi, Kenya; tel. (2) 621234; telex 22275; fax (2) 215991; e-mail uhnai@unesco.org; f. 1965 to execute UNESCO's regional science programme, and to assist in the planning and execution of national programmes. Dir Prof. P. B. VITTA.

Arab States

Regional Office for Education in the Arab States: POB 5244, ave Cité Sportive, Beirut, Lebanon; tel. (1) 850013; fax (1) 824854; e-mail uhbei@unesco.org; Dir K. BENSALAH.

Regional Office for Science and Technology in the Arab States: 8 Abdel Rahman Fahmy St, Garden City, Cairo 11511, Egypt; tel. (2) 3543036; telex 93722; fax (2) 3545296; e-mail uhcai@unesco.org; Dir ADNAN SHIHAB-ELDIN.

Asia and the Pacific

Principal Regional Office in Asia and the Pacific: 920 Sukhumvit Rd, POB 967, Prakanong Post Office, Bangkok 10110, Thailand; tel. (2) 391-0879; telex 20591; fax (2) 391-0866; Dir VÍCTOR ORDÓÑEZ.

Regional Office for Book Development in Asia and the Pacific: POB 2034, Islamabad 44000, Pakistan; tel. (51) 813308; telex 5886-54595; fax (51) 825341.

Regional Office for Science and Technology for South and Central Asia: UNESCO House, 8 Poorvi Marg, Vasant Vishar, New Delhi 110 057, India; tel. (11) 677310; telex 3165896; fax (11) 6873351; e-mail uhndl@unesco.org; Dir Prof. M. A. MOEGIADI.

Regional Office for Science and Technology for South-East Asia: UN Building (2nd Floor), Jalan M. H. Thamrin 14, Tromol Pos 1273/JKT, Jakarta 10002, Indonesia; tel. (21) 3141308; telex 61464; fax (21) 3150382; e-mail uhjak@unesco.org; Dir STEPHEN HILL.

Europe and North America

European Centre for Higher Education (CEPES): Palatul Kretulescu, Stirbei Voda 39, 70732 Bucharest, Romania; tel. (1) 6159956; telex 11658; fax (1) 3123567; e-mail uhbuc@unesco.org; Dir LESLEY WILSON (acting).

Regional Office for Science and Technology for Europe: Palazzo Loredan degli Ambasciatori, 1262/A Dorsoduro, 30123 Venice, Italy; tel. (41) 522-5535; telex 410095; fax (41) 528-9995; e-mail uhvni@unesco.org; Dir Dr VLADIMIR KOUZMINOV.

Latin America and the Caribbean

Office of the Caribbean Network of Educational Innovation for Development: POB 423, Bridgetown, Barbados; tel. 4274771; telex 2344; fax 4360094; e-mail uhbri@unesco.org.

Regional Centre for Higher Education in Latin America and the Caribbean (CRESALC): Ave Los Chorros, c/c Calle Aceuducto, Edif. Asovincar, Altos de Sebucan, Apdo 68394, Caracas 1062 A, Venezuela; tel. (2) 286-0721; telex 24642; fax (2) 286-2039; e-mail uhcar@unesco.org; Dir L. YARZABAL.

Regional Office for Culture in Latin America and the Caribbean: Apdo 4158, Havana 4, Cuba; tel. (7) 32-7741; telex 512154; fax (7) 33-3144; e-mail uhldo@unesco.org; Dir GLORIA LÓPEZ MORALES.

Regional Office for Education in Latin America and the Caribbean: Calle Enrique Delpiano 2058, Plaza Pedro de Valdivia, Casilla 3187, Santiago, Chile; tel. (2) 2049032; telex 340258; fax (2) 2091875; e-mail uhstg@unesco.org; Dir J. RIVERO HERRERA.

Regional Office for Science and Technology for Latin America and the Caribbean: Avda Brasil 2697 P. 4, Casilla 859, 11300 Montevideo, Uruguay; tel. 7072023; fax 7072140; e-mail uhmdc@unesco.org.uy; internet http://www.unesco.org.uy; Dir ENRIQUE MARTÍN-DEL-CAMPO.

Activities

UNESCO's activities are funded through a regular budget provided by contributions from member states and extrabudgetary funds from other sources, particularly UNDP, the World Bank, regional banks and other bilateral Funds-in-Trust arrangements. UNESCO co-operates with many other UN agencies and international non-governmental organizations.

In 1994–95 three main groups were identified as high-priority beneficiaries of UNESCO activities: least-developed countries, African member states and women. In addition, special attention was to be given to countries undergoing transition from centrally-planned to market economies, small-island states and countries emerging from conflict situations.

EDUCATION

Since its establishment UNESCO has devoted itself to promoting education in accordance with principles based on democracy and respect for human rights.

In March 1990 UNESCO, with other UN agencies, sponsored the World Conference on Education for All. 'Education for All' was subsequently adopted as a guiding principle of UNESCO's contribution to development. The promotion of access to learning opportunities throughout an individual's life is a priority for UNESCO's

1996–2001 programme of activities. UNESCO aims, initially, to foster basic education for all. The second part of its strategy is to renew and diversify education systems, including updating curricular programmes in secondary education, strengthening science and technology activities and ensuring equal access to education for girls and women. In December 1993 the heads of government of nine highly-populated developing countries (Bangladesh, Brazil, the People's Republic of China, Egypt, India, Indonesia, Mexico, Nigeria and Pakistan), meeting in Delhi, India, agreed to co-operate with the objective of achieving comprehensive primary education for all children and of expanding further learning opportunities for children and adults.

In 1994–95 further efforts were focused on extending educational opportunities and meeting the needs of remote, rural populations, cultural minorities and street children. Within the UN system, UNESCO is responsible for providing technical assistance and educational services within the context of emergency situations. This includes providing education to refugees and displaced persons, as well as assistance for the rehabilitation of national education systems. In Palestine, UNESCO collaborates with UNRWA (q.v.) to assist with the training of teachers, educational planning and rehabilitation of schools.

UNESCO is concerned with improving the quality, relevance and efficiency of higher education. It assists member states in reforming their national systems, organizes high-level conferences for Ministers of Education and other decision-makers, and disseminates research papers. During 1997–98 a series of regional meetings concerned with access to higher education was to be held prior to a world conference on Higher Education, scheduled to be convened in September 1998. The International Institute for Educational Planning and the International Bureau of Education (q.v.) undertake training, research and the exchange of information on aspects of education. A UNESCO Institute for Education, based in Hamburg, Germany, researches literacy activities and the evolution of adult learning systems.

In 1993 UNESCO established an International Commission on Education for the Twenty-First Century. The key elements under consideration were: education and culture; education and citizenship; education and social cohesion; education, work and employment; and education, research and science.

SCIENCE

Within this programme area, UNESCO is concerned with expanding the capacity of science and technologies for sustainable development purposes and ensuring sound environmental practices. In 1994 UNESCO published its first *World Science Report*, to place issues relating to science and technology in a global context. (A second report was published in 1996, and a third was to be published in 1998.)

UNESCO aims to improve the level of university teaching of the basic sciences through training courses, establishing national and regional networks and centres of excellence, and fostering co-operative research. In carrying out its mission, UNESCO relies on partnerships with non-governmental organizations and the world scientific communities. With the International Council of Scientific Unions and the Third World Academy of Sciences, UNESCO operates a short-term fellowship programme in the basic sciences and an exchange programme of visiting lecturers. UNESCO's engineering courses emphasize technology that is environmentally sound and/or that may offer alternative or renewable energy sources. In September 1996 UNESCO initiated a 10-year World Solar Programme, which aimed to promote the application of solar energy and to increase research, development and public awareness of all forms of ecologically-sustainable energy use.

In May 1997 the International Bioethics Committee, a group of specialists who meet under UNESCO auspices, approved a draft version of a Universal Declaration on the Human Genome and Human Rights, in an attempt to provide ethical guide-lines for developments in human genetics. The Declaration identified some 100,000 hereditary genes as 'common heritage', and committed states to promoting the dissemination of relevant scientific knowledge and co-operating in genome research. UNESCO is also sponsoring a joint UN programme on HIV and AIDS (UNAIDS).

UNESCO has over the years established various forms of intergovernmental co-operation concerned with the environmental sciences and research on natural resources, in order to support the recommendations of the June 1992 UN Conference on Environment and Development. The International Geological Correlation Programme, undertaken jointly with the International Union of Geological Sciences, aims to improve and facilitate global research of geological processes. In the context of the International Decade for Natural Disaster Reduction (declared in 1990), UNESCO has conducted scientific studies of natural hazards and means of mitigating their effects and has organized several disaster-related workshops. The International Hydrological Programme considers scientific aspects of water resources assessment and management; and the Intergovernmental Oceanographic Commission (IOC, q.v.) focuses on issues relating to oceans, shorelines and marine resources, in particular the role of the ocean in climate and global systems. The IOC is actively involved in the establishment of a Global Coral Reef Monitoring Network, and in preparations for the 1998 International Year of the Ocean. An initiative on Environment and Development in Coastal Regions and in Small Islands is concerned with ensuring environmentally-sound and sustainable development by strengthening management of the following key areas: freshwater resources; the mitigation of coastline instability; biological diversity; and coastal ecosystem productivity.

UNESCO's Man and the Biosphere Programme supports a world-wide network of biosphere reserves (comprising 337 sites in 85 countries in 1997), which aim to promote environmental conservation and research, education and training in biodiversity and problems of land use (including the fertility of tropical soils and the cultivation of sacred sites). Following the signing of the Convention to Combat Desertification in October 1994, UNESCO initiated an International Programme for Arid Land Crops, based on a network of existing institutions, to assist implementation of the Convention.

International Centre for Theoretical Physics: based in Trieste, Italy, the Centre brings together scientists from the developed and developing countries. With support from the Italian Government, the Centre has been operated jointly by the IAEA and UNESCO since 1970. At the end of 1995 administrative responsibility for the Centre was transferred to UNESCO, although IAEA remained a partner in the operations of the Centre. Each year it offers seminars followed by a research workshop, as well as short topical seminars, training courses, symposia and panels. Independent research is also carried out. The programme concentrates on solid-state physics, high-energy and elementary particle physics, physics of nuclear structure and reactions, applicable mathematics and, to a lesser extent, on physics of the earth and the environment, physics of energy, biophysics, microprocessors and physics of technology; Dir Prof. Miguel A. Virasoro (Argentina).

SOCIAL SCIENCES

UNESCO aims to contribute to the development of social sciences in member states, through co-operation in research, education, training and information exchange. UNESCO's work in this area also focuses on the development of principles such as democracy, pluralism and respect for human rights, as well as the promotion of peace.

In 1994 UNESCO initiated an international social science research programme, the Management of Social Transformations (MOST), to promote capacity-building in social planning at all levels of decision-making. UNESCO sponsors several research fellowships in the social sciences. In other activities UNESCO promotes the rehabilitation of underprivileged urban areas, the research of socio-cultural factors affecting demographic change, and the study of family issues.

UNESCO aims to assist the building and consolidation of peaceful and democratic societies. An international network of institutions and centres involved in research on conflict resolution is being established to support the promotion of peace. Other training, workshop and research activities have been undertaken in countries that have suffered conflict. The Associated Schools Project (comprising some 3,000 institutions in 120 countries at October 1994) has, for more than 40 years, promoted the principles of peace, human rights, democracy and international co-operation through education. An International Youth Clearing House and Information Service (INFOYOUTH) aims to increase and consolidate the information available on the situation of young people in society, and to heighten awareness of their needs, aspirations and potential among public and private decision-makers. UNESCO's programme also focuses on the educational and cultural dimensions of physical education and sport and their capacity to preserve and improve health.

Fundamental to UNESCO's mission is the rejection of all forms of discrimination. It disseminates scientific information aimed at combating racial prejudice, works to improve the status of women and their access to education, and promotes equality between men and women.

CULTURE

UNESCO's culture programme encompasses three broad areas of action: safeguarding, renewing and promoting the common cultural heritage; the study of cultural identities; and the role of culture in development.

UNESCO's World Heritage Programme, inaugurated in 1978, aims to protect historic sites and natural landmarks of outstanding universal significance, in accordance with the 1972 UNESCO Convention Concerning the Protection of the World Cultural and Natural Heritage, by providing financial aid for restoration, technical assistance, training and management planning. By October 1997 the 'World Heritage List' comprised 506 sites in 107 countries: for example, the Great Barrier Reef in Australia, the Galapagos Islands (Ecuador), Chartres Cathedral (France), the Taj Mahal at Agra

(India), Auschwitz concentration camp (Poland), the historic sanctuary of Machu Picchu (Peru), and the Serengeti National Park (Tanzania). In 1992 a World Heritage Centre was established to enable rapid mobilization of international technical assistance for the preservation of cultural sites. In addition, UNESCO supports efforts for the collection and safeguarding of humanity's non-material heritage, including oral traditions, music, dance and medicine. In co-operation with the International Council for Philosophy and Humanistic Studies, UNESCO is compiling a directory of endangered languages.

UNESCO was the leading agency for promoting the UN's World Decade for Cultural Development (1988–97). In the framework of the World Decade, UNESCO launched the Silk Roads Project, as a multi-disciplinary study of the interactions among cultures and civilizations along the routes linking Asia and Europe. Other regional projects undertaken considered the dynamic process of dialogue and exchange in forming cultural identities and promoted creativity and cultural life. UNESCO also established an International Fund for the Promotion of Culture, awarding two annual prizes for music and the promotion of arts.

UNESCO encourages the translation and publication of literary works, publishes albums of art, and produces records, audiovisual programmes and travelling art exhibitions. It supports the development of book publishing and distribution, including the free flow of books and educational material across borders, and the training of editors and managers in publishing. UNESCO is active in preparing and encouraging the enforcement of international legislation on copyright.

In December 1992 UNESCO established the World Commission on Culture and Development, to strengthen links between culture and development and to prepare a report on the issue.

COMMUNICATION, INFORMATION AND INFORMATICS

UNESCO's communications programme comprises three inter-related components concerned with the flow of information: a commitment to ensuring the wide dissemination of information, through the development of communications infrastructures and without impediments to freedom of expression or of the press; promotion of greater access to knowledge through international co-operation in the areas of information, libraries and archives; and efforts to harness informatics for development purposes and strengthen member states' capacities in this field. Within this framework, activities include assistance towards the development of legislation, training programmes and infrastructures for the media in countries where independent and pluralistic media are in the process of emerging; assistance, through professional organizations, in the monitoring of media independence, pluralism and diversity; promotion of exchange programmes and study tours, especially for young communications professionals from the least developed countries and central and eastern Europe; and improving access and opportunities for women in the media. In regions affected by conflict UNESCO supports efforts to establish and maintain an independent media service. This strategy is largely implemented through an International Programme for the Development of Communication (IPDC—see below). In Cambodia, Haiti and Mozambique UNESCO participated in the restructuring of the media in the context of national reconciliation.

In 1994–95 some 67% of UNESCO's communication budget was allocated to strengthening communications activities in developing countries. IPDC provides support to communication and media development projects in the developing world, including the establishment of news agencies and newspapers and training editorial and technical staff. In 1997 IPDC approved assistance worth US $2m. for 36 training and infrastructure projects in an effort to reduce the differences in technical competence between developing and industrialized countries. Since its establishment in 1982 IPDC has provided more than $73m. to finance some 600 projects.

The General Information Programme (PGI), which was established in 1976, provides a focus for UNESCO's activities in the fields of specialized information systems, documentation, libraries and archives. Under PGI, UNESCO aims to facilitate the elaboration of information policies and plans to modernize libraries and archives services; to encourage standardization; to train information specialists; and to establish specialized information networks. The objectives of the programme are accomplished by improving access to scientific literature; the holding of national seminars on information policies; the furthering of pilot projects, and preservation and conservation efforts under the Records and Archives Management Programme (RAMP); and the training of users of library and information services. UNESCO is participating in the reconstruction of the National and University Library in Bosnia and Herzegovina and in several national and regional projects to safeguard documentary heritage. PGI's mandate extends to trends and societal impacts of information technologies. In March 1997 the first International Congress on Ethical, Legal and Societal Aspects of Digital Information (InforEthics) was held in Monte Carlo, Monaco.

UNESCO supports the development of computer networking and the training of informatics specialists, in particular through its Intergovernmental Informatics Programme. The Programme's priorities include training in informatics, software development and research, the modernization of public administration and informatics policies, and the development of regional computer networks.

FINANCE

UNESCO's Regular Programme budget for the two years 1996–97 was US $518.4m., compared with $455.5m. for 1994–95.

PUBLICATIONS

(mostly in English, French and Spanish editions; Arabic, Chinese and Russian versions are also available in many cases)

Copyright Bulletin (quarterly).

International Social Science Journal (quarterly).

Museum International (quarterly).

Nature and Resources (quarterly).

Prospects (quarterly review on education).

UNESCO Courier (monthly, in 32 languages).

UNESCO Sources (monthly).

UNESCO Statistical Yearbook.

World Educational Report (biennial).

World Science Report (biennial).

Books, databases, video and radio documentaries, statistics, scientific maps and atlases.

INTERGOVERNMENTAL COMMITTEE FOR PHYSICAL EDUCATION AND SPORT—ICPES

Address: 7 place de Fontenoy, 75352 Paris, France.

Established by UNESCO in 1978 to serve as a permanent intergovernmental body in the field of physical education and sport.

The Committee is composed of 30 representatives of member states of UNESCO, elected by the General Conference.

Among its many activities aimed at further development of physical education and sport throughout the world, the Committee is responsible for supervising the planning and implementation of UNESCO's programme of activities in physical education and sport, promoting international co-operation in this area and facilitating the adoption and implementation of an International Charter of physical education and sport.

INTERNATIONAL BUREAU OF EDUCATION—IBE

Address: POB 199, 1211 Geneva 20, Switzerland.

Telephone: (22) 7981455; **telex:** 415771; **fax:** (22) 7981486.

Founded in 1925, the IBE became an intergovernmental organization in 1929 and was incorporated into UNESCO in 1969 as an international centre of comparative education. The Bureau provides information on developments and innovations in education; it has a library of 120,000 volumes, with almost 400,000 research reports on microfiche, and provides training courses in computerized documentation and librarianship. It publishes a quarterly review of education and newsletter, in addition to various reference works. The Council of the IBE is composed of representatives of 28 member states of UNESCO, designated by the General Conference. The International Conference on Education is held periodically.

Director: JUAN CARLOS TEDESCO.

INTERNATIONAL INSTITUTE FOR EDUCATIONAL PLANNING—IIEP

Address: 7–9 rue Eugène Delacroix, 75116 Paris, France.

Telephone: 1-45-03-77-00; **telex:** 620074; **fax:** 1-40-72-83-66.

The Institute was established by UNESCO in 1963 to serve as a world centre for advanced training and research in educational planning. Its purpose is to help all member states of UNESCO in their social and economic development efforts, by enlarging the fund of knowledge about educational planning and the supply of competent experts in this field.

Legally and administratively a part of UNESCO, the Institute is autonomous, and its policies and programme are controlled by its own Governing Board, under special statutes voted by the General Conference of UNESCO.

Chairman of Governing Board: LENNART WOHLGEMUTH.

Director: JACQUES HALLAK.

United Nations Industrial Development Organization—UNIDO

Address: Vienna International Centre, POB 300, 1400 Vienna, Austria.

Telephone: (1) 211310; **telex:** 135612; **fax:** (1) 232156; **e-mail:** unido-pinfo@unido.org; **internet:** http://www.unido.org.

UNIDO began operations in 1967, as an autonomous organization within the UN Secretariat, and became a specialized agency of the UN on 1 January 1986. Its objective is to promote and accelerate sustainable industrial development in developing countries. UNIDO aims to contribute to the stability of the global socio-economic system and promote equitable and sustainable industrialization.

MEMBERS

169 members: see Table on pp. 101–103.

Organization

(November 1997)

GENERAL CONFERENCE

The General Conference, which consists of representatives of all member states, meets once every two years. It is the chief policy-making body of the Organization, and reviews UNIDO's policy concepts, strategies on industrial development and budget. The seventh General Conference was held in Vienna, Austria, in December 1997.

INDUSTRIAL DEVELOPMENT BOARD

The Board consists of 53 members elected by the General Conference for a three-year period. It reviews the implementation of the approved work programme, the regular and operational budgets and other General Conference decisions.

PROGRAMME AND BUDGET COMMITTEE

The Committee, consisting of 27 members elected by the General Conference for a two-year term, assists the Industrial Development Board in preparing work programmes and budgets.

SECRETARIAT

The Secretariat comprises the office of the Director-General and six divisions, each headed by a Managing Director: Country Programmes and Funds Mobilization; Research and Publications; Human Resource, Enterprise and Private Sector Development; Industrial Sectors and Environment; Investment and Technology Promotion; and Administration. At September 1997 the Secretariat comprised 810 staff members.

Director-General: CARLOS ALFREDO MAGARIÑOS (Argentina).

FIELD REPRESENTATION

UNIDO field officers work in developing countries, at the level of Country Director, National Director, National Programme Officer and Junior Programme Officer. At September 1997 there were 42 field offices employing 948 staff members.

Activities

In its efforts to promote the advancement and integration of industry, UNIDO provides a global forum for addressing common obstacles to sustainable industrialization, for developing and assessing conventions, codes, norms and regulations, for disseminating new advances, policies and experiences in sustainable industrialization, for establishing international partnerships and networks and for developing comparable statistics and measures to provide criteria for industrial performance. In addition, UNIDO provides a range of services to governments, institutes and enterprises to enhance their capabilities to achieve UNIDO's overall aim of environmentally sustainable and equitable industrial development.

Between 1993 and 1997 UNIDO implemented a major restructuring programme in order to respond to changes in the global economy and industrial development. In December 1995 the General Conference, meeting in Vienna, Austria, approved the following set of development priorities, which formed the basis of a new conceptual and substantive framework for UNIDO activities:

(i) Promotion of economic co-operation between both developing and industrialized countries;
(ii) Dissemination of environmentally sustainable and energy-efficient industrial growth;
(iii) Development of small and medium-sized enterprises (SMEs);
(iv) Growth of global industrial competitiveness;
(v) Dissemination of new technologies;
(vi) Industrial development in rural areas;
(vii) Promotion of agro-industry in least-developed countries.

In 1996, as a result of the reforms, full or partial funding was secured for five new programmes focusing on: the formulation of industrial policies and strategies to encourage competitiveness; the establishment of international networks to promote the growth of SMEs; quality-control methods in food processing in sub-Saharan Africa; new techniques for mining and refining gold to prevent both environmental mercury pollution and the toxic metal pollution of water supplies in Africa; and the development of women's business skills.

The Conference agreed that special attention was to be given to the industrialization of developing countries in Africa, and in October 1996 UNIDO formally inaugurated the Alliance for Africa's Industrialization, which constituted the industrial sector element of the UN system-wide special initiative on Africa. The programme was to promote development of the continent's natural resources, strengthen labour resources and build government capacities in order to exploit new global markets, in particular in the agro-industrial sector.

In 1996 UNIDO implemented a number of normative activities that aimed to assist the industrial sector in developing countries and in countries with economies in transition to compete for international business. Some of the activities undertaken were: co-operation with the International Organization for Standardization to establish internationally-recognized accreditation bodies in developing countries; the construction of a UNIDO Industrial Development Index to measure industrial development on the basis of various indicators; the preparation of UNIDO guide-lines for the classification and certification of industrial science and technology parks; and the assessment of industrial performance through the use of existing technological, environmental and social parameters.

Since 1993 much of UNIDO's assistance to governments, agencies and private industrial institutions has aimed at developing a strong private sector. The percentage of UNIDO's private-sector counterparts doubled between 1993 and 1996 to reach some 50%, while technical co-operation projects involving the private sector accounted for some 80% of all projects undertaken in 1996. UNIDO also works with the private sector in an advisory and co-operative function. In 1996 UNIDO launched the International Business Advisory Council (IBAC), composed of international industrialists whose role it is to advise UNIDO on means of approaching industrialization and promoting awareness of the Organization's work. In the same year UNIDO undertook an initiative to establish National Industrial Business Councils in 12 developing countries. The Councils aim to assist UNIDO in developing and funding joint programmes with the private sector and in recognizing industrial business achievements through the use of international standards and conventions.

UNIDO provides advice to governmental agencies and industrial institutions to improve the management of human resources. The Organization also undertakes training projects to develop human resources in specific industries, and aims to encourage the full participation of women in economic progress through gender awareness programmes and practical training to improve women's access to employment and business opportunities. Between 1990 and 1995 UNIDO organized 473 training programmes, which were attended by 8,840 participants, of whom 1,614 were women.

In 1997 UNIDO helped to organize a number of conferences and forums to promote industrialization in developing countries. UNIDO supported the 13th Conference of African Ministers of Industry (Cami-13), held in Accra, Ghana, in May, which discussed methods to increase Africa's industrial development in the 21st century and to encourage greater participation by the private sector. UNIDO also sponsored an investment forum held in Yaoundé, Cameroon, in June, and a further UNIDO-sponsored forum was held in Abidjan, Côte d'Ivoire, in November. In the same year UNIDO established a programme worth US $312,000 under the Organization's Regional Africa Leather and Footwear Industry Scheme (Ralfis), which aimed to improve the quality of Zambia's leather goods, and opened a Cleaner Production Centre in Budapest, Hungary, to encourage increased industrial efficiency and to reduce health risks and environmental pollution from production methods in that country.

UNIDO also supports collaborative efforts between countries with complementary experience or resources in specific sectors, e.g. co-operative agreements in agro-industry between France and Brazil. A network of Investment Promotion Offices in Athens, Milan, Paris, Seoul, Tokyo, Vienna, Warsaw, Washington, DC, and Zürich publicize investment opportunities and provide information to investors. UNIDO also has two Industrial Co-operation Centres, in Moscow and Beijing, to enable foreign enterprises to participate in joint ventures. UNIDO is increasingly working to achieve investment promotion and transfer of technology and knowledge among developing countries.

UNIDO supports regional networks and centres of excellence, including the International Centre for Genetic Engineering and Biotechnology, based in Trieste (Italy) and New Delhi (India), the International Centre for Sciences and High Technology, in Trieste, and the Centre for the Application of Solar Energy, in Perth, Australia.

UNIDO also co-operates with other UN agencies. For example, it has collaborated with UNICEF on a project addressing iodine deficiency in the People's Republic of China; with ITC, UNCTAD and WTO on sustainable wood-processing; and with the World Bank regarding human resource development and enviromentally-sustainable industrial development.

FINANCE

UNIDO's total resources for the two years 1996–97 amounted to over US $385m., provided by regular and operational budgets as well as by contributions for technical co-operation projects. During 1996–97 funds for technical co-operation activities totalled some $202m. The regular budget for the two years 1996–97 amounted to approximately $158m. An operational budget of some $25m. was approved for the same period. The Industrial Development Fund is used by UNIDO to finance development projects which fall outside the usual systems of multilateral funding. On 1 January 1997 the USA, which provided some 22% of UNIDO's budget, withdrew from the organization; in December 1996 the United Kingdom, which provides 7.4% of the budget, announced its intention to withdraw from the organization, but this decision was reversed in July 1997.

PUBLICATIONS

Annual Report.
Environmental Technology Monitor (quarterly).
Industrial Africa (every 2 months).
Industrial Development Global Report (annually).
International Yearbook of Industrial Statistics (annually).
The Globalization of Industry: Implications for Developing Countries Beyond 2000.
UNIDOScope (monthly).
Several other publications and databases; numerous working papers and reports (listed in *UNIDO Links* as they appear).

Universal Postal Union—UPU

Address: Case postale, 3000 Berne 15, Switzerland.

Telephone: (31) 3503111; **telex:** 912761; **fax:** (31) 3503110; **e-mail:** ib.info@ib.upu.org; **internet:** http://ibis.ib.upu.org.

The General Postal Union was founded by the Treaty of Berne (1874), beginning operations in July 1875. Three years later its name was changed to the Universal Postal Union. In 1948 the UPU became a specialized agency of the UN.

MEMBERS

189 members: see Table on pp. 101–103.

Organization

(November 1997)

CONGRESS

The supreme body of the Union is Congress, which meets every five years. It focuses on general principles and broad policy issues. It is responsible for the Constitution and its General Regulations, changes in the provision of the Universal Postal Convention and Agreements, approval of the strategic plan and budget parameters, formulation of overall policy on technical co-operation and for elections and appointments. The 21st Congress was held in Seoul, Republic of Korea, in August–September 1994; the 22nd Congress was to be held in the People's Republic of China in 1999.

COUNCIL OF ADMINISTRATION

The Council, created by the Seoul Congress, 1994, to replace the existing Executive Council, meets annually at Berne. It is composed of 41 member countries of the Union elected by Congress on the basis of an equitable geographical distribution. It is responsible for supervising the affairs of the Union between Congresses, including the approval of proposals to modify provisions in the Universal Postal Convention and Special Agreements. The Council also considers policies that may affect other sectors, such as standardization and quality of service, provides a forum for considering the implications of governmental policies with respect to competition, deregulation, and trade-in-service issues for international postal services, and considers intergovernmental aspects of technical co-operation. The Council approves the Union's budget, supervises the activities of the International Bureau and takes decisions regarding UPU contacts with other international agencies and bodies. The Council is composed of the following six Committees: General Matters and Structure of the Union, Finance, Human Resources, Services and Standards (questions of policy and principle), Technical Co-operation, Seoul Postal Strategy.

POSTAL OPERATIONS COUNCIL (POC)

In accordance with the restructuring proposals approved in 1994, the Council replaced the Consultative Council for Postal Studies, from 1 January 1995. Its 40 member countries meet annually, generally at Berne. It is responsible for organizing studies of major problems affecting postal administrations in all UPU member countries, in the technical operations and economic fields and in the sphere of technical co-operation. The POC also adopts technical standards relating to the post, oversees technical aspects of co-operation, develops and monitors targets for service quality, revises postage charges for letter items, subject to the approval of the Council of Administration, between Congresses, and prepares the UPU's strategic plan. The responsibilities of the Council are conducted by the following Committees: Letter post; Parcel post; Financial services; Development of rapid/time-certain services; Quality of service; Marketing; Telematics development; Modernization; Postal development; and Seoul postal strategy.

INTERNATIONAL BUREAU

The day-to-day administrative work of UPU is executed through the International Bureau, located in Berne. It serves as an instrument of liaison, information and consultation for the postal administration of the member countries. The Bureau is responsible for strategic planning and programme budgeting, including the preparation of the strategic and operating plans under the authority of the POC, for monitoring the implementation of the plans, and for all financial reporting. It also supports the technical assistance programmes of the UPU and serves as an intermediary between the UPU, the UN, its agencies and other international organizations, customer organizations and private delivery services.

Director-General of the International Bureau: Thomas E. Leavey (USA).

Activities

The essential principles of the Union are the following:

(i) Formation of one single postal territory.

(ii) Unification of postal charges and weight steps.

(iii) Non-sharing of postage paid for ordinary letters between the sender country and the country of destination.
(iv) Guarantee of freedom of transit.
(v) Settlement of disputes by arbitration.
(vi) Establishment of a central office under the name of the International Bureau paid for by all members.
(vii) Periodical meeting of Congress.
(viii) Promotion of the development of international postal services and postal technical assistance to Union members.

The common rules applicable to the international postal service and to the letter-post provisions are contained in the Universal Postal Convention and its Detailed Regulations. Owing to their importance in the postal field and their historical value, these two Acts, together with the Constitution and the General Regulations, constitute the compulsory Acts of the Union. It is therefore not possible to be a member country of the Union without being a party to these Acts and applying their provisions.

The activities of the international postal service, other than letter mail, are governed by Special Agreements. These are binding only for the countries that have acceded to them. There are four such Agreements:

1. Agreement concerning Postal Parcels.
2. Agreement concerning Postal Money Orders.
3. Agreement concerning Giro Transfers.
4. Agreement concerning Cash on Delivery Items.

FINANCE

The 1997 approved budget amounted to 35.7m. Swiss francs. The Council agreed to maintain the regular budget at 35.7m. Swiss francs for 1998. All of the UPU's regular budget expenses are financed by member countries, based on a contribution class system. Members are listed in 11 classes, establishing the proportion that they should pay.

PUBLICATIONS

Union Postale (quarterly, in French, German, English, Arabic, Chinese, Spanish and Russian).

Other UPU publications are listed in *Liste des publications du Bureau international*; all are in French, some also in English, Arabic and Spanish.

World Health Organization—WHO

Address: Ave Appia, 1211 Geneva 27, Switzerland.

Telephone: (22) 7912111; **telex:** 415416; **fax:** (22) 7910746; **internet:** http://www.who.ch.

WHO was established in 1948 as the central agency directing international health work.

MEMBERS

191 members and two associate members: see Table on pp. 101–103.

Organization

(January 1998)

WORLD HEALTH ASSEMBLY

The Assembly meets in Geneva, once a year; it is responsible for policy making and the biennial programme and budget; appoints the Director-General, admits new members and reviews budget contributions.

EXECUTIVE BOARD

The Board is composed of 32 health experts designated by, but not representing, their governments; they serve for three years, and the World Health Assembly elects 10 or 11 member states each year to the Board. It meets at least twice a year to review the Director-General's programme, which it forwards to the Assembly with any recommendations that seem necessary. It advises on questions referred to it by the Assembly and is responsible for putting into effect the decisions and policies of the Assembly. It is also empowered to take emergency measures in case of epidemics or disasters.

SECRETARIAT

Director-General: Dr HIROSHI NAKAJIMA (Japan).

Assistant Directors-General: Dr HU CHING-LI (People's Republic of China), Dr AISSATOU KONE-DIABI (Senegal), Dr NIKOLAI P. NAPALKOV (Russia), Dr RALPH H. HENDERSON (USA), DENIS G. AITKEN (United Kingdom), Dr FERNANDO S. ANTEZANA (Bolivia), Dr FRANÇOISE VARET (France).

Note: In January 1998 the Executive Board nominated Dr GRO HARLEM BRUNDTLAND (Norway) as the new Director-General. Dr Brundtland was expected to take office on 21 July, subject to confirmation by member states in May.

REGIONAL OFFICES

Each of WHO's six geographical regions has its own organization consisting of a regional committee representing the member states and associate members in the region concerned, and a regional office staffed by experts in various fields of health.

Africa: POB 6, Brazzaville, Republic of the Congo; tel. 839111; telex 5217; fax 839400; Dir Dr EBRAHIM MALICK SAMBA.

Americas: Pan-American Sanitary Bureau, 525 23rd St, NW, Washington, DC 20037, USA; tel. (202) 861-3200; telex 248338; fax (202) 223-5971; Dir Sir GEORGE ALLEYNE.

Eastern Mediterranean: POB 1517, Alexandria 21511, Egypt; tel. (3) 4820223; telex 54028; fax (3) 4838916; Dir Dr HUSSEIN ABDUL-RAZZAQ GEZAIRY.

Europe: 8 Scherfigsvej, 2100 Copenhagen Ø, Denmark; tel. (1) 39-17-17-17; telex 15348; fax 39-17-18-18; Dir Dr JO ERIK ASVALL.

South-East Asia: World Health House, Indraprastha Estate, Mahatma Gandhi Rd, New Delhi 110 002, India; tel. (11) 3317804; telex 3165095; fax (11) 3318607; Dir Dr UTON MUCHTAR RAFEI.

Western Pacific: POB 2932, Manila 1000, Philippines; tel. (2) 5288001; telex 63260; fax (2) 5211036; Dir Dr SANG TAE HAN.

Activities

WHO's objective is stated in the constitution as 'the attainment by all peoples of the highest possible level of health'.

It acts as the central authority directing international health work, and establishes relations with professional groups and government health authorities on that basis.

It supports, on request from member states, programmes to promote health, prevent and control health problems, control or eradicate disease, train health workers best suited to local needs and strengthen national health systems. Aid is provided in emergencies and natural disasters.

A global programme of collaborative research and exchange of scientific information is carried out in co-operation with about 1,000 national institutions. Particular stress is laid on the widespread communicable diseases of the tropics, and the countries directly concerned are assisted in developing their research capabilities.

It keeps communicable and non-communicable diseases and other health problems under constant surveillance, promotes the exchange of prompt and accurate information, and administers the International Health Regulations. It sets standards for the quality control of drugs, vaccines and other substances affecting health.

It collects and disseminates health data and carries out statistical analyses and comparative studies in such diseases as cancer, heart disease and mental illness.

It receives reports on drugs observed to have shown adverse reactions in any country, and transmits the information to other member states. All available information on effects on human health of the pollutants in the environment is critically reviewed and published.

Co-operation among scientists and professional groups is encouraged, and the organization may propose international conventions and agreements. It assists in developing an informed public opinion on matters of health.

HEALTH FOR ALL

In May 1981 the 34th World Health Assembly adopted a Global Strategy in support of 'Health for all by the year 2000'. Through a broad consultation process involving all its partners, WHO is reviewing the policy of health for all, or the attainment by all citizens of the world of a level of health that will permit them to lead a socially and economically productive life. Primary health care is seen as the key to 'Health for all', with the following as minimum requirements:

Safe water in the home or within 15 minutes' walking distance, and adequate sanitary facilities in the home or immediate vicinity;

Immunization against diphtheria, pertussis (whooping cough), tetanus, poliomyelitis, measles and tuberculosis;

Local health care, including availability of at least 20 essential drugs, within one hour's travel;

Trained personnel to attend childbirth, and to care for pregnant mothers and children up to at least one year old.

The Ninth General Programme of Work, for the period 1996–2000, defines a policy framework for world action on health and the management and programme development of WHO itself.

In 1994 a new Division of Intensified Co-operation with Countries was established to strengthen WHO's capacity to respond to the requirements of individual countries and populations in greatest need. During 1995 the Division worked with 26 least-developed countries, with the aim of achieving intensified co-operation with all 48 UN-classified least-developed countries by 2000.

DISEASE PREVENTION AND CONTROL

One of WHO's major achievements was the eradication of smallpox. Following a massive international campaign of vaccination and surveillance (begun in 1958 and intensified in 1967), the last case was detected in 1977 and the eradication of the disease was declared in 1980. In February 1997, however, an increased number of monkeypox cases were reported in Zaire (now the Democratic Republic of the Congo), possibly owing to the discontinuation of immunization programmes against smallpox in the late 1970s. In May 1996 the World Health Assembly resolved that, pending a final endorsement, all remaining stocks of smallpox were to be destroyed on 30 June 1999, although 500,000 doses of smallpox vaccine, also effective against monkeypox, were to remain, along with a supply of the smallpox vaccine seed virus, in order to ensure that a further supply of the vaccine could be made available if required. In 1988 the World Health Assembly declared its commitment to the similar eradication of poliomyelitis by 2000; and in 1990 the Assembly also resolved to eliminate iodine deficiency (causing mental handicap) by 2000. In August 1996 WHO, UNICEF and Rotary International, together with other national and international partners, initiated a campaign to 'Kick Polio out of Africa', with the aim of immunizing more than 100m. children in 46 countries against the disease over a three-year period.

The objective of providing immunization for all children by 1990 was adopted by the World Health Assembly in 1977. Six diseases (measles, whooping cough, tetanus, poliomyelitis, tuberculosis and diphtheria) became the target of the Expanded Programme on Immunization (EPI), in which WHO, UNICEF and many other organizations collaborated. As a result of massive international and national efforts, the global immunization coverage increased from 20% in the early 1980s to the targeted rate of 80% by the end of 1990. This coverage signified that more than 100m. children in the developing world under the age of one had been successfully vaccinated against the targeted diseases, the lives of about 3m. children had been saved every year, and 500,000 annual cases of paralysis as a result of polio had been prevented. In 1992 the Assembly resolved to reach a new target of 90% immunization coverage with the six EPI vaccines; to introduce hepatitis B as a seventh vaccine; and to introduce the yellow fever vaccine in areas where it occurs endemically.

In September 1991 the Children's Vaccine Initiative (CVI) was launched, jointly sponsored by the Rockefeller Foundation, UNDP, UNICEF, the World Bank and WHO, to facilitate the development and provision of children's vaccines. The CVI has as its ultimate goal the development of a single oral immunization shortly after birth that will protect against all major childhood diseases. An International Vaccine Institute was established in Seoul, Republic of Korea, as part of the CVI, to provide scientific and technical services for the production of vaccines for developing countries. In September 1996 WHO, jointly with UNICEF, published a comprehensive survey, entitled *State of the World's Vaccines and Immunization*.

In 1995 WHO established the Division of Emerging, Viral and Bacterial ('Other Communicable') Diseases Surveillance and Control to strengthen the national and international capability to respond to the threats to public health from communicable diseases. The Division was to promote the development of national and international infrastructure and resources to recognize, monitor, prevent and control communicable diseases and emerging health problems, including antibiotic resistance. It also aimed to promote applied research on the diagnosis, epidemiology, prevention and control of communicable diseases and emerging health problems. In July 1996 WHO launched an interagency initiative to control an outbreak of cerebrospinal meningitis in Africa, which had caused some 15,000 deaths in the first half of that year. WHO was to provide technical assistance to enable countries to identify and control any outbreaks of the disease, and by November 16 African countries had declared their commitment to national action plans for the control of meningitis. In January 1997 an International Co-ordinating Group (ICG) was established to ensure the optimum use and rapid provision of the 14m. doses of vaccine available for epidemic control in 1997, following the enormous demand of the previous year.

The Division of Control of Tropical Diseases addresses malaria, dracunculiasis, Chagas disease, schistosomiasis, filariasis (lymphatic filariasis and onchocerciasis), leishmaniasis, dengue, dengue haemorrhagic fever and sleeping sickness. It provides active support for planning and implementing control programmes (based on global strategies for integrated tropical disease control) at regional, subregional and national levels. It takes part in mobilizing resources for disease control where needed, and co-ordinating national and international participation as appropriate. The Division promotes research and training that are directly relevant to control needs, and promotes the monitoring and evaluation of control measures. In January 1996 a new initiative to eliminate onchocerciasis became operational, with funding from the World Bank and with WHO as its executing agency. The African Programme for Onchocerciasis Control (APOC) aimed to benefit some 15m. people infected with the disease, which may cause blindness, in 16 participating African countries. APOC was to complement an existing control programme, initiated in 1974, which has eliminated onchocerciasis as a major public health risk in 11 west African countries. A Ministerial Conference on Malaria, organized by WHO, was held in October 1992, attended by representatives from 102 member countries. The Conference adopted a plan of action for the 1990s for the control of the disease, which kills between 1.5m. and 2.7m. people every year and affects a further 300m.–500m. Some 90% of all cases are in sub-Saharan Africa. At the end of 1995 38 African countries where malaria is endemic had prepared plans for malaria control in accordance with WHO's Global Malaria Control Strategy, which emphasized strengthening local capabilities, for example through training, for effective health control. In March 1997 it was reported that an African regional meeting of WHO had formulated a schedule aiming to control the prevalence of malaria throughout the entire region by 2030, through the establishment and completion of effective malaria-control programmes in all African countries. In May 1997 WHO announced that, with additional funding, a number of tropical diseases, including lymphatic filariasis and dracunculiasis, as well as malaria, could be controlled or eliminated.

In July 1994 WHO, together with the Sasakawa Memorial Health Foundation, organized an international conference on the elimination of leprosy, which was held in Hanoi, Viet Nam. As a result of a declaration adopted by the conference that committed all concerned parties to the elimination of leprosy by 2000, WHO established a Special Programme devoted to this objective. In October 1997 WHO announced that, while the use of a combination of three drugs (known as multi-drug therapy) had resulted in a reduction of 85% in the number of leprosy cases world-wide since 1985, some 2m. people were still suffering from the disease.

The WHO's Special Programme for Research and Training in Tropical Diseases, sponsored jointly by WHO, UNDP and the World Bank, was established in 1975, and involves a world-wide network of about 5,000 scientists working on the development and application of vaccines, new drugs, diagnostic kits and preventive measures, and an applied field research on practical community issues affecting the target diseases.

WHO's Programme for the Promotion of Environmental Health undertakes a wide range of initiatives to tackle the increasing threats to health and well-being from a changing environment, especially in relation to air pollution, water quality, sanitation, protection against radiation, management of hazardous waste, chemical safety and housing hygiene. Some 1,200m. people world-wide have no access to clean drinking water, while a further 2,900m. people are denied suitable sanitation systems. In rural areas, the emphasis continues to be on the provision and maintenance of safe and sufficient water supplies and adequate sanitation, the health aspects of rural housing, vector control in water resource management, and the safe use of agrochemicals. In urban areas, assistance is provided to identify local environmental health priorities and to improve municipal governments' ability to deal with environmental conditions and health problems in an integrated manner; promotion of the 'Healthy City' approach is a major component of the programme. Other Programme activities include environmental health information development and management, human resources development, environmental health planning methods, research and work on problems relating to global environment change, such as UV-radiation. A report considering the implications of climate change on human health, prepared jointly by WHO, WMO and UNEP (qq.v.), was published in July 1996. The WHO Global Strategy for Health and Environment, developed in response to the WHO Commission on Health and Environment which reported to the UN Conference on Environment and Development in June 1992, provides the framework for Programme activities.

WHO's work in the promotion of chemical safety is undertaken in collaboration with ILO and UNEP through the International

Programme on Chemical Safety (IPCS), the Central Unit for which is located in WHO. The Programme provides internationally-evaluated scientific information on chemicals, promotes the use of such information in national programmes, assists member states in establishment of their own chemical safety measures and programmes, and helps them strengthen their capabilities in chemical emergency preparedness and response and in chemical risk reduction. In April 1994 an Intergovernmental Forum on Chemical Safety (which was to be administered by WHO) was established to facilitate the review of intersectoral issues related to chemical safety and promote strategies and policies for environmentally-sound management of chemicals. In 1995 an Inter-organization Programme for the Social Management of Chemicals was established by UNEP, ILO, FAO, WHO, UNIDO and OECD, in order to strengthen international co-operation in the field of chemical safety.

WHO's Division of Diarrhoeal and Acute Respiratory Disease Control encourages national programmes aimed at reducing childhood deaths as a result of diarrhoea, particularly through the use of oral rehydration therapy and preventive measures. The Division is also seeking to reduce deaths from pneumonia in infants through the use of a simple case-management strategy involving the recognition of danger signs and treatment with an appropriate antibiotic. In September 1997 WHO, in collaboration with UNICEF, formally launched a programme advocating the Integrated Management of Childhood Illness (IMCI), following successful regional trials in more than 20 developing countries during 1996–97. IMCI recognizes that pneumonia, diarrhoea, measles, malaria and malnutrition cause some 70% of the 11m. childhood deaths each year, and recommends screening sick children for all five conditions, in order to enable health workers to reach a more accurate diagnosis than may be achieved from the results of a single assessment. Simultaneous screening in such a way could avoid the provision of inadequate treatment and the excessive or inadequate use of drugs.

In December 1995 WHO's Global Programme on AIDS (Acquired Immunodeficiency Syndrome), which began in 1987, was concluded. A Joint UN Programme on the human immunodeficiency virus (HIV) and AIDS—UNAIDS—became operational on 1 January 1996, sponsored jointly by WHO, the World Bank, UNICEF, UNDP, UNESCO and UNFPA. WHO established an Office of HIV/AIDS and Sexually-Transmitted Diseases in order to ensure the continuity of its global response to the problem, which included support for national control and education plans, improving the safety of blood supplies and improving the care and support of AIDS patients. In addition, the Office was to liaise with UNAIDS, which has its secretariat at WHO headquarters, and to make available WHO's research and technical expertise. At December 1996 WHO and UNAIDS estimated that 21.8m. adults and 830,000 children worldwide were infected with HIV/AIDS.

In 1995 WHO established a Global Tuberculosis Programme to address the emerging challenges of the TB epidemic. According to WHO estimates, one-third of the world's population is infected with TB and more than 3m. people die from the disease each year, prompting WHO to declare TB a global emergency. WHO provides technical support to all member countries, with special attention being given to those with high TB prevalence, to establish effective national tuberculosis control programmes. WHO's strategy for TB control includes the use of DOTS (directly observed treatment, short-course), standardized treatment guide-lines, and result accountability through routine evaluation of treatment outcomes. Simultaneously, WHO is encouraging research with the aim of further disseminating DOTS, adapting DOTS for wider use, developing new tools for prevention, diagnosis and treatment, and containing new threats such as the HIV/TB co-epidemic. In March 1997 WHO reported that even limited use of DOTS, which in 1996 had been employed in approximately 10% of cases world-wide, was resulting in the stabilization of the TB epidemic, and it was predicted that an increased use of the DOTS strategy could prevent 10m. deaths within 10 years.

'Inter-Health', an integrated programme to combat non-communicable diseases (such as those arising from an unhealthy diet), was initiated in 1990, with the particular aim of preventing an increase in the incidence of such diseases in developing countries.

WHO's programmes for diabetes mellitus, chronic rheumatic diseases and asthma assist with the development of national programmes, based upon goals and targets for the improvement of early detection, care and reduction of long-term complications. They also monitor the global epidemiological situation and co-ordinate multinational research activities concerned with the prevention and care of non-communicable diseases.

WHO's Cardiovascular Diseases Programme aims to prevent and control the major cardiovascular diseases, which are responsible for more than 14m. deaths each year. It is estimated that one-third of these deaths could have been prevented with existing scientific knowledge. In July 1994 WHO published a study as part of its ongoing research project monitoring coronary disease.

The Global Cancer Control Programme is concerned with the prevention of cancer, improving its detection and cure and ensuring care of all cancer patients in need. The WHO Human Genetics Programme manages genetic approaches for the prevention and control of common hereditary diseases and of those with a genetic predisposition representing a major health importance. The Programme also concentrates on the further development of genetic approaches suitable for incorporation into health care systems, as well as developing a network of international collaborating programmes.

FAMILY AND REPRODUCTIVE HEALTH

During 1995 WHO integrated its programmes relating to the health needs of individuals, families and groups throughout the life cycle and under different circumstances. Activities include newborn care; child health, including promoting and protecting the health and development of the child through such approaches as promotion of breast-feeding and use of the mother-baby package, as well as care of the sick child, including diarrhoeal and acute respiratory disease control and support to women and children in difficult circumstances; the promotion of safe motherhood and maternal health; adolescent health, including the promotion and development of young people and the prevention of specific health problems; women, health and development, including addressing issues of gender, sexual violence, and harmful traditional practices; and human reproduction, including research related to contraceptive technologies and effective methods. In addition, WHO aimed to provide technical leadership and co-ordination on reproductive health and to support countries in their efforts to ensure that people: experience healthy sexual development and maturation; have the capacity for healthy, equitable and responsible relationships; can achieve their reproductive intentions safely and healthily; avoid illnesses, diseases and injury related to sexuality and reproduction; and receive appropriate counselling, care and rehabilitation for diseases and conditions related to sexuality and reproduction.

FOOD AND NUTRITION

Adequate and safe food and nutrition is a priority programme area. WHO collaborates with FAO, the World Food Programme, UNICEF and other UN agencies in pursuing its objectives relating to nutrition and food safety. An estimated 780m. world-wide cannot meet basic needs for energy and protein, more than 2,000m. people lack essential vitamins and minerals, and 200m. children are estimated to be malnourished. In December 1992 WHO and FAO held an international conference on nutrition, at which a World Declaration and Plan of Action on Nutrition was adopted to make the fight against malnutrition a development priority. Following the conference, WHO promoted the elaboration and implementation of national plans of action on nutrition. In addition, WHO aims to identify and support countries with high levels of malnutrition. By 31 January 1996 a total of 98 countries had completed plans of action and a further 41 countries had plans under preparation. WHO aims to support the enhancement of member states' capabilities in dealing with their nutrition situations, and addressing scientific issues related to preventing, managing and monitoring protein-energy malnutrition; micronutrient malnutrition, including iodine deficiency disorders, vitamin A deficiency, and nutritional anaemia; and diet-related non-communicable diseases such as cancer and heart disease. In collaboration with other international agencies, WHO is implementing a comprehensive strategy for promoting appropriate infant, young child and maternal nutrition, and for dealing effectively with nutritional emergencies in large populations. Areas of emphasis include promoting health-care practices that enhance successful breast-feeding; appropriate complementary feeding; refining the use and interpretation of body measurements for assessing nutritional status; relevant information, education and training; and action to give effect to the International Code of Marketing of Breast-milk Substitutes. WHO's food safety programme aims to protect human health against risks associated with biological and chemical contaminants and additives in food. With FAO, WHO establishes food standards (through the work of the Codex Alimentarius Commission and its subsidiary committees) and evaluates food additives, pesticide residues and other contaminants and their implications for health. The programme provides expert advice on such issues as food-borne pathogens (e.g. listeria), production methods (e.g. aquaculture) and food biotechnology (e.g. genetic modification).

DRUGS

WHO's Action Programme on Essential Drugs is a central component of its Revised Drug Strategy and acts as WHO's operational arm to assist in the development and implementation by member states of their pharmaceutical policies, in the supply of essential drugs of good quality at low cost, and in the rational use of drugs. Other activities include global and national operational research in the pharmaceutical sector, and the development of technical tools for problem solving, management and evaluation. The Programme also has a strong advocacy and information role, promulgated through a periodical, the *Essential Drugs Monitor* (published in English, French, Spanish and Russian), an extensive range of technical publications, and an information dissemination programme targeting developing countries.

The Division of Drug Management and Policies supports national drug-regulatory authorities and drug-procurement agencies and facilitates international pharmaceutical trade through the exchange of technical information and the harmonization of internationally respected norms and standards. In particular, it publishes the International Pharmacopoeia, the Consultative List of International Nonproprietary Names for Pharmaceutical Substances, and annual and biennial reports of Expert Committees responsible for determining relevant international standards for the manufacture and specification of pharmaceutical and biological products in international commerce. It provides information on the safety and efficacy of drugs, with particular regard to counterfeit and substandard projects, to health agencies and providers of health care, and it maintains the pharmaceuticals section of the UN Consolidated List of Products whose Consumption and/or Sale have been Banned, Withdrawn, Severely Restricted or Not Approved by Governments. The WHO Model List of Essential Drugs is updated every two years and is complemented by corresponding model prescribing information.

The Programme on Traditional Medicine assesses those methods of traditional health care which are safe and effective, and encourages the incorporation of traditional practices into primary health-care systems. WHO works closely with Collaborating Centres for Traditional Medicines in 10 countries to increase understanding and awareness of this form of health care. In July 1996 a WHO scientific group of experts adopted a list of medicinal plants that are widely used in primary health care.

Within its Programme on Substance Abuse (PSA), which was established in 1990 in response to the global increase in substance abuse, WHO provides technical support to assist countries in formulating polices with regard to the prevention and reduction of the health and social effects of psychoactive substance abuse. PSA's sphere of activity includes epidemiological surveillance and risk assessment, advocacy and the dissemination of information, strengthening national and regional prevention and health promotion techniques and strategies, the development of cost-effective treatment and rehabilitation approaches, and also encompasses regulatory activities as required under the international drugs-control treaties in force. In November 1996 WHO hosted the first ever global scientific meeting on the health and social implications of the widespread use of amphetamine-type psychostimulants in both developed and developing countries. The Tobacco or Health Programme, which was incorporated into the PSA in May 1994, aims to reduce the use of tobacco, by educating tobacco-users and preventing young people from adopting the habit. In 1996 WHO published its first report on the tobacco situation world-wide. According to WHO, about one-third of the world's population aged over 15 years smoke tobacco, which causes approximately 3m. deaths each year (through lung cancer, heart disease, chronic bronchitis and other effects). In May the World Health Assembly approved a new five-year plan of action for national and international tobacco control programmes, international research, advocacy and public information activities.

HEALTH PROMOTION

A Division of Health Promotion, Education and Communication was established in May 1994 to implement the priority assigned to health promotion in the Ninth General Programme of Work. The Division promotes decentralized and community-based health programmes and is concerned with the challenge of population ageing and encouraging healthy life-styles and self-care. Several projects have been undertaken, in collaboration between WHO regional and country offices and other relevant organizations, including: the Global School Health Initiative, to bridge the sectors of health and education and to promote the health of school-age children; the Global Strategy for Occupational Health, to promote the health of the working population and the control of occupational health risks; Community-based Rehabilitation, which aimed to provide a more enabling environment for people with disabilities; and a communication strategy to provide training and support for health communications personnel and initiatives.

WHO's Division of Strengthening Health Services assists countries to expand and improve the functioning of their health infrastructure in order to ensure wider access to care, hospital services and health education. It works with countries to ensure continuity and quality of care at all levels, by well-trained health personnel. Under the UN's Special Initiative on Africa, launched in March 1996, WHO was mandated to co-ordinate international efforts to secure improvements in basic health care and to strengthen the management of health services and resources.

In March 1996 WHO's Centre for Health Development opened at Kobe, Japan. The Centre was to research health developments and other determinants to strengthen policy decision-making within the health sector.

In July 1997 the fourth International Conference on Health Promotion was held in Jakarta, Indonesia, where a declaration on 'Health Promotion into the 21st Century' was agreed.

EMERGENCY RELIEF

Within the UN system, WHO's Division of Emergency and Humanitarian Action co-ordinates the international response to emergencies and natural disasters in the health field, in close co-operation with other agencies and within the framework set out by the UN's Department of Humanitarian Affairs. In this context, WHO provides expert advice on epidemiological surveillance, control of communicable diseases, public health information and health emergency training. Its emergency preparedness activities include co-ordination, policy-making and planning, awareness-building, technical advice, training, publication of standards and guide-lines, and research. Its emergency relief activities include organizational support, the provision of emergency drugs and supplies and conducting technical emergency assessment missions. The Division's objective is to strengthen the national capacity of member states to reduce the adverse health consequences of disasters. In responding to emergency situations, WHO always tries to develop projects and activities that will assist the national authorities concerned in rebuilding or strengthening their own capacity to handle the impact of such situations. In 1996/97 WHO was a major participant in several international relief efforts, including in the Democratic Republic of the Congo, and throughout the Great Lakes region, to combat outbreaks of cholera and meningitis, particularly among the refugee population, in Indonesia, to provide assistance against the harmful environmental pollution caused by forest fires, in Gabon, to control an outbreak of Ebola haemorrhage fever, in Albania, to combat a poliomyelitis epidemic, in Tajikistan, to control an outbreak of typhoid fever, and in Iraq, to distribute emergency medical supplies and equipment under Security Council Resolution 986, permitting the sale of a limited amount of petroleum in return for essential supplies.

HEALTH DAYS

World Health Day is observed on 7 April every year, and is used to promote awareness of a particular health topic (Emerging Infectious Diseases, in 1997). World 'No Tobacco Day' is held every year on 31 May, and 'World AIDS Day' on 1 December.

ASSOCIATED AGENCY

International Agency for Research on Cancer: 150 Cours Albert Thomas, 69372 Lyon Cédex 08, France. Established in 1965 as a self-governing body within the framework of WHO, the Agency organizes international research on cancer. It has its own laboratories and runs a programme of research on the environmental factors causing cancer. Members: Australia, Belgium, Canada, Denmark, Finland, France, Germany, Italy, Japan, Netherlands, Norway, Russia, Sweden, Switzerland, United Kingdom, USA.

Director: Dr Paul Kleihues (Germany).

FINANCE

WHO's regular budget is provided by assessment of member states and associate members. An additional fund for specific projects is provided by voluntary contributions from members and other sources. Funds are received from UNDP for particular projects and from UNFPA for appropriate programmes.

A budget of US $842.7m. was approved for the two years 1996–97. Extra-budgetary funds were expected to amount to $993.7m. during this period. In May 1997 the Assembly resolved to maintain the regular budget at $842.7m. for 1998–99.

WHO Budget appropriations by region, 1996–97

Region	Amount (US dollars)	% of total budget
Africa	154,310,000	18.31
Americas	79,794,000	9.47
South-East Asia	96,220,000	11.42
Europe	50,837,000	6.03
Eastern Mediterranean	86,258,000	10.24
Western Pacific	76,709,000	9.10
Global and inter-regional	298,526,000	35.43
Total	842,654,000	100.00

Budget appropriations by purpose, 1996–97

Purpose	Amount (US dollars)	% of total budget
Governing bodies	21,600,000	2.56
Health policy and management	261,464,700	31.03
Health services development	162,871,000	19.33
Promotion and protection of health	131,146,000	15.56
Integrated control of disease	120,756,000	14.33
Administrative services	144,817,000	17.19
Total	842,654,000	100.00

PUBLICATIONS

Full catalogue of publications supplied free on request.

Bulletin of WHO (6 a year).

International Digest of Health Legislation (quarterly).

International Statistical Classification of Diseases and Related Health Problems, Tenth Revision, 1992–1994 (versions in 37 languages).

Weekly Epidemiological Record.

WHO Drug Information (quarterly).

World Health (6 a year in several languages).

World Health Forum (quarterly, in several languages).

World Health Statistics Quarterly.

World Health Statistics Annual.

Technical report series; catalogues of specific scientific, technical and medical fields available.

World Intellectual Property Organization—WIPO

Address: 34 chemin des Colombettes, 1211 Geneva 20, Switzerland.

Telephone: (22) 3389111; **telex:** 412912; **fax:** (22) 7335428; **internet:** http://www.wipo.int.

WIPO was established by a Convention signed in Stockholm in 1967, which came into force in 1970. It became a specialized agency of the UN in December 1974.

MEMBERS

165 members: see Table on pp. 101–103.

Organization

(December 1997)

GENERAL ASSEMBLY

The General Assembly is one of the three WIPO governing bodies, and is composed of all states that are party to the WIPO Convention and that are also members of any of the WIPO-administered Unions (see below). The Assembly meets in ordinary session once every two years to agree on programmes and budgets. It elects the Director-General, who is the executive head of WIPO.

CONFERENCE

All member states are represented in the Conference, which meets in ordinary session once every two years to adopt budgets and programmes.

CO-ORDINATION COMMITTEE

Countries belonging to the Committee are elected from among the member states of WIPO, the Paris and Berne Unions, and, *ex officio*, Switzerland. In July 1997 there were 68 members of the Committee. It meets in ordinary session once a year.

INTERNATIONAL BUREAU

The International Bureau, as WIPO's secretariat, prepares the meetings of the various bodies of WIPO and the Unions, mainly through the provision of reports and working documents. It organizes the meetings, and sees that the decisions are communicated to all concerned, and, as far as possible, that they are carried out.

The International Bureau implements projects and initiates new ones to promote international co-operation in the field of intellectual property. It acts as an information service and publishes reviews. It is also the depositary of most of the treaties administered by WIPO.

Director-General: Dr Kamil Idris (Sudan).

Deputy Director-General: François Curchod.

Activities

WIPO is responsible for promoting the protection of intellectual property throughout the world. Intellectual property comprises two principal branches: industrial property (patents and other rights in technological inventions, rights in trademarks, industrial designs, appellations of origin, etc.) and copyright and neighbouring rights (in literary, musical, artistic, photographic and audiovisual works).

WIPO administers various international treaties, of which the most important are the Paris Convention for the Protection of Industrial Property (1883) and the Berne Convention for the Protection of Literary and Artistic Works (1886). WIPO undertakes a programme of activities in the field of intellectual property, in order to promote creative intellectual activity and to facilitate the transfer of technology, especially to and among developing countries. WIPO also advises countries on obligations under the World Trade Organization's agreement on Trade-Related Aspects of Intellectual Property Rights (TRIPS).

CO-OPERATION WITH DEVELOPING COUNTRIES

WIPO carries out a substantial programme of development co-operation for the benefit of developing countries. The programme is directed towards: training of officials; the formulation or improvement of new national laws and regulations, regional treaties and different types of regional co-operation structures encouraging local inventive and artistic-creative activity; the teaching of intellectual property; the creation of measures to establish or expand the profession of intellectual property specialists; promoting exchange of experience and information among legislators and members of the judicial branch; giving advice on how to acquire access and disseminate information in patent documents; and promoting awareness of the importance of obtaining protection for inventions, trademarks, industrial designs and literary and artistic works.

These activities are supervised by the WIPO Permanent Committee for Development Co-operation Related to Industrial Property, membership of which is voluntary and carries no financial obligation with it. By July 1997 122 states were members of the Permanent Committee.

In the field of copyright, the main objectives of WIPO's co-operation with developing countries are: to encourage and increase the creation of literary and artistic works by their own nationals, and thereby to maintain their national culture in their own languages and/or corresponding to their own ethnic and social traditions and aspirations; and to improve the conditions of acquisition of the right to use or enjoy the literary and artistic works in which copyright is owned by foreigners. In order to achieve these objectives, most developing countries are in need of creating or modernizing domestic legislation and institutions, acceding to international treaties and having more specialists, all in the field of copyright.

Most of these development co-operation activities are kept under review by the WIPO Permanent Committee for Development Co-operation Related to Copyright and Neighbouring Rights, membership of which is voluntary and carries no financial obligation with it. By July 1997 this Committee had 109 states as members.

In both industrial property and copyright, WIPO's development co-operation consists mainly of advice, training and the furnishing of documents and equipment. The advice is given by the staff of WIPO, experts chosen by WIPO or international meetings called by WIPO. The training is individual (on-the-job) or collective (courses, seminars and workshops).

LEGAL AND TECHNICAL

WIPO prepares new treaties concerning the protection of intellectual property and undertakes the revision of existing treaties administered by the Organization. WIPO also carries out studies on issues in the field of intellectual property that could be the subject of model laws or guide-lines for implementation at the national or international levels.

WIPO administers international classifications established by treaties and relating to inventions, marks and industrial designs. Those classifications are subject to periodical revisions to ensure their improvement in terms of coverage and precision.

WIPO Permanent Committee on Industrial Property Information: composed of representatives of 118 states and five intergovernmental organizations (July 1997); encourages co-operation between national and regional industrial property offices; and monitors all matters concerning patent, trademark, documentation and information on industrial property.

SERVICES

WIPO maintains international registration services, which facilitate obtaining protection of intellectual property in the various countries of the world which participate in the international system for the administration of those services.

International registration of trademarks: operating since 1893; at 30 September 1996 780,701 registrations and renewals of trademarks had been made, of which 17,215 were made during the first nine months of 1996; publ. *WIPO Gazette of International Marks* (monthly).

International deposit of industrial designs: operating since 1928; at 30 September 1996 114,569 deposits had been made, of which 2,791 were made during the first nine months of 1996; publ. *International Designs Bulletin* (monthly).

International registration of appellations of origin: operating since 1966; by 30 September 1997 740 appellations had been registered; publ. *Les appellations d'origine* (irreg.).

International applications for patents: operating since 1978; at 30 September 1996 282,375 record copies of international applications for patents under the Patent Co-operation Treaty (PCT) had been received, of which 35,753 were received during the first nine months of 1996.

WIPO also maintains the WIPO Arbitration Centre, which became operational on 1 October 1994, to facilitate the settlement of intellectual property disputes between private parties.

PARIS AND BERNE CONVENTIONS

International Union for the Protection of Industrial Property (Paris Convention): the treaty was signed in Paris in 1883, and last revised in 1967; there were 143 member states at 10 December 1997. Member states must accord to nationals and residents of other member states the same advantages under their laws relating to the protection of inventions, trademarks and other subjects of industrial property as they accord to their own nationals.

International Union for the Protection of Literary and Artistic Works (Berne Union): the treaty was signed in Berne in 1886 and last revised in 1971; there were 127 member states at 10 December 1997. Member states must accord the same protection to the copyright of nationals of other member states as to their own. The treaty also prescribes minimum standards of protection, for example, that copyright protection generally continues throughout the author's life and for 50 years after. It includes special provision for the developing countries.

OTHER AGREEMENTS

International Protection of Industrial Property:

Madrid Agreement of 14 April 1891, for the Repression of False or Deceptive Indications of Source on Goods.

Madrid Agreement of 14 April 1891, Concerning the International Registration of Marks.

The Hague Agreement of 6 November 1925, Concerning the International Deposit of Industrial Designs.

Nice Agreement of 15 June 1957, Concerning the International Classification of Goods and Services for the Purposes of the Registration of Marks.

Lisbon Agreement of 31 October 1958, for the Protection of Appellations of Origin and their International Registration.

Locarno Agreement of 8 October 1968, Establishing an International Classification for Industrial Designs.

Patent Co-operation Treaty of 19 June 1970 (PCT).

Strasbourg Agreement of 24 March 1971, Concerning the International Patent Classification (IPC).

Vienna Agreement of 12 June 1973, Establishing an International Classification of the Figurative Elements of Marks.

Budapest Treaty of 28 April 1977, on the International Recognition of the Deposit of Micro-organisms for the Purposes of Patent Procedure.

Nairobi Treaty of 26 September 1981, on the Protection of the Olympic Symbol.

Trademark Law Treaty.

Protocol Relating to the Madrid Agreement Concerning the International Registration of Marks.

Eurasian Patent Convention.

Treaty on Intellectual Property in Respect of Integrated Circuits; not yet entered into force.

Special International Protection of the Rights of Performers, Producers of Phonograms and Broadcasting Organizations ('Neighbouring Rights'):

Rome Convention, 26 October 1961, for the Protection of Performers, Producers of Phonograms and Broadcasting Organizations.

Geneva Convention, 29 October 1971, for the Protection of Producers of Phonograms against Unauthorized Duplication of their Phonograms.

Brussels Convention, 21 May 1974, Relating to the Distribution of Programme-carrying Signals Transmitted by Satellite.

FINANCE

The budget for the two years 1996–97 amounted to approximately 300m. Swiss francs, compared with 235m. Swiss francs in 1994–95.

PUBLICATIONS

Les appellations d'origine (irregular, in French).

Industrial Property and Copyright (monthly in English and French; bimonthly in Spanish).

Intellectual Property in Asia and the Pacific (quarterly in English).

International Designs Bulletin (monthly in English and French).

Newsletter (irregular in Arabic, English, French, Portuguese, Russian and Spanish).

PCT Gazette (weekly in English and French).

PCT Newsletter (monthly in English).

WIPO Gazette of International Marks (monthly, in English and French).

A collection of industrial property and copyright laws and treaties; a selection of publications related to intellectual property.

World Meteorological Organization—WMO

Address: Case postale 2300, 41 ave Giuseppe Motta, 1211 Geneva 2, Switzerland.

Telephone: (22) 7308111; **telex:** 414199; **fax:** (22) 7342326; **internet:** http://www.wmo.ch.

The WMO started activities and was recognized as a Specialized Agency of the UN in 1951, operating in the fields of meteorology, climatology, operational hydrology and related fields, as well as their applications.

MEMBERS

184 members; see Table on pp. 101–103.

Organization

(December 1997)

WORLD METEOROLOGICAL CONGRESS

The supreme organ of the Organization, the Congress, is convened every four years and represents all members; it adopts regulations, and determines policy, programme and budget. Twelfth Congress: May–June 1995.

EXECUTIVE COUNCIL

The Council has 36 members and meets at least yearly to prepare studies and recommendations for the Congress; it supervises the implementation of Congress resolutions and regulations, informs members on technical matters and offers advice.

SECRETARIAT

The secretariat acts as an administrative, documentary and information centre; undertakes special technical studies; produces publications; organizes meetings of WMO constituent bodies; acts as a link between the meteorological and hydrometeorological services of the world, and provides information for the general public.

Secretary-General: Prof. G. O. P. Obasi (Nigeria).

Deputy Secretary-General: M. J. P. Jarraud.

REGIONAL ASSOCIATIONS

Members are grouped in six Regional Associations (Africa, Asia, Europe, North and Central America, South America and South-West Pacific), whose task is to co-ordinate meteorological activity within their regions and to examine questions referred to them by the Executive Council. Sessions are held at least once every four years.

TECHNICAL COMMISSIONS

The Technical Commissions are composed of experts nominated by the members of the Organization. Sessions are held at least once every four years. The Commissions cover the following areas: Basic Systems; Climatology; Instruments and Methods of Observation; Atmospheric Sciences; Aeronautical Meteorology; Agricultural Meteorology; Hydrology; Marine Meteorology.

Activities

WORLD WEATHER WATCH PROGRAMME

Combining facilities and services provided by the members, the Programme's primary purpose is to make available meteorological and related geophysical and environmental information enabling them to maintain efficient meteorological services. Facilities in regions outside any national territory (outer space, ocean areas and Antarctica) are maintained by members on a voluntary basis.

Antarctic Activities: co-ordinate WMO activities related to the Antarctic, in particular the surface and upper-air observing programme, plan the regular exchange of observational data and products needed for operational and research purposes, study problems related to instruments and methods of observation peculiar to the Antarctic, and develop appropriate regional coding practices. Contacts are maintained with scientific bodies dealing with Antarctic research and with other international organizations on aspects of Antarctic meteorology.

Data Management: This aspect of the Programme monitors the integration of the different components of the World Weather Watch (WWW) Programme, with the intention of increasing the efficiency of, in particular, the Global Observing System, the Global Data Processing System and the Global Telecommunication System. The Data Management component of the WWW Programme develops data handling procedures and standards for enhanced forms of data representation, in order to aid member countries in processing large volumes of meteorological data. It also supports the co-ordinated transfer of expertise and technology to developing countries.

Emergency Response Activities: assist national meteorological services to respond effectively to man-made environmental emergencies, particularly nuclear accidents, through the development, co-ordination and implementation of WMO/IAEA established procedures and response mechanisms for the provision and exchange of observational data and specialized transport model products.

Global Data Processing System: consists of World Meteorological Centres (WMCs) at Melbourne (Australia), Moscow (Russia) and Washington, DC (USA), 37 Regional/Specialized Meteorological Centres (RSMCs) and 183 National Meteorological Centres. The WMCs and RSMCs provide analyses, forecasts and warnings for exchange on the Global Telecommunications System. Some centres concentrate on the monitoring and forecasting of environmental quality and special weather phenomena, such as tropical cyclones, monsoons, droughts, etc., which have a major impact on human safety and national economies. These analyses and forecasts are designed to assist the members in making local and specialized forecasts.

Global Observing System: Simultaneous observations are made at more than 10,000 land stations. Meteorological information is also received from 3,000 aircraft, 7,200 ships, 700 fixed and drifting buoys and 10 polar orbiting and geostationary meteorological satellites. About 160 members operate some 1,100 ground stations equipped to receive picture transmissions from geostationary and polar-orbiting satellites.

Global Telecommunication System: provides telecommunication services for the rapid collection and exchange of meteorological information and related data; consists of (a) the Main Telecommunication Network (MTN), (b) six Regional Meteorological Telecommunication networks, and (c) the national telecommunication networks. The system operates through 174 National Meteorological Centres, 30 Regional Telecommunications Hubs and the three WMCs.

Instruments and Methods of Observation Programme: promotes the world-wide standardization of meteorological and geophysical instruments and methods of observation and measurement to meet agreed accuracy requirements. It provides related guidance material and training assistance in the use and maintenance of the instruments.

System Support Activity: provides guidance and support to members in the planning, establishment and operation of the WWW. It includes training, technical co-operation support, system and methodology support, operational WWW evaluations, advanced technology support, an operations information service, and the WWW referral catalogue.

Tropical Cyclone Programme: established in response to UN General Assembly Resolution 2733 (XXV), aims at the development of national and regionally co-ordinated systems to ensure that the loss of life and damage caused by tropical cyclones and associated floods, landslides and storm surges are reduced to a minimum. The programme supports the transfer of technology, and includes five regional tropical cyclone bodies, to improve warning systems and for collaboration with other international organizations in activities related to disaster mitigation.

WORLD CLIMATE PROGRAMME

Adopted by the Eighth World Meteorological Congress (1979), the World Climate Programme (WCP) comprises the following components: World Climate Data and Monitoring Programme (WCDMP), World Climate Applications and Services Programme (WCASP), World Climate Impact Assessment and Response Strategies Programme (WCIRP), World Climate Research Programme (WCRP). The WCP is supported by the Global Climate Observing System (GCOS), which provides comprehensive observation of the global climate system, involving a multi-disciplinary range of atmospheric, oceanic, hydrologic, cyrospheric and biotic properties and processes. The objectives of the WCP are: to use existing climate information to improve economic and social planning; to improve the understanding of climate processes through research, so as to determine the predictability of climate and the extent of man's influence on it; and to detect and warn governments of impending climate variations or changes, either natural or man-made, which may significantly affect critical human activities.

Co-ordination of the overall Programme is the responsibility of the WMO, along with direct management of the WCDMP and WCASP. The UN Environment Programme (q.v.) has accepted responsibility for the WCIRP, while the WCRP is jointly administered by WMO, the International Council of Scientific Unions (ICSU, q.v.) and UNESCO's Intergovernmental Oceanographic Commission. Other organizations involved in the Programme include FAO, WHO, and the Consultative Group on International Agricultural Research (CGIAR). The WCP Co-ordinating Committee co-ordinates the activities of the four components of the Programme and liaises with other international bodies concerned with climate. In addition, the WCP supports the WMO/UNEP Intergovernmental Panel on Climate Change (see below) and the implementation of international agreements, such as the Framework Convention on Climate Change (FCCC, see p. 42).

World Climate Applications and Services Programme (WCASP): promotes applications of climate knowledge in the areas of food production, water, energy (especially solar and wind energy), urban planning and building, human health, transport, tourism and recreation.

World Climate Data and Monitoring Programme (WCDMP): aims to make available reliable climate data for detecting and monitoring climate change for both practical applications and research purposes. The major projects are: the Climate Change Detection Project (CCDP); development of climate data bases; computer systems for climate data management (CLICOM); the World Data and Information Referral Service (INFOCLIMA); the Climate Monitoring System; and the Data Rescue (DARE) project.

World Climate Impact Assessment and Response Strategies Programme (WCIRP): aims to make reliable estimates of the socio-economic impact of climate changes, and to assist in forming national policies accordingly. It concentrates on: study of the impact of climate variations on national food systems; assessment of the impact of man's activities on the climate, especially through increasing the amount of carbon dioxide and other radiatively active gases in the atmosphere; and developing the methodology of climate impact assessments.

World Climate Research Programme (WCRP): organized jointly with the Intergovernmental Oceanographic Commission of UNESCO and the ICSU, to determine to what extent climate can be predicted, and the extent of man's influence on climate. Its three specific objectives are: establishing the physical basis for weather predictions over time ranges of one to two months; understanding and predicting the variability of the global climate over periods of several years; and studying the long-term variations and the response of climate to natural or man-made influence over periods of several decades. Studies include: changes in the atmosphere caused by emissions of carbon dioxide, aerosols and other gases; the effect of cloudiness on the radiation balance; the effect of ground water storage and vegetation on evaporation; the Arctic and Antarctic climate process; and the effects of oceanic circulation changes on the global atmosphere.

ATMOSPHERIC RESEARCH AND ENVIRONMENT PROGRAMME

This major programme aims to help members to implement research projects; to disseminate relevant scientific information; to draw the attention of members to outstanding research problems of major importance, such as atmospheric composition and environment changes; and to encourage and help members to incorporate the results of research into operational forecasting or other appropriate techniques, particularly when such changes of procedure require international co-ordination and agreement.

Global Atmosphere Watch (GAW): This is a world-wide system that integrates most monitoring and research activities involving the measurement of atmospheric composition, and is intended to serve as an early warning system to detect further changes in atmospheric concentrations of 'greenhouse' gases, changes in the ozone layer and in long-range transport of pollutants, including acidity and toxicity of rain, as well as the atmospheric burden of aerosols. The instruments of these globally standardized observations and related research are a set of 20 global stations in remote areas and, in order to address regional effects, some 200 regional stations measuring specific atmospheric chemistry parameters, such as ozone and acid deposition. GAW is the main contributor of data on chemical composition and physical characteristics of the atmosphere to the GCOS. Through GAW, WMO has collaborated with the UN Economic Commission for Europe (ECE) and has been responsible for the meteorological part of the Monitoring and Evaluation of the Long-range Transmission of Air Pollutants in Europe. In this respect, WMO has arranged for the establishment of two Meteorological Synthesizing Centres (Oslo, Norway, and Moscow, Russia) which provide daily analysis of the transport of pollution over Europe. The GAW also gives attention to atmospheric chemistry studies, prepares scientific assessments and encourages integrated environmental monitoring. Quality Assurance Science Activities Centres have been established to ensure an overall level of quality in GAW.

Physics and Chemistry of Clouds and Weather Modification Research Programme: encourages scientific research on cloud physics and chemistry, with special emphasis on interaction between clouds and atmospheric chemistry, as well as weather modification such as precipitation enhancement ('rain-making') and hail suppression. It provides information on world-wide weather modification projects, and guidance in the design and evaluation of experiments. It also studies the chemistry of clouds and their role in the transport, transformation and dispersion of pollution.

Tropical Meteorology Research Programme: aims at the promotion and co-ordination of members' research efforts into such important problems as monsoons, tropical cyclones, meteorological aspects of droughts in the arid zones of the tropics, rain-producing tropical weather systems, and the interaction between tropical and mid-latitude weather systems. This should lead to a better understanding of tropical systems and forecasting, and thus be of economic benefit to tropical countries.

Weather Prediction Research Programmes: The programmes assist members in exchanging the results of research on weather prediction and long-range forecasting by means of international conferences and technical reports and progress reports on numerical weather prediction, in order to improve members' weather services. The Programme on Very Short- and Short-range Weather Prediction Research is designed to promote and co-ordinate research activities by members, with a view to improving forecast accuracy over a period extending to three or four days. The Programme on Medium- and Long-range Weather Prediction Research is aimed at the improvement and better co-ordination of members' research activities in weather prediction beyond day four, including monthly and seasonal forecasting.

APPLICATIONS OF METEOROLOGY PROGRAMME

Agriculture Meteorology Programme: the study of weather and climate as they affect agriculture and forestry, the selection of crops and their protection from disease and deterioration in storage, soil conservation, phenology and physiology of crops and productivity and health of farm animals; the Commission for Agricultural Meteorology supervises the applications projects and also advises the Secretary-General in his efforts to co-ordinate activities in support of food production. There are also special activities in agrometeorology to monitor and combat drought and desertification, to apply climate and real-time weather information in agricultural planning and operations, and to help improve the efficiency of the use of human labour, land, water and energy in agriculture; close co-operation is maintained with FAO, centres of CGIAR and UNEP.

Aeronautical Meteorology Programme: to provide operational meteorological information required for safe, regular and efficient air navigation, as well as meteorological assistance to non-real-time activities of the aviation industry. The programme is implemented at global, regional and national levels by the Commission for Aeronautical Meteorology (CAeM) playing a major role, taking into account relevant meteorological developments in science and technology, studying aeronautical requirements for meteorological services, promoting international standardization of methods, procedures and techniques, and considering requirements for basic and climatological data as well as aeronautical requirements for meteorological observations and specialized instruments. Activities under this programme are carried out, where relevant, with the International Civil Aviation Organization (ICAO, q.v.) and in collaboration with users of services provided to aviation.

Marine Meteorology and Oceanography: operational monitoring of the oceans and the maritime atmosphere; collection, exchange, archival recording and management of marine data; processing of marine data, and the provision of marine meteorological and oceanographic services in support of the safety of life and property at sea and of the efficient and economic operation of all sea-based activities. The Commission for Marine Meteorology (CMM) has broad responsibilities in the overall management of the programme. Certain programme elements are undertaken, jointly with the Intergovernmental Oceanographic Commission, within the context of the Integrated Global Ocean Services System (IGOSS), the Global Ocean Observing System (GOOS) and the work of the Data Buoy Co-operation Panel (DBCP). Close co-operation also occurs with the International Maritime Organization (IMO, q.v.), as well as with other bodies both within and outside the UN system.

Public Weather Services Programme: a new programme, the purpose of which is to assist members to provide reliable and effective weather and related services for the benefit of the public. The main objectives of the programme are: to strengthen members' capabilities to meet the needs of the community through the provision of comprehensive weather and related services, with particular emphasis on public safety and welfare; and to foster a better understanding by the public of the capabilities of national meteorological services and how best to use their services.

HYDROLOGY AND WATER RESOURCES PROGRAMME

The overall objective of this major programme is to apply hydrology to meet the needs of sustainable development and use of water and related resources, for the mitigation of water-related disasters and for effective environment management at national and international levels. The Programme consists of three mutually supporting component programmes:

Operational Hydrology Programme (OHP)—Basic Systems: Deals with rational development and operation of hydrological services of members; water resources assessment; technology in operational hydrology; and capacity building in hydrology and water resources.

Operational Hydrology Programme (OHP)—Applications and Environment: Concentrates on water-related aspects of disaster mitigation through forecasting and hazard assessment; studies of the impact of climate change on water resources; effective use of operational hydrology in support of sustainable development, including the protection of the aquatic environment.

The above are both planned and executed under the auspices of the Commission for Hydrology (CHy), which brings together representatives of the world's hydrological and hydrometeorological services.

Programme on Water-Related Issues: ensures co-operation between WMO and other international organizations that have water-related programmes, including work related to water resources assessment and natural disaster reduction. It maintains particularly close links with UNESCO.

Specific suppport for the transfer of operational technology is provided through the Hydrological Operational Multipurpose System (HOMS).

Other WMO programmes contain hydrological elements, which are closely co-ordinated with the Hydrology and Water Resources Programme. These include the Tropical Cyclone Programme, the World Climate Programme, and the Global Energy and Water Budget Experiment of the World Climate Research Programme.

EDUCATION AND TRAINING PROGRAMME

The overall objective of this programme is to assist members in developing adequately trained staff to meet their responsibilities for providing meteorological and hydrological information services.

Activities include surveys of the training requirements of member states, the development of appropriate training programmes, the monitoring and improvement of the network of WMO Regional Meteorological Training Centres, the organization of training courses, seminars and conferences and the preparation of training materials. The Programme also arranges individual training programmes and the provision of fellowships. There are about 500 trainees in any one year. About 300 fellowships are awarded annually. Advice is given on training materials, resources and expertise between members. A Panel of Experts on Education and Training was set up by the Executive Council to serve as an advisory body on all aspects of technical and scientific education and of training in meteorology and operational hydrology.

TECHNICAL CO-OPERATION PROGRAMME

The objective of the WMO Technical Co-operation Programme is to assist developing countries in improving their meteorological and hydrological services so that they can serve the needs of their people more effectively. This is through improving, *inter alia*, their early warning systems for severe weather; their agricultural-meteorological services, to assist in more reliable and fruitful food production; and the assessment of climatological factors for economic planning. In 1995 the cost of the assistance to developing countries, administered or arranged by the Technical Co-operation Programme, was US $15.7m.

United Nations Development Programme (UNDP): WMO provides assistance in the development of national meteorological and hydrological services, in the application of meteorological and hydrological data to national economic development, and in the training of personnel. Assistance in the form of expert missions, fellowships and equipment was provided to 70 countries in 1995 at a cost of US $1.6m., financed by UNDP.

Voluntary Co-operation Programme (VCP): WMO assists members in implementing the World Weather Watch Programme to develop an integrated observing and forecasting system. Member governments contribute equipment, services and fellowships for training. In 1995 79 projects for equipment and 100 projects for fellowships were approved under this programme. The total cost of all VCP projects in 1995 was US $6.0m.

WMO also carries out assistance projects under Trust Fund arrangements, financed by national authorities, either for activities in their own country or in a beneficiary country and managed by UNDP, the World Bank and UNEP. Several such projects, at a cost of US $6.9m., were in progress in 1995.

Financial support from WMO's regular budget for fellowships, group training, technical conferences and study tours amounted to US $1.3m. in 1995.

CO-OPERATION WITH OTHER BODIES

As a Specialized Agency of the UN, WMO is actively involved in the activities of the UN system. In addition, WMO has concluded a number of formal agreements and working arrangements with international organizations both within and outside the UN system, at the intergovernmental and non-governmental level. As a result, WMO participates in major international conferences convened under the auspices of the UN or other organizations.

Intergovernmental Panel on Climate Change (IPCC): established in 1988 by UNEP and WMO; comprises some 2,500 scientists who meet regularly to assess scientific information on changes in climate. The IPCC aims to formulate a realistic response to climate change, based on a global scientific consensus, in order to influence governmental action. In December 1995 the IPCC presented evidence to 120 governments, demonstrating 'a discernible human influence on global climate'. The IPCC supports the adoption of legally-binding commitments to reduce the emission of so-called 'greenhouse' gases. In December 1997 delegates from 159 countries met at the third conference of parties to the FCCC, convened in Kyoto, Japan, in order to negotiate a global reduction of such emissions. Participants at the conference concluded an agreement, the Kyoto protocol, whereby the main industrial countries pledged to reduce annual emissions of the six most harmful gases by as much as 8% by 2012.

FINANCE

WMO is financed by contributions from members on a proportional scale of assessment. The assessed regular budget for the four years 1996–99 was 255.0m. Swiss francs (compared with 234.4m. Swiss francs for 1992–95). Outside this budget, WMO implements a number of projects as executing agency for the UNDP or else under trust-fund arrangements.

PUBLICATIONS

Annual Report.

WMO Bulletin (quarterly in English, French, Russian and Spanish).

Reports, technical regulations, manuals and notes and training publications.

Membership of the United Nations and its Specialized Agencies

(at November 1997, unless otherwise indicated)

	UN	IAEA[1]	IBRD[2]	IDA[2]	IFC[2]	IMF[2]	FAO[3]	IFAD[4]	IMO[5]	ICAO[6]	ILO	ITU[7]	UNESCO[8]	UNIDO	UPU[9]	WHO[10]	WMO[11]	WIPO[12]
Afghanistan	x	x	x	x	x	x	x	x		x	x	x	x	x	x	x	x	
Albania	x	x	x	x	x	x	x	x	x	x	x	x	x	x	x	x	x	x
Algeria	x	x	x	x	x	x	x	x	x	x	x	x	x	x	x	x	x	x
Andorra	x											x	x			x		x
Angola	x		x	x	x	x	x	x	x	x	x	x	x	x	x	x	x	x
Antigua and Barbuda	x		x		x	x	x	x	x	x	x	x	x		x	x	x	
Argentina	x	x	x	x	x	x	x	x	x	x	x	x	x	x	x	x	x	x
Armenia	x	x	x	x	x	x	x	x		x	x	x	x	x	x	x	x	x
Australia	x	x	x	x	x	x	x	x	x	x	x	x	x	x	x	x	x	x
Austria	x	x	x	x	x	x	x	x	x	x	x	x	x	x	x	x	x	x
Azerbaijan	x		x	x	x	x	x	x	x	x	x	x	x	x	x	x	x	x
Bahamas	x		x		x	x	x		x	x	x	x	x	x	x	x	x	x
Bahrain	x		x		x	x	x		x	x	x	x	x	x	x	x	x	x
Bangladesh	x	x	x	x	x	x	x	x	x	x	x	x	x	x	x	x	x	x
Barbados	x		x		x	x	x	x	x	x	x	x	x	x	x	x	x	x
Belarus	x	x	x		x	x				x	x	x	x	x	x	x	x	x
Belgium	x	x	x	x	x	x	x	x	x	x	x	x	x	x	x	x	x	x
Belize	x		x	x	x	x	x	x	x	x	x	x	x	x	x	x	x	
Benin	x		x	x	x	x	x	x	x	x	x	x	x	x	x	x	x	x
Bhutan	x		x	x		x	x	x		x		x	x	x	x	x		x
Bolivia	x	x	x	x	x	x	x	x	x	x	x	x	x	x	x	x	x	x
Bosnia and Herzegovina	x	x	x	x	x	x	x	x	x	x	x	x	x	x	x	x	x	x
Botswana	x		x	x	x	x	x	x		x	x	x	x	x	x	x	x	
Brazil	x	x	x	x	x	x	x	x	x	x	x	x	x	x	x	x	x	x
Brunei	x		x			x			x	x		x			x	x	x	x
Bulgaria	x	x	x		x	x	x		x	x	x	x	x	x	x	x	x	x
Burkina Faso	x		x	x	x	x	x	x		x	x	x	x	x	x	x	x	x
Burundi	x		x	x	x	x	x	x		x	x	x	x	x	x	x	x	x
Cambodia	x	x	x	x	x	x	x	x	x	x	x	x	x	x	x	x	x	x
Cameroon	x	x	x	x	x	x	x	x	x	x	x	x	x	x	x	x	x	x
Canada	x	x	x	x	x	x	x	x	x	x	x	x	x		x	x	x	x
Cape Verde	x		x	x	x	x	x	x	x	x	x	x	x	x	x	x	x	x
Central African Republic	x		x	x	x	x	x	x		x	x	x	x	x	x	x	x	x
Chad	x		x	x		x	x	x		x	x	x	x	x	x	x	x	x
Chile	x	x	x	x	x	x	x	x	x	x	x	x	x	x	x	x	x	x
China, People's Republic	x	x	x	x	x	x	x	x	x	x	x	x	x	x	x	x	x	x
Colombia	x	x	x	x	x	x	x	x	x	x	x	x	x	x	x	x	x	x
Comoros	x		x	x	x	x	x	x		x	x	x	x	x	x	x	x	
Congo, Democratic Republic	x	x	x	x	x	x	x	x	x	x	x	x	x	x	x	x	x	x
Congo, Republic	x		x	x	x	x	x	x	x	x	x	x	x	x	x	x	x	x
Costa Rica	x	x	x	x	x	x	x	x	x	x	x	x	x	x	x	x	x	x
Côte d'Ivoire	x	x	x	x	x	x	x	x	x	x	x	x	x	x	x	x	x	x
Croatia	x	x	x	x	x	x	x	x	x	x	x	x	x	x	x	x	x	x
Cuba	x	x					x	x	x	x	x	x	x	x	x	x	x	x
Cyprus	x	x	x	x	x	x	x	x	x	x	x	x	x	x	x	x	x	x
Czech Republic	x	x	x	x	x	x	x		x	x	x	x	x	x	x	x	x	x
Denmark	x	x	x	x	x	x	x	x	x	x	x	x	x	x	x	x	x	x
Djibouti	x		x	x	x	x	x	x	x	x	x	x	x	x	x	x	x	
Dominica	x		x	x	x	x	x	x	x		x	x	x	x	x	x	x	
Dominican Republic	x	x	x	x	x	x	x	x	x	x	x	x	x	x	x	x	x	
Ecuador	x	x	x	x	x	x	x	x	x	x	x	x	x	x	x	x	x	x
Egypt	x	x	x	x	x	x	x	x	x	x	x	x	x	x	x	x	x	x
El Salvador	x	x	x	x	x	x	x	x	x	x	x	x	x	x	x	x	x	x
Equatorial Guinea	x		x	x	x	x	x	x	x	x	x	x	x	x	x	x		x
Eritrea	x		x	x	x	x	x	x	x	x	x	x	x	x	x	x	x	x
Estonia	x	x	x		x	x	x		x		x	x	x		x	x	x	x
Ethiopia	x	x	x	x	x	x	x	x	x	x	x	x	x	x	x	x	x	
Fiji	x		x	x	x	x	x	x	x	x	x	x	x	x	x	x	x	x
Finland	x	x	x	x	x	x	x	x	x	x	x	x	x	x	x	x	x	x
France	x	x	x	x	x	x	x	x	x	x	x	x	x	x	x	x	x	x
Gabon	x	x	x	x	x	x	x	x	x	x	x	x	x	x	x	x	x	x
The Gambia	x		x	x	x	x	x	x	x	x	x	x	x	x	x	x	x	x
Georgia	x	x	x	x	x	x	x	x	x	x	x	x	x	x	x	x	x	x
Germany	x	x	x	x	x	x	x	x	x	x	x	x	x	x	x	x	x	x
Ghana	x	x	x	x	x	x	x	x	x	x	x	x	x	x	x	x	x	x
Greece	x	x	x	x	x	x	x	x	x	x	x	x	x	x	x	x	x	x
Grenada	x		x	x	x	x	x	x		x	x	x	x	x	x	x		
Guatemala	x	x	x	x	x	x	x	x	x	x	x	x	x	x	x	x	x	x
Guinea	x		x	x	x	x	x	x	x	x	x	x	x	x	x	x	x	x
Guinea-Bissau	x		x	x	x	x	x	x	x	x	x	x	x	x	x	x	x	x

continued

	UN	IAEA[1]	IBRD[2]	IDA[2]	IFC[2]	IMF[2]	FAO[3]	IFAD[4]	IMO[5]	ICAO[6]	ILO	ITU[7]	UNESCO[8]	UNIDO	UPU[9]	WHO[10]	WMO[11]	WIPO[12]
Guyana	x		x	x	x	x	x	x	x	x	x	x	x	x	x	x	x	x
Haiti	x	x	x	x	x	x	x	x	x	x	x	x	x	x	x	x	x	x
Honduras	x		x	x	x	x	x	x	x	x	x	x	x	x	x	x	x	x
Hungary	x	x	x	x	x	x	x		x	x	x	x	x	x	x	x	x	x
Iceland	x	x	x	x	x	x	x		x	x	x	x	x		x	x	x	x
India	x	x	x	x	x	x	x	x	x	x	x	x	x	x	x	x	x	x
Indonesia	x	x	x	x	x	x	x	x	x	x	x	x	x	x	x	x	x	x
Iran	x	x	x	x	x	x	x	x	x	x	x	x	x	x	x	x	x	
Iraq	x	x	x	x	x	x	x	x	x	x	x	x	x	x	x	x	x	x
Ireland	x	x	x	x	x	x	x	x	x	x	x	x	x	x	x	x	x	x
Israel	x	x	x	x	x	x	x	x	x	x	x	x	x	x	x	x	x	x
Italy	x	x	x	x	x	x	x	x	x	x	x	x	x	x	x	x	x	x
Jamaica	x	x	x		x	x	x	x	x	x	x	x	x	x	x	x	x	x
Japan	x	x	x	x	x	x	x	x	x	x	x	x	x	x	x	x	x	x
Jordan	x	x	x	x	x	x	x	x	x	x	x	x	x	x	x	x	x	x
Kazakhstan	x	x	x	x	x	x	x		x	x	x	x	x	x	x	x	x	x
Kenya	x	x	x	x	x	x	x	x	x	x	x	x	x	x	x	x	x	x
Kiribati			x	x	x	x				x		x	x		x	x		
Korea, Democratic People's Republic	x						x	x	x	x		x	x	x	x	x	x	x
Korea, Republic	x	x	x	x	x	x	x	x	x	x	x	x	x	x	x	x	x	x
Kuwait	x	x	x	x	x	x	x	x	x	x	x	x	x	x	x	x	x	
Kyrgyzstan	x		x	x	x	x	x	x		x	x	x	x	x	x	x	x	x
Laos	x		x	x	x	x	x	x		x	x	x	x	x	x	x	x	x
Latvia	x	x	x	x	x	x	x		x	x	x	x	x		x	x	x	x
Lebanon	x	x	x	x	x	x	x	x	x	x	x	x	x	x	x	x	x	x
Lesotho	x		x	x	x	x	x	x		x	x	x	x	x	x	x	x	x
Liberia	x	x	x	x	x	x	x	x	x	x	x	x	x	x	x	x	x	x
Libya	x	x	x	x	x	x	x	x	x	x	x	x	x	x	x	x	x	x
Liechtenstein		x										x			x	x		x
Lithuania	x	x	x		x	x	x		x	x	x	x	x	x	x	x	x	x
Luxembourg	x	x	x	x	x	x	x	x	x	x	x	x	x	x	x	x	x	x
Macedonia, former Yugoslav republic	x		x	x	x	x	x	x	x	x	x	x	x	x	x	x	x	x
Madagascar	x	x	x	x	x	x	x	x	x	x	x	x	x	x	x	x	x	x
Malawi	x		x	x	x	x	x	x	x	x	x	x	x	x	x	x	x	x
Malaysia	x	x	x	x	x	x	x	x	x	x	x	x	x	x	x	x	x	x
Maldives	x		x	x	x	x	x	x	x	x	x	x	x	x	x	x	x	
Mali	x	x	x	x	x	x	x	x		x	x	x	x	x	x	x	x	x
Malta	x	x	x			x	x	x	x	x	x	x	x	x	x	x	x	x
Marshall Islands	x	x	x	x	x	x				x		x	x			x		
Mauritania	x		x	x	x	x	x	x	x	x	x	x	x	x	x	x	x	x
Mauritius	x	x	x	x	x	x	x	x	x	x	x	x	x	x	x	x	x	x
Mexico	x	x	x	x	x	x	x	x	x	x	x	x	x	x	x	x	x	x
Micronesia, Federated States of	x		x	x	x	x				x		x				x	x	
Moldova	x	x	x	x	x	x	x	x		x	x	x	x	x	x	x	x	x
Monaco	x	x							x	x		x	x		x	x	x	x
Mongolia	x	x	x	x	x	x	x	x	x	x	x	x	x	x	x	x	x	x
Morocco	x	x	x	x	x	x	x	x	x	x	x	x	x	x	x	x	x	x
Mozambique	x		x	x	x	x	x	x	x	x	x	x	x	x	x	x	x	x
Myanmar	x	x	x	x	x	x	x	x	x	x	x	x	x	x	x	x	x	
Namibia	x		x		x	x	x	x	x	x	x	x	x	x	x	x	x	x
Nauru										x		x	x		x	x		
Nepal	x		x	x	x	x	x	x	x	x	x	x	x	x	x	x	x	x
Netherlands	x	x	x	x	x	x	x	x	x	x	x	x	x	x	x	x	x	x
New Zealand	x	x	x	x	x	x	x	x	x	x	x	x	x	x	x	x	x	x
Nicaragua	x	x	x	x	x	x	x	x	x	x	x	x	x	x	x	x	x	x
Niger	x	x	x	x	x	x	x	x		x	x	x	x	x	x	x	x	x
Nigeria	x	x	x	x	x	x	x	x	x	x	x	x	x	x	x	x	x	x
Norway	x	x	x	x	x	x	x	x	x	x	x	x	x	x	x	x	x	x
Oman	x		x	x	x	x	x	x	x	x	x	x	x	x	x	x	x	x
Pakistan	x	x	x	x	x	x	x	x	x	x	x	x	x	x	x	x	x	x
Palau	x		x	x	x	x			x							x		
Panama	x	x	x	x	x	x	x	x	x	x	x	x	x	x	x	x	x	x
Papua New Guinea	x		x	x	x	x	x	x	x	x	x	x	x	x	x	x	x	x
Paraguay	x	x	x	x	x	x	x	x	x	x	x	x	x	x	x	x	x	x
Peru	x	x	x	x	x	x	x	x	x	x	x	x	x	x	x	x	x	x
Philippines	x	x	x	x	x	x	x	x	x	x	x	x	x	x	x	x	x	x
Poland	x	x	x	x	x	x	x		x	x	x	x	x	x	x	x	x	x
Portugal	x	x	x	x	x	x	x	x	x	x	x	x	x	x	x	x	x	x
Qatar	x	x	x			x	x	x	x	x	x	x	x	x	x	x	x	x
Romania	x	x	x		x	x	x	x	x	x	x	x	x	x	x	x	x	x
Russia	x	x	x	x	x	x			x	x	x	x	x	x	x	x	x	x
Rwanda	x		x	x	x	x	x	x		x	x	x	x	x	x	x	x	x
Saint Christopher and Nevis	x		x	x	x	x	x	x			x		x	x	x	x		x
Saint Lucia	x		x	x	x	x	x	x	x	x	x	x	x	x	x	x	x	x

continued

	UN	IAEA[1]	IBRD[2]	IDA[2]	IFC[2]	IMF[2]	FAO[3]	IFAD[4]	IMO[5]	ICAO[6]	ILO	ITU[7]	UNESCO[8]	UNIDO	UPU[9]	WHO[10]	WMO[11]	WIPO[12]
Saint Vincent and the Grenadines	x		x	x		x	x	x	x	x	x	x	x	x	x	x		x
Samoa	x		x	x	x	x	x	x	x	x		x	x		x	x	x	x
San Marino										x	x	x	x		x	x		x
São Tomé and Príncipe	x		x	x		x	x	x	x	x	x	x	x	x	x	x	x	
Saudi Arabia	x	x	x	x	x	x	x	x	x	x	x	x	x	x	x	x	x	x
Senegal	x	x	x	x	x	x	x	x	x	x	x	x	x	x	x	x	x	x
Seychelles	x		x		x	x	x	x		x	x		x	x	x	x	x	
Sierra Leone	x	x	x	x	x	x	x	x	x	x	x	x	x	x	x	x	x	x
Singapore	x	x	x		x	x			x	x	x	x			x	x	x	x
Slovakia	x	x	x	x	x	x	x		x	x	x	x	x	x	x	x	x	x
Slovenia	x	x	x	x	x	x	x		x	x	x	x	x	x	x	x	x	x
Solomon Islands	x		x	x	x	x	x	x	x	x	x	x	x		x	x	x	
Somalia	x		x	x	x	x	x	x	x	x	x	x	x	x	x	x	x	x
South Africa	x	x	x	x	x	x	x	x	x	x	x	x	x		x	x	x	x
Spain	x	x	x	x	x	x	x	x	x	x	x	x	x	x	x	x	x	x
Sri Lanka	x	x	x	x	x	x	x	x	x	x	x	x	x	x	x	x	x	x
Sudan	x	x	x	x	x	x	x	x	x	x	x	x	x	x	x	x	x	x
Suriname	x		x			x	x	x	x	x	x	x	x	x	x	x	x	x
Swaziland	x		x	x	x	x	x	x		x	x	x	x	x	x	x	x	x
Sweden	x	x	x	x	x	x	x	x	x	x	x	x	x	x	x	x	x	x
Switzerland		x	x	x	x	x	x	x	x	x	x	x	x	x	x	x	x	x
Syria	x	x	x	x	x	x	x	x	x	x	x	x	x	x	x	x	x	
Tajikistan	x		x	x	x	x	x	x		x	x	x	x	x	x	x	x	x
Tanzania	x	x	x	x	x	x	x	x	x	x	x	x	x	x	x	x	x	x
Thailand	x	x	x	x	x	x	x	x	x	x	x	x	x	x	x	x	x	x
Togo	x		x	x	x	x	x	x	x	x	x	x	x	x	x	x	x	x
Tonga			x	x	x	x	x	x		x		x	x	x	x	x	x	
Trinidad and Tobago	x		x	x	x	x	x	x	x	x	x	x	x	x	x	x	x	x
Tunisia	x	x	x	x	x	x	x	x	x	x	x	x	x	x	x	x	x	x
Turkey	x	x	x	x	x	x	x	x	x	x	x	x	x	x	x	x	x	x
Turkmenistan	x		x		x	x	x		x	x		x	x	x	x	x	x	x
Tuvalu												x	x		x	x		
Uganda	x	x	x	x	x	x	x	x		x	x	x	x	x	x	x	x	x
Ukraine	x	x	x		x	x			x		x	x	x	x	x	x	x	x
United Arab Emirates	x	x	x	x	x	x	x	x	x	x	x	x	x	x		x	x	x
United Kingdom	x	x	x	x	x	x	x	x	x	x	x	x	x	x	x	x	x	x
USA	x	x	x	x	x	x	x	x	x	x	x	x			x	x	x	x
Uruguay	x	x	x		x	x	x	x	x	x	x	x	x	x	x	x	x	x
Uzbekistan	x	x	x	x	x	x				x	x	x	x	x	x	x	x	x
Vanuatu	x		x	x	x	x	x		x	x		x	x	x	x	x	x	
Vatican City		x										x			x			x
Venezuela	x	x	x		x	x	x	x	x	x	x	x	x	x	x	x	x	x
Viet Nam	x	x	x	x	x	x	x	x	x	x	x	x	x	x	x	x	x	x
Yemen	x	x	x	x	x	x	x	x	x	x	x	x	x	x	x	x	x	x
Yugoslavia[13]	x	x			x	x	x	x	x	x	x	x	x	x	x	x	x	x
Zambia	x	x	x	x	x	x	x	x		x	x	x	x	x	x	x	x	x
Zimbabwe	x	x	x	x	x	x	x	x	x	x	x	x	x	x	x	x	x	x

1 Membership has also been approved for Burkina Faso.
2 Membership as at 16 December 1997.
3 The Cook Islands and the European Union are members of FAO; Puerto Rico is an associate member. Membership as at 31 December 1997.
4 The Cook Islands is a member of IFAD.
5 Hong Kong and Macau are associate members of IMO.
6 The Cook Islands is a member of ICAO.
7 Members also include British Overseas Territories, French Overseas Territories and United States Territories. Membership as at 22 September 1997.
8 The Cook Islands and Niue are members of UNESCO; Aruba, the British Virgin Islands, Macau and the Netherlands Antilles are associate members.
9 Members also include British Overseas Territories and the Netherlands Antilles and Aruba.
10 The Cook Islands and Niue are members of WHO; Puerto Rico and Tokelau are associate members.
11 Members also include British Caribbean Territories, the Cook Islands, French Polynesia, Hong Kong, Macau, the Netherlands Antilles and Aruba, and New Caledonia.
12 Ethiopia was scheduled to become a member of WIPO in February 1998.
13 See p. 4 for details on Yugoslavia's status in the UN.

AFRICAN DEVELOPMENT BANK—ADB

Address: 01 BP 1387, Abidjan 01, Côte d'Ivoire.

Telephone: 20-44-44; **telex:** 22202; **fax:** 20-49-09.

Established in 1964, the Bank began operations in July 1966, with the aim of financing economic and social development in African countries.

AFRICAN MEMBERS

Algeria	Eritrea	Niger
Angola	Ethiopia	Nigeria
Benin	Gabon	Rwanda
Botswana	The Gambia	São Tomé and Príncipe
Burkina Faso	Ghana	Senegal
Burundi	Guinea	Seychelles
Cameroon	Guinea-Bissau	Sierra Leone
Cape Verde	Kenya	Somalia
Central African Republic	Lesotho	South Africa
Chad	Liberia	Sudan
Comoros	Libya	Swaziland
Congo, Democratic Republic	Madagascar	Tanzania
Congo, Republic	Malawi	Togo
Côte d'Ivoire	Mali	Tunisia
Djibouti	Mauritania	Uganda
Egypt	Mauritius	Zambia
Equatorial Guinea	Morocco	Zimbabwe
	Mozambique	
	Namibia	

There are also 24 non-African members.

Organization

(January 1998)

BOARD OF GOVERNORS

The highest policy-making body of the Bank. Each member country nominates one Governor, usually its Minister of Finance and Economic Affairs, and an alternate Governor or the Governor of its Central Bank. The Board meets once a year. It elects the Board of Directors and the President.

BOARD OF DIRECTORS

The Board consists of 18 members (of whom six are non-African and hold 33.33% of the voting power), elected by the Board of Governors for a term of three years; it is responsible for the general operations of the Bank. The Board meets on a weekly basis.

OFFICERS

The President is responsible for the organization and the day-to-day operations of the Bank under guidance of the Board of Directors. The President is elected for a five-year term and serves as the Chairman of the Board of Directors. Under a restructuring programme, which was approved by the Bank's Governors in January 1995, the number of Vice-Presidents was reduced from five to three.

The Bank's activities are divided into five sections (for northern, southern, eastern, western and central Africa) and there is a separate department for disbursements.

Executive President and Chairman of Board of Directors: OMAR KABBAJ (Morocco).

Secretary-General: CHEIKH I. FALL.

FINANCIAL STRUCTURE

The ADB Group of development financing institutions comprises the African Development Fund (ADF) and the Nigeria Trust Fund (NTF), which provide concessionary loans, and the African Development Bank itself. The group uses a unit of account (UA), which, in 1996, was valued at US $1.43796.

The capital stock of the Bank was at first exclusively open for subscription by African countries, with each member's subscription consisting of an equal number of paid-up and callable shares. In 1978, however, the Governors agreed to open the capital stock of the Bank to subscription by non-regional states on the basis of nine principles aimed at maintaining the African character of the institution. The decision was finally ratified in May 1982, and the participation of non-regional countries became effective on 30 December. It was agreed that African members should still hold two-thirds of the share capital, that all loan operations should be restricted to African members, and that the Bank's President should always be an African national. In 1996 the ADB's authorized capital was US $23,295m. At the end of 1996 subscribed capital was $22,835m. (of which the paid-up portion was $2,792m.).

Activities

At the end of 1996 total loan and grant approvals by the ADB Group since the beginning of its operations amounted to US $30,749m. Of that amount the public utilities sector received the largest proportion of assistance (24.0%), while industry received 23.2%, agriculture 19.7%, transport 15.4%, multi-sector activities 12.4%, and education and health projects 5.3%. In 1996 the group approved 31 loans and grants amounting to $803m.

A new credit policy, adopted in May 1995, effectively disqualified 39 low-income regional members, deemed to be non-creditworthy, from receiving non-concessional ADB financing, in an attempt to reduce the accumulation of arrears. The ADB Group estimated that its capital requirements for the period 1997–2001 would amount to US $46,500m. to allow for greater flexibility in its lending. During 1996 the Bank supported international efforts to address the problem of heavily indebted poor countries (HIPCs), and agreed to participate in a six-year initiative which aimed to encourage economic prospects in those countries while reducing outstanding debt and preventing its recurrence (see World Bank, p. 67).

The ADB contributed funds for the establishment in 1986 of the Africa Project Development Facility, which assists the private sector in Africa by providing advisory services and finance for entrepreneurs: it is managed by the International Finance Corporation (IFC—see p. 73). In 1989 the ADB, in co-ordination with IFC and UNDP, created the African Management Services Company (AMSCo) which provides management support and training to private companies in Africa.

The Bank also provides technical assistance to regional member countries in the form of experts' services, pre-investment feasibility studies, and staff training; much of this assistance is financed through bilateral aid funds contributed by non-African member states. The Bank's African Development Institute provides training for officials of regional member countries in order to enhance the management of Bank-financed projects and, more broadly, to strengthen national capacities for promoting sustainable development. In 1990 the ADB established the African Business Round Table (ABR), which is composed of the chief executives of Africa's leading corporations. The ABR aims to strengthen Africa's private sector, promote intra-African trade and investment, and attract foreign investment to Africa. The ABR is chaired by the ADB's Executive President. At its fourth annual meeting, held in Arusha, Tanzania, in March 1994, the ABR resolved to establish an African Investment Bank, in co-operation with the ADB, which was to provide financial services to African companies.

In 1990 a Memorandum of Understanding for the Reinforcement of Co-operation between the Organization of African Unity (OAU—q.v.), the UN's Economic Commission for Africa (q.v.) and the ADB was signed by the three organizations. A joint secretariat supports co-operation activities between the organizations.

AFRICAN DEVELOPMENT BANK (ADB)

The Bank makes loans at a variable rate of interest, which is adjusted twice a year (the rate was 7.31% per year at December 1996), plus a commitment fee of 1%. Loan approvals amounted to US $508.2m. for 11 loans in 1996.

AFRICAN DEVELOPMENT FUND (ADF)

The Fund commenced operations in 1974. It grants interest-free loans to African countries for projects with repayment over 50 years (including a 10-year grace period) and with a service charge of 0.75% per annum. Grants for project feasibility studies are made to the poorest countries.

In 1987 donor countries agreed on a fifth replenishment of the Fund's resources, amounting to US $2,800m. for 1988–90. In future 85% of available resources was to be reserved for the poorest countries (those with annual GDP per caput of less than $510, at 1985 prices). In 1991 a sixth replenishment of the Fund's resources amounting to $3,340m. was approved for 1991–93. Negotiations for the seventh replenishment of the Fund's resources commenced in May 1993. However, in May 1994, donor countries withheld any new funds owing to dissatisfaction with the Bank's governance. In May 1996, following the implementation of various institutional reforms to strengthen the Bank's financial management and decision-making capabilities and to reduce its administrative costs, an agreement was concluded on the seventh replenishment of the ADF. Donor countries pledged some $2,690m. for the period 1996–98. An additional allocation of $420m. was endorsed at a special donors' meeting held in Osaka, Japan, in June. Since the seventh replenishment came into effect in September 1996 the ADF has funded 19

ADB Loan and Grant Approvals by Region, 1995–96
(millions of UA)

Country	1995	%	1996	%
Central Africa	53.00	11.80	2.60	0.50
Gabon	53.00		—	
São Tomé and Príncipe	—		2.60	
East Africa	1.01	0.20	71.50	12.80
Eritrea	—		14.03	
Ethiopia	—		19.50	
Kenya	—		15.94	
Seychelles	1.01		—	
Uganda	—		22.03	
North Africa	386.15	85.90	354.46	63.40
Algeria	25.75		250.00	
Mauritania	—		16.70	
Morocco	150.00		60.41	
Sudan	1.55		—	
Tunisia	208.85		27.35	
Southern Africa	9.04	2.00	57.36	10.30
Malawi	—		5.00	
Mozambique	—		24.36	
Zambia	7.29		15.00	
Zimbabwe	1.75		13.00	
West Africa	0.55	0.10	72.62	13.00
Benin	—		18.00	
Côte d'Ivoire	—		29.00	
Gambia	—		4.00	
Ghana	—		7.53	
Nigeria	—		2.09	
Senegal	0.55		12.00	
Total	449.74	100.00	558.54	100.00

projects in 14 countries, and aims to offer concessional assistance to 42 African countries over the period 1996–98.

NIGERIA TRUST FUND (NTF)

The Agreement establishing the Nigeria Trust Fund was signed in February 1976 by the Bank and the Government of Nigeria. The Fund is administered by the Bank and its loans are granted for up to 25 years, including grace periods of up to five years, and carry 0.75% commitment charges and 4% interest charges. The loans are intended to provide financing for projects in co-operation with other lending institutions. The Fund also aims to promote the private sector and trade between African countries by providing information on African and international financial institutions able to finance African trade.

In 1996 the fund approved one loan amounting to US $8.63m., bringing the total amount committed since operations began to $320.27m. for 58 loans.

ASSOCIATED INSTITUTIONS

The ADB actively participated in the establishment of five associated institutions:

Africa Reinsurance Corporation—Africa-Re: Reinsurance House, 46 Marina, PMB 12765, Lagos, Nigeria; tel. (1) 66-52-82; telex 22647; fax (1) 66-88-02; f. 1977; started operations in 1978; its purpose is to foster the development of the insurance and reinsurance industry in Africa and to promote the growth of national and regional underwriting capacities. Africa-Re has an auth. cap. of US $30m., of which the ADB holds 10%. There are 12 directors, one appointed by the Bank. Mems: 41 countries and the ADB. Sec.-Gen. BAKARY KAMARA.

African Export-Import Bank—Afreximbank: POB 404 Gezira, 11568; World Trade Centre Building, 1191 Corniche el-Nil, Cairo 11221, Egypt; tel. (2) 5780282; telex 20003; fax (2) 5780277; f. 1993; aims to increase the volume of African exports and to expand intra-African trade by financing exporters and importers directly and indirectly through trade finance institutions, such as commercial banks; auth. cap. US $750m., subscribed cap. $495m. (at May 1994). Pres. CHRISTOPHER EDORDU (Nigeria); Exec. Sec. J. W. T. OTIENO.

Summary of Bank Group Activities (US $ million)

	1995	1996	Cumulative total*
ADB loans			
Number	11	11	725
Amount approved	668.53	508.18	19,941.39
Disbursements	1,058.37	1,007.94	13,308.52
ADF loans and grants			
Number	—	19	1,183
Amount approved	—	286.36	10,487.22
Disbursements	615.91	626.45	6,955.57
NTF loans			
Number	—	1	58
Amount approved	—	8.63	320.27
Disbursements	3.70	7.18	205.65
Group total			
Number	11	31	1,966
Amount approved	668.53	803.16	30,748.88
Disbursements	1,677.98	1,641.57	20,479.74

* Since the initial operations of the three institutions (1967 for ADB, 1974 for ADF and 1976 for NTF).

Association of African Development Finance Institutions—AADFI: c/o ADB, 01 BP 1387, Abidjan 01, Côte d'Ivoire; tel. 20-40-90; fax 22-73-44; e-mail adfi@AfricaOnline.co.ci; f. 1975; aims to promote co-operation among financial institutions in the region in matters relating to economic and social development, research, project design, financing and the exchange of information. Mems: 86 in 53 African and non-African countries. Pres. GERSHOM MUMBA; Sec.-Gen. Dr MAGATTE WADE.

Shelter-Afrique (Société pour l'habitat et le logement territorial en Afrique): Longonot Rd, POB 41479, Nairobi, Kenya; tel. (2) 722305; telex 25355; fax (2) 722024; f. 1982 to finance housing in ADB mem. countries. Share capital is US $300m., held by 28 African countries, the ADB, Africa-Re and the Commonwealth Development Corpn's. Dir P. M'BAYE.

Société Internationale Financière pour les Investissements et le Développement en Afrique—SIFIDA: 22 rue François-Perréard, BP 310, 1225 Chêne-Bourg/Geneva, Switzerland; tel. (22) 8692000; telex 418647; fax (22) 8692001; e-mail sifida@cortex.ch; f. 1970 by 120 financial and industrial institutions, including the ADB and the IFC. Following a restructuring at the end of 1995, the main shareholders are now Banque Nationale de Paris (BNP), SFOM (itself owned by BNP, Banque Bruxelles Lambert and Dresdner Bank) and the six banking affiliates of BNP/SFOM in West and Central Africa. SIFIDA is active in the fields of project and trade finance in Africa and also provides financial advisory services, notably in the context of privatizations and debt conversion; auth. cap. US $75m., subscribed cap. $7.5m. Chair. VIVIEN LÉVY-GARBOUA; Man. Dir PHILIPPE SÉCHAUD. Publ. *African Banking Directory* (annually).

PUBLICATIONS

Annual Report.

ADB Today (every 2 months).

African Development Report.

African Development Review.

Basic Information (annually).

Economic Research Papers.

Quarterly Operational Summary.

Statistical Handbook (annually).

Summaries of operations in each member country and various background documents.

ANDEAN COMMUNITY OF NATIONS

(COMUNIDAD ANDINA DE NACIONES—CAN)

Address: Avda Paseo de la República 3895, Lima 27; Casilla 18-1177, Lima 18, Peru.

Telephone: (1) 2212222; **telex:** 20104; **fax:** (1) 2213329; **e-mail:** info@junda.org.pe.

The organization, officially known as the Acuerdo de Cartagena (the Cartagena Agreement) and also known as the Grupo Andino (Andean Group) or the Pacto Andino (Andean Pact), was established in 1969. In March 1996 member countries signed a Reform Protocol of the Cartagena Agreement, according to which the Group was to be superseded by the Andean Community of Nations (CAN, generally referred to as the Andean Community), in order to promote greater economic, commercial and political integration, under a new Andean Integration System (Sistema Andina de Integración). The group covers an area of 4,710,000 sq km, with some 102m. inhabitants in early 1996.

MEMBERS

Bolivia Colombia Ecuador Peru Venezuela

Note: Chile withdrew from the Group in 1976. Panama has observer status with the Community.

Organization

(January 1998)

ANDEAN PRESIDENTIAL COUNCIL

The presidential summits, which had been held annually since 1989, were formalized under the 1996 Reform Protocol of the Cartagena Agreement as the Andean Presidential Council. The Council was to provide the political leadership of the Community.

COMMISSION

The Commission consists of a plenipotentiary representative from each member country, with each country holding the presidency in turn. The Commission is assisted by two Consultative Councils, each comprising four representatives from each country, elected respectively by national employers' organizations and by trades unions.

COUNCIL OF FOREIGN MINISTERS

The Council of Foreign Ministers meets annually or whenever it is considered necessary, to formulate common external policy and to co-ordinate the process of integration.

GENERAL SECRETARIAT

The General Secretariat (formerly the Junta) is the body charged with implementation of the Commission's decisions. It submits proposals to the Commission for facilitating the fulfilment of the Community's objectives. Members are appointed for a three-year term. They supervise technical officials assigned to the following Departments: External Relations, Agricultural Development, Press Office, Economic Policy, Physical Integration, Programme of Assistance to Bolivia, Industrial Development, Programme Planning, Legal Affairs, Technology. Under the reforms agreed in March 1996 the Secretary-General was to be elected by the Council of Foreign Ministers and was to have enhanced powers to adjudicate in disputes arising between member states.

Secretary-General: SEBASTIÁN ALEGRETT (Venezuela).

PARLIAMENT

Parlamento Andino: Carrera 7A, No 13–58, Of. 401, Santafé de Bogotá, Colombia; tel. (1) 2844191; telex 42380; fax (1) 2843270; f. 1979; comprises five members from each country, and meets in each capital city in turn; makes recommendations on regional policy. Exec. Sec.-Gen. Dr RUBÉN VÉLEZ NÚÑEZ.

COURT OF JUSTICE

Tribunal de Justicia del Acuerdo de Cartagena: Calle Roca 450, Casilla 17-07-9054, Quito, Ecuador; tel. (2) 529990; telex 21263; fax (2) 554543; f. 1979, began operating in 1984; its function is to resolve disputes and interpret legislation. It comprises five judges, one from each member country, appointed for a renewable period of six years. The Presidency is assumed annually by each judge in turn, by alphabetical order of country.

RESERVE FUND

Fondo Latinoamericano de Reservas—FLAR: Carrera 13, No. 27–47, 10°, Santafé de Bogotá, Colombia; tel. (1) 2858511; fax (1) 2881117; f. 1978 as the Fondo Andino de Reservas to support the balance of payments of member countries, provide credit, guarantee loans, and contribute to the harmonization of monetary and financial policies; adopted present name in 1991, in order to allow the admission of other Latin American countries. In 1992 the Fund began extending credit lines to commercial for export financing. It is administered by an Assembly of the ministers of finance and economy of the member countries, and a Board of Directors comprising the Presidents of the central banks of the member states. In October 1995 it was agreed to expand the Fund's capital from US $800m. to $1,000m. Exec. Pres. MIGUEL VELASCO BOSSHARD (Peru); Sec.-Gen. MANUEL MARTÍNEZ (Colombia).

DEVELOPMENT CORPORATION

Corporación Andina de Fomento—CAF: Torre Central, Avda Luis Roche, Altamira, Pisos 5°–10°, Apdo 5086, Caracas, Venezuela; tel. (2) 209-2111; telex 22587; fax (2) 284-5754; f. 1968, began operations in 1970; aims to encourage the integration of the Andean countries by specialization and an equitable distribution of investments. It conducts research to identify investment opportunities, and prepares the resulting investment projects; gives technical and financial assistance; and attracts internal and external credit. Auth. cap. US $2,000m., subscribed or underwritten by the governments of member countries, or by public-, semi-public and private-sector institutions authorized by those governments. In 1996 CAF loans granted to Andean countries totalled $2,250m. The Board of Directors comprises representatives of each country at ministerial level. Mems: the Andean Community, Brazil, Chile, Jamaica, Mexico, Panama, and Trinidad and Tobago. Exec. Pres. ENRIQUE GARCÍA RODRÍGUEZ (Bolivia).

Activities

In May 1979, at Cartagena, Colombia, the Presidents of the five member countries signed the 'Mandate of Cartagena', which envisaged greater economic and political co-operation, including the establishment of more sub regional development programmes (especially in industry). In May 1987 representatives of member countries signed the Quito Protocol, modifying the Cartagena Agreement. The protocol included a relaxation of the strict rules that had formerly been imposed on foreign investors in the region (see below). It came into force in May 1988.

In May 1989 the Presidents of four member countries, together with the Bolivian Minister of Foreign Affairs, undertook to revitalize the process of Andean integration, by withdrawing measures that obstructed the programme of trade liberalization, and by complying with tariff reductions that had already been agreed upon. In May 1990 another meeting of heads of state agreed to co-ordinate negotiations with creditors, improve co-operation in industrial development, and adopt a common policy on exports of energy. They also agreed to hold direct elections to the Andean Parliament.

In May 1991, in Caracas, Venezuela, a summit meeting of the Andean Group agreed the framework for the establishment of a subregional free-trade area on 1 January 1992 and for an Andean common market, to be in full operation by 1995 (see below, under Trade). The 'Caracas Declaration' also included a measure to elect the Andean Parliament by universal suffrage, and an 'open skies' agreement, giving airlines of the member countries equal rights to airspace and airport facilities within the Andean Group area.

In March 1996 another summit meeting, held in Trujillo, Peru, affirmed member countries' commitment to combat drugs-trafficking and indirectly condemned the decision of the USA to 'decertify' the Colombian anti-narcotics campaign (and thus to suspend financial assistance to that country). At the same meeting, member countries agreed to a substantial restructuring of the Andean Group. The heads of state signed the Reform Protocol of the Cartagena Agreement, establishing the Andean Community of Nations, which was to have more ambitious economic and political objectives than the previous Group. A new General Secretariat was to replace the existing Junta as the body responsible for implementing the Community's decision and was to be headed by a Secretary-General with greater executive and decision-making powers than at present. The initiation of these reforms was also designed to accelerate harmonization in economic matters, particularly the achievement of a common external tariff. However, the commitment of member countries to the Andean Community was brought into question later in 1996: in June the Bolivian President attended the summit meeting of the Mercado Común del Sur (Mercosur–see p. 239) and agreed the framework of a free-trade agreement with Mercosur on a unilateral basis (thus becoming an associate member of that grouping). Other countries, notably Venezuela, were reported to be seeking individual trade agreements with Mercosur, although in September the five countries agreed to negotiate with Mercosur as a bloc. In April 1997 the Peruvian Government announced its intention to withdraw from the Cartagena Agreement, owing to the group's failure to agree on the terms of Peru's full integration into the Community's trading system. Later in that month the heads of state of the four other Community members attended a summit meeting, in Sucre, Bolivia, and reiterated their commitment to strengthening regional integration. A high-level group of representatives was to be established to pursue negotiations with Peru regarding its future relationship with the Community. The presidential meeting also reaffirmed the Community's objective of strengthening relations with other economic groupings, and, in particular, resolved to negotiate a free-trade agreement with the members of Mercosur by the end of the year, and with Panama by 30 June 1998. The former agreement was intended to further the prospects of a Free Trade Area of the Americas, which the Community envisaged as comprising several subregional and bilateral agreements. A meeting of representatives of the Community and the European Union (EU) was held in the Netherlands earlier in April, and the summit meeting endorsed the objective of strengthening political and economic relations with the EU, as well as with members of APEC and ASEAN.

TRADE

Trade within the group increased by about 37% annually between 1978 and 1980. A council for customs affairs met for the first time in January 1982, aiming to harmonize national legislation within the group. In December 1984 the member states launched a new common currency, the Andean peso, aiming to reduce dependence on the US dollar and to increase regional trade. The new currency was to be backed by special contributions to the Fondo Andino de Reservas (now the Fondo Latinoamericano de Reservas) amounting to US $80m., and was to be 'pegged' to the US dollar, taking the form of financial drafts rather than notes and coins.

In May 1986 a new formula for trade among member countries was agreed, in order to restrict the number of products exempted from trade liberalization measures: under the new agreement each country could retain trade restrictions on up to 40 'sensitive' products.

The 'Caracas Declaration' of May 1991 established an Andean free-trade zone, which was to commence on 1 January 1992. Ecuador, with its highly protectionist system, was given a special dispensation whereby it was to abolish 50% of its tariffs by January 1992, with the remainder being removed by June of the same year. Heads of state also agreed in May 1991 to create a common external tariff (CET), to standardize member countries' trade barriers in their dealings with the rest of the world. In December 1991 heads of state defined four main levels of external tariffs (between 5% and 20%), with the intention that these would enter into effect in January 1992, but the conclusion of negotiations was delayed by Ecuador's request for numerous exceptions. Following the Peruvian Government's suspension of the Peruvian Constitution in April 1992, Venezuela suspended its diplomatic relations with Peru, and negotiations on the CET were halted. In August a request by Peru for a suspension of its rights and obligations under the Pact was approved. The other members then ratified the four-level CET (although Bolivia was to retain a two-level system).

Trade among member states increased steadily in the early 1990s, reaching a total value of US $4,600m. in 1994. In that year trade within the Andean Group accounted for 12.3% of member countries' exports, and in 1995 the proportion increased to 12.6%. In May 1994 an agreement was reached to introduce a four-tier structure of external tariffs from 1 January 1995; however, differences within the group remained. In November 1994 ministers of trade and integration, meeting in Quito, Ecuador, concluded a final agreement on the CET. The agreement, which came into effect in February 1995, covered 90% of the region's imports (the remainder to be incorporated by 1999), which were to be subject to the following tariff bands: 5% for raw materials; 10%–15% for semi-manufactured goods; and 20% for finished products. In order to reach an agreement, special treatment and exemptions were granted, while Peru, initially, was to remain a 'non-active' member of the accord: Bolivia was to maintain external tariffs of 5% and 10%, Ecuador was permitted to apply the lowest rate of 5% to an initial 800 industrial items, and Colombia and Venezuela were granted 230 items to be subject to special treatment for four years. In June 1997 an agreement was concluded to ensure Peru's continued membership of the Community, which provided for that country's integration into the group's free-trade zone. The Peruvian Government agreed to eliminate customs duties on some 2,500 products with immediate effect, and it was agreed that the process be completed by 2005. However, negotiations were to continue with regard to the replacement of Peru's single tariff on products from outside the region with the Community's scale of external duties.

During 1997 negotiations were pursued with representatives of Mercosur to formulate a free-trade agreement (see above); however, the two groups failed to conclude an accord by the initial deadline of 31 December 1997, owing to differences regarding tariff reductions and requirements in respect of local content for provisions covering rules of origin.

INDUSTRY

Negotiations began in 1970 for the formulation of joint industrial programmes, particularly in the petrochemicals, metal-working and motor vehicle industries, but disagreements over the allocation of different plants, and the choice of foreign manufacturers for co-operation, prevented progress and by 1984 the more ambitious schemes had been abandoned. Instead, emphasis was to be placed on assisting small and medium-sized industries, particularly in the agro-industrial and electronics sectors, in co-operation with national industrial organizations.

From 1971, in accordance with a Commission directive (Decision 24), foreign investors were required to transfer 51% of their shares to local investors in order to qualify for the preferential trade arrangements. Transfers were to be completed by 1989 for Colombia, Peru and Venezuela, and by 1994 for Bolivia and Ecuador. Foreign-owned companies were not to repatriate dividends of more than 14% (later raised to 20%), except with approval of the Commission. In addition, foreign investors were forbidden to participate in transport undertakings, public utilities, banking and insurance, and were not to engage in activities already adequately covered by existing national enterprises. In early 1985 individual Pact members began to liberalize these laws, recognizing that the Group's policy, by deterring foreign investors, had contributed to its collective foreign debt of some US $70,000m.

The Quito Protocol, modifying the Cartagena Agreement, was signed by members in May 1987 and entered into force one year later. It finally annulled Decision 24, and replaced it with Decision 220, allowing greater freedom for individual countries to establish their own rules on foreign investment. Each government was to decide which sectors were to be closed to foreign participation, and the period within which foreign investors must transfer a majority shareholding to local investors was extended to 30 years (37 years in Bolivia and Ecuador). In March 1991 Decision 220 was replaced by Decision 291, with the aim of further liberalizing foreign investment and stimulating an inflow of foreign capital and technology. External and regional investors were to be permitted to repatriate their profits (in accordance with the laws of the country concerned) and there was no stipulation that a majority share-holding must eventually be transferred to local investors. A further directive, adopted in March, covered the formation of 'Empresas Multinacionales Andinas' (multinational enterprises) in order to ensure that at least two member countries have a shareholding of 15% or more of the capital, including the country where the enterprise was to be based. These enterprises were entitled to participate in sectors otherwise reserved for national enterprises, subject to the same conditions as national enterprises in terms of taxation and export regulations, and to gain access to the markets of all member countries.

In November 1988 member states established a bank, the Banco Intermunicipal Andino, which was to finance public works.

In May 1995 the Group initiated a programme to promote the use of cheap and efficient energy sources and greater co-operation in the energy sector. The programme planned to develop a regional electricity grid.

AGRICULTURE

The Andean Agricultural Development Programme was formulated in 1976 within which 22 resolutions aimed at integrating the Andean agricultural sector were approved. In 1984 the Andean Food Security System was created to develop the agrarian sector, replace imports progressively with local produce, and improve rural living conditions.

TRANSPORT AND COMMUNICATIONS

In 1983 the Commission formulated a plan to assist Bolivia by giving attention to its problems as a land-locked country, particularly through improving roads connecting it with the rest of the region and with the Pacific. The Community has pursued efforts to improve and deregulate the transport and telecommunications sectors throughout the region.

Asociación de Empresas de Telecomunicaciones del Acuerdo Subregional Andino—ASETA: Calle La Pradera 510 y San Salvador, Casilla 10-1106042, Quito, Ecuador; tel. (2) 563-812; telex 22860; fax (2) 562-499; recommends to its members measures to improve telecommunications services, in order to contribute to the further integration of the countries of the Andean Group. Sec.-Gen. MARCELO LÓPEZ ARJONA.

SOCIAL DEVELOPMENT

Three Secretariats co-ordinate activities in social development and welfare. These are located in Santafé de Bogotá, Colombia (for education, science and culture), Lima, Peru (for health), and Quito, Ecuador (for labour affairs).

ASIA-PACIFIC ECONOMIC CO-OPERATION—APEC

Address: 438 Alexandra Rd, 19th Floor, Alexandra Point, Singapore 119958.

Telephone: 2761880; **fax:** 2761775; **e-mail:** info@mail.apecsec.org.sg; **internet:** http://www.apecsec.org.sg.

Asia-Pacific Economic Co-operation (APEC) was initiated in November 1989, in Canberra, Australia, as an informal consultative forum of the six ASEAN members and their six dialogue partners in the Pacific. Its aim is to promote multilateral economic co-operation on issues of trade and investment.

MEMBERS

Australia	Indonesia	Papua New Guinea
Brunei	Japan	Philippines
Canada	Korea, Republic	Singapore
Chile	Malaysia	Taiwan*
China, People's Republic	Mexico	Thailand
Hong Kong	New Zealand	USA

* Admitted as Chinese Taipei.

Organization

(January 1998)

ECONOMIC LEADERS' MEETINGS

The first meeting of APEC heads of government was convened in November 1993, in Seattle, USA. Subsequently, each annual meeting of APEC ministers of foreign affairs and of economic affairs has been followed by an informal gathering of the leaders of the APEC economies, at which the policy objectives of the grouping are discussed and defined. The 1997 meeting was held in Vancouver, Canada, in November, and the 1998 meeting was to be held in Malaysia.

MINISTERIAL MEETINGS

APEC ministers of foreign affairs and ministers of economic affairs meet annually. These meetings are hosted by the APEC Chair, which rotates each year, although it was agreed, in 1989, that alternate Ministerial Meetings were to be convened in an ASEAN member country. Senior officials meet regularly between Ministerial Meetings to co-ordinate and to administer the budgets and work programmes of APEC's committees and working groups.

During 1996 meetings were held of ministers concerned with human resource development (in Manila, the Philippines, in January) , finance (in Kyoto, Japan, in March), trade (in Christchurch, New Zealand, in July), sustainable development (in Manila, the Philippines, in July), energy (in Sydney, Australia, in August), telecommunications and information (in Gold Coast, Australia, in September), small and medium enterprises (SMEs) (in Cebu, the Philippines, in September) and regional science and technology co-operation (in Seoul, Republic of Korea, in November).

SECRETARIAT

In 1992 the Ministerial Meeting, held in Bangkok, Thailand, agreed to establish a permanent secretariat to support APEC activities, and approved an annual budget of US $2m. The Secretariat became operational in February 1993. The Executive Director is appointed from the member economy chairing the group and serves a one-year term.

Executive Director: Dato' NOOR ADLAN (Malaysia).

COMMITTEES AND GROUPS

Agricultural Technical Co-operation Experts' Group (ATC): f. 1995, recognized as a formal APEC grouping in October 1996; aims to promote co-operation in the following areas: conservation and utilization of plant and animal genetic resources; research, development and extension of agricultural biotechnology; marketing, processing and distribution of agricultural products; plant and animal quarantine and pest management; development of an agricultural finance system,; sustainable agriculture; and agricultural technology transfer and training.

Budget and Administrative Committee (BAC): f. 1993 to advise APEC senior officials on budgetary, administrative and managerial issues. The Committee reviews the operational budgets of APEC committees and groups, evaluates their effectiveness and conducts assessments of group projects.

Committee on Trade and Investment (CTI): f. 1993 on the basis of a Declaration signed by ministers meeting in Seattle, USA, in order to facilitate the expansion of trade and the development of a liberalized environment for investment among member countries. The CTI undertakes initiatives to improve the flow of goods, services and technology in the region.

Economic Committee: f. 1994 following an agreement, in November, to transform the existing *ad hoc* group on economic trends and issues into a formal committee. The Committee aims to enhance APEC's capacity to analyse economic trends and to research and report on issues affecting economic and technical co-operation in the region. In addition, the Committee is considering the environmental and development implications of expanding population and economic growth.

Ad Hoc Policy Level Group on Small and Medium Enterprises (PLG-SME): f. 1995 to oversee all APEC activities relating to SMEs; supported the establishment of an APEC Centre for Technical Exchange and Training for Small and Medium Enterprises, which was inaugurated at Los Baños, near Manila, the Philippines, in September 1996.

In addition, the following Working Groups promote and co-ordinate practical co-operation between member countries in different activities: Trade and investment data review; Trade promotion; Industrial science and technology; Human resources development; Regional energy co-operation; Marine resource conservation; Telecommunications; Transport; Tourism; and Fisheries.

ADVISORY COUNCIL

APEC Business Advisory Council (ABAC): an agreement to establish ABAC, comprising up to three representatives of the private sector from each APEC member economy, was concluded at the Ministerial Meeting held in November 1995. The first meeting of ABAC was convened in June 1996 in Manila, the Philippines, where a provisional secretariat for the Council was to be established. At the meeting, ABAC resolved to accelerate the liberalization of regional trade and agreed to focus its activities on infrastructure, SMEs and human resource development, regional communications and finance and cross-border investment. Chair. ROBERTO ROMULO (Philippines).

Activities

APEC was initiated in 1989 as a forum for informal discussion within the region and, in particular, to promote trade liberalization in the Uruguay Round of negotiations, which were being conducted under the General Agreement on Tariffs and Trade (GATT). The Seoul Declaration, adopted by ministers meeting in the Republic of Korea in November 1991, sets out the objectives of APEC as follows:

(i) To sustain the growth and development of the region for the common good of its peoples and, in this way, to contribute to the growth and development of the world economy;

(ii) To enhance the positive gains, both for the region and the world economy, resulting from increasing economic interdependence, including by encouraging the flow of goods, services, capital and technology;

(iii) To develop and strengthen the open multilateral trading system in the interest of Asia-Pacific and all other economies;

(iv) To reduce barriers to trade in goods and services and investment among participants in a manner consistent with GATT principles, where applicable, and without detriment to other economies.

The Declaration also specifies that APEC was to encourage private-sector participation in APEC activities, in order to maximize benefits of regional co-operation. APEC supports 'open regionalism' to encourage trade liberalization throughout the world economy, as well as amongst its members.

ASEAN countries were initially reluctant to support any more formal structure of the forum, or to admit new members, owing to concerns that it would undermine ASEAN's standing as a regional grouping and be dominated by powerful non-ASEAN economies. In August 1991 it was agreed to extend membership to the People's Republic of China, Hong Kong and Taiwan (subject to conditions imposed by the People's Republic of China, including that a Taiwanese official of no higher than vice-ministerial level should attend the annual meeting of ministers of foreign affairs).

In September 1992 APEC ministers, meeting in Bangkok, Thailand, agreed to establish a permanent secretariat. In addition, the meeting created an 11-member non-governmental Eminent Persons Group (EPG), which was to assess trade patterns within the region and propose measures to promote co-operation. The first EPG report was presented at the ministerial meeting in Seattle, USA, in November 1993. It proposed the creation of an Asia-Pacific Community, which would be a negotiating bloc to consult and co-operate with other regional economic groupings and counter any threat to economic growth. The proposal was supported by Australia and the USA, but was considered by the majority of APEC members to incorporate an overly-formalized vision of the grouping. Ministers did agree on a framework for expanding trade and investment among member countries, and to establish a permanent committee (the CTI, see above) to pursue these objectives.

In August 1994 the EPG published its second report, which proposed a timetable for the liberalization of all trade across the Asia-Pacific region: negotiations for the elimination of trade barriers were to commence in the year 2000 and be completed within 10 years in developed countries, 15 years in newly-industrialized economies and by 2020 in developing countries. Trade concessions could then be extended on a reciprocal basis to non-members in order to encourage world-wide trade liberalization rather than isolate APEC as a unique trading bloc. In November 1994 the meeting of APEC heads of government adopted the Bogor Declaration of Common Resolve, which endorsed the EPG's timetable for free and open trade and investment in the region by the year 2020. Malaysia expressed its dissension, however, by proposing that the timetable for the elimination of trade barriers be non-binding. Other issues incorporated into the Declaration included the implementation of GATT commitments in full and strengthening the multilateral trading system through the forthcoming establishment of the World Trade Organization (WTO), intensifying development co-operation in the Asia-Pacific region and expanding and accelerating trade and investment programmes.

During 1995 meetings of APEC officials and other efforts to substantiate the trade liberalization agreement revealed certain differences among members regarding the timetable and means of implementing the measures, which were to be agreed upon at the 1995 Economic Leaders' Meeting. The principal concern, expressed notably by the USA, focused on whether tariff reductions were to be achieved by individual trade liberalization plans or based on some reciprocal or common approach. In August the EPG issued a report, to be considered at the November Leaders' Meeting, which advocated acceleration of tariff reductions and other trade liberalization measures agreed under GATT, the establishment of a dispute mediation service to reduce and settle regional trade conflicts and a review of new trade groupings within the APEC region. Further proposals for the implementation of the Bogor Declaration objectives were presented, in September, by the Pacific Business Forum, comprising APEC business representatives. The recommendations included harmonization of product quality, the establishment of one-stop investment agencies in each APEC country, training and technology transfers and the implementation of visa-free business travel by 1999. In November 1995 the Ministerial Meeting decided to dismantle the EPG, although a similar advisory group may be irregularly constituted, and to establish an APEC Business Advisory Council consisting of private-sector representatives.

In April 1995 APEC ministers of finance, convening for their annual meeting, in Bali, Indonesia, discussed means to prevent currency instability, and requested the involvement of the IMF in a study of the impact of foreign-exchange instabilities on regional trade. The first meeting of an APEC Financiers' Group of bankers was held concurrently.

In November 1995, APEC heads of government, meeting in Osaka, Japan, adopted an Action Agenda as a framework to achieve the commitments of the Bogor Declaration. Part One of the Agenda identified action areas for the liberalization and facilitation of trade and investment, for example customs procedures, rules of origin and non-tariff barriers. It incorporated agreements that the process was to be comprehensive, consistent with WTO commitments, comparable among all APEC economies and non-discriminatory. Each member economy was to ensure the transparency of its laws, regulations and procedures that affect the flow of goods, services and capital among APEC economies and to refrain from implementing any trade protection measures. A second part of the Agenda was to provide a framework for further economic and technical co-operation between APEC members in areas such as energy, transport, infrastructure, SMEs and agricultural technology. In order to resolve a disagreement concerning the inclusion of agricultural products into the trade liberalization process, a provision for flexibility was incorporated into the Agenda, taking into account diverse circumstances and different levels of development in APEC member economies. Liberalization measures were to be implemented from January 1997 (i.e. three years earlier than previously agreed) and were to be subject to annual reviews. A Trade and Investment Liberalization and Facilitation Special Account was established to finance projects in support of the implementation of the Osaka Action Agenda. In May 1996 APEC senior officials met in Cebu, the Philippines, to consider the medium-term Individual Action Plans (IAPs) of tariff reductions, which had been submitted by all members, and to achieve some coherent approach to tariff liberalization prior to the Leaders' Meeting in November. Several IAPs were resubmitted at a meeting, in July, of APEC ministers of trade. That meeting was also concerned with APEC's role in ensuring the success of the first WTO ministerial conference, scheduled to be held in Singapore, in December.

In August 1996 APEC energy ministers convened for the first time, in Sydney, Australia, to discuss the major energy challenges confronting the region, and to provide support and guidance to the Working Group on regional energy co-operation. It was agreed to facilitate and encourage private investment in the regional power infrastructure and to observe a set of policy principles, including the reduction of energy subsidies and the application of environmentally-sound technologies. In September APEC ministers responsible for the telecommunications and information industry resolved to pursue efforts to develop an Asia-Pacific Information Infrastructure (APII), which was outlined at their first meeting, held in May 1995.

In November 1996 the Economic Leaders' Meeting, held in Subic Bay, the Philippines, approved the Manila Action Plan for APEC (MAPA), which had been formulated at the earlier Ministerial Meeting, held in Manila. MAPA incorporated the IAPs and other collective measures aimed at achieving the trade liberalization and co-operation objectives of the Bogor Declaration (see above), as well as the joint activities specified in the second part of the Osaka Agenda. The main issue of debate at the Meeting was a US proposal to eliminate tariffs and other barriers to trade in information technology products by 2000. The heads of government endorsed this objective and determined to support efforts to conclude an agreement to this effect at the forthcoming WTO conference; however, they insisted on the provision of an element of flexibility in achieving trade liberalization in this sector.

The 1997 Economic Leaders' Meeting, held in Vancouver, Canada, in November, was dominated by concern at the financial instability that had affected several Asian economies during 1997. The final declaration of the summit meeting endorsed a framework of measures which had been agreed by APEC deputy ministers of finance and central bank governors at an emergency meeting convened in the previous week in Manila, the Philippines. The meeting, attended by representatives of the IMF, the World Bank and the Asian Development Bank, committed all member economies receiving IMF assistance to undertake specified economic and financial reforms, and supported a separate Asian funding facility to supplement international financial assistance. The emergency mechanism was to be reviewed by finance officials in early 1998, having been endorsed by APEC heads of government. The principal item on the Vancouver summit agenda was an initiative to enhance trade liberalization, which, the grouping insisted, should not be undermined by the financial instability in Asia. At the earlier Ministerial Meeting the following nine economic sectors had been identified for 'early voluntary liberalization': environmental goods and services; fish and fish products; forest products; medical equipment and instruments; toys; energy; chemicals; gems and jewellery; and telecommunications. The heads of government subsequently requested the authorities in each member state to formulate details of tariff reductions in these sectors by mid-1998, with a view to implementing the measures in 1999. A further six potential priority sectors were to be reviewed by ministers during the forthcoming year. Despite these proposals, the meeting attracted some criticism for not having addressed the implementation of IAPs. A previously published report of ABAC had urged greater liberalization of trade by member economies and stricter monitoring of tariff reduction programmes. In Vancouver APEC Economic Leaders declared their support for an agreement to liberalize financial services (which was successfully negotiated under the auspices of the WTO in December 1997) and for the objective of reducing the emission of 'greenhouse gases', which was to be under consideration at a global conference in the following month. The summit meeting agreed that Peru, Russia and Viet Nam should be admitted to APEC in 1998, but imposed a 10-year moratorium on further expansion of the grouping.

PUBLICATIONS

APEC Economic Outlook (annually).

APEC Business Travel Handbook.

Selected APEC Documents (annually).

Guide to the Investment Regimes of the APEC Member Economies.

APEC Energy Statistics (annually).

Foreign Direct Investment and APEC Economic Integration (irregular).

Who is Who in Fish Inspection of APEC Economies (irregular).

The State of Economic and Technical Co-operation in APEC.

Working group reports, regional directories, other irregular surveys.

ASIAN DEVELOPMENT BANK—ADB

Address: 6 ADB Ave, Mandaluyong City 0401, Metro Manila, Philippines; POB 789, 0980 Manila, Philippines.

Telephone: (2) 6324444; **telex:** 63587; **fax:** (2) 6362444; **internet:** http://www.asianderbank.org.

The Bank commenced operations in December 1966. The Bank's principal functions are to provide loans and equity investments for the economic and social advancement of its developing member countries, to give technical assistance for the preparation and implementation of development projects and programmes and advisory services, to promote investment of public and private capital for development purposes, and to respond to requests from developing member countries for assistance in the co-ordination of their development policies and plans.

MEMBERS

There are 40 member countries and territories within the ESCAP region and 16 others (see list of subscriptions below).

Organization

(January 1998)

BOARD OF GOVERNORS

All powers of the Bank are vested in the Board, which may delegate its powers to the Board of Directors except in such matters as admission of new members, changes in the Bank's authorized capital stock, election of Directors and President, and amendment of the Charter. One Governor and one Alternate Governor are appointed by each member country. The Board meets at least once a year.

BOARD OF DIRECTORS

The Board of Directors is responsible for general direction of operations and exercises all powers delegated by the Board of Governors, which elects it. Of the 12 Directors, eight represent constituency groups of member countries within the ESCAP region (with about 65% of the voting power) and four represent the rest of the member countries. Each Director serves for two years and may be re-elected.

Three specialized committees (the Audit Committee, the Budget Review Committee and the Inspection Committee), each comprising six members, assist the Board of Directors to exercise its authority with regard to supervising the Bank's financial statements, approving the administrative budget, and reviewing and approving policy documents and assistance operations.

The President of the Bank, though not a Director, is Chairman of the Board.

Chairman of Board of Directors and President: MITSUO SATO (Japan).

Vice-President (Region East): PETER H. SULLIVAN (USA).

Vice-President (Finance and Administration): PIERRE UHEL (France).

Vice-President (Region West): BONG-SUH LEE (Republic of Korea).

ADMINISTRATION

The Bank had 1,939 staff on 31 December 1996.

A major reorganization of the Bank's administrative and operational structure came into effect on 1 January 1995, in order to strengthen the Bank's regional and country focus. The offices of the General Auditor, Post-Evaluation, Strategy and Policy, and Environment and Social Development report directly to the President of the Bank. The three Vice-Presidents are responsible for the following departments and divisions: Programmes (West), Agriculture and Social Sectors, Infrastructure, Energy and Financial Sectors, the Private Sector Group, the Economics and Development Centre; Programmes (East), Agriculture and Social Sectors, Infrastructure, Energy and Financial Sectors, Co-financing, the Office of Pacific Operations, Central Operations Services; and, the Office of the Secretary, the Office of the General Counsel, Budget, Personnel and Management Systems, Administrative Services, Controller's Department, Treasurer's Department, Information, Office of Computer Services.

There are Resident Missions in Bangladesh, Cambodia, India, Indonesia, Nepal, Pakistan and Viet Nam. In addition, there is a Bank Regional Mission in Vanuatu (for the South Pacific) and Representative Offices in Tokyo, Japan, Frankfurt am Main, Germany (for Europe), and Washington, DC, USA (for North America).

Secretary: D.C. AMERASINGHE (Sri Lanka).

General Counsel: BARRY METZGER (USA).

FINANCIAL STRUCTURE

The Bank's ordinary capital resources (which are used for loans to the more advanced developing member countries) are held and used entirely separately from its Special Funds resources (see below). A fourth General Capital Increase (GCI IV), amounting to US $26,318m. (or some 100%), was authorized in May 1994. At the final deadline for subscription to GCI IV, on 30 September 1996, 55 member countries had subscribed shares amounting to $24,675.4m.

At 31 December 1996 the position of subscriptions to the capital stock was as follows: authorized US $50,102.7m.; subscribed $49,368m.

The Bank also borrows funds from the world capital markets. Total borrowings during 1996 amounted to US $584m. (compared with $1,715m. in 1995).

In July 1986 the Bank abolished the system of fixed lending rates, under which ordinary operations loans had carried interest rates fixed at the time of loan commitment for the entire life of the loan. Under the new system the lending rate is adjusted every six months, to take into account changing conditions in international financial markets.

SPECIAL FUNDS

The Asian Development Fund (ADF) was established in 1974 in order to provide a systematic mechanism for mobilizing and administering resources for the Bank to lend on concessionary terms to the least-developed member countries. ADF loans are interest-free (although carry an annual service charge of 1%) and are repayable over a period of 35–40 years. At 30 December 1996 cumulative disbursements from ADF resources totalled US $11,981.3m.

Successive replenishments of the Fund's resources amounted to US $809m. for the period 1976–78, $2,150m. for 1979–82, $3,214m. for 1983–86, and $3,600m. for 1987–90. A further replenishment (ADF VI) was approved in December 1991, providing $4,200m. for the four years 1992–95. In January 1997 donor countries concluded an agreement for a seventh replenishment of the Fund's resources, which incorporated an agreed figure of $6,300m. for ADF operations during the period 1997–2000 and recommendations that new donor contributions initially amount to $2,610m. and that the commitment authority from non-donor resources total $3,300m., almost double the level set in the previous replenishment.

The Bank provides technical assistance grants from its Technical Assistance Special Fund (TASF). By the end of 1996, the Fund's total resources amounted to US $630.0m., including $85.7m. from direct voluntary contributions, of which $511.9m. had been utilized. The Japan Special Fund (JSF) was established in 1988 to provide finance for technical assistance by means of grants, in both the public and private sectors. The JSF aims to help developing member countries restructure their economies, enhance the opportunities for attracting new investment, and recycle funds. The Japanese Government had committed a total of 72,830m. yen (equivalent to $633.9m.) to the JSF by the end of 1996 (of which $326.5m. had been utilized).

Activities

Loans by the Bank are usually aimed at specific projects. In responding to requests from member governments for loans, the Bank's

SUBSCRIPTIONS AND VOTING POWER
(31 December 1996)

Country	Subscribed capital (% of total)	Voting power (% of total)
Regional:		
Afghanistan	0.035	0.385
Australia	5.952	5.119
Bangladesh	1.050	1.197
Bhutan	0.006	0.362
Cambodia	0.051	0.398
China, People's Republic	6.628	5.660
Cook Islands	0.003	0.359
Fiji	0.070	0.413
Hong Kong	0.560	0.805
India	6.512	5.567
Indonesia	5.602	4.839
Japan	16.054	13.200
Kazakhstan	0.830	1.021
Kiribati	0.004	0.360
Korea, Republic	5.182	4.503
Kyrgyzstan	0.308	0.603
Laos	0.014	0.369
Malaysia	2.801	2.598
Maldives	0.004	0.360
Marshall Islands	0.003	0.359
Micronesia, Federated States	0.004	0.360
Mongolia	0.015	0.370
Myanmar	0.560	0.805
Nauru	0.004	0.360
Nepal	0.151	0.478
New Zealand	1.580	1.621
Pakistan	2.241	2.150
Papua New Guinea	0.097	0.434
Philippines	2.451	2.318
Singapore	0.350	0.637
Solomon Islands	0.007	0.363
Sri Lanka	0.597	0.834
Taiwan	1.120	1.253
Thailand	1.400	1.478
Tonga	0.004	0.360
Tuvalu	0.001	0.358
Uzbekistan	0.693	0.911
Vanuatu	0.007	0.363
Viet Nam	0.351	0.638
(Western) Samoa	0.003	0.360
Sub-total	63.306	64.931
Non-regional:		
Austria	0.350	0.637
Belgium	0.350	0.637
Canada	5.381	4.662
Denmark	0.350	0.637
Finland	0.350	0.637
France	2.394	2.273
Germany	4.450	3.917
Italy	1.859	1.844
Netherlands	1.055	1.201
Norway	0.350	0.637
Spain	0.350	0.637
Sweden	0.350	0.637
Switzerland	0.600	0.837
Turkey	0.350	0.637
United Kingdom	2.101	2.038
USA	16.054	13.200
Sub-total	36.694	35.069
Total	100.000	100.000

staff assesses the financial and economic viability of projects and the way in which they fit into the economic framework and priorities of development of the country concerned. In 1987 the Bank adopted a policy of lending in support of programmes of sectoral adjustment, not limited to specific projects; such lending was not to exceed 15% of total Bank lending. In 1985 the Bank decided to expand its assistance to the private sector, hitherto comprising loans to development finance institutions, under government guarantee, for lending to small and medium-sized enterprises; a programme was formulated for direct financial assistance, in the form of equity and loans without government guarantee, to private enterprises. In addition, the Bank was to increase its support for financial institutions and capital markets and, where appropriate, give assistance for the privatization of public sector enterprises. In 1992 a Social Dimensions Unit was established as part of the central administrative structure of the Bank, which contributed to the Bank's increasing awareness of the importance of social aspects of development as essential components of sustainable economic growth. During the early 1990s the Bank also aimed to expand its role as project financier by providing assistance for policy formulation and review and promoting regional co-operation, while placing greater emphasis on individual country requirements.

Under the Bank's Medium-Term Strategic Framework for the period 1995–98 the following concerns were identified as strategic development objectives: promoting economic growth; reducing poverty; supporting human development (including population planning); improving the status of women; and protecting the environment. In 1995 the Bank resolved to promote sound development management, by integrating into its operations and projects the promotion of governance issues, such as capacity-building, legal frameworks and openness of information. Other policy initiatives adopted during the year included a new co-financing and guarantee policy to extend the use of guarantees and to provide greater assistance to co-financiers in order to mobilize more effectively private resources for development projects; a commitment to assess development projects for their impact on the local population and to avoid all involuntary resettlement where possible; the establishment of a formal procedure for grievances, under which the Board may authorize an inspection of a project, by an independent panel of experts, at the request of the affected community or group; and a policy to place greater emphasis on the development of the private sector, through the Bank's lending commitments and technical assistance activities. The Bank pursued these objectives throughout 1996 and incorporated components in support of good governance and capacity-building into an estimated 65% of all loan projects. During 1997 the Bank attempted to refine its policy on good governance by emphasizing the following two objectives: assisting the governments of developing countries to create conditions conducive to private-sector investment, for example through public-sector management reforms; and assisting those governments to identify and secure large-scale and long-term funding, for example through the establishment of joint public-private ventures and the formulation of legal frameworks.

In 1996 the Board approved the establisment of an ADB Institute (ADBI) to undertake research on development strategies and to conduct management training courses for administrators from developing member countries. The ADBI was to be located in Tokyo, Japan, and financed by the Japanese Government.

In 1996 the Bank approved 83 loans for projects in 21 developing member countries, amounting to US $5,545.08m. (compared with $5,504.39m. for 72 loans in 1995). Loans from ordinary capital resources totalled $3,879.45m., while loans from the ADF amounted to $1,665.63m. Private-sector operations approved amounted to $263.3m., which included direct loans without government guarantee of $156.0m. and equity investments of $107.3m. Disbursements of loans during 1996 amounted to $3,796.70m., compared with $3,587.02m. in the previous year.

During 1996 the transport and communications sector received the largest proportion (27%) of total loan approvals, while the energy sector received 22% and agriculture and natural resources 14% (see table).

In 1996 grants approved for technical assistance (e.g. project preparation, consultant services and training) amounted to US $174.9m. for 286 projects, with $58.7m. deriving from the Bank's ordinary resources and the TASF, $79.9m. from the JSF and $36.3m. from bilateral and multilateral sources. The Bank's Post-Evaluation Office prepares reports on completed projects, in order to assess achievements and problems.

The Bank co-operates with other international organizations active in the region, particularly the World Bank group, UNDP and the Asia-Pacific Economic Co-operation forum, and participates in meetings of aid donors for developing member countries. In 1996 the Bank signed a memorandum of understanding with the UN Industrial Development Organization, in order to strengthen co-operation between the two organizations.

BUDGET

Internal administrative expenses amounted to US $183.6m. in 1996, and was projected to total $199.5m. in 1997.

PUBLICATIONS

ADB Business Opportunities (monthly).

ADB Research Bulletin (2 a year).

ADB Review (6 a year).

Annual Report.

Asian Development Outlook (annually).

Asian Development Review (2 a year).
The Bank's Medium-Term Strategic Framework.
Key Indicators of Developing Asian and Pacific Countries (annually).
Loan, Technical Assistance and Private Sector Operations Approvals (monthly).
Loan and Technical Assistance Statistics Yearbook.
Project Profiles for Commercial Co-financing (quarterly).
Studies and reports, guidelines, sample bidding documents, staff papers.

BANK ACTIVITIES BY SECTOR

Sector	Loan Approvals (US $ million) 1996 Amount	1996 %	1968–96 %
Agriculture and natural resources	802.33	14.47	22.07
Energy	1,194.15	21.54	25.47
Finance	213.00	3.84	9.62
Industry and non-fuel minerals	222.00	4.06	3.80
Social infrastructure	731.10	13.18	15.27
Transport and communications	1,489.00	26.85	20.47
Multi-sector and others	893.50	16.11	3.29
Total	5,545.08	100.00	100.00

LENDING ACTIVITIES BY COUNTRY (US $ million)

Country	Loans approved in 1996: Ordinary Capital	ADF	Total
Bangladesh	—	256.40	256.40
Cambodia	0.00	105.00	105.00
China, People's Rep.	1,102.00	—	1,102.00
Cook Islands	—	5.00	5.00
India	788.00	—	788.00
Indonesia	884.30	67.80	952.10
Kazakhstan	50.00	20.00	70.00
Kyrgyzstan	—	80.00	80.00
Laos	—	91.70	91.70
Malaysia	26.30	—	26.30
Micronesia, Federated States	—	10.60	10.60
Mongolia	—	63.50	63.50
Nepal	36.50	252.70	289.20
Pakistan	332.00	283.00	615.00
Philippines	250.35	68.00	318.35
Sri Lanka	—	44.03	44.03
Thailand	330.00	—	330.00
Tonga	—	4.90	4.90
Uzbekistan	50.00	—	50.00
Vanuatu	—	10.00	10.00
Viet Nam	30.00	303.00	333.00
Total	3,879.45	1,665.63	5,545.08

LENDING ACTIVITIES (in %)

Country	1988–92 Ordinary Capital	1988–92 ADF	1993–96 Ordinary Capital	1993–96 ADF
Bangladesh	—	25.4	0.1	19.6
Bhutan	—	0.2	—	0.2
Cambodia	—	1.1	—	3.2
China, People's Rep.	12.3	—	31.5	—
Cook Islands	—	0.1	—	0.2
Fiji	0.4	—	—	—
India	24.9	—	17.0	—
Indonesia	31.0	5.7	26.6	4.1
Kazakhstan	—	—	1.3	0.7
Kiribati	—	0.0	—	—
Korea, Republic	0.9	—	—	—
Kyrgyzstan	—	—	—	2.9
Laos	—	3.5	—	5.6
Malaysia	3.1	—	1.0	—
Maldives	—	0.2	—	0.2
Marshall Islands	—	0.1	—	0.4
Micronesia, Federated States	—	—	—	0.3
Mongolia	—	0.5	—	5.0
Nepal	—	7.3	0.3	6.1
Pakistan	10.1	29.0	4.6	22.9
Papua New Guinea	0.6	2.4	—	0.5
Philippines	10.9	11.7	7.9	3.7
Solomon Islands	—	0.1	—	0.0
Sri Lanka	—	11.7	—	7.1
Thailand	5.5	—	9.1	—
Tonga	—	0.3	—	0.3
Uzbekistan	—	—	0.4	—
Vanuatu	—	0.1	—	0.2
Viet Nam	—	—	0.2	16.8
(Western) Samoa	—	0.6	—	0.0
Regional	0.3	—	—	—
Total	100.0	100.0	100.0	100.0
Value (US $ million)	13,978.5	6,428.3	14,343.4	5,594.7

Source: *ADB Annual Report 1996.*

ASSOCIATION OF SOUTH EAST ASIAN NATIONS—ASEAN

Address: 70A Jalan Sisingamangaraja, POB 2072, Jakarta 12110, Indonesia.

Telephone: (21) 7262410; **telex:** 47214; **fax:** (21) 7398234; **e-mail:** public@asean.or.id; **internet:** http://www.aseansec.org.

ASEAN was established in August 1967 at Bangkok, Thailand, to accelerate economic progress and to increase the stability of the South-East Asian region.

MEMBERS*

Brunei	Malaysia	Singapore
Indonesia	Myanmar	Thailand
Laos	Philippines	Viet Nam

* Cambodia, which was granted observer status of the organization in July 1995, was scheduled to become a full member in July 1997; however, its admission was postponed owing to internal conflict and adverse political conditions.

Organization

(January 1998)

SUMMIT MEETING

The highest authority of ASEAN, bringing together the heads of government of member countries. The first meeting was held in Bali, Indonesia, in February 1976; the second in Kuala Lumpur, Malaysia, in August 1977. A third summit meeting was held in Manila, the Philippines, in December 1987, and a fourth was held in Singapore in January 1992. Henceforth, summit meetings were to be held every three years, with an interim informal gathering of heads of government convened at least once. The fifth summit meeting was held in Bangkok, Thailand, in December 1995. The 30th anniversary of the founding of ASEAN was commemorated at an informal summit meeting held in Kuala Lumpur, Malaysia, in December 1997.

MINISTERIAL MEETINGS

The ministers of foreign affairs of member states meet annually, in each member country in turn, to formulate policy guidelines and to co-ordinate ASEAN activities. These meetings are followed by 'post-ministerial conferences' (PMCs), where ASEAN ministers of foreign affairs meet with their counterparts from countries that are 'dialogue partners' (see below) as well as from other countries. Ministers of economic affairs also meet about once a year, to direct ASEAN economic co-operation, and other ministers meet when necessary. Ministerial meetings are serviced by the committees described below.

STANDING COMMITTEE

The Standing Committee normally meets every two months. It consists of the minister of foreign affairs of the host country and ambassadors of the other members accredited to the host country.

SECRETARIATS

A permanent secretariat was established in Jakarta, Indonesia, in 1976 to form a central co-ordinating body. The Secretariat comprises the following five bureaux: general affairs; economic co-operation; functional co-operation; ASEAN co-operation unit and dialogue relations; and the AFTA unit. The Secretary-General holds office for a five-year term. In each member country day-to-day work is co-ordinated by an ASEAN national secretariat.

Secretary-General: RODOLFO SEVERINO (Philippines).

COMMITTEES AND SENIOR OFFICIALS' MEETINGS

Relevant ministerial meetings are serviced by the following three Committees: Culture and Information; Science and Technology; and Social Development. ASEAN political co-operation is directed by a Senior Officials' Meeting. Economic co-operation activities are administered by a Senior Economic Officials' Meeting. Other groups of senior officials meet to direct ASEAN activities concerned with drug issues and the environment. Matters relating to the civil service are considered by an ASEAN Conference (held every two years). ASEAN's various work programmes and activities are also supported by a network of subsidiary technical bodies comprising sub-committees, expert groups, *ad hoc* working groups and working parties.

To support the conduct of relations with other countries and international organizations, ASEAN committees (composed of heads of diplomatic missions) have been established in 12 foreign capitals: those of Australia, Belgium, Canada, France, Germany, India, Japan, the Republic of Korea, New Zealand, Switzerland, the United Kingdom and the USA.

Activities

ASEAN was established in 1967 with the signing of the ASEAN Declaration, otherwise known as the Bangkok Declaration, by the ministers of foreign affairs of Indonesia, Malaysia, the Philippines, Singapore and Thailand. Brunei joined the organization in January 1984, shortly after attaining independence. Viet Nam was admitted as the seventh member of ASEAN in July 1995; Laos and Myanmar joined in July 1997. The ASEAN Declaration sets out the objectives of the organization as follows:

(i) To accelerate economic growth, social progress and cultural development in the region through joint endeavours in the spirit of equality and partnership in order to strengthen the foundation for a prosperous and peaceful community of South East Asian nations;

(ii) To promote regional peace and stability through abiding respect for justice and the rule of law in the relationship among countries of the region and adherence to the principles of the United Nations Charter;

(iii) To promote active collaboration and mutual assistance on matters of common interest in the economic, social, cultural, technical, scientific and administrative fields;

(iv) To provide assistance to each other in the form of training and research facilities in the educational, professional, technical and administrative spheres;

(v) To collaborate more effectively for the greater utilization of their agriculture and industries, the expansion of their trade, including the study of the problems of international commodity trade, the improvement of their transportation and communication facilities and the raising of the living standards of their people;

(vi) To promote South-East Asian studies; and

(vii) To maintain close and beneficial co-operation with existing international and regional organizations with similar aims and purposes, and explore all avenues for even closer co-operation among themselves.

ASEAN's first summit meeting was held in Bali, Indonesia, in February 1976. Two major documents were signed:

Treaty of Amity and Co-operation, laying down principles of mutual respect for the independence and sovereignty of all nations; non-interference in the internal affairs of one another; settlement of disputes by peaceful means; and effective co-operation among the five countries. (Amended in 1987 by a Protocol which would allow other states within and outside the region to accede to the Treaty. Laos and Viet Nam signed the Treaty in July 1992; Myanmar became a signatory in July 1995.)

Declaration of Concord, giving guidelines for action in economic, social and cultural relations, including: the maintenance of political stability; the establishment of a 'Zone of Peace, Freedom and Neutrality' (ZOPFAN); the promotion of social justice and improvement of living standards; mutual assistance in the event of natural disasters; and co-operation in economic development.

TRADE

A Basic Agreement on the Establishment of ASEAN Preferential Trade Arrangements was concluded in 1977, but by mid-1987 the system covered only about 5% of trade between member states, since individual countries were permitted to exclude any 'sensitive' products from preferential import tariffs. In December 1987 the meeting of ASEAN heads of government resolved to reduce such exclusions to a maximum of 10% of the number of items traded and to a maximum of 50% of the value of trade, over the next five years (seven years for Indonesia and the Philippines).

In January 1992 heads of government, meeting in Singapore, signed an agreement to create an 'ASEAN Free Trade Area' (AFTA), by 2008. In accordance with the agreement, a common effective preferential tariff (CEPT) scheme came into effect in January 1993. The CEPT covered all manufactured products, including capital goods, and processed agricultural products (which together accounted for two-thirds of intra-ASEAN trade), but was to exclude unprocessed agricultural products. Tariffs were to be reduced to a maximum of 20% within a period of five to eight years and to 0%–5% during the subsequent seven to 10 years. Fifteen categories were designated for accelerated tariff reduction, including vegetable oils, rubber products, textiles, cement and pharmaceuticals. Member states were, however, still to be permitted exclusion for certain 'sensitive' products. In October 1993 ASEAN trade ministers agreed to modify the CEPT, with only Malaysia and Singapore having adhered to the original tariff reduction schedule. The new AFTA programme, under which all member countries except Brunei were scheduled to begin tariff reductions from 1 January 1994, substantially enlarged the number of products to be included in the tariff-reduction process (for example, unprocessed agricultural products) and reduced the list of products eligible for protection. In September 1994 ASEAN ministers of economic affairs agreed to accelerate the implementation of AFTA: tariffs were to be reduced to 0%–5% within seven to 10 years, or within five to eight years for products designated for accelerated tariff cuts. At the meeting, held in Chiang Mai, Thailand, ministers failed to adopt a unified approach to a proposal to create an APEC free-trade zone by 2020 that was to be discussed at a meeting of APEC ministers of foreign affairs in Jakarta, Indonesia, in November. In July 1995 Viet Nam was admitted as a member of ASEAN and was granted until the year 2006 to implement the AFTA trade agreements. In September 1995 ASEAN economy ministers, meeting in Brunei, advocated a further acceleration of the tariff reduction deadline, to 2000. The ministers emphasized the importance of maintaining momentum in trade liberalization, in order to ensure ASEAN's continued relevance in relation to other regional groupings. In December 1995 heads of government, convened in Bangkok, agreed to maintain the objective of achieving AFTA by 2003, while pursuing efforts to eliminate or reduce tariffs to less than 5% on the majority of products by 2000. Liberalization was to be extended to certain service industries, including banking, telecommunications and tourism. In July 1997 Laos and Myanmar became members of ASEAN and were granted a 10-year period, from January 1998, to comply with the AFTA schedule. In December 1997 ASEAN heads of government again agreed to accelerate the implementation of AFTA, but without specifying any new target date.

In June 1996 ASEAN's Working Group on Customs Procedures completed a draft legal framework for regional co-operation in order to simplify and to harmonize customs procedures, legislation and product classification. The customs agreement was to complement AFTA in facilitating intra-ASEAN trade. It was signed in March 1997 at the inaugural meeting of ASEAN finance ministers.

At meetings held in March and July 1991 ASEAN ministers discussed a proposal made by the Malaysian Government for the formation of an economic grouping, to be composed of ASEAN members, the People's Republic of China, Hong Kong, Japan, the Republic of Korea and Taiwan. In July 1993 ASEAN ministers of foreign affairs agreed a compromise, whereby the grouping was to be a caucus within APEC, although it was to be co-ordinated by ASEAN's meeting of economy ministers. In July 1994 ministers of foreign affairs of nine prospective members of the group held their first informal collective meeting; however, no progress was made towards forming the so-called East Asia Economic Caucus (EAEC). Japan's position on joining the EAEC remained to be established, owing to Japan's unwillingness to offend the USA, whose Government had expressed concerns that the grouping might undermine APEC by dividing the Asia-Pacific region. By late 1997 the EAEC had yet to be formally initiated.

SECURITY

In January 1992 ASEAN leaders agreed that there should be greater co-operation on security matters within the grouping, and that ASEAN's post-ministerial conferences (PMCs) should be used as a forum for discussion of questions relating to security with its dialogue partners and other countries. In July 1992 ASEAN's meeting of ministers of foreign affairs issued a statement calling for a peaceful resolution of the dispute concerning the Spratly Islands in the South China Sea, which are claimed, wholly or partly, by the People's Republic of China, Viet Nam, Taiwan, Brunei, Malaysia and the Philippines. (In February China had introduced legislation that defined the Spratly Islands as belonging to its territorial waters.) The ministers proposed a code of international conduct for the South China Sea, to be based on the principles contained in ASEAN's Treaty of Amity and Co-operation. At the ensuing PMC ASEAN requested the USA to maintain a military presence in the region, to compensate for the departure of its forces from the Philippines. The USA affirmed its commitment to maintaining the balance of security in South-East Asia. However, the issue of sovereignty of the Spratly Islands remained unresolved, and tensions in the region heightened in early 1995 owing to Chinese occupation of part of the disputed territory. Viet Nam's accession to ASEAN in July 1995, bringing all the Spratly Islands claimants except China and Taiwan into the grouping, was expected to strengthen ASEAN's position of negotiating a multilateral settlement on the Islands.

In December 1995 ASEAN heads of government, meeting in Bangkok, signed a treaty establishing a South-East Asia Nuclear-Weapon Free Zone. The treaty was also signed by Cambodia, Myanmar and Laos. It was extended to cover the offshore economic exclusion zones of each country. On ratification by all parties, the Treaty was to prohibit the manufacture or storage of nuclear weapons within the region. Individual signatories were to decide whether to allow port visits or transportation of nuclear weapons by foreign powers through territorial waters. The Treaty entered into force on 27 March 1997. ASEAN senior officials were mandated to oversee implementation of the Treaty pending the establishment of a permanent monitoring committee.

In July 1997 ASEAN ministers of foreign affairs reiterated their commitment to the principle of non-interference in the internal affairs of other countries. However, the group's efforts in Cambodia (see below) marked a significant shift in diplomatic policy towards one of 'constructive intervention', which had been proposed by the Malaysian Government in recognition of the increasing interdependence of the region.

ASEAN Regional Forum (ARF): In July 1993 the meeting of ASEAN ministers of foreign affairs sanctioned the establishment of a forum that was to discuss and co-operate on security issues within the region, and in particular was to ensure the involvement of the People's Republic of China in regional dialogue. The ARF was informally initiated during that year's PMC, comprising the ASEAN countries, its dialogue partners (at that time—Australia, Canada, the EC, Japan, the Republic of Korea, New Zealand and the USA), as well as the People's Republic of China, Laos, Papua New Guinea, Russia and Viet Nam. The first formal meeting of the ARF was conducted in July 1994 following the annual meeting of ASEAN ministers of foreign affairs, which was held in Bangkok, Thailand. The ministers presented proposals to improve security in the region, including exchanges of non-classified military information, co-operation in regional peace-keeping, nuclear non-proliferation and other confidence-building measures. It was agreed that ARF ministerial meetings would be convened each year following the gathering of ASEAN ministers. The 1995 meeting, held in Brunei, in August, attempted to define a framework for the future of the ARF. It was perceived as evolving in three stages: the promotion of confidence-building (including disaster relief and peace-keeping activities); the development of preventive diplomacy; and the elaboration of approaches to conflict. The 19 ministers of foreign affairs attending the meeting (Cambodia participated for the first time) recognized that the ARF was still in the initial stage of implementing confidence-building measures. The ministers, having conceded to a request by China not to discuss explicitly the Spratly Islands, expressed concern at overlapping sovereignty claims in the region. In a further statement, the ministers urged an 'immediate end' to the testing of nuclear weapons, then being undertaken by the French Government in the South Pacific region. The third ARF, convened in July 1996, which was attended for the first time by India and Myanmar, agreed a set of criteria and guiding principles for the future expansion of the grouping. In particular, it was decided that the ARF would only admit as participants countries that have a direct influence on the peace and security of the East Asia and Pacific region. The meeting supported the efforts of all claimants to territories in the South China Sea to resolve any disputes in accordance with international law, and recognized the importance of ending all testing of nuclear weapons in the region. The ARF that was held in July 1997 reviewed progress being made in developing the first two 'tracks' of the ARF process, through the structure of inter-sessional working groups and meetings. The Forum's consideration of security issues in the region was dominated by concern at the political situation in Cambodia; support was expressed for ASEAN mediation to restore stability within that country. Myanmar and Laos attended the ARF for the first time.

EXTERNAL RELATIONS

European Union: In March 1980 a co-operation agreement was signed between ASEAN and the European Community (EC, as the EU was known prior to its restructuring on 1 November 1993), which provided for the strengthening of existing trade links and increased co-operation in the scientific and agricultural spheres. A Joint Co-operation Committee met in November (and annually thereafter); it drew up a programme of scientific and technological co-operation, approved measures to promote contacts between industrialists from the two regions, and agreed on EC financing of ASEAN regional projects. An ASEAN-EC Business Council was launched in December 1983 to provide a forum for business representatives from the two regions and to identify joint projects. Three European Business Information Councils have since been established, in Malaysia, the Philippines and Thailand, in order to promote private-sector co-operation. The first meeting of ministers of economic affairs from ASEAN and EC member countries took place in October 1985.

In 1986 a joint group of experts on trade was set up, to examine problems of access to ASEAN markets and similar matters, and in 1987 joint investment committees were established in all the ASEAN capital cities. In December 1990 the Community adopted new guidelines on development co-operation, with an increase in assistance to Asia, and a change in the type of aid given to ASEAN members, emphasizing training, science and technology and venture capital, rather than assistance for rural development. At a meeting of ASEAN and EC ministers of foreign affairs, held in Luxembourg in June 1991, there was disagreement between the two sides over the EC's proposal to link economic agreements with trading partners to policies concerning human rights and environmental issues. In October 1992 the EC and ASEAN agreed to promote further trade between the regions, as well as bilateral investment, and made a joint declaration in support of human rights. The agreement was reached in spite of Portugal's threat to veto it in protest at the killing of demonstrators in East Timor by Indonesian security forces in November 1991. At the PMC, in July 1994, EU representatives assured ASEAN ministers of foreign affairs that there was no firm policy linkage of trade and regional aid to social and human rights issues. In September ministers of foreign affairs of the two groupings convened in Karlsruhe, Germany. The Ministerial Meeting confirmed ASEAN to be central to EU relations with the Asian region, and agreed to promote greater participation of the private sector. In May 1995 ASEAN and EU senior officials endorsed an initiative to convene an Asia-Europe Meeting (ASEM) in order to strengthen links between the two economic regions. (See chapter on the EU for ASEAN participation in ASEM.) In October 1995 an ASEAN-EU Eminent Persons Group was established to consider the future direction of ASEAN-EU relations. In November 1996 an EU-ASEAN Junior Managers Exchange Programme was initiated, as part of efforts to promote co-operation and understanding between the industrial and business sectors in both regions. In February 1997 a Ministerial Meeting was held in Singapore. Despite ongoing differences regarding human rights, in particular ASEAN's granting of full membership status to Myanmar and the situation in East Timor (which precluded the conclusion of a new co-operation agreement), the meeting issued a final joint declaration, committing both sides to strengthening co-operation and dialogue on economic, international and bilateral trade, security and social issues. A protocol to the 1980 co-operation agreement was signed, enabling the participation of Viet Nam in the dialogue process. In November 1997 a meeting of the Joint Co-operation Committee was postponed, following a dispute concerning the participation of Myanmar in the meeting as an observer.

People's Republic of China: Efforts to develop consultative relations between ASEAN and China were initiated in 1993. Joint Committees on economic and trade co-operation and on scientific and technological co-operation were subsequently established. The first formal consultations between senior officials of the two sides were held in April 1995. ASEAN representatives expressed serious concern at China's recent aggressive action in the Spratly Islands, in particular permitting illegal fishing activities and constructing a semi-permanent naval installation on one of the disputed reefs. In July China assured ASEAN ministers of foreign affairs that it would seek a peaceful resolution to the sovereignty dispute over the Islands, in accordance with international law. At the same time China reasserted its own territorial claims to the Islands. Despite ASEAN's continued concern at China's claims in the South China Sea, efforts have been pursued to strengthen relations between the two sides, and in July 1996 China was admitted to the PMC as a full dialogue partner. In February 1997 a Joint Co-operation Committee was established to co-ordinate the China-ASEAN dialogue and all aspects of relations between the two sides. In March Viet Nam protested at Chinese gas exploration activities in the disputed waters near the Paracel Islands and attempted to generate ASEAN support for its stance on the issue. In early April, however, the Chinese vessel was withdrawn from the area. Later in that month, at a meeting of ASEAN-Chinese senior officials, for the first time China agreed to discuss issues relating to the South China Sea at a multilateral forum, rather than limiting discussions to a bilateral basis. Relations between the two sides were further strengthened by China's expression of support for the expansion of the ASEAN grouping, by granting membership to Cambodia (subsequently postponed), Laos and Myanmar, and the decision to establish a joint business council to promote bilateral trade and investment. China participated in the informal summit meeting that was held in December, at the end of which both sides issued a joint statement affirming their commitment to resolving regional disputes through peaceful means.

Japan: The ASEAN-Japan Forum was established in 1977 to discuss matters of mutual concern in trade, investment, technology transfer and development assistance. Tariff cuts on certain ASEAN exports were made by Japan in 1985, but ASEAN members continued to criticize Japan's attitude and called for Japan to import more manufactured products rather than raw materials. The first ever meeting between ASEAN economic ministers and the Japanese Minister of International Trade and Industry was held in October 1992. At this meeting, and subsequently, ASEAN requested Japan to increase its investment in member countries and to make Japanese markets more accessible to ASEAN products in order to reduce the trade deficit with Japan. Japan agreed to extend ASEAN's privileges under its generalized system of tariffs until 2001. Since 1993 ASEAN-Japanese development and cultural co-operation has expanded under schemes including the Inter-ASEAN Technical Exchange Programme, the Japan-ASEAN Co-operation Promotion Programme and the ASEAN-Japan Friendship Programme. In December 1997 Japan, attending the informal summit meeting in Malaysia, agreed to improve market access for ASEAN products and to provide training opportunities for more than 20,000 young people in order to help develop local economies. A joint statement, issued after the meeting, committed both sides to greater co-operation and to the promotion of regional peace and stability.

Other countries: Under the ASEAN-Australia Economic Co-operation Programme, Australia gives financial support for ASEAN activities, and a joint Business Council was set up in 1980. A third phase of the Programme was initiated in mid-1994, with assistance amounting to $A32m. for the period to June 1998, which was to concentrate on projects in the environmental management, telecommunications, transport and agro-industrial sectors. Co-operation relations with New Zealand are based on the Inter-Institutional Linkages Programme and the Trade and Investment Promotion Programme, which mainly provide assistance in forestry development, dairy technology, veterinary management and legal aid training. An ASEAN-New Zealand Joint Management Committee was initiated in November 1993, in order to oversee the implementation of co-operation projects. The USA gives assistance for the development of small and medium-sized businesses and other projects, and supports a Center for Technology Exchange. In 1990 ASEAN and the USA established an ASEAN-US Joint Working Group, whose purpose is to review ASEAN's economic relations with the USA and to identify measures by which economic links could be strengthened. ASEAN-Canadian co-operation projects include fisheries technology, the telecommunications industry, use of solar energy, and a forest seed centre. A Joint Planning and Monitoring Committee was established in 1994 (and met for the first time in October 1995) to oversee projects at the planning and implementation levels. In July 1991 the Republic of Korea was accepted as a 'dialogue partner', and in December a joint ASEAN-Korea Chamber of Commerce was established. During 1995 co-operation projects concerned with human resources development, science and technology, agricultural development and trade and investment policies were implemented. The Republic of Korea participated in ASEAN's informal summit meeting in December 1997.

In July 1993 both India and Pakistan were accepted as sectoral partners: sectoral partners can participate in ASEAN meetings on certain sectors such as trade, transport and communications and tourism. An ASEAN-India Business Council was established, and met for the first time, in New Delhi, in February 1995. In December 1995 the ASEAN summit meeting agreed to enhance India's status to that of a full dialogue partner; India was formally admitted to the PMC in July 1996.

Indo-China: Pursuing the Association's decision from the outset to be a non-military, neutral grouping, diplomatic relations with the new communist governments in Indo-China were established in 1976. In 1981 ASEAN sponsored a UN conference on Kampuchea, and gave assurances that it would not, as a group, supply arms to any faction. In 1988–89 'informal' meetings were held by representatives of Viet Nam, Laos, ASEAN and the Kampuchean factions to discuss a possible political settlement in Kampuchea. ASEAN participated in the international conference on Cambodia (as it was now known) which was held in Paris, France, in July/August 1989, and in further negotiations held in Jakarta, Indonesia in February 1990, neither of which achieved a political settlement. In July 1990 ASEAN ministers urged the formation of a Supreme National Council (SNC), on which the Vietnamese-supported Government of Cambodia and the three opposition groups would be represented. A UN proposal for the formation of an SNC and the holding of elections, under UN supervision, was accepted by all the Cambodian factions in September. Following the mass return of Cambodian refugees and displaced people in 1992–93, ASEAN and Japan provided technical experts to assist in the resettlement of the returnees. In July 1994 ASEAN ministers of foreign affairs and their dialogue partner counterparts agreed to provide military training in order to assist the Cambodian Government to consolidate its position. In July 1995 Cambodia was accorded observer status. Co-operation between the two sides subsequently focused on issues relating to Cambodia's future admission to the grouping as a full member (for example, training courses for Cambodian officials). In May 1997 ASEAN ministers of foreign affairs confirmed that Cambodia, together with Laos and Myanmar, was to be admitted to the grouping in July of that year. In mid-July, however, Cambodia's membership was postponed owing to the deposition of the country's political administration, led by Prince Ranariddh, and the resulting civil unrest. Later in that month Cambodia's *de facto* leader, Second Prime Minister Hun Sen, agreed to ASEAN's pursuit of a mediation role in restoring stability in the country and in preparing for democratic elections. In early August the ministers of foreign affairs of Indonesia, the Philippines and Thailand, representing ASEAN, met Hun Sen to confirm these objectives; however, neither Prince Ranariddh's replacement nor his possible reinstatement was discussed.

In July 1992 Viet Nam and Laos signed ASEAN's Treaty on Amity and Co-operation: subsequently, the two countries participated in ASEAN meetings and committees as observers. Viet Nam was admitted as a full member of ASEAN in July 1995. In July 1994 an official delegation from Myanmar attended the annual meeting of ministers of foreign affairs, having been invited by the host Thai Government. The invitation was consistent with ASEAN's policy of pursuing limited 'constructive engagement' with Myanmar in order to encourage democracy in that country. In July 1995 Myanmar signed ASEAN's Treaty on Amity and Co-operation. In July 1996 ASEAN granted Myanmar observer status and admitted it to the ARF, despite the expression of strong reservations by (among others) the Governments of Australia, Canada and the USA, owing to the human rights situation in Myanmar. In November ASEAN heads of government, attending an informal summit meeting in Jakarta, Indonesia, agreed to admit Myanmar as a full member of the grouping at the same time as Cambodia and Laos. While Cambodia's membership was postponed, Laos and Myanmar were admitted to ASEAN in July 1997.

In May 1994 a proposal to establish a South-East Asian grouping was discussed by government officials and academics from the ASEAN member countries, Cambodia, Laos, Myanmar and Viet Nam. The initiative was to strengthen the region's cohesiveness, with greater co-operation on issues such as drug-trafficking, labour migration and terrorism, and to facilitate the process of future expansion of ASEAN. In December 1995 ASEAN heads of government and representatives of Cambodia, Laos and Myanmar (Viet Nam having become a member of ASEAN earlier in that year) agreed to pursue the initiative. In June 1996 ministers of these countries, and of the People's Republic of China, adopted a framework for ASEAN-Mekong Basin Development Co-operation. Groups of experts and senior officials were to be convened to consider funding issues and proposals to link the two regions, including a gas pipeline network, rail links and the establishment of a common time zone. In December 1996 the working group on rail links appointed a team of consultants to conduct a feasibility study of the proposals.

INDUSTRY

An ASEAN industrial projects scheme was initiated in 1976 to finance large-scale industrial infrastructure projects in the region. The ASEAN Industrial Complementation programme, begun in 1981, encourages member countries to produce complementary products in specific industrial sectors for preferential exchange among themselves, for example components to be used in the automobile industry (under the Brand-to-Brand Complementation scheme—BBC—established in 1988). The ASEAN—Chambers of Commerce and Industry (CCI) aims to enhance ASEAN economic and industrial co-operation, and the participation in these activities of the private sector. In 1994/95 it was agreed to establish a permanent ASEAN-CCI secretariat at the ASEAN Secretariat. An ASEAN industrial joint venture (AIJV), established in 1983, sets up projects with at least 40% participation by private sector companies from two or more ASEAN member states, to receive preferential trade treatment (in the form of tariff reductions of up to 90%) within the ASEAN region. In September 1994 changes to the AIJV scheme were formulated by ASEAN economic officials to bring it into line with tariff reductions anticipated under the CEPT arrangement and to maintain its margin of preference. In April 1995 a meeting of ASEAN economic ministers resolved to phase out the AIJV and the BBC. The ASEAN Consultative Committee on Standards and Quality (ACCSQ) aims to promote the understanding and implementation of quality concepts, which are considered to play an important role in strengthening the economic development of a member state and in helping to eliminate trade barriers. ACCSQ comprises three working groups: standards and information, conformance and assessment, and testing and calibration. In September 1994 the ACCSQ was recognized by the International Organization for Standardization as the standards organization for South-East Asia. In 1995 ACCSQ began to consider the elimination of technical barriers to trade, in order to facilitate the implementation of AFTA. In September 1994 an Ad-hoc Working Group on Intellectual Property Co-operation was established, with a mandate to formulate a framework agreement on intellectual property co-operation and to strengthen ASEAN activities towards intellectual property protection in the region.

In 1988 the ASEAN Fund was established, with capital of US $150m. (of which $15m. was contributed by the Asian Development Bank), to provide finance for portfolio investments in ASEAN countries, in particular for small and medium-sized companies.

FINANCE, BANKING AND INVESTMENT

In 1987 heads of government agreed to accelerate regional co-operation in this field, in order to support intra-ASEAN trade and investment; they adopted measures to increase the role of ASEAN currencies in regional trade, to assist negotiations on the avoidance of double taxation, and to improve the efficiency of tax and customs administrators. An ASEAN Reinsurance Corporation was established in 1988, with initial authorized capital of US $10m. In December 1995 the summit meeting proposed the establishment of an ASEAN Investment Area. Other measures to attract greater financial resource flows in the region, including an ASEAN Plan of Action for the Promotion of Foreign Direct Investment and Intra-ASEAN Investment, were implemented during 1996. In February 1997 ASEAN central bank governors agreed to strengthen efforts to combat currency speculation through the established network of foreign-exchange repurchase agreements. However, from mid-1997 several Asian currencies were undermined by speculative activities. Subsequent unsuccessful attempts to support the foreign-exchange rates contributed to a collapse in value of financial markets in some countries and to a reversal of the region's economic growth, at least in the short term, while governments undertook macro-economic structural reforms. In early December ASEAN ministers of finance, meeting in Malaysia, agreed to liberalize markets for financial services and to strengthen surveillance of member country economies in order to help prevent further deterioration of the regional economy. The ministers endorsed a proposal for the establishment of an Asian funding facility to provide emergency assistance in support of international credit and structural reform programmes. At the informal summit meeting held later in December, ASEAN leaders issued a joint statement in which they expressed the need for mutual support to counter the region's financial crisis and urged greater external assistance, in particular from the USA, Japan and the EU, to help overcome the situation and address the underlying problems. The heads of government also resolved to accelerate the implementation of the ASEAN Investment Area in order to promote intra-ASEAN trade and to enable the region to benefit from its economic competitiveness, resulting from the depreciation of its currencies.

AGRICULTURE

In October 1983 a ministerial agreement on fisheries co-operation was concluded, providing for the joint management of fish resources, the sharing of technology, and co-operation in marketing. In July 1994 a Conference on Fisheries Management and Development Strategies in the ASEAN region was held in Bangkok, Thailand. The Conference resolved to enhance fish production through the introduction of new technologies, aquaculture development, improvements of product quality and greater involvement by the private sector.

The first ASEAN Forestry Congress was held in October 1983 to discuss the state of the regional timber industry and the problems of forest depletion. Co-operation in forestry is focused on joint projects, funded by ASEAN's dialogue partners, which include a Forest Tree Seed Centre, an Institute of Forest Management and the ASEAN Timber Technology Centre.

In October 1993 ASEAN ministers of agriculture and forestry identified the following as priority areas for activity: strengthening food security in the region; promoting intra- and extra-ASEAN trade in agriculture, fishery and forestry products; technology generation and transfer; agricultural rural community and human resource development; private sector involvement and investment; management and conservation of natural resources for sustainable development; and strengthening ASEAN co-operation and joint approaches in addressing international and regional issues. ASEAN holds an emergency rice reserve, amounting to 53,000 metric tons, as part of its efforts to ensure food security in the region. There is an established ASEAN programme of training and study exchanges for farm workers, agricultural experts and members of agricultural co-operatives. In April 1995 representatives of the ASEAN Secretariat and private-sector groups met to co-ordinate the implementation of a scheme to promote the export of ASEAN agricultural and forestry products.

MINERALS AND ENERGY

In April 1994, a meeting on energy co-operation of the ASEAN economic ministers recognized the significance of energy and power development in sustaining the overall growth of the region's economies. A medium-term programme of action on energy co-operation, for the period 1995–99, includes measures to promote energy efficiency, the diversification of energy sources, training and research activities, and the exchange of information on energy policies among ASEAN members. In 1990 efforts to establish an ASEAN electricity grid were initiated. In July 1996 ASEAN ministers of energy, meeting in Kuala Lumpur, Malaysia, discussed the construction of a gas pipeline network linking all member countries. The ASEAN-EC Energy Management, Training and Research Centre (AEEMTRC), a co-operation project implemented with funding from the EU, based in Jakarta, Indonesia, conducts research, information, management and training activities in all aspects of energy, and publishes reference materials for the exchange of energy information. An ASEAN energy business forum is held annually and attended by representatives of the energy industry in the private and public sectors.

A Framework of Co-operation in Minerals was adopted by an ASEAN working group of experts in August 1993. The group has also developed a programme of action for ASEAN co-operation in the development and utilization of industrial minerals to promote the exploration and development of mineral resources in ASEAN member countries, the transfer of mining technology and expertise, the participation of the private sector in industrial mineral production. The programme of action is implemented by an ASEAN Regional Development Centre for Mineral Resources, which also conducts workshops and training programmes relating to the sector.

TRANSPORT AND COMMUNICATIONS

In March 1995 senior economic officials endorsed a plan of action for greater co-operation in the transport and communications sector. The plan identified the following as priority objectives for 1994–96: developing multi-modal transport; achieving interconnectivity in telecommunications; harmonizing road transport laws and regulations; improving air space management; developing ASEAN legislation for the carriage of dangerous goods and waste by land and sea; and human resources development. In 1994 preparations were under way for the establishment of two centres of excellence for the development of human resources in the railways and inland waterways sectors, to be located in Malaysia and Indonesia respectively. An Integrated Harbour Management Programme, which began operations in January 1994, conducts training activities for port managers and workers.

In October 1993 telecommunications companies from Indonesia, Malaysia and the Philippines agreed to reduce international telephone tariffs by 23%, effective 1 January 1994, and to improve the telecommunications infrastructure within a designated economic growth area comprising northern Malaysia, Indonesia's northern Sumatra and southern Thailand, referred to as the Northern Triangle. In 1994/95 ASEAN continued efforts to establish an ASEAN Postal Track and Trace System, in order to improve the region's express mail service.

SCIENCE AND TECHNOLOGY

In February 1994 ASEAN ministers of science and technology adopted a Plan of Action which was to be a framework for ASEAN co-operation in this sector for the period 1994–98. The Plan aims to achieve a high-level of intra-ASEAN co-operation, with the involvement of the private sector; to establish a network of science and technology infrastructure and programmes for human resources; to promote technology transfer; to enhance public awareness of the importance of science and technology for economic development; and to increase the level of co-operation in science and technology with the international community. ASEAN supports co-operation in food science and technology, meteorology and geophysics, microelectronics and information technology, biotechnology, non-conventional energy research, materials science and technology and marine science. There is an ASEAN Science Fund, used to finance policy studies in science and technology and to support information exchange and dissemination.

ENVIRONMENT

A ministerial meeting on the environment, held in April 1994, approved an ASEAN Strategic Plan of Action on the Environment (ASPEN) for the period 1994–98, which established long-term objectives on environmental quality and standards for the ASEAN region and aimed to enhance joint action to address environmental concerns. At the same time the ministers adopted standards for air quality and river water which were to be achieved by all ASEAN member countries by 2010. In June 1995 ministers agreed to co-operate in order to counter the problems of transboundary pollution. During 1997 efforts continued to establish an ASEAN Regional Centre for Biodiversity Conservation, which was to be based in the Philippines. In 1998 ASEAN was to convene a regional meeting to address the environmental problems resulting from forest fires, which had afflicted several countries in the region in mid-1997.

SOCIAL DEVELOPMENT

ASEAN concerns in social development include youth development, the role of women, health and nutrition, education, labour affairs and disaster management. In December 1993 ASEAN ministers responsible for social affairs adopted a Plan of Action for Children, which provided a framework for regional co-operation for the survival, protection and development of children in member countries. In 1994/95 the Committee on Social Development pursued efforts to establish an ASEAN Social Development Fund, which was endorsed in 1990 to finance regional social development projects. An ASEAN task force on AIDS has been created, and its first meeting was held in Jakarta in March 1993.

ASEAN supports efforts to combat drug abuse and illegal drugs-trafficking. It aims to promote education and drug-awareness campaigns throughout the region, and administers a project to strengthen the training of personnel involved in combating drug concerns. In October 1994 a meeting of ASEAN Senior Officials on Drug Matters approved a three-year plan of action on drug abuse, which provided a framework for co-operation in four priority areas: preventive drug education; treatment and rehabilitation; law enforcement; and research.

TOURISM

ASEAN co-operation in tourism aims to promote the region as a tourist destination, to develop human resources in the travel industry, to preserve ASEAN's cultural and environmental heritage and to promote intra-ASEAN travel. National Tourist Organizations from ASEAN countries meet regularly to assist in co-ordinating the region's tourist industry. In January 1995 the Tourist Organizations agreed to participate in a new tourism body, which was to include ASEAN private-sector organizations involved in the industry. A Tourism Forum is held annually to promote ASEAN's tourist industry.

CULTURE AND INFORMATION

The three-year 1994–97 programme for culture and information incorporated the following strategy priorities: promotion of the ASEAN image; development of source materials on culture for ASEAN studies; development of human resources; preservation and revitalization of the region's cultural heritage; utilization of technology; and adoption of themes. Regular workshops and festivals are held in visual and performing arts, youth music, radio, television and films, and print and interpersonal media. In addition, ASEAN administers a News Exchange and provides support for the training of editors, journalists and information officers. Projects administered under the Committee on Culture and Information are financed by an ASEAN Cultural Fund.

In July 1997 ASEAN ministers of foreign affairs endorsed the establishment of an ASEAN Foundation to promote awareness of the organization and greater participation in its activities.

PUBLICATIONS

Annual Report of the ASEAN Standing Committee.

ASEAN Insurance Journal.

ASEAN Journal on Science and Technology for Development (2 a year).

ASEAN Update (every 2 months).

Information Series and *Documents Series.*

BANK FOR INTERNATIONAL SETTLEMENTS—BIS

Address: Centralbahnplatz 2, 4002 Basel, Switzerland.
Telephone: (61) 2808080; **telex:** 962487; **fax:** (61) 2809100.

The Bank for International Settlements was founded pursuant to the Hague Agreements of 1930 to promote co-operation among national central banks and to provide additional facilities for international financial operations.

Organization

(January 1998)

GENERAL MEETING

The General Meeting is held annually in June and is attended by representatives of the central banks of countries in which shares have been subscribed. In September 1996 the BIS invited the central banks of nine transitional economies to join the organization. From 31 March 1997 the central banks of the following authorities were entitled to attend and vote at General Meetings of the BIS: Australia, Austria, Belgium, Brazil, Bulgaria, Canada, the People's Republic of China, the Czech Republic, Denmark, Estonia, Finland, France, Germany, Greece, Hong Kong, Hungary, Iceland, India, Ireland, Italy, Japan, the Republic of Korea, Latvia, Lithuania, Mexico, the Netherlands, Norway, Poland, Portugal, Romania, Russia, Saudi Arabia, Singapore, Slovakia, South Africa, Spain, Sweden, Switzerland, Turkey, the United Kingdom and the USA. The legal status of the Yugoslav issue of the Bank's capital remains in suspense. However, new shares have been issued, on an interim basis, to the central banks of four of the successor states of the former Yugoslavia, pending a comprehensive settlement of all outstanding issues.

BOARD OF DIRECTORS

The Board of Directors is responsible for the conduct of the Bank's operations at the highest level, and comprises the Governors in office of the central banks of Belgium, France, Germany, Italy, the United Kingdom and the USA, each of whom appoints another member of the same nationality. The statutes also provide for the election to the Board of not more than nine Governors of other member central banks: those of Canada, Japan, the Netherlands, Sweden and Switzerland are also members of the Board.

Chairman of the Board and President of the Bank: ALFONS VERPLAETSE (Belgium).

CHIEF EXECUTIVE OFFICER

General Manager: ANDREW CROCKETT (United Kingdom).

The Bank has a staff of about 470 employees, from 27 countries.

Activities

The BIS is an international financial institution whose special role is to promote the co-operation of central banks, and to fulfil the function of a 'central banks' bank'. Although it has the legal form of a company limited by shares, it is an international organization governed by international law, and enjoys special privileges and immunities in keeping with its role (a Headquarters Agreement was concluded with Switzerland in 1987). The participating central banks were originally given the option of subscribing the shares themselves or arranging for their subscription in their own countries: thus the BIS also has some private shareholders, but they have no right of participation in the General Meeting. Some 86% of the total share capital is in the hands of central banks and 14% is held by private shareholders.

FINANCE

The authorized capital of the Bank is 1,500m. gold francs, divided into 600,000 shares of 2,500 gold francs each.

Statement of Account*
(In gold francs; units of 0.29032258 . . . gram of fine gold—Art. 4 of the Statutes; 31 March 1997)

Assets		%
Gold	3,547,261,289	5.31
Cash on hand and on sight a/c with banks	384,413,644	0.58
Treasury bills	2,813,409,132	4.21
Time deposits and advances	43,311,812,901	64.84
Securities at term	16,535,287,225	24.76
Miscellaneous	200,780,131	0.30
Total	66,792,964,322	100.00

Liabilities		%
Authorized cap.: 1,500,000,000		
Issued cap.: 1,182,812,500 viz. 473,125 shares of which 25% paid up	323,203,125	0.48
Reserves	2,061,783,924	3.09
Deposits (gold)	3,836,401,223	5.74
Deposits (currencies)	58,260,349,475	87.23
Staff pension scheme	252,630,204	0.38
Miscellaneous	2,009,815,448	3.01
Dividend payable on 1 July 1996	48,780,923	0.07
Total	66,792,964,322	100.0

* Assets and liabilities in US dollars are converted at US $208 per fine ounce of gold (equivalent to 1 gold franc = US $1.94149 . . .) and all other items in currencies on the basis of market rates against the US dollar.

BANKING OPERATIONS

The BIS assists central banks in managing and investing their monetary reserves: in 1997 some 120 international financial institutions and central banks from all over the world had deposits with the BIS, which managed around 7% of world foreign exchange reserves.

The BIS uses the funds deposited with it partly for lending to central banks. Its credit transactions may take the form of swaps against gold; covered credits secured by means of a pledge of gold or marketable short-term securities; credits against gold or currency deposits of the same amount and for the same duration held with the BIS; unsecured credits in the form of advances or deposits; or standby credits, which in individual instances are backed by guarantees given by member central banks. In addition, the Bank undertakes operations in foreign exchange and in gold, both with central banks and with the markets.

In 1982, faced with the increasingly critical debt situation of some Latin American countries and the resultant threat to the viability of the international financial system, the BIS granted comparatively large-scale loans to central banks that did not number among its shareholders: the central banks of Argentina, Brazil and Mexico were granted bridging loans pending the disbursement of balance-of-payments credits extended by the IMF. These facilities amounted to almost US $3,000m., all of which had been repaid by the end of 1983. The Bank subsequently made similar loans, but with decreasing frequency. Since 1990 the BIS has contributed funds to bridging facilities arranged for the central banks of Venezuela, Guyana, Hungary, Romania, the former Yugoslav republic of Macedonia, Mexico (in 1995) and Thailand (in August 1997).

The BIS also engages in traditional types of investment: funds not required for lending to central banks are placed in the market as deposits with commercial banks and purchases of short-term negotiable paper, including Treasury bills. Such operations constitute a major part of the Bank's business.

Because the central banks' monetary reserves must be available at short notice, they can only be placed with the BIS at short term, for fixed periods and with clearly defined repayment terms. The BIS has to match its assets to the maturity structure and nature of its commitments, and must therefore conduct its business with special regard to maintaining a high degree of liquidity.

The Bank's operations must be in conformity with the monetary policy of the central banks of the countries concerned. It is not permitted to make advances to governments or to open current accounts in their name. Real estate transactions are also excluded.

INTERNATIONAL MONETARY CO-OPERATION

Governors of central banks meet for regular discussions at the BIS to co-ordinate international monetary policy and ensure orderly conditions on the international financial markets. There is close co-operation with the IMF and, since its membership includes central banks of eastern European countries, the BIS also provides a forum for contacts between East and West.

A Euro-currency Standing Committee was set up at the BIS in 1971 to provide the central bank Governors of the 'Group of Ten' industrialized countries (see p. 81) and Switzerland with information concerning the monetary policy aspects of the Euro-currency markets. Since 1982 it has provided a regular critical survey of the entire international credit system.

In 1974 the Governors of central banks of the Group of Ten and Switzerland set up the Basle Committee on Banking Supervision (whose secretariat is provided by the BIS) to co-ordinate banking supervision at the international level. The Committee pools information on banking supervisory regulations and surveillance systems, including the supervision of banks' foreign currency business, identifies possible danger areas and proposes measures to safeguard the banks' solvency and liquidity. In April 1997 the Committee published new guidelines that were intended to provide a comprehensive set of core principles relating to banking supervision.

The Bank also organizes and provides the secretariat for periodic meetings of experts, such as the Group of Computer Experts, the Group of Experts on Payment Systems and the Group of Experts on Monetary and Economic Data Bank Questions, which aims to develop a data bank service for the central banks of the Group of Ten countries and the BIS.

RESEARCH

The Bank's Monetary and Economic Department conducts research, particularly into monetary questions; collects and publishes data on international banking developments; and organizes a data bank for central banks. The BIS Annual Report provides an independent analysis of monetary and economic developments. Statistics on international banking and on external indebtedness are also published regularly.

AGENCY AND TRUSTEE FUNCTIONS

Since October 1986 the BIS has performed the functions of Agent for the private European Currency Unit (ECU) clearing and settlement system, in accordance with the provisions of successive agreements concluded between the ECU Banking Association (EBA), based in Paris, and the BIS, the most recent of which was signed and entered into force on 16 September 1996. Member banks of the EBA may be granted the status of clearing bank on the basis of criteria formulated by that body. At 1 May 1997 there were 49 clearing banks.

In April 1994 the BIS assumed new functions in connection with the rescheduling of Brazil's external debt, which had been agreed by the Brazilian Government in November 1993. In accordance with two collateral pledge agreements, the BIS acts in the capacity of collateral agent to hold and invest collateral for the benefit of the holders of certain US dollar-denominated bonds, maturing in 15 or 30 years, which have been issued by Brazil under the rescheduling arrangements. The Bank also acts as trustee for certain international governmental loans.

PUBLICATIONS

Annual Report.

Quarterly press release on international banking and financial market developments; half-yearly reports (jointly with the OECD) on external indebtedness.

CARIBBEAN COMMUNITY AND COMMON MARKET—CARICOM

Address: Bank of Guyana Building, POB 10827, Georgetown, Guyana.

Telephone: (2) 69281; **telex:** 2263; **fax:** (2) 67816.

CARICOM was formed in 1973 by the Treaty of Chaguaramas, signed in Trinidad, as a movement towards unity in the Caribbean; it replaced the Caribbean Free Trade Association (CARIFTA), founded in 1965.

MEMBERS

Antigua and Barbuda	Jamaica
Bahamas*	Montserrat
Barbados	Saint Christopher and Nevis
Belize	Saint Lucia
British Virgin Islands†	Saint Vincent and the Grenadines
Dominica	Suriname
Grenada	Trinidad and Tobago
Guyana	Turks and Caicos Islands†
Haiti‡	

* The Bahamas is a member of the Community but not the Common Market.

† The British Virgin Islands and the Turks and Caicos Islands were granted associate membership in 1991.

‡ Haiti was admitted to the Community in July 1997, although the final terms and conditions of its accession had yet to be concluded.

OBSERVERS

Anguilla	Dominican Republic
Aruba	Mexico
Bermuda	Netherlands Antilles
The Cayman Islands	Puerto Rico
Colombia	Venezuela

Organization

(January 1998)

HEADS OF GOVERNMENT CONFERENCE AND BUREAU

The Conference is the final authority of the Community and determines policy. It is responsible for the conclusion of treaties on behalf of the Community and for entering into relationships between the Community and international organizations and states. The Conference is also responsible for making the financial arrangements to meet the expenses of the Community, but has delegated this function to the Common Market Council of Ministers. Decisions of the Conference are generally taken unanimously. Heads of government meet annually.

At a special meeting of the Heads of Government Conference, held in Trinidad and Tobago in October 1992, participants decided to establish a Heads of Government Bureau, with the capacity to initiate proposals, to update consensus and to secure the implementation of CARICOM decisions. The Bureau was to consist of the Chairman of the Conference, as Chairman, as well as the incoming and outgoing Chairmen of the Conference, and the Secretary-General of the Conference, in the capacity of Chief Executive Officer.

COMMUNITY COUNCIL OF MINISTERS

At a special meeting of the Heads of Government Conference, held in Trinidad and Tobago in October 1992, it was agreed that a Caribbean Community Council of Ministers should be established to replace the existing Common Market Council of Ministers as the second highest organ of the Community. A Protocol amending the Treaty of Chaguaramas, to restructure the organs and institutions of the Community, was formally adopted at a meeting of CARICOM heads of government in February 1997 and was signed by all member states in July. The Community Council of Ministers consists of ministers responsible for community affairs, and any other government minister designated by member states. The Council is responsible for the development of the Community's strategic planning and co-ordination in the areas of economic integration, functional co-operation and external relations.

MINISTERIAL COUNCILS

The principal organs of the Community are assisted in their functions by the following bodies: the Council for Trade and Economic Development (COTED); the Council for Foreign and Community Relations (COFCOR); the Council for Human and Social Development (COHSOD); and the Council for Finance and Planning (COFAP). The Councils are responsible for formulating policies, promoting their implementation and supervising co-operation in the relevant areas.

SECRETARIAT

The Secretariat is the main administrative body of the Caribbean Community. The functions of the Secretariat are: to service meetings of the Community and of its Committees; to take appropriate follow-up action on decisions made at such meetings; to carry out studies on questions of economic and functional co-operation relating to the region as a whole; to provide services to member states at their request in respect of matters relating to the achievement of the objectives of the Community. The 1996–97 work programme of the Secretariat was divided into 15 sub-programmes: external economic and trade relations; co-ordination of economic policy and sectoral programmes; co-ordinated foreign and community relations; mobilization of resources from external agencies and the Caribbean Community technical assistance service; development and operation of the single market and economy; sustainable development; corporate services; financial planning, accounting and reporting (including budgeting and donor resources); organization development; information and communications; human resource development; health sector development; participation in the development of the Caribbean Community; legal and institutional framework; executive management.

Secretary-General: EDWIN W. CARRINGTON (Trinidad and Tobago).

Deputy Secretary-General: Dr CARLA BARNETT (Belize).

Activities

REGIONAL INTEGRATION

In 1989 CARICOM heads of government established the 15-member West Indian Commission to study regional political and economic integration. The Commission's final report, submitted in July 1992, recommended that CARICOM should remain a community of sovereign states (rather than a federation), but should strengthen the integration process and expand to include the wider Caribbean region. It recommended the formation of an Association of Caribbean States (ACS), to include all the countries within and surrounding the Caribbean Basin (see p. 259). The Heads of Government Conference that was held in October 1992 established an Inter-Governmental Task Force, which was to undertake preparations for a reorientation of CARICOM. In February 1993 it presented a draft Charter of Civil Society for the Community, which set out principles in the areas of democracy, government, parliament, freedom of the press and human rights. The Charter was signed by Community heads of government in February 1997. Suriname was admitted to the organization in July 1995. In July 1997 the Heads of Government Conference agreed to admit Haiti as a member with immediate effect, although the terms and conditions of its accession to the organization had yet to be negotiated.

CO-ORDINATION OF FOREIGN POLICY

Activities for the co-ordination of foreign policy include: strengthening of member states' position in international organizations; joint diplomatic action on issues of particular interest to the Caribbean; joint co-operation arrangements with third countries and organizations; and the negotiation of free-trade agreements with third countries and other regional groupings. This last area of activity has assumed increasing importance since the agreement in 1994 by almost all the governments of countries in the Americas to establish a 'Free Trade Area of the Americas' (FTAA) by 2005.

In 1990 a working group was established with Brazil, Colombia and Venezuela to consider ways of developing regional economic co-operation, including greater self-sufficiency in food, joint exploration for mineral resources, joint trading policies, and co-operation in communications and transport systems. In July 1991 Venezuela applied for membership of CARICOM, and offered a non-reciprocal free-trade agreement for CARICOM exports to Venezuela, over an initial five-year period. In October 1993 the newly-established Group of Three (Colombia, Mexico and Venezuela) signed joint agreements with CARICOM and Suriname on combating drugs-trafficking and environmental protection. In June 1994 CARICOM and Colombia concluded an agreement on trade, economic and technical co-operation, which, *inter alia* gives special treatment to the least-developed CARICOM countries. CARICOM has observer status in the Latin American Rio Group (see p. 271).

In 1992 Cuba applied for observer status within CARICOM, and in July 1993 a joint commission was inaugurated to establish closer ties between CARICOM and Cuba. In July 1997 the heads of government agreed to pursue consideration of a free-trade accord between the Community and Cuba. In February 1992 ministers of foreign affairs from CARICOM and Central American states met to discuss future co-operation, in view of the imminent conclusion of the North American Free Trade Agreement (NAFTA) between the USA, Canada and Mexico. It was agreed that a consultative forum would be established to discuss the possible formation of a Caribbean and Central American free-trade zone. In October 1993 CARICOM declared its support for NAFTA, but requested a 'grace period', during which the region's exports would have parity with Mexican products. In March 1994 CARICOM requested that it should be considered for early entry into NAFTA (which came into force in January 1994—see p. 203). In June the US Government announced proposals to remove all trade restrictions on textiles and garments from the Caribbean. In July 1996 the heads of government expressed strong concern over the complaint lodged with the World Trade Organization (WTO) by the USA, Ecuador, Guatemala and Honduras regarding the European Union's import regime on bananas, which gives preferential access to bananas from the ACP countries (see the EU, p. 176). CARICOM requested the US Government to withdraw its complaint and to negotiate a settlement. Nevertheless, WTO panel hearings on the complaint were initiated in September. Banana producers from the ACP countries were granted third-party status, at the insistence of the Eastern Caribbean ambassador to the EU, Edwin Laurent. In December a special meeting of the Heads of Government Conference was convened, in Barbados, in order to formulate a common position on relations with the USA, in particular with respect to measures to combat illegal drugs-trafficking, following reports that the US Government was planning to impose punitive measures against certain regional authorities, owing to their perceived failure to implement effective controls on illicit drugs. The Conference confirmed the need for comprehensive co-operation and technical assistance to combat the problem, but warned that any adverse measures implemented by the USA would undermine CARICOM–US relations. The Conference decided to establish a Caribbean Security Task Force to help formulate a single regional agreement on maritime interdiction, incorporating agreements already concluded by individual members.

South Africa's minister of agriculture and land affairs attended the 1996 Heads of Government Conference, at which proposals were announced to dispatch a ministerial trade and investment mission to South Africa in 1997, and to establish a joint CARICOM diplomatic mission in that country, in order to further relations with the Southern African region as a whole. Efforts to enhance relations with Japan were also pursued during 1996, and discussions were held regarding lines of credit and promotion of regional tourism.

In April 1997 CARICOM inaugurated a Regional Negotiating Machinery body to co-ordinate the region's external negotiations. The main focus of activities was to be the establishment of the FTAA, as well as other aspects of the forthcoming second summit meeting of the Americas (scheduled to be held in April 1998), ACP relations with the EU after the expiry of the Lome IV Convention in 2000, and multilateral trade negotiations under the WTO. In May 1997 CARICOM heads of government met the US President, Bill Clinton, to discuss issues of mutual concern. A partnership for prosperity and security was established at the meeting, and arrangements were instituted for annual consultations between the ministers of foreign affairs of CARICOM countries and the US Secretary of State. However, the Community failed to secure a commitment by the USA to grant the region's exports 'NAFTA-parity' status, or to guarantee concessions to the region's banana industry, following a temporary ruling of the WTO, issued in March, upholding the US trade complaint.

ECONOMIC CO-OPERATION

The Caribbean Community's main field of activity is economic integration, by means of a Caribbean Common Market which replaced the former Caribbean Free Trade Association. The Secretariat and the Caribbean Development Bank carry out research on the best means of facing economic difficulties, and meetings of the Chief Executives of commercial banks and of central bank officials are also held with the aim of strengthening regional co-operation.

During the 1980s the economic difficulties of member states hindered the development of intra-regional trade. At the annual Conference held in June/July 1987, the heads of government agreed to dismantle all obstacles to trade within CARICOM by October 1988. This was implemented as planned, but a three-year period was permitted during which 17 products from the member countries of the Organization of Eastern Caribbean States (OECS) would be allowed protection.

In July 1984 heads of government agreed to establish a common external tariff (CET) on certain products, such as steel, cement and fertilizers, in order to protect domestic industries, although implementation of the CET was considerably delayed (see below). They also urged the necessity of structural adjustment in the economies of the region, including measures to expand production and reduce imports. In 1989 the Conference of Heads of Government agreed to implement, by July 1993, a series of measures to encourage the creation of a single Caribbean market. These included the establishment of a CARICOM Industrial Programming Scheme; the bringing into operation of the CARICOM Enterprise Regime; abolition of passport requirements for CARICOM nationals travelling within the region; re-establishment of the MCF; full implementation of the CET by January 1991; full implementation of the rules of origin and the revised scheme for the harmonization of fiscal incentives; free movement of skilled workers; removal of all remaining regional barriers to trade; establishment of a regional system of air and sea transport; and the introduction of a scheme for regional capital movement. In November 1989 a CARICOM Export Development Council was established, and undertook a three-year export development project to stimulate trade within CARICOM and to promote exports outside the region.

In August 1990 CARICOM heads of government mandated the governors of CARICOM members' central banks to begin a study of the means to achieve a monetary union within CARICOM; they also institutionalized meetings of CARICOM ministers of finance and senior finance officials, to take place twice a year; and made a commitment to improvements in education, training and research. A *Regional Exporters' Directory* was published in 1990, and a regional trade fair was held in 1992.

The deadline of 1 January 1991 for the establishment of a CET was not achieved, and in July a new deadline of 1 October was set for those members which had not complied—Antigua and Barbuda, Belize, Montserrat, Saint Christopher and Nevis and Saint Lucia, whose governments feared that the tariff would cause an increase in the rate of inflation and damage domestic industries. This deadline was later (again unsuccessfully) extended to February 1992. The tariff, which imposed a maximum level of duty of 45% on imports (compared with a maximum rate of 20% imposed by members of the Andean Group and the Central American Common Market), was also criticized by the World Bank, the IMF and the US Government as being likely to reduce the region's competitiveness. At a special meeting, held in October 1992, CARICOM heads of government agreed to reduce the maximum level of tariffs to between 30% and 35%, to be in effect by 30 June 1993 (the level was to be further lowered, to 25%–30% by 1995). The Bahamas, however, was not party to these trading arrangements (since it is a member of the Community but not of the Common Market), and Belize was granted an extension for the implementation of the new tariff levels. At the Heads of Government Conference, held in July 1995 in Guyana, Suriname was admitted as a full member of CARICOM and acceded to the treaty establishing the common market. It was granted until 1 January 1996 for implementation of the tariff reductions.

The 1995 Heads of Government Conference approved additional measures to promote the single market. The free movement of skilled workers (mainly graduates from recognized regional institutions) was to be permitted from 1 January 1996. At the same time an agreement on the mutual protection and provision of social security benefits was to enter into force. The meeting also agreed to implement the 'open-sky' agreement enabling all CARICOM-owned and -controlled airlines to operate freely within the region.

In July 1996 the heads of government announced their objective of removing all remaining non-tariff barriers to intra-regional trade, such as licensing, quantitative restrictions, etc., by the end of 1996. The summit meeting also decided that CARICOM ministers of finance, central bank governors and planning agencies should meet more frequently to address single market issues and agreed to extend the provisions of free movement to sports people, musicians and others working in the arts and media. The leaders welcomed a report endorsing plans to establish a Caribbean Investment Fund (CIF), which was to have an initial capital of US $50m. and was to allocate some of its funds to member states of the Association of Caribbean States (ACS, q.v.) that do not belong to CARICOM. The purpose of the CIF was to be to mobilize foreign currency from extra-regional capital markets for investment in new or existing enterprises in the region. In July 1997 the heads of government, meeting in Montego Bay. Jamaica, agreed to accelerate economic integration, with the aim of completing a single market by 1999. It was noted that, as of 1 July 1997, all member states except Antigua and Barbuda had implemented the second phase of the CET, while four countries had implemented phase three, comprising a tariff of 0%–25%. Al members were expected to reach this stage by early 1998. At the meeting 11 member states signed Protocol II of the Treaty of Chaguaramas, which constituted a central element of a CARICOM single market and economy, providing for the right to establish enterprises, the provision of services and the movement of capital throughout participating countries.

INDUSTRY AND ENERGY

CARICOM aims to promote the development of joint ventures in exporting industries (particularly the woodwork, furniture, ceramics and foundry industries) through an agreement (reached in 1989) on an industrial programming scheme. Work on an investors' guide for each member state was completed in 1984. CARICOM's Export Development Council gives training and consultancy services to regional manufacturers. Regional manufacturers' exhibitions (CARIMEX) are held every three years. The Caribbean Trade Information System (CARTIS) comprises computer databases covering country and product profiles, trade statistics, trade opportunities, institutions and bibliographical information; it links the national trade centres of CARICOM members. A protocol relating to the CARICOM Industrial Programming Scheme (CIPS), approved in 1988, is the Community's instrument for promoting the co-operative development of industry in the region.

The Secretariat has established a national standards bureau in each member country to harmonize technical standards, and supervises the metrication of weights and measures.

The CARICOM Alternative Energy Systems Project provides training, assesses energy needs and conducts energy audits. Efforts in regional energy development are directed at the collection and analysis of data for national energy policy documents. A project document for the development of geothermal energy in the region was completed in 1990, and a reconnaissance study was started in the same year.

TRANSPORT, COMMUNICATIONS AND TOURISM

A Caribbean Confederation of Shippers' Councils represents the interests of regional exporters and importers. In July 1990 the Caribbean Telecommunications Union was established to oversee developments in regional telecommunications.

In 1988 a Consultative Committee on Caribbean Regional Information Systems (CCCRIS) was established to evaluate and monitor the functioning of existing information systems and to seek to co-ordinate and advise on the establishment of new systems.

A Summit of Heads of Government on Tourism, Trade and Transportation was held in Trinidad and Tobago, in August 1995, to which all members of the ACS and regional tourism organizations were invited. In 1997 CARICOM heads of government considered a number of proposals relating to air transportation, tourism, human resource development and capital investment, which had been identified by Community ministers of tourism as critical issues in the sustainable development of the tourist industry. The heads of government requested ministers to meet regularly to develop tourism policies, and in particular to undertake an in-depth study of human resource development issues in early 1998. A new fund to help train young people from the region in aspects of the tourist industry was inaugurated in July 1997, in memory of the former Prime Minister of Jamaica, Michael Manley.

AGRICULTURE

In 1985 the New Marketing Arrangements for Primary Agricultural Products and Livestock were instituted, with the aim of increasing the flow of agricultural commodities within the region. A computer-based Caribbean Agricultural Marketing Information System was initiated in 1987. The Caribbean Agricultural Research and Development Institute (CARDI), founded in 1975, devises and transfers appropriate technology for small-scale farmers, and provides training and advisory services. The Caribbean Food Corporation, established in 1976, implements joint-venture projects with investors from the private and public sectors.

At the CARICOM summit meeting in July 1996 it was agreed to undertake wide-ranging measures in order to modernize the agricultural sector and to increase the international competitiveness of Caribbean agricultural produce. The CARICOM Secretariat was to support national programmes with assistance in policy formulation, human resource development and the promotion of research and technology development in the areas of productivity, marketing, agri-business and water resources management. During 1997 CARICOM Governments continued to lobby against a complaint lodged at the WTO with regard to the EU's banana import regime (offering favourable conditions to ACP producers—see above) and to generate awareness of the economic and social importance of the banana industry to the region.

HEALTH AND EDUCATION

In 1986 CARICOM and the Pan-American Health Organization launched 'Caribbean Co-operation in Health' with projects to be undertaken in six main areas: environmental protection, including the control of disease-bearing pests; development of human resources; chronic non-communicable diseases and accidents; strengthening health systems; food and nutrition; maternal and child health care; and population activities. In early 1996 the Japanese Government approved a loan of US $0.5m. to assist CARICOM in the implementation of a health care programme aimed at children.

CARICOM educational programmes have included the improvement of reading in schools through assistance for teacher-training; and ensuring the availability of low-cost educational material throughout the region. A strategy for developing and improving technical and vocational education and training within each member state and throughout the region was completed and published in 1990. In July 1997 CARICOM heads of government adopted the recommendations of a ministerial committee, which identified priority measures for implementation in the education sector. These included the objective of achieving universal, quality secondary education and the enrolment of 15% of post-secondary students in tertiary education by 2005, as well as improved training in foreign languages and science and technology.

EMERGENCY ASSISTANCE

A Caribbean Disaster Emergency Response Agency was established in 1991, in Bridgetown, Barbados, to co-ordinate immediate disaster relief, primarily in the event of hurricanes. During 1997 CARICOM Governments remained actively concerned with the situation in Montserrat, which had suffered a series of massive volcanic eruptions. At the Heads of Government Conference in July, the Community pledged humanitarian, economic and technical assistance and resolved to help mobilize external assistance from regional and international donor countries and institutions.

ASSOCIATE INSTITUTIONS

Caribbean Council of Legal Education: Mona Campus, Kingston 7, Jamaica; tel. 92-71899; fax 92-73927; f. 1971; responsible for the training of members of the legal profession. Mems: govts of 15 countries and territories.

Caribbean Development Bank: POB 408, Wildey, St Michael, Barbados; tel. 431-1600; telex 2287; fax 426-7269; f. 1969 to stimulate regional economic growth through support for agriculture, industry, transport and other infrastructure, tourism, housing and education; cap. US $693.6m. (October 1995). In 1995 net approvals totalled $109.5m. and grant and loan disbursements $65.9m. In 1990 the Special Development Fund was replenished by $124m.; total resources at Dec. 1995 amounted to $1,107m. Mems: CARICOM states, and Anguilla, Canada, Cayman Islands, Colombia, France, Germany, Italy, Mexico, United Kingdom, Venezuela. Pres. Sir NEVILLE NICHOLLS.

Caribbean Examinations Council: The Garrison, St Michael 20, Barbados; tel. 436-6261; fax 429-5421; f. 1972; develops syllabuses and conducts examinations. Mems: govts of 16 English-speaking countries and territories.

Caribbean Meteorological Organization: POB 461, Port of Spain, Trinidad and Tobago; tel. 624-4481; fax 623-3634; e-mail cebcmo@carib-link.net; f. 1951 to co-ordinate regional activities in meteorology, operational hydrology and allied sciences; conducts training in meteorology and operational hydrology; became an associate institution of CARICOM in 1983. Mems: govts of 16 countries and territories. Co-ordinating Dir C. E. BERRIDGE.

Eastern Caribbean Central Bank: POB 89, Basseterre, St Christopher and Nevis; tel. 465-2537; telex 6828; fax 465-5615; f. 1983 by OECS governments; maintains regional currency (Eastern Caribbean dollar) and advises on the economic development of member states. Mems: Anguilla, Antigua and Barbuda, Dominica, Grenada, Montserrat, Saint Christopher and Nevis, Saint Lucia, Saint Vincent and the Grenadines. Gov. DWIGHT VENNER.

Organization of Eastern Caribbean States—OECS: POB 179, The Morne, Castries, Saint Lucia; tel. 22537; fax 31628; Economic Affairs Secretariat: POB 822, St John's, Antigua; f. 1981 by the seven states which formerly belonged to the West Indies Associated States (f. 1966). Aims to promote the harmonized development of trade and industry in member states; single market created on 1 January 1988. Principal institutions are: the Authority of Heads of Government (the supreme policy-making body), the Foreign Affairs Committee, the Defence and Security Committee, and the Economic Affairs Committee. There is an export development agency (based in Dominica). Mems: Antigua and Barbuda, Dominica, Grenada, Montserrat, Saint Christopher and Nevis, Saint Lucia, Saint Vincent and the Grenadines; assoc. mem.: British Virgin Islands. Dir-Gen. SWINBURNE LESTRADE.

Other Associate Institutions of CARICOM, in accordance with its constitution, are the University of Guyana, the University of the West Indies and an Assembly of Caribbean Community Parliamentarians. The establishment of a Caribbean Supreme Court is under consideration.

CENTRAL AMERICAN COMMON MARKET—CACM

(MERCADO COMÚN CENTROAMERICANO)

Address: 4A Avda 10-25, Zona 14, Apdo Postal 1237, 01901 Guatemala City, Guatemala.

Telephone: (2) 682151; **telex:** 6203; **fax:** (2) 681071.

CACM was established by the Organization of Central American States (ODECA, q.v.) under the General Treaty of Central American Economic Integration (Tratado General de Integración Económica Centroamericana) signed in Managua on 13 December 1960. It was ratified by all countries by September 1963.

MEMBERS

Costa Rica	El Salvador	Nicaragua
Guatemala	Honduras	

Organization

(January 1998)

MINISTERIAL MEETINGS

The organization's policy is formulated by regular meetings of Ministers and Vice-Ministers of Central American Integration; meetings of other ministers, and of presidents of central banks, also play an important part.

PERMANENT SECRETARIAT

Secretaría Permanente del Tratado General de Integración Económica Centroamericana—SIECA: provides institutional support for the Common Market, supervises the correct implementation of the legal instruments of economic integration, carries out relevant studies at the request of the Common Market authorities, and arranges meetings. There are departments covering the working of the Common Market; negotiations and external trade policy; physical integration; systems and statistics; finance and administration. There is also a unit for co-operation with the private sector and finance institutions and a legal consultative committee. In 1996 the Secretariat was in the process of establishing regional offices in each of the member countries. It was also envisaged that SIECA would open offices in third countries with which trade negotiations were under way.

Secretary-General: HAROLDO RODAS MELGAR.

Assistant Secretaries-General: Dr JUAN DANIEL ALEMÁN GURDIAN, GERARDO ZEPEDA BERMÚDEZ.

Activities

The General Treaty envisaged the eventual liberalization of intra-regional trade and the establishment of a free-trade area and a customs union. Economic integration in the region, however, has been hampered by ideological differences between governments, difficulties in internal supply, protectionist measures by overseas markets, external and intra-regional debts, adverse rates of exchange and high interest rates. Regular meetings of senior customs officials aim to increase co-operation, to develop a uniform terminology, and to recommend revisions of customs legislation. CACM member-countries also aim to pursue a common policy in respect of international trade agreements on commodities, raw materials and staples. SIECA participates in meetings with other regional organizations (such as SELA and ECLAC, q.v.) and represents the region at meetings of international organizations.

Under the Convention for Fiscal Incentives for Industrial Development, which came into operation in 1969, a wide range of tax benefits are applied to various categories of industries in the region, to encourage productivity. SIECA carries out studies on the industrial sector, compiles statistics, and provides information to member governments. It also analyses energy consumption in the region and assists governments in drawing up energy plans, aiming to reduce dependence on imported petroleum.

A co-ordinating commission supervises the marketing of four basic crops (maize, rice, beans and sorghum), recording and forecasting production figures and recommending minimum guarantee prices. Information on other crops is also compiled. A permanent commission for agricultural research and extension services monitors and co-ordinates regional projects in this field.

An agreement to establish a Central American Monetary Union was signed in 1964, with the eventual aim of establishing a common currency and aligning foreign exchange and monetary policies. The Central American Monetary Council, comprising the presidents of the member states' central banks, meets regularly to consider monetary policy and financial affairs. A Fund for Monetary Stabilization provides short-term financial assistance to members facing temporary balance-of-payments difficulties.

Trade within the region increased in value from US $33m. in 1960 to $1,129m. in 1980, but subsequently diminished every year until 1986, when it amounted to $406m. The decline was due to a number of factors: low prices for the region's main export commodities, and heavy external debts, both resulting in a severe shortage of foreign exchange; and intra-regional trade 'freezes' provoked by debts amounting to $700m. at mid-1986 (Guatemala and Costa Rica being the chief creditors, and Nicaragua and El Salvador the main debtors). In January 1986 a new CACM tariff and customs agreement came into effect, imposing standard import duties for the whole region (aimed at discouraging the import of non-essential goods from outside the region), and a uniform tariff nomenclature. Honduras, however, continued to insist on bilateral tariff agreements with other member countries. Honduras subsequently signed a temporary free-trade agreement with all the other member states. From 1987 intra-regional trade increased steadily and reached an estimated $1,600m. in 1996.

In June 1990 the presidents of the five CACM countries signed a declaration welcoming peace initiatives in El Salvador, Guatemala and Nicaragua, and appealing for a revitalization of CACM, as a means of promoting lasting peace in the region. In December the presidents committed themselves to the creation of an effective common market, proposing the opening of negotiations on a comprehensive regional customs and tariffs policy by March 1991, and the introduction of a regional 'anti-dumping' code by December 1991. They requested the support of multilateral lending institutions through investment in regional development, and the cancellation or rescheduling of member countries' debts. At the end of October 1993 the presidents of the CACM countries and Panama signed a protocol to the 1960 General Treaty, committing themselves to full economic integration in the region (with a common external tariff of 20% for finished products and 5% for raw materials and capital goods) and creating conditions for increased free trade. The countries agreed to accelerate the removal of internal non-tariff barriers, but no deadline was set. Full implementation of the protocol was to be 'voluntary and gradual', owing to objections on the part of Costa Rica and Panama. In May 1994, however, Costa Rica committed itself to full participation in the protocol. In March 1995 a meeting of the Central American Monetary Council discussed and endorsed a reduction in the tariff levels from 20% to 15% and from 5% to 1%. However, efforts to adopt this as a common policy were hindered by the implementation of these tariff levels by El Salvador on a unilateral basis, from 1 April, and the subsequent modifications by Guatemala and Costa Rica of their external tariffs.

In July 1996 Central American ministers of foreign affairs agreed to establish a Central American Institute for Higher Police Studies, in order to improve and modernize the region's police forces. The Institute was to be sited in San Salvador, the Salvadorean capital.

In May 1997 the Heads of State of CACM member countries, together with the Prime Minister of Belize, conferred with the US President, Bill Clinton, in San José, Costa Rica. The leaders resolved to establish a Trade and Investment Council to promote trade relations; however, Clinton failed to endorse a request from CACM members that their products receive preferential access to US markets, on similar terms to those from Mexico agreed under the NAFTA accord. During the year the Central American Governments pursued negotiations to conclude free-trade agreements with Mexico, Panama and the members of the Caribbean Community and Common Market (CARICOM). Nicaragua signed a bilateral accord with Mexico in December (Costa Rica already having done so in 1994).

In September 1997 CACM Heads of State, meeting in the Nicaraguan capital, signed the Managua Declaration in support of further regional integration and the establishment of a political union. A commission was to be established to consider all aspects of the policy and to formulate a timetable for the integration process.

In February 1993 the European Community (EC) signed a new framework co-operation agreement with the CACM member states extending the programme of economic assistance and political dialogue initiated in 1984; a further co-operation agreement with the European Union (as the EC had become) was signed in early 1996.

PUBLICATIONS

Anuario Estadístico Centroamericano de Comercio Exterior.

Carta Informativa (monthly).

Cuadernos de la SIECA (2 a year).

Estadísticas Macroeconómicas de Centroamérica (annually).

Series Estadísticas Seleccionadas de Centroamérica y Panamá (annually).

Institutions

FINANCE

Banco Centroamericano de Integración Económica—BCIE (Central American Bank for Economic Integration): Apdo Postal 772, Tegucigalpa, Honduras; tel. 372230; telex 1103; fax 370793; f. 1961 to promote the economic integration and balanced economic development of member countries; finances public and private development projects, particularly those related to industrialization and infrastructure. By June 1993 cumulative lending amounted to US $3,217m., mainly for roads, hydroelectricity projects, housing and telecommunications. Auth. cap. $2,000m. Pres. José Manuel Pacas. Publs *Annual Report, Revista de la Integración y el Desarrollo de Centroamérica.*

Consejo Monetario Centroamericano—CMCA (Central American Monetary Council): Apdo 5438, 1000 San José, Costa Rica; tel. 233-6044; telex 2234; fax 221-5643; f. 1964 by the presidents of Central American central banks, to co-ordinate monetary policies. Exec. Sec. Manuel Fontecha Ferrari. Publs *Boletín Estadístico* (annually), *Informe Económico* (annually).

TRADE AND INDUSTRY

Federación de Cámaras de Comercio del Istmo Centroamericano (Federation of Central American Chambers of Commerce): Avda Cuba y Calle 33, Apdo 74, Panamá 1, Panama; tel. 227-1233; fax 227-4186; e-mail cciap@panama.phoenix.net; internet http://www.panacamara.com; f. 1961; for planning and co-ordinating industrial and commercial exchanges and exhibitions. Pres. Edgardo R. Carles; Exec. Dir José Ramón Varela C.

Instituto Centroamericano de Administración de Empresas (Central American Institute for Business Administration): Apdo 960, 4050 Alajuela, Costa Rica; tel. 443-0506; telex 7040; fax 433-9101; f. 1964; provides postgraduate programme in business administration; executive training programmes; management research and consulting; second campus in Nicaragua; libraries of 75,000 vols. Rector Dr Brizzio Biondi-Morra.

Instituto Centroamericano de Investigación y Tecnología Industrial (Central American Research Institute for Industry): Apdo Postal 1552, Avda La Reforma 4-47, Zona 10, Guatemala City; tel. (2) 310631; telex 5312; fax (2) 317466; f. 1956 by the five Central American Republics, with assistance from the United Nations, to provide technical advisory services to regional governments and private enterprise. Dir (a.i.) Luis Fidel Cifuentes (Guatemala).

PUBLIC ADMINISTRATION

Instituto Centroamericano de Administración Pública—ICAP (Central American Institute of Public Administration): POB 10.025-1000, De la Heladería Pops en Curridabat 100 mts sur y 50 oeste, San José, Costa Rica; tel. 234-1011; telex 2180; fax 225-2049; e-mail icaper@sol.racsa.co.cr; internet http://www.icap.ac.cr; f. 1954 by the five Central American Republics and the United Nations, with later participation by Panama. The Institute aims to train the region's public servants, provide technical assistance and carry out research leading to reforms in public administration. Dir Dr Hugo Zelaya Cálix.

EDUCATION AND HEALTH

Confederación Universitaria Centroamericana (Central American University Confederation): Apdo 37, Ciudad Universitaria Rodrigo Facio, San José, Costa Rica; tel. 225-2744; fax 222-0478; f. 1948 to guarantee academic, administrative and economic autonomy for universities and to encourage regional integration of higher education; Council of 14 mems. Mems.: seven universities, in Costa Rica (two), El Salvador, Guatemala, Honduras, Nicaragua and Panama. Sec.-Gen. Dr Ronald Dormond (Costa Rica). Publs *Estudios Sociales Centroamericanas* (quarterly), *Cuadernos de Investigación* (monthly), *Carta Informativa de la Secretaría General* (monthly).

Instituto de Nutrición de Centroamérica y Panamá—INCAP (Institute of Nutrition of Central America and Panama): Apdo 1188, Carretera Roosevelt, Zona 11, 01901 Guatemala City, Guatemala; tel. (2) 723762; telex 5696; fax (2) 736529; e-mail hdelgado@.org.gt; f. 1949 to promote the development of nutritional sciences and their application and to strengthen the technical capacity of member countries to solve problems of food and nutrition; provides training and technical assistance for nutrition education and planning; conducts research. Divisions: agricultural and food sciences; nutrition and health; food and nutrition planning. Maintains library (including about 600 periodicals). Administered by the Pan American Health Organization (PAHO) and the World Health Organization. Mems: CACM mems and Belize and Panama. Dir Dr Hernán L. Delgado. Publs *Boletín ASI* (quarterly), annual report, compilations.

TRANSPORT AND COMMUNICATIONS

Comisión Centroamericana de Ferrocarriles—COCAFER (Central American Railways Commission): c/o SIECA, 4a Avda 10–25, Zona 14, Apdo Postal 1237, 01901 Guatemala City, Guatemala; tel. (2) 682151; telex 5676; fax (2) 681071.

Comisión Centroamericana de Transporte Marítimo—COCATRAM (Central American Commission of Maritime Transport): Cine Cabrera 2 c. al este 2½ c. al sur, Apdo 2423, Managua, Nicaragua; tel (2) 222754; fax (2) 222759; f. 1981. Sec. Gen. César Augusto Quiroz.

Comisión Técnica de las Telecomunicaciones de Centroamérica—COMTELCA (Technical Commission for Telecommunications in Central America): Apdo 1793, Tegucigalpa, Honduras; tel. 20-6666; fax 20-1197; f. 1966 to co-ordinate and improve the regional telecommunications network. Dir-Gen. Héctor L. Rodríguez.

Corporación Centroamericana de Servicios de Navegación Aérea—COCESNA (Central American Air Navigation Service Corporation): Apdo 660, Aeropuerto de Toncontín, Tegucigalpa, Honduras; tel. 331143; fax 331219; f. 1960; offers radar air traffic control services, aeronautical telecommunications services, flight inspections and radio assistance services for air navigation; administers the Central American Aeronautical School. Gen. Man. EDUARDO MARÍN J.

COMMON MARKET FOR EASTERN AND SOUTHERN AFRICA—COMESA

Address: Lotti House, Cairo Rd, POB 30051, Lusaka, Zambia.

Telephone: (1) 229726; **telex:** 40127; **fax:** (1) 225107; **e-mail:** comesa@comesa.zm.

Founded in 1993 as a successor to the Preferential Trade Area for Eastern and Southern Africa (PTA), which was established in 1981.

MEMBERS

Angola	Mauritius
Burundi	Mozambique*
Comoros	Namibia
Congo, Democratic Republic	Rwanda
Eritrea	Sudan
Ethiopia	Swaziland
Kenya	Tanzania
Lesotho*	Uganda
Madagascar	Zambia
Malawi	Zimbabwe

* Membership voluntarily suspended.

Organization

(January 1998)

AUTHORITY

The Authority of the Common Market is the supreme policy organ of COMESA, comprising Heads of State or of Government of member countries. The inaugural meeting of the Authority took place in Lilongwe, Malawi, in December 1994. The second summit meeting was held in Lusaka, Zambia, in April 1997.

COUNCIL OF MINISTERS

Each member government appoints a minister to participate in the Council. The Council monitors COMESA activities, including supervision of the Secretariat, recommends policy direction and development, and reports to the Authority.

A Committee of Governors of Central Banks advises the Authority and the Council of Ministers on monetary and financial matters.

SECRETARIAT

Secretary-General: JOEL ERASTUS MWENCHA (Kenya) (acting).

Activities

The COMESA treaty was signed by member states of the PTA in November 1993 and was scheduled to come into effect on being ratified by 10 countries. COMESA formally succeeded the PTA in December 1994 (by which time it had received 12 ratifications), with the aim of strengthening the process of regional economic integration that had been initiated under the PTA, in order to help member states achieve sustainable economic growth.

COMESA aims to establish a free-trade area by 2000, requiring full liberalization of trading practices, including the elimination of non-tariff barriers, to ensure the free movement of goods, services and capital within the Common Market. In April 1997 COMESA Heads of State agreed that a common external tariff would be implemented by 2004, to strengthen the establishment of a regional customs union, with a zero tariff on products originating from within the Common Market. COMESA aimed to formulate a common investment procedure to promote domestic, cross-border and direct foreign investment by ensuring the free movement of capital, services and labour.

The PTA aimed to facilitate intra-regional trade by establishing a clearing house to deal with credit arrangements and balance of payments issues. The clearing house became operational in February 1984 using the unit of account of the PTA (UAPTA) as its currency. (The UAPTA was valued at the rate of the IMF special drawing rights.) The clearing house, based in Harare, Zimbabwe, remained an integral part of the COMESA infrastructure. In April 1997 the Authority endorsed a proposal to replace UAPTA with a COMESA dollar, to be equivalent to the value of the US currency. An Automated System of Customs Data (ASYCUDA) has been established to facilitate customs administration in all COMESA member states. Through support for capacity-building activities and the establishment of other specialized institutions (see below) COMESA aims to reinforce its objectives of regional integration. The COMESA treaty envisaged the establishment of a sub-regional Court of Justice, to replace the PTA Tribunal; however, this had yet to be implemented in late 1997.

Co-operation programmes have been implemented by COMESA in the industrial, agricultural, energy and transport and communications sectors. A regional food security programme aimed to ensure adequate food supplies at all times. In 1997 COMESA Heads of State advocated that the food sector be supported by the immediate implementation of an irrigation action plan for the region. Other initiatives include a road customs declaration document, a regional customs bond guarantee scheme, third party motor vehicle insurance scheme and travellers cheques in the UAPTA unit of currency. A Trade Information Network, established under the PTA to disseminate information on the production and marketing of goods manufactured and traded in the region, was scheduled to be transformed into the COMESA Information Network (COMNET).

Since its establishment there have been concerns on the part of member states, as well as other regional non-member countries, in particular South Africa, of adverse rivalry between COMESA and the Southern African Development Community (SADC, q.v.) and of a duplication of roles. In December 1996 and January 1997 respectively, Lesotho and Mozambique suspended their membership of COMESA and announced their intention to withdraw from the organization owing to concerns that their continued participation in COMESA was incompatible with their SADC membership.

FINANCE

COMESA is financed by member states. Its administrative budget for 1996 amounted to US $4m. In April 1997 COMESA Heads of State concluded that the organization's activities were being undermined by lack of resources, and determined to expel countries which fail to pay membership dues over a five-year period.

COMESA INSTITUTIONS

COMESA Association of Commercial Banks: 101 Union Ave, POB 2940, Harare, Zimbabwe; tel. (4) 793911; telex 26166; fax (4) 730819; aims to strengthen co-operation between banks in the region; organizes training activities; conducts studies to harmonize banking laws and operations. Mems: commercial banking orgs in Burundi, Kenya, Malawi, Sudan, Tanzania, Uganda.

COMESA Leather and Leather Products Institute: POB 5538, Addis Ababa, Ethiopia; tel (1) 510361; fax (1) 512799; f. 1990 as the PTA Leather Institute. Mems: Govts of 16 COMESA mem. states.

COMESA Metallurgical Technology Centre: c/o 101 Union Ave, Harare, Zimbabwe; tel. (1) 793911; telex 26166; fax (1) 730819; conducts research, testing and evaluation of raw materials, training and the exchange of appropriate technologies in order to promote the local mineral resources sectors.

Compagnie de réassurance de la Zone d'échanges préférentiels—Zep-re (COMESA Reinsurance Co): Anniversary Towers,

University Way, POB 42769, Nairobi, Kenya; tel. (2) 212792; fax (2) 224102; f. 1993; provides local reinsurance services and training to personnel in the insurance industry; auth. cap. 20m. UAPTA; Man. Dir S. M. LUBASI.

Eastern and Southern African Trade and Development Bank: NSSF Bldg, Bishop's Rd, POB 48596, Nairobi, Kenya; tel. (2) 712260; fax (2) 711510; f. 1983 as PTA Development Bank; aims to mobilize resources and finance COMESA activities to foster regional integration; promotes investment and co-financing within the region; shareholders 15 COMESA mem. states and the African Development Bank; cap. p.u. US $82.9m. (Dec. 1995); Pres. MARTIN OGANG.

Federation of National Associations of Women in Business—FEMCOM; c/o COMESA Secretariat; f. 1993 to provide links between female business executives throughout the region and to promote greater awareness of relevant issues at policy level. FEMCOM was to be supported by a Revolving Fund for Women in Business.

PUBLICATIONS

COMESA Journal.

COMESA Trade Directory (annually).

COMESA Trade Information Newsletter (monthly).

Demand/supply surveys and reports.

THE COMMONWEALTH

Address: Commonwealth Secretariat, Marlborough House, Pall Mall, London, SW1Y 5HX, United Kingdom.

Telephone: (171) 839-3411; **telex:** 27678; **fax:** (171) 930-0827; **internet:** http://www.commonwealth.org.

The Commonwealth is a voluntary association of 50 independent states, comprising about one-quarter of the world's population. It includes the United Kingdom and most of its former dependencies, and former dependencies of Australia and New Zealand (themselves Commonwealth countries).

The evolution of the Commonwealth began with the introduction of self-government in Canada in the 1840s; Australia, New Zealand and South Africa became independent before the First World War. At the Imperial Conference of 1926 the United Kingdom and the Dominions, as they were then called, were described as 'autonomous communities within the British Empire, equal in status', and this change was enacted into law by the Statute of Westminster, in 1931.

The modern Commonwealth began with the entry of India and Pakistan in 1947, and of Sri Lanka (then Ceylon) in 1948. In 1949, when India decided to become a republic, the Commonwealth Heads of Government agreed to replace allegiance to the British Crown with recognition of the British monarch as Head of the Commonwealth, as a condition of membership. This was a precedent for a number of other members (see Heads of State and Heads of Government, below).

MEMBERS*

Antigua and Barbuda
Australia
Bahamas
Bangladesh
Barbados
Belize
Botswana
Brunei
Cameroon
Canada
Cyprus
Dominica
Fiji
The Gambia
Ghana
Grenada
Guyana
India
Jamaica
Kenya
Kiribati
Lesotho
Malawi
Malaysia
Maldives
Malta
Mauritius
Mozambique
Namibia
Nauru†
New Zealand
Nigeria
Pakistan
Papua New Guinea
Saint Christopher and Nevis
Saint Lucia
Saint Vincent and the Grenadines
Samoa
Seychelles
Sierra Leone
Singapore
Solomon Islands
South Africa
Sri Lanka
Swaziland
Tanzania
Tonga
Trinidad and Tobago
Tuvalu†
Uganda
United Kingdom
Vanuatu
Zambia
Zimbabwe

* Ireland, South Africa and Pakistan withdrew from the Commonwealth in 1949, 1961 and 1972 respectively. In October 1987 Fiji's membership was declared to have lapsed (following the proclamation of a republic there); it was readmitted on 1 October 1997. Pakistan rejoined the Commonwealth in October 1989 and South Africa rejoined in June 1994. Nigeria's membership was suspended in November 1995; Sierra Leone's participation in meetings of the Commonwealth was suspended in July 1997.

† Nauru and Tuvalu are special members of the Commonwealth; they have the right to participate in all activities except full Meetings of Heads of Government.

Dependencies and Associated States

Australia:
- Ashmore and Cartier Islands
- Australian Antarctic Territory
- Christmas Island
- Cocos (Keeling) Islands
- Coral Sea Islands Territory
- Heard Island and the McDonald Islands
- Norfolk Island

New Zealand:
- Cook Islands
- Niue
- Ross Dependency
- Tokelau

United Kingdom:
- Anguilla
- Bermuda
- British Antarctic Territory
- British Indian Ocean Territory
- British Virgin Islands
- Cayman Islands
- Channel Islands
- Falkland Islands
- Gibraltar
- Isle of Man
- Montserrat
- Pitcairn Islands
- St Helena
  - Ascension
  - Tristan da Cunha
- South Georgia and the South Sandwich Islands
- Turks and Caicos Islands

HEADS OF STATE AND HEADS OF GOVERNMENT

At the end of 1997 21 member countries were monarchies and 33 were republics. All Commonwealth countries accept Queen Elizabeth II as the symbol of the free association of the independent member nations and as such the Head of the Commonwealth. Of the 33 republics, the offices of Head of State and Head of Government were combined in 22: Botswana, Cameroon, Cyprus, The Gambia, Ghana, Guyana, Kenya, Kiribati, Malawi, Maldives, Mozambique, Namibia, Nauru, Nigeria, Seychelles, Sierra Leone, South Africa, Sri Lanka, Tanzania, Uganda, Zambia and Zimbabwe. The two offices were separated in the remaining 11: Bangladesh, Dominica, Fiji, India, Malta, Mauritius, Pakistan, Samoa, Singapore, Trinidad and Tobago and Vanuatu.

Of the monarchies, the Queen is Head of State of the United Kingdom and of 15 others, in each of which she is represented by a Governor-General: Antigua and Barbuda, Australia, the Bahamas, Barbados, Belize, Canada, Grenada, Jamaica, New Zealand, Papua New Guinea, Saint Christopher and Nevis, Saint Lucia, Saint Vincent and the Grenadines, Solomon Islands and Tuvalu. Brunei, Lesotho, Malaysia, Swaziland and Tonga are also monarchies, where the traditional monarch is Head of State.

The Governors-General are appointed by the Queen on the advice of the Prime Ministers of the country concerned. They are wholly independent of the Government of the United Kingdom.

HIGH COMMISSIONERS

Governments of member countries are represented in other Commonwealth countries by High Commissioners, who have a status equivalent to that of Ambassadors.

Organization

(January 1998)

The Commonwealth is not a federation: there is no central government nor are there any rigid contractual obligations such as bind members of the United Nations.

The Commonwealth has no written constitution but its members subscribe to the ideals of the Declaration of Commonwealth Principles (see below) unanimously approved by a meeting of heads of government in Singapore in 1971. Members also approved the 1977 statement on apartheid in sport (the Gleneagles Agreement); the 1979 Lusaka Declaration on Racism and Racial Prejudice (see below); the 1981 Melbourne Declaration on relations between developed and developing countries; the 1983 New Delhi Statement on Economic Action; the 1983 Goa Declaration on International Security; the 1985 Nassau Declaration on World Order; the Commonwealth Accord on Southern Africa (1985); the 1987 Vancouver Declaration on World Trade; the Okanagan Statement and Programme of Action on Southern Africa (1987); the Langkawi Declaration on the Environment (1989); the Kuala Lumpur Statement on Southern Africa (1989); the Harare Commonwealth Declaration (1991) (see below); the Ottawa Declaration on Women and Structural Adjustment (1991); the Limassol Statement on the Uruguay Round of multilateral trade negotiations (1993); the Millbrook Commonwealth Action Programme on the Harare Declaration (1995); and the Edinburgh Commonwealth Economic Declaration (1997).

MEETINGS OF HEADS OF GOVERNMENT

Meetings are private and informal and operate not by voting but by consensus. The emphasis is on consultation and exchange of views for co-operation. A communiqué is issued at the end of every meeting. Meetings are held every two years in different capitals in the Commonwealth. The 1997 meeting was held in Edinburgh, the United Kingdom, in October; the 1999 meeting was to be held in South Africa.

OTHER CONSULTATIONS

Meetings at ministerial and official level are also held regularly. Since 1959 finance ministers have met in a Commonwealth country in the week prior to the annual meetings of the IMF and the World Bank. Meetings on education, legal, women's and youth affairs are held at ministerial level every three years. Ministers of health hold annual meetings, with major meetings every three years, and ministers of agriculture meet every two years. Ministers of trade, labour and employment, industry, science and the environment also hold periodic meetings.

Senior officials—cabinet secretaries, permanent secretaries to heads of government and others—meet regularly in the year between meetings of heads of government to provide continuity and to exchange views on various developments.

COMMONWEALTH SECRETARIAT

The Secretariat, established by Commonwealth heads of government in 1965, operates as an international organization at the service of all Commonwealth countries. It organizes consultations between governments and runs programmes of co-operation. Meetings of heads of government, ministers and senior officials decide these programmes and provide overall direction.

The Secretariat is headed by a secretary-general (elected by heads of government), assisted by three deputy secretaries-general. One deputy is responsible for political affairs, one for economic and social affairs, and one for development co-operation (including the Commonwealth Fund for Technical Co-operation—see below). The Secretariat comprises 12 Divisions in the fields of political affairs; legal and constitutional affairs; information and public affairs; administration; economic affairs; human resource development; gender and youth affairs; science and technology; economic and legal advisory services; export and industrial development; management and training services; and general technical assistance services. It also includes a non-governmental organizations desk and a unit for strategic planning and evaluation.

Secretary-General: Chief E. CHUKWUEMEKA (EMEKA) ANYAOKU (Nigeria).

Deputy Secretary-General (Political): KRISHNAN SRINIVASAN (India).

Deputy Secretary-General (Economic and Social): Sir HUMPHREY MAUD (United Kingdom).

Deputy Secretary-General (Development Co-operation): EWAN (NICK) HARE (Canada).

BUDGET

The Secretariat's budget for 1996/97 was £10.45m.; a budget of £10.39m. was approved for 1997/98. Member governments meet the cost of the Secretariat through subscriptions on a scale related to income and population, similar to the scale for contributions to the United Nations.

Activities

INTERNATIONAL AFFAIRS

In 1977 Commonwealth heads of government reached an agreement on discouraging sporting links with South Africa, The Gleneagles Agreement on Sporting Contacts with South Africa, which was designed to express their abhorrence of that country's policy of apartheid. At their 1979 meeting in Lusaka, Zambia, the heads of government endorsed a nine-point plan to direct Zimbabwe-Rhodesia towards internationally recognized independence. The leaders also issued the Lusaka Declaration on Racism and Racial Prejudice as a formal expression of their abhorrence of all forms of racist policy.

In October 1985 heads of government, meeting at Nassau, Bahamas, issued the Nassau Declaration on World Order, reaffirming Commonwealth commitment to the United Nations, to international co-operation for development and to the eventual elimination of nuclear weapons. The same meeting issued the Commonwealth Accord on Southern Africa, calling on the South African authorities to dismantle apartheid and open dialogue with a view to establishing a representative government. The meeting also established a Commonwealth 'Eminent Persons Group'. It visited South Africa in February and March 1986 and attempted unsuccessfully to establish a dialogue between the South African Government and opposition leaders. In August the heads of government of seven Commonwealth countries (Australia, the Bahamas, Canada, India, the United Kingdom, Zambia and Zimbabwe) met to consider the Group's report, and (with the exception of the United Kingdom) agreed to adopt a series of measures to exert economic pressure on the South African Government, and to encourage other countries to adopt such measures.

In October 1987 heads of government, meeting at Vancouver, Canada, issued the Okanagan Statement and Programme of Action on Southern Africa, to strengthen the Commonwealth effort to end apartheid in South Africa. A Commonwealth Committee of Foreign Ministers on Southern Africa was established to provide impetus and guidance in furtherance of the objectives of the Statement. The meeting also issued the Vancouver Declaration on World Trade, condemning protectionism and reaffirming the leaders' commitment to work for a durable and just world trading system.

In October 1989 heads of government, meeting in Kuala Lumpur, Malaysia, issued the Langkawi Declaration on the Environment, a 16-point joint programme of action to combat environmental degradation and ensure sustainable development.

In October 1991 heads of government, meeting in Harare, Zimbabwe, issued the Harare Commonwealth Declaration, in which they reaffirmed their commitment to the Commonwealth Principles declared in 1971, and stressed the need to promote sustainable development and the alleviation of poverty. The Declaration placed emphasis on the promotion of democracy and respect for human rights and resolved to strengthen the Commonwealth's capacity to assist countries in entrenching democratic practices. The meeting also welcomed the political reforms introduced by the South African Government and urged all South African political parties to commence negotiations on a new constitution as soon as possible. The meeting endorsed measures on the phased removal of sanctions against South Africa. 'People-to-people' sanctions (including consular and visa restrictions, cultural and scientific boycotts and restrictions on tourism promotion) were removed immediately, with economic sanctions to remain in place until a constitution for a new democratic, non-racial state had been agreed. The sports boycott would continue to be repealed on a sport-by-sport basis, as each sport in South Africa became integrated and non-racial. The embargo on the supply of armaments would remain in place until a post-apartheid, democratic regime had been firmly established in South Africa. In December a group of six eminent Commonwealth citizens was dispatched to observe multi-party negotiations on the future of South Africa and to assist the process where possible. In October 1992, in a fresh attempt to assist the South African peace process, a Commonwealth team of 18 observers was sent to monitor political violence in the country. A second phase of the Commonwealth Mission to South Africa (COMSA) began in February 1993, comprising 10 observers with backgrounds in policing, the law, politics and public life. COMSA issued a report in May in which it urged a concerted effort to build a culture of political tolerance in South Africa. In a report on its third phase, issued in December 1993, COMSA appealed strongly to all political parties to participate in the transitional arrangements leading to democratic elections.

In October 1993 the Commonwealth heads of government, meeting in Limassol, Cyprus, agreed that a democratic and non-racial South Africa would be invited to join the organization. They endorsed the removal of all economic sanctions against South Africa, but agreed to retain the arms embargo until a post-apartheid, democratic government had been established. The summit meeting's communiqué urged a speedy withdrawal from Cyprus of all Turkish forces and settlers: this was the first time that the Commonwealth had taken sides so explicitly in the dispute over Cyprus. As an expression of the Commonwealth's collective support for the Uruguay Round of negotiations under GATT, the heads of government established a five-nation task force, which, in November, met with representatives of the Governments of France, Belgium, Germany, Switzerland, the United Kingdom, the USA and Japan to emphasize the importance of a successful and balanced conclusion to the Round.

In November 1995 Commonwealth heads of government, convened, in New Zealand, formulated and adopted the Millbrook Commonwealth Action Programme on the Harare Declaration, to promote adherence by member countries to the fundamental principles of democracy and human rights (as proclaimed in the 1991 Declaration). The Programme incorporated a framework of measures to be pursued in support of democratic processes and institutions, and actions to be taken in response to violations of the Harare Declaration principles, in particular the unlawful removal of a democratically-elected government. A Commonwealth Ministerial Action Group on the Harare Declaration (CMAG) was to be established to implement this process and to assist the member country involved to comply with the Harare principles. On the basis of this Programme, the leaders suspended Nigeria from the Commonwealth with immediate effect, following the execution by that country's military Government of nine environmental and human rights protesters and a series of other violations of human rights. The meeting determined to expel Nigeria from the Commonwealth if no 'demonstrable progress' had been made towards the establishment of a democratic authority by the time of the next summit meeting. In addition, the Programme formulated measures to promote sustainable development in member countries, which was considered to be an important element in sustaining democracy, and to facilitate consensus-building within the international community. Earlier in the meeting a statement was issued declaring the 'overwhelming majority' of Commonwealth governments to be opposed to nuclear-testing programmes being undertaken in the South Pacific region. However, in view of events in Nigeria, the issue of nuclear testing and disagreement among member countries did not assume the significance anticipated.

In December 1995 CMAG convened for its inaugural meeting in London. The Group, comprising the Ministers of Foreign Affairs of Canada, Ghana, Jamaica, Malaysia, New Zealand, South Africa, the United Kingdom and Zimbabwe, commenced by considering efforts to restore democratic government in the three Commonwealth countries under military regimes, i.e. The Gambia, Nigeria and Sierra Leone. At the second meeting of the Group, in April 1996, ministers commended the conduct of presidential and parliamentary elections in Sierra Leone and the announcement by The Gambia's military leaders to proceed with a transition to civilian rule. In June a three-member CMAG delegation visited The Gambia to reaffirm Commonwealth support of the transition process in that country and to identify possible areas of further Commonwealth assistance. In August the Gambian authorities issued a decree removing the ban on political activities and parties, although shortly afterwards prohibited certain parties and candidates involved in political life prior to the military take-over from contesting the elections. CMAG recommended that in such circumstances there should be no Commonwealth observers sent to either the presidential or parliamentary elections, which were held in September 1996 and January 1997 respectively. Following the restoration of a civilian Government in early 1997, CMAG requested the Commonwealth Secretary-General to extend technical assistance to The Gambia in order to consolidate the democratic transition process. In April 1996 it was noted that the human rights situation in Nigeria had continued to deteriorate. CMAG, having pursued unsuccessful efforts to initiate dialogue with the Nigerian authorities, outlined a series of punitive and restrictive measures (including visa restrictions on members of the administration, a cessation of sporting contacts and an embargo on the export of armaments) that it would recommend for collective Commonwealth action in order to exert further pressure for reform in Nigeria. Following a meeting of a high-level delegation of the Nigerian Government and CMAG in June, the Group agreed to postpone the implementation of the sanctions, pending progress on the dialogue. (Canada, however, determined, unilaterally, to impose the measures with immediate effect; the United Kingdom did so in accordance with a decision of the European Union to implement limited sanctions against Nigeria.) A proposed CMAG mission to Nigeria was postponed in August, owing to restrictions imposed by the military authorities on access to political detainees and other civilian activists in that country. In September the Group agreed to proceed with the visit and to delay further a decision on the implementation of sanction measures. CMAG, without the participation of the representative of the Canadian Government, undertook its ministerial mission in November. In March 1997 Canada suspended diplomatic relations with Nigeria, reportedly owing to frustration at the perceived inaction of CMAG. In July the Group reiterated the Commonwealth Secretary-General's condemnation of a military coup in Sierra Leone in May, and decided to suspend that country's participation in meetings of the Commonwealth pending the restoration of a democratic government.

In October 1997 Commonwealth heads of government, meeting in Edinburgh, the United Kingdom, endorsed CMAG's recommendation that the imposition of sanctions against Nigeria be held in abeyance pending the scheduled completion of a transition programme towards democracy by October 1998. It was also agreed that CMAG be formally constituted as a permanent organ to investigate abuses of human rights throughout the Commonwealth. Jamaica and South Africa were to be replaced as members of CMAG by Barbados and Botswana, respectively. The meeting adopted a final Declaration that focused on issues relating to global trade, investment and development and committed all member countries to free-market economic principles.

Political Affairs Division: assists consultation among member governments on international and Commonwealth matters of common interest. In association with host governments, it organizes the meetings of heads of government and senior officials. The Division services committees and special groups set up by heads of government dealing with political matters. The Secretariat has observer status at the United Nations, and the Division manages an office in New York to enable small states, which would otherwise be unable to afford facilities there, to maintain a presence at the United Nations. The Division monitors political developments in the Commonwealth and international progress in such matters as disarmament, the concerns of small states, dismantling of apartheid and the Law of the Sea. It also undertakes research on matters of common interest to member governments, and reports back to them. The Division is involved in diplomatic training and consular co-operation.

In 1990 Commonwealth Heads of Government mandated the Division to support the promotion of democracy by monitoring the preparations for and conduct of elections in member countries. By mid-1997 22 observer missions had been sent to monitor parliamentary, presidential or other elections at the request of the national governments. The Division also undertook preparatory missions in connection with these elections. In June 1995 the first meeting of a Commonwealth Election Management Programme was held in Namibia, attended by 32 officials from 14 countries. The meeting agreed to initiate a regular training programme on the conduct and management of elections. By mid-1997 a further four workshops had been held, resulting in the production of a document, entitled *Good Electoral Practice*.

LAW

Legal and Constitutional Affairs Division: promotes and facilitates co-operation and the exchange of information among member governments on legal matters. It administers, jointly with the Commonwealth of Learning, a distance training programme for legislative draftsmen and assists governments to reform national laws to meet the obligations of international conventions. The Division organizes the triennial meeting of ministers, Attorneys General and senior ministry officials concerned with the legal systems in Commonwealth countries. It has also initiated four Commonwealth schemes for co-operation on extradition, the protection of material cultural heritage, mutual assistance in criminal matters and the transfer of convicted offenders within the Commonwealth. It liaises with the Commonwealth Magistrates' and Judges' Association, the Commonwealth Legal Education Association, the Commonwealth Lawyers' Association (with which it helps to prepare the triennial Commonwealth Law Conference for the practising profession), the Commonwealth Association of Legislative Counsel, and with other international non-governmental organizations. The Division provides in-house legal advice for the Secretariat. The quarterly *Commonwealth Law Bulletin* reports on legal developments in and beyond the Commonwealth.

The Division's Commercial Crime Unit assists member countries to combat financial and organized crime, in particular transborder criminal activities, and promotes the exchange of information regarding national and international efforts to combat serious commercial crime through a quarterly publication, *Commonwealth Legal Assistance News,* and the *Crimewatch* bulletin. A Human Rights Unit aims to assist governments to strengthen national institutions and other mechanisms for the protection for human rights. It also organizes training workshops and promotes the exchange of relevant information among member countries.

ECONOMIC CO-OPERATION

Economic Affairs Division: organizes and services the annual meetings of Commonwealth ministers of finance and the ministerial group on small states and assists in servicing the biennial meetings of heads of government and periodic meetings of environment ministers. It engages in research and analysis on economic issues of interest to member governments and organizes seminars and conferences of government officials and experts. The Division initiated a major programme of technical assistance to enable developing Commonwealth countries to participate in the Uruguay Round of multilateral trade negotiations and has assisted the African, Caribbean and Pacific (ACP) group of countries in their trade negotiations with the European Union. It continues to help developing countries to strengthen their links with international capital markets and foreign investors. The Division also services groups of experts on economic affairs that have been commissioned by governments to report on, among other things, protectionism; obstacles to the North-South negotiating process; reform of the international financial and trading system; the debt crisis; management of technological change; the special needs of small states; the impact of change on the development process; environmental issues; women and structural adjustment; and youth unemployment. The Division co-ordinates the Secretariat's environmental work and manages the Iwokrama International Rainforest Programme.

The Division played a catalytic role in the establishment of a Commonwealth Equity Fund, initiated in September 1990, to allow developing member countries to improve their access to private institutional investment, and promoted a Caribbean Investment Fund. The Division supported the establishment of a Commonwealth Private Investment Initiative (CPII) to mobilize capital, on a regional basis, for investment in newly-privatized companies and in small- and medium-sized businesses in the private sector. The first regional fund under the CPII was launched in July 1996. The Commonwealth Africa Investment Fund (Comafin), was to be managed by the United Kingdom's official development institution, the Commonwealth Development Corporation, to assist businesses in 19 countries in sub-Saharan Africa, with initial resources of US $63.5m. In August 1997 a fund for the Pacific Islands was launched, with an initial capital of $15.0m. A $200m. South Asia Regional Fund was established at the Heads of Government Meeting in October. Initial market studies for a fund for the Caribbean states were undertaken during 1997.

The Economic Declaration that was signed by Commonwealth heads of government, meeting in Edinburgh, the United Kingdom, in October 1997, incorporated a provision for the establishment of a Trade and Investment Access Facility in order to assist developing member states in the process of international trade liberalization.

HUMAN RESOURCES

Human Resource Development Division: consists of two departments concerned with education and health. The Division co-operates with member countries in devising strategies for human resource development.

The **Education Department** arranges specialist seminars, workshops and co-operative projects and commissions studies in areas identified by ministers of education, whose three-yearly meetings it also services. Its present areas of emphasis include improving the quality of and access to basic education; strengthening the culture of science, technology and mathematics education in formal and non-formal areas of education; improving the quality of management in institutions of higher learning and basic education; improving the performance of teachers; strengthening examination assessment systems; and promoting the movement of students between Commonwealth countries. The Department also promotes multi-sectoral strategies to be incorporated in the development of human resources. Emphasis is placed on ensuring a gender balance, the appropriate use of technology, promoting good governance, addressing the problems of scale particular to smaller member countries, and encouraging collaboration between governments, the private sector and other non-governmental organizations.

The **Health Department** organizes ministerial, technical and expert group meetings and workshops, to promote co-operation on health matters, and the exchange of health information and expertise. The Department commissions relevant studies and provides professional and technical advice to member countries and to the Secretariat. It also supports the work of regional health organizations and promotes health for all people in Commonwealth countries.

Gender and Youth Affairs Division: consists of the Gender Affairs Department and the Commonwealth Youth Affairs Department.

The **Gender Affairs Department** is responsible for the implementation of the 1995 Commonwealth Plan of Action on Gender and Development, which was endorsed by the Heads of Government in order to achieve gender equality in the Commonwealth. The main objective of the Plan is to ensure that gender is incorporated into all policies, programmes, structures and procedures of member states and of the Commonwealth Secretariat. The Department is also addressing specific concerns such as the integration of gender issues into national budgetary processes, increasing the participation of women in politics and conflict prevention and resolution, and the promotion of human rights, including the elimination of violence against women and girls.

The **Youth Affairs Department** administers the Commonwealth Youth Programme (CYP), funded through separate voluntary contributions from governments, which seeks to promote the involvement of young people in the economic and social development of their countries. The CYP was awarded a budget of £2.1m. for 1996/97. It provides policy advice for governments and operates regional training programmes for youth workers and policy-makers through its centres in Africa, Asia, the Caribbean and the Pacific. It conducts a Youth Study Fellowship scheme, a Youth Project Fund, a Youth Exchange Programme (in the Caribbean), and a Youth Service Awards Scheme, holds conferences and seminars, carries out research and disseminates information. In May 1995 a Commonwealth Youth Credit Initiative was launched, in order to provide funds, training and advice to young entrepreneurs.

SCIENCE

Science and Technology Division: is partially funded and governed by the Commonwealth Science Council, consisting of 35 member governments, which aims to enhance the scientific and technological capabilities of member countries, through co-operative research, training and the exchange of information. Current priority areas of work are concerned with the promotion of sustainable development and cover biological diversity and genetic resources, water resources, and renewable energy.

TECHNICAL CO-OPERATION

Commonwealth Fund for Technical Co-operation (CFTC): f. in 1971 to facilitate the exchange of skills between member countries and to promote economic and social development. It is administered by the Commonwealth Secretariat and financed by voluntary subscriptions from member governments. The CFTC responds to requests from member governments for technical assistance, such as the provision of experts for short- or medium-term projects, advice on economic or legal matters, in particular in the areas of natural resources management and public-sector reform, and training programmes. The CFTC also administers the Langkawi awards for the study of environmental issues, which is funded by the Canadian Government. The CFTC budget for 1997/98 amounted to £26m. During 1995–97 more than 9,000 nationals from 49 Commonwealth developing countries trained under CFTC programmes, while more than 700 experts and consultants were assigned to projects in 45 countries. During that time CFTC also assisted six countries to define their maritime boundaries, 17 countries to develop their mineral and petroleum resources and undertook 84 export-promotion programmes.

CFTC activities are implemented by the following divisions:

Economic and Legal Advisory Services Division: serves as an in-house consultancy, offering advice to governments on macroeconomic and financial management, capital market and private-sector development, debt management, the development of natural resources, and the negotiation of maritime boundaries and fisheries access agreements;

Export and Industrial Development Division: advises on all aspects of export marketing and the development of tourism, industry, small businesses and enterprises. Includes an Agricultural Development Unit, which provides technical assistance in agriculture and renewable resources;

General Technical Assistance Services Division: provides short- and long-term experts in all fields of development;

Management and Training Services Division: provides integrated packages of consultancy and training to enhance skills in areas such as public sector reform and the restructuring of enterprises, and arranges specific country and overseas training programmes.

The Secretariat also includes an Administration Division, a Strategic Planning and Evaluation Unit, and an Information and Public Affairs Division, which produces information publications, and radio and television programmes, about Commonwealth co-operation and consultation activities.

SELECTED PUBLICATIONS

Commonwealth Currents (quarterly).
Commonwealth Declarations 1971–91.
Commonwealth Organisations (directory).
The Commonwealth Today.
In Common (quarterly newsletter of the Youth Programme).
International Development Policies (quarterly).
Link In to Gender and Development (2 a year)
Notes on the Commonwealth (series of reference leaflets).
Report of the Commonwealth Secretary-General (every 2 years).
The Commonwealth Yearbook.
Numerous reports, studies and papers (catalogue available).

Commonwealth Organizations

(In the United Kingdom, unless otherwise stated)

AGRICULTURE AND FORESTRY

CAB INTERNATIONAL (CABI): Wallingford, Oxon, OX10 8DE; tel. (1491) 832111; telex 847964; fax (1491) 833508; e-mail

C.Ogbourne@cabi.org; f. 1928; fmrly Commonwealth Agricultural Bureaux; an intergovernmental organization with 40 mem. countries, which aims to improve human welfare world-wide through the generation, dissemination and application of scientific knowledge in support of sustainable development. It places particular emphasis on agriculture, forestry, human health and the management of natural resources, with priority given to the needs of developing countries.

CABI compiles and publishes extensive information (in the form of abstract journals, newsletters, books, bibliographic and non-bibliographic data bases and maps) on aspects of agriculture, forestry, veterinary medicine, the environment and natural resources, Third World rural development, leisure, recreation and tourism, human nutrition, and human health. CABI's main data bases, CAB ABSTRACTS and CAB HEALTH may be accessed electronically on diskette, CD-ROM and magnetic tape. CABI undertakes research and development in innovative information systems, offers training in information management and other advice and practical assistance in the design and implementation of science-based information systems. CABI has regional offices in Kenya, Malaysia and Trinidad and Tobago. Dir-Gen. J. GILMORE.

Asia Regional Office: 19-21-1 Jalan SR 8/1, off Jalan Serdang Raya 43300 Seri Kembangan, Selangor DE, Malaysia; tel. (3) 9433641; fax (3) 9436400; Rep. Dr A. ZAMZAM MOHAMED.

The following are the four CABI scientific institutions:

International Institute of Biological Control: Silwood Park, Buckhurst Rd, Ascot, Berks, SL5 7TA; tel. (1334) 872999; telex 93121-02255; fax (1334) 875007; f. 1927; since 1983 its main research and admin. centre has been in the United Kingdom, with field stations in Kenya, Malaysia, Pakistan, Switzerland and Trinidad; its purpose is the promotion of biological means of pest control and their integration into sustainable pest-management systems through co-operative research, training and information, with an emphasis on the needs of the developing world. Dir Dr J. K. WAAGE. Publ. *Biocontrol News and Information* (quarterly).

International Institute of Entomology: 56 Queen's Gate, London, SW7 5JR; tel. (171) 584-0067; fax (171) 581-1676; f. 1913; undertakes research, training and development activities on insects and mites, relating to agriculture, horticulture and forestry; current emphasis on initiatives relevant to biodiversity and environmental change; undertakes identifications of insects and mites; conducts an extensive training programme. Dir Prof. VALERIE K. BROWN. Publs *Bulletin of Entomological Research* (quarterly), *Distribution Maps of Pests* (18 a year), bibliographies and monographs.

International Institute of Parasitology: 395A Hatfield Rd, St Albans, Herts, AL4 0XU; tel. (1727) 833151; telex 93121-02254; fax (1727) 868721; e-mail cabi-iip@cabi.org; f. 1929; conducts taxonomic and applied research on helminths (parasitic worms), particularly those of economic and medical importance, and on plant parasitic nematodes; provides advisory services and training. Dir Dr W. HOMINICK.

International Mycological Institute: Bakeham Lane, Egham, Surrey, TW20 9TY; tel. (1784) 470111; fax (1784) 470909; e-mail imi@cabi.org; f. 1920 for the collection and dissemination of information on the fungal, bacterial, virus and physiological disorders of plants; on opportunistic fungal diseases of man and animals; and on the taxonomy of fungi; undertakes identifications of fungi and plant pathogenic bacteria from all over the world; incorporates major collection of fungus cultures and a biodeterioration, industrial and environmental services centre; specializes in the areas of biodiversity, crop protection and industrial and environmental development; consultancy services, especially in industrial and environmental mycology, food spoilage by fungi, bacteria and yeasts, and surveys of plant diseases; holds training courses in the United Kingdom and in other countries. Dir Prof. D. L. HAWKSWORTH. Publs *Index of Fungi* (2 a year), *Mycological Papers* (4 or 5 a year), *Phytopathological Papers* (irregular), *Descriptions of Fungi and Bacteria* (4 sets a year), *Bibliography of Systematic Mycology* (2 a year), *Systema Ascomycetum* (2 a year), books on mycology and plant pathology.

Commonwealth Forestry Association: c/o Oxford Forestry Institute, South Parks Rd, Oxford, OX1 3RB; tel. (1865) 275072; fax (1865) 275074; f. 1921; produces, collects and circulates information relating to world forestry and the utilization of forest products and services and provides a means of communication in the Commonwealth and other interested countries. Mems: 1,500. Chair. Dr J. S. MAINI. Publs *Commonwealth Forestry Review* (quarterly), *Commonwealth Forestry Handbook*.

Standing Committee on Commonwealth Forestry: Forestry Commission, 231 Corstorphine Rd, Edinburgh, EH12 7AT; tel. (131) 314-6137; fax (131) 334-0442; e-mail libby.jones@forestry.gov.uk; f. 1923 to provide continuity between Confs, and to provide a forum for discussion on any forestry matters of common interest to mem. govts which may be brought to the Cttee's notice by any member country or organization; c. 50 mems. 1997 Conference: Victoria Falls, Zimbabwe. Sec. LIBBY JONES. Publ. *Newsletter* (quarterly).

COMMONWEALTH STUDIES

Institute of Commonwealth Studies: 28 Russell Sq., London, WC1B 5DS; tel. (171) 580-5876; fax (171) 255-2160; e-mail rowenak @sas.ac.uk; f. 1949 to promote advanced study of the Commonwealth; provides a library and meeting place for postgraduate students and academic staff engaged in research in this field; offers postgraduate teaching. Incorporates the Sir Robert Menzies Centre for Australian Studies. Dir PAT CAPLIN; Publs *Annual Report, Collected Seminar Papers, Newsletter, Theses in Progress in Commonwealth Studies.*

COMMUNICATIONS

Commonwealth Telecommunications Organization: Clareville House, 26–27 Oxendon St, London, SW1Y 4EL; tel. (171) 930-5516; telex 27328; fax (171) 930-4248; e-mail info@cto.int; f. 1967; aims to enhance the development of telecommunications in Commonwealth countries and contribute to the communications infrastructure required for economic and social devt, through a devt and training programme. Exec. Dir Dr DAVID SOUTER. Publ. *CTO Briefing* (quarterly).

EDUCATION AND CULTURE

Association of Commonwealth Universities (ACU): John Foster House, 36 Gordon Sq., London, WC1H 0PF; tel. (171) 387-8572; fax (171) 387-2655; e-mail pubinf@acu.ac.uk; f. 1913; holds major meetings of Commonwealth universities and their representatives; publishes factual information about Commonwealth universities and access to them; acts as a general information centre and provides an appointments advertising service; hosts a management consultancy service; supplies secretariats for the Commonwealth Scholarship Comm. in the United Kingdom and the Marshall Aid Commemoration Comm.; administers various other fellowship and scholarship programmes. Mems: 468 universities in 35 Commonwealth countries or regions. Sec.-Gen. Prof. MICHAEL GIBBONS. Publs include: *Commonwealth Universities Yearbook, ACU Bulletin of Current Documentation* (5 a year), *ACU: What it is and what it does* (annually), *Report of the Council of the ACU* (annually), *Quinquennial Report of the Secretary General to the Commonwealth Universities Congress, Awards for University Teachers and Research Workers, Awards for Postgraduate Study at Commonwealth Universities, Awards for First Degree Study at Commonwealth Universities, Awards for University Administrators and Librarians, Who's Who of Commonwealth University Vice-Chancellors, Presidents and Rectors of Commonwealth Universities, Appointments in Commonwealth Universities*, Student Information Papers (study abroad series).

Commonwealth Association for Education in Journalism and Communication—CAEJAC: c/o Faculty of Law, University of Western Ontario, London N6A 3K7, Canada; tel. (519) 6613348; fax (519) 6613790; e-mail caejc@julian.uwo.ca; f. 1985; aims to foster high standards of journalism and communication education and research in Commonwealth countries and to promote co-operation among institutions and professions. c. 700 mems in 32 Commonwealth countries. Pres. Prof. SYED ARABI IDID (Malaysia); Sec. Prof. ROBERT MARTIN. Publ. *CAEJAC Journal* (annually).

Commonwealth Association of Science, Technology and Mathematics Educators—CASTME: c/o Education Dept, Human Resource Development Division, Commonwealth Secretariat, Marlborough House, Pall Mall, London, SW1Y 5HX; tel. (171) 747-6282; telex 27678; fax (171) 747-6287; f. 1974; special emphasis is given to the social significance of education in these subjects. Organizes an Awards Scheme to promote effective teaching and learning in these subjects, and biennial regional seminars. Pres. (vacant); Hon. Sec. Dr VED GOEL. Publ. *CASTME Journal* (quarterly).

Commonwealth Council for Educational Administration and Management: c/o International Educational Leadership and Management Centre, School of Management, Lincoln University Campus, Brayford Pool, Lincoln, LN6 7TS; tel. (1522) 886071; fax (1522) 886023; f. 1970; aims to foster quality in professional development and links among educational administrators; holds nat. and regional confs, as well as visits and seminars. Mems: 60 affiliated groups representing 7,000 persons. Pres. Prof. ANGELA THODY. Publs *Newsletter* (quarterly), *International Directions in Education* (3 a year), *International Studies in Educational Administration* (2 a year).

Commonwealth Institute: Kensington High St, London, W8 6NQ; tel. (171) 603-4535; fax (171) 602-7374; e-mail info@commonwealth .org.uk; f. 1893 as the Imperial Institute; the centre for Commonwealth education and culture in the United Kingdom, the Inst. houses an Education Centre, a Commonwealth Resource and Literature Library and a Conference and Events Centre; organizes visual arts exhibitions; 'Commonwealth Experience' opened in 1997. Dir-Gen. DAVID FRENCH.

Commonwealth of Learning: 1285 West Broadway, Suite 600, Vancouver, British Columbia V6H 3X8, Canada; tel. (604) 775-8200; fax (604) 775-8210; e-mail info@col.org; f. 1987 by Commonwealth Heads of Government to promote and develop distance education and open learning. Pres. Dato' Dr GAJARAJ DHANARAJAN.

League for the Exchange of Commonwealth Teachers: 7 Lion Yard, Tremadoc Rd, London, SW4 7NQ; tel. (171) 498-1101; fax (171) 720-5403; f. 1901; promotes educational exchanges for a period of one year between teachers in Australia, the Bahamas, Barbados, Bermuda, Canada, Guyana, India, Jamaica, Kenya, Malawi, New Zealand, Pakistan, South Africa and Trinidad and Tobago. Dir PATRICIA SWAIN. Publs *Annual Report, Exchange Teacher* (annually), *Commonwealth Times* (2 a year).

HEALTH

Commonwealth Medical Association: BMA House, Tavistock Sq., London, WC1H 9JP; tel. (171) 383-6095; fax (171) 383-6195; e-mail 72242.3544@compuserve.com; f. 1962 for the exchange of information; provision of tech. co-operation and advice; formulation and maintenance of a code of ethics; provision of continuing medical education; devt and promotion of health education programmes; and liaison with WHO and the UN on health issues; meetings of its Council are held every three years. Mems: medical asscns in Commonwealth countries. Dir MARIANNE HASLEGRAVE; Sec. Dr J. D. J. HAVARD. Publ. *CommonHealth* (quarterly bulletin).

Commonwealth Pharmaceutical Association: 1 Lambeth High St, London, SE1 7JN; tel. (171) 735-9141; fax (171) 582-3401; e-mail eharden@compuserve.com; f. 1970 to promote the interests of pharmaceutical sciences and the profession of pharmacy in the Commonwealth; to maintain high professional standards, encourage links between members and the creation of nat. asscns; and to facilitate the dissemination of information. Holds confs (every four years) and regional meetings. Mems: 39 pharmaceutical asscns. Sec. PHILIP E. GREEN. Publ. *Quarterly Newsletter*.

Commonwealth Society for the Deaf: 134 Buckingham Palace Rd, London, SW1W 9SA; tel. (171) 259-0200; fax (171) 259-0300; promotes the health, education and general welfare of the deaf in developing Commonwealth countries; encourages and assists the development of educational facilities, the training of teachers of the deaf, and the provision of support for parents of deaf children; organizes visits by volunteer specialists to developing countries; provides audiological equipment and organises the training of audiological maintenance technicians; conducts research into the causes and prevention of deafness. CEO Brig. J. A. Davis. Publ. *Annual Report*.

Sight Savers International (Royal Commonwealth Society for the Blind): Grosvenor Hall, Bolnore Rd, Haywards Heath, West Sussex, RH16 4BX; tel. (1444) 412424; fax (1444) 415866; e-mail information@sightsaversint.org.uk; f. 1950 to prevent blindness and restore sight in developing countries, and to provide education and community-based training for incurably blind people; operates in collaboration with local partners, with high priority given to training local staff; Chair. DAVID THOMPSON; Dir RICHARD PORTER. Publ. *Horizons* (newsletter, 3 a year).

INFORMATION AND THE MEDIA

Commonwealth Broadcasting Association: Rm 312, BBC Yalding House, 152-156 Great Portland St, London, W1N 6AJ; tel. (171) 765-5151; fax (171) 765-5152; e-mail cba@bbc.co.uk; f. 1945; gen. confs are held every two years. Mems: 63 nat. public service broadcasting orgs in 53 Commonwealth countries. Pres. Dato' JAAGAR KAMIN; Sec.-Gen. ELIZABETH SMITH. Publs *COMBROAD* (quarterly), *Who's Who in Public Service Broadcasting in the Commonwealth—the Handbook of the CBA* (annually).

Commonwealth Institute: see under Education.

Commonwealth Journalists' Association: 17 Nottingham St, London, W1M 3RD; tel. (171) 486-3844; fax (171) 486-3822; f. 1978 to promote co-operation between journalists in Commonwealth countries, organize training facilities and confs, and foster understanding among Commonwealth peoples. Pres. MURRAY BURT; Exec. Dir LAWRIE BREEN.

Commonwealth Press Union (Association of Commonwealth Newspapers, News Agencies and Periodicals): 17 Fleet St, London, EC4Y 1AA; tel. (171) 583-7733; fax (171) 583-6868; e-mail 106156.3331@compuserve.com; f. 1950; promotes the welfare of the Commonwealth press by defending its freedom and providing training for journalists; organizes biennial confs. Mems: c. 1,000 newspapers, news agencies, periodicals in 42 Commonwealth countries. Pres. Sir DAVID ENGLISH; Dir ROBIN MACKICHAN. Publs *CPU News, Annual Report*.

LAW

Commonwealth Lawyers' Association: c/o The Law Society, 114 Chancery Lane, London, WC2A 1PL; tel. (171) 242-1222; telex 261203; fax (171) 831-0057; e-mail karen.brewer@lawsociety.org.uk; f. 1983 (fmrly the Commonwealth Legal Bureau); seeks to maintain and promote the rule of law throughout the Commonwealth, by ensuring that the people of the Commonwealth are served by an independent and efficient legal profession; upholds professional standards and promotes the availability of legal services; assists in organizing the triennial Commonwealth law confs. Pres. RODNEY HANSEN; Exec. Sec. JONATHAN GOLDSMITH. Publs. *The Commonwealth Lawyer*.

Commonwealth Legal Advisory Service: c/o British Institute of International and Comparative Law, Charles Clore House, 17 Russell Sq., London, WC1B 5DR; tel. (171) 636-5802; fax (171) 323-2016; e-mail bicl@dial.pipex.com; financed by the British Institute and by contributions from Commonwealth govts; provides research facilities for Commonwealth govts and law reform commissions. Legal Sec. Dr DEREK OBADINA.

Commonwealth Legal Education Association: Legal Division, Commonwealth Secretariat, Marlborough House, Pall Mall, London, SW1Y 5HX; tel. (171) 747-6410; fax (171) 930-0827; e-mail biicl@bbcnc.org.uk; f. 1971 to promote contacts and exchanges and to provide information. Gen. Sec. JOHN HATCHARD. Publs *Commonwealth Legal Education Association Newsletter* (2 a year), *Directory of Commonwealth Law Schools* (annually).

Commonwealth Magistrates' and Judges' Association: Uganda House, 58/59 Trafalgar Sq., London, WC2N 5DX; tel. (171) 976-1007; fax (171) 976-2395; e-mail cmja@btinternet.com; f. 1970 to advance the administration of the law by promoting the independence of the judiciary, to further education in law and crime prevention and to disseminate information; confs and study tours; corporate membership for asscns of the judiciary or courts of limited jurisdiction; assoc. membership for individuals. Pres. Chief Justice KIPLING DOUGLAS; Sec.-Gen.VIVIENNE CHIN. Publ. *Commonwealth Judicial Journal* (2 a year).

PARLIAMENTARY AFFAIRS

Commonwealth Parliamentary Association: Suite 700, Westminster House, 7 Millbank, London, SW1P 3JA; tel. (171) 799-1460; fax (171) 222-6073; e-mail hq.sec@comparlhq.co.uk; f. 1911 to promote understanding and co-operation between Commonwealth parliamentarians; organization: Exec. Cttee of 32 MPs responsible to annual Gen. Assembly; 140 brs throughout the Commonwealth; holds annual Commonwealth Parliamentary Confs and seminars; also regional confs and seminars; Sec.-Gen. ARTHUR DONAHOE. Publ. *The Parliamentarian* (quarterly).

PROFESSIONAL AND INDUSTRIAL RELATIONS

Commonwealth Association of Architects: 66 Portland Place, London, W1N 4AD; tel. (171) 636-8276; fax (171) 636-5472; f. 1964; an asscn of 39 socs of architects in various Commonwealth countries. Objects: to facilitate the reciprocal recognition of professional qualifications; to provide a clearing house for information on architectural practice, and to encourage collaboration. Plenary confs every three years; regional confs are also held. Exec. Dir GEORGE WILSON. Publs *Handbook, Objectives and Procedures: CAA Schools Visiting Boards, Architectural Education in the Commonwealth* (annotated bibliography of research), *CAA Newsnet* (3 a year), a survey and list of schools of architecture.

Commonwealth Association for Public Administration and Management—CAPAM: 1075 Bay St, Suite 402, Toronto, M5S 2B1, Canada; tel. (416) 920-3337; fax (416) 920-6574; e-mail 103350.3543@compuserve.com; f. 1994; aims to promote sound management of the public sector in Commonwealth countries and to assist those countries undergoing political or financial reforms. An awards scheme to reward innovation within the public sector was to be established in 1997. Pres. AHMAD SARJI (Malaysia); Exec. Dir ART STEVENSON (Canada).

Commonwealth Foundation: Marlborough House, Pall Mall, London, SW1Y 5HY; tel. (171) 930-3783; telex 27678; fax (171) 839-8157; f. 1966 to serve, support and link the 'unofficial' Commonwealth. The Foundation encourages development, knowledge, linkage and exchange within the Commonwealth, through the provision of grants to groups and individuals in the non-governmental, professional and cultural sectors. Awards an annual Commonwealth Writers' Prize. Funds are provided by Commonwealth govts. Chair. DONALD O. MILLS (Jamaica); Dir Dr HUMAYUN KHAN (Pakistan).

Commonwealth Trade Union Council: Congress House, 23–28 Great Russell St, London, WC1B 3LS; tel. (171) 631-0728; fax (171) 436-0301; e-mail ctuc-london@geo2.poptel.org.uk; f. 1979 to promote the interests of workers in the Commonwealth and encourage the development of trades unions in developing countries of the Commonwealth; provides assistance for training. Dir ARTHUR J. JOHNSTONE (United Kingdom). Publ. *Annual Report*.

SCIENCE AND TECHNOLOGY

Commonwealth Engineers' Council: c/o Institution of Civil Engineers, 1–7 Great George St, London, SW1P 3AA; tel. (171) 222-7722; fax (171) 222-7500; f. 1946; the Conf. meets every two years to provide an opportunity for engineering institutions of Commonwealth countries to exchange views on collaboration; there is a standing cttee on engineering education and training; organizes seminars on related topics. Sec. J. A. WHITWELL.

Commonwealth Geological Surveys Consultative Group: c/o Commonwealth Science Council, CSC Earth Sciences Programme, Marlborough House, Pall Mall, London, SW1Y 5HX; tel. (171) 839-3411; telex 27678; fax (171) 839-6174; e-mail comsci@gn.apc.org; f. 1948 to promote collaboration in geological, geochemical, geophysical and remote sensing techniques and the exchange of information. Geological Programme Officer Dr SIYAN MALOMO; Publ. *Earth Sciences Newsletter.*

SPORT

Commonwealth Games Federation: Walkden House, 3–10 Melton St, London, NW1 2EB; tel. (171) 383-5596; telex 9199156; fax (171) 383-5506; the Games were first held in 1930 and are now held every four years; participation is limited to competitors representing the mem. countries of the Commonwealth; held in Victoria, Canada, in 1994 and to be held in Kuala Lumpur, Malaysia, in 1998. Mems: 68 affiliated bodies. Pres. HRH The Prince EDWARD: Chair. MICHAEL FENNELL; Hon. Sec. DAVID DIXON.

YOUTH

Commonwealth Youth Exchange Council: 7 Lion Yard, Tremadoc Rd, London, SW4 7NQ; tel. (171) 498-6151; fax (171) 720-5403; f. 1970; promotes contact between groups of young people of the United Kingdom and other Commonwealth countries by means of educational exchange visits, provides information for organizers and allocates grants; 198 mem. orgs. Dir V. S. G. CRAGGS. Publs *Contact* (handbook), *Exchange* (newsletter), *Safety and Welfare* (guidelines for Commonwealth Youth Exchange groups).

Duke of Edinburgh's Award International Association: Award House, 7-11 St Matthew St, London, SW1P 2JT; tel. (171) 222-4242; fax (171) 222-4141; e-mail sect@intaward.org; f. 1956; offers a programme of leisure activities for young people, comprising service, expeditions, sport and skills; operates in more than 90 countries (not confined to the Commonwealth). International Sec.-Gen. PAUL ARENGO-JONES. Publs *Award World* (2 a year), *Annual Report*, handbooks and guides.

MISCELLANEOUS

British Commonwealth Ex-Services League: 48 Pall Mall, London, SW1Y 5JG; tel. (171) 973-7263; fax (171) 973-7308; links the ex-service organizations in the Commonwealth, assists ex-servicemen of the Crown and their dependants who are resident abroad; holds triennial confs. Grand Pres. HRH The Duke of EDINBURGH; Sec.-Gen. Lt-Col S. POPE.. Publ. *Annual Report.*

Commonwealth Countries League: 14 Thistleworth Close, Isleworth, Middlesex, TW7 4QQ; tel. (181) 737-3572; fax (181) 568-2495; f. 1925 to secure equal opportunities and status between men and women in the Commonwealth, to act as a link between Commonwealth women's orgs, and to promote and finance secondary education of disadvantaged girls of high ability in their own countries, through the CCL Educational Fund; holds meetings with speakers and an annual Conf., organizes the annual Commonwealth Fair for fund-raising; individual mems and affiliated socs in the Commonwealth. Sec.-Gen. SHEILA O'REILLY. Publ. *CCL Newsletter* (3 a year).

Commonwealth War Graves Commission: 2 Marlow Rd, Maidenhead, Berks, SL6 7DX; tel. (1628) 34221; telex 847526; fax (1628) 771208; f. 1917 (as Imperial War Graves Commission); provides for the marking and permanent care of the graves of Commonwealth Forces casualties in the wars of 1914–18 and 1939–45; maintains over 1.5m. graves in 147 countries and commemorates by name on memorials more than 760,000 who have no known grave or who were cremated. Mems: Australia, Canada, India, New Zealand, South Africa, United Kingdom. Pres. HRH The Duke of KENT; Dir-Gen. D. KENNEDY.

Joint Commonwealth Societies' Council: c/o Royal Commonwealth Society, 18 Northumberland Ave, London, WC2N 5BJ; tel. (171) 930-6733; fax (171) 930-9705; e-mail 106167.365@ compuserve.com; f. 1947; provides a forum for the exchange of information regarding activities of mem. orgs which promote understanding among countries of the Commonwealth; co-ordinates the distribution of the Commonwealth Day message by Queen Elizabeth; produces educational materials about the Commonwealth; mems: 16 unofficial Commonwealth organizations and four official bodies. Chair. Sir PETER MARSHALL; Sec. HELEN TRIDGELL.

Royal Commonwealth Society: 18 Northumberland Ave, London, WC2N 5BJ; tel. (171) 930-6733; fax (171) 930-9705; e-mail 106167.371@compuserve.com; f. 1868; to promote international understanding of the Commonwealth and its people; information service; library housed by Cambridge University Library. Chair. Sir MICHAEL MCWILLIAM; Sec.-Gen. Sir DAVID THORNE. Publs *Annual Report, Newsletter* (3 a year).

Royal Over-Seas League: Over-Seas House, Park Place, St James's St, London, SW1A 1LR; tel. (171) 408-0214; telex 268995; fax (171) 499-6738; f. 1910 to promote friendship and understanding in the Commonwealth; club houses in London and Edinburgh; membership is open to all British subjects and Commonwealth citizens. Chair. Sir GEOFFREY ELLERTON; Dir-Gen. ROBERT F. NEWELL. Publ. *Overseas* (quarterly).

The Victoria League for Commonwealth Friendship: 55 Leinster Square, London W2 4PW; tel. (171) 243-2633; fax (171) 229-2994; f. 1901; aims to further personal friendship among Commonwealth peoples and to provide hospitality for visitors; maintains Student House, providing accommodation for students from Commonwealth countries; has brs elsewhere in the UK and abroad. Pres. HRH Princess MARGARET, Countess of SNOWDON; Chair. COLIN WEBBER; Gen. Sec. JOHN ALLAN. Publ. *Annual Report.*

Declaration of Commonwealth Principles

Agreed by the Commonwealth Heads of Government Meeting at Singapore, 22 January 1971.

The Commonwealth of Nations is a voluntary association of independent sovereign states, each responsible for its own policies, consulting and co-operating in the common interests of their peoples and in the promotion of international understanding and world peace.

Members of the Commonwealth come from territories in the six continents and five oceans, include peoples of different races, languages and religions, and display every stage of economic development from poor developing nations to wealthy industrialized nations. They encompass a rich variety of cultures, traditions and institutions.

Membership of the Commonwealth is compatible with the freedom of member-governments to be non-aligned or to belong to any other grouping, association or alliance. Within this diversity all members of the Commonwealth hold certain principles in common. It is by pursuing these principles that the Commonwealth can continue to influence international society for the benefit of mankind.

We believe that international peace and order are essential to the security and prosperity of mankind; we therefore support the United Nations and seek to strengthen its influence for peace in the world, and its efforts to remove the causes of tension between nations.

We believe in the liberty of the individual, in equal rights for all citizens regardless of race, colour, creed or political belief, and in their inalienable right to participate by means of free and democratic political processes in framing the society in which they live. We therefore strive to promote in each of our countries those representative institutions and guarantees for personal freedom under the law that are our common heritage.

We recognize racial prejudice as a dangerous sickness threatening the healthy development of the human race and racial discrimination as an unmitigated evil of society. Each of us will vigorously combat this evil within our own nation.

No country will afford to regimes which practise racial discrimination assistance which in its own judgment directly contributes to the pursuit or consolidation of this evil policy. We oppose all forms of colonial domination and racial oppression and are committed to the principles of human dignity and equality.

We will therefore use all our efforts to foster human equality and dignity everywhere, and to further the principles of self-determination and non-racialism.

We believe that the wide disparities in wealth now existing between different sections of mankind are too great to be tolerated. They also create world tensions. Our aim is their progressive removal. We therefore seek to use our efforts to overcome poverty, ignorance and disease, in raising standards of life and achieving a more equitable international society.

To this end our aim is to achieve the freest possible flow of international trade on terms fair and equitable to all, taking into account the special requirements of the developing countries, and to encourage the flow of adequate resources, including governmental and private resources, to the developing countries, bearing in mind the importance of doing this in a true spirit of partnership and of establishing for this purpose in the developing countries conditions which are conducive to sustained investment and growth.

We believe that international co-operation is essential to remove the causes of war, promote tolerance, combat injustice, and secure development among the peoples of the world. We are convinced that the Commonwealth is one of the most fruitful associations for these purposes.

In pursuing these principles the members of the Commonwealth believe that they can provide a constructive example of the multinational approach which is vital to peace and progress in the modern world. The association is based on consultation, discussion and co-operation.

In rejecting coercion as an instrument of policy they recognize that the security of each member state from external aggression is a matter of concern to all members. It provides many channels for continuing exchanges of knowledge and views on professional, cultural, economic, legal and political issues among member states.

These relationships we intend to foster and extend, for we believe that our multi-national association can expand human understanding and understanding among nations, assist in the elimination of discrimination based on differences of race, colour or creed, maintain and strengthen personal liberty, contribute to the enrichment of life for all, and provide a powerful influence for peace among nations.

The Lusaka Declaration on Racism and Racial Prejudice

The Declaration, adopted by Heads of Government in 1979, includes the following statements:

United in our desire to rid the world of the evils of racism and racial prejudice, we proclaim our faith in the inherent dignity and worth of the human person and declare that:

(i) the peoples of the Commonwealth have the right to live freely in dignity and equality, without any distinction or exclusion based on race, colour, sex, descent, or national or ethnic origin;

(ii) while everyone is free to retain diversity in his or her culture and lifestyle this diversity does not justify the perpetuation of racial prejudice or racially discriminatory practices;

(iii) everyone has the right to equality before the law and equal justice under the law; and

(iv) everyone has the right to effective remedies and protection against any form of discrimination based on the grounds of race, colour, sex, descent, or national or ethnic origin.

We reject as inhuman and intolerable all policies designed to perpetuate apartheid, racial segregation or other policies based on theories that racial groups are or may be inherently superior or inferior.

We reaffirm that it is the duty of all the peoples of the Commonwealth to work together for the total eradication of the infamous policy of apartheid which is internationally recognized as a crime against the conscience and dignity of mankind and the very existence of which is an affront to humanity.

We agree that everyone has the right to protection against acts of incitement to racial hatred and discrimination, whether committed by individuals, groups or other organizations. . . .

Inspired by the principles of freedom and equality which characterise our association, we accept the solemn duty of working together to eliminate racism and racial prejudice. This duty involves the acceptance of the principle that positive measures may be required to advance the elimination of racism, including assistance to those struggling to rid themselves and their environment of the practice.

Being aware that legislation alone cannot eliminate racism and racial prejudice, we endorse the need to initiate public information and education policies designed to promote understanding, tolerance, respect and friendship among peoples and racial groups. . . .

We note that racism and racial prejudice, wherever they occur, are significant factors contributing to tension between nations and thus inhibit peaceful progress and development. We believe that the goal of the eradication of racism stands as a critical priority for governments of the Commonwealth committed as they are to the promotion of the ideals of peaceful and happy lives for their people.

Harare Commonwealth Declaration

The following are the major points of the Declaration adopted by Heads of Government at the meeting held in Harare, Zimbabwe, in 1991:

Having reaffirmed the principles to which the Commonwealth is committed, and reviewed the problems and challenges which the world, and the Commonwealth as part of it, face, we pledge the Commonwealth and our countries to work with renewed vigour, concentrating especially in the following areas: the protection and promotion of the fundamental political values of the Commonwealth; equality for women, so that they may exercise their full and equal rights; provision of universal access to education for the population of our countries; continuing action to bring about the end of apartheid and the establishment of a free, democratic, non-racial and prosperous South Africa; the promotion of sustainable development and the alleviation of poverty in the countries of the Commonwealth; extending the benefits of development within a framework of respect for human rights; the protection of the environment through respect for the principles of sustainable development which we enunciated at Langkawi; action to combat drugs trafficking and abuse and communicable diseases; help for small Commonwealth states in tackling their particular economic and security problems; and support of the United Nations and other international institutions in the world's search for peace, disarmament and effective arms control; and in the promotion of international consensus on major global political, economic and social issues.

To give weight and effectiveness to our commitments we intend to focus and improve Commonwealth co-operation in these areas. This would include strengthening the capacity of the Commonwealth to respond to requests from members for assistance in entrenching the practices of democracy, accountable administration and the rule of law.

In reaffirming the principles of the Commonwealth and in committing ourselves to pursue them in policy and action in response to the challenges of the 1990s, in areas where we believe that the Commonwealth has a distinctive contribution to offer, we the Heads of Government express our determination to renew and enhance the value and importance of the Commonwealth as an institution which can and should strengthen and enrich the lives not only of its own members and their peoples but also of the wider community of peoples of which they are a part.

THE COMMONWEALTH OF INDEPENDENT STATES—CIS

Address: 220000 Minsk, Kirava 17, Belarus.
Telephone: (172) 29-35-17; **fax** (172) 27-23-39.

The Commonwealth of Independent States is a voluntary association of 12 (originally 11) states, established at the time of the collapse of the USSR in December 1991.

MEMBERS

Armenia	Moldova
Azerbaijan	Russia
Belarus	Tajikistan
Georgia	Turkmenistan
Kazakhstan	Ukraine
Kyrgyzstan	Uzbekistan

Note: Azerbaijan signed the Alma-Ata Declaration (see below) on 21 December 1991, but on 7 October 1992 the Azerbaijan legislature voted against ratification of the foundation documents (see below) by which the Commonwealth of Independent States had been founded in December 1991. Azerbaijan, however, formally became a member of the CIS in September 1993, after the legislature voted in favour of membership. Georgia was admitted to the CIS in December 1993.

Organization

(January 1998)

COUNCIL OF HEADS OF STATE

This is the supreme body of the CIS, on which all the member states of the Commonwealth are represented at the level of head of state, for discussion of issues relating to the co-ordination of Commonwealth activities and the development of the Minsk Agreement (see below). Decisions of the Council are taken by common consent, with each state having equal voting rights. The Council meets no less than twice a year, although an extraordinary meeting may be convened on the initiative of the majority of Commonwealth heads of state.

COUNCIL OF HEADS OF GOVERNMENT

This Council convenes for meetings no less than once every three months; an extraordinary sitting may be convened on the initiative of a majority of Commonwealth heads of government. The two Councils may discuss and take necessary decisions on important domestic and external issues and may hold joint sittings.

Working and auxiliary bodies, composed of authorized representatives of the participating states, may be set up on a permanent or interim basis on the decision of the Council of Heads of State and the Council of Heads of Government.

SECRETARIAT

Executive Secretary: IVAN M. KOROTCHENYA.

The Minsk Agreement

The Minsk Agreement establishing a Commonwealth of Independent States was signed by the heads of state of Belarus, the Russian Federation and Ukraine on 8 December 1991. The text is as follows:

PREAMBLE

We, the Republic of Belarus, the Russian Federation and the Republic of Ukraine, as founder states of the Union of Soviet Socialist Republics (USSR), which signed the 1922 Union Treaty, further described as the high contracting parties, conclude that the USSR has ceased to exist as a subject of international law and a geopolitical reality.

Taking as our basis the historic community of our peoples and the ties which have been established between them, taking into account the bilateral treaties concluded between the high contracting parties;

striving to build democratic law-governed states; intending to develop our relations on the basis of mutual recognition and respect for state sovereignty, the inalienable right to self-determination, the principles of equality and non-interference in internal affairs, repudiation of the use of force and of economic or any other methods of coercion, settlement of contentious problems by means of mediation and other generally-recognized principles and norms of international law;

considering that further development and strengthening of relations of friendship, good-neighbourliness and mutually beneficial co-operation between our states correspond to the vital national interests of their peoples and serve the cause of peace and security;

confirming our adherence to the goals and principles of the United Nations Charter, the Helsinki Final Act and other documents of the Conference on Security and Co-operation in Europe;

and committing ourselves to observe the generally recognized internal norms on human rights and the rights of peoples, we have agreed the following:

ARTICLE 1

The high contracting parties form the Commonwealth of Independent States.

ARTICLE 2

The high contracting parties guarantee their citizens equal rights and freedoms regardless of nationality or other distinctions. Each of the high contracting parties guarantees the citizens of the other parties, and also persons without citizenship that live on its territory, civil, political, social, economic and cultural rights and freedoms in accordance with generally recognized international norms of human rights, regardless of national allegiance or other distinctions.

ARTICLE 3

The high contracting parties, desiring to promote the expression, preservation and development of the ethnic, cultural, linguistic and religious individuality of the national minorities resident on their territories, and that of the unique ethno-cultural regions that have come into being, take them under their protection.

ARTICLE 4

The high contracting parties will develop the equal and mutually beneficial co-operation of their peoples and states in the spheres of politics, the economy, culture, education, public health, protection of the environment, science and trade and in the humanitarian and other spheres, will promote the broad exchange of information and will conscientiously and unconditionally observe reciprocal obligations.

The parties consider it a necessity to conclude agreements on co-operation in the above spheres.

ARTICLE 5

The high contracting parties recognize and respect one another's territorial integrity and the inviolability of existing borders within the Commonwealth.

They guarantee openness of borders, freedom of movement for citizens and of transmission of information within the Commonwealth.

ARTICLE 6

The member states of the Commonwealth will co-operate in safeguarding international peace and security and in implementing effective measures for reducing weapons and military spending. They seek the elimination of all nuclear weapons and universal total disarmament under strict international control.

The parties will respect one another's aspiration to attain the status of a non-nuclear zone and a neutral state.

The member states of the Commonwealth will preserve and maintain under united command a common military-strategic space, including unified control over nuclear weapons, the procedure for implementing which is regulated by a special agreement.

They also jointly guarantee the necessary conditions for the stationing and functioning of and for material and social provision for the strategic armed forces. The parties contract to pursue a harmonized policy on questions of social protection and pension provision for members of the services and their families.

ARTICLE 7

The high contracting parties recognize that within the sphere of their activities, implemented on the equal basis through the common co-ordinating institutions of the Commonwealth, will be the following:

co-operation in the sphere of foreign policy;

co-operation in forming and developing the united economic area, the common European and Eurasian markets, in the area of customs policy;

co-operation in developing transport and communication systems;

co-operation in preservation of the environment, and participation in creating a comprehensive international system of ecological safety;

migration policy issues;

and fighting organized crime.

ARTICLE 8

The parties realize the planetary character of the Chernobyl catastrophe and pledge themselves to unite and co-ordinate their efforts in minimizing and overcoming its consequences.

To these ends they have decided to conclude a special agreement which will take consideration of the gravity of the consequences of this catastrophe.

ARTICLE 9

The disputes regarding interpretation and application of the norms of this agreement are to be solved by way of negotiations between the appropriate bodies, and, when necessary, at the level of heads of the governments and states.

ARTICLE 10

Each of the high contracting parties reserves the right to suspend the validity of the present agreement or individual articles thereof, after informing the parties to the agreement of this a year in advance.

The clauses of the present agreement may be addended to or amended with the common consent of the high contracting parties.

ARTICLE 11

From the moment that the present agreement is signed, the norms of third states, including the former USSR, are not permitted to be implemented on the territories of the signatory states.

ARTICLE 12

The high contracting parties guarantee the fulfilment of the international obligations binding upon them from the treaties and agreements of the former USSR.

ARTICLE 13

The present agreement does not affect the obligations of the high contracting parties in regard to third states.

The present agreement is open for all member states of the former USSR to join, and also for other states which share the goals and principles of the present agreement.

ARTICLE 14

The city of Minsk is the official location of the co-ordinating bodies of the Commonwealth.

The activities of bodies of the former USSR are discontinued on the territories of the member states of the Commonwealth.

The Alma-Ata Declaration

The Alma-Ata Declaration was signed by 11 heads of state on 21 December 1991 in the Kazakh capital, Alma-Ata (Almaty).

PREAMBLE

The independent states:

The Republic of Armenia, the Republic of Azerbaijan, the Republic of Belarus, the Republic of Kazakhstan, the Republic of Kyrgyzstan, the Republic of Moldova, the Russian Federation, the Republic of Tajikistan, the Republic of Turkmenistan, the Republic of Ukraine and the Republic of Uzbekistan;

seeking to build democratic law-governed states, the relations between which will develop on the basis of mutual recognition and respect for state sovereignty and sovereign equality, the inalienable right to self-determination, principles of equality and non-interference in the internal affairs, the rejection of the use of force, the threat of force and economic and any other methods of pressure, a peaceful settlement of disputes, respect for human rights and freedoms, including the rights of national minorities, a conscientious fulfilment of commitments and other generally recognized principles and standards of international law;

recognizing and respecting each other's territorial integrity and the inviolability of the existing borders;

believing that the strengthening of the relations of friendship, good neighbourliness and mutually advantageous co-operation, which has deep historic roots, meets the basic interests of nations and promotes the cause of peace and security;

being aware of their responsibility for the preservation of civilian peace and inter-ethnic accord;

being loyal to the objectives and principles of the agreement on the creation of the Commonwealth of Independent States;

are making the following statement:

THE DECLARATION

Co-operation between members of the Commonwealth will be carried out in accordance with the principle of equality through co-ordinating institutions formed on a parity basis and operating in the way established by the agreements between members of the Commonwealth, which is neither a state, nor a super-state structure.

In order to ensure international strategic stability and security, allied command of the military-strategic forces and a single control over nuclear weapons will be preserved, the sides will respect each other's desire to attain the status of a non-nuclear and (or) neutral state.

The Commonwealth of Independent States is open, with the agreement of all its participants, to the states—members of the former USSR, as well as other states—sharing the goals and principles of the Commonwealth.

The allegiance to co-operation in the formation and development of the common economic space, and all-European and Eurasian markets, is being confirmed.

With the formation of the Commonwealth of Independent States, the USSR ceases to exist. Member states of the Commonwealth guarantee, in accordance with their constitutional procedures, the fulfilment of international obligations, stemming from the treaties and agreements of the former USSR.

Member states of the Commonwealth pledge to observe strictly the principles of this declaration.

Agreement on Strategic Forces

The Agreement on Strategic Forces was concluded between the 11 members of the Commonwealth of Independent States on 30 December 1991.

PREAMBLE

Guided by the necessity for a co-ordinated and organized solution to issues in the sphere of the control of the strategic forces and the single control over nuclear weapons, the Republic of Armenia, the Republic of Azerbaijan, the Republic of Belarus, the Republic of Kazakhstan, the Republic of Kyrgyzstan, the Republic of Moldova, the Russian Federation, the Republic of Tajikistan, the Republic of Turkmenistan, the Republic of Ukraine and the Republic of Uzbekistan, subsequently referred to as 'the member states of the Commonwealth', have agreed on the following:

ARTICLE 1

The term 'strategic forces' means: groupings, formations, units, institutions, the military training institutes for the strategic missile troops, for the air force, for the navy and for the air defences; the directorates of the Space Command and of the airborne troops, and of strategic and operational intelligence, and the nuclear technical units and also the forces, equipment and other military facilities designed for the control and maintenance of the strategic forces of the former USSR (the schedule is to be determined for each state participating in the Commonwealth in a separate protocol).

ARTICLE 2

The member states of the Commonwealth undertake to observe the international treaties of the former USSR, to pursue a co-ordinated policy in the area of international security, disarmament and arms control, and to participate in the preparation and implementation of programmes for reductions in arms and armed forces. The member states of the Commonwealth are immediately entering into negotiations with one another and also with other states which were formerly part of the USSR, but which have not joined the Commonwealth, with the aim of ensuring guarantees and developing mechanisms for implementing the aforementioned treaties.

ARTICLE 3

The member states of the Commonwealth recognize the need for joint command of strategic forces and for maintaining unified control of nuclear weapons, and other types of weapons of mass destruction, of the armed forces of the former USSR.

ARTICLE 4

Until the complete elimination of nuclear weapons, the decision on the need for their use is taken by the President of the Russian Federation in agreement with the heads of the Republic of Belarus, the Republic of Kazakhstan and the Republic of Ukraine, and in consultation with the heads of the other member states of the Commonwealth.

Until their destruction in full, nuclear weapons located on the territory of the Republic of Ukraine shall be under the control of the Combined Strategic Forces Command, with the aim that they not be used and be dismantled by the end of 1994, including tactical nuclear weapons by 1 July 1992.

The process of destruction of nuclear weapons located on the territory of the Republic of Belarus and the Republic of Ukraine shall take place with the participation of the Republic of Belarus, the Russian Federation and the Republic of Ukraine under the joint control of the Commonwealth states.

ARTICLE 5

The status of strategic forces and the procedure for service in them shall be defined in a special agreement.

ARTICLE 6

This agreement shall enter into force from the moment of its signing and shall be terminated by decision of the signatory states or the Council of Heads of State of the Commonwealth.

This agreement shall cease to apply to a signatory state from whose territory strategic forces or nuclear weapons are withdrawn.

Note: At January 1996 an estimated 300 strategic nuclear warheads were reported to be stationed in Ukraine, while 20 remained in Belarus. All the warheads remaining in these countries and in Kazakhstan were to be removed to Russia during the first half of 1996.

An Agreement on Armed Forces and Border Troops was also concluded on 30 December 1991, which confirmed the right of member states to set up their own armed forces. It also appointed Commanders-in-Chief of the Armed Forces and of Border Troops who were to elaborate joint security procedures. In June 1993 CIS defence ministers agreed to abolish CIS joint military command and abandon efforts to maintain a unified defence structure. The existing CIS command was to be replaced, on a provisional basis, by the 'joint staff for co-ordinating military co-operation between the states of the Commonwealth'. It was widely reported that Russia had encouraged the decision to abolish the joint command. The Russian Government balked at the projected cost of a CIS joint military structure, while the Russian military leadership increasingly favoured bilateral military agreements with Russia's neighbours.

Chronology—1992

Jan. Heads of State meeting, Moscow. Commissions on Black Sea Fleet and Caspian Flotilla set up.

Inter-parliamentary Conference, Minsk. Agreement signed on legislative co-operation. Joint commissions established to co-ordinate action on economy, law, pensions, housing, energy and ecology.

Feb. Heads of Government meeting, Moscow. Five economic documents signed. Ukraine did not sign.

Heads of State meeting, Minsk. Agreement signed stipulating that the commander of strategic forces was subordinate to the Council of Heads of State. Eight states agreed on a unified command for general-purpose (i.e. non-strategic) armed forces for a transitional period of two years. Azerbaijan, Moldova and Ukraine insisted on setting up their own armed forces. Agreement reached on retaining rouble as common currency for trade between republics.

Agreement also reached on free movement of goods between republics.

March Heads of Government meeting, Moscow. Agreement reached on repayment of foreign debt of former USSR. Agreements also signed on pensions, joint tax policy and servicing of internal debt.

Heads of State meeting, Kiev. Commission to be established to examine resolution that 'all CIS member states are the legal successors of the rights and obligations of the former Soviet Union'. Agreement on status of border troops signed by five states. All participating states, except Turkmenistan, signed agreements on procedure for settling inter-state conflicts.

Apr. Publication of agreement whereby Armenia, Belarus, Kazakhstan, Kyrgyzstan, Russia, Tajikistan and Uzbekistan set up an Inter-Parliamentary Assembly. Eleven CIS republics join European Bank for Reconstruction and Development (EBRD, q.v.).

May Heads of State meeting, Tashkent. Five-Year Collective Security Agreement signed by Armenia, Kazakhstan, Russia, Tajikistan, Turkmenistan and Uzbekistan.

Heads of Government meeting, Tashkent. Agreement signed on repayment of inter-state debt and issue of balance-of-payments statements.

July Heads of State meeting, Moscow. Agreement to establish joint peacemaking forces to intervene in CIS disputes. Decision to establish economic court in Minsk. Documents also signed on legal succession to Soviet Union, and collective security.

Agreements concluded to establish an Inter-state Ecological Council and an Inter-state Television and Radio Company (ITRC).

Sept. First Inter-parliamentary Assembly, Bishkek. Delegations from Armenia, Belarus, Kazakhstan, Kyrgyzstan, Russia and Tajikistan.

Oct. Azerbaijan legislature voted against ratification of founding treaty of CIS, thereby effectively withdrawing from the Commonwealth.

Heads of State and Heads of Government meeting, Bishkek. Items under review included the formation of a Consultative Economic Council, formation of a single monetary system, a proposed CIS charter, the appointment of an Executive Secretary, the formation of the ITRC, the defence and stability of CIS external borders, and the status of strategic and nuclear forces.

1993

Jan. Heads of State meeting, Minsk. Formulated CIS Charter as a framework for closer co-operation, including a defence alliance, an inter-state court and an economic co-ordination committee. Of the 10 members, Ukraine, Moldova and Turkmenistan did not sign. All 10 members, however, endorsed the establishment of an inter-state bank to facilitate trade payments between the republics and co-ordinate monetary-credit policy. Russia was to hold 50% of shares in the bank, but decisions were to be made only with a two-thirds majority approval. A proposal by Russia to take over control of all nuclear weapons in the former USSR was rejected.

Feb. Meeting of heads of foreign economic departments, Moscow. Established the CIS Foreign Economic Council.

March Heads of Government meeting, Surgut. Petroleum and gas council created to guarantee energy supplies and invest in the Siberian petroleum industry. The council was to have a secretariat based in Tyumen, Siberia.

May Heads of State meeting, Moscow. All states, except Turkmenistan, signed a declaration of support for increased economic union.

June Council of Defence Ministers agreed to abolish the joint military command and to abandon efforts to maintain a unified CIS defence structure. Agreed on the establishment of a provisional joint staff for co-ordinating military co-operation between the members of the Commonwealth.

Sept. Protocol agreement to create a 'rouble zone' signed by Armenia, Belarus, Kazakhstan, Russia, Tajikistan and Uzbekistan. The Russian Central Bank was to be the only authority to issue roubles. Ukraine agreed to join the 'rouble zone' in mid-September.

Azerbaijan formally joined the CIS, following approval by its legislature.

Heads of State meeting, Moscow. Agreement on a framework for economic union, including the gradual removal of tariffs and a currency union. Ukraine and Turkmenistan did not sign the treaty. Establishment of a Bureau on Organized Crime, which was to be based in Moscow, agreed upon.

Dec. Georgia joined the CIS.

Council of Defence Ministers agreed to establish a secretariat to co-ordinate military co-operation as a replacement to the joint military command.

Turkmenistan admitted as a full member of the economic union.

1994

Jan. Meeting of council of border troop commanders, Ashkhabad (not attended by Moldova, Georgia or Tajikistan). Prepared a report on the issue of illegal migration and drug trade across the external borders of the CIS.

March Fourth plenary session of Inter-parliamentary Assembly, St Petersburg. Established a commission for the resolution of the conflicts in Nagornyi Karabakh and Abkhazia, and endorsed the use of CIS peace-keeping forces.

April Heads of State and Heads of Government meeting, Moscow. Ukraine admitted as an associate member of the CIS economic union. Agreement signed on establishment of free trade zone within the CIS. Agreement on the part of Russia to send peace-keeping forces to Georgia as part of CIS efforts to secure a settlement in the conflict in Abkhazia.

July Council of heads of customs committees, meeting in Moscow, approved a draft framework for customs legislation in CIS countries to facilitate the establishment of a free-trade zone. Framework approved by all participants except Turkmenistan.

Sept. Heads of Government meeting, Moscow. Agreed the establishment of an inter-state economic committee, which was to implement economic treaties adopted within the context of an economic union. Agreed the establishment of a payments union to improve the settlement of accounts.

Oct. Council of Defence Ministers approved the dispatch of some peace-keeping forces to Abkhazia.

Heads of State meeting, Moscow. Endorsed establishment of the inter-state economic committee and agreed it would be located in Moscow, with Russia contributing the majority of administrative costs in exchange for 50% of the voting rights. Convention on the rights of minorities adopted.

Fifth plenary session of Inter-parliamentary Assembly. Adopted a resolution to send groups of military observers to Abkhazia and Moldova. Inter-parliamentary peace-making commission on the conflict between Georgia and Abkhazia proposed initiating direct negotiations with the two sides in order to reach a peaceful settlement.

Nov. First session of the inter-state economic committee. Attended by representatives of all member states except Turkmenistan, which did not sign the agreement establishing the committee. Approved draft legislation regarding a customs union. Aleksey Bolshakov, a Russian, elected chairman of the committee.

Dec. Council of Defence Ministers enlarged the mandate of the commander of CIS collective peace-keeping forces in Tajikistan: when necessary, CIS military contingents can engage in combat operations without the prior consent of individual governments.

1995

Jan. Russia, Belarus and Kazakhstan signed an agreement establishing a customs union, which was to be implemented in two stages: firstly, the removal of trade restrictions and unifying trade and customs regulations, followed by the integration of economic, monetary and trade policies.

Feb. Heads of State meeting, Almaty. Adopted a non-binding memorandum on maintaining peace and stability. Signatories were to refrain from applying military, political, economic or other pressure on another member country, to seek the peaceful resolution of border or territorial disputes and not to support or assist separatist movements active in other member countries.

Session of the Inter-parliamentary Assembly established a new Council of CIS news agencies' heads, in order to promote the concept of a single information area.

March Tajikistan and Kyrgyzstan applied to join the customs union.

May Sixth plenary session of Inter-parliamentary Assembly. Approved several acts to improve co-ordination of legislation, including migration of labour, consumer rights, and the rights of prisoners of war.

Nov. Council of Defence Ministers authorized the establishment of a joint air defence system, to be co-ordinated largely by Russia. (By early 1998 all member states except Azerbaijan and Moldova were participating in the system.)

Heads of Government meeting, Moscow. Russia expressed its concern at the levels of non-payment of debts by CIS members (amounting to an estimated total of US $5,800m.), which was hindering further integration.

1996

Jan. Heads of State meeting, Moscow. Authorized a proposal by Georgia to impose sanctions against Abkhazia, in order to achieve a resolution of the conflict. Approved provisions on arrangements relating to collective peace-keeping operations; the training of military and civilian personnel for these operations was to commence in October. Approved the establishment of a Council of CIS Ministers of Internal Affairs, to promote co-operation between law-enforcement bodies of member states.

March Belarus, Kazakhstan, Kyrgyzstan and Russia agreed to establish a new common market for the free movement of goods, services, capital and labour. The 'New Union' was to be open to all CIS member countries and the Baltic states.

April Heads of Government meeting, Moscow. Approved a long-term plan for the integrated development of the CIS, incorporating measures for further socio-economic, military and political co-operation. Approved programme to combat organized crime within the CIS.

An agreement to establish a Commonwealth of Sovereign Republics, providing for the integration of foreign and defence policies and for the adoption of a single currency, was signed by Belarus and Russia.

May Heads of State meeting, Moscow. Issued a joint statement endorsing the re-election of the Russian President and the continuation of democratic reforms in that country.

Aug. Council of Defence Ministers condemned the political, economic and military threat implied in any expansion of NATO. The statement was not signed by Ukraine.

Sept. First meeting of the Inter-state Commission for Military Economic Co-operation. Approved a draft agreement on the export of military projects and services to third countries.

Oct. Heads of State meeting, Almaty. Emergency session to discuss the renewed fighting in Afghanistan and the threat to regional security. Requested the UN Security Council adopt measures to end the conflict.

Nov. Eighth plenary session of Inter-parliamentary Assembly (seventh held in February). Urged NATO countries to abandon plans for its expansion and called for a cessation of hostilities in Afghanistan.

1997

Feb. The Inter-state Economic Committee agreed to establish an Aviation Alliance to promote co-operation between the CIS civil aviation industries.

March Council of Defence Ministers approved the basic principles of a programme for greater military and technical co-operation and agreed on the extension of the peace-keeping mandates for CIS forces in Tajikistan and Abkhazia.

Heads of Government meeting, Moscow. With the exception of Georgia, all participants endorsed a programme of policy objectives for the CIS, including the establishment of a customs union and doubling intra-CIS trade by 2000.

Heads of State meeting, Moscow. Russia's President Yeltsin re-elected as chairman of the Council. Yeltsin admitted that many member states were suffering adverse economic conditions and that the CIS institutional structure had not been effective in promoting greater co-operation. Support for CIS reaffirmed during the meeting.

Oct. Seven Heads of Government signed a document on implementing the 'concept for the integrated economic development of the CIS', approved in March.

Heads of State meeting, Chişinău, Moldova. Russia was reportedly criticized by other country delegations for not implementing CIS agreements, hindering development of the organization and failing to resolve regional conflicts; Russia urged all member states to participate more actively in defining, adopting and implementing CIS policies. Participants agreed to consider means of accelerating economic integration at a meeting in January 1998.

CO-OPERATION COUNCIL FOR THE ARAB STATES OF THE GULF

Address: POB 7153, Riyadh 11462, Saudi Arabia.

Telephone: (1) 482-7777; **telex:** 403635; **fax:** (1) 482-9089.

More generally known as the Gulf Co-operation Council (GCC), the organization was established on 25 May 1981 by six Arab states.

MEMBERS

Bahrain	Oman	Saudi Arabia
Kuwait	Qatar	United Arab Emirates

Organization

(January 1998)

SUPREME COUNCIL

The Supreme Council is the highest authority of the GCC, comprises the heads of member states and meets annually in ordinary session, and in emergency session if demanded by two or more members. The Presidency of the Council is undertaken by each state in turn, in alphabetical order. The Supreme Council draws up the overall policy of the organization; it discusses recommendations and laws presented to it by the Ministerial Council and the Secretariat General in preparation for endorsement. The GCC's charter provides for the creation of a commission for the settlement of disputes between member states, to be attached to and appointed by the Supreme Council. In December 1997 the Supreme Council authorized the establishment of a 30-member Consultative Council, appointed by member states, to act as an advisory body.

MINISTERIAL COUNCIL

The Ministerial Council consists of the foreign ministers of member states, meeting every three months, and in emergency session if demanded by two or more members. It prepares for the meetings of the Supreme Council, and draws up policies, recommendations, studies and projects aimed at developing co-operation and co-ordination among member states in various spheres.

SECRETARIAT GENERAL

The Secretariat assists member states in implementing recommendations by the Supreme and Ministerial Councils, and prepares reports and studies, budgets and accounts. The Secretary-General is appointed by the Supreme Council for a renewable three-year term. In March 1996 the Ministerial Council approved a proposal that, in future, the position of Secretary-General be rotated among member states, in order to ensure equal representation. Assistant Secretary-Generals are appointed by the Ministerial Council upon the recommendation of the Secretary General. All member states contribute in equal proportions towards the budget of the Secretariat.

Secretary-General: Sheikh JAMIL IBRAHIM AL-HUJAYLAN (Saudi Arabia).

Assistant Secretary-General for Political Affairs: ABD AL-AZIZ ABD AR-RAHMAN BU ALI (Bahrain).

Assistant Secretary-General for Economic Affairs: Dr ABDULLAH SALEH AL-KHULAYFI (Qatar).

Assistant Secretary-General for Military Affairs: Maj.-Gen. FALEH ABDULLAH ASH-SHATTI (Kuwait).

Activities

The GCC was set up following a series of meetings of foreign ministers of the states concerned, culminating in an agreement on the basic details of its charter on 10 March 1981. The Charter was signed by the six heads of state on 25 May. It describes the organization as providing 'the means for realizing co-ordination, integration and co-operation' in all economic, social and cultural affairs. A series of ministerial meetings subsequently began to put the proposals into effect.

ECONOMIC CO-OPERATION

In November 1982 GCC ministers drew up a 'unified economic agreement' covering freedom of movement of people and capital, the abolition of customs duties, technical co-operation, harmonization of banking regulations and financial and monetary co-ordination. At the same time GCC heads of state approved the formation of a Gulf Investment Corporation, with capital of US $2,100m., to be based in Kuwait (see below). Customs duties on domestic products of the Gulf states were abolished in March 1983, and new regulations allowing free movement of workers and vehicles between member states were also introduced. A common minimum customs levy (of between 4% and 20%) on foreign imports was imposed in 1986. In May 1992 GCC trade ministers announced the objective of establishing a GCC common market by 2000. In September GCC ministers reached agreement on the application of a unified system of tariffs by March 1993. At a meeting of the Supreme Council, held in December 1992, however, it was decided to mandate GCC officials to formulate a plan for the introduction of common external tariffs, to be presented to the Council in December 1993. Only the tax on tobacco products was to be standardized from March 1993, at a rate of 50%. (In June 1996 ministers agreed to increase the customs tariff on tobacco products to 70%, effective from 1 July 1997.) In April 1994 ministers of finance agreed to pursue a gradual approach to unifying tariffs, which was to be achieved according to a schedule over two to three years. However, by the end of 1997 an agreement had yet to be concluded on the implementation of a unified external customs tariff.

In February 1987 the governors of the member states' central banks agreed in principle to co-ordinate their rates of exchange, and this was approved by the Supreme Council in November. It was subsequently agreed to link the Gulf currencies to a 'basket' of other currencies. In October 1990, following the Iraqi invasion of Kuwait, GCC Governments agreed to provide support for regional banks affected by the crisis. In April 1993 GCC central bank governors agreed to establish a joint banking supervisory committee, in order to devise rules for GCC banks to operate in other member states. They also decided to allow Kuwait's currency to become part of the GCC monetary system that was established following Iraq's invasion of Kuwait in order to defend the Gulf currencies. In December 1997 GCC heads of state authorized the guidelines that had been formulated to enable national banks to establish operations in other GCC states. These were to apply only to banks established at least 10 years previously with a share capital of more than US $100m.

TRADE AND INDUSTRY

In 1982 a ministerial committee was formed to co-ordinate trade policies and development in the region. Technical subcommittees were established to oversee a strategic food reserve for the member states, and joint trade exhibitions (which were generally held every year until responsibility was transferred to the private sector in 1996). In November 1986 the Supreme Council approved a measure whereby citizens of GCC member states were enabled to undertake certain retail trade activities in any other member state, with effect from 1 March 1987. The ministerial committee in charge of trade also forms the board of directors of the GCC Authority for Standards and Metrology, which approves minimum standards for goods produced in or imported to the region.

In 1985 the Supreme Council endorsed a common industrial strategy for the GCC states. It approved regulations stipulating that priority should be given to imports of GCC industrial products, and permitting GCC investors to obtain loans from GCC industrial development banks. In November 1986 resolutions were adopted on the protection of industrial products, and on the co-ordination of industrial projects, in order to avoid duplication. In March 1989 the Ministerial Council approved the Unified GCC Foreign Capital Investment Regulations, which aimed to attract foreign investment and to co-ordinate investments amongst GCC countries. Further guidelines to promote foreign investment in the region were formulated during 1997. In December 1992 the Supreme Council endorsed Patent Regulations for GCC member states to facilitate regional scientific and technological research.

AGRICULTURE

A unified agricultural policy for GCC countries was endorsed by the Supreme Council in November 1985. Between 1983 and 1990 ministers also approved proposals for harmonizing legislation relating to water conservation, veterinary vaccines, insecticides, fertilizers, fisheries and seeds. A permanent committee on fisheries aims to co-ordinate national fisheries policies, to establish designated fishing periods and to undertake surveys of the fishing potential in the Arabian (Persian) Gulf. Co-operation in the agricultural sector also extends to consideration of the water resources in the region.

TRANSPORT, COMMUNICATIONS AND INFORMATION

During 1985 feasibility studies were undertaken on new rail and road links between member states, and on the establishment of a joint coastal transport company. A scheme to build a 1,700-km railway to link all the member states and Iraq (and thereby the European railway network) was postponed, owing to its high cost (estimated at US $4,000m.). In November 1993 ministers agreed to request assistance from the International Telecommunications Union on the establishment of a joint telecommunications network, which had been approved by ministers in 1986. The region's telecommunications systems were to be integrated through underwater fibre-optic cables and a satellite-based mobile telephone network. In the mid-1990s, GCC ministers of information began convening on a regular basis with a view to formulating a joint external information policy. In November 1997 GCC interior ministers approved a simplified passport system to facilitate travel between member countries.

ENERGY

In 1982 a ministerial committee was established to co-ordinate hydrocarbons policies and prices. Ministers adopted a petroleum security plan to safeguard individual members against a halt in their production, to form a stockpile of petroleum products, and to organize a boycott of any non-member country when appropriate. In December 1987 the Supreme Council adopted a plan whereby a member state whose petroleum production was disrupted could 'borrow' petroleum from other members, in order to fulfil its export obligations.

During the early 1990s proposals were formulated to integrate the electricity networks of the six member countries. In the first stage of the plan the networks of Saudi Arabia, Bahrain, Kuwait and Qatar would be integrated; those of the United Arab Emirates (UAE) and Oman would be interconnected and finally linked to the others in the second stage, to be completed by 2003. In December 1997 GCC heads of state declared that work should commence on the first stage of the plan, under the management of an independent, commercial authority.

REGIONAL SECURITY

Although no mention of defence or security was made in the original charter, the summit meeting which ratified the charter also issued a statement rejecting any foreign military presence in the region. The Supreme Council meeting in November 1981 agreed to include defence co-operation in the activities of the organization: as a result, defence ministers met in January 1982 to discuss a common security policy, including a joint air defence system and standardization of weapons. In November 1984 member states agreed to form the Peninsula Shield Force for rapid deployment against external aggression, comprising units from the armed forces of each country under a central command to be based in Saudi Arabia.

In October 1987 (following an Iranian missile attack on Kuwait, which supported Iraq in its war against Iran) GCC ministers of foreign affairs issued a statement declaring that aggression against one member state was regarded as aggression against them all. In December the Supreme Council approved a joint pact on regional co-operation in matters of security. In August 1990 the Ministerial Council condemned Iraq's invasion of Kuwait as a violation of sovereignty, and demanded the withdrawal of all Iraqi troops from Kuwait. GCC ministers of defence met towards the end of August and put on alert the Peninsula Shield Force to counter any attempted invasion of Saudi Arabia by Iraq. During the crisis and the ensuing war between Iraq and a multinational force which took place in January and February 1991, the GCC developed closer links with Egypt and Syria, which, together with Saudi Arabia, played the most active role among the Arab countries in the anti-Iraqi alliance. In March the six GCC nations, Egypt and Syria formulated the 'Declaration of Damascus', which announced plans to establish a regional peace-keeping force. The Declaration also urged the abolition of all weapons of mass destruction in the area, and recommended the resolution of the Palestinian question by an international conference. In June 1991 Egypt and Syria, whose troops were to have formed the largest proportion of the peace-keeping force, announced their withdrawal from the project, reportedly as a result of disagreements with the GCC concerning the composition of the proposed force and the remuneration involved. A meeting of ministers of foreign affairs of the eight countries took place in July, but agreed only to provide mutual military assistance when necessary, thus apparently abandoning the establishment of a joint force. In June 1992 the GCC member states indicated that they had not completely abandoned the Declaration of Damascus, when they consented in principle to the convening of a summit conference on the pact, proposed by the Egyptian President. A meeting of the signatories of the Damascus Declaration, convened in September, adopted a joint statement on regional questions, including the Middle East peace process and the dispute between the UAE and Iran (see below), but rejected an Egyptian proposal to establish a series of rapid deployment forces which could be called upon to defend the interests of any of the eight countries. A meeting of GCC ministers of defence in November agreed to maintain the Peninsula Shield Force. In November 1993 GCC ministers of defence approved a proposal to expand the force from 8,000 to 17,000 troops and incorporate air and naval units. Ministers also agreed to strengthen the defence of the region by developing joint surveillance and early warning systems. A GCC military committee was established, and convened for the first time in April 1994, to discuss the implementation of the proposals. Joint military training exercises were conducted by forces of five GCC states (excluding Qatar) in northern Kuwait in March 1996. In December 1997 the Supreme Council approved plans that had been authorized by defence ministers in November for linking the region's military telecommunications networks and establishing a common early warning system.

In September 1992 the Ministerial Council endorsed the imposition by the USA, the United Kingdom, France and Russia of an air exclusion zone over southern Iraq in late August, which was designed to protect the population of that part of the country from attacks by the Iraqi armed forces. At the same meeting the Council expressed opposition to Iran's 'continued occupation' of islands claimed by the UAE: namely Abu Musa and the Greater and Lesser Tunb islands. In April 1993, Iran removed its restrictions on the movement of people to the island of Abu Musa, a development welcomed by the GCC states. Subsequently, the GCC has repeatedly confirmed its support for the UAE's sovereignty claim, condemned efforts by Iran to consolidate its presence on the islands and urged Iran to pursue peaceful means to end the dispute and refer the case to the International Court of Justice.

In late September 1992 a rift within the GCC was caused by an incident on the disputed border between Saudi Arabia and Qatar. Qatar's threat to boycott a meeting of the Supreme Council in December was allayed at the last minute as a result of mediation efforts by the Egyptian President. At the meeting, which was held in UAE, Qatar and Saudi Arabia agreed to establish a joint commission to demarcate the disputed border. The resolution of border disputes was the principal concern of GCC heads of state when they convened for their annual meeting in December 1994, in Bahrain. The Kuwaiti leader proposed the establishment of a GCC framework for resolving border disputes, consisting of bilateral negotiations between the concerned parties, mediated by a third GCC state.

In late November 1994 a security agreement, to counter regional crime and terrorism, was concluded by GCC states. The pact, however, was not signed by Kuwait, which claimed that a clause concerning the extradition of offenders was in contravention of its constitution; Qatar did not attend the meeting, held in Riyadh, owing to its ongoing dispute with Saudi Arabia (see above). At the summit meeting in December GCC heads of state expressed concern at the increasing incidence of Islamic extremist violence throughout the region. In April 1995 GCC interior ministers convened to discuss ongoing civil unrest in Bahrain; the ministers collectively supported measures adopted by the Bahraini Government to secure political and civil stability. The continuing unrest in Bahrain and the involvement of the Iranian Government in Bahraini domestic affairs remained issues of concern for the GCC throughout 1995 and 1996.

During 1995 the deterioration of relations between Qatar and other GCC states threatened to undermine the Council's solidarity. In December Qatar publicly displayed its dissatisfaction at the appointment, without a consensus agreement, of Saudi Arabia's nominee as the new Secretary-General by failing to attend the final session of the Supreme Council, held in Muscat, Oman. However, at a meeting of ministers of foreign affairs in March 1996, Qatar endorsed the new Secretary-General, following an agreement on future appointment procedures, and reasserted its commitment to the organization. In June Saudi Arabia and Qatar agreed to reactivate a joint technical committee in order to finalize the demarcation of their mutual border. In December Qatar hosted the annual GCC summit meeting; however, Bahrain refused to attend, owing to Qatar's 'unfriendly attitude' and the long-standing territorial dispute over the Hawar islands. The issue dominated the meeting, which agreed to establish a four-member committee to resolve the conflicting sovereignty claims. In January 1997 the ministers of foreign affairs of Kuwait, Oman, Saudi Arabia and the UAE, meeting in Riyadh, formulated a seven-point memorandum of understanding to ease tensions between Bahrain and Qatar. The two countries refused to sign the agreement; however, in March both sides announced their intention to establish diplomatic relations at ambassadorial level.

EXTERNAL RELATIONS

In June 1988 an agreement was signed by GCC and European Community (EC) ministers on economic co-operation (with effect from January 1990): the EC agreed to assist the GCC states in developing their agriculture and industry. A Joint Co-operation Council was established under the agreement, comprising EC and GCC ministers. In March 1990, at the first annual meeting of the Council, GCC and EC ministers of foreign affairs undertook to hold negotiations on a free-trade agreement. Discussions began in October, although any final accord would require the GCC to adopt a unified structure of customs duties. In early 1992 the agreement was jeopardized by the GCC's opposition to the EC's proposed tax on fossil fuels (in order to reduce pollution) which would have raised the price of a barrel of petroleum by an estimated US $10 by 2000. With the new US administration proposing a similar energy tax, in March 1993 GCC oil ministers threatened to restrict the supply of petroleum (the GCC countries control almost one-half of the world's petroleum reserves) in retaliation. In October 1995 an industrial conference was held in Muscat, Oman, which aimed to strengthen economic co-operation between European Union (EU, as the restructured EC was now known) and GCC member states, and to promote investment in both regions. In April 1996 the Joint Council advocated the conclusion of free-trade negotiations by 1998. In December 1997 GCC heads of state condemned statements issued by the European Parliament, as well as by other organizations, regarding human rights issues in member states and insisted they amounted to interference in GCC judicial systems.

In the early 1990s countries in the Far East overtook European countries and the USA as the GCC states' leading trading partners, with the largest amount of trade being conducted with Japan and China (followed by the USA and Germany).

In December 1991 GCC ministers of finance and of foreign affairs approved the establishment of an Arab Development Fund, which aimed to create greater political and economic stability in the region, and in particular was intended to assist Egypt and Syria, as a reward for their active military part in the Gulf War and their major role in the security force envisaged by the Declaration of Damascus. The GCC made it clear that those countries and organizations which had supported Iraq during its occupation of Kuwait would not be beneficiaries of the new fund. A starting capital of US $10,000m. was originally envisaged for the Fund, although by mid-1992 only $6,500m. had been pledged, with reports that the project had been scaled down. In May 1993 ministers of finance from the GCC states, Egypt and Syria, meeting in Qatar, failed to agree on the level of contributions to the Fund.

In September 1994 GCC ministers of foreign affairs decided to end the secondary and tertiary embargo on trade with Israel. In February 1995 a ministerial meeting of signatories of the Damascus Declaration adopted a common stand, criticizing Israel for its refusal to renew the nuclear non-proliferation treaty. In December 1996 the foreign ministers of the Damascus Declaration states, convened in Cairo, requested the USA to exert financial pressure on Israel to halt the construction of settlements on occupied Arab territory.

In May 1997 the Ministerial Council, meeting in Riyadh, expressed concern at Turkey's cross-border military operation in northern Iraq and urged a withdrawal of Turkish troops from Iraqi territory. In December the Supreme Council reaffirmed the need to ensure the sovereignty and territorial integrity of Iraq. At the same time, however, the Council expressed concern at the escalation of tensions in the region, owing to Iraq's failure to co-operate with the UN Special Commission. The Council noted the opportunity to strengthen relations with Iran, in view of political developments in that country.

In late June 1997 ministers of foreign affairs of the Damascus Declaration states agreed to pursue efforts to establish a free-trade zone throughout the region, which was to form the basis of a future Arab common market.

INVESTMENT CORPORATION

Gulf Investment Corporation (GIC): Joint Banking Center, Kuwait Real Estate Bldg, POB 3402, Safat 13035, Kuwait; tel. 2431911; telex 44002; fax 2448894; f. 1983 by the six member states of the GCC, each contributing US $350m. of the total capital of $2,100m.; total assets $10,245m., dep. $8,135m. (1995); investment chiefly in the Gulf region, financing industrial projects (including pharmaceuticals, chemicals, steel wire, aircraft engineering, aluminium, dairy produce and chicken-breeding). GIC provides merchant banking and financial advisory services, and in 1992 was appointed to advise the Kuwaiti Government on a programme of privatization. Chair. AHMED BIN HUMAID AT-TAYER; Gen. Man. HISHAM A. RAZZUQI. Publ. *The GIC Gazetteer* (annually).

Gulf International Bank: POB 1017, Al-Dowali Bldg, 3 Palace Ave, Manama 317, Bahrain; tel. 534000; fax 522633; f. 1976 by the six GCC states and Iraq; became a wholly-owned subsidiary of the GIC (without Iraqi shareholdings) in 1991; cap. US $450m., dep. $7,573.6m., total assets $8,982.9m. (Dec. 1996). Chair. IBRAHIM ABD AL-KARIM; Gen. Man. ABDULLAH AL-KUWAIZ.

PUBLICATIONS

GCC News (monthly).

Al-Ta'awun (periodical).

COUNCIL OF ARAB ECONOMIC UNITY

Address: PO Box 1, Mohammed Fareed, Cairo, Egypt.

Telephone: (2) 755321; **fax:** (2) 754090.

Established in 1957 by the Economic Council of the Arab League. The first meeting of the Council was held in 1964.

MEMBERS

Egypt	Palestine
Iraq	Somalia
Jordan	Sudan
Kuwait	Syria
Libya	United Arab Emirates
Mauritania	Yemen

Organization

(January 1998)

COUNCIL

The Council consists of representatives of member states, usually ministers of economy, finance and trade. It meets twice a year; meetings are chaired by the representative of each country for one year.

GENERAL SECRETARIAT

Entrusted with the implementation of the Council's decisions and with proposing work plans, including efforts to encourage participation by member states in the Arab Economic Unity Agreement. The Secretariat also compiles statistics, conducts research and publishes studies on Arab economic problems and on the effects of major world economic trends.

COMMITTEES

There are seven standing committees: preparatory, follow-up and Arab Common Market development; Permanent Delegates; budget; economic planning; fiscal and monetary matters; customs and trade planning and co-ordination; statistics. There are also seven *ad hoc* committees, including meetings of experts on tariffs, trade promotion and trade legislation.

Activities

A five-year work plan for the General Secretariat in 1986–90 was approved in December 1985. As in the previous five-year plan, it included the co-ordination of measures leading to a customs union subject to a unified administration; market and commodity studies; unification of statistical terminology and methods of data collection; studies for the formation of new joint Arab companies and federations; formulation of specific programmes for agricultural and industrial co-ordination and for improving road and railway networks.

ARAB COMMON MARKET

Members: Egypt, Iraq, Jordan, Libya, Mauritania, Syria and Yemen.

Based on a resolution passed by the Council in August 1964; its implementation is supervised by the Council and does not constitute a separate organization. Customs duties and other taxes on trade between the member countries were eliminated in annual stages, the process being completed in 1971. The second stage was to be the adoption of a full customs union, and ultimately all restrictions on trade between the member countries, including quotas, and restrictions on residence, employment and transport, were to be abolished. In practice, however, the trading of national products has not been freed from all monetary, quantitative and administrative restrictions.

Between 1978 and 1989, the following measures were undertaken by the Council for the development of the Arab Common Market:

Introduction of flexible membership conditions for the least developed Arab states (Mauritania, Somalia, Sudan and Yemen).

Approval in principle of a fund to compensate the least developed countries for financial losses incurred as a result of joining the Arab Common Market.

Approval of legal, technical and administrative preparations for unification of tariffs levied on products imported from non-member countries.

Formation of a committee of ministerial deputies to deal with problems in the application of market rulings and to promote the organization's activities.

Adoption of unified customs legislation and of an integrated programme aimed at enhancing trade between member states and expanding members' productive capacity.

MULTILATERAL AGREEMENTS

The Council has initiated the following multilateral agreements aimed at achieving economic unity:

Agreement on Basic Levels of Social Insurance.

Agreement on Reciprocity in Social Insurance Systems.

Agreement on Labour Mobility.

Agreement on Organization of Transit Trade.

Agreement on Avoidance of Double Taxation and Elimination of Tax Evasion.

Agreement on Co-operation in Collection of Taxes.

Agreement on Capital Investment and Mobility.

Agreement on Settlement of Investment Disputes between Host Arab Countries and Citizens of Other Countries.

JOINT VENTURES

A number of multilateral organizations in industry and agriculture have been formed on the principle that faster development and economies of scale may be achieved by combining the efforts of member states. In industries that are new to the member countries, Arab Joint Companies are formed, while existing industries are co-ordinated by the setting up of Arab Specialized Unions. The unions are for closer co-operation on problems of production and marketing, and to help companies deal as a group in international markets. The companies are intended to be self-supporting on a purely commercial basis; they may issue shares to citizens of the participating countries. The joint ventures are:

Arab Joint Companies (cap.=capital; figures in Kuwaiti dinars unless otherwise stated):

Arab Company for Drug Industries and Medical Appliances: POB 925161, Amman, Jordan; tel. (6) 821618; fax (6) 821649; cap. 60m.

Arab Company for Industrial Investment: POB 3385, Alwiyah, Baghdad, Iraq; tel. 718-9215; telex 212628; fax 718-0710; auth. cap. 150m.

Arab Company for Livestock Development: POB 5305, Damascus, Syria; tel. 666037; telex 11376; cap. 60m.

Arab Mining Company: POB 20198, Amman, Jordan; tel. (6) 663148; telex 21169; fax (6) 684114; cap. 120m.

Specialized Arab Unions and Federations:

Arab Co-operative Federation: POB 57640, Baghdad, Iraq; tel. (1) 888-8121; telex 2685.

Arab Federation of Chemical Fertilizers Producers: POB 23696, Kuwait.

Arab Federation of Engineering Industries: POB 509, Baghdad, Iraq; tel. 776-1101; telex 2724.

Arab Federation of Leather Industries: POB 2188, Damascus, Syria.

Arab Federation of Paper Industries: POB 5456, Baghdad, Iraq; tel. (1) 887-2384; telex 212205.

Arab Federation of Textile Industries: POB 620, Damascus, Syria.

Arab Federation of Travel Agents: POB 7090, Amman, Jordan.

Arab Seaports Federation: Basrah, Iraq.

Arab Sugar Federation: POB 195, Khartoum, Sudan.

Arab Union for Cement and Building Materials: POB 9015, Damascus, Syria; tel. (11) 6665070; telex 412602; fax (11) 6621525.

Arab Union of Fish Producers: POB 15064, Baghdad, Iraq; tel. 551-1261.

Arab Union of Food Industries: POB 13025, Baghdad, Iraq.

Arab Union of Land Transport: POB 926324, Amman, Jordan; tel. (6) 63153; telex 21118.

Arab Union of the Manufacturers of Pharmaceuticals and Medical Appliances: POB 811520, Amman 11181, Jordan; tel. (6) 654306; telex 21528; fax (6) 648141.

Arab Union of Railways: POB 6599, Aleppo, Syria; tel. (21) 220302; telex 331009.

General Arab Insurance Federation: POB 611, 11511 Cairo, Egypt; tel. 5743177; telex 93141; fax 762310.

PUBLICATIONS

Annual Bulletin for Arab Countries' Foreign Trade Statistics.

Annual Bulletin for Official Exchange Rates of Arab Currencies.

Arab Economic Unity Bulletin (2 a year).

Demographic Yearbook for Arab Countries.

Economic Report of the General Secretary (2 a year).

Guide to Studies prepared by Secretariat.

Progress Report (2 a year).

Statistical Yearbook for Arab Countries.

Yearbook for Intra-Arab Trade Statistics.

Yearbook of National Accounts for Arab Countries.

THE COUNCIL OF EUROPE

Address: 67075 Strasbourg Cédex, France.

Telephone: 3-88-41-20-00; **telex:** 870943; **fax:** 3-88-41-27-81; **internet:** http://www.coe.fr.

The Council was founded in May 1949 to achieve a greater unity between its members, to facilitate their social progress and to uphold the principles of parliamentary democracy, respect for human rights and the rule of law. Membership has risen from the original 10 to 40.

MEMBERS*

Albania
Andorra
Austria
Belgium
Bulgaria
Croatia
Cyprus
Czech Republic
Denmark
Estonia
Finland
France
Germany
Greece
Hungary
Iceland
Ireland
Italy
Latvia
Liechtenstein
Lithuania
Luxembourg
Macedonia, former Yugoslav republic
Malta
Moldova
Netherlands
Norway
Poland
Portugal
Romania
Russia
San Marino
Slovakia
Slovenia
Spain
Sweden
Switzerland
Turkey
Ukraine
United Kingdom

* Armenia, Azerbaijan, Belarus, Bosnia and Herzegovina and Georgia have applied for full membership. Canada, Japan and the USA have obtained observer status with the organization.

Organization

(January 1998)

COMMITTEE OF MINISTERS

The Committee consists of the ministers of foreign affairs of all member states (or their deputies); it decides with binding effect all matters of internal organization, makes recommendations to governments and draws up conventions and agreements; it also discusses matters of political concern, such as European co-operation, North-South relations and the protection of human rights, and considers possible co-ordination with other institutions, such as the European Union (EU) and the Organization for Security and Co-operation in Europe (OSCE). The Committee usually meets in April/May and November each year.

CONFERENCES OF SPECIALIZED MINISTERS

There are 19 Conferences of specialized ministers, meeting regularly for intergovernmental co-operation in various fields.

PARLIAMENTARY ASSEMBLY

President: Leni Fischer (Germany).

Chairman of the Socialist Group: Peter Schieder (Austria).

Chairman of the Group of the European People's Party: Dr Walter Schwimmer (Austria).

Chairman of the European Democratic (Conservative) Group: Jean Vailleix (France) (acting).

Chairman of the Liberal Democratic and Reformers' Group: Lord Russell-Johnston (United Kingdom).

Chairman of the Unified European Left Group: Jaakko Laakso (Finland).

Members are elected or appointed by their national parliaments from among the members thereof; political parties in each delegation follow the proportion of their strength in the national parliament. Members do not represent their governments; they speak on their own behalf. At January 1998 the Assembly had 286 members (and 286 substitutes): 18 each for France, Germany, Italy, Russia and the United Kingdom; 12 each for Poland, Spain, Turkey and Ukraine; 10 for Romania; seven each for Belgium, the Czech Republic, Greece, Hungary, the Netherlands and Portugal; six each for Austria, Bulgaria, Sweden and Switzerland; five each for Croatia, Denmark, Finland, Moldova, Norway and Slovakia; four each for Albania, Ireland and Lithuania; three each for Cyprus, Estonia, Iceland, Latvia, Luxembourg, the former Yugoslav republic of Macedonia, Malta and Slovenia; and two each for Andorra, Liechtenstein and San Marino. Israel and Canada have permanent observer status, while Armenia, Azerbaijan, Belarus, Bosnia and Herzegovina and Georgia have been granted special 'guest status'. (Belarus's special status was suspended in January 1997.)

The Assembly meets in ordinary session once a year. The session is usually divided into four parts, held in the last full week of January, April, June and September. The Assembly may submit recommendations to the Committee of Ministers, pass resolutions, and discuss reports on any matters of common European interest. It is also a consultative body to the Committee of Ministers, and elects the Secretary-General, the Deputy Secretary-General, the Clerk of the Assembly and the members of the European Court of Human Rights.

Standing Committee: Represents the Assembly when it is not in session, and may adopt Recommendations to the Committee of Ministers and Resolutions on behalf of the Assembly. Consists of the President, Vice-Presidents, Chairmen of the Political Groups, Chairmen of the Ordinary Committees and a number of ordinary members. Meets at least four times a year.

Ordinary Committees: political; economic and development; social, health and family affairs; legal and human rights; culture and education; science and technology; environment, regional planning and local authorities; migration, refugees and demography; rules of procedure; agriculture; parliamentary and public relations, budget and intergovernmental work programme; monitoring.

CONGRESS OF LOCAL AND REGIONAL AUTHORITIES OF EUROPE—CLRAE

The Congress was established in 1994, incorporating the former Standing Conference of Local and Regional Authorities, in order to protect and promote the political, administrative and financial autonomy of local and regional European authorities by encouraging central governments to develop effective local democracy. The Congress comprises two chambers—a Chamber of Local Authorities and a Chamber of Regions—with a total membership of 286 elected representatives. Annual sessions are mainly concerned with local government matters, regional planning, protection of the environment, town and country planning, and social and cultural affairs. A Standing Committee, drawn from all national delegations, meets between plenary sessions of the Congress; other working groups, appointed by the Chambers, meet regularly to consider specific issues: for example, inner city problems, education, rural development, and unemployment. *Ad hoc* conferences and steering committees are also held.

The Congress advises the Council's Committee of Ministers and the Parliamentary Assembly on all aspects of local and regional policy and co-operates with other national and international organizations representing local government. The Congress monitors implementation of the European Charter of Local Self-Government, which was opened for signature in 1985 and provides common standards for effective local democracy. Other legislative guidelines for the activities of local authorities and the promotion of democracy at local level include the 1980 European Outline Convention on Transfrontier Co-operation, and its Additional Protocol which was opened for signature in 1995, a Convention on the Participation of Foreigners in Public Life at Local Level (1992), and the European Charter for Regional or Minority Languages (1992). In addition, the European Urban Charter defines citizens' rights in European towns and cities, for example in the areas of transport, urban architecture, pollution and security.

President: Claude Haegi (Switzerland).

SECRETARIAT

Secretary-General: Daniel Tarschys (Sweden).

Deputy Secretary-General: Christian Krüger (Germany).

Clerk of the Parliamentary Assembly: Bruno Haller (France).

Activities

In an effort to harmonize national laws, to put the citizens of member countries on an equal footing and to pool certain resources and facilities, the Council has concluded a number of conventions and agreements covering particular aspects of European co-operation. Since 1989 the Council has undertaken to increase co-operation with countries of the former USSR and to facilitate their accession to the organization. In October 1997 heads of state or government of member countries convened for only the second time (the first meeting took place in Vienna, in October 1993—see below) with the aim of formulating a new social model to consolidate democracy throughout Europe. The meeting endorsed a Final Declaration and an Action Plan, which established priority areas for future Council activities, including fostering social cohesion; protecting civilian security; promoting human rights; enhancing joint measures to counter cross-border illegal trafficking; and strengthening democracy through education and other cultural activities.

HUMAN RIGHTS

The promotion and development of human rights is one of the major tasks of the Council of Europe. The European Convention for the Protection of Human Rights and Fundamental Freedoms was opened for signature in 1950. The Steering Committee for Human Rights is responsible for inter-governmental co-operation in human rights and fundamental freedoms; it works to strengthen the effectiveness of systems for protecting human rights, to identify potential threats and challenges to human rights, and to encourage education and provide information on the subject. It was responsible for the preparation of the European Ministerial Conference on Human Rights (1985), and an informal European Ministerial Conference on Human Rights (1990) and the elaboration of the European Convention for the Prevention of Torture, which entered into force in February 1989. The Convention provides for the establishment of an independent committee of experts, empowered to visit all places where persons are deprived of their liberty by a public authority. At the Council's first meeting of heads of state and of government, held in Vienna, Austria, in October 1993, members agreed to draw up new protocols to the Convention to establish cultural rights of minorities and to draw up a new framework convention for the protection of national minorities. The Framework Convention was adopted by the Council's Committee of Ministers in November 1994 and opened for signature on 1 February 1995. By November 1997 it had been signed by 37 member states and had received 15 ratifications. The Framework Convention was expected to enter into force on 1 February 1998 as the first ever legally-binding instrument devoted to the general protection of national minorities.

The Vienna summit meeting also agreed to restructure the control mechanism for the protection of human rights, mainly the procedure for the consideration of cases in order to reduce the length of time before a case is concluded. As a result, a new protocol (No. 11) to the European Convention was opened for signature by member states in May 1994. The existing institutions (see below) were to be replaced by a single Court of Human Rights, consisting of one judge for each contracting state. Cases were to be considered in Chambers. Committees of three judges in each Chamber were to be empowered to declare applications inadmissible. Chambers of seven judges were to pass judgment on cases deemed admissible for consideration. A Grand Chamber was to be established, consisting of 17 judges, who were to rule on difficult or important cases. In October 1997 the Council confirmed that the Protocol had been ratified by all member states, except Russia, and that it would enter into effect on 1 November 1998. In January 1998 the Parliamentary Assembly elected 31 judges for the new Court of Human Rights; elections for judges for the remaining eight contracting states were to be held in April.

European Commission of Human Rights

The Commission has 33 members. It is competent to examine complaints by a contracting party, or by an individual, non-governmental organization or group of individuals, that the European Convention for the Protection of Human Rights and Fundamental Freedoms has been violated. If the Commission decides to admit the application, it then ascertains the full facts of the case and places itself at the disposal of the parties in order to attempt to reach a friendly settlement. If no settlement is reached, the Commission sends a report to the Committee of Ministers, in which it establishes the facts and states an opinion as to whether there has been a violation of the Convention. It is then for the Committee of Ministers or, if the case is referred to it, the Court to decide whether or not a violation has taken place. By September 1997 more than 37,000 applications had been submitted.

A new single European Court of Human Rights, replacing the Commission and the existing Court (see below), was scheduled to become operational on 1 November 1998; however, the Commission was to continue to examine applications until October 1999.

President: Prof. Stefan Trechsel (Switzerland).

President of the First Chamber: Jane Liddy (Ireland).

President of the Second Chamber: Gro Hillestad Thune (Norway).

Secretary: Michele de Salvia (Italy).

European Court of Human Rights

The Court comprises 35 judges. It may consider a case only after the Commission has acknowledged the failure of efforts for a friendly settlement and has transmitted its report to the Committee of Ministers. The following may bring a case before the Court, provided that the High Contracting Party or Parties concerned have accepted its compulsory jurisdiction or, failing that, with the consent of the High Contracting Party or Parties concerned: the Commission, a High Contracting Party whose national is alleged to be a victim, a High Contracting Party which referred the case to the Commission, and a High Contracting Party against which the complaint has been lodged. Since 1 October 1994, when a new protocol to the Convention (No. 9) entered into force, an individual, a group of individuals or a non-governmental organization whose application has been declared admissable by the Commission, has been able, under certain conditions, to refer a case to the Court. In the event of dispute as to whether the Court has jurisdiction, the matter is settled by the Court. The judgment of the Court is final. The Court may, in certain circumstances, give advisory opinions at the request of the Committee of Ministers.

By September 1997 the Court had delivered 828 judgments and decisions since its creation in 1959.

In accordance with Protocol 11 to the European Convention, the functions of the Court were to be assumed by a new institution, with effect from 1 November 1998.

President: (vacant).

Registrar: Herbert Petzold (Germany).

European Social Charter

The European Social Charter, in force since 1965, is now applied in Austria, Belgium, Cyprus, Denmark, Finland, France, Germany, Greece, Iceland, Ireland, Italy, Luxembourg, Malta, the Netherlands, Norway, Poland, Portugal, Spain, Sweden, Turkey and the United Kingdom; it defines the rights and principles which are the basis of the Council's social policy, and guarantees a number of social and economic rights to the citizen, including the right to work, the right to form workers' organizations, the right to social security and social assistance, the right of the family to protection and the right of migrant workers to protection and assistance. In May 1988 the Charter was completed by an Additional Protocol which extends these rights. Two committees, comprising government and independent experts, supervise the parties' compliance with their obligations under the Charter. The Committee of Ministers may issue recommendations under the Charter. An Amending Protocol (1991) and an Additional Protocol (1995), which provide for a system of collective complaints, reinforce the Charter's control mechanism. A revised European Social Charter, which amended existing guarantees (for example, reinforcing non-discrimination rules) and incorporated new rights (such as protection for those without jobs and opportunities for workers with family responsibilities) was opened for signature in May 1996.

President of the Committee of Independent Experts: ROLF BIRK (Germany).

President of the Governmental Committee: MARIA-JOSEFINA LEITÃO (Portugal).

RACISM AND INTOLERANCE

In October 1993 heads of state and of government, meeting in Vienna, resolved to reinforce a policy to combat all forms of intolerance, in response to the increasing incidence of racial hostility and intolerance towards minorities in European societies. A European Commission against Racism and Intolerance (ECRI) was established by the summit meeting to analyse and assess the effectiveness of legal, policy and other measures taken by member states to combat these problems. Members of ECRI are designated by governments on the basis of their recognized expertise in the field. ECRI has undertaken a comparative study of the situation in all member states, and aims to assist governments to resolve problems identified. In addition, ECRI has formulated proposals to strengthen the non-discrimination clause of the European Convention on Human Rights, (Article 14), by means of an Additional Protocol.

In December 1994 a two-year European Youth Campaign was initiated to raise awareness among the public and to mobilize groups and individuals to achieve the goals of tolerance, equality, dignity and democracy. Non-governmental youth organizations, minorities and anti-racist groups have been the Council's main partners in the campaign. Since 1994 efforts to combat all forms of intolerance have been the priority of the Council of Europe's annual activity programmes. New projects have been initiated and existing ones reinforced, based on themes including education for democratic citizenship; media and intolerance; neighbourhood cultural life; intolerance and sexism; and history teaching in the new Europe.

MEDIA AND COMMUNICATIONS

In 1982 the Committee of Ministers adopted a Declaration on the freedom of expression and information, which, together with Article 10 of the European Convention on Human Rights (freedom of expression and information), forms the basis for the Council of Europe's mass media activities. Implementation of the Council of Europe's work programme concerning the media is undertaken by the Steering Committee on the Mass Media (CDMM), which comprises senior government officials and representatives of professional organizations, meeting in plenary session twice a year. The CDMM is mandated to devise concerted European policy measures and appropriate legal instruments. Its underlying aims are to further freedom of expression and information in a pluralistic democracy, and to promote the free flow of information and ideas. The CDMM is assisted by various specialist groups and committees. Policy and legal instruments have been developed on subjects including: exclusivity rights; disclosure of media ownership; protection of journalists in situations of conflict and tension; independence of public-service broadcasting, protection of rights holders; legal protection of encrypted television services. These policy and legal instruments (mainly in the form on non-binding recommendations addressed to member governments) are complemented by the publication of studies, analyses and seminar proceedings on topics of media law and policy. The CDMM has also prepared a number of international binding legal instruments, including the European Convention on Transfrontier Television (adopted in 1989 and ratified by 15 countries by December 1997) and the European Convention relating to questions on copyright law and other rights in the context of transfrontier broadcasting by satellite (signed by six member states by December 1996). In 1995 the CDMM embarked on work in new areas such as: access to official information; new communications technologies and their impact on human rights and democratic values; media and intolerance; and media in a pan-European perspective.

SOCIAL WELFARE

The European Code of Social Security and its Protocol entered into force in 1968; by 1996 the Code and Protocol had been ratified by Belgium, Germany, Luxembourg, the Netherlands, Norway, Portugal and Sweden, while the Code alone had been ratified by Cyprus, Denmark, France, Greece, Ireland, Italy, Spain, Switzerland, Turkey and the United Kingdom. These instruments set minimum standards for medical care and the following benefits: sickness, old-age, unemployment, employment injury, family, maternity, invalidity and survivor's benefit. A revision of these instruments, aiming to provide higher standards and greater flexibility, was completed for signature in 1990 and had been signed by 14 states by 1996.

The European Convention on Social Security, in force since 1977, now applies in Austria, Belgium, Italy, Luxembourg, the Netherlands, Portugal, Spain and Turkey; most of the provisions apply automatically, while others are subject to the conclusion of additional multilateral or bilateral agreements. The Convention is concerned with establishing the following four fundamental principles of international law on social security: equality of treatment, unity of applicable legislation, conservation of rights accrued or in course of acquisition, and payment of benefits abroad. In 1994 a Protocol to the Convention, providing for the enlargement of the personal scope of the Convention, was opened for signature. By the end of 1996 it had been signed by Austria, Greece and Luxembourg. Other specific issues may be studied by Ministerial Conferences.

A number of resolutions passed by the Committee of Ministers give guidance for intergovernmental action on particular aspects of social policy, welfare, employment policy or labour law. Recent recommendations prepared by the Steering Committee for Employment and Labour (CDEM) cover the promotion of small and medium-sized enterprises, the role of employment services and the issue of reconciling work and family life.

In 1996 the Steering Committee on Social Policy (CDPS) initiated a major project entitled 'Human Dignity and Social Exclusion' to consider aspects of housing, employment, health, social protection and education. The findings of the project and proposals for action were to be presented at a conference in early 1998. Ongoing activities of the CDPS concerned social policies in cities, the training of social workers, studies on the effects of youth unemployment on families, and on problems for social welfare arising from the crisis in the welfare state.

The Council of Europe operates annual social research programmes, in which groups of specialists make comparative studies in social welfare and labour, covering all member states.

HEALTH

Through a series of expert committees, the Council aims at ensuring constant co-operation in Europe in a variety of health-related fields, with particular emphasis on patients' rights, for example: equity in access to health care, quality assurance, health services for institutionalized populations (prisoners, elderly in homes), discrimination resulting from health status and education for health. These efforts are supplemented by the training of health personnel.

Improvement of blood transfusion safety and availability of blood and blood derivatives has been ensured through European Agreements and guidelines. Advances in this field and in organ transplantation are continuously assessed by expert committees. A computerized European network for the exchange of livers for patients in urgent need was scheduled to become operational in early 1998.

Sixteen states co-operate in establishing common standards regarding the use of pesticides, food additives, flavouring substances, and materials that come into contact with food. They also deal with pharmaceutical and cosmetic products, residues of veterinary drugs in food of animal origin, and wood protection products. A European Agreement on the restriction of the use of certain detergents in washing and cleaning products entered into force in 1971 (amended by a protocol, 1984).

In the co-operation group to combat drug abuse and illicit drug trafficking (Pompidou Group), 29 states work together, through meetings of ministers, officials and experts, to counteract drug abuse. The Group follows a multidisciplinary approach embracing in particular legislation, law enforcement, prevention, treatment, rehabilitation and data collection.

The Convention on the Elaboration of a European Pharmacopoeia (establishing legally binding standards for medicinal substances, auxiliary substances, pharmaceutical preparations and others articles) entered into force in May 1974: in 1997 25 states and the European Union were parties to the Convention; WHO and 15 European and non-European states participate as observers in the sessions of the European Pharmacopoeia Commission. In 1994 a network of some 90 national control laboratories for human and veterinary medicines was established.

In April 1997 the first international convention to control biomedicine was opened for signature at a meeting of health ministers of member states, in Oviedo, Spain. The so-called Convention for the Protection of Human Rights and the Dignity of Human Beings with Respect to the Applications of Biology and Medicine incorporated provisions on scientific research, the principle of informed patient consent, organ and tissue transplants and the prohibition of financial gain and disposal of a part of the human body. An Additional Protocol to the Convention, with regard to the prohibition of medical cloning of human beings, was approved by Council heads of state and government in October 1997 and was opened for signature in January 1998. Both documents were to be open to non-member states and were to be enforced by the European Court of Human Rights.

POPULATION AND MIGRATION

The European Convention on the Legal Status of Migrant Workers, in force since 1983, was applicable by 1995 to France, Italy, the Netherlands, Norway, Portugal, Spain, Sweden and Turkey. The Convention is based on the principle of equality of treatment for migrant workers and the nationals of the host country as to housing, working conditions, and social security. The Convention also upholds the principle of the right to family reunion. An international consultative committee, representing the parties to the Convention, monitors the application of the Convention.

During 1986–91 the European Committee on Migration was engaged on a multi-disciplinary project on community relations, which led to the adoption of a final report on community and ethnic relations in Europe. In 1996 work on the successor project entitled 'The Integration of Immigrants: Towards Equal Opportunities' was concluded and the results were presented at the sixth conference of European ministers responsible for migration affairs, held in Warsaw, Poland. A review of the implementation of community relations policies was also prepared for the Conference. In 1995 the Committee published a report on the situation of Roma/Gypsies in Europe, a subject for which it will have continuing responsibility, in co-ordination with other relevant Council of Europe bodies. The Committee is also jointly responsible, with the *ad hoc* Committee of Experts on the legal aspects of territorial asylum, refugees and stateless persons, for the examination of migration issues arising at the pan-European level.

The European Population Committee, an intergovernmental committee of scientists and government officials engaged in demography, monitors and analyses population trends throughout Europe and informs governments, research centres and the public of developments that may require political action. It compiles an annual statistical review of demographic developments (covering 45 European states) and publishes the results of studies of particular aspects of population, for example 'Ageing and its consequences for the socio-medical system' (1995) or 'Migration and Development Co-operation' (1994). In October 1996 a Mediterranean Conference on Population, Migration and Development, held in Palma de Mallorca, Spain, discussed demographic imbalances between the two sides of the Mediterranean, migration flows and future developments in the area of development and partnership.

SOCIAL DEVELOPMENT FUND

The Council of Europe Social Development Fund was created in 1956 (as the Resettlement Fund). In 1997 new articles of agreement, which were adopted in 1993, entered into force: these reinforced the primary aim of the Fund as the financing of projects to benefit refugees, migrants and displaced persons, and victims of natural or ecological disasters. As a secondary objective, it also funds social projects involving job creation, vocational training, social housing, education, health and the protection of the environment. At November 1996 there were 25 members states party to the agreement on the Fund; at the end of 1995 total loans granted since its inception amounted to ECU 9,323m.

EQUALITY BETWEEN WOMEN AND MEN

The Steering Committee for Equality between Women and Men (CDEG—an intergovernmental committee of experts) is responsible for encouraging action at both national and Council of Europe level to promote equality of rights and opportunities between the two sexes. Assisted by various specialist groups and committees, the CDEG is mandated to establish analyses, studies and evaluations, to examine national policies and experiences, to work out concerted policy strategies and measures for implementing equality and, as necessary, to prepare appropriate legal and other instruments. It is also responsible for preparing the European Ministerial Conferences on Equality between Women and Men, the fourth of which took place in November 1997. The main areas of CDEG activities are the comprehensive inclusion of the rights of women (for example, violence against women, forced prostitution, reproductive rights) within the context of human rights; the issue of equality and democracy, including the promotion of the participation of women in political and public life; projects aimed at studying the specific equality problems related to cultural diversity, migration and minorities; and the mainstreaming of equality into all policies and programmes at all levels of society.

LEGAL MATTERS

The European Committee on Legal Co-operation develops co-operation between member states in the field of law, with the objective of harmonizing and modernizing public and private law, including administrative law and the law relating to the judiciary. The Committee is responsible for expert groups which consider issues relating to administrative law, legal data processing, family law, nationality, incapacitated adults, and data protection. There are also committees concerned with the movement of persons and refugees, the protection of animals, the custody of children and the transmission of applications for legal aid. Numerous conventions have been adopted, on matters which include: information on foreign law; consular functions; bearer securities; state immunity; motorists' liability; adoption; nationality; animal protection; mutual aid in administrative matters; custody of children; data protection; insider trading; bankruptcy; and the legal status of non-governmental organizations.

In May 1990 the Committee of Ministers adopted a Partial Agreement to establish the European Commission for Democracy through Law, to be based in Venice, Italy. The Commission is composed of legal and political experts and is concerned with the guarantees offered by law in the service of democracy. In particular, it may supply opinions upon request, made through the Committee of Ministers, by the Parliamentary Assembly, the Secretary-General or any member states of the Council of Europe. Other states and international organizations may request opinions with the consent of the Committee of Ministers. The Commission may also conduct research on its own initiative. In 1997 the Commission was working on the following issues: constitutional justice; constitutional reforms; the consequences of state succession for nationality; legal foundations of foreign policy; the participation of persons belonging to minorities in public life; constitutional law and European integration; the composition of Constitutional Courts; and federal and regional states. The Commission has pursued its activities through the UniDem (University for Democracy) programme of seminars. In 1996 three seminars were held, concerning 'Local self-government, territorial autonomy and protection of minorities', 'Human rights and functioning of the democratic institutions in emergency situations' and the 'Constitutional heritage of Europe'.

With regard to crime, the European Committee on Crime Problems has prepared conventions on such matters as extradition, mutual assistance, recognition and enforcement of foreign judgments, the transfer of proceedings, the suppression of terrorism, the transfer of prisoners, the compensation to be paid to victims of violent crime, and search, seizure and confiscation of the proceeds from crime. In November 1996 the committee of Ministers adopted a Programme of Action against Corruption, which proposed criminal, civil and administrative law measures against corruption, to be implemented over a four-year period.

A Criminological Scientific Council, composed of specialists in law, psychology, sociology and related sciences, advises the Committee and organizes criminological research conferences. A Council for Penological Co-operation organizes regular high-level conferences of directors of prison administration and is responsible for collating statistical information on detention and community sanctions in Europe. The Council prepared new European Prison Rules in 1987 and European Rules on Community Sanctions (alternatives to imprisonment) in 1992.

EDUCATION, CULTURE AND HERITAGE

The European Cultural Convention covers education, culture, heritage, sport and youth. Programmes on education and culture are managed by the Council for Cultural Co-operation, assisted by four specialized committees.

The education programme consists of projects on 'Education for democratic citizenship', 'Learning and teaching about the history of Europe in the 20th century', and 'European university co-operation'. Other activities include: the annual European Schools Day Competition, organized in co-operation with the EU; the European Teacher Bursaries Scheme; the European Network of National Information Centres on Academic Mobility and Recognition, Legislative Reform Programme; and the European Documentation and Information System for Education (EUDISED).

In the field of cultural policy, a series of surveys of national policies are conducted. Surveys on the Netherlands and Finland were completed in 1994, on Italy and Estonia in 1995 and on Russia and Slovenia in 1996. A resources centre in support of cultural development policies was scheduled to become operational in early 1997. The European Convention on Cinematographic Co-production was opened for signature in October 1992. The Eurimages support fund helps to finance joint production of films. 'Cultural tourism' is encouraged by the devising of tourist routes of European cultural significance (e.g. routes illustrating baroque architecture, Cistercian monasteries and Viking settlements).

Conventions for the Protection of the Architectural Heritage and the Protection of the Archaeological Heritage provide a legal framework for European co-operation in these areas. The Cultural Heritage Committee maintains contact between authorities in charge of historic buildings and encourages public interest. The Committee's main activities include projects on heritage, landscapes and sites, the financing of architectural restoration, and technical assistance towards the enhancement of architectural heritage.

YOUTH

In 1972 the Council of Europe established the European Youth Centre (EYC) in Strasbourg. Following the changes in Europe in

1989 and the enlargement of the Council of Europe to include countries of central and eastern Europe, a second residential centre was created in Budapest in 1995. The activities of the centres are run with and by international non-governmental youth organizations, representing a wide range of interests, including politics, religion, socio-education, trade unions, students' groups, gay and lesbian organizations, conscripts and conscientious objectors, migrants, environmental groups and young people from rural and farming communities. They provide about 50 residential courses a year (study sessions, training courses, symposia) and a programme of 10 language courses. A notable feature of the EYC is its decision-making structure, by which decisions on its programme and general policy matters are taken by a Governing Board composed of an equal number of youth organizations and government representatives.

The European Youth Foundation (EYF) aims to provide financial assistance to European activities of non-governmental youth organizations and began operations in 1973. Since that time more than 200 organizations have received financial aid for carrying out international activities. The total number of young people taking part in meetings supported by the Foundation amounted to about 200,000 by 1995, coming from some 38 countries. More than 170m. French francs have been distributed.

The European Steering Committee for Intergovernmental Co-operation in the Youth Field conducts research in youth-related matters and prepares for ministerial conferences.

SPORT

The Committee for the Development of Sport, founded in November 1977, administers the Sports Fund. Its activities concentrate on the implementation of the European Sports Charter; the role of sport in society (e.g. medical, political, ethical and educational aspects); the provision of assistance in sports reform to new member states in central and eastern Europe; the practice of sport (activities, special projects, etc.); the diffusion of sports information; and co-ordination of sports research. The Committee is also responsible for preparing the conference of European ministers responsible for sport. In 1985 the Committee of Ministers adopted the European Convention on Spectator Violence and Misbehaviour at Sports Events. A Charter on Sport for Disabled Persons was adopted in 1986, an Anti-Doping Convention in 1989, and a Code of Sports Ethics in 1992. In 1996 the Committee for the Development of Sport adopted an Action Plan for Bosnia and Herzegovina, entitled 'Rehabilitation through Sport'.

ENVIRONMENT AND REGIONAL PLANNING

A Steering Committee for the Conservation and Management of the Environment and Natural Habitats was founded in 1962. It introduced a European Water Charter in 1968, a Soil Charter in 1974 and a Charter on Invertebrates in 1986. The Committee awards the European Diploma for protection of areas of European significance, supervises a network of biogenetic reserves, and maintains 'red lists' of threatened animals and plants.

At November 1996 30 member states, four non-members and the European Union had ratified a Convention on the Conservation of European Wildlife and Natural Habitats, which entered into force in June 1982 and gives total protection to 693 species of plants, 89 mammals, 294 birds, 43 reptiles, 21 amphibians, 115 freshwater fishes, 111 invertebrates and their habitats. The Council's NATUROPA Centre provides information and documentation on the environment, through periodicals and campaigns such as the Europe Nature Conservation Year (1995).

Regional disparities constitute a major obstacle to the process of European integration. Conferences of ministers of regional planning are held to discuss these issues. In 1994 they adopted a set of principles concerning the outlook for sustainable development and its implication for Europe beyond the year 2000.

EXTERNAL RELATIONS

Agreements providing for co-operation and exchange of documents and observers have been concluded with the United Nations and its agencies, and with most of the European inter-governmental organizations and the Organization of American States. Particularly close relations exist with the EU, OECD, Western European Union and the OSCE.

Israel and Canada are represented in the Parliamentary Assembly by observer delegations, and certain European and other non-member countries participate in or send observers to certain meetings of technical committees and specialized conferences at intergovernmental level. Full observer status with the Council was granted to the USA in 1995 and to Canada and Japan in 1996.

Relations with non-member states, other organizations and non-governmental organizations are co-ordinated within the Secretariat by the Directorate of Political Affairs.

The European Centre for Global Interdependence and Solidarity (the 'North–South Centre') was established in Lisbon, Portugal, in 1990, in order to provide a framework for European co-operation in this area and to promote pluralist democracy and respect for human rights. The Centre is co-managed by parliamentarians, governments, non-governmental organizations and local and regional authorities. Its activities are divided into three programmes: public information and media relations; education and training for global interdependence; and dialogue for global partnership. The Centre organizes workshops, seminars and training courses on global interdependence and convenes international colloquies on human rights.

During the early 1990s the Council of Europe established a number of programmes to assist the process of democratic reform in central and eastern European countries that had formerly been under communist rule (16 of which had become members of the Council by November 1996). The 'Demosthenes' programme makes available the expertise of the Council and its member states in the fields of pluralist democracy, human rights and the rule of law. The LODE programme gives assistance to central and eastern European countries in the restructuring of local government, while the Themis programme aims to assist in the transformation of the judicial system. Co-operation programmes also include workshops, training courses, scholarships, and study visits. In 1996 a new co-operation programme, the 'New Initiative', was launched to respond to the challenge of strengthening the democratic process in countries of the former USSR. In January 1997 the Council suspended the special guest status that had been granted to Belarus, having ruled that the new Constitition of that country failed to uphold democratic standards.

FINANCE

The budget is financed by contributions from members on a proportional scale of assessment (using population and gross domestic product as common indicators). The 1997 budget totalled £159m.

PUBLICATIONS

Activities Report (in French and English).

Catalogue of Publications (annually).

Congress of Local and Regional Authorities of Europe Newsletter (6 a year).

Europa40plus (electronic newsletter, monthly, in English and French).

European Cultural Diary (annually).

European Heritage (2 a year, in English, French and German).

The Europeans (electronic bulletin of the Parliamentary Assembly).

Naturopa (3 a year, in 4 languages).

Sports Information Bulletin (quarterly).

Strategy Bulletin (6 a year, in 5 languages).

ECONOMIC COMMUNITY OF WEST AFRICAN STATES—ECOWAS

Address: Secretariat Bldg, Asokoro, Abuja, Nigeria.

Telephone: (9) 5231858; **fax:** (9) 2637052.

The Treaty of Lagos, establishing ECOWAS, was signed in May 1975 by 15 states, with the object of promoting trade, co-operation and self-reliance in West Africa. Outstanding protocols bringing certain key features of the Treaty into effect were ratified in November 1976. Cape Verde joined in 1977. A revised ECOWAS treaty, designed to accelerate economic integration and to increase political co-operation, was drafted in 1991–92, and was signed in July 1993 (see below).

MEMBERS

Benin	Guinea	Niger
Burkina Faso	Guinea-Bissau	Nigeria
Cape Verde	Liberia	Senegal
Côte d'Ivoire	Mali	Sierra Leone
The Gambia	Mauritania	Togo
Ghana		

Organization

(February 1998)

CONFERENCE OF HEADS OF STATE AND GOVERNMENT

The Conference, the highest authority of ECOWAS, meets annually. The Chairman is drawn from the member states in turn. In August 1997 ECOWAS heads of state decided that the Conference should be convened twice each year to enhance monitoring and co-ordination of the Community's activities.

COUNCIL OF MINISTERS

The Council consists of two representatives from each country; a chairman is drawn from each country in turn. It meets twice a year, and is responsible for the running of the Community.

TRIBUNAL

The treaty provides for a Community Tribunal, whose composition and competence are determined by the Authority of Heads of State and Government; it interprets the provisions of the treaty and settles disputes between member states that are referred to it.

EXECUTIVE SECRETARIAT

The Executive Secretary is elected for a four-year term, which may be renewed once only.

Executive Secretary: Lansana Kouyaté (Guinea).

SPECIALIZED COMMISSIONS

There are six commissions:

(i) Trade, Customs, Immigration, Monetary and Payments;

(ii) Industry, Agriculture and Natural Resources;

(iii) Transport, Communications and Energy;

(iv) Social and Cultural Affairs;

(v) Administration and finance;

(vi) Information.

ECOWAS FUND FOR CO-OPERATION, COMPENSATION AND DEVELOPMENT

Address: BP 2704, blvd du 13 Janvier, Lomé, Togo.

Telephone: 216864; **telex:** 5339; **fax:** 218684.

The Fund is administered by a Board of Directors. The chief executive of the Fund is the Managing Director, who holds office for a renewable term of four years. There is a staff of 100. The authorized capital of the Fund is US $500m., of which $100m. has been called up, and $68.5m. is paid up (Oct. 1994). In 1988 agreements were reached with the African Development Bank and the Islamic Development Bank on the co-financing of projects and joint training of staff. Efforts are currently being undertaken to enhance the Fund's financial resources, by opening its capital to non-regional participants.

Managing Director: Samuel Kye Apea (Ghana).

Activities

ECOWAS aims to promote co-operation and development in economic, social and cultural activity, particularly in the fields for which specialized commissions (see above) are appointed, to raise the standard of living of the people of the member countries, increase and maintain economic stability, improve relations among member countries and contribute to the progress and development of Africa.

The treaty provides for compensation for states whose import duties are reduced through trade liberalization and contains a clause permitting safeguard measures in favour of any country affected by economic disturbances through the application of the treaty.

The treaty also contains a commitment to abolish all obstacles to the free movement of people, services and capital, and to promote: harmonization of agricultural policies; common projects in marketing, research and the agriculturally based industries; joint development of economic and industrial policies and elimination of disparities in levels of development; and common monetary policies.

Lack of success in many of ECOWAS' aims has been attributed to the existence of numerous other intergovernmental organizations in the region (in particular the francophone Communauté économique de l'Afrique de l'ouest, replaced by the Union économique et monétaire ouest-africaine in 1994, q.v.) and to member governments' lack of commitment, shown by their reluctance to implement policies at the national level, their failure to provide the agreed financial resources, and the absence of national links with the Secretariat. During the 1990s ECOWAS activities were increasingly dominated by its efforts to secure peace in Liberia (see below).

A revised treaty for the Community was drawn up by an ECOWAS Committee of Eminent Persons in 1991–92, and was signed at the ECOWAS summit conference that took place in Cotonou, Benin, in July 1993. The treaty, which was to extend economic and political co-operation among member states, designates the achievement of a common market and a single currency as economic objectives, while in the political sphere it envisages the establishment of a West African parliament, an economic and social council and an ECOWAS court of justice to replace the existing Tribunal and enforce Community decisions. The treaty also formally assigned the Community with the responsibility of preventing and settling regional conflicts. At the summit meeting, held in Abuja, Nigeria, in August 1994, ECOWAS heads of state and government signed a protocol agreement for the establishment of a regional parliament; however, no timetable was specified for this to be achieved. The meeting also adopted a Convention on Extradition of non-political offenders. At the end of July 1995 the new ECOWAS treaty was reported to have entered into effect, having received the required number of ratifications.

TRADE AND MONETARY UNION

Elimination of tariffs and other obstructions to trade among member states, and the establishment of a common external tariff, were planned over a transitional period of 15 years. At the 1978 Conference of Heads of State and Government it was decided that from 28 May 1979 no member state might increase its customs tariff on goods from another member. This was regarded as the first step towards the abolition of customs duties within the Community. During the first two years import duties on intra-community trade were to be maintained, and then eliminated in phases over the next eight years. Quotas and other restrictions of equivalent effect were to be abolished in the first 10 years. In the remaining five years all differences between external customs tariffs were to be abolished.

The 1980 Conference of Heads of State and Government decided to establish a free-trade area for unprocessed agricultural products and handicrafts from May 1981. Tariffs on industrial products made by specified community enterprises were also to be abolished from that date, but implementation was delayed by difficulties in defining the enterprises. From 1 January 1990 tariffs were lifted from 25 listed items manufactured in ECOWAS member states: by mid-1991 the number had increased to 90. Over the ensuing decade, tariffs on other industrial products were to be eliminated as follows: the 'most-developed' countries of ECOWAS (Côte d'Ivoire, Ghana, Nigeria and Senegal) were to abolish tariffs on 'priority' products within four years and on 'non-priority' products within six years; the second group (Benin, Guinea, Liberia, Sierra Leone and Togo) were to abolish tariffs on 'priority' products within six years, and on 'non-priority' products within eight years; and the 'least-developed' members (Burkina Faso, Cape Verde, The Gambia, Guinea-Bissau, Mali,

Mauritania and Niger) were to abolish tariffs on 'priority' products within eight years and on 'non-priority' products within 10 years.

In 1990 the Conference of Heads of State and Government agreed to adopt measures that would create a single monetary zone and remove barriers to trade in goods that originated in the Community. ECOWAS regards monetary union as necessary to encourage investment in the region, since it would greatly facilitate capital transactions with foreign countries. In September 1992 it was announced that, as part of efforts to enhance monetary co-operation and financial harmonization in the region, the West African Clearing House was to be restructured as the West African Monetary Agency (WAMA). As a specialized agency of ECOWAS, WAMA was to be responsible for administering an ECOWAS exchange rate system (EERS) and for establishing the single monetary zone. A credit guarantee scheme and travellers' cheque system were to be established in association with the EERS. The agreement establishing WAMA was signed by the Governors of the central banks of ECOWAS member states, meeting in Banjul, The Gambia, in March 1996. In July, the Conference agreed to impose a common value-added tax (VAT) on consumer goods, in order to rationalize indirect taxation and to stimulate greater intra-Community trade. In August 1997 ECOWAS heads of state and government appointed an *ad hoc* monitoring committee to promote and oversee the implementation of trade liberalization measures and the establishment of a single monetary zone by 2000. The Conference also authorized the introduction of the regional travellers' cheque scheme and determined that this should be operational by early 1998.

In December 1992 ECOWAS ministers agreed on the institutionalization of an ECOWAS trade fair, in order to promote trade liberalization and intra-Community trade. The first trade fair, which was held in Dakar, Senegal in May/June 1995, was attended by some 400 private businesses from the 16 member states. A second trade fair was scheduled to be held in Accra, Ghana, in February/March 1999.

TRAVEL, TRANSPORT AND COMMUNICATIONS

At the 1979 Conference of Heads of State a Protocol was signed relating to free circulation of the region's citizens and to rights of residence and establishment of commercial enterprises. The first provision (the right of entry without a visa) came into force in 1980. The second provision, allowing unlimited rights of residence, was signed in 1986 (although Nigeria indicated that unskilled workers and certain categories of professionals would not be allowed to stay for an indefinite period) and came into force in 1989. The third provision, concerning the right to establish a commercial enterprise in another member state was signed in 1990. In July 1992 the ECOWAS meeting of heads of state and government formulated a Minimum Agenda for Action for the implementation of Community agreements regarding the free movement of goods and people. Measures to be undertaken included removal of non-tariff barriers, the simplification of customs and transit procedures and a reduction in the number of control posts on international roads. By mid-1996 the ECOWAS summit meeting observed that few measures had been adopted by member states to implement the Minimum Agenda, and emphasized that it remained a central element of the Community's integration process. In April 1997 the Gambian and Senegalese finance and trade officials concluded an agreement on measures to facilitate the export of goods via Senegal to neighbouring countries, in accordance with ECOWAS protocols relating to inter-state road transit arrangements.

In August 1996 the initial phase of a programme to improve regional telecommunications was reported to have been completed. Some US $35m. had been granted for project financing in eight ECOWAS countries. A second phase of the programme, which aimed to modernize and expand the region's telecommunications services, was initiated by ECOWAS heads of state in August 1997.

A programme for the development of an integrated regional road network was adopted by the 1980 Conference. Under the programme, two major trans-regional roads were to be completed: the Trans-Coastal Highway, linking Lagos, Nigeria, with Nouackchott, Mauritania (4,767 km); and the Trans-Sahelian Highway, linking Dakar, Senegal, with N'Djamena, Chad (4,633 km). By mid-1993 about 88% of the trans-coastal route was complete, and about 78% of the trans-Sahelian route.

ECONOMIC AND INDUSTRIAL DEVELOPMENT

In November 1984 ECOWAS heads of state and government approved the establishment of a private regional investment bank, to be known as Ecobank Transnational Inc. The bank, which was based in Lomé, Togo, opened in March 1988. ECOWAS has a 10% share in the bank. By mid-1997 Ecobank affiliates were operating in Benin, Burkina Faso, Côte d'Ivoire, Ghana, Nigeria and Togo.

The West African Industrial Forum, sponsored by ECOWAS, is held every two years to promote regional industrial investment. The Secretariat is formulating a West African Industrial Master Plan. The first phase involved the compilation of an inventory of industrial enterprises, while the second phase was to comprise study of important industrial sub-sectors, prior to the drawing up of the Master Plan.

In September 1995 Nigeria, Ghana, Togo and Benin signed an agreement for the construction of a 400-km gas pipeline to connect Nigerian gas supplies to the other countries. The pipeline was expected to be completed in three years, under the management of a West African Pipeline Company.

In August 1997 the Conference of Heads of State and Government urged all member states to co-ordinate their long-term development programmes in order to formulate common objectives and to encourage greater economic growth in the region as a whole.

DEFENCE

At the third Conference of Heads of State and Government a protocol of non-aggression was signed. Thirteen members signed a protocol on mutual defence assistance at the 1981 Conference. Member states reaffirmed their commitment to refrain from aggression against one another at a summit conference in 1991. In 1990 a Standing Mediation Committee was formed to mediate in disputes between member states. The revised ECOWAS treaty, signed in July 1993, incorporates a separate provision for regional security, requiring member states to work towards the maintenance of peace, stability and security.

In July 1990 ECOWAS ministers attempted to mediate in civil conflict in Liberia. In August an ECOWAS Cease-fire Monitoring Group (ECOMOG—initially comprising about 4,000 troops from The Gambia, Ghana, Guinea, Nigeria and Sierra Leone) was dispatched to Liberia in an attempt to enforce a cease-fire between the rival factions there, to restore public order, and to establish an interim government, until elections could be held. In November a temporary cease-fire was agreed by the protagonists in Liberia, and an interim president was installed by ECOMOG. Following the signature of a new cease-fire agreement a national conference, organized by ECOWAS in March 1991, established a temporary government, pending elections to be held in early 1992. In June 1991 ECOWAS established a committee (initially comprising representatives of five member states, later expanded to nine) to co-ordinate the peace negotiations. In September, at a meeting in Yamoussoukro, Côte d'Ivoire, held under the aegis of the ECOWAS committee, two of the rival factions in Liberia agreed to encamp their troops in designated areas and to disarm under ECOMOG supervision. During the period preceding the proposed elections, ECOMOG was to occupy Liberian air and sea ports, and create a 'buffer zone' along the country's border with Sierra Leone. By September 1992, however, ECOMOG had been unable either to effect the disarmament of two of the principal military factions, the National Patriotic Front of Liberia (NPFL) and the United Liberation Movement of Liberia for Democracy (ULIMO), or to occupy positions in substantial areas of the country, as a result of resistance on the part of the NPFL. The proposed elections were consequently postponed indefinitely.

In October 1992 ECOMOG began offensive action against NPFL positions, with a campaign of aerial bombardment. In November ECOWAS imposed sanctions on the NPFL's territory, comprising a land, sea and air blockade, in response to the Front's refusal to comply with the Yamoussoukro accord of October 1991. In April 1993 ECOMOG announced that the disarmament of ULIMO had been completed, amid widespread accusations that ECOMOG had supported ULIMO against the NPFL, and was no longer a neutral force. An ECOWAS-brokered cease-fire agreement was signed in Cotonou, Benin, in late July, and took effect on 1 August. Under the agreement a neutral transitional government was to be formed, and there was to be a disarming of troops prior to the holding of fair and free elections, scheduled to take place in February 1994. In addition, ECOMOG was to be expanded. In September 1993 a 300-member UN observer mission (UNOMIL) was established in Liberia to work alongside ECOMOG in monitoring the disarmament process, as well as to verify the impartiality of ECOMOG. In March 1994 a transitional executive council was installed (elections now were to be conducted in September); however, continued fighting made the prospect of conducting elections increasingly untenable.

In September 1994 leaders of the country's main military factions, having negotiated with representatives of ECOWAS, the Organization of African Unity (OAU, q.v.) and the UN, signed an amendment to the Cotonou Agreement in Akosombo, Ghana. The agreement provided for a new five-member Council of State, in the context of a cease-fire, as a replacement to the expired interim executive authority, and established a new timetable for democratic elections. Negotiations for a peace settlement recommenced in November, in order to pursue the Akosombo agreement, with delegates from Liberia's six main armed factions, the OAU, the UN and countries constituting ECOWAS' Committee of Nine. In late December a new peace accord was signed by the main conflicting parties in Accra, Ghana. However, in early 1995 peace negotiations, conducted under ECOWAS auspices, collapsed, owing to disagreement on the composition of a new Council of State. In May, in an attempt to ease the political deadlock, ECOWAS heads of state and of government met leaders of the six main warring factions. The meeting, which was convened in Abuja, Nigeria, resolved that a greater commitment to the cease-fire and disarmament process needed to be demonstrated by all parties before the Council of State could be established. Under continuing pressure from the international community, the leaders of the Liberian factions signed a new peace accord, in Abuja, in August. This political development led to renewed efforts on the part of ECOWAS countries to strengthen ECOMOG. In September Burkina Faso agreed to send troops to join ECOMOG, and in October Nigeria, Ghana and Guinea pledged troop contributions to increase the force strength from 7,268 to 12,000. In accordance with the peace agreement, ECOMOG forces, with UNOMIL, were to be deployed throughout Liberia and along its borders to prevent the flow of arms into the country and to monitor the disarmament of the warring parties. In December an attack on ECOMOG troops, by a dissident ULIMO faction, disrupted the deployment of the multinational forces and the disarmament process, which was scheduled to commence in mid-January 1996. At least 16 members of the peace-keeping force were killed in the fighting that ensued. Clashes between ECOMOG and the ULIMO–J forces continued in the west of the country in late December 1995 and early January 1996, during which time 130 Nigerian members of ECOMOG were held hostage. In April, following a series of violations of the cease-fire, serious hostilities erupted in the Liberian capital, Monrovia, between government forces and dissident troops (see chapter on Liberia). An initial agreement to end the fighting, negotiated under ECOWAS auspices, was unsuccessful; however, it secured the release of several civilians and soldiers who had been taken hostage during the civil disruption. Later in April a further cease-fire agreement was concluded, under the aegis of the US Government, the UN and ECOWAS. In May ministers of foreign affairs of the countries constituting the ECOWAS Committee of Nine convened, in Accra, to consider the future of the peace process in Liberia. The Committee advocated that all armed factions be withdrawn from Monrovia and that ECOMOG troops be deployed throughout the capital in order to re-establish the city's 'safe-haven' status. According to the Committee's demands, all property, armaments and equipment seized unlawfully from civilians, ECOMOG and other international organizations during the fighting were to be returned, while efforts to disarm the warring factions and to pursue the restoration of democracy in the country were to be resumed. At the end of May the deployment of ECOMOG troops was initiated. In August a new cease-fire accord was signed by the leaders of the principal factions in Liberia, having been negotiated by the newly-appointed ECOWAS Chairman, President Abacha of Nigeria. The revised Abuja agreement envisaged the completion of the disarmament process by the end of January 1997, with elections to be held in May. The disarmament process began in late November 1996, and by the end of January 1997 ECOMOG confirmed that 23,000 of the targeted 30,000-35,000 soldiers had been disarmed (the original estimate of 60,000 troops having been revised, disputed by both faction leaders and ECOMOG officials once movement between factions was taken into account). The deadline for disarmament was extended by seven days, during which time a further 1,500 soldiers were reported to have been disarmed. However, vigilante attacks by remaining armed faction fighters continued and were condemned by the ECOMOG commander. In February, at the end of a meeting of the Committee of Nine, it was announced that presidential and legislative elections would be held on 30 May. Chief Tom Ikimi, the Chairman of the Committee, stated that ECOMOG would withdraw from Liberia six months after the election date, until which time it had proposed to offer security for the incoming government and to provide training for a new unified Liberian army, which would assume ECOMOG's duties on its departure. The Committee also agreed, in consultation with the Council of State, to replace the existing Electoral Commission with a new Commission comprising seven members, to reflect all aspects of Liberian society. Four members were to be civilians while the remaining members were to represent the three main factions: the NPFL, the Liberia Peace Council (LPC) and ULIMO. The Chairman would be selected from among the seven, in consultation with ECOWAS, which along with the UN and the OAU, would act as a 'technical adviser' to the Commission. In May elections were rescheduled to be held on 19 July, in order to allow sufficient time for planning, and for the repatriation of refugees wishing to vote and the registration of voters. ECOMOG deployed additional troops, who were joined by other international observers in ensuring that the elections were conducted in the necessary conditions of security. In early August several ECOWAS leaders celebrated the democratic transition of power in Liberia at the inauguration of Charles Taylor (formerly leader of the NPFL) as the newly-elected President. Some 11,000 ECOMOG troops were to remain in Liberia until early February 1998 in order to oversee the completion of the disarmament process.

On 25 May 1997 the democratically elected Sierra Leonean leader, President Ahmed Tejan Kabbah, was overthrown by a military coup involving officers of the national army and Revolutionary United Front (RUF) rebels. Nigerian forces based in Sierra Leone as part of a bilateral defence pact attempted to restore constitutional order. Their numbers were strengthened by the arrival of more than 700 Nigerian soldiers and two naval vessels which had been serving under the ECOMOG mandate in neighbouring Liberia. While the Nigerian Government insisted that the additional troops were acting as part of an ECOMOG operation, many commentators criticized the involvement of ECOMOG personnel in a Nigerian unilateral initiative, which they alleged had contradicted the humanitarian nature of the force's mandate. In early June the intervention of ECOMOG was supported by the UN and the OAU as well as the deposed President of Sierra Leone. On 2 June a naval bombardment of Freetown was launched from Nigerian naval vessels. At the end of that month ECOWAS ministers of foreign affairs convened in Conakry, Guinea, in an extraordinary meeting to consider the developments in Sierra Leone. The ministers agreed to pursue the objective of restoring a democratic government in Sierra Leone through dialogue and the imposition of economic sanctions. In July a four-member ministerial committee, comprising Côte d'Ivoire, Ghana, Guinea and Nigeria, together with representatives of the OAU, negotiated an agreement with the so-called Armed Forces Revolutionary Council (AFRC) in Sierra Leone to establish an immediate cease-fire and to pursue efforts towards the restoration of constitutional order. In August the ECOWAS Conference of Heads of State and Government reaffirmed the Community's condemnation of the removal of President Kabbah and officially endorsed a series of punitive measures against the AFRC authorities in order to accelerate the restoration of democratic government. The Conference mandated ECOMOG to maintain and monitor the cease-fire and to prevent all goods, excepting essential humanitarian supplies, from entering that country. It was also agreed that the committee on Sierra Leone include Liberia and be convened at the level of heads of state. In October the UN Security Council imposed an embargo on the sale or supply of armaments to Sierra Leone and authorized ECOWAS to ensure implementation of these measures. In September ECOMOG forces fired on container ships in the port of Freetown, which were suspected of violating the economic embargo. Subsequently, clashes occurred between ECOMOG troops and AFRC/RUF soldiers, in particular around the area of Freetown's international airport which had been seized by ECOMOG; further ECOMOG air attacks against commercial and military targets were also conducted, with the aim of upholding the international sanctions and in self-defence. Despite the escalation in hostilities, the Committee of Five pursued negotiations with the military authorities, and at the end of October both sides signed a peace agreement, in Conakry, Guinea, providing for the reinstatement of Kabbah's Government by April 1998, an immediate end to all fighting and the disarmament, demobilization and reintegration of all combatants under the supervision of a disarmament committee comprising representatives of ECOMOG, the military authorities and local forces loyal to former President Kabbah. In November 1997, however, the peace process was undermined by reports that ECOMOG forces had violated the cease-fire agreement following a series of air raids on Freetown, which ECOMOG claimed to have been in retaliation for attacks by AFRC/RUF-operated anti-aircraft equipment, and a demand by the AFRC authorities that the Nigerian contingent of ECOMOG leave the country. In mid-February 1998, following a series of offensive attacks against forces loyal to the military authorities, ECOMOG assumed control of Freetown and arrested several members of the AFRC/RUC regime.

In December 1997 an extraordinary meeting of ECOWAS heads of state and government was convened in Lomé, Togo, to consider the future stability and security of the region. It was agreed that a permanent mechanism be established for conflict prevention and the maintenance of peace. ECOWAS leaders also reaffirmed their commitment to pursuing dialogue to prevent conflicts, co-operating in the early deployment of peace-keeping forces and implementing measures to counter trans-border crime and the illegal trafficking of armaments and drugs. At the meeting ECOWAS leaders acknowledged ECOMOG's role in restoring constitutional order in Liberia and expressed their appreciation of the force's current efforts in Sierra Leone.

RURAL WATER RESOURCES

The ECOWAS programme for the development of village and pastoral water resources involves the creation of 3,200 water points throughout the region: 200 water points per member state. During the first phase of the programme (1992–96) attention was to be concentrated on the needs of the 10 member states most seriously affected or threatened by drought and desertification (Burkina Faso, Cape Verde, Guinea, Guinea Bissau, Mali, Mauritania, Niger, Nigeria, Senegal and Togo). The first phase of the programme was expected to cost US $40.7m., with international donors to provide the necessary resources.

AGRICULTURE AND FISHING

An Agricultural Development Strategy was adopted in 1982, aiming at sub-regional self-sufficiency by the year 2000. The strategy included plans for selecting seeds and cattle species, and called for solidarity among member states during international commodity negotiations. Seven seed selection and multiplication centres and eight livestock-breeding centres were designated in 1984.

In February 1993 ECOWAS signed an agreement with the EC concerning a grant of US $9.6m. to help with the development of the fishing industry in the ECOWAS region over a five-year period.

In November 1995 an agro-industrial forum, jointly organized by ECOWAS and the European Union, was held in Dakar, Senegal. The forum aimed to facilitate co-operation between companies in the two regions, to develop the agro-industrial sector in west Africa and to promote business opportunities.

SOCIAL PROGRAMME

Four organizations have been established within ECOWAS by the Executive Secretariat: the Organization of Trade Unions of West Africa, which held its first meeting in 1984; the West African Youth Association; the West African Universities' Association; and the West Africa Women's Association (whose statutes were approved by a meeting of ministers of social affairs in May 1987). Regional sports competitions are held annually. In 1987 ECOWAS member states agreed to establish a West African Health Organization.

INFORMATION AND MEDIA

In March 1990 ECOWAS ministers of information formulated a policy on the dissemination of information about ECOWAS throughout the region and the appraisal of attitudes of its population towards the Community. The ministers established a new information commission. In November 1991 a conference on press communication and African integration, organized by ECOWAS, recommended the creation of an ECOWAS press card, judicial safeguards to protect journalists, training programmes for journalists and the establishment of a regional documentation centre and data bank. In November 1994 the commission of social and cultural affairs, meeting in Lagos, Nigeria, endorsed a series of measures to promote west African integration. These included special radio, television and newspaper features, sporting events and other competitions or rallies.

FINANCE

ECOWAS is financed by contributions from member states, although there is a poor record of punctual payment of dues, which has hampered the work of the Secretariat. Arrears in contributions to the Secretariat were reported to total US $38.6m. at August 1997. Under the revised treaty, ECOWAS was to receive revenue from a community tax, based on the total value of imports from member countries. In July 1996 the summit meeting approved a protocol on a community levy, providing for the imposition of a 0.5% tax on the value of imports from a third country. Member states were requested to ratify the protocol, in order to enable its application with effect from 1 January 1997. In August 1997 the Conference of Heads of State and Government determined that the community levy should replace budgetary contributions as the organization's principal source of finance, although it had yet to be implemented by member states.

The 1993 budget amounted to 4,135m. francs CFA (approximately US $14.9m.).

EUROPEAN BANK FOR RECONSTRUCTION AND DEVELOPMENT—EBRD

Address: One Exchange Square, 175 Bishopsgate, London, EC2A 2EH, England.

Telephone: (171) 338-6000; **telex:** 8812161; **fax:** (171) 338-6100; **internet:** http://www.ebrd.com.

The EBRD was founded in May 1990 and inaugurated in April 1991. Its object is to contribute to the progress and the economic reconstruction of the countries of central and eastern Europe which undertake to respect and put into practice the principles of multi-party democracy, the rule of law, respect for human rights and a market economy.

MEMBERS

Countries of Operations:

Albania
Armenia
Azerbaijan
Bosnia and Herzegovina
Belarus
Bulgaria
Croatia
Czech Republic
Estonia
Georgia
Hungary
Kazakhstan
Kyrgyzstan
Latvia
Lithuania
Macedonia, former Yugoslav republic
Moldova
Poland
Romania
Russia
Slovakia
Slovenia
Tajikistan
Turkmenistan
Ukraine
Uzbekistan

European Union members*:

Austria
Belgium
Denmark
Finland
France
Germany
Greece
Ireland
Italy
Luxembourg
Netherlands
Portugal
Spain
Sweden
United Kingdom

EFTA members:

Iceland
Liechtenstein
Norway
Switzerland

Other countries:

Australia
Canada
Cyprus
Malta
Mexico
Morocco
Egypt
Israel
Japan
Republic of Korea
New Zealand
Turkey
USA

* The European Commission and the European Investment Bank are also shareholder members in their own right.

Organization

(February 1998)

BOARD OF GOVERNORS

The Board of Governors, representing all the shareholders of the Bank, is the highest authority of the EBRD.

BOARD OF DIRECTORS

There are 23 directors (each of whom has an alternate), who are responsible for the organization and operations of the EBRD. The Chairman of the Board of Directors is the President of the Bank.

ADMINISTRATION

The EBRD's operations are conducted by its Banking Department, headed by the First Vice-President. The other departments are: Finance; Personnel and administration; Project evaluation; Internal audit; Communications; and Offices of the Secretary-General, the General Counsel and the Chief Economist. A structure of country teams, industry teams and operations support units oversee the implementation of projects. The EBRD has 27 Resident Offices or other offices in 24 of its countries of operations.

President: (vacant).

First Vice-President: CHARLES FRANK (USA).

Activities

The Bank's authorized capital is ECU 10,000m. (approximately US $11,670m.), of which ECU 3,000m. was to be paid-in. In April 1996 EBRD shareholders, meeting in Sofia, Bulgaria, agreed to double the Bank's capital to ECU 20,000m. in order to enable the Bank to continue, and to enhance, its lending programme. It was agreed that 22.5% of the ECU 10,000m. of new resources, was to be paid-up, with the remainder as 'callable' shares. Contributions were to be paid over a 13-year period from April 1998.

The Bank aims to assist the transition of the economies of central and eastern European countries towards a market economy system, and to encourage private enterprise. The Agreement establishing the EBRD specifies that 60% of its lending should be for the private sector. The Bank helps the beneficiaries to undertake structural and sectoral reforms, including the dismantling of monopolies, decentralization, and privatization of state enterprises, so as to enable these countries to become fully integrated in the international economy. To this end, the Bank promotes the establishment and improvement of activities of a productive, competitive and private nature, particularly small and medium-sized enterprises. It mobilizes national and foreign capital, together with experienced management teams, and helps to develop an appropriate legal framework to support a market-orientated economy. The Bank provides extensive financial services, including loans, equity and guarantees. The Bank's founding Agreement specifies that all operations were to be undertaken in the context of promoting environmentally sound and sustainable development. It undertakes environmental audits and impact assessments in areas of particular concern, which enable the Bank to incorporate environmental action plans into any project approved for funding.

At the Bank's annual meeting in April 1993 the Board of Governors established an audit committee to investigate the Bank's financial operations. The committee's report, published in July, was critical of inefficient lending procedures and the extravagant internal use of funds. The Bank's President, Jacques Attali, announced his resignation in late June, in response to increasing criticism, but left office immediately after the publication of the report. The new President, Jacques de Larosière, was elected by the Bank's shareholders in August and took office at the end of September. De Larosière imposed administrative cost-reduction measures and initiated organizational changes in order to improve the Bank's effectiveness. A Task Force was established to consider the Bank's medium-term outlook. The group's report, which was approved by the Board of Directors in early 1994, proposed the following issues as medium-term operational priorities: focus on private-sector development; the EBRD to be active in all countries of operations; the need to reach local private enterprises; the importance of financial intermediaries; and a more active approach towards equity investment. These guidelines were endorsed at the EBRD's annual meeting, convened in St Petersburg, Russia, in April.

In the year ending 31 December 1996 the EBRD approved ECU 2,827m. for 119 projects, making a cumulative total of ECU 9,962m. approved for 450 projects since it commenced operations. During 1996 32% of all project financing approved was allocated to the financial and business sector, supporting privatizations or restructuring of the sector, the development of institutions and the expansion of trade financing services. The other main areas of project financing in the year were: the transport sector (17%), which included loans to upgrade railways in Romania, Russia and Poland, the rehabilitation and maintenance of the road network in Romania, and an emergency reconstruction project in Bosnia and Herzegovina; manufacturing (16%), mainly for the modernization of enterprises and supporting the process of privatization; and energy and power generation (16%). EBRD has helped to finance the commercial exploitation of petroleum in western Siberia, Russia, and supported the industry in other countries, while promoting environmental awareness throughout the energy sector.

A high priority is given to attracting external finance for Bank-sponsored projects, in particular in countries at advanced stages of transition, from governments, international financial institutions, commercial banks and export credit agencies. In 1996 those sources provided co-financing funds amounting to ECU 854m. for 52 projects. The EBRD's Technical Co-operation Funds Programme (TCFP) aims to facilitate access to the Bank's capital resources for countries of operations by providing support for project preparation, project implementation and institutional development. By December 1996 the TCFP had contributed ECU 101m. to support 154 projects (for which Bank financing totalled ECU 3,700m.). Resources for technical co-operation originate from regular TCFP contributions, specific agreements and contributions to Special Funds. The Baltic Investment Programme, which is administered by Nordic countries, consists of two special funds to co-finance investment and technical assistance projects in the private sectors of Baltic states. The Funds are open to contributions from all EBRD member states. The Russia Small Business Special Funds, established in October 1993, support local small- and medium-sized enterprises through similar investment and technical co-operation activities. Other financing mechanisms that the EBRD uses to address the needs of the region include Regional Venture Funds, which invest equity in privatized companies, in particular in Russia, and provide relevant management assistance, and the Central European Agency Lines, which disburse lines of credit to small-scale projects through local intermediaries. A TurnAround Management Programme (TAM) provides practical assistance to senior managers of industrial enterprises to facilitate the expansion of businesses in a market economy.

In February 1993 the Group of Seven industrialized countries officially proposed the establishment of a Nuclear Safety Account (NSA) to fund a multilateral programme of action for the improvement of safety in nuclear power plants of the former eastern bloc. The NSA, which was to be established and administered by the EBRD, was approved by the Bank's Board of Directors in March 1993. At 31 December 1996 14 countries and the European Commission had pledged funds amounting to ECU 257.4m. to the NSA. At that time projects to improve plants in Bulgaria, Lithuania, Russia and Ukraine were ongoing.

PROJECT FINANCING APPROVED BY SECTOR

	1996		Cumulative to 31 Dec. 1996	
	Number	Amount (ECU million)	Number	Amount (ECU million)
Agriculture, forestry, fishing	3	23	19	229
CEALs, co-financing lines and RVFs*	—	—	4	152
Commerce and tourism	4	135	17	259
Community/ social services	6	130	15	185
Construction	—	—	1	4
Energy/ power generation	10	447	37	1,295
Extractive industries	4	111	15	561
Finance and business	55	906	183	3,295
Manufacturing	21	447	74	1,284
Telecommunications	4	142	29	863
Transport	12	486	57	1,836
Total	119	2,827	450	9,962

* Central European Agency Lines, Regional Venture Funds.

PROJECT FINANCING APPROVED BY COUNTRY

	1996		Cumulative to 31 Dec. 1996	
	Number	Amount (ECU million)	Number	Amount (ECU million)
Albania	1	3	8	61
Armenia	—	—	3	77
Azerbaijan	1	11	4	81
Belarus	—	—	6	164
Bosnia and Herzegovina	1	27	1	27
Bulgaria	3	21	18	211
Croatia	8	157	15	339
Czech Republic	3	50	21	372
Estonia	4	25	15	149
Georgia	2	14	4	38
Hungary	7	133	47	1,072
Kazakhstan	2	73	3	172
Kyrgyzstan	1	2	6	88
Latvia	6	61	13	170
Lithuania	4	40	12	170
Macedonia, former Yugoslav republic	2	42	9	147
Moldova	1	3	8	109
Poland	8	234	49	934
Romania	9	252	30	831
Russia	30	918	84	2,495
Slovakia	5	94	19	440
Slovenia	2	36	16	326
Tajikistan	1	7	1	7
Turkmenistan	—	—	2	53
Ukraine	3	115	18	411
Uzbekistan	4	123	10	308
Regional	11	387	26	710
Total	119	2,827	450	9,962

Source: EBRD, *Annual Report 1996*.

PUBLICATIONS

Annual Report.

Environments in Transition (2 a year).

Transition Report (annual).

EUROPEAN FREE TRADE ASSOCIATION—EFTA

Address: 9-11 rue de Varembé, 1211 Geneva 20, Switzerland.

Telephone: (22) 7491111; **fax:** (22) 7339291.

Established in 1960, EFTA aimed to bring about free trade in industrial goods and to contribute to the liberalization and expansion of world trade. EFTA now serves as the structure through which three of its members participate in the European Economic Area (EEA), together with the 15 member states of the European Union (q.v.).

MEMBERS

Iceland	Norway
Liechtenstein	Switzerland

Three founder members subsequently left EFTA and joined the European Community (EC): Denmark (1973), the United Kingdom (1973) and Portugal (1986). Finland, formerly an associate member of EFTA, became a full member on 1 January 1986. Liechtenstein joined EFTA as a full member in September 1991, having hitherto had associate status through its customs union with Switzerland. Austria, Sweden (both founder members) and Finland left the Association on 31 December 1994 to become members of the European Union (as the EC had been restyled).

Organization

(January 1998)

EFTA COUNCIL

The Council is EFTA's governing body. The Chair is held for six months by each country in turn. The Council's decisions are binding on member states and must be unanimous. The Council is assisted by a substructure of committees and working groups.

EFTA STANDING COMMITTEES

Board of Auditors.

Budget Committee.

Committee of Members of Parliament of the EFTA Countries.

Committee of Origin and Customs Experts.

Committee on Technical Barriers to Trade.

Committee of Third Country Relations.

Committee of Trade Experts.

Consultative Committee.

Economic Committee.

Steering Committee of the Portuguese Fund.

MATTERS RELATED TO THE EEA

The treaty establishing the EEA, which entered into force in 1994 (see below), provided for an institutional structure to enhance its operations. An EEA Council, comprising ministers of all signatory countries, provides policy direction, while a Joint Committee, comprising representatives of the EFTA states in the EEA, the European Commission and EU member states, is responsible for the day-to-day management of EEA matters. A Standing Committee serves as the forum of consultation within EFTA, consisting of representatives from Iceland, Liechtenstein and Norway and observers from Switzerland. It is assisted by five Subcommittees and a number of Working Groups. An independent EFTA Surveillance Authority and an EFTA Court have also been established to provide judicial control.

SECRETARIAT

Address: 74 rue de Trèves, 1040 Brussels, Belgium.

Telephone: (2) 286-17-11; **fax:** (2) 286-17-50; **e-mail:** efta-mailbox@secrbru.efta.be; **internet:** http://www.efta.be.

Secretary-General: KJARTAN JÓHANNSSON (Iceland).

Deputy Secretaries-General: ALDO MATTEUCCI (Switzerland); GUTTORM VIK (Norway).

Activities

The creation of a single market including all the countries in Western Europe was the ultimate objective of EFTA when it was created in 1960. Member states were, however, not ready or able to accept the far-reaching political and economic implications of joining the EC, which was established in 1958. EFTA's first target, the creation of free trade in industrial goods between its members, was achieved by the end of 1966. By 1991 tariffs or import duties had been removed on all imports except agricultural products.

In 1972 EFTA member states signed bilateral agreements with the EC, which established free trade in most industrial goods between them from 1 July 1977. The last restrictions on free industrial trade were abolished from 1 January 1984. In April of that year ministers from all EFTA and EC member countries agreed on general guidelines for developing the EFTA-EC relationship. Their Declaration (known as the Luxembourg Declaration) recommended intensified efforts to promote the free movement of goods between their countries, and closer co-operation in a number of other fields, including research and development. In March 1989 the EFTA heads of government issued a declaration reaffirming their commitment to establish a European Economic Area (EEA), consisting of all the member states of EFTA and the EC. Formal negotiations on the establishment of the EEA commenced in June 1990, and the Agreement was signed in Oporto, Portugal, in May 1992. In December a Swiss referendum voted to oppose ratification of the EEA treaty. The ministers of trade of the remaining 18 member countries, however, signed an adjustment protocol in March 1993, allowing the EEA to be established without Switzerland. The EEA entered into force on 1 January 1994. Liechtenstein, which had been unable to become a member of the EEA as a result of its close legal and economic ties with Switzerland, joined the EEA on 1 May 1995, having amended its customs union agreement and secured the support of the majority of its population in a national referendum. The EEA Agreement provided for the removal of all restrictions on the movement of goods, persons, services and capital within the area, effectively extending the internal market of the EU to the three EFTA countries within the EEA. In addition, the Agreement provided for co-operation in areas such as the environment, social policy, education and training, tourism, culture, consumer protection and small- and medium-sized enterprises. To maintain homogeneity within the EEA, the Agreement is amended on a continuous basis to ensure that EU legislation is extended to the EFTA EEA grouping.

Although Portugal left EFTA in 1985, EFTA decided to maintain an industrial development fund for that country, which had been established in 1976, for the 25-year period originally foreseen. Declarations on co-operation were signed with Czechoslovakia, Hungary and Poland in June 1990; with Bulgaria, Estonia, Latvia, Lithuania and Romania in December 1991; with Slovenia in May 1992; with Albania in December 1992; with Egypt, Morocco and Tunisia in December 1995; with the former Yugoslav republic of Macedonia in March 1996; with the Palestine Liberation Organization in December 1996; and with Jordan and Lebanon in June 1997. Free-trade agreements have also been concluded with Turkey in December 1991; with Czechoslovakia in March 1992 (with protocols on succession with the Czech Republic and Slovakia in April 1993); with Israel in September 1992; with Poland and Romania in December 1992; and with Bulgaria and Hungary in March 1993. In July 1995 EFTA and Slovenia concluded a trade agreement covering industrial goods, processed agricultural products, and fish. Similar agreements were concluded with Estonia, Latvia and Lithuania in December, and with Morocco (which was granted a 12-year transitional period to phase out customs duties) in June 1997.

FINANCE

Net budget for 1997: 18.1m. Swiss francs.

PUBLICATIONS

EFTA Annual Report.

Factsheets, legal documents.

EUROPEAN SPACE AGENCY—ESA

Address: 8–10 rue Mario Nikis, 75738 Paris Cédex 15, France.

Telephone: 1-42-73-76-54; **telex:** 202746; **fax:** 1-42-73-75-60; **internet:** http://www.esa.int.

ESA was established in 1975 to provide for, and to promote, European co-operation in space research and technology, and their applications, for exclusively peaceful purposes. It replaced the European Space Research Organisation and the European Launcher Development Organisation (both founded in 1962).

MEMBERS*

Austria	Italy
Belgium	Netherlands
Denmark	Norway
Finland	Spain
France	Sweden
Germany	Switzerland
Ireland	United Kingdom

* Canada has signed an agreement for close co-operation with ESA, including representation on the ESA Council.

Organization

(January 1998)

Director-General: Antonio Rodotà (Italy).

COUNCIL

The Council is composed of representatives of all member states. It is responsible for formulating policy. In March 1997 the Council was convened at ministerial level and adopted a new industrial policy to strengthen ESA's competitiveness and its capacity for industrial innovation.

Chairman: Hugo Parr (Norway).

PROGRAMME BOARDS AND COMMITTEES

The Council is assisted in its work by five specialized Programme Boards, which oversee the management of the following ESA activities: Communication Satellite Programmes; Earth Observation; Microgravity; Ariane Launcher; and Manned Spaceflight. The other principal bodies of the ESA administrative structure are the Committees for Long-term Space Policy, Administration and Finance, Industrial Policy, Science Programme and International Relations.

ESA CENTRES

European Space Research and Technology Centre—ESTEC: Noordwijk, Netherlands. ESA's principal technical establishment, at which the majority of project teams are based, together with the space science department and the technological research and support engineers; provides the appropriate testing and laboratory facilities.

European Space Operations Centre—ESOC: Darmstadt, Germany. Responsible for all satellite operations and the corresponding ground facilities and communications networks.

European Space Research Institute—ESRIN: Frascati, Italy. Responsible for the corporate exploitation of Earth observation data from space.

European Astronaut Centre—EAC: Porz-Wahn, Germany. Co-ordinates all European astronaut activities, including the training of astronauts. In 1996 the Centre began to develop computer-based training courses for the ESA aspects of the International Space Station.

ESA also helps to maintain the Space Centre at Kourou, French Guiana, which is used for the Ariane launchers.

Activities

ESA's tasks are to define and put into effect a long-term European space policy of scientific research and technological development and to encourage all members to co-ordinate their national programmes with those of ESA to ensure that Europe maintains a competitive position in the field of space technology. ESA's basic activities cover studies on future projects, technological research, shared technical investments, information systems and training programmes. These, and the science programme, are mandatory activities to which all members must contribute; other programmes are optional and members may determine their own level of participation.

ESA is committed to pursuing international co-operation to achieve its objectives of developing the peaceful applications of space technology. ESA works closely with both the US National Aeronautics and Space Administration (NASA) and the Russian Space Agency. More recently it has developed a co-operative relationship with Japan, in particular in data relay satellites and the exchange of materials for the International Space Station. ESA has also concluded co-operation agreements with the Czech Republic, Greece, Hungary, Poland and Romania, providing for technical training and joint projects in the field of space science, Earth observation and telecommunications. ESA assists other developing and transitional countries to expand their space activities. It works closely with other international organizations, in particular the European Union and EUMETSAT (q.v.). ESA has observer status with the UN Committee on the Peaceful Uses of Outer Space and co-operates closely with the UN's Office of Outer Space Affairs, in particular through the organization of a training and fellowship programme.

SCIENCE

The first European scientific space programmes were undertaken under the aegis of ESRO, which launched seven satellites during 1968–72. The science programmes are mandatory activities of the Agency and form the basis of co-operation between member states. The first astronomical satellite (COS–B) was launched by ESA in August 1975. By early 1997 ESA had launched 12 scientific satellites and probes, among the most successful being the Giotto probe, launched in 1985 to study the composition of Halley's comet and reactivated in 1990 to observe the Grigg-Skjellerup comet in July 1992, and Hipparcos, which, between 1989 and 1993, determined the precise astronomic positions and distances of more than 1m. stars. In November 1995 ESA launched the Infrared Space Observatory, which has successfully conducted pre-planned scientific studies providing data on galaxy and star formation and on interstellar matter. ESA is collaborating with NASA in the Ulysses space project (a solar polar mission), the Solar and Helispheric Observatory (SOHO), launched in 1995 to study the internal structure of the sun, and the Hubble Space Telescope. In October 1997 the Huygens space probe was launched under the framework of a joint NASA–ESA project (the Cassini/Huygens mission) to study the planet Saturn and its largest moon, Titan. ESA's space missions are an integral part of its long-term science programme, Horizon 2000, which was initiated in 1984. In 1994 a new set of missions was defined, to enable the inclusion of projects using new technologies and participation in future international space activities, which formed the Horizon 2000 Plus extension covering the period 2005–16. Together they are called Horizons 2000. The revised strategy envisaged the introduction of a Small Mission for Advanced Research and Technology (SMART–1) to an asteroid or to the Moon in 2001 and a mission to the planet Mars in 2003.

The main projects being developed under the science programme in 1997 included the X-Ray Multimirror Mission (XMM), scheduled to be launched in late 1999; the relaunch of the Cluster spacecraft and satellites to study structures in the Earth's plasma environment, scheduled for 2000; the launch of the International Gamma Ray Laboratory (INTEGRAL) in 2001; the Rosetta mission for comet analysis, scheduled for 2003; and the launch of the Far Infrared and Submilletric Space Telescope (FIRST), scheduled for 2006.

OBSERVATION OF THE EARTH AND ITS ENVIRONMENT

ESA has contributed to the understanding and monitoring of the Earth's environment through its satellite projects. Since 1977 ESA has launched seven Meteosat spacecraft into geosynchronous orbit, which have provided continuous meteorological data, mainly for the purposes of weather forecasting. The Meteosat systems are financed and owned by EUMETSAT, but were operated by ESA until December 1995. In 1997 ESA was developing, in collaboration with EUMETSAT, a successor to the Meteosat weather satellites, which was scheduled to be operational by 2000.

In 1991 ESA launched the ERS–1 satellite, which carried sophisticated instruments to measure the Earth's surface and its atmosphere. A second ERS satellite was launched in April 1995 with the specific purpose of measuring the stratospheric and tropospheric ozone. An enhanced space mission (ENVISAT) was scheduled to assume the functions of the ERS project in 1999. It was also expected to provide greater information on the impact of human activities on the Earth's atmosphere, and land and coastal processes, and to monitor exceptional natural events, such as volcanic eruptions.

TELECOMMUNICATIONS

ESA commenced the development of communications satellites in 1968. These have since become the largest markets for space use and have transformed global communications, with more than 100 satellites circling the Earth for the purposes of telecommunications. The main series of operational satellites developed by ESA are the European Communications Satellites (ECS), based on the original orbital test satellite and used by EUTELSAT, and the Maritime Communications Satellites (MARECS), which have been leased for operations to INMARSAT (q.v.).

In 1989 ESA launched an experimental civilian telecommunications satellite, Olympus, to develop and demonstrate new broadcasting services. An Advanced Relay and Technology Mission Satellite (ARTEMIS) has been developed by ESA to test and operate new telecommunications techniques, and in particular to enable the relay of information directly between satellites. ARTEMIS was scheduled to be launched in 2000. In 1997 ESA, together with the EU and EUROCONTROL (q.v.), was implementing a satellite-based navigation system to be used for civilian aircraft and maritime services, similar to the two existing systems operational for military use. ESA was also working with the EU and representatives of the private sector to enhance the region's role in the development of electronic media infrastructure to meet the expanding global demand. ESA's broad objectives in this area were to expand and demonstrate the technological base of Europe's space industry in the fields of telecommunications, mobile communications, satellite navigation, multimedia and inter-satellite links, and to enable the industry to acquire a large share of the world market.

SPACE TRANSPORT SYSTEMS

In 1973 several European Governments adopted a programme to ensure that the future ESA had independent access to space, and determined to co-ordinate knowledge gained through national programmes to develop a space launcher. The resulting Ariane rocket was first launched in December 1979. The project, which incorporated four different launchers during the 1980s, subsequently became an essential element of ESA's programme activities and, furthermore, developed a successful commercial role in placing satellites into orbit. Since 1985 ESA has worked to develop Ariane–5, which was to be prototype for future launchers. In June 1996 the first qualification Ariane–5 rocket exploded on its inaugural flight, delaying the development project. The second launch was successfully conducted in October 1997. While ESA aims to pursue the development and exploitation of Ariane–5 during the early 2000s, it has already initiated preparation of a future generation launcher under the framework of its Future Space Transportation Investigation Programme (FESTIP).

MANNED SPACEFLIGHT AND MICROGRAVITY

European astronauts and scientists have gained access to space through Spacelab, which ESA developed and contributed as part of the US Space Shuttle Programme, and through joint missions on the Russian space station, Mir. The Spacelab project enabled ESA to conduct research in life and material sciences under microgravity conditions. In 1992 ESA launched a new automatic satellite, the European Retrievable Carrier (EURECA), to pursue microgravity studies. ESA has an ongoing programme of research in this field, and in 1997 initiated a new project to develop the facilities required for microgravity experiments to be conducted on the Columbus Orbiting Facility of the planned International Space Station (initiated by the US Government in 1984, and since developed as a joint project between five partners—Canada, Europe, Japan, Russia and the USA). The Facility was scheduled to be launched in 2002. ESA also envisages the development and launch of an Automated Transfer Vehicle to provide logistical support to the Space Station and, together with NASA, is pursuing studies for the possible development of a Crew Rescue Vehicle to ferry astronauts from the Station.

FINANCE

All member states contribute to ESA's mandatory programme activities, on a scale based on their national income, and are free to decide on their level of commitment in optional programmes, such as telecommunications, the Ariane project and future space station and platform projects. The 1998 budget totalled about ECU 2,600m., of which some ECU 630m. (24%) was for Earth Observation; ECU 574m. (22%) for launchers; ECU 370m. (14%) for manned spaceflight; and ECU 352m. (14%) for the science programme.

PUBLICATIONS

ESA Annual Report.

ECSL News (quarterly).

ESA Bulletin (quarterly).

Earth Observation Quarterly.

Microgravity News (3 a year).

Preparing for the Future (quarterly).

Reaching for the Skies (quarterly).

Scientific and technical reports, brochures, training manuals, conference proceedings.

THE EUROPEAN UNION—EU

No final decision has been made on a headquarters for the Union. Meetings of the principal organs take place in Brussels, Luxembourg and Strasbourg.

The European Coal and Steel Community (ECSC) was created by a treaty signed in Paris on 18 April 1951 (effective from 25 July 1952) to pool the coal and steel production of the six original members (see below). It was seen as a first step towards a united Europe. The European Economic Community (EEC) and European Atomic Energy Community (Euratom) were established by separate treaties signed in Rome on 25 March 1957 (effective from 1 January 1958), the former to create a common market and to approximate economic policies, the latter to promote growth in nuclear industries. The common institutions of the three Communities were established by a treaty signed in Brussels on 8 April 1965 (effective from 1 July 1967).

The EEC was formally changed to the European Community (EC) under the Treaty on European Union (effective from 1 November 1993), although in practice the term EC had been used for several years to describe the three Communities together. The new Treaty established a European Union (EU), which introduced citizenship thereof and aimed to increase intergovernmental co-operation in economic and monetary affairs; to establish a common foreign and security policy; and to introduce co-operation in justice and home affairs. The EU was placed under the supervision of the European Council (comprising Heads of State or Government of member countries), while the EC continued to exist, having competence in matters relating to the Treaty of Rome and its amendments.

MEMBERS

Austria	Germany*	Netherlands*
Belgium*	Greece	Portugal
Denmark	Ireland	Spain
Finland	Italy*	Sweden
France*	Luxembourg*	United Kingdom

* Original members. Denmark, Ireland and the United Kingdom joined on 1 January 1973, and Greece on 1 January 1981. In a referendum held in February 1982, the inhabitants of Greenland voted to end their membership of the Community, entered into when under full Danish rule. Greenland's withdrawal took effect from 1 February 1985. Portugal and Spain became members on 1 January 1986. Following the reunification of Germany in October 1990, the former German Democratic Republic immediately became part of the Community, although a transitional period was to be allowed before certain Community legislation took effect there. Austria, Finland and Sweden became members on 1 January 1995.

PERMANENT REPRESENTATIVES OF MEMBER STATES

Austria: 30 ave de Cortenbergh, 1040 Brussels; tel. (2) 282-11-11; telex 21407; fax (2) 230-79-30; MANFRED SCHEICH.

Belgium: 62 rue Belliard, 1040 Brussels; tel. (2) 233-21-11; fax (2) 233-10-75; FRANS VAN DAELE.

Denmark: 73 rue d'Arlon, 1040 Brussels; tel. (2) 233-08-11; telex 64434; fax (2) 230-93-84; POUL SKYTTE CHRISTOFFERSEN.

Finland: 100 rue de Trèves, 1040 Brussels; tel. (2) 287-84-11; fax (2) 287-84-00; ANTTI SATULI.

France: 14 place de Louvain, 1000 Brussels; tel. (2) 229-82-11; fax (2) 229-82-82; PIERRE DE BOISSIEU.

Germany: 19–21 rue J. de Lalaing, 1040 Brussels; tel. (2) 238-18-11; telex 21745; fax (2) 238-19-78; DIETRICH VON KYAW.

Greece: 25 rue Montoyer, 1040 Brussels; tel. (2) 551-56-11; fax (2) 551-56-51; PAVLOS APOSTOLIDIS.

Ireland: 89–93 rue Froissart, 1040 Brussels; tel. (2) 230-85-80; telex 26730; fax (2) 230-32-03; DENIS O'LEARY.

Italy: 9 rue du Marteau, 1040 Brussels; tel. (2) 220-04-11; fax (2) 219-34-49; LUIGI GUIDOBONO CAVALCHINI GAROFOLO.

Luxembourg: 75 ave de Cortenbergh, 1050 Brussels; tel. (2) 737-56-00; telex 21707; fax (2) 737-56-10; JEAN-JACQUES KASEL.

Netherlands: 48 ave Herrmann Debroux, 1160 Brussels; tel. (2) 679-15-11; fax (2) 679-17-75; BERNHARD R. BOT.

Portugal: 11–13 rue Marie-Thérèse, 1000 Brussels; tel. (2) 227-42-00; fax (2) 218-15-42; JOSÉ GREGÓRIO FARIA QUITERES.

Spain: 52 blvd du Régent, 1000 Brussels; tel. (2) 509-86-11; fax (2) 511-19-40; FRANCISCO JAVIER ELORZA CAVENGT.

Sweden: 30 square de Meeûs, 1000 Brussels; tel. (2) 289-56-11; fax (2) 289-56-00; FRANK BELFRAGE.

United Kingdom: 10 ave D'Auderghem, 1040 Brussels; tel. (2) 287-82-11; telex 24312; fax (2) 287-83-98; Sir STEPHEN WALL.

PERMANENT MISSIONS TO THE EUROPEAN UNION, WITH AMBASSADORS

(January 1998)

Afghanistan: 32 ave Raphaël, 75016 Paris, France; tel. 1-45-27-66-09; fax 1-45-24-46-87; Chargé d'affaires a.i.: DAOUD M. MIR.

Albania: 335 ave Louise, 1050 Brussels; tel. (2) 640-14-22; fax (2) 640-28-58; BASHKIM SELIM TRENOVA.

Algeria: 209 ave Molière, 1050 Brussels; tel. (2) 343-50-78; telex 25266; fax (2) 343-51-68; MISSOUM SBIH.

Andorra: 10 rue de la Montagne, 1000 Brussels; tel. (2) 513-28-06; fax (2) 513-39-34; MERITXELL MATEU I PI.

Angola: 182 rue Franz Merjay, 1180 Brussels; tel. (2) 346-18-80; telex 62635; fax (2) 344-08-94; JOSÉ GUERREIRO ALVES PRIMO

Antigua and Barbuda: 100 rue des Aduatiques, 1040 Brussels; tel. (2) 733-43-28; fax (2) 735-72-37; e-mail ecs.embassies@skynet.be; EDWIN P. J. LAURENT.

Argentina: 225 ave Louise (7e étage), Boîte 2, 1050 Brussels; tel. (2) 648-93-71; telex 23079; fax (2) 648-08-04; JUAN JOSÉ URANGA.

Armenia: 157 rue Franz Merjay, 1060 Brussels; tel. and fax (2) 346-56-67; V. CHITECHIAN.

Australia: 6–8 rue Guimard, 1040 Brussels; tel. (2) 231-05-00; telex 21834; fax (2) 230-68-02; DONALD KENYON.

Bahamas: 10 Chesterfield St, London, W1X 8AH, United Kingdom; tel. (171) 408-4488; fax (171) 499-9937; e-mail bahamas.hicom.lon@cableinet.co.uk; ARTHUR A. FOULKES.

Bangladesh: 29–31 rue Jacques Jordaens, 1050 Brussels; tel. (2) 640-55-00; telex 63189; fax (2) 646-59-98; ASM KHAIRUL ANAM.

Barbados: 78 ave Gén. Lartigue, 1200 Brussels; tel. (2) 732-17-37; fax (2) 732-32-66; MICHAEL I. KING.

Belize: 22 Harcourt House, 19 Cavendish Square, London, W1M 9AD, United Kingdom; tel. (171) 499-9728; fax (171) 491-4139; e-mail xgc19@pipex.dial.com; Dr URSULA H. BARROW.

Benin: 5 ave de l'Observatoire, 1180 Brussels; tel. (2) 374-91-92; telex 24568; fax (2) 375-83-26; ABOUDOU SALIOU.

Bhutan: 17–19 chemin du Champ d'Amier, 1209 Geneva, Switzerland; tel. (22) 7987971; telex 415447; fax (22) 7882593; JIGMI Y. THINLEY.

Bolivia: 176 ave Louise, Boîte 6, 1050 Brussels; tel. (2) 627-00-10; fax (2) 647-47-82; Chargé d'affaires a.i.: HORÁCIO BAZOBERRY.

Bosnia and Herzegovina: 9 rue Paul Lauters, 1050 Brussels; tel. (2) 644-00-47; fax (2) 644-16-98; Chargé d'affaires a.i.: HARIS LUKOVAC.

Botswana: 169 ave de Tervuren, 1150 Brussels; tel. (2) 735-20-70; telex 22849; fax (2) 735-63-18; SASALA CHASALA GEORGE.

Brazil: 350 ave Louise (6e étage), 1050 Brussels; tel. (2) 640-20-40; telex 24676; fax (2) 648-80-40; JORIO DAUSTER MAGALHÃES E SILVA.

Brunei: 238 ave F. D. Roosevelt, 1050 Brussels; tel. (2) 675-08-78; fax (2) 672-93-58; Dato' KASSIM DAUD.

Bulgaria: 7 ave Moscicki, 1180 Brussels; tel. (2) 374-84-68; fax (2) 374-91-88; NICOLA IVANOV KARADIMOV.

Burkina Faso: 16 place Guy d'Arezzo, 1180 Brussels; tel. (2) 345-99-12; telex 22252; fax (2) 345-06-12; YOUSSOUF OUÉDRAOGO.

Burundi: 46 square Marie-Louise, 1040 Brussels; tel. (2) 230-45-35; telex 23572; fax (2) 230-78-83; LÉONIDAS NDORICIMPA.

Cameroon: 131 ave Brugmann, 1060 Brussels; tel. (2) 345-18-70; telex 24117; fax (2) 344-57-35; ISABELLE BASSONG.

Canada: 2 ave de Tervuren, 1040 Brussels; tel. (2) 741-06-60; fax (2) 741-06-29; JEAN-PIERRE JUNEAU.

Cape Verde: 30 rue Antoine Labarre, 1050 Brussels; tel. (2) 646-90-25; fax (2) 646-33-85; JOSÉ LUÍS ROCHA.

Central African Republic: 416 blvd Lambermont, 1030 Brussels; tel. (2) 242-28-80; telex 22493; fax (2) 242-30-81; Chargé d'affaires a.i.: JEAN-PIERRE MBAZOA.

Chad: 52 blvd Lambermont, 1030 Brussels; tel. (2) 215-19-75; fax (2) 216-35-26; RAMADANE BARMA.

Chile: 326 ave Louise (23e étage), Boîte 22, 1050 Brussels; tel. (2) 640-30-24; fax (2) 646-42-77; e-mail misue@pophost.eunet.be; GONZALO ARENAS-VALVERDE.

China, People's Republic: 443–445 ave de Tervuren, 1150 Brussels; tel. (2) 771-33-09; fax (2) 779-28-95; SONG MINGJIANG.

Colombia: 96A ave F.D. Roosevelt, 1050 Brussels; tel. (2) 649-56-79; fax (2) 646-54-91; e-mail emeolbru@arcadis.be; JOSÉ ANTONIO VARGAS.

Comoros: 20 rue Marbeau, 75116 Paris, France; tel. 1-40-67-90-54; fax 1-40-67-72-96; MAHAMOUD SOILIH.

Congo, Democratic Republic: 30 rue Marie de Bourgogne, 1040 Brussels; tel. (2) 513-66-10; telex 21983; fax (2) 514-04-03; JUSTINE M'POYO-KASA VUBU.

Congo, Republic: 16–18 ave F. D. Roosevelt, 1050 Brussels: tel. (2) 648-38-56; telex 23677; fax (2) 648-42-13; PAUL A. MAPINGOU.

Costa Rica: 489 ave Louise (4e étage), 1050 Brussels; tel. (2) 640-55-41; fax (2) 648-31-92; MARIO CARVAJAL HERRERA.

Côte d'Ivoire: 234 ave F. D. Roosevelt, 1050 Brussels; tel. (2) 672-23-57; telex 21993; fax (2) 672-04-91; ANET N'ZI NANAN KOLIABO.

Croatia: 50 ave des Arts, Boîte 14, 1000 Brussels; tel. (2) 512-24-41; fax (2) 512-03-38; ŽELJKO MATIĆ.

Cuba: 77 rue Robert Jones, 1180 Brussels; tel. (2) 343-71-46; fax (2) 344-96-91; RENÉ MUJICA CANTELAR.

Cyprus: 2 square Ambiorix, 1000 Brussels; tel. (2) 735-35-10; fax (2) 735-45-52; MICHALIS ATTALIDES.

Czech Republic: 555 rue Engeland, 1180 Brussels; tel. (2) 375-93-34; fax (2) 375-22-46; e-mail eu.brussels@embassy.mzv.cz; JOSEF KREUTER.

Djibouti: 160 ave F. D. Roosevelt, 1050 Brussels; tel. (2) 646-41-51; telex 27242; fax (2) 646-44-59; AHMED OMAR FARAH.

Dominica: 100 rue des Aduatiques, 1040 Brussels; tel. (2) 733-43-28; fax (2) 735-72-37; e-mail ecs.embassies@skynet.be; EDWIN P. J. LAURENT.

Dominican Republic: 160A ave Louise, Boîte 19, 1050 Brussels; tel. (2) 646-08-40; fax (2) 640-95-61; CLARA QUIÑONES RODRÍGUEZ.

Ecuador: 363 ave Louise, 1050 Brussels; tel. (2) 644-30-50; fax (2) 644-28-13; ALFREDO PINOARGOTE CEVALLOS.

Egypt: 44 ave Léo Errera, 1180 Brussels; tel. (2) 345-52-53; telex 23716; fax (2) 343-65-33; MUHAMMAD CHABANE.

El Salvador: 171 ave de Tervuren, 1150 Brussels; tel. (2) 733-04-85; fax (2) 735-02-11; JOAQUÍN RODEZNA MUNGUIA.

Equatorial Guinea: 295 ave Brugmann, 1060 Brussels; tel. (2) 346-25-09; fax (2) 346-33-09; AURÉLIO MBA OLO ANDEME.

Eritrea: 15–17 ave de Wolvendael, 1180 Brussels; tel. (2) 644-24-01; fax (2) 644-23-99; ANDEBRHAN WELDEGIORGIS.

Estonia: 1 ave Isidore Gérard, 1160 Brussels; tel. (2) 779-07-55; fax (2) 779-28-17; PRIIT KOLBRE.

Ethiopia: 231 ave de Tervuren, Brussels; tel. (2) 771-32-94; fax (2) 771-49-14; PETER GABRIEL ROBLEH.

Fiji: 66 ave de Cortenbergh (7e étage), Boîte 7, 1000 Brussels; tel. (2) 736-90-50; fax (2) 736-14-58; KALIOPATE TAVOLA.

Gabon: 112 ave Winston Churchill, 1180 Brussels; tel. (2) 340-62-10; telex 23383; fax (2) 346-46-69; JEAN-ROBERT GOULONGANA.

The Gambia: 126 ave F. D. Roosevelt, 1050 Brussels; tel. (2) 640-10-49; telex 24344; fax (2) 646-32-77; ISMAILA B. CEESAY.

Georgia: 15 rue Vergote, 1030 Brussels; tel. (2) 732-85-50; fax (2) 732-85-47; ZURAB ABACHIDZE.

Ghana: 7 blvd Général Wahis, 1030 Brussels; tel. (2) 705-82-20; telex 22572; fax (2) 705-66-53; ALEX NTIM ABANKWA.

Grenada: 24 ave de la Toison d'Or, 1050 Brussels; tel. (2) 514-12-42; fax (2) 513-87-24; FABIAN A. REDHEAD.

Guatemala: 185 ave Winston Churchill, 1180 Brussels; tel. (2) 345-90-58; fax (2) 344-64-99; e-mail obguab@infoboard.be; CLAUDIO RIEDEL TELGE.

Guinea: 75 ave Roger Vandendriessche, 1150 Brussels; tel. (2) 771-01-26; fax (2) 762-60-36; NABY MOUSSA SOUMAH.

Guinea-Bissau: 70 ave F. D. Roosevelt, 1050 Brussels; tel. (2) 647-08-90; telex 63631; fax (2) 640-43-12; Chargé d'affaires: JOSÉ FONSECA.

Guyana: 12 ave du Brésil, 1000 Brussels; tel. (2) 675-62-16; fax (2) 675-55-98; e-mail embassy.guyana@skynet.be; HAVELOCK BREWSTER.

Haiti: 160A ave Louise, Boîte 4, 1050 Brussels; tel. (2) 649-73-81; fax (2) 640-60-80; YOLETTE AZOR-CHARLES.

Holy See: 5–9 ave des Franciscains, 1150 Brussels; tel. (2) 762-20-05; fax (2) 762-20-32; Apostolic Nuncio: Most Rev. GIOVANNI MORETTI, Titular Archbishop of Vartana.

Honduras: 3 ave des Gaulois (5e étage), 1040 Brussels; tel. (2) 734-00-00; fax (2) 735-26-26; IVÁN ROMERO MARTÍNEZ.

Hungary: 44 ave du Vert Chasseur, 1180 Brussels; tel. (2) 372-08-00; fax (2) 372-07-84; ENDRE JUHÁSZ.

Iceland: 1 rue Marie-Thérèse, 1040 Brussels; tel. (2) 219-90-90; telex 29459; fax (2) 219-94-30; GUNNAR SNORRI GUNNARSSON.

India: 217 chaussée de Vleurgat, 1050 Brussels; tel. (2) 640-91-40; telex 22510; fax (2) 648-96-38; e-mail eoibru@mail.interpac.be; C. DASGUPTA.

Indonesia: 38 blvd de la Woluwe, 1200 Brussels; tel. (2) 779-09-15; telex 20379; fax (2) 772-82-10; POEDJI KOENTARSO.

Iran: 415 ave de Tervuren, 1150 Brussels; tel. (2) 762-37-45; fax (2) 762-39-15; HAMID ABOUTALEBI.

Iraq: 131 ave de la Floride, 1180 Brussels; tel. (2) 374-59-92; telex 26414; fax (2) 374-76-15; Chargé d'affaires a.i.: SAAD MAGED.

Israel: 40 ave de l'Observatoire, 1180 Brussels; tel. (2) 373-55-00; fax (2) 373-56-17; EFRAÏM HALEVY.

Jamaica: 2 ave Palmerston, 1000 Brussels: tel. (2) 230-11-70; fax (2) 230-37-09; DOUGLAS A. C. SAUNDERS.

Japan: 58 ave des Arts (7e étage), Boîtes 13–14, 1040 Brussels; tel. (2) 513-92-00; fax (2) 513-32-41; TOMIHIKO KOBAYASHI.

Jordan: 104 ave F. D. Roosevelt, 1050 Brussels; tel. (2) 640-77-55; telex 55721; fax (2) 640-27-96; Dr UMAYYA TOUKAN.

Kenya: 1–5 ave de la Joyeuse Entrée, 1040 Brussels; tel. (2) 230-30-65; telex 62568; fax (2) 230-84-62; Dr P.M. MWANZIA.

Korea, Republic: 173–175 chaussée de la Hulpe, 1170 Brussels; tel. (2) 675-57-77; fax (2) 675-52-21; LEE JAI CHUN.

Kuwait: 43 ave F. D. Roosevelt, 1050 Brussels; tel. (2) 647-79-50; fax (2) 646-12-98; AHMAD A. AL-EBRAHIM.

Kyrgyzstan: 32 rue du Châtelain, 1050 Brussels; tel. (2) 627-19-16; fax (2) 627-19-00; Chargé d'affaires a.i.: SERGEI K. KASYMKULOV.

Laos: 74 ave Raymond Poincaré, 75116 Paris, France; tel. 1-45-53-02-98; telex 610711; fax 1-47-57-27-89; KHAMPHAN SIMMALAVONG.

Latvia: 39–41 rue d'Arlon, Boîte 6, 1000 Brussels; tel. (2) 282-03-60; fax (2) 282-03-69; IMANTS LIEGIS.

Lebanon: 2 rue Guillaume Stocq, 1050 Brussels; tel. (2) 649-94-60; telex 22547; fax (2) 649-90-02; JIHAD MORTADA.

Lesotho: 45 blvd Général Wahis, 1030 Brussels; tel. (2) 705-39-76; fax (2) 705-67-79; R. V. LECHESA.

Liberia: 50 ave du Château, 1081 Brussels; tel. and fax (2) 411-09-12; Chargé d'affaires a.i.: YOUNGOR TELEWODA.

Libya: 28 ave Victoria, 1050 Brussels; tel. (2) 649-21-12; telex 23398; HAMED AHMED ELHOUDERI.

Liechtenstein: Place du Congrès 1, 1000 Brussels; tel. (2) 229-39-00; fax (2) 219-35-45; Prince NIKOLAUS VON LIECHTENSTEIN.

Lithuania: 48 rue Maurice Liétart, 1150 Brussels; tel. (2) 771-01-40; fax (2) 771-45-97; ROMUALDAS KOLONAITIS.

Madagascar: 276 ave de Tervuren, 1150 Brussels; tel. (2) 770-17-26; telex 61197; fax (2) 772-37-31; JEAN OMER BERIZIKY.

Malawi: 15 rue de la Loi, 1040 Brussels; tel. (2) 231-09-80; telex 24128; fax (2) 231-10-66; JULIE NANYONI MPHANDE.

Malaysia: 414A ave de Tervuren, 1150 Brussels; tel. (2) 762-67-67; telex 26396; fax (2) 762-50-49; Dato' M. M. SATHIAH.

Maldives: 212 East 47th St, Apt 15B, New York, NY 10017, USA; tel. (212) 688-07-76; telex 960945.

Mali: 487 ave Molière, 1050 Brussels; tel. (2) 345-74-32; fax (2) 344-57-00; N'TJI LAÏCO TRAORÉ.

Malta: 44 rue Jules Lejeune, 1060 Brussels; tel. (2) 343-01-95; fax (2) 343-01-06; VICTOR CAMILLERI.

Mauritania: 6 ave de la Colombie, 1050 Brussels; tel. (2) 672-47-47; telex 26034; fax (2) 672-20-51; BOULLAH OULD MOGUEYE.

Mauritius: 68 rue des Bollandistes, 1040 Brussels; tel. (2) 733-99-88; fax (2) 734-40-21; PARRWIZ C. HOSSEN.

Mexico: 94 ave F.D. Roosevelt, 1050 Brussels; tel. (2) 629-07-11; fax (2) 672-93-12; e-mail mex-ue@pophost.eunet.be; MANUEL ARMENDÁRIZ ETCHEGARAY.

Mongolia: 18 ave Besme, 1190 Brussels; tel. (2) 344-69-74; fax (2) 344-32-15; JAGVARALYN HANIBAL.

Morocco: 29 blvd Saint-Michel, 1040 Brussels; tel. (2) 736-11-00; telex 21233; fax (2) 734-64-68; RACHAD BOUHLAL.

Mozambique: 97 blvd Saint-Michel, 1040 Brussels; tel. (2) 736-25-64; telex 65478; fax (2) 735-62-07; ÁLVARO O. DA SILVA.

Myanmar: Schumannstrasse 112, 53113 Bonn, Germany; tel. (228) 210091; telex 8869560; fax (228) 219316; U TUN NGWE.

Namibia: 454 ave de Tervuren, 1150 Brussels; tel. (2) 771-14-10; fax (2) 771-96-89; Dr ZEDEKIA J. NGAVIRUE.

Nepal: 24 ave F. D. Roosevelt, 1050 Brussels, Belgium; tel. (2) 649-40-48; fax (2) 649-84-54; e-mail rne.bru@skynet.be; KEDAR BHAKTA SHRESTHA.

New Zealand: 47–48 blvd du Régent, 1000 Brussels; tel. (2) 512-10-40; fax (2) 513-48-56; DEREK WILLIAM LEASK.

Nicaragua: 55 ave de Wolvendael, 1180 Brussels; tel. (2) 375-64-34; fax (2) 375-71-88; ALVARO PORTA BERMÚDEZ.

Niger: 78 ave F. D. Roosevelt, 1050 Brussels; tel. (2) 648-61-40; telex 22857; fax (2) 648-27-84; HOUSSEINI ABDOU-SALEYE.

Nigeria: 288 ave de Tervuren, 1150 Brussels; tel. (2) 762-52-00; fax (2) 762-37-63; ALABA OGUNSANWO.

Norway: 17 rue Archimède, 1000 Brussels; tel. (2) 234-11-11; fax (2) 234-11-50; EINAR M. BULL.

Oman: 50 ave d'Iéna, 75116 Paris, France; tel. 1-47-23-01-63; fax 1-47-23-77-10; MUNIR BIN ABDULNABI BIN YOUSUF MAKKI.

Pakistan: 57 ave Delleurs, 1170 Brussels; tel. (2) 673-80-07; telex 61816; fax (2) 675-83-94; RIAZ MOHAMED KHAN.

Panama: 8 blvd Brand Whitlock, 1150 Brussels; tel. (2) 733-90-89; fax (2) 733-77-79; e-mail epb@netropolis.be; VILMA E. RAMÍREZ.

Papua New Guinea: 430 ave de Tervuren, 1150 Brussels; tel. (2) 779-08-26; fax (2) 772-70-88; GABRIEL KOIBA PEPSON.

Paraguay: 522 ave Louise (3e étage), 1050 Brussels; tel. (2) 649-90-55; fax (2) 647-42-48; MANUEL MARIÁ CÁCERES.

Peru: 179 ave de Tervuren, 1150 Brussels; tel. (2) 733-33-19; fax (2) 733-48-19; e-mail embassy.of.peru@unicall.be; JOSÉ ANTONIO ARROSPIDE.

Philippines: 85 rue Washington, 1050 Brussels; tel. (2) 533-18-11; fax (2) 538-35-40; PACIFICO A. CASTRO.

Poland: 18 ave de l'Horizon, 1150 Brussels; tel. (2) 771-32-62; telex 20555; fax (2) 771-49-10; JAN TRUSZCZYNSKI.

Qatar: 71 ave F. D. Roosevelt, 1050 Brussels; tel. (2) 640-29-00; telex 63754; fax (2) 648-40-78; e-mail qatar@infonie.be; Chargé d'affaires a.i.: MOHAMED AL-HAIYKI.

Romania: 107 rue Gabrielle, 1180 Brussels; tel. (2) 344-41-45; fax (2) 344-24-79; CONSTANTIN ENE.

Russia: 56 ave Louis Lepoutre, 1060 Brussels; tel. (2) 343-03-39; fax (2) 346-24-53; e-mail misrusce@interpac.be; IVAN S. SILAYEV.

Rwanda: 1 ave des Fleurs, 1150 Brussels; tel. (2) 763-07-21; telex 26653; fax (2) 763-07-53; MANZI BAKURAMURZA.

Saint Christopher and Nevis: 100 rue des Aduatiques, 1040 Brussels; tel. (2) 733-43-28; fax (2) 735-72-37; e-mail ecs.embassies@skynet.be; EDWIN P. J. LAURENT.

Saint Lucia: 100 rue des Aduatiques, 1040 Brussels; tel. (2) 733-43-28; fax (12) 735-72-37; e-mail ecs.embassies@skynet.be; EDWIN P. J. LAURENT.

Saint Vincent and the Grenadines: 100 rue des Aduatiques, 1040 Brussels; tel. (2) 733-43-28; fax (12) 735-72-37; e-mail ecs.embassies@skynet.be; EDWIN P. J. LAURENT.

Samoa: 123 ave F. D. Roosevelt, Boîte 14, 1050 Brussels; tel. (2) 660-84-54; fax (2) 675-03-36; TAUILIILI UILI MEREDITH.

San Marino: 62 ave F.D. Roosevelt, 1050 Brussels; tel. and fax (2) 644-22-24; SAVINA ZAFFERANI.

São Tomé and Príncipe: 175 ave de Tervuren, 1150 Brussels; tel. and fax (2) 734-88-15; Chargé d'affaires: ANTÓNIO DE LIMA VIEGAS.

Saudi Arabia: 45 ave F. D. Roosevelt, 1050 Brussels; tel. (2) 649-57-25; fax (2) 647-24-92; NASSIR AL-ALASSAF.

Senegal: 196 ave F. D. Roosevelt, 1050 Brussels; tel. (2) 673-00-97; fax (2) 675-04-60; SALOUM KANDE.

Seychelles: 157 blvd du Jubilé, 1080 Brussels; tel. (2) 425-62-36; fax (2) 426-06-29; CLAUDE MOREL.

Sierra Leone: 410 ave de Tervuren, 1150 Brussels; tel. (2) 771-00-53; PETER J. KUYEMBEH.

Singapore: 198 ave F. D. Roosevelt, 1050 Brussels; tel. (2) 660-29-79; telex 26731; fax (2) 660-86-85; e-mail amb.eu@singembbru.be; PANG ENG FONG.

Slovakia: 118 ave Brugmann, 1190 Brussels; tel. (2) 346-26-05; fax (2) 343-67-30; e-mail pmsteul@pophost.eunet.be; EMIN KUCHAR.

Slovenia: 30 ave Marnix, 1000 Brussels; tel. (2) 512-44-66; fax (2) 512-09-97; e-mail mission.bruxelles@mzz-dkp.sigor.si; Dr BORIS CIZELJ.

Solomon Islands: 13 ave de L'Yser, Boîte 3, 1040 Brussels; tel. (2) 732-70-85; fax (2) 732-68-85; ROBERT SISILO.

Somalia: 26 rue Dumont d'Urville, 75116 Paris, France; tel. (1) 45-00-76-51; telex 611828; AHMED SHIRE MOHAMUD.

South Africa: 26 rue de la Loi, Boîtes 14–15, 1040 Brussels; tel. (2) 285-44-60; fax (2) 285-44-87; ELIAS LINKS.

Sri Lanka: 27 rue Jules Lejeune, 1050 Brussels; tel. (2) 344-53-94; fax (2) 344-67-37; Chargé d'affaires a.i. CASIE CHETTY.

Sudan: 124 ave F. D. Roosevelt, 1050 Brussels; tel. (2) 647-51-59; telex 24370; fax (2) 648-34-99; GALAL HASSAN ATABANI.

Suriname: 379 ave Louise, 1050 Brussels; tel. (2) 640-11-72; telex 62680; fax (2) 646-39-62; ELWOLD C. LEEFLANG.

Swaziland: 188 ave Winston Churchill, 1180 Brussels; tel. (2) 347-47-71; telex 26254; fax (2) 347-46-23; Dr THEMBAYENA A. DLAMINI.

Switzerland: 53 rue d'Arlon, Boîte 9, 1040 Brussels; tel. (2) 286-13-11; fax (2) 230-45-09; e-mail vertretung@brm.rep.admin.ch; ALEXIS P. LAUTENBERG.

Syria: 3 ave F. D. Roosevelt, 1050 Brussels; tel. (2) 648-01-35; telex 26669; fax (2) 646-40-18; Dr HANI HABEEB.

Tanzania: 363 ave Louise (7e étage), 1050 Brussels; tel. (2) 640-65-00; fax (2) 646-80-26; ALI ABEID KARUME.

Thailand: 2 square du Val de la Cambre, 1050 Brussels; tel. (2) 640-68-10; fax (2) 648-30-66; SOMKIATI ARIYAPRUCHYA.

Togo: 264 ave de Tervuren, 1150 Brussels; tel. (2) 770-17-91; telex 25093; fax (2) 771-50-75; KATI KORGA.

Tonga: 36 Molyneux St, London, W1H 6AB, United Kingdom; tel. (171) 724-5828; telex 8954094; fax (171) 723-9074; 'AKOSITA FINEANGANOFO.

Trinidad and Tobago: 14 ave de la Faisanderie, 1150 Brussels; tel. (2) 762-94-00; fax (2) 772-27-83; LINGSTON-LLOYD CUMBERBATCH.

Tunisia: 278 ave de Tervuren, 1150 Brussels; tel. (2) 771-73-95; telex 22078; fax (2) 771-94-33; TAHAR SIOUD.

Turkey: 4 rue Montoyer, 1000 Brussels; tel. (2) 513-28-36; fax (2) 511-0450; ULUÇ OZÜLKER.

Uganda: 317 ave de Tervuren, 1150 Brussels; tel. (2) 762-58-25; telex 62814; fax (2) 763-04-38; KAKIMA NTAMBI.

Ukraine: 7 rue Guimard, 1040 Brussels; fax (2) 512-40-45; IGOR MITYUKOV.

United Arab Emirates: 73 ave F. D. Roosevelt, 1050 Brussels; tel. (2) 640-60-00; fax (2) 646-24-73; ABDEL HADI ABDEL WAHID AL-KHAJA.

USA: 40 blvd du Régent, Boîte 3, 1000 Brussels; tel. (2) 513-44-50; fax (2) 511-20-92; A. VERNON WEAVER.

Uruguay: 22 ave F. D. Roosevelt, 1050 Brussels; tel (2) 640-11-69; telex (2) 24663; fax (2) 648-29-09; e-mail uruemb@infoboard.be; GUILLERMO VALLES.

Venezuela: 10 ave F. D. Roosevelt, 1050 Brussels; tel. (2) 639-03-40; fax (2) 647-88-20; LUIS XAVIER GRISANTI.

Viet Nam: 130 ave de la Floride, 1180 Brussels; tel. (2) 374-91-33; fax (2) 374-93-76; HUYNH ANH DZUNG.

Yemen: 44 rue Van Eyck, 1000 Brussels; tel. (2) 646-52-90; fax (2) 646-29-11; GAZEM A. K. AL-AGHBARI.

Yugoslavia: 11 ave Emile Demot, 1000 Brussels; tel. (2) 649-83-65; telex 26156; fax (2) 649-08-78; DRAGOSLAV JOVANOVIĆ.

Zambia: 469 ave Molière, 1060 Brussels; tel. (2) 343-56-49; telex 63102; fax (2) 347-43-33; ISAIAH ZIMBA CHABALA.

Zimbabwe: 11 square Joséphine Charlotte, 1200 Brussels; tel. (2) 762-58-08; telex 24133; fax (2) 762-96-05; SIMBARASHE S. MUMBENGEGWI.

Summary of the Treaty establishing the European Economic Community (Treaty of Rome)

(effective from 1 January 1958)

PART I. PRINCIPLES

The aim of the Community is, by establishing a Common Market and progressively approximating the economic policies of the member states, to promote throughout the Community a harmonious development of economic activities, a continuous and balanced expansion, an increased stability, an accelerated raising of the standard of living and closer relations between its member states. With these aims in view, the activities of the Community will include:

(a) the elimination between member states of customs duties and of quantitative restrictions in regard to the importation and exportation of goods, as well as of all other measures with equivalent effect;

(b) the establishment of a common customs tariff and a common commercial policy towards third countries;

(c) the abolition between member states of the obstacles to the free movement of persons, services and capital;

(d) the inauguration of a common agricultural policy;

(e) the inauguration of a common transport policy;

(f) the establishment of a system ensuring that competition shall not be distorted in the Common Market;

(g) the application of procedures that will make it possible to co-ordinate the economic policies of member states and to remedy disequilibria in their balance of payments;

(h) the approximation of their respective municipal law to the extent necessary for the functioning of the Common Market;

(i) the creation of a European Social Fund in order to improve the possibilities of employment for workers and to contribute to the raising of their standard of living;

(j) the establishment of a European Investment Bank intended to facilitate the economic expansion of the Community through the creation of new resources; and

(k) the association of overseas countries and territories with the Community with a view to increasing trade and to pursuing jointly their effort toward economic and social development.

Member states, acting in close collaboration with the institutions of the Community, shall co-ordinate their respective economic policies to the extent that is necessary to attain the objectives of the Treaty; the institutions of the Community shall take care not to prejudice the internal and external financial stability of the member states. Within the field of application of the Treaty and without prejudice to certain special provisions which it contains, any discrimination on the grounds of nationality shall be hereby prohibited.

The Common Market shall be progressively established in the course of a transitional period of 12 years. This transitional period shall be divided into three stages of four years each.

PART II. BASES OF THE COMMUNITY

Free Movement of Goods

Member states shall refrain from introducing between themselves any new import or export customs duties, or charges with equivalent effect, and from increasing such duties or charges as they apply in their commercial relations with each other. Member states shall progressively abolish between themselves all import and export customs duties, charges with an equivalent effect, and also customs duties of a fiscal nature. Independently of these provisions, any member state may, in the course of the transitional period, suspend in whole or in part the collection of import duties applied by it to products imported from other member states, or may carry out the foreseen reductions more rapidly than laid down in the Treaty if its general economic situation and the situation of the sector so concerned permit.

A common customs tariff shall be established, which, subject to certain conditions (especially with regard to the Italian tariff), shall be at the level of the arithmetical average of the duties applied in the four customs territories (i.e. France, Germany, Italy and Benelux) covered by the Community. This customs tariff shall be applied in its entirety not later than at the date of the expiry of the transitional period. Member states may follow an independent accelerating process similar to that allowed for reduction of inter-Community customs duties.

Member states shall refrain from introducing between themselves any new quantitative restrictions or measures with equivalent effect, and existing restrictions and measures shall be abolished not later than at the end of the first stage of the transitional period. These provisions shall not be an obstacle to prohibitions or restrictions in respect of importation, exportation or transit which are justified on grounds of public morality, health or safety, the protection of human or animal life or health, the preservation of plant life, the protection of national treasures of artistic, historic or archaeological value or the protection of industrial and commercial property. Such prohibitions or restrictions shall not, however, constitute either a means of arbitrary discrimination or a disguised restriction on trade between member states. Member states shall progressively adjust any state monopolies of a commercial character in such a manner as will ensure the exclusion, at the end of the transitional period, of all discrimination between the nationals of member states in regard to conditions of supply and marketing of goods. These provisions shall apply to any body by means of which a member state shall *de jure* or *de facto*, either directly or indirectly, control or appreciably influence importation or exportation between member states, and also to monopolies assigned by the state. In the case of a commercial monopoly which is accompanied by regulations designed to facilitate the marketing or the valorization of agricultural products, it should be ensured that in the application of these provisions equivalent guarantees are provided in respect of the employment and standard of living of the producers concerned.

The obligations incumbent on member states shall be binding only to such extent as they are compatible with existing international agreements.

Agriculture

The Common Market shall extend to agriculture and trade in agricultural products. The common agricultural policy shall have as its objectives:

(a) the increase of agricultural productivity by developing technical progress and by ensuring the rational development of agricultural production and the optimum utilization of the factors of production, particularly labour;

(b) the ensurance thereby of a fair standard of living for the agricultural population;

(c) the stabilization of markets;

(d) regular supplies;

(e) reasonable prices in supplies to consumers.

Due account must be taken of the particular character of agricultural activities, arising from the social structure of agriculture and from structural and natural disparities between the various agricultural regions; of the need to make the appropriate adjustments gradually; and of the fact that in member states agriculture constitutes a sector which is closely linked with the economy as a whole. With a view to developing a common agricultural policy during the transitional period and the establishment of it not later than at the end of the period, a common organization of agricultural markets shall be effected.

Free Movement of Persons, Services and Capital

Workers: The free movement of workers shall be ensured within the Community not later than at the date of the expiry of the transitional period, involving the abolition of any discrimination based on nationality between workers of the member states as regards employment, remuneration and other working conditions. This shall include the right to accept offers of employment actually made, to move about freely for this purpose within the territory of the member states, to stay in any member state in order to carry on an employment in conformity with the legislative and administrative provisions governing the employment of the workers of that state, and to live, on conditions which shall be the subject of implementing regulations laid down by the Commission, in the territory of a member state after having been employed there. (These provisions do not apply to employment in the public administration.)

In the field of social security, the Council shall adopt the measures necessary to effect the free movement of workers, in particular, by introducing a system which permits an assurance to be given to migrant workers and their beneficiaries that, for the purposes of qualifying for and retaining the rights to benefits and of the calculation of these benefits, all periods taken into consideration by the respective municipal law of the countries concerned shall be added together, and that these benefits will be paid to persons resident in the territories of the member states.

Right of Establishment: Restrictions on the freedom of establishment of nationals of a member state in the territory of another member state shall be progressively abolished during the transitional period, nor may any new restrictions of a similar character be introduced. Such progressive abolition shall also extend to restrictions on the setting up of agencies, branches or subsidiaries. Freedom of establishment shall include the right to engage in and carry on non-wage-earning activities and also to set up and manage enterprises and companies under the conditions laid down by the law of the country of establishment for its own nationals, subject to the provisions of this Treaty relating to capital.

Services: Restrictions on the free supply of services within the Community shall be progressively abolished in the course of the transitional period in respect of nationals of member states who are established in a state of the Community other than that of the person to whom the services are supplied; no new restrictions of a similar character may be introduced. The Council, acting by a unanimous vote on a proposal of the Commission, may extend the benefit of these provisions to cover services supplied by nationals of any third country who are established within the Community.

Particular services involved are activities of an industrial or artisan character and those of the liberal professions.

Capital: Member states shall during the transitional period progressively abolish between themselves restrictions on the movement of capital belonging to persons resident in the member states, and also any discriminatory treatment based on the nationality or place of residence of the parties or on the place in which such capital is invested. Current payments connected with movements of capital between member states shall be freed from all restrictions not later than at the end of the first stage of the transitional period.

Member states shall endeavour to avoid introducing within the Community any new exchange restrictions which affect the movement of capital and current payments connected with such movements, and making existing rules more restrictive.

Transport

With a view to establishing a common transport policy, the Council of Ministers shall, acting on a proposal of the Commission and after consulting the Economic and Social Committee and the European Parliament, lay down common rules applicable to international transport effected from or to the territory of a member state or crossing the territory of one or more member states, conditions for the admission of non-resident carriers to national transport services within a member state and any other appropriate provisions. Until these have been enacted and unless the Council of Ministers gives its unanimous consent, no member state shall apply the various provisions governing this subject at the date of the entry into force of this Treaty in such a way as to make them less favourable, in their direct or indirect effect, for carriers of other member states by comparison with its own national carriers.

Any discrimination which consists in the application by a carrier, in respect of the same goods conveyed in the same circumstances, of transport rates and conditions which differ on the ground of the country of origin or destination of the goods carried, shall be abolished in the traffic of the Community not later than at the end of the second stage of the transitional period.

A Committee with consultative status, composed of experts appointed by the governments of the member states, shall be established and attached to the Commission, without prejudice to the competence of the transport section of the Economic and Social Committee.

PART III. POLICY OF THE COMMUNITY

Common Rules

Enterprises: The following practices by enterprises are prohibited: the direct or indirect fixing of purchase or selling prices or of any other trading conditions; the limitation of control of production, markets, technical development of investment; market-sharing or the sharing of sources of supply; the application to parties to transactions of unequal terms in respect of equivalent supplies, thereby placing them at a competitive disadvantage; the subjection of the conclusion of a contract to the acceptance by a party of additional supplies which, either by their nature or according to commercial usage, have no connection with the subject of such contract. The provisions may be declared inapplicable if the agreements neither impose on the enterprises concerned any restrictions not indispensable to the attainment of improved production, distribution or technical progress, nor enable enterprises to eliminate competition in respect of a substantial proportion of the goods concerned.

Dumping: If, in the course of the transitional period, the Commission, at the request of a member state or of any other interested party, finds that dumping practices exist within the Common Market, it shall issue recommendations to the originator of such practices with a view to bringing them to an end. Where such practices continue, the Commission shall authorize the member state injured to take protective measures of which the Commission shall determine the conditions and particulars.

Re-importation within the Community shall be free of all customs duties, quantitative restrictions or measures with equivalent effect.

Aid granted by States: Any aid granted by a member state or granted by means of state resources which is contrary to the purposes of the treaty is forbidden. The following shall be deemed to be compatible with the Common Market:

(a) aids of a social character granted without discrimination to individual consumers;

(b) aids intended to remedy damage caused by natural calamities or other extraordinary events;

(c) aids granted to the economy of certain regions of the Federal German Republic affected by the division of Germany, to the extent that they are necessary to compensate for the economic disadvantages caused by the division.

The following may be deemed to be compatible with the Common Market:

(a) aids intended to promote the economic development of regions where the standard of living is abnormally low or where there exists serious under-employment;

(b) aids intended to promote the execution of important projects of common European interest or to remedy a serious economic disturbance of the economy of a member state;

(c) aids intended to facilitate the development of certain activities or of certain economic regions, provided that such aids do not change trading conditions to such a degree as would be contrary to the common interest;

(d) such other categories of aids as may be specified by a decision of the Council of Ministers acting on a proposal of the Commission.

The Commission is charged to examine constantly all systems of aids existing in the member states, and may require any member state to abolish or modify any aid which it finds to be in conflict with the principles of the Common Market.

Fiscal Provisions: A member state shall not impose, directly or indirectly, on the products of other member states, any internal charges of any kind in excess of those applied directly or indirectly to like domestic products. Furthermore, a member state shall not impose on the products of other member states any internal charges of such a nature as to afford indirect protection to other productions. Member states shall, not later than at the beginning of the second stage of the transitional period, abolish or amend any provisions existing at the date of the entry into force of the Treaty which are contrary to these rules. Products exported to any member state may not benefit from any drawback on internal charges in excess of those charges imposed directly or indirectly on them. Subject to these conditions, any member states which levy a turnover tax calculated by a cumulative multi-stage system may, in the case of internal charges imposed by them on imported products or of drawbacks granted by them on exported products, establish average rates for specific products or groups of products.

Approximation of Laws: The Council, acting by means of a unanimous vote on a proposal of the Commission, shall issue directives for the approximation of such legislative and administrative provisions of the member states as have a direct incidence on the establishment or functioning of the Common Market. The European Parliament and the Economic and Social Committee shall be consulted concerning any directives whose implementation in one or more of the member states would involve amendment of legislative provisions.

Economic Policy

Balance of Payments: Member states are charged to co-ordinate their economic policies in order that each may ensure the equilibrium of its overall balance of payments and maintain confidence in its currency, together with a high level of employment and stability of prices. In order to promote this co-ordination, a Monetary Committee is established.

Each member state engages itself to treat its policy with regard to exchange rates as a matter of common interest. Where a member state is in difficulties or seriously threatened with difficulties as regards its balance of payments as a result either of overall disequilibrium of the balance of payments or of the kinds of currency at its disposal, and where such difficulties are likely, in particular, to prejudice the functioning of the Common Market or the progressive establishment of the common commercial policy, the Commission shall examine the situation and indicate the measures which it recommends to the state concerned to adopt; if this action proves insufficient to overcome the difficulties, the Commission shall, after consulting the Monetary Committee, recommend to the Council of Ministers the granting of mutual assistance. This mutual assistance may take the form of:

(a) concerted action in regard to any other international organization to which the member states may have recourse;

(b) any measures necessary to avoid diversions of commercial traffic where the state in difficulty maintains or re-establishes quantitative restrictions with regard to third countries;

(c) the granting of limited credits by other member states, subject to their agreement.

Furthermore, during the transitional period, mutual assistance may also take the form of special reductions in customs duties or enlargements of quotas. If the mutual assistance recommended by the Commission is not granted by the Council, or if the mutual assistance granted and the measures taken prove insufficient, the Commission shall authorize the state in difficulties to take measures of safeguard, of which the Commission shall determine the conditions and particulars. In the case of a sudden balance-of-payments crisis, any member state may take immediate provisional measures of safeguard, which must be submitted to the consideration of the Commission as soon as possible. On the basis of an opinion of the Commission and after consulting the Monetary Committee, the Council may decide that the state concerned shall amend, suspend or abolish such measures.

Commercial Policy: Member states shall co-ordinate their commercial relations with third countries in such a way as to bring about, not later than at the expiry of the transitional period, the conditions necessary to the implementation of a common policy in the matter of external trade. After the expiry of the transitional period, the common commercial policy shall be based on uniform principles, particularly in regard to tariff amendments, the conclusion of tariff or trade agreements, the alignment of measures of liberalization, export policy and protective commercial measures, including measures to be taken in cases of dumping or subsidies. The Commission will be authorized to conduct negotiations with third countries. As from the end of the transitional period, member states shall, in respect of all matters of particular interest in regard to the Common Market, within the framework of any international organizations of an economic character, only proceed by way of common action. The Commission shall for this purpose submit to the Council of Ministers proposals concerning the scope and implementation of such common action. During the transitional period, member states shall consult with each other with a view to concerting their action and, as far as possible, adopting a uniform attitude.

Social Policy

Social Provisions: Without prejudice to the other provisions of the Treaty and in conformity with its general objectives, it shall be the aim of the Commission to promote close collaboration between member states in the social field, particularly in matters relating to employment, labour legislation and working conditions, occupational and continuation training, social security, protection against occupational accidents and diseases, industrial hygiene, the law as to trade unions and collective bargaining between employers and workers.

Each member state shall in the course of the first stage of the transitional period ensure and subsequently maintain the application of the principle of equal pay for men and women.

The European Social Fund: See p. 181.

The European Investment Bank: See p. 162.

PART IV. OVERSEAS COUNTRIES AND TERRITORIES

The member states agree to bring into association with the Community the non-European countries and territories which have special relations with Belgium, France, Italy and the Netherlands in order to promote the economic and social development of these countries and territories and to establish close economic relations between them and the Community as a whole.

Member states shall, in their commercial exchanges with the countries and territories, apply the same rules which they apply among themselves pursuant to the Treaty. Each country or territory shall apply to its commercial exchanges with member states and with other countries and territories the same rules which it applied in respect of the European state with which it has special relations. Member states shall contribute to the investments required by the progressive development of these countries and territories.

Customs duties on trade between member states and the countries and territories are to be progressively abolished according to the same timetable as for trade between the member states themselves. The countries and territories may, however, levy customs duties which correspond to the needs of their development and to the requirements of their industrialization or which, being of a fiscal nature, have the object of contributing to their budgets.

(The Convention implementing these provisions is concluded for a period of five years only from the date of entry into force of the Treaty.)

PART V. INSTITUTIONS OF THE COMMUNITY

Provisions Governing Institutions

For the achievement of their aims and under the conditions provided for in the Treaty, the Council and the Commission shall adopt regulations and directives, make decisions and formulate recommendations or opinions. Regulations shall have a general application and shall be binding in every respect and directly applicable in each member state. Directives shall bind any member state to which they are addressed, as to the result to be achieved, while leaving to domestic agencies a competence as to form and means. Decisions shall be binding in every respect for the addressees named therein. Recommendations and opinions shall have no binding force.

Financial Provisions

Estimates shall be drawn up for each financial year for all revenues and expenditures of the Community and shall be shown in the budget.

The revenues of the budget shall comprise the financial contributions of member states assessed by reference to a fixed scale.

The Commission shall implement the budget on its own responsibility and within the limits of the appropriations made. The Council of Ministers shall:

(a) lay down the financial regulations specifying, in particular, the procedure to be adopted for establishing and implementing the budget, and for rendering and auditing accounts;

(b) determine the methods and procedure whereby the contributions by member states shall be made available to the Commission; and

(c) establish rules concerning the responsibility of pay-commissioners and accountants and arrange for the relevant supervision.

PART VI. GENERAL AND FINAL PROVISIONS

Member states shall, in so far as is necessary, engage in negotiations with each other with a view to ensuring for the benefit of their nationals:

(a) the protection of persons as well as the enjoyment and protection of rights under the conditions granted by each state to its own nationals;

(b) the elimination of double taxation within the Community;

(c) the mutual recognition of companies, the maintenance of their legal personality in cases where the registered office is transferred from one country to another, and the possibility for companies subject to the municipal law of different member states to form mergers; and

(d) the simplification of the formalities governing the reciprocal recognition and execution of judicial decisions and arbitral awards.

Within a period of three years after the date of the entry into force of the Treaty, member states shall treat nationals of other member states in the same manner, as regards financial participation by such nationals in the capital of companies, as they treat their own nationals, without prejudice to the application of the other provisions of the Treaty.

The Treaty shall in no way prejudice the system existing in member states in respect of property.

The provisions of the Treaty shall not detract from the following rules:

(a) no member state shall be obliged to supply information the disclosure of which it considers contrary to the essential interests of its security.

(b) any member state may take the measures which it considers necessary for the protection of the essential interests of its security, and which are connected with the production of or the trade in arms, ammunition and war material; such measures shall not, however, prejudice conditions of competition in the Common Market in respect of products not intended for specifically military purposes.

The list of products to which (b) applies shall be determined by the Council in the course of the first year after the date of entry into force of the Treaty. The list may be subsequently amended by the unanimous vote of the Council on a proposal of the Commission.

Member states shall consult one another for the purpose of enacting in common the necessary provisions to prevent the functioning of the Common Market from being affected by measures which a member state may be called upon to take in case of serious internal disturbances affecting public order, in case of war or in order to carry out undertakings into which it has entered for the purpose of maintaining peace and international security.

In the course of the transitional period, where there are serious difficulties which are likely to persist in any sector of economic activity or difficulties which may seriously impair the economic situation in any region, any member state may ask for authorization to take measures of safeguard in order to restore the situation and adapt the sector concerned to the Common Market economy.

The provisions of the Treaty shall not affect those of the Treaty establishing the European Coal and Steel Community, nor those of the Treaty establishing the European Atomic Energy Community; nor shall they be an obstacle to the existence or completion of regional unions between Belgium and Luxembourg, and between Belgium, Luxembourg and the Netherlands, in so far as the objectives of these regional unions are not achieved by the application of this Treaty.

The government of any member state of the Commission may submit to the Council proposals for the revision of the Treaty.

Any European state may apply to become a member of the Community.

The Community may conclude with a third country, a union of states or an international organization agreements creating an association embodying reciprocal rights and obligations, joint actions and special procedures.

The Treaty is concluded for an unlimited period.

OTHER TREATIES

The following additional treaties have been signed by the members of the European Union:

Treaty Instituting a Single Council and a Single Commission of the European Communities: signed in Brussels on 8 April 1965 by the six original members.

Treaty Modifying Certain Budgetary Arrangements of the European Communities and of the Treaty Instituting a Single Council and a Single Commission of the European Communities: signed in Luxembourg on 22 April 1970 by the six original members.

Treaty Concerning the Accession of the Kingdom of Denmark, Ireland, the Kingdom of Norway and the United Kingdom of Great Britain to the European Economic Community and the European Atomic Energy Community: signed in Brussels on 22 January 1972 (amended on 1 January 1973, owing to the non-accession of Norway).

Treaty of Accession of the Hellenic Republic to the European Economic Community and to the European Atomic Energy Community: signed in Athens on 28 May 1979.

Treaty of Accession of the Portuguese Republic and the Kingdom of Spain to the European Economic Community and to the European Atomic Energy Community: signed in Lisbon and Madrid on 12 June 1985.

Treaty Concerning the Accession of the Kingdom of Norway, the Republic of Austria, the Republic of Finland and the Kingdom of Sweden to the European Union: signed in Corfu on 24 June 1994 (amended on 1 January 1995, owing to the non-accession of Norway).

(Accession of new members to the European Coal and Steel Community is enacted separately, by a Decision of the European Council.)

THE SINGLE EUROPEAN ACT

On 1 July 1987 amendments to the Treaty of Rome, in the form of the 'Single European Act', came into effect, following ratification by all the member states. The Act contained provisions which aimed to complete by 1992 the creation of a single Community market—'an area without internal frontiers in which the free movement of goods, persons, services and capital is ensured'. Other provisions increased Community co-operation in research and technology, social policy (particularly the improvement of working conditions), economic and social cohesion (reduction of disparities between regions), environmental protection, creation of economic and monetary union, and foreign policy. It allowed the Council of Ministers to take decisions by a qualified majority vote on matters which previously, under the Treaty of Rome, had required unanimity: this applied principally to matters relating to the establishment of the internal market (see below under the heading Council of Ministers). The Act increased the powers of the European Parliament to delay and amend legislation, although the Council retained final decision-making powers. The Act also provided for the establishment of a secretariat for European political co-operation on matters of foreign policy.

TREATY ON EUROPEAN UNION ('THE MAASTRICHT TREATY')

The Treaty, which further amends and extends the scope of the Treaty of Rome as well as establishing a European Union, was approved by EC heads of government at Maastricht, the Netherlands, in December 1991, signed in February 1992 and ratified in all member states by October 1993; it came into effect on 1 November 1993. At the meeting of the European Council in December 1992, it was agreed that Denmark was to be exempted from certain central provisions of the Treaty, including those regarding monetary union, European citizenship and defence (subject to approval by a second Danish referendum, which ratified the Treaty in May 1993).

Below is given the introductory section of the Treaty ('Common Provisions'), which establishes the principles elaborated in the remainder of the document.

A protocol to the Treaty was approved and a separate agreement signed by all member states except the United Kingdom on social policy, based on the Social Charter of 1989 (see 'Social Policy', p. 170).

COMMON PROVISIONS

Article A

By this Treaty, the High Contracting Parties establish among themselves a European Union, hereinafter called 'the Union'.

This Treaty marks a new stage in the process of creating an ever closer union among the peoples of Europe, in which decisions are taken as closely as possible to the citizen.

The Union shall be founded on the European Communities, supplemented by the policies and forms of co-operation established by this Treaty. Its task shall be to organize, in a manner demonstrating consistency and solidarity, relations between the Member States and between their peoples.

Article B

The Union shall set itself the following objectives:

to promote economic and social progress which is balanced and sustainable, in particular through the creation of an area without internal frontiers, through the strengthening of economic and social cohesion[1] and through the establishment of economic and monetary union[2], ultimately including a single currency in accordance with the provisions of this Treaty;

to assert its identity on the international scene, in particular through the implementation of a common foreign and security policy including the eventual framing of a common defence policy, which might in time lead to a common defence;

to strengthen the protection of the rights and interests of the nationals of its Member States through the introduction of a citizenship of the Union;

to develop close co-operation on justice and home affairs;

to maintain in full the *acquis communautaire*[3] and build on it with a view to considering, through the procedure referred to in Article N (2), to what extent the policies and forms of cooperation introduced by this Treaty may need to be revised with the aim of ensuring the effectiveness of the mechanisms and the institutions of the Community.

The objectives of the Union shall be achieved as provided in this Treaty and in accordance with the conditions and the timetable set out therein while respecting the principle of subsidiarity as defined in Article 3b of the Treaty establishing the European Community[4].

Article C

The Union shall be served by a single institutional framework which shall ensure the consistency and the continuity of the activities carried out in order to attain its objectives while respecting and building upon the *acquis communautaire.*

The Union shall in particular ensure the consistency of its external activities as a whole in the context of its external relations, security, economic and development policies. The Council and the Commission shall be responsible for ensuring such consistency. They shall ensure the implementation of these policies, each in accordance with its respective powers.

Article D

The European Council shall provide the Union with the necessary impetus for its development and shall define the general political guidelines thereof.

The European Council shall bring together the Heads of State or Government of the Member States and the President of the Commission. They shall be assisted by the Ministers for Foreign Affairs of the Member States and by a Member of the Commission. The European Council shall meet at least twice a year, under the chairmanship of the Head of State or Government of the Member State which holds the Presidency of the Council.

The European Council shall submit to the European Parliament a report after each of its meetings and a yearly written report on the progress achieved by the Union.

Article E

The European Parliament, the Council, the Commission and the Court of Justice shall exercise their powers under the conditions and for the purposes provided for, on the one hand, by the provisions of the Treaties establishing the European Communities and of the subsequent Treaties and Acts modifying and supplementing them and, on the other hand, by the provisions of this Treaty.

Article F

(1) The Union shall respect the national identities of its Member States, whose systems of government are founded on the principles of democracy.

(2) The Union shall respect fundamental rights, as guaranteed by the European Convention for the Protection of Human Rights and Fundamental Freedoms signed in Rome on 4 November 1950 and as they result from the constitutional traditions common to the Member States, as general principles of Community law.

(3) The Union shall provide itself with the means necessary to attain its objectives and carry through its policies.

[1] See 'Structural Actions', p. 180, for plans to establish a 'cohesion fund'.

[2] See 'Economic Co-operation', p. 172.

[3] The term used to describe collectively all the secondary legislation approved by the Commission and the Council of Ministers under the provisions of the founding treaties and their subsequent amendments.

[4] The Treaty on European Union amends Article 3 of the Treaty establishing the EEC, inserting Article 3b:

'The Community shall act within the limits of the powers conferred upon it by this Treaty and of the objectives assigned to it therein.

In areas which do not fall within its exclusive competence, the Community shall take action, in accordance with the principle of subsidiarity, only if and in so far as the objectives of the proposed action cannot be sufficiently achieved by the member states and can therefore, by reason of the scale or effects of the proposed action, be better achieved by the Community.

Any action by the Community shall not go beyond what is necessary to achieve the objectives of this Treaty.'

TREATY OF AMSTERDAM

The Treaty of Amsterdam (Amending the Treaty on European Union, the Treaties Establishing the European Communities and Certain Related Acts) was agreed at the intergovernmental conference held in Amsterdam, the Netherlands, in June 1997, signed by EU ministers of foreign affairs in October, and was expected to be ratified by member states during 1998. Among other things, it included a chapter on employment, thus making a high level of employment one of the major objectives of the EU; incorporated into the Treaty the protocol based on the Social Charter of 1989, following the decision of the Government of the United Kingdom to subscribe to it with effect from May 1997; also incorporated the Schengen Agreement (see p. 168) on the freedom of movement of persons across internal EU boundaries into the Treaty; enhanced the foreign policy role of the EU, to be co-ordinated by the Secretary-General of the Council; and instituted a process of institutional reforms, expanding the use of qualified majority voting by the Council and awarding greater responsibilities to the European Parliament, which would make the structure of the EU more efficient, with a view to the admittance of further member countries.

Union Institutions

Originally each of the Communities had its own Commission (High Authority in the case of the ECSC) and Council, but a treaty transferring the powers of these bodies to a single Commission and a single Council came into effect in 1967.

EUROPEAN COMMISSION

Address: 200 rue de la Loi, 1049 Brussels, Belgium.

Telephone: (2) 299-11-11; **telex:** 21877; **fax:** (2) 295-01-38; **internet:** http://europa.eu.int.

MEMBERS OF THE COMMISSION

(with their responsibilities: December 1997*)

President: JACQUES SANTER (Luxembourg): Common foreign and security policy and human rights; Monetary matters; Institutional matters.

Vice-Presidents†:

Sir LEON BRITTAN (United Kingdom): External relations with North America, Australia, New Zealand, Japan, People's Republic of China, Republic of Korea, Hong Kong, Macau, Taiwan; Common commercial policy; Relations with OECD and WTO.

MANUEL MARÍN (Spain): External relations with Southern Mediterranean countries, the Near and Middle East, Latin America and Asia (except Japan, People's Republic of China, Republic of Korea, Hong Kong, Macau, Taiwan), including development aid matters.

Other Members:

MARTIN BANGEMANN (Germany): Industrial Affairs; Information and Telecommunications technologies.

KAREL VAN MIERT (Belgium): Competition.

HANS VAN DEN BROEK (Netherlands): External relations with Central and Eastern Europe and the former Soviet Union, Mongolia, Turkey, Cyprus, Malta, other European countries; Common foreign and security policy and human rights (with the President); External diplomatic missions.

JOÃO DE DEUS PINHEIRO (Portugal): External relations with the countries of Africa, the Caribbean and the Pacific, South Africa, the Lomé Convention, including development aid matters.

PADRAIG FLYNN (Ireland): Employment and social affairs; Relations with the Economic and Social Committee.

MARCELINO OREJA (Spain): Relations with the European Parliament; Relations with member states on transparency, communication, and information; Culture and audio-visual media policy; Publications office; Institutional questions.

EDITH CRESSON (France): Science, research and development; Joint Research Centre; Education, training and youth.

RITT BJERREGAARD (Denmark): Environment; Nuclear safety.

MONIKA WULF-MATHIES (Germany): Regional policies; Relations with the Committee of the Regions.

NEIL KINNOCK (United Kingdom): Transport, including trans-European networks.

MARIO MONTI (Italy): Internal market; Financial services and financial integration; Customs; Taxation.

EMMA BONINO (Italy): Fisheries; Consumer policy; EC Humanitarian Office (ECHO).

YVES-THIBAULT DE SILGUY (France): Economic and financial affairs; Monetary matters (with the President); Credit and investments; Statistical office.

CHRISTOS PAPOUTSIS (Greece): Energy and Euratom Supply Agency; Small and medium-sized enterprises (SMEs); Tourism.

ANITA GRADIN (Sweden): Immigration; Justice and home affairs; Relations with the Ombudsman; Financial control; Fraud prevention.

FRANZ FISCHLER (Austria): Agriculture and rural development.

ERKKI LIIKANEN (Finland): Budget; Personnel and administration; Translation and in-house computer services.

* The new composition of the European Commission was approved by the European Parliament on 18 January 1995 by 416 votes to 103 (with 59 abstentions). It formally took office on 24 January.

† Elected on 1 February 1995 by a ballot of the Commissioners.

The functions of the Commission are fourfold: to ensure the application of the provisions of the Treaties and of the provisions enacted by the institutions of the Communities in pursuance thereof; to formulate recommendations or opinions in matters which are the subject of the Treaties, where the latter expressly so provides or where the Commission considers it necessary; to dispose, under the conditions laid down in the Treaties, of a power of decision of its own and to participate in the preparation of acts of the Council of the European Union and of the European Parliament; and to exercise the competence conferred on it by the Council of the European Union for the implementation of the rules laid down by the latter.

The Commission may not include more than two members having the nationality of the same state; the number of members of the Commission may be amended by a unanimous vote of the Council of the European Union. In the performance of their duties, the members of the Commission are forbidden to seek or accept instructions from any Government or other body, or to engage in any other paid or unpaid professional activity.

The members of the Commission are appointed by the Governments of the member states acting in common agreement for a renewable term of five years (although the last Commission was, exceptionally, appointed for the two-year period 1993–94 only); from January 1995, under the terms of the Treaty on European Union, the nominated President and other members of the Commission must be approved as a body by the European Parliament before they can take office. Once approved, the Commission may nominate one or two of its members as Vice-President. Any member of the Commission, if he or she no longer fulfils the conditions required for the performance of his or her duties, or commits a serious offence, may be declared removed from office by the Court of Justice. The Court may furthermore, on the petition of the Council of the European Union or of the Commission itself, provisionally suspend any member of the Commission from his or her duties.

ADMINISTRATION

Offices are at the address of the European Commission: 200 rue de la Loi, 1049 Brussels, Belgium; tel. (2) 299-11-11; telex 21877; fax (2) 295-01-22 (unless otherwise stated).

Secretariat-General of the Commission: Sec.-Gen. CARLO TROJAN.

Forward Studies Unit: Dir-Gen. (vacant).

Inspectorate-General: Dir-Gen. MARIA PIA FILIPPONE.

Legal Service: Dir-Gen. JEAN-LOUIS DEWOST.

Spokesman's Service: Spokesman NIKOLAUS VAN DER PAS.

Joint Interpreting and Conference Service: Head of Service ROCCO TANZILLI.

Statistical Office (EUROSTAT): Bâtiment Jean Monnet, rue Alcide de Gasperi, 2920 Luxembourg; tel. 4301 33107; telex 3423; fax 4301 33015; Dir-Gen. YVES FRANCHET.

Translation Service: Dir-Gen. COLETTE FLESCH.

Informatics Directorate: Bâtiment Jean Monnet, rue Alcide de Gasperi, 2920 Luxembourg; tel. 43011; telex 3423; Dir-Gen. COLETTE FLESCH.

Security Office: Dir PIETER DE HAAN.

Directorates-General:

I (External Relations: Commercial Policy and Relations with North America, the Far East, Australia and New Zealand): Dir-Gen. HANS-FRIEDRICH BESELER

IA (External Relations: Europe and New Independent States, Common Foreign and Security Policy and External Missions): Dir-Gen. GÜNTER BURGHARDT.

IB (External Relations: Southern Mediterranean, Middle East, Latin America, South and South-East Asia and North-South Co-operation): Dir-Gen. ENRICO CIOFFI.

II (Economic and Financial Affairs): Dir-Gen. GIOVANNI RAVASIO.

III (Industry): Dir-Gen. STEFANO MICOSSI.

IV (Competition): Dir-Gen. ALEXANDER SCHAUB.

V (Employment, Industrial Relations and Social Affairs): Dir-Gen. ALLAN LARSSON.

VI (Agriculture): Dir-Gen. GUY LEGRAS.

VII (Transport): Dir-Gen. ROBERT COLEMAN.

VIII (Development): Dir-Gen. PHILIP LOWE.

IX (Personnel and Administration): Dir-Gen. STEFFEN SMIDT.

X (Information, Communication, Culture and Audiovisual Media): Dir-Gen. SPYROS PAPPAS.

XI (Environment, Nuclear Safety and Civil Protection): Dir-Gen. JAMES CURRIE.

XII (Science, Research and Development): Dir-Gen. JORMA ROUTTI.

Joint Research Centre: Dir-Gen. HUGH RICHARDSON (acting).

XIII (Telecommunications, Information Market and Exploitation of Research): Dir-Gen. ROBERT VERRUE.

XIV (Fisheries): Dir-Gen. ANTÓNIO CAVACO.

XV (Internal Market and Financial Services): Dir-Gen. JOHN F. MOGG.

XVI (Regional Policy and Cohesion): Dir-Gen. ENEKO LANDÁBURU ILLARRAMENDI.

XVII (Energy): Dir-Gen. PABLO BENAVIDES SALAS.

XIX (Budgets): Dir-Gen. JEAN-PAUL MINGASSON.

XX (Financial Control): Dir-Gen. ISABELLA VENTURA (Financial Controller of the Commission).

XXI (Customs and Indirect Taxation): Dir-Gen. MICHEL VANDEN ABEELE.

XXII (Education, Training and Youth): Dir-Gen. THOMAS O'DWYER.

XXIII (Enterprise Policy, Distributive Trades, Tourism and Co-operatives): Dir-Gen. GUY CRAUSER.

XXIV (Consumer Policy and Health Protection): Dir-Gen. HORST REICHENBACH.

European Community Humanitarian Office (ECHO): Dir ALBERTO NAVARRO.

Euratom Supply Agency: Dir-Gen. MICHAEL GOPPEL.

Office for Official Publications of the European Union: 2 rue Mercier, 2985 Luxembourg; tel. 29291; fax 495719; Dir-Gen. LUCIEN EMRINGER.

THE EUROPEAN COUNCIL

The heads of state or of government of the member countries meet at least twice a year, in the member state which currently exercises the presidency of the Council of the European Union, or in Brussels.

Until 1975 summit meetings were held less frequently, on an *ad hoc* basis, usually to adopt major policy decisions regarding the future development of the Community. In answer to the evident need for more frequent consultation at the highest level, it was decided at the summit meeting in Paris in December 1974 to hold the meetings on a regular basis, under the rubric of the European Council. There was no provision made for the existence of the European Council in the Treaty of Rome, but its position was acknowledged and regularized in the Single European Act (1987). Its role was further strengthened in the Treaty on European Union, which entered into force on 1 November 1993. As a result of the Treaty, the European Council became directly responsible for common policies within the fields of Common Foreign and Security Policy and Justice and Home Affairs.

COUNCIL OF THE EUROPEAN UNION

General Secretariat: 170 rue de la Loi, 1048 Brussels, Belgium.

Telephone: (2) 285-61-11; **telex:** 21711; **fax:** (2) 285-73-97.

Secretary-General: JÜRGEN TRUMPF.

The Council of the European Union (until 1994 known formally as the Council of Ministers of the European Community and still frequently referred to as the Council of Ministers) is the only institution that directly represents the member states. It is the Community's principal decision-making body, acting on proposals made by the Commission, and is responsible for ensuring the co-ordination of the general economic policies of the member states and for taking the decisions necessary to implement the Treaties. The Council is composed of representatives of the member states, each Government delegating to it one of its members, according to the subject to be discussed. These meetings are generally referred to as the Agriculture Council, Telecommunications Council, etc. The Foreign Affairs, Economics and Finance ('ECOFIN') and Agriculture Councils normally meet once a month. The office of President is exercised for a term of six months by each member of the Council in rotation (in 1998, January–June: the United Kingdom; July–December: Austria). Meetings of the Council are convened and chaired by the President, acting on his or her own initiative or at the request of a member or of the Commission.

The Treaty of Rome prescribed three types of voting: simple majority, qualified majority and unanimity. The votes of its members are weighted as follows: France, Germany, Italy and the United Kingdom 10; Spain 8; Belgium, Greece, the Netherlands and Portugal 5; Austria and Sweden 4; Denmark, Finland and Ireland 3; Luxembourg 2. Out of a total number of votes of 87, 62 are required for a qualified majority decision, making 26 votes sufficient for a blocking minority. During negotiations for enlargement of the EU, an agreement was reached, in March 1994, on new rules regulating voting procedures in the expanded Council, in response to concerns on the part of Spain and the United Kingdom that their individual influence would be diminished. Under the 'Ioannina compromise' (named after the Greek town where the agreement was concluded) 23–25 opposing votes were to be sufficient to continue debate of legislation for a 'reasonable period' until a consensus decision is reached. Amendments to the Treaty of Rome (the Single European Act), effective from July 1987, restricted the right of 'veto', and were expected to accelerate the development of a genuine common market: they allowed proposals relating to the dismantling of barriers to the free movement of goods, persons, services and capital to be approved by a majority vote in the Council, rather than by a unanimous vote. Unanimity would still be required, however, for certain areas, including harmonization of indirect taxes, legislation on health and safety, veterinary controls, and environmental protection; individual states would also retain control over immigration rules, prevention of terrorism and drugs-trafficking. The Treaty of Amsterdam, which was expected to be ratified during 1998, was to extend the use of qualified majority voting to limited policy areas.

The Single European Act introduced a 'co-operation procedure' whereby a proposal adopted by a qualified majority in the Council must be submitted to the European Parliament for approval: if the Parliament rejects the Council's common position, unanimity shall be required for the Council to act on a second reading, and if the Parliament suggests amendments, the Commission must re-examine the proposal and forward it to the Council again. A 'co-decision procedure' was introduced in 1993 by the Treaty on European Union. The procedure allows a proposal to be submitted for a third reading by a so-called 'Conciliation Committee', composed equally of Council representatives and members of the European Parliament. The Treaty of Amsterdam was to simplify the co-decision procedure, and extend it to matters previously resolved under the co-operation procedure, although the latter was to remain in place for matters concerning economic and monetary union.

Under the Treaty of Amsterdam, the Secretary-General of the council was also to take the role of 'high representative', responsible for the co-ordination of common foreign and security policy. The Secretary-General was to be supported by a policy planning and early warning unit.

PERMANENT REPRESENTATIVES

Preparation and co-ordination of the Council's work is entrusted to a Committee of Permanent Representatives (COREPER), meeting in Brussels, consisting of the ambassadors of the member countries to the Union. A staff of national civil servants assists each ambassador.

EUROPEAN PARLIAMENT

Address: Centre Européen, Plateau du Kirchberg, 2929 Luxembourg.

Telephone: 43001; **telex:** 2894; **fax:** 437009; **internet:** http://www.europarl.eu.int.

PRESIDENT AND MEMBERS
(January 1998)

President: José-María Gil-Robles Gil Delgado (Spain).

Members: 626 members, apportioned as follows: Germany 99 members; France, Italy and the United Kingdom 87 members each; Spain 64; the Netherlands 31; Belgium, Greece and Portugal 25 each; Sweden 22; Austria 21; Denmark and Finland 16 each; Ireland 15; Luxembourg 6. Members are elected for a five-year term by direct universal suffrage by the citizens of the member states. Members sit in the Chamber in political, not national, groups.

The tasks of the European Parliament are: amending legislation, scrutinizing the Union budget and exercising a measure of democratic control over the executive organs of the European Communities, the Commission and the Council. It has the power to dismiss the Commission by a vote of censure. Increases in parliamentary powers have been brought about through amendments to the Treaty of Rome. The Single European Act, which entered into force on 1 July 1987, introduced, in certain circumstances where the Council normally adopts legislation through majority voting, a co-operation procedure involving a second parliamentary reading, enabling Parliament to amend legislation. Community agreements with third countries require parliamentary approval. The Treaty on European Union, which came into force in November 1993, introduced the co-decision procedure, permitting a third parliamentary reading (see Council of the European Union, above). The Treaty also gives Parliament the right to veto legislation, and allows Parliament a vote of approval for a new Commission. Parliament appoints the European Ombudsman. The Treaty of Amsterdam, which was expected to enter into force during 1998, was to expand and simplify Parliament's Legislative role.

Political Groupings

	Distribution of seats (November 1997)
Party of European Socialists	215
Group of the European People's Party	180
Union for Europe	56
European Liberal Democratic and Reformist Party	41
Confederal Group of the European United Left-Nordic Green Left	33
Green Group	27
Group of the European Radical Alliance	20
The Independent Europe of the Nations Group	18
Non-attached	36
Total	626

Parliament has an annual session, divided into about 12 one-week meetings, normally held in Strasbourg, France. The session opens with the March meeting. Committees and political group meetings and additional sittings of Parliament are held in Brussels.

The budgetary powers of Parliament (which, with the Council, forms the Budgetary Authority of the Communities) were increased to their present status by a treaty of 22 July 1975. Under this treaty, it can amend non-agricultural spending and reject the draft budget, acting by a majority of its members and two-thirds of the votes cast.

The Parliament is run by a Bureau comprising the President, 14 Vice-Presidents elected from its members by secret ballot to serve for two-and-a-half years, and the four members of the College of Quaestors. Parliament has 20 specialized committees, which deliberate on proposals for legislation put forward by the Commission before Parliament's final opinion is delivered by a resolution in plenary session.

There are Standing Committees on Foreign Affairs, Security, and Defence Policies; Agriculture and Rural Development; Budgets; Budgetary Control; Economic and Monetary Affairs and Industrial Policy; Research, Technological Development and Energy; External Economic Relations; Legal Affairs and Citizens' Rights; Social Affairs and Employment; Regional Policy; Transport and Tourism; Environment, Public Health and Consumer Protection; Culture, Youth, Education and the Media; Development and Co-operation; Fisheries; Rules of Procedure, the Verification of Credentials and Immunities; Institutional Affairs; Petitions; Women's Rights; Civil Liberties and Internal Affairs.

The first direct elections to the European Parliament took place in June 1979, and Parliament met for the first time in July. The second elections were held in June 1984 (with separate elections held in Portugal and Spain in 1987, following the accession of these two countries to the Community), the third in June 1989, and the fourth elections were held in June 1994. Direct elections to the European Parliament were held in Sweden in September 1995, and in Austria and Finland in October 1996.

COURT OF JUSTICE OF THE EUROPEAN COMMUNITIES

Address: Palais de la Cour de Justice, 2925 Luxembourg.

Telephone: 43031; **telex:** 2510; **fax:** 4303-2600.

The task of the Court of Justice is to ensure the observance of law in the interpretation and application of the Treaties setting up the three Communities. The 15 Judges and the nine Advocates General are appointed for renewable six-year terms by the Governments of the member states. The President of the Court is elected by the Judges from among their number for a renewable term of three years. The majority of cases are dealt with by one of the six chambers, each of which consists of a President of Chamber and two or four Judges. The Court may sit in plenary session in cases of particular importance or when a member state or Community institution that is a party to the proceedings so requests. The Court has jurisdiction to award damages. It may review the legality of acts (other than recommendations or opinions) of the Council or the Commission and is competent to give judgment on actions by a member state, the Council or the Commission on grounds of lack of competence, of infringement of an essential procedural requirement, of infringement of a Treaty or of any legal rule relating to its application, or of misuse of power. The Court of Justice may hear appeals, on a point of law only, from the Court of First Instance.

The Court is also empowered to hear certain other cases concerning the contractual and non-contractual liability of the Communities and disputes between member states in connection with the objects of the Treaties. It also gives preliminary rulings at the request of national courts on the interpretation of the Treaties, of Union legislation, and of the Brussels Convention on Jurisdiction and the Enforcement of Judgments in Civil and Commercial Matters. During 1996 423 new cases were brought before the Court, of which 256 were cases referred to it for preliminary rulings by the national courts of the member states and 28 were appeals from the Court of First Instance. In the same period 193 judgments were delivered and 349 cases completed.

Composition of the Court (in order of precedence, as at 18 December 1997).

G. C. Rodríguez Iglesias, President of the Court of Justice.

C. Gulmann, President of the Third and Fifth Chambers.

G. Cosmas, First Advocate General.

H. Ragnemalm, President of the Fourth and Sixth Chambers.

M. Wathelet, President of the First Chamber.

R. Schingten, President of the Second Chamber.

G. F. Mancini, Judge.

J. C. Moitinho de Almeida, Judge.

F. G. Jacobs, Advocate General.

G. Tesauro, Advocate General.

P. J. G. Kapteyn, Judge.

J. L. Murray, Judge.

D. A. O. Edward, Judge.

A. M. La Pergola, Advocate General.

J.-P. Puissochet, Judge.

P. Léger, Advocate General.

G. Hirsch, Judge.

P. Jann, Judge.

L. Sevón, Judge.

N. Fennelly, Advocate General.

D. Ruiz-Jarabo Colomer, Advocate General.

K. M. Ioannou, Judge.

Jean Mischo, Advocate General.

S. Alber, Advocate General.

R. Grass, Registrar.

COURT OF FIRST INSTANCE OF THE EUROPEAN COMMUNITIES

Address: blvd Konrad Adenauer, 2925 Luxembourg.

Telephone: 43031; **telex:** 60216; **fax:** 4303-2100.

By a decision of 24 October 1988, as amended by decisions of 8 June 1993 and 7 March 1994, the European Council, exercising powers conferred upon it by the Single European Act, established a Court of First Instance with jurisdiction to hear and determine cases brought by natural or legal persons and which had hitherto been dealt with by the Court of Justice.

Composition of the Court of First Instance (in order of precedence, with effect from 1 October 1997 to 31 August 1998)

A. Saggio, President of the Court of First Instance.

A. Kalogeropoulos, President of Chamber.

V. Tiili, President of Chamber.

P. Lindh, President of Chamber.

J. Azizi, President of Chamber.

C. P. Briët, Judge.

B. Vesterdorf, Judge.

R. García-Valdecasas y Fernández, Judge.

K. Lenaerts, Judge.

C. W. Bellamy, Judge.

A. Potocki, Judge.

R. Moura-Ramos, Judge.

J. D. Cooke, Judge.

M. Jaeger, Judge.

J. Pirrung, Judge.

H. Jung, Registrar.

COURT OF AUDITORS OF THE EUROPEAN COMMUNITIES

Address: 12 rue Alcide de Gasperi, 1615 Luxembourg.

Telephone: 4398-45518; **telex:** 3512; **fax:** 4398-46430; **e-mail:** euraud@eca.eu.int; **internet:** http://www.eca.eu.int.

The Court of Auditors was created by the Treaty of Brussels, which was signed on 22 July 1975, and commenced its duties in late 1977. It was given the status of an institution on a par with the Commission, the Council, the Court of Justice and the Parliament by the Treaty on European Union. It is the institution responsible for the external audit of the resources managed by the three Communities. It consists of 15 members who are appointed for six-year terms by unanimous decision of the Council of the European Union, after consultation with the European Parliament. The members elect the President from among their number for a term of three years.

The Court is organized and acts as a collegiate body. It adopts its decisions by a majority of its members. Each member, however, has a direct responsibility for the audit of certain sectors of Union activities.

The Court examines the accounts of all expenditure and revenue of the European Communities and of any body created by them in so far as the relevant constituent instrument does not preclude such examination. It examines whether all revenue has been received and all expenditure incurred in a lawful and regular manner and whether the financial management has been sound. The audit is based on records, and if necessary is performed directly in the institutions of the Communities, in the member states and in other countries. In the member states the audit is carried out in co-operation with the national audit bodies. The Court of Auditors draws up an annual report after the close of each financial year. The Court provides the Parliament and the Council with a statement of assurance as to the reliability of the accounts, and the legality and regularity of the underlying transactions. It may also, at any time, submit observations on specific questions (usually in the form of special reports) and deliver opinions at the request of one of the institutions of the Communities. It assists the European Parliament and the Council in exercising their powers of control over the implementation of the budget, in particular in the framework of the annual discharge procedure, and gives its prior opinion on the financial regulations, on the methods and procedure whereby the budgetary revenue is made available to the Commission, and on the formulation of rules concerning the responsibility of authorizing officers and accounting officers and concerning appropriate arrangements for inspection.

President: Bernhard Friedmann (Germany).

Audit Group I: Barry Desmond; Kalliopi Nikolaou; Maarten Engwirda.

Audit Group II: Patrick Everard; Armindo de Jesus de Sousa Ribeiro; Antoni Castells; Jørgen Mohr; François Colling.

Audit Group III: Giorgio Clemente; Jan. O Karlsson; Aunus Salmi; Jean-François Bernicot.

Audit Development and Reports (ADAR) Group: Hubert Weber.

Statement of Assurance (SoA) Group: John Wiggins.

Secretary-General: Edouard Ruppert.

EUROPEAN INVESTMENT BANK

Address: 100 blvd Konrad Adenauer, 2950 Luxembourg.

Telephone: 43791; **telex:** 3530; **fax:** 437704; **internet:** http://www.eib.org.

The European Investment Bank (EIB) was created in 1958 by the six founder member states of the European Economic Community. At December 1997 the capital subscribed by the 15 member states totalled ECU 62,013m., of which 7.5% was paid-in or to be paid-in. Capital structure at 31 December 1995 was as follows: France, Germany, Italy and the United Kingdom 17.8% each; Spain 6.5%; Belgium and the Netherlands 4.9% each; Sweden 3.3%; Denmark 2.5%; Austria 2.4%; Finland 1.4%; Greece 1.3%; Portugal 0.9%; Ireland 0.6%; Luxembourg 0.1%. The bulk of the EIB's resources comes from borrowings, principally public bond issues or private placements on capital markets inside and outside the Union. In 1996 the Bank borrowed ECU 17,572m., compared with ECU 12,395m. in 1995. Some 92% of resources raised in 1996 was in EU currencies.

The EIB's principal task is defined in Article 130 of the Treaty of Rome: working on a non-profit basis, the Bank makes or guarantees loans for investment projects which contribute to the balanced and steady development of EU member states. Throughout the Bank's history, priority has been given to financing investment projects which further regional development within the Community. The EIB also finances projects that improve communications, protect and improve the environment, promote urban development, strengthen the competitive position of industry and encourage industrial integration within the Union, support the activities of small and medium-sized enterprises (SMEs), and help ensure the security of energy supplies. The EIB also provides finance for developing countries in Africa, the Caribbean and the Pacific, under the terms of the Lomé Convention (q.v.); for countries in the Mediterranean region, under co-operation agreements; and for countries in central and eastern Europe.

The European Investment Fund (EIF) was founded in 1994 by the EIB (which was to provide 40% of the Fund's ECU 2,000m. authorized capital), the European Communities (EC—represented by the Commission; 30%) and a group of 76 banks and financial institutions from throughout the EU (30%). The EIF's purpose is to assist SMEs and provide guarantees for the long-term financing of European infrastructure projects, particularly for Trans-European Networks (TENs) in the fields of transport, energy transmission and telecommunications. By early 1996, the EIB had subscribed ECU 800m., the EC ECU 600m. and the financial institutions ECU 386m.

In 1996 total financing contracts signed by the EIB both inside and outside the European Union, amounted to ECU 23,200m., compared with ECU 21,408m. in 1995. Loans agreed for projects within member states in 1996 totalled ECU 20,946m. Trans-European transport and energy infrastructures accounted for 31.0%, environment 28.2%, energy 19.1% and industry and services 21.5%. Operations outside the Union totalled ECU 2,254m., compared with ECU 2,805m. in 1995.

The Board of Governors of the EIB, which usually meets only once a year, lays down general directives on credit policy, approves the annual report and accounts and decides on capital increases. The Board of Directors has sole power to take decisions in respect of loans, guarantees and borrowings. Its members are appointed by the Governors for a renewable five-year term following nomination by the member states. The day-to-day management of operations is the responsibility of the Management Committee, which is the EIB's collegiate executive body and recommends decisions to the Board of Directors. It comprises the Bank's President and six Vice-Presidents, nominated for renewable six-year terms by the Board of Directors and approved by the Board of Governors. The President presides over meetings of the Board of Directors.

Board of Governors: One minister (usually the minister of finance) from each member state.

Board of Directors: Twenty-five directors and 13 alternates (senior officials from finance or economic ministeries, public-sector banks or credit institutions), appointed for a renewable five-year term, of whom 24 and 12 respectively are nominated by the member states; one director and one alternate are nominated by the Commission of the European Communities.

Management Committee:

President: Sir BRIAN UNWIN.

Vice-Presidents: WOLFGANG ROTH, PANAGIOTIS-LOUKAS GENNIMATAS, MASSIMO PONZELLINI, LUIS MARTÍ, ARIANE OBOLENSKY, RUDOLF DE KORTE, CLAES DE NEERGAARD.

FINANCE CONTRACTS SIGNED (ECU million)

	1995		1996	
Recipient	Amount	%	Amount	%
Austria	242	1.3	490	2.3
Belgium	665	3.6	657	3.1
Denmark	825	4.4	688	3.3
Finland	179	1.0	302	1.4
France	2,207	11.9	2,509	12.0
Germany	2,715	14.6	3,022	14.4
Greece	525	2.8	721	3.4
Ireland	327	1.8	189	0.9
Italy	3,435	18.5	4,121	19.7
Luxembourg	79	0.4	—	—
Netherlands	319	1.7	766	3.7
Portugal	1,232	6.6	1,294	6.2
Spain	2,818	15.1	2,553	12.2
Sweden	273	1.5	847	4.0
United Kingdom	2,244	12.1	2,386	11.4
Other*	519	2.8	403	1.9
EU total	18,603	100.0	20,946	100.0
ACP-Overseas countries and territories	430	15.3	396	17.6
South Africa	45	1.6	56	2.5
Mediterranean	1,038	37.0	681	30.2
Central and Eastern Europe	1,005	35.8	1,076	47.7
Latin America and Asia	288	10.3	45	2.0
Non-EU total	2,805	100.0	2,254	100.0
Total	21,408	—	23,200	—

* Projects of direct benefit to the Union but located outside the member states.

CONSULTATIVE BODIES

ECONOMIC AND SOCIAL COMMITTEE

Address: 2 rue Ravenstein, 1000 Brussels.

Telephone: (2) 546-90-11; **telex:** 25983; **fax:** (2) 513-48-93; **internet:** http://www.esc.eu.int.

The Committee is advisory and is consulted by the Council of the European Union or by the European Commission, particularly with regard to agriculture, free movement of workers, harmonization of laws and transport, as well as legislation adopted under the Euratom Treaty. In certain cases consultation of the Committee by the Commission or the Council is mandatory. In addition, the Committee has the power to deliver opinions on its own initiative.

The Committee has 222 members: 24 each from France, Germany, Italy and the United Kingdom, 21 from Spain, 12 each from Austria, Belgium, Greece, the Netherlands, Portugal and Sweden, nine from Denmark, Finland and Ireland, and six from Luxembourg. One-third represent employers, one-third employees, and one-third various interest groups (e.g. agriculture, small enterprises, consumers). The Committee is appointed for a renewable term of four years by the unanimous vote of the Council of the European Union. Members are nominated by their governments, but are appointed in their personal capacity and are not bound by any mandatory instructions. The Committee is served by a permanent and independent General Secretariat, headed by the Secretary-General.

President: TOM JENKINS.

Vice-Presidents: JOHANNES JASCHICK, GIACOMO REGALDO.

Secretary-General: ADRIANO GRAZIOSI.

COMMITTEE OF THE REGIONS

Address: 79 rue Belliard, 1040 Brussels.

Telephone: (2) 282-22-11; **fax:** (2) 282-20-85.

The Treaty on European Union provided for a committee to be established, with advisory status, comprising representatives of regional and local bodies throughout the EU. The first meeting of the Committee was held in March 1994. It may be consulted on EU proposals concerning economic and social cohesion, trans-European networks, public health, education and culture, and may issue an opinion on any issue with regional implications. The Committee meets in plenary session five times a year.

The number of members of the Committee is equal to that of the Economic and Social Committee (see above). Members are appointed for a renewable term of four years by the Council, acting unanimously on the proposals from the respective member states. The Committee elects its principal officers from among its members for a two-year term.

President: PASQUAL MARAGALL I MARA (Spain).

First Vice-President: JACQUES BLANC (France).

ECSC CONSULTATIVE COMMITTEE

The Committee is advisory and is attached to the Commission. It advises the Commission on matters relating to the coal and steel industries of the Union. Its members are appointed by the Council of the European Union for two years and are not bound by any mandate from the organizations that designated them in the first place.

There are 84 members representing, in equal proportions, producers, workers and consumers and dealers in the coal and steel industries.

OTHER ADVISORY COMMITTEES

There are advisory committees dealing with all aspects of EU policy. Consultation with some committees is compulsory in the procedure for drafting EC legislation.

In addition to the consultative bodies listed above there are several hundred special interest groups representing every type of interest within the Union. All these hold unofficial talks with the Commission.

OTHER INSTITUTIONS

European Monetary Institute—EMI: Postfach 102 031, Eurotower, Kaiserstrasse 29, 60020 Frankfurt a.M., Germany; tel. (69) 27-22-70; fax (69) 27-227-227.

Established on 1 January 1994, under Stage II of the process of economic and monetary union under the Treaty on European Union ('The Maastricht Treaty'). The EMI's members are the central banks of the EU member states. Its purpose is to strengthen the co-ordination of monetary policies of the member states with a view to ensuring price stability and by making the necessary preparations required for the establishment of the European System of Central Banks (ESCB), for the conduct of a single monetary policy and the creation of a single currency, the Euro. The EMI was scheduled to be replaced by the ESCB at the start of Stage II, on 1 January 1999.

President: WILLEM DUISENBERG (Netherlands).

Director-General: ROBERT RAYMOND (France).

Secretary-General: HANSPETER K. SCHELLER.

European Environment Agency—EEA: 6 Kongens Nytorv, 1050 Copenhagen K, Denmark; tel. 33-36-71-00; fax 33-36-71-99; e-mail eea@eea.eu.int; internet: http://www.eea.eu.int.

Became operational in 1994, having been approved in 1990, to gather and supply information to assist the implementation of Community policy on environmental protection and improvement. The Agency's annual budget amounts to ECU 16.7m. The Agency publishes a report on the state of the environment every three years.

Chairman of the Management Board: F. DEREK A. OSBORN (United Kingdom).

Executive Director: DOMINGO JIMÉNEZ-BELTRÁN (Spain).

European Monitoring Centre for Drugs and Drug Addiction: Palacete Mascarenhas, Rua da Cruz de Sta. Apolónia 23-25, 1100 Lisbon, Portugal; tel. (1) 811-30-00; fax (1) 813-17-11; internet: http://www.emcdda.org.

Became fully operational at the end of 1995, with the aim of providing member states with objective, reliable and comparable information on drugs and drug addiction in order to assist in combatting the problem. The Centre co-operates with other European and international organizations and non-Community countries. The Centre's first *Annual Report on the State of the Drugs Problem in Europe* was published in October 1996. A newsletter, 'Drugnet Europe', is published every two months.

President: FRANZ-JOSEF BINDERT (Germany).

Executive Director: GEORGES ESTIEVENART (France).

European Agency for the Evaluation of Medicinal Products (EMEA): 7 Westferry Circus, Canary Wharf, London, E14 4HB, United Kingdom; tel. (171) 418-8400; fax (171) 418-8416; e-mail mail@emea.eudra.org; internet http://www.eudra.org.

Established in 1993 for the authorization and supervision of medicinal products for human and veterinary use. Became operational in 1994 with a budget of ECU 7.72m.

Chairman of the Management Board: STRACHAN HEPPELL (United Kingdom).

Executive Director: FERNAND SAUER (France).

European Training Foundation: Villa Gualino, Viale Settimio Severo 65, 10133 Turin, Italy; tel. (11) 630-22-22; fax (11) 630-22-00; e-mail info@etf.it; internet http://www.etf.it.

Established in 1990 with the aim of contributing to the development of the vocational training systems of designated central and eastern European countries. The Foundation incorporates initial and continuing vocational training, as well as retraining for adults and young people.

Director: PETER DE ROOIJ.

European Foundation for the Improvement of Living and Working Conditions: Wyattville Rd, Loughlinstown, Shankill, Co Dublin, Ireland; tel. (1) 204-3100; telex 30726; fax (1) 282-6456; e-mail postmaster@eurofound.ie.

Established in 1975 to develop strategies for the medium- and long-term improvement of living and working conditions.

Director: CLIVE J. PURKISS (United Kingdom).

Office for Harmonization in the Internal Market (Trade Marks and Designs)—OHIM: Avda de Aguilera 20, 03080 Alicante, Spain; tel. (6) 513-91-00; fax (6) 513-91-73; internet http://europa.eu.int.

Established in 1993.

President: JEAN-CLAUDE COMBALDIEU.

Activities of the Community

AGRICULTURE

Co-operation in the Community is at its most highly-organized in the area of agriculture. The objectives of the Common Agricultural Policy (CAP) are described in the Treaty of Rome (see p. 155). The markets for agricultural products have been progressively organized following three basic principles: (i) unity of the market (products must be able to circulate freely within the Community and markets must be organized according to common rules); (ii) Community preference (products must be protected from low-cost imports and from fluctuations on the world market); (iii) common financial responsibility: the European Agricultural Guidance and Guarantee Fund (EAGGF) finances, through its Guarantee Section, all public expenditure intervention, storage costs, marketing subsidies and export rebates.

From 1969 the operation of the CAP was hindered by the unstable monetary situation. A system of 'monetary compensatory amounts' (MCAs) was therefore introduced, in order to compensate for currency fluctuations, although, in practice, it led to wide variations in prices within the Community. In 1989 the relative stability of currencies made it possible to abolish MCAs for all countries that were full members of the European Monetary System (EMS). In December 1992 the MCA system was replaced by new agrimonetary arrangements, under which the ECU was to be the unit of account for agricultural prices and was to be convertible with national currencies at the central rate of fixed currencies within the narrow band of the EMS or the average market rate of the other 'floating' currencies. From 2 August 1993, when the fluctuation margin of the ERM was enlarged to 15% owing to persisting currency disturbances, the agrimonetary rules applicable to floating currencies were applied to the currencies of all member states.

Agricultural prices are, in theory, fixed each year at a common level for the Community as a whole, taking into account the rate of inflation and the need to discourage surplus production of certain commodities. Export subsidies are paid to enable farmers to sell produce at the lower world market prices without loss. These subsidies account for some 50% of agricultural spending.

When market prices of certain cereals, sugar, some fruits and vegetables, dairy produce and meat fall below a designated level the Community intervenes, and buys a certain quantity which is then stored until prices recover. During the 1980s expanding production led to food surpluses, costly to maintain, particularly in dairy produce, beef, cereals and wine, and to the destruction of large quantities of fruit and vegetables.

Agriculture is by far the largest item on the Community budget, accounting for about two-thirds of annual expenditure, mainly for supporting prices through the EAGGF Guarantee Section (appropriations for which amounted to ECU 41,305m., or 47.1% of the total budget, in 1997). A system of 'stabilizers' was introduced in February 1988, imposing an upper limit on the production of certain products. Any over-production would result in a decrease in the guaranteed intervention price for the following year. Similar 'stabilizers' were later imposed on production of oilseeds, protein feed crops, wine, sugar, fruit and vegetables, tobacco, olive oil, cotton and mutton. The existing system of milk production quotas was extended until 1992.

In 1990 the CAP came under attack in the 'Uruguay Round' of negotiations on the General Agreement on Tariffs and Trade (GATT, see WTO). The US Government demanded massive reductions in the EC's agricultural and export subsidies, on the grounds that they disrupted world markets. In November Community ministers of agriculture agreed to accept proposals by the Commission for a reduction of 30% in agricultural subsidies over a 10-year period. In 1990 increasing surpluses of cereals, beef and dairy products were again reported, and a decline in international wheat prices increased the cost to the Community of exporting surplus wheat. In May 1992, on the basis of proposals made by the Commission in 1991, ministers adopted a number of reforms, which aimed to transfer the Community's agricultural support from upholding prices to maintaining farmers' incomes, thereby removing the incentive to over-produce. Intervention prices were reduced by 29% for cereals, 15% for beef and poultry, and 5% for dairy products. Farmers were to be compensated for the price reductions by receiving additional grants, which, in the case of crops, took the form of a subsidy per hectare of land planted. To qualify for these subsidies, arable farmers (except for those with the smallest farms) were to be obliged to remove 15% of their land from cultivation (the 'set-aside' scheme). Incentives were to be given for alternative uses of the withdrawn land (e.g. forestry). The reform meant that prices payable for cereals would be reduced to the level of those prevailing in the international market.

In May 1992 the US Government threatened to impose a large increase in import tariffs on European products, in retaliation against subsidies paid by the EC to oilseed producers, which, the US Government claimed, led to unfair competition for US exports of soya beans. In November, however, agreement was reached between the USA and the European Commission: the USA agreed that limits should be imposed on the area of EC land on which cultivation of oilseed was permitted. The USA also agreed to accept a reduction of 21% in the volume and 36% in the value of the EC's subsidized exports of farm produce, over a six-year period (the amounts being based on average production during 1986–90). These agreements formed the basis of the GATT agricultural accord which was concluded as part of the Uruguay Round trade agreement in mid-December 1993.

The Commission estimated that between September 1992 and the end of July 1993, as a result of the turmoil in the exchange rate mechanism (see below), an extra ECU 1,500m. was spent in price support payments to farmers through the 'green' currencies system. In February 1995 ministers adopted a new agrimonetary regime, which limited the amount of compensation paid to farmers as a result of currency fluctuations. Further amendments, introduced in June, abandoned the existing common exchange rate, used to calculate compensation payments, and introduced two rates: one for currencies linked to the Deutsche Mark and one for all other EU currencies. Attempts by some member states to reform the system further were unsuccessful, and in October ministers agreed that national governments would be permitted to compensate farmers who had suffered loss of income as a result of currency fluctuations. In June 1997 it was reported that cereal farmers had been overcompensated by some ECU 8,500m. over the previous four years as a result of inaccurate price-reduction forecasts. In June 1995 the guaranteed intervention price for beef was decreased by 5%, and that for cereals by 7.5%. Other product prices remained unchanged. In September ministers agreed to reduce the level of compulsory 'set-aside' for 1996/97 to 10%, in response to much lower food surpluses in the EU and high world prices for cereal crops. In February 1996 the Commission adopted the agricultural price scheme proposals for 1996/97 which cut cereal intervention prices, to take account of interest rate reductions, and introduced measures to encourage the grain legume sector. It was also agreed that discussions on long-term price and quota policy with regard to the milk sector would begin in 1997. The 1992 CAP reforms, rises in world prices and other factors resulted in underspending in the agriculture budget, it was revealed in March 1996. This was to be used to help to finance infrastructure investment in the EU. In July agriculture ministers agreed on a reduction in the 'set-aside' rate for cereals from 10% to 5%. Fruit and vegetable production subsidies were fixed at no more than 4% of the value of total marketed production, rising to 4.5% in 1999. The aim was to improve competitiveness in the European market and avoid the widespread destruction of surplus fruit and vegetables that had taken place in recent years. The cereals harvest in 1996 was 201m. metric tons, and the annual total was forecast to rise to 214m. by 2005. The Commission is allowed to recover from member states sums that they have paid out under the CAP without sufficient guarantees of legitimacy or without adequate regard to control and verification. By November 1996 a total of ECU 787m. was being recovered from 10 member states under a decision taken by the Commission in March of that year. The largest sums, totalling ECU 415m., related to milk quotas in Italy, Spain and Greece.

In July 1994 Community ministers adopted measures to prevent the spread of the disease bovine spongiform encephalopathy (BSE) by imposing strict controls on carcass beef trade, extending the time-scale for the prohibition of exports from diseased herds from two years to six years. The agreement temporarily resolved a dispute whereby Germany had attempted to impose a unilateral ban on beef exports from the United Kingdom, provoking that country to seek a judicial ruling on the action by the European Court of Justice. Despite a relaxation in the rules to allow the export of UK beef from any animal under 30 months old, three German Länder imposed a ban on UK beef imports. New fears about possible links between BSE and Creutzfeldt-Jakob disease (CJD), which affects humans, led to a collapse in consumer confidence in the European beef market in early 1996. In March the Commission accepted that member countries could unilaterally stop imports of UK beef on health grounds, pending a decision by a committee of scientific and veterinary experts from all member states. By late March 12 EU countries had banned UK beef imports, and at the end of the month the Commission agreed a ban on exports from the United Kingdom of live cattle, beef and beef products. In late May the UK Government proposed a programme of selective slaughter as a means of eradicating BSE from the national herd. At the European Council meeting held in June, the United Kingdom agreed to the slaughter of 120,000 animals born since 1989, and new legislation to ensure that meat and bonemeal were excluded from the manufacture of animal feeds. In return, the ban on UK beef exports would be gradually removed. By July European beef consumption had fallen by an average of 11%, with the largest decrease, 30%, recorded in Germany. At the end of 1996 the Commission was estimated to have spent some ECU 1,500m., including ECU 850m. as compensation paid to beef farmers, on dealing with the consequences of the BSE crisis. Meanwhile, the UK Government abandoned the planned cull, proposing instead a much smaller slaughter scheme. This provoked widespread anger in other EU member states, and in July the European Court of Justice rejected the UK Government's application for the beef export ban to be suspended.

In August 1996 evidence emerged that BSE could be transmitted from cows to their calves and it seemed likely that the EU would demand the slaughter of further cattle in the United Kingdom. In October the Commission proposed a compulsory ear-tagging and 'passport' system for logging the identity and movement of cattle throughout the EU, and a voluntary labelling system for beef and beef products. In the same month EU ministers of agriculture agreed measures to provide an additional ECU 500m. to farmers affected by the BSE crisis and to reduce beef surpluses. In December the UK Government yielded to the European Commission's demand for an additional cull of more than 100,000 cattle. The Commission also stated that the United Kingdom was to submit plans for a certified BSE-free herd scheme, to provide computerized evidence that cattle herds had had no contact with other animals infected with BSE, before a phased removal of the embargo could begin. In June 1997 the United Kingdom's plans for monitoring and preventing BSE were judged by the Commission to be inadequate. However, in September the Scientific Veterinary Committee confirmed that a successful automated certified herd scheme had been used in Northern Ireland for nine years. The rest of the United Kingdom was expected to have implemented a similar system by March 1998. In July 1997 the United Kingdom was reported by the Commission to be engaging in the illegal export of beef, while in late June the Commission commenced infringement proceedings against 10 EU countries accused of evading the full implementation of hygiene procedures for the eradication of BSE. The UK Government, which had already taken steps to exclude the parts of animals considered most likely to carry BSE (such as the brain and spinal cord), threatened to impose import controls on beef suppliers unless the same measures were enforced in other countries. In July agriculture ministers voted, by a narrow margin, to introduce a complete ban on the use, for any purpose, of 'specified risk materials' (SRMs) from cattle, sheep and goats. The ban was to come into effect on 1 January 1998. In August the USA requested that US tallow manufacturers be temporarily exempted from the ban, claiming that the USA was free from BSE and that compliance with the new regulations could cause shortages within the pharmaceutical and cosmetics industries. In December the USA announced the extension of an existing ban on EU beef and lamb, in a move that was considered by some to be retaliatory. The Commission voted to postpone the introduction of the ban on SRMs until April 1998, later delayed further until July, as a result of opposition from a number of EU member states, particularly Germany, in addition to that from the USA. In protest at the delay, the United Kingdom imposed a unilateral ban on imports of all beef products breaching UK meat safety regulations. In January 1998 the Commission endorsed a proposal to ease the export ban on British beef, to allow the export of deboned beef from Northern-Irish herds certified as BSE-free. The proposal was subject to approval by EU ministers of agriculture and veterinary experts. In February the Commission announced plans to exempt from the ban on SRMs those countries able to prove that they had a low incidence of BSE infection.

In June 1995 the Agricultural Council agreed to new rules on the welfare of livestock during transport. The agreement, which came into effect in 1996, limited transport of livestock to a maximum of eight hours in any 24-hour period, and stipulated higher standards for their accommodation and care while in transit. In January 1996 the Commission proposed a ban on veal crates, which was to come into effect on 1 January 1998 for new buildings, and which was to be implemented within a further 10 years in all other cases.

During 1995–97 there was widespread speculation that the CAP would have to undergo dramatic reform to prevent possible economic problems and political upheaval following the proposed expansion of the EU into the less agriculturally-developed countries of central and eastern Europe. In July 1997 the Commission outlined proposals for reform of the CAP as part of its 'Agenda 2000', concerning the enlargement of the EU and the Community's budget after 2000. The plans envisaged the abolition of the 'set-aside' system and the use of the cold-storage method of intervention as an emergency measure only. Guaranteed prices and subsidies were to be progressively eliminated and replaced by direct annual payments to low-income farmers, thereby removing incentives for over-production and allowing compliance with WTO rules. Under the proposals, a limit was to be imposed on payments made to farmers, to prevent large-scale producers from receiving excessive compensation, while farmers were to be encouraged to adopt environmentally sound production methods in order to qualify for funds. Aid payments were also to be made available to support rural tourism and small enterprises.

FISHERIES

The Common Fisheries Policy (CFP) came into effect in January 1983 after seven years of negotiations, particularly concerning the problem of access to fishing-grounds. In 1973 a 10-year agreement had been reached, whereby member states could have exclusive access to waters up to six nautical miles (11.1 km) or, in some cases, 12 miles from their shores; 'historic rights' were reserved in certain cases for foreign fishermen who had traditionally fished within a country's waters. In 1977 the Community set up a 200-mile (370-km) fishing zone around its coastline (excluding the Mediterranean) within which all members would have access to fishing. The 1983 agreement confirmed the 200-mile zone and allowed exclusive national zones of six miles with access between six and 12 miles from the shore for other countries according to specified 'historic rights'. Rules furthering conservation (e.g. standards for fishing tackle) are imposed under the policy, with checks by a Community fisheries inspectorate. Total allowable catches are fixed annually by species, divided into national quotas under the renewable Multi-annual Guidance Programme (MAGP). In late 1990 it was reported that stocks of certain species of fish in EC waters had seriously diminished, and a reduction in quotas was agreed, together with the imposition of a compulsory eight-day period in each month during which fishermen in certain areas (chiefly the North Sea) would stay in port, with exemptions for fishermen using nets with larger meshes that would allow immature fish to escape. In 1992 the compulsory non-fishing period was increased to 135 days between February and December (with similar exemptions). In December of that year EC ministers agreed to extend the CFP for a further 10-year period.

The proposals put forward in May 1996 by the European Commission for the fourth MAGP, covering 1997–2002, envisaged catch reductions of up to 40% for species most at risk, and set targets and detailed rules for restructuring fishing fleets in the EU. The draft MAGP IV failed to gain approval at the meeting of fisheries ministers held in November 1996. In particular, the proposed reduction in the number of fishing vessels provoked anger in many member countries. The UK Government said in October it would not accept additional limits on catches without action to stop 'quota-hopping', in which UK-registered boats are bought by operators in other EU countries (mainly Spain and the Netherlands), which are thus able to gain part of the UK fishing quotas. In March the European Court of Justice had ruled against the UK Government in its attempt to prevent 'quota-hopping'. The agreement on 1997 quotas, reached by fisheries ministers in December 1996, represented a compromise between the Commission's desire to impose severe cuts in quotas to protect scarce stocks and the demands of EU Governments, anxious to defend the interests of their fishermen. Ministers also agreed upon the establishment of a satellite monitoring system, which was to be used to verify the fishing activities of boats greater than 20m in length. The new system was to be introduced gradually from 1 June 1998. In April 1997, following a number of concessions by the Commission, ministers approved MAGP IV. The programme fixed catch reductions at 30% for species most at risk and at 20% for other over-fished species.

The organization of fish marketing involves common rules on quality and packing, and a system of guide prices established annually by the Council. Fish are withdrawn from the market if prices fall too far below the guide price, and compensation may then be paid to the fishermen. Export subsidies are paid to enable the export of fish onto the lower-priced world market, and import levies are imposed to prevent competition from low-priced imports. A new import regime was adopted by Community fisheries ministers in April 1993, to take effect from 15 May. The regime, which was to be reviewed after two years, enabled regional fishermen's associations to increase prices to a maximum of 10% over the Community's reference price, although this was to apply to both EU and imported fish.

Agreements have been signed with other countries (Norway, Sweden, Canada and the USA) allowing reciprocal fishing rights and other advantages, and with some African countries which receive assistance in building up their fishing industries in return for allowing EU boats to fish in their waters. Following the withdrawal of Greenland from the Community in February 1985, Community vessels retained fishing rights in Greenland waters, in exchange for financial compensation under a 10-year agreement. In 1992 fisheries agreements with Estonia, Latvia, Lithuania and Argentina were initialled; and in 1993 an agreement was reached with Mauritania to benefit Spanish fishermen in the Canary Islands. Under a four-year agreement signed with Morocco in November 1995, the size of catches by EU vessels fishing in Moroccan waters was to be reduced by 20%–40% for various species, and the EU was to provide financial compensation for Morocco amounting to ECU 355m. In 1995 relations with Canada were severely strained by a dispute concerning Spanish boats, which, Canada claimed, were breaking rules, established by the Northwest Atlantic Fisheries Organization (q.v.), to prevent overfishing of Greenland halibut. In mid-April the EU and Canada reached agreement on an increased quota for EU fishermen, and extra inspection and surveillance measures were introduced to ensure that fishing limits were observed. Following the publication of an independent scientific report in April 1996, which warned that herring stocks were in danger of being totally eradicated, the EU and Norway agreed an emergency measure to reduce by 50% catches in the North Sea and the waters around Denmark. In June 1997 the Commission voted to counteract the 'dumping' of low-cost Norwegian salmon imports on the EU market, by accepting a five-year accord, negotiated with the Norwegian Government, compelling Norway to sell its salmon at a fixed minimum price and to set its export growth to the EU at no more than 12% in the first year, and 10% per year thereafter. Norway also agreed to a voluntary increase in the export duty on Norwegian salmon imports.

In December 1994 the EU fisheries ministers concluded a final agreement on the revised CFP, allowing Spain and Portugal to be integrated into the CFP by 1 January 1996. A compromise accord was reached regarding access to waters around Ireland and off south-west Great Britain (referred to as the 'Irish box') by means of which up to 40 Spanish vessels were granted access to 80,000 sq miles of the 90,000 sq mile area. However, the accord was strongly opposed by Irish and British fishermen. In April 1995 seven Spanish vessels were seized by the Irish navy, allegedly for fishing illegally in the Irish Sea. In October fisheries ministers agreed a regime to control fishing in the 'Irish box', introducing stricter controls, and instituting new surveillance measures.

SCIENCE AND TECHNOLOGY

In the amendments to the Treaty of Rome, effective from July 1987, a section on research and technology was included for the first time, defining the extent of Community co-operation in this area. Most of the funds allocated to research and technology are granted to companies or institutions that apply to participate in EU research programmes. The fourth framework programme for 1994–98 was to include new areas: research into transport systems, and socio-economic projects concerning the urban environment, social exclusion and education. The new programme aimed to focus on important technologies of benefit to many industrial sectors, and to improve dissemination of research and development findings. The programme, which had a budget of ECU 12,300m., was approved by the European Parliament in April 1994. In January 1996 the Commission proposed that additional research funds for the programme, of up to ECU 700m., should be concentrated on five priority areas: aeronautics, clean cars, multimedia software, intermodal transport and environmental technologies. In March 1996 the budget was increased by a further ECU 800m., as a result of the accession of Austria, Finland and Sweden in January 1995. Ministers responsible for scientific research, meeting in December, agreed on additional funding of ECU 100m., including ECU 35m. for research on transmissible spongiform encephalopathies. The fifth framework programme, covering the period 1999–2003, was proposed by the Commission in April 1997. The programme aimed to focus on the economic and social priorities of those living in the EU and on strengthening the capacity of the EU for scientific and technological research. In January 1998 it was suggested that the new programme should concentrate on four main areas: preservation of the ecosystem, management of living resources, the information society and competitive and sustainable growth. A budget of ECU 14,000m. was to be allocated to the programme. In 1997 research and development projects were allocated a total of ECU 3,500m. in the EU budget.

The Community's own Joint Research Centre (JRC), following a reorganization in 1996, comprises seven institutes, based at Ispra (Italy), Geel (Belgium), Karlsruhe (Germany), Seville (Spain) and Petten (Netherlands). The institutes' work covers: nuclear measurements; transuranium elements; advanced materials; remote sensing applications; the environment; systems engineering and informatics; safety technology; and prospective technological studies. Under the fourth framework programme (1994–98), the budget for the JRC was increased to ECU 900m. Proposed funding under the fifth framework programme (1999–2003) amounted to ECU 815m.

The European Strategic Research Programme for Research and Development in Information Technology ('ESPRIT'), inaugurated in 1984, concentrates on five key areas: advanced micro-electronics; software technology; advanced information processing; office automation; and computer integrated manufacturing. The programme is financed half by the EU and half by the participating research institutes, universities and industrial companies. In November 1997 a research project to develop technology to improve the methods used to locate and deactivate landmines under the ESPRIT programme was announced by the Commission. The project was to be allocated a budget of ECU 15m.

In 1987 the Community began a joint programme of research and development in advanced communications technology in Europe (RACE), aiming to establish an integrated broad-band telecommunications network. The successor programme, Advanced Communications Technologies and Services (ACTS), became effective in September 1994.

As part of a programme on telematic systems, 172 research and development projects were initiated in 1992. The programme, which involved more than 1,000 organizations, was concerned with the establishment of trans-European networks between administrations and the development of data communications systems for transport, health care, flexible and distance learning, libraries, linguistic engineering and rural areas.

The Community supports biotechnological research, aiming to promote the use of modern biology in agriculture and industry. In 1995 the EU's biotechnology programme ('BRIDGE') involved 60 projects, conducted by 528 research bodies, with a budget of

ECU 73m. Other programmes have focused on agro-industrial research, and food sciences and technology.

In 1985 the Council adopted a programme of basic research in industrial technologies ('BRITE'), aiming to develop new methods for the benefit of existing industries, such as aeronautics, chemicals, textiles and metalworking. A 'Euram' research programme covered raw materials and advanced materials. A new programme of research and development in the areas of materials and raw materials, design and manufacturing, and aeronautics was allocated a budget of ECU 670m. in 1990–94.

In March 1996 research–industry task forces established by the Commission presented a report identifying priority topics for European research: the car of tomorrow; educational software and multimedia; new generation aircraft; vaccines and viral diseases; trains and railway systems of the future; intermodal transport; maritime systems; and environment, with a particular focus on water. An action plan to encourage innovation was approved in November by the Commission. The plan aimed to create a legal, regulatory and financial framework more favourable to innovation, and to strengthen links between business and research.

In July 1997 the European Parliament approved the Life Patent Directive, a proposal aiming to harmonize European rules on gene patenting in order to promote research into genetic diseases, despite objections regarding the ethical implications.

Research in the fields of energy and the environment is described below under the appropriate headings.

The EU also co-operates with non-member countries (particularly EFTA states) in bilateral research projects. The Commission and 19 European countries (including the members of the EU as individuals) participate in the 'Eureka' programme of research in advanced technology (see p. 302). The Community research and development information service ('Cordis') disseminates findings in this field and comprises eight databases. The 'Value' programme funds the publication and dissemination of technical reports from specific research projects. From 1994 a European Technology Assessment Network was developed in order to improve the dissemination of technological research findings.

ENERGY

The treaty establishing the European Atomic Energy Community ('Euratom') came into force on 1 January 1958, to encourage the growth of the nuclear energy industry in the Community by conducting research, providing access to information, supplying nuclear fuels, building reactors and establishing common laws and procedures for the nuclear industry. A common market for nuclear materials was introduced in 1959, and there is a common insurance scheme against nuclear risks. In 1977 the Commission began granting loans on behalf of Euratom to finance investment in nuclear power stations and the enrichment of fissile materials. An agreement with the International Atomic Energy Authority entered into force in 1977, to facilitate co-operation in research on nuclear safeguards and controls. The EU's Joint Research Centre (see under Science and Technology) conducts research on nuclear safety and the management of radioactive waste.

The Joint European Torus (JET) is an experimental thermonuclear machine designed to pioneer new processes of nuclear fusion, using the 'Tokamak' system of magnetic confinement to heat gases to very high temperatures and bring about the fusion of tritium and deuterium nuclei. Switzerland is also a member of the JET project. Since 1974 work has been proceeding at Culham in the United Kingdom, and the project was formally inaugurated in April 1984. In 1988 work began with representatives of Japan, the former USSR and the USA on the joint design of an International Thermonuclear Experimental Reactor (ITER). Construction of a demonstration reactor was not expected to begin until the 21st century.

The Commission has consistently urged the formation of an effective overall energy policy. The 'Thermie' programme, initiated in 1990, fosters the development of new technologies in the energy sector; in January 1998 the Commission announced plans to provide ECU 140m. to fund more than 200 energy projects. The five-year 'SAVE' programme, introduced in 1991, emphasized the improvement of energy efficiency, reduction of the energy consumption of vehicles, and the use of renewable energy. A second five-year programme, SAVE II, was initiated in 1995. It was to continue the work of the first programme, and also aimed to establish energy efficiency as a criterion for all EU projects. In May 1996 energy ministers decided that the budget for SAVE II should be ECU 45m., instead of the ECU 150m. proposed by the Commission.

In 1990 Community legislation on the completion of the 'internal energy market' was adopted: it aimed to encourage the sale of electricity and gas across national borders in the Community, by opening national networks to foreign supplies, obliging suppliers to publish their prices, and co-ordinating investment in energy. Energy ministers reached agreement in June 1996 on rules for the liberalization of the electricity market, which was to be carried out progressively, with 22% of the market opened up initially, rising to about 33% within six years. In December 1997 the Council agreed rules to allow the gas market to be opened up in three stages, over a period of 10 years. Twenty per cent of the market was to be liberalized within two years, with the proportion rising to 28% after five years and some 33% after 10 years. In the first instance those consuming 25m. cu m of gas per annum were to be eligible to benefit from liberalization, but this threshold was to decrease to 15m. cu m within five years and to 5m. cu m within 10 years. The scheme was to allow the largest gas suppliers to receive temporary exemptions from trade liberalization if the presence of competitors should cause demand for supplies to drop below the amount which the distributor was contracted to purchase in the long term.

In October 1990 the Council agreed that emissions of carbon dioxide should be stabilized at their 1990 level by 2000. It established the ALTENER programme, which aimed to increase the contribution of renewable energy sources (RES) within the Community. The programme finished at the end of 1997, having supported 278 projects since 1993, at a cost of ECU 26.9m. A further programme, ALTENER II, was initiated in 1997 and was allocated a budget of ECU 22m. for a two-year period. A green paper on ways of promoting RES in the EU was issued in November 1996. These sources (such as wind, solar, biomass and small-scale hydropower) at that time provided less than 6% of total energy produced in the EU. A report published in November 1997 committed the Commission to increasing the use of RES to 12% by 2010. The paper proposed a strategy which could result in a reduction in carbon dioxide emissions of 402 metric tons each year by 2010, along with significant savings on fuel costs and a large number of employment opportunities. In December 1997, in the context of the third conference of parties to the UN Framework Convention on Climate Change (held in Kyoto, Japan), the EU adopted a target to reduce greenhouse gas emissions by 8% between 2008 and 2012, in comparison with 1990 levels.

Energy ministers from the EU member states and 12 Mediterranean countries agreed at a meeting held in June 1996 in Trieste, Italy, to develop a Euro-Mediterranean gas and electricity network. The first Euro-Mediterranean Energy Forum was held in May 1997.

In 1997 it was agreed to help a number of eastern European countries to overcome energy problems by means of the Interstate Oil and Gas to Europe programme (INOGATE), which was to receive ECU 50m. over a five-year period in order to improve energy flows in eastern Europe and increase the access of newly-independent countries to European markets. INOGATE forms part of the TACIS programme (see under External Relations).

INDUSTRY

Industrial co-operation was the earliest activity of the Community. The treaty establishing the European Coal and Steel Community (ECSC) came into force in July 1952, and by the end of 1954 nearly all barriers to trade in coal, coke, steel, pig-iron and scrap iron had been removed. The ECSC treaty was due to expire in July 2002, and in 1991 the Council agreed that, by that date, the provisions of the ECSC treaty should be incorporated in the EEC treaty, on the grounds that it was no longer appropriate to treat the coal and steel sectors separately.

In the late 1970s and 1980s, measures were adopted to restructure the steel industry in response to a dramatic reduction in world demand for steel. These included production capacity quotas and a reduction of state subsidies. In November 1992 the Commission announced a three-year emergency programme to further restructure the industry, following a reduction of 30% in steel prices over the previous two years. Limits were to be placed on steel imports from central and eastern Europe to avoid further depression of prices. In December 1993 ministers approved aid totalling ECU 7,000m. to achieve a further reduction of 5.5m. metric tons in annual capacity at state-owned steel plants in Germany, Italy, Portugal and Spain. The industry failed to achieve the required reduction in capacity of 19m. tons (by mid-1994 reductions of only 11m. tons had been assured), and in October 1994 the Commission decided to abandon the restructuring plan, although the social measures, which allocated ECU 240m. to compensate for job losses, were to be maintained. The Commission's report on the coal and steel industries in 1995 demonstrated that capital expenditure in the steel industry amounted to ECU 3,312m., some 21.6% higher than in 1994, while output of crude steel totalled 155.8m. tons, reversing the downward trend of previous years. Coal production continued to decline in 1995. The ECSC operating budget for 1997 was set at ECU 265.5m., which included increased funds for social aid and for research. In December 1996 the Commission adopted a new code on steel aid, for the period 1997–2002, which stipulated the conditions whereby member states may grant aid to steel companies, namely for research and development, for environmental protection and for full or partial closures of capacity. In October 1997 the Commission announced plans to finance, using ECSC reserves, research of benefit to the coal and steel industries amounting to some ECU 40m. each year, after the expiry of the ECSC Treaty in 2002.

The European textile and clothing industry has been seriously affected by overseas competition over an extended period. The Community participates in the Multi-fibre Arrangement (MFA, see WTO), to limit imports from low-cost suppliers overseas. A proposal by the Commission in October 1996 to accelerate liberalization of the textiles and clothing market in the EU provoked anger among industry leaders in member states, because no reciprocal concessions, in the form of removal of trade barriers, were being obtained from the major textile-exporting countries in other parts of the world. The Commission plans to include several 'sensitive' categories in the second stage of the MFA phasing-out of trade barriers, which was due to start in January 1998. These categories include woollen yarns and fabrics, gloves, and synthetic ropes. Another proposal by the Commission, regarding duties on imports of unfinished cotton fabrics to counter alleged 'dumping' by several developing countries, was opposed by nine EU member states. The proposal was aimed at helping weaving industries (mainly in France and Italy), which have been adversely affected by the developing countries' practice of sharply undercutting their prices. Fabric finishers claimed that the provisional duties, of between 3% and 36%, would cause more job losses in the industry than the 'dumping'. In 1995 the EU imported about 250,000 metric tons of unfinished cotton fabric but produced only 95,500 tons. Duties were provisionally introduced, for a period of six months, in late 1996, but were removed in May 1997. However, in July it was reported that a further investigation into suspected 'dumping' was being undertaken.

Production in EU member states' shipyards has fallen drastically since the 1970s, mainly as a result of competition from shipbuilders in the Far East. In the first half of the 1980s a Council directive allowed for subsidies to help to reorganize the shipbuilding industry and to increase efficiency, but subsequently rigorous curbs on state aid to the industry were introduced. The permitted maximum percentage of state aid for shipbuilding was reduced from 28% of the value of each vessel in 1987 to 9% in 1992. In July 1994 the EU signed an accord with Japan, the USA, the Republic of Korea and the Nordic countries to end subsidies to the shipbuilding industry from 1996, although this was subject to ratification by individual member states. Subsidies still available in several EU countries in 1996 were known to be higher than the official ceiling, and state aid was also given for industrial restructuring (for example, for modernization of east German shipyards) and for rescuing state-owned yards in difficulties (as was the case in Spain). In October 1997 the Commission proposed to maintain state aid until the end of 2000. Member countries approved operating aid totalling some ECU 5,000m. in 1990–95.

The Commission has made a number of proposals on a joint strategy for developing the information technology industry in Europe, particularly in view of the superiority of Japan and the USA in the market for advanced electronic circuits. The ESPRIT research programme (see under Science and Technology) aims to build the technological foundations for a fully competitive European industry. In 1990 proposals were adopted by the Council on the co-ordinated introduction of a European public paging system and of cellular digital land-based mobile communications. In 1991 the Council adopted a directive requiring member states to liberalize their rules on the supply of telecommunications terminal equipment, thus ending the monopolies of national telecommunications authorities. In the same year the Council adopted a plan for the gradual introduction of a competitive market in satellite communications. In October 1995 the Commission adopted a directive liberalizing the use of cable telecommunications, requiring members states to permit a wide range of services, in addition to television broadcasts, on such networks. The EU market for mobile telephone networks was opened to full competition as a result of a directive adopted by the Commission in January 1996, according to which member states were to abolish all exclusive and special rights in this area, and establish open and fair licensing procedures for digital services. The number of subscribers to cellular networks in the EU grew from 12m. to more than 20m. during 1995. The telecommunications market was to be fully deregulated by 1998, although extensions to the deregulation schedule were agreed for a number of member states. In October 1997 the Commission announced plans to commence legal proceedings against those member states which had not yet adopted the legislation necessary to permit the liberalization of the telecommunications market. Spain agreed to bring forward the full deregulation of its telecommunications market from January 2003 to 1998, which meant that all the major EU telecommunications markets were to be open to competition from 1998 onwards. Greece and Ireland have until 2000 to liberalize their telecommunications markets. Portugal's market will be open from 2003.

Harmonization of national company law to form a common legal structure has led to the adoption of directives concerning disclosure of information, company capital, internal mergers, the accounts of companies and of financial institutions, division of companies, the qualification of auditors, single-member private limited companies, mergers, take-over bids, and the formation of joint ventures. The Community Patent Convention was signed in 1975, subject to ratification by all member states. In June 1997 the Commission published a consultative document containing proposals that aimed to simplify the European patent system through the introduction of a unitary Community patent, thereby removing the need to file patent applications with individual member states. An Office for Harmonization in the Internal Market (OHIM), based in Alicante, Spain, was established in December 1993, and is responsible for the registration of Community trade marks and ensuring that they receive uniform protection throughout the EU. As part of the process of completing the internal market, numerous directives have been adopted on the technical harmonization and standardization of products (e.g. on safety devices in motor vehicles, labelling of foodstuffs and of dangerous substances, and classification of medicines).

The liberalization of Community public procurement formed an important part of the establishment of the internal market. A directive on public supplies contracts (effective from 1 January 1989, or from 1 March 1992 in Greece, Portugal and Spain) stipulated that major purchases of supplies by public authorities should be offered for tender throughout the community; while public contracts for construction or civil engineering works in excess of ECU 5m. were to be offered for tender throughout the EC from 19 July 1990 (1 March 1992 for Greece, Portugal and Spain). From 1 January 1993 the liberalization of procurement was extended to include public utilities in the previously excluded sectors of energy, transport, drinking-water and telecommunications.

In September 1990 new regulations entered into force concerning mergers of large companies that might create unfair competition. In July 1996 the Commission proposed an extension of its authority to oversee merger operations, to include smaller mergers and joint ventures overseen by national regulators. The Commission planned to have authority over operations involving companies with combined global turnover of more than ECU 2,000m. and turnover within the EU of ECU 150m.; however, the proposal was widely opposed.

The Business Co-operation Centre, established in 1973, supplies information to businesses and introduces businesses from 70 different countries wishing to co-operate or form links. The Business Co-operation Network (BC-Net) links enterprises, both public and private, that wish to form alliances with others (e.g. licensing agreements), on a confidential basis. BC-Net includes enterprises in EFTA member states, Poland and Australia. In September 1995 a Commission report outlined proposals to improve the business environment for small and medium-sized enterprises (SMEs) in the EU, continuing work on improving fiscal policies and access to finance, in addition to measures aimed at reducing delays in payments and the costs of international transactions. The European Investment Bank (see p. 162) provides finance for small businesses by means of 'global loans' to financial intermediaries. A mechanism providing small businesses with subsidized loans was approved by ministers in April 1992. In March 1996 the Commission agreed new guidelines for state aid to SMEs. Aid for the acquisition of patent rights, licences, expertise, etc., would now be allowed at the same level as that for tangible investment. In July 1997 the I-TEC scheme was inaugurated, with a budget of ECU 7.5m., in order to encourage SMEs to invest in new technology. A network of 39 'Euro-Info-Centres' (aimed particularly at small businesses) began work in 1987, and a total of 248 such Centres were in operation in 1996.

A review of EU industry, published in early 1996, showed that EU companies had been losing world market share in many areas, especially in electronics, mechanical engineering and automotive equipment. It appeared that there was too much emphasis on basic research at the expense of commercial innovation. A study, published by the Commission in October, criticized industry in the EU for its structural weaknesses and the fact that, since 1960, only 10m. jobs in industry had been created in the EU (half the number created in Japan and less than one-fifth the number in the USA). The study cited high costs of labour, telecommunications and energy as being major contributory factors in the EU's declining share of export markets. Ministers of industry, meeting in November, decided to promote the use of benchmarking techniques to improve the competitiveness of European industry. They also reached political agreement on the third multiannual programme (1997–2000) for SMEs, reducing the budget from ECU 140m. to ECU 127m.

TRANSPORT AND INTERNAL MOVEMENT

The establishment of a common transport policy is stipulated in the Treaty of Rome (see p. 155), with the aim of gradually standardizing national regulations which hinder the free movement of traffic within the Community, such as the varying safety and licensing rules, diverse restrictions on the size of lorries, and frontier-crossing formalities.

Measures on the abolition of customs formalities at intra-community frontiers were completed by mid-1991, and entered into force at the beginning of January 1993. However, disagreements remained among member governments concerning the free movement of persons: discussions continued in 1992 on the abuse of open frontiers by organized crime, particularly for drugs-trafficking; on extradition procedures; and on rules of asylum and immigration. By late 1993 nine member states had signed the 'Schengen Agreement' (originally signed by five members at Schengen, Luxembourg, in June 1990, following the failure of a 1985 agreement signed at the same location), abolishing frontier controls on the free movement of persons from the beginning of 1993. Delay in the establishment of the Schengen Information System (SIS), providing a computer network on criminals and illegal immigrants for use by the police forces of signatory states, resulted in postponement of implementation of the new agreement. Seven countries agreed to implement the Agreement with effect from 26 March 1995 (Belgium, France, Germany, Luxembourg, the Netherlands, Portugal and Spain). Frontier controls at airports on travellers between the seven countries were dismantled during a three-month transition period from that date. However, following the transition period, which ended on 1 July 1995, the French Government announced that it would retain land border controls for a further six months, claiming that drugs-trafficking and illegal immigration had increased as a result of the Agreement. In March 1996 France decided to lift its border controls with Spain and Germany, in line with the Schengen Agreement, while maintaining controls on borders with the Benelux countries, mainly because of its anxieties about drugs being brought in from the Netherlands via Belgium and Luxembourg. Italy joined the 'Schengen Group' on 26 October 1997, and Austria was to join on 1 December. Border controls for both countries were expected to be removed by 1 April 1998. Denmark, Finland and Sweden (and non-EU members Norway and Iceland) were admitted as observers of the accord as from 1 May 1996. The latter agreement was framed in such a way as to enable the three countries to accede to the Schengen Agreement in the future without adversely affecting the border-free zone provided by the Nordic Passport Union (see Nordic Council, p. 200). Ireland and the United Kingdom remain outside the 'Schengen Group'. In June 1997 the Commission published details of an action plan to achieve a single market, which envisaged the abolition of all EU internal border controls by 1 January 1999. The Treaty of Amsterdam (signed in October 1997), which incorporated the Schengen Agreement, was also to permit the United Kingdom and Ireland to maintain permanent jurisdiction over their borders and rules of asylum and immigration.

In 1986 transport ministers agreed on a system of Community-wide permits for commercial vehicles, to allow easier crossing of frontiers, and in 1993 they agreed on measures concerning road haulage. A common tax system for trucks using EC roads was to lead to full liberalization of road 'cabotage'—whereby road hauliers may provide services in the domestic market of another member state—by 1998. In 1991 directives were adopted by the Council on the compulsory use of safety belts in vehicles of less than 3.5 metric tons. Further regulations were to be introduced regarding the fitting of seatbelts in minibuses and coaches following approval by the Commission in mid-1996. In November 1997 the Commission proposed a regulation to compel member governments to pay damages if they should fail to clear serious obstructions, such as truck blockades, which hinder the free movement of goods, and so disrupt the operation of a single market.

In the late 1980s ministers of transport approved measures to contribute to the liberalization of air transport within the Community. In 1990 ministers agreed to make further reductions in guaranteed quotas for a country's airlines on routes to another country, and to liberalize air cargo services. In 1992 they approved an 'open skies' arrangement that would allow any EC airline to operate domestic flights within another member state (with effect from 1 April 1997). In June 1996 the ministers of transport approved a mandate for the Commission to negotiate an 'open skies' agreement with the USA, under which a common EU–US aviation area would be created. The Commission decided in mid-1996 to investigate co-operation agreements between European and American airlines in case these breached EU rules on competition. In July 1994, despite the recommendations of a 'Committee of Wise Men' (established by the Commission in 1993) for tighter controls on subsidies awarded to airlines, as part of efforts to increase competitiveness within the industry, the Commission approved substantial subsidies that had been granted by the French and Greek governments to their respective national airlines. In response to strong opposition by other member states, in particular the United Kingdom, the Commission insisted that the subsidies be conditional on the application of restructuring measures and certain competition guarantees. Subsequently the Commission specified that state assistance could be granted to airlines 'in exceptional, unforeseen circumstances, outside the control of the company'. In February 1996 the Commission approved a substantial subsidy granted by the Spanish Government to the Spanish national airline, Iberia.

In 1986 progress was made towards the establishment of a common maritime transport policy, with the adoption of regulations on unfair pricing practices, safeguard of access to cargoes, application of competition rules, and the eventual phasing-out of unilateral cargo reservation and discriminatory cargo-sharing arrangements. In December 1990 the Council approved, in principle, the freedom for shipping companies to provide maritime transport anywhere within the Community.

In 1989 the Commission approved proposals on railway policy with the aim of achieving greater integration, including technical harmonization (e.g. standardization of track gauges and signalling) and guaranteed rights of transit for joint ventures between railways of different member states. The Commission published a white paper in July 1996 containing proposals for revitalizing railways in the EU, and making them more efficient. The key points of the proposed strategy were the separation of infrastructure and operations, clarification of financial relations between the railways and the state, to permit independent financial management; the introduction of market forces and the creation of trans-European 'freight freeways'; and the removal of obstacles that hinder the process of integrating rail systems. Rail operators from EU member countries met in Brussels in October to discuss plans for a European network of 'freight freeways' capable of competing with road haulage. One of the first of six routes to be considered was to run from Rotterdam, Antwerp and Hamburg through Germany and Austria to Milan.

The PACT (pilot action for combined transport) scheme was instigated in 1992 and had funded 65 combined transport projects (where goods are moved by at least two forms of transport without unloading) on 22 routes by July 1996, when the Commission approved plans to extend the programme from 1997 to 2001, with an additional budget of ECU 35m.

The Commission's white paper on growth, competitiveness and employment, which was issued in December 1993, proposed the establishment of trans-European networks (TENs) to improve transport, telecommunications and energy infrastructure throughout the Community. The priority transport projects for development under this scheme include high-speed rail links from Paris–Strasbourg and Munich–Berlin, a rail and road tunnel through the Brenner pass in Italy and a motorway linking Lisbon–Valladolid. Most of the finance for the schemes is to be provided by individual member states, although some ECU 25,000m. was to be made available for such projects from the EU budget in 1994–99. In January 1997 the Commission revealed that ECU 325m. was to be made available for TENs projects in that year. In April plans to extend the TENs scheme into central and eastern Europe were disclosed. ECU 100m. was to be provided for such projects under the PHARE (Poland/Hungary Aid for Restructuring of Economies) assistance programme (see under External Relations, below). A project to develop a motorway providing a Berlin–Kiev link began in May, aided by a grant of ECU 68m. from the PHARE programme.

Ministers responsible for postal services met in November 1996 and discussed plans to liberalize mail deliveries in member states. The Commission wanted direct mail deliveries and cross-border services, representing 20% of all services, to be liberalized within five years, but there was strong opposition to this proposal from several member countries, especially France and Italy, and the ministers failed to reach agreement.

JUSTICE AND HOME AFFAIRS

Under the Treaty on European Union, member states of the EU undertook to co-operate, for the first time, in the areas of justice and home affairs, particularly in relation to the free movement of people between member states. Issues of common interest were defined as asylum policy; border controls; immigration; drug addiction; fraud; judicial co-operation in civil and criminal matters; customs co-operation; and police co-operation for the purposes of combating terrorism, drugs-trafficking and other serious forms of international crime. A European Police Office (Europol), to facilitate the exchange of information between police forces, was to be established in The Hague, the Netherlands. However, agreement on implementation of the Convention was delayed by a dispute among member states concerning the role of the European Court of Justice with regard to Europol. The United Kingdom, in particular, objected to the proposed role of the Court in settling legal disputes arising from Europol operations. The special Europol unit dealing with the trafficking of illicit drugs and nuclear and radioactive materials began work in 1994. Europol later had its mandate extended to cover illegal immigrants and stolen vehicles. In December 1997 the Council approved a further extension, to include investigation into child pornography. A European Council meeting in June 1996 finally resolved the outstanding disagreements relating to the establishment of Europol. By the end of 1996 Europol had carried out work on 2,150 cases. The EU convention on extradition, signed by ministers of justice in September 1996 prior to ratification by national governments, simplified and accelerated procedures, reduced the number of cases where extradition can be refused, and made it easier to extradite members of criminal organizations. In November 1997 the Commission made a proposal to extend European law in order to allow civil and commercial judgments made in the courts of member states to be enforced across the whole of the EU. In February 1994 the Commission issued a document concerning the formulation of a comprehensive EU policy on asylum and immigration. In September 1995, as part of a policy of achieving a common visa regime for non-EU nationals, ministers agreed a common list of 101 countries, citizens of which required visas to enter the EU. Further progress on this issue was delayed by the desire of some member states to retain existing bilateral visa agreements.

EDUCATION, CULTURE AND BROADCASTING

The Treaty of Rome, although not covering education directly, gave the Community the role of establishing general principles for implementing a common vocational training policy. The Treaty on European Union urged greater co-operation on education policy, including the encouragement of exchanges and mobility for students and teachers, and of distance learning, and development of European studies.

The postgraduate European University Institute was founded in Florence in 1976, with departments of history, economics, law and political and social sciences, together with a European Policy Unit and a European Culture Research Centre. In 1995/96 there were 330 research students and 45 professional posts. The Commission provided ECU 4.75m. towards the Institute's budget for 1996.

In September 1980 an educational information network, 'Eurydice', began operations, with a central unit in Brussels and national units providing data on the widely varying systems of education within member states. In 1987 the Council adopted a European Action Scheme for the Mobility of University Students ('Erasmus'). The scheme was expanded to include EFTA member states from 1992. During 1987–94 Erasmus supported educational exchanges for 300,000 students and 50,000 teachers. The 'Lingua' programme promoted the teaching of foreign languages in the Community, with a budget of ECU 200m. for 1990–94. From 1 January 1995 the Erasmus and Lingua schemes were incorporated into a new Community programme, Socrates, which was to be effective during 1995–99, with a budget of ECU 850m. The programme was to pursue the Community's activities of promoting co-operation and the exchange of information between member states with regard to education, as well as the mobility of students, especially in higher education. The Trans-European Mobility Programme for University Studies (TEMPUS) was launched in 1990 to foster co-operation between institutions of higher education and their counterparts in central and eastern Europe, as part of their wider aid programme to those countries (see below). By May 1993 TEMPUS had supported 637 projects, involving more than 10,000 teachers and 6,400 students in 1,800 institutions. Under the second phase of the scheme (TEMPUS II) for 1994–98 the former Soviet republics were eligible to participate in the scheme. It also sought to provide support for the restructuring of higher education in countries of central and eastern Europe participating in the PHARE programme (see External Relations, below).

From 1 January 1995 the Leonardo da Vinci programme for vocational training became effective, with a budget of ECU 620m. for 1995–99. The priority areas for project proposals under the programme in 1997 were: the acquisition of new skills; forging links between business and educational or training establishments; combating social exclusion; the promotion of investment in human resources; and promoting access to skills and the development of vocational skills through information technology, in the context of lifelong learning.

The EU directive on the recognition of diplomas, which came into effect in January 1991, had enabled at least 11,000 people to work in another member state, according to a report covering 1991–94.

Under the Community's programme for conserving the European architectural heritage, 100 projects were approved in 1995, with a budget of ECU 4.7m. In March 1995 the Commission initiated the Raphael programme, which aimed to promote the cultural heritage of Europe, by developing links between cultural institutions and improving training. The programme had a budget of ECU 30m. for the period 1997–2000. A total of 91 projects were selected during 1997 for funding of ECU 9.4m. under the Raphael programme. In 1997 the Kaleidoscope programme, which encourages European cultural exchanges and other cultural projects, supported 128 projects with a total of ECU 6.8m. In 1996 the Ariane programme was established to promote reading and to provide public access to books.

A programme to improve awareness of information technology, promote understanding of the benefits and possible risks of the 'Information Society', and identify opportunities for the use of new technologies, particularly in relation to disadvantaged social groups, was proposed by the Commission in December 1996. The ECU 45m. programme was to operate from 1997 to the end of 2001. A further information technology scheme was initiated in September 1997, with a budget of ECU 13m., to examine new methods for the promotion of learning among children aged between four and eight years. The scheme formed part of the ESPRIT research programme (see under Science and Technology).

In 1989 ministers of foreign affairs adopted a directive (television without frontiers) establishing minimum standards for television programmes which could be broadcast freely throughout the Community: limits were placed on the amount of time devoted to advertisements, a majority of programmes broadcast were to be from the Community, where practicable, and governments were to be allowed to forbid the transmission of programmes considered morally harmful. The 'Media' programme was introduced in 1991 to provide financial support to the television and film industry. During 1991–95 it provided funds for some 5,000 projects, including professional training, the production of programmes and films with a European dimension and the transnational distribution of programmes. A second programme, 'Media II', was initiated in January 1996 with a planned budget of ECU 310m. for the five-year period 1996–2000. In 1993 ministers approved a measure to ensure copyright protection for television programmes broadcast across borders by means of satellite and cable transmission. In December 1997 the Commission suggested that the need to amend the regulatory framework of broadcasting rules might arise in the future, owing to the increasing convergence of the television, telecommunications and information technology industries. The Commission's conclusions were to be published in June 1998.

SOCIAL POLICY

The Single European Act, which entered into force in 1987, added to the original Treaty of Rome articles which emphasized the need for 'economic and social cohesion' in the Community, i.e. the reduction of disparities between the various regions, principally through the existing 'structural funds'—the European Regional Development Fund, the European Social Fund, and the Guidance Section of the European Agricultural Guidance and Guarantee Fund (for details of these funds, as well as the Cohesion Fund, which became operational in 1993, see p. 180). In 1988 the Council declared that Community operations through the structural funds, the European Investment Bank and other financial instruments should have five priority objectives: (i) promoting the development and structural adjustment of the less-developed regions (where gross domestic product per caput is less than 75% of the Community average); (ii) converting the regions, frontier regions or parts of regions seriously affected by industrial decline; (iii) combating long-term unemployment among people above the age of 25; (iv) providing employment for young people (aged under 25); (v) with a view to the reform of the common agricultural policy: speeding up the adjustment of agricultural structures and promoting the development of rural areas.

In 1989 the Commission proposed a Charter on the Fundamental Social Rights of Workers (Social Charter), covering freedom of movement, fair remuneration, improvement of working conditions, the right to social security, freedom of association and collective wage agreements, the development of participation by workers in management, and sexual equality. The Charter was approved by the heads of government of all Community member states except the United Kingdom in December. On the insistence of the United Kingdom, the chapter on social affairs of the Treaty on European Union, negotiated in December 1991, was omitted from the Treaty to form a separate protocol. In May 1997 the new UK Government approved the Social Charter, which was to be incorporated into the Treaty of Amsterdam, signed in October. The Treaty, which was expected to be ratified in 1998, was also to include a new chapter on employment.

A number of Community directives have been adopted on equal rights for women in pay, access to employment and social security, and the Commission has undertaken legal proceedings against several member states before the European Court of Justice for infringements. In 1991–95 the third Community Action Programme on the Promotion of Equal Opportunities for Women was undertaken, involving action by national governments in combating unemployment among women; bringing about equal treatment for men and women in occupational social schemes (e.g. sick pay and pensions) and in self-employed occupations, including agriculture; and legislation on parental leave. A Fourth Action Programme, with a budget of ECU 30m. for the five-year period 1996–2000, aims to ensure that the question of equality is integrated into all relevant policy issues. In December 1997 the Council adopted a directive on sex discrimination cases, whereby the plaintiff and defendant were to share the burden of proof. Legislation was to be introduced in member states by 1 January 2000. Numerous directives on health and safety in the workplace have been adopted by the Community. The creation of a Major Accident Hazards Bureau (MAHB) was announced by the Commission in February 1996. Based at the Joint Research Centre at Ispra in Italy, its purpose is to help prevent industrial accidents in the EU. In June 1993 the Working Time directive was approved, restricting the working week to 48 hours, except where overtime arrangements are agreed with trade unions. In October ministers adopted a directive limiting the number of hours worked by young people. The United Kingdom secured a dispensation to delay implementation of these latter measures for four years. The directive, which also prescribed minimum rest periods and a minimum of four weeks' paid holiday a year, had to be implemented by 23 November 1996, three years after its enactment. The original version exempted certain categories of employee from the maximum 48-hour week rule, including those in the transport sector, fishermen and junior hospital doctors, but in July 1997 the Commission published a report that proposed extending the directive to cover these groups as well. In September 1994 ministers adopted the first directive to be approved under the Social Charter, concerning the establishment of mandatory works councils in multinational companies. After lengthy negotiations, it was agreed that the legislation was to be applied in companies employing more than 1,000 people, of whom 150 worked in at least two EU member states. The United Kingdom was excluded from the directive; however, UK companies operating in other European countries were to participate in the scheme (although without counting UK-based employees towards the applicability thresholds). The directive came into force in September 1996, but by mid-1996 more than 140 companies had already concluded voluntary agreements to inform and consult with their employees. In April 1996 the Commission proposed that part-time, fixed-term and temporary employees should receive comparable treatment to permanent, full-time employees. A directive ensuring equal treatment for part-time employees was adopted by the Council in December 1997. The directive on parental leave, the second directive to be adopted under the Social Charter, provided for a statutory minimum of three months' unpaid leave to allow parents to care for young children, and was adopted in June 1996. In December 1997, following the UK Government's approval of the Social Charter in May, the Council adopted amendments extending the two directives to include the United Kingdom. The UK Government was to implement the directives within a period of two years.

The European Confidence Pact for Employment was launched by the Commission in January 1996. This was a comprehensive strategy to combat unemployment involving a common approach by public authorities, employers and employees. The European Council, meeting in Florence in June, resolved to give new impetus to job creation, in line with the Confidence Pact, and invited each member state to select candidate areas for pilot local employment pacts. An employment body, EURES, operates as a network of 450 advisers who have access to two European databases listing job vacancies in the EU and in Norway and Iceland. It was launched in November 1994, and in its first 10 months of operating it handled 180,000 contacts with job-seekers. The rate of unemployment across the Community averaged 10.8% of the labour force at mid-1997. An employment summit was held in Luxembourg in November 1997, with the aim of promoting job creation. The conference focused on four themes: employability, entrepreneurship, equal opportunities and adaptability, and committed member governments to providing training or work placements for unemployed young people within six months, and for the long-term unemployed within 12 months. Member states also agreed to reduce taxation on labour-intensive service industries from 1 July 1998, and to produce a national action plan for employment, to be discussed at the European Council meeting in June 1998.

EU activities regarding disability include the HELIOS programme for disabled people, which focuses on the issues of mobility, integration and independence and a 'technology initiative for disabled and elderly people' (TIDE), which aims to develop technologies that improve the living conditions of the groups concerned.

The European Voluntary Service was established in 1996 as a pilot scheme to enable young people aged 18–25 to take part in a range of projects of benefit to the community in a country other than their own. The Eurathlon programme awarded grants to a total of 175 sports projects in 1996. The projects covered 50 different sports and were selected by independent national committees and a European jury.

The European Foundation for the Improvement of Living and Working Conditions (Dublin), established in 1975, undertakes four-year research programmes. Under the Treaty on European Union, the EU assumed responsibility for addressing the problem of drug addiction, and a European Monitoring Centre for Drugs and Drug Addiction was established in Lisbon, Portugal, in 1995 (see 'Other Institutions'). A programme to promote co-operation between member states in action against drug dependency was adopted by ministers of health, meeting in November 1996. The ECU 27m. programme covers the period 1996–2000.

CONSUMER PROTECTION

The Community's second Consumer Protection Programme was approved by the Council in 1981, based on the principles of the first programme: protection of health and safety, with procedures for withdrawal of goods from the market; standardization of rules for food additives and packaging; rules for machines and equipment; and authorization procedures for new products. The second programme also included measures for monitoring the quality and durability of products, improving after-sale service, legal remedies for unsatisfactory goods and services, and the encouragement of consumer associations.

In 1993 a three-year action plan was inaugurated, with the aim of strengthening consumer power in the single market. The plan's priorities were: to consolidate legislation; to improve dissemination of consumer information; to facilitate access to small claims' courts; and to increase customer security in cross-frontier payments and after-sales service. The Consumers' Consultative Council represents European consumers' organizations, and gives opinions on consumer matters. In October 1996 the Commission issued a further plan covering the period until 1998 and containing some new priorities, including the protection of consumer interests in the supply of public utilities, improving consumer confidence in foodstuffs, strengthening consumer representation and developing consumer policies in central and eastern Europe.

In June 1996 the Commission published its proposed directive on the sale of consumer goods and associated guarantees, aimed at improving the degree of protection when products or after-sales services fail to reach expectations. In November ministers approved a Commission directive which would enable a consumer body in one member state to take action in another in connection with breaches of certain EU laws such as those on consumer credit, package holidays, and misleading advertising. In May 1997 the Commission proposed in a report on telecommunications services that from 1 January 2000 customers should be able to keep the same telephone numbers if they changed service provider.

In February 1997 the Commission extended the function of its directorate-general on consumer policy to incorporate consumer health protection, in order to ensure that sufficient importance be given to food safety, particularly owing to consumer concerns resulting from the BSE crisis (see under Agriculture). In June the Commission announced that a Scientific Steering Committee was to be established to provide advice regarding consumer health issues.

ENVIRONMENT POLICY

The Community's fifth environmental action programme (1993–2000), entitled 'Towards Sustainability', aims to address the root causes of environmental degradation, by raising public awareness and changing the behaviour of authorities, enterprises and the general public. The programme targets the following sectors: industry (aiming for improved resource management and production standards); energy (reducing emissions of carbon dioxide and other pollutants, by improving energy efficiency); transport (investment in public transport, cleaner fuels); agriculture (reducing pollution, encouraging tree-planting); and tourism (controls on new and existing tourist developments).

Directives have been adopted, obliging member states to introduce regulations on air and water pollution (e.g. 'acid rain', pollution by fertilizers and pesticides, and emissions from vehicles), the transport of hazardous waste across national boundaries, waste treatment, noise abatement and the protection of natural resources; and guaranteeing freedom of access to information on the environment held by public authorities. The fifth environmental action programme focuses on anticipating environmental problems, with initiatives expected on improved resource management by industry, more effective management of mass tourism, and the development of environmental policies in agriculture.

The Community's programme of research and technological development on the environment, carried out on a shared-cost basis by various scientific institutions, covers the EU's participation in global change programmes; technologies and engineering for the environment; research on economic and social aspects of environmental issues; and technological and natural hazards. The programme is open to all European countries. A separate programme covers research in marine science and technology. In 1990 the EC established a European Environment Agency (EEA, see p. 164) to monitor environmental issues. The agency became operational in November 1994.

In 1985 the Community (and a number of individual member states) signed an international agreement, the Vienna Convention for the Protection of the Ozone Layer, and in 1987 the Community signed a protocol to the treaty, controlling the production of chlorofluorocarbons. In 1990 ministers of the environment undertook to ban production, import and use of chlorofluorocarbons altogether by mid-1997: in 1992 the date was brought forward to the end of 1995. In 1990 they agreed to stabilize emissions of carbon dioxide, believed to be responsible for 'global warming', at 1990 levels by the year 2000 (2005 for the United Kingdom). In December 1997, at the third conference of parties to the UN Framework Convention on Climate Change (held in Kyoto, Japan), agreement was reached to reduce greenhouse gas emissions by 8% between 2008 and 2012 in member states, in comparison with 1990 levels.

The Eco-Management and Audit Scheme (EMAS) is a voluntary scheme, launched in April 1995, in which participating industrial companies undergo an independent audit of their environmental performance.

In June 1996 the Commission agreed a strategy, drawn up in collaboration with the European petroleum and car industries, for reducing harmful emissions from road vehicles by between 60% and 70% by 2010. In June 1997 environment ministers agreed measures to lower the allowable limits for sulphur, benzenes and aromatics in petrol and diesel fuel by 2000. An action programme for the protection and management of groundwater resources was adopted by the Commission in July. Member states were to be asked to prepare national programmes to identify, map and protect groundwater resources. Also in July, the Commission decided to take the United Kingdom to the European Court of Justice for not fully implementing the drinking water directive, which came into force in 1985. In December 1997 the Council agreed upon a target to reduce the volume of waste disposed in landfill sites.

Rules governing the sale of genetically engineered foods were agreed by ministers in November 1996, despite objections from some countries, principally Germany and Austria, and strong opposition from environmental campaigners. The rules were amended in June 1997 when the Commission adopted measures to compel member countries to label all food products containing genetically modified organisms.

A regulation revising EU laws on trade in wild animals and plants was adopted by ministers of the environment in December 1996. It was to tighten controls and improve enforcement of restrictions on trade in endangered species.

The Commission announced in July 1997 that it was to provide some ECU 90.2m. to help to finance 188 environmental projects in that year. The projects were to concentrate on three specific areas: environment (particularly waste disposal and the treatment of water); nature (for example the conservation of natural habitats for wildlife); and third countries (focusing on projects in Russia and the Mediterranean basin).

FINANCIAL SERVICES AND CAPITAL MOVEMENTS

A directive on Community banking, adopted in 1977, laid down common prudential criteria for the establishment and operation of banks in member states. A second banking directive, adopted in 1989, aimed to create a single community licence for banking, whereby the authorization initially given to a bank by its country of origin is automatically valid for the whole Community: in other words, a bank established in one member country can open branches in any other. The directive entered into force on 1 January 1993. Related measures were subsequently adopted with the aim of ensuring the capital adequacy of credit institutions, and the prevention of 'money-laundering' by criminals. In September 1993 ministers approved a directive on a bank deposit scheme to protect account-holders: banks were to be obliged to raise protection to 90% on the first ECU 20,000 in an account from 1 January 1995.

In 1992 the third insurance co-ordination directives, relating to life assurance and non-life insurance, were adopted, creating a framework for an integrated Community insurance market. The directives provide greater access to insurance companies and customers to the European market, guarantee greater protection for purchasers of life assurance policies and prohibit substantive control of rates. The directives came into effect on 1 July 1994.

In May 1993 ministers adopted a directive on investment services, which (with effect from 1 January 1996) allows credit institutions to offer investment services in any member state, on the basis of a licence held in one state.

Freedom of capital movement and the creation of a uniform financial area were regarded as vital for the completion of the internal market by 1992. In 1987, as part of the liberalization of the flow of capital, a Council directive came into force, whereby member states were obliged to remove restrictions on three categories of transactions: long-term credits related to commercial transactions; acquisition of securities; and the admission of securities to capital markets. In June 1988 the Council of Ministers approved a directive whereby all restrictions on capital movements (financial loans and credits, current and deposit account operations, transactions in securities and other instruments normally dealt in on the money market) were removed by 1 July 1990 (except in Belgium, Greece, Ireland, Luxembourg, Portugal and Spain, which were permitted to exercise certain restrictions until the end of 1992). In September 1995 the Council adopted measures to eliminate excessive fees and delays in transfers of funds between banks in member states. In November 1997 the Commission adopted proposals to co-ordinate tax policy among member states. The measures included a code of conduct on corporate taxation and were to lead to the simplification of methods used to transfer royalty and interest payments between member countries and to prevent the withholding of taxes.

ECONOMIC CO-OPERATION

A report on the economic situation is presented annually by the Commission, analysing recent developments and short- and medium-term prospects. Economic policy guidelines for the following year are adopted annually by the Council.

The following objectives for the end of 1973 were agreed by the Council in 1971, as the first of three stages towards European economic and monetary union:

> the narrowing of exchange rate margins to 2.25%; creation of a medium-term pool of reserves; co-ordination of short- and medium-term economic and budgetary policies; a joint position on international monetary issues; harmonization of taxes; creation of the European Monetary Co-operation Fund (EMCF); creation of the European Regional Development Fund.

The narrowing of exchange margins (the 'snake') came into effect in 1972; but Denmark, France, Ireland, Italy and the United Kingdom later floated their currencies, with only Denmark permanently returning to the arrangement. Sweden and Norway also linked their currencies to the 'snake'; but Sweden withdrew from the arrangement in August 1977, and Norway withdrew in December 1978.

The European Monetary System (EMS) came into force in March 1979, with the aim of creating closer monetary co-operation, leading to a zone of monetary stability in Europe, principally through an exchange rate mechanism (ERM), supervised by the ministries of finance and the central banks of member states. Not all Community members participated in the ERM: Greece did not join, Spain joined only in June 1989, the United Kingdom in October 1990 and Portugal in April 1992. To prevent wide fluctuations in the value of members' currencies against each other, the ERM fixed for each currency a central rate in European Currency Units (ECUs, see below), based on a 'basket' of national currencies; a reference rate in relation to other currencies was fixed for each currency, with established fluctuation margins (until July 1993 6% for the Portuguese escudo and the Spanish peseta, 2.25% for others). Central banks of the participating states intervened by buying or selling currencies when the agreed margin was likely to be exceeded. Each member placed 20% of its gold reserves and dollar reserves respectively into the EMCF, and received a supply of ECUs to regulate central bank interventions. Short- and medium-term credit facilities were given to support the balance of payments of member countries. The EMS was initially put under strain by the wide fluctuations in the exchange rates of non-Community currencies and by the differences in economic development among members, which led to nine re-alignments of currencies in 1979–83. Subsequently greater stability was achieved, with only two realignments of currencies between 1984 and 1988. In September 1992, however, the Italian and Spanish currencies were devalued, by 7% and 5% respectively, within the ERM, and Italian and British membership was suspended; in November the Portuguese and Spanish currencies were both devalued by 6% within the ERM. In May 1993 the Spanish and Portuguese currencies were further devalued (by 8% and 6.5%, respectively). In late July, as a result of intensive currency speculation on European financial markets (forcing the weaker currencies to the very edge of their permitted margins), the ERM almost collapsed. In response to the crisis, EC finance ministers decided to widen the fluctuation margins allowed for each currency to 15%, except in the cases of Germany and the Netherlands, which agreed to maintain their currencies within the original 2.25% limits. The 15% margins were regarded as allowing for so much fluctuation in exchange rates as to represent a virtual suspension of the ERM; however, some countries, notably France and Belgium, expressed determination to adhere as far as possible to the original 'bands' in order to fulfil the conditions for eventual monetary union. In practice, during 1994, most currencies remained within the former 2.25% and 6% bands. Austria became a member of the EMS in January 1995, and its currency was subject to ERM conditions. While Sweden decided to remain outside the EMS, Finland joined in October 1996. In November the Italian lira was readmitted to the ERM.

In September 1988 a committee (chaired by Jacques Delors, the President of the European Commission, and comprising the governors of member countries' central banks, representatives of the European Commission and outside experts) was established to discuss European monetary union. The resulting 'Delors plan' was presented to heads of government in June 1989, and they agreed to begin the first stage of the process of monetary union—the drafting of a treaty on the subject—in 1990. The Intergovernmental Conference on Economic and Monetary Union was initiated in December 1990, and continued to work (in parallel with the Intergovernmental Conference on Political Union) throughout 1991, with monthly meetings at ministerial level. The Intergovernmental Conference was responsible for the drafting of the economic and monetary provisions of the Treaty on European Union, which was agreed by the European Council in December 1991 and which came into force on 1 November 1993 (see p. 158). The principal feature of the Treaty's provisions on economic and monetary union (EMU) was the gradual introduction of a single currency, to be administered by a single central bank. During the remainder of Stage I, member states were to adopt programmes for the 'convergence' of their economies and ensure the complete liberalization of capital movements. Stage II began on 1 January 1994, and included the establishment of a European Monetary Institute (EMI), replacing the EMCF and comprising governors of central banks and a president appointed by heads of government (see 'Other Institutions'). Heads of government were to decide, not later than 31 December 1996, whether a majority of member states fulfilled the necessary conditions for the adoption of a single currency: if so, they were to establish a date for the beginning of Stage III, but if no date for this had been set by the end of 1997, Stage III was to begin on 1 January 1999, and was to be confined to those members which did fulfil the necessary conditions. After the establishment of a starting date for Stage III, the European Central Bank (ECB) and a European System of Central Banks were to be set up to replace the EMI. During Stage III, exchange rates were to be irrevocably fixed, and a single currency introduced. Member states that had not fulfilled the necessary conditions for the adoption of a single currency would be exempt from participating. The United Kingdom was to be allowed to make a later, separate decision on whether to proceed to Stage III, while Denmark reserved the right to submit its participation in Stage III to a referendum. The near-collapse of the ERM in July 1993 cast serious doubts on the agreed timetable for monetary union, although in October the EC heads of government reaffirmed their commitment to that objective by the end of the century.

In December 1995 the European Council, meeting in Madrid, confirmed that Stage III of Economic and Monetary Union was planned to begin on 1 January 1999. The existing economic conditions for member states wishing to enter Stage III (including an annual budget deficit of no more than 3% of annual gross domestic product—GDP—and total public debt of no more than 60% of annual GDP) were also confirmed. The meeting also decided that the proposed single currency would be officially known as the 'Euro'. Participants in EMU were to be selected in early 1998, on the basis of economic performance during 1997. In October 1996 the Commission issued a draft regulation on a proposed 'stability pact', intended to ensure that member countries maintained strict budgetary discipline during Stage III of monetary union. Another draft regulation formed the legal framework for the Euro, confirming that it would be the single currency of participating countries from 1 January 1999. During a transitional period of up to three years, national currencies would remain in circulation, having equivalent legal status to the Euro. The communication outlined the main features of a new ERM, which would act as a 'waiting room' for countries preparing to join the single currency. Member countries remaining outside the monetary system, whether or not by choice, would still be part of the single market.

Although all 15 members of the EU endorsed the principle of monetary union, with France and Germany the most ardent supporters, the United Kingdom and also Sweden and Denmark were known to have political doubts about joining. In October 1997 both the United Kingdom and Sweden confirmed that they would not participate in EMU from 1999. The EMI declared in November 1996 that the majority of member states did not fulfil the necessary conditions for the adoption of a single currency. This statement contrasted with a report by the Commission, which forecast that only three countries—the United Kingdom, Greece and Italy—would fail to meet the criteria for joining the new ERM. In October 1997 the Commission reported that Greece alone would fail to fulfil the conditions required for the adoption of a single currency.

Technical preparations for the Euro were politically agreed during the meeting of the European Council in Dublin in December 1996. The heads of government endorsed the new ERM and the legal framework for the Euro and reached agreement on the proposed 'stability pact'. Nevertheless, there was continuing disagreement between some member states about the rules governing monetary union, and in particular about the planned timetable. Controversy arose in May 1997 over plans by the German Government to revalue gold reserves in an apparent attempt to improve its 1997 budget. In June the European Council, meeting in Amsterdam, reached final agreement on the content of the 'stability pact', which included a resolution on growth, following demands by the newly-elected French Government that a commitment be made to employment. In September finance ministers agreed that the conversion rates for national currencies joining EMU were to be fixed in May 1998, at the same time as an announcement to confirm the countries eligible to participate in the single currency.

The European Currency Unit

With the creation of the European Monetary System (EMS) a new monetary unit, the European Currency Unit (ECU) was adopted. Its value and composition were identical to those of the European Unit of Account (EUA) already used in the administrative fields of the Community. The ECU is a composite monetary unit, in which the relative value of each currency is determined by the gross national product and the volume of trade of each country.

The ECU, which has been assigned the function of the unit of account used by the European Monetary Co-operation Fund, is also used as the denominator for the exchange rate mechanism; as the denominator for operations in both the intervention and the credit mechanisms; and as a means of settlement between monetary authorities of the European Community.

From April 1979 onwards the ECU was also used as the unit of account for the purposes of the common agricultural policy. From 1981 it replaced the EUA in the general budget of the Community; the activities of the European Development Fund under the Lomé Convention; the balance sheets and loan operations of the European Investment Bank; and the activities of the European Coal and Steel Community. It is now the only unit of account used in the Community.

In June 1985 measures were adopted by the governors of the Community's central banks, aiming to strengthen the EMS by expanding the use of the ECU, e.g. by allowing international monetary institutions and the central banks of non-member countries to become 'other holders' of ECUs.

In June 1989 it was announced that, with effect from 20 September, the Portuguese and Spanish currencies were to be included in the composition of the ECU. From that date the amounts of the national currencies included in the composition of the ECU were to be 'weighted' as follows (in percentages): Belgian franc 7.6; Danish krone 2.45; French franc 19.0; Deutsche Mark 30.1; Greek drachma 0.8; Irish pound 1.1; Italian lira 10.15; Luxembourg franc 0.3; Netherlands guilder 9.4; Portuguese escudo 0.8; Spanish peseta 5.3; United Kingdom pound sterling 13.0. The composition of the ECU 'basket' of currencies was 'frozen' with the entry into force of the Treaty on European Union on 1 November 1993. This was not affected by the accession to the EU of Austria, Finland and Sweden; consequently those countries' currencies are not represented in the ECU 'basket'. As part of Stage III of the process of economic and monetary union (EMU), the ECU was to be replaced by a single currency, the Euro. Designs for the Euro bank notes, and the symbol for the single currency, were presented by the EMI at the European Council meeting in Dublin in December 1996, and designs for the Euro coins were presented at the European Council meeting in Amsterdam in June 1997. The notes and coins would not be in circulation until 2002, and the Euro was gradually to replace the national currencies of participating countries in the first half of that year. A payments settlement system, called Target (Trans-European Automated Real-time Gross Settlement Express Transfer), was to be introduced for countries participating in EMU, but the question of whether banks of non-participating countries should be given access to Target was still under discussion.

The ECU's value in national currencies is calculated and published daily. Its value on 27 February 1998 was US $1.0888.

External Relations

The EU has diplomatic relations in its own right with many countries (see p. 152), and with international organizations, and participates as a body in international conferences on trade and development, such as the 'Uruguay Round' of trade negotiations, under the General Agreement on Tariffs and Trade (GATT—see WTO, p. 244). It has observer status at the United Nations. Agreements have been signed with numerous countries and groups of countries, allowing for co-operation in trade and other matters. The Union is also a party to various international conventions (in some of these to the exclusion of the individual member states).

Under the Single European Act, which came into force on 1 July 1987 (amending the Treaty of Rome), it was formally stipulated for the first time that member states should inform and consult each other on foreign policy matters (as was already, in practice, often the case).

The Treaty on European Union, which came into force on 1 November 1993, allows for joint action by member governments in matters of foreign and security policy, and envisages the eventual formation of a common defence policy, with the possibility of a common defence force. The Western European Union (WEU, q.v.), to which all EU members except Denmark, Greece and Ireland belong, is to be developed as the 'defence component' of the Union, but member states' existing commitments to NATO are to be honoured. Common foreign and security policy is the province of the EU (as opposed to the EC), and decisions in this field are made by the European Council and the Council of the European Union.

CENTRAL AND EASTERN EUROPE

During the late 1980s the extensive political changes and reforms in eastern European countries led to a strengthening of links with the EC. Agreements on trade and economic co-operation were concluded with Hungary (1988), Poland (1989), the USSR (1989), Czechoslovakia (1988—on trade only—and 1990), Bulgaria (1990), the German Democratic Republic (GDR—1990) and Romania (1990). In July 1989 the EC was entrusted with the co-ordination of aid from member states of the Organisation for Economic Co-operation and Development (OECD) to Hungary and Poland ('Operation PHARE'—Poland/Hungary Aid for Restructuring of Economies): this programme was subsequently extended to include Albania, Bulgaria, the Czech Republic, Slovakia, Romania and the Baltic states. Community heads of government agreed in December 1989 to establish a European Bank for Reconstruction and Development (EBRD, q.v.), with participation by member states of the OECD and the Council for Mutual Economic Assistance, to promote investment in eastern Europe; the EBRD began operations in April 1991. In June 1995 the European Council agreed to provide total funding under the PHARE programme of ECU 6,693m. to central and eastern European countries in the period 1995–99.

In August 1991 the EC formally recognized the independence of the Baltic republics (Estonia, Latvia and Lithuania), and in December the PHARE programme was extended to them. Trade and co-operation agreements with the three Baltic states were signed in May 1992. In 1991 the EC established a programme providing technical assistance to the Commonwealth of Independent States (TACIS). In 1994 Mongolia also became eligible for assistance. The programme aimed to assist in the development of successful market economies and to foster pluralism and democracy, by providing expertise and training. In 1996–99 ECU 2,224m. was to be made available under the TACIS programme.

'Europe Agreements' between the EC and Czechoslovakia, Hungary and Poland were signed in December 1991, with the aim of establishing a free-trade area within 10 years and developing political co-operation. The agreements with Hungary and Poland came into effect on 1 February 1994; in April both countries submitted formal applications for EU membership. In June 1991 the EC established diplomatic relations with Albania, and in May 1992 an agreement on trade and co-operation with Albania was signed. Europe Agreements were initialled with Romania in October, and with Bulgaria in March 1993. In June 1993 the European Council approved measures to accelerate the opening of EC markets to goods from central and eastern European countries, with customs duties on many industrial items to be removed by the end of 1994. In September 1993 a co-operation agreement with Slovenia came into force. Further developments in relations with Slovenia were delayed by demands from the Italian Government for a settlement of a dispute concerning property confiscated from ethnic Italians in Slovenia in the 1940s. However, a Europe Agreement was signed in June 1996, after Italy's new Government agreed to withdraw that country's objections, following a compromise agreement. Slovenia then formally applied for EU membership. The Interim Agreement, implementing the agreement signed in June, was due to come into force on 1 January 1997 and provided for the gradual establishment of a free-trade area during a transitional period of six years. On 1 February 1995 Europe Agreements between the EU and Bulgaria, the Czech Republic, Romania and Slovakia entered into force. In June 1996 the Commission decided that 2002 was the earliest probable date for the Czech Republic, Poland and Hungary to become members of the EU.

In February 1994 the EU Council of Ministers agreed to pursue closer economic and political relations with Ukraine, following an agreement by that country to renounce control of nuclear weapons on its territory. A partnership and co-operation agreement was signed by the two sides in June. In December EU ministers of finance approved a loan totalling ECU 85m., conditional on Ukraine's implementation of a strategy to close the Chornobyl (Chernobyl) nuclear power plant. An Interim Trade Agreement with Ukraine came into force in February 1996. A partnership and co-operation agreement was successfully concluded with Russia at the European Council meeting of heads of government in June 1994. An Interim Agreement on trade concessions was initiated in July 1995, after a six-month delay, owing to EU disapproval of Russia's violent repression of an independence movement in Chechnya. This agreement came into effect in February 1996, giving EU exporters improved access to the Russian market for specific products, including cars and alcoholic beverages, and at the same time abolishing quantitative restrictions on some Russian exports to the EU. In November 1994 a partnership and co-operation agreement was signed with Moldova. Similar agreements were signed with Kazakhstan in January 1995, with Kyrgyzstan in February 1995, with Georgia, Armenia and Azerbaijan in January 1996 and with Uzbekistan in July 1996. Free-trade agreements with the Baltic states were finalized by the EU in July 1994, and came into effect on 1 January 1995. In June 1995 the EU concluded Europe Agreements with the three Baltic states. In October Latvia submitted a formal application for EU membership. In December Estonia and Lithuania also submitted membership applications.

As part of the EU's common foreign and security policy, a Conference on Stability in Europe was convened in Paris, in May 1994 to discuss the prevention of ethnic and territorial conflicts in central and eastern Europe. In particular, the conference sought to secure bilateral 'good-neighbour' accords between nine European countries that were regarded as potential future members of the EU (Bulgaria, the Czech Republic, Estonia, Hungary, Latvia, Lithuania, Poland, Romania and Slovakia). These countries, together with EU member states and other European countries (including Belarus, Moldova, Russia and Ukraine), signed a 'Stability Pact' in Paris in March 1995.

In March 1997 the Commission agreed to extend the PHARE programme in order to provide specific assistance to applicant countries in central and eastern Europe, by helping such countries to implement the reform required to fulfil the criteria for EU membership. In July the Commission published a report, entitled 'Agenda 2000', which proposed that accession negotiations should commence with the Czech Republic, Estonia, Hungary, Poland and Slovenia, while it was recommended that discussions with Bulgaria, Latvia, Lithuania, Romania and Slovakia be deferred, owing to the need for further economic or democratic reform in those countries. The report acknowledged that it was also necessary for the EU to be restructured in order to ensure its successful operation following expansion, after the failure of negotiations leading to the Treaty of Amsterdam, approved in June, to reach agreement upon the issue of institutional reform. An intergovernmental conference was expected to be convened after 2000 to formulate plans for the required reform. Ministers of foreign affairs, meeting in Luxembourg in December, endorsed the 'Agenda 2000' proposals, and membership negotiations were scheduled to commence on 31 March 1998. A European Conference was expected to take place in the same month, to be attended by representatives of all applicant countries.

Following the introduction on 1 July 1990 of monetary, economic and social union between the Federal Republic of Germany and the GDR, and the formal integration of the two countries on 3 October, Community legislation was introduced within the former GDR over a transitional period.

A co-operation agreement was signed with Yugoslavia in 1980 (but not ratified until April 1983), allowing tariff-free imports and Community loans. New financial protocols were signed in 1987 and 1991. However, EC aid was suspended in July 1991, following the declarations of independence by the Yugoslav republics of Croatia and Slovenia, and the subsequent outbreak of civil conflict. Efforts were made in the ensuing months by EC ministers of foreign affairs to negotiate a peaceful settlement between the Croatian and Serbian factions, and a team of EC observers was maintained in Yugoslavia from July onwards, to monitor successive cease-fire agreements. In September the EC initiated a conference, attended by representatives of the Yugoslav federal and republican governments, in an attempt to end the conflict. In October the EC proposed a plan for an association of independent states, to replace the Yugoslav federation: this was accepted by all the Yugoslav republics except Serbia, which demanded a redefining of boundaries to accommodate within Serbia all predominantly Serbian areas. In November the application of the Community's co-operation agreements with Yugoslavia was suspended (with exemptions for the republics which co-operated in the peace negotiations). In January 1992 the Community granted diplomatic recognition to the former Yugoslav republics of Croatia and Slovenia, and in April it recognized Bosnia and Herzegovina, while withholding recognition from Macedonia (owing to pressure from the Greek Government, which feared that the existence of an independent Macedonia would imply a claim on the Greek province of the same name). In May EC ambassadors were withdrawn from Belgrade, in protest at Serbia's support for aggression by Bosnian Serbs against other ethnic groups in Bosnia and Herzegovina, and in the same month the Community imposed a trade embargo on Serbia and Montenegro.

New proposals for a settlement of the Bosnian conflict, submitted by EC and UN mediators in early 1993, were accepted by the Bosnian Croats and by the Bosnian Government in March, but rejected by the Bosnian Serbs. In June the European Council pledged more rigorous enforcement of sanctions against Serbia. In July, at UN/EC talks in Geneva, all three parties to the Bosnian war agreed on a plan to divide Bosnia and Herzegovina into three separate republics; however, the Bosnian Government rejected the proposals for the share of territory to be allotted to the Muslims.

In April 1994, following a request from EU ministers of foreign affairs, a Contact Group, consisting of France, Germany, the United Kingdom, the USA and Russia, was initiated to undertake peace negotiations. The following month ministers of foreign affairs of the USA, Russia and the EU (represented by five member states) jointly endorsed a proposal to divide Bosnia and Herzegovina in proportions of 49% to the Bosnian Serbs and 51% to the newly-established Federation of Muslims and Croats. The proposal was rejected by the Bosnian Serb assembly in July and had to be abandoned after the Muslim-Croat Federation withdrew its support subsequent to the Bosnian Serb vote. In July the EU formally assumed political control of Mostar, a town in southern Bosnia and Herzegovina, in order to restore the city's administrative infrastructure and secure peace.

Negotiations towards a trade and co-operation agreement with Croatia began in June 1995, but talks were suspended in early August, following Croatia's military offensive in the Krajina region, which was strongly criticized by the EU. Despite some criticism of US policy towards the former Yugoslavia (notably by France), in September the EU supported US-led negotiations in Geneva to devise a plan to end the conflict in Bosnia and Herzegovina. The plan closely resembled the previous proposals of the Contact Group: two self-governing entities were to be created within Bosnia and Herzegovina, with 51% of territory being allocated to the Muslim-Croat Federation, and 49% to Bosnian Serbs. The proposals were finally agreed after negotiations in Dayton, USA, in November 1995, and an accord was signed in Paris in December. In September EU ministers endorsed a plan to provide financial aid valued at some US $2,000m. to Bosnia and Herzegovina and other parts of the former Yugoslavia for post-war reconstruction. In January 1996 the EU announced its intention to recognize Yugoslavia (Serbia and Montenegro), despite the opposition of the USA. The Commission concluded a memorandum of understanding in late 1996 with the authorities of Bosnia and Herzegovina for aid worth $190m. for programmes to help the return of refugees, restructure the economy, bolster democracy, and strengthen infrastructure. This aid was in addition to existing EU humanitarian programmes for the former Yugoslavia.

In December 1993 six member states of the EU formally recognized the former Yugoslav republic of Macedonia (FYRM) as an independent state, but in February 1994 Greece imposed a commercial embargo against the FYRM, on the grounds that the use of the name and symbols (e.g. on the state flag) of 'Macedonia' was a threat to Greek national security. In March, however, ministers of foreign affairs of the EU decided that the embargo was in contravention of EU law, and in mid-April the Commission commenced legal proceedings in the European Court of Justice against Greece. In September 1995 Greece and the FYRM began a process of normalizing relations, after the FYRM agreed to change the design of its state flag. In October Greece ended its economic blockade of the FYRM, and in November the Council of the European Union authorized the Commission to begin negotiating a trade and co-operation agreement with the FYRM.

In March 1997 the EU sent two advisory delegations to Albania to help to restore order when the collapse of a number of 'pyramid' investment schemes led to violent unrest and political instability in that country. The EU stated that technical advice had been offered to the Albanian Government prior to the collapse, with the aim of introducing legislation to ban such schemes, but that it had been rejected. A request by the Albanian Government for the deployment of EU peace-keeping troops was refused, but it was announced in early April that the EU was to provide humanitarian aid of some ECU 2m., to be used for emergency relief in Albania.

OTHER EUROPEAN COUNTRIES

The members of the European Free Trade Association (EFTA) concluded bilateral free trade agreements with the EEC and the ECSC during the 1970s. Customs duties for the majority of products were abolished in July 1977. On 1 January 1984 the last tariff barriers were eliminated, thus establishing full free trade for industrial products between the Community and EFTA members. Some EFTA members subsequently applied for membership of the EC: Austria in 1989, Sweden in 1991, Finland, Switzerland and Norway in 1992. Formal negotiations on the creation of a 'European Economic Area' (EEA), a single market for goods, services, capital and labour among EC and EFTA members, began in June 1990, and were concluded in October 1991. The agreement was signed in May 1992 (after a delay caused by a ruling of the Court of Justice of the EC that a proposed joint EC-EFTA court, for adjudication in disputes, was incompatible with the Treaty of Rome: EFTA members then agreed to concede jurisdiction to the Court of Justice on cases of competition involving both EC and EFTA members, and to establish a special joint committee for other disputes). In a referendum in December Swiss voters rejected ratification of the agreement, and the remaining 18 countries signed an adjustment protocol in March 1993, allowing the EEA to be established without Switzerland (which was to have observer status). The EEA entered into force on 1 January 1994. Formal negotiations on the accession to the EU of Austria, Finland and Sweden began on 1 February, and those on Norway's membership started on 1 April. Negotiations were concluded with Austria, Finland and Sweden on 1 March 1994, and with Norway on 16 March, having been delayed by issues concerning the fisheries sector. Heads of government of the four countries signed treaties of accession to the EU in June, which were to come into effect from 1995, subject to approval by a national referendum in each country. Accession to the EU was endorsed by the electorates of Austria, Finland and Sweden in June, October and November respectively. Norway's accession was rejected by a referendum conducted at the end of November. Austria, Finland and Sweden became members of the EU on 1 January 1995. Liechtenstein, which became a full member of EFTA in September 1991, joined the EEA on 1 May 1995. Negotiations conducted with Switzerland since 1992 on the formulation of a new bilateral economic arrangement have proceeded slowly. The main obstacles to an agreement have concerned Switzerland's work permit quotas for EU citizens, and the weight limit on trucks passing through its territory. In January 1998 Switzerland agreed to abolish this weight limit and instead impose road haulage taxes on trucks weighing 40 metric tons or more. In December 1996 it was reported that Switzerland had agreed to phase out the use of work permit quotas within six years of a treaty being signed.

THE MIDDLE EAST AND THE MEDITERRANEAN

Association agreements, intended to lead to customs union or possible accession, were signed between the Community and Greece (1961), Turkey (1963), Malta (1970) and Cyprus (1972). The agreements established free access to the Community market for most industrial products and tariff reductions for most agricultural products. Annexed were financial protocols under which the Community was to provide concessional finance to these countries. Aid to Turkey was suspended, owing to the violation of human rights there following the coup in 1980. In 1987 Turkey applied for membership of the Community. In 1989 the European Commission stated that, for formal negotiations on Turkish membership to take place it would be necessary for Turkey to restructure its economy, improve its observance of human rights, and harmonize its relations with Greece. Negotiations in early 1995 to conclude a customs union agreement with Turkey were obstructed by the opposition of Greece. In early March, however, Greece removed its veto on the customs union, having received assurance on the accession of Cyprus to the EU. Ratification of the agreement by the European Parliament was delayed until mid-December, owing to concern over issues of human rights, in particular the policies of the Turkish Government towards the Kurdish population in Turkey. Under the agreement, Turkey was to receive some ECU 1,400m. in grants and loans in 1995–99. In July 1990 Cyprus and Malta made formal applications to join the Community. In June 1993 the European Commission approved the eligibility of both countries to join the community, but in November 1996 Malta's new Labour Government announced its intention to 'freeze' its membership application, and instead to try to negotiate a free-trade agreement. Throughout 1996 and 1997 the EU, along with the USA, took part in extensive diplomatic activity in order to facilitate Cyprus' accession as a single entity. In March 1997 Turkey received assurances that its application for membership would be considered on equal terms with that of any other country. However, in July the Commission published 'Agenda 2000', a report which recommended that accession negotiations should begin with the (Greek) Cypriot Government, while talks with Turkey were to be postponed indefinitely. In December ministers of foreign affairs, meeting in Luxembourg, endorsed the report's proposals, and accession talks with Cyprus were scheduled to take place at the end of March 1998. A European Conference for all applicant countries was to be held in the same month, but Turkey rejected an invitation, amid threats to withdraw its application. A trade agreement with Andorra entered into force on 1 January 1991, establishing a customs union between the EC and Andorra for industrial products, and allowing duty-free access to the EC for certain Andorran agricultural products. Negotiations on a similar agreement with San Marino were concluded in December 1991.

Co-operation agreements came into force with Israel in 1975, with the Maghreb countries (Algeria, Morocco and Tunisia) in 1976 and with the Mashreq countries (Egypt, Jordan, Lebanon and Syria) in 1977, covering free access to the Community market for industrial products, customs preferences for certain agricultural products, and financial aid in the form of grants and loans from the European Investment Bank. A non-preferential co-operation agreement was negotiated with the Yemen Arab Republic in 1984 (extended to cover the whole of the recently-unified Republic of Yemen in 1992). In April 1997 a further co-operation accord, incorporating commitments to democratic principles and a respect for human rights, was approved. In July 1987 Morocco applied to join the Community, but its application was rejected on the grounds that it is not a European country. In July 1995 the EU and Tunisia signed an association agreement, which aimed to eliminate duties and other trade barriers on most products over a transitional 12-year period. In the short term the agreement provided for an increase in quotas for certain agricultural exports from Tunisia to the EU. Association agreements have also been signed with Morocco (February 1996) and Jordan (November 1997). In March 1997 the Commission commenced negotiations with the Algerian Government, with the aim of concluding an association agreement which would incorporate commitments towards human rights and democracy. In January and February 1998 EU delegations visited Algeria to express concern at the escalating violence in that country. Preliminary negotiations towards association agreements have also taken place with Egypt and Syria.

Three protocols were negotiated in 1987 on assistance to Israel for the period 1987–91; however, approval of these protocols was delayed by the European Parliament until October 1988, as a protest against Israel's response to unrest in the occupied territories of the West Bank and the Gaza Strip. In January 1989 the Community and Israel eliminated the last tariff barriers to full free trade for industrial products. In November 1995 the EU and Israel signed an association agreement, establishing more extensive political dialogue between the two parties and providing trade concessions. In September 1993, following the signing of the Israeli-Palestine Liberation Organization (PLO) peace agreement, the EC committed ECU 33m. in immediate humanitarian assistance. In addition, a five-year assistance programme for the period 1994–98 was proposed, which was to consist of ECU 500m. in grants and loans to improve the economic and social infrastructure in the Occupied Territories. In October 1996 ministers of foreign affairs agreed to appoint a special envoy to the Middle East in order to promote a peaceful settlement. In July 1997 the special envoy, Miguel Angel Moratinos (hitherto the Spanish ambassador to Israel), negotiated a meeting between the PLO leader, Yasser Arafat, and the Israeli Minister of Foreign Affairs, David Levy, where it was agreed to resume the peace talks which had been suspended since March. Meanwhile, a Euro-Mediterranean Interim Association Agreement on Trade and Co-operation was signed with the PLO in January. The agreement confirmed existing trade concessions offered to the Palestinians since 1986 and provided for free trade to be introduced during an initial five-year period.

Talks were held with Iran in April 1992 on the establishment of a co-operation accord. In December the Council of Ministers recommended that a 'critical dialogue' be undertaken with Iran, owing to the country's significance to regional security. In April 1997 the 'critical dialogue' was suspended, following a German court ruling that found the Iranian authorities responsible for ordering the murder of four Kurdish dissidents in Berlin in 1992. Germany and the Netherlands recalled their ambassadors from Iran, and urged other EU member states to do likewise. In late April 1997 ministers of foreign affairs resolved to restore diplomatic relations with Iran, in order to protect the strong trading partnership. However, diplomatic relations were not resumed until November, as EU ministers reversed their decision to return diplomats to Teheran, owing to the Iranian Government's reluctance to readmit the German and Dutch ambassadors.

In June 1995 the European Council endorsed a proposal to reform and strengthen the Mediterranean policy of the EU, on the basis of a strategic communication approved by the Commission in October 1994. The initiative envisaged the establishment of a Euro-Mediterranean Economic Area (EMEA) by 2010, preceded by a gradual liberalization of trade within the region. It also aimed to formulate common rules regarding intellectual property, company and banking laws and rules of origin. The Council approved financial support amounting to ECU 4,685.5m. for the Maghreb and Mashreq agreement countries, as well as for Israel (including the Palestinian Territories), Cyprus, Malta, Turkey and Libya, for the period 1995–99. In November 1995 representatives of these countries (with the exception of Libya) and the EU finalized agreement on the EMEA at a conference held in Barcelona, Spain. The conference also agreed to extend co-operation on issues of energy and water resources, and on immigration and drugs-trafficking. The final accords also included commitments by Mediterranean countries to uphold democracy and to work towards the peaceful settlement of disputes and the renunciation of terrorism. In April 1997 a second Euro-Mediterranean Conference of ministers of foreign affairs was held in Malta.

In June 1988 an agreement was signed with the countries of the Gulf Co-operation Council (GCC), providing for co-operation in industry, energy, technology and other fields. Negotiations on a full free-trade pact began in October 1990, but it was expected that any agreement would involve transition periods of some 12 years for the reduction of European tariffs on 'sensitive products' (i.e. petrochemicals).

Contacts with the Arab world in general take place within the framework of the 'Euro-Arab Dialogue', established in 1973 to provide a forum for discussion of economic issues through working groups on specific topics. Following a decision in 1989 to reactivate the Dialogue, meetings were suspended in 1990 as a result of Iraq's invasion of Kuwait. In April 1992 senior EC and Arab officials agreed to resume the process.

LATIN AMERICA

A non-preferential trade agreement was signed with Uruguay in 1974, and economic and commercial co-operation agreements with Mexico in 1975 and Brazil in 1980. A five-year co-operation agreement with the members of the Central American Common Market and with Panama entered into force in 1987, as did a similar agreement with the member countries of the Andean Group (now the Andean Community). Co-operation agreements were signed with Argentina and Chile in 1990, and in that year tariff preferences were approved for Bolivia, Colombia, Ecuador and Peru, in support of those countries' efforts to combat drugs-trafficking. In May 1992 an interinstitutional co-operation agreement was signed with the Southern Common Market (Mercosur); in June the EC and the member states of the Andean Group (Bolivia, Colombia, Ecuador, Peru and Venezuela) initialled a new co-operation agreement, which was to broaden the scope of economic and development co-operation and enhance trade relations, and a new co-operation agreement was signed with Brazil. In April 1997 the EU extended further trade benefits to the countries of the Andean Community. In July 1993 the EC introduced a tariff regime to limit the import of bananas from Latin America, in order to protect the banana-producing countries of the ACP group, linked to the EC by the Lomé Convention (see below). In June 1995 a Commission communication advocated greater economic co-operation with Cuba. This policy was strongly supported by a resolution of the European Parliament in January 1996, but was criticized by the US Government, which continued to maintain an economic embargo against Cuba (see Canada and the USA, below). In July 1997 the EU and Mexico concluded a co-operation agreement and an interim agreement on trade.

In April 1994 ministers of foreign affairs of the EU and the Rio Group (q.v.) held their fourth meeting since formal dialogue was initiated in 1990. A final declaration issuing from the meeting, in São Paulo, Brazil, consisted of a joint commitment to protect human rights and to promote social development and the principles of free trade. The Rio Group ministers, however, rejected any imposition of social or environmental conditional terms on to trading agreements. A bilateral fisheries agreement was concluded in May between the EU and Argentina. The five-year accord secured greater access for the EU to fishing stocks and opened up the European market to fish exports from Argentina.

In late December 1994 the EU and Mercosur signed a joint declaration that was aimed at promoting trade liberalization and greater political co-operation between the groups. In September 1995, at a meeting in Montevideo, Uruguay, a framework agreement on the establishment of a free-trade regime between the two organizations was initialled by representatives of Mercosur and the EU. The agreement was formally signed in December.

ASIA AND AUSTRALASIA

Non-preferential co-operation agreements were signed with the EC by India (1973 and 1981), Bangladesh (1976), Sri Lanka (1975) and Pakistan (1976 and 1986). A trade agreement was signed with the People's Republic of China in 1978, and renewed and expanded in May 1985. A co-operation agreement was signed with the countries of the Association of South East Asian Nations (ASEAN) in 1980. In October 1992 the EC and ASEAN reached a further agreement on co-operation between the two groupings in spite of Portugal's threat to veto the agreement in protest at the killing of demonstrators in East Timor by Indonesian security forces in November 1991. (See p. 114 for the EU's relations with ASEAN.) In June 1989, following the violent repression of the Chinese pro-democracy movement by the Chinese Government, the EC imposed economic sanctions on China. In October 1990 it was decided that relations with China should be 'progressively normalized'. In November 1994 a China-Europe International Business School was initiated in Shanghai. Regular meetings continued to be held between Chinese and EU representatives, which focused on issues relating to human rights, economic reforms in China and bilateral trade relations. The EU has supported China's increased involvement in the international community and, in particular, its application for membership of the WTO. In October 1997 the EU and the Republic of Korea signed an agreement regarding a reciprocal opening of markets for telecommunications equipment, following a protracted dispute, which had led the EU to lodge a complaint with the WTO. In September 1997, however, the Commission submitted a further complaint to the WTO, accusing the Republic of Korea of tax discrimination against European spirits exporters. In September 1997 the EU joined the Korean Peninsular Energy Development Organization (KEDO), an initiative to increase nuclear safety and reduce the risk of nuclear proliferation from the energy programme of the Democratic People's Republic of Korea. In June 1992 the EC signed trade and co-operation agreements with Mongolia and Macau, with respect for democracy and human rights forming the basis of envisaged co-operation. A co-operation accord was formally signed by Viet Nam and the EU in July 1995, in which the EU agreed to increase quotas for Vietnamese textile products, to support the country's efforts to join the WTO and to provide aid for environmental and public management projects. The agreement, which entered into force on 1 June 1996, incorporated a commitment by Viet Nam to guarantee human rights and a procedure for the gradual repatriation of some 40,000 Vietnamese refugees from Germany, who had lost their legal status after German reunification. A permanent EU mission to Viet Nam was established in February 1996. In October 1997 the EU agreed to increase Viet Nam's textile quotas by some 30%, in exchange for improved market access for EU exports. The revised quotas were expected to be introduced in early 1998. In July 1996 a European Business Information Centre was opened in Malaysia, with the object of promoting trade. In October the EU imposed strict limits on entry visas for Myanma senior officials, because of Myanmar's continuing failure to respect human rights. This followed Myanmar's refusal to allow the European Commission to send a mission to investigate allegations of forced labour. In March 1997 EU ministers of foreign affairs agreed to revoke Myanmar's special trade privileges under the Generalized System of Preferences (GSP). The Commission proposed in June 1996 that relations between the EU and India should be strengthened, within the framework of the Partnership Co-operation Agreement signed in 1983. Non-preferential co-operation agreements were signed with Laos and Cambodia in November 1996.

Textiles exports by Asian countries have caused concern in the EU, owing to the depressed state of its own textiles industry. During 1982 bilateral negotiations were held under the Multi-fibre

Arrangement (MFA, see WTO) with Asian producers, notably Hong Kong, the Republic of Korea and Macau. Agreements were eventually reached involving cuts in clothing quotas and 'anti-surge' clauses to prevent flooding of European markets. In 1986 new bilateral negotiations were held and agreements were reached with the principal Asian textile exporters, for the period 1987–91 (later extended to December 1993, when the 'Uruguay Round' of GATT negotiations was finally concluded): in most cases a slight increase in quotas was permitted by the EC. As a result of the trade accord reached under the Uruguay Round, the MFA was to be progressively eliminated, in four stages, over a 10-year period. In January 1995 bilateral textiles agreements, signed by the EU with India, Pakistan and the People's Republic of China, specified certain trade liberalization measures to be undertaken, including an increase of China's silk export quota to 38,000 metric tons and a removal of trade barriers on small-business and handloom textile products from India, while including commitments from the Asian countries to greater efforts to combat textile and design fraud.

The first Asia-Europe meeting (ASEM) was held in March 1996 in Bangkok, Thailand. A wide range of political, economic and co-operation issues was discussed by representatives of the EU member countries and 10 East Asian countries. It was agreed to launch an Asia-Europe Partnership for Greater Growth, in order to expand trade, investment and technology transfer. An Asia-Business Forum was to be formed, as well as an Asia-Europe Foundation in Singapore to promote educational and cultural exchanges. The EU-Korea Framework Agreement was initialled, and Malaysia was appointed to oversee the building of an integrated Asian electric rail network which was to link Singapore to Europe via China. Issues of human and labour rights threatened to provoke confrontation, but this was averted by the topics being relegated to a single sentence in the final statement. ASEM was to reconvene in the United Kingdom in April 1998, and in the Republic of Korea in 2000. In February 1997 ministers of foreign affairs participating in ASEM held their first meeting, in Singapore. In November, however, it was reported that EU ministers of finance were to boycott their inaugural meeting, to be held that month, owing to demands by Asian nations that Myanmar be represented

Numerous discussions have been held since 1981 on the Community's increasing trade deficit with Japan, amounting to some ECU 25,100m. in 1993, and on the failure of the Japanese market to accept more European exports. In July 1991 the heads of government of Japan and of the EC signed a joint declaration on closer co-operation in both economic and political matters; annual meetings of heads of government were to take place. In the same month an agreement was reached on limiting exports of Japanese cars to the EC: the Community's imports from Japan were to be 'frozen' at the current level of 1.23m. cars per year until the end of 1999, after which no restrictions would be imposed by the EC. The agreement did not include vehicles produced in Europe by Japanese companies. In September 1994 a 1.3% increase of Japan's car export quota was agreed, although this figure was substantially lower than that sought by Japanese negotiators. In October 1995 the EU secured an agreement to establish a WTO dispute panel to consider Japan's trade restrictions on alcohol, which were consequently judged to discriminate against European manufacturers of alcoholic spirits. Japan's restrictive trading practices in several sectors, and its treatment of foreign shipping companies using Japanese ports, continued to be a source of disagreement between the EU and Japan during much of 1996. However, the fifth annual meeting between the EU and Japan, held in Tokyo in September, appeared to facilitate more constructive dialogue. The European office of the EU-Japan Industrial Co-operation Centre was opened in Brussels in June 1996; the aim of the Centre, which was established in 1987 as a joint venture between the Japanese Government and the European Commission, was to boost industrial co-operation between the EU and Japan and foster business contacts between companies and universities. The Vulcanus programme, launched in June 1995 by the European Commission and the Japanese Ministry of International Trade and Industry, aims to foster links with Japan through the hosting of Japanese advanced students by European companies.

Regular consultations are held with Australia at ministerial level. In January 1996 the Commission proposed a framework agreement to formalize the EU's trade and political relationship with Australia. However, in September negotiations were suspended, following the Australian Government's objections to the human rights clause contained in all EU international agreements. In June 1997 a joint declaration was signed, committing both sides to greater political, cultural and economic co-operation. Despite intensive negotiations between the EU and the New Zealand Government in 1996, no conclusion was reached regarding import duties. In March 1997 New Zealand took the case to the WTO.

CANADA AND THE USA

A framework agreement for commercial and economic co-operation between the Community and Canada was signed in Ottawa in July 1976, and this was superseded in 1990 by a Declaration on EC-Canada Relations. In 1995 relations with Canada were strained as a result of a dispute regarding fishing rights in the north-west Atlantic Ocean. An agreement on a new division of quotas between EU and Canadian fishermen was concluded in April (see above under Fisheries). In February 1996 the Commission proposed closer ties with Canada, and an action plan covering, among other things, early warning to avoid trade disputes, elimination of trade barriers, and promotion of business contacts. An action plan and joint political declaration were signed in Ottawa in December. In 1996 and 1997 negotiations took place between the EU and Canada over the use of leg-hold traps in the Canadian hunting and fur industry. In July 1997 an agreement was reached, limiting their use.

A number of specific agreements have been concluded between the Community and the USA: a co-operation agreement on the peaceful use of atomic energy entered into force in 1959, and agreements on environmental matters and on fisheries came into force in 1974 and 1984 respectively. Additional agreements provide for co-operation in other fields of scientific research and development, while bilateral contacts take place in many areas not covered by a formal agreement.

The USA has frequently criticized the Common Agricultural Policy, which it sees as creating unfair competition for American exports by its system of export refunds and preferential agreements. A similar criticism has been levelled at Community subsidies to the steel industry. In October 1985 and September 1986 agreements were reached on Community exports of steel to the USA until September 1989 (subsequently extended until March 1992). In January 1993 the USA announced the imposition of substantial duties on imports of steel from 19 countries, including seven EC member states, as an 'anti-dumping' measure. Meanwhile, a further trade dispute emerged between the EC and the USA regarding public procurement of services (e.g. telecommunications, transport and power). A partial agreement was reached in April, with both sides allowing greater access to foreign firms tendering for public-sector contracts. The EC refused to compromise with regard to the telecommunications sector, and the USA implemented sanctions directed at the European telecommunications industry. The EC responded in kind in June, although Germany came to a controversial separate arrangement with the USA, whereby it unilaterally abandoned the agreed retaliatory sanctions. In early December the EC and the USA undertook intensive trade negotiations, which facilitated the conclusion of GATT's Uruguay Round of talks by the deadline of 15 December. In April 1994 the EU and the USA finalized an agreement to liberalize public procurement contracts. The agreement excluded access to the telecommunications sector, but incorporated the supply of services for the generation and distribution of power. It was to become effective in early 1996.

A 'Transatlantic Declaration' on EC–US relations was agreed in November 1990: the two parties agreed to consult each other on important matters of common interest, and to increase formal contacts. In May 1993 the fifth EC–US transatlantic ministerial meeting, a forum for discussion of geopolitical rather than trade issues, was held in Washington. The talks were dominated by the conflict in Bosnia and Herzegovina. A new Trans-Atlantic Agenda for EU–US relations was signed by the US President and the Presidents of the European Commission and European Council at a meeting in Madrid, Spain, in December 1995. In 1995 the USA filed a complaint with the WTO against the EU's banana import regime (see Lomé Convention, below). In October 1996 EU ministers of foreign affairs agreed to pursue in the WTO a complaint regarding the effects on European businesses of the USA's trade embargo against Cuba, formulated in the Helms–Burton Act. In April 1997 the EU and the USA approved a temporary resolution of the Helms-Burton dispute, whereby the US Administration was to limit the application of sanctions in return for a formal suspension of the WTO case. A final settlement had been scheduled for October, but the deadline passed without agreement. In mid-1996 the US Congress had adopted legislation imposing an additional trade embargo (threatening sanctions against any foreign company investing more than US $40m. in energy projects in a number of prescribed states, including Iran and Libya), the presence of which further complicated the EU–US debate in September 1997, when a French petroleum company, Total, provoked US anger, owing to its proposed investment in an Iranian natural gas project. In July the EU became involved in intensive negotiations with the US aircraft company, Boeing, over fears that its planned merger with McDonnell Douglas would harm European interests. In late July the EU approved the merger, after Boeing accepted concessions demanded by the Commission, including an agreement to dispense with exclusivity clauses for 20-year supply contracts and to maintain McDonnell Douglas as a separate company for a period of 10 years. In June the EU and the USA agreed to introduce a mutual recognition agreement, which was to enable goods (including medicines, pharmaceutical products, telecommunications equipment and electrical apparatus) undergoing tests in Europe to be marketed in the USA or Canada without the need for further testing. Meanwhile, negotiations took place throughout 1997 regarding the enforcement of

European meat hygiene regulations (see under Agriculture), the labelling of genetically-engineered food products (see under Environment Policy) and a gradual ban on the use of steel-jawed leg-traps. In May 1997 the WTO upheld a US complaint against the EU's ban on imports of hormone-treated beef, which had led to a retaliatory US ban on meat imports from the EU.

GENERALIZED PREFERENCES

In July 1971 the Community introduced a system of generalized tariff preferences (GSP) in favour of developing countries, ensuring duty-free entry to the EC of all otherwise dutiable manufactured and semi-manufactured industrial products, including textiles—but subject in certain circumstances to preferential limits. Preferences, usually in the form of a tariff reduction, are also offered on some agricultural products. In 1980 the Council agreed to the extension of the scheme for a second decade (1981–90): at the same time it adopted an operational framework for industrial products, which gives individual preferential limits based on the degree of competitiveness of the developing country concerned. From the end of 1990 an interim scheme was in operation, pending the introduction of a revised scheme based on the outcome of the 'Uruguay Round' of GATT negotiations on international trade (which were finally concluded in December 1993). Since 1977 the Community has progressively liberalized GSP access for the least-developed countries by according them duty-free entry on all products and by exempting them from virtually all preferential limits. In 1992–93 the GSP was extended to Albania, the Baltic states, the CIS and Georgia; in September 1994 it was extended to South Africa.

In December 1994 the European Council adopted a new, revised GSP to operate in the four-year period 1995–98. It was to provide additional trade benefits to encourage the introduction by governments of environmentally sound policies and of internationally-recognized labour standards. Conversely, a country's preferential entitlement may be withdrawn, for example, if it undertook forced labour or failed to apply adequate controls on the trafficking of drugs. Under the new scheme preferential tariffs were to amount to 85% of the common customs duty for very sensitive products (for example, most textile products), and 70% or 35% for products classified as sensitive (for example, chemicals, electrical goods). The common customs duty was to be suspended for non-sensitive products (for example, paper, books, cosmetics). In accordance with the EU's foreign policy objective of focusing on the development of the world's poorest countries, duties were eliminated in their entirety for 49 least-developed countries. Duties were also to be suspended for a further five Latin American countries, conditional on their conduct of campaigns against the production and trade of illegal drugs.

AID TO DEVELOPING AND NON-EU COUNTRIES

The main channels for Community aid to developing countries are the Lomé Convention (see below) and the Mediterranean Financial Protocols, but technical and financial aid, and assistance for refugees, training, trade promotion and co-operation in industry, energy, science and technology is also provided to about 30 countries in Asia and Latin America. The EC International Investment Partners facility, established in 1988, promotes private-sector investment in Asian, Latin American and Mediterranean countries, especially in the form of joint ventures. The European Community Humanitarian Office (ECHO) was established in 1991 with a mandate to co-ordinate emergency aid provided by the Community and became fully operational in early 1993. ECHO finances operations conducted by non-governmental organizations and international agencies, with which it works in partnership. In 1996 the EU provided humanitarian aid worth ECU 512m. The main areas of operation were Rwanda, Burundi and the Democratic Republic of the Congo (ECU 205.4m.) and the former Yugoslavia (ECU 187m.). In June 1995 EU finance ministers agreed to contribute ECU 500m. during 1996–99 to fund the European Reconstruction and Development Programme for South Africa.

THE LOMÉ CONVENTION

The First Lomé Convention (Lomé I), which was concluded at Lomé, Togo, in February 1975 and came into force on 1 April 1976, replaced the Yaoundé Conventions and the Arusha Agreement (under which some of the former overseas possessions of France and the United Kingdom retained privileged access to the European market, together with financial assistance). Lomé I was designed to provide a new framework of co-operation, taking into account the varying needs of developing African, Caribbean and Pacific (ACP) countries. The Second Lomé Convention came into force on 1 January 1981. The Third Lomé Convention came into force on 1 March 1985 (trade provisions) and 1 May 1986 (aid). The Fourth Lomé Convention, which had a 10-year commitment period, was signed in December 1989: its trade provisions entered into force on 1 March 1990, and the remainder entered into force in September 1991. At the end of 1997 71 ACP states were parties to the Convention.

ACP-EU Institutions

Council of Ministers: one minister from each signatory state; one co-chairman from each of the two groups; meets annually.

Committee of Ambassadors: one ambassador from each signatory state; chairmanship alternates between the two groups; meets at least every six months.

Joint Assembly: EU and ACP are equally represented; attended by parliamentary delegates from each of the ACP countries and an equal number of members of the European Parliament; one co-chairman from each of the two groups; meets twice a year.

Secretariat of the ACP-EU Council of Ministers: 175 rue de la Loi, 1048 Brussels; tel. (2) 285-61-11; fax (2) 285-62-50.

Centre for the Development of Industry (CDI): 52 ave Herrmann Debroux, 1160 Brussels, Belgium; tel. (2) 679-18-11; telex 61427; fax (2) 675-26-03; f. 1977 to encourage and support the creation, expansion and restructuring of industrial companies (mainly in the fields of manufacturing and agro-industry) in the ACP states by promoting co-operation between ACP and European companies, in the form of financial, technical or commercial partnership, management contracts, licensing or franchise agreements, sub-contracts, etc.; Dir SURENDRA SHARMA.

Technical Centre for Agricultural and Rural Co-operation: Postbus 380, 6700 AJ Wageningen, Netherlands; tel. (317) 467100; telex 30169; fax (317) 460067; f. 1983 to provide ACP states with better access to information, research, training and innovations in agricultural development and extension; Dir Dr R. D. COOKE.

ACP Institutions

ACP Council of Ministers.

ACP Committee of Ambassadors.

ACP Secretariat: ACP House, 451 ave Georges Henri, Brussels, Belgium; tel. (2) 743-06-00; fax (2) 735-55-73; Sec.-Gen. NG'ANDU PETER MAGANDE (Zambia).

The ACP States

Angola	Liberia
Antigua and Barbuda	Madagascar
Bahamas	Malawi
Barbados	Mali
Belize	Mauritania
Benin	Mauritius
Botswana	Mozambique
Burkina Faso	Namibia
Burundi	Niger
Cameroon	Nigeria
Cape Verde	Papua New Guinea
Central African Republic	Rwanda
Chad	Saint Christopher and Nevis
Comoros	Saint Lucia
Congo, Democratic Republic	Saint Vincent and the Grenadines
Congo, Republic	Samoa
Côte d'Ivoire	São Tomé and Príncipe
Djibouti	Senegal
Dominica	Seychelles
Dominican Republic	Sierra Leone
Equatorial Guinea	Solomon Islands
Eritrea	Somalia
Ethiopia	South Africa*
Fiji	Sudan
Gabon	Suriname
The Gambia	Swaziland
Ghana	Tanzania
Grenada	Togo
Guinea	Tonga
Guinea-Bissau	Trinidad and Tobago
Guyana	Tuvalu
Haiti	Uganda
Jamaica	Vanuatu
Kenya	Zambia
Kiribati	Zimbabwe
Lesotho	

*Partial membership (see below).

Under the First Lomé Convention (Lomé I), the Community committed ECU 3,052.4m. for aid and investment in developing countries. Provision was made for over 99% of ACP (mainly agricultural) exports to enter the EC market duty free, while certain products which compete directly with Community agriculture were given preferential treatment but not free access: for certain commodities, such as sugar, imports of fixed quantities at internal Community prices were guaranteed. The Stabex (Stabilization of Export Earnings) scheme was designed to help developing countries to withstand fluctuations in the price of their agricultural products, by paying compensation for reduced export earnings. The Convention also provided for Community funds to help finance projects in ACP countries through grants and loans from the European Investment Bank (EIB, q.v.) and from the European Development Fund (EDF), which is not included in the Community budget (except for its administrative expenditure) but is financed separately by the member states.

The Second Lomé Convention (1981–85) envisaged Community expenditure of ECU 5,530m.: it extended some of the provisions of Lomé I, and introduced new fields of co-operation. One of the most important innovations was a scheme (Sysmin), similar to Stabex, to safeguard exports of mineral products. Other chapters concerned new rules on investment protection, migrant labour, fishing, sea transport, and co-operation in energy policy and agricultural development.

Negotiations for a Third Lomé Convention began in October 1983. Lomé III, which came into force on 1 March 1985 (trade provisions) and 1 May 1986 (aid), made commitments of ECU 8,500m., including loans of ECU 1,100m. from the European Investment Bank. Innovations included an emphasis on agriculture and fisheries, and measures to combat desertification; assistance for rehabilitating existing industries or sectoral improvements; improvements in the efficiency of the Stabex system (now covering a list of 48 agricultural products) and of Sysmin; simplification of the rules of origin of products exported to the EC; an undertaking to promote private investment; co-operation in transport and communications, particularly shipping; cultural and social co-operation; restructuring of emergency aid, and more efficient procedures for technical and financial assistance.

The Fourth Lomé Convention entered partially into force (trade provisions) on 1 March 1990, and fully into force on 1 September 1991. It was to cover the 10-year period 1990–99. The budget for financial and technical co-operation for 1990–95 amounted to ECU 12,000m., of which ECU 10,800m. was from the EDF (including ECU 1,500m. for Stabex and ECU 480m. for Sysmin) and ECU 1,200m. from the EIB. The budget for the second five years was ECU 14,625m., of which ECU 12,967m. was from the EDF, and ECU 1,658m. from the EIB. Under the fourth Convention the obligation of most of the ACP states to contribute to the replenishment of STABEX resources, including the repayment of transfers made under the first three Conventions, was removed. In addition, special loans made to ACP member countries were to be cancelled, except in the case of profit-orientated businesses. Other innovations included the provision of assistance for structural adjustment programmes (amounting to ECU 1,150m.); increased support for the private sector, environmental protection, and control of growth in population; and measures to avoid increasing the recipient countries' indebtedness (e.g. by providing Stabex and Sysmin assistance in the form of grants, rather than loans).

COMMITMENTS MADE UNDER THE LOMÉ CONVENTION
(ECU million)

	1995	1996*
Trade promotion	57.6	8.7
Cultural and social development	163.8	69.5
Education and training	40.7	38.6
Water engineering, urban infrastructure and housing	65.8	22.7
Health	57.3	8.1
Economic infrastructure (transport and communications)	236.8	104.3
Development of production	471.2	122.9
Rural production	93.4	24.6
Industrialization	286.3	51.7
Campaigns on specific themes[1]	91.5	46.5
Exceptional aid, Stabex	334.2	121.3
Rehabilitation	161.0	47.2
Disasters	33.7	-9.7
Stabex	131.1	78.8
AIDS	9.6	3.9
Refugees and returnees	-1.2	1.0
Other[2]	256.5	170.0
Total	1,520.0	596.7

* Provisional figures.

[1] Including desertification and drought, natural disasters, major endemic and epidemic diseases, hygiene and basic health, endemic cattle diseases, energy-saving research, sectoral imports programmes and long-term operations.

[2] Including information and documentation, seminars, programmes and general technical co-operation, general studies, multi-sectoral programmes, delegations, public buildings and project-linked multi-sectoral technical co-operation (all projects).

Source: European Commission, *General Report* (1996).

On 1 July 1993 the EC introduced a regime covering the import of bananas into the Community. This was designed to protect the banana industries of ACP countries (mostly in the Caribbean), which were threatened by the availability of cheaper bananas, produced by countries in Latin America. The new regime guaranteed 30% of the European market to ACP producers, and established an annual quota of 2m. metric tons for bananas imported from Latin America, which would incur a uniform duty of 20%, while imports above this level were to be subject to a tariff of ECU 850 per ton. In February 1994 a dispute panel of GATT upheld a complaint, brought by five Latin American countries, that the EU banana import regime was in contravention of free-trade principles. An agreement was reached in March, under which the EU increased the annual quota for Latin American banana imports to 2.1m. tons with effect from October 1994, and to 2.2m. tons in 1995. However, in 1995 the USA, supported by Guatemala, Honduras and Mexico (and subsequently by Ecuador), filed a complaint with the WTO against the EU's banana regime. In May 1997 the WTO concluded that the EU banana import regime violated 19 free-trade regulations. The EU presented an appeal against the ruling in July, but in September the WTO's dispute settlement body endorsed the original verdict. However, the allocation of preferential tariffs to ACP producers, covered by a waiver since late 1994, was upheld. In October 1997 the EU agreed to amend its banana import regime to comply with the WTO ruling. An arbitration report, published in January 1998, compelled the EU to implement changes by 1 January 1999. In January 1998 the Commission proposed maintaining the existing quotas and duty tariffs while replacing the disallowed import licensing regime with a further quota of 353,000 tons per year to allow for the enlargement of the EU.

In early September 1993 the Community announced plans to revise and strengthen its relations with the ACP countries under the Lomé Convention. Amendment of the Convention was to be guided by three objectives: the promotion of democracy, the rule of law and good governance in ACP countries; open dialogue, avoiding paternalistic or colonial attitudes; and the simplification of the Convention's mechanisms. In May 1994 representatives of EU member states and ACP countries initiated the mid-term review of the Lomé IV Convention. The Community reiterated its intention to maintain the Convention as an aid instrument but emphasized that stricter conditions relating to the awarding of aid would be imposed, based on standards of human rights, human resource development and environmental protection. However, negotiations between EU and ACP states were adjourned in February 1995, owing to disagreements among EU states concerning reimbursement of the EDF in the period 1995–2000. In June the European Council agreed to provide ECU 14,625m. for the second phase of the Lomé IV Convention, of which ECU 12,967m. was to be allocated from the EDF and ECU 1,658m. in loans from the EIB. Agreement was also reached on revision of the 'country-of-origin' rules for manufactured goods, a new protocol on the sustainable management of forest resources and a joint declaration on support for the banana industry. The agreement was subsequently endorsed by an EU–ACP ministerial group, and the revised Convention was signed in November, in Mauritius. In March 1997 the Commission proposed granting debt relief assistance of ECU 25m. each year for the period 1997–2000 to the 11 heavily-indebted poor countries (as identified by the World Bank and the IMF) forming part of the ACP Group. Funding was to be used to support international efforts to reduce debt and encourage the economic prospects of such countries.

In June 1995 negotiations opened with a view to concluding a wide-ranging trade and co-operation agreement with South Africa, including the eventual creation of a free-trade area (FTA). In March 1997 the Commission approved a Special Protocol for South Africa's accession to the Lomé Convention, and in April South Africa attained partial membership. Full membership was withheld, as South Africa was not regarded as, in all respects, a developing country, and was therefore not entitled to aid provisions. A special provision was introduced into the revised Lomé IV Convention to allow Somalia to accede, should constitutional government be established in that country prior to the expiry of the Convention.

Intensive debate has been taking place since 1995 on the future relations between the ACP states and the EU, in view of the increasingly global nature of the EU's foreign policies, and particularly the growing emphasis it is placing on relations with central and eastern Europe and countries of the Mediterranean rim. In November 1996 the Commission published a consultative document to consider the options for future ACP–EU relations. The document focused on the areas of trade, aid and politics, and included proposals to encourage competitiveness, to support private-sector investment and to enhance democracy. The report suggested abolishing or restructuring Stabex and Sysmin, and considered altering the grouping of the ACP states for the purpose of implementing economic agreements. The ultimate aim of the document was to foster conditions in which the EU and the ACP countries could co-exist as equal partners. In November 1997 the first summit of heads of state of ACP countries was held in Libreville, Gabon. The ACP council of ministers prepared a mandate for negotiations towards a renewed Lomé Convention, which was approved by the Commission in January 1998. Negotiations on the renewal of the Lomé pact, or on some new form of agreement, were due to start in September.

Finance

THE COMMUNITY BUDGET

The general budget of the European Union covers all EEC and Euratom expenditure and the administrative expenditure of the ECSC. The Commission is responsible for implementing the budget. (The ECSC, like the EIB, has its own resources and conducts its own financial operations.) Under the Council decision of 24 June 1988 all revenue (except that expressly designated for supplementary research and technological development programmes) is used without distinction to finance all expenditure, and all budget expenditure must be covered in full by the revenue entered in the budget. Any amendment of this decision requires the unanimous approval of the Council and must be ratified by the member states. The Treaty of Rome requires member states to release funds to cover the appropriations entered in the budget.

Each Community institution draws up estimates of its expenditure, and sends them to the Commission before 1 July of the year preceding the financial year (1 January–31 December) in question. The Commission consolidates these estimates in a preliminary draft budget, which it sends to the Council by 1 September. Expenditure is divided into two categories: that necessarily resulting from the Treaties (compulsory expenditure) and other (non-compulsory) expenditure. The draft budget must be approved by a qualified majority in the Council, and presented to Parliament by 5 October. Parliament may propose modifications to compulsory expenditure, and may (within the limits of the 'maximum rate of increase', dependent on growth of member states' gross national product—GNP—and budgets) amend non-compulsory expenditure. The budget must normally be declared finally adopted 75 days after the draft is presented to Parliament. If the budget has not been adopted by the beginning of the financial year, monthly expenditure may amount to one-twelfth of the appropriations adopted for the previous year's budget. The Commission may (even late in the year during which the budget is being executed) revise estimates of revenue and expenditure, by presenting supplementary and/or amending budgets.

BUDGET EXPENDITURE APPROPRIATIONS FOR THE ACTIVITIES OF THE EUROPEAN COMMISSION
(ECU million)

	1996	1997
Administration		
Expenditure relating to persons working with the institution	1,732.3	1,806.9
Buildings, equipment and miscellaneous operating expenditure	354.1	373.5
Expenditure resulting from special functions carried out by the institution	253.6	253.7
Data-processing	94.8	93.8
Staff and administrative expenditure of EC delegations	197.2	201.8
Other expenditure	64.8	68.3
Total	2,696.7	2,798.0
Operations		
EAGGF Guarantee section	41,328.0	41,305.0
Structural operations, other agricultural and regional operations, transport and fisheries	29,410.6	31,838.0
Training, youth, culture, audiovisual media, information and other social operations	819.7	793.0
Energy, Euratom nuclear safeguards and environment	217.4	185.7
Consumer protection, internal market, industry and trans-European networks	821.5	887.2
Research and technological development	3,183.1	3,500.0
Co-operation with developing countries and other third countries	5,727.6	5,899.5
Common foreign and security policy	62.0	30.0
Repayments, guarantees and reserves	827.0	415.0
Operations—Total	82,396.9	84,853.4
Grand total	85,093.6	87,651.4

Note: The other Community institutions were allocated budgetary resources of ECU 1,486.9m. in 1996 and ECU 1,485.5m. in 1997. These funds were to be supplemented by the institutions' own resources.

Expenditure under the general budget is financed by 'own resources', comprising agricultural duties (on imports of agricultural produce from non-member states), customs duties, application of value-added tax (VAT) on goods and services, and (since 1988) a levy based on the GNP of member states. Member states are obliged to collect 'own resources' on the Community's behalf. From May 1985 arrangements were introduced for the correction of budgetary imbalances, as a result of which the United Kingdom received compensation in the form of reductions in VAT payments. In 1988 it was decided by the Community's heads of government to set a maximum amount for 'own resources' that might be called up in any one year.

REVENUE (ECU million)

Source of revenue	1996	1997
Agricultural duties	808.8	873.4
Sugar and isoglucose levies	1,210.4	1,366.0
Customs duties	13,068.9	13,559.0
Own resources collection costs	–1,508.8	–1,579.9
VAT own resources	35,595.8	34,587.8
GNP-based own resources	21,084.4	32,947.2
Balance of VAT and GNP own resources from previous years	833.7	0.0
Budget balance from previous year	9,215.2	0.0
Other revenue	720.0	612.0
Total	81,028.4	82,365.5

Source: European Commission, *General Report* (1996).

MEMBER STATES' PAYMENTS*

Country	Contribution for 1996 (ECU million)	% of total
Austria	2,077.5	2.9
Belgium	2,804.6	3.9
Denmark	1,379.1	1.9
Finland	1,100.1	1.5
France	12,553.3	17.4
Germany	21,632.7	30.0
Greece	1,047.9	1.5
Ireland	669.9	0.9
Italy	8,619.0	11.9
Luxembourg	156.9	0.2
Netherlands	4,274.8	5.9
Portugal	1,030.3	1.4
Spain	4,552.4	6.3
Sweden	2,097.8	2.9
United Kingdom	8,154.2	11.3
Total	72,150.5	100.0

* Figures are provisional. The revised total is ECU 80,308.4 million.

The general budget contains the expenditures of the six main Community institutions—the Commission, the Council, Parliament, the Court of Justice, the Court of Auditors, and the Economic and Social Committee and the Committee of the Regions—of which Commission expenditure (covering administrative costs and expenditure on operations) forms the largest proportion. The Common Agricultural Policy accounts for about 50% of total expenditure, principally in agricultural guarantees. In 1988 it was decided (as part of a system of budgetary discipline agreed by the Council) that the rate of increase in spending on agricultural guarantees between 1988 and a given year was not to exceed 74% of the growth rate of Community GNP during the same period. In December 1992 it was agreed to increase the ceiling on Community expenditure from 1.2% of the EC's combined GNP to 1.27% in 1999 (the ceiling for 1995 was 1.21%, and for 1996 1.22%). In December 1994, taking into account the enlargement of the EU to 15 countries (from 1 January 1995) it was agreed to set a level of maximum expenditure at ECU 75,500m. in 1995, increasing to ECU 87,000m. in 1999, at constant 1992 prices.

STRUCTURAL ACTIONS

The Community's 'structural actions' comprise the Guidance Section of the European Agricultural Guidance and Guarantee Fund, the European Regional Development Fund, the European Social Fund and the Cohesion Fund. There is also a financial instrument for fisheries guidance, commitments for which amounted to ECU 450m.

in 1996. In accordance with the Single European Act (1987), reforms of the Community's structural funds were adopted by the Council with effect from 1 January 1989, with the aim of more accurate identification of priority targets, and greater selectivity to enable action to be concentrated in the least-favoured regions (see Social Policy, p. 170). Commitments for the structural funds were to double, in real terms, by 1993 from their 1987 level of ECU 7,200m. In December 1992 it was agreed that total 'structural' expenditure would be increased to ECU 30,000m. per year by 1999, at constant 1992 prices. Commitments in the 1996 budget totalled ECU 29,131m.

Cohesion Fund

The Treaty on European Union and its protocol on economic and social cohesion provided for the establishment of a 'cohesion fund', which began operating on 1 April 1993, with a budget of ECU 1,500m. for the first year. This was to subsidize projects in the fields of the environment and trans-European energy and communications networks in member states with a per caput GNP of less than 90% of the Community average (in practice, this was to mean Greece, Ireland, Portugal and Spain). Commitments under the fund in the budget appropriations for 1996 amounted to ECU 2,444m. The fund's total budget for the period 1993–99 was ECU 15,500m.

European Agricultural Guidance and Guarantee Fund (EAGGF)—Guidance Section

Created in 1962, the European Agricultural Guidance and Guarantee Fund is administered by the Commission. The Guidance section covers expenditure on Community aid for projects to improve farming conditions in the member states. It includes aid for poor rural areas and the structural adjustment of rural areas, particularly in the context of the reform of the common agricultural policy (CAP). This aid is usually granted in the form of financial contributions to programmes also supported by the member governments themselves. Commitments of ECU 3,772m. were budgeted for in 1996.

European Regional Development Fund—ERDF

Payments began in 1975. The Fund is intended to compensate for the unequal rate of development in different regions of the Community, by encouraging investment and improving infrastructure in 'problem regions'. The 1996 budget included an allocation of ECU 11,883.7m. for the Fund's commitments.

European Social Fund

The Fund (established in 1960) provides resources with the aim of combating long-term unemployment and facilitating the integration into the labour market of young people and the socially disadvantaged. It also supports schemes to help workers to adapt to industrial changes. The 1996 budget allocated ECU 7,145.8m. for the Fund's commitments.

PUBLICATIONS*

Bulletin of the European Union (10 a year).

The Courier (every 2 months, on ACP-EU affairs).

European Economy (every 6 months, with supplements).

European Voice (weekly).

General Report on the Activities of the European Union (annually).

Official Journal of the European Communities.

Publications of the European Communities (quarterly).

Information sheets, background reports and statistical documents.

* Most publications are available in all the official languages of the Union. They are obtainable from the Office for Official Publications of the European Communities, 2 rue Mercier, 2985 Luxembourg; tel. 29291; telex 1324; fax 495719.

THE FRANC ZONE

Address: Direction Générale des Services Etrangers (Service de la Zone Franc), Banque de France, 39 rue Croix-des-Petits-Champs, 75049, Paris Cédex 01, France.

Telephone: 1-42-92-31-46; **telex:** 220932; **fax:** 1-42-92-39-88.

MEMBERS

Benin	Equatorial Guinea
Burkina Faso	French Republic*
Cameroon	Gabon
Central African Republic	Guinea-Bissau
Chad	Mali
The Comoros	Niger
Republic of the Congo	Senegal
Côte d'Ivoire	Togo

* Metropolitan France, Mayotte, St Pierre and Miquelon and the Overseas Departments and Territories.

The Franc Zone embraces all those countries and groups of countries whose currencies are linked with the French franc at a fixed rate of exchange and who agree to hold their reserves mainly in the form of French francs and to effect their exchange on the Paris market. Each of these countries or groups of countries has its own central issuing bank and its currency is freely convertible into French francs. This monetary union is based on agreements concluded between France and each country or group of countries.

Apart from Guinea and Mauritania, all of the countries that formerly comprised French West and Equatorial Africa are members of the Franc Zone. The former West and Equatorial African territories are still grouped within the currency areas that existed before independence, each group having its own currency issued by a central bank.

A number of states left the Franc Zone during the period 1958–73: Guinea, Tunisia, Morocco, Algeria, Mauritania and Madagascar.

The Comoros, formerly a French Overseas Territory, did not join the Franc Zone following its unilateral declaration of independence in 1975. However, francs CFA were used as the currency of the new state and the Institut d'émission des Comores continued to function as a Franc Zone organization. In 1976 the Comoros formally assumed membership. In July 1981 the Banque centrale des Comores replaced the Institut d'émission des Comores, establishing its own currency, the Comoros franc. The island of Mayotte, however, has remained under French administration as an Overseas Collectivité Territoriale, using the French franc as its unit of currency.

Equatorial Guinea, a former Spanish possession, joined the Franc Zone in January 1985, and Guinea-Bissau, a former Portuguese territory, joined in May 1997.

During the late 1980s and early 1990s the economies of the African Franc Zone countries were adversely affected by increasing foreign debt and by a decline in the prices paid for their principal export commodities. The French Government, however, refused to devalue the franc CFA, as recommended by the IMF. In 1990 the Franc Zone governments agreed to develop economic union, with integrated public finances and common commercial legislation. In April 1992, at a meeting of Franc Zone ministers, a treaty was signed on the insurance industry whereby a regulatory body for the industry was to be established: the Conférence Intrafricaine des Marchés d'Assurances (CIMA). Under the treaty, which was to be effective from 31 December 1992, a council of Franc Zone ministers responsible for the insurance industry was also to be established with its secretariat in Libreville, Gabon. (A code of conduct for members of CIMA came into effect in early 1995.) At the meeting held in April 1992 ministers also agreed that a further council of ministers was to be created with the task of monitoring the social security systems in Franc Zone countries. A programme drawn up by Franc Zone finance ministers concerning the harmonization of commercial legislation in member states through the establishment of l'Organisation pour l'Harmonisation du Droit des Affaires en Afrique (OHADA), was approved by the Franco-African summit in October. A treaty to align corporate and investment regulations was signed by 11 member countries at the annual meeting with France in October 1993. Devaluations of the franc CFA and the Comoros franc were agreed by CFA central banks in January 1994 (see below). Following the devaluation the CFA countries embarked on programmes of economic adjustment, including restrictive fiscal and wage policies and other monetary, structural and social measures, designed to stimulate growth and to ensure eligibility for development assistance from international financial institutions. France established a special development fund of FFr 300m. to alleviate the immediate social consequences of the devaluation, and announced substantial debt cancellations. In April the French Government announced assistance amounting to FFr 10,000m. over three years to Franc Zone countries undertaking structural adjustment programmes. The IMF, which had strongly advocated a devaluation of the franc CFA, and the World Bank approved immediate soft-credit loans, technical assistance and cancellations or rescheduling of debts. In June 1994 Heads of State (or representatives) of African Franc Zone countries convened in Libreville, Gabon, to review the effects of the currency realignment. The final communiqué of the meeting urged further international support for the countries' economic development efforts. In April 1995 Franc Zone finance ministers, meeting in Paris, recognized the positive impact of the devaluation on agricultural export sectors, in particular in west African countries, though central African countries, it was noted, were still afflicted by serious economic difficulties. In September 1995 the Franc Zone member countries and the French Government agreed to establish a research and training institution, Afristat, which was to support national statistical organizations in order to strengthen economic management capabilities in participating states. In April 1997 finance ministers met to review the economies of member states. Capital entries (private investment and public development aid) along with tax and wage policies and an increase in exports were found to have contributed to economic growth. Improvements were continuing within a programme supported by the IMF and the World Bank, though ministers stated that economic development efforts were not sufficiently supported by the private sector, with the average rate of investment remaining at 10% of GDP. The adoption of a charter to encourage private investors was discussed, but postponed pending an investigation into proposals made by UEMOA and CEMAC. The co-operation agreement permitting Guinea-Bissau's membership of the Franc Zone, to come into effect on 2 May, was also signed. In the same month delegates from OHADA met donors in Guinea-Bissau, aiming to raise funds worth US $50m. over a 12-year period, to allow them to train commercial court judges, provide information for businesses and cover administration costs.

EXCHANGE REGULATIONS

Currencies of the Franc Zone are freely convertible into the French franc at a fixed rate, through 'operations accounts' established by agreements concluded between the French Treasury and the individual issuing banks. It is backed fully by the French Treasury, which also provides the issuing banks with overdraft facilities.

The monetary reserves of the CFA countries are normally held in French francs in the French Treasury. However, the Banque centrale des états de l'Afrique de l'ouest (BCEAO) and the Banque des états de l'Afrique centrale (BEAC) are authorized to hold up to 35% of their foreign exchange holdings in currencies other than the franc. Exchange is effected on the Paris market. Part of the reserves earned by richer members can be used to offset the deficits incurred by poorer countries.

Regulations drawn up in 1967 provided for the free convertibility of currency with that of countries outside the Franc Zone. Restrictions were removed on the import and export of CFA banknotes, although some capital transfers are subject to approval by the governments concerned.

When the French Government instituted exchange control to protect the French franc in May 1968, other Franc Zone countries were obliged to take similar action in order to maintain free convertibility within the Franc Zone. The franc CFA was devalued following devaluation of the French franc in August 1969. Since March 1973 the French authorities have ceased to maintain the franc-US dollar rate within previously agreed margins, and, as a result, the value of the franc CFA has fluctuated on foreign exchange markets in line with the French franc.

In August 1993, as a result of the financial turmoil regarding the European exchange rate mechanism and the continuing weakness of the French franc, the BCEAO and the BEAC decided to suspend repurchasing of francs CFA outside the Franc Zone. Effectively this signified the withdrawal of guaranteed convertibility of the franc CFA with the French franc. In January 1994 the franc CFA was devalued by 50%, and the Comoros franc by 33.3%.

CURRENCIES OF THE FRANC ZONE

French franc (= 100 centimes): used in Metropolitan France, in the Overseas Departments of Guadeloupe, French Guiana, Martinique, Réunion, and in the Overseas Collectivités Territoriales of Mayotte and St Pierre and Miquelon.

1 franc CFA = 1 French centime. CFA stands for Communauté financière africaine in the West African area and for Coopération financière en Afrique centrale in the Central African area. Used in the monetary areas of West and Central Africa respectively.

1 Comoros franc = 1.333 French centimes (1 French franc = 75 Comoros francs). Used in the Comoros, where it replaced the franc CFA in 1981.

1 franc CFP = 5.5 French centimes. CFP stands for Comptoirs français du Pacifique. Used in New Caledonia, French Polynesia and the Wallis and Futuna Islands.

WEST AFRICA

Union économique et monétaire ouest-africaine—UEMOA: Ouagadougou, Burkina Faso; f. 1994; replaced the Communauté économique de l'Afrique de l'ouest–CEAO; promotes regional monetary and economic convergence, and aims to improve regional trade by facilitating the movement of labour and capital between member states. The first meeting of heads of state of UEMOA member countries, held in May 1996 in Ouagadougou, agreed to establish a customs union with effect from 1 January 1998. A preferential tariff scheme, eliminating duties on most local products and reducing by 30% import duties on many Community-produced industrial goods, became operational on 1 July 1996; in addition, from 1 July, a community solidarity tax of 0.5% was imposed on all goods from third countries sold within the Community, in order to strengthen UEMOA's capacity to promote economic integration. In June 1997 the second meeting of UEMOA heads of state and government agreed to reduce import duties on industrial products originating in the Community by a further 30%. The meeting also confirmed that Côte d'Ivoire's stock exchange was to be transformed into the Bourse Régional des Valeurs Mobilières serving the UEMOA sub-region, in order to further economic integration. The Bourse was scheduled to commence operations in January 1998. At the meeting UEMOA heads of state adopted a declaration on peace and security in the region. In November 1997 UEMOA ministers of finance agreed to postpone the establishment of a customs union until 1 January 2000, when a five-band system of tariffs of between 0% and 20% was to become effective. Mems: Benin, Burkina Faso, Côte d'Ivoire, Guinea-Bissau, Mali, Niger, Senegal and Togo. Chair. BLAISE COMPAORÉ (Burkina Faso).

Union monétaire ouest-africaine—UMOA (West African Monetary Union): established by Treaty of November 1973, entered into force 1974; in 1990 the UMOA Banking Commission was established, which is responsible for supervising the activities of banks and financial institutions in the region, with the authority to prohibit the operation of a banking institution. UMOA constitutes an integral part of UEMOA.

Banque centrale des états de l'Afrique de l'ouest—BCEAO: ave Abdoulaye Fadiga, BP 3108, Dakar, Senegal; tel. 23-16-15; telex 21815; fax 23-93-35; f. 1962 by Benin, Burkina Faso, Côte d'Ivoire, Mali, Niger, Senegal and Togo (in co-operation with France) in order to manage the franc CFA; central bank of issue for the mems of UEMOA; cap. and res 657,592m. francs CFA (Dec. 1995). Gov. CHARLES KONAN BANNY (Côte d'Ivoire); Sec.-Gen. MICHEL K. KLOUSSEH (Togo). Publs *Annual Report, Notes d'Information et Statistiques* (monthly), *Annuaire des banques, Bilan des banques et établissements financiers* (annual).

Banque ouest-africaine de développement—BOAD: 68 ave de la Libération, BP 1172, Lomé, Togo; tel. 21-42-44; telex 5289; fax 21-52-67; f. 1973 to promote the balanced development of mem. states and the economic integration of West Africa; cap. 18,100m. francs CFA (Dec. 1995). A Guarantee Fund for Private Investment in west Africa, established jtly by BOAD and the European Investment Bank, was inaugurated in Dec. 1994. The Fund, which had an initial capital of 8,615.5m. francs CFA, aimed to guarantee medium- and long-term credits to private sector businesses in the region. Mems: Benin, Burkina Faso, Côte d'Ivoire, Guinea-Bissau, Mali, Niger, Senegal, Togo. Chair. BONI YAYI (Benin); Vice-Chair. ALPHA TOURÉ. Publ. *Rapport Annuel, BOAD-INFO* (every 3 months).

CENTRAL AFRICA

Union douanière et économique de l'Afrique centrale—UDEAC (Customs and Economic Union of Central Africa): BP 969, Bangui, Central African Republic; tel. 61-09-22; telex 5254; fax 61-21-35; f. 1966 by the Brazzaville Treaty of 1964 (revised in 1974); forms customs union, with free trade between mems and a common external tariff for imports from other countries. UDEAC has a common code for investment policy and a Solidarity Fund to counteract regional disparities of wealth and economic development. UDEAC priority areas are transport and communication, agriculture, food and environment, industry, and research. UDEAC comprises six technical depts and one admin. dept, with 85 employees. Mems: Cameroon, Central African Republic, Chad, Republic of the Congo, Equatorial Guinea, Gabon. Sec.-Gen. THOMAS DAKAYI KAMGA (Cameroon). Publ. *Bulletin de liaison du DEP* (every 3 months).

At a summit meeting in December 1981, UDEAC leaders agreed in principle to form an economic community of Central African states (Communauté économique des états d'Afrique centrale—CEEAC), to include UDEAC members and Burundi, Rwanda, São Tomé and Príncipe and Zaire (now Democratic Republic of the Congo). CEEAC (q.v.) began operations in 1985.

In March 1994 UDEAC leaders signed a treaty for the establishment of a Communauté économique et monétaire en Afrique centrale (CEMAC), which was to promote the process of sub-regional integration within the framework of an economic union and a monetary union. In August 1996 a meeting of CEMAC heads of state, scheduled to be held in Pointe-Noire, Republic of the Congo, was cancelled. In February 1998 UDEAC leaders, meeting in Libreville, Gabon, agreed that the union should be superseded by CEMAC. A meeting of CEMAC heads of state was scheduled to be held in Malabo, Equatorial Guinea, in December.

Banque de développement des états de l'Afrique centrale (BDEAC): place du Gouvernement, BP 1177, Brazzaville, Republic of the Congo; tel. 83-02-12; telex 5306; fax 83-02-66; f. 1975; cap. 19,735m. francs CFA (June 1996); shareholders: Cameroon, Central African Republic, Chad, Republic of the Congo, Gabon, Equatorial Guinea, ADB, BEAC, France, Germany and Kuwait; Dir-Gen. JEAN-MARIE MBIOKA.

Banque des états de l'Afrique centrale (BEAC): ave Mgr François Xavier Vogt, BP 1917, Yaoundé, Cameroon; tel. 23-40-30; telex 8343; fax 23-33-29; f. 1973 as the central bank of issue of Cameroon, the Central African Republic, Chad, the Republic of the Congo, Equatorial Guinea and Gabon; a monetary market, incorporating all national financial institutions of the BEAC countries, came into effect on 1 July 1994; cap. and res 204,933m. francs CFA (Dec. 1995). Gov. JEAN-FÉLIX MAMALEPOT, Publs *Rapport annuel, Etudes et statistiques* (monthly).

CENTRAL ISSUING BANKS

Banque centrale des Comores: place de France, BP 405, Moroni, Comoros; tel. (73) 1002; telex 0994213; fax (73) 0349; f. 1981; Gov. SAÏD AHMED SAÏD ALI.

Banque centrale des états de l'Afrique de l'ouest: see above.

Banque des états de l'Afrique centrale: see above.

Banque de France: 39 rue Croix-des-Petits-Champs, BP 140-01, 75049 Paris, France; tel. 1-42-92-42-92; telex 220932; fax 1-42-96-04-23; f. 1800; bank of issue for Metropolitan France; Gov. JEAN-CLAUDE TRICHET; Dep. Govs DENIS FERMAN, HERVÉ HANNOUN.

Institut d'émission des départements d'outre-mer: Cité du Retiro, 35/37 rue Boissy d'Anglas, 75379 Paris Cédex 08, France; tel. 1-40-06-41-41; issuing authority for the French Overseas Departments and the French Overseas Collectivité Territoriale of St Pierre and Miquelon; Pres. DENIS FERMAN; Dir-Gen. ANTOINE POUILLIEUTE; Dir GILLES AUDREN.

Institut d'émission d'outre-mer: Cité du Retiro, 35/37 rue Boissy d'Anglas, 75379 Paris Cédex 08, France; tel. 1-40-06-41-41; issuing authority for the French Overseas Territories and the French Overseas Collectivité Territoriale of Mayotte; Pres. DENIS FERMAN; Dir-Gen. ANTOINE POUILLIEUTE; Dir GILLES AUDREN.

FRENCH ECONOMIC AID

France's connection with the African Franc Zone countries involves not only monetary arrangements, but also includes comprehensive French assistance in the forms of budget support, foreign aid, technical assistance and subsidies on commodity exports.

Official French financial aid and technical assistance to developing countries is administered by the following agencies:

Caisse française de développement—CFD (fmrly the Caisse centrale de coopération économique—CCCE): Cité du Retiro, 35/37 rue Boissy d'Anglas, 75379 Paris Cédex 08, France; tel. 1-40-06-31-31; telex 212632; f. 1941. French development bank which lends money to member states and former member states of the Franc Zone and several other states, and executes the financial operations of the FAC (see below). Following the devaluation of the franc CFA in January 1994, the French Government cancelled some 25,000m. French francs in debt arrears owed by member states to the CFD. The CFD established a Special Fund for Development and the Exceptional Facility for Short-term Financing to help alleviate the immediate difficulties resulting from the devaluation. A total of FFr 4,600m. of financial assistance was awarded to Franc Zone countries in 1994. In early 1994 the CFD made available funds totalling 2,420m. francs CFA to assist the establishment of CEMAC (see above); Dir-Gen. ANTOINE POUILLIEUTE.

Fonds d'aide et de coopération—FAC: 20 rue Monsieur, 75007 Paris, France; tel. 1-53-69-00-00; fax 1-53-69-43-82; in 1959 FAC took over from FIDES (Fonds d'investissement pour le développement économique et social) the administration of subsidies and loans from the French Government to the former French African states. FAC is administered by the Ministry of Co-operation, which allocates budgetary funds to it.

INTER-AMERICAN DEVELOPMENT BANK—IDB

Address: 1300 New York Ave, NW, Washington, DC 20577, USA.

Telephone: (202) 623-1000; **fax:** (202) 623-3096; **internet:** http://www.iadb.org.

The Bank was founded in 1959 to promote the individual and collective development of regional developing member countries through the financing of economic and social development projects and the provision of technical assistance. Membership was increased in 1976 and 1977 to include countries outside the region.

MEMBERS

Argentina	El Salvador	Panama
Austria	Finland	Paraguay
Bahamas	France	Peru
Barbados	Germany	Portugal
Belgium	Guatemala	Slovenia
Belize	Guyana	Spain
Bolivia	Haiti	Suriname
Brazil	Honduras	Sweden
Canada	Israel	Switzerland
Chile	Italy	Trinidad and Tobago
Colombia	Jamaica	United Kingdom
Costa Rica	Japan	USA
Croatia	Mexico	Uruguay
Denmark	Netherlands	Venezuela
Dominican Republic	Nicaragua	
Ecuador	Norway	

Organization

(January 1998)

BOARD OF GOVERNORS

All the powers of the Bank are vested in a Board of Governors, consisting of one Governor and one alternate appointed by each member country (usually ministers of finance or presidents of central banks). The Board meets annually, with special meetings when necessary.

BOARD OF EXECUTIVE DIRECTORS

The Board of Executive Directors is responsible for the operations of the Bank. It establishes the Bank's policies, approves loan and technical co-operation proposals that are submitted by the President of the Bank, and authorizes the Bank's borrowings on capital markets.

There are 12 executive directors and 12 alternates. Each Director is elected by a group of two or more countries, except the Directors representing Canada and the USA. The USA holds 34.7% of votes on the Board, proportional to its contribution to the Bank's capital. The Board has four standing committees, relating to: Board matters and evaluation; Policy; Budget, financial policies and audit; and Programming.

ADMINISTRATION

In 1994 the Bank reorganized its administrative structure, in order to improve management accountability and efficiency, to strengthen country focus and regional co-operation and to address the region's priorities. The Bank now comprises three Regional Operations Departments, as well as the following departments: Finance; Legal; Secretariat; Strategic Planning and Operational Policy; Integration and Regional Programmes; Private Sector; Social Programmes and Sustainable Development; and Administrative. In addition, there are External Relations, Controller's and Auditor General's Offices and an Evaluation Office. The Bank has country offices in each of its borrowing member states, and a special office in Europe, located in Paris. At the end of 1995 there were 1,646 Bank staff.

President: ENRIQUE V. IGLESIAS (Uruguay).

Executive Vice-President: NANCY BIRDSALL (USA).

Activities

Loans are made to governments, and to public and private entities for specific economic and social development projects and for sectoral reforms. These loans are repayable in the currencies lent and their terms range from 15 to 40 years. Total lending authorized by the Bank by the end of 1995 amounted to US $78,213m. During 1995 the Bank approved 73 loans totalling $7,304m., compared with 70 loans amounting to $5,255m. in 1994. Disbursements on authorized loans amounted to $4,818m., compared with $3,040m. in 1994.

The subscribed ordinary capital stock, including inter-regional capital, which was merged into it in 1987, totalled US $66,398.7m. at the end of 1995, of which $3,480.8m. was paid-in and $62,917.9m.

was callable. The callable capital constitutes, in effect, a guarantee of the securities which the Bank issues in the capital markets in order to increase its resources available for lending. Replenishments are made every four years. During 1987 and 1988 agreement on a seventh replenishment of the Bank's capital was delayed by the US Government's demands for a restructuring of lending policies. Previously, a simple majority of directors' votes was sufficient to ensure the approval of a loan; developing member countries had nearly 54% of the voting power. The USA now proposed that a 65% majority should be necessary, thus giving the USA and Canada combined a virtual power of veto. In March 1989 it was agreed that authorized capital should be increased by $26,500m. to a total of some $61,000m., with effect from 17 January 1990. The proposal for loan approvals by a 65% majority was not accepted, but it was agreed that opposition by one shareholder could delay approval of a loan for two months, opposition by two for another five months, while opposition by three shareholders, holding at least 40% of the votes, could delay approval by a further five months, after which approval was to be decided by a simple majority of shareholders. In July 1995 the eighth general increase of the Bank's authorized capital was ratified by member countries: the Bank's resources were to be increased by $41,000m. to $102,000m.

In 1995 the Bank borrowed the equivalent of US $2,746m. on the international capital markets, bringing total borrowings outstanding to $26,338m. at the end of the year. Net earnings during 1995 amounted to $521m. in ordinary capital resources and $84m. from the Fund for Special Operations (see below), and at the end of the year the Bank's total reserves were $6,500m.

The Fund for Special Operations enables the Bank to make concessional loans for economic and social projects where circumstances call for special treatment, such as lower interest rates and longer repayment terms than those applied to loans from the ordinary resources. The Board of Governors approved US $200m. in new contributions to the Fund in 1990, and in 1995 authorized $1,000m. in extra resources for the Fund. During 1995 the Fund made 21 loans totalling $795m. (compared with 21 loans totalling $543m. in 1994).

In January 1993 a Multilateral Investment Fund was established to promote private investment in the region. The 21 Bank members who signed the initial draft agreement in 1992 to establish the Fund pledged to contribute US $1,200m. The Fund's activities are undertaken through three separate facilities concerned with technical co-operation, human resources development and small enterprise development. During 1995 the Fund approved $66m. for 36 projects.

An increasing number of donor countries have placed funds under the Bank's administration for assistance to Latin America, outside the framework of the Ordinary Resources and the Bank's Special Operations. By the end of 1995 19 countries had established 37 trust funds with the Bank. These include the Social Progress Trust Fund (set up by the USA in 1961); the Venezuelan Trust Fund (set up in 1975); the Japan Special Fund (1988); and other funds administered on behalf of Austria, Argentina, Belgium, Canada, Denmark, France, Germany, Israel, Italy, Japan, the Netherlands, Norway, Portugal, Spain, Sweden, Switzerland, the United Kingdom and the EU. A Program for the Development of Technical Co-operation was established in 1991, which is financed by European countries and the EU. Total cumulative lending from all these trust funds was $1,636m. by the end of 1995. During 1995 they approved $16.4m. in loans.

Distribution of loans (US $ million)

Sector	1995	%	1961–95	%
Productive Sectors				
Agriculture and fisheries	507	6.9	12,271	15.7
Industry, mining and tourism	310	4.2	8,565	10.9
Science and technology	284	3.9	1,403	1.8
Physical Infrastructure				
Energy	245	3.4	15,559	19.9
Transportation and communications	847	11.6	10,544	13.5
Social Infrastructure				
Health and sanitation	801	11.0	8,045	10.3
Urban development	328	4.5	4,265	5.4
Education	107	1.5	2,813	3.6
Social investment	1,439	19.7	2,116	2.7
Environment	31	0.4	1,095	1.4
Microenterprise	25	0.3	218	0.3
Other				
Public-sector reform	2,005	27.5	7,715	9.9
Export financing	25	0.3	1,496	1.9
Other	350	4.8	2,108	2.7
Total	7,304	100.0	78,213	100.0

Following the capital increase approved in 1989, the Bank was to undertake sectoral lending for the first time, devoting up to 25% of its financing in 1990–93 to loans which would allow countries to make policy changes and improve their institutions. An environmental protection division was also formed in 1989. In 1993 a six-member task force undertook a comprehensive review of the Bank's operations. The task force's report, which it presented to the Board of Executive Directors in December, included the following recommendations: that country offices should be given greater responsibility throughout the project cycle; that more emphasis should be placed on development results, as opposed to lending targets; that there should be increased training for the personnel involved in implementing projects; and that lending to social and poverty reduction programmes should be expanded. A high-level Social Agenda Policy Group was created during 1993 with a remit to investigate the most effective means of supporting social reform in borrowing countries. Under the eighth general increase of the Bank's resources priority areas of operation were designated as poverty reduction and social equity; modernization of state organs; and the environment. During 1995 an inter-departmental working group on poverty was established, in order to identify policies and projects likely to be effective in reducing poverty.

The Bank provides technical co-operation to help member countries to identify and prepare new projects, to improve loan execution, to strengthen the institutional capacity of public and private agencies, and to facilitate the transfer of experience and technology among regional programmes. In 1995 the Bank approved 270 technical co-operation operations, totalling US $115m.

The IDB has created an Inter-American Institute for Social Development (INDES), which is designed to train senior officials in modern techniques for improving social policies and social services, with poverty reduction as the ultimate objective. INDES began operating in 1995 and aimed to provide training for 4,000 officials from government and non-governmental organizations over the subsequent four years.

AFFILIATED INSTITUTIONS

Instituto para la Integración de América Latina y el Caribe (Institute for the Integration of Latin America and the Caribbean): Esmeralda 130, 16° and 17°, Casilla de Correo 39, Sucursal 1, 1401 Buenos Aires, Argentina; tel. (1) 320-1850; fax (1) 320-1865; e-mail int/inl@iadb.org; f. 1965 under the auspices of the Inter-American Development Bank: it became an independent entity in 1991. The Institute undertakes research on all aspects of regional integration and co-operation and issues related to international trade, hemispheric integration and relations with other regions and countries of the world. Activities come under four main headings: regional and national technical co-operation projects on integration; policy fora; integration fora; and journals and information. A Documentation Center holds 80,000 documents, 10,000 books and 50 periodical titles. Dir JUAN JOSÉ TACCONE. Publs *Integración y Comercio* (4 a year), *Newsletter* (monthly).

Inter-American Investment Corporation—IIC: 1300 New York Ave, NW, Washington, DC 20577, USA; tel. (202) 623-3900; fax (202) 623-3815; f. 1986 as a legally autonomous affiliate of the Inter-American Development Bank, to promote private-sector investment in the region. The IIC's initial capital stock was US $200m., of which 55% was contributed by developing member nations, 25.5% by the USA, and the remainder by non-regional members. Emphasis is placed on investment in small and medium-sized enterprises. In 1995 the IIC approved equity investments and loans totalling $36.6m. for 14 private-sector transactions. Gen. Man. JOHN RAHMING (acting). Publ. *Annual Report*.

PUBLICATIONS

Annual Report (annually, in English, Spanish, Portuguese and French).

Annual Report on the Environment and Natural Resources (in English and Spanish).

Economic and Social Progress in Latin America (annually, in English, Spanish, Portuguese and French).

Proceedings of the Annual Meeting of the Board of Directors of the IDB and IIC (annually, in English, Spanish, Portuguese and French).

The IDB (monthly, in English and Spanish).

Brochure series, occasional papers, reports.

Yearly and cumulative disbursements, 1961–95 (US $ million; after cancellations and exchange adjustments)

Country	Total Amount		Ordinary Capital		Fund for Special Operations		Funds in Administration	
	1995	1961–95	1995	1961–95	1995	1961–95	1995	1961–95
Argentina	1,070.6	6,995.8	1,053.4	6,418.4	17.2	528.4	—	49.0
Bahamas	8.3	150.4	8.3	148.4	—	—	—	2.0
Barbados	7.1	169.6	7.1	107.8	—	42.8	—	19.0
Bolivia	133.4	1,908.6	79.3	1,003.1	54.1	835.6	—	69.9
Brazil	491.3	8,460.4	437.3	7,015.0	54.0	1,314.6	—	130.8
Chile	65.2	4,338.3	65.2	4,092.4	—	203.3	—	42.6
Colombia	173.2	5,202.5	162.9	4,464.2	10.3	676.1	—	62.2
Costa Rica	143.8	1,448.6	143.8	969.0	—	351.3	—	128.3
Dominican Republic	113.8	1,111.3	79.6	432.8	30.5	596.4	3.7	82.1
Ecuador	243.1	2,560.5	184.4	1,660.3	58.7	811.6	—	88.6
El Salvador	124.5	1,365.5	94.5	551.2	30.0	679.4	—	134.9
Guatemala	43.9	1,221.2	26.4	651.4	17.5	509.6	—	60.2
Guyana	21.8	328.2	—	121.5	21.8	199.8	—	6.9
Haiti	74.1	297.6	—	—	74.1	291.1	—	6.5
Honduras	80.8	1,356.9	35.9	517.5	44.9	788.5	—	50.9
Jamaica	53.8	995.4	42.8	671.8	—	163.0	11.0	160.6
Mexico	985.4	8,723.4	979.6	8,123.6	—	559.0	5.8	40.8
Nicaragua	121.5	888.1	30.8	235.8	90.7	600.9	—	51.4
Panama	90.9	937.1	85.7	629.2	5.2	275.1	—	32.8
Paraguay	92.2	799.5	63.0	308.7	29.2	478.7	—	12.1
Peru	271.7	2,828.1	271.7	2,212.0	—	393.1	—	223.0
Suriname	0.1	18.2	0.1	16.5	—	1.7	—	—
Trinidad and Tobago	101.4	435.0	97.4	389.9	2.0	27.8	2.0	17.3
Uruguay	68.2	1,091.4	67.5	945.7	0.7	103.9	—	41.8
Venezuela	224.3	2,177.4	224.3	2,003.1	—	101.4	—	72.9
Regional	13.9	1,728.1	13.9	1,534.4	—	180.2	—	13.5
Total	4,818.3	57,537.1	4,254.9	45,223.7	540.9	10,713.3	22.5	1,600.1

Source: *Annual Report*, 1995.

INTERNATIONAL CHAMBER OF COMMERCE—ICC

Address: 38 Cours Albert 1er, 75008 Paris, France.

Telephone: 1-49-53-28-28; **telex:** 650770; **fax:** 1-49-53-29-42; **internet:** http://www.iccwbo.org.

The ICC was founded in 1919 to promote free trade and private enterprise, provide practical services and represent business interests at governmental and inter-governmental levels.

MEMBERS

At September 1996 membership consisted of about 5,500 individual corporations and 1,700 organizations (mainly trade and industrial organizations and chambers of commerce). By December 1996 National Committees or Councils had been formed in 62 countries and territories to co-ordinate ICC objectives and functions at the national level.

Argentina
Australia
Austria
Bangladesh
Belgium
Brazil
Burkina Faso
Cameroon
Canada
Chile
China, People's Republic
Colombia
Côte d'Ivoire
Cyprus
Denmark
Ecuador
Egypt
Finland
France
Germany
Greece
Hungary
Iceland
India
Indonesia
Iran
Ireland
Israel
Italy
Japan
Jordan
Korea, Republic
Kuwait
Lebanon
Lithuania
Luxembourg
Madagascar
Mexico
Morocco
Netherlands
Nigeria
Norway
Pakistan
Peru
Portugal
Saudi Arabia
Senegal
Singapore
South Africa
Spain
Sri Lanka
Sweden
Switzerland
Syria
Taiwan*
Togo
Tunisia
Turkey
United Kingdom
USA
Uruguay
Venezuela
Yugoslavia

* Admitted as Chinese Taipei.

Organization

(January 1998)

COUNCIL

The Council is the governing body of the organization. It is composed of members nominated by the National Committees and meets twice a year.

President: Helmut D. Maucher (Switzerland).

Vice-President: Adnan Kassar (Lebanon).

EXECUTIVE BOARD

The Executive Board consists of 12–15 members appointed by the Council on the recommendation of the President and six *ex-officio* members. Members serve for a three-year term, one-third of the members retiring at the end of each year. It ensures close direction of ICC activities and meets at least three times each year.

INTERNATIONAL SECRETARIAT

The ICC secretariat is based at International Headquarters in Paris, with additional offices maintained in Geneva and New York principally for liaison with the United Nations and its agencies.

Secretary-General: Maria Livanos Cattaui.

NATIONAL COMMITTEES AND GROUPS

Each affiliate is composed of leading business organizations and individual companies. It has its own secretariat, monitors issues of concern to its national constituents, and draws public and government attention to ICC policies.

CONGRESS

The ICC's supreme assembly, to which all member companies and organizations are invited to send senior representatives. Congresses are held every three years, in a different place on each occasion, with up to 2,000 participants. The 31st Congress was held in Mexico in October 1993, and the 32nd Congress was held in Shanghai, People's Republic of China, in April 1997.

CONFERENCE

Conferences with about 350 participants take place in non-Congress years. The ninth Conference was held in Marrakesh, Morocco, in May 1992, and the tenth in New Delhi, India, in March 1995.

Activities

The various Commissions of the ICC (listed below) are composed of practising businessmen and experts from all sectors of economic life, nominated by National Committees. ICC recommendations must be adopted by a Commission following consultation with National Committees, and then approved by the Council or Executive Board, before they can be regarded as official ICC policies. Meetings of Commissions are generally held twice a year. Working Parties are frequently constituted by Commissions to undertake specific projects and report back to their parent body. Officers of Commissions, and specialized Working Parties, often meet in the intervals between Commission sessions. The Commissions produce a wide array of specific codes and guidelines of direct use to the world business community; draw up statements and initiatives for presentation to governments and international bodies; and comment constructively and in detail on proposed actions by intergovernmental organizations that are likely to affect business.

ICC works closely with other international organizations. ICC members, the heads of UN economic organizations and the OECD convene for annual discussions on the world economy. The Commission on International Trade Policy campaigns against protectionism in world trade and in support of the World Trade Organization (WTO, q.v.). The ICC also works closely with the European Union, commenting on EU directives and making recommendations on, for example, tax harmonization and laws relating to competition.

ICC plays a part in combating international crime connected with commerce. The ICC International Maritime Bureau combats maritime fraud, for example insurance fraud and the theft of cargoes. The ICC Counterfeiting Intelligence Bureau was established in 1985 to investigate counterfeiting in trade-marked goods, copyrights and industrial designs. Commercial disputes are submitted to the ICC International Court of Arbitration.

Policy and Technical Commissions:

Commission on Air Transport
Commission on Banking Technique and Practice
Commission on Computing, Telecommunications and Information Policy
Commission on Energy
Commission on Environment
Commission on Financial Services
Commission on Insurance
Commission on Intellectual and Industrial Property
Commission on International Arbitration
Commission on International Commercial Practice
Commission on International Trade and Investment Policy
Commission on Law and Practices Relating to Competition
Commission on Maritime and Surface Transport
Commission on Marketing, Advertising and Distribution
Commission on Taxation

Bodies for the Settlement of Disputes:

International Centre for Technical Expertise
International Court of Arbitration
International Maritime Arbitration Organization

Other Bodies:

ICC Centre for Maritime Co-operation
ICC Corporate Security Services
ICC Counterfeiting Intelligence Bureau
ICC Institute of International Business Law and Practice
ICC International Maritime Bureau
ICC-WTO Economic Consultative Committee
International Bureau of Chambers of Commerce

FINANCE

The International Chamber of Commerce is a private organization financed partly by contributions from National Committees and other members, according to the economic importance of the country which each represents, and partly by revenue from fees for various services and from sales of publications.

PUBLICATIONS

Annual Report.

Handbook.

ICC Contact (newsletter).

ICC International Court of Arbitration Bulletin.

IGO Report.

Numerous publications on general and technical business and trade-related subjects.

INTERNATIONAL CONFEDERATION OF FREE TRADE UNIONS—ICFTU

Address: 155 blvd Emile Jacqmain, 1210 Brussels, Belgium.

Telephone: (2) 224-02-11; **fax:** (2) 218-84-15; **internet:** http://www.icftu.org.

ICFTU was founded in 1949 by trade union federations which had withdrawn from the World Federation of Trade Unions (see p. 243). It aims to promote the interests of working people and to secure recognition of workers' organizations as free bargaining agents; to reduce the gap between rich and poor; and to defend fundamental human and trade union rights. During 1996 it campaigned for the adoption by the World Trade Organization of a social clause, with legally-binding minimum labour standards. See also the World Confederation of Labour (p. 242).

MEMBERS

195 organizations in 137 countries with 124m. members (Nov. 1996).

Organization

(January 1998)

WORLD CONGRESS

The Congress, the highest authority of ICFTU, normally meets every four years. The 16th Congress was held in Brussels, Belgium, in June 1996.

Delegations from national federations vary in size according to membership. The Congress examines past activities, maps out future plans, elects the Executive Board and the General Secretary, considers the functioning of the regional machinery, examines financial reports and social, economic and political situations. It works through plenary sessions and through technical committees which report to the plenary sessions.

EXECUTIVE BOARD

The Board meets not less than once a year, for about three days, usually at Brussels, or at the Congress venue; it comprises 53 members elected by Congress and nominated by areas of the world. The General Secretary is an *ex-officio* member. After each Congress the Board elects a President and at least seven Vice-Presidents.

The Board considers administrative questions; hears reports from field representatives, missions, regional organizations and affiliates, and makes resultant decisions; and discusses finances, applications for affiliation, and problems affecting world labour. It elects a steering committee of 19 to deal with urgent matters between Board meetings.

PERMANENT COMMITTEES

Steering Committee. Administers the General Fund, comprising affiliation fees, and the International Solidarity Fund, constituting additional voluntary contributions.

Economic and Social Committee.

Human and Trade Union Rights Committee.

***ICFTU/ITS Education Working Party.**

***ICFTU/ITS Working Group on Young Workers' Questions.**

***ICFTU/ITS Working Party on Multinational Companies.**

Peace, Security and Disarmament Committee.

Projects Committee.

Women's Committee.

*A joint body of the ICFTU and International Trade Secretariats.

SECRETARIAT

The headquarters staff numbers 75, comprising some 25 different nationalities.

The six departments are: Economic and Social Policy; Trade Union Rights; Projects, Co-ordination and Education (comprising units for Projects and Trade Union Education); Equality (including Youth); Finance and Administration; Press and Publications. There are also the Co-ordination Unit for Central and Eastern Europe, the Electronic Data Processing Unit, Personnel, Co-ordination and Regional Liaison Desks for the Americas, Africa and Asia.

General Secretary: WILLIAM (BILL) JORDAN (United Kingdom).

BRANCH OFFICES

ICFTU Geneva Office: 46 avenue Blanc, 1202 Geneva, Switzerland; tel. (22) 7384202; fax (22) 7381082; Dir GUY RYDER.

ICFTU United Nations Office: Room 404, 104 East 40th St, New York, NY 10016, USA.

There are also Permanent Representatives accredited to FAO (Rome) to the UN, UNIDO and IAEA (Vienna) and to UNEP and UNCHS (Habitat) (Nairobi).

REGIONAL ORGANIZATIONS

ICFTU African Regional Organization—AFRO: Utalii House, Uhuru Highway, POB 67273, Nairobi, Kenya; Pres. MADIA DIOP (Senegal); Gen. Sec. ANDREW KAILEMBO (Tanzania).

ICFTU Asian and Pacific Regional Organization—APRO: Trade Union House, 3rd Floor, Shenton Way, Singapore 068810; tel. (65) 2226294; fax (65) 2217380; e-mail icftu@singnet.com.sg; Pres. KEN G. DOUGLAS; Gen. Sec. TAKASHI IZUMI.

Inter-American Regional Organization of Workers—ORIT: Avda Andrés Eloy Blanco (Este 2), Ed. José Vargas 15°, Apdo 14264, Los Caobos, Caracas, Venezuela; tel. (2) 5749752; fax (2) 5748502; f. 1951; Pres. DICK MARTIN; Gen. Sec. LUIS ANDERSON.

There are Field Representatives in various parts of Africa. In addition, a number of Project Planners for development co-operation travel in different countries.

FINANCE

Affiliated federations pay a standard fee of 6,211 Belgian francs (1998), or its equivalent in other currencies, per 1,000 members per annum, which covers the establishment and routine activities of the ICFTU headquarters in Brussels, and partly subsidizes the regional organizations.

An International Solidarity Fund was set up in 1956 to assist unions in developing countries, and workers and trade unionists victimized by repressive political measures. It provides legal assistance and supports educational activities. In cases of major natural disasters affecting workers token relief aid is granted.

PUBLICATIONS

Survey of Violations of Trade Union Rights (annually).

Trade Union World (official journal, monthly).

These periodicals are issued in English, French and Spanish. In addition the Congress report is issued in English. Numerous other publications on labour, economic and trade union training have been published in various languages.

Associated International Trade Secretariats

Education International (EI): 155 blvd Emile Jacqmain (8ème étage), 1210 Brussels, Belgium; tel. (2) 224-06-11; fax (2) 224-06-06; e-mail educint@infoboard.be; internet http://www.ei-ie.org; f. 1993 by merger of the World Confederation of Organizations of the Teaching Profession (f. 1952) and the International Federation of Free Teachers' Unions (f. 1951). Mems: 278 national orgs of teachers' trade unions representing 23m. members in 148 countries and territories. Holds Congress (every three years): 1995 in Zimbabwe; 1998 in USA. Pres. MARY HATWOOD FUTRELL (USA); Sec.-Gen. FRED VAN LEEUWEN (Netherlands). Publs *El Monitor* (monthly), *Magazine* (quarterly) (both in English, French and Spanish).

International Federation of Building and Woodworkers: POB 1897, 1215 Geneva 15 Aéroport, Switzerland; tel. (22) 7880888; fax (22) 7880716; e-mail info@ifbww.org; f. 1934. Mems: national unions with a membership of 11.7m. workers. Organization: Congress, Executive Committee. Pres. ROEL DE VRIES (Netherlands); Sec.-Gen. ULF ASP (Sweden). Publ. *Bulletin* (8 a year).

International Federation of Chemical, Energy, Mine and General Workers' Unions—ICEM: 109 ave Emile de Béco, 1050 Brussels, Belgium; tel. (2) 626-20-20; fax (2) 648-43-16; e-mail icem@geoz.poptel.org.uk; internet http://www.icem.org; f. 1995 by merger of the International Federation of Chemical, Energy and General Workers' Unions (f. 1907) and the Miners' International Federation (f. 1890). Mems: 403 trade unions covering approximately 20m. workers in 113 countries. Main sectors cover energy industries; chemicals; pharmaceuticals and biotechnology; mining and extraction; pulp and paper; rubber; ceramics; glass; building materials; and environmental services. Pres. HANS BERGER; Gen. Sec. VICTOR THORPE. Publs *ICEM Info* (quarterly), *ICEM Focus on Health, Safety and Environment* (2 a year), *ICEM Update* (Irregular).

International Federation of Commercial, Clerical, Professional and Technical Employees—FIET: 15 ave de Balexert, 1219 Châtelaine-Geneva, Switzerland; tel. (22) 9790311; telex 418736; fax (22) 7965321; e-mail 100441:1236@compuserve.com; internet http://www.fiet.org; f. 1904. Mems: 410 national unions of non-manual workers comprising 11.5m. people in 125 countries. Holds World Congresses (every four years): 1995 in Vienna, Austria; has seven trade sections (for bank workers, insurance workers, workers in social insurance and health care, commercial workers, salaried employees in industry, hairdressers and workers in property services), regional organizations for Europe, Western Hemisphere, Asia and Africa. Pres. GARY NEBEKER; Sec.-Gen. PHILIP J. JENNINGS (UK). Publs *FIETNET NEWS* (16 a year), *FIET INFO* (every two months, in English, French, German and Spanish).

International Federation of Journalists: 266 rue Royale, 1201 Brussels, Belgium; tel. (2) 223-22-65; telex 61275; fax (2) 219-29-76; e-mail ifj@pophost.eunet.be; internet http://www.ifj.org; f. 1952 to link national unions of professional journalists dedicated to the freedom of the press, to defend the rights of journalists, and to raise professional standards; it conducts surveys, assists in trade union training programmes, organizes seminars and provides information; it arranges fact-finding missions in countries where press freedom is under pressure, and issues protests against the persecution and detention of journalists and the censorship of the mass media. Mems: 107 unions in 96 countries, comprising 420,000 individuals. Pres. JENS LINDE (Denmark); Gen. Sec. AIDAN WHITE (UK). Publs *IFJ Direct Line* (every two months), *IFJ Information* (annually, in English, French and Spanish).

International Graphical Federation: 17 rue des Fripiers, Galerie du Centre (Bloc 2), 1000 Brussels, Belgium; tel. (2) 223-02-20; telex 222044; fax (2) 223-18-14; e-mail igf-fgi@enter.org; f. 1949. Mems: 104 national organizations in 67 countries, covering more than 2m. individuals. Holds Congress (every four years). Pres. RENÉ VAN TILBORG; Gen. Sec. (vacant). Publs *Journal of the IGF* (2 a year), *INFOGRAF* (quarterly), reports.

International Metalworkers' Federation: Route des Acacias 54 bis, 1227 Geneva, Switzerland; tel. (22) 3085050; telex 423298; fax (22) 3085055; e-mail imf@iprolink.ch; f. 1893. Mems: national organizations covering 16m. workers in 92 countries. Holds Congress (every four years); has four regional offices; six industrial departments; World Company Councils for unions in multinational corporations. Pres. K. ZWICKEL (Germany); Gen. Sec. MARCELLO MALENTACCHI. Publ. *IMF News* (monthly, seven languages), *Metal* (quarterly).

International Textile, Garment and Leather Workers' Federation: rue Joseph Stevens 8, 1000 Brussels, Belgium; tel. (2) 512-26-06; fax (2) 511-09-04; e-mail itglwf@compuserve.com; f. 1970. Mems: 220 unions covering 8.25m. workers in 120 countries. Pres. D. LAMBERT (UK); Gen. Sec. NEIL KEARNEY (Ireland). Publ. *ITGLWF Newsletter* (quarterly).

International Transport Workers' Federation: 49-60 Borough Rd, London, SE1 1DS, United Kingdom; tel. (171) 403-2733; telex 8811397; fax (171) 357-7871; e-mail info@itf.org.uk; internet http://www.itf.org.uk; f. 1896. Mems: national trade unions covering 5m. workers in more than 100 countries. Holds Congress (every four years); has eight Industrial Sections. Pres. JAMES HUNTER; Gen. Sec. DAVID COCKROFT (UK). Publ. *ITF News* (monthly).

International Union of Food, Agricultural, Hotel, Restaurant, Catering, Tobacco and Allied Workers' Associations: 8 rampe du Pont-Rouge, 1213 Petit-Lancy, Switzerland; tel. (22) 7932233; fax (22) 7932238; e-mail iuf@iuf.org; f. 1920. Mems: 331 affiliated organizations covering about 2.6m workers in 112 countries. Holds Congress (every five years). Pres. WILLY VIJVERMAN (Belgium); Gen. Sec. RON OSWALD. Publs bi-monthly bulletins.

Media and Entertainment International—MEI: 207 rue Royale, 1210 Brussels; tel. (2) 223-55-37; fax (2) 223-55-38; e-mail mei@pophost.eunet.be; internet http://www.mei-its.org; f. 1993, by merger of International Secretariat for Arts, Mass Media and Entertainment Trade Unions (ISETU) and the International Federation of Audio-visual Workers (FISTAV); Pres. TONY LENNON; Gen. Sec. JAMES WILSON.

Postal, Telegraph and Telephone International—PTTI: 38 ave du Lignon, 1219 Geneva, Switzerland; tel. (22) 7968311; fax (22) 7963975; f. 1920. Mems: national trade unions covering 4.6m.

workers in 119 countries. Holds Congress (every four years). Pres. CURT PERSSON (Sweden); Gen. Sec. PHILIP BOWYER. Publs *PTTI News* (six languages, monthly), *PTTI Studies* (four languages, quarterly).

Public Services International: 45 ave Voltaire, BP9, 01211 Ferney-Voltaire, France; tel. 4-50-40-64-64; fax 4-50-40-73-20; e-mail psi@world-psi.org; internet http://www.world-psi.org; f. 1907; Mems: 499 unions and professional associations covering 20m. workers in 130 countries. Holds Congress (every five years). Pres. WILLIAM LUCY (USA); Gen. Sec. HANS ENGELBERTS (Netherlands). Publ. *Focus* (quarterly).

Universal Alliance of Diamond Workers: Lange Kievitstraat 57/B (Bus 1), 2018 Antwerp, Belgium; tel. (3) 232-48-60; fax (3) 232-40-09; f. 1905. Mems: 110,000 in eight countries. Pres. G. HONING (Netherlands); Gen. Sec. JEF HOYMANS (Belgium).

INTERNATIONAL OLYMPIC COMMITTEE

Address: Château de Vidy, 1007 Lausanne, Switzerland.

Telephone: (21) 6216111; **telex:** 454024; **fax:** (21) 6216354.

The International Olympic Committee was founded in 1894 to ensure the regular celebration of the Olympic Games.

Organization

(February 1998)

INTERNATIONAL OLYMPIC COMMITTEE

The International Olympic Committee (IOC) is a non-governmental international organization comprising 111 members, who are representatives of the IOC in their countries and not their countries' delegates to the IOC. The members meet in session at least once a year.

The IOC is the final authority on all questions concerning the Olympic Games and the Olympic movement. There are 197 recognized National Olympic Committees, which are the sole authorities responsible for the representation of their respective countries at the Olympic Games. The IOC may give recognition to International Federations which undertake to adhere to the Olympic Charter, and which govern sports that comply with the IOC's criteria.

A Supreme Council of International Sport Arbitration has been established to hear cases brought by competitors.

EXECUTIVE BOARD

The session of the IOC delegates to the Executive Board the authority to manage the IOC's affairs. The President of the Board is elected for an eight-year term, and is eligible for re-election for successive terms of four years. The Vice-Presidents are elected for four-year terms, and may be re-elected after a minimum interval of four years. Members of the Board are elected to hold office for four years. The Executive Board generally meets four to five times per year.

President: JUAN ANTONIO SAMARANCH (Spain).

Vice-Presidents: PÁL SCHMITT (Hungary); RICHARD W. POUND (Canada); ANITA DEFRANTZ (USA); KÉBA MBAYE (Senegal).

Members of the Board:
RICHARD KEVAN GOSPER (Australia)
THOMAS BACH (Germany)
CHIHARU IGAYA (Japan)
KIM UN YONG (Republic of Korea)
MARC HODLER (Switzerland)
JACQUES ROGGE (Belgium)

ADMINISTRATION

The administration of the IOC is under the authority of the Director-General and the Secretary-General, who are appointed by the Executive Board, on the proposal of the President.

Director-General: FRANÇOIS CARRARD.

Secretary-General: FRANÇOISE ZWEIFEL.

Activities

The fundamental principles of the Olympic movement are:

Olympism is a philosophy of life, exalting and combining, in a balanced whole, the qualities of body, will and mind. Blending sport with culture and education, Olympism seeks to create a way of life based on the joy found in effort, the educational value of good example and respect for universal fundamental ethical principles.

Under the supreme authority of the IOC, the Olympic movement encompasses organizations, athletes and other persons who agree to be guided by the Olympic Charter. The criterion for belonging to the Olympic movement is recognition by the IOC.

The goal of the Olympic movement is to contribute to building a peaceful and better world by educating youth through sport practised without discrimination of any kind and in the Olympic spirit, which requires mutual understanding with a spirit of friendship, solidarity and fair-play.

The activity of the Olympic movement is permanent and universal. It reaches its peak with the bringing together of the athletes of the world at the great sport festival, the Olympic Games.

The Olympic Charter is the codification of the fundamental principles, rules and bye-laws adopted by the IOC. It governs the organization and operation of the Olympic movement and stipulates the conditions for the celebration of the Olympic Games.

THE GAMES OF THE OLYMPIAD

The Olympic Summer Games take place during the first year of the Olympiad (period of four years) which they are to celebrate. They are the exclusive property of the IOC, which entrusts their organization to a host city seven years in advance.

1896	Athens	1960	Rome
1900	Paris	1964	Tokyo
1904	St Louis	1968	Mexico City
1908	London	1972	Munich
1912	Stockholm	1976	Montreal
1920	Antwerp	1980	Moscow
1924	Paris	1984	Los Angeles
1928	Amsterdam	1988	Seoul
1932	Los Angeles	1992	Barcelona
1936	Berlin	1996	Atlanta
1948	London	2000	Sydney
1952	Helsinki	2004	Athens
1956	Melbourne		

The programme of the Games must include at least 15 of the total number of Olympic sports (sports governed by recognized International Federations and admitted to the Olympic programme by decision of the IOC at least seven years before the Games). The Olympic summer sports are: archery, athletics, badminton, baseball, basketball, boxing, canoeing, cycling, equestrian sports, fencing, football, gymnastics, handball, field hockey, judo, modern pentathlon, rowing, shooting, swimming (including water polo and diving), table tennis, tennis, volleyball, weight-lifting, wrestling, yachting.

OLYMPIC WINTER GAMES

The Olympic Winter Games comprise competitions in sports practised on snow and ice. From 1994 onwards, they were to be held in the second calendar year following that in which the Games of the Olympiad take place.

1924	Chamonix	1972	Sapporo
1928	St Moritz	1976	Innsbruck
1932	Lake Placid	1980	Lake Placid
1936	Garmisch-Partenkirchen	1984	Sarajevo
1948	St Moritz	1988	Calgary
1952	Oslo	1992	Albertville
1956	Cortina d'Ampezzo	1994	Lillehammer
1960	Squaw Valley	1998	Nagano
1964	Innsbruck	2002	Salt Lake City
1968	Grenoble		

The Winter Games may include skiing, skating, ice hockey, bobsleigh, luge and biathlon.

FINANCE

The operational budget for the International Olympic Committee for 1997 was 36,985m. Swiss francs.

INTERNATIONAL ORGANIZATION FOR MIGRATION—IOM

Address: 17 route des Morillons, Case postale 71, 1211 Geneva 19, Switzerland.

Telephone: (22) 7179111; **fax:** (22) 7986150; **e-mail:** telex@genera.iom.ch; **internet:** http://www.iom.ch.

The Intergovernmental Committee for Migration (ICM) was founded in 1951 as a non-political and humanitarian organization with a predominantly operational mandate, including the handling of orderly and planned migration to meet specific needs of emigration and immigration countries; and the processing and movement of refugees, displaced persons and other individuals in need of international migration services to countries offering them resettlement opportunities. In 1989 ICM's name was changed to the International Organization for Migration (IOM).

MEMBERS

Albania	Ecuador	Norway
Angola	Egypt	Pakistan
Argentina	El Salvador	Panama
Armenia	Finland	Paraguay
Australia	France	Peru
Austria	Germany	Philippines
Bangladesh	Greece	Poland
Belgium	Guatemala	Portugal
Bolivia	Haiti	Senegal
Bulgaria	Honduras	Slovakia
Canada	Hungary	Sri Lanka
Chile	Israel	Sweden
Colombia	Italy	Switzerland
Costa Rica	Japan	Tajikistan
Croatia	Kenya	Thailand
Cyprus	Korea, Republic	Uganda
Czech Republic	Liberia	USA
Denmark	Luxembourg	Uruguay
Dominican Republic	Netherlands	Venezuela
	Nicaragua	Zambia

Observers: Afghanistan, Belarus, Belize, Bosnia and Herzegovina, Brazil, Cape Verde, Democratic Republic of the Congo, Georgia, Ghana, Guinea, Guinea-Bissau, Holy See, India, Indonesia, Iran, Ireland, Jamaica, Jordan, Kyrgyzstan, Latvia, Lithuania, Madagascar, Malta, Mexico, Moldova, Morocco, Mozambique, Namibia, New Zealand, Romania, Russia, Rwanda, San Marino, São Tomé and Príncipe, Slovenia, Somalia, South Africa, Sovereign Military Order of Malta, Spain, Sudan, Tanzania, Tunisia, Turkey, Ukraine, United Kingdom, Viet Nam, Yugoslavia, Zimbabwe.

Organization

(January 1998)

IOM is governed by a Council which is composed of representatives of all member governments, and has the responsibility for making final decisions on policy, programmes and financing. An Executive Committee of 10 member governments elected by the Council prepares the work of the Council and makes recommendations on the basis of reports from the Sub-Committee on Budget and Finance and the Sub-Committee on the Co-ordination of Transport. IOM had a network of 74 offices in 1995.

Director General: JAMES N. PURCELL, Jr. (USA).

Deputy Director General: NARCISA DE LEON ESCALER (Philippines).

Activities

IOM aims to provide assistance to member governments in meeting the operational challenges of migration, to advance understanding of migration issues, to encourage social and economic development through migration and to work towards effective respect of the human dignity and well-being of migrants. It provides a full range of migration assistance to, and sometimes *de facto* protection of, migrants, refugees, displaced persons and other individuals in need of international migration services. This includes recruitment, selection, processing, medical examinations, and language and cultural orientation courses, placement, activities to facilitate reception and integration and other advisory services. IOM co-ordinates its refugee activities with the UN High Commissioner for Refugees (UNHCR, q.v.) and with governmental and non-governmental partners. In May 1997 IOM and UNHCR signed a memorandum of understanding which aimed to facilitate co-operation between the two organizations. During 1996 IOM assisted some 749,309 people, of whom 734,576 were humanitarian migrants, 6,956 national migrants and 7,777 were registered as qualified human resources. Between 1 February 1952 and 31 July 1997 IOM provided assistance to a total of 10,006,364 migrants.

IOM programmes are divided into four main areas.

HUMANITARIAN MIGRATION

Under its humanitarian migration programmes, IOM provides assistance to persons fleeing conflict situations, to refugees being resettled in third countries or repatriated, to stranded individuals and unsuccessful asylum seekers returning home, to internally and externally displaced persons, to other persons compelled to leave their homelands, to individuals seeking to reunite with other members of their families and to migrants involved in regular migration. IOM provides these individuals with secure, reliable, cost-effective services, including counselling, document processing, medical examination, transportation, language training and cultural orientation and integration assistance. Humanitarian migration activities also include the provision of emergency assistance to persons affected by conflict and post-conflict situations. IOM offers its services to vulnerable populations in need of evacuation, resettlement or return, both in the initial phases of an emergency and during the transition from emergency humanitarian relief, through a period of rehabilitation, to longer-term reconstruction and development efforts. During 1996 IOM co-operated with UNHCR to co-ordinate the return of more than 470,000 refugees to Rwanda. In recent years IOM has increasingly assisted in the return home and reintegration of demobilized soldiers, police officials, and their dependents. In 1997 IOM provided assistance to demobilized soldiers and their families in Angola; by the end of August IOM had helped to resettle some 30,000 soldiers and 60,000 dependents.

MIGRATION FOR DEVELOPMENT

IOM's programmes of migration for development aim to contribute towards alleviating economic and social problems through recruitment and selection of high-level workers and professionals to fill positions in priority sectors of the economy in developing countries for which qualified persons are not available locally (particularly in Latin America and Africa), taking into account national development priorities as well as the needs and concerns of receiving communities. Under the programmes for the Transfer of Qualified Human Resources IOM screens candidates, identifies employment opportunities and provides reintegration assistance. Selection Migration programmes help qualified professionals migrate to countries in need of specific expertise when the country cannot find the required skills from within or through the return of nationals. Integrated Experts programmes provide temporary expatriate expertise to states for up to six years: these experts transfer their skills to their working partners and contribute directly to productive output. Programmes of Intraregional Co-operation in the field of qualified human resources encourage collective self-reliance among developing countries by fostering the exchange of governmental experts and the transfer of professionals and technicians within a given region. IOM maintains recruitment offices throughout the world. In November 1996 IOM established a Return of Qualified Nationals programme to facilitate the employment of refugees returning to Bosnia and Herzegovina. By August 1997 some 200 professionals had been placed in jobs in that country.

TECHNICAL CO-OPERATION

Through its technical co-operation programmes IOM offers advisory services on migration to governments, intergovernmental agencies and non-governmental organizations. They aim to assist in the formation and implementation of effective and coherent migration policy, legislation and administration. IOM technical co-operation also focuses on capacity building projects such as training courses for government migration officials, and analysis of and suggestions for solving emerging migration problems.

MIGRATION DEBATE, RESEARCH AND INFORMATION

IOM furthers the understanding of migration through regional and international seminars and conferences which bring together those concerned with migration issues in order to develop practical solutions on current migration problems. Recent topics have included migrant women, migrant trafficking, migration and development, undocumented migrants, the impact of migration on social structures, migration and health. Research on migration relates not only to the migration process but also to the specific situation and needs of the migrant as an individual human being. IOM has developed mechanisms to gather information on potential migrants' attitudes and motivations, as well as on situations which could lead to irregular migration flows. Trends in international migration point to information as an essential resource for individuals making life-changing decisions about migrating; for governments setting migration policies; for international, regional or non-governmental organizations designing migration programmes; and for researchers, the media and individuals analyzing and reporting on migration. IOM gathers information on migration to meet these growing demands. It also designs and implements information campaigns which provide potential migrants with a more accurate picture of migration realities, in order to prevent unsuccessful or unnecessary migration.

INTERNATIONAL CENTRE FOR MIGRATION AND HEALTH

Address: 11 route du Nant-d'Avril, 1214 Geneva, Vernier, Switzerland; tel. (22) 7831080; fax (22) 7831087; e-mail icmh@iom.int.

Established in March 1995, by IOM and the University of Geneva, with the support of WHO, to respond to the growing needs for information, documentation, research, training and policy development in migration health. In August 1996 was designated a WHO collaborating centre for health-related issues among people displaced by disasters.

Co-ordinator: Dr MANUEL CARBALLO.

FINANCE

The IOM budget for 1997 amounted to US $221.1m. for operations and 34.1m. Swiss francs for administration.

PUBLICATIONS

International Migration (quarterly).

IOM Latin American Journal (3 a year).

IOM News (every 2 months, in English, French and Spanish).

Migration and Health Quarterly Newsletter.

Report by the Director General (in English, French and Spanish).

Trafficking in Migrants (quarterly).

INTERNATIONAL RED CROSS AND RED CRESCENT MOVEMENT

The International Red Cross and Red Crescent Movement is a world-wide independent humanitarian organization, comprising two bodies working at an international level: one in time of armed conflict, the International Committee of the Red Cross (ICRC), founded in 1863; and the other in peace time, the International Federation of Red Cross and Red Crescent Societies (the Federation), founded in 1919, and 171 National Red Cross and Red Crescent Societies working mainly at national level. International Red Cross Day is observed on 8 May each year.

Organization

INTERNATIONAL CONFERENCE

The supreme deliberative body of the Movement, the Conference comprises delegations from the ICRC, the Federation and the National Societies, and of representatives of States Parties to the Geneva Conventions (see below). The Conference's function is to determine the general policy of the Movement and to ensure unity in the work of the various bodies. It usually meets every four to five years, and is hosted by the National Society of the country in which it is held. The 26th International Conference, due to be held in November/December 1991 in Budapest, Hungary, was postponed; it was finally convened in December 1995, in Geneva, Switzerland.

STANDING COMMISSION

The Commission meets at least twice a year in ordinary session. It promotes harmony in the work of the Movement, and examines matters which concern the Movement as a whole. It is formed of two representatives of the ICRC, two of the Federation, and five members of National Societies elected by the Conference.

COUNCIL OF DELEGATES

The Council comprises delegations from the National Societies, from the ICRC and from the Federation. The Council is the body where the representatives of all the components of the Movement meet to discuss matters that concern the Movement as a whole.

Fundamental Principles of the Movement

Humanity. The International Red Cross and Red Crescent Movement, born of a desire to bring assistance without discrimination to the wounded on the battlefield, endeavours, in its international and national capacity, to prevent and alleviate human suffering wherever it may be found. Its purpose is to protect life and health and to ensure respect for the human being. It promotes mutual understanding, friendship, co-operation and lasting peace amongst all peoples.

Impartiality. It makes no discrimination as to nationality, race, religious beliefs, class or political opinions. It endeavours to relieve the suffering of individuals, being guided solely by their needs, and to give priority to the most urgent cases of distress.

Neutrality. In order to continue to enjoy the confidence of all, the Movement may not take sides in hostilities or engage in controversies of a political, racial, religious or ideological nature.

Independence. The Movement is independent. The National Societies, while auxiliaries in the humanitarian services of their governments and subject to national laws, must retain their autonomy so that they may always be able to act in accordance with the principles of the Movement.

Voluntary Service. It is a voluntary relief movement not prompted by desire for gain.

Unity. There can be only one Red Cross or Red Crescent Society in any one country. It must be open to all. It must carry on its humanitarian work throughout the territory.

Universality. The International Red Cross and Red Crescent Movement, in which all National Societies have equal status and share equal responsibilities and duties in helping each other, is worldwide.

International Committee of the Red Cross—ICRC

Address: 19 avenue de la Paix, 1202 Geneva, Switzerland.

Telephone: (22) 7346001; **telex:** 414226; **fax:** (22) 7332057; **internet:** http://www.icrc.org.

Organization

(February 1998)

INTERNATIONAL COMMITTEE

The ICRC is an independent institution of a private character. The Assembly of the International Committee is exclusively composed of Swiss nationals. Members are co-opted, and their total number may not exceed 25. The international character of the ICRC is based on its mission and not on its composition.

President: CORNELIO SOMMARUGA.

Vice-Presidents: ERIC ROETHLISBERGER, ANNE PETITPIERRE.

EXECUTIVE BOARD

The Executive Board, which meets weekly, is responsible for the implementation of all guidelines issued, and decisions made, by the International Committee in accordance with the Geneva Conventions and their Additional Protocols. It carries out the Committee's daily business and supervises the three structures which oversee the ICRC's activities: the Directorate for General Affairs, the Directorate of Operations and the Directorate for International Law and Policy. The seven members of the Executive Board are elected by the Assembly of the International Committee for renewable four-year terms. At February 1998 the ICRC employed about 8,000 people, of whom 90% were working in the field among its 55 delegations.

President: CORNELIO SOMMARUGA.

Members: ERIC ROETHLISBERGER, JACQUES FORSTER, ERNST A. BRUGGER, JEAN DE COURTEN (Director of Operations), YVES SANDOZ (Director for International Law and Policy), PAUL GROSSRIEDER (Director for General Affairs).

Activities

The International Committee of the Red Cross was founded in 1863, in Geneva, by Henry Dunant and four of his friends. The original purpose of the Committee was to assist wounded soldiers on the battlefield. The ICRC promoted the foundation in each country of the world of National Committees of the Red Cross or Red Crescent, which later became the National Societies of the Red Cross or Red Crescent. The present activities of the ICRC consist in giving legal protection and material assistance to military and civilian victims of wars (international wars, internal strife and disturbances). In 1990 the ICRC was granted the status of an observer at the United Nations General Assembly.

As well as providing medical aid and emergency food supplies in many countries, the ICRC plays an important part in monitoring prison conditions and in tracing missing persons, and in disseminating humanitarian principles in an attempt to protect non-combatants from violence. In January 1991 the World Campaign for the Protection of War Victims was initiated. This campaign aimed to draw attention to the large numbers of civilians who are killed or injured as a result of armed conflict in which they are not directly involved. At the end of August 1993 the ICRC held an international conference at which a Declaration for the Protection of War Victims was adopted to confirm adherence to the fourth Geneva Convention. In December 1995 the 26th International Conference of the Red Cross and Red Crescent was held in Geneva, organized jointly by the ICRC and the International Federation of Red Cross and Red Crescent Societies (q.v.) and attended by representatives of 143 governments. The Conference considered the following main themes: protection of the civilian population in periods of armed conflict; international humanitarian law applicable to armed conflicts at sea; principles and action in international humanitarian assistance and protection; strengthening national capacities to provide humanitarian and development assistance; and protection to the most vulnerable. At the same time the ICRC presented its newly-created Advisory Service, which was intended to assist national authorities in their implementation of humanitarian law. The Advisory Service was to provide a basis for consultation, analysis and harmonization of leglislative texts and help states create the structures required to ensure greater respect for humanitarian law. It became fully operational in January 1996. A Documentation Centre for exchanging information on what national measures exist and what is being done to promote the law in the different states has been established. It is open to all states and National Societies, as well as interested institutions and the general public.

In April 1993 the ICRC organized a symposium in Montreux, Switzerland, to consider the use of anti-personnel mines. The ICRC has continued to convene experts to consider the issue in the context of incorporating the use of anti-personnel mines into the review of the 1980 UN Convention on prohibitions or restrictions on the use of conventional weapons. In February 1994 the ICRC issued a report for the review of the Convention. This included a recommendation for the adoption of an additional protocol on the use of laser weapons, which cause permanent blindness or irreparable damage. In October 1995 a session of the Review Conference on the Convention adopted a Protocol, which, as a binding instrument of humanitarian law, prohibits the use and transfer of these weapons. In May 1996 the Conference approved an amended protocol on prohibitions or restrictions on the use of land-mines. The ICRC subsequently resolved to continue its efforts to achieve a world-wide ban on the use of land-mines, and other anti-personnel devices. In October the ICRC supported an International Strategy Conference, organized by the Canadian Government in Ottawa, which was the first formal meeting of states committed to a comprehensive ban on land-mines. In September 1997 the ICRC participated in an international conference, held in Oslo, Norway, at which a Convention was adopted, prohibiting 'the use, stockpiling, production and transfer of anti-personnel mines' and ensuring their destruction. The treaty was opened for signature in December. In November the Swiss Government announced that it was to establish a Geneva International Centre for Humanitarian Mine Clearance, in co-operation with the United Nations and the ICRC, to co-ordinate the destruction of land-mines world-wide.

Examples of recent ICRC activities include the following:

Africa: visits to detainees; food and medical assistance, including public health services, war surgery, programmes for the rehabilitation of the disabled, food distribution; and agricultural and veterinary programmes to improve the self-sufficiency of vulnerable and displaced populations. Major operations in 1996 and 1997 covered Angola, Burundi, Liberia, Mali, Rwanda, Sierra Leone, Somalia, Sudan and the former Zaire. The ICRC has undertaken tracing activities to reunite Rwandan families: at September 1997 some 11,266 children had been returned to their families by the ICRC and a further 10,000 children in camps remained on an ICRC register. From October 1996 the ICRC provided assistance in the former Zaire to meet the needs of the mass movement of Rwandan refugees and Zaireans after the outbreak of civil war.

Latin America: protection and relief activities in favour of the civilian population, prisoners of war and detainees in the context of the armed conflict between Ecuador and Peru in early 1996, as well as in various situations of internal violence, such as in Colombia, Peru, Haiti and Mexico; the dissemination of the fundamental principles of international humanitarian law, in particular in the training of armed forces. Between December 1996 and April 1997 the ICRC undertook to provide assistance, including the provision of food and medical and psychological care to civilians being unlawfully detained at the Japanese ambassador's residence in Lima, Peru. The ICRC also helped to organize negotiations to secure the release of hostages.

Asia: medical assistance to hospitals in Afghanistan; manufacture of artificial limbs and fitting of amputees in Afghanistan and Cambodia; protection of detainees and prisoners in Afghanistan, India, Bhutan, Sri Lanka, the Philippines and Indonesia (including East Timor); tracing missing relatives among families affected by armed conflicts in Afghanistan, Sri Lanka, Cambodia; food and non-food assistance to particularly vulnerable categories of victims, and water and sanitation programmes in Afghanistan, Indonesia and Sri Lanka. Emergency supplies were airlifted to Kabul in February 1996, in an effort to assist the 1m. residents of the Afghan capital besieged by renewed hostilities.

Middle East: visits to detainees in Israel and the Israeli-occupied territories and monitoring the implementation of the fourth Geneva Convention; visits to detainees and prisoners in Iraq, Kuwait, Yemen, Morocco and the Western Sahara; sanitation and orthopaedic programmes in Iraq; acting as a neutral intermediary in the search for people missing since the 1991 Gulf War.

Europe and Transcaucasia: medical aid, protection of civilian population, relief assistance, support to local hospitals and visits to detainees in the former Yugoslavia, Albania, Armenia, Azerbaijan and Georgia; tracing activities in the former Yugoslavia; acting as a neutral intermediary and providing a 'message service' in Bosnia and Herzegovina; promoting awareness of the dangers of anti-personnel devices; visits to prisoners in Northern Ireland; assistance to persons in Chechnya and the surrounding republics affected by the outbreak of hostilities with Russian authorities in late 1994. (In December 1996 the ICRC withdrew from Chechnya following the unlawful killing of six ICRC humanitarian workers.)

THE GENEVA CONVENTIONS

In 1864, one year after its foundation, the ICRC submitted to the states called to a Diplomatic Conference in Geneva a draft international treaty for 'the Amelioration of the Condition of the Wounded in Armies in the Field'. This treaty was adopted and signed by twelve states, which thereby bound themselves to respect as neutral wounded soldiers and those assisting them. This was the first Geneva Convention.

With the development of technology and weapons, the introduction of new means of waging war, and the manifestation of certain phenomena (the great number of prisoners of war during World War I; the enormous number of displaced persons and refugees during World War II; the internationalization of internal conflicts in recent years) the necessity was felt of having other international treaties to protect new categories of war victims. The ICRC, for more than 134 years, has been the leader of a movement to improve and complement international humanitarian law.

There are now four Geneva Conventions, adopted on 12 August 1949: I—to protect wounded and sick in armed forces on land, as well as medical personnel; II—to protect the same categories of people at sea, as well as the shipwrecked; III—concerning the treatment of prisoners of war; IV—for the protection of civilians in time of war; and there are two Additional Protocols of 8 June 1977, for the protection of victims in international armed conflicts (Protocol

I) and in non-international armed conflicts (Protocol II).

By February 1998 188 states were parties to the Geneva Conventions; 150 were parties to Protocol I and 142 to Protocol II.

FINANCE

The ICRC's work is financed by a voluntary annual grant from governments parties to the Geneva Conventions, voluntary contributions from National Red Cross and Red Crescent Societies and by gifts and legacies from private donors. The ICRC's various budgets for 1998 amounted to some 775m. Swiss francs.

PUBLICATIONS

Annual Report (editions in English, French and Spanish).

The Geneva Conventions: texts and commentaries.

ICRC News (weekly, French, English, Spanish and German editions).

International Review of the Red Cross (every 2 months, French, English, Russian, Arabic and Spanish editions).

The Protocols Additional.

Various publications on subjects of Red Cross interest (medical studies, international humanitarian law, etc.).

International Federation of Red Cross and Red Crescent Societies

Address: 17 chemin des Crêts, Petit-Saconnex, CP 372, 1211 Geneva 19, Switzerland.

Telephone: (22) 7304222; **telex:** 412133; **fax:** (22) 7330395; **e-mail:** secretariat@ifrc.org; **internet:** http://www.ifrc.org.

The Federation was founded in 1919 (as the League of Red Cross Societies). It is the world federation of all Red Cross and Red Crescent Societies. The general aim of the Federation is to inspire, encourage, facilitate and promote at all times all forms of humanitarian activities by the National Societies, with a view to the prevention and alleviation of human suffering, and thereby contribute to the maintenance and promotion of peace in the world.

MEMBERS

National Red Cross and Red Crescent Societies in 171 countries in August 1997, with a total of 123m. members and volunteers.

Organization

(January 1998)

GENERAL ASSEMBLY

The General Assembly is the highest authority of the Federation and meets every two years in commission sessions (for development, disaster relief, health and community services, and youth) and plenary sessions. It is composed of representatives from all National Societies that are members of the Federation.

President: Dr Mario Villarroel Lander (Venezuela).

EXECUTIVE COUNCIL

The Council, which meets every six months, is composed of the President of the Federation, nine Vice-Presidents and 16 National Societies elected by the Assembly. Its functions include the implementation of decisions of the General Assembly; it also has powers to act between meetings of the Assembly.

ASSEMBLY AND FINANCE COMMISSIONS

Development Commission.
Disaster Relief Commission.
Finance Commission.
Health and Community Services Commission.
Youth Commision.

The Advisory Commissions meet, in principle, twice a year, just before the Executive Council. Members are elected by the Assembly under a system that ensures each Society a seat on one Commission.

SECRETARIAT

Secretary-General: George Weber (Canada).

Treasurer-General: Bengt Bergmann (Sweden).

Activities

RELIEF

The Secretariat assumes the statutory responsibilities of the Federation in the field of relief to victims of natural disasters, refugees and civilian populations who may be displaced or exposed to abnormal hardship. This activity has three main aspects:

(i) Relief Operations: for the co-ordination of relief operations on the international level and execution by the National Society of the stricken country or by the Federation itself;

(ii) Supply, Logistics and Warehouses: for the co-ordination and purchase, transport and warehousing of relief supplies;

(iii) Disaster Preparedness: for co-ordination of assistance to National Societies situated in disaster-prone areas in the study and execution of practical measures calculated to prevent disasters and diminish their effects.

SERVICES TO NATIONAL SOCIETIES

The Secretariat promotes and co-ordinates assistance to National Societies in developing their basic structure and their services to the community. The Secretariat is equipped to advise Societies in the fields of health, social welfare, information, nursing, first aid and training; and the operation of blood programmes. It also promotes the establishment and development of educational and service programmes for children and youth.

The Federation maintains close relations with many inter-governmental organizations, the United Nations and its Specialized Agencies, and with non-governmental organizations, and represents member Societies in the international field. The Federation has permanent observer status with the United Nations.

FINANCE

The permanent Secretariat of the Federation is financed by the contributions of member Societies on a pro-rata basis. Each relief action is financed by separate, voluntary contributions, and development programme projects are also financed on a voluntary basis.

PUBLICATIONS

Annual Report.

Handbook of the International Red Cross and Red Crescent Movement (with the ICRC).

Red Cross, Red Crescent (quarterly, English, French and Spanish).

Weekly News.

World Disasters Report (annual).

Newsletters on several topics; various guides and manuals for Red Cross and Red Crescent activities.

INTERNATIONAL SEABED AUTHORITY

Address: 14–20 Port Royal St, Kingston, Jamaica.

Telephone: 922-9105; **fax:** 922-0195; **internet:** http://www.isa.org.jm.

The Authority was established in November 1994, upon the entry into force of the 1982 United Nations Convention on the Law of the Sea. The Authority is the institute through which states party to the Convention organize and control activities in the international seabed area beyond the limits of national jurisdiction, particularly with a view to administering the resources of that area. It functions as an autonomous international organization in relationship with the UN. All states party to the Convention are members of the Authority; there were 137 members at December 1997.

Organization

(January 1998)

ASSEMBLY

The Assembly is the supreme organ of the Authority, consisting of representatives of all member states. It formulates policies, approves the budget and elects Council members. The first session of the Assembly was initiated in November 1994 and was continued at a meeting in February/March 1995. The session was concluded in August 1995, having failed to reach agreement on the composition of the Council (see below) and to elect a Secretary-General of the Authority. In March 1996 the Assembly concluded the first part of its second session, having constituted the 36-member Council and elected, by consensus, the first Secretary-General of the Authority.

COUNCIL

The Council acts as the executive organ of the Authority. It consists of 36 members, of whom 18 are elected from four 'major interest groups'—the four states who are the largest investors in sea-bed minerals, the four major importers of sea-bed minerals, the four major land-based exporters of the same minerals, and six developing countries representing special interests—while 18 are elected on the principle of equitable representation. The Council aims to reach decisions by consensus agreement, failing which a vote may be conducted, although any decision has to be approved by the majority within each of the four member groups, or chambers.

LEGAL AND TECHNICAL COMMISSION

The 21-member Commission (originally it was to comprise 15 members) assists the Council by making recommendations concerning sea-bed activities, assessing the environmental implications of activities in the area and proposing measures to protect the marine environment. Under the terms of the agreement on the implementation of Part XI of the Convention, the Commission was to undertake the functions of a proposed economic planning commission until the Council decides otherwise or until the approval of the first work plan for mineral exploitation of the deep sea-bed. These functions include reviewing trends and factors affecting supply, demand and prices of materials that may be derived from the deep sea-bed area.

FINANCE COMMITTEE

The Committee, comprising 15 members, was established to make recommendations to the Assembly and the Council on all financial and budgetary issues.

SECRETARIAT

The Secretariat provides administrative services to all the bodies of the Authority and implements the relevant work programmes. It comprises Offices of Resources and Environmental Monitoring, Legal Affairs, and Administration and Management. Under the terms of the agreement on the implementation of Part XI of the Convention (see below), the Secretariat was to undertake the functions of the Enterprise, which was to carry out deep sea-bed mining operations, through joint ventures.

Secretary-General: SATYA N. NANDAN (Fiji).

The Law of the Sea Convention

The third UN Conference on the Law of the Sea (UNCLOS) began its work in 1973, with the aim of regulating maritime activities by defining zones and boundaries, ensuring fair exploitation of resources, and providing machinery for settlement of disputes. Negotiations, involving more than 160 countries, continued until 1982, having been delayed in 1981 when the newly-elected US Government decided to review its policy. The UN Convention on the Law of the Sea was finally adopted by UNCLOS in April 1982; 130 states voted in its favour, while the USA, Israel, Turkey and Venezuela voted against, and there were 17 abstentions, including the then Federal Republic of Germany, the USSR and the United Kingdom. The Convention was opened for signing in December for a two-year period: by 1984 159 states had signed, but the USA, the United Kingdom and the Federal Republic of Germany refused to sign. The 60th ratification of the Convention was received in November 1993, and by October 1995 81 states had ratified, acceded or succeeded to the Convention. The main provisions of the Convention are as follows:

Coastal states are allowed sovereignty over their territorial waters of up to 12 nautical miles in breadth; foreign vessels are to be allowed 'innocent passage' through these waters.

Ships and aircraft of all states are allowed 'transit passage' through straits used for international navigation.

Archipelagic states (composed of islands) have sovereignty over a sea area enclosed by straight lines drawn between the outermost points of the islands.

Coastal states have sovereign rights in a 200-mile exclusive economic zone with respect to natural resources and jurisdiction over certain activities (such as protection and preservation of the environment), and rights over the adjacent continental shelf up to 350 miles from the shore under specified circumstances.

All states have freedom of navigation, overflight, scientific research and fishing on the high seas, but must co-operate in measures to conserve living resources.

A 'parallel system' is to be established for exploiting the international sea-bed, where all activities are to be supervised by the International Seabed Authority.

States are bound to control pollution and co-operate in forming preventive rules, and incur penalties for failing to combat pollution.

Marine scientific research in the zones under national jurisdiction is subject to the prior consent of the coastal state, but consent may be denied only under specific circumstances.

States must submit disputes on the application and interpretation of the Convention to a compulsory procedure entailing decisions binding on all parties. An International Tribunal for the Law of the Sea is to be established.

The USA and other industrialized nations witheld their support, owing to Part XI of the Convention, concerning the provisions for exploitation of the international ocean bed, and particularly the minerals to be found there (chiefly manganese, cobalt, copper and nickel), envisaged as the 'common heritage of mankind'. It was argued that those countries which possess adequate technology for deep-sea mining would be insufficiently represented in the new Authority; the operations of private mining consortia, according to the objectors, would be unacceptably limited by the stipulations that their technology should be shared with a supranational mining venture (the 'Enterprise'), and that production should be limited in order to protect land-based mineral producers. In July 1994 the UN General Assembly adopted an agreement amending the implementation of Part XI of the Convention. Under the new agreement, which aimed to counter the objections of the industrialized nations, there was to be no mandatory transfer of technology, the Enterprise was to operate according to commercial principles and there were to be no production limits, although a compensation fund was to assist land-based producers adversely affected by sea-bed mining. An agreement on the implementation of the provisions of the Convention relating to the conservation and management of straddling and highly migratory fish stocks was opened for signature in December 1995 and was to enter into force after ratification by 30 countries.

FINANCE

The Authority's budget is the responsibility of the Finance Committee. The provisional UN budget appropriation for the Authority for the two-year period 1996–97 was US $1.3m. Thereafter, the administrative expenses of the Authority were to be met by assessed contributions of its members.

PUBLICATION

Annual Report of the Secretary-General.

ASSOCIATED INSTITUTIONS

The following were also established under the terms of the Convention:

Commission on the Limits of the Continental Shelf: Division for Ocean Affairs and the Law of the Sea, Room DC2-0470, United

Nations, New York, NY, USA; tel. (212) 963-3951; fax (212) 963-5847; e-mail doalos@un.org; 21 members of the Commission were elected, for a five-year term, in March 1997; responsible for making recommendations regarding the establishment of the outer limits of the continental shelf of a coastal state, where the limit extends beyond 200 nautical miles (370 km).

International Tribunal for the Law of the Sea: Wexstrasse 4, 20354 Hamburg, Germany; tel. (40) 356070; fax (40) 35607245; e-mail itlos@itlos.hamburg.de; inaugurated in October 1996; 21 judges; responsible for interpreting the Convention and ruling on disputes brought by states party to the Convention on matters within its jurisdiction. **Registrar:** GRITAKUMAR E. CHITTY.

ISLAMIC DEVELOPMENT BANK

Address: POB 5925, Jeddah 21432, Saudi Arabia.

Telephone: (2) 6361400; **telex:** 601137; **fax:** (2) 6366871.

The Bank is an international financial institution that was established following a conference of Ministers of Finance of member countries of the Organization of the Islamic Conference (OIC, q.v.), held in Jeddah in December 1973. Its aim is to encourage the economic development and social progress of member countries and of Muslim communities in non-member countries, in accordance with the principles of the Islamic *Shari'a* (sacred law). The Bank formally opened in October 1975.

MEMBERS

There are 51 members.

Organization

(January 1998)

BOARD OF GOVERNORS

Each member country is represented by a governor, usually its Minister of Finance, and an alternate. The Board of Governors is the supreme authority of the Bank, and meets annually.

BOARD OF EXECUTIVE DIRECTORS

The Board consists of 11 members, five of whom are appointed by the five largest subscribers to the capital stock of the Bank; the remaining six are elected by Governors representing the other subscribers. Members of the Board of Executive Directors are elected for three-year terms. The Board is responsible for the direction of the general operations of the Bank.

President of the Bank and Chairman of the Board of Executive Directors: Dr AHMED MUHAMMAD ALI.

Bank Secretary: Dr ABD AR-RAHIM OMRANA.

FINANCIAL STRUCTURE

The authorized capital of the Bank is 6,000m. Islamic Dinars (divided into 600,000 shares, having a value of 10,000 Islamic Dinars each). The Islamic Dinar (ID) is the Bank's unit of account and is equivalent to the value of one Special Drawing Right of the IMF (SDR 1 = US $1.36521 at 30 September 1997).

Subscribed capital amounts to ID 4,000m.

Activities

The Bank adheres to the Islamic principle forbidding usury, and does not grant loans or credits for interest. Instead, its methods of financing are: provision of interest-free loans (with a service fee), mainly for infrastructural projects which are expected to have a marked impact on long-term socio-economic development; provision of technical assistance (e.g. for feasibility studies); equity participation in industrial and agricultural projects; leasing operations, involving the leasing of equipment such as ships, and instalment sale financing; and profit-sharing operations. Funds not immediately needed for projects are used for foreign trade financing, particularly for importing commodities to be used in development (i.e. raw materials and intermediate industrial goods, rather than consumer goods); priority is given to the import of goods from other member countries (see table). The Longer-term Trade Financing Scheme, introduced in 1987/88, provides financing for the export of non-traditional and capital goods. In addition, the Special Assistance Account provides emergency aid and other assistance, with particular emphasis on education in Islamic communities in non-member countries.

By 17 May 1996 the Bank had approved a total of ID 3,025.56m. for project financing and technical assistance, a total of ID 8,559.57m. for foreign trade financing, and ID 364.81m. for special assistance operations, excluding amounts for cancelled operations.

SUBSCRIPTIONS (million Islamic Dinars, as at 17 May 1996)

Afghanistan	5.00	Malaysia	79.56
Albania	2.50	Maldives	2.50
Algeria	124.26	Mali	4.92
Azerbaijan	4.92	Mauritania	4.92
Bahrain	7.00	Morocco	24.81
Bangladesh	49.29	Mozambique	2.50
Benin	4.92	Niger	12.41
Brunei	12.41	Oman	13.78
Burkina Faso	12.41	Pakistan	124.26
Cameroon	12.41	Palestine Liberation Organization	9.85
Chad	4.92	Qatar	49.23
Comoros	2.50	Saudi Arabia	997.17
Djibouti	2.50	Senegal	12.42
Egypt	49.23	Sierra Leone	2.50
Gabon	14.77	Somalia	2.50
The Gambia	2.50	Sudan	19.69
Guinea	12.41	Syria	5.00
Guinea-Bissau	2.50	Tunisia	9.85
Indonesia	124.26	Turkey	315.47
Iran	349.97	Turkmenistan	2.50
Iraq	13.05	Uganda	12.41
Jordan	19.89	United Arab Emirates	283.03
Kuwait	496.64	Yemen	24.81
Kyrgyzstan	2.50	**Total**	3,753.77
Lebanon	4.92		
Libya	400.00		

Operations approved, Islamic year 1416 (30 May 1995–17 May 1996)

Type of operation	Number of operations	Total amount (million Islamic Dinars)
Ordinary operations	66	344.01
Project financing	57	342.12
Technical assistance	9	1.89
Trade financing operations*	77	627.59
Special assistance operations	37	7.77
Total†	180	979.36

* Including import trade financing, the Longer-term Trade Financing Scheme, and the Islamic Bank's Portfolio.

† Excluding cancelled operations.

During the Islamic year AH 1416 (30 May 1995 to 17 May 1996) the Bank approved a total of ID 979.36m., for 180 operations.

The Bank approved 26 loans in the year ending 17 May 1996, amounting to ID 79.16m. (compared with 16 loans, totalling ID 57.51m., in the previous year). These loans supported projects concerned with infrastructural improvements, for example of roads, canals, water-supply and rural electrification, the construction of schools and health centres, and agricultural developments.

During the year 72% of loan financing was directed to least-developed member countries under a Special Account, providing concessionary terms. Loans financed by this Account are charged an annual service fee of 0.75%, compared with 2.5% for ordinary loans, and have a repayment period of 25–30 years, compared with 15–25 years.

During AH 1416 the Bank approved nine technical assistance operations for eight countries in the form of grants and loans, amounting to ID 1.9m.

Import trade financing approved during the Islamic year 1416 amounted to ID 395m. for 54 operations in nine member countries. By the end of that year cumulative import trade financing amounted to ID 8,560m., of which 42.1% was for imports of crude petroleum, 28% for intermediate industrial goods, 9% for vegetable oil and

Project financing and technical assistance by sector, Islamic year 1416

Sector	Number of Operations	Amount (million Islamic Dinars)	%
Agriculture and agro-industry	13	64.03	18.6
Industry and mining	4	28.34	8.2
Transport and communications	10	70.30	20.4
Public utilities	18	113.67	33.0
Social sectors	18	65.52	19.0
Other*	3	2.16	0.6
Total†	66	344.01	100.0

* Mainly approved amounts for Islamic banks.
† Excluding cancelled operations.

6.1% for refined petroleum products. Financing approved under the Longer-term Trade Financing Scheme amounted to ID 59.88m. for 13 operations in six countries in AH 1416. In the same year the Bank's Portfolio for Investment and Development, established in AH 1407 (1986–87), approved 10 operations amounting to US $248.5m. Since its introduction, the Portfolio has approved 75 net financing operations in 17 member countries, amounting to $1,129m.

Under the Bank's Special Assistance Account, 37 operations were approved during the year, amounting to ID 7.77m., providing assistance primarily in the education and health sectors; of the total financing, 32 operations provided for Muslim communities in non-member countries. The Bank's scholarships programme sponsored 283 students from 38 countries during the year to 17 May 1996. The Merit Scholarship Programme, initiated in AH 1411 (1990–91), aims to develop scientific, technological and research capacities in member countries through advanced studies and/or research. Since the beginning of the programme 93 scholars have been placed in academic centres of excellence in Australia, Europe and the USA. The Bank's Programme for Technical Co-operation aims to mobilize technical capabilities among member countries and to promote the exchange of expertise, experience and skills. During AH 1416 60 projects were implemented under the programme. The Bank also undertakes the distribution of meat sacrificed by Muslim pilgrims: during the year meat from 430,560 head of sheep and 7,022 head of cattle and of camels was distributed to the needy in 27 member countries.

Disbursements during the year ending 17 May 1996 totalled ID 418m., bringing the total cumulative disbursements since the Bank began operations to ID 8,518m.

The Bank's Unit Investment Fund became operational in 1990, with the aim of mobilizing additional resources and providing a profitable channel for investments conforming to *Shari'a*. The initial issue of the Fund was US $100m., with a minimum subscription of $100,000. An additional issue of $100m. became effective on 1 January 1994; the first tranche of an additional issue of $300m. was launched in early 1995, bringing the Fund's subscribed capital to $275m. at 31 December 1995. The Fund finances mainly private-sector industrial projects in middle-income countries.

SUBSIDIARY ORGANS

Islamic Corporation for the Insurance of Investment and Export Credit—ICIEC: POB 15722, Jeddah 21454, Saudi Arabia; tel. (2) 6361400; telex 607509; fax (2) 6379504; e-mail kgazzah@isdb.org.sa; f. 1994; aims to promote trade and the flow of investments among member countries of the OIC; auth. cap. ID 100m., subscribed cap. ID 76.5m. (May 1996). Man. Dr ABDEL RAHMAN A. TAHA. Mems: 15 OIC member states.

Islamic Research and Training Institute: POB 9201, Jeddah 21413, Saudi Arabia; tel. (2) 6361400; telex 601137; fax (2) 6378927; f. 1982 for research enabling economic, financial and banking activities to conform to Islamic law, and to provide training for staff involved in development activities in the Bank's member countries. During the Islamic year 1416 the Institute undertook 10 research studies on economic, financial and general development issues relevant to the Bank's member states. The Institute also organized seminars and workshops, and held training courses aimed at furthering the expertise of government and financial officials in Islamic developing countries. Dir Dr MABID ALI AL-JARHI. Publs *Annual Report*, *Islamic Economic Studies*.

PUBLICATION

Annual Report.

LEAGUE OF ARAB STATES

Address: Arab League Bldg, Tahrir Square, Cairo, Egypt.

Telephone: (2) 5750511; **telex:** 92111; **fax:** (2) 5775626.

The League of Arab States (more generally known as the Arab League) is a voluntary association of sovereign Arab states, designed to strengthen the close ties linking them and to co-ordinate their policies and activities and direct them towards the common good of all the Arab countries. It was founded in March 1945 (see Pact of the League, p. 199).

MEMBERS

Algeria	Lebanon	Somalia
Bahrain	Libya	Sudan
Comoros	Mauritania	Syria
Djibouti	Morocco	Tunisia
Egypt	Oman	United Arab Emirates
Iraq	Palestine*	Yemen
Jordan	Qatar	
Kuwait	Saudi Arabia	

* Palestine is considered an independent state, as explained in the Charter Annex on Palestine, and therefore a full member of the League.

Organization

(January 1998)

COUNCIL

The supreme organ of the Arab League, the Council consists of representatives of the member states, each of which has one vote, and a representative for Palestine. Unanimous decisions of the Council shall be binding upon all member states of the League; majority decisions shall be binding only on those states which have accepted them.

The Council may, if necessary, hold an extraordinary session at the request of two member states. Invitations to all sessions are extended by the Secretary-General. The ordinary sessions are presided over by representatives of the member states in turn.

The Council is supported by technical and specialized committees which advise on financial and administrative affairs, information affairs and legal affairs. In addition, specialized ministerial councils have been established to formulate common policies for the regulation and the advancement of co-operation in the following areas: information; home affairs; legal affairs; health; housing; social affairs; transport; the youth and sports sectors; environmental affairs; and telecommunications.

GENERAL SECRETARIAT

The administrative and financial offices of the League. The Secretariat carries out the decisions of the Council, and provides financial and administrative services for the personnel of the League. General departments comprise: the Bureau of the Secretary-General, Arab Affairs, Economic Affairs, International Affairs, Palestine Affairs, Legal Affairs, Military Affairs, Social and Cultural Affairs, Information Affairs and Financial and Administrative Affairs. In addition, there are Units for Internal Auditing and Institutional Development, a Documentation and Information Centre, Arab League Centres in Tunis and, for Legal and Judicial Research, in Beirut and a Principal Bureau for the Boycott of Israel, based in Damascus, Syria (see below).

The Secretary-General is appointed by the League Council by a two-thirds majority of the member states, for a five-year, renewable term. He appoints the Assistant Secretaries-General and principal officials, with the approval of the Council. He has the rank of ambassador, and the Assistant Secretaries-General have the rank of ministers plenipotentiary.

Secretary-General: Dr AHMAD ESMAT ABD AL-MEGUID (Egypt).

Assistant Secretaries-General:

Economic Affairs: Dr ABD AR-RAHMAN AS-SOUHAIBANI (Saudi Arabia).

Financial and Administrative Affairs: Dr ALI ABDULKARIM (Yemen).

Head of Arab League Centre, Tunis: NOUREDDINE HACHED (Tunisia).

Head of the Bureau of the Secretary-General: AHMAD IBRAHIM ADEL (Egypt).

Information Affairs: MUHAB MUQBEL (Egypt).

International Affairs: MUHAMMAD ZAKARIA ISMAIL (Syria).

Military Affairs: MUHAMMAD SAID BIN HASSAN EL-BERIQDAR (Syria).

Palestine Affairs: SAID KAMAL (Palestine).

Social and Cultural Affairs: DHAW ALI SIWEDAN (Libya).

DEFENCE AND ECONOMIC CO-OPERATION

Groups established under the Treaty of Joint Defence and Economic Co-operation, concluded in 1950 to complement the Charter of the League.

Arab Unified Military Command: f. 1964 to co-ordinate military policies for the liberation of Palestine.

Economic and Social Council: to compare and co-ordinate the economic policies of the member states; supervises the activities of the Arab League's specialized agencies. The Council is composed of ministers of economic affairs or their deputies; decisions are taken by majority vote. The first meeting was held in 1953.

Joint Defence Council: supervises implementation of those aspects of the treaty concerned with common defence. Composed of foreign and defence ministers; decisions by a two-thirds majority vote of members are binding on all.

Permanent Military Commission: established 1950; composed of representatives of army general staffs; main purpose: to draw up plans of joint defence for submission to the Joint Defence Council.

ARAB DETERRENT FORCE

Created in June 1976 by the Arab League Council to supervise successive attempts to cease hostilities in Lebanon, and afterwards to maintain the peace. The mandate of the Force has been successively renewed. The Arab League Summit Conference in October 1976 agreed that costs were to be paid in the following percentage contributions: Saudi Arabia and Kuwait 20% each, the United Arab Emirates 15%, Qatar 10% and other Arab states 35%.

OTHER INSTITUTIONS OF THE LEAGUE

Other bodies established by resolutions adopted by the Council of the League:

Administrative Tribunal of the Arab League: f. 1964; began operations 1966.

Arab Fund for Technical Assistance to African Countries: f. 1975 to provide technical assistance for development projects by providing African and Arab experts, grants for scholarships and training, and finance for technical studies. Exec. Sec. HASSAN ABADI (Egypt).

Higher Auditing Board: comprises representatives of seven member states, elected every three years; undertakes financial and administrative auditing duties.

Investment Arbitration Board: examines disputes between member states relating to capital investments.

Special Bureau for Boycotting Israel: POB 437, Damascus, Syria; f. 1951 to prevent trade between Arab countries and Israel, and to enforce a boycott by Arab countries of companies outside the region that conduct trade with Israel. Commr-Gen. ZUHEIR AQUIL (Syria).

SPECIALIZED AGENCIES

All member states of the Arab League are also members of the Specialized Agencies, which constitute an integral part of the Arab League. (See also entries on the Arab Fund for Economic and Social Development, the Arab Monetary Fund, the Council of Arab Economic Unity and the Organization of Arab Petroleum Exporting Countries.)

Arab Administrative Development Organization (ARADO): POB 2692 Al-Horreia, Heliopolis, Cairo, Egypt; tel. (2) 4175401; fax (2) 4175407; e-mail arado@idsc.gov.eg; f. 1961 (as Arab Organization of Administrative Sciences), although became operational in 1969; administration development, training, consultancy, research and studies, information, documentation; promotes Arab and international co-operation in administrative sciences; includes Arab Network of Administrative Information; 20 Arab state members; Library of 20,000 volumes, 380 periodicals. Dir-Gen. Dr AHMAD SAKR ASHOUR. Publs *Arab Journal of Administration* (biannual), *Management Newsletter* (quarterly), research series, training manuals.

Arab Atomic Energy Agency (AAEA): 4 rue Mouaouiya ibn Abi Soufiane, Al-Menzah 8, POB 402, 1004 Tunis, Tunisia; tel. (1) 709464; fax (1) 711330; e-mail aaea@aaea.org.tn; f. 1988 to co-ordinate research into the peaceful uses of atomic energy. Dir-Gen. Prof. Dr MAHMOUD FOUAD BARAKAT (Egypt). Publ. *The Atom and Development* (quarterly); other publs in the field of nuclear sciences and their applications in industry, biology, medicine, agriculture and seawater desalination.

Arab Bank for Economic Development in Africa (Banque arabe pour le développement économique en Afrique—BADEA): Sayed Abdel-Rahman el-Mahdi Ave, POB 2640, Khartoum, Sudan; tel. (11) 773646; telex 22248; fax (11) 770600; f. 1973 by Arab League; provides loans and grants to African countries to finance development projects; paid-up capital US $1,145.8m. (Oct. 1997). In 1997 the Bank approved loans and grants totalling $ 99.7m. By October 1997 total loans and grants approved since funding activities began in 1975 amounted to $1,944.6m. Subscribing countries: all countries of Arab League, except the Comoros, Djibouti, Somalia and Yemen; recipient countries: all countries of Organization of African Unity (q.v.), except those belonging to the Arab League. Chair. AHMED ABDALLAH AL-AKEIL (Saudi Arabia); Dir.-Gen. MEDHAT SAMI LOTFY (Egypt). Publs *Annual Report, Co-operation for Development,* Studies on Afro-Arab co-operation, periodic brochures.

Arab Centre for the Study of Arid Zones and Dry Lands (ACSAD): POB 2440, Damascus, Syria; tel. (11) 5323087; telex 412697; fax (11) 5323063; f. 1971 to conduct regional research and development programmes related to water and soil resources, plant and animal production, agro-meteorology, and socio-economic studies of arid zones. The Centre holds conferences and training courses and encourages the exchange of information by Arab scientists. Dir-Gen. Dr HASSAN SEOUD.

Arab Industrial Development and Mining Organization: rue France, Zanagat Al Khatawat, POB 8019, Rabat, Morocco; tel. (7) 772600; telex 36763; fax (7) 772188; f. 1990 by merger of Arab Industrial Development Organization, Arab Organization for Mineral Resources and Arab Organization for Standardization and Metrology.

Arab Labour Organization: POB 814, Cairo, Egypt; f. 1965 for co-operation between member states in labour problems; unification of labour legislation and general conditions of work wherever possible; research; technical assistance; social insurance; training, etc.; the organization has a tripartite structure: governments, employers and workers. Dir-Gen. BAKR MAHMOUD RASOUL (Iraq). Publs *ALO Bulletin* (monthly), *Arab Labour Review* (quarterly), *Legislative Bulletin* (annually), series of research reports and studies concerned with economic and social development issues in the Arab world.

Arab League Educational, Cultural and Scientific Organization—ALECSO: POB 1120, Tunis, Tunisia; tel. (1) 784-466; telex 18825; fax (1) 784-965; f. 1970 to promote and co-ordinate educational, cultural and scientific activities in the Arab region. Regional units: Arab Centre for Arabization, Translation, Authorship, and Publication—Damascus, Syria; Institute of Arab Manuscript—Cairo, Egypt; Institute of Arab Research and Studies—Cairo, Egypt; Khartoum Institute for Arabic Language—Khartoum, Sudan; and the Arabization Co-ordination Bureau—Rabat, Morocco. Dir-Gen. MOHAMED ALMILI IBRAHIMI (Algeria). Publs *Arab Journal of Culture, Arab Journal of Science, Arab Bulletin of Publications, Statistical Yearbook, Journal of the Institute of Arab Manuscripts, Arab Magazine for Information Science.*

Arab Maritime Transport Academy: POB 1029, Alexandria, Egypt; tel. (3) 5602366; telex 54160; fax (3) 5602144; f. 1989 by merger; 130 teaching staff. Dir-Gen. Dr GAMAL EL-DIN MOUKHTAR. Publs *Maritime Technology* (every 2 months), *News Bulletin, Bulletin of Maritime Transport Information Analysis* (monthly), *Current Awareness Bulletin* (monthly), *Journal of the Arab Maritime Transport Academy* (2 a year).

Arab Organization for Agricultural Development: St no. 7, Al-Amarat, POB 474, Khartoum, Sudan; tel. (11) 472176; telex 22554; fax (11) 471402; f. 1970; began operations in 1972 to contribute to co-operation in agricultural activities, and in the development of natural and human resources for agriculture; compiles data, conducts studies, training and food security programmes; includes Arab Institute of Forestry and Range, Arab Centre for Information and Early Warning, and Arab Centre for Agricultural Documentation. Dir-Gen. Dr YAHIA BAKOUR. Publs *Agricultural Statistics Yearbook, Annual Report on Agricultural Development, the State of Arab Food Security* (annually), *Agriculture and Development in the Arab World* (quarterly), *Accession Bulletin* (every 2 months), monthly newsletter.

Arab Satellite Communications Organization: POB 1038, Riyadh, 11431 Saudi Arabia; tel. (1) 464-6666; fax (1) 465-6983; f. 1976; operates the ARABSAT project, under which the first two satellites were launched in 1985, for the improvement of telephone, telex, data transmission and radio and television in Arab countries; a third satellite was launched in February 1992 with a 10-year operational life, and two more satellites were under construction in early 1993. Dir-Gen. SAAD IBN ABD AL-AZIZ AL-BADNA (Saudi Arabia).

Arab States Broadcasting Union—ASBU: POB 250, 1080 Tunis Cedex; 6 rue des Entrepreneurs, zone industrielle Charguia 2, Ariana Aéroport, Tunisia; tel. (1) 703854; telex 13398; fax (1) 704203; f. 1969 to promote Arab fraternity, co-ordinate and study broadcasting subjects, to exchange expertise and technical co-operation in broadcasting; conducts training and audience research. Mems: 21 Arab radio and TV stations and eight foreign associates. Sec.-Gen. RAOUF BASTI. Publ. *ASBU Review* (quarterly).

Inter-Arab Investment Guarantee Corporation: POB 23568, Safat 13096, Kuwait; tel. 4844500; telex 22562; fax 4815741; f. 1975; insures Arab investors for non-commercial risks, and export credits for commercial and non-commercial risks; undertakes research and other activities to promote inter-Arab trade and investment; authorized capital 25m. Kuwaiti dinars (Dec. 1995). Mems: 22 Arab governments. Dir-Gen. MAMOUN I. HASSAN. Publs *News Bulletin* (monthly), *Arab Investment Climate Report* (annually).

External Relations

ARAB LEAGUE OFFICES AND INFORMATION CENTRES ABROAD

Established by the Arab League to co-ordinate work at all levels among Arab embassies abroad.

Austria: Grimmelshausengasse 12, 1030 Vienna.

Belgium: 89 ave Winston Churchill, 1180 Brussels.

Brazil: Shis-Qi, Conj. 2, Casa 2, 71600 Brasília, DF.

Canada: 170 Laurier Ave West, Suite 604, Ottawa, K1P 5VS.

China, Peoples's Republic: 14 Liang Male, 1-14-2 Taynan Diplomatic Building, Beijing 100600.

Ethiopia: POB 5768, Addis Ababa.

France: 114 blvd Malesherbes, 75017 Paris.

Germany: Rheinallee 23, 53173 Bonn.

India: 137 Neeti Bagh, New Delhi 110 049.

Italy: Piazzale delle Belle Arti 6, 00196 Rome.

Russia: 28 Koniouch Kovskaya, Moscow.

Senegal: BP 3805, Dakar.

Spain: Paseo de la Castellana 180, 6°, 28046 Madrid.

Tunisia: 93 rue Louis Bray, el-Khadra, 1003 Tunis.

United Kingdom: 52 Green St, London W1Y 3RH.

USA: 1100 17th St, NW, Suite 602, Washington, DC 20036; 747 Third Ave, New York, NY 10017 (UN Office).

Record of Events

1945 Pact of the Arab League signed, March.

1946 Cultural Treaty signed.

1950 Joint Defence and Economic Co-operation Treaty.

1952 Agreements on extradition, writs and letters of request, nationality of Arabs outside their country of origin.

1953 Formation of Economic and Social Council. Convention on the privileges and immunities of the League.

1954 Nationality Agreement.

1956 Agreement on the adoption of a Common Tariff Nomenclature.

1962 Arab Economic Unity Agreement.

1964 First Summit Conference of Arab kings and presidents, Cairo, January. First meeting of Economic Unity Council, June. Arab Common Market approved by Arab Economic Unity Council, August. Second Summit Conference welcomed establishment of Palestine Liberation Organization (PLO), September.

1965 Arab Common Market established, January.

1969 Fifth Summit Conference, Rabat. Call for mobilization of all Arab nations against Israel.

1977 Tripoli Declaration, December. Decision of Algeria, Iraq, Libya and Yemen PDR to boycott League meetings in Egypt in response to President Sadat's visit to Israel.

1979 Council meeting in Baghdad, March: resolved to withdraw Arab ambassadors from Egypt; to recommend severance of political and diplomatic relations with Egypt; to suspend Egypt's membership of the League on the date of the signing of the peace treaty with Israel; to transfer the headquarters of the League to Tunis; to condemn US policy regarding its role in concluding the Camp David agreements and the peace treaty; to halt all bank loans, deposits, guarantees or facilities, as well as all financial or technical contributions and aid to Egypt; to prohibit trade exchanges with the Egyptian state and with private establishments dealing with Israel.

1981 In November the 12th Summit Conference, held in Fez, Morocco, was suspended after a few hours, following disagreement over a Saudi Arabian proposal known as the Fahd Plan, which included not only the Arab demands on behalf of the Palestinians, as approved by the UN General Assembly, but also an implied *de facto* recognition of Israel.

1982 Twelfth Summit Conference reconvened, Fez, September: adopted a peace plan, which demanded Israel's withdrawal from territories occupied in 1967, and removal of Israeli settlements in these areas; freedom of worship for all religions in the sacred places; the right of the Palestinian people to self-determination, under the leadership of the PLO; temporary UN supervision for the West Bank and the Gaza Strip; the creation of an independent Palestinian state, with Jerusalem as its capital; and a guarantee of peace for all the states of the region by the UN Security Council.

1983 The summit meeting due to be held in November was postponed owing to members' differences of opinion concerning Syria's opposition to Yasser Arafat's chairmanship of the PLO, and Syrian support of Iran in the war against Iraq.

1984 In March an emergency meeting established an Arab League committee to encourage international efforts to bring about a negotiated settlement of the Iran–Iraq war. In May ministers of foreign affairs adopted a resolution urging Iran to stop attacking non-belligerent ships and installations in the Gulf region: similar attacks by Iraq were not mentioned.

1985 In August an emergency Summit Conference was boycotted by Algeria, Lebanon, Libya, Syria and the People's Democratic Republic of Yemen, while of the other 16 members only nine were represented by their heads of state. Two commissions were set up to mediate in disagreements between Arab states (between Jordan and Syria, Iraq and Syria, Iraq and Libya, and Libya and the PLO).

1986 In July King Hassan of Morocco announced that he was resigning as chairman of the next League Summit Conference, after criticism by several Arab leaders of his meeting with the Israeli Prime Minister earlier that month. A ministerial meeting, held in October, condemned any attempt at direct negotiation with Israel.

1987 An extraordinary Summit Conference was held in November, mainly to discuss the war between Iran and Iraq. Contrary to expectations, the participants (including President Assad of Syria) unanimously agreed on a statement expressing support for Iraq in its defence of its legitimate rights, and criticizing Iran for its procrastination in accepting the UN Security Council Resolution No. 598 of July 1987, which had recommended a cease-fire in the Iran–Iraq war and negotiations on a settlement of the conflict. The meeting also stated that the resumption of diplomatic relations with Egypt was a matter to be decided by individual states.

1988 In June a Summit Conference agreed to provide finance for the PLO to continue the Palestinian uprising in Israeli-occupied territories. It reiterated the Arab League's demand for the convening of an international conference, attended by the PLO, to seek to bring about a peaceful settlement in the Middle East (thereby implicitly rejecting recent proposals by the US Government for a conference that would exclude the PLO).

1989 In January (responding to the deteriorating political situation in Lebanon) an Arab League mediation group, comprising six ministers of foreign affairs, began discussions with the two rival Lebanese governments on the possibility of a political settlement in Lebanon. At a Summit Conference, held in May, Egypt was readmitted to the League. The Conference expressed support for the chairman of the PLO, Yasser Arafat, in his recent peace proposals made before the UN General Assembly, and reiterated the League's support for proposals that an international conference should be convened to discuss the rights of Palestinians: in so doing, it accepted UN Security Council Resolutions 242 and 338 on a peaceful settlement in the Middle East and thus gave tacit recognition to the State of Israel. The meeting also supported Arafat in rejecting Israeli proposals for elections in the Israeli-occupied territories of the West Bank and the Gaza Strip. A new mediation committee, comprising the heads of state of Algeria, Morocco and Saudi Arabia, was established, with a six-month mandate to negotiate a cease-fire in Lebanon, and to reconvene the Lebanese legislature with the aim of holding a presidential election and restoring constitutional government in Lebanon. In September the principal factions in

Lebanon agreed to observe a cease-fire, and the surviving members of the Lebanese legislature (originally elected in 1972) met at Taif, in Saudi Arabia, in October, and approved the League's proposed 'charter of national reconciliation' (see chapter on Lebanon).

1990 In May a Summit Conference, held in Baghdad, Iraq (which was boycotted by Syria and Lebanon), criticized recent efforts by Western governments to prevent the development of advanced weapons technology in Iraq. In August an emergency Summit Conference was held to discuss the invasion and annexation of Kuwait by Iraq. Twelve members (Bahrain, Djibouti, Egypt, Kuwait, Lebanon, Morocco, Oman, Qatar, Saudi Arabia, Somalia, Syria and the United Arab Emirates) approved a resolution condemning Iraq's action, and demanding the withdrawal of Iraqi forces from Kuwait and the reinstatement of the Government. The 12 states expressed support for the Saudi Arabian Government's invitation to the USA to send forces to defend Saudi Arabia; they also agreed to impose economic sanctions on Iraq, and to provide troops for an Arab defensive force in Saudi Arabia. The remaining member states, however, condemned the presence of foreign troops in Saudi Arabia, and their ministers of foreign affairs refused to attend a meeting, held at the end of August, to discuss possible solutions to the crisis. The dissenting countries also rejected the decision, taken earlier in the year, to return the League's headquarters from Tunis to Cairo. None the less, the official transfer of the League's headquarters to Cairo took place on 31 October. In November King Hassan of Morocco urged the convening of an Arab Summit Conference, in an attempt to find an 'Arab solution' to Iraq's annexation of Kuwait. However, the divisions in the Arab world over the issue meant that conditions for such a meeting could not be agreed.

1991 The first meeting of the Arab League since August 1990 took place in March, attended by representatives of all 21 member nations, including Iraq. Discussion of the recently-ended war against Iraq was avoided, in an attempt to re-establish the unity of the League. In September, despite deep divisions between member states, resulting from Iraq's invasion of Kuwait, particularly between Iraq and Kuwait, and Egypt and Jordan, it was agreed that a committee should be formed to co-ordinate Arab positions in preparation for the US-sponsored peace talks between Arab countries and Israel (which began in late October). (In the event, an *ad hoc* meeting, attended by Egypt, Jordan, Syria, the PLO, Saudi Arabia—representing the Gulf Co-operation Council (GCC), and Morocco—representing the Union of the Arab Maghreb, was held in October, prior to the start of the talks.) In early December the League expressed solidarity with Libya, which was under international pressure to extradite two Libyan government agents who were suspected of involvement in the explosion which destroyed a US passenger aircraft over Lockerbie, United Kingdom, in December 1988.

1992 In early 1992 the League was involved in mediation efforts between the warring factions in Somalia to bring about a cease-fire. In March the League appointed a committee to seek to resolve the disputes betwen Libya and the USA, the United Kingdom and France over the Lockerbie explosion and the explosion which destroyed a French passenger aircraft over the Sahara (in Niger) in September 1989. The League condemned the UN's decision, at the end of March, to impose sanctions against Libya, and appealed for a negotiated solution. In September the League's Council issued a condemnation of Iran's alleged occupation of three islands in the Persian (Arabian) Gulf that were claimed by the United Arab Emirates, and decided to refer the issue to the United Nations.

1993 In April the Council approved the creation of a committee to consider the political and security aspects of water supply in Arab countries. In the same month the League pledged its commitment to the Middle East peace talks, but warned that Israel's continued refusal to repatriate the Palestinians who were stranded in Lebanon remained a major obstacle to the process. The League sent an official observer to the independence referendum in Eritrea, held in April. In September the Council admitted the Comoros as the 22nd member of the League. Following the signing of the Israeli-PLO peace accord in September the Council convened in emergency session, at which it approved the agreement, despite opposition from some members, notably Syria. In November it was announced that the League's boycott of commercial activity with Israel was to be maintained.

1994 In January the US Secretary of Commerce met with the League's Secretary-General in an attempt to negotiate an end to the secondary and tertiary boycott against Israel, by which member states refuse to trade with international companies which have investments in Israel. In September the Council endorsed a recommendation that the United Nations conduct a census of Palestinian refugees. The Council also considered the establishment of a regional court of justice, which had been discussed prior to the meeting by Arab ministers of foreign affairs. The League condemned a decision of the GCC, announced in late September, to end the secondary and tertiary trade embargo against Israel, in the absence of any such action taken by the League. A statement issued by the League insisted that the embargo could be removed only on the decision of the Council.

1995 In January the League's Secretary-General advocated the creation of a free-trade area among Arab states in order, partly, to counter proposals for a regional market that would include Israel. In March Arab ministers of foreign affairs approved a resolution urging Israel to renew the Nuclear Non-Proliferation Treaty (NPT). The resolution stipulated that failure by Israel to do so would cause Arab states to seek to protect legitimate Arab interests by alternative means. At an extraordinary session of the Council, which was convened in early May, the League condemned a decision by Israel to confiscate Arab-owned land in East Jerusalem for resettlement, and requested that the UN Security Council meet to consider the issue. Arab heads of state and government were scheduled to convene in emergency session later in that month to formulate a collective response to the action. However, the meeting was postponed, following an announcement by the Israeli Government that it was suspending its expropriation plans. In September the Council discussed plans for a regional court of justice and for an Arab Code of Honour to prevent the use of force in disputes between Arab states. The Council expressed its support for the Algerian Government in its efforts to combat Muslim separatist violence. In October the League was reported to be in financial difficulties, owing to the non-payment of contributions by seven member states. At that time undisputed arrears amounted to US $80.5m. In November the Arab League dispatched 44 observers to oversee elections in Algeria as part of an international monitoring team.

1996 In March, following protests by Syria and Iraq that extensive construction work in southern Turkey was restricting water supply in the region, the Council determined that the waters of the Euphrates and Tigris rivers be shared equitably between the three countries. In April an emergency meeting of the Council issued a further endorsement of Syria's position in the dispute with Turkey. The main objective of the meeting, which was convened at the request of Palestine, was to attract international attention to the problem of radiation from an Israeli nuclear reactor. The Council requested an immediate technical inspection of the site by the UN, and further demanded that Israel be obliged to sign the NPT to ensure the eradication of its nuclear weaponry. In June a Summit Conference was convened, the first since 1990, in order to formulate a united Arab response to the election, in May, of a new government in Israel and to the prospects for peace in the Middle East. The Conference, which was attended by heads of state of 13 countries and senior representatives of seven others (Iraq was excluded from the meeting in order to ensure the attendance of the Gulf member states), aimed to assure the international community of the commitment of Arab states to the peace process. Israel was urged to honour its undertaking to withdraw from the Occupied Territories, including Jerusalem, and to respect the establishment of an independent Palestinian state, in order to ensure the success of the peace process. A final communiqué of the meeting warned that Israeli co-operation was essential to prevent Arab states' reconsidering their participation in the peace process and the re-emergence of regional tensions. Meanwhile, there were concerns over increasing inter-Arab hostility, in particular between Syria and Jordan, owing to the latter's relations with Israel and allegations of Syrian involvement in recent terrorist attacks against Jordanian targets. In early September the League condemned US missile attacks against Iraq as an infringement of that country's sovereignty. In addition, it expressed concern at the impact on Iraqi territorial integrity of Turkish intervention in the north of Iraq. Later in that month the League met in emergency session, following an escalation of civil unrest in Jerusalem and the Occupied Territories. The League urged the UN Security Council to prevent further alleged Israeli aggression against the Palestinians. In November the League criticized Israel's settlement policy, and at the beginning of December convened in emergency session to consider measures to end any expansion of the Jewish population in the West Bank and Gaza.

1997 On 1 March the Council met in emergency session, in response to the Israeli Government's decision to proceed with construction of a new settlement at Har Homa (Jabal Abu-Ghuneim) in East Jerusalem. The Council pledged its commitment to seeking a reversal of the decision and urged the international community to support this aim. At the end of March ministers of foreign affairs of Arab League states agreed to end all efforts to secure normal diplomatic relations with Israel (although binding agreements already in force with Egypt, Jordan and Palestine were exempt) and to close diplomatic offices and missions while construction work continued in East Jerusalem. In addition, ministers recommended reactivating the economic boycott against Israel until comprehensive peace was achieved in the region and suspending Arab participation in the multilateral talks that were initiated in 1991 to further the peace process. Earlier in the year, in February, the Economic and Social Council ratified a programme to facilitate and develop inter-Arab trade through the reduction and eventual elimination of customs duties. The Council agreed to supervise the process and formally to review implementation of the programme twice a year. In June a 60-member delegation from the Arab League participated in an international mission to monitor legislative elections in Algeria. In the same month the League condemned Turkey's military incursion into northern Iraq and demanded a withdrawal of Turkish troops from Iraqi territory. In September ministers of foreign affairs of member states advocated a gradual removal of international sanctions against Libya, and agreed that member countries should permit international flights to leave Libya for specific humanitarian and religious purposes and when used for the purposes of transporting foreign nationals. Ministers also voted to pursue the decision, adopted in March, not to strengthen relations with Israel. Several countries urged a formal boycott of the forthcoming Middle East and North Africa economic conference, in protest at the lack of progress in the peace process (for which the League blamed Israel, which was due to participate in the conference). However, the meeting upheld a request by the Qatari Government, the host of the conference, and resolved that each member should decide individually whether to attend. In the event, only seven Arab League countries participated in the conference, which was held in Doha in mid-November, while the Secretary-General of the League decided not to attend as the organization's official representative. In November the League criticized the decision of the US Government to impose economic sanctions against Sudan. The League also expressed concern at the tensions arising from Iraq's decision not to co-operate fully with UN weapons inspectors, and held several meetings with representatives of the Iraqi administration in an effort to secure a peaceful conclusion to the impasse. (In early 1998 the Secretary-General of the League condemned the use or threat of force against Iraq and continued to undertake diplomatic efforts to secure Iraq's compliance with UN Security Council resolutions.)

PUBLICATIONS

Arab Perspectives— Sh'oun Arabiyya (monthly).

Journal of Arab Affairs (monthly).

Bulletins of treaties and agreements concluded among the member states, essays, regular publications circulated by regional offices.

The Pact of the League of Arab States

(22 March 1945)

Article 1. The League of Arab States is composed of the independent Arab States which have signed this Pact.

Any independent Arab state has the right to become a member of the League. If it desires to do so, it shall submit a request which will be deposited with the Permanent Secretariat-General and submitted to the Council at the first meeting held after submission of the request.

Article 2. The League has as its purpose the strengthening of the relations between the member states; the co-ordination of their policies in order to achieve co-operation between them and to safeguard their independence and sovereignty; and a general concern with the affairs and interests of the Arab countries. It has also as its purpose the close co-operation of the member states, with due regard to the organization and circumstances of each state, on the following matters:

(*a*) Economic and financial affairs, including commercial relations, customs, currency, and questions of agriculture and industry.

(*b*) Communications: this includes railways, roads, aviation, navigation, telegraphs and posts.

(*c*) Cultural affairs.

(*d*) Nationality, passports, visas, execution of judgments, and extradition of criminals.

(*e*) Social affairs.

(*f*) Health problems.

Article 3. The League shall possess a Council composed of the representatives of the member states of the League; each state shall have a single vote, irrespective of the number of its representatives.

It shall be the task of the Council to achieve the realization of the objectives of the League and to supervise the execution of agreements which the member states have concluded on the questions enumerated in the preceding article, or on any other questions.

It likewise shall be the Council's task to decide upon the means by which the League is to co-operate with the international bodies to be created in the future in order to guarantee security and peace and regulate economic and social relations.

Article 4. For each of the questions listed in Article 2 there shall be set up a special committee in which the member states of the League shall be represented. These committees shall be charged with the task of laying down the principles and extent of co-operation. Such principles shall be formulated as draft agreements, to be presented to the Council for examination preparatory to their submission to the aforesaid states.

Representatives of the other Arab countries may take part in the work of the aforesaid committees. The Council shall determine the conditions under which these representatives may be permitted to participate and the rules governing such representation.

Article 5. Any resort to force in order to resolve disputes arising between two or more member states of the League is prohibited. If there should rise among them a difference which does not concern a state's independence, sovereignty, or territorial integrity, and if the parties to the dispute have recourse to the Council for the settlement of this difference, the decision of the Council shall then be enforceable and obligatory.

In such a case, the states between whom the difference has arisen shall not participate in the deliberations and decisions of the Council.

The Council shall mediate in all differences which threaten to lead to war between two member states, or a member state and a third state, with a view to bringing about their reconciliation.

Decisions of arbitration and mediation shall be taken by majority vote.

Article 6. In case of aggression or threat of aggression by one state against a member state, the state which has been attacked or threatened with aggression may demand the immediate convocation of the Council.

The Council shall by unanimous decision determine the measures necessary to repulse the aggression. If the aggressor is a member state, its vote shall not be counted in determining unanimity.

If, as a result of the attack, the government of the state attacked finds itself unable to communicate with the Council, that state's representative in the Council shall have the right to request the convocation of the Council for the purpose indicated in the foregoing paragraph. In the event that this representative is unable to communicate with the Council, any member state of the League shall have the right to request the convocation of the Council.

Article 7. Unanimous decisions of the Council shall be binding upon all member states of the League; majority decisions shall be binding only upon those states which have accepted them.

In either case the decisions of the Council shall be enforced in each member state according to its respective basic laws.

Article 8. Each member state shall respect the systems of government established in the other member states and regard them as exclusive concerns of those states. Each shall pledge to abstain from any action calculated to change established systems of government.

Article 9. States of the League which desire to establish closer co-operation and stronger bonds than are provided by this Pact may conclude agreements to that end.

Treaties and agreements already concluded or to be concluded in the future between a member state and another state shall not be binding or restrictive upon other members.

Article 10. The permanent seat of the League of Arab States is established in Cairo. The Council may, however, assemble at any other place it may designate.

Article 11. The Council of the League shall convene in ordinary session twice a year, in March and in September. It shall convene in extraordinary session upon the request of two member states of the League whenever the need arises.

Article 12. The League shall have a permanent Secretariat-General which shall consist of a Secretary-General, Assistant Secretaries, and an appropriate number of officials.

The Council of the League shall appoint the Secretary-General by a majority of two-thirds of the states of the League. The Secretary-General, with the approval of the Council, shall appoint the Assistant Secretaries and the principal officials of the League.

The Council of the League shall establish an administrative regulation for the functions of the Secretariat-General and matters relating to the Staff.

The Secretary-General shall have the rank of Ambassador and the Assistant Secretaries that of Ministers Plenipotentiary.

Article 13. The Secretary-General shall prepare the draft of the budget of the League and shall submit it to the Council for approval before the beginning of each fiscal year.

The Council shall fix the share of the expenses to be borne by each state of the League. This share may be reconsidered if necessary.

Article 14. (confers diplomatic immunity on officials).

Article 15. The first meeting of the Council shall be convened at the invitation of the head of the Egyptian Government. Thereafter it shall be convened at the invitation of the Secretary-General.

The representatives of the member states of the League shall alternately assume the presidency of the Council at each of its ordinary sessions.

Article 16. Except in cases specifically indicated in this Pact, a majority vote of the Council shall be sufficient to make enforceable decisions on the following matters:

(*a*) Matters relating to personnel.

(*b*) Adoption of the budget of the League.

(*c*) Establishment of the administrative regulations for the Council, the Committees, and the Secretariat-General.

(*d*) Decisions to adjourn the sessions.

Article 17. Each member state of the League shall deposit with the Secretariat-General one copy of every treaty or agreement concluded or to be concluded in the future between itself and another member state of the League or a third state.

Article 18. (deals with withdrawal).

Article 19. (deals with amendment).

Article 20. (deals with ratification).

ANNEX REGARDING PALESTINE

Since the termination of the last great war, the rule of the Ottoman Empire over the Arab countries, among them Palestine, which has become detached from that Empire, has come to an end. She has come to be autonomous, not subordinate to any other state.

The Treaty of Lausanne proclaimed that her future was to be settled by the parties concerned.

However, even though she was as yet unable to control her own affairs, the Covenant of the League (of Nations) in 1919 made provision for a regime based upon recognition of her independence.

Her international existence and independence in the legal sense cannot, therefore, be questioned, any more than could the independence of the Arab countries.

Although the outward manifestations of this independence have remained obscured for reasons beyond her control, this should not be allowed to interfere with her participation in the work of the Council of the League.

The states signatory to the Pact of the Arab League are therefore of the opinion that, considering the special circumstances of Palestine and until that country can effectively exercise its independence, the Council of the League should take charge of the selection of an Arab representative from Palestine to take part in its work.

ANNEX REGARDING CO-OPERATION WITH COUNTRIES WHICH ARE NOT MEMBERS OF THE COUNCIL OF THE LEAGUE

Whereas the member states of the League will have to deal in the Council as well as in the committees with matters which will benefit and affect the Arab world at large;

And whereas the Council has to take into account the aspirations of the Arab countries which are not members of the Council and has to work toward their realization;

Now therefore, it particularly behoves the states signatory to the Pact of the Arab League to enjoin the Council of the League, when considering the admission of those countries to participation in the committees referred to in the Pact, that it should do its utmost to co-operate with them, and furthermore, that it should spare no effort to learn their needs and understand their aspirations and hopes; and that it should work thenceforth for their best interests and the safeguarding of the future with all the political means at its disposal.

NORDIC COUNCIL

Address: Store Strandstraede 18, POB 3043, 1021 Copenhagen, Denmark.

Telephone: 33-96-04-00; **fax:** 33-11-18-70; **internet:** http://www.norden.org.

The Nordic Council was founded in 1952 for co-operation between the Nordic parliaments and governments. The four original members were Denmark, Iceland, Norway and Sweden; Finland joined in 1955, and the Faroe Islands and Åland Islands were granted representation in 1970 within the Danish and Finnish delegations respectively. Greenland had separate representation within the Danish delegation from 1984. Co-operation was first regulated by a Statute, and subsequently by the Helsinki Treaty of 1962. The Nordic region has a population of about 24 million.

MEMBERS

Denmark (with the autonomous territories of the Faroe Islands and Greenland)	Finland (with the autonomous territory of the Åland Islands)	Norway
	Iceland	Sweden

Organization

(January 1998)

COUNCIL

The Nordic Council is not a supranational parliament, but a forum for co-operation between the parliaments and governments of the Nordic countries. The Nordic Council of Ministers (see below) coordinates the activities of the governments of the Nordic countries when decisions are to be implemented.

The Council comprises 87 members, elected annually by and from the parliaments of the respective countries (Denmark 16 members; Faroes 2; Greenland 2; Finland 18; Åland 2; Iceland 7; Norway 20; Sweden 20). The various parties are proportionately represented in accordance with their representation in the national parliaments. Sessions of the Council consider proposals submitted by Council members, by the Council of Ministers or national governments. The sessions also follow up the outcome of past decisions and the work of the various Nordic institutions. The Plenary Assembly, which convenes once a year, is the highest body of the Nordic Council. Government representatives may participate in the Assembly, but do not have the right to vote.

The Council has initiated and overseen extensive efforts to strengthen Nordic co-operation at the political, economic and social level. The intensification of co-operation among European countries, particularly since the mid-1980s, and the dissolution of the former Soviet Union created new challenges for the Nordic Council and Council of Ministers. In 1995 the Nordic Council, meeting in Reykjavík, Iceland, endorsed new guidelines for policy and administrative reform, in response to the region's political developments. Subsequently the Council's activities have focused on the following three areas: intra-Nordic co-operation, with the emphasis on cultural, education and research co-operation; co-operation with the EU and the European Economic Area, where the aim was jointly to promote Nordic values and interests in a broader European context; and co-operation with the Adjacent Areas, i.e. the Baltic States, north-west Russia and the Arctic Area/Barents Sea, where Nordic governments are committed to furthering democracy, security and sustainable development.

STANDING COMMITTEES

Council members are assigned to the following Standing Committees, corresponding to the Council's three pillars for co-operation: the Committee on Nordic Affairs; the Committee on the Adjacent Areas; and the Committee on European Affairs.

PRESIDIUM

The day-to-day work of the Nordic Council is directed by a Presidium, consisting of 11 members of national legislatures. The Presidium is the Council's highest decision-making body between sessions. The Presidium secretariat is headed by a Council Director. Each delegation to the Nordic Council has a secretariat at its national legislature.

PUBLICATIONS

Norden the Top of Europe (monthly newsletter in English, German and French).

The Nordic Council (handbook).

Politik i Norden (newsletter, in the languages of the region).

Yearbook of Nordic Statistics (in English and Swedish).

Books and pamphlets on Nordic co-operation; summaries of Council sessions.

NORDIC COUNCIL OF MINISTERS

Address: Store Strandstraede 18, 1255 Copenhagen K, Denmark.

Telephone: 33-96-02-00; **fax:** 33-96-02-02.

The Governments of Denmark, Finland, Iceland, Norway and Sweden co-operate through the Nordic Council of Ministers. This co-operation is regulated by the Treaty of Co-operation between Denmark, Finland, Iceland, Norway and Sweden of 1962 (amended in 1971, 1974, 1983, 1985 and 1993) and the Treaty between Denmark, Finland, Iceland, Norway and Sweden concerning cultural co-operation of 1971 (amended in 1983 and 1985). Although the Prime Ministers do not meet formally within the Nordic Council of Ministers, they have decided to take a leading role in overall Nordic co-operation. The Ministers of Defence and Foreign Affairs do not meet within the Council of Ministers. These ministers, however, meet on an informal basis.

MEMBERS

Denmark Finland Iceland Norway Sweden

Greenland, the Faroe Islands and the Åland Islands also participate as autonomous regions.

Organization

(January 1998)

COUNCIL OF MINISTERS

The Nordic Council of Ministers holds formal and informal meetings and is attended by ministers with responsibility for the subject under discussion. Each member state also appoints a minister in its own cabinet as Minister for Nordic Co-operation.

Decisions of the Council of Ministers must be unanimous, except for procedural questions, which may be decided by a simple majority of those voting. Abstention constitutes no obstacle to a decision. Decisions are binding on the individual countries, provided that no parliamentary approval is necessary under the constitution of any of the countries. If such approval is necessary, the Council of Ministers must be so informed before its decision.

Meetings are concerned with: agreements and treaties, guidelines for national legislation, recommendations from the Nordic Council, financing joint studies, setting up Nordic institutions.

The Council of Ministers reports each year to the Nordic Council on progress in all co-operation between member states, as well as on future plans.

SECRETARIAT

The Office of the Secretary-General is responsible for co-ordination and legal matters (including co-ordination of work related to the European integration process and to the development of eastern Europe).

The work of the Secretariat is divided into the following departments:

Cultural and educational co-operation, research, advanced education, computer technology;

Budget and administration;

Environmental protection, finance and monetary policy, fisheries, industry and energy, regional policy, agriculture and forestry;

Information;

Labour market issues, social policy and health care, occupational environment, consumer affairs, equal opportunities.

Secretary-General: Søren Christensen (Denmark).

COMMITTEES

Nordic Co-operation Committee: for final preparation of material for the meetings of Ministers of Nordic Co-operation.

Senior Executives' Committees: prepare the meetings of the Council of Ministers and conduct research at its request. There are a number of sub-committees. The Committees cover the subjects listed under the Secretariat (above).

Activities

ECONOMIC CO-OPERATION

Economic co-operation is undertaken in the following areas: freer markets for goods and services; measures on training and employment; elimination of trade barriers; liberalization of capital movements; research and development; export promotion; taxes and other levies; and regional policy.

Nordic Development Fund: f. 1989; supports activities by national administrations for overseas development with resources amounting to SDR 500m.

Nordic Industrial Fund: f. 1973 to provide grants, subsidies and loans for industrial research and development projects of interest to more than one member country.

Nordic Investment Bank: founded under an agreement of December 1975 to provide finance and guarantees for the implementation of investment projects and exports; authorized and subscribed capital 2,400m. IMF special drawing rights. The main sectors of the Bank's activities are energy, metal and wood-processing industries (including petroleum extraction) and manufacturing. In 1982 a separate scheme for financing investments in developing countries was established. In 1997 an Environmental Loan Facility was established to facilitate environmental investments in the Nordic Adjacent Areas.

Nordic Project Fund: f. 1982 to strengthen the international competitiveness of Nordic exporting companies, and to promote industrial co-operation in international projects (e.g. in environmental protection).

NORDTEST: f. 1973 as an inter-Nordic agency for technical testing and standardization of methods and of laboratory accreditation.

RELATIONS WITH THE EU AND EASTERN EUROPE

In 1991 the theme 'Norden in Europe' was regarded as an area of high priority for the coming years by the Council. Nordic co-operation would be used to co-ordinate member countries' participation in the western European integration process, based on EC and EC/EFTA co-operation. Since 1995, when Finland and Sweden acceded to the European Union (joining Denmark, already a member of that organization), Europe and the EU have been an integrated part of the work of Nordic co-operation.

Since 1991 the Nordic Council of Ministers has developed its co-operation relating to the Baltic countries and north-west Russia, in order to contribute to peace, security and stability in Europe. Co-operation measures aim to promote democracy, the establishment of market economies, respect for civil rights and the responsible use of resources in these areas. The Nordic 'Working Programme of the Adjacent Areas' comprises the following three major components: Nordic Information Offices in Tallinn, Riga, Vilnius and St Petersburg, which co-ordinate Nordic projects and activities, promote regional contact at all levels and provide information about the Nordic countries in general and Nordic co-operation specifically; the Nordic-Baltic Scholarship Scheme, which awards grants to students, teachers, scientists, civil servants and parliamentarians; and the Nordic Council of Ministers Project Activities, which in 1997 was to fund 31 projects within the cultural, educational, industrial, housing, agricultural and environmental sectors.

COMMUNICATIONS AND TRANSPORT

The main areas of co-operation have been concerned with international transport, the environment, infrastructure, road research, transport for the disabled and road safety.

EMPLOYMENT

In 1954 an agreement entered into force on a free labour market between Denmark, Finland, Norway and Sweden. Iceland became a party to the agreement in 1982 and the Faroe Islands in 1992. In 1982 an agreement on worker training and job-oriented rehabilitation came into effect. There is a joint centre for labour market training at Övertorneå in Sweden. A convention on the working environment was signed in 1989. The Nordic Institute for Advanced Training in Occupational Health is based in Helsinki, Finland.

GENDER EQUALITY

A Nordic co-operation programme on equality between women and men began in 1974. The main areas of co-operation have been working conditions, education, social welfare and family policy, housing and social planning, and women's participation in politics. In 1995–2000 the main areas of concern were the integration of equality aspects into all areas of society (i.e. 'mainstreaming'), the role of men, and the means of securing equal access for women and men to economic and political processes.

ENVIRONMENT

A new Nordic Strategy for the Environment, adopted in February 1996 for the period 1996–2000, constitutes the overall guidelines for Nordic co-operation in this field. In the Nordic region priority was to be given to nature conservation and the integration of environmental considerations into sectors such as fisheries, agriculture and forestry, finance and energy. Support for the solution of environmental problems was accorded high priority in relation to the areas adjacent to the Nordic region, with monitoring and assessment the key elements of its strategy for the Arctic region. The Nordic countries promote a high level of ambition as the basis for the environmental work conducted in the EU and at an international level.

ENERGY AND INDUSTRY

Co-operation in the energy sector focuses on energy-saving, energy and the environment, the energy market, and the introduction of new and renewable sources of energy.

CONSUMER AFFAIRS

The main areas of co-operation are in safety legislation, consumer education and information and consumers' economic and legal interests.

FOOD AND NUTRITION

Co-operation in this sector began in 1982, and includes projects in food legislation, diet and nutrition, toxicology, risk evaluation and food controls.

AGRICULTURE AND FISHERIES

In 1995 a five-year programme for Nordic co-operation in agriculture and forestry was approved for the period 1996–2000, identifying the following as areas of future co-operation activities: quality production; management of genetic resources; development of regions dependent on agriculture and forestry; and sustainable forestry. Efforts to develop co-operation in both the fisheries and agriculture and forestry sectors have been undertaken with the aim of integrating environmental aspects into the relevant policies and strategies. The four-year programme of co-operation in the Nordic fisheries sector for 1997–2000 aims to strengthen fisheries regulation, management, and research and development. It emphasizes the environmental aspects of the industry, such as the influence of land-based pollution on the sea and the integration of environmentally-compatible techniques into fishing and the on-shore industry.

LAW

The five countries have similar legal systems and tend towards uniformity in legislation and interpretation of law. Much of the preparatory committee work within the national administrations on new legislation involves consultation with the neighbour countries.

Citizens of one Nordic country working in another are in many respects given the status of nationals. In all the Nordic countries they already have the right to vote in local elections in the country of residence. The changing of citizenship from one Nordic country to another has been simplified, and legislation on marriage and on children's rights amended to achieve the greatest possible parity.

There are special extradition facilities between the countries and further stages towards co-operation between the police and the courts have been adopted. In October 1996 justice ministers of the Nordic countries agreed to strengthen police co-operation in order to counter an increase in violent crime perpetrated by gangs. Emphasis is also placed on strengthening co-operation to combat the sexual abuse of children.

There is a permanent Council for Criminology and a Nordic Institute for Maritime Law in Oslo.

REGIONAL POLICY

Under a joint programme, covering the period 1995–99, the Council of Ministers agreed to develop cross-border co-operation between the Nordic countries and co-operation with the EU and the Baltic countries and to give greater priority to exchanging knowledge and information.

SOCIAL WELFARE AND HEALTH

Existing conventions and other co-operation directives ensure that Nordic citizens have the same rights, benefits and obligations in each Nordic country, with regard to sickness, parenthood, occupational injury, unemployment, disablement and old-age pension. Uniform provisions exist concerning basic pension and supplementary pension benefits when moving from one Nordic country to another. In June 1993 Nordic representatives signed an agreement providing for a common Nordic labour market for health professionals. Numerous joint initiatives have been undertaken in the social welfare and health sectors within the framework of the co-operating institutions.

Institutions:
Nordic Centre for the Development of Aids and Appliances for the Handicapped;
Nordic Committee on Disability;
Nordic Committee on Social Security Statistics;
Nordic Council for Alcohol and Drug Research, Helsinki, Finland;
Nordic Council on Medicines, Uppsala, Sweden;
Nordic Education Programme for Social Service Development, Gothenburg, Sweden;
Nordic Medico-statistical Committee;
Nordic School of Public Health, Gothenburg, Sweden;
Nordic Staff Training Centre for Deaf-blind Services, Dronninglund, Denmark;
Scandinavian Institute of Dental Materials.

EDUCATIONAL AND SCIENTIFIC CO-OPERATION

Education: Nordic co-operation in the educational field includes the objective content and means of education, the structure of the educational system and pedagogical development work.

The Nordic Council of Ministers finances the following co-operating bodies, permanent institutions and joint programmes:

- Nordic-Baltic Scholarship Scheme
- Nordic Folk Academy
- Nordic Institute in Finland
- Nordic Language and Literature Courses
- NORDPLUS (Nordic Programme for Mobility of University Students and Teachers)
- Nordic programmes for mobility of pupils, students, and teachers at primary and secondary school level (NORDPLUS-Junior and others)
- Nordic School Data Network
- Nordic Summer University
- Programme of Action for Nordic Language Co-operation
- Steering Committee for Nordic Co-operation on General and Adult Education
- Steering Committee for Nordic Co-operation in Higher Education
- Steering Committee for Nordic Educational Co-operation (primary and secondary school)

Research: Nordic co-operation in research comprises information on research activities and research findings, joint research projects, joint research institutions, the methods and means in research policy, the organizational structure of research and co-ordination of the national research programmes.

Much of the research co-operation activities at the more permanent joint research institutions consists of establishing science contacts in the Nordic areas by means of grants, visiting lecturers, courses and symposia.

The research institutions and research bodies listed below receive continuous financial support via the Nordic cultural budget. In many cases, these joint Nordic institutions ensure a high international standard that would otherwise have been difficult to maintain at a purely national level.

- Nordic Academy for Advanced Study
- Nordic Committee for Bioethics
- Nordic Council for Scientific Information and Research Libraries
- Nordic Folklore Network
- Nordic Institute of Asian Studies
- Nordic Institute of Maritime Law
- Nordic Institute for Theoretical Physics
- Nordic Programme for Arctic Research
- Nordic Sami Institute
- Nordic Science Policy Council
- Nordic Vulcanological Institute
- Research Programme on the Nordic Countries and Europe

Cultural activities: Cultural co-operation is concerned with artistic and other cultural exchange between the Nordic countries; activities relating to libraries, museums, radio, television, and film; promotion of activities within organizations with general cultural aims, including youth and sports organizations; the improvement of conditions for the creative and performing arts; and encouragement for artists and cultural workers. Exhibitions and performances of Nordic culture are organized abroad.

Joint projects include:

- Fund for Mobility of Young Nordic Artists—SLEIPNIR
- Nordic Amateur Theatre Council
- Nordic Art Centre
- Nordic Co-operation in Athletics
- Nordic Council Literature Prize

Nordic Council Music Prize
Nordic Documentation Centre for Mass Communication Research
Nordic Film and Television Fund
Nordic House in the Faroe Islands
Nordic House in Reykjavík
Nordic Institute in Åland
Nordic Institute of Contemporary Art
Nordic Institute in Greenland
Nordic Literature and Libraries Committee
Nordic Music Committee
Nordic Theatre and Dance Committee
Nordic Visual Art Committee
Steering Committee on Culture and Mass Media
Steering Committee on Nordic Cultural Projects Abroad

NORDIC CULTURAL FUND

The Nordic Cultural Fund was established through a separate agreement between the governments of the Nordic countries in 1966, and began operating in 1967, with the aim of supporting the needs of cultural life in the Nordic countries. A Board of 11 members administers and distributes the resources of the Fund and supervises its activities. Five of the members are appointed by the Nordic Council and five by the Nordic Council of Ministers (of culture and education), for a period of two years. The autonomous territories (the Åland islands, the Faroe Islands and Greenland) are represented by one member on the Board, appointed alternately by the Nordic Council and the Nordic Council of Ministers. The Fund is located within and administered by the Secretariat of the Nordic Council of Ministers. It considers applications for assistance for research, education and general cultural activities; grants may also be awarded for the dissemination of information concerning Nordic culture within and outside the region.

FINANCE

Joint expenses are divided according to an agreed scale in proportion to the relative national product of the member countries. The 1998 proposed budget of the Nordic Council of Ministers amounted to 696m. Danish kroner. Various forms of co-operation are also financed directly from the national budgets.

NORTH AMERICAN FREE TRADE AGREEMENT—NAFTA

Address (US headquarters): 14th St, Constitution Ave NW, Room 2061, Washington, DC, USA.

Telephone: (202) 482-5438; **fax:** (202) 482-0148; **e-mail:** info@nafta.org; **internet:** http://www.nafta.net.

The North American Free Trade Agreement (NAFTA) grew out of the free-trade agreement between the USA and Canada that was signed in January 1988 and came into effect on 1 January 1989. Negotiations on the terms of NAFTA, which includes Mexico in the free-trade area, were concluded in October 1992 and the Agreement was signed in December. The accord was ratified in November 1993 and entered into force on 1 January 1994.

MEMBERS

Canada	Mexico	USA

MAIN PROVISIONS OF THE AGREEMENT

Under NAFTA almost all restrictions on trade and investment between Canada, Mexico and the USA were to be gradually removed over a 15-year period. Most tariffs were eliminated immediately on agricultural trade between the USA and Mexico, with tariffs on 6% of agricultural products (including corn, sugar, and some fruits and vegetables) to be abolished over the 15 years. Tariffs on automobiles and textiles were to be phased out over 10 years in all three countries. Mexico was to open its financial sector to US and Canadian investment, with all restrictions to be removed by 2007. Barriers to investment were removed in most sectors, with exemptions for petroleum in Mexico, culture in Canada and airlines and radio communications in the USA. Mexico was to liberalize government procurement, removing preferential treatment for domestic companies over a 10-year period. In transport, heavy goods vehicles were to have complete freedom of movement between the three countries by 2000. An interim measure, whereby transport companies could apply for special licences to travel further within the borders of each country than the existing limit of 20 miles (32 km), was postponed in December 1995, shortly before it was scheduled to come into effect. The postponement was due to concerns, on the part of the US Government, relating to the implementation of adequate safety standards by Mexican truck-drivers.

In the case of a sudden influx of goods from one country to another that adversely affects a domestic industry, the Agreement makes provision for the imposition of short-term 'snap-back' tariffs.

Disputes are to be settled in the first instance by intergovernmental consultation. If a dispute is not resolved within 30 to 40 days, a government may call a meeting of the ministerial, three-member Free Trade Commission. If the Commission is unable to settle the issue a panel of experts in the relevant field is appointed to adjudicate. By September 1996 some 80 trade disputes had been submitted to the Free Trade Commission for adjudication, mostly by private-sector companies. In June of that year Canada and Mexico announced their decision to refer the US 'Helms-Burton' legislation on trade with Cuba to the Commission. They claimed that the legislation, which provides for punitive measures against foreign companies that engage in trade with Cuba, imposed undue restrictions on Canadian and Mexican companies and was, therefore, in contravention of NAFTA. However, at the beginning of 1997 enactment of the Helms-Burton legislation was suspended for a period of six months by the US administration. In April it was suspended for a further six months as part of a compromise agreement with the European Union (see p. 177).

In December 1994 NAFTA members issued a formal invitation to Chile to seek membership of the Agreement. Formal discussions on Chile's entry began in June 1995, but were stalled in December when the US Congress failed to approve 'fast-track' negotiating authority for the US Government, which was to have allowed the latter to negotiate a trade agreement with Chile, without risk of incurring a line-by-line veto from the US Congress. In February 1996 Chile began high-level negotiations with Canada on a wide-ranging bilateral free-trade agreement. Chile, which already had extensive bilateral trade agreements with Mexico, was regarded as advancing its position with regard to NAFTA membership by means of the proposed accord with Canada. The bilateral agreement, which provided for the extensive elimination of customs duties by 2002, was signed in November 1996 and ratified by Chile in July 1997. In September the US Government requested the support of the House of Representatives in its appeal to Congress for 'fast-track' negotiating authority; however, in November the Government was obliged to request the removal of the 'fast-track' proposal from the legislative agenda, owing to insufficient support within Congress.

Formal negotiations aiming to create a Free Trade Area of the Americas (FTAA) were expected to begin in March 1998 in Santiago, Chile. The proposed FTAA was to exist alongside other regional trade associations, including NAFTA.

ADDITIONAL AGREEMENTS

During 1993, as a result of domestic pressure, the new US Government negotiated two 'side agreements' with its NAFTA partners, which were to provide safeguards for workers' rights and the environment. A labour commission was established to monitor implementation of labour accords and to foster co-operation in that area. The North American Council for Environmental Co-operation (CEC) was initiated to combat pollution, to ensure that economic development was not environmentally damaging and to monitor compliance with national and NAFTA environmental regulations. Panels of experts, with representatives from each country, were established to adjudicate in cases of alleged infringement of workers' rights or environmental damage. The panels were given the power to impose fines and trade sanctions, but only with regard to the USA and Mexico; Canada, which was opposed to such measures, was to enforce compliance with NAFTA by means of its own legal system.

In February 1996 the CEC consented for the first time to investigate a complaint brought by environmentalists regarding non-compliance with domestic legislation on the environment. Mexican environmentalists claimed that a company that was planning to build a pier for tourist ships (a project that was to involve damage to a coral reef) had not been required to supply adequate environmental impact studies. The CEC was limited to presenting its findings in such a case, as it could only make a ruling in the case of complaints brought by one NAFTA government against another. The CEC allocates the bulk of its resources to research undertaken to support compliance with legislation and agreements on the environment. However, in October 1997 NAFTA ministers of the environment, meeting in Montréal, Canada, approved a new structure for the CEC's activities. The CEC's main objective was to be the provision of advice concerning the environmental impact of trade issues. It was also agreed that the CEC was further to promote trade in environmentally-sound products and to encourage private-sector investment in environmental trade issues.

With regard to the NAFTA 'side agreement' concerning protection of labour rights, National Administration Offices have been established in each of the three countries in order to monitor labour issues and to address complaints about non-compliance with domestic labour legislation. However, punitive measures in the form of trade sanctions or fines (up to US $20m.) may only be imposed in the specific instances of contravention of national legislation regarding child labour, a minimum wage or health and safety standards. A Commission for Labour Co-operation has been established in Dallas, USA. It incorporates a council of labour ministers of the three NAFTA countries.

In August 1993 the USA and Mexico agreed to establish a Border Environmental Co-operation Commission to monitor the environmental impact of the Agreement on the US–Mexican border area, where industrial activity was expected to intensify. The Commission is located in Ciudad Juaŕez, Mexico. In October 1993 the USA and Mexico concluded an agreement to establish a North American Development Bank (Nadbank), which was to finance environmental and infrastructure projects along the US–Mexican border. Both countries were expected to contribute US $225m. in paid-up capital to cover loans and guarantees over a four-year period.

North American Council for Environmental Co-operation (CEC): 393 rue St Jacques West, Montréal, Québec H2Y IN9, Canada; tel. (514) 350-4300; fax (514) 350-4314; f. 1994; Exec. Dir VÍCTOR LICHTINGER (Mexico).

NORTH ATLANTIC TREATY ORGANIZATION—NATO

Address: 1110 Brussels, Belgium.

Telephone: (2) 707-41-11; **telex:** 23867; **fax:** (2) 707-45-79; **internet:** http://www.nato.int.

The Atlantic Alliance was established on the basis of the 1949 North Atlantic Treaty as a defensive political and military alliance of a group of European states (then numbering 10) and the USA and Canada. The Alliance aims to provide common security for its members through co-operation and consultation in political, military and economic fields, as well as scientific and other non-military aspects. The objectives of the Alliance are implemented by NATO. Following the collapse of the communist governments in central and eastern Europe, from 1989 onwards, and the dissolution of the Warsaw Pact (which had hitherto been regarded as the Alliance's principal adversary) in 1991, NATO has undertaken a fundamental transformation of its structures and policies to meet the new security challenges in Europe (see below).

MEMBERS*

Belgium	Iceland	Spain
Canada	Italy	Turkey
Denmark	Luxembourg	United Kingdom
France	Netherlands	USA
Germany	Norway	
Greece	Portugal	

* Greece and Turkey acceded to the Treaty in 1952, and the Federal Republic of Germany in 1955. France withdrew from the integrated military structure of NATO in 1966, although remaining a member of the Atlantic Alliance; in 1996 France resumed participation in some, but not all, of the military organs of NATO. Spain acceded to the Treaty in 1982, but remained outside the Alliance's integrated military structure; in 1996 the Spanish Government decided to participate fully in a reformed military structure of NATO.

Organization

(February 1998)

NORTH ATLANTIC COUNCIL

The Council, the highest authority of the Alliance, is composed of representatives of the 16 member states. It meets at the level of Permanent Representatives, ministers of foreign affairs, or heads of state and government, and, at all levels, has effective political and decision-making authority. Ministerial meetings are held at least twice a year. At the level of Permanent Representatives the Council meets at least once a week.

The Secretary-General of NATO is Chairman of the Council, and each year a minister of foreign affairs of a member state is nominated honorary President, following the English alphabetical order of countries.

Decisions are taken by common consent and not by majority vote. The Council is a forum for wide consultation between member governments on major issues, including political, military, economic and other subjects, and is supported by the Political Committee, the Military Committee and other subordinate bodies.

PERMANENT REPRESENTATIVES

Belgium: THIERRY DE GRUBEN
Canada: DAVID WRIGHT
Denmark: GUNNAR RIBERHOLDT
France: GÉRARD ERRERA
Germany: Dr HERMANN Freiherr VON RICHTHOFEN
Greece: GEORGE SAVVAIDES
Iceland: THORSTEINN INGÓLFSSON
Italy: GIOVANNI JANNUZZI
Luxembourg: PAUL SCHULLER
Netherlands: NICOLAAS HENDRIK BIEGMANN
Norway: LEIF MEVIK
Portugal: ANTÓNIO MARTINS DA CRUZ
Spain: JAVIER CONDE DE SARO.
Turkey: ONUR ÖYMEN
United Kingdom: Sir JOHN GOULDEN
USA: ALEXANDER R. VERSHBOW

DEFENCE PLANNING COMMITTEE

Most defence matters are dealt with in the Defence Planning Committee, composed of representatives of all member countries except France. The Committee provides guidance to NATO's military authorities and, within the field of its responsibilities, has the same functions and authority as the Council. Like the Council, it meets regularly at ambassadorial level and assembles twice a year in ministerial sessions, when member countries are represented by their ministers of defence.

OTHER COMMITTEES

There are also committees for political affairs, economics, nuclear matters, armaments, defence review, science, the environment, infrastructure, logistics, communications, civil emergency planning, information and cultural relations, and civil and military budgets. In addition, other committees consider specialized subjects such as NATO pipelines, European air space co-ordination, etc. Since 1992 most of these committees consult on a regular basis with representatives from central and eastern European countries.

INTERNATIONAL SECRETARIAT

The Secretary-General is Chairman of the North Atlantic Council, the Defence Planning Committee, the Nuclear Planning Group, and the Committee on the Challenges of Modern Society. He is the head of the International Secretariat, with staff drawn from the member countries. He proposes items for NATO consultation and is generally responsible for promoting consultation and co-operation in accordance with the provisions of the North Atlantic Treaty. He is empowered to offer his help informally in cases of disputes between member countries, to facilitate procedures for settlement.

Secretary-General: Dr JAVIER SOLANA MADARIAGA (Spain).

Deputy Secretary-General: SERGIO BALANZINO (Italy).

There is an Assistant Secretary-General for each of the divisions listed below.

PRINCIPAL DIVISIONS

Division of Political Affairs: maintains political liaison with national delegations and international organizations. Prepares reports on political subjects for the Secretary-General and the Council, and provides the administrative structure for the management of the Alliance's political responsibilities, including arms control. Asst Sec.-Gen. KLAUS-PETER KLAIBER (Germany).

Division of Defence Planning and Policy: studies all matters concerning the defence of the Alliance, and co-ordinates the defence review and other force planning procedures of the Alliance. Asst Sec.-Gen. ANTHONY CRAGG (UK).

Division of Defence Support: promotes the most efficient use of the Allies' resources in the production of military equipment and its standardization. Asst Sec.-Gen. NORMAN W. RAY (USA).

Division of Infrastructure, Logistics and Civil Emergency Planning: supervises the technical and financial aspects of the infrastructure programme. Provides guidance, co-ordination and support to the activities of NATO committees or bodies active in the field of consumer logistics and civil emergency planning. Asst Sec.-Gen. HERPERT VAN FOREEST (Netherlands).

Division of Scientific and Environmental Affairs: advises the Secretary-General on scientific matters of interest to NATO.

Responsible for promoting and administering scientific exchange programmes between member countries, research fellowships, advanced study institutes and special programmes of support for the scientific and technological development of less-advanced member countries. Asst Sec.-Gen. YVES SILLARD (France).

Military Organization

MILITARY COMMITTEE

Composed of the allied Chiefs-of-Staff, or their representatives, of all member countries: the highest military body in NATO under the authority of the Council. Meets at least twice a year at Chiefs-of-Staff level and remains in permanent session with Permanent Military Representatives. It is responsible for making recommendations to the Council and Defence Planning Committee on military matters and for supplying guidance on military questions to Supreme Allied Commanders and subordinate military authorities.

In December 1995 France agreed to rejoin the Military Committee, which it formally left in 1966.

Chairman: Gen. KLAUS NAUMANN (Germany).

Deputy Chairman: Lt-Gen. NICHOLAS B. KEHOE (USA).

INTERNATIONAL MILITARY STAFF

Director: Lt-Gen. G. J. FOLMER (Netherlands).

COMMANDS

Allied Command Europe (ACE): Casteau, Belgium—Supreme Headquarters Allied Powers Europe—SHAPE. Supreme Allied Commander Europe—SACEUR: Gen. WESLEY CLARK (USA).

Allied Command Atlantic (ACLANT): Norfolk, Virginia, USA. Supreme Allied Commander Atlantic—SACLANT: Gen. JOHN J. SHEEHAN (USA).

ALLIED COMMAND EUROPE RAPID REACTION CORPS—ARRC

Bielefeld, Germany; Commander: Lt-Gen. Sir MICHAEL WALKER (UK).

Activities

The common security policy of the members of the North Atlantic Alliance is to safeguard peace through the maintenance of political solidarity and adequate defence at the lowest level of military forces needed to deter all possible forms of aggression. Each year, member countries take part in a Defence Review, designed to assess their contribution to the common defence in relation to their respective capabilities and constraints. Allied defence policy is reviewed periodically by ministers of defence.

Since the 1980s the Alliance has been actively involved in co-ordinating policies with regard to arms control and disarmament issues designed to bring about negotiated reductions in conventional forces, intermediate and short-range nuclear forces and strategic nuclear forces.

Political consultations within the Alliance take place on a permanent basis, under the auspices of the North Atlantic Council (NAC), on all matters affecting the common security interests of the member countries, as well as events outside the North Atlantic Treaty area.

Co-operation in scientific and technological fields as well as co-operation on environmental challenges takes place in the NATO Science Committee and in its Committee on the Challenges of Modern Society. Both these bodies operate an expanding international programme of science fellowships, advance study institutes and research grants.

At a summit meeting of the Conference on Security and Co-operation in Europe (CSCE, now renamed as the Organization for Security and Co-operation in Europe, OSCE, see p. 212) in November 1990, the member countries of NATO and the Warsaw Pact signed an agreement limiting Conventional Armed Forces in Europe (CFE), whereby conventional arms would be reduced to within a common upper limit in each zone. The two groups also issued a Joint Declaration, stating that they were no longer adversaries and that none of their weapons would ever be used 'except in self-defence'. Following the dissolution of the USSR in December 1991, the eight former Soviet republics with territory in the area of application of the CFE Treaty committed themselves to honouring its obligations in June 1992. The Treaty entered retroactively into full force from 17 July (Armenia was unable to ratify it until the end of July, and Belarus until the end of October). In March 1992, under the auspices of the CSCE, the ministers of foreign affairs of the NATO and of the former Warsaw Pact countries (with Russia, Belarus, Ukraine and Georgia taking the place of the USSR) signed the 'Open Skies' treaty. Under this treaty, aerial reconnaissance missions by one country over another were to be permitted, subject to regulation. At the summit meeting of the OSCE in December 1996 the signatories of the CFE Treaty agreed to begin negotiations on a revised treaty governing conventional weapons in Europe. In July 1997 the CFE signatories concluded an agreement on Certain Basic Elements for Treaty Adaptation, which provided for substantial reductions in the maximum levels of conventional military equipment at national and territorial level, replacing the previous bloc-to-bloc structure of the Treaty.

In October 1991 NATO defence ministers endorsed the US decision to withdraw and destroy all its nuclear artillery shells and nuclear warheads for its short-range ballistic missiles in Europe. The ministers also agreed to reduce NATO's stock of airborne nuclear bombs by 50%. These and other measures were to reduce NATO's nuclear arsenal in Europe by 80%.

An extensive review of NATO's structures was initiated in June 1990, in response to the fundamental changes taking place in central and eastern Europe. A ministerial session of the NAC, in June 1991, welcomed the reforms undertaken in central and eastern Europe, noted the increased security of Europe as a whole, and urged greater co-operation between all European states, by means of 'a network of interlocking institutions and relationships'. It acknowledged the role of the CSCE, the European Community (EC) and the Western European Union (WEU) in this context, while at the same time reaffirming NATO's own scope and purpose. In November NATO heads of government, convened in Rome, recommended a radical restructuring of the organization in order to meet the demands of the new security environment, which was to involve further reductions in military forces in Europe, active involvement in international peace-keeping operations, increased co-operation with other international institutions and close co-operation with its former adversaries, the USSR and the countries of eastern Europe. The basis for NATO's new force structure was incorporated into a new Strategic Concept, which was adopted in the Rome Declaration issuing from the summit meeting. The concept provided for the maintenance of a collective defence capability, with a reduced dependence on nuclear weapons. Substantial reductions in the size and levels of readiness of NATO forces were undertaken, in order to reflect the Alliance's strictly defensive nature, and forces were reorganized within a streamlined integrated command structure. Forces were categorized into immediate and rapid reaction forces (including the ACE Rapid Reaction Corps—ARRC, which was inaugurated in October 1992), main defence forces and augmentation forces, which may be used to reinforce any NATO region or maritime areas for deterrence, crisis management or defence. Further reform of the Alliance's command structure was under discussion in 1996, with a reduction in the number of military commands and headquarters proposed. In December 1995 France announced that it was to resume participation in some of NATO's military organs (France had completely withdrawn from NATO's military structure in 1966), while delaying full military reintegration until certain conditions, allowing for greater European influence within the Alliance, were met. In October 1997 the French Government stated that it was not yet ready to reintegrate into the military structure, but would not obstruct any reorganization of the Alliance. In November 1996 the Spanish legislature voted to approve Spain's full integration into NATO's military structure in the light of the Alliance's proposed internal restructuring and with a reassertion of Spain's non-nuclear status. Discussions on a new command structure were hindered during 1997 by bilateral disagreements within the Alliance, notably between the United Kingdom and Spain regarding Spanish restrictions on the use of Gibraltar for military manoeuvres. In early December the United Kingdom withdrew its opposition to the establishment of a NATO command in Spain, enabling the Military Committee to approve a new command structure, but warned that it would obstruct Spain's planned integration into NATO'S military structure if no permanent solution to the use of Gibraltar bases was reached. The NAC, meeting at ministerial level in mid-December, endorsed the new military structure, which envisaged a reduction in the number of NATO command headquarters from 65 to 20, and instructed the military authorities of the Alliance to formulate a plan for the transitional process.

In January 1994 NATO heads of state and government welcomed the entry into force of the Maastricht Treaty, establishing the European Union (EU, superseding the EC). The Treaty included an agreement on the development of a common foreign and security policy, which was intended to be a mechanism to strengthen the European pillar of the Alliance. Regular joint NATO-WEU meetings are convened to discuss means of strengthening practical co-operation between the two groupings. In May 1995 NATO's ministers of foreign affairs supported a decision by WEU's Council of Ministers to improve the Union's operational capabilities through new mechanisms and force structures, which could be employed within the framework of NATO. In November the first memorandum of understanding between the two organizations was signed, to provide for full access to each other's communications capabilities; and in May 1996 NATO and WEU signed a security agreement concerning the safeguarding of classified material provided by either organization.

In June 1996 NATO ministers of foreign affairs reached agreement on the implementation of the 'Combined Joint Task Force (CJTF) concept', which had been adopted in January 1994. Measures were to be taken to establish the 'nuclei' of these task forces at certain NATO headquarters, which would provide the basis for missions that could be activated at short notice for specific purposes such as crisis management and peace-keeping. It was also agreed to make CJTFs available for operations undertaken by WEU. In conjunction with this, WEU was to be permitted to make use of Alliance hardware and capabilities (in practice, mostly belonging to the USA) subject to the endorsement of the NAC. This development represented the evolving construction of a European Security and Defence Identity (EDSI) within NATO. In November 1996 NATO and the European Commission met at a senior level for the first time in order to discuss a joint strategy for the enlargement of the Alliance and the EU respectively, to include former eastern bloc countries (see below). In order to support an integrated security structure in Europe, NATO also co-operates with the OSCE and has provided assistance for the development of the latter's conflict prevention and crisis management activities.

The enlargement of NATO, through the admission of new members from the former USSR and eastern and central European countries, was considered to be a progressive means of contributing to the enhanced stability and security of the Euro-Atlantic area. In January 1994 NATO heads of state and government reaffirmed this objective. However, the contentious nature of the issue, in particular the strong opposition on the part of the Russian Government to NATO's expansion, has resulted in a more cautious approach than was initially envisaged. In December 1996 NATO ministers of foreign affairs announced that invitations to join the Alliance would be issued to some former eastern bloc countries at a summit meeting that was to be held in Madrid in mid-1997. The NATO Secretary-General and member governments subsequently began intensive diplomatic efforts to secure Russia's tolerance of these developments. It was agreed that no nuclear weapons or large numbers of troops would be deployed on the territory of any new member country in the former Eastern bloc. In March 1997 the Presidents of the USA and Russia met to pursue negotiations on the future of Russian relations with NATO and to discuss further arms control measures. In May NATO and Russia signed the Founding Act on Mutual Relations, Co-operation and Security, which provided for enhanced Russian participation in all NATO decision-making activities, equal status in peace-keeping operations and representation at the Alliance headquarters at ambassadorial level, as part of a recognized shared political commitment to maintaining stability and security throughout the Euro-Atlantic region. A NATO-Russian Permanent Joint Council was established under the Founding Act, and met for the first time in July; the Council provided each side the opportunity for consultation and participation in the other's security decisions, but without a right of veto. At the end of May, NATO ministers of foreign affairs, meeting in Sintra, Portugal, concluded an agreement with Ukraine providing for enhanced co-operation between the two sides; the so-called Charter on a Distinctive Relationship was signed at the NATO summit meeting held in Madrid, Spain, in July. At that time NATO heads of state and government formally invited the Czech Republic, Hungary and Poland to begin accession negotiations, with the aim of extending membership to those countries in April 1999. Romania and Slovenia were expected to be invited to join the Alliance before 2000, while the meeting also recognized the Baltic States as aspiring members. During 1997 concern was expressed on the part of some member governments with regard to the cost of expanding the Alliance; however, in November the initial cost of incorporating the Czech Republic, Hungary and Poland into NATO was officially estimated at US $1,300m. over a 10-year period, which was widely deemed to be an acceptable figure. The Madrid summit meeting in July endorsed the establishment of a Mediterranean Co-operation Group to enhance NATO relations with Egypt, Israel, Jordan, Mauritania, Morocco and Tunisia. The Group was to provide a forum for regular political dialogue between the two groupings and to promote co-operation in training, scientific research and information exchange.

EURO-ATLANTIC PARTNERSHIP COUNCIL—EAPC

The EAPC was inaugurated on 30 May 1997 as a successor to the North Atlantic Co-operation Council (NACC), that had been established in December 1991 as an integral part of NATO's new Strategic Concept, to provide a forum for consultation on political and security matters with the countries of central and eastern Europe, including the former Soviet republics. An EAPC Council was to meet monthly at ambassadorial level and twice a year at ministerial level. It was to be supported in its work by a steering committee and a political committee. The EAPC was to pursue the NACC Work Plan for Dialogue, Partnership and Co-operation and incorporate it into a new Work Plan, which was to include an expanded political dimension of consultation and co-operation among participating states. The Partnership for Peace (PfP) programme, which was established in January 1994 within the framework of the NACC, was to remain an integral element of the new co-operative mechanism. The PfP incorporated practical military and defence-related co-operation activities that had originally been part of the NACC Work Plan. Participation in the PfP requires an initial signature of a framework agreement, establishing the common principles and objectives of the partnership, the submission of a presentation document, indicating the political and military aspects of the partnership and the nature of future co-operation activities, and thirdly, the development of individual partnership programmes establishing country-specific objectives. In June 1994 Russia, which had previously opposed the strategy as being the basis for future enlargement of NATO, signed the PfP framework document, which included a declaration envisaging an 'enhanced dialogue' between the two sides. Despite its continuing opposition to any enlargement of NATO, in May 1995 Russia agreed to sign a PfP Individual Partnership Programme, as well as a framework document for NATO-Russian dialogue and co-operation beyond the PfP. During 1994 a partnership co-ordination cell, incorporating representatives of all partnership countries, became operational in Mons, Belgium. The cell, which was under the authority of the NAC, was to conduct military co-ordination and planning in order to implement PfP programmes. The first joint military exercises with countries of the former Warsaw Pact were conducted in September. NATO began formulating a PfP Status of Forces Agreement (SOFA) to define the legal status of Allies' and partners' forces when they are present on each other's territory; the PfP SOFA was opened for signature in June 1995. The new EAPC was to provide a framework for the development of an enhanced PfP programme, which NATO envisaged would become an essential element of the overall European security structure. Accordingly, the military activities of the PfP were to be expanded to include all Alliance missions and incorporate all NATO committees into the PfP process, thus providing for greater co-operation in crisis management, civil emergency planning and training activities. In addition, all PfP member countries were to participate in the CJTF concept through a structure of Partners Staff Elements, working at all levels of the Alliance military structure. Defence ministers of NATO and partner countries were to meet regularly to provide the political guidance for the enhanced Planning and Review Process of the PfP. By December 1997 27 countries were participating in the PfP.

PEACE-KEEPING ACTIVITIES

A meeting of the NATO ministers of foreign affairs which took place in Oslo, Norway, in June 1992 announced the Alliance's readiness to support peace-keeping operations under the aegis of the CSCE on a case-by-case basis: NATO would make both military resources and expertise available to such operations. In July NATO, in co-operation with WEU, undertook a maritime operation in the Adriatic Sea to monitor compliance with the UN Security Council's resolutions imposing sanctions against the Yugoslav republics of Serbia and Montenegro. In October NATO was requested to provide, staff and finance the military headquarters of the United Nations peace-keeping force in Bosnia and Herzegovina, the UN Protection Force in Yugoslavia (UNPROFOR). In November the UN Security Council gave the NATO/WEU operation in the Adriatic powers to stop and search ships suspected of flouting the blockade of Serbia and Montenegro. (The NATO/WEU maritime blockade was formally terminated in October 1996.) In December 1992 NATO ministers of foreign affairs expressed the Alliance's readiness to support peace-keeping operations under the authority of the UN Security Council; in that month NATO began formal military planning of operations designed to help bring an end to hostilities in Bosnia and Herzegovina. From April 1993 NATO fighter and reconnaissance aircraft began patrolling airspace over Bosnia and Herzegovina in order to enforce the UN prohibition of military aerial activity over the country. In addition, from July NATO aircraft provided protective cover for UNPROFOR troops operating in the 'safe areas' established by the UN Security Council. In August the North Atlantic Council endorsed operational plans to conduct air attacks, at the request of the UN, to defend the designated 'safe areas'. NATO began to formulate options for air attacks, which subsequently served as some deterrent against attacks on the 'safe areas', and in February 1994 conducted the first of several aerial strikes against artillery positions that were violating heavy-weapons exclusion zones imposed around 'safe areas' and threatening the civilian populations. Throughout the conflict the Alliance also provided transport, communications and logistics to support UN humanitarian assistance in the region.

The peace accord for the former Yugoslavia, which was initialled in Dayton, USA, in November 1995, and signed in Paris in December, provided for the establishment of a NATO-led Implementation Force (IFOR) to ensure compliance with the treaty, in accordance with a strictly defined timetable and under the authority of a UN Security Council mandate. In early December a joint meeting of allied foreign and defence ministers endorsed the military structure for the peace mission, entitled Operation Joint Endeavour, which was to involve approximately 60,000 troops from 31 NATO and non-NATO countries. The Operation was to include a Russian contingent, under an agreement that granted Russia access to the consultation and decision-making processes affecting participating troops. The mission was to be under the overall authority of the Supreme Allied Commander Europe, with the Commander of the ARRC providing command on the ground. The operation was to serve three separate sectors—the North, with force headquarters in Tuzla; the South-West, with forces based in Gornji Vakuf; and the South-East, based in Mostar—under immediate US, British and French command, respectively. A small contingent of specialist troops and technicians was dispatched immediately to prepare for the arrival of IFOR. IFOR, which constituted NATO's largest military operation ever, formally assumed responsibility for peace-keeping in Bosnia and Herzegovina from the UN on 20 December.

By mid-1996 the military aspects of the Dayton peace agreement had largely been implemented under IFOR supervision. The former warring parties had withdrawn behind agreed lines of separation by the end of January, and by the end of March the majority of the prisoners of war held by the different factions had been released. Territory was exchanged between the two Bosnian 'entities', although IFOR was criticized for failing to prevent widespread destruction in suburbs of Sarajevo that were being vacated by Bosnian Serbs on the transfer of the districts to Bosnian Federation control (see chapter on Bosnia and Herzegovina). Substantial progress was achieved in the demobilization of soldiers and militia and in the cantonment of heavy weaponry. However, in August and September the Bosnian Serbs obstructed IFOR weapons inspections and the force was obliged to threaten the Serbs with strong military retaliation to secure access to the arms sites. During 1996 IFOR personnel undertook many activities relating to the civilian reconstruction of Bosnia and Herzegovina, including the repair of roads, railways and bridges; reconstruction of schools and hospitals; delivery of emergency food and water supplies; and emergency medical transportation. IFOR also co-operated with, and provided logistical support for, the Office of the High Representative of the International Community in Bosnia and Herzegovina, which was charged with overseeing implementation of the civilian aspects of the Bosnian peace accord. IFOR assisted the OSCE in preparing for and overseeing the all-Bosnia legislative elections that were held in September. IFOR also provided security for displaced Bosnians who crossed the inter-entity boundary in order to vote in their towns of origin. In December NATO ministers of foreign affairs approved a follow-on force for Bosnia and Herzegovina, with an 18-month mandate, to be known as the Stabilization Force (SFOR). SFOR was to be about one-half the size of IFOR, but was to retain 'the same unity of command and robust rules of engagement' as the previous force. However, NATO failed to give SFOR an increased mandate to pursue and arrest indicted war criminals, whose prosecution at the International Criminal Tribunal for the Former Yugoslavia (see p.21), in The Hague, was widely regarded as essential for the success of the Bosnian peace process. SFOR became operational on 20 December. Its principal objective was to maintain a safe environment at a military level to ensure that the civil aspects of the Dayton peace accord could be fully implemented, including the completion of the de-mining process, the repatriation of refugees and preparations for municipal elections. In July 1997 NATO heads of government expressed their support for a more determined implementation of SFOR's mandate permitting the arrest of people sought by the International Criminal Tribunal for the Former Yugoslavia if they were discovered within the normal course of duties. A few days later troops serving under SFOR seized two former Serb officials who had been indicted on charges of genocide. One man died in the assault. In December two Croats suspected of having committed war crimes were arrested by SFOR officers. From mid-1997 SFOR assisted efforts by the Bosnian Serb President, Biljana Plavšić, to maintain the security and territorial integrity of the Republika Srpska in the face of violent opposition from nationalist supporters of the former President, Radovan Karadžić, based in Pale. In August NATO authorized SFOR to use force to prevent the use of the local media to incite violence, following attacks on multinational forces by Serb nationalists during attempts to regain control of police buildings. In October SFOR seized radio and television transmitters, which had allegedly been exploited by Karadžić supporters. In November SFOR provided the general security framework, as well as logistical and communications assistance, in support of the OSCE's supervision of legislative elections that were conducted in the Republika Srpska. In December NATO ministers of defence confirmed that SFOR would be maintained at its current strength of some 31,000 troops until the expiry of its mandate in June 1998, and that subsequently some form of international military presence in Bosnia and Herzegovina was essential. An agreement on a successor operation to SFOR was concluded in February 1998.

NATO AGENCIES

1. Civilian production and logistics organizations responsible to the Council:

Central European Operating Agency—CEOA: Versailles, France; f. 1957 to supervise the integrated military pipeline network in central Europe.

Nato Airborne Early Warning and Control Programme Management Organisation—NAPMO: Brunssum, Netherlands; f. 1978 to manage the procurement aspects of the NATO Airborne Early Warning and Control System.

NATO Consultation Command and Control Organization—NC3O: Brussels, Belgium; f. 1997 by restructuring of the NATO Communications and Information Systems Organization and the Tri-Service Group on Communications and Electronics; decides on policies and interoperability, supervises planning and implementation, and operates and maintains communications and information systems for tactical and strategic integrated services, including voice, data, fax, video (tele)conferencing and automated command and control capability for crisis management, consultation of the NATO nations and the command and control of NATO forces.

NATO European Fighter Aircraft Development, Production and Logistics Management Organisation—NEFMO: Munich, Germany; f. 1987; mems: Germany, Italy, Spain, United Kingdom.

NATO HAWK Management Office: 26 rue Galliéni, 92500 Rueil-Malmaison, France; tel. 1-47-08-75-00; telex 634176; fax 1-47-52-10-99; f. 1959 to supervise the multinational production and upgrading programmes of the HAWK surface-to-air missile system in Europe; Gen. Man. Gen. F. BARTONE.

NATO Maintenance and Supply Agency—NAMSA: Luxembourg; f. 1958; supplies spare parts and logistic support for a number of jointly-used weapon systems, missiles and electronic systems; all member nations except Iceland participate.

NATO MRCA Development and Production Management Organisation—NAMMO: Munich, Germany; f. 1969 to supervise development and production of the Multi-Role Combat Aircraft project; mems: Germany, Italy, United Kingdom.

2. Responsible to the Military Committee:

Allied Communications Security Agency—ACSA: Brussels, Belgium; f. 1953.

Allied Data Systems Interoperability Agency—ADSIA: Brussels, Belgium; f. 1979 to improve interoperability within the NATO Command, Control and Information Systems.

Allied Long Lines Agency—ALLA: Brussels, Belgium; f. 1951 to formulate policies to meet the long lines communications requirements of NATO.

Allied Naval Communications Agency—ANCA: London, United Kingdom; f. 1951 to establish reliable communications for maritime operations.

Allied Radio Frequency Agency—ARFA: Brussels, Belgium; f. 1951 to establish policies concerned with military use of the radio frequency spectrum.

Allied Tactical Communications Agency—ATCA: Brussels, Belgium; f. 1972 to establish policies concerned with tactical communications for land and air operations.

Military Agency for Standardization—MAS: Brussels, Belgium; f. 1951 to improve military standardization of equipment for NATO forces.

NATO Defense College—NADEFCOL: Rome, Italy; f. 1951 to train officials for posts in NATO organizations or in national ministries.

Research and Technology Organization—RTO: 7 rue Ancelle, Neuilly-sur-Seine, France; tel. 1-55-61-22-00; telex 610176; fax 1-55-61-22-99; f. 1996 by merger of the Advisory Group for Aerospace Research and Development and the Defence Research Group; brings together scientists and engineers from member countries for exchange of information and research co-operation; provides scientific and technical advice for the Military Committee, for other NATO bodies and for member nations; comprises a Research and Technology Board and a Research and Technology Agency, responsible for implementing RTO's work programme.

3. Responsible to Supreme Allied Commander Atlantic (SACLANT):

SACLANT Undersea Research Centre—SACLANTCEN: La Spezia, Italy; f. 1962 for research in submarine detection and oceanographic problems.

4. Responsible to Supreme Allied Commander Europe (SACEUR):

SHAPE Technical Centre—STC: The Hague, Netherlands; f. 1960 to provide scientific and technical advice, originally on the formation of an integrated air defence system, subsequently on a broader programme covering force capability and structure; command and control; communications.

FINANCE

As NATO is an international, not a supra-national, organization, its member countries themselves decide the amount to be devoted to their defence effort and the form which the latter will assume. Thus, the aim of NATO's defence planning is to develop realistic military plans for the defence of the alliance at reasonable cost. Under the annual defence planning process, political, military and economic factors are considered in relation to strategy, force requirements and available resources. The procedure for the co-ordination of military plans and defence expenditures rests on the detailed and comparative analysis of the capabilities of member countries. All installations for the use of international forces are financed under a common-funded infrastructure programme. In accordance with the terms of the Partnership for Peace strategy, partner countries undertake to make available the necessary personnel, assets, facilities and capabilities to participate in the programme. The countries also share the financial cost of military exercises in which they participate.

PUBLICATIONS

NATO publications (in English and French, with some editions in other languages) include:

NATO Basic Fact Sheets.

NATO Facts and Figures.

NATO Final Communiqués.

NATO Handbook.

NATO Review (quarterly in 11 languages; annual edition in Icelandic).

Economic and scientific publications.

ORGANISATION FOR ECONOMIC CO-OPERATION AND DEVELOPMENT—OECD

Address: 2 rue André-Pascal, 75775 Paris Cédex 16, France.

Telephone: 1-45-24-82-00; **telex:** 640048; **fax:** 1-45-24-85-00; **internet:** http://www.oecd.org.

OECD was founded in 1961, replacing the Organisation for European Economic Co-operation (OEEC) which had been established in 1948 in connection with the Marshall Plan. It constitutes a forum where representatives of the governments of the industrialized democracies discuss and attempt to co-ordinate their economic and social policies.

MEMBERS

Australia	Hungary	Norway
Austria	Iceland	Poland
Belgium	Ireland	Portugal
Canada	Italy	Spain
Czech Republic	Japan	Sweden
Denmark	Republic of Korea	Switzerland
Finland	Luxembourg	Turkey
France	Mexico	United Kingdom
Germany	Netherlands	USA
Greece	New Zealand	

The European Commission also takes part in OECD's work.

Organization

(January 1998)

COUNCIL

The governing body of OECD is the Council on which each member country is represented. The Council meets from time to time (usually once a year) at the level of government ministers, and regularly at official level, when it comprises the heads of Permanent Delegations to OECD (diplomatic missions headed by ambassadors). It is responsible for all questions of general policy and may establish subsidiary bodies as required to achieve the aims of the Organisation. Decisions and recommendations of the Council are adopted by mutual agreement of all its members. The Chairman of the Council at ministerial level is a member of government from the country elected to the chairmanship for that year. The Chairman of the Council at official level is the Secretary-General.

Heads of Permanent Delegations (with ambassadorial rank):

Australia: RALPH HILLMAN
Austria: PETER JANKOWITSCH
Belgium: PIERRE-DOMINIQUE SCHMIDT
Canada: KIMON VALASKAKIS
Czech Republic: JAROMÍR PRIVRATSKY
Denmark: FLEMMING HEDEGAARD
Finland: ILKKA RISTIMAKI
France: MARIE-CLAUDE CABANA
Germany: WERNER KAUFMANN-BÜHLER
Greece: SPYROS LIOUKAS
Hungary: LÁSZLÓ BALOGH
Iceland: SVERRIR HAUKUR GUNNLAUGSSON
Ireland: PATRICK O'CONNOR
Italy: ALESSANDRO VATTANI
Japan: YOSHIJI NOGAMI
Republic of Korea: BOHN-YOUNG KOO
Luxembourg: PAUL MERTZ
Mexico: FRANCISCO SUÁREZ DAVILA
Netherlands: EGBERT JACOBS
New Zealand: RICHARD WOODS
Norway: MARTIN ØLBERG
Poland: JAN WORONIECKI
Portugal: JORGE DE LEMOS GODINHO
Spain: JOSÉ LUIS FEITO HIGUERUELA
Sweden: ANDERS FERM
Switzerland: JEAN-PIERRE ZEHNDER
Turkey: AKIN ALPTUNA
United Kingdom: PETER VEREKER
USA: AMY BONDURANT

Participant with Special Status:

European Commission: PIERGIORGIO MAZZOCCHI (Italy).

EXECUTIVE COMMITTEE

Each year the Council designates 14 of its members to form the Executive Committee which prepares the work of the Council. It is also called upon to carry out specific tasks where necessary. Apart from its regular meetings, the Committee meets occasionally in special sessions attended by senior government officials.

SECRETARIAT

The Council, the committees and other bodies in OECD are assisted by an independent international secretariat headed by the Secretary-General. In 1996 a new position, that of Executive Director (responsible for the management of administrative support services), was created.

Secretary-General: DONALD J. JOHNSTON (Canada).

Deputy Secretaries-General: KUMIHARU SHIGEHARA (Japan), THORVALD MOE (Norway), SALVATORE ZECCHINI (Italy).

Executive Director: JEAN-JACQUES NOREAU (Canada).

AUTONOMOUS AND SEMI-AUTONOMOUS BODIES

Centre for Educational Research and Innovation—CERI: f. 1968; includes all member countries. Dir THOMAS J. ALEXANDER (see also under Education, Employment, Labour and Social Affairs, below).

Club du Sahel: f. 1976; an informal forum of donor countries and member states of the Permanent Inter-State Committee on Drought Control in the Sahel (see p. 262). Dir ROY STACEY.

Development Centre: f. 1962; includes all member countries except Australia and New Zealand. Pres. JEAN BONVIN (see also under Development Co-operation, below).

European Conference of Ministers of Transport (see p. 311).

International Energy Agency (see p. 211).

Nuclear Energy Agency (see p. 211).

Activities

The greater part of the work of OECD, which covers all aspects of economic and social policy, is prepared and carried out in about 200 specialized bodies (Committees, Working Parties, etc.); all members are normally represented on these bodies, except on those of a restricted nature. Participants are usually civil servants coming either from the capitals of member states or from the Permanent Delegations to OECD.

ECONOMIC POLICY

The main organ for the consideration and direction of economic policy among the member countries is the Economic Policy Committee, which comprises governments' chief economic advisors and central bankers, and meets two or three times a year to review the economic and financial situation and policies of member countries. It has several working parties and groups, the most important of which are Working Party No. 1 on Macro-Economic and Structural Policy Analysis, Working Party No. 3 on Policies for the Promotion of Better International Payments Equilibrium and the Working Group on Short-Term Economic Prospects.

The Economic and Development Review Committee is responsible for the annual examination of the economic situation of each member country. Usually, a report is issued each year on each country, after an examination carried out by a panel of representatives of a number of other member countries; this process of mutual examination has been extended also to other branches of the Organisation's work (agriculture, manpower and social affairs, scientific policy and development aid efforts).

ENERGY

Work in the field of energy includes co-ordination of members' energy policies, assessment of short-, medium- and long-term energy prospects; a long-term programme of energy conservation, development of alternative energy sources and energy research and development; a system of information on the international oil and energy markets; and improvement of relations between oil-producing and oil-consuming countries. This work is carried out in OECD's International Energy Agency (IEA, see below), as well as within the context of OECD as a whole under the Committee for Energy Policy. Co-operation in the development of nuclear power is undertaken by the Nuclear Energy Agency (see below).

DEVELOPMENT CO-OPERATION

The Development Assistance Committee (DAC) consists of representatives of the main OECD capital-exporting countries; it discusses methods for making national resources available for assisting countries and areas in the process of economic development anywhere in the world, and for expanding and improving the flow of development assistance and other long-term funds. In May 1996 DAC recommended that foreign aid be assessed on the basis of its economic and social impact, in order to increase the efficiency of development assistance and to stimulate donor funding. In May 1997 DAC approved new guidelines for development assistance aiming to promote peace and prevent conflict.

The Group on North-South Economic Issues deals with the wide range of subjects involved in economic relationships between OECD countries and developing countries. It is particularly concerned with the treatment of these issues in the various fora of international economic discussion, such as UNCTAD.

A Technical Co-operation Committee has the task of drawing up and supervising the programmes of technical assistance arranged for the benefit of member countries, or areas of member countries, in the process of development.

The OECD Development Centre (a semi-autonomous body) was set up in 1962 for the collection and dissemination of information in the field of economic development, research into development problems and the training of specialists both from the industrialized and developing countries.

The OECD Centre for Co-operation with Economies in Transition (CCET) was established in 1990 to assist central and eastern European countries in their transition to a market economy and to pluralistic democracy. The Centre, which in 1997 had a budget of some 93.5m. French francs, has since expanded its activities to assist all newly-independent republics of the former Soviet Union, Mongolia and Viet Nam. The Centre designs and manages OECD's programme of activities in support of economic reform in these countries and acts as a focal point for access to OECD expertise, as well as for all contacts with the participating countries and with other international organizations working in the same field. The Centre operates a Register of information and statistical data, which is used to analyse assistance efforts and to promote multilateral collaboration. The Centre's Partners in the Transition Programme was initiated in 1991 to address the specific reform needs of the Czech Republic, Hungary, Poland and Slovakia. In June 1994 the Council agreed to commence negotiations for accession to the OECD with these countries. The Czech Republic became a member of the organization in November 1995; Hungary and Poland joined in March and July 1996 respectively. Following the conclusion of a co-operation agreement between the OECD and Russia in June 1994, the Centre developed a programme specifically for that country. The programme aimed to facilitate the development of macroeconomic stabilization and the development of market-orientated institutions and structures. In May 1996 Russia applied to join the OECD. In May 1997 OECD agreed to establish a Liaison Committee to strengthen economic co-operation with Russia and to promote the liberalization of its economy, prior to that country's accession. Other country-specific programmes have been developed for Bulgaria, Romania and Slovenia.

During 1995 the OECD broadened its policy dialogue with 'dynamic non-member countries'. Two new programmes were initiated: the Programme of Dialogue and Co-operation with China and the Emerging Market Economy Forum.

INTERNATIONAL TRADE

The activities of the Trade Committee are aimed at maintaining the degree of trade liberalization achieved, avoiding the emergence of new trade barriers, and improving further the liberalization of trade on a multilateral and non-discriminatory basis. These activities include examination of issues concerning trade relations among member countries as well as relations with non-member countries, in particular developing countries, countries of central and east Europe and the former Soviet Union. The existing procedures allow, inter alia, any member country to obtain prompt consideration and discussions by the Trade Committee of trade measures taken by another member country which adversely affect its own interests. The Committee also considers the challenges that are presented to the existing international trading system by the process of globalization of production and markets and the ensuing deeper integration of national economies. OECD provided support to the multilateral trade negotiations conducted under the General Agreement on Tariffs and Trade (GATT), assisting member countries to analyse the effects of the trade accords and promoting its global benefits. Following the conclusion of the negotiations in December 1993, and the entry into force of the World Trade Organization (WTO) agreements in 1995, OECD has continued to study and assess aspects of the international trade agenda, such as integrating emerging market economies into the international trading system, trade and environment, trade and competition policy, trade and investment and trade and industry. In 1993 OECD ministers adopted the first set of procedural guidelines to help governments to improve the compatibility of trade and environment policies.

FINANCIAL, FISCAL AND ENTERPRISE AFFAIRS

The progressive abolition of obstacles to the international flow of services and capital is the responsibility of various OECD Committees, with the overall objective of promoting the efficient functioning of markets and enterprises and strengthening the multilateral framework for trade and investments. The Committee on Capital Movements and Invisible Transactions monitors the implementation of the Codes of Liberalization of Invisible Transactions and of Capital Movements. The Committee on International Investment and Multinational Enterprises prepared a Code of Behaviour (called 'Guidelines') for multinational enterprises, on the basis of recommendations of member governments. A Declaration on International Investment and Multinational Enterprises, while non-binding, contains commitments on the conduct and treatment of foreign-owned enterprises established in member countries. The harmonization of national competition policies and procedures for international mergers is reviewed by the Committee on Competition and Policy. A Committee on Financial Markets aims to support policies to improve structural and regulatory conditions in financial markets, to promote international trade in financial services, to promote the integration of non-member countries into the global financial system and to improve financial statistics. The Committee on Fiscal Affairs has recently focused its efforts on the tax implications of the globalization of national economies. Its activities include promoting the removal of tax barriers and monitoring the implementation and impact of major tax reforms. Other specialized committees have been set up to deal with tourism, consumer policy and insurance.

In May 1995 the OECD Council initiated negotiations for a Multilateral Agreement on Investment (MAI), which was to provide a framework for international investment, incorporating high standards for the liberalization of investment regimes and protection and effective dispute settlement procedures. The Agreement was expected to be concluded by mid-1998.

In May 1997 the OECD Council endorsed plans to introduce a global ban on the corporate bribery of public officials. A convention on commercial corruption was signed in December, and was expected to enter into force by the end of 1998.

FOOD, AGRICULTURE AND FISHERIES

The Committee for Agriculture reviews major developments in agricultural policies, deals with the adaptation of agriculture to changing economic conditions, elaborates forecasts of production and market prospects for the major commodities, promotes the use of sustainable practices in the sector, holds consultations on import and export practices and assesses implications of world developments in food and agriculture for member countries' policies. A separate Fisheries Committee carries out similar tasks in its own sector.

ENVIRONMENT

The basic structure of OECD's work in this field is outlined by its 'Environmental Strategy for the 1990s', which aims to integrate environmental and economic decision-making, to improve environmental performance (including the reduction of pollution) and to expand international co-operation. Responsibility for implementing the programme lies principally with the Environment Policy Committee and other inter-committee working groups. OECD has supported international efforts to implement Agenda 21, a framework for environmentally sustainable development that was adopted at the UN Conference on Environment and Development in June 1992. Other technical assistance is provided to decision-makers at national level to promote the incorporation of environmental concerns into new policies, regulations, etc. Countries are encouraged to implement activities to reduce pollution and to manage waste; their compliance with internationally-agreed standards is monitored through a programme of Country Environmental Peformance Reviews. A central part of OECD's environment programme focuses on chemicals, specifically the prevention and reduction of risks to health and the environment from chemicals, the harmonization of policies and regulations relating to chemicals, the promotion of integrated approaches to chemical testing, data and management extending OECD expertise in this field to non-member countries. A Joint Session of Trade and Environment Experts considers interrelated issues, such as the effects of trade liberalization on the environment, processes and production methods and the harmonization of environmental policies and requirements.

OECD's Group on Urban Affairs is concerned with economic, social and administrative issues in cities, as well as ecological aspects of the built-up environment.

SCIENCE, TECHNOLOGY AND INDUSTRY

The principal objective of the Directorate for Science, Technology and Industry is to enhance member countries' understanding of how scientific development, technology and structural change may contribute to economic growth, employment and social development. The Committee for Scientific and Technological Policy reviews national and international policy issues relating to the sector and promotes the development of national science systems to expand scientific training and education, and to involve all elements of the scientific community in the formulation and funding of science projects. A Megascience Forum was established in 1992 to strengthen co-operation in specific disciplines, e.g. global change and oceanography. At a ministerial meeting of the Committee, convened in September 1995, the Forum's mandate was extended for a further three years; it was to inform governments and assist in the planning of large science projects and review policy issues relevant to the successful implementation of multilateral projects. The meeting also formulated a set of principles to facilitate international technical co-operation involving enterprises, which was subsequently adopted by the Council.

The Committee for Information, Computer and Communications Policy monitors developments in telecommunications and information technology and their impact on competitiveness and productivity, promotes the development of new rules (e.g. guidelines on information security), and analyses trade and liberalization issues. In 1995 OECD initiated a study of the development of the global information infrastructure and its effect on economic and social systems.

The Industry Committee regularly reviews industrial policies, trends and the situation in industry in member countries; since 1990 reviews have also been undertaken in some central and eastern European countries and dynamic Asian economies. The Committee is also concerned with subsidies, structural adjustment, the implication of globalization, i.e. transborder operations, of industrial enterprises and regional development policies. A working party on small and medium-sized enterprises (SMEs) conducts an ongoing review on the contribution of SMEs to growth and employment in member and non-member countries. The Maritime Transport and Steel Committees aim to promote multilateral solutions to sectoral friction and instability based on the definition and monitoring of rules. In June 1994 negotiations between leading ship-building nations, conducted under OECD auspices, concluded a multilateral agreement to end state subsidies to the industry. In 1996 failure by the US Congress to ratify the agreement disrupted its entry into force.

EDUCATION, EMPLOYMENT, LABOUR AND SOCIAL AFFAIRS

The Employment, Labour and Social Affairs Committee is concerned with the development of labour market and selective employment policies to ensure the utilization of human capital at the highest possible level and to improve the quality and flexibility of working life as well as the effectiveness of social policies. The Committee's work covers such issues as the role of women in the economy, industrial relations, international migration and the development of an extensive social data base. In June 1994 the ministerial meeting endorsed an employment policy, which comprised proposals to combat the high level of unemployment throughout member states, including enhanced labour flexibility, improving training opportunities and expanding labour market policies. In 1995, following the publication of the OECD Job Study, consideration focused on the policy implications of an ageing population and on indicators of human capital investment.

The Committee for Education relates decision-making to educational, social and economic policy and evaluates the implications of policy for the allocation and use of resources. The Committee reviews educational trends, develops statistics and indicators, and analyses policies for education and training at all levels: pre-school to higher and adult education and training. Together, the Employment, Labour and Social Affairs and Education Committees seek to provide for greater integration of labour market and educational policies and the prevention of social exclusion.

A separate Rural Development Programme focuses on economic and social development in rural areas and the welfare of rural populations, and reviews policies which affect these areas.

The OECD's Centre for Educational Research and Innovation (CERI) promotes the development of research activities in education together with experiments of an advanced nature designed to test innovations in educational systems and to stimulate research and development.

RELATIONS WITH OTHER INTERNATIONAL ORGANIZATIONS

Under a Protocol signed at the same time as the OECD Convention, the European Commission generally takes part in the work of OECD. EFTA may also send representatives to OECD meetings. Formal relations exist with a number of other international organizations, including the ILO, FAO, IMF, IBRD, UNCTAD, IAEA and the Council of Europe. A few non-governmental organizations have been granted consultative status, notably the Business and Industry Advisory Committee to OECD (BIAC) and the Trade Union Advisory Committee to OECD (TUAC).

FINANCE

In 1995 OECD's total budget amounted to 1,701.7m. French francs, of which some 61.7% was funded by regular contributions from member states and the remainder by special income or project participants.

PUBLICATIONS

Activities of OECD (Secretary-General's Annual Report).

Agricultural Outlook (annually).

Energy Balances (quarterly).

Energy Prices and Taxes (quarterly).

Financial Market Trends (3 a year).

Financial Statistics (Part 1 (domestic markets): monthly; Part 2 (international markets): monthly; Part 3 (OECD member countries): 25 a year).

Foreign Trade Statistics (monthly).

Higher Education Management (3 a year).

Indicators of Industrial Activity (quarterly).

Main Developments in Trade (annually).

Main Economic Indicators (monthly).

National Accounts Quarterly.

OECD Economic Outlook (2 a year).

OECD Economic Studies (2 a year).

OECD Economic Surveys (annually for each country).

OECD Employment Outlook (annually).

The OECD Observer (every 2 months).

Oil and Gas Statistics (quarterly).

PEB Exchange (newsletter of the Programme on Educational Building, 3 a year).

Quarterly Labour Force Statistics.

Science, Technology, Industry Review (2 a year).

Short-term Economic Indicators: Transition Economies (quarterly).

Numerous specialized reports, working papers, books and statistics on economic and social subjects (about 130 titles a year, both in English and French) are also published.

International Energy Agency—IEA

Address: 2 rue André Pascal, 75775 Paris Cédex 16, France.

The Agency was set up by the Council of OECD in 1974 to develop co-operation on energy questions among participating countries.

MEMBERS

Australia	Greece	Portugal
Austria	Ireland	Spain
Belgium	Italy	Sweden
Canada	Japan	Switzerland
Denmark	Luxembourg	Turkey
Finland	Netherlands	United Kingdom
France	New Zealand	USA
Germany	Norway	

The European Commission is also represented.

Organization

(January 1998)

GOVERNING BOARD

Composed of ministers or senior officials of the member governments. Decisions may be taken by a weighted majority on a number of specified subjects, particularly concerning emergency measures and the emergency reserve commitment; a simple weighted majority is required for procedural decisions and decisions implementing specific obligations in the agreement. Unanimity is required only if new obligations, not already specified in the agreement, are to be undertaken.

The Governing Board is assisted by a Coal and an Oil Industry Advisory Board, composed of industrial executives.

SECRETARIAT

The Secretariat comprises the following five Offices: Long-Term Co-operation; Non-member Countries; Oil Markets and Emergency Preparedness; Economics, Statistics and Information Systems; and Energy Technology and Research and Development.

Executive Director: ROBERT PRIDDLE (United Kingdom).

Activities

The Agreement on an International Energy Programme was signed in November 1974 and formally entered into force in January 1976. The Programme commits the participating countries of the International Energy Agency to share petroleum in emergencies, to strengthen their long-term co-operation in order to reduce dependence on petroleum imports, to increase the availability of information on the petroleum market and to develop relations with the petroleum-producing and other petroleum-consuming countries.

An emergency petroleum-sharing plan has been established, and the IEA ensures that the necessary technical information and facilities are in place so that it can be readily used in the event of a reduction in petroleum supplies. The IEA undertakes emergency response reviews and workshops, and publishes an Emergency Management Manual to facilitate a co-ordinated response to a severe disruption in petroleum supplies. A separate division monitors and reports on short-term developments in the petroleum market. It also considers other related issues, including international crude petroleum pricing, petroleum trade and stock developments and investments by major petroleum-producing countries.

The IEA Long-Term Co-operation Programme is designed to strengthen the security of energy supplies and promote stability in world energy markets. It provides for co-operative efforts to conserve energy, to accelerate the development of alternative energy sources by means of both specific and general measures, to step up research and development of new energy technologies and to remove legislative and administrative obstacles to increased energy supplies. Regular reviews of member countries' efforts in the fields of energy conservation and accelerated development of alternative energy sources assess the effectiveness of national programmes in relation to the objectives of the Agency.

The IEA also reviews the energy situation in non-member countries, in particular the petroleum-producing countries of the Middle East and central and eastern European countries. In the latter states the IEA has provided technical assistance for the development of national energy legislation and energy efficiency projects. In 1995 the IEA completed a major study of the energy policies of Russia, following the largest single-country review ever undertaken by the Agency.

The IEA aims to contribute to the energy security of member countries through energy technology and research and development projects, in particular those concerned with energy efficiency, conservation and protection of the environment. The IEA promotes international collaboration in this field and the participation of energy industries to facilitiate the application of new technologies, through effective transfer of knowledge, technology innovation and training. Member states adopt Implementing Agreements, which provide mechanisms for collaboration and information exchange in specific areas, for example electric vehicle technologies, electric demand-side management and photovoltaic power systems. Non-member states are encouraged to participate in these Agreements with associate status. The Agency sponsors conferences, symposia and workshops to further enhance international co-operation among member and non-member countries.

The Office of Economics, Statistics and Information Systems examines the world energy situation and major energy developments and collects and disseminates data on energy generation and new forms of energy.

PUBLICATIONS

Coal Information (annually).

Electricity Information (annually).

Gas and Oil Information (annually).

Oil Market Report (monthly).

World Energy Outlook (annually).

OECD Nuclear Energy Agency—NEA

Address: Le Seine Saint-Germain, 12 blvd des Îles, 92130 Issy-les-Moulineaux, France.

Telephone: 1-45-24-82-00; **telex:** 640048; **fax:** 1-45-24-11-10.

The NEA was established in 1958 to further the peaceful uses of nuclear energy. Originally a European agency, it has since admitted OECD members outside Europe.

MEMBERS

All members of OECD (except New Zealand and Poland).

Organization

(January 1998)

STEERING COMMITTEE FOR NUCLEAR ENERGY

Chairman: CHRISTIAN PRETTRE (France).

SECRETARIAT

Director-General: LUIS ENRIQUE ECHAVARRI (Spain).

Deputy Director-General: SAMUEL THOMPSON (USA).

Deputy Director (Science and Computer Processing): PHILIPPE SAVELLI (France).

Deputy Director (Safety and Regulation): MAKOTO TAKAHASHI (Japan).

MAIN COMMITTEES

Committee on Nuclear Regulatory Activities;
Committee on Radiation Protection and Public Health;
Committee on the Safety of Nuclear Installations;
Committee for Technical and Economic Studies on Nuclear Energy Development and the Fuel Cycle;
Group of Governmental Experts on Third Party Liability in the Field of Nuclear Energy;
Nuclear Science Committee;
Radioactive Waste Management Committee.

Activities

The main purpose of the Agency is to promote international co-operation within the OECD area for the development and application of nuclear power for peaceful purposes through international research and development projects and exchange of scientific and technical experience and information. The Agency also maintains a continual survey with the co-operation of other organizations, notably the International Atomic Energy Agency (IAEA, see p. 65), of world uranium resources, production and demand, and of economic and technical aspects of the nuclear fuel cycle.

A major part of the Agency's work is devoted to the safety and regulation of nuclear power, including co-operative studies and projects related to the prevention of nuclear accidents and the long-term safety of radioactive waste disposal systems.

JOINT PROJECTS

Analogue Studies in the Alligator Rivers Region: an international research project, initiated in 1995 as an extension to the original Alligator Rivers Analogue Project, which was established in 1987 to gain further insight into the long-term physical and chemical processes likely to influence the transport of radionuclides through rock masses. Research involves the study of geochemical and hydrogeological processes responsible for the mobilization and fixation of uranium in the vicinity of the Koongarra deposit in Australia, which may resemble those processes acting upon high-level radioactive waste disposal facility.

Chemical Thermodynamic Database: the objective of this project, set up in 1983, is to compile fundamental chemical thermodynamic data which permit the quantification of mass transfers in chemical reactions occurring in ground water and in water-rock reactions. Such data can be used in geochemical modelling of waste disposal systems performance assessments to predict the concentration of radioelements under various conditions.

Decommissioning of Nuclear Installations: this co-operative programme, set up in 1985, provides for an exchange of scientific and technical information to develop the operational experience and data base needed for the future decommissioning of large nuclear power plants and other nuclear fuel cycle facilities. The Programme is administered by a Liaison Committee, while technical discussions and exchanges are undertaken in the context of a Technical Advisory Group. In 1997 the Programme comprised 31 projects in 13 countries.

Halden Reactor Project: Halden, Norway; experimental boiling heavy water reactor, which became an OECD project in 1958. From 1964, under successive agreements with participating countries, the reactor has been used for long-term testing of water reactor fuels and for research into automatic computer-based control of nuclear power stations. Some 100 nuclear energy research institutions and authorities in 19 countries support the project.

Incident Reporting System—IRS: introduced in 1980 to exchange experience in operating nuclear power plants in OECD member countries and to improve nuclear safety by facilitating feedback of this experience to nuclear regulatory authorities, utilities and manufacturers. Since 1995 the IRS has operated in conjunction with the IAEA.

Information System on Occupational Exposure—ISOE: initiated in 1991; ISOE databases contain annual collective dose information on more than 360 reactors in 20 countries; the system also contains information from 35 nuclear reactors which are either defunct or actively decommissioning.

Rasplav Project: initiated in 1994, in Moscow, Russia, to study the behaviour of molten corium in a reactor pressure vessel during a severe accident. Seventeen countries participate in the project.

COMMON SERVICE

NEA Data Bank: f. 1978 in succession to the Computer Programme Library and the Neutron Data Compilation Centre, the Data Bank allows participating countries to share large computer programmes used in reactor calculations, and nuclear data applications. It also operates as one of a worldwide network of four nuclear data centres.

FINANCE

The Agency's budget for 1996 amounted to 81m. French francs.

PUBLICATIONS

Annual Report.

NEA Newsletter (2 a year).

Nuclear Energy Data (annually).

Nuclear Law Bulletin (2 a year).

Reports and proceedings.

ORGANIZATION FOR SECURITY AND CO-OPERATION IN EUROPE—OSCE

Address: 1010 Vienna, Kärntner Ring 5–7, Austria.

Telephone: (1) 514-36-190; **telex:** 112966; **fax:** (1) 514-36-99; **e-mail:** pm-dga@osce.or.at; **internet:** http://www.osceprag.cz.

The OSCE was established in 1972 as the Conference on Security and Co-operation in Europe (CSCE), providing a multilateral forum for dialogue and negotiation. It produced the Helsinki Final Act of 1975 on East–West relations. The areas of competence of the CSCE were expanded by the Charter of Paris for a New Europe (1990), which transformed the CSCE from an *ad hoc* forum to an organization with permanent institutions, and the Helsinki Document 1992 (see 'Activities'). In December 1994 the summit conference adopted the new name of OSCE, in order to reflect the Organization's changing political role and strengthened secretariat. The OSCE has 55 participating states and comprises all the recognized countries of Europe, and Canada, the USA and all the former republics of the USSR.

PARTICIPATING STATES

Albania[1]	Greece	Portugal
Andorra[2]	Hungary	Romania
Armenia[3]	Iceland	Russia[9]
Austria	Ireland	San Marino
Azerbaijan[3]	Italy	Slovakia[6]
Belarus[3]	Kazakhstan[3]	Slovenia[5]
Belgium	Kyrgyzstan[3]	Spain
Bosnia and Herzegovina[4]	Latvia[7]	Sweden
Bulgaria	Liechtenstein	Switzerland
Canada	Lithuania[7]	Tajikistan[3]
Croatia[5]	Luxembourg	Turkey
Cyprus	Macedonia, former Yugoslav republic[8]	Turkmenistan[3]
Czech Republic[6]	Malta	Ukraine[3]
Denmark	Moldova[3]	United Kingdom
Estonia[7]	Monaco	USA
Finland	Netherlands	Uzbekistan[3]
France	Norway	Vatican City (Holy See)
Georgia[5]	Poland	Yugoslavia[10]
Germany		

[1] Admitted as participating state of the CSCE in June 1991.
[2] Admitted as participating state in April 1996.
[3] Admitted as participating state in January 1992.
[4] Admitted as participating state in April 1992.
[5] Admitted as participating state in March 1992.
[6] The Czech Republic and Slovakia succeeded Czechoslovakia on 1 January 1993.
[7] Admitted as participating state in September 1991.
[8] Admitted as participating state in October 1995.
[9] Russia assumed the USSR's seat following the dissolution of the USSR in December 1991.
[10] The Federal Republic of Yugoslavia (Serbia and Montenegro) was suspended from the CSCE in July 1992.

THE HELSINKI FINAL ACT

The Final Act comprises four main sections:

(i) covers security in Europe, including commitments to non-aggression and respect for human rights.

(ii) covers co-operation in the fields of economics, science and technology, and the environment.

(iii) covers co-operation in humanitarian and other related fields, including promotion of cultural exchanges and the free movement of people.

(iv) comprises a commitment to continue the process of consultation and increased co-operation between CSCE countries, by means of 'follow-up' conferences.

Organization

(January 1998)

SUMMIT CONFERENCES

Heads of state or government of OSCE participating states normally meet every two years to set priorities and political orientation of the Organization. The most recent conference was held in Lisbon, Portugal, in December 1996.

MINISTERIAL COUNCIL

The Ministerial Council (formerly the Council of Foreign Ministers) comprises ministers of foreign affairs of member states. It is the central decision-making and governing body of the OSCE and meets at least once a year.

SENIOR COUNCIL

The Senior Council (formerly the Council of Senior Officials—CSO) is responsible for the supervision, management and co-ordination of OSCE activities. Member states are represented by senior political officers, who convene at least twice a year in Prague, Czech Republic, and once a year as the Economic Forum.

PERMANENT COUNCIL

The Council, which is based in Vienna, is responsible for day-to-day operational tasks. Members of the Council, comprising the permanent representatives of member states to the OSCE, convene weekly. The Council is the regular body for political consultation and decision-making, and may be convened for emergency purposes.

FORUM FOR SECURITY CO-OPERATION—FSC

The FSC, comprising representatives of delegations of member states, meets weekly in Vienna to negotiate and consult on measures aimed at strengthening security and stability throughout Europe. Its main objectives are negotiations on arms control, disarmament, and confidence- and security-building; regular consultations and intensive co-operation on matters related to security; and the further reduction of the risks of conflict. The FSC is also responsible for the implementation of confidence- and security-building measures (CSBMs); the preparation of seminars on military doctrine; the holding of annual implementation assessment meetings; and the provision of a forum for the discussion and clarification of information exchanged under agreed CSBMs.

CHAIRMAN-IN-OFFICE—CIO

The CIO is vested with overall responsibility for executive action. The position is held by a minister of foreign affairs of a member state for a one-year term. The CIO may be assisted by a troika, consisting of the preceding, current and succeeding chairpeople; *ad hoc* steering groups; or personal representatives, who are appointed by the CIO with a clear and precise mandate to assist the CIO in dealing with a crisis or conflict.

Chairman-in-Office: (until 31 December 1998) BRONISŁAW GEREMEK (Poland).

SECRETARIAT

The Secretariat consists of the following four departments: the Department for CIO Support, responsible for the preparation of meetings, contacts with international organizations, press relations and public information; the Conflict Prevention Centre, responsible for overall support of OSCE activities in early warnings, conflict prevention and crisis management, and provides operational support for OSCE missions; the Department of Conference Services, responsible for conference and interpretation services, documentation and protocol; and the Department for Administration and Budget, responsible for administrative services, personnel and financial control. There are 75 permanent staff.

The position of Secretary-General was established in December 1992 and the first appointment to the position was made in June 1993. The Secretary-General is the representative of the CIO and is responsible for the management of OSCE structures and operations.

Secretary-General: GIANCARLO ARAGONA (Italy).

HIGH COMMISSIONER ON NATIONAL MINORITIES

Address: POB 20062, Prinsessegracht 22, 2514 AP The Hague, Netherlands.

Telephone: (70) 312 55 00; **fax:** (70) 363 59 10; **e-mail:** cscehcnm@euronet.nl.

The establishment of the office of High Commissioner on National Minorities was proposed in the 1992 Helsinki Document, and endorsed by the Council of Foreign Ministers in Stockholm in December 1992. The role of the High Commissioner is to identify ethnic tensions that might endanger peace, stability or relations between OSCE participating states, and to promote their early resolution. The High Commissioner may issue an 'early warning' for the attention of the Senior Council of an area of tension likely to degenerate into conflict. The High Commissioner is appointed by the Ministerial Council, on the recommendation of the Senior Council, for a three-year term.

High Commissioner: MAX VAN DER STOEL (Netherlands).

OFFICE FOR DEMOCRATIC INSTITUTIONS AND HUMAN RIGHTS—ODIHR

Address: Krucza 36/Wspolna 6, 00-522 Warsaw, Poland.

Telephone: (22) 625-70-40; **fax:** (22) 625-43-57; **e-mail:** office@odihr.osce.waw.pl.

The ODIHR, which was originally called the Office for Free Elections with a mandate to promote multiparty democracy, was assigned major new tasks under the Helsinki Document 1992, including responsibility for promoting human rights, democracy and the rule of law. The Office provides a framework for the exchange of information on and the promotion of democracy-building, respect for human rights and elections within OSCE states. In addition, it co-ordinates the monitoring of elections and provides expertise and training on constitutional and legal matters.

Director: GERARD STOUDMANN (Switzerland).

PARLIAMENTARY ASSEMBLY

Address: Radhusstraede 1, 1466 Copenhagen K, Denmark.

Telephone: 33-32-94-00; **fax:** 33-32-55-05; **e-mail:** oscepa@centrum.dk.

The OSCE Parliamentary Assembly, which is comprised of parliamentarians from participating countries, was inaugurated in July 1992, and meets annually. It is supported by a secretariat in Copenhagen, Denmark.

President: JAVIER RUPEREZ-RUBIO (Spain).

Secretary-General: SPENCER OLIVER.

COURT OF CONCILIATION AND ARBITRATION

Address: 266 route de Lausanne, 1292 Chambesy, Geneva, Switzerland.

Telephone: (22) 7580025; **fax:** (22) 7582510.

The establishment of the Court of Conciliation and Arbitration was agreed in 1992 and effected in 1994. OSCE states that have ratified the OSCE Convention on Conciliation and Arbitration may submit a dispute to the Court for settlement by the Arbitral Tribunal or the Conciliation Commission.

JOINT CONSULTATIVE GROUP (JCG)

The states that are party to the Treaty on Conventional Armed Forces in Europe (CFE), which was concluded within the CSCE framework in 1990, established the Joint Consultative Group (JCG). The JCG, which meets in Vienna, addresses questions relating to compliance with the Treaty; enhancement of the effectiveness of the Treaty; technical aspects of the Treaty's implementation; and disputes arising out of its implementation. There are currently 30 states participating in the JCG.

Activities

In July 1990 heads of government of the NATO member countries proposed to increase the role of the CSCE 'to provide a forum for wider political dialogue in a more united Europe'. In November heads of government of the participating states signed the Charter of Paris for a New Europe, which undertook to strengthen pluralist democracy and observance of human rights, and to settle disputes between participating states by peaceful means. At the summit meeting the Treaty on Conventional Armed Forces in Europe (CFE), which had been negotiated within the framework of the CSCE, was signed by the member states of NATO (q.v.) and of the Warsaw Pact. The Treaty limits non-nuclear air and ground armaments in the signatory countries. It was decided at the same meeting to establish a secretariat in Prague, Czechoslovakia, which was opened in February 1991. (The secretariat was moved to Vienna, Austria, in 1993.) It was also decided to create a Conflict Prevention Centre, which was established in Vienna, Austria, in March 1991, and an Office for Free Elections (later renamed the Office for Democratic Institutions and Human Rights), which was established in July in Warsaw, Poland. In April parliamentarians from the CSCE countries agreed on the creation of a pan-European parliamentary assembly. The assembly was to consist of 245 parliamentary delegates from all of the CSCE countries and was to have a consultative role. Its first session was held in Budapest, Hungary, in July 1992.

The Council of Foreign Ministers met for the first time in Berlin, Germany, in June 1991. At the meeting a mechanism for consultation and co-operation in the case of emergency situations was adopted. This mechanism was to be implemented by the Council of Senior Officials (CSO, which was subsequently renamed the Senior Council). A separate mechanism regarding the prevention of the outbreak of conflict was also adopted, whereby a country can demand an explanation of 'unusual military activity' in a neighbouring country. These mechanisms were utilized in July in relation to the armed conflict in Yugoslavia between the Republic of Croatia and the Yugoslav Government. The CSCE appealed to all parties involved in the conflict to uphold a cease-fire. In mid-August a meeting of the CSO resolved to reinforce the CSCE's mission in Yugoslavia considerably and requested all the parties involved in the conflict to begin negotiations as a matter of urgency. In September the CSO agreed to impose an embargo on the export of armaments to Yugoslavia. In October the CSO resolved to establish an observer mission to monitor the observance of human rights in Yugoslavia.

The third CSCE Conference on Human Dimensions (the CSCE term used with regard to issues concerning human rights and welfare) was held in Moscow in September 1991. The Conference formulated an accord which empowers CSCE envoys to investigate reported abuses of human rights in any CSCE country, either at the request of the country concerned, or if six participating states deem such an investigation necessary.

At the second meeting of the Council of Foreign Ministers, held in Prague in January 1992, it was agreed that the Conference's rule of decision-making by consensus was to be altered to allow the CSO to take appropriate action against a participating state 'in cases of clear and gross violation of CSCE commitments'. This development was precipitated by the conflict in Yugoslavia, where the Yugoslav Government was held responsible by the majority of CSCE states for the continuation of hostilities. It was also agreed at the meeting that the CSCE should undertake fact-finding and conciliation missions to areas of tension, with the first such mission to be sent to Nagornyi Karabakh, the largely Armenian-populated enclave in Azerbaijan.

In March 1992 CSCE participating states reached agreement on a number of confidence-building measures, including commitments to exchange technical data on new weapons systems; to report activation of military units; and to prohibit military activity involving very large numbers of troops or tanks. Later in that month at a meeting of the Council of Foreign Ministers, which opened the Helsinki Follow-up Conference, the members of NATO and the former members of the Warsaw Pact (with Russia, Belarus, Ukraine and Georgia taking the place of the USSR) signed the Open Skies Treaty. Under the treaty, aerial reconnaissance missions by one country over another were permitted, subject to regulation. An Open Skies Consultative Commission was subsequently established. Its meetings are serviced by the OSCE secretariat.

The Federal Republic of Yugoslavia (Serbia and Montenegro) was suspended from the CSCE immediately prior to the summit meeting of heads of state and government that took place in Helsinki, Finland, in July 1992. The summit meeting adopted the Helsinki Document 1992, in which participating states defined the terms of future CSCE peace-keeping activities. Conforming broadly to UN practice, peace-keeping operations would be undertaken only with the full consent of the parties involved in any conflict and only if an effective cease-fire were in place. The CSCE may request the use of the military resources of NATO, WEU, the EU, the CIS or other international bodies. (NATO and WEU had recently changed their constitutions to permit the use of their forces for CSCE purposes.) France had opposed the USA's suggestion to make NATO the CSCE's main military arm, and a compromise was reached, whereby NATO would be requested to provide military support on a case-by-case basis. The Helsinki Document declared the CSCE a 'regional arrangement' in the sense of Chapter VIII of the UN's Charter, which states that such a regional grouping should attempt to resolve a conflict in the region before referring it to the Security Council. In December 1993 a Permanent Committee (now renamed as the Permanent Council) was established, in Vienna, providing for greater political consultation and dialogue through its weekly meetings. In December 1994 the summit conference endorsed the organization's role as the primary instrument for early warning, conflict prevention and crisis management in the region, and adopted a 'Code of Conduct on Politico-Military Aspects of Security', which set out principles to guide the role of the armed forces in democratic societies. The summit conference that was held in Lisbon, Portugal, in December 1996 agreed to adapt the CFE Treaty, in order to further arms reduction negotiations on a national and territorial basis. The conference also adopted the 'Lisbon Declaration on a Common and Comprehensive Security Model for Europe for the 21st Century', committing all parties to pursuing measures to ensure regional security. A Security Model Committee was established and began to meet regularly during 1997 to consider aspects of the Declaration, including the identification of risks and challenges to future European security; enhancing means of joint co-operative action within the OSCE framework in the event of non-compliance with OSCE commitments by participating states; considering other new arrangements within the OSCE framework that could reinforce security and stability in Europe; and defining a basis of co-operation between the OSCE and other relevant organizations to co-ordinate security enforcement.

Under the Dayton peace accord for the former Yugoslavia, which was concluded in late 1995, the OSCE was assigned the tasks of supervising post-war Bosnian elections; drafting arms-control agreements for the former Yugoslavia; and monitoring the observance of human rights in Bosnia and Herzegovina. In August 1996 the head of the OSCE mission in Bosnia and Herzegovina postponed Bosnian municipal elections until the first half of 1997, on the grounds that he was not satisfied with the manner in which voter registration was being conducted. The municipal elections were to have been held in September 1996, simultaneously with legislative and cantonal elections. The OSCE mission to organize and oversee the Bosnian national elections, which were held on 14 September, was the largest-ever operation undertaken by the organization, with some 1,200 electoral observers deployed. The OSCE certified the election results at the end of the month, in spite of widespread allegations of serious voting irregularities (see chapter on Bosnia and Herzegovina). In October the OSCE decided to postpone the Bosnian municipal elections until mid-1997; in March 1997 the elections were again rescheduled and were to be held in September. In mid-December 1996 the Government of the Federal Republic of Yugoslavia invited the OSCE to verify the results of municipal elections that had been held in Serbia in November (the opposition coalition was protesting over the Government's annulment of victories that they had gained in 14 towns, including the capital, Belgrade). The OSCE delegation issued a report at the end of the month that supported the opposition's demands that the original election results be reinstated.

In April 1997 the OSCE monitored legislative and municipal elections in Croatia, including the Eastern Slavonia, Baranja and Western Srem (Sirmiun) region under UN administration. In June the Permanent Council agreed to increase the OSCE presence in Croatia from 14 to 250 staff officers, and to enhance the mission's capacity to protect human rights, in particular the rights of minorities, and to monitor the implementation of legislation and other commitments concerning the return and treatment of refugees and displaced persons, under a new mandate extending until 31 December 1998. The process of voter registration for the Bosnian elections commenced in May 1997, and was concluded at the end of June. At that time some 2.4m voters had been registered through 480 OSCE-supervised centres in Bosnia and Herzegovina, Croatia and the Federal Republic of Yugoslavia, and through an Out-of-Country Voting office, in Vienna, Austria, which was jointly operated by OSCE and the International Organization for Migration. More than 2,000 OSCE personnel supervised the elections that took place as scheduled in mid-September. OSCE monitors also observed presidential and legislative elections in Serbia held later in September, and the presidential poll in Montenegro in October. In November OSCE representatives supervised voting in legislative elections in the Republika Srpska and confirmed that they had been conducted fairly.

In December 1994 OSCE heads of state and government authorized the establishment of a 3,000-strong peace-keeping force for the Nagornyi Karabakh region, which was the focus of a conflict between Armenia and Azerbaijan. However, in the absence of a formal cease-fire and the start of peace negotiations, the proposed force was not dispatched. The OSCE continued to provide a framework for discussions between the two countries through its 11-nation Minsk Group, which from early 1997 was co-chaired by France, Russia and the USA. The principles of a negotiated settlement, based on self-determination and the territorial integrity of Armenia and Azerbaijan, were formulated in a separate document at the Lisbon summit meeting in December 1996. However, Armenia refused to accept the terms of the settlement. In April 1997 the Minsk Group declared its commitment to intensifying efforts to achieve a political settlement. By October both governments were reported to have agreed on OSCE proposals, which recognized Nagornyi Karabakh as an autonomous area within Azerbaijan, although it was to maintain a reduced strength armed force, and demanded the withdrawal of Karabakh Armenian troops from certain strategic areas under the supervision of OSCE forces.

In late 1996 the OSCE declared the constitutional referendum held in Belarus in November to be illegal and urged that country's Government to ensure political freedoms and respect for human rights. An OSCE fact-finding mission visited Belarus in April 1997 and recommended the establishment of a permanent presence in that country. This was agreed in principle with the Belarusian authorities in June. In April the OSCE opened a new mission office in Tskhinvali, Georgia, in order to observe the human rights situation following the conflict in the autonomous region of Abkhazia and to oversee the distribution of humanitarian supplies.

In January 1995 Russia agreed to an OSCE proposal to send a fact-finding mission to assist in the conflict between the Russian authorities and an independence movement in Chechnya. The mission, which arrived in Groznyi (now Dzhokar Ghala), the Chechen capital, in late January, criticized the Russian army for using excessive force against Chechen rebels and civilians; reported that violations of human rights had been perpetrated by both sides in the conflict; and urged Russia to enforce a cease-fire in Groznyi to allow the delivery of humanitarian supplies by international aid agencies to the population of the city. In May the Russian military authorities in Chechnya and the Chechen rebels took part in peace negotiations that were mediated by the newly-established OSCE Assistance Group; however, the talks collapsed after only several hours of discussion. The Assistance Group brokered a cease-fire agreement between the Russian military authorities in Chechnya and the Chechen rebels in July. A 'special observer commission', composed of representatives of all sides and the OSCE, was established to supervise implementation of the agreement. A further peace accord was signed, under the auspices of the OSCE, in May 1996, but the truce was broken in July. A more conclusive cease-fire agreement was signed by the two parties to the conflict in August (see chapter on the Russian Federation). In January 1997 the OSCE assisted in the preparation and monitoring of general elections conducted in Chechnya. The Assistance Group remained in the territory to help with post-conflict rehabilitation, including the promotion of democratic institutions and respect for human rights.

In June 1996 the OSCE reported serious fraudulence in the conduct of the general election in Albania. In October OSCE monitors, dispatched to observe the local elections, withdrew from Albania following demands by the Albanian Government to reduce their number to a level deemed unacceptable by the OSCE. In March 1997 the OSCE agreed to dispatch a fact-finding mission to Albania to help restore political and civil stability, which had been undermined by the collapse of a national pyramid saving scheme at the start of the year. The former Austrian Chancellor, Franz Vranitzky, was appointed to lead the mission, as the Personal Representative of the OSCE Chairman. Vranitzky, together with representatives of the EU, negotiated an agreement between Albania's President Berisha and opposition parties to hold elections in mid-1997 and to establish a government of national reconciliation. At the end of March the Permanent Council agreed to establish an OSCE presence in Albania, and confirmed that the organization should provide the framework for co-ordinating other international efforts to help restore order, security and respect for human rights. The OSCE endorsed proposals by several European countries to send peace-keeping forces to Albania in order to facilitate the safe delivery of humanitarian supplies and to create a secure environment for all international efforts. The establishment of a temporary multinational protection force was authorized by the UN Security Council at the end of March. Vranitzky continued to lead OSCE efforts in Albania, which focused on reaching a political consensus on new legislation for the conduct of the forthcoming elections. A compromise agreement was announced in mid-May and Vranitzky later confirmed that all of the main political parties would contest the elections. More than 500 OSCE observers provided technical electoral assistance and helped to monitor the voting which took place at the end of June and in early July, under the protection of some 6,500 troops of the eight-nation force. In spite of some outbreaks of violence, the OSCE declared its satisfaction with the conduct of the elections. The withdrawal of the multinational forces began in late July, although it was agreed that the OSCE would maintain a presence in the country.

At the end of 1997 there were 10 OSCE missions, with the objectives of conflict prevention and crisis management: in Bosnia and Herzegovina, Croatia, Estonia, Georgia, Latvia, the former Yugoslav republic of Macedonia, Moldova, Tajikistan, Ukraine, and Kosovo, Sandjak and Vojvodina (Federal Republic of Yugoslavia).

Japan and the Republic of Korea have the status of 'partners for co-operation' with the OSCE, while Algeria, Egypt, Israel, Morocco and Tunisia are 'Mediterranean partners for co-operation'. Consultations are held with these countries in order to discuss security issues of common concern.

FINANCE

All activities of the institutions, negotiations, *ad hoc* meetings and missions are financed by contributions from member states. The budget for 1996 amounted to some 553.2m. Austrian Schillings (approximately US $55m.), of which some 46% was allocated to the OSCE's activities in Bosnia and Herzegovina.

PUBLICATIONS

OSCE Handbook (annually).

OSCE Newsletter (monthly).

ORGANIZATION OF AFRICAN UNITY—OAU

Address: POB 3243, Addis Ababa, Ethiopia.

Telephone: (1) 517700; **telex:** 21046; **fax:** (1) 513036.

The Organization was founded in 1963 to promote unity and solidarity among African states.

FORMATION

There were various attempts at establishing an inter-African organization before the OAU Charter was drawn up. In November 1958 Ghana and Guinea (later joined by Mali) drafted a Charter which was to form the basis of a Union of African States. In January 1961 a conference was held at Casablanca, attended by the heads of state of Ghana, Guinea, Mali, Morocco, and representatives of Libya and of the provisional government of the Algerian Republic (GPRA). Tunisia, Nigeria, Liberia and Togo declined the invitation to attend. An African Charter was adopted and it was decided to set up an African Military Command and an African Common Market.

Between October 1960 and March 1961 three conferences were held by French-speaking African countries, at Abidjan, Brazzaville and Yaoundé. None of the 12 countries which attended these meetings had been present at the Casablanca Conference. These conferences led eventually to the signing in September 1961, at Tananarive, of a charter establishing the Union africaine et malgache, later the Organisation commune africaine et mauricienne (OCAM).

In May 1961 a conference was held at Monrovia, Liberia, attended by the heads of state or representatives of 19 countries: Cameroon, Central African Republic, Chad, Congo Republic (ex-French), Côte d'Ivoire, Dahomey, Ethiopia, Gabon, Liberia, Madagascar, Mauritania, Niger, Nigeria, Senegal, Sierra Leone, Somalia, Togo, Tunisia and Upper Volta. They met again (with the exception of Tunisia and with the addition of the ex-Belgian Congo Republic) in January 1962 at Lagos, Nigeria, and set up a permanent secretariat and a standing committee of finance ministers, and accepted a draft charter for an Organization of Inter-African and Malagasy States.

It was the Conference of Addis Ababa, held in 1963, which finally brought together African states despite the regional, political and linguistic differences which divided them. The foreign ministers of 32 African states attended the Preparatory Meeting held in May: Algeria, Burundi, Cameroon, Central African Republic, Chad, Congo (Brazzaville) (now Republic of the Congo), Congo (Léopoldville) (now Democratic Republic of the Congo), Côte d'Ivoire, Dahomey (now Benin), Ethiopia, Gabon, Ghana, Guinea, Liberia, Libya, Madagascar, Mali, Mauritania, Morocco, Niger, Nigeria, Rwanda, Senegal, Sierra Leone, Somalia, Sudan, Tanganyika (now Tanzania), Togo, Tunisia, Uganda, the United Arab Republic (Egypt) and Upper Volta (now Burkina Faso).

The topics discussed by the meeting were: (i) creation of the Organization of African States; (ii) co-operation among African states in the following fields: economic and social; education, culture and science; collective defence; (iii) decolonization; (iv) apartheid and racial discrimination; (v) effects of economic grouping on the economic development of Africa; (vi) disarmament; (vii) creation of a Permanent Conciliation Commission; and (viii) Africa and the United Nations.

The Heads of State Conference which opened on 23 May drew up the Charter of the Organization of African Unity, which was then signed by the heads of 30 states on 25 May 1963. The Charter was essentially functional and reflected a compromise between the concept of a loose association of states favoured by the Monrovia Group and the federal idea supported by the Casablanca Group, and in particular by Ghana.

SUMMARY OF OAU CHARTER

Article I. Establishment of the Organization of African Unity. The Organization to include continental African states, Madagascar, and other islands surrounding Africa.

Article II. Aims of the OAU:

1. To promote unity and solidarity among African states.

2. To intensify and co-ordinate efforts to improve living standards in Africa.

3. To defend sovereignty, territorial integrity and independence of African states.

4. To eradicate all forms of colonialism from Africa.

5. To promote international co-operation in keeping with the Charter of the United Nations.

Article III. Member states adhere to the principles of sovereignty, non-interference in internal affairs of member states, respect for territorial integrity, peaceful settlement of disputes, condemnation of political subversion, dedication to the emancipation of dependent African territories, and international non-alignment.

Article IV. Each independent sovereign African state shall be entitled to become a member of the Organization.

Article V. All member states shall have equal rights and duties.

Article VI. All member states shall observe scrupulously the principles laid down in Article III.

Article VII. Establishment of the Assembly of Heads of State and Government, the Council of Ministers, the General Secretariat, and the Commission of Mediation, Conciliation and Arbitration.

Articles VIII–XI. The Assembly of Heads of State and Government co-ordinates policies and reviews the structure of the Organization.

Articles XII–XV. The Council of Ministers shall prepare conferences of the Assembly, and co-ordinate inter-African co-operation. All resolutions shall be by simple majority.

Articles XVI–XVIII. The General Secretariat. The Administrative Secretary-General and his staff shall not seek or receive instructions from any government or other authority external to the Organization. They are international officials responsible only to the Organization.

Article XIX. Commission of Mediation, Conciliation and Arbitration. A separate protocol concerning the composition and nature of this Commission shall be regarded as an integral part of the Charter.

Articles XX–XXII. Specialized Commissions shall be established, composed of Ministers or other officials designated by Member Governments. Their regulations shall be laid down by the Council of Ministers.

Article XXIII. The Budget shall be prepared by the Secretary-General and approved by the Council of Ministers. Contributions shall be in accordance with the scale of assessment of the United Nations. No Member shall pay more than 20% of the total yearly amount.

Article XXIV. Texts of the Charter in African languages, English and French shall be equally authentic. Instruments of ratification shall be deposited with the Government of Ethiopia.

Article XXV. The Charter shall come into force on receipt by the Government of Ethiopia of the instruments of ratification of two-thirds of the signatory states.

Article XXVI. The Charter shall be registered with the Secretariat of the United Nations.

Article XXVII. Questions of interpretation shall be settled by a two-thirds majority vote in the Assembly of Heads of State and Government.

Article XXVIII. Admission of new independent African states to the Organization shall be decided by a simple majority of the Member States.

Articles XXIX–XXXIII. The working languages of the Organization shall be African languages, English, French, Arabic and Portuguese. The Secretary-General may accept gifts and bequests to the Organization, subject to the approval of the Council of Ministers. The Council of Ministers shall establish privileges and immunities to be accorded to the personnel of the Secretariat in the territories of Member States. A State wishing to withdraw from the Organization must give a year's written notice to the Secretariat. The Charter may only be amended after consideration by all Member States and by a two-thirds majority vote of the Assembly of Heads of State and Government. Such amendments will come into force one year after submission.

MEMBERS*

Algeria	Eritrea	Nigeria
Angola	Ethiopia	Rwanda
Benin	Gabon	São Tomé and Príncipe
Botswana	The Gambia	Senegal
Burkina Faso	Ghana	Seychelles
Burundi	Guinea	Sierra Leone
Cameroon	Guinea-Bissau	Somalia
Cape Verde	Kenya	South Africa
Central African Republic	Lesotho	Sudan
Chad	Liberia	Swaziland
The Comoros	Libya	Tanzania
Congo, Democratic Republic†	Madagascar	Togo
Congo, Republic	Malawi	Tunisia
Côte d'Ivoire	Mali	Uganda
Djibouti	Mauritania	Zambia
Egypt	Mauritius	Zimbabwe
Equatorial Guinea	Mozambique	
	Namibia	
	Niger	

* The Sahrawi Arab Democratic Republic (SADR–Western Sahara) was admitted to the OAU in February 1982, following recognition by 26 of the 50 members, but its membership was disputed by Morocco and other states which claimed that a two-thirds majority was needed to admit a state whose existence was in question. Morocco withdrew from the OAU with effect from November 1985.

† Known as Zaire between 1971 and 1997.

Organization

(January 1998)

ASSEMBLY OF HEADS OF STATE

The Assembly of Heads of State and Government meets annually to co-ordinate policies of African states. Resolutions are passed by a two-thirds majority, procedural matters by a simple majority. A chairman is elected at each meeting from among the members, to hold office for one year.

Chairman (1997/98): Robert Mugabe (Zimbabwe).

COUNCIL OF MINISTERS

Consists of ministers of foreign affairs and others and meets twice a year, with provision for extraordinary sessions. Each session elects its own Chairman. Prepares meetings of, and is responsible to, the Assembly of Heads of State.

GENERAL SECRETARIAT

The permanent headquarters of the organization. It carries out functions assigned to it in the Charter of the OAU and by other agreements and treaties made between member states. Departments: Political; Finance; Education, Science, Culture and Social Affairs; Economic Development and Co-operation; Administration and Conferences. The Secretary-General is elected for a four-year term by the Assembly of Heads of State.

Secretary-General: Salim Ahmed Salim (Tanzania).

ARBITRATION COMMISSION

Commission of Mediation, Conciliation and Arbitration: Addis Ababa; f. 1964; consists of 21 members elected by the Assembly of Heads of State for a five-year term; no state may have more than one member; has a Bureau consisting of a President and two Vice-Presidents, who shall not be eligible for re-election. Its task is to hear and settle disputes between member states by peaceful means.

SPECIALIZED COMMISSIONS

There are specialized commissions for economic, social, transport and communications affairs; education, science, culture and health; defence; human rights; and labour.

BUDGET

Member states contribute in accordance with their United Nations assessment. No member state is assessed for an amount exceeding 20% of the yearly regular budget of the Organization. The biennial budget for 1996-98 was US $61.45m. At July 1996 member states owed some $53m. in outstanding contributions.

Principal Events, 1987–97

1987

July The 23rd Assembly of Heads of State reiterated its demands that Western countries should impose economic sanctions against South Africa. It renewed the mandate of the special OAU committee which had been attempting to resolve the dispute between Chad and Libya. It also discussed the spread of the disease AIDS in Africa; and approved the establishment of an African Commission on Human and People's Rights (q.v.), now that the African Charter on Human and People's Rights (approved in 1981) had been ratified by a majority of member states.

Nov. A summit meeting on the subject of Africa's substantial external debt (then estimated to total US $200,000m.) was held in Addis Ababa (but was attended by only 10 heads of state and government). The meeting issued a statement requesting the conversion of past bilateral loans into grants, a 10-year suspension of debt-service payments, reduction of interest rates and the lengthening of debt-maturity periods. It asked that creditors should observe the principle that debt-servicing should not exceed a 'reasonable and bearable' percentage of the debtor country's export earnings. A 'contact group' was established to enlist support for an international conference on African debt.

1988

May The Assembly of Heads of State recognized that no conference on debt was likely to be held in 1988, owing to the reluctance of creditors to participate. It condemned the links with South Africa still maintained by some African countries, and protested at the recently-reported unauthorized disposal of toxic waste in Africa by industrial companies from outside the continent.

Aug. The OAU organized an international conference in Oslo, Norway, on refugees and displaced persons in southern Africa.

1989

Jan. A meeting on apartheid, organized by the OAU, resulted in the formation of an African Anti-Apartheid Committee.

May The OAU Chairman, President Traoré of Mali, undertook a mission of mediation between the governments of Mauritania and Senegal, following ethnic conflict between the citizens of the two countries.

July The Assembly of Heads of State discussed the Namibian independence process, and urged that the UN should ensure that the forthcoming elections there would be fairly conducted. They again requested that an international conference on Africa's debts should be held.

Sept.–Dec. The newly-elected OAU Chairman, Hosni Mubarak, and the newly-appointed OAU Secretary-General, Salim Ahmed Salim, attempted to mediate in the dispute between Mauritania and Senegal. In November a mediation committee, comprising representatives of six countries, visited Mauritania and Senegal.

1990

March A monitoring group was formed by the OAU to report on events in South Africa. The OAU urged the international community to continue imposing economic sanctions on South Africa.

July The Assembly of Heads of State reviewed the implications for Africa of recent socio-economic and political changes in Eastern Europe, and of the European Community's progress towards monetary and political union.

1991

June The Assembly of Heads of State signed the treaty on the creation of an African Economic Community (AEC). The treaty was to enter into force after ratification by two-thirds of OAU member states. The Community was to be established by 2025, beginning with a five-year stage during which measures would be taken to strengthen existing economic groupings. The meeting also established a committee of heads of state to assist national reconciliation in Ethiopia; and gave a mandate to the OAU Secretary-General to undertake a mission to assist in restoring political stability in Somalia.

1992

Feb.–March The OAU was involved, together with the UN and the Organization of the Islamic Conference (OIC, q.v.), in mediation between the warring factions in Mogadishu, Somalia. The OAU subsequently continued to assist in efforts to achieve a peace settlement in Somalia.

May An OAU mission was dispatched to South Africa to monitor the continued violence in that country.

June–July Proposals were advanced at the Assembly of Heads of State, held in Dakar, Senegal, for a mechanism to be established within the OAU for 'conflict management, prevention and resolution'. These proposals were accepted in principle, but operational details were to be elaborated at a later stage.

Oct. The Ad Hoc Committee on Southern Africa met in Gaborone, Botswana, to discuss a report compiled by a team of OAU experts on practical steps to be taken towards the democratization of South Africa. Plans to send a mission to monitor the Mozambican peace accord were announced.

Nov. An International Conference on Assistance to African Children, which was organized by the OAU with assistance from UNICEF, was held in Dakar, Senegal. The Conference aimed to focus awareness on the plight of many of Africa's children and to encourage African countries to honour commitments made at the UN World Summit for Children in 1991, whereby governments were to allocate greater resources to programmes benefiting children.

1993

Feb. A session of the Council of Ministers discussed the OAU's serious financial crisis. The meeting agreed to allocate US $250,000 to the creation of a conflict prevention bureau, and a further $250,000 for the purposes of monitoring elections.

May A Pan-African Conference on Reparations for the suffering caused by colonialism in Africa, organized by the OAU together with the Nigerian Government, was held in Abuja. The Conference appealed to those countries which had benefited from the colonization of Africa and the use of Africans as slaves (particularly European countries and the USA) to make reparations to Africans and their descendants, either in the form of capital transfers, or cancellation of debt.

June Eritrea was admitted as the 52nd member of the OAU. The 29th Assembly of Heads of State resolved to establish a mechanism for conflict prevention and resolution. The mechanism's primary objective was to be anticipation and prevention of conflict. In cases where conflicts had already occurred, the OAU was to undertake peace-making and peace-building activities, including the deployment of civilian or military monitoring missions. However, in the case of a conflict seriously degenerating, assistance would be sought from the United Nations.

July A seminar on the AEC was held in Addis Ababa, Ethiopia, concerned with the popularization of the treaty establishing the Community. Lack of resources emerged as one of the main barriers to the actual creation of the Community.

Sept. The OAU announced the immediate removal of economic sanctions against South Africa, following the approval by that country's Parliament of a bill to establish a transitional executive council prior to the democratic elections, scheduled to be conducted in April 1994.

Oct. The OAU Secretary-General condemned an attempted military coup in Burundi, in which the President and six Cabinet ministers were killed, and the subsequent civil unrest.

Nov. A summit conference of African ministers of foreign affairs, conducted in Addis Ababa, resolved to establish an OAU protection and observation mission to Burundi, consisting of 180 military personnel and 20 civilians, and appealed for international financial and material support to assist the mission. The ministers approved the principles for the establishment of a mechanism for conflict prevention, management and resolution. The meeting suggested that 5% of the OAU budget, but not less than US $1m., be allocated for an OAU Peace Fund to finance the mechanism, and that $0.5m. be made available for 1993.

Dec. A meeting of 11 African Heads of State approved the establishment of the Peace Fund and called for contributions from the international community. A draft statement of the mechanism for conflict prevention, management and resolution, issued by the OAU Secretary-General, expressed support for the efforts to resolve the conflict in Somalia and emphasized the need to promote national reconciliation.

1994

Feb. The Council of Ministers, at its 59th ordinary session, reaffirmed its support for the results of elections in Burundi, which were conducted in 1993, and endorsed the establishment of an OAU mission to promote dialogue and national reconciliation in that country. The Council condemned anti-government forces for the escalation of violence in Angola.

April The OAU mission to South Africa participated as observers of the electoral process. An OAU delegation visited Nigeria and Cameroon to investigate the border dispute between the two countries.

May South Africa was admitted as the 53rd member of the OAU.

June Consultations with each of the conflicting parties in Rwanda were conducted by the OAU. The Assembly of Heads of State, meeting in Tunis, approved a code of conduct for inter-African relations, in order to strengthen political consultation and co-operation for the promotion of security and stability in the region. Nine countries were nominated to serve on the central committee (organ) of the mechanism for conflict prevention, management and resolution. The military component of the OAU mission in Burundi was now deployed in that country, and its mandate was extended until mid-September. (The mission has subsequently been granted three-monthly extensions of its mandate.)

Nov. The Secretary-General, noting the Organization's serious financial situation, warned that most activities of the regular budget for 1994/95 would have to be suspended. Certain sanctions were to be imposed on any country that had not paid its contribution in full by 1 June 1995.

1995

March An extraordinary session of the Council of Ministers, held in Cairo, Egypt, adopted an Agenda for Action, which aimed to stimulate African economic and social development. The document emphasized the importance of peace, democratic government and stability in achieving development targets. It also assessed Africa's role in the world economy and the need for structural reforms of countries' economies, in particular in view of agreements reached under the GATT Uruguay Round of trade negotiations. The OAU, together with representatives of the UN and the Commonwealth Secretariat, dispatched a special mission to Sierra Leone, in order to assess means of facilitating the peace process in that country.

April A meeting of the conflict mechanism's central organ, held in Tunis, Tunisia, reviewed OAU peace initiatives. The meeting urged OAU member states to offer humanitarian aid to consolidate the peace process in Angola and for further OAU assistance for the rehabilitation and reconstruction of Somalia. A seminar, organized jointly by the OAU and the International Committee of the Red Cross, assembled military and civil experts in Yaoundé, Cameroon, to discuss the issue of land-mines.

May An 81-member OAU observer group was deployed to monitor a general election in Ethiopia. The group confirmed that the electoral process had been 'free and fair'.

June Faced with the threat of sanctions, which included a prohibition on full participation in the forthcoming summit and on the election of a country's nationals to key positions in the Organization, member states paid some US $20m. in owed contributions during the month (leaving an estimated total deficit of $38m.). At the 31st Assembly of Heads of State, held in Addis Ababa, Ethiopia, later in the month, the Secretary-General observed that the OAU's peace-keeping role had been severely affected by the failure of member states to pay their contributions. Sanctions were to be imposed on those countries which had failed to pay 25% of their arrears by the end of June. (Liberia and Somalia were exempted from this deadline.) The meeting endorsed a proposal to establish a conflict management centre, provisionally in Cairo, Egypt, to strengthen the OAU's role in conflict prevention. The situation in warring African countries was discussed, as well as the problem of large-scale refugee and displaced populations in the region. In addition, member states urged the international community to end the application of sanctions against Libya.

Sept. An extraordinary meeting of the conflict mechanism's central organ condemned the attempted assassination of Egypt's President Mubarak prior to the 31st Heads of State meeting in June. The committee censured Sudan for protecting the alleged perpetrators of the attack and for supporting other terrorist elements in the country.

Oct. OAU observers monitored the conduct of elections in Zanzibar and attempted to mediate between the parties when the vote failed to secure a decisive result.

Nov. Ten member states (Angola, Central African Republic, Chad, Comoros, Equatorial Guinea, Guinea-Bissau, Niger, São Tomé and Príncipe, Seychelles and Sierra Leone) lost their full rights to participate in the organization, having failed to pay, in full or part, their accumulated contribution arrears, amounting to US $16.5m. A 50-member OAU observer group was deployed to monitor elections in Algeria, as part of an international team.

1996

Feb. The Council of Ministers reiterated the OAU's readiness to promote and support dialogue and reconciliation in Burundi. However, the meeting did not support military intervention in that country, despite a UN report proposing international co-operation with the OAU to establish a stand-by force for Burundi.

March The UN Secretary-General launched a system-wide Special Initiative on Africa, which was based on the development objectives outlined in the OAU Agenda for Action (see above). Funds were to be allocated under the Initiative to strengthen the OAU's capacity for conflict prevention, management and resolution.

May-June The OAU assisted the International Peace Academy to conduct a meeting of international organizations, in Cape Town, South Africa, to promote the OAU's conflict mechanism, under the theme of 'Civil Society and Conflict Management in Africa'.

July The 32nd Assembly of Heads of State agreed to support a plan, formulated earlier that month by the Governments of Tanzania, Uganda and Ethiopia, to send troops to Burundi in a peace-keeping capacity. The Assembly requested logistical and financial support from the international community for the initiative. In a separate declaration OAU leaders expressed their support for Boutros Boutros-Ghali's candidacy for a second term as the UN Secretary-General. The endorsement was opposed by the President of Rwanda, Pasteur Bizimungu, who condemned the lack of UN protection afforded to his country during the civil unrest in 1994. At the end of the meeting it was announced that member states still owing contributions to the organization were to be exempt from sanctions measures until the end of the year, provided that they pay 30% of their arrears by 31 July. (Burundi, Liberia, Sierra Leone and Somalia were to be exempt until March 1997.) At the end of July, following a military coup in Burundi, the OAU endorsed a decision of seven east and central African states to impose economic sanctions against the new regime.

Aug. The US Government granted US $2.9m. to the OAU Peace Fund, in support of conflict prevention and resolution.

Oct. The OAU Secretary-General cautiously endorsed a US proposal to establish an African military force for the protection of civilian populations in areas of conflict. A regional committee of the OAU declared its support for the continuation of the economic embargo against Burundi.

Nov. An OAU delegation, meeting with the heads of state of eight African countries in Nairobi, Kenya, supported the establishment of an international humanitarian force, to be sent to Zaire (although this was never deployed).

Dec. The OAU President, in an attempt to overcome the impasse reached regarding the election of a new UN Secretary-General (owing to US opposition to Boutros-Ghali), confirmed that African nations should propose alternative candidates for the position.

1997

Jan. The UN and the OAU appointed Muhamed Sahnoun as a joint Special Representative for the Great Lakes Region.

Feb. The 65th session of the Council of Ministers, meeting in Libya, expressed its support of that country in the face of sanctions imposed upon it by the international community. The OAU welcomed the newly-elected Secretary-General of the UN, the Ghanaian, Kofi Annan. The situation in Zaire was discussed and an extraordinary summit of the OAU's conflict management mechanism was scheduled for March. Further donations to the OAU Peace Fund were requested.

March A special summit of the OAU Organ on conflict management and resolution, which was attended by delegations from both the Zairean Government and the rebel Alliance des forces démocratiques pour la libération du Congo-Zaïre, called for an immediate cease-fire and concluded a provisional agreement for negotiations between the two sides based on a five-point plan that had been formulated by Sahnoun and approved by the UN Security Council in February.

June The Assembly of Heads of State, meeting in Harare, Zimbabwe, condemned the military coup in Sierra Leone, which took place in May, and endorsed the intervention of ECOMOG troops in order to restore a democratic government in that country. The OAU stated that future coups in the continent would not be tolerated, and the importance of universal human rights to be established across Africa was reiterated throughout the meeting. The first meeting between ministers of the OAU and the European Union was held in New York, USA. The inaugural meeting of the African Economic Community also took place.

July The UN Development Programme donated US $3m. to the OAU conflict management mechanism. An OAU observer group was deployed to monitor elections in Liberia.

Aug. The OAU appointed a special envoy to the Comoros, Pierre Yere, following a declaration of independence by separatists on the islands of Anjouan and Mohéli.

Nov. A group of OAU military observers was dispatched to the Comoros.

Dec. The OAU organized a conference, held in Addis Ababa, Ethiopia, which aimed to resolve the dispute between the Comoran Government and the secessionists. OAU ministers of justice adopted a protocol approving the creation of an African court on human and people's rights.

Specialized Agencies

African Accounting Council: POB 11223, Kinshasa, Democratic Republic of the Congo; f. 1979; provides assistance to institutions in member countries on standardization of accounting; promotes education, further training and research in accountancy and related areas of study. Publ. *Information and Liaison Bulletin* (every two months).

African Bureau for Educational Sciences: 29 ave de la Justice, BP 1764, Kinshasa I, Democratic Republic of the Congo; tel. (12) 22006; telex 21166; f. 1973 to conduct educational research. Publs *Bulletin d'Information* (quarterly), *Revue africaine des sciences de l'éducation* (2 a year), *Répertoire africain des institutions de recherche* (annually).

African Civil Aviation Commission—AFCAC: 15 blvd de la République, BP 2356, Dakar, Senegal; tel. 23-20-30; telex 61182; fax 23-26-61; f. 1969 to encourage co-operation in all civil aviation activities; promotes co-ordination and better utilization and development of African air transport systems and the standardization of aircraft, flight equipment and training programmes for pilots and mechanics; organizes working groups and seminars, and compiles statistics. Pres. Capt. SHETTIMA ABBA-GANA (Nigeria); Sec. A. CHEIFFOU (acting).

Pan-African News Agency—PANA: BP 4650, Dakar, Senegal; tel. 24-14-10; fax 24-13-90; regional headquarters in Khartoum, Sudan; Lusaka, Zambia; Kinshasa, Democratic Republic of the Congo; Lagos, Nigeria; Tripoli, Libya; began operations in May 1983; receives information from national news agencies and circulates news in English and French. Following financial problems, plans to restructure the agency at a cost of US $4.7m., in order to allow shares to be held by the private sector, were announced in June 1997. Capital was to be increased by 25,000 shares, while the agency was to be renamed PANA Presse. Co-ordinator BABACAR FALL. Publ. *PANA Review*.

Pan-African Postal Union—PAPU: POB 6026, Arusha, Tanzania; tel. (57) 8603; telex 42096; fax (57) 8606; f. 1980 to extend members' co-operation in the improvement of postal services. Sec.-Gen. GEZAHEGNE GEBREWOLD (Ethiopia). Publ. *PAPU Bulletin*.

Pan-African Railways Union: BP 687, Kinshasa, Democratic Republic of the Congo; tel. (12) 23861; telex 21258; f. 1972 to standardize, expand, co-ordinate and improve members' railway services; the ultimate aim is to link all systems; main organs: Gen. Assembly, Exec. Bd, Gen. Secr., five tech. cttees. Mems in 30 African countries. Pres. TOM MMARI; Sec.-Gen. ROBERT GEBE NKANA (Malawi).

Pan-African Telecommunications Union: POB 7248, Kinshasa, Democratic Republic of the Congo; f. 1977; co-ordinates devt of telecommunications networks and services in Africa.

Supreme Council for Sports in Africa: BP 1363, Yaoundé, Cameroon; tel. and fax 23-95-80; telex 8295. Sec.-Gen. Dr AWOTURE ELEYAE (Nigeria). Publs *SCSA News* (6 a year), *African Sports Movement Directory* (annually).

ORGANIZATION OF AMERICAN STATES—OAS

(ORGANIZACIÓN DE LOS ESTADOS AMERICANOS—OEA)

Address: 17th St and Constitution Ave, NW, Washington, DC 20006, USA.

Telephone: (202) 458-3000; **telex:** 64128-24838; **fax:** (202) 458-3967.

The OAS was founded at Bogotá, Colombia, in 1948 (succeeding the International Union of American Republics, founded in 1890) to foster peace, security, mutual understanding and co-operation among the nations of the Western Hemisphere.

MEMBERS

Antigua and Barbuda	Guyana
Argentina	Haiti
Bahamas	Honduras
Barbados	Jamaica
Belize	Mexico
Bolivia	Nicaragua
Brazil	Panama
Canada	Paraguay
Chile	Peru
Colombia	Saint Christopher and Nevis
Costa Rica	Saint Lucia
Cuba*	Saint Vincent and the Grenadines
Dominica	Suriname
Dominican Republic	Trinidad and Tobago
Ecuador	USA
El Salvador	Uruguay
Grenada	Venezuela
Guatemala	

* The Cuban Government was suspended from OAS activities in 1962.

Permanent Observers: Algeria, Angola, Austria, Belgium, Croatia, Cyprus, Czech Republic, Egypt, Equatorial Guinea, Finland, France, Germany, Greece, the Holy See, Hungary, India, Israel, Italy, Japan, the Republic of Korea, Lebanon, Morocco, the Netherlands, Pakistan, Poland, Portugal, Romania, Russia, Saudi Arabia, Spain, Switzerland, Tunisia, Ukraine, the United Kingdom and the European Union.

Organization

(January 1998)

GENERAL ASSEMBLY

The Assembly meets annually and may also hold special sessions when convoked by the Permanent Council. As the supreme organ of the OAS, it decides general action and policy.

MEETINGS OF CONSULTATION OF MINISTERS OF FOREIGN AFFAIRS

Meetings are held to consider problems of an urgent nature and of common interest to member states; they may be held at the request of any member state.

PERMANENT COUNCIL

The Council meets regularly throughout the year at OAS headquarters. It is composed of one representative of each member state with the rank of ambassador; each government may accredit alternate representatives and advisers and when necessary appoint an interim representative. The office of Chairman is held in turn by each of the representatives, following alphabetical order according to the names of the countries in Spanish. The Vice-Chairman is determined in the same way, following reverse alphabetical order. Their terms of office are three months.

The Council acts as an organ of consultation and oversees the maintenance of friendly relations between members. It supervises the work of the OAS and promotes co-operation with a variety of other international bodies including the United Nations. The official languages are English, French, Portuguese and Spanish.

INTER-AMERICAN COUNCIL FOR INTEGRAL DEVELOPMENT—CIDI

The Council was established in 1996, replacing the Inter-American Economic and Social Council and the Inter-American Council for Education, Science and Culture. Its aim is to promote co-operation among the countries of the region, in order to accelerate economic and social development. CIDI's work focuses on eight areas: social development and education; cultural development; the generation of productive employment; economic diversification, integration and trade liberalization; strengthening democratic institutions; the exchange of scientific and technological information; the development of tourism; and sustainable environmental development. CIDI comprises three committees: a special committee on trade, a social development committee and an inter-American committee for sustainable development.

Executive Secretary: LEONEL ZÚÑIGA (Mexico).

INTER-AMERICAN JURIDICAL COMMITTEE

Address: Rua Senador Vergueiro 81, Rio de Janeiro, RJ, Brazil; tel. (21) 285-7997; fax (21) 225-4600.

The Committee is composed of 11 jurists, nationals of different member states, elected for a period of four years, with the possibility of re-election. The Committee's purposes are: to serve as an advisory body to the Organization on juridical matters; to promote the progressive development and codification of international law; and to study juridical problems relating to the integration of the developing countries in the hemisphere, and, in so far as may appear desirable, the possibility of attaining uniformity in legislation.

Secretary: MANOEL TOLOMEI MOLETTA.

INTER-AMERICAN COMMISSION ON HUMAN RIGHTS

The Commission was established in 1960 and comprises seven members. It promotes the observance and protection of human rights in the member states of the OAS; it examines and reports on the human rights situation in member countries, and provides consultative services.

President: ALVARO TIRADO.

INTER-AMERICAN COURT OF HUMAN RIGHTS

Address: POB 6906-1000, San José, Costa Rica; tel. 234-0581; fax 234-0584.

The Court was established in 1978, as an autonomous judicial institution whose purpose is to apply and interpret the American Convention on Human Rights (which entered into force in 1978 and had been ratified by 23 OAS member states by the end of July 1991). The Court comprises seven jurists from OAS member states.

Secretary: MANUEL E. VENTURA-ROBLES.

GENERAL SECRETARIAT

The Secretariat, the central and permanent organ of the Organization, performs the duties entrusted to it by the General Assembly, Meetings of Consultation of Ministers of Foreign Affairs and the Councils.

Secretary-General: CÉSAR GAVIRIA TRUJILLO (Colombia).

Assistant Secretary-General: CHRISTOPHER THOMAS (Trinidad and Tobago).

Record of Events

1826 First Congress of American States, convened by Simón Bolívar at Panama City. The Treaty of Perpetual Union, League and Confederation was signed by Colombia, the United Provinces of Central America, Peru, and Mexico.

1889–90 First International Conference of American States (Washington) founded the International Union of American Republics and established a central office, the Commercial Bureau, the purpose of which was the 'prompt collection and distribution of commercial information'.

1910 Fourth Conference (Buenos Aires) changed the organization's name to Union of American Republics. The name of its principal organ was changed from Commercial Bureau to Pan American Union.

1923 Fifth Conference (Santiago, Chile) changed the title to Union of Republics of the American Continent, with the Pan American Union as its permanent organ.

1928 Sixth Conference (Havana): the Governing Board and Pan American Union were prohibited from exercising political functions.

1945 Inter-American Conference on Problems of War and Peace: Mexico City.
The Act of Chapultepec established a system of Continental Security for the American States.

1947 The Inter-American Treaty of Reciprocal Assistance set up a joint security pact for the defence of the Western Hemisphere against attack from outside and for internal security.

1948 Ninth Conference (Bogotá). Member Governments signed the Charter of the Organization of American States.

1954 The OAS adopted the Declaration of Solidarity for the Preservation of the Political Integrity of the American States against the Intervention of International Communism.

1959 An Act was passed by 21 American States to establish the Inter-American Development Bank (q.v.).

1962 Cuba was suspended from the OAS, which supported the USA in its demand for the removal of missile bases in Cuba.

1964 The OAS mediated in dispute between USA and Panama, and voted for sanctions against Cuba by 15 votes to 4 (Bolivia, Chile, Mexico and Uruguay).

1965 An Inter-American Peace Force was created in reaction to events in the Dominican Republic.

1967 A treaty for the establishment of a Latin American nuclear-free zone was signed in Mexico City.
In April a regional summit conference agreed to create a Latin American Common Market based on existing integration systems LAFTA and CACM.

1969 El Salvador and Honduras called on the OAS to investigate alleged violation of human rights of Salvadoreans in Honduras. A committee was sent to investigate after fighting broke out. Observers from OAS member nations supervised cease-fire and exchange of prisoners.

1970 Entry into force of the Protocol of Buenos Aires, establishing the General Assembly as the highest body of the OAS, replacing the Inter-American Conferences, and the three Councils as its main organs. The General Assembly held two special sessions to establish the new system and to discuss other current problems, in particular kidnapping and extortion.

1971 First regular session of the General Assembly of the OAS at San José, Costa Rica, in April.

1976 Sixth General Assembly; chief resolutions concerned human rights, the US Trade Act of 1974 and transnational enterprises. It also resolved to hold a Special Assembly to review matters concerning inter-American co-operation for development. The Assembly proclaimed a Decade of Women 1976–85: Equality, Development and Peace. Honduras and El Salvador signed the Act of Managua to end a series of border incidents between them.

1979 The Inter-American Court of Human Rights was formally established in San José, Costa Rica, its members installed, and the statutes governing its operation were adopted.

1980 The Permanent Council met in July and passed a resolution condemning the military coup in Bolivia and deploring the interruption of the return to democracy there. In November the 10th General Assembly named Argentina, Chile, El Salvador, Haiti, Paraguay and Uruguay as countries of special concern with regard to human rights violations (but avoided condemning them outright after Argentina threatened to withdraw from the organization if this was done).

1981 In February ministers of foreign affairs urged Ecuador and Peru to stop military operations in their border area: both countries agreed to a cease-fire monitored by a committee composed of representatives of Argentina, Brazil, Chile and the USA.

1982 In May ministers of foreign affairs urged Argentina and the United Kingdom to cease hostilities over the Falkland (Malvinas) Islands and to resume negotiations for a peaceful settlement of the conflict, taking into account Argentina's 'rights of sovereignty' and the interests of the islanders.

1984 In November the General Assembly discussed the political crisis in Central America and the increasing foreign debts incurred by Latin American countries; it agreed to attempt to 'revitalize' the OAS during the next year, so that the Organization could play a more effective part in solving regional problems.

1985 In December amendments to the OAS Charter were adopted by the General Assembly (subject to ratification by two-thirds of the member states, which was expected to take several years). The amendments increased the executive powers of the OAS Secretary-General, who would henceforth be allowed to take the initiative in bringing before the Permanent Council matters that 'might threaten the peace and security of the hemisphere or the development of the member states', something which previously only a member country had been permitted to do. The OAS also gained greater powers of mediation through an amendment allowing the Permanent Council to try to resolve a dispute between members, whether or not all the parties concerned had (as previously stipulated) agreed to take the matter before the OAS.

1986 In November the General Assembly passed a resolution expressing 'strong concern' over the United Kingdom's decision, in the previous month, to establish an exclusive 'conservation and management zone' extending for 150 nautical miles around the Falkland Islands. The Assembly also expressed its support for the negotiations conducted by the Contadora Group with the aim of bringing about peace in Central America.

1987 Following the signing in August of the 'Esquipulas II' agreement (in which the heads of government of Costa Rica, El Salvador, Guatemala, Honduras and Nicaragua agreed to implement a cease-fire between government forces and rebel groups, an amnesty for rebels, and democratic political processes) the Secretary-General of the OAS was invited to serve as a member of the international commission which was established to oversee compliance with the agreement.

1988 The OAS Secretary-General was invited to witness negotiations held in March between the Nicaraguan Government and rebel forces, and, following the signing of a cease-fire agreement with effect from 1 April, he continued to serve as a member of the verification commission established by the agreement. In November the Protocol of Cartagena, containing amendments to the OAS Charter, entered into force.

1989 In May ministers of foreign affairs met to consider the situation in Panama (where the Government had declared the recent elections invalid following an apparent victory by its opponents) and instructed a four-member group, comprising the OAS Secretary-General and three ministers, to attempt to bring about democratic reforms in Panama. The mission made five visits to Panama, but failed to bring about a transfer of power.

The OAS Secretary-General was invited to observe the electoral process in Nicaragua (where elections were due to be held in February 1990), and in July 1989 he established a team of observers for this purpose. The OAS Secretary-General, together with the UN Secretary-General, was requested to verify the dismantling of the Nicaraguan resistance forces, as agreed upon by Central American heads of state in August. In December the OAS adopted a resolution deploring the USA's invasion of Panama two days previously, and urging that hostilities should cease immediately.

1990 Following the elections held in Nicaragua in February, OAS observers were invited to remain in the country during the transitional period leading to the inauguration of the new President in April. OAS observers were sent to elections in the Dominican Republic in May and in Guatemala in November. An electoral assistance and observation mission was sent to Haiti for the elections in December.

1991 Electoral assistance and observer missions were sent to Suriname and Paraguay for elections held in those countries in May. In June the General Assembly approved a resolution on representative democracy, authorizing the Secretary-General to convoke the Permanent Council immediately in the case of the abandonment of democratic procedures or the overthrow of a democratically elected government in a member state. The Permanent Council would, in turn, have the power to convene a meeting of OAS ministers of foreign affairs within 10 days. This procedure was invoked following the overthrow by a military coup of the democratically elected Government in Haiti at the end of September. An *ad hoc* meeting of ministers of foreign affairs imposed trade and diplomatic sanctions on Haiti and sent a mission to attempt to persuade the military leaders to restore the deposed President, Fr Jean-Bertrand Aristide, to his position.

1992 In February an agreement was negotiated and signed by Haitian legislative leaders and the deposed President Aristide, under OAS auspices, to provide the basis for a return to democratic government. This agreement was not ratified by the Haitian authorities. The OAS set up a special committee to monitor and report on compliance with the trade embargo decreed by the ministers of foreign affairs.

Following the suspension of constitutional government by the President of Peru in April, an *ad hoc* meeting of ministers of foreign affairs was convened (in accordance with the procedures for the preservation of representative democracy established by the OAS General Assembly in 1991), and a mission was sent to that country.

The 22nd General Assembly was held in the Bahamas in May, as well as two sessions of the *ad hoc* meeting of ministers of foreign affairs to consider the situations in Haiti and Peru. In August an international mission, led by the Secretary-General of the OAS, visited Haiti for discussions on a political solution there. An *ad hoc* meeting of ministers of foreign affairs in December approved a resolution urging all OAS and UN member states to adopt measures to implement fully the trade embargo against Haiti, particularly the suspension of supplies of petroleum, weapons and munitions, and to 'freeze' the state assets of Haiti. A large OAS electoral assistance mission was sent to Peru in November to monitor the election of a Constituent Congress. The installation of the democratic Congress in the following month was recognized by the *ad hoc* meeting of ministers of foreign affairs, which was then adjourned.

At the 16th special session of the General Assembly, held in December, the Protocol of Washington was adopted as an amendment to the OAS Charter. The resolution on representative democracy (see 1991, above) was incorporated into the Charter, as part of this Protocol, as a provision for the suspension of any member whose democratic government had been overthrown by force. The General Assembly also incorporated into the purposes and principles of the Organization's Charter the eradication of extreme poverty.

1993 An OAS mission was sent to Paraguay in March to observe preparations for, and the holding of, the May general election. An *ad hoc* meeting of ministers of foreign affairs was convened in May, following the suspension of the Constitution and dissolution of Congress by the President of Guatemala. In June the Guatemalan Constitutional Court declared the positions of President and Vice-President vacant, and a new president was elected by congress, in accordance with the Constitution. After taking note of these positive developments, the *ad hoc* meeting was adjourned.

In January the Secretary-General appointed as his representative for Haiti the special representative of the UN Secretary-General. The representative continued talks with the *de facto* Government and oversaw the establishment of a joint OAS–UN civilian mission in February. The peace plan agreed on Governor's Island, off New York, was negotiated under OAS–UN auspices, and was signed in July by the country's governing military leader and the deposed President, Fr Jean-Bertrand Aristide. In mid-October the 270 OAS–UN monitors were evacuated from the country, having been directly threatened by the civil unrest that accompanied the approach of the peace agreement's deadline of 30 October for the return of Aristide.

Further amendments to the OAS Charter were made by the General Assembly in June, through the approval of the Protocol of Managua (see above). Other measures were introduced to improve the delivery of technical co-operation to member states, as part of the Organization's commitment to the eradication of extreme poverty.

1994 In February an OAS delegation, including the Secretary-General, monitored presidential elections in Costa Rica as part of a team of international observers.

In late March the new Secretary-General, César Gaviria Trujillo (formerly President of Colombia), was elected; he took office in September, announcing that his principal objective was the achievement of a free trade area covering the whole of the Americas.

In May OAS countries were reported to be divided on the use of military intervention in Haiti, with only the USA, Argentina and Anguilla in favour of it. A UN-OAS joint civilian mission (MICIVIH), comprising human rights monitors, was expelled from Haiti in July. At the General Assembly, held in June, the reinforcement of sanctions against Haiti was approved, with the Secretary-General urging compliance. The measures ended following the restoration of President Aristide in October. In December the OAS and the UN issued a joint appeal to the international community for humanitarian and reconstruction assistance totalling US $77m. to help secure democracy in Haiti over a six-month period.

The OAS participated in the Summit of the Americas, which was convened in Miami, USA, in December, and agreed to organize a special regional conference on the prevention of terrorism. The Summit endorsed the concept of a Free Trade Area of the Americas (FTAA), which was to be achieved by 2005.

1995 In February the Inter-American Commission on Human Rights declared that it considered the US embargo on the supply of food and medicine to Cuba to be a violation of international humanitarian law and of OAS principles. The issue was, among others, considered at the General Assembly meeting held in June, in Port-au-Prince, Haiti. Some support was expressed among OAS member states for the readmission of Cuba into the organization. Also in June, the OAS participated in a meeting of Latin American trade ministers, convened in Denver, USA, to discuss the FTAA. The OAS, with the Inter-American Development Bank, was to take the lead in technical efforts to pursue the goal of the FTAA.

A 300-member OAS team monitored legislative and municipal elections, held in Haiti in June and July.

1996 In June a resolution referring the US 'Helms-Burton' legislation, allowing punitive measures against foreign companies that traded with Cuba, to the Inter-American Juridical Committee was supported by a large majority of OAS member states (23; 10 countries abstained and the USA voted against). The General Assembly also approved resolutions regarding the secure future of the Panama Canal (the control of which was to be transferred from the USA to Panama on 31 December 1999) and the development of tourism in the region (an OAS Intersectoral Tourist Unit was to be established). The Permanent Council was charged with implementing the measures approved at the Specialized Inter-American Conference on Terrorism that had been held in Peru in April. The General Assembly endorsed the organization of the first high-level meeting on social development and the proposal by the Secretary-General to create an OAS Specialized Unit on Social Development, in order to assist in the fight against poverty and discrimination. In August the Inter-American Juridical Committee ruled that the 'Helms-Burton' legislation did not conform to international law.

1997 The General Assembly meeting held in Lima, Peru, in June, resolved to limit the stockpiling of conventional weapons and to clear all land-mines from the region within the medium term. The establishment of an inter-American co-operation programme to combat corruption was also approved. In October two OAS observers monitoring elections in Colombia were taken hostage by the Ejército de Liberación Nacional guerrilla movement, which reportedly was concerned about the Organization's neutrality.

FINANCE

The OAS budget for 1997 amounted to US $100.6m., while the budget for 1998 totalled $91m.

PUBLICATIONS

(in English and Spanish)

Américas (6 a year).
Annual Report.
Catalog of Publications (annually).
Ciencia Interamericana (quarterly).
La Educación (quarterly).
Statistical Bulletin (quarterly).
Numerous cultural, legal and scientific reports and studies.

SPECIALIZED ORGANIZATIONS OF THE OAS

Inter-American Children's Institute: Avda 8 de Octubre 2904, Casilla Correos 16212, Montevideo, Uruguay; tel. (2) 4872150; fax (2) 4873242; e-mail iin@chasque.apc.org; f. 1927 to achieve better health, education, social legislation, social services and statistics; conducts research on problems relating to children and the family; provides technical assistance to governments in establishing institutions to protect the welfare of children. Dir-Gen. RODRIGO QUINTANA (Chile). Publ. *Boletín* (quarterly).

Inter-American Commission of Women: General Secretariat of the OAS, 17th St and Constitution Ave, NW, Washington, DC 20006, USA; tel. (202) 458-6084; fax (202) 458-6094; f. 1928 for the extension of civil, political, economic, social and cultural rights for women. Pres. VILMA QUEZADA MARTÍNEZ (Honduras).

Inter-American Indian Institute: Av. de las Fuentes 106, Col. Jardines del Pedregal 01900 México, DF, Mexico; tel. (5) 595-8410; fax (5) 652-0089; f. 1940; conducts research on the situation of the indigenous peoples of America; assists the exchange of information; promotes indigenist policies in member states aimed at the elimination of poverty and development within Indian communities, and to secure their position as ethnic groups within a democratic society. Dir Dr JOSÉ MANUEL DEL VAL (Mexico); Exec. Co-ordinator EVANGELINA MENDIZABAL. Publs *América Indígena* (quarterly), *Anuario Indigenista*.

Inter-American Institute for Co-operation on Agriculture: Apdo 55–2200 Coronado, San José, Costa Rica; tel. 2290222; telex 2144; fax 2294741; f. 1942 (as the Inter-American Institute of Agricultural Sciences: new name 1980); supports the efforts of member states to improve agricultural development and rural well-being; encourages co-operation between regional organizations, and provides a forum for the exchange of experience. Dir-Gen. CARLOS AQUINO GONZÁLEZ (Dominican Republic). Publ. *Comuniica* (quarterly).

Pan American Health Organization: 525 23rd St, NW, Washington, DC 20037, USA; tel. (202) 974-3000; telex 248338; fax (202) 974-3663; e-mail webmaster@paho.org; f. 1902; co-ordinates regional efforts to improve health; maintains close relations with national health organizations and serves as the Regional Office for the Americas of the World Health Organization. Dir Sir GEORGE ALLEYNE (Barbados).

Pan-American Institute of Geography and History: Ex-Arzobispado 29, 11860 México, DF, Mexico; tel. (5) 277-5888; fax (5) 271-6172; f. 1928; co-ordinates and promotes the study of cartography, geophysics, geography, history, anthropology, archaeology, and other related scientific studies. Pres. Dr JORGE SALVADOR LARA (Ecuador); Sec.-Gen. CHESTER ZELAYA-GOODMAN (Costa Rica). Publs *Boletín Aéreo, Revista Cartográfica, Revista Geográfica, Revista de Historia de América, Revista de Arqueología Americana, Revista Geofísica, Folklore Americano, Boletín de Antropologia Americana.*

ASSOCIATED ORGANIZATIONS

Inter-American Defense Board: 2600 16th St, NW, Washington, DC 20441, USA; tel. (202) 939-6600; works in liaison with member governments to plan and train for the common defence of the western hemisphere; operates the Inter-American Defense College. Chair. Maj.-Gen. JOHN C. THOMPSON (USA).

Inter-American Nuclear Energy Commission: General Secretariat of the OAS, 17th St and Constitution Ave, NW, Washington, DC 20006, USA; tel. (202) 458-3368; telex 64128; fax (202) 458-3167; f. 1959 to assist member countries in developing and co-ordinating nuclear energy research; organizes periodic conferences and gives fellowships and financial assistance to research institutions. Exec. Sec. SITOO MUKERJI (Canada).

ORGANIZATION OF ARAB PETROLEUM EXPORTING COUNTRIES—OAPEC

Address: POB 20501, Safat 13066, Kuwait.

Telephone: 4844500; **telex:** 22166; **fax:** 4815747; **e-mail:** oapec@kuwait.net; **internet:** http://www.kuwait.net/~oapec.

OAPEC was established in 1968 to safeguard the interests of members and to determine ways and means for their co-operation in various forms of economic activity in the petroleum industry. In 1996 member states accounted for 25.7% of total world petroleum production.

MEMBERS

Algeria	Kuwait	Syria
Bahrain	Libya	United Arab Emirates
Egypt*	Qatar	
Iraq	Saudi Arabia	

* Egypt's membership was suspended in April 1979, but restored in May 1989.

Organization

(January 1998)

MINISTERIAL COUNCIL

The Council consists normally of the ministers of petroleum of the member states, and forms the supreme authority of the Organization, responsible for drawing up its general policy, directing its activities and laying down its governing rules. It meets twice yearly, and may hold extraordinary sessions. Chairmanship is on an annual rotation basis.

EXECUTIVE BUREAU

Assists the Council to direct the management of the Organization, approves staff regulations, reviews the budget, and refers it to the Council, considers matters relating to the Organization's agreements and activities and draws up the agenda for the Council. The Bureau comprises one senior official from each member state. Chairmanship is by rotation. The Bureau convenes at least three times a year.

GENERAL SECRETARIAT

Secretary-General: ABD AL-AZIZ AT-TURKI (Saudi Arabia).

Besides the Office of the Secretary-General, there are four departments: Finance and Administrative Affairs, Information and Library, Technical Affairs and Economics. The last two form the Arab Centre for Energy Studies (which was established in 1983). At the end of 1997 there were 21 professional staff members and 30 general personnel at the General Secretariat.

JUDICIAL TRIBUNAL

The Tribunal comprises seven judges from Arab countries. Its task is to settle differences in interpretation and application of the OAPEC Agreement, arising between members and also between OAPEC and its affiliates; disputes among member countries on petroleum activities falling within OAPEC's jurisdiction and not under the sovereignty of member countries; and disputes that the Ministerial Council decides to submit to the Tribunal.

President: FARIS AL-WAGAYAN.

Registrar: RIAD AD-DAOUDI.

Activities

OAPEC co-ordinates different aspects of the Arab petroleum industry through the joint undertakings described below. It co-operates with the League of Arab States and other Arab organizations, and attempts to link petroleum research institutes in the Arab states. It organizes or participates in conferences and seminars, many of which are held jointly with non-Arab organizations in order to enhance Arab and international co-operation.

OAPEC provides training in technical matters and in documentation and information. The General Secretariat also conducts technical and feasibility studies and carries out market reviews. It provides information through a library, 'databank' and the publications listed below.

The invasion of Kuwait by Iraq in August 1990, and the subsequent international embargo on petroleum exports from Iraq and Kuwait, severely disrupted OAPEC's activities. In December the OAPEC Council decided to establish temporary headquarters in Cairo while Kuwait was under occupation. The Council resolved to reschedule overdue payments by Iraq and Syria over a 15-year period, and to postpone the Fifth Arab Energy Conference from mid-1992 to mid-1994. The Conference was held in Cairo, Egypt, in May 1994, attended by OAPEC ministers of petroleum and energy, senior officials from nine other Arab states and representatives of regional and international organizations. The Sixth Conference was scheduled to be held in Damascus, Syria, in 1998. In June 1994 OAPEC returned to its permanent headquarters in Kuwait.

During 1995 the General Secretariat organized the 14th training programme relating to the fundamentals of the petroleum and gas industry, held in April, a workshop on the application of new technologies to the production of hydrocarbons, held in the Netherlands, in September, and a seminar on pipeline transportation of hydrocarbons in Arab countries, held in November. The Secretariat also convened a meeting of energy information specialists from the Arab countries, as part of its efforts to develop an integrated resource base, or 'databank' to serve the information needs of the sector throughout the region.

FINANCE

The 1998 budget, approved by the Council in December 1997, amounted to 1,447,000 Kuwaiti dinars (KD). In addition, a budget of 118,800 KD was approved for the Judicial Tribunal.

OAPEC-SPONSORED VENTURES

Arab Maritime Petroleum Transport Company—AMPTC: POB 22525, Safat 13086, Kuwait; tel. 4844500; telex 22180; fax 4842996; f. 1973 to undertake transport of crude petroleum, gas, refined products and petro-chemicals, and thus to increase Arab participation in the tanker transport industry; auth. cap. US $200m. Gen. Man. SULEIMAN AL-BASSAM.

Arab Petroleum Investments Corporation—APICORP: POB 448, Dhahran Airport 31932, Saudi Arabia; tel. 864-7400; telex 870068; fax 898-1883; f. 1975 to finance investments in petroleum and petrochemicals projects and related industries in the Arab world and in developing countries, with priority being given to Arab joint ventures. Projects financed include gas liquefaction plants, petrochemicals, tankers, oil refineries, pipelines, exploration, detergents, fertilizers and process control instrumentation; auth. cap. US $1,200m.; subs. cap. $460m. (31 Dec. 1996). Shareholders: Kuwait, Saudi Arabia and United Arab Emirates (17% each), Libya (15%), Iraq and Qatar (10% each), Algeria (5%), Bahrain, Egypt and Syria (3% each). Chair. ABDULLAH A. AZ-ZAID; Gen.-Man. Dr NUREDDIN FARRAG.

Arab Company for Detergent Chemicals—ARADET: POB 27864, el-Monsour, Baghdad, Iraq; tel. (1) 541-9893; telex 213675; f. 1981 to implement two projects in Iraq; APICORP and the Iraqi Government each hold 32% of shares in the co; auth. cap. 72m. Iraqi dinars.

Arab Petroleum Services Company—APSCO: POB 12925, Tripoli, Libya; tel. (21) 45861; telex 20405; fax (21) 3331930; f. 1977 to provide petroleum services through the establishment of companies specializing in various activities, and to train specialized personnel; auth. cap. 100m. Libyan dinars; subs. cap. 15m. Libyan dinars. Chair. AYYAD AD-DALI; Gen.-Man. ISMAIL AL-KORAITLI.

Arab Drilling and Workover Company: POB 680, Suani Rd, km 3.5, Tripoli, Libya; tel. (21) 800064; telex 20361; fax (21) 805945; f. 1980; auth. cap. 12m. Libyan dinars; Gen. Man. MUHAMMAD AHMAD ATTIGA.

Arab Geophysical Exploration Services Company—AGESCO: POB 84224, Tripoli, Libya; tel. (21) 800031; telex 20716; fax (21) 800032; f. 1985; auth. cap. 12m. Libyan dinars; Gen. Man. AYYAD AD-DALI.

Arab Well Logging Company—AWLCO: POB 6225, Baghdad, Iraq; tel. (1) 541-8259; telex 213688; f. 1983; provides well-logging services and data interpretation; auth. cap. 7m. Iraqi dinars.

Arab Petroleum Training Institute—APTI: POB 6037, Al-Tajeyat, Baghdad, Iraq; tel. (1) 551-3135; telex 212728; fax (1) 521-

0526; f. 1978 to provide instruction in many technical aspects of the oil industry. Since Dec. 1994 the Institute has been placed under the trusteeship of the Iraqi Government. Dir HAZIM B. ASAD (acting).

Arab Shipbuilding and Repair Yard Company—ASRY: POB 50110, Hidd, Bahrain; tel. 671111; telex 8455; fax 670236; e-mail asryco@batelco.com.bh; f. 1974 to undertake repairs and servicing of vessels; operates a 500,000 dwt dry dock in Bahrain; two floating docks operational since 1992. Capital (auth. and subs.) US $340m. Chair. Sheikh DAIJ BIN KHALIFA AL-KHALIFA; Chief Exec. MOHAMED M. AL-KHATEEB.

PUBLICATIONS

Energy Resources Monitor (quarterly, Arabic).

OAPEC Monthly Bulletin (Arabic and English editions).

OAPEC Statistical Bulletin (Arabic and English editions).

Oil and Arab Co-operation (quarterly, Arabic).

Secretary-General's Annual Report (Arabic and English editions).

Papers, studies, conference proceedings.

ORGANIZATION OF THE ISLAMIC CONFERENCE—OIC

Address: Kilo 6, Mecca Rd, POB 178, Jeddah 21411, Saudi Arabia.

Telephone: (2) 680-0800; **telex:** 601366; **fax:** (2) 687-3568.

The Organization was formally established in May 1971, when its Secretariat became operational, following a summit meeting of Muslim heads of state at Rabat, Morocco, in September 1969, and the Islamic Foreign Ministers' Conference in Jeddah in March 1970, and in Karachi, Pakistan, in December 1970.

MEMBERS

Afghanistan	Iran	Qatar
Albania	Iraq	Saudi Arabia
Algeria	Jordan	Senegal
Azerbaijan	Kazakhstan	Sierra Leone
Bahrain	Kuwait	Somalia
Bangladesh	Kyrgyzstan	Sudan
Benin	Lebanon	Suriname
Brunei	Libya	Syria
Burkina Faso	Malaysia	Tajikistan
Cameroon	Maldives	Togo
Chad	Mali	Tunisia
The Comoros	Mauritania	Turkey
Djibouti	Morocco	Turkmenistan
Egypt	Mozambique	Uganda
Gabon	Niger	United Arab Emirates
The Gambia	Nigeria*	Uzbekistan
Guinea	Oman	Yemen
Guinea-Bissau	Pakistan	
Indonesia	Palestine	

* Nigeria renounced its membership of the OIC in May 1991; however, the OIC has not formally recognized this decision.

Note: Observer status has been granted to Bosnia and Herzegovina, the Central African Republic, Côte d'Ivoire, Guyana, the Muslim community of the 'Turkish Republic of Northern Cyprus', the Moro National Liberation Front (MNLF) of the southern Philippines, the United Nations, the Non-Aligned Movement, the League of Arab States, the Organization of African Unity, the Economic Co-operation Organization, the Union of the Arab Maghreb and the Co-operation Council for the Arab States of the Gulf.

Organization

(January 1998)

SUMMIT CONFERENCES

The supreme body of the Organization is the Conference of Heads of State, which met in 1969 at Rabat, Morocco, in 1974 at Lahore, Pakistan, and in January 1981 at Mecca, Saudi Arabia, when it was decided that summit conferences would be held every three years in future. Seventh Conference: Casablanca, Morocco, December 1994; eighth Conference: Teheran, Iran, December 1997. The ninth Conference was to be held in Doha, Qatar, in 2000.

CONFERENCE OF MINISTERS OF FOREIGN AFFAIRS

Conferences take place annually, to consider the means for implementing the general policy of the Organization, although they may also be convened for extraordinary sessions.

SECRETARIAT

The executive organ of the Organization, headed by a Secretary-General (who is elected by the Conference of Ministers of Foreign Affairs for a four-year term, renewable only once) and four Assistant Secretaries-General (similarly appointed).

Secretary-General: AZEDDINE LARAKI (Morocco).

At the summit conference in January 1981 it was decided that an International Islamic Court of Justice should be established to adjudicate in disputes between Muslim countries. Experts met in January 1983 to draw up a constitution for the court, but by 1998 it was not yet in operation.

SPECIALIZED COMMITTEES

Al-Quds Committee: f. 1975 to implement the resolutions of the Islamic Conference on the status of Jerusalem (Al-Quds); it meets at the level of foreign ministers; maintains the Al-Quds Fund; Chair. King HASSAN II of Morocco.

Standing Committee for Economic and Commercial Co-operation (COMCEC): f. 1981; Chair. SÜLEYMAN DEMIREL (Pres. of Turkey).

Standing Committee for Information and Cultural Affairs (COMIAC): f. 1981; Chair. ABDOU DIOUF (Pres. of Senegal).

Standing Committee for Scientific and Technological Co-operation (COMSTECH): f. 1981; Chair. FAROOQ A. LEGHARI (Pres. of Pakistan).

Islamic Commission for Economic, Cultural and Social Affairs: f. 1976.

Permanent Finance Committee.

Other committees comprise the Committee of Islamic Solidarity with the Peoples of the Sahel, the Six-Member Committee on the Situation of Muslims in the Philippines, the Six-Member Committee on Palestine, the *ad hoc* Committee on Afghanistan, the OIC contact group on Bosnia and Herzegovina, and the OIC contact group on Jammu and Kashmir.

Activities

The Organization's aims, as proclaimed in the Charter that was adopted in 1972, are:

(i) To promote Islamic solidarity among member states;

(ii) To consolidate co-operation among member states in the economic, social, cultural, scientific and other vital fields, and to arrange consultations among member states belonging to international organizations;

(iii) To endeavour to eliminate racial segregation and discrimination and to eradicate colonialism in all its forms;

(iv) To take necessary measures to support international peace and security founded on justice;

(v) To co-ordinate all efforts for the safeguard of the Holy Places and support of the struggle of the people of Palestine, and help them to regain their rights and liberate their land;

(vi) To strengthen the struggle of all Muslim people with a view to safeguarding their dignity, independence and national rights; and

(vii) To create a suitable atmosphere for the promotion of co-operation and understanding among member states and other countries.

The first summit conference of Islamic leaders (representing 24 states) took place in 1969 following the burning of the Al Aqsa Mosque in Jerusalem. At this conference it was decided that Islamic governments should 'consult together with a view to promoting close co-operation and mutual assistance in the economic, scientific, cultural and spiritual fields, inspired by the immortal teachings of Islam'. Thereafter the foreign ministers of the countries concerned met annually, and adopted the Charter of the Organization of the Islamic Conference in 1972.

At the second Islamic summit conference (Lahore, Pakistan, 1974), the Islamic Solidarity Fund was established, together with a committee of representatives which later evolved into the Islamic Commission for Economic, Cultural and Social Affairs. Subsequently, numerous other subsidiary bodies have been set up (see below).

ECONOMIC CO-OPERATION

A general agreement for economic, technical and commercial co-operation came into force in 1981, providing for the establishment of joint investment projects and trade co-ordination. This was followed by an agreement on promotion, protection and guarantee of investments among member states. A plan of action to strengthen economic co-operation was adopted at the third Islamic summit conference in 1981, aiming to promote collective self-reliance and the development of joint ventures in all sectors. In May 1993 the OIC committee for economic and commercial co-operation, meeting in Istanbul, agreed to review and update the 1981 plan of action.

A meeting of ministers of industry was held in February 1982, and agreed to promote industrial co-operation, including joint ventures in agricultural machinery, engineering and other basic industries. The fifth summit conference, held in 1987, approved proposals for joint development of modern technology, and for improving scientific and technical skills in the less developed Islamic countries. In December 1988 it was announced that a committee of experts, established by the OIC, was to draw up a 10-year programme of assistance to developing countries (mainly in Africa) in science and technology.

CULTURAL CO-OPERATION

The Organization supports education in Muslim communities throughout the world, and was instrumental in the establishment of Islamic universities in Niger and Uganda (see below). It organizes seminars on various aspects of Islam, and encourages dialogue with the other monotheistic religions. Support is given to publications on Islam both in Muslim and Western countries.

In March 1989 the Conference of Ministers of Foreign Affairs denounced as an apostate the author of the controversial novel *The Satanic Verses* (Salman Rushdie), demanded the withdrawal of the book from circulation, and urged member states to boycott publishing houses that refused to comply.

HUMANITARIAN ASSISTANCE

Assistance is given to Muslim communities affected by wars and natural disasters, in co-operation with UN organizations, particularly UNHCR. The countries of the Sahel region (Burkina Faso, Cape Verde, Chad, The Gambia, Guinea, Guinea-Bissau, Mali, Mauritania, Niger and Senegal) receive particular attention as victims of drought. In April 1993 member states pledged US $80m. in emergency assistance for Muslims affected by the war in Bosnia and Herzegovina (see below for details of subsequent assistance).

POLITICAL CO-OPERATION

The Organization is also active at a political level. From the beginning it called for vacation of Arab territories by Israel, recognition of the rights of Palestinians and of the Palestine Liberation Organization (PLO) as their sole legitimate representative, and the restoration of Jerusalem to Arab rule. The 1981 summit conference called for a *jihad* (holy war—though not necessarily in a military sense) 'for the liberation of Jerusalem and the occupied territories'; this was to include an Islamic economic boycott of Israel. In 1982 Islamic ministers of foreign affairs decided to establish Islamic offices for boycotting Israel and for military co-operation with the PLO. The 1984 summit conference agreed to reinstate Egypt (suspended following the peace treaty signed with Israel in 1979) as a member of the OIC, although the resolution was opposed by seven states.

The fifth summit conference, held in January 1987, discussed the continuing Iran–Iraq war, and agreed that the Islamic Peace Committee should attempt to prevent the sale of military equipment to the parties in the conflict. The conference also discussed the conflicts in Chad and Lebanon, and requested the holding of a United Nations conference to define international terrorism, as opposed to legitimate fighting for freedom.

In August 1990 a majority of ministers of foreign affairs condemned Iraq's recent invasion of Kuwait, and demanded the withdrawal of Iraqi forces. In August 1991 the Conference of Ministers of Foreign Affairs obstructed Iraq's attempt to propose a resolution demanding the repeal of economic sanctions against the country. The sixth summit conference, held in Senegal in December 1991, reflected the divisions in the Arab world that resulted from Iraq's invasion of Kuwait and the ensuing war. Twelve heads of state did not attend, sending representatives, reportedly to register protest at the presence of Jordan and the PLO at the conference, both of which had given support to Iraq. Disagreement also arose between the PLO and the majority of other OIC members when it was proposed to cease the OIC's support for the PLO's *jihad* in the Arab territories occupied by Israel. The proposal, which was adopted, represented an attempt to further the Middle East peace negotiations.

In August 1992 the UN General Assembly approved a non-binding resolution, introduced by the OIC, that requested the UN Security Council to take increased action, including the use of force, in order to defend the non-Serbian population of Bosnia and Herzegovina (some 43% of Bosnians being Muslims) from Serbian aggression, and to restore its 'territorial integrity'. The OIC Conference of Ministers of Foreign Affairs, which was held in Jeddah, Saudi Arabia, in early December, demanded anew that the UN Security Council take all necessary measures against Serbia and Montenegro, including military intervention, in accordance with Article 42 of the UN Charter, in order to protect the Bosnian Muslims. In early February 1993 the OIC appealed to the Security Council to remove the embargo on armaments to Bosnia and Herzegovina with regard to the Bosnian Muslims, to allow them to defend themselves from the Bosnian Serbs, who were far better armed.

A report by an OIC fact-finding mission, which in February 1993 visited Azad Kashmir while investigating allegations of repression of the largely Muslim population of the Indian state of Jammu and Kashmir by the Indian armed forces, was presented to the 1993 Conference. The meeting urged member states to take the necessary measures to persuade India to cease the 'massive human rights violations' in Jammu and Kashmir and to allow the Indian Kashmiris to 'exercise their inalienable right to self-determination'. In September 1994 ministers of foreign affairs, meeting in Islamabad, Pakistan, urged the Indian Government to grant permission for an OIC fact-finding mission, and for other human rights groups, to visit Jammu and Kashmir (which it had continually refused to do) and to refrain from human rights violations of the Kashmiri people. The ministers agreed to establish a contact group on Jammu and Kashmir, which was to provide a mechanism for promoting international awareness of the situation in that region and for seeking a peaceful solution to the dispute. In December OIC heads of state approved a resolution condemning reported human rights abuses by Indian security forces in Kashmir.

In July 1994 the OIC Secretary-General visited Afghanistan and proposed the establishment of a preparatory mechanism to promote national reconciliation in that country. In mid-1995 Saudi Arabia, acting as a representative of the OIC, pursued a peace initiative for Afghanistan and issued an invitation for leaders of the different factions to hold negotiations in Jeddah.

A special ministerial meeting on Bosnia and Herzegovina was held in July 1993, at which seven OIC countries committed themselves to making available up to 17,000 troops to serve in the UN Protection Force in the former Yugoslavia (UNPROFOR), to assist the United Nations in providing adequate protection and relief to the victims of war in Bosnia and Herzegovina. The meeting also decided to dispatch immediately a ministerial mission to persuade influential governments to support the OIC's demands for the removal of the arms embargo on Bosnian Muslims and the convening of a restructured international conference to bring about a political solution to the conflict. At the end of September 1994 ministers of foreign affairs of nine countries constituting the OIC contact group on Bosnia and Herzegovina, meeting in New York, resolved to prepare an assessment document on the issue, and to establish an alliance with its Western counterpart (comprising France, Germany, Russia, the United Kingdom and the USA). The two groups met in Geneva, Switzerland, in January 1995. In December 1994 OIC heads of state, convened in Morocco, proclaimed that the UN arms embargo on Bosnia and Herzegovina could not be applied to the Muslim authorities of that Republic, and requested the support of the international community for the continued presence of a UN force in the area. The Conference also resolved to review economic relations between OIC member states and any country that supported Serbian activities. An aid fund was established, to which member states were requested to contribute between US $500,000 and US $5m., in order to provide further humanitarian and economic assistance to Bosnian Muslims. In relation to wider concerns the conference adopted a Code of Conduct for Combating International Terrorism, in an attempt to control Muslim extremist groups. The code commits states to ensuring that militant groups do not use their territory for planning or executing terrorist activity against other states, in addition to states refraining from direct support or participation in acts of terrorism. In a further resolution the OIC supported the decision by Iraq to recognize Kuwait, but advocated that Iraq comply with all UN Security Council decisions.

In July 1995 the OIC contact group on Bosnia and Herzegovina (at that time comprising Egypt, Iran, Malaysia, Morocco, Pakistan, Saudi Arabia, Senegal and Turkey), meeting in Geneva, declared the UN arms embargo against Bosnia and Herzegovina to be 'invalid'. Several Governments, including that of Malaysia, subsequently announced their willingness officially to supply weapons and other military assistance to the Bosnian Muslim forces. In September a meeting of all OIC ministers of defence and foreign affairs endorsed the establishment of an 'assistance mobilization group' which was to supply military, economic, legal and other assistance to Bosnia and Herzegovina. In a joint declaration the ministers also demanded the return of all territory seized by Bosnian Serb forces, the continued NATO bombing of Serb military targets, and that the city of Sarajevo be preserved under a Muslim-led Bosnian Government. In November the OIC Secretary-General endorsed the peace accord for the former Yugoslavia, which was signed, in Dayton, USA, by leaders of all the conflicting factions, and reaffirmed the commitment of Islamic states to participate in efforts to implement the accord. In the following month the OIC Conference of Ministers of Foreign Affairs, convened in Conakry, Guinea, requested the full support of the international community to reconstruct Bosnia and Herzegovina through humanitarian aid as well as economic and technical co-operation. Ministers declared that Palestine and the establishment of fully-autonomous Palestinian control of Jerusalem were issues of central importance for the Muslim world. The Conference urged the removal of all aspects of occupation and the cessation of the construction of Israeli settlements in the occupied territories. In addition, the final statement of the meeting condemned Armenian aggression against Azerbaijan, registered concern at the persisting civil conflict in Afghanistan, demanded the elimination of all weapons of mass destruction and pledged support for Libya (affected by the US trade embargo).

In December 1996 OIC ministers of foreign affairs, meeting in Jakarta, Indonesia, urged the international community to apply pressure on Israel in order to ensure its implementation of the terms of the Middle East peace process. The ministers reaffirmed the importance of ensuring that the provisions of the Dayton Peace Agreement for the former Yugoslavia were fully implemented, called for a peaceful settlement of the Kashmir issue, demanded that Iraq fulfil its obligations for the establishment of security, peace and stability in the region and proposed that an international conference on peace and national reconciliation in Somalia be convened. The ministers elected a new Secretary-General, Azeddine Laraki, who confirmed that the organization would continue to develop its role as an international mediator. In March 1997, at an extraordinary summit held in Pakistan, OIC heads of state and of government reiterated the organization's objective of increasing international pressure on Israel to ensure the full implementation of the terms of the Middle East peace process. An 'Islamabad Declaration' was also adopted, which pledged to increase co-operation between members of the OIC. In June both the OIC and the Islamic World League condemned the decision by the US House of Representatives to recognize Jerusalem as the Israeli capital. The Secretary-General of the OIC issued a statement rejecting the US decision as counter to the role of the USA as sponsor of the Middle East peace plan. In December OIC heads of state attended the eighth summit conference, held in Iran. The Teheran Declaration, issued at the end of the conference, demanded the liberation of the Israeli-occupied territories and the creation of an autonomous Palestinian state. The conference also appealed for a cessation of the conflicts in Afghanistan, and between Armenia and Azerbaijan. It was requested that the UN sanctions against Libya be removed and that the US legislation threatening sanctions against foreign companies investing in energy projects in certain countries (including Iran and Libya), introduced in July 1996, be dismissed as invalid. In addition, the Declaration encouraged the increased participation of women in OIC activities.

SUBSIDIARY ORGANS

International Commission for the Preservation of Islamic Cultural Heritage (ICPICH): POB 24, 80692 Beşiktaş, İstanbul, Turkey; tel. (212) 2591742; fax (212) 2584365; e-mail ircica@ihlas.net.tr; f. 1982. Sec. Prof. Dr EKMELEDDİN İHSANOĞLU (Turkey).

Islamic Centre for the Development of Trade: Complexe Commercial des Habous, ave des FAR, BP 13545, Casablanca, Morocco; tel. (2) 314974; telex 46296; fax (2) 310110; e-mail icdt@icdt.org; internet http://www.icdt.org; f. 1983 to encourage regular commercial contacts, harmonize policies and promote investments among OIC mems. Dir BADRE EDDINE ALLALI. Publs *Tijaris: International and Inter-Islamic Trade Magazine* (quarterly), *Inter-Islamic Trade Report* (annual).

Islamic Institute of Technology (IIT): GPO Box 3003, Board Bazar, Gazipur, Dhaka, Bangladesh; tel. (2) 980-0960; telex 642739; fax (2) 980-0970; e-mail dg@iit.bangla.net; f. 1981 to develop human resources in OIC mem. states, with special reference to engineering, technology, tech. and vocational education and research; capacity of 224 full-time and 57 part-time staff and 1,000 students; library of 18,000 vols. Dir-Gen. Prof. A. M. PATWARI. Publs *News Bulletin* (annually), reports, human resources development series.

Islamic Jurisprudence Academy: Jeddah, Saudi Arabia; f. 1982. Sec.-Gen. Sheikh MOHAMED HABIB BELKHOJAH.

Islamic Solidarity Fund: c/o OIC Secretariat, POB 178, Jeddah 21411, Saudi Arabia; tel. (2) 680-0800; telex 601366; fax (2) 687-3568; f. 1974 to meet the needs of Islamic communities by providing emergency aid and the finance to build mosques, Islamic centres, hospitals, schools and universities. Chair. Sheikh NASIR ABDULLAH BIN HAMDAN; Exec. Dir ABDULLAH HERSI.

Islamic University of Niger: BP 11507, Niamey, Niger; tel. 723903; telex 8266; fax 733796; f. 1984; provides courses of study in *Shar'ia* (Islamic law) and Arabic language and literature; also offers courses in pedagogy and teacher training; receives grants from Islamic Solidarity Fund and contributions from OIC member states; Rector Prof. ABDELALI OUDHRIRI.

Islamic University in Uganda: POB 2555, Mbale, Uganda; tel. (45) 33417; telex 66176; fax (45) 3034; Kampala Liaison Office: POB 7689, Kampala; tel. (41) 236874; fax (41) 254576; f. 1988 to meet the educational needs of Muslim populations in English-speaking Africa; financed by OIC. Prin. Officer Prof. MAHDI ADAMU.

Research Centre for Islamic History, Art and Culture (IRCICA): POB 24, Beşiktaş 80692, İstanbul, Turkey; tel. (212) 2591742; telex 26484; fax (212) 2584365; e-mail ircica@ihlas.net.tr; f. 1980; library of 50,000 vols. Dir-Gen. Prof. Dr EKMELEDDİN İHSANOĞLU. Publ. *Newsletter* (3 a year).

Statistical, Economic and Social Research and Training Centre for the Islamic Countries: Attar Sok 4, GOP 06700, Ankara, Turkey; tel. (312) 4686172; telex 18944838; fax (312) 4673458; e-mail sesrtcic-f@servis.net.tr; f. 1978. Dir-Gen. Dr ŞADI CINDORUK.

SPECIALIZED INSTITUTIONS

International Islamic News Agency (IINA): King Khalid Palace, Madinah Rd, POB 5054, Jeddah, Saudi Arabia; tel. (2) 665-8561; telex 601090; fax (2) 665-9358; e-mail iina@mail.gcc.com.bh; f. 1972. Dir-Gen. ABDULWAHAB KASHIF.

Islamic Development Bank: See p. 194.

Islamic Educational, Scientific and Cultural Organization (ISESCO): Hay Ryad, BP 2275, Rabat 10104, Morocco; tel. (7) 772433; telex 32645; fax (7) 777459; f. 1982. Dir-Gen. Dr ABDULAZIZ BIN OTHMAN AL-TWAIJRI. Publs *ISESCO Newsletter* (quarterly), *Islam Today* (2 a year), *ISESCO Triennial*.

Islamic States Broadcasting Organization (ISBO): POB 6351, Jeddah 21442, Saudi Arabia; tel. (2) 672-1121; telex 601442; fax (2) 672-2600; f. 1975. Sec.-Gen. HUSSEIN AL-ASKARY.

AFFILIATED INSTITUTIONS

International Association of Islamic Banks (IAIB): King Abdulaziz St, Queen's Bldg, 23rd Floor, Al-Balad Dist, POB 23425, Jeddah 21426, Saudi Arabia; tel. (2) 643-1276; fax (2) 644-7239; f. 1977 to link financial institutions operating on Islamic banking principles; activities include training and research; mems: 192 banks and other financial institutions in 34 countries. Sec.-Gen. SAMIR A. SHAIKH.

Islamic Chamber of Commerce and Industry: POB 3831, Clifton, Karachi 75600, Pakistan; tel. (21) 5874756; telex 27272; fax (21) 5870765; e-mail icci@paknet3.ptc.pk; f. 1979 to promote trade and industry among member states; comprises nat. chambers or feds of chambers of commerce and industry. Sec.-Gen. AQEEL AHMAD AL-JASSEM.

Islamic Committee for the International Crescent: c/o OIC, Kilo 6, Mecca Rd, POB 178, Jeddah 21411, Saudi Arabia; tel. (2) 680-0800; telex 601366; fax (2) 687-3568; f. 1979 to attempt to alleviate the suffering caused by natural disasters and war. Sec.-Gen. Dr AHMAD ABDALLAH CHERIF.

Islamic Solidarity Sports Federation: POB 6040, Riyadh 11442, Saudi Arabia; tel. and fax (1) 482-2145; telex 404760; f. 1981. Sec.-Gen. Dr MOAMMAD SALEH GAZDAR.

Organization of Islamic Capitals and Cities (OICC): POB 13621, Jeddah 21414, Saudi Arabia; tel. (2) 698-6651; fax (2) 698-1053; f. 1980 to promote and develop co-operation among OICC mems, to preserve their character and heritage, to implement planning guidelines for the growth of Islamic cities and to upgrade standards of public services and utilities in those cities. Sec.-Gen. ABDULQADIR HAMZAK KOSHAK.

Organization of the Islamic Shipowners' Association: POB 14900, Jeddah 21434, Saudi Arabia; tel. (2) 663-7882; telex 607303; fax (2) 660-4920; f. 1981 to promote co-operation among maritime cos in Islamic countries. Sec.-Gen. Dr ABDULLATIF A. SULTAN.

ORGANIZATION OF THE PETROLEUM EXPORTING COUNTRIES—OPEC

Address: Obere Donaustrasse 93, 1020 Vienna, Austria.

Telephone: (1) 211-12-0; **telex:** 134474; **fax:** (1) 216-43-20; **e-mail:** info@opec.org.; **internet:** http://www.opec.org.

OPEC was established in 1960 to link countries whose main source of export earnings is petroleum; it aims to unify and co-ordinate members' petroleum policies and to safeguard their interests generally. The OPEC Fund for International Development is described on p. 230.

OPEC's share of world petroleum production was 40.2% in 1996 (compared with 44.6% in 1980 and 54.7% in 1974). It is estimated that OPEC members possess more than 75% of the world's known reserves of crude petroleum, of which about two-thirds are in the Middle East. In 1996 OPEC members possessed about 42.3% of known reserves of natural gas.

MEMBERS

Algeria	Kuwait	Saudi Arabia
Indonesia	Libya	United Arab Emirates
Iran	Nigeria	Venezuela
Iraq	Qatar	

Organization

(January 1998)

CONFERENCE

The Conference is the supreme authority of the Organization, responsible for the formulation of its general policy. It consists of representatives of member countries, who examine reports and recommendations submitted by the Board of Governors. It approves the appointment of Governors from each country and elects the Chairman of the Board of Governors. It works on the unanimity principle, and meets at least twice a year.

President: ABDULLAH BIN HAMAD AL-ATTIYA (Qatar).

BOARD OF GOVERNORS

The Board directs the management of the Organization; it implements resolutions of the Conference and draws up an annual budget. It consists of one governor for each member country, and meets at least twice a year.

MINISTERIAL MONITORING COMMITTEE

The Committee (f. 1988) is responsible for monitoring price evolution and ensuring the stability of the world petroleum market. As such, it is charged with the preparation of long-term strategies, including the allocation of quotas to be presented to the Conference. The Committee consists of all national representatives, and is normally convened four times a year. A Ministerial Monitoring Sub-committee, reporting to the Committee on production and supply figures, was established in 1993.

ECONOMIC COMMISSION

A specialized body operating within the framework of the Secretariat, with a view to assisting the Organization in promoting stability in international prices for petroleum at equitable levels; consists of a board, national representatives and a commission staff; meets at least twice a year.

SECRETARIAT

Secretary-General: Dr RILWANU LUKMAN (Nigeria).

Research Division: comprises three departments:

Data Services Department: Computer Section maintains and expands information services to support the research activities of the Secretariat and those of member countries. Statistics Section collects, collates and analyses statistical information from both primary and secondary sources.

Energy Studies Department: Conducts a continuous programme for research in energy and related matters; monitors, forecasts and analyses developments in the energy and petrochemical industries; and evaluates hydrocarbons and products and their non-energy uses.

Petroleum Market Analysis Department: Analyses economic and financial issues of significant interest; in particular those related to international financial and monetary matters, and to the international petroleum industry.

Division Head: Dr SHOKRI M. GHANEM.

Administration and Human Resources Department: Responsible for all organization methods, provision of administrative services for all meetings, personnel matters, budgets accounting and internal control; **Head:** ABBAS N. AFSHAR.

OPECNA and Information Department: Formed in 1990 by the merging of the former Public Information Department and the OPEC News Agency (OPECNA, f. 1980). Responsible for a central public relations programme; production and distribution of publications, films, slides and tapes; and communication of OPEC objectives and decisions to the world at large; operates a daily on-line news service; **Head:** FAROUK MUHAMMED (acting).

Legal Office: Undertakes special and other in-house legal studies and reports to ascertain where the best interests of the Organization and member countries lie; **Head:** AHMED ABDULAZIZ.

Office of the Secretary-General: Provides the Secretary-General with executive assistance in maintaining contacts with governments, organizations and delegations, in matters of protocol and in the preparation for and co-ordination of meetings; **Head:** Dr NAFRIZAL SIKUMBANG.

Record of Events

1960 The first OPEC Conference was held in Baghdad in September, attended by representatives from Iran, Iraq, Kuwait, Saudi Arabia and Venezuela.

1961 Second Conference, Caracas, January. Qatar was admitted to membership; a Board of Governors was formed and statutes agreed.

1962 Fourth Conference, Geneva, April and June. Protests were addressed to petroleum companies against price cuts introduced in August 1960. Indonesia and Libya were admitted to membership.

1965 In July the Conference reached agreement on a two-year joint production programme, implemented from 1965 to 1967, to limit annual growth in output to secure adequate prices.

1967 Abu Dhabi was admitted to membership.

1969 Algeria was admitted to membership.

1970 Twenty-first Conference, Caracas, December. Tax on income of petroleum companies was raised to 55%.

1971 A five-year agreement was concluded in February between the six producing countries in the Gulf and 23 international petroleum companies (Teheran Agreement). Nigeria was admitted to membership.

1972 In January petroleum companies agreed to adjust petroleum revenues of the largest producers after changes in currency exchange rates (Geneva Agreement).

1973 OPEC and petroleum companies concluded an agreement whereby posted prices of crude petroleum were raised by 11.9% and a mechanism was installed to make monthly adjustments to prices in future (Second Geneva Agreement). Negotiations with petroleum companies on revision of the Teheran Agreement collapsed in October, and the Gulf states unilaterally declared 70% increases in posted prices, from US $3.01 to $5.11 per barrel.

Thirty-sixth Conference, Teheran, December. The posted price was to increase by nearly 130%, from US $5.11 to $11.65 per barrel, from 1 January 1974. Ecuador was admitted to full membership and Gabon became an associate member.

1974 As a result of Saudi opposition to the December price increase, prices were held at current level for first quarter (and subsequently for the remainder of 1974). Abu Dhabi's membership was transferred to the United Arab Emirates (UAE). A meeting in June increased royalties charged to petroleum companies from 12.5% to 14.5% in all member states except Saudi Arabia. A meeting in September increased governmental take by about 3.5% through further increases in royalties on equity crude to 16.67% and in taxes to 65.65%, except in Saudi Arabia.

1975 OPEC's first summit conference was held in Algiers in March. Gabon was admitted to full membership.

A ministerial meeting in September agreed to raise prices by 10% for the period until June 1976.

1976 The OPEC Special Fund for International Development was created in May.
In December 11 member states endorsed a rise in basic prices of 10% as of 1 January 1977, and a further 5% rise as of 1 July 1977. However, Saudi Arabia and the UAE decided to raise their prices by 5% only.

1977 Following an earlier waiver by nine members of the 5% second stage of the price increase agreed at Doha, Saudi Arabia and the UAE announced in July that they would both raise their prices by 5%. As a result, a single level of prices throughout the organization was restored. Because of continued disagreements between the 'moderates', led by Saudi Arabia and Iran, and the 'radicals', led by Algeria, Libya and Iraq, the year's second Conference at Caracas, December, was unable to settle on an increase in prices.

1978 At the fifty-first Conference, held in June, it was agreed that price levels should remain stable until the end of the year. In December it was decided to raise prices in four instalments, in order to compensate for the effects of the depreciation of the US dollar. These would bring a rise of 14.5% over nine months, but an average increase of 10% for 1979.

1979 At an extraordinary meeting in Geneva in March members decided to raise prices by 9%. In June the Conference agreed minimum and maximum prices which seemed likely to add between 15% and 20% to import bills of consumer countries. The December Conference agreed in principle to convert the OPEC Fund into a development agency with its own legal personality.

1980 In June the Conference decided to set the price for a marker crude at US $32 per barrel, and that the value differentials which could be added above this ceiling (on account of quality and geographical location) should not exceed $5 per barrel. The planned OPEC summit meeting in Baghdad in November was postponed indefinitely because of the Iran–Iraq war, but the scheduled price-fixing meeting of petroleum ministers went ahead in Bali in December, with both Iranians and Iraqis present. A ceiling price of $41 per barrel was fixed for premium crudes.

1981 In May attempts to achieve price reunification were made, but Saudi Arabia refused to increase its US $32 per barrel price unless the higher prices charged by other countries were lowered. Most of the other OPEC countries agreed to cut production by 10% so as to reduce the surplus. An emergency meeting in Geneva in August again failed to unify prices, although Saudi Arabia agreed to reduce production by 1m. barrels per day (b/d), with the level of output to be reviewed monthly. In October OPEC countries agreed to increase the Saudi marker price to $34 per barrel, with a ceiling price of $38 per barrel.

1982 The continuing world glut of petroleum forced prices below the official mark of US $34 per barrel in some producer countries. In March an emergency meeting of petroleum ministers was held in Vienna and agreed (for the first time in OPEC's history) to defend the Organization's price structure by imposing an overall production ceiling of 18m. b/d. At the same time Saudi Arabia announced a reduction in its own production to 7m. b/d. In December the Conference agreed to limit OPEC production to 18.5m. b/d in 1983 but postponed the allocation of national quotas pending consultations among the respective governments.

1983 In January an emergency meeting of petroleum ministers, fearing a collapse in world petroleum prices, decided to reduce the production ceiling to 17.5m. b/d (itself several million b/d above actual current output) but failed to agree on individual production quotas or on adjustments to the differentials in prices charged for the high-quality crude petroleum produced by Algeria, Libya and Nigeria compared with that produced by the Gulf States. In February Nigeria cut its prices to US $30 per barrel, following a collapse in its production. To avoid a 'price war' OPEC set the official price of marker crude at $29 per barrel, and agreed to maintain existing differentials among the various OPEC crudes at the level agreed on in March 1982, with the temporary exception that the differentials for Nigerian crudes should be $1 more than the price of the marker crude. It also agreed to maintain the production ceiling of 17.5m. b/d and allocated quotas for each member country except Saudi Arabia, which was to act as a 'swing producer' to supply the balancing quantities to meet market requirements.

1984 In October the production ceiling was lowered to 16m. b/d. In December price differentials for light (more expensive) and heavy (cheaper) crudes were slightly altered in an attempt to counteract price-cutting by non-OPEC producers, particularly Norway and the United Kingdom.

1985 In January members (except Algeria, Iran and Libya) effectively abandoned the marker price system. During the year production in excess of quotas by OPEC members, unofficial discounts and barter deals by members, and price cuts by non-members (such as Mexico, which had hitherto kept its prices in line with those of OPEC) contributed to a weakening of the market.

1986 During the first half of the year prices dropped to below US $10 per barrel. In April ministers agreed to set OPEC production at 16.7m. b/d for the third quarter of 1986 and at 17.3m. b/d for the fourth quarter. Algeria, Iran and Libya dissented. Discussions were also held with non-member countries (Angola, Egypt, Malaysia, Mexico and Oman), which agreed to co-operate in limiting production, but the United Kingdom refused to reduce its petroleum production levels. In August all members, with the exception of Iraq (which demanded to be allowed the same quota as Iran and, when this was denied it, refused to be a party to the agreement), agreed upon a return to production quotas, with the aim of cutting production to 14.8m. b/d (about 16.8m. b/d including Iraq's production) for the ensuing two months. This measure resulted in an increase in prices to about $15 per barrel, which was extended until the end of the year. In December members (with the exception of Iraq) agreed to return to a fixed pricing system at a level of $18 per barrel as the OPEC reference price, with effect from 1 February 1987. OPEC's total production for the first and second quarters of 1987 was not to exceed 15.8m. b/d.

1987 In June, with prices having stabilized, the Conference decided that production during the third and fourth quarters of the year should be limited to 16.6m. b/d (including Iraq's production). However, total production continued to exceed the agreed levels. In December ministers decided to extend the existing agreement for the first half of 1988, although Iraq, once more, refused to participate.

1988 By March petroleum prices had fallen below US $15 per barrel. In April non-OPEC producers offered to reduce the volume of their petroleum exports by 5% if OPEC members would do the same. Saudi Arabia, however, refused to accept further reductions in production, saying that existing quotas should first be more strictly enforced. In June the previous production limit (15.06m. b/d, excluding Iraq's production) was again renewed for six months, in the hope that increasing demand would be sufficient to raise prices. By October, however, petroleum prices were below $12 per barrel. OPEC members (excluding Iraq) were estimated to be producing about 21m. b/d. In November a new agreement was reached, limiting total production (including that of Iraq) to 18.5m. b/d, with effect from 1 January 1989. Iran and Iraq finally agreed to accept identical quotas.

1989 In June (when prices had returned to about US $18 per barrel) ministers agreed to increase the production limit to 19.5m. b/d for the second half of 1989. However, Kuwait and the UAE indicated that they would not feel bound to observe this limit. In September the production limit was again increased, to 20.5m. b/d, and in November the limit for the first half of 1990 was increased to 22m. b/d.

1990 In May those members that had been exceeding their quotas declared that they would reduce their production to the agreed limit, in response to a decline in prices of some 25% since the beginning of the year. By late June, however, it was reported that total production had decreased by only 400,000 b/d, and prices remained at about US$14 per barrel. In July Iraq threatened to take military action against Kuwait unless it reduced its petroleum production. In the same month OPEC members agreed to raise prices to $21 per barrel, and to limit output to 22.5m. b/d. In August, however, Iraq invaded Kuwait, and petroleum exports by the two countries were halted by an international embargo. Petroleum prices immediately increased to exceed $25 per barrel. Later in the month an informal consultative meeting of OPEC ministers placed the July agreement in abeyance, and permitted a temporary increase in production of petroleum, of between 3m. and 3.5m. b/d (mostly by Saudi Arabia, the UAE and Venezuela). In September and October prices fluctuated in response to political developments in the Gulf region, reaching a point in excess of $40 per barrel in early October, but falling to about $25 per barrel by the end of the month. In December a meeting of OPEC members voted to maintain the high levels of production and to reinstate the quotas that had been agreed in July, once the Gulf crisis was over. During the period August 1990–February 1991 Saudi Arabia increased its petroleum output from 5.4m. to 8.5m. b/d. Seven of the other OPEC states also produced in excess of their agreed quotas. It was estimated that OPEC producers' revenues from petroleum sales rose by 40% in 1990, owing to increased prices and panic buying by consumer countries.

1991 In the first quarter OPEC members were producing about 23m. b/d, and the average price of petroleum was US $19 per barrel, before dropping further to $17.5 per barrel in the second quarter. In an attempt to reach the target of a minimum reference price of $21 per barrel, ministers agreed in March to reduce production from 23m. b/d to 22.3m. b/d, although Saudi Arabia refused to return to its pre-August 1990 quota. In June ministers decided to maintain the ceiling of 22.3m. b/d into the third quarter of the year, since Iraq and Kuwait were still unable to export their petroleum. In September it was agreed that OPEC members' production for the last quarter of 1991 should be raised to 23.65m. b/d, and in November the OPEC Conference decided to maintain the increased production ceiling during the first quarter of 1992. From early November, however, the price of petroleum declined sharply, with demand less than anticipated as a result of continuing world recession and a mild winter in the northern hemisphere.

1992 The Ministerial Monitoring Committee, meeting in February, decided to impose a production ceiling of 22.98m. b/d with immediate effect. The agreement was, however, repudiated by both Saudi Arabia, which stated that it would not abide by its allocated quota of 7.9m. b/d, and Iran, unhappy that the production ceiling had not been set lower. In May it was agreed to continue the production restriction of 22.98m. b/d during the third quarter of 1992. In addition, Kuwait, which was resuming production in the wake of the extensive damage inflicted on its oil-wells by Iraq during the Gulf War, was granted a special dispensation to produce without a fixed quota. During the first half of 1992 member states' petroleum output consistently exceeded agreed levels, with Saudi Arabia and Iran (despite its stance on reducing production) the principal over-producers. In June, at the UN Conference on Environment and Development, OPEC's Secretary-General expressed its member countries' strong objections to the tax on fossil fuels (designed to reduce pollution) proposed by the EC. In September negotiations between OPEC ministers in Geneva were complicated by Iran's alleged annexation of Abu Musa and two other islands in the territorial waters of the UAE. However, agreement was reached on a production ceiling of 24.2m. b/d for the final quarter of 1992, in an attempt to raise the price of crude petroleum to the OPEC target of $21 per barrel. At a ministerial meeting in late November Ecuador formally resigned from OPEC, the first country ever to do so, citing as reasons the high membership fee and OPEC's refusal to increase Ecuador's quota. At the meeting, agreement was reached on a production ceiling of 24.58m. b/d for the first quarter of 1993 (24.46m. b/d, excluding Ecuador).

1993 In mid-February a quota was set for Kuwait for the first time since the onset of the Gulf crisis. Kuwait agreed to a quota of 1.6m. b/d (400,000 less than current output) from 1 March, on the understanding that it would be substantially increased in the third quarter of the year. The quota for overall production from 1 March was set at 23.58m. b/d. A Ministerial Monitoring Sub-committee was established to ensure compliance with quotas. In June OPEC ministers decided to 'roll over' the overall quota of 23.58m. b/d into the third quarter of the year. However, Kuwait rejected its new allocation of 1.76m. b/d, demanding a quota of at least 2m. In July discussions between Iraq and the UN on the possible supervised sale of Iraqi petroleum depressed petroleum prices to below $16 per barrel. The Monitoring Sub-committee, meeting with the OPEC President in August, urged member states to adhere to their production quotas (which were exceeded by a total of 1m. b/d in July). At the end of September an extraordinary meeting of the Conference was convened in Geneva. Members agreed on a raised production ceiling of 24.52m. b/d, to be effective for six months from 1 October. Kuwait accepted a quota of 2m. b/d, which brought the country back into the production ceiling mechanism. Iran agreed on an allocation of 3.6m. b/d, while Saudi Arabia consented to freeze production at current levels. The accord was intended effectively to lower production by ensuring that countries did not exceed their quotas, and thus boost petroleum prices which remained persistently low. In November the Conference rejected any further reduction in production. Prices subsequently fell below the $14 level, owing partly to a decision by Iraq to allow the UN to monitor its weapons programme (a move that would consequently lead to a repeal of the UN embargo on Iraqi petroleum exports) and reached a low point of $12.87 per barrel.

1994 Prices remained depressed during the first quarter of the year. In March, the Ministerial Monitoring Committee opted to maintain the output quotas, agreed in September 1993, until the end of the year, and urged non-OPEC producers to freeze their production levels. (Iraq failed to endorse the agreement, since it recognizes only the production agreement adopted in July 1990.) At the meeting Saudi Arabia resisted a proposal from Iran and Nigeria, both severely affected by declines in petroleum revenue, to reduce its production by 1m. b/d in order to boost prices. In June the Conference endorsed the decision to maintain the existing production ceiling, and stated that there would be no further meeting of the Conference until November, in an attempt to emphasize that the production agreement would remain in effect until the end of 1994. Ministers acknowledged that there had been a gradual increase in petroleum prices in the second quarter of the year, with an average basket price of $15.6 per barrel for that period. Political disruption in Nigeria, including a strike by petroleum workers, was considered to be the principal factor contributing to the price per barrel rising above $19 in August. In November OPEC ministers endorsed a proposal by Saudi Arabia to maintain the existing production quota, of 24.52m. b/d, until the end of 1995. At the Conference ministers elected Dr Rilwanu Lukman of Nigeria as the new Secretary-General, with effect from January 1995.

1995 In January it was reported that Gabon was reconsidering its membership of the Organization, owing to difficulties in meeting its budget contribution. During the first half of the year Gabon consistently exceeded its quota of 287,000 b/d, by 48,000 b/d, and the country failed to send a delegate to the ministerial Conference in June. At mid-1995 efforts were continuing in order to assess different options regarding the issue of membership subscriptions, including Gabon's proposal that they be linked to production; however, the problem remained unresolved. At the June Conference ministers expressed concern at OPEC's falling share of the world petroleum market. The Conference criticized the high level of North Sea production, by Norway and the United Kingdom, and urged collective production restraint in order to stimulate prices. In November the Conference agreed to extend the existing production quota, of 24.52m. b/d, for a further six months, in order to stabilize prices. During the year, however, output remained in excess of the production quotas, by between 500,000 b/d and 1.06m. b/d according to different estimates, and averaged some 25.58m. b/d.

1996 The possibility of a UN-Iraqi agreement permitting limited petroleum sales dominated OPEC concerns in the first half of the year and contributed to price fluctuations in the world markets. By early 1996 output by OPEC countries was estimated to be substantially in excess of quota levels; however, the price per barrel remained relatively buoyant (the average basket price reaching US $21 in March), owing largely to unseasonal cold weather in the northern hemisphere (stimulating demand). In May a memorandum of understanding was signed between Iraq and the UN to allow the export of petroleum, up to a value of $2,000m. over a six-month period, in order to fund humanitarian relief efforts within that country. In June the ministerial Conference agreed to increase the overall output ceiling by 800,000 b/d, i.e. the anticipated level of exports from Iraq in the first six months of the agreement. A proposal, endorsed by Iran, to raise the individual country quotas failed to win support, while a comprehensive reduction in output, in order to accommodate the Iraqi quota without adjusting the existing production ceiling, was also rejected, notably by Saudi Arabia and Venezuela, concerned to retain their shares of production. At the meeting Gabon's withdrawal from the Organization was confirmed. As a result of these developments, the new ceiling was set at 25.03m. b/d. It was agreed that, under the Monitoring Sub-committee, stricter efforts would be made to endorse the production agreement and to act against countries that persistently exceed their quotas. Independent market observers expressed concern that, without any formal agreement to reduce overall production and given the actual widespread violation of the quota system, the renewed export of Iraqi petroleum would substantially depress petroleum prices. However, the markets remained stable as implementation of the UN-Iraqi agreement was delayed. In September the monitoring group acknowledged that members were exceeding their production quotas, but declined to impose any punitive measures (owing to the steady increase in petroleum prices). In late November the Conference agreed to maintain the existing production quota for a further six months. Also in November, Iraq accepted certain disputed technical terms of the UN agreement (for example, the freedom of movement of UN inspectors), enabling the export of petroleum to commence in December.

1997 During the first half of the year petroleum prices declined, reaching a low of US $16.7 per barrel in early April, owing to the Iraqi exports, depressed world demand and persistent overproduction. In June OPEC's ministerial Conference agreed to extend the existing production ceiling, of 25.03m. b/d, for a further six-month period. Member states resolved to adhere to their individual quotas in order to reduce the cumulative excess production of an estimated 2m. b/d; however, Venezuela, which (some sources claimed) was producing almost 800,000 b/d over its quota of 2.4m. b/d, declined to co-operate. An escalation in political tensions in the Gulf region in October, in particular Iraq's reluctance to co-operate with UN inspectors, prompted an increase in the price of crude petroleum to some $21.2 per barrel. Price fluctuations ensued, although there was a general downward trend. In November the OPEC ministerial Conference, meeting in Jakarta, Indonesia, approved a proposal by Saudi Arabia, to increase the overall production ceiling by some 10%, with effect from 1 January 1998, in order to meet the perceived stable world demand and to reflect more accurately current output levels. At the same time the Iranian Government announced its intention to increase its production capacity and maintain its share of the quota by permitting foreign companies to conduct petroleum exploration in Iran.

1998 At the start of the year there was widespread concern that the decision to increase production to 27.5m. b/d, together with the prospect of a decline in demand from Asian economies that had been undermined by extreme financial difficulties and speculation that a new Iraqi agreement with the UN would provide for petroleum exports of up to US $3,000m. every 180 days, was having an adverse effect on prices, which declined to $14.78 per barrel in late January. An emergency meeting of the Monitoring Sub-committe was arranged for the end of that month to consider means of easing the pressure on prices, although the Saudi Government indicated that it would not attend.

FINANCE

The budget for 1997 amounted to 215.3m. Austrian Schillings.

PUBLICATIONS

Annual Report.

Facts and Figures.

OPEC Annual Statistical Bulletin.

OPEC Bulletin (monthly).

OPEC at a Glance.

OPEC General Information and Chronology.

OPEC Official Resolutions and Press Releases.

OPEC Review (quarterly).

OPEC FUND FOR INTERNATIONAL DEVELOPMENT

Address: POB 995, 1011 Vienna, Austria.

Telephone: (1) 515-64-0; **telex:** 131734; **fax:** (1) 513-92-38.

The Fund was established by OPEC member countries in 1976.

MEMBERS

Member countries of OPEC (q.v.).

Organization

(January 1998)

ADMINISTRATION

The Fund is administered by a Ministerial Council and a Governing Board. Each member country is represented on the Council by its minister of finance. The Board consists of one representative and one alternate for each member country.

Chairman, Ministerial Council: MAR'IE MOHAMMED (Indonesia).

Chairman, Governing Board: Dr SALEH AL-OMAIR (Saudi Arabia).

Director-General of the Fund: Dr YESUFU SEYYID ABDULAI (Nigeria).

FINANCIAL STRUCTURE

The resources of the Fund, whose unit of account is the US dollar, consist of contributions by OPEC member countries, and income received from operations or otherwise accruing to the Fund.

The initial endowment of the Fund amounted to US $800m. Its resources have been replenished three times, and have been further increased by the profits accruing to seven OPEC member countries through the sales of gold held by the International Monetary Fund. The pledged contributions to the OPEC Fund amounted to US $3,435.0m. at the end of 1996, and paid-in contributions totalled $2,848.6m.

Activities

The OPEC Fund for International Development is a multilateral agency for financial co-operation and assistance. Its objective is to reinforce financial co-operation between OPEC member countries and other developing countries through the provision of financial support to the latter on appropriate terms, to assist them in their economic and social development. The Fund was conceived as a collective financial facility which would consolidate the assistance extended by its member countries; its resources are additional to those already made available through other bilateral and multilateral aid agencies of OPEC members. It is empowered to:

(*a*) Provide concessional loans for balance-of-payments support;

(*b*) Provide concessional loans for the implementation of development projects and programmes;

(*c*) Make contributions and/or provide loans to eligible international agencies; and

(*d*) Finance technical assistance and research through grants.

The eligible beneficiaries of the Fund's assistance are the governments of developing countries other than OPEC member countries, and international development agencies whose beneficiaries are developing countries. The Fund gives priority to the countries with the lowest income.

The Fund may undertake technical, economic and financial appraisal of a project submitted to it, or entrust such an appraisal to an appropriate international development agency, the executing national agency of a member country, or any other qualified agency. Most projects financed by the Fund have been co-financed by other development finance agencies. In each such case, one of the co-financing agencies may be appointed to administer the Fund's loan in association with its own. This practice has enabled the Fund to extend its lending activities to more than 95 countries over a short period of time and in a simple way, with the aim of avoiding duplication and complications. As its experience grew, the Fund increasingly resorted to parallel, rather than joint financing, taking up separate project components to be financed according to its rules and policies. In addition, it started to finance some projects completely on its own. These trends necessitated the issuance in 1982 of guidelines for the procurement of goods and services under the Fund's loans, allowing for a margin of preference for goods and services of local origin or originating in other developing countries: the general principle of competitive bidding is, however, followed by the Fund. The loans are not tied to procurement from Fund member countries or from any other countries. The margin of preference for goods and services obtainable in developing countries is allowed on the request of the borrower and within defined limits. Fund assistance in the form of programme loans has a broader coverage than project lending. Programme loans are used to stimulate an economic sector or sub-sector, and assist recipient countries in obtaining inputs, equipment and spare parts.

The Fund's twelfth lending programme, covering a two-year period effective from 1 January 1996, was approved in June 1995. Besides extending loans for project and programme financing and balance of payments support, the Fund also undertakes other operations, including grants in support of technical assistance and other activities (mainly research), and financial contributions to other international institutions.

By the end of December 1996 the Fund had extended 688 loans since operations began in 1976, totalling US $3,431.8m., of which $2,442.1m. (or 71.2%) was for project financing, $724.2m. (21.1%) was for balance-of-payments support and $265.5m. (7.7%) was for programme financing.

Direct loans are supplemented by grants to support technical assistance, food aid and research. By the end of December 1996, 403 grants, amounting to US $231.4m., had been extended, including

OPEC FUND COMMITMENTS AND DISBURSEMENTS IN 1996
(US $ million).

	Commit-ments	Disburse-ments
Lending operations:	159.20	92.80
Project financing	146.20	89.79
Programme financing	13.00	3.00
Grant Programme	2.32	3.01
Technical assistance	1.44	1.79
Research and other activities	0.19	0.09
Emergency aid	0.65	1.08
Project preparation facility	0.05	0.05
Total	161.52	95.80

$83.6m. to the Common Fund for Commodities (established by UNCTAD), and a special contribution of $20m. to the International Fund for Agricultural Development (IFAD). In addition, the Fund had committed $971.9m. to other international institutions by the end of 1996, comprising OPEC members' contributions to the resources of IFAD, and irrevocable transfers in the name of its members to the IMF Trust Fund. By the end of 1996 73.1% of total commitments had been disbursed.

During the year ending 31 December 1996 the Fund's total commitments amounted to US $161.5m. (compared with $196.8m. in 1995). These commitments included 28 project loans, amounting to $146.2m., and one loan to finance a commodity import programme in the Republic of Congo, totalling $13.0m. The largest proportion of project loans (24.1%) was for improvements in the education sector in six countries, including the rehabilitation of primary schools in Angola, the expansion of higher science and technology education in Pakistan and the upgrading of textbook printing facilities in Mauritania. The transportation sector received 18.7% of loans, to finance road rehabilitation and improvements in Madagascar and Haiti and international airport upgrading projects in Nepal and Ethiopia. Water supply and sewerage loans (18.5% of the total) were awarded to finance projects in Burkina Faso, São Tomé and Príncipe, Cambodia, India and Honduras. Four health projects (13.4%) were approved: to build or rehabilitate hospitals and health centres in the Democratic People's Republic of Korea, Jamaica and Peru and to provide universal access to medical and dental treatment at primary care level in Ghana. Loans for the agriculture and agro-industry sector (11.0%) went to finance four projects, including an irrigation scheme in Laos, rural infrastructure development in Guinea and Tanzania, and agricultural development in Senegal. The energy sector received 8.4% of lending, supporting the repair and expansion of electricity generation in São Tomé and Príncipe and a rural electrification scheme in Viet Nam. National development banks accounted for 4.6%, with lines of credit being extended to Kenya, for on-lending to small enterprises, and to Maldives, to provide financial services to the populations of the Southern Atolls. A multi-purpose project loan was extended to The Gambia in support of urban development.

During 1996 the Fund approved US $2.32m. for 18 grants, of which $1.4m. was for technical assistance activities, $185,000 for research, $650,000 in emergency assistance to the Great Lakes region of Africa, Yemen and the West Bank and Gaza Strip and $50,000 in project preparation.

Project loans approved in 1996 (US $ million)

Region and country		Loans approved
Africa		63.20
Angola	Education	7.49
Benin	Education	4.00
Burkina Faso	Water supply and sewerage	6.70
Ethiopia	Transportation	10.00
The Gambia	Urban infrastructure	2.00
Ghana	Health	6.55
Guinea	Agriculture and agro-industry	4.00
Kenya	National development banks	5.20
Madagascar	Transportation	2.40
Mauritania	Education	3.20
São Tomé and Príncipe	Energy	2.23
	Water supply and sewerage	1.29
Senegal	Agriculture and agro-industry	4.04
Tanzania	Agriculture and agro-industry	4.10
Asia and Oceania		67.00
Cambodia	Water supply and sewerage	4.00
India	Water supply and sewerage	10.00
Korea, Democratic People's Republic	Health	6.00
Laos	Agriculture and agro-industry	4.00
Lebanon	Education	4.00
Maldives	National development banks	1.50
Nepal	Transportation	11.00
Pakistan	Education	10.00
Sri Lanka	Education	6.50
Viet Nam	Energy	10.00
Latin America and the Caribbean		16.00
Haiti	Transportation	4.00
Honduras	Water supply and sewerage	5.00
Jamaica	Health	2.00
Peru	Health	5.00
Total		146.20

PUBLICATIONS

Annual Report (in Arabic, English, French and Spanish).
OPEC Aid and OPEC Aid Institutions—A Profile (annually).
OPEC Fund Newsletter (3 a year).
Occasional books and papers.

PACIFIC COMMUNITY

Address: BP D5, 98848 Nouméa Cédex, New Caledonia.

Telephone: 26-20-00; **fax:** 26-38-18; **e-mail:** spc@spc.org.nc; **internet:** http://www.spc.org.nc/.

In February 1947 the Governments of Australia, France, the Netherlands, New Zealand, the United Kingdom and the USA, signed an agreement to establish the South Pacific Commission, which came into effect in July 1948. (The Netherlands withdrew from the Commission in 1962, when it ceased to administer the former colony of Dutch New Guinea, now Irian Jaya, part of Indonesia.) In October 1997 the 37th South Pacific Conference, convened in Canberra, Australia, agreed to rename the organization the Pacific Community, with effect from 6 February 1998. The Secretariat of the Pacific Community (SPC) provides technical advice, training and assistance in economic, social and cultural development to 22 countries and territories of the Pacific region. As a non-political organization, its main areas of activity cover agriculture, fisheries, forestry, community health, socio-economic and statistical services, and community education services. It serves a population of about 6.8m., scattered over some 30m. sq km, more than 98% of which is sea.

MEMBERS

American Samoa	Northern Mariana Islands
Australia	Palau
Cook Islands	Papua New Guinea
Fiji	Pitcairn Islands
France	Samoa
French Polynesia	Solomon Islands
Guam	Tokelau
Kiribati	Tonga
Marshall Islands	Tuvalu
Federated States of Micronesia	United Kingdom*
Nauru	USA
New Caledonia	Vanuatu
New Zealand	Wallis and Futuna Islands
Niue	

* The United Kingdom withdrew from the organization in 1996; however, it renewed its membership with effect from 1 January 1998.

Organization

(February 1998)

SOUTH PACIFIC CONFERENCE

The Conference is the governing body of the Community and is composed of representatives of all member countries and territories. According to an organizational review of the South Pacific Commission, which was implemented in 1997, the main responsibilities of the Conference are to appoint the Director-General, to determine major national or regional policy issues in the areas of competence of the organization and to note changes to the Financial and Staff Regulations approved by the Committee of Representatives of Governments and Administrations (CRGA). From 1997 the Conference, which was previously held annually, was to be convened every two years.

COMMITTEE OF REPRESENTATIVES OF GOVERNMENTS AND ADMINISTRATIONS (CRGA)

This Committee comprises representatives of all member states and territories, having equal voting rights. With effect from 1998 it was to meet annually (previously twice a year) to consider the work programme evaluation conducted by the Secretariat and to discuss any changes proposed by the Secretariat in the context of regional priorities; to consider and approve any policy issues for the organization presented by the Secretariat or by member countries and territories; to consider applicants and make recommendations for the post of Director-General; to approve the administrative and work programme budgets; to approve amendments to the Financial and Staff Regulations; and to conduct annual performance evaluations of the Director-General.

SECRETARIAT

The Secretariat is headed by a Director-General (previously the Secretary-General) and two Deputy Directors-General (previously the Directors of Programmes and of Services). Three Divisions, each headed by a Director, cover Marine Resource Development, Socio-Economic Development and Health and the activities administered by the Community's regional office in Fiji. The organization has more than 180 staff members.

Director-General: Dr Robert Dun (Australia).

Deputy Directors-General: Dr Jimmie Rodgers (Solomon Islands), Lourdes Pangelinan (Guam).

Regional Office: Private Mail Bag, Suva, Fiji; tel. 370733; fax 370021; e-mail spcsuva@spc.org.fj.

Activities

The Community provides, on request of its member countries, technical assistance, advisory services, information and clearing-house services. The organization also conducts regional conferences and technical meetings, as well as training courses, workshops and seminars at the regional or country level. It provides small grants-in-aid and awards to meet specific requests and needs of members. In November 1996 the Conference agreed to establish a specific Small Islands States fund to provide technical services, training and other relevant activities. The Conference also endorsed a series of organizational reforms, on the basis of a review conducted earlier in the year. The reforms were implemented during 1997. From 1 January 1997 the Commission assumed responsibility for the maritime programme and telecommunications policy activities of the South Pacific Forum Secretariat (q.v.). The organization is also responsible for a South Pacific Forests and Trees Support Project, which is concerned with natural forest management and conservation, agroforestry and development and the use of tree and plant resources, and for a regional project relating to the sustainable management of forests and agroforestry.

AGRICULTURE

The Community's agriculture programme, which is based in Suva, Fiji, aims to promote land and agricultural management practices that are both economically and environmentally sustainable; to strengthen national capabilities to reduce losses owing to crop pests (insects, pathogens and weeds) and animal diseases already present and to prevent the introduction of new pests and diseases; to facilitate trade through improved quarantine procedures; and to improve access to, and use of, sustainable development information for all. The programme incorporates the following five main policy units: agriculture programme management, to ensure overall management and co-ordination; general agriculture, including advice on general agriculture and specific activities in crop diversification, such as coconut technology development, and the provision of agricultural training; plant protection, through the implementation of regional research and technical support projects; animal health and animal production; and the provision of advice and information on agricultural concerns and sustainable development.

FISHERIES

The Community aims to support and co-ordinate the sustainable development and management of inshore fisheries resources in the region, to undertake scientific research in order to provide member governments with relevant information for the sustainable development and management of tuna and billfish resources in and adjacent to the South Pacific region, and to provide data and analytical services to national fisheries departments. The main components of the Community's fisheries activities are the Coastal Fisheries Programme (CFP) and the Oceanic Fisheries Programme (OFP). The CFP is divided into five sections: capture—to provide practical, field-based training, through the services of experts in support of captive fisheries development activities; post-harvest—to offer advice and training in order to improve handling practices, storage, seafood product development, quality control and marketing; training—to improve manpower development and assist in the co-ordination of fisheries training; resource assessment—to assist with the design and implementation of inshore resources surveys, programmes for the collection, analysis and interpretation of fishery statistics, and other activities directed towards the acquisition of information necessary for sound management of national fishery resources; and an information section. The Community also implements a Womens' Fisheries Development Project, which assists women from coastal fishing communities to participate more effectively in, and benefit from, fisheries activities, particularly in the post-harvest, processing industry. The OFP consists of the Tuna and Billfish Research Section Project, the South Pacific Regional Tuna Resource Assessment and Monitoring Project, which was to promote the sustainable management of tuna fisheries in the region through continuous scientific monitoring, and a Fisheries Statistics Section, which maintains a database of industrial tuna fisheries in the region. The OFP contributed research and statistical information to a multilateral high-level conference that was convened in Majuro, the Marshall Islands, in June 1997, to formulate a framework for the conservation and management of highly migratory fish stocks in the Western and Central Pacific.

COMMUNITY HEALTH

The Community Health Services programme aims to implement health promotion programmes; to assist regional authorities to strengthen health information systems and to promote the use of new technology for health information development and disease control (for example, through the Public Health Surveillance and Disease Control Programme); to promote efficient health services management; and to help all Pacific Islanders to attain a level of health and quality of life that will enable them to contribute to the development of their communities. The Community Health Services also work in the areas of non-communicable diseases and nutrition, in particular the high levels of diabetes and heart disease in parts of the region, environmental health, through the improvement of water and sanitation facilities, and to reduce the incidence of HIV/AIDS and other sexually-transmitted diseases. The division is responsible for implementing a Pacific Regional Vector-Borne Diseases Project that was established in 1996, with particular emphasis on Fiji, Vanuatu and the Solomon Islands.

SOCIO-ECONOMIC AND STATISTICAL SERVICES

The statistics programme assists governments and administrations in the region to provide effective and efficient national statistical services through the provision of training activities, a statistical information service and other advisory services. A Regional Conference of Statisticians facilitates the integration and co-ordination of statistical services throughout the region.

The Population/Demographic Programme aims to assist governments effectively to utilize and incorporate data into the formulation of development policies and programmes and to provide technical support in population, demographic and development issues to member governments, other Community programmes and organizations active in the region. The Programme organizes national workshops in population and development planning, provides short-term professional attachments, undertakes demographic research and analysis and disseminates information.

The Rural Development Programme promotes active participation of the rural population and encourages the use of traditional practices and knowledge in the formulation of rural development projects and income-generating activities. The Rural Technology Programme aims to provide technical assistance, advice and monitoring of pilot regional programmes, with emphasis on technologies to generate renewable energy in rural areas, to help achieve environmentally-sustainable development.

The Youth and Adult Education Programme provides non-formal education and support for youth, community workers and young adults in community development subjects. It also advises and assists the Pacific Youth Council in promoting a regional youth identity. The Community implements its cultural affairs and conservation programme mainly through the Council of Pacific Arts. A Pacific Women's Resource Bureau aims to promote the social, economic and cultural advancement of women in the region by assisting governments and regional organizations to include women in the development planning process. The Bureau also provides technical and advisory services, advocacy and management support training to groups concerned with women in development and gender and development, and supports the production and exchange of information regarding women.

INFORMATION AND COMMUNICATION SERVICES

These include a Publication Section, which produces documentation in English and French; an Interpretation and Translation Section; Computer Services, to support the use of computers in the processing and exchange of information both within and beyond the organization; and a Library, which acts as a centre for the collection, holding and dissemination of regional development information published by the Community.

COMMUNITY EDUCATION SERVICES

All Community activities in this area are administered by the regional office in Suva, Fiji. A Community Education Training Centre (CETC) conducts a seven-month training course for up to 36 women community workers annually, with the objective of training women in methods of community development so that they can help others to achieve better living conditions for island families and communities. A Regional Media Centre provides training, technical assistance and production materials in all areas of the media for member countries and territories, Community work programmes, donor projects and regional non-governmental organizations. The Centre comprises a radio broadcast unit, a graphic design and publication unit and a TV and video unit.

FINANCE

The organization's budget is divided into administrative and work programme budgets. The administrative budget is funded by assessed contributions from member states, while the work programme is financed in part by assessed contributions, but in the main by voluntary contributions from industrialized member governments, other governments, aid agencies and other sources. The approved administrative budget for 1997 amounted to US $2.8m. The work programme budget for the year amounted to $13.0m.

PUBLICATIONS

Annual Report.

Fisheries Newsletter (quarterly).

Pacific Aids Alert Bulletin (quarterly).

Pacific Island Nutrition (quarterly).

Regional Tuna Bulletin (quarterly).

Report of the South Pacific Conference.

Women's Newsletter (quarterly).

Technical publications, statistical bulletins, advisory leaflets and reports.

SOUTH PACIFIC FORUM

MEMBERS

Australia	Niue
Cook Islands	Palau
Fiji	Papua New Guinea
Kiribati	Samoa
Marshall Islands	Solomon Islands
Federated States of Micronesia	Tonga
Nauru	Tuvalu
New Zealand	Vanuatu

The South Pacific Forum is the gathering of Heads of Government of the independent and self-governing states of the South Pacific. Its first meeting was held on 5 August 1971, in Wellington, New Zealand. It provides an opportunity for informal discussions to be held on a wide range of common issues and problems and meets annually or when issues require urgent attention. The Forum has no written constitution or international agreement governing its activities nor any formal rules relating to its purpose, membership or conduct of meeting. Decisions are always reached by consensus, it never having been found necessary or desirable to vote formally on issues. In October 1994 the Forum was granted observer status by the General Assembly of the United Nations.

From 1989 onwards, each Forum was followed by 'dialogues' with representatives of other countries that were influential in the region. In 1995 'dialogue partners' comprised Canada, the People's Republic of China, France, Japan, the United Kingdom, the USA, the Republic of Korea and the European Union. In October the Forum Governments suspended France's 'dialogue' status, following that country's resumption of the testing of nuclear weapons in French Polynesia. France was reinstated as a 'dialogue partner' in September 1996. In January 1997 Malaysia became the ninth dialogue partner, and was invited to participate in the post-forum dialogue, to be held in the Cook Islands in September.

The South Pacific Nuclear-Free Zone Treaty (Treaty of Rarotonga), prohibiting the acquisition, stationing or testing of nuclear weapons in the region, came into effect in December 1986, following ratification by eight states. The USSR signed the protocols to the treaty (whereby states possessing nuclear weapons agree not to use or threaten to use nuclear explosive devices against any non-nuclear party to the Treaty) in December 1987 and ratified them in April 1988; the People's Republic of China did likewise in December 1987 and October 1988 respectively. The other three major nuclear powers, however, intimated that they did not intend to adhere to the Treaty. In July 1993 the Forum petitioned the USA, the United Kingdom and France, asking them to reconsider their past refusal to sign the Treaty in the light of the end of the 'Cold War'. In July

1995, following the decision of the French Government to resume testing of nuclear weapons in French Polynesia, members of the Forum resolved to increase diplomatic pressure on the three Governments to sign the Treaty. In October the United Kingdom, the USA and France announced their intention to accede to the Treaty, by mid-1996. While the decision was approved by the Forum, it urged the Governments to sign with immediate effect, thus accelerating the termination of France's testing programme. Following France's decision, announced in January 1996, to end the programme four months earlier than scheduled, representatives of the Governments of the three countries signed the Treaty in March.

In 1990 five of the Forum's smallest island member states formed an economic sub-group to address their specific concerns, in particular economic disadvantages resulting from a poor resource base, absence of a skilled work-force and lack of involvement in world markets. Representatives from Kiribati, the Cook Islands, Nauru, Niue and Tuvalu, which constitute the group, meet regularly. In September 1997 the 28th Forum, convened in Rarotonga, the Cook Islands, endorsed the inclusion of the Marshall Islands as the sixth member of the Smaller Island States sub-group.

The 19th Forum, held in September 1988 in Tonga, discussed the threat posed to low-lying island countries in the region (such as Kiribati, Tonga and Tuvalu) by the predicted rise in sea-level caused by heating of the earth's atmosphere as a result of pollution (the 'greenhouse effect'). The Forum agreed to establish a network of stations to monitor climatic change in the Pacific region. The meeting also agreed to seek multilateral (rather than bilateral) negotiations with Japan on fishing rights in the Pacific.

The 20th Forum, held in July 1989 in Tarawa, Kiribati, discussed the problem of drift-net fishing, as practised by the Japanese and Taiwanese fleets, which was reported to have increased tuna catches in the region to considerably more than the agreed maximum sustainable level, while also indiscriminately destroying many other marine species. In November members adopted a regional convention banning the practice.

The 21st Forum, held in August 1990 in Vanuatu, welcomed announcements made by Japan and Taiwan in the previous month that they would suspend drift-net fishing in the region. The members criticized the US Government's proposal to use the US external territory of Johnston Atoll for the destruction of chemical weapons. The meeting urged industrialized countries to reduce the emission of gases that contribute to the 'greenhouse effect'. A ministerial committee was established to monitor political developments in New Caledonia, in co-operation with the French authorities.

The 22nd Forum took place in Pohnpei, Federated States of Micronesia, in July 1991. It issued a strong condemnation of French testing of nuclear weapons in the region. The Forum examined the report of the ministerial committee on New Caledonia, and instructed the committee to visit New Caledonia annually. However, this proposal was rejected by the French Government.

The 23rd Forum, held in Honiara, Solomon Islands, in July 1992, welcomed France's suspension of its nuclear-testing programme until the end of the year, but urged the French Government to make the moratorium permanent. Forum members discussed the decisions made at the UN Conference on Environment and Development held in June, and approved the Cook Islands' proposal to host a 'global conference for small islands'. The Niue Fisheries Surveillance and Law Enforcement Co-operation Treaty was signed by members, with the exception of Fiji, Kiribati and Tokelau, which were awaiting endorsement from their legislatures. The treaty provides for co-operation in the surveillance of fisheries resources and in defeating drug-trafficking and other organized crime.

At the 24th Forum, held in Yaren, Nauru, in August 1993 it was agreed that effective links needed to be established with the broader Asia-Pacific region, with participation in Asia-Pacific Economic Co-operation (APEC), where the Forum has observer status, to be utilized to the full. The Forum urged an increase in intra-regional trade and asked for improved opportunities for Pacific island countries exporting to Australia and New Zealand. New Caledonia's right to self-determination was supported. Environmental protection measures and the rapid growth in population in the region, which was posing a threat to economic and social development, were also discussed by the Forum delegates.

The 25th Forum was convened in Brisbane, Australia, in August 1994 under the theme of 'Managing Our Resources'. In response to the loss of natural resources as well as of income-earning potential resulting from unlawful logging of timber by foreign companies, Forum members agreed to impose stricter controls on the exploitation of forestry resources and to begin negotiations to standardize monitoring of the region's resources. The Forum also agreed to strengthen its promotion of sustainable exploitation of fishing stocks, reviewed preparations of a convention to control the movement and management of radioactive waste within the South Pacific and discussed the rationalization of national airlines, on a regional or sub-regional basis, to reduce operational losses.

The 26th Forum, held in Mantang, Papua New Guinea, in September 1995, was dominated by extreme hostility on the part of Forum Governments to the resumption of testing of nuclear weapons by France in the South Pacific region. The decision to recommence testing, announced by the French Government in June, had been instantly criticized by Forum Governments. The 26th Forum reiterated their demand that France stop any further testing, and resolved to reconsider France's 'dialogue' status with the Forum if the tests continued (see above). The Forum also condemned the People's Republic of China for conducting nuclear tests in the region. The meeting endorsed a draft Code of Conduct on the management and monitoring of indigenous forest resources in selected South Pacific countries, which had been initiated at the 25th Forum; however, while the six countries concerned committed themselves to implementing the Code through national legislation, its signing was deferred, owing to an initial unwillingness on the part of Papua New Guinea and Solomon Islands. The Forum did adopt a treaty to ban the import into the region of all radioactive and other hazardous wastes, and to control the transboundary movement and management of these wastes (the so-called Waigani Convention). The Forum agreed to reactivate the ministerial committee on New Caledonia, comprising Fiji, Nauru and Solomon Islands, which was to monitor political developments in that territory prior to its referendum on independence, scheduled to be held in 1998. In addition, the Forum resolved to implement and pursue means of promoting economic co-operation and long-term development in the region. In December 1995 Forum finance ministers, meeting in Port Moresby, Papua New Guinea, discussed the issues involved in the concept of 'Securing Development Beyond 2000' and initiated an assessment project to further trade liberalization efforts in the region.

The 27th Forum, held in Majuro, the Marshall Islands, in September 1996, supported the efforts of the French Government to improve relations with countries in the South Pacific and agreed to readmit France to the post-Forum dialogue. The region's economy was a predominant point of discussion at the 27th Forum. The meeting recognized the importance of responding to the liberalization of the global trading system by reviewing the region's tariff policies, and of assisting members in attracting investment for the development of the private sector. The Forum advocated that a meeting of economy ministers of member countries be held each year. The Forum was also concerned with environmental issues: in particular, it urged the ratification and implementation of the Waigani Convention by all member states, the formulation of an international, legally-binding agreement to reduce gas emissions, and the promotion of regional efforts to conserve marine resources and to protect the coastal environment. In July 1996 the Forum's ministerial committee on New Caledonia visited the territory (although Nauru was prevented by the French Government from participating in the mission owing to Nauru's severing of diplomatic relations with France over the issue of nuclear-weapons testing). The Forum requested the committee to pursue contacts with all parties in New Caledonia and to continue to monitor preparations for the 1998 referendum.

In July 1997 a meeting of Forum economy ministers, convened in Cairns, Australia, formulated an Action Plan to encourage the flow of foreign investment into the region by committing members to economic reforms, good governance and the implementation of multilateral trade and tariff policies. The meeting also commissioned a formal study of the establishment of a free-trade agreement between Forum island states. The 28th Forum, held in Rarotonga, the Cook Islands, in September, considered the economic challenges confronting the region, but failed to conclude a common policy position on mandatory targets for the emission of so-called 'greenhouse gases', which some members considered to be a threat to low-lying islands in the region, owing to an ongoing dispute between Australia and other Forum Governments.

South Pacific Forum Secretariat

Address: Ratu Sukuna Rd, GPO Box 856, Suva, Fiji.

Telephone: 312600; **telex:** 2229; **fax:** 301102; **internet:** http://www.forumsec.org.fj.

The South Pacific Bureau for Economic Co-operation (SPEC) was established by an agreement signed on 17 April 1973, at the third meeting of the South Pacific Forum in Apia, Western Samoa (now Samoa). SPEC was renamed the South Pacific Forum Secretariat in 1988.

Organization

(February 1998)

COMMITTEE

The Committee is the Secretariat's executive board. It comprises representatives and senior officials from all member countries. It meets twice a year, immediately before the meetings of the South Pacific Forum and at the end of the year, to discuss in detail the Secretariat's work programme and annual budget.

SECRETARIAT

The Secretariat undertakes the day-to-day activities of the Forum. It is headed by a Secretary-General, with a staff of 77 drawn from the member countries.

Secretary-General: Noel Levi (Papua New Guinea).

Deputy Secretary-General: Anthony Slatyer (Australia).

Activities

The Secretariat's aim is to enhance the economic and social well-being of the people of the South Pacific, in support of the efforts of national governments. It also services the meetings of the Forum, disseminates its views and co-ordinates activities with other regional organizations.

During 1995 an extensive review of the structure and role of the Secretariat was undertaken. Subsequent reorganization of the Secretariat was authorized at the Forum Officials' Committee in August/September 1996 and came into effect on 1 January 1997. The revised structure comprised the following four Divisions, all of which adopted an expanded policy advisory role: Corporate Services; Development and Economic Policy; Trade and Investment; and Political and International Affairs.

The Secretariat's trade activities cover trade promotion, the identification and development of export-orientated industries, and the negotiation of export opportunities. The South Pacific Regional Trade and Economic Co-operation Agreement (SPARTECA), which came into force in 1981, aims to redress the trade deficit of the South Pacific countries with Australia and New Zealand. It is a non-reciprocal trade agreement under which Australia and New Zealand offer duty-free and unrestricted access or concessional access for specified products originating from the developing island member countries of the Forum. In 1985 Australia agreed to further liberalization of trade by abolishing (from the beginning of 1987) duties and quotas on all Pacific products except steel, cars, sugar, footwear and garments. In August 1994 New Zealand expanded its import criteria under the agreement by reducing the rule of origin requirement for garment products from 50% to 45% of local content. In response to requests from Fiji, Australia agreed to widen its interpretation of the agreement by accepting as being of local content manufactured products that consist of goods and components of 50% Australian content.

The Secretariat also investigates the prospects for closer economic co-operation between members, and has conducted market surveys in Japan and the USA, and surveys on regional industry. It provides support for national and regional trade promotion and trade information services. In March 1992 the Secretariat's economic development division organized a meeting of Forum members with developed countries and international aid organizations, which discussed economic development, human resources development, the provision of aid and policy formulation in the region. The Industrial Development and Training Project, which is administered by the Trade and Investment Division, was initiated in 1992, and provides advisory services and funds industrial training placements for Pacific islanders in industrialized countries. Under the new structure of the Secretariat the Division was expanded to address import management and trade policy issues. In mid-1995 the Forum Secretariat and Japan completed a feasibility study on the establishment of a South Pacific economic exchange support centre in Tokyo. The so-called Pacific Islands' Centre, was inaugurated in October 1996 (see below). A similar undertaking with the People's Republic of China was under consideration.

The South Pacific Forum established the Pacific Forum Line and the Association of South Pacific Airlines (see below), as part of its efforts to promote co-operation in regional transport. On 1 January 1997 the work of the Forum Maritime Programme, which includes assistance for regional maritime training and for the development of regional maritime administrations and legislation, was transferred to the regional office of the South Pacific Commission (renamed the Pacific Community from February 1998) at Suva. At the same time responsibility for the Secretariat's civil aviation activities was transferred to individual countries, to be managed at a bilateral level.

In 1991 the Telecommunications Division assisted in the installation of the region's first solar-powered satellite earth station in Funafuti, Tuvalu. In May 1994 the Division established the Executive Development Programme to conduct training courses and management workshops for telecommunications executives in the region. Under the restructuring, it was agreed to terminate the technical programmes of the Telecommunications Division, with effect from 1 January 1997, and to transfer the Division's policy activities to the South Pacific Commission.

The Secretariat's Energy Division provided advice on and assistance with renewable energy technologies, conservation, and the purchase, transport and storage of petroleum. In addition, the Secretariat administered a solar electrification programme for rural areas, partly financed by the European Union (EU). All energy programmes remained at the Secretariat following the restructuring, pending a decision on their permanent reallocation.

The Secretariat services the Pacific Group Council of ACP states receiving assistance from the EU under the Lomé Convention (q.v.), and in early 1993 a joint unit was established within the Secretariat headquarters to assist Pacific ACP countries and regional organizations in submitting projects to the EU for funding. In October 1994 the Secretariat signed an agreement with representatives of the EU for the establishment of a Pacific Regional Agricultural Programme. The four-year programme was to be funded under the Lomé IV Pacific Regional Programme, with the aim of improving agricultural productivity in the region. The Secretariat also manages a regional disaster relief fund and a Fellowship Scheme to provide in-service training in island member and ASEAN countries. A Short-Term Advisory Service provides short-term consultancy services on a wide range of economic issues.

BUDGET

The Governments of Australia and New Zealand each contribute one-third of the annual budget and the remaining third is equally shared by the other member Governments. Extra-budgetary funding is contributed mainly by Australia, New Zealand, Japan, the EU and France. In December 1996 Forum officials approved a budget of $F 14.1m. for the Secretariat's 1997 work programme.

Associated and Affiliated Organizations

Association of South Pacific Airlines—ASPA: POB 9817, Nadi Airport, Nadi, Fiji; tel. 723526; fax 720196; f. 1979 at a meeting of airlines in the South Pacific, convened to promote co-operation among the member airlines for the development of regular, safe and economical commercial aviation within, to and from the South Pacific. Mems: 14 regional airlines, three associates. Pres. Richard Gates; Sec.-Gen. George E. Faktaufon.

Pacific Forum Line: POB 796, Auckland, New Zealand; tel. (9) 356-2333; telex 60460; fax (9) 356-2330; e-mail pflnz@pflnz.co.nz; f. 1977 as a joint venture by South Pacific countries, to provide shipping services to meet the special requirements of the region; operates three container vessels; conducts shipping agency services in Australia, Fiji, New Zealand and Samoa, and stevedoring in Samoa. Chair. T. Tufui; CEO W. J. MacLennan.

Pacific Islands' Centre (PIC): Akasaka Twin Tower, Main Bldg, 1st Floor, 2-17-22 Akasaka, Minato-ku, Tokyo 107-0052, Japan; tel. (3) 3585-8419; fax (3) 3585-8637; f. 1996 to promote and to facilitate trade, investment and tourism among Forum members and Japan; Dir Yoshiaki Kotaki.

South Pacific Forum Fisheries Agency—FFA: POB 629, Honiara, Solomon Islands; tel. (677) 21124; telex 66336; fax (677) 23995; f. 1978 by the South Pacific Forum to promote co-operation in fisheries among coastal states in the region; collects and disseminates information and advice on the living marine resources of the region, including the management, exploitation and development of these resources; provides assistance in the areas of law (treaty negotiations, drafting legislation, and co-ordinating surveillance and enforcement), fisheries development, research, economics, computers, and information management. On behalf of its member countries, the FFA administers a multilateral fisheries treaty, under which vessels from the USA operate in the region, in exchange for an annual payment. Dir VICTORIO UHERBELAN. Publs *FFA News Digest* (every two months), *FFA Reports*.

South Pacific Trade Commission: Suite 3003, Piccadilly Tower, 133 Castlereagh St, Sydney, NSW 2000, Australia; tel. (2) 9283-5933; fax (2) 9283-5948; e-mail info@sptc.gov.au; f. 1979; assists Pacific Island Governments and business communities to identify market opportunities in Australia and promotes investment in the Pacific Island countries. Senior Trade Commr CHRISTOPHER WARD. Publ. *Australian Newsletter* (monthly).

PUBLICATIONS

Annual Report.

Forum News (quarterly).

Forum Secretariat Directory of Aid Agencies.

South Pacific Trade Directory.

SPARTECA (guide for Pacific island exporters).

Reports of Forum and Bureau meetings; profiles of Forum member countries.

SOUTHERN AFRICAN DEVELOPMENT COMMUNITY—SADC

Address: SADC Bldg, Private Bag 0095, Gaborone, Botswana.
Telephone: 351863; **telex:** 2555; **fax:** 372848.

The first Southern African Development Co-ordination Conference (SADCC) was held at Arusha, Tanzania, in July 1979, to harmonize development plans and to reduce the region's economic dependence on South Africa. On 17 August 1992 the 10 member countries of the SADCC signed a treaty establishing the Southern African Development Community (SADC), which replaced the SADCC. The treaty places binding obligations on member countries, with the aim of promoting economic integration towards a fully developed common market. A tribunal was to be established to arbitrate in the case of disputes between member states arising from the treaty. By September 1993 all of the member states had ratified the treaty; it came into effect on 5 October. South Africa and Mauritius joined the SADC after that date; the Democratic Republic of the Congo and Seychelles became members in September 1997.

MEMBERS

Angola	Mauritius	Swaziland
Botswana	Mozambique	Tanzania
Congo, Democratic Republic	Namibia	Zambia
Lesotho	Seychelles	Zimbabwe
Malawi	South Africa	

TREATY ESTABLISHING THE SADC

The Treaty declares the following aims:

(i) deeper economic co-operation and integration, on the basis of balance, equality and mutual benefit, providing for cross-border investment and trade, and freer movement of factors of production, goods and services across national boundaries;

(ii) common economic, political and social values and systems, enhancing enterprise competitiveness, democracy and good governance, respect for the rule of law and human rights, popular participation, and the alleviation of poverty; and

(iii) strengthened regional solidarity, peace and security, in order for the people of the region to live and work in harmony.

Organization

(January 1998)

SUMMIT MEETING

The meeting is held annually and is attended by Heads of State and Government or their representatives. It is the supreme policy-making organ of the SADC.

COUNCIL OF MINISTERS

Representatives of SADC member countries at ministerial level meet at least twice a year; in addition, special meetings are held to co-ordinate regional policy in a particular field by, for example, ministers of energy and ministers of transport.

CONFERENCES ON CO-OPERATION

A conference with the SADC's 'international co-operating partners' (donor governments and international agencies) is held annually to review progress in the various sectors of the SADC programme and to present new projects requiring assistance.

SECRETARIAT

Executive Secretary: KAIRE MBUENDE (Namibia).

SECTORAL CO-ORDINATION OFFICES

Agricultural and Natural Resources Research and Training: Private Bag 0033, Gaborone, Botswana; tel. 328780; telex 2752; fax 328965.

Culture and Information: Ministry of Information, Avda Francisco Orlando Magumbwe 750, Maputo, Mozambique; tel. (1) 493423; telex 6487; fax (1) 493427.

Employment and Labour: POB 32186, Lusaka, Zambia; tel. (1) 223154; telex 40686; fax (1) 227251.

Energy: rua Gil Vicente No. 2, Luanda, Angola; tel. 345288; telex 4090; fax 343003.

Environment and Land Management: Ministry of Agriculture, Co-operatives and Marketing, POB 24, Maseru 100, Lesotho; tel. 312158; telex 4414; fax 310190.

Finance and Investment: Private Bag X115, Pretoria, 0001, South Africa; tel. (12) 3155693; fax (12) 219580.

Food, Agriculture and Natural Resources: 88 Rezende St, POB 4046, Harare, Zimbabwe; tel. (4) 736051; telex 22440; fax (4) 795345.

Human Resources Development: Dept of Economic Planning and Statistics, POB 602, Mbabane, Swaziland; tel. 46344; telex 3020; fax 46407.

Industry and Trade: POB 9491, Dar es Salaam, Tanzania; tel. (51) 31455; telex 41686; fax (51) 46919.

Inland Fisheries, Wildlife and Forestry: Ministry of Forestry and Natural Resources, Private Bag 350, Lilongwe 3, Malawi; tel. 782600; telex 44465; fax 780260.

Livestock Production and Animal Disease Control: Private Bag 0032, Gaborone, Botswana; tel. 350620; telex 2543; fax 303744.

Marine Fisheries and Resources: Private Bag 13355, Windhoek, Namibia; tel. (61) 2053911; fax (61) 224566.

Mining: Ministry of Mines and Mineral Development, POB 31969, Lusaka, Zambia; tel. (1) 251719; telex 40539; fax (1) 252095; e-mail sadc-mcu@zamnet.zm.

Southern African Centre for Co-operation in Agricultural Research (SACCAR): Private Bag 00108, Gaborone, Botswana; tel. 328847; telex 2752; fax 328806; Dir Dr BRUNO NDUNGURU.

Southern African Transport and Communications Commission (SATCC): CP 2677, Maputo, Mozambique; tel. (1) 420246; telex 6606; fax (1) 420213; Dir SEVENIN KAOMBWE (acting).

Tourism: Ministry of Tourism, Sports and Culture, POB 52, Maseru 100, Lesotho; tel. 313034; telex 4228; fax 310194.

Activities

In July 1979 the first Southern African Development Co-ordination Conference was attended by delegations from Angola, Botswana, Mozambique, Tanzania and Zambia, with representatives from donor governments and international agencies; the group was later joined by Lesotho, Malawi, Swaziland and Zimbabwe, and Namibia became a member in 1990.

In April 1980 a regional economic summit conference was held in Lusaka, Zambia, and the Lusaka Declaration, a statement of strategy entitled 'Southern Africa: Towards Economic Liberation', was approved, together with a programme of action allotting specific studies and tasks to member governments (see list of co-ordinating offices, above). The members aimed to reduce their dependence on South Africa for rail and air links and port facilities, imports of raw materials and manufactured goods, and the supply of electric power. In 1985, however, an SADCC report noted that since 1980 the region had become still more dependent on South Africa for its trade outlets, and the 1986 summit meeting, although it recommended the adoption of economic sanctions against South Africa, failed to establish a timetable for doing so.

In January 1992 a meeting of the SADCC Council of Ministers approved proposals to transform the organization into a fully integrated economic community, and in mid-August the treaty establishing the SADC (see above) was signed. South Africa became a member of the SADC in August 1994, thus strengthening the objective of regional co-operation and economic integration.

A possible merger between the SADC and the Preferential Trade Area for Eastern and Southern African States (PTA), which consisted of all the members of the SADC apart from Botswana and had similar aims of enhancing economic co-operation, was rejected by the SADC's Executive Secretary in January 1993. He denied that the two organizations were duplicating each other's work, as had been suggested. In August 1994 SADC heads of state, meeting in Gaborone, Botswana, advocated that, in order to minimize any duplication of activities, the PTA be divided into two sections: a southern region, incorporating all SADC members, and a northern region. It was emphasized that there would not be a merger between the two groupings. Concerns of regional rivalry with the PTA's successor, the Common Market for Eastern and Southern Africa (COMESA, q.v.), were ongoing in 1995. In July SADC heads of state and government agreed to hold a joint SADC/COMESA summit meeting on the future of the two organizations. In August 1996 an SADC–COMESA ministeral meeting advocated the continued separate functioning of the two organizations.

In September 1994 the first meeting of ministers of foreign affairs of the SADC and the European Union (EU) was held in Berlin, Germany. The two sides agreed to establish working groups to promote closer trade, political, regional and economic co-operation. In particular, a declaration issued from the meeting specified joint objectives, including a reduction of exports of weapons to southern Africa and of the arms trade within the region, promotion of investment in the region's manufacturing sector and support for democracy at all levels. A consultative meeting between representatives of the SADC and EU was held in February 1995, in Lilongwe, Malawi, at which both groupings resolved to strengthen security in the southern African region. The meeting proposed initiating mechanisms to prevent conflicts and to maintain peace, and agreed to organize a conference to address the problems of drugs-trafficking and cross-border crime in the region. A second SADC–EU ministerial meeting, held in Namibia in October 1996, endorsed a Regional Indicative Programme to enhance co-operation between the two organizations over the next five years.

In April 1997 the SADC announced the establishment of a Parliamentary Forum to promote democracy, human rights and good governance throughout the region. Membership was to be open to national parliaments of all SADC countries, and was to offer fair representation for women. Representatives were to serve for a period of five years. The Parliamentary Forum, with its headquarters in Windhoek, Namibia, was to receive funds from member parliaments, governments and charitable and international organizations.

REGIONAL SECURITY

In November 1994 SADC ministers of defence, meeting in Arusha, Tanzania, approved the establishment of a regional rapid-deployment peace-keeping force, which could be used to contain regional conflicts or civil unrest in member states. In April 1997 the newly-formed peace-keeping force commenced a training programme which aimed to inform troops from nine SADC countries of UN peace-keeping doctrines, procedures and strategies. The exercise took place in Zimbabwe at a cost of US $900,000, provided by the British Government and the Zimbabwe National Army.

In June 1996 SADC heads of state and government, meeting in Gaborone, Botswana, inaugurated a new Organ on Politics, Defence and Security, which was expected to enhance co-ordination of national policies and activities in these areas. The objectives of the body were, *inter alia,* to safeguard the people and development of the region against instability arising from civil disorder, inter-state conflict and external aggression; to undertake conflict prevention, management and resolution activities, by mediating in inter-state and intra-state disputes and conflicts, pre-empting conflicts through an early-warning system and using diplomacy and peace-keeping to achieve sustainable peace; to promote the development of a common foreign policy, in areas of mutual interest, and the evolution of common political institutions; to develop close co-operation between the police and security services of the region; and to encourage the observance of universal human rights, as provided for in the charters of the UN and OAU. The summit meeting elected the Zimbabwean President, Robert Mugabe, to chair the Organ. The Zambian President, Frederick Chiluba, failed to attend the meeting, owing to his Government's concern that the new body was empowered to interfere in the country's internal affairs. In October the Organ convened, at summit level, to consider measures to promote the peace process in Angola.

At the 1997 summit meeting, held in Blantyre, Malawi, in September, heads of state and of governments signed a declaration prohibiting the use, stockpiling and production of land-mines.

TRANSPORT AND COMMUNICATIONS

At the SADC's inception transport was seen as the most important area to be developed, on the grounds that, as the Lusaka Declaration noted, without the establishment of an adequate regional transport and communications system, other areas of co-operation become impractical. Priority was to be given to the improvement of road and railway services into Mozambique, so that the landlocked countries of the region could transport their goods through Mozambican ports instead of South African ones. The Southern African Transport and Communications Commission (SATCC) was established, in Maputo, Mozambique, in order to undertake SADC's activities in this sector. The successful distribution of emergency supplies in 1992/93, following a severe drought in the region, was reliant on improvements made to the region's infrastructure in recent years. The facilities of 12 ports in southern Africa, including South Africa, were used to import some 11.5m. metric tons of drought-related commodities, and the SADC co-ordinated six transport corridors to ensure unobstructed movement of food and other supplies. In 1997 Namibia announced plans, supported by the SADC, to establish a rail link with Angola in order to form a trade route similar to that created in Mozambique, on the western side of southern Africa.

In 1993/94 208 of the SADC's 446 development projects were in the transport and communications sector, amounting to US $6,934.1m., or 81% of total project financing. These projects aimed to address missing links and over-stretched sections of the regional network, as well as to improve efficiency, operational co-ordination and human resource development, such as management training projects. Other sectoral objectives were to ensure the compatibility of technical systems within the region and to promote the harmonization of regulations relating to intra-regional traffic and trade.

Port rehabilitation projects in 1993/94 were centred on Maputo and Nacala ports, in Mozambique, and Lobito, in Angola. The SADC promotes greater co-operation in the civil aviation sector, in order to improve efficiency and to reverse a steady decline in the region's airline industries. Within the telecommunications sector efforts have been made to increase the capacity of direct exchange lines and international subscriber dialling (ISD) services. An SADC Expedited Mail Service operates in the postal services sector. The SATCC's Technical Unit oversees the region's meteorological services and issues a regular *Drought-Watch for Southern Africa* bulletin, a monthly *Drought Overview* bulletin and forewarnings of impending natural disasters.

During 1995 the SATCC undertook a study of regional transport and communications to provide a comprehensive framework and strategy for future courses of action. The study was compiled using analysis and data of existing infrastructure, their viability and trading use. A task force was also established to identify measures to simplify procedures at border crossings throughout southern Africa.

FOOD, AGRICULTURE AND NATURAL RESOURCES

The food, agriculture and natural resources sector covers eight sub-sectors: agricultural research and training; inland fisheries; forestry; wildlife; marine fisheries and resources; food security; livestock production and animal disease control; and environment and land management. At July 1994 funding required for 101 projects in this sector was US $658.8m., of which $354.0m. had been secured. The importance of this sector is evident in the fact that, according to SADC figures, agriculture contributes one-third of the region's GNP, accounts for 26% of total earnings of foreign exchange and employs some 80% of the labour force. A new integrated strategy for the sector was prepared in 1992 and was adopted by ministers of agriculture and natural resources in January 1993. The sector's principal objectives are regional food security, agricultural development and natural resource development.

The Southern African Centre for Co-operation in Agricultural Research (SACCAR), in Gaborone, Botswana, which began operations in 1985, co-ordinates SADC efforts in this field of activity. It aims to strengthen national agricultural research systems, in order to improve management, increase productivity, promote the development and transfer of technology to assist local farmers, and improve training. Examples of activity include: a sorghum and millet improvement programme; a land and water management research programme; a root crop research network; agroforestry research, implemented in Malawi, Tanzania, Zambia and Zimbabwe; and a grain legume improvement programme, comprising separate research units for groundnuts, beans and cowpeas. The SADC's Plant Genetic Resources Centre was established in 1988, near Lusaka, Zambia, to collect, conserve and utilize indigenous and exotic plant genetic resources and to develop appropriate management practices.

The sector aims to promote inland and marine fisheries as an important, sustainable source of animal protein. Marine fisheries are also considered to be a potential source of income of foreign exchange. In May 1993 the first formal meeting of SADC ministers of marine fisheries convened in Namibia, and it was agreed to hold annual meetings. The development of fresh water fisheries is focused on aquaculture projects, and their integration into rural community activities. In 1995 efforts were initiated for regional fisheries capacity-building and for the management of shared water bodies. The environment and land management sub-sector is concerned with sustainability as an essential quality of development. Following the severe drought in the region in 1991/92, the need for water resources development has become a priority. The sector also undertakes projects for the conservation and sustainable development of forestry and wildlife, the control of animal diseases and the improvement of livestock production.

Under the food security programme, the Harare-based Regional Early Warning System aims to anticipate and prevent food shortages through the provision of information relating to the food security situation in member states. As a result of the drought crisis experience, SADC member states have agreed to inform the food security sector of their food and non-food requirements on a regular basis, in order to assess the needs of the region as a whole. A regional food reserve project was also to be developed. In June 1995 the SADC appealed for US $270m. of aid from western countries in order to combat the effects of drought, which had afflicted food production in the region. The Regional Early Warning System predicted that the region's total maize output would decrease by 41% in 1995, from the level of the previous year's harvest, to only 12m. metric tons, leaving a basic food requirement deficit of 3.5m. tons. By 1997 the situation had greatly improved and the SADC Food Security Bulletin announced that sufficient cereal was available for both normal consumption and the reserve fund, leaving a surplus of 1.33m. tons.

ENERGY

Areas of activity in the energy sector include: joint petroleum exploration, training programmes for the petroleum sector and studies for strategic fuel storage facilities; promotion of the use of coal; development of hydroelectric power and the co-ordination of SADC generation and transmission capacities; new and renewable sources of energy, including pilot projects in solar energy; assessment of the environmental and socio-economic impact of wood-fuel scarcity and relevant education programmes; and energy conservation. In July 1995 SADC energy ministers approved the establishment of a Southern African Power Pool, an arrangement whereby all member states were to be linked into a single electricity grid. (Several grids are already integrated and others are being rehabilitated.) At the same time, ministers endorsed a Protocol to promote greater co-operation in energy development within the SADC. On receiving final approval and signature by member states, the Protocol was to replace the energy sector with an Energy Commission, responsible for 'demand-side' management, pricing, ensuring private-sector involvement and competition, training and research, collecting information, etc.

TRADE, INDUSTRY AND MINING

Under the treaty establishing the SADC, efforts were to be undertaken to achieve regional economic integration. The trade and industry sector aims to facilitate this by the creation of an enabling investment and trade environment in SADC countries, the establishment of a single regional market, by progressively removing barriers to the movement of goods, services and people, and the promotion of cross-border investment. The sector supports programmes for industrial research and development and standardization and quality assurance. A new sector of finance and investment has been established to mobilize industrial investment resources and to co-ordinate economic policies and the development of the financial sector. During 1995 work continued on the preparation of two Protocols on trade co-operation and finance and investment, which were to provide the legal framework for integration. In August 1996 SADC member states (except Angola) signed a Protocol providing for the establishment of a free-trade area, through the gradual elimination of tariff barriers over an eight-year period, at a summit meeting held in Lesotho. The Protocol was to come into effect following its ratification by two-thirds of member states. By August 1997 the Protocol had been signed by five member countries.

In January 1992 a new five-year strategy for the promotion of mining in the region was approved, with the principal objective of stimulating local and foreign investment in the sector to maximize benefits from the region's mineral resources. In December 1994 the SADC held a mining forum, jointly with the EU, in Lusaka, Zambia, with the aim of demonstrating to potential investors and promoters the possibilities of mining exploration in the region. Other objectives of the mining sector are the improvement of industry training, increasing the contribution of small-scale mining, reducing the illicit trade in gemstones and gold, increasing co-operation in mineral exploration and processing, and minimizing the adverse impact of mining operations on the environment. Of the 31 mining projects planned at July 1994 (amounting to US $30.9m.), 11 were for overall co-ordination of the industry and five for environmental protection.

HUMAN RESOURCES DEVELOPMENT

The SADC helps to supply the region's requirements in skilled manpower by providing training in the following categories: high-level managerial personnel; agricultural managers; high- and medium-level technicians; artisans; and instructors. The sector aims to harmonize and strengthen the education and training systems in the SADC through initiatives such as the determination of active labour market information systems and institutions in the region, improving education policy analysis and formulation, the standardization of curricula and examinations and addressing issues of teaching and learning materials in the region. It has also initiated a programme of distance education to enable greater access to education, and operates the SADC's scholarship and training awards programme.

CULTURE AND INFORMATION

A new culture and information sector was established in 1990, and is co-ordinated by Mozambique. Following the ratification of the new treaty establishing the Community, the sector was expected to emphasize regional socio-cultural development as part of the process of greater integration. The SADC Press Trust was established, in Harare, Zimbabwe, to disseminate information about the SADC and to articulate the concerns and priorities of the region. Public education initiatives have commenced to encourage the involvement of people in the process of regional integration and development, as well as to promote democratic and human rights' values. A four-year programme, entitled the SADC Festival on Arts and Culture, was initiated in 1994. The following events were to be held: a music festival, in Zimbabwe, in 1995; a theatre festival, in Mozambique, in 1996; an arts and crafts regional exposition, in Namibia, in 1997; and a dance festival, in Tanzania, in 1998.

TOURISM

The sector's current programme is to promote tourism within the context of national and regional socio-economic development objectives. It comprises four components: tourism product development; tourism marketing and research; tourism services; and human resources development and training. The SADC has promoted tourism for the region at trade fairs in Europe, and has initiated a project to provide a range of promotional material. By September 1993 a project to design a standard grading classification system for tourist accommodation in the region was completed, with the assistance of the World Tourism Organization, and the Council approved its implementation. The sector also aims to stimulate and assess the potential of intra-regional tourism, which is considered to be a major element of regional integration. In an attempt to further promote tourism in the region, SADC ministers have approved the establishment of a new tourism body, to be administered jointly by SADC officials and private-sector operators. The Regional Tourism Organization for Southern Africa (RETOSA) was to assist member states to formulate tourism promotion policies and strategies. In June 1996 SADC ministers of tourism, meeting in Maputo, Mozambique, agreed on funding to assist the establishment of RETOSA.

FINANCE

SADC PROJECT FINANCING BY SECTOR (July 1994)

Sector	Number of projects	Total cost (US $ million)	Funding secured (US $ million)*
Culture and information	6	14.30	4.44
Energy	60	820.22	673.63
Food, agriculture and natural resources			
Agricultural research and training	16	126.92	79.91
Inland fisheries	12	69.18	33.19
Food security	10	63.17	18.27
Forestry	16	117.29	50.40
Wildlife	11	68.15	53.74
Livestock production and animal disease control	18	126.65	85.54
Environment and land management	12	80.06	32.80
Marine fisheries and resources	6	7.38	0.15
Industry and trade	11	12.63	2.84
Human resources development	21	45.23	17.11
Mining	31	30.91	14.75
Tourism	8	4.67	1.96
Transport and communications	208	6,934.10	3,238.10
Total	446	8,520.86	4,306.83

* Includes both local and foreign resources.

PUBLICATIONS

SACCAR Newsletter (quarterly).

SADC Annual Report.

SADC Energy Bulletin.

SATCC Bulletin (quarterly).

SKILLS.

SPLASH.

SOUTHERN COMMON MARKET—MERCOSUR/MERCOSUL

(MERCADO COMÚN DEL SUR/MERCADO COMUM DO SUL)

Address: Edificio Mercosur, Rincón 575 P 12, 11000 Montevideo, Uruguay.

Telephone: (2) 964590; **fax:** (2) 964591.

Mercosur (known as Mercosul in Portuguese) was established in March 1991 by the heads of state of Argentina, Brazil, Paraguay and Uruguay with the signature of the Treaty of Asunción. The primary objective of the Treaty is to achieve the economic integration of member states by means of a free flow of goods and services between member states, the establishment of a common external tariff, the adoption of common commercial policy, and the co-ordination of macroeconomic and sectoral policies. The Ouro Preto Protocol, which was signed in December 1994, conferred on Mercosur the status of an international legal entity with the authority to sign agreements with third countries, group of countries and international organizations.

MEMBERS

Argentina Brazil Paraguay Uruguay

In 1996 Chile negotiated a free-trade agreement with Mercosur. This association agreement came into effect on 1 October. On 11 October Bolivia also signed a free-trade agreement (see below); an agreement extending associate membership to Bolivia was endorsed in December.

Organization

(January 1998)

COMMON MARKET COUNCIL

The Common Market Council (Consejo Mercado Común) is the highest organ of Mercosur and is responsible for leading the integration process and for taking decisions in order to achieve the objectives of the Asunción Treaty.

COMMON MARKET GROUP

The Common Market Group (Grupo Mercado Común) is the executive body of Mercosur and is responsible for implementing concrete measures to further the integration process. The Group is assisted by an Administrative Secretariat.

Administrative Secretary: MANUEL OLARREAGA.

TRADE COMMISSION

The Trade Commission has competence for the area of joint commercial policy and, in particular, is responsible for monitoring the operation of the common external tariff (see below). The Brasília Protocol may be referred to for the resolution of trade disputes between member states.

JOINT PARLIAMENTARY COMMISSION

The Joint Parliamentary Commission (Comisión Parliamentaria Conjunto) is made up of parliamentarians from the member states and is charged with accelerating internal national procedures to implement Mercosur decisions, including the harmonization of country legislation.

CONSULTATIVE ECONOMIC AND SOCIAL FORUM

The Consultative Economic and Social Forum is made up of representatives from the business community and trade unions in the member countries and has a consultative role in relation to Mercosur.

Activities

Mercosur's free-trade zone entered into effect on 1 January 1995, with tariffs removed from 85% of intra-regional trade. A regime of gradual removal of duties on a list of special products was agreed, with Argentina and Brazil given four years to complete this process while Paraguay and Uruguay were allowed five years. Regimes governing intra-zonal trade in the automobile and sugar sectors remained to be negotiated. Mercosur's customs union also came into force at the start of 1995, comprising a common external tariff of 0–20%. A list of exceptions from the common external tariff was also agreed; these products were to lose their special status and be subject to the general tarification concerning foreign goods by 2006. The value of intra-Mercosur trade increased from US $9,400m. in 1994 to $15,300m. in 1995, and was estimated to have tripled during the period 1991–95.

In June 1995 Mercosur ministers responsible for the environment held a meeting at which they agreed to harmonize environmental legislation and to form a permanent sub-group of Mercosur. In December Mercosur and the EU signed a framework agreement for commercial and economic co-operation, which provides for co-operation in the economic, trade, industrial, scientific, institutional and cultural fields and the promotion of wider political dialogue on issues of mutual interest.

At the summit meeting in December 1995 the presidents affirmed the consolidation of free trade as Mercosur's 'permanent and most urgent goal'. To this end they agreed to prepare norms of application for Mercosur's customs code, accelerate paper procedures and increase the connections between national computerized systems. It was also agreed to increase co-operation in the areas of agriculture, industry, mining, energy, communications, transport and tourism, and finance. At this meeting Argentina and Brazil reached an agreement aimed at overcoming their dispute regarding the trade in automobiles between the two countries. They agreed that cars should have a minimum of 60% domestic components and that Argentina should be allowed to complete its balance of exports of cars to Brazil, which had earlier imposed a unilateral quota on the import of Argentine cars. (A comprehensive agreement covering the automobile sector was still under negotiation in late 1997 and was expected to come into force at the beginning of 2000.) In May 1996 Mercosur parliamentarians met with the aim of harmonizing legislation on patents in member countries.

In December 1996 Mercosur heads of state, meeting in Fortaleza, Brazil, approved agreements on harmonizing competition practices (by 2001), on the integration of educational opportunities for post-graduates and human resources training, on the standardization of trading safeguards applied against third-country products (by 2001) and for intra-regional cultural exchanges. An Accord on Subregional Air Services was signed at the meeting (including by the heads of state of Bolivia and Chile) to liberalize civil transport throughout the region. In addition, the heads of state endorsed texts on consumer rights that were to be incorporated into a Mercosur Consumers' Defence Code and agreed to consider the establishment of a bank to finance the integration and development of the region.

In June 1996 the Joint Parliamentary Commission agreed that Mercosur should endorse a 'Democratic Guarantee Clause', whereby a country would be prevented from participation in Mercosur unless democratic, accountable institutions were in place. The clause was adopted by the Mercosur heads of state at the summit meeting that was held in San Luis de Mendoza, in Argentina, later in the month. The presidents approved the entry into Mercosur of Bolivia and Chile as associate members. An Economic Complementation Accord with Bolivia, which includes Bolivia in Mercosur's free-trade zone, but not in the customs union, was signed in December 1995 and was to come into force on 1 January 1997. In December 1996 the Accord was extended until 30 April 1997, when a free-trade zone between Bolivia and Mercosur was to become operational. Measures of the free-trade agreement, which was signed in October 1996, were to be implemented over a transitional period commencing on 28 February 1997 (revised from 1 January). Chile's Economic

Complementation Accord with Mercosur entered into effect on 1 October 1996, with duties on most products to be removed over a 10-year period (Chile's most sensitive products were given 18 years for complete tariff elimination). Chile was also to remain outside the customs union, but was to be involved in other integration projects, in particular infrastructure projects designed to give Mercosur countries access to both the Atlantic and Pacific Oceans (Chile's Pacific coast was regarded as Mercosur's potential link to the economies of the Far East).

In June 1997 the first meeting of tax administrators and customs officials of Mercosur member countries was held, with the aim of enhancing information exchange and promoting joint customs inspections. Later in that month Mercosur heads of state convened in Asunción, Paraguay. The meeting reaffirmed the group's intention to pursue trade negotiations with the EU, Mexico and the Andean Community, as well as to negotiate a single economic bloc in discussions with regard to the establishment of a Free Trade Area of the Americas (FTAA). Chile and Bolivia were to be incorporated into these negotiations. Mercosur supports the FTAA, but has proposed a more gradual approach to its establishment, and in particular to further tariff reductions, than that favoured by the USA. Negotiations on the FTAA were scheduled to commence in April 1998. In September 1997 representatives of the EU and Mercosur expressed their intention of concluding a free-trade accord by 1999. During 1997 Mercosur's efforts towards regional economic integration were threatened by Brazil's adverse external trade balance and its Government's measures to counter the deficit, which included the imposition of import duties on certain products. In November the Brazilian Government announced that it was to increase its import tariff by 3%, in a further effort to improve its external balance. The measure was endorsed by Argentina as a means of maintaining regional fiscal stability. The new external tariff, which was to remain in effect until 31 December 2000, was formally adopted by Mercosur heads of state at a meeting held in Montevideo, Uruguay, in December 1997. At the same time a separate Protocol was signed providing for the liberalization of trade in services and government purchases over a 10-year period. In order to strengthen economic integration throughout the region, Mercosur leaders agreed that Chile, while still not a full member of the organization, be integrated into the Mercosur political structure, with equal voting rights. The meeting failed to conclude a single trading policy with Mexico, although Argentina, Paraguay and Uruguay resolved to renew their existing bilateral trade agreements with that country. Mercosur heads of state also acknowledged that the initial timetable of concluding a free-trade accord with the members of the Andean Community by 31 December 1997 could not be achieved, but declared their commitment to future economic integration between the two groupings.

FINANCE

In December 1996 the Mercosur summit meeting approved a budget of US $1.2m. for the Mercosur secretariat, to be contributed by the four full member countries.

PUBLICATION

Boletín Oficial del Mercosur (quarterly).

WESTERN EUROPEAN UNION—WEU

Address: 4 rue de la Régence, 1000 Brussels, Belgium

Telephone: (2) 513-4365; **fax:** (2) 511-3519; **internet:** http://www.weu.int.

Based on the Brussels Treaty of 1948, the Western European Union (WEU) was set up in 1955. WEU is an intergovernmental organization for European co-operation in the field of security and defence. It seeks to define common positions and harmonize the policies of its member states. WEU now has a dual objective: being developed as the defence component of the European Union, and as the means of strengthening the European pillar of the Atlantic Alliance under NATO.

MEMBERS*

Belgium	Luxembourg
France	Netherlands
Germany	Portugal
Greece	Spain
Italy	United Kingdom

* WEU has invited the other members of the EU to join the organization. In November 1992 Denmark and Ireland took up observer status. At the same time Iceland, Norway and Turkey were granted associate membership, which allowed them to participate fully in WEU's activities. In May 1994 associate partnership status was granted to Bulgaria, the Czech Republic, Estonia, Hungary, Latvia, Lithuania, Poland, Romania and Slovakia. Slovenia became the 10th associate partner in June 1996. Following their accession to the EU on 1 January 1995, Austria, Finland and Sweden took up observer status.

Organization

(January 1998)

COUNCIL

The Council of Western European Union consists of representatives nominated by each member country—in some cases this is the ambassador resident in Brussels or the permanent representative to NATO. As supreme authority of WEU, it is responsible for formulating policy and issuing directives to WEU's intergovernmental bodies. The Council meets at least twice a year at ministerial level, and at permanent (ambassadorial) level as often as required (usually twice a month). The Permanent Council, chaired by the Secretary-General, co-ordinates the activities of various working groups, principally the Special Working Group (SWG) for politico-military issues and the Defence Representatives Group (DRG) for more specifically military issues. The Presidency of the Council is rotated between members on a six-monthly basis.

SECRETARIAT-GENERAL

Secretary-General: José Cutileiro (Portugal).

SUBSIDIARY BODIES

WEU Institute for Security Studies: 43 ave du Président Wilson, 75775 Paris Cédex 16, France; tel. 1-53-67-22-00; fax 1-47-20-81-78; e-mail weu-iss@compuserve.com; f. 1990; Dir Guido Lenzi (Italy).

WEU Satellite Centre: Avda de Cádiz, Edif. 457, Base Aérea de Torrejón, 28850 Torrejón de Ardoz, Spain; tel. (1) 6777999; fax (1) 6777228; f. 1993; supplies information resulting mainly from space imagery for the general surveillance of areas of interest to WEU, used, for example, in support of treaty verification, arms control, maritime surveillance and environmental monitoring.

ASSEMBLY

Address: 43 ave du Président Wilson, 75775 Paris Cédex 16, France; tel. 1-53-67-22-00; fax 1-53-67-22-01; e-mail 100315.240@compuserve.com; internet http://www.weu.int/assembly/welcome.html.

The Assembly of Western European Union is composed of the representatives of the Brussels Treaty powers to the Parliamentary Assembly of the Council of Europe. It meets at least twice a year, usually in Paris. The Assembly may proceed on any matter regarding the application of the Brussels Treaty and on any matter submitted to the Assembly for an opinion by the Council. Resolutions may be adopted in cases where this form is considered appropriate. When so directed by the Assembly, the President transmits such resolutions to international organizations, governments and national parliaments. An annual report is presented to the Assembly by the Council.

President: Luís Maria de Puig (Spain).

Clerk: Henri Burgelin (France).

PERMANENT COMMITTEES OF THE ASSEMBLY

There are permanent committees on: Defence Questions and Armaments; General Affairs; Scientific Questions; Budgetary Affairs and Administration; Rules of Procedure and Privileges; and Parliamentary and Public Relations.

Activities

The Brussels Treaty was signed in 1948 by Belgium, France, Luxembourg, the Netherlands and the United Kingdom. It foresaw the potential for international co-operation in Western Europe and provided for collective defence and collaboration in economic, social and cultural activities. Within this framework, NATO and the Council of Europe (see chapters) were formed in 1949.

On the collapse in 1954 of plans for a European Defence Community, a nine-power conference was convened in London to try to reach a new agreement. This conference's decisions were embodied in a series of formal agreements drawn up by a ministerial conference held in Paris in October 1954. The agreements entailed: arrangements for the Brussels Treaty to be strengthened and modified to include the Federal Republic of Germany and Italy, the ending of the occupation regime in the Federal Republic of Germany, and the invitation to the latter to join NATO. These agreements were ratified on 6 May 1955, on which date the seven-power Western European Union came into being.

Article V of the modified Brussels Treaty stipulates: 'If any of the High Contracting Parties should be the object of an armed attack in Europe, the other High Contracting Parties will, in accordance with the provisions of article 51 of the Charter of the United Nations, afford the Party so attacked all the military and other aid and assistance in their power.' This article exceeds the Washington Treaty establishing NATO, which does not provide for the same automatic military assistance by the allies.

A meeting of ministers of defence and of foreign affairs, held in Rome in October 1984, agreed to 'reactivate' WEU by restructuring its organization and by holding more frequent ministerial meetings, in order to harmonize members' views on defence questions, arms control and disarmament, developments in East-West relations, Europe's contribution to the Atlantic alliance, and European armaments co-operation.

In October 1987 the Council adopted a 'Platform on European Security Interests', declaring its intention to develop a 'more cohesive European defence identity', while affirming that 'the substantial presence of US conventional and nuclear forces plays an irreplaceable part in the defence of Europe'. The document also resolved to improve consultations and extend co-ordination in defence and security matters, and to use existing resources more effectively by expanding bilateral and regional military co-operation.

During the international crisis caused by Iraq's invasion and annexation of Kuwait in August 1990, WEU co-ordinated the military presence of member states in the Persian (Arabian) Gulf region; it subsequently co-ordinated members' mine-clearing operations in the Gulf, and played a part in bringing humanitarian aid to Kurdish displaced persons in northern Iraq.

In April 1990 the Council of ministers of foreign affairs and defence discussed the implications of recent political changes in central and eastern Europe, and mandated WEU to develop contacts with democratically elected governments there. WEU dispatched fact-finding missions to Hungary, Czechoslovakia, Poland, Romania, Bulgaria, Estonia, Latvia and Lithuania in late 1990 and early 1991. An extraordinary meeting of WEU's Ministerial Council with the ministers of defence and foreign affairs of those countries, held in Bonn, Germany, in June 1992, agreed on measures to enhance co-operation. The ministers were to meet annually, while a forum of consultation was to be established between the WEU Council and the ambassadors of the countries concerned, which was to meet at least twice a year. The focus of consultations was to be the security structure and political stability of Europe; the future development of the CSCE (now the OSCE); and arms control and disarmament, in particular the implementation of the Treaty on Conventional Armed Forces in Europe (the CFE Treaty) and the 'Open Skies' Treaty (see NATO for both). In May 1994 the Council of Ministers, meeting in Luxembourg, issued the Kirchberg Declaration, according the nine eastern and central European countries concerned (including the Czech Republic and Slovakia, which were the legal successors to Czechoslovakia) the status of associate partners of WEU, thereby suspending the forum of consultation.

The EC Treaty on European Union, which was agreed at Maastricht, in the Netherlands, in December 1991, and entered into force on 1 November 1993, refers to WEU as an 'integral part of the development of European Union' and requests WEU 'to elaborate and implement decisions and actions of the Union which have defence implications'. The Treaty also commits EU member countries to the 'eventual framing of a common defence policy which might in time lead to a common defence'. A separate declaration, adopted by WEU member states in Maastricht, defines WEU's role as being the defence component of the European Union but also as the instrument for strengthening the European pillar of the Atlantic Alliance, thus maintaining a role for NATO in Europe's defence and retaining WEU's identity as distinct from that of the EU. In January 1993 WEU's Council and Secretariat-General moved to Brussels (from Paris and London, respectively), in order to promote closer co-operation with both the EU and NATO, which have their headquarters there. In November 1994 a WEU ministerial meeting in Noordwijk, the Netherlands, adopted a set of preliminary conclusions on the formulation of a Common European Defence Policy. The role and place of WEU in further European institutional arrangements were addressed by the EU's Intergovernmental Conference, which commenced in March 1996. The process was concluded in June 1997 with no agreement having been reached on a proposal made by the French and German Governments to integrate WEU into the EU decision-making structure (the United Kingdom being the main opponent).

The Petersberg Declaration, which issued from the extraordinary ministerial meeting of June 1992, gave WEU a genuine operational capacity for the first time: member states declared that they were prepared to make available military units from the whole spectrum of their conventional armed forces for military tasks conducted under the authority of WEU. In addition to contributing to the common defence in accordance with Article V of the modified Brussels Treaty, three categories of missions have been identified for the possible employment of military units under the aegis of WEU: humanitarian and rescue tasks; peace-keeping tasks; and crisis management, including peace-making. The Petersberg Declaration stated that the WEU was prepared to support peace-keeping activities of the CSCE and UN Security Council on a case-by-case basis. A WEU planning cell was established in Brussels in October, which was to be responsible for preparing contingency plans for the employment of forces under WEU auspices for humanitarian operations, peace-keeping and crisis-management activities. It was expected that the same military units identified by member states for deployment under NATO would be used for military operations under WEU: this arrangement was referred to as 'double-hatting'. In May 1995 WEU ministers of defence and foreign affairs, convened in Lisbon, Portugal, agreed to strengthen WEU's operational capabilities through new structures and mechanisms, including the establishment of a politico-military group to advise on crises and crisis management, a Situation Centre able to monitor WEU operations and support decisions taken by the Council, and an Intelligence Section within the planning cell. WEU rules of engagement, with a view to implementing the missions identified in the Petersberg Declaration, were to be formulated. In May 1996 WEU ministers resolved to strengthen further WEU operational capabilities. It was agreed that 'neutral' observer countries be invited to participate in any peace-keeping operation. In late 1994 NATO and WEU initiated joint efforts to develop and implement the concept of Combined Joint Task Forces (CJTFs), which was to provide separable, but not separate, military capabilities that could be employed by either organization. In May 1996 NATO and WEU signed a security agreement, which provided for the protection and shared use of classified information. In June NATO ministers agreed on a framework of measures to enable the implementation of the CJTF concept and the development of a European Security and Defence Identity within its military structure. WEU was to be permitted to request the use of a CJTF headquarters for an operation under its command and to use Alliance planning capabilities and military infrastructure. During 1997 NATO and WEU pursued efforts to enhance co-operation and consultation between the two groupings and to implement the CJTF concept.

From mid-July 1992 warships and aircraft of WEU members undertook a monitoring operation in the Adriatic Sea, in co-ordination with NATO, to ensure compliance with the UN Security Council's resolutions imposing a trade and armaments embargo on Serbia and Montenegro. In mid-November the UN Security Council gave the NATO/WEU operation the power to search vessels suspected of attempting to flout the embargo. In June 1993 the Councils of WEU and NATO agreed to establish a unified command for the operation, which was to implement a Security Council resolution to strengthen the embargo against Serbia and Montenegro. Under the agreement, the Councils were to exert joint political control, and military instructions were to be co-ordinated within a joint *ad hoc* headquarters. In April WEU ministers offered civil assistance to Bulgaria, Hungary and Romania in enforcing the UN embargo on the Danube. A monitoring mission, consisting of some 270 experts and 10 patrol boats, began operations in June. In June 1996 the NATO/WEU naval monitoring mission in the Adriatic Sea was suspended, following the decision of the UN Security Council to remove the embargo on the delivery of armaments to the former Yugoslavia. At that time more than 73,000 ships had been challenged, and 5,800 inspected, under the operation. WEU provides assistance for the administration of Mostar, Bosnia and Herzegovina, for which the EU assumed responsibility in July 1994. In mid-1997 WEU dispatched a small team of police officers to Albania to help reinforce the security environment in that country.

In May 1992 France and Germany announced that they would establish a joint defence force, the 'Eurocorps', which was to be based in Strasbourg, France, and which was intended to provide a basis for a European army under the aegis of WEU. This development caused concern among some NATO member countries, particularly the USA and United Kingdom, which feared that it represented a fresh attempt (notably on the part of France, which is outside NATO's military structure) to undermine the Alliance's role in Europe. In November, however, France and Germany stated that troops from the joint force could serve under NATO military command. This principle was recognized in an agreement signed in January 1993, which established links between the proposed joint force and NATO's military structure. In June 1993 Belgium opted to participate in the Eurocorps, but threatened to withdraw in

November if Dutch was not recognized as an official language of the force; this was later endorsed. In December 1993 Spain agreed to provide troops for the force. Luxembourg agreed to participate in May 1994. Eurocorps formally became operational on 30 November 1995. In May France, Italy, Spain and Portugal announced the establishment of two new forces, which were to be at the disposal of WEU as well as NATO and the UN: EUROFOR, consisting of up to 14,000 ground troops, to be based in Florence, Italy; and EUROMARFOR, a maritime force serving the Mediterranean.

PUBLICATIONS

Account of the Session (2 a year).

Annual Report of the Council.

Assembly of Western European Union: Texts adopted and Brief Account of the Session (2 a year).

Chaillot Papers (WEU Institute for Security Studies).

Assembly documents and reports.

WORLD CONFEDERATION OF LABOUR—WCL

Address: 33 rue de Trèves, 1040 Brussels, Belgium.

Telephone: (2) 230-62-95; **telex:** 26966; **fax:** (2) 230-87-22.

Founded in 1920 as the International Federation of Christian Trade Unions (IFCTU); reconstituted under present title in 1968. (See also the International Confederation of Free Trade Unions and the World Federation of Trade Unions.)

MEMBERS

Affiliated national federations and trade union internationals; about 21m. members in 102 countries.

Organization

(January 1998)

CONGRESS

The supreme and legislative authority. The most recent meeting was held in November 1993 in Mauritius. Congress consists of delegates from national confederations and trade internationals. Delegates have votes according to the size of their organization. Congress receives official reports, elects the Executive Board, considers the future programme and any proposals.

CONFEDERAL BOARD

The Board meets annually, and consists of 38 members (including 18 representatives of national confederations and 11 representatives of trade internationals) elected by Congress from among its members for four-year terms. It issues executive directions and instructions to the Secretariat.

SECRETARIAT-GENERAL

Secretary-General: Carlos Luis Custer (Argentina).

REGIONAL OFFICES

Africa: ODSTA, BP 4401, Lomé, Togo. Pres. F. Kikongi.

Asia: Brotherhood of Asian Trade Unionists (BATU), 1839 Dr Antonio Vasquez St, Malate, Manila, Philippines; tel. (2) 500709; telex 521-8335; fax (2) 973908. Pres. J. Tan.

Latin America: Latin-American Confederation of Workers, Apdo 6681, Caracas 1010, Venezuela; tel. (32) 720878; fax (32) 720463. Sec.-Gen. Emilio Maspero.

North America: c/o National Alliance of Postal and Federal Employees, 1628 11th St, NW, Washington, DC 20001, USA.

INTERNATIONAL INSTITUTES OF TRADE UNION STUDIES

Africa: Fondation panafricaine pour le développement économique, social et culturel (Fopadesc), Lomé, Togo.

Asia: BATU Social Institute, Manila, Philippines.

Latin America:

Instituto Andino de Estudios Sociales, Lima, Peru.

Instituto Centro-Americano de Estudios Sociales (ICAES), San José, Costa Rica.

Instituto del Cono Sur (INCASUR), Buenos Aires, Argentina.

Instituto de Formación del Caribe, Willemstad, Curaçao, Netherlands Antilles.

Universidad de Trabajadores de América Latina (UTAL).

FINANCE

Income is derived from affiliation dues, contributions, donations and capital interest.

PUBLICATIONS

Labor Press and Information Bulletin (6 a year; in English, French, German, Dutch and Spanish).

Flash (in English, French, German, Dutch and Spanish).

Reports of Congresses; Study Documents.

International Trade Union Federations

International Federation of Textile and Clothing Workers: 27 Koning Albertlaan, 9000 Ghent, Belgium; tel. (91) 22-57-01; fax (91) 20-45-59; f. 1901. Mems: unions covering 400,000 workers in 19 countries. Organization: Congress (every three years), Bureau, Secretariat. Pres. J. Jouret (Belgium); Gen. Sec. J. Gysen (Netherlands).

International Federation of Trade Unions of Employees in Public Service—INFEDOP: 33 rue de Trèves, 1040 Brussels, Belgium; tel. (2) 230-38-65; fax (2) 231-14-72; e-mail info@infedop-eurofedop.com; f. 1922. Mems: national federations of workers in public service, covering 4m. workers. Organization: World Congress (at least every five years), World Confederal Board (meets every year), 10 Trade Groups, Secretariat. Pres. Filip Wieers (Belgium); Sec.-Gen. Bert van Caelenberg (Belgium). Publ. *Servus* (monthly).

EUROFEDOP: 33 rue de Trèves, 1040 Brussels, Belgium.

International Federation of Trade Unions of Transport Workers—FIOST: Galerie Agora, 105 rue du Marché aux Herbes, bte 38/40, 1000 Brussels, Belgium; tel. (2) 549-07-62; fax (2) 512-85-91; f. 1921. Mems: national federations in 28 countries covering 600,000 workers. Organization: Congress (every four years), Committee (meets twice a year), Executive Board. Pres. Michel Bovy (Belgium); Exec. Sec. Dirk Uyttenhove (Belgium). Publ. *Labor* (6 a year).

World Confederation of Teachers: 33 rue de Trèves, 1040 Brussels, Belgium; tel. (2) 285-47-00; telex 26966; fax (2) 230-87-22; e-mail wct@cmt-wcl.org; f. 1963. Mems: national federations of unions concerned with teaching. Organization: Congress (every four years), Council (at least once a year), Steering Committee. Pres. L. van Beneden; Sec.-Gen. G. de la Haye.

World Federation of Agriculture and Food Workers: 33 rue de Trèves, 1040 Brussels, Belgium; tel. (2) 230-60-90; fax (2) 230-87-22; f. 1982 (merger of former World Federation of Agricultural Workers and World Federation of Workers in the Food, Drink, Tobacco and Hotel Industries). Mems: national federations covering 2,800,000 workers in 38 countries. Organization: Congress (every five years), World Board, Daily Management Board. Exec. Sec. J. Gómez Cerda. Publ. *Labor* (8 a year).

World Federation of Building and Woodworkers Unions: POB 414 Kromme Nieuwgracht 22, 3500 Utrecht, Netherlands; tel. (3405) 97711; fax (3405) 71101; f. 1936. Mems: national federations covering 2,438,000 workers in several countries. Organization: Congress, Bureau, Permanent Secretariat. Pres. A. Desloovere; Sec.-Gen. Dick van de Kamp (Netherlands). Publ. *Bulletin.*

World Federation of Clerical Workers: 33 rue de Trèves, 1040 Brussels, Belgium; tel. (2) 285-47-00; fax (2) 230-87-22; f. 1921. Mems: national federations of unions and professional associations covering 600,000 workers in 38 countries. Organization: Congress (every four years), Council, Executive Board, Secretariat. Sec. Piet Nelissen. Publ. *Labor.*

World Federation of Industry Workers: 33 rue de Trèves, 1040 Brussels, Belgium; e-mail dirk.uyttenhove@cmt-wcl.org; f. 1985. Mems: regional and national federations covering about 500,000 workers in 30 countries. Organization: Congress (every five years), World Board (every year), Executive Committee, six World Trade Councils. Pres. L. Dusoleil; Sec.-Gen. M. André. Publ. *Labor.*

WORLD COUNCIL OF CHURCHES—WCC

Address: 150 route de Ferney, POB 2100, 1211 Geneva 2, Switzerland.

Telephone: (22) 7916111; **telex:** 415730; **fax:** (22) 7910361.

The Council was founded in 1948 to promote co-operation between Christian Churches and to prepare for a clearer manifestation of the unity of the Church.

MEMBERS

There are 335 member Churches in more than 100 countries, of which 35 are associate members. Chief denominations: Anglican, Baptist, Congregational, Lutheran, Methodist, Moravian, Old Catholic, Orthodox, Presbyterian, Reformed and Society of Friends. The Roman Catholic Church is not a member but sends official observers to meetings.

Organization

(January 1998)

ASSEMBLY

The governing body of the World Council, consisting of delegates of the member Churches, it meets every seven or eight years to frame policy and consider some main theme. The seventh Assembly was held at Canberra, Australia, in February 1991.

Presidium: Prof. Dr Anna Marie Aagaard (Denmark), Bishop Vinton R. Anderson (USA), Bishop Leslie Boseto (Solomon Islands), Priyanka Mendis (Sri Lanka), Rev. Eunice Santana (Puerto Rico), Pope Shenouda III (Egypt), Dr Aaron Tolen (Cameroon).

CENTRAL COMMITTEE

Appointed by the Assembly to carry out its policies and decisions, the Committee consists of 150 members chosen from Assembly delegates. It meets annually.

Moderator: His Holiness Aram I, Catholicos of Cilicia (Lebanon).

Vice-Moderators: Ephorus Dr Soritua Nababan (Indonesia), Pastora Nélida Ritchie (Argentina).

EXECUTIVE COMMITTEE

Consists of the Presidents, the Officers and 15 members chosen by the Central Committee from its membership to prepare its agenda, expedite its decisions and supervise the work of the Council between meetings of the Central Committee. Meets every six months.

GENERAL SECRETARIAT

The General Secretariat implements the policies laid down by the WCC, and co-ordinates the work of the programme units described below. It includes Offices of Communication, Management and Finance, and for Church and Ecumenical Relations, Interreligious Relations and Programme Co-ordination. The General Secretariat is also responsible for the Ecumenical Centre Library and an Ecumenical Institute, at Bossey, which provides training in ecumenical leadership.

General Secretary: Rev. Dr Konrad Raiser (Germany).

Activities

The work of the WCC is undertaken by four programme units:

UNITY AND RENEWAL

This unit brings together the concern for the search for visible unity and lay participation towards inclusive community; renewal through worship and spirituality; ecumenical theological education; and reflection on justice, peace and the integrity of creation.

CHURCHES IN MISSION: HEALTH, EDUCATION, WITNESS

This unit focuses on the Churches' Action for Health; mission and evangelism in unity; community and justice; gospel and cultures; and education for all God's people.

JUSTICE, PEACE AND CREATION

This unit constitutes the base for concerns relating to Justice, Peace and the Integrity of Creation (JPIC) as a conciliar process; Economy, ecology and sustainable society (ECOS); the Programme to Combat Racism (PCR), including issues of indigenous peoples and land rights; international affairs and human rights; women; and youth.

SHARING AND SERVICE

This unit is concerned with sharing ecumenical resources; understanding diakonia (deaconship); meeting urgent human need, including emergencies and refugees; advocacy and action with the poor; and equipping and linking churches in service.

FINANCE

The WCC's total budget for 1996 amounted to 103m. Swiss francs. The main contributors are the churches and their agencies, with funds for certain projects contributed by other organizations.

PUBLICATIONS

Catalogue of periodicals, books and audio-visuals.

Ecumenical News International (weekly).

Ecumenical Review (quarterly).

International Review of Mission (quarterly).

WORLD FEDERATION OF TRADE UNIONS—WFTU

Address: Branická 112, 14700 Prague 4, Czech Republic.

Telephone: (2) 462140; **telex:** 121645; **fax:** (2) 461378; **e-mail:** wftu@mbox.vol.cz.

The Federation was founded in 1945, on a world-wide basis. A number of members withdrew from the Federation in 1949 to establish the International Confederation of Free Trade Unions (see p. 186). (See also the World Confederation of Labour, p. 242.)

MEMBERS

In 1996 there were 131m. members, organized in 92 affiliated or associated national federations and six Trade Unions Internationals, in 120 countries.

Organization

(January 1998)

WORLD TRADE UNION CONGRESS

The Congress meets every five years. It reviews WFTU's work, endorses reports from the executives, and elects the General Council. The size of the delegations is based on the total membership of national federations. The Congress is also open to participation by non-affiliated organizations. The 13th Congress, held in Damascus, Syria, in November 1994 was attended by 418 participants representing more than 300m. workers in 84 countries.

GENERAL COUNCIL

The General Council meets three times between Congresses, and comprises members and deputies elected by Congress from nominees of national federations. Every affiliated or associated organization and Trade Unions International has one member and one deputy member.

The Council receives reports from the Presidential Council, approves the plan and budget and elects officers.

PRESIDENTIAL COUNCIL

The Presidential Council meets twice a year and conducts most of the executive work of WFTU. It elects the President each year from among its members.

President (1997/98): Nguyen Van Tu (Viet Nam).

SECRETARIAT

The Secretariat consists of the General Secretary, the Deputy General Secretary and five secretaries. It is appointed by the General Council and is responsible for general co-ordination, regional activities, national trade union liaison, press and information, administration and finance.

WFTU has regional offices in New Delhi, India (for the Asia-Pacific region), Havana, Cuba (covering the Americas), Dakar, Senegal, (for Africa), Damascus, Syria (for the Middle East) and in Moscow, Russia (covering the CIS countries).

General Secretary: ALEKSANDR ZHARIKOV (Russia).

BUDGET

Income is derived from affiliation dues, which are based on the number of members in each trade union federation.

PUBLICATION

Flashes from the Trade Unions (fortnightly, in English, French and Spanish; monthly in Arabic and Russian).

Trade Unions Internationals

The following autonomous Trade Unions Internationals (TUIs) are associated with WFTU:

Trade Unions International of Agriculture, Food, Commerce, Textile and Allied Workers: c/o POB 50, Central International Post, Moscow, Russia; tel. and fax (95) 938-82-63; f. 1997 by merger of the TUI of Agricultural, Forestry and Plantation Workers (f. 1949), the TUI of Food, Tobacco, Hotel and Allied Industries Workers (f. 1949), the TUI of Workers in Commerce (f. 1959) and the TUI of Textile, Clothing, Leather and Fur Workers (f. 1949). Pres. FREDDY HUCK (France); Gen. Sec. DMITRII DOZORIN (Russia).

Trade Unions International of Public and Allied Employees: 5E Rani Jhansi Rd, New Delhi 110 055, India; tel. (11) 3555321; fax (11) 7775130; f. 1949. Mems: 34m. in 152 unions in 54 countries. Branch Commissions: State, Municipal, Postal and Telecommunications, Health, Banks and Insurance. Gen. Sec. SUKOMAL SEN (India) (acting). Publ. *Information Bulletin* (in three languages).

Trade Unions International of Transport Workers: Tengerszem U. 21/B, 1142 Budapest, Hungary; tel. (1) 3707796; fax (1) 1890413; f. 1949. Mems: 160 unions from 67 countries. Pres. NASR ZARIF MOUHREZ (Syria); Gen. Sec. JÓZSEF TÓTH. Publ. *TUI Reporter* (every 2 months, in English and Spanish).

Trade Unions International of Workers of the Building, Wood and Building Materials Industries (Union Internationale des Syndicats des Travailleurs du Bâtiment, du Bois et des Matériaux de Construction—UITBB): Box 281, 00101 Helsinki, Finland; tel. (9) 6931130; telex 121394; fax (9) 6931020; f. 1949. Mems: 78 unions in 60 countries, grouping 17m. workers. Pres. R. BRUN (France); Sec.-Gen. J. DINIS. Publ. *Bulletin*.

Trade Unions International of Workers in the Chemical, Energy, Oil, Metal and Allied Industries: c/o Kopernika 36/40, 00924 Warsaw, Poland; tel. (22) 268049; fax (22) 6358688; new organization to be formally established in 1998 by merger of the TUI of Chemical, Oil and Allied Workers (f. 1950), the TUI of Energy Workers (f. 1949) and the TUI of Workers in the Metal Industry (f. 1949). Gen. Sec. of the Preparatory Commission EUGENIUSZ MIELNICKI (Poland).

World Federation of Teachers' Unions: 5E Rani Jhansi Rd, New Delhi 110 055, India; tel. (11) 3555321; fax (11) 7775130; f. 1946. Mems: 132 national unions of teachers and educational and scientific workers in 85 countries, representing over 25m. individuals. Pres. LESTURUGE ARIYAWANSA (Sri Lanka); Gen. Sec. MRINMOY BHATTACHARYYA (India). Publ. *FISE-Infos* (quarterly, in English, French and Spanish).

WORLD TRADE ORGANIZATION—WTO

Address: Centre William Rappard, rue de Lausanne 154, 1211 Geneva, Switzerland.

Telephone: (22) 7395111; **telex:** 412324; **fax:** (22) 7395458; **internet:** http://www.wto.org.

The WTO is the legal and institutional foundation of the multilateral trading system. It was established on 1 January 1995, as the successor to the General Agreement on Tariffs and Trade (GATT).

MEMBERS*

Angola
Antigua and Barbuda
Argentina
Australia
Austria
Bahrain
Bangladesh
Barbados
Belgium
Belize
Benin
Bolivia
Botswana
Brazil
Brunei
Bulgaria
Burkina Faso
Burundi
Cameroon
Canada
Central African Republic
Chad
Chile
Colombia
Congo, Democratic Republic
Congo, Republic
Costa Rica
Côte d'Ivoire
Cuba
Cyprus
Czech Republic
Denmark
Djibouti
Dominica
Dominican Republic
Ecuador
Egypt
El Salvador
Fiji
Finland
France
Gabon
The Gambia
Germany
Ghana
Greece
Grenada
Guatemala
Guinea
Guinea-Bissau
Guyana
Haiti
Honduras
Hong Kong
Hungary
Iceland
India
Indonesia
Ireland
Israel
Italy
Jamaica
Japan
Kenya
Korea, Republic
Kuwait
Lesotho
Liechtenstein
Luxembourg
Macau
Madagascar
Malawi
Malaysia
Maldives
Mali
Malta
Mauritania
Mauritius
Mexico
Mongolia
Morocco
Mozambique
Myanmar
Namibia
Netherlands
New Zealand
Nicaragua
Niger
Nigeria
Norway
Pakistan
Panama
Papua New Guinea
Paraguay
Peru
Philippines
Poland
Portugal
Qatar
Romania
Rwanda
Saint Christopher and Nevis
Saint Lucia
Saint Vincent and the Grenadines
Senegal
Sierra Leone
Singapore
Slovakia
Slovenia
Solomon Islands
South Africa
Spain
Sri Lanka
Suriname
Swaziland
Sweden
Switzerland
Tanzania
Thailand
Togo
Trinidad and Tobago
Tunisia
Turkey
Uganda
United Arab Emirates
United Kingdom
USA
Uruguay
Venezuela
Zambia
Zimbabwe

* The European Community also has membership status.

Note: At the end of September 1997 a further 29 governments had requested to join the WTO, and their applications were under consideration by accession working parties.

Organization

(February 1998)

MINISTERIAL CONFERENCE

The Ministerial Conference is the highest authority of the WTO. It is composed of representatives of all WTO members at ministerial level, and may take decisions on all matters under any of the multilateral trade agreements. The Conference is required to meet at least every two years; the first Conference was held in December 1996, in Singapore.

GENERAL COUNCIL

The Council, which is also composed of representatives of all WTO members, is required to report to the Ministerial Conference and conducts much of the day-to-day work of the WTO. The Council convenes as the Dispute Settlement Body, to oversee the trade dispute settlement procedures, and as the Trade Policy Review Body, to conduct regular reviews of the trade policies of WTO members. The Council delegates responsibility to three other major Councils: for trade-related aspects of intellectual property rights, for trade in goods and for trade in services.

Chairman: JOHN WEEKES (Canada).

SECRETARIAT

In 1996 the WTO Secretariat comprised some 450 staff. Its responsibilities include the servicing of WTO delegate bodies, with respect to negotiations and the implementation of agreements, undertaking accession negotiations for new members and providing technical support and expertise to developing countries.

Director-General: RENATO RUGGIERO (Italy).

Activities

The Final Act of the Uruguay Round of GATT multilateral trade negotiations, which were concluded in December 1993, provided for extensive trade liberalization measures and for the establishment of a permanent structure to oversee international trading procedures. The Final Act was signed in April 1994, in Marrakesh, Morocco. At the same time a separate accord, the Marrakesh Declaration, was signed by the majority of GATT contracting states, endorsing the establishment of the WTO. The essential functions of the WTO are: to administer and facilitate the implementation of the results of the Uruguay Round; to provide a forum for multilateral trade negotiations; to administer the trade dispute settlement procedures; to review national trade policies; and to co-operate with other international institutions, in particular the IMF and World Bank, in order to achieve greater coherence in global economic policy-making.

The WTO Agreement contains some 29 individual legal texts and more than 25 additional Ministerial declarations, decisions and understandings, which cover obligations and commitments for member states. All these instruments are based on a few fundamental principles, which form the basis of the WTO Agreement. An integral part of the Agreement is 'GATT 1994', an amended and updated version of the original GATT Agreement of 1947, which was formally concluded at the end of 1995. Under the 'most-favoured nation' (MFN) clause, members are bound to grant to each other's products treatment no less favourable than that accorded to the products of any third parties. A number of exceptions apply, principally for customs unions and free-trade areas and for measures in favour of and among developing countries. The principle of 'national treatment' requires goods, having entered a market, to be treated no less favourably than the equivalent domestically-produced goods. Secure and predictable market access, to encourage trade, investment and job creation, may be determined by 'binding' tariffs, or customs duties. This process means that a tariff level for a particular product becomes a commitment by a member state, and cannot be increased without compensation negotiations with its main trading partners. Other WTO agreements also contribute to predictable trading conditions by demanding commitments from member countries and greater transparency of domestic laws and national trade policies. By permitting tariffs, whilst adhering to the guidelines of being non-discriminatory, the WTO aims to promote open, fair and undistorted competition.

The WTO aims to encourage development and economic reform among the increasing number of developing countries and countries with economies in transition participating in the international trading system. These countries, particularly the least-developed states, have been granted transition periods and greater flexibility to implement certain WTO provisions. Industrial member countries are encouraged to assist developing nations by their trading conditions and by not expecting reciprocity in trade concession negotiations.

Finally, the WTO Agreement recognizes the need to protect the environment and to promote sustainable development. A new Committee on Trade and Environment was established to identify the relationship between trade policies, environmental measures and sustainable development and to recommend any appropriate modifications of the multilateral trading provisions.

The final declaration issued from the Ministerial Conference in December 1996 incorporated a text on the contentious issue of core labour standards, although it was emphasized that the relationship between trade and labour standards was not part of the WTO agenda. The text recognized the International Labour Organization's competence in establishing and dealing with core labour standards and endorsed future WTO/ILO co-operation. The declaration also included a plan of action on measures in favour of the world's least-developed countries, to assist these countries in enhancing their trading opportunities. At the Conference representatives of some 28 countries signed a draft Information Technology Agreement (ITA), which aimed to eliminate tariffs on the significant global trade in IT products by 2000. By late February 1997 some 39 countries representing the required 90% share of the world's IT trade had consented to implement the ITA. It was signed in March, and was to cover the following main product categories: computers; telecommunications products; semiconductors or manufacturing equipment; software; and scientific instruments. Tariff reductions in these sectors were to be undertaken in four stages, commencing in July, and subsequently on 1 January each year, providing for the elimination of all tariffs by the start of 2000.

AGRICULTURE

The Final Act of the Uruguay Round extended previous GATT arrangements for trade in agricultural products through new rules and commitments to ensure more predictable and fair competition in the sector. All quantitive measures limiting market access for agricultural products were to be replaced by tariffs (i.e. a process of 'tariffication'), enabling more equal protection and access opportunities. All tariffs on agricultural items were to be reduced by 36% by developed countries, over a period of six years, and by 24% by developing countries (excluding least-developed member states) over 10 years. A special treatment clause applies to 'sensitive' products (mainly rice) in four countries, for which limited import restrictions may be maintained. Efforts to reduce domestic support measures for agricultural products were to be based on calculations of total aggregate measurements of support (Total AMS) by each member state. A 20% reduction in Total AMS was required by developed countries, over six years, and 13%, over 10 years, by developing countries. No reduction was required of least-developed countries. Developed member countries are required to reduce the value and quantity of direct export subsidies by 36% and 21% respectively (on 1986–90 levels) over six years. For developing countries these reductions were to be two-thirds those of developed nations, over 10 years. A specific concern of least-developed and net-food importing developing countries, which had previously relied on subsidized food products, was to be addressed through other food aid mechanisms and assistance for agricultural development. The situation was to be monitored by WTO's Committee on Agriculture. The Agreement on the Application of Sanitary and Phytosanitary Measures aims to regulate world-wide standards of food safety and animal and plant health in order to encourage the mutual recognition of standards and conformity to facilitate trade in these products. The Agreement includes provisions on control inspection and approval procedures. In September 1997 a dispute panel of the WTO ruled that the EU's ban on imports of hormone-treated beef from the USA and Canada was in breach of international trading rules, in the first case to be brought under the Agreement. (In January 1998 the Appellate Body upheld the panel's ruling but expressed its support for restrictions to ensure food standards if there is adequate scientific evidence of risks to human health.)

TEXTILES AND CLOTHING

From 1974 the Multi-fibre Arrangement (MFA) provided the basis of international trade concerning textiles and clothing, enabling the major importers to establish quotas and protect their domestic industries, through bilateral agreements, against more competitive low-cost goods from developing countries. MFA restrictions that were in place on 31 December 1994 were carried over into the new agreement and were to be phased out through integration into GATT 1994, under which they would be subject to the same rules applying to other industrial products. This was to be achieved in four stages: products accounting for 16% of the total volume of textiles and clothing imports (at 1990 levels) were to be integrated from 1 January 1995; a further 17% on 1 January 1998; and not less than a further 18% on 1 January 2002, with all remaining products to be integrated by 1 January 2005.

TRADE IN SERVICES

The General Agreement on Trade in Services (GATS), which was negotiated during the GATT Uruguay Round, is the first set of multilaterally-agreed and legally-enforceable rules and disciplines ever negotiated to cover international trade in services. The GATS comprises a framework of general rules and disciplines, annexes addressing special conditions relating to individual sectors and national schedules of market access commitments. A Council for Trade in Services oversees the operation of the agreement.

The GATS framework consists of 29 articles, including the following set of basic obligations: total coverage of all internationally-traded services; national treatment, i.e. according services and service suppliers of other members no less favourable treatment than that accorded to domestic services and suppliers; MFN treatment (see above), with any specific exemptions to be recorded prior to the implementation of the GATS, with a limit of 10 years duration; transparency, requiring publication of all relevant national laws and legislations; bilateral agreements on recognition of standards and qualifications to be open to other members who wish to negotiate accession; no restrictions on international payments and transfers; progressive liberalization to be pursued; and market access and national treatment commitments to be bound and recorded in national schedules. These schedules, which include exemptions to the MFN principles, contain the negotiated and guaranteed conditions under which trade in services is conducted and are an integral part of the GATS.

Annexes to the GATS cover the movement of natural persons, permitting governments to negotiate specific commitments regarding the temporary stay of people for the purpose of providing a service; the right of governments to take measures in order to ensure the integrity and stability of the financial system; the role of telecommunications as a distinct sector of economic activity and as a means of supplying other economic activities; and air transport services, excluding certain activities relating to traffic rights.

At the end of the Uruguay Round governments agreed to continue negotiations in the following areas: basic telecommunications, maritime transport, movement of natural persons and financial services.

The Protocol to the GATS relating to movement of natural persons was concluded in July 1995. In May 1996 the USA withdrew from negotiations to conclude an agreement on maritime transport services. At the end of June the participating countries agreed to suspend the discussions and to recommence negotiations in 2000. Efforts to negotiate a multilateral agreement on financial services by the initial deadline of 30 June 1995 failed and were subsequently pursued for a further month. At the end of July some 29 members signed an interim agreement to grant greater access to the banking, insurance, investment and securities sectors from August 1996. Negotiations to strengthen the agreement and to extend it to new signatories (including the USA, which had declined to sign the July 1995 agreement, claiming lack of reciprocity by some Asian countries) commenced in April 1997 and required each country to submit proposals for national deregulation in the financial services sectors. A final agreement was successfully concluded in mid-December, with 102 countries endorsing the elimination of restrictions on access to the financial services sectors from 1 March 1999 and to subject those services to legally-binding rules and disciplines. Further negotiations were scheduled to commence in 2000. Negotiations on trade in basic telecommunications began in May 1994 and were scheduled to conclude in April 1996. Before the final deadline, however, the negotiations were suspended, owing to US concerns, which included greater access to satellite telecommunications markets in Asia and greater control over foreign companies operating from the domestic markets. An agreement was finally concluded by the new deadline of 15 February 1997. Accordingly the largest telecommunications markets, i.e. the USA, the EU and Japan, were to eliminate all remaining restrictions on domestic and foreign competition in the industry by 1 January 1998 (although delays were granted to Spain, until December 1998, Ireland, until 2000, and Greece and Portugal, until 2003). The majority of the 69 signatories to the accord also agreed on common rules to ensure that fair competition could be enforced by the WTO disputes settlement mechanism, and pledged their commitment to establishing a regulatory system for the telecommunications sector and guaranteeing transparency in government licensing. The agreement entered into force on 5 February 1998, having been rescheduled, owing to the delay on the part of some signatory countries (then totalling 72 states) in ratifying the accord and incorporating the principles of industry regulation into national legislation.

INTELLECTUAL PROPERTY RIGHTS

The WTO Agreement on Trade-Related Aspects of Intellectual Property Rights (TRIPS) recognizes that widely varying standards in the protection and enforcement of intellectual property rights and the lack of multilateral disciplines dealing with international trade in counterfeit goods have been a growing source of tension in international economic relations. The TRIPS agreement aims to ensure that nationals of member states receive equally favourable treatment with regard to the protection of intellectual property and that adequate standards of intellectual property protection exist in all WTO member countries. These standards are largely based on the obligations of the Paris and Berne Conventions of WIPO (see p. 97), however, the agreement aims to expand and enhance these where necessary, for example: computer programmes, to be protected as literary works for copyright purposes; definition of trade marks eligible for protection; stricter rules of geographical indications of consumer products; a 10-year protection period for industrial designs; a 20-year patent protection available for all inventions; tighter protection of layout design of integrated circuits; and protection for trade secrets and 'know-how' with a commercial value.

Under the agreement member governments are obliged to provide procedures and remedies to ensure the effective enforcement of intellectual property rights. Civil and administrative procedures outlined in the TRIPS include provisions on evidence, injunctions, judicial authority to order the disposal of infringing goods, and criminal procedures and penalties, in particular for trade-mark counterfeiting and copyright piracy. A one-year period was envisaged for developed countries to bring their legislation and practices into conformity with the agreement. Developing countries were to do so in five years (or 10 years if an area of technology does not already have patent protection) and least-developed countries in 11 years. A Council for Trade-Related Property Rights monitors the compliance of governments with the agreement and its operation.

LEGAL FRAMEWORK

In addition to the binding agreements mentioned above, WTO aims to provide a comprehensive legal framework for the international trading system. Under GATT 1994 'anti-dumping' measures are permitted against imports of a product with an export price below its normal value, if these imports are likely to cause damage to a domestic industry. The WTO agreement provides for greater clarity and more-detailed rules determining the application of these measures and determines settlement procedures in disputes relating to anti-dumping actions taken by WTO members. In general, anti-dumping measures were to be limited to five years. WTO's Agreement on Subsidies and Countervailing Measures is intended to expand on existing GATT agreements. It classifies subsidies into three categories: prohibited, which may be determined by the Dispute Settlement Body and must be immediately withdrawn; actionable, which must be withdrawn or altered if the subsidy is found to cause adverse effects on the interests of other members; and non-actionable, for example subsidies involving assistance to industrial research, assistance to disadvantaged regions or adaptation of facilities to meet new environmental requirements. The Agreement also contains provisions on the use of duties to offset the effect of a subsidy (so-called countervailing measures) and establishes procedures for the initiation and conduct of investigations into this action. Countervailing measures must generally be terminated within five years of their imposition. Least-developed countries, and developing countries with gross national product per capita of less than US $1,000, are exempt from disciplines on prohibited export subsidies; however, these were to be eliminated by 2003 in all other developing countries and by 2002 in countries with economies in transition.

WTO members may take safeguard actions to protect a specific domestic industry from a damaging increase of imported products. However, the WTO agreement aims to clarify criteria for imposing safeguards, their duration (normally to be no longer than four years, which may be extended to eight years) and consultations on trade compensation for the exporting countries. At 1 December 1995 50 member states had notified the Committee on Safeguards of the WTO Secretariat of their existing domestic safeguard legislations, as required under the agreement. Any measures to protect domestic industries through voluntary export restraints or other market-sharing devices must be phased out by the end of 1998, or a year later for one specific safeguard measure, subject to mutual agreement of the members directly concerned. Safeguard measures are not applicable to products from developing countries as long as their share of imports of the product concerned does not exceed 3%.

Further legal arrangements act to ensure the following: that technical regulations and standards (including testing and certification procedures) do not create unnecessary obstacles to trade; that import licensing procedures are transparent and predictable; that the valuation of goods for customs purposes are fair and uniform; that GATT principles and obligations apply to import preshipment inspection activities; the fair and transparent administration of rules of origin; and that no investment measures which may restrict or distort trade may be applied. A Working Group on Notification Obligations and Procedures aims to ensure that members fulfil their notification requirements, which facilitate the transparency and surveillance of the trading rules.

PLURILATERAL AGREEMENTS

The majority of GATT agreements became multilateral obligations when the WTO became operational in 1995; however, four agreements, which have a selective group of signatories, remained in effect. These so-called plurilateral agreements, the Agreement on Trade in Civil Aircraft, the Agreement on Government Procurement, the International Dairy Agreement and the International Bovine Meat Agreement, aim to increase international co-operation and fair and open trade and competition in these areas. Each of the agreements establish their own management bodies, which are required to report to the General Council.

TRADE POLICY REVIEW MECHANISM

The mechanism, which was established provisionally in 1989, was given a permanent role in the WTO. Through regular monitoring and surveillance of national trade policies the mechanism aimed to increase the transparency and understanding of trade policies and practices and to enable assessment of the effects of policies on the world trading system. In addition, it was to record efforts being made by governments to bring domestic trade legislation into conformity with WTO provisions and to implement WTO commitments. Reviews are conducted in the Trade Policy Review Body on the basis of a policy statement of the government under review and an independent report prepared by the WTO Secretariat. During 1995 15 reviews were undertaken. Under the mechanism the world's four largest traders, the European Union, the USA, Japan and Canada, were to be reviewed every two years. Special groups were established to examine new regional free-trade arrangements and the trade policies of acceding countries. In February 1996 a single Committee on Regional Trade Agreements was established, superseding these separate working parties. The Committee aimed to ensure that these groupings contribute to the process of global trade liberalization and to study the implications of these arrangements on the multilateral system. At the Ministerial Conference, held in December 1996, it was agreed to establish a new working group to conduct a study of transparency in government procurement practices.

SETTLEMENT OF DISPUTES

A separate annex to the WTO agreement determines a unified set of rules and procedures to govern the settlement of all WTO disputes, substantially reinforcing the GATT procedures. WTO members are committed not to undertake unilateral action against perceived violations of the trade rules, but to seek recourse in the dispute settlement mechanism and abide by its findings.

The first stage of the process requires bilateral consultations between the members concerned in an attempt to conclude a mutually-acceptable solution to the issue. These may be undertaken through the good offices and mediation efforts of the Director-General. Only after a consultation period of 60 days may the complainant ask the General Council, convened as the Dispute Settlement Body (DSB), to establish an independent panel to examine the case, which then does so within the terms of reference of the agreement cited. Each party to the dispute submits its arguments and then presents its case before the panel. Third parties which notify their interest in the dispute may also present views at the first substantive meeting of the panel. At this stage an expert review group may be appointed to provide specific scientific or technical advice. The panel submits sections and then a full interim report of its findings to the parties, who may then request a further review involving additional meetings. A final report should be submitted to the parties by the panel within six months of its establishment, or within three months in cases of urgency, including those related to perishable goods. Final reports are normally adopted by the DSB within 60 days of issuance. In the case of a measure being found to be inconsistent with the relevant WTO agreement the panel recommends ways in which the member may bring the measure into conformity with the agreement. However, under the WTO mechanism either party has the right to appeal against the decision and must notify the DSB of its intentions before adoption of the final report. Appeal proceedings, which are limited to issues of law and the legal interpretation covered by the panel report, are undertaken by three members of the Appellate Body within a maximum period of 90 days. The report of the Appellate Body must be unconditionally accepted by the parties to the dispute (unless there is a consensus within the DSB against its adoption). If the recommendations of the panel or appeal report are not implemented immediately, or within a 'reasonable period' as determined by the DSB, the parties are obliged to negotiate mutually-acceptable compensation pending full implementation. Failure to agree compensation may result in the DSB authorizing the complainant to suspend concessions or obligations against the other party. In any case the DSB monitors the implementation of adopted recommendations or rulings, while any outstanding cases remain on its agenda until the issue is resolved. Agreement on the composition of the Appellate Body was finally concluded in late November 1995. By September 1997 101 trade disputes had been brought before the WTO, more than one-third of which had been initiated by the USA. Panel and Appellate Body investigations under way at that time included consideration of access to the Japanese domestic markets for imports of photographic film (a complaint brought by the USA), Indonesia's national car programme (following complaints by the EU, Japan and the USA) and the USA's import prohibition on certain shrimp and shrimp products (brought by India, Malaysia, Pakistan and Thailand). In September the Appellate Body upheld a complaint against the EU's banana import regime (brought by Ecuador, Guatemala, Honduras, Mexico and the USA), which granted preferential market access to Caribbean-produced goods.

CO-OPERATION WITH OTHER ORGANIZATIONS

WTO is mandated to pursue co-operation with the IMF and the World Bank, as well as with other multilateral organizations, in order to achieve greater coherence in global economic policy-making. In November 1994 the preparatory committee of the WTO resolved not to incorporate the new organization into the UN structure as a specialized agency. Instead, co-operation arrangements with the IMF and World Bank were to be developed. In addition, efforts were pursued to enhance co-operation with UNCTAD in research, trade and technical issues. The Directors-General of the two organizations agreed to meet at least twice a year in order to develop the working relationship. In particular, co-operation was to be undertaken in WTO's special programme of activities for Africa, which aimed to help African countries expand and diversify their trade and benefit from the global trading system.

International Trade Centre UNCTAD/WTO: Palais des Nations, 1211 Geneva 10, Switzerland; tel. (22) 7300111; telex 414119; fax (22) 7334439; f. 1964 by GATT; jointly operated with the UN (through UNCTAD) since 1968; ITC works with developing countries in product and market development, the development of trade support servcies, trade information, human resource development, international purchasing and supply management, and needs assessment and programme design for trade promotion.

In 1984 it became an executing agency of the UN Development Programme (UNDP, see p. 38), directly responsible for carrying out UNDP-financed projects related to trade promotion. Publs *International Trade Forum* (quarterly), market studies, handbooks etc.

Executive Director: J. DENIS BÉLISLE.

FINANCE

The WTO's 1996 budget amounted to 115m. Swiss francs (approximately US $93m.), financed by contributions from members in proportion to their share of total trading conducted by WTO members.

PUBLICATIONS

Annual Report (2 volumes).

WTO Focus (monthly).

OTHER INTERNATIONAL ORGANIZATIONS

OTHER INTERNATIONAL ORGANIZATIONS

Agriculture, Food, Forestry and Fisheries

(For organizations concerned with agricultural commodities, see Commodities, p. 256)

African Timber Organization—ATO: BP 1077, Libreville, Gabon; tel. 732928; telex 5620; fax 734030; f. 1976 to enable members to study and co-ordinate ways of ensuring the optimum utilization and conservation of their forests. Mems: Angola, Cameroon, Central African Republic, Democratic Republic of the Congo, Republic of the Congo, Côte d'Ivoire, Equatorial Guinea, Gabon, Ghana, Liberia, Nigeria, São Tomé and Príncipe, Tanzania. Sec.-Gen. MOHAMMED LAWAL GARBA. Publs *ATO Information Bulletin* (quarterly), *International Magazine of African Timber* (2 a year).

Asian Vegetable Research and Development Center: POB 42, Shanhua, Tainan 741, Taiwan; tel. (6) 5837801; telex 73560; fax (6) 5830009; e-mail avrdcbox@netra.avrdc.org.tw; internet http://www.avrdc.org.tw; f. 1971; aims to enhance the nutritional well-being and raise the incomes of the poor in rural and urban areas of developing countries, through improved varieties and methods of vegetable production, marketing and distribution, taking into account the need to preserve the quality of the environment; the Centre has an experimental farm, laboratories, gene-bank, greenhouses, quarantine house, insectarium, library and weather station and provides training for research and production specialists in tropical vegetables; exchanges and disseminates vegetable germplasm through regional centres in the developing world; serves as a clearing-house for vegetable research information and undertakes scientific publishing. Mems: Australia, France, Germany, Japan, Republic of Korea, Philippines, Taiwan, Thailand, USA. Dir-Gen. Dr SAMSON C. S. TSOU. Publs *Progress Report, Newsletter, Tropical Vegetable Information Service Newsletter* (2 a year), *Technical Bulletin, Proceedings, Centerpoint,* working papers.

Caribbean Food and Nutrition Institute: UWI Campus, St. Augustine, Trinidad and Tobago; tel. 662-7025; fax 662-5511; f. 1967 to serve the governments and people of the region and to act as a catalyst among persons and organizations concerned with food and nutrition through research and field investigations, training in nutrition, dissemination of information, advisory services and production of educational material. Mems: all English-speaking Caribbean territories, including the mainland countries of Belize and Guyana. Dir Dr ADELINE WYNANTE PATTERSON. Publs *Cajanus* (quarterly), *Nyam News* (monthly), *Nutrient-Cost Tables* (quarterly), educational material.

Collaborative International Pesticides Analytical Council Ltd.—CIPAC: c/o Dr A. Martijn, 't Gotink 7, 7261 VE Ruurlo, Netherlands; tel. and fax (573) 452851; f. 1957 to organize international collaborative work on methods of analysis for pesticides used in crop protection. Mems: in 46 countries. Chair. Dr F. SÁNCHEZ RASERO (Spain); Sec. Dr A. MARTIJN (Netherlands).

Dairy Society International—DSI: 7185 Ruritan Drive, Chambersburg, PA 17201, USA; tel. (717) 375-4392; f. 1946 to foster the extension of dairy and dairy industrial enterprise internationally through an interchange and dissemination of scientific, technological, economic, dietary and other relevant information; organizer and sponsor of the first World Congress for Milk Utilization. Mems: in 50 countries. Pres. JAMES E. CLICK (USA); Man. Dir G. W. WEIGOLD (USA). Publs *DSI Report to Members, DSI Bulletin, Market Frontier News, Dairy Situation Review.*

Desert Locust Control Organization for Eastern Africa: POB 30223, Nairobi, Kenya; tel. 501704; fax 505137; f. 1962 to promote most effective control of desert locust in the region and to carry out research into the locust's environment and behaviour; conducts pesticides residue analysis; assists member states in the monitoring and extermination of other migratory pests such as the quelea-quelea (grain-eating birds), the army worm and the tsetse fly; bases at Asmara (Eritrea), Dire Dawa (Ethiopia), Mogadishu and Hargeisa (Somalia), Nairobi (Kenya), Khartoum (Sudan), Arusha (Tanzania), Kampala (Uganda) and Djibouti. Mems: Djibouti, Eritrea, Ethiopia, Kenya, Somalia, Sudan, Tanzania, Uganda. Dir Dr A. H. M. KARRAR; Co-ordinator C. K. MUINAMIA. Publs *Desert Locust Situation Reports* (monthly), *Annual Report,* technical reports.

European and Mediterranean Plant Protection Organization: 1 rue Le Nôtre, 75016 Paris, France; tel. 1-45-20-77-94; fax 1-42-24-89-43; e-mail hq@eppo.fr; f. 1951, present name adopted in 1955; aims to promote international co-operation between government plant protection services and in preventing the introduction and spread of pests and diseases of plants and plant products. Mems: governments of 38 countries and territories. Chair. R. PETZOLD; Dir-Gen. I. M. SMITH. Publs *EPPO Bulletin, Data Sheets on Quarantine Organisms, Guidelines for the Efficacy Evaluation of Pesticides, Crop Growth Stage Keys, Summary of the Phytosanitary Regulations of EPPO Member Countries, Reporting Service.*

European Association for Animal Production (Fédération européenne de zootechnie): Via A. Torlonia 15A, 00161 Rome, Italy; tel. (6) 44238013; fax (6) 44241466; e-mail zoorec@mnet.it; f. 1949 to help improve the conditions of animal production and meet consumer demand; holds annual meetings. Mems: associations in 37 member countries. Pres. Prince P. ZU SOLMS-LICH (Germany). Publ. *Livestock Production Science* (16 a year).

European Association for Research on Plant Breeding—EUCARPIA: c/o POB 315, 6700 AH Wageningen, Netherlands; e-mail marjo.dejeu@users.pv.wau.nl; f. 1956 to promote scientific and technical co-operation in the plant breeding field. Mems: 1,000 individuals, 64 corporate mems; 12 sections and several working groups. Pres. Prof. G. T. SCARASCIA MUGNOZZA (Italy); Sec. Dr Ir M. J. DE JEU (Netherlands). Publ. *Bulletin.*

European Confederation of Agriculture: 23 rue de la Science, 1040 Brussels, Belgium; tel. (2) 230-43-80; fax (2) 230-46-77; f. 1889 as International Confederation, re-formed in 1948 as European Confederation; represents the interests of European agriculture in the international field; social security for independent farmers and foresters in the member countries; currently giving priority to developing relations with the countries of central and eastern Europe. Mems: 300 mems. from 30 countries. Pres. HANS JONSSON (Sweden); Gen. Sec. CHRISTOPHE HÉMARD (France). Publs *CEA Dialog, Annual Report.*

European Grassland Federation: c/o Dr W. H. Prins, Hollandseweg 382, 6705 BE Wageningen, Netherlands; tel. (317) 417811; fax (317) 416386; e-mail w.h.prins@inter.nl.net; f. 1963 to facilitate and maintain liaison between European grassland organizations and to promote the interchange of scientific and practical knowledge and experience; general meeting is held every two years and symposia at other times. Mems: 27 full and nine corresponding member countries in Europe. Pres. Prof. G. NAGY; Sec. Dr W. H. PRINS. Publ. *Proceedings.*

European Livestock and Meat Trading Union: 81A rue de la Loi, 1040 Brussels, Belgium; tel. (2) 230-46-03; fax (2) 230-94-00; e-mail uecbv@pophost.eunet.be; f. 1952 to study problems of the European livestock and meat trade and inform members of all legislation affecting it, and to act as an international arbitration commission; conducts research on agricultural markets, quality of livestock, and veterinary regulations. Mems: national organizations in Austria, Belgium, Denmark, Finland, France, Germany, Greece, Hungary, Ireland, Italy, Luxembourg, Netherlands, Norway, Poland, Portugal, Spain, Sweden, Switzerland, United Kingdom; corresponding mems in Czech Republic, Slovenia and Federal Republic of Yugoslavia; and the European Association of Livestock Markets. Pres. A. ANORO; Sec.-Gen. J.-L. MERIAUX.

Inter-American Association of Agricultural Librarians, Documentalists and Information Specialists (Asociación Interamericana de Bibliotecarios, Documentalistas y Especialistas en Información Agrícolas—AIBDA): c/o IICA-CIDIA, Apdo 55-2200 Coronado, Costa Rica; tel. 229-0222; fax 229-4741; e-mail aibda@iica.ac.cr; f. 1953 to promote professional improvement of its members through technical publications and meetings, and to promote improvement of library services in agricultural sciences. Mems: about 400 in 29 countries and territories. Pres. SUZANA SPERRY; Exec. Sec. MICHAEL SNARSKIS. Publs *Boletín Informativo* (3 a year), *Boletín Especial* (irregular), *Revista AIBDA* (2 a year), *AIBDA Actualidades* (4 or 5 a year).

Inter-American Tropical Tuna Commission—IATTC: Scripps Institution of Oceanography, 8604 La Jolla Shores Drive, La Jolla, CA 92037-1508, USA; tel. (619) 546-7100; fax (619) 546-7133; e-mail jjoseph@iattc.ucsd.edu; f. 1950; two programmes, the Tuna-Billfish Programme and the Tuna-Dolphin Programme. The Tuna-Billfish Programme investigates the biology of the tunas and related species of the eastern Pacific Ocean to determine the effects of fishing and natural factors on stocks; recommends appropriate conservation measures to maintain stocks at levels which will afford maximum sustainable catches; the Tuna-Dolphin Programme monitors dolphin levels and the number of deaths caused to dolphins by tuna-fishers, in order to recommend measures to maintain dolphin stocks; promotes fishing methods that avoid the needless killing of dolphins; investigates the effect of various fishing methods on different species of fish and other aquatic animals. Mems: Costa Rica, Ecuador, France, Japan, Nicaragua, Panama, USA, Vanuatu, Venezuela. Dir JAMES JOSEPH. Publs *Bulletin* (irregular), *Annual Report.*

International Association for Cereal Science and Technology: Wiener Strasse 22A, POB 77, 2320 Schwechat, Austria; tel. (1) 707-72-02; telex 133316; fax (1) 707-72-04; e-mail gen.sec@icc.or.at; f. 1955 (as the International Association for Cereal Chemistry; name changed 1984) to standardize the methods of testing and analysing cereals and cereal products. Mems: 38 member states. Sec.-Gen. Dr Dipl. Ing. HELMUT GLATTES (Austria).

International Association for Vegetation Science: Wilhelm-Weber-Str. 2, 37073 Göttingen, Germany; tel. (551) 395700; fax (551) 392287; e-mail hdiersc@gwdg.de; f. 1938. Mems: 1,330 from 70 countries. Chair. Prof. Dr E. O. BOX; Sec. Prof. Dr H. DIERSCHKE. Publs *Phytocoenologia, Vegetatio, Journal of Vegetation Science.*

International Association of Agricultural Economists: 1211 West 22nd St, Suite 216, Oak Brook, IL 60521-2197, USA; tel. (708) 571-9393; fax (708) 571-9580; e-mail farmfnd@interaccess.com; f. 1929 to foster development of the sciences of agricultural economics and further the application of the results of economic investigation in agricultural processes and the improvement of economic and social conditions relating to agricultural and rural life. Mems: in 96 countries. Pres. ROBERT L. THOMPSON (USA); Sec. and Treas. WALTER J. ARMBRUSTER (USA). Publs *Agricultural Economics* (8 a year), *IAAE Newsletter* (2 a year).

International Association of Agricultural Information Specialists: c/o Margot Bellamy, CAB International, Wallingford, Oxon OX10 8DE, United Kingdom; tel. (1491) 832111; fax (1491) 833508; e-mail m.bellamy@cabi.org; f. 1955 to promote agricultural library science and documentation, and the professional interests of agricultural librarians and documentalists; affiliated to the International Federation of Library Associations and to the Fédération Internationale de Documentation. Mems: 600 in 84 countries. Pres. Dr J. VAN DER BURG (Netherlands); Sec.-Treas. MARGOT BELLAMY (UK). Publs *Quarterly Bulletin, IAALD News, World Directory of Agricultural Information Resource Centres.*

International Association of Horticultural Producers: Postbus 93099, 2509 AB The Hague, Netherlands; tel. (70) 3041234; fax (70) 3470956; f. 1948; represents the common interests of commercial horticultural producers in the international field by frequent meetings, regular publications, press-notices, resolutions and addresses to governments and international authorities; authorizes international horticultural exhibitions. Mems: national associations in 25 countries. Pres. O. KOCH; Gen. Sec. Drs J. B. M. ROTTEVEEL. Publ. *Yearbook of International Horticultural Statistics.*

International Bee Research Association: 18 North Rd, Cardiff, CF1 3DY, United Kingdom; tel. (1222) 372409; fax (1222) 665522; e-mail ibra@cardiff.ac.uk; f. 1949 to further bee research and provide an information service for bee scientists and bee-keepers worldwide. Mems: 1,200 in 130 countries. Dir RICHARD JONES; Asst Dir Dr PAMELA MUNN. Publs *Bee World* (quarterly), *Apicultural Abstracts* (quarterly), *Journal of Apicultural Research* (quarterly).

International Centre for Integrated Mountain Development: POB 3226, Kathmandu, Nepal; tel. (1) 525313; fax (1) 524509; e-mail dits@icimod.org.np; f. 1983 with the primary objective of promoting the sustained well-being of mountain communities through effective socioeconomic development policies and programmes, and through the sound management of fragile mountain habitats, especially in the Hindu Kush-Himalayan region, covering all or parts of Afghanistan, Bangladesh, Bhutan, China, India, Myanmar, Nepal and Pakistan; international staff of 30; Dir-Gen. EGBERT PELINCK.

International Centre for Tropical Agriculture (Centro Internacional de Agricultura Tropical—CIAT): Apdo Aéreo 6713, Cali, Colombia; tel. (57) 2445-0000; fax (57) 2445-0073; e-mail CIAT@cgnet.com; f. 1967 to contribute to the alleviation of hunger and poverty in tropical developing countries by using new techniques in agriculture research and training focuses on production problems of the tropics concentrating on field beans, cassava, rice and tropical pastures. Dir-Gen. GRANT M. SCOBIE. Publs *Annual Report, Growing Affinities* (2 a year), *Pasturas Tropicales* (3 a year), catalogue of publications.

International Commission for the Conservation of Atlantic Tunas—ICCAT: Estebanez Calderón 3, 28020 Madrid, Spain; tel. (1) 5793352; telex 46330; fax (1) 5715299; f. 1969 under the provisions of the International Convention for the Conservation of Atlantic Tunas (1966) to maintain the populations of tuna and tuna-like species in the Atlantic Ocean and adjacent seas at levels that will permit the maximum sustainable catch; collects statistics, conducts studies. Mems: 24 contracting parties. Pres. Dr A. RIBEIRO LIMA (Portugal); Exec. Sec. Dr ANTONIO FERNANDEZ. Publs *ICCAT Newsletter, Statistical Bulletin* (annually), *Data Record* (annually).

International Commission of Sugar Technology: c/o Dr H. van Malland, 97199 Ochsenfurt, Marktbreiter Str. 74, Germany; tel. (9331) 91450; fax (9331) 91462; f. 1949 to discuss investigations and promote scientific and technical research work. Pres. of Scientific Cttee. Prof. G. VACCARI (Italy); Sec.-Gen. Dr HENK VAN MALLAND.

International Committee for Animal Recording: Via A. Torlonia 15A, 00161 Rome, Italy; tel. (6) 44238013; fax (6) 44241466; e-mail zoorec@rmnet.it; f. 1951 to extend and improve the work of recording and to standardize methods. Mems: in 40 countries. Pres. W. M. G. WISMANS (Netherlands).

International Crops Research Institute for the Semi-Arid Tropics—ICRISAT: Patancheru, Andhra Pradesh, India; tel. (40) 596161; telex 422203; fax (40) 241239; e-mail icrisat@cgnet.com; internet http://www.cgiar.org/icrisat; f. 1972 as world centre for genetic improvement of sorghum, millet, pigeonpea, chickpea and groundnut, and for research on the management of resources in the world's semi-arid tropics; research covers all physical and socio-economic aspects of improving farming systems on unirrigated land. Dir SHAUKI M. BARGHOUTI (Jordan). Publs *ICRISAT Report* (annually), *SAT News* (2 a year), *International Chickpea and Pigeonpea Newsletter, International Arachis Newsletter, International Sorghum and Millet Newsletter* (annually), information and research bulletins.

International Dairy Federation: 41 Square Vergote, 1030 Brussels, Belgium; tel. (2) 733-98-88; fax (2) 733-04-13; e-mail info@fil-idf.org; internet http://www.fil-idf.org; f. 1903 to link all dairy associations in order to encourage the solution of scientific, technical and economic problems affecting the dairy industry. Mems: national committees in 34 countries. Sec.-Gen. E. HOPKIN (UK). Publs *Bulletin of IDF, IDF Standards.*

International Federation of Agricultural Producers—IFAP: 21 rue Chaptal, 75009 Paris, France; tel. 1-45-26-05-53; fax 1-48-74-72-12; e-mail 101476.3474@compuserve.com; f. 1946 to represent, in the international field, the interests of agricultural producers; to exchange information and ideas and help develop understanding of world problems and their effects upon agricultural producers; to encourage efficiency of production, processing, and marketing of agricultural commodities; holds conference every two years. National farmers' organizations and agricultural co-operatives of 55 countries are represented in the Federation. Pres. GRAHAM BLIGHT (Australia); Sec.-Gen. DAVID KING. Publs *IFAP Newsletter* (bimonthly), *Proceedings of General Conferences.*

International Federation of Beekeepers' Associations—APIMONDIA: Corso Vittorio Emanuele 101, 00186 Rome, Italy; tel. and fax (6) 6852286; telex 612533; e-mail apimondia@mclink.it; f. 1949; collects and brings up to date documentation concerning international beekeeping; studies the particular problems of beekeeping through its permanent committees; organizes international congresses, seminars, symposia and meetings; stimulates research into new techniques for more economical results; co-operates with other international organizations interested in beekeeping, in particular with FAO. Mems: 56 associations from 52 countries. Pres. RAYMOND BORNECK; Sec.-Gen. RICCARDO JANNONI-SEBASTIANINI. Publs *Apiacta* (quarterly, in English, French, German and Spanish), *Dictionary of Beekeeping Terms,* AGROVOC (thesaurus of agricultural terms), studies.

International Hop Growers' Convention: c/o Inštitut za hmeljarstvo in pivovarstvo, 3310 Žalec, Slovenia; tel. (63) 715214; telex 36314; fax (63) 717163; e-mail martin.pavlovic@uni-lj.si; internet http://www.bf.uni-lj.si/iae/mp/cich.htm; f. 1950 to act as a centre for the collection of data on hop production, and to conduct scientific, technical and economic commissions. Mems: national associations in Australia, Belgium, Bulgaria, Czech Republic, France, Germany, New Zealand, Poland, Russia, Slovakia, Slovenia, Spain, Ukraine, United Kingdom, USA, Federal Republic of Yugoslavia. Pres. FRANTIŠEK CHVALOVSKÝ; Gen. Sec. Dr MARTIN PAVLOVIĆ. Publ. *Hopfen-Rundschau* (fortnightly).

International Institute for Sugar Beet Research: 47 rue Montoyer, 1040 Brussels, Belgium; tel. (2) 509-15-33; telex 21287; fax (2) 512-65-06; f. 1932 to promote research and exchange of information, by organizing meetings and study groups. Mems: 555 in 29 countries. Pres. of the Admin. Council J. A. ESTEBAN BASELGA; Sec.-Gen. L. WEICKMANS.

International Institute of Tropical Agriculture—IITA: Oyo Rd, PMB 5320, Ibadan, Nigeria; tel. (2) 241-2626; telex 31417; fax (874) 177-2276; e-mail iita@cgnet.com; f. 1967; principal financing arranged by the Consultative Group on International Agricultural Research (CGIAR), co-sponsored by the FAO, the IBRD and the UNDP. The research programmes comprise crop management, improvement of crops (cereals, legumes and root crops) and plant protection; training programme for researchers in tropical agriculture; library of 75,000 vols and data base of 95,500 records. Dir-Gen. Dr LUKAS BRADER. Publs *Annual Report, IITA Research* (quarterly), technical bulletins, research reports.

International Livestock Research Institute—ILRI: POB 30709, Nairobi, Kenya; tel. 632311; telex 22040; fax 631499; f. 1995, to supersede the International Laboratory for Research on Animal Diseases and the International Livestock Centre for Africa; conducts laboratory and field research on animal health (in particular, animal trypanosomiasis and theileriosis), the conservation of genetic resources, production systems analysis, natural resource management, livestock policy analysis and strengthening national research capacities; undertakes training programmes for scientists and technicians; specialized science library. Dir Dr HANK FITZHUGH. Publs *Annual Report, Livestock Research for Development* (newsletter, 2 a year).

International Maize and Wheat Improvement Centre—CIMMYT: Lisboa 27—Col Juarez, Apdo Postal 6-641, 06600 México, DF, Mexico; tel. (5) 7269091; fax (5) 7267558; e-mail cimmyt@alphac.cimmyt.mx; conducts world-wide research programme for increasing production of maize, wheat and triticale in developing countries. Dir-Gen. Prof. TIMOTHY REEVES.

International Organization for Biological Control of Noxious Animals and Plants: IOBC Permanent Secretariat, AGROPOLIS, Ave Agropolis, 34394 Montpellier Cédex 5, France; e-mail iobc@agropolis.fr; f. 1955 to promote and co-ordinate research on the more effective biological control of harmful organisms; re-organized in 1971 as a central council with world-wide affiliations and largely autonomous regional sections in different parts of the world: the West Palaearctic (Europe, North Africa, the Middle East), the Western Hemisphere, South-East Asia, Pacific Region and Tropical Africa. Pres. Dr J. WAAGE (UK); Sec.-Gen. Dr E. WAJNBERG (France). Publs *Entomophaga* (quarterly), *Newsletter*.

International Organization of Citrus Virologists: c/o C. N. Roistacher, Dept of Plant Pathology, Univ. of California, Riverside, CA 92521, USA; tel. (909) 684-0934; fax (909) 684-4324; f. 1957 to promote research on citrus virus diseases at international level by standardizing diagnostic techniques and exchanging information. Mems: 250. Chair. R. F. LEE; Sec. C. N. ROISTACHER.

International Red Locust Control Organization for Central and Southern Africa: POB 240252, Ndola, Zambia; tel. 615684; telex 30072; fax 614285; e-mail locust@zamnet.zm; f. 1971 to control locusts in eastern, central and southern Africa, and assists in the control of African army-worm and quelea-quelea. Mems: nine countries. Dir E. K. BYARUHANGA. Publs *Annual Report, Monthly Report* and scientific reports.

International Regional Organization of Plant Protection and Animal Health (Organismo Internacional Regional de Sanidad Agropecuaria—OIRSA): Calle Ramón Belloso, Final Pasaje Isolde, Col. Escalón, San Salvador, El Salvador; tel. 223-2391; fax 298-2119; f. 1953 for the prevention of the introduction of animal and plant pests and diseases unknown in the region; research, control and eradication programmes of the principal pests present in agriculture; technical assistance and advice to the ministries of agriculture and livestock of member countries; education and qualification of personnel. Mems: Belize, Costa Rica, Dominican Republic, El Salvador, Guatemala, Honduras, Mexico, Nicaragua, Panama. Exec. Dir CELIO HUMBERTO BARRETO.

International Rice Research Institute—IRRI: POB 933, Manila 1099, Philippines; tel. (2) 845-0563; telex 22456; fax (2) 891-1292; internet http://www.cgiar.org/irri; f. 1960; conducts research on rice, aiming to develop technology that is of environmental, social and economic benefit, and to enhance national rice research systems; maintains a library to collect and provide access to the world's technical rice literature; publishes and disseminates research results; conducts regional rice research projects in co-operation with scientists in rice-producing countries; offers training in rice research methods and techniques; organizes international conferences and workshops. Dir-Gen. Dr ROBERT HAVENER (acting). Publs *Annual Program Report, Annual Corporate Report, Rice Literature Update, International Rice Research Notes, IRRI Hotline*.

International Scientific Council for Trypanosomiasis Research and Control: PM Bag 2359, Lagos, Nigeria; tel. (1) 633289; telex 22199; fax (1) 2636093; f. 1949 to review the work on tsetse and trypanosomiasis problems carried out by organizations and workers concerned in laboratories and in the field; to stimulate further research and discussion and to promote co-ordination between research workers and organizations in the different countries in Africa, and to provide a regular opportunity for the discussion of particular problems and for the exposition of new experiments and discoveries.

International Seed Testing Association: Reckenholz, POB 412, 8046 Zürich, Switzerland; tel. (1) 3713133; fax (1) 3713427; e-mail istach@iprolink.ch; f. 1906 (reconstituted 1924) to promote uniformity and accurate methods of seed testing and evaluation in order to facilitate efficiency in production, processing, distribution and utilization of seeds; organizes triennial conventions, meetings, workshops, symposia and training courses. Mems: 65 countries. Exec. Sec. H. SCHMID; Hon. Sec. Treas. Prof. A. LOVATO (Italy). Publs *Seed Science and Technology* (3 a year), *ISTA News Bulletin* (3 a year).

International Sericultural Commission: 25 quai JeanJacques Rousseau, 69350 La Mulatière, France; tel. 4-78-50-41-98; fax 4-78-86-09-57; f. 1948 to encourage the development of silk production. Library of 1,215 vols. Mems: governments of Brazil, Egypt, France, India, Indonesia, Japan, Lebanon, Madagascar, Romania, Thailand, Tunisia, Turkey. Sec.-Gen. Dr GÉRARD CHAVANCY (France). Publ. *Sericologia* (quarterly).

International Service for National Agricultural Research—ISNAR: POB 93375, 2509 AJ The Hague, Netherlands; tel. (70) 349-61-00; telex 33746; fax (70) 381-96-77; e-mail isnar@cgnet.com; internet http://www.cgiar.org/isnar; f. 1980 by the Consultative Group on International Agricultural Research (q.v.) to strengthen national agricultural research systems in developing countries by promoting appropriate research policies, sustainable research institutions, and improved research management; provides advisory service, training, research services and information. Chair. AMIR MUHAMMED; Dir-Gen. STEIN BIE.

International Society for Horticultural Science: Kardinaal Merclerlaan 92, 3001 Leuven, Belgium; tel. (16) 22-94-27; fax (16) 22-94-50; e-mail ishs@agr.kuleuven.ac.be; f. 1959 to co-operate in the research field. Mems: 54 member-countries, 265 organizations, 3,050 individuals. Pres. Prof. Dr SANSAVINI (Italy); Exec. Dir Ir J. VAN ASSCHE (Belgium). Publs *Chronica Horticulturae* (4 a year), *Acta Horticulturae, Scientia Horticulturae* (monthly), *Horticultural Research International*.

International Society for Soilless Culture—ISOSC: POB 52, 6700 AB Wageningen, Netherlands; tel. (317) 413809; fax (317) 423457; f. 1955 as International Working Group on Soilless Culture, to promote world-wide distribution and co-ordination of research, advisory services, and practical application of soilless culture (hydroponics); international congress held every four years (9th congress: Jersey, Channel Islands, April 1996). Mems: 450 from 69 countries. Pres. RICK S. DONNAN (Australia); Sec.-Gen. Ing. Agr. ABRAM A. STEINER. Publ. *ISOSC Proceedings* (every 4 years).

International Society of Soil Science: c/o Institute of Soil Science, University of Agriculture, Gregor-Mendel-Strasse 33, 1180 Vienna, Austria; tel. (1) 310-60-26; fax (1) 310-60-27; e-mail isss@edv1.boku.ac.at; internet http://www.cirad.fr/isss/aiss.html; f. 1924. Mems: 8,000 individuals and associations in 163 countries. Pres. Prof. A. RUELLAN (France); Sec.-Gen. Prof. Dr W. E. H. BLUM (Austria). Publ. *Bulletin* (2 a year).

International Union of Forestry Research Organizations—IUFRO: 1131 Vienna, Seckendorff-Gudent-Weg 8, Austria; tel. (1) 877-01-51; fax (1) 877-93-55; e-mail iufro@forvie.ac.at; f. 1892. Mems: 700 organizations in 115 countries, involving more than 15,000 scientists. Pres. Dr JEFFREY BURLEY (UK); Sec. HEINRICH SCHMUTZENHOFER (Austria). Publs *Annual Report, IUFRO News* (quarterly), *IUFRO World Series, IUFRO Paper Series* (occasional).

International Whaling Commission—IWC: The Red House, Station Rd, Histon, Cambridge, CB4 4NP, United Kingdom; tel. (1223) 233971; fax (1223) 232876; f. 1946 under the International Convention for the Regulation of Whaling, for the conservation of the world whale stocks; aims to review the regulations covering the operations of whaling, to encourage research relating to whales and whaling, to collect and analyse statistical information and to study and disseminate information concerning methods of increasing whale stocks; a ban on commercial whaling was passed by the Commission in July 1982, to take effect three years subsequently (although, in some cases, a phased reduction of commercial operations was not completed until 1988). An assessment of the effects on whale stocks of this ban was under way in the early 1990s, and a revised whale-management procedure was adopted in 1992, to be implemented only after the development of a complete whale management scheme, including arrangements for data collection and an inspection and monitoring scheme; Iceland left the IWC in June 1992 and Norway resumed commercial whaling in 1993. Mems: governments of 41 countries. Chair. MICHAEL CANNY (Ireland); Sec. Dr R. GAMBELL. Publ. *Annual Report*.

Joint Organization for the Control of Desert Locust and Bird Pests (Organisation commune de lutte anti-acridienne et de lutte antiaviaire—OCLALAV): BP 1066, route des Pères Maristes, Dakar, Senegal; tel. 32-32-80; fax 32-04-87; f. 1965 to destroy insect pests, in particular the desert locust, and grain-eating birds, in particular the quelea-quelea, and to sponsor related research projects. Mems: Benin, Burkina Faso, Cameroon, Chad, Côte d'Ivoire, The Gambia, Mali, Mauritania, Niger, Senegal. Dir-Gen. ABDULLAHI OULD SOUEÏD AHMED. Publ. *Bulletin* (monthly).

North Pacific Anadromous Fish Commission: 6640 Northwest Marine Drive, Vancouver, BC V6T 1X2, Canada; tel. (604) 228-1128; fax (604) 228-1135; e-mail wmorris@unixg.ubc.ca; f. 1993. Mems: Canada, Japan, Russia, USA. Exec. Dir IRINA G. SHESTAKOVA. Publs *Annual Report, Newsletter* (2 a year), *Statistical Yearbook, Scientific Bulletin*.

Northwest Atlantic Fisheries Organization: POB 638, Dartmouth, NS B2Y 3Y9, Canada; tel. (902) 468-5590; fax (902) 468-5538; e-mail nafo@fox.nstn.ca; f. 1979 (formerly International Commission for the Northwest Atlantic Fisheries); aims at optimum use, management and conservation of resources, promotes research and compiles statistics. Pres. A. V. RODIN (Russia); Exec. Sec. Dr L. I. CHEPEL. Publs *Annual Report, Statistical Bulletin, Journal of Northwest Atlantic Fishery Science, Scientific Council Reports, Scientific Council Studies, Sampling Yearbook, Proceedings*.

World Association for Animal Production: Via A. Torlonia 15A, 00161 Rome, Italy; tel. (6) 44238013; fax (6) 44241466; e-mail zoorec@rmnet.it; f. 1965; holds world conference on animal production every five years; encourages, sponsors and participates in regional meetings, seminars and symposia. Pres. Prof. Ing. K. HAN (Republic of Korea); Sec.-Gen. J. BOYAZOGLU (Greece). Publ. *News Items* (2 a year).

World Association of Veterinary Food-Hygienists: Federal Institute for Health Protection of Consumers and Veterinary Medicine (BgVV), Diedersdorfer Weg 1, 12277 Berlin, Germany; tel. (30) 8412-2101; fax (30) 8412-2951; e-mail p.teufel@bgvv.de; f. 1955 to promote hygienic food control and discuss research. Mems: national asscns in 40 countries. Pres. Prof. PAUL TEUFEL; Sec. Treas. Dr L. ELLERBROEK.

World Association of Veterinary Microbiologists, Immunologists and Specialists in Infectious Diseases: Ecole Nationale Vétérinaire d'Alfort, 7 ave du Général de Gaulle, 94704 Maisons-Alfort Cédex, France; tel. 1-43967021; fax 1-43967022; f. 1967 to facilitate international contacts in the fields of microbiology, immunology and animal infectious diseases. Pres. Prof. CH. PILET (France). Publs *Comparative Immunology, Microbiology and Infectious Diseases*.

World Ploughing Organization—WPO: Søkildevej 17, 5270 Odense N, Denmark; tel. 65978006; fax 65932440; f. 1952 to promote World Ploughing Contest in a different country each year, to improve techniques and promote better understanding of soil cultivation practices through research and practical demonstrations; arranges tillage clinics world-wide to improve the use of new techniques. Affiliates in 28 countries. Gen. Sec. CARL ALLESO. Publs *WPO Handbook* (annual), *WPO Bulletin of News and Information* (irregular).

World's Poultry Science Association: c/o Dr P. C. M. Simons, Centre for Applied Poultry Research, 'Het Spelderholt', POB 31, 7360 AA Beckbergen, Netherlands; tel. (55) 506-6534; fax (55) 506-4858; f. 1912 to exchange knowledge in the industry, to encourage research and teaching, to publish information relating to production and marketing problems; to promote World Poultry Congresses and co-operate with governments. Mems: individuals in 95 countries, branches in 55 countries. Pres. ANURADHA DESAI (India); Sec. Dr P. C. M. SIMONS (Netherlands). Publ. *The World Poultry Science Journal* (4 a year).

World Veterinary Association: Rosenlunds Allé 8, 2720 Vanlose, Denmark; tel. 38-71-01-56; fax 38-71-03-22; e-mail wva@ddd.dk; f. 1959 as a continuation of the International Veterinary Congresses; organizes quadrennial congress. Mems: organizations in 76 countries and 19 organizations of veterinary specialists as associate members. Pres. Dr APOSTOLOS T. RANTSIOS (Greece); Exec. Sec. Dr LARS HOLSAAE. Publs *WVA Bulletin, World Veterinary Directory*.

Arts and Culture

Europa Nostra—Association of Non-Governmental Organizations for the Protection of Europe's Architectural and Natural Heritage: Lange Voorhout 35, 2514 EC The Hague, Netherlands; tel. (70) 3560333; fax (70) 3617865; f. 1963; a large grouping of organizations and individuals concerned with the protection and enhancement of the European architectural and natural heritage and of the European environment; has consultative status with the Council of Europe. Mems: more than 200 mem. organizations, more than 100 allied mems, more than 40 supporting bodies, more than 900 individual mems. Pres. HRH The Prince Consort of Denmark; Exec. Pres. DANIEL CARDON DE LICHTBUER (Belgium); Sec.-Gen. ANTONIO MARCHINI CAMIA (Italy).

European Association of Conservatoires, Music Academies and Music High Schools: c/o Conservatoire de Paris, 209 ave Jean-Jaurès, 75019 Paris, France; tel. 1-40-40-46-03; fax 1-40-40-46-09; f. 1953 to establish and foster contacts and exchanges between members. Mems: 112. Pres. IAN HORSBRUGH; Gen. Sec. MARC-OLIVIER DUPIN.

European Centre for Culture (Centre Européen de la Culture): Villa Moynier, 122B rue de Lausanne, 1202 Geneva, Switzerland; tel. (22) 7322803; telex 289917; fax (22) 7384012; f. 1950 to contribute to the union of Europe by encouraging cultural pursuits, providing a meeting place, and conducting research in the various fields of European Studies; holds conferences on European subjects, European documentation and archives. Groups the Secretariats of the European Association of Music Festivals and the Association of Institutes of European Studies. Pres. JEAN-FRED BOURQUIN (Switzerland); Sec.-Gen. CLAUS HÄSSIG. Publs *Transeuropéennes* (quarterly), *Newsletter* (2 a year), *Season* (annually), *Festivals* (annually).

European Society of Culture: Guidecca 54P (Calle Michelangelo, Villa Hériot), 30133 Venice, Italy; tel. (41) 5230210; fax (41) 5231033; f. 1950 to unite artists, poets, scientists, philosophers and others through mutual interests and friendship in order to safeguard and improve the conditions required for creative activity; library of 10,000 volumes. Mems: national and local centres, and 2,000 individuals, in 60 countries. Pres. Prof. VINCENZO CAPPELLETTI (Italy); Gen. Sec. Dott. MICHELLE CAMPAGNOLO-BOUVIER.

Inter-American Music Council (Consejo Interamericano de Música—CIDEM): 2511 P St NW, Washington, DC 20007, USA; f. 1956 to promote the exchange of works, performances and information in all fields of music, to study problems relative to music education, to encourage activity in the field of musicology, to promote folklore research and music creation, to establish distribution centres for music material of the composers of the Americas, etc. Mems: national music societies of 33 American countries. Sec.-Gen. EFRAÍN PAESKY.

International Association of Art: Maison de l'UNESCO, 1 rue Miollis, 75732 Paris Cédex 15, France; tel. 1-45-68-26-55; fax 1-45-67-22-87; f. 1954. Mems: 104 national committees. Pres. UNA WALKER; Sec.-Gen. J. C. DE SALINS. Publ. *IAA Newsletter* (quarterly).

International Association of Art Critics: 11 rue Berryer, 75008 Paris, France; tel. 1-42-56-17-53; fax 1-42-56-08-42; internet http://www.aagif.fr.sermadiras; f. 1949 to increase co-operation in plastic arts, promote international cultural exchanges and protect the interests of members. Mems: 3,600, in 69 countries. Pres. KIM LEVIN (USA); Sec.-Gen. RAMON TIO BELLIDO (France). Publs *Annuaire, Newsletter* (quarterly).

International Association of Bibliophiles: Bibliothèque nationale de France, 58 rue Richelieu, 75084 Paris Cédex 02, France; fax 1-47-03-75-70; internet http://web.cnam.fr/abu; f. 1963 to create contacts between bibliophiles and to encourage book-collecting in different countries; to organize or encourage congresses, meetings, exhibitions, the award of scholarships, the publication of a bulletin, yearbooks, and works of reference or bibliography. Mems: 450. Pres. ANTHONY R. A. HOBSON (UK); Sec.-Gen. JEAN-MARC CHATELAIN (France). Publ. *Le Bulletin du Bibliophile*.

International Association of Literary Critics: 38 rue du Faubourg St-Jacques, 75014 Paris, France; tel. 1-40-51-33-00; telex 206963; fax 1-43-54-92-99; f. 1969; national centres in 34 countries; organizes congresses. Pres. ROBERT ANDRÉ. Publ. *Revue* (2 a year).

International Association of Museums of Arms and Military History—IAMAM: c/o Dr C. Gaier, Musée d'Armes de Liège, Quai de Maastricht 8, 4000 Liège, Belgium; tel. (4) 221-94-16; fax (4) 221-94-01; f. 1957; links museums and other scientific institutions with public collections of arms and armour and military equipment, uniforms, etc.; triennial conferences and occasional specialist symposia. Mems: 252 institutions in 50 countries. Pres. CLAUDE GAIER (Belgium); Sec.-Gen. BAS KIST (Netherlands). Publs *Directory of Museums of Arms and Military History, The Mohonk Courier*.

International Board on Books for Young People—IBBY: Nonnenweg 12, Postfach, 4003 Basel, Switzerland; tel. (61) 2722917; fax (61) 2722757; e-mail ibby@eye.ch; f. 1953 to support and link bodies in all countries connected with children's book work; to encourage the distribution of good children's books; to promote scientific investigation into problems of juvenile books; to organize educational aid for developing countries; presents the Hans Christian Andersen Award every two years to a living author and a living illustrator whose work is an outstanding contribution to juvenile literature, and the IBBY-Asahi Reading Promotion Award annually to an organization that has made a significant contribution towards the encouragement of reading; sponsors International Children's Book Day (2 April). Mems: national sections and individuals in 61 countries. Pres. CARMEN DIANA DEARDEN (Venezuela); Sec. LEENA MAISSEN. Publs *Bookbird* (quarterly, in English), *Congress Papers, IBBY Honour List* (every 2 years); special bibliographies.

International Centre for the Study of the Preservation and Restoration of Cultural Property—ICCROM: Via di San Michele 13, 00153 Rome, Italy; tel. (6) 585-531; fax (6) 5855-3349; e-mail iccrom@iccrom.org; internet http://www.icomos.org/iccrom; f. 1959; assembles documents on preservation and restoration of cultural property; stimulates research and proffers advice; organizes missions of experts; undertakes training of specialists and organizes regular courses on (i) Architectural Conservation; (ii) Conservation of Mural Paintings; (iii) Scientific Principles of Conservation; (iv) Conservation of Paper. Mems: 93 countries. Dir-Gen. MARC LAENEN. Publ. *Newsletter* (annually, English and French).

International Centre of Films for Children and Young People—Centre international des films pour les enfants et les jeunes—CIFEJ: 3774 rue Saint-Denis, Bureau 200, Montréal, PQ H2W 2M1, Canada; tel. (514) 284-9388; fax (514) 284-0168; e-mail cifej@odyssee.net; internet http://www.odyssee.net/cifej; f. 1955; a clearing house for information about: entertainment films (cinema and television) for children and young people, influence of films on the young, and regulations in force for the protection and education of young people; promotes production and distribution of suitable films and their appreciation. The CIFEJ prize is awarded at selected film festivals. Mems: 157 mems from 52 countries. Exec. Dir MICHELLE BISCHOFF. Publ. *CIFEJ Info* (monthly).

International Committee for the Diffusion of Arts and Literature through the Cinema (Comité international pour la diffusion des arts et des lettres par le cinéma—CIDALC): 24 blvd Poissonnière, 75009 Paris, France; tel. 1-42-46-13-60; f. 1930 to promote the creation and release of educational, cultural and documentary films and other films of educational value in order to contribute to closer understanding between peoples; awards medals and prizes for films of exceptional merit. Mems: national committees in 19 countries. Pres. JEAN-PIERRE FOUCAULT (France); Sec.-Gen. MARIO VERDONE (Italy). Publs *Annuaire CIDALC, Cinéma éducatif et cultural*.

International Comparative Literature Association: c/o M. Schmeling, Allg. u. Vergl. Literaturwissenschaft, Univ. des Saarlandes, POB 151150, 66041 Saarbrücken, Germany; tel. (681) 302-2750; fax (681) 302-2210; f. 1954 to work for the development of the comparative study of literature in modern languages. Member societies and individuals in 62 countries. Sec. M. SCHMELING. Publ. *ICLA Bulletin* (twice a year).

International Confederation of Societies of Authors and Composers—World Congress of Authors and Composers: 11 rue Keppler, 75116 Paris, France; tel. 1-47-20-81-01; fax 1-47-23-02-66; f. 1926 to protect the rights of authors and composers; documentation centre; organizes biennial congress. Mems: 165 member societies from 90 countries. Sec.-Gen. JEAN-ALEXIS ZIEGLER.

International Council of Graphic Design Associations—ICOGRADA: POB 398, London, W11 4UG, United Kingdom; tel. (171) 603-8494; fax (171) 371-6040; e-mail 106065.2235@compuserve.com; internet http://www.csiac.org; f. 1963; aims to raise standards of graphic design, to exchange information, and to organize exhibitions and congresses; maintains library, slide collection and archive. Mems: 62 associations in 38 countries. Pres. JOSÉ KORN BRUZZONE; Sec.-Gen. MARY MULLIN. Publs *Newsletter* (quarterly), *Graphic Design World Views, Regulations and Guidelines governing International Design Competitions, Model Code of Professional Conduct*.

International Council of Museums—ICOM: Maison de l'UNESCO, 1 rue Miollis, 75732 Paris Cédex 15, France; tel. 1-47-34-05-00; telex 270602; fax 1-43-06-78-62; e-mail secretariat@icom.org; f. 1946 to further international co-operation among museums and to advance museum interests; maintains with UNESCO the organization's documentation centre. Mems: 13,000 individuals and institutions from 145 countries. Pres. SAROJ GHOSE (India); Sec.-Gen. ELISABETH DES PORTES (France). Publ. *ICOM News—Nouvelles de l'ICOM—Noticias del ICOM* (quarterly).

International Council on Monuments and Sites—ICOMOS: 162 Blvd E. Jacqmain, POB 60, 1210 Brussels, Belgium; tel. (2) 207-75-94; fax (2) 203-09-64; internet http://www.icomos.org; f. 1965 to promote the study and preservation of monuments and sites; to arouse and cultivate the interest of public authorities, and people of every country in their monuments and sites and in their cultural heritage; to liaise between public authorities, departments, institutions and individuals interested in the preservation and study of monuments and sites; to disseminate the results of research into the problems, technical, social and administrative, connected with the conservation of the architectural heritage, and of centres of historic interest; holds triennial General Assembly and Symposium. Mems: c. 5,300; 14 international committees, 84 national committees. Pres. LEO VAN NISPEN; Sec.-Gen. JEAN-LOUIS LUXEN (Belgium). Publ. *ICOMOS Newsletter* (quarterly).

International Federation for Theatre Research: Flat 9, 118 Avenue Rd, London, W3 8QG, United Kingdom; tel. (1227) 764000; fax (1227) 827164; e-mail m.j.anderson@ukc.ac.uk; f. 1955 by 21 countries at the International Conference on Theatre History, London. Pres. Prof. ERIKA FISCHER-LICHTE; Joint Secs-Gen. Prof. MICHAEL J. ANDERSON, Prof. JEAN-MARC LARRUE. Publs *Theatre Research International* (in association with Oxford University Press) (3 a year), *Bulletin* (2 a year).

International Federation of Film Archives: c/o Christian Dimitriu, rue Defacqz 1, 1000 Brussels, Belgium; tel. (2) 538-30-65; fax (2) 534-47-47; f. 1938 to encourage the creation of archives in all countries for the collection and conservation of the film heritage of each land; to facilitate co-operation and exchanges between these film archives; to promote public interest in the art of the cinema; to aid research in this field and to compile new documentation; conducts research; publishes manuals, etc.; holds annual congresses. Mems in 60 countries. Pres. MICHELLE AUBERT (France); Sec.-Gen. ROGER SMITHER (UK).

International Federation of Film Producers' Associations: 33 ave des Champs-Elysées, 75008 Paris, France; tel. 1-42-25-62-14; fax 1-42-56-16-52; f. 1933 to represent film production internationally, to defend its general interests and promote its development, to study all cultural, legal, economic, technical and social problems of interest to the activity of film production. Mems: national associations in 25 countries. Pres. AURELIO DE LAURENTIIS (Italy); Dir-Gen. ANDRÉ CHAUBEAU (France).

International Institute for Children's Literature and Reading Research (Internationales Institut für Jugendliteratur und Leseforschung): 1040 Vienna, Mayerhofgasse 6, Austria; tel. (1) 50-50-35-90; fax (1) 50-50-35-90; f. 1965 as an international documentation, research and advisory centre of juvenile literature and reading; maintains specialized library; arranges conferences and exhibitions; compiles recommendation lists. Mems: individual and group members in 28 countries. Pres. Dr HILDE HAWLICEK; Dir KARIN SOLLAT. Publs *1000 & 1 Buch* (6 a year in co-operation with the Austrian Ministry of Education, *INFO: Lesen*.

International Institute for Conservation of Historic and Artistic Works: 6 Buckingham St., London, WC2N 6BA, United Kingdom; tel. (171) 839-5975; fax (171) 976-1564; e-mail 100731.1565@compuserve.com; f. 1950. Mems: 3,350 individual, 450 institutional members. Pres. AGNES Gräfin BALLESTREM; Sec.-Gen. DAVID BOMFORD. Publ. *Studies in Conservation* (quarterly).

International Liaison Centre for Cinema and Television Schools (Centre international de liaison des écoles de cinéma et de télévision): 8 rue Thérésienne, 1000 Brussels, Belgium; tel. (2) 511-98-39; fax (2) 511-00-35; e-mail hverh.cilect@skynet.be; internet http://www.-leland.stanford.edu/~hbreit/cilect; f. 1955 to link higher teaching and research institutes and to improve education of makers of films and television programmes; organizes conferences, student film festivals, training programme for developing countries. Mems: 103 institutions in 52 countries. Pres. GUSTAVO MONTIEL (Mexico); Exec. Sec. HENRY VERHASSELT (Belgium). Publ. *Newsletter*.

International Music Council—IMC: Maison de l'UNESCO, 1 rue Miollis, 75732 Paris Cédex 15, France; tel. 1-45-68-25-50; fax 1-43-06-87-98; e-mail imc-cim@compuserve.com; f. 1949 to foster the exchange of musicians, music (written and recorded), and information between countries and cultures; to support traditional music, contemporary composers and young professional musicians. Mems: 30 international non-governmental organizations, national committees in 65 countries. Pres. FRANS DE RUITER (Netherlands); Sec.-Gen. GUY HUOT.

Members of IMC include:

European Festivals Association: 120B rue de Lausanne, 1202 Geneva, Switzerland; tel. (22) 7386873; fax (22) 7384012; e-mail aef@vtx.ch; f. 1952; aims to maintain high artistic standards and the representative character of art festivals; holds annual General Assembly. Mems: 71 regularly-held music festivals in 26 European countries, Israel, Japan and Mexico. Pres. FRANS DE RUITER. Publ. *Festivals* (annually).

International Association of Music Libraries, Archives and Documentation Centres—IAML: c/o Cataloguing Dept, Carleton Univ. Library, 1125 Colonel By Drive, Ottawa, ON K1S 5B6, Canada; tel. (613) 520-2600; fax (613) 520-3583; e-mail alisonhall@carleton.ca; f. 1951. Mems: 2,003 institutions and individuals in 58 countries. Pres. VESLEMÖY HEINTZ (Sweden); Sec.-Gen. ALISON HALL (Canada). Publ. *Fontes artis musicae* (quarterly).

International Council for Traditional Music: Dept of Music–MC 1815, Columbia University, 2960 Broadway, New York, NY 10027; tel. (212) 678-0332; telex 220094; fax (212) 678-2513; f. 1947 (as International Folk Music Council) to further the study, practice, documentation, preservation and dissemination of traditional music of all countries; conferences held every two years. Mems: 1,350. Pres. Dr ANTHONY SEEGAR (USA); Sec.-Gen. Prof. DIETER CHRISTENSEN (USA). Publs *Yearbook for Traditional Music, Bulletin* (2 a year), *Directory of Traditional Music* (every 2 years).

International Federation of 'Jeunesses Musicales': Palais des Beaux-Arts, 10 rue Royale, 1000 Brussels, Belgium; tel. (2) 513-97-74; fax (2) 514-47-55; e-mail fiym@arcadis.be; f. 1945 to enable young people to develop musically across all boundaries and to stimulate contacts between member countries. Mems: organizations in 53 countries. Sec.-Gen. DAG FRANZÉN.

International Federation of Musicians: 21 bis rue Victor Massé, 75009 Paris, France; tel. 1-45-26-31-23; fax 1-45-26-31-57; e-mail 106340.1224@compuserve.com; f. 1948 to promote and protect the interests of musicians in affiliated unions; promotes international exchange of musicians. Mems: 50 unions totalling 200,000 individuals in 43 countries. Pres. JOHN MORTON (UK); Gen. Sec. JEAN VINCENT (France).

International Institute for Traditional Music: Winkler Str. 20, 14193 Berlin, Germany; tel. (30) 826-28-53; fax (30) 825-99-91; e-mail iitm@netmbx.netmbx.de; f. 1963 to promote traditional folk music and non-European traditional music; annual festival. Mems from 20 countries. Dir Prof. MAX PETER BAUMANN. Publs *The World of Music* (3 a year), *Intercultural Music Studies* (book series), *Traditional Music of the World* (CD/MC series), *Musikbogen*.

International Jazz Federation: c/o Jan A. Byrczek, 117 W 58th St, Ste 12G, New York, NY 10019, USA; tel. (212) 581-7188; f. 1969 to promote the knowledge and appreciation of jazz throughout the world; arranges jazz education conferences and competitions for young jazz groups; encourages co-operation among national societies. Mems: national organizations and individuals in 24 countries. Pres. Arnvid Meyer (Denmark); Exec. Dir Jan A. Byrczek. Publ. *Jazz Forum* (6 a year).

International Music Centre (Internationales Musikzentrum—IMZ): 1230 Vienna, Speisinger Str. 121–127, Austria; tel. (1) 889-03-15; fax (1) 889-03-15-77; e-mail imz@magnet.at; internet http://www.imz.magnet.at/imz; f. 1961 for the study and dissemination of music through the technical media (film, television, radio, gramophone); organizes congresses, seminars and screenings on music in the audio-visual media; courses and competitions to strengthen the relationship between performing artists and the audio-visual media. Mems: 110 ordinary mems and 30 associate mems in 33 countries, including 50 broadcasting organizations. Pres. Avril Macrory (UK); Sec.-Gen. Franz A. Patay (Austria). Publ. *IMZ-Bulletin* (6 a year in English, French and German).

International Society for Contemporary Music: c/o Gaudeamus, Swammerdamstraat 38, 1091 RV Amsterdam, Netherlands; tel. 6947349; fax 6947258; f. 1922 to promote the development of contemporary music and to organize annual World Music Days. Member organizations in 48 countries. Pres. Arne Mellnas; Sec.-Gen. Henk Heuvelmans.

World Federation of International Music Competitions: 104 rue de Carouge, 1205 Geneva, Switzerland; tel. (22) 3213620; fax (22) 7811418; e-mail fmcim@iprolink.ch; f. 1957 to co-ordinate the arrangements for affiliated competitions, to exchange experience, etc.; a General Assembly is held every May. Mems: 107. Pres. Renate Ronnefeld; Sec.-Gen. Jacques Haldenwang.

International PEN (A World Association of Writers): 9–10 Charterhouse Bldgs, Goswell Rd, London, EC1M 7AT, United Kingdom; tel. (171) 253-4308; fax (171) 253-5711; e-mail intpen@gn.apc.org; f. 1921 to promote co-operation between writers. There are 130 centres throughout the world, with total membership about 13,500. International Pres. Ronald Harwood; International Sec. Alexandre Blokh. Publ. *PEN International* (2 a year in English, French and Spanish, with the assistance of UNESCO).

International Theatre Institute—ITI: Maison de l'UNESCO, 1 rue Miollis, 75732 Paris Cédex 15, France; tel. 1-45-68-26-50; fax 1-45-66-50-40; e-mail secretariat@iti-worldwide.org; internet http://iti-worldwide.org; f. 1948 to facilitate cultural exchanges and international understanding in the domain of the theatre; conferences, publications, etc. Mems: 87 member nations, each with an ITI national centre. Pres. Kim Jeong-Ok (Republic of Korea); Sec.-Gen. André-Louis Perinetti.

International Typographic Association: c/o Nordic Trade Centre, Eggerstedstrasse 13, 24103 Kiel, Germany; tel. (431) 97-406-23; fax (431) 97-83-67; f. 1957 to co-ordinate the ideas of those whose profession or interests are concerned with the art of typography and to obtain effective international legislation to protect type designs. Mems: 400 in 25 countries. Pres. Ernst-Erich Marhencke. Publs *TypoGraphic News* (quarterly), *Letter Letter* (2 or 3 times a year), *Journal of Typographic Metaphysics*.

Pan-African Writers' Association: POB C450, Cantonments, Accra, Ghana; tel. 773062; fax 773042; f. 1989 to link African creative writers, defend the rights of authors and promote awareness of literature. Sec.-Gen. Atukwei Okai (Ghana); Dep. Sec.-Gen. Mahamadu Traoré Diop (Senegal).

Royal Asiatic Society of Great Britain and Ireland: 60 Queen's Gardens, London, W2 3AF, United Kingdom; tel. (171) 724-4742; f. 1823 for the study of history and cultures of the East. Mems: c. 1,000, branch societies in Asia. Dir P. M. Vaughan; Sec. L. Collins. Publ. *Journal* (3 a year).

Society of African Culture: 25 bis rue des Ecoles, 75005 Paris, France; tel. 1-43-54-15-88; fax 1-43-25-96-67; f. 1956 to create unity and friendship among scholars in Africa for the encouragement of their own cultures. Mems: national asscns and individuals in 44 countries and territories. Pres. Aimé Césaire; Sec.-Gen. Christiane Yandé Diop. Publ. *La Revue Présence Africaine* (2 a year).

United Towns Organization: 22 rue d'Alsace, 92532 Levallois-Perret Cédex, France; tel. 1-47-39-36-86; telex 610472; fax 1-47-39-36-85; f. 1957 by Le Monde Bilingue (f. 1951); aims to set up permanent links between towns throughout the world, leading to social, cultural, economic and other exchanges favouring world peace, understanding and development; involved in sustainable development and environmental activities at municipal level; mem. of the Habitat II follow-up group. Mems: 4,000 local and regional authorities throughout the world. World Pres. Daby Diagne; Dir-Gen. Michel Bescond. Publs *Cités Unies* (quarterly, French, English and Spanish), *UTO News* (6 a year in English, French, German, Italian and Spanish).

World Crafts Council: 19 Race Course Ave, Colombo 7, Sri Lanka; tel. (1) 695831; fax (1) 692554; f. 1964; aims to strengthen the status of crafts as a vital part of cultural life, to link crafts people around the world, and to foster wider recognition of their work. Mems: national organizations in more than 80 countries. Pres. Siva Obeyesekere. Publs *Annual Report, Newsletter* (2 a year).

Commodities

African Groundnut Council: Trade Fair Complex, Badagry Expressway Km 15, POB 3025, Lagos, Nigeria; tel. (1) 880982; telex 21366; fax (1) 880982; f. 1964 to advise producing countries on marketing policies. Mems: The Gambia, Mali, Niger, Nigeria, Senegal, Sudan. Chair. E. T. Ibanga (Nigeria); Exec. Sec. Elhadj Mour Mamadou Samb (Senegal). Publ. *Groundnut Review*.

African Oil Palm Development Association—AFOPDA: 15 BP 341, Abidjan 15, Côte d'Ivoire; tel. 25-15-18; f. 1985; seeks to increase production of, and investment in, palm oil. Mems: Benin, Cameroon, Democratic Republic of the Congo, Côte d'Ivoire, Ghana, Guinea, Nigeria, Togo. Exec. Sec. Baudelaire Sourou.

African Petroleum Producers' Association: POB 1097, Brazzaville, Republic of the Congo; tel. 83-64-63; telex 5552; fax 83-67-99; f. 1987 by African petroleum-producing countries to reinforce co-operation among regional producers and to stabilize prices; council of ministers responsible for the hydrocarbons sector meets every two years. Mems: Algeria, Angola, Benin, Cameroon, Democratic Republic of the Congo, Republic of the Congo, Côte d'Ivoire, Egypt, Equatorial Guinea, Gabon, Libya, Nigeria. Publ. *APPA Bulletin* (2 a year).

Asian and Pacific Coconut Community: POB 1343, 3rd Floor, Lina Bldg, Jalan H. R. Rasuna Said Kav. B7., Kuningan, Jakarta 10002, Indonesia; tel. (21) 5221712; telex 62209; fax (21) 5221714; e-mail apcc@indo.net.id; internet http://www.apcc.org.sg; f. 1969 to promote, co-ordinate, and harmonize all activities of the coconut industry towards better production, processing, marketing and research. Mems: Fiji, India, Indonesia, Malaysia, Federated States of Micronesia, Papua New Guinea, Philippines, Samoa, Solomon Islands, Sri Lanka, Thailand, Vanuatu, Viet Nam; assoc. mem.: Palau. Exec. Dir P. G. Punchihewa. Publs *Cocomunity* (2 a month), *CORD* (2 a year), *Statistical Yearbook, Cocoinfo International* (2 a year).

Association of Coffee Producing Countries: Suite B, 5th Floor, 7/10 Old Park Lane, London, W1Y 3LJ, United Kingdom; tel. (171) 493-4790; fax (171) 355-1690; f. 1993; aims to co-ordinate policies of coffee production and to co-ordinate the efforts of producer countries to secure a stable situation in the world coffee market. Mems 28 African, Asian and Latin American countries. Pres. Ambassador Rubens Antônio Barbosa (Brazil); Sec.-Gen. Robério Oliveira Silva.

Association of Natural Rubber Producing Countries—ANRPC: Bangunan Getah Asli, 148 Jalan Ampang, 7th Floor, 50450 Kuala Lumpur, Malaysia; tel. (3) 2611900; telex 30953; fax (3) 2613014; f. 1970 to co-ordinate the production and marketing of natural rubber, to promote technical co-operation amongst members and to bring about fair and stable prices for natural rubber. A joint regional marketing system has been agreed in principle. Seminars, meetings and training courses on technical and statistical subjects are held. Mems: India, Indonesia, Malaysia, Papua New Guinea, Singapore, Sri Lanka, Thailand. Sec.-Gen. J. Lalithambika; Publs *Quarterly Statistical Bulletin, ANRPC News*.

Association of Tin Producing Countries (ATPC): Menara Dayabumi, 4th Floor, Jalan Sultan Hishamuddin, 50050 Kuala Lumpur, Malaysia; tel. (3) 2747620; telex 32721; fax (3) 2740669; f. 1983; promotes co-operation in marketing of tin, supports research, compiles and analyses data. Mems: Bolivia, People's Republic of China, Democratic Republic of the Congo, Indonesia, Malaysia, Nigeria; observer: Brazil.

Cocoa Producers' Alliance: POB 1718, Western House, 8–10 Broad St, Lagos, Nigeria; tel. (1) 2635506; telex 28288; fax (1) 2635684; f. 1962 to exchange technical and scientific information; to discuss problems of mutual concern to producers; to ensure adequate supplies at remunerative prices; to promote consumption. Mems: Brazil, Cameroon, Côte d'Ivoire, Dominican Republic, Ecuador, Gabon, Ghana, Malaysia, Nigeria, São Tomé and Príncipe, Togo, Trinidad and Tobago. Sec.-Gen. Djeumo Silas Kamga.

Common Fund for Commodities: Postbus 74656, 1070 BR, Amsterdam, Netherlands; tel. (20) 575-4949; telex 12331; fax (20) 676-0231; e-mail 106202.241@compuserve.com; f. 1989 as the result of an UNCTAD agreement; provides financial support for international buffer stocks and internationally co-ordinated national stocks (through its first account) and finances commodity development measures (through its second account), such as research, marketing, productivity improvements and vertical diversification, with the aim of increasing the long-term competitiveness of particular commodities; paid-in capital US $174.5m. Mems 103 countries and the EU. Man. Dir (also Chief Exec. and Chair.) Rolf Boehake.

European Aluminium Association: 12 ave de Broqueville, 1150 Brussels, Belgium; tel. (2) 755-63-11; fax (2) 779-05-31; f. 1981 to encourage studies, research and technical co-operation, to make representations to international bodies and to assist national associations in dealing with national authorities. Mems: individual producers of primary aluminium, 16 national groups for wrought producers, the Organization of European Aluminium Smelters, representing producers of secondary aluminium, and the European Aluminium Foil Association, representing foil rollers and converters. Sec.-Gen. DICK DERMER. Publs *Annual Report, EAA Quarterly Report*.

European Association for the Trade in Jute and Related Products: Adriaan Goekooplaan 5, 2517 JX The Hague, Netherlands; tel. (70) 354-68-11; fax (70) 351-27-77; f. 1970 to maintain contacts between national associations and carry out scientific research; to exchange information and to represent the interests of the trade. Mems: enterprises in Belgium, Denmark, France, Germany, Italy, Netherlands, Spain, Sweden, Switzerland, United Kingdom. Sec.-Gen. H. J. J. KRUIPER.

European Committee of Sugar Manufacturers: 182 ave de Tervueren, 1150 Brussels, Belgium; tel. (2) 762-07-60; fax (2) 771-00-26; e-mail cefs@infoboard.be; f. 1954 to collect statistics and information, conduct research and promote co-operation between national organizations. Mems: national associations in Austria, Belgium, Denmark, Finland, France, Germany, Greece, Ireland, Italy, Netherlands, Portugal, Spain, Sweden, Switzerland, United Kingdom. Pres. RENATO PICCO; Dir-Gen. JULES BEAUDUIN.

Group of Latin American and Caribbean Sugar Exporting Countries—GEPLACEA: Ejército Nacional 373, 1°, 11520 México DF, Mexico; tel. (5) 250-7566; telex 01771042; fax (5) 250-7591; f. 1974 to serve as a forum of consultation on the production and sale of sugar; to contribute to the adoption of agreed positions at international meetings on sugar; to provide training and the transfer of technology; to exchange scientific and technical knowledge on agriculture and the sugar industry; to co-ordinate the various branches of sugar processing; to co-ordinate policies of action in order to achieve fair and remunerative prices. Mems: 23 Latin American and Caribbean countries (accounting for about 45% of world sugar exports and 66% of world cane sugar production). Exec. Sec. LUIS CUSTODIO COTTA.

Inter-African Coffee Organization—IACO: BP V210, Abidjan, Côte d'Ivoire; tel. 21-61-31; telex 22406; fax 21-62-12; f. 1960 to adopt a common policy on the marketing of coffee; aims to collaborate on research and improvement in the quality of exports. Mems: 25 coffee-producing countries in Africa. Pres. Dr ABEL RWENDEIRE, (Uganda); Sec.-Gen. AREGA WORKU (Ethiopia). Publs temporarily suspended.

International Cadmium Association: 42 Weymouth St, London, W1N 3LQ, United Kingdom; tel. (171) 499-8425; telex 261286; fax (171) 486-4007; f. 1976; covers all aspects of the production and use of cadmium and its compounds; includes almost all producers and users of cadmium outside the USA. Chair. JEAN FEUILLAT (Belgium); Dir J. K. ATHERTON (UK).

International Cocoa Organization—ICCO: 22 Berners St, London, W1P 3DB, United Kingdom; tel. (171) 637-3211; telex 28173; fax (171) 631-0114; f. 1973 under the first International Cocoa Agreement, 1972 (renewed in 1975 and 1980; the fourth agreement entered into force in January 1987; it was extended, without its economic clauses, for two years from October 1990, and again to 30 September 1993). ICCO supervises the implementation of the agreement, and provides member governments with conference facilities and up-to-date information on the world cocoa economy and the operation of the agreement (price-stabilizing activities were suspended in March 1990). Negotiations on a fifth agreement were concluded in July 1993, under the auspices of UNCTAD, which came into force in February 1994. Exec. Dir EDOUARD KOUAMÉ (Côte d'Ivoire); Council Chair. 1997/98 TIM MORDAN (UK). Publs *Quarterly Bulletin of Cocoa Statistics, Annual Report, World Cocoa Directory, Cocoa Newsletter*, studies on the world cocoa economy.

International Coffee Organization: 22 Berners St, London, W1P 4DD, United Kingdom; tel. (171) 580-8591; telex 267659; fax (171) 580-6129; e-mail library@intercaf.win-uk.net; internet http://www.ico.org; f. 1963 under the International Coffee Agreement, 1962, which was renegotiated in 1968, 1976, 1983 and 1994. The objectives of the 1994 Agreement are to improve international co-operation and provide a forum for intergovernmental consultations on coffee matters; to facilitate international trade in coffee by the collection, analysis and dissemination of statistics; to act as a centre for the collection, exchange and publication of coffee information; to promote studies in the field of coffee; and to encourage an increase in coffee consumption. Mems: 48 exporting and 18 importing countries. Chair. of Council FERNANDO MONTES (Honduras); Exec. Dir CELSIUS A. LODDER (Brazil).

International Confederation of European Sugar Beet Growers: 29 rue du Général Foy, 75008 Paris, France; tel. 1-44-69-41-80; fax 1-42-93-28-93; f. 1925 to act as a centre for the co-ordination and dissemination of information about beet sugar production and the industry; to represent the interests of sugar beet growers at an international level. Member associations in Austria, Belgium, Czech Republic, Denmark, Finland, France, Germany, Greece, Hungary, Ireland, Italy, Netherlands, Poland, Slovakia, Spain, Sweden, Switzerland, United Kingdom. Pres. D. DUCROQUET (France); Sec.-Gen. H. CHAVANES (France).

International Cotton Advisory Committee: 1629 K St, NW, Suite 702, Washington, DC 20006, USA; tel. (202) 463-6660; telex 408272789; fax (202) 463-6950; e-mail secretariat@icac.org; f. 1939 to observe developments affecting the world cotton situation; to collect and disseminate statistics; to suggest to the governments represented any measures for the furtherance of international collaboration in maintaining and developing a sound world cotton economy; and to provide a forum for international discussions on cotton prices. Mems: 40 countries. Exec. Dir Dr LAWRENCE H. SHAW. Publs *Cotton: Review of the World Situation, Cotton: World Statistics, The ICAC Recorder*.

International Grains Council: 1 Canada Sq., Canary Wharf, London, E14 5AE, United Kingdom; tel. (171) 513-1122; fax (171) 513-0630; f. 1949 as International Wheat Council, present name adopted in 1995; responsible for the administration of the Grains Trade Convention of the International Grains Agreement, 1995; aims to further international co-operation in all aspects of trade in grains, to promote international trade in grains, and to secure the freest possible flow of this trade in the interests of members, particularly developing member countries; and to contribute to the stability of the international grain market; acts as forum for consultations between members, and provides comprehensive information on the international grain market and factors affecting it. Mems: 32 countries and the EU. Exec. Dir. G. DENIS. Publs *World Grain Statistics* (annually), *Wheat and Coarse Grain Shipments* (annually), *Report for the Fiscal Year* (annually), *Grain Market Report* (monthly).

International Jute Organization—IJO: 145 Monipuriparu, Old Airport Rd, Dhaka 1215, Bangladesh; tel. (2) 9125581; fax (2) 9125248; f. 1984 in accordance with an agreement made by 48 producing and consuming countries in 1982, under the auspices of UNCTAD (new agreement negotiated in 1989, to expire in April 2000); aims to improve the jute economy and the quality of jute and jute products through research and development projects and market promotion. Mems: five exporting and 20 importing countries, as well as the European Union. Exec. Dir K. M. RABBANI (Bangladesh); Dir HENRI L. JASON (France). Publ. *Jute* (quarterly).

International Lead and Zinc Study Group: 2 King St, London, SW1Y 6OP, United Kingdom; tel. (171) 839-8550; telex 299819; fax (171) 930-4635; e-mail 2542@compuserve.com; f. 1959, for intergovernmental consultation on world trade in lead and zinc; conducts studies and provides information on trends in supply and demand. Mems: 32 countries. Chair. T. TOBIN (Ireland); Sec.-Gen. F. LABRO. Publ. *Lead and Zinc Statistics* (monthly).

International Molybdenum Association: Unit 7, Hackford Walk, 119–123 Hackford Rd, London, SW9 0QT, United Kingdom; tel. (171) 582-2777; fax (171) 582-0556; f. 1989; collates statistics, promotes the use of molybdenum, monitors health and environmental issues. Pres. U. KRYNITZ; Sec.-Gen. MICHAEL MABY.

International Natural Rubber Organization—INRO: POB 10374, 50712 Kuala Lumpur, Malaysia; tel. (3) 2486466; telex 31570; fax (3) 2486485; f. 1980 to stabilize natural rubber prices by operating a buffer stock, and to seek to ensure an adequate supply, under the International Natural Rubber Agreement (1979), which entered into force in April 1982, and was extended for two years in 1985; a second agreement came into effect in 1988, to expire in Dec. 1993 but was extended to Dec. 1995; a third agreement was adopted in Feb. 1995. Mems: 21 importing countries (including the European Union) and six exporting countries (Côte d'Ivoire, Indonesia, Malaysia, Nigeria, Sri Lanka and Thailand). Exec. Dir PONG SONO (Thailand).

International Olive Oil Council: Principe de Vergara 154, 28002 Madrid, Spain; tel. (91) 5630071; fax (91) 5631263; e-mail iooc@mad.servicom.es; f. 1959 to administer the International Agreement on Olive Oil and Table Olives, which aims to promote international co-operation in connection with problems of the world economy for olive products; to prevent unfair competition; to encourage the production and consumption of, and international trade in, olive products, and to reduce the disadvantages due to fluctuations of supplies on the market. Mems: of the 1986 Agreement (Fourth Agreement, amended and extended in 1993): eight mainly producing countries, one mainly importing country, and the European Commission. Dir FAUSTO LUCHETTI. Publs *Information Sheet of the IOOC* (fortnightly, French and Spanish), *OLIVAE* (5 a year, in English, French, Italian and Spanish), *National Policies for Olive Products* (annually).

International Pepper Community: 4th Floor, Lina Bldg, Jalan H. R. Rasuna Said, Kav. B7, Kuningan, Jakarta 12920, Indonesia; tel. (21) 5224902; fax (21) 5224905; e-mail ipc@indo.net.id; f. 1972 for promoting pepper and co-ordinating activities relating to the pepper economy, with a view to achieving optimum economic development. Mems: Brazil, India, Indonesia, Malaysia, Federated States of Micronesia, Sri Lanka, Thailand. Exec. Dir Dr S. N. DARWIS. Publs *Pepper Statistical Yearbook, International Pepper News* (quarterly), *Directory of Pepper Exporters, Weekly Prices Bulletin.*

International Platinum Association: 60313 Frankfurt-am-Main, Kroegerstr. 5, Germany; tel. (69) 287941; fax (69) 283601; links principal producers and fabricators of platinum. Pres. EDWARD HASLAM; Man. Dir MARCUS NURDIN.

International Rubber Study Group: 8th Floor, York House, Empire Way, Wembley, HA9 0PA, United Kingdom; tel. (181) 903-7727; fax (181) 903-2848; f. 1944 to provide a forum for the discussion of problems affecting synthetic and natural rubber and to provide statistical and other general information on rubber. Mems: 20 governments. Sec.-Gen. M. E. CAIN. Publs *Rubber Statistical Bulletin* (monthly), *International Rubber Digest* (monthly), *Proceedings of International Rubber Forums* (annually), *World Rubber Statistics Handbook, Key Rubber Indicators, Rubber Statistics Yearbook* (annually), *Outlook for Elastomers* (annually).

International Silk Association: 34 rue de la Charité, 69002 Lyon, France; tel. 4-78-42-10-79; fax 4-78-37-56-72; f. 1949 to promote closer collaboration between all branches of the silk industry and trade, develop the consumption of silk and foster scientific research; collects and disseminates information and statistics relating to the trade and industry; organizes biennial Congresses. Mems: employers' and technical organizations in 40 countries. Pres. ADOLF FAES (Switzerland); Gen. Sec. R. CURRIE. Publs *ISA Newsletter* (monthly), congress reports, standards, trade rules, etc.

International Spice Group: c/o Commonwealth Secretariat, Marlborough House, Pall Mall, London, SW1Y 5HX, United Kingdom; tel. (171) 839-3411; telex 27678; fax (171) 930-0827; f. 1983 to provide forum for producers and consumers of spices, and to attempt to increase the consumption of spices; under arrangement adopted in 1991 (subject to acceptance by member govts), secretariat services were to be transferred to the International Trade Centre (UNCTAD/WTO). Mems: 33 producer countries, 15 importing countries. Chair. HERNAL HAMILTON (Jamaica).

International Sugar Organization: 1 Canada Sq., Canary Wharf, London, E14 5AA, United Kingdom; tel. (171) 513-1144; fax (171) 513-1146; e-mail iso@sugar.org.uk.; administers the International Sugar Agreement (1992); the agreement does not include measures for stabilizing markets. Mems: 50 countries. Exec. Dir Dr P. BARON. Publs *Sugar Year Book, Monthly Statistical Bulletin, Market Report and Press Summary, Quarterly Market Review.*

International Tea Committee Ltd: Sir John Lyon House, 5 High Timber St, London, EC4V 3NH, United Kingdom; tel. (171) 248-4672; fax (171) 329-6955; f. 1933 to administer the International Tea Agreement; now serves as a statistical and information centre; in 1979 membership was extended to include consuming countries. Producer Mems: national tea boards or associations of Bangladesh, India, Indonesia, Japan, Kenya, Malawi, Sri Lanka, Zimbabwe; Consumer Mems: United Kingdom Tea Assn, Tea Assn of the USA Inc., Comité Européen du Thé and the Tea Council of Canada; Assoc. Mems: Netherlands and UK ministries of agriculture, Cameroon Development Corpn. Chair. M. J. BUNSTON; Chief Exec. Sec. PETER ABEL. Publs *Bulletin of Statistics* (annually), *Statistical Summary* (monthly).

International Tea Promotion Association: POB 20064, Tea Board of Kenya, Nairobi, Kenya; tel. (2) 220241; telex 987-22190; fax (2) 331650; f. 1979. Mems: eight countries (Bangladesh, Indonesia, Kenya, Malawi, Mauritius, Mozambique, Tanzania, Uganda). Pres. GEORGE M. KIMANI; Liaison Officer NGOIMA WA MWAURA. Publ. *International Tea Journal* (2 a year).

International Tobacco Growers' Association: POB 125, East Grinstead, West Sussex, RH18 5FA, United Kingdom; tel. (1342) 823549; fax (1342) 825502; f. 1984 to provide forum for the exchange of views and information of interest to tobacco producers. Mems: 17 countries producing over 80% of the world's internationally traded tobacco. Pres. ALBERT JOHNSON (USA); Chief Exec. DAVID WALDER (UK).

International Tropical Timber Organization: International Organizations Center, 5th Floor, Pacifico-Yokohama, 1-1-1, Minato-Mirai, Nishi-ku, Yokohama 220, Japan; tel. (45) 223-1110; fax (45) 223-1111; f. 1985 under the International Tropical Timber Agreement (1983); a new treaty, ITTA 1994, came into force in 1997; provides forum for consultation and co-operation between countries that produce and consume tropical timber, in order to strike a balance between utilization and conservation; facilitates progress towards 'the objective for the year 2000' (all trade in tropical timber to be derived from sustainably managed resources by the year 2000); promotes research and development, reforestation and forest management, further processing of tropical timber in producing countries, and establishment of market intelligence and economic information; no economic provision is made for price stabilization. Mems: 25 producing and 21 consuming countries and the EU. Exec. Dir Dr FREEZAILAH BIN CHE YEOM (Malaysia).

International Tungsten Industry Association: Unit 7, Hackford Walk, 119–123 Hackford Rd, London, SW9 0QT, United Kingdom; tel. (171) 582-2777; fax (171) 582-0556; f. 1988 (fmrly Primary Tungsten Asscn, f. 1975); promotes use of tungsten, collates statistics, prepares market reports, monitors health and environmental issues. Mems: 56. Pres. P. KÄHLERT; Sec.-Gen. MICHAEL MABY.

International Vine and Wine Office: 18 rue d'Aguesseau, 75008 Paris, France; tel. 1-44-94-80-80; telex 281196; fax 1-42-66-90-63; e-mail 101675.2013@compuserve.com; f. 1924 to study all the scientific, technical, economic and human problems concerning the vine and its products; to spread knowledge by means of its publications; to assist contacts between researchers and establish international research programmes. Mems: 46 countries. Dir-Gen. GEORGES DUTRUC-ROSSET. Publs *Bulletin de l'OIV* (every 2 months), *Lettre de l'OIV* (monthly), *Lexique de la Vigne et du Vin, Recueil des méthodes internationales d'analyse des vins, Code international des Pratiques oenologiques, Codex oenologique international,* numerous scientific publications.

IWS International Pty Ltd: Wool House, 369 Royal Parade, Parkville, Victoria, 3052 Australia; tel. (3) 9341-9111; fax (3) 9341-9273; internet http://www.wool.com.au; f. 1937 as the International Wool Secretariat; operates globally to build demand for wool on behalf of member states. Activities include wool product marketing; process technology and product development; technical servicing; quality control and economic and market research. IWS owns and licences Woolmark, a symbol of quality in pure wool products. Mems: branches or offices in 34 countries. Chair ALEC MORRISON.

Lead Development Association International: 42 Weymouth St, London, W1N 3LQ, United Kingdom; tel. (171) 499-8422; telex 261286; fax (171) 493-1555; f. 1954; provides authoritative information on the use of lead and its compounds; maintains a library and abstracting service in collaboration with the Zinc Development Association (see below). Financed by lead producers and users in the United Kingdom, Europe and elsewhere. Dir Dr D. N. WILSON (UK).

Mutual Assistance of the Latin American Government Oil Companies (Asistencia Recíproca Petrolera Estatal Latinoamericana—ARPEL): Javier de Viana 2345, Casilla de correo 1006, 11200 Montevideo, Uruguay; tel. (2) 406993; telex 22560; fax (2) 409207; f. 1965 to study and recommend the implementation of mutually beneficial agreements among members in order to promote technical and economic development; to further Latin American integration; to promote the interchange of technical assistance and information; to plan congresses, lectures, and meetings concerning the oil industry. Mems: state enterprises in Argentina, Bolivia, Brazil, Canada, Chile, Colombia, Costa Rica, Cuba, Ecuador, Jamaica, Mexico, Nicaragua, Paraguay, Peru, Suriname, Trinidad and Tobago, Uruguay, Venezuela. Sec.-Gen. ANDRÉS TIERNO ABREU. Publ. *Boletín Técnico.*

Sugar Association of the Caribbean (Inc.): 80 Abercromby St, Port of Spain, Trinidad; tel. 636-2311; fax 636-2847; f. 1942. Mems: national sugar cos of Barbados, Belize, Guyana, Jamaica and Trinidad and Tobago, and Sugar Asscn of St Kitts–Nevis–Anguilla. Chair. KARL JAMES; Sec. A. MOHAMMED. Publs *SAC Handbook, SAC Annual Report, Proceedings of Meetings of WI Sugar Technologists.*

Union of Banana-Exporting Countries—UPEB: Apdo 4273, Bank of America, piso 7, Panamá 5, Panama; tel. 636266; telex 2468; fax 648355; e-mail iicapan@pan.gbm.net; f. 1974 as an intergovernmental agency to assist the cultivation and marketing of bananas and secure prices; collects statistics and compiles bibliographies. Mems: Colombia, Costa Rica, Guatemala, Honduras, Nicaragua, Panama, Venezuela. Exec. Dir J. ENRIQUE BETANCOURT. Publs *Informe UPEB, Fax UPEB, Anuario de Estadísticas,* bibliographies.

West Africa Rice Development Association—WARDA: 01 BP 2551 Bouaké 01, Côte d'Ivoire; tel. 63-45-14; telex 69138; fax 63-47-14; e-mail warda@cgnet.com; f. 1970; undertakes research on rice for West Africa; maintains research stations in Côte d'Ivoire, Nigeria and Senegal; provides training and consulting services; revenue: US $9.4m. in 1996. WARDA is a member of the network of agricultural research centres supported by the World Bank's Consultative Group on International Agricultural Research (CGIAR, q.v.). Mems: Benin, Burkina Faso, Cameroon, Chad, Côte d'Ivoire, The Gambia, Ghana, Guinea, Guinea-Bissau, Liberia, Mali, Mauritania, Niger, Nigeria, Senegal, Sierra Leone, Togo. Dir-Gen. Dr KANAYO F. NWANZE (Nigeria); Exec. Asst P.-JUSTIN KOUKA. Publs *Annual Report, Directory of Rice Scientists in West Africa, Current Contents at WARDA* (monthly).

West Indian Sea Island Cotton Association (Inc.): c/o Barbados Agricultural Development Corporation, Fairy Valley, Christ Church, Barbados. Mems: organizations in Antigua-Barbuda, Barbados, Montserrat, St Christopher and Nevis, St Vincent and the Grenadines. Pres. E. LEROY WARD; Sec. MICHAEL I. EDGHILL.

World Federation of Diamond Bourses: 62 Pelikaanstraat, 2018 Antwerp, Belgium; tel. (3) 234-07-78; fax (3) 226-40-73; f. 1947 to protect the interests of affiliated organizations and their individual members and to settle or arbitrate in disputes. Mems: 21 bourses in 13 countries. Pres. E. IZHAKOFF (USA); Sec.-Gen. G. GOLDSCHMIDT (Belgium).

World Gold Council: 1 rue de la Rôtisserie, 1204 Geneva, Switzerland; tel. (22) 3119666; fax (22) 3108160; internet http://www.gold.org; f. 1987 as worldwide international association of gold producers, to promote the demand for gold. Chair. D. M. MORLEY; CEO ELLIOT M. HOOD.

Zinc Development Association: 42 Weymouth St, London, W1N 3LQ, United Kingdom; tel. (171) 499-6636; telex 261286; fax (171) 493-1555; provides authoritative advice on the uses of zinc, its alloys and its compounds; maintains a library in collaboration with the Lead Development Association (q.v.). Affiliate: Zinc Pigment Development Association. Financed by zinc producers and users in Europe and North America. Chair. J. SOUTHERN (UK).

Development and Economic Co-operation

African Capacity Building Foundation: Southampton Life Centre, 7th Floor, Jason Moyo Ave/Second St, POB 1562, Harare, Zimbabwe; tel. (4) 738520; fax (4) 702915; f. 1991 by the World Bank, UNDP, the African Development Bank, African and non-African governments; assists African countries to strengthen and build local capacity in economic policy analysis and development management. Exec. Sec. ABEL L. THOAHLANE.

African Training and Research Centre in Administration for Development (Centre africain de formation et de recherche administratives pour le développement—CAFRAD): ave Mohamed V, BP 310, Tangier, 90001 Morocco; tel. 942652; fax 941415; e-mail cafradt@mail.sis.net.ma; f. 1964 by agreement between Morocco and UNESCO; undertakes research into administrative problems in Africa, documentation of results, provision of a consultation service for governments and organizations; holds frequent seminars. Mems: 26 African countries. Pres. MESSAOUD MANSOURI; Dir-Gen. Dr MOHAMED AHMED WALI. Publs *African Administrative Studies* (2 a year), *Directory of African Consultants, CAFRAD News* (2 a year, in English, French and Arabic).

Afro-Asian Rural Reconstruction Organization—AARRO: No. 2, State Guest Houses Complex, Chanakyapuri, New Delhi 110 021, India; tel. (11) 6877783; telex 72326; fax (11) 6115937; e-mail aarrohq@hub.nic.in; f. 1962 to act as a catalyst for co-operative restructuring of rural life in Africa and Asia; and to explore collectively opportunities for co-ordination of efforts for promoting welfare and eradicating hunger, thirst, disease, illiteracy and poverty among the rural people. Activities include collaborative research on development issues; training; the exchange of information; international conferences and seminars; and awarding 100 individual training fellowships at nine institutes in Egypt, India, Japan, the Republic of Korea and Taiwan. Mems: 11 African, 14 Asian countries, and one African associate. Sec.-Gen. Dr BAHAR MUNIP. Publs *Annual Report, Journal of Rural Reconstruction, Rural Reconstruction* (2 a year), *AARRO Newsletter* (4 a year).

Agence de coopération culturelle et technique: 13 quai André Citroën, 75015 Paris, France: tel. 1-44-37-33-00; telex 201916; fax 1-45-79-14-98; f. 1970; promotes co-operation among French-speaking countries in the areas of education, culture, science and technology. Technical and financial assistance has been given to projects in every member country, mainly to aid rural people. Mems: 44 countries and territories. Sec.-Gen. JEAN-LOUIS ROY (Canada). Publs *Lettre de la Francophonie* (monthly), *AGECOP Liaison* (6 a year).

Amazonian Co-operation Council: Avda Prolongación Primavera 654, Chacarilla, Lima 33, Peru; tel. (1) 449-9084; fax (1) 449-8718; f. 1978 by signature of the Amazon Region Co-operation Treaty; aims to promote the harmonious development of the Amazon territories of signatory countries; Lima Declaration on Sustainable Development signed by ministers of foreign affairs in December 1995. Mems: Bolivia, Brazil, Colombia, Ecuador, Guyana, Peru, Suriname, Venezuela.

Arab Authority for Agricultural Investment and Development—AAAID: POB 2102, Khartoum, Sudan; tel. 773752; telex 23017; fax 772600; f. 1976 to accelerate agricultural development in the Arab world and to ensure food security; acts principally by equity participation in agricultural projects in Iraq, Sudan and Tunisia; authorized capital US $ 501.8m., paid-in capital US $ 334.6m. (Dec. 1995). Mems: Algeria, Egypt, Iraq, Jordan, Kuwait, Mauritania, Morocco, Oman, Qatar, Saudi Arabia, Somalia, Sudan, Syria, Tunisia, United Arab Emirates. Pres. YOUSIF ABDAL LATIF ALSERKAL. Publ. *Annual Report.*

Arab Co-operation Council: Amman, Jordan; f. 1989 to promote economic co-operation between member states, including free movement of workers, joint projects in transport, communications and agriculture, and eventual integration of trade and monetary policies. Mems: Egypt, Iraq, Jordan, Yemen. Sec.-Gen. HELMI NAMRAR (Egypt).

Arab Fund for Economic and Social Development—AFESD: POB 21923, Safat, 13080 Kuwait; tel. 4844500; telex 22153; fax 4815750; f. 1968; participates in the financing of economic and social development projects in Arab states by issuing loans on concessional terms to governments and public or private institutions; by encouraging directly or indirectly the investment of public and private capital in projects consistent with development; and by providing technical assistance in the various fields of economic development. The Fund's authorized capital amounts to 800m. Kuwaiti dinars (KD); at the end of 1996 paid-up capital was KD 663.04m; loans approved during 1996 totalled KD 266.4m. Mems: 21 Arab countries. Dir-Gen. and Chair. of Bd of Dirs ABDLATIF YOUSOUF AL-HAMAD.

Arab Gulf Programme for the United Nations Development Organizations—AGFUND: POB 18371, Riyadh 11415, Saudi Arabia; tel. (1) 4416240; fax (1) 4412963; e-mail agfund@khaleej.net.bh; f. 1981 to provide grants for projects in mother and child care carried out by United Nations organizations, Arab non-governmental organizations and other international bodies, and co-ordinate assistance by the nations of the Gulf; financing comes mainly from member states, all of which are members of OPEC. Mems: Bahrain, Iraq, Kuwait, Oman, Qatar, Saudi Arabia, UAE. Pres. HRH Prince TALAL IBN ABD AL-AZIZ AL-SAUD.

Arab Monetary Fund: POB 2818, Abu Dhabi, United Arab Emirates; tel. 215000; telex 22989; fax 326454; f. 1977 to encourage Arab economic integration and development, by assisting member states' balance of payments, co-ordinating their monetary policies, and promoting stability of exchange rates. The Fund provides loans, loan guarantees and technical assistance; its unit of account is the Arab Accounting Dinar (AAD), equivalent to three IMF Special Drawing Rights. Authorized capital AAD 600m., subscribed capital AAD 326m. and paid-up capital AAD 323.8m. (Dec. 1995); loans in 1995 amounted to AAD 25.62m. Mems: 20 Arab countries. Dir-Gen. Dr JASSM AL-MANNAI.

Arab Trade Financing Program (ATFP): POB 26799, Abu Dhabi, United Arab Emirates; tel. (2) 316999; telex 24166; fax (2) 316793; e-mail iatinhq@emirates.net.ae; f. 1989 to develop and promote trade among Arab countries and to enhance the competitive ability of Arab exporters; operates by extending lines of credit to 83 national agencies (designated by the monetary authorities of 18 Arab countries) for exports and imports. The ATFP's authorized capital is US $500m. The ATFP is working on the establishment of an Inter-Arab Trade Information Network. Chief Exec. and Chair. Dr JASSIM A. AL -MANNAI.

Association of Caribbean States—ACS: 11–13 Victoria Ave, POB 660, Port of Spain, Trinidad and Tobago; tel. 623-2782; fax 623-2679; e-mail acs-aec@trinidad.net; internet acs-aec.org; f. 1994 by the Governments of the 13 CARICOM countries (q.v.) and Colombia, Costa Rica, Cuba, the Dominican Republic, El Salvador, Guatemala, Haiti, Honduras, Mexico, Nicaragua, Suriname and Venezuela. Aims to promote economic integration and co-operation in the region; to co-ordinate participation in multilateral forums; to undertake concerted action to protect the environment, particularly the Caribbean Sea; and to co-operate in the areas of science and technology, health, transport, education and culture. Policy is determined by a Council of Ministers and implemented by a Secretariat based in Port of Spain, Trinidad and Tobago. The Third Ordinary Meeting of the Council of Ministers was held in Cartagena de Indias, Colombia, in November 1997. The meeting approved the objectives for 1998, which included the establishment of a Sustainable Tourist Zone, the development of a programme to link both air and sea transport within the region, and the creation of a facility to provide assistance in the event of natural disasters. The establishment of a special fund to support technical co-operation projects was also approved. In addition to the 25 signatory states there are 2 associate members, while a further 13 countries have observer status. Sec.-Gen. SIMÓN MOLINA-DUARTE.

Association of Development Financing Institutions in Asia and the Pacific—ADFIAP: Skyland Plaza, Sen. Gil J. Puyat Ave, City of Makati 1200, Metro Manila, Philippines; tel. (2) 816-1672; fax (2) 817-6498; e-mail opp@adfiap.globalden.com; f. 1976 to promote the interests and economic development of the respective countries of its member institutions, through development financing. Mems: 81 institutions in 35 countries. Chair. ASWIN KONGSIRI (Thailand); Sec.-Gen. ORLANDO P. PEÑA (Philippines). Publs *Asian Banking Digest, Journal of Development Finance* (2 a year), *ADFIAP Newsletter,* surveys.

Benelux Economic Union: 39 rue de la Régence, 1000 Brussels, Belgium; tel. (2) 519-38-11; fax (2) 513-42-06; f. 1960 to bring about the economic union of Belgium, Luxembourg and the Netherlands; aims to introduce common policies in the field of cross-border co-operation; structure comprises: Committee of Ministers; Council; Court of Justice; Consultative Inter-Parliamentary Council; the Economic and Social Advisory Council; and the General Secretariat;

Secs-Gen. B. M. J. HENNEKAM (Netherlands), MARIE-ROSE BERNA (Luxembourg), LUC VANDAMME (Belgium). Publs *Benelux Newsletter, Bulletin Benelux.*

Black Sea Economic Co-operation—BSEC: I Hareket Köşkü, Dolmabahçe Sarayı, Beşiktaş 80680, İstanbul, Turkey; tel. (212) 227-73-00; fax (212) 227-7306; f. 1992. Priority areas of activity: transport and communications; energy; environmental protection; tourism; trade and industrial co-operation; agriculture and agro-industry; health care and pharmaceutics; science and technology; banking and finance. There is a BSEC Business Council and a Black Sea Trade and Development Bank was to be established in Thessaloniki, Greece. Mems: Albania, Armenia, Azerbaijan, Bulgaria, Georgia, Greece, Moldova, Romania, Russia, Turkey, Ukraine; observers: Austria, Egypt, Israel, Italy, Poland, Slovakia, Tunisia. Dir YEVGENI KUTOVOI.

Caritas Internationalis (International Confederation of Catholic Organizations for charitable and social action): Palazzo San Calisto, 00120 Città del Vaticano; tel. (6) 69887197; fax (6) 69887237; e-mail ci.comm@caritas.va; f. 1950 to study problems arising from poverty, their causes and possible solutions; national member organizations undertake assistance and development activities. The Confederation co-ordinates emergency relief and development projects, and represents members at international level. Mems: 135 national organizations. Pres. Mgr AFFONSO GREGORY, Bishop of Imperatriz (Brazil); Sec.-Gen. LUC TROUILLARD. Publs. *Caritas Matters* (quarterly), *Emergency Calling* (2 a year).

Caribbean Council for Europe: Nelson House, 8/9 Northumberland St, London, WC2N 5RA, United Kingdom; tel. (171) 976-1493; telex 22914; fax (171) 976-1541; f. 1992 by the Caribbean Association of Industry and Commerce and other regional organizations, to represent the interests of the Caribbean private sector in the European Union; organizes regular Europe/Caribbean Conference. Chair. JOHN BOWERS.

Central European Free Trade Association: f. 1992, entered into force 1993; free-trade agreement covering a number of sectors. Mems: Czech Republic, Hungary, Poland, Slovakia, Slovenia.

Colombo Plan: 12 Melbourne Ave, Colombo 4, Sri Lanka; tel. (1) 581853; telex 21537; fax (1) 581754; f. 1950 by seven Commonwealth countries, to encourage economic and social development in Asia and the Pacific. The Plan comprises the Programme for Public Administration, to provide training for officials in the context of a market-orientated economy; the Programme for Private Sector Development, which organizes training programmes to stimulate the economic benefits of development of the private sector; a Drug Advisory Programme, to encourage regional co-operation in efforts to control drug-related problems, in particular through human resources development; a programme to establish a South-South Technical Co-operation Data Bank, to collate, analyse and publish information in order to facilitate south-south co-operation; and a Staff College for Technician Education (see below). All programmes are voluntarily funded; developing countries are encouraged to become donors and to participate in economic and technical co-operation activities among developing members. Publs *Annual Report,* Consultative Committee proceedings (every 2 years).

Colombo Plan Staff College for Technician Education: POB 7500, Domestic Airport Post Office, NAIA, Pasay City 1300, Metro Manila, Philippines; tel. (2) 6310991; fax (2) 6310996; e-mail cpscdir@sunl.dost.gov.ph; f. 1973 with the support of member Governments of the Colombo Plan; aims to enhance the development of technician education systems in developing member countries. Dir Dr BERNARDO F. ADIVISO. Publ. *CPSC Quarterly.*

Communauté économique des états de l'Afrique centrale—CEEAC (Economic Community of Central African States): BP 2112, Libreville, Gabon; tel. 73-35-48; telex 5480; f. 1983; operational 1 January 1985; aims to promote co-operation between member states by abolishing trade restrictions, establishing a common external customs tariff, linking commercial banks, and setting up a development fund, over a period of 12 years; combat drug abuse; and to promote regional security. Budget (1993): US $3.5m. Membership comprises the states belonging to UDEAC (q.v.), those belonging to the Economic Community of the Great Lakes Countries, and São Tomé and Príncipe. Sec.-Gen. KASASA MUTATI CHINYATA (Democratic Republic of the Congo).

Conference of Regions in North-West Europe: POB 107, 8000 Bruges 1, Belgium; f. 1955 to co-ordinate regional studies with a view to planned development in the area around the North Sea and in the Scheldt, Meuse and Rhine valleys; also compiles cartographical documents. Mems: individual scholars and representatives of planning offices in Belgium, France, Germany, Luxembourg, Netherlands and the United Kingdom. Pres. ANGUS MACMILLAN (UK); Sec.-Gen. Prof. I. B. F. KORMOSS (Belgium).

Conseil de l'Entente (Entente Council): 01 BP 3734, Abidjan 01, Côte d'Ivoire; tel. 33-28-35; telex 23558; fax 33-11-49; f. 1959 to promote economic development in the region. The Council's Mutual Aid and Loan Guarantee Fund (Fonds d'Entraide et de Garantie des Emprunts) finances development projects, including agricultural projects, support for small and medium-sized enterprises, vocational training centres, research into new sources of energy and building of hotels to encourage tourism. Fund budget (1992): 1,746m. francs CFA. Mems: Benin, Burkina Faso, Côte d'Ivoire, Niger, Togo. Administrative Sec. of Fund PAUL KAYA. Publs *Entente africaine* (quarterly), *Rapport d'activité* (annually).

Communauté économique du bétail et de la viande du Conseil de l'Entente (Livestock and Meat Economic Community of the Entente Council): BP 638 Ouagadougou, Burkina Faso; tel. (3) 30-62-66; telex 5329; f. 1970 to promote the production, processing and marketing of livestock and meat; negotiates between members and with third countries on technical and financial co-operation and co-ordinated legislation; attempts to co-ordinate measures to combat drought and cattle diseases. Mems: states belonging to the Conseil de l'Entente. Exec. Sec. Dr ELIE LADIKPO.

Council of American Development Foundations—SOLIDARIOS: Calle 6 No. 10 Paraiso, Apdo Postal 620, Santo Domingo, Dominican Republic; tel. (809) 549-5111; fax (809) 544-0550; f. 1972; exchanges information and experience, arranges technical assistance, raises funds to organize training programmes and scholarships; administers development fund to finance programmes carried out by members through a loan guarantee programme; provides consultancy services. Member foundations provide technical and financial assistance to low-income groups for rural, housing and microenterprise development projects. Mems: 28 institutional mems in 14 Latin American and Caribbean countries. Pres. JOSÉ MANUEL ARAYA; Sec.-Gen. ENRIQUE A. FERNÁNDEZ P. Publs *Solidarios* (quarterly), *Annual Report.*

Developing Eight — D-8: Atik Ali Paşa Yalısı, Çırağan Cad. 80, Beşiktaş, İstanbul, Turkey; tel. (212) 2275610; fax (212) 2275613; inaugurated at a meeting of Heads of State in June 1997; aims to foster economic co-operation between member states and to strengthen the role of developing countries in the global economy; project areas include trade and industry, agriculture, human resources, telecommunications, rural development, and privatizations, banking and Islamic insurance. Second summit meeting convened in Dhaka, Bangladesh, in December 1997. Mems: Bangladesh, Egypt, Iran, Indonesia, Malaysia, Nigeria, Pakistan, Turkey.

Economic Community of the Great Lakes Countries (Communauté économique des pays des Grands Lacs—CEPGL): POB 58, Gisenyi, Rwanda; tel. 40228; telex 602; f. 1976; main organs: annual Conference of Heads of State, Council of Ministers of Foreign Affairs, Permanent Executive Secretariat, Consultative Commission, Security Commission, three Specialized Technical Commissions. There are four specialized agencies: a development bank, the Banque de Développement des États des Grands Lacs (BDEGL) at Goma, Democratic Republic of the Congo; an energy centre at Bujumbura, Burundi; the Institute of Agronomic and Zootechnical Research, Gitega, Burundi; and a regional electricity company (SINELAC) at Bukavu, Democratic Republic of the Congo. Two extraordinary summit meetings were held in 1994 to discuss security concerns in the region and efforts to revive economic co-operation activities. Mems: Burundi, Democratic Republic of the Congo, Rwanda. Publs *Grands Lacs* (quarterly review), *Journal* (annually).

Economic Co-operation Organization—ECO: 1 Golbou Alley, Kamraniyeh, POB 14155-6176, Teheran, Iran; tel. (21) 2831731; fax (21) 2831734; f. 1985 (as successor to Regional Co-operation for Development, a tripartite body comprising Iran, Pakistan and Turkey; f. 1964); aims to promote regional economic co-operation between member states. Main areas of co-operation are transport (including the construction of road and rail links), communications, trade, energy (including the interconnection of power grids in the region), minerals, environmental issues, industry and agriculture, with long-term priorities defined in terms of action plans; comprises three regional institutions; ECO Shipping Company, ECO Chamber of Commerce, ECO Insurance College, and three specialized agencies: ECO Cultural Institute, ECO Science Foundation (in Pakistan) and ECO Consultancy and Engineering Company (also in Pakistan). Three further institutions were to be established: an ECO Trade and Development Bank in Turkey, an ECO Re-insurance Company in Pakistan and an ECO Air Company in Iran; a protocol on a preferential tariff arrangement was signed in 1991; an agreement on Transit Trade and Visa Simplification for ECO corporate travellers was signed in 1995. Summits held annually. Mems: Afghanistan, Azerbaijan, Iran, Kazakhstan, Kyrgyzstan, Pakistan, Tajikistan, Turkey, Turkmenistan, Uzbekistan. Dir S. M. HASAN ZAIDI; Sec.-Gen. ONDER OZAR (Turkey).

Food Aid Committee: c/o International Grains Council, 1 Canada Square, Canary Wharf, London, E14 5AE, United Kingdom; tel. (171) 513-1122; fax (171) 513-0630; f. 1967; responsible for administration of the Food Aid Convention (1995), a constituent element of the International Grains Agreement (1995); monitors execution of members' obligations and provides forum for discussion on food aid issues. The 23 donor members are pledged to supply 5.3m. metric tons of grain suitable for human consumption annually to developing countries, mostly as gifts: in practice aid has usually exceeded 10m. tons annually. Exec. Dir G. DENIS. Publ. *Report on shipments* (annually).

Gambia River Basin Development Organization (Organisation de mise en valeur du fleuve Gambie—OMVG): BP 2353, 13 passage Leblanc, Dakar, Senegal; tel. 22-31-59; telex 51487; fax 22-59-26; f. 1978 by Senegal and The Gambia; Guinea joined in 1981 and Guinea-Bissau in 1983. An agricultural plan for the integrated development of the Kayanga/Geba and Koliba/Corubal river basins commenced in 1993 and was extended to encompass an agro-sylvo-pastoral project (to commence in the near future); work on a hydraulic development plan for the Gambia river commenced in late 1996 and was to be completed by mid-1998; a study to connect the national electric grids of the four member states, and a feasibility study for the construction of four hydroelectric dams was also to be undertaken; maintains documentation centre. Exec. Sec. MAMADOU NASSIROU DIALLO.

Group of Three—G3: f. 1993 by Colombia, Mexico and Venezuela to remove restrictions on trade between the three countries. The trade agreement covers market access, rules of origin, intellectual property, trade in services, and government purchases, and entered into force in early 1994. Tariffs on trade between member states were to be removed on a phased basis. Co-operation was also envisaged in employment creation, the energy sector and the fight against cholera.

Indian Ocean Commission—IOC: Q4, Ave Sir Guy Forget, BP 7, Quatre Bornes, Mauritius; tel. 425-9564; fax 425-1209; f. 1982 to promote regional co-operation, particularly in economic development; principal projects under way in the early 1990s (at a cost of 11.6m. francs CFA) comprised tuna-fishing development, protection and management of environmental resources and strengthening of meterological services, with assistance principally from the EU; tariff reduction is also envisaged. Permanent technical committees cover: tuna-fishing; regional industrial co-operation; regional commerce; tourism; environment; maritime transport; handicrafts; labour; sports. The IOC organizes an annual regional trade fair. Mems: Comoros, France (representing the French Overseas Department of Réunion), Madagascar, Mauritius, Seychelles. Sec.-Gen. (vacant). Publ. *La Gazette de la Commission de l'Océan Indien*.

Indian Ocean Rim Association for Regional Co-operation—IORARC: Mauritius; the first intergovernmental meeting of countries in the region to promote an Indian Ocean Rim initiative was convened in March 1995; charter to establish the Asscn signed at a ministerial meeting in March 1997; aims to promote regional economic co-operation through trade, investment, infrastructure, tourism, science and technology. Mems: Australia, India, Indonesia, Kenya, Madagascar, Malaysia, Mauritius, Mozambique, Oman, Singapore, South Africa, Sri Lanka, Tanzania and Yemen.

Inter-American Planning Society (Sociedad Interamericana de Planificación—SIAP): c/o Revista Interamericana de Planificacion, Casilla 01-05-1978, Cuenca, Ecuador; tel. (7) 823-860; fax (7) 823-949; f. 1956 to promote development of comprehensive planning as a continuous and co-ordinated process at all levels. Mems: institutions and individuals in 46 countries. Pres. Arq. HERMES MARROQUÍN (Guatemala); Exec. Sec. LUIS E. CAMACHO (Colombia). Publs *Correo Informativo* (quarterly), *Inter-American Journal of Planning* (quarterly).

Intergovernmental Authority on Development—IGAD: BP 2653, Djibouti; tel. 354050; fax 356994; e-mail IGAD@intnet.dj; f. 1996 to supersede the Intergovernmental Authority on Drought and Development, f. 1986 to co-ordinate measures to combat the effects of drought and desertification. IGAD has an expanded mandate to co-ordinate and harmonize policies in the areas of infrastructure development, food security, environmental protection, conflict prevention and resolution, and humanitarian affairs. Mems: Djibouti, Eritrea, Ethiopia, Kenya, Somalia, Sudan, Uganda. Exec. Sec. Dr TEKESTE GHEBRAY (Eritrea).

International Bank for Economic Co-operation—IBEC: 107815 GSP Moscow B-78, 11 Masha Poryvaeva St, Russia; tel. (95) 975-38-61; telex 411391; fax 975-22-02; f. 1963 by members of the Council for Mutual Economic Assistance (dissolved in 1991), as a central institution for credit and settlements; following the decision in 1989–91 of most member states to adopt a market economy, the IBEC abandoned its system of multilateral settlements in transferable roubles, and (from 1 January 1991) began to conduct all transactions in convertible currencies. The Bank provides credit and settlement facilities for member states, and also acts as an international commercial bank, offering services to commercial banks and enterprises. Authorized capital ECU 400m., paid-up capital ECU 143.5m., reserves ECU 164.8m. (Dec. 1996). Mems: Bulgaria, Cuba, Czech Republic, Hungary, Mongolia, Poland, Romania, Russia, Slovakia, Viet Nam. Chair. VITALI S. KHOKHLOV; Man. Dirs A. ORASCU, V. SYTNIKOV, E. BOURDAKOV, L. RUSMICH.

International Co-operation for Development and Solidarity—CIDSE: 16 rue Stévin, Bte 6, 1040 Brussels, Belgium; tel. (2) 230-77-22; telex 64208; fax (2) 230-70-82; e-mail euro-cidse@cidse.be; f. 1967 to link Catholic development organizations and assist in co-ordination of projects, obtaining co-financing and providing information. Mems: 16 Catholic agencies in 12 countries and territories. Pres. BERNARD HOLZER; Sec.-Gen. Dr KOENRAAD VERHAGEN.

International Investment Bank: 107078 Moscow, 7 Masha Poryvaeva St, Russia; tel. (95) 975-40-08; telex 411358; fax (95) 975-20-70; f. 1970 by members of the CMEA (q.v.) to grant credits for joint investment projects and the development of enterprises; following the decision in 1989–91 of most member states to adopt a market economy, the Bank conducted its transactions (from 1 January 1991) in convertible currencies, rather than in transferable roubles. The Bank focuses on production and scientific and technical progress. By the end of 1996 the Bank had approved financing of some ECU 7,000m. for 159 projects. Authorized capital ECU 1,300m., paid-up capital ECU 214.5m., reserves ECU 233m. (Dec. 1996). Mems: Bulgaria, Cuba, Czech Republic, Hungary, Mongolia, Poland, Romania, Russia, Slovakia, Viet Nam. Chair. I. NOVIKOV.

Lake Chad Basin Commission: BP 727, N'Djamena, Chad; tel. 52-41-45; telex 5251; fax 52-41-37; e-mail lake!lcbc@sdntcd.undp.org; f. 1964 to encourage co-operation in developing the Lake Chad region and to promote the settlement of regional disputes. Work programmes emphasize the regulation of the utilization of water and other natural resources in the basin; the co-ordination of natural resources development projects and research; in 1988–92 a border demarcation exercise concerning all five member states was conducted. Annual summit of heads of state. Mems: Cameroon, Central African Republic, Chad, Niger, Nigeria. Exec. Sec. ABUBAKAR BOBBOI JAURO.

Latin American Association of Development Financing Institutions (Asociación Latinoamericana de Instituciones Financieras de Desarrollo—ALIDE): Apdo Postal 3988, Paseo de la República 3211, Lima 100, Peru; tel. (1) 4422400; fax (1) 4428105; e-mail postmaster@alide.org.pe; internet http://www.rcp.net.pe/usr/alide; f. 1968 to promote co-operation among regional development financing bodies. Mems: 73 active, 12 associate and 13 collaborating (banks and financing institutions and development organizations in 22 Latin American countries, Canada, Slovenia, Spain and Portugal). Pres. Dr NOEL LEZAMA MARTINEZ; Sec.-Gen. CARLOS GARATEA YORI. Publs *ALIDE Bulletin* (6 a year), *ALIDE NOTICIAS Newsletter* (12 a year), *Annual Report, Latin American Directory of Development Financing Institutions*.

Latin American Economic System (Sistema Económico Latinoamericano—SELA): Apdo 17035, Avda Francisco de Miranda, Torre Europa, piso 4, Chacaito, Caracas 1010, Venezuela; tel. (2) 905-5111; fax (2) 951-6953; e-mail difsela@true.net; internet http://www.sela.org; f. 1975 by the Panama Convention; aims to accelerate the economic and social development of its members through intra-regional co-operation, and to provide a permanent system of consultation and co-ordination in economic and social matters; conducts studies; provides library, information service and data bases on regional co-operation. The Latin American Council meets annually at ministerial level and high-level regional consultation and co-ordination meetings are held; there are also Action Committees and a Permanent Secretariat. Mems: 27 counries. The following organizations have also been created within SELA:

Latin American and Caribbean Trade Information and Foreign Trade Support Programme (PLACIEX): Lima, Peru.

Latin American Commission for Science and Technology (COLCYT): Caracas, Venezuela.

Multinational Fertilizer Marketing Enterprise (MULTIFERT): Panama City, Panama.

Latin American Fisheries Development Organization (OLDEPESCA): Lima, Peru.

Latin American Handicraft Co-operation Programme (PLACART): Caracas, Venezuela.

Latin American Technological Information Network (RITLA): Brasilia, Brazil.

Perm. Sec. CARLOS MONETA (Argentina). Publ. *Capítulos del SELA* (quarterly).

Latin American Integration Association – LAIA (Asociación Latinoamericana de Integración – ALADI): Cebollatí 1461, Casilla 577, Montevideo, Uruguay; tel. (2) 495915; telex 26944; fax (2) 490649; e-mail aladi@chasque.apc.org; f. 1980 as successor to the Latin American Free Trade Association (f. 1960); aims to establish an area of economic preferences, in order to promote trade throughout Latin America, with the eventual objective of establishing a regional common market. Mems divided into three categories: most developed (Argentina, Brazil, Mexico); intermediate (Chile, Colombia, Peru, Uruguay, Venezuela); least developed (Bolivia, Ecuador, Paraguay). Sec-Gen. ANTÔNIO DE CERQUEIRA ANTÚNES (Brazil). Publs *ALADI News* (monthly), *Nuestro Perfil* (monthly), other reports, studies, texts of agreements.

Liptako-Gourma Integrated Development Authority: POB 619, ave M. Thevenond, Ouagadougou, Burkina Faso; tel. (3) 30-61-48; telex 5247; f. 1972; scope of activities includes water infrastructure, telecommunications and construction of roads and railways; in 1986 undertook study on development of water resources in the basin of the Niger river (for hydroelectricity and irrigation). Mems: Burkina Faso, Mali, Niger. Dir-Gen. GISANGA DEMBÉLÉ (Mali).

Mano River Union: Private Mail Bag 133, Delco House, Lightfoot Boston St, Freetown, Sierra Leone; tel. (22) 226883; f. 1973 to establish a customs and economic union between member states to accelerate development via integration. A common external tariff was instituted in October 1977. Intra-union free trade was officially introduced in May 1981, as the first stage in progress towards a customs union. An industrial development unit was set up in 1980 to identify projects and encourage investment. Construction of the Monrovia-Freetown-Conakry highway was partially completed by 1990. The Union was inactive for three years until mid-1994, owing to disagreements regarding funding. In January 1995 a Mano River Centre for Peace and Development was established, which was to be temporarily based in London. The Centre aims to provide a permanent mechanism for conflict prevention and resolution, and monitoring of human rights violations, and to promote sustainable peace and development following a peaceful resolution of the conflicts currently under way in the region. Decisions are taken at meetings of a joint ministerial council formed by the ministers of member states. Mems: Guinea, Liberia, Sierra Leone. Dir Dr KABINEH KOROMAH (Sierra Leone).

Mekong River Commission: Kasatsuk Bridge, Rama I Rd, Bangkok 10330, Thailand; tel. (2) 225-0029; fax (2) 225-2796; e-mail wolfgang@mozart.inet.co.th; f. 1995, as successor to the Committee for Co-ordination of Investigations of the Lower Mekong Basin (f. 1957); aims to co-ordinate the sustainable development, utilization and conservation of the resources of the Mekong River Basin for navigational and non-navigational purposes, in order to assist the social and economic development of member states, while at the same time preserving the ecological balance of the basin. Mems: Cambodia, Laos, Thailand, Viet Nam. CEO YASUNOBU MATOBA.

Niger Basin Authority (Autorité du bassin du Niger): BP 729, Niamey, Niger; tel. 723102; fax 735310; f. 1964 (as River Niger Commission; name changed 1980) to harmonize national programmes concerned with the River Niger Basin and to execute an integrated development plan; activities comprise: statistics; navigation regulation; hydrological forecasting; environmental control; infrastructure and agro-pastoral development; and arranging assistance for these projects. Mems: Benin, Burkina Faso, Cameroon, Chad, Côte d'Ivoire, Guinea, Mali, Niger, Nigeria. Exec. Sec. OTHMAN MUSTAPHA (Nigeria). Publ. *Bulletin*.

Organization for the Development of the Senegal River (Organisation pour la mise en valeur du fleuve Sénégal—OMVS): 46 rue Carnot, BP 3152, Dakar, Senegal; tel. 22-36-79; telex 51670; fax 23-47-62; f. 1972 to use the Senegal river for hydroelectricity, irrigation and navigation. The Djama dam in Senegal provides a barrage to prevent salt water from moving upstream, and the Manantali dam in Mali is intended to provide a reservoir for irrigation of about 400,000 ha of land and (eventually) for production of hydroelectricity and provision of year-round navigation for ocean-going vessels. In 1991 an agreement was signed whereby a company, l'Agence de gestion pour les ouvrages communs (AGOC) was formed; member states were to hold 75% of the capital and 25% by private shareholders. Work was to begin in 1996 on a hydro-electric power station on the Senegal River: international donors were to provide US $520m. for the project which was due for completion in 1999. Mems: Mali, Mauritania, Senegal; Guinea has held observer status since 1987. Chair. ALPHA OUMAR KONARE.

Organization for the Management and Development of the Kagera River Basin (Organisation pour l'aménagement et le développement du bassin de la rivière Kagera): BP 297, Kigali, Rwanda; tel. (7) 84665; telex 0909 22567; fax (7) 82172; f. 1978; envisages joint development and management of resources, including the construction of an 80-MW hydroelectric dam at Rusumo Falls, on the Rwanda-Tanzania border, a 2,000-km railway network between the four member countries, road construction (914 km), and a telecommunications network between member states (financed by US $16m. from the African Development Bank). A tsetse-fly control project began in 1990. Budget (1992) US $2m. Mems: Burundi, Rwanda, Tanzania, Uganda. Exec. Sec. JEAN-BOSCO BALINDA.

Pacific Basin Economic Council—PBEC: 900 Fort St Mall No. 1080, Honolulu, HI 96813-3721, USA; tel. (808) 521-9044; fax (808) 521-8530; f. 1967; an association of business representatives which aims to promote business opportunities in the region in order to enhance overall economic development; to advise governments and to serve as a liaison between business leaders and government officials; encourages business relationships and co-operation among members; holds business symposia. Mems: 19 country economic committees (Australia, Canada, Chile, People's Republic of China, Colombia, Ecuador, Fiji, Hong Kong, Indonesia, Japan, Republic of Korea, Mexico, New Zealand, Peru, Philippines, Russia, Taiwan, Thailand, USA). Chair. GARY L. TOOKER; Sec.-Gen. ROBERT G. LEES.

Pacific Economic Co-operation Council—PECC: 4 Nassim Rd, Singapore 258372; tel. 7379823; fax 7379824; e-mail peccsec@pacific.net.sg; f. 1980; an independent, policy-orientated organization of senior research, government and business representatives from 23 economies in the Asia-Pacific region; aims to foster economic development in the region by providing a forum for discussion and co-operation in a wide range of economic areas; general meeting every 2 years. Mems: the ASEAN states, Australia, Canada, Chile, the People's Republic of China, Colombia, Hong Kong, Japan, the Republic of Korea, Mexico, New Zealand, Peru, Russia, Taiwan, USA and the South Pacific Forum; French Pacific Territories (assoc. mem.); Dir-Gen. LEUNG PAK-CHUNG. Publs *PECC Link* (quarterly), *Pacific Economic Outlook* (annually).

Pan-African Institute for Development—PAID: BP 4056, Douala, Cameroon; tel. 42-10-61; telex 6048; fax 42-43-35; f. 1964; gives training to people involved with development at grassroots, intermediate and senior levels coming from African countries (47 countries in 1994); emphasis in education is given to: women in development; promotion of small and medium-sized enterprises; involvement of local populations in development; preparation of projects for regional co-operation; income-generating activities; financial analysis and management; applied research, local project support and specialized training. There are four regional institutes: Central Africa (Douala), Sahel (Ouagadougou, Burkina Faso) (French-speaking), West Africa (Buéa, Cameroon), Eastern and Southern Africa (Kabwe, Zambia) (English-speaking), and a European office in Geneva. Sec.-Gen. FAYA KONDIANO. Publs *Newsletter* (2 a year), *PAID Report* (quarterly).

Pan American Development Foundation—PADF: 2600 16th St, NW, Washington, DC 20006-4202, USA; tel. (202) 458-3969; fax (202) 458-6316; f. 1962 to improve economic and social conditions in Latin America and the Caribbean through providing low-interest credit for small-scale entrepreneurs, vocational training, improved health care, agricultural development and reforestation, and strengthening local non-governmental organizations; provides emergency disaster relief and reconstruction assistance. Mems: foundations and institutes in 30 countries. Exec. Dir PETER REITZ. Publ. *PADF Newsletter* (2 a year).

Permanent Inter-State Committee on Drought Control in the Sahel—CILSS: POB 7049, Ouagadougou, Burkina Faso; tel. 306758; telex 5263; fax 306757; f. 1973; works in co-operation with UN Sudano-Sahelian Office (UNSO, q.v.); aims to combat the effects of chronic drought in the Sahel region (where the deficit in grain production was estimated at 1.7m. metric tons for 1988), by improving irrigation and food production, halting deforestation and creating food reserves; maintains Institut du Sahel at Bamako (Mali) and centre at Niamey (Niger). Budget (1995): 318.5m. francs CFA. Mems: Burkina Faso, Cape Verde, Chad, The Gambia, Guinea-Bissau, Mali, Mauritania, Niger, Senegal. Chair. (1997–2000) Pres. YAHYA A. J. J. JAMMEH (The Gambia); Exec. Sec. CISSÉ MARIAM K. SIDIBE. Publ. *Reflets Sahéliens* (quarterly).

Permanent Tripartite Commission for East African Co-operation: International Conference Centre, Arusha, Tanzania; f. 1993, by agreement between the heads of state of Kenya, Tanzania and Uganda, to promote greater regional co-operation (previously pursued under the East African Community, f. 1967; dissolved 1977); agreement to establish a secretariat was signed in Nov. 1994; initial areas for co-operation were to be trade and industry, security, immigration and promotion of investment; further objectives were the elimination of trade barriers and ensuring the free movement of people and capital within the grouping; secretariat inaugurated in March 1996. Exec. Sec. FRANCIS KIRIMI MUTHAURA.

Population Council: 1 Dag Hammarskjöld Plaza, New York, NY 10017, USA; tel. (212) 339-0500; telex 9102900660; fax (212) 755-6052; e-mail pubinfo@popcouncil.org; internet http://www.popcouncil.org; f. 1952; aims to improve reproductive health and achieve a balance between people and resources; analyses demographic trends; conducts biomedical research to develop new contraceptives; works with private and public agencies to improve the quality of family planning and reproductive health services; helps governments to influence demographic behaviour. Five regional offices, in India, Mexico, Egypt, Kenya and Senegal. Additional office in Washington, DC, USA, carries out world-wide operational research and activities for the prevention of HIV and AIDS. Chair. ELIZABETH J. MCCORMACK; Pres. MARGARET CATLEY-CARLSON. Publs *Studies in Family Planning* (quarterly), *Population and Development Review* (quarterly), *Population Briefs* (quarterly).

Society for International Development: Via Panisperna 207, 00184 Rome, Italy; tel. (6) 4872172; fax (6) 4872170; e-mail info@sidint.org; internet http://www.waw.be/sid; f. 1957; a global network of individuals and institutions concerned with development that is participative, pluralistic and sustainable; mobilizes and strengthens civil society groups by actively building partnerships among them and with other sectors; fosters local initiatives and new forms of social experimentation. Mems: over 6,000 in 115 countries and 77 local chapters. Pres. Boutros Boutros-Ghali (Egypt); Sec.-Gen. Roberto Savio. Publs *Development* (quarterly), *Bridges* (bimonthly newsletter).

South Asian Association for Regional Co-operation—SAARC: GPO Box 4222, Kathmandu, Nepal; tel. (1) 221785; telex 2561; fax (1) 227033; e-mail saarc@mos.com.np; f. 1985 by the leaders of seven South Asian nations, to improve regional co-operation, particularly in economic development. There are 11 technical committees covering: agriculture and forestry; education, culture and sports; health, population and child welfare; environment and meteorology; rural development (including the SAARC Youth Volunteers Programme); tourism; transport; science and technology; communications; women in development; prevention of drugs-trafficking and drug abuse. In addition, SAARC is committed to achieving the eradication of poverty in the region and has endorsed an Agenda of Action to help achieve this by 2002. Conventions were signed in 1987 on measures to counter terrorism and in 1990 on narcotic drugs and psychotropic substances. SAARC operates an Agricultural Information Centre (Dhaka, Bangladesh), and a Food Security Reserve to supply emergency food requirements; it also offers fellowships, scholarships and chairs, an audio-visual exchange programme and a youth volunteers programme. There is a SAARC Tuberculosis Centre in Kathmandu, a SAARC Documentation Centre in New Delhi, India, and a SAARC Meteorological Research Centre in Dhaka, Bangladesh. SAARC associations of parliamentarians and political parties were formed in 1992. In April 1993 ministers signed the SAARC Preferential Trading Arrangement (SAPTA), which came into effect in December 1995. A South Asian Development Fund was established in 1996. The SAARC charter stipulates that decisions should be made unanimously, and that 'bilateral and contentious issues' should not be discussed; summit meetings of heads of governments are held every two years and ministers of foreign affairs meet at least twice a year. Mems: Bangladesh, Bhutan, India, Maldives, Nepal, Pakistan, Sri Lanka. Sec.-Gen. Naeem U. Hasan (Pakistan). Publs *SAARC Newsletter* (monthly), *SPECTRUM* (irregularly).

South Centre: Chemin du Champ-d'Anier 17–19, BP 228, 1211 Geneva 19, Switzerland; tel. (22) 7983433; fax (22) 7988531; e-mail south@southcentre.org.; f. 1990 as a follow-up mechanism of the South Commission (f. 1987); 1995 established as an intergovernmental body that aims to promote South–South solidarity and co-operation by generating ideas and action-oriented proposals on major policy issues for consideration by collective institutions and intergovernmental organizations of the South and individual governments. Chair. Dr Julius Nyerere. Publ. *South Letter* (quarterly).

Union of the Arab Maghreb (Union du Maghreb arabe—UMA): 26–27 rue Okba, Agdal, Rabat, Morocco; tel. (7) 772668; telex 36488; fax (7) 772693; f. 1989; aims to encourage joint ventures and to create a single market; structure comprises a council of heads of state (meeting annually), a council of ministers of foreign affairs, a consultative council of 30 delegates from each country, and a UMA judicial court, and four specialized ministerial commissions. Chairmanship rotates annually between heads of state. By 1995 joint projects that had been approved or were under consideration included: free movement of citizens within the region; joint transport undertakings, including road and railway improvements; establishment of the Maghreb Investment and Foreign Trade Bank to fund joint agricultural and industrial projects (with a capital of US $500m.); and the creation of a customs union. In April 1994 the Supreme Council agreed to undertake measures to establish a free trade zone, and to set up a Maghrebian Agency for Youth Tourism and a Maghrebian Union of Sport. Sec.-Gen. Mohamed Amamou (Tunisia). Mems: Algeria, Libya, Mauritania, Morocco, Tunisia.

Vienna Institute for Development and Co-operation (Wiener Institut für Entwicklungsfragen und Zusammenarbeit): Weyrgasse 5, 1030 Vienna, Austria; tel. (1) 713-35-94; fax (1) 713-35-94-73; e-mail vidc@magnet.at; f. 1987 (fmrly Vienna Institute for Development, f. 1964); disseminates information on the problems and achievements of developing countries; encourages increased aid-giving and international co-operation; conducts research. Pres. Franz Vranitzky; Dir Erich Andlik. Publs *Report Series*, *Echo*.

World University Service—WUS: 383 Los Jardines, Nuñoa, Santiago de Chile, Chile; tel. (2) 272375; fax (2) 2724002; f. 1920; links students, faculty and administrators in post-secondary institutions concerned with economic and social development, and seeks to protect their academic freedom and autonomy; seeks to extend technical, personal and financial resources of post-secondary institutions to under-developed areas and communities; provides scholarships at university level for refugees, displaced people, and returnees, and supports informal education projects for women; the principle is to assist people to improve and develop their own communities. WUS is independent and is governed by an assembly of national committees. Pres. Caleb Fundanga (Zambia); Sec.-Gen. Ximena Erazo. Publs *WUS News, WUS and Human Rights* (quarterly).

Economics and Finance

African Centre for Monetary Studies: 15 blvd Franklin Roosevelt, BP 4128, Dakar, Senegal; tel. 821-93-80; telex 61256; fax 822-73-43; began operations 1978; aims to promote better understanding of banking and monetary matters; to study monetary problems of African countries and the effect on them of international monetary developments; seeks to enable African countries to co-ordinate strategies in international monetary affairs. Established as an organ of the Association of African Central Banks (AACB) as a result of a decision by the OAU Heads of State and Government. Mems: all mems of AACB (q.v.). Chair. Patrice Djamboleka Loma Okitongono (Democratic Republic of the Congo); Dir Antoine Ndiaye (acting).

African Insurance Organization: BP 5860, Douala, Cameroon; tel. 42-47-58; fax 43-20-08; f. 1972 to promote the expansion of the insurance and reinsurance industry in Africa, and to increase regional co-operation; holds annual conference, and arranges meetings for reinsurers, brokers, consultants, supervisory authorities and actuaries in Africa; has established African insurance 'pools' for aviation, petroleum and fire risks, and has created associations of African insurance educators, supervisory authorities and insurance brokers and consultants. Sec.-Gen. Y. Aseffa.

Asian Clearing Union—ACU: c/o Central Bank of the Islamic Republic of Iran, POB 11365/8531, Teheran, Iran; tel. (21) 2842076; telex 216868; fax (21) 2847677; e-mail acusecret@neda.net; f. 1974 to provide clearing arrangements, whereby members settle payments for intra-regional transactions among the participating central banks, on a multilateral basis, in order to economize on the use of foreign exchange and promote the use of domestic currencies in trade transactions among developing countries; part of ESCAP's Asian trade expansion programme; the Central Bank of Iran is the Union's agent; in September 1995 the ACU unit of account was changed from SDR to US dollars, with effect from 1 January 1996. Mems: central banks of Bangladesh, India, Iran, Myanmar, Nepal, Pakistan, Sri Lanka. Gen. Man. Mohammad Firouzdor. Publs *Annual Report, Newsletter* (monthly).

Asian Reinsurance Corporation: 17th Floor, Tower B, Chamnan Phenjati Business Center, 65 Rama 9 Rd, Huaykwang, Bangkok 10310, Thailand; tel. (2) 245-2169; telex 87231; fax (2) 248-1377; f. 1979 by ESCAP with UNCTAD, to operate as a professional reinsurer, giving priority in retrocessions to national insurance and reinsurance markets of member countries, and as a development organization providing technical assistance to countries in the Asia-Pacific region; cap. (auth.) US $15m., (p.u.) US $5m. Mems: Afghanistan, Bangladesh, Bhutan, People's Republic of China, India, Iran, Republic of Korea, Philippines, Sri Lanka, Thailand. Gen. Man. A. S. Malabanan.

Association of African Central Banks: 15 blvd Franklin Roosevelt, BP 4128, Dakar, Senegal; tel. 821-93-80; telex 61256; fax 822-73-43; f. 1968 to promote contacts in the monetary and financial sphere in order to increase co-operation and trade among member states; to strengthen monetary and financial stability on the African continent. Mems: 36 African central banks representing 47 states. Chair. Jean Claude Masangu Mulongo.

Association of African Tax Administrators: POB 13255, Yaoundé, Cameroon; tel. 22-41-57; fax 23-18-55; f. 1980 to promote co-operation in the field of taxation policy, legislation and administration among African countries. Mems: 18 states. Exec. Sec. Owona Pascal-Baylon.

Association of Asian Confederation of Credit Unions: POB 24-171, Bangkok 10240, Thailand; tel. (2) 374-3170; fax (2) 374-5321; links and promotes credit unions in Asia, provides research facilities and training programmes. Mems in Bangladesh, Hong Kong, Indonesia, Japan, Republic of Korea, Malaysia, Philippines, Sri Lanka, Taiwan, Thailand. Gen. Man. Ranjith Hettiarachichi. Publs *ACCU News* (every 2 months), *Annual Report and Directory*.

Association of European Institutes of Economic Research (Association d'instituts européens de conjoncture économique): 3 place Montesquieu, BP 4, 1348 Louvain-la-Neuve, Belgium; tel. (10) 47-41-52; fax (10) 47-39-45; f. 1955; provides a means of contact between member institutes; organizes two meetings yearly, at which discussions are held on the economic situation and on a special theoretical subject. Mems: 40 institutes in 20 European countries. Admin. Sec. Paul Olbrechts.

Centre for Latin American Monetary Studies (Centro de Estudios Monetarios Latinoamericanos): Durango 54, Col. Roma, Del. Cuauhtémoc, 06700 México, DF, Mexico; tel. and fax (5) 533-03-00; e-mail cemlainf@mail.internet.com.mx.; f. 1952; organizes technical training programmes on monetary policy, development finance, etc., applied research programmes on monetary and central banking policies and procedures, regional meetings of banking officials. Mems: 30 associated members (Central Banks of Latin America and the Caribbean), 32 co-operating members (supervisory institutions of the region and non-Latin American Central Banks). Dir SERGIO GHIGLIAZZA. Publs *Bulletin* (every 2 months), *Monetaria* (quarterly), *Money Affairs* (2 a year), *Banking Supervision Bulletin* (3 a year).

Comité Européen des Assurances: 3 bis rue de la Chaussée d'Antin, 75009 Paris, France; tel. 1-44-83-11-83; fax 1-47-70-03-75; internet http://www.cea.assur.org; f. 1953 to represent the interests of European insurers, to encourage co-operation between members, to allow the exchange of information and to conduct studies. Mems: national insurance associations of 29 countries. Pres. HERBERT SCHIMETSCHEK (Austria); Sec.-Gen. FRANCIS LOHEAC (France). Publs *CEA INFO—Euro Brief* (every 2 months), *European Insurance in Figures* (annually), *The European Life Insurance Market* (every 2 years).

Econometric Society: Dept of Economics, Northwestern University, Evanston, IL 60208, USA; tel. (847) 491-3615; f. 1930 to promote studies that aim at a unification of the theoretical-quantitative and the empirical-quantitative approach to economic problems. Mems: 7,000. Exec. Dir and Sec. JULIE P. GORDON. Publ. *Econometrica* (6 a year).

European Federation of Finance House Associations—Eurofinas: 267 ave de Tervuren, 1150 Brussels, Belgium; tel. (2) 778-05-60; fax (2) 778-05-79; f. 1959 to study the development of instalment credit financing in Europe, to collate and publish instalment credit statistics, to promote research into instalment credit practice; mems: finance houses and professional associations in Austria, Belgium, Finland, France, Germany, Ireland, Italy, Netherlands, Norway, Portugal, Spain, Sweden, Switzerland, United Kingdom. Chair. GREGORIO D'OTTAVIANO (Italy); Sec.-Gen. MARC BAERT. Publs *Eurofinas Newsletter* (monthly), *Annual Report, Study Reports*.

European Federation of Financial Analysts Societies: 3 rue d'Antin, 75002 Paris, France; tel. 1-42-98-02-00; fax 1-42-98-02-02; f. 1962 to co-ordinate the activities of all European associations of financial analysts. Biennial congress: Barcelona, Spain, 1996. Mems: 10,700 in 17 societies. Chair. J.-G. DE WAEL.

European Financial Management and Marketing Association: 16 rue d'Aguesseau, 75008 Paris, France; tel. 1-47-42-52-72; telex 280288; fax 1-47-42-56-76; f. 1971 to link financial institutions by organizing seminars, conferences and training sessions and an annual World Convention, and by providing documentation services. Mems: 145 European financial institutions. Pres. BERNARD THIOLON; Sec.-Gen. MICHEL BARNICH (acting). Publ. *Newsletter*.

European Venture Capital Association: 6 Minervastraat, Box 6, 1930 Zaventem, Belgium; tel. (2) 715-00-20; fax (2) 725-07-04; e-mail evca@evca.com; internet http://www.evca.com; f. 1983 to link venture capital companies within Europe and to encourage joint investment projects, particularly in support of small and medium-sized businesses; holds annual symposium, seminars and training courses. Mems: over 350 in more than 30 countries. Sec.-Gen. SERGE RAICHER.

Fédération Internationale des Bourses de Valeurs—FIBV (International Federation of Stock Exchanges): 22 boulevard de Courcelles, 75017 Paris, France; tel. 1-44-01-05-45; fax 1-47-54-94-22; f. 1961; assumes a leadership role in advocating the benefits of self-regulation in the regulatory process, offers a platform for closer collaboration between member exchanges, promotes enhanced ethical and professional behaviour in the securities industry. Mems: 51 and 42 corresponding exchanges. Pres. MANUEL ROBLEDA; Sec-Gen. GERRIT H. DE MAREZ OYENS.

Fonds Africain de Garantie et de Co-opération Economique—FAGACE (African Guarantee and Economic Co-operation Fund): BP 2045, Cotonou, Benin; tel. 300376; telex 5024; fax 300284; commenced operations in 1981; guarantees loans for development projects, provides loans and grants for specific operations and supports national and regional enterprises. Cap. 7,750m. francs CFA. Mems: Benin, Burkina Faso, Central African Republic, Côte d'Ivoire, Mali, Niger, Rwanda, Senegal, Togo. Dir-Gen. SOULEYMANE GADO.

International Accounting Standards Committee—IASC: 167 Fleet St, London, EC4A 2ES, United Kingdom; tel. (171) 353-0565; fax (171) 353-0562; f. 1973 to formulate and publish in the public interest accounting standards to be observed in the presentation of financial statements and to promote worldwide acceptance and observance, and to work for the improvement and harmonization of regulations, accounting standards and procedures relating to the presentation of financial statements. Mems: 118 accounting bodies representing more than 1.7m. accountants in 87 countries. Chair. MICHAEL SHARPE; Sec.-Gen. Sir BRYAN CARSBERG. Publs *Statements of International Accounting Standards, Exposure Drafts, IASC Insight* (4 a year), *IASC Update* (3 a year), *Bound Volume of International Accounting Standards* (annually), *Annual Review*.

International Association for Research in Income and Wealth: Dept of Economics, New York University, 269 Mercer St, Room 700, New York, NY 10003, USA; tel. (212) 924-4386; fax (212) 366-5067; f. 1947 to further research in the general field of national income and wealth and related topics by the organization of biennial conferences and by other means. Mems: approx. 425. Chair. RICHARD RUGGLES (USA); Exec. Sec. JANE FORMAN (USA). Publ. *Review of Income and Wealth* (quarterly).

International Association of Islamic Banks: Queen's Bldg, 23rd Floor, Al Balad Dist., POB 9707, Jeddah 21423, Saudi Arabia; tel. (2) 643-1276; fax (2) 644-7239; f. 1977 to link Islamic banks, which do not deal at interest but operate on a profit-/loss-sharing basis; activities include training and research. Mems: 42 banks and financial institutions in 18 countries. Chair. Prince MOHAMED AL-FAISAL AL-SAUD; Sec.-Gen. SAMIR ABID SHAIKH.

International Bureau of Fiscal Documentation: Sarphatistraat 600, POB 20237, 1000 HE Amsterdam, Netherlands; tel. (20) 6267726; telex 13217; fax (20) 6228658; e-mail ibfd@ibfd.nl; f. 1938 to supply information on fiscal law and its application; library on international taxation. Pres. J. F. AVERY JONES; Man. Dir H. M. A. L. HAMAEKERS. Publs *Bulletin for International Fiscal Documentation, European Taxation, International VAT Monitor, Supplementary Service to European Taxation* (all monthly), *Tax News Service* (fortnightly); studies, data bases, regional tax guides.

International Centre for Local Credit: Koninginnegracht 2, 2514 AA The Hague, Netherlands; tel. (70) 3750850; fax (70) 3454743; f. 1958 to promote local authority credit by gathering, exchanging and distributing information and advice on member institutions and on local authority credit and related subjects; studies important subjects in the field of local authority credit. Mems: 22 financial institutions in 14 countries. Pres. F. NARMON (Belgium); Sec.-Gen. P. P. VAN BESOUW (Netherlands). Publs *Bulletin, Newsletter* (quarterly).

International Economic Association: 23 rue Campagne Première, 75014 Paris, France; tel. 1-43-27-91-44; telex 264918; fax 1-42-79-92-16; f. 1949 to promote international collaboration for the advancement of economic knowledge and develop personal contacts between economists, and to encourage provision of means for the dissemination of economic knowledge. Member associations in 59 countries. Pres. Prof. JACQUES DRÈZE; Sec.-Gen. Prof. JEAN-PAUL FITOUSSI (France).

International Federation of Accountants: 114 West 47th St, Suite 2410, New York, NY 10036, USA; tel. (212) 302-5952; fax (212) 302-5964; e-mail judymccrudden@ifac.org; internet http://www.ifac.org; f. 1977 to develop a co-ordinated worldwide accounting profession with harmonized standards. Mems: accountancy bodies in 82 countries. Pres. BERTIL EDLUND (Sweden); Gen. Dir JOHN GRUNER (USA). Publ. *Codification of International Standards on Auditing*.

International Fiscal Association: World Trade Center, POB 30215, 3001 DE Rotterdam, Netherlands; tel. (10) 4052990; fax (10) 4055031; e-mail n.gensecr@ifa.nl; internet http://www.ifa.nl; f. 1938 to study international and comparative public finance and fiscal law, especially taxation; holds annual congresses. Mems in 90 countries and national branches in 47 countries. Pres. Prof S. O. LODIN (Sweden); Sec.-Gen. J. FRANS SPIERDIJK (Netherlands). Publs *Cahiers de Droit Fiscal International, Yearbook of the International Fiscal Association, IFA Congress Seminar Series*.

International Institute of Public Finance: University of the Saar, PO Box 151150, 66041 Saarbrücken, Germany; fax (681) 302-4369; e-mail iipf@rz.uni-fb.de; f. 1937; a private scientific organization aiming to establish contacts between people of every nationality, whose main or supplementary activity consists in the study of public finance; holds one meeting a year devoted to a certain scientific subject. Pres. ROBERT HAVEMAN (USA).

International Organization of Securities Commissions—IOSCO; CP 171, Tour de la Bourse, 800 Square Victoria, Suite 4510, Montreal H4Z 1C8, Canada; tel. (514) 875-8278; fax (514) 875-2669; e-mail mail@oicv.iosco.org; internet http://www.iosco.org; f. 1988 to develop securities markets and co-ordinate regulation. Mems: national securities commissions and similar agencies in 110 countries. Sec.-Gen. PAUL GUY. Publ. *IOSCO News* (3 a year).

International Savings Banks Institute: 1–3 rue Albert Gos, POB 355, 1211 Geneva 25, Switzerland; tel. (22) 3477466; telex 428702; fax (22) 3467356; f. 1924 to act as an intelligence and liaison centre for savings banks. Mems: 127 savings banks and savings banks associations in 92 countries. Pres. Dr ALAIN LE RAY; Gen. Man. J. M. PESANT (France). Publs (in English, French and German) *Savings Banks International* (quarterly), *International Savings Banks Directory, International Business Directory*.

International Securities Market Association: Rigistr. 60, PO Box, 8033 Zürich, Switzerland; tel. (1) 3634222; telex 815812; fax (1) 3637772; f. 1969 for discussion of questions relating to the international securities market, to issue rules governing their functions, and to maintain a close liaison between the primary and secondary markets in international securities. Mems: 838 banks and major financial institutions in 48 countries. Chair. RIJNHARD W.

F. VAN TETS (Netherlands); Chief Exec. and Sec.-Gen. JOHN L. LANGTON (Switzerland). Publs *International Bond Manual*, daily Eurobond listing, electronic price information, weekly Eurobond guide, ISMA formulae for yield, members' register, ISMA quarterly comment, reports, etc.

International Union for Housing Finance: Suite 400, 111 East Wacker Drive, Chicago, IL 60601-4389, USA; tel. (312) 946-8200; fax (312) 946-8202; e-mail iuhf@wwa.com; internet http://www.housingfinance.org; f. 1914 to foster world-wide interest in savings and home-ownership and co-operation among members; to encourage comparative study of methods and practice in housing finance; to encourage appropriate legislation on housing finance. Mems: 350 in 71 countries, 8 regional affiliates. Sec.-Gen. DONALD R. HOLTON. Publs *Housing Finance International* (quarterly), *Directory, International Housing Finance Factbook* (every 2 years), *IUHFI Newsletter* (3 a year).

Latin American Banking Federation (Federación Latinoamericana de Bancos—FELABAN): Apdo Aéreo 091959, Santafé de Bogotá, DE8, Colombia; tel. 2560875; fax 6111153; f. 1965 to co-ordinate efforts towards a wide and accelerated economic development in Latin American countries. Mems: 19 Latin American national banking associations. Pres. of Board HERNÁN SOMERVILLE SENN; Sec.-Gen. Dra MARICIELO GLEN DE TOBÓN (Colombia).

West African Clearing House: Kissy House, 54 Siaka Stevens St, PMB 218, Freetown, Sierra Leone; tel. 224485; telex 3368; fax 223943; f. 1975; administers transactions between its 10 member central banks in order to promote sub-regional trade and monetary co-operation; scheduled to be restructured as the West African Monetary Agency (see under ECOWAS). Mems: Banque Centrale des Etats de l'Afrique de l'Ouest (serving Benin, Burkina Faso, Côte d'Ivoire, Mali, Niger, Senegal, Togo) and the central banks of Cape Verde, The Gambia, Ghana, Guinea, Guinea-Bissau, Liberia, Mauritania, Nigeria and Sierra Leone. Exec. Sec. Dr EMMANUEL O. AKINNIFESI (Nigeria).

World Council of Credit Unions—WOCCU: POB 2982, 5810 Mineral Point Rd, Madison, WI 53701, USA; tel. (608) 231-7130; fax (608) 238-8020; f. 1970 to link credit unions and similar co-operative financial institutions and assist them in expanding and improving their services; provides technical and financial assistance to credit union associations in developing countries. Mems: 37,000 credit unions in 87 countries. CEO CHRISTOPHER BAKER. Publs *WOCCU Annual Report* (annually), *WOCCU Statistical Report, Perspectives* (12 a year).

Education

African Association for Literacy and Adult Education: POB 50768, Finance House, 6th Floor, Loita St, Nairobi, Kenya; tel. (2) 222391; telex 22096; fax (2) 340849; f. 1984, combining the former African Adult Education Association and the AFROLIT Society (both f. 1968); aims to promote adult education and literacy in Africa, to study the problems involved, and to allow the exchange of information; programmes are developed and implemented by 'networks' of educators; holds Conference every three years. Mems: 28 national education associations and 300 institutions in 33 countries. Chair. Dr ANTHONY SETSABI (Lesotho); Sec.-Gen. PAUL WANGOOLA (Uganda). Publs *The Spider Newsletter* (quarterly, French and English), *Journal* (2 a year).

Agence Francophone pour l'Enseignement Supérieur et la Recherche (AUPELF–UREF): BP 400, succ. Côte-des-Neiges, Montréal, Canada H3S 2S7; tel. (514) 343-6630; fax (514) 343-2107; e-mail rectorat@aupelf.refer.org; internet http://www.refer.qc.ca; f. 1961; aims: documentation, co-ordination, co-operation, exchange. Mems: 355 institutions. Pres. MICHEL GERVAIS (Canada); Dir-Gen. and Rector MICHEL GUILLOU (France). Publs *Universités* (quarterly), *UREF Actualités* (every 2 months), yearbooks (Francophone universities, Professors from francophone universities, Departments of French studies worldwide).

Asian Confederation of Teachers: 2nd Floor, Wisma DTC, 3455-B Jalan Sultansh Zainab, 15050 Kota Bharu, Kelatan, Malaysia; f. 1990. Pres. MUHAMMAD MUSTAPHA; Sec.-Gen. LAM WAH-HUI.

Association for Childhood Education International: 11501 Georgia Ave, Suite 315, Wheaton, MD 20902, USA; tel. (301) 942-2443; fax (301) 942-3012; f. 1892 to work for the education of children (from infancy through early adolescence) by promoting desirable conditions in schools, raising the standard of teaching, co-operating with all groups concerned with children, informing the public of the needs of children. Mems: 12,000. Pres. SUE WORTHAM; Exec. Dir GERALD C. ODLAND. Publs *Childhood Education* (6 a year), *ACEI Exchange Newsletter* (6 a year), *Journal of Research in Childhood Education* (2 a year), books on current educational subjects (3 a year).

Association Montessori Internationale: Koninginneweg 161, 1075 CN Amsterdam, Netherlands; tel. (20) 6798932; e-mail ami@xs4all.nl; f. 1929 to propagate the ideals and educational methods of Dr Maria Montessori on child development, without racial, religious or political prejudice; organizes training courses for teachers in 15 countries. Pres. G. J. PORTIELJE; Sec. RENILDE MONTESSORI. Publ. *Communications* (quarterly).

Association of African Universities: POB 5744, Accra North, Ghana; tel. (21) 774495; telex 2284; fax (21) 774821; f. 1967 to promote exchanges, contact and co-operation among African university institutions and to collect and disseminate information on research and higher education in Africa. Mems: 132 university institutions. Sec.-Gen. Prof. NARCISO MATOS (Mozambique). Publs *AAU Newsletter* (3 a year), *Directory of African Universities* (every 2 years).

Association of Arab Universities: POB 401, Jubeyha, Amman, Jordan; tel. (6) 845131; telex 23855; fax (6) 832994; f. 1964. Mems: 138 universities. Sec.-Gen. Dr EHAB ISMAIL. Publ. *AARU Bulletin* (annually and quarterly, in Arabic).

Association of Caribbean University and Research Institutional Libraries—ACURIL: Apdo postal 23317, San Juan 00931, Puerto Rico; tel. 764-0000; fax 763-5685; e-mail vtorres@upracd.upr.clu.edu; f. 1968 to foster contact and collaboration between member universities and institutes; conferences, meetings, seminars, etc.; circulation of information through newsletters, bulletins; facilitates co-operation and the pooling of resources in research; encourages exchange of staff and students. Mems: 250. Exec.-Sec. ONEIDA R. ORTIZ. Publ. *Newsletter* (2 a year).

Association of European Universities (Association des Universités Européennes; formerly the Conférence permanente des recteurs, présidents et vice-chanceliers des universités européennes—CRE): 10 rue du Conseil Général, 1211 Geneva 4, Switzerland; tel. (22) 3292644; fax (22) 3292821; e-mail cre@uniza.unige.ch.; f. 1959; holds two conferences a year, a General Assembly every four years, and training seminars for university executive heads; also involved in special programmes: a history of the university in Europe in four volumes; a joint university programme on institutional development with Latin American universities (*Columbus*); a European university-industry forum, co-sponsored by CRE and the Round Table of European Industrialists; a programme of environmental education and research (*Copernicus*); a programme for the evaluation of institutional strategies for quality. Mems: 520 universities in 39 countries. Pres. Prof. JOSEP M. BRICALL; Sec.-Gen. Dr ANDRIS BARBLAN. Publ. *CRE-Info* (quarterly).

Association of South-East Asian Institutions of Higher Learning—ASAIHL: Secretariat, Ratasastra Bldg 2, Chulalongkorn University, Henri Dunant Rd, Bangkok 10330, Thailand; tel. (2) 251-6966; fax (2) 253-7909; e-mail oninnat@chula.ac.th; f. 1956 to promote the economic, cultural and social welfare of the people of South-East Asia by means of educational co-operation and research programmes; and to cultivate a sense of regional identity and interdependence; collects and disseminates information, organizes discussions. Mems: 160 university institutions in 14 countries. Pres. Pehin Dato ABU BAKAR APONG (Brunei); Sec.-Gen. Dr NINNAT OLANVORAVUTH. Publs *Newsletter, Handbook* (every 3 years).

Catholic International Education Office: 60 rue des Eburons, 1000 Brussels, Belgium; tel. (2) 230-72-52; fax (2) 230-97-45; e-mail oiec@pophost.eunet.be; f. 1952 for the study of the problems of Catholic education throughout the world; co-ordination of the activities of members; and representation of Catholic education at international bodies. Mems: 96 countries, 16 assoc. mems, 13 collaborating mems, 5 corresponding mems. Pres. Mgr A. SARR; Sec.-Gen. ANDRÉS DELGADO HERNÁNDEZ. Publs *OIEC Bulletin* (every 3 months in English, French and Spanish), *OIEC Tracts on Education*.

Catholic International Federation for Physical and Sports Education: 22 rue Oberkampf, 75011 Paris, France; tel. 1-43-38-50-57; f. 1911 to group Catholic associations for physical education and sport of different countries and to develop the principles and precepts of Christian morality by fostering meetings, study and international co-operation. Mems: 14 affiliated national federations representing about 2.8m. members. Pres. ACHILLE DIEGENANT (Belgium); Sec.-Gen. JACQUES GAUTHERON (France).

Comparative Education Society in Europe: Institut für Augemeine Pädagogik, Humboldt-Universität zu Berlin, Unter den Linden 6, 10099 Berlin, Germany; tel. (30) 20934094; fax (30) 20931006; e-mail juergen.schriewer@educat.hu-berlin.de; f. 1961 to promote teaching and research in comparative and international education; the Society organizes conferences and promotes literature. Mems in 49 countries. Pres. Prof. J. SCHRIEWER (Belgium); Sec. and Treasurer Prof. M. A. PEREYRA (Spain). Publ. *Newsletter* (quarterly).

European Bureau of Adult Education: Hotel d'Entitats, Empordà 33, 08020 Barcelona, Spain; tel. (93) 2780294; fax (93) 2780174; e-mail eaea@mx3.redestb.es; internet http://www.vsy.fi/eaea; f. 1953 as a clearing-house and centre of co-operation for all groups concerned with adult education in Europe. Mems: 150 in 18 countries. Pres. P. FEDERIGHI (Italy); Dir W. BAX. Publs *Conference*

Reports, Directory of Adult Education Organisations in Europe, Newsletter, Survey of Adult Education Legislation, Glossary of Terms.

European Cultural Foundation: Jan van Goyenkade 5, 1075 HN Amsterdam, Netherlands; tel. (20) 6760222; fax (20) 6752231; e-mail ecsinfo@pi.net; f. 1954 as a non-governmental organization, supported by private sources, to promote activities of mutual interest to European countries, concerning culture, education, environment, East-West cultural relations, media, cultural relations with the countries of the Mediterranean, issues regarding cultural pluralism; national committees in 22 countries; transnational network of institutes and centres: European Institute of Education and Social Policy, Paris; Institute for European Environmental Policy, London, Madrid and Paris; Association for Innovative Co-operation in Europe (AICE), Brussels; EURYDICE Central Unit (the Education Information Network of the European Community), Brussels; European Institute for the Media, Düsseldorf; European Foundation Centre, Brussels; Fund for Central and East European Book Projects, Amsterdam; Institute for Human Sciences, Vienna; East West Parliamentary Practice Project, Amsterdam; Centre Européen de la Culture, Geneva. A grants programme, for European co-operation projects is also conducted. Pres. HRH Princess MARGRIET of the Netherlands; Sec.-Gen. Dr R. STEPHAN. Publs *Annual Report, Newsletter* (3 a year).

European Federation for Catholic Adult Education: Bildungshaus Mariatrost, Kirchbergstrasse 18, A-8044 Graz, Austria; tel. (316) 39-11-31-35; fax (316) 39-11-31-30; f. 1963 to strengthen international contact between members, to assist international research and practical projects in adult education; to help communications between its members and other international bodies; holds conference every two years. Pres. Prof. Mag. KARL KALCSICS (Austria).

European Foundation for Management Development: 40 rue Washington, 1050 Brussels, Belgium; tel. (2) 648-03-85; fax (2) 646-07-68; e-mail info@efmd.be; internet http://www.efmd.be; f. 1971 through merger of European Association of Management Training Centres and International University Contact for Management Education; aims to help improve the quality of management development and disseminate information within the economic, social and cultural context of Europe and promote international co-operation. Mems: more than 390 institutions in 41 countries world-wide (26 in Europe). Pres. GERARD VAN SCHAIK; Dir-Gen. BERNADETTE CONRATHS. Publs *Forum* (3 a year), *Guide to European Business Schools and Management Centres* (annually).

European Union of Arabic and Islamic Scholars: c/o Dipartimento di studi e ricerche su Africa e Paesi arabi, Istituto universitario orientale, Piazza S. Domenico Maggiore 12, 80134 Naples, Italy; tel. (81) 5517840; fax (81) 5515386; f. 1964 to organize congresses of Arabic and Islamic Studies; congresses are held every two years. Mems: 270 in 25 countries. Pres. Prof. WILFERD MADELUNG; Sec. Prof. CARMELA BAFFIONI.

Graduate Institute of International Studies (Institut universitaire de hautes études internationales): POB 36, 132 rue de Lausanne, Geneva, Switzerland; tel. (22) 7311730; telex 412151; fax (22) 7384306; f. 1927 to establish a centre for advanced studies in international relations of the present day, juridical, historical, political and economic. Library of 147,000 vols. Dir Prof. ALEXANDER SWOBODA; Sec.-Gen. J.-C. FRACHEBOURG.

Inter-American Centre for Research and Documentation on Vocational Training (Centro Interamericano de Investigación y Documentación sobre Formación Profesional—CINTERFOR): Avda Uruguay 1238, Casilla de correo 1761, Montevideo, Uruguay; tel. (2) 920557; telex 22573; fax (2) 921305; f. 1964 by the International Labour Organisation (q.v.) for mutual help among the Latin American and Caribbean countries in planning vocational training; services are provided in documentation, research, exchange of experience; holds seminars and courses. Dir PEDRO DANIEL WEINBERG. Publs *Bulletin* (4 a year), *Documentation* (2 a year), *SIRFO Flash* (quarterly), *Bibliographical Series, Studies, Monographs and Abstracts.*

Inter-American Confederation for Catholic Education (Confederación Interamericana de Educación Católica): Calle 78 No 12–16 (ofna 101), Apdo Aéreo 90036, Santafé de Bogotá 8 DE, Colombia; tel. 255-3676; fax (1) 2550513; f. 1945 to defend and extend the principles and rules of Catholic education, freedom of education, and human rights; organizes congress every three years. Pres. SALVADOR VALLE; Gen. Sec. OSCAR MONTOYA. Publ. *Educación Hoy.*

International Association for Educational and Vocational Guidance—IAEVG: c/o Kathleen M. V. Hall, Training and Employment Agency, Gloucester House, 57 Chichester St, Belfast BT1 4RA, United Kingdom; tel. (1232) 252299; fax (1232) 252266; f. 1951 to contribute to the development of vocational guidance and promote contact between persons associated with it. Mems: 40,000 from 60 countries. Pres. Prof. JOSÉ FERREIRA MARQUES (Portugal); Sec.-Gen. KATHLEEN HALL (UK). Publs *Bulletin* (2 a year), *Newsletter* (3 a year).

International Association for the Development of Documentation, Libraries and Archives in Africa: Villa 2547 Dieuppeul II, BP 375, Dakar, Senegal; tel. 24-09-54; f. 1957 to organize and develop documentation and archives in all African countries. Mems: national asscns, institutions and individuals in 48 countries. Sec.-Gen. ZACHEUS SUNDAY ALI (Nigeria).

International Association of Papyrologists: Fondation Egyptologique Reine Elisabeth, Parc du Cinquantenaire 10, 1040 Brussels, Belgium; tel. (2) 741-73-64; f. 1947; Mems: about 500. Pres. Prof. HANS-ALBERT RUPPRECHT (Germany); Sec. Prof. ALAIN MARTIN (Belgium).

International Association of Physical Education in Higher Education: Institut Supérieur d'Education Physique, Bâtiment B21, Université de Liège au Sart Tilman, 4000 Liège, Belgium; tel. (4) 366-38-90; fax (4) 366-29-01; e-mail mpieron@ulg.ac.be; f. 1962; organizes congresses, exchanges, and research in physical education. Mems: institutions in 51 countries. Sec.-Gen. Dr MAURICE PIERON.

International Association of Universities—IAU/International Universities Bureau—IUB: 1 rue Miollis, 75732 Paris Cédex 15, France; tel. 1-45-68-25-45; telex 270602; fax 1-47-34-76-05; e-mail iau@unesco.org; f. 1950 to allow co-operation at the international level among universities and other institutions of higher education; provides clearing-house services and operates the joint IAU/UNESCO Information Centre on Higher Education; conducts meetings and research on issues concerning higher education. Mems: about 600 universities and institutions of higher education in some 150 countries; assoc. mems: 20 international and national university organizations. Pres. WATARU MORI; Sec.-Gen. FRANZ EBERHARD. Publs *Higher Education Policy* (quarterly), *IAU Newsletter* (every 2 months), *International Handbook of Universities* (every 2 years), *Issues in Higher Education* (monographs), *World Academic Database* (CD-ROM, annually), *World List of Universities* (every 2 years).

International Association of University Professors and Lecturers—IAUPL: c/o F. Mauro, 18 rue du Docteur Roux, 75015 Paris, France; f. 1945 for the development of academic fraternity amongst university teachers and research workers; the protection of independence and freedom of teaching and research; the furtherance of the interests of all university teachers; and the consideration of academic problems. Mems: federations in 17 countries. Sec.-Gen. F. MAURO.

International Baccalaureate Organization—IBO: Route des Morillons 15, Grand-Saconnex 1218, Geneva, Switzerland; tel. (22) 7910274; fax (22) 7910277; e-mail ibhq@ibo.org; f. 1967 to plan curricula and an international university entrance examination, the International Baccalaureate, recognized by major universities world-wide; offers the Primary Years Programme for children aged between 3 and 12 and the Middle Years Programme for students in the 11–16 age range; Mems: 770 participating schools in 95 countries. Pres. of Council GREG CRAFTER (Australia); Dir-Gen. ROGER M. PEEL.

International Council for Adult Education: 720 Bathurst St, Suite 500, Toronto, Ont, Canada M5S 2R4; tel. (416) 588-1211; telex 06-986766; fax (416) 588-5725; e-mail icae@web.net; internet http://www.web.net/icae; f. 1973 to promote the education of adults in relation to the need for healthy growth and development of individuals and communities; undertakes research and training; organizes seminars, the exchange of information, and co-operative publishing; maintains resource centre with extensive material on literacy, adult education and development education; General Assembly meets every four years. Mems: seven regional organizations and 95 national associations in 80 countries. Pres. LALITA RAMDAS. Publs *Convergence, ICAE News.*

International Council for Open and Distance Education—ICDE: Gjerdrums Vei 12, 0486 Oslo, Norway; tel. 22-95-06-30; fax 22-95-07-19; e-mail icde@icde.no; internet http://www.icde.org; f. 1938 (name changed 1982); furthers distance (correspondence) education by promoting research, encouraging regional links, providing information and organizing conferences. Mems: institutions, corporations and individuals in 120 countries. Pres. A. ROCHA TRINDADE (Portugal); Sec.-Gen. REIDAR ROLL (Norway). Publ. *Open Praxis* (2 a year).

International Federation for Parent Education: 1 ave Léon Journault, 92311 Sèvres Cédex, France; tel. 1-45-07-21-64; fax 1-46-26-69-27; f. 1964 to gather in congresses and colloquia experts from different scientific fields and those responsible for family education in their own countries and to encourage the establishment of family education where it does not exist. Mems: 120. Pres. MONEEF GUITOUNI (Canada). Publ. *Lettre de la FIEP* (2 a year).

International Federation of Catholic Universities (Fédération internationale d'universités catholiques—FIUC) 21 rue d'Assas, 75270 Paris Cédex 06, France; tel. 1-44-39-52-26; fax 1-44-39-52-28; e-mail fiuc@icp.fr; f. 1948; to ensure a strong bond of mutual assistance among all Catholic universities in the search for truth; to help to solve problems of growth and development, and to co-operate with other international organizations. Mems: 182 in 41 countries. Pres. ANDREW GONZALEZ (Philippines); Sec.-Gen. VINCENT HANSSENS (Belgium). Publ. *Quarterly Newsletter.*

International Federation of Library Associations and Institutions—IFLA: POB 95312, 2509 CH The Hague, Netherlands; tel. (70) 3140884; fax (70) 3834827; e-mail ifla.hq@ifla.nl; f. 1927 to promote international co-operation in librarianship and bibliography. Mems: 139 associations, 1,072 institutions and 294 individual members in 146 countries. Pres. CHRISTINE DESCHAMPS; Sec.-Gen. LEO VOOGT. Publs *IFLA Council Report* (every 2 years), *IFLA Directory, IFLA Journal, International Cataloguing and Bibliographic Control* (quarterly), *IFLA Professional Reports.*

International Federation of Organizations for School Correspondence and Exchange: Via Torino 256, 10015 Ivrea, Italy; tel. (125) 234433; fax (125) 234761; e-mail fioces@toz.flashnet.it; f. 1929; aims to contribute to the knowledge of foreign languages and civilizations and to bring together young people of all nations by furthering international scholastic correspondence. Mems: comprises 78 national bureaux of scholastic correspondence and exchange in 21 countries. Pres. ALBERT V. RUTLER (Malta); Gen. Sec. LIVIO TONSO (Italy).

International Federation of Physical Education (Fédération internationale d'éducation physique—FIEP): 4 Cleevecroft Ave, Bishops Cleeve, Cheltenham, GL52 4JZ, United Kingdom; tel. and fax (1242) 673674; f. 1923; studies physical education on scientific, pedagogic and aesthetic bases in order to stimulate health, harmonious development or preservation, healthy recreation, and the best adaptation of the individual to the general needs of social life; organizes international congresses and courses, and awards research prize. Mems: from 112 countries. Pres. JOHN C. ANDREWS. Publ. *FIEP Bulletin* (trilingual edition in French, English and Spanish, 3 times a year).

International Federation of Teachers of Modern Languages: Seestrasse 247, 8038 Zürich, Switzerland; tel. (1) 4855251; telex 815250; fax (1) 4825054; f. 1931; holds meetings on every aspect of foreign-language teaching; has consultative status with UNESCO. Mems: 33 national and regional language associations and six international unilingual associations (teachers of English, French, German, Italian and Spanish). Pres. MICHAEL CANDELIER; Sec.-Gen. DENIS CUNNINGHAM. Publ. *FIPLV World News* (quarterly in English, French and Spanish).

International Federation of University Women: 8 rue de l'Ancien Port, 1201 Geneva, Switzerland; tel. (22) 7312380; fax (22) 7380440; e-mail ifuw@iprolink.ch; internet http://www.ifuw.org; f. 1919 to promote understanding and friendship among university women of the world; to encourage international co-operation; to further the development of education; to represent university women in international organizations; to encourage the full application of members' skills to the problems which arise at all levels of public life. Affiliates: 67 national associations with over 161,000 mems. Pres. Dr ELIZABETH M. E. POSKITT (UK). Publs *IFUW News* (6 a year), triennial report.

International Federation of Workers' Education Associations: c/o AOF Postboks 8703, Youngstorget, 0028 Oslo 1, Norway; tel. 22-03-12-88; fax 22-03-12-70; e-mail jmehlum@online.no; f. 1947 to promote co-operation between non-governmental bodies concerned with workers' education, through clearing-house services, exchange of information, publications, international seminars, conferences, summer schools, etc. Pres. DAN GALLIN (Switzerland); Gen. Sec. JAN MEHLUM (Norway).

International Institute for Adult Literacy Methods: POB 19395/6194, 5th Floor, Golfam St, 19156 Teheran, Iran; tel. (21) 2220313; f. 1968 by UNESCO and the Government of Iran, to collect, analyse and distribute information on activities concerning methods of literacy training and adult education; sponsors seminars; maintains documentation service and library on literacy and adult education. Dir Dr MOHAMMAD REZA HAMIDIZADE. Publs *Selection of Adult Education Issues* (monthly), *Adult Education and Development* (quarterly), *New Library Holdings* (quarterly).

International Institute of Philosophy—IIP (Institut international de philosophie—IIP): 8, rue Jean-Calvin, 75005 Paris, France; tel. 1-43-36-39-11; f. 1937 to clarify fundamental issues of contemporary philosophy in annual meetings and to promote mutual understanding among thinkers of different backgrounds and traditions; a maximum of 115 members are elected, chosen from all countries and representing different tendencies. Mems: 100 in 39 countries. Pres. TOMONOBU IMAMICHI (Japan); Sec.-Gen. P. AUBENQUE (France). Publs *Bibliography of Philosophy* (quarterly), *Proceedings* of annual meetings, *Chroniques, Philosophy and World Community* (series), *Philosophical Problems Today, Controverses philosophiques.*

International Institute of Public Administration: 2 ave de l'Observatoire, 75272 Paris Cédex 06; tel. 1-44-41-85-00; telex 270229; fax 1-44-41-86-19; e-mail iiap.bib@wanadoo.fr; f. 1966; trains high-ranking civil servants from abroad; administrative, economic, financial and diplomatic programmes; Africa, Latin America, Asia, Europe and Near East departments; research department, library of 80,000 vols; Documentation Centre. Dir M. MAUS. Publs *Revue française d'administration publique* (quarterly).

International Reading Association: 800 Barksdale Rd, POB 8139, Newark, DE 19714-8139, USA; tel. (302) 731-1600; fax (302) 731-1057; internet http://www.reading.org; f. 1956 to improve the quality of reading instruction at all levels, to promote the habit of lifelong reading, and to develop every reader's proficiency. Mems: 95,000 in 99 countries. Pres. JOHN J. PIKULSKI; Publs *The Reading Teacher* (8 a year), *Journal of Adolescent and Adult Literacy* (8 a year), *Reading Research Quarterly, Lectura y Vida* (quarterly in Spanish), *Reading Today* (6 a year).

International Schools Association—ISA: CIC CASE 20, 1211 Geneva 20, Switzerland; tel. (22) 7336717; f. 1951 to co-ordinate work in international schools and promote their development; member schools maintain the highest standards and accept pupils of all nationalities, irrespective of race and creed. ISA carries out curriculum research; convenes annual conferences on problems of curriculum and educational reform; organizes occasional teachers' training workshops and specialist seminars. Mems: 85 schools throughout the world. Pres. JAMES MCLELLAN. Publs *Education Bulletin* (2 a year), *ISA Magazine* (annually), *Conference Report* (annually), curriculum studies (occasional).

International Society for Business Education: Hunderupvej 122A, 5230 Odense M, Denmark; tel. 66-12-19-66; fax 66-14-57-94; f. 1901 to encourage international exchange of information and organize international courses and congresses on business education; 2,200 mems, national organizations and individuals in 19 countries. Pres. ANDREW MOORE (UK); Dir ERIK LANGE (Denmark). Publ. *International Review for Business Education.*

International Society for Education through Art: c/o Diederik Schönau, CITO, POB 1109, 6801 BC Arnhem, Netherlands; fax (26) 3521202; e-mail insea@cito.nl; f. 1951 to unite art teachers throughout the world, to exchange information and to co-ordinate research into art education; organizes international congresses and exhibitions of children's art. Pres. KIT GRAUER (Canada). Publ. *INSEA News* (3 a year).

International Society for Music Education: ICRME, University of Reading, Bulmershe Court, Reading, RG6 1HY, United Kingdom; tel. (118) 9318846; fax (118) 9318846; f. 1953 to organize international conferences, seminars and publications on matters pertaining to music education; acts as advisory body to UNESCO in matters of music education. Mems: national committees and individuals in 60 countries. Pres. ANA LUCIA FREGA (Argentina); Sec.-Gen. JOAN THERENS (Canada). Publs *ISME Newsletter, Journal.*

International Society for the Study of Medieval Philosophy: Collège Mercier, place du Cardinal Mercier 14, 1348 Louvain-la-Neuve, Belgium; tel. (10) 47-48-07; fax (10) 47-82-85; e-mail accademia.belgio@hella.stm.it; internet http://www.isp.ucl.ac.be/siepm/siepm.html; f. 1958 to promote the study of medieval thought and the collaboration between individuals and institutions concerned in this field; organizes international congresses. Mems: 569. Pres. Prof. DAVID LUSCOMBE (United Kingdom); Sec. Prof JACQUELINE HAMESSE (Belgium). Publ. *Bulletin de Philosophie Médiévale* (annually).

International Youth Library (Internationale Jugendbibliothek): 81247 Munich, Schloss Blutenburg, Germany; tel. (89) 8912110; fax (89) 8117553; e-mail bib@ijb.de; f. 1948, since 1953 an associated project of UNESCO, to promote the international exchange of children's literature and to provide study opportunities for specialists in children's books; maintains a library of 460,000 volumes in about 120 languages. Dir Dr BARBARA SCHARIOTH. Publs *The White Ravens, IJB Report,* catalogues.

League of European Research Libraries—LIBER: c/o Prof. Esko Häkli, Helsinki University Library, National Library of Finland, POB 15, 00014 Helsinki, Finland; tel. (9) 191-22721; fax (9) 191-2719; f. 1971 to establish close collaboration between the general research libraries of Europe, and national and university libraries in particular; and to help in finding practical ways of improving the quality of the services these libraries provide. Mems: 310 libraries and individuals in 33 countries. Pres. Prof. ESKO HÄKLI; Sec. Dr ANN MATHESON (UK). Publ. *LIBER Quarterly.*

Organization of Ibero-American States for Education, Science and Culture (Organización de Estados Iberoamericanos para la Educación, la Ciencia y la Cultura): Calle Bravo Murillo, No 38, 28015 Madrid, Spain; tel. (1) 594-44-42; fax (1) 594-32-86; e-mail oeimad@oei.es; f. 1949 (as the Ibero-American Bureau of Education); provides information on education, science and culture; encourages exchanges and organizes training courses; the General Assembly (at ministerial level) meets every four years. Mems: governments of 20 countries. Sec.-Gen. JOSÉ TORREBLANCA PRIETO. Publ. *Revista Iberoamericana de Educacion* (quarterly).

Organization of the Catholic Universities of Latin America (Organización de Universidades Católicas de América Latina—

ODUCAL): c/o Dr J. A. Tobías, Universidad del Salvador, Viamonte 1856, CP 1056, Buenos Aires, Argentina; tel. (1) 813-1408; fax (1) 812-4625; f. 1953 to assist the social, economic and cultural development of Latin America through the promotion of Catholic higher education in the continent. Mems: 43 Catholic universities in Argentina, Bolivia, Brazil, Chile, Colombia, Dominican Republic, Ecuador, Guatemala, Mexico, Panama, Paraguay, Peru, Puerto Rico, Uruguay, Venezuela. Pres. Dr JUAN ALEJANDRO TOBÍAS (Argentina); Publs *Anuario; Sapientia; Universitas.*

Southeast Asian Ministers of Education Organization—SEAMEO: Darakarn Bldg, 920 Sukhumvit Rd, Bangkok 10110, Thailand; tel. (2) 391-0144; telex 22683; fax (2) 381-2587; f. 1965 to promote co-operation among the Southeast Asian nations through projects in education, science and culture; SEAMEO has 14 regional centres including: BIOTROP for tropical biology, in Bogor, Indonesia; INNOTECH for educational innovation and technology, and a Non-Formal Education Programme (SNEP), at Quezon City, Philippines; an Open-Learning Centre in Indonesia; RECSAM for education in science and mathematics, in Penang, Malaysia; RELC for languages, in Singapore; RIHED for higher education development in Bangkok, Thailand; SEARCA for graduate study and research in agriculture, in Los Baños, Philippines; SPAFA for archaeology and fine arts in Bangkok, Thailand; TROPMED for tropical medicine and public health with regional centres in Indonesia, Malaysia, Philippines and Thailand and a central office in Bangkok; VOCTECH for vocational and technical education; and the SEAMO Training Centre in Ho Chi Minh City, Viet Nam. Mems: Brunei, Cambodia, Indonesia, Laos, Malaysia, Philippines, Singapore, Thailand, Viet Nam. Assoc. mems: Australia, Canada, France, Germany, Netherlands, New Zealand. Pres. Dr RICARDO GLORIA (Philippines); Dir Dr SUPARAK RACHAINTRA. Publs *Annual Report, SEAMEO Forum, SEAMEO Update, Calendar of Activities, SEAMO Directory, Catalogue of Publications.*

Union of Latin American Universities (Unión de Universidades de América Latina—UDUAL): Edificio UDUAL, Apdo postal 70-232, Ciudad Universitaria, Del. Coyoacán, 04510 México, DF, Mexico; tel. (5) 622-0991; telex 1764112; fax (5) 616-1414; f. 1949 to organize the interchange of professors, students, research fellows and graduates and generally encourage good relations between the Latin American universities; arranges conferences, conducts statistical research; centre for university documentation. Mems: 165 universities. Pres. Dr JORGE BROVETO (Uruguay); Sec.-Gen. Dr ABELARDO VILLEGAS (Mexico). Publs *Universidades* (2 a year), *Gaceta UDUAL* (quarterly), *Censo* (every 2 years).

Universal Esperanto Association: Nieuwe Binnenweg 176, 3015 BJ Rotterdam, Netherlands; tel. (10) 4361044; fax (10) 4361751; e-mail uea@inter.nl.net; f. 1908 to assist the spread of the international language, Esperanto, and to facilitate the practical use of the language. Mems: 56 affiliated national associations and 20,591 individuals in 117 countries. Pres. Prof. LEE CHONG-YEONG (Republic of Korea); Gen. Sec. MICHELA LIPARI (Italy). Publs *Esperanto* (monthly), *Kontakto* (every 2 months), *Jarlibro* (yearbook), *Esperanto Documents.*

World Association for Educational Research: Universiteit Gent, Pedagogisch Laboratorium, 1 Henri Dunantlaan, 9000 Ghent, Belgium; tel. (9) 164-63-78; fax (9) 264-64-90; e-mail vhenderi@rug.ac.be; f. 1953, present title adopted 1977; aims to encourage research in educational sciences by organizing congress, issuing publications, the exchange of information, etc. Member societies and individual members in 50 countries. Pres. Prof. Dr W. MITTER; Gen. Sec. Prof. Dr M.-L. VAN HERREWEGHE (Belgium). Publ. *Communicationes* (2 a year).

World Education Fellowship: 22A Kew Gardens, Kew, Richmond, TW9 3HD, United Kingdom; tel. (181) 940-0131; f. 1921 to promote education for international understanding, and the exchange and practice of ideas together with research into progressive educational theories and methods. Sections and groups in 20 countries. Chair. CHRISTINE WYKES; Sec. ROSEMARY CROMMELIN. Publ. *The New Era in Education* (3 a year).

World Union of Catholic Teachers (Union Mondiale des Enseignants Catholiques—UMEC): Piazza San Calisto 16, 00120 Città del Vaticano; tel. 698-87286; f. 1951; encourages the grouping of Catholic teachers for the greater effectiveness of the Catholic school, distributes documentation on Catholic doctrine with regard to education, and facilitates personal contacts through congresses, seminars, etc., nationally and internationally. Mems: 32 organizations in 29 countries. Pres. ARNOLD BACKX; Sec.-Gen. MICHAEL EMM. Publ. *Nouvelles de l'UMEC.*

Environmental Conservation

BirdLife International: Wellbrook Ct, Girton Rd, Cambridge, CB3 0NA, United Kingdom; tel. (1223) 277318; fax (1223) 277200; e-mail birdlife@birdlife.org.uk; internet http://www.surfnet.fi/birdlife/int/index.html; f. 1922 as the International Council for Bird Preservation; a global partnership of organizations that determines status of bird species throughout the world and compiles data on all endangered species; identifies conservation problems and priorities; initiates and co-ordinates conservation projects and international conventions. Partners in 53 countries; representatives in around 50 more. Chair. GERARD A. BERTRAND; Dir Dr MICHAEL RANDS (UK). Publs *Bird Red Data Book, World Birdwatch* (quarterly), *Bird Conservation Series* and study reports.

Friends of the Earth International: Prins Hendrikkade 48, POB 19199, 1000 GD Amsterdam, Netherlands; tel. (20) 6221369; telex 918023; fax (20) 6392181; e-mail foeint@antenna.nl; internet http://www.xs4all-nl/~foeint; f. 1971 to promote the conservation, restoration and rational use of the environment and natural resources through public education and campaigning. Mems: 56 national groups. Publ. *FoE Link* (6 a year).

Greenpeace International: Keizersgracht 176, 1016 DW Amsterdam, Netherlands; tel. (20) 5236222; fax (20) 5236200; e-mail greenpeace international@green2.greenpeace.org; internet http://www.greenpeace.org; f. 1971 to campaign for the protection of the environment; aims to bear witness to environmental destruction, and to demonstrate solutions for positive change. Mems: offices in 34 countries. Chair. CORNELIA DURRANT; Exec. Dir THILO BODE.

International Commission for the Protection of the Rhine against Pollution: 56003 Koblenz, Hohenzollernstrasse 18, POB 309, Germany; tel. (261) 12495; telex 862499; fax (261) 36572; e-mail iksr@rz-online.de; f. 1950 to prepare and commission research to establish the nature of the pollution of the Rhine; to propose measures of protection and ecological rehabilitation of the Rhine to the signatory governments. Mems: 23 delegates from France, Germany, Luxembourg, Netherlands, Switzerland and the EU. Pres. D. MOYEN; Sec. J. P. WIERIKS. Publ. *Annual Report.*

International Council on Metals and the Environment: 294 Albert St, Suite 506, Ottawa, ON K1P 6E6, Canada; tel. (613) 235-4263; fax (613) 235-2865; e-mail info@icme.com; internet http://www.icme.com; f. 1991 by mining companies to promote responsible environmental practices and policies in the mining, use, recycling and disposal of non-ferrous and precious metals. Mems: companies from six continents representing about 60% of the western world's production of copper, lead, nickel, silver and zinc. Chair. JAIME LOMELIN (Mexico); Sec.-Gen. GARY NASH (Canada). Publ. *ICME Newsletter* (quarterly).

International Waterfowl and Wetlands Research Bureau: Slimbridge, Glos, GL2 7BX, United Kingdom; tel. (453) 890624; telex 437145; fax (453) 890697; f. 1954 to stimulate and co-ordinate research on and conservation of waterfowl and their wetland habitats, particularly through the Ramsar Convention; co-ordinates research, wetland and waterfowl management, and training by institutes and individuals (professional and amateur) throughout the world; alerts governments and organizations when wetlands are threatened. Mems: 40 countries. Dir Dr MICHAEL MOSER. Publs *IWRB News* (every 6 months), *Annual Report,* conference proceedings.

South Pacific Environment Programme—SPREP: POB 240, Apia, Samoa; tel. 21929; fax 20231; e-mail sprep@talofa.net; f. 1978 by the South Pacific Commission (where it was based), the South Pacific Forum, ESCAP and UNEP; formally established as an independent institution in June 1993 when members signed the *Agreement Establishing SPREP*; aims to promote regional co-operation in environmental matters, to assist members to protect and improve their shared environment, and to help members to work towards sustainable development; responsible for implementation of the South Pacific Biodiversity Conservation Programme, a five-year project funded by the UN's Global Environment Facility. Mems: 22 Pacific islands, Australia, France, New Zealand, USA. Dir TAMARII P. TUTANGATA (Cook Islands). Publs *SPREP Newsletter* (quarterly), *CASOLink* (quarterly), *La letter de l'environnement* (quarterly), *Climate Change and Sea Level Rise* (quarterly).

World Conservation Union—IUCN: rue Mauverney 28, 1196 Gland, Switzerland; tel. (22) 9990001; fax (22) 9990002; e-mail mail@hq.iucn.org; internet http://www.iucn.org; f. 1948, as the International Union for Conservation of Nature and Natural Resources, to promote the conservation of natural resources, to secure the conservation of nature, and especially of biological diversity, as an essential foundation for the future; to ensure wise use of the earth's natural resources in an equitable and sustainable way; to guide the development of human communities towards ways of life in enduring harmony with other components of the biosphere, developing programmes to protect and sustain the most important and threatened species and eco-systems and assisting governments to devise and carry out conservation projects; maintains a conservation library and documentation centre and units for monitoring traffic in wildlife. Comprises six Commissions of some 1,000 specialists: the Commission on Ecosystem Management, the Commission on Education and Communication, the Commission on Environmental Law, the Commission on Environmental, Economic and

Strategic Planning, the World Commission on Protected Areas and the Species Survival Commission. Mems: 74 governments, 105 government agencies, 626 national and 56 international non-governmental organizations and 34 affiliates. Pres. YOLANDA KAKABADSE (Ecuador); Dir-Gen. DAVID MCDOWELL (New Zealand). Publs *Annual Report, Red List of Threatened Animals, United Nations List of National Parks and Protected Areas, World Conservation* (3–4 a year).

World Society for the Protection of Animals: 2 Langley Lane, London, SW8 1TJ, United Kingdom; tel. (171) 793-0540; fax (171) 793-0208; f. 1981, incorporating the World Federation for the Protection of Animals (f. 1950) and the International Society for the Protection of Animals (f. 1959); promotes animal welfare and conservation by humane education, practical field projects, international lobbying and legislative work. Chief Exec. ANDREW DICKSON.

World Wide Fund for Nature—WWF: ave de Mont-Blanc, 1196 Gland, Switzerland; tel. (22) 3649111; fax (22) 3643239; e-mail userid@wwfnet.org; internet http://www.panda.org; f. 1961 (as World Wildlife Fund); aims to conserve nature and ecological processes by preserving genetic, species and ecosystem diversity; to ensure the sustainable use of resources; to reduce pollution and wasteful consumption of resources and energy. Mems: 25 national organizations, and six associates. Pres. Syed BABAR ALI (Pakistan); Dir-Gen. Dr CLAUDE MARTIN. Publs *Annual Review, WWF News* (quarterly).

Government and Politics

African Association for Public Administration and Management: POB 48677, Nairobi, Kenya; tel. (2) 52-19-44; fax (2) 52-18-45; e-mail aapam@tt.sasa.union.org; f. 1971 to provide senior officials with a forum for the exchange of ideas and experience, to promote the study of professional techniques and encourage research in particular African administrative problems. Mems: over 500 corporate and individual. Pres WILLIAM N. WAMALWA; Sec.-Gen. Dr IJUKA KABUMBA. Publs *Newsletter* (quarterly), *Annual Seminar Report, African Journal of Public Administration and Management,* studies.

Afro-Asian Peoples' Solidarity Organization—AAPSO: 89 Abdel Aziz Al-Saoud St, POB 11559-61 Manial El-Roda, Cairo, Egypt; tel. (2) 3636081; telex 92627; fax (2) 3637361; e-mail aapso@idsc.gov.eg; f. 1957; acts among and for the peoples of Africa and Asia in their struggle for genuine independence, sovereignty, socio-economic development, peace and disarmament; congress held every four years. Mems: national committees and affiliated organizations in 66 countries and territories, assoc. mems in 15 European countries. Pres. Dr MOURAD GHALEB; Sec.-Gen. NOURI ABDEL-RAZZAK (Iraq). Publs *Solidarity Bulletin* (monthly), *Development and Socio-Economic Progress* (quarterly).

Agency for the Prohibition of Nuclear Weapons in Latin America and the Caribbean (Organismo para la Proscripción de las Armas Nucleares en la América Latina y el Caribe—OPANAL): Temístocles 78, Col. Polanco, CP 11560, México, DF, Mexico; tel. (5) 280-4923; fax (5) 280-2965; f. 1969 to ensure compliance with the Treaty for the Prohibition of Nuclear Weapons in Latin America (Treaty of Tlatelolco), 1967; to ensure the absence of all nuclear weapons in the application zone of the Treaty; to contribute to the movement against proliferation of nuclear weapons; to promote general and complete disarmament; to prohibit all testing, use, manufacture, acquisition, storage, installation and any form of possession, by any means, of nuclear weapons. The organs of the Agency comprise the General Conference, meeting every two years, the Council, meeting every two months, and the secretariat. Holds General Conference every two years. Mems: 30 states which have fully ratified the Treaty: Antigua and Barbuda, Argentina, Bahamas, Barbados, Belize, Bolivia, Brazil, Chile, Colombia, Costa Rica, Dominica, Dominican Republic, Ecuador, El Salvador, Grenada, Guatemala, Haiti, Honduras, Jamaica, Mexico, Nicaragua, Panama, Paraguay, Peru, Saint Vincent and the Grenadines, Suriname, Trinidad and Tobago, Uruguay and Venezuela. The Treaty has two additional Protocols: the first signed and ratified by France, the Netherlands, the UK and the USA; the second signed and ratified by China, the USA, France, the UK and Russia. Sec.-Gen. ENRIQUE ROMÁN-MOREY (Peru).

ANZUS: c/o Dept of Foreign Affairs and Trade, Locked Bag 40, Queen Victoria Terrace, Canberra, ACT 2600, Australia; tel. (2) 6261-9111; telex 62007; fax (2) 6273-3577; the ANZUS Security Treaty was signed in 1951 by Australia, New Zealand and the USA, and ratified in 1952 to co-ordinate partners' efforts for collective defence for the preservation of peace and security in the Pacific area, through the exchange of technical information and strategic intelligence, and a programme of exercises, exchanges and visits. In 1984 New Zealand refused to allow visits by US naval vessels that were either nuclear-propelled or potentially nuclear-armed, and this led to the cancellation of joint ANZUS military exercises: in 1986 the USA formally announced the suspension of its security commitment to New Zealand under ANZUS. Instead of the annual ANZUS Council meetings, bilateral talks were subsequently held every year between Australia and the USA. ANZUS continued to govern security relations between Australia and the USA, and between Australia and New Zealand; security relations between New Zealand and the USA were the only aspect of the treaty to be suspended. Senior-level contacts between New Zealand and the USA resumed in 1994.

Association of Secretaries General of Parliaments: c/o Committee Office, House of Commons, London, SW1, United Kingdom; tel. (171) 219-3259; f. 1938; studies the law, practice and working methods of different Parliaments and proposes measures for improving those methods and for securing co-operation between the services of different Parliaments; operates as a consultative body to the Inter-Parliamentary Union (q.v.), and assists the Union on subjects within the scope of the Association. Mems: about 200 representing about 90 countries. Pres. JACQUES OLLÉ-LAPRUNE (France); Joint Sec. Y. AZAD (UK). Publ. *Constitutional and Parliamentary Information* (2 a year).

Atlantic Treaty Association: 10 rue Crevaux, 75116 Paris, France; tel. 1-45-53-28-80; fax 1-47-55-49-63; f. 1954 to inform public opinion on the North Atlantic Alliance and to promote the solidarity of the peoples of the North Atlantic; holds annual assemblies, seminars, study conferences for teachers and young politicians. Mems: national associations in the 16 member countries of NATO (q.v.); 16 assoc. mems from central and eastern Europe. Chair. THEODOSSIS GEORGIOU (Greece); Sec.-Gen. ALFRED CAHEN (France).

Baltic Council: f. 1993 by the Baltic Assembly comprising 60 parliamentarians from Estonia, Latvia and Lithuania; Council of Ministers of the three Baltic countries to co-ordinate policy in the areas of foreign policy, justice, the environment, education and science.

Celtic League: 11 Hilltop View, Farmhill, Braddan, Isle of Man; tel. (1624) 627128; f. 1961 to foster co-operation between the six Celtic nations (Ireland, Scotland, Man, Wales, Cornwall and Brittany), especially those who are actively working for political autonomy by non-violent means; campaigns politically on issues affecting the Celtic countries; monitors military activity in the Celtic countries; co-operates with national cultural organizations to promote the languages and culture of the Celts. Mems: approx. 1,400 individuals in the Celtic communities and elsewhere. Chair. CATHAL Ó LUAIN; Gen. Sec. J. B. MOFFAT. Publ. *Carn* (quarterly).

Central European Initiative—CEI: c/o Ambassador Dr ISTVÀN BALOGH, Chair. of the National Co-ordinators, Ministry for Foreign Affairs, Bem rakpart 47, Budapest, Hungary; f. 1989 as 'Pentagonal' group of central European countries (Austria, Czechoslovakia, Italy, Hungary, Yugoslavia); became 'Hexagonal' with the admission of Poland in July 1991; present name adopted in March 1992, when Croatia and Slovenia replaced Yugoslavia as members (Bosnia and Herzegovina and the former Yugoslav republic of Macedonia subsequently became members); the Czech Republic and Slovakia became separate mems in January 1993; Albania, Belarus, Bulgaria, Romania and Ukraine joined the CEI in June 1996 and Moldova in November; 1996 Summit: Graz, Austria, in November. The Initiative aims to encourage regional and bilateral co-operation, working within the OSCE (q.v.).

Christian Democrat International: 16 rue de la Victoire, Boîte 1, 1060 Brussels, Belgium; tel. (2) 537-13-22; fax (2) 537-93-48; f. 1961 to serve as a platform for the co-operation of political parties of Christian Social inspiration. Mems: parties in 64 countries (of which 47 in Europe). Sec.-Gen. JAVIER RUPEREZ. Publs *DC-Info* (quarterly), *Human Rights* (5 a year), *Documents* (quarterly).

Comunidade dos Países de Língua Portuguesa (Community of Portuguese-Speaking Countries): rua S. Caetano 32, 1200 Lisbon, Portugal; tel. (1) 392-8560; fax (1) 392-8588; f. 1996; aims to produce close political, economic, diplomatic and cultural links between Portuguese-speaking countries and to strengthen the influence of the Lusophone commonwealth within the international community. Mems: Angola, Brazil, Cape Verde, Guinea-Bissau, Mozambique, Portugal, São Tomé e Príncipe; East Timor has observer status. Exec. Sec. MARCOLINO MOCO (Angola).

Council of the Baltic Sea States: c/o Ministry for Foreign Affairs, Gustav Adolf storg 1, POB 16121, 103 23 Stockholm; f. 1992 to intensify co-operation between member states. Mems: Denmark, Estonia, Finland, Germany, Iceland, Latvia, Lithuania, Norway, Poland, Russia, Sweden, the EU.

Eastern Regional Organization for Public Administration—EROPA: POB 198, University of the Philippines, Diliman, Quezon City, Metro Manila, Philippines; tel. (2) 9295411; fax (2) 9283861; f. 1960 to promote regional co-operation in improving knowledge, systems and practices of governmental administration to help accelerate economic and social development; organizes regional conferences, seminars, special studies, surveys and training programmes. There are three regional centres: Training Centre (New Delhi),

Local Government Centre (Tokyo), Development Management Centre (Seoul). Mems: 13 countries, 103 organizations/groups, 368 individuals. Chair. Dr TAN SRI MAZLAN BIN AHMAD (Malaysia); Sec.-Gen. PATRICIA A. STO TOMAS (Philippines). Publs *EROPA Bulletin* (quarterly), *Asian Review of Public Administration* (every 6 months).

European Movement: European Action Centre, place du Luxembourg 1, 1040 Brussels, Belgium; tel. (2) 512-44-44; fax (2) 512-66-73; f. 1947 by a liaison committee of representatives from European organizations, to study the political, economic and technical problems of a European Union and suggest how they can be solved; to inform and lead public opinion in the promotion of integration. Conferences have led to the creation of the Council of Europe, College of Europe, etc. Mems: national councils and committees in Austria, Belgium, Croatia, Cyprus, Czech Republic, Denmark, France, Germany, Greece, Hungary, Ireland, Italy, Luxembourg, former Yugoslav republic of Macedonia, Malta, Netherlands, Norway, Poland, Portugal, Romania, Slovakia, Slovenia, Spain, Switzerland, Turkey, United Kingdom, Yugoslavia; and several international social and economic organizations. Pres. VALÉRY GISCARD D'ESTAING (France); Sec.-Gen. PIER VIRGILIO DASTOLI (Italy). Publ. *Lettre du Mouvement Européen* (6 a year).

European Union of Women—EUW: Auklands, Gloucester Rd, Thornbury, Bristol, BS12 1JH, United Kingdom; tel. (1454) 413865; fax (1454) 412490; f. 1955 to increase the influence of women in the political and civic life of their country and of Europe. Mems: national organizations in 19 countries. Pres. ANGELA GUILLAUME; Sec.-Gen. PAM RICKARDS.

European Young Christian Democrats—EYCD: 16 rue de la Victoire, 1060 Brussels, Belgium; tel. (2) 537-41-47; fax (2) 534-50-28; f. 1947; holds monthly seminars and meetings for young political leaders; conducts training in international political matters. Mems: 28 national organizations in 25 European countries. Pres. ENRICO LETTA (Italy); Sec.-Gen. MARC BERTRAND (Belgium). Publ. *EYCD File* (6 a year).

General Secretariat of the Central American Integration System (Secretario General del Sistema de la Integración Centroamericano—SG-SICA): Paseo General Escalón No. 5353, San Salvador, El Salvador; tel. 263-3166; fax 263-1340; internet http://www.sicanet.org.sv; f. 1951 as Organization of Central American States, present name adopted in 1991; aims to achieve Central American integration, with peace, liberty, democracy, development and respect for human rights as the guiding principles; co-ordinates the integration process in the political, economic, social and environmental areas towards the stated objective. Mems: Costa Rica, El Salvador, Guatemala, Honduras, Nicaragua. Gen. Sec. ERNESTO LEAL SÁNCHEZ (Nicaragua).

Hansard Society for Parliamentary Government: St Philips Bldg North, Sheffield St, London, WC2A 2EX, United Kingdom; tel. (171) 955-7478; fax (171) 955-7492; f. 1944 to promote political education and research and the informed discussion of all aspects of modern parliamentary government. Dir DAVID HARRIS. Publ. *Parliamentary Affairs—A Journal of Comparative Politics* (quarterly).

Inter-African Socialists and Democrats: 6 rue al-Waquidi 1004, al-Menzah IV, Tunis, Tunisia; tel. 231-138; telex 15415; f. 1981 (as Inter-African Socialist Organization; name changed 1988). Chair. ABDOU DIOUF (Senegal); Sec.-Gen. SADOK FAYALA (Tunisia).

International Alliance of Women: 9/10 Queen St, Melbourne, Vic 3000, Australia; tel. (3) 9629-3653; fax (3) 9629-2904; e-mail toddsec@surfnetcity.com.au; f. 1904 to obtain equality for women in all fields and to encourage women to take up their responsibilities; to join in international activities. Mems: 78 national affiliates in 67 countries. Pres. PATRICIA GILES. Publ. *International Women's News* (quarterly).

International Association for Community Development: 179 rue du Débarcadère, 6001 Marcinelle, Belgium; tel. (71) 44-72-78; fax (71) 47-11-04; organizes annual international colloquium for community-based organizations. Sec.-Gen. PIERRE ROZEN. Publ. *IACD Newsletter* (2 a year).

International Association of Educators for World Peace: POB 3282, Mastin Lake Station, Huntsville, AL 35810, USA; tel. (205) 534-5501; fax (205) 536-1018; e-mail mercieca@hiwaay.net; f. 1969 to develop the kind of education which will contribute to the promotion of peaceful relations at personal, community and international levels, to communicate and clarify controversial views in order to achieve maximum understanding and to help put into practice the Universal Declaration of Human Rights. Mems: 25,000 in 102 countries. Pres. Dr SURYA NATH PRASAD (India); Exec. Vice-Pres. Dr CHARLES MERCIECA (USA); Sec.-Gen. Dr JOACHIM SCHUSTER (Germany). Publs *Peace Progress* (annually), *IAEWP Newsletter* (6 a year), *Peace Education* (2 a year).

International Commission for the History of Representative and Parliamentary Institutions: c/o John Rogister, Dept of History, 43–46 North Bailey, Durham DH1 3EX, United Kingdom; fax (191) 374-4754; f. 1936. Mems: 300 individuals in 31 countries. Pres. JOHN ROGISTER (UK); Sec. JOHN H. GREVER (USA). Publs *Parliaments, Estates and Representation* (annually), studies.

International Democrat Union: 32 Smith Square, London, SW1P 3HH, United Kingdom; tel. (171) 222-0847; fax (171) 222-1459; e-mail 100066.2502@compuserve.com; f. 1983; group of centre-right political parties; holds conference every six months. Mems: 29 political parties in 28 countries, four assoc. mems. Exec. Sec. GRAHAM WYNN.

International Federation of Resistance Movements: c/o R. Maria, 5 rue Rollin, 75005 Paris, France; tel. 1-43-26-84-29; f. 1951; supports the medical and social welfare of former victims of fascism; works for peace, disarmament and human rights, against fascism and neo-fascism. Mems: 82 national organizations in 29 countries. Pres. ALIX LHOTE (France); Sec.-Gen. Prof. ILYA KREMER (Russia). Publs *Feville d'information* (in French and German), *Cahier d'informations médicales, sociales et juridiques* (in French and German).

International Institute for Peace: Möllwaldplatz 5, 1040 Vienna, Austria; tel. (1) 504-43-76; fax (1) 505-32-36; f. 1957; non-governmental organization with consultative status at ECOSOC (see UN) and UNESCO; studies interdependence as a strategy for peace, conflict prevention and the transformation of central and eastern Europe. Mems: individuals and corporate bodies invited by the executive board. Pres. ERWIN LANC (Austria); Dir Prof. LEV VORONKOV (Russia). Publs *Peace and the Sciences* (quarterly, in English), occasional papers (2 or 3 a year, in English and German).

International Institute for Strategic Studies: 23 Tavistock St, London, WC2E 7NQ, United Kingdom; tel. (171) 379-7676; fax (171) 836-3108; f. 1958; concerned with the study of the role of force in international relations, including problems of international strategy, the ethnic, political and social sources of conflict, disarmament and arms control, peace-keeping and intervention, defence economics, etc.; independent of any government. Mems: 3,000. Dir Dr JOHN M. CHIPMAN. Publs *Survival* (quarterly), *The Military Balance* (annually), *Strategic Survey* (annually), *Adelphi Papers* (10 a year), *Strategic Comments* (10 a year).

International Lesbian and Gay Association—ILGA: 81 rue Marché-au-charbon, 1000 Brussels 1, Belgium; tel. and fax (2) 502-24-71; e-mail ilga@ilga.org; f. 1978; works to remove legal, social and economic discrimination against homosexual women and men throughout the world; co-ordinates political action at an international level; co-operates with other supportive movements. 1997 world conference: Cologne, Germany. Mems: 300 national and regional associations in 75 countries. Secs-Gen JENNIFER WILSON, JORDI PETIT. Publ. *ILGA Bulletin* (quarterly).

International Peace Bureau: 41 rue de Zürich, 1201 Geneva, Switzerland; tel. (22) 7316429; fax (22) 7389419; e-mail ipb@gn.apc.org; internet http://www.ial.ch/ipb; f. 1892; promotes international co-operation for general and complete disarmament and the non-violent solution of international conflicts; co-ordinates and represents peace movements at the UN; conducts projects on the abolition of nuclear weapons and the role of non-governmental organizations in conflict prevention/resolution. Mems: 158 peace organizations in 40 countries. Pres. Maj. BRITT THEORIN; Sec.-Gen. COLIN ARCHER. Publs *Geneva Monitor* (every 2 months), *IPB Geneva News*.

International Political Science Association: c/o Prof. John Coakley, Dept. of Politics, Univ. College Dublin, Belfield, Dublin 4, Ireland; tel. (1) 706-8182; fax (1) 706-1171; e-mail ipsa@ucd.ie; internet http://www.ucd.ie/~ipsa/index.html; f. 1949; aims to promote the development of political science. Mems: 41 national associations, 100 institutions, 1,350 individual mems. Pres. Prof. THEODORE J. LOWI (USA); Sec.-Gen. JOHN COAKLEY. Publs *Participation* (3 a year), *International Political Science Abstracts* (6 a year), *International Political Science Review* (quarterly).

International Union of Local Authorities: POB 90646, 2509 LP, The Hague, Netherlands; tel. (70) 3066066; fax (70) 3500496; e-mail iula@iula-hq.nl; f. 1913 to promote local government, improve local administration and encourage popular participation in public affairs. Functions include organization of conferences, seminars, and biennial international congress; servicing of specialized committees (municipal insurance, wholesale markets, subsidiary corporations); development of intermunicipal relations to provide a link between local authorities of countries; maintenance of a permanent office for the collection and distribution of information on municipal affairs. Mems in over 100 countries; seven regional sections. Pres. NORBERT BURGER (Germany); Sec.-Gen. ANDREW HORGAN.

International Union of Young Christian Democrats—IUYCD: 16 rue de la Victoire, 1060 Brussels, Belgium; tel. (2) 537-77-51; fax (2) 534-50-28; f. 1962. Mems: national organizations in 59 countries and territories. Sec.-Gen. MARCOS VILLASMIL (Venezuela). Publs *IUYCD Newsletter* (fortnightly), *Debate* (quarterly).

Inter-Parliamentary Union: place du Petit-Saconnex, CP 438, 1211 Geneva 19, Switzerland; tel. (22) 9194150; fax (22) 7333141; e-mail postbox@mail.ipu.org; f. 1889; brings together representatives of the legislatures of sovereign states. As the focal point for world-wide parliamentary dialogue, the IPU works for peace and co-operation among peoples and for the firm establishment of representative institutions; holds two conferences annually, bringing together MPs to study political, economic, social and cultural problems and sustainable human development. The Union operates a Programme for the Study and Promotion of Representative Institutions, and co-ordinates a technical co-operation programme to help strengthen the infrastructures of legislatures in developing countries. It also defends the human rights of parliamentarians, and promotes the participation of women in political life. Budget (1997) 9.7m. Swiss francs. Mems: 137 Inter-Parliamentary Groups. Assoc. Mems: the Andean Parliament, the Latin American Parliament and the Parliamentary Assembly of the Council of Europe. Pres. of Inter-Parliamentary Council MIGUEL ANGEL MARTÍNEZ (Spain); Sec.-Gen. PIERRE CORNILLON (France). Publs. *Inter-Parliamentary Bulletin* (2 a year), *World Directory of Parliaments* (annually), *Chronicle of Parliamentary Elections* (annually), *Parliaments of the World: A Reference Compendium*.

Inuit Circumpolar Conference: 170 Laurier Ave West, Suite 504, Ottawa, ON K1P 5V5, Canada; tel. (613) 563-2642; fax (613) 565-3089; f. 1977 to protect the indigenous culture, environment and rights of the Inuit people (Eskimoes), and to encourage co-operation among the Inuit; conferences held every three years. Mems: Inuit communities in Canada, Greenland, Alaska and Russia. Pres. ROSEMARIE KUPTANA. Publ. *ICC Arctic Policy Review*.

Jewish Agency for Israel: POB 92, 48 King George St, Jerusalem, Israel; tel. (2) 20-22-22; fax (2) 20-23-03; f. 1929; reconstituted 1971 as an instrument through which world Jewry could develop a national home. Constituents are: World Zionist Organization, United Israel Appeal, Inc. (USA), and Keren Hayesod. Chair. Exec. AVRAHAM BURG; Chair. Bd. CHARLES GOODMAN.

Latin American Parliament (Parlamento Latinoamericano): Avda Abancay 210, Casilla 6041, Lima, Peru; tel. (1) 462-8083; fax (1) 462-5165; f. 1965; permanent democratic institution, representative of all existing political trends within the national legislative bodies of Latin America; aims to promote the movement towards economic, political and cultural integration of the Latin American republics, and to uphold human rights, peace and security. Publs *Acuerdos, Resoluciones de las Asambleas Ordinarias* (annually), *Revista del Parlamento Latinoamericano* (annually); statements and agreements.

Liberal International: 1 Whitehall Place, London, SW1A 2HD, United Kingdom; tel. (171) 839-5905; fax (171) 925-2685; e-mail worldlib@cix.compulink.co.uk; f. 1947; world union of 71 liberal parties in 52 countries; co-ordinates foreign policy work of member parties, and promotes freedom, tolerance, democracy, international understanding, protection of human rights and market-based economics; has consultative status at ECOSOC of United Nations and the Council of Europe. Pres. FRITS BOLKESTEIN (Netherlands); Sec.-Gen. JULIUS MAATEN. Publ. *London Aerogramme* (monthly).

Non-aligned Movement: c/o Permanent Representative of Colombia to the UN, New York, NY 10017, USA (no permanent secretariat); tel. (212) 355-7776; fax (212) 371-2813; f. 1961 by a meeting of 25 Heads of State, aiming to link countries which refused to adhere to the main East-West military and political blocs; co-ordination bureau established in 1973; works for the establishment of a new international economic order, and especially for better terms for countries producing raw materials; maintains special funds for agricultural development, improvement of food production and the financing of buffer stocks; 'South Commission' (q.v.) promotes co-operation between developing countries; seeks changes in the United Nations to give developing countries greater decision-making power; in October 1995 member states urged the USA to lift its economic embargo against Cuba; summit conference held every three years, twelfth conference of heads of state and government was to be held in Pretoria, South Africa, in 1998. Mems: 113 countries. Chair. Pres. ERNESTO SAMPER PIZANO (Colombia).

North Atlantic Assembly: 3 place du Petit Sablon, 1000 Brussels, Belgium; tel. (2) 513-28-65; telex 24809; fax (2) 514-18-47; internet gopher://marvin.nc3a.nato.int:70/11/other-international/naa; f. 1955 as the NATO Parliamentarians' Conference; name changed 1966; the inter-parliamentary assembly of the North Atlantic Alliance; holds two plenary sessions a year and meetings of committees (Political, Defence and Security, Economic, Scientific and Technical, Civilian Affairs) where parliamentarians from North America, western Europe and eastern Europe (associate delegates) examine the problems confronting the Alliance and European security issues in general. Pres. KARSTEN VOIGT (Germany); Sec.-Gen. PETER CORTERIER (Germany).

Open Door International (for the Economic Emancipation of the Woman Worker); 16 rue Américaine, 1060 Brussels, Belgium; tel. (2) 537-67-61; f. 1929 to obtain equal rights and opportunities for women in the whole field of work. Mems in 10 countries. Hon. Sec. ADÈLE HAUWEL (Belgium).

Organization for the Prohibition of Chemical Weapons—OPCW: TS-OPCW, Johan de Wittlaan 32, 2517JR The Hague, Netherlands; f. 1997 to oversee implementation of the Chemical Weapons Convention, which aims to ban the development, production, stockpiling and use of chemical weapons. The Convention was negotiated under the auspices of the UN Conference on Disarmament and opened for signature in January 1993; it entered into force in April 1997, at which time the OPCW was inaugurated. Controlled by an Executive Council, comprising representatives of all founding mems; undertakes mandatory inspections of member states party to the Convention. Provisional 1997 budget: US $52m. Dir-Gen. JOSÉ MAURICIO BUSTANI (Brazil).

Organization of Solidarity of the Peoples of Africa, Asia and Latin America (Organización de Solidaridad de los Pueblos de Africa, Asia y América Latina—OSPAAAL): Apdo 4224, Havana 10400, Cuba; tel. (7) 30-5510; fax (7) 33-3985; telex 512259; f. 1966 at the first Conference of Solidarity of the Peoples of Africa, Asia and Latin America, to unite, co-ordinate and encourage national liberation movements in the three continents, to oppose foreign intervention in the affairs of sovereign states, colonial and neo-colonial practices, and to fight against racialism and all forms of racial discrimination; favours the establishment of a new international economic order. Mems: organizations in Angola, Congo, Guatemala, Guinea, Democratic Republic of Korea, Palestine, Puerto Rico, South Africa, Syria and Viet Nam. Sec.-Gen. Dr RAMÓN PEZ FERRO. Publ. *Tricontinental* (every 3 months, in English and Spanish).

Organization of the Cooperatives of America (Organización de las Cooperativas de América): Apdo postal 241263, Carrera 11, No. 86-32 Of. 101, Santafé de Bogotá, DC, Colombia; tel. 6103296; telex 45103; fax 610912; f. 1963 for improving socio-economic, cultural and moral conditions through the use of the co-operative system; works in every country of the continent; regional offices sponsor plans of activities based on the most pressing needs and special conditions of individual countries. Mems: organizations in 23 countries and territories. Pres. Dr ARMANDO TOVAR PARADA; Exec. Sec. Dr CARLOS JULIO PINEDA. Publs *OCA News* (monthly), *América Cooperativa* (every 4 months).

Parliamentary Association for Euro-Arab Co-operation: 21 rue de la Tourelle, 1040 Brussels, Belgium; tel. (2) 231-13-00; fax (2) 231-06-46; e-mail paeac@medea.be; f. 1974 as an association of 650 parliamentarians of all parties from the national parliaments of the Council of Europe countries and from the European Parliament, to promote friendship and co-operation between Europe and the Arab world; Executive Committee holds annual joint meetings with Arab Inter-Parliamentary Union; represented in Council of Europe, Western European Union and European Parliament; works for the progress of the Euro-Arab Dialogue and a settlement in the Middle East which takes into account the national rights of the Palestinian people. Joint Chair. EDITHA LIMBACH (Germany), HENNING GJELLEROD (Denmark); Sec.-Gen. JEAN-MICHEL DUMONT (Belgium). Publs *Information Bulletin* (quarterly), *Euro-Arab Political Fact Sheets* (2 a year).

Rio Group: f. 1987 at a meeting in Acapulco, Mexico, of eight Latin American government leaders, who agreed to establish a 'permanent mechanism for joint political action'; additional countries subsequently joined the Group (see below); holds annual summit meetings at presidential level. At the ninth presidential summit (Quito, Ecuador, September 1995) a 'Declaration of Quito' was adopted, which set out joint political objectives, including the strengthening of democracy; combating corruption, drugs-production and -trafficking and 'money laundering'; and the creation of a Latin American and Caribbean free trade area by 2005 (supporting the efforts of the various regional groupings). In September 1996 the summit meeting strongly condemned recent US legislation (the 'Helms-Burton' Act), which provides for sanctions against foreign companies that trade with Cuba. The Rio Group holds annual ministerial conferences with the European Union. Mems: Argentina, Bolivia, Brazil, Chile, Colombia, Ecuador, Mexico, Panama, Paraguay, Peru, Uruguay, Venezuela.

Party of the European Socialists: 97–113 rue Belliard, 1047 Brussels, Belgium; tel. (2) 284-29-78; fax (2) 230-17-66; f. 1974 as the Confederation of the Socialist Parties of the EC; affiliated to the Socialist International (q.v.). Mems: 21 full member parties, two associate, 12 with observer status. Chair. RUDOLF SCHARPING (Germany); Sec.-Gen. JEAN FRANÇOIS VALLIN (France).

Socialist International: Maritime House, Clapham, London, SW4 0JW, United Kingdom; tel. (171) 627-4449; telex 261735; fax (171) 720-4448; e-mail socint@gn.apc.org; internet http://www.gn.apc.org/socint; f. 1864; the world's oldest and largest association of political parties, grouping democratic socialist, labour and social democratic parties from every continent; provides a forum for political action, policy discussion and the exchange of ideas; works with many international organizations and trades unions (particularly members of ICFTU, q.v.); holds Congress every three years; the Council meets twice a year, and regular conferences and meetings of party leaders are also held; committees and councils on a variety of subjects and in different regions meet frequently. Mems: 66 full member parties, 25 consultative and 8 observer parties in 85 countries. There are three fraternal organizations and nine associated organizations, including: the Party of European Socialists (PES), the Group of the PES at the European Parliament and the International Federation of the Socialist and Democratic Press (q.v.). Pres. PIERRE MAUROY (France); Gen. Sec. LUIS AYALA (Chile); Publ. *Socialist Affairs* (quarterly).

International Falcon Movement—Socialist Educational International: 3 rue Quinaux, 1030 Brussels, Belgium; tel. (2) 215-79-27; fax (2) 245-00-83; f. 1924 to promote international understanding, develop a sense of social responsibility and to prepare children and adolescents for democratic life; co-operates with several institutions concerned with children, youth and education. Mems: about 1m.; 62 co-operating organizations in all countries. Pres. JESSI SÖRENSEN (Denmark); Sec.-Gen. ODETTE LAMBERT (Belgium). Publs *IFM-SEI Bulletin* (quarterly), *IFM-SEI Documents, Flash Infos* (6 a year), *Asian Regional Bulletin, Latin American Regional Bulletin.*

International Union of Socialist Youth: 1070 Vienna, Neustiftgasse 3, Austria; tel. (1) 523-12-67; fax (1) 526-958-49; e-mail iusy@blackbox.ping.at; f. 1907 as Socialist Youth International (present name from 1946) to educate young people in the principles of free and democratic socialism and further the co-operation of democratic socialist youth organizations; conducts international meetings, symposia, etc. Mems: 121 youth and student organizations in 87 countries. Pres. NICOLA ZINGARETTI; Gen. Sec. ALFREDO LAZZERETTI. Publs *IUSY Newsletter, FWG News, IUSY—You see us in Action.*

Socialist International Women: Maritime House, Old Town, Clapham, London, SW4 0JW, United Kingdom; tel. (171) 627-4449; telex 261735; fax (171) 720-4448; f. 1907 to strengthen relations between its members, to exchange experience and views, to promote the understanding among women of the aims of democratic socialism, to promote programmes to oppose any discrimination in society and to work for human rights in general and for development and peace. Mems: 96 organizations. Pres. ANNE-MARIE LIZIN; Gen. Sec. MARLÈNE HAAS. Publ. *Women and Politics* (quarterly).

Sommet francophone (la Francophonie): c/o Agence de co-opération culturelle et technique, 13 quai André-Citroën, 75015 Paris, France; tel. 1-44-37-33-00; fax 1-45-79-14-98; conference of Heads of State convened every two years to promote co-operation throughout the French-speaking world (1995: Cotonou, Benin; 1997: Hanoi, Viet Nam). Mems: Governments of 49 countries. Sec.-Gen. BOUTROS BOUTROS-GHALI (Egypt).

Stockholm International Peace Research Institute—SIPRI: Frösunda, 169 70 Solna, Sweden; tel. (8) 655-97-00; fax (8) 655-97-33; e-mail sipri@sipri.se; f. 1966; studies relate to international security and arms control, e.g. peace-keeping and regional security, chemical and biological warfare, production and transfer of arms, military expenditure, etc. About 50 staff mems, half of whom are researchers. Dir Dr ADAM DANIEL ROTFELD (Poland); Chair. Prof. DANIEL TARSCHYS (Sweden). Publs *SIPRI Yearbook: Armaments, Disarmament and International Security*, monographs and research reports.

Transparency International: Heylstrasse 33, 10825 Berlin, Germany; tel. (30) 787-5908; fax (30) 787-5707; e-mail ti@transparency.de; internet http://www.transparency.de; f. 1993; aims to promote governmental adoption of anti-corruption practices and accountability at all levels of the public sector; aims to ensure international business transactions conducted with integrity and without resort to corrupt practices. Formulates an annual Corruption Perception Index. Chair. Dr PETER EIGEN.

Trilateral Commission: 345 East 46th St, New York, NY 10017, USA; tel. (212) 661-1180; fax (212) 949-7268; (also offices in Paris and Tokyo); f. 1973 by private citizens of western Europe, Japan and North America, to encourage closer co-operation among these regions on matters of common concern; by analysis of major issues the Commission seeks to improve public understanding of such problems, to develop and support proposals for handling them jointly, and to nurture the habit of working together in the 'trilateral' area. The Commission issues 'task force' reports on such subjects as monetary affairs, political co-operation, trade issues, the energy crisis and reform of international institutions. Mems: about 335 individuals eminent in academic life, industry, finance, labour, etc.; those currently engaged as senior government officials are excluded. Chairmen PAUL A. VOLCKER, OTTO GRAF LAMBSDORFF, KIICHI MIYAZAWA (acting); Dirs CHARLES B. HECK, PAUL REVAY, TADASHI YAMAMOTO. Publs *Task Force Reports, Triangle Papers.*

Unrepresented Nations' and Peoples' Organization—UNPO: Javastraat, 40A, 2585 AP, Netherlands; tel. (70) 360-3318; fax (70) 360-3346; e-mail unpo@unpo.nl; f. 1991 to provide an international forum for indigenous and other unrepresented peoples and minorities; provides training in human rights, law, diplomacy and public relations to UNPO members; provides conflict resolution services. Mems: 50 peoples and minorities. Gen.-Sec. TSERING JAMPA (acting).

War Resisters' International: 5 Caledonian Rd, London, N1 9DX, United Kingdom; tel. (171) 278-4040; fax (171) 278-0444; e-mail warresisters@gn.apc.org; f. 1921; encourages refusal to participate in or support wars or military service, collaborates with movements that work for peace and non-violent social change. Mems: approx. 150,000. Chair. JØRGEN JOHANSEN; Secs HOWARD CLARK, DOMINIQUE SAILLARD. Publ. *Peace News* (monthly).

Women's International Democratic Federation: c/o Union of French Women, 25 rue du Charolais, 75012 Paris, France; tel. 1-40-01-90-90; fax 1-40-01-90-81; f. 1945 to unite women regardless of nationality, race, religion and political opinion, so that they may work together to win and defend their rights as citizens, mothers and workers, to protect children and to ensure peace and progress, democracy and national independence. Structure: Congress, Secretariat and Executive Committee. Mems: 122 organizations in 93 countries as well as individual mems. Pres. SYLVIE JAN (France); Vice-Pres. MAYADA ABBASSI (Palestine). Publs *Women of the Whole World* (6 a year), *Newsletter*.

World Council of Indigenous Peoples: 100 Argyle Ave, 2nd Floor, Ottawa, K2P 1B6, Canada; tel. (613) 230-9030; fax (613) 230-9340; f. 1975 to promote the rights of indigenous peoples and to support their cultural, social and economic development. The Council comprises representatives of indigenous organizations from five regions: North, South and Central America, Pacific-Asia and Scandinavia; a general assembly is held every three years. Pres. CONRADO JORGE VALIENTE. Publ. *WCIP Newsletter* (4–6 a year).

World Disarmament Campaign: 45–47 Blythe St, London, E2 6LN, United Kingdom; tel. (171) 729-2523; f. 1980 to encourage governments to take positive and decisive action to end the arms race, acting on the four main commitments called for in the Final Document of the UN's First Special Session on Disarmament; aims to mobilize people of every country in a demand for multilateral disarmament, to encourage consideration of alternatives to the nuclear deterrent for ensuring world security, and to campaign for a strengthened role for the UN in these matters. Chair. Dr FRANK BARNABY, Dr TONY HART. Publ. *World Disarm!* (6 a year).

World Federalist Movement: 777 UN Plaza, New York, NY 10017, USA; tel. (212) 599-1320; fax (212) 599-1332; e-mail wfm@igc.apc.org; f. 1947 to achieve a just world order through a strengthened United Nations; to acquire for the UN the authority to make and enforce laws for peaceful settlement of disputes, and to raise revenue under limited taxing powers; to establish better international co-operation in areas of environment, development and disarmament and to promote federalism throughout the world. Mems: 25,000 in 41 countries. Pres. Sir PETER USTINOV; Exec. Dir WILLIAM R. PACE. Publ. *World Federalist News* (quarterly).

World Federation of United Nations Associations—WFUNA: c/o Palais des Nations, 1211 Geneva 10, Switzerland; tel. (22) 7330730; telex 412962; fax (22) 7334838; f. 1946 to encourage popular interest and participation in United Nations programmes, discussion of the role and future of the UN, and education for international understanding. Plenary Assembly meets every two years; WFUNA founded International Youth and Student Movement for the United Nations (q.v.). Mems: national associations in 80 countries. Pres. HASHIM ABDUL HALIM (India); Sec.-Gen. L. H. HORACE PERERA (Sri Lanka) (acting). Publ. *WFUNA News*.

World Peace Council: Lönnrotinkatu 25A/V, 00180 Helsinki 18, Finland; tel. 693-1044; fax 693-3703; e-mail 100144.1501@compuserve.com; f. 1950 at the Second World Peace Congress, Warsaw. Principles: the prevention of nuclear war; the peaceful co-existence of the various socio-economic systems in the world; settlement of differences between nations by negotiation and agreement; complete disarmament; elimination of colonialism and racial discrimination; respect for the right of peoples to sovereignty and independence. Mems: Representatives of national organizations, groups and individuals from 140 countries, and of 30 international organizations; Executive Committee of 40 mems elected by world assembly held every 3 years (1993 assembly: Basel, Switzerland). Pres. ALBERTINA SISULU; Exec. Sec. SADHAN MUKHERJEE. Publ. *Peace Courier* (monthly).

Industrial and Professional Relations

See also the chapters on ICFTU, WCL and WFTU.

Arab Federation of Petroleum, Mining and Chemicals Workers: POB 5339, Tripoli, Libya; tel. (2) 608501; fax (2) 608989; f. 1961 to establish industrial relations policies and procedures for the guidance of affiliated unions; promotes establishment of trade unions in the relevant industries in countries where they do not exist. Publs *Arab Petroleum* (monthly), specialized publications and statistics.

Association for Systems Management: POB 38370, Cleveland, OH 44138-0370, USA; tel. (216) 243-6900; fax (216) 234-2930; f. 1947; an international professional organization for the advancement and self-renewal of information systems professionals throughout business and industry. Mems: 6,500 in 35 countries. Pres. William Munch; Dir Bob La Prad. Publ. *Journal of Systems Management.*

European Association for Personnel Management: c/o ANDCP, 29 ave Hoche, 75008 Paris, France; tel. 1-45-63-03-65; fax 1-42-56-41-15; e-mail eamp@eamp.org; f. 1962 to disseminate knowledge and information concerning the personnel function of management, to establish and maintain professional standards, to define the specific nature of personnel management within industry, commerce and the public services, and to assist in the development of national associations. Mems: 22 national associations. Sec.-Gen. Armand Nella (France); Pres. Pedro Neudes (Portugal).

European Civil Service Federation: Ave d'Aderghem, 1040 Brussels, Belgium; tel. (2) 230-84-33; fax (2) 230-69-05; f. 1962 to foster the idea of a European civil service of staff of international organizations operating in western Europe or pursuing regional objectives; upholds the interests of civil service members. Mems: local cttees in 12 European countries and individuals in 66 countries. Sec.-Gen. L. Rijnoudt. Publ. *Eurechos.*

European Federation of Conference Towns: POB 182, 1040 Brussels, Belgium; tel. (2) 732-69-54; fax (2) 732-58-62; lays down standards for conference towns; provides advice and assistance to its members and other organizations holding conferences in Europe; undertakes publicity and propaganda for promotional purposes; helps conference towns to set up national centres. Exec. Dir Aline Legrand.

European Federation of Lobbying and Public Affairs (Fédération Européenne du Lobbying et Public Affairs—FELPA): rue du Trône 61, 1050 Brussels, Belgium; tel. (2) 511-74-30; fax (2) 511-12-84; aims to enhance the development and reputation of the industry; encourages professionals active in the industry to sign a code of conduct outlining the ethics and responsibilities of people involved in lobbying or public relations work with the institutions of the EU. Pres. Y. de Lespinay.

European Industrial Research Management Association—EIRMA: 34 rue de Bassano, 75008 Paris, France; tel. 1-47-23-00-66; fax 1-47-20-05-30; f. 1966 under auspices of the OECD (q.v.); a permanent body in which European science-based firms meet to discuss and study industrial research policy and management and take joint action in trying to solve problems in this field. Mems: 170 in 18 countries. Pres. Prof. S. Barabaschi; Gen. Sec. B. A. Watkinson. Publs *Annual Report, Conference Reports, Working Group Reports.*

European Trade Union Confederation (Confédération Européenne des Syndicats): 155 blvd Emile Jacquain, 1210 Brussels, Belgium; tel. (2) 224-04-11; fax (2) 224-04-54; f. 1973; comprises 61 national trade union confederations and 14 European industrial federations in 28 European countries, representing 53.6m. workers; holds congress every four years. Gen. Sec. Emilio Gabaglio.

Federation of International Civil Servants' Associations: Palais des Nations, 1211 Geneva 10, Switzerland; tel. (22) 7988400; telex 412962; fax (22) 7330096; e-mail 100306.3212@compuserve.com; f. 1952 to co-ordinate policies and activities of member associations and unions, to represent staff interests before inter-agency and legislative organs of the UN and to promote the development of an international civil service. Mems: 26 associations and unions consisting of staff of UN organizations, 22 consultative associations and eight inter-organizational federations with observer status. Pres. Walter P. Scherzer. Publs *Annual Report, FICSA Newsletter, FICSA Update, FICSA circulars.*

Graphical International Federation: Valeriusplein 30, 1075 BJ Amsterdam, Netherlands; tel. (20) 671-32-79; fax (20) 675-13-31; f. 1925. Mems: national federations in 15 countries, covering 100,000 workers. Pres. L. van Haudt (Belgium); Sec.-Gen. R. E. van Kesteren (Netherlands).

International Association of Conference Interpreters: 10 ave de Sécheron, 1202 Geneva, Switzerland; tel. (22) 9081540; fax (22) 7324151; e-mail 100665.2456@compuserve.com; f. 1953 to represent professional conference interpreters, ensure the highest possible standards and protect the legitimate interests of members. Establishes criteria designed to improve the standards of training and recognizes schools meeting the required standards. Has consultative status with the UN and several of its agencies. Mems: 2,300 in 53 countries. Pres. Malick Sy (Switzerland); Exec. Sec. Josyane Cristina. Publs *Code of Professional Conduct, Yearbook* (listing interpreters), etc.

International Association of Conference Translators: 15 route des Morillons, 1218 Le Grand-Saconnex, Geneva, Switzerland; tel. (22) 7910666; fax (22) 7885644; e-mail aitc@atge.automail.com; f. 1962; represents revisers, translators, précis writers and editors working for international conferences and organizations, to protect the interests of those in the profession and help maintain high standards; establishes links with international organizations and conference organizers. Mems: 419 in 33 countries. Pres. Geneviève Sériot (Switzerland); Exec. Sec. Debra Bénard (USA). Publs *Directory, Bulletin.*

International Association of Crafts and Small and Medium-Sized Enterprises—IACME: c/o Centre patronal, 2 ave Agassi, CP 1215, 1001 Lausanne, Switzerland; tel. (21) 3197111; fax (21) 3197910; f. 1947 to defend undertakings and the freedom of enterprise within private economy, to develop training, to encourage the creation of national organizations of independent enterprises and promote international collaboration, to represent the common interests of members and to institute exchange of ideas and information. Mems: organizations in 26 countries. Chair. Mario Secca; Gen. Sec. Jacques Desgraz.

International Association of Medical Laboratory Technologists: Adolf Fredriks Kyrkogata 11, 111 37 Stockholm, Sweden; tel. (8) 10-30-31; fax (8) 10-90-61; e-mail mhaag@iamlt.se; internet http://www.iamlt.se; f. 1954 to allow discussion of matters of common professional interest; to promote national organizations of medical laboratory technologists; to raise training standards and to standardize training in different countries in order to facilitate free exchange of labour; holds international congress every second year. Mems: 200,000 in 37 countries. Pres. Marja Kaarina Koskinen; Exec. Dir Margareta Haag. Publ. *MedTecInternational* (2 a year).

International Association of Mutual Insurance Companies: 114 rue La Boëtie, 75008 Paris, France; tel. 1-42-25-84-86; fax 1-42-56-04-49; f. 1963 for the establishment of good relations between its members and the protection of the general interests of private insurance based on the principle of mutuality. Mems: over 250 in 25 countries. Pres. E. J. Aldeweireldt (Belgium); Sec.-Gen. A. Tempelaere (France). Publs *Mutuality* (2 a year), *AISAM Dictionary, Newsletter* (3 a year).

International Confederation of Executive and Professional Staffs (Confédération internationale des cadres): 30 rue de Gramont, 75002 Paris, France; telex 215116; f. 1950 to represent the interests of managerial and professional staff and to improve their material and moral status. Mems: national organizations in Austria, Belgium, Denmark, France, Germany, Italy, Luxembourg, Netherlands, Norway, Portugal, Spain, Sweden, UK, and international professional federations for chemistry and allied industries (FICCIA), mines (FICM), transport (FICT), metallurgical industries (FIEM), agriculture (FIDCA) and insurance (AECA). There are affiliated members in Hungary and Slovenia. Pres. Henry Bordes-Pages (France); Sec.-Gen. Fleming Friis Larsen (Denmark). Publ. *Cadres.*

International European Construction Federation: 9 rue La Pérouse, 75116 Paris, France; tel. 1-47-20-80-74; telex 613456; f. 1905. Mems: 25 national employers' organizations in 18 countries. Pres. Paul Willemen (Belgium); Sec.-Gen. Eric Lepage (France). Publ. *L'Entreprise Européenne.*

International Federation of Actors: Guild House, Upper St Martin's Lane, London, WC2H 9EG, United Kingdom; tel. (171) 379-0900; fax (171) 379-8260; f. 1952. Mems: 63 performers' unions in 47 countries. Pres. Tomas Bolme (Sweden); Gen. Sec. Katherine Sand.

International Federation of Air Line Pilots' Associations: Interpilot House, Gogmore Lane, Chertsey, Surrey, KT16 9AP, United Kingdom; tel. (1932) 571711; fax (1932) 570920; e-mail admin@ifalpa; f. 1948 to aid in the establishment of fair conditions of employment; to contribute towards safety within the industry; to provide an international basis for rapid and accurate evaluation of technical and industrial aspects of the profession. Mems: 89 associations, over 100,000 pilots. Pres. Capt. R. J. McInnis; Exec. Dir T. V. Middleton.

International Federation of Business and Professional Women: Studio 16, Cloisters Business Centre, 8 Battersea Park Rd, London, SW8 4BG, United Kingdom; tel. (171) 738-8323; fax (171) 622-8528; f. 1930 to promote interests of business and professional women and secure combined action by them. Mems: national federations, associate clubs and individual associates, totalling more than 200,000 mems in over 100 countries. Pres. Sylvia G. Perry; Dir Tamara Martinez. Publ. *BPW News International* (monthly).

International Industrial Relations Association: c/o International Labour Office, 1211 Geneva 22, Switzerland; tel. (22) 7996841; fax (22) 7998541; e-mail mennie@ilo.org; f. 1966 to encourage development of national associations of specialists, facilitate the spread of information, organize conferences, and to promote internationally planned research, through study groups and regional meetings; a World Congress is held every three years. Mems: 38 associations, 45 institutions and 1,500 individuals. Pres. Prof. Tiziano Treu; Sec.

W. R. Simpson. Publs *IIRA Bulletin* (3 a year), *IIRA Membership Directory, IIRA Congress proceedings.*

International Organisation of Employers—IOE: 26 chemin de Joinville, BP 68, 1216 Cointrin/Geneva, Switzerland; tel. (22) 7981616; telex 415463; fax (22) 7988862; f. 1920, reorganized 1948; aims to establish and maintain contacts between members and to represent their interests at the international level; to promote free enterprise; and to assist the development of employers' organizations. General Council meets annually; there is an Executive Committee and a General Secretariat. Mems: 122 federations in 119 countries. Chair. Jean-Jacques Oechslin (France); Sec.-Gen. Costas Kapartis (Cyprus). Publ. *The Free Employer*.

International Organization of Experts—ORDINEX: 19 blvd Sébastopol, 75001 Paris, France; tel. 1-40-28-06-06; fax 1-40-28-03-13; f. 1961 to establish co-operation between experts on an international level. Mems: 600. Pres. Pierre Royer (France); Sec.-Gen. Santa Bertinotti; Publ. *General Yearbook*.

International Public Relations Association—IPRA: Cardinal House, Wolsey Rd, KT8 9EL, United Kingdom; tel. (181) 481-7634; fax (181) 481-7648; f. 1955 to provide for an exchange of ideas, technical knowledge and professional experience among those engaged in international public relations, and to foster the highest standards of professional competence. Mems: 1,000 in 73 countries. Pres. Roger Hayes. Publs *Newsletter* (4 a year), *International Public Relations Review* (4 a year), *Members' Manual* (annually).

International Society of City and Regional Planners—ISoCaRP: Mauritskade 23, 2514 HD The Hague, Netherlands; tel. (70) 3462654; fax (70) 3617909; e-mail isocarp@bart.nl; internet http://www.soc.hitech.ac.jp/isocarp; f. 1965 to promote better planning practice through the exchange of knowledge. Mems: 450 in 57 countries. Pres. Halûk Alatan (Turkey); Sec.-Gen. Peter Jonquière (Netherlands). Publs *News Bulletin* (4 a year), *Bulletin* (2 a year).

International Union of Architects: 51 rue Raynouard, 75016 Paris, France; tel. 1-45-24-36-88; fax 1-45-24-02-78; e-mail uia@uia.architects.org; internet http://www.uia-architects.org; f. 1948; holds triennial congress. Mems: 106 countries. Pres. Sara Topelson de Grinberg (Mexico); Sec.-Gen. Vassilis Sgoutas (Greece). Publ. *Lettre d'informations* (monthly).

Latin American Federation of Agricultural and Food Industry Workers (Federación Latinoamericana de Trabajadores Campesinos y de la Alimentación): Apdo 1422, Caracas 1010a, Venezuela; tel. (32) 721549; telex 29873; fax (32) 720463; f. 1961 to represent the interests of agricultural workers and workers in the food and hotel industries in Latin America. Mems: national unions in 28 countries and territories. Sec.-Gen. José Lasso. Publ. *Boletín Luchemos* (quarterly).

Nordic Industry Workers' Federation (Nordiska IndustriarbetareFederationen): Vasagatan 11, 9 tr, Box 1127, 111 81 Stockholm, Sweden; tel. (8) 7966100; fax (8) 114179; f. 1901 to promote collaboration between affiliates in Denmark, Finland, Iceland, Norway and Sweden; supports sister unions economically and in other ways in labour market conflicts. Mems: 408,000 in 17 unions. Pres. Sune Ekbåge (Sweden); Sec. Arne Lökken (Sweden).

Organisation of African Trade Union Unity—OATUU: POB M386, Accra, Ghana; tel. 772574; telex 2673; fax 772621; f. 1973 as a single continental trade union org, independent of international trade union organizations; has affiliates from all African trade unions. Congress, composed of four delegates from all affiliated trade union centres, meets at least every four years as supreme policy-making body; General Council, composed of one representative from all affiliated trade unions, meets annually to implement Congress decisions and to approve annual budget. Mems: trade union movements in 52 independent African countries. Sec.-Gen. Hassan Sunmonu (Nigeria). Publ. *Voices of African Workers*.

Pan-African Employers' Confederation: c/o Federation of Kenya Employers, POB 48311, Nairobi, Kenya; tel. (2) 721929; telex 22642; fax (2) 721990; f. 1986 to link African employers' organizations and to represent them at the UN, the International Labour Organisation and the OAU. Pres. Hedi Jiliani (Tunisia); Sec.-Gen. Tom Diju Owuor (Kenya).

World Federation of Scientific Workers: 1–7 Great George St, London, SW1P 3AA, United Kingdom; tel. (171) 222-7722; e-mail 100764.1427@compuserve.com; f. 1946 to improve the position of science and scientists, to assist in promoting international scientific co-operation and to promote the use of science for beneficial ends; studies and publicizes problems of general, nuclear, biological and chemical disarmament; surveys the position and activities of scientists. Member organizations in 37 countries, totalling over 500,000 mems. Sec.-Gen. S. Davison (UK). Publ. *Scientific World* (quarterly in English, Esperanto, German and Russian).

World Movement of Christian Workers—WMCW: 124 blvd du Jubilé, 1080 Brussels, Belgium; tel. (2) 421-58-40; fax (2) 421-58-49; e-mail mmtc@skynet.be; f. 1961 to unite national movements that advance the spiritual and collective well-being of workers; general assembly every four years. Mems: 49 affiliated movements in 42 countries. Sec.-Gen. Norbert Klein. Publ. *Infor-WMCW*.

World Union of Professions (Union mondiale des professions libérales): 38 rue Boissière, 75116 Paris, France; tel. 1-44-05-90-15; fax 1-44-05-90-71; f. 1987 to represent and link members of the liberal professions. Mems: 27 national inter-professional organizations, two regional groups and 12 international federations. Pres. Alain Tinayre.

Law

African Bar Association: POB 3451, 29 La Tebu St, East Cantonments, Accra, Ghana; f. 1971; aims to uphold the rule of law, to maintain the independence of the judiciary, and to improve legal services. Pres. Charles Idehen (Nigeria).

African Society of International and Comparative Law: Private Bag 520, Kairaba ave KSMD, Banjul, The Gambia; tel. 375476; fax 375469; f. 1986; promotes public education on law and civil liberties; aims to provide a legal aid and advice system in each African country, and to facilitate the exchange of information on civil liberties in Africa. Ninth annual conference: Abidjan, Côte d'Ivoire, 1997. Pres. Mohamed Bedjaoui; Sec. Emile Yakpo (Ghana). Publs *Newsletter* (every 2 months), *African Journal of International and Comparative Law* (quarterly).

Asian-African Legal Consultative Committee: 27 Ring Rd, Lajpat Nagar-IV, New Delhi 110 024, India; tel. 6415280; fax 6221344; f. 1956 to consider legal problems referred to it by member countries and to be a forum for Afro-Asian co-operation in international law and economic relations; provides background material for conferences, prepares standard/model contract forms suited to the needs of the region; promotes arbitration as a means of settling international commercial disputes; trains officers of member states; has permanent UN observer status. Mems: 44 states. Pres. Dr M. Javad Zarif (Iran); Sec.-Gen. Tang Cheng Yuan (China).

Council of the Bars and Law Societies of the European Community—CCBE: 40 rue Washington, 1050 Brussels, Belgium; tel. (2) 640-42-74; fax (2) 647-79-41; f. 1960; the officially recognized organization in the European Union for the legal profession; liaises both among the bars and law societies themselves and between them and the Community institutions and the European Economic Area; also maintains contact with other international organizations of lawyers. The CCBE's principal objective is to study all questions affecting the legal profession in member states and to harmonize professional practice. Mems: 17 delegations from EU and EEA countries, and observers from Cyprus, the Czech Republic, Hungary, Slovakia, Switzerland and Turkey. Pres. Ramon Mullerat; Sec.-Gen. Caroline Goemans-Dorny.

Hague Conference on Private International Law: Scheveningseweg 6, 2517 KT The Hague, Netherlands; tel (70) 3633303; fax (70) 3604867; f. 1893 to work for the unification of the rules of private international law, Permanent Bureau f. 1955. Mems: 30 European and 15 other countries. Sec.-Gen. J. H. A. van Loon.

Institute of International Law (Institut de droit international): c/o IUHEI, 132 rue de Lausanne, CP 36, 1211 Geneva 21, Switzerland; tel. (22) 7311730; f. 1873 to promote the development of international law by endeavouring to formulate general principles in accordance with civilized ethical standards, and by giving assistance to genuine attempts at the gradual and progressive codification of international law. Mems: limited to 132 members and associates from all over the world. Sec.-Gen. Christian Dominicé (Switzerland). Publ. *Annuaire de l'Institut de Droit international.*

Inter-African Union of Lawyers: 12 rue du Prince Moulay Abdullah, Casablanca, Morocco; tel. (2) 271017; fax (2) 204686; f. 1980; holds congress every three years. Pres. Abdelaziz Benzakour (Morocco); Sec.-Gen. François Xavier Agondjo-Okawe (Gabon). Publ. *L'avocat africain* (2 a year).

Inter-American Bar Association: 815 15th St, NW, Suite 921, Washington, DC 20005-2201, USA; tel. (202) 393-1217; fax (202) 393-1241; f. 1940 to promote the rule of law and to establish and maintain relations between associations and organizations of lawyers in the Americas. Mems: 90 associations and 3,500 individuals in 27 countries. Sec.-Gen. Louis G. Ferrant (USA). Publs *Newsletter* (quarterly), *Conference Proceedings.*

Intergovernmental Committee of the Universal Copyright Convention: Division of Creativity, Cultural Industries and Copyright, UNESCO, 7 place de Fontenoy, 75700 Paris, France; tel. 1-45-68-47-05; telex 204461; fax 1-45-68-55-89; e-mail mbastide@unesco.org; established to study the application and operation of the Universal Copyright Convention and to make preparations for periodic revisions of this Convention; and to study any other problems concerning the international protection of copyright, in co-operation with various international organizations. Mems: 18 states. Chair. 1997–99 Mayer Gabay (Israel). Publ. *Copyright Bulletin* (quarterly).

International Association for the Protection of Industrial Property: Bleicherweg 58, Postfach, 8027 Zürich 27, Switzerland; tel. (1) 2041212; fax (1) 2041200; e-mail generalsecretariat@aippi.org; f. 1897 to encourage legislation regarding the international protection of industrial property and the development and extension of international conventions, and to make comparative studies of existing legislation with a view to its improvement and unification; holds triennial congress. Mems: 7,500 (national and regional groups and individual mems) in 103 countries. Exec. Pres. LUIZ LEONARDOS (Brazil); Sec.-Gen. Dr MARTIN J. LUTZ (Switzerland). Publs *Yearbook*, reports.

International Association of Democratic Lawyers: c/o Amar Bentoumi, 9 blvd Ziroud Youcef, 16000 Algiers, Algeria; tel. and fax (2) 737533; f. 1946 to facilitate contacts and exchange between lawyers, to encourage study of legal science and international law and support the democratic principles favourable to maintenance of peace and co-operation between nations; promotes the preservation of the environment; conducts research on labour law, private international law, agrarian law, etc.; consultative status with UN. Mems: in 96 countries. Pres. AMAR BENTOUMI (Algeria); Sec.-Gen. JITENDRA SHARMA (India). Publs *International Review of Contemporary Law*, in French, English and Spanish (every 6 months).

International Association of Juvenile and Family Court Magistrates: Molenstraat 15, 4851 SG Ulvenhout, Netherlands; tel. (76) 561240; fax (76) 5311169; e-mail j.vandergoes@tip.nl; f. 1928 to consider questions concerning child welfare legislation and to encourage research in the field of juvenile courts and delinquency. Activities: international congress, study groups and regional meetings. Mems: 23 national associations. Pres. J. ZERMATTEN (Switzerland); Gen.-Sec. J. VAN DER GOES (Netherlands).

International Association of Law Libraries: POB 5709, Washington, DC 20016-1309, USA; tel. (804) 924-3384; fax (804) 982-2232; e-mail bkjolstad@unog.ch; f. 1959 to encourage and facilitate the work of librarians and others concerned with the bibliographic processing and administration of legal materials. Mems: 600 from more than 50 countries (personal and institutional). Pres. LARRY B. WENGER (USA); Sec. BRITT S. M. KJOLSTAD (Switzerland). Publs *International Journal of Legal Information* (3 a year).

International Association of Lawyers: 25 rue du Jour, 75001 Paris, France; tel. 1-45-08-82-34; fax 1-45-08-82-31; e-mail 100771.2060@compuserve.com; f. 1927 to promote the independence and freedom of lawyers, and defend their ethical and material interests on an international level; to contribute to the development of international order based on law. Mems: 250 asscns and 3,000 lawyers in over 100 countries. Pres. BERNARD CAHEN (France).

International Association of Legal Sciences (Association internationale des sciences juridiques): c/o CISS, 1 rue Miollis, 75015 Paris, France; tel. 1-45-68-25-59; fax 1-43-06-87-98; f. 1950 to promote the mutual knowledge and understanding of nations and the increase of learning by encouraging throughout the world the study of foreign legal systems and the use of the comparative method in legal science. Governed by a president and an executive committee of 11 members known as the International Committee of Comparative Law. National committees in 47 countries. Sponsored by UNESCO. Pres. Prof. WLADIMIR TOUMANOV (Russia); Sec.-Gen. M. LEKER (Israel).

International Association of Penal Law: BP 1146, 64013 Pau, Université Cédex, France; tel. 5-59-80-75-56; fax 5-59-80-75-59; f. 1924 to establish collaboration between those from different countries who are working in penal law, studying criminology, and promoting the theoretical and practical development of an international penal law. Mems: 1,500. Pres. Prof. M. C. BASSIOUNI; Sec.-Gen. Dr H. EPP. Publ. *Revue Internationale de Droit Pénal* (bi-annual).

International Bar Association: 271 Regent St, London, W1R 7PA, United Kingdom; tel. (171) 629-1206; fax (171) 409-0456; f. 1947; a non-political federation of national bar associations and law societies; aims to discuss problems of professional organization and status; to advance the science of jurisprudence; to promote uniformity and definition in appropriate fields of law; to promote administration of justice under law among peoples of the world; to promote in their legal aspects the principles and aims of the United Nations. Mems: 154 member organizations in 164 countries, 17,500 individual members in 173 countries. Pres. DESMOND FERNANDO (Sri Lanka); Exec. Dir PAUL HODDINOTT (UK). Publs *International Business Lawyer* (11 a year), *International Bar News* (3 a year), *International Legal Practitioner* (quarterly), *Journal of Energy and Natural Resources Law* (quarterly).

International Commission of Jurists: POB 216, 81A ave de Châtelaine, 1219 Châtelaine/Geneva, Switzerland; tel. (22) 9793805; fax (22) 9793801; e-mail bovay@icj.org; f. 1952 to promote the understanding and observance of the rule of law and the protection of human rights throughout the world; maintains Centre for the Independence of Judges and Lawyers (f. 1978); contributes to the elaboration of international human rights instruments and their adoption and implementation by governments. Mems: 81 sections and affiliates. Pres. MICHAEL D. KIRBY (Australia); Sec.-Gen. ADAMA DIENG. Publs *CIJL Yearbook, The Review, ICJ Newsletter*, special reports.

International Commission on Civil Status: 3 place Arnold, 67000 Strasbourg, France; f. 1950 for the establishment and presentation of legislative documentation relating to the rights of individuals, and research on means of simplifying the judicial and technical administration concerning civil status. Mems: governments of Austria, Belgium, France, Germany, Greece, Italy, Luxembourg, Netherlands, Portugal, Spain, Switzerland, Turkey, United Kingdom. Pres. A. DAINOTTO (Italy); Sec.-Gen. J. MASSIP (France).

International Copyright Society: 8000 Munich 80, Rosenheimer Strasse 11, Germany; tel. (89) 480-03-00; telex 522306; fax (89) 480-03-408; f. 1954 to enquire scientifically into the natural rights of the author and to put the knowledge obtained to practical application all over the world, in particular in the field of legislation. Mems: 393 individuals and corresponding organizations in 52 countries. Pres. Prof. Dr REINHOLD KREILE; Gen. Sec. Dr MARTIN VOGEL. Publs *Schriftenreihe* (61 vols), *Yearbook*.

International Council of Environmental Law: 53113 Bonn, Adenauerallee 214, Germany; tel. (228) 2692-240; fax (228) 2692-250; e-mail 100651.317@compuserve.com; f. 1969 to exchange information and expertise on legal, administrative and policy aspects of environmental questions. Exec. Governors Dr WOLFGANG BURHENNE, Dr ABDULBAR AL-GAIN. Publs *Directory, References, Environmental Policy and Law*.

International Criminal Police Organization—INTERPOL: BP 6041, 69411 Lyon Cédex 06, France; tel. 4-72-44-70-00; telex 301987; fax 4-72-44-71-63; internet http://www.interpol-pr.com; f. 1923, reconstituted 1946; aims to promote and ensure the widest possible mutual assistance between police forces within the limits of laws existing in different countries, to establish and develop all institutions likely to contribute to the prevention and suppression of ordinary law crimes; co-ordinates activities of police authorities of member states in international affairs, centralizes records and information regarding international criminals; operates a telecommunications network of 176 stations. The General Assembly is held annually. Mems: official bodies of 177 countries. Pres. TOSHINORI KANEMOTO (Japan); Sec.-Gen. RAYMOND E. KENDALL (United Kingdom). Publs *International Criminal Police Review* (6 a year), *International Crime Statistics*.

International Customs Tariffs Bureau: 38 rue de l'Association, 1000 Brussels, Belgium; tel. (2) 501-87-74; fax (2) 218-30-25; the executive instrument of the International Union for the Publication of Customs Tariffs; f. 1890, to translate and publish all customs tariffs in five languages—English, French, German, Italian, Spanish. Mems: 71. Pres. F. ROELANTS (Belgium); Dir RICHARD J. PERKINS. Publs *International Customs Journal, Annual Report*.

International Development Law Institute: Via di San Sebastianello 16, 00187 Rome, Italy; tel. (6) 697-9261; telex 622381; fax (6) 678-1946; e-mail idli@idli.org; internet http://www.idli.org; f. 1983; designs and conducts courses and seminars for lawyers, legal advisors and judges from developing countries, central and eastern Europe and the former USSR; also provides in-country training workshops; training programme addresses legal skills, international commercial law, economic law reform, governance and the role of the judiciary. Dir L. MICHAEL HAGER.

International Federation for European Law—FIDE: Via Nicolò Tartaglia 5, 1-00197 Rome, Italy; fax (6) 8080731; f. 1961 to advance studies on European law among members of the European Community by co-ordinating activities of member societies and by organizing conferences every two years. Mems: 12 national associations. Pres. FRANCESCO CAPOTORIL; Sec.-Gen. Prof. P.-C. MÜLLER-GRAFF.

International Federation of Senior Police Officers: 26 rue Cambacères, 75008 Paris, France; tel. 1-49-27-40-67; fax 1-49-24-01-13; f. 1950 to unite policemen of different nationalities, adopting the general principle that prevention should prevail over repression, and that the citizen should be convinced of the protective role of the police; seeks to develop methods, and studies problems of traffic police. Set up International Centre of Crime and Accident Prevention, 1976. established International Association against Counterfeiting, 1994. Mems: 34 national organizations. Sec.-Gen. JEAN-PIERRE HAVRIN (France). Publ. *International Police Information* (every 3 months, French, German and English).

International Institute for the Unification of Private Law—UNIDROIT: Via Panisperna 28, 00184 Rome, Italy; tel. (6) 69941372; fax (6) 69941394; f. 1926 to undertake studies of comparative law, to prepare for the establishment of uniform legislation, to prepare drafts of international agreements on private law and to organize conferences and publish works on such subjects; holds international congresses on private law and meetings of organizations concerned with the unification of law; library of 215,000 vols. Mems: governments of 58 countries. Pres. LUIGI FERRARI BRAVO (Italy); Sec.-Gen. MALCOLM EVANS (UK). Publs *Uniform Law Review*

(4 a year), *Digest of Legal Activities of International Organizations, News Bulletin* (quarterly), etc.

International Institute of Space Law—IISL: 3–5 rue Mario Nikis, 75015 Paris, France; tel. 1-45-67-42-60; telex 205917; fax 1-42-73-21-20; f. 1959 at the XI Congress of the International Astronautical Federation; organizes annual Space Law colloquium; studies juridical and sociological aspects of astronautics and makes awards. Mems: individuals from many countries. Pres. NANDARI JASENTULYIANA (acting). Publs *Proceedings of Annual Colloquium on Space Law, Survey of Teaching of Space Law in the World.*

International Juridical Institute: Permanent Office for the Supply of International Legal Information, Spui 186, 2511 BW, The Hague, Netherlands; tel. (70) 3460974; fax (70) 3625235; f. 1918 to supply information on any matter of international interest, not being of a secret nature, respecting international, municipal and foreign law and the application thereof. Pres. A. V. M. STRUYCKEN; Dir A. L. G. A. STILLE.

International Law Association: Charles Clore House, 17 Russell Sq., London, WC1B 5DR, United Kingdom; tel. (171) 323-2978; fax (171) 323-3580; f. 1873 for the study and advancement of international law, public and private; the promotion of international understanding and goodwill. Mems: 4,000 in 50 regional branches; 25 international cttees. Pres. Prof. Judge BENGT BROMS (Finland); Chair. Exec. Council Lord SLYNN OF HADLEY (UK); Sec.-Gen. DAVID J. C. WYLD (UK).

International Maritime Committee (Comité Maritime International): Markgravestraat 9, 2000 Antwerp, Belgium; tel. (3) 227-35-26; fax (3) 227-35-28; f. 1897 to contribute to the unification of maritime law by means of conferences, publications, etc. and to encourage the creation of national associations; work includes drafting of conventions on collisions at sea, salvage and assistance at sea, limitation of shipowners' liability, maritime mortgages, etc. Mems: national associations in 50 countries. Pres. PATRICK GRIGGS (United Kingdom); Administrator LEO DELWAIDE. Publs *CMI Newsletter, Year Book.*

International Nuclear Law Association: 29 sq. de Meeûs, 1000 Brussels, Belgium; tel. (2) 547-58-41; fax (2) 503-04-40; f. 1972 to promote international studies of legal problems related to the peaceful use of nuclear energy, particularly the protection of man and the environment; holds conference every two years. Mems: 450 in 30 countries. Sec.-Gen. V. VERBRAEKEN.

International Penal and Penitentiary Foundation: c/o Dr K. Hobe, Bundesministerium der Justiz, 10104 Berlin, Germany; tel. (30) 20259226; fax (30) 20259525; f. 1951 to encourage studies in the field of prevention of crime and treatment of delinquents. Mems in 23 countries (membership limited to three people from each country) and corresponding mems. Pres. JORGE DE FIGUEIREDO DIAS (Portugal); Sec.-Gen. KONRAD HOBE (Germany).

International Police Association—IPA: 1 Fox Rd, West Bridgford, Nottingham, NG2 6AJ, United Kingdom; tel. (115) 945-5985; fax (115) 982-2578; f. 1950 to exchange professional information, create ties of friendship between all sections of police service, organize group travel, studies, etc. Mems: 260,000 in over 50 countries. International Sec.-Gen. A. F. CARTER.

International Society for Labour Law and Social Security: ILO, CP 500, 1211 Geneva 22, Switzerland; fax (22) 7996260; e-mail servais@ilo.org; f. 1958 to encourage collaboration between specialists; holds World Congress every three years as well as irregular regional congresses (Europe, Africa, Asia and Americas). Mems: 1,000 in 67 countries. Pres. Prof. AMÉRICO PLÁ RODRÍGUEZ (Argentina); Sec.-Gen. J.-M. SERVAIS (Belgium).

International Union of Latin Notaries (Unión Internacional del Notariado Latino): Via Locatelli 5, 20124 Milan, Italy; f. 1948 to study and standardize notarial legislation and promote the progress, stability and advancement of the Latin notarial system. Mems: organizations and individuals in 67 countries. Sec. EMANUELE FERRARI. Publ. *Revista Internacional del Notariado* (quarterly), *Notarius International.*

Law Association for Asia and the Pacific—LAWASIA: GPO Box 3275, NT House, 11th Floor, 22 Mitchell St, Darwin, Northern Territory 0800, Australia; tel. (8) 8946-9500; fax (8) 8946-9505; e-mail lawasia@lawasia.asn.au; internet http://lawasia.asn.au; f. 1966 to promote the administration of justice, the protection of human rights and the maintenance, reform and development of the rule of law within the region, to advance the standard of legal education, to promote uniformity within the region in appropriate fields of law and to advance the interests of the legal profession. Holds a biennial conference (1999–Seoul, Republic of Korea). Mems: national orgs in 24 countries; 2,500 individual, firm and corporate mems in more than 65 countries. Sec.-Gen. ROSLYN WEST (Australia). Publs *Directory* (annually), *LAWASIA Newsletter Update* (quarterly), *Directory* (annually), *Journal* (annually).

Permanent Court of Arbitration: Carnegieplein 2, 2517 KJ The Hague, Netherlands; tel. (70) 3024242; fax (70) 3024167; f. by the Convention for the Pacific Settlement of International Disputes (1899, 1907) to enable immediate recourse to be made to arbitration for international disputes which cannot be settled by diplomacy, to facilitate the solution of disputes by international inquiry and conciliation commissions. Mems: governments of 84 countries. Sec.-Gen. HANS JONKMAN (Netherlands).

Society of Comparative Legislation: 28 rue Saint-Guillaume, 75007 Paris, France; tel. 1-44-39-86-23; fax 1-44-39-86-28; f. 1869 to study and compare laws of different countries, and to investigate practical means of improving the various branches of legislation. Mems: 600 in 48 countries. Pres. XAVIER BLANC-JOUVAN (France); Sec.-Gen. MARIE-ANNE GALLOT LE LORIER (France). Publs *Revue Internationale de Droit Comparé* (quarterly).

Union of Arab Jurists: POB 6026, Al-Mansour, Baghdad, Iraq; tel. (1) 8840051; fax (1) 8849973; f. 1975 to facilitate contacts between Arab lawyers, to safeguard the Arab legislative and judicial heritage; to encourage the study of Islamic jurisprudence; and to defend human rights. Mems: national jurists asscns in 15 countries. Sec.-Gen. SHIBIB LAZIM AL-MALIKI. Publ. *Al-Hukuki al-Arabi* (Arab Jurist).

Union of International Associations: 40 rue Washington, 1050 Brussels, Belgium; tel. (2) 640-41-09; telex 65080; fax (2) 646-05-25; f. 1907, present title adopted 1910; aims to facilitate the evolution of the activities of the world-wide network of non-profit organizations, especially non-governmental and voluntary associations; collects information on such organizations and makes this information available; promotes research on the legal, administrative and other problems common to these associations. Mems: 200 in 54 countries. Pres. M. MERLE (France); Sec.-Gen. JACQUES RAEYMAECKERS (Belgium). Publs *Transnational Associations* (6 a year), *International Congress Calendar* (quarterly), *Yearbook of International Organizations, International Organization Participation* (annually), *Global Action Network* (annually), *Encyclopedia of World Problems and Human Potential, Documents for the Study of International Non-Governmental Relations, International Congress Science* series, *International Association Statutes* series, *Who's Who in International Organizations.*

World Jurist Association—WJA: 1000 Connecticut Ave, NW, Suite 202, Washington, DC 20036, USA; tel. (202) 466-5428; telex 440456; fax (202) 452-8540; e-mail wja@geocities.com; internet http://www.geocities.com/capitolhill/4165; f. 1963; promotes the continued development of international law and legal maintenance of world order; holds biennial world conferences, World Law Day, demonstration trials; organizes research programmes. Mems: lawyers, jurists and legal scholars in 155 countries. Pres. LUCIO GHIA (Italy); Exec. Vice-Pres. MARGARETHA M. HENNEBERRY (USA). Publs *The World Jurist* (English, every 2 months), Research Reports, *Law and Judicial Systems of Nations,* 3rd revised edn (directory), *World Legal Directory, Law / Technology* (quarterly), *World Law Review* Vols I–V (World Conference Proceedings), *The Chief Justices and Judges of the Supreme Courts of Nations* (directory), etc.

World Association of Judges—WAJ: 1000 Connecticut Ave, NW, Suite 202, Washington, DC 20036, USA; tel. (202) 466-5428; telex 440456; fax (202) 452-8540; f. 1966 to advance the administration of judicial justice through co-operation and communication among ranking jurists of all countries. Pres. Prince BOLA AJIBOLA (Nigeria).

World Association of Law Professors—WALP: 1000 Connecticut Ave, NW, Suite 202, Washington, DC 20036, USA; tel. (202) 466-5428; telex 440456; fax (202) 452-8540; f. 1975 to improve scholarship and education in dealing with matters related to international law; Pres. SERAFIN V. C. GUINGONA (Philippines).

World Association of Lawyers—WAL: 1000 Connecticut Ave, NW, Suite 202, Washington, DC 20036, USA; tel. (202) 466-5428; telex 440456; fax (202) 452-8540; f. 1975 to develop international law and improve lawyers' effectiveness in dealing with it; Pres. JACK STREETER (USA).

Medicine and Health

Council for International Organisations of Medical Sciences—CIOMS: c/o WHO, ave Appia, 1211 Geneva 27, Switzerland; tel. (22) 7913406; telex 415416; fax (22) 7910746; f. 1949; general assembly every three years. Mems: 104 organizations. Pres. Prof JOHN H. BRYANT; Sec.-Gen. Dr Z. BANKOWSKI. Publs *Calendar of International and Regional Congresses* (annual), *Proceedings of CIOMS, Round Table Conferences, International Nomenclature of Diseases.*

MEMBERS OF CIOMS

Members of CIOMS include the following:

FDI World Dental Federation: 7 Carlisle St, London, W1V 5RG, United Kingdom; tel. (171) 935-7852; fax (171) 486-0183; f. 1900.

Mems: 93 national dental associations and 21 affiliates. Pres. H. ERNI (Switzerland); Exec. Dir Dr P. Å. ZILLÉN (Sweden). Publs *International Dental Journal* (every 2 months) and *FDI World* (every 2 months).

International Academy of Legal and Social Medicine: c/o 49A ave Nicolai, BP 8, 4802 Verviers, Belgium; tel. and fax (87) 22-98-21; f. 1938; holds an international Congress and General Assembly every three years, and interim meetings. Mems in 50 countries. Perm. Sec. and Treas. ELISABETH FRANCSON. Publs *Acta Medicinae Legalis et Socialis* (annually), *Newsletter* (3 a year).

International Association for the Study of the Liver: c/o Prof. June W. Halliday, Queensland Institute of Medical Research, The Bancroft Centre, PO Royal Brisbane Hospital, Brisbane, Australia 4029; tel. (7) 3362-0373; fax (7) 3362-0191; Pres. Prof. JOHN TERBLANCHE; Sec. Prof. JUNE W. HALLIDAY.

International Association of Allergology and Clinical Immunology: Health Science Center, State Univ. of New York at Stony Brook, Stony Brook, NY 11794, USA; tel. (414) 276-6445; fax (414) 276-3349; f. 1945 to further work in the educational, research and practical medical aspects of allergic and immunological diseases; 1997 Congress: Cancun, Mexico. Mems: 42 national societies. Pres. ALBERT OEHLING (Spain); Sec.-Gen. ALLEN KAPLAN (USA); Exec. Sec. R. IBER (USA). Publ. *Allergy and Clinical Immunology News* (6 a year).

International College of Surgeons: 1516 N. Lake Shore Drive, Chicago, IL 60610, USA; tel. (312) 642-3555; fax (312) 787-1624; f. 1935, as a world-wide federation of surgeons and surgical specialists for the advancement of the art and science of surgery, to create a common bond among the surgeons of all nations and promote the highest standards of surgery without regard to nationality, creed, or colour; sends teams of surgeons to developing countries to teach local surgeons; provides research and scholarship grants, organizes surgical congresses around the world; manages the International Museum of Surgical Science in Chicago. Mems: about 14,000 in 111 countries. Pres. Prof. PEDRO A. RUBIO (USA); Exec. Dir J. THOMAS VIALL (USA). Publ. *International Surgery* (quarterly).

International Diabetes Federation: 1 rue Defacqz, 1000 Brussels, Belgium; tel. (2) 538-55-11; fax (2) 538-51-14; e-mail idf@idf.org; internet http://www.idf.org; f. 1949 to help in the collection and dissemination of information regarding diabetes and to improve the welfare of people suffering from that disease. Mems: 147 associations in 122 countries. Pres. MARIA L. DEALVA; Exec. Dir HILARY WILLIAMS. Publs *IDF Diabetes Voice* (quarterly), *IDF Bulletin* (quarterly).

International Federation of Clinical Neurophysiology: c/o Prof. G. Caruso, Clinica Neurologica, Univ. di Napoli 'Federico II', Via S. Panini S, 80131 Naples, Italy; tel. (81) 746-3793; fax (81) 546-9861. f. 1949 to attain the highest level of knowledge in the field of electro-encephalography and clinical neurophysiology in all the countries of the world. Mems: 48 organizations. Pres. Prof. MARC NUWER; Sec. Prof. HIROSHI SHIBASAKI. Publs *The EEG Journal* (monthly), *Evoked Potentials* (every 2 months), *EMG and Motor Control* (every 2 months).

International Federation of Oto-Rhino-Laryngological Societies: Oosterveldlaan 24, 2610 Wilrijk, Belgium; tel. and fax (3) 443-36-11; e-mail ifos@uia.ua.ac.be; f. 1965 to initiate and support programmes to protect hearing and prevent hearing impairment; Congresses every four years. Pres. G. J. MCCAFFERTY (Australia); Sec.-Gen. P. W. ALBERTI. Publ. *IFOS Newsletter* (4 a year).

International Federation of Physical Medicine and Rehabilitation: Rehabilitation Unit, Royal Melbourne Hospital, Chester St, Moonee Ponds 3039, Victoria, Australia; tel. (3) 9342-4509; fax (3) 9342-4617; f. 1952 to link national societies, organize conferences (every four years) and disseminate information to developing countries. Latest conference: Sydney, Australia, 1995. Pres. Dr R. OAKESHOTT; Sec. Dr Prof. P. DISLER.

International Federation of Surgical Colleges: c/o Prof. S. W. A. Gunn, La Panetiere, 1279 Bogis-Bossey, Switzerland; tel. (22) 7762161; fax (22) 7766417; f. 1958 to encourage high standards in surgical training; co-operates with the World Health Organization in developing countries; conducts international symposia; receives volunteers to serve as surgical teachers in developing countries; provides journals and text books for needy medical schools; offers travel grants. Mems: colleges or associations in 45 countries, and 420 individual associates. Pres. Prof. JOHN TERBLANCHE (South Africa); Hon. Sec. Prof. S. W. A. GUNN. Publ. *World Journal of Surgery*.

International League of Associations for Rheumatoloy: c/o Dr J. Sergent, Chief Medical Officer, Vanderbilt Univ., 3810 Nashville, TN 37232-5545, USA; tel. (615) 343-9324; fax (615) 343-6478; f. 1927 to promote international co-operation for the study and control of rheumatic diseases; to encourage the foundation of national leagues against rheumatism; to organize regular international congresses and to act as a connecting link between national leagues and international organizations. Mems: 13,000. Pres. Dr ROBERTO ARINOVICHE (Chile); Sec.-Gen. Dr JOHN SERGENT (USA). Publs *Annals of the Rheumatic Diseases* (in the UK), *Revue du Rhumatisme* (in France), *Reumatismo* (in Italy), *Arthritis and Rheumatism* (in the USA), etc.

International Leprosy Association: Sasakawa Hall 6F, 3-12-12 Hita, Minato-ku, Tokyo 108, Japan; tel. (3) 452-8281; fax (3) 452-8283; f. 1931 to promote international co-operation in work on leprosy, from which about 15m. people in the world are suffering. Thirteenth International Congress, The Hague, 1988. Sec. Dr YO YUASA (Japan). Publ. *International Journal of Leprosy and Other Mycobacterial Diseases* (quarterly).

International Pediatric Association: c/o Univ. of Rochester School of Medicine and Dentistry, Dept. of Pediatrics (Rm 4-8104), 601 Elmwood, Rochester NY 14642-8777, USA; tel. (716) 275-0225; fax (716) 273-1038; f. 1912; holds triennial congresses and regional and national workshops. Mems: 135 national paediatric societies in 131 countries, 9 regional affiliate societies, 9 paediatric specialty societies. Pres. Prof. GAVIN C. ARNEIL (Scotland); Exec. Dir Dr ROBERT J. HAGGERTY. Publ. *International Child Health* (quarterly).

International Rehabilitation Medicine Association: 1333 Moursund Ave, A-221, Houston, TX 77030, USA; tel. (713) 799-5086; fax (713) 799-5058; f. 1968. Mems: 2,005 in 72 countries. Pres. Prof. M. GRABOIS (USA). Publ. *News and Views* (quarterly).

International Rhinologic Society: c/o Prof. Clement, ENT-Dept, AZ-VUB, Laarbeeklaan 101, 1090 Brussels, Belgium; tel. (2) 477-60-02; fax (2) 477-64-23; e-mail knoctp@az.vub.ac.be; f. 1965; holds congress every four years. Pres. EUGENE B. KERN (USA); Sec. Prof. P. A. R. CLEMENT (Belgium). Publ. *Rhinology*.

International Society and Federation of Cardiology: 34 rue de l'Athénée, CP 117, 1211 Geneva 12, Switzerland; tel. (22) 3476755; fax (22) 3471028; e-mail iofc@compuserve.com; f. 1978 through merger of the International Society of Cardiology and the International Cardiology Federation; aims to promote the study, prevention and relief of cardiovascular diseases through scientific and public education programmes and the exchange of materials between its affiliated societies and foundations and with other agencies having related interests. Organizes World Congresses every four years. Mems: national cardiac societies and heart foundations in 78 countries. Pres. Dr A. BAYÉS DE LUNA; Sec. Dr M. A. MARTÍNEZ-RÍOS (Mexico); Exec. Sec. M. B. DE FIGUEIREDO. Publ. *Heartbeat* (quarterly).

International Society of Audiology: University Hospital Rotterdam, Audiological Centre, Molewaterplein 40, 3015 GD Rotterdam, Netherlands; tel. (10) 463-4586; fax (10) 463-3102; f. 1952. Mems: 300 individuals. Pres. Prof. G. MEUCHER; Gen. Sec. Dr J. VERSCHUURE. Publ. *Audiology* (every 2 months).

International Society of Dermatopathology: Inga Ellzey Practice Group Inc., 1398 Semoran Blvd, Suite 102, Casselberry, FL 32707, USA; f. 1958; holds quinquennial congress. Pres. Dr TERENCE RYAN; Sec.-Gen. Dr MARIA DURAN.

International Society of Internal Medicine: Dept. of Medicine, Regionalspital, 4900 Langenthal, Switzerland; tel. (62) 9163102; fax (62) 9164155; e-mail r.streuli@rsl.ch; f. 1948 to encourage research and education in internal medicine. Mems: 37 national societies, 3,000 individuals in 54 countries. Congresses: Manila, Philippines 1996; Lima, Peru 1998. Pres. Prof. AKIHIRO IGATA (Japan); Sec. Prof. ROLF A. STREULI (Switzerland).

International Union against Cancer: 3 rue du Conseil Général, 1205 Geneva, Switzerland; tel. (22) 3201811; telex 429724; fax (22) 3201810; e-mail info@uicc.ch; internet http://www.uicc.ch; f. 1933 to promote on an international level the campaign against cancer in its research, therapeutic and preventive aspects; organizes International Cancer Congress every four years; administers the American Cancer Society International Cancer Research Fellowships, the International Cancer Research Technology Transfer Fellowships, the Yamagiwa-Yoshida Memorial International Cancer Study Grants and the International Oncology Nursing Fellowships; conducts worldwide programmes of campaign organization, public education and patient support, detection and diagnosis, epidemiology and prevention, professional education, tobacco and cancer, treatment of cancer and tumour biology. Mems: voluntary national organizations, private or public cancer research and treatment organizations and institutes and governmental agencies in more than 80 countries. Pres. Dr N. GRAY (Australia); Sec.-Gen. Dr G. P. MURPHY (USA); Exec. Dir A. J. TURNBULL. Publs *UICC International Directory of Cancer Institutes and Organizations* (every 4 years), *International Journal of Cancer* (18 a year), *UICC News* (quarterly), *International Calendar of Meetings on Cancer* (2 a year).

Latin American Association of National Academies of Medicine: Col 7 No 60–15, Santafé de Bogotà, Colombia; tel. (1) 2493122; fax (1) 2128670; f. 1967. Mems: nine national Academies. Pres. Dr PLUTARCO NARANJO (Peru); Sec. Dr ALBERTO CÁRDENAS-ESCOVAR (Colombia).

Medical Women's International Association: 50931 Cologne, Herbert-Lewin-Strasse 1, Germany; tel. (221) 4004558; fax (221)

4004557; e-mail mwi@aol.com; f. 1919 to facilitate contacts between medical women and to encourage their co-operation in matters connected with international health problems. Mems: national associations in 44 countries, and individuals. Pres. Dr FLORENCE MANGUYU (Kenya); Sec.-Gen. CAROLYN MOTZEL (Germany). Publ. *MWIA Update* (3 a year).

Organisation panafricaine de lutte contre le SIDA—OPALS: 15/21 rue de L'Ecole de Médecine, 75006 Paris, France; tel. 1-43-26-72-28; fax 1-43-29-70-93; f. 1988; disseminates information relating to the treatment and prevention of AIDS; provides training of medical personnel; promotes co-operation between African medical centres and specialized centres in the USA and Europe. Publ. *OPALS Liaison.*

World Federation for Medical Education: University of Edinburgh Centre for Medical Education, 11 Hill Square, Edinburgh, EH8 9DR, United Kingdom; tel. (131) 650-6209; telex 727742; fax (131) 650-6537; f. 1972; promotes and integrates medical education world-wide; links regional and international associations, and has official relations with WHO, UNICEF, UNESCO, UNDP and the World Bank. Pres. Prof. H. J. WALTON.

World Federation of Associations of Paediatric Surgeons: c/o Prof. J. Boix-Ochoa, Clinica Infantil 'Vall d'Hebrón', Departamento de Cirugía Pediátrica, Valle de Hebrón, s/n, Barcelona 08035, Spain; f. 1974. Mems: 50 associations. Pres. Prof. W. MAIER; Sec. Prof. J. BOIX-OCHOA.

World Federation of Neurology: London Neurological Centre, 110 Harley St, London, W1N 1AF, United Kingdom; tel. (171) 935-3546; fax (171) 935-4172; e-mail 100675.761@compuserve.com; f. 1955 as International Neurological Congress, present title adopted 1957. Aims to assemble members of various congresses associated with neurology, and organize co-operation of neurological researchers. Organizes Congress every four years. Mems: 23,000 in 70 countries. Pres. Lord WALTON OF DETCHANT (UK); Sec.-Treas. F. CLIFFORD ROSE (UK). Publs *Journal of the Neurological Sciences, World Neurology* (quarterly).

World Medical Association: 28 ave des Alpes, 01210 Ferney-Voltaire, France; tel. 450-40-75-75; fax 450-40-59-37; e-mail wma@iprolink.fr; f. 1947 to achieve the highest international standards in all aspects of medical education and practice, to promote closer ties among doctors and national medical associations by personal contact and all other means, to study problems confronting the medical profession and to present its views to appropriate bodies. Structure: annual General Assembly and Council (meets twice a year). Mems: 65 national medical associations. Pres. Dr A. AZWAR (Indonesia); Sec.-Gen. Dr D. HUMAN (South Africa). Publ. *The World Medical Journal* (6 a year).

World Organization of Gastroenterology: II Medizinische Klinik und Poliklinik der Technischen Universität München, Ismaninger Str. 22, 81675 Munich, Germany; tel. (89) 41402250; fax (89) 41404871; f. 1958 to promote clinical and academic gastroenterological practice throughout the world, and to ensure high ethical standards. Mems in 80 countries. Sec.-Gen. MEINHARD CLASSEN.

World Psychiatric Association: López Ibor Clinic, Nueva Zelanda 44, 28035 Madrid, Spain; tel. (1) 3737361; f. 1961 for the exchange of information concerning the problems of mental illness and the strengthening of relations between psychiatrists in all countries; organizes World Psychiatric Congresses and regional and inter-regional scientific meetings. Mems: 120,000 psychiatrists in 85 countries. Sec.-Gen. Dr JUAN ENRIQUE MEZZICH (Spain).

ASSOCIATE MEMBERS OF CIOMS

Associate members of CIOMS include the following:

Asia Pacific Academy of Ophthalmology: c/o Prof. Arthur S. M. Lim, Eye Clinic Singapura, 6A Napier Rd, 02-38 Gleneagles Annexe Block Gleneagles Hospital, Singapore 258500; tel. 466-6666; fax 733-3360; f. 1956; holds congress every two years. Pres. S. SELVARAJAH (Malaysia); Sec.-Gen. Prof. ARTHUR S. M. LIM (Singapore).

International Association of Medicine and Biology of the Environment: c/o 115 rue de la Pompe, 75116 Paris, France; tel. 1-45-53-45-04; fax 1-45-53-41-75; f. 1971 with assistance from the UN Environment Programme; aims to contribute to the solution of problems caused by human influence on the environment; structure includes 13 technical commissions. Mems: individuals and organizations in 73 countries. Hon. Pres. Prof. R. DUBOS; Pres. Dr R. ABBOU.

International Committee of Military Medicine: 79 rue Saint-Laurent, 4000 Liège, Belgium; tel. (4) 222-21-83; fax (4) 222-21-50; f. 1921. Mems: official delegates from 88 countries. Pres. Maj.-Gen. Dr LU ZENGQI (China); Sec.-Gen. Lt.-Col Dr M. COOLS (Belgium). Publ. *Revue Internationale des Services de Santé des Forces Armées* (quarterly).

International Congress on Tropical Medicine and Malaria: congress held every four years to work towards the solution of the problems concerning malaria and tropical diseases; 1996 congress: Japan. Pres. Dr S. SORNMANI.

International Council for Laboratory Animal Science—ICLAS: Division of Comparative Medicine, Univ. of Texas South-western Medical Center at Dallas, 5323 Harry Hines Blvd, Dallas, Texas 75235, USA; tel. (214) 648-3218; fax (214) 648-2659; e-mail spakes@mednet.swmed.edu; f. 1956. Pres. J. MAISIN (Belgium); Sec.-Gen. Prof. STEVEN PAKES (USA).

International Federation of Clinical Chemistry: Dept of Clinical Biochemistry, Royal Prince Alfred Hospital, Camperdown, 2050 Sydney, Australia; tel. (2) 9515-5246; fax (2) 9515-7931; e-mail thirion@ifccts.u-nancy.fr; f. 1952. Mems: 72 national societies (about 33,000 individuals). Pres. Prof. M. MCQUEEN (Canada); Sec. Dr J. WHITFIELD (Australia). Publs *Journal* (every 2 months), *Annual Report.*

International Medical Society of Paraplegia: National Spinal Injuries Centre, Stoke Mandeville Hospital, Aylesbury, Bucks, HP21 8AL, United Kingdom; tel. (1296) 315866; fax (1296) 315268; e-mail imsop/-stokemandeville@Bucks.net; Pres. Dr HANS L. FRANKEL; Hon. Sec. Prof. J. J. WYNDALE. Publ. *Spinal Cord.*

International Society of Blood Transfusion: Gateway House, Picadilly South, Manchester M60 7LP, United Kingdom; tel. (161) 236-2263; fax (161) 236-0519; f. 1937. Mems: about 1,300 in 100 countries. Pres. S. LEONG (Hong Kong); Sec.-Gen. H. GUNSON (UK). Publ. *Transfusion Today* (quarterly).

Rehabilitation International: 25 East 21st St, New York, NY 10010, USA; tel. (212) 420-1500; telex 446412; fax (212) 505-0871; f. 1922 to improve the lives of disabled people through the exchange of information and research on equipment and methods of assistance; organizes international conferences and co-operates with UN agencies and other international organizations. Mems: organizations in 92 countries. Pres. Dr ARTHUR O'REILLY; Sec.-Gen. SUSAN PARKER. Publs *International Rehabilitation Review, Rehabilitación* (2 a year).

Transplantation Society: c/o Dr Felix Rapaport, PR Transplant Program, University Hospital, Health Science Centre, State Univ. of New York at Stony Brook, Stony Brook, NY 11794-8192, USA; tel. (516) 444-2209; fax (516) 444-3831; e-mail rapaport@surg.som.sunysb.edu; Sec. EDUARDO A. SANTIAGO-DELPÍN.

World Federation of Associations of Clinical Toxicology Centres and Poison Control Centres: c/o Prof. Jacques Descotes, Centre anti-poisons, Pavilion N, Hôpital Edouard Herriot, 69009 Lyon, France. Pres. Prof. A. FURTADO RAHDE; Sec. Prof. JACQUES DESCOTES.

OTHER ORGANIZATIONS

Aerospace Medical Association: 320 So. Henry St, Alexandria, VA 22314, USA; tel. (703) 739-2240; fax (703) 739-9652; e-mail rrayman@asma.org; f. 1929 as Aero Medical Association; to advance the science and art of aviation and space medicine; to establish and maintain co-operation between medical and allied sciences concerned with aerospace medicine; to promote, protect, and maintain safety in aviation and astronautics. Mems: individual, constituent and corporate in 75 countries. Pres. ROBERT R. MCMEEKIN (USA); Exec. Vice-Pres. RUSSELL B. RAYMAN (USA). Publ. *Aviation Space and Environmental Medicine* (monthly).

Asian-Pacific Dental Federation: 242 Tanjong Katong Rd, Singapore 437030; tel. 3453125; fax 3442116; e-mail bibi@pacific.net.sq; f. 1955 to establish closer relationship among dental associations in Asian and Pacific countries and to encourage research on dental health in the region; holds congress every year. Mems: 19 national associations. Sec.-Gen. Dr OLIVER HENNEDIGE. Publ. *Asian Dentist* (every 2 months).

Association for Paediatric Education in Europe: c/o Dr Claude Billeaud, Dept. Néonatal Médicine, Maternité-CHU Pellegrin, 33076 Bordeaux, France; fax 5-56-79-60-38; e-mail claude.billeaud@neonata.u-bordeaux2.fr; internet http://www.atinternet.com/apee; f. 1970 to promote research and practice in educational methodology in paediatrics. Mems: 80 in 20 European countries. Pres. Dr MARION CROUCHMAN (UK); Sec.-Gen. Dr CLAUDE BLLEAUD (France).

Association of National European and Mediterranean Societies of Gastroenterology—ASNEMGE: Gastroenterology Unit, 18th Floor, Guy's Tower, Guy's Hospital, London, SE1 9RT, United Kingdom; tel. (171) 955-4564; fax (171) 955-4230; f. 1947 to facilitate the exchange of ideas between gastroenterologists and disseminate knowledge; organizes International Congress of Gastroenterology every four years. Mems in 30 countries, national societies and sections of national medical societies. Pres. Prof. CONSTANTINE ARVANITAKIS; Sec. Prof. R. H. DOWLING (UK).

Balkan Medical Union: 1 rue G. Clémenceau, 70148 Bucharest, Romania; tel. 613-78-57; fax 312-15-70; f. 1932; studies medical problems, particularly ailments specific to the Balkan region, to promote a regional programme of public health; enables exchange of information between doctors in the region; organizes research programmes and congresses. Mems: doctors and specialists from Albania, Bulgaria, Cyprus, Greece, Moldova, Romania, Turkey and the former Yugoslav republics. Pres. Prof. NIKI AGNANTIS (Greece); Sec.-Gen. (1997–2000) Prof. Dr VASILE CÂNDEA (Romania). Publs *Archives de l'union médicale Balkanique* (4 a year), *Bulletin de l'union médicale Balkanique* (6 a year), *Annuaire*.

European Association for Cancer Research: c/o Dr M. R. Price, Cancer Research Laboratories, University of Nottingham, University Park, Nottingham, NG7 2RD, United Kingdom; tel. (115) 9513418; fax (115) 9515115; f. 1968 to facilitate contact between cancer research workers and to organize scientific meetings in Europe. Mems: over 1,500 in more than 40 countries in and outside Europe. Pres. Sir WALTER BODMER (UK); Sec. Dr M. R. PRICE (UK).

European Association for Health Information and Libraries—EAHIL: 60 rue de la Concorde, 1050 Brussels, Belgium; tel. (2) 511-80-63; fax (2) 511-80-63; e-mail elizabeth.husem@psykiatri.uio.no; f. 1987; serves professionals in health information and biomedical libraries in Europe; holds biennial conferences of medical and health librarians. Pres. ELISABETH HUSEM (Norway); Sec. TONY MCSEÁN (UK). Publs *Newsletter to European Health Librarians* (quarterly), conference proceedings.

European Association for the Study of Diabetes: 40223 Düsseldorf, Merowingerstr. 29, Germany; tel. (211) 316738; fax (211) 3190987; e-mail easd@uni-duesseldorf.de; internet http://www.uni-duesseldorf.de/www/easd; f. 1965 to support research in the field of diabetes, to promote the rapid diffusion of acquired knowledge and its application; holds annual scientific meetings within Europe. Mems: 5,500 in 101 countries, not confined to Europe. Pres. Prof. M. BERGER (Germany); Exec. Dir Dr VIKTOR JOERGENS. Publ. *Diabetologia* (13 a year).

European Association of Internal Medicine: Dept de Médecine Interne, ave Hippocrate 10, 1200 Brussels, Belgium; tel. (2) 764-10-55; fax (2) 764-36-97; f. 1969 to promote internal medicine on the ethical, scientific and professional level; to bring together European specialists and establish communication between them; to organize congresses and meetings; and to provided information. Mems: 400 in 20 European countries. Pres. Prof. Y. LE TALLEC (France); Sec. Prof. M. LAMBERT (Belgium). Publ. *European Journal of Internal Medicine* (quarterly).

European Association of Radiology: c/o Prof. A. Baert, Universitaire Ziekenhuizen, Gasthuisberg, Herestraat 49, 3000 Leuven, Belgium; tel. (16) 33-84-27; fax (16) 33-84-24; e-mail jenny.bonnast@uz.kuleuven.ac.be; f. 1962 to develop and co-ordinate the efforts of radiologists in Europe by promoting radiology in both biology and medicine, studying its problems, developing professional training and establishing contact between radiologists and professional, scientific and industrial organizations. Mems: national associations in 35 countries. Sec.-Gen. Prof. Dr PETER VOCK.

European Association of Social Medicine: Corso Vittorio Emanuele 92, 10121 Turin, Italy; f. 1953 to provide co-operation between national associations of preventive medicine and public health. Mems: associations in 10 countries. Pres. Dr JEAN-PAUL FOURNIER (France); Sec.-Gen. Prof. Dr ENRICO BELLI (Italy).

European Brain and Behaviour Society: c/o Dr S. J. Sara, Université Paris VI, Institut des Neurosciences, 75005 Paris, France; f. 1969; holds two conferences a year. Sec.-Gen. Dr SUSAN J. SARA.

European Healthcare Management Association: Vergemount Hall, Clonskeagh, Dublin 6, Ireland; tel. (1) 2839299; fax (1) 2838653; e-mail ehma@iol.ie; f. 1966; aims to improve health care in Europe by raising standards of managerial performance in the health sector; fosters co-operation between health service organizations and institutions in the field of health-care management education and training. Mems: 225 in 30 countries. Pres. Prof. T. E. D. VAN DER GRINTEN; Dir PHILIP C. BERMAN; Publs *Newsletter* (every 2 months), *Directory* (annually).

European League against Rheumatism: Witikonerstr. 15, 8032 Zürich, Switzerland; tel. (1) 3839690; fax (1) 3839810; f. 1947 to co-ordinate research and treatment of rheumatic complaints, conducted by national societies; holds annual symposia, and congress every four years. Mems in 35 countries. Exec. Sec. F. WYSS. Publ. *Rheumatology in Europe* (in English, French and German).

European Organization for Caries Research—ORCA: c/o Dr C. M. Pine, Dept of Dental Health, Univ. of Dundee, Park Place, Dundee, DD1 4HR, United Kingdom; tel. (1382) 635960; f. 1953 to promote and undertake research on dental health, encourage international contacts, and make the public aware of the importance of care of the teeth. Mems: research workers in 23 countries. Pres. Prof. D. M. O'MULLANE (Ireland); Sec.-Gen. Dr C. M. PINE (UK).

European Orthodontic Society: Flat 31, 49 Hallam St, London, W1N 5LL, United Kingdom; tel. and fax (171) 935-2795; f. 1907 (name changed in 1935) to advance the science of orthodontics and its relations with the collateral arts and sciences. Mems: 2,250 in 67 countries. Sec. Prof. J. MOSS. Publ. *European Journal of Orthodontics* (6 a year).

European Union of Medical Specialists: 20 ave de la Couronne, Brussels 1050, Belgium; tel. (2) 649-51-64; fax (2) 640-37-30; e-mail uems@optimet.be; f. 1958 to safeguard the interests of medical specialists. Mems: two representatives each from Austria, Belgium, Denmark, Finland, France, Germany, Greece, Iceland, Ireland, Italy, Luxembourg, Netherlands, Norway, Portugal, Spain, Sweden, Switzerland, United Kingdom. Pres. Dr L. HARVEY (UK); Sec.-Gen. Dr R. PEIFFER (Belgium).

Eurotransplant Foundation: POB 2304, 2301 CH Leiden, Netherlands; tel. (71) 5795795; fax (71) 5790057; f. 1967; co-ordinates the exchange of organs for transplants in Germany, Austria, Belgium, Luxembourg and the Netherlands; keeps register of almost 15,000 patients with all necessary information for matching with suitable donors in the shortest possible time; organizes transport of the organ and the transplantation; collaboration with similar organizations in western and eastern Europe. Dirs Dr B. COHEN, Dr G. G. PERSIJN.

Federation of French-Language Obstetricians and Gynaecologists (Fedération des gynécologues et obstetriciens de langue française): Clinique Baudelocque, 123 blvd de Port-Royal, 75674 Paris Cédex 14, France; tel. 1-42-34-11-43; fax 1-42-34-12-31; f. 1920 for the scientific study of phenomena having reference to obstetrics, gynaecology and reproduction in general. Mems: 1,500 in 50 countries. Pres. Prof. H. BOSSART (Switzerland); Gen. Sec. Prof. J. R. ZORN (France). Publ. *Journal de Gynécologie Obstétrique et Biologie de la Reproduction* (8 a year).

Federation of the European Dental Industry: 50858 Cologne, Kirchweg 2, Germany; tel. (221) 9486280; fax (221) 483428; f. 1957 to promote the interests of the dental industry. Mems: national associations in Austria, Belgium, Denmark, France, Germany, Italy, Netherlands, Spain, Sweden, Switzerland, United Kingdom. Pres. and Chair. Dr M. MAILLEFER (Switzerland); Sec. HARALD RUSSEGGER (Germany).

General Association of Municipal Health and Technical Experts: 83 ave Foch, BP 3916, 75761 Paris Cédex 16, France; tel. 1-53-70-13-53; fax 1-53-70-13-40; f. 1905 to study all questions related to urban and rural health—the control of preventable diseases, disinfection, distribution and purification of drinking water, construction of drains, sewage, collection and disposal of household refuse, etc. Mems in 35 countries. Pres. M. AFFHOLDER; Sec.-Gen. M. LASALMONIE (France). Publ. *TSM-Techniques, Sciences, Méthodes* (monthly).

Inter-American Association of Sanitary and Environmental Engineering: Rua Nicolau Gagliardi 354, 05429-010 São Paulo, SP, Brazil; tel. (11) 212-4080; fax (11) 814-2441; f. 1948 to assist the development of water supply and sanitation. Mems: 24 countries. Exec. Dir LUIZ AUGUSTO DE LIMA PONTES. Publs *Revista Ingeniería Sanitaria* (quarterly), *Desafío* (quarterly).

International Academy of Aviation and Space Medicine: Medical Dept, Air New Zealand, Private Bag 92007, Auckland, New Zealand; tel. (9) 2563523; fax (9) 2563969; f. 1955; to facilitate international co-operation in research and teaching in the fields of aviation and space medicine. Mems: in 40 countries. Sec.-Gen. Dr A. G. DAWSON.

International Academy of Cytology: 79104 Freiburg, Burgunderstr. 1, Germany; tel. (761) 270-3012; fax (761) 3122; f. 1957 to facilitate international exchange of information on specialized problems of clinical cytology, to stimulate research and to standardize terminology. Mems: 2,400. Pres. HARUBUMI KATO; Sec. VOLKER SCHNEIDER. Publ. *Acta Cytologica, Analytical and Quantitative Cytology and Histology* (both every 2 months).

International Agency for the Prevention of Blindness: Grosvenor Hall, Bolnore Rd, Haywards Heath, West Sussex, RH16 4BX, United Kingdom; tel. and fax (1444) 458810; f. 1975 umbrella organization whose objectives include advocacy and information sharing on prevention of blindness; aims to encourage the formation of national prevention of blindness committees and programmes; in official relationship with WHO. Pres. Dr R. PARARAJASEGARAM. Publ. *IAPB News*.

International Anatomical Congress: c/o Prof. Dr Wolfgang Kühnel, Institut für Anatomie, Medizinische Universität zu Lübeck, Ratzeburger Allee 160, 23538 Lübeck, Germany; tel. (451) 500 4030; fax (451) 500 4034; f. 1903; runs congresses for anatomists from all over the world to discuss research, teaching methods and terminology in the fields of gross and microscopical anatomy, histology, cytology, etc. Pres. J. ESPERENCA-PINE (Portugal); Sec.-Gen. Prof. Dr WOLFGANG KÜHNEL (Germany).

International Association for Child and Adolescent Psychiatry and Allied Professions: c/o Prof. Kosuke Yamazaki, Tokai Univ. School of Medicine, Dept of Psychiatry, Bohseidai, Isehara, Kanagawaken 259 11, Japan; tel. (463) 93-11-21; fax (463) 94-55-32; f. 1937 to promote scientific research in the field of child psychiatry by collaboration with allied professions. Mems: national associations and individuals in 44 countries. Sec.-Gen. Prof. KOSUKE YAMAZAKI. Publs *The Child in the Family (Yearbook of the IACAPP), Newsletter*.

International Association for Dental Research: 1619 Duke St, Alexandria, VA 22314, USA; tel. (703) 548-0066; fax (703) 548-1883; f. 1920 to encourage research in dentistry and related fields, and to publish the results; holds annual meetings, triennial conferences and divisional meetings. Pres. JOHN GREENSPAN; Exec. Dir Dr JOHN J. CLARKSON.

International Association of Agricultural Medicine and Rural Health: Saku Central Hospital, 197 Usuda-machi, Minami-saku-Gun, Nagano 384-03, Japan; tel. (267) 82-3131; fax (267) 82-7533; e-mail sakuchp@valley.or.jp; f. 1961 to study the problems of medicine in agriculture in all countries and to prevent the diseases caused by the conditions of work in agriculture. Mems: 405. Pres. Prof. J. TÉNYI (Hungary); Sec.-Gen. Dr SHOSUI MATSUSHIMA (Japan) (acting).

International Association of Applied Psychology: c/o Dr M. Knowles, Monash Univ., Dept of Administrative Studies, Clayton, Vic. 3168, Australia; f. 1920, present title adopted in 1955; aims to establish contacts between those carrying out scientific work on applied psychology, to promote research and the adoption of measures contributing to this work. Mems: 2,000 in 90 countries. Pres. Prof. H. C. TRIANDIS (USA); Sec.-Gen. Dr M. C. KNOWLES (Australia). Publ. *Applied Psychology: An International Review* (quarterly).

International Association of Asthmology—INTERASMA: c/o Prof. Hugo Neffen, Irigoyen Freyre 2670, 3000 Santa Fé, Argentina; tel. (42) 537-638; fax (42) 56-07-73; e-mail interasm@neffen.satlink@.net; f. 1954 to advance medical knowledge of bronchial asthma and allied disorders. Mems: 1,100 in 54 countries. Pres. Prof. C. BANOV (USA); Sec./Treas. Prof. H. NEFFEN. Publs *Journal of Investigative Allergology and Clinical Immunology* (every 2 months), *Allergy and Clinical Immunology International* (every 2 months).

International Association of Gerontology: Gerontology Centre of Semmelweis University of Medicine, Rökk Szilárd utca 13, 1085 Budapest, Hungary; tel. (1) 2699158; fax (1) 1188476; f. 1950 to promote research and training in all fields of gerontology and to protect interests of gerontologic societies and institutions. Mems: 55 national societies in 51 countries. Pres. Prof. Dr EDIT BEREGI; Sec.-Gen. Dr ISTVÁN GERGELY. Publ. *Newsletter* (annually).

International Association of Group Psychotherapy: c/o Dr E. Hopper, 11 Heath Mansions, The Mount, London NW3 6SN, United Kingdom; f. 1954; holds congresses every three years. Mems: in 35 countries. Pres. Dr E. HOPPER; Sec. Dr C. SANDAHL (Sweden). Publs *Newsletter, Yearbook of Group Psychotherapies*.

International Association of Hydatidology: Florida 460, Piso 3, 1005 Buenos Aires, Argentina; tel. (1) 322-3431; fax (1) 325-8231; f. 1941. Mems: 800 in 40 countries. Pres. Dr MIGUEL PÉREZ GALLARDO (Spain); Sec.-Gen. Prof. Dr RAUL MARTÍN MENDY (Argentina). Publs *Archivos Internacionales de la Hidatidosis* (every 4 years), *Boletín de Hidatidosis* (quarterly).

International Association of Logopedics and Phoniatrics: 6 ave de la Gare, 1003 Lausanne, Switzerland; fax (21) 3112025; f. 1924 to promote standards of training and research in human communication disorders in all countries, to establish information centres and communicate with kindred organizations. Mems: 400 individuals and 60 societies from 36 countries. Pres. Prof. N. KOTBY. Publ. *Folia Phoniatrica et Logopedica* (6 a year).

International Association of Oral and Maxillofacial Surgeons: c/o Medical College of Virginia, PO Box 980 410, Richmond, VA 23298-0410, USA; tel. (804) 828-8515; fax (804) 828-1753; f. 1963 to advance the science and art of oral and maxillofacial surgery; organizes biennial international conference. Mems: 2,000. Pres. RUDOLF FRIES (Austria); Exec. Dir DANIEL M. LASKIN (USA). Publs *International Journal of Oral and Maxillofacial Surgery* (every 2 months), *Newsletter* (every 6 months).

International Brain Research Organization—IBRO: 51 blvd de Montmorency, 75016 Paris, France; f. 1958 to further all aspects of brain research. Mems: 45 corporate, 15 academic and 51,000 individual. Pres. Prof. D. P. PURPURA (USA); Sec.-Gen. Dr D. OTTOSON. Publs *IBRO News, Neuroscience* (bi-monthly), *IBRO Membership Directory*.

International Bronchoesophagological Society: Mayo Clinic, 13400 E. Shea Blvd, Scottsdale, AZ 85259, USA; f. 1951 to promote by all means the progress of bronchoesophagology and to provide a forum for discussion among broncho-esophagologists of various specialities; holds congress every three years. Mems: 500 in 37 countries. Exec. Sec. Dr DAVID SANDERSON.

International Bureau for Epilepsy: POB 21, 2100 AA Heemstede, Netherlands; tel. (23) 5237411; fax (23) 5470119; e-mail ibe@xs4all.nl; f. 1961 to collect and disseminate information about social and medical care for people with epilepsy; to organize international and regional meetings; to advise and answer questions on social aspects of epilepsy. Mems: 40 national epilepsy organizations. Sec.-Gen. MICHAEL D. HILLS. Publ. *International Epilepsy News* (quarterly).

International Cell Research Organization: c/o UNESCO, SC/BSC, 1 rue Miollis, 75015 Paris, France; e-mail icro@unesco.org; f. 1962 to create, encourage and promote co-operation between scientists of different disciplines throughout the world for the advancement of fundamental knowledge of the cell, normal and abnormal; organizes every year eight to ten international laboratory courses on modern topics of cell and molecular biology and biotechnology for young research scientists in important research centres all over the world. Mems: 400. Pres. Prof. E. CARAFOLI (Switzerland); Exec. Sec. Prof. G. N. COHEN (France).

International Centre for Diarrhoeal Disease Research Bangladesh: GPO Box 128, Dhaka 1000, Bangladesh; tel. (2) 603236; telex 675612; fax (2) 871686; f. 1960; undertakes research, training and information dissemination on diarrhoeal diseases, with particular reference to developing countries; supported by 45 governments and international organizations. Dir Prof. DEMISSIE HABTE. Publs *Annual Report, ICDDR, B News* (quarterly), *Journal of Diarrhoeal Diseases Research* (quarterly), *Glimpse* (quarterly).

International Chiropractors' Association: 1110 North Glebe Rd, Suite 1000, Arlington, VA 22201, USA; tel. (703) 528-5000; f. 1926 to promote advancement of the art and science of chiropractic. Mems: 7,000 individuals in addition to affiliated associations. Pres. FRED BARGE; Exec. Vice-Pres. RON HENRIKSON. Publs *International Review of Chiropractic* (every 2 months), *ICA Today* (every 2 months).

International Commission on Occupational Health: Dept of Community, Occupational and Family Medicine, MD3, National University Hospital, Lower Kent Ridge Rd, Singapore 119074; tel. (65) 874 4985; fax (65) 779 1489; f. 1906 (present name 1985) to study and prevent pathological conditions arising from industrial work; arranges congresses on occupational medicine and the protection of workers' health; provides information for public authorities and learned societies. Mems: 1,900 from 92 countries. Pres. Prof.J.-F. CAILLARD (France); Sec.-Gen. Prof. J. JEYARATNAM (Singapore). Publ. *Newsletter* (quarterly).

International Commission on Radiological Protection—ICRP: POB 35, Didcot, OX11 0RJ, United Kingdom; tel. (1235) 833929; fax (1235) 832832; f. 1928 to provide technical guidance and promote international co-operation in the field of radiation protection; committees on Radiation Effects, Secondary Limits, Protection in Medicine, and the application of recommendations. Mems: about 70. Chair. Prof. R. H. CLARKE (UK); Scientific Sec. Dr H. SMITH (UK). Publ. *Annals of the ICRP*.

International Committee of Catholic Nurses: 43 Square Vergote, 1030 Brussels, Belgium; tel. (2) 732-10-50; fax (2) 734-84-60; f. 1933 to group professional Catholic nursing associations; to represent Christian thought in the general professional field at international level; to co-operate in the general development of the profession and to promote social welfare. Mems: 49 full, 20 corresponding mems. Pres. EILEEN LAMB; Gen. Sec. ANN VERLINDE. Publ. *Nouvelles / News / Nachrichten* (every 4 months).

International Council for Physical Fitness Research—ICPFR: Cosell Center for Physical Education and Health Promotion, Hebrew University of Jerusalem, Givat Ram, Jerusalem 91904, Israel; tel. (2) 6584430; fax (2) 6585308; f. 1964 to construct international standardized physical fitness tests, to encourage research based upon the standardized tests and to encourage research to enhance participation in physical activity. Mems: in 25 countries. Pres. Prof. HILLEL RUSKIN; Sec. Treas. Prof. ALBRECHT L. CLAESSENS.

International Council of Nurses—ICN: 3 place Jean-Marteau, 1201 Geneva, Switzerland; tel. (22) 8090100; fax (22) 8090101; f. 1899 to allow national associations of nurses to share their common interests, working together to develop the contribution of nursing to the promotion of health. Quadrennial congresses are held. Mems: 112 national nurses' associations. Pres. Dr MARGRETTA MADDEN STYLES (USA); Exec. Dir JUDITH OULTON. Publ. *The International Nursing Review* (6 a year, in English).

International Cystic Fibrosis (Mucoviscidosis) Association: Avda Campanar 106-3a-6a, 46015 Valencia, Spain; tel. (6) 346-1414; fax (6) 349-4047; e-mail fq@vlc.servicom.es; f. 1964 to disseminate current information on cystic fibrosis in those areas of the world where the disease occurs and to stimulate the work of scientific and medical researchers attempting to discover its cure. Conducts annual medical symposia. Mems: 41 national organizations; 14 associate mems. Pres. IAN THOMPSON (Canada); Sec. AISHA RAMOS (Spain).

International Epidemiological Association—IEA: Suite 840, 111 Market Place, Baltimore, MD 21202-6709, USA; tel. (410) 223-1600; fax (410) 223-1620; e-mail harmenia@jhsph.edu; f. 1954. Mems: 2,237. Pres. and Chair. Dr RODOLFO SARACCI; Sec. Prof. HAROUTUNE ARMENIAN. Publ. *International Journal of Epidemiology* (6 a year).

International Federation for Hygiene, Preventive Medicine and Social Medicine: 79 ave du Général Leclerc, 54000 Vandoeuvre-les-Nancy, France; tel. 83-51-07-19; f. 1951. Twelfth Conference: Montreal, Canada, 1989. Mems: national associations and individual members in 74 countries. Pres. Prof. R. SENAULT; Sec.-Gen. Dr ERNST MUSIL (Austria). Publ. *Bulletin.*

International Federation for Medical and Biological Engineering: c/o Prof. Jos A. E. Spaan, Faculty of Medicine, Meibergdreef 15, 1105 AZ Amsterdam, Netherlands; tel. (20) 566-5200; fax (20) 691-7233; e-mail ifmbe@amc.uva.nl; internet http://www.vub.vub.oc.be/~ifmbe/ifmbe-html; f. 1959. Mems: organizations in 40 countries. Sec.-Gen. Prof. JOS A. E. SPAAN (Netherlands).

International Federation for Medical Psychotherapy: c/o Prof. E. Heim, Tannackstr. 3, 3653 Oberhofen, Switzerland; tel. and fax (33) 2431141; e-mail senf-blum@t-online.de; f. 1946 to further research and teaching of psychotherapy, to organize international congresses. Mems: some 6,000 psychotherapists from around 40 countries, 36 societies. Pres. Dr EDGAR HEIM (Switzerland); Sec.-Gen. Prof. Dr WOLFGANG SENE (Germany).

International Federation of Fertility Societies: c/o R. Harrison, Rotunda Hospital, Dublin, Ireland; f. 1951 to study problems of fertility and sterility. Sec.-Gen. R. HARRISON.

International Federation of Gynecology and Obstetrics: 27 Sussex Place, Regent's Park, London, NW1 4RG, United Kingdom; tel. (171) 723-2951; fax (171) 258-0737; f. 1954; aims to improve standards in gynaecology and obstetrics, to promote better health care for women, and to facilitate the exchange of information and perfect methods of teaching; organizes international congresses. Membership: national societies in 98 countries. Pres. of Bureau Prof. M. FATHALLA (Egypt); Sec.-Gen. Prof. HO KEI MA (Hong Kong). Publ. *Journal.*

International Federation of Multiple Sclerosis Societies: 10 Heddon St, London, W1R 7LJ, United Kingdom; tel. (171) 734-9120; fax (171) 287-2587; f. 1965 to co-ordinate the work of 34 national multiple sclerosis organizations throughout the world, to encourage scientific research in this and related neurological diseases, to aid member societies in helping individuals who are in any way disabled as a result of these diseases, to collect and disseminate information and to provide counsel and active help in furthering the development of voluntary national multiple sclerosis organizations. Pres. JAMES R. CANTALUPO; Administrator PAULINE CROWE. Publs *Federation Update* (2 a year), *MS Research in Progress* (every 2 years), *MS Management* (2 a year), *Therapeutic Claims in MS* (annually).

International Federation of Ophthalmological Societies: c/o Dr Bruce E. Spivey, Northwestern Healthcare, 980 North Michigan Ave, Suite 1500, Chicago, IL 60611, USA; tel. (312) 335-6035; fax (312) 335-6030; f. 1953; holds international congress every four years. Pres. Prof. A. NAKAJIMA (Japan); Sec. Dr BRUCE E. SPIVEY.

International Federation of Thermalism and Climatism: Centre thermal, ave des Bains, 1400 Yverdon-les-Bains, Switzerland; f. 1947. Mems in 26 countries. Pres. Dr G. EBRARD; Gen. Sec. M. CLAUDE OGAY.

International Hospital Federation: 4 Abbots Place, London, NW6 4NP, United Kingdom; tel. (171) 372-7181; fax (171) 328-7433; e-mail 101662.1262@compuserve.co; f. 1947 for information exchange and education in hospital and health service matters; represents institutional health care in discussions with WHO; conducts conferences and courses on management and policy issues. Mems in five categories: national hospital and health service organizations, professional associations, regional organizations and individual hospitals; individual mems; professional and industrial mems; honorary mems. Dir-Gen. Dr E. N. PICKERING. Publs *Yearbook, Journal, Newsletter.*

International League against Epilepsy: c/o Dr Peter Wolf, Klinik Mara I, Epilepsie-Zentrum Bethel, Maraweg 21, 33617 Bielefeld, Germany; tel. (521) 144-4897; fax (521) 144-4637; e-mail pwo@mara.de; f. 1909 to link national professional associations and to encourage research, including classification and anti-epileptic drugs; collaborates with the International Bureau for Epilepsy (q.v.) and with WHO. Mems: 62 associations. Pres. JEROME EUGEL, Jr (USA); Sec.-Gen. P. WOLF.

International Medical Association for the Study of Living Conditions and Health: National Centre of Hygiene, Medical Ecology and Nutrition, blvd D. Nestorov 15, 1431 Sofia, Bulgaria; f. 1951 to co-ordinate research in a wide range of subjects relating to living, working and environmental conditions which favour humanity's healthy physical and moral development; holds international congresses. Mems: doctors in 35 countries. Pres. Prof. T. TASHEV (Bulgaria). Publs *Acta Medica et Sociologica,* congress and conference reports.

International Narcotics Control Board—INCB: 1400 Vienna, POB 500, Austria; tel. (1) 213-45-42-77; telex 135612; fax (1) 213-45-58-67; f. 1961 by the Single Convention on Narcotic Drugs to supervise the implementation of the drug control treaties by governments. Mems: 13 individuals. Pres. Prof. HAMID GHODSE (Iran); Sec. HERBERT SCHAEPE (Germany). Publ. *Annual Report* (with three statistical supplements).

International Opticians' Association: 113 Eastbourne Mews, London, W2 6LQ, United Kingdom; tel. (171) 258-0240; fax (171) 724-1175; f. 1951 to promote the science of, and to maintain and advance standards and effect co-operation in optical dispensing.

International Organization for Medical Physics: c/o Prof. Hans Svensson, Radiation Physics Dept, Univ. Hospital, 90185 Umea, Sweden; tel. (90) 785-3891; fax (90) 785-1588; f. 1963 to organize international co-operation in medical physics, to promote communication between the various branches of medical physics and allied subjects, to contribute to the advancement of medical physics in all its aspects and to advise on the formation of national organizations. Mems: national organizations of medical physics in 56 countries. Pres. Prof. KEITH BODDY (UK); Sec.-Gen. Prof. HANS SVENSSON. Publ. *Medical Physics World.*

International Pharmaceutical Federation: Andries Bickerweg 5, 2517 JP The Hague, Netherlands; tel. (70) 3631925; fax (70) 3633914; e-mail a.davidson@fipinl; f. 1912; aims to represent and serve pharmacy and pharmaceutical sciences world-wide; holds Assembly of Pharmacists every two years, International Congress every year. Mems: 84 national pharmaceutical organizations in 62 countries, 100 associate collective mems, 4,500 individuals. Dir A. W. DAVIDSON. Publ. *International Pharmacy Journal* (every 2 months).

International Psycho-Analytical Association: Broomhills, Woodside Lane, London, N12 8UD, United Kingdom; tel. (181) 446-8324; fax (181) 445-4729; e-mail 100450.1362; f. 1908 to hold meetings to define and promulgate the theory and teaching of psychoanalysis, to act as a forum for scientific discussions, to control and regulate training and to contribute to the interdisciplinary area which is common to the behavioural sciences. Mems: 9,292. Pres. Dr R. HORACIO ETCHEGOYEN; Sec. Prof. ANA MARIA ANDRADE DE AZEVEDO. Publs *Bulletin, Newsletter.*

International Society for Cardiovascular Surgery: 13 Elm St, POB 1565, Manchester, MA 01944-0865, USA; tel. (508) 526-8330; fax (508) 526-4018; e-mail iscvs@prri.com; f. 1950 to stimulate research in the diagnosis and therapy of cardiovascular diseases and to exchange ideas on an international basis. Sec.-Gen. MALCOLM O. PERRY (USA). Publ. *Cardiovascular Surgery.*

International Society for Oneiric Mental Imagery Techniques: c/o André Virel, 24 rue Jean Colly, 75013 Paris, France; tel. 1-44-23-74-58; fax 1-47-00-16-63; f. 1968; a group of research workers, technicians and psychotherapists using oneirism techniques under waking conditions, with the belief that a healing action cannot be dissociated from the restoration of creativity. Mems: in 17 countries. Pres. Dr ANDRÉ VIREL (France); Vice-Pres. ODILE DORKEL (France).

International Society of Art and Psychopathology: c/o Dr G. Roux, 27 rue du mal Joffre, 64000 Pau, France; tel. and fax 1-59-27-69-74; f. 1959 to bring together the various specialists interested in the problems of expression and artistic activities in connection with psychiatric, sociological and psychological research, as well as in the use of methods applied to other fields than that of mental illness. Mems: 625. Pres. Dr G. ROUX (France); Sec.-Gen. Dr J. VERDEAU-PAILLÈS (France).

International Society of Developmental Biologists: c/o Paul van der Saag, Hubrecht Laboratorium, Uppsalalaan 8, 3584 CT, Utrecht, Netherlands; tel. (30) 2510-211; e-mail directie@niob.knaw.nl; f. 1911 as International Institute of Embryology. Objects: to promote the study of developmental biology and to promote international co-operation among the investigators in this field. Mems: 850 in 33 countries. Pres. Prof. PETER GRUSS (Germany); Sec.-Treas. Prof. SIEGFRIED DE LAAT. Publ. *Mechanisms of Development.*

International Society of Lymphology: POB 245063, University of Arizona, 1501 North Campbell Ave, Room 4406, Tucson, AZ 85724-5063, USA; tel. (520) 626-6118; fax (520) 626-0822; e-mail lymph@u.arizona.edu; f. 1966 to further progress in lymphology through personal contact and exchange of ideas among members. Mems: 400 in 43 countries. Pres. E. FÖLDI (Germany); Sec.-Gen. M. H. WITTE (USA). Publ. *Lymphology* (quarterly).

International Society of Neuropathology: c/o Dr Janice Anderson, Dept of Histopathology, Addenbrooke's Hospital, Hills Rd, Cambridge CB2 200, United Kingdom. Pres. Prof. GEORG W. KREUTZBERG; Sec.-Gen. Dr JANICE ANDERSON.

International Society of Orthopaedic Surgery and Traumatology: 40 rue Washington, 1050 Brussels, Belgium; tel. (2) 648-68-23; telex 65080; fax (2) 649-86-01; f. 1929; congresses are convened every three years. Mems: 101 countries, 3,000 individuals. Pres. CHARLES SORBIE (Canada); Sec.-Gen. ANTHONY J. HALL (UK). Publ. *International Orthopaedics* (every 2 months).

International Society of Radiology: Dept of Radiology, Helsinki University Central Hospital, Meilahti Clinics, 00290 Helsinki, Finland; tel. 471-24-80; fax 471-44-04; f. 1953 to promote radiology world-wide. International Commissions on Radiation Units and

Measurements, on Radiation Protection, on Radiological Education and on Rules and Regulations; organizes biannual International Congress of Radiology; collaborates with WHO. Mems: 68 national radiological societies. Sec. C. G. STANDERTSKJÖLD-NORDENSTAM.

International Society of Surgery: Netzibodenstr. 34, 4133 Pratteln, Switzerland; tel. (61) 8114770; fax (61) 8114775; e-mail 101762.1434@compuserve.com; f. 1902; organizes congresses: 38th World Congress of Surgery, Vienna, Austria, August 1999. Mems: 3,500. Admin. Dir. VICTOR BERTSCHI; Sec.-Gen. Prof. THOMAS RÜEDI. Publ. *World Journal of Surgery* (every 2 months).

International Union against Tuberculosis and Lung Disease: 68 blvd St Michel, 75006 Paris, France; tel. 1-44-32-03-60; fax 1-43-29-90-87; e-mail iuatldparis@compuserve.com; f. 1920 to co-ordinate the efforts of anti-tuberculosis and respiratory disease associations, to mobilize public interest, to assist control programmes and research around the world, to collaborate with governments and WHO, to promote conferences. Mems: associations in 165 countries, 3,000 individual mems. Pres. Prof. S. SUPCHAROEN; Exec. Dir Dr NILS BILLO. Publs *The International Journal of Tuberculosis and Lung Disease* (in English with summaries in French and Spanish; incl. conference proceedings), *Newsletter*.

International Union for Health Promotion and Education: Immeuble le Berry, 2 rue Auguste Comte, 92170 Vanves, France; tel. 1-46-45-00-59; fax 1-46-45-00-45; e-mail iuhpemcl@worldnet.fr; f. 1951; provides an international network for the exchange of practical information on developments in health promotion and education; promotes research into effective methods and techniques in health promotion and education and encourages professional training in health promotion and education for health workers, teachers, social workers and others; holds regional and world conferences. Mems: in 90 countries. Pres. Dr SPENCER HAGARD (UK). Publ. *International Journal of Health Promotion and Education* (quarterly).

International Union of Therapeutics: c/o Prof. A. Pradalier, Hôpital Louis Mourier, 178 rue des Renouillers, 92700 Colombes, France; tel. 1-47-60-67-05; f. 1934; international congresses every other year. Mems: 500 from 22 countries. Pres. Prof. A. PRADALIER; Gen. Sec. Prof. P. LECHAT.

Middle East Neurosurgical Society: c/o Dr Fuad S. Haddad, Neurosurgical Department, American University Medical Centre, POB 113-6044, Beirut, Lebanon; tel. 347348; telex 20801; fax 342517; e-mail gfhaddad@aub.edu.lb; f. 1958 to promote clinical advances and scientific research among its members and to spread knowledge of neurosurgery and related fields among all members of the medical profession in the Middle East. Mems: 684 in nine countries. Pres. Dr FUAD S. HADDAD; Hon. Sec. Dr GEDEON MOHASSEB.

Organization for Co-ordination and Co-operation in the Struggle against Endemic Diseases (Organisation de coordination et de coopération pour la lutte contre les grandes endémies—OCCGE): 01 BP 153, Bobo-Dioulasso 01, Burkina Faso; tel. 97-01-55; fax 97-00-99; e-mail sq@pegase.occge.bf; f. 1960; conducts research, provides training and maintains a documentation centre and computer information system. Mems: governments of Benin, Burkina Faso, Côte d'Ivoire, Mali, Mauritania, Niger, Senegal, Togo. Pres. ABDOULAYE RHALY; Sec.-Gen. Dr YOUSSOUF KANE. Publs *Rapport annuel, OCCGE Info* (3 a year), *Bulletin Bibliographique* (quarterly).

Research centres:

Centre de Recherches sur les Méningites et les Schistosomiases: BP 10 887, Niamey, Niger; tel. 72-39-69.

Centre Muraz: 01 BP 153, Bobo-Dioulasso 01, Burkina Faso; tel. 97-01-02; fax 97-04-57; f. 1939; multi-discipline research centre with special interest in biology and epidemiology of tropical diseases and training of health workers. Dir Prof. PHILIPPE VAN DE PERRE.

Centre Régional de Recherches entomologiques: Cotonou, Benin.

Institut de Recherche sur la Tuberculose et les Infections respiratoires aigües: Nouakchott, Mauritania.

Institut d'Ophtalmologie tropicale africaine—IOTA: BP 248, Bamako, Mali; tel. 22-34-21; fax 22-51-86; e-mail hug10@caluacom.fr; f. 1953; eye care, clinical, operational and epidemiological research, training; Dir Dr PIERRE HUGUET.

Institut Marchoux: BP 251, Bamako, Mali; tel. 22-51-31; fax 22-28-45; research, epidemiology and training on leprosy, dermatology, surgery. Dir Dr JACQUES MILLAN.

Institut Pierre Richet: BP 1500, Bouaké 01, Côte d'Ivoire; tel. 63-37-46; fax 63-27-38; e-mail carneval@bouake2.orsrom.ci; f. 1974; research on trypanosomiasis, onchocerciasis, malaria and vector control; maintains a geographical information system; Dir Dr PIERRE CARNEVALE.

Office de Recherches sur l'Alimentation et la Nutrition africaine: BP 2089, Dakar, Senegal; tel. 22-58-92; Dir Dr MAKHTAR N'DIAYE.

In 1990 it was announced that the West African Health Community was to be amalgamated with the Organization for Co-ordination and Co-operation in the Struggle against Endemic Diseases to form the West African Health Organization, covering all the member states of ECOWAS (subject to ratification by member states).

Organization for Co-ordination in the Struggle against Endemic Diseases in Central Africa (Organisation de coordination pour la lutte contre les endémies en Afrique Centrale—OCEAC): BP 288, Yaoundé, Cameroon; tel. 23-22-32; telex 8411; fax 23-00-61; f. 1965 to standardize methods of controlling endemic diseases, to co-ordinate national action, and to negotiate programmes of assistance and training on a regional scale. Mems: Cameroon, Central African Republic, Chad, Republic of the Congo, Equatorial Guinea, Gabon. Pres. JEAN RÉMY PENDY BOUYIKI; Sec.-Gen. Dr AUGUSTE BILONGO MANENE. Publ. *Bulletin de Liaison et de Documentation* (quarterly).

Pan-American Association of Ophthalmology: 1301 South Bowen Rd, Suite 365, Arlington, TX 76013, USA; tel. (817) 265-2831; fax (817) 275-3961; e-mail paa@flash.net; f. 1939 to promote friendship and dissemination of scientific information among the profession throughout the Western Hemisphere; holds annual meetings. Mems: national ophthalmological societies and other bodies in 39 countries. Pres. Dr JUAN VERDAGUER (Chile); Exec. Dir Dr FRANCISCO MARTINEZ CASTRO (Mexico). Publs *Ojo-Eye-Olho* (2 a year), *El Noticiero* (quarterly).

Pan-Pacific Surgical Association: 1360 South Beretania, Suite 304, Honolulu, HI 96814, USA; tel. (808) 593-1180; fax (808) 593-1176; f. 1929 to bring together surgeons to exchange scientific knowledge relating to surgery and medicine, and to promote the improvement and standardization of hospitals and their services and facilities; congresses are held every two years. Mems: 2,716 regular, associate and senior mems from 44 countries. Chair. WILLIAM H. MONTGOMERY.

Society of French-speaking Neuro-Surgeons (Société de neurochirurgie de langue française): Hôpital d'Enfants de la Timone, 13385 Marseille, France; f. 1949; holds annual convention and congress. Mems: 700 in numerous countries. Pres. M. CHOUX (France); Sec. J. LAGARRIGUE (France). Publ. *Neuro-Chirurgie* (6 a year).

World Association for Disaster and Emergency Medicine: c/o Safar Centre for Resuscitation Research, Univ. of Pittsburgh, 3434 Fifth Ave, Pittsburgh, PA 15260, USA; tel. (412) 383-1904; fax (412) 624-0943; f. 1976 to improve the world-wide delivery of emergency and humanitarian care in mass casualty and disaster situations through training, symposia, publications and emergency missions. Mems: 600 in 62 countries. Pres. STEVEN ROTTMAN (USA); Hon. Sec. Prof. W. DICK (Germany). Publ. *Prehospital and Disaster Medicine*.

World Association of Societies of (Anatomic and Clinical) Pathology—WASP: c/o Japan Clinical Pathology Foundation for International Exchange, Sakura-Sugamo Bldg 7F, Sugamo 2-11-1, Toshima-ku, Tokyo 170, Japan; tel. (3) 3918-8161; fax (3) 3949-6168; f. 1947 to link national societies and to co-ordinate their scientific and technical means of action; and to promote the development of anatomic and clinical pathology, especially by convening conferences, congresses and meetings, and by the interchange of publications and personnel. Membership: 54 national associations. Pres. PETER B. HERDSON; Sec. WALTER TIMPERLEY. Publ. *Newsletter* (quarterly).

World Confederation for Physical Therapy: 4A Abbots Place, London, NW6 4NP, United Kingdom; tel. (171) 328-5448; fax (171) 624-7579; f. 1951; represents physical therapy internationally; encourages high standards of physical therapy education and practice; promotes exchange of information among members, and the development of a scientific professional base through research; aims to contribute to the development of informed public opinion regarding physical therapy. Mems: 67 organizations. Pres. Prof. D. P. G. TEAGER; Sec.-Gen. B. J. MYERS. Publ. *Newsletter* (2 a year).

World Council of Optometry—WCO: 10 Knaresborough Place, London, SW5 0TG, United Kingdom; tel. (171) 370-4765; fax (171) 373-1143; f. 1927 to co-ordinate efforts to provide a good standard of ophthalmic optical (optometric) care throughout the world; enables exchange of ideas between different countries; a large part of its work is concerned with optometric education, and advice upon standards of qualification. The WCO also interests itself in legislation in relation to optometry throughout the world. Mems: 70 optometric organizations in 47 countries and four regional groups. Pres. ROLAND DES GROSEILLIERS; Sec. D. A. LEASON. Publ. *Interoptics* (quarterly).

World Federation for Mental Health: 1021 Prince St, Alexandria, VA 22314, USA; tel. (703) 838-7543; fax (703) 684-5968; f. 1948 to promote among all nations the highest possible standard of mental health; to work with agencies of the United Nations in promoting mental health; to help other voluntary associations in the improvement of mental health services. Mems: 337 national or international associations in 115 countries. Pres. BEVERLY B. LONG (USA); Dir-Gen. Dr EUGENE B. BRODY. Publ. *Newsletter* (quarterly).

World Federation of Neurosurgical Societies: c/o Prof. Edward R. Laws, Dept. of Neurological Surgery, Univ. of Virginia, Box 212, Health Science Center, Charlottesville, VA 22908, USA; tel. (804) 924-2650; fax (804) 924-5894; f. 1957 to assist the development of neurosurgery and to help the formation of associations; to assist the exchange of information and to encourage research. Mems: 57 societies representing 56 countries. Pres. Prof. ARMANDO BASSO; Sec. Prof. EDWARD R. LAWS, Jr.

World Federation of Occupational Therapists: c/o Carolyn Webster, Disabilities Services Comm., PO Box 441, West Perth, 6872 Western Australia, Australia; tel. (8) 9426-9325; fax (8) 9426-9380; f. 1952 to further the rehabilitation of the physically and mentally disabled by promoting the development of occupational therapy in all countries; to facilitate the exchange of information and publications; to promote research in occupational therapy; international congresses are held every four years. Mems: national professional associations in 46 countries, with total membership of approximately 100,000. Pres. BARBARA TYLDESLY (UK); Hon. Sec. CAROLYN WEBSTER (Australia). Publ. *Bulletin* (2 a year).

World Federation of Public Health Associations: c/o Diane Kuntz, American Public Health Asscn, 1015 15th St, NW, Washington, DC 20005, USA; tel. (202) 789-5696; fax (202) 789-5681; e-mail diane.kuntz@msmail.apha.org; internet http://www.apha.org/apha.wfpha; f. 1967. Triennial Congress: Atlanta, GA, USA,1991. Mems: 45 national public health associations. Exec. Sec. DIANE KUNTZ (USA). Publs *WFPHA News* (in English), and occasional technical papers.

World Federation of Societies of Anaesthesiologists—WFSA: Dept of Anaesthetics, SKZ/AZR, Sh 3.601, Dr Molewaterplein 60, 3015 GJ Rotterdam, Netherlands; tel. (10) 463-6754; fax (10) 463-6804; e-mail meursing@anes.azr.nl; f. 1955 to make available the highest standards of anaesthesia to all peoples of the world. Mems: 102 national societies. Pres. Prof. M. D. VICKERS (UK); Sec. Dr A. E. E. MEURSING; Publs *World Anaesthesia Newsletter* (2 a year), *Annual Report, Anaesthesia Worldwide* (4 a year).

Posts and Telecommunications

African Posts and Telecommunications Union: ave Patrice Lumumba, BP 44, Brazzaville, Republic of the Congo; tel. 832778; telex 5212; fax 832779; f. 1961 to improve postal and telecommunication services between member administrations. Mems: 11 countries. Sec.-Gen. MAHMOUDOU SAMOURA.

Asia-Pacific Telecommunity: No. 12/49, Soi 5, Chaengwattana Rd, Thungsonghong, Bangkok 10210, Thailand; tel. (2) 573-0044; fax (2) 573-7479; e-mail apthq@mozart.inet.co.th; f. 1979 to cover all matters relating to telecommunications in the region. Mems: Afghanistan, Australia, Bangladesh, Brunei, the People's Republic of China, India, Indonesia, Iran, Japan, the Republic of Korea, Laos, Malaysia, Maldives, Myanmar, Nauru, Nepal, Pakistan, the Philippines, Singapore, Sri Lanka, Thailand, Viet Nam; assoc. mems: Cook Islands, Hong Kong; two affiliated mems each in Indonesia, Japan and Thailand, three in the Republic of Korea, four in Hong Kong, one in Maldives and six in the Philippines.

Asian-Pacific Postal Union: Post Office Bldg, 1000 Manila, Philippines; tel. (2) 470760; fax (2) 407448; f. 1962 to extend, facilitate and improve the postal relations between the member countries and to promote co-operation in the field of postal services. Mems: 23 countries. Chair. SOMBUT UTHAISANG (Thailand); Dir IRINEO V. INTIA. Publs *Annual Report, Exchange Program of Postal Officials, Newsletter.*

European Conference of Postal and Telecommunications Administrations: Ministry of Transport and Communications, 49 ave Syngrou, 117 80 Athens, Greece; tel. (1) 9236494; telex 216369; fax (1) 9237133; f. 1959 to strengthen relations between member administrations and to harmonize and improve their technical services; set up Eurodata Foundation, for research and publishing. Mems: 26 countries. Sec. Z. PROTOPSALTI. Publ. *Bulletin*.

European Telecommunications Satellite Organization—EUTELSAT: Tour Maine Montparnasse, 33 ave du Maine, 75755 Paris Cédex 15 , France; tel. 1-45-38-47-47; telex 203823; fax 1-45-38-37-00; f. 1977 to operate satellites for fixed and mobile communications in Europe; operates an eight-satellite system, incorporating four EUTELSAT I and four EUTELSAT II satellites. Mems: public and private telecommunications operations in 33 countries. Dir-Gen. JEAN GRENIER.

INMARSAT—International Mobile Satellite Organization: 99 City Rd, London, EC1Y 1AX, United Kingdom; tel. (171) 728-1000; telex 297201; fax (171) 728-1044; internet http://www.inmarsat.org/inmarsat; f. 1979 to provide (from February 1982) global communications for shipping via satellites on a commercial basis; satellites in geo-stationary orbit over the Atlantic, Indian and Pacific Oceans provide telephone, telex, facsimile, telegram, low to high speed data services and distress and safety communications for ships of all nations and structures such as oil rigs; in 1985 the operating agreement was amended to include aeronautical communications, and in 1988 amendments were approved which allow provision of global land-mobile communications. Organs: Assembly of all Parties to the Convention (every 2 years); council of representatives of 22 national telecommunications administrations; executive Directorate. Mems: 79 countries. Chair. of Council DIETER EXNER; Dir-Gen. WARREN GRACE.

International Telecommunications Satellite Organization—INTELSAT: 3400 International Drive, NW, Washington, DC 20008-3098, USA; tel. (202) 944-6800; telex 892707; fax (202) 944-7860; f. 1964 to establish a global commercial satellite communications system. Assembly of Parties attended by representatives of member governments, meets every two years to consider policy and long-term aims and matters of interest to members as sovereign states. Meeting of Signatories to the Operating Agreement held annually. Twenty-four INTELSAT satellites in geosynchronous orbit provide a global communications service; INTELSAT provides most of the world's overseas traffic. Mems: 141 governments. Dir-Gen. and CEO IRVING GOLDSTEIN.

Pacific Telecommunications Council: 2454 Beretania St, 302 Honolulu, HI 96826, USA; tel. (808) 941-3789; fax (808) 944-4874; e-mail info@ptc.org; f. 1980 to promote the development, understanding and beneficial use of telecommunications and information systems/services throughout the Pacific region; provides forum for users and providers of communications services; sponsors annual conference and seminars. Mems: 600 (corporate, government, academic and individual). Pres. JANE HURD; Exec. Dir RICHARD J. BARBER. Publ. *Pacific Telecommunications Review* (quarterly).

Postal Union of the Americas, Spain and Portugal (Unión Postal de las Américas, España y Portugal): Calle Cebollatí 1468/70, Casilla de Correos 20.042, Montevideo, Uruguay; tel. (2) 400070; fax (2) 405046; internet upaepadinet.com.uy; f. 1911 to extend, facilitate and study the postal relationships of member countries. Mems: 26 countries. Sec.-Gen. MARIO FELMER KLENNER (Chile).

Press, Radio and Television

Asia-Pacific Broadcasting Union—ABU: POB 1164, Jalan Pantai Bahru, 59700 Kuala Lumpur, Malaysia; tel. (3) 2823592; telex 32227; fax (3) 2825292; e-mail sg@abu.org.my; internet http://www.abu.org.my/abu; f. 1964 to assist in the development of radio and television in the Asia/Pacific area, particularly in its use for educational purposes. Mems: 45 full, 29 additional and 26 associates in 50 countries and territories. Pres. Dato' JAAFAR KAMIN (Malaysia); Sec.-Gen. HUGH LEONARD. Publs *ABU News* (every 2 months), *ABU Technical Review* (every 2 months).

Association for the Promotion of the International Circulation of the Press—DISTRIPRESS: 8002 Zürich, Beethovenstrasse 20, Switzerland; tel. (1) 2024121; fax (1) 2021025; f. 1955 to assist in the promotion of the freedom of the press throughout the world, supporting and aiding UNESCO in promoting the free flow of ideas. Organizes meetings of publishers and distributors of newspapers, periodicals and paperback books, to promote the exchange of information and experience among members. Mems: 458. Pres. CHRIS HADZOPOULOS (Greece); Man. HEINZ E. GRAF (Switzerland). Publs *Distripress Gazette, Who's Who.*

Association of European Journalists: 5300 Bonn 2, Kastanienweg 26, Germany; tel. and fax (228) 321712; f. 1963 to participate actively in the development of a European consciousness; to promote deeper knowledge of European problems and secure appreciation by the general public of the work of European institutions; and to facilitate members' access to sources of European information. Mems: 1,500 individuals and national associations in 15 countries. Sec.-Gen. GUENTHER WAGENLEHNER.

Association of Private European Cable Operators: 1 blvd Anspach, boîte 25, 1000 Brussels, Belgium; tel. (2) 223-25-91; fax (2) 223-06-96; f. 1995 aims to promote the interests of independent cable operators and to ensure exchange of information on cable and telecommunications; carries out research on relevant technical and legal questions. Mems: 27 organizations in 19 countries. Pres. M. DE SUTTER.

Broadcasting Organization of Non-aligned Countries—BONAC: c/o Cyprus Broadcasting Corporation, POB 4824, 1397 Nicosia, Cyprus; tel. (2) 422231; telex 2333; fax (2) 314050; e-mail rik@cybc.com.cy; f. 1977 to ensure an equitable, objective and comprehensive flow of information through broadcasting; Secretariat moves to the broadcasting organization of host country. Mems: in 102 countries.

European Alliance of Press Agencies: c/o Agence Belga, rue F. Pelletier 8B, 1030 Brussels, Belgium; tel. (2) 743-13-11; fax (2) 735-

18-74; f. 1957 to assist co-operation among members and to study and protect their common interests; annual assembly. Mems in 30 countries. Sec.-Gen. RUDI DE CEUSTER.

European Broadcasting Union—EBU: Ancienne-Route 17A, CP 67, 1218 Grand-Saconnex, Geneva, Switzerland; tel. (22) 7172111; telex 415700; fax (22) 7172481; f. 1950 in succession to the International Broadcasting Union; a professional association of broadcasting organizations, supporting the interests of members and assisting the development of broadcasting in all its forms; activities include the Eurovision news, programme exchanges (linking 58 television services in 47 countries) and the Euroradio music exchanges. Mems: 118 active (European) and associate in 80 countries. Pres. Prof. A. SCHARF (Germany); Sec.-Gen. JEAN BERNARD MÜNCH (Switzerland). Publs *EBU Technical Review* (quarterly), *Diffusion* (quarterly).

IFRA: Washingtonplatz 1, 64287 Darmstadt, Germany; tel. (6151) 7336; fax (6151) 733800; f. 1961 as Inca-Fiej Research Asscn to develop methods and techniques for the newspaper industry; to evaluate standard specifications for raw materials for use in newspaper production; to investigate economy and quality improvements for newspaper printing and publishing. Mems: 1,122 newspapers, 410 suppliers. Pres. MICHAEL RINGIER; Man. Dir G. W. BOETTCHER. Publ. *Newspaper Techniques* (monthly in English, French and German).

Inter-American Press Association (Sociedad Interamericana de Prensa): 2911 NW 39th St, Miami, FL 33142, USA; tel. (305) 634-2465; telex 522873; fax (305) 635-2272; f. 1942 to guard the freedom of the press in the Americas; to promote and maintain the dignity, rights and responsibilities of the profession of journalism; to foster a wider knowledge and greater interchange among the peoples of the Americas. Mems: 1,400. Exec. Dir JULIO E. MUÑOZ, Publ. *IAPA News*.

International Association of Broadcasting (Asociación Internacional de Radiodifusión—AIR): Cnel Brandzen 1961, Office 402, 11200 Montevideo, Uruguay; tel. and fax (2) 488121; telex 31173; f. 1946 to preserve free and private broadcasting; to promote co-operation between the corporations and public authorities; to defend freedom of expression. Mems: national associations of broadcasters. Pres. Dr LUIS H. TARSITANO; Dir-Gen. Dr HÉCTOR OSCAR AMENGUAL. Publ. *La Gaceta de AIR* (every 2 months).

International Association of Sound Archives: c/o Albrecht Häfner, Südwestfunk, Documentation and Archives Dept, 76522 Baden-Baden, Germany; tel. (7221) 923487; fax (7221) 922094; e-mail haefner@swf.de; f. 1969; involved in the preservation and exchange of sound and audiovisual recordings, and in developing recording techniques; holds annual conference. Mems: 380 individuals and institutions in 48 countries. Sec.-Gen. ALBRECHT HÄFNER. Publs. *IASA Journal* (2 a year), *IASA Information Bulletin* (quarterly).

International Catholic Union of the Press (Union catholique internationale de la presse—UCIP): 37–39 rue de Vermont, Case Postale 197, 1211 Geneva 20, Switzerland; tel. (22) 7340017; fax (22) 7340053; f. 1927 to link all Catholics who influence public opinion through the press, to inspire a high standard of professional conscience and to represent the interest of the Catholic press at international organizations. Mems: Federation of Catholic Press Agencies, Federation of Catholic Journalists, Federation of Catholic Dailies, Federation of Catholic Periodicals, Federation of Teachers in the Science and Technics of Information, Federation of Church Press Associations, Federation of Book Publishers, seven regional asscns. Pres. GÜNTHER MEES; Sec.-Gen. JOSEPH CHITTILAPPILLY (India). Publ. *UCIP-Information*.

International Council for Film, Television and Audiovisual Communication: 1 rue Miollis, 75732 Paris Cédex 15, France; tel. 1-45-68-25-56; fax 1-45-67-28-40; f. 1958 to arrange meetings and co-operation generally. Mems: 36 international film and television organizations. Pres. JEAN ROHCH; Exec. Sec. L. PATRY. Publ. *Letter of Information* (monthly).

International Council of French-speaking Radio and Television Organizations (Conseil international des radios-télévisions d'expression française): 52 blvd Auguste-Reyers, 1044 Brussels, Belgium; tel. (2) 732-45-85; telex 25324; fax (2) 732-62-40; f. 1978 to establish links between French-speaking radio and television organizations. Mems: 46 organizations. Pres. GERVAIS MENDO; Sec.-Gen. ABDELKADER MARZOUKI (Tunisia).

International Federation of Press Cutting Agencies: Streulistr. 19, POB 8030 Zürich, Switzerland; tel. (1) 3888200; fax (1) 3888201; f. 1953 to improve the standing of the profession, prevent infringements, illegal practices and unfair competition; and to develop business and friendly relations among press cuttings agencies throughout the world. Annual meeting, 1997: India. Mems: 71 agencies. Pres. JOACHIM VON BEUST (Germany); Gen. Sec. Dr DIETER HENNE (Switzerland).

International Federation of the Cinematographic Press—FIPRESCI: 80797 Munich, Schleissheimerstr. 83, Germany; tel. (89) 182303; telex 5214674; fax (89) 184766; e-mail keder@fipresci.muc.de; f. 1930 to develop the cinematographic press and promote cinema as an art; organizes international meetings and juries in film festivals. Mems: national organizations or corresponding members in 68 countries. Pres. DEREK MALCOLM (UK); Sec.-Gen. KLAUS EDER (Germany).

International Federation of the Periodical Press—FIPP: Queens House, 55/56 Lincoln's Inn Fields, London, WC2A 3LJ, United Kingdom; tel. (171) 404-4169; fax (171) 404-4170; e-mail fipp.nemo@nemo-geis.com; f. 1925; works through national associations to promote optimum conditions for the development of periodical publishing; fosters formal and informal alliances between magazine publishers. Mems: 33 national asscns representing 2,500 publishing cos and 75 international publishing cos and assoc. mems. Pres. and CEO PER R. MORTENSEN; Chair. KENGO TANAKA (Japan). Publ. *Magazine World* (6 a year).

International Federation of the Socialist and Democratic Press: CP 737, 20101 Milan, Italy; tel. (2) 8050105; f. 1953 to promote co-operation between editors and publishers of socialist newspapers; affiliated to the Socialist International (q.v.). Mems: about 100. Sec. UMBERTO GIOVINE.

International Institute of Communications: Tavistock House South, Tavistock Sq., London, WC1H 9LF, United Kingdom; tel. (171) 388-0671; fax (171) 380-0623; f. 1969 (as the International Broadcast Institute) to link all working in the field of communications, including policy makers, broadcasters, industrialists and engineers; holds local, regional and international meetings, undertakes research and publishes journal. Mems: over 1,000 corporate, institutional and individual. Pres. HENRI PIGEAT; Exec. Dir VICKI MACLEOD.

International Maritime Radio Association: South Bank House, Black Prince Rd, London, SE1 7SJ, United Kingdom; tel. (171) 587-1245; fax (171) 587-1436; f. 1928 to study and develop means of improving marine radio communications and radio aids to marine navigation. Mems: over 50 organizations and companies are involved in marine electronics in the areas of radio communications and navigation. The member companies are located in the major maritime nations of the world. Pres. S. KUNITOMO (Japan); Sec.-Gen. and Chair. of Technical Cttee M. P. FOX.

International Organization of Journalists: Calle Mayor 81, Madrid 28013, Spain; tel. (1) 24224243; fax (1) 24223853; f. 1946 to defend the freedom of the press and of journalists and to promote their material welfare. Activities include the maintenance of international training centres and international recreation centres for journalists. Mems: national organizations and individuals in 120 countries. Pres. ARMANDO S. ROLLEMBERG; Sec.-Gen. GERARD GATINOT. Publs *The World of Journalists* (quarterly, in English, French and Spanish), *IOJ Newsletter* (2 a month, in Arabic, English, French, Russian and Spanish).

International Press Institute—IPI: Spiegelgasse 2/29, 1010 Vienna, Austria; tel. (1) 5129011; fax (1) 5129014; e-mail ipi.vienna@xpoint.at; f. 1951 as a non-governmental organization of editors, publishers and news broadcasters who support the principles of a free and responsible press; activities: defence of press freedom, regional meetings of members, training programmes, research and library; annual World Congress. Mems: about 2,000 from 100 countries. Chair. EUGENE L. ROBERTS (USA); Dir JOHANN FRITZ (Austria). Publs *IPI Report* (quarterly), *World Press Freedom Review* (annually).

International Press Telecommunications Council: 8 Sheet St, Windsor, Berks, SL4 1BG, United Kingdom; tel. (1753) 833728; fax (1753) 833750; f. 1965 to safeguard and promote the interests of the Press on all matters relating to telecommunications; keeps its members informed of current and future telecommunications developments. The Council meets three times a year and maintains four committees and 10 working parties. Mems: 44 press associations, newspapers, news agencies and industry vendors. Chair. KEITH KINCAID; Man. Dir DAVID ALLEN. Publs *IPTC Spectrum* (2 a year), *IPTC Mirror* (monthly).

Latin-American Catholic Press Union: Apdo Postal 17-21-178, Quito, Ecuador; tel. (2) 548046; fax (2) 501658; f. 1959 to co-ordinate, promote and improve the Catholic press in Latin America. Mems: national asscns and local groups in most Latin American countries. Pres. ISMAR DE OLIVEIRA SOARES (Brazil); Sec. CARLOS EDUARDO CORTÉS (Colombia).

Organization of Asia-Pacific News Agencies—OANA: c/o Xinhua News Agency, 57 Xuanwumen Xidajie, Beijing 100803, People's Republic of China; tel. (10) 3074762; fax (10) 3072707; f. 1961 to promote co-operation in professional matters and mutual exchange of news, features, etc. among the news agencies of Asia and the Pacific via the Asia-Pacific News Network (ANN). Mems: Anadolu Ajansi (Turkey), Antara (Indonesia), APP (Pakistan), Bakhtar (Afghanistan), BERNAMA (Malaysia), BSS (Bangladesh), ENA (Bangladesh), Hindustan Samachar (India), IRNA (Iran), ITAR-TASS (Russia), Kaz-TAG (Kazakhstan), KABAR (Kyrgyzstan), KCNA (Korea, Democratic People's Republic), KPL (Laos),

Kyodo (Japan), Lankapuvath (Sri Lanka), Montsame (Mongolia), PNA (Philippines), PPI (Pakistan), PTI (India), RSS (Nepal), Samachar Bharati (India), TNA (Thailand), UNB (Bangladesh), UNI (India), Viet Nam News Agency, Xinhua (People's Republic of China), Yonhap (Republic of Korea). Pres. GUO CHAOREN; Sec.-Gen. YU JIAFU.

Press Foundation of Asia: POB 1843, 1500 Roxas Blvd, Manila, Philippines; tel. (2) 598633; telex 27674; fax (2) 5224365; f. 1967; an independent, non-profit making organization governed by its newspaper members; acts as a professional forum for about 200 newspapers in Asia; aims to reduce cost of newspapers to potential readers, to improve editorial and management techniques through research and training programmes and to encourage the growth of the Asian press; operates *Depthnews* feature service. Mems: 200 newspapers. Exec. Chair. EUGENIO LOPEZ (Philippines); Dir-Gen. MOCHTAR LUBIS (Indonesia). Publs *Pressasia* (quarterly), *Asian Women* (quarterly).

Reporters sans Frontières: 5 rue Geoffroy Marie, 75009 Paris, France; tel. 1-44-83-84-84; fax 1-45-23-11-51; e-mail rsf@cavanet.calvacom.fr/rsf/; internet http://www.calvacom.fr/rsf/; f. 1985 to defend press freedoms throughout the world; generates awareness of violations of press freedoms and supports journalists under threat or imprisoned as a result of their work. Mems in 77 countries. Dir ROBERT MENARD. Publs *Quarterly Digest, La Lettre de Reporters sans Frontières* (2 a month).

Union of National Radio and Television Organizations of Africa—URTNA: 101 rue Carnot, BP 3237, Dakar, Senegal; tel. 21-16-25; telex 51650; fax 22-51-13; f. 1962; co-ordinates radio and television services, including monitoring and frequency allocation, the exchange of information and coverage of national and international events among African countries; maintains programme exchange centre (Nairobi, Kenya), technical centre (Bamako, Mali), a centre for rural radio studies (Ouagadougou, Burkina Faso) and a centre for the exchange of television news in Algiers, Algeria. Mems: 49 organizations and six associate members. Sec.-Gen. EFOÉ ADODO MENSAH. Publ. *URTNA Review* (English and French, 2 a year).

World Association for Christian Communication—WACC: 357 Kennington Lane, London, SE11 5QY, United Kingdom; tel. (171) 582-9139; telex 8812669; fax (171) 735-0340; internet http://www.oneworld.org/wacc/; f. 1975; works among churches, church-related organizations and individuals to promote more effective use of all forms of media (including radio, television, newspapers, books, film, cassettes, dance, drama etc.) for proclaiming the Christian gospel, particularly with reference to ethical and social issues. Mems in 61 countries. Pres. RANDY L. NAYLOR; Gen.-Sec. CARLOS A. VALLE. Publs *Action* newsletter (10 a year), *Media Development* (quarterly).

World Association of Newspapers: 25 rue d'Astorg, 75008 Paris, France; tel. 1-47-42-85-00; fax 1-47-42-49-48; e-mail tbalding@nemo.geis.com; f. 1948 to defend the freedom of the press, to safeguard the ethical and economic interests of newspapers and to study all questions of interest to newspapers at international level. Mems: 57 national organizations in 53 countries, individual publishers in 90 others, and 17 news agencies. Pres. JAYME SIROTSKY (Brazil); Dir-Gen. TIMOTHY BALDING. Publ. *Newsletter*.

Religion

Agudath Israel World Organisation: Hacherut Sq, POB 326, Jerusalem 91002, Israel; tel. (2) 5384357; fax (2) 5383634; f. 1912 to help solve the problems facing Jewish people all over the world in the spirit of the Jewish tradition; holds World Rabbinical Council (every five years), and an annual Central Council comprising 100 mems nominated by affiliated organizations. Mems: over 500,000 in 25 countries. Sec.-Gen. A. HIRSCH (Jerusalem). Publs *Hamodia* (Jerusalem daily newspaper), *Jewish Tribune* (London, weekly), *Jewish Observer* (New York, monthly), *Dos Yiddishe Vort* (New York, monthly), *Coalition* (New York), *Perspectives* (Toronto, monthly), *La Voz Judia* (Buenos Aires, monthly), *Jüdische Stimme* (Zürich, monthly).

All Africa Conference of Churches—AACC: POB 14205, Waiyaki Way, Nairobi, Kenya; tel. (2) 441483; telex 22175; fax (2) 443241; e-mail aacc-secretariat@maf.org; f. 1958; an organ of co-operation and continuing fellowship among Protestant, Orthodox and independent churches and Christian Councils in Africa. 1997 Assembly: Addis Ababa, Ethiopia. Mems: 147 churches and affiliated Christian councils in 39 African countries. Pres. The Very Rev. Prof. KWESI DICKSON (Ghana); Gen. Sec. Canon CLEMENT JANDA (Uganda). Publs *ACIS/APS Bulletin, ACLCA News, Tam Tam*.

Alliance Israélite Universelle; 45 rue La Bruyère, 75425 Paris Cédex 09, France; tel. 1-53-32-88-55; fax 1-48-74-51-33; e-mail aiu@imaginet.fr; f. 1860 to work for the emancipation and moral progress of the Jews; maintains 40 schools in eight countries; library of 120,000 vols. Mems: 8,000 in 16 countries. Pres. ADY STEG; Dir JEAN-JACQUES WAHL (France). Publs *Cahiers de l'Alliance Israélite Universelle* (3 a year, in French), *The Alliance Review* (in English), *Les Nouveaux Cahiers* (quarterly, in French).

Bahá'í International Community: Bahá'í World Centre, POB 155, 31 001 Haifa, Israel; tel. (4) 8358394; telex 46626; fax 8358522; f. 1844 in Persia to promote the unity of mankind and world peace through the teachings of the Bahá'í religion, including the equality of men and women and the elimination of all forms of prejudice; maintains schools for children and adults worldwide, and maintains educational and cultural radio stations in the USA, Asia and Latin America; has 30 publishing trusts throughout the world. Governing body: Universal House of Justice (nine mems elected by 175 National Spiritual Assemblies). Mems: in 126,904 centres (190 countries and 45 dependent territories or overseas departments). Sec.-Gen. ALBERT LINCOLN (USA). Publs *Bahá'í World* (annually), *One Country* (quarterly, in 6 languages).

Baptist World Alliance: 6733 Curran St, McLean, VA 22101-6005, USA; tel. (703) 790-8980; fax (703) 893-5160; e-mail bwa@bwanet.org; f. 1905; aims to unite Baptists, lead in evangelism, respond to people in need and defend human rights. Mems: 191 Baptist unions and conventions comprising 42m. people in 200 countries and territories. Pres. Dr NILSON DO AMARAL FANINI (Brazil); Gen. Sec. Dr DENTON LOTZ. Publ. *The Baptist World* (quarterly).

Caribbean Conference of Churches: POB 616, Bridgetown, Barbados; tel. (246) 427-2681; fax (246) 429-2075; e-mail ccc-barbados@fcci.geomail.org; f. 1973; holds Assembly every five years; conducts study and research programmes and supports education and community projects. Mems: 34 churches. Gen. Sec. Rev. Dr MONRELLE T. WILLIAMS.

Christian Conference of Asia: Pak Tin Village, Mei Tin Rd, Shatin, NT, Hong Kong; tel. 26911068; fax 26924378; f. 1959 (present name adopted 1973) to promote co-operation and joint study in matters of common concern among the Churches of the region and to encourage interaction with other regional Conferences and the World Council of Churches. Mems: 119 churches and 16 national councils of churches. Gen. Sec. Dr FELICIANO V. CARIÑO. Publ. *CCA News* (quarterly).

Christian Peace Conference: 130 00, Prague 3, POB 136, Prokopova 4, Czech Republic; tel. (2) 279722; fax (2) 276853; f. 1958 as an international movement of theologians, clergy and lay-people, aiming to bring Christendom to recognize its share of guilt in both world wars and to dedicate itself to the service of friendship, reconciliation and peaceful co-operation of nations, to concentrate on united action for peace and justice, and to co-ordinate peace groups in individual churches and facilitate their effective participation in the peaceful development of society. It works through five continental associations, regional groups and member churches in many countries. Moderator Prof. MARTIN RUMSCHEIDT; Co-ordinator Canon KENYON E. WRIGHT. Publs *CPC News Bulletin* (10 a year in English and German), occasional *Study Volume*.

Conference of European Churches—CEC: POB 2100, 150 route de Ferney, 1211 Geneva 2, Switzerland; tel. (22) 7916111; telex 415730; fax (22) 7916227; e-mail re@wcc-coe.org; f. 1959 as a regional ecumenical organization for Europe and a meeting-place for European churches, including members and non-members of the World Council of Churches; assemblies every few years. Mems: 122 Protestant, Anglican, Orthodox and Old Catholic churches in all European countries. Gen. Sec. Rev. Dr KEITH CLEMENTS. Publs *Monitor*, CEC communiqués.

Conference of International Catholic Organizations: 37–39 rue de Vermont, 1202 Geneva, Switzerland; tel. (22) 7338392; f. 1927 to encourage collaboration and agreement between the different Catholic international organizations in their common interests, and to contribute to international understanding; organizes international assemblies and meetings to study specific problems. Permanent commissions deal with human rights, the new international economic order, social problems, the family health, education, etc. Mems: 36 Catholic international organizations. Administrator PAUL MORAND (Switzerland).

Consultative Council of Jewish Organizations—CCJO: 420 Lexington Ave, New York, NY 10170, USA; tel. (212) 808-5437; f. 1946 to co-operate and consult with the UN and other international bodies directly concerned with human rights and to defend the cultural, political and religious rights of Jews throughout the world. Sec.-Gen. WARREN GREEN (USA).

European Baptist Federation: Postfach 610340, 22423 Hamburg, Germany; tel. (40) 5509723; fax (40) 5509725; e-mail office@ebf.org; f. 1949 to promote fellowship and co-operation among Baptists in Europe; to further the aims and objects of the Baptist World Alliance; to stimulate and co-ordinate evangelism in Europe; to provide for consultation and planning of missionary work in Europe and elsewhere in the world. Mems: 49 Baptist Unions in European countries and the Middle East. Pres. DAVID COFFEY; Sec.-Treas. Rev. KARL-HEINZ WALTER (Germany).

European Evangelical Alliance: Postfach 23 (OM), 1037 Vienna, Austria; tel. (1) 714-91-51; fax (1) 713-83-82; e-mail 100341.550@

compuserve.com; f. 1953 to promote understanding among evangelical Christians in Europe and to stimulate evangelism. Mems: 25 national alliances from 24 countries, 6 pan-European asscns. Pres. DEREK COPLEY (UK); Sec. STUART MCALLISTER.

Friends World Committee for Consultation: 4 Byng Place, London, WC1E 7JH, United Kingdom; tel. (171) 388-0497; fax (171) 383-4644; internet http://www.quaker.org/fwcc/; f. 1937 to encourage and strengthen the spiritual life within the Religious Society of Friends (Quakers); to help Friends to a better understanding of their vocation in the world; to promote consultation among Friends of all countries; representation at the United Nations as a non-governmental organization. Mems: appointed representatives and individuals from 64 countries. Gen. Sec. THOMAS TAYLOR. Publs *Friends World News* (2 a year), *Calendar of Yearly Meetings* (annually), *Quakers around the World* (handbook).

International Association for Religious Freedom—IARF: 2 Market St, Oxford OX1 3EF, United Kingdom; tel. (1865) 202-744; fax (1865) 202-746; e-mail iarf@interfaith-center.org; f. 1900 as a world community of religions, subscribing to the principle of openness and to respect for fundamental human rights; conducts intercultural encounters, inter-religious dialogues, a social service network and development programme. Regional conferences and triennial congress. Mems: 70 groups in 25 countries. Pres. NATALIE GULBRANDSEN (USA); Gen. Sec. Rev. Dr ROBERT TRAER (Germany). Publ. *IARF World* (2 a year).

International Association of Buddhist Studies: c/o Prof. Oskar von Hinüber, Orientalisches Seminar, Indologie, Humboldstr. 5, Freiburg 79102, Germany; tel. (761) 203-3158; fax (761) 203-3152; f. 1976; holds international conference every three or four years; supports studies of Buddhist life and literature. Gen. Sec. OSKAR VON HINÜBER. Publ. *Journal* (2 a year).

International Council of Christians and Jews: 64629 Heppenheim, Werlestrasse 2, Postfach 1129, Germany; tel. (6252) 5041; fax (6252) 68331; f. 1955 to promote mutual respect and co-operation; holds annual international colloquium, seminars, meetings for young people and for women; forum for Jewish–Christian–Muslim relations established. Mems: national councils in 28 countries. Pres. Dr MARTIN STÖHR; Chair. Exec. Cttee Sir SIGMUND STERNBERG; Sec.-Gen. Rev. FRIEDHELM PIEPER.

International Council of Jewish Women: 24–32 Stephenson Way, London, NW1 2JW, United Kingdom; tel. (171) 388-8311; fax (171) 387-2110; e-mail hq@icjw.demon.co.uk; f. 1912 to promote friendly relations and understanding among Jewish women throughout the world; exchanges information on community welfare activities, promotes volunteer leadership, sponsors field work in social welfare and fosters Jewish education. Mems: affiliates totalling over 1.5m. members in 46 countries. Pres. JUNE JACOBS. Publs *Newsletter, Links around the World* (2 a year, English and Spanish).

International Fellowship of Reconciliation: Spoorstraat 38–40, 1815 BK Alkmaar, Netherlands; tel. (72) 512-30-14; fax (72) 515-11-02; e-mail office@ifor.ccmail.compuserve.com; internet http://www.gn.apc.org/ifor/; f. 1919; international, spiritually-based movement committed to active non-violence as a way of life and as a means of transformation, to create justice and restore community. Branches, affiliates and groups in more than 50 countries. Gen. Sec. JOHANNA S. M. KOOKE. Publ. *Reconciliation International* (every 2 months), *Patterns in Reconciliation* (2 a year), *Non-violence Training in Africa* (3 a year), *Cross the Lines / Franchir les lignes* (3 a year).

International Humanist and Ethical Union: Nieuwegracht 69A, 3512 LG Utrecht, Netherlands; tel. (30) 231-21-55; fax (30) 236-41-69; e-mail r.thielman@apc.nl; f. 1952 to bring into association all those interested in promoting ethical and scientific humanism. Mems: national organizations and individuals in more than 51 countries. Pres Prof. VERN BULLOUGH (USA), JANE WYNNE WILLSON (UK), Dr R. A. P. TIELMAN (Netherlands). Publ. *International Humanist News* (quarterly).

International Organization for the Study of the Old Testament: Faculteit der Godgeleerdheid, POB 9515, 2300 RA Leiden, Netherlands; tel. (71) 5272577; fax (71) 5272571; f. 1950. Holds triennial congresses. Pres. Prof. M. SAEBØ (Norway); Sec. Prof. A. VAN DER KOOIJ (Netherlands). Publ. *Vetus Testamentum* (quarterly).

Latin American Council of Churches (Consejo Latinoamericano de Iglesias—CLAI): Casilla 85–22, Av. Patria 640 y Amazonas, Of. 1001, Quito, Ecuador; tel. (2) 561-539; telex 21150; fax (2) 504-377; e-mail felipe@clai.ecx.ec; f. 1982. Mems: 97 churches in 19 countries, and nine associated organizations. Gen. Sec. Rev. FELIPE ADOLF.

Latin American Episcopal Council: Apartado Aéreos 5278 y 51086, Santafé de Bogotá, Colombia; tel. 6121620; telex 41388; fax 6121929; f. 1955 to study the problems of the Roman Catholic Church in Latin America; to co-ordinate Church activities. Mems: the Episcopal Conferences of Central and South America and the Caribbean. Pres. Archbishop OSCAR ANDRÉS RODRÍGUEZ MARADIAGA (Honduras); Sec.-Gen. Bishop JORGE E. JIMÉNEZ CARVAJAL (Colombia). Publ. *CELAM* (6 a year).

Lutheran World Federation: 150 route de Ferney, 1211 Geneva 2, Switzerland; tel. (22) 7916111; fax (22) 7988616; f. 1947; communion of 124 Lutheran Churches of 69 countries. Current activities: inter-church aid; relief work in various areas of the globe; service to refugees including resettlement; aid to missions; theological research, conferences and exchanges; scholarship aid in various fields of church life; inter-confessional dialogue with Roman Catholic, Seventh-day Adventist, Anglican and Orthodox churches; religious communications projects and international news and information services; Ninth Assembly: Hong Kong, 1997. Pres. Rt Rev. CHRISTIAN KRAUSSE (Germany); Gen. Sec. Rev. Dr ISHMAEL NOKO (Zimbabwe). Publs *Lutheran World Information* (English and German, every 2 weeks), *LWF Today* (quarterly) and *LWF Documentation* (English and German, 2–3 a year).

Middle East Council of Churches: Makhoul St, Deep Bldg, POB 5376, Beirut, Lebanon; tel. and fax 344894; telex 22662; f. 1974. Mems: 24 churches. Pres. Patriarch IGNATIUS ZAKKA I IWAS, Patriarch IGNATIUS IV, Rt Rev. SAMIR KAFITY, Archbishop YOUSUF EL-KHOURY; Gen. Sec. Rev. Dr RIAD JARJOUR. Publs *MECC News Report* (monthly), *Al Montada News Bulletin* (quarterly, in Arabic), *Courrier oecuménique du Moyen-Orient* (quarterly), *MECC Perspectives* (3 a year).

Moral Re-Armament: Mountain House, Caux, 1824 Vaud, Switzerland; tel. (21) 9629111; fax (21) 9629355; e-mail caux@caux.ch; internet http://www.caux.ch; other international centres at Panchgani, India, Petropolis, Brazil, London and Tirley Garth, UK, and Gweru, Zimbabwe; f. 1921; aims: a new social order for better human relations and the elimination of political, industrial and racial antagonism. Legally incorporated bodies in 20 countries. Pres. of Swiss foundation MARCEL GRANDY. Publs *Changer* (French, 6 a year), *For a Change* (English, 6 a year), *Caux Information* (German, monthly).

Muslim World League (Rabitat al-Alam al-Islami): POB 537–538, Mecca, Saudi Arabia; tel. (2) 5422733; telex 540009; fax (2) 5436619; f. 1962; aims to advance Islamic unity and solidarity, and to promote world peace and respect for human rights; provides financial assistance for education, medical care and relief work; has 30 offices throughout the world. Sec.-Gen. Sheikh Prof. Dr ABD' ALLAH BIN SALEH EL-OBEID. Publs *Majalla al-Rabita* (monthly, Arabic), *Akhbar al-Alam al Islami* (weekly, Arabic), *Journal* (monthly, English).

Opus Dei (Prelature of the Holy Cross and Opus Dei): Viale Bruno Buozzi 73, 00197 Rome, Italy; tel. (6) 808961; f. 1928 by Blessed Josemaría Escrivá de Balaguer to spread, at every level of society, a profound awakening of consciences to the universal calling to sanctity and apostolate in the course of members' own professional work. Mems: 79,027 Catholic laypeople and 1,611 priests. Bishop Prelate Most Rev. JAVIER ECHEVARRÍA. Publ. *Romana, Bulletin of the Prelature* (every six months).

Pacific Conference of Churches: POB 208, 4 Thurston St, Suva, Fiji; tel. 311277; f. 1961; organizes assembly every five years, as well as regular workshops, meetings and training seminars throughout the region. Mems: 36 churches and councils. Moderator Pastor REUBEN MAGEKON; Gen. Sec. Rev. VALAMOTU PALU (acting). Publ. *PCC News* (quarterly).

Pax Romana International Catholic Movement for Intellectual and Cultural Affairs—ICMICA; and International Movement of Catholic Students—IMCS: 7 rue des Alpes, POB 1062, 1701 Fribourg, Switzerland; tel. (26) 322-74-82; fax (26) 322-74-83; e-mail pax.romana@edu.mcnet.ch; f. 1921 (IMCS), 1947 (ICMICA), to encourage in members an awareness of their responsibilities as people and Christians in the student and intellectual milieux; to promote contacts between students and graduates throughout the world and co-ordinate the contribution of Catholic intellectual circles to international life. Mems: 80 student and 60 intellectual organizations in 80 countries. ICMICA—Pres. MARY J. MWINGIRA (Tanzania); Gen. Sec. ANSELMO LEE SEONG-HOON (Republic of Korea); IMCS—Gen. Secs WALTER PRYSTHON (Brazil), ROLAND RANAIVOARISON (Madagascar). Publ. *Convergence* (every 4 months).

Salvation Army: International HQ, 101 Queen Victoria St, London, EC4P 4EP, United Kingdom; tel. (171) 236-5222; telex 8954847; fax (171) 236-4981; internet http://www.salvationarmy.org; f. 1865 to spread the Christian gospel and relieve poverty; emphasis is placed on the need for personal discipleship, and to make its evangelism effective it adopts a quasi-military form of organization. Social, medical and educational work is also performed in the 99 countries where the Army operates. Pres. Gen. PAUL RADER; Chief of Staff Commissioner EARLE MAXWELL. Publs 132 periodicals in 31 languages.

Soroptimist International: 87 Glisson Rd, Cambridge, CB1 2HG, United Kingdom; tel. (1223) 311833; fax (1223) 467951; f. 1921 to maintain high ethical standards in business, the professions, and other aspects of life; to strive for human rights for all people and, in particular, to advance the status of women; to develop friendship and unity among Soroptimists of all countries; to contribute to international understanding and universal friendship. Convention held every 4 years, 1999: Helsinki, Finland. Mems: 95,000 in 3,000 clubs in 112 countries and territories. International Pres. PATRICIA D. DANIELS (USA); Exec. Officer JANET BILTON. Publ. *International Soroptimist* (quarterly).

Theosophical Society: Adyar, Chennai 600 020, India; tel. (44) 4912815; f. 1875; aims at universal brotherhood, without distinction of race, creed, sex, caste or colour; study of comparative religion, philosophy and science; investigation of unexplained laws of nature and powers latent in man. Mems: 35,000 in 70 countries. Pres. RADHA S. BURNIER; Int. Sec. CONRAD JAMIESON. Publs *The Theosophist* (monthly), *Adyar News Letter* (quarterly), *Brahmavidya* (annually).

United Bible Societies: 7th Floor, Reading Bridge House, Reading, RG1 8PJ, United Kingdom; tel. (118) 950-0200; fax (118) 950-0857; f. 1946. Mems: 97 Bible Societies and 27 Bible Society Offices at work throughout the world. Pres. Dr SAMUEL ESCOBAR (Peru/USA); Gen. Sec. Rev. Dr JOHN D. ERICKSON (USA). Publs *United Bible Societies Bulletin, The Bible Translator* (quarterly), *The Bible Distributor, Prayer Booklet* (annually), *World Report* (monthly).

Watch Tower Bible and Tract Society: 25 Columbia Heights, Brooklyn, New York, NY 11201, USA; tel. (718) 560-5600; fax (718) 560-5619; f. 1881; 104 branches; serves as legal agency for Jehovah's Witnesses, whose membership is 5.2m. Pres. MILTON G. HENSCHEL; Sec. and Treas. LYMAN SWINGLE. Publs *The Watchtower* (2 a month, in 125 languages), *Awake!* (2 a month, in 80 languages).

World Alliance of Reformed Churches (Presbyterian and Congregational): Box 2100, 150 route de Ferney, 1211 Geneva 2, Switzerland; tel. (22) 7916238; telex 415730; fax (22) 7916505; f. 1970 by merger of WARC (Presbyterian) (f. 1875) with International Congregational Council (f. 1891) to promote fellowship among Reformed, Presbyterian and Congregational churches. Mems: 211 churches in 104 countries. Pres. Prof. CHOAN-SENG SONG; Gen. Sec. Prof. MILAN OPOCENSKY (Czech Republic). Publs *Reformed World* (quarterly), *Up-Date*.

World Christian Life Community: Borgo S. Spirito 8, Casella Postale 6139, 00195 Rome, Italy; tel. (6) 6868079; f. 1953 as World Federation of the Sodalities of our Lady (first group founded 1563) as a lay movement (based on the teachings of Ignatius Loyola) to integrate Christian faith and daily living. Mems: groups in 55 countries representing about 100,000 individuals. Pres. JOSÉ MARÍA RIERA; Exec. Sec. ROSWITHA COOPER. Publ. *Progressio* (every 2 months in English, French, Spanish).

World Conference on Religion and Peace: 777 United Nations Plaza, New York, NY 10017, USA; tel. (212) 687-2163; fax (212) 983-0566; f. 1970 to co-ordinate education and action of various world religions for world peace and justice. Mems: religious organizations and individuals in 100 countries. Sec.-Gen. Dr WILLIAM VENDLEY. Publ. *Religion for Peace*.

World Congress of Faiths: 2 Market St, Oxford OX1 3EF, United Kingdom; tel. (1865) 202751; fax (1865) 202746; f. 1936 to promote a spirit of fellowship among mankind through an understanding of each other's religion, to bring together people of all nationalities, backgrounds and creeds in mutual respect and tolerance, to encourage the study and understanding of issues arising out of multi-faith societies, and to promote welfare and peace. Mems: about 800. Vice-Pres Rev. Dr EDWARD CARPENTER, Prof. KEITH WARD; Chair. MARCUS BRAYBROOKE. Publ. *World Faiths Encounter* (3 a year).

World Evangelical Fellowship: 141 Middle Rd 05-05, GSM Bldg, Singapore 188976, Singapore; tel. 3397900; fax 3383756; e-mail 100012.345@compuserve.com; f. 1951, on reorganization of World Evangelical Alliance (f. 1846); an int. grouping of national and regional bodies of evangelical Christians; encourages the organization of national fellowships and assists national mems in planning their activities. Mems: national evangelical asscns in 110 countries. International Dir. AUGUSTIN B. VENCER, Jr. Publs *Evangelical World* (monthly), *Evangelical Review of Theology* (quarterly).

World Fellowship of Buddhists: 616 Benjasiri Pk, Soi Medhinivet off Soi Sukhumvit 24, Bangkok 10110, Thailand; f. 1950 to promote strict observance and practice of the teachings of the Buddha; holds General Conference every 2 years; has 123 regional centres in 37 countries. Pres. SANYA DHARMASAKTI; Hon. Gen. Sec. PRASERT RUANGSKUL. Publ. *WFB Review* (quarterly).

World Hindu Federation: c/o Dr Jogendra Jha, Pashupati Kshetra, Kathmandu, Nepal; tel. (1) 470182; telex 2326; fax (1) 470131; f. 1981 to promote and preserve Hindu philosophy and culture; to protect the rights of Hindus, particularly the right to worship. Executive Board meets annually. Mems: in 45 countries and territories. Sec.-Gen. Dr JOGENDRA JHA. Publ. *Vishwa Hindu* (monthly).

World Jewish Congress: 501 Madison Ave, New York, NY 10022, USA; tel. (212) 755-5770; fax (212) 755-5883; f. 1936; a voluntary association of representative Jewish communities and organizations throughout the world, aiming to foster the unity of the Jewish people and to ensure the continuity and development of their heritage. Mems: Jewish communities in 84 countries. Pres. EDGAR M. BRONFMAN; Sec.-Gen. ISRAEL SINGER. Publs *Gesher* (Hebrew quarterly, Israel), *Boletín Informativo OJI* (fortnightly, Buenos Aires).

World Methodist Council: International Headquarters, POB 518, Lake Junaluska, NC 28745, USA; tel. (704) 456-9432; fax (704) 456-9433; f. 1881 to deepen the fellowship of the Methodist peoples, to encourage evangelism, to foster Methodist participation in the ecumenical movement, and to promote the unity of Methodist witness and service. Mems: 73 churches in 108 countries, comprising 32m. individuals. Chair. FRANCES ALGUIRE; Gen. Sec. JOE HALE (USA). Publ. *World Parish* (6 a year).

World Sephardi Federation: 13 rue Marignac, 1206 Geneva, Switzerland; tel. (22) 3473313; telex 427569; fax (22) 3472839; f. 1951 to strengthen the unity of Jewry and Judaism among Sephardi and Oriental Jews, to defend and foster religious and cultural activities of all Sephardi and Oriental Jewish communities and preserve their spiritual heritage, to provide moral and material assistance where necessary and to co-operate with other similar organizations. Mems: 50 communities and organizations in 33 countries. Pres. NESSIM D. GAON; Sec.-Gen. SHIMON DERY.

World Student Christian Federation: 5 route des Morillons, Grand-Saconnex, 1218 Geneva, Switzerland; tel. (22) 7988953; telex 415730; fax (22) 7982370; f. 1895 to proclaim Jesus Christ as Lord and Saviour in the academic community, and to present students with the claims of the Christian faith over their whole life. Gen. Assembly every four years. Mems: 67 national Student Christian Movements, and 34 national correspondents. Chair. DEBORA SPINI (Italy); Secs-Gen. CLARISSA BALAN-SYCIP (Philippines), KANGWA MABULUKI (Zambia).

World Union for Progressive Judaism: 838 Fifth Ave, New York, NY 10021, USA; tel. (212) 249-0100; fax (212) 650-4099; f. 1926; promotes and co-ordinates efforts of Reform, Liberal, Progressive and Reconstructionist congregations throughout the world; supports new congregations; assigns and employs rabbis; sponsors seminaries and schools; organizes international conferences; maintains a youth section. Mems: organizations and individuals in 30 countries. Pres. AUSTIN BEUTEL; Exec. Dir Rabbi RICHARD G. HIRSCH (Israel). Publs *News Updates, International Conference Reports, European Judaism* (bi-annual).

World Union of Catholic Women's Organisations: 18 rue Notre-Dame-des-Champs, 75006 Paris, France; tel. 1-45-44-27-65; fax 1-42-84-04-80; e-mail wucwosec@netcomuk.co.uk; f. 1910 to promote and co-ordinate the contribution of Catholic women in international life, in social, civic, cultural and religious matters. Mems: 25m. Pres.-Gen. MARÍA EUGENIA DÍAZ DE PFENNICH (Mexico); Sec.-Gen. GILLIAN BADCOCK (UK). Publ. *Newsletter* (quarterly in four languages).

Science

International Council of Scientific Unions—ICSU: 51 blvd de Montmorency, 75016 Paris, France; tel. 1-45-25-03-29; telex 630 553; fax 1-42-88-94-31; e-mail icsu@lmcp.jussieu.fr; f. 1919 as International Research Council; present name adopted 1931; new statutes adopted 1996; to co-ordinate international co-operation in theoretical and applied sciences and to promote national scientific research through the intermediary of affiliated national organizations; General Assembly of representatives of national and scientific members meets every three years to formulate policy. The following committees have been established: Cttee on Science for Food Security, Scientific Cttee on Antarctic Research, Scientific Cttee on Oceanic Research, Cttee on Space Research, Scientific Cttee on Water Research, Scientific Cttee on Solar-Terrestrial Physics, Cttee on Science and Technology in Developing Countries, Cttee on Data for Science and Technology, Programme on Capacity Building in Science, Scientific Cttee on Problems of the Environment, Steering Cttee on Genetics and Biotechnology and Scientific Cttee on International Geosphere-Biosphere Programme. The following services and Inter-Union Committees and Commissions have been established: Federation of Astronomical and Geophysical Data Analysis Services, Inter-Union Commission on Frequency Allocations for Radio Astronomy and Space Science, Inter-Union Commission on Radio Meteorology, Inter-Union Commission on Spectroscopy, Inter-Union Commission on Lithosphere. National mems: academies or research councils in 95 countries; Scientific mems and assocs: 25 international unions (see below) and 28 scientific associates. Pres. W. ARBER; Sec.-Gen. H. A. MOONEY. Publs *ICSU Yearbook, Science International* (quarterly), *Annual Report*.

UNIONS FEDERATED TO THE ICSU

International Astronomical Union: 98 bis blvd d'Arago, 75014 Paris, France; tel. 1-43-25-83-58; fax 1-43-25-26-16; e-mail iau@iap.fr; f. 1919 to facilitate co-operation between the astronomers of various countries and to further the study of astronomy in all its branches; last General Assembly was held in 1994 in The Hague, Netherlands. Mems: organizations in 61 countries, and 8,000 individual mems. Pres. Prof. L. WOLTJER (France); Gen. Sec. Prof. I. APPENZELLER (Germany). Publ. *IAU Information Bulletin* (2 a year).

International Geographical Union—IGU: Dept of Geography, University of Bonn, 53115 Bonn, Meckenheimer Allee 166, Germany; tel. (228) 739287; fax (228) 739272; f. 1922 to encourage the study of problems relating to geography, to promote and co-ordinate research requiring international co-operation, and to organize international congresses and commissions. Mem. countries: 80, and 12 associates. Pres. Prof. BRUNO MESSERLI (Switzerland); Sec.-Gen. Prof. ECKART EHLERS (Germany). Publ. *IGU Bulletin* (1–2 a year).

International Mathematical Union: c/o IMPA, Estrada Dona Castorina 110, Jardim Botânico, Rio de Janeiro, RJ 22460, Brazil; tel. (21) 529-5000; fax (21) 512-4115; e-mail imu@impa.br; f. 1952 to support and assist the International Congress of Mathematicians and other international scientific meetings or conferences; to encourage and support other international mathematical activities considered likely to contribute to the development of mathematical science—pure, applied or educational. Mems: 60 countries. Pres. DAVID MUNFORD; Sec.-Gen. Prof. JACOB PALIS, Jr.

International Union for Pure and Applied Biophysics: Dept of Biochemistry and Molecular Biology, University of Leeds, Leeds, LS2 9JT, United Kingdom; tel. (113) 2333023; fax (113) 2333167; e-mail a.c.t.north@leeds.ac.uk; f. 1961 to organize international co-operation in biophysics and promote communication between biophysics and allied subjects, to encourage national co-operation between biophysical societies, and to contribute to the advancement of biophysical knowledge. Mems: 45 adhering bodies. Pres. D. A. D. PARRY (New Zealand); Sec.-Gen. Prof. A. C. T. NORTH (UK). Publ. *Quarterly Reviews of Biophysics.*

International Union of Biochemistry and Molecular Biology: Institute for Biophysical Chemistry and Biochemistry, Technical University Berlin, Franklinstr. 29, 10587 Berlin, Germany; tel. (30) 314-24205; fax (30) 314-24783; e-mail kleinkauf@chem.tu-berlin.de; f. 1955 to sponsor the International Congresses of Biochemistry, to co-ordinate research and discussion, to organize co-operation between the societies of biochemistry and molecular biology, to promote high standards of biochemistry and molecular biology throughout the world and to contribute to the advancement of biochemistry and molecular biology in all its international aspects. Mems: 65 bodies. Pres. W. WHELAN (USA); Gen. Sec. Prof. Dr H. KLEINKAUF (Germany).

International Union of Biological Sciences: 51 blvd de Montmorency, 75016 Paris, France; tel. 1-45-25-00-09; telex 630553; fax 1-45-25-20-29; e-mail iubs@paris7.jussieu.fr; f. 1919. Mems: 41 national bodies, 80 scientific bodies. Exec. Dir Dr T. YOUNES. Publs *Biology International* (2 a year, plus special issues), *IUBS Monographs, IUBS Methodology, Manual Series*.

International Union of Crystallography: c/o M. H. Dacombe, 2 Abbey Sq., Chester, CH1 2HU, United Kingdom; tel. (1244) 345431; fax (1244) 344843; f. 1947 to facilitate international standardization of methods, of units, of nomenclature and of symbols used in crystallography; and to form a focus for the relations of crystallography to other sciences. Mems in 40 countries. Pres. Prof. E. N. BAKER (New Zealand); Gen. Sec. S. LARSEN (Denmark); Exec. Sec. M. H. DACOMBE. Publs *Acta Crystallographica, Journal of Applied Crystallography, Journal of Synchroton Radiation, International Tables for Crystallography, World Directory of Crystallographers, IUCr/OUP Crystallographic Symposia, IUCr/OUP Monographs on Crystallography, IUCr/OUP Texts on Crystallography.*

International Union of Geodesy and Geophysics—IUGG: 18 ave Edouard Belin, 31401 Toulouse Cédex 4, France; tel. 5-61-33-28-89; telex 530776; fax 5-61-25-30-98; e-mail balmino.uggi@cnes.fr; internet http://www.obs-mip.fr/uggi/; f. 1919; federation of seven associations representing Geodesy, Seismology and Physics of the Earth's Interior, Physical Sciences of the Ocean, Volcanology and Chemistry of the Earth's Interior, Hydrological Sciences, Meteorology and Atmospheric Physics, Geomagnetism and Aeronomy, which meet at the General Assemblies of the Union. In addition, there are Joint Committees of the various associations either among themselves or with other unions. The Union organizes scientific meetings and also sponsors various permanent services, to collect, analyse and publish geophysical data. Mems: in 75 countries. Pres. Prof. PETER WYLLIE (USA); Sec.-Gen. Dr G. BALMINO. Publs *IUGG Yearbook, Geodetic Bulletin* (quarterly), *International Bibliography of Geodesy* (irregular), *International Seismological Summary* (annually), *Bulletin Volcanologique* (2 a year), *Bulletin mensuel du Bureau Central Sismologique* (monthly), *Bulletin de l'Association Internationale d'Hydrologie Scientifique* (quarterly), *International Bibliography of Hydrology, Catalogue des Volcans Actifs* (both irregular).

International Union of Geological Sciences—IUGS: Norges Geologiske Undersøkelse, POB 3006, 7002 Trondheim, Norway; tel. (7) 90-43-15; telex 55417; fax (7) 90-43-04; e-mail iugs.secretariat .ngu.no; internet http://www.iugs.org/; f. 1961 to encourage the study of geoscientific problems, facilitate international and inter-disciplinary co-operation in geology and related sciences, and support the quadrennial International Geological Congress. IUGS organizes international meetings and co-sponsors joint programmes, including the International Geological Correlation Programme (with UNESCO). Mems from 95 countries. Pres. Prof. U. G. CORDANI (Brazil); Sec.-Gen. LEIV EIRIKSSONS (Norway).

International Union of Immunological Societies: Dept of Surgery, University of Edinburgh Medical School, Teviot Place, Edinburgh, EH8 9AG, United Kingdom; tel. (131) 650-3557; fax (131) 667-6190; f. 1969; holds triennial international congress. Mems: national societies in 50 countries and territories. Pres. TOMIO TADA; Sec.-Gen. KEITH JAMES.

International Union of Microbiological Societies—IUMS: Institut de Biologie Moléculaire et Cellulaire du CNRS, 15 rue Descartes, 67084 Strasbourg, France; tel. 3-88-41-70-22; fax 3-88-61-06-80; f. 1930. Mems: 106 national microbiological societies. Pres. P. HELENA MÄKELÄ (Finland); Sec.-Gen. MARC H. V. VAN REGENMORTEL. Publs *International Journal of Systematic Bacteriology* (quarterly), *International Journal of Food Microbiology* (every 2 months), *Advances in Microbial Ecology* (annually), *World Journal of Microbiology and Biotechnology* (every 2 months), Archives of Virology.

International Union of Nutritional Sciences: c/o Prof. Galal, UCLA School of Public Health, International Health Program, 10833 Le Conte Ave, POB 951772, Los Angeles, CA 90095-1772, USA; tel. (310) 2069639; fax (310) 7941805; e-mail ogalal@ucla.edu; f. 1946 to promote international co-operation in the scientific study of nutrition and its applications, to encourage research and exchange of scientific information by holding international congresses and issuing publications. Mems: 67 organizations. Pres. Dr B. A. UNDERWOOD (USA); Sec.-Gen. Prof. OSMAN M. GALAL. Publs *Annual Report, IUNS Directory, Newsletter.*

International Union of Pharmacology: Dept of Physiology and Pharmacology, Univ. of Strathclyde, 204 George St, Glasgow G1 1XW, United Kingdom; tel. (141) 552-4400; fax (141) 552-2562; f. 1963 to promote international co-ordination of research, discussion and publication in the field of pharmacology, including clinical pharmacology, drug metabolism and toxicology; co-operates with WHO in all matters concerning drugs and drug research; holds international congresses. Mems: 52 national and four regional societies. Pres. T. GODFRAIND (Belgium); Sec.-Gen. W. C. BOWMAN (UK). Publ. *TIPS (Trends in Pharmacological Sciences).*

International Union of Physiological Sciences: IUPS Secretariat, LGN, Bâtiment CERVI, Hôpital de la Pitié-Salpêtrière, 83 blvd de l'Hôpital, 75013 Paris, France; tel. 1-42-17-75-37; fax 1-42-17-75-75; f. 1955. Mems: 50 national, six assoc., four regional, two affiliated and 14 special mems. Pres. Prof. MASAO ITO (Japan); Sec. Prof. DENIS NOBLE.

International Union of Psychological Science: c/o Prof. P. L.-J. Ritchie, Ecole de psychologie, Université d'Ottawa, 145 Jean-Jacques-Lussier, CP 450, Succ. A, Ottawa, ON KIN 6N5, Canada; tel (613) 562-5289; fax (613) 562-5169; f. 1951 to contribute to the development of intellectual exchange and scientific relations between psychologists of different countries. Mems: 62 national and 10 affiliate organizations. Pres. Prof. GÉRY D'YDEWALLE (Belgium); Sec.-Gen. Prof. P. L.-J. RITCHIE (Canada). Publs *International Journal of Psychology* (quarterly), *The IUPsyS Directory* (irregular).

International Union of Pure and Applied Chemistry—IUPAC: Bank Court Chambers, 2–3 Pound Way, Templars Square, Cowley, Oxford, OX4 3YF, United Kingdom; tel. (1865) 747744; fax (1865) 747510; f. 1919 to organize permanent co-operation between chemical associations in the member countries, to study topics of international importance requiring regulation, standardization or codification, to co-operate with other international organizations in the field of chemistry and to contribute to the advancement of all aspects of chemistry. Biennial General Assembly. Mems: in 40 countries. Pres. Prof. A. E. FISCHLI (Switzerland); Sec.-Gen. Dr E. D. BECKER (USA). Publs *Chemistry International* (bi-monthly), *Pure and Applied Chemistry* (monthly).

International Union of Pure and Applied Physics: CEN Sacley, 91191 Gif-sur-Yvette Cédex, France; tel. 1-69-08-84-18; fax 1-69-08-76-36; e-mail turlay@frcpnll.in2p3.fr; f. 1922 to promote and encourage international co-operation in physics. Mems: in 47 countries. Pres. Y. YAMAGUCHI (Japan); Sec.-Gen. Dr RENÉ TURLAY (France).

International Union of Radio Science: c/o University of Ghent (LEA), Sint-Pietersnieuwstraat 41, 9000 Ghent, Belgium; tel. (9) 264-33-20; fax (9) 264-35-93; e-mail helev@intec.rug.ac.be; f. 1919 to stimulate and co-ordinate, on an international basis, studies in radio, telecommunications and electronics; to promote research and disseminate the results; to encourage the adoption of common methods of measurement, and the standardization of measuring instruments; and to stimulate studies of the scientific aspects of telecommunications using electromagnetic waves. There are 46 national committees. Pres. T. B. A. SENIOR (USA); Sec.-Gen. Prof. P. LAGASSE (Belgium). Publs *The Radio Science Bulletin* (quarterly), *Modern Radio Science* (every 3 years), *Review of Radio Science* (every 3 years).

International Union of the History and Philosophy of Science: Division of the History of Science: Centre d'Histoire des

Sciences et des Techniques, 15 ave des Tilleuls, 4000 Liège, Belgium; tel. (4) 366-94-79; fax (4) 366-94-47; e-mail chstulg@vml.ulg.ac.be; Division of the History of Logic, Methodology and Philosophy of Science: Dept of Philosophy, University of Turku, 20500 Turku 50, Finland; f. 1954 to promote research into the history and philosophy of science. There are 36 national committees. DHS Council: Pres. Prof. W. SHEA (Canada); Sec. Prof. R. HALLEUX. DLMPS Council: Pres. Prof. J. E. FENSTAD (Norway); Sec. E. SOBER (USA).

International Union of Theoretical and Applied Mechanics: Technical University of Vienna, 1040 Vienna, Wiedner Hauptstr. 8-10, E201, Austria; fax (1) 587-60-93; f. 1947 to form a link beween persons and organizations engaged in scientific work (theoretical or experimental) in mechanics or in related sciences; to organize international congresses of theoretical and applied mechanics, through a standing Congress Committee, and to organize other international meetings for subjects falling within this field; and to engage in other activities meant to promote the development of mechanics as a science. Mems: from 45 countries. Pres. Prof. W. SCHIEHLEN (Germany); Sec.-Gen. Prof. M. HAYES (Ireland); Publs *Annual Report, Newsletter*.

OTHER ORGANIZATIONS

Association for the Taxonomic Study of the Flora of Tropical Africa: National Botanic Garden of Belgium, Domein von Bouchout, 1860 Meise, Belgium; tel. (2) 269-39-05; fax (2) 270-15-67; e-mail jrammeloo@br.fgov.be; f. 1950 to facilitate co-operation and liaison between botanists engaged in the study of the flora of tropical Africa south of the Sahara including Madagascar; maintains a library. Mems: about 800 botanists in 63 countries. Sec.-Gen. Prof. J. RAMMELOO. Publs *AETFAT Bulletin* (annual), *Proceedings*.

Association of European Atomic Forums—FORATOM: 15–17 rue Belliard, 1040 Brussels, Belgium; tel. (2) 502-45-95; fax (2) 502-39-02; e-mail foratom@skynet.be; internet http://www.foratom.org; f. 1960; holds periodical conferences. Mems: atomic 'forums' in Austria, Belgium, Czech Republic, Finland, France, Germany, Italy, Netherlands, Spain, Sweden, Switzerland and the United Kingdom. Pres. STIG SANDKLEF; Sec.-Gen. Dr W.-J. SCHMIDT-KÜSTER. Publ. *Almanac* (annually).

Association of Geoscientists for International Development—AGID: Institute of Geoscience, University of São Paulo, 11348 São Paulo, 05422-970 Brazil; tel. (11) 818-4232; fax (11) 210-4958; e-mail neellert@bruspvm; f. 1974 to encourage communication between those interested in the application of the geosciences to international development; to give priority to the developing countries in these matters; to organize meetings and publish information; affiliated to the International Union of Geological Sciences (q.v.) and the Economic and Social Council of the United Nations. Mems: in 149 countries (2,000 individuals, and 57 institutions). Exec. Officer KATIA MELLITO. Publ. *AGID News* (quarterly).

Council for the International Congresses of Entomology: c/o FAO, POB 3700 MCPO, 1277 Makati, Philippines; tel. (2) 8134229; fax (2) 8127725; f. 1910 to act as a link between quadrennial congresses and to arrange the venue for each congress; the committee is also the entomology section of the International Union of Biological Sciences (q.v.). Chair. Dr M. J. WHITTAM (Australia); Sec. Dr J. OLIVER (USA).

European Association of Geoscientists and Engineers: Laan van Vollenhove 3039, POB 298, 3700 AG Zeist, Netherlands; tel. (30) 6962655; fax (30) 6962640; e-mail eage@pobox.ruu.nl; f. 1997 by merger of European Asscn of Exploration Geophysicists and Engineers (f. 1951) and the European Asscn of Petroleum Geoscientists and Engineers (f. 1988); these two organizations have become, respectively, the Geophysical and the Petroleum Divisions of the EAGE; aims to promote the applications of geoscience and related subjects, to foster communication, fellowship and co-operation between those working or studying in the fields; organizes conferences, workshops, education programmes and exhibitions and seeks global co-operation with other organizations having similar objectives. Mems approx. 5,000 in 95 countries throughout the world. Pres. J. SMETHURST; Sec. J.-C. GROSSET. Publs *Geophysical Prospecting* (6 a year), *First Break* (monthly), *Petroleum Geoscience* (quarterly).

European Molecular Biology Organization—EMBO: 6900 Heidelberg 1, Postfach 1022.40, Meyerhofstr. 1, Germany; tel. (6221) 383031; telex 461613; fax (6221) 384879; e-mail embo@embl heidelberg.dr; f. 1964 to promote collaboration in the field of molecular biology; to establish fellowships for training and research; to establish a European Laboratory of Molecular Biology where a majority of the disciplines comprising the subject will be represented. Mems: 950. Chair. Prof. W. NEUPERT (Germany); Sec.-Gen. Prof. W. GEHRING (Switzerland). Publ. *EMBO Journal* (24 a year).

European Organization for Nuclear Research—CERN: European Laboratory for Particle Physics, 1211 Geneva 23, Switzerland; tel. (22) 7676111; telex 419000; fax (22) 7676555; internet http://www.cern.ch/; f. 1954 to provide for collaboration among European states in nuclear research of a pure scientific and fundamental character; the work of CERN is for peaceful purposes only and concerns subnuclear, high-energy and elementary particle physics; it is not concerned with the development of nuclear reactors or fusion devices. Council comprises two representatives of each member state. Major experimental facilities: Synchro-Cyclotron (of 600 MeV), Proton Synchrotron (of 25–28 GeV), Super Proton Synchrotron (of 450 GeV), and a Large Electron-Positron Collider (LEP) of 27 km circumference (of 50 GeV per beam). Budget (1997) 870.1m. Swiss francs. Mems: Austria, Belgium, Czech Republic, Denmark, Finland, France, Germany, Greece, Hungary, Italy, Netherlands, Norway, Poland, Portugal, Slovakia, Spain, Sweden, Switzerland, United Kingdom; Observers: Israel, Japan, Russia, Turkey, USA, European Commission, UNESCO. Dir-Gen. Prof. CHRISTOPHER LLEWELLYN SMITH (UK). Publs *CERN Courier* (monthly), *Annual Report, Scientific Reports*.

European-Mediterranean Seismological Centre: c/o LDG, BP 12, 91680 Bruyères-le-Châtel, France; tel. 1-69-26-78-14; telex 681862; fax 1-69-26-70-00; f. 1976 for rapid determination of seismic hypocentres in the region; maintains data base. Mems: institutions in 21 countries. Pres. C. BROWITT; Sec.-Gen. B. FEIGNIER. Publ. *Newsletter* (quarterly).

Federation of Arab Scientific Research Councils: POB 13027, Al Karkh/Karadat Mariam, Baghdad, Iraq; tel. 5381090; telex 212466; f. 1976 to encourage co-operation in scientific research, to promote the establishment of new institutions and plan joint regional research projects. Mems: national science bodies in 15 countries. Sec.-Gen. Dr TAHA AL-NUEIMI. Publs *Journal, Newsletter*.

Federation of Asian Scientific Academies and Societies—FASAS: c/o Indian National Science Academy, Bahadur Shah Zafar Marg, New Delhi 110 002, India; tel. (11) 3232066; fax (11) 3235648; e-mail insa@giasdl01.vsnl.net.in; f. 1984 to stimulate regional co-operation and promote national and regional self-reliance in science and technology, by organizing meetings, training and research programmes and encouraging the exchange of scientists and of scientific information. Mems: national scientific academies and societies from Afghanistan, Australia, Bangladesh, People's Republic of China, India, Republic of Korea, Malaysia, Nepal, New Zealand, Pakistan, Philippines, Singapore, Sri Lanka, Thailand. Pres. Prof. C. S. DAYRIT Philippines); Sec. Prof. INDIRA NATH (India).

Federation of European Biochemical Societies: c/o Prof. V. Turk, Dept of Biochemistry, Jozef Stefan Institute, Jamova 39, 61000 Ljubljana, Slovenia; tel. (61) 1257080; telex 31296; fax (61) 273594; f. 1964 to promote the science of biochemistry through meetings of European biochemists, provision of fellowships and advanced courses and issuing publications. Mems: 40,000 in 32 societies. Chair. Dr L. THELANDER; Sec.-Gen. Prof. V. TURK. Publs *European Journal of Biochemistry, FEBS Letters, FEBS Bulletin*.

Foundation for International Scientific Co-ordination (Fondation 'Pour la science', Centre international de synthèse): 12 rue Colbert, 75002 Paris, France; tel. 1-42-97-50-68; fax 1-42-97-46-46; e-mail synthese@filnet.fr; f. 1924. Dirs MICHEL BLAY, ERIC BRIAN; Publs *Revue de Synthèse, Revue d'Histoire des Sciences, Semaines de Synthèse, L'Evolution de l'Humanité*.

Intergovernmental Oceanographic Commission: UNESCO, 1 rue Miollis, 75732 Paris Cédex 15, France; tel. 1-45-68-39-83; telex 204461; fax 1-45-68-58-10; f. 1960 to promote scientific investigation of the nature and resources of the oceans through the concerted action of its members. Mems: 125 governments. Chair. GEOFFREY HOLLAND (Canada); Exec. Sec. Dr GUNNAR KULLENBERG. Publs *IOC Technical Series* (irregular), IOC *Manuals* and *Guides* (irregular), *IOC Workshop Reports* (irregular) and *IOC Training Course Reports* (irregular), annual reports.

International Academy of Astronautics—IAA: 6 rue Galilee, POB 1268–16, 75766 Paris Cédex 16, France; tel. 1-47-23-82-15; telex 651767; fax 1-47-23-82-16; f. 1960; fosters the development of astronautics for peaceful purposes, holds scientific meetings and makes scientific studies, reports, awards and book awards; maintains 19 scientific cttees and a multilingual terminology data base (20 languages). Mems: 681, and 382 corresponding mems, in basic sciences, engineering sciences, life sciences and social sciences, from 57 countries. Sec.-Gen. Dr JEAN-MICHEL CONTANT. Publ. *Acta Astronautica* (monthly).

International Association for Earthquake Engineering: Kenchiku Kaikan, 3rd Floor, 5-26-20, Shiba, Minato-ku, Tokyo 108, Japan; tel. (3) 453-1281; fax (3) 453-0428; f. 1963 to promote international co-operation among scientists and engineers in the field of earthquake engineering through exchange of knowledge, ideas and results of research and practical experience. Mems: national cttees in 39 countries. Pres. THOMAS PAULAY (New Zealand); Sec.-Gen. Dr TSUNEO KATAYAMA.

International Association for Ecology—INTECOL: Savannah River Ecology Laboratory, Drawer E, Aiken, SC 29802, USA; tel. (803) 725-2472; fax (803) 725-3309; f. 1967 to provide opportunities for communication between ecologists; to co-operate with organizations and individuals having related aims and interests; to encourage studies in the different fields of ecology; affiliated to the International Union of Biological Sciences (q.v.). Mems: 35 national and international ecological societies, and 1,000 individuals. Pres. A. Miyawaki (Japan); Sec.-Gen. R. Sharitz (USA).

International Association for Mathematical Geology: c/o T. A. Jones, POB 2189, Houston, TX 77252-2189, USA; tel. (713) 966-3046; fax (713) 966-6336; f. 1968 for the preparation and elaboration of mathematical models of geological processes; the introduction of mathematical methods in geological sciences and technology; assistance in the development of mathematical investigation in geological sciences; the organization of international collaboration in mathematical geology through various forums and publications; educational programmes for mathematical geology; affiliated to the International Union of Geological Sciences (q.v.). Mems: c. 600. Pres. Dr R. A. Olea (USA); Sec.-Gen. Dr T. A. Jones (USA). Publs *Mathematical Geology* (8 a year), *Computers and Geosciences* (10 a year), *Non-renewable Resources* (quarterly), *Newsletter* (2 a year).

International Association for Mathematics and Computers in Simulation: c/o Free University of Brussels, Automatic Control, CP 165, ave F. D. Roosevelt 50, 1050 Brussels, Belgium; tel. (2) 650-20-97; fax (2) 650-35-64; f. 1955 to further the study of mathematical tools and computer software and hardware, analogue, digital or hybrid computers for simulation of soft or hard systems. Mems: 1,100 and 27 assoc. mems. Pres. R. Vichnevetsky (USA); Sec. Prof. Raymond Hanus. Publs *Mathematics and Computers in Simulation* (6 a year), *Applied Numerical Mathematics* (6 a year), *Journal of Computational Acoustics*.

International Association for the Physical Sciences of the Ocean—IAPSO: POB 820440, Vicksburg, MS 39182-0440, USA; tel. (601) 636-1363; fax (601) 629-9640; e-mail camfield@vicksburg.com; f. 1919 to promote the study of scientific problems relating to the oceans and interactions occurring at its boundaries, chiefly in so far as such study may be carried out by the aid of mathematics, physics and chemistry; to initiate, facilitate and co-ordinate research; to provide for discussion, comparison and publication; affiliated to the International Union of Geodesy and Geophysics (q.v.). Mems: 81 member states. Pres. Dr Robin D. Muench (USA); Sec.-Gen. Dr Fred E. Camfield (USA). Publ. *Publications Scientifiques* (irregular).

International Association for Plant Physiology—IAPP: c/o Dr D. Graham, Division of Food Science and Technology, CSIRO, POB 52, North Ryde, NSW, Australia 2113; tel. (2) 9490-8333; telex 23407; fax (2) 9490-3107; e-mail douglasgraham@dfst.csiro.au; f. 1955 to promote the development of plant physiology at the international level through congresses, symposia and workshops, by maintaining communication with national societies and by encouraging interaction between plant physiologists in developing and developed countries; affiliated to the International Union of Biological Sciences (q.v.). Pres. Prof. S. Miyachi; Sec.-Treas. Dr D. Graham.

International Association for Plant Taxonomy: Botanisches Museum, 14191 Berlin, Königin Luisestr. 6–8, Germany; tel. (30) 8300-6218; e-mail iapt@zedat.fu-berlin.de; internet http://www.bgbm.fu-berlin.de/iapt; f. 1950 to promote the development of plant taxonomy and encourage contacts between people and institutes interested in this work; affiliated to the International Union of Biological Sciences (q.v.). Mems: institutes and individuals in 85 countries. Pres. D. A. Nicolson (USA); Sec.-Gen. W. Greuter (Germany). Publs *Taxon* (quarterly), *Regnum vegetabile* (irregular).

International Association of Biological Standardization: Biostandards, CP 456, 1211 Geneva 4, Switzerland; fax (22) 702-93-55; f. 1955 to connect producers and controllers of immunological products (sera, vaccines, etc.) for the study and the development of methods of standardization; supports international organizations in their efforts to solve problems of standardization. Mems: 500. Pres. F. Horaud (France); Sec.-Gen. D. Gaudry (France). Publs *Newsletter* (quarterly), *Biologicals* (quarterly).

International Association of Botanic Gardens: c/o Prof. J. E. Hernández-Bermejo, Córdoba Botanic Garden, Avda de Linneo, s/n, 14004 Córdoba, Spain; tel. (57) 200077; fax (57) 295333; f. 1954 to promote co-operation between scientific collections of living plants, including the exchange of information and specimens; to promote the study of the taxonomy of cultivated plants; and to encourage the conservation of rare plants and their habitats; affiliated to the International Union of Biological Sciences (q.v.). Pres. Prof. Kunio Iwatsuki (Japan); Sec. Prof. J. Esteban Hernández-Bermejo (Spain).

International Association of Geodesy: Dept. of Geophysics, Juliane Maries Vej 30, 2100 Copenhagen Oe, Denmark; tel. (45) 3582-0582; fax (45) 3536-5357; f. 1922 to promote the study of all scientific problems of geodesy and encourage geodetic research; to promote and co-ordinate international co-operation in this field; to publish results; affiliated to the International Union of Geodesy and Geophysics (q.v.). Mems: national committees in 73 countries. Pres. K. P. Schwarz (Canada); Sec.-Gen. C. C. Tscherning (Denmark). Publs *Journal of Geodesy, Travaux de l'AIG*.

International Association of Geomagnetism and Aeronomy—IAGA: c/o Dr JoAnn Joselyn, NOAA Space Environment Center, 325 Broadway, Boulder, CO 80303, USA; tel. (303) 497-5147; fax (303) 494-0980; e-mail jjoselyn@sec.noaa.gov; f. 1919 for the study of questions relating to geomagnetism and aeronomy and the encouragement of research; holds General and Scientific Assemblies every two years; affiliated to the International Union of Geodesy and Geophysics (IUGG, q.v.). Mems: the countries which adhere to the IUGG. Pres. M. Kono (Japan); Sec.-Gen. Dr JoAnn Joselyn. Publs *IAGA Bulletin* (including annual *Geomagnetic Data), IAGA News* (annually).

International Association of Hydrological Sciences: Dept of Geography, Wilfrid Laurier Univ., Waterloo, ON N2L 3C5, Canada; tel. (519) 884-1970; fax (519) 846-0968; e-mail 44iahs@mach1.wlu.ca; internet http://www.wlu.ca/~wwwiahs/index.html; f. 1922 to promote co-operation in the study of hydrology and water resources. Pres. Dr J. C. Rodda (UK); Sec.-Gen. Dr Gordon J. Young (Canada). Publs *Journal* (every 2 months), *Newsletter* (3 a year).

International Association of Meteorology and Atmospheric Sciences—IAMAS: Dept of Physics, Univ. of Toronto, Toronto, ON M5S 1A7, Canada; f. 1919; permanent commissions on atmospheric ozone, radiation, atmospheric chemistry and global pollution, dynamic meteorology, polar meteorology, clouds and precipitation, climate, atmospheric electricity, planetary atmospheres and their evolution, and meteorology of the upper atmosphere; general assemblies held once every four years; special assemblies held once between general assemblies; affiliated to the International Union of Geodesy and Geophysics (q.v.). Pres. Prof. R. Duce (USA); Sec.-Gen. Prof. R. List (Canada).

International Association of Sedimentologists: c/o Prof. A. Strasser, Institut de Géologie, Pérolles, 1700 Fribourg, Switzerland; tel. (26) 3008978; fax (26) 3009742; e-mail andreas.strasser@unifr.ch; f. 1952; affiliated to the International Union of Geological Sciences (q.v.). Mems: 2,200. Pres. Prof. A. Bosellini (Italy); Gen. Sec. Prof. A. Strasser (Switzerland). Publ. *Sedimentology* (every 2 months).

International Association of Theoretical and Applied Limnology (Societas Internationalis Limnologiae): Dept of Biology, University of Alabama, Tuscaloosa, AL 35487-0206, USA; tel. (205) 348-1793; fax (205) 348-1403; f. 1922; study of physical, chemical and biological phenomena of lakes and rivers; affiliated to the International Union of Biological Sciences (q.v.). Mems: about 3,200. Pres. C. W. Burns (New Zealand); Gen. Sec. and Treas. Robert G. Wetzel (USA).

International Association of Volcanology and Chemistry of the Earth's Interior—IAVCEI: c/o Australian Geological Survey Organisation, GPO Box 378, Canberra, ACT 2601, Australia; tel. (6) 2499377; fax (6) 2499983; f. 1919 to examine scientifically all aspects of volcanology; affiliated to the International Union of Geodesy and Geophysics (q.v.). Pres. G. Heiken (USA); Sec.-Gen. R. W. Johnson (Australia). Publs *Bulletin of Volcanology, Catalogue of the Active Volcanoes of the World, Proceedings in Volcanology*.

International Association of Wood Anatomists: Herbarium Division, University of Utrecht, Netherlands; tel. 030-532643; f. 1931 for the purpose of study, documentation and exchange of information on the structure of wood. Mems: 500 in 61 countries. Exec. Sec. B. J. H. Ter Welle. Publ. *IAWA Journal*.

International Association on Water Quality: Duchess House, 20 Masons Yard, Duke St, London, SW1Y 6BU, United Kingdom; tel. (171) 839-8390; fax (171) 839-8299; e-mail 100065.3664@compuserve.com; f. 1965 to encourage international communication, co-operative effort, and a maximum exchange of information on water quality management; to sponsor conferences; to publish research reports. Mems: 52 national, 544 corporate and 5,668 individuals. Pres. Dr T. M. Keinath; Exec. Dir A. Milburn. Publs *Water Research* (monthly), *Water Science and Technology* (24 a year), *Water Quality International* (6 a year), *Yearbook, Scientific and Technical Reports*.

International Astronautical Federation—IAF: 3–5 rue Mario-Nikis, 75015 Paris, France; tel. 1-45-67-42-60; telex 205917; fax 1-42-73-21-20; f. 1950 to foster the development of astronautics for peaceful purposes at national and international levels. The IAF has created the International Academy of Astronautics (IAA) and the International Institute of Space Law (IISL). Mems: 129 national astronautical societies in 45 countries. Pres. Alvaro Azcarraga (Spain); Exec. Sec. B. Woessner (acting).

International Biometric Society: c/o Dr E. Barath, Chair. of Statistics, 2103 Gödöllö, Hungary; tel. (28) 310-694; fax (28) 330-336; f. 1947 for the advancement of quantitative biological science through the development of quantitative theories and the application, development and dissemination of effective mathematical and statistical techniques; the Society has 16 regional organizations and 16 national groups, is affiliated with the International Statistical Institute and the World Health Organization, and constitutes the Section of Biometry of the International Union of Biological Sciences (q.v.). Mems: over 6,000 in more than 60 countries. Pres. Prof.

B. MORGAN (UK); Sec. Dr E. BARATH (Hungary). Publs *Biometrics* (quarterly), *Biometric Bulletin* (quarterly).

International Botanical Congress: c/o Dr Peter Hoch, Missouri Botanical Garden, PO Box 299, St Louis, MO 63166-0299, USA; tel. (314) 577-5175; fax (314) 577-9589; e-mail ibc16@mobot.org; f. 1864 to inform botanists of recent progress in the plant sciences; the Nomenclature Section of the Congress attempts to provide a uniform terminology and methodology for the naming of plants; other Divisions deal with developmental, metabolic, structural, systematic and evolutionary, ecological botany; genetics and plant breeding; next Congress: St Louis, 1999; affiliated to the International Union of Biological Sciences (q.v.). Sec. Dr PETER HOCH.

International Bureau of Weights and Measures: Pavillon de Breteuil, 92312 Sèvres Cédex, France; tel. 1-45-07-70-70; fax 1-45-34-20-21; e-mail info@bipm.fr; f. 1875 for the international unification of physical measures; establishment of fundamental standards and of scales of the principal physical dimensions; preservation of the international prototypes; determination of national standards; precision measurements in physics. Mems: 48 states. Pres. J. KOVALEVSKY (France); Sec. W. R. BLEVIN (Austria).

International Cartographic Association: 136 bis rue de Grenelle, 75700 Paris 07 SP, France; tel. 1-43-98-82-95; fax 1-43-98-84-00; f. 1959 for the advancement, instigation and co-ordination of cartographic research involving co-operation between different nations. Particularly concerned with furtherance of training in cartography, study of source material, compilation, graphic design, drawing, scribing and reproduction techniques of maps; organizes international conferences, symposia, meetings, exhibitions. Mems: 80 nations. Pres. MICHAEL WOOD. Publ. *ICA Newsletter* (2 a year).

International Centre of Insect Physiology and Ecology: POB 30772, Nairobi, Kenya; tel. (2) 802501; fax (2) 803360; e-mail icipe@cgnet.com; f. 1970; specializes in research and development of environmentally sustainable and affordable methods of managing tropical arthropod plant pests and disease vectors, and in the conservation and utilisation of biodiversity of insects of commercial and ecological importance; administers the Pest Management Research and Development Network, which operates in several African countries and encourages the site-specific development and testing of improved methods for control of plant pests and disease vectors. Dir-Gen. Dr HANS RUDOLPH HERREN. Publs *Insect Science and its Application* (quarterly), *Annual Report*.

International Commission for Optics: Institut d'Optique/CNRS, POB 147, 91403 Orsay Cédex, France; tel. 1-69-35-87-41; fax 1-69-35-87-00; internet http://www.ico-optics.org; f. 1948 to contribute to the progress of theoretical and instrumental optics, to assist in research and to promote international agreement on specifications; Gen. Assembly every three years. Mems: committees in 44 territories. Pres. Prof. T. ASAKURA (Japan); Sec.-Gen. Dr P. CHAVEL (France). Publ. *ICO Newsletter*.

International Commission for Plant-Bee Relationships: c/o Prof. I. Williams, Entomology-Nematology Dept, Rothamsted Experimental Station, Harpenden, Herts, AL5 2JQ, United Kingdom; f. 1950 to promote research and its application in the field of bee botany, and collect and spread information; to organize meetings, etc., and collaborate with scientific organizations; affiliated to the International Union of Biological Sciences (q.v.). Mems: 175 in 34 countries. Pres. Prof. INGRID WILLIAMS; Sec. Dr J. N. TASEI.

International Commission for the Scientific Exploration of the Mediterranean Sea (Commission internationale pour l'exploration scientifique de la mer Méditerranée—CIESM): 16 blvd de Suisse, 98000 Monaco; tel. 93-30-38-79; fax 92-16-11-95; internet http://www.ciesm.org; f. 1919 for scientific exploration and sustainable management of the Mediterranean Sea; includes 16 scientific committees. Mems: 23 member countries, 2,500 scientists. Pres. SAS The Prince RAINIER III of MONACO; Sec.-Gen. Prof. F. DOUMENGE; Dir-Gen. Prof. F. BRIAND.

International Commission on Physics Education: c/o Prof. J. Barojas, POB 55534, 09340 México DF, Mexico; tel. (5) 686-35-19; f. 1960 to encourage and develop international collaboration in the improvement and extension of the methods and scope of physics education at all levels; collaborates with UNESCO and organizes international conferences. Mems: appointed triennially by the International Union of Pure and Applied Physics. Sec. Prof. J. BAROJAS.

International Commission on Radiation Units and Measurements—ICRU: 7910 Woodmont Ave, Suite 800, Bethesda, MD 20814, USA; tel. (301) 657-2652; fax (301) 907-8768; f. 1925 to develop internationally acceptable recommendations regarding: (1) quantities and units of radiation and radioactivity, (2) procedures suitable for the measurement and application of these quantities in clinical radiology and radiobiology, (3) physical data needed in the application of these procedures. Makes recommendations on quantities and units for radiation protection (see below, International Radiation Protection Association). Mems: from about 18 countries. Chair. A. ALLISY; Sec. R. S. CASWELL. Publs *Reports*.

International Commission on Zoological Nomenclature: c/o The Natural History Museum, Cromwell Rd, London, SW7 5BD, United Kingdom; tel. (171) 938-9387; e-mail iczn@nhm.ac.uk; f. 1895; has judicial powers to determine all matters relating to the interpretation of the International Code of Zoological Nomenclature and also plenary powers to suspend the operation of the Code where the strict application of the Code would lead to confusion and instability of nomenclature; the Commission is responsible also for maintaining and developing the Official Lists and Official Indexes of Names in Zoology; affiliated to the International Union of Biological Sciences (q.v.). Pres. Prof. A. MINELLI (Italy); Exec. Sec. Dr P. K. TUBBS (UK). Publs *International Code of Zoological Nomenclature, Bulletin of Zoological Nomenclature, Official Lists and Indexes of Names and Works in Zoology, Towards Stability in the Names of Animals*.

International Council for Scientific and Technical Information: 51 blvd de Montmorency, 75016 Paris, France; tel. 1-45-25-65-92; fax 1-42-15-12-62; e-mail icsti@dial.oleane.com; internet http://www.icsti.nrc.ca/icsti; f. 1984 as the successor to the International Council of Scientific Unions Abstracting Board (f. 1952); aims to increase accessibility to scientific and technical information; fosters communication and interaction among all participants in the information transfer chain. Mems: 50 organizations. Pres. DAVID RUSSON (UK); Gen. Sec. CLAUDE PATOU (France).

International Council for the Exploration of the Sea—ICES: Palægade 2–4, 1261 Copenhagen K, Denmark; tel. 33-15-42-25; fax 33-93-42-15; e-mail ices.info@ices.dk; f. 1902 to encourage and facilitate marine research on the utilization and conservation of living resources and the environment in the North Atlantic Ocean and its adjacent seas; to publish and disseminate results of research; to advise member countries and regulatory commissions. Gen. Sec. Prof. C. C. E. HOPKINS. Publs *ICES Journal of Marine Science, ICES Marine Science Symposia, ICES Fisheries Statistics, ICES Cooperative Research Reports, ICES Oceanographic Data Lists and Inventories, ICES Techniques in Marine Environmental Sciences, ICES Identification Leaflets for Plankton, ICES Identification Leaflets for Diseases and Parasites of Fish and Shellfish, ICES / CIEM Information*.

International Council of Psychologists: Dept. of Psychology, Southwest Texas State University, San Marcos, TX 78666, USA; tel. (512) 245-7605; fax (512) 245-3153; f. 1941 to advance psychology and the application of its scientific findings throughout the world; holds annual conventions. Mems: 1,200 qualified psychologists. Sec.-Gen. Dr JOHN M. DAVIS. Publs *International Psychologist* (quarterly), *World Psychology* (quarterly).

International Council of the Aeronautical Sciences: c/o Netherlands Association of Aeronautical Engineers (NVvL), Anthony Fokkerweg 2, 1059 Amsterdam, Netherlands; tel. (20) 5113618; fax (20) 5113210; f.1957 to encourage free interchange of information on all phases of mechanical flight; holds biennial Congresses. Mems: national associations in 32 countries. Pres. Prof. RICHARD H. PETERSEN (USA); Exec. Sec. FRED STERK.

International Earth Rotation Service: Central Bureau, Paris Observatory, 61 ave de l'Observatoire, 75014 Paris, France; tel. 1-40-51-22-26; fax 1-40-51-22-91; e-mail iers@obspm.fr; f. 1988 (fmrly International Polar Motion Service and Bureau International de l'Heure); maintained by the International Astronomical Union and the International Union of Geodesy and Geophysics; defines and maintains the international terrestrial and celestial reference systems; determines earth orientation parameters (terrestrial and celestial co-ordinates of the pole and universal time) connecting these systems; monitors global geophysical fluids; organizes collection, analysis and dissemination of data. Pres. Directing Board Prof. C. REIGBER.

International Federation for Cell Biology: c/o Dr Ivan Cameron, Dept of Cellular and Structural Biology, Univ. of Texas Health Science Center, 7703 Floyd Curl Drive, San Antonio, Texas 78229, USA; f. 1972 to foster international co-operation, and organize conferences. Pres. Dr JUDIE WALTON; Sec.-Gen. Dr IVAN CAMERON. Publs *Cell Biology International* (monthly), reports.

International Federation of Operational Research Societies: Bldg 321, Technical University of Denmark, 2800 Lyngby, Denmark; tel. 45-25-34-10; fax 45-88-13-97; f. 1959 for development of operational research as a unified science and its advancement in all nations of the world. Mems: about 30,000 individuals, 44 national societies, four kindred societies. Pres. Prof. PETER BELL (Canada); Sec. HELLE R. WELLING. Publs *International Abstracts in Operational Research, IFORS Bulletin, International Transactions in Operational Research*.

International Federation of Science Editors: School for Scientific Communication, Mario Negri Sud, Via Nazionale, 66030 Santa Maria Imbaro, Italy; tel. (872) 570316; fax (872) 570317; f. 1978; links editors in different branches of science with the aim of improving scientific writing, editing and communication internationally. Pres. MIRIAM BALABAU (Italy).

International Federation of Societies for Electron Microscopy: Electron Microscope Unit, University of Sydney, Sydney, NSW 2006, Australia; tel. (2) 9351-2351; fax (12) 9552-1967; e-mail djhc@emu.su.oz.au; f. 1955. Mems: representative organizations of 40 countries. Gen.-Sec. D. J. H. COCKAYNE (Australia).

International Food Information Service: UK Office (IFIS Publishing), Lane End House, Shinfield, Reading, RG2 9BB, United Kingdom; tel. (1734) 883895; fax (1734) 885065; e-mail ifis@ifis.org; f. 1968; board of governors comprises two members each from CAB-International (UK), ZADI (Zentralstelle für Agrardokumentation und-information) (Germany), the Institute of Food Technologists (USA), and the Centrum voor Landbouwpublikaties en Landbouwdocumentaties (Netherlands); collects and disseminates information on all disciplines relevant to food science, food technology and human nutrition. Gen. Man. Dr JOHN R. METCALFE; Man. Dir (IFIS GmbH) BIANCA SCHNEIDER. Publ. *Food Science and Technology Abstracts* (monthly).

International Foundation of the High-Altitude Research Stations Jungfraujoch and Gornergrat: Sidlerstrasse 5, 3012 Berne, Switzerland; tel. (31) 6314052; fax (31) 6314405; e-mail debrunner@phim.unibe.ch; f. 1931; international research centre which enables scientists from many scientific fields to carry out experiments at high altitudes. Six countries contribute to support the station: Austria, Belgium, Germany, Italy, Switzerland, United Kingdom. Pres. Prof. H. DEBRUNNER.

International Glaciological Society: Lensfield Rd, Cambridge, CB2 1ER, United Kingdom; tel. (1223) 355974; f. 1936 to stimulate interest in and encourage research into the scientific and technical problems of snow and ice in all countries. Mems: 850 in 29 countries. Pres. Dr BJÖRN WOLD (Norway); Sec.-Gen. C. S. L. OMMANNEY. Publs *Journal of Glaciology* (3 a year), *Ice* (News Bulletin—3 a year), *Annals of Glaciology*.

International Hydrographic Organization: 4 quai Antoine 1er, BP 445, Monte Carlo, 98011 Monaco; tel. 93-10-81-00; fax 93-10-81-40; e-mail info@ihb.mc; f. 1921 to link the hydrographic offices of its member governments and co-ordinate their work with a view to rendering navigation easier and safer on all the seas of the world; to obtain as far as possible uniformity in charts and hydrographic documents; to foster the development of electronic chart navigation; to encourage the adoption of the best methods of conducting hydrographic surveys and improvements in the theory and practice of the science of hydrography, and to encourage surveying in those parts of the world where accurate charts are lacking; to extend and facilitate the application of oceanographic knowledge for the benefit of navigators and specialists in marine sciences; to render advice and assistance to developing countries upon request, facilitating their application for financial aid from the UNDP and other aid organizations for creation or extension of their hydrographic capabilities; to fulfil the role of world data centre for bathymetry; provides computerized Tidal Constituent Data Bank and IHO Data Centre for Digital Bathymetry; organizes quinquennial conference. Mems: 64 states. Directing Committee: Pres. Rear-Adm. GIUSEPPE ANGRISANO (Italy); Dirs Commodore N. GUY (South Africa), Commodore J. LEECH (Australia). Publs *International Hydrographic Review* (2 a year), *International Hydrographic Bulletin* (monthly), *IHO Yearbook*.

International Institute of Refrigeration: 177 blvd Malesherbes, 75017 Paris, France; tel. 1-42-27-32-35; fax 1-47-63-17-98; e-mail iifiir@ibm.net; f. 1908 to further the development of the science of refrigeration and its applications on a world-wide scale; to investigate, discuss and recommend any aspects leading to improvements in the field of refrigeration; maintains FRIDOC data-base (available on diskette). Mems: 55 national, 1,500 associates. Dir L. LUCAS (France). Publs *Bulletin* (every 2 months), *International Journal of Refrigeration* (8 a year), books, proceedings, recommendations.

International Mineralogical Association: Institute of Mineralogy, University of Marburg, 3550 Marburg, Germany; tel. 28-5617; telex 482372; fax 285831; f. 1958 to further international co-operation in the science of mineralogy; affiliated to the International Union of Geological Sciences (q.v.). Mems: national societies in 31 countries. Sec. Prof. S. S. HAFNER.

International Organization of Legal Metrology: 11 rue Turgot, 75009 Paris, France; tel. 1-48-78-12-82; telex 215463; fax 1-42-82-17-27; f. 1955 to serve as documentation and information centre on the verification, checking, construction and use of measuring instruments, to determine characteristics and standards to which measuring instruments must conform for their use to be recommended internationally, and to determine the general principles of legal metrology. Mems: governments of 50 countries. Dir B. ATHANÉ (France). Publ. *Bulletin* (quarterly).

International Palaeontological Association: c/o Prof. D. L. Bruton, Palentologisk Museum, Sars Gate 1, 0562 Oslo, Norway; tel. 22-85-16-58; fax 22-85-18-10; f. 1933; affiliated to the International Union of Geological Sciences and the International Union of Biological Sciences (q.v.). Pres. Dr CHANG MEE-MANN (China); Sec.-Gen. D. L. BRUTON (Norway). Publs *Lethaia* (quarterly), *Directory*.

International Peat Society: Kuokkalantie 4, 40420 Jyskä, Finland; tel. (14) 674042; fax (14) 677405; e-mail peatsocinternat@peatsoc.pp.fi; f. 1968 to encourage co-operation in the study and use of mires, peatlands, peat and related material, through international meetings, research groups and the exchange of information. Mems: 16 National Cttees, research institutes and other organizations, and individuals from 35 countries. Pres. Dr JENS DIETER BECKER-PLATEN (Germany); Sec.-Gen. RAIMO SOPO (Finland). Publs *IPS Bulletin* (annually), *International Peat Journal* (every 2 years).

International Phonetic Association—IPA: Dept of Linguistics, University of Victoria, POB 3045, Victoria, V84 3P4, Canada; e-mail esling@uvic.ca; f. 1886 to promote the scientific study of phonetics and its applications. Mems: 800. Sec. J. H. ESLING (Canada). Publ. *Journal* (2 a year).

International Photobiology Association: c/o Dr Tom Dubbelman, POB 9503, 2300 RA Leiden, Netherlands; tel. (71) 276053; fax (71) 276125; e-mail tmardubbelman@biochemistry.medfac.leidenuniv.nl; f. 1928; stimulation of scientific research concerning the physics, chemistry and climatology of non-ionizing radiations (ultra-violet, visible and infra-red) in relation to their biological efffects and their applications in biology and medicine; 18 national committees represented; affiliated to the International Union of Biological Sciences (q.v.). International Congresses held every four years. Pres. Prof. PILL SOON SONG; Sec.-Gen. Dr TOM DUBBELMAN.

International Phycological Society: c/o Harbor Branch Oceanographic Institute, 5600 Old Dixie Highway, Fort Pierce, FL 34946, USA; fax (407) 468-0757; f. 1961 to promote the study of algae, the distribution of information, and international co-operation in this field. Mems: about 1,000. Pres. M. D. GUIRY; Sec. M. D. HANISAK. Publ. *Phycologia* (every 2 months).

International Primatological Society: c/o Dr D. Fragaszy, Dept of Psychology, Univ. of Georgia, Athens, GA 30602, USA; tel. (706) 542-3036; fax (706) 542-3275; e-mail cmspsy37@uga.cc.uga.edu; f. 1964 to promote primatological science in all fields. Mems: about 1,500. Pres. Dr T. NISHIDA; Sec.-Gen. Dr D. FRAGASZY.

International Radiation Protection Association—IRPA: POB 662, 5600 AR Eindhoven, Netherlands; tel. (40) 247-33-55; fax (40) 243-50-20; e-mail irpa.exof@sbd.tue.nl; f. 1966 to link individuals and societies throughout the world concerned with protection against ionizing radiations and allied effects, and to represent doctors, health physicists, radiological protection officers and others engaged in radiological protection, radiation safety, nuclear safety, legal, medical and veterinary aspects and in radiation research and other allied activities. Mems: 16,000 in 42 societies. Pres. Prof. K. DUFTSCMID (Austria); Sec.-Gen. C. J. HUYSKENS (Netherlands). Publ. *IRPA Bulletin*.

International Society for General Semantics: POB 728, Concord, CA 94522, USA; tel. (510) 798-0311; f. 1943 to advance knowledge of and inquiry into non-Aristotelian systems and general semantics. Mems: 2,000 individuals in 40 countries. Pres. D. DAVID BOURLAND, Jr (USA); Exec. Dir PAUL D. JOHNSTON (USA).

International Society for Human and Animal Mycology—ISHAM: c/o PHLS Mycology Reference Laboratory, Dept of Microbiology, Univ. of Leeds, Leeds LS2 9JT, United Kingdom; tel. (113) 233-5600; fax (113) 233-5587; f. 1954 to pursue the study of fungi pathogenic for man and animals; holds congresses (1994 Congress: Adelaide, Australia). Mems: 1,050 from 71 countries. Pres. Prof. J. MULLER; Sec.-Gen. Prof. E. G. V. EVANS. Publ. *Journal of Medical and Veterinary Mycology* (6 a year).

International Society for Rock Mechanics: c/o Laboratório Nacional de Engenharia Civil, 101 Av. do Brasil, 1799 Lisboa Codex, Portugal; tel. (1) 8482131; telex 16760; fax (1) 8497660; e-mail isrm@lnec.pt; f. 1962 to encourage and co-ordinate international co-operation in the science of rock mechanics; to assist individuals and local organizations to form national bodies; to maintain liaison with organizations that represent related sciences, including geology, geophysics, soil mechanics, mining engineering, petroleum engineering and civil engineering. The Society organizes international meetings and encourages the publication of the results of research in rock mechanics. Mems: c. 6,000. Pres. Prof. SHUNSUKE SAKURAI; Sec.-Gen. JOSÉ DELGADO RODRIGUES. Publ. *News Journal* (3 a year).

International Society for Stereology: c/o Dr Jens R. Nyengaard, Stereological Research Laboratory, Bartholin Bldg, Aarhud Univ., 8000 Århus C, Denmark; tel. 89-49-36-54; fax 89-49-36-50; f. 1961; an interdisciplinary society gathering scientists from metallurgy, geology, mineralogy and biology to exchange ideas on three-dimensional interpretation of two-dimensional samples (sections, projections) of their material by means of stereological principles; ninth Congress: Copenhagen, Denmark, 1995. Mems: 300. Pres. BENTE PAKKENBER; Treas. JENS R. NYENGAARD.

International Society for Tropical Ecology: c/o Botany Dept, Banaras Hindu University, Varanasi, 221 005 India; tel. (542) 317099; telex 545304; fax (542) 317074; f. 1956 to promote and develop the science of ecology in the tropics in the service of humanity; to publish a journal to aid ecologists in the tropics in communication of their findings; and to hold symposia from time to time to summarize the state of knowledge in particular or general fields of tropical ecology. Mems: 500. Sec. Prof. J. S. SINGH (India); Editor Prof. K. P. SINGH. Publ. *Tropical Ecology* (2 a year).

International Society of Biometeorology: School of Earth Sciences, Macquarie Univ., Sydney, NSW 2109, Australia; tel. (2) 9850-8399; fax (2) 9850-8428; f. 1956 to unite all biometeorologists working in the fields of agricultural, botanical, cosmic, entomological, forest, human, medical, veterinarian, zoological and other branches of biometeorology. Mems: 350 individuals, nationals of 46 countries. Pres. Dr ANDRIS AULICIEMS (Australia); Sec. Dr PAUL J. BEGGS (Australia). Publs *Biometeorology* (Proceedings of the Congress of ISB), *International Journal of Biometeorology* (quarterly), *Biometeorology Bulletin*.

International Society of Criminology: 4–14 rue Ferrus, 75014 Paris, France; tel. 1-45-88-00-23; f. 1934 to promote the development of the sciences in their application to the criminal phenomenon. Mems: in 63 countries. Sec.-Gen. GEORGES PICCA. Publ. *Annales internationales de Criminologie* (2 a year).

International Union for Quaternary Research—INQUA: c/o G. Kroon, Netherlands Institute of Applied Geoscience, National Geological Survey, Secretariat Dept Geo-mapping, POB 157, 2000 Haarlem, Netherlands; tel. (23) 5300261; fax (23) 5367064; e-mail g.kroon@nitg.tno.nl; f. 1928 to co-ordinate research on the Quaternary geological era throughout the world. Pres. Prof. STEPHEN C. PORTER (USA); Sec. GERRY KROON (Netherlands).

International Union of Food Science and Technology: 3110 Seneca Drive, Oakville, Ontario, L6L 1B2, Canada; tel. (905) 827-3492; fax (905) 827-9213; e-mail iufost@inforamp-net; internet http://www.inforamp.net/-iufost; f. 1970; sponsors international symposia and congresses. Mems: 60 national groups. Pres. P. A. BIACS (Hungary); Sec.-Gen. J. P. MEYERS (Canada). Publ. *IUFOST Newsline* (3 a year).

Nordic Molecular Biology Association: c/o H. Prydz, Biotechnology Centre of Oslo, Univ. of Oslo, Gaustadalleen 21, 0371 Oslo, Norway; tel. 22-95-87-54; fax 22-69-41-30; organizes congress every two years, symposia. Mems: 1,000 in Denmark, Finland, Iceland, Norway, Sweden. Chair. HANS PRYDZ (Norway); Sec. LENE SVITH. Publ. *NOMBA Bulletin* (2 a year).

Pacific Science Association: 1525 Bernice St, POB 17801, Honolulu, HI 96817; tel. (808) 848-4139; fax (808) 847-8252; f. 1920 to promote co-operation in the study of scientific problems relating to the Pacific region, more particularly those affecting the prosperity and well-being of Pacific peoples; sponsors Pacific Science Congresses and Inter-Congresses. Mems: institutional representatives from 35 areas, scientific societies, individual scientists. Ninth Inter-Congress: Taipei, Taiwan, Nov. 1998; 19th Congress: Sydney, Australia, 1997. Pres. Dr AKITA ARIMA (Japan); Exec. Sec. Dr L. G. ELDREDGE. Publ. *Information Bulletin* (2 a year).

Pan-African Union of Science and Technology: POB 2339, Brazzaville, Republic of the Congo; tel. 832265; telex 5511; fax 832185; f. 1987 to promote the use of science and technology in furthering the development of Africa; organizes triennial congress. Pres. Prof. EDWARD AYENSU; Sec.-Gen. Prof. LÉVY MAKANY.

Pugwash Conferences on Science and World Affairs: 63A Great Russell St, London, WC1B 3BJ, United Kingdom; tel. (171) 405-6661; fax (171) 831-5651; f. 1957 to organize international conferences of scientists to discuss problems arising from development of science, particularly the dangers to mankind from weapons of mass destruction. Mems: national Pugwash groups in 38 countries. Pres. Prof. JOSEPH ROTBLAT; Sec.-Gen. Prof. FRANCESCO CALOGERO. Publs *Pugwash Newsletter* (quarterly), *Annals of Pugwash*, proceedings of Pugwash conferences, monographs.

Scientific, Technical and Research Commission—STRC: Nigerian Ports Authority Bldg, PMB 2359, Marina, Lagos, Nigeria; tel. (1) 2633289; fax (1) 2636093; f. 1965 to succeed the Commission for Technical Co-operation in Africa (f. 1954). Supervises the Inter-African Bureau for Animal Resources (Nairobi, Kenya), the Inter-African Bureau for Soils (Lagos, Nigeria) and the Inter-African Phytosanitary Commission (Yaoundé, Cameroon) and several joint research projects. The Commission provides training in agricultural man., and conducts pest control programmes. Exec. Sec. Prof. JOHNSON A. EKPERE.

Unitas Malacologica (Malacological Union): Dr E. Gittenberger, Nationaal Natuurhistorisch Museum, POB 9517, 2300 RA Leiden, Netherlands; tel. (71) 5687614; fax (71) 5687666; f. 1962 to further the study of molluscs; affiliated to the International Union of Biological Sciences (q.v.); holds triennial congress. Mems: 400 in over 30 countries. Pres. Dr R. BIELER (USA); Sec. Dr E. GITTENBERGER (Netherlands). Publ. *UM Newsletter* (2 a year).

World Organisation of Systems and Cybernetics—WOSC: c/o Prof. R. Vallée, 2 rue de Vouillé, 75015 Paris, France; tel. 1-45-33-62-46; f. 1969 to act as clearing-house for all societies concerned with cybernetics and systems, to aim for the recognition of cybernetics as fundamental science, to organize and sponsor international exhibitions of automation and computer equipment, congresses and symposia, and to promote and co-ordinate research in systems and cybernetics; sponsors an honorary fellowship and awards a Norbert Weiner memorial gold medal. Mems: national and international societies in 30 countries. Pres. Prof. S. BEER (UK); Dir-Gen. Prof. R. VALLÉE (France). Publs *Kybernetes, the International Journal of Cybernetics and Systems*.

Social Sciences

International Council for Philosophy and Humanistic Studies—ICPHS: Maison de l'UNESCO, 1 rue Miollis, 75732 Paris Cédex 15, France; tel. 1-45-68-26-85; fax 1-40-65-94-80; f. 1949 under the auspices of UNESCO to encourage respect for cultural autonomy by the comparative study of civilization and to contribute towards international understanding through a better knowledge of humanity; to develop international co-operation in philosophy, humanistic and kindred studies and to encourage the setting up of international organizations; to promote the dissemination of information in these fields; to sponsor works of learning, etc. Mems: organizations (see below) representing 145 countries. Pres. JEAN D'ORMESSON (France); Sec.-Gen. TILO SCHABERT (Germany). Publs *Bulletin of Information* (biennially), *Diogenes* (quarterly).

UNIONS FEDERATED TO THE ICPHS

International Academic Union: Palais des Académies, 1 rue Ducale, 1000 Brussels, Belgium; tel. (2) 550-22-00; fax (2) 550-22-05; f. 1919 to promote international co-operation through collective research in philology, archaeology, art history, history and social sciences. Mems: academic institutions in 42 countries. Pres. A. RONCAGLIA (Italy); Sec.-Gen. P. ROBERTS-JONES.

International Association for the History of Religions: c/o Prof. Michael Pye, FG Religionswissenschaft, Philipps-Universität, Lieligstrasse 37, 35032 Marburg, Germany; tel. (6421) 283662; fax (6421) 283944; e-mail pye@mailer.uni-marburg.de; f. 1950 to promote international collaboration of scholars, to organize congresses and to stimulate research. Mems: 24 countries. Pres. MICHAEL PYE; Sec.-Gen. Prof. ARMIN W. GEERTZ.

International Committee for the History of Art: 13 rue de Seine, 75006 Paris, France; f. 1930 by the 12th International Congress on the History of Art, for collaboration in the scientific study of the history of art. International congress every five years, and two colloquia between congresses. Mems: National Committees in 34 countries. Pres. Prof. RONALD DE LEEUW (Netherlands); Sec. PHILIPPE SENECHAL (France). Publs *Bibliographie d'histoire de l'Art* (quarterly), *Corpus international des vitraux, Bulletin du CIHA*.

International Committee of Historical Sciences: 44 rue de l'Amiral Mouchez, 75014 Paris, France; f. 1926 to work for the advancement of historical sciences by means of international co-ordination; an international congress is held every five years. Mems: 53 national committees, 22 affiliated international organizations and 18 internal commissions. Pres. IVAN T. BEREND (USA); Sec.-Gen. FRANÇOIS BÉDARIDA (France). Publ. *Bulletin d'Information du CISH*.

International Congress of African Studies: c/o School of Oriental and African Studies, Thornhaugh St, London, WC1H OXG, United Kingdom; tel. (171) 323-6035; fax (171) 323-6118; f. 1962.

International Federation for Modern Languages and Literatures: c/o D. A. Wells, Dept of German, Birkbeck College, Malet St, London, WC1E 7HX, United Kingdom; tel. (171) 631-6103; fax (171) 383-3729; f. 1928 to establish permanent contact between historians of literature, to develop or perfect facilities for their work and to promote the study of modern languages and literature. Congress every three years. Mems: 19 associations, with individual mems in 98 countries. Sec.-Gen. D. A. WELLS (UK).

International Federation of Philosophical Societies: c/o I. Kuçuradi, Ahmet Rasim Sok. 8/4, Çankaya, 06550 Ankara, Turkey; tel. (312) 2351219; fax (312) 4410297; f. 1948 under the auspices of UNESCO, to encourage international co-operation in the field of philosophy; holds World Congress of Philosophy every five years. Mems: 120 societies from 50 countries; 27 international societies. Pres. F. MIRÓ QUESADA (Peru); Sec.-Gen. IOANNA KUÇURADI (Turkey). Publs *International Bibliography of Philosophy, Chroniques de Philosophie, Contemporary Philosophy, Philosophical Problems Today, Philosophy and Cultural Development*.

International Federation of Societies of Classical Studies: c/o Prof. F. Paschoud, 6 chemin Aux Folies, 1293 Bellevue, Switzerland; tel. and fax (22) 7742656; f. 1948 under the auspices of UNESCO. Mems: 79 societies in 44 countries. Pres. C. J. CLASSEN; Sec. Prof. F. PASCHOUD (Switzerland). Publs *L'Année Philologique, Thesaurus linguae Latinae*.

International Musicological Society: CP 1561, 4001 Basel, Switzerland; fax (1) 9231027; e-mail mwsba@mws.unizh.ch; f. 1927;

international congresses every five years. Pres. STANLEY SADIE (UK); Sec.-Gen. DOROTHEA BAUMANN (Switzerland). Publ. *Acta Musicologica* (2 a year).

International Union for Oriental and Asian Studies: Közraktar u. 12A 11/2, 1093 Budapest, Hungary; f. 1951 by the 22nd International Congress of Orientalists under the auspices of UNESCO, to promote contacts between orientalists throughout the world, and to organize congresses, research and publications. Mems: in 24 countries. Sec.-Gen. Prof. GEORG HAZAI. Publs *Philologiae Turcicae Fundamenta, Materialien zum Sumerischen Lexikon, Sanskrit Dictionary, Corpus Inscriptionum Iranicarum, Linguistic Atlas of Iran, Matériels des parlers iraniens, Turcology Annual, Bibliographie égyptologique.*

International Union of Anthropological and Ethnological Sciences: c/o Prof. E. Sunderland, University College of North Wales, Bangor, Gwynedd, LL57 2EF, United Kingdom; tel. (1248) 354036; fax (1248) 355830; f. 1948 under the auspices of UNESCO; has 19 international research commissions. Mems: institutions and individuals in 100 countries. Pres. Prof. VINSON H. SUTLIVE (USA); Sec.-Gen. Prof. E. SUNDERLAND (UK). Publ. *IUAES Newsletter* (3 a year).

International Union of Prehistoric and Protohistoric Sciences: c/o Prof. J. Bourgeois, Dept of Archaeology and Ancient History of Europe, University of Ghent, Blandijnberg 2, 9000 Ghent, Belgium; tel. (9) 264-41-06; fax (9) 264-41-73; e-mail jbourbeo@allserv.rug.ac.be; f. 1931 to promote congresses and scientific work in the fields of pre- and proto-history. Mems: 120 countries. Pres. Prof. A. M. RADMILLI (Italy); Sec.-Gen. Prof. J. BOURGEOIS (Belgium).

Permanent International Committee of Linguists: Instituut voor Nederlandse Lexicologie, Matthias de Vrieshof 2, 2311 BZ Leiden, Netherlands; tel. (71) 5141648; fax (71) 5272115; e-mail secretariaat@rulxha.leidenuniv.nl; f. 1928; to further linguistic research, to co-ordinate activities undertaken for the advancement of linguistics, and to make the results of linguistic research known internationally; holds Congress every five years. Mems: 48 countries and two international linguistic organizations. Pres. S. A. WURM (Australia); Sec.-Gen. P. G. J. VAN STERKENBURG (Netherlands). Publs *Linguistic Bibliography* (annually).

OTHER ORGANIZATIONS

African Social and Environmental Studies Programme: Box 44777, Nairobi, Kenya; tel. (2) 747960; fax (2) 740817; f. 1968; develops and disseminates educational material on social and environmental studies, and education for all in eastern and southern Africa. Mems: 18 African countries. Chair. Prof. WILLIAM SENTEZA-KAJUBI; Exec. Dir Prof. PETER MUYANDA MUTEBI. Publs *African Social Studies Forum* (2 a year), teaching guides.

Arab Towns Organization: PO Box 4954, Safat 13050, Kuwait; tel. 4849705; fax 4849322; f. 1967 to help Arab towns in solving problems, preserving the natural environment and cultural heritage; runs a fund to provide loans on concessional terms for needy members, and an Institute for Urban Development (AUDI) based in Riyadh, Saudi Arabia; provides training courses for officials of Arab municipalities and holds seminars on urban development and other relevant subjects; offers awards for preservation of Arabic architecture. Mems: 380 towns. Dir-Gen. WASSEL MANSOUR; Sec.-Gen. ABD AL-AZIZ Y. AL-ADASANI. Publ. *Al-Madinah Al-Arabiyah* (every 2 months).

Association for the Study of the World Refugee Problem—AWR: Piazzale di Porta Pia 121, 00198 Rome, Italy; tel. (6) 44250159; f. 1951 to promote and co-ordinate scholarly research on refugee problems. Mems: 475 in 19 countries. Pres. FRANCO FOSCHI (Italy); Sec.-Gen. ALDO CLEMENTE (Italy). Publs *AWR Bulletin* (quarterly) in English, French, Italian and German; treatises on refugee problems (17 vols).

Council for the Development of Social Research in Africa—CODESRIA: BP 3304, Dakar, Senegal; tel. 25-98-22; telex 61339; fax 24-12-89; f. 1973; promotes research, provides conferences, working groups and information services. Mems: research institutes and university faculties in African countries. Exec. Sec. (vacant). Publs *Africa Development* (quarterly), *CODESRIA Bulletin* (quarterly), *Index of African Social Science Periodical Articles* (annually), directories of research.

Council for Research in Values and Philosophy: c/o Prof. G. F. McLean, School of Philosophy, Catholic University of America, Washington, DC 20064, USA; tel. (202) 319-5636; fax (202) 319-6089; e-mail cua-rvp@cua.edu; internet http://www.cua.edu/www/org/rvp; f. 1948. Mems: 33 teams from 24 countries. Pres. Prof. KENNETH L. SCHMITZ (Canada); Sec.-Gen. Prof. GEORGE F. MCLEAN (USA).

Eastern Regional Organisation for Planning and Housing: PAM Centre 4 and 6 Jalang Tangsi, 50480 Kuala Lumpur, Malaysia; tel. (3) 298-4136; fax (3) 718-3931; f. 1958 to promote and co-ordinate the study and practice of housing and regional town and country planning. Offices in Japan, India and Indonesia. Mems: 77 organizations and 315 individuals in 14 countries. Sec.-Gen. JOHN KOH SENG SIEW. Publs *EAROPH News and Notes* (monthly), *Town and Country Planning* (bibliography).

English-Speaking Union of the Commonwealth: Dartmouth House, 37 Charles St, Berkeley Sq., London, W1X 8AB, United Kingdom; tel. (171) 493-3328; fax (171) 495-6108; e-mail esu@mailbox.ulcc.ac.uk; f. 1918 to promote international understanding between Britain, the Commonwealth, the United States and Europe, in conjunction with the ESU of the USA. Mems: 70,000 (incl. USA). Chair. Baroness BRIGSTOCKE; Dir-Gen. VALERIE MITCHELL. Publ. *Concord.*

European Association for Population Studies: POB 11676, 2502 AR The Hague, Netherlands; tel. (70) 3565200; telex 31138; fax (70) 3647187; e-mail eaps@nidi.nl; f. 1983 to foster research and provide information on European population problems; organizes conferences, seminars and workshops. Mems: demographers from 40 countries. Exec. Sec. GIJS BEETS. Publ. *European Journal of Population/Revue Européenne de Démographie* (quarterly).

European Co-ordination Centre for Research and Documentation in Social Sciences: 1010 Vienna, Grünangergasse 2, Austria; tel. (1) 512-43-33-0; fax (1) 512-53-66-16; f. 1963 for promotion of contacts between East and West European countries in all areas of social sciences. Activities include co-ordination of international comparative research projects; training of social scientists in problems of international research; organization of conferences; exchange of information and documentation; administered by a Board of Directors (23 social scientists from East and West) and a permanent secretariat in Vienna. Pres. ØRJAR ØYEN (Norway); Dir L. KIUZADJAN. Publs *Vienna Centre Newsletter, ECSSID Bulletin*, and books.

European Society for Rural Sociology: c/o M. Villa, Centre for Rural Research, Univ. of Trondheim, 7055 Dragvoll, Norway; tel. 7359-1729; fax 7359-1275; f. 1957 to further research in, and co-ordination of, rural sociology and provide a centre for documentation of information. Mems: 300 individuals, institutions and associations in 29 European countries and nine countries outside Europe. Pres. Prof. GÖRAN DJURFELDT (Sweden); Sec. MARIANN VILLA (Norway). Publ. *Sociologia Ruralis* (quarterly).

Experiment in International Living: POB 595, Main St, Putney, VT 05346, USA; tel. (802) 387-4210; fax (802) 387-5783; f. 1932 as an international federation of non-profit educational and cultural exchange institutions, to create mutual understanding and respect among people of different nations, as a means of furthering peace. Mems: organizations in 25 countries. Dir ROBIN BITTERS.

Institute for International Sociological Research: POB 50858, Cologne 40, Wiener Weg 6, Germany; tel. (221) 486019; f. 1964; diplomatic and international affairs, social and political sciences, moral and behavioural sciences, arts and literature. Mems: 132 Life Fellows, 44 Assoc. Fellows; 14 research centres; affiliated institutes: Academy of Diplomacy and International Affairs, International Academy of Social and Moral Sciences, Arts and Letters. Pres., Chair. Exec. Cttee and Dir-Gen. Consul Dr EDWARD S. ELLENBERG. Publs *Diplomatic Observer* (monthly), *Newsletter, Bulletin* (quarterly), *Annual Report*, etc.

International African Institute: School of Oriental and African Studies, Thornhaugh St, Russell Sq., London, WC1H 0XG, United Kingdom; tel. (171) 323-6035; fax (171) 323-6118; f. 1926 to promote the study of African peoples, their languages, cultures and social life in their traditional and modern settings; international seminar programme brings together scholars from Africa and elsewhere; links scholars so as to facilitate research projects, especially in the social sciences. Mems: 1,500 in 97 countries. Chair. Prof. GEORGE C. BOND; Dir Prof. PAUL SPENCER. Publs *Africa* (quarterly), *Africa Bibliography* (annually).

International Association for Mass Communication Research: c/o Prof. Dr Cees J. Hamelink, IAMCR Administrative Office, Baden Powellweg 109-111, 1069 LD Amsterdam, Netherlands; tel. (20) 6101581; fax (20) 6104821; f. 1957 to stimulate interest in mass communication research and the dissemination of information about research and research needs, to improve communication practice, policy and research and training for journalism, to provide a forum for researchers and others involved in mass communication to meet and exchange information. Mems: over 2,000 in 65 countries. Pres. Prof. Dr CEES J. HAMELINK (Netherlands); Sec.-Gen. Dr ROBIN CHEESMAN (Denmark).

International Association of Applied Linguistics: c/o Prof. Andrew D. Cohen, ESL/ILASLL, 130 Klaeber Court, University of Minnesota, 320 16th Ave SE, Minneapolis, MN 55455, USA; tel. (612) 624-3806; fax (612) 624-4579; e-mail adcohen@tc.umn.edu; f. 1964; organizes seminars on applied linguistics, and a World Congress every three years. Mems: associations in 38 countries. Pres. Prof. CHRISTOPHER CANDLIN (Australia). Sec.-Gen. Prof. ANDREW D. COHEN (USA). Publs. *AILA Review* (annually), *AILA News* (quarterly).

International Association of Metropolitan City Libraries—INTAMEL: c/o Frances Schwenger, Metropolitan Toronto Reference Library, 789 Yonge St, Toronto, Ontario, Canada M4W 2G8; tel. (416) 393-7215; fax (416) 393-7229; f. 1967. Mems: 93 libraries in 28 countries. Sec. and Treas. FRANCES SCHWENGER.

International Committee for Social Sciences Information and Documentation: c/o Dr A. F. Marks, Herengracht 410 (Swidoc), 1017BX Amsterdam, Netherlands; tel. (20) 6225061; fax (20) 6238374; f. 1950 to collect and disseminate information on documentation services in social sciences, to help improve documentation, to advise societies on problems of documentation and to draw up rules likely to improve the presentation of all documents. Members from international associations specializing in social sciences or in documentation, and from other specialized fields. Sec.-Gen. ARNAUD F. MARKS (Netherlands). Publs *International Bibliography of the Social Sciences* (annually), *Newsletter* (2 a year).

International Council on Archives: 60 rue des Francs-Bourgeois, 75003 Paris, France; tel. 1-40-27-63-06; fax 1-42-72-20-65; e-mail 100640.54@compuserve.com; f. 1948. Mems: 1,394 in 158 countries; work includes conservation, training, automation, development of standards for description of archives; nine regional branches. Pres. WANG GANG; Sec.-Gen. CHARLES KECSKEMETI (France). Publs *Archivum* (annually), *Janus* (2 a year), *ICA Bulletin* (2 a year), *Directory* (annually).

International Ergonomics Association: BP 2025, 3500 HA Utrecht, Netherlands; tel. (30) 35-44-55; fax (30) 35-76-39; f. 1957 to bring together organizations and persons interested in the scientific study of human work and its environment; to establish international contacts among those specializing in this field, co-operate with employers' associations and trade unions in order to encourage the practical application of ergonomic sciences in industries, and promote scientific research in this field. Mems: 17 federated societies. Pres. ILKKA KUORINKA (Finland); Sec.-Gen. Prof. D. P. ROOKMAAKER. Publ. *Ergonomics* (monthly).

International Federation for Housing and Planning: Wassenaarseweg 43, 2596 CG The Hague, Netherlands; tel. (70) 3244557; fax (70) 3282085; e-mail ifhp.nl@inter.nl.net; internet http://www.ifhp.org; f. 1913 to study and promote the improvement of housing, the theory and practice of town planning inclusive of the creation of new agglomerations and the planning of territories at regional, national and international levels; world congress and international conference held every 2 years. Mems: 200 organizations and 300 individuals in 65 countries. Pres. IRENE WIESE-VON OFEN (Germany); Sec.-Gen. E. E. VAN HYLCKAMA VLIEG (Netherlands). Publ. *Newsletter* (4 a year).

International Federation of Institutes for Socio-religious Research: 1 place Montesquieu, Bte 13, 1348 Louvain-la-neuve, Belgium; f. 1958; federates centres engaged in undertaking scientific research in order to analyse and discover the social and religious phenomena at work in contemporary society. Mems: institutes in 26 countries. Pres. Canon Fr. HOUTART (Belgium); Sec. F. GENDEBIEN. Publ. *Social Compass (International Review of Sociology of Religion)* (quarterly, in English and French).

International Federation of Social Science Organizations: Via dei Laghi 14, 00198 Rome, Italy; tel. and fax (6) 884-8943; f. 1979 to assist research and teaching in the social sciences, and to facilitate co-operation and enlist mutual assistance in the planning and evaluation of programmes of major importance to members. Mems: 23 organizations. Pres. Prof. CARMENCITA T. AGUILAR; Sec.-Gen. Prof. J. BLAHOZ. Publs *Newsletter, International Directory of Social Science Organizations.*

International Federation of Vexillological Associations: Box 580, Winchester, MA 01890, USA; tel. (718) 729-9410; fax (718) 721-4817; f. 1967 to promote through its member organizations the scientific study of the history and symbolism of flags, and especially to hold International Congresses every two years and sanction international standards for scientific flag study. Mems: 39 institutions and associations in 27 countries. Pres. Prof. MICHEL LUPANT (Belgium); Liaison Officer WHITNEY SMITH. Publs *Recueil* (every 2 years), *The Flag Bulletin* (every 2 months), *Info FIAV* (every 4 months).

International Institute for Ligurian Studies: Museo Bicknell, via Romana 39, 18012 Bordighera, Italy; tel. (184) 263601; fax (184) 266421; f. 1947 to conduct research on ancient monuments and regional traditions in the north-west arc of the Mediterranean (France and Italy). Library of 80,000 vols. Mems: in France, Italy, Spain, Switzerland. Dir Prof. CARLO VARALDO (Italy).

International Institute of Administrative Sciences: 1 rue Defacqz, POB 11, 1000 Brussels, Belgium; tel. (2) 538-91-65; fax (2) 537-97-02; e-mail iias@infoboard.be; f. 1930 for comparative examination of administrative experience in the various countries; research and programmes for improving administrative law and practices and for technical assistance; library of 15,000 vols; consultative status with UN, UNESCO and ILO; international congresses. Mems: 45 mem. states, 62 national sections, 11 international governmental organizations, 64 corporate mems, 14 individual members. Pres. DAVID BROWN (Canada); Dir-Gen. TURKIA OULD DADDAH (Mauritania). Publs *International Review of Administrative Sciences* (quarterly), *Interadmin* (3 a year).

International Institute of Sociology: c/o Facoltà di Scienze Politiche, Università di Roma 'La Sapienza', Piazzale A. Moro 5, 00185 Rome, Italy; tel. (6) 3451017; fax (6) 3451017; f. 1893 to enable sociologists to meet and study sociological questions. Mems: 300, representing 45 countries. Pres. PAOLO AMMASSARI (Italy); Gen. Sec. ALAN HEDLEY. Publ. *The Annals of the IIS.*

International Numismatic Commission: Coins and Medals Dept, British Museum, London, WC1B 3DG, United Kingdom; tel. (171) 323-8227; fax (171) 323-8171; f. 1936; enables co-operation between scholars studying coins and medals. Mems: numismatic organizations in 35 countries. Pres. C. MORRISSON (France); Sec. ANDREW BURNETT.

International Peace Academy: 777 United Nations Plaza, New York, NY 10017, USA; tel. (212) 949-8480; fax (212) 983-8246; e-mail ipa@ipapost.ipacademy.org; internet http://www.ipacademy.org/; f. 1967 to educate government officials in the procedures needed for conflict resolution, peace-keeping, mediation and negotiation, through international training seminars and publications; off-the-record meetings are also conducted to gain complete understanding of a specific conflict. Chair. RITA E. HAUSER; Pres. OLARA A. OTUNNU. Publs *Annual Report, Newsletter* (2 a year).

International Peace Research Association: c/o Information Unit, Peace Research Bonn, Beethovenallee 4, 53173 Bonn, Germany; tel. (228) 356032; fax (228) 356050; e-mail ipra@bonn.IZSOZ.de; f. 1964 to encourage interdisciplinary research on the conditions of peace and the causes of war. Mems: 150 corporate, five regional branches, 1,007 individuals, in 95 countries. Sec.-Gen. KARLHEINZ KOPPE (Germany). Publ. *IPRA Newsletter* (4 a year).

International Social Science Council—ISSC: Maison de l'UNESCO, 1 rue Miollis, 75732 Paris Cédex 15, France; tel. 1-45-68-27-98; fax 1-43-06-87-98; e-mail issclak@zcc.net; f. 1952; since 1973 a federation of the organizations listed below. Aims: the advancement of the social sciences throughout the world and their application to the major problems of the world; the spread of co-operation at an international level between specialists in the social sciences. ISSC has a Standing Committee for Conceptual and Terminological Analysis (COCTA); and programmes on International Human Dimensions of Global Environmental Change (IHDP), co-sponsored by the International Council of Scientific Unions (q.v.), Comparative Research on Poverty (CROP) and Conflict Early Warning System Research (CEWS). Pres. ELSE ØYEN (Norway); Sec.-Gen. LESZEK A. KOSINSKI (Canada).

Associations Federated to the ISSC

(details of these organizations will be found under their appropriate category elsewhere in the International Organizations section)

International Association of Legal Sciences (p. 275).
International Economic Association (p. 264).
International Federation of Social Science Organizations (p. 295).
International Geographical Union (p. 288).
International Institute of Administrative Sciences (p. 295).
International Law Association (p. 276).
International Peace Research Association (p. 295).
International Political Science Association (p. 270).
International Sociological Association (see below).
International Union for the Scientific Study of Population (p. 296).
International Union of Anthropological and Ethnological Sciences (p. 294).
International Union of Psychological Science (p. 288).
World Association for Public Opinion Research (p. 296).
World Federation for Mental Health (p. 282).

International Society of Social Defence and Humane Criminal Policy: c/o Centro nazionale di prevenzione e difesa sociale, Piazza Castello 3, 20121 Milan, Italy; tel. (2) 86460714; fax (2) 72008431; e-mail cnpds.ispac@iol.it; f. 1945 to combat crime, to protect society and to prevent citizens from being tempted to commit criminal actions. Mems in 34 countries. Pres. SIMONE ROZES (France); Sec.-Gen. EDMONDO BAUTI LIBERATI (Italy). Publ. *Cahiers de défense sociale* (annually).

International Sociological Association: c/o Faculty of Political Sciences and Sociology, Universidad Complutense, 28223 Madrid, Spain; tel. (1) 3527650; fax (1) 3524945; e-mail isa@sis.ucm.es; internet http://www.ucm.es/info/isa; f. 1949 to promote sociological knowledge, facilitate contacts between sociologists, encourage the dissemination and exchange of information and facilities and stimulate research; has 50 research committees on various aspects of sociology; holds World Congresses every four years (14th Congress:

Montreal, Canada, 1998). Pres. I. WALLERSTEIN (USA); Exec. Sec. IZABELA BARLINSKA. Publs *Current Sociology* (3 a year), *International Sociology* (4 a year), *Sage Studies in International Sociology* (based on World Congress).

International Statistical Institute: POB 950, Prinses Beatrixlaan 428, 2270 AZ Voorburg, Netherlands; tel. (70) 3375737; fax (70) 3860025; e-mail isi@cs.vu.nl; f. 1885; devoted to the development and improvement of statistical methods and their application throughout the world; administers among others a statistical education centre in Calcutta in co-operation with the Indian Statistical Institute; executes international research programmes. Mems: 1,900 ordinary mems; 10 hon. mems; 110 ex-officio mems; 75 corporate mems; 45 affiliated organizations; 32 national statistical societies. Pres. W. VAN ZWET; Dir Permanent Office M. P. R. VAN DEN BROECKE. Publs *Bulletin of the International Statistical Institute* (proceedings of biennial sessions), *International Statistical Review* (3 a year), *Short Book Reviews* (3 a year), *Statistical Theory and Method Abstracts* (quarterly), *ISI Newsletter* (quarterly), *Directories* (every 2 years).

International Studies Association: Social Science 324, Univ. of Arizona, Tucson, AZ 85721, USA; tel. (520) 621-7715; fax (520) 621-5780; e-mail isa@arizona.edu; internet http://www.isanet.org; f. 1959; links those whose professional concerns extend beyond their own national boundaries (government officials, representatives of business and industry, and scholars). Mems: 3,500 in 60 countries. Pres. JAMES CAPORASO; Exec. Dir THOMAS J. VOLGY. Publs *International Studies Quarterly, ISA Newsletter, ISA Notes.*

International Union for the Scientific Study of Population: 34 rue des Augustins, 4000 Liège, Belgium; tel. (4) 222-40-80; telex 42648; fax (4) 222-38-47; e-mail fdevpop1@vm1.ulg.ac.be; f. 1928 to advance the progress of quantitative and qualitative demography as a science. Mems: 1,725 in 128 countries. Pres. JOSÉ ALBERTO M. DE CARVALHO. Publs *IUSSP Newsletter* and books on population.

Mensa International: 15 The Ivories, 6–8 Northampton St, London, N1 2HY, United Kingdom; tel. (171) 226-6891; fax (171) 226-7059; f. 1946 to identify and foster intelligence for the benefit of humanity. Members are individuals who score in a recognized intelligence test higher than 98% of people in general: there are 100,000 mems world-wide. Pres. Chair. VELMA JEREMIAH (USA); Exec. Dir E. J. VINCENT (UK). Publ. *Mensa International Journal* (monthly).

Third World Forum: 39 Dokki St, POB 43, Orman, Cairo, Egypt; tel. (2) 3488092; fax (2) 3480668; e-mail isabry@idsc1.gov.eg; f. 1973 to link social scientists and others from the developing countries, to discuss alternative development policies and encourage research; undertaking Egypt 2020 research project. Regional offices in Egypt, Mexico, Senegal and Sri Lanka. Mems: individuals in more than 50 countries. Chair. ISMAIL-SABRI ABDALLA.

World Association for Public Opinion Research: c/o The School of Journalism and Mass Communication, University of North Carolina, CB 3365, Howell Hall, Chapel Hill, NC 27599-3365, USA; tel. (919) 962-6396; fax (919) 962-4079; e-mail kcole@unc.edu; f. 1947 to establish and promote contacts between persons in the field of survey research on opinions, attitudes and behaviour of people in the various countries of the world; to further the use of objective, scientific survey research in national and international affairs. Mems: 460 from 50 countries. Sec. KATHERINE COLE. Publs *WAPOR Newsletter* (quarterly), *International Journal of Public Opinion* (quarterly).

World Society for Ekistics: c/o Athens Centre of Ekistics, 24 Strat. Syndesmou St, 106 73 Athens, Greece; tel. (1) 3623216; telex fax (1) 3629337; f. 1965; aims to promote knowledge and ideas concerning human settlements through research, publications and conferences; to recognize the benefits and necessity of an interdisciplinary approach to the needs of human settlements. Pres. CHARLES M. CORREA; Sec.-Gen. P. PSOMOPOULOS.

Social Welfare and Human Rights

African Commission on Human and People's Rights: Kairaba Ave, POB 673, Banjul, The Gambia; tel. 392962; telex 2346; fax 390764; f. 1987; meets twice a year for 10 days in March and Oct.; the Commission comprises 11 members. Its mandate is to monitor compliance with the African Charter on Human and People's Rights (ratified in 1986), and it investigates claims of human rights abuses perpetrated by govts that have ratified the Charter. Claims may be brought by other African govts, the victims themselves, or by a third party. Pres. ISAAC NGUEMA; Sec. GERMAIN BARICAKO (Burundi).

Aid to Displaced Persons and its European Villages: 35 rue du Marché, 4500 Huy, Belgium; tel. (85) 21-34-81; f. 1957 to carry on and develop work begun by the Belgian association Aid to Displaced Persons; aims to provide material and moral aid for refugees; European Villages established at Aachen, Bregenz, Augsburg, Berchem-Ste-Agathe, Spiesen, Euskirchen, Wuppertal as centres for refugees. Pres. J. EECKHOUT (Belgium).

Amnesty International: 1 Easton St, London, WC1X 8DJ, United Kingdom; tel. (171) 413-5500; telex 28502; fax (171) 956-1157; e-mail amnestyis@gn.apc.org; internet http://www.amnesty.org/; f. 1961; an independent worldwide movement, campaigning impartially for the release of all prisoners of conscience, fair and prompt trials for all political prisoners, the abolition of torture and the death penalty and the end of extrajudicial executions and 'disappearances'; also opposes abuses by opposition groups (hostage-taking, torture and arbitrary killings); financed by donations. Mems: 1.1m. in over 150 countries; 4,349 locally organized groups in over 80 countries; nationally organized sections in 54 countries. Sec.-Gen. PIERRE SANÉ (Senegal). Publs *International Newsletter* (monthly), *Annual Report*, other country reports.

Anti-Slavery International: Stableyard, Broomgrove Rd, London, SW9 9TL, United Kingdom; tel. (171) 924-9555; fax (171) 738-4110; e-mail antislavery@gn.apc.org; f. 1839 to eradicate slavery and forced labour in all their forms, to promote the well-being of indigenous peoples, and to protect human rights in accordance with the Universal Declaration of Human Rights, 1948. Mems: 1,800 members in 30 countries. Chair. REGGIE NORTON; Dir MIKE DOTTRIDGE. Publs *Annual Report, Anti-Slavery Reporter* (4 a year), special reports on research.

Associated Country Women of the World: Vincent House, Vincent Sq., London, SW1P 2NB, United Kingdom; tel. (171) 834-8635; f. 1933; aims to aid the economic and social development of countrywomen and home-makers of all nations; to promote international goodwill and understanding; and to work to alleviate poverty, and promote good health and education. Mems: several million. Gen. Sec. ANNA FROST. Publ. *The Countrywoman* (quarterly).

Association Internationale de la Mutualité (International Association for Mutual Benefit Funds): 8–10 rue de Hesse, 1204 Geneva, Switzerland; tel. (22) 3114528; fax (22) 3114541; f. 1950; aims to develop the sound management of mutual benefits funds, primarily in health insurance, in all countries. Mems: 45 health finance orgs in 23 countries. Pres. GEERT JAN HAMILTON (Netherlands); Sec.-Gen. TIMOTHY NATER (USA).

Aviation sans frontières—ASF: Brussels National Airport, Brucargo 706, POB 7513/14, 1931 Brucargo, Belgium; tel. (2) 722-35-35; fax (2) 722-36-00; f. 1980 to make available the resources of the aviation industry to humanitarian organizations, for carrying supplies and equipment at minimum cost, both on long-distance flights and locally. Mems: about 200 pilots and other airline staff. Pres. LEON DIDDEN.

Catholic International Union for Social Service: 31 rue de la Citronelle, 1348 Louvaine-la-Neuve, Belgium; tel. (10) 45-25-13; f. 1925 to develop social service on the basis of Christian doctrine; to unite Catholic social schools and social workers' associations in all countries to promote their foundation; to represent at the international level the Catholic viewpoint as it affects social service. Mems: 172 schools of social service, 26 associations of social workers, 52 individual members. Exec. Sec. ALEXANDRE CARLSON. Publs *Service Social dans le monde* (quarterly), *News Bulletin, Bulletin de Liaison, Boletín de Noticias* (quarterly).

Co-ordinating Committee for International Voluntary Service—CCIVS: Maison de l'UNESCO, 1 rue Miollis, 75732 Paris Cédex 15, France; tel. 1-45-68-27-31; fax 1-42-73-05-21; f. 1948; acts as an information centre and co-ordinating body for youth voluntary service organizations all over the world. Affiliated mems: 142 organizations. Pres. T. PICQUART; Dir N. WATT. Publs *News from CCIVS* (4 a year), handbook, directories.

EIRENE—International Christian Service for Peace: 56503 Neuwied, Postfach 1322, Germany; tel. (2631) 83790; fax (2631) 31160; e-mail eirene-intcoln.comlink.apc.org; f. 1957; works in Africa and Latin America (professional training, apprenticeship programmes, agricultural work and co-operatives), Europe and the USA (volunteer programmes in co-operation with peace groups). Gen. Sec. EKKEHARD FRICKE.

European Federation for the Welfare of the Elderly—EURAG: Wielandg. 7, 1 Stock, 8010 Graz, Austria; tel. (316) 81-46-08; fax (316) 81-47-67; f. 1962 for the exchange of experience among member associations; practical co-operation among member organizations to achieve their objectives in the field of ageing; representation of the interests of members before international organizations; promotion of understanding and co-operation in matters of social welfare; to draw attention to the problems of old age. Mems: organizations in 25 countries. Pres. EDMÉE MANGERS-ANEN (Luxembourg); Sec.-Gen. GREGOR HAMMERL (Austria). Publs (in English, French, German and Italian) *EURAG Newsletter* (quarterly), *EURAG Information* (monthly).

Federation of Asian Women's Associations—FAWA: Centro Escolar University, 9 Mendiola St, San Miguel, Manila, Philippines;

tel. 741-04-46; f. 1959 to provide closer relations, and bring about joint efforts among Asians, particularly among the women, through mutual appreciation of cultural, moral and socio-economic values. Mems: 415,000. Pres. MADELEINE BORDALLO (Guam); Sec. EVELINA McDONALD (Guam). Publ. *FAWA News Bulletin* (every 3 months).

Interamerican Conference on Social Security (Conferencia Interamericano de Seguridad Social—CISS): Calle San Ramon s/n Unidad Independencia, Apdo 99089, San Jerónimo Lidice, 10100 México DF, Mexico; tel. (5) 595-01-77; fax (5) 683-85-24; e-mail ciss@data.net.mx; internet http://www.ciss.org.mx; f. 1942 to contribute to the development of social security in the countries of the Americas and to co-operate with social security institutions. CISS bodies are: the General Assembly, the Permanent Interamerican Committee on Social Security, the Secretariat General, the American Commissions of Social Security and the Interamerican Center for Social Security Studies. Mems: social security institutions in 35 countries. Pres. GENARO BORREGO ESTRADA (Mexico); Sec.-Gen. MARIA ELVIRA CONTRERAS SAUCEDO (Mexico). Publs *Social Security Journal,* monographs, study series.

International Abolitionist Federation: 16 rue Cassette, 75006 Paris, France; f. 1875 for the abolition of the organization and exploitation of prostitution by public authorities, sex discrimination, and for the rehabilitation of the victims of traffic and prostitution; holds international congress every three years and organizes regional conferences to raise awareness regarding the cultural, religious and traditional practices which affect adversely the lives of women and children. Affiliated organizations in 17 countries. Corresponding mems in 40 countries. Pres. BRIGITTE POLONOVSKI (Switzerland); Exec. Sec. HÉLÈNE SACKSTEIN (France). Publ. *IAF Information* (3 a year).

International Association against Noise: Hirschenplatz 7, 6004 Lucerne, Switzerland; tel. (41) 513013; fax (41) 529093; f. 1959 to promote noise-control at an international level; to promote co-operation and the exchange of experience and prepare supranational measures; issues information, carries out research, organizes conferences, and assists national anti-noise associations. Mems: 17, and three associate mems. Pres. KAREL NOVOTNÝ (Czech Republic); Sec. Dr WILLY AECHERLI (Switzerland).

International Association of Children's International Summer Villages—CISV International: Mea House, Ellison Place, Newcastle upon Tyne, NE1 8XS, United Kingdom; tel. (191) 232-4998; fax (191) 261-4710; e-mail cisvio@dial.pipex.com; f. 1950 to conduct International Camps for children and young people between the ages of 11 and 18. Mems: 40,268. International Pres. DAVID LISTER; Sec.-Gen. JOSEPH G. BANKS. Publs *CISV News* (2 a year), *Annual Report, Local Work Magazine* (2 a year), *Interspectives* (annually).

International Association for Education to a Life without Drugs (Internationaler Verband für Erziehung zu suchtmittelfreiem Leben—IVES): c/o W. Stuber, Lerchenweg 13, 4912 Aarwangen, Switzerland; tel. and fax (62) 9222673; f. 1954 (as the International Association for Temperance Education) to promote international co-operation in education on the dangers of alcohol and drugs; collection and distribution of information on drugs; maintains regular contact with national and international organizations active in these fields; holds conferences. Mems: 77,000 in 10 countries. Pres. WILLY STUBER; Sec. ULJAS SYVÄNIEMI.

International Association for Suicide Prevention: c/o Ms M. Campos, IASP Central Administrative Office, 1725 West Harrison St, Suite 955, Chicago, IL 60612, USA; tel. (312) 942-7208; fax (312) 942-2177; f. 1960 to establish an organization where individuals and agencies of various disciplines and professions from different countries can find a common platform for interchange of acquired experience, literature and information about suicide; disseminates information; arranges special training; encourages and carries out research; organizes the Biannual International Congress for Suicide Prevention. Mems: 340 individuals and societies, in 55 countries of all continents. Pres. Prof. Dr ROBERT GOLDNEY. Publ. *Crisis* (quarterly).

International Association of Schools of Social Work: 1010 Vienna, Palais Palfy, Josefplatz 6, Austria; tel. (1) 513-4297; fax (1) 513-8468; f. 1928 to provide international leadership and encourage high standards in social work education. Mems: 1,600 schools of social work in 70 countries, and 25 national associations of schools. Pres. Dr RALPH GARBER (Canada); Sec.-Gen. VERA MEHTA (India). Publs *International Social Work* (quarterly), *Directory of Members, IASSW News.*

International Association of Workers for Troubled Children and Youth: 22 rue Halevy, 59000 Lille, France; tel. 3-20-93-70-16; fax 3-20-09-18-39; f. 1951 to promote the profession of specialized social workers for troubled children and youth; to provide a centre of information about child welfare and encourage co-operation between the members; 1997 Congress: Brescia, Italy. Mems: national and regional public or private associations from 22 countries and individual members in many other countries. Pres. GUSTAVO VELASTEGUI (France); Sec.-Gen. ISABELLE PERSOONS (Belgium).

International Catholic Migration Commission: CP 96, 37–39 rue de Vermont, 1211 Geneva 20, Switzerland; tel. (22) 7334150; telex 414122; fax (22) 7347929; f. 1951; offers migration aid programmes to those who are not in a position to secure by themselves their resettlement elsewhere; grants interest-free travel loans; assists refugees on a worldwide basis, helping with all social and technical problems. Sub-committees dealing with Europe and Latin America. Mems: in 85 countries. Pres. MICHAEL WHITELEY (Australia); Sec.-Gen. Dr ANDRÉ N. VAN CHAU (USA). Publs *Annual Report, Migrations, Migration News, ICMC Today.*

International Centre for Childhood and the Family (Centre international de l'enfance et de la famille): Château de Longchamp, carrefour de Longchamp, Bois de Boulogne, 75016 Paris, France; tel. 1-44-30-20-00; fax 1-45-25-73-67; e-mail cidef@compuserve.com; f. 1997 by merger of the International Children's Centre and the Institute for Childhood and the Family; serves as a national and international centre of excellence for health and social issues affecting children and families, a national reference centre for childhood immunizations and a WHO collaborating centre on child, adolescent and family health and on immunization; facilitates co-operation between researchers, professionals, decision-makers and other associations and institutions in the field; provides documentation centre, publications and bibliographical data base. Pres. of Admin. Council Prof. BERNARD DEBRÉ; Dir-Gen. Dr OLIVER BRASSEUR. Publ. *L'enfant en milieu tropical* (5 a year).

International Christian Federation for the Prevention of Alcoholism and Drug Addiction: 20A Ancienne Route, Apt. No 42, 1218 Grand-Saconnex, Geneva, Switzerland; tel. (22) 7888158; fax (22) 7888136; e-mail jonathan@iprolink.ch; f. 1960, reconstituted 1980 to promote worldwide education and remedial work through the churches, to co-ordinate Christian concern about alcohol and drug abuse, in co-operation with the World Council of Churches and WHO. Chair. KARIN ISRAELSSON (Sweden); Gen. Sec. JONATHAN N. GNANADASON.

International Civil Defence Organisation: 10–12 chemin de Surville, 1213 Petit-Lancy-Geneva, Switzerland; tel. (22) 7934433; fax (22) 7934428; f. 1931, present statutes in force 1972; aims to intensify and co-ordinate on a world-wide scale the development and improvement of organization, means and techniques for preventing and reducing the consequences of natural disasters in peacetime or of the use of weapons in time of conflict. Sec.-Gen. SADOK ZNAÏDI (Tunisia). Publs *International Civil Defence Journal* (quarterly, in English, French, Spanish, Russian and Arabic).

International Commission for the Prevention of Alcoholism and Drug Dependency: 12501 Old Columbia Pike, Silver Spring, MD 20904-6600 USA; tel. (301) 680-6719; telex 440186; fax (301) 680-6090; f. 1952 to encourage scientific research on intoxication by alcohol, its physiological, mental and moral effects on the individual, and its effect on the community; ninth World Congress, Hamburg, Germany, 1994. Mems: individuals in 90 countries. Exec. Dir THOMAS R. NESLUND. Publ. *ICPA Quarterly.*

International Council of Voluntary Agencies: CP 216, 1211 Geneva 21, Switzerland; tel. (22) 7326600; fax (22) 9080770; f. 1962 to provide a forum for voluntary humanitarian and development agencies. Mems: 98 non-governmental organizations. Chair. TRYGVE G. NORDBY; Exec. Dir RUDOLPH VON BERNUTH. Publs *Annual Report, ICVA Forum* (monthly).

International Council of Women: c/o 13 rue Caumartin, 75009 Paris, France; tel. 1-47-42-19-40; fax 1-42-66-26-23; f. 1888 to bring together in international affiliation National Councils of Women from all continents for consultation and joint action in order to promote equal rights for men and women and the integration of women in development and in decision-making; five standing committees. Mems: 78 national councils. Pres. PNINA HERZOG; Sec.-Gen. MARIE-CHRISTINE LAFARGUE.

International Council on Alcohol and Addictions: CP 189, 1001 Lausanne, Switzerland; tel. (21) 3209865; fax (21) 3209817; e-mail icaa@pingnet.ch; f. 1907; organizes training courses, congresses, symposia and seminars in different countries. Mems: affiliated organizations in 74 countries, as well as individual members. Pres. Dr IBRAHIM AL-AWAJI (Saudi Arabia); Exec. Dir Dr EVA TONGUE (UK). Publs *ICAA News* (quarterly), *Alcoholism* (2 a year).

International Council on Disability: c/o Rehabilitation International, 25 East 21st St, New York, NY 10010, USA; tel. (212) 420-1500; telex 446412; f. 1953 to assist the UN and its specialized agencies to develop a well co-ordinated international programme for rehabilitation of the handicapped. Mems: 66 organizations. Pres. SHEIKH AL-GHANIM; Sec.-Gen. SUSAN HAMMERMAN.

International Council on Jewish Social and Welfare Services: 75 rue de Lyon, 1211 Geneva 13, Switzerland; tel. (22) 3449000; fax (22) 3457013; f. 1961; functions include the exchange of views and information among member agencies concerning the problems of

Jewish social and welfare services including medical care, old age, welfare, child care, rehabilitation, technical assistance, vocational training, agricultural and other resettlement, economic assistance, refugees, migration, integration and related problems; representation of views to governments and international organizations. Mems: six national and international organizations. Exec. Sec. CHERYL MARINER.

International Council on Social Welfare: 380 St Antoine St West, Suite 3200, Montreal H2Y 3X7, Canada; tel. (514) 287-3280; fax (514) 987-1567; e-mail icswintl@web.apc.org; f. 1928 to provide an international forum for the discussion of social work and related issues; to promote interest in social welfare; holds international conference every two years; provides documentation and information services. Mems: 68 national committees, 25 international organizations. Pres. DIRK JARRE (Germany); Sec.-Gen. SIRPA UTRIAINEN (Finland). Publs *International Social Work* (quarterly), *ICSW Newsletter* (quarterly).

International Dachau Committee: 95 ave des Ortolans, 1170 Brussels, Belgium; f. 1958 to perpetuate the memory of the political prisoners of Dachau; to manifest the friendship and solidarity of former prisoners whatever their beliefs or nationality; to maintain the ideals of their resistance, liberty, tolerance and respect for persons and nations; and to maintain the former concentration camp at Dachau as a museum and international memorial. Sec.-Gen. JEAN SAMUEL. Publ. *Bulletin Officiel du Comité International de Dachau* (2 a year).

International Federation of the Blue Cross: CP 6813, 3001 Bern, Switzerland; tel. (31) 3005860; fax (31) 3005869; f. 1877 to aid the victims of intemperance and drug addicts, and to take part in the general movement against alcoholism. Pres. Pastor RAYMOND BASSIN (Switzerland); Gen. Sec. HANS RÜTTIMAN.

International Federation of Disabled Workers and Civilian Handicapped: 53173 Bonn, Beethovenallee 56–58, Germany; tel. (228) 95640; fax (228) 9564312; e-mail fimitic@t-online.de; f. 1953 to bring together representatives of the disabled and handicapped into an international non-political organization under the guidance of the disabled themselves; to promote greater opportunities for the disabled; to create rehabilitation centres; to act as a co-ordinating body for all similar national organizations. Mems: national groups from 28 European countries, and corresponding mems from eight countries. Pres. MARCEL ROYEZ (France); Gen. Sec. MARIJA ŠTIGLIC (Germany). Publs *Bulletin, Nouvelles.*

International Federation of Educative Communities: Freyastrasse 14, 8004 Zürich, Switzerland; tel. (1) 2983434; fax (1) 2983435; f. 1948 under the auspices of UNESCO to co-ordinate the work of national associations, and to promote the international exchange of knowledge and experience in the field of childcare. Mems: national associations from 20 European countries, Israel, Canada, the USA and South Africa. Pres. ROBERT SOISSON (Luxembourg); Gen. Sec. THOMAS MÄCHLER (Switzerland). Publ. *Bulletin* (2 a year).

International Federation of Human Rights Leagues—FIDH: 17 passage de la Main d'Or, 75011 Paris, France; tel. 1-43-55-25-28; fax 1-43-55-18-80; e-mail fidh@hol.fr; internet http://www.fidh.imaginet.fr; f. 1922; promotes the implementation of the Universal Declaration of Human Rights and other instruments of human rights protection; aims to raise awareness and alert public opinion to issues of human rights violations and undertakes investigation and observation missions, training and uses its consultative and observer status to lobby international authorities. Mems 105 national leagues in more than 80 countries. Pres. PATRICK BAUDOUIN. Publs *Lettre* (2 a month), monthly mission reports.

International Federation of Social Workers—IFSW: PO Box 4649, Sofienberg, 0506 Oslo, Norway; tel. 22-03-11-52; fax 22-03-11-14; e-mail secr.gen@ifsw.org; internet http://www.ifsw.org; f. 1928 as International Permanent Secretariat of Social Workers; present name adopted 1950; aims to promote social work as a profession through international co-operation concerning standards, training, ethics and working conditions; organizes international conferences; represents the profession at the UN and other international bodies; supports national associations of social workers. Mems: national associations in 61 countries. Pres. ELIS ENVALL (Sweden); Sec.-Gen. TOM JOHANNESEN (Norway).

International League against Racism and Antisemitism: CP 1754, 1211 Geneva 1, Switzerland; tel. (22) 7310633; fax (22) 7370634; e-mail licra@mnet.ch; f. 1927; mems in 17 countries. Pres. PIERRE AIDENBAUM (France).

International League for Human Rights: 432 Park Avenue South, 11th Floor, New York, NY 10016, USA; tel. (212) 684-1221; fax (212) 684-1696; f. 1942 to implement political, civil, social, economic and cultural rights contained in the Universal Declaration of Human Rights adopted by the United Nations and to support and protect defenders of human rights world-wide. Mems: individuals, national affiliates and correspondents throughout the world. Exec. Dir CHARLES H. NORCHI. Publs *In-Brief, Human Rights Bulletin,* human rights reports.

International League of Societies for Persons with Mental Handicap (European Association): Galeries de la Toison d'Or, 29 chaussée d'Ixelles, Ste 393/35, 1050 Brussels, Belgium; tel. (2) 502-28-15; fax (2) 502-80-10; e-mail secretariat@ilsmh-ea.be; f. 1988 to promote the interests of the mentally handicapped without regard to nationality, race or creed; furthers co-operation between national bodies; organizes congresses. Mems: 19 societies in the 15 EU member states.

International Planned Parenthood Federation—IPPF: Regent's College, Inner Circle, Regent's Park, London, NW1 4NS, United Kingdom; tel. (171) 487-7900; telex 919573; fax (171) 487-7950; f. 1952; aims to promote and support sexual and reproductive health and family planning services throughout the world, and to increase understanding of population problems; offers technical assistance and training; collaborates with other international organizations and provides information. Mems: independent family planning associations in over 150 countries. Pres. Dr ATTIYA INAYATULLAH; Sec.-Gen. INGAR BRUEGGEMANN. Publs *People and the Planet* (quarterly), *Planned Parenthood Challenges* (2 a year), *Medical Bulletin* (every 2 months), *Open File* (monthly), *Annual Report.*

International Prisoners Aid Association: c/o Dr Ali, Department of Sociology, University of Louisville, Louisville, KY 40292, USA; tel. (502) 588-6836; fax (502) 852-7042; f. 1950; to improve prisoners' aid services for rehabilitation of the individual and protection of society. Mems: national federations in 29 countries. Pres. Dr WOLFGANG DOLEISCH (Austria); Exec. Dir Dr BADR-EL-DIN ALI. Publ. *Newsletter* (3 a year).

International Scout and Guide Fellowship—ISGF: 9 rue du Champ de Mars, bte 14, 1050 Brussels, Belgium; tel. (2) 511-46-95; fax (2) 511-84-36; e-mail isgf@azcadis.be; f. 1953 to help adult scouts and guides to keep alive the spirit of the Scout and Guide Promise and Laws in their own lives; to bring that spirit into the communities in which they live and work; to establish liaison and co-operation between national organizations for former scouts and guides; to encourage the founding of an organization in any country where no such organization exists; to promote friendship amongst former scouts and guides throughout the world. Mems: 80,000 in 43 member states. Chair. of Committee MILES KINCHIN; Sec.-Gen. NAÏC PIRARD. Publ. *World Gazette Mondiale* (quarterly).

International Social Security Association: Case Postale No. 1, 1211 Geneva 22, Switzerland; tel. (22) 7996617; telex 415647; fax (22) 7986385; f. 1927 to promote the development of social security through the improvement of techniques and administration. Mems: 340 institutions in 127 countries. Pres. KARL GUSTAF SCHERMAN (Sweden); Sec.-Gen. DALMER HOSKINS (USA). Publs *International Social Security Review* (quarterly, English, French, German, Spanish), *Trends in Social Security* (quarterly), *African News Sheet* (English and French), *Asian News Sheet, Social Security Documentation* (African, Asian, European and American series).

International Social Service: 32 quai du Seujet, 1201 Geneva, Switzerland; tel. (22) 7317454; fax (22) 7380949; e-mail iss.gs@span.ch; f. 1921 to aid families and individuals whose problems require services beyond the boundaries of the country in which they live and where the solution of these problems depends upon co-ordinated action on the part of social workers in two or more countries; to study from an international standpoint the conditions and consequences of emigration in their effect on individual, family, and social life. Operates on a non-sectarian and non-political basis. Mems: branches in 14 countries, five affiliated offices, and correspondents in some 100 other countries. Pres. Prof. Dr RAINER FRANK (Germany); Sec.-Gen. DAMIEN NGABONZIZA.

International Union of Family Organisations: 28 place Saint-Georges, 75009 Paris, France; tel. 1-48-78-07-59; fax 1-42-82-95-24; f. 1947 to bring together all organizations throughout the world which are working for family welfare; conducts permanent commissions on standards of living, housing, marriage guidance, work groups on family movements, rural families, etc.; there are six regional organizations: the Pan-African Family Organisation (Rabat, Morocco), the North America organization (Montreal, Canada), the Arab Family Organisation (Tunis, Tunisia), the Asian Union of Family Organisations (New Delhi, India), the European regional organization (Berne, Switzerland) and the Latin American Secretariat (Curitiba, Brazil). Mems: national associations, groups and governmental departments in more than 55 countries. Pres. MARIA TERESA DA COSTA MACEDO (Portugal).

International Union of Societies for the Aid of Mental Health: CSM, BP 323, 40107 Dax Cédex, France; tel. 5-58-91-48-38; fax 5-58-91-46-84; f. 1964 to group national societies and committees whose aim is to help mentally handicapped or maladjusted people. Gen. Pres Dr DEMANGEAT; Gen. Sec. Dr MINARD.

International Union of Tenants: Box 7514, 10392 Stockholm, Sweden; tel. (8) 791-02-50; fax (8) 20-43-44; e-mail nic.nilsson@hyresgasterna.se; f. 1955 to collaborate in safeguarding the interests of tenants; participates in activities of UNCHS (Habitat); has working groups for EC matters, eastern Europe, developing countries and for future development; holds annual council meeting and triennial congress. Mems: national tenant organizations in 24 European countries, Australia, Benin, Canada, Ecuador, India, Kenya, New Zealand, Tanzania and Uganda. Chair. JAN DANNEMANN; Sec. NIC NILSSON. Publ. *The Global Tenant* (quarterly).

Inter-University European Institute on Social Welfare—IEISW: 179 rue du Débarcadère, 6001 Marcinelle, Belgium; tel. (71) 36-62-73; f. 1970 to promote, carry out and publicize scientific research on social welfare and community work. Chair. Board of Dirs JACQUES HOCHEPIED (Belgium); Gen. Sec. P. ROZEN (Belgium). Publ. *COMM.*

Lions Clubs International: 300 West 22nd St, Oak Brook, IL 60523-8842, USA; tel. (630) 571-5466; telex 297236; fax (630) 571-8890; e-mail lions@lionsclubs.org; internet http://www.lionsclubs.org; f. 1917 to foster understanding among people of the world; to promote principles of good government and citizenship; and an interest in civic, cultural, social and moral welfare; to encourage service-minded people to serve their community without financial reward. Mems: 1.43m. with over 42,500 clubs in 184 countries and geographic areas. Exec. Admin. (vacant). Publ. *The Lion* (10 a year, in 20 languages).

Médecins sans frontières—MSF: 39 rue de la Tourelle, 1040 Brussels, Belgium; tel. (2) 280-18-81; fax (2) 280-01-73; f. 1971; composed of physicians and other members of the medical profession; aims to provide medical assistance to victims of war and natural disasters, and medium-term programmes of nutrition, immunization, sanitation, public health, and rehabilitation of hospitals and dispensaries. Centres in France, Luxembourg, the Netherlands, Spain and Switzerland; delegate offices in other European countries, North America and Asia. Int. Sec. JEAN-MARIE KINDERMANS.

Pan Pacific and South East Asia Women's Association—PPSEAWA: 707 Kent Rd, Kenilworth, IL 60043, USA; f. 1928 to strengthen the bonds of peace by fostering better understanding and friendship among women in this region, and to promote co-operation among women for the study and improvement of social conditions; holds international conference every three years. Pres. Dr ELIZABETH-LOUISE GIRARDI. Publ. *PPSEAWA Bulletin*.

Rotary International: 1560 Sherman Ave, Evanston, IL 60201, USA; tel. (847) 866-3000; fax (847) 328-8554; f. 1905 to carry out activities for the service of humanity, to promote high ethical standards in business and professions and to further international understanding, goodwill and peace. Mems: over 1,195,000 in 28,200 Rotary Clubs in 154 countries and 35 regions. Pres. LUIS VICENTE GIAY; Gen. Sec. GEOFFREY LARGE (USA). Publs *The Rotarian* (monthly, English), *Revista Rotaria* (bi-monthly, Spanish).

Service Civil International—SCI: Draakstraat 37, 2018 Antwerp, Belgium; tel. (3) 235-94-73; fax (3) 235-29-73; f. 1920 to promote peace and understanding through voluntary service projects (work-camps, local groups, long-term community development projects and education). Mems: 10,000 in 22 countries; projects in 20 countries. Pres. HELEN HONEYMAN. Publ. *Action* (quarterly).

Society of Saint Vincent de Paul: 5 rue du Pré-aux-Clercs, 75007 Paris, France; tel. 1-44-55-36-55; fax 1-42-61-72-56; f. 1833 to conduct charitable activities such as child care, youth work, work with immigrants, adult literacy programmes, residential care for the sick, handicapped and elderly, social counselling and work with prisoners and the unemployed—all conducted through personal contact. Mems: over 875,000 in 132 countries. Pres. CÉSAR A. NUÑES-VIANA; Sec.-Gen. PIERRE BONNASSIES. Publ. *Vincenpaul* (quarterly, in French, English and Spanish).

SOLIDAR: 28 rue le Titien, 1040 Brussels, Belgium; tel. (2) 743-05-73; fax (2) 743-05-89; e-mail solidar@compuserve.com; frmly International Workers' Aid f. 1951; an association of independent development and social welfare agencies based in Europe, which are linked to the labour and democratic socialist movements; aims to contribute to the creation of radical models of economic and social development, and to advance practical solutions that enable people in all parts of the world to have increased control over their own future. Mems: 19 agencies in 14 countries. Pres. Dr MANFRED RAGATI; Sec.-Gen. GIAMPI ALPHADEFF.

World Blind Union: c/o CBC ONCE, 18 La Coruña, 28020 Madrid, Spain; tel. (1) 5713675; fax (1) 5715777; e-mail umc@once.es; f. 1984 (amalgamating the World Council for the Welfare of the Blind and the International Federation of the Blind) to work for the prevention of blindness and the welfare of blind and visually-impaired people; encourages development of braille, talking book programmes and other media for the blind; rehabilitation, training and employment; prevention and cure of blindness in co-operation with the International Agency for the Prevention of Blindness; co-ordinates aid to the blind in developing countries; conducts studies on technical, social and educational matters, maintains the Louis Braille birthplace as an international museum. Mems in 140 countries. Pres. EUCLID HERIE (Canada); Sec.-Gen. PEDRO ZURITA (Spain). Publs *World Blind* (2 a year, in English, English Braille and on cassette, in Spanish and Spanish Braille and on cassette and in French).

World Federation of the Deaf—WFD: POB 65, Ilkantie 4, 00401 Helsinki, Finland; tel. 58031; fax 5803770; f. 1951 aims to serve deaf people and their national organizations, and to represent the interests of deaf people in international forums, such as the UN system; to achieve the goal of full participation by deaf people in society; encourages deaf people to set up and run their own organizations. Priority is given to the promotion of the recognition and use of national sign languages; human rights; the education of deaf people; and deaf people in the developing world. Mems: 110 member countries. Pres. LIISA KAUPPINEN. Publ. *WFD News* (quarterly).

World ORT Union: ORT House, 126 Albert St, London, NW1 7NE, United Kingdom; tel. (171) 446-8500; fax (171) 446-8650; f. 1880 for the development of industrial, agricultural and artisan skills among Jews; now, a highly developed educational and training organization active in over 60 countries throughout the world; conducts vocational training programmes for adolescents and adults, including instructors' and teachers' education and apprenticeship training in more than 40 countries, including technical assistance programmes in co-operation with interested governments. Mems: committees in over 40 countries. Dir-Gen. Dr ELLEN ISLER. Publs *Annual Report, Frontline News, What in the World is ORT*.

World Veterans Federation: 17 rue Nicolo, 75116 Paris, France; tel. 1-40-72-61-00; fax 1-40-72-80-58; e-mail 101727.1446 compuserve.com; f. 1950 to maintain international peace and security by the application of the San Francisco Charter and helping to implement the Universal Declaration of Human Rights and related international conventions, to defend the spiritual and material interests of war veterans and war victims. It promotes practical international co-operation in disarmament, human rights problems, economic development, rehabilitation of the handicapped, accessibility of the man-made environment, legislation concerning war veterans and war victims, and development of international humanitarian law; in 1986 established International Socio-Medical Information Centre (United Kingdom) for psycho-medical problems resulting from stress. Regional committees for Africa, Asia and the Pacific, and Europe and Standing Committee on Women. Mems: national organizations in 72 countries, representing about 27m. war veterans and war victims. Pres. BJÖRN EGGE (Norway); Sec.-Gen. SERGE WOURGAFT (France). Publs special studies (disarmament, human rights, rehabilitation).

Zonta International: 557 W. Randolph St, Chicago, IL 60661-2206, USA; tel. (312) 930-5848; fax (312) 930-0951; f. 1919; executive service organization; international and community service projects to promote the status of women. Mems: 36,000 in 67 countries. Pres. JOSEPHINE G. COOKE; Exec. Dir JANET HALSTEAD. Publ. *The Zontian* (quarterly).

Sport and Recreations

Arab Sports Confederation: POB 62997, Riyadh 11442, Saudi Arabia; tel. (1) 482-9427; telex 403099; fax (1) 482-3196; f. 1976 to encourage regional co-operation in sport. Mems: 20 national Olympic Committees, 36 Arab sports federations. Pres. Prince FAISAL BIN FAHD ABD AL-AZIZ; Sec.-Gen. OTHMAN M. AL-SAAD. Publ. *Annual Report*.

Fédération Aéronautique Internationale (International Aeronautical Federation): 93 blvd du Montparnasse, 75006 Paris, France; tel. 1-49-54-38-92; fax 1-49-54-38-88; e-mail sec@fai.org; f. 1905 to encourage all aeronautical sports; organizes world championships and makes rules through Air Sports Commissions; endorses world aeronautical and astronautical records. Mems: in 74 countries and territories. Pres. EILIF NESS; Sec.-Gen. MAX BISHOP. Publ. *Air Sports International*.

General Association of International Sports Federations—GAISF: 4 blvd du Jardin Exotique, Monte Carlo, Monaco; tel. 93-50-74-13; fax 93-25-28-73; e-mail gaist@mcn.mc; f. 1967 to act as a forum for the exchange of ideas and discussion of common problems in sport; to collect and circulate information; to provide secretarial and translation services for members, organize meetings and provide technical documentation and consultancy services. Mems: 88 international sports organizations; Pres. Dr UN YONG KIM; Sec.-Gen. PETER TALLBERG (Finland). Publs *Calendar of International Sports Competitions* (2 a year), *Sportime Magazine* (quarterly, in English and French), *GAISF Calendar, Sport and Education* and *Sport and Media*.

International Amateur Athletic Federation: 17 rue Princesse Florestine, BP 359, 98007 Monte Carlo Cédex, Monaco; tel. 93-30-70-70; fax 93-15-95-15; e-mail headquarters@iaaf.org; f. 1912 to ensure co-operation and fairness among members, and to combat discrimination in athletics; to affiliate national governing bodies, to compile athletic competition rules and to organize championships at all levels; to settle disputes between members, and to conduct a programme of development for members who need coaching, judging courses, etc., and to frame regulations for the establishment of World, Olympic and other athletic records. Mems: national asscns in 209 countries and territories. Pres. PRIMO NEBIOLO (Italy); Gen. Sec. ISTVÁN GYULAI (Hungary). Publs *IAAF Handbook* (every 2 years), *IAAF Review* (quarterly), *IAAF Directory* (annually, in English and French), *IAAF Technical Quarterly, New Studies in Athletics* (quarterly).

International Amateur Boxing Association: 10321 Berlin, PO Box 700141, Germany; tel. (30) 4236766; fax (30) 4235943; e-mail aibaoffice@t-online.de; f. 1946 as the world body controlling amateur boxing for the Olympic Games, continental, regional and inter-nation championships and tournaments in every part of the world. Mems: 189 national asscns. Pres. Prof. A. CHOWDHRY (Pakistan); Sec.-Gen. KARL-HEINZ WEHR (Germany). Publ. *World Amateur Boxing Magazine* (quarterly).

International Amateur Radio Union: POB 310905, Newington, CT 06131-0905, USA; tel. (860) 594-0200; fax (860) 594-0259; f. 1925 to link national amateur radio societies and represent the interests of two-way amateur radio communication. Mems: 150 national amateur radio societies. Pres. RICHARD L. BALDWIN; Sec. LARRY E. PRICE.

International Amateur Swimming Federation (Fédération Internationale de Natation Amateur—FINA): 9 ave de Beaumont, 1012 Lausanne, Switzerland; tel. (21) 3126602; fax (21) 3126610; internet http://www.fina.org; f. 1908 to promote amateur swimming and swimming sports internationally; to administer rules for swimming sports, for competitions and for establishing records; to organize world championships and FINA events; development programme to increase the popularity and quality of aquatic sports. Mems: 139 federations. Pres. MUSTAPHA LARFAOUI (Algeria); Dir CORNEL MARCULESCU. Publs *Handbook* (every 2 years), *FINA News* (monthly), *World of Swimming* (quarterly).

International Archery Federation (Fédération internationale de tir à l'arc—FITA): 135 ave de Cour, 1007 Lausanne, Switzerland; tel. (21) 6143050; fax (21) 6143055; e-mail fita@worldcom.ch; f. 1931 to promote international archery; organizes world championships and Olympic tournaments; Biennial Congress: France, 1999. Mems: national amateur associations in 117 countries. Pres. JAMES L. EASTON (USA); Sec.-Gen. GIUSEPPE CINNIRELLA (Italy). Publs *Information FITA* (monthly), *The Arrow* (bulletin, quarterly), *The Target* (annually).

International Automobile Federation (Fédération Internationale de l'Automobile—FIA): 8 place de la Concorde, 75008 Paris, France; tel. 1-43-12-44-55; fax 1-43-12-44-67; internet http://www.fia.com; f. 1904; manages world motor sport and organizes international championships. Mems: 143 national automobile clubs or asscns in 113 countries. Pres. MAX MOSLEY; Sec.-Gen. (Sport) PIERRE DE CONINCK; Sec.-Gen. (Tourism) JACQUES SARRUT.

International Badminton Federation—IBF: 4 Manor Park, MacKenzie Way, Cheltenham, Gloucestershire, GL51 9TX, United Kingdom; tel. (1242) 234904; telex 5131720; fax (1242) 221030; f. 1934 to oversee the sport of badminton world-wide. Mems: affiliated national organizations in 131 countries and territories. Pres. LU SHENGRONG; Exec. Dir DAVID SHAW (UK). Publs *World Badminton* (quarterly), *Statute Book* (annually).

International Basketball Federation (Fédération Internationale de Basketball): PO Box 700607, 81306 Munich, Germany; tel. (49) 7481580; fax (49) 74815833; e-mail secretariat@office.fiba.com; internet http://www.fiba.com; f. 1932 as International Amateur Basketball Federation (present name adopted 1989); aims to promote, supervise and direct international basketball; organizes quadrennial congress. Mems: affiliated national federations in 206 countries. Sec.-Gen. BORISLAV STANKOVIC. Publs *FIBA Bulletin* (2 a year), *FIBA Media Guide*.

International Canoe Federation: Dozsa György ut. 1-3, 1143 Budapest, Hungary; tel. (1) 363-4832; fax (1) 157-5643; e-mail icf-hq-budapest@mail.datanet.hu; internet http://www.datanet.hu/icf-hq; f. 1924; administers canoeing at the Olympic Games; promotes canoe/kayak activity in general. Mems: 100 national federations. Pres. SERGI ORSI; Sec.-Gen. OTTO BONN.

International Council for Health, Physical Education, Recreation, Sport and Dance: 1900 Association Drive, Reston, VA 20191, USA; tel. (800) 213-7193; f. 1958 to encourage the development of programmes in health, physical education, recreation, sport and dance throughout the world, by linking teaching professionals in these fields.

International Cricket Council: Lord's Cricket Ground, London, NW8 8QN, United Kingdom; tel. (171) 266-1818; fax (171) 266-1777; f. 1909; governing body for international cricket. Annual conference. Mems: Australia, England, India, New Zealand, Pakistan, South Africa, Sri Lanka, West Indies, Zimbabwe; and 23 associate and 13 affiliate mems. Chief Exec. D. L. RICHARDS.

International Cycling Union: 37 route de Chavannes, 1007 Lausanne, Switzerland; tel. (21) 6260080; telex 450112; fax (21) 6260088; e-mail admin@uci.ch; f. 1900 to develop, regulate and control all forms of cycling as a sport. Mems: 172 federations. Pres. HEIN VERBRUGGEN (Netherlands). Publ. *International Calendar* (annually).

International Equestrian Federation: CP 157, ave Mon-Repos 24, 1000 Lausanne 5, Switzerland; tel. (21) 3125656; telex 4548029; fax (21) 3128677; f. 1921; administers equestrian events at the Olympic Games. Sec.-Gen. Dr BO HELANDER.

International Federation of Associated Wrestling Styles: 17 ave Juste-Olivier, 1006 Lausanne, Switzerland; tel. (21) 3128426; telex 455958; fax (21) 3236073; e-mail sandner@iat.uni-leipzig.de; internet http://www.uni-leipzig.de/~iat/fila/fila1.htm; f. 1912 to encourage the development of amateur wrestling and promote the sport in countries where it is not yet practised; to further friendly relations between all members; to oppose any form of political, racial or religious discrimination. Mems: 139 federations. Pres. MILAN ERCEGAN; Sec.-Gen. MICHEL DUSSON. Publs *News Bulletin, Wrestling Revue*.

International Federation of Association Football (Fédération Internationale de Football Association—FIFA): Hitzigweg 11, POB 85, 8030 Zürich, Switzerland; tel. (1) 3849595; telex 817240; fax (1) 3849696; internet http://www.fifa.com; f. 1904 to promote the game of association football and foster friendly relations among players and national associations; to control football and uphold the laws of the game as laid down by the International Football Association Board; to prevent discrimination of any kind between players; and to provide arbitration in any disputes between national associations; organizes World Cup competition every four years. Mems: 198 national associations, six regional confederations. Pres. Dr JOÃO HAVELANGE (Brazil); Gen. Sec. J. S. BLATTER (Switzerland). Publs *FIFA News* (monthly), *FIFA Magazine* (every 2 months) (both in English, French, Spanish and German).

International Federation of Park and Recreation Administration—IFPRA: The Grotto, Lower Basildon, Reading, Berkshire, RG8 9NE, United Kingdom; tel. (1491) 874222; fax (1491) 874059; f. 1957 to provide a world centre where members of government departments, local authorities, and all organizations concerned with recreational services can discuss relevant matters. Mems: 300 in over 40 countries. Gen. Sec. ALAN SMITH (UK).

International Fencing Federation: 32 rue La Boëtie, 75008 Paris, France; tel. 1-45-61-14-72; fax 1-45-63-46-85; f. 1913; administers fencing at the Olympic Games. Mems: 96 national federations. Pres. RENÉ ROCH; Sec.-Gen. JENO KAMUTI.

International Gymnastic Federation: rue des Oeuches 10, CP 359, 2740 Moutier 1, Switzerland; tel. (32) 4946410; fax (32) 4946419; f. 1881 to promote the exchange of official documents and publications on gymnastics. Mems: 124 affiliated federations. Pres. BRUNO GRANDI; Gen. Sec. NORBERT BUECHE (Switzerland). Publ. *Bulletin* (3 a year), *World of Gymnastics Magazine* (3 a year).

International Hockey Federation: 1 ave des Arts, Boîte 5, 1210 Brussels, Belgium; tel. (2) 219-45-37; telex 63393; fax (2) 219-47-61; f. 1924 to fix the rules of outdoor and indoor hockey for all affiliated national associations; to control the game of hockey and indoor hockey; to control the organization of international tournaments, such as the Olympic Games and the World Cup. Mems: 120 national associations. Pres. JUAN ANGEL CALZADO; Sec.-Gen. ELS VAN BREDA-VRIESMAN. Publ. *World Hockey* (quarterly).

International Judo Federation: 12 rue Maamoun, 1082 Tunis, Tunisia; tel. (1) 781-057; fax (1) 801-517; e-mail dhouib@gnet.tn; internet http://www.ijf.org; f. 1951 to promote cordial and friendly relations between members; to protect the interests of judo throughout the world; to organize World Championships and the judo events of the Olympic Games; to develop and spread the techniques and spirit of judo throughout the world. Pres. YONG SUNG PARK (Republic of Korea); Gen. Sec. Dr HEDI DHOUIB (Tunisia).

International Paralympic Committee: Residentie Lodewijk 1, Abdijbekestraat 4B Bus 6, 8200 Sint Andries, Belgium; tel. (50) 38-93-40; fax (50) 39-01-19; f. 1989; responsible for organizing the paralympic games for sportspeople with disabilities, which are held alongside the Olympic Games; Pres. Dr ROBERT STEADWARD (Canada); Sec.-Gen. MIGUEL SAGARRA (Spain).

International Philatelic Federation: Zollikerstrasse 128, 8008 Zürich, Switzerland; tel. (1) 4223839; fax (1) 3831446; f. 1926 to promote philately internationally. Pres. D. N. JATIA; Sec.-Gen. M. L. HEIRI.

International Rowing Federation (Fédération internationale des Sociétés d'Aviron—FISA): 135 ave de Cour, CP 18, 1000 Lausanne 3, Switzerland; tel. (21) 6178373; fax (21) 6178375; e-mail fisa@ping.ch; f. 1892 to establish contacts between rowers in all countries and to draw up racing rules; world controlling body of the sport of rowing. Mems: national federations in 103 countries. Pres. DENIS OSWALD; Sec.-Gen. and Exec. Dir MATTHEW SMITH. Publs *FISA Directory* (annually), *FISA Info* (quarterly), *FISA Coach* (quarterly).

International Shooting Union: 80336 Munich, Bavariaring 21, Germany; tel. (89) 531012; fax (89) 5309481; f. 1907 to promote and guide the development of the amateur shooting sports; to organize

World Championships; to control the organization of continental and regional championships; to supervise the shooting events of the Olympic and Continental Games under the auspices of the International Olympic Committee. Mems: 149 federations in 144 countries. Pres. OLEGARIO VÁZQUEZ-RAÑA (Mexico); Sec.-Gen. HORST G. SCHREIBER (Germany). Publs *UIT Journal, International Shooting Sport* (6 a year).

International Skating Union—ISU: chemin de Primerose 2, 1007 Lausanne, Switzerland; tel. (21) 6126666; fax (21) 6166677; e-mail info@isu.ch; f. 1892; holds regular conferences. Mems: 70 national federations in 55 countries. Pres. OTTAVIA CINQUANTA; Gen.-Sec. FREDI SCHMID.

International Ski Federation: 3653 Oberhofen am Thunersee, Switzerland; tel. (33) 2446161; fax (33) 2435353; f. 1924 to further the sport of skiing; to prevent discrimination in skiing matters on racial, religious or political grounds; to organize World Ski Championships and regional championships and, as supreme international skiing authority, to establish the international competition calendar and rules for all ski competitions approved by the FIS, and to arbitrate in any disputes. Mems: 94 national ski associations. Pres. MARC HODLER (Switzerland); Sec.-Gen. GIAN-FRANCO KASPER (Switzerland). Publ. *FIS Bulletin* (4 times a year).

International Table Tennis Federation: 53 London Rd, St Leonards-on-Sea, East Sussex, TN37 6AY, United Kingdom; tel. (1424) 721414; fax (1424) 431871. Pres. XU YINSHENG.

International Tennis Federation: Palliser Rd, Barons Court, London, W14 9EN, United Kingdom; tel. (171) 381-8060; telex 919253; fax (171) 381-3989; f. 1913 to govern the game of tennis throughout the world and promote its teaching; to preserve its independence of outside authority; to produce the Rules of Tennis, to promote the Davis Cup Competition for men, the Fed. Cup for women, 15 cups for veterans, the World Youth Cup for players of 16 years old and under, and the NTT World Junior Tennis Tournament for players of 14 years old and under; to organize tournaments. Mems: 126 full and 70 associate. Pres. BRIAN TOBIN. Publs *World of Tennis* (annually), *ITF News* (monthly).

International Volleyball Federation (Fédération Internationale de Volleyball—FIVB): ave de la Gare 12, 1001 Lausanne, Switzerland; tel. (21) 3208932; telex 455234; fax (21) 3208865; e-mail info@mail.fivb.ch; f. 1947 to encourage, organize and supervise the playing of volleyball; organizes biennial congress. Mems: 214 national federations. Pres. Dr RUBÉN ACOSTA HERNÁNDEZ; Dir ALAIN COUPAT. Publs *VolleyWorld* (every 2 months), *X-Press* (monthly).

International Weightlifting Federation: PF 614, 1374 Budapest, Hungary; tel. (1) 1530530; telex 227553; fax (1) 1530199; f. 1905 to control international weightlifting; to set up technical rules and to train referees; to supervise World Championships, Olympic Games, regional games and international contests of all kinds; to supervise the activities of national and continental federations; to register world records. Mems: 160 national organizations. Pres. GOTTFRIED SCHÖDL (Austria); Gen. Sec. TAMÁS AJAN (Hungary). Publs *IWF Constitution and Rules* (every 4 years), *World Weightlifting* (quarterly).

International World Games Association: Hazeveld 24, 2761 XJ Zevenhuizen, Netherlands; tel. (1802) 3363; fax (1802) 3792; f. 1980; organizes World Games every four years, comprising 25 sports that are not included in the Olympic Games. Sec.-Gen. J. A. P. KOREN.

International Yacht Racing Union: 27 Broadwall, London, SE1 9PL, United Kingdom; tel. (171) 928-6611; telex 2794; fax (171) 401-8304; f. 1907; controlling authority of sailing in all its forms throughout the world; establishes and amends international yacht racing rules, organizes the Olympic Yachting Regatta and other championships. Mems: 117 national yachting federations. Pres. PAUL HENDERSON; Sec.-Gen. ARVE SUNDHEIM.

Union of European Football Associations—UEFA: chemin de la Redoute 54, 1260 Nyon, Switzerland; tel. (22) 9944444; fax (22) 9944488; f. 1954. Mems: 50 national associations. Pres. LENNART JOHANSSON; Sec.-Gen. GERHARD AIGNER.

World Boxing Organization: 412 Colorado Ave, Aurora, IL 60506, USA; tel. (630) 897-4765; fax (630) 897-1134; f. 1962; regulates professional boxing.

World Bridge Federation: 56 route de Vandoeuvres, 1253 Geneva, Switzerland; tel. (22) 7501541; telex 422887; fax (22) 7501620; f. 1958 to promote the game of contract bridge throughout the world, federate national bridge associations in all countries, conduct bridge associations in all countries, conduct world championships competitions, establish standard bridge laws. Mems: 89 countries. Pres. ERNESTO D'ORSI (Brazil). Publ. *World Bridge News* (quarterly).

World Chess Federation (Fédération Internationale des Echecs—FIDE): POB 166, 1000 Lausanne 4, Switzerland; tel. (21) 3103900; f. 1924; controls chess competitions of world importance and awards international chess titles. Mems: national orgs in more than 150 countries. Publs *President's Circular Letter* (5 a year), *FIDA Forum* (every 2 months), *International Rating List*.

World Squash Federation Ltd: 6 Havelock Rd, Hastings, East Sussex, TN43 1BP, United Kingdom; tel. (1424) 429245; fax (1424) 429250; f. 1966. Mems: 111 national organizations. Exec. Dir EDWARD J. WALLBUTTON.

World Underwater Federation: Viale Tiziano 74, 00196 Rome, Italy; tel. (6) 36858480; fax (6) 36858490; f. 1959 to develop underwater activities; to form bodies to instruct in the techniques of underwater diving; to perfect existing equipment and encourage inventions and to experiment with newly marketed products, suggesting possible improvements; to organize international competitions. Mems: organizations in 90 countries. Pres. ACHILLE FERRERO (Italy); Sec. PIERRE DERNIER (Belgium). Publs *International Year Book of CMAS, Scientific Diving: A Code of Practice,* manuals.

Technology

International Union of Technical Associations and Organizations (Union Internationale des Associations et Organismes Techniques—UATI): UNESCO House, 1 rue Miollis, 75015 Paris Cédex 15, France; tel. 1-45-68-27-70; telex 204461; fax 1-43-06-29-27; e-mail uati@unesco.org; f. 1951 (fmrly Union of International Technical Associations) under the auspices of UNESCO; aims to promote and co-ordinate activities of member organizations and represent their interests; facilitates relations with international organizations, notably UN agencies, receives proposals and makes recommendations on the establishment of new international technical associations. Mems: 25 organizations. Chair. MICHEL SAILLARD (France). Publ. *UATI Magazine* (2 a year).

MEMBER ORGANIZATIONS

Members of UATI include the following:

International Association for Hydraulic Research: c/o Delft Hydraulics, Rotterdamseweg 185, POB 177, 2600 MH Delft, Netherlands; tel. (15) 285-85-85; fax (15) 285-85-82; e-mail iahr@wldelft.nl; f. 1935; holds biennial congresses. Mems: 2,150 individual, 200 corporate. Sec.-Gen. H. J. OVERBEEK (Netherlands). Publs *AHR Bulletin, Journal of Hydraulic Research, Proceedings of Biennial Conferences*.

International Association of Lighthouse Authorities: 20 ter rue Schnapper, 78100 St Germain en Laye, France; tel. 1-34-51-70-01; telex 695499; fax 1-34-51-82-05; e-mail aismiala@easynet.fr; f. 1957; holds technical conference every four years; working groups study special problems and formulate technical recommendations, guidelines and manuals. Mems in 80 countries. Sec.-Gen. TORSTEN KRUUSE. Publ. *Bulletin* (quarterly).

International Bridge, Tunnel and Turnpike Association: 2120 L St, NW, Suite 305, Washington, DC 20037, USA; tel. (202) 659-4620; telex 275445; fax (202) 659-0500; e-mail ibtta@ibtta.org; f. 1932. Pres. JAMES K. BROOKSHIRE, Jr; Exec. Dir. NEIL D. SCHUSTER. Publ. *Tollways* (monthly).

International Commission of Agricultural Engineering—CIGR: Rijksstation voor Landbouwtechniek, 115 Van Gansberghelaan, 9820 Merelbeke, Belgium; tel. (9) 252-18-21; fax (9) 252-42-34; e-mail rvl.cigr@pophost.eunet.be; f. 1930. Mems: associations from 40 countries, individual mems from six countries. Pres. Prof. O. KITANI (Japan); Sec.-Gen. J. DAELEMANS (Belgium). Publs *Bulletin de la CIGR, Newsletter* (quarterly), technical reports.

International Commission on Glass: Stazione Sperimentale del Vetro, Via Briati 10, 30141 Murano, Venice, Italy; tel. (41) 739422; fax (41) 739420; e-mail spevet@unive.it; f. 1950 to co-ordinate research in glass and allied products, exchange information and organize conferences. Mems: 26 organizations. Pres. D. PYE; Sec.-Gen. F. NICOLETTI.

International Commission on Irrigation and Drainage: 48 Nyaya Marg, Chanakyapuri, New Delhi 110 021, India; tel. (11) 3016837; telex 3165920; fax (11) 3015962; f. 1950; holds triennial congresses. Mems: 64 national committees. Pres. ALY M. SHADY (Canada); Sec.-Gen. M. A. CHITALE (India). Publs *Bulletin* (2 a year), *Bibliography* (annually), *World Irrigation, Multilingual Technical Dictionary, World Flood Control,* technical books.

International Committee of Foundry Technical Associations: Konradstr. 9, POB 7190, 8023 Zürich, Switzerland; tel. (1) 2719090; fax (1) 2719292; e-mail gerster@jgp.ch; Pres. W. KUHLGATZ; Gen. Sec. Dr J. GERSTER.

International Federation for the Theory of Machines and Mechanisms: PO Box 444, Univ. of Oulu, 90571 Oulu, Finland; tel. (8) 553-2050; fax 8) 553-2026; e-mail tatu@me.oulu.fi; f. 1969; study of robots, man-machine systems, etc. Pres. J. ANGELES; Sec.-Gen. T. LEINONEN. Publ. *Mechanism and Machine Theory*.

International Federation of Automatic Control—IFAC: 2361 Laxenburg, Schlossplatz 12, Austria; tel. (2236) 71447; fax (2236) 72859; e-mail secr@ifac.co.at; internet http://www.ifac-control.org; f. 1957 to serve those concerned with the theory and application of automatic control and systems engineering. Mems: 48 national associations. Pres. Prof. YONG ZAI LU (China); Sec. G. HENCSEY. Publs *Automatica and Control Engineering Practice* (bi-monthly), *Newsletter* and affiliated journals.

International Gas Union: c/o N.V. Nederlandse Gasunie, POB 19, 9700 MA Groningen, Netherlands; tel. (50) 5212999; fax (50) 5255951; e-mail secr.igu@gasnie.nl; internet http://www.igu.org; f. 1931 to study all aspects and problems of the gas industry with a view to promoting international co-operation and the general improvement of the industry. Mems: national organizations in 55 countries. Pres. C. DÉTOURNÉ (France); Sec.-Gen. J. F. MEEDER (Netherlands).

International Institute of Welding: c/o J. G. Hicks, Abington Hall, Abington, Cambridge, CB1 6AL, United Kingdom; tel. (1223) 891162; fax (1223) 894180; f. 1948. Mems: 52 societies in 40 countries. Pres. RAÚL TIMERMAN (Argentina); Sec.-Gen. J. G. HICKS (UK). Publ. *Welding in the World* (7 a year).

International Measurement Confederation: POB 457, 1371 Budapest 5, Hungary; tel. (1) 153-1562; fax (1) 156-1215. Sec.-Gen. T. KEMENY.

International Navigation Association: Graaf de Ferraris, 11e étage, Bte 3, 156 blvd Emile Jacqmain, 1000 Brussels, Belgium; tel. (2) 553-71-60; fax (2) 553-71-55; e-mail navigation-aipcn-pianc @tornado.be; internet http://www.tornado.be/~navigation-aipcn-pianc/; f. 1885; fmrly Permanent International Assoc. of Navigation Congresses (PIANC); fosters progress in the construction, maintenance and operation of inland and maritime waterways, of inland and maritime ports and of coastal areas; publishes information in this field, undertakes studies, organizes international and national meetings. Congresses are held every four years. Mems: 40 governments, 2,780 others. Pres. Ir. R. DE PAEPE; Sec.-Gen. C. VAN BEGIN. Publs *Bulletin* (quarterly), *Illustrated Technical Dictionary* (in 6 languages), technical reports, Congress papers.

International Union for Electricity Applications: Espace Elec. CNIT, BP 10, 92053 Paris-la-Défense, France; tel. 1-41-26-56-48; fax 1-41-26-56-49; e-mail uie@semaphore.fr; internet http://www .uie.org; f. 1953, present title adopted 1994. Aims to study all questions relative to electricity applications, except commercial questions; links national groups and organizes international congresses on electricity applications. Mems: national committees and corporate members in 18 countries. Pres. W. WARING (UK); Gen. Sec. G. VANDERSCHUEREN (Belgium).

International Union of Air Pollution Prevention and Environmental Protection Associations: 136 North St, Brighton, BN1 1RG, United Kingdom; tel. (1273) 326313; fax (1273) 735802; e-mail cleanair@mistral.co.uk; f. 1963; organizes triennial World Clean Air Congress and regional conferences for developing countries (several a year). Pres. Dr A. D. SURRIDGE (South Africa); Dir-Gen. TOM CROSSETT. Publs *IUAPPA Newsletter* (quarterly), *Clean Air around the World.*

International Union of Producers and Distributors of Electrical Energy: 28 rue Jacques Ibert, 75858 Paris Cédex 17, France; tel. 1-40-42-37-08; telex 616305; fax 1-40-42-60-52; f. 1925; aims to study all questions relating to the production, transmission and distribution of electrical energy, to promote the image of and defend the interests of the electricity supply industry. Mems: 53 countries. Pres. LENNART LUNDBERG; Exec. Dir GEORGES LUCENET. Publs *Mediawatt, Watt's New* (newsletter).

International Union of Testing and Research Laboratories for Materials and Structures: Ecole Normale Supérieure, Pavillon des Jardins, 61 ave du Président Wilson, 94235 Cachan Cédex, France; tel. 1-47-40-23-97; fax 1-47-40-01-13; f. 1947 for the exchange of information and the promotion of co-operation on experimental research concerning structures and materials, for the study of research methods with a view to improvement and standardization. Mems: laboratories and individuals in 73 countries. Pres. Prof. F. H. WITTMANN (Switzerland); Sec.-Gen. M. BRUSIN (France). Publ. *Materials and Structures—Testing and Research* (10 a year).

World Energy Council: 34 St James's St, London, SW1A 1HD, United Kingdom; tel. (171) 930-3966; telex 264707; fax (171) 925-0452; f. 1924 to link all branches of energy and resources technology and maintain liaison between world experts; holds congresses every three years. Mems: 99 committees. Pres. M. GÓMEZ DE PABLOS (Spain); Sec.-Gen. I. D. LINDSAY (UK). Publs energy supply and demand projections, resources surveys, technical assessments, reports.

World Road Association (PIARC): La Grande Arche, Paroi Nord, Niveau 1, 92055 La Défense Cédex, France; tel. 1-47-96-81-21; fax 1-49-00-02-02; f. 1909 as the Permanent International Association of Road Congresses; aims to promote the construction, improvement, maintenance, use and economic development of roads; organizes technical committees and study sessions. Mems: governments, public bodies, organizations and private individuals in 100 countries. Pres. V. MAHBUB (Mexico); Sec.-Gen. M. B. FAUVEAU (France). Publs *Bulletin, Technical Dictionary, Lexicon,* technical reports.

OTHER ORGANIZATIONS

African Organization of Cartography and Remote Sensing: 5 Route de Bedjarah, BP 102, Hussein Dey, Algiers, Algeria; tel. (2) 77-79-34; telex 65474; fax (2) 77-79-34; f. 1988 by amalgamation of African Association of Cartography and African Council for Remote Sensing; aims to encourage the development of cartography and of remote sensing by satellites; organizes conferences and other meetings, promotes establishment of training institutions; four regional training centres (in Burkina Faso, Kenya, Nigeria and Tunisia). Mems: national cartographic institutions of 24 African countries. Sec.-Gen. UNIS MUFTAH.

African Regional Centre for Technology: Imm. Fahd, 17th Floor, blvd Djilly Mbaye, BP 2435, Dakar, Senegal; tel. 23-77-12; telex 61282; fax 23-77-13; f. 1980 to encourage the development of indigenous technology and to improve the terms of access to imported technology; assists the establishment of national centres. Dep. Exec. Dir Dr OUSMANE KANE. Publs *African Technodevelopment, Alert Africa.*

Bureau International de la Recupération et du Recyclage (Bureau of International Recycling): 24 rue du Lombard, Box 14, 1000 Brussels, Belgium; tel. (2) 514-21-80; fax (2) 514-12-26; e-mail bir.sec@skynet.be; f. 1948 as the world federation of the reclamation and recycling industries, to promote international trade in scrap iron and steel, non-ferrous metals, paper, textiles, plastics and glass. Mems: associations and individuals in 53 countries. Dir-Gen. FRANCIS VEYS.

ECMA—Standardizing Information and Communication Systems: 114 rue de Rhône, 1204 Geneva, Switzerland; tel. (22) 8496000; fax (22) 8496001; e-mail helpdesk@ecma.ch; f. 1961 to develop, in co-operation with the appropriate national, European and international organizations, as a scientific endeavour and in the general interest, standards and technical reports in order to facilitate and standardize the use of information processing and telecommunications systems; and to promulgate various standards applicable to the functional design and use of these systems. Mems: 28 ordinary and 18 associate. Sec.-Gen. JAN VAN DEN BELD. Publs *ECMA Standards, ECMA Memento.*

EUREKA: 19H ave des Arts, Bte 5, 1000 Brussels, Belgium; tel. (2) 229-22-40; fax (2) 218-79-06; e-mail eureka.secretariat@es .eureka.be; f. 1985; aims to promote collaboration between member countries of non-military research and development activities; enables joint development of technology and supports systematic use of standardization in new technology sectors. Mems: 26 in 25 countries. Sec.-Gen. L. J. A. M. VAN DEN BERGEN.

European Convention for Constructional Steelwork—ECCS: 32/36 ave des Ombrages, bte 20, 1200 Brussels, Belgium; tel. (2) 762-04-29; fax (2) 762-09-35; e-mail eccs@steelconstruct.com; internet http://www.steelconstruct.com; f. 1955 for the consideration of problems involved in metallic construction. Member organizations in Austria, Belgium, Denmark, Croatia, Czech Republic, Finland, France, Germany, Greece, Italy, Japan, Republic of Korea, Luxembourg, Netherlands, Norway, Portugal, Romania, Slovenia, Spain, Sweden, Switzerland, Turkey, United Kingdom, USA. Gen. Sec. R. V. SALKIN.

European Federation of Chemical Engineering: c/o Institution of Chemical Engineers, Davis Bldg, 165–189 Railway Terrace, Rugby, Warwickshire, CV21 3HQ, United Kingdom; tel. (1788) 578214; telex 311780; fax (1788) 560833; f. 1953 to encourage co-operation in Europe between non-profit-making scientific and technical societies for the advancement of chemical engineering and its application in the process industries. Mems: 65 societies in 25 European countries; 15 corresponding societies in other countries.

European Federation of Corrosion: 1 Carlton House Terrace, London, SW1Y 5DB, United Kingdom; tel. (171) 839-4071; telex 8814813; fax (171) 839-1702; f. 1955 to encourage co-operation in research on corrosion and methods of combating it. Member societies in 20 countries. Hon. Secs R. MAS (France), G. KREYSA (Germany), J. A. CATTERALL (UK).

European Federation of National Engineering Associations—FEANI: 21 rue du Beau Site, 1050 Brussels, Belgium; tel (2) 639-03-90; fax (2) 639-03-99; f. 1951 to affirm the professional identity of the engineers of Europe; to strive for the unity of the engineering profession in Europe. Mems: 27 mem. countries. Pres. Sir JOHN CULLEN (UK); Sec.-Gen. PIERRE-E. DE BOIGNE (France). Publ. *FEANI News.*

European Metal Union: Einsteinbaan 1, POB 2600, 3430 GA Nieuwegein, Netherlands; tel. (30) 605-33-44; fax (30) 605-31-15; e-mail info@metaalunie.nl; f. 1954 as International Union of Metal; aims to provide liaison between national craft organizations and small and medium-sized enterprises in the metal industry; to represent members' interests at a European level; to exchange information and ideas on related subjects, such as vocational training, quality assurance, European legislation, and normalization and standardization. Mems: national federations from Austria, Belgium,

Germany, Luxembourg, Netherlands and Switzerland. Pres. WILLEMIEN VAN GARDINGEN (Netherlands); Sec. HARM-JAN KEIJER (Netherlands).

European Organisation for the Exploitation of Meteorological Satellites—EUMETSAT: 64295 Darmstadt, Am Kavalleriesand 31, Germany; tel. (6151) 8077; telex 419320; fax (6151) 807555; internet http://www.eumetsat.de; f. 1986; maintains and exploits European systems of meteorological satellites, including the Meteosat programme for gathering weather data. Mems: 17 European countries. Pres. JORMA RIISSANEN (Finland); Gen. Dir Dr TILLMANN MOHR.

European Organization for Civil Aviation Equipment—EUROCAE: 17 rue Hamelin, 75783 Paris Cédex 16, France; tel. 1-45-05-71-88; telex 611045; fax 1-45-05-72-30; f. 1963; studies and advises on problems related to the equipment used in aeronautics and assists international bodies in the establishment of international standards. Mems: 70 manufacturers, organizations and research bodies. Pres. Sir JOHN CHARNLEY; Sec.-Gen. FRANCIS GRIMAL.

Eurospace: 16 rue Hamelin, 75116 Paris, France; tel. (1) 47-55-83-00; fax (1) 47-55-63-30; e-mail eurospac@micronet.fr; f. 1961; an association of European aerospace industrial companies, banks, press organizations and national associations for promoting space activity in the fields of telecommunication, television, aeronautical, maritime, meteorological, educational and press usage satellites, as well as launchers (conventional and recoverable). The Association carries out studies on the legal, economic, technical and financial aspects. It acts as an industrial adviser to the European Space Agency. Mems (direct or associate) in Belgium, Denmark, Finland, France, Germany, Italy, Netherlands, Norway, Spain, Sweden, Switzerland, United Kingdom. Pres. Prof. ERNESTO VALLERANI; Sec.-Gen. ALAIN GAUBERT.

Inter-African Committee for Hydraulic Studies—CIEH: 01 BP 369, Ouagadougou, Burkina Faso; tel. 30-71-12; telex 5277; f. 1960 to ensure co-operation in hydrology, hydrogeology, climatology, urban sanitation and other water sciences, through exchange of information and co-ordination of research and other projects; administrative budget (1988/89): 110m. francs CFA; investment budget 400m. francs CFA. Mems: 13 African countries. Sec.-Gen. AMADOU DIAW. Publs *Bulletin de Liaison technique* (quarterly), research studies.

International Association for Bridge and Structural Engineering: ETH—Hönggerberg, 8093 Zürich, Switzerland; tel. (1) 6332647; fax (1) 3712131; e-mail secretariat@iabse.ethz.ch; internet http://www.iabse.ethz.ch; f. 1929 to exchange knowledge and advance the practice of structural engineering world-wide. Mems: 3,500 government departments, local authorities, universities, institutes, firms and individuals in 90 countries. Pres. KLAUS OSTENFELD (Denmark); Exec. Dir A. GOLAY. Publs *Structural Engineering International* (quarterly), *Congress Report, IABSE Report, Structural Engineering Documents.*

International Association for Cybernetics (Association Internationale de Cybernétique): Palais des Expositions, ave Sergent Vrithoff 2, 5000 Namur, Belgium; tel. (81) 71-71-71; fax (81) 71-71-00; e-mail cyb@info.fundp.ac.be; f. 1957 to ensure liaison between research workers engaged in various sectors of cybernetics, to promote the development of the science and of its applications and to disseminate information about it. Mems: firms and individuals in 42 countries. Chair. J. RAMAEKERS; Gen. Sec. CARINE AIGRET. Publ. *Cybernetica* (quarterly).

International Association of Technological University Libraries: c/o Heriot-Watt University Library, Riccarton, Edinburgh, EH14 4AS, United Kingdom; tel. (131) 451-3570; fax (131) 451-3164; f. 1955 to promote co-operation between member libraries and stimulate research on library problems. Mems: 202 university libraries in 39 countries. Pres. Dr NANCY FJÄLLBRANT (Sweden); Sec. MICHAEL BREAKS (UK). Publs *IATUL Proceedings, IATUL Newsletter.*

International Cargo Handling Co-ordination Association—ICHCA: 71 Bondway, London, SW8 1SH, United Kingdom; tel. (171) 793-1022; fax (171) 820-1703; e-mail info@ichca.org.uk; f. 1952 to foster economy and efficiency in the movement of goods from origin to destination. Mems: 2,000 in 90 countries. Pres. GADI SASSOWER (Israel); Chief Exec. PETER E. WIGGINTON. Publs *Cargo Today* (bimonthly), *International Bulk Journal, World of Cargo Handling* (annual review), *Who's Who in Cargo Handling* (annually), *Buyers' Guide to Manufacturers* (annually).

International Colour Association: c/o Dr C. van Trigt, Philips Lighting, POB 80020, 5600 JM, Eindhoven, Netherlands; tel. (40) 2262788; fax (40) 22755861; f. 1967 to encourage research in colour in all its aspects, disseminate the knowledge gained from this research and promote its application to the solution of problems in the fields of science, art and industry; holds international congresses and symposia. Mems: organizations in 21 countries. Pres. Dr L. RONCHI (Italy); Sec. Dr C. VAN TRIGT (Netherlands).

International Commission on Illumination—CIE: Kegelgasse 27, 1030 Vienna, Austria; tel. (1) 714-31-87-0; fax (1) 713-08-38-18; e-mail ciecb@ping.at; f. 1900 as International Commission on Photometry, present name 1913; aims to provide an international forum for all matters relating to the science and art of light and lighting; to exchange information; to develop and publish international standards, and to provide guidance in their application. Mems: 40 national committees and 12 individuals. Gen. Sec. C. HERMANN. Publs standards, technical reports.

International Commission on Large Dams: 151 blvd Haussmann, 75008 Paris, France; tel. 1-40-42-67-33; fax 1-40-42-60-71; f. 1928; holds triennial congresses; 1997 congress: Florence, Italy. Mems in 83 countries. Pres. T. P. C. VAN ROBBROECK (South Africa); Sec.-Gen. JACQUES LECORNU. Publs *Technical Bulletin* (3/4 a year), *World Register of Dams, World Register of Mine and Industrial Wastes, Technical Dictionary on Dams,* studies.

International Committee on Aeronautical Fatigue—ICAF: c/o Prof. O. Buxbaum, Fraunhofer-Institut für Betriebsfestigkeit LBF, 64289 Darmstadt, Bartningstrasse 47, Germany; tel. (6151) 7051; fax (6151) 705214; f. 1951 for collaboration on fatigue of aeronautical structures among aeronautical bodies and laboratories by means of exchange of documents and by organizing periodical conferences. Mems: national centres in 13 countries. Sec. Prof. O. BUXBAUM (Germany).

International Conference on Large High-Voltage Electric Systems—CIGRE: 21 rue d'Artois, 75008 Paris, France; tel. 1-53-89-12-90; fax 1-53-89-12-99; e-mail cigre@world-net.sct.fr; internet http://www.worldnet.net/~cigre; f. 1921 to facilitate and promote the exchange of technical knowledge and information between all countries in the general field of electrical generation and transmission at high voltages; holds general sessions (every two years), symposia. Mems: 5,000 in 79 countries. Pres. M. CHAMIA; Sec.-Gen. Y. THOMAS (France). Publ. *Electra* (every 2 months).

International Council for Building Research, Studies and Documentation—CIB: Postbox 1837, 3000 BV Rotterdam, Netherlands; tel. (10) 411-02-40; fax (10) 433-43-72; e-mail secretariat@cibworld.nl; f. 1953 to encourage and facilitate co-operation in building research, studies and documentation in all aspects. Mems: governmental and industrial organizations and qualified individuals in 70 countries. Pres. Prof. C. SJÖSTROM (Sweden); Sec.-Gen. W. J. P. BAKENS. Publs *Information Bulletin* (bi-monthly), conference proceedings and technical, best practice and other reports.

International Electrotechnical Commission—IEC: 3 rue de Varembé, POB 131, 1211 Geneva 20, Switzerland; tel. (22) 9190211; telex 414121; fax (22) 9190300; e-mail info@iec.ch; internet http://www.iec.ch; f. 1906 as the authority for world standards for electrical and electronic engineering: its standards are used as the basis for regional and national standards, and are used in preparing specifications for international trade. Mems: national committees representing all branches of electrical and electronic activities in more than 50 countries. Gen.-Sec. A. M. RAEBURN. Publs *International Standards and Reports, IEC Bulletin, Annual Report, IEC Yearbook, Catalogue of Publications.*

International Special Committee on Radio Interference: British Electrotechnical Committee, British Standards Institution, 389 Chiswick High Rd, London, W4 4AL, United Kingdom; tel. (181) 996-9000; fax (181) 996-7400; f. 1934; special committee of the IEC to promote international agreement on the protection of radio reception from interference by equipment other than authorized transmitters; recommends limits of such interference and specifies equipment and methods of measurement; determines requirements for immunity of sound and TV broadcasting receivers from interference and the impact of safety regulations on interference suppression. Mems: national committees of IEC and seven other international organizations. Sec. A. G. HORSBURGH.

International Federation for Information and Documentation: POB 90402, 2509 LK The Hague, Netherlands; tel. (70) 314-06-71; fax (70) 314-06-67; e-mail fid@python.konbib.nl; f. 1895; aims to promote, through international co-operation, research in and development of information science; information management and documentation; and improvement of all the processes involved in the entire life-cycle of data, information and knowledge in all fields; regional commissions for Latin America, North America and the Caribbean, Asia and Oceania, Western, Eastern and Southern Africa, North Africa and the Near East, and for Europe. Mems: 62 national, five international, 330 institutional or individual. Pres. MARTHA STONE; Exec. Dir (vacant). Publs *International Forum on Information and Documentation* (quarterly), *FID News Bulletin* (monthly), *FID/ET Newsletter* (quarterly), *FID Directory* (every 2 years).

International Federation for Information Processing: Hofstrasse 3, 2361 Laxenburg, Austria; tel. (2236) 73616; fax (2236) 736169; e-mail ifip@ifip.or.at; f. 1960 to promote information science and technology; to stimulate research, development and application of information processing in science and human activities; to further the dissemination and exchange of information on information processing; to encourage education in information processing; to advance international co-operation in the field of information processing. Mems: 46 national organizations representing 64 countries. Pres. B. SENDOV (Bulgaria); Exec. Dir PLAMEN NEDKOV.

International Federation of Airworthiness—IFA: 58 Whiteheath Ave, Ruislip, Middx, HA4 7PW, United Kingdom; tel. (1895) 672504; fax (1895) 676656; f. 1964 to provide a forum for the exchange of international experience in maintenance, design and operations; holds annual conference; awards international aviation scholarship annually. Mems: 120, comprising 50 airlines, 17 airworthiness authorities, 23 aerospace manufacturing companies, 17 service and repair organizations, three consultancies, six professional societies, two aviation insurance companies, one aircraft leasing company, and the Flight Safety Foundation (USA). Pres. M. C. BEARD (USA); Exec. Dir J. W. SAULL (UK). Publ. *IFA News* (quarterly).

International Federation of Automotive Engineering Societies: c/o IMechE, 1 Birdcage Walk, London SW1H 9JJ, United Kingdom; tel. (171) 222-7899; telex 917944; fax (171) 333-4557; f. 1947 to promote the technical development of automotive engineering, passenger cars, trucks, engineering and research; congresses every two years. Mems: national organizations in 26 countries. Sec.-Gen. Dr ERIC LUCKEY. Publ. *Bulletin*.

International Federation of Consulting Engineers: 13C ave du Temple, POB 86, 1000 Lausanne 12, Switzerland; tel. (21) 6544411; fax (21) 6535432; e-mail fidic@pobox.com; f. 1913 to encourage international co-operation and the setting up of standards for consulting engineers. Mems: national associations in 67 countries, comprising some 500,000 design professionals. Pres. J. M. STEYN LAUBSCHER.

International Federation of Hospital Engineering: Via Michelino 69, 40127 Bologna, Italy; tel. and fax (51) 6332288; f. 1970 to promote internationally the standards of hospital engineering and to provide for the interchange of knowledge and ideas. Mems: 106. Pres. PAUL ERIK REE (Denmark); Gen. Sec. COSIMO PIPOLI (Italy).

International Information Management Congress: 1650 38th St, Suite 205W, Boulder, CO 80301, USA; tel. (303) 440-7085; fax (303) 440-7234; internet http://www.iimc.org; f. 1962 to promote co-operation in document-based information management; to provide an international clearing-house for information, exchange publications and encourage the establishment of international standards; to promote international product exhibitions, seminars and conventions. Mems: 30 associations, 80 regular and 350 affiliate mems from 64 countries. Exec. Dir PAUL CARMEN (USA). Publ. *Document World* (every 2 months).

International Institute of Seismology and Earthquake Engineering: Building Research Institute, Ministry of Construction, 1 Tatehara, Tsukuba-shi, Ibaraki Pref., Japan; tel. (298) 64-2151; fax (298) 64-6777; e-mail iisee@kenken.go.jp; f. 1962 to work on seismology and earthquake engineering for the purpose of reducing earthquake damage in the world; trains seismologists and earthquake engineers from the earthquake-prone countries and undertakes surveys, research, guidance and analysis of information on earthquakes and related matters. Mems: 69 countries. Dir M. MIZUNO.

International Institution for Production Engineering Research: 10 rue Mansart, 75009 Paris, France; tel. 1-45-26-21-80; fax 1-40-16-40-75; f. 1951 to promote by scientific research the study of the mechanical processing of all solid materials including checks on efficiency and quality of work. Mems: 230 active, 113 corresponding and 131 assoc. in 40 countries. Pres. H. J. J. KALS (Netherlands); Sec.-Gen. M. VÉRON (France). Publ. *Annals*.

International Iron and Steel Institute—IISI: 120 rue Col Bourg, 1140 Brussels, Belgium; tel. (2) 702-89-00; fax (2) 702-88-99; e-mail steel@iisi.be; f. 1967 to promote the welfare and interest of the world's steel industries; to undertake research in all aspects of steel industries; to serve as a forum for exchange of knowledge and discussion of problems relating to steel industries; to collect, disseminate and maintain statistics and information; to serve as a liaison body between international and national steel organizations. Mems: in over 50 countries. Sec.-Gen. LENHARD J. HOLSCHUH.

International Organization for Standardization: POB 56, 1 rue de Varembé, 1211 Geneva 20, Switzerland; tel. (22) 7490111; telex 412205; fax (22) 7333430; e-mail central@isocs.iso.ch; internet http://www.iso.ch/; f. 1947 to reach international agreement on industrial and commercial standards. Mems: national standards bodies of 86 countries. Pres. EBERHARD MÖLLMANN; Sec.-Gen. LAWRENCE D. EICHER. Publs *ISO International Standards, ISO Memento* (annually), *ISO 9000 News* (6 a year), *ISO Bulletin* (monthly).

International Research Group on Wood Preservation: Box 5607, 114 86 Stockholm, Sweden; tel. (8) 10-14-53; fax (8) 10-80-81; f. 1965 as Wood Preservation Group by OECD; independent since 1969; consists of five sections; holds plenary annual meeting. Mems: 315 in 51 countries. Pres. Prof. JOHN N. R. RUDDICK (Canada); Sec.-Gen. JÖRAN JERMER (Sweden). Publs technical documents and books, *Annual Report*.

International Rubber Research and Development Board—IRRDB: Brickendonbury, Hertford, SG13 8NP, United Kingdom; tel. (1992) 584966; fax (1992) 504267; f. 1937. Mems: 15 research institutes. Sec. KEVIN P. JONES.

International Society for Photogrammetry and Remote Sensing: c/o Mr L. W. Fritz, Martin Marietta Corporation, PO Box 8048-13A24, Philadelphia, PA 19101, USA; tel. (610) 531-3205; fax (510) 889-3296; f. 1910; holds congress every four years, and technical symposia. Mems: 81 countries. Pres. SHUNJI MURAI (Japan); Sec.-Gen. LAWRENCE W. FRITZ (USA). Publs *International Archives of Photogrammetry and Remote Sensing, Photogrammetria*.

International Society for Soil Mechanics and Foundation Engineering: University Engineering Dept, Trumpington St, Cambridge, CB2 1PZ, United Kingdom; tel. (1223) 355020; fax (1223) 359675; f. 1936 to promote international co-operation among scientists and engineers in the field of geotechnics and its engineering applications; maintains 28 technical committees; holds quadrennial international conference, regional conferences and specialist conferences. Mems: 18,000 individuals, 70 national societies. Pres. Prof. M. B. JAMIOLKOWSKI; Gen. Sec. Dr R. PARRY. Publs *Newsletter* (quarterly), *Lexicon of Soil Mechanics Terms* (in eight languages).

International Solar Energy Society: Wiesentalstrasse 50, 79115 Freiburg, Germany; tel. (761) 459060; fax (761) 4590699; f. 1954 to foster science and technology relating to the applications of solar energy, to encourage research and development, to promote education and to gather, compile and disseminate information in this field; holds international conferences; four regional offices (Africa, Asia/Pacific, Europe, South America). Mems: 4,650 in 95 countries. Pres. Prof. EDUARDO DE OLIVEIRAS FERNANDES (Portugal); Exec. Dir. BURKHARD HOLDER (Germany). Publs *Journal* (monthly), *Newsletter* (2 a year), *Sunworld* (quarterly).

International Solid Wastes Association—ISWA: Laederstraede 9, 2nd Floor, 1201 Copenhagen K, Denmark; tel. 33-91-44-91; fax 33-91-91-88; e-mail iswa@inet.uni-c.dk; internet http://www.iswa.org; f. 1970; organizes conferences and establishes technical working groups. Pres. HAAKEN RYLANDER (Sweden); Man. Dir SUZANNE ARUP VELTZÉ (Denmark) (acting).

International Tin Research Institute Ltd: Kingston Lane, Uxbridge, Middx, UB8 3PJ, United Kingdom; tel. (1895) 272406; fax (1895) 251841; f. 1932, privatized in 1995; provides technological support for the tin-producing and -consuming industries world-wide. Facilities include: soldering, electroplating, metallography, and chemical and analytical laboratories; a technical enquiry and information service; research is conducted to support existing uses of tin and to develop new applications. Dir RODNEY BEDDER. Publs *Soldering Bits, Market Monitor, ITRAlert* (all quarterly).

International Union for Vacuum Science, Technique and Applications: c/o Prof. J. S. Colligon, Dept of Electronic and Electrical Engineering, University of Salford, Salford, M5 4WT, United Kingdom; tel. (161) 745-5247; telex 668680; fax (161) 745-5999; f. 1958; collaborates with the International Standards Organization in defining and adopting technical standards; holds triennial International Vacuum Congress and International Conference on Solid Surfaces; administers the Welch Foundation scholarship for postgraduate research in vacuum science and technology; scientific divisions for surface science, applied surface science, thin film, vacuum science, electronic materials, nanometer structures, plasma science and technique and vacuum metallurgy; steering committee on nanometer science and technology. Mems: organizations in 30 countries. Pres. Prof. J. L. ROBINS (Australia); Sec.-Gen. Prof. JOHN S. COLLIGON (UK). Publ. *News Bulletin* (quarterly).

International Water Resources Association: University of New Mexico, 1915 Roma NE, Albuquerque, NM 87131-1436, USA; tel. (505) 277-9400; fax (505) 277-9405; e-mail iwra@unm.edu; f. 1972 to promote collaboration in and support for international water resources programmes; holds conferences; conducts training in water resources management. Pres. GLENN E. STOUT (USA); Sec.-Gen. VICTOR DE KOSINSKY (Belgium). Publ. *Water International* (quarterly).

International Water Supply Association: 1 Queen Anne's Gate, London, SW1H 9BT, United Kingdom; tel. (171) 957-4567; fax (171) 222-7243; f. 1947 to co-ordinate technical, legal and administrative aspects of public water supply; congresses held every two years. Mems: national organizations, water authorities and individuals in 95 countries. Pres. PIERRE GIACASSO (Switzerland); Sec.-Gen. M. J. SLIPPER (UK). Publs *Aqua* (6 a year), *Water Supply* (4 a year).

Latin-American Energy Organization (Organización Latinoamericana de Energía–OLADE): Av. Occidental, OLADE Bldg, Sector San Carlos, POB 17-11-6413 CCI, Quito, Ecuador; tel. (2) 598-122; fax (2) 539-684; f. 1973 to act as an instrument of co-operation in using and conserving the energy resources of the region. Mems: 25 Latin-American and Caribbean countries. Exec. Sec. LUIZ AUGUSTO DA FONSECA. Publs *Energy Magazine, Energy Update*.

Latin-American Iron and Steel Institute: Benjamín 2944, 5° piso, Las Condes, Santiago, Chile; tel. (2) 233-0545; fax (2) 233-0768;

e-mail ilafa@entelchile.net; f. 1959 to help achieve the harmonious development of iron and steel production, manufacture and marketing in Latin America; conducts economic surveys on the steel sector; organizes technical conventions and meetings; disseminates industrial processes suited to regional conditions; prepares and maintains statistics on production, end uses, prices, etc., of raw materials and steel products within this area. Hon. mems 30; mems 68; assoc. mems 63; Chair. PAULO D. VILLARES; Sec.-Gen. ANÍBAL GÓMEZ. Publs *Acero Latinoamericano* (every 2 months), *Siderurgia Latinoamericana* (monthly), *Statistical Year Book, Directory of Latin American Iron and Steel Companies* (every 2 years).

Regional Centre for Services in Surveying, Mapping and Remote Sensing: POB 18118, Nairobi, Kenya; tel. (2) 803320; telex 25258; fax (2) 802767; f. 1975 to provide services in the professional techniques of map-making, and the application of satellite and remote sensing data in resource analysis and development planning; undertakes research and provides advisory services to African governments. Mems: 14 signatory and 10 non-signatory governments. Dir-Gen. Prof. SIMON NDYETABULA.

Regional Centre for Training in Aerospace Surveys: PMB 5545, Ile-Ife, Nigeria; tel. (36) 230050; telex 34262; fax (36) 230481; f. 1972 for training, research and advisory services; administered by the ECA. Mems: eight governments. Dir J. A. OGUNLAMI.

Regional Council of Co-ordination of Central and East European Engineering Organizations: c/o MTESZ, 1055 Budapest, Kossuth Lajos tér 6–8, Hungary; tel. (1) 153-3333; telex 225792; fax (1) 153-0317; f. 1992. Hon. Pres. JÁNOS TÓTH.

World Association of Industrial and Technological Research Organizations—WAITRO: c/o Danish Technological Institute, POB 141, 2630 Taastrup, Denmark; tel. 43-50-43-50; telex 33146; fax 43-50-72-50; e-mail waifro@dti.dk; internet http://www.waitro.dti.dk; f. 1970 by the UN Industrial Development Organization to encourage co-operation in industrial and technological research, through financial assistance for training and joint activities, arranging international seminars, and allowing the exchange of information. Mems: 200 research institutes in 80 countries. Pres. Dr HANI MULKI (Jordan); Contact MOSES MENGU. Publs *WAITRO News* (quarterly), *WAITRO Outline*.

World Association of Nuclear Operators—WANO-CC: Kings Bldgs, 16 Smith Sq., London, SW1P 3JG, United Kingdom; tel. (171) 828-2111; fax (171) 828-6691; f. 1989 by operators of nuclear power plants; aims to improve the safety and operability of nuclear power plants by exchange of operating experience; four regional centres (in France, Japan, Russia and the USA) and a co-ordinating centre in the UK. Mems in 34 countries. Dir (Co-ordinating Centre) V. J. MADDEN.

World Bureau of Metal Statistics: 27A High St, Ware, Herts, SG12 9BA, United Kingdom; tel. (1920) 461274; telex 317210; fax (1920) 464258; f. 1949; statistics of production, consumption, stocks, prices and international trade in copper, lead, zinc, tin, nickel, aluminium and several other minor metals. Gen. Man. J. L. T. DAVIES. Publs *World Metal Statistics* (monthly), *World Tin Statistics* (monthly), *World Nickel Statistics* (monthly), *World Metal Statistics Yearbook, World Metal Statistics Quarterly Summary, World Stainless Steel Statistics* (annually), *World Wrought Copper Statistics* (annually).

World Federation of Engineering Organizations—WFEO: 1–3 Birdcage Walk, London, SW1P 9JJ, United Kingdom; tel. (171) 222-7512; fax (171) 222-0812; f. 1968 to advance engineering as a profession in the interests of the world community; to foster co-operation between engineering organizations throughout the world; to undertake special projects through co-operation between members and in co-operation with other international bodies. Mems: 80 national, nine international. Pres. C. E. BAUER (Argentina); Sec.-Gen. JOHN C. MACKENZIE. Publ. *WFEO Newsletter* (twice a year).

World Petroleum Congresses: 61 New Cavendish St, London, W1M 8AR, United Kingdom; tel. (171) 467-7137; fax (171) 255-1472; f. 1933 to provide an international congress as a forum for petroleum science, technology, economics and management; to publish the proceedings, and to undertake related information and liaison activities; Permanent Council includes 47 member countries; 15th Congress: Beijing, China, October 1997. Pres. Ir D. VAN DER MEER (Netherlands); Dir-Gen. PAUL TEMPEST (UK).

Tourism

Alliance Internationale de Tourisme: CP 6120, 1211 Geneva, Switzerland; tel. (22) 7352727; fax (22) 7352326; e-mail ait@aitgva.ch; internet http://www.aitgva.ch; f. 1898, present title adopted 1919; represents motoring organizations and touring clubs around the world; aims to study all questions relating to international touring and to suggest reforms, to encourage the development of tourism and all matters concerning the motorist, traffic management, the environment, road safety, consumer protection and to defend the interests of touring associations. Mems: 132 associations totalling 100m. members in 98 countries. Pres. P. NOUWEN (Netherlands); Dir Gen. P. DOGGWILER (Switzerland).

Caribbean Tourism Organization: 2nd Floor, Sir Frank Walcott Bldg, Culloden Farm Complex, St Michael, Barbados; tel. 427-5242; fax 429-3065; e-mail ctobar@caribsurf.com; offices in New York (tel. (212) 635-9530), Canada (tel. (6) 485-7827) and London (tel. (171) 222-4335); f. 1951 to encourage tourism in the Caribbean region (present name 1989). Mems: 33 Caribbean governments and 400 allied mems. Sec.-Gen. JEAN HOLDER.

East Asia Travel Association: c/o Japan National Tourist Organization, 2-10-1 Yurakucho, Chiyoda-ku, Tokyo, Japan; tel. (3) 3216-2910; telex 24132; fax (3) 3214-7680; f. 1966 to promote tourism in the East Asian region, encourage and facilitate the flow of tourists to that region from other parts of the world, and to develop regional tourist industries by close collaboration among members. Mems: six national tourist organizations and one travel association. Pres. ICHIRO TANAKA; Sec.-Gen. JOÃO MANUEL COSTA ANTUNES.

European Travel Commission: 61 rue du Marché aux Herbes, 1000 Brussels, Belgium; tel. (2) 504-03-03; fax (2) 514-18-43; f. 1948 to promote tourism in and to Europe, to foster co-operation and the exchange of information, to organize research. Mems: national tourist organizations of 28 European countries. Exec. Dir WALTER LEU (Switzerland).

International Association of Scientific Experts in Tourism: Varnbüelstrasse 19, 9000 St Gallen, Switzerland; tel. (71) 2242530; fax (71) 2242536; f. 1949 to encourage scientific activity by its members; to support tourist institutions of a scientific nature; to organize conventions. Mems: 400 from 40 countries. Pres. Prof. Dr PETER KELLER (Switzerland); Gen. Sec. Dr HANSPETER SCHMIDHAUSER (Switzerland). Publ. *The Tourist Review* (quarterly).

International Congress and Convention Association: Entrada 121, 1096 EB Amsterdam, Netherlands; tel. (20) 690-11-71; fax (20) 699-07-81; e-mail icca@icca.nl; f. 1963 to establish worldwide co-operation between all involved in organizing congresses, conventions and exhibitions (including travel agents, airlines, hotels, congress centres, professional congress organizers, tourist and convention bureaux and ancillary congress services); organizes professional training. Mems: 492 meeting experts from 71 countries. Pres. PIETER VAN DER HOEVEN; Exec. Dir. TOM HULTON. Publ. *International Meetings News* (quarterly).

International Federation of Tourist Centres: c/o G. van Lijf, Kleine Staat 1, 6211 Maastricht, Netherlands; tel. (43) 3280820; fax (43) 3213746; f. 1949. Mems: Austria, Belgium, France, Germany, Finland, Italy, Liechtenstein, Netherlands, Norway, Sweden, Switzerland, United Kingdom. Pres. G. VAN LIJF (Netherlands).

International Ho-Re-Ca: Blumenfeldstrasse 20, 8046 Zürich, Switzerland; tel. (1) 3775111; fax (1) 3718909; f. 1949 to bring together national associations of hotel, restaurant and café proprietors to further the interests of the trade, international tourism, etc. Mems: 29 national organizations. Pres. MOHAMED A. NABI (Egypt); Gen. Sec. Dr XAVER FREI (Switzerland).

International Hotel and Restaurant Association: 251 rue du Faubourg St Martin, 75010 Paris, France; tel. 1-44-89-94-00; fax 1-40-36-73-30; e-mail members@ih-ra.com; f. 1946 to act as the leader and authority on matters affecting the international hotel industry, to promote its interests and to contribute to its growth, profitability and quality of the industry worldwide; membership extended to restaurants in 1996. Mems: 120 national hospitality associations, 100 national and international hotel and restaurant chains; also independent hotels and restaurant and allied members. Pres. (1998) ERIC P. PFEFFER (USA); Sec.-Gen. CHRISTIANE CLECH. Publs *Hotels* (monthly), *International Hotel Guide* (annually), *Action IHRA* (every 3 months).

Latin-American Confederation of Tourist Organizations—COTAL: Viamonte 640, 8°, 1053 Buenos Aires, Argentina; tel. (1) 322-4003; fax (1) 393-5696; f. 1957 to link Latin American national associations of travel agents and their members with other tourist bodies around the world. Mems: in 21 countries and affiliate mems in 55 countries. Pres. GONZALO RUEDA; Exec. Dir EDUARDO E. PANTANO. Publ. *Revista COTAL* (every 2 months).

Pacific Asia Travel Association—PATA: 1 Montgomery St, Suite 1000, San Francisco, CA 94104, USA; tel. (415) 986-4646; telex 170685; fax (415) 986-3458; e-mail PataHQ@ix.netcom.com; f. 1951; aims to promote travel to and between the countries of the Pacific Rim; annual Conference in March/April; regional offices in Singapore, Sydney and Monaco; holds annual conference, seminars. Mems: more than 2,200 governments, carriers, tour operators and hotels. Publs *PATA Travel News* (monthly), *PATA Annual Statistical Report, Quarterly Statistical Report*.

Tourism Council of the South Pacific: POB 13119, Suva, Fiji; tel. 304177; fax 301995; e-mail spice@is.com.fj; internet http://www.tcsp.com; aims to foster regional co-operation in the development and promotion of tourism in the island nations of the South Pacific; receives EU funding and undertakes sustainable activities. Mems: Cook Islands, Fiji, French Polynesia, Kiribati, New Caledonia, Niue, Papua New Guinea, Samoa, Solomon Islands, Tonga, Tuvalu, Vanuatu; Chief Exec. LEVANI TUINABUA.

Tourism International Co-operative and Associated: c/o CWS Ltd, POB 53, New Century House, Manchester M60 4ES, United Kingdom; tel. (161) 827-5151; fax (161) 832-6388; f. 1992. Mems: 15 organizations. Pres. MICHAEL GRINDOD; Sec.-Gen. RAYMOND STELANDRE (Belgium). Publ. *TICA News*.

Universal Federation of Travel Agents' Associations—UFTAA: 1 ave des Castelans, Stade Louis II-Entrée H, 98000 Monaco; tel. 92-05-28-29; fax 92-05-29-87; e-mail uftaamc@sunnyworld.mc; f. 1966 to unite travel agents' associations, to represent the interests of travel agents at the international level, to help in international legal differences; issues literature on travel, etc. Mems: national associations of travel agencies in 104 countries. Sec.-Gen. BIRGER BÄCKMAN.

World Association of Travel Agencies: 14 rue Ferrier, 1202 Geneva, Switzerland; tel. (22) 7314760; telex 412837; fax (22) 7328161; e-mail watahq@iprolink.ch; internet http://www.watanetwork.kenpubs.co.uk; f. 1949 to foster the development of tourism, to help the rational organization of tourism in all countries, to collect and disseminate information and to participate in all commercial and financial operations which will foster the development of tourism. Individual travel agencies may use the services of the world-wide network of 200 members. Pres. ADEL ZAKI (Egypt); Sec.-Gen. MARCO AGUSTONI (Switzerland). Publ. *WATA Gazette* (quarterly).

World Tourism Organization: Calle Capitán Haya 42, 28020 Madrid, Spain; tel. (1) 5710628; telex 42188; fax (1) 5713733; e-mail omt@dial.eunet.es; f. 1975 to promote travel and tourism; undertakes technical co-operation, and the protection of tourists and tourist facilities; provides training and information (including statistics). There are six regional commissions and a General Assembly is held every two years. Mems: governments of 120 countries; also four associate members, one observer, and over 300 affiliated mems. Sec.-Gen. FRANCESCO FRANGIALLI.

World Travel and Tourism Council—WTTC: 20 Grosvenor Pl., London, SW1X 7TT, United Kingdom; tel. (171) 838-9400; fax (171) 838-9050; e-mail 106174.3247@compuserve.com; f. 1989; promotes the development of the travel/tourist industry; analyses impact of tourism on employment levels and local economies and promotes greater expenditure on tourism infrastructure. Pres. GEOFFREY H. LIPMAN.

Trade and Industry

African Regional Organization for Standardization: POB 57363, Nairobi, Kenya; tel. (2) 224561; fax (2) 794338; f. 1977 to promote standardization, quality control, certification and metrology in the African region, formulate regional standards, and co-ordinate participation in international standardization activities. Mems: 24 states. Sec.-Gen. ZAWDU FELLEKE. Publs *ARSO Newsletter* (2 a year), *ARSO Catalogue of Standards* (annually).

Arab Iron and Steel Union—AISU: BP 4, Chéraga, Algiers, Algeria; tel. (2) 371579; telex 71158; fax (2) 371975; f. 1972 to develop commercial and technical aspects of Arab steel production by helping member associations to commercialize their production in Arab markets, guaranteeing them high quality materials and intermediary products, informing them of recent developments in the industry and organizing training sessions. Mems: 73 companies in 13 Arab countries. Gen. Sec. MUHAMMAD LAID LACHGAR. Publs *Arab Steel Review* (monthly), *Information Bulletin* (2 a month), *Directory* (annually).

Asian Productivity Organization: 4-14 Akasaka, 8-chome, Minato-ku, Tokyo 107, Japan; tel. (3) 34087221; telex 26477; fax (3) 34087220; e-mail apo@gol.com; internet http://www.apo-tokyo.com; f. 1961 to strengthen the productivity movement in the Asian and Pacific region and disseminate technical knowledge. Mems: 18 countries. Sec.-Gen. YANAGI KENICHI. Publs *APO News* (monthly), *Annual Report, APO Productivity Journal* (2 a year), *Directory of National Productivity Organizations in APO member countries* (irregular).

Association of African Trade Promotion Organizations—AATPO: Pavillion International, BP 23, Tangier, Morocco; tel. (9) 41687; telex 33695; fax (9) 41536; f. 1975 under the auspices of the OAU and the ECA to foster regular contact between African states in trade matters and to assist in the harmonization of their commercial policies in order to promote intra-African trade; conducts research and training; organizes meetings and trade information missions. Mems: 26 states. Sec.-Gen. Prof. ADEYINKA W. ORIMALADE. Publs *FLASH: African Trade* (monthly), *Directory of Trade Information Sources in Africa, Directory of State Trading Organizations, Directory of Importers and Exporters of Food Products in Africa.*

Association of European Chambers of Commerce and Industry (EUROCHAMBRES): 5 rue d'Archimède, 1000 Brussels, Belgium; tel. (2) 282-08-50; fax (2) 230-00-38; e-mail eurocham@mail.interpac.be; internet http://www.eurochambres.be; f. 1958 to promote the exchange of experience and information among its members and to bring their joint opinions to the attention of the institutions of the European Union; conducts studies and seminars. Mems: 15 full and 17 affiliated mems and one corresponding mem; Pres. ANTONI NEGRE I VILLAVECCHIA (Spain); Sec.-Gen. FRANK FRIEDRICH (Germany).

Cairns Group: c/o Department of Foreign Affairs and Trade, R. G. Casey Bldg, John McEwen Crescent, Barton, ACT 2600, Australia; f. 1986 by major agricultural exporting countries, aiming to bring about reforms in international agricultural trade, including reductions in export subsidies, in barriers to access and in internal support measures; represents members' interests in WTO negotiations. Mems: Argentina, Australia, Brazil, Canada, Chile, Colombia, Fiji, Hungary, Indonesia, Malaysia, New Zealand, Paraguay, Philippines, South Africa, Thailand, Uruguay. Chair. TIM FISCHER (Australia).

Caribbean Association of Industry and Commerce—CAIC: Musson Bldg, Hincks St, POB 259, Bridgetown, Barbados; tel. (809) 436-6385; telex 2473; fax (809) 436-9937; f. 1955; aims to encourage economic development through the private sector; undertakes research, training, assistance for small enterprises, and export promotion. Mems: chambers of commerce and enterprises in 17 countries and territories. Exec. Dir FELIPE NAGUERA. Publ. *CAIC News* (2 a month), *Business Wave* (6 a year).

Committee for European Construction Equipment—CECE: 101 rue de Stassart, 1050 Brussels, Belgium; tel. (2) 512-72-02; fax (2) 502-54-42; f. 1959 to further contact between manufacturers, to improve market conditions and productivity and to conduct research into techniques. Mems: representatives from Belgium, Finland, France, Germany, Italy, Netherlands, Spain, Sweden, United Kingdom. Pres. J. GUIGNABODET (France); Sec.-Gen. D. BARRELL (UK).

Committee of European Foundry Associations: 2 rue de Bassano, 75783 Paris Cédex 16, France; tel. 1-47-23-55-50; fax 1-47-20-44-15; f. 1953 to safeguard the common interests of European foundry industries; to collect and exchange information. Mems: associations in 14 countries. Sec.-Gen. H. CHAPOTOT.

Confederation of Asia-Pacific Chambers of Commerce and Industry: 7th Floor, 3 Sungshou Rd, Taipei 110, Taiwan; tel. (2) 27255663; fax (2) 27255665; e-mail cacci@stsvr.showtower.com.tw; f. 1966; holds biennial conferences to examine regional co-operation; undertakes liaison with governments in the promotion of laws conducive to regional co-operation; serves as a centre for compiling and disseminating trade and business information; encourages contacts between businesses; conducts training and research. Mems: national chambers of commerce and industry of Australia, Bangladesh, Brunei, Hong Kong, India, Indonesia, Japan, Republic of Korea, Malaysia, New Zealand, Pakistan, Papua New Guinea, Philippines, Singapore, Sri Lanka, Taiwan, Thailand, Viet Nam; also affiliate and special mems. Dir-Gen. JOHNSON C. YEN. Publs *CACCI Profile* (monthly), *CACCI Journal of Commerce and Industry* (2 a year).

Confederation of International Soft Drinks Associations—CISDA: 35 blvd Louis Schmidt, BP 14, 1040 Brussels, Belgium; tel. (2) 735-37-49; fax (2) 732-51-02; e-mail mail@unesda-cisda.org; f. 1961 to promote co-operation among the national associations of soft drinks manufacturers on all industrial and commercial matters, to stimulate the sales and consumption of soft drinks, to deal with matters of interest to all member associations and to represent the common interests of member associations; holds a congress every year. Gen. Sec. ALAIN BEAUMONT.

Consumers International: 24 Highbury Crescent, London, N5 1RX, United Kingdom; tel. (171) 226-6663; fax (171) 354-0607; f. 1960 as International Organization of Consumers' Unions—IOCU; links consumer groups worldwide through information networks and international seminars; supports new consumer groups and represents consumers' interests at the international level; five regional offices. Mems: 215 associations in 93 countries. Dir-Gen. JULIAN EDWARDS. Publs *Consumer Currents* (10 a year), *World Consumer* (4 a year), *Consumidores y Desarollo* (10 a year), *Consommation-Developpement* (4 a year).

European Association of Advertising Agencies: 5 rue St Quentin, 1000 Brussels, Belgium; tel. (2) 280-16-03; fax (2) 230-09-66; f. 1960 to maintain and to raise the standards of service to advertisers of all European advertising agencies, and to strive towards uniformity in fields where this would be of benefit; to serve the interests of all agency members in Europe. Mems: 16 national advertising agency associations and 24 multinational agency groups. Pres. ALBERT WINNINGHOFF (Netherlands); Sec.-Gen. STIG CARLSON (Sweden). Publ. *Next Steps* (monthly).

European Association of Manufacturers of Radiators—EURORAD: Konradstr. 9, 8023 Zürich, Switzerland; tel. (1)

2719090; fax (1) 2719292; f. 1966 to represent the national associations of manufacturers of radiators made of steel and cast iron, intended to be attached to central heating plants and which convey heat by natural convection and radiation without the need for casing. Mems: in 12 countries. Pres. G. VANDENSCHRIECK (Belgium); Gen. Sec. K. EGLI (Switzerland).

European Association of National Productivity Centres: 60 rue de la Concorde, 1050 Brussels, Belgium; tel. (2) 511-71-00; f. 1966 to enable members to pool knowledge about their policies and activities, specifically as regards the relative importance of various productivity factors, and the ensuing economic and social consequences. Mems: 19 European centres. Pres. KLAUS DIECKHOFF; Sec.-Gen. A. C. HUBERT. Publs *EPI* (quarterly), *EUROproductivity* (monthly), *Annual Report.*

European Brewery Convention: POB 510, 2380 BB Zoeterwoude, Netherlands; tel. (71) 545-60-47; fax (71) 541-00-13; e-mail ebc@syntegra.net; f. 1947, present name adopted 1948; aims to promote scientific co-ordination in malting and brewing. Mems: national associations in Austria, Belgium, Bulgaria, Czech Republic, Denmark, Finland, France, Germany, Hungary, Ireland, Italy, Netherlands, Norway, Portugal, Slovakia, Slovenia, Spain, Sweden, Switzerland, United Kingdom. Pres. P. VAN EERDE (Netherlands); Sec.-Gen. Mrs M. VAN WIJNGAARDEN (Netherlands).

European Chemical Industry Council: ave E. van Nieuwenhuyse 4, 1160 Brussels, Belgium; tel. (2) 676-72-11; telex 62444; fax (2) 676-73-00; f. 1972; represents and defends the interests of the chemical industry relating to legal and trade policy, internal market, environmental and technical matters; liaises with intergovernmental organizations; provides secretariat for some 84 product sector groups. Mems: 16 national federations; Dir.-Gen. Dr HUGO LEVER; Sec.-Gen. JEAN-MARIE DEVOS.

European Committee for Standardization (Comité européen de normalisation—CEN): 36 rue de Stassart, 1050 Brussels, Belgium; tel. (2) 550-08-11; fax (2) 550-08-19; f. 1961 to promote European standardization so as to eliminate obstacles caused by technical requirements in order to facilitate the exchange of goods and services. Mems: 19 national standards bodies, 6 associated and 14 affiliated bodies in central and eastern Europe and 3 corresponding organizations. Sec.-Gen. YEORG HONGLER.

European Committee of Associations of Manufacturers of Agricultural Machinery: 19 rue Jacques Bingen, 75017 Paris, France; tel. 1-47-66-02-20; telex 640362; fax 1-40-54-95-60; f. 1959 to study economic and technical problems, to protect members' interests and to disseminate information. Mems: Austria, Belgium, Denmark, Finland, France, Germany, Italy, Netherlands, Norway, Spain, Sweden, Switzerland, United Kingdom. Pres. J. CASTELLANO (Spain); Sec.-Gen. H. VINCENT (France).

European Committee of Textile Machinery Manufacturers: POB 190, 2700-AD Zoetermeer, Netherlands; tel. (79) 531-100; fax (79) 531-365; f. 1952; promotes general interests of the industry. Mems: organizations in Belgium, France, Germany, Italy, Netherlands, Spain, Switzerland, United Kingdom. Pres. Dr F. PAETZOLD (Germany); Gen. Sec. R. BICKER CAARTEN.

European Confederation of Iron and Steel Industries—EUROFER: 211 rue du Noyer, 1000 Brussels, Belgium; tel. (2) 738-79-20; fax (2) 736-30-01; e-mail mail@eurofer.be; f. 1976; a confederation of national federations and companies in the European steel industry which aims to foster co-operation between the member federations and companies and to represent their common interests to the EU and other international organizations. Mems: Austria, Belgium, Finland, France, Germany, Ireland, Italy, Luxembourg, Netherlands, Portugal, Spain, Sweden, United Kingdom; assoc. mems from countries of central and eastern European countries. Dir-Gen. D. VON HÜLSEN.

European Confederation of Paint, Printing Ink and Artists' Colours Manufacturers' Associations: ave E. van Nieuwenhuyse 4, 1160 Brussels, Belgium; tel. (2) 676-7480; fax (2) 676-7490; e-mail cepe@mail.interpac.be; f. 1951 to study questions relating to paint and printing ink industries, to take or recommend measures for their development and interests, to exchange information. Mems: national associations in 17 European countries. Pres. F. J. RANKL; Gen. Sec. J. SCHODER.

European Confederation of Woodworking Industries: Hof-ter-Vleestdreef, bus 4, 3-1070 Brussels, Belgium; tel. (2) 556-25-85; fax (2) 556-25-95; e-mail euro.wood.fed@skynet.be; f. 1952 to act as a liaison between national organizations, to undertake research and to defend the interests of the industry. Mems: national federations in 18 European countries and European sectoral organizations in woodworking. Pres. B. CASTELLINI (Italy); Sec.-Gen. Dr G. VAN STEERTEGEM.

European Federation of Associations of Insulation Enterprises: Karl Liebknecht Str. 33, 10178 Berlin, Germany; tel. (30) 242-68-63; fax (30) 242-55-97; f. 1970; groups the organizations in Europe representing insulation firms including thermal insulation, sound-proofing and fire-proofing insulation; aims to facilitate contacts between member associations, to study any problems of interest to the profession, to safeguard the interests of the profession and represent it in international forums. Mems: professional organizations in 15 European countries. Chair. T. WREDE.

European Federation of Associations of Particle Board Manufacturers: Hof-ter-Vleestdreef 5, 1070 Brussels, Belgium; tel. (2) 556-25-89; fax (2) 556-25-94; e-mail euro.wood.fed@skynet.be; f. 1958 to develop and encourage international co-operation in the particle board industry. Pres. F. DE COCK; Sec.-Gen. G. VAN STEERTEGEM (Belgium). Publs *Annual Report,* technical documents.

European Federation of Handling Industries: POB 179, Kirchenweg 4, 8032 Zürich, Switzerland; tel. (1) 3844844; telex 816519; fax (1) 3844848; f. 1953 to facilitate contact between members of the profession, conduct research, standardize methods of calculation and construction and promote standardized safety regulations. Mems: organizations in 14 European countries. Pres. Prof. RÜDIGER FRANKE; Sec. Dr K. MEIER (Switzerland).

European Federation of Management Consultants' Associations: 145 rue Royale, 1000 Brussels, Belgium; tel. (2) 223-04-13; fax (2) 223-06-74; e-mail feaco@mail.interpac.be; f. 1960 to bring management consultants together and promote a high standard of professional competence in all European countries concerned, by encouraging discussions of, and research into, problems of common professional interest. Mems: 25 associations. Pres. and Chair. GIL GIDRON; Exec. Sec. ANNE-MARIE BURSELL.

European Federation of Plywood Industry: 30 ave Marceau, 75008 Paris, France; f. 1957 to organize joint research between members of the industry at international level. Mems: associations in 14 European countries. Pres. P. OJANPÄÄ (Finland); Sec.-Gen. PIERRE LAPEYRE.

European Federation of Tile and Brick Manufacturers: Obstgartenstrasse 28, 8035 Zürich, Switzerland; tel. (1) 3619650; fax (1) 3610205; f. 1952 to co-ordinate research between members of the industry, improve technical knowledge, encourage professional training. Mems: associations in Austria, Belgium, Czech Republic, Denmark, Finland, France, Germany, Greece, Hungary, Ireland, Italy, Netherlands, Norway, Poland, Portugal, Slovakia, Spain, Sweden, Switzerland, Tunisia, United Kingdom. Chair. Dr W. REITHOFER; Dir Dr W. P. WELLER.

European Furniture Manufacturers Federation: 35 chaussé de Haecht, 1210 Brussels; tel. (2) 223-39-64; e-mail u.e.a.@euronet.be; f. 1950 to determine and support general interests of the European furniture industry and to facilitate contacts between members of the industry. Mems: organizations in Belgium, Denmark, Finland, France, Germany, Italy, Netherlands, Norway, Portugal, Slovenia, Spain, Sweden, Switzerland, United Kingdom. Pres. J. ENGELS; Sec.-Gen. B. DE TURCK.

European General Galvanizers Association: Craudace House, Godstone Rd, Caterham, Surrey, CR3 6RE, United Kingdom; tel. (1883) 331277; fax (1883) 331287; f. 1955 to promote co-operation between members of the industry, especially in improving processes and finding new uses for galvanized products. Mems: associations in Austria, Czech Republic, Belgium, Denmark, Finland, France, Germany, Italy, Netherlands, Norway, Spain, Sweden, Switzerland, United Kingdom. Pres. J. F. WOOLRIDGE (UK).

European Glass Container Manufacturers' Committee: Northumberland Rd, Sheffield, S10 2UA, United Kingdom; tel. (1742) 686201; fax (1742) 681073; f. 1951 to facilitate contacts between members of the industry, inform them of legislation regarding it. Mems: representatives from 15 European countries. Sec. D. K. BARLOW (UK).

European Organization for Quality—EOQ: POB 5032, 3001 Berne, Switzerland; tel. (31) 3206166; fax (31) 3206828; e-mail eoq@aey.ch; internet http://www.eoq.org; f. 1956 to encourage the use and application of quality management with the intent to improve quality, reduce costs and increase productivity; organizes annual congress for the exchange of information, documentation, etc. Member organizations in 30 European countries. Pres. OTTO NEUMAYER. Publs *European Quality* (6 a year), *Annual Report.*

European Packaging Federation: c/o Institut Français de l'Emballage et du Conditionnement IFEC, 33 rue Louis Blanc, 93582 St-Ouen Cédex, France; tel. 1-40-11-22-12; fax 1-40-11-01-06; f. 1953 to encourage the exchange of information between national packaging institutes and to promote technical and economic progress. Mems: organizations in Austria, Belgium, Denmark, Finland, France, Germany, Hungary, Italy, Netherlands, Poland, Spain, Switzerland, United Kingdom. Pres. Prof. DIETER BERNDT (Germany); Sec.-Gen. PAUL F. H. JANSSEN (Netherlands).

European Patent Office—EPO: 80331 Munich, Erhardtstrasse 27, Germany; tel. (89) 2399-0; telex 523656; fax (89) 2399 4560; f. 1977 to grant European patents according to the Munich convention of 1973; conducts searches and examination of patent applications. Mems: Austria, Belgium, Denmark, Finland, France, Germany,

Greece, Ireland, Italy, Liechtenstein, Luxembourg, Monaco, Netherlands, Portugal, Spain, Sweden, Switzerland, United Kingdom. Pres. INGO KOBER (Germany); Chair. Admin. Council JULIAN ALVAREZ ALVAREZ. Publs *Annual Report, Official Journal* (monthly), *European Patent Bulletin, European Patent Applications, Granted Patents.*

European Society for Opinion and Marketing Research—ESOMAR: J. J. Viottastraat 29, 1071 JP Amsterdam, Netherlands; tel. (20) 664-21-41; fax (20) 664-29-22; e-mail mail@esomar.nl; internet http://www.esomar.nl; f. 1948 to further professional interests and encourage high technical standards. Mems: about 3,500 in 90 countries. Pres. MARIO VAN HAMERSVELD (Netherlands); Dir-Gen. JUERGEN SCHWOERER. Publs *Marketing and Research Today* (quarterly), *Newsbrief* (monthly), *ESOMAR Directory* (annually).

European Union of Coachbuilders: 46 Woluwedal, bte 14, 1200 Brussels, Belgium; tel. (2) 778-62-00; fax (2) 778-62-22; f. 1948 to promote research on questions affecting the industry, exchange information, and establish a common policy for the industry. Mems: national federations in Belgium, France, Germany, Italy, Luxembourg, Netherlands, Switzerland, United Kingdom. Pres. G. BAETEN (Belgium); Sec.-Gen. HILDE VANDER STICHELE (Belgium).

European Union of the Natural Gas Industry—EUROGAS: 4 ave Palmerston, 1000 Brussels, Belgium; tel. (2) 237-11-11; fax (2) 230-62-91; e-mail eurogas@arcadis.be. Mem. organizations in Austria, Belgium, Denmark, Finland, France, Germany, Ireland, Italy, Netherlands, Spain, Sweden, Switzerland, United Kingdom. Pres. G. H. B. VERBERG (Netherlands); Gen. Sec. P. CLAUS (Belgium).

Federation of European Marketing Research Associations—FEMRA: Studio 38, Wimbledon Business Centre, Riverside Road, London, SW17 0BA, United Kingdom; tel. (181) 879-0709; fax (181) 947-2637; f. 1965 to facilitate contacts between researchers; main specialist divisions: European chemical marketing research; European technological forecasting; paper and related industries; industrial materials; automotive; textiles; methodology; information technology. Mems: 500. Pres. DAVID A. CLARK (Belgium).

General Union of Chambers of Commerce, Industry and Agriculture for Arab Countries: POB 11-2837, Beirut, Lebanon; tel. and fax 862841; f. 1951 to foster Arab economic collaboration, to increase and improve production and to facilitate the exchange of technical information in Arab countries. Mems: chambers of commerce, industry and agriculture in 21 Arab countries. Gen. Sec. BURHAN DAJANI. Publs *Arab Economic Report, Al-Omran Al-Arabi* (every 2 months), economic papers, proceedings.

Global Crop Protection Federation—GCPF: ave Louise 143, 1050 Brussels, Belgium; tel. (2) 542-0410; fax (2) 542-0419; e-mail gcp@pophost.eunet.be; internet http://www.gcpf.org; f. 1960 as European Group of National Asscns of Pesticide Manufacturers; international body since 1967; present name adopted in 1996. Aims to harmonize national and international regulations concerning crop protection products, to support the development of the industry and to promote observation of the FAO Code of Conduct on the Distribution and Use of Pesticides. Mems: national asscns in 62 countries. Dir-Gen. K. P. VLAHODIMOS.

Gulf Organization for Industrial Consulting: POB 5114, Doha, Qatar; tel. 858888; telex 4619; fax 831465; f. 1976 by the Gulf Arab states to encourage industrial co-operation among Gulf Arab states, and to pool industrial expertise and encourage joint development of projects; undertakes feasibility studies, market diagnosis, assistance in policy-making, legal consultancies, project promotion, promotion of small and medium industrial investment profiles and technical training; maintains industrial data bank. Mems: member states of Gulf Co-operation Council (q.v.). Sec.-Gen. Dr ABDULRAHMAN A. AL-JAFARY. Publs *GOIC Monthly Bulletin* (in Arabic), *Al Ta'awon al Sina'e* (quarterly, in Arabic and English).

Inter-American Commercial Arbitration Commission: OAS Administrative Bldg, Rm 211, 19th and Constitution Ave, NW, Washington, DC 20006, USA; tel. (202) 458-3249; fax (202) 458-3293; f. 1934 to establish an inter-American system of arbitration for the settlement of commercial disputes by means of tribunals. Mems: national committees, commercial firms and individuals in 22 countries. Dir Gen. Dr GUILLERMO FERNÁNDEZ DE SOTO.

International Advertising Association Inc: 521 Fifth Ave, Suite 1807, New York, NY 10175, USA; tel. (212) 557-1133; fax (212) 983-0455; e-mail iaaglobal@worldnet.att.net; internet http://www.iaaglobal.org; f. 1938; a global partnership of advertisers, agencies, the media and other marketing communications professionals; aims to protect freedom of commercial speech and consumer choice. Mems: more than 3,600 in 95 countries. World Congress held every 2 years, 1998: Cairo, Egypt. Pres. SENYON KIM (Republic of Korea); Dir-Gen. NORMAN VALE (USA). Publs *IAA Membership Directory and Annual Report, IAA World News.*

International Association of Buying Groups: 5300 Bonn 1, Vongelsingsstr. 43, Germany; tel. (228) 985840; fax (228) 9858410; f. 1951 for research, documentation and compilation of statistics; holds congress every three years. Mems: 80 buying groups in 12 countries. Sec.-Gen. Dr GÜNTER OLESCH.

International Association of Congress Centres (Association internationale des palais de Congrès—AIPC): c/o Muzejski prostor, Jezuitski trg 4, POB 19, 41000 Zagreb, Croatia; tel. (41) 433-722; telex 22398; f. 1958 to unite conference centres fulfilling certain criteria, to study the administration and technical problems of international conferences, to promote a common commercial policy and co-ordinate all elements of conferences. Mems: 73 from 29 countries. Pres. MATTHIAS FUCHS; Sec.-Gen. RADOVAN VOLMUT (Yugoslavia). Publ. list of principal conferences of the world (3 a year).

International Association of Department Stores: 4 rue de Rome, 75008 Paris, France; tel. 1-42-94-02-02; fax 1-42-94-02-04; e-mail iads@worldnet.fr; f. 1928 to conduct research, exchange information and statistics on management, organization and technical problems; centre of documentation. Mems: large-scale retail enterprises in Andorra, Belgium, Denmark, Finland, France, Germany, Ireland, Italy, Lebanon, Netherlands, Singapore, Spain, Switzerland, United Kingdom; associate mems in Czech Republic. Pres. R. BENEDICK (Switzerland); Gen. Sec. M. DE GROOT VAN EMBDEN (Netherlands). Publ. *Retail News Letter* (monthly).

International Association of Electrical Contractors: 5 rue Hamelin, 75116 Paris, France; tel. 1-44-05-84-20; fax 1-44-05-84-05. Pres. MIGUEL SERAFIO CALVO; Gen. Sec. DENIS HANNOTIN.

International Association of Insurance and Reinsurance Intermediaries (Bureau International des Producteurs d'Assurances et de Réassurances—BIPAR): 40 ave Albert-Elisabeth, 1200 Brussels, Belgium; tel. (2) 735-60-48; fax (2) 732-14-18; e-mail bipar@skynet.be; f. 1937. Mems: 47 associations from 29 countries, representing approx. 250,000 brokers and agents. Pres. KURT SEDLER; Dir HARALD KRAUSS. Publ. *EU Bulletin* (4 a year).

International Association of Scholarly Publishers: c/o Tønnes Bekker-Nielsen, Aarhus Universitetsforlag, 8000 Århus C, Denmark; tel. 86-19-70-33; fax 86-19-84-33; f. 1972 for the exchange of information and experience on scholarly and academic publishing by universities and others; assists in the transfer of publishing skills to developing countries. Mems: 139 in 40 countries. Pres. TØNNES BEKKER-NIELSEN (Denmark); Sec.-Gen. CHRISTOPHER HUDSON (USA). Publs *IASP Newsletter* (every 2 months), *International Directory of Scholarly Publishers.*

International Association of the Soap, Detergent and Maintenance Products Industry: 49 sq. Marie-Louise, 1000 Brussels, Belgium; tel. (2) 230-83-71; fax (2) 230-82-88; e-mail a.i.s.e@euronet.be; f. 1967 to promote in all fields the manufacture and use of a wide range of cleaning products, polishes, bleaches, disinfectants and insecticides, to develop the exchange of statistical information and to study technical, scientific, economic and social problems of interest to its members. Mems: 31 national asscns in 25 countries. Pres. H. R. BIRCHER; Sec. P. COSTA (Belgium).

International Association of Textile Dyers and Printers: POB 518, 3900 AM Veenendaal, Netherlands; tel. (318) 564-488; fax (318) 564-487; e-mail krl@pi.net; f. 1967 to defend and promote the interests of members in international affairs and to provide a forum for discussion of matters of mutual interest. Mems: national trade associations representing dyers and printers in nine countries. Pres. M. L. FOX (UK); Sec.-Gen. C. LODIERS (Netherlands).

International Booksellers Federation—IBF: rue du Grand Hospice 34a, 1000 Belgium; tel. (2) 223-49-40; fax (2) 223-49-41; e-mail eurobooks@skynet.be; f. 1956 to promote the booktrade and the exchange of information and to protect the interests of booksellers when dealing with other international organizations; special committees deal with questions of postage, resale price maintenance, book market research, advertising, customs and tariffs, the problems of young booksellers, etc. Mems: 200 in 22 countries. Pres. YVONNE STEINBERGER; Sec.-Gen. CHRISTIANE VUIDAR. Publs *IBF-bulletin* (2 a year), *Booksellers International.*

International Bureau for the Standardization of Man-Made Fibres (BISFA): 4 ave van Nieuwenhuyse, 1160 Brussels, Belgium; tel. (2) 676-74-55; fax (2) 676-74-54; f. 1928 to examine and establish rules for the standardization, classification and naming of various categories of man-made fibres. Mems: 49. Sec.-Gen. A. KRIEGER.

International Butchers' Confederation: 4 Bte, 10 rue Jacques de Lalaing, 1040 Brussels, Belgium; tel. (2) 230-38-76; fax (2) 230-34-51; f. 1907; aims to defend the interests of small and medium-sized enterprises in the meat trading and catering industry. Pres. ANTON KARL; Sec.-Gen. THEO WERSHOVEN.

International Confederation for Printing and Allied Industries—INTERGRAF: 18 sq. Marie-Louise, bte 25, 1040 Brussels, Belgium; tel. (2) 230-86-46; fax (2) 231-14-64; f. 1983 (formerly EUROGRAF, f. 1975) to defend the common interests of the printing and allied interests in member countries. Mems: federations in 20 countries. Pres. MARTIN HANDGRAAF; Sec.-Gen. GEOFFREY WILSON.

International Confederation of Art Dealers: 32 rue Ernest Allard, 1000 Brussels, Belgium; f. 1936 to co-ordinate the work of associations of dealers in works of art and paintings and to contribute to artistic and economic expansion. Mems: associations in 18 countries. Pres. R. OTTO (Austria).

International Co-operative Alliance—ICA: 15 route des Morillons, 1218 Grand-Saconnex, Geneva, Switzerland; tel. (22) 929-88-88; telex 415620; fax (22) 798-41-22; e-mail ica@coop.org; internet http://www.coop.org; f. 1895 for the pursuit of co-operative aims. A General Assembly and four Regional Assemblies meet every two years, on an alternating basis; a 20-member ICA Board controls the affairs of the organization between meetings of the General Assembly. Specialized bodies have been established to promote co-operative activities in the following fields: agriculture, banking, fisheries, consumer affairs, energy, tourism, communications, co-operative research, health, human resources, wholesale distribution, housing, insurance, women's participation and industrial and artisanal and service producers' co-operatives. Mems: 224 affiliated national orgs, with a total membership of more than 750m. individuals in 93 countries and seven int. orgs. Pres. ROBERTO RODRIGUES (Brazil); Dir-Gen. BRUCE THORDARSON (Canada). Publs *Review of International Co-operation* (quarterly), *ICA News* (every 2 months), *Co-op Dialogue* (2 a year).

International Council of Shopping Centres: 665 Fifth Ave, New York, NY 10022, USA; tel. (212) 421-8181; telex 128185; fax (212) 486-0849; f. 1957 as a trade association for the shopping centre industry, to promote professional standards of performance in the development, construction, financing, leasing and management of shopping centres throughout the world; organizes training courses; gives awards for new centres. Exec. Vice-Pres. JOHN T. RIORDAN.

International Council of Societies of Industrial Design—ICSID: Yrjönkatu 11E, 00120 Helsinki, Finland; tel. (9) 607611; fax (9) 607875; f. 1957 to encourage the development of high standards in the practice of industrial design; to improve and expand the contribution of industrial design throughout the world. Mems: 151 in 48 countries. Pres. AUGUSTO MORELLO (Italy); Sec.-Gen. KAARINA POHTO. Publs *ICSID News, World Directory of Design Schools.*

International Council of Tanners: POB 36, Northampton, NN6 8DN, United Kingdom; tel. and fax (1604) 820-461; f. 1926 to study all questions relating to the leather industry and maintain contact with national associations. Mems: national tanners' organizations in 36 countries. Pres. COLIN CHAFFER (Australia); Sec. Dr ROBERT L. SYKES (UK).

International Exhibitions Bureau: 56 ave Victor Hugo, Paris 16e, France; tel. 1-45-00-38-63; f. 1928, revised by Protocol 1972, for the authorization and registration of international exhibitions falling under the 1928 Convention. Mems: 84 states. Pres. OLE PHILIPSON; Sec.-Gen. VICENTE GONZALES LOSCERTALES.

International Federation of Associations of Textile Chemists and Colourists—IFATCC: Postfach 403, 4153 Reinach 1, Switzerland; e-mail markuskrayer@chbs.mhs.ciba.com; f. 1930 for liaison on professional matters between members; and the furtherance of scientific and technical collaboration in the development of the textile finishing industry and the colouring of materials. Mems: in 21 countries. Pres. JOHN HANSEN (Denmark); Sec. MARKUS KRAYER (Switzerland).

International Federation of Grocers' Associations—IFGA: Falkenplatz 1, 3001 Berne, Switzerland; tel. (31) 3024249; fax (31) 3017646; f. 1927; initiates special studies and works to further the interests of members having special regard to new conditions resulting from European integration and developments in consuming and distribution. Mems: 500,000. Sec.-Gen. PETER SCHUETZ (Switzerland).

International Federation of Pharmaceutical Manufacturers Associations—IFPMA: 30 rue de St Jean, POB 9, 1211 Geneva 18, Switzerland; tel. (22) 3401200; fax (22) 3401380; f. 1968 for the exchange of information and international co-operation in all questions of interest to the pharmaceutical industry, particularly in the field of health legislation, science and research; development of ethical principles and practices and co-operation with national and international organizations, governmental and non-governmental. Mems: the national pharmaceutical associations of 56 countries and one regional association (representing Latin America). Pres. SEÁN LANCE (UK); Vice-Pres LODEWIJK DE VINK (USA), TADASHI SUZUKI (Japan). Publ. *Health Horizons* (3 a year).

International Federation of the Phonographic Industry: 54 Regent St, London, W1R 5PJ, United Kingdom; tel. (171) 878-7900; fax (171) 878-7950; e-mail info@ifpi.org; f. 1933; represents the interests of record producers by campaigning for the introduction, improvement and enforcement of copyright and related rights legislation and co-ordinating the recording industry's anti-piracy activities. Mems: 1,100 in over 70 countries. Chair. DAVID FINE; Chief Exec NIC GARNETT.

International Fertilizer Industry Association: 28 rue Marbeuf, 75008 Paris, France; tel. 1-42-25-27-07; telex 640481; fax 1-42-25-24-08. Pres. C. E. CHILDERS; Sec.-Gen. L. M. MAENE.

International Fragrance Association—IFRA: 8 rue Charles-Humbert, 1205 Geneva, Switzerland; tel. (22) 3213548; fax (22) 7811860; e-mail ifra@dial.eunet.ch; f. 1973 to collect and study scientific data on fragrance materials and to make recommendations on their safe use. Mems: national associations in 14 countries. Pres. Dr J. ADAMS; Sec.-Gen. Dr F. GRUNDSCHOBER.

International Fur Trade Federation: 2 The Quintet, Churchfield Rd, Walton-on-Thames, KT12 2TZ, United Kingdom; tel. (1932) 232866; fax (1932) 232656; f. 1949 to promote and organize joint action by fur trade organizations for promoting, developing and protecting trade in fur skins and/or processing thereof. Mems: 33 organizations in 28 countries. Exec. Officer J. BAILEY.

International Group of National Associations of Manufacturers of Agrochemical Products: 79A ave Albert Lancaster, 1180 Brussels, Belgium; tel. (2) 375-68-60; telex 62120; f. 1967 to encourage the rational use of chemicals in agriculture, the harmonization of national and international legislation, and the respect of industrial property rights; encourages research on chemical residues and toxicology. Mems: associations in 50 countries. Dir-Gen. HANS G. VAN LOEPER.

International Meat Secretariat (Office International de la Viande): 64 rue Taitbout, 75009 Paris, France; tel. 1-42-80-04-72; fax 1-42-80-67-45.

International Organization for Motor Trades and Repairs: Kosterijland 15, 3981 AJ Bunnik, Netherlands; tel. (30) 6595301; fax (30) 6564982; e-mail iomtr@rdc.nl; internet http://www.rdc.nliomtr; f. 1947 to collect and disseminate information about all aspects of the retail motor industry; to hold meetings and congresses. Mems: 37 associations in 24 countries. Pres. P. CABRAL (Portugal); Exec. Dir H. W. G. VAN DIJK (Netherlands). Publ. *Newsletter*.

International Organization of Motor Manufacturers: 4 rue de Berri, 75008 Paris; tel. 1-43-59-00-13; fax 1-45-63-84-41; e-mail oica@club-internet.fr; f. 1919 to co-ordinate and further the interests of the automobile industry, to promote the study of economic and other matters affecting automobile construction; to control automobile manufacturers' participation in international exhibitions in Europe. Full mems: manufacturers' associations of 16 European countries, China, Japan, the Republic of Korea and the USA. Assoc. mems: four importers' associations. Corresponding mems: seven automobile associations. Pres. C. ESPINOSA (Spain); Gen. Sec. J. M. MULLER. Publ. *Yearbook of the World's Motor Industry*.

International Organization of the Flavour Industry—IOFI: 8 rue Charles-Humbert, 1205 Geneva, Switzerland; tel. (22) 3213548; fax (22) 7811860; e-mail iofi@dial.eunet.ch; f. 1969 to support and promote the flavour industry; active in the fields of safety evaluation and regulation of flavouring substances. Mems: national associations in 21 countries. Pres. Dr S. M. A. LECCHINI; Sec.-Gen. F. GRUNDSCHOBER. Publs *Documentation Bulletin* (monthly), *Information Letters, Code of Practice*.

International Publishers' Association: 3 ave de Miremont, 1206 Geneva, Switzerland; tel. (22) 3463018; fax (22) 3475717; e-mail secretariat@ipa-uie.org; f. 1896 to defend the freedom of publishers, promote their interests and foster international co-operation; helps the international trade in books and music, works on international copyright, and translation rights. Mems: 74 professional book publishers' organizations in 65 countries and music publishers' associations in 20 countries. Pres. ALAIN GRÜND; Sec.-Gen. J. ALEXIS KOUTCHOUMOW.

International Rayon and Synthetic Fibres Committee: 4 ave E. van Nieuwenhuyse, 1160 Brussels, Belgium; tel. (2) 676-74-55; fax (2) 676-74-54; f. 1950 to improve the quality and use of man-made fibres and of products made from fibres. Mems: national associations and individual producers in 19 countries. Pres. G. A. CAMPBELL; Dir-Gen. C. PURVIS (UK). Publ. *Statistical Booklet* (annual).

International Shopfitting Organisation: Schmelzbergstr. 56, 8044 Zürich, Switzerland; tel. (1) 2678100; fax (1) 2678150; f. 1959 to promote interchange of ideas between individuals and firms concerned with the common interests of shopfitting. Mems: companies in 16 countries. Pres. U. FAETCH; Sec. PETRA ISENBERG.

International Textile Manufacturers Federation—ITMF: Am Schanzengraben 29, Postfach, 8039 Zürich, Switzerland; tel. (1) 2017080; telex 817578; fax (1) 2017134; f. 1904, present title adopted 1978. Aims to protect and promote the interests of its members, to disseminate information, and encourage co-operation. Mems: national textile trade associations in about 50 countries. Pres. HERVÉ GIRAUD (Turkey); Dir-Gen. Dr HERWIG STROLZ (Austria). Publs *State of Trade Report* (quarterly), *Statistics* (annually).

International Union of Marine Insurance: Löwenstr. 19, POB 6333, 8023 Zürich, Switzerland; tel. (1) 2116040; fax (1) 2211165; f. 1873 to collect and distribute information on marine insurance on a world-wide basis. Mems: 53 associations. Pres. NICHOLAS ADAMANTIADIS (Greece); Gen. Sec. Dr ALEXANDER VON ZIEGLER.

International Wool Textile Organisation: 63 Albert Drive, London, SW19 6LB, United Kingdom; tel. (181) 788-8876; fax (181) 788-5171; f. 1929 to link wool textile organizations in member-countries and represent their interests; holds annual International

Wool Conference. Mems: in 28 countries. Pres. H. GRUNZKE (Germany); Sec.-Gen. W. H. LAKIN (UK).

International Wrought Copper Council: 6 Bathurst St, Sussex Sq., London, W2 2SD, United Kingdom; tel. (171) 724-7465; fax (171) 724-0308; f. 1953 to link and represent copper fabricating industries, and to represent the views of copper consumers to raw material producers; organizes specialist activities on technical work and the development of copper. Mems: 18 national groups in Europe, Australia, Japan and Malaysia, 4 assoc. mems. Chair. TETSURO KAWAKAMI; Sec.-Gen. S. N. PAYTON.

Liaison Group of the European Mechanical, Electrical, Electronic and Metalworking Industries: 99 rue de Stassart, 1050 Brussels, Belgium; tel. (2) 511-34-84; fax (2) 512-99-70; e-mail secretariat@orgalime.be; f. 1954 to provide a permanent liaison between the mechanical, electrical and electronic engineering, and metalworking industries of member countries. Mems: 24 trade associations in 16 West European countries. Pres. ED DE HAAS (Netherlands); Sec.-Gen. PATRICK KNOX-PEEBLES.

Union of Industrial and Employers' Confederations of Europe—UNICE: 40 rue Joseph II, 1000 Brussels, Belgium; tel. (2) 237-65-11; fax (2) 231-14-45; e-mail main@unice.be; f. 1958; aims to ensure that European Community policy-making takes account of the views of European business; committees and working groups work out joint positions in the various fields of interest to business and submit them to the Community institutions concerned. The Council of Presidents (of member federations) lays down general policy; the Executive Committee (of Directors-General of member federations) is the managing body; and the Committee of Permanent Delegates, consisting of federation representatives in Brussels, ensures permanent liaison with members. Mems: 20 industrial and employers' federations from the EU member states, and 13 federations from non-EU countries. Pres. FRANÇOIS PERIGOT; Sec.-Gen. ZYGMUNT TYSZKIEWICZ. Publ. *UNICE Information* (every 2 months), *Compendium of Position Papers* (2 a year).

Union of International Fairs: 35 bis, rue Jouffroy d'Abbans, 75017 Paris, France; tel. 1-42-67-99-12; telex 644097; fax 1-42-27-19-29; f. 1925 to increase co-operation between international fairs, safeguard their interests and extend their operations; holds annual congress and educational seminars. The Union has defined the conditions to be fulfilled to qualify as an international fair, and is concerned with the standards of the fairs. It studies improvements which could be made in the conditions of the fairs and organizes training seminars. Mems: 172 organizers with 546 approved events, 26 assoc. mems in 67 countries. Pres. DIETER EBERT (German); Sec.-Gen. GERDA MARQUARDT (France).

World Council of Management—CIOS: c/o RKW, 6236 Eschborn, Düsseldorfstr. 40, POB 5867, Germany; tel. (6196) 495366; telex 4072755; fax (6196) 495304; f. 1926 to promote the understanding of the principles and the practice of the methods of modern management; to organize conferences, congresses and seminars on management; to exchange information on management techniques; to promote training programmes. Mems: national organizations in 45 countries. Pres. JOHN DIEBOLU (USA); Sec. HERBERT MÜLLER (Germany). Publ. *Newsletter*.

World Customs Organization—WCO: 26–38 rue de l'Industrie, 1040 Brussels, Belgium; tel. (2) 508-42-11; fax (2) 508-42-40; f. 1952 as Customs Co-operation Council; an independent intergovernmental body that aims to enhance the effectiveness and efficiency of customs administrations in the areas of compliance with trade regulations; the protection of society; and revenue collection. Mems: governments of 145 countries or territories. Chair. G. LUDLOW (New Zealand); Sec.-Gen. J. W. SHAVER (USA). Publ. *WCO News* (2 a year).

World Federation of Advertisers: 18–24 rue des Colonies, Bte 6, 1000 Brussels; tel. (2) 5025740; fax (2) 5025666; e-mail info@wfa.be; internet http://www.wfa.be/; f. 1953; promotes and studies advertising and its related problems. Mems: associations in 35 countries and 28 international companies. Pres. MALCOLM EARNSHAW; Dir-Gen. BERNHARD ADRIAENSENS.

World Packaging Organisation: 42 ave de Versailles, 75016 Paris, France; tel. 1-42-88-29-74; fax 1-45-25-02-73; f. 1967 to provide a forum for the exchange of knowledge of packaging technology and, in general, to create conditions for the conservation, preservation and distribution of world food production; holds annual congress and competition. Mems: Asian, North American, Latin American, European and South African packaging federations. Pres. G. K. TOWNSHEND (UK); Gen. Sec. PIERRE J. LOUIS (France).

World Trade Centers Association: One World Trade Center, Suite 7701, New York, NY 10048, USA; tel. (212) 432-2626; telex 285472; fax (212) 488-0064; internet http://www.wtca.org/; f. 1968 to promote trade through the establishment of world trade centres, including education facilities, information services and exhibition facilities; operates an electronic trading and communication system (World Trade Center Network). Mems: trade centres, chambers of commerce and other organizations in 89 countries. Pres. GUY F. TOZZOLI; Chair. TADAYOSHI YAMADA. Publs *WTCA News* (monthly), *World Traders* (quarterly).

Transport

African Airlines Association: POB 20116, Nairobi, Kenya; tel. (2) 502645; fax (2) 502504; f. 1968 to give African air companies expert advice in technical, financial, juridical and market matters; to improve air transport in Africa through inter-carrier co-operation; and to develop manpower resources. Mems: 34 national carriers.

Airports Council International—ACI: POB 16, 1215 Geneva 15-Airport, Switzerland; tel. (22) 7984141; fax (22) 7880909; f. 1991, following merger of Airport Operators Council International and International Civil Airports Association; aims to represent and develop co-operation among airports of the world. Mems: 477 operating more than 1,200 airports in 150 countries and territories. Chair. JEAN FLEURY; Dir-Gen. JONATHAN HOWE.

Arab Air Carriers' Organization—AACO: PO Box 13-5468, Beirut, Lebanon; tel. 861297; fax 603140; e-mail aaco@dn.net.lb; f. 1965 to co-ordinate and promote co-operation in the activities of Arab airline companies. Mems: 16 Arab air carriers. Pres. Gen. OMAR ALI RIDA (Syria); Sec.-Gen. ABDUL WAHAB TEFFAHA.

Arab Union of Railways: POB 6599, Aleppo, Syria; tel. 220302; telex 331009; f. 1979 to stimulate co-operation between railways in Arab countries, to co-ordinate their activities and to ensure the interconnection of Arab railways with each other and with international railways; holds symposium every two years. Mems: 19 railways companies, railway infrastructure companies and associated organizations. Chair. TAHAR AZAIEZ; Gen. Sec. MOURHAF SABOUNI. Publs *Al Sikak Al Arabiye* (Arab Railways, quarterly), *Statistics of Arab Railways* (annually), *Glossary of Railway Terms* (Arabic, English, French and German).

Association of Asia Pacific Airlines: 5/F Corporate Business Centre, 151 Paseo de Roxas, 1226 Makati, Philippines; tel. (2) 8403191; fax (2) 8103518; e-mail aapahdq@aapa.org.ph; f. 1966 as Orient Airlines Asscn; present name adopted in April 1997; member carriers exchange information and plan the development of the industry within the region by means of commercial, technical and management information committees. Mems: Air New Zealand, Air Niugini, All Nippon Airways, Ansett Australia, Asiana Airlines, Cathay Pacific Airways Ltd, China Airlines, Dragonair, EVA Airways, Garuda Indonesia, Japan Airlines, Korean Air, Malaysia Airlines, Philippine Airlines, Qantas Airways Ltd, Royal Brunei Airlines, Singapore Airlines and Thai Airways International. Dir.-Gen. RICHARD T. STIRLAND. Publs *Annual and Statistical Report, Orient Aviation*.

Association of European Airlines: 350 ave Louise, Bte 4, 1050 Brussels, Belgium; tel. (2) 627-06-00; telex 22918; fax (2) 648-40-17; f. 1954 to carry out research on political, commercial, economic and technical aspects of air transport; maintains statistical data bank. Mems: 26 airlines. Pres. JÜRGEN WEBER (Germany); Sec.-Gen. KARL-HEINZ NEUMEISTER.

Baltic and International Maritime Council—BIMCO: Bagsvaerdvej 161, 2880 Bagsvaerd, Denmark; tel. 44-44-45-00; telex 19086; fax 44-44-44-50; e-mail mailbox@bimco.dk; internet http://www.bimco.dk; f. 1905 to unite shipowners and other persons and organizations connected with the shipping industry. Mems: in 115 countries, representing over 50% of world merchant tonnage. Pres. RONALD BERGMAN (Sweden); Sec.-Gen. FINN FRANDSEN.

Central Commission for the Navigation of the Rhine: Palais du Rhin, Place de la République, 67000 Strasbourg, France; tel. 3-88-52-20-10; fax 3-88-32-10-72; f. 1815 to ensure free movement of traffic and standard river facilities to ships of all nations; draws up navigational rules, standardizes customs regulations, arbitrates in disputes involving river traffic, approves plans for river maintenance work; there is an administrative centre for social security for boatmen, and a tripartite commission for labour conditions. Mems: Belgium, France, Germany, Netherlands, Switzerland. Pres. MATTHIAS KRAFT (Switzerland); Sec.-Gen. ALAIN DEMENTHON (France).

Danube Commission: Benczúr utca 25, 1068 Budapest, Hungary; tel. (1) 352-1835; fax (1) 352-1839; f. 1948; supervises implementation of the convention on the regime of navigation on the Danube; holds annual sessions; approves projects for river maintenance, supervises a uniform system of traffic regulations on the whole navigable portion of the Danube and on river inspection. Mems: Austria, Bulgaria, Hungary, Romania, Russia, Slovakia, Ukraine, Yugoslavia. Pres. E. MITROVA (Slovakia); Dir-Gen. H. STRASSER. Publs *Basic Regulations for Navigation on the Danube, Hydrological Yearbook, Statistical Yearbook,* proceedings of sessions.

European Civil Aviation Conference—ECAC: 3 bis Villa Emile-Bergerat, 92522 Neuilly-sur-Seine Cédex, France; tel. 1-46-41-85-45; fax 1-46-24-18-18; e-mail 101575.1313@compuserve.com; f. 1955; aims to promote the continued development of a safe, efficient and sustainable European transport system. Mems: 36 European states. Pres. ANDRÉ ANER; Exec. Sec. RAYMOND BENJAMIN.

European Conference of Ministers of Transport—ECMT: 2 rue André Pascal, 75113 Paris Cédex 16, France; tel. 1-45-24-82-00; fax 1-45-24-97-42; f. 1953 to achieve the maximum use and most rational development of European inland transport. Council of Ministers of Transport meets annually; Committee of Deputy Ministers meets three times a year and is assisted by Subsidiary Bodies concerned with: General Transport Policy, Railways, Roads, Inland Waterways, Investment, Road and Traffic Signs and Signals, Urban Safety, Economic Research, and other matters. Shares Secretariat staff with OECD (q.v.). Mems: 31 European countries; Associate Mems: Australia, Canada, Japan, New Zealand, Russia, USA. Sec.-Gen. G. AURBACH.

European Organisation for the Safety of Air Navigation—EUROCONTROL: 96 rue de la Fusée, 1130 Brussels, Belgium; tel. (2) 729-90-11; telex 21173; fax (2) 729-90-44; internet http://www.eurocontrol.be; f. 1963 principal objective is the development of a coherent and co-ordinated air traffic control system in Europe; comprises two organs: the Permanent Commission for the Safety of Air Navigation (policy-making), and the Agency for the Safety of Air Navigation (executive); there are directorates, covering human resources and finance matters and a general secretariat. A special organizational structure covers the management of the European Air Traffic Control Harmonization and Integration Programme. EUROCONTROL also operates the Experimental Centre (at Brétigny-sur-Orge, France), the Institute of Air Navigation Services (in Luxembourg), the Central Route Charges Office, the Central Flow Management Unit (both in Brussels) and the Upper Area Control Centre (in Maastricht, Netherlands). Budget (1997) ECU 457m. Mems: Austria, Belgium, Bulgaria, Croatia, Cyprus, Czech Republic, Denmark, France, Germany, Greece, Hungary, Ireland, Italy, Luxembourg, Malta, Netherlands, Norway, Portugal, Romania, Slovakia, Slovenia, Spain, Sweden, Switzerland, Turkey, United Kingdom. Dir-Gen. YVES LAMBERT (France).

European Passenger Train Time-Table Conference: Direction générale des chemins de fer fédéraux suisses, Hochschulstrasse 6, 3030 Berne, Switzerland; f. 1923 to arrange international passenger connections by rail and water and to help obtain easing of customs and passport control at frontier stations. Mems: rail and steamship companies and administrations. Administered by the Directorate of the Swiss Federal Railways. Pres. Dr B. WEIBEL.

European Railway Wagon Pool—EUROP: SNCB, Département Transport, 85 rue de France, 1060 Brussels, Belgium; tel. (2) 525-41-30; telex 24607; fax (2) 525-38-99; f. 1953 for the common use of wagons put into the pool by member railways. Mems: national railway administrations of Austria, Belgium, Denmark, France, Germany, Italy, Luxembourg, Netherlands, Switzerland. Managing railway: Belgian Railways. Pres. J. DEKEMPENEER.

Institute of Air Transport: 103 rue la Boétie, 75008 Paris, France; tel. 1-43-59-38-68; telex 642584; fax 1-43-59-47-37; f. 1945 as an international centre of research on economic, technical and policy aspects of air transport, and on the economy and sociology of transport and tourism; acts as economic and technical consultant in carrying out research requested by members on specific subjects; maintains a data bank, a library and a consultation and advice service; organizes training courses on air transport economics. Mems: organizations involved in air transport, production and equipment, universities, banks, insurance companies, private individuals and government agencies in 79 countries. Dir-Gen. JACQUES PAVAUX. Publs (in French and English), *ITA Press* (2 a month), *ITA Studies and Reports* (quarterly), *Aviation Industry Barometer* (quarterly).

Intergovernmental Organization for International Carriage by Rail: Gryphenhübeliweg 30, 3006 Berne, Switzerland; tel. (31) 3511762; fax (31) 3511164; e-mail otif@otif.ch; f. 1893 as Central Office for International Carriage by Rail, present name adopted 1985; aims to establish and develop a uniform system of law governing the international carriage of passengers, luggage and goods by rail in member states, which between them have a total of 240,000 km of railway lines. Mems: 39 states. Dir-Gen. M. BURGMANN. Publ. *Bulletin des Transports Internationaux ferroviaires* (every 2 months, in French and German).

International Air Transport Association—IATA: 33 route de l'Aéroport, CP 416, 1215 Geneva 15, Switzerland; tel. (22) 7992525; fax (22) 7983553; e-mail information@iata.org; internet http://www.iata.org; f. 1945 to represent and serve the airline industry. Aims to promote safe, reliable and secure air services; to assist the industry to attain adequate levels of profitability while developing cost-effective operational standards; to promote the importance of the industry to global social and economic development; and to identify common concerns and represent the industry in addressing these at regional and international level. Maintains regional offices in Amman, Brussels, Dakar, London, Nairobi, Santiago, Singapore and Washington, DC. Mems: 258 airline cos. Dir-Gen. PIERRE JEANNIOT; Corporate Sec. LORNE CLARK. Publ. *Airlines International* (every 2 months).

International Association for the Rhine Vessels Register—IVR: Vasteland 12E, 3011 BL Rotterdam (POB 23210, 3001 KE Rotterdam), Netherlands; tel. (10) 4116070; fax (10) 4129091; f. 1947 for the classification of Rhine ships, the organization and publication of a Rhine ships register and for the unification of general average rules, etc. Mems: shipowners and associations, insurers and associations, shipbuilding engineers, average adjusters and others interested in Rhine traffic. Gen. Sec. T. K. VAN DEN HEUVEL.

International Association of Ports and Harbors: Kono Bldg, 1-23-9 Nishi-Shimbashi, Minato-ku, Tokyo 105, Japan; tel. (3) 3591-4261; fax (3) 3580-0364; e-mail iaph@msn.com; f. 1955 to increase the efficiency of ports and harbours through the dissemination of information relative to the fields of port organization, management, administration, operation, development and promotion; to encourage the growth of water-borne commerce; holds conference every two years. Mems: 350 in 85 states. Pres. JEAN SMAGGHE (France); Sec.-Gen. HIROSHI KUSAKA (Japan). Publs *Ports and Harbors* (10 a year), *Membership Directory* (annually).

International Chamber of Shipping: Carthusian Court, 12 Carthusian St, London, EC1M 6EB, United Kingdom; tel. (171) 417-8844; fax (171) 417-8877; f. 1921 to co-ordinate the views of the international shipping industry on matters of common interest, in the policy-making, technical and legal fields of shipping operations. Mems: national associations representative of free-enterprise shipowners and operators in 33 countries, covering 50% of world merchant shipping. Sec.-Gen. J. C. S. HORROCKS.

International Container Bureau: 167 rue de Courcelles, 75017 Paris, France; tel. 1-47-66-03-90; fax 1-47-66-08-91; f. 1933 to group representatives of all means of transport and activities concerning containers, to promote combined door-to-door transport by the successive use of several means of transport; to examine and bring into effect administrative, technical and customs advances and to centralize data on behalf of its members. Mems: 800. Sec.-Gen. JEAN REY. Publ. *Container Bulletin*.

International Federation of Freight Forwarders' Associations: Baumackerstr. 24, POB 8050 Zürich, Switzerland; tel. (1) 3116511; fax (1) 3119044; e-mail 101623.1324@compuserve.com; internet http://www.fiata.com; f. 1926 to protect and represent its members at international level. Mems: 95 organizations and more than 2,500 associate members in 145 countries. Pres. ABDELMALEK DAHMANI; Dir MARCO A. SANGALETTI. Publ. *FIATA Review* (every 2 months).

International Rail Transport Committee (Comité international des transports ferroviaires—CIT): Direction générale des Chemins de fer fédéraux suisses, Division juridique, 6 Hochschulstrasse, 3030 Berne, Switzerland; tel. (512) 202806; telex 991212; fax (512) 203457; e-mail henri.trdliet@sbb.ch; f. 1902 for the development of international law relating to railway transport on the basis of the Convention concerning International Carriage by Rail (COTIF) and its Appendices (CIV, CIM), and for the adoption of standard rules on other questions relating to international transport law. Mems: 300 transport undertakings in 37 countries. Pres. M. WEIBEL (Switzerland); Sec. M. LEIMGRUBER (Switzerland).

International Railway Congress Association: Section 10, 85 rue de France, 1060 Brussels, Belgium; tel. (2) 520-78-31; telex 46-20424; fax (2) 525-40-84; f. 1885 to facilitate the progress and development of railways by holding periodical congresses and by issuing publications. Mems: governments, railway administrations and national or international organizations. Pres. E. SCHOUPPE; Sec.-Gen. A. MARTENS. Publ. *Rail International* (monthly).

International Road Federation—IRF: Washington office: 2600 Virginia Ave, NW, Suite 208, Washington, DC 20037, USA; tel. (202) 338-4641; fax (202) 338-8104; e-mail irf@irfnet.org; Geneva Office: 63 rue de Lausanne, 1202 Geneva, Switzerland; tel. (22) 7317150; fax (22) 7317158; e-mail irf@dial.eunet.ch; f. 1948 to encourage the development and improvement of highways and highway transportation; organizes World Highway Conferences. Mems: 70 national road associations and 500 individual firms and industrial associations. Dir-Gen. (Washington) RICHARD B. ROBERTSON; Dir-Gen. (Geneva) M. W. WESTERHUIS. Publs *World Road Statistics* (annually, Geneva), *World Highways* (8 a year).

International Road Safety: POB 40, 8005 Luxembourg-Bertrange; tel. 31-83-41; fax 31-14-60; f. 1959 for exchange of ideas and material on road safety; organizes international action and congresses; assists non-member countries. Mems: 60 national organizations. Pres. Prof. L. NILLES (Luxembourg); Sec.-Gen. MARTINE PETERS. Publ. *Revue-Pri* (3 a year).

International Road Transport Union—IRU: Centre International, 3 rue de Varembé, BP 44, 1202 Geneva, Switzerland; tel. (22) 9182700; telex 412813; fax (22) 9182741; e-mail iru@iru.org; f. 1948 to study all problems of road transport, to promote unification and simplification of regulations relating to road transport, and to develop the use of road transport for passengers and goods. Mems: 160 national federations for road transport and interested groups, in 65 countries. Sec.-Gen. MARTIN MARMY.

International Shipping Federation: Carthusian Court, 12 Carthusian St, London, EC1M 6EB, United Kingdom; tel. (171) 417-8844; fax (171) 417-8877; f. 1909 to consider all personnel questions affecting the interests of shipowners; responsible for Shipowners' Group at conferences of the International Labour Organisation. Mems: national shipowners' organizations in 32 countries. Pres. J. KELLY (UK); Dir J. C. S. HORROCKS; Sec. D. A. DEARSLEY.

International Union for Inland Navigation: 7 quai du Général Koenig, 67085 Strasbourg Cédex, France; tel. 3-88-36-28-44; fax 3-88-37-04-82; f. 1952 to promote the interests of inland waterways carriers. Mems: national waterways organizations of Austria, Belgium, France, Germany, Italy, Luxembourg, Netherlands, Switzerland. Pres. PH. GRULOIS (Belgium); Sec. M. RUSCHER. Publs annual and occasional reports.

International Union of Public Transport: 19 ave de l'Uruguay, 1000 Brussels, Belgium; tel. (2) 673-61-00; fax (2) 660-10-72; f. 1885 to study all problems connected with the urban and regional public passenger transport industry. Mems: 505 public transport systems in 60 countries, 347 contractors and services and 660 personal members. Pres. JEAN-PAUL BAILLY (France); Sec.-Gen. PIERRE LACONTE. Publs *Public Transport International* (every 2 months), *Biblio-Express* (every 2 months), *EuroExpress, UITP Express, Compendium of Statistics*, congress reports, bibliographies.

International Union of Railways—UIC: 16 rue Jean-Rey, 75015 Paris, France; tel. 1-44-49-20-20; telex 270835; fax 1-44-49-20-29; f. 1922 for the harmonization of railway operations and the development of international rail transport; compiles information concerning economic, management and technical aspects of railways; organizes international conferences. Mems: 120 railways. Pres. ADAM WIELADEK; Chief Exec. PHILIPPE ROUMEGUÈRE. Publs *Rail International*, jointly with the International Railway Congress Association (IRCA) (monthly, in English, French and German), *International Railway Statistics* (annually), *Activities Reports, UIC Panorama* (newsletter).

Northern Shipowners' Defence Club (Nordisk Skibsrederforening): Kristinelundv. 22, POB 3033 El., 0207 Oslo, Norway; tel. 22-13-56-00; telex 76825; fax 22-43-00-35; e-mail post@nordisk-skibsrederforenig.no; f. 1889 to assist members in disputes over charter parties, contracts, sale and purchase, taking the necessary legal steps on behalf of members and bearing the cost of such claims. Members are mainly Finnish, Swedish and Norwegian and some non-Scandinavian shipowners, representing about 1,800 ships and drilling rigs with gross tonnage of about 50 million. Man. Dir NICHOLAS HAMBRO; Chair. FRIDTJOF LORENTZEN. Publ. *A Law Report of Scandinavian Maritime Cases* (annually).

Organisation for the Collaboration of Railways: Hozà 63–67, 00681 Warsaw, Poland; tel. (22) 6573600; fax (22) 6573654; f. 1956; aims to improve standards and co-operation in railway traffic between countries of Europe and Asia; promotes co-operation on issues relating to traffic policy and economic and environmental aspects of railway traffic; ensures enforcement of the following agreements: Convention concerning international passenger traffic by railway; Regulation concerning the use of wagons in international traffic; International passenger tariff; Standard transit tariff to the convention concerning international goods traffic by rail; and contracts referring to the international transport of passengers and goods. Aims to elaborate and standardize general principles for international transport law. Conference of Ministers of member countries meets annually; Conference of Gen. Dirs of Railways meets at least once a year. Mems: ministries of transport of the Albania, Azerbaijan, Belarus, Bulgaria, People's Republic of China, Cuba, Czech Republic, Estonia, Georgia, Hungary, Iran, Kazakhstan, Democratic People's Republic of Korea, Kyrgyzstan, Latvia, Lithuania, Moldova, Mongola, Poland, Romania, Russia, Slovakia, Tajikistan, Turkmenistan, Ukraine, Uzbekistan, Viet Nam. Chair. Dr ANDRZEJ GOLASZEWSKI (Poland). Publ. *OSShD Journal* (every 2 months, in Chinese, German and Russian).

Pan American Railway Congress Association (Asociación del Congreso Panamericano de Ferrocarriles): Av. 9 de Julio 1925, 13°, 1332 Buenos Aires, Argentina; tel. (1) 381-4625; telex 22507; fax (1) 814-1823; f. 1907; present title adopted 1941; aims to promote the development and progress of railways in the American continent; holds Congresses every three years. Mems: government representatives, railway enterprises and individuals in 21 countries. Pres. JUAN CARLOS DE MARCHI (Argentina); Gen. Sec. CAYETANO MARLETTA RAINIERI (Argentina). Publ. *Technical Bulletin* (every 2 months).

Union of European Railway Industries—UNIFE: 221 ave Louise, 1050 Brussels, Belgium; tel. (2) 626-12-60; fax (2) 626-12-61; e-mail unife@pophost.eunet.be; f. 1975 to represent companies concerned in the manufacture of railway equipment in Europe, in order to represent their collective interests towards all European and international organizations concerned. Mems: 140 companies in 14 countries of; Chair. KAARE VAGNER; Dir Gen. MARC HONINCKX.

World Airlines Clubs Association: c/o IATA, Suite 2000, 2000 Peel St, Montréal, Québec, Canada H3A 2R4; tel. (514) 844-6311; fax (514) 844-5286; internet http://www.waca.org/; f. 1966; holds a General Assembly annually, regional meetings, international events and sports tournaments. Mems: clubs in 38 countries. Man. AUBREY WINTERBOTHAM. Publs *WACA World, WACA Contact, WACA World News*, annual report.

Youth and Students

Asian Students' Association: 511 Nathan Rd, 1/F, Kowloon, Hong Kong; tel. 23880515; fax 27825535; f. 1969; aims to promote students' solidarity in struggling for democracy, self-determination, peace, justice and liberation; conducts campaigns, training of activists, and workshops on human rights and other issues of importance.There are Student Commissions for Peace, Education and Human Rights. Mems: 34 national or regional student unions, four observers. Secretariat: LINA CABAERO (Philippines), STEVEN GAN (Malaysia), CHOW WING-HANG (Hong Kong). Publs *Movement News* (monthly), *ASA News* (quarterly).

Council of European National Youth Committees—CENYC: 517–519 Chaussée de Wavre, 1040 Brussels, Belgium; tel. (2) 648-91-01; fax (2) 648-96-40; f. 1963 to further the consciousness of European youth and to represent the National Co-ordinating Committees of youth work vis-à-vis European and international institutions. Activities include research on youth problems in Europe; projects, seminars, study groups, study tours; the Council provides a forum for the exchange of information, experiences and ideas between members, and represents European youth organizations in relations with other regions; furthers contact between young people in eastern and western Europe. Mems: 32 national councils in 30 countries. Sec.-Gen. WILLY BORSUS (Belgium). Publ. *CENYC Scene* (quarterly).

Council on International Educational Exchange: 205 East 42nd St, New York, NY 10017, USA; tel. (212) 661-1414; telex 423227; fax (212) 972-3231; e-mail strooboff@ciee.org; f. 1947; issues International Student Identity Card entitling holders to discounts and basic insurance; arranges overseas work and study programmes for students; co-ordinates summer work programme in the USA for foreign students; administers programmes for teachers and other professionals, sponsors conferences on educational exchange; operates a voluntary service programme. Mems: 307 colleges, universities and international educational organizations. Pres. and CEO STEVAN TROOBOFF. Publs include *Work, Study, Travel Abroad: The Whole World Handbook, Update, Volunteer!, High-School Student's Guide to Study, Travel and Adventure Abroad*.

European Law Students' Association—ELSA: 1 rue Defacqz, 1050 Brussels, Belgium; tel. (2) 5345679; fax (2) 5346586; f. 1981 to foster mutual understanding and promote social responsibility of law students and young laywers. Publs *ELSA Law Review, Legal Studies in Europe*.

International Association for the Exchange of Students for Technical Experience—IAESTE: c/o Prof. Sfeir, Dean School of Engineering and Architecture, LAU, POB 13-5053, Beirut, Lebanon; tel. (3) 617232; fax (3) 867098; e-mail asfeir@lau.edu.lb; 1948. Mems: 49 national committees. Gen. Sec. Prof. A. A. SFEIR. Publs *Activity Report, Annual Report*.

International Association of Dental Students: c/o FDI World Dental Federation, 7 Carlisle St, London, W1V 5RG, United Kingdom; tel. (171) 935 7852; fax (171) 486 0183; f. 1951 to represent dental students and their opinions internationally, to promote dental student exchanges and international congresses. Mems: 60,000 students in 45 countries (and 15,000 corresponding mems). Pres. CHRISTOPHER ORR (UK); Sec.-Gen. LIZ STOCKWELL; Publ. *IADS Newsletter* (3 a year).

International Association of Students in Economics and Management (AIESEC): 40 rue Washington, 1050 Brussels, Belgium; tel. (2) 646-24-20; fax (2) 646-37-64; e-mail aiesec@ai.aiesec.org; f. 1948; promotes international and cultural understanding through international exchange programmes, while developing leadership skills in its members. Mems: 50,000 from some 740 higher education institutions in 87 countries. Pres. MARIANNE KNUTH. Publ. *International Link* (magazine).

International Federation of Medical Students' Associations: Institute of Social Medicine, Academisch Medisch Centrum, Meibergdreef 15, 1105 Amsterdam, Netherlands; tel. (20) 5665366; fax (20) 6972316; e-mail f.w.hilhorst@amc.uva.nl; f. 1951 to promote international co-operation in professional treatment and the achievement of humanitarian ideals; provides forum for medical students; standing committees on professional exchange, electives exchange, medical education, public health, refugees and AIDS; organizes annual General Assembly. Mems: 57 associations. Sec.-Gen. MIA HILHORST. Publ. *IFMSA Newsletter* (4 a year).

International Pharmaceutical Students' Federation: Andries Bickerweg 5, 2517 JP The Hague, Netherlands; tel. (70) 363-19-25; fax (70) 363-39-14; e-mail ipsf@fip.nl; f. 1949 to study and promote the interests of pharmaceutical students and to encourage international co-operation. Mems: 34 full mems from national organizations and 22 assoc. mems from national or local organizations. Pres. ALISON SUTHERLAND; Sec.-Gen. DIDI GEORNARAS. Publ. *IPSF News Bulletin* (3 a year).

International Union of Students: POB 58, 17th November St, 110 01 Prague 01, Czech Republic; tel. 2312812; telex 122858; fax 2316100; f. 1946 to defend the rights and interests of students and strive for peace, disarmament, the eradication of illiteracy and of all forms of discrimination; operates research centre, sports and cultural centre and student travel bureau; activities include conferences, meetings, solidarity campaigns, relief projects, award of 30–40 scholarships annually, travel and exchange, sports events, cultural projects. Mems: 140 organizations from 115 countries. Pres. JOSEF SKALA; Vice-Pres. MARTA HUBIČKOVÁ; Gen. Sec. GIORGOS MICHAELIDES (Cyprus). Publs *World Student News* (quarterly), *IUS Newsletter, Student Life* (quarterly), *DE—Democratization of Education* (quarterly).

International Young Christian Workers: 11 rue Plantin, 1070 Brussels, Belgium; tel. (2) 521-69-83; fax (2) 521-69-44; e-mail jociycw@skynet.be; internet http://www.skynet.be/sky34197; f. 1925, on the inspiration of the Priest-Cardinal Joseph Cardijn; aims to educate young workers to take on present and future responsibilities in their commitment to the working class, and to confront all the situations which prevent them from fulfilling themselves. Pres. HELIO ALVES (Brazil); Sec.-Gen. DOMINADOR OLAVERE (Philippines). Publs *International INFO* (3 a year), *IYCW Bulletin* (quarterly).

International Youth and Student Movement for the United Nations—ISMUN: c/o Palais des Nations, 16 ave Jean-Tremblay, 1211 Geneva 10, Switzerland; tel. (22) 7985850; fax (22) 7334838; f. 1948 by the World Federation of United Nations Associations, independent since 1949; an international non-governmental organization of students and young people dedicated especially to supporting the principles embodied in the United Nations Charter and Universal Declaration of Human Rights; encourages constructive action in building economic, social and cultural equality and in working for national independence, social justice and human rights on a worldwide scale; regional offices in Austria, France, Ghana, Panama and the USA. Mems: associations in 53 countries. Sec.-Gen. JAN LÖNN. Publs *ISMUN Newsletter* (monthly).

International Youth Hostel Federation: 9 Guessens Rd, Welwyn Garden City, Herts., AL8 6QW, United Kingdom; tel. (1707) 324170; fax (1707) 323980; f. 1932; facilitates international travel by members of the various youth hostel associations and advises and helps in the formation of youth hostel associations in all countries where no such organizations exist; records over 32m. overnight stays annually in over 4,500 youth hostels. Mems: 60 national associations with 3.7m. individual members; 17 associated national organizations. Pres. FRIEDRICH MUTH (Germany); Sec.-Gen. RAWDON LAU (Hong Kong). Publs *Annual Report, Guidebook on World Hostels* (annually), *Manual, News Bulletin*.

Junior Chamber International (JCI), Inc.: 400 University Drive (POB 140-577), Coral Gables, FL 33114-0577, USA; tel. (305) 446-7608; fax (305) 442-0041; e-mail jciwhq@ix.netcom.com; f. 1944 to encourage and advance international understanding and goodwill. Junior Chamber organizations throughout the world provide young people with opportunities for leadership training, promoting goodwill through international fellowship, solving civic problems by arousing civic consciousness and discussing social, economic and cultural questions. Mems: 400,000 in 90 countries. Pres. PETRI NISKANEN (1998); Sec.-Gen. BENNY ELLERBE. Publ. *JCI News* (quarterly, in English and more than six other languages).

Latin American and Caribbean Confederation of Young Men's Christian Associations (Confederación Latinoamericana y del Caribe de Asociaciones Cristianas de Jóvenes): Culpina 272, 1406 Buenos Aires, Argentina; tel. (1) 637-4727; fax (1) 637-4867; f. 1914; aims to encourage the moral, spiritual, intellectual, social and physical development of young men; to strengthen the work of national Associations and to sponsor the establishment of new Associations. Mems: affiliated YMCAs in 25 countries (comprising 350,000 individuals). Pres. GERARDO VITUREIRA (Uruguay); Gen. Sec. NORBERTO D. RODRÍGUEZ (Argentina). Publs *Diecisiete/21* (bulletin), technical articles and other studies.

Pan-African Youth Movement (Mouvement pan-africain de la jeunesse): 19 rue Debbih Chérif, BP 72, Didouch Mourad, 16000 Algiers, Algeria; tel. and fax (2) 71-64-71; telex 61244; f. 1962; aims to mobilize and sensitize African youth to participate in socio-economic and political development and democratization; organizes conferences and seminars, youth exchanges, youth festivals. Mems: youth groups in 52 African countries and liberation movements. Publ. *MPJ News* (quarterly).

World Alliance of Young Men's Christian Associations: 12 clos Belmont, 1208 Geneva; tel. (22) 8495100; fax (22) 8495110; e-mail office@ymca.int; internet http://www.ymca.int; f. 1855 to unite the National Alliances of Young Men's Christian Associations throughout the world. Mems: national alliances and related associations in 128 countries. Pres. DAVID KWANG-SUN SUH (Republic of Korea); Sec.-Gen. JOHN W. CASEY (USA). Publ. *YMCA World* (quarterly).

World Assembly of Youth: Ved Bellahøj 4, 2700 Brønshøj, Copenhagen, Denmark; tel. 38-60-77-70; fax 38-60-57-97; f. 1949 as co-ordinating body for youth councils and organizations; organizes conferences, training courses and practical development projects. Pres. Datuk ALI RUSTAM; Sec.-Gen. HEIKKI PAKARINEN. Publs. *WAY Information* (every 2 months), *Youth Roundup* (monthly), *WAY Forum* (quarterly).

World Association of Girl Guides and Girl Scouts: World Bureau, Olave Centre, 12c Lyndhurst Rd, London, NW3 5PQ, United Kingdom; tel. (171) 794-1181; fax (171) 431-3764; f. 1928 to promote unity of purpose and common understanding in the fundamental principles of the Girl Guide and Girl Scout Movement throughout the world and to encourage friendship and mutual understanding among girls and young women world-wide; World Conference meets every three years. Mems: about 9m. individuals in 136 organizations. Chair. World Board HEATHER BRANDON; Dir World Bureau JAN HOLT. Publs *Triennial Report, Trefoil Round the World, Our World News*.

World Council of Service Clubs: POB 193, 651 05 Karstad, Sweden; e-mail woco@kd.gd.se; f. 1946 to provide a means of exchange of information and news for furthering international understanding and co-operation, to facilitate the extension of service clubs, and to create in young people a sense of civic responsibility. Mems: more than 3,000 clubs (in 83 countries. Sec.-Gen. FILIP GILLE.

World Federation of Democratic Youth—WFDY: POB 147, 1389 Budapest, Hungary; tel. (1) 154-095; telex 22-7197; fax (1) 352-746; f. 1945 to strive for peace and disarmament and joint action by democratic and progressive youth movements in support of national independence, democracy, social progress and youth rights; to support liberation struggles in Asia, Africa and Latin America; and to work for a new and more just international economic order. Mems: 195 organizations in 115 countries. Pres. ANDILE YAWA (South Africa). Publs *WFDY News* (monthly, in English, French and Spanish), *World Youth* (irregular, in English, French and Spanish).

World Organization of the Scout Movement: Case Postale 241, 1211 Geneva 4, Switzerland; tel. (22) 3204233; fax (22) 7812053; e-mail worldbureau@world.scout.org; f. 1922 to promote unity and understanding of scouting throughout the world; to develop good citizenship among young people by forming their characters for service, co-operation and leadership; to provide aid and advice to members and potential member associations. The World Scout Bureau (Geneva) has regional offices in Chile, Costa Rica, Egypt, Kenya and the Philippines (the European Region has its office in Brussels). Mems: over 25m. in 215 countries and territories. Sec.-Gen. Dr JACQUES MOREILLON (Switzerland). Publs *World Scouting News* (every 2 months), *Triennial Report*.

World Union of Jewish Students: POB 7914, 91077 Jerusalem, Israel; tel. (2) 610133; telex 25615; fax (2) 610741; e-mail wujs@jer1.il; f. 1924; organization for national student bodies concerned with educational and political matters, where possible in co-operation with non-Jewish student organizations, UNESCO, etc.; divided into six regions; organizes Congress every three years. Mems: 52 national unions representing over 1,500,000 students. Chair. CLAUDE KANDIYOTI; Admin. Dr MARCUS BLUM. Publs *Hamitzdeh, WUJS Report*.

World Young Women's Christian Association—World YWCA: 16 Ancienne Route, 1218 Grand-Saconnex, Geneva, Switzerland; tel. (22) 9296040; fax (22) 9296044; e-mail worldoffice@worldywca.org; f. 1894 for the linking together of national YWCAs (now in 88 countries) for their mutual help and development and the initiation of work in countries where the Association does not yet exist; works for international understanding, for improved social and economic conditions and for basic human rights for all people. Pres. ANITA ANDERSSON; Gen. Sec.MUSIMBI KANYORO. Publs *Annual Report, Advocacy Newsletter, Common Concern*.

Youth for Development and Co-operation—YDC: Rijswijkstrasse 141, 1062 HN Amsterdam, Netherlands; tel. (20) 614-25-10; fax (20) 617-55-45; e-mail ydc@geo2.geonet.de; aims to strengthen youth structures that promote new co-operation between young people in the industrialized and developing worlds, in order to achieve development that is environmentally sustainable and socially just; seminars, conferences and campaigns on issues related to youth and development (employment, young women, structural adjustment programmes etc.) Mems: 51 organizations. Sec.-Gen. B. AUER. Publ. *FLASH Newsletter* (irregular).

PART TWO
Afghanistan–Jordan

AFGHANISTAN

Introductory Survey

Location, Climate, Language, Religion, Flag, Capital

The Islamic State of Afghanistan (or Islamic Emirate of Afghanistan, as it was unilaterally renamed by Taliban in late 1997) is a land-locked country in south-western Asia. Its neighbours are Turkmenistan, Uzbekistan and Tajikistan to the north, Iran to the west, the People's Republic of China to the north-east and Pakistan to the east and south. The climate varies sharply between the highlands and lowlands; the temperature in the south-west in summer reaches 48.8°C (120°F), but in the winter, in the Hindu Kush mountains of the north-east, it falls to −26°C (−15°F). Of the many languages spoken in Afghanistan, the principal two are Pashtu and Dari (a dialect of Farsi or Iranian). The majority of Afghans are Muslims of the Sunni sect; there are also minority groups of Hindus, Sikhs and Jews. The state flag has three equal horizontal stripes, of black, white and green, with the inscription 'Allahu Akbar ('God is Great') centred on the black stripe and the inscription 'La Illaha Illa Allah Wa Muhammad Ur-Rusul Allah' ('There is no God but Allah, and Muhammad is his Prophet') centred on the white stripe. In October 1997 the Taliban administration in Kabul unilaterally decided to change the state flag: henceforth, it was to be plain white with, in the centre, an Arabic inscription in green lettering reading 'There is no God but Allah, and Muhammad is the Prophet of Allah'. The capital is Kabul.

Recent History

The last King of Afghanistan, Mohammad Zahir Shah, reigned from 1933 to 1973. His country was neutral during both World Wars and became a staunch advocate of non-alignment. In 1953 the King's cousin, Lt-Gen. Sardar Mohammad Daud Khan, was appointed Prime Minister and, securing aid from the USSR, initiated a series of economic plans for the modernization of the country. In 1963 Gen. Daud resigned and Dr Mohammad Yusuf became the first Prime Minister not of royal birth. He introduced a new democratic Constitution in the following year, which combined Western ideas with Islamic religious and political beliefs, but the King never allowed political parties to operate. Afghanistan made little progress under the succeeding Prime Ministers.

In July 1973, while King Zahir was in Italy, the monarchy was overthrown by a coup, in which the main figure was the former Prime Minister, Gen. Daud. The 1964 Constitution was abolished and Afghanistan was declared a republic. Daud renounced his royal titles and took office as Head of State, Prime Minister and Minister of Foreign Affairs and Defence.

A Loya Jirgah (Supreme National Tribal Assembly), appointed from among notable tribal elders by provincial governors, was convened in January 1977 and adopted a new Constitution, providing for presidential government and a one-party state. Daud was elected to continue as President for six years and the Loya Jirgah was then dissolved. In March President Daud formed a new civilian Government, nominally ending military rule. However, during 1977 there was growing discontent with Daud, especially within the armed forces, and in April 1978 a coup, known (from the month) as the 'Saur Revolution', ousted the President, who was killed with several members of his family. Nur Mohammad Taraki, imprisoned leader of the formerly banned People's Democratic Party of Afghanistan (PDPA), was released and installed as President of the Revolutionary Council and Prime Minister. The country was renamed the Democratic Republic of Afghanistan, the year-old Constitution was abolished and no political parties other than the communist PDPA were allowed to function. Afghanistan's already close relations with the USSR were further strengthened. However, opposition to the new regime led to armed insurrection, particularly by fiercely traditionalist Muslim rebel tribesmen (known, collectively, as the *mujahidin*), in almost all provinces, and the flight of thousands of refugees to Pakistan and Iran. In spite of purges of the army and civil service, Taraki's position became increasingly insecure, and in September 1979 he was ousted by Hafizullah Amin, who had been Deputy Prime Minister and Minister of Foreign Affairs since March. Amin's imposition of rigorous communist policies was unsuccessful and unpopular. In December he was removed and killed in a coup which was supported by the entry into Afghanistan of about 80,000 combat troops from the USSR. This incursion by Soviet armed forces into a traditionally non-aligned neighbouring country aroused world-wide condemnation. Babrak Karmal, a former Deputy Prime Minister under Taraki, was installed as the new Head of State, having been flown into Kabul by a Soviet aircraft from virtual exile in eastern Europe.

Riots, strikes and inter-factional strife and purges continued into 1980 and 1981. Sultan Ali Keshtmand, hitherto a Deputy Prime Minister, replaced Karmal as Prime Minister in June 1981. In the same month the regime launched the National Fatherland Front (NFF), incorporating the PDPA and other organizations, with the aim of promoting national unity. Despite a series of government reshuffles carried out in the early 1980s, the PDPA regime continued to fail to win widespread popular support. Consequently, the Government attempted to broaden the base of its support: in April 1985 it summoned a Loya Jirgah, which ratified a new Constitution for Afghanistan; a non-PDPA member was appointed Chairman of the NFF in May 1985; elections were held between August 1985 and March/April 1986 for new local government organs (it was claimed that 60% of those elected were non-party members), and several non-party members were appointed to high-ranking government posts between December 1985 and February 1986.

In May 1986 Dr Najibullah (the former head of the state security service, KHAD) succeeded Karmal as General Secretary of the PDPA. Karmal retained the lesser post of President of the Revolutionary Council. In the same month Dr Najibullah announced the formation of a collective leadership comprising himself, Karmal and Prime Minister Keshtmand. In November, however, Karmal was relieved of all party and government posts. Haji Muhammad Chamkani, formerly First Vice-President (and a non-PDPA member), became Acting President of the Revolutionary Council, pending the introduction of a new constitution and the establishment of a permanent legislature.

In December 1986 an extraordinary plenum of the PDPA Central Committee approved a policy of national reconciliation, involving negotiations with opposition groups, and the proposed formation of a coalition government of national unity. In early January 1987 a Supreme Extraordinary Commission for National Reconciliation, led by Abd ar-Rahim Hatif (the Chairman of the National Committee of the NFF), was formed to conduct the negotiations. The NFF was renamed the National Front (NF), and became a separate organization from the PDPA. The new policy of reconciliation won some support from former opponents, but the seven-party *mujahidin* alliance (Ittehad-i-Islami Afghan Mujahidin, Islamic Union of Afghan Mujahidin—IUAM) refused to observe the cease-fire or to participate in negotiations, while continuing to demand a complete and unconditional Soviet withdrawal.

In July 1987, as part of the process of national reconciliation, several important developments occurred: a law permitting the formation of other political parties (according to certain provisions) was introduced; Dr Najibullah announced that the PDPA would be prepared to share power with representatives of opposition groups in the event of the formation of a coalition government of national unity; and the draft of a new Constitution was approved by the Presidium of the Revolutionary Council. The main innovations incorporated in the draft Constitution were: the formation of a multi-party political system, under the auspices of the NF; the formation of a bicameral legislature, called the Meli Shura (National Assembly), composed of a Sena (Senate) and a Wolasi Jirgah (House of Representatives); the granting of a permanent constitutional status to the PDPA; the bestowal of unlimited power on the President, who was to hold office for seven years; and the reversion of the name of the country from the Democratic Republic to the Republic of Afghanistan. A Loya Jirgah ratified the new Constitution in November.

A further round of local elections throughout the country began in August 1987. A considerable number of those elected were reported to be non-PDPA members. On 30 September

Dr Najibullah was unanimously elected as President of the Revolutionary Council, and Haji Muhammad Chamkani resumed his former post as First Vice-President. In order to strengthen his position, Dr Najibullah ousted all the remaining supporters of the former President, Babrak Karmal, from the Central Committee and Politburo of the PDPA in October. In the following month a Loya Jirgah unanimously elected Dr Najibullah as President of the State.

In April 1988 elections were held to both houses of the new National Assembly, which replaced the Revolutionary Council. Although the elections were boycotted by the *mujahidin*, the Government left vacant 50 of the 234 seats in the House of Representatives, and a small number of seats in the Senate, in the hope that the guerrillas would abandon their armed struggle and present their own representatives to participate in the new administration. The PDPA itself won only 46 seats in the House of Representatives, but was guaranteed support from the NF, which gained 45, and from the various newly-recognized left-wing parties, which won a total of 24 seats. In May Dr Muhammad Hasan Sharq (a non-PDPA member and a Deputy Prime Minister since June 1987) replaced Sultan Ali Keshtmand as Prime Minister, and in June a new Council of Ministers was appointed.

On 18 February 1989, following the completion of the withdrawal of Soviet troops from Afghanistan (see below), Najibullah implemented a government reshuffle, involving the replacement of non-communist ministers with loyal PDPA members. On the same day, the Prime Minister, Dr Sharq (who had been one of the main promoters of the policy of national reconciliation), resigned from his post and was replaced by the former Prime Minister, Sultan Ali Keshtmand. Following the declaration of a state of emergency by Najibullah (citing allegations of repeated violations of the Geneva accords by Pakistan and the USA) on 19 February, a PDPA-dominated 20-member Supreme Council for the Defence of the Homeland was established. The Council, which was headed by President Najibullah and was composed of ministers, Politburo members and high-ranking military figures, assumed full responsibility for the country's economic, political and military policies (although the Council of Ministers continued to function).

In early March 1990 the Minister of Defence, Lt-Gen. Shahnawaz Tanay, with the alleged support of the air force and some divisions of the army, led an unsuccessful coup attempt against Najibullah's Government. Following the defeat of the conspirators, Najibullah carried out thorough purges of PDPA and army leaders and decided to revert rapidly to some form of constitutional civilian government. On 20 May the state of emergency was lifted; the Supreme Council for the Defence of the Homeland was disbanded; and a new Council of Ministers, under the premiership of Fazle Haq Khalikyar, was appointed. At the end of the month a Loya Jirgah was convened in Kabul, which ratified constitutional amendments, greatly reducing Afghanistan's socialist orientation; ending the PDPA's and the NF's monopoly over executive power and paving the way for democratic elections acceptable to everyone in Afghanistan; introducing greater political and press freedom; encouraging the development of the private sector and further foreign investment; lessening the role of the State and affording greater prominence to Islam. The extensive powers of the presidency were, however, retained. In addition, in late June the PDPA changed its name to the Homeland Party (HP—Hizb-i Watan), and dissolved the Politburo and the Central Committee, replacing them with an Executive Board and a Central Council, respectively. The party adopted a new programme, of which the hallmark was hostility to ideology. Najibullah was unanimously elected as Chairman of the HP. An important factor in Najibullah's decision to continue with, and to extend, the process of national reconciliation was the fact that the USSR's own internal problems meant that the Soviet administration was unwilling to sustain, for much longer, the supplies of arms, goods and credits that were helping to uphold the Kabul regime.

Fighting between the *mujahidin* and Afghan army units had begun in the eastern provinces after the 1978 coup and was aggravated by the implementation of social and economic reforms by the new administrations. The Afghan army relied heavily upon Soviet military aid in the form of weapons, equipment and expertise, but morale and resources were severely affected by defections to the rebels' ranks: numbers fell from about 80,000 men in 1978 to about 40,000 in 1985. A vigorous recruitment drive and stricter conscription regulations, implemented by Dr Najibullah in June 1986, failed to increase the size of the Afghan army to any great extent, and the defections continued.

During 1984–89 the guerrilla groups, which had been poorly armed at first, received ever-increasing support (both military and financial) from abroad, notably from the USA (which began to supply them with sophisticated anti-aircraft weapons in 1986), the United Kingdom and the People's Republic of China. Despite the Government's decision to seal the border with Pakistan, announced in September 1985, and the strong presence of Soviet forces there, foreign weapons continued to reach the guerrillas via Pakistan. Many of the guerrillas established bases in the North-West Frontier Province of Pakistan (notably in the provincial capital, Peshawar). Major efforts were made by the Government to enlist the support of border tribes by offering important concessions, financial inducements and guns in return for their support. From 1985 the fighting intensified, especially in areas close to the border between Afghanistan and Pakistan. There were many violations of the border, involving shelling, bombing and incursions into neighbouring airspace. The general pattern of the war, however, remained the same: the regime held the main towns and a few strategic bases, and relied on bombing of both military and civilian targets, and occasional attacks in force, together with conciliatory measures such as the provision of funds for local development, while the rebel forces dominated rural areas and were able to cause serious disruption.

With the civil war came famine in parts of Afghanistan, and there was a mass movement of population from the countryside to Kabul (whose population increased from about 750,000 in 1978 to 1,424,400, according to UN figures, in July 1988), and of refugees to Pakistan and Iran. In mid-1988 a UNHCR estimate assessed the number of Afghan refugees in Pakistan at 3.15m., and the number in Iran at 2.35m. Supply convoys were often prevented from reaching the cities, owing to the repeated severing of major road links by the guerrillas. Kabul, in particular, began to suffer from severe shortages of food and fuel, which were only partially alleviated by airlifts of emergency supplies, organized by the UN, the USSR and India. As a result of the increasing danger and hardship, a number of countries, including the USA, the UK, the Federal Republic of Germany and Japan, temporarily closed their embassies in the capital.

From 1980 extensive international negotiations took place to try to achieve the complete withdrawal of Soviet forces from Afghanistan. Between June 1982 and September 1987, seven rounds of indirect talks, the last in several phases, took place between the Afghan and Pakistani Ministers of Foreign Affairs in Geneva, under the auspices of the UN. In October 1986 the USSR made a token withdrawal of six regiments (6,000–8,000 men) from Afghanistan. As a result of the discussions in Geneva, an agreement was finally signed on 14 April 1988. The Geneva accords consisted of five documents: detailed undertakings by Afghanistan and Pakistan, relating to non-intervention and non-interference in each other's affairs; international guarantees of Afghan neutrality (with the USA and the USSR as the principal guarantors); arrangements for the voluntary and safe return of Afghan refugees from Pakistan and Iran; a document linking the preceding documents with a timetable for a Soviet withdrawal; and the establishment of a UN monitoring force, to be known as the United Nations Good Offices Mission in Afghanistan and Pakistan (UNGOMAP) and to be based in Kabul and Islamabad, which was to monitor both the Soviet troop departures and the return of the refugees. The withdrawal of Soviet troops (numbering 100,000, according to Soviet figures, or 115,000, according to Western sources) commenced on 15 May.

Neither the *mujahidin* nor Iran played any role in the formulation of the Geneva accords, and, in spite of protests by Pakistan, the accords did not incorporate an agreement regarding the composition of an interim coalition government in Afghanistan, or the 'symmetrical' cessation of Soviet aid to Najibullah's regime and US aid to the *mujahidin*. Therefore, despite the withdrawal of the Soviet troops, the supply of weapons to both sides was not halted, and the fighting continued. Pakistan repeatedly denied accusations, made by the Afghan and Soviet Governments, that it had violated the accords by continuing to harbour Afghan guerrillas and to act as a conduit for arms supplies to the latter from various sympathizers. At the end of November 1988 Soviet officials held direct talks with representatives of the *mujahidin* in Peshawar, Pakistan, the first such meeting since the start of the 10-year conflict. High-level discussions were held in early December in Saudi Arabia between

Prof. Burhanuddin Rabbani, the Chairman of the IUAM, and the Soviet ambassador to Afghanistan. These discussions collapsed, however, when the *mujahidin* leaders reiterated their demand that no members of Najibullah's regime should be incorporated in any future Afghan government, while the Soviet officials continued to insist on a government role for the PDPA. In spite of the unabated violence, the USSR, adhering to the condition specified in the Geneva accords, had withdrawn all of its troops from Afghanistan by mid-February 1989.

In mid-1988 the *mujahidin* had intensified their military activities, attacking small provincial centres and launching missiles against major cities, several of which were unsuccessfully besieged. By the end of 1990, owing mainly to their lack of organization and limited experience of modern strategic warfare, the *mujahidin* had failed to achieve any significant military successes and their limited control was confined to rural areas (including several small provincial capitals). The guerrillas also failed to make any important advances on the political front. Talks between the IUAM and the Iranian-based Hizb-i Wahadati-i Islami (Islamic Unity Party), an alliance of eight Shi'ite Afghan resistance groups, repeatedly failed to reach any agreement as to the composition of a broadly-based interim government. Consequently, in February 1989 the IUAM convened its own Shura (Assembly) in Rawalpindi, Pakistan, at which an interim government-in-exile (known as the Afghan Interim Government, AIG) was elected. The AIG, however, was officially recognized by only four countries. It also failed to gain any substantial support or recognition from the guerrilla commanders, who were beginning to establish their own unofficial alliances inside the country. In March, however, the AIG received a form of diplomatic recognition, when it was granted membership of the Organization of the Islamic Conference (OIC). In addition, in June the US Government appointed a special envoy to the *mujahidin*, with the rank of personal ambassador. In mid-1989 the unity of the *mujahidin* forces was seriously weakened by an increase in internecine violence between the various guerrilla groups, while the AIG was riven by disputes between the moderates and the fundamentalists. The USA, Saudi Arabia and Pakistan began to reduce financial aid and military supplies to the IUAM in Peshawar, and to undertake the difficult task of delivering weapons and money directly to guerrilla commanders and tribal leaders inside Afghanistan.

Following extensive negotiations with the regional powers involved in the crisis, the UN Secretary-General made a declaration in May 1991, setting out five principles for a settlement, the main points of which were: recognition of the national sovereignty of Afghanistan; the right of the Afghan people to choose their own government and political system; the establishment of an independent and authorized mechanism to oversee free and fair elections to a broadly-based government; a UN-monitored cease-fire; and the donation of sufficient financial aid to facilitate the return of the refugees and internal reconstruction. The declaration received the approval of the Afghan and Pakistani Governments, but was rejected by the AIG.

On the domestic front, the Afghan Government continued its efforts to advance the process of national reconciliation in 1990–91, through further promises of local autonomy to various guerrilla leaders and through several meetings with moderate groups within the ranks of the Peshawar-based *mujahidin* who were disillusioned with their fundamentalist colleagues in the ineffective and divided AIG.

Reflecting its disenchantment with the guerrilla cause, the US Government reduced aid to the *mujahidin* by one-third, to US $200m., in 1991. New military campaigns were launched by the *mujahidin* in the second half of 1990 in an attempt to impress their international supporters, disrupt the return of refugees and obstruct contacts between the Government and the moderates. At the end of March 1991, following more than two weeks of heavy fighting, the south-eastern city of Khost was captured by the *mujahidin*, representing the most severe reversal sustained by the Government since the Soviet withdrawal. The *mujahidin* also carried out attacks on Gardez, Jalalabad, Ghazni, Qandahar and Herat in 1991, and communications between cities and with the Soviet border were severed.

An unexpected breakthrough towards resolving the Afghan crisis occurred in mid-September 1991, when the USA and the USSR announced that they would stop supplying arms to the warring factions, and would encourage other countries (namely Pakistan, Saudi Arabia and Iran) to do likewise, by 1 January 1992. Although both the Afghan Government and the *mujahidin* welcomed this pledge, neither side showed any sign of implementing the proposed cease-fire, and, indeed, the fighting intensified around Kabul. In February 1992, however, the peace process was given a major boost when Pakistan made it clear that, rather than continuing actively to encourage the *mujahidin,* through arms supplies and training, it was urging all the guerrilla factions to support the five-point UN peace plan (see above). In doing so, Pakistan was effectively abandoning its insistence on the installation of a fundamentalist government in Kabul. There were growing fears, none the less, that the peace process might be placed in jeopardy by an increase in ethnic divisions within both the government forces and a number of *mujahidin* groups, between the majority Pashtuns and minority groups such as the Tajiks and Uzbeks. As a result of a mutiny staged by Uzbek militia forces in the Afghan army, under the command of Gen. Abdul Rashid Dostam, the northern town of Mazar-i-Sharif was captured by the *mujahidin* in March.

On 16 April 1992 events took an unexpected turn when Najibullah was forced to resign by his own ruling party, following the capture of the strategically-important Bagram air base and the nearby town of Charikar, only about 50 km north of Kabul, by the Jamiat-i Islami guerrilla group under the command of the Tajik general, Ahmad Shah Masoud. Najibullah went into hiding in the capital, under UN protection, while one of the Vice-Presidents, Abd ar-Rahim Hatif, assumed the post of acting President. Within a few days of Najibullah's downfall, every major town in Afghanistan was under the control of different coalitions of *mujahidin* groups co-operating with disaffected army commanders. Masoud was given orders by the guerrilla leaders in Peshawar to secure Kabul. On 25 April the forces of both Masoud and of Gulbuddin Hekmatyar, the leader of a rival guerrilla group, the Pashtun-dominated Hizb-i Islami, whose men were massed to the south of the capital, entered Kabul. The army surrendered its key positions, and immediately the city was riven by *mujahidin* faction-fighting. The military council that had, a few days earlier, replaced the Government handed over power to the *mujahidin*. Having discarded the UN's proposal to form a neutral body, the guerrilla leaders in Peshawar agreed to establish a 51-member interim Islamic Jihad Council, composed of military and religious leaders, which was to assume power in Kabul. The leader of the small, moderate Jebha-i-Nejat-i-Melli (National Liberation Front), Prof. Sibghatullah Mojaddedi, was to chair the Islamic Jihad Council for two months, after which period a 10-member Leadership Council, comprising *mujahidin* chiefs and presided over by the head of the Jamiat-i Islami, Prof. Burhanuddin Rabbani, would be set up for a period of four months. Within the six months a special council was to meet to designate an interim administration which was to hold power for up to a year pending elections.

Mojaddedi arrived in Kabul on 28 April 1992 as the President of the new interim administration. The Islamic Jihad Council was not, however, supported by Hekmatyar, whose radical stance differed substantially from Mojaddedi's more tolerant outlook. At the end of the month Hekmatyar's forces lost control of their last stronghold in the centre of Kabul. Within a few weeks the Government of the newly-proclaimed Islamic State of Afghanistan had won almost universal diplomatic recognition, and by early May about one-half of the Islamic Jihad Council had arrived in the capital. An acting Council of Ministers was formed, in which Masoud was given the post of Minister of Defence and the premiership was set aside for Ustad Abdol Sabur Farid, a Tajik commander from the Hizb-i Islami (Hekmatyar declined to accept the post). As part of the process of 'Islamization', the death penalty was introduced, alcohol and narcotics were banned and the wearing of strict Islamic dress by all women was enforced. Despite Mojaddedi's repeated pleas to Hekmatyar and his followers to lay down their arms, Hekmatyar, who was particularly angered by the presence of Gen. Dostam's Uzbek forces in the capital, continued to bombard Kabul with artillery and indiscriminate rocket launches from various strongholds around the city, killing and wounding scores of citizens.

On 28 June 1992 Mojaddedi surrendered power to the Leadership Council, which immediately offered Burhanuddin Rabbani the presidency of the country and the concomitant responsibility for the interim Council of Ministers for four months, as set forth in the Peshawar Agreement (see above). In early July Ustad Abdol Sabur Farid, a close colleague of Hekmatyar, assumed the premiership, which had been held open for him since late April. On assuming the presidency Rabbani announced the adoption of a new Islamic flag, the establishment of an economic council, which was to tackle the country's severe economic problems, and the appointment of a commission to draw up a new Constitution. A Deputy President was appointed in late July. In early August the withdrawal of the members of the Hizb-i Islami faction led by Maulvi Muhammad Yunus Khalis from the Leadership Council revealed serious rifts within the Government. A further problem was the continuing inter-*mujahidin* violence in Kabul. Within days the violence had escalated into a full-scale ground offensive, launched by Hekmatyar's forces against the capital. The airport was closed down, hundreds of people were killed or wounded, and tens of thousands of civilians fled Kabul in fear of their lives. In response President Rabbani expelled Hekmatyar from the Leadership Council and dismissed Prime Minister Farid. Hekmatyar demanded the expulsion of the 75,000 Uzbek militia from Kabul as a precondition to peace talks, alleging that Gen. Dostam was still closely allied to former members of the communist regime. At the end of the month a cease-fire agreement was reached between Rabbani and Hekmatyar and, after a few days of relative peacefulness the airport was reopened. Sporadic fighting involving various *mujahidin* and militia groups (notably Gen. Dostam's Uzbek forces) continued, however, in Kabul itself and in the provinces throughout the remainder of the year. At the end of October the Leadership Council agreed to extend Rabbani's tenure of the presidency by two months. On 30 December a special advisory council, known as the Resolution and Settlement Council (Shura-e Ahl-e Hal wa Aqd), which was composed of 1,335 tribal leaders, was convened in Kabul. The Council elected Rabbani, who was the sole candidate, as President of the country for a period of a further two years. In early January 1993 200 members of the advisory council were selected to constitute the future membership of the country's legislature.

The establishment of the advisory council and the re-election of President Rabbani provoked yet further heavy fighting in Kabul and other provinces in early 1993. Owing to the worsening violence, all of the Western diplomats had left the capital by the end of January. In early March, however, President Rabbani, Hekmatyar, Mojaddedi and leaders of other major *mujahidin* factions held negotiations in Islamabad, at the end of which a peace accord was signed. Under the terms of the accord, an interim Government was to be established, which would hold power for 18 months; President Rabbani was to remain as Head of State, and Hekmatyar (or his nominee) was to assume the premiership of the acting Council of Ministers; a cease-fire was to be imposed with immediate effect; legislative elections were to be held within six months; a 16-member defence commission was to be formed, which would be responsible for the establishment of a national army; and all weaponry was to be seized from the warring factions in an attempt to restore peace and order. The peace accord was officially approved and signed by the Governments of Pakistan, Saudi Arabia and Iran.

Confronted with the difficult task of satisfying the demands of all the *mujahidin* groups, Hekmatyar was not able to present a new Council of Ministers until late May 1993 (it was sworn in the following month). Each *mujahidin* faction was allocated two ministerial posts, with further positions left vacant for other representatives (representatives from General Dostam's group of Uzbek militiamen were offered two posts in July). One of Hekmatyar's most noteworthy decisions in the formation of the new Council of Ministers was to remove one of his most powerful rivals, Ahmad Shah Masoud, from the crucial post of Minister of Defence. The new Prime Minister promised to hold a general election by October. The temporary headquarters of the Government were situated in Charasiab, Hekmatyar's military base, about 25 km south of Kabul.

Despite the signing of the Islamabad peace accord in March 1993, the violence between the various *mujahidin* groups did not cease, and hundreds of people continued to be killed and wounded. The interim Government was beset by internal dissension and proved rather ineffectual in the administration of the war-torn country. Hekmatyar refused to co-operate with Rabbani, and frequently demanded the President's immediate and unconditional resignation. In September, however, it was reported that a new draft Constitution (known as the Basic Law) had been drawn up and approved by a special commission, in preparation for the holding of a general election. The fighting intensified in late December, when Gen. Dostam transferred his allegiance to his hitherto arch-enemy, Hekmatyar, and the supporters of the two combined to confront the forces of Rabbani and Ahmad Shah Masoud. The violence spread throughout the provinces, resulting in large numbers of military and civilian casualties and the internal displacement of thousands of people. Various unsuccessful attempts were made in 1994 by neighbouring countries and by international organizations, such as the UN and the OIC, to achieve a negotiated settlement between the main warring factions. In late June the Supreme Court ruled that Rabbani could retain the presidency for a further six months, but failed to grant a similar extension to Hekmatyar's premiership. President Rabbani's extended term in office expired at the end of December. However, he did not resign, owing to, according to various sources, the continuation of the civil war and the lack of a suitable replacement for the post.

In the latter half of 1994, a new, hitherto unknown, militant grouping emerged in Afghanistan, known as Taliban (the plural form of 'Talib', meaning 'seeker of religious knowledge'). The movement, comprising an estimated 25,000 fighters (the majority of whom were reported to be young Pashtun graduates of fundamentalist Islamic schools established by Afghan refugees in Pakistan), advocated the adoption of extremist practices, including the complete seclusion of women from society. Although initially claiming that it had no interest in actually assuming power in Afghanistan, Taliban, which was led by Mola Mohammad Omar, won a major victory in October, when it captured the city of Qandahar from the forces of Hekmatyar, which had hitherto dominated the southern provinces of the country. In February 1995 Taliban routed Hekmatyar's men from their headquarters in Charasiab, and within a month it controlled 10 provinces, mostly in southern and south-eastern Afghanistan. However, Taliban retreated from its advance on Kabul when Rabbani's troops launched a massive counter-offensive. By mid-1995, with both Taliban and Hekmatyar's men held in check, President Rabbani and his supporters were enjoying an unprecedented level of authority and confidence in Kabul and its environs. This was reflected in Rabbani's reneging on his earlier promise of standing down from the presidency in late March and in the growing number of countries that were considering reopening their embassies in the Afghan capital (the Indian embassy reopened in May). In mid-1995 talks were held between Rabbani and Taliban, but relations between the two sides remained extremely strained. In early September Taliban achieved a notable gain when it captured the key north-western city of Herat and the surrounding province from government forces. Taliban's resurgence apparently provoked an attack on the Pakistani embassy in Kabul by hundreds of pro-Government demonstrators protesting against Pakistan's alleged support for the student militia; the embassy was destroyed by fire, one employee was killed and a number wounded (including the ambassador himself). In response, the Afghan ambassador to Pakistan and six other Afghan diplomats were expelled from Islamabad. In October Taliban launched a massive ground and air assault on Kabul, but by early January 1996 had failed to breach the capital's defences. The constant bombardment of the besieged city, however, resulted in hundreds of civilian deaths, and the road blockades around the capital caused serious shortages of vital supplies.

Despite the holding of exploratory negotiations between the Rabbani Government and major opposition parties in the first quarter of 1996, the fighting in and around Kabul intensified. The President's attempts at conciliation finally proved successful, however, in late May when, in a critical development (known as the Mahipar Agreement), he persuaded Hekmatyar to rejoin the Government. Hekmatyar's forces arrived in the capital during May to defend the city against Taliban. In late June Hekmatyar resumed the post of Prime Minister and President Rabbani appointed a new Council of Ministers in early July, which was to hold power for a period of six–12 months pending the staging of a general election. In addition, under the terms of the Mahipar Agreement, a Constitution to cover the interim period was drawn up and published.

The political situation was radically altered in late September 1996 when, as a culmination of two weeks of sweeping military advances (including the capture of the crucial eastern city of Jalalabad), Taliban seized control of Kabul following fierce clashes with government troops, who fled northwards together with the deposed Government. One of Taliban's first actions in the captured capital was the summary execution of the former President, Najibullah, and his brother. On assuming power, Taliban declared Afghanistan a 'complete' Islamic state and appointed an interim Council of Ministers, led by Mola Mohammad Rabbani, to administer the country (of which they now controlled about two-thirds). Pakistan, which was widely suspected of actively aiding the Islamic militia, was the first country officially to recognize the new regime. (By mid-November, however, few other countries or international organizations had followed suit—neither the UN, India, Russia nor Iran had given official recognition to the Taliban administration.) Taliban imposed a strict and intimidatory Islamic code—women were not permitted to enter employment or be educated beyond the age of 10; television, non-religious music, gambling and alcohol were all banned; amputations and public stonings were enforced as forms of punishment; compulsory attendance at mosques by all men was introduced; and women were ordered into purdah.

In mid-October 1996 the former Minister of Defence, Ahmad Shah Masoud, and his troops repulsed the Taliban forces and regained some lost territory in the Panjshir Valley to the north of Kabul. Taliban's hopes that the opposition would remain divided were thwarted following the formation of a powerful military and logistical alliance by Gen. Dostam, Masoud and the leader of the Hizb-i Wahadat-i Islami, Gen. Abdol Karim Khalili. Gen. Dostam, who controlled six northern provinces, apparently decided to establish this unlikely alliance after cease-fire talks between himself and Taliban broke down. By late October the anti-Taliban forces, whose leaders were now collectively known as the Supreme Council for the Defence of Afghanistan (the headquarters of which were situated in Gen. Dostam's stronghold of Mazar-i-Sharif), had launched a concerted offensive against Kabul in the hope of ousting the Islamic militia. Despite repeated calls for a cease-fire from various foreign governments and the UN and despite complaints by Amnesty International regarding civilian casualties and abuses of human rights, the fighting between Taliban and the allied opposition continued into January 1997, with both sides claiming to have made advances and to have gained the upper hand. In mid-January a working group on Afghanistan, comprising representatives from Taliban, Rabbani's Government and from the Supreme Council for the Defence of Afghanistan, met in Islamabad, under the auspices of the UN, to discuss the crisis. Following the rapid collapse of these talks, Taliban launched an unexpected offensive, advancing north and capturing Bagram air base and the provincial capital of Charikar. By late January Taliban had made significant military gains and had pushed the front line to about 100 km north of Kabul. In an attempt to halt Taliban's advance northwards, Gen. Dostam's forces used explosives to block the vital Salang Highway, the main link between northern and southern Afghanistan. In response, Taliban moved westwards, but was stopped at the Shibar Pass by Hizb-i Wahadat-i Islami forces. The situation underwent a dramatic development in mid-May when, following the defection of the Uzbek Gen. Abdul Malik Pahlawan and his men to Taliban, the latter was able to capture the strategically-important northern town of Mazar-i-Sharif with relatively little bloodshed. Gen. Dostam was reported to have fled to Turkey, and his position as leader of the National Islamic Movement was assumed by Gen. Malik. Taliban now controlled about 90% of the country, including all of the major towns and cities. Its position was also strengthened around this time by Pakistan's decision to be the first country to accord formal recognition to the Taliban Government (closely followed by Saudi Arabia and the United Arab Emirates). Taliban's control of Mazar-i-Sharif, however, was extremely short-lived, and within only three days of entering the town it was in full retreat. It appeared that Gen. Malik's tenuous alliance with Taliban had collapsed almost immediately and his troops, together with Shi'ite militia, forced the newcomers out after ferocious fighting. Taliban was soundly routed and by early June its forces had retreated almost 200 km south of Mazar-i-Sharif. The regional aspect of the Afghan conflict was highlighted at the beginning of June by Taliban's decision to close down the Iranian embassy in Kabul; the Iranian Government was widely suspected of actively aiding the anti-Taliban northern alliance. The alliance was reported to have been expanded and strengthened in early June by the inclusion of the forces of Hekmatyar and of the Mahaz-i-Melli-i-Islami, led by Pir Sayed Ahmad Gailani. This new coalition, which superseded the Supreme Council for the Defence of Afghanistan, was known as the United Islamic Front for the Salvation of Afghanistan (UIFSA). Despite the arrival of thousands of reinforcements from training camps in Pakistan (many of whom were, however, inexperienced teenagers), Taliban suffered a series of military defeats in northern Afghanistan, and by late July the UIFSA forces were within firing range of Kabul, having recaptured Charikar and the air base at Bagram. In the same month the UN Security Council demanded a cease-fire and an end to all foreign intervention in Afghanistan. In mid-1997 it was widely believed that Taliban was supported by Pakistan and Saudi Arabia; on the opposing side, to various degrees, were ranged Iran, India, the Central Asian states (which feared the encroachment of Taliban's fundamentalism) and Russia.

In mid-August 1997 it was reported that the UIFSA had appointed a new Government, based in Mazar-i-Sharif, with Rabbani continuing as President. Abdorrahim Ghafurzai as Prime Minister, Ahmad Shah Masoud as Minister of Defence and Gen. Abdul Malik as Minister of Foreign Affairs. The former Prime Minister in the anti-Taliban administration, Gulbuddin Hekmatyar, refused to recognize the new Government. Within a few days of its appointment, however, seven members of the new Government, including Prime Minister Ghafurzai, were killed in an aeroplane crash. In late August the anti-Taliban opposition alliance appointed Abdolghaffur Rawanfarhadi as new Prime Minister.

In September 1997 the main battlefront moved northwards from Kabul when Taliban launched an offensive in an attempt to recapture Mazar-i-Sharif. Following fierce fighting Taliban was forced to lift the siege and retreat in early October. Meanwhile, in mid-September Gen. Dostam was reported to have returned to Mazar-i-Sharif from Turkey, and in the following month the member parties of the UIFSA re-elected him as commander of the forces of the alliance and appointed him as Vice-President of the anti-Taliban administration. However, there were reports of a bitter rivalry between Gen. Dostam and Gen. Abdul Malik and skirmishes between their respective forces. Dostam's battle for supremacy with his rival led him to make overtures to Taliban, including offers of exchanges of prisoners of war. Gen. Dostam also accused Gen. Malik of having massacred about 3,000 Taliban prisoners earlier in the year. By late November Gen. Dostam had reassumed the leadership of the National Islamic Movement, ousting Gen. Malik. In late October Taliban unilaterally decided to change the country's name to the Islamic Emirate of Afghanistan and altered the state flag, moves that were condemned by the opposition alliance and all of Afghanistan's neighbours (with the exception of Pakistan). In early December a three-day peace conference was held in Esfahan, Iran, and, although boycotted by Taliban, was attended by representatives of all other parties (both religious and military) involved in the Afghan conflict. In mid-December the UN Security Council issued a communiqué expressing its concern at the alleged massacres of civilians and prisoners of war being perpetrated by various factions in Afghanistan.

Government

Following the collapse of Najibullah's regime in April 1992, a provisional *mujahidin* Government was established in Kabul. For the first two months, Prof. Sibghatullah Mojaddedi held the post of acting President and headed a 51-member executive body, known as the Islamic Jihad Council, which appointed an interim Council of Ministers in early May. On 28 June Mojaddedi, in line with the proposals set out in the Peshawar Agreement (see History), surrendered the presidency to Prof. Burhanuddin Rabbani, who presided over another executive body, called the Leadership Council. Rabbani was granted power until October, when his tenure of the presidency was extended for a further two months. In December he was elected as President of the country for a two-year term. Following the signing of a peace accord by the majority of *mujahidin* groups in Islamabad in March 1993, an interim multi-faction Government, which was to hold power for 18 months, was established just south of Kabul in June. In January 1996 Rabbani remained in the presidency, despite the official expiry of his tenure of office, and there seemed no prospect of any elections being held in the near future, owing to the continuing civil war.

In September 1996, however, the extremist Islamic militia Taliban seized control of Kabul and Rabbani's Government fled north. On assuming power, Taliban declared Afghanistan a 'complete' Islamic state and appointed an interim Council of Ministers to administer the country (of which they now controlled about two-thirds). Pakistan was the first country officially to recognize the new regime, but by the end of 1997 few other countries or international organizations—including the UN, India, Russia and Iran—had followed suit.

The 31 provinces of Afghanistan are each administered by an appointed governor.

Defence

Prior to the collapse of Najibullah's regime in April 1992, every able-bodied Afghan male (excepting religious scholars and preachers) between the ages of 15 and 40 years was obliged by law to serve four years in the army (with a break of three years at the end of the second year), which was estimated to number 40,000 men in June 1991, but conscription was difficult to enforce and desertions were frequent. Equipment and training were provided largely by the USSR. The withdrawal of Soviet troops was completed in February 1989. The Afghan air force, which numbered an estimated 5,000, was equipped with supersonic jet aircraft. Paramilitary forces included a gendarmerie (Sarandoy) of about 20,000, a state security service (KHAD) of around 25,000, a border guard of about 20,000 and numerous regional militias; police security forces come under the Ministry of the Interior (gendarmarie) and the Ministry of State Security (KHAD). A Special Guard was formed to defend the capital city in 1988. Budgeted defence expenditure in 1990 was 22,000m. afghanis (US $430m.).

Following the installation of a *mujahidin* Government in Kabul in April 1992, it was announced that all the military bodies of the former communist regime, including the army, Sarandoy, KHAD, the border guard and all the regional militias, were to be dissolved and combined with the *mujahidin* to form a new national Islamic military force. In mid-1993, as part of the Islamabad Peace Accord of March 1993, a 16-member defence commission was formed with the responsibility of establishing a national army.

According to Russian estimates, Taliban controlled an army of about 40,000 men in late 1996.

Economic Affairs

According to government figures, Afghanistan's gross national product (GNP) in 1986/87 amounted to US $3,156m., an increase of 5.2% compared with 1985/86, and GNP per head stood at $155–$160. In 1990/91, according to UN estimates, gross domestic product (GDP) in purchasers' values, measured at 1978 prices, totalled 114,800m. afghanis, a decrease of 3.1% compared with the previous year. According to the United Nations Development Programme (UNDP), Afghanistan's GDP per head, in terms of purchasing power parity, was an estimated $700 in 1991 and $819 in 1992, compared with $755 in 1960.

Agriculture (including hunting, forestry and fishing), according to UN estimates, contributed 64.4% of GDP in 1993, while the value of agricultural output in that year decreased by 8.6%, compared with the previous year. According to the FAO, 68.9% of the economically active population were employed in the agricultural sector in 1996. In that year wheat production was estimated at 1.7m. metric tons. The principal commercial products of the sector are fruit and nuts (which accounted for around 39.7% of total export earnings, according to the IMF, in 1990/91), wool and cotton, and processed hides and skins. According to UNDP, cereal imports totalled 156,000 tons in 1992, compared with 322,000 metric tons in 1990. The value of food aid reached US $5.1m. in 1992.

According to UN estimates, the industrial sector (including mining, manufacturing, construction and power) contributed 20% of GDP in 1993, while the value of industrial output in that year decreased by 11.4%, compared with the previous year.

Mining and quarrying employed about 1.5% of the settled labour force in 1979. Natural gas is the major mineral export (accounting for about 23.6% of total export earnings, according to the IMF, in 1988/89). Salt, hard coal, copper, lapis lazuli, barytes and talc are also mined. In addition, Afghanistan has small reserves of petroleum and iron ore.

Manufacturing employed about 10.9% of the settled labour force in 1979. Afghanistan's major manufacturing industries include food products, cotton textiles, chemical fertilizers, cement, leather and plastic goods.

Energy is derived principally from petroleum (which is imported from Iran and republics of the former USSR) and coal. The Government plans to increase internal sources of energy by establishing hydro- and thermal electric power stations. In early 1996 Afghanistan signed an agreement that could eventually lead to the construction of a high-pressure natural gas pipeline across the country, which would transport gas from Turkmenistan to Pakistan. In October 1997 the US petroleum company Unocal established a consortium which proposed to build a US $2,000m.-pipeline.

In 1989, according to the IMF, Afghanistan recorded a visible trade deficit of US $371.2m., and there was a deficit of $143.3m. on the current account of the balance of payments. In 1992, according to UN figures, the principal source of imports (62.7%) was the former USSR, which was also the principal market for exports (71.7%). The main exports were natural gas, fruit (dried and fresh) and nuts, carpets and rugs, Karakul fur skins and cotton. The major imports are vehicles and spare parts, petroleum products, fertilizers, basic manufactured goods and foodstuffs (notably wheat). In late 1995 it was announced that trade tariffs were to be reduced between the member states of the Economic Co-operation Organization (ECO, see p. 260), which Afghanistan joined in late 1992.

In 1987 the Government estimated that financial contributions from the USSR constituted 40% of the country's civilian budget. In 1988/89 the USSR and other member countries of the Council for Mutual Economic Assistance (CMEA) were to contribute 97% (USSR 81%) of foreign aid to Afghanistan, which totalled an estimated US $223.3m., an increase of 14.5% compared with 1987/88. In 1994, according to UN figures, Afghanistan received $139.7m. in bilateral official development assistance and $88.8m. in multilateral official development assistance. In 1997 the European Union (EU) was the largest single aid donor to Afghanistan. In 1987 Afghanistan's total external debt was $1,499m.

It is extremely difficult to provide an accurate economic profile of Afghanistan, owing to the continuing civil war, population movements, communication problems and lack of reliable official statistics. Government figures often appear highly optimistic. Both the agricultural and industrial sectors have been severely disrupted by the unrest. The *mujahidin* Government, which came to power in April 1992, was faced with immense economic problems, including serious food and fuel shortages, a collapsed industrial sector, a severely-damaged infrastructure, the difficulties of thousands of refugees returning to their ravaged farms and fields studded with mines, and high inflation (according to one source, inflation reached an estimated 56.7% in 1991). The new Government established an economic council, made urgent appeals for international assistance and held talks with Pakistan and other members of the ECO regarding trade co-operation. Requests for foreign aid, however, were jeopardized to some extent by the continuing bitter infighting between rival guerrilla and militia groups and by the fact that Afghanistan was now the world's leading producer of opium (overtaking Myanmar in 1994). According to certain Western sources, the area of land in Afghanistan currently under poppy cultivation has increased by more than 50% since 1990. In 1997, according to UN estimates, about 1m. Afghans were involved in the opium trade. UN field surveys indicated that about 165,000 acres of arable land was under poppy cultivation. In 1996 Afghanistan produced about 2,250 metric tons of raw opium, most of which was exported to Pakistan, Russia and Europe. In October 1995 the UN launched an appeal to the international community for emergency humanitarian assistance of US $124m. for 1996 for Afghanistan; however, by the end of 1996, only about 52% of this sum had been achieved. There appeared little prospect of an improvement in Afghanistan's economic situation following Taliban's seizure of power in Kabul in September 1996, particularly taking into account the subsequent introduction of a decree banning women from working (with the exception of a small number of medical staff). Levels of aid to Afghanistan fell markedly in 1997, partly in response to Taliban's harsh treatment of women and other abuses of human rights. The UN's appeal for humanitarian assistance of US $133m. for Afghanistan in 1997 seemed highly unlikely to achieve even one-half of this amount. In late 1997 the World Food Programme launched an emergency operation to help people facing starvation in the impoverished central province of Bamian.

In early 1997 UNHCR reported that between 1988 and 1996 about 2.56m. Afghan refugees had returned to their homeland from Pakistan and around 1.33m. from Iran.

Social Welfare

Serious damage was reported to have been caused to health and social welfare facilities by the disturbances from 1980 onwards. The estimated average life expectancy at birth in 1997 stood at only 43 years for males and 44 for females, by far the lowest in Asia. In that year there were 163 deaths of children under 12 months old for every 1,000 live births, the highest infant mortality rate in Asia. In 1993 cholera was reported to have reached epidemic proportions in Afghanistan, and in 1997 a UN-organized polio vaccination campaign was carried out. In 1990, according to UNDP estimates, public expenditure on health was equivalent to 1.6% of GDP. In 1987, according to UN figures, there were 2,957 physicians (2 per 10,000 population), 329 dentists and 2,135 nursing personnel in Afghanistan. In 1988 government officials assessed the combined total of medical centres and hospitals at 196.

In late 1997 the UN faced major criticism after WHO supported Taliban in establishing separate facilities for women in Kabul's medical institutions.

Education

Primary education, which is officially compulsory, begins at seven years of age and lasts for six years. Secondary education, beginning at 13 years of age, lasts for a further six years. As a proportion of the school-age population, the total enrolment at primary and secondary schools was equivalent to 36% (males 49%; females 22%) in 1995. Primary enrolment in that year was equivalent to an estimated 48% of children in the relevant age-group (boys 63%; girls 32%), while the enrolment ratio at general secondary schools was equivalent to 22% (boys 32%; girls 11%).

Afghanistan has one of the highest levels of adult illiteracy in Asia, with an average rate (excluding the nomadic population) of 68.5% (males 52.8%; females 85.0%) in 1995, according to estimates by UNESCO.

Since 1979 higher education has been disrupted by the departure of many teaching staff from Afghanistan. In 1980 it was reported that up to 80% of university staff had fled their posts. In the late 1980s more than 15,000 Afghan students and trainees were receiving education at establishments in the USSR and other Eastern bloc countries. In March 1992, following the collapse of communism in eastern Europe and the dissolution of the USSR, the Afghan Government announced that all Afghan students in Russia, Uzbekistan, Tajikistan and Kazakhstan were to continue their education, on the basis of protocols signed with the former Soviet Union. In 1988 there were eight vocational colleges, 15 technical colleges and five universities (including an Islamic university in Kabul) in Afghanistan.

Following its seizure of power in late September 1996, Taliban banned education for girls over the age of 10, closed all the women's institutes of higher education and planned to draw up a new Islamic curriculum for boys' schools. In late 1997, however, there were still two co-educational universities functioning in Afghanistan (in areas not under Taliban control), one of which was situated in Bamian.

Public Holidays

The Afghan year 1376 runs from 21 March 1997 to 20 March 1998, and the year 1377 runs from 21 March 1998 to 20 March 1999.

1998: 30 January (Id al-Fitr, end of Ramadan), 21 March (Nauroz: New Year's Day, Iranian calendar), 8 April* (Id al-Adha, Feast of the Sacrifice), 18 April (Liberation Day), 27 April (Revolution Day), 1 May (Workers' Day), 7 May* (Ashura, Martyrdom of Imam Husayn), 7 July* (Roze-Maulud, Birth of Prophet Muhammad), 18 August (Independence Day), 20 December* (first day of Ramadan).

1999: 19 January* (Id al-Fitr, end of Ramadan), 21 March (Nauroz: New Year's Day, Iranian calendar), 28 March* (Id al-Adha, Feast of the Sacrifice), 18 April (Liberation Day), 26 April* (Ashura, Martyrdom of Imam Husayn), 27 April (Revolution Day), 1 May (Workers' Day), 26 June * (Roze-Maulud, Birth of Prophet Muhammad), 18 August (Independence Day), 9 December* (first day of Ramadan).

* These holidays are dependent on the Islamic lunar calendar and may vary by one or two days from the dates given.

Weights and Measures

The metric system has been officially adopted but traditional weights are still used. One 'seer' equals 16 lb (7.3 kg).

Statistical Survey

Source (unless otherwise stated): Central Statistics Authority, Block 4, Macroraion, Kabul; tel. (93) 24883.

Area and Population

AREA, POPULATION AND DENSITY

Area (sq km)	652,225*
Population (census results)	
23 June 1979†	
Males	6,712,377
Females	6,338,981
Total	13,051,358
Population (official estimates at mid-year)‡	
1984	17,672,000
1985	18,136,000
1986	18,614,000
Density (per sq km) at mid-1986	28.5

* 251,773 sq miles.

† Figures exclude nomadic population, estimated to total 2,500,000. The census data also exclude an adjustment for underenumeration, estimated to have been 5% for the urban population and 10% for the rural population.

‡ These data include estimates for nomadic population (2,734,000 in 1983), but take no account of emigration by refugees. Assuming an average net outflow of 703,000 persons per year in 1980–85, the UN Population Division has estimated Afghanistan's total mid-year population (in '000) as: 14,519 in 1985; 14,529 in 1986; 14,709 in 1987 (Source: UN, *World Population Prospects: 1988)*. In 1988, according to UNHCR estimates, the total Afghan refugee population numbered 5.5m., of whom 3.15m. were living in Pakistan and 2.35m. in Iran.

Population (official estimates, excluding nomads, at mid-year): 15,219,000 in 1987; 15,513,000 in 1988; 15,814,000 in 1989; 16,121,000 in 1990; 16,433,000 in 1991; 16,750,000 in 1992; 17,080,000 in 1993; 17,420,000 in 1994.

PROVINCES (estimates, March 1982)*

	Area (sq km)	Population	Density (per sq km)	Capital (with population)
Kabul	4,585	1,517,909	331.1	Kabul (1,036,407)
Kapesa†	1,871	262,039	140.1	Mahmudraki (1,262)
Parwan	9,399	527,987	56.2	Sharikar (25,117)
Wardag†	9,023	300,796	33.3	Maidanshar (2,153)
Loghar†	4,652	226,234	48.6	Baraiki Barak (1,164)‡
Ghazni	23,378	676,416	28.9	Ghazni (31,985)
Paktia	9,581	506,264	52.8	Gardiz (10,040)
Nangarhar	7,616	781,619	102.6	Jalalabad (57,824)
Laghman	7,210	325,010	45.0	Mehterlam (4,191)
Kunar	10,479	261,604	25.0	Asadabad (2,196)
Badakhshan	47,403	520,620	10.9	Faizabad (9,564)
Takhar	12,376	543,818	43.9	Talukan (20,947)
Baghlan	17,109	516,921	30.2	Baghlan (41,240)
Kunduz	7,827	582,600	74.4	Kunduz (57,112)
Samangan	15,465	273,864	17.7	Aibak (5,191)
Balkh	12,593	609,590	48.4	Mazar-i-Sharif (110,367)
Jawzjan	25,553	615,877	24.1	Shiberghan (19,969)
Fariab	22,279	609,703	27.3	Maymana (40,212)
Badghis	21,858	244,346	11.2	Kalainow (5,614)
Herat	61,315	808,224	13.2	Herat (150,497)
Farah	47,788	245,474	5.1	Farah (19,761)
Neemroze	41,356	108,418	2.6	Zarang (6,809)
Helmand	61,829	541,508	8.8	Lashkargha (22,707)

PROVINCES (estimates, March 1982)* — *continued*

	Area (sq km)	Population	Density (per sq km)	Capital (with population)
Qandahar	47,676	597,954	12.5	Qandahar (191,345)
Zabul	17,293	187,612	10.8	Qalat (6,251)
Uruzgan	29,295	464,556	15.5	Terincot (3,534)
Ghor	38,666	353,494	9.1	Cheghcheran (3,126)
Bamian	17,414	280,859	16.1	Bamian (7,732)
Paktika	19,336	256,470	13.3	Sheran (1,469)
Total	652,225	13,747,786	21.1	

* Population figures refer to settled inhabitants only, excluding kuchies (nomads), estimated at 2,600,000 for the whole country.
† Formed in 1981.
‡ The capital of Loghar Province was later changed to Pul-i-Alam.

PRINCIPAL TOWNS (estimated population at March 1982)

Kabul (capital)	1,036,407	Kunduz	57,112
Qandahar	191,345	Baghlan	41,240
Herat	150,497	Maymana	40,212
Mazar-i-Sharif	110,367	Pul-i-Khomri	32,695
Jalalabad	57,824	Ghazni	31,985

Estimated population at July 1988: Kabul 1,424,400; Qandahar 225,500; Herat 177,300; Mazar-i-Sharif 130,600 (Source: UN, *Demographic Yearbook 1991*).

BIRTHS AND DEATHS (UN estimates, annual averages)

	1980–85	1985–90	1990–95
Birth rate (per 1,000)	48.9	47.5	50.2
Death rate (per 1,000)	23.0	22.8	21.8

Expectation of life (UN estimates, years at birth, 1990–95): 43.5 (males 43.0; females 44.0).

Source: UN, *World Population Prospects: The 1994 Revision.*

ECONOMICALLY ACTIVE POPULATION*
(ISIC Major Divisions, persons aged 8 years and over, 1979 census)

	Males	Females	Total
Agriculture, hunting, forestry and fishing	2,358,821	10,660	2,369,481
Mining and quarrying	57,492	1,847	59,339
Manufacturing	170,908	252,465	423,373
Electricity, gas and water	11,078	276	11,354
Construction	50,670	416	51,086
Wholesale and retail trade	135,242	2,618	137,860
Transport, storage and communications	65,376	867	66,243
Other services	716,511	32,834	749,345
Total	3,566,098	301,983	3,868,081

* Figures refer to settled population only and exclude 77,510 persons seeking work for the first time (66,057 males; 11,453 females).

Agriculture

PRINCIPAL CROPS ('000 metric tons)

	1994	1995	1996
Wheat*	2,050	2,170	1,700
Rice (paddy)*	350	300	300
Barley*	258	274	180
Maize*	500	530	360
Millet*	31	33	22
Potatoes*	265	280	235
Pulses*	41	44	35
Sesame seed*	24	24	24
Cottonseed	44†	44*	44*
Cotton (lint)	22†	22*	22*
Vegetables*	445	475	380
Watermelons*	90	90	90
Cantaloupes and other melons*	22	22	22
Grapes*	330	330	330
Sugar cane*	38	38	38
Sugar beets*	1	1	1
Apples*	18	18	18
Peaches and nectarines*	14	14	14
Plums*	34	35	35
Oranges*	12	12	12
Apricots*	37	38	38
Other fruit*	169	168	168

* FAO estimate(s). † Unofficial figure.

Source: FAO, *Production Yearbook.*

LIVESTOCK (FAO estimates, '000 head, year ending 30 September)

	1994	1995	1996
Horses	300	300	300
Mules	23	23	23
Asses	1,160	1,160	1,160
Cattle	1,500	1,500	1,500
Camels	265	265	265
Sheep	17,000	18,000	14,300
Goats	2,560	2,715	2,200

Poultry (FAO estimates, million): 9 in 1994; 9 in 1995; 7 in 1996.

Source: FAO, *Production Yearbook.*

LIVESTOCK PRODUCTS (FAO estimates, '000 metric tons)

	1994	1995	1996
Beef and veal	65	65	65
Mutton and lamb	137	145	117
Goat meat	27	29	24
Poultry meat	16	17	14
Other meat	11	11	11
Cows' milk	300	300	300
Sheep's milk	238	253	201
Goats' milk	48	51	41
Cheese	19	20	16
Butter and ghee	12	12	11
Hen eggs	17	18	18
Honey	3	3	3
Wool:			
greasy	18	19	16
clean	10	11	9
Cattle hides	11	11	11
Sheepskins	22	23	18
Goatskins	4	4	4

Source: FAO, *Production Yearbook.*

Forestry

ROUNDWOOD REMOVALS
(FAO estimates, '000 cu m, excluding bark)

	1992	1993	1994
Sawlogs, veneer logs and logs for sleepers*	856	856	856
Other industrial wood	686	730	778
Fuel wood	4,946	5,264	5,617
Total	6,488	6,850	7,251

* Assumed to be unchanged from 1976.

Source: FAO, *Yearbook of Forest Products*.

SAWNWOOD PRODUCTION (FAO estimates, '000 cu m)

	1974	1975	1976
Coniferous (softwood)	360	310	380
Broadleaved (hardwood)	50	20	20
Total	410	330	400

1977–94: Annual production as in 1976 (FAO estimates).

Source: FAO, *Yearbook of Forest Products*.

Fishing

(FAO estimates, '000 metric tons, live weight)

	1993	1994	1995
Total catch	1.2	1.3	1.3

Source: FAO, *Yearbook of Fishery Statistics*.

Mining

('000 metric tons, unless otherwise indicated)

	1992	1993	1994
Hard coal*	8	7†	6†
Gypsum (crude)‡	3	n.a.	n.a.
Natural gas (petajoules)*†	7	7	7

* Twelve months beginning 21 March of year stated.

† Estimate.

‡ Data from the US Bureau of Mines.

Source: UN, *Industrial Commodity Statistics Yearbook*.

Industry

SELECTED PRODUCTS
(year ending 20 March, '000 metric tons, unless otherwise indicated)

	1986/87	1987/88	1988/89
Margarine	3.5	3.3	1.8
Vegetable oil	4	n.a.	n.a.
Wheat flour*	187	203	166
Wine ('000 hectolitres)*	289	304	194
Soft drinks ('000 hectolitres)	8,500	10,300	4,700
Woven cotton fabrics (million sq metres)	58.1	52.6	32.1
Woven woollen fabrics (million sq metres)	0.4	0.3	0.3
Footwear—excl. rubber ('000 pairs)*	613	701	607
Rubber footwear ('000 pairs)*	2,200	3,200	2,200
Nitrogenous fertilizers†	56	57	55
Cement	103	104	70
Electric energy (million kWh)*‡	1,171	1,257	1,109

* Production in calendar years 1986, 1987 and 1988.

† Production in year ending 30 June.

‡ Provisional.

Nitrogenous fertilizers (year ending 30 June): 42 in 1992/93; 40 in 1993/94; 49 in 1994/95.

Cement: 100 in 1989/90; 100 in 1990/91; 109 in 1991/92.

Electric energy (provisional, million kWh): 703 in 1992/93; 695 in 1993/94; 687 in 1994/95.

Sources: UN, *Industrial Commodity Statistics Yearbook* and *Statistical Yearbook for Asia and the Pacific*.

Finance

CURRENCY AND EXCHANGE RATES

Monetary Units

100 puls (puli) = 2 krans = 1 afghani (Af).

Sterling and Dollar Equivalents (30 September 1997)

£1 sterling = 4,846.2 afghanis;
US $1 = 3,000.0 afghanis;
10,000 afghanis = £2.063 = $3.333.

Exchange Rate

The foregoing information refers to the official exchange rate. The official rate was maintained at US $1 = 50.60 afghanis between September 1981 and March 1996. From 1 April 1996 a rate of US $1 = 3,000 afghanis has been in operation. However, this rate is applicable to only a limited range of transactions. There is also a market-determined rate, which was US $1 = 20,280 afghanis in June 1997.

BUDGET (million afghanis, year ending 20 March)

	1983/84	1984/85
Current revenue	34,744	37,615
Taxes	13,952	17,081
Non-taxes	20,792	20,534
Current expenditure	37,760	43,177
Capital expenditure	5,433	8,000

Source: UN, *Statistical Yearbook for Asia and the Pacific*.

BANK OF AFGHANISTAN RESERVES* (US $ million at December)

	1989	1990	1991
IMF special drawing rights	10.63	9.02	6.67
Reserve position in IMF	6.41	6.97	7.01
Foreign exchange	226.65	250.41	221.22
Total	243.69	266.40	234.89

* Figures exclude gold reserves, totalling 965,000 troy ounces since 1980. Assuming a gold price of 12,850 afghanis per ounce, these reserves were officially valued at US $245.06 million in December of each year 1985–91.

1992 (US $ million at December): IMF special drawing rights 4.37; Reserve position in IMF 6.78.

1993 (US $ million at December): IMF special drawing rights 2.76; Reserve position in IMF 6.77.

1994 (US $ million at December): IMF special drawing rights 1.40; Reserve position in IMF 7.19.

1995 (US $ million at December): Reserve position in IMF 7.33.

1996 (US $ million at December): Reserve position in IMF 7.09.

Source: IMF, *International Financial Statistics.*

MONEY SUPPLY (million afghanis at 21 December)

	1989	1990	1991
Currency outside banks	222,720	311,929	454,750
Private sector deposits at Bank of Afghanistan	12,838	13,928	19,368
Demand deposits at commercial banks	11,699	18,217	n.a.

Source: IMF, *International Financial Statistics.*

COST OF LIVING
(retail price index, excluding rent; base: 1990 = 100)

	1989	1990	1991
All items	70.5	100.0	156.7

Source: IMF, *International Financial Statistics.*

NATIONAL ACCOUNTS
('000 million afghanis at constant 1978 prices)

Gross Domestic Product by Economic Activity

	1991	1992	1993
Agriculture, hunting, forestry and fishing	59.9	62.7	57.3
Mining and quarrying Manufacturing Electricity, gas and water	29.2	14.3	12.3
Construction	7.0	5.8	5.5
Wholesale and retail trade, restaurants and hotels	11.1	10.5	10.1
Transport, storage and communications	4.8	4.5	2.0
Finance, insurance, real estate and business services	2.1	2.0	1.8
GDP in purchasers' values	114.1	99.8	89.0

Source: UN, *Statistical Yearbook for Asia and the Pacific.*

BALANCE OF PAYMENTS (US $ million)

	1987	1988	1989
Exports of goods f.o.b.	538.7	453.8	252.3
Imports of goods f.o.b.	−904.5	−731.8	−623.5
Trade balance	−365.8	−278.0	−371.2
Exports of services	35.6	69.6	8.2
Imports of services	−156.3	−120.0	−103.4
Balance on goods and services	−486.5	−328.4	−466.4
Other income received	19.2	23.3	20.1
Other income paid	−11.3	−11.5	−7.9
Balance on goods, services and income	−478.6	−316.6	−454.2
Current transfers received	311.7	342.8	312.1
Current transfers paid	—	—	−1.2
Current balance	−166.9	26.2	−143.3
Investment liabilities	−33.9	−4.1	−59.6
Net errors and omissions	211.6	−47.7	182.8
Overall balance	10.8	−25.6	−20.1

Source: IMF, *International Financial Statistics.*

OFFICIAL DEVELOPMENT ASSISTANCE (US $ million)

	1992	1993	1994
Bilateral	130.2	110.7	139.7
Multilateral	74.2	116.6	88.8
Total	204.3	227.2	228.5
Grants	206.9	222.6	228.6
Loans	−2.6	4.6	−0.1
Per caput assistance (US $)	12.2	13.3	13.1

Source: UN, *Statistical Yearbook for Asia and the Pacific.*

External Trade

PRINCIPAL COMMODITIES (US $ '000, year ending 20 March)

Imports c.i.f.	1980/81	1981/82	1983/84*
Wheat	798	18,100	38,251
Sugar	40,833	50,328	25,200
Tea	28,369	n.a.	23,855
Cigarettes	5,114	7,219	12,755
Vegetable oil	17,320	26,332	30,481
Drugs	4,497	4,195	3,768
Soaps	9,991	17,256	8,039
Tyres and tubes	16,766	12,764	28,823
Textile yarn and thread	16,800	24,586	n.a.
Cotton fabrics	873	6,319	n.a.
Rayon fabrics	6,879	9,498	n.a.
Other textile goods	52,546	49,036	n.a.
Vehicles and spare parts	89,852	141,062	n.a.
Petroleum products	124,000	112,093	n.a.
Footwear (new)	2,058	5,275	5,317
Bicycles	2,042	488	1,952
Matches	1,171	1,542	1,793
Sewing machines	140	285	266
Electric and non-electric machines	2,333	765	n.a.
Chemical materials	7,464	6,636	n.a.
Agricultural tractors	1	8,280	n.a.
Fertilizers	8,325	3,300	3,904
Used clothes	2,523	1,875	5,334
Television receivers	5,391	3,241	10,139
Other items	106,662	92,307	n.a.
Total	551,748	622,416	846,022

* Figures for 1982/83 are not available.

Total imports c.i.f. (US $ million, year ending 20 March): 616 in 1991/92; 700 in 1992/93; 740 in 1993/94. Source: UN, *Statistical Yearbook for Asia and the Pacific.*

Exports f.o.b.	1988/89	1989/90	1990/91
Fruit and nuts	103,400	110,200	93,300
Karakul fur skins	6,100	3,600	3,000
Natural gas	93,200	n.a.	n.a.
Wool	30,900	5,500	9,600
Carpets	39,100	38,000	44,000
Cotton	8,000	5,300	2,500
Total (incl. others)	394,700	235,900	235,100

Source: IMF, *International Financial Statistics.*

Total exports f.o.b. (US $ million, year ending 20 March): 188 in 1992/92; 200 in 1992/93; 180 in 1993/94. Source: UN, *Statistical Yearbook for Asia and the Pacific.*

PRINCIPAL TRADING PARTNERS (estimates, US $ million)

Imports	1992	1993	1994
ASEAN members	77	59	47
Singapore	57	37	20
SAARC members	57	50	57
India	37	32	25
Pakistan	18	17	28
Other Asian countries			
China, People's Republic	26	36	30
Hong Kong	25	30	26
Japan	96	101	89
Korea, Republic	33	33	n. a.
Western Europe	68	69	67
Eastern Europe and the former USSR	4	57	17
Total (incl. others)	593	638	602

Exports	1992	1993	1994
SAARC members	11	11	12
India	5	2	2
Pakistan	6	9	10
Other Asian countries			
China, People's Republic	2	2	11
Japan	1	1	1
Western Europe	48	37	29
Eastern Europe and the former USSR	2	618	7
USA	2	3	6
Total (incl. others)	359	872	296

Source: UN, *Statistical Yearbook for Asia and the Pacific.*

Transport

ROAD TRAFFIC (estimates, '000 motor vehicles in use)

	1994	1995	1996
Passenger cars	31.0	31.0	31.0
Commercial vehicles	25.0	25.0	25.0

Source: IRF, *World Road Statistics.*

CIVIL AVIATION ('000)

	1991	1992	1993
Kilometres flown	4,000	4,000	4,000
Passengers carried	212	212	n. a.
Passenger-km	205,000	205,000	197,000
Freight ton-km	8,000	n. a.	n. a.

Source: UN, *Statistical Yearbook for Asia and the Pacific.*

Tourism

	1991	1992	1993
Tourist arrivals ('000)	8	6	6
Tourist receipts (US $ million)	1	1	1

Source: UN, *Statistical Yearbook.*

Communications Media

	1992	1993	1994
Radio receivers ('000 in use)	2,045	2,080	2,230
Television receivers ('000 in use)	160	175	185
Daily newspapers	16	n.a.	15

Source: UNESCO, *Statistical Yearbook.*

Telephones ('000 main lines in use): 35* in 1989; 36 in 1990; 37* in 1991. Source: UN, *Statistical Yearbook.*

* Estimate.

Education

(1994)

	Institutions	Teachers	Pupils
Elementary	1,753*	20,055	1,161,444
Secondary†	n.a.	17,548	497,762

* 1993 figure.

† Figures refer to general education only, excluding vocational training (teachers 1,262 in 1980; pupils 12,410 in 1980, 14,532 in 1981).

Pre-primary: 263 institutions (1988); 1,505 teachers (1986); 19,660 pupils (1988).

Higher education (1990): 1,342 teachers, 24,333 students.

1994: 1,312,197 elementary pupils; 512,851 general secondary pupils.

Source: UNESCO, *Statistical Yearbook.*

Directory

The Constitution

Immediately after the coup of 27 April 1978 (the Saur Revolution), the 1977 Constitution was abolished. Both Nur Muhammad Taraki (Head of State from April 1978 to September 1979) and his successor, Hafizullah Amin (September–December 1979), promised to introduce new constitutions, but these leaders were removed from power before any drafts had been prepared by special commissions which they had appointed. On 21 April 1980 the Revolutionary Council ratified the Basic Principles of the Democratic Republic of Afghanistan. These were superseded by a new Constitution ratified in April 1985. Another new Constitution was ratified during a meeting of a Loya Jirgah (Supreme National Tribal Assembly), held on 29–30 November 1987. This Constitution was amended in May 1990. The following is a summary of the Constitution as it stood in May 1990.

GENERAL PROVISIONS

The fundamental duty of the State is to defend the independence, national sovereignty and territorial integrity of the Republic of Afghanistan. National sovereignty belongs to the people. The people exercise national sovereignty through the Loya Jirgah and the Meli Shura.

Foreign policy is based on the principle of peaceful co-existence and active and positive non-alignment. Friendship and co-operation are to be strengthened with all countries, particularly neighbouring and Islamic ones. Afghanistan abides by the UN Charter and the Universal Declaration of Human Rights and supports the struggle against colonialism, imperialism, Zionism, racism and fascism. Afghanistan favours disarmament and the prevention of the proliferation of nuclear and chemical weapons. War propaganda is prohibited.

Islam is the religion of Afghanistan and no law shall run counter to the principles of Islam.

Political parties are allowed to be formed, providing that their policies and activities are in accordance with the provisions of the Constitution and the laws of the country. A party that is legally formed cannot be dissolved without legal grounds. Judges and prosecutors cannot be members of a political party during their term of office.

Pashtu and Dari are the official languages.

The capital is Kabul.

The State shall follow the policy of understanding and co-operation between all nationalities, clans and tribes within the country to ensure equality and the rapid development of backward regions.

The family constitutes the basic unit of society. The State shall adopt necessary measures to ensure the health of mothers and children.

The State protects all forms of legal property, including private property. The hereditary right to property shall be guaranteed according to Islamic law.

For the growth of the national economy, the State encourages foreign investment in the Republic of Afghanistan and regulates it in accordance with the law.

RIGHTS AND DUTIES OF THE PEOPLE

All subjects of Afghanistan are equal before the law. The following rights are guaranteed: the right to life and security, to complain to the appropriate government organs, to participate in the political sphere, to freedom of speech and thought, to hold peaceful demonstrations and strikes, to work, to free education, to protection of health and social welfare, to scientific, technical and cultural activities, to freedom of movement both within Afghanistan and abroad, to observe the religious rites of Islam and of other religions, to security of residence and privacy of communication and correspondence, and to liberty and human dignity.

In criminal cases, an accused person is considered innocent until guilt is recognized by the court. Nobody may be arrested, detained or punished except in accordance with the law.

Every citizen is bound to observe the Constitution and the laws of the Republic of Afghanistan, to pay taxes and duties to the State in accordance with the provisions of the law, and to undertake military service, when and as required.

LOYA JIRGAH

This is the highest manifestation of the will of the people of Afghanistan. It is composed of: the President and Vice-Presidents, members of the Meli Shura (National Assembly), the General Prosecutor, the Council of Ministers, the Attorney-General, his deputies and members of the Attorney-General's Office, the chairman of the Constitution Council, the heads of the provincial councils, representatives from each province, according to the number of their representatives in the Wolasi Jirgah (House of Representatives), elected by the people by a general secret ballot, and a minimum of 50 people, from among prominent political, scientific, social and religious figures, appointed by the President.

The Loya Jirgah is empowered: to approve and amend the Constitution; to elect the President and to accept the resignation of the President; to consent to the declaration of war and armistice; and to adopt decisions on major questions regarding the destiny of the country. The Loya Jirgah shall be summoned, opened and chaired by the President. Sessions of the Loya Jirgah require a minimum attendance of two-thirds of the members. Decisions shall be adopted by a majority vote. In the event of the dissolution of the Wolasi Jirgah (House of Representatives), its members shall retain their membership of the Loya Jirgah until a new Wolasi Jirgah is elected. Elections to the Loya Jirgah shall be regulated by law and the procedure laid down by the Loya Jirgah itself.

THE PRESIDENT

The President is the Head of State and shall be elected by a majority vote of the Loya Jirgah for a term of seven years. No person can be elected as President for more than two terms. The President is accountable, and shall report, to the Loya Jirgah. The Loya Jirgah shall be convened to elect a new President 30 days before the end of the term of office of the outgoing President. Any Muslim citizen of the Republic of Afghanistan who is more than 40 years of age can be elected as President.

The President shall exercise the following executive powers: the supreme command of the armed forces; the ratification of the resolutions of the Meli Shura; the appointment of the Prime Minister; the approval of the appointment of ministers, judges and army officials; the granting of citizenship and the commuting of punishment; the power to call a referendum, to proclaim a state of emergency, and to declare war (with the consent of the Loya Jirgah). Should a state of emergency continue for more than three months, the consent of the Loya Jirgah is imperative for its extension.

In the event of the President being unable to perform his duties, the presidential functions and powers shall be entrusted to the first Vice-President. In the event of the death or resignation of the President, the first Vice-President shall ask the Loya Jirgah to elect a new President within one month. In the event of resignation, the President shall submit his resignation directly to the Loya Jirgah.

MELI SHURA

The Meli Shura (National Assembly) is the highest legislative organ of the Republic of Afghanistan. It consists of two houses: the Wolasi Jirgah (House of Representatives) and the Sena (Senate). Members of the Wolasi Jirgah (representatives) are elected by general secret ballot for a legislative term of five years. Members of the Sena (senators) are elected and appointed in the following manner: two people from each province are elected for a period of five years; two people from each provincial council are elected by the council for a period of three years; and the remaining one-third of senators are appointed by the President for a period of four years.

The Meli Shura is vested with the authority: to approve, amend and repeal laws and legislative decrees, and to present them to the President for his signature; to interpret laws; to ratify and annul international treaties; to approve socio-economic development plans and to endorse the Government's reports on their execution; to approve the state budget and to evaluate the Government's report on its execution; to establish and make changes to administrative units; to establish and abolish ministries; to appoint and remove Vice-Presidents, on the recommendation of the President; and to endorse the establishment of relations with foreign countries and international organizations. The Wolasi Jirgah also has the power to approve a vote of confidence or no confidence in the Council of Ministers or one of its members.

At its first session, the Wolasi Jirgah elects, from among its members, an executive committee, composed of a chairman, two deputy chairmen and two secretaries, for the whole term of the legislature. The Sena elects, from among its members, an executive committee, composed of a chairman for a term of five years, and two deputy chairmen and two secretaries for a term of one year.

Ordinary sessions of the Meli Shura are held twice a year and do not normally last longer than three months. An extraordinary session can be held at the request of the President, the chairman of either house, or one-fifth of the members of each house. The houses of the Meli Shura can hold separate or joint sessions. Sessions require a minimum attendance of two-thirds of the members of each house and decisions shall be adopted by a majority vote. Sessions are open, unless the houses decide to meet in closed sessions.

The following authorities have the right to propose the introduction, amendment or repeal of a law in either house of the Meli Shura: the President, the standing commissions of the Meli Shura, at least one-tenth of the membership of each house, the Council of Ministers, the Supreme Court, and the office of the Attorney-General.

If the decision of one house is rejected by the other, a joint committee, consisting of an equal number of members from both houses, shall be formed. A decision by the joint committee, which will be agreed by a two-thirds majority, will be considered valid after approval by the President. If the joint committee fails to resolve differences, the matter shall be discussed in a joint session of the Meli Shura, and a decision reached by a majority vote. The decisions that are made by the Meli Shura are enforced after being signed by the President.

After consulting the chairman of the Wolasi Jirgah, the chairman of the Sena, the Prime Minister, the Attorney-General and the chairman of the Constitution Council, the President can declare the dissolution of the Wolasi Jirgah, stating his justification for doing so. Re-elections shall be held within 3 months of the dissolution.

COUNCIL OF MINISTERS

The Council of Ministers is composed of: a Prime Minister, deputy Prime Ministers and Ministers. The Council of Ministers is appointed by the Prime Minister. It is empowered: to formulate and implement domestic and foreign policies; to formulate economic development plans and state budgets; and to ensure public order.

The Council of Ministers is dissolved under the following conditions: the resignation of the Prime Minister, chronic illness of the Prime Minister, the withdrawal of confidence in the Council of Ministers by the Meli Shura, the end of the legislative term, or the dissolution of the Wolasi Jirgah or the Meli Shura.

THE JUDICIARY

(See section on the Judicial System.)

THE CONSTITUTION COUNCIL

The responsibilities of this body are: to evaluate and ensure the conformity of laws, legislative decrees and international treaties with the Constitution; and to give legal advice to the President on constitutional matters. The Constitution Council is composed of a chairman, a vice-chairman and eight members, who are appointed by the President.

LOCAL ADMINISTRATIVE ORGANS

For the purposes of local administration, the Republic of Afghanistan is divided into provinces, districts, cities and wards. These administrative units are led, respectively, by governors, district administrators, mayors and heads of wards. In each province a provincial council and district councils are formed in accordance with the law. Provincial councils and district councils each elect a chairman and a secretary from among their members. The term of office of a provincial council and a district council is three years.

FINAL PROVISIONS

Amendments to the Constitution shall be made by the Loya Jirgah. Any amendment shall be on the proposal of the President, or on the proposal of one-third and the approval of two-thirds of the members of the Meli Shura. Amendment to the Constitution during a state of emergency is not allowed.

Note: Following the downfall of Najibullah's regime in April 1992, a provisional *mujahidin* Government assumed power in Kabul. In July an acting executive body, known as the Leadership Council, appointed a special commission to draw up a new and more strictly Islamic Constitution. In September 1993 it was reported that a draft Constitution had been approved by the commission, in preparation for the holding of a general election.

In May 1996, following the signing of the Mahipar Agreement between President Burhanuddin Rabbani and Gulbuddin Hekmatyar, a Constitution to cover the interim period pending the holding of a general election was drawn up and published. The main provisions of the **Constitution of the Interim Period** are as follows:

General provision: Afghanistan is an Islamic country where all aspects of the life of the people shall be conducted according to the tenets of Shari'a.

President: The President is the Head of State and exercises the highest executive power; the President is the supreme commander of the armed forces and his approval is required for the appointment of all civil and military officials; the President is authorized to declare war or peace (on the advice of the Council of Ministers or an Islamic Shura), to approve death sentences or grant pardons, to summon and dismiss a Shura, and to sign international treaties. In the event of the President's death, the presidential functions and powers shall be entrusted to the President of the Supreme Court until a new Head of State can be appointed.

Council of Ministers: The Council of Ministers, under the leadership of the Prime Minister, shall discuss and make decisions regarding government policy (both internal and external), the annual budget and administrative regulations, all of which shall be referred to the President for his assent.

According to the Iranian news agency, IRNA, in early October 1996 the Pakistani political party, Jamiat-e-Ulema-e-Islam, had prepared a draft Constitution for Afghanistan at the request of Taliban, which had seized control of the capital in late September.

The Government

Following the collapse of Najibullah's regime in April 1992, a provisional *mujahidin* Government was established in Kabul. For the first two months, Prof. Sibghatullah Mojaddedi held the post of acting President and headed a 51-member executive body, known as the Islamic Jihad Council, which appointed an interim Council of Ministers in early May. On 28 June Mojaddedi, in accordance with the proposals formulated in the Peshawar Agreement (see History), surrendered the presidency to Prof. Burhanuddin Rabbani, who presided over another executive body, called the Leadership Council. Rabbani held power until the end of October, when his tenure of the presidency was extended for a further two months. On 30 December a special advisory council elected Rabbani, unopposed, as President of the country for a period of a further two years. Following the signing of a peace accord by the majority of *mujahidin* groups in Islamabad in March 1993, an interim multi-faction Government was established, about 25 km south of Kabul, in June. In June 1994 the Supreme Court extended Rabbani's presidency for a further six months. When this six-month period ended in early 1995, Rabbani continued to exercise power.

In late September 1996 Rabbani's Government was ousted from power by Taliban, which captured the capital and installed a strict Islamic regime. An interim Council of Ministers was appointed, but Taliban gave no indication of when elections would be held. The Taliban Government won little international recognition (the UN refused to recognize it) and former President Rabbani continued to be acknowledged by many as the rightful leader of Afghanistan.

HEAD OF STATE

(July 1997)

President: Prof. BURHANUDDIN RABBANI.

Vice-President: Mawlawi MOHAMMAD NABI MOHAMMADI.

INTERIM COUNCIL OF MINISTERS*

(July 1997)

Prime Minister: GULBUDDIN HEKMATYAR.

First Deputy Prime Minister: Eng. QOTBODDIN HELAL.

Minister of Defence: Lt-Gen. WAHIDOLLAH SABA'UN.

Minister of Internal Affairs: MOHAMMAD YUNUS QANUNI.

Minister of Foreign Affairs: ABDORRAHIM GHAFURZAI.

Minister of Water and Power: Eng. SAYD MOHAMMAD AYUB.

Minister of Information and Culture: QEYAMODDIN KASHAF.

Minister of Agriculture: SEKANDER QIYAM.

Minister of Housing and City Construction: Eng. ABDOL SALAM HASHEMI.

Minister of Education: Eng. AHMAD SHAH AHMADZAY.

Minister of Finance: ABDUL HADI ARGHANDEWAL.

Minister of Planning: Hojjat-ol Islam SAYD MOHAMMAD ALI JAWID.

Minister of Martyrs and the Disabled: Mawlawi SAMIOLLAH NAJEBI.

Minister of Commerce: Hojjat-ol Islam SAYD HOSAYN ALEMI BALKHI.

Minister of Labour and Social Affairs: Lt-Gen. SAYD HOSAYN ANWARI.

Minister of State for Foreign Affairs: Dr NAJIBULLAH LAFRA'I.

* Note: In mid-August 1997 it was reported that the anti-Taliban opposition coalition known as the United Islamic Front for the Salvation of Afghanistan (UIFSA) had appointed a new Government, with Prof. BURHANUDDIN RABBANI continuing as President, ABDORRAHIM GHAFURZAI as Prime Minister, AHMAD SHAH MASOUD as Minister of Defence and Gen. ABDUL MALIK PAHLAWAN as Minister of Foreign Affairs. The former Prime Minister in the anti-Taliban administration, GULBUDDIN HEKMATYAR, refused to recognize the new Government. Within a few days of its appointment, however, seven members of the new Government, including Prime Minister Ghafurzai, were killed in an aeroplane crash. In late August the anti-Taliban opposition alliance appointed ABDOLGHAFFUR RAWANFARHADI as new Prime Minister, and in September Gen. ABDUL RASHID DOSTAM

was appointed Vice-President of the UIFSA administration. In December it was reported that the following appointments had been made in Rabbani's Government: GHULAM HUSAYN SHAHAQ as Minister of Labour and Social Affairs, Eng. MOHAMMAD IBRAHIM ADIL as Minister of Construction Affairs, Eng. AL-SAYED AHMAD MUSAVI as Minister of Water and Power, SAYED ABDULHADI BALKHI as Government Adviser, MUHAMMAD AWAZ FIKRAT as Deputy Minister of Trade, and Mr MA'SUMYAR as Deputy Minister of Higher Education.

TALIBAN INTERIM COUNCIL OF MINISTERS
(December 1997)

Chairman: Haji Mola MOHAMMAD RABBANI.

Deputy Chairman: Mawlawi ABDOL KABIR.

Minister of Foreign Affairs: Alhaj Mola MOHAMMAD HASAN AKHOND.

Minister of Finance: Mola MOHAMMAD AMIN AHMADI.

Minister of Civil Aviation: Mola AKHTAR MANSUR.

Minister of Communications: Alhaj Mola ALAHDAD ZAHED.

Minster of Water and Power: Mola MOHAMMAD ISA AKHUND.

Minister of Internal Affairs: Mola KHAIROLLAH KHAIRKHAH.

Minister of Public Works: Mola ALAHDAD AKHOND.

Minister of Justice: Alhaj Mola NORUDDIN TORABI.

Minister of Light Industries and Food: Mawlawi HAMDOLLAH ZAHED.

Minister of Agriculture and Animal Husbandry: Mawlawi ABDOL LATIF MANSUR.

Minister of Religious Guidance and Endowment: Mawlawi HAFEZ MOHEBOLLAH.

Minister of Education: Alhaj Mawlawi ABDUL SALAAM HANIFI.

Minister of Information and Culture: Mola AMIR KHAN MOTAQI.

Minister of Rural Development: Mawlawi SEDIQOLLAH.

Minister of Planning: Qari DIN MOHAMMAD.

Minister of Refugees' Repatriation: Mawlawi ABDORRAQIB.

Minister of Martyrs and the Disabled: Mawlawi ABDOL BAQI.

Minister of Mines and Industries: Mawlawi AHMAD JAN.

Minister of Borders: Mawlawi JALALODDIN HAQQANI.

Minister of Labour and Social Welfare: Mawlawi MOHAMMAD MIR.

Minister of Logistics: Mawlawi YAR MOHAMMAD.

Minister of National Defence: Alhaj Mola OBAIDOLLAH AKHOND.

Minister of Security: Mola MOHAMMAD FAZEL.

Minister of Public Health: Mola MOHAMMAD ABAS AKHOND.

Minister of Higher Education: Mawlawi HAMDOLLAH NOMANI.

Minister without Portfolio: Mawlawi GHIASODDIN.

Deputy Minister for the Promotion of Virtue and the Suppression of Vice: Mawlawi INAYATULLAH BALIGH.

MINISTRIES

Office of the Council of Ministers: Shar Rahi Sedarat, Kabul; tel. (93) 26926.

Office of the Prime Minister: Shar Rahi Sedarat, Kabul; tel. (93) 26926.

Ministry of Agriculture and Land Reform: Jamal Mina, Kabul; tel. (93) 41151.

Ministry of Border Affairs: Shah Mahmud Ghazi Ave, Kabul; tel. (93) 21793.

Ministry of Civil Aviation and Tourism: POB 165, Ansari Wat, Kabul; tel. (93) 21015.

Ministry of Commerce: Darulaman Wat, Kabul; tel. (93) 41041; telex 234.

Ministry of Communications: Puli Bagh-i-Omomi, Kabul; tel. (93) 21341; telex 297.

Ministry of Construction Affairs: Micro-Rayon, Kabul; tel. (93) 63701.

Ministry of Defence: Darulaman Wat, Kabul; tel. (93) 41232; telex 325.

Ministry of Education and Training: Mohd Jan Khan Wat, Kabul; tel. (93) 20666.

Ministry of Energy: Micro-Rayon, Kabul; tel. (93) 25109.

Ministry of Finance: Shar Rahi Pashtunistan, Kabul; tel. (93) 26041.

Ministry of Foreign Affairs: Shah Mahmud Ghazi St, Shar-i-Nau, Kabul; tel. (93) 25441; telex 232.

Ministry of Higher and Vocational Education: Jamal Mina, Kabul; tel. (93) 40041; f. 1978.

Ministry of Information and Culture: Mohd Jan Khan Wat, Kabul.

Ministry of Internal Affairs: Shar-i-Nau, Kabul; tel. (93) 32441.

Ministry of Islamic Affairs: Kabul.

Ministry of Justice: Shar Rahi Pashtunistan, Kabul; tel. (93) 23404.

Ministry of Light Industries and Foodstuffs: Ansari Wat, Kabul; tel. (93) 41551.

Ministry of Mines and Industries: Shar Rahi Pashtunistan, Kabul; tel. (93) 25841; telex 260.

Ministry of Planning: Shar-i-Nau, Kabul; tel. (93) 21273.

Ministry of Public Health: Micro-Rayon, Kabul; tel. (93) 40851.

Ministry of Transport: Ansari Wat, Kabul; tel. (93) 25541.

Ministry of Water Resources Development and Irrigation: Darulaman Wat, Kabul; tel. (93) 40743.

Legislature

MELI SHURA*
(National Assembly)

The Meli Shura, which was established in 1987 and replaced the Revolutionary Council, is composed of two houses: the Wolasi Jirgah (House of Representatives) and the Sena (Senate). Elections were held to both houses in April 1988.

Wolasi Jirgah

Representatives were elected for five years. Of the total 234 seats, 184 were contested in the general election in April 1988. The remaining 50 seats were reserved for members of the opposition.

Sena

The Sena comprised 192 members. One-third of its members were elected for five years, one-third were elected for three years, and one-third were appointed for three years. At the general election in 1988, 115 senators were elected, while the majority of the remaining 77 seats were filled by senators appointed by the President. A small number of seats were reserved for members of the opposition.

* Following the downfall of Najibullah's regime in April 1992, an interim *mujahidin* Government took power in Kabul and both houses of the Meli Shura were dissolved. A High State Council (HSC) was formed, which was to meet regularly, under the chairmanship of the President, to discuss and make decisions regarding matters of national importance.

Political Organizations

The following were the principal *mujahidin* and militia groups operating in 1997:

The seven below were formerly members of a grand alliance, formed in 1985 and called the Ittehad-i-Islami Afghan Mujahidin (Islamic Union of Afghan Mujahidin—IUAM), based in Peshawar, Pakistan:

Three moderate/traditionalist groups:

Harakat-i-Inqilab-i-Islami (Islamic Revolutionary Movement): Pashtun; supports Taliban; Leader Mawlawi MOHAMMAD NABI MOHAMMADI; c. 25,000 supporters (estimate).

Jebha-i-Nejat-i-Melli (National Liberation Front): Pashtun; Leader Prof. Hazrat SIBGHATULLAH MOJADDEDI; Sec.-Gen. ZABIHOLLAH MOJADDEDI; c. 15,000 supporters (estimate).

Mahaz-i-Melli-i-Islami (National Islamic Front): Pashtun; Leader Pir SAYED AHMAD GAILANI; Dep. Leader HAMED GAILANI; c. 15,000 supporters (estimate).

Four Islamic fundamentalist groups:

Hizb-i Islami Gulbuddin (Islamic Party Gulbuddin): Pashtun/Turkmen/Tajik; Leader GULBUDDIN HEKMATYAR; c. 50,000 supporters (estimate).

Hizb-i Islami Khalis (Islamic Party Khalis): Pashtun; Leader Maulvi MUHAMMAD YUNUS KHALIS; c. 40,000 supporters (estimate).

Ittehad-i-Islami (Islamic Union): Pashtun; Leader Prof. ABD AR-RASUL SAYEF; Dep. Leader AHMAD SHAH AHMADZAY; c. 18,000 supporters (estimate).

Jamiat-i Islami (Islamic Society): Turkmen/Uzbek/Tajik; Leaders Prof. BURHANUDDIN RABBANI, Gen. AHMAD SHAH MASOUD; Sec.-Gen. ENAYATOLLAH SHADAB; c. 60,000 supporters (estimate).

In June 1987 eight Afghan Islamic (Shi'ite) factions (based in Teheran, Iran) formed the **Hizb-i Wahadat-i Islami** (Islamic Unity Party; Chair. of Political Committee Hojjat-ol Islam MOHAMMAD AKBARI; Chair. of Supreme Council ALEMI BALKHI; Sec.-Gen. ABDOL KARIM KHALILI), comprising: the **Afghan Nasr Organization** (Hazara; c. 50,000 supporters), the **Guardians of Islamic Jihad**

of Afghanistan, the **United Islamic Front of Afghanistan,** the **Islamic Force of Afghanistan,** the **Dawa Party of Islamic Unity of Afghanistan,** the **Harakat-e Eslami Afghanistan** (the Islamic Movement of Afghanistan; Pashtun/Tajik/Uzbek; Leader: Ayatollah MOHAMMAD ASEF MOHSENI; Dep. Leader SAYD MOHAMMAD ALI JAWED; c. 20,000 supporters), the **Hezbollah** (c. 4,000 supporters), and the **Islamic Struggle for Afghanistan.**

National Islamic Movement (Jonbesh-e Melli-e Eslami): f. 1992; formed mainly from troops of former Northern Command of the Afghan army; predominantly Uzbek/Tajik/Turkmen/Ismaili and Hazara Shi'ite; Leader Gen. ABDUL RASHID DOSTAM; 65,000–150,000 supporters.

Taliban: headquarters in Qandahar; emerged in 1994; Islamic fundamentalist; mainly Sunni Pashtuns; Leader Mola MOHAMMAD OMAR; Dep. Leader Mola WAKIL AHMAD; c. 40,000 armed supporters.

Diplomatic Representation

By the end of 1992 many of the embassies had been temporarily closed down and the diplomatic staff had left Kabul, owing to the continuing unrest in the capital.

EMBASSIES IN AFGHANISTAN

Austria: POB 24, Zarghouna Wat, Kabul; tel. (93) 32720; telex 218; Ambassador: (vacant).

Bangladesh: Kabul; tel. (93) 25783; Chargé d'affaires a.i.: MAHMOOD HASAN.

Bulgaria: Wazir Akbar Khan Mena, Kabul; tel. (93) 20683; telex 22249; Ambassador: VALENTIN PETKOV GATSINSKI.

China, People's Republic: Shah Mahmud Wat, Shar-i-Nau, Kabul; tel. (93) 20446; Chargé d'affaires a.i.: ZHANG DELIANG.

Cuba: Shar Rahi Haji Yaqub, opp. Shar-i-Nau Park, Kabul; tel. (93) 30863; Ambassador: REGINO FARINAS CANTERO.

Czech Republic: Taimani Wat, Kala-i-Fatullah, Kabul; tel. (93) 32082.

France: Shar-i-Nau, Kabul; tel. (93) 23631; Ambassador-at-large: DIDIER LEROY.

Germany: Wazir Akbar Khan Mena, POB 83, Kabul; tel. (93) 22432; telex 249; Ambassador: (vacant).

Hungary: POB 830, Sin 306–308, Wazir Akbar Khan Mena, Kabul; tel. (93) 24281; Ambassador: MIHÁLY GOLUB.

India: Malalai Wat, Shar-i-Nau, Kabul; tel. (93) 30557; Chargé d'affaires a.i.: A. S. TOOR.

Indonesia: POB 532, Wazir Akbar Khan Mena, District 10, Zone 14, Road Mark Jeem House 93, Kabul; tel. (93) 20586; telex 239; Ambassador: HAVID ABDUL GHANI.

Iran: Shar-i-Nau, Kabul; tel. (93) 26255; Ambassador: GHOLAMREZA HADDADI. (Closed down by Taliban administration in June 1997.)

Iraq: POB 523, Wazir Akbar Khan Mena, Kabul; tel. (93) 24797; Ambassador: BURHAN KHALIL GHAZAL.

Italy: POB 606, Khoja Abdullah Ansari Wat, Kabul; tel. (93) 24624; telex 55; Chargé d'affaires a.i.: Mr CALAMAI.

Japan: POB 80, Wazir Akbar Khan Mena, Kabul; tel. (93) 26844; telex 216; Chargé d'affaires a.i.: KEIKI HIRAGA.

Korea, Democratic People's Republic: Wazir Akbar Khan Mena, House 28, Sarak 'H' House 103, Kabul; tel. (93) 22161; Ambassador: OH IN YONG.

Libya: 103 Wazir Akbar Khan Mena, Kabul; tel. (93) 25947; Ambassador: ALI AL-BARUQ AL-SHARIFI.

Mongolia: Wazir Akbar Khan Mena, Sarak 'T' House 8714, Kabul; tel. (93) 22138; Ambassador: (vacant).

Pakistan: Kabul; Ambassador: AZIZ AHMAD KHAN.

Poland: Gozargah St, POB 78, Kabul; tel. (93) 42461; Chargé d'affaires: Prof. ANDRZEJ WAWRZYNIAK.

Russia: Darulaman Wat, Kabul; tel. (93) 41541; Ambassador: BORIS NIKOLAYEVICH PASTUKHOV.

Saudi Arabia: Kabul; Chargé d'affaires: SALMAN MUHAMMAD AL-UMARI.

Slovakia: Taimani Wat, Kala-i-Fatullah, Kabul; tel. (93) 32082.

Sudan: Kabul.

Turkey: Shar-i-Nau, Kabul; tel. (93) 20072; Chargé d'affaires a.i.: SALEH AHSAN.

United Kingdom: Karte Parwan, Kabul; tel. (93) 88888; Ambassador: (vacant).

USA: Wazir Akbar Khan Mena, Kabul; tel. (93) 62230; Chargé d'affaires a.i.: JON D. GLASSMANN.

Viet Nam: 3 Nijat St, Wazir Akbar Khan Mena, Kabul; tel. (93) 26596; Ambassador: NGUYEN NGOC SINH.

Yugoslavia: POB 53, 923 Main Rd, Wazir Akbar Khan Mena, Kabul; tel. (93) 61671; telex 272; Chargé d'affaires a.i.: VELIBOR DULOVIĆ.

Judicial System

The functions and structure of the judiciary are established in Articles 107–121 of the Constitution ratified by the Loya Jirgah in November 1987 and amended in May 1990.

The courts apply the provisions of the Constitution and the laws of Afghanistan, and, in cases of ambivalence, will judge in accordance with the rules of Shari'a (Islamic religious law). Trials are held in open session except when circumstances defined by law deem the trial to be held in closed session. Trials are conducted in Pashtu and Dari or in the language of the majority of the inhabitants of the locality. The right to speak in court in one's mother tongue is guaranteed to the two sides of the lawsuit.

The judiciary comprises the Supreme Court and those courts which are formed in accordance with the directives of the law. The State may establish specialized courts within the unified system of the judiciary.

The highest judicial organ is the Supreme Court, which consists of a President, Vice-President and judges, all of whom are appointed by the Head of State in accordance with the law. It supervises the judicial activities of the courts and ensures the uniformity of law enforcement and interpretation by those courts.

Death sentences are carried out after ratification by the Head of State.

President of the Supreme Court: MOHAMMAD SHAH FAZLI.

The public prosecutor's office consists of the Attorney-General's office and those other attorneys' offices which are formed in accordance with the directives of the law. The Attorney-General supervises the activities of all the attorney offices, which are independent of local organs and answerable only to the Attorney-General himself. The Attorney-General and his deputies, who are appointed by the Head of State in accordance with the law, supervise the implementation and observance of all laws.

Attorney-General: SAYED ABDORRAZAQ MOSAMEM (acting).

Deputy Attorney-General: ABDUL HADY KHALILZIA.

Following the collapse of Najibullah's regime and the installation of a *mujahidin* Government in Kabul in April 1992, a judicial system fully based on the rules of Shari'a was expected to be incorporated in the *mujahidin's* new Constitution. In an apparent attempt to improve security in Kabul, special courts were established by the *mujahidin* administration to prosecute 'people who violate homes, honour, children and property'.

Following its seizure of power in the capital in September 1996, Taliban imposed a strict Islamic code of conduct on Kabul, including the introduction of stonings, lashings, amputations and the death penalty as punishment for various crimes.

Taliban President of the Supreme Court: Mawlawi JALILOLLAH MOWLAWIZADA.

Taliban Vice-Presidents of the Supreme Court: Mawlawi NUR MOHAMMAD SAQEB, Mawlawi ABDOL SATAR SEDIQI, Mawlawi RAFIOLLAH MO'AZEN.

Religion

The official religion of Afghanistan is Islam. Muslims comprise 99% of the population, approximately 80% of them of the Sunni and the remainder of the Shi'ite sect. There are small minority groups of Hindus, Sikhs and Jews.

ISLAM

The High Council of Ulema and Clergy of Afghanistan: Kabul; f. 1980; 7,000 mems; Gen. Dir Alhaj GHOLAM SARWAR MANZUR; Dep. Dirs ABDUL AZIZE QIASARI, MOHAMMED MUSA TAHERI.

The Press

Some of the following newspapers and periodicals have not always appeared on a regular basis.

PRINCIPAL DAILIES

Anis: (Friendship): Kabul; f. 1927; evening; independent; Dari and Pashtu; news and literary articles; Chief Editor MOHAMMAD S. KHARNIKASH; circ. 25,000.

Badakhshan: Faizabad; f. 1945; Dari and Pashtu; Chief Editor HADI ROSTAQI; circ. 3,000.

Bedar: Mazar-i-Sharif; f. 1920; Dari and Pashtu; Chief Editor ROZEQ FANI; circ, 2,500.

Dariz: Kabul.

Ettehadi-Baghlan: Baghlan; f. 1930; Dari and Pashtu; Chief Editor Shafiqullah Moshfeq; circ. 1,200.

Hewad (Homeland): Kabul; f. 1959; Dari and Pashtu; state-owned; Editor-in-Chief Amir Afghanpur; circ. 12,200.

Ittifak Islam: Herat; Dari and Pashtu.

Jawzjan: Jawzjan; f. 1942; Dari and Pashtu; Chief Editor A. Rahem Hamro; circ. 1,500.

Kabul New Times: POB 983, Ansari Wat, Kabul; tel. (93) 61847; f. 1962 as Kabul Times, renamed 1980; English; state-owned; Editor-in-Chief M. Seddiq Rahpoe; circ. 5,000.

Nangarhor: Jalalabad; f. 1919; Pashtu; Chief Editor Morad Sangarmal; circ. 1,500.

Sanae: Parwan; f. 1953; Dari and Pashtu; Chief Editor G. Sakhi Eshanzada; circ. 1,700.

Seistan: Farah; f. 1947; Dari and Pashtu; Editor-in-Chief M. Anwar Mahal; circ. 1,800.

Shahadat: organ of the Hizb-i Islami Gulbuddin.

Shahr: Kabul.

Tulu-i-Afghan: Qandahar; f. 1924; Pashtu; Chief Editor Taher Shafeq; circ. 1,500.

Wolanga: Paktia; f. 1943; Pashtu; Chief Editor M. Anwar; circ. 1,500.

PERIODICALS

Afghanistan: Historical Society of Afghanistan, Kabul; tel. (93) 30370; f. 1948; quarterly; English and French; historical and cultural; Editor Maliha Zafar.

Afghanistan Today: Block 106, Ansari Wat, Kabul; tel. (93) 61868; telex 333; f. 1985; every 2 months; state-owned; socio-political, economics and cultural; CEO Karim Hoqouq; circ. 10,500.

Ahbar: Baihaki Book Publishing and Import Institute, Kabul; illustrated monthly; Dari and Pashtu; publ. by Rossiiskoye Informatsionnoye Agentstvo-Novosti.

Akhbar-e-Hafta: Kabul; f. 1989; weekly; Editor Zaher Tanin.

Aryana: ISA Academy of Sciences, Kabul; tel. (93) 25106; f. 1943; quarterly; Pashtu and Dari; culture, history, ethnography, socio-economics; Editor Sayed Amin Mujahed.

Awaz: Kabul; f. 1940; monthly; Pashtu and Dari; radio and television programmes; Editor Nasir Tohori; circ. 20,000.

Erfan: Ministry of Education and Training, Mohd Jan Khan Wat, Kabul; tel. (93) 21612; f. 1923; every two months; Dari and Pashtu; education, psychology, mathematics, religion, literature and technology; Chief Editor Mohammad Qasem Hilaman; circ. 7,500.

Ershad-e-Islam (Islamic Precepts): Kabul; f. 1987; publ. by the Ministry of Islamic Affairs; Editor Muhammad Salem Khares.

Gharjestan: Kabul; f. 1988; every two months; political and cultural; for the people of Hazara.

Gorash: Ministry of Information and Culture, Mohd Jan Khan Wat, Kabul; f. 1979; weekly; Turkmen; Chief Editor S. Misediq Amini; circ, 1,000.

Haqiqat-e-Sarbaz: Ministry of Defence, Kabul; f. 1980; 3 a week; Dari and Pashtu; Chief Editor Mer Jamaluddin Fakhr; circ. 18,370.

Helmand: Bost; f. 1954; 2 a week; Pashtu; Editor-in-Chief M. Omer Farhat Balegh; circ. 1,700.

Herat: Ministry of Information and Culture, Mohd Jan Khan Wat, Kabul; f. 1923; monthly; Dari and Pashtu; Chief Editor Jalil Shabger Foladyon.

Kabul: Afghanistan Academy of Sciences, Research Centre for Languages and Literature, Akbar Khan Mena, Kabul; f. 1931; monthly; Pashtu; literature and language research; Editor N. M. Saheem.

Kar: POB 756, Kabul; tel. (93) 25629; telex 372; monthly; publ. by the Central Council of the National Union of Afghanistan Employees; Editor-in-Chief Aziz Ahmad Nasir; circ. 2,500.

Kunar Periodical Journal: Asadabad; f. 1987; Pashtu; news and socio-economic issues; circ. 5,000.

Meli Jabha: Kabul; weekly.

Mojahed: Kabul; weekly; organ of the Jamiat-i Islami.

Mojala-e-Ariana (Light): Kabul; f. 1978; monthly; Dari and Pashtu; Editor-in-Chief Rashid Ashti; circ. 1,000.

Muhasel-e-Emroz (Today's Student): Kabul; f. 1986; monthly; state-owned; juvenile; circ. 5,000.

Nengarhar: Kabul; f. 1919; weekly; Pashtu; Editor-in-Chief Karim Hashimi; circ. 1,500.

Palwasha: Kabul; f. 1988; fortnightly; Editor-in-Chief Shah Zaman Breed.

Pamir: Micro-Rayon, Kabul; tel. (93) 20585; f. 1952; fortnightly; Dari and Pashtu; combined organ of the Kabul Cttee and Municipality; Chief Editor Enayet Pozhohan Gurdani; circ. 30,000.

Payam-e-Haq: Kabul; f. 1953; monthly; Dari and Pashtu; Editor-in-Chief Farah Shah Mohibi; circ. 1,000.

Samangon: Aibak; f. 1978; weekly; Dari; Editor-in-Chief M. Mohsen Hassan; circ. 1,500.

Sawad (Literacy): Kabul; f. 1954; monthly; Dari and Pashtu; Editor-in-Chief Malem Gol Zadron; circ. 1,000.

Seramiasht: POB 3066, Afghan Red Crescent Society, Puli Artal, Kabul; tel. (93) 32853; telex 318; f. 1958; quarterly; Dari, Pashtu and English; Editor-in-Chief Sayed Assadullah Stoman; circ. 1,000.

Shariat: Kabul; weekly; central organ of Taliban.

Sob: Kabul; tel. (93) 25240; f. 1979; weekly; Balochi; Editor-in-Chief Walimuhammad Rokhshoni; circ. 1,000.

Talim wa Tarbia (Education): Kabul; f. 1954; monthly; publ. by Institute of Education.

Urdu (Military): Kabul; f. 1922; quarterly; Dari and Pashtu; military journal; issued by the Ministry of Defence; Chief Editor Khalilulah Akbari; circ. 500.

Yulduz (Star): Ministry of Information and Culture, Mohd Jan Khan Wat, Kabul; f. 1979; weekly; Uzbek and Turkmen; Chief Editor Ekhan Bayoni; circ. 2,000.

Zeray: Afghanistan Academy of Sciences, Research Centre for Languages and Literature, Akbar Khan Mena, Kabul; f. 1938; weekly; Pashtu; Pashtu folklore, literature and language; Editor Muhammad Nasser; circ. 1,000.

Zhwandoon (Life): Kabul; tel. (93) 26849; f. 1944; weekly; Pashtu and Dari; illustrated; Editor Rohela Rosekh Khorami; circ. 1,400.

NEWS AGENCIES

Bakhtar Information Agency (BIA): Ministry of Information and Culture, Mohd Jan Khan Wat, Kabul; tel. (93) 24089; telex 210; f. 1939; Dir-Gen. Abdol Hafiz Mansur.

Foreign Bureaux

Česká tisková kancelář (ČTK) (Czech Republic): POB 673, Kabul; tel. (93) 23419; telex 79.

The following foreign agencies are also represented in Kabul: Rossiiskoye Informatsionnoye Agentstvo—Novosti (RIA—Novosti; Russia) and Tanjug (Yugoslavia).

PRESS ASSOCIATIONS

Journalists' Association: Kabul; f. 1991; Chair. Amir Afghanpur; Dep. Chair. Habib Shams, Lt Faruq.

Union of Journalists of Afghanistan: Wazir Akbar Khan Mena, St 13, Kabul; f. 1980; Pres. Mohammad Yusuf Ayina.

Publishers

Afghan Book: POB 206, Kabul; f. 1969; books on various subjects, translations of foreign works on Afghanistan, books in English on Afghanistan and Dari language textbooks for foreigners; Man. Dir Jamila Ahang.

Afghanistan Today Publishers: POB 983, c/o The Kabul New Times, Ansari Wat, Kabul; tel. (93) 61847; publicity materials; answers enquiries about Afghanistan.

Balhaqi Book Publishing and Importing Institute: POB 2025, Kabul; tel. (93) 26818; f. 1971 by co-operation of the Government Printing House, Bakhtar News Agency and leading newspapers; publishers and importers of books; Pres. Muhammad Anwar Numyalai.

Book Publishing Institute: Herat; f. 1970 by co-operation of Government Printing House and citizens of Herat; books on literature, history and religion.

Book Publishing Institute: Qandahar; f. 1970; supervised by Government Printing House; mainly books in Pashtu language.

Educational Publications: Ministry of Education and Training, Mohd Jan Khan Wat, Kabul; tel. (93) 21716; textbooks for primary and secondary schools in the Pashtu and Dari languages; also three monthly magazines in Pashtu and in Dari.

Franklin Book Programs Inc: POB 332, Kabul.

Historical Society of Afghanistan: Kabul; tel. (93) 30370; f. 1931; mainly historical and cultural works and two quarterly magazines: *Afghanistan* (English and French), *Aryana* (Dari and Pashtu); Pres. Ahmad Ali Motamedi.

Institute of Geography: Kabul University, Kabul; geographical and related works.

International Center for Pashtu Studies: Kabul; f. 1975 by the Afghan Govt with the assistance of UNESCO; research work on the Pashtu language and literature and on the history and culture of the Pashtu people; Pres. and Assoc. Chief Researcher J. K. HEKMATY; publs *Pashtu* (quarterly).

Kabul University Press: Kabul; tel. (93) 42433; f. 1950; textbooks; two quarterly scientific journals in Dari and in English, etc.

Research Center for Linguistics and Literary Studies: Afghanistan Academy of Sciences, Akbar Khan Mena, Kabul; tel. (93) 26912; f. 1978; research on Afghan languages (incl. Pashtu, Dari, Balochi and Uzbek) and Afghan folklore; Pres. Prof. MOHAMMED R. ELHAM; publs *Kabul* (Pashtu), *Zeray* (Pashtu weekly) and *Khurasan* (Dari).

Government Publishing House

Government Printing House: Kabul; tel. (93) 26851; f. 1870 under supervision of the Ministry of Information and Culture; four daily newspapers in Kabul, one in English; weekly, fortnightly and monthly magazines, one of them in English; books on Afghan history and literature, as well as textbooks for the Ministry of Education; 13 daily newspapers in 13 provincial centres and one journal and also magazines in three provincial centres; Dir MUHAMMAD AYAN AYAN.

Broadcasting and Communications

Following its capture of Kabul in September 1996, Taliban banned television and closed down the station. It also renamed Radio Afghanistan the Voice of Shari'a. In November, however, it was reported that the pro-Rabbani Radio Afghanistan was broadcasting daily, in Dari and Pashtu, from Talukan, the capital of Takhar province in northern Afghanistan.

Afghan Radio, TV and Film: POB 544, Ansari Wat, Kabul; tel. (93) 20355; telex 24288; under the supervision of the Ministry of Information and Culture; Voice of Shari'a home service in Dari and Pashtu (10 hours daily); home service in Uzbek, Turkmen, Nurestani and Pashai (50 minutes daily); foreign service in Urdu and English (30 minutes daily); Gen. Pres. Ustad Mawlawi MOHAMMED ESAQ NIZAMI; Pres. of Planning and Foreign Relations Eng. ABDUL RAHMAN.

Finance

(cap. = capital; auth. = authorized; p.u. = paid up; res = reserves; m. = million; brs = branches; amounts in afghanis unless otherwise stated)

BANKING

In June 1975 all banks were nationalized. There are no foreign banks operating in Afghanistan.

Da Afghanistan Bank (Central Bank of Afghanistan): Ibne Sina Wat, Kabul; tel. (93) 24075; telex 22223; f. 1939; main functions: banknote issue, foreign exchange regulation, credit extensions to banks and leading enterprises and companies, govt and private depository, govt fiscal agency; cap. 4,000m., res 5,299m., dep. 15,008m. (1985); Pres. Mawlawi ABDORRAHMAN ZAHED; Vice-Pres. Mawlawi ABDORRAB; 65 brs.

Agricultural Development Bank of Afghanistan: POB 414, Cineme Pamir Bldg, Jade Maiwand, Kabul; tel. (93) 24459; telex 274; f. 1959; makes available credits for farmers, co-operatives and agro-business; aid provided by IBRD and UNDP; cap. 666.8m., res 498.7m., total resources 3,188.3m. (March 1987); Chair. Dr M. KABIAR; Pres. Dr ABDULLAH NAQSHBANDI.

Banke Milli Afghan (Afghan National Bank): Jana Ibn Sina, Kabul; tel. (93) 25451; telex 22231; f. 1932; cap. p.u. 1,000m., res 100.7m., total resources 6,954.8m. (1986); Chair. ABDUL WAHAB ASSEFI; Pres. ELHAMUDDIN QIAM; 16 brs.

Export Promotion Bank of Afghanistan: 24 Mohd Jan Khan Wat, Kabul; tel. (93) 24447; telex 202; f. 1976; provides financing for exports and export-orientated investments; total assets 12,904.1m. (March 1987); Pres. MOHAMMAD YAQUB NEDA; Vice-Pres. BURHANUDDIN SHAHIM.

Industrial Development Bank of Afghanistan: POB 14, Shar-i-Nau, Kabul; tel. (93) 33336; f. 1973; provides financing for industrial development; cap. 10,500m. (1996); Pres. M. A. AZIZ MAHJOOR.

Mortgage and Construction Bank: Bldg No. 2, First Part Jade Maiwand, Kabul; tel. (93) 23341; f. 1955 to provide short- and long-term building loans; auth. cap. 200m.; cap. p.u. 100m. (1987); Pres. FAIZ MUHAMMAD ALOKOZI.

Pashtany Tejaraty Bank (Afghan Commercial Bank): Mohd Jan Khan Wat, Kabul; tel. (93) 26551; telex 243; f. 1954 to provide short-term credits, forwarding facilities, opening letters of credit, purchase and sale of foreign exchange; cap. p.u. 1,000m., dep. 7,085.7m., total assets 19,826.4m. (1987); Chair. Dr BASIR RANJBAR; Pres. and CEO ZIR GUL WARDAK; 14 brs.

INSURANCE

There is one national insurance company:

Afghan National Insurance Co: Wazir Akbar Khan Wat, Sarak B, Bldg No. 221, POB 329, Kabul; tel. (93) 21271; telex 231; f. 1964; mem. of Asian Reinsurance Corpn; marine, aviation, fire, motor and accident insurance; cap. 750m.; Pres. S. B. AHMAD BASIR; Claims Man. Eng. A. S. ALIZAI.

No foreign insurance companies are permitted to operate in Afghanistan.

Trade and Industry

CHAMBERS OF COMMERCE AND INDUSTRY

Afghan Chamber of Commerce and Industry: Mohd Jan Khan Wat, Kabul; tel. (93) 26796; telex 245; Gen. Head GOLABODDIN SHERZAI.

Federation of Afghan Chambers of Commerce and Industry: Darulaman Wat, Kabul; f. 1923; includes chambers of commerce and industry in Ghazni, Qandahar, Kabul (Chair. Mr KARIMZADA), Herat (Chair. Mr SIDIQI), Mazar-i-Sharif, Fariab, Jawzjan, Kunduz, Jalalabad and Andkhoy; Pres. ABDOLRAHMAN AHADI; Deputy Pres. MUHAMMAD HAKIM.

INDUSTRIAL AND TRADE ASSOCIATIONS

Afghan Carpet Exporters' Guild: POB 3159, Darulaman Wat, Kabul; tel. (93) 41765; telex 234; f. 1967; a non-profit-making, independent organization of carpet manufacturers and exporters; Pres. ZIAUDDIN ZIA; c. 1,000 mems.

Afghan Cart Company: POB 61, Zerghona Maidan, Kabul; tel. (93) 31068; telex 24257; f. 1988; the largest export/import company in Afghanistan; imports electrical goods, machinery, metal, cars, etc.; exports raisins, carpets, medical herbs, wood, animal hides, etc.

Afghan Fruit Processing Co: POB 261, Industrial Estate, Puli Charkhi, Kabul; tel. (93) 65186; telex 24261; f. 1960; exports raisins, other dried fruits and nuts.

Afghan Raisin and Other Dried Fruits Institute: POB 3034, Sharara Wat, Kabul; tel. (93) 30463; telex 48; exporters of dried fruits and nuts; Pres. NAJMUDDIN MUSLEH.

Afghan Wool Enterprises: Shar-i-Nau, Kabul; tel. (93) 31963.

Afghanistan Karakul Institute: POB 506, Puli Charkhi, Kabul; tel. (93) 61852; telex 234; f. 1967; exporters of furs; Pres. G. M. BAHEER.

Afghanistan Plants Enterprise: POB 122, Puli Charkhi, Kabul; tel. (93) 31962; exports medicines, plants and spices.

Handicraft Promotion and Export Centre: POB 3089, Sharara Wat, Kabul; tel. (93) 32935; telex 234; Pres. MOMENA RANJBAR.

Parapamizad Co Ltd: Jadai Nader Pashtoon, Sidiq Omar Market, POB 1911, Kabul; tel. (93) 22116; export/import co; Propr PADSHAH SARBAZ.

TRADE UNIONS

National Union of Afghanistan Employees (NUAE): POB 756, Kabul; tel. (93) 23040; telex 372; f. 1978, as Central Council of Afghanistan Trade Unions, to establish and develop the trade union movement, including the formation of councils and organizational cttees in the provinces; name changed in 1990; composed of seven vocational unions; 300,000 mems; Pres. A. HABIB HARDAMSHAID; Vice-Pres. ASADOLLAH POYA.

Artists' Union: Kabul; tel. (93) 23195; Chair. NASIM KHUSHGAWAR.

Balkh Council of Trade Unions: Mazar-i-Sharif; Pres. MUHAMMAD KABIR KARGAR.

Central Council of the Union of Craftsmen: Kabul; f. 1987; c. 58,000 mems.

Commerce and Transport Employees' Union: Kabul; Gen. Sec. AHMAD ZIA SIDDIQI.

Construction Employees' Union: Kabul; Gen. Sec. AMINULLAH.

Kabul Union of Furriers: Kabul; Leader ABD AL-KHALIQ.

Mines and Industries Employees' Union: Kabul; Gen. Sec. MOHAMMED AMIN.

Nangarhar Council of Trade Unions: Jalalabad; Deputy Chair. MUQREBUDDIN KARGAR.

Public Health Employees' Union: Kabul; Pres. Prof. M. RAHIM KHUSHDEL.

Public Services Employees' Union: Kabul; Gen. Sec. ABDUL MEJJER TEMORY.

Science and Culture Employees' Union: Kabul; Gen. Sec. T. HABIBZAI.

Traders' Union of Afghanistan: Kabul; Chair. REZWANQOL TAMANA.

Union of Peasant Co-operatives of the Republic of Afghanistan (UPCRA): POB 3272, Dehmazang, Kabul; tel. (93) 42683; telex 241; 1,370,000 mems; Chair. FAZULLAH ALBURZ.

Weaving and Sewing Employees' Union: Kabul; Gen. Sec. A. W. KARGAR.

Writers' Union of Afghanistan: Kabul; Chair. MOHAMMAD AZAM RAHNAWARD ZARYAB; Vice-Chair. ABDOLLAH BAKHTIANI, AKBAR KARKAR.

Transport

RAILWAYS

In 1977 the Government approved plans for the creation of a railway system. The proposed line (of 1,815 km) was to connect Kabul to Qandahar and Herat, linking with the Iranian State Railways at Islam Quala and Tarakun, and with Pakistan Railways at Chaman. By 1997 however, work had not yet begun on the proposed railway.

A combined road and rail bridge was completed across the Amu-Dar'ya (Oxus) river in 1982, linking the Afghan port of Hairatan with the Soviet port of Termez. There were also plans for a 200-km railway line from Hairatan to Pul-i-Khomri, 160 km north of Kabul, but work had not begun by 1997.

ROADS

In 1986 there were 22,000 km of roads. All-weather highways now link Kabul with Qandahar and Herat in the south and west, Jalalabad in the east and Mazar-i-Sharif and the Amu-Dar'ya river in the north. In July 1992 Afghanistan signed an agreement with Pakistan and Uzbekistan regarding co-operation in the construction and repair of highways.

Afghan International Transport Company: Kabul.

Afghan Container Transport Company Ltd: POB 3234, Shar-i-Nau, Kabul; tel. (93) 23088; telex 17.

Afghan Transit Company: POB 530, Ghousy Market, Mohd Jan Khan Wat, Kabul; tel. (93) 22654; telex 76.

Land Transport Company: Khoshal Mena, Kabul; tel. (93) 20345; f. 1943; commercial transport within Afghanistan.

The Milli Bus Enterprise: Ministry of Transport, Ansari Wat, Kabul; tel. (93) 25541; state-owned and -administered; 721 buses; Pres. Eng. AZIZ NAGHABAN.

Salang-Europe International Transport and Transit: Kabul; f. 1991 as joint Afghan/Soviet co; 500 vehicles.

INLAND WATERWAYS

There are 1,200 km of navigable inland waterways, including the Amu-Dar'ya (Oxus) river. River ports on the Amu-Dar'ya are linked by road to Kabul.

CIVIL AVIATION

There are international airports at Kabul and Qandahar, and 30 local airports are located throughout the country.

Ministry of Civil Aviation and Tourism: POB 165, Ansari Wat, Kabul; tel. (93) 21015; Deputy Dir-Gen. of Civil Aviation RAZ MOHAMMAD ALAMI.

Ariana Afghan Airlines: POB 76, Afghan Air Authority Bldg, Ansari Wat, Kabul; tel. (93) 280784; telex 228; f. 1955; merged with Bakhtar Afghan Airlines Co Ltd in 1985; internal services between Kabul and 18 regional locations; external services to Europe, the Middle East and Asia; Head Mola RAHMATOLLAH.

Balkh Airlines: Mazar-i-Sharif; f. 1996; passenger and cargo flights to Pakistan, Iran and Central Asian republics; Owner Gen. ABDUL RASHID DOSTAM.

Khyber Afghan Airlines: Jalalabad; Owner Haji ABDUL QADEER.

Pameer Airlines: Bagram; flights to Iran, India, Russia, Albania, Bulgaria and the UAE.

Taliban Airways Co.

Tourism

Afghanistan's potential attractions for the foreign visitor include: Bamian, with its high statue of Buddha and thousands of painted caves; Bandi Amir, with its suspended lakes; the Blue Mosque of Mazar; Herat, with its Grand Mosque and minarets; the towns of Qandahar and Girishk; Balkh (ancient Bactria), 'Mother of Cities', in the north; Bagram, Hadda and Surkh Kotal (of interest to archaeologists); and the high mountains of the Hindu Kush. In 1993 there were an estimated 6,000 foreign visitors and tourist receipts amounted to around US $1m.

Afghan Tour: Ansari Wat, Shar-i-Nau, Kabul; tel. (93) 30152; official travel agency supervised by ATO; Pres. MOHD KAZIM WARDAK (acting).

Afghan Tourist Organization (ATO): Ansari Wat, Shar-i-Nau, Kabul; tel. (93) 30323; f. 1958; Pres. MOHD KAZIM WARDAK (acting).

ALBANIA

Introductory Survey

Location, Climate, Language, Religion, Flag, Capital

The Republic of Albania lies in south-eastern Europe. It is bordered by Yugoslavia to the north and north-east, by the former Yugoslav republic of Macedonia to the east, by Greece to the south and by the Adriatic and Ionian Seas (parts of the Mediterranean Sea) to the west. The climate is Mediterranean throughout most of the country. The sea plays a moderating role, although frequent cyclones in the winter months make the weather unstable. The average temperature is 14°C (57°F) in the north-east and 18°C (64°F) in the south-west. The language is Albanian, the principal dialects being Gheg (north of the Shkumbini river) and Tosk (in the south). The literary language is being formed on the basis of a strong fusion of the two dialects, with the phonetic and morphological structure of Tosk prevailing. An official ban on religious worship was in effect between 1967 and 1990. Before 1946 Islam was the predominant faith, and there were small groups of Christians (mainly Roman Catholic in the north and Eastern Orthodox in the south). The national flag (proportions 7 by 5) is red, with a two-headed black eagle in the centre. The capital is Tirana (Tiranë).

Recent History

On 28 November 1912, after more than 400 years of Turkish rule, Albania declared its independence under a provisional Government. The country was occupied by Italy in 1914 but its independence was re-established in 1920. Albania was declared a republic in 1925 and Ahmet Beg Zogu was elected President. He was proclaimed King Zog in 1928 and reigned until the occupation of Albania by Italy in April 1939. Albania was united with Italy for four years, before being occupied by German forces in 1943; the Germans withdrew one year later.

The communist-led National Liberation Front (NLF), established with help from Yugoslav communists in 1941, was the most successful wartime resistance group and took power on 29 November 1944. Elections in December 1945 were based on a single list of candidates, sponsored by the communists. The new regime was led by Enver Hoxha, who had been the head of the Albanian Communist Party (ACP) since 1943. King Zog was deposed and the People's Republic of Albania was proclaimed on 11 January 1946. The ACP was renamed the Party of Labour of Albania (PLA) in 1948, the NLF having been succeeded by the Democratic Front of Albania (DFA) in 1945.

The communist regime developed close relations with Yugoslavia, including a monetary and customs union, until the latter's expulsion from the Cominform (a Soviet-sponsored body co-ordinating the activities of European communist parties) in 1948. Albania, fearing Yugoslav expansionism, became a close ally of the USSR and joined the Moscow-based Council for Mutual Economic Assistance (CMEA) in 1949. Hoxha resigned as Head of Government in 1954 but retained effective national leadership as First Secretary of the PLA. Albania joined the Warsaw Treaty Organization (Warsaw Pact) in 1955, but relations with the USSR deteriorated when Soviet leaders attempted a *rapprochement* with Yugoslavia. The Albanian leadership declared its support for the People's Republic of China in the Sino-Soviet ideological dispute, prompting the USSR to suspend relations with Albania in 1961. Albania established increasingly close relations with China, ended participation in the CMEA in 1962 and withdrew from the Warsaw Pact in 1968. However, following the improvement of relations between China and the USA after 1972, and the death of Mao Zedong, the Chinese leader, in 1976, Sino-Albanian relations progressively deteriorated. In 1974 the Albanian Minister of Defence, Gen. Beqir Balluku, was dismissed; in 1975 he was executed for alleged involvement in a Chinese-inspired conspiracy against the Government. In 1978 Albania declared its support for Viet Nam in its dispute with China, prompting the Chinese Government to suspend all economic and military co-operation with Albania.

A new Constitution was adopted in December 1976, and the country was renamed the People's Socialist Republic of Albania. In December 1981 Mehmet Shehu, Chairman of the Council of Ministers (Prime Minister) since 1954, died as a result of a shooting incident. It was officially reported that he had committed suicide, but other sources suggested his involvement in a leadership struggle with Hoxha, and there were subsequent allegations that he had been executed. Following the death of Shehu, a new Government was formed under Adil Çarçani, hitherto the First Deputy Chairman. Feçor Shehu, the Minister of the Interior and a nephew of Mehmet Shehu, was not reappointed. In November 1982 Ramiz Alia replaced Haxhi Lleshi as President of the Presidium of the People's Assembly (Head of State). A number of former state and PLA officials, including Feçor Shehu and two other former ministers, were reportedly executed in September 1983.

Enver Hoxha died in April 1985, and was succeeded as First Secretary of the PLA by Alia. In March 1986 Nexhmije Hoxha, widow of Enver Hoxha, was elected to the chairmanship of the General Council of the DFA. Alia was re-elected as First Secretary of the PLA and as President of the Presidium of the People's Assembly in November 1986 and February 1987, respectively. In the latter month Adil Çarçani was reappointed Chairman of the Council of Ministers.

In November 1989, on the 45th anniversary of Albania's liberation from Nazi occupation, an amnesty for certain prisoners was declared. A number of political detainees, including some who had been imprisoned for having attempted to flee the country and others convicted on charges of agitation and propaganda against the State, were among those to benefit. (In previous years similar amnesties had excluded political prisoners.)

In December 1989 and January 1990 a number of anti-Government demonstrations were reported to have taken place, particularly in the northern town of Shkodër. In late January, while continuing to deny the reports of internal unrest, Alia announced proposals for limited political and economic reforms, including the introduction of a system of multi-candidate elections (although the leading role of the PLA was to be maintained). Limitations on the terms of office of certain party and state officials were to be imposed, and the powers of the PLA's local organizations were to be expanded. Extensive reforms of the judicial system were approved by the People's Assembly in May, shortly before a visit to Tirana by the UN Secretary-General, Javier Pérez de Cuéllar. The Ministry of Justice was re-established, and the number of capital offences were considerably reduced. Although Albania was to remain a secular state, the practice of religion was henceforth to be tolerated. Furthermore, Albanians were to be granted the right to a passport for the purposes of foreign travel, while the penalty for attempting to flee the country illegally was reduced. In July there was renewed unrest, when anti-Government demonstrators occupied the streets of Tirana and were violently dispersed by the security forces. More than 5,000 Albanians subsequently took refuge in foreign embassies. Although they were denounced by the Albanian authorities, the refugees were nevertheless granted permission to leave the country. A multinational relief operation, co-ordinated by the UN, facilitated the safe evacuation of the Albanians, most of whom ultimately travelled to the Federal Republic of Germany. Meanwhile, the membership of both the Council of Ministers and the Political Bureau of the PLA had been reorganized; a number of prominent anti-reformists were among those replaced.

In November 1990, in response to increasing domestic pressure, Alia announced proposals for more radical political reforms, urging that the leading role of the PLA be redefined. The new electoral procedure was confirmed, requiring the presentation of at least two candidates for every polling centre at the 1991 elections. A special commission was established to examine the need for amendments to the Constitution. In December 1990 it was announced that elections to the People's Assembly were to take place in February 1991 and that the establishment of independent political parties was to be permitted. In mid-December 1990, however, anti-Government demonstrators clashed with the security forces in several cities. Nexhmije Hoxha resigned from the chairmanship of the General Council of the DFA, and was replaced by Çarçani (who was, in turn, replaced in mid-1991). In the same month a reallocation of ministerial portfolios was effected, in which several uncompromising ministers were replaced. Further government changes followed in late January 1991.

On 20 February 1991, following widespread anti-Government demonstrations, Alia declared presidential rule. An eight-member Presidential Council was established, and a provisional Council of Ministers was appointed. Çarçani was replaced as Chairman of the Council of Ministers by Fatos Nano, a progressive economist, who had been appointed Deputy Chairman at the end of January. In late February unrest finally ended, owing, in part, to an increased use of force by the authorities to quell the protests.

Meanwhile, following pressure from the newly-established opposition parties, the elections had been postponed until the end of March 1991 to allow political organizations more time to prepare. Despite these concessions, an increasing number of ethnic Greek Albanians attempted to leave the country; by mid-January more than 5,000 had crossed the border into Greece. Furthermore, by early March it was estimated that as many as 20,000 Albanians had sailed to Italy, after seizing vessels in Albanian ports.

In mid-March 1991 a general amnesty for all political prisoners was declared. The first stage of the multi-party elections to the People's Assembly duly took place on 31 March, and the second and third rounds of voting were held on 7 and 14 April. The PLA and affiliated organizations won 169 of the 250 seats, while the Democratic Party of Albania (DPA) secured 75 seats, and the Democratic Union of the Greek Minority (OMONIA) obtained five seats. The victory of the PLA, amid allegations of electoral malpractice, prompted dismay in some urban areas, where support for the DPA had been strong. Widespread protests ensued, and in Shkodër four people, including a local DPA leader, were killed when the security forces opened fire on demonstrators.

In late April 1991 an interim Constitution replaced that of 1976, pending the drawing up of a new draft constitution. The country was renamed the Republic of Albania, and the post of executive President, who was to be elected by two-thirds of votes cast in the People's Assembly, was created. Alia was subsequently elected to the new post, defeating the only other candidate, Namik Dokle, also of the PLA; all the opposition deputies abstained from voting. In early May Nano was reappointed Chairman of the Council of Ministers, and the Government was again reorganized. In accordance with the provisions of the interim Constitution, President Alia resigned from the leadership of the PLA. In mid-May, however, the newly-established Union of Independent Trade Unions of Albania (UITUA) initiated a general strike in support of demands for substantial pay increases and for the resignation of the Government. A hunger strike by a group of miners at Valias, in response to the Government's continued rejection of union demands, attracted widespread support.

In early June 1991 the continuing general strike forced the resignation of Nano's Government. A Government of National Stability was subsequently formed, with Ylli Bufi (hitherto Minister of Food) as Chairman of the Council of Ministers. The coalition included representatives of the PLA, the DPA, the Albanian Republican Party (ARP), the Social Democratic Party (SDP) and the Agrarian Party (AP). Gramoz Pashko, a prominent member of the DPA, was appointed Deputy Chairman of the Council of Ministers and Minister of the Economy. At its 10th Congress, which took place later in June, the PLA was renamed the Socialist Party of Albania (SPA).

In August 1991, following a further seaborne exodus of migrants to Italy, the ports of Albania were placed under military control. Several vessels were refused entry by the Italian authorities, while many of the Albanians who had succeeded in disembarking were subsequently repatriated. Later that month Manush Myftiu, a former Deputy Chairman of the Council of Ministers, and another former senior official were arrested on charges of abuse of power. Further opposition demonstrations were staged in subsequent weeks; in October protesters demanded the resignation of President Alia. Strikes in various sectors, particularly the fuel supply industry, also continued. In early December the Chairman of the DPA, Dr Sali Berisha, announced the withdrawal of party members from the coalition Government, despite opposition from other prominent DPA officials. The withdrawal of the seven DPA representatives, following the expulsion of three ARP ministers who had criticized the administration, forced Bufi's Government to resign. President Alia subsequently appointed an interim Government, principally composed of non-party specialists, under a new Prime Minister, Vilson Ahmeti (hitherto Minister of Food); new elections were to take place in March 1992. Following widespread food riots in December 1991, draft legislation on public order was introduced in the Assembly at the end of January 1992, proposing the establishment of an intervention force to apprehend rioters and looters.

A new electoral law, which was approved by the People's Assembly in early February 1992, reduced the number of deputies in the Assembly from 250 to 140, of whom 100 were to be elected by majority vote from single-member constituencies, while the remaining deputies were to be elected according to a system of proportional representation. Under provisions that defined legitimate political parties, OMONIA, as an organization representing an ethnic minority, was prohibited from contesting the forthcoming general election, prompting widespread protest from the Greek minority. At the general election, which was conducted in two rounds on 22 and 29 March, the DPA secured 92 of the 140 contested seats, while the SPA obtained 38 seats, the SDP seven seats, the Union for Human Rights Party (UNHRP—supported by the minority Greek and Macedonian communities) two seats and the ARP one seat. According to official figures, 90% of the electorate participated. Following the defeat of the SPA, Alia resigned as President on 3 April. A few days later the new People's Assembly elected Berisha to the presidency. Berisha subsequently appointed a coalition Government, headed by Aleksander Meksi, a member of the DPA. In addition to the premiership, the DPA held 14 ministerial portfolios, while the SDP and ARP were allocated one portfolio each.

In July 1992 an amendment to the law on political organizations effectively banned the Albanian Communist Party. At the end of that month the DPA secured 43% of the total votes cast in the country's first multi-party local elections since the Second World War, while the SPA recovered some of the support that it had lost in the March general election, with 41% of the votes. In September divisions within the DPA resulted in the defection of a number of prominent party members, who had accused the Berisha administration of becoming increasingly right-wing and authoritarian, to form a new political grouping, the Democratic Alliance Party (DAP).

In 1992 a number of former communist officials were detained, including Nexhmije Hoxha, who had been arrested on charges of corruption. In February 1993 the former Prime Minister, Vilson Ahmeti, was placed under house arrest, following charges of corruption; further allegations concerning abuse of power resulted in the arrest of another former Prime Minister, Fatos Nano (who was now President of the SPA), in July. Nexhmije Hoxha was imprisoned for nine years in January 1993, having been convicted of embezzling state funds; in May her sentence was increased by two years. In August Alia was arrested on charges of abuse of power. Later that month Ahmeti was sentenced to two years' imprisonment. The trial of Nano commenced in April 1994, despite an international campaign on his behalf, organized by the SPA, and a European Parliament resolution appealing for his release. Nano was convicted of misappropriation of state funds during his premiership in 1991, and was sentenced to 12 years' imprisonment. In July 1994 Alia, who had denied the charges against him, was sentenced to nine years' imprisonment for abuse of power and violating the rights of citizens. (In July 1995, however, under the terms of a general amnesty, Alia, and a further 30 political prisoners, were released.)

In late July 1994 the SPA deputies unsuccessfully proposed a motion of no confidence in the People's Assembly against the Government. In October the draft Constitution was finally presented to Berisha, but failed to obtain the requisite two-thirds' majority approval in the People's Assembly, and was consequently submitted for endorsement at a national referendum. As a result of Berisha's personal campaign in support of the draft Constitution (which was to vest additional powers in the President, and reduce those of the legislature), the referendum was widely perceived as a vote of confidence in his leadership. At the referendum, which took place on 6 November with the participation of 84.4% of the electorate, the draft Constitution was rejected by 53.9% of the voters, prompting demands for a general election (on the grounds that the administration lacked a popular mandate). Later that month Dhimiter Anagnosti, the Minister of Culture, Youth and Sport, resigned, citing his personal opposition to Prime Minister Meksi. In early

December Berisha effected an extensive reorganization of the Council of Ministers. On the following day the ARP, which held only one seat in the People's Assembly, withdrew from the governing coalition. The SDP split into two factions; a new grouping, known as the Union of Social Democrats (USD—led by the new Minister of Culture, Youth and Sport, Teodor Laco), remained in the coalition, while the SDP withdrew.

In March 1995 the Chairman of the DPA, Eduard Selami, was removed from his post at an extraordinary party congress for opposing Berisha's efforts to organize a further referendum on the draft Constitution. Selami's accusations concerning Berisha's abuse of his position reinforced widespread discontent at the perceived corruption in the latter's administration. Public discontent at the slow pace of economic recovery in Albania was demonstrated by the continued flow of illegal immigrants to Italy, which, in May, deployed troops along its coast in an attempt to stem the influx. In that month the Albanian Government also assigned 300 troops to prevent people from leaving the country by sea.

In June 1995 Ilir Hoxha, the son of Enver Hoxha, was convicted on charges of inciting national hatred, after condemning leaders of the DPA in a newspaper interview. In September the People's Assembly adopted a 'Genocide Law' prohibiting those in power under the former communist regime from holding public office until the year 2002 (thereby banning a large number of prospective candidates, including incumbent SPA deputies, from contesting legislative elections in 1996). In the same month the Minister of Justice dismissed three Supreme Court judges, owing to their alleged activities under the communist regime. The Chairman of the Supreme Court, Zef Brozi (who had previously accused the Government of exerting undue pressure on the judiciary), challenged the Minister's authority to dismiss employees of the court and refused to accept the decision. The security forces were subsequently deployed around the Supreme Court to prevent the three judges from entering the building. Brozi had aroused the disapproval of the Government earlier in the year, when he recommended a review of Fatos Nano's case and advocated his release. The Government had subsequently adopted an amendment to the penal code, which was widely believed to be aimed at prolonging Nano's imprisonment. As a result of this amendment, in September the Supreme Court was forced to reject Nano's appeal. On the next day, following a ruling against him by the Constitutional Court, which declared his previous suspension of lower court verdicts to be illegal, Brozi was dismissed as Chairman of the Supreme Court by the People's Assembly, and replaced by his deputy, Avin Shehu. The SPA deputies boycotted the People's Assembly, in protest at Brozi's dismissal and the Government's alleged infringement of the independence of the judiciary.

In November 1995 a parliamentary commission initiated an inquiry following the discovery of a mass grave near the border town of Shkodër. Families of the deceased urged the prosecution service to initiate charges against former members of the communist regime, including Alia, who had allegedly been responsible for the killing by border guards of nationals attempting to flee the country in 1990–92. Also in November 1995 the People's Assembly approved legislation requiring senior civil servants to be investigated for their activities under the communist regime. In December 14 prominent former members of the communist regime were arrested on charges of involvement in the execution, internment and deportation of citizens for political reasons. (In May 1996 three of the former officials received death sentences, which were later commuted to terms of imprisonment, while the remaining defendants also received custodial terms in August and September of that year.) In February 1996 Alia was detained in connection with the killing of demonstrators in Shkodër in April 1991 and the border incidents. Later that month a bomb exploded in central Tirana, killing four people. It was reported that two senior officials of the former secret police, the Sigurimi, had been arrested in connection with the attack, which was later attributed by the Government to a communist terrorist organization, known as Albanian Justice Revenge.

Following increasing division within the SPA, in March 1996 a liberal faction left the organization to form the Albanian New Socialist Party. Later that month the Government invited international representatives to observe the legislative elections, which were scheduled to take place in late May. The first round of the elections (which was preceded by SPA allegations of intimidation by the security forces) took place on 26 May; following alleged incidents of electoral irregularities, however, the principal opposition parties, including the SPA, the SDP and the DAP, withdrew from the poll and issued a statement rejecting the election results. A subsequent SPA demonstration held in protest at the alleged malpractices was violently dispersed by the security forces. The second round of the elections took place on 2 June; as a result of opposition demands for a boycott, only 59.4% of the electorate participated in the poll (compared with 89% in the first round). According to official results, the DPA secured 101 of the 115 directly-elected seats (25 seats were to be allocated proportionately). However, international observers, who included representatives of the Organization for Security and Co-operation in Europe (OSCE, formerly the Conference on Security and Co-operation in Europe—CSCE, see p. 212), claimed that widespread malpractice and intimidation of voters had been perpetrated and urged the Government to conduct fresh elections, while SPA deputies initiated a hunger strike in an attempt to oblige Berisha to annul the results. Berisha rejected the allegations of government malpractice, and agreed to conduct further elections in only 17 constituencies. The principal opposition parties (which demanded that fresh elections be held, under international supervision, in all constituencies) continued their electoral boycott. Consequently, the DPA won all the seats contested in the partial elections, which took place on 16 June, thereby securing a total of 122 of the 140 seats in the People's Assembly. The SPA won 10 of the remaining seats, while the UHRP and the ARP each acquired three and the National Front two. (The SPA, however, refused to recognize the new legislature and boycotted the inaugural session of the People's Assembly.) The OSCE subsequently issued a report, stating that the elections had failed to meet international legal standards. In early July Aleksander Meksi, who had been reappointed to the office of Prime Minister, formed a new Council of Ministers, principally comprising members of the DPA; the ARP, the Christian Democratic Party and the USD were also represented. Later that month a parliamentary commission was established to investigate the reported electoral violations.

In August 1996 the Government established a permanent Central Election Commission, prior to local government elections, which were scheduled to take place in October; the main opposition parties subsequently nominated a number of representatives to the Commission. Despite continued division within the SPA, Nano (who remained in prison) was re-elected as Chairman at a party congress in late August. In the local government elections, which took place in two rounds in late October, the DPA secured the highest number of votes in 58 of the 64 municipalities and in 267 of the 309 communes. Shortly before the elections, the OSCE had withdrawn its observers, after Berisha objected to one of its members, who, he claimed, was biased against the DPA. Nevertheless, observers from the Council of Europe (see p. 140) declared that, despite some irregularities, the elections had been conducted fairly. Also in October four political activists (who had been arrested in March) were convicted and received custodial terms for attempting to reconstitute a communist party in contravention of the Constitution. In January 1997 Nexhmije Hoxha was released (her term of imprisonment had twice been reduced under successive presidential amnesties).

In January 1997 the collapse of several widely-popular 'pyramid' financial investment schemes (which had offered high rates of interest), resulting in huge losses of individual savings, prompted violent anti-Government demonstrations, particularly in Tirana and the southern town of Vlorë. It was widely believed that members of the Government were associated with the 'pyramid' schemes, which had allegedly financed widespread illegal activities. The People's Assembly subsequently adopted legislation prohibiting the 'pyramid' schemes. However, the Government increased efforts to suppress the protests (which were supported by a newly-established opposition alliance, Forum for Democracy): large numbers of demonstrators were arrested, while prominent opposition members were publicly assaulted by the security forces. At the end of January the People's Assembly granted Berisha emergency powers to mobilize special army units to restore order. It was reported that several people were killed in ensuing violent clashes between security forces and protesters (who continued to demand the resignation of Berisha and state reimbursement for the financial losses that they had incurred). At the end of February, however, Berisha (whose mandate was due to expire in April) was nominated as the presidential candidate for the DPA. On 3 March he was re-elected unopposed for a second five-year term (with the SPA continuing to boycott the People's Assembly).

Following an escalation in hostilities between insurgents (who seized armaments from military depots) and government troops in the south of the country, Berisha declared a national state of emergency at the beginning of March 1997, empowering security forces to shoot demonstrators and imposing total official censorship. However, insurgent groups gained control of the southern towns of Vlorë, Sarandë and Gjirokastër, while it was reported that large numbers of government forces had deserted or defected to join the rebels. Following negotiations with representatives of nine principal opposition parties, Berisha signed an agreement whereby an interim coalition government was to be installed, pending elections in June, and offered an amnesty to rebels who surrendered to the authorities. A former SPA mayor of Gjirokastër, Bashkim Fino, was appointed to the office of Prime Minister. Berisha subsequently approved the formation of a Government of National Reconciliation, which included representatives of eight opposition parties. (The DAP had withdrawn from the negotiations, after its proposal that the interior portfolio be allocated to an opposition member was rejected.) Despite these concessions, the insurgency continued, reaching the northern town of Tropojë and Tirana (where rebels seized the airport). All those detained in Tirana central prison, including Nano and Alia, were released; Nano was subsequently granted an official pardon by Berisha. The evacuation of western European and US nationals from Tirana and Durrës was impeded by the rebels, who exchanged fire with foreign troops effecting the evacuation. Extreme hardship and concern that the fighting would escalate into widespread civil conflict prompted thousands of Albanians to flee to Italy (where the Italian authorities announced they would be permitted to remain for a maximum of three months). Later in March, however, Italian naval authorities were ordered to intercept boats transporting Albanian refugees, in an effort to halt the exodus. At the end of the month an Italian vessel patrolling coastal waters struck and sank a boat of Albanian refugees; some 83 Albanians were reported to have died. A judicial inquiry into the incident was subsequently initiated.

In late March 1997 it was reported that government forces had regained control of Tirana; the south of the country was controlled by insurgent groups opposed to the Government, while the north was largely held by paramilitary units loyal to Berisha. Following mediation by the Italian Government and an OSCE special envoy, Franz Vranitzky, southern rebel leaders, grouped in a self-designated 'national committee for public salvation', agreed to abandon hostilities in return for guarantees of amnesty. However, the rebels subsequently refused to surrender their armaments, and demanded that further legislative elections take place. The Government of National Reconciliation requested military assistance in the restoration of civil order, and in late March Fino attended a meeting of European Union (EU, see p. 152) foreign ministers in Rome to appeal for the establishment of a multinational force which would supervise humanitarian aid operations in Albania. (A number of European Governments, including those of Italy and France, had already pledged military support.) At the end of March the UN Security Council endorsed an OSCE proposal that member states be authorized to contribute troops to the force. In early April Fino visited Gjirokastër to initiate discussions with rebel leaders (although Berisha refused to support negotiations with the insurgents); Fino also held discussions in Gjirokastër with the Italian Prime Minister, Prof. Romano Prodi, regarding Italian efforts to organize the creation of the multi-national force. Fino subsequently conducted discussions in Athens with the Greek Prime Minister, Konstantinos Simitis, concerning Greece's contribution to the contingent. Following the Italian legislature's approval of the participation of Italian troops, the 5,915-member Multinational Protection Force for Albania was established, with an official mission (known as Operation Alba) to facilitate the distribution of humanitarian assistance; the Italian contingent numbered 2,500, and the French 1,000, while Turkey, Greece, Spain, Romania, Austria and Denmark also contributed troops. The Multinational Protection Force (which had a mandate to remain in the country for three months) began to arrive in mid-April, and was subsequently deployed in regions under government control in northern and central Albania. After negotiations between Italian forces and insurgents at Vlorë, the leader of the 'national committee for public salvation', Ekeren Osmani, announced that he would co-operate with the Italian troops.

At the beginning of April 1997 the SPA ended its boycott of the People's Assembly, which subsequently voted to end press restrictions that had been imposed under the state of emergency in March. Later in April the National Council of the DPA endorsed Berisha's leadership of the party and removed a number of dissident members who had demanded his resignation. In the same month Berisha rejected a decision by the Government of National Reconciliation to remove the Deputy Minister of the Interior, Gen. Agim Shehu (who was an ally of Berisha) from his post. The son of King Zog and claimant to the throne, Leka Zogu, who returned to Albania in April, with the support of the pro-monarchist Legality Movement Party, urged that a referendum on the restoration of the monarchy take place; the principal political parties had already agreed that such a referendum be conducted. In early May the People's Assembly adopted legislation regulating the operation of the 'pyramid' investment schemes. Following mediation by Vranitzky, the leaders of 10 major political parties agreed that further elections would take place by the end of June. However, negotiations between the parties regarding the drafting of a new electoral code ended in failure, owing to disagreement over the number of parliamentary deputies who would be elected by proportional representation. Later in May the DPA submitted to the People's Assembly legislation on a new electoral system, which was approved, despite a further parliamentary boycott by SPA deputies; under the new legislation, the number of deputies in the People's Assembly was to be increased from 140 to 155, of whom 115 were to be directly elected and 40 elected on the basis of proportional representation. After Vranitzky mediated further discussions between the parties, he announced that the elections would take place on 29 June; the percentage of the total vote required for representation in the People's Assembly was reduced from 4% to 3%. The SPA and its allied parties indicated that they would boycott the elections unless the DPA agreed to a number of demands, including the appointment of a central electoral commission by the Government of National Reconciliation (rather than by Berisha), guarantees that international observers would monitor the elections, and the reformation of the country's security system. However, the opposition parties subsequently agreed to participate in the elections, after Berisha complied with the stipulation that the central electoral commission be appointed by the interim Government. The establishment of a 17-member central electoral commission, chaired by a member of the DPA, was announced later in May.

Election campaigning was marred by a number of violent incidents, including a number of bomb explosions in Tirana. In early June 1997 an unknown assailant attempted to assassinate Berisha at a rally near Durrës. Later that month the UN Security Council voted to extend the mandate of the Multinational Protection Force to mid-August. Leaders of the DPA and SPA signed an agreement in Rome pledging to abide by the results of the elections. On 29 June the first round of voting in the elections to the People's Assembly took place; a referendum on the restoration of the monarchy was conducted on the same day. Despite the presence of the Multi-national Protection Force, some three people were killed in violent incidents during the voting. A further electoral ballot took place in 32 constituencies on 6 July. OSCE observers, who had monitored the voting, subsequently declared the electoral process to have been conducted satisfactorily. Later in July the central electoral commission announced that the SPA had secured 101 seats in the People's Assembly, while the DPA had won 29 seats; the SPA and its allied parties (the SDP, the Democratic Alliance Party, the AP and the UHRP) thereby secured the requisite two-thirds majority for the approval of constitutional amendements, which they had proposed earlier that month. At the referendum, 66.7% of the electorate voted in favour of retaining a republic, while only 33.3% voted in favour of the restoration of the monarchy; the Legality Movement Party subsequently claimed that the results were invalid and accused the electoral commission of malpractice. On 24 July, following Berisha's resignation, the Secretary-General of the SPA, Dr Rexhep Mejdani, was elected President by the People's Assembly. Parliamentary deputies also voted to end the state of emergency, which had been imposed in March. The SPA proposed Nano to the office of Prime Minister, and a new Council of Ministers was appointed, which comprised representatives of the SPA and its allied parties, and retained Fino in the post of Deputy Prime Minister. At the end of July the new Government submitted a programme for the restoration of civil order and economic reconstruction, which received a vote of confidence in the People's Assembly. The legislature also voted in favour of auditing the existing 'pyramid' schemes and investigating those that had been dissolved, in an effort to reimburse lost savings. At an international conference on Albania, which was convened in Rome, delegates pledged support for the political and economic reconstruction of the country.

In early August 1997 the National Council of the DPA removed a number of prominent officials from the party. In the same month the Government dispatched troops to the south of the country, in an effort to restore order in major towns that were under the control of rebel forces. It was subsequently announced that Vlorë had been recaptured and a number of rebel forces arrested; the Minister of the Interior ordered that all the armaments that had been looted during the unrest be surrendered to the authorities. By mid-August the mandate of the Multinational Protection Force had officially ended and the contingent had left Albania. Foreign advisers subsequently returned to the country to assist the Government in the reorganization of the military and security services, under the terms of existing bilateral treaties; the Albanian Minister of Defence signed a further agreement with his Italian counterpart, providing for Italian assistance in the reconstruction of the Albanian armed forces. In late August a number of prominent officials and members of the armed forces, including the army Chief of Staff, the head of the security services and the Governor of the Central Bank, were replaced as part of an extensive reorganization of public services.

At the end of August 1997 the Constitutional Court upheld the results of the referendum in which voters had rejected the restoration of the monarchy, following a legal challenge by monarchists (who had accused the central electoral commission of malpractice). At the beginning of September, following pressure from Albania, the Italian Government extended until the end of November the deadline for the repatriation of some 15,000 Albanian refugees who had been granted temporary humanitarian residence in the country. (The deadline had already earlier been extended until the end of August.) In early September the People's Assembly established a parliamentary commission which was to draft a new constitution in accordance with the amendments proposed by the SPA; the new constitution was to be submitted to a referendum in March 1998. Later in September an SPA member, Gafur Mazreku, shot and wounded an opposition deputy, following acrimony during a parliamentary session on proposals to raise value-added tax. Mazreku was subsequently charged with attempted murder, and the incident further exacerbated relations between the SPA and the DPA. In October Berisha was re-elected Chairman of the DPA. In the same month Alia and a further three former senior officials were acquitted of genocide by a Tirana court (upholding a ruling of the Supreme Court), on the grounds that the charge did not exist under the penal legislation of the former communist Government.

Meanwhile, in foreign relations, following the rift with the People's Republic of China in the mid-1970s, Albania began to improve relations with Western European nations, while maintaining its policy of self-reliance. The gradual relaxation of isolationist policies culminated in 1990, in a declaration of Albania's desire to establish good relations with all countries, irrespective of their social system. Until 1990 Albania remained hostile to the USSR; in July of that year, however, Albania and the USSR formally agreed to restore diplomatic relations. Diplomatic relations between Albania and the USA were re-established in March 1991 (they had been suspended since 1946), while diplomatic links between Albania and the United Kingdom were restored in May. In April 1996 the USA and Albania pledged to continue military co-operation, envisaging the establishment of a US military training centre in Albania.

Albania's relations with neighbouring Greece and Yugoslavia have been strained. In August 1987 Greece formally ended the technical state of war with Albania, which had been in existence since 1945. However, the status of the Greek minority in Albania, unofficially estimated to number between 200,000 and 400,000, remained a sensitive issue. Relations between Albania and Greece deteriorated in 1993, owing to Greece's deportation of some 20,000 Albanian immigrants and to the alleged mistreatment of the Greek minority in southern Albania. Relations between the two states were exacerbated further in April 1994, following a violent border incident in which two Albanian guards were killed by unidentified opponents; a series of diplomatic expulsions ensued on both sides, and the border situation remained tense, with a number of reports of minor skirmishes. In May six prominent members of the ethnic Greek organization, OMONIA, were arrested, following the alleged seizure by Albanian police of weapons and 'anti-constitutional' documents. Greece subsequently protested at the actions of the Albanian authorities by vetoing the provision of funds from the EU to Albania and by increasing the deportations of illegal Albanian immigrants. In September five of the six members of OMONIA were convicted on a number of charges, including espionage and the illegal possession of weapons, and received custodial sentences. Following the verdict, Greece and Albania recalled their mutual ambassadors. In addition, the Greek Government submitted formal protests to the UN and the EU regarding Albania's perceived maltreatment of its ethnic Greek population and closed the important Kakavija border crossing, which had hitherto been used by Albanian migrant workers. One of the OMONIA defendants, Irakli Sirmo, was pardoned in December, following a reduction in tension between the two countries (in November Greece had withdrawn its veto on EU aid to Albania). In early February 1995 the four remaining OMONIA prisoners were released. Later that month the OSCE suspended its inquiries into the alleged persecution of the Greek minority in Albania, on the grounds that there was no case to answer. In March relations between Albania and Greece improved dramatically, following a two-day official visit to Albania by the Greek Minister of Foreign Affairs. In June the Albanian Government approved a new education bill, which recognized the right of ethnic minorities to their own language and culture. In March 1996 the Greek President, Konstantinos Stefanopoulos, visited Albania for discussions, during which a co-operation agreement was signed, apparently resolving outstanding issues of concern between the two nations. In August of that year the Greek authorities expelled some 3,500 Albanian migrants. In August 1997 the Ministers of Foreign Affairs of Albania and Greece signed an agreement whereby Albanian migrant workers in Greece would receive temporary work permits.

Relations with Yugoslavia deteriorated sharply in early 1989, when many ethnic Albanian demonstrators were killed during renewed unrest in the Yugoslav province of Kosovo (where the population was principally composed of ethnic Albanian Muslims). In April 1993 it was reported that 10 Albanians had been killed by Yugoslav guards while unwittingly crossing the border. As a result of increasing tension in this area, in the following month the Albanian Government requested the establishment of a UN peace-keeping mission in Kosovo to protect Albanians there. This was refused, however, and Kosovo remained a focus of political and ethnic tension. In March 1994 President Berisha appealed to the international community to make any relaxation of the sanctions against Yugoslavia dependent on a settlement in Kosovo, and again requested that UN monitors be dispatched to the region. No measures to this end were carried out, however, and in May informal discussions between Yugoslav and Albanian officials in Belgrade ended in failure. Throughout 1995 Berisha continued to appeal for a settlement in Kosovo and expressed particular concern in August about the settlement of Krajina Serb refugees in Kosovo by Yugoslavia. The insurgency in southern Albania in early 1997 (see above) prompted concern among western European Governments that armaments seized by the rebels might also be used to support an insurrection by ethnic Albanians in Kosovo. In early November 1997, following a meeting between Prime Minister Nano and the Yugoslav President, Slobodan Milošević, it was announced that relations between Albania and Yugoslavia were to be normalized (although Milošević emphasized during the discussions that the unrest in Kosovo remained an internal issue of Yugoslavia).

In February 1993 Albania refused to accept an application by the former Yugoslav republic of Macedonia (FYRM) for membership of the CSCE, and it was only in April that Albania officially recognized the existence of the republic as an independent state. Albania was concerned at the oppression of the large ethnic Albanian minority in the FYRM, who constituted about 21% of the population and the majority of whom were Muslims. Relations between the two countries deteriorated in the course of the year, owing to a number of shooting incidents on the border. In March 1994, however, Albania urged Greece to end its economic embargo on the FYRM.

Albania was granted observer status at the 1990 CSCE summit meeting, and became a full member of the organization in June 1991. In February 1988 Albania attended a meeting of Balkan ministers responsible for foreign affairs, which took place in Yugoslavia. At the conference, the first involving representatives of all six Balkan nations for more than 50 years, the participants agreed that ministerial delegations should meet on a regular basis in order to discuss multilateral co-operation. In May 1992 the newly-elected President Berisha made a tour of Europe. In the same month, Albania and the EC signed a 10-year agreement on trade and co-operation. In June Albania, together with 10 other countries (including six of the former Soviet republics), signed a pact to establish the Black Sea Economic Co-operation Group (see p. 260), envisaging the creation of a Black Sea economic zone that would complement the EC. In December Albania was granted membership of the Organization of the Islamic Conference (OIC, see p. 224), and in the same month applied to join NATO (see p. 204), thus becoming the first former Warsaw Pact country formally to seek membership of the Western alliance. Albania joined NATO's 'partnership for peace' programme of military co-operation in April 1994. Albania was admitted to the Council of Europe in July 1995, having agreed to adopt a new Constitution and to take measures to fulfil the Council's requirements concerning human rights.

Government

Under the interim constitutional legislation adopted in April 1991 and the electoral law approved in February 1992, legislative power is vested in the unicameral People's Assembly. The People's Assembly comprises 155 deputies, of whom 115 are directly elected by a simple majority and 40 elected on the basis of proportional representation. The President of the Republic is Head of State, and is elected by the People's Assembly. Executive authority is held by the Council of Ministers, whose Chairman is Head of Government. The Chairman of the Council of Ministers is appointed by the President and ministers are appointed by the President upon the Chairman's recommendation. For the purposes of local government, Albania is divided into 36 districts *(rrethe),* which comprise 309 communes. Administrative affairs in each district are conducted by multi-party executive committees.

Defence

In August 1996 the total strength of the armed forces was 54,000 (including 22,050 conscripts): army 45,000, air force 6,500 and navy 2,500. The paramilitary forces numbered 13,500 (including an internal security force of 5,000 and a people's militia of 3,500). Defence expenditure in 1995 was estimated at 5,100m. lekë. Military service is compulsory and lasts for 12 months. In March 1997 insurgent groups opposed to the Government gained control of the south of the country, and large numbers of government forces defected to join the rebels. In April the Multinational Protection Force for Albania, comprising troops from Italy and a further seven European nations, was deployed in the country to assist in the restoration of order. Following the departure of the contingent in August, the armed forces were to be reconstructed with assistance from European Governments, particularly those of Greece and Italy.

Economic Affairs

In 1995, according to World Bank estimates, Albania's gross national product (GNP), measured at average 1993–95 prices, was US $2,199m., equivalent to $670 per head. During 1985–94, it was estimated, GNP per head decreased, in real terms, at an average annual rate of 6.0%. In 1985–95 the population increased by an annual average of 1.0%. Albania's gross domestic product (GDP) declined, in real terms, by an average of 2.7% per year in 1990–95. However, real GDP increased by 9.4% in 1994 and by 8.9% in 1995.

Agriculture (including forestry and fishing) contributed an estimated 55.9% of GDP in 1995. Some 53.4% of the labour force were engaged in the sector in 1996. In 1988 co-operatives accounted for almost 75% of agricultural output; from 1990, however, an increasing degree of private enterprise was permitted. By mid-1995, according to government estimates, 96% of total farm land had been redistributed to private ownership. In August 1995 a law allowing the sale and purchase of farm land was enacted. The principal crops are wheat, sugar beet, maize, potatoes, barley and sorghum. Agricultural GDP increased by an annual average of 5.7% in 1990–95, and by 10.6% in 1995.

Industry (comprising mining, manufacturing, construction and utilities) accounted for an estimated 21.3% of GDP in 1995 and employed 22.5% of the labour force in 1989. Principal contributors to industrial output include mining, energy generation and food-processing. Construction was the fastest-growing sector in recent years, with output expanding by 30% in 1993, by 15% in 1994, and by 12.5% in 1995. Industrial GDP declined at an average rate of 16.8% per year during 1990–95 (but increased by 6.0% in 1995).

Albania is one of the world's largest producers of chromite (chromium ore), possessing Europe's only significant reserves (an estimated 37m. metric tons of recoverable ore, constituting about 5% of total world deposits). The mining sector has been centred on chromite and copper since the closure of nickel and iron ore operations, together with more than one-half of the country's coal mines, in 1990. Albania has petroleum resources and its own refining facilities, and there has been considerable foreign interest in the exploration of both onshore and offshore reserves since 1991. (The acceptance of foreign capital in order to establish joint ventures was authorized in 1990.)

As in the mining sector, output in manufacturing has declined sharply since 1990. The Enterprise Restructuring Agency, established in 1993, acquired more than 30 state industrial enterprise, in which employment was reduced from a pre-1992 level of about 50,000 to less than 7,000 by the end of 1995.

Hydroelectric generation accounted for more than 80% of total electricity production in 1988. A serious drought in 1988–90, however, led to problems in the hydroelectric sector.

Services employed 21.5% of the labour force in 1989 and provided an estimated 22.7% of GDP in 1995. In real terms, the combined GDP of the service sectors increased by an average of 3.9% per year during 1990–95; it grew by an estimated 7.7% in 1995.

In 1996 Albania recorded a visible trade deficit of US $678.3m., and there was a deficit of $107.3m. on the current account of the balance of payments. In 1995, according to the IMF, Albania's principal trading partners were Italy (supplying 37.9% of total imports and taking 51.5% of exports) and Greece (26.8% and 9.9%, respectively). The principal exports in 1995 were miscellaneous manufactured articles (accounting for 45.6% of the total), inedible crude materials and basic manufactures. The main imports in that year were food, beverages and tobacco (22.3% of the total), basic manufactures, and machinery and transport equipment.

Albania's overall budget deficit for 1995 was estimated at 23,110m. lekë (10.3% of GDP). At the end of 1995 Albania's total external debt was US $708.7m., of which $556.7m. was long-term public debt. In that year the cost of servicing the debt was equivalent to 0.9% of the value of exports of goods and services. Remittances from Albanians working abroad totalled $266m. in 1994. Foreign aid and remittances together contributed 40% of GDP in 1993. In 1991–96 the average annual rate of inflation was 55.0%; consumer prices increased by 12.7% in 1996. In 1995 the average rate of unemployment was 16.9% of the domestic labour force. An estimated 17.6% of the Albanian labour force were working abroad in that year.

Having reversed its long-standing policy of economic self-sufficiency, in 1991 Albania became a member of the World Bank, the IMF and the newly-established European Bank for Reconstruction and Development (EBRD, see p. 148).

In late 1991, despite reforms to the centralized economy implemented in that year (permitting limited free enterprise and beginning a programme of comprehensive land redistribution), Albania was experiencing a serious economic crisis. In 1992 the newly-elected Government introduced an extensive programme of economic reforms, providing for the transfer to private ownership of farm land, state-owned companies and housing, and the abolition of trade restrictions and price controls. A strict programme of high interest rates, reduced subsidies, banking reforms and trade liberalization, supported by the IMF, was successful in reducing the massive budget deficit, controlling inflation and stabilizing the currency. Nevertheless, illicit trade was believed to account for a high proportion of total revenue, while the country remained dependent on remittances from Albanian emigrants and foreign aid to support the current account of the balance of payments. The Government's failure to reform the state banking sector, despite warnings from the IMF and World Bank, encouraged the development of informal financial markets, with the establishment of a number of 'pyramid' investment schemes (which offered exceptionally high monthly rates of interest). In early 1997 the collapse of the 'pyramid' schemes, resulting in huge losses of individual savings, precipitated escalating civil unrest. By March armed insurgents, demanding the resignation of the President, had gained control of much of the south of the country; the hostilities between rebels and government forces resulted in damage to infrastructure and the suspension of legitimate economic activity in the greater part of the country. The extreme hardship of the civilian population was compounded by increasing food shortages, necessitating emergency assistance from the EU; a Multinational Protection Force (see Recent History) was deployed in the country to assist in the restoration of civil order. The unrest resulted in a contraction of GDP, and a rapid increase in inflation and the budgetary deficit. Following elections at the end of June, the new government reached agreement with the IMF later that year on the adoption of a three-year economic programme, which was to be financed by emergency assistance from the IMF; primary objectives were to contain the budgetary deficit, control the collection of taxes and customs duties, audit the remaining 'pyramid' schemes and reimburse investors for financial losses, and reform the banking sector. At a conference of donor nations in October, the international community pledged some $670m. to support government investment and economic measures to be undertaken under the initial six months of the programme.

Social Welfare

All medical services are provided free of charge, and medicines are supplied free to infants of up to one year of age. In 1993 the number of hospitals totalled 40, and there were 10,500 beds available. In the same year there was one doctor for every 735 persons. Kindergartens and nursery schools receive large subsidies. Women are entitled to 180 to 360 days' maternity leave, receiving 80% of their salary. There is a non-contributory state social insurance system for all workers, with 70%–100% of salary being paid during sick leave, and a pension system for the old and disabled. Retirement pensions represent 70% of the average monthly salary. Men retire between the ages of 55 and 65 years, and women between 50 and 60. Legislation relating to social assistance for the unemployed entered into force in November 1991. Municipalities and communes became responsible for social assistance in mid-1993. Of total current expenditure in the 1995 state budget, 13,999m. lekë (23.9%) was for social security, 2,504m. lekë (4.3%) for unemployment insurance, and 3,698m. lekë (6.3%) for social assistance.

Education

Education in Albania is provided free at primary and secondary level. Approximately 35% of children aged three to six years attended nursery school in 1994, compared with 59% in 1990. Children between the ages of six and 14 years attend an 'eight-year school', which is compulsory. In 1994 enrolment at primary schools was equivalent to 98% of children in the relevant age-group (boys 98%; girls 99%). In 1990/91 about 75% of pupils leaving the 'eight-year school' proceeded to secondary education. In 1995 secondary education was undergoing restructuring to a system comprising two alternative levels. The second level lasts for five years and qualifies students for management-level employment or higher studies. In 1994 enrolment at secondary schools was equivalent to only 36% of children in the relevant age-group (boys 36%; girls 37%), compared with 78% in 1990. In 1995 there were eight universities and two institutes of higher education. In 1994/95 about 2.4% of secondary school-leavers continued into higher education.

Government expenditure on education amounted to 5,893m. lekë in 1994.

Public Holidays

1998: 1 January (New Year's Day), 30 January* (Small Bayram, end of Ramadan), 8 March (International Women's Day), 8 April* (Great Bayram, Feast of the Sacrifice), 10–13 April (Catholic Easter), 20 April (Orthodox Easter), 28 November (Independence and Liberation Day), 25 December (Christmas Day).

1999: 1 January (New Year's Day), 19 January* (Small Bayram, end of Ramadan), 8 March (International Women's Day), 28 March* (Great Bayram, Feast of the Sacrifice), 2–5 April (Catholic Easter), 12 April (Orthodox Easter), 28 November (Independence and Liberation Day), 25 December (Christmas Day).

* These holidays are dependent on the Islamic lunar calendar and may vary by one or two days from the dates given.

Weights and Measures

The metric system is in force.

Statistical Survey

Source (unless otherwise stated): Institute of Statistics (Drejtoria e Statistikës), Tirana.

Area and Population

AREA, POPULATION AND DENSITY

Area (sq km)	
Land	27,398
Inland water	1,350
Total	28,748*
Population (census results)	
January 1979	2,591,000
2 April 1989	
Males	1,638,900†
Females	1,543,500†
Total	3,182,417
Population (official estimate at 1 January)	
1993	3,165,925
Density (per sq km) at 1 January 1993	110.1

* 11,100 sq miles. † Provisional.

Ethnic Groups (census of 2 April 1989): Albanian 3,117,601; Greek 58,758; Macedonian 4,697; Montenegrin, Serb, Croat, etc. 100; others 1,261.

DISTRICTS (estimated population at 1 January 1993)

	Population
Berat	136,939
Bulqizë	43,363
Delvinë	29,926
Devoll	37,744
Dibër	91,916
Durrës	162,846
Elbasan	215,240
Fier	208,646
Gjirokastër	60,547
Gramsk	42,087
Has	21,271
Kavajë	85,120
Kolonjë	25,089
Korçë	171,205
Krujë	59,997
Kucovë	40,035
Kukës	78,061
Lac	50,712
Lezhë	65,075
Librazhd	75,300
Lushnjë	136,865
Malesia e Madhe	43,924
Mallakastër	36,287
Mat	75,436
Mirditë	49,900
Peqin	29,831
Përmet	36,979
Pogradec	72,203
Pukë	47,621
Sarandë	53,730
Shkodër	195,424
Skrapar	44,339
Telepe	42,365
Tiranë	384,010
Tropojë	44,761
Vlorë	171,131
Total	3,165,925

PRINCIPAL TOWNS (population at mid-1990)

Tiranë (Tirana, the capital)	244,200
Durrës (Durazzo)	85,400
Elbasan	83,300
Shkodër (Scutari)	81,900
Vlorë (Vlonë or Valona)	73,800
Korçë (Koritsa)	65,400
Fier	45,200
Berat	43,800
Lushnjë	31,500
Kavajë	25,700
Gjirokastër	24,900
Kuçovë*	22,300

* This town was known as Qyteti Stalin during the period of Communist rule, but has since reverted to its former name.

Source: *Statistical Directory of Albania.*

BIRTHS, MARRIAGES AND DEATHS*

	Registered live births		Registered marriages		Registered deaths	
	Number	Rate (per 1,000)	Number	Rate (per 1,000)	Number	Rate (per 1,000)
1986	76,435	25.3	25,718	8.5	17,369	5.7
1987	79,696	25.9	27,370	8.9	17,119	5.6
1988	80,241	25.5	28,174	9.0	17,027	5.4
1989	78,862	24.7	27,655	8.6	18,168	5.7
1990	82,125	25.2	28,992	8.9	18,193	5.6
1991	77,361	23.8	24,853	7.6	17,743	5.4

Registered deaths: 17,238 (5.1 per 1,000) in 1992; 16,639 (4.9 per 1,000) in 1993.

* From 1990 rates are based on unrevised estimates of mid-year population.

Expectation of life (years at birth, 1989/90): 72.2 (Males 69.3; Females 75.4).

Source: *Statistical Yearbook of the PSR of Albania, Statistical Yearbook of Albania* and UN, *Demographic Yearbook.*

ECONOMICALLY ACTIVE POPULATION
(ISIC Major Divisions, 1989 census)

	Males	Females	Total
Agriculture, hunting, forestry and fishing	399,810	399,249	799,059
Mining and quarrying; Manufacturing; Electricity, gas and water	160,833	118,155	278,988
Construction	41,979	7,312	49,291
Trade, restaurants and hotels	22,171	26,447	48,618
Transport, storage and communications	36,324	8,109	44,433
Financing, insurance, real estate and business services; Community, social and personal services	119,279	100,905	220,184
Activities not adequately defined	10,293	6,798	17,091
Total employed	790,689	666,975	1,457,664

Source: ILO, *Yearbook of Labour Statistics.*

1995 (annual averages, '000 persons): Total domestic employment 1,145; Emigrant workers 295; Unemployed 233; Labour force 1,672 (males 885, females 787). Source: IMF, *Albania—Recent Economic Developments* (April 1997).

Agriculture

PRINCIPAL CROPS ('000 metric tons)

	1994	1995	1996
Wheat and spelt	420	405	305
Barley	9	7	4
Maize	193	216	192
Rye	4	4	4
Oats	20	13	15
Sorghum*	20	17	17
Potatoes	89	130	137
Dry beans	18	20	23
Sunflower seed	1	2	2
Olives	30	39	45
Tomatoes	127	150	140
Other vegetables*	300	300	300
Watermelons*	20	20	20
Grapes	44	55	64
Sugar beet	60	67	74
Apples	10	10	10*
Pears*	5	5	5
Peaches and nectarines*	3	3	3
Plums*	6	6	6
Oranges	5	6	6*
Other fruits and berries*	21	21	21
Tree-nuts*	4	4	4
Tobacco (leaves)	4	6	6

* FAO estimate(s).

Source: FAO, *Production Yearbook*.

LIVESTOCK ('000 head, year ending September)

	1994	1995	1996
Horses*	58	58	58
Mules*	25	25	25
Asses*	113	113	113
Cattle	820	840	850
Pigs	99	100	1,100
Sheep	2,400	2,480	2,500
Goats	1,717	1,650	1,900

Poultry (million): 4 in 1994; 4 in 1995; 4 in 1996.

* FAO estimates.

Source: FAO, *Production Yearbook*.

LIVESTOCK PRODUCTS ('000 metric tons)

	1994	1995	1996
Beef and veal	51	56	71
Mutton and lamb	12*	15*	27
Goat meat	15	15	15
Pig meat	20	20	23
Poultry meat	4	4	4
Cows' milk	647	791	893
Sheep's milk	73	82	90
Goats' milk	83	96	96†
Cheese†	1	1	1
Butter†	2	2	2
Poultry eggs	14*	17*	17†
Wool:			
greasy	3	4	4
scoured (clean)†	2	2	2
Cattle hides†	6	7	7
Sheep and lamb skins†	4	4	4
Goat and kid skins†	3	3	3

* Unofficial figure. † FAO estimate(s).

Source: FAO, *Production Yearbook*.

Forestry

ROUNDWOOD REMOVALS ('000 cubic metres, excl. bark)

	1992*	1993	1994
Industrial wood	1,000	57	64
Fuel wood	1,556	538	346
Total	2,556	595	409

* FAO estimates.

Source: FAO, *Yearbook of Forest Products*.

SAWNWOOD PRODUCTION ('000 cubic metres, incl. railway sleepers)

	1992*	1993	1994
Coniferous (softwood)	86	1	2
Broadleaved (hardwood)	296	3	3
Total	382	4	5

* FAO estimates.

Source: FAO, *Yearbook of Forest Products*.

Fishing

(FAO estimates, metric tons, live weight)

	1993	1994	1995
Inland waters	1,211	1,290	1,249
Mediterranean Sea	1,789	1,910	1,851
Total catch	3,000	3,200	3,100

* FAO estimates.

Source: FAO, *Yearbook of Fishery Statistics*.

Mining

('000 metric tons, unless otherwise indicated)

	1992	1993	1994
Lignite (brown coal)	366	215	169
Crude petroleum	585	568	535
Natural gas (million cu metres)	102	82	52
Copper ore†‡	3.4	8.0	2.2
Nickel ore (metric tons)†§	150	75	—
Chromium ore†	16	24	31
Cobalt ore (metric tons)*†§	20	10	10

* Provisional or estimated production.

† Figures refer to the metal content of ores.

‡ Data from *World Metal Statistics* (London).

§ Data from the US Bureau of Mines.

Source: mainly UN, *Industrial Commodity Statistics Yearbook*.

1995: Lignite ('000 metric tons) 120; Crude petroleum ('000 metric tons) 521; Natural gas (million cu metres) 28 (Source: IMF, *Albania—Recent Economic Developments,* April 1997).

Industry

SELECTED PRODUCTS
('000 metric tons, unless otherwise indicated)

	1992	1993	1994
Wheat flour	208	115	44
Raw sugar	1	—	3†
Wine ('000 hectolitres)	120	90	50
Cigarettes (million)	1,393	1,395	929
Footwear ('000 pairs)	1,200	n.a.	n.a.
Veneer sheets ('000 cubic metres)†	10	10	10
Plywood ('000 cubic metres)†	6	6	6
Mechanical wood pulp†	2	2	2
Chemical wood pulp†	14	14	14
Paper and paperboard†	44	44	44
Sulphuric acid	11	6	4
Caustic soda (Sodium hydroxide)	—	1	n.a.
Nitrogenous fertilizers (a)‡	110	21	9
Phosphatic fertilizers (b)‡	22	9	11
Soap	2	4	3
Motor spirit (petrol)	45	46	39
Kerosene	41	29	29
Gas-diesel (distillate fuel) oil	116	148	111
Residual fuel oils*	127	105	82
Lubricating oils*	3	3	1
Petroleum bitumen (asphalt)*	11	19	34
Coke*	22	—	—
Cement	197	198	240
Ferro-chromium	22	35	34
Crude steel	—	9	19
Copper (unrefined)§	2.3	2.3	1.5
Television receivers ('000)	1	n.a.	n.a.
Electric energy (million kWh)*	3,357	3,482	3,904

* Provisional or estimated production.

† FAO estimate(s).

‡ Production in terms of (a) nitrogen or (b) phosphoric acid.

§ Data from *World Metal Statistics* (London).

Source: mainly UN, *Industrial Commodity Statistics Yearbook*.

1995 ('000 metric tons, unless otherwise indicated): Raw sugar 3 (FAO estimate); Wine 17; Phosphatic fertilizers 14; Soap 2; Motor spirit 43; Kerosene 29; Gas-diesel oil 106; Cement 238; Ferro-chromium 43; Copper (unrefined) 3; Electric energy (million kWh) 4,414.

1996 ('000 metric tons): Raw sugar 3 (FAO estimate); Wine 17.

Sources (for 1995 and 1996): FAO, *Production Yearbook*; IMF, *Albania—Recent Economic Developments* (April 1997).

Finance

CURRENCY AND EXCHANGE RATES

Monetary Units

100 qindarka (qintars) = 1 new lek.

Sterling and Dollar Equivalents (30 September 1997)

£1 sterling = 238.1 lekë;
US $1 = 147.4 lekë;
1,000 lekë = £4.200 = $6.784.

Average Exchange Rate (lekë per US $)

1994	94.62
1995	92.70
1996	104.50

STATE BUDGET (million lekë)

Revenue	1993	1994	1995
Tax revenue	22,736	35,965	39,679
Turnover tax/value-added tax	4,991	4,959	5,587
Taxes on income and profits	4,582	4,140	3,979
Social security contributions	3,208	6,384	9,245
Import duties and export taxes	3,642	6,260	6,231
Excise taxes	4,348	9,495	10,404
Other revenue	9,349	10,084	14,345
Profit transfer from Bank of Albania	1,250	400	5,926
Income from budgetary institutions	1,105	2,054	3,965
Counterpart sales revenue	4,476	4,194	2,468
Privatization receipts	916	2,200	309
Total	32,086	46,049	54,024

Expenditure	1993	1994	1995
Current expenditure	38,582	52,125	58,684
Wages	8,586	12,045	14,692
Social security contributions	1,534	3,397	3,746
Interest	2,941	4,405	4,984
Operational and maintenance	7,589	10,585	12,231
Subsidies	2,443	2,225	1,304
Price subsidies	2,443	1,975	1,304
Social security	7,302	10,821	13,999
Unemployment insurance	4,756	2,367	2,504
Social assistance	1,390	4,156	3,698
Enterprise restructuring	1,152	549	139
Capital expenditure (investment)	11,853	16,134	18,450
Total	50,435	68,259	77,134

Source: IMF, *Albania—Recent Economic Developments* (April 1997).

INTERNATIONAL RESERVES (US $ million at 31 December)

	1994	1995	1996
Gold*	20.85	24.30	42.50
IMF special drawing rights	0.30	0.14	0.75
Reserve position in IMF	0.01	0.01	0.01
Foreign exchange	204.50	240.90	280.10
Total	225.66	265.35	323.36

* Valued at market-related prices.

Source: IMF, *International Financial Statistics*.

MONEY SUPPLY ('000 million lekë at 31 December)

	1994	1995	1996
Currency outside banks	27.63	41.91	47.81
Demand deposits at deposit money banks	11.41	17.35	42.59
Total money	39.04	59.25	90.41

Source: IMF, *International Financial Statistics*.

COST OF LIVING (Consumer price index; base: 1992 = 100)

	1994	1995	1996
Food	214.3	228.5	263.0
All items (incl. others)	226.7	244.4	275.5

Source: UN, *Monthly Bulletin of Statistics*.

NATIONAL ACCOUNTS (million lekë at current prices)

Gross Domestic Product by Economic Activity

	1993	1994	1995
Agriculture	68,487	103,517	125,725
Industry*	17,363	23,315	25,859
Construction	11,344	17,877	22,085
Transport	3,876	6,268	7,296
Other services	24,269	36,914	43,780
GDP in purchasers' values	125,339	187,891	224,745
GDP at constant 1990 prices	12,309	13,466	14,667

* Comprising mining, manufacturing, electricity, gas and water.

Source: IMF, *Albania—Recent Economic Developments* (April 1997).

BALANCE OF PAYMENTS (US $ million)

	1994	1995	1996
Exports of goods f.o.b.	141.3	204.9	243.7
Imports of goods f.o.b.	-601.0	-679.7	-922.0
Trade balance	-459.7	-474.8	-678.3
Exports of services	79.1	98.8	129.2
Imports of services	-132.5	-156.5	-189.4
Balance on goods and services	-513.1	-532.5	-738.5
Other income received	55.1	72.0	83.7
Other income paid	-41.3	-28.4	-11.9
Balance on goods, services and income	-499.3	-488.9	-666.7
Current transfers received	347.5	521.2	595.9
Current transfers paid	-5.5	-43.8	-36.5
Current balance	-157.3	-11.5	-107.3
Capital account (net)	—	389.4	4.8
Direct investment from abroad	53.0	70.0	90.1
Other investment assets	-97.3	-97.0	-138.6
Other investment liabilities	84.5	-384.0	110.0
Net errors and omissions	123.9	53.7	96.9
Overall balance	6.8	20.6	55.9

Source: IMF, *International Financial Statistics*.

External Trade

PRINCIPAL COMMODITIES (million lekë)

Imports c.i.f.	1988	1989	1990
Machinery and equipment	1,160.9	1,070.0	1,174.8
Fuels, minerals and metals	742.3	984.1	931.0
Chemical products	409.7	458.0	354.0
Raw materials of plant or animal origin	347.2	573.8	385.7
Unprocessed foodstuffs	86.5	104.0	203.1
Processed foodstuffs	262.4	274.0	382.3
Non-foodstuffs of mass consumption	204.3	296.0	319.1
Total (incl. others)	3,217.4	3,792.0	3,795.3

Exports f.o.b.	1988	1989	1990
Fuels, minerals and metals	1,404.2	1,647.3	1,063.8
Raw materials of plant or animal origin	329.3	437.0	350.2
Unprocessed foodstuffs	62.1	50.3	44.6
Processed foodstuffs	431.4	521.5	456.0
Non-foodstuffs of mass consumption	246.3	295.4	269.2
Total (incl. others)	2,549.2	3,029.2	2,273.3

Source: *Statistical Yearbook of Albania*.

Total imports f.o.b. (US $ million): 455.9 in 1990; 281.0 in 1991; 540.5 in 1992; 601.5 in 1993; 601.0 in 1994; 679.7 in 1995; 922.0 in 1996.

Total exports f.o.b. (US $ million): 322.1 in 1990; 73.0 in 1991; 70.0 in 1992; 111.6 in 1993; 141.3 in 1994; 204.9 in 1995; 243.7 in 1996.

Source: IMF, *International Financial Statistics*.

PRINCIPAL TRADING PARTNERS (% of total trade)

Imports f.o.b.	1993	1994	1995
Austria	0.9	1.5	2.0
Belgium-Luxembourg	1.0	1.0	1.6
Bulgaria	5.7	8.2	8.0
China, People's Republic	0.5	1.1	0.0
France	8.7	1.9	1.2
Germany	12.4	5.5	4.6
Greece	18.5	24.0	26.8
Hungary	1.2	0.5	0.7
Italy	31.2	35.0	37.9
Morocco	3.1	n.a.	0.0
Switzerland	1.7	0.9	0.7
Turkey	3.0	4.6	4.1
USA	2.5	0.2	0.3
Yugoslavia (former)	4.6	4.5	0.0
Total (incl. others)	100.0	100.0	100.0

Exports f.o.b	1993	1994	1995
Austria	1.0	2.4	0.9
Belgium-Luxembourg	6.1	4.3	5.4
France	1.8	2.1	2.3
Germany	4.3	4.8	6.1
Greece	18.0	10.4	9.9
Italy	41.0	52.1	51.5
Japan	1.4	1.4	0.7
Netherlands	0.3	0.1	2.1
Switzerland	1.3	0.6	1.0
Turkey	1.4	0.7	6.2
USA	3.7	11.1	3.4
Yugoslavia (former)	13.6	6.0	0.0
Total (incl. others)	100.0	100.0	100.0

Source: IMF, *Albania—Recent Economic Developments* (April 1997).

Transport

RAILWAYS (traffic)*

	1988	1989	1990
Passengers carried ('000)	10,966	11,724	11,908
Passengers-km (million)	703.0	752.4	779.2
Freight carried ('000 metric tons)	7,659	8,048	6,646
Freight ton-km (million)	626.4	674.2	584.0

* Figures refer to operations by the Ministry of Transport only.

Source: *Statistical Directory of Albania*.

ROAD TRAFFIC (motor vehicles in use at 31 December)

	1994	1995	1996
Passenger cars	67,960	58,692	67,031
Buses and coaches	8,149	6,651	6,926
Lorries and vans	42,271	25,790	27,132
Road tractors	8,842	3,334	2,835
Motorcycles and mopeds	14,339	6,946	5,541

Source: International Road Federation, *World Road Statistics*.

SHIPPING

Merchant Fleet (registered at 31 December)

	1994	1995	1996
Number of vessels	24	32	33
Displacement ('000 gross registered tons)	59.1	63.0	43.4

Source: Lloyd's Register of Shipping, *World Fleet Statistics*.

International Sea-borne Freight Traffic
('000 metric tons)

	1988	1989	1990
Goods loaded	1,090	1,112	1,065
Goods unloaded	644	659	664

Source: UN, *Monthly Bulletin of Statistics*.

CIVIL AVIATION (traffic on scheduled services)

	1994
Passengers carried ('000)	9
Passenger-km (million)	2

Source: UN, *Statistical Yearbook*.

Tourism

	1992	1993	1994
Tourist arrivals*	28,430	45,152	28,439
Tourist receipts (US $ million)	9	8	5

* International tourist arrivals at hotels and similar establishments.

Source: UN, *Statistical Yearbook*.

Communications Media

	1992	1993	1994
Radio receivers ('000 in use)	583	600	650
Television receivers ('000 in use)	290	300	310
Telephones ('000 main lines in use)	45	43	48
Telefax stations (number in use)	600	n.a.	n.a.
Daily newspapers:			
Number	4	n.a.	3
Average circulation ('000 copies)	165	n.a.	185

Book production (1991): 381 titles (including 18 pamphlets).

Sources: UN, *Statistical Yearbook*, and UNESCO, *Statistical Yearbook*.

Education

(1994/95, unless otherwise indicated)

	Institutions	Teachers	Students		
			Males	Females	Total
Pre-primary	2,668	4,428	n.a.	n.a.	80,348
Primary	1,782	30,893	285,155	265,582	550,737
Secondary					
General	162*	4,965	33,403	39,813	73,216
Vocational	259*	1,400	14,251	6,363	20,614
Higher†‡	10	1,774	14,116	16,069	30,185
Universities, etc.‡	n.a.	1,596	8,656	10,430	19,086
Other‡	n.a.	178	1,143	523	1,666

* 1990 figure.

† Figures for students include those enrolled at distance-learning institutions, totalling 9,433 (males 4,317; females 5,116).

‡ 1993/94 figures.

Sources: Ministry of Education, Tirana, and UNESCO, *Statistical Yearbook*.

Directory

The Constitution

The Constitution adopted on 28 December 1976 was declared invalid in April 1991, following the adoption of interim constitutional legislation. A draft constitution was rejected by more than one-half of the voters in a national referendum held on 6 November 1994.

On 30 April 1991 the People's Assembly adopted the Law on the Major Constitutional Provisions of the People's Assembly of the Republic of Albania, which was, in effect, an interim organic law. In late 1997 a parliamentary commission was established to draft a new constitution, which was to be submitted to a national referendum in March 1998.

THE SOCIAL ORDER

The Political Order

Articles 1–9. The Republic of Albania is a parliamentary republic. The Republic is a juridical and democratic state which observes and defends the rights and freedoms of its citizens.

The fundamental principle of state organization is the separation of legislative, executive and judicial powers. The people exercise their power through their representative organs, which are elected by free, universal, direct and secret ballot.

Legislative power belongs to the People's Assembly; the Head of State is the President of the Republic; the supreme body of executive power is the Council of Ministers; judicial power is exercised by courts, which are independent and guided only by the provisions of the law.

Albania recognizes and guarantees those fundamental rights and freedoms that are proclaimed in international law, including those of national minorities. Judicial norms must be applied equally to all state bodies, political parties and other groups and organizations. All citizens are equal under the law.

Political pluralism is a fundamental condition of democracy in Albania. Political parties are entirely separate from the State and are prohibited from activities in military bodies, state ministries, diplomatic representations abroad, judicial institutions and other state bodies.

Albania is a secular state. The State observes the freedom of religious belief and creates conditions to exercise it.

The Economic Order

Articles 10–14. The country's economy is based on diverse systems of ownership, freedom of economic activity and the regulatory role of the State. All kinds of ownership are protected by law. Foreign persons may gain the right to ownership and are guaranteed the right to carry out independent economic activity in Albania, to form joint economic ventures and to repatriate profits.

All citizens are liable for contributions to state expenditure in relation to their income.

SUPREME BODIES OF STATE POWER

The People's Assembly

Articles 15–23. The People's Assembly is the supreme body of state power and sole law-making body. It defines the main directions of the domestic and foreign policy of the State. It approves and amends the Constitution and is competent to declare war and ratify or annul international treaties. It elects its Presidency which is composed of a Chairman and two Deputy Chairmen. It also elects the President of the Republic of Albania, the Supreme Court, the Attorney-General and his or her deputies. It controls the activity of state radio and television, the state news agency and other official information media.

The People's Assembly is composed of at least 140 deputies, elected for a period of four years.

The President of the Republic of Albania

Articles 24–32. The President of the Republic is Head of State and is elected by the People's Assembly, in a secret ballot, and by a two-thirds majority of the votes of all the deputies. The term of office is five years. No person is to hold the office of President for more than two successive terms. The President may not occupy any other post while fulfilling the functions of President.

The President guarantees the observation of the Constitution and legislation adopted by the People's Assembly; he appoints the Chairman of the Council of Ministers and accepts his or her resignation; he exercises the duties of the People's Assembly when the legislature is not in session.

The President is Commander-in-Chief of the Armed Forces and Chairman of the Council of Defence. The Council of Defence is responsible for organizing the country's resources to ensure the territorial defence of the Republic. Its members are proposed by the President and approved by the People's Assembly.

The Supreme Organs of State Administration

Articles 33–41. The Council of Ministers is the supreme executive and legislative body. It directs activity for the realization of the domestic and foreign policies of the State and directs and controls the activity of ministries, other central organs of state administration and local organs of administration. It is composed of the Chairman, Vice-Chairmen, Ministers and other persons defined by law. The Chairman of the Council of Ministers is appointed by the President; Ministers are appointed by the President upon the recommendation of the Chairman. The composition of the Council of Ministers is approved by the People's Assembly. Members of the Council of Ministers may not have any other state or professional function.

The Chairman and Vice-Chairmen of the Council of Ministers constitute the Presidency of the Council of Ministers.

FINAL PROVISIONS

Articles 42–46. The creation, organization and activity of the local organs of power, administration, courts and the Attorney-General are made according to existing legal provisions, except those invalidated by the Law on Major Constitutional Provisions. Drafts for amendments to the Law on Major Constitutional Provisions may be proposed by the President of the Republic, the Council of Ministers or one-quarter of the deputies of the People's Assembly. The adoption of amendments requires a two-thirds majority of all deputies. The provisions of the Law on Major Constitutional Provisions operate until the adoption of the Constitution of the Republic of Albania, which will be drafted by the Special Commission appointed by the People's Assembly. The Constitution of the People's Socialist Republic of Albania, adopted on 28 December 1976, is invalidated.

The Government

(December 1997)

HEAD OF STATE

President of the Republic: Dr REXHEP MEJDANI (elected 24 July 1997).

COUNCIL OF MINISTERS

A coalition of the Socialist Party of Albania (SPA), the Social Democratic Party of Albania (SDP), the Democratic Alliance Party (DAP), the Agrarian Party (AP), the Union for Human Rights Party (UHRP), and independents.

Prime Minister: FATOS NANO (SPA).

Minister of State for the Council of Ministers: KASTRIOT ISLAMI (SPA).

Deputy Prime Minister: BASHKIM FINO (SPA).

Minister of Foreign Affairs: PASKAL MILO (SPA).

Minister of Defence: SABIT BROKAJ (SPA).

Minister of the Interior: NERITAN CEKA (DAP).

Minister of the Public Economy and Privatization: YLLI BUFI (SPA).

Minister of Labour, Social Affairs and Women: ELMAZ SHERIFI (SPA).

Minister of Agriculture and Food: LUFTER XHUVELI (AP).

Minister of Finance: ARBEN MALAJ (SPA).

Minister of Trade and Tourism: SHAQIR VUKAJ (SPA).

Minister of Public Affairs and Transport: GAQO APOSTOLI (SDP).

Minister of Education and Science: ETHEM RUKA. (SPA).

Minister of Culture, Youth and Sports: ARTA DADE (SPA).

Minister of Health and the Environment: LEONARD SOLIS (UHRP).

Minister of State for Legislative Reform and Relations with the People's Assembly: ARBEN IMAMI (DAP).

Minister of State for Co-operation and Economic Development: ERMELINDA MEKSI (SPA).

Minister of Justice: THIMIO KONDI (Independent).

Secretary of State for Euro-Atlantic Integration: MAQO LAKRORI (SPA).

Secretary of State for Defence: PERIKLI TETA (DAP).

Secretary of State for the Interior: NDRE LEGISI (SPA).

Secretary of State for Local Government: LUSH PERPALI (SPA).

MINISTRIES

Council of Ministers: Këshilli i Ministrave, Tirana; tel. (42) 28210; telex 4201; fax (42) 27888.

Ministry of Agriculture and Food: Ministria e Bujqësisë dhe Ushqimit, Tirana; tel. and fax (42) 23917; telex 4209.

Ministry of Culture, Youth and Sports: Ministria e Kulturës, Bulevardi Zhan D'Ark, Tirana; tel. (42) 29715; fax (42) 27878.

Ministry of Defence: Ministria e Mbrojtjes, Tirana; tel. (42) 28428; fax (42) 27944.

Ministry of Education and Science: Ministria e Arsimit dhe Sporteve, Tirana; tel. (42) 26307; telex 4203; fax (42) 28304.

Ministry of Energy and Mining: Ministria e Rezervave Minerale dhe Energjisë, Skenderbeg 2, Tirana; tel. (42) 27617; telex 4204; fax (42) 34052.

Ministry of Finance: Ministria e Financave, Tirana; tel. (42) 28405; telex 4297; fax (42) 28494.

Ministry of Foreign Affairs: Ministria e Punëve të Jashtme, Tirana; tel. (42) 34600; telex 2164; fax (42) 32971.

Ministry of Health and the Environment: Ministria e Shendetesisë dhe Mbrojtjes së Ambjentit, Tirana; tel. (42) 28303; telex 4205; fax (42) 34632.

Ministry of Higher Education: c/o Këshilli i Ministrave, Tirana.

Ministry of the Interior: Tirana; tel. (42) 28167; fax (42) 27520.

Ministry of Justice: Ministria e Drejtësisë, Tirana; tel. (42) 28378; fax (42) 28359.

Ministry of Labour, Social Affairs and Women: Ministria e Punës dhe Ndihmës Sociale, Rruga e Kavajes, Tirana; tel. (42) 28340; fax (42) 27779.

Ministry of Public Affairs and Transport: Bulevardi Zhan D'Ark, Tirana; tel. (42) 32445; telex 4290; fax (42) 27931.

Ministry of the Public Economy and Privatization: c/o Këshilli i Ministrave, Tirana.

Ministry of Trade and Tourism: Ministria e Industrisë, Tregtisë e Transporteve, Tirana; tel. (42) 34668; telex 2152; fax (42) 34658.

Legislature

KUVENDI POPULLOR

(People's Assembly)

President (Speaker): SKENDER GJINUSHI.

Deputy President: NAMIK DOKLE.

General Election, 29 June and 6 July 1997

Party	Seats
Socialist Party of Albania	101
Democratic Party of Albania	29
Social Democratic Party of Albania	8
Union for Human Rights Party	4
National Front Party	3
Democratic Alliance Party	2
Legality Movement Party	2
Albanian Republican Party	1
Party of National Unity	1
Agrarian Party	1
Independents	3
Total	155

Political Organizations

Agrarian Party (AP): Rruga Budi 6, Tirana; tel. (42) 27481; fax (42) 27481; f. 1991; Chair. LUFTER XHUVELI.

Albanian Conservative Party (Partia Konservatore Shqiptare): Tirana; Chair. ARMANDO RUCO.

Albanian Green Party (Partia e Blertë Shqiptare): POB 749, Tirana; tel. and fax (42) 33309; f. 1991; campaigns on environmental issues; Chair. NEVRUZ MALUKA; Sec. SHYQRI KONDI.

Albanian Helsinki Forum (Forum Shqiptar i Helsinkit): Tirana; f. 1990; mem. International Federation of Helsinki; Chair. Prof. Arben Puto.

Albanian Liberal Party (Partia Liberale Shqiptare): Tirana; f. 1991; Chair. Valter File.

Albanian National Democratic Party (Partia Nacional Demokratike): Tirana; f. 1991; Chair. Fatmir Çekani.

Albanian Nationalist Party: Tirana; f. 1993.

Albanian New Socialist Party: Tirana; f. 1996 by former mems of the SPA.

Albanian Republican Party (ARP) (Partia Republikane Shqiptare—PRS): Tirana; f. 1991; Gen. Council of 54 mems, Steering Commission of 21 mems; Chair. Sabri Godo; Vice-Chair. Fatmir Mediu; Sec. Cerciz Mingomatas.

Albanian Women's Federation (Forum i Grus Shqiptare): Tirana; tel. (42) 28309; f. 1991; independent organization uniting women from various religious and cultural backgrounds; Chair. Diana Çuli.

Alternative Republican Party: Tirana; f. 1993.

Çamëria Political and Patriotic Association (Shoqata Politike-Patriotike Çamëria): Tirana; supports the rights of the Çam minority (an Albanian people) in northern Greece; f. 1991; Chair. Dr Abaz Dojaka.

Christian Democratic Party of Albania (CDPA): Rruga Dëshmorët e 4 Shkurtit, Tirana; tel. (42) 30042; fax (42) 34024; f. 1991; Pres. Zef Bushati; Gen.-Sec. Gasper Molni.

Democratic Alliance Party (DAP): Tirana; f. 1992 by former members of the DPA; Chair. Neritan Çeka; Sec.-Gen. Edmond Dragoti.

Democratic Movement of the Unification of Albanians: f. 1993.

Democratic Party of Albania (DPA) (Partia Demokratike të Shqipërisë—PDS): Rruga Punetoret e Rilndjes; Tirana; tel. (42) 28525; fax (42) 28463; f. 1990; committed to liberal-democratic ideals and market economics; Chair. Dr Sali Berisha; Sec.-Gen. Ridvan Bode.

Democratic Prosperity Party (Partia e Prosperitetit Demokratik): Tirana; f. 1991; Chair. Yzeir Fetahu.

Democratic Party of the Right: Tirana; Leader Petrit Kalakula.

Democratic Union of the Greek Minority (OMONIA—Bashkimia Demokratik i Minoritet Grek): Tirana; f. 1991; electoral regulations of 1992 forbade it participating in elections, as the party of an ethnic minority; Chair. Jorgo Labovitjadhi.

Democratic Unity Party (Partia e Bashkimit Demokratik): Tirana; Chair. Xhevdet Libohova.

Independent Party (Partia Indipendente): Tirana; f. 1991; Chair. Edmond Gjokrushi.

Legality Movement Party (Partia Lëvizja e Legalitetit): Tirana; f. 1992; monarchist; Chair. Guri Durollari.

Movement for Democracy (Levizja per Democraci): Tirana; f. 1997 by former mems of the DPA; Leader Dashamir Shehi.

National Committee of the War Veterans of the Anti-Fascist National Liberation War of the Albanian People (Komiteti Kombëtar i Veteranëve të Luftës Antifashiste Nacional Çlirimtare të Popullit Shqiptar): Rruga Dëshmorët e 4 Shkurtit, Tirana; f. 1957; Chair. Pirro Dodbiba; Gen. Sec. Qamil Poda.

National Front (Balli Kombëtar): c/o Kuvendi Popullor, Tirana; Chair. Hysen Selfo.

National Progress Party (Partia e Perparimit Kombëtar): Tirana; f. 1991; Chair. Myrto Xhaferri.

Party of National Unity (Partia e Unitetit Kombëtar): Rruga Alqi Kondi, Tirana; tel. (42) 27498; fax (42) 23929; f. 1991; Chair. of Steering Cttee Idajet Beqiri.

People's Party (Partia Popullore): Tirana; f. 1991; aims to eradicate Communism; Chair. Bashkim Driza.

Republican Party: Tirana; Chair. Fatmir Mediu.

Social Democratic Party of Albania (SDP) (Partia Social Demokratike e Shqipërise—PSDS): Rruga Asim Vokshi 26, Tirana; tel. (42) 26540; fax (42) 27485; f. 1991; advocates gradual economic reforms and social justice; 100-member National Managing Council; Chair. Paskal Milo; Gen.-Sec. Dhori Kule.

Social Justice Party (Partia e Drejtesise Shogerore): Tirana.

Social Labour Party of Albania (Partia Socialpuntore Shqiptare): Burrel; f. 1992; Pres. Ramadan Ndreka.

Socialist Party of Albania (SPA) (Partia Socialiste e Shqipërisë—PSS): Tirana; tel. (42) 27409; telex 4291; fax (42) 27417; f. 1941 as Albanian Communist Party, renamed Party of Labour of Albania (PLA) in 1948, adopted present name in 1991; until 1990 the only permitted political party in Albania; now rejects Marxism-Leninism and claims commitment to democratic socialism and a market economy; Managing Cttee of 81 mems, headed by Presidency of 15 mems; 130,000 mems and candidate mems; Chair. Prof. Dr Rexhep Mejdani; Sec. Pandeli Majko; 110,000 mems.

Union for Human Rights Party (UHRP) (Partia për Mbrojtjen e te Drejtave te Njeriut—PBDNj): Tirana; f. 1992; represents the Greek and Macedonian minorities; Chair. Vasil Melo; Sec.-Gen. Thoma Mico.

Union of Social Democrats (USD): Tirana; f. 1995; breakaway faction from the SDP; Leader Teodor Laco.

Diplomatic Representation

EMBASSIES IN ALBANIA

Bosnia and Herzegovina: Tirana; Chargé d'affaires a.i.: Muharem Zejnulahu.

Bulgaria: Rruga Skënderbeu 12, Tirana; tel. (42) 33155; Ambassador: Stefan Naumov.

China, People's Republic: Rruga Skënderbeu 57, Tirana; tel. (42) 32077; telex 2148; Ambassador: Tao Miaofa.

Cuba: Tirana; tel. (42) 25176; telex 2155; Ambassador: Julio C. Cancio Ferrer.

Czech Republic: Rruga Skënderbeu 4, Tirana; tel. (42) 34004; telex 2162; fax (42) 32159; Chargé d'affaires a.i.: Imrich Sedlák.

Egypt: Rruga Skënderbeu 43, Tirana; tel. (42) 33022; telex 2156; Ambassador: Karam.

France: Rruga Skënderbeu 14, Tirana; tel. (42) 34250; telex 2150; Ambassador: Jacques Faure.

Germany: Rruga Skënderbeu 8, Tirana; tel. (42) 32050; telex 2254; fax (42) 33497; Ambassador: Hannspeter Disdorn.

Greece: Rruga Frederik Shiroka 3, Tirana; tel. (42) 34290; fax (42) 34443; Ambassador: Constanin Prevedourakis.

Holy See: Rruga e Durrësit 13, Tirana; tel. (42) 33516; fax (42) 32001; Apostolic Nuncio: (vacant).

Hungary: Rruga Skënderbeu 16, Tirana; tel. (42) 32238; telex 2257; fax (42) 33211; Ambassador: Ferenc Póka.

Italy: Rruga Lek Dukagjini, Tirana; tel. (42) 34343; telex 2166; fax (42) 32507; Ambassador: Marcello Spatafora.

Korea, Democratic People's Republic: Tirana; tel. (42) 22258; Ambassador: Kim U-Jong.

Libya: Rruga Donika Kastrioti 9, Tirana; tel. (42) 28101; fax (42) 32098; Bureau Chief: Abdelhamit Farhat.

Macedonia, former Yugoslav republic: Skënderbeu 3/6, Tirana; tel. and fax (42) 33036; Ambassador: Nikola Todorcevski.

Poland: Rruga e Durrësit 123, Tirana; tel. (42) 34190; fax (42) 33464; Chargé d'affaires a.i.: Artur Tomaszewski.

Romania: Rruga Themistokli Gërmenji 2, Tirana; tel. (42) 32287; Ambassador: Filip Teodorescu.

Russia: Rruga Asim Zeneli 5, Tirana; tel. (42) 34500; telex 2121; fax (42) 32253; Ambassador: Igor A. Saprykin.

Switzerland: Rruga e Elbasanit 81, Tirana; tel. (42) 34890; fax (42) 34889; Chargé d'affaires: Christian Hauswirth.

Turkey: Rruga Konferenca e Pezës 31, Tirana; tel. (42) 33399; fax (42) 32719; Ambassador: Metin Ornekol.

United Kingdom: Rruga Skënderbeu 12, Tirana; tel. and fax (42) 34973; Ambasssador: Andrew Tesoriere.

USA: Rruga Labinoti 103, Tirana; tel. (42) 32875; fax (42) 32222; Chargé d'affaires: Robert Cekuta.

Yugoslavia: Rruga e Durrësit 192–196, Tirana; tel. and fax (42) 23042; telex 2167; Ambassador: Nikola Todorčevski.

Judicial System

The judicial structure comprises District Courts, Appeal Courts (one for every 36 District Courts), the Supreme Court and the Constitutional Court. Military tribunals are held at the Supreme Court, and at District and Appeal Courts. The officials of the District Courts and the Appeal Courts are nominated by a Higher Judicial Council, which is presided over by the President of the Republic.

The Supreme Court: The Supreme Court has jurisdiction over both the Appeal Courts and District Courts. The Chairman and other members of the Supreme Court are elected by the People's Assembly.

Chairman of the Supreme Court: Avin Shehu.

The Constitutional Court: The Constitutional Court arbitrates on constitutional issues, and determines, *inter alia*, the conformity of proposed legislation with the Constitution. It is empowered to prohibit the activities of political organizations on constitutional grounds, and also formulates legislation regarding the election of the President of the Republic. The Constitutional Court comprises nine members, of whom five are elected by the People's Assembly and four are appointed by the President of the Republic.

Chairman of the Constitutional Court: RUSTEM GJATA.

Attorneys' offices are state organs, which control the application of legislation from ministries, and other central and local organs. The Attorney-General is appointed by the People's Assembly on the recommendation of the President of the Republic.

Attorney-General: ALUSH DRAGOSHI.

Religion

All religious institutions were closed by the Government in 1967 and the practice of religion was prohibited. In May 1990, however, the prohibition on religious activities was revoked, religious services were permitted, and, from 1991, mosques and churches began to be reopened. Transitional legislation, adopted in April 1991 to replace the 1976 Constitution, states that Albania is a secular state which observes 'freedom of religious belief and creates conditions in which to exercise it'. On the basis of declared affiliation in 1945, it is estimated that some 70% of the population are of Muslim background (mainly Sunni or adherents of the liberal Bektashi order), 20% Eastern Orthodox Christian (mainly in the south) and some 10% Roman Catholic Christian (mainly in the north). During 1991 the small number of Albanian Jews emigrated to Israel.

ISLAM

Albanian Islamic Community (Bashkesia Islame e Shqipërisë): Rruga Puntoret e Rilindjes, Tirana; f. 1991; Chair. HAFIZ H. SABRI KOÇI; Grand Mufti of Albania HAFIZ SALIH TERMAT HOXHA.

Bektashi Sect

World Council of Elders of the Bektashis: Tirana; f. 1991; Chair. RESHAT Baba BARDHI.

CHRISTIANITY

The Eastern Orthodox Church

Orthodox Autocephalous Church of Albania (Kisha Orthodhokse Autoqefale të Shqipërisë): Rruga Kavaja 151, Tirana; tel. (42) 42271; fax (42) 32109; the Albanian Orthodox Church was proclaimed autocephalous at the Congress of Berat in 1922, its status was approved in 1929 and it was recognized by the Ecumenical Patriarchate in Istanbul (Constantinople), Turkey, in 1936; the Serbian, Macedonian and Greek churches do not recognize its separate existence; Archbishop ANASTAS JANULATOS.

The Roman Catholic Church

Many Roman Catholic churches have been reopened since 1990, and in September 1991 diplomatic relations were restored with the Holy See. Albania comprises two archdioceses, four dioceses and one apostolic administration. At 31 December 1995 there were an estimated 540,507 adherents in the country, representing about 15% of the total population.

Bishops' Conference: Conferenza Episcopale dell'Albania, Kryeipeshkëvi, Shkodër; tel. (224) 3353; Pres. Most Rev. FRANO ILLIA, Archbishop of Shkodër.

Archbishop of Durrës-Tirana: Most Rev. RROK K. MIRDITA., Arqipeshkvia, Rruga Labinoti, Vilar e Gjermaneve 3, Tirana; tel. (42) 32082; fax (42) 30727.

Archbishop of Shkodër: Most Rev. FRANO ILLIA, Kryeipeshkëvi, Sheshi Gijon Pali II, Shkodër; tel. (224) 2741.

The Press

Until 1991 the Press was controlled by the Party of Labour of Albania, now the Socialist Party of Albania (SPA), and adhered to a strongly Marxist-Leninist line. From 1991 many new periodicals and newspapers were established by the newly emerging independent political organizations. In 1994 there were some 400 newspapers and periodicals in publication.

PRINCIPAL DAILIES

Koha Jonë (Our Time): Tirana; f. 1991; independent; Editor-in-Chief BEN BLUSHI; circ. 400,000.

Rilindja Demokratike (Democratic Revival): Rruga Fortuzi, Tirana; tel. (42) 29609; fax (42) 42329; f. 1991; organ of the DPA; Editor-in-Chief LORENC LIGORI; circ. 50,000.

Zëri i Popullit (The Voice of the People): Bulevardi Zhan D'Ark, Tirana; tel. (42) 22192; telex 4251; fax (42) 27813; f. 1942; daily, except Mon.; organ of the SPA; Editor-in-Chief LUAN RAMA; circ. 105,000.

PERIODICALS

Tirana

Agrovizion: Rruga d'Istria, Tirana: tel. (42) 26147; f. 1992; 2 a week; agricultural economic policies, new technology in farming, advice for farmers; circ. 3,000.

Albania: Tirana; f. 1991; weekly; organ of the Albanian Green Party; environmental issues.

Albanian Daily News: Rruga Hile Mosi, 5, Tirana; tel. and fax (42) 27639; e-mail adn@icc.al.eu.org; internet http://www.albaniannews.com.; f. 1995; fax (42) 32035; weekly English-language newspaper; Editor ARBEN LESKAJ.

Alternativa SD: Tirana; f. 1991; 2 a week; organ of the Social Democratic Party.

Arbër: Tirana; f. 1992; fortnightly; social, literary and artistic review.

The Balkans: Tirana; f. 1993; humorous review; Editor-in-Chief NIKO NIKOLLA.

Balli i Kombit (The Head of the Nation): Tirana; f. 1991.

Bashkimi Kombëtar: Bulevardi Zhan D'Ark, Tirana; tel. (42) 28110; f. 1943; Editor-in-Chief QEMAL SAKAJEVA; circ. 30,000.

Çamëria—Vatra Amtare (Çamëria—Maternal Hearth): Tirana; f. 1991; weekly; organ of the Çamëria Political and Patriotic Association.

Drita (The Light): Rruga Konferenca e Pezës 4, Tirana; tel. (42) 27036; f. 1960; weekly; publ. by Union of Writers and Artists of Albania; Editor-in-Chief BRISEIDA MEMA; circ. 31,000.

Ekonomia Botërore (World Economics): Tirana; f. 1991; monthly; independent.

Fatosi (The Valiant): Tirana; tel. (42) 23024; f. 1959; fortnightly; literary and artistic magazine for children; Editor-in-Chief XHEVAT BEQARAJ; circ. 21,200.

Filmi (The Film): Tirana; f. 1992; monthly; illustrated cinema review.

Gazeta Shqiptare (Albanian Gazette): Tirana; independent; Editor CARLO BOLLINO.

Hosteni (The Goad): Tirana; f. 1945; fortnightly; political review of humour and satire; publ. by the Union of Journalists; Editor-in-Chief NIKO NIKOLLA.

The Hour of Albania: Rruga Dëshmorët e 4 Shkurtit, Tirana; tel. (42) 42042; fax (42) 34024; weekly; organ of the Christian Democratic Party of Albania; Editor-in-Chief Dr FAIK LAMA; circ. 3,000.

Kombi (The Nation): Rruga Alqi Kondi, Tirana; tel. (42) 27498; fax (42) 23929; f. 1991; 2 a week; organ of the Party of National Unity; circ. 15,000.

Kushtrim Brezash (Clarion Call of Generations): Tirana; f. 1992; weekly; organ of the National Committee of the War Veterans of the Anti-Fascist National Liberation War of the Albanian People.

Liria: Tirana.

Mbrojtja (The Defence): Tirana; f. 1991; monthly; publ. by the Ministry of Defence; Editor-in-Chief XHELADIN ÇELMETA.

Mësuesi (The Teacher): Tirana; f. 1961; weekly; publ. by the Ministry of Education and Science; Editor-in-Chief THOMA QENDRO.

Ndërtuesi (The Builder): Tirana; quarterly

Official Gazette of the Republic of Albania: Kuvendi Popullore, Tirana; tel. (42) 28668; telex 4298; fax (42) 27949; f. 1945; occasional government review.

Panorama Agroushqimore (Agro-food Panorama): Rruga d'Istria, Tirana; f. 1921, publ. under several names; monthly; specialist agricultural magazine; circ. 3,000.

Pasqyra (The Mirror): Bulevardi Zhan D'Ark, Tirana; f. 1991 to replace *Puna* (Labour—f. 1945); 2 a week; also 4 times a year in French; organ of the Confederation of Albanian Trade Unions; Editor-in-Chief KRISTAQ LAKA.

Patrioti (The Patriot): Tirana; f. 1992; organ of the Elez Isufi Patriotic Association; Editor-in-Chief VEDIP BRENSHI.

Përmbledhje Studimesh (Collection of Studies): Tirana; quarterly; summaries in French.

Populli Po: Tirana.

Progresi (Progress): Rruga Budi 6, Tirana; tel. (42) 27481; fax (42) 27481; f. 1991; 2 a week; organ of the Agrarian Party.

Republika: Bulevardi Zhan D'Ark 66, Tirana; tel. and fax (42) 25988; f. 1991; 2 a week; organ of the Albanian Republican Party; Editor-in-Chief YLLI RAKIPI.

Revista Pedagogjike: Naim Frasheri St 37, Tirana; fax (42) 23860; f. 1945; quarterly; organ of the Institute of Pedagogical Studies; educational development, psychology, didactic; Editor STAVRI LLAMBIRI; circ. 8,000.

Rinia e Lire (Free Youth): Tirana; f. 1992; organ of the Albanian Free Youth Federation.

Shëndeti (Health): M. Duri 2, Tirana; tel. (42) 27803; fax (42) 27803; f. 1949; monthly; publ. by the National Directorate of Health Education; issues of health and welfare, personal health care; Editors-in-Chief KORNELIA GJATA, AGIM XHUMARI.

Shqiptarja e Re (The New Albanian Woman): Tirana; f. 1943; monthly; political and socio-cultural review; Editor-in-Chief VALENTINA LESKAJ.

Sindikalisti (Trade Unionists): Tirana; f. 1991; newspaper; organ of the Union of Independent Trade Unions of Albania; Editor-in-Chief VANGJEL KOZMAI.

Skena dhe Ekrani (Stage and Screen): Tirana; quarterly; cultural review.

Spektër (The Spectre): Tirana; f. 1991; illustrated independent monthly; in Albanian and Italian.

Sporti (Sport): Rruga e Kavajës 23, Sheshi Ataturk, 2908 Tirana; tel. and fax (42) 23577; f. 1935; 2 a week; publ. by the Ministry of Culture, Youth and Sports; Editor BESNIK DIZDARI; circ. 10,000.

Studenti (The Student): Tirana; f. 1967; weekly.

Tirana: Tirana; f. 1987; independent; 2 a week; publ. by Tirana District SPA.

Tregtia e Jashtme Popullore (Albanian Foreign Trade): Rruga Konferenca e Pezës 6, Tirana; tel. (42) 22934; telex 2179; f. 1961; 6 a year; in English and French; organ of the Albanian Chamber of Commerce; Editor AGIM KORBI.

Tribuna Demokratike (Democratic Tribune): Tirana.

Tribuna e Gazetarit (The Journalist's Tribune): Tirana; 6 a year; publ. by the Union of Journalists of Albania; Editor NAZMI QAMILI.

Ushtria dhe Koha (Army and Time): Tirana; f. 1993; monthly; publ. by the Ministry of Defence; Editor-in-Chief AGRON MANÇE.

Zeri i Atdheut (The Voice of the Country): Tirana; f. 1992; weekly.

Other Towns

Adriatiku (Adriatic): Durrës; f. 1967; independent; 2 a week.

Dibra: Dibër; f. 1991; independent; 2 a week.

Egnatia: Berat; f. 1991; independent; 2 a week.

Korçë Demokratike (Democratic Korça): Korça; f. 1992; organ of the Democratic Party of Albania; weekly.

Ore (The Clock): Shkodër; f. 1992; independent; 2 a week.

Universi Rinor (The Youth Universe): Korçë; f. 1991.

Zëri i Vlorës (The Voice of Vlorë): Vlorë; f. 1967; 2 a week; Editor-in-Chief DASHO METODASHAJ.

NEWS AGENCIES

Albanian Telegraphic Agency (ATA): Bulevardi Zhan D'Ark 23, Tirana; tel. (42) 22929; telex 2142; fax (42) 34230; f. 1929; domestic and foreign news; brs in provincial towns and in Kosovo, Yugoslavia; Dir-Gen. FRROK CUPI.

Foreign Bureau

Xinhua (New China) News Agency (People's Republic of China): Rruga Zef Jubani 3, Apt 903, Tirana; tel. (42) 33139; fax (42) 33139; Bureau Chief LI JIYU.

PRESS ASSOCIATIONS

League of Journalists of Albania (Lidhja e Gazetarëve të Shqipërisë): Tirana.

Union of Journalists of Albania (Bashkimi i Gazetarëve të Shqipërisë): Tirana; tel. (42) 28020; f. 1949; Chair. MARASH HAJATI; Sec.-Gen. YMER MINXHOZI.

Publishers

Agjensia Qëndrore e Tregtimit të Librit Artistik dhe Shkencor (Central Agency of the Artistic and Scientific Book Trade): Tirana; tel. and fax (42) 27246.

Bota Sportive: Tirana; f. 1991; sports.

Botime të Akademisë së Shkencave të RSH: Tirana; publishing house of the Albanian Academy of Sciences.

Botime te Universitetit Bujqësor te Tiranës: Kamzë, Tirana; publishing house of the Agricultural University of Tirana.

Botime të Shtëpisë Botuese 8 Nëntori: Tirana; tel. (42) 28064; f. 1972; books on Albania and other countries, political and social sciences, translations of Albanian works into foreign languages, technical and scientific books, illustrated albums, etc.; Dir XHEMAL DINI.

Dituria Publishing House: Rruga Dervish Hima 32, Tirana; tel. and fax (42) 25882; f. 1991; dictionaries, calendars, encyclopaedias, social sciences, biographies, fiction and non-fiction; Gen. Dir PETRIT YMERI.

Dora d'Istria: Tirana; f. 1991.

Fan Noli: Tirana; tel. (42) 42739; f. 1991; Albanian and foreign literature.

Globus: Tirana; f. 1991.

Hasan Tahsini: Tirana; f. 1991; humorous literature.

Qendr e Informacionit për Bujsinë dhe Ushqimin (Information Centre for Agriculture and Food): Rruga d'Istria, Tirana; tel. (42) 26147; f. 1970; publishes various agricultural periodicals; Gen. Dir SALI ÇELA.

Shtëpia Botuese e Librit Shkollor: Tirana; tel. (42) 22331; f. 1967; educational books; Dir SHPËTIM BOZDO.

Shtëpia Botuese 'Libri Universitar': Rruga Dora d'Istria, Tirana; tel. (42) 25659; telex 2211; fax (42) 29268; f. 1988; publishes university textbooks on science, medicine, engineering, geography, history, literature, foreign languages, economics, etc.; Dir MUSTAFA FEZGA.

Shtëpia Botuese e Lidhjes së Shkrimtarëve: Konferenca e Pezës 4, Tirana; tel. (42) 22691; fax (42) 25912; f. 1990; artistic and documentary literature; Dir ZIJA ÇELA.

Shtëpia Botuese Naim Frashëri: Tirana; tel. (42) 27906; f. 1947; fiction, poetry, drama, criticism, children's literature, translations; Dir GAQO BUSHAKA.

Union of Writers and Artists Publishing House: Tirana; f. 1991; fiction, poetry incl. foreign literature and works by the Albanian diaspora.

WRITERS' UNIONS

Independent Union of Writers (Bashkimi i Shkrimtarëve te Pavarur): Tirana; f. 1991; Chair. AGIM SHEHU.

Union of Writers and Artists of Albania (Lidhja e Shkrimtarëve dhe e Artistëve të Shqipërisë): Rruga Konferenca e Pezës 4, Tirana; tel. (42) 29689; f. 1945; 26 brs; 1,750 mems; Chair. BARDHYL LONDO.

Broadcasting and Communications

TELECOMMUNICATIONS

State Department of Posts and Telecommunications: Rruga Myslym Shyri 42, Tirana; tel. (42) 27204; fax (42) 33772; e-mail kote@dshpt.tirana.al; Gen. Dir HYDAJET KOPANI; Man. Dir FREDERIK KOTE.

BROADCASTING

In 1991 state broadcasting was removed from political control and made subordinate to the Parliamentary Commission for the Media.

Radiotelevisioni Shqiptar: Rruga Ismail Qemali 11, Tirana; tel. (42) 28310; fax (42) 27745; f. 1938; Chair. YLLI PANGO; Dir-Gen. ALBERT MINGA.

Radio

Radio Tirana: Rruga Ismail Qemali 11, Tirana; tel. (42) 28310; telex 4158; fax (42) 27745; two channels broadcast 24 hours of internal programmes daily from Tirana; regional stations in Korçë, Gjirokastër, Kukës and Shkodër; in 1991 radio broadcasts in Macedonian began in the area of Korçë; in Gjirokastër, programmes in Greek are broadcast for 45 minutes daily; external service broadcasts for 20 hours daily in eight languages; Gen. Dir MARTIN LEKA; Dir of External Service SADI PETRELA.

Television

Alba Television: International Centre of Culture, QNK, Tirana; private television station; broadcasts suspended Aug. 1997; Dir PAULIN SHKJEZI.

Finance

(cap. = capital; dep. = deposits; res = reserves; m. = million; brs = branches; amounts in lekë)

BANKING

Central Bank

Bank of Albania: Sheshi Skënderbeu 1, Tirana; tel. (42) 22752; telex 2153; fax (42) 23558; f. 1992; res 5,677.5m., dep. 42,786.0m. (Dec. 1995); Gov. SHKELQIM CANI.

State Banks

National Commercial Bank of Albania: Bulevardi Zhan D'Ark, Tirana; tel. (42) 28315; telex 2118; fax (42) 28715; f. 1993, following merger of National Bank of Albania and Commercial Bank of

Albania; cap. 3,552.0m., dep. 25,133.4m. (Dec. 1995); Pres. and Dir-Gen. SPIRO BRUMBULLI; 37 brs.

Rural Commercial Bank: Bulevardi Zhan D'Ark, Tirana; tel. (42) 27080; fax (42) 28331; scheduled for transfer to private ownership.

Savings Bank of Albania: Rruga Deshmoret e 4 Shkurtit 6, Tirana; tel. (42) 23695; telex 2192; fax (42) 30013; f. 1991; 100% state-owned; cap. 250m., res 180.4m., dep. 15,594.3m. (Dec. 1993); Gen. Man. ARTAN SANTO; 37 brs.

Other Banks

Arab-Albanian Islamic Bank: Dëshmorët e Kombit 8, Tirana; tel. (42) 28460; telex 2259; fax (42) 28387; jt venture with National Commercial Bank.

Dardania Bank: Dëshmorët e Kombit 'VEVE' Center, Tirana; tel. (42) 28759; telex 2298; fax (42) 42566; f. 1994; privately-owned.

Italian-Albanian Bank: Tirana; jt venture between the National Commercial Bank and Banca di Roma.

INSURANCE

Insurance Institute of Albania (Instituti i Sigurimeve të Shqipërisë): Rruga Dibres 91, Tirana; tel. (42) 34170; telex 2245; fax (42) 34180; f. 1991; all types of insurance; Gen. Dir QEMAL DISHA; 28 brs.

STOCK EXCHANGE

Albanian Stock Exchange: Sheshi Skënderbeu 1, Tirana; f. 1996.

Trade and Industry

PRIVATIZATION AGENCY

National Agency for Privatization (NAP): Tirana; tel. and fax (42) 27933; govt agency under the control of the Council of Ministers; prepares and proposes the legal framework concerning privatization procedures and implementation; Dir NIKO GLOZHENI.

SUPERVISORY ORGANIZATION

Albkontroll: Rruga Skënderbeu 45, Durrës; tel. (52) 23377; telex 2181; fax (52) 22791; f. 1962; brs throughout Albania; independent control body for inspection of goods for import and export, means of transport, etc.; Gen. Man. STEFAN BOSHKU; 15 brs.

DEVELOPMENT ORGANIZATIONS

Albanian Centre for Foreign Investment Promotion (ACFIP): Bulevardi Zhan D'Ark, Tirana; tel. (42) 28439; fax (42) 42133; govt agency to promote foreign investment in Albania and to provide practical support to foreign investors; Vice-Pres. ARBEN PAPARISTO.

Enterprise Restructuring Agency (Agjensia e Ristrukturimit te Ndermarrjeve): Rruga e Durresit 83, Tirana; tel. (42) 27878; fax (42) 25730; govt agency established to assist state-owned enterprises to become privately owned by offering enterprise sector surveys, strategic plans and consultations; provides technical assistance; Dir ADRIATIK BANKJA.

CHAMBERS OF COMMERCE

Union of Chambers of Commerce and Industry of Albania: Rruga Kavajes 6, Tirana; tel. and fax (42) 22934; f. 1958; Pres. ANTON LEKA.

Durrës Chamber of Commerce: Durrës; f. 1988; promotes trade with southern Italy.

Gjirokastër Chamber of Commerce: Gjirokastër; f. 1988; promotes trade with Greek border area.

Shkodër Chamber of Commerce: Shkodër; promotes trade with Yugoslav border area.

There are also chambers of commerce in Korçë, Kukës, Peshkopi, Pogradec, Sarandë and Vlorë.

UTILITIES

Ministry of Energy and Mining: see section on The Government (ministries).

Electricity

Korporata Elektroenergjetike Shquiptare (KESH): Biloky 'Vasil Shanto', Tirana; tel. (42) 28434; fax (42) 32046; state corpn for the generation, transmission, distribution and export of electrical energy; controlled by the Ministry of Mineral Resources and Energy; scheduled for transfer to private ownership; Chair. BASHKIM QATIPI; Gen. Dir Dr NAKO HOBDARI.

MAJOR COMPANIES

Until 1990 foreign trade was a state monopoly in Albania, and was conducted solely through foreign trade organizations. Since 1990 the foreign trade organizations have no longer been the sole institutions authorized to engage in foreign trade.

Agroeksport: Rruga 'Reshit Collaku' 9, Tirana; tel. (42) 23871; telex 2262; fax (42) 34357; fmrly foreign trade org.; exports tobacco, medicinal herbs; imports rice, edible oil, sugar, flour and other foodstuffs; Gen. Man. MEHMET SHIJAKU.

Agrokoop: Rruga 4 Shkurti 6, Tirana; tel. (42) 23871; telex 2248; fax (42) 34357; fmrly foreign trade org.; specializes in foodstuffs and consumer goods.

Albbaker: Tirana; f. 1992 to aid the reorganization, restoration and development of Albania's copper industry.

Albchrome: Bulquza; state-owned mining and smelting group; Gen. Dir RAMADAN DISHA.

Albkoop: Rruga 4 Shkurti 6, Tirana; tel. (42) 24179; telex 2187; f. 1986; fmrly foreign trade org.; import and export of consumer goods, incl. clothing, textiles, handicrafts, stationery, jewellery; Gen. Man. ISMAIL ÇELA.

Albpetrol: Tirana; Chair. Dr FOTAQ DIAMANTI; Gen.-Dir GJERGJ KERRI.

Alimpeks: Tirana; f. 1991; fmrly foreign trade org.; exports tobacco and foodstuffs; imports raw materials, chemicals, foodstuffs, etc.; Dir MASAR KELLISI.

Arteksportimport: Rruga 4 Shkurti 6, Tirana; tel. (42) 26417; telex 2154; fax (42) 25578; f. 1989; fmrly foreign trade org.; exports handicrafts and light industrial products; imports raw materials for chemical and textile industries; Gen. Man. TEFIK KOKONA.

Dibërimpeks: Peshkopi; f. 1990; former regional foreign trade org.; handles border trade with Yugoslavia and the former Yugoslav republic of Macedonia; minerals and agricultural products.

Durrësimpeks: Rruga Skënderbeu 177, Durrës; tel. (52) 22199; telex 2181; f. 1988; former regional foreign trade org.; handles border trade with southern Italy (Puglia); industrial and agricultural goods; Dir TAQO KOSTA.

Eksimagra: Rruga Gjon Muzaka, Tirana; tel. (42) 23128; telex 2111; f. 1989; fmrly foreign trade org.; exports fresh vegetables and fruit, figs, pheasants, etc.; imports meat, cereals, edible fats, packaging, etc.

Gjirokastërimpeks: Rruga Kombëtare 55, Gjirokastër; tel. 707; f. 1988; former regional foreign trade org.; handles border trade with Greece; industrial and agricultural goods.

Industrialimpeks: Rruga 4 Shkurti 6, Tirana; tel. (42) 26123; telex 2112; fmrly foreign trade org.; exports copper wires, furniture, kitchenware, paper, timber, wooden articles, cement, etc.; imports fabrics, cement, chemicals, paper, cardboard, school and office items, etc.; Gen. Man. FARUK BOROVA.

Korçaimpeks: Blokn Demokracia Pall. 2B, Korçë; tel. and fax (82) 42457; f. 1990; former regional foreign trade org.; handles border trade with Greece.

Kukësimpeks: Kukës; former regional foreign trade org.; handles trade with Yugoslavia and the former Yugoslav republic of Macedonia; Dir ASIM BARUTI.

Makinaimpeks: Rruga 4 Shkurti 6, Tirana; tel. (42) 25220; telex 2128; fmrly foreign trade org.; imports vehicles, factory installations, machinery and parts; exports explosives; Gen. Man. AFRIM BALLKA.

Mandimpeks: Rruga Lek Dukagjini, Tirana; tel. (42) 34508; fmrly foreign trade org.; imports metals, concrete, paints and design materials; exports cement, marble and ceramics.

Mekalb: Rruga e Durrësit 83, Tirana; tel. (42) 25444; telex 2102; fax (42) 34304; f. 1990; fmrly foreign trade org.; imports machine tools, metal products, spare parts for cars and agricultural machinery, food products, etc.; Gen. Dir BASHKIM JUPI.

Minergoimpeks: Rruga Marcel Cachin, Tirana; tel. (42) 22148; telex 2238; f. 1990; fmrly foreign trade org.; exports products of the mining, metallurgical and petroleum industries; imports machinery and equipment, lubricating oils and raw materials; Gen. Man. QAZIM QAZAMI.

Pogradecimpeks: Pogradec; former regional foreign trade org.; handles border trade with the former Yugoslav republic of Macedonia.

Sarandaimpeks: Sarandë; former regional foreign trade org.; handles trade with Corfu and regions of southern Greece.

Transshqip (Transalbania): Rruga 4 Shkurti 6, Tirana; tel. (42) 27429; telex 2131; fax (42) 27605; f. 1960; fmrly foreign trade org.; transport and forwarding of foreign trade goods by sea, road and rail; agents in Durrës, Vlorë and at Albanian border crossings.

Vloraimpeks: Vlorë; former regional foreign trade org.; handles trade and economic co-operation with southern Italy; industrial and agricultural goods.

TRADE UNIONS

Until 1991 independent trade-union activities were prohibited, the official trade unions being represented in every work and production centre. During 1991, however, independent unions were established. The most important of these was the Union of Independent Trade Unions of Albania (UITUA). Other unions were established for workers in various sectors of the economy.

Confederation of Albanian Trade Unions (Konfederata e Sindikatave të Shqipërisë—KSSh): Bulevardi Zhan D'Ark, Tirana; f. 1991 to replace the official Central Council of Albanian Trade Unions (f. 1945); includes 17 trade union federations representing workers in different sectors of the economy; Chair. of Man. Council KASTRIOT MUÇO.

Union of Independent Trade Unions of Albania (Bashkimi i Sindikatave të Pavarura të Shqipërisë–BSPSh): Tirana; f. 1991; Chair. VALER XHEKA.

Other Trade Unions

Agricultural Trade Union Federation (Federata Sindikale e Bujqesise): Tirana; f. 1991; Leaders ALFRED GJOMO, NAZMI QOKU.

Autonomous Union of Public-Service Workers: Tirana; f. 1992; Chair. MINELLA KURETA.

Free and Independent Miners' Union (Sindikata e Lire dhe e Pavarur e Minatoreve): Tirana; f. 1991; Chair. GEZIM KALAJA.

Independent Trade Union Federation of Workers in the Artistic Articles, Handicrafts, Glassware and Ceramics Industries: Tirana; f. 1991.

Independent Trade Union Federation of the Food Industry: Tirana; f. 1991.

Independent Trade Union of Dock Workers: Durrës; f. 1992.

Independent Trade Union of Radio and Television: Tirana; f. 1991; represents interests of media workers.

Trade Union of Army and Police Civilians: Tirana; f. 1994.

Trade Union Federation of Education and Science Workers: Tirana; f. 1991; represents teachers and academics.

Trade Union Federation of Health Workers: Tirana; Chair. MINELLA MANO.

Union of Oil Industry Workers: seceded from the Confederation of Albanian Trade Unions in 1991; represents workers in the petroleum and natural gas industry; Chair. MENPOR XHEMALI.

Transport

RAILWAYS

In 1994 there were approximately 720 km of railway track, with lines linking Tirana–Vlorë–Durrës, Durrës–Kavajë–Rrogozhinë–Elbasan–Librazhd–Prenjas–Pogradec, Rrogozhinë–Lushnjë–Fier–Ballsh, Milot–Rrëshen, Vlorë–Laç–Lezhë–Shkodër and Selenicë–Vlorë. There are also standard-gauge lines between Fier and Selenicë and between Fier and Vlorë. A 50-km international freight link between Shkodër and Titograd (now Podgorica), Montenegro (Yugoslavia), opened in September 1986.

Albanian Railways: Durrës; tel. (52) 22311; telex 4250; fax (52) 22037; Gen. Dir FERDINAND XHAFERRI; Deputy Gen. Dirs ALEKSANDËR SHELDIA, PETRAQ PANO.

ROADS

In 1996 the road network comprised an estimated 18,000 km of classified roads, including 3,225 km of main roads and 4,300 km of secondary roads; about 30% of the total network was paved in 1995. All regions are linked by the road network, but many roads in mountainous districts are unsuitable for motor transport. Private cars were banned in Albania until 1991, but many have since been imported (estimated at over 120,000 by the end of 1993). A three-year public investment plan, which was initiated in 1995, included substantial funds for the rehabilitation of the road network; the principal projects were the creation of east–west (Durrës–Kapshtice) and north–south highways.

SHIPPING

At December 1996 Albania's merchant fleet had 33 vessels, with a total displacement of 43,356 grt. The chief ports are those in Durrës, Vlorë, Sarandë and Shëngjin. In 1996 the port of Himare, which was closed in 1991, was reopened. Ferry services have been established between Durrës and three Italian ports (Trieste, Bari and Ancona) and between Sarandë and the Greek island of Corfu. There is also a service between Vlorë and Brindisi (Italy).

Adetare Shipping Agency Ltd: Durrës; tel. (52) 23883; telex 4133; fax (52) 23666.

Albanian State Shipping Enterprise: Porti Detar, Durrës; tel. (52) 22233; telex 4148; fax (52) 229111.

CIVIL AVIATION

There is a small international airport at Rinas, 25 km from Tirana. Reconstruction of the airport, funded by a German business consortium, began in 1996. In 1995 some 200,000 passengers were expected to use the airport. There is no regular internal air service.

Albanian Airlines Mak: Rruga Durresit 202, Tirana; tel. (42) 27606; fax (42) 39414; f. 1992 as Albanian Airlines, a jt venture between the Albanian state-owned air agency, Albtransport, and the Austrian airline, Tyrolean Airways; acquired in 1995 by the Kuwaiti co, Aviation World Mak, and assumed present name; scheduled services to Germany, Italy and Turkey; Commercial Man. HANS MOOK.

Arberia Airways: Tirana; f. 1992.

Tourism

In 1994 there were 28,439 international tourist arrivals at hotels and similar establishments in Albania, compared with 45,192 in the previous year. In 1993 receipts from tourism totalled about US $8m., but in 1994 the total declined to $5m. The main tourist centres include Tirana, Durrës, Sarandë, Shkodër and Pogradec. The Roman amphitheatre at Durrës is one of the largest in Europe. The ancient towns of Apollonia and Butrint are important archaeological sites and there are many other towns of historic interest. However, expansion of the tourist industry has as yet been limited by the inadequacy of Albania's infrastructure and a lack of foreign investment in the development of new facilities.

Albturist: Bulevardi Zhan D'Ark 8, Tirana; tel. (42) 27958; telex 2148; fax (42) 34295; brs in main towns and all tourist centres; 28 hotels throughout the country; Dir-Gen. BESNIK PELLUMBI.

Committee for Development and Tourism: Tirana; govt body.

ALGERIA

Introductory Survey

Location, Climate, Language, Religion, Flag, Capital

The Democratic and People's Republic of Algeria lies in north Africa, with the Mediterranean Sea to the north, Mali and Niger to the south, Tunisia and Libya to the east, and Morocco and Mauritania to the west. The climate on the Mediterranean coast is temperate, becoming more extreme in the Atlas mountains immediately to the south. Further south is part of the Sahara, a hot and arid desert. Temperatures in Algiers, on the coast, are generally between 9°C (48°F) and 29°C (84°F), while in the interior they may exceed 50°C (122°F). Arabic is the official language but French is still widely used. There is a substantial Berber-speaking minority. Islam is the state religion, and almost all Algerians are Muslims. The national flag (proportions 3 by 2) has two equal vertical stripes, of green and white, with a red crescent moon and a five-pointed red star superimposed in the centre. The capital is Algiers (el-Djezaïr).

Recent History

Algeria was conquered by French forces in the 1830s and annexed by France in 1842. For most of the colonial period, official policy was to colonize the territory with French settlers, and many French citizens became permanent residents. Unlike most of France's overseas possessions, Algeria was not formally a colony but was 'attached' to metropolitan France. However, political and economic power within Algeria was largely held by the white settler minority, as the indigenous Muslim majority did not have equal rights.

On 1 November 1954 the principal Algerian nationalist movement, the Front de libération nationale (FLN), began a war for national independence, in the course of which about 1m. Muslims were killed or wounded. Despite resistance from the Europeans in Algeria, the French Government agreed to a cease-fire in March 1962 and independence was declared on 3 July 1962. In August the Algerian provisional Government transferred its functions to the Political Bureau of the FLN, and in September a National Constituent Assembly was elected (from a single list of FLN candidates) and the Republic proclaimed. A new Government was formed, with Ahmed Ben Bella, founder of the FLN, as Prime Minister. As a result of the nationalist victory, about 1m. French settlers emigrated from Algeria.

A draft Constitution, providing for a presidential regime with the FLN as the sole party, was adopted by the Constituent Assembly in August 1963. In September the Constitution was approved by popular referendum and Ben Bella was elected President. Under his leadership, economic reconstruction was begun and the foundation was laid for a single-party socialist state. However, the failure of the FLN to function as an active political force left real power with the bureaucracy and the army. In June 1965 the Minister of Defence, Col Houari Boumedienne, deposed Ben Bella in a bloodless coup and took control of the State as President of a Council of the Revolution, which was composed of 26 members, chiefly army officers.

Boumedienne encountered considerable opposition from left-wing members of the FLN, but by 1971 the Government was confident enough to adopt a more active social policy. French petroleum interests were nationalized and an agrarian reform programme was initiated. In mid-1975 Boumedienne announced a series of measures to consolidate the regime and enhance his personal power, including the drafting of a National Charter and a new Constitution, and the holding of elections for a President and National People's Assembly. Following public discussion of the National Charter, which formulated the principles and plans for creating a socialist system and maintaining Islam as the state religion, a referendum was held in June 1976, at which the Charter was adopted by 98.5% of the electorate. In November a new Constitution (incorporating the principles of the Charter) was approved by another referendum, and in December Boumedienne was elected President unopposed, winning more than 99% of the votes cast. The new formal structure of power was completed in February 1977 by the election of FLN members to the National People's Assembly.

In December 1978 President Boumedienne died, and the Council of the Revolution (now comprising only eight members) took over the Government. An FLN Congress in January 1979 adopted a new party structure, electing a Central Committee, which was envisaged as the highest policy-making body both of the party and of the nation as a whole: this Committee was to choose a party Secretary-General, who would automatically become the sole presidential candidate. The Committee was also to elect an FLN Political Bureau (nominated by the Secretary-General). The Committee's choice of Col Ben Djedid Chadli, commander of Oran military district, as presidential candidate was endorsed by a national referendum in February, and was regarded as a compromise between liberal and radical aspirants. Unlike Boumedienne, Chadli appointed a Prime Minister, Col Muhammad Abd al-Ghani (who also retained his post as Minister of the Interior), anticipating constitutional changes that were approved by the National People's Assembly in June and which included the obligatory appointment of a Prime Minister. In June 1980 the FLN authorized Chadli to form a smaller Political Bureau, with more limited responsibilities, thereby increasing the power of the President. Membership of the National People's Assembly was increased to 281 for the legislative elections of March 1982, when the electorate was offered a choice of three candidates per seat.

At a presidential election, held in January 1984, Chadli's candidature was endorsed by 95.4% of the electorate. Immediately after his re-election, Chadli reorganized the Government, and appointed a new Prime Minister, Abd al-Hamid Brahimi. In 1985 Chadli initiated a public debate on Boumedienne's National Charter, and this resulted in the adoption of a new National Charter at a special FLN Congress in December. The revised Charter, which envisaged a state ideology based on the twin principles of socialism and Islam, and encouraged the development of the private sector, was approved by a referendum in January 1986. The number of seats in the National People's Assembly was increased to 295, all candidates being nominated by the FLN, for a general election in February 1987. In July of that year the National People's Assembly adopted legislation to permit the formation of local organizations without prior government approval: a ban remained, however, on associations that were deemed to oppose the policies of the Charter or to threaten national security.

In 1987, in response to a decline in the price of petroleum and an increase in Algeria's external debt, the Government introduced austerity measures and began to remove state controls from various sectors of the economy. In December President Chadli announced a series of administrative reforms, designed to improve the efficiency of Algeria's bureaucratic procedures.

During the 1980s the Government incurred criticism from a number of different groups. In 1985 22 Berber cultural and human rights activists were imprisoned after being convicted of belonging to illegal organizations, while 18 alleged supporters of the former President Ben Bella were also detained. In 1986 riots occurred at Constantine and Sétif, following protests by students against inadequate facilities. In 1987 several leading members of an Islamist fundamentalist group were killed by the security forces, and some 200 other members of the group were given prison sentences. From mid-1988 severe unemployment, high prices, and shortages of essential supplies (resulting from the Government's economic austerity measures) provoked a series of strikes, and in early October rioting erupted in Algiers, spreading to Oran and Annaba: a six-day state of emergency was imposed, and (according to official sources) 159 people were killed during confrontations with government forces, while more than 3,500 were arrested. In response to the unrest, Chadli proposed constitutional amendments that would allow non-FLN candidates to participate in elections, and make the Prime Minister answerable to the National People's Assembly, rather than to the President. In November these reforms were approved by a referendum. In the same month Chadli appointed Col Kasdi Merbah, hitherto the Minister of Health, as Prime Minister, and a new Council of Ministers (of whom fewer than one-half had previously held government office) was formed. Also in November, Chadli relinquished the post of Secretary-General of the FLN. In December he was elected President for a third term of office, obtaining 81% of the votes cast.

In February 1989 a new Constitution, signifying the end of the one-party socialist state, was approved by referendum. The formation of political associations outside the FLN was henceforth to be permitted, while the armed forces were no longer allocated a role in the development of socialism. The executive, legislative and judicial functions of the State were separated and subjected to the supervision of a Constitutional Council. In July legislation permitting the formation of political parties became effective (although parties were still required to be licensed by the Government): by mid-1991 a total of 47 political parties had been registered, including an Islamist fundamentalist party, the Front islamique du salut (FIS), the Mouvement pour la démocratie en Algérie (MDA), which had been founded by Ben Bella in 1984, the Parti d'avant-garde socialiste (renamed Ettahaddi in 1993), the Parti social-démocrate and the Berber Rassemblement pour la culture et la démocratie (RCD). Other legislation that was adopted in July 1989 further reduced state control of the economy, allowed the expansion of investment by foreign companies, and ended the state monopoly of the press (while leaving the principal newspapers under the control of the FLN). Despite these changes, strikes and riots continued during 1989, in protest at alleged official corruption and the Government's failure to improve living conditions. In September Chadli again appointed a new Prime Minister, Mouloud Hamrouche (hitherto a senior official in the presidential office), who made extensive changes to the Council of Ministers. A programme of economic liberalization was announced by the new Government. Municipal and provincial elections, scheduled to take place in December, were postponed until the following June, to allow the newly-registered parties time to organize. A new electoral law, adopted in March 1990, introduced a system of partial proportional representation for local elections.

In early 1990 widespread strikes and demonstrations occurred, some of which were attributable to the increasing influence of Islamist fundamentalism. At the local elections, held in June, the principal Islamist party, the FIS, received some 55% of total votes cast, while the FLN obtained about 32%. In July, following disagreement within the FLN concerning the pace of economic and political reform, the Prime Minister and four other ministers resigned from the party's Political Bureau. In the same month the Council of Ministers was reorganized, and the defence portfolio was separated from the presidency for the first time since 1965. Also in July, Chadli acceded to the demands of the FIS for an early general election, announcing that it was to take place in early 1991. In August 1990 a general amnesty permitted the release of thousands of 'political' prisoners, and in September the former President, Ben Bella, was allowed to return from exile.

In December 1990 the National People's Assembly adopted a law providing that, after 1997, Arabic would be Algeria's only official language and that the use of French and Berber in schools and in official transactions would be punished by substantial fines. In response, more than 100,000 people demonstrated in Algiers against political and religious intolerance.

In March 1991 the Union Générale des Travailleurs Algériens (UGTA), although affiliated to the FLN, organized a two-day general strike, the country's first since independence, in protest against recent price rises. The Government reacted by announcing increases in subsidies and other benefits. In April President Chadli announced that Algeria's first multi-party general election would take place in late June. The FIS argued that a presidential election should be held simultaneously with, or shortly after, the general election, and in May organized an indefinite general strike and held demonstrations, demanding the resignation of President Chadli and changes in the electoral laws. The violent confrontations that occurred in June between Islamist activists and the security forces resulted in between 20 and 50 fatalities. In response, President Chadli declared a state of emergency and postponed the general election. He also announced that he had accepted the resignation of the Prime Minister and his Government. The former Minister of Foreign Affairs, Sid-Ahmad Ghozali, was appointed Prime Minister. Following a further week of unrest, the FLN and the FIS reached a compromise, according to which the strike was abandoned and legislative and presidential elections were to be held before the end of 1991. In mid-June Ghozali appointed a new Council of Ministers, consisting mainly of political independents. In late June, following further violent incidents between Islamists and the security forces, President Chadli resigned from his post as Chairman of the FLN. In early July army units arrested about 700 Islamists and occupied the headquarters of the FIS. Among those arrested were the President of the FIS, Abbasi Madani, who had earlier threatened to launch a jihad ('holy war') if the state of emergency were not ended, and the party's Vice-President, Ali Belhadj; the two men were charged with armed conspiracy against the State. In late September the state of emergency was revoked.

In October 1991, following the National People's Assembly's decision to enact a revised electoral law, President Chadli announced that the multi-party general election would take place in December. The revisions that were made to the electoral system included an increase in the number of seats in the Assembly, from 295 to 430, and a lowering of the minimum age for electoral candidates from 35 years to 28 years. On 26 December, in the first round of voting in the general election, at which 231 of the 430 seats in the National People's Assembly were won outright, the FIS gained 188 seats (with 47.5% of the votes cast), the Front des forces socialistes (FFS) won 25 seats, the FLN just 15, and independents three. The FLN alleged that there had been widespread intimidation and electoral malpractice on the part of the FIS. A second round of voting, in the 199 remaining constituencies where no candidate had obtained an absolute majority, was scheduled for 16 January 1992. On 4 January the National People's Assembly was dissolved by presidential decree, and on 11 January President Chadli resigned. On the following day the High Security Council, comprising the Prime Minister, three generals and two senior ministers, cancelled the second round of voting, and on 14 January a five-member High Council of State (HCS) was appointed to act as a collegiate presidency until the expiry of Chadli's term of office in December 1993, at the latest. The most influential figure in the HCS was believed to be Maj.-Gen. Khaled Nezzar, the Minister of Defence, but its Chairman was Muhammad Boudiaf, a veteran of the war of independence who had been in exile since 1964. The other members of the HCS were Ali Haroun (the Minister of Human Rights), Sheikh Tejini Haddam (the Rector of the Grand Mosque in Paris) and Ali Kafi (President of the war veterans' association, the Organisation nationale des moudjahidine—ONM); Ghozali was not included, although he remained Prime Minister. The constitutional legality of the HCS was disputed by all the political parties, including the FLN. The 188 FIS deputies who had been elected in December 1991 formed a 'shadow' Assembly and demanded a return to legality.

Amid sporadic outbreaks of violence, the security forces took control of the FIS offices in early February 1992. The HCS declared a 12-month state of emergency, detention centres were opened in the Sahara, and the FIS claimed that 150 people had been killed, and as many as 30,000 detained, since the military-sponsored take-over. In March the FIS was officially dissolved by the Government.

In April 1992 Boudiaf, as Chairman of the HCS, announced the creation of a National Human Rights' Monitoring Centre (to replace the Ministry of Human Rights) and a 60-member National Consultative Council (NCC), which was to meet each month in the building of the suspended Assembly, although it enjoyed no legislative powers. In the same month the trial of Maj.-Gen. Mustafa Beloucif, a former senior defence ministry official accused of embezzlement, was regarded as evidence of a genuine desire on Boudiaf's part to eradicate corruption. In June Boudiaf proposed the establishment of a National Patriotic Rally, with committees in every village and workplace, to prepare for genuine multi-party democracy, and promised a constitutional review, the dissolution of the FLN and a presidential election. Moreover, he ordered the release of 2,000 FIS detainees, despite the fact that the security forces continued to be the target of frequent attack.

On 27 June 1992 the FIS leaders, Madani and Belhadj, were brought before a military tribunal in Blida, accused of conspiracy against the State, but, following the withdrawal of the defence lawyers from the court, the trial was adjourned until July. On 29 June Boudiaf was assassinated while making a speech in Annaba. The HCS ordered an immediate inquiry into the assassination, for which the FIS denied all responsibility. Ali Kafi succeeded Boudiaf as Chairman of the HCS, and Redha Malek, the Chairman of the NCC, was appointed as a new member of the HCS. In June 1995 Lt Lembarek Boumâarafi was sentenced to death for Boudiaf's assassination. However, the trial revealed little new information, and some observers remained sceptical about the authorities' insistence that Boumâarafi had acted alone.

On 8 July 1992 Ghozali resigned in order to enable Kafi to appoint his own Prime Minister. He was replaced by Belaid Abd es-Salam, who, for almost 20 years after independence, had directed Algeria's petroleum and gas policy. In mid-July Abd es-Salam appointed a new Council of Ministers.

In late July 1992 Madani and Belhadj were sentenced to 12 years' imprisonment. Violent protest demonstrations erupted in Algiers and quickly spread to other cities. In mid-August Ali Kafi appealed for a multi-party dialogue to be held in September, in an attempt to end civil strife. However, the Government attracted widespread criticism for reinforcing its emergency powers to repress any person or organization whose activities were deemed to represent a threat to stability. On 26 August there was a bomb explosion at Algiers airport, in which nine people were killed and many injured. The FIS denied any involvement in the incident. Political manoeuvring and attempts at reconciliation continued against a background of escalating violence throughout the country. In early December the Government imposed a curfew in the capital and in the six neighbouring departments.

In February 1993 the state of emergency was renewed for an indefinite period. Nevertheless, there was subsequently an assassination attempt against Maj.-Gen. Nezzar, followed by a series of attacks on other senior government officials. In May large demonstrations, organized principally by the UGTA, took place in Algiers, Constantine and Oran, to protest against terrorism and to demand that there be no negotiation with its perpetrators. In June the HCS appealed for a 'general mobilization' against terrorism, but in the same month Abd es-Salam expressed his willingness to open a dialogue with the militants. Meanwhile, violence continued unabated and several prominent officials were assassinated in July. Moreover, in what appeared to be a change of tactics, terrorist attacks were increasingly targeted against intellectual and civilian figures.

In March 1993 Kafi had met representatives of the ONM and the FLN to discuss, *inter alia*, possible formulae for a transitional period and the amendment of the Constitution. In June the HCS announced that it would dissolve itself at the end of December, and that a modern democracy and free market economy would be created within three years of that date.

In July 1993 Liamine Zéroual (a retired general) replaced Maj.-Gen. Nezzar as Minister of Defence, although Nezzar retained his position within the HCS. In August Redha Malek, while also retaining his post within the HCS, was appointed to replace Abd es-Salam as Prime Minister; the economic policies of the latter had shown no indication of benefiting the country. On the same day, Kasdi Merbah, the former Prime Minister and now leader of the Mouvement algérien pour la justice et le développement, was assassinated, together with several of his staff. In September Malek appointed a new Council of Ministers. He stated that the resolute stance against terrorism would be maintained, and rejected the possibility of dialogue with its perpetrators. In the following month Maj.-Gen. Nezzar announced that he would be withdrawing from political life following the expiry of the mandate of the HCS. Also in October, the HCS appointed an eight-member National Dialogue Commission (NDC), which included three generals and which was charged with the preparation of a political conference to organize the gradual transition to an elected and democratic form of government. In mid-December it was announced that the HCS would not be disbanded until a new presidential body had been elected at the NDC conference in January 1994. However, all the main political parties (with the exception of the moderate Islamist party, Hamas) boycotted the conference. Liamine Zéroual was subsequently appointed as Head of State for a three-year term by the HCS, on the apparent recommendation of an eight-man High Security Council (composed mainly of senior army officers), and inaugurated on 31 January. Plans for a three-year transitional period, leading to a presidential election, and for the appointment of a National Transition Council were approved by the NDC. Zéroual retained the defence portfolio, and the Council of Ministers remained unchanged. In February Ali Djeddi and Abdelkader Boukhamkham, representing the second tier in the FIS leadership, were released from prison, and rumours circulated that divisions had occurred within the military as a result of high-ranking members of the regime, including President Zéroual, making contact with imprisoned Islamist leaders in an attempt to establish dialogue with them. Redha Malek, who was known to be opposed to any compromise with the Islamist militants, resigned as Prime Minister on 11 April; Mokdad Sifi, the erstwhile Minister of Equipment, was appointed in his place. Only 12 ministers retained their portfolios in the new Council of Ministers, announced in mid-April, and the majority of new officials appointed were technocrats or senior civil servants. In May, in an apparent attempt to strengthen his authority, Zéroual carried out a number of major changes to high-ranking military posts, including the appointment of Maj.-Gen. Ahmed Gaïd, who was believed to be one of the President's close associates, as Commander of the Land Force. In the same month the President inaugurated the National Transition Council (NTC), an interim legislature of 200 appointed members, the aim of which was to provide a forum for debate pending legislative elections. Most of the 21 parties that agreed to participate in the NTC were virtually unknown except for Hamas, and the 22 seats that were allocated to major parties remained vacant. Also in May, a group of six 'independent national figures', including former President Ahmed Ben Bella, was commissioned by Zéroual to promote dialogue with the Islamist militants and other opposition groups.

In August 1994 members of the FLN, the Parti du renouveau algérien (PRA), the MDA, Nahdah and Hamas engaged in national dialogue with the Government; the meetings were boycotted, however, by Ettahaddi, the FFS and the RCD. At further negotiations, held in early September, discussion focused on two letters sent to the President by Abbasi Madani, which allegedly offered a 'truce'. Madani and Belhadj were released from prison in mid-September and placed under house arrest; three other leading Islamists were also freed. The Secretary of State for National Solidarity and the Family, Leila Aslaoui, resigned in protest at their release. However, the FIS did not participate in the next round of national dialogue later that month, declaring that negotiations could take place only after the granting of a general amnesty, the rehabilitation of the FIS and the repeal of the state of emergency. The radical Groupe islamique armé (GIA) threatened reprisals if the FIS entered into dialogue with the regime, and intensified its campaign of violence against secular society. The militant group warned children and teachers not to attend school, and continued to destroy educational institutions. In addition to the upheaval caused by Islamist terrorism, the Berber RCD urged a boycott of the start of the school year, and in September a general strike was staged by Berber activists in the Kabyle, in protest at the exclusion of the Berber language, Tamazight, from the syllabus and at the prospect of the FIS's entering the national dialogue. In May 1995 the RCD welcomed the establishment of a government body to oversee the teaching of Tamazight in schools and universities (commencing in October) and to promote its use in the official media. The Mouvement culturel berbère, however, appealed for the continuation of the school boycott and continued to demand that Tamazight be recognized as an official language.

In October 1994 President Zéroual announced that a presidential election would be held before the end of 1995. The announcement was welcomed by many, but others questioned the purpose of any elections if the FIS were not included in the political process. In November representatives from most of the major Algerian parties, including the FIS, attended a two-day conference in Rome, Italy, organized by the Sant' Egidio Catholic community to foster discussion about the crisis in Algeria. The Sant' Egidio pact, endorsed by all the participants at a meeting in Rome in January 1995, rejected the use of violence to achieve or maintain power, and urged the Algerian regime to repeal the state of emergency and thereby facilitate negotiations between all parties. In April Zéroual resumed bilateral discussions with the legalized opposition parties in preparation for the presidential election. Talks with the FLN and the FFS quickly collapsed, however, as they rejected the prospect of participating in an election in which the FIS were excluded. In May the Government issued an electoral decree (promulgated by the NTC in mid-July), stipulating that presidential candidates would be required to obtain the endorsement of 75,000 signatures from at least 25 provinces in order to qualify. There was speculation that the Government was still engaged in dialogue with the FIS leaders, who had once again reportedly been placed under house arrest (in March) and reimprisoned in June. The prospect of a *rapprochement* between the Government and the FIS appeared imminent when, in early July, the anti-Islamist Minister of the Interior, Abderrahmane Cherif, was dismissed from his post and replaced by a technocrat, Mustapha Benmansour. However, shortly afterwards Zéroual reaffirmed his commitment to ending Islamist terrorist activity by military means. In mid-July a co-founder of the FIS and prominent opposition spokesman in France, Sheikh Sahraoui, was assassinated in a mosque in Paris. The FIS blamed the Algerian security forces for the murder, although some analysts considered it more likely to have been perpetrated by the GIA, angered by the dialogue between the Government and the FIS. The incident coincided with Zéroual's announcement that dialogue with the FIS had failed.

In August 1995 President Zéroual declared that the presidential election would take place on 16 November. As many as 40 people subsequently presented themselves as candidates for the presidency, although in October it was announced that only four had succeeded in attaining the required number of signatures: President Zéroual; Saïd Saadi, Secretary-General of the RCD; Nourreddine Boukrouh, leader of the PRA; and Sheikh Mahfoud Nahnah, leader of Hamas. Redha Malek (the former Prime Minister), who had established an anti-Islamist political party (the Alliance national républicaine) earlier in the year, failed to qualify as a presidential candidate. The FLN, the FFS and the FIS, meanwhile, urged voters to boycott the election. Notwithstanding their appeal, 75.7% of the electorate voted at the election, which was monitored by observers from the Organization of African Unity (OAU), the Arab League and the UN. President Zéroual won 61.0% of the valid votes cast, followed by Sheikh Mahfoud Nahnah (25.6%), Saïd Saadi (9.6%) and Nourreddine Boukrouh (3.8%). Despite initial suggestions that the election had not been conducted fairly, most opposition parties subsequently accepted the legitimacy of President Zéroual's victory. Zéroual was inaugurated on 27 November. On the same day a high-ranking military official was shot and killed in a suburb of Algiers. Shortly afterwards, despite this assassination, the Government announced the closure of the last of seven detention centres (all of which had opened since February 1992), thereby releasing as many as 650 prisoners, many of whom were Islamist sympathizers. In late December Ahmed Ouyahia, a career diplomat, replaced Mokdad Sifi as Prime Minister. In early January 1996 Ouyahia appointed a new Government, which included two members of Hamas and a dissident leader of the FIS. Notably, Muhammad Dembri was replaced as Minister of Foreign Affairs by Ahmed Attaf (hitherto Secretary of State for Co-operation and Maghreb Affairs).

In January 1996 the FLN elected Boualem Benhamouda as its new Secretary-General, in place of Abd al-Hamid Mehiri, whose leadership had been questioned following his appeal for a boycott of the November 1995 presidential election. On his appointment, Benhamouda strove to distance the FLN from the Sant' Egidio pact, and in February he announced that the party was prepared to enter into dialogue with the Government. In the following month, although internal divisions in the FFS had resulted in the restructuring of the party, Hocine Aït Ahmad was re-elected as its leader. In April, in an attempt to foster national reconciliation, President Zéroual held bilateral discussions with more than 50 influential individuals, including leaders of trade unions, opposition parties and organizations. Notably, the FIS was not invited to participate. In the following month Zéroual announced his intention to hold legislative elections in early 1997. In addition, he proposed that a referendum be held on constitutional reform, prior to the elections. Recommended amendments to the Constitution included measures increasing the powers of the President, while limiting his tenure to a maximum of two consecutive mandates, creating a second parliamentary chamber, to be known as the Council of the Nation (one-third of whose members would be chosen by the President), establishing a State Council and a High State Court, and, significantly, banning political parties that were based on religion, language, gender or regional differences. It was also suggested that the electoral law be revised to allow for a system of full proportional representation. Several opposition parties reiterated their plea that the Government resume negotiations with the FIS, and argued that constitutional reform should be undertaken only after legislative elections. A government-sponsored conference on national concord, held in mid-September (following inconclusive bilateral discussions in July), was attended by some 1,000 delegates, including representatives of the FLN, Nahdah and Hamas; however, the conference was boycotted by the FFS, the RCD, Ettahaddi and the MDA. Owing to their lack of support, Zéroual subsequently withdrew his offer to include members of opposition parties in an expanded Council of Ministers and NTC. The constitutional amendments were duly approved by referendum on 28 November. According to official sources, some 79.8% of the electorate participated in the referendum, of whom 85.8% voted in favour of the changes; however, a number of opposition parties disputed the results, claiming that the Government had manipulated the figures concerning the rate of participation and the votes cast in favour. The constitutional amendments were promulgated in December.

In mid-February 1997 President Zéroual announced that elections to the National People's Assembly would take place in late May or early June. Shortly afterwards the NTC adopted restrictive legislation concerning political parties in accordance with the amended Constitution (see above). The new electoral law, replacing the majority system with proportional representation, was also adopted. Later in February Abdelkader Bensalah, the President of the NTC, formed a new centrist grouping, the Rassemblement national démocratique (RND), which was originally to have been led by Adb al-Hak Benhamouda (see below). The RND received support from a wide range of organizations, including trade unions, anti-Islamist groups and the influential ONM, and was closely linked with President Zéroual and the Government. In the following months several more political parties emerged, while certain existing parties changed their names to comply with the new legislation. Notably, Hamas became the Mouvement de la société pour la paix (MSP).

In April 1997 representatives of Algeria's principal opposition parties (including the FIS) attended a conference in Madrid, Spain, convened by Spanish non-governmental organizations, to discuss the situation in Algeria. During the conference the FIS strongly condemned the massacre of civilians by the GIA and it appealed to the Algerian Government to initiate dialogue with the banned opposition.

Some 39 political parties contested the elections to the National People's Assembly on 5 June 1997. The FIS and Ettahaddi appealed for a boycott of the elections, while the MDA was banned from participating after failing to comply with the new legislation concerning political parties. (Later in June the MDA and several small political groupings were formally dissolved by the Government as they had not conformed with this legislation.) As the preliminary results of the elections began to emerge, opposition leaders complained of irregularities during the electoral process, and accused officials of manipulating the results in favour of the RND. International observers were critical of the conduct of the elections and commented that the rate of voter participation (officially estimated at 65.5% of the electorate) seemed unrealistically high. According to the final official results, announced by the Constitutional Council, the RND won 156 of the Assembly's 380 seats, followed by the MSP (69), the FLN (62), Nahdah (34), the FFS (20), the RCD (19), and other small political groupings and independent candidates. In mid-June President Zéroual asked Ahmed Ouyahia (who had tendered his resignation following the election) to form a new Government. Later in the month Ouyahia announced a new Council of Ministers, comprising members of the RND, the FLN and the MSP. Meanwhile, the newly-formed National People's Assembly convened for the first time in mid-June.

In July 1997 Abdelkader Hachani, a high-ranking member of the FIS, was formally sentenced to five years' imprisonment and three years' deprivation of his civil rights; Hachani was released immediately as he had been in custody for five years. Shortly afterwards Abbasi Madani was conditionally released following a hearing at a military tribunal. The release of the two leaders was widely interpreted as a conciliatory gesture by the Government towards the Islamist opposition. In late August Kofi Annan, the UN Secretary-General, angered the Algerian Government by suggesting that the UN might consider some form of intervention in Algeria in order to stem the violence, which had escalated dramatically. In early September Madani responded by writing Annan an open letter offering to appeal for an immediate truce. Shortly afterwards Madani was once again confined to house arrest. (Annan subsequently announced tha the UN would not be considering intervention in Algeria.) In late September the Armée islamique du salut (AIS, the armed wing of the FIS) declared a cease-fire, effective from 1 October, in an attempt to expose members of the GIA as the principal perpetrators of the recent civilian massacres. The GIA admitted responsibility for the massacres, which it insisted were 'God's work'. The FIS appealed to the Government to respond to the AIS truce by offering a general amnesty, repealing the state of emergency and holding a national conference on reconciliation.

Elections to regional and municipal authorities in Algeria took place on 23 October 1997. According to official results, the RND won more than one-half of the seats contested, followed by the FLN (20.8%), the MSP (10.3%), and other smaller parties. All the main opposition parties, including the FLN and the MSP, accused the authorities of manipulating the results in favour of the RND and disputed the reported high rate of voter participation, which was officially estimated at some 66.2% of the electorate. In the following weeks several thousand people demonstrated in Algiers to protest against the alleged electoral fraud. In late December the Government announced the appointment of the Council of the Nation. Of the Council's 96 seats indirectly elected by regional and municipal authorities, 80 were won by the RND, followed by the FLN (10), the FFS (4) and the MSP (2); President Zéroual appointed the remaining 48 members. The RND thus became the dominant party in both parliamentary chambers.

In mid-1994 it was reported that about 490 death sentences had been imposed and a total of 26 official executions carried out since the institution in February 1993 of three special courts to try suspects accused of terrorist offences. (The courts were abolished in February 1995, however, following strong criticism of alleged cases of abuse of human rights.) It remained unclear whether the FIS actively supported the GIA (the most prominent and radical Islamic militant group) in its attacks on members of the security forces, local government and the judiciary, as well as prominent public figures, intellectuals, journalists and ordinary civilians. In March 1994 an attack by Islamist militants on the high-security Tazoult prison, near Batna, resulted in the release of more than 1,000 political prisoners. Certain towns and entire neighbourhoods in some cities were virtually controlled by Islamist militants, and the increasing number of murders of foreign nationals (60 killings, the majority carried out by the GIA, in the year to September 1994) led several countries to advise their citizens to leave. In response to the rise in violence, the security forces intensified their campaign against the armed Islamist groups, resorting to air attacks, punitive raids, torture and psychological warfare. Thousands of militants were killed during 1994, including the GIA leader in February and his successor in September. In October the human rights organization Amnesty International condemned the Algerian security forces for the widespread use of torture and the systematic killing of suspected Islamist militants as an alternative to arrest.

The violence continued unabated in 1995 and 1996, and both the Islamist militants and the security forces appeared determined to match the other in the intensity of their attacks. The GIA claimed responsibility for a car-bomb explosion in Algiers in late January 1995, in which 42 people were killed and more than 280 injured. In the following month the security forces shot and killed 96 prisoners (18 of whom were Islamists) during an alleged mass escape attempt at Serkadji prison in Algiers. In March another car-bomb attack left 63 people injured in a suburb of Algiers; in the same month the security forces claimed to have killed as many as 1,300 Islamists in a week-long campaign in the Ain Defla, Jijel and Médéa regions. In the months preceding the presidential election the GIA intensified its campaign of violence: between May and November car-bomb attacks occurred at regular intervals throughout Algeria, resulting in nearly 100 deaths and injuring many more. In September Boubaker Belkaïd, a former Minister of the Interior, became the third high-ranking civil servant to be assassinated by Islamist militants since early 1992. Also in September 13 presumed GIA members were tried in Brussels, Belgium, on a number of charges associated with the armed struggle in Algeria. Seven of the accused received prison sentences ranging from three months to five years. The spate of car-bomb attacks intensified during late 1995 and early 1996, and in February the Government imposed harsh censorship measures on the media in an attempt to suppress reports on the extent of the violence. There was an escalation of violent attacks in mid-1996. Meanwhile, internal divisions in the GIA led to the expulsion of its leader, Djamel Zitouni, in July. Zitouni, who had controlled the GIA since October 1994, was assassinated shortly afterwards, most probably by rivals in the GIA. In August, in an attempt to restore order to the capital, President Zéroual took the unprecedented step of promoting the Governor of Algiers to the rank of minister with extraordinary functions. None the less, in the same month Islamist militants launched a series of ambushes in which as many as 80 civilians were brutally killed. Many more died as a result of isolated armed attacks and bomb explosions. The security forces, meanwhile, became increasingly aggressive in their attempts to eliminate the armed opposition. In late January 1997 the Secretary-General of the UGTA, Abd al-Hak Benhamouda (who had recently announced his intention to establish a centrist political party), was shot dead in Algiers. Although an Islamist group claimed responsibility for the assassination, there was speculation that it may have been perpetrated by opponents within the regime. The level of violence continued unabated during the following months, with civilians increasingly becoming the target of attacks by armed Islamists. There were numerous massacres in villages to the south and west of Algiers, resulting in the deaths of hundreds of civilians and the kidnapping of many young women for 'temporary marriage'. The security forces appeared unable or unwilling to prevent the bloodshed; on several occasions the military failed to assist the local population during massacres in the vicinity of army barracks. An estimated 300 civilians were killed in late August during a massacre in the Blida region; in mid-September another 200 died during an attack on a suburb of Algiers. The leader of the AIS subsequently declared a cease-fire effective from 1 October (see above); however, the GIA continued to target the civilian population. In late October Saïd Bey, the head of the first military region around Algiers (the site of some of the worst attacks on civilians in the previous months) was replaced by Rabeh Boughaba, who had been actively involved in the negotiations that led to the AIS truce. Meanwhile, the security forces intensified their offensives against Islamist bases. It was widely accepted that by late 1997 as many as 75,000 people, victims of political violence, had been killed since February 1992. In January 1998, following a dramatic increase in the massacre of civilians, the European Union (EU) sent a ministerial-level delegation to Algeria to investigate the security situation.

During the late 1970s and early 1980s the protracted struggle in Western Sahara embittered Algeria's relations with France, which supported the claims of Morocco. Algeria also criticized French military intervention elsewhere in Africa, while further grievances were the trade imbalance in favour of the former colonial power, and recurrent disputes over the price of Algerian exports of gas to France; the French Government's determination to reduce the number of Algerians residing in France was another source of contention. In 1986 the French Government co-operated with the Algerian Government by expelling 13 members of the MDA, and in 1986–88 it suppressed three MDA newspapers that were being published in France. In 1987 the Algerian Government agreed to release the assets of former French settlers, which had been 'frozen' since independence, and to allow former settlers to sell their land to the Algerian State; in return, financial assistance was provided by France. The Algerian army's coup in January 1992 was welcomed by the French Government, which was rumoured to have been consulted beforehand. French economic and political support for the Algerian Government increased in early 1993, following the appointment of Edouard Balladur as Prime Minister of France. Alleged Islamist militants residing in France continued to be prosecuted, and in August 1994, following the killing of five French embassy employees in Algiers, 26 suspected Algerian extremists were interned in northern France; 20 of them were subsequently expelled to Burkina Faso. In September the French embassy in Algiers confirmed that entry visas would be issued to Algerians only in exceptional cases. By November, when the number of French nationals killed by Islamist militants in Algeria had reached 21, the French Government was urging its citizens to evacuate Algeria. An Air France aircraft was hijacked in Algiers in December by members of the GIA, resulting in the deaths of three passengers and, later, in the killing of the hijackers by French security forces when the aircraft landed in Marseilles, France. In retaliation, the GIA 'declared war' on France.

In early 1995 French police made a series of arrests across France in an attempt to dismantle support networks for Islamist militants in Algeria and Tunisia; however, this did not prevent the GIA from embarking on a ruthless campaign of violence in France in the following months. The GIA claimed responsibility for numerous bomb attacks across France between July and November, in which seven people were killed and more than 160 injured. The French authorities made a number of arrests and, in a widely-publicized attempted arrest, shot and killed an Algerian-born French resident, whom they alleged to be a leading figure in the bombing campaign. French authorities sought extradition orders for further suspects in Sweden and

Britain. In November the French authorities arrested several alleged Islamist militants in France and seized explosive devices, reportedly foiling an imminent bomb attack in Lille. Meanwhile, British police arrested two Algerian nationals suspected of involvement in the French bomb attacks. In mid-October relations between Algeria and France deteriorated following President Zéroual's cancellation of a meeting with the French President, Jacques Chirac, which was scheduled to take place later in the month at the UN headquarters in New York. Zéroual allegedly decided to cancel the meeting because of France's 'malevolent' attitude towards Algeria; however, President Chirac countered that the meeting had merely been 'postponed' after he had rejected Zéroual's request for the event to receive extensive coverage in the mass media. Relations between the two countries improved in December, when Philippe Séguin, the President of the French National Assembly, held talks with Zéroual in Algiers, and in January 1996, when Ahmed Attaf made his first official visit to France in his capacity as Algeria's Minister of Foreign Affairs. French nationals in Algeria continued to be the target of attacks by Islamist militants, and in March seven French clergymen were abducted by the GIA, who threatened their execution if Islamist detainees in France were not released. The clergymen were killed in May, despite apparent efforts by the French Ministry of Foreign Affairs to negotiate their release. In late July Hervé de Charette, the French Minister of Foreign Affairs, made an official visit to Algeria, the first ministerial-level visit for three years. However, the success of the visit was marred by the assassination in early August of Pierre Claverie, the French Roman Catholic Bishop of Oran, only hours after meeting de Charette. Moreover, in early December four people were killed and at least 45 were injured as a result of a bomb explosion on a passenger train in Paris, prompting speculation that the GIA had resumed its campaign of violence in France. The French authorities subsequently arrested numerous suspected Islamist activists.

Relations with Spain were affected during the early 1980s by Spain's support for Morocco in the Western Sahara dispute, and by mutual suspicion that each country was harbouring opponents of the other's Government. In 1987 Algeria and Spain concluded an agreement allowing closer supervision of Algerian dissidents in Spain and of members of Euskadi ta Askatasuna (ETA, the Basque separatist movement) in Algeria; later in that year, an MDA activist was expelled from Spain, and in early 1989 Algeria expelled 16 ETA members.

During the 1980s Algeria attempted to achieve a closer relationship with the other countries of the Maghreb (Libya, Mauritania, Morocco and Tunisia). In March 1983 Algeria and Tunisia signed the Maghreb Fraternity and Co-operation Treaty, establishing a basis for the creation of the long-discussed 'Great Arab Maghreb'; Mauritania signed the treaty in December. Relations with Morocco, however, continued to be affected by the dispute over Western Sahara. In May 1988 Algeria and Morocco re-established diplomatic relations at ambassadorial level (relations had been severed in 1976). In June 1988 the five Heads of State of the Maghreb countries met in Algiers, and announced the formation of a Maghreb commission, to examine areas of regional integration. In February 1989 the five leaders signed a treaty establishing the Union of the Arab Maghreb (UAM, see p. 263), with the aim of encouraging economic co-operation and eventually establishing a full customs union.

The Algerian army's intervention in January 1992, to prevent an FIS victory in the general election, was welcomed by nearly all Arab Governments (particularly Egypt), with the exception of Sudan. In February the Minister of Foreign Affairs, Lakhdar Brahimi, visited member states of the Gulf Co-operation Council (GCC, see p. 136) to explain the reasons behind the coup and to highlight Algeria's economic plight. Of Algeria's fellow Maghreb countries, Tunisia and Morocco were relieved that the establishment of a neighbouring fundamentalist state had been pre-empted, and diplomatic relations remained cordial.

In March 1993 the Algerian Government severed diplomatic relations with Iran and recalled its ambassador from Sudan, in protest at the alleged complicity of the two countries in terrorist activities in Algeria. In August 1994, however, Algerian–Sudanese relations improved somewhat when the Heads of State of the two countries met for the first time since the incident.

Morocco imposed entry visas on Algerian nationals in August 1994, following the murder of two Spanish tourists in a Moroccan hotel, allegedly by Algerian Islamist extremists. Algeria reciprocated by temporarily closing the border between the two countries and imposing entry visas on Moroccan nationals. Tensions eased slightly in September when Algeria announced the appointment of a new ambassador to Morocco, and in early 1995 Algerian–Moroccan negotiations commenced on the development of bilateral co-operation. However, in December King Hassan of Morocco expressed his disapproval at Algeria's alleged continuing support for the independence of Western Sahara, and he demanded that UAM activities be suspended. A UAM summit meeting, scheduled for later that month, was subsequently postponed. In December 1996 the Ministers of the Interior of Algeria and Morocco held a meeting in Rabat, prompting speculation of a *rapprochement* between the two countries.

In February 1995 the GIA claimed responsibility for an attack on a Tunisian border post, during which six Tunisian border guards were killed. The Tunisian Government initially denied that the incident had actually taken place; however, it later accepted that the guards had been killed, most probably by Islamist militants. Security measures were subsequently increased along the common border.

Relations between Algeria and the USA—which had been strained because of Algeria's objection to the contact, albeit low-level, maintained by the USA with the FIS in case of its future integration into the political system—improved in March 1996, when Robert Pelletreau, the US Assistant Secretary of State, held talks with President Zéroual in Algiers. This constituted the first visit by a senior US official since 1992. In December 1996 Anwar Haddam, the FIS spokesman in the USA, was taken into custody by US immigration officials pending his deportation.

Algeria's relations with Germany (strained by the presence of FIS spokesman Rabah Kebir in Germany) improved in March 1996 when Werner Hoyer, Germany's Secretary of State for Foreign Affairs, visited Algeria. Hoyer was the first senior German official to visit Algeria since 1989. Although Kebir was granted political refugee status in Germany in October 1996, the German authorities strove to demonstrate their intolerance of armed Islamists in the country, and in April they arrested four Algerian nationals (including two sons of Abbasi Madani) and charged them with belonging to a criminal organization and smuggling arms and explosives to Islamist terrorist groups in Algeria. In June 1997 the two men were found guilty of the charges and sentenced to short terms of imprisonment.

In December 1996 Algeria commenced discussions with officials of the EU on Algeria's admission to the Euro-Mediterranean free-trade zone; negotiations were expected to continue until at least 1999.

Government

Under the 1976 Constitution (with modifications adopted by the National People's Assembly in June 1979 and with further amendments approved by popular referendum in November 1988, February 1989 and in November 1996), Algeria is a multi-party state, with parties subject to approval by the Ministry of the Interior. The Head of State is the President of the Republic, who is elected by universal adult suffrage for a five-year term, renewable once. The President presides over a Council of Ministers and a High Security Council. The President must appoint a Prime Minister as Head of Government, who appoints a Council of Ministers. The legislature consists of the National People's Assembly and the Council of the Nation. The members of the National People's Assembly are elected by universal, direct, secret suffrage for a five-year term. Two-thirds of the members of the Council of the Nation are elected by indirect, secret suffrage from regional and municipal authorities; the remainder are appointed by the President of the Republic. The Council's term in office is six years; one-half of its members are replaced every three years. Both the Head of Government and the parliamentary chambers may initiate legislation. Legislation must be deliberated upon respectively by the National People's Assembly and the Council of the Nation before promulgation. The country is divided into 48 departments (*wilayat*), which are, in turn, sub-divided into communes. Each *wilaya* and commune has an elected assembly.

A new electoral law, adopted in March 1990, introduced a system of partial proportional representation for local elections, whereby any list of candidates obtaining more than 50% of the votes would win all the seats. If no party secured the requisite majority, the winning list would be allocated one-half of the seats, the remainder being distributed proportionately among other parties that had received a minimum of 7% of the votes. In April 1991 the National People's Assembly approved further revisions of the electoral law. These stipulated that, for elections to the Assembly, a second round of voting would take place in constituencies where no candidate gained at least 50% of the votes cast in the first round; limited the number of proxy votes to one per person; and raised the number of constituencies from 290 to 542, each of which would elect one representative. In October the National Assembly approved a new electoral law providing for an increase in the number of seats in the Assembly from 295 to 430, the imposition of further limitations on proxy voting, and the lowering of the minimum age for electoral candidates from 35 years to 28 years. In February 1997 the National Transition Council adopted a new electoral law, allowing for a system of full proportional representation. In March a further law was adopted, providing for a bicameral legislature: the National People's Assembly and the Council of the Nation (the new upper chamber), with 380 and 144 members respectively.

Defence

In August 1997 the estimated strength of the armed forces was 124,000 (including 75,000 conscripts), comprising an army of 107,000, a navy of about 7,000 and an air force of 10,000. The 1997 defence budget was estimated at 94,000m. dinars. Military service is compulsory for 18 months, and there are paramilitary forces of 41,200, controlled by the Ministry of the Interior.

Economic Affairs

In 1995, according to estimates by the World Bank, Algeria's gross national product (GNP), measured at average 1993–95 prices, was US $44,609m., equivalent to $1,600 per head. During 1985–95, it was estimated, GNP per head declined, in real terms, at an average annual rate of 2.6%. Over the same period, the population increased by an annual average of 2.5%. Algeria's gross domestic product (GDP) increased, in real terms, by an annual average of 0.2% in 1985–95. Real GDP declined by 1.1% in 1994, but rose by an estimated 4.1% in 1995.

Agriculture (including forestry and fishing) is an important sector of the Algerian economy, employing 23.8% of the country's total labour force in 1996 and providing an estimated 11.3% of GDP in 1995. The principal crops are wheat, barley and potatoes. Olives, citrus fruits and grapes are also grown. During 1985–95 agricultural GDP increased at an average annual rate of 3.0%. Agricultural GDP declined by 11.1% in 1994; however, it increased by 20.0% in 1995.

Industry (including mining, manufacturing, construction and power) contributed an estimated 50.7% of GDP in 1995, and engaged 31.2% of the employed population in 1987. During 1985–95 industrial GDP decreased by an annual average of 0.3%. It declined by 2.0% in 1994, but rose by 2.6% in 1995.

The mining sector engaged only 1.6% of the employed population in 1987, but provides almost all of Algeria's export earnings. The major mineral exports are petroleum and natural gas. In November 1996 a 1,400-km gas pipeline became fully operational, transporting natural gas from Algeria to Spain. Reserves of iron ore, phosphates, lead and zinc are also exploited. In addition, Algeria has deposits of antimony, tungsten, manganese, mercury, copper and salt. The exploitation of gold reserves was expected to commence in the late 1990s. Mining provided an estimated 18.2% of GDP in 1992. In real terms, the GDP of the mining sector declined at an estimated average rate of 2.5% per year during 1985–88, but increased by an annual average of 2.3% in 1988–92.

Manufacturing engaged 12.2% of the employed population in 1987 and provided an estimated 11.5% of GDP in 1995; the most important sectors, measured by gross value of output, are food-processing, machinery and transport equipment, and textiles. During 1985–95 the GDP of the manufacturing sector declined by an annual average of 7.3%. The rate of decline was 4.4% in 1994 and 2.4% in 1995.

Energy is derived principally from natural gas and petroleum. However, nuclear power is exploited as an additional source of energy; the first nuclear reactor was installed in 1989. Imports of fuel and energy comprised only 1.6% of the value of merchandise imports in 1995.

Services engaged 46.0% of the employed labour force in 1987 and provided an estimated 38.0% of GDP in 1995. During 1985–95 the combined GDP of the service sectors increased, in real terms, at an estimated average rate of 0.9% per year. Services GDP rose by 2.5% in 1994 and by 3.3% in 1995.

In 1991 Algeria recorded a visible trade surplus of US $5,468m., and there was a surplus of $2,367m. on the current account of the balance of payments. In 1994 Algeria recorded a trade deficit of $1,005m. In that year the principal source of imports continued to be France (providing 24.8% of the total), while Italy was the principal market for exports (17.9%). Other major trading partners were the USA, Spain and Germany. The principal exports in 1994 were mineral fuels, lubricants, etc., which accounted for 97.1% of total export revenue (petroleum and derivatives 65.0%, gas 31.2%). Other exports included vegetables, tobacco, hides and dates. The principal imports in 1994 were food and live animals, machinery and transport equipment, and basic manufactures.

The 1997 administrative budget envisaged a deficit of 64,700m. dinars. Algeria's total external debt at the end of 1995 amounted to US $32,610m., of which $30,442m. was long-term public debt. The cost of debt-servicing represented 35.5% of export earnings (goods and services) in that year. The annual rate of inflation averaged 18.5% in 1985–95. Consumer prices increased by an average of 29.8% in 1995. An estimated 28% of the labour force were unemployed in 1997.

Algeria is a member of the Union of the Arab Maghreb (see p. 263), which aims to promote economic integration of member states, and also of the Organization of the Petroleum Exporting Countries (OPEC, see p. 227).

Despite the implementation of the 1990–94 Development Plan, which was aimed at liberalizing and diversifying the economy, by 1994 Algeria was experiencing an economic crisis, not least because of its continued dependence on the export of crude petroleum, the international price of which had not recovered to the level recorded in the early 1980s. In April, therefore, the Government came to an agreement with the IMF to implement a stabilization programme, including a 40% currency devaluation and a substantial rise in interest rates, in return for a stand-by credit of US $1,040m. The agreement enabled Algeria to reschedule $5,000m. of its total debt with the 'Paris Club' of official creditors in June; the IMF's approval of another credit in mid-1995 led to the further rescheduling of Algeria's foreign debt with both the 'Paris Club' and the 'London Club' of commercial creditors. Meanwhile, in October 1994 the Government took a first step towards freeing the exchange rate when it announced that in future the value of the dinar would be set by matching available 'hard' currency with demand from commercial banks. In the following year the Government outlined plans to support the medium-term adjustment and structural reform programme: it would liberalize trade and payments, eliminate subsidies on energy products and food, and privatize certain state-owned companies. In September 1997 the Government announced a three-year strategy to address some of the country's most pressing issues, notably the high level of unemployment, the housing shortage and the economy's dependence on the export of hydrocarbons. The plan envisaged the creation of some 1.2m. jobs, the construction of 800,000 new housing units, the restructuring of the financial sector and the substantial increase in non-hydrocarbon exports. It also sought to attract foreign investment in the refinery and petrochemicals sector. It was anticipated that the slow pace of the privatization programme would be accelerated following the announcement in August 1997 that the Daewoo Corporation of the Republic of Korea planned to invest $2,000m. in Algeria over a five-year period, and the Algerian Government's pledge to inaugurate a stock exchange in Algiers before 1998. Severe drought led to a particularly poor harvest of cereals in 1997; however, the increase in cereal imports was offset by higher than expected revenue from the export of hydrocarbons.

Social Welfare

Since 1974 all Algerian citizens have had the right to free medical care. In 1984 there were 9,056 physicians (4.3 per 10,000 population), 2,596 dentists, 1,174 pharmacists and 474 midwifery personnel working in the country. In 1995 the administrative budget allocated 21,280m. dinars (2.9% of total administrative expenditure) to health.

Education

Education, in the national language (Arabic), is officially compulsory for nine years between six and 15 years of age. Primary education begins at the age of six and lasts for six years. Secondary education begins at 12 years of age and lasts for up to six years (comprising two cycles of three years each). In 1994 the total enrolment at primary and secondary schools was equivalent to 84% of the school-age population (89% of boys; 79% of girls). Enrolment at primary schools in that year included an estimated 95% of children in the relevant age-group (99% of boys; 91% of girls). Enrolment at secondary schools in 1994 included 55% of children in the relevant age-group (59% of boys; 52% of girls). Some 12.5% of total planned expenditure in the 1997 administrative budget was allocated to education and training. Priority is being given to teacher-training, to the development of technical and scientific teaching programmes, and to adult literacy and training schemes. In addition to the 10 universities, there are seven other *centres universitaires* and a number of technical colleges. In 1992 a total of 303,111 students were enrolled in higher education. In 1995, according to UNESCO estimates, the average rate of adult illiteracy was 38.4% (males 26.1%; females 51.0%).

Public Holidays

1998: 1 January (New Year), 30 January* (Id al-Fitr, end of Ramadan), 8 April* (Id al-Adha, Feast of the Sacrifice), 28 April* (Islamic New Year), 1 May (Labour Day), 7 May* (Ashoura), 19 June (Ben Bella's Overthrow), 5 July (Independence), 7 July* (Mouloud, Birth of Muhammad), 1 November (Anniversary of the Revolution), 17 November* (Leilat al-Meiraj, Ascension of Muhammad), 20 December* (Ramadan begins).

1999: 1 January (New Year), 19 January* (Id al-Fitr, end of Ramadan), 28 March* (Id al-Adha, Feast of the Sacrifice), 17 April* (Islamic New Year), 26 April* (Ashoura), 1 May (Labour Day), 19 June (Ben Bella's Overthrow), 26 June* (Mouloud, Birth of Muhammad), 5 July (Independence), 1 November (Anniversary of the Revolution), 6 November* (Leilat al-Meiraj, Ascension of Muhammad), 9 December*(Ramadan begins).

* Religious holidays, which are dependent on the Islamic lunar calendar, may differ by one or two days from the dates given.

Weights and Measures

The metric system is in force.

Statistical Survey

Source (unless otherwise stated): Office National des Statistiques, 8 rue des Moussebiline, BP 55, Algiers; tel. (2) 64-77-90; telex 52620.

Area and Population

AREA, POPULATION AND DENSITY

Area (sq km)	2,381,741*
Population (census results)†	
12 February 1977 (provisional)	16,948,000
20 April 1987	23,038,942
Population (official estimates at mid-year)†	
1994	27,561,000
1995	28,548,000
1996	29,168,000
Density (per sq km) at mid-1996	12.2

* 919,595 sq miles.
† Excluding Algerian nationals residing abroad, numbering an estimated 828,000 at 1 January 1978.

POPULATION BY WILAYA (ADMINISTRATIVE DISTRICT)
(provisional census results, April 1987)*

	Population
Adrar	216,931
el-Asnam (ech-Cheliff)	679,717
Laghouat	215,183
Oum el-Bouaghi (Oum el-Bouagul)	402,683
Batna	757,059
Béjaia	697,669
Biskra (Beskra)	429,217
Béchar	183,896
Blida (el-Boulaïda)	704,462
Bouira	525,460
Tamanrasset (Tamenghest)	94,219
Tébessa (Tbessa)	409,317
Tlemcen (Tilimsen)	707,453
Tiaret (Tihert)	574,786
Tizi-Ouzou	931,501
Algiers (el-Djezaïr)	1,687,579
Djelfa (el-Djelfa)	490,240
Jijel	471,319
Sétif (Stif)	997,482
Saida	235,240
Skikda	619,094
Sidi-Bel-Abbès	444,047
Annaba	453,951
Guelma	353,329
Constantine (Qacentina)	662,330
Médéa (Lemdiyya)	650,623
Mostaganem (Mestghanem)	504,124
M'Sila	605,578
Mascara (Mouaskar)	562,806
Ouargla (Wargla)	286,696
Oran (Ouahran)	916,678
el-Bayadh	155,494
Illizi	19,698
Bordj Bou Arreridj	429,009
Boumerdes	646,870
el-Tarf	276,836
Tindouf	16,339
Tissemsilt	227,542
el-Oued	379,512
Khenchela	243,733
Souk-Ahras	298,236
Tipaza	615,140
Mila	511,047
Ain-Defla	536,205
Naama	112,858
Ain-Temouchent	271,454
Ghardaia	215,955
Relizane	545,061
Total	22,971,558

* Excluding Algerian nationals abroad, estimated to total 828,000 at 1 January 1978.

PRINCIPAL TOWNS (estimated population at 1 January 1983)

Algiers (el-Djezaïr, capital)	1,721,607	Tlemcen (Tilimsen)	146,089
Oran (Ouahran)	663,504	Skikda	141,159
Constantine (Qacentina)	448,578	Béjaia	124,122
Annaba	348,322	Batna	122,788
Blida (el-Boulaïda)	191,314	El-Asnam (ech-Cheliff)	118,996
Sétif (Stif)	186,978	Boufarik	112,000*
Sidi-bel-Abbès	146,653	Tizi-Ouzou	100,749
		Médéa (Lemdiyya)	84,292

* 1977 figure.

April 1987 (census results, not including suburbs): Algiers 1,483,000; Oran 590,000; Constantine 438,000.

BIRTHS AND DEATHS (UN estimates, annual averages)

	1980–85	1985–90	1990–95
Birth rate (per 1,000)	40.6	33.9	29.1
Death rate (per 1,000)	10.4	7.8	6.4

Expectation of life (UN estimates, years at birth, 1990–95): 67.1 (males 66.0; females 68.3).

Source: UN, *World Population Prospects: The 1994 Revision.*

1993 (provisional): Registered live births 776,000 (birth rate 28.8 per 1,000); Registered deaths 166,000 (death rate 6.2 per 1,000).

1994 (provisional): Registered live births 776,000 (birth rate 28.2 per 1,000); Registered deaths 180,000 (death rate 6.5 per 1,000).

Note: Figures refer to the Algerian population only and exclude live-born infants dying before registration of birth. Birth registration is estimated to be at least 90% complete, but death registration is incomplete.

ECONOMICALLY ACTIVE POPULATION (1987 census)*

	Males	Females	Total
Agriculture, hunting, forestry and fishing	714,947	9,753	724,699
Mining and quarrying	64,685	3,142	67,825
Manufacturing	471,471	40,632	512,105
Electricity, gas and water	40,196	1,579	41,775
Construction	677,211	12,372	689,586
Trade, restaurants and hotels	376,590	14,399	390,990
Transport, storage and communications	207,314	9,029	216,343
Financing, insurance, real estate and business services	125,426	17,751	143,178
Community, social and personal services	945,560	234,803	1,180,364
Activities not adequately defined	149,241	83,718	232,959
Total employed	3,772,641	427,183	4,199,824
Unemployed	1,076,018	65,260	1,141,278
Total labour force	4,848,659	492,443	5,341,102

* Employment data relate to persons aged 6 years and over; those for unemployment relate to persons aged 16 to 64 years. Estimates have been made independently, so the totals may not be the sum of the component parts.

Mid-1996 (estimates in '000): Agriculture, etc. 2,153; Total labour force 9,041 (Source: FAO, *Production Yearbook*).

Agriculture

PRINCIPAL CROPS ('000 metric tons)

	1994	1995	1996
Wheat	714	1,500	2,800
Barley	234	585	1,690
Oats	15	53	110
Potatoes	716	1,200	1,500
Pulses	38	39	50
Rapeseed*	99	99	100
Olives	170	131	313
Tomatoes	695	859	718
Pumpkins, squash and gourds	100	100*	100*
Cucumbers and gherkins	40	41*	41*
Green chillies and peppers	80	133*	133*
Onions (dry)	248	314	313
Carrots	158	132	129
Other vegetables	424	423	424
Melons and watermelons	401	400*	400*
Grapes	120	159	132
Dates	317	285	361
Apples	49	64	74
Pears	36	37*	37*
Peaches and nectarines	36	45*	45*
Oranges	253	227	237
Tangerines, mandarins, clementines and satsumas	100	78	80
Apricots	43	43*	43*
Other fruits	130	125	124
Tobacco (leaves)	4	3	4

* FAO estimate(s).

Source: FAO, *Production Yearbook*.

LIVESTOCK ('000 head, year ending September)

	1994	1995	1996
Sheep	17,842	17,302	17,565
Goats	2,544	2,780	2,895
Cattle	1,269	1,267	1,228
Horses	67	67*	67*
Mules	81	82*	82*
Asses	226	230*	230*
Camels	114	115*	115*

* FAO estimate.

Poultry (million): 89 in 1994; 90 in 1995; 90 in 1996.

Source: FAO, *Production Yearbook*.

LIVESTOCK PRODUCTS ('000 metric tons)

	1994	1995	1996
Beef and veal	101	101	104
Mutton and lamb	169	170	175
Goat meat*	8	8	9
Poultry meat*	202	202	202
Other meat	9	10	9
Cows' milk*	530	530	530
Sheep's milk*	220	220	220
Goats' milk*	125	125	125
Poultry eggs*	150	150	150
Honey*	2	2	2
Wool:			
greasy*	50	50	50
clean*	26	26	26
Cattle hides*	13	13	13
Sheepskins*	29	26	27
Goatskins*	2	2	2

* FAO estimates.

Source: FAO, *Production Yearbook*.

Forestry

ROUNDWOOD REMOVALS ('000 cubic metres, excluding bark)

	1992	1993*	1994*
Sawlogs, veneer logs and logs for sleepers	46	90	64
Other industrial wood*	252	258	264
Fuel wood*	1,990	2,035	2,081
Total	2,288	2,383	2,409

* FAO estimates.

Sawnwood production ('000 cubic metres, incl. railway sleepers): 13 per year (FAO estimates) in 1980–94.

Source: FAO, *Yearbook of Forest Products*.

Fishing

('000 metric tons, live weight)

	1993	1994	1995
European pilchard (sardine)	67.3*	95.8*	59.0
Other fishes	29.6*	36.0*	44.3
Crustaceans and molluscs	5.0*	3.6*	3.0
Total catch	101.9	135.4	106.2
Inland waters	0.3	0.4	0.3
Mediterranean Sea	101.6	135.0	105.9

* FAO estimate.

Source: FAO, *Yearbook of Fishery Statistics*.

Mining

('000 metric tons, unless otherwise indicated)

	1992	1993	1994
Hard coal*	15	20	20
Crude petroleum	36,333	35,086	35,330
Natural gas (petajoules)	2,038	2,102	1,996
Iron ore:			
gross weight	2,568	2,316	2,016
metal content	1,364	1,250	1,089
Lead ores or concentrates†	1.5	1.5	1.1
Zinc concentrates†	7.5	6.8	5.6
Mercury (metric tons)	469	458	n.a.
Phosphate rock	1,173	717	763
Salt (unrefined)	103	59	75
Gypsum (crude)	48	n.a.	n.a.

* Provisional or estimated data.

† Figures refer to the metal content of ores or concentrates.

Source: UN, *Industrial Commodity Statistics Yearbook* and *Monthly Bulletin of Statistics*.

Industry

SELECTED PRODUCTS ('000 metric tons, unless otherwise indicated)

	1992	1993	1994
Olive oil (crude)	27	22	14
Refined sugar	192	201	193
Wine	50*	65	50
Beer ('000 hectolitres)	337	421	398
Soft drinks ('000 hectolitres)	1,048	1,007	901
Cigarettes (metric tons)	16,426	16,260	16,345
Cotton yarn—pure and mixed	27.0	n.a.	n.a.
Woven cotton fabrics (million metres)	69.7	n.a.	n.a.
Woven woollen fabrics (million metres)	7.9	n.a.	n.a.
Footwear—excl. rubber ('000 pairs)	9,040	7,171	6,467
Nitrogenous fertilizers	88†	79	n.a.
Phosphate fertilizers	154	204	179
Naphthas‡	4,300	4,400	4,500
Motor spirit (petrol)	2,272	2,469	2,907
Kerosene‡	110	129	200
Jet fuel‡	350	350	900
Distillate fuel oils	7,960	7,543	6,896
Residual fuel oils	5,700	5,827	5,810
Lubricating oils‡	130	140	140
Petroleum bitumen (asphalt)‡	230	240	250
Liquefied petroleum gas:			
from natural gas plants	4,530	4,570	4,510
from petroleum refineries	530	430	520
Cement	7,093	6,951	6,093
Pig-iron for steel-making	930	925	919
Crude steel (ingots)	768	798	772
Zinc—unwrought	29.4	29.7	20.1
Refrigerators for household use ('000)	317	183	119
Radio receivers ('000)	238	109	107
Television receivers ('000)	141	157	94
Buses and coaches—assembled (number)	1,008	596	468
Lorries—assembled (number)	2,434	2,304	1,230
Electric energy (million kWh)	18,286	19,415	19,888

* Unofficial figure.

† Production in terms of nitrogen. Source: FAO, *Quarterly Bulletin of Statistics*.

‡ Provisional or estimated data.

Source: mainly UN, *Industrial Commodity Statistics Yearbook*.

1995 ('000 metric tons): Olive oil 15; Wine 50*.
1996 ('000 metric tons): Olive oil 48; Wine 50*.

* FAO estimate.

(Source: FAO, *Production Yearbook*.)

Finance

CURRENCY AND EXCHANGE RATES

Monetary Units

100 centimes = 1 Algerian dinar (AD).

Sterling and Dollar Equivalents (30 September 1997)

£1 sterling = 93.734 dinars;
US $1 = 58.025 dinars;
1,000 Algerian dinars = £10.67 = $17.23.

Average Exchange Rate (dinars per US $)

1994	35.059
1995	47.663
1996	54.749

ADMINISTRATIVE BUDGET (estimates, million AD)

Expenditure	1985	1986	1987*
Presidency	611.8	640.0	585.0
National defence	4,793.1	5,459.0	5,805.0
Foreign affairs	583.5	619.3	583.0
Light industry	137.6	149.5	132.0
Housing and construction	359.4	460.9	439.0
Finance	1,252.4	1,446.1	1,613.0
Home affairs	n.a.	3,543.0	4,003.0
Commerce	130.6	146.8	148.0
Youth and sport	403.6	446.6	396.0
Information	350.8	384.8	373.0
Ex-servicemen	2,984.5	3,289.0	3,192.0
Culture and tourism	218.3	258.2	226.0
Agriculture and fishing	766.0	838.1	772.0
Health	2,720.6	3,518.3	3,961.0
Transport	373.7	414.0	413.0
Justice	477.4	556.4	668.0
Professional training	1,397.9	1,539.8	1,562.0
Religious affairs	363.7	403.1	473.0
Public works	690.8	784.1	697.0
Education	11,026.7	13,626.7	15,886.0
Higher education and scientific research	2,764.4	2,931.6	3,494.0
Heavy industry	94.6	108.3	107.0
Water, environment and forests	798.3	866.0	810.0
Energy and petrochemicals industries	201.5	220.9	216.0
Planning and land development	n.a.	165.9	—
Social protection	476.7	530.1	501.0
Extra expenditure	25,197.5	23,384.4	15,779.0
Total (incl. others)	62,200.0	67,000.0	63,000.0

* As announced in November 1985. A revised administrative budget, announced in April 1986, projected total expenditure of 59,500 million AD.

1988 (million AD): Revenue 103,000; Administrative expenditure 64,500.
1989 (million AD): Revenue 114,700; Administrative expenditure 71,900.
1990 (million AD): Revenue 136,500; Administrative expenditure 84,000.
1991 (million AD): Revenue 195,300; Administrative expenditure 118,300.
1992 (million AD): Revenue 322,700; Administrative expenditure 396,800.
1993 (million AD): Revenue 335,600; Administrative expenditure 503,900.
1994 (million AD): Revenue 474,100; Administrative expenditure 613,700.
1995 (million AD): Revenue 586,500; Administrative expenditure 734,900 (Health 21,280, Education and training 86,800).
1996 (million AD): Revenue 749,200; Administrative expenditure 848,600.
1997 (million AD): Revenue 881,500; Administrative expenditure 946,200 (Education 118,200).

INVESTMENT BUDGET (million AD)

Expenditure	1988
Hydrocarbons	700
Manufacturing industries	1,300
Mines and energy (incl. rural electrification)	1,000
Agriculture and water projects	7,450
Services	135
Economic and administrative infrastructure	8,369
Education and training	7,100
Social and cultural infrastructures	3,294
Construction	2,142
Infrastructure and training linked to the reform of state enterprises	470
Grants to new enterprises	150
Financial restructuring of state enterprises	3,400
Total (incl. others)	47,500

Source: *Al-Moudjahid*.

CENTRAL BANK RESERVES (US $ million at 31 December)

	1994	1995	1996
Gold*	285	290	281
IMF special drawing rights	23	1	5
Foreign exchange	2,651	2,004	4,230
Total	2,959	2,295	4,516

* Valued at SDR 35 per troy ounce.

Source: IMF, *International Financial Statistics*.

MONEY SUPPLY (million AD at 31 December)*

	1993	1994	1995
Currency outside banks	211,310	222,990	249,770
Demand deposits at deposit money banks	188,930	196,450	210,780
Checking deposits at post office	40,980	48,500	53,740
Private sector demand deposits at treasury	5,680	7,890	4,820
Total money (incl. others)	450,320	485,650	520,290

* Figures are rounded to the nearest 10 million dinars.

Source: IMF, *International Financial Statistics.*

COST OF LIVING (Consumer Price Index for Algiers; average of monthly figures; base: 1990 = 100)

	1993	1994	1995
Food	187.8	265.4	347.1
All items (incl. others)	199.8	257.8	334.6

Source: UN, *Monthly Bulletin of Statistics.*

NATIONAL ACCOUNTS

National Income and Product (million AD at current prices)

	1987	1988	1989
Compensation of employees	125,754.4	137,647.5	156,145.1
Operating surplus	92,417.5	99,899.8	142,711.2
Domestic factor incomes	218,171.9	237,547.3	298,856.3
Consumption of fixed capital	32,525.2	32,621.8	33,050.1
Gross domestic product (GDP) at factor cost	250,697.1	270,169.1	331,906.4
Indirect taxes, *less* subsidies	62,009.0	64,437.5	71,553.8
GDP in purchasers' values	312,706.1	334,606.6	403,460.2
Net factor income from abroad	−7,267.7	−11,744.7	−13,178.4
Reinsurance (net)	−76.0	—	—
Gross national product	305,362.4	322,861.9	390,281.8
Less Consumption of fixed capital	32,525.2	32,621.8	33,050.1
National income in market prices	272,837.2	290,240.1	357,231.7
Other current transfers from abroad (net)	2,358.2	2,067.7	3,850.4
National disposable income	275,195.4	292,307.8	361,082.1

Expenditure on the Gross Domestic Product
('000 million AD at current prices)

	1993	1994	1995
Government final consumption expenditure	198.8	247.1	309.8
Private final consumption expenditure	636.4	825.6	1,089.9
Increase in stocks	−9.3	41.7	54.9
Gross fixed capital formation	330.5	426.2	580.0
Total domestic expenditure	1,156.4	1,540.6	2,034.6
Exports of goods and services	261.6	349.4	539.8
Less Imports of goods and services	255.9	418.6	612.7
GDP in purchasers' values	1,162.1	1,471.4	1,961.7

Source: IMF, *International Financial Statistics.*

Gross Domestic Product by Economic Activity
(estimates, million AD at current prices)

	1990	1991	1992
Agriculture, hunting, forestry and fishing	28,393	42,579	59,618
Mining and quarrying	78,603	120,437	172,295
Manufacturing	49,015	75,682	109,106
Electricity, gas and water	9,414	15,192	22,898
Construction	80,800	127,392	187,456
Trade, restaurants and hotels	53,498	82,216	117,957
Transport, storage and communications	28,019	45,877	70,164
Finance, insurance, real estate and business services	20,473	33,248	50,413
Public administration and defence	60,223	94,146	137,351
Other services	7,322	12,011	18,394
GDP at factor cost	415,760	648,779	945,652
Indirect taxes, *less* subsidies	81,240	86,221	93,348
GDP in purchasers' values	497,000	735,000	1,039,000

Source: UN Economic Commission for Africa, *African Statistical Yearbook.*

BALANCE OF PAYMENTS (US $ million)

	1989	1990	1991
Exports of goods f.o.b.	9,534	12,965	12,330
Imports of goods f.o.b.	−8,390	−8,786	−6,862
Trade balance	1,144	4,179	5,468
Exports of services	496	497	393
Imports of services	−1,214	−1,321	−1,163
Balance on goods and services	425	3,355	4,698
Other income received	111	73	70
Other income paid	−2,157	−2,341	−2,618
Balance on goods, services and income	−1,622	1,087	2,151
Current transfers received	603	400	269
Current transfers paid	−62	−67	−53
Current balance	−1,081	1,420	2,367
Direct investment abroad	−8	−5	−50
Direct investment from abroad	12	–	12
Other investment assets	−97	−229	−145
Other investment liabilities	848	−860	−837
Net errors and omissions	−448	−336	−299
Overall balance	−774	−10	1,047

Source: IMF, *International Financial Statistics.*

External Trade

Note: Data exclude military goods. Exports include stores and bunkers for foreign ships and aircraft.

PRINCIPAL COMMODITIES (distribution by SITC, US $ million)

Imports c.i.f.	1992	1993	1994
Food and live animals	2,121.1	2,155.5	2,848.9
Dairy products and birds' eggs	641.6	654.0	540.8
Milk and cream	558.7	569.4	493.7
Cereals and cereal preparations	772.8	904.2	1,324.1
Wheat and meslin (unmilled)	320.9	353.8	602.4
Meal and flour of wheat, etc.	231.8	281.3	323.2
Sugar, sugar preparations and honey	178.3	253.3	298.1
Sugar and honey	177.3	253.3	297.3
Coffee, tea, cocoa and spices	165.8	113.9	336.7
Coffee and coffee substitutes	56.9	105.8	308.2
Crude materials (inedible) except fuels	331.0	386.0	378.6
Animal and vegetable oils, fats and waxes	292.8	184.2	222.9
Fixed vegetable oils and fats	248.9	153.1	188.7
Chemicals and related products	922.3	895.4	1,027.0
Medicinal and pharmaceutical products	442.6	366.7	509.8
Medicaments (incl. veterinary)	406.6	334.7	473.9

Imports c.i.f. — *continued*	1992	1993	1994
Basic manufactures	1,859.6	1,905.6	2,087.4
Rubber manufactures	130.4	180.3	140.8
Non-metallic mineral manufactures	206.5	194.7	246.0
Iron and steel	824.2	740.3	913.6
Bars, rods, angles, shapes and sections	313.2	254.0	418.2
Bars and rods (excl. wire rod)	218.8	161.0	335.9
Tubes, pipes and fittings	271.3	224.8	325.3
Machinery and transport equipment	2,646.6	2,784.1	2,572.2
Power-generating machinery and equipment	199.5	355.6	398.5
Machinery specialized for particular industries	418.0	241.2	232.9
General industrial machinery, equipment and parts	767.0	974.1	739.5
Heating and cooling equipment	190.1	251.4	158.2
Telecommunications and sound equipment	179.0	135.9	134.1
Other electrical machinery, apparatus, etc.	452.0	508.4	507.9
Switchgear, etc., and parts	122.7	164.0	217.3
Road vehicles and parts*	394.1	351.7	348.2
Miscellaneous manufactured articles	306.9	299.9	321.8
Total (incl. others)	8,647.8	8,785.3	9,598.7

* Excluding tyres, engines and electrical parts.

Exports f.o.b.	1992	1993	1994
Mineral fuels, lubricants, etc.	10,759.1	9,679.2	8,342.0
Petroleum, petroleum products, etc.	7,051.9	6,339.7	5,585.5
Crude petroleum oils, etc.	4,806.7	4,448.7	3,924.5
Refined petroleum products	2,161.2	1,828.8	1,617.0
Motor spirit (petrol) and other light oils	691.4	539.8	564.2
Gas oils (distillate fuels)	779.7	677.0	494.1
Residual fuel oils	669.1	587.8	485.2
Gas (natural and manufactured)	3,643.6	3,329.9	2,677.6
Liquefied petroleum gases	2,574.8	2,198.8	1,773.9
Petroleum gases, etc., in the gaseous state	1,068.7	1,131.0	903.7
Total (incl. others)	11,136.8	10,097.7	8,593.8

Source: UN, *International Trade Statistics Yearbook*.

PRINCIPAL TRADING PARTNERS (US $ million)*

Imports c.i.f.	1992	1993	1994
Austria	174.7	172.5	286.6
Belgium-Luxembourg	256.7	164.6	214.7
Brazil	41.0	79.4	126.4
Canada	179.5	120.0	156.5
China, People's Republic	157.1	248.0	383.1
France	2,097.0	2,240.6	2,376.3
Germany	752.2	469.1	517.1
Indonesia	55.2	216.5	240.2
Italy	1,242.4	952.1	931.4
Japan	385.0	375.9	254.0
Morocco	96.9	84.8	120.6
Netherlands	121.1	159.5	109.6
New Zealand	59.1	96.7	76.9
Spain	832.2	926.2	901.3
Switzerland	87.4	69.8	91.8
Tunisia	123.7	122.5	138.5
Turkey	131.0	108.5	250.4
United Kingdom	96.9	119.1	132.0
USA	954.2	1,311.5	1,371.9
Total (incl. others)	8,647.8	8,785.3	9,598.7

Exports f.o.b.	1992	1993	1994
Austria	206.9	67.2	161.2
Belgium-Luxembourg	796.0	627.8	528.5
Brazil	351.0	443.8	195.2
Canada	33.2	158.2	174.1
France	2,037.8	1,688.6	1,326.2
Germany	524.0	504.2	524.8
Italy	2,414.6	2,219.7	1,535.1
Morocco	136.5	70.7	101.3
Netherlands	896.0	784.5	885.0
Portugal	157.8	284.7	285.0
Russia	126.2	126.3	40.0
Singapore	58.1	154.2	59.9
Spain	846.1	679.2	650.2
Tunisia	78.3	62.2	113.1
United Kingdom	377.4	192.4	140.0
USA	1,553.4	1,608.7	1,414.0
Total (incl. others)	11,136.8	10,097.7	8,593.8

* Imports by country of production; exports by country of last consignment.

Source: UN, *International Trade Statistics Yearbook*.

1995 (US $ million): Imports c.i.f. 10,250; Exports f.o.b. 10,240 (source: UN, *Monthly Bulletin of Statistics*).

Transport

RAILWAYS (traffic)

	1990	1991	1992
Passengers carried ('000)	53,664	57,841	58,422
Freight carried ('000 metric tons)	12,357	11,939	11,112
Passenger-km (million)	2,991	3,192	2,904
Freight ton-km (million)	2,690	2,710	2,523

ROAD TRAFFIC (estimates, '000 motor vehicles in use)

	1993	1994	1995
Passenger cars	797	850	871
Commercial vehicles	478	516	566

Source: IRF, *World Road Statistics*.

SHIPPING

Merchant Fleet (registered at 31 December)

	1994	1995	1996
Number of vessels	148	151	151
Total displacement ('000 grt)	935.8	980.5	982.5

Source: Lloyd's Register of Shipping, *World Fleet Statistics*.

International Sea-borne Freight Traffic (estimates, '000 metric tons)

	1991	1992	1993
Goods loaded	59,430	61,577	63,110
Goods unloaded	15,100	15,600	15,700

Source: UN Economic Commission for Africa, *African Statistical Yearbook*.

CIVIL AVIATION (traffic on scheduled services)

	1992	1993	1994
Kilometres flown (million)	27	36	36
Passengers carried ('000)	3,551	3,254	3,241
Passenger-km (million)	3,234	2,901	2,706
Total ton-km (million)	310	296	268

Source: UN, *Statistical Yearbook*.

Tourism

FOREIGN TOURIST ARRIVALS BY COUNTRY OF ORIGIN

	1994	1995	1996
France	38,581	26,349	35,214
Germany	2,416	1,398	1,467
Italy	8,788	2,791	2,541
Libya	11,014	7,698	6,349
Morocco	180,673	4,797	2,067
Spain	2,137	1,621	1,826
Tunisia	56,805	24,207	19,966
Total (incl. others)	336,226	97,650	93,491

Source: Ministère du Tourisme et de l'Artisanat.

Communications Media

	1992	1993	1994
Radio receivers ('000 in use)	6,160	6,310	6,450
Television receivers ('000 in use)	2,000	2,100	2,150
Telephones ('000 main lines in use)	962	1,068	1,122
Telefax stations (number in use)	5,000	5,500	4,140
Mobile cellular telephones (subscribers)	4,781	4,781	1,350
Daily newspapers			
Number	5	n.a.	6
Average circulation ('000 copies)	1,000	n.a.	1,250

Sources: UNESCO, *Statistical Yearbook*, and UN, *Statistical Yearbook*.

Education

(1995/96)

	Institutions	Teachers	Pupils
Primary	17,186	169,010	4,617,000
Middle	2,921	98,187	1,691,561
Secondary	1,033	52,210	853,303

Source: Ministère de l'Education nationale.

Higher education (1992/93): Teachers 19,291; Students 303,111 (Source: UNESCO, *Statistical Yearbook*).

Directory

The Constitution

A new Constitution for the Democratic and People's Republic of Algeria, approved by popular referendum on 19 November 1976, was promulgated on 22 November 1976. The Constitution was amended by the National People's Assembly on 30 June 1979. Further amendments were approved by referendum on 3 November 1988, on 23 February 1989, and on 28 November 1996. The main provisions of the Constitution, as amended, are summarized below:

The preamble recalls that Algeria owes its independence to a war of liberation which led to the creation of a modern sovereign state, guaranteeing social justice, equality and liberty for all. It emphasizes Algeria's Islamic, Arab and Amazigh heritage, and stresses that, as an Arab Mediterranean and African country, it forms an integral part of the Great Arab Maghreb.

FUNDAMENTAL PRINCIPLES OF THE ORGANIZATION OF ALGERIAN SOCIETY

The Republic

Algeria is a popular, democratic state. Islam is the state religion and Arabic is the official national language.

The People

National sovereignty resides in the people and is exercised through its elected representatives. The institutions of the State consolidate national unity and protect the fundamental rights of its citizens. The exploitation of one individual by another is forbidden.

The State

The State is exclusively at the service of the people. Those holding positions of responsibility must live solely on their salaries and may not, directly or by the agency of others, engage in any remunerative activity.

Fundamental Freedoms and the Rights of Man and the Citizen

Fundamental rights and freedoms are guaranteed. All discrimination on grounds of sex, race or belief is forbidden. Law cannot operate retrospectively and a person is presumed innocent until proved guilty. Victims of judicial error shall receive compensation from the State.

The State guarantees the inviolability of the home, of private life and of the person. The State also guarantees the secrecy of correspondence, the freedom of conscience and opinion, freedom of intellectual, artistic and scientific creation, and freedom of expression and assembly.

The State guarantees the right to form political associations (on condition that they are not based on differences in religion, language, race, gender or region), to join a trade union, the right to strike, the right to work, to protection, to security, to health, to leisure, to education, etc. It also guarantees the right to leave the national territory, within the limits set by law.

Duties of Citizens

Every citizen must respect the Constitution, and must protect public property and safeguard national independence. The law sanctions the duty of parents to educate and protect their children, as well as the duty of children to help and support their parents. Every citizen must contribute towards public expenditure through the payment of taxes.

The National Popular Army

The army safeguards national independence and sovereignty.

Principles of Foreign Policy

Algeria subscribes to the principles and objectives of the UN. It advocates international co-operation, the development of friendly relations between states, on the basis of equality and mutual interest, and non-interference in the internal affairs of states.

POWER AND ITS ORGANIZATION

The Executive

The President of the Republic is Head of State, Head of the Armed Forces and responsible for national defence. He must be of Algerian origin, a Muslim and more than 40 years old. He is elected by universal, secret, direct suffrage. His mandate is for five years, and is renewable once. The President embodies the unity of the nation. The President presides over meetings of the Council of Ministers. He decides and conducts foreign policy and appoints the Head of Government, who is responsible to the National People's Assembly. The Head of Government must appoint a Council of Ministers. He drafts, co-ordinates and implements his government's programme, which he must present to the Assembly for ratification. Should the Assembly reject the programme, the Head of Government and the Council of Ministers resign, and the President appoints a new Head of Government. Should the newly-appointed Head of Government's programme be rejected by the Assembly, the President dissolves the Assembly, and a general election is held. Should the President be unable to perform his functions, owing to a long and serious illness, the President of the Council of the Nation assumes the office for a maximum period of 45 days (subject to the approval of a two-thirds majority in the National People's Assembly and the Council of the Nation). If the President is still unable to perform his functions after 45 days, the Presidency is declared vacant by the Constitutional Council. Should the Presidency fall vacant, the President of the Council of the Nation temporarily assumes the office and organizes presidential elections within 60 days. He may not himself be a candidate in the election. The President presides over a High Security Council which advises on all matters affecting national security.

The Legislature

The legislature consists of the National People's Assembly and the Council of the Nation. The members of the National People's Assembly are elected by universal, direct, secret suffrage for a five-year term. Two-thirds of the members of the Council of the Nation are elected by indirect, secret suffrage from regional and municipal authorities; the remainder are appointed by the President of the Republic. The Council's term in office is six years; one-half of its members are replaced every three years. The deputies enjoy parliamentary immunity. The legislature sits for two ordinary sessions per year, each of not less than four months' duration. The commissions of the legislature are in permanent session. The two parliamentary chambers may be summoned to meet for an extraordinary session on the request of the President of the Republic, or of the Head of Government, or of two-thirds of the members of the National People's Assembly. Both the Head of Government and the parliamentary chambers may initiate legislation. Legislation must be deliberated upon respectively by the National People's Assembly and the Council of the Nation before promulgation. Any text passed by the Assembly must be approved by three-quarters of the members of the Council in order to become legislation.

The Judiciary

Judges obey only the law. They defend society and fundamental freedoms. The right of the accused to a defence is guaranteed. The Supreme Court regulates the activities of courts and tribunals, and the State Council regulates the administrative judiciary. The Higher Court of the Magistrature is presided over by the President of the Republic; the Minister of Justice is Vice-President of the Court. All magistrates are answerable to the Higher Court for the manner in which they fulfil their functions. The High State Court is empowered to judge the President of the Republic in cases of high treason, and the Head of Government for crimes and offences.

The Constitutional Council

The Constitutional Council is responsible for ensuring that the Constitution is respected, and that referendums, the election of the President of the Republic and legislative elections are conducted in accordance with the law. The Constitutional Council comprises nine members, of whom three are appointed by the President of the Republic, two elected by the National People's Assembly, two elected by the Council of the Nation, one elected by the Supreme Court and one elected by the State Council. The Council's term in office is six years; the President of the Council is appointed for a six-year term and one-half of the remaining members are replaced every three years.

The High Islamic Council

The High Islamic Council is an advisory body on matters relating to Islam. The Council comprises 15 members and its President is appointed by the President of the Republic.

Constitutional Revision

The Constitution can be revised on the initiative of the President of the Republic (subject to approval by the National People's Assembly and by three-quarters of the members of the Council of the Nation), and must be approved by national referendum. Should the Constitutional Council decide that a draft constitutional amendment does not in any way affect the general principles governing Algerian society, it may permit the President of the Republic to promulgate the amendment directly (without submitting it to referendum) if it has been approved by three-quarters of the members of both parliamentary chambers. Three-quarters of the members of both parliamentary chambers, in a joint sitting, may propose a constitutional amendment to the President of the Republic who may submit it to referendum. The basic principles of the Constitution may not be revised.

The Government

HEAD OF STATE

President and Minister of Defence: LIAMINE ZÉROUAL (appointed 30 January 1994; elected President 16 November 1995).

COUNCIL OF MINISTERS

(December 1997)

A coalition of the Rassemblement national démocratique (RND), the Front de libération nationale (FLN) and the Mouvement de la société pour la paix (MSP).

Prime Minister: AHMED OUYAHIA (RND).

Minister of Foreign Affairs: AHMED ATTAF (RND).

Minister of Justice: MUHAMMAD ADAMI (RND).

Minister of the Interior, Local Communities and the Environment : MUSTAPHA BENMANSOUR (RND).

Minister of Finance: ABDELKRIM HARCHAOUI (RND).

Minister of Energy and Mines: YOUCEF YOUSFI (RND).

Minister of Equipment and of National and Regional Development: ABDERRAHMANE BELAYAT (FLN).

Minister of Industry and Restructuring: ABEDELMAJID MENASRA (MSP).

Minister of War Veterans: SAÏD ABADOU (RND).

Minister of National Education: BOUBEKEUR BENBOUZID (RND).

Minister of Higher Education and Scientific Research: AMAR TOU (FLN).

Minister of Small and Medium-sized Enterprises: BOUGUERRA SOLTANI (MSP).

Minister of Health and Population: YAHIA GUIDOUM (RND).

Minister of Labour, Social Affairs and Vocational Training: HACÈNE LASKRI (RND).

Minister of Agriculture and Fisheries: BOULAHAOUADJEB BENALIA (FLN).

Minister of Tourism and Handicrafts: ABDELKADER BENGRINA (MSP).

Minister of Posts and Telecommunications: MUHAMMAD SALAH YOUYOU (RND).

Minister of Religious Affairs: BOUABDELLAH GHLAMALLAH (RND).

Minister of Housing: ABDELKADER BOUNEKRAF (FLN).

Minister of Transport: SID AHMED BOULIL (MSP).

Minister of Commerce: BAKHTI BELAIB (RND).

Minister of National Solidarity and the Family: RABEA MECHERNENE (RND).

Minister of Youth and Sports: MUHAMMAD AZIZ DEROUAZ (RND).

Minister of Communications and Culture, and Spokesman for the Government: HABIB CHAWKI HAMRAOUI (RND).

Minister of Parliamentary Affairs: MUHAMMAD KECHOUD (RND).

Minister Delegate to the Prime Minister in charge of the governorship of Algiers: CHERIF RAHMANI (RND).

Minister Delegate at the Office of the Prime Minister: AMAR ZEGRAR (RND).

Minister Delegate at the Office of the Prime Minister: ABDELKADER TAFFAR (RND).

Minister Delegate to the Minister of Finance in charge of the Budget: ALI BRAHITI (RND).

Minister Delegate to the Prime Minister in charge of Administrative Reform and the Civil Service: AHMED NOUI (RND).

Minister Delegate to the Minister of Foreign Affairs in charge of Co-operation and Maghreb Affairs: LAHCENE MOUSSAOUI (RND).

Secretary of State in charge of the Algerian Community Abroad: TEDJINI SALAOUANDJI (RND).

Secretary-General of the Government: MAHFOUD LACHEB.

In addition, there are seven Secretaries of State without independent portfolio (three from the MSP, three from the FLN and one from the RND).

MINISTRIES

Office of the President: Présidence de la République, el-Mouradia, Algiers; tel. (2) 69-15-15; telex 66044; fax (2) 69-15-95.

Office of the Prime Minister: rue Docteur Saâdane, Algiers; tel. (2) 73-23-40; telex 66066; fax (2) 71-79-27.

Ministry of Agriculture and Fisheries: 4 route des Quatre Canons, Algiers; tel. (2) 71-17-12; telex 66127; fax (2) 61-57-39.

Ministry of Commerce: rue Docteur Saâdane, Algiers; tel. (2) 73-23-40; telex 55273; fax (2) 73-54-18.

Ministry of Communications and Culture: Palais de la Culture, Les Annassers, Kouba, Algiers; tel. (2) 69-22-01; telex 65666; fax (2) 68-40-41.

Ministry of Defence: Les Tagarins, el-Biar, Algiers; tel. (2) 71-15-15; telex 66424; fax (2) 64-67-26.

Ministry of Energy and Mines: 80 ave Ahmed Ghermoul, Algiers; tel. (2) 67-33-00; telex 65092; fax (2) 65-27-83.

Ministry of Equipment and of National and Regional Development: BP 86, Ex Grand Séminaire, Kouba, Algiers; tel. (2) 58-65-50; telex 62560; fax (2) 58-50-38.

Ministry of Finance: Immeuble Maurétania, place du Pérou, Algiers; tel. (2) 71-13-66; telex 55073; fax (2) 73-42-76.

Ministry of Foreign Affairs: place Mohamed Seddik Benyahia, el-Mouradia, Algiers; tel. (2) 69-23-33; telex 66242; fax (2) 69-21-61.

Ministry of Health and Population: 125 rue Abd ar-Rahmane Laâla, el-Madania, Algiers; tel. (2) 68-29-00; telex 65316; fax (2) 66-24-13.

Ministry of Higher Education and Scientific Research: 11 rue Doudou Mokhtar, Algiers; tel. (2) 91-12-56; telex 61381; fax (2) 91-11-97.

Ministry of Housing: 137 rue Didouche Mourad, Algiers; tel. (2) 74-07-22; telex 66223; fax (2) 74-53-83.

Ministry of Industry and Restructuring: Immeuble le Colisée, 4 rue Ahmed Bey, Algiers; tel. (2) 60-11-44; telex 67947; fax (2) 69-32-35.

Ministry of the Interior, Local Communities and the Environment: 18 rue Docteur Saâdane, Algiers; tel. (2) 73-23-40; telex 66341; fax (2) 73-43-67.

Ministry of Justice: 8 place Bir Hakem, el-Biar, Algiers; tel. (2) 92-41-83; telex 61606; fax (2) 92-25-60.

Ministry of Labour, Social Affairs and Vocational Training: 14 blvd Mohamed Belouizdad, Algiers; tel. (2) 68-33-66; telex 65534; fax (2) 66-28-11.

Ministry of National Education: 8 ave de Pékin, Algiers; tel. (2) 69-20-98; telex 66638; fax (2) 60-67-57.

Ministry of Posts and Telecommunications: 4 blvd Krim Belkacem, Algiers; tel. (2) 71-12-20; telex 52020; fax (2) 71-76-84.

Ministry of Religious Affairs: 4 rue de Timgad, Hydra, Algiers; tel. (2) 60-85-55; telex 66118; fax (2) 60-09-36.

Ministry of Small and Medium-sized Enterprises: Immeuble le Colisée, 4 rue Ahmed Bey, Algiers; tel. (2) 23-97-11; fax (2) 69-72-73.

Ministry of Tourism and Handicrafts: 7 rue des Frères Ziata, el-Mouradia, Algiers; tel. (2) 60-59-60; telex 67758; fax (2) 59-06-64.

Ministry of Transport: 119 rue Didouche Mourad, Algiers; tel. (2) 74-06-99; telex 66137; fax (2) 74-33-95.

Ministry of War Veterans: 2 ave du Lt. Med Benarfa, el-Biar, Algiers; tel. (2) 92-23-55; telex 61370; fax (2) 92-35-16.

Ministry of Youth and Sports: 3 rue Mohamed Belouizdad, Algiers; tel. (2) 66-33-50; telex 65054; fax (2) 68-41-71.

President and Legislature

PRESIDENT

Presidential Election, 16 November 1995

Candidate	Votes	% of votes
LIAMINE ZÉROUAL	7,088,618	61.01
Sheikh MAHFOUD NAHNAH	2,971,974	25.58
SAÏD SAADI	1,115,796	9.60
NOURREDDINE BOUKROUH	443,144	3.81
Total*	11,619,532	100.00

* Excluding 467,749 spoilt votes.

ASSEMBLÉE NATIONALE POPULAIRE

President: ABDELKADER BENSALAH.

General Election, 5 June 1997

	Seats
Rassemblement national démocratique (RND)	156
Mouvement de la société pour la paix (MSP)	69
Front de libération nationale (FLN)	62
Nahdah	34
Front des forces socialistes (FFS)	20
Rassemblement pour la culture et la démocratie (RCD)	19
Independent	11
Parti des travailleurs (PT)	4
Parti républicain progressif (PRP)	3
Union pour la démocratie et les libertés (UDL)	1
Parti social-libéral (PSL)	1
Total	380

Constitutional amendments, approved by national referendum in November 1996, provided for the establishment of a second parliamentary chamber, the Council of the Nation. In late December 1997 two-thirds of the Council's 144 members were indirectly elected by regional and municipal authorities: the RND won 80 seats, followed by the FLN (10), the FFS (4) and the MSP (2). The remaining 48 members were appointed by the President of the Republic.

Political Organizations

Until 1989 the FLN was the only legal party in Algeria. The February 1989 amendments to the Constitution permitted the formation of other political associations, with some restrictions. The right to establish political parties was guaranteed by constitutional amendments in November 1996; however, political associations based on differences in religion, language, race, gender or region were proscribed. Some 39 political parties contested the legislative elections which took place in June 1997. The most important political organizations are listed below.

Alliance centriste et démocrate (ACD): Algiers; f. 1990 as an informal alliance to unite social-democratic and central candidates for electoral purposes; includes:

Association populaire pour l'unité et l'action (APUA): BP 85, Bachdjarah, 116 rue de Tripoli, Hussein-Dey, Algiers; tel. (2) 77-91-05; telex 65645; fax (2) 77-64-64; f. 1990 as a legal party but formally dissolved by Govt in June 1997; Leader AL-MAHDI ABBES ALLALOU.

Front national de renouvellement (FNR): Algiers; Leader ZINEDDINE CHERIFI.

Parti national pour la solidarité et le développement (PNSD): Cité du 5 juillet 11, No. 22, Constantine; Leader MOHAMED CHERIF TALEB.

Parti social-démocrate (PSD): 8 rue des Frères Adder, Algiers; tel. (2) 51-39-13; f. 1989; centre party; advocates economic liberalization; Leader ABDERRAHMANE ABJERID; Sec.-Gen. ABD AL-KADER BOUZAR.

Parti social-libéral (PSL): 52 rue Didouche Mourad, Algiers; tel. (2) 63-12-60; Leader AHMAD KHELIL.

Alliance nationale républicaine: Algiers; f. 1995; anti-Islamist; Leader REDHA MALEK.

Bloc national: rue Boukhachba Bouamama, el-Menéa, Ghardaia; tel. (9) 83-31-10; f. 1990 as Parti d'unité arabe islamique-démocratique (PUAID); adopted current name in 1997; advocates creation of a pan-Arab state under Islamic law; Leader BELHADJ KHALIL HARFI.

El-Oumma (The Community): 2 place el-Qods, Hydra, Algiers; tel. (2) 60-04-65; f. 1990 as a legal party but formally dissolved by Govt in June 1997; advocates the application of Islam in political life; Leader BENYOUSSEF BEN KHEDDA.

Ettahaddi: 67 blvd Krim Belkacem, Algiers; tel. (2) 71-89-92; f. 1993 to replace Parti d'Avant-Garde Socialiste (Communist); Leader HACHÉMI CHERIF.

Front des forces socialistes (FFS): 56 ave Souidani Boudjemaâ, 16000 Algiers; tel. (2) 59-33-13; f. 1963; revived 1990; Leader HOCINE AÏT AHMAD.

Front islamique du salut (FIS): Algiers; f. 1989; aims to emphasize the importance of Islam in political and social life; formally dissolved by the Algiers Court of Appeal in March 1992; Leader ABBASI MADANI.

Front de libération nationale (FLN): 7 rue du Stade, Hydra, Algiers; tel. (2) 59-21-49; telex 53931; f. 1954; sole legal party until 1989; socialist in outlook, the party is organized into a Secretariat, a Political Bureau, a Central Committee, Federations, Kasmas and cells; under the aegis of the FLN are various mass political organizations, including the Union Nationale de la Jeunesse Algérienne (UNJA) and the Union Nationale des Femmes Algériennes (UNFA); Sec.-Gen. BOUALEM BENHAMOUDA.

Mouvement algérien pour la justice et le développement (MAJD): Villa Laibi, Lot. Kapiot No. 5, Bouzaréah, Algiers; tel. (2) 60-58-00; fax (2) 78-78-72; f. 1990; reformist party supporting policies of fmr Pres. Boumedienne; Leader ABD AL-KADER MERBAH.

Mouvement pour la démocratie en Algérie (MDA): 31 rue Didouche Mourad, Algiers; tel. (2) 61-08-78; f. 1990 as a legal party but formally dissolved by Govt in June 1997; Leader AHMAD BEN BELLA; Sec.-Gen. KHALED BENSMAIL.

Mouvement pour la démocratie et la citoyenneté (MDC): Tizi-Ouzou; f. 1997 by dissident members of the FFS; Leader SAÏD KHELIL.

Mouvement de la société pour la paix (MSP): 163 Hassiba Ben Bouali, Algiers; f. as Hamas; adopted current name in 1997; moderate Islamic party, favouring the gradual introduction of an Islamic state; Leader Sheikh MAHFOUD NAHNAH.

Nahdah: Algiers; fundamentalist Islamist group; Leader Sheikh ABDULLAH DJABALLAH.

Parti démocratique progressif (PDR): Algiers; f. 1990 as a legal party; Leader SACI MABROUK.

Parti du renouveau algérien (PRA): 29 rue des Frères Bouatik, el-Biar, Algiers; tel. (2) 56-62-78; Leader NOURREDDINE BOUKROUH.

Parti républicain progressif (PRP): 10 rue Ouahrani Abou-Mediêne, Cité Seddikia, Oran; tel. (5) 35-79-36; f. 1990 as a legal party; Sec.-Gen. SLIMANE CHERIF.

Parti des travailleurs (PT): Algiers; workers' party; Leader LOUISA HANOUNE.

Rassemblement algérien: 22 rue Abri Arezki, Hydra, Algiers; tel. (2) 59-33-43; f. 1990 as Rassemblement arabique-islamique (RAI); adopted current name in 1997; aims to increase the use of Arabic in social and cultural life; Leader ME LAID GRINE.

Rassemblement pour la culture et la démocratie (RCD): 87A rue Didouche Mourad, Algiers; tel. (2) 73-62-01; telex 67256; fax (2) 73-62-20; f. 1989; secular party; advocates recognition of the Berber language, Tamazight, as a national language; Sec.-Gen. SAÏD SAADI.

Rassemblement national démocratique (RND): Algiers; f. 1997; centrist party; Chair. ABDELKADER BENSALAH.

Union pour la démocratie et les libertés (UDL): Algiers; f. 1997; Leader ABDELKRIM SEDDIKI.

Diplomatic Representation

EMBASSIES IN ALGERIA

Angola: 14 rue Marie Curie, el-Biar, Algiers; tel. (2) 92-54-41; telex 61620; fax (2) 79-74-41; Ambassador: JOSÉ CÉSAR AUGUSTO.

Argentina: 26 rue Finaltieri, el-Biar, Algiers; tel. (2) 92-34-23; telex 55260; fax (2) 92-34-43; Ambassador: GERÓNIMO CORTES FUNES.

Austria: rue les Vergers, Villa 136, Bir Mourad Rais, Algiers; tel. (2) 56-26-99; telex 62302; fax (2) 56-73-52; Ambassador: CHRISTIAN BERLAKOVITS.

Belgium: 22 chemin Youcef Tayebi, el-Biar, Algiers; tel. (2) 92-24-46; telex 61365; fax (2) 92-50-36; Ambassador: DIRK LETTENS.

Benin: 36 Lot. du Stade, Birkhadem, Algiers; tel. (2) 56-52-71; telex 62307; Ambassador: LEONARD ADJIN.

Brazil: 10 chemin Laroussi Messaoud Les Glycines, BP 186, Algiers; tel. (2) 74-95-75; telex 67156; fax (2) 74-96-87; Ambassador: SÉRGIO THOMPSON-FLORES.

Bulgaria: 13 blvd Col Bougara, Algiers; tel. (2) 23-00-14; fax (2) 23-05-33; Ambassador: MARIN DIMITROV TODOROV.

Burkina Faso: 10 rue du Vercors, Air de France, el-Hammadia, Algiers; tel. (2) 94-26-77; telex 61200; fax (2) 94-25-35.

Cameroon: 34 rue Yahia Mazouni, 16011 el-Biar, Algiers; tel. (2) 92-11-24; telex 61356; fax (2) 92-11-25; Chargé d'affaires: Dr FRANCIS NGANTCHA.

Canada: BP 225, 16000 Alger-Gare, 27 bis rue des Frères Benhafid, Algiers; tel. (2) 69-16-11; fax (2) 69-39-20; Ambassador: JACQUES NOISEUX.

Chad: Villa No. 18, Cité DNC, chemin Ahmed Kara, Hydra, Algiers; tel. (2) 69-26-62; fax (2) 69-26-63; Ambassador: El-Hadj MAHAMOUD ADJI.

China, People's Republic: 34 blvd des Martyrs, Algiers; tel. (2) 69-27-24; telex 66193; fax (2) 69-29-62; Ambassador: LI QINGYU.

Congo, Democratic Republic: 5 rue Saint Georges, Kouba, Algiers; tel. (2) 59-12-27; telex 62545; Ambassador: IKAKI BOMELE MOLINGO.

Congo, Republic: 111 Parc Ben Omar, Kouba, Algiers; tel. (2) 58-68-00; telex 62433; Ambassador: PIERRE N'GAKA.

Côte d'Ivoire: Immeuble 'Le Bosquet', Le Paradou, BP 710 Hydra, Algiers; tel. (2) 69-23-78; telex 66152; fax (2) 69-36-83; Ambassador: GUSTAVE OUFFOUE-KOUASSI.

Cuba: 22 rue Larbi Alik, Hydra, Algiers; tel. (2) 69-21-48; telex 52963; fax (2) 69-32-81; Ambassador: RAFAEL POLANCO BRAHOJOS.

Czech Republic: BP 258, Villa Koudia, 3 chemin Zyriab, Algiers; tel. (2) 23-00-56; telex 66281; fax (2) 23-01-31; Chargé d'affaires a.i.: JOSEF BUZALKA.

Denmark: 12 ave Emile Marquis, Lot. Djenane el-Malik, 16035 Hydra, BP 384, 16000 Alger-Gare, Algiers; tel. (2) 69-22-34; telex 66270; fax (2) 69-28-46; Ambassador: HERLUF HANSEN.

Egypt: BP 297, 8 chemin Abdel-Kader Gadouche, 16300 Hydra, Algiers; tel. (2) 60-16-73; telex 66058; fax (2) 60-29-52; Ambassador: IBRAHIM YOUSSRI.

Finland: BP 256, 16035 Hydra, Algiers; tel. (2) 69-12-92; telex 66296; fax (2) 69-16-37; Ambassador: JAN GROOP.

France: chemin Abd al-Kader Gadouche, Hydra, Algiers; tel. (2) 69-24-88; telex 66076; fax (2) 69-13-69; Ambassador: ALFRED SIEFER-GAILLARDIN.

Gabon: BP 125, Rostomia, 21 rue Hadj Ahmed Mohamed, Hydra, Algiers; tel. (2) 69-24-00; telex 61282; fax (2) 60-25-46; Ambassador: YVES ONGOLLO.

Germany: BP 664, 165 chemin Sfindja, Algiers; tel. (2) 74-19-56; telex 56043; fax (2) 74-05-21; Ambassador: JOACHIM BROUDRÉ-GRÖGER.

Ghana: 62 rue des Frères Benali Abdellah, Hydra, Algiers; tel. (2) 60-64-44; telex 62234; fax (2) 69-28-56; Ambassador: GEORGE A. O. KUGBLENU.

Greece: 60 blvd Col Bougara, Algiers; tel. (2) 60-08-55; telex 66071; fax (2) 69-16-55; Ambassador: IOANNIS DRAKOULARAKOS.

Guinea: 43 blvd Central Saïd Hamdine, Hydra, Algiers; tel. (2) 60-06-11; telex 66208; fax (2) 60-04-68; Ambassador: MAMADY CONDÉ.

Guinea-Bissau: 17 rue Ahmad Kara, BP 32, Colonne Volrol, Hydra, Algiers; tel. (2) 60-01-51; telex 62210; fax (2) 60-97-25; Ambassador: JOSÉ PEREIRA BATISTA.

Holy See: 1 rue Noureddine Mekiri, 16090 Bologhine, Algiers (Apostolic Nunciature); tel. (2) 69-13-79; fax (2) 59-22-37; Apostolic Nuncio: Most Rev. ANTONIO SOZZO, Titular Archbishop of Concordia.

Hungary: BP 68, 18 ave des Frères Oughlis, el-Mouradia, Algiers; tel. (2) 69-79-75; fax (2) 69-81-86; Chargé d'affaires: Dr LÁSZLÓ MÁRTON.

India: 14 rue des Abassides, el-Biar, 16030 Algiers; tel. (2) 92-34-44; telex 61526; fax (2) 92-40-11; e-mail eoialg.ist.cerist.dz; Ambassador: JAYANT PRASAD.

Indonesia: BP 62, 16 chemin Abdel-Kader Gadouche, 16070 el-Mouradia, Algiers; tel. (2) 69-20-11; telex 67912; fax (2) 69-39-31; Ambassador: LILLAHI GRAHANA SIDHARTA.

Iraq: 4 rue Abri Arezki, Hydra, Algiers; tel. (2) 69-31-25; telex 66098; fax (2) 69-10-97; Ambassador: ABD AL-KARIM AL-MULLA.

Italy: 18 rue Muhammad Ouidir Amellal, el-Biar, Algiers; tel. (2) 92-23-30; telex 61357; fax (2) 79-37-66; Ambassador: ANTONIO BADINI.

Japan: 1 chemin el-Bakri, el-Biar, Algiers; tel. (2) 91-20-04; telex 61389; fax (2) 91-20-46; Ambassador: YOSHIHISA ARA.

Jordan: 6 rue du Chenoua, Algiers; tel. (2) 60-20-31; telex 66089; Ambassador: KHALED ABIDAT.

Korea, Democratic People's Republic: 49 rue Hamlia, Bologhine, Algiers; tel. (2) 62-39-27; telex 61165; Ambassador: PAK HO IL.

Korea, Republic: 12 rue No 1 chemin des Crêtes, Hydra, Algiers; tel. (2) 69-36-20; fax (2) 69-16-03; Chargé d'affaires a.i.: SEE-YOUNG LEE.

Kuwait: chemin Abd al-Kader Gadouche, Hydra, Algiers; tel. (2) 59-31-57; telex 66628; Ambassador: YOUSSEFF ABDULLAH AL-AMIZI.

Lebanon: 9 rue Kaïd Ahmad, el-Biar, Algiers; tel. (2) 78-20-94; telex 61354; Ambassador: SALHAD NASRI.

Libya: 15 chemin Cheikh Bachir Ibrahimi, Algiers; tel. (2) 92-15-02; telex 52700; fax (2) 92-46-87; Ambassador: ABDEL-MOULA EL-GHADHBANE.

Madagascar: 22 rue Abd al-Kader Aouis, 16090 Bologhine, BP 65, Algiers; tel. (2) 95-03-74; fax (2) 95-17-76; Chargé d'affaires: MODESTE RANDRIANARIVONY.

Mali: Villa 15, Cité DNC/ANP, chemin Ahmed Kara, Algiers; tel. (2) 69-13-51; telex 66109; fax (2) 69-20-82; Ambassador: CHEICK S. DIARRA.

Malta: Bureau 24, Niv C, Hotel El Aurassi, Algiers; tel. (2) 63-19-74; telex 66371; Ambassador: ALFRED A. ZARB.

Mauritania: 107 Lot. Baranès, Air de France, Bouzaréah, Algiers; tel. (2) 79-21-39; telex 61455; fax (2) 78-42-74; Ambassador: SID AHMED OULD BABAMINE.

Mexico: BP 329, 21 rue du Commandant Amar Azzouz, el-Biar, Alger-Gare, Algiers; tel. (2) 92-40-23; telex 61641; fax (2) 92-34-51; Ambassador: HÉCTOR E. PÉREZ GALLARDO.

Morocco: 8 rue des Cèdres, el-Mouradia, Algiers; tel. (2) 60-74-08; telex 66159; fax (2) 60-59-00; Ambassador: ABD AL-KRIM SEMMAR.

Netherlands: BP 72, 23 chemin Cheikh Bachir Ibrahimi, el-Biar, Algiers; tel. (2) 92-28-28; telex 61364; fax (2) 92-37-70; Ambassador: CORN. W. A. DE GROOT.

Niger: 54 rue Vercors Rostamia Bouzaréah, Algiers; tel. (2) 78-89-21; telex 61371; fax (2) 78-97-13; Ambassador: GOUROUZA OUMAROU.

Nigeria: BP 629, 27 bis rue Blaise Pascal, Algiers; tel. (2) 69-18-49; telex 61093; fax (2) 69-11-75; Ambassador: ALIYU MOHAMMED.

Oman: 53 rue Djamel Eddine, El Afghani, Bouzaréah, Algiers; tel. (2) 94-13-10; telex 61335; fax (2) 94-13-75; Ambassador: HELLAL AS-SIYABI.

Pakistan: BP 404, 14 ave Souidani Boudjemâa, Algiers; tel. (2) 69-37-81; telex 66277; fax (2) 69-22-12; Ambassador: M. ASLAM RIZVI.

Poland: 37 ave Mustafa Ali Khodja, el-Biar, Algiers; tel. (2) 92-25-53; telex 52562; fax (2) 92-14-35; Ambassador: ANDRZEJ BILIK.

Portugal: 7 rue Mohamed Khoudi, el-Biar, Algiers; tel. (2) 78-48-20; fax (2) 92-54-14; Ambassador: EDUARDO MANUEL FERNANDES.

Qatar: BP 118, 7 chemin Doudou Mokhtar, Algiers; tel. (2) 92-28-56; telex 66342; fax (2) 92-24-15; Ambassador: HOCINE ALI EDDOUSRI.

Romania: 24 rue Abri Arezki, Hydra, Algiers; tel. (2) 60-08-71; telex 66156; fax (2) 69-36-42; Ambassador: EMILIAN MANCIUR.

Russia: 7 chemin du Prince d'Annam, el-Biar, Algiers; tel. (2) 92-31-39; telex 61561; fax (2) 92-28-82; Ambassador: ALEKSANDR ADSENYONOK.

Saudi Arabia: 62 rue Med. Drafini, chemin de la Madeleine, Hydra, Algiers; tel. (2) 60-35-18; telex 61389; Ambassador: HASAN FAQQI.

Senegal: BP 379, Alger-Gare, 1 chemin Mahmoud Drarnine, Hydra, Algiers; tel. (2) 69-16-27; telex 67743; fax (2) 69-26-84; Ambassador: SAÏDOU NOUROU.

Slovakia: BP 84, 7 chemin du Ziryab, Didouche Mourad, 16006 Algiers; tel. (2) 22-01-31; fax (2) 23-00-51; Chargé d'affaires a.i.: TOMÁŠ FELIX.

Spain: 46 bis rue Mohamed Chabane, el-Biar, Algiers; tel. (2) 92-27-13; telex 61266; fax (2) 92-27-19; Ambassador: RICARDO ZALACAIN.

Sudan: 8 Shara Baski Brond, el-Yanabia, Bir Mourad Rais, Algiers; tel. (2) 60-95-35; fax (2) 69-30-19.

Sweden: rue Olof Palme, Nouveau Paradou, Hydra, Algiers; tel. (2) 69-23-00; telex 66046; fax (2) 69-19-17; Ambassador: GÖRAN WIDE.

Switzerland: 27 blvd Zirout Youcef, 16000 Alger-Gare, Algiers; tel. (2) 73-73-10; telex 56042; fax (2) 73-81-58; Ambassador: H. REIMANN.

Syria: Domaine Tamzali, 11 chemin A. Gadouche, Hydra, Algiers; tel. (2) 91-20-26; telex 61368; fax (2) 91-20-30; Ambassador: ABELJABER ALDAHAK.

Tunisia: 11 rue du Bois de Boulogne, el-Mouradia, Algiers; tel. (2) 60-13-88; telex 66164; fax (2) 69-23-16; Ambassador: M'HEDI BACCOUCHE.

Turkey: Villa dar el Ouard, chemin de la Rochelle, blvd Col Bougara, Algiers; tel. (2) 69-12-57; telex 66244; fax (2) 69-31-61; Ambassador: UMIT PAMIR.

United Arab Emirates: BP 454, 19 rue des Frères Benhafid, Hydra, Algiers; tel. (2) 69-25-74; telex 67911; fax (2) 59-37-70; Ambassador: TARIQ AL-HAIDAN.

United Kingdom: BP 43, Résidence Cassiopée, Bâtiment B, 7 chemin des Glycines, 16000 Alger-Gare, Algiers; tel. (2) 23-00-68; telex 66151; fax (2) 23-00-67; Ambassador: FRANÇOIS GORDON.

USA: BP 549, 4 chemin Cheikh Bachir Ibrahimi, 16000 Alger-Gare, Algiers; tel. (2) 60-11-86; telex 66047; fax (2) 60-39-79; e-mail amembalg@ist.cerist.dz; Ambassador: CAMERON HUME.

Venezuela: BP 813, 3 impasse Ahmed Kara, Algiers; tel. (2) 69-38-46; telex 66642; fax (2) 69-35-55; Ambassador: HELIODORO CLAVERIE.

Viet Nam: 30 rue de Chenoua, Hydra, Algiers; tel. (2) 69-27-52; telex 66053; Ambassador: TRAN XUAN MAN.

Yemen: Villa 19, Cité DNC, rue Ahmed Kara, Hydra, Algiers; tel. (2) 69-30-85; telex 66037; fax (2) 69-17-58; Ambassador: GASSEM ASKAR DJEBRANE.

Yugoslavia: BP 366, 7 rue des Frères Benhafid, Hydra, Algiers; tel. (2) 69-12-18; telex 66076; fax (2) 69-34-72; Chargé d'affaires a.i.: DIMITRIJE BABIĆ.

Judicial System

The highest court of justice is the Supreme Court (Cour suprême) in Algiers. Justice is exercised through 183 courts (tribunaux) and 31 appeal courts (cours d'appel), grouped on a regional basis. The Cour des comptes was established in 1979. Algeria adopted a penal code in 1966, retaining the death penalty. In February 1993 three special courts were established to try suspects accused of terrorist offences; however, the courts were abolished in February 1995. Constitutional amendments, introduced in November 1996, provided for the establishment of a High State Court (empowered to judge the President of the Republic in cases of high treason, and the Head of Government for crimes and offences), and a State Council to regulate the administrative judiciary. In addition, a Conflicts Tribunal is to be established to adjudicate in disputes between the Supreme Court and the State Council.

Supreme Court: ave du 11 Décembre 1960, Ben Aknoun, Algiers; fax (2) 92-44-89.

President of Supreme Court: A. NASRI.

Procurator-General: M. DAHMANI.

Religion

ISLAM

Islam is the official religion, and the whole Algerian population, with a few rare exceptions, is Muslim.

Superior Islamic Council: place Cheikh Abd al-Hamid ibn Badis, Algiers.

President of the Superior Islamic Council: AHMAD HAMANI.

CHRISTIANITY

The European inhabitants, and a few Arabs, are generally Christians, mostly Roman Catholics.

The Roman Catholic Church

Algeria comprises one archdiocese and three dioceses (including one directly responsible to the Holy See). In December 1995 there were an estimated 3,200 adherents in the country.

Bishops' Conference: Conférence Episcopale Régionale du Nord de l'Afrique, 13 rue Khélifa-Boukhalfa, 16000 Alger-Gare, Algiers; tel. (2) 74-41-22; fax (2) 73-41-78; f. 1985; Pres. Most Rev. HENRI TEISSIER, Archbishop of Algiers; Sec.-Gen. Fr ROMAN STÄGER.

Archbishop of Algiers: Most Rev. HENRI TEISSIER, Archevêché, 13 rue Khélifa-Boukhalfa, 16000 Alger-Gare, Algiers; tel. (2) 73-41-22; fax (2) 73-41-78.

Protestant Church

Protestant Church of Algeria: 31 rue Reda Houhou, 16000 Alger-Gare, Algiers; tel. and fax (2) 71-62-38; three parishes; 1,500 mems; Pastor Dr HUGH G. JOHNSON.

The Press

DAILIES

L'Authentique: Algiers; French.

Al-Badil: Algiers; relaunched 1990; MDA journal in French and Arabic; circ. 130,000.

Ach-Cha'ab (The People): 1 place Maurice Audin, Algiers; f. 1962; FLN journal in Arabic; Dir KAMEL AVACHE; circ. 24,000.

Al-Djeza'ir El-Youm: Algiers; Arabic; circ. 54,000.

Horizons: 20 rue de la Liberté, Algiers; tel. (2) 73-47-25; telex 66310; fax (2) 73-61-34; f. 1985; evening; French; circ. 35,000.

Al-Joumhouria (The Republic): 6 rue Bensenouci Hamida, Oran; f. 1963; Arabic; Editor BOUKHALFA BENAMEUR; circ. 20,000.

Le Journal: Algiers; f. 1992; French.

El Khabar: Maison de la Presse 'Tahar Djaout', 1 rue Bachir Attar, place du 1er mai, Algiers; tel. (2) 66-12-01; telex 65484; fax (2) 66-19-27; f. 1990; Arabic; Gen. Man. CHERIF REZKI; circ. 200,000.

Liberté: 37 rue Larbi Ben M'Hidi, BP 178, Alger-Gare, Algiers; tel. (2) 69-25-88; fax (2) 69-35-46; French; independent; Dir-Gen. ABROUS OUTOUDERT.

Al-Massa: Maison de la Presse, Abdelkader Safir Kouba, Algiers; tel. (2) 59-54-19; fax (2) 59-64-57; f. 1977; evening; Arabic; circ. 45,000.

Le Matin: Maison de la Presse, 1 rue Bachir Attar, 16016 Algiers; tel. (2) 66-07-08; fax (2) 66-20-97; French.

Al-Moudjahid (The Fighter): 20 rue de la Liberté, Algiers; f. 1965; govt journal in French and Arabic; Dir ZOUBIR ZEMZOUM; circ. 392,000.

An-Nasr (The Victory): BP 388, Zone Industrielle, La Palma, Constantine; tel. (4) 93-92-16; f. 1963; Arabic; Editor ABDALLAH GUETTAT; circ. 340,000.

L'Opinion: Algiers; French.

Le Soir d'Algérie: Algiers; f. 1990; evening; independent information journal in French; Editors ZOUBIR SOUISSI, MAAMAR FARRAH.

La Tribune: Algiers, f. 1994; current affairs journal in French; Editor BAYA GACEMI.

El Watan: Maison de la Presse, 1 rue Bachir Attar, 16016 Algiers; tel. (2) 68-21-83; fax (2) 68-21-87; French; Dir OMAR BELHOUCHET.

WEEKLIES

Algérie Actualité: 2 rue Jacques Cartier, 16000 Algiers; tel. (2) 63-54-20; telex 66475; f. 1965; French; Dir KAMEL BELKACEM; circ. 250,000.

Al-Hadef (The Goal): Constantine; tel. (4) 93-92-16; f. 1972; sports; French; Editor-in-Chief LARBI MOHAMED ABBOUD; circ. 110,000.

La Nation: Algiers; French; Editor SALIMA GHEZALI; circ. 60,000.

Révolution Africaine: 5 place Emir Abdelkader, 16400 Algiers; tel. (2) 64-04-71; telex 56126; fax (2) 61-19-96; current affairs journal in French; socialist; Dir FERRAH ABDELALI; circ. 50,000.

El Wadjh al-Akhar (The Other Face): Algiers; Arabic.

OTHER PERIODICALS

Al-Acala: 4 rue Timgad, Hydra, Algiers; tel. (2) 60-85-55; telex 66118; fax (2) 60-09-36; f. 1970; published by the Ministry of Religious Affairs; fortnightly; Editor MUHAMMAD AL-MAHDI.

Algérie Médicale: 3 blvd Zirout Youcef, Algiers; f. 1964; publ. of Union médicale algérienne; 2 a year; circ. 3,000.

Alouan (Colours): 119 rue Didouche Mourad, Algiers; f. 1973; cultural review; monthly; Arabic.

Bibliographie de l'Algérie: Bibliothèque Nationale d'Algérie, BP 127, Hamma el-Annasser, 16000 Algiers; tel. (2) 67-18-67; fax (2) 67-29-99; f. 1963; lists books, theses, pamphlets and periodicals published in Algeria; 2 a year; Arabic and French; Dir-Gen. MOHAMED AÏSSA OUMOUSSA.

Ach-Cha'ab ath-Thakafi (Cultural People): Algiers; f. 1972; cultural monthly; Arabic.

Ach-Chabab (Youth): Algiers; journal of the UNJA; bi-monthly; French and Arabic.

Al-Djeich (The Army): Office de l'Armée Nationale Populaire, 3 chemin de Gascogne, Algiers; f. 1963; monthly; Algerian army review; Arabic and French; circ. 10,000.

Journal Officiel de la République Algérienne Démocratique et Populaire: Saint-Charles, Les Vergers, Bir Mourad Rais, Algiers; tel. (2) 54-35-06; telex 65180; fax (2) 54-35-12; f. 1962; French and Arabic.

Nouvelles Economiques: 6 blvd Amilcar Cabral, Algiers; f. 1969; publ. of Institut Algérien du Commerce Extérieur; monthly; French and Arabic.

Révolution et Travail: 1 rue Abdelkader Benbarek, place du 1er mai, Algiers; tel. (2) 66-73-53; telex 65051; fax (2) 65-82-21; journal of UGTA (central trade union) with Arabic and French editions; monthly; Editor-in-Chief LAKHDARI MOHAMED LAKHDAR.

Revue Algérienne du Travail: Algiers; f. 1964; labour publication; quarterly; French.

Ath-Thakafa (Culture): BP 96, 2 place Cheikh ben Badis, Algiers; tel. (2) 62-20-73; f. 1971; every 2 months; cultural review; Editor-in-Chief CHEBOUB OTHMANE; circ. 10,000.

NEWS AGENCIES

Algérie Presse Service (APS): 4 rue Zouieche, Kouba, Algiers; tel. (2) 77-79-28; telex 66577; fax (2) 59-77-59; f. 1962.

Foreign Bureaux

Agence France-Presse (AFP): 6 rue Abd al-Karim el-Khettabi, Algiers; tel. (2) 63-62-01; telex 67427; Chief YVES LEERS.

Agencia EFE (Spain): 4 ave Pasteur, 15000 Algiers; tel. (2) 71-85-59; telex 66458; fax (2) 73-77-62; Chief MANUEL OSTOS LÓPEZ.

Agenzia Nazionale Stampa Associata (ANSA) (Italy): 4 ave Pasteur, Algiers; tel. (2) 63-73-14; telex 66467; fax (2) 61-25-84; Rep. CARLO DI RENZO.

Associated Press (AP) (USA): BP 769, 4 ave Pasteur, Algiers; tel. (2) 63-59-41; telex 67365; fax (2) 63-59-42; Rep. RACHID KHIARI.

Bulgarska Telegrafna Agentsia (BTA) (Bulgaria): Algiers; Chief GORAN GOTEV.

Informatsionnoye Telegrafnoye Agentstvo Rossii—Telegrafnoye Agentstvo Suverennykh Stran (ITAR—TASS) (Russia): 21 rue de Boulogne, Algiers; Chief KONSTANTIN DUDAREV.

Reuters (UK): Algiers; tel. (2) 74-70-53; telex 67756; fax (2) 74-53-75.

Rossiyskoye Informatsionnoye Agentstvo—Novosti (RIA—Novosti) (Russia): Algiers; Chief Officer YURII S. BAGDASAROV.

Xinhua (New China) News Agency (People's Republic of China): 32 rue de Carthage, Hydra, Algiers; tel. and fax (2) 69-27-12; telex 67950; Chief WANG LIANZHI.

Wikalat al-Maghreb al-Arabi (Morocco) and the Middle East News Agency (Egypt) are also represented.

Publishers

Entreprise Nationale du Livre (ENAL): 3 blvd Zirout Youcef, BP 49, Algiers; tel. and fax (2) 73-58-41; telex 53845; f. 1966 as Société Nationale d'Edition et de Diffusion, name changed 1983; publishes books of all types, and imports, exports and distributes printed material, stationery, school and office supplies; Pres. and Dir-Gen. HASSEN BENDIF.

Office des Publications Universitaires: 1 place Centrale de Ben Aknoun, Algiers; tel. (2) 78-87-18; telex 61396; publishes university textbooks.

Broadcasting and Communications

RADIO

Arabic Network: transmitters at Adrar, Aïn Beïda, Algiers, Béchar, Béni Abbès, Djanet, El Goléa, Ghardaia, Hassi Messaoud, In Aménas, In Salah, Laghouat, Les Trembles, Ouargla, Reggane, Tamanrasset, Timimoun, Tindouf.

French Network: transmitters at Algiers, Constantine, Oran and Tipaza.

Kabyle Network: transmitter at Algiers.

Radio Algérienne: 21 blvd des Martyrs, Algiers; tel. (2) 59-07-00; fax (2) 60-58-14; govt-controlled; Dir-Gen. ABDELKADER LALMI.

TELEVISION

The principal transmitters are at Algiers, Batna, Sidi-Bel-Abbès, Constantine, Souk-Ahras and Tlemcen. Television plays a major role in the national education programme.

Télévision Algérienne: 21 blvd des Martyrs, Algiers; tel. (2) 60-23-00; fax (2) 60-19-22; Dir-Gen. BRAHIM BELBAHRI.

Finance

(cap. = capital; res = reserves; dep. = deposits; brs = branches; m. = million; amounts in Algerian dinars)

BANKING

Central Bank

Banque d'Algérie: 38 ave Franklin Roosevelt, Algiers; tel. (2) 23-02-32; telex 66499; fax (2) 23-01-50; f. 1963 as Banque Centrale d'Algérie; present name adopted 1990; cap. 40m.; bank of issue; Gov. ABDELOUAHAB KERAMANE; Sec.-Gen. FERHAT MECIBAH; 50 brs.

Nationalized Banks

Banque Extérieure d'Algérie (BEA): BP 344, Alger-Gare, 11 blvd Col Amirouche, Algiers; tel. (2) 71-12-52; telex 67488; fax (2) 63-93-34; f. 1967; cap. 1,600m., res 4,001m., total assets 318,420m. (Dec. 1994); chiefly concerned with energy and maritime transport sectors; Chair. MOHAMED BENHALIMA; Dir-Gen. HOCINE HANNACHI; 80 brs.

Banque du Maghreb Arabe pour l'Investissement et le Commerce: 21 blvd des Trois Frères Bouadou, Bir Mourad Rais, Algiers; tel. (2) 56-04-46; telex 62266; fax (2) 56-60-12; owned by the Algerian Govt (50%) and the Libyan Govt (50%); Pres. HAKIKI; Dir-Gen. IBRAHIM ALBISHARY.

Banque Nationale d'Algérie (BNA): 8 blvd Ernesto Ché Guévara, 16000 Alger-Gare, Algiers; tel. (2) 71-55-64; telex 61227; fax (2) 71-47-59; f. 1966; cap. 8,000m., res 10,227m., dep. 68,920m., total assets 228,892m. (Dec. 1995); specializes in industry, transport and trade sectors; Chair. and Man. Dir MUHAMMAD TERBECHE; 163 brs.

Al-Baraka Bank of Algeria (ABA): 11 rue Ahmed Kara, Saïd Hamdine, Hydra, Algiers; tel. (2) 69-32-76; telex 67928; fax (2) 59-01-68; f. 1991; Algeria's first Islamic financial institution; owned by the Jeddah-based Al-Baraka Investment and Development Co (50%) and the local Banque de l'Agriculture et du Développement Rural (BADR) (50%); Chair. MOHAMED TEWFIK AL-MAGHARIBI; Gen. Man. MOHAMED SEDDIK HAFID.

Crédit Populaire d'Algérie (CPA): BP 1031, 2 blvd Col Amirouche, 16000 Algiers; tel. (2) 64-96-60; telex 56061; fax (2) 64-97-29; f. 1966; cap. 13,600m. (Dec. 1996); specializes in light industry, construction and tourism; Chair. and Gen. Man. MADJID NASSOU; 117 brs.

Development Banks

Banque de l'Agriculture et du Développement Rural (BADR): BP 484, 17 blvd Col Amirouche, Algiers; tel. (2) 64-72-64; telex 66658; fax (2) 61-55-51; f. 1982; cap. 2,200m., res 1,942m., dep. 103,939m. (Dec. 1993); finance for the agricultural sector; Chair. and Man. Dir MOURAD DAMARDJI; 270 brs.

Banque Algérienne de Développement (BAD): 12 blvd Col Amirouche, Algiers; tel. (2) 73-89-50; telex 55220; fax (2) 74-51-36; f. 1963; cap. 100m. (1994), dep. 3,596.5m. (Dec. 1984); a public establishment with fiscal sovereignty; aims to contribute to Algerian economic development through long-term investment programmes; Chair. SASSI AZIZA; Dir-Gen. MUHAMMAD KERKEBANE; 4 brs.

Banque de Développement Local (BDL): 5 rue Gaci Amar, Staouéli, Wilaya de Tipaza; tel. (2) 39-28-01; telex 71171; fax (2) 39-23-51; f. 1985; regional development bank; cap. 500m. (1992); Dir-Gen. MUHAMMAD MALEK; 14 brs.

Caisse Nationale d'Epargne et de Prévoyance (CNEP): 42 blvd Khélifa Boukhalfa, Algiers; tel. (2) 71-33-53; telex 65286; fax (2) 71-70-22; f. 1964; savings and housing bank; Dir-Gen. ABDELKRIM NAAS.

Private Banks

First Private Bank of Algeria: Algiers; f. 1997.

Union Bank: Algiers; f. 1995; cap. 100m.; principal shareholder Brahim Hadjas; Pres. ABDERRAHMANE HADJ NACER.

Foreign Banks
(Representative offices)

Beogradska Banka (Yugoslavia): 12 rue Ali Azil, Algiers; tel. (2) 63-56-19; fax (2) 79-69-42.

Crédit Lyonnais (France): BP 268, 2 blvd Mohamed Khemisti, Algiers; tel. (2) 73-30-74; telex 56160; fax (2) 73-30-76; Dir PHILIPPE BRICQ.

Société Générale (France): BP 294, Villa No. 1, 2 rue le Paradou, Hydra, Algiers; tel. (2) 59-49-21; telex 66569; fax (2) 60-04-87; Dir JEAN-PAUL COURT.

INSURANCE

Insurance is a state monopoly; however, in 1997 regulations were being drafted to permit private companies to enter the Algerian insurance market.

Caisse Nationale de Mutualité Agricole: 24 blvd Victor Hugo, Algiers; tel. (2) 73-46-31; telex 56033; fax (2) 73-31-07; f. 1972; Dir-Gen. YAHIA CHERIF BRAHIM; 47 brs.

Compagnie Algérienne d'Assurance: 48 rue Didouche Mourad, Algiers; tel. (2) 64-54-32; telex 56051; fax (2) 64-20-15; f. 1963 as a public corpn; Pres. ALI DJENDI.

Compagnie Centrale de Réassurance: 21 blvd Zirout Youcef, Algiers; tel. (2) 73-80-20; telex 55091; fax (2) 73-80-60; f. 1973; general; Chair. DJAMEL-EDDINE CHOUAÏB CHOUITER.

Société Nationale d'Assurances (SNA): 5 blvd Ernesto Ché Guévara, Algiers; tel. (2) 71-47-60; telex 61309; fax (2) 71-22-16; f. 1963; state-sponsored co; Pres. KACI AISSA SLIMANE; Chair. and Gen. Man. LATROUS AMARQ.

Trade and Industry

DEVELOPMENT ORGANIZATIONS

Engineering Environment Consult (EEC): BP 395, Alger-Gare, 50 rue Khélifa Boukhalfa, Algiers; tel. (2) 73-33-90; telex 65153; fax (2) 73-24-81; f. 1982; Dir-Gen. MUHAMMAD BENTIR.

Entreprise Nationale de Développement des Industries Alimentaires (ENIAL): 2 rue Ahmed Aït Muhammad, Algiers; tel. (2) 76-51-42; telex 54816; Dir-Gen. MOKRAOUI.

Entreprise Nationale de Développement des Industries d'Articles de Sport, Jouets et Instruments de Musique (DEJIMAS): 5 rue Abane Ramdane, Algiers; tel. (2) 63-22-17; telex 52873; Dir-Gen. FAROUK NADI.

Entreprise Nationale de Développement des Industries Manufacturières (ENEDIM): 22 rue des Fusillés, El Anasser, Algiers; tel. (2) 68-13-43; telex 65315; fax (2) 67-55-26; f. 1983; Dir-Gen. FODIL.

Entreprise Nationale de Développement et de Recherche Industriels des Matériaux de Construction (ENDMC): BP 78, 35000 Algiers; tel. (2) 41-50-70; telex 63352; f. 1982; Dir-Gen. A. TOBBAL.

Institut National de la Production et du Développement Industriel (INPED): 126 rue Didouche Mourad, Boumerdès; tel. (2) 41-52-50; telex 52488.

CHAMBERS OF COMMERCE

Chambre Française de Commerce et d'Industrie en Algérie (CFCIA): 1 rue Lieutenant Mohamed Touileb, Algiers; tel. (2) 73-28-28; fax (2) 63-75-33; f. 1965; Pres. JEAN-PIERRE DEQUEKER; Dir JEAN-FRANÇOIS HEUGAS.

Chambre Algérienne de Commerce et d'Industrie (CACI): BP 100, Palais Consulaire, rue Amilcar Cabral, Algiers; tel. (2) 57-55-55; telex 61345; fax (2) 57-70-25; f. 1980; Dir-Gen. MOHAMED CHAMI.

INDUSTRIAL AND TRADE ORGANIZATIONS

Association Nationale des Fabrications et Utilisateurs d'Emballages Métalliques: BP 245, rue de Constantine, Algiers; telex 64415; Pres. OTHMANI.

Groupement pour l'Industrialisation du Bâtiment (GIBAT): BP 51, 3 ave Colonel Driant, 55102 Verdun, France; tel. 29-86-09-76; fax 29-86-20-51; Dir JEAN MOULET.

Institut Algérien de Normalisation et de Propriété Industrielle (INAPI): 5–7 rue Abou Hamou Moussa, 16000 Algiers; tel. (2) 63-51-80; telex 66409; fax (2) 61-09-71; f. 1973; Dir-Gen. DJENIDI BENDAOUD.

Institut National Algérien du Commerce Extérieur (COMEX): 6 blvd Anatole-France, Algiers; tel. (2) 62-70-44; telex 52763; Dir-Gen. SAAD ZERHOUNI.

Institut National des Industries Manufacturières (INIM): 35000 Boumerdès; tel. (2) 81-62-71; telex 68462; fax (2) 82-56-62; f. 1973; Dir-Gen. HOCINE HASSISSI.

STATE TRADING ORGANIZATIONS

Since 1970 all international trading has been carried out by state organizations, of which the following are the most important:

Entreprise Nationale d'Approvisionnement en Bois et Dérivés (ENAB): BP 166, Alger-Gare, 2 blvd Muhammad V, Algiers; tel. (2) 63-85-32; telex 66470; fax (2) 61-10-89; wood and derivatives and other building materials; Dir-Gen. El-Hadj REKHROUKH.

Entreprise Nationale d'Approvisionnement en Outillage et Produits de Quincaillerie Générale (ENAOQ): 6 rue Amar Semaous, Hussein-Dey, Algiers; tel. (2) 77-45-03; telex 65566; tools and general hardware; Dir-Gen. ALI HOCINE.

Entreprise Nationale d'Approvisionnements en Produits Alimentaires (ENAPAL): Algiers; tel. (2) 76-10-11; telex 64278; f. 1983; monopoly of import, export and bulk trade in basic foodstuffs; brs in more than 40 towns; Chair. LAID SABRI; Man. Dir BRAHIM DOUAOURI.

Entreprise Nationale d'Approvisionnement et de Régulation en Fruits et Légumes (ENAFLA): BP 42, 12 ave des Trois Frères Bouadou, Bir Mourad Rais, Algiers; tel. (2) 54-10-10; telex 62113; fax (2) 56-79-59; f. 1983; division of the Ministry of Commerce; fruit and vegetable marketing, production and export; Man. Dir RÉDHA KHELEF.

Office Algérien Interprofessionel des Céréales (OAIC): 5 rue Ferhat-Boussaad, Algiers; tel. (2) 73-26-01; telex 65056; fax (2) 73-22-11; f. 1962; monopoly of trade in wheat, rice, maize, barley and products derived from these cereals; Gen. Man. LAÏD TALAMALI.

Office National de la Commercialisation des Produits Viti-Vinicoles (ONCV): 112 Quai-Sud, Algiers; tel. (2) 73-72-75; telex 56063; fax (2) 73-72-97; f. 1968; monopoly of importing and exporting products of the wine industry; Man. Dir S. MEBARKI.

UTILITIES

Société Nationale de l'Electricité et du Gaz (SONELGAZ): 2 blvd Colonel Krim Belkacem, Algiers; tel. (2) 74-82-60; telex 66381; fax (2) 61-54-77; monopoly of production, distribution and transportation of electricity and transportation and distribution of natural gas; Gen. Man. AÏSSA ABDELKRIM BENGHANEM.

Electricity

Entreprise Nationale de Travaux d'Electrification: Villa Malwall, Ain d'Heb, Médéa; tel. (3) 50-61-27; telex 74061; f. 1982; study of electrical infrastructure; Dir-Gen. ABD AL-BAKI BELABDOUN.

Gas

Entreprise Nationale des Gaz Industriels (ENGI): BP 247, route de Baraki, Gué de Constantine, Algiers; tel. (2) 77-85-81; fax (2) 77-11-94; production and distribution of gas; Gen. Man. LAHOCINE BOUCHERIT.

PETROLEUM COMPANIES

Société Nationale pour la Recherche, la Production, le Transport, la Transformation et la Commercialisation des Hydrocarbures (SONATRACH): 10 rue du Sahara, Hydra, Algiers; tel. (2) 60-70-00; telex 62106; f. 1963; exploration, exploitation, transport and marketing of petroleum, natural gas and their products; Dir-Gen. ABDELMAJID ATTAR (acting).

In May 1980 SONATRACH was disbanded, and its functions were divided among 12 companies (including SONATRACH itself). The other 11 were:

Entreprise Nationale de Canalisation (ENAC): Algiers; tel. (2) 70-35-90; telex 42939; piping; Dir-Gen. HAMID MAZRI.

Entreprise Nationale de Distribution et de Commercialisation des Produits Pétroliers (NAFTAL): BP 73, route des Dusses, Cheraga, Algiers; tel. (2) 36-09-69; telex 53876; fax (2) 37-57-11; f. 1987; international marketing and distribution of petroleum products; Gen. Man. NORDINE CHEROUATY.

Entreprise Nationale d'Engineering Pétrolier (ENEP): 2 blvd Muhammad V, Algiers; tel. (2) 64-08-37; telex 66493; fax (2) 63-71-83; design and construction for petroleum-processing industry; Gen. Man. MUSTAPHA MEKIDECHE.

Entreprise Nationale de Forage (ENAFOR): BP 211, 30500 Hassi Messaoud, Algiers; tel. (2) 73-71-35; telex 44077; fax (2) 73-22-60; drilling; Dir-Gen. ABD AR-RACHID ROUABAH.

Entreprise Nationale de Génie Civil et Bâtiments (GCB): BP 23, route de Corso, Boudouaou, Algiers; tel. (2) 84-65-26; telex 68213; fax (2) 84-60-09; civil engineering; Dir-Gen. ABD EL-HAMID ZERGUINE.

Entreprise Nationale de Géophysique (ENAGEO): BP 140, Hassi Messaoud, Ouargla; tel. (9) 73-77-00; telex 42703; fax (9) 73-72-12; geophysics; Dir-Gen. RABAH DJEDDI.

Entreprise Nationale des Grands Travaux Pétroliers (ENGTP): BP 09, Zone Industrielle, Reghaïa, Boumerdes; tel. (2) 85-24-50; telex 68150; fax (2) 85-14-70; f. 1980; major industrial projects; Dir-Gen. B. DRIAD.

Entreprise Nationale de la Pétrochimie (ENIP): BP 215, Skikda; telex 87098; fax (8) 75-74-41; petrochemicals and fertilizers.

Entreprise Nationale des Plastiques et de Caoutchouc (ENPC): BP 452, rue des Frères Meslim, Aïn Turk, Sétif; tel. (5) 90-64-99; telex 86040; fax (5) 90-05-65; production and marketing of rubber and plastics; Dir-Gen. MAHIEDDINE ECHIKH.

Entreprise Nationale de Services Petroliers (ENSP): BP 83, Hassi Messaoud, Ouargla; tel. (9) 73-73-33; telex 44026; fax (9) 73-82-01; oil-well services; Dir-Gen. A. GASMI.

Entreprise Nationale des Travaux aux Puits (ENTP): BP 71, In-Amenas, Illizi; telex 44052; oil-well construction; Dir-Gen. ABD AL-AZIZ KRISSAT.

PRINCIPAL TRADE UNIONS

Union Générale des Travailleurs Algériens (UGTA): Maison du Peuple, place du 1er mai, Algiers; tel. (2) 66-89-47; telex 65051; f. 1956; 800,000 mems; Sec.-Gen. ABDELMADJID SIDI SAID (acting).

There are 10 national 'professional sectors' affiliated to UGTA. These are:

Secteur Alimentation, Commerce et Tourisme (Food, Commerce and Tourist Industry Workers): Gen. Sec. ABD AL-KADER GHRIBLI.

Secteur Bois, Bâtiments et Travaux Publics (Building Trades Workers): Gen. Sec. LAIFA LATRECHE.

Secteur Education et Formation Professionnelle (Teachers): Gen. Sec. SAÏDI BEN GANA.

Secteur Energie et Pétrochimie (Energy and Petrochemical Workers): Gen. Sec. ALI BELHOUCHET.

Secteur Finances (Financial Workers): Gen. Sec. MUHAMMAD ZAAF.

Secteur Information, Formation et Culture (Information, Training and Culture).

Secteur Industries Légères (Light Industry): Gen. Sec. ABD AL-KADER MALKI.

Secteur Industries Lourdes (Heavy Industry).

Secteur Santé et Sécurité Sociale (Health and Social Security Workers): Gen. Sec. ABD AL-AZIZ DJEFFAL.

Secteur Transports et Télécommunications (Transport and Telecommunications Workers): Gen. Sec. EL-HACHEMI BEN MOUHOUB.

Al-Haraka al-Islamiyah lil-Ummal al-Jazarivia (Islamic Movement for Algerian Workers): Tlemcen; f. 1990; based on teachings of Islamic faith and affiliated to the FIS.

Union Nationale des Paysans Algériens (UNPA): f. 1973; 700,000 mems; Sec.-Gen. AÏSSA NEDJEM.

Transport

RAILWAYS

A new authority, Infrafer (Entreprise Publique Economique de Réalisation des Infrastructures Ferroviaires), was established in 1987 to take responsibility for the construction of new track. In the following year a project to build an underground railway network in Algiers was revived in a modified form. Work on the first 12.5-km section of the 26-km line of the network, which was to be constructed by local companies with foreign assistance, began in 1990. It was projected that the line would take 10 years to complete.

Infrafer (Entreprise Publique Economique de Réalisation des Infrastructures Ferroviaires): BP 208, 35300 Rouiba; tel. (2) 85-27-47; telex 68152; fax (2) 85-17-55; f. 1987; Pres. and Dir-Gen. K. BENMAMI.

Société Nationale des Transports Ferroviaires (SNTF): 21–23 blvd Muhammad V, Algiers; tel. (2) 71-15-10; telex 66333; fax (2) 74-81-90; f. 1976 to replace Société Nationale des Chemins de Fer Algériens; 4,290 km of track, of which 301 km are electrified and 1,055 km are narrow gauge; daily passenger services from Algiers to the principal provincial cities and services to Tunisia and Morocco; Dir-Gen. ABDELADIM BENALLEGUE.

ROADS

In 1995 there were 102,424 km of roads and tracks, of which 608 km were motorways, 25,332 km were main roads and 23,357 km were secondary roads. The French administration built a good road system (partly for military purposes), which, since independence, has been allowed to deteriorate in parts. New roads have been built linking the Sahara oil fields with the coast, and the Trans-Sahara highway is a major project. The first 360-km stretch of the highway, from Hassi Marroket to Aïn Salah, was opened in 1973, and the next section, ending at Tamanrasset, was opened in 1978. In 1996 it was estimated that the cost of renovating the national road system would total US $4,124m.

Société Nationale des Transports Routiers (SNTR): 27 rue des Trois Frères Bouadou, Bir Mourad Rais, Algiers; tel. (2) 54-06-00; telex 62120; fax (2) 56-53-73; f. 1967; holds a monopoly of goods transport by road; Chair. El-Hadj HAOUSSINE; Dir-Gen. ESSAID BENDAKIR.

Société Nationale des Transports des Voyageurs (SNTV): Algiers; tel. (2) 66-00-52; telex 52603; f. 1967; holds monopoly of long-distance passenger transport by road; Man. Dir M. DIB.

SHIPPING

Algiers is the main port, with anchorage of between 23 m and 29 m in the Bay of Algiers, and anchorage for the largest vessels in Agha Bay. The port has a total quay length of 8,380 m. There are also important ports at Annaba, Arzew, Béjaia, Djidjelli, Ghazaouet, Mostaganem, Oran, Skikda and Ténés. Petroleum and liquefied gas are exported through Arzew, Béjaia and Skikda. Algerian crude petroleum is also exported through the Tunisian port of La Skhirra. In December 1996 Algeria's merchant fleet totalled 151 vessels, amounting to 982,528 grt.

Compagnie Algéro-Libyenne de Transports Maritimes (CALTRAM): 19 rue des Trois Frères Bouadou, Bir Mourad Rais, Algiers; tel. (2) 57-17-00; telex 62150; fax (2) 54-21-04; Dir-Gen. M. ZITOUNI.

Entreprise Nationale de Réparations Navales (ERENAV): quai no. 12, Ex d'Aurey, Algiers; tel. (2) 64-00-10; telex 66650; fax (2) 64-60-93; f. 1987; ship repairs; Dir-Gen. MOHAMED MOSLI.

Entreprise Nationale de Transport Maritime de Voyageurs—Algérie Ferries (ENTMV): BP 467, 5,6 Jawharlal Nehru, Algiers; tel. (2) 74-04-85; telex 55100; fax (2) 64-88-76; f. 1987 as part of restructuring of SNTM-CNAN; responsible for passenger transport; operates car ferry services between Algiers, Annaba, Skikda, Alicante, Marseilles and Oran; Dir-Gen. A. CHERIET.

Entreprise Portuaire d'Alger (EPAL): BP 259, 2 rue d'Angkor, Alger-Gare, Algiers; tel. (2) 71-54-39; telex 61275; fax (2) 71-54-52; f. 1982; responsible for management and growth of port facilities and sea pilotage; Dir-Gen. ALI FERRAH.

Entreprise Portuaire d'Annaba (EPAN): BP 1232, Môle de la Cigogne-Quai nord, Annaba; tel. (8) 86-31-31; telex 81652; fax (8) 86-54-15; Man. Dir D. SALHI.

Entreprise Portuaire d'Arzew (EPA): BP 46, 7 rue Larbi Tebessi, Arzew; tel. (6) 37-24-91; telex 12919; fax (6) 47-57-23; Man. Dir CHAIB OUMEUR.

Entreprise Portuaire de Béjaia (EPB): BP 94, Môle de la Casbah, Béjaia; tel. (5) 21-18-07; telex 83055; fax (5) 22-25-79; Man. Dir M. BOUMSILA.

Entreprise Portuaire de Djen-Djen (EPDJ): BP 87, El Achouat, Djen-Djen, Djidjelli; tel. (5) 45-94-63; telex 84060; fax (5) 45-90-72; f. 1984; Man. Dir MOHAMED ATMANE.

Entreprise Portuaire de Ghazaouet (EPG): BP 217, Enceinte Portuaire Môle de Batna, 13400 Ghazaouet; tel. (7) 32-13-45; telex 18836; fax (7) 32-12-55; Man. Dir B. ABDELMALEK.

Entreprise Portuaire de Mostaganem (EPM): BP 131, quai du Port, Mostaganem; tel. (6) 21-14-11; telex 14097; fax (6) 21-78-05; Dir M. CHERIF.

Entreprise Portuaire d'Oran (EPO): BP 106, 6 blvd Mimouni Lahcène, Oran; tel. (6) 39-26-25; telex 22422; fax (6) 39-53-52; Man. Dir M. S. LOUHIBI.

Entreprise Portuaire de Skikda (EPS): BP 65, 46 ave Rezki Rahal, Skikda; tel. (8) 75-68-27; telex 87840; fax (8) 75-20-15; Man. Dir M. Lemrabet.

Entreprise Portuaire de Ténès (EPT): BP 18, 02200 Ténès; tel. (3) 76-72-76; telex 78090; fax (3) 76-61-77; Man. Dir K. el-Hamri.

NAFTAL Direction Aviation Maritime: BP 70, Aéroport Houari Boumedienne, Dar-el-Beïda, Algiers; tel. (2) 50-86-23; telex 64579; fax (2) 50-74-81; Dir Zerrouk ben Merabet.

Société Générale Maritime (GEMA): 2 rue J. Nehru, Algiers; tel. (2) 74-73-00; telex 56079; fax (2) 74-76-73; f. 1987 as part of restructuring of SNTM-CNAN; responsible for merchant traffic; Dir-Gen. Abdullah Seriai.

Société Nationale de Transport Maritime et Compagnie Nationale Algérienne de Navigation (SNTM-CNAN): BP 280, 2 quai no. 9, Nouvelle Gare Maritime, Algiers; tel. (2) 71-14-78; telex 66581; fax (2) 61-59-64; f. 1963; state-owned co which owns and operates fleet of freight ships; rep. office in Marseilles and rep. agencies in Antwerp, Valencia and the principal ports in many other countries; Gen. Man. Ghazi Regaïnia.

Société Nationale de Transports Maritimes des Hydrocarbures et des Produits Chimiques (SNTM-HYPROC): BP 60, Arzew, 31200 Oran; tel. (6) 37-30-99; telex 12097; fax (6) 37-28-30; f. 1982; Dir-Gen. Chaïb Oumeur.

CIVIL AVIATION

Algeria's main airport, Houari Boumedienne, 20 km from Algiers, is a class A airport of international standing. At Constantine, Annaba, Tlemcen and Oran there are also airports that meet international requirements. There are, in addition, 65 aerodromes, of which 20 are public, and a further 135 airstrips connected with the petroleum industry.

Air Algérie (Entreprise Nationale d'Exploitation des Services Aériens): BP 858, 1 place Maurice Audin, Immeuble el-Djazair, Algiers; tel. (2) 74-24-28; telex 67145; fax (2) 74-44-25; f. 1953 by merger; state-owned from 1972; internal services and extensive services to Europe, North and West Africa, and the Middle East; Sec.-Gen. Ali Djeraba; Dir-Gen. Faysal Khalil.

Air Maghreb: planned consortium of the national airlines of Algeria, Libya, Mauritania, Morocco and Tunisia; the merger of the airlines has been delayed indefinitely.

Tourism

Algeria's tourist attractions include the Mediterranean coast, the Atlas mountains and the desert. In 1996 a total of 93,491 tourists visited Algeria, compared with 722,682 in 1991. Receipts from tourism totalled about US $64m. in 1990. In 1996 there were 737 hotels, with a total of 64,937 beds.

Entreprise de Gestion Touristique du Centre (EGT CENTRE): 70 rue Hassiba Ben-Bouali, Algiers; tel. (2) 67-03-05; telex 66165; fax (2) 67-49-00; Dir-Gen. Salah Eddine Senni.

Office National du Tourisme (ONT): 2 rue Ismail Kerrar, Algiers; tel. (2) 71-29-82; telex 55362; fax (2) 71-29-85; f. 1990; state institution; oversees tourism development policy; Dir-Gen. Saddek Zerrouk.

ONAT-TOUR (Opérateur National Algérien de Tourism): 25–27 rue Khélifa-Boukhalfa, 16000 Algiers; tel. (2) 74-33-76; telex 66383; fax (2) 74-32-14; f. 1962; Dir-Gen. Abid Keramane.

Société de Développement de l'Industrie Touristique en Algérie (SODITAL): 72 rue Asselah Hocine, Algiers; f. 1989; Dir-Gen. Noureddine Salhi.

ANDORRA

Introductory Survey

Location, Climate, Language, Religion, Flag, Capital

The Principality of Andorra lies in the eastern Pyrenees, bounded by France and Spain, and is situated roughly midway between Barcelona and Toulouse. The climate is alpine, with much snow in winter and a warm summer. The official language is Catalan, but French and Spanish are also widely spoken. Most of the inhabitants profess Christianity, and about 94% are Roman Catholics. The civil flag (proportions 3 by 2) has three equal vertical stripes, of blue, yellow and red. The state flag has, in addition, the state coat of arms (a quartered shield above the motto *Virtus unita fortior*) in the centre of the yellow stripe. The capital is Andorra la Vella.

Recent History

Owing to the lack of distinction between the authority of the General Council (Consell General) of Andorra and the Co-Princes (Coprínceps) who have ruled the country since 1278, the Andorrans encountered many difficulties in their attempts to gain international status for their country and control over its essential services.

Until 1970 the franchise was granted only to third-generation Andorran males who were more than 25 years of age. Thereafter, women, persons aged between 21 and 25, and second-generation Andorrans were allowed to vote in elections to the General Council. In 1977 the franchise was extended to include all first-generation Andorrans of foreign parentage who were aged 28 and over. The electorate remained small, however, when compared with the size of the population, and Andorra's foreign residents (who comprised 69.2% of the total population at December 1995) increased their demands for political and nationality rights. Immigration is on a quota system, being restricted primarily to French and Spanish nationals intending to work in Andorra.

Prior to 1993, political parties were not directly represented in the General Council, but there were loose groupings with liberal and conservative sympathies. The country's only political organization, the Partit Democràtic d'Andorra (PDA), was technically illegal, and in the 1981 elections to the General Council the party urged its supporters to cast blank votes.

During discussions on institutional reform, held in 1980, representatives of the Co-Princes and the General Council agreed that an executive council should be formed, and that a referendum should be held on changes to the electoral system. In January 1981 the Co-Princes formally requested the General Council to prepare plans for reform, in accordance with these proposals. After the December elections to the General Council, in January 1982 the new legislature elected Oscar Ribas Reig as Head of Government (Cap de Govern). Ribas Reig appointed an executive body of six ministers, who expressed their determination to provide Andorra with a written constitution, to defend local industry and to encourage private investment. The formation of the executive body, known as the Govern, constituted the separation of powers between an executive and a legislature, and represented an important step towards institutional reform.

Severe storm damage in November 1982, and the general effects of the world-wide economic recession, led to a controversial vote by the General Council, in August 1983, in favour of the introduction of income tax, in an effort to alleviate Andorra's budgetary deficit and to provide the Government with extra revenue for development projects. Subsequent government proposals for an indirect tax on bank deposits, hotel rooms and property sales encountered strong opposition from financial and tourism concerns, and prompted the resignation of the Government in April 1984. Josep Pintat Solans, a local business executive, was elected unopposed by the General Council as Head of Government in May. In August, however, the Ministers of Finance and of Industry, Commerce and Agriculture resigned, following disagreements concerning the failure to implement economic reforms (including the introduction of income tax).

At the December 1985 elections to the General Council the electorate was increased by about 27%, as a result of the newly-introduced lower minimum voting age of 18 years. The Council re-elected Josep Pintat Solans as Head of Government in January 1986, when he won the support of 27 of its 28 members.

In September 1986 President François Mitterrand of France and the Bishop of Urgel, Dr Joan Martí Alanis (respectively the French and Spanish Co-Princes), met in Andorra to discuss the principality's status in relation to the European Community (EC, now European Union—EU—see p. 152), as well as the question of free exchange of goods between the members of the EC and Andorra, following Spain's admission to the Community in January of that year.

In April 1987 the Consejo Sindical Interregional Pirineos-Mediterráneo, a collective of French and Spanish trade unions, in conjunction with the Andorran Asociación de Residentes Andorranos, began to claim rights, including those of freedom of expression and association and the right to strike, on behalf of 20,000 of its members who were employed as immigrant workers in Andorra.

Further proposals for institutional reforms were approved by the General Council in October 1987. The transfer to the Andorran Government of responsibility for such matters as public order was proposed, while the authority of the Co-Princes in the administration of justice was recognized. The drafting of a constitution for Andorra was also envisaged. The implementation of the reforms was, however, dependent on the agreement of the Co-Princes.

Municipal elections were held in December 1987, at which 80% of the electorate voted; however, the number of citizens eligible to vote represented only 13% of Andorra's total population. For the first time, the election campaign involved the convening of meetings and the use of the media, in addition to traditional canvassing. Although Andorra then had no political parties as such, four of the seven seats were won by candidates promoting a conservative stance.

In April 1988 Andorra enacted legislation recognizing the Universal Declaration of Human Rights, adopted by the UN General Assembly in 1948. In June 1988 the first Andorran trade union was established by two French union confederations, the Confédération Française Democratique du Travail and Force Ouvrière, and by the Spanish Unión General de Trabajadores. (There were about 26,000 salaried workers in Andorra at this time, 90% of whom were of French or Spanish origin.) In the following month, however, the General Council unanimously rejected the formation of the union, as it did not recognize workers' right of association and prohibited the existence of any union.

Elections to the General Council took place in December 1989, at which more than 80% of the registered electorate (of 7,185 voters) participated. In January 1990 the new Council elected the reformist Ribas Reig as Head of Government, with the support of 22 members. In June the General Council voted unanimously to establish a special commission to draft a constitution. The proposed document was to promulgate popular sovereignty and to constitutionalize the Co-Princes. In April 1991 representatives of the Co-Princes agreed to recognize popular sovereignty in Andorra and to permit the drafting of a constitution, which would be subject to approval by referendum. In September, however, Ribas Reig was threatened with a vote of 'no confidence' by traditionalist members of the Council. There followed a period of political impasse, during which no official budget was authorized for the principality. In January 1992, following small, but unprecedented, public demonstrations in protest against the political deadlock, Ribas Reig and the General Council resigned. A general election took place in April, at which 82% of the electorate (of 8,592 voters) voted. The result was, however, inconclusive, necessitating a second round of voting one week later, following which supporters of Ribas Reig controlled 17 of the 28 seats. Accordingly, Ribas Reig was re-elected as Head of Government.

At a referendum held in March 1993, in which 75.7% of the 9,123 eligible voters participated, 74.2% of Andorrans approved the draft Constitution. The document was signed by the two Co-Princes in April, and was promulgated on 4 May. Under its provisions, the Co-Princes remained as Heads of State, but with greatly reduced powers, while Andorran nationals were afforded full sovereignty and (together with foreigners who had lived in Andorra for at least 20 years) were authorized to form and to join political parties and trade unions. The Constitution also provided for the establishment of an independent judiciary, and permitted the principality to formulate its own foreign policy and to join international organizations. The Co-Princes were to retain a right of veto over treaties with France and Spain that affected Andorra's borders or security.

The first general election under the terms of the new Constitution took place on 12 December 1993. Fourteen of the General Council's 28 members were directly elected from the single national constituency, the remainder being elected by Andorra's seven parishes (two for each parish). No party won an overall majority of seats, the largest number (eight) being secured by Ribas Reig's Agrupament Nacional Democràtic (AND—the successor to the PDA); Nova Democratica (ND) and the Unió Liberal (UL) each won five seats. Some 80.8% of the registered electorate (of 9,675) participated in the election. In January 1994 Ribas Reig was re-elected Head of Government, supported by the AND and the ND, together with the two representatives of the Iniciatíva Democratica Nacional (IDN). He announced that it would be a priority of his administration to restore economic growth by means of financial reforms and infrastructural development. Opposition to Ribas Reig's proposed budget and tax legislation, however, led in November to the adoption by the General Council of a motion expressing 'no confidence' in the Government. Ribas Reig immediately submitted his resignation; Marc Forné Molne, the leader of the UL, was subsequently elected Head of Government, and was inaugurated in late December.

Forné Molne's Government lacked an overall majority in the General Council; however, the support of councillors from regional political organizations enabled the Government to adopt more than 30 acts (between December 1994 and July 1996), including controversial legislation regarding foreign nationals (see Economic Affairs). Municipal elections, at which some 77.7% of the electorate voted, took place in December 1995. Bibiana Rossa (a former Minister of Health) became the first woman in Andorra to be elected to the office of mayor (of Canillo). After being censured twice in one year by the General Council, Forné Molne was obliged to announce that a general election would be held in early 1997. Elections to the General Council took place on 16 February 1997, at which 81.6% of the registered electorate (of 10,837 voters) participated. Forné Molne's UL won an overall majority of seats (18 of 28); six seats were secured by the AND, while the ND and the IDN won two each. In April Forné Molne announced the formation of a new, expanded Govern.

Following the referendum of March 1993, Andorra formally applied for membership of the Council of Europe (see p. 140). In June the Andorran Government signed a treaty of co-operation with France and Spain that explicitly recognized the sovereignty of Andorra. In the following month Andorra became the 184th member of the UN. In late 1993 France and Spain established embassies in Andorra, and Andorra subsequently opened embassies in Madrid and Paris. In September 1997 Jacques Chirac made his first official visit to Andorra in his capacity of President of France. During the visit Chirac affirmed his intention to assume his responsibilities as a Co-Prince of Andorra, in accordance with the Constitution.

Government

Andorra is a co-principality, under the suzerainty of the President of France and the Spanish Bishop of Urgel. However, since May 1993, when the Constitution of the Principality of Andorra was promulgated, these positions have been almost purely honorary.

The General Council comprises 28 councillors, who are elected by universal suffrage for a four-year period. Two councillors are directly elected by each of the seven parishes of Andorra, and the remainder by a single national constituency. At its opening session the Council elects as its head the Speaker (Syndic General) and the Deputy Speaker (Subsyndic General), who cease to be members of the Council on their election. The General Council elects the Head of Government, who appoints ministers to the Govern.

Andorra is divided into seven parishes, each of which is administered by a Communal Council. Communal councillors are elected for a four-year term by direct universal suffrage. At its opening session each Communal Council elects two consuls, who preside over it.

Defence

Andorra has no defence budget.

Economic Affairs

In 1994 Andorra's national revenue totalled an estimated US $1,016m., equivalent to $15,805 per head. Traditionally an agricultural country, Andorra's principal crops are tobacco and potatoes; livestock-rearing is also of importance. However, the agricultural sector accounted for less than 1% of total employment in 1997, and Andorra is dependent on imports of foodstuffs to satisfy domestic requirements.

Industry in Andorra includes the manufacture of cigars and cigarettes, together with the production of textiles, leather goods, wood products and processed foodstuffs. Iron, lead, alum and stone are also produced. Including construction, industry provided 21.3% of total employment in 1997.

The country's hydroelectric power plant supplies only about one-quarter of domestic needs, and Andorra is dependent on imports of electricity and other fuels from France and Spain. Andorra's total electricity consumption in 1995 amounted to 324.3m. kWh.

After 1945 Andorra's economy expanded rapidly, as a result of the co-principality's development as a market for numerous European and overseas goods, owing to favourable excise conditions. The trade in low-duty consumer items and tourism are therefore the most important sources of revenue. An estimated 8m. tourists visited Andorra in 1995. The absence of income tax and other forms of direct taxation favoured the development of Andorra as a 'tax haven'. The banking sector makes a significant contribution to the economy.

Andorra's external trade is dominated by the import of consumer goods destined for sale to visitors. In 1996 imports were valued at 135,460m. pesetas and exports at 5,883m. pesetas. Spain and France are Andorra's principal trading partners, respectively providing 40.5% and 30.8% of imports and taking 49.9% and 39.4% of exports in 1996.

In 1994 Andorra recorded a budgetary deficit of 2,721m. pesetas. For 1997 expenditure was projected at 27,665m. pesetas and revenue at 27,450m. pesetas. In the absence of direct taxation, the Government derives its revenue from levies on imports and on financial institutions, indirect taxes on petrol and other items, stamp duty and the sale of postage stamps. There is reportedly no unemployment in Andorra: the restricted size of the indigenous labour force necessitates high levels of immigration.

In March 1990 Andorra approved a trade agreement with the EC (effective from July 1991), allowing for the establishment of a customs union with the EC, which enabled Andorran companies to sell non-agricultural goods to the EU market without being subject to the external tariffs levied on third countries. Andorra benefits from duty-free transit for goods imported via EU countries. Potential impediments to growth in Andorra, none the less, remain the narrow economic base and the inability of the agricultural and manufacturing sectors to fulfil domestic needs. As part of initiatives to establish Andorra as a major financial centre, a law regulating financial services was approved in November 1993. Banks were required to invest as much as 4% of their clients' deposits in a fund intended to alleviate the public debt, in accordance with legislation approved in mid-1994. Controversial legislation was adopted in 1996 to allow certain foreign nationals to become 'nominal residents' (individuals who, for the purposes of avoiding taxation, establish their financial base in Andorra), on condition that they pay an annual levy of some 1m. pesetas, in addition to a deposit. The practice of granting this status (without the levy) had been suspended in 1992; however, in the mid-1990s those already accorded nominal residency were estimated to contribute 90% of Andorra's bank deposits. Plans were announced in 1997 to remove restrictions on foreign investment in Andorra, which currently limit investors to holding a maximum of one-third of the capital of any Andorran business. In October Andorra's request to commence negotiations for membership of the World Trade Organization (WTO, see p. 244) was approved by the WTO General Council.

Social Welfare

In 1994 there was one hospital in Andorra, providing 2.2 beds per 1,000 inhabitants, and 132 registered medical practitioners. The 1997 budget allocated some 2,398m. pesetas (8.7% of total expenditure) to welfare and health services. A formal system of social security was established in 1966–68, and provides for sickness benefits, old-age pensions and workers' insurance. Contributions are made both by employers and workers.

Education

Education is compulsory for children of between six and 16 years of age, and is provided free of charge by Catalan-, French- and Spanish-language schools. Six years of primary education are followed by four years of secondary schooling. University education is undertaken abroad, although there are two centres for vocational training in Andorra. In 1996/97 there were a total of 9,344 pupils (4,754 boys; 4,590 girls) attending Andorra's 33 schools. The 1997 budget allocated some 4,434m. pesetas (16.0% of total expenditure) to education, youth and sports.

Public Holidays

1998: 1 January (New Year's Day), 6 January (Epiphany), 14 March (Constitution Day), 10 April (Good Friday), 13 April (Easter Monday), 1 May (Labour Day), 1 June (Whit Monday), 15 August (Assumption), 8 September (National Holiday), 1 November (All Saints' Day), 8 December (Immaculate Conception), 25 December (Christmas), 26 December (St Stephen's Day).

1999: 1 January (New Year's Day), 6 January (Epiphany), 14 March (Constitution Day), 2 April (Good Friday), 5 April (Easter Monday), 1 May (Labour Day), 24 May (Whit Monday), 15 August (Assumption), 8 September (National Holdiay), 1 November (All Saints' Day), 8 December (Immaculate Conception), 25 December (Christmas), 26 December (St Stephen's Day).

Each Parish also holds its own annual festival, which is taken as a public holiday, usually lasting for three days, in July, August or September.

Weights and Measures

The metric system is in force.

Statistical Survey

Source (unless otherwise stated): Servei d'Estudis, Ministeri de Finances, Govern d'Andorra, Carrer Prat de la Creu 62–64, Andorra la Vella.

AREA AND POPULATION

Area: 467.76 sq km (180.6 sq miles).

Population (December 1996): 64,479 (males 33,852; females 30,627); comprising 20,331 Andorrans, 28,656 Spanish, 6,886 Portuguese, 4,352 French and 4,254 others. *Capital:* Andorra la Vella, population 21,721.

Births, Marriages and Deaths (1996): Registered live births 700; Registered marriages 123; Registered deaths 197.

Employment (July 1997): Agriculture, forestry and fishing 201; Industry (incl. construction) 6,074; Services 20,601; Other 1,640; Total 28,516.

AGRICULTURE

Principal Crop (metric tons, 1996): Tobacco 1,023.2.

Livestock (1997): Cattle 1,243; Sheep 2,102; Horses 909; Goats 562.

FINANCE

Currency and Exchange Rates: French and Spanish currencies are both in use. *French currency:* 100 centimes = 1 franc. *Sterling and Dollar Equivalents* (30 September 1997): £1 sterling = 9.583 francs; US $1 = 5.932 francs; 1,000 French francs = £104.35 = $168.57. *Average Exchange Rate* (francs per US dollar): 5.5520 in 1994; 4.9915 in 1995; 5.1155 in 1996. *Spanish currency:* 100 céntimos = 1 peseta. *Sterling and Dollar Equivalents* (30 September 1997): £1 sterling = 240.97 pesetas; US $1 = 149.17 pesetas; 1,000 Spanish pesetas = £4.150 = $6.704. *Average Exchange Rate* (pesetas per US dollar): 133.96 in 1994; 124.69 in 1995; 126.66 in 1996.

Budget (million pesetas, 1997): *Expenditure:* Head of Government's Office 1,799, Ministry of the Interior 2,346, Ministry of the Environment and Tourism 1,796, Ministry of the Presidency 368, Ministry of Foreign Affairs 471, Ministry of Finance 666, Ministry of Territorial Development 6,116, Ministry of Education, Youth and Sports 4,434, Ministry of the Economy 845, Ministry of Welfare and Public Health 2,398, Ministry of Culture 759, Transfers to local authorities 5,667, Total 27,665; *Revenue:* Indirect taxes on commodities 20,850, Other taxes 1,818, Administrative fees and charges, sales and other receipts 981, Property income 3,714, Total (incl. others) 27,450.

EXTERNAL TRADE

Principal Commodities (million pesetas, 1996): *Imports:* Live animals and animal products 9,739 (Milk and dairy products; eggs; natural honey 5,589); Prepared foodstuffs; beverages, spirits and vinegar; tobacco and manufactured substitutes 26,013 (Alcoholic and non-alcoholic beverages 7,569; Tobacco 10,772); Mineral products 6,119 (Mineral fuels and oils, etc. 4,979); Products of chemical or allied industries 12,325 (Perfumery products and toiletries 8,508); Wood pulp, etc.; paper and paperboard and articles thereof 4,266; Textiles and textile articles 10,360 (Non-knitted clothing and accessories 5,133); Base metals and articles thereof 4,449; Machinery and mechanical appliances; electrical equipment; sound and television apparatus 19,077 (Boilers, non-electric machinery and mechanical appliances 5,875; Electrical machinery and appliances; sound and television apparatus 13,202); Vehicles, aircraft, vessels and associated transport equipment 10,283 (Passenger motor cars, tractors and other road vehicles 10,166); Optical, photographic, cinematographic, precision and medical instruments, etc.; clocks and watches; musical instruments 6,281; Total (incl. others) 135,460. *Exports:* Prepared foodstuffs; beverages, spirits and vinegar; tobacco and manufactured substitutes 277 (Alcoholic and non-alcoholic beverages 252); Products of chemical or allied industries 253 (Perfumery products and toiletries 193); Raw hides and skins, leather, furskins and articles thereof; saddlery and harness; travel goods, handbags, etc. 244 (Leather objects 227); Wood pulp, etc.; paper and paperboard and articles thereof 676 (Printed matter 613); Textiles and textile articles 809 (Non-knitted clothing and accessories 726); Machinery and mechanical appliances; electrical equipment; sound and television apparatus 1,154 (Boilers, non-electric machinery and mechanical appliances 375; Electrical machinery and appliances; sound and television apparatus 779); Vehicles, aircraft, vessels and associated transport equipment 1,201 (Passenger motor cars, tractors and other road vehicles 1,190); Furniture, bed linen, etc.; lighting devices 276; Total (incl. others) 5,883.

Principal Trading Partners (million pesetas, 1996): *Imports:* China, People's Republic 1,616; France 41,715; Germany 5,853; Italy 4,437; Japan 3,867; Netherlands 1,954; Spain 54,899; Switzerland 2,593; United Kingdom 5,302; USA 5,413; Total (incl. others) 135,460. *Exports:* Belgium-Luxembourg 127; France 2,320; Germany 77; Portugal 138; Spain 2,937; Switzerland 76; Total (incl. others) 5,883.

TRANSPORT

Road Traffic (registered motor vehicles, 1995): Passenger cars 35,941; Commercial vehicles 4,014; Transport vehicles 159.

TOURISM

Tourist Arrivals (1993): Passenger cars entering from Spain 1,531,038; Passenger cars entering from France 565,124.

COMMUNICATIONS MEDIA

Radio Receivers (1994): 14,000 in use.

Television Receivers (1994): 24,000 in use.

Source: UNESCO, *Statistical Yearbook*.

Daily Newspapers (1997): 2 titles published.

Telephones (main lines in use, 1996): 30,964.

Telefax Stations (number in use, 1992): 1,280 (Source: UN, *Statistical Yearbook*).

Mobile Cellular Telephones (subscribers, 1994): 780 (Source: UN, *Statistical Yearbook*).

EDUCATION*

Enrolment (1996/97): 3- to 6-year-olds 2,270; 7- to 15-year-olds 5,304; 16 and over 1,770; Total 9,344.

* Part of the educational systems is undertaken by Spain and France.

Directory

The Constitution

The Constitution of the Principality of Andorra came into force on 4 May 1993, having been approved by the Andorran people in a referendum on 14 March. The official name of the independent state is Principat d'Andorra. The Constitution asserts that Andorra is 'a Democratic and Social independent state abiding by the Rule of Law', and defines the fundamental rights, freedoms and obligations of Andorran citizens and delineates the functions and competences of the organs of state.

In accordance with Andorran tradition, the Co-Princes (Coprínceps), respectively the Bishop of Urgel and the President of the French Republic, are titular Heads of State.

The legislature is the General Council (Consell General), one-half of whose members are elected from a single national constituency, the remainder being elected to represent Andorra's seven parishes (Parròquies); members are elected to the General Council for four years. Elections are on the basis of direct universal adult suffrage. The ruling organ of the General Council is the Sindicatura, headed by a Speaker (Syndic General).

The Govern (the executive organ of state) is directed by the Head of Government (Cap de Govern), who is elected by the General Council (and formally appointed by the Co-Princes) and who must command the support of the majority of the legislature's members. The Head of Government nominates government ministers, who may not at the same time be members of the General Council. The Head of Government is restricted to two consecutive full terms of office.

The Constitution defines the composition and powers of the judiciary, the highest organ of which is the Higher Court of Justice.

The Constitution defines the functions of the communal councils (Comuns), which are the organs of representation and administration of the parishes.

Revision of the Constitution shall require the approval of two-thirds of the members of the General Council and ratification by a referendum.

The Constitutional Court is the supreme interpreter of the Constitution. Its decisions are binding for public authorities and for individuals.

The Government

(December 1997)

HEADS OF STATE

Episcopal Co-Prince: Dr Joan Martí Alanis, Bishop of Urgel.

French Co-Prince: Jacques Chirac.

GOVERN

Head of Government: Marc Forné Molne.

Minister of the Presidency: Estanislau Sangrà Cardona.

Minister of Foreign Affairs: Albert Pintat Santolària.

Minister of Finance: Susangna Arasanz Serra.

Minister of the Economy: Enric Casadevall Medrano.

Minister of Agriculture: Josep Garrallà Rossell.

Minister of the Interior: Lluís Montanya Tarrés.

Minister of Welfare and Public Health: Josep Goicoechea Utrillo.

Minister of Education, Youth and Sports: Carme Sala Sansa.

Minister of Environment and Tourism: Enric Pujal Areny.

Minister of Culture: Pere Canturri Montanya.

MINISTRIES

All ministries are situated in Andorra la Vella.

Legislature

CONSELL GENERAL
(General Council)

Syndic General (Speaker): Josep Dalleres (AND).

General Election, 16 February 1997

Party	Seats
Unió Liberal (UL)	18
Agrupament Nacional Democràtic (AND)	6
Nova Democratica (ND)	2
Iniciatíva Democratica Nacional (IDN)	2
Total	28

Political Organizations

The establishment of political parties was sanctioned under the Constitution that was promulgated in May 1993.

Agrupament Nacional Democràtic (AND): Andorra la Vella; tel. 821930; fax 864368; internet http://www.mypic.ad/and; f. 1979; fmrly Partit Democràtic d'Andorra; Leader Ladislau Baró.

Coalició Nacional Andorrana (CNA): Andorra la Vella; f. 1993.

Iniciatíva Democratica Nacional (IDN): Plaça Rebés 1, 2°, Andorra la Vella; tel. 866406; fax 866306; f. 1993; Leader Vicenç Mateu.

Nova Democratica (ND): Andorra la Vella; f. 1993; Leader Jaume Bartomeu.

Unió Liberal (UL): Andorra la Vella; f. 1993; Leader Marc Forné Molne.

Diplomatic Representation

EMBASSIES IN ANDORRA

France: Carrer-les-Canals 38–40, POB 155, Andorra la Vella; tel. 820809; Ambassador: Jean Mazeo.

Spain: Carrer Prat de la Creu 34, Andorra la Vella; tel. 820500; fax 868500; Ambassador: José Paz Agueras.

Judicial System

The 1993 Constitution guarantees the independence of the judiciary.

Judicial power is vested, in the first instance, in the Magistrates' Courts (Batllia) and in the Judges' Tribunal (Tribunal de Batlles), the criminal-law courts (Tribunal de Corts) and the Higher Court of Justice (Tribunal Superior de la Justícia). The judiciary is represented, directed and administered by the Higher Council of Justice (Consell Superior de la Justícia), whose five members are appointed for single terms of six years. Final jurisdiction, in constitutional matters, is vested in the Constitutional Court (Tribunal Constitucional), whose four members hold office for no more than two consecutive eight-year terms.

The Press

In 1994 the average weekly circulation of the local press totalled 10,000.

Butlletí Oficial de Principat d'Andorra: Andorra la Vella; official govt gazette.

Correu Andorrà: Andorra la Vella; tel. 822500; fax 822938; Dir Cristina Cornella; circ. 2,000.

Diari d'Andorra: Avinguda Riberaygua 39, Andorra la Vella; tel. 863700; fax 863800; f. 1991; daily; local issues; Catalan; Editor Manuel M. Pujadas; circ. 3,000.

El Periòdic: Andorra la Vella; daily.

Poble Andorra: Carretera de la Comella, Andorra la Vella; tel. 822506; telex 211; fax 826696; f. 1974; weekly; Dir M. Carme Grau; circ. 3,000.

Broadcasting and Communications

RADIO

Radio Andorra: Baixada del Molí, Andorra la Vella; tel. 873777; fax 864999; f. 1991 as an Andorran-owned commercial public broadcasting service, to replace two stations which closed in 1981, following the expiry of their contracts with French and Spanish companies; Dir ENRIC CASTELLET.

TELEVISION

In 1994 Andorra was able to receive broadcasts from seven television stations (excluding channels received by satellite or cable).

Andorra Televisió: Baixada del Molí, Andorra la Vella; tel 873777; fax 864999; f. 1995 as an Andorran-owned commercial public broadcasting service; Dir ENRIC CASTELLET.

Antena 7: Avinguda les Escoles 16, Escaldes-Engordany; tel. 824433; telex 427; fax 826088; private co; in 1987 began to transmit one hour of Andorran-interest programmes from the Spanish side of the border.

Finance

(cap. = capital; res = reserves; dep. = deposits; m. = million; brs = branches; amounts in Spanish pesetas)

In 1993 there were seven banks, with a total of 53 branches, operating in Andorra.

PRINCIPAL BANKS

Banc Agricol i Comercial d'Andorra SA: POB 49, Avinguda Fiter i Rossell, 4 bis, Escaldes-Engordany; tel. 873333; telex 201; fax 863905; f. 1930; cap. 4,500m., res 19,610m., dep. 228,451m. (Dec. 1996); Pres. MANUEL CERQUEDA-DONADEU; Dir and Gen. Man. JOSEP MONTAÑÉS ALSO; 9 brs.

Banc Internacional d'Andorra SA: POB 8, Avinguda Meritxell 32, Andorra la Vella; tel. 820607; telex 206; fax 829980; f. 1958; affiliated to Banco de Bilbao, Spain; cap. 7,056m., res 15,029m., dep. 401,312m. (Dec. 1996); Chair. JOAN MORA FONT; Gen. Man. MANUEL DOMINGO NARVARTE; 4 brs.

Banca Mora SA: POB 8, Plaça Coprínceps 2, Escaldes-Engordany; tel. 820607; telex 222; fax 829980; f. 1952; subsidiary of Banc Internacional d'Andorra SA; cap. 1,512m., res 7,349m., dep. 178,607m. (Dec. 1996); Chair. FRANCESC MORA FONT; Man. Dir JORDI ARISTOT MORA; 7 brs.

Banca Privada d'Andorra SA: POB 25, Avinguda Carlemany 119, Escaldes-Engordany; tel. 873500; telex 202; fax 873517; f. 1958; fmrly Banca Cassany SA; cap. 2,400m., res 766m., dep. 58,636m. (Dec. 1996); Dir JOAN PAU MIQUEL PRATS; Sec. IGNÀSI MARTÍN; 4 brs.

Banca Reig SA: Avinguda Verge de Canòlich 43, Sant Julià de Lòria; tel. 841074; telex 240; fax 841833; f. 1956; cap. 2,000m., res 8,631m., dep. 134,158m. (Dec. 1995); Pres. JULIÀ REIG RIBO; Man. Dir JOSEP MARIA PALLEROLA SEGON; 7 brs.

Crèdit Andorrà: Avinguda Princep Benlloch 25, Andorra la Vella; tel. 820326; telex 200; fax 829325; f. 1955; cap. 10,000m., res 37,230m., dep. 482,016m. (Dec. 1996); Chair. A. PINTAT; Man. Dir P. ROQUET; 14 brs.

Transport

RAILWAYS

There are no railways in Andorra, but the nearest stations are Ax-les-Thermes, L'Hospitalet and La Tour de Carol, in France (with trains from Toulouse and Perpignan), and Puigcerdá, in Spain, on the line from Barcelona. There is a connecting bus service from all four stations to Andorra.

ROADS

A good road connects the Spanish and French frontiers, passing through Andorra la Vella. In 1994 there were 269 national roads, 198 of which were tarmacked.

CIVIL AVIATION

There is an airport at Seo de Urgel in Spain, 20 km from Andorra la Vella.

Tourism

Andorra has attractive mountain scenery, and winter sports facilities are available at five skiing centres. Tourists are also attracted by Andorra's duty-free shopping facilities. In 1994 there were 350 hotels and hostels in Andorra. An estimated 8m. tourists visited Andorra in 1995.

Ministeri de Medi Ambient i Turisme: Carrer Prat de la Creu 62–64, Andorra la Vella; tel. 829345; fax 860184; e-mail turisme@andorra.ad.

Sindicat d'Iniciativa Oficina de Turisme: Carrer Dr Vilanova, Andorra la Vella; tel. 820214; fax 825823.

ANGOLA

Introductory Survey

Location, Climate, Language, Religion, Flag, Capital

The Republic of Angola lies on the west coast of Africa. The Cabinda district is separated from the rest of the country by the estuary of the River Congo and territory of the Democratic Republic of the Congo (DRC—formerly Zaire), with the Republic of the Congo lying to its north. Angola is bordered by the DRC to the north, Zambia to the east and Namibia to the south. The climate is tropical, locally tempered by altitude. There are two distinct seasons (wet and dry) but little seasonal variation in temperature. It is very hot and rainy in the coastal lowlands but temperatures are lower inland. The official language is Portuguese, but African languages (mainly Umbundo, Kimbundo, Kikongo, Chokwe and Ganguela) are also in common use. Much of the population follows traditional African beliefs, although a majority profess to be Christians, mainly Roman Catholics. The flag (proportions 3 by 2) has two equal horizontal stripes, of red and black; superimposed in the centre, in gold, are a five-pointed star, half a cog-wheel and a machete. The capital is Luanda.

Recent History

Formerly a Portuguese colony, Angola became an overseas province in 1951. African nationalist groups began to form in the 1950s and 1960s, including the Movimento Popular de Libertação de Angola (MPLA) in 1956, the Frente Nacional de Libertação de Angola (FNLA) in 1962 and the União Nacional para a Independência Total de Angola (UNITA) in 1966. There was an unsuccessful nationalist rebellion in 1961. Severe repression ensued but, after a new wave of fighting in 1966, nationalist guerrilla groups were able to establish military and political control in large parts of eastern Angola and to press westward. Following the April 1974 *coup d'état* in Portugal, Angola's right to independence was recognized, and negotiations between the Portuguese Government and the nationalist groups began in September. After the formation of a common front by these groups, it was agreed that Angola would become independent in November 1975.

In January 1975 a transitional Government was established, comprising representatives of the MPLA, the FNLA, UNITA and the Portuguese Government. However, violent clashes between the MPLA and the FNLA occurred in March, as a result of the groups' political differences, and continued throughout the country. By the second half of 1975 control of Angola was effectively divided between the three major nationalist groups, each aided by foreign powers. The MPLA (which held the capital) was supported by the USSR and Cuba, the FNLA by Zaire and Western powers (including the USA), while UNITA was backed by South African forces. The FNLA and UNITA formed a united front to fight the MPLA.

The Portuguese Government proclaimed Angola independent from 11 November 1975, transferring sovereignty to 'the Angolan people' rather than to any of the liberation movements. The MPLA proclaimed the People's Republic of Angola and the establishment of a government in Luanda under the presidency of the movement's leader, Dr Agostinho Neto. The FNLA and UNITA proclaimed the People's Democratic Republic of Angola and a coalition government, based in Nova Lisboa (renamed Huambo). The involvement of South African and Cuban troops caused an international furore. By the end of February 1976, however, the MPLA, aided by Cuban technical and military expertise, had effectively gained control of the whole country. South African troops were withdrawn from Angola in March, but Cuban troops remained to assist the MPLA regime in countering guerrilla activity by the remnants of the defeated UNITA forces.

In May 1977 an abortive coup, led by Nito Alves (a former minister), resulted in a purge of state and party officials, severely hampering the task of national reconstruction. In December the MPLA was restructured as a political party, the Movimento Popular de Libertação de Angola—Partido do Trabalho (MPLA—PT), but further divisions became evident in December 1978, when President Neto abolished the post of Prime Minister and ousted several other ministers.

President Neto died in September 1979, and José Eduardo dos Santos, hitherto the Minister of Planning, was unanimously elected party leader and President by the MPLA—PT Central Committee. President dos Santos continued to encourage strong links with the Soviet bloc, and led campaigns to eliminate corruption and inefficiency. Elections to the National People's Assembly, which replaced the Council of the Revolution, were first held in 1980. Fresh elections, due to be held in 1983, were postponed until 1986, owing to political and military problems.

The MPLA—PT Government's recovery programme was continually hindered by security problems. Although the FNLA rebel movement reportedly surrendered to the Government in 1984, UNITA conducted sustained and disruptive guerrilla activities, mainly in southern and central Angola, throughout the 1980s. In addition, forces from South Africa, which was providing UNITA with considerable military aid, made numerous armed incursions over the Angolan border with Namibia, ostensibly in pursuit of guerrilla forces belonging to the South West Africa People's Organisation (SWAPO), which was supported by the Angolan Government. In July 1983 regional military councils were established in the provinces affected by the fighting. Although the Government's military campaign against UNITA appeared to be increasingly successful during 1985, the rebels' position was strengthened in April 1986, when US military aid began to arrive. A visit to the European Parliament by Dr Jonas Savimbi, the President of UNITA, in October failed to improve the international standing of the group. The US Government, however, continued to provide covert military aid to UNITA during the period 1987–90. Nevertheless, UNITA was excluded from a series of major peace negotiations which commenced in May 1988. In July and August Savimbi travelled to the USA and to several European and African capitals to seek support for UNITA's demands to be included in the negotiations. Although movement for a negotiated settlement between the MPLA—PT Government and UNITA then gathered momentum, UNITA's position became vulnerable in August, when a cease-fire between Angola and South Africa was declared and when South African troops were reportedly withdrawn from Angola. UNITA, which openly refused to adhere to the cease-fire, continued to be active. Following the conclusion of the New York accords on Angola and Namibia in December, whereby South Africa undertook to discontinue its military support for UNITA (see below), the US Government renewed its commitment to the rebels.

During late 1988 peace initiatives emerged from within Africa with regard to the Angolan civil war. Several African states (including Zaire) were involved in efforts, supported by the USA, to pressurize the Angolan Government into negotiating an internal settlement with UNITA. In December the UN Security Council established the UN Angola Verification Mission (UNAVEM), to verify the withdrawal of Cuban troops from Angola (see below).

In early February 1989 the Angolan Government offered a 12-month amnesty to members of the rebel organization; UNITA, restating its aim of entering into a transitional coalition government with the MPLA—PT as a prelude to multi-party elections, responded to the amnesty by launching a major offensive against Angolan government targets. This was abandoned shortly afterwards, following the intercession of President Houphouët-Boigny of Côte d'Ivoire. In early March President dos Santos announced that he was willing to attend a regional summit conference on the Angolan civil war; Savimbi, in turn, announced that he would honour a unilateral moratorium on offensive military operations until mid-July. In mid-May eight African Heads of State attended a conference in Luanda, at which President dos Santos presented a peace plan that envisaged the cessation of US aid to UNITA and offered the rebels reintegration into society; this was rejected by UNITA. Nevertheless, in mid-June both President dos Santos and Savimbi attended a conference at Gbadolite, in Zaire, convened by the Zairean President, Mobutu Sese Seko, at which 18 African Heads of State were present. President Mobutu succeeded in mediating a peace agreement between the Angolan Government and UNITA, in accordance with which a cease-fire came into effect on 24 June. The full terms of the accord were not, however, made public at that time, and it subsequently became apparent that these were interpreted differently by each party. Within one week, each side had accused the other of violating the cease-fire, and in late August Savimbi announced a resumption of hostilities.

In September 1989, after boycotting a conference of eight African Heads of State in Kinshasa, Zaire, at which the June peace accord had been redrafted, Savimbi announced a series of counter-proposals, envisaging the creation of an African peace-keeping force, to supervise a renewed cease-fire, and the commencement of negotiations between UNITA and the Angolan Government, with the objective of agreeing a settlement that would lay the foundation of a multi-party democracy in Angola. In early October, following a meeting with President Bush of the USA, Savimbi agreed to resume peace talks with the Angolan Government, with President Mobutu of Zaire acting as mediator. In late December President dos Santos proposed a peace plan that envisaged some political reform, but did not include provisions for a multi-party political system; the plan was rejected by UNITA.

During early 1990 fighting intensified between government troops and the UNITA rebels in the Mavinga region of southern Angola, a UNITA stronghold. Initially, the government forces made substantial advances. In April UNITA agreed to respect an immediate cease-fire and requested direct discussions with the Government: exploratory talks between representatives of the two sides were held in Portugal later that month. During May UNITA guerrillas succeeded in regaining control of Mavinga, and in the following month the Government announced that it was to withdraw its troops from the region as a gesture of goodwill.

In early July 1990 the Central Committee of the MPLA—PT announced that the Government would allow Angola to 'evolve towards a multi-party system', thus conceding one of UNITA's principal demands. In late October the Central Committee proposed a general programme of reform, including the replacement of the party's official Marxist-Leninist ideology with a commitment to 'democratic socialism', the legalization of political parties, the transformation of the army from a party institution to a state institution, the introduction of a market economy, a revision of the Constitution and the holding of multi-party elections in 1994, following a population census. These proposals were formally approved by the third Congress of the MPLA—PT in December. However, the Government and UNITA continued to disagree over the timing of elections and the status of UNITA pending the elections. UNITA insisted on immediate political recognition as a precondition for a cease-fire, and the holding of elections by the end of 1991.

In late March 1991 the People's Assembly approved legislation permitting the formation of political parties. On 1 May, as a result of the series of talks that commenced in April 1990, the Government and UNITA concluded a peace agreement in Estoril, Portugal. The agreement provided for a cease-fire from midnight on 15 May, which was to be monitored by a joint political and military commission, comprising representatives from the MPLA—PT, UNITA, the UN, Portugal, the USA and the USSR. A new national army of 50,000 men was to be established, comprising equal numbers of government and UNITA soldiers. Free and democratic elections were to be held by the end of 1992. In early May 1991 the Government approved legislation allowing all exiles one year in which to return to Angola. The cease-fire took effect, according to plan, on 15 May, despite an intensification of hostilities prior to that date. On 31 May the Government and UNITA signed a formal agreement in Lisbon, Portugal, ratifying the Estoril agreement. Meanwhile, all Cuban troops had been withdrawn from Angola, but the UN Security Council agreed to prolong the presence of the UN Angola Verification Mission (as UNAVEM II), with a mandate to ensure implementation of the peace accords. In July the Standing Commission of the People's Assembly approved a new amnesty law, under the terms of which amnesty would be granted for all crimes against state security as well as for military and common law offences committed before 31 May 1991.

A reshuffle of the Council of Ministers in July 1991 included the appointment of Fernando José França van-Dúnem to the post of Prime Minister, thus reintroducing the premiership to the Government. Supreme executive power remained, however, with the President.

At the end of September 1991 Savimbi returned to Luanda for the first time since the civil war began in 1975; UNITA headquarters were transferred to the capital from Jamba in October. In the following month President dos Santos announced that legislative and presidential elections were to take place in September 1992, subject to the extension of state administration to areas still under UNITA control and the confinement of all UNITA forces to assembly points by mid-December 1991. In January 1992, on the recommendation of the joint political and military commission, a monitoring task group was established in order to oversee the implementation of the peace agreement. The creation of the group, which included members of the Government, UNITA and UNAVEM II, followed growing concern over the reported decline in the number of government and UNITA troops in confinement areas and the reoccupation of territory by UNITA forces.

Representatives of the Government and 26 political parties met in Luanda in January 1992 to discuss the transition to multi-party democracy; the Government rejected demands to convene a national conference on the transition process. UNITA boycotted the meeting, but in February it held talks with the Government, at which agreement was reached on various points of electoral procedure. It was agreed that the elections would be conducted on the basis of proportional representation, with the President elected for a five-year term, renewable for a maximum of three terms. The legislature would be a national assembly, elected for a four-year term. In early April the People's Assembly adopted electoral legislation incorporating these decisions and providing for the creation of a national assembly of 223 members (90 to be elected in 18 provincial constituencies and the remainder from national lists).

Signs of internal conflict within UNITA became apparent in early March 1992 with the announcement that two of its leading members, Gen. Miguel N'Zau Puna and Gen. Tony da Costa Fernandes, had resigned. In February the two men had secretly left Angola for Paris, France, from where they issued statements denouncing Savimbi as a dictator and claiming that he was maintaining a clandestine force of some 20,000 troops near the Namibian border.

In mid-April 1992 the Supreme Court approved UNITA's registration as a political party. In early May the MPLA—PT held an extraordinary congress to prepare for the forthcoming elections. The delegates voted to enlarge the membership of the Central Committee to allow the inclusion of prominent dissidents who had returned to the party. The Central Committee recommended that the Political Bureau further expand its membership with a view to broadening the base of the party's support. During the congress the delegates also voted to remove the suffix Partido do Trabalho (Party of Labour or Workers' Party) from the organization's official name. In late August the legislature approved a further revision of the Constitution, removing the remnants of the country's former Marxist ideology, and deleting the words 'People's' and 'Popular' from the Constitution and from the names of official institutions. The name of the country was changed from the People's Republic of Angola to the Republic of Angola.

Increased tension and outbreaks of violence in the period preceding the general election, which was due to be held on 29 and 30 September 1992, seriously threatened to disrupt the electoral process. In early September secessionist groups in Cabinda province, the enclave which provides most of Angola's petroleum revenue, intensified attacks on government troops. Following an offensive by guerrilla forces of the Frente de Libertação do Enclave de Cabinda (FLEC), government troops effectively lost control of Cabinda City for several days. In the same month, clashes between UNITA and government forces in Bié province resulted in the seizure of Kuito airport by UNITA.

On 27 September 1992 the government Forças Armadas Populares de Libertação de Angola (FAPLA) and the UNITA forces were formally disbanded, and the new national army, the Forças Armadas de Angola (FAA), was officially established. However, the process of training and incorporating FAPLA and UNITA troops into the new 50,000-strong national army had been hindered by delays in the demobilization programme. By 28 September fewer than 10,000 soldiers were ready to be sworn in as members of the FAA. Tens of thousands of government troops were reported to be awaiting demobilization or to have abandoned confinement areas, owing to poor conditions and non-payment of wages. Military observers reported that only a small percentage of UNITA soldiers had been demobilized, and that UNITA retained a heavily armed and disciplined force.

Presidential and legislative elections were held, as scheduled, on 29 and 30 September 1992. When preliminary results indicated victory in the elections to the new National Assembly for the MPLA, Savimbi accused the Government of electoral fraud, withdrew his troops from the FAA, and demanded the suspension of the official announcement of the election results until an inquiry into the alleged electoral irregularities had been conducted. According to the provisions of the electoral law, a second round of the presidential election was required to be held between dos Santos and Savimbi, as neither candidate had secured 50% of the votes cast in the first round. Savimbi, who had retreated to the UNITA-dominated province of Huambo, agreed to participate in this second round on the condition that it be conducted by the UN, while the Government insisted that the election should not take place until UNITA had satisfied the conditions of the Estoril peace agreement by transferring its troops to assembly points or to the FAA.

Following the announcement, on 17 October 1992, of the official results of the elections, which the UN had declared to have been free and fair, violence broke out between MPLA and UNITA supporters in the cities of Luanda and Huambo. By the end of October hostilities had spread throughout Angola, with the majority of UNITA's demobilized soldiers returning to arms. In early November several senior UNITA officials, including Elias Salupeto Pena (the senior UNITA representative on the joint political and military commission) and Jeremias Chitunda (Vice-President of UNITA), were reported to be among those killed in the renewed conflict. On 10 November UN diplomats met Savimbi in Huambo province, in an attempt to negotiate a peaceful solution to the political and military crisis. On 20 November Savimbi issued a statement in which he agreed to abide by the results of the September elections, although he maintained that the ballot had been fraudulent. UNITA, however, failed to attend an all-party national conference, convened on the following day in Luanda, on the grounds that the safety of a UNITA delegation could not be guaranteed. Subsequently dos Santos announced that the new National Assembly, which was to be formed in accordance with the results of the September elections, would be inaugurated on 26 November. On that day delegations from the Government and UNITA met in Namibe in an effort to resolve the crisis. A joint communiqué was issued, declaring full acceptance of the validity of the May 1991 Estoril peace agreement and the intention to implement immediately a nation-wide cease-fire. However, UNITA's 70 elected deputies failed to attend the inauguration of the National Assembly. On 27 November dos Santos announced the appointment of Marcolino José Carlos Moco, the Secretary-General of the MPLA, as Prime Minister. At the end of November, in violation of the recently-signed Namibe accord, hostilities broke out in the north of the country. On 2 December a new Council of Ministers was announced, including minor ministerial positions for members of the FNLA, the Fórum Democrático Angolano, the Partido Renovador Social and the Partido de Aliança de Juventude, Operários e Camponêses de Angola. In addition, one full and four deputy ministerial posts were reserved for UNITA, which was allowed a week to join the Government. UNITA subsequently issued a statement nominating a number of its officials to the reserved posts. According to a statement by the Prime Minister, however, the appointment of UNITA officials to the Government was entirely dependent upon the implementation of the Estoril peace agreement.

In December 1992 government forces launched a major nation-wide offensive against UNITA, in an effort to regain territory lost to the rebels in the wake of the September elections, when UNITA assumed control of some 65% of the country. By mid-January 1993 UNITA forces had been ousted from most major towns, but had captured the petroleum-producing centre of Soyo, on the Zaire border (the occupation of which was estimated to cost the Government some US $2m. per day in lost revenue). In late January peace talks between UNITA and the Government, convened by the UN, were conducted in Addis Ababa, Ethiopia, with Portugal, Russia and the USA attending as observers. Following two months of intense fighting for control of the country's second largest city, Huambo (a traditional UNITA stronghold), the Government confirmed in early March that it had withdrawn its forces. Some 10,000 people were thought to have died in the conflict. On 12 March the UN Security Council adopted a resolution condemning UNITA's violations of the peace accords. Peace talks, which resumed in Abidjan, Côte d'Ivoire, in mid-April, were frustrated by UNITA's insistence that a UN peace-keeping force be deployed prior to the negotiation of a formal cease-fire. The talks were finally suspended indefinitely on 21 May. On 19 May, prompted by UNITA's intransigence and apparent lack of commitment to peace, the US President, Bill Clinton, had announced that the USA was to recognize the Angolan Government. In June, in a move reflecting an improvement in their diplomatic relations, Angola and South Africa agreed to upgrade their respective diplomatic missions in Pretoria and Luanda to embassies. In the same month a US embassy was opened in Luanda. In mid-July the UN Security Council reiterated demands that UNITA cease military activity and abide by the results of the September 1992 elections, warning that an embargo would be enforced against UNITA unless an effective cease-fire had been established by 15 September. In early August the FAA launched a major bombing campaign against Huambo. In response, UNITA intensified its attacks on the besieged government garrison in the central city of Kuito. On 9 August, in recognition of the Government's 'legitimate right of self-defence', the United Kingdom lifted its arms embargo against the Angolan Government (which had been in force since independence in 1975). Later in the month the Government signed an agreement with the World Food Programme, providing for a six-month emergency food operation, which was intended to reach almost 2m. people suffering the consequences of the civil war. On 14 September UNITA announced that it would implement a unilateral cease-fire, to begin on 20 September, thus prompting the UN Security Council to delay its deadline for imposing an embargo against UNITA until 25 September. However, despite UNITA's claims that it was observing the cease-fire, diplomatic sources reported an intensification of UNITA activity beyond the UN deadline. Consequently, on 26 September the UN imposed an arms and petroleum embargo against UNITA. Observers calculated, however, that clandestine supplies of arms and petroleum from Zaire, in addition to UNITA's existing arms stockpiles, would ensure that the rebels' military capacity could be sustained for some years, despite the embargo. Further UN sanctions, including the expulsion of UNITA representatives from foreign capitals and the freezing of the rebels' assets abroad, were to be imposed on 1 November if UNITA should fail to cease hostilities.

Diplomatic efforts, made during late September and early October 1993, to effect a resumption of peace talks continued to falter, owing to UNITA's refusal to comply with the Government's demand that, as a precondition to talks, the rebels withdraw from territory seized since the September 1992 elections. However, in mid-October 1993 the Government reportedly abandoned this demand. According to the Government's revised terms, UNITA was required to accept unequivocally the results of the September 1992 elections, the terms of the 1991 Estoril peace agreement and all subsequent UN Security Council resolutions. At the same time, the UN Secretary-General's special representative, Alioune Blondin Beye, reported that a reduction in hostilities was facilitating the distribution of relief aid, including consignments to the besieged city of Kuito. In late October exploratory peace talks began in Lusaka, Zambia, between the UN, the official observer nations, and representatives of the Government and UNITA. On 1 November Beye informed the UN Security Council that UNITA had agreed to withdraw its forces to UN-monitored confinement areas. In response, the UN agreed to delay the imposition of further sanctions against UNITA until 15 December, on condition that the rebels comply with their undertakings.

Direct talks between UNITA and the Government, which had been adjourned in May, resumed in Lusaka in mid-November 1993. By 10 December agreement had reportedly been reached on issues concerning the demobilization and confinement of UNITA troops, the surrender of UNITA weapons to the UN, and the integration of UNITA generals into the FAA. On 15 December the UN Security Council extended the mandate of UNAVEM II for a further three months and agreed to another postponement of additional sanctions against UNITA. The Lusaka talks resumed in January 1994, and that month an agreement was announced on the formation of a national police force of 26,700 members, of which UNITA was to provide 5,500, to be formed under UN supervision. Further talks culminated in the signing, on 17 February, of a document on national reconciliation incorporating five fundamental principles. Acceptance of the September 1992 election results by both sides was also reaffirmed.

The resignation of the Minister of Finance prompted a wider reorganization of the Council of Ministers in March 1994, including the creation of a new Ministry of Economic Planning. On 16 March the UN Security Council extended the mandate of UNAVEM II until 31 May. Progress at the Lusaka peace talks slowed as discussions moved on to the issue of the participation of UNITA in central and local government. Negotiations on the distribution of ministerial posts appeared to have reached an impasse in mid-March, and Beye announced at the end of March that negotiations would instead move on to discuss the conclusion of the electoral process: the second round of presidential elections between dos Santos and Savimbi. In early May agreement was officially confirmed regarding these elections, although some related issues remained to be discussed, including the role of the independent observers. Further talks, concerning the issues of UNITA's representation in the Council of Ministers and the status of Savimbi, reached an impasse in May. The talks took place against a background of intensified hostilities, particularly in Kuito and Malanje. On 31 May the UN Security Council extended the mandate of UNAVEM II until 30 June, when it was to reconsider the role of the UN if a peace accord had not been reached. In mid-June agreement was reached on the extension of state administration throughout the entire national territory. Talks continued in Lusaka in late June, culminating in the signing of an 18-point document on national reconciliation. At the same time, government forces were reported to have gained complete control of Kuito, ending an 18-month siege of the city by UNITA forces.

In early July 1994 President Mandela of South Africa hosted talks in Pretoria between the Presidents of Angola, Mozambique and Zaire. The discussions concentrated on allegations of Zairean support for UNITA and resulted in the re-establishment of a joint defence and security commission between Angola and Zaire, with the aim of curbing the supply of armaments to the rebels. In early August UNITA acceded to government insistence that its officials be permitted to participate in government institutions only after the total demilitarization of the movement. An 11-point procedural accord, enabling discussions on full reconciliation, was signed on 9 August. In mid-August UNITA officially acknowledged that it had lost control of the diamond-mining centre of Kafunfo (in the north-east of the country), an important source of funds for UNITA. Government troops were also reported to have taken control of the strategic diamond-producing town of Catoca, close to the border with Zaire, in a campaign to drive UNITA out of Lunda-Norte province.

Throughout July and August 1994 the question of the governorship of Huambo continued to constitute the main obstacle to the furtherance of the peace talks. On 8 September UNITA reportedly accepted a proposal by mediators for the allocation to UNITA of government positions that included some 170 posts in central and local administration but excluded the governorship of Huambo. On 9 September the UN Security Council announced that additional sanctions would not be imposed on UNITA. In mid-September the Government and UNITA agreed on the general principles governing the mandate of a new UN Angola Verification Mission—UNAVEM III. At the end of September, following successive extensions since July, the UN Security Council further extended the mandate of UNAVEM II until 31 October and urged both sides to sign a peace accord by 15 October. However, talks continued throughout October, concentrating on the replacement of the joint political and military commission with a new joint commission—to be chaired by Beye and comprise representatives of the Government and UNITA and observers from the USA, Russia and Portugal—and the issue of Savimbi's security. A peace accord was finally initialled on 31 October, and dos Santos and Savimbi were to sign it on 15 November in Lusaka. However, an intensified military campaign by the Government, which resulted in the seizure in early November of Soyo and the UNITA stronghold of Huambo, threatened to jeopardize the peace accord, and UNITA indicated that it was no longer disposed to sign the treaty. On 15 November, following mediation by President Mandela, government and UNITA generals signed a truce in Lusaka, which was to remain in force until 22 November, when a permanent cease-fire was to come into force. The formal signing of the peace accord was postponed until 20 November, to allow outstanding issues to be discussed. Despite the absence of Savimbi, the formal signing of the Lusaka peace accord took place on the designated date, with the Secretary-General of UNITA, Eugênio Antonino Ngolo Manuvakola, signing on behalf of the rebels, and the Minister of Foreign Affairs, Dr Venâncio da Silva Moura, signing for the Government. However, hostilities continued beyond 22 November, notably in Huambo and in Bié province, and each side accused the other of violations of the permanent cease-fire.

In December 1994 the UN Security Council extended the mandate of UNAVEM II until 8 February 1995, when it was to be superseded by UNAVEM III, on condition that the cease-fire was observed. In January 1995, in the light of continuing fighting, a meeting took place at Chipipa, in Huambo province, between the Chief of General Staff of the FAA and his UNITA counterpart, at which agreement was reached on an immediate cessation of hostilities nation-wide, the disengagement of opposing troops (particularly in sensitive areas such as Huambo and Uíge), the release of prisoners of war and the creation of conditions to allow the free movement of people and goods. Despite these undertakings, hostilities continued.

In early February 1995 the UN Security Council adopted a resolution creating UNAVEM III (see p. 54). The new mission, the initial mandate of which was to expire in early August, was to comprise a military peace-keeping force of some 7,000 troops, in addition to 350 civilian staff. However, the deployment of UNAVEM III remained conditional on the cessation of hostilities and the disengagement of government and UNITA forces. Also in February the UN conducted an appeal for humanitarian aid in excess of US $200m. to provide emergency assistance for more than 3m. people, to support the demobilization and reintegration of former combatants, and to finance a programme to clear the country of an estimated 10m. land-mines.

At UNITA's party congress held at Bailundo, in Huambo province, in February 1995, agreement was reached to accept the terms of the Lusaka peace accord and to endorse a proposed meeting between Savimbi and dos Santos. However, there were reports of division within the party concerning commitment to the peace process. These were supported in late February by the testimony of Col Isaac Zabarra, secretary to UNITA's military council, who, having surrendered to the FAA, alleged that Savimbi had privately rejected the peace accord and intended to prepare a major military offensive.

In March 1995 both the Government and UNITA came under criticism in a report made to the UN Security Council by the UN Secretary-General, Dr Boutros Boutros-Ghali, who accused the two sides of a lack of goodwill in implementing the peace process, and reiterated the conditions for the deployment of UNAVEM III, which required strict observance of the cease-fire. The report, which followed continued and widespread violations of the truce, set a deadline of 25 March for the two sides to demonstrate a genuine commitment to the peace process. It also appealed for preparations to be expedited to enable the prompt transfer of UNITA troops into the FAA. On 28 March, following a meeting of the joint commission, Beye announced that the initial stage of troop disengagement had been completed, allowing arrangements to proceed for the deployment of UNAVEM III. In the following month Beye confirmed that the majority of UNAVEM III personnel would begin arriving in early May. In late April the joint commission reported a significant reduction in violations of the cease-fire and a concomitant increase in the free movement of people and goods. However, at the same time Boutros-Ghali indicated that the fragility of the cease-fire and reports of military preparations, including the acquisition of arms from abroad, remained serious causes of concern.

In early May 1995, in what represented an important development in the peace process, dos Santos and Savimbi met in Lusaka for direct talks. The meeting, which had been achieved as the result of mediation by Beye, concluded with the ratification of the Lusaka peace accord. Notably, Savimbi recognized the status of dos Santos as President of Angola, addressing him as such, and pledged his full co-operation in the reconstruction of the nation. The two leaders agreed to accelerate the consolidation of the cease-fire, to create conditions for the deployment of UNAVEM III, to expedite the integration of UNITA troops into the FAA, and to establish a government of unity based on the provisions of the Lusaka accord (subsequent to the demobilization of the UNITA forces). Dos Santos requested that Savimbi nominate immediately the UNITA appointees to the new government.

In June 1995 the MPLA announced its decision to propose a revision of the Constitution to create two new posts of Vice-President, of which one was to be offered to Savimbi, conditional upon the prior disbanding of UNITA forces. The other vice-presidency was to be assumed by the then President of the National Assembly, Fernando José França van-Dúnem. Later that month Savimbi, who had publicly expressed his intention to accept the vice-presidency, declared the war in Angola to be at an end and appealed to neighbouring nations to prevent the traffic of arms to the country. In July the National Assembly approved the proposal that the Constitution be reformed to create the two new vice-presidential positions, and Boutros-Ghali announced that the deployment of UNAVEM III personnel, which had fallen seriously behind schedule, would be completed by the end of August. In late July, at ongoing discussions between delegations of the Government and UNITA concerning the implementation of military aspects of the Lusaka accord, it was agreed that the FAA should be enlarged to 90,000 troops. Other issues under discussion included the formation of a fourth, non-combatant branch of the FAA, which would engage in public works projects.

Direct talks between dos Santos and Savimbi resumed in August 1995 in Franceville, Gabon. At the meeting Savimbi agreed in principle to accept the vice-presidency but requested that the offer be formally extended to UNITA. The Government duly complied. Earlier in August the UN Security Council had extended the mandate of UNAVEM III until February 1996. In September the joint commission expressed concern at continuing violations of the cease-fire. However, in the following month, figures issued by UNAVEM III revealed that recorded cease-fire violations had decreased by approximately 50% between July and September. In late September the Government signed a four-month cease-fire agreement with FLEC-Renovada, a faction of FLEC, the secessionist group in Cabinda province. It was anticipated that the agreement, which followed an offensive by FLEC-Renovada on Cabinda City in the previous month, would facilitate the negotiation, between the Government and all factions of FLEC, of a pact aimed at national reconciliation. Discussions concerning the implementation of the military aspects of the Lusaka accord continued in October and November.

In late September 1995 dos Santos and Savimbi met for direct talks in Brussels, Belgium, immediately prior to the convention there of an international donors' conference on Angola. Reportedly the two leaders discussed the presentation of an appeal for assistance totalling some US $650m. towards Angola's national rehabilitation and reconciliation programme. However, at the conference donors exceeded the requested sum, pledging a total of $997.5m., of which $200m. was to be allocated to emergency humanitarian assistance. The cantonment of UNITA forces began officially in late November. However, continued hostilities were reported that month, including confrontations in the diamond-producing areas of the north-east and in the Cabinda enclave. In early December, following concerted military operations by government forces aimed at occupying UNITA-controlled territory in Zaire province, UNITA suspended the confinement of its troops. In the light of this set-back, and in an effort to promote confidence in the peace process in advance of discussions, to be conducted that month, with US President Clinton, dos Santos promptly introduced a number of conciliatory measures, including the withdrawal of government troops from positions seized in Zaire province, and the confinement, which began the following month, of the paramilitary Rapid Intervention Force. In addition, dos Santos cancelled the Government's contract with Executive Outcomes, a South African company ostensibly providing military advisers to give logistical support to the FAA, but condemned by UNITA as mercenaries in active service, in direct contravention of the Lusaka accord, which forbids mercenary support for either side. In early January 1996 Executive Outcomes confirmed that its representatives had departed from Angola. Later that month UNITA resumed the process of confining its troops. However, in the same month the US Permanent Representative at the UN, Dr Madeleine Albright, warned that further delay would prompt the international community to withdraw its support for the peace process. In response, Savimbi pledged to confine a total of 16,500 UNITA troops by 8 February, when the UN Security Council was to review the mandate of UNAVEM III. By that date, however, UNITA had succeeded in confining only some 8,200 troops, prompting the UN Security Council to renew the mandate of UNAVEM III for a reduced term of only three months. In late January, following discussions conducted in Brazzaville, the Congo, the Government and FLEC–Renovada agreed to extend the cease-fire accord secured in September 1995. Discussions were to continue in pursuit of a definitive cease-fire agreement.

In March 1996 discussions between dos Santos and Savimbi, conducted in Libreville, Gabon, resulted in agreement on the establishment of a government of national unity, in accordance with the provisions of the Lusaka accord, by the end of July. Savimbi presented dos Santos with a proposal listing the UNITA nominees who would participate in such a government, while dos Santos in turn presented Savimbi with a formal invitation to assume the vice-presidency. (Later that month, however, Savimbi demanded the inclusion of other opposition parties in the government of national unity, presenting as a condition to his own participation the inclusion in the new administration of the President of the FNLA, Holden Roberto.) Agreement was also reached in Libreville on the formation of the unified national army, which, it was envisaged, would be concluded in June. In subsequent talks conducted that month between representatives of the Government and UNITA it was agreed that 18 UNITA generals would be appointed to command posts in the new unified FAA, of which nine would be in the army and another nine in the non-combatant 'fourth branch'. It was also established that 26,300 of UNITA's total force of some 62,000 would be integrated into the FAA. In late March the Government began the phased withdrawal to barracks of its troops.

On 8 May 1996, in the light of further delays in the peace process, the UN Security Council extended the mandate of UNAVEM III by just two months. That month the National Assembly approved an amnesty law pardoning all crimes against internal state security committed since the signing of the Estoril peace agreement. In late May, following negotiations between the Government and UNITA, agreement was reached on a programme to integrate UNITA troops into the FAA. Selection of UNITA personnel was to begin on 1 June. During May Savimbi introduced further conditions for his acceptance of the vice-presidency and expressed his intention to retain control of diamond-producing areas in north-eastern Angola. In mid-May the Government and a Cabinda secessionist faction, FLEC-Forças Armadas Cabindesas (FLEC-FAC), signed an agreement outlining the principles of a cease-fire. However, following renewed fighting later that month between government troops and the secessionists, the leader of FLEC-FAC, Henrique N'zita Tiago, declared that a definitive cease-fire would only follow the withdrawal of the FAA from Cabinda.

In mid-1996 public protest at deteriorating economic conditions and the high level of corruption within the state apparatus placed increasing political pressure on dos Santos, who responded in early June with the dismissal of the Moco administration. Moco was succeeded as Prime Minister by the President of the National Assembly (and former Prime Minister), Fernando José França van-Dúnem. A new Government was sworn in on 8 June, with only limited changes to the previous administration.

On 11 July 1996 the UN Security Council extended the mandate of UNAVEM III by a further three months. In mid-August the Government approved the disbursement of US $65m. to finance the reintegration of as many as 100,000 government and UNITA soldiers into civilian society. A further $66m. was required from international donors to complete the programme. In late August, following its party congress, UNITA issued a communiqué declining the appointment of Savimbi to the position of national Vice-President. Savimbi, who had publicly rejected the post earlier that month, subsequently reaffirmed his decision. UNITA did not propose the appointment of another of its officials to the post, and in September Beye confirmed that the offer of the vice-presidency had become void.

In October 1996 delays in the implementation of the provisions of the Lusaka accord prompted the UN Security Council to threaten the imposition of sanctions against UNITA unless it met certain requirements by 20 November, including the surrender of weapons and the designation of those UNITA troops to be integrated into the FAA. In the following month the National Assembly adopted a constitutional revision extending its mandate, which was due to expire that month, for a period of between two and four years, pending the establishment of suitable conditions for the conduct of free and fair elections. On 11 December the UN Security Council extended the mandate of UNAVEM III until 28 February 1997, when the peace-keeping force was due to complete its mandate and begin withdrawing from Angola. Despite assertions by UNITA that it had fully disarmed in accordance with the terms of the Lusaka accord, UNAVEM III expressed concern in December 1996 that some 15,705 UNITA troops had deserted confinement areas. At the same time UN sources reported the existence of a residual

UNITA force of some 15,000 well-armed troops in central and north-eastern Angola. Despite these apparent obstacles to the further implementation of the peace accord, the Government announced in the same month that the UNITA deputies who had been elected in 1992 would join the National Assembly in mid-January 1997, and that the new government of national unity and reconciliation would be inaugurated on 25 January.

On 12 January 1997 dos Santos confirmed his acceptance of UNITA's nominees to the new government. However, following the failure of the UNITA deputies to join the National Assembly in mid-January, the Government postponed the inauguration of the new administration. In February UNITA asserted that it would only send its deputies and government nominees to the capital if the Government first agreed to negotiate a draft programme for the government of national unity and reconciliation. In mid-March the Government conceded to UNITA's demand and agreement was reached later that month on a basic programme. In the light of Savimbi's rejection of the vice-presidency, discussions concerning the special status to be conferred on him resulted, in early April, in an agreement according the UNITA leader the official title of 'leader of the opposition'. Subsequent to the arrival of the full contingent of UNITA deputies and government nominees in Luanda, on 11 April the new Government of National Unity and Reconciliation was inaugurated, although the ceremony was not attended by Savimbi who maintained that his personal security could not be guaranteed. As envisaged, UNITA assumed the ministerial portfolios of geology and mines, trade, health, and hotels and tourism, and a further seven deputy ministerial posts. Ten minor political parties were also represented in the 87-member Government.

In May 1997 the Angolan Government officially recognized the new Government of Laurent-Désiré Kabila in the Democratic Republic of the Congo (formerly Zaire). The Angolan Government had actively supported Kabila's rebels during the civil war in Zaire, while UNITA, which relied on Zaire as a conduit for exporting diamonds and importing arms, had reportedly sent some 2,000 troops to support President Mobutu. In the light of the defeat of UNITA's main ally, the Government subsequently launched a military offensive on UNITA strongholds in the north-eastern provinces of Lunda Sul and Lunda Norte in what appeared to be an attempt to eradicate UNITA as a military force. UNITA claimed that the FAA was contravening the Lusaka accord by attempting to restore control of the areas by force. In early 1997 Savimbi had reiterated his assertion that UNITA would not relinquish control of these diamond-producing regions, which industry sources estimated to earn UNITA some US $500m. per annum.

On 30 June 1997 the UN Security Council unanimously approved the UN Secretary-General's recommendations that UNAVEM III be discontinued and replaced by a scaled-down observer mission, the United Nations Observer Mission in Angola (MONUA), with a seven-month mandate to oversee the implementation of the remaining provisions of the Lusaka accord, including the reinstatement of state administration throughout the country. MONUA began operating on 1 July. The remaining UNAVEM III personnel were to be withdrawn gradually. In late July the UN again condemned UNITA's failure to adhere to the Lusaka accord and threatened to impose further sanctions on the movement, including travel restrictions, if it did not take irreversible steps towards fulfilling its obligations. A deadline of 15 August was set by which date UNITA was to give a full account of its military strength and to allow for the disarmament of its troops and the extension of state administration into those areas under its control. In addition, UNITA was required to transform its radio station, Voz da Resistência do Galo Negro, from an instrument of propaganda into a non-partisan station. According to government estimates, UNITA forces numbered some 25,000–35,000, whereas UNITA claimed to retain a force of only 2,963 'police'. By 15 August UNITA had failed to meet the requirements stipulted by the UN, which on 28 August unanimously adopted new sanctions. However, the implementation of the resolution was delayed until 30 September, allowing UNITA a further opportunity to resume the peace process. In addition, the withdrawal of some 2,650 UN military personnel was postponed until the end of October. At the end of August UNITA announced that it intended to comply with the demands of the UN in order to avoid the imposition of new sanctions.

In September 1997 the restoration of state administration proceeded in several districts, and, despite unsatisfactory progress in the demobilization of UNITA's residual force, was sufficient to prompt the UN Security Council, at the end of that month, to postpone the implementation of the sanctions for a further 30 days. In early October UNITA ceded control of one of the country's principal diamond mines, at Luzamba in Lunda Norte, to the Government.

In July 1997 government delegations from Angola and the Republic of the Congo met in Cabinda to discuss the security situation along the border between the Angolan exclave and the Congo, in the light of armed clashes between Angolan soldiers and FLEC separatists apparently operating from Congolese territory. The talks resulted in proposals to strengthen border security, including the establishment of a joint police force, comprising representatives from both countries and UNHCR. However, in October it became evident that FAA troops were actively supporting the former Marxist ruler of the Congo, Gen. Denis Sassou-Nguesso, in his attempts to overthrow the Government of President Pascal Lissouba. Angola's involvement had been prompted by attacks on Cabinda by FLEC and UNITA forces operating from bases in the Congo provided by Lissouba. In mid-October Sassou-Nguesso's Cobra militia, with Angolan assistance, succeeded in securing his return to power in the Congo.

Throughout the 1980s Angola supported proposals for the attainment of independence by Namibia, following a UN-supervised cease-fire and elections. From 1982, however, South Africa and the USA insisted that a withdrawal of South African troops from Namibia should be conditional on the withdrawal of Cuban forces from Angola. In December 1983 South Africa proposed a complete withdrawal of its forces from Angola, on condition that the Angolan Government undertook to prevent SWAPO and Cuban forces from entering the area vacated by the South African troops. Angola accepted the proposal, and a cease-fire was established in the occupied area in early 1984, although some South African forces remained inside Angolan territory. In September President dos Santos proposed a peace plan for Namibia, envisaging a phased withdrawal of the majority of Cuban troops from Angola, to begin only after the procedure leading to Namibian independence was under way, and conditional on the evacuation of the remaining South African forces from Angola. However, differences between South Africa and Angola concerning the timetable for (and the extent of) the Cuban withdrawal prevented the conclusion of the agreement. During 1987 and early 1988 South African forces became increasingly active in Angola and Namibia, despite a demand by the UN Security Council for an unconditional withdrawal.

From the mid-1980s Angolan relations with the USA deteriorated. In July 1985 the US Congress repealed legislation, adopted in 1976, prohibiting US military support for UNITA. In early 1986 Savimbi secured covert aid from the USA, which was to continue until 1990. In April 1987 Angola and the USA resumed discussions concerning a negotiated settlement over Namibia. Angola's readiness to establish good relations with the USA was reflected in the change in the direction of the Government's economic policy, indicated in August by dos Santos' announcement that Angola was applying for membership of the IMF. In March 1988, prompted by a state of military deadlock, a series of negotiations began between Angola, Cuba, the USA and the USSR. Major discussions also began in May between Angola, Cuba and South Africa, with the unofficial mediation of the USA. By mid-July the participants had agreed to a document containing 14 'essential principles' for a peaceful settlement, which provided for independence for Namibia, in accordance with the terms of the UN Security Council's Resolution 435 (see chapter on Namibia, Vol. II), and for the withdrawal of Cuban troops from Angola. A cease-fire was instigated on 8 August, and South African troops were evacuated from Angola later that month. Negotiations concerning the timetable for Cuban withdrawal from Angola were finally concluded on 22 December in New York, USA. A bilateral agreement was signed by Angola and Cuba, and a tripartite accord by Angola, Cuba and South Africa: Cuba undertook to complete a phased withdrawal of its estimated 50,000 troops from Angola by July 1991, while 1 April 1989 was designated as the date of commencement for a seven-month transition process, culminating in a general election in November, in preparation for Namibian independence. (Namibia became independent on 21 March 1990.) Angola, Cuba and South Africa were to establish a joint commission, in which the USA and the USSR would be represented as observers. All prisoners of war were to be exchanged, and the signatories of the tripartite accord were to refrain from supporting subversive organizations in each other's territories (the latter clause necessitated the curtailment of South African aid to UNITA). The UN Security Council authorized the creation of UNAVEM to monitor the Cuban troop redeployment and withdrawal. By late May 1991 all Cuban troops had been withdrawn from Angola.

In February 1985 Angola and Zaire signed a defence and security agreement which included an undertaking that neither country would allow its territory to be used as a base for attacks against the other and established a joint defence and security commission to monitor the security of their common border. The efficacy of this agreement was brought into question in March 1986, when it appeared that a UNITA raid on Andrada, in northern Angola, had been launched from Zaire. The two countries reaffirmed the terms of the 1985 agreement at talks held in July 1986. Zaire's tacit complicity with Savimbi was, however, indicated by the spread of UNITA activity in the area that borders Zaire in late 1986 and early 1987, and by the reputed use of Zairean territory by the US Government to transfer military aid to UNITA during the late 1980s. Although efforts by Zaire to mediate in the armed conflict in Angola during 1988 were resisted by President dos Santos (owing to Zaire's alleged support for UNITA), relations between Angola and Zaire improved in 1989, and from mid-1989 President Mobutu of Zaire played a prominent role in initiatives to achieve a settlement to the Angolan civil war. Renewed allegations of Zairean support for UNITA led to the re-establishment, in mid-1994, of the joint defence and security commission, with the aim of curbing the supply of weapons to the rebels (see above).

In July 1996 Angola was among the five lusophone African countries which, together with Portugal and Brazil, formed the Comunidade dos Países de Língua Portuguesa (CPLP, see p. 269), a Portuguese-speaking commonwealth seeking to achieve collective benefits from co-operation in technical, cultural and social matters.

Government

In March 1991 and in the first half of 1992 the Government of the Movimento Popular de Libertação de Angola—Partido do Trabalho (MPLA—PT) introduced a series of far-reaching amendments to the 1975 Constitution, providing for the establishment of a multi-party democracy (hitherto, no other political parties, apart from the ruling MPLA—PT, had been permitted). According to the amendments, legislative power was to be vested in the National Assembly, with 223 members elected for four years on the basis of proportional representation. Executive power was to be held by the President, who was to be directly elected for a term of five years (renewable for a maximum of three terms). As Head of State and Commander-in-Chief of the armed forces, the President was to govern with the assistance of an appointed Council of Ministers.

For the purposes of local government, the country is divided into 18 provinces, each administered by an appointed Governor.

Legislative elections, held in September 1992, resulted in victory for the MPLA. However, in the presidential election, which was held at the same time, the MPLA's candidate and incumbent President, José Eduardo dos Santos, narrowly failed to secure the 50% of the votes necessary to be elected President. Following a resumption of hostilities between UNITA and government forces, the conduct of a second round of presidential elections was held in abeyance, with dos Santos remaining in the presidency. The inauguration of the National Assembly took place, in the absence of UNITA's 70 delegates, in late November 1992. In accordance with the terms of the Lusaka peace accord of November 1994, in April 1997 a new Government of National Unity and Reconciliation was inaugurated in which UNITA held four portfolios. The second round of presidential elections having been abandoned, Savimbi was accorded the official title of 'leader of the opposition'. Meanwhile, in November 1996 the National Assembly had adopted a constitutional revision extending the parliamentary mandate, which was due to expire that month, for a period of between two and four years in order to allow for the establishment of suitable conditions for the conduct of elections.

Defence

In December 1990 the governing party, the Movimento Popular de Libertação de Angola—Partido do Trabalho (MPLA—PT), agreed to terminate the party's direct link with the armed forces. In accordance with the peace agreement concluded by the Government and the União Nacional para a Independência Total de Angola (UNITA) in May 1991 (see Recent History), a new 50,000-strong national army, the Forças Armadas de Angola (FAA), was to be established, comprising equal numbers of government forces, the Forças Armadas Populares de Libertação de Angola (FAPLA), and UNITA soldiers. The formation of the FAA was to coincide with the holding of a general election in late September 1992. Pending the general election, a ceasefire between FAPLA and UNITA forces, which commenced in mid-May 1991, was monitored by a joint political and military commission, comprising representatives of the MPLA—PT, UNITA, the UN, Portugal, the USA and the USSR. This commission was to oversee the withdrawal of FAPLA and UNITA forces to specific confinement areas, to await demobilization. Although not all troops had entered the confinement areas, demobilization began in late March 1992. Military advisers from Portugal, France and the United Kingdom were to assist with the formation of the new national army. However, the demobilization process and the formation of the FAA fell behind schedule and were only partially completed by the end of September and the holding of the general election. Following the election, UNITA withdrew its troops from the FAA, alleging electoral fraud on the part of the MPLA, and hostilities resumed. Following the signing of the Lusaka peace accord in November 1994, preparations for the confinement and demobilization of troops, and the integration of the UNITA contingent into the FAA, resumed. In mid-1995 agreement was reached between the Government and UNITA on the enlargement of the FAA to comprise a total of 90,000 troops, and discussions began concerning the potential formation of a fourth, non-combatant branch of the FAA, which would engage in public works projects. The internment of UNITA forces began in November 1995. In March 1996 agreement was reached that the unified FAA would include 26,300 UNITA troops. The process of selecting UNITA troops for integration into the FAA began in June. In December the UN Angola Verification Mission (UNAVEM III) expressed concern that, of a total of 70,336 UNITA troops registered at confinement areas, some 15,705 had deserted. At that time UN sources reported the existence of a residual UNITA force estimated at 15,000 well-armed troops operating in central and north-eastern Angola. In mid-1997 the Government estimated that UNITA's residual force numbered some 25,000–30,000 troops, while UNITA claimed to have retained a force of only 2,963 'police'. In early October UNITA was still in the process of demobilizing its residual force.

In August 1997 the FAA had an estimated total strength of 110,500: army 98,000, navy 1,500 and air force 11,000. In addition, there was a paramilitary force numbering an estimated 15,000. By May 1997 some 10,600 UNITA soldiers had been integrated into the FAA.

The defence budget for 1997 was estimated at US $295m.

Economic Affairs

In 1995, according to estimates by the World Bank, Angola's gross national product (GNP), measured at average 1993–95 prices, was US $4,422m., equivalent to $410 per head. During 1985–95 GNP per head declined, in real terms, by an estimated average annual rate of 4.0%, although it increased by 6.8% in 1994 and by an estimated 13.2% in 1995. During 1985–95 Angola's population increased by an average annual rate of 3.0%. Angola's gross domestic product (GDP) increased, in real terms, by an average of 0.9% per year in 1985–95. However, real GDP rose by 7.7% in 1994 and by an estimated 12.5% in 1995.

Agriculture, forestry and fishing contributed 17.1% of GDP in 1994, and an estimated 16.5% in 1995. An estimated 73.8% of the total working population were employed in the agricultural sector in 1995. The principal cash crops are coffee and sugar cane. The main subsistence crops are cassava, bananas, maize and sweet potatoes. During 1985–95 agricultural GDP increased at an average rate of 1.0% per year; it rose by 12.0% in 1994 and by an estimated 15.1% in 1995.

Industry (including mining, manufacturing, construction and power) provided 55.0% of GDP in 1994, and an estimated 52.8% in 1995. Industrial GDP increased, in real terms, at an average rate of 3.9% in 1985–95; it rose by 9.3% in 1994 and by an estimated 13.7% in 1995. Industry employed an estimated 10.5% of the labour force in 1991.

Mining contributed 51.2% of GDP in 1994, with petroleum production (including liquefied petroleum gas) accounting for an estimated 50.0% of GDP. Angola's principal mineral exports are petroleum and diamonds. In addition, there are reserves of iron ore, copper, lead, zinc, gold, manganese, phosphates, salt and uranium.

The manufacturing sector provided 2.4% of GDP in 1994. According to the World Bank, during 1985–95 the GDP of the sector declined at an average annual rate of 11.0%; it declined by 8.8% in 1994 and by an estimated 3.0% in 1995. The principal branch of manufacturing is petroleum refining. Other manufacturing activities include food-processing, brewing, textiles and construction materials.

Energy is derived mainly from hydroelectric power. Angola's power potential exceeds its requirements.

Services accounted for 27.9% of GDP in 1994. In real terms, the combined GDP of the service sectors declined at an average rate of 2.5% per year in 1985–95; it rose by 3.2% in 1994 and by an estimated 9.7% in 1995. The service sectors employed an estimated 20.1% of the labour force in 1991.

In 1994 Angola recorded an estimated visible trade surplus of US $1,369m., while there was an estimated deficit of $872m. on the current account of the balance of payments. In 1989 the principal source of imports (18.1%) was Portugal; other major suppliers were the Federal Republic of Germany and the Netherlands. In 1992 the principal market for exports (66.5%) was the USA; other notable purchasers were the United Kingdom, France and the Netherlands. The principal exports in 1993 were petroleum and petroleum products, accounting for 97.4% of total export earnings. The principal imports in 1985 were foodstuffs, transport equipment, electrical equipment and base metals.

The 1997 state budget envisaged balanced expenditure and revenue of 694,600,000m. readjusted kwanza. Angola's total external debt at the end of 1995 was US $11,482m., of which $9,533m. was long-term public debt. In that year the cost of debt-servicing was equivalent to 12.5% of the value of exports of goods and services. The annual rate of inflation averaged 1,380% in 1993, 972% in 1994 and 3,661% in 1995.

Angola is a member of both the Common Market for Eastern and Southern Africa (COMESA, see p. 124) and the Southern African Development Community (SADC, see p. 236), which was formed with the aim of reducing the economic dependence of southern African states on South Africa.

Since independence, exploitation of Angola's extensive mineral reserves, hydroelectric potential and abundant fertile land has been severely impaired by internal conflict, as well as an acute shortage of skilled personnel. Angola's prospects depend greatly on a definitive resolution of the civil strife, the successful reintegration of the displaced population and the rehabilitation of the country's devastated infrastructure. In 1995 rapid devaluation of the new kwanza prompted the introduction of a new currency, the 'readjusted' kwanza. In 1996 the Government introduced a reform programme aimed at lowering the rate of inflation and decreasing the discrepancy between the official and parallel exchange rates. In that year the IMF announced that it was to provide US $75m. in a three-year emergency programme under an enhanced structural adjustment facility. In mid-1997 UNITA was still in control of the majority of the country's diamond-producing areas. However, with the fall that year in the Congo and the Democratic Republic of the Congo (formerly Zaire) of governments sympathetic to UNITA, as well as the threat of further UN sanctions against the movement, the prospect of the Government gaining control of this vital resource improved significantly. In 1997 the development of the petroleum sector continued apace. In August the French company Elf Aquitaine announced the discovery of one of Africa's largest ever petroleum fields, with estimated reserves of 3,500m. barrels. With increasing international investment in the sector, Angola's total daily output of crude petroleum was expected to reach 1.25m. barrels early in the next century.

Social Welfare

Medical care is provided free of charge, but its availability is limited by a shortage of trained personnel and medicines. At independence there were 24 hospitals in Angola (eight of them in Luanda), but these were left without trained staff. In 1981 there were 460 foreign physicians in the country, mainly from Cuba, and a major training programme produced about 1,000 Angolan paramedics per year, helping to spread basic medical knowledge to village communities. In 1993 Angola had 31 hospitals, 246 health centres and 1,288 health posts, with a total of 12,297 beds. There were 630 doctors and 5,780 paramedics working in the country. The 1997 budget allocated an estimated 12,600,000m. readjusted kwanza (1.8% of total expenditure) to health. A scheme to rehabilitate the national referral hospital, Américo Boavida, towards which the EC and Italy provided US $28m., commenced in 1989. War veterans receive support from the Ministry of Defence.

Education

Education is officially compulsory for eight years, between seven and 15 years of age, and is provided free of charge by the Government. Primary education begins at six years of age and lasts for four years. Secondary education, beginning at the age of 10, lasts for up to seven years, comprising a first cycle of four years and a second of three years. In 1973, under Portuguese rule, primary school pupils numbered only 300,000, but by 1991/92 there were 989,443 pupils. Enrolment at secondary schools (including students receiving vocational instruction and teacher-training) increased from 57,829 in 1970 to 218,987 in 1991/92. As a proportion of the school-age population, the total enrolment at primary and secondary schools was 45% in 1991. Higher education is being encouraged. The only university, Agostinho Neto University in Luanda, had 5,736 students in 1986/87. The number of students attending courses at the university and other equivalent institutions in 1991/92 was 6,331. Much education is now conducted in vernacular languages rather than Portuguese. At independence the estimated rate of adult illiteracy was more than 85%. A national literacy campaign was launched in 1976, and the average rate of adult illiteracy in 1990 was estimated by UNESCO to be 58.3% (males 44.4%, females 71.5%). The 1997 budget allocated an estimated 19,800,000m. readjusted kwanza (2.9% of total expenditure) to education.

In March 1991 the People's Assembly approved legislation permitting the foundation of private educational establishments.

Public Holidays

1998: 1 January (New Year's Day), 4 February (Anniversary of the outbreak of the armed struggle against Portuguese colonialism), 27 March (Victory Day), 14 April (Youth Day)*, 1 May (Workers' Day), 1 August (Armed Forces' Day)*, 17 September (National Hero's Day, birthday of Dr Agostinho Neto), 11 November (Independence Day), 1 December (Pioneers' Day)*, 10 December (Anniversary of the Foundation of the MPLA), 25 December (Family Day).

1999: 1 January (New Year's Day), 4 February (Anniversary of the outbreak of the armed struggle against Portuguese colonialism), 27 March (Victory Day), 14 April (Youth Day)*, 1 May (Workers' Day), 1 August (Armed Forces' Day)*, 17 September (National Hero's Day, birthday of Dr Agostinho Neto), 11 November (Independence Day), 1 December (Pioneers' Day)*, 10 December (Anniversary of the Foundation of the MPLA), 25 December (Family Day).

* Although not officially recognized as public holidays, these days are popularly treated as such.

Weights and Measures

The metric system is in force.

Statistical Survey

Source (unless otherwise stated): Instituto Nacional de Estatística, Luanda.

Area and Population

AREA, POPULATION AND DENSITY

Area (sq km)	1,246,700*
Population (census results)	
30 December 1960	4,480,719
15 December 1970	
Males	2,943,974
Females	2,702,192
Total	5,646,166
Population (official estimates at mid-year)	
1993	10,916,000
1994	11,233,000
1995	11,561,000
Density (per sq km) at mid-1995	9.3

* 481,354 sq miles.

DISTRIBUTION OF POPULATION BY DISTRICT
(provisional estimates, mid-1995)

	Area (sq km)	Population	Density (per sq km)
Luanda	2,418	2,002,000	828.0
Huambo	34,274	1,687,000	49.2
Bié	70,314	1,246,000	17.7
Malanje	87,246	975,000	11.2
Huíla	75,002	948,000	12.6
Uíge	58,698	948,000	16.2
Benguela	31,788	702,000	22.1
Cuanza-Sul	55,660	688,000	12.4
Cuanza-Norte	24,110	412,000	17.1
Moxico	223,023	349,000	1.6
Lunda-Norte	102,783	311,000	3.0
Zaire	40,130	247,000	6.2
Cunene	88,342	245,000	2.8
Cabinda	7,270	185,000	25.4
Bengo	31,371	184,000	5.9
Lunda-Sul	56,985	160,000	2.8
Cuando-Cubango	199,049	137,000	0.7
Namibe	58,137	135,000	2.3
Total	1,246,600	11,561,000	9.3

PRINCIPAL TOWNS (population at 1970 census)

Luanda (capital)	480,613*	Benguela	40,996
Huambo (Nova Lisboa)	61,885	Lubango (Sá da Bandeira)	31,674
Lobito	59,258	Malanje	31,559

* 1982 estimate: 1,200,000.

Source: Direcção dos Serviços de Estatística, Luanda.

BIRTHS AND DEATHS (UN estimates, annual averages)

	1980–85	1985–90	1990–95
Birth rate (per 1,000)	50.8	51.3	51.3
Death rate (per 1,000)	22.8	21.3	19.2

Expectation of life (UN estimates, years at birth, 1990–95): 46.5 (males 44.9; females 48.1).

Source: UN, *World Population Prospects: The 1994 Revision.*

ECONOMICALLY ACTIVE POPULATION
(estimates, '000 persons, 1991)

	Males	Females	Total
Agriculture, etc.	1,518	1,374	2,892
Industry	405	33	438
Services	644	192	836
Total labour force	2,567	1,599	4,166

Source: UN Economic Commission for Africa, *African Statistical Yearbook.*

Mid-1996 (estimates in '000): Agriculture, etc. 3,811; Total (incl. others) 5,171. Source: FAO, *Production Yearbook.*

Agriculture

PRINCIPAL CROPS ('000 metric tons)

	1994	1995	1996
Wheat	3†	3†	5*
Rice (paddy)	21	23*	25*
Maize	201	211†	398†
Millet and sorghum	60	61†	102*
Potatoes	27	30*	33*
Sweet potatoes*	180	185	190
Cassava (Manioc)	2,379	2,400*	2,500*
Dry beans	162	170*	175*
Groundnuts (in shell)*	20	22*	23*
Sunflower seed*	11	10	10
Cottonseed†	8	8	8
Cotton (lint)†	4	4	4
Palm kernels*	16	16	16
Palm oil*	52	52	52
Vegetables*	249	256	263
Citrus fruit*	79	80	82
Pineapples*	34	36	38
Bananas*	285	290	295
Other fruits*	29	30	31
Sugar cane*	240	330	330
Coffee (green)†	2	3	5
Tobacco (leaves)*	4	4	4
Sisal*	1	1	1

* FAO estimate(s). † Unofficial figure(s).

Source: FAO, *Production Yearbook.*

LIVESTOCK ('000 head, year ending September)

	1994*	1995	1996
Cattle	3,000	3,000	3,309
Pigs	790	800	810*
Sheep	240	240†	245*
Goats	1,450	1,460†	1,470*

Poultry (million): 6* in 1994; 6* in 1995; 7* in 1996.

* FAO estimate(s). † Unofficial figure.

Source: FAO, *Production Yearbook.*

LIVESTOCK PRODUCTS (FAO estimates, '000 metric tons)

	1994	1995	1996
Beef and veal	53	53	57
Goat meat	4	4	4
Pig meat	22	22	22
Poultry meat	7	7	7
Other meat	6	6	7
Cows' milk	146	147	162
Cheese	1	1	1
Poultry eggs	4	4	4
Honey	21	22	23
Cattle hides	8	8	9

Source: FAO, *Production Yearbook*.

Forestry

ROUNDWOOD REMOVALS
(FAO estimates, '000 cubic metres, excluding bark)

	1992	1993	1994
Sawlogs, veneer logs and logs for sleepers*	66	66	66
Other industrial wood	832	865	898
Fuel wood	5,480	5,652	5,830
Total	6,378	6,583	6,794

* Annual output assumed to be unchanged since 1990.

Source: FAO, *Yearbook of Forest Products*.

SAWNWOOD PRODUCTION
(FAO estimates, '000 cubic metres, including railway sleepers)

	1992	1993	1994
Total	5	5	5

Source: FAO, *Yearbook of Forest Products*.

Fishing

('000 metric tons, live weight)

	1993	1994	1995
Freshwater fishes	7.0	7.0	6.0
Cunene horse mackerel	44.0	29.5	25.3
Sardinellas	12.4	19.7	34.2
Other marine fishes (incl. unspecified)	15.7	19.6	27.2
Total fish	79.0	75.8	92.7
Crustaceans and molluscs	1.7	2.1	1.1
Total catch	80.7	77.9	93.8

Source: FAO, *Yearbook of Fishery Statistics*.

Mining

('000 metric tons, unless otherwise indicated)

	1992	1993	1994
Crude petroleum	26,000	25,200	25,250*
Natural gas (petajoules)*	7	7	7
Salt (unrefined)†	20	30	30
Diamonds ('000 carats):†			
Industrial	80	15	30
Gem	1,100	130	270
Gypsum (crude)†	57	50	50

* Estimate(s).

† Data from the US Bureau of Mines.

Source: UN, *Industrial Commodity Statistics Yearbook*.

Industry

SELECTED PRODUCTS
('000 metric tons, unless otherwise indicated)

	1992	1993	1994
Raw sugar	33*	20*	20†
Cigarettes (million)‡	2,400	n.a.	n.a.
Plywood ('000 cubic metres)*§	10	10	10
Chemical wood pulp*§	15	15	15
Jet fuels§	160	162	160
Motor spirit (petrol)§	110	110	105
Kerosene§	50	52	50
Distillate fuel oils§	330	325	320
Residual fuel oils§	650	645	640
Cement‖	370	n.a.	n.a.
Crude steel‖	10	9	9
Electric energy (million kWh)§	1,855	1,855	1,865

* Data from the FAO.

† Data from the International Sugar Organization (London).

‡ Data from the US Department of Agriculture.

§ Estimates.

‖ Data from the US Bureau of Mines.

Source: UN, *Industrial Commodity Statistics Yearbook*.

Finance

CURRENCY AND EXCHANGE RATES

Monetary Units

100 lwei = 1 readjusted kwanza.

Sterling and Dollar Equivalents (21 July 1997)

£1 sterling = 444,670 readjusted kwanza;
US \$1 = 265,000 readjusted kwanza;
1,000,000 readjusted kwanza = £2.249 = \$3.774.

Average Exchange Rate (new kwanza per US \$)

1992	457
1993	4,832
1994	175,672

Note: An official exchange rate of US \$1 = 29.62 kwanza was introduced in 1976 and remained in force until September 1990. In that month the kwanza was replaced, at par, by the new kwanza. At the same time, it was announced that the currency was to be devalued by more than 50%, with the exchange rate adjusted to US \$1 = 60 new kwanza, with effect from 1 October 1990. This rate remained in force until 18 November 1991, when a basic rate of US \$1 = 90 new kwanza was established. The currency underwent further devaluation, by 50% in December 1991, and by more than 67% on 15 April 1992, when a basic rate of US \$1 = 550 new kwanza was established. In February 1993 the currency was again devalued, when a basic rate of US \$1 = 7,000 new kwanza was established. In April 1993 this was adjusted to US \$1 = 4,000 new kwanza, and in October to US \$1 = 6,500 new kwanza, a devaluation of 38.5%. Following a series of four devaluations in February and March 1994, a rate of US \$1 = 35,000 new kwanza was established in late March. In April 1994 the introduction of a new method of setting exchange rates resulted in an effective devaluation, to US \$1 = 68,297 new kwanza, and provided for an end to the system of multiple exchange rates. Further substantial devaluations followed, and in July 1995 a 'readjusted' kwanza, equivalent to 1,000 new kwanza, was introduced. The currency, however, continued to depreciate. In July 1997 the currency was again devalued, when a basic rate of US \$1 = 265,000 'readjusted' kwanza was established.

BUDGET ('000 million new kwanza)

Revenue	1992	1993*	1994*
Tax revenue	924.4	10,300	256,800
Income tax	606.3	6,800	187,400
Petroleum corporate tax	265.5	2,900	75,600
Petroleum transaction tax	292.5	3,900	106,600
Tax on goods and services	173.1	2,100	54,500
Petroleum sector	150.0	1,800	49,700
Diamond sector	12.7	100	200
Taxes on foreign trade	130.3	700	11,200
Other taxes	14.7	700	3,600
Stamp tax	14.1	300	2,500
Total (incl. others)	941.0	10,500	260,900

* Figures are rounded.

Expenditure*	1992	1993	1994
Defence	230	4,700	150,600
Public order	205	2,500	90,500
Education	155	1,000	10,900
Health	80	800	14,600
Social security	200	900	6,100
Foreign relations	—	200	8,400
General administration	195	3,300	124,000
Total (incl. others)	2,445	16,400	427,100

* Figures are rounded.

Source: IMF, *Angola—Recent Economic Developments* (December 1995).

1995 (estimates, million new kwanza): Total revenue 3,880,103,863.2; Total expenditure 4,793,863,326.3.

COST OF LIVING

(Consumer Price Index for Luanda; base: 1991 = 100)

	1992	1993	1994
Food	408.9	6,856.0	70,425
Clothing	224.5	n.a.	n.a.
Rent, fuel and light	298.5	n.a.	n.a.
All items (incl. others)	399.1	5,904.5	61,982

Source: ILO, *Yearbook of Labour Statistics*.

NATIONAL ACCOUNTS

Composition of the Gross National Product (US $ million)

	1987	1988	1989
Gross domestic product (GDP) at factor cost	6,482	6,877	7,682
Indirect taxes	94	95	117
Less Subsidies	189	122	93
GDP in purchasers' values	6,386	6,850	7,706
Net factor income from abroad	−402	−938	−1,079
Gross national product	5,984	5,912	6,627

Gross Domestic Product by Economic Activity

(million kwanza at current prices)

	1992	1993	1994
Agriculture, forestry and fishing	1,086.6	9,075.3	122,480.0
Mining	1,381.6	11,360.8	367,085.0
Processing industry	120.9	983.2	16,877.0
Electricity and water	1.8	16.9	239.0
Construction	86.3	550.9	10,504.0
Trade	380.2	3,460.3	57,332.0
Transport and communications	89.5	832.8	13,466.0
Financial services	312.0	2,952.3	95,497.0
Other services	529.7	3,375.2	33,969.0
Sub-total	3,988.6	32,607.7	717,449.0
Import duties	130.3	683.2	10,916.0
GDP in purchasers' values	4,118.9	33,290.9	728,365.0

BALANCE OF PAYMENTS (US $ million)

	1992	1993	1994*
Exports of goods f.o.b.	3,833	2,900	3,002
Imports of goods f.o.b.	−1,988	−1,463	−1,633
Trade balance	1,845	1,437	1,369
Services (net)	−2,302	−1,874	−1,860
Balance on goods and services	−457	−437	−491
Interest payments (net)	−504	−583	−549
Unrequited transfers (net)	102	166	169
Current balance	−859	−854	−872
Direct investment abroad	−385	−549	−576
Direct investment from abroad	673	851	902
Other long-term capital (net)	−604	−783	−450
Short-term capital (net) Net errors and omissions	−165	−383	−326
Overall balance	−1,340	−1,718	−1,321

* Estimates.

Source: IMF, *Angola—Recent Economic Developments* (December 1995).

External Trade

SELECTED COMMODITIES

Imports (million kwanza)	1983	1984	1985
Animal products	1,315	1,226	1,084
Vegetable products	2,158	3,099	2,284
Fats and oils	946	1,006	1,196
Food and beverages	2,400	1,949	1,892
Industrial chemical products	1,859	1,419	1,702
Plastic materials	431	704	454
Paper products	376	380	411
Textiles	1,612	1,816	1,451
Base metals	1,985	3,730	2,385
Electrical equipment	3,296	2,879	2,571
Transport equipment	2,762	2,240	3,123
Total (incl. others)	20,197	21,370	19,694

Total Imports (million kwanza): 18,691 in 1986; 13,372 in 1987; 29,845 in 1988; 34,392 in 1989 (Source: UN, *Monthly Bulletin of Statistics*).

Exports (US $ million)	1991	1992	1993
Crude petroleum	3,161	3,490	2,750
Refined petroleum products	56	66	63
Diamonds	190	250	63
Total (incl. others)	3,449	3,833	2,900

Source: IMF, *Angola—Recent Economic Developments* (December 1995).

PRINCIPAL TRADING PARTNERS (US $ million)

Imports c.i.f.	1987	1988	1989
Belgium-Luxembourg	17.9	22.9	99.9
Brazil	55.8	119.2	104.0
France	63.3	8.8	114.1
German Dem. Repub.	35.2	34.7	41.9
Germany, Fed. Repub.	51.0	149.0	178.4
Italy	19.0	19.3	35.2
Japan	8.1	39.7	34.5
Netherlands	20.6	148.3	160.5
Portugal	51.4	171.4	206.8
Spain	4.8	53.2	55.6
United Arab Emirates	70.5	25.1	23.1
United Kingdom	9.1	26.7	32.9
Total (incl. others)	442.6	987.9	1,139.6

Total Imports (US $ million): 1,139.5 in 1990; 457.9 in 1991; 728.7 in 1992.

Exports f.o.b.	1990	1991	1992
Austria	62.8	—	—
Belgium-Luxembourg	231.9	45.9	106.0
Brazil	80.0	210.2	46.0
Canada	28.1	37.1	—
Chile	76.7	22.2	—
China, People's Republic	—	—	63.0
France	456.3	290.4	300.0
Germany	40.4	21.0	—
Gibraltar	72.8	12.5	—
Italy	143.9	82.6	37.0
Netherlands	414.0	206.2	167.1
Portugal	88.8	87.8	75.5
Singapore	—	—	49.0
Spain	2.5	40.5	50.1
United Kingdom	21.5	144.3	316.0
USA	2,067.6	2,094.6	2,460.0
Yugoslavia	—	62.2	—
Total (incl. others)	3,910.3	3,409.7	3,697.5

Source: UN, *International Trade Statistics Yearbook*.

Transport

GOODS TRANSPORT ('000 metric tons)

	1988	1989	1990
Road	1,056.7	690.1	867.3
Railway	580.9	510.3	443.2
Water	780.8	608.6	812.1
Air	24.6	10.5	28.3
Total	2,443.0	1,819.5	2,150.9

Sources: Instituto Nacional de Estatística; Ministério de Transporte e Comunicações.

PASSENGER TRANSPORT ('000 journeys)

	1988	1989	1990
Road	12,699.2	32,658.7	48,796.1
Railway	6,659.7	6,951.2	6,455.8
Water	151.8	163.2	223.8
Air	608.9	618.4	615.9
Total	20,119.6	40,391.5	56,091.6

Sources: Instituto Nacional de Estatística; Ministério de Transporte e Comunicações, Luanda.

ROAD TRAFFIC (estimates, motor vehicles in use at 31 December)

	1993	1994	1995
Passenger cars	174,000	180,000	197,000
Lorries and vans	30,900	32,100	26,000
Total	204,900	212,100	223,000

Source: IRF, *World Road Statistics*.

SHIPPING

Merchant Fleet (registered at 31 December)

	1994	1995	1996
Number of vessels	112	112	113
Total displacement (grt)	89,591	89,594	81,856

Source: Lloyd's Register of Shipping, *World Fleet Statistics*.

International Sea-borne Freight Traffic
(estimates, '000 metric tons)

	1989	1990	1991
Goods loaded	19,980	21,102	23,288
Goods unloaded	1,235	1,242	1,261

Source: UN Economic Commission for Africa, *African Statistical Yearbook*.

CIVIL AVIATION (traffic on scheduled services)

	1992	1993	1994
Kilometres flown (million)	10	9	13
Passengers carried ('000)	440	334	519
Passenger-km (million)	1,196	948	1,594
Total ton-km (million)	147	113	197

Source: UN, *Statistical Yearbook*.

Tourism

	1992	1993	1994
Tourist arrivals ('000)	40	21	11
Tourist receipts (US $ million)	n.a.	20	13

Source: UN, *Statistical Yearbook*.

Communications Media

	1992	1993	1994
Radio receivers ('000 in use)	282	295	320
Television receivers ('000 in use)	62	68	70
Telephones ('000 main lines in use)	49	53	n.a.

Book production: 47 titles (books 35, pamphlets 12) and 419,000 copies (books 338,000, pamphlets 81,000) in 1985; 14 titles (all books) and 130,000 copies in 1986.

Daily newspapers: 4 (estimated circulation 115,000) in 1990; 4 (estimated circulation 116,000) in 1992; 4 (estimated circulation 117,000) in 1994.

Sources: UNESCO, *Statistical Yearbook*; UN, *Statistical Yearbook*.

Education

(1991/92)

	Teachers	Pupils
Pre-primary	n.a.	214,867
Primary	31,062*	989,443
Secondary:		
general	5,138†	196,099
teacher training	280‡	10,772
vocational	286†	12,116
Higher	787	6,331

* Figure for school year 1990/91.
† Figure for school year 1989/90.
‡ Figure for school year 1987/88.

Source: mainly UNESCO, *Statistical Yearbook*.

Directory

The Constitution

The MPLA regime adopted an independence Constitution for Angola in November 1975. It was amended in October 1976, September 1980, March 1991, April and August 1992, and November 1996. The main provisions of the Constitution, as amended, are summarized below:

BASIC PRINCIPLES

The Republic of Angola shall be a sovereign and independent state whose prime objective shall be to build a free and democratic society of peace, justice and social progress. It shall be a democratic state based on the rule of law, founded on national unity, the dignity of human beings, pluralism of expression and political organization, respecting and guaranteeing the basic rights and freedoms of persons, whether as individuals or as members of organized social groups. Sovereignty shall be vested in the people, which shall exercise political power through periodic universal suffrage.

The Republic of Angola shall be a unitary and indivisible state. Economic, social and cultural solidarity shall be promoted between all the Republic's regions for the common development of the entire nation and the elimination of regionalism and tribalism.

Religion

The Republic shall be a secular state and there shall be complete separation of the State and religious institutions. All religions shall be respected.

The Economy

The economic system shall be based on the coexistence of diverse forms of property—public, private, mixed, co-operative and family—and all shall enjoy equal protection. The State shall protect foreign investment and foreign property, in accordance with the law. The fiscal system shall aim to satisfy the economic, social and administrative needs of the State and to ensure a fair distribution of income and wealth. Taxes may be created and abolished only by law, which shall determine applicability, rates, tax benefits and guarantees for taxpayers.

Education

The Republic shall vigorously combat illiteracy and obscurantism and shall promote the development of education and of a true national culture.

FUNDAMENTAL RIGHTS AND DUTIES

The State shall respect and protect the human person and human dignity. All citizens shall be equal before the law. They shall be subject to the same duties, without any distinction based on colour, race, ethnic group, sex, place of birth, religion, level of education, or economic or social status.

All citizens aged 18 years and over, other than those legally deprived of political and civil rights, shall have the right and duty to take an active part in public life, to vote and be elected to any state organ, and to discharge their mandates with full dedication to the cause of the Angolan nation. The law shall establish limitations in respect of non-political allegiance of soldiers on active service, judges and police forces, as well as the electoral incapacity of soldiers on active service and police forces.

Freedom of expression, of assembly, of demonstration, of association and of all other forms of expression shall be guaranteed. Groupings whose aims or activities are contrary to the constitutional order and penal laws, or that, even indirectly, pursue political objectives through organizations of a military, paramilitary or militarized nature shall be forbidden. Every citizen has the right to a defence if accused of a crime. Individual freedoms are guaranteed. Freedom of conscience and belief shall be inviolable. Work shall be the right and duty of all citizens. The State shall promote measures necessary to ensure the right of citizens to medical and health care, as well as assistance in childhood, motherhood, disability, old age, etc. It shall also promote access to education, culture and sports for all citizens.

STATE ORGANS

President of the Republic

The President of the Republic shall be the Head of State, Head of Government and Commander-in-Chief of the Angolan armed forces. The President of the Republic shall be elected directly by a secret universal ballot and shall have the following powers:

to appoint and dismiss the Prime Minister, Ministers and other government officials determined by law;

to appoint the judges of the Supreme Court;

to preside over the Council of Ministers;

to declare war and make peace, following authorization by the National Assembly;

to sign, promulgate and publish the laws of the National Assembly, government decrees and statutory decrees;

to preside over the National Defence Council;

to decree a state of siege or state of emergency;

to announce the holding of general elections;

to issue pardons and commute sentences;

to perform all other duties provided for in the Constitution.

National Assembly

The National Assembly is the supreme state legislative body, to which the Government is responsible. The National Assembly shall be composed of 223 deputies, elected for a term of four years. The National Assembly shall convene in ordinary session twice yearly and in special session on the initiative of the President of the National Assembly, the Standing Commission of the National Assembly or of no less than one-third of its deputies. The Standing Commission shall be the organ of the National Assembly that represents and assumes its powers between sessions.

Government

The Government shall comprise the President of the Republic, the ministers and the secretaries of state, and other members whom the law shall indicate, and shall have the following functions:

to organize and direct the implementation of state domestic and foreign policy, in accordance with decision of the National Assembly and its Standing Commission;

to ensure national defence, the maintenance of internal order and security, and the protection of the rights of citizens;

to prepare the draft National Plan and General State Budget for approval by the National Assembly, and to organize, direct and control their execution;

The Council of Ministers shall be answerable to the National Assembly. In the exercise of its powers, the Council of Ministers shall issue decrees and resolutions.

Judiciary

The organization, composition and competence of the courts shall be established by law. Judges shall be independent in the discharge of their functions.

Local State Organs

The organs of state power at provincial level shall be the Provincial Assemblies and their executive bodies. The Provincial Assemblies shall work in close co-operation with social organizations and rely on the initiative and broad participation of citizens. The Provincial Assemblies shall elect commissions of deputies to perform permanent or specific tasks. The executive organs of Provincial Assemblies shall be the Provincial Governments, which shall be led by the Provincial Governors. The Provincial Governors shall be answerable to the President of the Republic, the Council of Ministers and the Provincial Assemblies.

National Defence

The State shall ensure national defence. The National Defence Council shall be presided over by the President of the Republic, and its composition shall be determined by law. The Angolan armed forces, as a state institution, shall be permanent, regular and non-partisan. Defence of the country shall be the right and the highest indeclinable duty of every citizen. Military service shall be compulsory. The forms in which it is fulfilled shall be defined by the law.

Note: In accordance with the terms of the Lusaka peace accord of November 1994, in April 1997 a new Government of National Unity and Reconciliation was inaugurated in which UNITA held four portfolios. In November 1996 the National Assembly adopted a constitutional revision extending the parliamentary mandate, which was due to expire that month, for a period of between two and four years in order to allow for the establishment of suitable conditions for the conduct of elections.

The Government

HEAD OF STATE

President: José Eduardo dos Santos (assumed office 21 September 1979).

COUNCIL OF MINISTERS
(November 1997)

Prime Minister: Fernando José França van-Dúnem.
Minister of Defence: Gen. Pedro Sebastião.
Minister of the Interior: Santana André Pitra Petroff.
Minister of Foreign Affairs: Dr Venâncio da Silva Moura.
Minister of Territorial Administration: Fernando Faustino Muteka.
Minister of Finance: Mário de Alcantara Monteiro.
Minister of Economic Planning: Emanuel Moreira Carneiro.
Minister of Petroleum: Albina Faria de Assis Pereira Africano.
Minister of Industry: Manuel Diamantino Borges Duque.
Minister of Agriculture and Rural Development: Carlos António Fernandes.
Minister of Fisheries: Maria de Fátima Monteiro Jardim.
Minister of Geology and Mines: Marcos Samondo.
Minister of Public Works and Urbanization: (vacant).
Minister of Transport: André Luís Brandão.
Minister of Trade: Victorino Domingos Hossi.
Minister of Health: Anastacio Ruben Sikatu.
Minister of Education: António Burity da Silva Neto.
Minister of Assistance and Social Reintegration: Albino Malungo.
Minister of Culture: Ana Maria de Oliveira.
Minister of Youth and Sports: José da Rocha Sardinha de Castro.
Minister of Justice: Dr Paulo Tchipilica.
Minister of Public Administration, Employment and Social Welfare: Dr António Domingos Pitra Costa Neto.
Minister of Information: Dr Pedro Hendrik Vaal Neto.
Minister of Science and Technology: Francisco Mubengai.
Minister of Post and Telecommunications: Licínio Tavares Ribeiro.
Minister of Women's Affairs: Dra Joana Lima Ramos Baptista Cristiano.
Minister of War Veterans: Pedro José van-Dúnem.
Minister of Hotels and Tourism: Jorge Alicerces Valentim.
Minister of Energy and Water: João Moreira Pinto Saraiva.

SECRETARY OF STATE
(November 1997)

Secretary of State for Coffee: Gilberto Buta Lutukuta.

MINISTRIES

Office of the President: Luanda; telex 3072.

Ministry of Agriculture and Rural Development: Avda Norton de Matos 2, Luanda; telex 3322.

Ministry of Assistance and Social Reintegration: Luanda.

Ministry of Culture: Luanda.

Ministry of Defence: Rua Silva Carvalho ex Quartel General, Luanda; telex 3138.

Ministry of Economic Planning: Luanda.

Ministry of Education: Avda Comandante Jika, CP 1281, Luanda; tel. (2) 321592; telex 4121; fax (2) 321592.

Ministry of Energy and Water: Luanda.

Ministry of Finance: Avda 4 de Fevereiro, Luanda; tel. (2) 344628; telex 3363.

Ministry of Fisheries: Avda 4 de Fevereiro 25, Predio Atlântico, Luanda; tel. (2) 392782; telex 3273.

Ministry of Foreign Affairs: Avda Comandante Jika, Luanda; telex 3127.

Ministry of Geology and Mines: CP 1260, Luanda.

Ministry of Health: Rua Diogo Cão, Luanda.

Ministry of Hotels and Tourism: Luanda.

Ministry of Industry: Luanda.

Ministry of Information: Luanda.

Ministry of the Interior: Avda 4 de Fevereiro, Luanda.

Ministry of Justice: Largo do Palácio, Luanda.

Ministry of Petroleum: Avda 4 de Fevereiro 105, CP 1279, Luanda; tel. (2) 337448; telex 3300.

Ministry of Post and Telecommunications: Luanda.

Ministry of Public Administration, Employment and Social Welfare: Rua 17 de Setembro 32, CP 1986, Luanda; tel. (2) 339656; telex 4147; fax (2) 339054.

Ministry of Public Works and Urbanization: Luanda.

Ministry of Science and Technology: Luanda.

Ministry of Territorial Administration: Luanda.

Ministry of Trade: Largo Kinaxixi 14, Luanda; tel. (2) 344525; telex 3282.

Ministry of Transport: Avda 4 de Fevereiro 42, CP 1250-C, Luanda; tel. (2) 370061; telex 3108.

Ministry of War Veterans: Luanda.

Ministry of Women's Affairs: Luanda.

Ministry of Youth and Sports: Luanda.

PROVINCIAL GOVERNORS*

Bengo: Ezelino Mendes.

Benguela: Dumilde das Chagas Simões Rangel.

Bié: Luís Paulino dos Santos.

Cabinda: José Amaro Tati.

Cuando-Cubango: Manuel Gama.

Cuanza-Norte: Manuel Pedro Pacavira.

Cuanza-Sul: Francisco José Ramos da Cruz.

Cunene: Pedro Mutinde.

Huambo: Paulo Kassoma.

Huíla: Kundi Paihama.

Luanda: José Aníbal Lopes Rocha.

Lunda-Norte: Manuel Francisco Gomes Maiato.

Lunda-Sul: Gonçalves Manuel Manvumbra.

Malanje: Flavio Fernandes.

Moxico: João Ernesto dos Santos (Liberdade).

Namibe: Joaquim da Silva Matias.

Uíge: Kananito Alexandre.

Zaire: Ludi Kissassunda.

*All Governors are ex-officio members of the Government.

President and Legislature

PRESIDENT*

Presidential Election, 29 and 30 September 1992

	Votes	% of votes
José Eduardo dos Santos (MPLA)	1,953,335	49.57
Dr Jonas Malheiro Savimbi (UNITA)	1,579,298	40.07
António Alberto Neto (PDA)	85,249	2.16
Holden Roberto (FNLA)	83,135	2.11
Honorato Lando (PDLA)	75,789	1.92
Luís dos Passos (PRD)	59,121	1.47
Bengui Pedro João (PSD)	38,243	0.97
Simão Cacete (FPD)	26,385	0.67
Daniel Júlio Chipenda (Independent)	20,646	0.52
Anália de Victória Pereira (PLD)	11,475	0.29
Rui de Victória Pereira (PRA)	9,208	0.23
Total	3,940,884	100.00

NATIONAL ASSEMBLY

President: ROBERTO DE ALMEIDA.

Legislative Election, 29 and 30 September 1992

	Votes	% of votes	Seats†
MPLA	2,124,126	53.74	129
UNITA	1,347,636	34.10	70
FNLA	94,742	2.40	5
PLD	94,269	2.39	3
PRS	89,875	2.27	6
PRD	35,293	0.89	1
AD Coalition	34,166	0.86	1
PSD	33,088	0.84	1
PAJOCA	13,924	0.35	1
FDA	12,038	0.30	1
PDP—ANA	10,620	0.27	1
PNDA	10,281	0.26	1
CNDA	10,237	0.26	—
PSDA	19,217	0.26	—
PAI	9,007	0.23	—
PDLA	8,025	0.20	—
PDA	8,014	0.20	—
PRA	6,719	0.17	—
Total	3,952,277	100.00	220

* Under the terms of the electoral law, a second round of presidential elections was required to take place in order to determine which of the two leading candidates from the first round would be elected. However, a resumption of hostilities between UNITA and government forces prevented a second round of presidential elections from taking place. The electoral process was to resume only when the provisions of the Estoril peace agreement, concluded in May 1991, had been fulfilled. However, provision in the Lusaka peace accord of November 1994 for the second round of presidential elections was not pursued.

† According to the Constitution, the total number of seats in the National Assembly is 223. On the decision of the National Electoral Council, however, elections to fill three seats reserved for Angolans abroad were abandoned.

Political Organizations

Aliança Democrática de Angola: Leader SIMBA DA COSTA.

Angolan Alliance and Hamista Party.

Angolan Democratic Coalition (AD Coalition): Pres. EVIDOR QUIELA (acting).

Angolan Democratic Confederation: f. 1994; Chair. GASPAR NETO.

Angolan Democratic Unification: Leader EDUARDO MILTON SIVI.

Associação Cívica Angolana (ACA): f. 1990; Leader JOAQUIM PINTO DE ANDRADE.

Centro Democrático Social (CDS): Pres. MATEUS JOSÉ; Sec.-Gen. DELFINA FRANCISCO CAPCIEL.

Christian Democratic Convention: Leader GASPAR NETO.

Democratic Civilian Opposition: f. 1994; opposition alliance including:

Convenção Nacional Democrata de Angola (CNDA): Leader PAULINO PINTO JOÃO.

Frente Nacional de Libertação de Angola (FNLA): f. 1962; Pres. HOLDEN ROBERTO.

Frente para a Democracia (FPD): Leader NELSO PESTANA; Sec.-Gen. FILOMENO VIEIRA LOPES.

Movimento de Defesa dos Interesses de Angola—Partido de Consciência Nacional: Leader ISIDORO KLALA.

National Ecological Party of Angola: Leader SUKAWA DIZIZEKO RICARDO.

National Union for Democracy: Leader SEBASTIÃO ROGERIO SUZAMA.

Partido Renovador Social (PRS):

Party of Solidarity and the Conscience of Angola: Leader FERNANDO DOMBASSI QUIESSE.

Fórum Democrático Angolano (FDA): Leader JORGE REBELO PINTO CHICOTI.

Frente de Libertação do Enclave de Cabinda (FLEC): f. 1963; comprises several factions, claiming total forces of c. 5,000 guerrillas, seeking the secession of Cabinda province; mem. groups include:

Frente Democrática de Cabinda (FDC).

Frente de Libertação do Enclave de Cabinda–Forças Armadas Cabindesas (FLEC–FAC): Chair. HENRIQUE TIAGO N'ZITA; Chief-of-Staff (FAC) Commdr ESTANISLAU MIGUEL BOMBA.

Frente de Libertação do Enclave de Cabinda–Renovada (FLEC–R): Pres. ANTÓNIO BENTO BEMBE.

Movimento Amplo para a Democracia: Leader FRANCISCO VIANA.

Movimento Popular de Libertação de Angola (MPLA) (People's Movement for the Liberation of Angola): Luanda; telex 3369; f. 1956; in 1961–74, as MPLA, conducted guerrilla operations against Portuguese rule; governing party since 1975; known as Movimento Popular de Libertação de Angola—Partido do Trabalho (MPLA—PT) (People's Movement for the Liberation of Angola—Workers' Party) 1977–92; in Dec. 1990 replaced Marxist-Leninist ideology with commitment to 'democratic socialism'; Chair. JOSÉ EDUARDO DOS SANTOS; Sec.-Gen. LOPO FORTUNATO FERREIRA DO NASCIMENTO.

Movimento de Unidade Democrática para a Reconstrução (Mudar): Leader MANUEL DOS SANTOS LIMA.

National Union for the Light of Democracy and Development of Angola: Pres. MIGUEL MUENDO; Sec.-Gen. DOMINGOS CHIZELA.

Partido de Aliança de Juventude, Operários e Camponêses de Angola (PAJOCA) (Angolan Youth, Workers' and Peasants' Alliance Party): Leader MIGUEL JOÃO SEBASTIÃO.

Partido para a Aliança Popular: Leader CAMPOS NETO.

Partido Angolano Independente (PAI): Leader ADRIANO PARREIRA.

Partido Democrático Angolano (PDA): Leader ANTÓNIO ALBERTO NETO.

Partido Liberal Democrata (PLD): Leader ANÁLIA DE VICTÓRIA PEREIRA.

Partido Nacional Democrata de Angola (PNDA): Sec.-Gen. PEDRO JOÃO ANTÓNIO.

Partido Reformador de Angola (PRA): Leader RUI DE VICTÓRIA PEREIRA.

Partido Renovador Democrático (PRD): Leader LUÍS DOS PASSOS.

Partido Republicano Conservador de Angola (PRCA): Leader MARTINHO MATEUS.

Partido Social Democrata (PSD): Leader BENGUI PEDRO JOÃO.

Partido do Trabalho de Angola (PTA): Leader AGOSTINHO PALDO.

Patriotic Front: f. 1995; opposition alliance including:

Partido Angolano Liberal (PAL): Leader MANUEL FRANCISCO LULO (acting).

Partido Democrático Liberal de Angola (PDLA): Leader HONORATO LANDO.

Partido Democrático para o Progresso—Aliança Nacional de Angola (PDP—ANA): Leader MFUFUMPINGA NLANDU VICTOR.

Partido Social Democrata de Angola (PSDA): Leader ANDRÉ MILTON KILANDONOCO.

Peaceful Democratic Party of Angola: Leader ANTÓNIO KUNZOLAKO.

Unangola: Leader ANDRÉ FRANCO DE SOUSA.

União Nacional para a Independência Total de Angola (UNITA): f. 1966 to secure independence from Portugal; later received Portuguese support to oppose the MPLA; UNITA and the Frente Nacional de Libertação de Angola conducted guerrilla campaign against the MPLA Govt with aid from some Western nations, 1975–76; supported by South Africa until 1984 and in 1987–88, and by USA after 1986; support drawn mainly from Ovimbundu ethnic group; Pres. Dr JONAS MALHEIRO SAVIMBI; Sec.-Gen. PAULO LUKAMBA 'GATO'.

United Front for the Salvation of Angola: Leader JOSÉ AUGUSTO DA SILVA COELHO.

Vofangola: Leader LOMBY ZUENDOKI.

Diplomatic Representation

EMBASSIES IN ANGOLA

Algeria: Luanda; Ambassador: HANAFI OUSSEDIK.

Belgium: Avda 4 de Fevereiro 93, CP 1203, Luanda; tel. (2) 336437; telex 3356; fax (2) 336438; Ambassador: PAUL A. C. TAVERNIERS.

Brazil: Rua Houari Boumedienne 132, CP 5428, Luanda; tel. (2) 344848; telex 3365; Ambassador: PAULO DYRCEU PINHEIRO.

Bulgaria: Rua Fernão Mendes Pinto 35, CP 2260, Luanda; tel. (2) 321010; telex 2189; Chargé d'affaires a.i.: LILO TOCHEV.

Cape Verde: Rua Alexandre Peres 29, Luanda; tel. (2) 333211; telex 3247; Ambassador: JOSÉ LUÍS JESUS.

China, People's Republic: Rua Houari Boumedienne 196, Luanda; tel. (2) 344185; Ambassador: ZHANG BAOSHENG.

Congo, Democratic Republic: Rua Cesario Verde 24, Luanda; tel. (2) 361953; Ambassador: MUNDINDI DIDI KILENGO.

Congo, Republic: Rua 4 de Fevereiro 3, Luanda; Ambassador: ANATOLE KHONDO.

Côte d'Ivoire: Rua Karl Marx 43, Luanda; tel. (2) 390150; Ambassador: JEAN-MARIE KACOU GERVAIS.

Cuba: Rua Che Guevara 42, Luanda; tel. (2) 339165; telex 3236; Ambassador: NARCISCO MARTÍN MORA.

Czech Republic: Rua Amílcar Cabral 5, CP 2691, Luanda; tel. (2) 334456.

Egypt: Rua Comandante Stona 247, Luanda; tel. (2) 321590; telex 3380; Ambassador: ANWAR DAKROURY.

France: Rua Reverendo Pedro Agostinho Neto 31–33, Luanda; tel. (2) 334335; fax (2) 391949; Ambassador: ANDRÉ CIRA.

Gabon: Avda 4 de Fevereiro 95, Luanda; tel. (2) 372614; telex 3263; Ambassador: RAPHAËL NKASSA-NZOGHO.

Germany: Avda 4 de Fevereiro 120, CP 1295, Luanda; tel. (2) 334516; telex 2096; fax (2) 334516; Ambassador: HELMUT VAN EDIG.

Ghana: Rua Cirilo da Conceição e Silva 5, CP 1012, Luanda; tel. (2) 339222; telex 2051; fax (2) 338235; Chargé d'affaires a.i.: E. OBENG KUFUOR.

Guinea: Luanda; telex 3177.

Holy See: Rua Luther King 123, CP 1030, Luanda (Apostolic Delegation); tel. (2) 336289; fax (2) 332378; Apostolic Delegate: Most Rev. ALDO CAVALLI, Titular Archbishop of Vibo Valentia.

Hungary: Rua Comandante Stona 226-228, Luanda; tel. (2) 32313; telex 3084; fax (2) 322448; Ambassador: Dr GÁBOR TÓTH.

India: Prédio dos Armazens Carrapas 81, 1°, D, 6040, Luanda; tel. (2) 345398; telex 3233; fax (2) 342061; Ambassador: BALDEV RAJ GHULIANI.

Italy: Edif. Importang 7°, Rua Kinaxixi, Luanda; tel. (2) 393533; telex 3265; Ambassador: FRANCESCO LANATA.

Korea, Democratic People's Republic: Rua Cabral Moncada 116–120, CP 599, Luanda; tel. (2) 395575; fax (2) 332813; Ambassador: HYON SOK.

Morocco: Largo 4 de Fevereiro 3, Luanda; tel. (2) 338847.

Mozambique: Luanda; tel. (2) 330811; Ambassador: M. SALESSIO.

Namibia: Rua dos Coqueiros, Luanda; tel. (2) 396281; fax (2) 339234.

Netherlands: Edif. Secil, Avda 4 de Fevereiro 42, CP 3624, Luanda; tel. (2) 333540; telex 3051; fax (2) 333699; Ambassador: H. KROON.

Nigeria: Rua Houari Boumedienne 120, CP 479, Luanda; tel. (2) 340084; telex 3014; Ambassador: GABRIEL SAM AKUMAFOR.

Poland: Rua Comandante N'zaji 21–23, CP 1340, Luanda; tel. (2) 323086; telex 3222; Ambassador: JAN BOJKO.

Portugal: Rua Karl Marx 50, CP 1346, Luanda; tel. (2) 333027; telex 3370; Ambassador: RAMALHO ORTIGÃO.

Romania: Ramalho Ortigão 30, Alvalade, Luanda; tel. and fax (2) 321076; telex 2085; Ambassador: MARIN ILIESCU.

Russia: Rua Houari Boumedienne 170, CP 3141, Luanda; tel. (2) 345028; Ambassador: YURII KAPRALOV.

São Tomé and Príncipe: Rua Armindo de Andrade 173–175, Luanda; tel. (2) 345677; Ambassador: ARIOSTO CASTELO DAVID.

Slovakia: Rua Amílcar Cabral 5, CP 2691, Luanda; tel. (2) 334456.

South Africa: Rua Manuel Fernandes Caldeira 6B, CP 6212 Luanda; tel. (2) 397301; fax (2) 396788; Chargé d'affaires a.i.: ROGER BALLARD-TREMEER.

Spain: Avda 4 de Fevereiro 95, 1°, CP 3061, Luanda; tel. (2) 391187; telex 2621; fax (2) 391188; Ambassador: RAFAEL FERNÁNDEZ-PITA Y GONZÁLEZ.

Sweden: Rua Garcia Neto 9, Luanda; tel. (2) 340424; telex 3126; Ambassador: LENA SUND.

Switzerland: Avda 4 de Fevereiro 129, 2°, CP 3163, Luanda; tel. (2) 338314; fax (2) 336878; Chargé d'affaires a.i.: ARNOLDO LARDI.

Tanzania: Rua Joaquim Kapango 57–63, Luanda; tel. (2) 330536.

United Kingdom: Rua Diogo Cão 4, CP 1244, Luanda; tel. (2) 392991; telex 3130; fax (2) 333331; Ambassador: ROGER D. HART.

USA: Rua Houari Boumedienne 32, Miramar, CP 6468, Luanda; tel. (2) 346418; Ambassador: BILL RICHARDSON.

Viet Nam: Rua Comandante N'zaji 66–68, CP 75, Luanda; tel. (2) 323388; telex 3226; Ambassador: NGUYEN HUY LOI.

Yugoslavia: Rua Comandante N'zaji 25–27, Luanda; tel. (2) 321421; fax (2) 321724; Chargé d'affaires a.i.: BRANKO MARKOVIĆ.

Zambia: Rua Rei Katyavala 106–108, CP 1496, Luanda; tel. (2) 331145; telex 3439; Ambassador: BONIFACE ZULU.

Zimbabwe: Edif. do Ministério de Transportes e Comunicações, Avda 4 de Fevereiro 42, CP 428, Luanda; tel. (2) 332338; telex 3275; fax (2) 332339; Ambassador: B. G. CHIDYAUSIKU.

Judicial System

There is a Supreme Court and Court of Appeal in Luanda. There are also civil, criminal and military courts.

Chief Justice of the Supreme Court: JOÃO FELIZARDO.

Religion

Much of the population follows traditional African beliefs, although a majority profess to be Christians, mainly Roman Catholics.

CHRISTIANITY

Conselho de Igrejas Cristãs em Angola (Council of Christian Churches in Angola): Rua Amílcar Cabral 182, 1° andar, CP 1659, Luanda; tel. (2) 330415; fax (2) 393746; f. 1977; 14 mem. churches; five assoc. mems; one observer; Pres. Rev. ALVARO RODRIGUES; Gen. Sec. Rev. AUGUSTO CHIPESSE.

Protestant Churches

Evangelical Congregational Church in Angola (Igreja Evangélica Congregacional em Angola: CP 551, Huambo; tel. 3087; 100,000 mems; Gen. Sec. Rev. JÚLIO FRANCISCO.

Evangelical Pentecostal Church of Angola (Missão Evangélica Pentecostal de Angola): CP 219, Porto Amboim; 13,600 mems; Sec. Rev. JOSÉ DOMINGOS CAETANO.

United Evangelical Church of Angola (Igreja Evangélica Unida de Angola): CP 122, Uíge; 11,000 mems; Gen. Sec. Rev. A. L. DOMINGOS.

Other active denominations include the African Apostolic Church, the Church of Apostolic Faith in Angola, the Church of Our Lord Jesus Christ in the World, the Evangelical Baptist Church, the Evangelical Church in Angola, the Evangelical Church of the Apostles of Jerusalem, the Evangelical Reformed Church of Angola, the Kimbanguist Church in Angola and the United Methodist Church.

The Roman Catholic Church

Angola comprises three archdioceses and 12 dioceses. At 31 December 1995 an estimated 44.7% of the total population were adherents.

Bishops' Conference: Conferência Episcopal de Angola e São Tomé, CP 3579, Luanda; tel. (2) 343686; fax (2) 345504; f. 1967; Pres. Cardinal ALEXANDRE DO NASCIMENTO, Archbishop of Luanda.

Archbishop of Huambo: Most Rev. FRANCISCO VITI, Arcebispado, CP 10, Huambo; tel. 2371.

Archbishop of Luanda: Cardinal ALEXANDRE DO NASCIMENTO, Arcebispado, CP 87, 1230-C, Luanda; tel. (2) 334640; fax (2) 334433.

Archbishop of Lubango: Most Rev. MANUEL FRANKLIN DA COSTA, Arcebispado, CP 231, Lubango; tel. 20405; fax 23547.

The Press

The press was nationalized in 1976.

DAILIES

Diário da República: CP 1306, Luanda; official govt bulletin.

O Jornal de Angola: Rua Rainha Ginga 18–24, CP 1312, Luanda; tel. (2) 338947; telex 3341; fax (2) 333342; f. 1923; Dir-Gen. ADELINO MARQUES DE ALMEIDA; mornings and Sun.; circ. 41,000.

Newspapers are also published in several regional towns.

PERIODICALS

Angola Norte: CP 97, Malanje; weekly.

A Célula: Luanda; political journal of MPLA; monthly.

Comércio Actualidade: Rua da Missão 85, CP 6375, Luanda; tel. (2) 334060; fax (2) 392216.

Correio da Semana: Rua Rainha Ginga 18–24, CP 1213, Luanda; f. 1992; owned by *O Jornal de Angola*; weekly. Editor-in-Chief MANUEL DIONISIO.

Jornal de Benguela: CP 17, Benguela; 2 a week.

Lavra & Oficina: CP 2767-C, Luanda; tel. (2) 322155; f. 1975; journal of the Union of Angolan Writers; monthly; circ. 5,000.

M: Luanda; f. 1996; MPLA publ.

Militar: Luanda; f. 1993; Editor-in-Chief CARMO NETO.

Novembro: CP 3947, Luanda; tel. (2) 331660; monthly; Dir ROBERTO DE ALMEIDA.

O Planalto: CP 96, Huambo; 2 a week.

A Voz do Trabalhador: Avda 4 de Fevereiro 210, CP 28, Luanda; telex 3387; journal of União Nacional de Trabalhadores Angolanos (National Union of Angolan Workers); monthly.

NEWS AGENCIES

ANGOP: Rua Rei Katiavala 120, Luanda; tel. (2) 334595; telex 4162; Dir-Gen. and Editor-in-Chief AVELINO MIGUEL.

Foreign Bureaux

Agence France-Presse (AFP): Prédio Mutamba, CP 2357, Luanda; tel. (2) 334939; telex 3334; Bureau Chief MANUELA TEIXEIRA.

Allgemeiner Deutscher Nachrichtendienst (ADN) (Germany): CP 3193, Luanda; telex 3323; Correspondent GUDRUN GROSS.

Informatsionnoye Telegrafnoye Agentstvo Rossii—Telegrafnoye Agentstvo Suverennykh Stran (ITAR—TASS) (Russia): Rua Marechal Tito 75, CP 3209, Luanda; tel. (2) 342524; telex 3244; Correspondent VLADIMIR BORISOVICH BUYANOV.

Inter Press Service (IPS) (Italy): c/o Centro de Imprensa Anibal de Melo, Rua Cequeira Lukoki 124, Luanda; tel. (2) 334895; fax: (2) 393445; Correspondent CHRIS SIMPSON.

Prensa Latina (Cuba): Rua D. Miguel de Melo 92-2, Luanda; tel. (2) 336804; telex 3253; Chief Correspondent LUÍS MANUEL SÁEZ.

Reuters (UK): c/o Centro de Imprensa Anibal de Melo, Rua Cequeira Lukoki 124, Luanda; tel. (2) 334895; fax (2) 393445; Correspondent CRISTINA MULLER.

Rossiyskoye Informatsionnoye Agentstvo—Novosti (RIA—Novosti) (Russia): Luanda; Chief Officer VLADISLAV Z. KOMAROV.

Xinhua (New China) News Agency (People's Republic of China): Rua Karl Marx 57-3, andar E, Bairro das Ingombotas, Zona 4, Luanda; tel. (2) 332415; telex 4054; Correspondent ZHAO XIAOZHONG.

Publishers

Empresa Distribuidora Livreira (EDIL), UEE: Rua da Missão 107, CP 1245, Luanda; tel. (2) 334034.

Neográfica, SARL: CP 6518, Luanda; publ. *Novembro*.

Nova Editorial Angolana, SARL: CP 1225, Luanda; f. 1935; general and educational; Man. Dir POMBO FERNANDES.

Offsetográfica Gráfica Industrial Lda: CP 911, Benguela; tel. 32568; f. 1966; Man. FERNANDO MARTINS.

Government Publishing House

Imprensa Nacional, UEE: CP 1306, Luanda; f. 1845; Gen. Man. Dr ANTÓNIO DUARTE DE ALMEIDA E CARMO.

Broadcasting and Communications

TELECOMMUNICATIONS

Empresa Pública de Telecomunicações (EPTEL), UEE: Rua I Congresso 26, CP 625, Luanda; tel. (2) 392285; telex 3012; fax (2) 391688; international telecommunications.

RADIO

Rádio Nacional de Angola: Rua Comandante Jika, CP 1329, Luanda; tel. (2) 320192; telex 3066; fax (2) 324647; broadcasts in Portuguese, English, French, Spanish and vernacular languages (Chokwe, Kikongo, Kimbundu, Kwanyama, Fiote, Ngangela, Luvale, Songu, Umbundu); Dir-Gen. AGOSTINHO VIEIRA LOPES.

Luanda Antena Comercial (LAC): Praceta Luther King 5, Luanda; tel. (2) 396229.

TELEVISION

Televisão Popular de Angola (TPA): Rua Ho Chi Minh, CP 2604, Luanda; tel. (2) 320025; telex 3238; fax (2) 391091; f. 1975; state-controlled; Man. Dir CARLOS CUNHA.

Finance

(cap. = capital; res = reserves; dep. = deposits; m. = million; brs = branches; amounts in old kwanza)

BANKING

All banks were nationalized in 1975. In 1995 the Government authorized the creation of private banks.

Central Bank

Banco Nacional de Angola: Avda 4 de Fevereiro 151, CP 1298, Luanda; tel. (2) 399141; telex 3005; fax (2) 393179; f. 1976 to replace Banco de Angola; bank of issue; cap. and res 7,657m.; dep. 111,975m. (1983); Gov. SEBASTIÃO BASTOS LAVRADOR.

Commercial Banks

Banco de Crédito Comercial e Industrial: CP 1395, Luanda.

Banco de Poupança e Crédito (BPC): Largo Saydi Mingas, CP 1343, Luanda; tel. (2) 339158; telex 4149; fax (2) 393790; cap. 10,000m. (Dec. 1992); Chair. AMILCAR S. AZEVEDO SILVA; brs throughout Angola.

Caixa de Crédito Agro-Pecuario e Pescas (CCAPP): f. 1991; assumed commercial operations of Banco Nacional de Angola in 1996.

Development Bank

Banco de Comércio e Indústria SARL: Avda 4 de Fevereiro 86, CP 1395, Luanda; tel. (2) 333684; telex 2009; fax (2) 333823; f. 1991; provides loans to businesses in all sectors; cap. 1,000m., dep. 424,591.3m. (1992); Chair. PEDRO MAIANGALA PUNA; 2 brs.

Investment Bank

Banco Africano de Investimento (BAI): Luanda; f. 1996; Govt of Angola holds 39% share of US $35m. joint capital stock; Pres. AGUINALDO JAIME.

Foreign Banks

Banco Espírito Santo e Comercial de Lisboa SA: 5-3°, Rua Cirilo da Conceição Silva, CP 1471, Luanda; tel. (2) 392287; telex 3400; fax (2) 391484; Rep. JOSÉ RIBEIRO DA SILVA.

Banco de Fomento e Exterior SA: Edifício BPA, 7° andar, Rua Dr Alfredo Troni, Luanda; Man. TERESA MATEUS.

Banco Totta e Açores SA: Avda 4 de Fevereiro 99, CP 1231, Luanda; tel. (2) 334257; telex 2015; fax (2) 333233; Gen. Man. Dr MÁRIO NELSON MAXIMINO.

INSURANCE

Empresa Nacional de Seguros e Resseguros de Angola (ENSA), UEE: Avda 4 de Fevereiro 93, CP 5778, Luanda; tel. (2) 332991; telex 3087.

Trade and Industry

SUPERVISORY BODY

National Supplies Commission: Luanda; f. 1977 to combat sabotage and negligence.

CHAMBERS OF COMMERCE

Angolan Chamber of Commerce and Industry: Largo do Kinaxixi 14, 1° andar, CP 92, Luanda; tel. (2) 344506; telex 3283.

Associação Comercial de Luanda: Edifício Palácio de Comércio, 1° andar, CP 1275, Luanda; tel. (2) 322453.

STATE TRADING ORGANIZATIONS

Angomédica, UEE: Rua Dr Américo Boavida 85/87, CP 2698, Luanda; tel. (2) 363765; fax (2) 362336; f. 1981 to import pharmaceutical goods; Gen. Dir Dr FÁTIMA SAIUNDO.

Direcção dos Serviços de Comércio (Dept of Trade): Largo Diogo Cão, CP 1337, Luanda; f. 1970; brs throughout Angola.

Epmel, UEE: Rua Karl Marx 35–37, Luanda; tel. (2) 330943; industrial agricultural machinery.

Exportang, UEE: Rua dos Enganos 1A, CP 1000, Luanda; tel. (2) 332363; telex 3318; co-ordinates exports.

Importang, UEE: Calçada do Município 10, CP 1003, Luanda; tel. (2) 337994; telex 3169; f. 1977; co-ordinates majority of imports; Dir-Gen. SIMÃO DIOGO DA CRUZ.

Maquimport, UEE: Rua Rainha Ginga 152, CP 2975, Luanda; tel. (2) 339044; telex 4175; f. 1981 to import office equipment.

Mecanang, UEE: Rua dos Enganos, 1°–7° andar, CP 1347, Luanda; tel. (2) 390644; telex 4021; f. 1981 to import agricultural and construction machinery, tools and spare parts.

STATE INDUSTRIAL ENTERPRISES

Companhia do Açúcar de Angola: 77 Rua Direita, Luanda; production of sugar.

Companhia Geral dos Algodões de Angola (COTONANG): Avda da Boavista, Luanda; production of cotton textiles.

Empresa Abastecimento Técnico Material (EMATEC), UEE: Largo Rainha Ginga 3, CP 2952, Luanda; tel. (2) 338891; telex 3349; technical and material suppliers to the Ministry of Defence.

Empresa Açucareira Centro (OSUKA), UEE: Estrada Principal do Lobito, CP 37, Catumbela; tel. 24681; telex 08268; sugar industry.

Empresa Açucareira Norte (ACUNOR), UEE: Rua Robert Shilds, Caxito, Bengo; tel. 71720; sugar production.

Empresa Angolana de Embalagens (METANGOL), UEE: Rua Estrada do Cacuaco, CP 151, Luanda; tel. (2) 370680; production of non-specified metal goods.

Empresa de Cimento de Angola (CIMANGOLA), UEE: Avda 4 de Fevereiro 42, Luanda; tel. (2) 371190; telex 3142; f. 1954; 69% state-owned; cement production; exports to several African countries.

Empresa de Construção de Edificações (CONSTROI), UEE: Rua Alexandre Peres, CP 2566, Luanda; tel. (2) 333930; telex 3165; construction.

Empresa de Pesca de Angola (PESCANGOLA), UEE: Luanda; f. 1981; state fishing enterprise, responsible to Ministry of Fisheries.

Empresa de Rebenefício e Exportação do Café de Angola (CAFANGOL), UEE: Avda 4 de Fevereiro 107, CP 342, Luanda; tel. (2) 337916; telex 2137; f. 1983; nat. coffee-processing and trade org.

Empresa de Tecidos de Angola (TEXTANG), UEE: Rua N'gola Kiluanji-Kazenga, CP 5404, Luanda; tel. (2) 381134; telex 4062; production of textiles.

Empresa Nacional de Cimento (ENCIME), UEE: CP 157, Lobito; tel. (711) 2325; cement production.

Empresa Nacional de Comercialização e Distribuição de Produtos Agrícolas (ENCODIPA): Luanda; central marketing agency for agricultural produce; numerous brs throughout Angola.

Empresa Nacional de Diamantes de Angola (ENDIAMA), UEE: Rua Major Kanhangulo 100, Luanda; tel. (2) 392336; telex 3046; fax (2) 337276; f. 1981 as the sole diamond-mining concession; commenced operations 1986; Dir-Gen. AUGUSTO PAULINO ALMEIDA NETO.

Empresa Nacional de Ferro de Angola (FERRANGOL): Rua João de Barros 26, CP 2692, Luanda; tel. (2) 373800; iron production; Dir ARMANDO DE SOUSA (MACHADINHO).

Empresa Nacional de Manutenção (MANUTECNICA), UEE: Rua 7, Avda do Cazenga 10, CP 3508, Luanda; tel. (2) 383646; assembly of machines and specialized equipment for industry.

Empresa Texteis de Angola (ENTEX), UEE: Avda Comandante Kima Kienda, CP 5720, Luanda; tel. (2) 336182; telex 3086; weaving and tissue finishing.

Fina Petróleos de Angola SARL: CP 1320, Luanda; tel. (2) 336855; telex 3246; fax (2) 391031; f. 1957; petroleum production, refining and exploration; operates Luanda petroleum refinery, Petrangol, with capacity of 32,000 b/d; also operates Quinfuquena terminal; Man. Dir CARLOS ALVES.

Siderurgia Nacional, UEE: CP Zona Industrial do Forel das Lagostas, Luanda; tel. (2) 373028; telex 3178; f. 1963, nationalized 1980; steelworks and rolling mill plant.

Sociedade Nacional de Combustíveis de Angola (SONANGOL): Rua I Congresso do MPLA, CP 1318, Luanda; tel. (2) 331690; telex 3148; f. 1976 for exploration, production and refining of crude petroleum, and marketing and distribution of petroleum products; sole concessionary in Angola, supervises on- and offshore operations of foreign petroleum cos; holds majority interest in jt ventures with Cabinda Gulf Oil Co (Cabgoc), Fina Petróleos de Angola and Texaco Petróleos de Angola; Dir-Gen. JOAQUIM DAVID.

Sociedade Unificada de Tabacos de Angola, Lda (SUT): Rua Deolinda Rodrigues 530/537, CP 1263, Luanda; tel. (2) 360180; telex 3237; fax (2) 362138; f. 1919; tobacco products; Gen. Man. Dr MANUEL LAMAS.

UTILITIES

Electricity

Empresa Nacional de Construções Eléctricas (ENCEL), UEE: Rua Comandante Che Guevara 185/7, Luanda; tel. (2) 391630; fax (2) 331411; f. 1982; electric energy.

Empresa Nacional de Electricidade (ENE), UEE: Edifício Geominas, 6°–7° andar, CP 772, Luanda; tel. (2) 321529; telex 3170; fax (2) 323382; f. 1980; production and distribution of electricity; Dir-Gen. Eng. MARIO FERNANDO PONTES MOREIRA FONTES.

TRADE UNIONS

Angolan General Independent and Free Trade Union Confederation: Chair. MANUEL DIFUILA.

União Nacional de Trabalhadores Angolanos (UNTA) (National Union of Angolan Workers): Avda 4 de Fevereiro 210, CP 28, Luanda; telex 3387; f. 1960; Sec.-Gen. PASCOAL LUVUALU; 600,000 mems.

Transport

The transport infrastructure has been severely dislocated by the civil war.

RAILWAYS

The total length of track operated was 2,952 km in 1987. There are plans to extend the Namibe line beyond Menongue and to construct north–south rail links.

Caminhos de Ferro de Angola: Avda 4 de Fevereiro 42, CP 1250-C, Luanda; tel. (2) 339794; telex 3224; fax (2) 339976; f. 1975; nat. network operating four fmrly independent systems covering 2,952 track-km; Nat. Dir R. M. DA CONCEIÇÃO JUNIOR.

Amboim Railway: Porto Amboim; f. 1922; 123 track-km; Dir A. GUIA.

Benguela Railway (Companhia do Caminho de Ferro de Benguela): Rua Praça 11 Novembro 3, CP 32, Lobito; tel. (711) 22645; telex 2922; fax (711) 22865; f. 1903, line completed 1928; owned 90% by Tank Consolidated Investments (a subsidiary of Société Générale de Belgique), 10% by Govt of Angola; line carrying passenger and freight traffic from the port of Lobito across Angola, via Huambo and Luena, to the border of the Democratic Republic of the Congo (fmrly Zaire) where it connects with that country's railway system, which, in turn, links with Zambia Railways, thus providing the shortest west coast route for central African trade; 1,394 track-km; guerrilla operations by UNITA suspended all international traffic from 1975, with only irregular services from Lobito to Huambo being operated; a declaration of intent to reopen the cross-border lines was signed in April 1987 by Angola, Zambia and Zaire, and the rehabilitation of the railway was a priority of a 10-year programme, planned by the SADCC (now SADC), to develop the 'Lobito corridor'; In 1997 an Italian company, Tor di Vale, began a US $450m. programme of repairs to the railway. Minimum repairs allowing the resumption of freight traffic were expected to take three years to complete, to be followed by further modernization, including the reconstruction of 22 passenger stations; Dir-Gen. LUKOKI SEBASTIÃO.

Luanda Railway (Empresa de Caminho de Ferro de Luanda, UEE): CP 1250-C, Luanda; tel. (2) 370061; telex 3108; f. 1886; serves an iron, cotton and sisal-producing region between Luanda and Malanje; reconstruction of Luanda-Dombo rail link completed April 1997, rehabilitation of Dombo-Malanje section due for completion end 1997; 536 track-km; Man. A. ALVARO AGANTE.

Namibe Railway: CP 130, Lubango; f. 1905; main line from Namibe to Menongue, via Lubango; br. lines to Chibia and iron ore mines at Cassinga; 899 track-km; Gen. Man. J. SALVADOR.

ROADS

In 1995 Angola had 72,626 km of roads, of which 7,955 km were main roads and 15,571 km were secondary roads. About 25% of roads were paved. In 1997 the state-owned road construction and maintenance company, the Instituto de Estradas de Angola, reported that 80% of the country's road network was in disrepair and that the cost of rebuilding the roads and bridges damaged during the civil conflict would total some US $4,000m.

SHIPPING

The main harbours are at Lobito, Luanda and Namibe; the commercial port of Porto Amboim, in Cuanza-Sul province, has been closed for repairs since 1984. The expansion of port facilities in Cabinda was due to begin in late 1995 and was expected to be completed within two years. In May 1983 a regular shipping service began to operate between Luanda and Maputo (Mozambique). Under the emergency transport programme launched in 1988, refurbishment work was to be undertaken on the ports of Luanda and Namibe. The first phase of a 10-year SADCC (now SADC) programme to develop the 'Lobito corridor', for which funds were pledged in January 1989, was to include the rehabilitation of the ports of Lobito and Benguela.

Angonave—Linhas Marítimas de Angola, UEE: Rua Serqueira 31, CP 5953, Luanda; tel. (2) 330144; telex 3313; national shipping line; Dir-Gen. FRANCISCO VENÂNCIO.

Cabotang—Cabotagem Nacional Angolana, UEE: Avda 4 de Fevereiro 83A, Luanda; tel. (2) 373133; telex 3007; operates off the coasts of Angola and Mozambique; Dir-Gen. JOÃO OCTAVIO VAN-DÚNEM.

Empresa Portuaria do Lobito, UEE: Avda da Independência, CP 16, Lobito; tel. (711) 2710; telex 8233; long-distance sea transport.

Empresa Portuaria de Moçâmedes—Namibe, UEE: Rua Pedro Benje 10A and 10C, CP 49, Namibe; tel. (64) 60643; long-distance sea transport; Dir HUMBERTO DE ATAIDE DIAS.

Linhas Marítimas de Angola, UEE: Rua Serqueira 31, CP 5953, Luanda; tel. (2) 30144; telex 3313.

Secil Marítima SARL, UEE: Avda 4 de Fevereiro 42, 1° andar, CP 5910, Luanda; tel. (2) 335230; telex 3060.

CIVIL AVIATION

Air Nacoia: Rua Comandante Che Guevara 67, 1° andar, Luanda; tel. and fax (2) 395477; f. 1993; Pres. SALVADOR SILVA.

TAAG—Linhas Aéreas de Angola: Rua da Missão 123, CP 79, Luanda; tel. (2) 332485; telex 3442; fax (2) 393548; f. 1939; internal scheduled passenger and cargo services, and services from Luanda to destinations within Africa and to Europe, South America and the Caribbean; Chair. JÚLIO SAMPAIO ALMEIDA; Gen. Dir ABEL ANTÓNIO LOPES.

Angola Air Charter: Aeroporto Internacional 4 de Fevereiro, CP 5433, Luanda; tel. (2) 350559; fax (2) 392229; f. 1992; subsidiary of TAAG.

Transafrik International: Rua Joaquim Kapango, CP 2839, Luanda; tel. (2) 352141; telex 4159; fax (2) 351723; f. 1986; operates contract cargo services mainly within Africa; Man. Dir ERICH F. KOCH; Gen. Man. PIMENTAL ARAUJO.

Tourism

National Tourist Agency: Palácio de Vidro, CP 1240, Luanda; tel. (2) 372750.

ANTARCTICA

Source: Scientific Committee on Antarctic Research, Scott Polar Research Institute, Lensfield Rd, Cambridge, CB2 1ER, England; tel. (1223) 362061; fax (1223) 336549.

The Continent of Antarctica is estimated to cover 13,661,000 sq km. There are no indigenous inhabitants, but a number of permanent research stations have been established. W. S. Bruce, of the Scottish National Antarctic Expedition (1902–04), established a meteorological station on Laurie Island, South Orkney Islands, on 1 April 1903. After the expedition, this was transferred to the Argentine authorities (the British Government having declined to operate the station), who have maintained the observatory since 22 February 1904 (see Orcadas, below). The next permanent stations were established in 1944 by the United Kingdom, and then subsequently by other countries.

Wintering Stations

(The following list includes wintering stations south of latitude 60° occupied during austral winter 1997)

	Latitude	Longitude
ARGENTINA		
General Belgrano II, Bertrab Nunatak, Luitpold Coast	77° 52′ S	34° 37′ W
Esperanza, Hope Bay	63° 24′ S	57° 00′ W
Teniente Jubany, King George Island	62° 14′ S	58° 40′ W
Vicecomodoro Marambio, Seymour Island	64° 14′ S	56° 37′ W
Orcadas, Laurie Island	60° 44′ S	44° 44′ W
General San Martín, Barry Island	68° 08′ S	67° 06′ W
AUSTRALIA		
Casey, Vincennes Bay, Budd Coast	66° 18′ S	110° 32′ E
Davis, Ingrid Christensen Coast	68° 36′ S	77° 58′ E
Mawson, Mac. Robertson Land	67° 36′ S	62° 52′ E

In a report published in 1997 the Australian Government's advisory body on the Antarctic proposed that future research work might be concentrated at the Davis station, thus enabling Casey and Mawson to be leased to other countries or to strictly regulated tour operators.

	Latitude	Longitude
BRAZIL		
Comandante Ferraz, King George Island	62° 05′ S	58° 24′ W
CHILE		
Capitán Arturo Prat, Greenwich Island	62° 30′ S	59° 41′ W
General Bernardo O'Higgins, Cape Legoupil	63° 19′ S	57° 54′ W
Presidente Eduardo Frei, King George Island	62° 12′ S	58° 58′ W
PEOPLE'S REPUBLIC OF CHINA		
Chang Cheng (Great Wall), King George Island	62° 13′ S	58° 58′ W
Zhongshan, Princess Elizabeth Land	69° 22′ S	76° 23′ E
FRANCE		
Dumont d'Urville, Terre Adélie	66° 40′ S	140° 01′ E

A new research station, Concorde (at Dome C—75° 06′ S 123° 23′ E), is currently under construction as a joint venture with Italy.

	Latitude	Longitude
GERMANY		
Neumayer, Ekstrømisen	70° 39′ S	8° 15′ W
INDIA		
Maitri, Schirmacheroasen	70° 46′ S	11° 44′ E
JAPAN		
Dome Fuji	77° 19′ S	39° 42′ E
Syowa, Ongul	69° 00′ S	39° 35′ E
REPUBLIC OF KOREA		
King Sejong, King George Island	62° 13′ S	58° 47′ W
NEW ZEALAND		
Scott Base, Ross Island	77° 51′ S	166° 45′ E
POLAND		
Henryk Arctowski, King George Island	62° 09′ S	58° 28′ W
RUSSIA		
Bellingshausen, King George Island	62° 12′ S	58° 58′ W
Mirnyy, Queen Mary Land	66° 33′ S	93° 01′ E
Molodezhnaya, Enderby Land	67° 40′ S	45° 51′ E
Novolazarevskaya, Prinsesse Astrid Kyst	70° 46′ S	11° 50′ E
SOUTH AFRICA		
SANAE, Vesleskarvet	71° 41′ S	2° 50′ W
UKRAINE		
Vernadsky, Argentine Islands	65° 15′ S	64° 16′ W
UNITED KINGDOM		
Halley, Brunt Ice Shelf, Caird Coast	75° 35′ S	26° 15′ W
Rothera, Adelaide Island	67° 34′ S	68° 07′ W

In May 1990 the UK built an airstrip at the Rothera scientific station.

	Latitude	Longitude
USA		
McMurdo, Ross Island	77° 51′ S	166° 40′ E
Palmer, Anvers Island	64° 46′ S	64° 03′ W
South Pole (Amundsen-Scott)	South Pole	
URUGUAY		
Artigas, King George Island	62° 11′ S	58° 51′ W

Territorial Claims

Territory	Claimant State
Antártida Argentina	Argentina
Australian Antarctic Territory	Australia
British Antarctic Territory	United Kingdom
Dronning Maud Land	Norway
Ross Dependency	New Zealand
Terre Adélie	France
Territorio Chileno Antártico	Chile

These claims are not recognized by the USA or Russia. No formal claims have been made in the sector of Antarctica between 90° W and 150° W.

See also Article 4 of the Antarctic Treaty below.

Research

Scientific Committee on Antarctic Research (SCAR) of the **International Council of Scientific Unions (ICSU):** Secretariat: Scott Polar Research Institute, Lensfield Rd, Cambridge, CB2 1ER, England; tel. (1223) 362061; fax (1223) 336549; f. 1958 to initiate, promote and co-ordinate scientific research in the Antarctic, and to provide scientific advice to the Antarctic Treaty System; 25 full mems; seven assoc. mems.

President: Prof. A. C. ROCHA-CAMPOS (Brazil).

Vice-Presidents: Dr R. H. RUTFORD (USA), Prof. O. ORHEIM (Norway), Prof. P. G. QUILTY (Australia), Dr F. J. DAVEY (New Zealand).

Executive Secretary: Dr P. D. CLARKSON.

The Antarctic Treaty

The Treaty (summarized below) was signed in Washington, DC, on 1 December 1959 by the 12 nations co-operating in the Antarctic during the International Geophysical Year, and entered into force on 23 June 1961. The Treaty made provision for a review of its terms, 30 years after ratification; however, no signatory to the Treaty has requested such a review.

Article 1. Antarctica shall be used for peaceful purposes only.

Article 2. On freedom of scientific investigation and co-operation.

Article 3. On exchange of information and personnel.

Article 4. i. Nothing contained in the present Treaty shall be interpreted as:

(a) a renunciation by any Contracting Party of previously asserted rights of or claims to territorial sovereignty in Antarctica;

(b) a renunciation or diminution by any Contracting Party of any basis of claim to territorial sovereignty in Antarctica which it may have whether as a result of its activities or those of its nationals in Antarctica, or otherwise;

(c) prejudicing the position of any Contracting Party as regards its recognition or non-recognition of any other State's right of or claim or basis of claim to territorial sovereignty in Antarctica.

ii. No acts or activities taking place while the present Treaty is in force shall constitute a basis for asserting, supporting or denying a claim to territorial sovereignty in Antarctica or create any rights of sovereignty in Antarctica. No new claim, or enlargement of an existing claim, to territorial sovereignty in Antarctica shall be asserted while the present Treaty is in force.

Article 5. Any nuclear explosions in Antarctica and the disposal there of radioactive waste material shall be prohibited.

Article 6. On geographical limits and rights on high seas.

Article 7. On designation of observers and notification of stations and expeditions.

Article 8. On jurisdiction over observers and scientists.

Article 9. On consultative meetings.

Articles 10–14. On upholding, interpreting, amending, notifying and depositing the Treaty.

ORIGINAL SIGNATORIES

Argentina	France	South Africa
Australia	Japan	USSR (former)
Belgium	New Zealand	United Kingdom
Chile	Norway	USA

ACCEDING STATES

Austria, Brazil, Bulgaria, Canada, the People's Republic of China, Colombia, Cuba, the Czech Republic, Denmark, Ecuador, Finland, Germany, Greece, Guatemala, Hungary, India, Italy, the Democratic People's Republic of Korea, the Republic of Korea, the Netherlands, Papua New Guinea, Peru, Poland, Romania, Slovakia, Spain, Sweden, Switzerland, Turkey, Uruguay.

Brazil, the People's Republic of China, Ecuador, Finland, Germany, India, Italy, the Republic of Korea, the Netherlands, Peru, Poland, Spain, Sweden and Uruguay have achieved consultative status under the Treaty, by virtue of their scientific activity in Antarctica.

ANTARCTIC TREATY CONSULTATIVE MEETINGS

Meetings of representatives from all the original signatory nations of the Antarctic Treaty and acceding nations accorded consultative status (26 in 1997), are held every one to two years to discuss scientific, environmental and political matters. The 21st meeting was held in Christchurch, New Zealand, in May 1997, and the 22nd was to take place in Tromsø, Norway, in May–June 1998. The representatives elect a Chairman and Secretary. Committees and Working Groups are established as required.

Among the numerous measures which have been agreed and implemented by the Consultative Parties are several designed to protect the Antarctic environment and wildlife. These include Agreed Measures for the Conservation of Antarctic Flora and Fauna, the designation of Specially Protected Areas and Sites of Special Scientific Interest, and a Convention for the Conservation of Antarctic Seals. A Convention on the Conservation of Antarctic Marine Living Resources, concluded at a diplomatic conference in May 1980, entered into force in April 1982.

A Convention on the Regulation of Antarctic Mineral Resource Activities (the Wellington Convention) was adopted in June 1988 and was opened for signature on 25 November 1988. To enter into force, the Wellington Convention required the ratification of 16 of the Consultative Parties (then numbering 22). However, France and Australia opposed the Convention, which would permit mineral exploitation (under stringent international controls) in Antarctica, and proposed the creation of an Antarctic wilderness reserve. An agreement was reached at the October 1989 consultative meeting, whereby two extraordinary meetings were to be convened in Chile in November 1990, one to discuss the protection of the environment and the other to discuss the issue of liability for environmental damage within the framework of the Wellington Convention. In September 1990 the Government of New Zealand, which played a major role in drafting the Wellington Convention, reversed its policy, stating that it was no longer willing to ratify the Convention. At the same time, it introduced legislation in the New Zealand House of Representatives to ban all mining and prospecting activities from its territories in Antarctica. At the extraordinary meetings, which were held in Chile in November–December, the Consultative Parties failed to reach an agreement regarding the protection of Antarctica's environment. However, a draft protocol was approved. This formed the basis for a further meeting in Madrid, Spain, in April 1991. France, Australia and 16 other countries supported a permanent ban on mining, whereas the USA, the United Kingdom, Japan, Germany and four others were in favour of a moratorium. Subsequently, however, Japan and Germany transferred their allegiance to the Australian-French initiative, exerting considerable pressure on the USA and the United Kingdom, whose position became increasingly isolated. Agreement was eventually reached on a ban on mining activity for 50 years, and mechanisms for a review of the ban after 50 years, or before if all Parties agree. This agreement is embodied in Article 7 of the Protocol on Environmental Protection to the Antarctic Treaty, which was adopted by the Antarctic Treaty Parties in October 1991, immediately prior to the 16th Antarctic Treaty Consultative Meeting. By late 1997 the Protocol had been ratified by all 26 Consultative Parties, and entered into force on 14 January 1998. Thus there can only be mining in the Antarctic only with the consent of all the present Consultative Parties and, even then, only when a regulatory regime is in place. The first four annexes to the Protocol, providing for environmental impact assessment, conservation of fauna and flora, waste disposal, and monitoring of marine pollution, entered into force with the Protocol, but the fifth annex, on area protection, agreed after the adoption of the Protocol, has yet to take effect. A sixth annex on environmental liability is currently being negotiated.

At a meeting of the International Whaling Commission (see p. 253), held in Mexico in May 1994, it was agreed to establish a whale sanctuary around Antarctica below 40° S. The sanctuary, which was expected to protect about 80% of the world's remaining whales from commercial hunting, came into effect in December.

In May 1997 the World Meteorological Organization (see p. 98) suggested that long-term prospects for the rate of depletion of the ozone layer over Antarctica might be improving, but that strong statistical evidence of such a trend might not become apparent for at least five years. There has been speculation that the recent calving of a 1,300-sq. km. iceberg from the Larsen ice-shelf at the northern Antarctic Peninsula may have been attributable to the normal cycle of loss by calving; however, there is stronger evidence that the disintegration of a further considerable area of the ice shelf during the past 50 years was the result of climate warming. International opinion has been divided as to whether such examples of regional warming of the climate might be repeated elsewhere in Antarctica, and over the extent to which these effects might be indicative of climate warming on a global scale.

ANTIGUA AND BARBUDA

Introductory Survey

Location, Climate, Language, Religion, Flag, Capital

The country comprises three islands: Antigua (280 sq km—108 sq miles), Barbuda (161 sq km—62 sq miles) and the uninhabited rocky islet of Redonda (1.6 sq km—0.6 sq mile). They lie along the outer edge of the Leeward Islands chain in the West Indies. Barbuda is the most northerly (40 km—25 miles north of Antigua), and Redonda is 40 km south-west of Antigua. The French island of Guadeloupe lies to the south of the country, the British dependency of Montserrat to the south-west and Saint Christopher and Nevis to the west. The climate is tropical, although tempered by constant sea breezes and the trade winds, and the mean annual rainfall of 1,000 mm (40 ins) is slight for the region. The temperature averages 27°C (81°F) but can rise to 33°C (93°F) during the hot season between May and October. English is the official language but an English patois is commonly used. The majority of the inhabitants profess Christianity, and are mainly adherents of the Anglican Communion. The national flag consists of an inverted triangle centred on a red field; the triangle is divided horizontally into three unequal bands, of black, blue and white, with the black stripe bearing a symbol of the rising sun in gold. The capital is St John's, on Antigua.

Recent History

Antigua was colonized by the British in the 17th century. The island of Barbuda, formerly a slave stud farm for the Codrington family, was annexed to the territory in 1860. Until December 1959 Antigua and other nearby British territories were administered, under a federal system, as the Leeward Islands. The first elections under universal adult suffrage were held in 1951. The colony participated in the West Indies Federation, which was formed in January 1958 but dissolved in May 1962.

Attempts to form a smaller East Caribbean Federation failed, and most of the eligible colonies subsequently became Associated States in an arrangement that gave them full internal self-government while the United Kingdom retained responsibility for defence and foreign affairs. Antigua attained associated status in February 1967. The Legislative Council was replaced by a House of Representatives, the Administrator became Governor and the Chief Minister was restyled Premier.

In the first general election under associated status, held in February 1971, the Progressive Labour Movement (PLM) ousted the Antigua Labour Party (ALP), which had held power since 1946, by winning 13 of the 17 seats in the House of Representatives. George Walter, leader of the PLM, replaced Vere C. Bird, Sr, as Premier. However, a general election in February 1976 was won by the ALP, with 11 seats, while the seat representing Barbuda was won by an independent. Vere Bird, the ALP's leader, again became Premier, while Lester Bird, one of his sons, became Deputy Premier.

In 1975 the Associated States agreed that they would seek independence separately. In the 1976 elections the PLM campaigned for early independence while the ALP opposed it. In September 1978, however, the ALP Government declared that the economic foundation for independence had been laid, and a premature general election was held in April 1980, when the ALP won 13 of the 17 seats. There was strong opposition in Barbuda to gaining independence as part of Antigua, and at local elections in March 1981 the Barbuda People's Movement (BPM), which continued to campaign for secession from Antigua, won all the seats on the Barbuda Council. However, the territory finally became independent, as Antigua and Barbuda, on 1 November 1981, remaining within the Commonwealth. The grievances of the Barbudans concerning control of land and devolution of power were unresolved, although the ALP Government had made concessions, yielding a certain degree of internal autonomy to the Barbuda Council. The Governor, Sir Wilfred Jacobs, became Governor-General, while the Premier, Vere Bird, Sr, became the country's first Prime Minister.

Following disagreements within the opposition PLM, George Walter, the former Premier, formed his own political party, the United People's Movement (UPM), in 1982. In April 1984 at the first general election since independence, divisions within the opposition allowed the ALP to win all of the 16 seats that it contested. The remaining seat, representing Barbuda, was retained by an unopposed independent (who subsequently formed the Barbuda National Party—BNP). A new opposition party, the National Democratic Party (NDP), was formed in Antigua in 1985. In April 1986 it merged with the UPM to form the United National Democratic Party (UNDP). George Walter declined to play any significant public role in the UNDP, and Dr Ivor Heath, who had led the NDP, was elected leader of the new party.

In November 1986 controversy surrounding a rehabilitation scheme at the international airport on Antigua led to an official inquiry, which concluded that Vere Bird, Jr (a senior minister and the eldest son of the Prime Minister), had acted 'in a manner unbecoming a minister of government' by awarding part of the contract to a company with which he was personally involved. The affair divided the ALP, with eight ministers (including Lester Bird, the Deputy Prime Minister) demanding the resignation of Vere Bird, Jr, and Prime Minister Bird refusing to dismiss him. The rifts within the ALP and the Bird family continued into 1988, when new allegations of corruption by government members were made, this time implicating Lester Bird.

At a general election in March 1989 the ALP remained the ruling party by retaining 15 of the 16 seats that it had held in the previous House of Representatives. The UNDP won more than 30% of all the votes cast, but only one seat. The Barbuda seat was won by the BPM.

In April 1990 the Government of Antigua and Barbuda received a diplomatic note of protest from the Government of Colombia regarding the sale of weapons to the Medellín cartel of drugs-traffickers in Colombia. The weapons had originally been sold by Israel to Antigua and Barbuda but, contrary to regulation, were then immediately shipped on to Colombia in April 1989. It was assumed that this could have occurred only with official connivance. The communication from the Colombian Government implicated Vere Bird, Jr. The Prime Minister eventually agreed to establish a judicial inquiry, as a result of demands from Lester Bird. In October the Chamber of Commerce recommended the resignation of the Government. In November a news agency obtained a copy of the unpublished report of the judicial inquiry, which accused Antigua and Barbuda of having become 'engulfed in corruption'. The Governments of the United Kingdom, the USA and Israel were similarly accused of neglecting to take action to prevent the sale of armaments. The report also revealed the activities of a number of British mercenaries on Antigua, involved in the training of paramilitary forces employed by Colombian drugs-trafficking organizations. In the same month, acting upon the recommendations of the report, the Government of Antigua and Barbuda dismissed Vere Bird, Jr, and banned him for life from holding office in the Government, and also dismissed the head of the defence force, Col Clyde Walker.

Discontent within the ALP (including dissatisfaction with the leadership of Vere Bird, Sr), provoked a serious political crisis in early 1991. The Minister of Finance, John St Luce, resigned in February, after claiming that his proposals for a restructuring of government were ignored by the Prime Minister. A subsequent reorganization of cabinet portfolios (in which Lester Bird lost his deputy premiership) provoked the immediate resignation of three ministers. In September, however, Lester Bird and John St Luce accepted invitations from the Prime Minister to rejoin the Cabinet.

In early 1992 the Government's position was further undermined by a series of demonstrations and strikes in support of demands for the immediate resignation of Vere Bird, Sr. The protests were provoked by further reports of corruption. In April the Antigua Caribbean Liberation Movement (ACLM), the PLM and the UNDP consolidated their opposition to the Government by merging to form the United Progressive Party (UPP). In response to mounting public pressure, the ALP convened in May to elect a new leader. However, Vere Bird, Sr, retained the post, following an inconclusive result after the two candidates,

Lester Bird and John St Luce, received an equal number of votes. In August further controversy arose when proposed anti-corruption legislation (which had been recommended following the Colombian arms scandal in 1991) was withdrawn as a result of legal intervention by the Prime Minister.

On 10 June 1993 James (later Sir James) Carlisle took office as Governor-General, replacing Sir Wilfred Jacobs. In September the ALP convened in order to organize further leadership elections. As a result of the vote, Lester Bird became leader of the party, while Vere Bird, Jr, was elected to the position of Chairman.

At a general election in March 1994 the ALP remained the ruling party, although with a reduced majority. The ALP secured 11 seats, the UPP won five and the BPM retained the Barbuda seat. Following the election, Lester Bird assumed the premiership. Although some criticism was expressed regarding inaccuracies in the electoral register and the fact that the opposition was not permitted access to the state-owned media during its campaign, the election was generally thought to have been free and fair.

Controversy continued to surround the Government in 1995. In February of that year an ALP activist, Leonard Aaron, was arrested and charged with threatening to murder Tim Hector, editor of an opposition newspaper, *The Outlet*. It was reported that Hector's house had been burgled on several occasions, when documents and tapes containing allegedly incriminating information relating to members of the Government had been stolen. Aaron was subsequently released, following the intervention of the Prime Minister. Furthermore, in May the Prime Minister's brother, Ivor Bird, was arrested following an incident in which he collected luggage at V. C. Bird International Airport from a Barbadian citizen from Venezuela, which contained 12 kg of cocaine. The opposition newspaper, *The Outlet*, claimed to have evidence that Bird had collected luggage at the airport from the same man on at least three previous occasions. His subsequent release from police custody, upon payment of a fine of EC $200,000, attracted considerable criticism. In an attempt to improve the country's increasingly negative reputation as a centre for drugs-trafficking activities, the Government proposed legislation in early 1996 which aimed to curb the illegal drugs trade. Moreover, later that year Wrenford Ferrance, a former financial controller at the Organization of Eastern Caribbean States (OECS—see p. 122), was appointed to the newly-created position of Special Adviser to the Government on 'money laundering' and on the control of illicit drugs.

In September 1995 Antigua and Barbuda suffered extensive damage when the islands were struck by Hurricane Luis. The storm, which caused damage estimated at US $300m., seriously affected some 75% of buildings on the islands and left almost one-half of the population homeless. Discussions between the Government and the World Bank, the IMF and other financial institutions took place in late 1995, in an attempt to resolve some of the economic problems caused by the hurricane.

A major cabinet reorganization, effected in May 1996, was controversial because of the appointment to the post of Special Adviser to the Prime Minister of Vere Bird, Jr, who had been declared unfit for public office following a judicial inquiry in 1990 (see above).

In September 1996 Molwyn Joseph resigned as Minister of Finance over allegations that he had used his position in order to evade the payment of customs duties on the import of a vintage motor car. His resignation followed a demonstration by members of the opposition at Joseph's office, at which the UPP leader, Baldwin Spencer, and seven other party members, including Tim Hector, were arrested (charges brought against them were later dismissed). A further demonstration took place at the end of the month, attended by some 10,000 people, in support of demands for a full inquiry into the affair and for the organization of an early general election. In early December, however, Joseph was reinstated in the Cabinet, assuming the new post of Minister of Planning and Environment; the appointment was vehemently condemned by the opposition.

In March 1997 the opposition BPM defeated the ALP's ally, the New Barbuda Development Movement, in elections to the Barbuda Council, winning all five of the contested seats and thus gaining control of all the seats in the nine-member Council. In the same month the High Court upheld a constitutional motion presented by the UPP leader, Baldwin Spencer, seeking the right of expression on the state-owned radio and television station (denied to the opposition during the electoral campaign in March 1994). In late May and early June the UPP boycotted sittings of the House of Representatives (the first legislative boycotts in the country's history) during a parliamentary debate on a proposed US $300m.-tourism development on Guiana Island, which was to be constructed by a Malaysian company. The boycott was staged on the grounds that the Prime Minister had failed to publish the proposals for public discussion prior to the parliamentary debate. The opposition also claimed that the 2,000-room hotel project would have adverse effects on the island's ecology. The project was, none the less, endorsed by the legislature. In September Baldwin Spencer applied to the High Court to have the hotel project agreement declared illegal and unconstitutional. The following month the UPP organized a march, in which thousands of people took part in support of a demand for a referendum on the controversial scheme. Meanwhile, in August *The Outlet* published further allegations regarding government-supported drugs-trafficking, including a claim that a Colombian drug cartel had contributed US $1m. to the ALP's election campaign in 1994. In response, Prime Minister Lester Bird stated that he intended to sue the opposition newspaper and he obtained a High Court injunction in early September prohibiting it from publishing further material relating to the damaging allegations.

In February 1997 the Government announced that four Russian and one Ukrainian 'offshore' banks were to be closed down, owing to 'irregularities' in their operations (they were suspected of 'laundering' substantial amounts of money for the Russian mafia). Wrenford Ferrance, the government Special Adviser, stated that, since the country's 'offshore' banking system (which had expanded rapidly in the mid-1990s) was showing signs of weakness through lack of regulation, no new 'offshore' banking applications would be accepted until new legislation was passed. In April Ferrance was appointed to the post of superintendent of 'offshore' banks and insurance companies and director of international business corporations; the appointment was criticized by the opposition on the grounds that Ferrance did not have banking experience and was not an established civil servant. Following the collapse, under suspicious circumstances, of the Antigua-based European Union Bank in August, the 51 remaining 'offshore' banks in Antigua and Barbuda were requested to submit full details of their operations in an attempt to combat further fraud.

In foreign relations the ALP Government follows a policy of non-alignment, although the country has strong links with the USA, and actively assisted in the US military intervention in Grenada in October 1983 as a member of the OECS. Antigua and Barbuda is also a member of the Caribbean Community and Common Market (CARICOM—see p. 119), but in 1988 proved to be one of the main opponents of closer political federation within either organization. The Government did, however, agree to the reduction of travel restrictions between OECS members (which took effect in January 1990). Following a period of political unrest in Haiti in mid-1994 the Government of Antigua and Barbuda agreed to accept 2,000 refugees from that country. In mid-1997 Antigua and Barbuda appointed its first ambassador to Cuba, serving on a non-resident basis.

Government

Antigua and Barbuda is a constitutional monarchy. Executive power is vested in the British sovereign, as Head of State, and exercised by the Governor-General, who represents the sovereign locally and is appointed on the advice of the Antiguan Prime Minister. Legislative power is vested in Parliament, comprising the sovereign, a 17-member Senate and a 17-member House of Representatives. Members of the House are elected from single-member constituencies for up to five years by universal adult suffrage. The Senate is composed of 11 members (of whom one must be an inhabitant of Barbuda) appointed on the advice of the Prime Minister, four appointed on the advice of the Leader of the Opposition, one appointed at the discretion of the Governor-General and one appointed on the advice of the Barbuda Council. Government is effectively by the Cabinet. The Governor-General appoints the Prime Minister and, on the latter's recommendation, selects the other ministers. The Prime Minister must be able to command the support of a majority of the House, to which the Cabinet is responsible. The Barbuda Council has nine seats, with partial elections held every two years.

Defence

There is a small defence force of 150 men (army 125, navy 25). The US Government leases two military bases on Antigua. Antigua and Barbuda participates in the US-sponsored Regional

Security System. Military expenditure in 1997 was projected to total an estimated EC $9.0m.

Economic Affairs

In 1994, according to estimates by the World Bank, Antigua and Barbuda's gross national product (GNP), measured at average 1992–94 prices, was US $453m., equivalent to US $6,970 per head. During 1985–94, it was estimated, GNP per head increased, in real terms, at an average annual rate of 2.7%. The country's gross domestic product (GDP) increased, in real terms, at an average annual rate of 5.0% in 1985–95. According to the Eastern Caribbean Central Bank, real GDP increased by 5.5% in 1994, but declined by an estimated 3.8% in 1995. GDP growth was projected to be 4.5% in 1996. Between 1985 and 1995 the population increased at an annual average rate of 0.5%.

Agriculture (including forestry and fishing) engaged 3.9% of the labour force in 1991. The sector contributed an estimated 3.6% of GDP in 1995. Agricultural GDP decreased, in real terms, by 1.0% in 1994 and by 5.1% in 1995. The principal crops are cucumbers, pumpkins, sweet potatoes, mangoes, coconuts, limes, melons and the speciality 'Antigua Black' pineapple. Lobster, shrimp and crab farms are in operation, and further projects to develop the fishing industry were undertaken in the mid-1990s.

Industry (comprising mining, manufacturing, construction and utilities) employed 18.9% of the labour force in 1991 and provided an estimated 17.9% of GDP in 1995. The principal industrial activity is construction, accounting for 11.6% of total employment in 1991. Industrial GDP declined, in real terms, at an estimated average rate of 0.3% per year during 1991–95.

Mining and quarrying employed only 0.2% of the labour force in 1991 and contributed 1.7% of GDP in 1995.

The manufacturing sector consists of some light industries producing garments, paper, paint, furniture, food and beverage products, and the assembly of household appliances and electrical components for export. Manufacturing contributed 1.9% of GDP in 1995, when the construction sector provided some 9.9%. The real GDP of the manufacturing sector declined by 14.0% in 1995; however, construction activity increased by 27.4% in that year (mainly owing to rehabilitation projects necessitated by Hurricane Luis).

Most of the country's energy production is derived from imported fuel. Imports of mineral fuels accounted for 9.9% of total imports in 1991. However, this included petroleum products for re-export to neighbouring islands.

Services provided 70.2% of employment in 1991 and 78.4% of GDP in 1995. The combined GDP of the service sectors increased, in real terms, at an average rate of 4.4% per year during 1991–94, but declined by 5.1% in 1995. Tourism is the main economic activity, and by the early 1990s this sector provided approximately 35% of employment, and accounted (directly and indirectly) for some 70% of GDP. The industry, however, was severely affected by Hurricane Luis in 1995, resulting in a decline of 16.4% in the sector's output for that year. In 1995 receipts from tourism were estimated at US $319m., a reduction of 19.1% compared with the previous year. Tourist arrivals decreased by 9.4% in 1995, to total 462,114. Most tourists are from Europe, particularly the United Kingdom (38% in 1995), the USA (35%), Canada and other Caribbean countries (17%).

In 1994 Antigua and Barbuda recorded a visible trade deficit of US $253.7m. and a deficit of US $18.0m. on the current account of the balance of payments. The country's principal trading partners are the other members of CARICOM (see p. 119), the USA, the United Kingdom and Canada. In 1987 the USA provided 29.5% of total imports and was also one of the main markets for exports (mainly re-exports).

For the financial year ending 31 March 1996 there was an estimated budgetary deficit of EC $66m. The 1997/98 budget proposals envisaged total expenditure of EC $442m., compared with revenue of EC $390m., resulting in a deficit of EC $52m. Debt-servicing costs were expected to account for EC $72.6m. By the end of 1996 total external debt amounted to EC $1,187m. The annual rate of inflation averaged 4.5% in 1985–91. The estimated average rate was 3.5% in 1994 and 2.9% in 1995.

Antigua and Barbuda is a member of CARICOM, the OECS, the Organization of American States (see p. 122), and is a signatory of the Lomé Conventions with the EU (see p. 178).

In the 1980s and 1990s the Government sought to diversify the economy, which is dominated by tourism. In May 1993 the Senate approved legislation to allow the establishment of a free-trade zone, to encourage the manufacture of goods for export, in the north-east of Antigua. Consumption taxes were introduced in January 1995 to coincide with the implementation of the CARICOM common external tariff. The new taxes, however, proved extremely unpopular and resulted in large-scale demonstrations and widespread industrial action in early 1995. In April 1996 the Government introduced an economic austerity programme, which included a two-year 'freeze' of the salaries of public-sector employees and a reduction of 10% in government ministers' earnings. The budget proposals for 1997/98 appeared to indicate a relaxation of fiscal policy, suggesting economic recovery since the pay 'freeze' implemented in the previous year.

Social Welfare

There are two state welfare schemes, both funded by contributions from employers and employees. The Social Security Scheme provides pensions and benefits for maternity, disability and sickness, while the Medical Benefits Scheme awards grants for the treatment of specific chronic diseases. Antigua has a 220-bed general hospital and 25 health centres and clinics. In May 1997 work began on the construction of a new hospital near St John's; the project was estimated to cost EC $80m. and was to be financed by a US company. In 1990 there was one physician for every 3,750 inhabitants.

Education

Education is compulsory for 12 years between five and 16 years of age. Primary education begins at the age of five and normally lasts for seven years. Secondary education, beginning at 12 years of age, lasts for five years, comprising a first cycle of three years and a second cycle of two years. In 1987/88 there were 43 primary and 15 secondary schools; the majority of schools are administered by the Government. In 1991/92 some 9,298 primary school pupils and 5,845 secondary school pupils were enrolled. Teacher training and technical training are available at the State Island College. An extra-mural department of the University of the West Indies offers several foundation courses leading to higher study at branches elsewhere. The adult literacy rate in Antigua and Barbuda is more than 90%, one of the highest rates in the Eastern Caribbean. Current government expenditure on education in 1993/94 was projected at EC $37.1m., equivalent to 12.8% of total budgetary expenditure.

Public Holidays

1998: 1 January (New Year's Day), 10 April (Good Friday), 13 April (Easter Monday), 4 May (Labour Day), 1 June (Whit Monday), 6 July (CARICOM Day), 3–4 August (Carnival), 1 November (Independence Day), 25–26 December (Christmas).

1999: 1 January (New Year's Day), 2 April (Good Friday), 5 April (Easter Monday), 3 May (Labour Day), 24 May (Whit Monday), 5 July (CARICOM Day), 2–3 August (Carnival), 1 November (Independence Day), 25–26 December (Christmas).

Weights and Measures

The imperial system is in use but a metrication programme is being introduced.

Statistical Survey

Source (unless otherwise stated): Ministry of Finance and Social Security, High St, St John's; tel. 462-4860; fax 462-1622.

AREA AND POPULATION

Area: 441.6 sq km (170.5 sq miles).

Population: 65,525 (males 31,054, females 34,471) at census of 7 April 1970; 62,922 (provisional result) at census of 28 May 1991; 64,353 (official estimate) at mid-1995.

Density (estimate, mid-1995): 145.7 per sq km.

Principal Town: St John's (capital), population 22,342 at 1991 census.

Births, Marriages and Deaths (registrations, 1994): Live births 1,217 (birth rate 19.0 per 1,000); Marriages (1987) 343 (marriage rate 5.4 per 1,000); Deaths 415 (death rate 6.5 per 1,000).

Expectation of Life (estimate, years at birth, 1995): 73. Source: *The Commonwealth Yearbook*.

Employment (persons aged 15 years and over, census of 28 May 1991): Agriculture, forestry and fishing 1,040; Mining and quarrying 64; Manufacturing 1,444; Electricity, gas and water 435; Construction 3,109; Trade, restaurants and hotels 8,524; Transport, storage and communications 2,395; Finance, insurance, real estate and business services 1,454; Community, social and personal services 6,406; Activities not adequately defined 1,882; Total employed 26,753 (males 14,564, females 12,189). Source: ILO, *Yearbook of Labour Statistics*.

AGRICULTURE, ETC.

Principal Crops (FAO estimates, '000 metric tons, 1996): Vegetables 1; Melons 1; Mangoes 1; Other fruits 6. Source: FAO, *Production Yearbook*.

Livestock (FAO estimates, '000 head, year ending September 1996): Asses 1; Cattle 16; Pigs 2; Sheep 12; Goats 12. Source: FAO, *Production Yearbook*.

Livestock Products (FAO estimates, '000 metric tons, 1996): Beef and veal 1; Cows' milk 6. Source: FAO, *Production Yearbook*.

Fishing (metric tons, live weight): Total catch 580 in 1993; 629 in 1994; 470 (Marine fishes 352, Caribbean spiny lobster 71, Stromboid conchs 47) in 1995. Source: FAO, *Yearbook of Fishery Statistics*.

INDUSTRY

Production (estimates, 1988): Rum 4,000 hectolitres; Wines and vodka 2,000 hectolitres; Electric energy (1994) 97m. kWh. Source: UN, *Industrial Commodity Statistics Yearbook*.

FINANCE

Currency and Exchange Rates: 100 cents = 1 Eastern Caribbean dollar (EC $). *Sterling and US Dollar equivalents* (30 September 1997): £1 sterling = EC $4.362; US $1 = EC $2.700; EC $100 = £22.93 = US $37.04. *Exchange rate*: Fixed at US $1 = EC $2.700 since July 1976.

Budget (estimates, EC $ million, year ending 31 March 1996): *Revenue:* Recurrent 284.8 (Tax 246.1, Non-tax 38.7), Capital 4.2; External grants 0.6; Total 289.6. *Expenditure:* Recurrent 305.9 (Wages and salaries 155.7); Capital 49.5; Total 355.4.

International Reserves (US $ million at 31 December 1996): IMF special drawing rights 0.01; Foreign exchange 47.73; Total 47.74. Source: IMF, *International Financial Statistics*.

Money Supply (EC $ million at 31 December 1996): Currency outside banks 68.06; Demand deposits at deposit money banks 187.25; Total money (incl. others) 255.39. Source: IMF, *International Financial Statistics*.

Cost of Living (Consumer Price Index; base: 1990 = 100): 93.5 in 1989; 100.0 in 1990; 105.7 in 1991. Source: ILO, *Yearbook of Labour Statistics*.

Expenditure on the Gross Domestic Product (provisional, EC $ million at current prices, 1995): Government final consumption expenditure 291.2; Private final consumption expenditure 703.6; Gross capital formation 632.2; *Total domestic expenditure* 1,627.1; Exports of goods and services 1,163.7; *Less* Imports of goods and services 1,435.6; *GDP in purchasers' values* 1,355.2. Source: IMF, *Antigua and Barbuda—Statistical Annex* (August 1996).

Gross Domestic Product by Economic Activity (estimates, EC $ million at current prices, 1995): Agriculture, hunting, forestry and fishing 43.5; Mining and quarrying 20.6; Manufacturing 22.7; Electricity and water 52.9; Construction 119.3; Trade 119.4; Restaurants and hotels 136.4; Transport and communications 215.8; Finance, insurance, real estate and business services 98.0; Government services 217.9; Other community, social and personal services 154.7; *Sub-total* 1,201.0; *Less* Imputed bank service charges 59.7; *GDP at factor cost* 1,141.2; Indirect taxes, *less* subsidies 213.9; GDP in purchasers' values 1,355.2. Source: IMF, *Antigua and Barbuda—Statistical Annex* (August 1996).

Balance of Payments (US $ million, 1994): Exports of goods f.o.b. 44.45; Imports of goods f.o.b. −298.12; *Trade balance* −253.67; Exports of services 396.31; Imports of services −134.93; *Balance on goods and services* 7.71; Other income received 4.26; Other income paid −30.81; *Balance on goods, services and income* −18.84; Current transfers received 10.36; Current transfers paid −9.47; *Current balance* −17.95; Capital account (net) 5.91; Direct investment from abroad 24.81; Portfolio investment assets −1.38; Other investment assets −16.67; Other investment liabilities 2.83; Net errors and omissions 10.53; *Overall balance* 8.08. Source: IMF, *International Financial Statistics*.

EXTERNAL TRADE

Principal Commodities (US $ million, 1991): *Imports:* Food and live animals 30.4; Beverages and tobacco 8.2; Mineral fuels, lubricants, etc. 24.3; Chemicals 15.3; Basic manufactures 66.5; Machinery and transport equipment 65.8; Miscellaneous manufactured articles 30.2. Total (incl. others) 245.9. *Exports:* Food and live animals 1.1; Mineral fuels, lubricants, etc. 10.0; Chemicals 2.8; Basic manufactures 3.3; Machinery and transport equipment 12.0; Miscellaneous manufactured articles 9.9; Total (incl. others) 39.8. Source: UN, *International Trade Statistics Yearbook*.

Principal Trading Partners (EC $ million, 1987): *Imports:* Italy 166.5; Trinidad and Tobago 42.5; United Kingdom 70.6; USA 197.0; Total (incl. others) 666.9. *Exports:* CARICOM 24.7; United Kingdom 4.7; USA 8.1; Total (incl. others) 52.5. Source: OECS, *Digest of Trade Statistics*.

TRANSPORT

Road Traffic (registered vehicles, 1994): Passenger motor cars 15,100; Commercial vehicles 4,800. Source: UN, *Statistical Yearbook*.

Shipping (international freight traffic, '000 metric tons, 1990): Goods loaded 28; Goods unloaded 113 (Source: UN, *Monthly Bulletin of Statistics*). *Arrivals* (vessels, 1987): 3,940. *Merchant Fleet* (registered at 31 December): 520 vessels (total displacement 2,176,204 grt) in 1996. (Source: Lloyd's Register of Shipping, *World Fleet Statistics*).

Civil Aviation (traffic on scheduled services, 1994): Kilometres flown (million) 11; Passengers carried ('000) 1,000; Passenger-km (million) 240; Total ton-km (million) 22. Source: UN, *Statistical Yearbook*.

TOURISM

Foreign Tourist Arrivals: 496,583 in 1993; 510,102 in 1994; 462,114 (191,401 visitors by air, 234,773 cruise-ship passengers, 17,974 yacht passengers, 17,967 visitors to private houses, etc.) in 1995.

Tourist Receipts (US $ million): 353.5 in 1993; 394.4 in 1994; 318.9 in 1995.

Source: IMF, *Antigua and Barbuda—Statistical Annex* (August 1996).

COMMUNICATIONS MEDIA

Daily Newspaper (1990): 1 (estimated circulation 6,000)*.

Non-Daily Newspapers (1990): 4*.

Radio Receivers (1994): 28,000 in use*.

Television Receivers (1994): 24,000 in use*.

Telephones (1996): 27,556 in use.

Telefax stations (year ending 31 March 1991): 350 in use (Source: UN, *Statistical Yearbook*).

* Source: UNESCO, *Statistical Yearbook*.

EDUCATION

Pre-primary (1983): 21 schools; 23 teachers; 677 pupils.

Primary (1987/88): 43 schools; 446 teachers; 9,298 students (1991/92).

Secondary (1991/92): 15 schools (1987/88); 400 teachers (estimate); 5,845 students.

Tertiary (1986): 2 colleges; 631 students.

Directory

The Constitution

The Constitution, which came into force at the independence of Antigua and Barbuda on 1 November 1981, states that Antigua and Barbuda is a 'unitary sovereign democratic state'. The main provisions of the Constitution are summarized below:

FUNDAMENTAL RIGHTS AND FREEDOMS

Regardless of race, place of origin, political opinion, colour, creed or sex, but subject to respect for the rights and freedoms of others and for the public interest, every person in Antigua and Barbuda is entitled to the rights of life, liberty, security of the person, the enjoyment of property and the protection of the law. Freedom of movement, of conscience, of expression (including freedom of the press), of peaceful assembly and association is guaranteed and the inviolability of family life, personal privacy, home and other property is maintained. Protection is afforded from discrimination on the grounds of race, sex, etc., and from slavery, forced labour, torture and inhuman treatment.

THE GOVERNOR-GENERAL

The British sovereign, as Monarch of Antigua and Barbuda, is the Head of State and is represented by a Governor-General of local citizenship.

PARLIAMENT

Parliament consists of the Monarch, a 17-member Senate and the House of Representatives composed of 17 elected members. Senators are appointed by the Governor-General: 11 on the advice of the Prime Minister (one of whom must be an inhabitant of Barbuda), four on the advice of the Leader of the Opposition, one at his own discretion and one on the advice of the Barbuda Council. The Barbuda Council is the principal organ of local government in that island, whose membership and functions are determined by Parliament. The life of Parliament is five years.

Each constituency returns one Representative to the House who is directly elected in accordance with the Constitution.

The Attorney-General, if not otherwise a member of the House, is an ex-officio member but does not have the right to vote.

Every citizen over the age of 18 is eligible to vote.

Parliament may alter any of the provisions of the Constitution.

THE EXECUTIVE

Executive authority is vested in the Monarch and exercisable by the Governor-General. The Governor-General appoints as Prime Minister that member of the House who, in the Governor-General's view, is best able to command the support of the majority of the members of the House, and other ministers on the advice of the Prime Minister. The Governor-General may remove the Prime Minister from office if a resolution of no confidence is passed by the House and the Prime Minister does not either resign or advise the Governor-General to dissolve Parliament within seven days.

The Cabinet consists of the Prime Minister and other ministers and the Attorney-General.

The Leader of the Opposition is appointed by the Governor-General as that member of the House who, in the Governor-General's view, is best able to command the support of a majority of members of the House who do not support the Government.

CITIZENSHIP

All persons born in Antigua and Barbuda before independence who, immediately prior to independence, were citizens of the United Kingdom and Colonies automatically become citizens of Antigua and Barbuda. All persons born outside the country with a parent or grandparent possessing citizenship of Antigua and Barbuda automatically acquire citizenship as do those born in the country after independence. Provision is made for the acquisition of citizenship by those to whom it would not automatically be granted.

The Government

Head of State: HM Queen ELIZABETH II (succeeded to the throne 6 February 1952).

Governor-General: Sir JAMES CARLISLE (took office 10 June 1993).

CABINET
(December 1997)

Prime Minister and Minister of Foreign Affairs, Social Services, Civil Aviation and International Transport and Information: LESTER BIRD.

Minister of Finance, and of Agriculture, Fisheries and Lands: JOHN ST LUCE.

Minister of Health and Civil Service Affairs: SAM AYMER.

Minister of Trade, Industry, Commerce and Consumer Affairs: HILROY HUMPHREYS.

Minister of Justice: CLARE ROBERTS.

Minister of Planning and Environment: MOLWYN JOSEPH.

Minister of Home Affairs and Labour: ADOLPHUS ELEAZER FREELAND.

Minister of Education, Youth, Sports and Community Development: BERNARD PERCIVAL.

Minister of Tourism and Culture: Dr RODNEY WILLIAMS.

Minister of Public Works, Utilities and Energy: ROBIN YEARWOOD.

Minister of State in the Office of the Prime Minister with responsibility for Housing: HENDERSON SIMON.

MINISTRIES

Office of the Prime Minister: Factory Rd, St John's; tel. 462-4956; telex 2127; fax 462-3225.

Ministry of Agriculture, Fisheries and Lands: Queen Elizabeth Highway, St John's.

Ministry of Education, Youth, Sports and Community Development: Church St, St John's; tel. 462-4959; telex 2122; fax 462-4970.

Ministry of Finance and Social Security: High St, St John's; tel. 462-4860; fax 462-1622.

Ministry of Health and Civil Service Affairs: St John's St, St John's; tel. 462-1600; fax 462-5003.

Ministry of Home Affairs and Labour: Redcliffe St, St John's; tel. 462-0011.

Ministry of Justice: Hadeed Bldg, Redcliffe St, St John's; tel. 462-0017.

Ministry of Public Works, Utilities and Energy: St John's St, St John's; tel. 462-0894.

Ministry of Tourism and Culture: Queen Elizabeth Highway, St John's; tel. 462-0787; telex 2087; fax 462-2836.

Legislature

PARLIAMENT

Senate

President: MILLICENT PERCIVAL.

There are 17 nominated members.

House of Representatives

Speaker: BRIDGETTE HARRIS.

Ex-Officio Member: The Attorney-General.

Clerk: L. DOWE.

General Election, 8 March 1994

Party	Votes cast	%	Seats
Antigua Labour Party	14,763	54.4	11
United Progressive Party	11,852	43.7	5
Barbuda People's Movement	367	1.4	1
Others	134	0.5	—
Total	27,116	100.0	17

Political Organizations

Antigua Labour Party (ALP): St Mary's St, St John's; tel. 462-1059; f. 1968; Leader LESTER BIRD; Chair. VERE BIRD, Jr.

Barbuda Independence Movement: Codrington; f. 1983 as Organisation for National Reconstruction, re-formed 1988; advocates self-government for Barbuda; Pres. ARTHUR SHABAZZ-NIBBS.

Barbuda National Party: Codrington; Leader ERIC BURTON.

Barbuda People's Movement (BPM): Codrington; campaigns for separate status for Barbuda; Parliamentary Leader THOMAS HILBOURNE FRANK; Chair. FABIAN JONES.

New Barbuda Development Movement: Codrington; linked with the Antigua Labour Party.

People's Democratic Movement (PDM): St John's; f. 1995; Leader HUGH MARSHALL.

United Progressive Party (UPP): St John's; f. 1992 by merger of the Antigua Caribbean Liberation Movement (f. 1979), the Progressive Labour Movement (f. 1970) and the United National Democratic Party (f. 1986); Leader BALDWIN SPENCER; Dep. Leader TIM HECTOR; Chair. VINCENT DERRICK.

Diplomatic Representation

EMBASSIES AND HIGH COMMISSION IN ANTIGUA AND BARBUDA

China, People's Republic: The Heritage Hotel, POB 1446, St John's; tel. 462-1125; (Ambassador resident in Barbados).

United Kingdom: British High Commission Office, Price Waterhouse Centre, 11 Old Parham Rd, POB 483, St John's; tel. 462-0008; fax 462-2806; (High Commissioner resident in Barbados).

Venezuela: Cross and Redcliffe Sts, POB 1201, St John's; tel. 462-1574; telex 2161; fax 462-1570; Ambassador: ALBERTO GARANTÓN.

Judicial System

Justice is administered by the Eastern Caribbean Supreme Court, based in Saint Lucia, which consists of a High Court of Justice and a Court of Appeal. One of the Court's Puisne Judges is resident in and responsible for Antigua and Barbuda, and presides over the Court of Summary Jurisdiction on the islands. There are also Magistrates' Courts for lesser cases.

Chief Justice: Sir VINCENT FLOISSAC.

Solicitor-General: LEBRECHT HESSE.

Attorney-General: RADFORD HILL.

Religion

The majority of the inhabitants profess Christianity, and the largest denomination is the Church in the Province of the West Indies (Anglican Communion).

CHRISTIANITY

Antigua Christian Council: POB 863, St John's; tel. 462-0261; f. 1964; five mem. churches; Pres. Most Rev. Dr ORLAND U. LINDSAY (Anglican Church); Exec. Sec. EDRIS ROBERTS.

The Anglican Communion

Anglicans in Antigua and Barbuda are adherents of the Church in the Province of the West Indies. The diocese of the North Eastern Caribbean and Aruba comprises 12 islands: Antigua, Saint Christopher (St Kitts), Nevis, Anguilla, Barbuda, Montserrat, Dominica, Saba, St Maarten/St Martin, Aruba, St Bartholomew and St Eustatius; the total number of Anglicans is about 60,000. The See City and the headquarters of the Provincial Secretariat is St John's.

Bishop of the North Eastern Caribbean and Aruba and Archbishop of the West Indies: Most Rev. ORLAND U. LINDSAY, Bishop's Lodge, POB 23, St John's; tel. 462-0151; fax 462-2090; e-mail dioceseneca@candw.ag.

The Roman Catholic Church

The diocese of St John's-Basseterre, suffragan to the archdiocese of Castries (Saint Lucia), includes Anguilla, Antigua and Barbuda, the British Virgin Islands, Montserrat and Saint Christopher and Nevis. At 31 December 1995 there were an estimated 15,035 adherents in the diocese. The Bishop participates in the Antilles Episcopal Conference (whose Secretariat is based in Port of Spain, Trinidad).

Bishop of St John's-Basseterre: Rt Rev. DONALD J. REECE, Chancery Offices, POB 836, St John's; tel. 461-1135; fax 462-2383.

Other Christian Churches

Antigua Baptist Association: POB 277, St John's; tel. 462-1254; Pres. IVOR CHARLES.

Evangelical Lutheran Church: Woods Centre, POB W77, St John's; tel. 462-2896; e-mail kehld@candw.ag; Pastors M. HENRICH, D. KEHL.

Methodist Church: c/o POB 863, St John's; Superintendent Rev. ELOY CHRISTOPHER.

There are also Pentecostal, Seventh-day Adventist, Moravian, Nazarene, Salvation Army and Wesleyan Holiness places of worship.

The Press

Antigua Today: St John's; f. 1993; weekly; publ. by Wadadli Productions Ltd; Editor BARRYMORE STEVENS.

Business Expressions: POB 774, St John's; tel. 462-0743; fax 462-4575; monthly; organ of the Antigua and Barbuda Chamber of Commerce and Industry.

Daily Observer: Fort Rd, POB 1318, St John's; fax 462-5561; Publr SAMUEL DERRICK; Editor WINSTON DERRICK.

The Nation: Ministry of Information, Cross St, POB 590, St John's; tel. 462-0010; weekly; Editor GEORGE E. JOSEPH; circ. 1,500.

The Outlet: Cross and Tanner Sts, POB 493, St John's; tel. 462-4425; f. 1975; weekly; publ. by the Antigua Caribbean Liberation Movement (founder member of the United Progressive Party in 1992); Editor TIM HECTOR; circ. 5,500.

The Sentinel: Long St, POB 402, St John's; tel. 462-5500; fax 462-4084; Editor BEVERLEY P. MAXIME.

The Worker's Voice: Emancipation House, 46 North St, POB 1281, St John's; tel. 462-0090; f. 1943; weekly; official organ of the Antigua Labour Party and the Antigua Trades and Labour Union; Editor NOEL THOMAS; circ. 6,000.

FOREIGN NEWS AGENCY

Inter Press Service (IPS) (Italy): Old Parham Rd, St John's; tel. 462-3602; Correspondent LOUIS DANIEL.

Publishers

Antigua Printing and Publishing Ltd: POB 670, St John's; tel. 462-1265; fax 462-6200.

Wadadli Productions Ltd: POB 571, St John's; tel. 462-4489.

Broadcasting and Communications

TELECOMMUNICATIONS

Telephone services are provided by the Antigua Public Utilities Authority (see Trade and Industry).

RADIO

ABS Radio: POB 590, St John's; tel. 462-3602; telex 2127; f. 1956; subsidiary of Antigua and Barbuda Broadcasting Service (see Television, below); Programme Man. D. L. PAYNE.

Caribbean Radio Lighthouse: POB 1057, St John's; tel. 462-1454; e-mail cradiolight@candw.ag; f. 1975; religious broadcasts; operated by Baptist Int. Mission Inc. (USA); Dir CURTIS L. WAITE.

Caribbean Relay Co Ltd: POB 1203, St John's; tel. 462-0994; fax 462-0487; e-mail cm-crc@candw.ag; jtly-operated by British Broadcasting Corpn and Deutsche Welle.

Radio ZDK: Grenville Radio Ltd, POB 1100, St John's; tel. 462-1100; f. 1970; commercial; Programme Dir IVOR BIRD; CEO E. PHILIP.

TELEVISION

Antigua and Barbuda Broadcasting Service (ABS): Directorate of Broadcasting and Public Information, POB 590, St John's; tel. 462-0010; fax 462-4442; Dir-Gen. HOLLIS HENRY; CEO DENIS LEANDRO; subsidiary:

ABS Television: POB 1280, St John's; tel. 462-0010; fax 462-1622; f. 1964; Programme Man. JAMES TANNY ROSE.

CTV Entertainment Systems: 25 Long St, St John's; tel. 462-0346; fax 462-4211; cable television co; transmits 12 channels of US television 24 hours per day to subscribers; Programme Dir J. COX.

Finance

(cap. = capital; res = reserves; dep. = deposits; brs = branches)

BANKING

The Eastern Caribbean Central Bank (see p. 122), based in Saint Christopher, is the central issuing and monetary authority for Antigua and Barbuda.

Antigua Barbuda Investment Bank Ltd: High St and Corn Alley, POB 1679, St John's; tel. 480-2700; telex 2039; fax 480-2750; e-mail aob@candw.ag; f. 1990; cap. EC $4.7m., res EC $1.9m., dep. EC $84.9m. (Sept. 1995); two subsidiaries: Antigua Overseas Bank Ltd and ABI Trust Ltd; Chair. EUSTACE FRANCIS; Man. Dir McALISTER ABBOTT; 2 brs.

Antigua Commercial Bank: St Mary's and Thames Sts, POB 95, St John's; tel. 462-1217; telex 2175; fax 462-1220; f. 1955; auth. cap. EC $5m.; Man. JOHN BENJAMIN; 2 brs.

Antigua and Barbuda Development Bank: 27 St Mary's St, POB 1279, St John's; tel. 462-0838; fax 462-0839; f. 1974; Man. S. ALEX OSBORNE.

Bank of Antigua: 1000 Airport Blvd, Coolidge, POB 315, St John's; tel. 462-4282; fax 462-4718; 1 br.

Foreign Banks

Bank of Nova Scotia (Canada): High St, POB 342, St John's; tel. 480-1500; telex 2118; fax 480-1554; Man. J. A. BATTERTON.

Barclays Bank PLC (UK): High St, POB 225, St John's; tel. 480-5000; telex 2135; fax 462-4910; Man. WINSTON ST AGATHE; 2 brs.

Canadian Imperial Bank of Commerce: 28 High St, POB 28, St John's; tel. 462-0836; telex 2150; Man. G. R. HILTS.

Royal Bank of Canada: High and Market Sts, POB 252, St John's; tel. 462-0325; telex 2120; offers a trustee service.

Swiss American Bank Ltd: High St, POB 1302, St John's; tel. 462-4460; telex 2181; fax 462-0274; f. 1983; cap. US $1.0m., res US $2.1m., dep. US $31.9m. (Dec. 1993); Gen. Man. JOHN GREAVES; 3 brs.

In mid-1997 there were 51 registered 'offshore' banks in Antigua and Barbuda.

INSURANCE

Several foreign companies have offices in Antigua. Local insurance companies include the following:

Diamond Insurance Co Ltd: St Mary's St, POB 489, St John's; tel. 462-3474; telex 2173.

General Insurance Co Ltd: Upper Redcliffe St, POB 340, St John's; tel. 462-2346; fax 462-4482.

Sentinel Insurance Co Ltd: Coolidge, POB 207, St John's; tel. 462-4603.

State Insurance Corpn: Redcliffe St, POB 290, St John's; tel. 462-0110; telex 2177; fax 462-2649; Gen. Man. ROLSTON BARTHLEY.

Trade and Industry

DEVELOPMENT ORGANIZATIONS

Barbuda Development Agency: St John's; economic development projects for Barbuda; Chair. HAKIM AKBAR.

Development Control Authority: St John's.

Industrial Development Board: Newgate St, St John's; tel. 462-1038; f. 1984 to stimulate investment in local industries.

St John's Development Corporation: Redcliffe St, POB 1473, St John's; tel. 462-3925; fax 462-3931; f. 1986; manages the Heritage Quay tourist complex.

CHAMBER OF COMMERCE

Antigua and Barbuda Chamber of Commerce and Industry Ltd: Redcliffe St, POB 774, St John's; tel. 462-0743; fax 462-4575; f. 1944 as Antigua Chamber of Commerce Ltd; name changed as above in 1991, following the collapse of the Antigua and Barbuda Manufacturers' Assn; Pres. CLARVIS JOSEPH.

INDUSTRIAL AND TRADE ASSOCIATIONS

Antigua Cotton Growers' Association: Dunbars, St John's; tel. 462-4962; telex 2122; Chair. FRANCIS HENRY; Sec. PETER BLANCHETTE.

Antigua Fisheries Corpn: St John's; partly funded by the Antigua and Barbuda Development Bank; aims to help local fishermen.

Antigua Sugar Industry Corpn: Gunthorpes, POB 899, St George's; tel. 462-0653.

Private Sector Organization of Antigua and Barbuda: St John's.

EMPLOYERS' ORGANIZATION

Antigua Employers' Federation: Factory Rd, POB 298, St John's; tel. 462-0449; fax 462-0449; f. 1950; 120 mems; Chair. JOSEPH BENJAMIN; Sec. HENDERSON BASS.

UTILITIES

Antigua Public Utilities Authority (APUA): St Mary's St, POB 416, St John's ; tel. 480-7000; fax 462-2782; provides electricity, water and telephone services.

TRADE UNIONS

Antigua and Barbuda Public Service Association (ABPSA): POB 1285, St John's; Pres. JAMES SPENCER; Gen. Sec. ELLOY DE FREITAS; 550 mems.

Antigua Trades and Labour Union (ATLU): 46 North St, St John's; tel. 462-0090; f. 1939; affiliated to the Antigua Labour Party; Pres. WILLIAM ROBINSON; Gen. Sec. (vacant); about 10,000 mems.

Antigua Workers' Union (AWU): Freedom Hall, Newgate St, St John's; tel. 462-2005; f. 1967 after a split with ATLU; not affiliated to any party; Pres. MALCOLM DANIEL; Gen. Sec. KEITHLYN SMITH; 10,000 mems.

National Assembly of Workers: Cross St, St John's; affiliated to the Antigua Caribbean Liberation Movement (founder member of the United Progressive Party in 1992).

Transport

ROADS

There are 384 km (239 miles) of main roads and 781 km (485 miles) of secondary dry-weather roads. A road improvement project was undertaken in 1992 with aid from the People's Republic of China.

SHIPPING

The main harbour is the St John's Deep Water Harbour. It is used by cruise ships and a number of foreign shipping lines. There are regular cargo and passenger services internationally and regionally. At Falmouth, on the south side of Antigua, is a former Royal Navy dockyard in English Harbour. The harbour is now used by yachts and private pleasure craft.

Antigua Port Authority: Deep Water Harbour, POB 1052, St John's; tel. 462-1273; telex 2179; fax 462-2510; Port Dir EMIL SWEENEY.

Caribbean Link: High St, St John's; tel. 462-3000; f. 1987; operates high-speed passenger and cargo ferry; scheduled services to 10 islands; Dirs DON MARSHALL, KEVIN BELIZAIRE.

Vernon Edwards Shipping Co: Thames St, POB 82, St John's; tel. 462-2034; telex 2129; fax 462-2035; weekly cargo service to Dominica.

CIVIL AVIATION

Antigua's V.C. Bird (formerly Coolidge) International Airport, 9 km (5.6 miles) north-east of St John's, is modern and accommodates jet-engined aircraft. There is a small airstrip at Codrington on Barbuda. Antigua and Barbuda Airlines, a nominal company, controls international routes, but services to Europe and North America are operated by American Airlines (USA), Continental Airlines (USA), Lufthansa (Germany) and Air Canada. Antigua and Barbuda is a shareholder in, and the headquarters of, the regional airline, LIAT. Other regional services are operated by BWIA (Trinidad and Tobago) and Air BVI (British Virgin Islands).

LIAT (1974) Ltd: POB 819, V.C. Bird Int. Airport; tel. 462-0700; telex 2124; fax 462-4736; f. 1956 as Leeward Islands Air Transport Services, jointly-owned by 11 regional Govts; privatized in 1995; shares are held by the Govts of Antigua and Barbuda, Montserrat, Grenada, Barbados, Trinidad and Tobago, Jamaica, Guyana, Dominica, Saint Lucia, Saint Vincent and the Grenadines and Saint Christopher and Nevis (30.8%), BWIA (29.2%), LIAT employees (13.3%) and private investors (26.7%); scheduled passenger and cargo services to 26 destinations in the Caribbean; charter flights are also undertaken; Chair. AZIZ HADEED; CEO GILLES FILIATREAULT.

Carib Aviation Ltd: V.C. Bird Int. Airport; tel. 462-3147; fax 462-3125; e-mail caribav@candw.ag; charter co; operates regional services.

Regal Air: V.C. Bird Int. Airport.

Tourism

Tourism is the country's main industry. Antigua offers a reputed 365 beaches, the annual attractions of an international sailing regatta and Carnival week, and the historic Nelson's Dockyard in English Harbour (a national park since 1985). Barbuda is less developed but is noted for its beauty, wildlife and beaches of pink sand. In 1986 the Government established the St John's Development Corporation to oversee the redevelopment of the capital as a commercial duty-free centre, with extra cruise-ship facilities. In 1995 there were 462,114 tourist arrivals, including 234,773 cruise-ship passengers. In that year some 38% of stop-over visitors came from Europe (particularly the United Kingdom), 35% from the USA, 17% from other Caribbean countries and 6% from Canada. In 1995 there were a total of 3,462 hotel rooms.

Antigua Department of Tourism: Long and Thames Sts, POB 363, St John's; tel. 462-0029; fax 462-2483; Dir of Tourism (vacant).

Antigua Hotels and Tourist Association (AHTA): Lower St Mary's St, POB 454, St John's; tel. 462-3703; fax 462-3702; Chair. PETER RAMRATTAN; Pres. CHARLES V. HAWLEY.

ARGENTINA

Introductory Survey

Location, Climate, Language, Religion, Flag, Capital

The Argentine Republic occupies almost the whole of South America south of the Tropic of Capricorn and east of the Andes. It has a long Atlantic coastline stretching from Uruguay and the River Plate to Tierra del Fuego. To the west lie Chile and the Andes mountains, while to the north are Bolivia, Paraguay and Brazil. Argentina also claims the Falkland Islands (known in Argentina as the Islas Malvinas), South Georgia, the South Sandwich Islands and part of Antarctica. The climate varies from sub-tropical in the Chaco region of the north to sub-arctic in Patagonia, generally with moderate summer rainfall. Temperatures in Buenos Aires are usually between 5°C (41°F) and 29°C (84°F). The language is Spanish. The great majority of the population profess Christianity: more than 90% are Roman Catholics and about 2% Protestants. The national flag (proportions 14 by 9) has three equal horizontal stripes, of light blue (celeste), above white, above light blue. The state flag (proportions 2 by 1) has the same design with, in addition, a gold 'Sun of May' in the centre of the white stripe. The capital is Buenos Aires.

Recent History

During the greater part of the 20th century, government in Argentina has tended to alternate between military and civilian rule. In 1930 Hipólito Yrigoyen, a member of the reformist Unión Cívica Radical (UCR), who in 1916 had become Argentina's first President to be freely elected by popular vote, was overthrown by an army coup, and the country's first military regime was established. Civilian rule was restored in 1932, only to be supplanted by further military intervention in 1943. A leading figure in the new military regime, Col (later Lt-Gen.) Juan Domingo Perón Sosa, won a presidential election in 1946. As President, he established the Peronista party in 1948 and pursued a policy of extreme nationalism and social improvement, aided by his second wife, Eva ('Evita') Duarte de Perón, whose popularity (particularly among industrial workers and their families) greatly enhanced his position and contributed to his re-election as President in 1951. In 1954, however, his promotion of secularization and the legalization of divorce brought him into conflict with the Roman Catholic Church. In September 1955 President Perón was deposed by a revolt of the armed forces. He went into exile, eventually settling in Spain, from where he continued to direct the Peronist movement.

Following the overthrow of Perón, Argentina entered another lengthy period of political instability. Political control continued to pass between civilian (mainly Radical) and military regimes during the late 1950s and the 1960s. This period was also characterized by increasing guerrilla activity, particularly by the Montoneros, a group of left-wing Peronist sympathizers, and urban guerrilla groups intensified their activities in 1971 and 1972.

Congressional and presidential elections were conducted in March 1973. The Frente Justicialista de Liberación, a Peronist coalition, won control of the National Congress (Congreso Nacional), while the presidential election was won by the party's candidate, Dr Héctor Cámpora, who assumed the office in May. However, Cámpora resigned in July, to enable Gen. Perón, who had returned to Argentina in June, to contest a fresh presidential election. In September Perón was returned to power, with more than 60% of the votes. He took office in October, with his third wife, María Estela ('Isabelita') Martínez de Perón, as Vice-President.

General Perón died in July 1974 and was succeeded as President by his widow. The Government's economic austerity programme and the soaring rate of inflation caused widespread strike action and prompted dissension among industrial workers. This increasingly chaotic situation resulted in demands for the resignation of 'Isabelita' Perón. In March 1976 the armed forces, led by Gen. Jorge Videla (Commander of the Army), overthrew the President and installed a three-man junta: Gen. Videla was sworn in as President. The junta made substantial alterations to the Constitution, dissolved Congress, suspended all political and trade union activity and removed most government officials from their posts. Several hundred people were arrested, while 'Isabelita' Perón was detained and later went into exile.

The new military regime launched a successful, although ferocious, offensive against left-wing guerrillas and opposition forces. The imprisonment, torture and murder of many people who were suspected of left-wing political activity by the armed forces provoked domestic and international protests against violations of human rights. Repression eased in 1978, after all armed opposition had been eliminated.

In March 1981 Gen. Roberto Viola, a former member of the junta, succeeded President Videla and made known his intention to extend dialogue with political parties as a prelude to an eventual return to democracy. Owing to ill health, he was replaced in December by Lt-Gen. Leopoldo Galtieri, the Commander-in-Chief of the Army, who attempted to cultivate popular support by continuing the process of political liberalization which had been initiated by his predecessor.

In April 1982, in order to distract attention from an increasingly unstable domestic situation, and following unsuccessful negotiations with the United Kingdom in February over Argentina's long-standing sovereignty claim, President Galtieri ordered the invasion of the Falkland Islands (Islas Malvinas) (see chapter on the Falkland Islands, Vol. II). The United Kingdom recovered the islands after a short conflict, in the course of which about 750 Argentine lives were lost. Argentine forces surrendered in June 1982, but no formal cessation of hostilities was declared until October 1989. Humiliated by the defeat, Galtieri was forced to resign, and the members of the junta were replaced. The army, under the control of Lt-Gen. Cristino Nicolaides, installed a retired general, Reynaldo Bignone, as President in July 1982. The armed forces were held responsible for the disastrous economic situation, and the transfer of power to a civilian government was accelerated. Moreover, in 1983 a Military Commission of Inquiry into the Falklands conflict concluded in its report that the main responsibility for Argentina's defeat lay with members of the former junta, who were recommended for trial. Galtieri was sentenced to imprisonment, while several other officers were put on trial for corruption, murder and insulting the honour of the armed forces. Meanwhile, in August 1983 the regime approved the Ley de Pacificación Nacional, an amnesty law which granted retrospective immunity to the police, the armed forces and others for political crimes that had been committed over the previous 10 years.

In February 1983 the Government announced that general and presidential elections would be held on 30 October. At the elections, the UCR defeated the Peronist Partido Justicialista (PJ), attracting the votes of many former Peronist supporters. The UCR won 317 of the 600 seats in the presidential electoral college, and 129 of the 254 seats in the Chamber of Deputies (Cámara de Diputados), although the PJ won a narrow majority of provincial governorships. Dr Raúl Alfonsín, the UCR candidate, took office as President on 10 December. President Alfonsín promptly announced a radical reform of the armed forces, which led to the immediate retirement of more than one-half of the military high command. In addition, he repealed the Ley de Pacificación Nacional and ordered the court martial of the first three military juntas to rule Argentina after the coup of 1976, for offences including abduction, torture and murder. Public opposition to the former military regime was reinforced by the discovery and exhumation of hundreds of bodies from unmarked graves throughout the country. (It was believed that 15,000–30,000 people had 'disappeared' during the so-called 'dirty war' between the former military regime and its opponents from 1976 until 1983.) In December the Government announced the formation of the National Commission on the Disappearance of Persons to investigate the events of the 'dirty war'. The trial of the former leaders began in April 1985. Several hundred prosecution witnesses gave testimonies which revealed the systematic atrocities and the campaign of terror perpetrated by the former military leaders. In December four of the accused were acquitted, but sentences were imposed on the remaining five, including sentences of life imprisonment for Gen. Videla and Adm. Eduardo Massera. The court martial of the members of the junta that had held power during the Falklands conflict was conducted concurrently with the trial of the former military leaders. In May 1986 all three members of the junta were found guilty of negligence and received prison sentences, including a term of 12 years for Galtieri.

In late 1986 the Government sought approval for the Punto Final ('Full Stop') Law, whereby civil and military courts were to begin new judicial proceedings against members of the armed forces accused of violations of human rights, within a 60-day period ending on 22 February 1987. The pre-emptive nature of the legislation provoked widespread popular opposition but was, nevertheless, approved by Congress in December 1986. However, in May 1987, following a series of minor rebellions at army garrisons throughout the country, the Government announced new legislation, known as the Obediencia Debida ('Due Obedience') law, whereby an amnesty was to be declared for all but senior ranks of the police and armed forces. Therefore, under the new law, of the 350–370 officers hitherto due to be prosecuted for alleged violations of human rights, only 30–50 senior officers were now to be tried. The legislation provoked great controversy, and was considered to be a decisive factor in the significant gains made by the PJ at gubernatorial and legislative elections conducted in September. The UCR's defeat was also attributed to its imposition, in July, of an unpopular economic programme of strict austerity measures.

Two swiftly-suppressed army rebellions in January and December 1988 (led by Lt-Col Aldo Rico and Col Mohamed Ali Seineldín respectively) demonstrated continuing military disaffection. In both incidents, the rebel military factions demanded higher salaries for soldiers, an increase in the military budget and some form of amnesty for officers awaiting trial for violations of human rights during the 'dirty war'.

In January 1989 the army quickly repelled an attack by 40 left-wing activists on a military base at La Tablada, in which 39 lives were lost. Many of the guerrilla band were identified as members of the Movimiento Todos por la Patria.

In the campaign for the May 1989 elections, Carlos Saúl Menem headed the Frente Justicialista de Unidad Popular (FREJUPO) electoral alliance, comprising his own PJ grouping, the Partido Demócrata Cristiano (PDC) and the Partido Intransigente (PI). On 14 May the Peronists were guaranteed a return to power, having secured, together with the two other members of the FREJUPO alliance, 48.5% of the votes cast in the presidential election and 310 of the 600 seats in the electoral college. The Peronists were also victorious in the election for 127 seats (one-half of the total) in the Chamber of Deputies, winning 45% of the votes and 66 seats, in contrast to the 29% (41 seats) obtained by the UCR.

The failure of attempts by the retiring and incoming administrations to collaborate, and the reluctance of the Alfonsín administration to continue in office with the prospect of further economic embarrassment, left the nation in a political vacuum. Menem was due to take office as President on 10 December 1989, but the worsening economic situation compelled Alfonsín to resign five months earlier than scheduled. Menem took office on 8 July.

Rumours of a possible amnesty, agreed between the newly-elected Government and military leaders, prompted the organization of a massive demonstration in support of human rights in Buenos Aires in September 1989. In October, however, the Government issued decrees whereby 210 officers, NCOs and soldiers who had been involved in the 'dirty war', the governing junta during the Falklands conflict (including Gen. Galtieri) and leaders of three recent military uprisings (including Lt-Col Rico and Col Seineldín) were pardoned.

Economic affairs dominated the latter half of 1989 and much of 1990. The Minister of the Economy, Nestór Rapanelli, introduced several measures, including the devaluation of the austral, but these failed to reverse the trend towards hyperinflation, and Rapanelli resigned in December 1989. His successor, Antonio Erman González, introduced a comprehensive plan for economic readjustment, incorporating the expansion of existing plans for the transfer to private ownership of many state-owned companies, the rationalization of government-controlled bodies, and the restructuring of the nation's financial systems. In August 1990 González appointed himself head of the Central Bank and assumed almost total control of the country's financial structure. Public disaffection with the Government's economic policy was widespread. Failure to contain the threat of hyperinflation led to a loss in purchasing power, and small-scale food riots and looting became more frequent. The Government's rationalization programme proved, predictably, unpopular with public-sector employees, and industrial action and demonstrations, organized from within the sector with the backing of trade unions, political opposition parties and human rights organizations, were well supported.

In August 1990, following a formal declaration by the PI and the PDC of their intention to leave the 1989 (FREJUPO) alliance, Menem announced his readiness to enter into electoral alliances with centre-right parties for congressional elections due to be held in 1991.

Widespread public concern at the apparent impunity of military personnel increased following President Menem's suggestion that a further military amnesty would be granted before the end of 1990, and was exacerbated by rumours of escalating military unrest (which were realized in December 1990 when 200–300 rebel soldiers staged a swiftly-suppressed uprising at the Patricios infantry garrison in Buenos Aires). A second round of presidential pardons was announced in late December. More than 40,000 demonstrators gathered in Buenos Aires to protest against the release of former military leaders, including Gen. Videla, Gen. Viola and Adm. Massera. Critics and political opponents dismissed claims, made by the President, that such action was essential for the effective 'reconciliation' of the Argentine people. In mid-1991 it was announced that the number of armed forces personnel was to be reduced by an estimated 20,000 men; military spending was also to be restricted.

During 1991 the popularity and the political reputation of President Menem were dramatically undermined by the highly-publicized deterioration in marital relations between the President and his wife, Zulema Yoma, and by a succession of corruption scandals in which members of the Yoma family were implicated. In January 1991 Menem was obliged to reorganize the Cabinet, following allegations that government ministers and officials had requested bribes from US businessmen during the course of commercial negotiations. Later in the month, the President was forced to implement a second cabinet reshuffle when his economic team, headed by Antonio Erman González, resigned following a sudden spectacular decline in the value of the austral in relation to the US dollar.

In mid-1991, following congressional approval of an amendment to the electoral law, it was announced that gubernatorial and congressional elections would take place later in the year. In the first two rounds of voting, the Peronists were unexpectedly successful, wresting the governorship of San Juan from the provincial Bloquista party on 11 August, and securing control of nine of the 12 contested provinces (including the crucial province of Buenos Aires) on 8 September. The third and fourth rounds of voting, on 27 October and 1 December respectively, proved less successful for the PJ. Overall, however, the Peronists secured control of 14 of the 24 contested territories and increased their congressional representation by seven seats, compared with a five-seat reduction in the congressional representation of the UCR.

The success of the Peronist campaign was widely attributed to the popularity of the Minister of the Economy, Domingo Cavallo, and the success of the economic policies that he had implemented since January 1991, when he succeeded Antonio Erman González. New economic measures, announced in February and March, included the abolition of index-linked wage increases and, most dramatically, the announcement that the austral would become freely convertible from 1 April. This new economic initiative soon achieved considerable success in reducing inflation, and impressed international finance organizations sufficiently to secure the negotiation of substantial loan agreements. In October the President issued a comprehensive decree ordering the removal of almost all of the remaining bureaucratic apparatus of state regulation of the economy, and in November the Government announced plans to accelerate the transfer to private ownership of the remaining public-sector concerns. Continuing economic success in 1992 helped to secure agreements for the renegotiation of repayment of outstanding debts with the Government's leading creditor banks and with the 'Paris Club' of Western creditor governments.

However, in November 1992 the Confederación General del Trabajo (CGT—General Confederation of Labour) organized a one-day general strike, in protest at the Government's continuing programme of economic austerity. The strike, which was well-supported in the provinces but only partially observed in the capital, was precipitated by revelations that senior government officials were to receive pay increases of as much as 200%.

Meanwhile, President Menem sought to consolidate his own position and to increase the popularity of his party in the months preceding legislative elections scheduled for late 1993, at which the Peronists hoped to make significant gains in order to facilitate Menem's wish to effect a constitutional amendment that would allow him to pursue a second, consecutive presidential term. In December 1992 the President reorganized the Cabinet, replacing three unpopular ministers with close associates.

Legislative elections to renew 127 seats in the Chamber of Deputies, conducted on 3 October 1993, were won convincingly by the ruling PJ party, with 42.3% of the votes, while the UCR obtained 30% of the votes. Small gains were made by the right-wing Movimiento por la Dignidad y la Independencia (Modin), led by former army rebel Aldo Rico, which received 5.7% of the votes. The performance of the Peronists, however, by no means guaranteed the two-thirds majority necessary in the lower house to approve the need for constitutional reform sought by Menem, although the President's hopes were encouraged by the Senate's approval of the reform proposal in late October.

An unexpected development in early November 1993 was the return to political prominence of former President Raúl Alfonsín. While UCR opposition to Menem's presidential ambitions had remained vociferous, several prominent opposition leaders, notably Alfonsín, feared that the UCR would be excluded from negotiations on constitutional reform, should the unorthodox political manoeuvring of the Peronists, largely orchestrated by the President of the Senate, Menem's brother Eduardo, succeed in propelling the reform proposal through the legislature. Alfonsín, also anxious to avoid another humiliating defeat for the UCR at a national referendum which Menem had elected to organize in late 1993 on the question of constitutional reform, entered into a dialogue with the President, which resulted in a declaration, in early November, that a framework for consensual reform had been negotiated, apparently in return for Menem's postponement of the referendum and acceptance of modified reform proposals. Hopes for the successful conclusion of a bilateral agreement on constitutional reform were further encouraged, later in November, by the election of Alfonsín to the presidency of the UCR. The terms of the agreement, detailing the central reform issues of the possibility of re-election of the President for one consecutive term, a reduction in the presidential term, to four years, the abolition of the presidential electoral college, the creation of the post of co-ordinating minister to fulfil a prime-ministerial function, an increase in the number of seats in the Senate and a reduction in the length of the mandate of all senators, a reform of the procedure for judicial appointments, the removal of religious stipulations from the terms of eligibility for presidential candidates, and the abolition of the President's power to appoint the mayor of the federal capital, were endorsed by the UCR national convention in early December, and the need for constitutional reform was approved by Congress later in the month. Elections to a 305-member constituent assembly were to be conducted in April 1994. Menem immediately declared his intention to seek re-election in 1995.

Elections to the Constituent Assembly took place 10 April 1994. While the Peronists won the largest share of the vote (37.8%—136 seats), they failed to secure an absolute majority in the Assembly. The election results also represented a disappointment for the UCR, which won only 19.9% of the votes, equivalent to 75 seats in the Assembly. A centre-left coalition, Frente Grande, established in mid-1993 to contest the October 1993 legislative elections, emerged unexpectedly as the third political force (with 12.5% of the votes and 31 seats), having campaigned against institutionalized corruption. The Assembly was inaugurated in May 1994, and by mid-August it had successfully incorporated the crucial recommendations of the December 1993 constitutional reform pact between the PJ and the UCR (see above) into the 1853 Constitution. On 24 August 1994 a new Constitution containing 19 new articles, 40 amendments to existing articles and a new chapter on civil rights and guarantees, was duly promulgated. An electoral timetable was also established by the Assembly, with presidential, legislative and provincial elections all scheduled for May 1995. In December 1994 the Senate approved the new electoral code providing for the direct election of a president and a vice-president and for a second round of voting for the first- and second-placed candidates in the event of a closely contested election.

In January 1995 Carlos Ruckauf, the Minister of the Interior, was named as President Menem's running mate for the new post of vice-president. Menem's campaign for re-election concentrated on the economic success of his previous administration and, despite the increasingly precarious condition of the economy during 1995 (see below), was sufficiently successful to secure 49.9% of the votes at the presidential election conducted on 14 May, thereby exceeding the 45% of votes needed to avoid a second round of voting. José Octavio Bordón, the candidate of the Frente del País Solidario (Frepaso—a centre-left alliance of socialist, communist, Christian Democrat and dissident Peronist groups formed in late 1994) was second with 29.3% of the votes, ahead of the UCR candidate, Horacio Massaccesi, who received 17.0% of the votes. The Peronists were also successful in nine of the 14 gubernatorial contests; however, Frepaso, with almost 35% of the votes, won the largest share of the 130 contested seats in the Chamber of Deputies at legislative elections conducted concurrently, and significantly increased its representation in the Senate (as did the Peronists) largely at the expense of the UCR. (In September 1995 Raúl Alfonsín resigned as UCR party leader in response to dwindling popular support for the party's policies; Rodolfo Terragno was elected as his successor in November.) Menem was inaugurated as President for a four-year term on 8 July 1995. The composition of a largely unaltered Cabinet was announced simultaneously. Eduardo Bauzá was appointed to the new post of Secretary-General of the Presidency, while the former environment and social development secretariats assumed full ministerial status. The Peronists continued to perform well at gubernatorial elections conducted in late 1995, but suffered an unexpected defeat at senatorial elections in the capital on 8 October at which the Peronist candidate was beaten into third place by the Frepaso and UCR candidates respectively. Menem's executive power was increased in February 1996 when Congress endorsed the Administrative Reform Act, enabling the Government to merge certain state agencies and reduce public expenditure considerably.

Meanwhile the Government's ongoing programme of economic austerity continued to provoke violent opposition, particularly from the public sector, where redundancies and a 'freeze' on salaries had been imposed in many provinces. A protest march in the capital in July 1994 and a general strike in August were organized by two of Argentina's dissident trade union confederations, the Congreso de los Trabajadores Argentinos (CTA) and the Movimiento de Trabajadores Argentinos (MTA), and were well supported despite opposition from the country's largest trade union confederation, the CGT. However, in late August a 12-month moratorium on appointments in the public sector was announced, as were plans to privatize several more state enterprises. In March 1995 the Government presented an economic consolidation programme aimed at protecting the Argentine currency against devaluation and supporting the ailing banking sector, which had been adversely affected by the financial crisis in Mexico in late 1994. Subsequent austerity measures adopted by provincial governments, together with a dramatic increase in the rate of unemployment, provoked widespread social unrest in the city of Córdoba in mid-1995 (prompting the resignation of the incumbent Governor six months before the scheduled inauguration of the Governor-elect) and in the province of Río Negro in September. The publication of official unemployment figures for July of 18.6% prompted Menem to announce, in early August, a series of employment initiatives. General strikes organized in April and September were only partially observed, principally in those provinces already experiencing social unrest.

In February 1996 a television programme revealed that Domingo Cavallo, the Minister of the Economy, had paid a minimal amount of income tax in 1994. Cavallo, whose economic reform programme had concentrated on combating tax evasion and corruption, denounced the claims and insisted that he was the victim of a campaign to discredit him. Cavallo's position was undermined further in March 1996, when President Menem dismissed one of Cavallo's close associates, Haroldo Grisanti, the Postmaster-General (indicted on charges of fraudulent actions against the public administration), and when responsibility for telecommunications was transferred from the Ministry of the Economy to the Secretary-General of the Presidency. In addition, Menem announced that a tripartite council of business, trade union and government representatives would be established to propose measures to counter the problems of unemployment and recession; Menem subsequently conceded that the council would be limited to a consultatory role following strong objections by Cavallo. Later in the month Jorge Rodríguez, hitherto Minister of Education and Culture, was appointed

Secretary-General of the Presidency in place of Eduardo Bauzá, who had resigned citing ill health. Meanwhile, internal divisions in Frepaso led to the resignation from the alliance in February of José Octavio Bordón (the Frepaso presidential candidate in the 1995 elections); shortly afterwards Bordón resigned from the leadership of his own party (Política Abierta para la Integridad Social), and from the Senate.

In June 1996 the Government suffered a serious political defeat when a UCR candidate, Fernando de la Rúa, won almost 40% of the votes cast in the first direct elections for the Mayor of the Federal District of Buenos Aires; a Frepaso candidate secured 26.5% of the votes, while the incumbent Peronist Mayor, Jorge Domínguez, received only 18% of the ballot. In concurrent elections to the 60-member Constituent Assembly (which was charged with drafting a constitution for the newly-autonomous Federal District of Buenos Aires), Frepaso candidates secured 25 seats, the UCR 19, the PJ 11 and the recently-formed Nueva Dirigencia (ND, led by a former Peronist, Gustavo Béliz) five. The results were widely believed to reflect growing discontent with the Government's inability to redress the problems of recession and high levels of unemployment. In July the Government was again undermined by the resignations of Rodolfo Barra, the Minister of Justice (who had been criticized for the slow progress made in resolving anti-semitic attacks and who had subsequently conceded that he had belonged to a fascist group in his youth), and that of Oscar Camilión, the Minister of Defence, whose parliamentary immunity was to be removed to allow investigations in connection with the illegal sale of armaments to Ecuador and Croatia. More significant, however, was the dismissal of Domingo Cavallo from the post of Minister of the Economy, following months of bitter dispute with the President and other cabinet members. Roque Fernández, hitherto President of the Central Bank, assumed the economy portfolio. Meanwhile, Cavallo became increasingly vociferous in his attacks against the integrity of certain cabinet members, and, in October, as Menem launched a well-publicized campaign against corruption after the discovery of wide-scale malpractice within the customs service, Cavallo accused the Government of having links with organized crime.

Meanwhile, industrial unrest continued during 1996, and in August a 24-hour general strike, organized by the CGT, the MTA and the CTA, received widespread support. A 36-hour strike in September was also widely observed, and was supported by Frepaso, the UCR and several Peronist deputies and senators. None the less, in that month taxation and austerity measures secured congressional approval, albeit with significant amendments. In October relations between the Government and the trade unions deteriorated, following the submission to Congress of controversial labour reform legislation. In mid-December, owing to the slow pace at which debate on the bill was progressing in Congress, President Menem carried out his threat to introduce part of the reforms by decree. Three decrees were signed, radically altering labour contracts; however, in January 1997 a court declared the decrees unconstitutional.

In January 1997 there was public outcry at the mafia-style murder of José Luis Cabezas, an investigative news photographer who had been examining alleged links between drugs-traffickers and policemen in the province of Buenos Aires, as well as between certain provincial officials and Alfredo Yabrán, a controversial businessman whom Domingo Cavallo had accused of corruption. Policemen from the province of Buenos Aires and Yabrán's chief of security were subsequently implicated in the murder. In March Eduardo Duhalde, the Peronist Governor of the province of Buenos Aires, initiated a radical reorganization of the provincial police in an attempt to avert attention from the politically sensitive issue of corruption, with which the PJ was increasingly associated. Nevertheless, in June Elías Jassan, the Minister of Justice, tendered his resignation after admitting maintaining links with Yabrán, having previously denied that he had ever met him.

The popularity of the PJ was undermined further by an upsurge in social and industrial unrest during 1997, which was primarily the result of widespread discontent with proposed labour reforms, reductions in public expenditure and the high level of unemployment. In May violent protests erupted across Argentina as police clashed with thousands of demonstrators who had occupied government buildings and blockaded roads and bridges. During one incident as many as 100 people were injured in a confrontation between border police and recently-dismissed sugar workers in the province of Jujuy. Protests in the province subsided following pledges by the Governor of Jujuy to create an additional 12,500 jobs; however, in August there were renewed protests in Jujuy as prospects for the unemployed failed to improve. Meanwhile, in July some 30,000 people demonstrated in the capital to protest at the high level of unemployment, which was estimated at more than 17%. However, a general strike in August, organized by the MTA and the CTA, was only partially observed and was not supported by the CGT, which in May was reported to have reached a compromise agreement with the Government concerning labour reforms.

In July 1997 Gustavo Béliz of the ND and Domingo Cavallo announced the launch of Acción por la República–ND, an alliance to contest the forthcoming congressional elections. In the following month the leaders of Frepaso and the UCR confirmed that they had agreed to an electoral pact, known as the Alianza por el Trabajo, la Justicia y la Educación (ATJE), in order to present joint lists in certain constituencies, notably in the province of Buenos Aires. The popularity of the ATJE was enhanced by the selection of José Luis Machinea, a former President of the Central Bank, to devise its economic programme.

At the mid-term congressional elections, held on 26 October 1997, the UCR and Frepaso (in both separate and joint lists) won 45.6% of the votes and 61 of the 127 seats contested, in contrast to the 36.3% (51 seats) obtained by the PJ; of the remaining 15 seats, three were secured by Acción por la República–ND. The PJ thus lost its overall majority in the Chamber of Deputies (its total number of seats in the Chamber being reduced to 118), while the UCR and Frepaso together increased their representation to 110 seats. More significant was the PJ's poor performance in the critical constituency of the province of Buenos Aires, where it received only 41.3% of the votes, compared with the ATJE's 48.3%. Indeed, the popularity of Graciela Fernández Meijide, a former Frepaso senator who had headed the ATJE list in the province of Buenos Aires, threatened to undermine the chances of a PJ victory at the presidential election in 1999.

Detailed accounts of the murders of as many as 2,000 political detainees during the 'dirty war' were contained in a book written by a retired Lt-Commander which was published in March 1995. Renewed public outrage prompted the current military high command to issue an unprecedented admission of the crimes committed by the armed forces during this period. Public expressions of regret for these actions were also conveyed by the heads of the navy, the army and the air force in April and May 1995. In addition, in April 1996 the Catholic Church expressed regret and asked for forgiveness for the role taken by some of its members during the dictatorship.

In May 1985 a treaty was formally ratified by representatives of the Argentine and Chilean Governments, concluding the territorial dispute over three small islands in the Beagle Channel, south of Tierra del Fuego. The islands were awarded to Chile, while Argentine rights to petroleum and other minerals in the disputed waters were guaranteed. In August 1991 Argentina and Chile reached a settlement regarding disputed claims to territory in the Antarctic region; however, the sovereignty of the territory remained under dispute, necessitating the signing of an additional protocol in late 1996. The protocol was expected to receive congressional approval in Argentina and Chile in early 1998.

Full diplomatic relations were restored with the United Kingdom in February 1990, following senior-level negotiations in Madrid, Spain. The improvement in relations between Argentina and the United Kingdom prompted the European Community (now European Union) to sign a new five-year trade and co-operation agreement with Argentina in April. In November Argentina and the United Kingdom concluded an agreement for the joint administration of a comprehensive protection programme for the lucrative South Atlantic fishing region. Subsequent agreements to regulate fishing in the area were concluded in December 1992 and November 1993. A diplomatic accord, signed in September 1991, significantly reduced military restrictions in the region, which the United Kingdom had imposed on Argentina following the Falklands conflict. The question of sovereignty over the disputed islands was not resolved. The results of preliminary seismic investigations (published in late 1993), which indicated rich petroleum deposits in the region, were expected to further complicate future negotiations. However, a comprehensive agreement on exploration was signed by both countries in New York in September 1995. Meanwhile, negotiations on fishing rights in the region remained tense. Anglo-Argentine relations improved in late 1996 when Lt-Gen.

Martín Balza, the Chief of Staff of the Argentinian Army, became the first high-ranking Argentinian military official to visit the United Kingdom since 1982. Both countries vigorously denied allegations, made in October, that a secret agreement had been concluded earlier to relax the United Kingdom's arms embargo on Argentina in return for petroleum concessions in the South Atlantic. Relations between Argentina and the United Kingdom were consolidated further in January 1997 when the two countries agreed to resume negotiations on a long-term fisheries accord. Moreover, in late 1997 President Menem was invited to make an official visit to the United Kingdom during 1998.

In late 1996 the Argentine Government suggested, for the first time, that it might consider shared sovereignty of the Falkland Islands with the United Kingdom. The proposal was firmly rejected by the British Government and by the Falkland Islanders, who reiterated their commitment to persuading the UN Special Political and Decolonization Committee to adopt a clause allowing the Islanders the right to self-determination.

In March 1991 the Presidents of Argentina, Brazil, Paraguay and Uruguay signed the Asunción treaty in Paraguay. Under the terms of the treaty, the four Presidents confirmed their commitment to the creation of a Southern Common Market, Mercosur (Mercado Común del Sur), by the end of 1994. Mercosur duly came into effect on 1 January 1995, following the signing, by the Presidents of the four member nations, of the Ouro Prêto Protocol, in Brazil, in December 1994. While a complete common external tariff was not expected until 2006, customs barriers on 80%–85% of mutually exchanged goods were removed immediately.

Relations with Brazil deteriorated in August 1997 when President Menem publicly criticized Brazil's request to be allocated a permanent seat on the UN Security Council, arguing that it would lead to a regional imbalance. However, the two countries subsequently settled their dispute by agreeing to request that Latin American countries be granted more than one permanent seat on the Security Council. Meanwhile, during a visit to Argentina in October, President Bill Clinton of the USA confirmed that he had asked the US Congress to declare Argentina a 'special non-NATO ally', which would afford Argentina privileged access to US surplus defence supplies and certain military funding.

In late 1996 a criminal investigation was begun in Spain regarding the torture, disappearance and killing of several hundred Spanish citizens in Argentina during 1976–83. A parallel investigation was instigated into the abduction of 54 children of Spanish victims during this period. In October 1997 Adolfo Scilingo, a former Argentine military official, was arrested in Madrid, Spain, after admitting to his involvement in the 'dirty war'. During that year a Spanish High Court judge issued international arrest warrants for several other Argentine officers, including Adm. Massera and Gen. Galtieri.

Government

For administrative purposes Argentina comprises 1,617 municipalities located in 22 provinces, the Federal District of Buenos Aires, and the National Territory of Tierra del Fuego.

Legislative power is vested in the bicameral Congress (Congreso): the Chamber of Deputies (Cámara de Diputados) has 257 members, elected by universal adult suffrage for a term of four years (with approximately one-half of the seats renewable every two years). In accordance with the amended Constitution, promulgated in August 1994, beginning in 1995 legislative elections will provide for an expanded Senate (Senado), with three members from each of the 22 provinces, the Federal District of Buenos Aires and the National Territory of Tierra del Fuego, with a reduced, six-year term of office, while the President will be directly elected for a four-year term, renewable once. Each province has its own elected Governor and legislature, concerned with all matters not delegated to the Federal Government.

Defence

Conscription was ended on 1 April 1995. The total strength of the regular armed forces in August 1997 was estimated at 73,000, comprising a 41,000-strong army with a further 375,000 trained reservists, a 20,000-strong navy and an air force of 12,000 men. There were also paramilitary forces numbering 31,240 men. Budget forecasts for 1998 envisaged defence expenditure of 4,900m. new pesos.

Economic Affairs

In 1995, according to estimates by the World Bank, Argentina's gross national product (GNP), measured at average 1993–95 prices, was US $278,431m., equivalent to $8,030 per head. During 1985–95, it was estimated, GNP per head increased, in real terms, at an average annual rate of 1.9%. Over the same period, Argentina's population increased by an annual average of 1.3%. The country's gross domestic product (GDP) increased, in real terms, by an annual average of 5.7% during 1990–95. Real GDP declined by 4.6% in 1995, but increased by an estimated 4.3% in 1996.

Agriculture (including forestry and fishing) contributed 6% of GDP in 1995 and employed an estimated 10.8% of the labour force in 1996. The principal cash crops are wheat, maize, sorghum and soybeans. Beef production is also important. During 1990–95 agricultural GDP increased by an annual average of 0.5%.

Industry (including mining, manufacturing, construction and power) engaged 25.3% of the employed labour force in 1991 and provided 31% of GDP in 1995. During 1990–95 industrial GDP increased, in real terms, by an estimated annual average of 5.9%, but in 1995 it declined by an estimated 6%.

Mining contributed 1.8% of GDP in 1992, and employed 0.4% of the working population in 1991. Argentina has substantial deposits of petroleum and natural gas, as well as steam coal and lignite. In early 1995 preliminary construction work began on the country's largest ever mining project. The Bajo de la Alumbrera open-pit gold and copper mine was expected to be fully operational in 1997. The GDP of the mining sector increased, in real terms, at an average rate of 2.4% per year during 1985–92.

Manufacturing contributed 20.0% of GDP in 1994, and employed 17.3% of the working population in 1991. In 1993 the most important branches of manufacturing, measured by gross value of output, were food products and beverages (accounting for 26.4% of the total), chemical products (10.5%), transport equipment (9.9%) and petroleum refineries. During 1985–95 manufacturing GDP increased, in real terms, by an estimated annual average of 1.4%. Manufacturing output declined by 6.9% in 1995, but increased by 5.7% in 1996.

Energy is derived principally from hydroelectric power (responsible for the production of 42.7% of total electricity in 1995) and coal. In 1996 11.4% of Argentina's total energy requirements were produced by its two nuclear power stations. In 1995 imports of mineral fuels comprised 3.3% of the country's total energy requirements.

Services engaged 62.7% of the employed labour force in 1991 and accounted for 63% of GDP in 1995. The combined GDP of the service sectors increased, in real terms, at an estimated average rate of 6.4% per year during 1990–95.

In 1996 Argentina recorded a visible trade surplus of US $1,612m., although there was a deficit of $4,013m. on the current account of the balance of payments. In 1995 the principal source of imports (20.9%) was the USA, just ahead of Brazil (20.7%), which was the principal market for exports (26.2%). Other major trading partners in 1995 were Italy, Chile, Germany, Spain, the Netherlands and France. The principal exports in 1995 were petroleum and petroleum products, vegetable fats and oils, cereals, chemicals and related products, prepared animal fodder, and meat and meat preparations. The principal imports were machinery and transport equipment (particularly road vehicles and parts), chemical and mineral products, and basic manufactures.

In 1994 there was a budget deficit of 1,885.7m. new Argentine pesos, equivalent to 0.7% of GDP. Argentina's total external debt was US $89,747m. at the end of 1995, of which $62,181m. was long-term public debt. In that year the total cost of debt-servicing was equivalent to 34.7% of revenue from exports of goods and services. The annual rate of inflation averaged 32.2% in 1990–95, although consumer prices increased by an annual average of only 0.2% in 1996. An estimated 20.2% of the labour force in Gran Buenos Aires were unemployed in May 1995 and record national unemployment of 18.6% (equivalent to 2.2m. workers) was reported in the same month. By May 1997, however, national unemployment had declined to 16.1%.

During 1986–90 Argentina signed a series of integration treaties with neighbouring Latin American countries, aimed at increasing bilateral trade and establishing the basis for a Latin American economic community. Argentina is a member of ALADI (see p. 261) and of Mercosur (see p. 239).

Economic growth in Argentina in the 1980s was hampered primarily by massive external debt obligations, limited access to financial aid and a scarcity of raw materials. In 1989, however, the IMF approved a stand-by loan of US $1,400m. in recognition of the austerity measures adopted under the Menem administration. Further deregulation of the economy, and the success of new economic measures introduced by the Government in the early 1990s (including a programme of privatization), drastically reduced inflation and helped to secure agreements to reschedule debt repayments and the disbursement of loans from international financial organizations. Attempts to support the Argentine peso in the aftermath of the collapse of the Mexican currency in early 1995 imposed severe restrictions on public expenditure, which, together with a dramatic rise in the rate of unemployment, led to widespread social unrest. Real GDP declined by 4.6% in 1995, but in 1996 (in which year the IMF approved a stand-by loan of $1,041m.) economic growth of 4.3% was recorded. A considerable increase in investment (notably in the agricultural and mining sectors) was expected to contribute to strong economic growth in 1997; however, despite a record cereals harvest and a rise in the volume of exports, the trade deficit widened during that year, largely owing to a surge in imports and low international prices for petroleum and other primary products. Meanwhile, government priorities for the late 1990s included eliminating the fiscal deficit, improving the quality of public expenditure and reducing the level of unemployment, which had provoked further social unrest in 1996–97.

Social Welfare

Social welfare benefits comprise three categories: retirement, disability and survivors' pensions; family allowances; and health insurance. The first is administered by the Administración Nacional de Seguridad Social (part of the Ministry of Labour and Social Security) and funded by compulsory contributions from all workers, employed and self-employed, over 18 years of age. The second is supervised by the Administración Nacional de Seguridad Social and funded by employers. The third is administered by the Administración Nacional del Seguro de Salud, by means of public funds, and may be provided only by authorized public institutions. Work insurance is the responsibility of the employer. In 1993 the Government approved reforms to the pension system, which offered contributors a choice between privately-managed and state-operated schemes. In the case of privately-managed pension funds (Administradoras de Fondos de Jubilación y Pensión—AFJPs), employees set aside 11% of their monthly salaries, 7.5% of which goes toward retirement. On retirement (at 65 years of age for men and 60 years of age for women), employees can use these funds to purchase an annuity from an insurance company or begin to withdraw funds at a specified monthly rate. Pension managers are required to maintain sufficient reserves to honour a minimum pension guaranteed by the Government. AFJPs are monitored by a government supervisory body. There is considerable foreign participation in the management of the AFJPs and the country's three most successful funds, Consolidar, Máxima and Siembra, have strong links with Dresdner Bank AG, Deutsche Bank AG and Citibank NA, respectively. Government expenditure on social welfare in 1992 was 13,826.2m. new Argentine pesos. Budget forecasts for 1994 envisaged increases in expenditure on health and social security of 3.7% and 1.9% respectively.

In 1984 there were 80,100 physicians working in Argentina, equivalent to 27 for every 10,000 inhabitants: the best doctor-patient ratio of any country in Latin America. In 1995 there were 155,822 hospital beds in Argentina.

Education

Education from pre-school to university level is available free of charge. Education is officially compulsory for all children at primary level, between the ages of six and 14 years. Secondary education lasts for between five and seven years, depending on the type of course: the normal certificate of education (bachillerato) course lasts for five years, whereas a course leading to a technical or agricultural bachillerato lasts for six years. Technical education is supervised by the Consejo Nacional de Educación Técnica. The total enrolment at primary and secondary schools in 1996 was estimated at 99.4% and 67.2% of the school-age population, respectively. Non-university higher education, usually leading to a teaching qualification, is for three or four years, while university courses last for four years or more. There are 36 state universities and 48 private universities. Expenditure on education by all levels of government in 1994 was 10,471m. pesos (14.0% of total public expenditure).

According to estimates by UNESCO, the average rate of adult illiteracy in 1995 was only 3.8%.

Public Holidays

1998: 1 January (New Year's Day), 10 April (Good Friday), 1 May (Labour Day), 25 May (Anniversary of the 1810 Revolution), 8 June (for Occupation of the Islas Malvinas), 22 June (for Flag Day), 9 July (Independence Day), 17 August (Death of Gen. José de San Martín), 12 October (Columbus Day), 25 December (Christmas).

1999: 1 January (New Year's Day), 2 April (Good Friday), 1 May (Labour Day), 25 May (Anniversary of the 1810 Revolution), 14 June (for Occupation of the Islas Malvinas), 21 June (for Flag Day), 9 July (Independence Day), 16 August (for Death of Gen. José de San Martín), 11 October (for Columbus Day), 25 December (Christmas).

Weights and Measures

The metric system is in force.

Statistical Survey

Sources (unless otherwise stated): Instituto Nacional de Estadística y Censos, Avda Julio A. Roca 609, 1067 Buenos Aires; tel. (1) 349-9652; fax (1) 349-9621; e-mail ces@indec.mecon.ar; internet http://www.indec.mecon.ar; and Banco Central de la República Argentina, Reconquista 266, 1003 Buenos Aires; tel. (1) 394-8111; telex 1137; fax (1) 334-5712.

Area and Population

AREA, POPULATION AND DENSITY

Area (sq km)	2,780,400*
Population (census results)†	
22 October 1980	27,949,480
15 May 1991	
Males	15,937,980
Females	16,677,548
Total	32,615,528
Population (official estimates at mid-year)	
1994	34,320,000
1995	34,768,455
1996	35,220,000
Density (per sq km) at mid-1996	12.7

* 1,073,518 sq miles. The figure excludes the Falkland Islands (Islas Malvinas) and Antarctic territory claimed by Argentina.

† Figures exclude adjustment for underenumeration, estimated to have been 1% at the 1980 census and 0.9% at the 1991 census.

PROVINCES (census of 15 May 1991)

	Area (sg km)	Population*	Density (per sq km)	Capital
Buenos Aires—Federal District	200	2,965,403	14,827.0	
Buenos Aires—Province	307,571	12,594,974	40.9	La Plata
Catamarca	102,602	264,234	2.6	San Fernando del Valle de Catamarca
Chaco	99,633	839,677	8.4	Resistencia
Chubut	224,686	357,189	1.6	Rawson
Córdoba	165,321	2,766,683	16.7	Córdoba
Corrientes	88,199	795,594	9.0	Corrientes
Entre Ríos	78,781	1,020,257	13.0	Paraná
Formosa	72,066	398,413	5.5	Formosa
Jujuy	53,219	512,329	9.6	San Salvador de Jujuy
La Pampa	143,440	259,996	1.8	Santa Rosa
La Rioja	89,680	220,729	2.5	La Rioja
Mendoza	148,827	1,412,481	9.5	Mendoza
Misiones	29,801	788,915	26.5	Posadas
Neuquén	94,078	388,833	4.1	Neuquén
Río Negro	203,013	506,772	2.5	Viedma
Salta	155,488	866,153	5.6	Salta
San Juan	89,651	528,715	5.9	San Juan
San Luis	76,748	286,458	3.7	San Luis
Santa Cruz	243,943	159,839	0.7	Río Gallegos
Santa Fe	133,007	2,798,422	21.0	Santa Fe
Santiago del Estero	136,351	671,988	4.9	Santiago del Estero
Tucumán	22,524	1,142,105	50.7	San Miguel de Tucumán
Territory				
Tierra del Fuego	21,571	69,369	3.2	Ushuaia
Total	2,780,400	32,615,528	11.7	Buenos Aires

* Excluding adjustment for underenumeration.

PRINCIPAL TOWNS (provisional population, census of 15 May 1991)

Buenos Aires (capital)	2,960,976*	Corrientes	257,766
Córdoba	1,148,305	Bahía Blanca	255,145
La Matanza	1,111,811	Resistencia	228,199
Rosario	894,645	Paraná	206,848
Morón	641,541	Posadas	201,943
Lomas de Zamora	572,769	Santiago del Estero	189,490
La Plata	520,647	San Salvador de Jujuy	181,318
Mar del Plata	519,707	Neuquén	167,078
Quilmes	509,445	Formosa	153,855
San Miguel de Tucumán	470,604	San Fernando	141,496
Lanús	466,755	Río Cuarto	133,741
General San Martín	407,506	Comodoro Rivadavia	123,672
Salta	367,099	Mendoza	121,739
Avellaneda	346,620	San Juan	119,492
Santa Fe	342,796	Concordia	116,491
San Isidro	299,022	San Nicolás	114,752
Vicente López	289,142	San Fernando del Valle de Catamarca	110,269

* Figure for urban agglomeration: 10,686,163.

BIRTHS AND DEATHS

	Registered live births		Registered deaths	
	Number	Rate (per 1,000)	Number	Rate (per 1,000)
1988	680,605	21.6	254,953	8.1
1989	667,058	20.9	252,302	7.9
1990	678,644	21.0	259,683	8.0
1991	694,776	21.1	255,609	7.8
1992	678,761	20.3	262,287	7.9
1993	667,518	19.8	267,286	7.9
1994	707,869	20.7	260,245	7.6
1995	658,735	18.9	268,997	7.7

Marriages: 186,337 (marriage rate 5.7 per 1,000) in 1990; 158,805 (provisional figure—marriage rate 4.6 per 1,000) in 1995.

Source: mainly UN, *Demographic Yearbook* and *Population and Vital Statistics Report*.

Expectation of life (UN estimates, years at birth, 1990–95): 72.1 (males 68.6; females 75.7). Source: UN, *World Population Prospects: The 1994 Revision*.

ECONOMICALLY ACTIVE POPULATION
(persons aged 14 years and over, census of 15 May 1991)

	Males	Females	Total
Agriculture, hunting, forestry and fishing	1,142,674	222,196	1,364,870
Mining and quarrying	43,905	3,525	47,430
Manufacturing	1,590,713	546,090	2,136,803
Electricity, gas and water	92,469	11,318	103,787
Construction	818,831	17,617	836,448
Wholesale and retail trade, restaurants and hotels	1,730,600	808,702	2,539,302
Transport, storage and communication	583,938	54,024	637,962
Finance, insurance, real estate and business services	432,264	222,757	655,021
Community, social and personal services	1,459,492	2,464,552	3,924,044
Activities not adequately described	81,013	41,648	122,661
Total employed	7,975,899	4,392,429	12,368,328
Unemployed	447,488	386,384	833,872
Total labour force	8,423,387	4,778,813	13,202,200

1995 (provisional figures, sample survey, persons aged 15 years and over): Total active population 14,345,171 (males 9,087,075; females 5,258,096) (Source: ILO, *Yearbook of Labour Statistics*).

Mid-1996 (estimates in '000): Agriculture, etc. 1,497; Total labour force 13,829 (Source: FAO, *Production Yearbook*).

Agriculture

PRINCIPAL CROPS ('000 metric tons)

	1994	1995	1996
Wheat	11,306	9,185	15,200
Rice (paddy)	608	926	974
Barley	344	386	411
Maize	10,360	11,404	10,466
Rye	54	40	39
Oats	357	260	259
Millet	53	65	45
Sorghum	2,148	1,649	2,132
Potatoes	2,366	1,914	2,000*
Sweet potatoes	371	336	340
Cassava (Manioc)	150	160	160*
Dry beans	198	238	224
Other pulses	84	57	57
Soybeans	11,720	12,134	12,654
Groundnuts (in shell)	299†	339†	464
Sunflower seed	4,095	5,604	5,300
Linseed	152	151	80*
Cottonseed	338	619	729
Cotton (lint)	230	367	432
Olives	77	89	92
Tomatoes	790	920	740
Pumpkins, squash and gourds	420	415	400*
Onions (dry)	458	491	460*
Carrots	205	210*	210*
Watermelons*	129	130	130
Grapes	2,497	2,855	2,728
Sugar cane*	15,500	17,400	17,600
Apples	1,070	937	1,147†
Pears	365	320	513†
Peaches and nectarines	244	199	159†
Oranges	747	788	759
Tangerines, mandarins, clementines and satsumas	422	385	462
Lemons and limes	681	729	713
Grapefruit and pomelos	229	204	203
Bananas	142	171	170*
Tea (made)	50	42	40
Tobacco (leaves)	82	79	98

* FAO estimate(s). † Unofficial figure.

Source: FAO, *Production Yearbook*.

LIVESTOCK ('000 head, year ending September)

	1994	1995	1996
Horses*	3,300	3,300	3,300
Cattle	53,157	52,649	54,000
Pigs	3,300	3,100	3,100
Sheep	23,500†	21,626†	17,000
Goats	3,978	3,547	4,000*

Chickens (million)*: 51 in 1994; 55 in 1995; 64 in 1996.
Ducks (million)*: 2 in 1994; 2 in 1995; 2 in 1996.
Turkeys (million)*: 3 in 1994; 3 in 1995; 3 in 1996.

* FAO estimate(s). † Unofficial figure.

Source: FAO, *Production Yearbook*.

LIVESTOCK PRODUCTS ('000 metric tons)

	1994	1995	1996
Beef and veal	2,484	2,453	2,471
Mutton and lamb	85	81	64
Goat meat*	8	7	7
Pig meat	181	163	184
Horse meat*	50	50	50
Poultry meat	566	608	641
Cows' milk	8,018	8,792	9,176†
Butter	43	51	50†
Cheese	385	405	370†
Hen eggs	249	270	270*
Wool:			
greasy	88	80	70*
scoured	48†	44†	39*
Cattle hides (fresh)*	356	348	350

* FAO estimate(s). †Unofficial figure.

Source: FAO, *Production Yearbook*.

Forestry

ROUNDWOOD REMOVALS ('000 cubic metres, excl. bark)

	1992	1993	1994*
Sawlogs, veneer logs and logs for sleepers	3,446	2,393	2,393
Pulpwood	3,536	3,145	3,145
Other industrial wood	595	323	323
Fuel wood	4,288	5,822	5,822
Total	11,865	11,683	11,683

* FAO estimates.

Source: FAO, *Yearbook of Forest Products*.

SAWNWOOD PRODUCTION
('000 cubic metres, incl. railway sleepers)

	1992	1993	1994*
Coniferous (softwood)	309	360	360
Broadleaved (hardwood)	1,163	638	638
Total	1,472	998	998

* FAO estimates.

Source: FAO, *Yearbook of Forest Products*.

Fishing

('000 metric tons, live weight)

	1993	1994	1995
Freshwater fishes	11.8	11.8	11.8
Southern blue whiting	109.8	86.1	104.2
Argentine hake	422.2	435.8	574.3
Other marine fishes	174.4	195.8	247.7
Crustaceans	18.4	21.4	7.8
Argentine shortfin squid	193.7	196.9	199.0
Other molluscs	1.9	1.7	3.9
Total catch	932.2	949.5	1,148.8
Inland waters	12.7	12.8	13.3
Atlantic Ocean	919.5	936.6	1,135.5

Source: FAO, *Yearbook of Fishery Statistics.*

1996 (estimate): Total catch 1,225,958 metric tons.

Mining

('000 metric tons, unless otherwise indicated)

	1992	1993	1994
Hard coal	215	167	348
Crude petroleum	28,617	30,485	34,278
Natural gas ('000 terajoules)	899*	925	996
Iron ore†	2.5	1.4	28.2
Lead ore†	18.0	11.8	10.0
Zinc ore†	41.0	31.4	26.9
Silver ore (metric tons)	45.4	42.7	38.0
Uranium ore (metric tons)†	123	126	79
Gold ore (kilograms)†	1,106	937	899

* Estimate.

† Figures refer to the metal content of ores and concentrates.

Source: mainly UN, *Industrial Commodity Statistics Yearbook.*

1995 (estimates, '000 metric tons, unless otherwise stated): Crude petroleum ('000 cu metres) 41,739; Natural gas (million cu metres) 30,467; Zinc ore 32.1; Iron ore 0.3; Gold ore (kilograms) 837; Silver ore (metric tons) 47.8; Lead ore 10.5; Uranium ore (metric tons) 68.

1996 (estimates, '000 metric tons, unless otherwise stated): Crude petroleum ('000 cu metres) 45,549; Natural gas (million cu metres) 34,650; Zinc ore 31.1; Gold ore (kilograms) 723; Silver ore (metric tons) 50.4; Lead ore 11.3; Uranium ore (metric tons) 27.

Industry

SELECTED PRODUCTS ('000 metric tons, unless otherwise indicated)

	1992	1993	1994
Wheat flour	3,118	3,137	3,291
Beer ('000 hectolitres)	9,518	10,305	11,293
Cigarettes (million units)	1,845	1,929	1,975
Paper and paper products	977	927	970
Wood pulp, sulphate and soda	379	515*	554*
Non-cellulosic continuous fibres†	32.0	34.9	37.0
Sulphuric acid	219	206	199
Rubber tyres for motor vehicles ('000)	5,628	6,243	7,329
Portland cement	5,051	5,647	6,306
Distillate fuel oils	9,401	9,502	8,793
Residual fuel oils	3,370	3,089	2,748
Motor spirit (petrol)	670†	811	986
Kerosene	465†	357	346
Liquefied petroleum gas:			
from natural gas plants	813	913	681
from petroleum refineries	816	752	869
Passenger motor vehicles ('000 units)	221	287	338
Refrigerators ('000 units)	554	688	494
Washing machines	756	801	702
Television receivers ('000)	1,386	1,612	1,523‡
Electric energy (million kWh)	56,273†	62,530	66,196†

* FAO estimate.

† Provisional figure(s).

‡ Source: UN Economic Commission for Latin America and the Caribbean.

Source: mainly UN, *Industrial Commodity Statistics Yearbook.*

1995 ('000 metric tons, unless otherwise indicated): Wheat flour 3,240; Beer ('000 hectolitres) 10,422; Cigarettes (million units) 1,963; Paper and paper products 1,021; Sulphuric acid 226; Rubber tyres for motor vehicles ('000) 7,174; Portland cement 5,477; Television receivers ('000) 949; Refrigerators ('000 units) 389; Washing machines ('000 units) 458; Passenger motor vehicles ('000 units) 227.

1996 ('000 metric tons, unless otherwise indicated): Wheat flour 3,481*; Beer ('000 hectolitres) 10,286; Cigarettes (million units) 1,971; Paper and paper products 1,123*; Sulphuric acid 220*; Rubber tyres for motor vehicles ('000) 7,593; Portland cement 5,117; Television receivers ('000) 1,089; Washing machines ('000 units) 524; Passenger motor vehicles ('000 units) 269.

* Provisional figure.

Finance

CURRENCY AND EXCHANGE RATES

Monetary Units:

100 centavos = 1 nuevo peso argentino (new Argentine peso).

Sterling and Dollar Equivalents (30 September 1997)

£1 sterling = 1.6146 nuevos pesos;
US $1 = 99.95 centavos;
100 nuevos pesos = £61.94 = $100.05.

Average Exchange Rate (pesos argentinos per US $)

1994 0.99901
1995 0.99975
1996 0.99966

Note: The nuevo peso argentino was introduced on 1 January 1992, replacing the austral at a rate of 1 nuevo peso = 10,000 australes. The austral had been introduced on 15 June 1985, replacing the peso argentino at the rate of 1 austral = 1,000 pesos argentinos. The peso argentino, equal to 10,000 former pesos, had itself been introduced on 1 June 1983. Some figures in this survey may be in terms of australes.

BUDGET ('000 million australes)*

Revenue	1990	1991	1992
Taxation	64,559	180,294	257,431
Taxes on income, profits, etc.	1,712	4,519	8,409
Social security contributions	31,121	89,696	131,694
Taxes on property	3,581	8,610	6,860
Domestic taxes on goods and services	14,187	50,050	78,952
Value-added tax	6,895	24,941	54,971
Excises	6,733	23,452	21,851
Taxes on international trade and transactions	10,181	15,908	21,772
Import duties	1,659	5,992	14,493
Export duties	5,994	2,966	1,334
Property income	1,386	8,829	8,428
Administrative fees and charges, etc.	1,342	6,638	7,869
Other current revenue	4,306	6,159	4,598
Capital revenue	3,002	16,763	21,736
Total revenue	74,595	218,683	300,062

Expenditure†	1990	1991	1992
General public services	5,417	16,003	21,081
Defence	4,975	14,498	17,961
Public order and safety	3,814	12,500	15,977
Education	6,815	19,182	12,887
Health	2,059	5,040	5,424
Social security and welfare	33,387	91,680	138,262
Housing and community amenities	263	569	656
Recreational, cultural and religious affairs and services	288	621	1,019
Economic affairs and services	9,235	23,153	32,220
Agriculture, forestry and fishing	581	1,921	3,233
Fuel and energy	1,788	5,304	10,771
Transportation and communication	4,095	9,784	11,968
Mining, manufacturing and construction	928	2,084	2,077
Other purposes	6,683	23,526	27,406
Interest payments	6,159	22,402	26,218
Sub-total	72,936	206,772	272,893
Adjustment to cash basis	–110	–286	–176
Total expenditure	72,826	206,486	272,717
Current	69,451	201,219	264,463
Capital	3,375	5,267	8,254

* Budget figures refer to the consolidated accounts of the central Government, including special accounts, government agencies and the national social security system. The budgets of provincial and municipal governments are excluded.

† Excluding net lending ('000 million australes): 4,222 in 1990; 11,824 in 1991; 14,280 in 1992.

Source: IMF, *Government Finance Statistics Yearbook.*

INTERNATIONAL RESERVES (US $ million at 31 December)

	1994	1995	1996
Gold*	1,651	1,679	1,611
IMF special drawing rights	563	539	399
Foreign exchange	13,764	13,749	17,705
Total	15,978	15,967	19,715

* Valued at US $377 per troy ounce in 1994, at $384 per ounce in 1995 and at $368 per ounce in 1996.

Source: IMF, *International Financial Statistics.*

MONEY SUPPLY (million new pesos at 31 December)

	1994	1995	1996
Currency outside banks	11,229	11,162	11,758
Demand deposits at commercial banks	5,133	5,471	7,318
Total money	16,362	16,633	19,076

Source: IMF, *International Financial Statistics.*

COST OF LIVING (Consumer Price Index for Buenos Aires metropolitan area; annual averages; base: 1988 = 100)

	1994	1995	1996
Food	270,038	277,693	276,443
Clothing	192,512	188,651	181,480
Housing	309,091	324,517	325,439
All items (incl. others)	310,967	321,465	321,966

NATIONAL ACCOUNTS (million new pesos at current prices)

Expenditure on the Gross Domestic Product

	1994	1995	1996
Final consumption expenditure	232,557	229,018	245,704
Gross capital formation	56,256	50,429	52,426
Total domestic expenditure	288,813	279,447	298,130
Exports of goods and services	18,919	24,247	27,491
Less Imports of goods and services	26,087	24,152	28,262
GDP in purchasers' values	281,645	279,543	297,359
GDP at constant 1990 prices	96,864	92,428	96,363

Source: IMF, *International Financial Statistics.*

Gross Domestic Product by Economic Activity

	1990	1991	1992
Agriculture, forestry and fishing	5,599	12,420	13,577
Mining and quarrying	1,972	3,733	4,067
Manufacturing	18,464	44,115	49,541
Electricity, gas and water	1,328	2,924	3,826
Construction	3,064	8,422	12,107
Trade, restaurants and hotels	10,750	28,725	34,929
Transport and communications	3,614	9,429	11,719
Finance, insurance, real estate and business services	10,239	27,675	38,133
Community, social and personal services	14,679	44,876	59,022
Sub-total	69,709	182,050	226,921
Less imputed bank service charge	786	1,152	283
GDP in purchasers' values	68,922	180,898	226,638

Source: UN, *National Accounts Statistics.*

BALANCE OF PAYMENTS (US $ million)

	1994	1995	1996
Exports of goods f.o.b.	15,840	20,964	23,774
Imports of goods f.o.b.	–20,078	–18,726	–22,162
Trade balance	–4,238	2,238	1,612
Exports of services	2,669	2,924	3,302
Imports of services	–5,529	–5,099	–5,738
Balance on goods and services	–7,098	63	–824
Other income received	3,099	4,423	4,628
Other income paid	–6,297	–7,364	–8,151
Balance on goods, services and income	–10,296	–2,878	–4,347
Current transfers received	541	542	429
Current transfers paid	–223	–110	–95
Current balance	–9,978	–2,446	–4,013
Direct investment abroad	–127	–155	–205
Direct investment from abroad	3,068	4,181	4,285
Portfolio investment assets	–185	64	–1,296
Portfolio investment liabilities	4,772	5,069	11,808
Other investment assets	530	–13,250	–7,589
Other investment liabilities	1,115	4,347	426
Net errors and omissions	–16	12	–8
Overall balance	–821	–2,178	3,408

Source: IMF, *International Financial Statistics.*

External Trade

PRINCIPAL COMMODITIES (distribution by SITC, US $ '000)

Imports c.i.f.	1993	1994	1995
Food and live animals	792,386	992,607	969,714
Crude materials (inedible) except fuels	540,243	591,619	714,088
Mineral fuels, lubricants, etc.	410,621	645,657	859,003
Petroleum, petroleum products, etc.	273,393	487,133	623,960
Refined petroleum products	230,181	382,372	475,807
Chemicals and related products	2,299,714	2,933,092	3,482,325
Organic chemicals	679,783	866,994	1,053,378
Medicinal and pharmaceutical products	356,371	495,061	488,826
Artificial resins, plastic materials, etc.	446,934	535,438	679,265
Products of polymerization, etc.	295,188	337,577	426,948
Basic manufactures	2,284,408	2,854,621	3,023,691
Paper, paperboard and manufactures	450,844	524,493	665,675
Textile yarn, fabrics, etc.	444,106	485,520	428,685
Iron and steel	368,755	487,569	514,292
Machinery and transport equipment	8,439,424	11,188,152	8,930,586
Power-generating machinery and equipment	533,023	660,762	767,264
Machinery specialized for particular industries	931,568	1,132,190	814,516
General industrial machinery, equipment and parts	1,050,495	1,559,845	1,691,779
Office machines and automatic data-processing equipment	666,400	927,403	707,632
Automatic data-processing machines, etc.	482,350	670,504	469,076
Telecommunications and sound equipment	1,151,088	1,495,055	1,028,653
Other electrical machinery, apparatus, etc.	1,332,950	1,504,753	1,338,292
Road vehicles and parts*	2,328,285	3,330,590	2,118,971
Passenger motor cars (excl. buses)	844,534	1,394,468	773,204
Motor vehicles for goods transport, etc.	264,650	558,680	310,998
Goods vehicles (lorries and trucks)	242,385	519,705	284,389
Parts and accessories for cars, buses, lorries, etc.*	876,185	968,052	867,733
Miscellaneous manufactured articles	1,873,078	2,236,232	1,996,847
Total (incl. others)	16,772,936	21,581,084	20,121,674

Exports f.o.b.	1993	1994	1995
Food and live animals	5,338,956	5,584,425	7,214,582
Meat and meat preparations	748,198	918,088	1,229,138
Fresh, chilled or frozen meat	472,591	627,906	848,098
Boneless meat (bovine)	327,903	470,400	653,341
Meat and edible meat offals, prepared or preserved	275,593	289,991	381,013
Fish and fish preparations	706,597	725,169	914,291
Fish, fresh (live or dead), chilled or frozen	302,256	365,653	501,564
Cereals and cereal preparations	1,536,630	1,456,331	2,017,775
Wheat (including spelt) and meslin, unmilled	734,865	669,979	1,005,372
Maize (corn), unmilled	525,341	491,845	682,289
Vegetables and fruit	594,487	699,238	1,034,940
Fruit and nuts, fresh or dried	237,191	275,728	444,813
Feeding-stuff for animals	1,451,123	1,348,966	1,254,639
Oilcake and other residues	1,401,727	1,301,788	1,196,120
Crude materials (inedible) except fuels	938,493	1,446,894	1,767,938
Oil seeds and oleaginous fruit	687,816	943,600	875,059
Soya beans	547,150	690,463	535,966
Textile fibres and waste	130,504	318,971	582,196
Cotton	26,509	179,153	437,489
Mineral fuels, lubricants, etc.	1,241,843	1,657,123	2,175,369
Petroleum, petroleum products, etc.	1,174,738	1,580,964	2,088,659
Crude petroleum	527,361	1,125,573	1,591,855
Refined petroleum products	606,179	413,556	435,540
Animal and vegetable oils, fats and waxes	1,063,123	1,518,934	2,077,340
Fixed vegetable oils and fats	1,048,045	1,498,542	2,043,852
Soya bean oil	599,590	859,437	942,993
Sunflower seed oil	355,579	546,835	973,681
Chemicals and related products	694,678	918,947	1,314,779
Basic manufactures	1,796,615	2,095,484	2,972,490
Leather, leather manufactures and dressed furskins	721,522	876,354	989,161
Leather	598,760	733,416	893,786
Iron and steel	432,468	467,998	731,961
Tubes, pipes and fittings	290,907	273,386	334,442
'Seamless' tubes and pipes	267,706	261,574	315,006
Machinery and transport equipment	1,443,895	1,770,733	2,275,227
Road vehicles and parts*	662,187	863,390	1,233,141
Parts and accessories for cars, buses, lorries, etc.*	369,747	456,722	546,161
Miscellaneous manufactured articles	429,793	642,324	889,997
Total (incl. others)	13,117,758	15,838,665	20,962,590

* Excluding tyres, engines and electrical parts.

Source: UN, *International Trade Statistics Yearbook*.

PRINCIPAL TRADING PARTNERS (US $ '000)

Imports c.i.f.	1993	1994	1995
Belgium-Luxembourg	331,610	591,830	231,440
Brazil	3,568,453	4,285,915	4,174,537
Canada	87,875	132,701	273,529
Chile	701,981	828,851	513,815
China, People's Republic	214,839	217,081	607,891
France (incl. Monaco)	738,662	1,072,187	1,040,038
Germany	1,023,548	1,382,413	1,250,648
Hong Kong	387,049	489,686	75,869
Italy	980,918	1,431,177	1,259,042
Japan	668,488	619,847	710,823
Korea, Republic	525,590	503,344	362,145
Mexico	235,489	260,723	376,424
Netherlands	224,821	352,064	210,807
Singapore	200,897	265,826	109,072
Spain	509,760	865,760	929,733
Sweden	116,120	168,283	252,633
Switzerland-Liechtenstein	164,060	177,854	236,078
United Kingdom	258,271	351,843	412,900
USA	3,858,597	4,928,321	4,206,624
Uruguay	570,815	789,099	279,283
Total (incl. others)	16,772,934	21,581,063	20,121,655

Exports f.o.b.	1993	1994	1995
Belgium-Luxembourg	165,391	153,274	237,457
Bolivia	177,989	192,372	254,024
Brazil	2,814,207	3,654,849	5,484,131
Chile	591,892	998,849	1,475,133
China, People's Republic	163,250	224,671	285,741
Colombia	112,832	123,210	233,408
Egypt	135,418	151,493	228,526
France (incl. Monaco)	208,341	215,621	318,513
Germany	625,144	605,481	649,865
Hong Kong	155,831	204,818	288,960
Iran	248,168	228,755	509,563
Italy	505,098	654,360	736,449
Japan	466,792	445,246	457,289
Malaysia	73,417	132,584	259,267
Mexico	219,392	273,672	144,380
Netherlands	1,270,067	1,179,560	1,191,261
Paraguay	357,800	498,494	631,378
Peru	222,246	288,602	275,578
South Africa*	80,481	184,762	339,970
Spain	504,437	592,399	714,048
United Kingdom	162,021	222,427	310,126
USA	1,276,829	1,719,400	1,803,421
Uruguay	511,960	649,841	653,724
Venezuela	229,096	211,197	377,736
Total (incl. others)	13,114,404	15,803,260	20,962,561

* Southern African Customs Union, also including Botswana, Lesotho, Namibia and Swaziland.

Source: UN, *International Trade Statistics Yearbook*.

Transport

RAILWAYS (traffic)

	1993	1994	1995
Passengers carried (million)*	216	248	349
Freight carried ('000 tons)*	9,259	13,174	15,197
Passenger-km (million)	5,836	6,460	n.a.
Freight ton-km (million)	4,477	6,613	7,613

1996*: Freight ton-km (million) 8,506.

* Source: Secretaría de Obras Públicas y Transporte.

ROAD TRAFFIC (motor vehicles in use)

	1993	1994	1995
Passenger cars	4,556,000	4,426,706	4,665,329
Commercial vehicles	n.a.	1,203,908	1,181,569

Source: Secretaría de Obras Públicas y Transporte.

SHIPPING

Merchant Fleet (registered at 31 December)

	1994	1995	1996
Number of vessels	468	471	480
Total displacement ('000 grt)	715.7	594.9	586.3

Source: Lloyd's Register of Shipping, *World Fleet Statistics*.

International Sea-borne Freight Traffic ('000 metric tons)

	1993	1994	1995
Goods loaded	38,032	40,025	48,538
Goods unloaded	10,831	14,202	15,146

Source: Secretaría de Obras Públicas y Transporte.

CIVIL AVIATION (scheduled airline traffic)

	1993	1994	1995
Passengers carried ('000)	6,191	6,359	6,798
Passenger-km (million)	9,272	11,305	12,190
Kilometres flown (million)	78	90	113
Freight ('000 metric tons)	120	123	109
Total ton-km (million)*	1,117	1,289	n.a.

Source: UN, *Statistical Yearbook*.

Source: Secretaría de Obras Públicas y Transporte.

Tourism

	1994	1995	1996
Tourist arrivals ('000)	3,866	4,101	4,286
Tourist receipts (million new pesos)	3,970	4,306	4,572

Source: Secretaría de Turismo de la Nación.

Communications Media

	1992	1993	1994
Radio receivers ('000 in use)	22,600	22,700	23,000
Television receivers ('000 in use)	7,300	7,420	7,500
Telephones* ('000 main lines in use)	3,682	4,092	4,834
Telefax stations* ('000 in use)	25	30	n.a.
Mobile cellular telephones* ('000 subscribers)	46.6	115.8	202.2
Daily newspapers	190	n.a.	187
Books (number of titles)	7,365	7,848	9,640

* Year ending September.

Sources: mainly UNESCO, *Statistical Yearbook*, and UN, *Statistical Yearbook*.

1995: Telephones ('000 main lines in use) 5,532; Mobile cellular telephones ('000 subscribers) 340.7; Books (number of titles) 9,511.

1996: Telephones ('000 main lines in use) 6,120; Mobile cellular telephones ('000 subscribers) 667.0; Books (number of titles) 9,913.

Education

(1996)

	Institutions*	Students	Teachers†
Pre-primary	14,064	1,116,951	65,708
Primary	27,146	5,250,329	295,488
Secondary	7,623	2,594,329	238,791
Universities‡	36	790,775*	n.a.
Colleges of higher education	1,795	391,778	43,921

* Provisional.

† 1994 figures.

‡ State universities only.

Source: Ministerio de Cultura y Educación.

Directory

The Constitution

The return to civilian rule in 1983 represented a return to the principles of the 1853 Constitution, with some changes in electoral details. In August 1994 a new Constitution was approved, which contained 19 new articles, 40 amendments to existing articles and the addition of a chapter on New Rights and Guarantees. The Constitution is summarized below:

DECLARATIONS, RIGHTS AND GUARANTEES

Each province has the right to exercise its own administration of justice, municipal system and primary education. The Roman Catholic religion, being the faith of the majority of the nation, shall enjoy state protection; freedom of religious belief is guaranteed to all other denominations. The prior ethnical existence of indigenous peoples and their rights, as well as the common ownership of lands they traditionally occupy, are recognized. All inhabitants of the country have the right to work and exercise any legal trade; to petition the authorities; to leave or enter the Argentine territory; to use or dispose of their properties; to associate for a peaceable or useful purpose; to teach and acquire education, and to express freely their opinion in the press without censorship. The State does not admit any prerogative of blood, birth, privilege or titles of nobility. Equality is the basis of all duties and public offices. No citizens may be detained, except for reasons and in the manner prescribed by the law; or sentenced other than by virtue of a law existing prior to the offence and by decision of the competent tribunal after the hearing and defence of the person concerned. Private residence, property and correspondence are inviolable. No one may enter the home of a citizen or carry out any search in it without his consent, unless by a warrant from the competent authority; no one may suffer expropriation, except in case of public necessity and provided that the appropriate compensation has been paid in accordance with the provisions of the laws. In no case may the penalty of confiscation of property be imposed.

LEGISLATIVE POWER

Legislative power is vested in the bicameral Congreso (Congress), comprising the Cámara de Diputados (Chamber of Deputies) and the Senado (Senate). The Chamber of Deputies has 257 directly-elected members, chosen for four years and eligible for re-election; approximately one-half of the membership of the Chamber shall be renewed every two years. Until October 1995 the Senate had 48 members, chosen by provincial legislatures for a nine-year term, with one-third of the seats renewable every three years. Since October 1995 elections have provided for a third senator, elected by provincial legislatures. By 2001 the members of the expanded Senate will henceforth serve a six-year term.

The powers of Congress include regulating foreign trade; fixing import and export duties; levying taxes for a specified time whenever the defence, common safety or general welfare of the State so requires; contracting loans on the nation's credit; regulating the internal and external debt and the currency system of the country; fixing the budget and facilitating the prosperity and welfare of the nation. Congress must approve required and urgent decrees and delegated legislation. Congress also approves or rejects treaties, authorizes the Executive to declare war or make peace, and establishes the strength of the Armed Forces in peace and war.

EXECUTIVE POWER

Executive power is vested in the President, who is the supreme head of the nation and controls the general administration of the country. The President issues the instructions and rulings necessary for the execution of the laws of the country, and himself takes part in drawing up and promulgating those laws. The President appoints, with the approval of the Senate, the judges of the Supreme Court and all other competent tribunals, ambassadors, civil servants, members of the judiciary and senior officers of the Armed Forces and bishops. The President may also appoint and remove, without reference to another body, his cabinet ministers. The President is Commander-in-Chief of all the Armed Forces. The President and Vice-President are elected directly for a four-year term, renewable only once.

JUDICIAL POWER

Judicial power is exercised by the Supreme Court and all other competent tribunals. The Supreme Court is responsible for the internal administration of all tribunals. In April 1990 the number of Supreme Court judges was increased from five to nine.

PROVINCIAL GOVERNMENT

The 22 provinces, the Federal District of Buenos Aires and the National Territory of Tierra del Fuego retain all the power not delegated to the Federal Government. They are governed by their own institutions and elect their own governors, legislators and officials.

The Government

HEAD OF STATE

President of the Republic: CARLOS SAÚL MENEM (took office 8 July 1989, re-elected 14 May 1995).

Vice-President of the Republic: CARLOS FEDERICO RUCKAUF.

CABINET
(December 1997)

Cabinet Chief: CARLOS FEDERICO RUCKAUF.

Minister of the Interior: CARLOS CORACH.

Minister of Foreign Affairs and Worship: GUIDO DI TELLA.

Minister of Education and Culture: SUSANA DECIBE.

Minister of Defence: JORGE DOMÍNGUEZ.

Minister of the Economy and Public Works: ROQUE BENJAMÍN FERNÁNDEZ.

Minister of Labour and Social Security: ANTONIO ERMAN GONZÁLEZ.

Minister of Health and Social Welfare: ALBERTO JOSÉ MAZZA.

Minister of Justice: RAÚL GRANILLO OCAMPO.

Secretary-General of the Presidency: ALBERTO KOHAN.

MINISTRIES

General Secretariat to the Presidency: Balcarce 50, 1064 Buenos Aires; tel. (1) 46-9841.

Ministry of Defence: Avda Paseo Colón 255, 9°, 1063 Buenos Aires; tel. (1) 343-1560; fax (1) 331-7745.

Ministry of the Economy and Public Works: Hipólito Yrigoyen 250, 1310 Buenos Aires; tel. (1) 342-6411; telex 21952; fax (1) 331-7426.

Ministry of Education and Culture: Pizzurno 935, 1020 Buenos Aires; tel. (1) 42-4551; telex 22646; fax (1) 812-8905.

Ministry of Foreign Affairs and Worship: Reconquista 1088, 1003 Buenos Aires; tel. (1) 311-0071; telex 27051; fax (1) 311-5730.

Ministry of Health and Social Welfare: 9 de Julio 1925, 1332 Buenos Aires; tel. (1) 381-8911; telex 25064; fax (1) 381-2182.

Ministry of the Interior: Balcarce 50, 1064 Buenos Aires; tel. (1) 46-9841; fax (1) 331-6376.

Ministry of Justice: Gelly y Obes 2289, 1425 Buenos Aires; tel. (1) 803-4051; fax (1) 803-3955.

Ministry of Labour and Social Security: Leandro N. Alem 650, 1001 Buenos Aires; tel. (1) 311-2913; telex 18007; fax (1) 312-7860.

President and Legislature

PRESIDENT

Election, 14 May 1995

Candidates	Votes	% votes cast
CARLOS SAÚL MENEM (PJ)	8,686,685	49.92
JOSÉ OCTAVIO BORDÓN (Frepaso)	5,095,974	29.29
HORACIO MASSACCESI (UCR)	2,956,101	16.99
Others	661,246	3.80
Total	17,400,006	100.00

CONGRESO

Cámara de Diputados
(Chamber of Deputies)

President: ALBERTO PIERRI.

The Chamber has 257 members, who hold office for a four-year term, with approximately one-half of the seats renewable every two years.

Legislative Elections, 26 October 1997*

	Seats
Partido Justicialista (PJ)	118
Unión Cívica Radical (UCR) / Frente del País Solidario (Frepaso)	110†
Others	29
Total	257

* The table indicates the distribution of the total number of seats, following the elections for 127 seats.

† In 1997 Frepaso and the UCR formed an electoral alliance, the Alianza para el Trabajo, la Justícia y la Educación, and presented joint lists in 13 of the 24 electoral districts.

Senado
(Senate)

President: EDUARDO MENEM.

Distribution of Seats, November 1997*

	Seats
Partido Justicialista (PJ)	36
Unión Cívica Radical (UCR)	15
Frente del País Solidario (Frepaso)	2
Provincial parties	10
Total	63

* Until October 1995 the Senate comprised 48 members, who were nominated by the legislative bodies of the Federal District, the National Territory, and each province (two Senators for each), with the exception of Buenos Aires, which elected its Senators by means of a special Electoral College. The Senate's term of office was nine years, with one-third of the seats renewable every three years. Since October 1995 elections have provided for an expanded Senate (three members from each region) with a six-year term of office. By November 1997 the Senate comprised 63 members; seven provinces had yet to nominate additional Senators.

PROVINCIAL ADMINISTRATORS
(December 1997)

Mayor of the Federal District of Buenos Aires: FERNANDO DE LA RÚA.

Governor of the Province of Buenos Aires: EDUARDO DUHALDE.

Governor of the Province of Catamarca: ARNOLDO CASTILLO.

Governor of the Province of Chaco: ANGEL ROZAS.

Governor of the Province of Chubut: CARLOS MAESTRO.

Governor of the Province of Córdoba: RAMÓN BAUTISTA MESTRE.

Governor of the Province of Corrientes: RAÚL ROMERO FERIS.

Governor of the Province of Entre Ríos: JORGE PEDRO BUSTI.

Governor of the Province of Formosa: GILDO INSFRÁN.

Governor of the Province of Jujuy: CARLOS FERRARO.

Governor of the Province of La Pampa: RUBÉN HUGO MARIN.

Governor of the Province of La Rioja: ANGEL MAZA.

Governor of the Province of Mendoza: ARTURO LAFALLA.

Governor of the Province of Misiones: FEDERICO RAMÓN PUERTA.

Governor of the Province of Neuquén: FELIPE SAPAG.

Governor of the Province of Río Negro: PABLO VERANI.

Governor of the Province of Salta: JUAN CARLOS ROMERO.

Governor of the Province of San Juan: JORGE ALBERTO ESCOBAR.

Governor of the Province of San Luis: ADOLFO RODRÍGUEZ SAA.

Governor of the Province of Santa Cruz: NÉSTOR KIRSCHNER.

Governor of the Province of Santa Fe: JORGE OBEID.

Governor of the Province of Santiago del Estero: CARLOS JUÁREZ.

Governor of the Province of Tucumán: ANTONIO BUSSI.

Governor of the Territory of Tierra del Fuego: JOSÉ ESTABILLO.

Political Organizations

Acción por la República–Nueva Dirigencia: Buenos Aires; f. 1997; electoral alliance; Leaders DOMINGO CAVALLO, GUSTAVO BÉLIZ.

Nueva Dirigencia (ND): Buenos Aires; f. 1996; centre-right; Leader GUSTAVO BÉLIZ.

Alianza para el Trabajo, la Justícia y la Educación (ATJE): Buenos Aires; f. 1997; electoral alliance comprising the UCR and Frepaso.

Frente del País Solidario (Frepaso): Buenos Aires; internet http://www.visit-ar.com/nuevoespacio/frepaso.htm; f. 1994; centre-left coalition of socialist communist and Christian Democrat groups; Leader CARLOS ÁLVAREZ.

Unión Cívica Radical (UCR): Buenos Aires; tel. (1) 49-0036; telex 21326; moderate; f. 1890; Pres. RODOLFO TERRAGNO; 1,410,000 mems.

Movimiento por la Dignidad y la Independencia (Modin): Buenos Aires; f. 1991; right-wing; Leader Col ALDO RICO.

Movimiento de Integración y Desarrollo (MID): Buenos Aires; f. 1963; Leader ARTURO FRONDIZI; 145,000 mems.

Movimiento al Socialismo (MAS): Chile 1362, 1098 Buenos Aires; tel. (1) 381-2718; fax (1) 381-2976; e-mail mas@giga.com.ar; Leaders RUBÉN VISCONTI, LUIS ZAMORA; 55,000 mems.

Partido Comunista de Argentina: Buenos Aires; f. 1918; Leader PATRICIO ECHEGARAY; Sec.-Gen. ATHOS FAVA; 76,000 mems.

Partido Demócrata Cristiano (PDC): Combate de los Pozos 1055, 1222 Buenos Aires; fax (1) 26-3413; f. 1954; Leader ESIO ARIEL SILVEIRA; 85,000 mems.

Partido Demócrata Progresista (PDP): Chile 1934, 1227 Buenos Aires; Leader RAFAEL MARTÍNEZ RAYMONDA; 97,000 mems.

Partido Intransigente: Buenos Aires; f. 1957; left-wing; Leaders Dr OSCAR ALENDE, LISANDRO VIALE; Sec. MARIANO LORENCES; 90,000 mems.

Partido Justicialista (PJ): Buenos Aires; Peronist party; f. 1945; Pres. CARLOS SAÚL MENEM; 3m. mems; three factions within party:

Frente Renovador, Justicia, Democracia y Participación—Frejudepa: f. 1985; reformist wing; Leaders CARLOS SAÚL MENEM, ANTONIO CAFIERO, CARLOS GROSSO.

Movimiento Nacional 17 de Octubre: Leader HERMINIO IGLESIAS.

Oficialistas: Leaders JOSÉ MARÍA VERNET, LORENZO MIGUEL.

Partido Nacional de Centro: Buenos Aires; f. 1980; conservative; Leader RAÚL RIVANERA CARLES.

Partido Nacionalista de los Trabajadores (PNT): Buenos Aires; f. 1990; extreme right-wing; Leader ALEJANDRO BIONDINI.

Partido Obrero: Ayacucho 444, Buenos Aires; tel. (1) 953-3824; fax (1) 953-7164; f. 1982; Trotskyist; Leaders JORGE ALTAMIRA, CHRISTIAN RATH; 61,000 mems.

Partido Popular Cristiano: Leader JOSÉ ANTONIO ALLENDE.

Partido Socialista Democrático: Rivadavia 2307, 1034 Buenos Aires; Leader AMÉRICO GHIOLDI; 39,000 mems.

Partido Socialista Popular: f. 1982; Leaders GUILLERMO ESTÉVEZ BOERO, EDGARDO ROSSI; 60,500 mems.

Política Abierta para la Integridad Social (PAIS): Buenos Aires; f. 1994 following split with the PJ.

Unión del Centro Democrático (UCeDé): Buenos Aires; f. 1980 as coalition of eight minor political organizations to challenge the 'domestic monopoly' of the populist movements; Leader ÁLVARO ALSOGARAY.

Unión para la Nueva Mayoría: Buenos Aires; f. 1986; centre-right; Leader JOSÉ ANTONIO ROMERO FERIS.

The following political parties and groupings contested the 1995 presidential elections: Alianza del Sur, Corriente Patria Libre, Frente para la Coincidencia Patriótica (Frecopa), Movimiento Democrático del Pueblo Antidemocrático (Modepa), Movimiento de Trabajadores Socialistas, Partido Humanista and the Partido Socialista Auténtico (PSA).

Other parties and groupings include: Afirmación Peronista, Alianza Socialista, Confederación Socialista Argentina, Cruzada Renovadora (San Juan), Frente Cívica y Socialista (Catamarca), Fuerza Republicana (Tucumán), Movimiento Línea Popular, Movimiento Patriótico de Liberación, Movimiento Peronista, Movimiento Popular Neuquino, Movimiento Popular (Tierra del Fuego), Partido Autonomista (Corrientes), Partido Bloquista de San Juan, Partido Conservador Popular, Partido Izquierda Nacional, Partido Liberal (Corrientes), Partido Obrero Comunista Marxista-Leninista, Partido Socialista Auténtico, Partido Socialista Unificado and Renovador de Salta.

The following political parties and guerrilla groups are illegal:

Intransigencia y Movilización Peronista: Peronist faction; Leader NILDA GARRES.

Movimiento Todos por la Patria (MTP): left-wing movement.

Partido Peronista Auténtico (PPA): f. 1975; Peronist faction; Leaders MARIO FIRMENICH, ÓSCAR BIDEGAIN, RICARDO OBREGÓN CANO.

Partido Revolucionario de Trabajadores: political wing of the **Ejército Revolucionario del Pueblo (ERP)**; Leader LUIS MATTINI.

Triple A—Alianza Anticomunista Argentina: extreme right-wing; Leader ANÍBAL GORDON (in prison).

Diplomatic Representation

EMBASSIES IN ARGENTINA

Algeria: Montevideo 1889, 1021 Buenos Aires; tel. (1) 815-1271; telex 22467; fax (1) 815-8837; Ambassador: ABDELKADER RASHI.

Armenia: Avda Roque S. Peña 570, 3°, 1035 Buenos Aires; tel. (1) 345-2051; fax (1) 343-2467; Ambassador: VAHAN TER-GHEVONDIAN.

Australia: Villanueva 1400, 1426 Buenos Aires; tel. (1) 777-6580; fax (1) 772-3349; Ambassador: WARWICK WEEMAES.

Austria: French 3671, 1425 Buenos Aires; tel. (1) 802-7195; fax (1) 805-4016; Ambassador: Dr WOLFGANG KRIECHBAUM.

Belgium: Defensa 113, 8°, 1065 Buenos Aires; tel. (1) 331-0066; telex 22070; fax (1) 311-0814; Ambassador: PAUL DUQUÉ.

Bolivia: Corrientes 545, 2°, 1043 Buenos Aires; tel. (1) 394-6042; telex 24362; Ambassador: AGUSTÍN SAAVEDRA WEISE.

Brazil: Arroyo 1142, 1007 Buenos Aires; tel. (1) 44-0035; telex 21158; fax (1) 814-4085; Ambassador: LUIZ FELIPE DE SEIXAS CORREA.

Bulgaria: Mariscal A. J. de Sucre 1568, 1428 Buenos Aires; tel. (1) 781-8644; telex 21314; fax (1) 786-6273; Ambassador: VASSILIY TAKEV.

Canada: Tagle 2828, 1425 Buenos Aires; tel. (1) 805-3032; telex 21383; fax (1) 806-1209; Ambassador: ROBERT ROCHON.

Central African Republic: Marcelo T. de Alvear 776, Edif. Charcas, Buenos Aires; tel. (1) 312-2051.

Chile: Tagle 2762, 1425 Buenos Aires; tel. (1) 802-7020; telex 21669; Ambassador: CARLOS FIGUEROA SERRANO.

China, People's Republic: Avda Crisólogo Larralde 5349, 1431 Buenos Aires; tel. (1) 543-8862; telex 22871; Ambassador: TANG YONGGUI.

Colombia: Carlos Pellegrini 1363, 3°, 1011 Buenos Aires; tel. (1) 325-0494; fax (1) 322-9370; Ambassador: VÍCTOR G. RICARDO.

Congo, Democratic Republic: Madero 2882, Buenos Aires; tel. (1) 792-9989; telex 22324; Ambassador: BADASSA-BAHADUKA.

Costa Rica: Uruguay 292, 14°G, 1015 Buenos Aires; tel. (1) 49-4731; telex 21394; Ambassador: FERNANDO SALAZAR NAVARRETE.

Cuba: Virrey del Pino 1820, 1426 Buenos Aires; tel. (1) 782-9049; fax (1) 786-7713; Ambassador: NICOLÁS RODRÍGUEZ ASTIAZARAÍN.

Czech Republic: Avda Figueroa Alcorta 3240, 1425 Buenos Aires; tel. (1) 801-3804; telex 22748.

Denmark: Avda Leandro N. Alem 1074, 9°, 1001 Buenos Aires; tel. (1) 312-6901; telex 22173; fax (1) 312-7857; Ambassador: LEIF DONDE.

Dominican Republic: Avda Santa Fe 1206, 2°C, 1059 Buenos Aires; tel. (1) 41-4669; Ambassador: JESÚS M. HERNÁNDEZ SÁNCHEZ.

Ecuador: Quintana 585, 9° y 10°, 1129 Buenos Aires; tel. (1) 804-0073; Ambassador: LUIS VALENCIA RODRÍGUEZ.

Egypt: Juez Tedín 2795, 1425 Buenos Aires; tel. (1) 801-6145; Ambassador: HASSAN I. ABDEL HADI.

El Salvador: Avda Santa Fe 882, 12°A, 1059 Buenos Aires; tel. (1) 394-7628; Ambassador: HORACIO TRUJILLO.

Finland: Avda Santa Fe 846, 5°, 1059 Buenos Aires; tel. (1) 312-0600; fax (1) 312-0670; Ambassador: ERKKI KIVIMÄKI.

France: Cerrito 1399, 1010 Buenos Aires; tel. (1) 819-2930; telex 24300; fax (1) 819-1235; Ambassador: PAUL DIJOUD.

Gabon: Avda Figueroa Alcorta 3221, 1425 Buenos Aires; tel. (1) 801-9840; telex 18577; Ambassador: J.-B. EYI-NKOUMOU.

Germany: Villanueva 1055, 1426 Buenos Aires; tel. (1) 778-2500; telex 21668; fax (1) 778-2550; Ambassador: Dr WIEGAND PABSCH.

Greece: Avda Roque S. Peña 547, 4°, 1035 Buenos Aires; tel. (1) 34-4598; telex 22426; fax (1) 34-2838; Ambassador: APOSTOLOS ANNINOS.

Guatemala: Avda Santa Fe 830, 5°, 1059 Buenos Aires; tel. (1) 313-9160; fax (1) 313-9181; Ambassador: LESLIE MISHAAN DE KIRKVOORDE.

Haiti: Avda Figueroa Alcorta 3297, 1425 Buenos Aires; tel. (1) 802-0211; Ambassador: FRANK PAUL.

Holy See: Avda Alvear 1605, 1014 Buenos Aires; tel. (1) 813-9697; fax (1) 815-4097; Apostolic Nuncio: Most Rev. UBALDO CALABRESI, Titular Archbishop of Fundi (Fondi).

Honduras: Paraná 275, 4°, Of. 7, 1017 Buenos Aires; tel. (1) 813-2800; fax (1) 371-4885; Ambassador: RAFAEL LEIVA VIVAS.

Hungary: Coronel Díaz 1874, 1425 Buenos Aires; tel. (1) 822-0767; telex 22843; fax (1) 805-3918; Ambassador: KÁROLY MISLEY.

India: Córdoba 950, 4°, 1054 Buenos Aires; tel. (1) 393-4001; telex 23413; fax (1) 393-4063; Ambassador: M. K. KHISHA.

Indonesia: Mariscal Ramón Castilla 2901, 1425 Buenos Aires; tel. (1) 807-2211; telex 18704; fax (1) 802-4448; Chargé d'affaires: EDDY S. SURYODININGRAT.

Iran: Avda Figueroa Alcorta 3229, 1425 Buenos Aires; tel. (1) 802-1470; telex 21288; fax (1) 805-4409; Ambassador: HADI SOLEIMANPOUR (recalled August 1994).

Ireland: Suipacha 1380, 2°, 1011 Buenos Aires; tel. (1) 325-8588; fax (1) 325-7572; Ambassador: ART AGNEW.

Israel: Arroyo 910, 1007 Buenos Aires; tel. (1) 325-2502; telex 17106; Ambassador: ITSHAK SHEFI.

Italy: Billinghurst 2577, 1425 Buenos Aires; tel. (1) 802-0071; telex 21961; Ambassador: LUDOVICO INCISA DI CAMERANA.

Japan: Bouchard 547, 17°, Buenos Aires; tel. (1) 318-8200; fax (1) 318-8210; Ambassador: AGUSTIN YOSHIO FUJIMOTO.

Korea, Republic: Avda del Libertador 2257, 1425 Buenos Aires; tel. (1) 802-9665; telex 22294; Ambassador: SANG CHIN LEE.

Lebanon: Avda del Libertador 2354, 1425 Buenos Aires; tel. (1) 802-4492; telex 22866; fax (1) 802-2909; Ambassador: RIAD KANTAR.

Libya: Cazadores 2166, 1428 Buenos Aires; tel. (1) 788-3760; fax (1) 788-9394; Chargé d'affaires a.i.: ASSED MOHAMED ALMUTAA.

Malaysia: Villanueva 1040-1048, 1062 Buenos Aires; tel. (1) 776-0504; Ambassador: DENNIS JOACHIM IGNATIUS.

Mexico: Larrea 1230, 1117 Buenos Aires; tel. (1) 821-7172; telex 21869; fax (1) 821-7251; Ambassador: JESÚS PUENTE LEYVA.

Morocco: Mariscal Ramón Castilla 2952, 1425 Buenos Aires; tel. (1) 801-8154; fax (1) 802-0136; e-mail sifamabueno@tournet.com.ar; Chargé d'affaires a.i.: ABDELLAH DGHOUHGI.

Netherlands: Avda de Mayo 701, 19°, 1084 Buenos Aires; tel. (1) 334-3474; telex 21824; fax (1) 334-2717; Ambassador: A. J. A. M. NOOIJ.

Nicaragua: Corrientes 2548, 4°I, 1426 Buenos Aires; tel. (1) 951-3463; telex 23481; Ambassador: ARIEL RAMÓN GRANERA SACASA.

Nigeria: Rosales 2674, 1636 Olivos, Buenos Aires; tel. (1) 771-6541; telex 23565; Ambassador: OKON EDET UYA.

Norway: Esmeralda 909, 3°B, 1007 Buenos Aires; tel. (1) 312-2204; telex 22811; fax (1) 315-2831; Ambassador: ERIK TELLMANN.

Pakistan: Gorostiaga 2176, 1426 Buenos Aires; tel. (1) 782-7663; Ambassador: ZAFAR HABIB.

Panama: Avda Santa Fe 1461, 5°, 1060 Buenos Aires; tel. (1) 42-8543; Ambassador: MARÍA ESTHER VILLALAZ DE ARIAS.

Paraguay: Avda Las Heras 2545, 1425 Buenos Aires; tel. (1) 802-3826; fax (1) 801-0657; Ambassador: OSCAR FACUNDO YNSFRÁN.

Peru: Avda del Libertador 1720, 1425 Buenos Aires; tel. (1) 802-2000; telex 17807; Ambassador: ALFONSO GRADOS BERTORINI.

Philippines: Juramento 1945, 1428 Buenos Aires; tel. (1) 781-4173; Ambassador: SIME D. HIDALGO.

Poland: Alejandro M. de Aguado 2870, 1425 Buenos Aires; tel. (1) 802-9681; fax (1) 802-9683; Ambassador: ANDRZEJ WRÓBEL.

Portugal: Córdoba 315, 3°, 1054 Buenos Aires; tel. (1) 311-2586; telex 22736; Ambassador: ANTÓNIO BAPTISTA MARTINS.

Romania: Arroyo 962-970, 1007 Buenos Aires; tel. and fax (1) 322-2630; telex 24301; Ambassador: STELIAN OANCEA.

Russia: Rodríguez Peña 1741, 1021 Buenos Aires; tel. (1) 813-1552; telex 22147; fax (1) 812-1794; Ambassador: IAN A. BURLIAY.

Saudi Arabia: Alejandro M. de Aguado 2881, 1425 Buenos Aires; tel. (1) 802-4735; telex 23291; Ambassador: FUAD A. NAZIR.

Slovakia: Avda Figueroa Alcorta 3240, 1425 Buenos Aires; tel. (1) 786-0692; fax (1) 786-0938; Ambassador: MARIÁN MASARIK.

South Africa: Marcelo T. de Alvear 590, 8°, 1058 Buenos Aires; tel. (1) 317-2900; fax (1) 317-2951; Ambassador: AUBREY X. NKOMO.

Spain: Mariscal Ramón Castilla 2720, 1425 Buenos Aires; tel. (1) 802-6031; telex 21660; fax (1) 802-0719; Ambassador: CARLOS CARDERERA SOLER.

Sweden: Corrientes 330, 3°, 1378 Buenos Aires; tel. (1) 311-3088; telex 21340; fax (1) 311-8052; Ambassador: ANDERS SANDSTRÖM.

Switzerland: Avda Santa Fe 846, 10°, 1059 Buenos Aires; tel. (1) 311-6491; fax (1) 313-2998; Ambassador: JEAN-MARC BOILLAT.

Syria: Calloa 956, 1023 Buenos Aires; tel. (1) 42-2113; Ambassador: ABDUL HASSIB ITSWANI.

Thailand: Virrey del Pino 2458, 6°, 1426 Buenos Aires; tel. (1) 785-6504; Ambassador: VICHIEN CHATSUWAN.

Turkey: 11 de Setiembre 1382, 1426 Buenos Aires; tel. (1) 788-3239; fax (1) 784-9179; e-mail iyihava@ba.net; Ambassador: SENCAR ÖZSOY.

United Kingdom: Dr Luis Agote 2412/52, 1425 Buenos Aires; tel. (1) 803-7070; fax (1) 803-1731; e-mail ukembarg@starnet.net.ar; Ambassador: WILLIAM MARSDEN.

USA: Avda Colombia 4300, 1425 Buenos Aires; tel. (1) 774-7611; telex 18156; fax (1) 775-4205; Ambassador: TERENCE TODMAN.

Uruguay: Avda Las Heras 1907, 1127 Buenos Aires; tel. (1) 803-6030; telex 25526; Ambassador: ADOLFO CASTELLS MENDIVIL.

Venezuela: Virrey Loreto 2035, 1428 Buenos Aires; tel. (1) 788-4944; telex 26306; fax (1) 784-4311; Ambassador: REINALDO LEANDRO RODRÍGUEZ.

Yugoslavia: Marcelo T. de Alvear 1705, 1060 Buenos Aires; tel. (1) 41-2860; telex 21479; Ambassador: RUDOLF HAZURAN.

Judicial System

SUPREME COURT

Corte Suprema: Talcahuano 550, 4°, 1013 Buenos Aires; tel. (1) 40-0837; fax (1) 40-2270.

The nine members of the Supreme Court are appointed by the President, with the agreement of at least two-thirds of the Senate. Members are dismissed by impeachment.

President: JULIO SALVADOR NAZARENO.

Justices: CARLOS SANTIAGO FAYT, AUGUSTO CÉSAR BELLUSCIO, ENRIQUE SANTIAGO PETRACCHI, EDUARDO MOLINÉ O'CONNOR, ADOLFO VÁZQUEZ, ANTONIO BOGGIANO, GUILLERMO A. F. LÓPEZ, GUSTAVO A. BOSSERT.

OTHER COURTS

Judges of the lower, national or further lower courts are appointed by the President, with the agreement of the Senate, and are dismissed by impeachment. From 1999, however, judges are to retire on reaching 75 years of age.

The Federal Court of Appeal in Buenos Aires has three courts: civil and commercial, criminal, and administrative. There are six other courts of appeal in Buenos Aires: civil, commercial, criminal, peace, labour, and penal-economic. There are also federal appeal courts in: La Plata, Bahía Blanca, Paraná, Rosario, Córdoba, Mendoza, Tucumán and Resistencia. In August 1994, following constitutional amendments, the Office of the Attorney-General was established as an independent entity and a Council of Magistrates was created.

The provincial courts each have their own Supreme Court and a system of subsidiary courts. They deal with cases originating within and confined to the provinces.

Attorney-General: OSCAR LUJÁN FAPPIANO.

Religion

CHRISTIANITY

More than 90% of the population are Roman Catholics and about 2% are Protestants.

Federación Argentina de Iglesias Evangélicas (Argentine Federation of Evangelical Churches): José María Moreno 873, 1424 Buenos Aires; tel. (1) 922-5356; f. 1958; 29 mem. churches; Pres. Rev. RODOLFO ROBERTO REINICH (Evangelical Church of the River Plate); Exec. Sec. Rev. ENRIQUE LAVIGNE.

The Roman Catholic Church

Argentina comprises 13 archdioceses, 51 dioceses (including one each for Uniate Catholics of the Ukrainian rite, of the Maronite rite and of the Armenian rite) and three territorial prelatures. The Archbishop of Buenos Aires is also the Ordinary for Catholics of Oriental rites, and the Bishop of San Gregorio de Narek en Buenos Aires is also the Apostolic Exarch of Latin America and Mexico for Catholics of the Armenian rite.

Bishops' Conference: Conferencia Episcopal Argentina, Calle Suipacha 1034, 1008 Buenos Aires; tel. (1) 328-2015; fax (1) 328-9570; f. 1959; Pres. Mgr ESTANISLAO ESTEBAN KARLIC, Archbishop of Paraná.

Armenian Rite

Bishop of San Gregorio de Narek en Buenos Aires: VARTAN WALDIR BOGHOSSIAN, Charcas 3529, 1425 Buenos Aires; tel. (1) 824-1613; fax (1) 827-1975; e-mail exarmal@usa.net; internet http://www.geocities.com/Athens/Forum 4643.

Latin Rite

Archbishop of Bahía Blanca: RÓMULO GARCÍA, Avda Colón 164, 8000 Bahía Blanca; tel. (91) 22-070; fax (91) 55-0707.

Archbishop of Buenos Aires: Cardinal ANTONIO QUARRACINO, Arzobispado, Rivadavia 415, 1002 Buenos Aires; tel. (1) 343-3925; fax (1) 334-8373.

Archbishop of Córdoba: Cardinal RAÚL FRANCISCO PRIMATESTA, Hipólito Yrigoyen 98, 5000 Córdoba; tel. (51) 22-1015; fax (51) 22-9317.

Archbishop of Corrientes: DOMINGO SALVADOR CASTAGNA, 9 de Julio 1543, 3400 Corrientes; tel. and fax (783) 22436.

Archbishop of La Plata: CARLOS GALÁN, Arzobispado, Calle 14, 1009, 1900 La Plata; tel. (21) 25-1656; fax (21) 25-8269.

Archbishop of Mendoza: JOSÉ MARÍA ARANCIBIA, Catamarca 98, 5500 Mendoza; tel. (61) 23-3862; fax (61) 29-5415.

Archbishop of Paraná: Mgr ESTANISLAO ESTEBAN KARLIC, Monte Caseros 77, 3100 Paraná; tel. (43) 31-1440; fax (43) 23-0372; e-mail arzparan@satlink.com.ar.

Archbishop of Resistencia: CARMELO JUAN GIAQUINTA, Bartolomé Mitre 363, Casilla 35, 3500 Resistencia; tel. and fax (722) 34573.

Archbishop of Rosario: EDUARDO VICENTE MIRÁS, Córdoba 1677, 2000 Rosario; tel. (41) 25-1298; fax (41) 25-1207.

Archbishop of Salta: MOISÉS JULIO BLANCHOUD, España 596, 4400 Salta; tel. (87) 21-4306.

Archbishop of San Juan de Cuyo: ITALO SEVERINO DI STÉFANO, Bartolomé Mitre 240 Oeste, 5400 San Juan de Cuyo; tel. (64) 22-2578; fax (64) 22-6261.

Archbishop of Santa Fe de la Vera Cruz: EDGARDO GABRIEL STORNI, Avda General López 2720, 3000 Santa Fe; tel. (42) 59-5791; fax (42) 59-4491.

Archbishop of Tucumán: ARSENIO RAÚL CASADO, Avda Sarmiento 895, 4000 San Miguel de Tucumán; tel. (81) 22-6345; fax (81) 31-0617.

Maronite Rite

Bishop of San Charbel en Buenos Aires: CHARBEL MERHI, Eparquía Maronita, Paraguay 834, 1057 Buenos Aires; tel. (1) 311-7299; fax (1) 321-8348.

Ukrainian Rite

Bishop of Santa María del Patrocinio en Buenos Aires: ANDRÉS SAPELAK, Ramón L. Falcón 3950, Casilla 28, 1407 Buenos Aires; tel. (1) 671-4192.

The Anglican Communion

The Iglesia Anglicana del Cono Sur de América (Anglican Church of the Southern Cone of America) was formally inaugurated in Buenos Aires in April 1983. The Church comprises six dioceses: Argentina, Northern Argentina, Chile, Paraguay, Peru with Bolivia, and Uruguay. The Primate is the Bishop of Northern Argentina.

Bishop of Argentina: Rt Rev. DAVID LEAKE, 25 de Mayo 282, 1002 Buenos Aires; Casilla 4293, 1000 Correo Central, Buenos Aires; tel. (1) 342-4618; fax (1) 331-0234.

Bishop of Northern Argentina: Rt Rev. MAURICE SINCLAIR, Casilla 187, 4400 Salta; jurisdiction extends to Jujuy, Salta, Tucumán, Catamarca, Santiago del Estero, Formosa and Chaco; tel. (87) 31-1718; fax (87) 31-2622.

Protestant Churches

Convención Evangélica Bautista Argentina (Baptist Evangelical Convention): Rivadavia 3461, 1203 Buenos Aires; tel. (1) 864-2711; Pres. JUAN CALCAGNI.

Iglesia Evangélica Congregacionalista (Evangelical Congregational Church): Perón 525, 3100 Paraná; tel. (43) 21-6172; f. 1924; 100 congregations, 8,000 mems, 24,000 adherents; Supt Rev. REYNOLDO HORSTT.

Iglesia Evangélica Luterana Argentina (Evangelical Lutheran Church of Argentina): Ing. Silveyra 1639-41, 1607 Villa Adelina, Buenos Aires; tel. (1) 766-7948; fax (1) 766-7948; f. 1905; 30,000 mems; Pres. WALDOMIRO MAILI.

Iglesia Evangélica del Río de la Plata (Evangelical Church of the River Plate): Mariscal Sucre 2855, 1428 Buenos Aires; tel. (1) 787-0436; fax (1) 787-0335; e-mail ierp@wamani.apc.org; f. 1899; 50,000 mems; Pres. RODOLFO R. REINICH.

Iglesia Evangélica Metodista Argentina (Methodist Church of Argentina): Rivadavia 4044, 3°, 1205 Buenos Aires; tel. (1) 982-3712; fax (1) 981-0885; e-mail iema@iema.wamani.apc.org; f. 1836; 6,040 mems, 9,000 adherents, seven regional superintendents; Bishop ALDO M. ETCHEGOYEN; Exec. Sec.-Gen. Board DANIEL A. FAVARO.

JUDAISM

Delegación de Asociaciones Israelitas Argentinas—DAIA (Delegation of Argentine Jewish Associations): Ayacucho 632, 6°, 1026 Buenos Aires; tel. (1) 375-4729; f. 1935; there are about 250,000 Jews in Argentina, mostly in Buenos Aires; Pres. Dr RUBÉN E. BERAJA; Sec.-Gen. Dr JOSÉ KESTELMAN.

The Press

PRINCIPAL DAILIES

Buenos Aires

Ambito Financiero: Avda Paseo Colón 1196, 1063 Buenos Aires; tel. (1) 349-1500; telex 17721; fax (1) 349-1580; f. 1976; morning (Mon.–Fri.); business; Dir JULIO A. RAMOS; circ. 130,000.

Buenos Aires Herald: Azopardo 455, 1107 Buenos Aires; tel. (1) 342-1535; fax (1) 334-7917; f. 1876; English; morning; independent; Editor-in-Chief ANDREW GRAHAM-YOOLL; circ. 20,000.

Boletín Oficial de la República Argentina: Suipacha 767, 1008 Buenos Aires; tel. (1) 322-3982; fax (1) 322-3982; f. 1893; morning (Mon.–Fri.); official records publication; Dir RUBÉN ANTONIO SOSA; circ. 15,000.

Clarín: Piedras 1743, 1140 Buenos Aires; tel. (1) 307-0330; fax (1) 309-7559; f. 1945; morning; independent; Dir ERNESTINA LAURA HERRERA DE NOBLE; circ. 600,000 (daily), 1.1m. (Sunday).

Crónica: Avda Juan de Garay 130, 1063 Buenos Aires; tel. (1) 361-1001; fax (1) 361-4237; f. 1963; morning and evening; Dir MARIO ALBERTO FERNÁNDEZ (morning), RICARDO GANGEME (evening); circ. 330,000 (morning), 190,000 (evening), 450,000 (Sunday).

El Cronista Comercial: Honduras 5663, 1414 Buenos Aires; tel. (1) 778-6789; fax (1) 778-6727; f. 1908; morning; Dirs NÉSTOR SCIBONA, EDUARDO EURNEKIAN; circ. 100,000.

Diario Popular: Beguerestain 142, 1872 Sarandí, Avellaneda, Buenos Aires; tel. (1) 204-2778; fax (1) 205-2376; f. 1974; morning; Dir ALBERTO ALBERTENGO; circ. 145,000.

La Gaceta: Beguerestain 182, 1870 Avellaneda, Buenos Aires; Dir RICARDO WEST OCAMPO; circ. 35,000.

La Nación: Bouchard 551, 1106 Buenos Aires; tel. (1) 313-1600; telex 18558; fax (1) 313-1210; f. 1870; morning; independent; Dir BARTOLOMÉ MITRE; circ. 210,648.

Página 12: Avda Belgrano 671, 1092 Buenos Aires; tel. (1) 334-7203; fax (1) 334-2330; f. 1987; morning; independent; Dir ERNESTO TIFFENBERG; Editor FERNANDO SOKOLOWICZ; circ. 280,000.

La Prensa: Azopardo 715, 1107 Buenos Aires; tel. (1) 349-1000; fax (1) 349-1001; f. 1869; morning; independent; Dir FLORENCIO ALDREY IGLESIAS; circ. 100,000.

La Razón: Río Cuarto 1242, 1168 Buenos Aires; tel. (1) 303-2270; fax (1) 303-1233; f. 1992; evening; Dir OSCAR MAGDALENA; circ. 180,000.

El Sol: Hipólito Yrigoyen 122, Quilmes, 1878 Buenos Aires; tel. and fax (1) 253-4595; f. 1927; Dir RODRIGO GHISANI; circ. 25,000.

Tiempo Argentino: Buenos Aires; tel. (1) 28-1929; telex 22276; Editor Dr TOMÁS LEONA; circ. 75,000.

PRINCIPAL PROVINCIAL DAILIES

Catamarca

La Unión: San Martín 671, 4700 Catamarca; tel. (833) 36666; fax (833) 30218; f. 1928; morning; Dir RODOLFO ISAAC SUÁREZ.

Chaco

El Territorio: Carlos Pellegrini 211–231, Casilla 320, 3500 Resistencia; f. 1919; morning; Dir RAÚL ANDRÉS AGUIRRE; circ. 15,000.

Chubut

Crónica: Impresora Patagónica, Namuncurá 122, 9000 Comodoro Rivadavia; tel. (97) 47-1200; fax (97) 47-1780; f. 1962; morning; Dir Dr DIEGO JOAQUÍN ZAMIT; circ. 15,000.

Córdoba

Comercio y Justicia: Mariano Moreno 378, 5000 Córdoba; tel. and fax (51) 22-1473; telex 51563; f. 1939; morning; economic and legal news; Editor PABLO EGUÍA; circ. 10,000.

La Voz del Interior: Avda Colón 37-39, 5000 Córdoba; tel. (51) 24-2385; telex 51602; fax (51) 24-4104; f. 1904; morning; independent; Dir LUIS EDUARDO REMONDA; circ. 95,000.

Corrientes

El Litoral: Hipólito Yrigoyen 990, 3400 Corrientes; tel. (783) 22227; fax (783) 27445; f. 1960; morning; Dir JORGE A. FARIZANO; circ. 25,000.

El Territorio: Avda Quaranta 4307, 3300 Posadas; tel. and fax (752) 52100; telex 76134; f. 1925; Dir ÁLVARO CAYETANO CAAMAÑO; circ. 22,000 (Mon.–Fri.), 28,000 (Sunday).

Entre Ríos

El Diario: Buenos Aires y Urquiza, 3100 Paraná; tel. (43) 23-1000; telex 45108; fax (43) 24-2839; f. 1914; morning; democratic; Dir Dr LUIS F. ETCHEVEHERE; circ. 25,000.

El Heraldo: Quintana 46, 3200 Concordia; tel. (45) 21-5304; telex 46508; fax (45) 21-1397; f. 1915; evening; Editor Dr CARLOS LIEBERMANN; circ. 10,000.

Provincia de Buenos Aires

El Atlántico: Bolívar 2975, 7600 Mar del Plata; tel. (23) 35462; f. 1938; morning; Dir OSCAR ALBERTO GASTIARENA; circ. 20,000.

La Capital: Avda Champagnat 2551, 7600 Mar del Plata; tel. (23) 78-8490; telex 39884; fax (23) 78-1038; f. 1905; Dir FLORENCIO ALDREY IGLESIAS; circ. 32,000.

El Día: Avda A. Diagonal 80, 817-21, 1900 La Plata; tel. (21) 25-0101; fax (21) 23-2996; f. 1884; morning; independent; Dir RAÚL E. KRAISELBURD; circ. 54,868.

Ecos Diarios: Calle 62, No 2486, 7630 Necochea; tel. (262) 30754; fax (262) 24114; f. 1921; morning; independent; Dir GUILLERMO IGNACIO; circ. 6,000.

La Nueva Provincia: Sarmiento 54–64, 8000 Bahía Blanca; tel. (91) 59-0000; fax (91) 59-0001; f. 1898; morning; independent; Dir DIANA JULIO DE MASSOT; circ. 36,000 (Mon.–Fri.), 55,000 (Sunday).

La Voz del Pueblo: Avda San Martín 991, 7500 Tres Arroyos; tel. (983) 30680; fax (938) 30682; f. 1902; morning; independent; Dir ALBERTO JORGE MACIEL.

Río Negro

Río Negro: 9 de Julio 733, 8332, Gen. Roca, Río Negro; tel. (941) 30501; fax (941) 30517; f. 1912; morning; Editor NÉLIDA RAJNERI DE GAMBA.

Salta

El Tribuno: Avda Ex Combatientes de Malvinas 3890, 4400 Salta; tel. (87) 24-0000; telex 65126; fax (87) 24-1382; f. 1949; morning; Dir ROBERTO EDUARDO ROMERO; circ. 26,697.

San Juan

Diario de Cuyo: Mendoza 380 Sur, 5400 San Juan; tel. (64) 29-0016; fax (64) 29-0004; f. 1947; morning; independent; Dir FRANCISCO MONTES; circ. 25,000.

San Luis

El Diario de La República: Junín 741, 5700 San Luis; tel (652) 22037; fax (652) 28770; f. 1966; Dir ZULEMA A. RODRÍGUEZ SAA DE DIVIZIA.

Santa Fe

La Capital: Sarmiento 763, 2000 Rosario; tel. (41) 20-1100; fax (41) 20-1114; f. 1867; morning; independent; Dir CARLOS MARÍA LAGOS; circ. 93,920.

El Litoral: Avda 25 de Mayo 3536, 3000 Santa Fe; tel. (42) 50-2500; fax (42) 50-2530; f. 1918; morning; independent; Dir GUSTAVO VÍTTORI; circ. 40,000.

Santiago del Estero

El Liberal: Libertad 263, 4200 Santiago del Estero; tel. (85) 22-4400; telex 64114; fax (85) 22-4538; f. 1898; morning; Editors JOSÉ LUIS CASTIGLIONE, Dr JULIO CÉSAR CASTIGLIONE; circ. 30,000.

Tucumán

La Gaceta: Mendoza 654, 4000 San Miguel de Tucumán; tel. (81) 31-1111; telex 61208; fax (81) 31-1597; f. 1912; morning; independent; Dir ENRIQUE GARCÍA HAMILTON; circ. 80,552.

WEEKLY NEWSPAPER

El Informador Público: Uruguay 252, 3°F, 1015 Buenos Aires; tel. (1) 476-3551; fax (1) 342-2628; f. 1986.

PERIODICALS

Aeroespacio: Casilla 37, Sucursal 12B, 1412 Buenos Aires; tel. (1) and fax 774-9310; f. 1940; bimonthly, aeronautics; Dir JORGE A. CUADROS; circ. 24,000.

Billiken: Azopardo 579, 1307 Buenos Aires; tel. (1) 30-7040; telex 21163; f. 1919; weekly; children's magazine; Dir CARLOS SILVEYRA; circ. 240,000.

Casas y Jardines: Sarmiento 643, 1382 Buenos Aires; tel. (1) 45-1793; f. 1932; every 2 months; houses and gardens; publ. by Editorial Contémpora SRL; Dir NORBERTO M. MUZIO.

Chacra y Campo Moderno: Editorial Atlántida, SA, Azopardo 579, 1307 Buenos Aires; tel. (1) 331-4591; fax (1) 331-3272; f. 1930; monthly; farm and country magazine; Dir CONSTANCIO C. VIGIL; circ. 35,000.

Claudia: Avda Córdoba 1345, 12°, Buenos Aires; tel. (1) 42-3275; telex 9229; fax (1) 814-3948; f. 1957; monthly; women's magazine; Dir ANA TORREJÓN; circ. 150,000.

El Economista: Avda Córdoba 632, 2°, 1054 Buenos Aires; tel. (1) 322-7360; fax (1) 322-8157; f. 1951; weekly; financial; Dir Dr D. RADONJIC; circ. 37,800.

Fotografía Universal: Muniz 1327/49, Buenos Aires; monthly; circ. 39,500.

Gente: Azopardo 579, 3°, 1307 Buenos Aires; tel. (1) 33-4591; telex 21163; f. 1965; weekly; general; Dir JORGE DE LUJÁN GUTIÉRREZ; circ. 133,000.

El Gráfico: Azopardo 579, 3°, 1307 Buenos Aires; tel. (1) 33-4591; telex 21163; f. 1919; weekly; sport; Dir CONSTANCIO C. VIGIL; circ. 127,000.

Guía Latinoamericana de Transportes: Florida 8287 esq. Portinari, 1669 Del Viso (Ptdo de Pilar), Provincia de Buenos Aires; tel. (1) 320-7004; fax (1) 307-1956; f. 1968; every 2 months; travel information and timetables; Editor Dr ARMANDO SCHLECKER HIRSCH; circ. 7,500.

Humor: Venezuela 842, 1095 Buenos Aires; tel. (1) 334-5400; telex 9072; fax (1) 11-2700; f. 1978; every 2 weeks; satirical revue; Editor ANDRÉS CASCIOLI; circ. 180,000.

Legislación Argentina: Talcahuano 650, 1013 Buenos Aires; tel. (1) 371-0528; e-mail jurispru@lvd.com.ar; f. 1958; weekly; law; Dir RICARDO ESTÉVEZ BOERO; circ. 15,000.

Mercado: Rivadavia 877, 2°, 1067 Buenos Aires; tel. (1) 342-3322; fax (1) 343-7880; f. 1969; monthly; business; Dir MIGUEL ANGEL DIEZ; circ. 28,000.

Mundo Israelita: Pueyrredón 538, 1°B, 1052 Buenos Aires; tel. (1) 961-7999; fax (1) 961-0763; f. 1923; weekly; Editor Dr JOSÉ KESTELMAN; circ. 26,000.

Nuestra Arquitectura: Sarmiento 643, 5°, 1382 Buenos Aires; tel. (1) 45-1793; f. 1929; every 2 months; architecture; publ. by Editorial Contémpora SRL; Dir NORBERTO M. MUZIO.

Para Ti: Azopardo 579, 1307 Buenos Aires; tel. (1) 331-4591; telex 21163; fax (1) 331-3272; f. 1922; weekly; women's interest; Dir ANÍBAL C. VIGIL; circ. 104,000.

Pensamiento Económico: Avda Leandro N. Alem 36, 1003 Buenos Aires; tel. (1) 331-8051; telex 18542; fax (1) 331-8055; f. 1925; quarterly; review of Cámara Argentina de Comercio; Dir Lic. PEDRO NAÓN ARGERICH.

La Prensa Médica Argentina: Junín 845, 1113 Buenos Aires; tel. (1) 961-9793; fax (1) 961-9494; f. 1914; monthly; medical; Editor Dr P. A. LÓPEZ; circ. 8,000.

Prensa Obrera: Ayacucho 444, Buenos Aires; tel. (1) 953-3824; fax (1) 953-7164; f. 1982; weekly; publication of Partido Obrero; circ. 16,000.

La Semana: Sarmiento 1113, 1041 Buenos Aires; tel. (1) 35-2552; telex 18213; general; Editor DANIEL PLINER.

La Semana Médica: Arenales 3574, 1425 Buenos Aires; tel. (1) 824-5673; f. 1894; monthly; Dir Dr EDUARDO F. MELE; circ. 7,000.

Siete Días Ilustrados: Avda Leandro N. Alem 896, 1001 Buenos Aires; tel. (1) 32-6010; f. 1967; weekly; general; Dir RICARDO CÁMARA; circ. 110,000.

Técnica e Industria: Rodríguez Peña 694, 5°, 1020 Buenos Aires; tel. (1) 46-3193; f. 1922; monthly; technology and industry; Dir E. R. FEDELE; circ. 5,000.

Visión: French 2820, 2°A, 1425 Buenos Aires; tel. (1) 825-1258; fax (1) 827-1004; f. 1950; fortnightly; Latin American affairs, politics; Editor LUIS VIDAL RUCABADO.

Vosotras: Avda Leandro N. Alem 896, 3°, 1001 Buenos Aires; tel. (1) 32-6010; f. 1935; women's weekly; Dir ABEL ZANOTTO; circ. 33,000. Monthly supplements: **Labores:** circ. 130,000; **Modas:** circ. 70,000.

NEWS AGENCIES

Agencia TELAM, SA: Bolívar 531, 1066 Buenos Aires; tel. (1) 342-2161; telex 21077; fax (1) 331-4235; Dir OMAR CERIGLIANO.

Diarios y Noticias (DYN): Chacabuco 314, 10°, 1069 Buenos Aires; tel. (1) 343-4931; fax (1) 342-3043; Editor SANTIAGO GONZÁLEZ.

Noticias Argentinas, SA (NA): Suipacha 570, 3°B, 1008 Buenos Aires; tel. (1) 394-7522; telex 18363; fax (1) 394-7648; f. 1973; Dir LUIS FERNANDO TORRES.

Foreign Bureaux

Agence France-Presse (AFP): Corrientes 456, 3°, Of. 34/37, 1366 Buenos Aires; tel. (1) 394-8169; telex 24349; fax (1) 393-9912; Bureau Chief JEAN VIREBAYRE.

Agencia EFE (Spain): Guido 1770, 1016 Buenos Aires; tel. (1) 812-9596; telex 17568; fax (1) 819-4388; Bureau Chief JOSÉ ANTONIO RODRÍGUEZ COUCEIRO.

Agenzia Nazionale Stampa Associata (ANSA) (Italy): Avda Eduardo Madero 940/942, 24°, 1106 Buenos Aires; tel. and fax (1) 313-4449; telex 24214; Bureau Chief RICARDO BENOZZO.

Associated Press (AP) (USA): Bouchard 551, 5°, Casilla 1296, 1106 Buenos Aires; tel. (1) 311-0081; telex 121053; fax (1) 311-0082; Bureau Chief WILLIAM H. HEATH.

Deutsche Presse-Agentur (dpa) (Germany): Buenos Aires; tel. (1) 394-0990; Bureau Chief HASSO RAMSPECK.

Informatsionnoye Telegrafnoye Agentstvo Rossii-Telegrafnoye Agentstvo Suverennykh Stran (ITAR-TASS) (Russia): Avda Córdoba 652, 11°E, 1054 Buenos Aires; tel. (1) 392-2044; Dir ISIDORO GILBERT.

Inter Press Service (IPS) (Italy): Corrientes 456, 8°, Of. 87, Edif. Safico, 1068 Buenos Aires; tel. (1) 394-0829; telex 24712; Bureau Chief RAMÓN M. GORRIARÁN; Correspondent GUSTAVO CAPDEVILLA.

Magyar Távirati Iroda (MTI) (Hungary): Marcelo T. de Alvear 624, 3° 16, 1058 Buenos Aires; tel. (1) 312-9596; telex 17106; Correspondent ENDRE SIMÓ.

Prensa Latina (Cuba): Corrientes 456, 2°, Of. 27, Buenos Aires; tel. (1) 394-0565; telex 24410; Correspondent MARIO HERNÁNDEZ DEL LLANO.

Reuters (United Kingdom): Avda Eduardo Madero 940, 25°, 1106 Buenos Aires; tel. (1) 318-0600; fax (1) 318-0698; Dir CARLOS PÍA MANGIONE.

United Press International (UPI) (USA): Avda Belgrano 271, Casilla 796, Correo Central 1000, 1092 Buenos Aires; tel. (1) 34-5501; telex 350-1225; fax (1) 334-1818; Dir ALBERTO J. SCHAZÍN.

Xinhua (New China) News Agency (People's Republic of China): Tucumán 540, 14°, Apto D, 1049 Buenos Aires; tel. (1) 313-9755; telex 23643; Bureau Chief JU QINGDONG.

The following are also represented: Central News Agency (Taiwan), Interpress (Poland), Jiji Press (Japan).

PRESS ASSOCIATION

Asociación de Entidades Periodísticas Argentinas (ADEPA): Chacabuco 314, 3°, 1069 Buenos Aires; tel. (1) 334-3705; fax (1) 334-3707; f. 1962; Pres. LUIS FÉLIX ETCHEVEHERE.

Publishers

Editorial Abril, SA: Francisco Acuña de Figueroa 1753, 1180 Buenos Aires; tel. (1) 862-4022; telex 22630; f. 1961; fiction, non-fiction, children's books, textbooks; Dir ROBERTO M. ARES.

Editorial Acme, SA: Santa Magdalena 635, 1277 Buenos Aires; tel. (1) 28-2014; f. 1949; general fiction, children's books, agriculture, textbooks; Man. Dir EMILIO I. GONZÁLEZ.

Aguilar, Altea, Taurus, Alfaguara, SA de Ediciones: Beazley 3860, 1437 Buenos Aires; tel. (1) 91-4111; fax (1) 953-3716; f. 1946; general, literature, children's books; Gen. Man. ENRIQUE DE POLANCO.

Editorial Albatros, SACI: Hipólito Yrigoyen 3920, 1208 Buenos Aires; tel. (1) 982-5439; fax (1) 981-1161; f. 1967; technical, non-fiction, social sciences, sport, children's books, medicine and agriculture; Pres. ANDREA INÉS CANEVARO.

Amorrortu Editores, SA: Paraguay 1225, 7°, 1057 Buenos Aires; tel. (1) 393-8812; fax (1) 325-6307; f. 1967; anthropology, religion, economics, sociology, philosophy, psychology, pschoanalysis, current affairs; Man. Dir HORACIO DE AMORRORTU.

Angel Estrada y Cía, SA: Bolívar 462-66, 1066 Buenos Aires; tel. (1) 331-6521; telex 17990; fax (1) 331-6527; f. 1869; textbooks, children's books; Gen. Man. OSCAR DOMECQ.

El Ateneo Pedro García S.A.L.E., Librería Editorial: Patagones 2463, 1282 Buenos Aires; tel. (1) 942-9002; telex 18522; fax (1) 942-9162; f. 1912; medicine, engineering, economics and general; Pres. JORGE IGNACIO LETEMENDIA; Dir ADRIANA HIDALGO SOLA DE HUFFMANN.

Editorial Atlántida, SA: Azopardo 579, 1307 Buenos Aires; tel. (1) 331-4591; telex 21163; fax (1) 331-3341; f. 1918; fiction and non-fiction, children's books; Founder CONSTANCIO C. VIGIL; Man. Dir ALFREDO J. VERCELLI.

Ediciones La Aurora: Buenos Aires; tel. and fax (1) 941-8940; f. 1925; general, religion, spirituality, theology, philosophy, psychology, history, semiology, linguistics; Dir Dr HUGO O. ORTEGA.

Biblioteca Nacional de Maestros: c/o Ministry of Education and Culture, Pizzurno 935, Planta baja, 1020 Buenos Aires; tel. (1) 811-0275; Dir GRACIELA PERRONE.

Centro Editor de América Latina, SA: Salta 38, 3°, 1074 Buenos Aires; tel. (1) 35-9449; f. 1967; literature, history; Man. Dir JOSÉ B. SPIVACOW.

Editorial Claretiana: Lima 1360, 1138 Buenos Aires; tel. (1) 27-9250; fax (1) 27-4015; f. 1956; Catholicism; Dir EDUARDO RIGHETTI.

Editorial Claridad, SA: Viamonte 1730, 1°, 1055 Buenos Aires; tel. (1) 371-6402; fax (1) 375-1659; e-mail eheliasta@impsat1.com.ar; internet http://www.talksa.claridad; f. 1922; literature, biographies, social science, politics, reference, dictionaries; Pres. Dra ANA MARÍA CABANELLAS.

Club de Lectores: Avda de Mayo 624, 1084 Buenos Aires; tel. (1) 34-6251; f. 1938; non-fiction; Dir JUAN MANUEL FONTENLA.

Club de Poetas: Casilla 189, 1401 Buenos Aires; f. 1975; poetry and literature; Exec. Dir JUAN MANUEL FONTENLA.

Editorial Columba, SA: Sarmiento 1889, 5°, 1044 Buenos Aires; tel. (1) 45-4297; f. 1953; classics in translation, 20th century; Man. Dir CLAUDIO A. COLUMBA.

Editorial Contémpora, SRL: Sarmiento 643, 5°, 1382 Buenos Aires; tel. (1) 45-1793; architecture, town-planning, interior decoration and gardening; Dir NORBERTO C. MUZIO.

Cosmopolita, SRL: Piedras 744, 1070 Buenos Aires; tel. and fax (1) 361-8049; f. 1940; science and technology; Man. Dir RUTH F. DE RAPP.

Ediciones Depalma, SRL: Talcahuano 494, 1013 Buenos Aires; tel. (1) 371-7306; fax (1) 371-6913; f. 1944; periodicals and books covering law, politics, sociology, philosophy, history and economics; Dir ROBERTO SUARDÍAZ; Man. ALBERTO BARÓN.

Editorial Difusión, SA: Sarandi 1065–67, Buenos Aires; tel. (1) 941-0088; f. 1937; literature, philosophy, religion, education, textbooks, children's books; Dir DOMINGO PALOMBELLA.

Edicial, SA: Rivadavia 739, 1002 Buenos Aires; tel. (1) 342-8481; fax (1) 343-1151; f. 1931; general non-fiction; Man. Dir J. A. MUSSET.

Emecé Editores, SA: Alsina 2048, 1090 Buenos Aires; tel. (1) 954-0105; fax (1) 953-4200; f. 1939; fiction, non-fiction, biographies, history, art, essays; Pres. ALFREDO DEL CARRIL.

Espasa Calpe Argentina, SA: Buenos Aires; tel. (1) 342-0073; fax (1) 345-1776; f. 1937; literature, science, dictionaries; publ. *Colección Austral*; Dir GUILLERMO SCHAUELZON.

EUDEBA—Editorial Universitaria de Buenos Aires: Rivadavia 1573, 1033 Buenos Aires; tel. (1) 383-4064; fax (1) 383-2202; f. 1958; university text books and general interest publications; Gen. Man. Dr CARLOS ALBERTO O. CRUZ.

Fabril Editora, SA: Buenos Aires; tel. (1) 21-3601; f. 1958; non-fiction, science, arts, education and reference; Editorial Man. ANDRÉS ALFONSO BRAVO; Business Man. RÓMULO AYERZA.

Editorial Glem, SACIF: Avda Caseros 2056, 1264 Buenos Aires; tel. (1) 26-6641; f. 1933; psychology, technology; Pres. JOSÉ ALFREDO TUCCI.

Editorial Guadalupe: Mansilla 3865, 1425 Buenos Aires; tel. (1) 822-4164; fax (1) 805-4112; f. 1895; social sciences, religion, anthropology, children's books, and pedagogy; Man. Dir P. LUIS O. LIBERTI.

Editorial Heliasta, SRL: Viamonte 1730, 1°, 1055 Buenos Aires; tel. (1) 371-6402; fax (1) 375-1659; e-mail eheliasta@impsat1.com.ar; f. 1944; literature, biography, dictionaries, legal; Pres. Dra ANA MARÍA CABANELLAS.

Editorial Hemisferio Sur, SA: Pasteur 743, 1028 Buenos Aires; tel. (1) 952-9825; fax (1) 952-8454; f.1966; agriculture, veterinary and food science; Man. Dir ADOLFO JULIÁN PEÑA.

Editorial Hispano-Americana, SA (HASA): Alsina 731, 1087 Buenos Aires; tel. (1) 331-5051; f. 1934; science and technology; Pres. Prof. HÉCTOR OSCAR ALGARRA.

Editorial Inter-Médica, SAICI: Junín 917, 1°, Casilla 4625, 1113 Buenos Aires; tel. (1) 961-9234; fax (1) 961-5572; f. 1959; science, medicine, dentistry, psychology, odontology, veterinary; Pres. JORGE MODYEIEVSKY.

Editorial Inter-Vet, SA: Avda de los Constituyentes 3141, Buenos Aires; tel. (1) 51-2382; f. 1987; veterinary; Pres. JORGE MODYEIEVSKY.

Kapelusz Editora, SA: Moreno 372, 1091 Buenos Aires; tel. (1) 342-6450; fax (1) 331-9352; f. 1905; textbooks, psychology, pedagogy, children's books; Gen. Man. TOMÁS CASTILLO.

Editorial Kier, SACIFI: Avda Santa Fe 1260, 1059 Buenos Aires; tel. and fax (1) 811-0507; f. 1907; Eastern doctrines and religions, astrology, parapsychology, tarot, I Ching, occultism, cabbala, freemasonry and natural medicine; Pres. HECTOR S. PIBERNUS; Mans SERGIO PIBERNUS, OSVALDO PIBERNUS, CRISTINA GRIGNA.

Ediciones Librerías Fausto: Corrientes 1316, 1043 Buenos Aires; tel. (1) 476-4919; telex 22146; fax (1) 476-3914; f. 1943; fiction and non-fiction; Man. RAFAEL ZORRILLA.

Carlos Lohlé, SA: Tacuarí 1516, 1139 Buenos Aires; tel. (1) 27-9969; f. 1953; philosophy, religion, belles-lettres; Dir FRANCISCO M. LOHLÉ.

Editorial Losada, SA: Moreno 3362/64, 1209 Buenos Aires; tel. (1) 863-8608; fax (1) 864-0434; f. 1938; general; Pres. JOSÉ JUAN FERNÁNDEZ REGUERA.

Ediciones Macchi, SA: Alsina 1535/37, 1088 Buenos Aires; tel. (1) 46-2506; fax (1) 46-0594; f. 1947; economic sciences; Pres. RAÚL LUIS MACCHI; Dir JULIO ALBERTO MENDONÇA.

Editorial Médica Panamericana, SA: Marcelo T. de Alvear 2143, 1122 Buenos Aires; tel. (1) 821-5520; fax (1) 11-1196; f. 1962; health sciences; Pres. HUGO BRIK.

Ediciones Nueva Visión, SAIC: Tucumán 3748, 1189 Buenos Aires; tel. (1) 864-5050; fax (1) 863-5980; f. 1954; psychology, education, social sciences, linguistics; Man. Dir HAYDÉE P. DE GIACONE.

Editorial Paidós: Defensa 599, 1°, 1065 Buenos Aires; tel. (1) 331-2275; fax (1) 345-6769; f. 1945; social sciences, medicine, philosophy, religion, history, literature, textbooks; Man. Dir MARITA GOTTHEIL.

Plaza y Janés, SA: Buenos Aires; tel. (1) 86-6769; popular fiction and non-fiction; Man. Dir JORGE PÉREZ.

Editorial Plus Ultra, SA: Callao 575, 1022 Buenos Aires; tel. (1) 374-2953; f. 1964; literature, history, textbooks, law, economics, politics, sociology, pedagogy, children's books; Man. Editors RAFAEL ROMÁN, LORENZO MARENGO.

Schapire Editor, SRL: Uruguay 1249, 1016 Buenos Aires; tel. (1) 812-0765; fax (1) 815-0369; f. 1941; music, art, theatre, sociology, history, fiction; Dir MIGUEL SCHAPIRE DALMAT.

Editorial Sigmar, SACI: Belgrano 1580, 7°, 1093 Buenos Aires; tel. (1) 383-3045; fax (1) 11-2662; f. 1941; children's books; Man. Dir ROBERTO CHWAT.

Editorial Sopena Argentina, SACI e I: 1091 Buenos Aires; tel. (1) 38-7182; f. 1918; dictionaries, classics, chess, health, politics, history, children's books; Exec. Pres. DANIEL CARLOS OLSEN.

Editorial Stella: Viamonte 1984, 1056 Buenos Aires; tel. (1) 46-0346; general non-fiction and textbooks; owned by Asociación Educacionista Argentina.

Editorial Sudamericana, SA: Humberto 545, 1°, 1103 Buenos Aires; tel. (1) 362-2128; telex 25644; fax (1) 362-7364; f. 1939; general fiction and non-fiction; Gen. Man. JAIME RODRÍGUEZ.

Editorial Troquel, SA: Dr E. Finochietto 473, 1143 Buenos Aires; tel. (1) 27-1116; fax (1) 23-9350; f. 1954; general literature, and textbooks; Pres. GUSTAVO A. RESSIA.

PUBLISHERS' ASSOCIATION

Cámara Argentina de Publicaciones: Reconquista 1011, 6°, 1003 Buenos Aires; tel. (1) 311-6855; f. 1970; Pres. AGUSTÍN DOS SANTOS; Man. LUIS FRANCISCO HOULIN.

Broadcasting and Communications

Secretaría de Comunicaciones: Sarmiento 151, 4°, 1000 Buenos Aires; tel. (1) 318-9410; telex 21706; fax (1) 318-9432; co-ordinates 30 stations and the international service; Sec. Dr GERMÁN KAMMERATH.

Subsecretaría de Planificación y Gestión Tecnológica: Sarmiento 151, 4°, 1000 Buenos Aires; tel. (1) 311-5909; telex 21706; Under-Sec. Ing. LEONARDO JOSÉ LEIBSON.

Subsecretaría de Radiocomunicaciones: Sarmiento 151, 4°, 1000 Buenos Aires; tel. (1) 311-5909; telex 21706; Under-Sec. Ing. ALFREDO R. PARODI.

Subsecretaría de Telecomunicaciones: Sarmiento 151, 4°, 1000 Buenos Aires; tel. (1) 311-5909; telex 21706; Under-Sec. JULIO I. GUILLÁN.

Comité Federal de Radiodifusión (COMFER): Suipacha 765, 9°, 1008 Buenos Aires; tel. (1) 394-1349; fax (1) 394-6866; f. 1972; controls various technical aspects of broadcasting and transmission of programmes; Head JOSÉ AIELLO.

TELECOMMUNICATIONS

Cámara de Informática y Comunicaciones de la República Argentina (CICOMRA): Avda Córdoba 744, 2°, 1054 Buenos Aires; tel. (1) 325-8839; fax (1) 325-9604; e-mail cicomra@starnet.net.ar.

Comisión Nacional de Comunicaciones (CNC): Perú 103, 9°, 1067 Buenos Aires; tel. (1) 347-9242; fax (1) 347-9244; Pres. Dr ROBERTO CATALÁN.

Cía Ericsson SACI: Avda Madero, 1020 Buenos Aires; tel. (1) 319-5500; fax (1) 315-0629; Dir-Gen. Ing. ROLANDO ZUBIRÁN.

Cía de Radiocomunicaciones Móviles SA: Tucumán 744, 9°, 1049 Buenos Aires; tel. (1) 325-5006; fax (1) 325-5334; Pres. Lic. MAURICIO E. WIOR.

Telecom Argentina: Avda Congreso 3942, 1°, 1430 Buenos Aires; tel. (1) 968-1569; fax (1) 968-1420; e-mail rkustra@starnet.net.ar; Man. Ing. RUBÉN KUSTRA.

Telecomunicaciones Internacionales de Argentina TELINTAR SA: 25 de Mayo 457, 7°, 1002 Buenos Aires; tel. (1) 318-0500; fax (1) 313-4924; e-mail mlamas@telintar.com.ar; Sec.-Gen. Dr MARCELO MIGUEL LAMAS.

Telefónica de Argentina SA (TASA): Tucumán 1, 17°, 1049 Buenos Aires; tel. (1) 345-5772; fax (1) 345-5771; e-mail gabello@telefonica.com.ar; Man. Ing. EDUARDO A. GAGELLONI.

RADIO

There are three privately-owned stations in Buenos Aires and 72 in the interior. There are also 37 state-controlled stations, four provincial, three municipal and three university stations. The principal ones are Radio Antártida, Radio Argentina, Radio Belgrano, Radio Ciudad de Buenos Aires, Radio Excelsior, Radio Mitre, Radio El Mundo, Radio Nacional, Radio del Plata, Radio Rivadavia and Radio Splendid, all in Buenos Aires.

Servicio Oficial de Radiodifusión (SOR): Maipú 555, 1006 Buenos Aires; tel. (1) 325-1969; fax (1) 325-9433; Dir JULIO E. MAHARBIZ; controls:

Cadena Argentina de Radiodifusión (CAR): Avda Entre Ríos 149, 3°, 1079 Buenos Aires; tel. (1) 325-9100; fax (1) 325-9433; groups all national state-owned commercial stations which are operated directly by the Subsecretaría Operativa.

LRA Radio Nacional de Buenos Aires: Maipú 555, 1006 Buenos Aires; tel. (1) 325-9100; telex 21250; fax (1) 325-9433; f. 1937; Dir JULIO E. MAHARBIZ.

Radiodifusión Argentina al Exterior (RAE): Maipú 555, 1006 Buenos Aires; tel. (1) 325-6368; fax (1) 325-9433; f. 1958; broadcasts in 8 languages to all areas of the world; Dir-Gen. PERLA DAMURI.

Asociación de Radiodifusoras Privadas Argentinas (ARPA): Cangallo 1561, 8°, 1037 Buenos Aires; tel. (1) 35-4412; f. 1958; an association of all but 3 of the privately-owned commercial stations; Pres. EVARISTO R. E. ALONSO.

TELEVISION

There are 44 television channels, of which 29 are privately-owned and 15 are owned by provincial and national authorities. The national television network is regulated by the Comité Federal de Radiodifusión (see above).

The following are some of the more important television stations in Argentina: Argentina Televisora Color LS82 Canal 7, LS83 Telearte SA, LS84 Televisión Federal, SA: Channel II TV (Telefé), LS85 ArTeAr SA, Telenueva, Teledifusora Bahiense, Telecor, Dicor Difusión Córdoba, TV Universidad Nacional Córdoba, and TV Mar del Plata.

Asociación de Teleradiodifusoras Argentinas (ATA): Avda Córdoba 323, 6°, 1054 Buenos Aires; tel. (1) 312-4208; fax (1) 315-4681; e-mail ata@giga.com.ar; f. 1959; association of 22 private television channels; Pres. LUIS HUMBERTO TARSITANO.

ATC—Argentina Televisora Color LS82 TV Canal 7: Avda Figueroa Alcorta 2977, 1425 Buenos Aires; tel. (1) 802-6001; fax (1) 802-9878; state-controlled channel; Dir RENÉ JOLIVET.

LS83 (Telearte SA): México 990, 1097 Buenos Aires; tel. (1) 801-3065; private channel; Dir ALEJANDRO RAMAY.

LS84 Televisión Federal, SA: Channel II TV (Telefé): Pavón 2444, 1248 Buenos Aires; tel. (1) 941-9549; telex 22780; fax (1) 942-6773; leased to a private concession in 1992; Pres. PEDRO SIMONCINI.

LS85: Canal 13 (ArTeAr SA): Lima 1261, 1138 Buenos Aires; tel. (1) 27-3661; fax (1) 331-8573; f. 1989; leased to a private concession in 1992; Dir-Gen. LUCIO PAGLIARO.

Finance

(cap. = capital; res = reserves; dep. = deposits; m. = million; amounts in australes—₳ or nuevos pesos argentinos—$, unless otherwise stated)

BANKING

In early 1995 there were four public banks, 30 municipal banks, 62 domestic private banks, 31 foreign private banks and 39 co-operative banks. By mid-1995 it was reported that the total number of commercial banks in operation had decreased to 130.

Central Bank

Banco Central de la República Argentina: Reconquista 266, 1003 Buenos Aires; tel. (1) 348-3500; telex 23942; fax (1) 325-4860; f. 1935 as a central reserve bank; it has the right of note issue; all capital is held by the State; Gov. ROQUE BENJAMIN FERNÁNDEZ; Pres. PEDRO POU.

Government-owned Commercial Banks

Banco de la Ciudad de Buenos Aires: Florida 302, 1313 Buenos Aires; tel. (1) 329-8600; telex 22365; fax (1) 112-098; municipal bank; f. 1878; cap. $6.9m., res $172.0m., dep. $1,403.4m. (Oct. 1995); Chair. HORACIO CHIGHIZOLA; 31 brs.

Banco de Mendoza, SA: Gutiérrez 51, 5500 Mendoza; tel. (61) 25-1200; telex 55204; fax (61) 25-4749; f. 1934; provincial bank; cap. $87.8m., res $11.5m., dep. $808.3m. (June 1993); Pres. NICOLÁS E. CANET; 24 brs.

Banco de la Nación Argentina: Bartolomé Mitre 326, 1036 Buenos Aires; tel. (1) 343-1011; telex 9189; fax (1) 112-067; f. 1891; national bank; cap. $288.0m., res $1,606.5m., dep. $8,349.0m. (Dec. 1995); Pres. Dr ROQUE MACCARONE; 543 brs.

Banco de la Pampa: Carlos Pellegrini 255, 6300 Santa Rosa; tel. (954) 51000; telex 83106; fax (954) 51096; f. 1958; cap. and res $92.7m., dep. $644m. (Nov. 1996); Pres. NÉSTOR MARIO BOSIO; 59 brs.

Banco de Previsión Social: Avda España 1275, 5500 Mendoza; tel. (61) 25-5200; fax (61) 38-0544; cap. and res $44.9m., dep. $167.1m. (June 1992); Pres. RITO LUIS IRAÑETA.

Banco de la Provincia de Buenos Aires: Avda San Martín 137, 1004 Buenos Aires; tel. (1) 331-2561; telex 18276; fax (1) 331-5154; f. 1822; provincial bank; cap. and res $1,125.5m., dep. $5,299.0m. (Dec. 1995); Pres. RODOLFO ANÍBAL FRIGERI; 330 brs.

Banco de la Provincia del Chubut: Rivadavia 615, 9103 Rawson; tel. (965) 82506; dep. $170.0m., total assets $456.8m. (May 1995); Principal Officer FREDERICO G. POLAK.

Banco de la Provincia de Córdoba: San Jerónimo 166, 5000 Córdoba; tel. (51) 20-7200; telex 51756; fax (51) 22-9718; f. 1873; provincial bank; cap. $47.6m., res $142.8m., dep. $1,036.1 (Dec. 1994); Pres. LUIS FELIPE FERRARO; 180 brs.

Banco de la Provincia de Jujuy: Alvear 999, 4600 San Salvador de Jujuy; tel. (882) 23003; telex 66129; dep. $87.9m., total assets $134.8m. (May 1995); Pres. Dr ARMANDO EDUARDO FERNÁNDEZ.

Banco de la Provincia del Neuquén: Avda Argentina 41/45, 8300 Neuquén; tel. (99) 34221; telex 84128; fax (99) 40439; f. 1960; dep. $232.8m., total assets $388.6m. (March 1995); Pres. OMAR SANTIAGO NEGRETTI; 21 brs.

Banco de la Provincia de Río Negro: 25 de Mayo 99, 8500 Viedma; tel. (920) 24130; dep. $110.4m., total assets $373.0m. (May 1995); Pres. ANTONIO TROMER.

Banco de la Provincia de San Luis: Rivadavia 602, 5700 San Luis; tel. (652) 25013; fax (652) 24943; dep. $88.8m., total assets $107.8m. (May 1995); Principal Officer SALVADOR OMAR CAMPO.

Banco de la Provincia de Santa Cruz: Avda General Roca 802, 9400 Río Gallegos; tel. (966) 20845; dep. $211.7m., total assets $382.1m. (June 1995); Govt Admin. EDUARDO LABOLIDA.

Banco de la Provincia de Santiago del Estero: Avda Belgrano 529 Sur, 4200 Santiago del Estero; tel. (85) 22-2300; dep. $69.9m., total assets $101.6m. (Jan. 1995); Pres. AMÉRICO DAHER.

Banco de la Provincia de Tucumán: San Martín 362, 4000 San Miguel de Tucumán; tel. (81) 31-1709; dep. $164.7m., total assets $359.5m. (March 1995); Govt Admin. EMILIO APAZA.

Banco Provincial de Salta: España 550, 4400 Salta; tel. (87) 31-1254; telex 65119; fax (87) 31-0020; f. 1887; dep. $40.7m., total assets $125.0m. (June 1995); Pres. Dr REYNALDO ALFREDO NOGUEIRA; 19 brs.

Banco de Santa Fe: San Martín 715, 2000 Rosario; tel. (42) 40151; telex 41751; f. 1874; provincial bank; dep. $40.7m., total assets $773.3m. (June 1995); Chair. FERNANDO JUAN VINALS.

Banco Social de Córdoba: 27 de Abril 185, 1°, 5000 Córdoba; tel. (51) 22-3367; dep. $187.3m., total assets $677.3m. (June 1995); Pres. Dr JAIME POMPAS.

Banco del Territorio Nacional de Tierra del Fuego, Antártida e Islas del Atlántico Sur: San Martín, esq. Roca, 9410 Ushuaia; tel. (901) 24087; national bank; cap. and res $21.8m., dep. $54.2m. (June 1992); Pres. OSVALDO MANUEL RODRÍGUEZ.

Private Commercial Banks

Banco BI Creditanstalt, SA: Bouchard 547, 24°, 1106 Buenos Aires; tel. (1) 319-8400; telex 20194; fax (1) 319-8296; f. 1971; fmrly Banco Interfinanzas; cap. and res $20.0m., dep. $120.0m. (Sept. 1995); Pres. Dr MIGUEL ANGELINO.

Banco Baires, SA: San Martín 215, 1004 Buenos Aires; tel. (1) 394-5851; telex 24199; fax (1) 325-8548; f. 1956 as Baires Exchange House, adopted current name in 1992 following merger with Banco Mediterráneo, SA; cap. $11.6m., res $1.3m., dep. $56.5m. (Dec. 1994); Pres. G. ANÍBAL MENÉNDEZ.

Banco BanSud, SA: Sarmiento 355, 1041 Buenos Aires; tel. (1) 348-6500; telex 18907; fax (1) 325-5641; f. 1995 after merger of Banesto Banco Shaw, SA and Banco del Sud, SA; cap. $44.4m., res $293.0m., dep. $1,151.2m. (June 1996); Pres. LEONARDO ANIDJAR; 39 brs.

Banco del Buen Ayre, SA: Bartolomé Mitre 899, 1036 Buenos Aires; tel. (1) 382-2001; telex 18883; fax (1) 476-0228; cap. and res $31.0m., dep. $116.8m. (June 1992); f. 1980; Pres. MARCOS GARFUNKEL.

Banco Comercial Israelita, SA: Bartolomé Mitre 702, Rosario, 2000 Santa Fe; tel. (41) 25-5440; telex 41818; fax (41) 25-5430; f. 1921; cap. $0.5m., res $27.0m., dep. $191.3 (March 1995); Pres. Ing. DAVID CZARNY; 4 brs.

Banco de Corrientes: 9 de Julio 1099, esq. San Juan, 3400 Corrientes; tel. (783) 79200; telex 74106; fax (783) 79283; f. 1951 as Banco de la República de Corrientes; adopted current name in 1993, after transfer to private ownership; cap. and res $38.5m., dep. $126.7m. (June 1995); Pres. JUAN RAMÓN BRANCHI; 33 brs.

Banco de Crédito Argentino, SA: Reconquista 2, 1003 Buenos Aires; tel. (1) 331-1394; telex 18077; fax (1) 334-7219; f. 1887; cap. $52.4m., res $143.4m., dep. $1,440.5m. (June 1996); merged with Banco Financiero Argentino in 1987; Chair. FERNANDO DE SANTIBAÑES; 122 brs.

Banco Crédito Provincial SA: Calle 7, esq. 50, Casilla 54, 1900 La Plata; tel. (21) 25-7008; telex 31126; fax (21) 25-5578; f. 1911; cap. $2.5m., res $40.5m., dep. $160.5m. (June 1995); Pres. ANTONIO R. FALABELLA; 47 brs.

Banco de Entre Ríos SA: Monte Caseros 128, 3100 Paraná; tel. (43) 23-1200; telex 45134; fax (43) 21-1221; f. 1935; provincial bank; transferred to private ownership in 1995; cap. $34.2m., res $0.1m., dep. $500.4m. (June 1996); Pres. EDMUNDO JUSTO MUGURUZA; 29 brs.

Banco Federal Argentino, SA: Sarmiento 401, 1041, Buenos Aires; tel. (1) 394-1011; telex 17026; fax (1) 394-2273; f. 1969; cap. and res $19.1m., dep. $137.9m. (March 1993); Pres. JORGE F. CHRISTENSEN; 19 brs.

Banco Florencia, SA: Reconquista 353, 1003 Buenos Aires; tel. (1) 325-5949; telex 25232; fax (1) 325-5849; f. 1984; cap. and res $8.8m., dep. $11.8m. (Dec. 1993); Chair. ALBERTO BRUNET; Vice-Chair. JORGE GONZÁLEZ.

Banco Francés del Río de la Plata SA: Reconquista 199, 1003 Buenos Aires; tel. (1) 331-7071; telex 9119; fax (1) 953-8009; f. 1886; cap. $128.2m., res $286.7m., dep. $1,907.1m. (June 1996); Pres. Dr LUIS ROQUE OTERO MONSEGUR; 75 brs.

Banco de Galicia y Buenos Aires SA: Juan D. Perón 407, Casilla 86, 1038 Buenos Aires; tel. (1) 394-7080; telex 23906; fax (1) 393-1603; internet http://www.bancogalicia.com.ar; f. 1905; cap. and res $441.4m., dep. $3,595.8m. (June 1996); Chair. EDUARDO J. ESCASANY; 207 brs.

Banco General de Negocios, SA: Esmeralda 120/38, 1035 Buenos Aires; tel. (1) 394-3187; telex 24077; fax (1) 334-6422; f. 1978; cap. $38.0m., res $11.5m., dep. $230.1m. (Dec. 1995); Chair. JOSÉ E. ROHM.

Banco Israelita de Cordoba, SA: Ituzaingó 60, 5000 Córdoba; tel. (51) 21-2041; telex 51837; fax (51) 24-3616; f. 1942; cap. $9.0m., res $18.3m., dep. $160.5m. (June 1995); Pres. ARNOLDO LEVIN; 15 brs.

Banco Macro, SA: Sarmiento 735, 1041 Buenos Aires; tel. (1) 325-2330; telex 18679; fax (1) 325-6935; f. 1988; cap. and res $10.3m., dep. $29.3m. (June 1992); Pres. JORGE HORACIO BRITO.

Banco Mariva, SA: Sarmiento 500, 1041 Buenos Aires; tel. (1) 331-7571; telex 22849; fax (1) 322-6814; f. 1980; cap $30.0m., res $10.0m., dep. $206.3m. (Dec.1994); Pres. RICARDO MAY.

Banco Mercantil Argentino, SA: Corrientes 629, 1324 Buenos Aires; tel. (1) 334-9999; telex 9122; fax (1) 111-1448; f. 1923; cap. and res $50.5m., dep. $374.8m. (Dec. 1994); Pres. NOEL WERTHEIN; 60 brs.

Banco Popular Argentino: Florida 201, esq. Juan D. Perón, 1005 Buenos Aires; tel. (1) 320-2800; telex 9220; fax (1) 331-5427; f. 1887; cap. and res $32.7m., dep. $188.6m. (Dec. 1993); Gen. Man. JOSÉ LUIS CAMPOS; 22 brs.

Banco Popular Financiero: Sobremonte 801, Casilla 5800, Río Cuarto, Córdoba; tel. (586) 30001; telex 54507; f. 1964; cap. and res $8.8m., dep. $41.2m. (June 1992); Pres. JOSÉ OSVALDO TRAVAGLIA; Vice-Pres. HUGO RICARDO LARDONE.

Banco de la Provincia de Misiones, SA: Santa Fe 1630, 1300 Posadas; tel. (752) 32250; transferred to private ownership in 1995; dep. $159.3m., total assets $504.4m. (May 1995); Pres. RICARDO MAZLUMIAN.

Banco Quilmes, SA: Juan D. Perón 564, 2°, 1038 Buenos Aires; tel. (1) 331-8111; telex 18955; fax (1) 334-5235; f. 1907; cap. $81.7m., res $55.4m., dep. $1,161.8m. (June 1995); Pres. Dr PEDRO O. FIORITO; 90 brs.

Banco República: Sarmiento 336, 1041 Buenos Aires; tel. (1) 331-8385; telex 17330; fax (1) 331-8402; f. 1974; cap. and res $63.3m., dep. $728.1m. (Dec. 1993); Chair. BENITO JAIME LUCINI.

Banco Río de la Plata, SA: Bartolomé Mitre 480, 1036 Buenos Aires; tel. (1) 340-1000; telex 9215; fax (1) 340-1554; f. 1908; cap. and res $687.7m., dep. $2,821.6m. (June 1996); Pres. J. GREGORIO PÉREZ COMPAÑO; 175 brs.

Banco Roberts, SA: 25 de Mayo 258, 1002 Buenos Aires; tel. (1) 342-0061; telex 24159; fax (1) 331-3960; f. 1978; cap. $140.2m., res $48.1m., dep. $1,477.1m. (June 1996); Pres. JORGE A. HEINZE; 38 brs.

Banco del Suquía, SA: 25 de Mayo 160, 5000 Córdoba; tel. (51) 22-2048; telex 51451; fax (51) 22-9366; f. 1961; cap. $58.6m., res $39.4m., dep. $613.9m. (June 1996); Pres. VITO REMO ROGGIO; Gen. Man. JUAN CARLOS IRAZUSTA; 47 brs.

Banco UNB, SA: 25 de Mayo 459, 1002 Buenos Aires; tel. (1) 312-7370; telex 18452; fax (1) 312-9202; f. 1988; cap. and res $41.3m., dep. $202.9m. (Sept. 1994); Pres. RAFAEL BONASSO.

Banco de Valores, SA: Sarmiento 310, 1041 Buenos Aires; tel. (1) 345-1900; telex 28168; fax (1) 334-1731; f. 1978; cap. and res $14.6m., dep. $67.8m. (March 1993); Pres. HÉCTOR N. FERNÁNDEZ SAAVEDRA; 1 br.

Banco Velox, SA: San Martín 298, 1004 Buenos Aires; tel. (1) 320-0200; telex 23882; fax (1) 393-7672; f. 1983; cap. and res $48.0m., dep. $283.5m. (June 1997); Pres. JUAN PEIRANO; 8 brs.

Nuevo Banco del Chaco, SA: Güemes 40, 3500 Resistencia; tel. (722) 24888; telex 17717; f. 1958 as Banco del Chaco; transferred to private ownership and adopted current name in 1994; cap. $10.5m., dep. $45.4m. (June 1995); 28 brs.

Nuevo Banco de Formosa: 25 de Mayo 102, 3600 Formosa; tel. (717) 26030; transferred to private ownership in 1995; dep. $145.3m., total assets $235.7m. (May 1995); Pres. JOSÉ MANUEL PABLO VIUDES.

Co-operative Banks

Banco Almafuerte Cooperativo Ltdo: Avda de Mayo 600, 1085 Buenos Aires; tel. (1) 346-0700; telex 23368; fax (1) 331-3414; f. 1978; cap. $18.4m., res $28.7m., dep. $250.1m. (Dec.1994); Pres. Dr ELIAS FARAH; 27 brs.

Banco Mayo Cooperativo Ltdo: Sarmiento 706, 1041 Buenos Aires; tel. (1) 326-4774; telex 17394; fax (1) 326-8080; f. 1978; cap. $79.0m., res $31.2m., dep. $689.5m. (June 1996); Pres. and Gen. Man. RUBÉN E. BERAJA; 75 brs.

Banco Nueva Era Cooperativo Ltdo: Avda Córdoba 1690, 1055 Buenos Aires; tel. (1) 811-6868; fax (1) 811-7112; f. 1979; cap. and res $14,350m., dep. $59,313m. (Dec. 1993); Pres. RODOLFO E. FERNÁNDEZ DIAZ; 12 brs.

Banco Patricios: Florida 101, 1005 Buenos Aires; tel. (1) 331-1786; telex 23175; fax (1) 331-6887; cap. and res $19.1m., dep. $144.0m. (Dec. 1993); Pres. Dr ALBERTO SPOLSKI.

Banco Roco Cooperativo Ltdo: 25 de Mayo 122, 1002 Buenos Aires; tel. (1) 342-0051; telex 21149; fax (1) 331-6596; f. 1961; cap. and res $10.8m., dep. $58.1m. (Dec. 1992); Pres. ALFREDO B. ARREGUI.

Other National Banks

Banco Hipotecario Nacional: Defensa 130, 1065 Buenos Aires; tel. (1) 331-2778; fax (1) 334-9743; f. 1886; mortgage bank; cap. and res $322.4m., dep. $83.6m. (April 1992); Govt Admin. HORACIO JOSÉ AGUSTÍN ALVAREZ RIVERO; 23 brs.

Banco Nacional de Desarrollo: 25 de Mayo 145, 1002 Buenos Aires; tel. (1) 331-2091; telex 9179; fax (1) 334-9315; f. 1944; development bank; cap. and res $568.6m., dep. $158.4m. (1991); Pres. HUGO RICARDO AVELLANEDA.

Caja Nacional de Ahorro y Seguro: Hipólito Yrigoyen 1770, 1308 Buenos Aires; tel. (1) 372-5860; telex 22642; fax (1) 372-6080; f. 1915; transferred to private ownership in April 1994; savings bank and insurance institution; cap. and res $143.5m., dep. $307.6m. (May 1994); Pres. Dr CARLOS AUGUSTO FONT; 44 brs.

Foreign Banks

ABN Amro Bank N.V. (Netherlands): Florida 361, 1005 Buenos Aires; tel. (1) 394-1022; telex 24302; fax (1) 322-0603; f. 1914; cap. and res $37.7m., dep. $94.5m. (June 1992); Gen. Man. CÉSAR A. DEYMONNAZ.

Banca Nazionale del Lavoro, SA—BNL (Italy): Juncal 1319, 1005 Buenos Aires; tel. (1) 814-4866; telex 24028; fax (1) 814-4864; cap. and res $102.6m., dep. $562.2m. (June 1992); took over Banco de Italia y Río de la Plata in 1987; Pres. ANGELO DE TRAGEACHE.

Banco do Brasil, SA (Brazil): Sarmiento 487, Casilla 2684, 1041 Buenos Aires; tel. (1) 394-9273; telex 24197; fax (1) 394-9577; f. 1960; cap. and res $33.9m., dep. $2.0m. (June 1992); Gen. Man. HÉLIO TESTONI.

Banco Crédit Lyonnais Argentina, SA: Bartolomé Mitre 531, Casilla 1001, 1036 Buenos Aires; tel. (1) 343-7841; telex 20093; fax (1) 342-6090; f. 1960 as Banco Tornquist, SA, acquired by Crédit Lyonnais (France) in 1981, adopted current name in 1993; cap. and res $73.2m., dep. $594.3m. (Dec. 1993); Pres. ROBERT GANNE; 24 brs.

Banco do Estado de São Paulo (Brazil): Tucumán 821, Casilla 2177, 1049 Buenos Aires; tel. (1) 325-9533; telex 17837; fax (1) 325-9527; cap. and res $11.7m., dep. $6.7m. (June 1992); Gen. Man. CARLOS ALBERTO BERGAMASCO.

Banco Europeo para América Latina (BEAL), SA: Juan D. Perón 338, 1038 Buenos Aires; tel. (1) 331-6544; telex 20071; fax (1) 331-2010; e-mail bealbsa@inter.prov.com; f. 1914; cap. and res $60m., dep. $121m. (Nov. 1996); Gen. Mans JEAN PIERRE SMERD, KLAUS KRÜGER.

Banco Exterior, SA—Argentina: Avda Leandro N. Alem 356, 11°, 1003 Buenos Aires; tel. (1) 313-3633; telex 17710; fax (1) 313-0354; f. 1980; cap. and res ₳91,735m., dep. ₳488,960m. (Dec. 1991); Gen. Man. GUILLERMO ROTHLISBERGER.

Banco Exterior, SA (Spain): Corrientes 441, 4°, 1317 Buenos Aires; tel. (1) 394-1766; telex 23228; fax (1) 325-1666; cap. and res $11.0m., dep. $12.9m. (Dec. 1993); Pres. IÑIGO DE LA SOTA.

Banco Itaú, SA (Brazil): Reconquista 590, 1003 Buenos Aires; tel. (1) 325-6683; telex 23547; fax (1) 325-6711; cap. and res $20.2m., dep. $1.2m. (June 1992); Gen. Man. JOÃO DE FARIA BURNIER.

Banco Real, SA (Brazil): San Martín 480, 1004 Buenos Aires; tel. (1) 394-3357; fax (1) 394-3345; cap. $22.6m., dep. $11.5m. (Sept. 1994); Gen. Man. CÉSAR ONOFRE SÁNCHEZ.

Banco de Santander-Argentina (Spain): Avda Leandro N. Alem 356, 12°, 1003 Buenos Aires; tel. (1) 319-9100; telex 9117; fax (1) 319-9192; f. 1964; cap. and res $20.9m., dep. $16.8m. (June 1992); Gen. Man. JOSÉ ÁLVAREZ PARRA.

Banco Sudameris Argentina, SA: Juan D. Perón 500, 1038 Buenos Aires; tel.(1) 329-5200; telex 9186; fax (1) 331-2793; f. 1912; cap. and res $62.5m., dep. $330.2m. (Dec. 1995); Exec.-Dir CARLOS GONZÁLEZ TABOADA.

Banco Supervielle-Société Générale, SA: Reconquista 300, 1003 Buenos Aires; tel. (1) 322-9354; telex 9108; fax (1) 394-3960; f. 1887 as Banco Supervielle de Buenos Aires, SA, adopted current name in 1979; cap. and res $70.7m., dep. $323.3m. (Dec. 1995); Chair. and Gen. Man. YVES THIEFFRY; 24 brs.

Bank of America, NT & SA (USA): 25 de Mayo 537, 1002 Buenos Aires; tel. (1) 319-2699; telex 9145; fax (1) 319-2658; f. 1940; cap. and res ₳308.9m., dep. ₳518.2m. (Jan. 1989); Pres. RODOLFO ALBORELLI.

Bank of New York, SA (USA): 25 de Mayo, 9°, 1002 Buenos Aires; tel. (1) 334-0630; cap. and res $25.8m., dep. $18.1m. (June 1992); Pres. EMILIO JORGE CARDENAS.

Bank of Tokyo-Mitsubishi, Ltd (Japan): Corrientes 420, 1043 Buenos Aires; tel. (1) 322-7087; telex 22099; fax (1) 322-6607; f. 1956; cap. and res $20m., dep. $81m. (Sept. 1994); Gen. Man. KAZUO OMI.

BankBoston NA (USA): Florida 99, 1005 Buenos Aires; tel. (1) 346-2000; telex 21139; fax (1) 346-3200; f. 1784; cap. $344.1m., dep. $1,846.0m. (June 1995); total assets $4,300m. (Sept. 1996); Pres. Ing. MANUEL SACERDOTE; 43 brs.

Banque Nationale de Paris, SA (France): 25 de Mayo 471, 1002 Buenos Aires; tel. (1) 318-0318; telex 21178; fax (1) 311-1368; f. 1981; cap. and res $29.4m., dep. $86.7m. (June 1992); Gen. Man. CHISLAIN DE BEAUCÉ.

Barclays Bank International PLC (United Kingdom): Bouchard 547, 26°, 1106 Buenos Aires; tel. (1) 315-3370; telex 22080; fax (1) 315-3374; f. 1979; cap. and res ₳160.5m., dep. ₳4.2m. (Jan. 1989); Rep. JUAN MARTÍN.

Chase Manhattan Bank (USA): Arenales 707, 5°, 1061 Buenos Aires; tel. (1) 319-2400; telex 9138; fax (1) 319-2416; f. 1904; cap. and res $46.3m., dep. $12,387m. (Sept. 1992); Gen. Man. MARCELO PODESTÁ.

Citibank, NA (USA): Colón 58, Bahía Blanca, 8000 Buenos Aires; tel. (1) 331-8281; telex 81757; f. 1914; cap. and res $172.8m., dep. $660.8m. (June 1992); Pres. RICARDO ANGLES; Vice-Pres. GUILLERMO STANLEY; 16 brs.

Deutsche Bank Argentina, SA (Germany): Bartolomé Mitre 401, Casilla 995, 1036 Buenos Aires; tel. (1) 343-2510; telex 9115; fax (1) 343-3536; f. 1960; cap. and res $123.6m., dep. $801.0m. (June 1994); Gen. Man. GERARDO GREISER; 47 brs.

Lloyds Bank (Bank of London and South America) Ltd (United Kingdom): Tronador 4890, 13°, Casilla 128, 1003 Buenos Aires; tel. (1) 335-3551; telex 21558; fax (1) 342-7487; f. 1862; subsidiary of Lloyds Bank TSB Group; cap. and res $108.1m., dep. $583.4m. (Sept. 1997); Gen. Man. for Argentina COLIN J. MITCHELL; 31 brs.

Morgan Guaranty Trust Co of New York (USA): Corrientes 411, 1043 Buenos Aires; tel. and fax (1) 325-8046; telex 18451; cap. and res $29.1m., dep. $11.6m. (June 1992); Gen. Man. JOSÉ MCLOUGHLIN.

Republic National Bank of New York (USA): Bartolomé Mitre 343, 1036 Buenos Aires; tel. (1) 343-0161; telex 9237; fax (1) 331-6064; cap. and res $17.2m., dep. $13.6m. (March 1994); Gen. Man. ALBERTO MUCHNICK.

Royal Bank of Canada: Avda del Libertador 602, 18°, 1001 Buenos Aires; tel. (1) 814-5140; fax (1) 814-5227; f. 1869; cap. and res $18.1m., dep. $45.8m. (June 1992); Regional Rep. R. H. STREETON; 2 brs.

Bankers' Associations

Asociación de Bancos Argentinos (ADEBA): San Martín 229, 10°, 1004 Buenos Aires; tel. (1) 394-1430; fax (1) 394-6340; e-mail adeba@datamarkets.com.ar; f. 1972; Pres. EDUARDO J. ESCASANY; 31 mems.

Asociación de Bancos del Interior de la República Argentina (ABIRA): Corrientes 538, 4°, 1043 Buenos Aires; tel. (1) 394-3439; telex 28273; fax (1) 394-5682; f. 1956; Pres. Dr JORGE FEDERICO CHRISTENSEN; Dir RAÚL PASSANO; 30 mems.

Asociación de Bancos de Provincia de la República Argentina (ABAPRA): Florida 470, 1°, 1005 Buenos Aires; tel. (1) 322-6321; telex 24015; fax (1) 322-6721; f. 1959; Pres. JOSÉ MANUEL PABLO VIUDES; Man. LUIS B. BUCAFUSCO; 31 mems.

Asociación de Bancos de la República Argentina (ABRA): Reconquista 458, 2°, 1358 Buenos Aires; tel. (1) 394-6452; fax (1) 322-9642; e-mail abradir@satlink.com; f. 1919; Pres. JULIO J. GÓMEZ; Exec. Dir ADALBERTO BARBOSA; 72 mems.

Federación de Bancos Cooperativos de la República Argentina (FEBANCOOP): Maipú 374, 9°/10°, 1006 Buenos Aires; tel. (1) 394-9949; telex 23650; f. 1973; Pres. OMAR C. TRILLO; Exec. Sec. JUAN CARLOS ROMANO; 32 mems.

STOCK EXCHANGES

Mercado de Valores de Buenos Aires, SA: 25 de Mayo 367, 8°–10°, 1002 Buenos Aires; tel. (1) 313-6021; telex 17445; fax (1) 313-4472; internet http://www.merval.sba.com.ar; Pres. HÉCTOR J. BACQUÉ.

There are also stock exchanges at Córdoba, Rosario, Mendoza and La Plata.

Supervisory Authority

Comisión Nacional de Valores (CNV): Hipólito Yrigoyen 250, 10°, 1310 Buenos Aires; tel. (1) 342-1919; fax (1) 331-0639; monitors capital markets; Pres. GUILLERMO HARTNECK.

INSURANCE

Superintendencia de Seguros de la Nación: Avda Julio A. Roca 721, 1°, 1067 Buenos Aires; tel. (1) 331-9821; fax (1) 331-8733; f. 1938; Superintendent Dr ALBERTO ANGEL FERNÁNDEZ.

In December 1993 there were 249 insurance companies operating in Argentina, of which 11 were foreign. The following is a list of those offering all classes or a specialized service.

La Agrícola, SA: Corrientes 447, Buenos Aires; tel. (1) 394-5031; f. 1905; associated co La Regional; all classes; Pres. LUIS R. MARCO; First Vice-Pres. JUSTO J. DE CORRAL.

Aseguradora de Créditos y Garantías, SA: Corrientes 415, 4°, 1043 Buenos Aires; tel. (1) 394-4661; fax (1) 394-7292; f. 1965; Dir FÉLIX DE BARRIO; Gen. Man. Dr ANÍBAL E. LÓPEZ.

Aseguradora de Río Negro y Neuquén: Avda Alem 503, Cipolletti, Río Negro; f. 1960; all classes; Gen. Man. ERNESTO LÓPEZ.

Aseguradores de Cauciones, SA: Paraguay 580, 1057 Buenos Aires; tel. (1) 318-3700; telex 27032; fax (1) 318-3799; f. 1968; all classes; Pres. Dr AGUSTÍN DE VEDIA; Gen. Man. Lic. CARLOS A. POMESANO.

Aseguradores Industriales, SA: Juan D. Perón 650, 6°, 1038 Buenos Aires; tel. (1) 46-5425; f. 1961; all classes; Exec. Pres. Dir LUIS ESTEBAN LOFORTE.

La Austral: Buenos Aires; tel. (1) 42-9881; telex 21078; fax (1) 953-4459; f. 1942; all classes; Pres. RODOLFO H. TAYLOR.

Colón, Cía de Seguros Generales, SA: San Martín 548–550, 1004 Buenos Aires; tel. (1) 393-5069; telex 23923; f. 1962; all classes; Gen. Man. L. D. STÜCK.

Columbia, SA: Juan D. Perón 690, 1038 Buenos Aires; tel. (1) 325-0208; fax (1) 326-1392; f. 1918; all classes; Pres. MARTA BLANCO; Gen. Man. HORACIO H. PETRILLO.

El Comercio, Cía de Seguros a Prima Fija, SA: Corrientes 415, 3° y 5°, 1043 Buenos Aires; tel. (1) 394-9111; fax (1) 393-1207; f. 1889; all classes; Pres. DONALD JOSÉ SMITH BALMACEDA; Man. PABLO DOMINGO F. LONGO.

Cía Argentina de Seguros de Créditos a la Exportación, SA: Corrientes 345, 7°, 1043 Buenos Aires; tel. (1) 313-3048; telex 24207; fax (1) 313-2919; f. 1967; covers credit and extraordinary and political risks for Argentine exports; Pres. LUIS ORCOYEN; Gen. Man. Dr MARIANO A. GARCÍA GALISTEO.

Cía Aseguradora Argentina, SA: Avda Roque S. Peña 555, 1035 Buenos Aires; tel. (1) 30-1571; telex 22876; fax (1) 30-5973; f. 1918; all classes; Man. GUIDO LUTTINI; Vice-Pres. ALBERTO FRAGUIO.

La Continental, Cía de Seguros Generales SA: Corrientes 655, 1043 Buenos Aires; tel. (1) 393-8051; telex 121832; fax (1) 325-7101; f. 1912; all classes; Pres. RAÚL MASCARENHAS.

La Franco-Argentina, SA: Buenos Aires; tel. (1) 30-3091; telex 17291; f. 1896; all classes; Pres. Dr GUILLERMO MORENO HUEYO; Gen. Man. Dra HAYDÉE GUZIAN DE RAMÍREZ.

Hermes, SA: Edif. Hermes, Bartolomé Mitre 754/60, 1036 Buenos Aires; tel. (1) 331-4506; fax (1) 343-5552; f. 1926; all classes; Pres. DIONISIO KATOPODIS; Gen. Man. FRANCISCO MARTÍN ZABALO.

India, Cía de Seguros Generales SA: Avda Roque S. Peña 730, 1035 Buenos Aires; tel. (1) 328-6001; fax (1) 328-5602; f. 1950; all classes; Pres. ALFREDO JUAN PRIESSE; Vice-Pres. Dr RAÚL ALBERTO GUARDIA.

Instituto Italo-Argentino de Seguros Generales, SA: Avda Roque S. Peña 890, 1035 Buenos Aires; tel. (1) 320-9200; fax (1) 320-9229; f. 1920; all classes; Pres. ALEJANDRO A. SOLDATI.

La Meridional, Cía Argentina de Seguros SA: Juan D. Perón 646, 1038 Buenos Aires; tel. (1) 331-0941; fax (1) 331-0959; f. 1949; life and general; Pres. GUILLERMO V. LASCANO QUINTANA; Gen. Man. PETER HAMMER.

Plus Ultra, Cía Argentina de Seguros, SA: San Martín 548–50, 1004 Buenos Aires; tel. (1) 393-5069; telex 23923; f. 1956; all classes; Gen. Man. L. D. STÜCK.

La Primera, SA: Blvd Villegas y Oro, Trenque Lauquén, Prov. Buenos Aires; tel. (1) 393-8125; all classes; Pres. ENRIQUE RAÚL U. BOTTINI; Man. Dr RODOLFO RAÚL D'ONOFRIO.

La Rectora, SA: Corrientes 848, 1043 Buenos Aires; tel. (1) 394-6081; f. 1951; all classes; Pres. PEDRO PASCUAL MEGNA; Gen. Man. ANTONIO LÓPEZ BUENO.

La República Cía Argentina de Seguros Generales, SA: San Martín 627/29, 1374 Buenos Aires; tel. (1) 314-1000; fax (1) 318-8778; f. 1928; group life and general; Pres. JUAN E. CAMBIASO; Gen. Man. EDUARDO ESCAFFI.

Sud América Terrestre y Marítima Cía de Seguros Generales, SA: Avda Roque S. Peña 530, 1035 Buenos Aires; tel. (1) 340-5100; telex 24256; fax (1) 340-5380; f. 1919; all classes; Pres. EMA SÁNCHEZ DE LARRAGOITI; Vice-Pres. ALAIN HOMBREUX.

La Unión Gremial, SA: Mitre 665/99, 2000 Rosario, Santa Fe; tel. (41) 26-2900; fax (41) 25-9802; f. 1908; general; Pres. EDUARDO IGNACIO LLOBET.

La Universal: Buenos Aires; tel. (1) 42-9881; telex 21078; fax (1) 953-4459; f. 1905; all classes; Pres. RODOLFO H. TAYLOR.

Zurich-Iguazú Cía de Seguros, SA: San Martín 442, 1004 Buenos Aires; tel. (1) 329-0400; f. 1947; all classes; Pres. RAMÓN SANTAMARINA.

Reinsurance

Instituto Nacional de Reaseguros: Avda Julio A. Roca 694, 1067 Buenos Aires; tel. (1) 334-0084; telex 21170; fax (1) 334-5588; f. 1947; reinsurance in all branches; Pres. and Man. REINALDO A. CASTRO.

Insurance Associations

Asociación Argentina de Cías de Seguros: 25 de Mayo 565, 2°, 1002 Buenos Aires; tel. (1) 312-7790; fax (1) 312-6300; e-mail aacrsa@mbox.servicenet.com.ar; f. 1894; 76 mems; Pres. ROBERTO F. E. SOLLITTO.

Asociación de Entidades Aseguradoras Privadas de la República Argentina (EAPRA): San Martín 201, 7°, 1004 Buenos Aires; fax (1) 394-3881; f. 1875; asscn of 12 foreign insurance cos operating in Argentina; Pres. Dr PIERO ZUPPELLI; Sec. BERNARDO VON DER GOLTZ.

Trade and Industry

GOVERNMENT AGENCIES

Cámara de Exportadores de la República Argentina: Avda Roque S. Peña 740, 1°, 1035 Buenos Aires; tel. (1) 328-8556; fax (1) 328-1003; e-mail contacto@cera.org.ar; internet http://www.cera.org.ar; f. 1943 to promote exports; 700 mems.

Consejo Federal de Inversiones: San Martín 871, 1004 Buenos Aires; tel. (1) 313-5557; telex 21180; fax (1) 313-4486; federal board to co-ordinate domestic and foreign investment and provide technological aid for the provinces; Sec.-Gen. Ing. JUAN JOSÉ CIÁCERA.

Dirección de Producción Forestal (DPF): Avda Paseo Colón 982, anexo jardin, 1063 Buenos Aires; tel. (1) 349-2124; fax (1) 349-2102; assumed the responsibilities of the national forestry commission (Instituto Forestal Nacional—IFONA) in 1991, following its dissolution; supervised by the Secretaría de Agricultura, Ganadería y Pesca; maintains the Centro de Documentación e Información Forestal; Library Man. NILDA E. FERNÁNDEZ.

Instituto de Desarrollo Económico y Social (IDES): Araoz 2838, 1425 Buenos Aires; tel. (1) 804-4949; fax (1) 804-5856; e-mail ides@clasco.edu.ar; f. 1961; investigation into social sciences; 700 mems; Pres. ALFREDO MONZA; Sec. JUAN CARLOS GÓMEZ SABAINI.

Junta Nacional de Granos: Avda Paseo Colón 359, 1063 Buenos Aires; tel. (1) 30-0641; telex 21793; national grain board; supervises commercial practices and organizes the construction of farm silos and port elevators; Pres. JORGE CORT.

Secretaría de Agricultura, Ganadería y Pesca: Avda Paseo Colón 922, primera planta, Of. 146, 1063 Buenos Aires; tel. (1) 349-2291; fax (1) 349-2292; f. 1871; undertakes regulatory, promotional, advisory and administrative responsibilities on behalf of the meat, livestock and fisheries industries; Sec. FELIPE C. SOLA.

Sindicatura General de Empresas Públicas: Lavalle 1429, 1048 Buenos Aires; tel. (1) 49-5415; fax (1) 476-4054; f. 1978; to exercise external control over wholly-or partly-owned public enterprises; Pres. ALBERTO R. ABAD.

DEVELOPMENT ORGANIZATIONS

Instituto Argentino del Petróleo: Maipú 645, 3°, 1006 Buenos Aires; tel. (1) 393-5494; fax (1) 325-8009; f. 1957; established to promote the development of petroleum exploration and exploitation; Pres. Ing. E. J. ROCCHI.

Secretario de Programación Económica: Hipólito Yrigoyen 250, 8°, Of. 819, Buenos Aires; tel. (1) 349-5710; fax (1) 349-5714; f. 1961 to formulate national long-term development plans; Sec. Dr JUAN JOSÉ LACH.

Sociedad Rural Argentina: Florida 460, 1005 Buenos Aires; tel. (1) 322-3431; telex 23414; fax (1) 326-5091; f. 1866; private org. to promote the development of agriculture; Pres. ENRIQUE C. CROTTO; 9,400 mems.

CHAMBERS OF COMMERCE

Cámara Argentina de Comercio: Avda Leandro N. Alem 36, 1003 Buenos Aires; tel. (1) 331-8051; telex 18542; fax (1) 331-8055; f. 1924; Pres. JORGE L. DI FIORI.

Cámara de Comercio, Industria y Producción de la República Argentina: Florida 1, 4°, 1005 Buenos Aires; tel. (1) 331-0813; telex 18693; fax (1) 331-9116; f. 1913; Pres. JOSÉ CHEDIEK; Vice-Pres Dr FAUSTINO S. DIÉGUEZ, Dr JORGE M. MAZALAN; 1,500 mems.

Cámara de Comercio Exterior de la Federación Gremial del Comercio e Industria de Rosario: Avda Córdoba 1868, 2000 Rosario, Santa Fe; tel. and fax (41) 25-7147; e-mail ccer@commerce.com.ar; internet http://www.commerce.com.ar; f. 1958; deals with imports and exports; Pres. AGUSTÍN ÁLVAREZ: Vice-Pres. EDUARDO C. SALVATIERRA; 150 mems.

Similar chambers are located in most of the larger centres and there are many foreign chambers of commerce.

INDUSTRIAL AND TRADE ASSOCIATIONS

Asociación de Importadores y Exportadores de la República Argentina: Avda Belgrano 124, 1°, 1092 Buenos Aires; tel. (1) 342-0010; telex 25761; fax (1) 342-1312; f. 1966; Pres. HÉCTOR MARCELLO VIDAL; Man. ESTELIA D. DE AMATI.

Asociación de Industriales Textiles Argentinos: Buenos Aires; tel. (1) 373-2256; fax (1) 373-2351; f. 1945; textile industry; Pres. BERNARDO ABRAMOVICH; 250 mems.

Asociación de Industrias Argentinas de Carnes: Buenos Aires; tel. (1) 322-5244; telex 17304; meat industry; refrigerated and canned beef and mutton; Pres. JORGE BORSELLA.

Asociación Vitivinícola Argentina: Güemes 4464, 1425 Buenos Aires; tel. (1) 774-3370; f. 1904; wine industry; Pres. LUCIANO COTUMACCIO; Man. Lic. MARIO J. GIORDANO.

Cámara de Sociedades Anónimas: Florida 1, 3°, 1005 Buenos Aires; tel. (1) 342-9013; fax (1) 342-9225; Pres. Dr ALFONSO DE LA FERRERE; Man. CARLOS ALBERTO PERRONE.

Centro de Exportadores de Cereales: Bouchard 454, 7°, 1106 Buenos Aires; tel. (1) 311-1697; fax (1) 312-6924; f. 1943; grain exporters; Pres. RAUL S. LOEH.

Confederaciones Rurales Argentinas: México 628, 2°, 1097 Buenos Aires; tel. (1) 261-1501; Pres. ARTURO J. NAVARRO.

Coordinadora de Actividades Mercantiles Empresarias: Buenos Aires; Pres. OSVALDO CORNIDE.

Federación Lanera Argentina: Avda Paseo Colón 823, 5°, 1063 Buenos Aires; tel. (1) 300-7661; fax (1) 361-6517; f. 1929; wool industry; Pres. JULIO AISENSTEIN; Sec. RICHARD VON GERSTENBERG; 80 mems.

EMPLOYERS' ORGANIZATION

Unión Industrial Argentina (UIA): Avda Leandro N. Alem 1067, 11°, 1001 Buenos Aires; tel. (1) 313-4474; fax (1) 313-2413; e-mail uia01@act.net.ar; f. 1887; re-established in 1974 with the fusion of the Confederación Industrial Argentina (CINA) and the Confederación General de la Industria; following the dissolution of the CINA in 1977, the UIA was formed in 1979; asscn of manufacturers, representing industrial corpns; Pres. CLAUDIO SEBASTIANI; Sec.-Gen. Dr JOSÉ I. DE MENDIGUREN.

UTILITIES

Agua y Energía Eléctrica Sociedad del Estado (AyEE): Avda Leandro N. Alem 1134, 1001 Buenos Aires; tel. (1) 311-6364; telex 22613; fax (1) 312-2236; f. 1947; scheduled for transfer to private ownership; state water and electricity board; Principal Officer HAROLDO H. GRISANTI.

Electricity

Comisión Nacional de Energía Atómica (CNEA): Avda del Libertador 8250, 1429 Buenos Aires; tel. (1) 70-4181; telex 21388; fax (1) 544-9252; f. 1950; scheduled for transfer to private ownership; Pres. ANIBAL NÚÑEZ (acting).

Comisión Técnica Mixta de Salto Grande (CTMSG): Avda Leandro N. Alem 449, 1003 Buenos Aires; operates Salto Grande hydroelectric station, which has an installed capacity of 650 MW; joint Argentine-Uruguayan project.

Consejo Consultivo Nacional de Energía Atómica: Buenos Aires; f. 1987 to advise the CNEA's Pres. (see above) in the preparation of studies and projects concerned with the reorganization of nuclear activities.

Entidad Binacional Yacyretá: Avda Eduardo Madero 942, 21–22°, 1106 Buenos Aires; tel. (1) 315-2750; telex 22659; co-ordinates the hydroelectic project at Yaciretá on the Paraná river, undertaken jointly by Argentina and Paraguay. When completed it will be one of the world's largest hydroelectric complexes, with a generating capacity of 2,700 MW. The project was scheduled for privatization in the late 1990s.

ESEBA, SA: Calle 48, No. 786, La Plata; former state electricity company operating in the province of Buenos Aires; transferred to private ownership in 1997 and divided into six business units: two generators, three distributors and one transmission co; installed capacity of 1,089 MW.

Hidroeléctrica Norpatagónica, SA (HIDRONOR): Avda Leandro N. Alem 1074, 1001 Buenos Aires; tel. (1) 312-6031; telex 18097; fax (1) 313-0734; formerly the largest producer of electricity in Argentina; responsible for developing the hydroelectric potential of the Limay and neighbouring rivers; transferred to private ownership in 1992 and divided in to the following companies:

Central Hidroeléctrica Alicurá, SA: Avda Leandro N. Alem 712, 7°, 1001 Buenos Aires.

Central Hidroeléctrica Cerros Colorados, SA: Avda Leandro N. Alem 690, 12°, 1001 Buenos Aires.

Central Hidroeléctrica El Chocón, SA: Suipacha 268, 9°, Of. A, Buenos Aires.

Hidroeléctrica Piedra del Aguila, SA: Avda Tomás Edison 1251, 1104 Buenos Aires; tel. (1) 315-2586; fax (1) 317-5174; Pres. Dr Uriel Federico O'Farrell; Gen. Man. Ignacio J. Rosner.

Transener, SA: Avda Paseo Colón 728, 6°, 1063 Buenos Aires; tel. (1) 342-6925; fax (1) 342-7147; energy transmission co.

Hidroeléctrica Pichi Picún Leufu, SA: Avda Leandro N. Alem 1074, 6°, Buenos Aires; fax (1) 313-0734; state-owned co, responsible for the construction of the Pichi Picún dam; Pres. Ing. Alberto A. Hevia; Vice-Pres. Dr Carlos E. Basanta.

Servicios Eléctricos del Gran Buenos Aires, SA: Balcarce 184, 1002 Buenos Aires; tel. (1) 331-1901; Principal Officer Carlos A. Mattausch.

Gas

Gas del Estado, SA: Alsina 1169, 1069 Buenos Aires; tel. (1) 37-2091; operates integrated natural-gas network and produces liquefied gas and by-products.

Water

Obras Sanitarias de la Nación: Marcelo T. de Alvear 1840, 1122 Buenos Aires; tel. (1) 41-1081; fax (1) 41-4050; sanitation; transferred to private ownership in 1992.

TRADE UNIONS

Congreso de los Trabajadores Argentinos (CTA): Buenos Aires; dissident trade union confederation.

Confederación General del Trabajo—CGT (General Confederation of Labour): Buenos Aires; f. 1984; Peronist; represents approximately 90% of Argentina's 1,100 trade unions; Sec.-Gen. Gerardo Martínez.

Movimiento de Trabajadores Argentinos (MTA): Buenos Aires; dissident trade union confederation.

Transport

Subsecretaría de Energía y Puertos: Hipólito Yrigoyen 250, Buenos Aires; tel. (1) 349-8005; Under-Sec. Ing. Héctor Mirkin.

Secretaría de Obras Públicas y Transporte: Hipólito Yrigoyen 250, 12°, 1310 Buenos Aires; tel. (1) 349-7254; fax (1) 349-7201; Sec. Ing. Armando Guibert.

Secretaría de Transporte Metropolitano y de Larga Distancia: Hipólito Yrigoyen 250, 12°, 1310 Buenos Aires; tel. (1) 349-7162; fax (1) 349-7146; Under-Sec. Dr Armando Canosa.

Secretaría de Transporte Aero-Comercial: Hipólito Yrigoyen 250, 12°, 1310 Buenos Aires; tel. (1) 349-7203; fax (1) 349-7206; Under-Sec. Arq. Fermín Alarcia.

Dirección de Estudios y Proyectos: Hipólito Yrigoyen 250, 12°, 1310 Buenos Aires; tel. (1) 349-7127; fax (1) 349-7128; Dir Ing. José Luis Jagodnik.

RAILWAYS

Lines: General Belgrano (narrow-gauge), General Roca, General Bartolomé Mitre, General San Martín, Domingo Faustino Sarmiento (all wide-gauge), General Urquiza (medium-gauge) and Línea Metropolitana, which controls the railways of Buenos Aires and its suburbs. There are direct rail links with the Bolivian Railways network to Santa Cruz de la Sierra and La Paz; with Chile, through the Las Cuevas–Caracoles tunnel (across the Andes) and between Salta and Antofagasta; with Brazil, across the Paso de los Libres and Uruguayana bridge; with Paraguay (between Posadas and Encarnación by ferry-boat); and with Uruguay (between Concordia and Salto). In 1991 there were 34,509 km of tracks. In the Buenos Aires commuter area 270.4 km of wide-gauge track and 52 km of medium gauge track are electrified.

Plans for the eventual total privatization of Ferrocarriles Argentinos (FA) were initiated in 1991, with the transfer to private ownership of the Rosario-Bahía Blanca grain line and with the reallocation of responsibility for services in Buenos Aires to the newly-created Ferrocarriles Metropolitanos, prior to its privatization.

In early 1993 central government funding for the FA was suspended and responsibility for existing inter-city passenger routes was devolved to respective provincial governments. However, owing to lack of resources, few provinces have successfully assumed the operation of services, and many trains have been suspended. At the same time, long-distance freight services were sold as six separate 30-year concessions (including lines and rolling stock) to private operators. By late 1996 all freight services had been transferred to private management, with the exception of Ferrocarril Belgrano, SA, which was in the process of undergoing privatization. The Buenos Aires commuter system was divided into eight concerns (one of which incorporates the underground railway system) and was offered for sale to private operators as 10- or 20-year (subsidized) concessions. The railway network is currently regulated by the National Commission for Transport Regulation.

Ferrocarriles Argentinos (FA): Avda Ramos Mejía 1302, Buenos Aires; tel. (1) 318-3593; fax (1) 313-3129; f. 1948 with the nationalization of all foreign property; autonomous body but policies established by the Secretaría de Obras Públicas y Transporte; dismantled and responsibilities transferred in 1993 (see above); Trustee Dr Lucas M. Ordóñez; Gen. Man. P. Suárez.

Ferrocarriles Metropolitanos, SA (FEMESA): Bartolomé Mitre 2815, Buenos Aires; tel. (1) 865-4135; fax (1) 861-8757; f. 1991 to assume responsibility for services in the capital; 820 km of track; Pres. Matías Ordóñez; concessions to operate services have been awarded to:

Metrovías.

Trainmet.

Ferrovías.

Cámara de Industriales Ferroviarios: Alsina 1609, 1°, Buenos Aires; tel. (1) 371-5571; private org. to promote the development of Argentine railway industries; Pres. Ing. Ana María Guibaudi.

The following consortia were awarded 30-year concessions to operate rail services, during 1991–94:

Consorcio Nuevo Central Argentino (CNCA): Buenos Aires; operates freight services on the Bartolomé Mitre lines; 5,011 km of track; Pres. H. Urquia.

Ferrocarril Buenos Aires al Pacífico/San Martín (BAP): Avda Santa Fe 4636, 3°, Buenos Aires; tel. (1) 778-2486; operates services on much of the San Martín line, and on 706 km of the Sarmiento line; 6,106 km of track; Pres. Lic. Horacio Vivacqua.

Ferrocarril General Belgano, SA (FGB): Maipú 88, 1084 Buenos Aires; tel. and fax (1) 343-7220; f. 1993; operates freight services; Pres. Dr Ignacio A. Ludveña.

Ferrocarril Mesopotámico General Urquiza (FMGU): Avda Santa Fe 4636, 3°, Buenos Aires; tel. (1) 778-2486; operates freight services on the Urquiza lines; 2,272 km of track; Pres. Lic. Horacio Vivacqua.

Ferroexpreso Pampeano (FEPSA): Bouchard 680, 9°, Buenos Aires; tel. (1) 318-4900; operates services on the Rosario–Bahía Blanca grain lines; 5,193 km of track; Pres. Ing. Juan Jorge Asconape.

Ferrosur Roca (FR): Bouchard 680, 8°, Buenos Aires; tel. (1) 318-3930; operates services on the Roca lines; 3,343 km of track; Pres. Amelia Lacroze de Fortabat.

Buenos Aires also has an underground railway system:

Subterráneos de Buenos Aires: Bartolomé Mitre 3342, 1201 Buenos Aires; tel. (1) 862-6844; telex 18979; fax (1) 864-0633; f. 1913; became completely state-owned in 1951; fmrly controlled by the Municipalidad de la Ciudad de Buenos Aires; responsibility for operations was transferred, in 1993, to a private consortium (Metrovías) with a 20-year concession; five underground lines totalling 36.5 km, 63 stations, and a 7.4 km light rail line with 13 stations, which was inaugurated in 1987; Chair. S. C. Cirigliano.

ROADS

In 1996 there were 218,276 km of roads, of which 29.1% were paved. Four branches of the Pan-American highway run from Buenos Aires to the borders of Chile, Bolivia, Paraguay and Brazil. In 1996 9,932 km of main roads were under private management. Construction work on a 41-km bridge across the River Plate (linking Punta Lara in Argentina with Colonia del Sacramento in Uruguay) was scheduled to begin in mid-1998.

Dirección Nacional de Vialidad: Avda Julio A. Roca 378, Buenos Aires; tel. (1) 343-2838; fax (1) 343-7292; controlled by the Secretaría de Transportes; Gen. Man. Ing. ELIO VERGARA.

Asociación Argentina de Empresarios Transporte Automotor (AAETA): Bernardo de Yrigoyen 330, 6°, 1072 Buenos Aires; Pres. LUIS CARRAL.

Federación Argentina de Entidades Empresarias de Autotransporte de Cargas (FADEAC): Avda de Mayo 1370, 3°, 1372 Buenos Aires; tel. (1) 383-3635; Pres. ROGELIO CAVALIERI IRIBARNE.

There are several international passenger and freight services including:

Autobuses Sudamericanos, SA: Bernardo de Yrigoyen 1370, 1°, 1401 Buenos Aires; tel. (1) 307-1956; telex 23891; fax (1) 307-1956; f. 1928; international bus services; car and bus rentals; charter bus services; Pres. ARMANDO SCHLECKER HIRSCH; Gen. Man. MIGUEL ANGEL RUGGIERO.

INLAND WATERWAYS

There is considerable traffic in coastal and river shipping, mainly carrying petroleum and its derivatives.

Dirección Nacional de Construcciones Portuarias y Vías Navegables: Avda España 221, 4°, Buenos Aires; tel. (1) 361-5964; responsible for the maintenance and improvement of waterways and dredging operations; Dir Ing. ENRIQUE CASALS DE ALBA.

SHIPPING

There are more than 100 ports, of which the most important are Buenos Aires, Quequén and Bahía Blanca. There are specialized terminals at Ensenada, Comodoro Rivadavia, San Lorenzo and Campana (petroleum); Bahía Blanca, Rosario, Santa Fe, Villa Concepción, Mar del Plata and Quequén (cereals); and San Nicolás and San Fernando (raw and construction materials). In 1996 Argentina's merchant fleet totalled 87 vessels amounting to 1,803,798 grt.

Administración General de Puertos: Avda Ing. Huergo 431, Buenos Aires; tel. (1) 342-5621; fax (1) 331-0298; f. 1956; state enterprise for direction, administration and exploitation of all national sea- and river-ports; scheduled for transfer to private ownership; Supervisor Lic. RAFAEL E. CONEJERO; Gen. Man. Ing. EDUARDO KLUZ.

Capitanía General del Puerto: Avda Julio A. Roca 734, 2°, 1067 Buenos Aires; tel. (1) 34-9784; f. 1967; co-ordination of port operations; Port Captain Capt. PEDRO TARAMASCO.

Administración General de Puertos (Santa Fe): Duque 1 Cabacera, Santa Fe; tel. (42) 41732; telex 48149.

Consorcio de Gestión del Puerto de Bahía Blanca: Avda Dr Mario M. Guido s/n, 8103 Provincia de Buenos Aires; tel. (91) 57-3213; telex 81849; Pres. JOSÉ E. CONTE; Sec.-Gen. CLAUDIO MARCELO CONTE.

Terminales Portuarias Argentinas: Buenos Aires; operates one of five recently privatized cargo and container terminals in the port of Buenos Aires.

Terminales Río de la Plata: Buenos Aires; operates one of five recently privatized cargo and container terminals in the port of Buenos Aires.

Empresa Líneas Marítimas Argentinas, SA (ELMA): Corrientes 389, 1327 Buenos Aires; tel. (1) 312-9245; telex 22317; fax (1) 311-7954; f. 1941 as state-owned org.; transferred to private ownership in 1994; operates vessels to northern Europe, the Mediterranean, west and east coasts of Canada and the USA, Gulf of Mexico, Caribbean ports, Brazil, Pacific ports of Central and South America, Far East, northern and southern Africa and the Near East; Pres. Dr L. A. J. OLAIZOLA.

Other private shipping companies operating on coastal and overseas routes include:

Antártida Pesquera Industrial: Moreno 1270, 5°, 1091 Buenos Aires; tel. (1) 381-0167; telex 18477; fax (1) 381-0519; Pres. J. M. S. MIRANDA; Man. Dir J. R. S. MIRANDA.

Astramar Cía Argentina de Navegación, SAC: Buenos Aires; tel. (1) 311-3678; telex 22782; fax (1) 311-7534; Pres. ENRIQUE W. REDDIG.

Bottacchi SA de Navegación: Maipú 509, 2°, 1006 Buenos Aires; tel. (1) 392-7411; telex 22639; fax (1) 11-1280; Pres. ANGEL L. M. BOTTACCHI.

Maruba S. en C. por Argentina: Maipú 535, 7°, 1006 Buenos Aires; tel. (1) 322-7173; telex 24147; fax (1) 322-3353; Chartering Man. R. J. DICKIN.

Yacimientos Petrolíferos Fiscales (YPF): Avda Roque S. Peña 777, 1364 Buenos Aires; tel. (1) 46-7271; telex 21792; privatization finalized in 1993; Pres. NELLS LEÓN.

CIVIL AVIATION

Argentina has 10 international airports (Aeroparque Jorge Newbery, Córdoba, Corrientes, El Plumerillo, Ezeiza, Jujuy, Resistencia, Río Gallegos, Salta and San Carlos de Bariloche). Ezeiza, 35 km from Buenos Aires, is one of the most important air terminals in Latin America. The privatization of more than 30 airports was under consideration in 1997.

Aerolíneas Argentinas: Bouchard 547, 9°, Buenos Aires; tel. (1) 317-3201; fax (1) 317-3581; f. 1950; transfer to private ownership initiated in 1990; services to North and Central America, Europe, the Far East, New Zealand, South Africa and destinations throughout South America; the internal network covers the whole country; passengers, mail and freight are carried; Pres. MANUEL MORÁN.

Austral Líneas Aéreas (ALA): L. Alem 1134, 4°, Buenos Aires; tel. (1) 317-3922; fax (1) 317-3991; f. 1971; transferred to state ownership in 1980 to prevent financial collapse; transferred to private ownership in 1987; domestic flights linking 27 cities in Argentina; Pres. Ing. NÉSTOR FARIAS BOUVIER.

CATA Líneas Aéreas S.A.C.I.F.I.: Cerrito 1320, 3°, 1010 Buenos Aires; tel. (1) 812-3390; fax (1) 325-0506; domestic passenger flights; Pres. ROQUE PUGLIESE.

Líneas Aéreas Entre Ríos: 25 de Mayo 119, 3100 Paraná, Entre Ríos; tel. (43) 21-6375; fax (43) 24-3320; f. 1967; scheduled domestic passenger services; Pres. DOMINGO DATO.

Líneas Aéreas del Estado (LADE): Perú 710, Buenos Aires; tel. (1) 362-1853; fax (1) 361-5437; Pres. J.C. HRUBIK.

Líneas Aéreas Privadas Argentinas (LAPA): Avda Santa Fe 1970, 2°, 1123 Buenos Aires; tel. (1) 812-0953; telex 9031; fax (1) 814-2100; f. 1976; domestic scheduled passenger services; an international route to Uruguay is under negotiation; Pres. GUSTAVO ANDRÉS DEUTSCH.

Transporte Aéreo Costa Atlántica (TACA): Bernardo de Yrigoyen 1370, 1°, Ofs 25-26, 1138 Buenos Aires; tel. (1) 307-1956; fax (1) 307-8899; f. 1956; domestic and international passenger and freight services between Argentina and Bolivia, Brazil and the USA; Pres. Dr ARMANDO SCHLECKER HIRSCH.

Transportes Aéreos Neuquén: Diagonal 25 de Mayo 180, 8300 Neuquén; tel. (99) 423076; fax (99) 488926; domestic routes; Pres. JOSÉ CHALÉN; Gen. Man. PATROCINIO VALVERDE MORAIS.

Valls Líneas Aéreas: Río Grande, Tierra del Fuego; f. 1995; operates three routes between destinations in southern Argentina, Chile and the South Atlantic islands.

Tourism

Argentina's superb tourist attractions include the Andes mountains, the lake district centred on Bariloche (where there is a National Park), Patagonia, the Atlantic beaches and Mar del Plata, the Iguazú falls, the Pampas and Tierra del Fuego. Tourist arrivals in Argentina in 1996 totalled 4,285,648. In the same year tourist receipts were US $4,572m.

Secretaría de Turismo de la Nación: Suipacha 1111, 20°, 1368 Buenos Aires; tel. (1) 312-5611; telex 24882; fax (1) 313-6834; internet http://www//turismo.gov.ar; Sec. FRANCISCO MAYORGA.

Asociación Argentina de Agencias de Viajes y Turismo (AAAVYT): Viamonte 640, 10°, 1053 Buenos Aires; tel. (1) 325-4691; fax (1) 322-9641; f. 1951; Pres. HUGO E. COPERTARI; Gen. Man. JOSÉ A. NAVARRO.

ARMENIA

Introductory Survey

Location, Climate, Language, Religion, Flag, Capital

The Republic of Armenia (formerly the Armenian Soviet Socialist Republic) is situated in south-west Transcaucasia, on the north-eastern border of Turkey. Its other borders are with Iran to the south, Azerbaijan to the east, and Georgia to the north. The Nakhichevan Autonomous Republic, an Azerbaijani territory, is situated to the south, separated from the remainder of Azerbaijan by Armenian territory. The climate is typically continental: dry, with wide temperature variations. Winters are cold, the average January temperature in Yerevan being –3°C (26°F), but summers can be very warm, with August temperatures averaging 25°C (77°F), although high altitude moderates the heat in much of the country. Precipitation is low in the Yerevan area (annual average 322 mm), but much higher in the mountains. The official language is Armenian, the sole member of a distinct Indo-European language group. It is written in the Armenian script. Kurdish is used in broadcasting and publishing for some 56,000 Kurds inhabiting Armenia. Most of the population are adherents of Christianity, the largest denomination being the Armenian Apostolic Church. There are also Russian Orthodox, Protestant, Islamic and Yazidi communities. The national flag (approximate proportions 3 by 2) consists of three equal horizontal stripes, of red, blue and orange. The capital is Yerevan.

Recent History

Although Armenia was an important power in ancient times, for much of its history it has been ruled by foreign states. In 1639 Armenia was partitioned, with the larger, western part being annexed by Turkey and the eastern region becoming part of the Persian Empire. In 1828, after a period of Russo–Persian conflict, eastern Armenia was ceded to the Russian Empire by the Treaty of Turkmanchai, and subsequently became a province of the empire. At the beginning of the 20th century Armenians living in western, or Anatolian, Armenia, under Ottoman rule, were subject to increasing persecution by the Turks. As a result of brutal massacres and deportations (particularly in 1915), the Anatolian lands were largely emptied of their Armenian population, and it was estimated that during the period 1915–22 some 1.5m. Armenians perished. After the collapse of Russian imperial power in 1917, Russian Armenia joined the anti-Bolshevik Transcaucasian Federation, which included Georgia and Azerbaijan. This collapsed when threatened by Turkish forces, and on 28 May 1918 Armenia was proclaimed an independent state. Without Russian protection, however, the newly-formed republic was almost defenceless against Turkish expansionism and was forced to cede the province of Kars and other Armenian lands to Turkey. Armenia was recognized as an independent state by the Allied Powers and by Turkey in the Treaty of Sèvres, signed on 10 August 1920. However, the rejection of the Treaty by the new Turkish ruler, Mustafa Kemal, left Armenia vulnerable to renewed Turkish threats. In September Turkish troops attacked Armenia, but they were prevented from establishing full control over the country by the invasion of Armenia, from the east, by Russian Bolshevik troops, and the founding, on 29 November 1920, of a Soviet Republic of Armenia. In December 1922 the republic became a member, together with Georgia and Azerbaijan, of the Transcaucasian Soviet Federative Socialist Republic (TSFSR), which, in turn, became a constituent republic of the USSR. In 1936 the TSFSR was dissolved and Armenia became a full union republic of the USSR.

Although many Armenians suffered under communist rule, advances were made in economic and social development. During the period of tsarist rule Russian Armenia had been an underdeveloped region of the empire, with very little infrastructure; however, in the Armenian Soviet Socialist Republic (SSR), the authorities implemented a policy of forced modernization, which expanded communications and introduced industrial plants. Literacy and education were also improved. A programme to collectivize agriculture, initiated on a voluntary basis in 1928, engendered little enthusiasm; collectivization was enforced in 1930, and many thousands of peasants who still opposed it were deported. Armenians experienced further suffering during the Stalinist purges of the late 1930s, in which thousands of people were executed or imprisoned. Unlike many western parts of the USSR during the Second World War (1939–45), Armenia was not occupied by German forces following their invasion of the USSR in June 1941. Consequently, the republic provided an essential source of labour for the Soviet economy, and as many as 600,000 Armenians served in the Soviet armies (of whom an estimated 350,000 were killed). In the immediate post-war period the Soviet Government gave priority to developing the industrial sector in Armenia, while also expanding the agricultural collectivization programme. In the late 1940s an estimated 150,000 Armenians of the 'diaspora' returned to the republic.

The Soviet leader Mikhail Gorbachev's policies of *perestroika* and *glasnost* (introduced following his accession to power in 1985) had little initial impact in Armenia. The first manifestations of the new policies were campaigns against corruption in the higher echelons of the Communist Party of Armenia (CPA). On a more public level, environmental problems became a focus for popular protest. The first demonstrations against ecological degradation took place in September 1987, but the demands of protesters soon began to include the redress of historical and political grievances.

Of the historical and ethnic issues discussed in late 1987 and early 1988, the most significant was the status of Nagornyi Karabakh, an autonomous oblast (region) within neighbouring Azerbaijan, largely populated by (non-Muslim) Armenians, control of which had been ceded to Azerbaijan in 1921 (see chapter on Azerbaijan). Demands for the incorporation of Nagornyi Karabakh into the Armenian SSR began within the enclave itself in early 1988. In February as many as 1m. people took part in demonstrations in Yerevan, the Armenian capital, in support of these demands. The demonstrations were organized by Yerevan intellectuals, who formed a group known as the Karabakh Committee. In response to increased unrest within Armenia, many Azerbaijanis began to leave the republic. Rumours of ill-treatment of the refugees led to anti-Armenian riots in Sumgait (Azerbaijan) in late February, in which 26 Armenians died. This event provoked further Armenian anger, which was compounded by the decision of the Presidium of the USSR's Supreme Soviet (legislature) not to transfer Nagornyi Karabakh to Armenia. Strikes and rallies continued under the leadership of the officially-outlawed Karabakh Committee, and the inability of the local authorities to control the unrest led to the dismissal, in May, of the First Secretary (leader) of the CPA. In December, however, the issue of Nagornyi Karabakh was temporarily subordinated to the problems of overcoming the effects of a severe earthquake which had struck northern Armenia. The city of Leninakan (now Gyumri) was seriously damaged, while the village of Spitak was completely destroyed. Some 25,000 people were reported to have been killed and many thousands more were made homeless. In the chaos following the earthquake the members of the Karabakh Committee were arrested, ostensibly for interfering in relief work. They were released only in May 1989, after huge demonstrations took place, protesting against their continued internment. Meanwhile, in January 1989, the Soviet Government had formed a Special Administration Committee of the Council of Ministers to administer Nagornyi Karabakh, although the enclave remained under formal Azerbaijani jurisdiction.

Throughout 1989 unrest continued both in Armenia and within Nagornyi Karabakh, but there were other significant political developments within the republic. *Glasnost* allowed a much fuller examination of Armenian history and culture, and several unofficial groups, concerned with both cultural and political issues, were formed. In May the *yerakuyn*, the national flag of independent Armenia, was flown again, and 28 May, the anniversary of the establishment of independent Armenia, was declared a national day. However, internal politics continued to be dominated by events in Nagornyi Karabakh. In September Azerbaijan implemented an economic blockade against Armenia, seriously affecting the reconstruction programme required after the 1988 earthquake (hitherto almost 90% of

Armenia's imports from other republics of the USSR had arrived via Azerbaijan). In November 1989 the Special Administration Committee was disbanded, and Azerbaijan resumed control over Nagornyi Karabakh. This prompted the Armenian Supreme Soviet to declare the enclave part of a 'unified Armenian Republic'. In January 1990 this declaration was declared unconstitutional by the USSR's Supreme Soviet. The Armenian Supreme Soviet responded by granting itself the power to veto any legislation approved by the central authorities.

The increasing disillusionment among Armenians with the Soviet Government was apparently responsible for the low level of participation in the elections to the Armenian Supreme Soviet, which took place in May–July 1990. No party achieved an overall majority, but the Pan-Armenian National Movement (PNM), the successor to the Karabakh Committee, was the largest single party, with some 35% of the seats in the legislature. Supported by other non-communist groups, Levon Ter-Petrossian, a leader of the PNM, defeated Vladimir Movsissian, the First Secretary of the CPA, in elections to the chairmanship of the Supreme Soviet. Vazgen Manukian, also a leader of the PNM, was appointed Prime Minister. On 23 August the legislature adopted a declaration of sovereignty, including a claim to the right to maintain armed forces and a demand for international recognition that the Turkish massacres of Armenians in 1915 constituted genocide. The Armenian SSR was renamed the Republic of Armenia. The new Government began to establish political and commercial links with the Armenian diaspora, and several prominent exiles returned to the republic. In late November 1990 the CPA, after heated debate, voted to become an independent organization within the Communist Party of the Soviet Union (CPSU).

The Armenian Government refused to enter into the negotiations between Soviet republics on a new treaty of union, which took place in late 1990 and early 1991, and officially boycotted the referendum on the renewal of the USSR, which was held in March 1991 in nine of the other republics. Instead, the legislature decided to conduct a referendum on Armenian secession from the USSR, to be held in September. Initially, it was planned that the referendum would be conducted within the provisions of the Soviet law on secession, adopted in April by the all-Union Supreme Soviet. This entailed a transitional period of at least five years before full independence could be achieved.

In late April 1991 there was an escalation of tension in the Nagornyi Karabakh region. The Armenian Government continued to deny any direct involvement in the violence, claiming that the attacks were outside its control, being organized by units of the ethnic Armenian 'Nagornyi Karabakh self-defence forces'. However, Azerbaijan countered that Armenia was, in fact, playing an aggressive role in the conflict, making reference to 'Armenian expeditionary forces'. In a further complication, Armenia suggested that the Soviet leadership was supporting Azerbaijan, following the latter's agreement to sign the new union treaty, and punishing Armenia for its moves towards independence, for its refusal to take part in discussions on the union treaty and for its nationalization of CPA property.

The moderate policies of the new PNM-led Government, especially in developing relations with Turkey, attracted criticism from more extreme nationalist groups, notably the Union for National Self-Determination (UNS), which continued to seek the recovery of lands lost to Turkey after the First World War. The CPA attacked the Government for its willingness to promote relations with Turkey, as did the Armenian Revolutionary Federation (ARF, or Dashnaktsutyun, which had formed the Government of independent Armenia during 1918–20). The CPA also strongly opposed the idea of secession, while the ARF advocated a more gradual process towards independence. The UNS campaigned for immediate secession, which was in breach of the constitutional procedure.

The attempted coup in Moscow, and subsequent events of August 1991, forced the Government to accelerate the moves towards secession, and provided further support for those advocating complete independence for Armenia. The response of the Armenian leadership to the overthrow of President Gorbachev on 19 August was initially cautious, with Ter-Petrossian stressing the need for maximum restraint. The referendum on independence took place, as scheduled, on 21 September. According to official returns, 94.4% of the electorate took part, and 99.3% of voters supported Armenia's becoming 'an independent, democratic state outside the Union'. On 23 September, instead of conforming to the Soviet law on secession, the Supreme Soviet declared Armenia to be an independent state. Meanwhile, in early September, a congress of the CPA voted to dissolve the party.

The independence declaration was followed, on 16 October 1991, by elections to the post of President of the Republic. There were six candidates in the election, but it was won overwhelmingly by the incumbent, Ter-Petrossian (with some 87% of the total votes). The President continued to demand international recognition of Armenia, but on 18 October, with the leaders of seven other Soviet republics, he signed a treaty to establish an economic community, stressing, however, that it did not encroach on Armenia's political independence, and refusing to sign a new treaty on political union. The Armenian leadership did, nevertheless, join the Commonwealth of Independent States (CIS, see p. 132), and signed the founding Alma-Ata Declaration, on 21 December. In early 1992 Armenia was admitted to the Conference on Security and Co-operation in Europe (CSCE, subsequently renamed the Organization for Security and Co-operation in Europe—OSCE—see p. 212) and the UN.

Economic conditions in Armenia deteriorated alarmingly during 1992, and there were widespread shortages of foodstuffs and fuel. The situation was exacerbated not only by the continuing conflict in Nagornyi Karabakh (see below), but also by the fighting in neighbouring Georgia (impeding supplies to Armenia), and the ongoing economic blockade by Azerbaijan (and its ally, Turkey). Compounding the economic crisis was the enormous influx of refugees from Nagornyi Karabakh and Azerbaijan. By late 1992 the population of Yerevan was believed to have increased to almost twice its pre-conflict size. There were also growing signs of public dissatisfaction with the Ter-Petrossian administration, and in mid-August mass rallies were staged in Yerevan to demand the President's resignation. In the same month, however, a proposal to hold a referendum to decide the President's future was rejected during an emergency session of the legislature.

In February 1993 there were further large-scale rallies in Yerevan, at which demonstrators protested at the continuing energy crisis and reiterated demands for Ter-Petrossian to resign. Earlier in the month Ter-Petrossian had dismissed the Prime Minister, Khosrov Arutyunian, following disagreements over economic and social policy. A new Council of Ministers was subsequently announced; it was headed by Hrant Bagratian, who was widely known as an economic reformist.

Armenia's economic crisis deteriorated further during 1993. In 1993/94 Armenians endured their third successive winter without heating or lighting for long periods. Popular resentment against Ter-Petrossian's leadership increased, and hundreds of thousands of Armenians were reported to have emigrated, owing to the level of economic hardship. In July 1994 opposition parties organized a number of anti-Government protests in Yerevan, and later in the year thousands of people participated in a series of rallies, which were organized at regular intervals by the Union of Civic Accord (UCA), an association of opposition groups. Within the legislature—now known as the Supreme Council—opposition deputies were vocal in criticizing PNM-supported proposals for the new Constitution (under discussion since late 1992), which envisaged extensive presidential powers and a restricted role for the legislature.

The assassination, in December 1994, of the former Mayor of Yerevan, Ambartsum Galstian, prompted the Government to effect a number of measures aimed at eliminating terrorism. By far the most radical of these was the suspension, in late December, of the leading opposition party, the ARF. The party was officially charged with having engaged in 'terrorist activities, political murders and drugs-trafficking'. A number of ARF members were arrested and put on trial, while publications associated with the party were ceased. (In late 1997 the ARF remained suspended.) Anti-Government forces condemned these measures and monthly rallies were organized by the UCA in early 1995 in protest at official harassment of opposition activists.

Armenia's first post-Soviet legislative elections were held on 5 July 1995 (with a second round of voting taking place on 27 July). Thirteen parties and organizations contested the 190 seats of the new National Assembly under a mixed system of voting (150 seats to be filled by majority vote and the remaining 40 by proportional representation on the basis of party lists). Nine parties, including the ARF, were barred from participation. The Republican bloc (an alliance of six groups, led by the PNM) won an overwhelming majority of the seats in the Assembly (119). Eight seats were won by the Shamiram Women's Party, while the revived CPA achieved seven. The UNS took three seats and the ARF, despite the official ban, succeeded in winning one seat. Forty-five independent candidates won representation in the Assembly. The election was monitored by 185 international observers; some irregularities were reported by the delegation of the OSCE. Opposition parties contested the authenticity of the election results. In late July President Ter-Petrossian appointed the new Government, in which Hrant Bagratian remained as Prime Minister. A referendum on the new Armenian Constitution was held simultaneously with the general election. Of the 56% of the electorate who participated in the plebiscite, some 68% voted in favour of the Constitution, which granted wide-ranging executive authority to the President.

The presidential election was held on 22 September 1996. Ter-Petrossian was the candidate of the Republican bloc, while five opposition parties united to support Vazgen Manukian, the Chairman of the National Democratic Union (NDU). The leader of the CPA, Sergei Badalian, and a former presidential aide, Ashot Manucharian, also contested the election. Preliminary results indicated that Ter-Petrossian had been re-elected; however, the opposition alleged that widespread electoral malpractice had been perpetrated, and several thousand opposition supporters staged protest rallies in Yerevan, demanding the President's resignation. International observers reported that there had been serious irregularities in the electoral proceedings, which cast doubt on the validity of the result; in particular, discrepancies between the number of votes cast and the number of officially-registered ballot papers had emerged. On 25 September supporters of Manukian stormed the National Assembly building, injuring, among others, the Chairman and his deputy. A temporary ban on rallies was imposed, and large numbers of opposition supporters, including parliamentary deputies, were arrested; it was subsequently reported that some of them had been charged in connection with the clashes, and the trials of those arrested continued throughout 1997. According to the final election results, Ter-Petrossian received 51.8% of votes cast, while Manukian secured 41.3% (although he achieved a significantly higher percentage than Ter-Petrossian in Yerevan), Badalian 6.3% and Manucharian less than 1% of the votes. In October Manukian and Manucharian submitted an appeal to the Constitutional Court that the election results be declared invalid and that new elections be held; Ter-Petrossian announced that he was prepared to resign if the court ruled in favour of the opposition. Despite the decision in November by the Constitutional Court to reject the appeal, opposition parties maintained their demand for fresh elections. A number of them had also boycotted the elections to the new bodies of local government, established by the Constitution in 1995, which were held earlier in that month. The resignation of Hrant Bagratian as Prime Minister, allegedly in response to opposition to his programme of economic reforms, was announced in November. He was replaced by Armen Sarkissian, and a government reorganization was carried out.

Sarkissian resigned in March 1997 on grounds of ill health, and was replaced by Robert Kocharian, the President of Nagornyi Karabakh, in what was regarded as an attempt by Ter-Petrossian to reduce the pressure from opposition parties to hold fresh presidential elections. Nevertheless, tension within the republic persisted and in March seven opposition parties, including the NDU and the ARF, formed an alliance, the Union of National Accord, to campaign for new presidential and legislative elections. Protest rallies, attended by several thousand people, were organized in support of these demands by the opposition alliance in April and May, but a nation-wide demonstration against government policies in June failed to attract a significant turn-out. Earlier in that month Ter-Petrossian carried out a minor reorganization of government ministries.

Disagreements within the ruling PNM, which had developed since the re-election of Ter-Petrossian in September 1996, became apparent in mid-1997. The decision by the National Assembly in June to approve draft legislation on the compulsory conscription into military service of all men between the ages of 18 and 27 resulted in the resignation of the Chairman of the legislature, Babken Ararktsian, who had opposed the legislation on the grounds that the Ministry of Defence had unduly influenced the Assembly. However, following the intervention of Ter-Petrossian, who stated that discussion of the bill was to be postponed until late 1997, Ararktsian resumed his position. Tension resurfaced at the PNM's annual congress in July, when the Mayor of Yerevan, Vano Siradeghian, defeated Eduard Yegorian in elections to the chairmanship of the party. Yegorian subsequently left the party, amidst bitter recriminations, claiming to have the support of a significant proportion of its members. In October it was announced that the opposition Union of National Accord was to be disbanded. Failure to achieve its aim of fresh presidential and legislative elections was cited as the reason for its dissolution.

The proclamation of Armenia's independence in September 1991 led to an escalation of hostilities in the disputed enclave of Nagornyi Karabakh. In that month the territory declared itself an independent republic. A cease-fire agreement, signed in late September, was not observed, and the violence only intensified following the dissolution of the USSR in December. In January 1992 the President of Azerbaijan, Ayaz Mutalibov, placed the region under direct presidential rule; in the same month Azerbaijani forces surrounded and attacked Stepanakert, the capital of Nagornyi Karabakh, while the Armenians laid siege to Shusha, a town with a mainly Azerbaijani population. In May the Nagornyi Karabakh self-defence forces (which the Armenian Government continued to claim to be operating without its military support) captured Shusha, thereby gaining complete control of the enclave and ending the bombardment of Stepanakert. With the capture of the strategically-important Lachin valley, the Armenian militia then succeeded in opening a 'corridor' inside Azerbaijan, linking Nagornyi Karabakh with Armenia proper.

In June 1992 Azerbaijani forces launched a sustained counter-offensive in Nagornyi Karabakh, recapturing villages both inside and around the enclave, and expelling several thousand inhabitants, thus exacerbating the already urgent refugee crisis. Efforts resumed in July and August to organize a peace conference (which was to be held in Minsk, Belarus, under the aegis of the CSCE), but no significant progress was made. In early August Azerbaijani forces resumed the bombardment of Stepanakert. In response to the escalation of attacks and ensuing military gains by Azeri forces, the Nagornyi Karabakh legislature declared a state of martial law, and a state defence committee, in close alignment with the Ter-Petrossian administration, replaced the enclave's government.

In early 1993 the military situation in Nagornyi Karabakh was reversed, as Armenian forces undertook a series of successful offensives, regaining territory that they had lost in 1992 and also taking control of large areas of Azerbaijan surrounding the enclave. With the capture of the Kelbajar district of Azerbaijan in April 1993, the Armenians succeeded in creating a second 'corridor' linking the enclave with Armenia and effectively securing the whole swath of Azerbaijani territory extending south to the Lachin 'corridor'. Many thousands of Azeris fled or were expelled from their homes. The Armenian position was only strengthened by the growing political turmoil in Azerbaijan in mid-1993 (q.v.), and by late June Armenian forces had secured full control of Nagornyi Karabakh.

The Armenian seizure of Azerbaijani territory prompted widespread international condemnation, particularly by neighbouring Turkey and Iran, the latter fearing a massive influx of refugees from south-western Azerbaijan. Resolutions adopted by the UN Security Council, demanding the withdrawal of Armenian forces from Azerbaijan, went unheeded; by late August 1993 as much as 20% of Azerbaijan's total territory was reported to have been captured by the Nagornyi Karabakh Armenian forces. In late October the Turkish leadership stated that no normalization of relations between Turkey and Armenia could occur until Armenian aggression in Azerbaijan had ceased. In the same month the Armenian Government appeared to have endorsed the CSCE 'Minsk Group's' schedule for achieving a lasting peace. Nevertheless, in late October hostilities reintensified: yet more Azerbaijani territory came under the control of the Armenians, who had extended their operations as far south as the Azerbaijan-Iran border. Azeri forces launched a major new counter-offensive in December, recapturing some of the territory that they had lost to the Armenians during the year. A series of cease-fire agreements was reached in the first half of 1994, but none was lasting. In February it was reported that as many as 18,000 people had been killed since 1988, with a further 25,000 wounded. The number of displaced Azeris was now believed to have exceeded 1m.

However, in early May 1994, following protracted mediation by the CSCE and Russia, a new cease-fire agreement was signed by the Ministers of Defence of Armenia and Azerbaijan and representatives of Nagornyi Karabakh. Although some violations of the cease-fire were subsequently reported, the agreement was formalized in late July. Ter-Petrossian held talks with the President of Azerbaijan, Heydar Aliyev, in Moscow in early September. Although agreement was reached on some key provisions of a future peace treaty, Aliyev stated that his willingness to negotiate such an accord depended on the unconditional withdrawal of Armenian forces from occupied Azerbaijani territory. Negotiations were held at regular intervals throughout 1995 under the aegis of the 'Minsk Group'. However, progress towards reaching a political settlement was hampered by Azerbaijan's demand for the return of Lachin and Shusha regions, as well as by its apparent unwillingness to recognize the Nagornyi Karabakh leadership as an equal party in the negotiations. Nevertheless, the cease-fire continued to be observed, with only sporadic violations reported, and in May the three sides carried out a large-scale exchange of prisoners of war. Presidents Ter-Petrossian and Aliyev met in October (in New York, for the 50th anniversary celebrations of the UN), and direct discussions, held in conjunction with the OSCE negotiations, were initiated in December.

Ter-Petrossian and Aliyev met, together with President Shevardnadze of Georgia, in April 1996 in Luxembourg, where they signed an agreement on partnership and co-operation with the European Union (EU, see p. 152), and affirmed their commitment to the 1994 cease-fire. A further exchange of prisoners of war occurred in May 1996. Little progress was made in the negotiations in the following months, and elections to the post of President of Nagornyi Karabakh, held on 24 November, were condemned by Azerbaijan and criticized by the 'Minsk Group' as a hindrance to the peace process. Robert Kocharian, the incumbent President, was re-elected with some 86% of the vote. He subsequently appointed Leonard Petrossian as Prime Minister.

In December 1996 Ter-Petrossian and Aliyev attended an OSCE summit meeting in Lisbon, Portugal. Following demands by Azerbaijan, the OSCE Chairman issued a statement that recommended three principles which would form the basis of a future political settlement in the enclave: the territorial integrity of Armenia and Azerbaijan; the legal status of Nagornyi Karabakh, which would be granted broad autonomy within Azerbaijan; and security guarantees for the population of Nagornyi Karabakh. Armenia, however, refused to accept the terms of the statement.

Relations between the two countries deteriorated in early 1997, when Azerbaijan accused Armenia of illegally obtaining weapons from Russia, in contravention of the Conventional Forces in Europe treaty. Armenia retaliated by issuing a statement denying the accusations, and claimed that Azerbaijan had been stockpiling weapons in preparation for a military assault on Nagornyi Karabakh. In April Armenia withdrew from the direct negotiations, that were being held in conjunction with the OSCE talks, and this was followed by a series of clashes on the Armenian–Azerbaijani border, which left many people killed and wounded. Negotiations under the auspices of the OSCE continued, however, and it was reported in late May that new proposals for a settlement to the conflict had been offered to the participants. Fresh elections to the post of President of Nagornyi Karabakh on 1 September, which were called following the appointment of Kocharian as Prime Minister of Armenia, were won by Arkadyi Gukasian, with some 90% of the vote, but were criticized by the international community. Gukasian reportedly rejected the OSCE peace settlement on the grounds that the proposals presupposed Azerbaijan's sovereignty over the enclave. However, in late September it was reported that Armenia had accepted, in principle, the OSCE's plan for a stage-by-stage settlement of the conflict, which entailed the withdrawal of Armenian forces from six districts around Nagornyi Karabakh, to be followed by a decision on the status of the Shusha and Lachin 'corridors', and on the status of Nagornyi Karabakh itself. A statement by President Ter-Petrossian that Nagornyi Karabakh could neither hope to gain full independence, nor be united with Armenia, was severely condemned by opposition parties, and appeared to indicate a significant change in policy on the part of the President. Presidents Ter-Petrossian and Aliyev, meeting during the Council of Europe summit in Strasbourg, France, in October, reaffirmed their commitment to a peaceful resolution of the conflict, and reportedly were in favour of French proposals for a further meeting in Moscow.

Armenia's relations with Russia in 1997 focused on the ratification by the Armenian legislature in April of a treaty allowing Russia to maintain military bases in Armenia for a period of 25 years, and on the signing of a treaty of 'friendship, co-operation and mutual understanding' in August, during a state visit by Ter-Petrossian to Moscow. The possibility that Armenia might join the Union of Belarus and Russia was also raised in mid-1997, and reportedly attracted widespread support; however, Ter-Petrossian declared that ratification of the Armenian–Russian friendship treaty was necessary before any discussion on joining the Union could take place. Armenia's relations with Georgia were furthered by the visit of the Georgian President, Eduard Shevardnadze, in May, during which several co-operation agreements were signed.

Government

Under the Constitution of 1995, the President of the Republic is Head of State and Supreme Commander-in-Chief of the armed forces, but also holds broad executive powers. The President is directly elected for a term of five years (and for no more than two consecutive terms of office). The President appoints the Prime Minister and, on the latter's recommendation, the members of the Government. Legislative power is vested in the 131-member National Assembly, which is elected for a four-year term by universal adult suffrage. (The National Assembly that was elected in July 1995 comprised 190 deputies, in accordance with the electoral law in existence before the adoption of the new Constitution.) For administrative purposes, Armenia is divided into 11 regions (*marz*), including the capital, Yerevan. The regions are subdivided into communities (*hamaynk*).

Defence

Following the dissolution of the USSR in December 1991, Armenia became a member of the Commonwealth of Independent States and its collective security system. The country also began to establish its own armed forces (estimated to number some 60,000 by August 1997). Military service is compulsory and lasts for 18 months. Some mobilization of reserves by conscription was reported. There is also a paramilitary force of an estimated 1,000, attached to the Ministry of Internal Affairs. In August 1997 there were approximately 4,300 Russian troops stationed on Armenian territory. The budget for 1996 allocated an estimated US $92m. to defence. In October 1994 Armenia joined NATO's 'Partnership for Peace' programme of military co-operation (see p. 206).

Economic Affairs

In 1995, according to estimates by the World Bank, Armenia's gross national product (GNP), measured at average 1993–95 prices, was US $2,752m., equivalent to $730 per head. During 1985–95, it was estimated, GNP per head declined at an average annual rate of 15.1% in real terms, while the population increased by an annual average of 1.2%. Over the same period, it was estimated, Armenia's gross domestic product (GDP) decreased, in real terms, by an average of 11.4% annually. However, in 1995 GDP increased by 6.9% and in 1996 it grew by 5.8%.

Agriculture and forestry contributed an estimated 32.1% of GDP and employed 33.9% of the working population in 1995. The principal crops are potatoes and other vegetables, cereals and fruit. Private farms accounted for some 95% of agricultural production in September 1996. By late 1996 privatization of arable land was near to completion. During 1990–95, according to estimates by the World Bank, agricultural GDP declined, in real terms, by an annual average of 0.6%. The GDP of the sector declined by 12.0% in 1994, but grew by 5.1% in 1995.

In 1995 industry (including mining, manufacturing, construction and power) contributed 40.8% of GDP and employed 30.8% of the working population. According to the World Bank, industrial GDP increased by an annual average of 5.1% during 1980–90. However, during 1990–95 industrial GDP declined by an average of 28.7% annually. The GDP of the sector declined, in real terms, by 20.0% in 1994. However, growth of an estimated 1.0% was achieved in 1995.

Armenia's mining sector has not yet been extensively developed. Copper, molybdenum, gold, silver and iron are extracted on a small scale, and there are reserves of lead and zinc. There are also substantial, although largely unexploited, reserves of mineral salt, calcium oxide and carbon. Production of gold decreased significantly in the 1990s, but the Government hoped to encourage a recovery in the industry, following the conclusion of an agreement with a US company to develop new extraction facilities in 1996.

In 1993 the principal branches of manufacturing, measured by gross value of output, were food-processing and beverages (accounting for 18.2% of the total), machinery and metal products (16.9%), textiles (5.7%), and professional and scientific equipment (5.6%). Shortages of energy and raw materials in the mid-1990s resulted in a change of emphasis in industrial production, with the production of textiles and jewellery, for example, increasing, while traditional industries declined.

Armenia is heavily dependent on imported energy. The two principal suppliers of energy products are Russia (petroleum and derivatives) and Turkmenistan (natural gas). It is, however, thought probable that Armenia has significant reserves of petroleum and natural gas. Hydroelectricity was the only significant domestic source of energy in 1994, providing 63.1% of Armenia's electricity supply. The country's sole nuclear power station, at Medzamor, was closed following the earthquake of 1988. However, in late 1995, in view of Armenia's worsening energy crisis, the station's second generating unit resumed operations, following restoration work. By 1995, with the recommissioning of the Medzamor power station, hydroelectricity provided only 35% of the country's electricity supply, and nuclear power contributed 5.5%. The nuclear share increased to 44.6% in the first six months of 1996. In 1996 proposals were made for the construction of a new nuclear power plant, scheduled for completion in 2010. Imports of energy products comprised 31.3% of the value of merchandise imports in 1995.

The services sector contributed an estimated 23.5% of GDP in 1995, according to the World Bank, and engaged 35.2% of the labour force in that year. During 1980–90 the GDP of the sector increased by an annual average of 4.6%. However, services GDP declined by an average of 19.7% annually during 1990–95. In 1995 the GDP of the sector increased by an estimated 22.5%.

In 1996 Armenia recorded a visible trade deficit of US $468.3m., while the deficit on the current account of the balance of payments was $319.4m. In 1995 the principal source of imports was Russia; other main sources were Turkmenistan, the USA, Iran and Georgia. In that year the major market for exports was Russia. Other important purchasers were Turkmenistan, Iran and Belgium. The principal exports in 1995 were pearls, precious and semi-precious stones, precious metals, imitation jewellery and coin; machinery and electrical equipment; and base metals. The principal imports in that year were mineral products, vegetable products, and live animals and animal products.

In 1995 there was a budgetary deficit of 51,658m. drams (equivalent to 9.9% of GDP). At the end of 1995 Armenia's total external debt was estimated to be US $373.5m., of which $300.4m. was long-term public debt. In that year the cost of debt-servicing was equivalent to 2.9% of the value of exports of goods and services. The average annual rate of inflation was 4,964.3% in 1994, 175.5% in 1995 and 18.7% in 1996. In the year to March 1997 consumer prices increased by only 3.9%. In July 1997 some 166,760 people were officially registered as unemployed (about 11% of the labour force).

Armenia is a member of the IMF, the World Bank and the European Bank for Reconstruction and Development (EBRD, see p. 148). It is also a member of the Black Sea Economic Co-operation organization (BSEC, see p. 260), and is pursuing membership of the World Trade Organization (WTO, see p. 244).

The collapse of the Soviet central planning system and internal trading structures exacerbated an already critical economic situation in Armenia. The decline was compounded by the severe effects of the earthquake in 1988 and of the conflict in Nagornyi Karabakh, which resulted in a massive influx of refugees from the enclave and from Azerbaijan. The economic blockade of Armenia by Azerbaijan and, subsequently, Turkey, as well as the civil war in Georgia, resulted in widespread shortages of food and fuel, and a concomitant decline in industrial production, owing to a lack of essential raw materials. A wide-ranging programme of economic reforms was initiated in the early 1990s, which included price liberalization, the promotion of privatization and a rationalization of the taxation system. By 1994 the first signs of economic recovery were observed, with growth in GDP and a decrease in the rate of inflation. The Government expanded its reform programme in the mid-1990s, to include a review of public-sector administration and expenditure, and reform of the energy sector. New agreements, which provided for the supply to Armenia of nuclear fuel and electricity, were concluded with Russia and Iran, respectively, in 1997, and a further agreement was reached with a Russian company, Gazprom, and an international energy corporation concerning deliveries of natural gas and the upgrading of Armenia's gas infrastructure. The privatization programme was well advanced by late 1997, and it was estimated that some 60% of the republic's enterprises had been privatized by October. The agricultural sector had largely passed into private ownership by late 1996, but restructuring of the industrial sector was less extensive. The collection of taxation revenue was expected to improve in 1998, following the introduction of legislative amendments. Reforms were also being pursued in the health and education sectors. Loan agreements to support the Government's reform programme were concluded with the IMF and the World Bank in 1996 and 1997, respectively, and were an indication of the international financial community's confidence in Armenia's continued economic recovery.

Social Welfare

Much of Armenia's expenditure on health and welfare services has been directed towards the victims of the 1988 earthquake, which caused an estimated 25,000 deaths and 8,500m. roubles' worth of damage. However, the collapse of the USSR and the escalation of the conflict in Nagornyi Karabakh encouraged a large number of refugees to flee to Armenia, creating new demands of social expenditure at a time of restricted government revenue. Furthermore, the adaptation to a market economy and the economic blockade on the country also exacerbated the situation. In 1992 it was estimated that about one-seventh of the population was 'in need' (excluding refugees—estimated at some 350,000). The Government sought to control social expenditure by targeting resources, as well as encouraging private and voluntary involvement.

In 1995 life expectancy at birth was 68 years for males and 74 years for females. A Pension Fund was created in August 1991. It was later merged with the Employment Fund, to create the Pension and Employment Fund, which, in 1992, was the only extrabudgetary fund remaining in Armenia. In June 1996 615,055 people were in receipt of state pensions, of which 58.3% were provided on account of old age. In 1993 there was one physician for every 261 people. In 1995 there were 90 hospital beds per 10,000 inhabitants. Current expenditure on health by all levels of government in 1993 was 32,744m. roubles.

Education

Education is compulsory for nine years, to be undertaken between the ages of six and 17 years. Until the early 1990s the general education system conformed to that of the centralized Soviet system, but extensive changes were then introduced, with greater emphasis placed on Armenian history and culture. Primary education usually begins at seven years of age and lasts for three years. Secondary education, beginning at 10 years of age, comprises a first cycle of five years and a second of two years. In 1993 total enrolment at primary and secondary schools was equivalent to 87% of the school-age population (82% of males; 91% of females). Primary enrolment in that year was equivalent to 90% of children in the relevant age-group (87% of males; 93% of females), while the comparable ratio for secondary enrolment was 85% (80% of males; 90% of females). Most instruction in higher institutions is in Armenian, although Russian is widely taught as a second language. In addition to Yerevan State University and the recently-established State Engineering University, higher education is provided at 13 institutes of higher education, with a total enrolment, in the 1996/97 academic year, of 35,640 students. Current expenditure on education by all levels of government in 1996 was 3,418.6m. drams. In 1989, according to census results, the rate of adult illiteracy in Armenia was 1.2% (males 0.6%; females 1.9%).

Public Holidays

1998: 1–2 January (New Year), 6 January (Christmas), 7 April (Motherhood and Beauty Day), 24 April (Armenian Genocide Commemoration Day), 9 May (Victory Day), 28 May (Independence Day), 5 July (Constitution Day), 21 September (Referendum Day), 7 December (Day of Remembrance of the 1988 Earthquake).

1999: 1–2 January (New Year), 6 January (Christmas), 7 April (Motherhood and Beauty Day), 24 April (Armenian Genocide Commemoration Day), 9 May (Victory Day), 28 May (Independence Day), 5 July (Constitution Day), 21 September (Referendum Day), 7 December (Day of Remembrance of the 1988 Earthquake).

Weights and Measures

The metric system is in force.

Statistical Survey

Principal sources: IMF, *Armenia, Economic Review, Recent Economic Developments* and *International Financial Statistics: Supplement on Countries of the Former Soviet Union*; World Bank, *Statistical Handbook: States of the Former USSR* and *World Tables*.

Area and Population

AREA, POPULATION AND DENSITY

Area (sq km)	29,800*
Population (census results)†	
17 January 1979	3,037,259
12 January 1989	
Males	1,619,308
Females	1,685,468
Total	3,304,776
Population (official estimates at 1 January)	
1995	3,754,300
1996	3,766,400
1997	3,782,400
Density (per sq km) at 1 January 1997	126.9

* 11,500 sq miles.

† Figures refer to *de jure* population. The *de facto* total at the 1989 census was 3,287,677.

POPULATION BY NATIONALITY
(permanent inhabitants, 1989 census)

	%
Armenian	93.3
Azerbaijani	2.6
Kurdish	1.7
Russian	1.5
Others	0.9
Total	100.0

PRINCIPAL TOWNS
(estimated population at 1 July 1990)

Yerevan (capital) 1,254,400; Gyumri (formerly Leninakan) 206,600; Vanadzor (formerly Kirovakan) 170,200.

Source: UN, *Demographic Yearbook*.

BIRTHS, MARRIAGES AND DEATHS

	Registered live births		Registered marriages		Registered deaths	
	Number	Rate (per 1,000)	Number	Rate (per 1,000)	Number	Rate (per 1,000)
1988	74,707	22.1	26,581	7.9	35,567	10.5
1989	75,250	21.6	27,257	7.8	20,853	6.0
1990	79,882	22.5	28,233	8.0	21,993	6.2
1991	77,825	21.5	28,023	7.8	23,425	6.5
1992	70,581	19.1	22,955	6.2	25,824	7.0
1993	59,041	15.8	21,514	5.8	27,500	7.4
1994	51,143	13.6	17,074	4.6	24,648	6.6

1996 (provisional): Live births 48,900; Marriages 14,200; Deaths 25,200.

Expectation of life (years at birth, 1995): Males 68; Females 74 (Source: World Bank, *World Development Indicators*).

EMPLOYMENT ('000 persons)

	1993	1994	1995
Material sphere	1,133	1,077	1,057
Agriculture and forestry	522	504	493
Industry*	363	355	352
Construction	117	97	96
Transport and communications†	31	30	28
Trade and catering‡	70	64	63
Other activities	31	24	24
Non-material sphere	411	410	398
Transport and communications†	25	25	22
Education, culture and art	181	181	178
Science	24	25	24
Health, physical culture and social welfare	83	84	82
Housing and personal services	60	58	57
General administration	30	29	n.a.
Insurance	8	8	7
Total	1,544	1,488	1,456

* Comprising manufacturing (except printing and publishing), mining and quarrying, electricity, gas, water, logging and fishing.

† Transport and communications servicing material production are included in activities of the material sphere. Other branches of the sector are considered to be non-material services.

‡ Including material supply and procurement.

Agriculture

PRINCIPAL CROPS ('000 metric tons)

	1994	1995	1996
Wheat	147	154	168
Barley	66	82	105
Maize	5	4	5
Potatoes	400	451	423
Pulses	4	4	5
Cabbages	60*	65*	82
Tomatoes	244*	252*	180
Cauliflowers*	3	3	3
Cucumbers and gherkins*	18	25	25
Onions (dry)	20*	22*	39
Garlic*	8	9	8
Peas (green)*	3	3	3
Carrots	8*	9*	12
Other vegetables	56*	63*	77
Grapes	202	142	158
Apples*	30	96	118
Pears*	3	8	10
Peaches and nectarines*	5	10	15
Plums*	8	17	16
Apricots*	4	15	18
Almonds†	2	2	2
Tobacco (leaves)†	2	2	n.a.

* Unofficial figure(s). † FAO estimates.

Source: FAO, *Production Yearbook*.

LIVESTOCK ('000 head, year ending September)

	1994	1995	1996
Horses*	9	8	8
Asses*	3	3	3
Cattle	502	504	497
Pigs	81	82	79
Sheep	721†	623*	548
Goats	15†	13†	13

Poultry (unofficial figures, million): 3 in 1994; 3 in 1995; 3 in 1996).

* FAO estimate(s). † Unofficial figure.

Source: FAO, *Production Yearbook.*

LIVESTOCK PRODUCTS ('000 metric tons)

	1994	1995	1996
Beef and veal	29	30	32*
Mutton and lamb	8	7	6
Pig meat	6	5	4
Poultry meat	3	7	9*
Cows' milk	408	420	400
Sheep's milk	7*	8*	10
Cheese†	15	15	15
Hen eggs*	11	11	11
Wool:			
greasy	2†	2†	1
clean†	1	1	1

* Unofficial figure(s). † FAO estimate(s).

Source: FAO, *Production Yearbook.*

Fishing

(FAO estimates, metric tons, live weight)

	1993	1994	1995
Common carp	1,870	1,780	1,840
Goldfish	250	250	260
Silver carp	260	250	260
Rainbow trout	370	350	360
Whitefishes	1,680	1,600	1,660
Other fishes	120	120	120
Total catch	4,550	4,350	4,500

Source: FAO, *Yearbook of Fishery Statistics.*

Mining

('000 metric tons)

	1992	1993	1994
Salt (unrefined)	61	45	47
Gypsum (crude)	69	50	35

Source: UN, *Industrial Commodity Statistics Yearbook.*

Industry

SELECTED PRODUCTS ('000 metric tons, otherwise indicated)

	1992	1993	1994
Margarine	2.0	0.1	n.a.
Refined soya oil	2	n.a.	n.a.
Wheat flour	299	290	279
Ethyl alcohol ('000 hectolitres)	9	8	7
Wine ('000 hectolitres)	258	274	227
Beer ('000 hectolitres)	149	70	70
Mineral water ('000 hectolitres)	77	38	48
Soft drinks ('000 hectolitres)	30	16	13
Cigarettes (million)	3,927	1,878	2,014
Wool yarn—pure and mixed (metric tons)	2,000	500	200
Cotton yarn—pure and mixed (metric tons)	5,400	1,000	400
Woven cotton fabrics (million sq metres)	5	2	n.a.
Silk fabrics ('000 sq metres)	3,681	4,016	629
Woven woollen fabrics ('000 sq metres)	2,900	800	400
Carpets ('000 sq metres)	404	200	35
Leather footwear ('000 pairs)	5,661	3,517	1,612
Caustic soda (Sodium hydroxide)	15	5	4
Synthetic rubber	11.7	0.4	2.1
Non-cellulosic continuous fibres (metric tons)	400	300	200
Rubber tyres ('000)[1]	97	65	104
Rubber footwear ('000 pairs)	515	350	205
Quicklime	6	3	3
Cement	368	198	122
Aluminium plates, sheets, strip and foil	7.3	0.7	1.1
Domestic washing machines ('000)	9	—	n.a.
Radio receivers ('000)	50	8	n.a.
Lorries (number)	3,171	1,247	446
Bicycles ('000)	27	16	8
Watches ('000)	6	1	3
Clocks ('000)[2]	1,149	384	362
Electric energy (million kWh)	9,003	6,294	5,658

[1] For road motor vehicles.

[2] Including electric clocks.

Source: UN, *Industrial Commodity Statistics Yearbook.*

1995: Wine ('000 hectolitres) 121.5; Cement ('000 metric tons) 228; Electric energy (million kWh) 5,561 (Source: IMF, *Republic of Armenia—Recent Economic Developments and Selected Issues,* November 1996).

Finance

CURRENCY AND EXCHANGE RATES

Monetary Units

100 louma = 1 dram.

Sterling and Dollar Equivalents (31 July 1997)

£1 sterling = 823.09 drams;
US $1 = 502.65 drams;
1,000 drams = £1.215 = $1.989.

Average exchange rate (drams per US $)

1994 288.65
1995 405.91
1996 414.04

Note: The dram was introduced on 22 November 1993, replacing the Russian (formerly Soviet) rouble at a conversion rate of 1 dram = 200 roubles. The initial exchange rate was set at US $1 = 14.3 drams, but by the end of the year the rate was $1 = 75 drams. Following the dissolution of the USSR in December 1991, Russia and several other former Soviet republics retained the rouble as their monetary unit. The average interbank market rate in 1992 was $1 = 222.1 Russian roubles. After the introduction of the dram, Russian currency continued to circulate in Armenia. The rouble had been withdrawn from circulation by March 1994.

STATE BUDGET (million drams)*

Revenue	1993	1994	1995
Tax revenue	625	24,431	66,457
Value-added tax	196	5,076	17,019
Excises	46	836	2,388
Enterprise profits tax	174	10,712	23,868
Personal income tax	63	2,275	6,826
Land tax	—	405	1,721
Customs duties	7	789	2,707
Payroll taxes	108	2,836	10,680
Other taxes	31	1,502	900
Other revenue	293	5,179	18,346
Grants	207	22,146	19,031
Total	1,125	51,756	103,834

Expenditure	1993	1994	1995
Current expenditure	2,319	64,134	117,557
Wages	293	3,443	13,528
Subsidies	652	24,032	4,916
Interest	29	3,642	16,112
Transfers	283	7,484	28,597
Goods and services	1,063	25,533	54,404
Health and education	376	3,931	12,866
Other	686	21,602	41,538
Capital expenditure	309	17,913	35,359
Net lending	685	531	2,575
Total	3,313	82,578	155,492

* Figures refer to the consolidated accounts of republican and local authorities, including the operations of the Pension and Employment Fund.

1997 (million drams): Revenue 128,000; Expenditure 151,900.

INTERNATIONAL RESERVES (US $ million at 31 December)

	1994	1995	1996
Gold*	2.44	10.46	12.82
IMF special drawing rights	0.28	44.33	41.50
Reserve position in IMF	0.01	0.01	0.01
Foreign exchange	31.99	55.24	114.14
Total	34.72	110.04	168.47

Source: IMF, *International Financial Statistics.*

MONEY SUPPLY (million drams at 31 December)

	1994	1995	1996
Currency outside banks	10,056	24,601	34,784
Demand deposits at commercial banks	3,978	6,232	5,190
Total money (incl. others)	14,200	30,935	40,052

Source: IMF, *International Financial Statistics.*

COST OF LIVING

(Consumer Price Index; base: December 1992 = 100)

	1994	1995	1996
All items	86,355	237,947	282,384

Source: IMF, *International Financial Statistics.*

NATIONAL ACCOUNTS (million drams at current prices)

Expenditure on the Gross Domestic Product

	1993	1994	1995
Government final consumption expenditure	754	21,086	58,336
Private final consumption expenditure	3,962	176,885	545,056
Increase in stocks	−109	6,012	11,859
Gross fixed capital formation	525	37,855	94,365
Total domestic expenditure	5,132	241,838	709,616
Exports of goods and services	1,511	73,569	124,965
Less Imports of goods and services	2,563	136,747	324,775
Sub-total	4,080	178,661	509,805
Statistical discrepancy*	185	8,404	12,451
GDP in purchasers' values	4,265	187,065	522,256

* Referring to the difference between the sum of the expenditure components and official estimates of GDP, compiled from the production approach.

Source: IMF, *International Financial Statistics.*

Gross Domestic Product by Economic Activity (provisional)

	1994	1995
Agriculture and forestry	81,364	167,475
Industry*	54,495	164,834
Construction	12,508	48,368
Transport and communications	2,765	17,687
Trade and catering	8,314	42,927
Others	27,603	80,994
Total	187,049	522,285

* Principally mining, manufacturing, electricity, gas and water.

BALANCE OF PAYMENTS (US $ million)

	1994	1995	1996
Exports of goods f.o.b.	237.9	270.9	290.4
Imports of goods f.o.b.	−418.7	−673.9	−758.8
Trade balance	−180.8	−403.0	−468.3
Exports of services	13.4	28.6	77.7
Imports of services	−40.5	−52.3	−128.5
Balance on goods and services	−208.0	−426.7	−519.1
Other income received	n.a.	1.6	64.4
Other income paid	−3.8	−14.6	−44.7
Balance on goods, services and income	−211.8	−439.7	−499.5
Current transfers received	106.2	161.9	194.5
Current transfers paid	−0.7	−1.7	−14.4
Current balance	−106.2	−279.4	−319.4
Capital account (net)	5.7	8.1	13.4
Direct investment from abroad	8.0	—	17.6
Portfolio investment assets	n.a.	—	0.0
Portfolio investment liabilities	n.a.	—	9.9
Other investment assets	35.3	−11.5	77.4
Other investment liabilities	42.2	152.9	177.0
Net errors and omissions	−12.8	70.8	1.8
Overall balance	−27.8	−59.2	−22.5

Source: IMF, *International Financial Statistics.*

External Trade

PRINCIPAL COMMODITIES (US $ million)

Imports c.i.f.	1994	1995
Live animals and animal products	46.1	63.3
Vegetable products	64.3	85.6
Animal or vegetable fats and oils; prepared edible fats; animal or vegetable waxes	11.9	25.1
Prepared foodstuffs; beverages, spirits and vinegar; tobacco and manufactured substitutes	32.4	51.5
Mineral products	161.0	224.7
Products of chemical or allied industries	9.1	55.4
Textiles and textile articles	8.6	7.8
Natural or cultured pearls, precious and semi-precious stones, precious metals and articles thereof; imitation jewellery; coin	31.8	62.4
Base metals and articles thereof	3.6	15.9
Machinery and mechanical appliances; electrical equipment; sound and television apparatus	8.0	49.6
Total (incl. others)	393.8	673.9

Exports f.o.b.	1994	1995
Prepared foodstuffs; beverages, spirits and vinegar; tobacco and manufactured substitutes	12.9	12.6
Mineral products	17.8	28.8
Products of chemical or allied industries	3.9	14.5
Plastics, rubber and articles thereof	7.9	10.8
Textiles and textile articles	15.8	15.2
Footwear, headgear, umbrellas, walking-sticks, whips, etc.; prepared feathers; artificial flowers; articles of human hair	15.9	5.4
Articles of stone, plaster, cement, asbestos, mica, etc.; ceramic products; glass and glassware	12.7	2.1
Natural or cultured pearls, precious and semi-precious stones, precious metals and articles thereof; imitation jewellery; coin	75.2	89.6
Base metals and articles thereof	9.4	30.5
Machinery and mechanical appliances; electrical equipment; sound and television apparatus	30.9	39.1
Vehicles, aircraft, vessels and associated transport equipment	1.7	11.4
Miscellaneous manufactured articles	5.5	3.4
Total (incl. others)	215.5	270.9

1996 (US $ million): Total imports c.i.f. 857.2; Total exports f.o.b. 290.6 (Source: IMF, *International Financial Statistics*).

PRINCIPAL TRADING PARTNERS (US $ million)

Imports c.i.f.	1993	1994	1995
Belgium	2.9	1.4	15.6
France	0.9	10.7	16.3
Georgia	19.5	17.8	61.9
Germany	0.3	6.9	11.3
Iran	15.8	42.5	89.8
Italy	31.1	8.9	22.4
Netherlands	0.3	8.3	6.0
Russia	77.9	112.2	135.1
Turkmenistan	64.1	n.a.	n.a.
USA	26.9	96.1	114.4
Total (incl. others)	254.1	393.8	673.9

Exports f.o.b.	1993	1994	1995
Belarus	1.9	0.7	0.9
Belgium	14.9	25.9	30.8
Georgia	3.2	2.9	2.7
Germany	0.3	6.6	10.1
Iran	5.5	14.6	35.0
Netherlands	0.1	0.7	5.3
Russia	58.5	83.9	88.5
Switzerland	0.4	2.5	3.1
Turkmenistan	57.0	65.7	68.6
Total (incl. others)	156.1	215.5	270.9

Transport

RAILWAYS (traffic)

	1991	1992	1993
Passenger-km (million)	320	446	435
Freight ton-km (million)	4,177	1,280	451

Source: UN, *Statistical Yearbook*.

Communications Media

	1992	1994*
Television receivers ('000 in use)	n.a.	800
Book production†:		
Titles	n.a.	224
Copies ('000)	n.a.	1,739
Daily newspapers:		
Titles	7	7
Average circulation ('000 copies)	84‡	80‡
Non-daily newspapers:		
Titles	57	n.a.
Average circulation ('000 copies)	200‡	n.a.
Other periodicals:		
Titles	40	n.a.
Average circulation ('000 copies)	5,064	n.a.

* Figures for 1993 are not available.
† Including pamphlets (27 titles and 83,000 copies in 1994).
‡ Provisional.

Source: UNESCO, *Statistical Yearbook*.

Telephones ('000 main lines in use): 578 in 1992; 583 in 1993; 587 in 1994 (Source: UN, *Statistical Yearbook*).

Telefax stations (number in use): 180 in 1992; 220 in 1993; 300 in 1994 (Source: UN, *Statistical Yearbook*).

Education

(1993/94, unless otherwise indicated)

	Institutions	Teachers	Students
Pre-primary	n.a.	11,966	93,052
Primary	n.a.	n.a.	193,915
Secondary:			
General	1,456*	n.a.	359,084
Vocational		n.a.	21,029
Higher schools (incl. universities)	15*	5,473†	35,640*

* 1996/97. † 1991/92.

Sources: Ministry of Education and Science; UNESCO, *Statistical Yearbook*.

Directory

The Constitution

The Constitution was approved by some 68% of the electorate in a national referendum, held on 5 July 1995. It replaced the amended Soviet Constitution of 1978. The following is a summary of the new Constitution's main provisions:

GENERAL PROVISIONS OF CONSTITUTIONAL ORDER

The Republic of Armenia is an independent democratic state; its sovereignty is vested in the people, who execute their authority through free elections, referendums and local self-government institutions and officials, as defined by the Constitution. Referendums, as well as elections of the President of the Republic, the National Assembly and local self-government bodies, are carried out on the basis of universal, equal, direct suffrage by secret ballot. Through the Constitution and legislation, the State ensures the protection of human rights and freedoms, in accordance with the principles and norms of international law. A multi-party political system is guaranteed. The establishment of political parties is a free process, but the activities of political parties must not contravene the Constitution and the law. The right to property is recognized and protected. Armenia conducts its foreign policy based on the norms of international law, seeking to establish neighbourly and mutually beneficial relations with all countries. The State ensures the protection of the environment, historical and cultural monuments, as well as cultural values. The official language is Armenian.

FUNDAMENTAL HUMAN AND CIVIL RIGHTS AND FREEDOMS

The acquisition and loss of citizenship are prescribed by law. A citizen of the Republic of Armenia may not be simultaneously a citizen of another country. The rights, liberties and duties of citizens of Armenia, regardless of nationality, race, sex, language, creed, political or other convictions, social origin, property and other status, are guaranteed. No one shall be subject to torture or cruel treatment. Every citizen has the right to freedom of movement and residence within the republic, as well as the right to leave the republic. Every citizen has the right to freedom of thought, speech, conscience and religion. The right to establish or join associations, trade unions, political organizations, etc., is guaranteed, as is the right to strike for protection of economic, social and labour interests. Citizens of the republic who have attained 18 years of age are entitled to participate in state government through their directly-elected representatives or by expression of free will.

Every citizen has the right to social insurance in the event of old age, disability, sickness, widowhood, unemployment, etc. Every citizen has the right to education. Education is provided free at elementary and secondary state educational institutions. Citizens belonging to national minorities have the right to preserve their traditions and to develop their language and culture. Everyone charged with a penal offence has the right to be presumed innocent until proved guilty. The advocacy of national, racial and religious hatred, and the propagation of violence and war, are prohibited.

THE PRESIDENT OF THE REPUBLIC

The President of the Republic of Armenia ensures the observance of the Constitution and the effective operation of the legislative, executive and juridical authorities. The President is the guarantor of the independence, territorial integrity and security of the republic. He/she is elected by citizens of the republic for a period of five years. Any person who has the right to participate in elections, has attained the age of 35 years, and has been a resident citizen of Armenia for the preceding 10 years is eligible for election to the office of President. No person may be elected to the office for more than two successive terms.

The President signs and promulgates laws adopted by the National Assembly, or returns draft legislation to the National Assembly for reconsideration; may dismiss the National Assembly and declare special elections to it, after consultation with the Prime Minister and the Chairman of the National Assembly; appoints and dismisses the Prime Minister; appoints and dismisses the members of the Government, upon the recommendation of the Prime Minister; appoints civil service officials; establishes deliberation bodies; represents Armenia in international relations, co-ordinates foreign policy, concludes international treaties, signs international treaties ratified by the National Assembly, and ratifies agreements between governments; appoints and recalls diplomatic representatives of Armenia to foreign countries and international organizations, and receives the credentials of diplomatic representatives of foreign countries; appoints the Procurator General, as nominated by the Prime Minister; appoints members and the Chairman of the Constitutional Court; is the Supreme Commander-in-Chief of the armed forces; takes decisions on the use of the armed forces; grants titles of honour; and grants amnesties to convicts.

THE NATIONAL ASSEMBLY

Legislative power in the Republic of Armenia is executed by the National Assembly. The Assembly comprises 131 deputies, elected for a four-year term*. Any person who has attained the age of 25 years and has been a permanent resident and citizen of Armenia for the preceding five years is eligible to be elected a deputy.

The National Assembly deliberates and enacts laws; has the power to express a vote of 'no confidence' in the Government; confirms the state budget, as proposed by the Government; supervises the implementation of the state budget; elects its Chairman (Speaker) and two Deputy Chairmen; appoints the Chairman and Deputy Chairman of the Central Bank, upon the nomination of the President; appoints members of the Constitutional Court.

At the suggestion of the President of the Republic, the National Assembly declares amnesties; ratifies or declares invalid international treaties; and declares war. Upon the recommendation of the Government, the National Assembly confirms the territorial and administrative divisions of the republic.

THE GOVERNMENT

Executive power is realized by the Government of the Republic of Armenia, which is composed of the Prime Minister and the Ministers. The Prime Minister is appointed by the President; upon the recommendation of the Prime Minister, the President appoints the remaining Ministers. The Prime Minister directs the current activities of the Government and co-ordinates the activities of the Ministers.

The Government presents the programme of its activities to the National Assembly for approval; presents the draft state budget to the National Assembly for confirmation, ensures implementation of the budget and presents a report on its implementation to the National Assembly; manages state property; ensures the implementation of state fiscal, loan and tax policies; ensures the implementation of state policy in the spheres of science, education, culture, health care, social security and environmental protection; ensures the implementation of defence, national security and foreign policies; and takes measures to strengthen adherence to the laws, to ensure the rights and freedoms of citizens, and to protect public order and the property of citizens.

JUDICIAL POWER

In the Republic of Armenia the courts of general competence are the tribunal courts of first instance, the review courts and the Court of Appeal. There are also economic, military and other courts. The guarantor of the independence of judicial bodies is the President of the Republic. He/she is the Head of the Council of Justice. The Minister of Justice and the Procurator General are the Deputy Heads of the Council of Justice. Fourteen members appointed by the President of the Republic for a period of five years are included in the Council. The Constitutional Court is composed of nine members, of whom the National Assembly appoints five and the President of the Republic appoints four. The Constitutional Court, *inter alia*, determines whether decisions of the National Assembly, decrees and orders of the President, and resolutions of the Government correspond to the Constitution; decides, prior to ratification of an international treaty, whether the obligations created in it correspond to the Constitution; resolves disputes relating to referendums and results of presidential and legislative elections; and decides on the suspension or prohibition of the activity of a political party.

TERRITORIAL ADMINISTRATION AND LOCAL SELF-GOVERNMENT

The administrative territorial units of the Republic of Armenia are: regions and communities. Regions are comprised of rural and urban communities. Local self-government takes place in the communities. Bodies of local self-government, community elders and the community head (city mayor or head of village) are elected for a three-year period to administer community property and solve issues of community significance. State government is exercised in the regions. The Government appoints and dismisses regional governors, who carry out the Government's regional policy and co-ordinate the performance of regional services by state executive bodies. The city of Yerevan has the status of a region.

* At the legislative elections of July 1995, 189 of 190 deputies were elected to the National Assembly; this was in accordance with the electoral law applicable before the Constitution entered into force.

The Government

HEAD OF STATE

President: LEVON TER-PETROSSIAN (elected 16 October 1991, re-elected 22 September 1996).

GOVERNMENT

(December 1997)

Prime Minister: ROBERT KOCHARIAN.

Minister of Energy: GAGIK MARTIROSSIAN.

Minister of Urban Planning and Construction: FELIKS PIRUMIAN.

Minister of Foreign Affairs: ALEXANDER ARZUMANIAN.

Minister of Social Security: HRANUSH HAKOPIAN.

Minister of Health: GAGIK STAMBOLTSIAN.

Minister of Justice: MARAT ALEKSANIAN.

Minister of Local Government Affairs: GALOUST GAMAZIAN.

Minister of Parliamentary Affairs: ARSEN KAMALIAN.

Minister of Agriculture and Food Supplies: VLADIMIR MOVSISSIAN.

Minister of the Environment and Natural Resources: SARKIS SHAKHAZIZIAN.

Minister of Industry and Trade: GARNIK NANAGULIAN.

Minister of Education and Science: ARTASHES PETROSSIAN.

Minister of Communications: GRIGOR POGHPATIAN.

Minister of Culture, Youth and Sport: ARMEN SMBATIAN.

Minister of Internal Affairs and National Security: SERGE SARKISSIAN.

Minister of Defence: VAZGEN SARKISSIAN.

Minister of Transport: HENRIK KOCHINIAN.

Minister of Finance and the Economy: ARMEN DARBINIAN.

Minister of Privatization: PAVEL KALTAKHCHIAN.

Mayor of Yerevan: VANO SIRADEGHIAN.

Minister-Chief of Staff of Government: GAGIK SHAHBAZIAN.

Head of the State Commission for Statistics and Data: EDUARD AGHADJANOV.

Head of the State Commission for Tax Inspection: PAVEL SAFARIAN.

MINISTRIES

Office of the Prime Minister: 375010 Yerevan, Republic Sq. 1, Government House; tel. (2) 52-03-60; fax (2) 15-10-35.

Ministry of Agriculture and Food Supplies: 375010 Yerevan, Republic Sq. 1, Government House; tel. (2) 52-46-41; fax (2) 15-10-86.

Ministry of Communications: 375002 Yerevan, Sarian St 22; tel. (2) 52-66-32; fax (2) 15-14-46.

Ministry of Culture, Youth and Sport: 375010 Yerevan, Tumanian St 5; tel. (2) 56-19-20; fax (2) 52-39-22.

Ministry of Defence: Yerevan, Proshian Settlement, Shaush St 60G; tel. (2) 35-78-22; fax (2) 52-65-60.

Ministry of Education and Science: 375010 Yerevan, Movses Khorenatsi St 13; tel. (2) 52-66-02; fax (2) 15-11-50.

Ministry of Emergency Situations: Yerevan.

Ministry of Energy: 375010 Yerevan, Republic Sq. 1, Government House 2; tel. (2) 52-19-64; fax (2) 15-16-87.

Ministry of the Environment and Natural Resources: 375012 Yerevan, Moskovian St 35; tel. (2) 53-07-41; fax (2) 53-49-02.

Ministry of Finance and the Economy: 375010 Yerevan, Melik-Adamian St 1; tel. (2) 52-54-22; fax (2) 15-11-54.

Ministry of Foreign Affairs: 375010 Yerevan, Republic Sq. 1, Government House; tel. (2) 52-35-31; fax (2) 15-10-42.

Ministry of Health: 375001 Yerevan, Tumanian St 8; tel. (2) 58-24-13; fax (2) 15-10-97.

Ministry of Industry and Trade: 375008 Yerevan, Terian St 69; tel. (2) 56-25-91; fax (2) 15-16-75.

Ministry of Internal Affairs and National Security: Yerevan.

Ministry of Justice: 375010 Yerevan, Parliament St 8; tel. (2) 58-21-57.

Ministry of Local Government Affairs: Yerevan; tel (2) 52-52-74.

Ministry of Privatization: 375010 Yerevan, Republic Sq., Government House 2.

Ministry of Social Security: 375009 Yerevan, Terian St 69; tel. (2) 56-53-21; fax (2) 15-19-20.

Ministry of Transport: 375015 Yerevan, Zakian St 10; tel. (2) 56-33-91; fax (2) 52-76-36.

Ministry of Urban Planning and Construction: 375010 Yerevan, Republic Sq. 1, Government House; tel. (2) 52-52-74; fax (2) 15-10-36.

President and Legislature

PRESIDENT

Presidential Election, 22 September 1996

	% of votes
LEVON TER-PETROSSIAN (Pan-Armenian National Movement)	51.8
VAZGEN MANUKIAN (National Democratic Union)	41.3
SERGEI BADALIAN (Communist Party of Armenia)	6.3
ASHOT MANUCHARIAN (Scientific-Industrial and Civic Union of Armenia)	0.6
Total	100.00

NATIONAL ASSEMBLY

Chairman: BABKEN ARARKTSIAN.

Deputy Chairmen: KARAPET RUBINIAN, ARA SAHAKIAN.

General Election, 5 and 27 July 1995

Parties and blocs	Seats by proportional representation	Single-member constituency seats	Total seats
Republican bloc*	20	99	119
Shamiram Women's Party	8	—	8
Communist Party of Armenia	6	1	7
National Democratic Union	3	2	5
Union for National Self-Determination	3	—	3
Ramkavar-Azatakan Liberal Democratic Party	—	1	1
Armenian Revolutionary Federation	—	1	1
Independents	—	45	45
Total	40	150†	190†‡

* A coalition of the Pan-Armenian National Movement, the Republican Party of Armenia, the Armenian Christian Democratic Union, the Hnchak Armenian Social Democratic Party, the Armenian Liberal Democratic Party and the Intellectual Armenia Union.

† One seat remained vacant, to be filled at a later date.

‡ Under the existing electoral law, the National Assembly comprised 190 deputies; however, the new Constitution (approved in a national referendum on 5 July 1995) provided for an Assembly of 131 deputies (effective from the next general election, due to be held in 1999).

Political Organizations

Armenian Christian Democratic Union: Yerevan, Nubarashen St 16; tel. (2) 47-68-68; Chair. AZAD ARSHAKIAN.

Armenian Democratic Agricultural Party: Yerevan, Kutuzov St 1/7; tel. (2) 26-40-03; Chair. TELMAN DILANIAN.

Armenian Democratic Party: Yerevan, Koriun St 14; tel. (2) 52-52-73; f. 1992 by elements of former Communist Party of Armenia; Chair. ARAM SARKISSIAN.

Armenian Monarchists Party: Aparan, Garegin Nejdeh St 13/11; tel. (520) 85-20; Chair. TIGRAN PETROSSIAN.

Armenian National Party: Yerevan; f. 1996.

Armenian Revolutionary Federation (ARF) (Hai Heghapokhakan Dashnaktsutyun): 375025 Yerevan, Myasnyak Ave 2; f. 1890; formed the ruling party in independent Armenia, 1918–20; prohibited under Soviet rule, but continued its activities in other countries; permitted to operate legally in Armenia from 1991; suspended in December 1994; 40,000 mems; Chair. RUBEN HAGOBIAN, VAHAN HOVHANISSIAN.

Azatutyun (Freedom): Yerevan; f. 1997; liberal, right-wing; Leader HRANT BAGRATIAN.

Communist Party of Armenia: Yerevan, Marshal Baghramian St 10; tel. (2) 56-79-33; fax (2) 53-38-55; f. 1920; dissolved 1991, relegalized 1992; c. 50,000 mems; Chair. SERGEI BADALIAN.

Haykandoukht Women's Party: Yerevan; Leader ARMENOUHI KAZARIAN.

Hnchak Armenian Social Democratic Party: Yerevan, Aghbiur Serob St 7; tel. (2) 27-33-15; Chair. YEGHIA NAJARIAN.

National Democratic Union: Yerevan, Abovian St 12; tel. (2) 52-60-06; f. 1991 as a splinter party of the PNM; Leader DAVIT VARDANIAN; Chair. VAZGEN MANUKIAN.

Pan-Armenian National Movement (PNM) (Haiots Hamazgaien Sharjoum): 375019 Yerevan, Marshal Baghramian St 14; tel. (2) 52-03-31; f. 1989 as the Armenian Pan-national Movement, renamed 1995; Pres. LEVON TER-PETROSSIAN; Chair. VANO SIRADEGHIAN.

Ramkavar-Azatakan Liberal Democratic Party: 375009 Yerevan, Koryun St 19A; tel. (2) 52-64-03; fax (2) 52-53-23; f. 1905; Leader HARUTYUN KARAPETIAN.

Republican Party of Armenia: Yerevan, Tumanian St 23; tel. (2) 58-00-31; fax (2) 56-60-34; f. 1990 following a split in the UNS; 13 territorial orgs; 2,000 mems; Chair. ASHOT NAVASARDIAN.

Shamiram Women's Party: Yerevan; f. 1995.

Union for National Self-Determination (UNS): 375013 Yerevan, Gregory the Illuminator St 15; tel. (2) 52-55-38; Chair. PARUIR HAIRIKIAN.

Diplomatic Representation

EMBASSIES IN ARMENIA

China, People's Republic: 375019 Yerevan, Marshal Baghramian St 12; tel. (2) 56-00-67; fax (2) 15-11-43; Ambassador: YANG KERONG.

Egypt: Yerevan, Pionerakan St 72, Hotel Hrazdan, 10th Floor; tel. (2) 53-73-04; fax (2) 15-11-60; Chargé d'affaires a.i.: Dr AHMAD FUAD RASLAN.

France: 375015 Yerevan, Grigor Lussavorich St 8; tel. (2) 56-11-03; fax (2) 15-11-05; Ambassador: MICHEL LEGRAS.

Georgia: Yerevan; Ambassador: REVAZ BARAMIDZE.

Germany: Yerevan, Pionerakan St 72, Hotel Hrazdan, 7th Floor; tel. (2) 53-67-74; telex 243138; fax (2) 15-11-12; Ambassador: CAROLA MÜLLER-HOLTKEMPER.

Greece: Yerevan, Pionerakan St 72, Hotel Hrazdan, 5th Floor; tel. (2) 53-00-51; fax (2) 15-11-70; Ambassador: YAKOVOS SPETSIOS.

Iran: Yerevan, Budaghian St 1; tel. (2) 52-98-30; fax (2) 15-13-85; Ambassador: HAMID REZA ISFAHANI.

Lebanon: Yerevan.

Russia: Yerevan, Grigor Lussavorich St 13A; tel. (2) 56-74-27; fax (2) 50-52-37; Ambassador: ANDREI URNOV.

Syria: Yerevan.

Ukraine: Yerevan; Ambassador: OLEKSANDR BOZHKO.

United Kingdom: Yerevan, Charents St 28; tel. (2) 15-18-41; fax (2) 15-18-07; Ambassador: Dr JOHN MITCHINER.

USA: 375019 Yerevan, Marshal Baghramian St 18; tel. (2) 15-15-51; telex 243137; fax (2) 15-15-50; Ambassador: PETER TOMSEN.

Judicial System

Chairman of the Constitutional Court: GAGIK ARUTYUNIAN.

Chairman of the Supreme Court: T. K. BARSEGIAN.

Procurator General: GENRIKH KHACHATRIAN.

Religion

The major religion is Christianity. The Armenian Apostolic Church is the leading denomination and was widely identified with the movement for national independence. There are also Russian Orthodox and Islamic communities, although the latter have lost adherents as a result of the departure of large numbers of Muslim Azerbaijanis from the republic. Most Kurds are also adherents of Islam, although some are Yazidis.

GOVERNMENT AGENCY

Council for the Affairs of the Armenian Church: 375001 Yerevan, Abovian St 3; tel. (2) 56-46-34; fax (2) 56-41-81; Chair. LYUDVIG KHACHATRIAN.

CHRISTIANITY

Armenian Apostolic Church: Echmiadzin; tel. (59) 15-11-98; four dioceses in Armenia, three in other ex-Soviet republics and 25 dioceses and bishoprics in the rest of the world; 7m. members worldwide (some 4m. in Armenia); 15 monasteries and three theological seminaries in Armenia; Supreme Patriarch GAREGIN I (NESHAN SARKISSIAN), Catholicos of All Armenians.

The Roman Catholic Church

Armenian Rite

Armenian Catholics in Eastern Europe are under the jurisdiction of an Ordinary (equivalent to a bishop with direct authority). At 31 December 1995 there were an estimated 159,000 adherents within this jurisdiction, including about 30,000 in Armenia itself.

Ordinary: Most Rev. NERSES TER-NERSESSIAN (Titular Archbishop of Sebaste), Gyumri, Atarbeghian St 82; tel. (69) 22-115; fax (69) 21-839.

Latin Rite

The Apostolic Administrator of the Caucasus is the Apostolic Nuncio (Ambassador of the Holy See) to Georgia, Armenia and Azerbaijan, who is resident in Tbilisi, Georgia.

The Press

In 1994, according to UNESCO, there were seven daily newspapers. There were 57 non-daily newspapers published in Armenia in 1992. There were also 40 periodicals published in that year, with a combined average circulation of 5.1m. copies.

PRINCIPAL NEWSPAPERS

In Armenian except where otherwise stated.

Ankakhutiun (Independence): 375013 Yerevan, Gregory the Illuminator St 15; tel. (2) 58-18-64; daily; organ of the Union for National Self-Determination; Editor PARUIR HAIRIKIAN.

Aravot: 375023 Yerevan, Arshakunyats Ave 2, 10th Floor; tel (2) 52-87-52; Editor A. ABRAMIAN.

Avangard: 375023 Yerevan, Arshakunyats Ave 2; f. 1923; 3 a week; organ of the Youth League of Armenia; Editor M. K. ZOHRABIAN.

Azg (The Nation): 375010 Yerevan, Hanrapetutian St 47; tel. (2) 52-16-35; f. 1990; Editor S. SARKISSIAN.

Bravo: Yerevan, Abovian St 12, Hotel Yerevan; tel. (2) 55-44-05; weekly; Editor K. KAZARIAN.

Eis Express: Yerevan, Zarian St 22, 2nd Floor; tel. (2) 25-26-83; weekly; Editor E. NAGDALIAN.

Epokha (Epoch): 375023 Yerevan, Arshakunyats Ave 2; f. 1938; fmrly *Komsomolets*; weekly; Russian; organ of the Youth League of Armenia; Editor V. S. GRIGORIAN.

Golos Armenii (The Voice of Armenia): 375023 Yerevan, Arshakunyats Ave 2, 7th Floor; tel. (2) 52-77-23; f. 1934 as *Kommunist;* 3 a week; Russian; Editor F. NASHKARIAN.

Grakan Tert (Literary Paper): 375019 Yerevan, Marshal Baghramian St 3; tel. (2) 52-05-94; f. 1932; weekly; organ of the Union of Writers; Editor F. H. MELOIAN.

Hanrapetakan: Yerevan, Tumanian St 23; tel. (2) 58-00-31; fax (2) 56-60-34; publ. by the Republican Party of Armenia.

Hayastan (Armenia): 375023 Yerevan, Arshakunyats Ave 2; tel. (2) 52-84-50; f. 1920; 6 a week; Russian; Editor G. ABRAMIAN.

Hayastani Hanrapetutyun (Republic of Armenia): 375023 Yerevan, Arshakunyats Ave 2, 13th–14th Floors; f. 1990; tel. and fax (2) 52-69-74; 6 a week; also in Russian (as *Respublika Armeniya*); Editor M. HARUTYUNIAN.

Hayk (Armenia): 375023 Yerevan, Arshakunyats Ave 2, 11th Floor; tel. (2) 52-77-01; weekly; organ of the Pan-Armenian National Movement; Editor V. DAVTIAN; circ. 30,000.

Hayots Ashkhar: Yerevan, Tumanian St 38; tel. (2) 53-88-65; Editor G. MKRTCHIAN.

Hazatamart (The Battle for Freedom): 375070 Yerevan, Atarbekian 181; organ of the Armenian Revolutionary Federation; Editor M. MIKAYELIAN.

Hnchak Hayastani (The Bell of Armenia): 375019 Yerevan, Lord Byron St 12; weekly.

Marzakan Hayastan: 375023 Yerevan, Arshakunyats Ave 5; tel. (2) 52-62-41; weekly; Editor S. MOURADIAN.

Molorak: 375023 Yerevan, Arshakunyats Ave 5; tel. (2) 52-62-12; daily; Editor H. GHAGHRINIAN.

Respublika Armenia: 375023 Yerevan, Arshakunyats Ave 2, 9th Floor; tel. (2) 52-69-69; Editor A. KHANBABIAN.

Ria Taze (New Way): Yerevan; 2 a week; Kurdish.

Vozny (Hedgehog): 375023 Yerevan, Arshakunyats Ave 2, 12th Floor; tel. (2) 52-63-83; f. 1954; Editor A. SAHAKIAN.

Yerevanyan Orer (Yerevan Days): Yerevan; Editor M. AIRAPETIAN.

Yerkir (Country): 375009 Yerevan, Yeznik Koghbatsi St 50A; tel. (2) 53-05-70; daily; organ of the Armenian Revolutionary Federation; suspended Dec. 1994.

Yerokoyan Yerevan (Evening Yerevan): 375023 Yerevan, Arshakunyats Ave 2, 10th Floor; tel. (2) 52-97-52; weekly; organ of Yerevan City Council; Editor N. YENGIBARIAN.

Yeter: Yerevan, Manukian St 5; tel. (2) 55-34-13; weekly; Editor G. KAZARIAN.

Zroutsakits: 375023 Yerevan, Arshakunyats Ave 2, 2nd Floor; tel. (2) 52-84-30; weekly; Editor M. MIRIDJANIAN.

PRINCIPAL PERIODICALS

Aghbiur (Source): Yerevan; f. 1923, fmrly *Pioner;* monthly; for teenagers; Editor T. V. TONOIAN.

Armenian Kommersant: Yerevan, Koriuny St 19A; tel. (2) 52-79-77; monthly; Editor M. VARTANIAN.

Aroghchapakutyun (Health): 375001 Yerevan, Tumanian St 8; f. 1956; monthly; journal of the Ministry of Health; Editor M. A. MURADIAN.

Arvest (Art): 375001 Yerevan, Tumanian St 5; f. 1932, fmrly *Sovetakan Arvest* (Soviet Art); monthly; publ. by the Ministry of Culture, Youth and Sport; Editor G. A. AZAKELIAN.

Chetvertaya Vlast: Yerevan, Abovian St 12, Hotel Yerevan, Room 105; tel. (2) 59-73-81; monthly; Editor A. GEVORKIAN.

Ekonomika (Economics): Yerevan, Vardanants St 2; tel. (2) 52-27-95; f. 1957; monthly; organ of the Ministry of Finance and the Economy; Editor R. H. SHAKHKULIAN; circ. 1,500–2,000.

Garun (Spring): 375015 Yerevan, Karmir Banaki St 15; tel. (2) 56-29-56; f. 1967; monthly; independent; fiction and socio-political issues; Editor L. Z. ANANIAN.

Gitutyun ev Tekhnika (Science and Technology): 375048 Yerevan, pr. Komitasa 49/3; tel. (2) 23-37-27; f. 1963; quarterly; journal of the Research Institute of Scientific-Technical Information and of Technological and Economic Research; Dir M. B. YEDILIAN; Editor M. A. CHUGURIAN; circ. 1,000.

Hayastani Ashkhatavoruhi (Working Women of Armenia): Yerevan; f. 1924; monthly; Editor A. G. CHILINGARIAN.

Hayreniky Dzayn (Voice of the Motherland): Yerevan; f. 1965; weekly; organ of the Armenian Committee for Cultural Relations with Compatriots Abroad; Editor L. H. ZAKARIAN.

Iravounk: 375009 Yerevan, Yeznik Koghbatsu St 50A; tel. (2) 53-27-30; monthly; Editor H. BABUKHANIAN.

Literaturnaya Armeniya (Literature of Armenia): 375019 Yerevan, Marshal Baghramian St 3; tel. (2) 56-36-57; f. 1958; monthly; journal of the Union of Writers; fiction; Russian; Editor A. M. NALBANDIAN.

Nork: Yerevan; f. 1934; fmrly *Sovetakan Grakanutyun* (Soviet Literature); monthly; journal of the Union of Writers; fiction; Russian; Editor R. G. OVSEPIAN.

Novoye Vremya: 375023 Yerevan, Arshakunyats Ave 2, 3rd Floor; tel. (2) 52-29-61; 2 a week; Editor R. SATIAN.

Veratsnvats Hayastan (Reborn Armenia): Yerevan; f. 1945 as *Sovetakan Hayastan* (Soviet Armenia); monthly; journal of the Armenian Committee for Cultural Relations with Compatriots Abroad; fiction; Editor V. A. DAVITIAN.

The Yerevan Times: 375009 Yerevan, Isaahakian St 28, 3rd Floor; tel. (2) 52-82-70; fax (2) 15-17-38; e-mail yertime@armpress.arminco.com; weekly; English; Editor T. HAKOBIAN.

NEWS AGENCIES

Armenpress (Armenian Press Agency): 375009 Yerevan, Isaahakian St 28, 4th Floor; tel. (2) 52-67-02; fax (2) 15-17-38; e-mail root@armpress.arminco.com; state information agency, transformed into state joint-stock company in 1997; Dir T. HAKOBIAN.

Noyan Tapan (Noah's Ark): 375009 Yerevan, Isaahakian St 28, 3rd Floor; tel. and fax (2) 52-42-18; Dir TIGRAN HARUTYUNIAN.

Past: 375023 Yerevan, Arshakunyats Ave 2, 15th Floor; tel. (2) 53-86-18; Dir T. NAGDALIAN.

Snark: 375009 Yerevan, Isaahakian St 28, 1st Floor; tel. (2) 52-99-42; fax (2) 56-22-51; Dir V. OGHANIAN.

Publishers

In 1994 a total of 224 titles (books and pamphlets) were published.

Academy of Sciences Publishing House: 375019 Yerevan, Marshal Baghramian St 24G; Dir KH. H. BARSEGHIAN.

Anait: Yerevan; art publishing.

Arevik (Sun Publishing House): 375009 Yerevan, Isaahakian St 28; political, scientific, fiction for children; Dir V. S. KALANTARIAN.

Hayastan (Armenia Publishing House): 375009 Yerevan, Isaahakian St 91; tel. (2) 52-85-20; f. 1921; political and fiction; Dir DAVID SARKISSIAN.

Haykakan Hanragitaran (Armenian Encyclopedia): 375001 Yerevan 1, Tumanian St 17; tel. (2) 52-43-41; f. 1967; encyclopaedias and other reference books; Editor K. S. KHUDAVERDIAN.

Luys (Enlightenment Publishing House): Yerevan, Kirov St 19A; textbooks; Dir S. M. MOVSISSIAN.

Nairi: Yerevan, Teryana St 91; fiction; Dir H. H. FELEKHIAN.

Broadcasting and Communications

State Television and Radio Broadcasting: 375025 Yerevan, A. Manukian St 5; tel. (2) 55-50-33; Chair. (vacant).

Armenian Radio: 375025 Yerevan, A. Manukian St 5; tel. (2) 55-80-10; telex 243260; fax (2) 55-15-13; 3 programmes; broadcasts inside the republic in Armenian, Russian and Kurdish; external broadcasts in Armenian, Russian, Kurdish, Azeri, Arabic, English, French, Spanish and Farsi; transformed into state joint-stock company in 1997.

Armenian Television: 375025 Yerevan, A. Manukian St 5; tel. (2) 55-20-91; fax (2) 55-15-13; broadcasts in Armenian and occasionally in Russian; transformed into state joint-stock company in 1997.

Finance

(cap. = capital; res = reserves; dep. = deposits; m. = million; brs = branches; amounts in drams, unless otherwise stated)

BANKING

Central Bank

Central Bank of the Republic of Armenia: 375010 Yerevan, Nalbandian St 6; tel. (2) 58-38-41; telex 243327; fax (2) 56-04-41; cap. 5m., res 1,528m., dep 4,640m. (Dec. 1995); Chair. Dr BAGRAT ASATRIAN.

Commercial Banks

In late 1996 there were reported to be 33 commercial banks in operation in Armenia. Some of the most influential of these are listed below:

Ardshinbank (ASHB): 375010 Yerevan, Deghatan St 3; tel. (2) 52-85-13; telex 243241; fax (2) 15-11-55; f. 1922, reorganized as joint-stock commercial bank for industry and construction in 1992; largest bank in Armenia; cap. 1,518.2m., res 213.6m., dep. 3,699.1m. (Dec. 1996); Chair. ARAM ANDREASSIAN; 35 brs.

Armaviabank: 375014 Yerevan, Sevaki St 1; tel. (2) 28-88-57; telex 243113; fax (2) 28-19-40.

Armenian Development Bank: 375000 Yerevan, Paronian St 21/7; tel. (2) 53-00-94; telex 243324; fax (2) 53-03-12.

Armenian Economy Development Bank (Armeconombank): 375002 Yerevan, Amirian St 23/1; tel. (2) 56-27-05; telex 243274; fax (2) 56-27-05; incorporated as joint-stock co in 1992; corporate banking; total assets US $12m. (Nov. 1997); Chair. of Bd ARMEN MARTIROSSIAN; 26 brs.

Armenian Import-Export Bank (Armimpexbank): 375010 Yerevan, Nalbandian St 2; tel. (2) 58-99-06; telex 243352; fax (2) 56-59-58; f. 1992 by reorganization of Armenian br. of the Vneshekonombank of the former USSR; joint-stock co with foreign shareholding; cap. US $1.3m., dep. US $13.2m. (Nov. 1996); Chair. of Bd E. ARABKHANIAN; 10 brs.

Armenian Joint-Stock Agrobank (Armagrobank): 375015 Yerevan, M. Khorenatsi St 7A; tel. (2) 53-53-47; telex 243159; fax (2) 90-71-24; incorporated as joint-stock co in 1992; cap. 279m.; 49 brs.

Arminvestbank: 375010 Yerevan, Vardanants St 13; tel. (2) 52-37-18; telex 243134; fax (2) 15-15-45.

Credit-Yerevan Commercial Joint-Stock Bank: 375010 Yerevan, Amirian 2/8; tel. (2) 58-90-65; telex 243244; fax (2) 15-18-20; f. 1993; cap. US $1.1m. (Nov. 1997); Pres. MARTIN HOVHANNISIAN.

Midland Bank of Armenia: Yerevan; f. 1996; cap. US $4m.

Shirakinvestbank: 377500 Gyumri, G. Njdeh St 7; tel. (69) 36-21-4; telex 243245; fax (69) 06-16-9; f. 1996; cap. 144m., res 11m., dep. 307m. (Dec. 1996); Chair. MAMIKON GINOSIAN; Pres. HOVHANNES GRIGORIAN.

Savings Bank

State Joint-Stock Savings Bank of Armenia (Armsavingsbank): 375079 Yerevan, Mikoian St 20; tel. (2) 64-46-00; telex 243383; fax (2) 63-40-60; reorganized 1996; cap. 915m., dep. 1,242m. (Oct. 1996); Chair. H. MANDAKUNI; 35 regional brs.

COMMODITY AND STOCK EXCHANGES

Adamand Stock Exchange: Adamand.

Gyumri Stock Exchange: Gyumri.

Yerevan Commodity and Raw Materials Exchange: 375051 Yerevan, Aram Khachaturian St 31/1; tel. (2) 25-26-00; fax (2) 25-09-93; f. 1991; authorized cap. 5m.; Gen. Man. ARA ARZUMANAIAN.

Yerevan Stock Exchange: 375002 Yerevan, Sarian St 22; tel. (2) 53-58-23; fax (2) 15-15-48; f. 1993; Pres. Dr SEDRAK SEDRAKIAN.

Trade and Industry

CHAMBER OF COMMERCE

Chamber of Commerce and Industry of the Republic of Armenia: 375033 Yerevan, Hanrapetutian St 39; tel. (2) 56-54-38; telex 243322; fax (2) 56-50-71; Chair. ASHOT SARKISSIAN.

INDUSTRIAL AND TRADE ASSOCIATION

Armenintorg—Armenian State Foreign Economic and Trade Association: 375012 Yerevan, Hr. Kochar St 25; tel. (2) 22-43-10; telex 243323; fax (2) 22-00-34; f. 1987; import and export of all types of goods, marketing, consultancy, auditing and other services, conducts training programmes, arranges international exhibitions and trade fairs; Gen. Dir ARAM NAZUKIAN; 20 employees.

EMPLOYERS' ORGANIZATIONS

Armenian Business Forum: Yerevan; tel. (2) 52-75-43; fax (2) 52-43-32; f. 1991; promotes joint ventures, foreign capital investments; Pres. VAHE JAZMADARIAN.

Armenian Union of Industrialists and Entrepreneurs: Yerevan; Chair. ARAM VARDANIAN.

TRADE UNIONS

Confederation of Armenian Trade Unions: 375010 Yerevan, Hanrapetutian Sq.; tel. (2) 58-42-78; fax (2) 15-18-78; Chair. MARTIN ARUTYUNIAN.

Transport

RAILWAYS

In 1992 there were 825 km of railway track, on which Armenia Railways was operating about 100 diesel electric locomotives and 80 diesels. There are international lines to Iran and Georgia; lines to Azerbaijan and Turkey remained closed in October 1997, as a result of those countries' continuing economic blockade of Armenia.

Armenia Railways: 375005 Yerevan, Tigran the Great St 50; f. 1992 following the dissolution of the former Soviet Railways; Pres. V. V. ASRIYANTS.

Metropolitan Railway

Yerevan Metro: 375033 Yerevan, Marshal Baghramian St 76; tel. (2) 27-45-43; fax (2) 15-13-95; f. 1981; Gen. Man. H. BEGLARIAN.

ROADS

In 1995 there were an estimated 7,720 km of roads in Armenia (3,990 km of highways and 3,730 km of secondary roads). Some 40% of the network was estimated to be in poor condition and in need of repair. In 1996 plans were made to upgrade existing roads, and to construct some 1,400 km of new roads over the next four years, with financial assistance from various international organizations. As a result of the economic blockade imposed in 1989 by Azerbaijan (and subsequently reinforced by Turkey), the Kajaran highway linking Armenia with Iran has emerged as Armenia's most important international road connection; in December 1995 a permanent road bridge over the Araks river was opened, strengthening this link. In mid-1997 a bus route to Syria was opened—the first overland route between the two countries.

CIVIL AVIATION

In 1991 the Armenian Airlines Company, which was an integral part of the USSR Ministry of Civil Aviation, was restructured as the State Airlines Company of Armenia, using aircraft from the Aeroflot fleet. A new joint-venture company was established to handle air freight. In 1993 the company's name reverted to Armenian Airlines. In 1997 the Government approved proposals to privatize the airline.

Armenian Airlines: 375042 Yerevan, Zvarnots Airport; tel. (2) 77-59-20; fax (2) 15-13-93; f. 1993; operates scheduled and charter passenger services to countries of the CIS, Europe and the Middle East; Dir V. YARALOV.

AUSTRALIA

Introductory Survey

Location, Climate, Language, Religion, Flag, Capital

The Commonwealth of Australia occupies the whole of the island continent of Australia, lying between the Indian and Pacific Oceans, and its offshore islands, principally Tasmania to the south-east. Australia's nearest neighbour is Papua New Guinea, to the north. In the summer (November–February) there are tropical monsoons in the northern part of the continent (except for the Queensland coast), but the winters (July–August) are dry. Both the north-west and north-east coasts are liable to experience tropical cyclones between December and April. In the southern half of the country, winter is the wet season; rainfall decreases rapidly inland. Very high temperatures, sometimes exceeding 50°C (122°F), are experienced during the summer months over the arid interior and for some distance to the south, as well as during the pre-monsoon months in the north. The official language is English. Indigenous languages are spoken by Aboriginal and Torres Strait Islander peoples. In 1996 70.3% of the population professed Christianity (of whom 38.1% were Roman Catholic and 31.0% Anglican). The national flag (proportions 2 by 1) is blue, with a representation of the United Kingdom flag in the upper hoist, a large seven-pointed white star in the lower hoist and five smaller white stars, in the form of the Southern Cross constellation, in the fly. The capital, Canberra, lies in one of two enclaves of federal territory known as the Australian Capital Territory (ACT).

Recent History

Since the Second World War, Australia has played an important role in Asian affairs, and has strengthened its political and economic ties with Indonesia, and the other countries of South-East Asia, and with Japan. The country co-operates more closely than formerly with the USA (see ANZUS, p. 269), and has given much aid to Asian and Pacific countries.

At the election of December 1949 the ruling Australian Labor Party (ALP) was defeated by the Liberal Party, in coalition with the Country Party. In January 1966 Sir Robert Menzies resigned after 16 years as Prime Minister, and was succeeded by Harold Holt, who was returned to office at elections in December of that year. However, Holt died in December 1967. His successor, Senator John Gorton, took office in January 1968 but resigned, after losing a vote of confidence, in March 1971. William McMahon was Prime Minister from March 1971 until December 1972, when, after 23 years in office, the Liberal-Country Party coalition was defeated at a general election for the House of Representatives. The ALP, led by Gough Whitlam, won 67 of the 125 seats in the House. Following a conflict between the Whitlam Government and the Senate, both Houses of Parliament were dissolved in April 1974, and a general election was held in May. The ALP was returned to power, although with a reduced majority in the House of Representatives. However, the Government failed to gain a majority in the Senate, and in October 1975 the Opposition in the Senate obstructed legislative approval of budget proposals. The Government was not willing to consent to a general election over the issue, but in November the Governor-General, Sir John Kerr, intervened and took the unprecedented step of dismissing the Government. A caretaker Ministry was installed under Malcolm Fraser, the Liberal leader, who formed a coalition Government with the Country Party. This coalition gained large majorities in both Houses of Parliament at a general election in December 1975, but the majorities were progressively reduced at general elections in December 1977 and October 1980.

Fraser's coalition Government was defeated by the ALP at a general election in March 1983. Robert (Bob) Hawke, who had replaced William (Bill) Hayden as Labor leader in the previous month, became the new Prime Minister and immediately organized a meeting of representatives of government, employers and trade unions to reach agreement on a prices and incomes policy (the 'Accord') that would allow economic recovery. Hawke called a general election for December 1984, 15 months earlier than necessary, and the ALP was returned to power with a reduced majority in the House of Representatives. The opposition coalition between the Liberal Party and the National Party (formerly known as the Country Party) collapsed in April 1987, when 12 National Party MPs withdrew from the agreement and formed the New National Party (led by the right-wing Sir Johannes Bjelke-Petersen, the Premier of Queensland), while the remaining 14 National Party MPs continued to support their leader, Ian Sinclair, who wished to remain within the alliance. Parliament was dissolved in June, in preparation for an early general election in July. The election campaign was dominated by economic issues. The ALP was returned to office with an increased majority, securing 86 of the 148 seats in the House of Representatives. The Liberal and National Parties announced the renewal of the opposition alliance in August. Four months later, Bjelke-Petersen was forced to resign as Premier of Queensland, under pressure from National Party officials.

During 1988 the Hawke Government suffered several defeats at by-elections, seemingly as a result of a decline in living standards and an unpopular policy of wage restraint. The ALP narrowly retained power at state elections in Victoria, but was defeated in New South Wales, where it had held power for 12 years. In May 1989 the leader of the Liberal Party, John Howard, was replaced by Andrew Peacock, and Charles Blunt succeeded Ian Sinclair as leader of the National Party. In July a commission of inquiry into alleged corruption in Queensland published its report. The Fitzgerald report documented several instances of official corruption and electoral malpractice by the Queensland Government, particularly during the administration of Bjelke-Petersen. Following the publication of the report, support for the National Party within Queensland declined once more, and in December the ALP defeated the National Party in the state election (the first time that it had defeated the National Party in Queensland since 1957). By the end of 1991 four former members of the Queensland Cabinet and the former chief of the state's police force had received custodial sentences. The trial of Bjelke-Petersen, initially on charges of perjury and corruption but subsequently of perjury alone, resulted in dismissal of the case, when the jury failed to reach a verdict.

In August 1989 the popularity of the Hawke Government was further damaged by a dispute between the major domestic airlines and the airline pilots' federation. The pilots had resigned *en masse* when both Ansett and Australian Airlines, with government approval, had rejected their claim for a 29.5% increase in wages. In September Hawke announced that the Government was to award substantial compensation to the airlines. In November the airlines intensified overseas recruitment initiatives, while maintaining a very limited service. By February 1990 the airlines claimed to have restored their operations, and in March the remaining rebel pilots ended their strike.

In February 1990 Hawke announced that a general election for the House of Representatives and for 40 of the 76 seats in the Senate was to be held on 24 March. The Government's position in the period preceding the election had been strengthened by the ALP's victory in Queensland in December 1989, the removal of an unpopular Labor leadership in Western Australia and its replacement by the first female Premier, Dr Carmen Lawrence, and by the support that it secured from environmental groups as a result of its espousal of 'green' issues. Although the opposition parties won the majority of the first-preference votes in the election for the House of Representatives, the endorsement of the environmental groups delivered a block of second-preference votes to the ALP, which was consequently returned to power, albeit with a reduced majority, securing 78 of the 148 seats. Following its defeat, Peacock immediately resigned as leader of the Liberal Party and was replaced by Dr John Hewson, a former professor of economics. Blunt lost his seat in the election and was succeeded as leader of the National Party by Timothy Fischer.

In September 1990, at a meeting of senior ALP members, government proposals to initiate a controversial programme of privatization were endorsed, effectively ending almost 100 years of the ALP's stance against private ownership. In October plans for constitutional and structural reform were approved in principle by the leaders of the six state and two territory governments. The proposed reforms envisaged the creation of national standards in regulations and services. They also aimed to alleviate the financial dependence of the states and territories on the Federal Government. These suggested reforms, however, encountered strong opposition from sections of the public services, the trade unions and the business community. In July 1991 the leaders of the federal and state Governments finally agreed to reforms in the country's systems of marketing, transport, trade and taxation, with the aim of creating a single national economy from 1992.

In April 1991, as a result of preliminary investigations by a Royal Commission into the financial dealings of the Labor Government of Western Australia in the 1980s, Brian Burke, the former state Premier, resigned as Australia's ambassador to Ireland and the Holy See. Owing to the alleged irregularities, more than $A1,000m. of public funds were believed to have been lost. In May the Premier of New South Wales called a state election, 10 months earlier than was necessary, in an attempt to capitalize on the problems of Labor administrations at federal and state level. However, the Liberal-National Party Government lost its overall majority and was able to retain power only with the support of independent members of the state legislature.

In June 1991, following months of divisions within the ALP, Hawke narrowly defeated a challenge to his leadership from Paul Keating, the Deputy Prime Minister and Treasurer, who accused the Prime Minister of reneging on a promise to resign in his favour before the next general election. This cast doubt on Hawke's credibility, as he had assured Parliament and the public in 1990 that he would continue as leader for the whole of the parliamentary term. Following his defeat, Keating resigned. In December Hawke dismissed John Kerin, Keating's replacement as Treasurer, following a series of political and economic crises. Hawke called another leadership election, but, on this occasion, he was defeated by Keating, who accordingly became Prime Minister. A major reorganization of the Cabinet followed. John Dawkins, a staunch supporter of Keating, was appointed Treasurer.

Following the ALP's recent defeat in state elections in Tasmania, the party encountered further embarrassment in April 1992, when a by-election in Melbourne to fill the parliamentary seat vacated by Bob Hawke was won by a local football club coach, standing as an independent candidate. In May the Prime Minister suffered another set-back, when Graham Richardson, the Minister for Transport and Communications, resigned, owing to his implication in a scandal involving a relative who was alleged to have participated in an illegal scheme whereby Taiwanese investors were able to secure US residency rights via the Marshall Islands. In the following month Nick Greiner, the Liberal-National Premier of New South Wales, was obliged to resign, as a result of accusations of corruption. In August, however, he was exonerated by the state's Supreme Court.

Meanwhile, Brian Burke, the former Premier of Western Australia, had been arrested. It was alleged that, during his term of office, he had misappropriated more than $A17,000 from a parliamentary expense account. In October 1992 the conclusions of the inquiry into the ALP's alleged involvement in corrupt practices in Western Australia were released. The Royal Commission was highly critical of the improper transactions between successive governments of Western Australia and business entrepreneurs. The conduct of Brian Burke drew particular criticism. (In July 1994 Burke received a prison sentence of two years upon conviction on four charges of fraud; he was released in February 1995, but was sentenced to three years' imprisonment in February 1997 for the theft of $A122,000 from ALP funds.) Furthermore, in February 1995 Ray O'Connor, Premier of Western Australia between 1982 and 1983, received a prison sentence of 18 months, having been found guilty of the theft in 1984 of $A25,000, intended as a donation to the Liberal Party. He was released in August 1995.

In September 1992 John Bannon became the seventh state Premier since 1982 to leave office in disgrace. The resignation of the ALP Premier of South Australia was due to a scandal relating to attempts to offset the heavy financial losses incurred by the State Bank of South Australia. At state elections in Queensland in mid-September, the ALP administration of Wayne Goss was returned to power. In the following month, however, the ruling ALP was defeated in state elections in Victoria. Furthermore, in November a new financial scandal emerged: the federal Treasurer was alleged to have suppressed information pertaining to the former ALP Government of Victoria which, in a clandestine manner prior to the state elections, was believed to have exceeded its borrowing limits.

By late 1992, therefore, the ALP's prospects of being returned to office at the forthcoming general election appeared to have been seriously damaged. Proposals for radical tax and economic reforms (in particular the proposed introduction of a goods and services tax—GST) that were advocated by the federal opposition leader, Dr John Hewson, attracted much attention. At state elections in Western Australia in February 1993, the incumbent Labor Government was defeated. Dr Carmen Lawrence was replaced as Premier by Richard Court of the Liberal-National coalition.

Nevertheless, at the general election, held on 13 March 1993, the ALP was unexpectedly returned to office, for a fifth consecutive term, having secured 80 of the 147 seats in the House of Representatives. The new Government, appointed later that month, included many younger members, although several senior ministers were retained. John Dawkins resigned as Treasurer in December 1993. A government reorganization followed, in which Dawkins was replaced by Ralph Willis.

In January 1994 the Government was embarrassed by the resignation of the Minister of Industry, Technology and Regional Development, Alan Griffiths, as a result of allegations that public funds and ALP resources had been misappropriated in order to meet the private business debts incurred by his Melbourne sandwich shop. In the following month Ros Kelly, the Minister for Environment, Sport and Territories and close associate of the Prime Minister, yielded to pressure to resign, owing to a scandal relating to the alleged use of community sports grants to attempt to influence voters in vulnerable ALP-held constituencies prior to the 1993 general election. In March 1994 Graham Richardson, the Minister for Health, resigned. In the ensuing government reorganization, Dr Carmen Lawrence, former Premier of Western Australia, joined the Cabinet as Minister for Health.

In May 1994 Dr John Hewson was replaced as leader of the Liberal Party by Alexander Downer, a supporter of the monarchy. Downer was therefore expected to lead the campaign against Paul Keating's proposal that Australia become a republic by the year 2001 (see below). In January 1995, however, Downer resigned. The party leadership was resumed by John Howard, also a monarchist.

National attention was focused on the issue of immigration and on the rising levels of organized crime in September 1994 when John Newman, an ALP member of the New South Wales Parliament and outspoken critic of local Asian criminal syndicates, was shot dead outside his Sydney home. This unprecedented murder of a serving Australian politician gave rise to concern for the country's tradition of relative freedom from ethnic tensions.

At state elections in New South Wales in March 1995 the ALP defeated the ruling Liberal-National coalition. Robert (Bob) Carr was appointed Premier. At a federal by-election in Canberra, however, the ALP suffered a serious reverse when, for the first time in 15 years, the seat fell to the Liberal Party. In July, at state elections in Queensland, the ALP Government of Wayne Goss was narrowly returned to office, only to be ousted following a by-election defeat in February 1996. In June 1995, meanwhile, the Deputy Prime Minister, Brian Howe, who intended to retire at the next general election, announced his resignation from the Cabinet. He was replaced by the Minister for Finance, Kim Beazley.

At the general election held on 2 March 1996 the Liberal-National coalition achieved a decisive victory, securing a total of 94 of the 148 seats in the House of Representatives. The ALP won only 49 seats. In the Senate the minor parties and independent members retained the balance of power. John Howard of the Liberal Party became Prime Minister, and immediately promised to give priority to the issues of industrial relations, the transfer to partial private ownership of the state telecommunications company, Telstra, and to expanding relations with Asia. The leader of the National Party, Tim Fischer, was appointed Deputy Prime Minister and Minister for Trade. Paul Keating was replaced as leader of the ALP by Kim Beazley.

The massacre in Tasmania of 35 people by a lone gunman in April 1996 obliged the new Government immediately to address the question of firearms ownership and to confront the powerful gun lobby. At the Prime Minister's initiative, the various state and territory governments reached agreement upon the implementation of a uniform ban on assault weapons.

In August 1996, in an unprecedented display of violence, demonstrators protesting against proposed budget cuts stormed the Parliament building in Canberra. Clashes between the police and the protesters resulted in many injuries. Meanwhile, fears for Australia's tradition of racial tolerance continued to grow. In October Pauline Hanson, a newly-elected independent member of the House of Representatives, aroused much controversy when, in a speech envisaging 'civil war', she reiterated her demands for the ending of immigration from Asia and for the elimination of special funding for Aboriginal people. The Prime Minister attracted criticism for his failure to issue a direct denunciation of the views of Pauline Hanson, a former member of the Liberal Party. The increasingly bitter debate also damaged Australia's image in the countries of Asia, a vital source of investment and of tourist revenue. In March 1997, moreover, the One Nation Party was established by Pauline Hanson and rapidly attracted support. In May, while attending a fund-raising rally in Perth, Pauline Hanson was besieged by more than 1,000 opponents. Larger protests against her policies followed in Melbourne and Canberra. Meanwhile, after his initial weak response, the Prime Minister condemned the views of the founder of the One Nation Party. In August, as fears for Australian revenue from Asian investment, trade and tourism grew, the Government issued a document on foreign policy, in which Pauline Hanson's views were strongly repudiated and in which Australia's commitment to racial equality was reiterated. In order to counter the negative impact of the activities of the One Nation Party, a special diplomatic unit was established. In November 1997, furthermore, former Prime Ministers Hawke, Keating and Whitlam published a statement denouncing Pauline Hanson.

In July 1997 the Minister for Small Business and Consumer Affairs was obliged to resign amid controversy over a conflict of interest. In September a scandal arising from apparently illicit claims for parliamentary travel allowances led to further resignations, and in October the Prime Minister announced major changes in the composition of his Government. These included the removal of the employment portfolio from Senator Amanda Vanstone, the post being regarded as of vital importance as the next general election approached and as the issue of unemployment remained a principal concern. In October Senator Cheryl Kernot, leader of the Australian Democrats Party, announced her defection to the ALP, from where she hoped better to oppose the Liberal-National Government.

In May 1987 Australia and the United Kingdom (UK) began a joint operation to ascertain the extent of plutonium contamination resulting from British nuclear weapons testing at Maralinga in South Australia between 1956 and 1963. Many Australians were highly critical of the UK's apparent disregard for the environmental consequences of the tests and of the British authorities' failure to make adequate arrangements to protect the local Aboriginal people, who were now campaigning for a thorough decontamination of their traditional lands. In June 1993 Australia announced its acceptance of $A45m. in compensation from the British Government for the cost of the decontamination. In December 1994 the displaced Aboriginal people and the federal Government reached agreement on a compensation settlement of $A13.5m., to be spent on health, employment and infrastructural projects.

The sensitive issue of Aboriginal land rights was addressed by the Government in August 1985, when it formulated proposals for legislation that would give Aboriginal people inalienable freehold title to national parks, vacant Crown land and former Aboriginal reserves, in spite of widespread opposition from state governments (which had previously been responsible for their own land policies), from mining companies and from the Aboriginal people themselves, who were angered by the Government's withdrawal of its earlier support for the Aboriginal right to veto mineral exploitation. In October 1985 Ayers Rock, in the Northern Territory, was officially transferred to the Mutijulu Aboriginal community, on condition that continuing access to the rock (the main inland tourist attraction) be guaranteed. In 1986, however, the Government abandoned its pledge to impose such federal legislation on unwilling state governments, and this led to further protests from Aboriginal leaders. In June 1991 the Government imposed a permanent ban on mining at an historical Aboriginal site in the Northern Territory.

An important precedent was established in June 1992, when the High Court overruled the concept of *terra nullius* (unoccupied land) by recognizing the existence of land titles that predated European settlement in 1788 in cases where a close association with the land in question had been continued; however, land titles legally acquired since 1788 were to remain intact. As a result of the 'Mabo' decision of 1992 (named after the Aboriginal claimant, Eddie Mabo), in December 1993 Parliament approved the Native Title Act, historic legislation granting Aboriginal people the right to claim title to their traditional lands. Despite the Prime Minister's personal involvement in the issue, the legislation aroused much controversy, particularly in Western Australia (vast areas of the state being vacant Crown land) where rival legislation to replace native title rights with lesser rights to traditional land usage, such as access for ceremonial purposes only, had been enacted. In March 1995 the High Court declared the Native Title Act to be valid, rejecting as unconstitutional Western Australia's own legislation. The ruling was expected to have widespread implications for the mining industry.

In October 1996, following protracted delays in the development of a valuable zinc mine in Queensland owing to Aboriginal land claims, the Howard Government announced proposals to amend the Native Title Act to permit federal ministers to overrule Aboriginal concerns if a project of 'major economic benefit' to Australia were threatened. Other proposed amendments included the simplification of the process of negotiation between potential developers and Aboriginal claimants. In December the Larrakia people of the Northern Territory presented a claim under the Native Title Act. The area in question incorporated the city of Darwin and was thus the first such claim to encompass a provincial capital. In the same month the federal High Court upheld an appeal by two Aboriginal communities in Queensland (including the Wik people of Cape York) against an earlier ruling that prevented them from submitting a claim to land leased by the state Government to cattle and sheep farmers. The Court's decision, known as the Wik judgment, was expected to encourage similar challenges to 'pastoral' leases, which covered 40% of Australia. Vociferous protests from farmers, who were strongly opposed to the co-existence of native title and pastoral leases, followed.

In April 1997 the first native title deed to be granted on mainland Australia was awarded to the Dunghutti people of New South Wales. In the same month the Prime Minister announced the introduction of legislation to clarify the issue of land tenure; a 10-point plan was to be drawn up in consultation with state governments and with representatives of the Aboriginal community. In September the Government introduced the Wik Native Title Bill, which was subsequently passed by the House of Representatives. In November, however, the Senate questioned the constitutional validity of the proposed legislation, whereby pastoralists' rights and activities would prevail over, but not extinguish (as had been assumed), the Aboriginal people's rights to Native Title.

In November 1987 an official commission of inquiry into the cause of the high death rate among Aboriginal prisoners recommended immediate government action, and in July 1988 it was announced that 108 cases remained to be investigated. In August 1988 a UN report accused Australia of violating international human rights in its treatment of the Aboriginal people. In November the Government announced an enquiry into its Aboriginal Affairs Department, following accusations, made by the opposition coalition, of nepotism and misuse of funds. The commission of inquiry published its first official report in February 1989. Following the report's recommendations, the Government announced the creation of a $A10m. programme to combat the high death rate among Aboriginal prisoners. In October an unofficial study indicated that Aboriginal people, although accounting for only 1% of the total population of Australia, comprised more than 20% of persons in prison. In May 1991 the report of the Royal Commission into Aboriginal Deaths in Custody was published, after three years of investigation. The report outlined evidence of racial prejudice in the police force and included more than 300 recommendations for changes in policies relating to Aboriginal people, aimed at improving relations between the racial groups of Australia and granting Aboriginal people greater self-determination and access to land ownership. In June Parliament established a Council for Aboriginal Reconciliation. In March 1992, Aboriginal deaths in custody having continued, radical plans for judicial, economic and social reforms, aimed at improving the lives of Aboriginal people, were announced. The Government made an immediate allocation of $A150m.; a total of $A500m. was to be made available over the next 10 years. In February 1993 the human rights organization, Amnesty International, issued a highly critical report on the prison conditions of Aboriginal people. In March 1996 Amnesty International claimed that Australia had made little progress with regard to its treatment of Aboriginal prisoners.

In July 1996 the Roman Catholic Church issued an apology for its role in the forcible removal from their parents of tens of thousands of Aboriginal children, in a controversial practice of placement in white foster homes, where many were abused. This policy of assimilation had continued until the late 1960s. In August 1996 the new Governor-General, Sir William Deane, urged all state parliaments to affirm their support for reconciliation with the Aboriginal people. The legislature of South Australia was the first to do so, in November. In May 1997 the publication of the findings of a two-year inquiry into the removal of as many as 100,000 Aboriginal children from their families had profound political repercussions. The author of the report, a distinguished former judge and President of the Human Rights and Equal Opportunities Commission, urged the Government to issue a formal apology to the 'stolen generation'. At a conference on reconciliation at the end of the month, the Prime Minister made an unexpected personal apology. The Government, however, repudiated the commission's assertion that the policy of assimilation had been tantamount to genocide and rejected recommendations that compensation be paid to victims. In July 1997, furthermore, with more than 1,000 claims pending, the federal High Court ruled that a group of Aboriginal applicants could not sue for compensation for their removal from their parents.

In foreign affairs, the Hawke and Keating Governments placed greater emphasis on links with South-East Asia. This policy was continued by John Howard, who pledged to expand relations with Asia. In January 1989 Hawke proposed the creation of an Asia-Pacific Economic Co-operation forum (APEC, see p. 108) to facilitate the exchange of services, tourism and direct foreign investment in the region. The inaugural APEC conference took place in Canberra in November 1989.

Australian relations with Indonesia, which had been strained since the Indonesian annexation of the former Portuguese colony of East Timor in 1976, improved in August 1985, when Hawke made a statement recognizing Indonesian sovereignty over the territory, but subsequently deteriorated, following the publication in a Sydney newspaper, in April 1986, of an article containing allegations of corruption against the Indonesian President, Gen. Suharto. Relations between Australia and Indonesia improved in December 1989, when they signed an accord regarding joint exploration for petroleum and gas reserves in the Timor Gap, an area of sea forming a disputed boundary between the two countries. Portugal, however, withdrew its ambassador from Canberra in protest, and in February 1991 instituted proceedings against Australia at the International Court of Justice. In June 1995 the Court refused to invalidate the exploration treaty. In April 1992 Paul Keating's visit to Indonesia, the new Prime Minister's first official overseas trip, aroused controversy, owing to the repercussions of the massacre of unarmed civilians in East Timor by Indonesian troops in November 1991. On another visit to Jakarta in June 1994, the Australian Prime Minister attempted to concentrate on economic issues. In July 1995, owing to strong opposition in Australia, Indonesia was obliged to withdraw the appointment as ambassador to Canberra of Lt-Gen. (retd) Herman Mantiri, a former Chief of the General Staff of the Armed Forces and an apparent supporter of the November 1991 Dili massacre. Nevertheless, in December 1995 Australia and Indonesia unexpectedly signed a joint security treaty. In March 1996 a new Indonesian ambassador took up his appointment in Canberra, and in September, following a visit to Jakarta by John Howard, Indonesia accepted Australia's ambassador-designate. Meanwhile, the investigation into the deaths of six Australia-based journalists in East Timor in 1975 had been reopened, and in June 1996 a government report concluded that they had been murdered by Indonesian soldiers. In October 1996, as Canberra continued to fail to denounce the Suharto Government's violations of human rights, Australian senators from all parties urged the Government to withdraw its recognition of Indonesian sovereignty over East Timor. In March 1997 Australia and Indonesia signed a treaty defining their seabed and 'economic zone' boundaries.

A crisis in Australia's relations with Malaysia arose in late 1993, when Keating described the Malaysian Prime Minister as a 'recalcitrant' for his failure to attend the APEC summit meeting in Seattle, USA, in November. Relations subsequently improved, however, and in January 1996 Keating paid the first official visit to Malaysia by an Australian Prime Minister since 1984. In March 1996, furthermore, the Malaysian Prime Minister travelled to Brisbane for a meeting with his newly-elected Australian counterpart. During an official visit to Hanoi in April 1994 Keating had discussions with his Vietnamese counterpart. Australia's relations with the People's Republic of China continued to be strained by the issue of China's nuclear-testing programme, and deteriorated further in September 1996 when the Dalai Lama, the exiled spiritual leader of Tibet, was received in Sydney by the Prime Minister. In March 1997, however, the Australian Prime Minister began a six-day official visit to China, where he had discussions with Premier Li Peng.

The viability of the ANZUS military pact, which was signed in 1951, linking Australia, New Zealand and the USA, was disputed by the US Government following the New Zealand Government's declaration, in July 1984, that vessels which were believed to be powered by nuclear energy, or to be carrying nuclear weapons, would be barred from the country's ports. Hawke did not support the New Zealand initiative, and Australia continued to participate with the USA in joint military exercises from which New Zealand had been excluded. However, the Hawke Government declined directly to endorse US retaliation against New Zealand, and in 1986 stated that Australia regarded its 'obligations to New Zealand as constant and undiminishing'. In late 1988 Australia signed a 10-year agreement with the USA, extending its involvement in the management of US-staffed military bases in Australia. In March 1987 proposals for an ambitious new defence strategy were published, following the recommendations of a government commissioned report advocating a comprehensive restructuring of the country's military forces, on the basis of greater self-reliance. The cost of the plan, however, was estimated at $A25,000m. over 15 years. In September 1990 Australia and New Zealand signed an agreement to establish a joint venture to construct as many as 12 naval frigates to patrol the South Pacific. In February 1994 the USA announced its decision to resume senior-level contacts with New Zealand. In July 1996 Australia and the USA upgraded their defence alliance. Training facilities were to be expanded, and major joint military exercises were to be held in Queensland in early 1997.

Owing to Australian opposition to French test explosions of nuclear weapons at Mururoa Atoll (French Polynesia) in the South Pacific Ocean, a ban on uranium sales to France was introduced in 1983. However, in August 1986 the Government announced its decision to resume uranium exports, claiming that the sanction had been ineffective and that the repeal of the ban would increase government revenue. In December Australia ratified a treaty declaring the South Pacific area a nuclear-free zone. France's decision, in April 1992, to suspend its nuclear-testing programme was welcomed by Australia. In June 1995, however, the French President's announcement that the programme was to be resumed provoked outrage throughout the Pacific region. The Australian ambassador to France was recalled, and the French consulate in Perth was destroyed in an arson attack. Further widespread protests followed the first of the new series of tests in September. Australia's relations with the UK were strained by the British Government's refusal to join the condemnation of France's policy. The final test was conducted in January 1996. On an official visit to Paris in September, the Australian Minister for Foreign Affairs adopted a conciliatory stance (which drew much criticism from anti-nuclear groups). A ban on new contracts for the supply of uranium to France, imposed in September 1995, was removed in October 1996. Meanwhile, Australia remained committed to achieving the elimination of all nuclear testing. In August, following a veto of the draft text by India and Iran at the UN Conference on Disarmament in Geneva, Australia took the initiative in leading an international effort to secure the passage of the Comprehensive Test Ban Treaty. In an unusual procedure, the Treaty was referred to the UN General Assembly, which voted overwhelmingly in its favour in September.

Relations with neighbouring Pacific island states were strained in mid-1997. In July Australia was embarrassed by the unauthorized publication of a secret official document in which certain regional politicians were described as corrupt and incompetent. At a meeting of the South Pacific Forum in September, the member countries failed to reach agreement on a common policy regarding mandatory targets for the reduction of emissions of the so-called 'greenhouse gases'. The low-lying nation of Tuvalu was particularly critical of Australia's refusal to compromise, the Australian Prime Minister declaring that the Pacific islands' concerns over rising sea levels were exaggerated.

Australia's relations with Papua New Guinea were strained in early 1997 as a result of the latter's decision to engage the services of a group of mercenaries in the Government's operations against secessionists on the island of Bougainville. Fearing for the stability of the South Pacific region, the Australian Prime Minister denounced the use of foreign forces as unacceptable. As the crisis escalated (see chapter on Papua New Guinea), Australia continued its attempts to mediate, while reportedly placing its troops on alert. Following the suspension of the mercenaries' contract by the Prime Minister of Papua New Guinea in March, Australia remained committed to a peaceful settlement of the Bougainville dispute, and in November 1997 offered a venue for the next round of peace talks. In the same month Australian forces played a leading role in drought-relief operations in Papua New Guinea.

In March 1986 Australia's constitutional links with the UK were reduced by the Australia Act, which abolished the British Parliament's residual legislative, executive and judicial controls over Australian state law. In February 1992, shortly after a visit by Queen Elizabeth, Paul Keating caused a furore by accusing the UK of abandoning Australia to the Japanese threat during the Second World War. Following a visit to the UK in September 1993, Keating announced that Australia was to become a republic by the year 2001, subject to approval by referendum. It was envisaged that Australia would remain within the Commonwealth and that the head of state would be appointed by the Prime Minister, with the approval of a two-thirds majority of Parliament. The President would hold the same powers as the Governor-General, and would serve a single five-year term. Sir William Deane succeeded William Hayden as Governor-General in February 1996, the former's term of office being scheduled to expire at the end of the year 2000. Although John Howard personally favoured the retention of the monarchy, in 1996 the new Prime Minister announced plans for a constitutional convention, prior to the holding of a referendum on the issue if necessary. In an unexpected development in January 1997, the Deputy Prime Minister put forward proposals for the removal from the Constitution of all references to the monarch and for the transfer of the Queen's functions to Australia's Chief Justice. Voluntary postal voting to select, from among 609 candidates, the 76 delegates who were to attend the constitutional convention (scheduled for February 1998) commenced in November 1997. The complex system of preferential voting, however, appeared to give rise to much confusion, particularly in New South Wales where a total of 174 candidates were contesting 20 places at the forthcoming convention. In addition to the official groupings, the Australian Republican Movement (ARM) and Australians for a Constitutional Monarchy (ACM), numerous other republican and monarchist, as well as individual, candidates were standing for election.

Government

Australia comprises six states and three territories. Executive power is vested in the British monarch and exercised by the monarch's appointed representative, the Governor-General, who normally acts on the advice of the Federal Executive Council (the Ministry), led by the Prime Minister. The Governor-General appoints the Prime Minister and, on the latter's recommendation, other Ministers. (Proposals for the establishment of a republic were announced in 1993—see above.)

Legislative power is vested in the Federal Parliament. This consists of the monarch, represented by the Governor-General, and two chambers elected by universal adult suffrage (voting is compulsory). The Senate has 76 members (12 from each state and two each from the Northern Territory and the Australian Capital Territory), who are elected by a system of proportional representation for six years when representing a state, with half the seats renewable every three years, and for a term of three years when representing a territory. The House of Representatives has 148 members, elected for three years (subject to dissolution) from single-member constituencies. The Federal Executive Council is responsible to Parliament.

Each state has a Governor, representing the monarch, and its own legislative, executive and judicial system. The state governments are essentially autonomous, but certain powers are placed under the jurisdiction of the Federal Government. All states except Queensland have an Upper House (the Legislative Council) and a Lower House (the Legislative Assembly or House of Assembly). The chief ministers of the states are known as Premiers, as distinct from the Federal Prime Minister. The Northern Territory (self-governing since 1978) and the Australian Capital Territory (self-governing since 1988) have unicameral legislatures, and each has a government led by a Chief Minister. The Jervis Bay Territory is not self-governing.

Defence

Australia's defence policy is based on collective security, and it is a member of the British Commonwealth Strategic Reserve and of ANZUS, with New Zealand and the USA. Australia also participates in the Five Powers Defence Arrangements, with New Zealand, Malaysia, Singapore and the United Kingdom. In August 1997 Australia's armed forces numbered 57,400 (army 25,400, navy 14,300, air force 17,700). Defence expenditure for 1998 was budgeted at $A10,400m. Service in the armed forces is voluntary.

Economic Affairs

In 1995, according to estimates by the World Bank, Australia's gross national product (GNP), measured at average 1993–95 prices, was US $337,909m., equivalent to US $18,720 per head. It was estimated that Australia's GNP per head increased, in real terms, at an average rate of 1.4% per year between 1985 and 1995. Over the same period, the population increased by an average annual rate of 1.4%. The country's gross domestic product (GDP) increased, in real terms, by an annual average of 3.5% in 1990–95.

Agriculture (including forestry, hunting and fishing) contributed 3.3% of GDP in 1994/95, and engaged 5.1% of the employed labour force in August 1996. The principal crops are wheat, fruit, sugar and cotton, and Australia is the world's leading producer of wool (exports of which totalled $A4,030m. in 1994/95). The export of wine is of increasing importance, rising from 10m. litres in 1986 to 155m. litres in 1996/97. The value of wine exports was projected to reach $A700m. in 1997/98. Beef production is also important, contributing an estimated 12.6% of the value of gross farm output in 1995/96. During 1980–90 agricultural GDP increased by an annual average rate of 3.3%. Between 1991/92 and 1995/96 the sector's GDP rose by an average rate of 1.2% annually. The sector recovered from drought in 1995/96, and an excellent wheat harvest, of 23.6m. metric tons, was achieved in 1996/97.

Industry (comprising mining, manufacturing, construction and utilities) employed 22.5% of the working population in 1996, and provided 29.6% of GDP in 1994/95. Industrial GDP increased at an average rate of 2.8% per year between 1980 and 1990, and by 3.4% between 1991/92 and 1995/96.

The mining sector employed less than 1.1% of the working population in 1996, and contributed 4.3% of GDP in 1994/95. Australia is one of the world's leading exporters of coal. Earnings from coal and related products in 1995/96 reached $A7,837m., more than 10.3% of total export receipts in that year. The other principal minerals extracted are iron ore, gold, silver, petroleum and natural gas. Bauxite, zinc, copper, titanium, nickel, tin, lead, zirconium and diamonds are also mined. Between 1991/92 and 1995/96 the GDP of the mining sector increased by an annual average rate of 3.0%

Manufacturing contributed 15.5% of GDP in 1994/95. The sector employed 13.4% of the working population in 1996. Measured by the value of sales, the principal branches of manufacturing in 1994/95 were food, beverages and tobacco (21.2%), equipment and machinery (19.7%), metal products (17.9%), petroleum, coal and chemical products (15.7%), printing, publishing and recording (7.0%) and wood and paper products (5.9%). The sector's GDP grew by an annual average rate of 3.4% between 1991/92 and 1995/96.

Energy is derived principally from petroleum, natural gas and coal. Production of petroleum rose from 29,583m. litres in 1993/94 to 31,301m. litres in 1994/95, while that of black coal increased from 177.9m. metric tons in 1993/94 to 191.9m. tons in 1994/95.

The services sector provided 67.2% of GDP in 1994/95, and engaged 72.1% of the employed labour force in 1996. The tourism industry is of growing significance. The number of visitor arrivals rose from 3.7m. in 1995 to almost 4.2m. in 1996, when tourist receipts reached $A16,101m. It was estimated that in 1993/94 the tourism sector contributed 6.6% of GDP and accounted for 6.9% of total employment.

In 1996 Australia recorded a visible trade deficit of US $891m., and there was a deficit of US $15,870m. on the current account of the balance of payments. In the year ending 30 June 1996 the principal source of imports was the USA (22.6%), followed by Japan (13.9%). Japan was the principal market for exports in that year (21.6%), followed by the Republic of Korea (8.7%) and New Zealand (7.4%). Other major trading partners are the United Kingdom, Singapore, Taiwan, the People's Republic of China and Germany. The principal exports were metalliferous ores (sales of gold being of increasing significance), coal, machinery, non-ferrous metals, textile fibres (mainly wool), and meat (mainly beef). The principal imports were machinery and transport equipment, basic manufactures, and chemicals and related products.

In the 1996/97 financial year a budgetary surplus of $A474m. (including net lending) was projected, compared with a deficit of $A5,045m. in 1995/96 (equivalent to 1.0% of GDP). The Government aimed to achieve a fiscal surplus of $A1,000m. by 1998/99. In late 1995 Australia's net external debt stood at $A260,000m. (equivalent to 57% of annual GDP). An estimated 8.6% of the labour force were unemployed in 1996, the rate rising to 8.7% in the third quarter of 1997. The annual rate of inflation averaged 4.8% in 1986–95 and 2.6% in 1996. Consumer prices declined by 0.3% in the 12 months to September 1997.

Australia is a member of the Asian Development Bank (see p. 110), the South Pacific Forum (see p. 233) and the Pacific Community (formerly the South Pacific Commission—see p. 232). In 1989 Australia played a major role in the creation of the Asia-Pacific Economic Co-operation group (APEC, see p. 108), which aimed to stimulate economic development in the region. Australia is also a member of the OECD (see p. 208) and of the International Grains Council (see p. 257).

Upon taking office in March 1996, the Howard Government confirmed its determination to achieve fiscal balance, while upholding its promise to introduce no new or higher taxes. One of the principal aims of the administration's programme was the partial transfer to the private sector of Telstra, the state-owned telecommunications company. This sale of one-third of the company's assets took place in November 1997, raising revenue of $A14,300m. The incoming Government was also committed to the deregulation of the labour market. The 1996/97 budget, announced in August 1996, incorporated drastic reductions in expenditure. Social welfare programmes were severely curtailed, and the number of public servants was to be reduced, entailing thousands of job losses. Although there was greater fiscal support for low-income families, certain tax concessions were abolished. The 1997/98 budget, presented in May 1997, was less austere. Nevertheless, the high level of unemployment remained a cause for concern, as did the low rate of domestic savings. Meanwhile, Australia's general competitiveness in the global market contined to decline. The gradual weakening of the Australian dollar during 1997 was expected to raise relative earnings from exports and from tourism. In the latter part of 1997, however, the Asian financial crisis threatened to depress Australian's major export markets. GDP expanded by 4.2% in 1995/96 and by an estimated 3.25% in 1996/97. A growth rate of 3.75% was projected for 1997/98.

Social Welfare

Australia provides old-age, invalid and widows' pensions, unemployment, sickness and supporting parents' benefits, family allowances and other welfare benefits and allowances. Reciprocal welfare agreements operate between Australia and New Zealand and the United Kingdom. In 1993/94 Australia had 1,142 hospitals, with a total of 78,298 beds. In 1995/96 there were 30,800 general practitioners and 15,000 specialist practitioners. There were 160,500 nurses registered in the country. The desert interior is served by the Royal Flying Doctor Service. Expenditure on health by all levels of government in 1994/95 was estimated at $A26,339m. Public expenditure on social security and welfare (including housing and community amenities) totalled an estimated $A48,897m. in 1996/97.

In February 1984 the Government introduced a system of universal health insurance, known as Medicare, whereby every Australian is protected against the costs of medical and hospital care. Where medical expenses are incurred, Medicare covers patients for 85% of the government-approved Schedule Fee for services. For private in-patients in hospitals, 75% of the Schedule Fee for services is payable. The Medicare scheme is financed in part by a 1.7% levy on taxable incomes above a certain level.

Education

Education is the responsibility of each of the states and the Federal Government. It is compulsory, and available free of charge, for all children from the ages of six to 15 years (16 in Tasmania). Primary education generally begins at six years of age and lasts for six years. Secondary education, beginning at the age of 12, usually lasts for five years. As a proportion of children in the relevant age-groups, the enrolment ratios in 1993 were 98% in primary schools and 81% in secondary schools. In 1995 there were 1,361,287 children enrolled in government primary schools and 846,566 in secondary schools, while 901,484 children were attending private schools (472,394 primary and 429,090 secondary). Special services have been developed to fulfil the requirements of children living in the remote 'outback' areas, notably Schools of the Air, using two-way receiver sets. A system of one-teacher schools and correspondence schools also helps to satisfy these needs. Under a major reform programme initiated in 1988, the binary system of universities and colleges of advanced education was replaced by a unified national system of fewer and larger institutions. In 1991 there were 44 publicly-funded institutions. In 1995 students totalled 604,177. Most courses last from three to six years. Expenditure on education by all levels of government in the financial year 1994/95 was $A22,594m.

Public Holidays*

1998: 1 January (New Year's Day), 26 January (Australia Day), 10–13 April (Easter), 25 April (Anzac Day), 8 June (Queen's Official Birthday), 25–28 December (Christmas Day, Boxing Day).

1999 (provisional): 1 January (New Year's Day), 26 January (Australia Day), 2–5 April (Easter), 25 April (Anzac Day), 7 June (Queen's Official Birthday), 27–28 December (Christmas Day, Boxing Day).

* National holidays only. Some states observe these holidays on different days.

There are also numerous individual state holidays.

Weights and Measures

The metric system is in force.

Statistical Survey

Source (unless otherwise stated): Australian Bureau of Statistics, POB 10, Belconnen, ACT 2616; tel. (2) 6252-7911; fax (2) 6251-6009.

Area and Population

AREA, POPULATION AND DENSITY

Area (sq km)	7,682,300*
Population (census results)†	
6 August 1991	
Males	8,361,798
Females	8,485,512
Total	16,847,310
6 August 1996 (provisional)	
Total	17,892,423
Population (official estimates at mid-year)†	
1994	17,838,000
1995	18,054,000
1996 (provisional)	18,289,000
Density (per sq km) at mid-1996	2.4

* 2,966,151 sq miles.

† Census results exclude, and estimates include, an adjustment for under-enumeration, estimated to have been 1.9% in 1991. Estimates also exclude overseas visitors in Australia and include Australian residents temporarily overseas. On this basis, the adjusted census total was 17,317,800 (provisional) in 1991.

STATES AND TERRITORIES (30 June 1995)

	Area (sq km)	Estimated Population	Density (per sq km)
New South Wales (NSW)	801,600	6,115,000	7.6
Victoria	227,600	4,502,000	19.8
Queensland	1,727,200	3,277,000	1.9
South Australia	984,000	1,474,000	1.5
Western Australia	2,525,500	1,732,000	0.7
Tasmania	67,800	473,000	7.0
Northern Territory	1,346,200	174,000	0.1
Australian Capital Territory (ACT)	2,400*	304,000	126.7
Total	7,682,300	18,054,000†	2.4

* Includes Jervis Bay Territory. Following the ACT's attainment of self-government in November 1988, the Jervis Bay Territory (part of the ACT since 1915) became a separate territory. It has an area of 70 sq km and a population of about 800.

† Includes populations of Jervis Bay Territory, Christmas Island and the Cocos (Keeling) Islands.

PRINCIPAL TOWNS (estimated population at 30 June 1993)*

Canberra (national capital)	325,400†
Sydney (capital of NSW)	3,719,000
Melbourne (capital of Victoria)	3,187,500
Brisbane (capital of Queensland)	1,421,700
Perth (capital of W Australia)	1,221,300
Adelaide (capital of S Australia)	1,070,200
Newcastle	455,700
Gold Coast	300,200
Wollongong	250,100
Hobart (capital of Tasmania)	193,300
Geelong	151,800
Sunshine Coast	133,500
Townsville	121,700

* Figures refer to metropolitan areas, each of which normally comprises a municipality and contiguous urban areas.

† Including Queanbeyan, in NSW.

BIRTHS, MARRIAGES AND DEATHS*

	Registered live births		Registered marriages		Registered deaths	
	Number	Rate (per 1,000)	Number	Rate (per 1,000)	Number	Rate (per 1,000)
1988	246,193	14.9	116,816	7.1	119,866	7.2
1989	250,853	14.9	117,176	7.0	124,232	7.4
1990	262,648	15.4	116,959	6.9	120,062	7.0
1991	257,247	14.9	113,869	6.6	119,146	6.9
1992	264,151	15.1	114,752	6.6	123,660	7.1
1993	260,229	14.7	113,255	6.4	121,599	6.9
1994	258,051	14.5	111,174	6.2	126,709	7.1
1995	256,190	14.2	n.a.	6.1	125,133	6.9

* Data are tabulated by year of registration rather than by year of occurrence.

Expectation of life (years at birth, 1995): males 75.4, females 81.1.

PERMANENT AND LONG-TERM MIGRATION*
(year ending 31 December)

	1992	1993	1994
Permanent			
Arrivals	107,390	76,330	69,770
Departures	29,120	27,910	27,280
Other long-term			
Arrivals	126,780	127,440	137,600
Departures	115,160	113,190	112,710

* Persons intending to remain in Australia, or Australian residents intending to remain abroad, for 12 months or more. Figures are rounded to the nearest 10.

ECONOMICALLY ACTIVE POPULATION
('000 persons aged 15 years and over, excluding armed forces, at August)

	1994	1995	1996
Agriculture, forestry and fishing	405.5	411.6	430.2
Mining	85.5	84.7	89.1
Manufacturing	1,117.4	1,114.7	1,118.3
Electricity, gas and water supply	89.9	84.0	68.7
Construction	571.5	603.3	601.3
Wholesale trade	491.4	509.3	490.5
Retail trade	1,171.1	1,202.4	1,255.9
Accommodation, cafes and restaurants	362.3	390.5	375.8
Transport and storage	374.6	384.4	395.9
Communication services	139.0	150.8	173.1
Finance and insurance	312.6	315.1	314.4
Property and business services	706.9	795.7	805.2
Government administration and defence	352.2	379.9	370.4
Education	546.8	580.1	580.8
Health and community services	707.6	750.0	765.1
Cultural and recreational services	183.1	194.3	183.9
Personal and other services	300.4	305.1	316.5
Total employed (incl. others)	7,917.8	8,252.9	8,358.2
Unemployed	834.9	744.6	784.4
Total labour force	8,776.8	9,027.5	9,142.6
Males	5,051.0	5,150.2	5,212.4
Females	3,725.7	3,873.0	3,930.2

Source: Department of Employment, Education, Training and Youth Affairs (DEETYA), Canberra.

Agriculture

PRINCIPAL CROPS ('000 metric tons)

	1994	1995	1996
Wheat	9,036	17,263	23,497
Rice (paddy)	1,042	1,016	951
Barley	2,913	6,252	6,075
Maize	204	242	317
Oats	924	1,937	1,616
Sorghum	931	1,272	1,555
Potatoes	1,185	1,122	1,122*
Dry peas	240	547	379
Other pulses	1,005	1,941	1,807
Soybeans (Soya beans)	81	27	73
Sunflower seed	105	112	87
Rapeseed	264	561	616
Cottonseed	466	474	595
Cotton (lint)	329	335	420
Cabbages	71	72	72*
Tomatoes	340	425	425*
Cauliflower*	90	90	90
Pumpkins, squash and gourds*	78	80	80
Onions (dry)	200	246	246*
Green peas*	95	100	100
Carrots*	175	185	185
Watermelons*	70	70	70
Grapes	920	767	1,050
Sugar cane	34,920	37,597	40,649
Apples	307	317	342
Pears	142†	145†	160
Peaches and nectarines	80†	80†	80*
Oranges	517	436	436*
Pineapples	139	134	152†
Bananas	208	219	225†

* FAO estimate(s). † Unofficial figure.

Source: FAO, *Production Yearbook*.

LIVESTOCK ('000 head at 31 March)

	1994	1995	1996
Horses*	250	240	240
Cattle	25,758	25,736	26,952
Pigs	2,775	2,653	2,663
Sheep	132,569	123,210	126,320
Goats	232	220*	220*
Chickens	68,701	65,593	65,000*

* FAO estimate(s).

Source: mainly FAO, *Production Yearbook*.

LIVESTOCK PRODUCTS ('000 metric tons)

	1994	1995	1996
Beef and veal	1,825	1,803	1,702
Mutton and lamb	648	604	555
Goat meat*	12	11	11
Pig meat	344	351	329
Horse meat*	22	22	22
Poultry meat	491	489	490
Cows' milk	8,327	8,460	8,986
Butter	143	135	142
Cheese	234	216	261
Hen eggs*	180	163	155
Honey	26	19	19*
Wool:			
greasy	831	732	714
clean*	570	540	540
Cattle hides*	207	207	207
Sheepskins*	148	144	126

* FAO estimate(s).

Note: Figures for meat and milk refer to the 12 months ending 30 June of the year stated.

Source: FAO, *Production Yearbook*.

Forestry

ROUNDWOOD REMOVALS ('000 cubic metres, excl. bark)

	1992	1993	1994
Sawlogs, veneer logs and logs for sleepers	8,149	8,819	9,789
Pulpwood	7,925	8,276	8,314
Other industrial wood	580	564	559
Fuel wood*	2,898	2,898	2,898
Total	19,552	20,557	21,560

* FAO estimates.

Source: FAO, *Yearbook of Forest Products*.

SAWNWOOD PRODUCTION ('000 cubic metres, incl. sleepers)

	1992	1993	1994
Coniferous (softwood)	1,570	1,660	1,898
Broadleaved (hardwood)	1,471	1,527	1,616
Total	3,041	3,187	3,514

Source: FAO, *Yearbook of Forest Products*.

Fishing

('000 metric tons, live weight, year ending 30 June)

	1992/93	1993/94	1994/95
Inland waters	5.1	5.5	5.3
Indian Ocean*	133.3	115.7	114.2
Pacific Ocean*	108.0	101.1	100.0
Total catch	246.4	222.3	219.5

* FAO estimates.

Source: FAO, *Yearbook of Fishery Statistics*.

Mining*

(year ending 30 June, '000 metric tons, unless otherwise indicated)

	1992/93	1993/94	1994/95
Coal (black)	177,970	177,874	191,903
Coal, brown (lignite)	47,912	49,684	50,679
Bauxite	40,946	43,306	45,384
Mineral sands†	2,118	2,252	2,375
Iron ore (incl. pellets)	115,703	123,631	137,525
Lead concentrate	856	873	766
Zinc concentrate‡	2,011	1,890	1,699
Copper concentrate and precipitate§	1,262	1,338	1,133
Antimony (metric tons)‖	1,701¶	1,700**	1,700††
Cadmium (refined, metric tons)‡‡	1,000¶	951**	910††
Cobalt (metric tons)‡‡	1,600¶	1,700**	2,100††
Manganese ore and concentrate§§	1,715	2,045	n.a.
Titanium (ilmenite concentrate only)	1,870	1,769	n.a.
Tin (metric tons)§§	7,048	7,972	n.a.
Crude petroleum (incl. condensate, million litres)	30,592	29,583	31,301
Natural gas (million cu m)	23,953	24,855	28,176
Gold (kg)	244,595	255,757	243,213
Silver (metric tons)§§	1,086	1,055	n.a.
Nickel§§	68	72	n.a.
Tungsten (metric tons)‡‡	23	11	n.a.
Uranium (metric tons)	2,704§§	2,751§§	2,232‖‖
Diamonds ('000 carats)§§	42,199	39,909	n.a.

* Figures for metallic minerals represent metal contents based on chemical assay, except figures for bauxite, iron and manganese, which are in terms of gross quantities produced.
† Includes ilmenite, beneficiated ilmenite, leucoxene, monazite, rutile and zircon.
‡ Includes zinc-lead concentrate.
§ Excluding copper concentrate of South Australia.
‖ Data from *World Metal Statistics* (London). (Source: UN, *Industrial Commodity Statistics Yearbook.*)
¶ January–December 1992.
** January–December 1993.
†† January–December 1994.
‡‡ Estimated by US Bureau of Mines (Source: UN, *Industrial Commodity Statistics Yearbook*).
§§ Source: Australian Bureau of Agricultural and Resource Economics (ABARE), ACT. Figures for 1993/94 are provisional.
‖‖ Sales of uranium (contained in uranium oxide).

Industry

SELECTED PRODUCTS

(year ending 30 June, '000 metric tons, unless otherwise indicated)

	1993/94	1994/95	1995/96
Pig-iron	7,209	7,449	7,553
Blooms and slabs from continuous casting	7,627	7,807	7,950
Aluminium—unwrought*†	1,384	1,285‡	n.a.
Copper—unwrought†	351	281‡	n.a.
Lead—unwrought*†	220	206‡	n.a.
Zinc—unwrought*†	316	312‡	n.a.
Tin—unwrought (metric tons)*†	190	455‡	n.a.
Motor spirit (petrol—million litres)†	17,724	17,911‡	n.a.
Fuel oil (million litres)†	2,263	2,431‡	n.a.
Diesel-automotive oil (million litres)†	11,063	11,365‡	n.a.
Industrial and marine fuel (million litres)†	95	129‡	n.a.
Electric motors ('000)	2,990	3,099	2,850
Clay bricks (million)	1,814	1,860	1,458
Sulphuric acid	833	n.a.	n.a.
Superphosphate	1,344	1,590‡	n.a.
Refrigerators ('000)	460	408	414
Woven man-made fibres ('000 sq metres)	184,885	185,171	149,066
Woven cotton fabrics (incl. towelling, '000 sq metres)	49,864	51,938	63,886
Woven woollen fabrics (incl. blanketing, '000 sq metres)	7,893	8,189	6,523
Cotton yarn (metric tons)	33,780	37,643	36,955
Wool yarn (metric tons)	21,016	23,093	20,063
Textile floor coverings ('000 sq metres)	46,910	47,258	42,683
Electricity (million kWh)	161,813	165,063	167,543
Cement	6,733	7,124	6,397
Concrete—ready-mixed ('000 cu m)	15,267	15,892	14,556
Newsprint	411	423	445
Motor vehicles ('000)	321	328	328
Wheat flour§	1,321‖	1,403¶	n.a.
Plastics in primary forms	1,147	1,240	1,222
Non-laminated particle board ('000 sq metres)	752	846	804
Domestic washing machines ('000)	326	305	297
Confectionery	179.2	182.4	187.0
Beer (million litres)	1,752	1,788	1,742
Tobacco and cigarettes (metric tons)	23,273	23,083	20,390

* Primary refined metal only.
† Source: Australian Bureau of Agricultural and Resource Economics (ABARE), ACT.
‡ Provisional figure.
§ Source: UN, *Industrial Commodity Statistics Yearbook*.
‖ January–December 1993.
¶ January–December 1994.

Finance

CURRENCY AND EXCHANGE RATES

Monetary Units

100 cents = 1 Australian dollar ($A).

Sterling and US Dollar Equivalents (30 September 1997)

£1 sterling = $A2.231;
US $1 = $A1.381;
$A100 = £44.83 = US $72.42.

Average Exchange Rate (US $ per Australian dollar)

1994	0.7317
1995	0.7415
1996	0.7829

COMMONWEALTH GOVERNMENT BUDGET
($A million, year ending 30 June)

Revenue	1994/95	1995/96	1996/97*
Tax revenue	105,671	116,358	125,028
Direct taxes	76,656	85,470	92,630
Individuals	54,647	60,414	65,940
Companies	15,588	18,252	19,700
Indirect taxes, etc.	29,015	30,888	32,398
Sales Tax	11,624	12,955	13,890
Excise	12,001	12,849	13,360
Non-tax revenue	4,743	5,302	5,132
Interest	1,790	1,403	1,123
Total	110,413	121,660	130,160

Expenditure†	1994/95	1995/96	1996/97*
Defence	9,731	10,011	10,027
Education	10,134	10,644	11,064
Health	17,144	18,634	19,408
Social security and welfare	43,607	46,699	48,897
Economic services	8,320	8,628	7,767
Public-debt interest	7,994	9,126	9,781
General purpose transfers to other governments	15,068	13,798	16,797
Other	10,044	9,165	5,945
Total	122,042	126,705	129,686

* Forecasts.
† Including net lending ($A million): −1,592 in 1994/95; −5,272 in 1995/96; −6,123 in 1996/97.
Source: Commonwealth of Australia, *Budget Statement, 1996/97*.

STATE GOVERNMENT FINANCES*
($A million, year ending 30 June)

	Receipts		Expenditure	
	1992/93†	1993/94‡	1992/93†	1993/94‡
New South Wales	23,062	22,780	23,723	24,786
Victoria	16,425	17,314	18,291	22,129
Queensland	12,313	12,636	11,463	11,773
South Australia	6,135	6,433	7,035	6,555
Western Australia.	6,751	6,930	7,421	7,635
Tasmania.	2,115	2,083	2,249	2,208
Northern Territory	1,404	1,412	1,473	1,540
Australian Capital Territory	1,249	1,199	1,275	1,293

* Including all state government authorities.
† Provisional figures.
‡ Estimates.

OFFICIAL RESERVES (US $ million at 31 December)

	1994	1995	1996
Gold*	3,023	3,055	2,918
IMF special drawing rights	73	55	37
Reserve position in IMF	506	502	482
Foreign exchange	10,706	11,340	14,016
Total	14,308	14,952	17,453

* Valued at market-related prices.
Source: IMF, *International Financial Statistics*.

MONEY SUPPLY ($A million at 31 December)

	1994	1995	1996
Currency outside banks	18,208	19,092	19,628
Demand deposits at trading and savings banks	60,496	64,772	75,801
Total money (incl. others)	78,763	83,899	95,641

Source: IMF, *International Financial Statistics*.

COST OF LIVING (Consumer Price Index*; base: 1990 = 100)

	1993	1994	1995
Food	107.3	108.7	112.9
Fuel and light	115.7	116.7	117.6
Clothing.	105.0	104.1	104.4
Rent†	91.7	92.2	101.6
All items (incl. others)	106.1	108.1	113.2

* Weighted average of six state capitals.
† Including expenditure on maintenance and repairs of dwellings.
Source: ILO, *Yearbook of Labour Statistics*.

1996: Food 116.1; All items 116.1 (Source: UN, *Monthly Bulletin of Statistics*).

NATIONAL ACCOUNTS ($A million, year ending 30 June)

National Income and Product (at current prices)

	1993/94	1994/95	1995/96
Compensation of employees	210,955	223,960	239,954
Operating surplus	103,344	108,603	117,149
Domestic factor incomes	314,299	332,563	357,103
Consumption of fixed capital	65,121	66,658	68,615
Gross domestic product (GDP) at factor cost	379,420	399,221	425,718
Indirect taxes	57,396	62,539	66,493
Less Subsidies	6,392	6,144	6,157
GDP in purchasers' values	430,424	455,616	486,054
Net factor income from abroad	−14,147	−15,964	−17,641
Gross national product	416,276	439,652	468,413
Less Consumption of fixed capital	65,121	66,658	68,615
National income in market prices	351,155	372,994	399,798

Expenditure on the Gross Domestic Product (at current prices)

	1993/94	1994/95	1995/96
Government final consumption expenditure	77,444	80,220	83,708
Private final consumption expenditure	266,478	283,983	303,766
Increase in stocks	575	2,525	3,450
Gross fixed capital formation	87,205	96,905	97,602
Statistical discrepancy	271	1,686	−419
Total domestic expenditure	431,973	465,319	488,107
Exports of goods and services	82,361	86,381	97,600
Less Imports of goods and services	83,910	96,084	99,653
GDP in purchasers' values	430,424	455,616	486,054
GDP at constant 1989/90 prices	400,431	415,710	431,654

Gross Domestic Product by Economic Activity
(at constant 1989/90 prices)

	1992/93*	1993/94*	1994/95
Agriculture, hunting, forestry and fishing	15,897	16,347	13,558
Mining and quarrying	16,999	17,295	17,967
Manufacturing	56,191	60,533	64,623
Electricity, gas and water	12,935	13,114	13,449
Construction	23,462	24,867	27,033
Wholesale and retail trade	62,200	65,173	70,949
Transport, storage and communications	31,463	33,879	37,191
Finance, insurance, real estate and business services	48,336	47,968	50,732
Ownership of dwellings	37,749	38,925	40,444
Public administration and defence	15,020	15,095	15,226
Other community, recreational and personal services (incl. restaurants and hotels)	60,026	61,887	65,032
Sub-total	380,278	395,083	416,204
Import duties	4,268	4,534	5,314
Less Imputed bank service charge	8,070	7,546	7,545
Statistical discrepancy	3,560	6,466	1,737
GDP in purchasers' values	380,036	398,537	415,710

* Figures are provisional. Revised totals (in $A million) are: 381,684 in 1992/93; 400,431 in 1993/94.

BALANCE OF PAYMENTS (US $ million)

	1994	1995	1996
Exports of goods f.o.b.	47,331	53,145	60,064
Imports of goods f.o.b.	−50,611	−57,311	−60,955
Trade balance	−3,280	−4,166	−891
Exports of services	14,085	15,978	18,424
Imports of services	−15,248	−16,906	−18,495
Balance on goods and services	−4,442	−5,095	−962
Other income received	4,131	5,080	5,794
Other income paid	−16,053	−19,026	−20,808
Balance on goods, services and income	−16,364	−19,040	−15,977
Current transfers received	1,180	1,338	1,481
Current transfers paid	−1,533	−1,405	−1,374
Current balance	−16,717	−19,107	−15,870
Capital account (net)	313	537	884
Direct investment abroad	−5,243	−4,092	−3,140
Direct investment from abroad	3,881	14,251	6,321
Portfolio investment assets	−547	−1,483	−1,008
Portfolio investment liabilities	14,522	2,219	10,067
Other investment assets	1,318	−3,382	−4,700
Other investment liabilities	−3,642	12,459	10,322
Net errors and omissions	5,154	−1,006	−415
Overall balance	−960	396	2,460

Source: IMF, *International Financial Statistics*.

FOREIGN INVESTMENT ($A million, year ending 30 June)

Inflow	1992/93	1993/94	1994/95
EU—United Kingdom	3,533	8,654	2,130
—Other	849	4,376	2,649
Switzerland	31	258	−253
USA	10,297	8,878	2,148
Japan	−3,057	−1,622	756
Other OECD countries	834	1,436	326
ASEAN*	−1,137	961	−376
Other countries	1,676	3,677	−141
Unallocated	5,316	2,342	16,234
Total	18,342	28,960	23,473

Outflow	1992/93	1993/94	1994/95
United Kingdom	1,011	3,686	1,728
New Zealand	1,195	264	1,437
USA	685	3,475	−2,103
Japan	−206	2,828	−3,479
Other OECD countries	−458	1,840	495
Papua New Guinea	146	257	21
ASEAN*	778	531	815
Other countries	366	7	773
Unallocated	504	2,889	666
Total	4,021	15,777	353

* Brunei, Indonesia, Malaysia, the Philippines, Singapore and Thailand.

External Trade

PRINCIPAL COMMODITIES ($A million, year ending 30 June)

Imports f.o.b.	1993/94	1994/95	1995/96
Food and live animals	2,478	2,821	2,894
Beverages and tobacco	467	522	503
Crude materials (inedible) except fuels	1,595	1,794	1,576
Mineral fuels, lubricants, etc.	3,441	3,668	4,312
Petroleum, petroleum products, etc.	3,392	3,608	4,234
Animal and vegetable oils, fats and waxes	203	232	268
Chemicals and related products	7,045	8,009	8,901
Organic chemicals	1,615	1,795	1,919
Medicinal and pharmaceutical products	1,427	1,562	1,830
Basic manufactures	9,445	10,908	11,040
Paper, paperboard and manufactures	1,518	1,859	1,942
Textile yarn, fabrics, etc.	2,246	2,454	2,359
Machinery and transport equipment	28,911	35,160	36,484
Power-generating machinery and equipment	1,690	1,769	1,998
Machinery specialized for particular industries	3,061	3,792	3,924
General industrial machinery and equipment and parts	3,638	4,299	4,470
Office machines and automatic data-processing machines	4,828	5,728	6,032
Telecommunications and sound-recording and reproducing apparatus and equipment	2,538	3,362	3,759
Other electrical machinery, apparatus, appliances and parts	4,051	4,909	5,315
Road vehicles	7,108	8,678	7,980
Other transport equipment	1,620	2,050	2,514
Miscellaneous manufactured articles	9,798	10,708	11,035
Clothing and accessories	1,480	1,637	1,766
Professional, scientific and controlling instruments and apparatus	1,707	1,834	1,910
Other commodities and transactions	1,086	797	806
Total	64,470	74,619	77,819

Exports f.o.b.	1993/94	1994/95	1995/96
Food and live animals	12,967	12,565	15,250
Meat and meat preparations	4,044	3,661	3,293
Dairy products and birds' eggs	1,287	1,413	1,672
Cereals and cereal preparations	3,206	2,522	4,927
Sugars, sugar preparations and honey	1,316	1,729	1,710
Beverages and tobacco	506	551	646
Crude materials (inedible) except fuels	12,917	14,072	14,741
Textile fibres and waste*	3,977	4,594	4,056
Metalliferous ores and metal scrap	7,315	7,604	8,669

Exports f.o.b. — *continued*	1993/94	1994/95	1995/96
Mineral fuels, lubricants, etc.	11,116	11,245	12,601
Coal, coke and briquettes	7,255	6,938	7,837
Petroleum, petroleum products, etc.	2,676	2,952	3,195
Gas (natural and manufactured)	1,185	1,355	1,569
Animal and vegetable oils, fats and waxes	207	263	235
Chemicals and related products	2,351	2,678	3,002
Basic manufactures	7,911	9,022	9,830
Iron and steel	1,496	1,580	1,756
Non-ferrous metals	3,900	4,518	5,043
Machinery and transport equipment	7,502	8,137	9,684
Office machines and automatic data-processing machines	1,370	1,589	1,899
Other machinery	4,033	4,502	5,301
Transport equipment	2,098	2,046	2,483
Miscellaneous manufactured articles	2,106	2,314	2,707
Other commodities and transactions	6,965	6,205	7,304
Non-monetary gold (excl. gold ores and concentrates)	5,269	4,699	5,625
Total	64,548	67,051	75,999

* Excluding wool tops.

PRINCIPAL TRADING PARTNERS ($A million, year ending 30 June)

Imports f.o.b.	1993/94	1994/95	1995/96
Canada	1,055	1,278	1,557
China, People's Republic	3,120	3,649	4,010
France	1,542	1,754	1,867
Germany	3,759	4,861	4,862
Hong Kong	801	923	970
Indonesia	1,105	1,198	1,522
Italy	1,617	2,026	2,231
Japan	11,700	12,777	10,817
Korea, Republic	1,882	2,028	2,293
Malaysia	1,103	1,421	1,636
Netherlands	664	712	702
New Zealand	3,201	3,554	3,591
Papua New Guinea	1,296	1,125	1,220
Saudi Arabia	593	750	873
Singapore	1,792	2,246	2,612
Sweden	1,072	1,426	1,617
Switzerland	818	991	966
Taiwan	2,362	2,570	2,585
Thailand	794	970	1,005
United Arab Emirates	617	627	475
United Kingdom	3,698	4,439	4,882
USA	14,017	16,044	17,572
Total (incl. others)	69,275	74,619	77,819

Exports f.o.b.	1993/94	1994/95	1995/96
Canada	1,149	1,150	1,261
China, People's Republic	2,590	2,963	3,777
France	792	794	724
Germany	1,006	1,083	1,151
Hong Kong	2,797	2,632	3,070
India	865	979	1,184
Indonesia	1,906	2,113	2,779
Italy	1,052	1,250	1,281
Japan	15,924	16,282	16,419
Korea, Republic	4,706	5,250	6,609
Malaysia	1,759	2,033	2,296
Netherlands	703	707	694
New Zealand	4,009	4,790	5,591
Papua New Guinea	954	932	1,040
Philippines	699	839	1,074
Singapore	3,197	3,643	3,551
Taiwan	2,757	3,102	3,446
Thailand	1,278	1,560	1,778
United Kingdom	2,901	2,275	2,826
USA	5,075	4,643	4,601
Total (incl. others)	64,548	67,051	75,999

Transport

RAILWAYS*

	1992/93	1993/94	1994/95
Passengers carried ('000)	401,394	407,170	n.a.
Freight carried ('000 metric tons)	203,168	216,639	214,986
Freight ton-km (million)	56,555	74,093	68,037

* Traffic on government railways only.

ROAD TRAFFIC ('000 vehicles registered at 30 June)

	1993	1994	1995
Passenger vehicles	8,050.0	8,208.8	8,391.5
Light commercial vehicles and trucks	2,089.8	2,198.6	2,246.7
Motor cycles	291.7	291.8	297.2

SHIPPING

Merchant Fleet (registered at 31 December)

	1994	1995	1996
Number of vessels	628	627	625
Total displacement ('000 grt)	3,012.2	2,853.1	2,717.9

Source: Lloyd's Register of Shipping, *World Fleet Statistics*.

INTERNATIONAL SEA-BORNE TRAFFIC ('000 metric tons, year ending 30 June)

	1990/91	1991/92	1992/93
Goods loaded	304,439	316,729	327,097
Goods unloaded	32,202	34,396	38,757

CIVIL AVIATION

	1991/92	1992/93	1993/94
Domestic services			
Passengers carried ('000)	18,476.2	18,577.8	19,997.3
Passenger-km (million)	19,059.9	18,997.0	21,114.5
Freight carried (metric tons)	137,900	144,100	153,100
International services*			
Km flown ('000)	136,533	160,520	168,865
Passengers carried	4,468,149	5,222,783	5,817,263
Passenger-km ('000)	28,396,869	33,189,062	37,341,545
Freight carried (metric tons)	172,790	197,249	218,194
Mail carried (metric tons)	8,324	8,737	10,031

* Refers only to services operated by Qantas Airways Ltd.

Domestic services (1994/95, provisional): Passengers carried ('000) 23,422.8; Passenger-km (million) 25,268.9.

Tourism

VISITOR ARRIVALS BY COUNTRY OF ORIGIN*

	1994	1995	1996
Canada	54,218	58,370	61,119
China, People's Republic	29,175	42,593	53,968
Germany	122,613	124,176	125,402
Hong Kong	109,355	131,702	153,204
Indonesia	105,591	134,958	154,451
Japan	720,937	782,671	813,113
Korea, Republic	110,704	167,975	227,850
Malaysia	94,979	108,186	134,408
New Zealand	480,214	538,377	671,889
Papua New Guinea	37,998	42,286	43,482
Singapore	187,540	202,366	222,819
Taiwan	142,512	151,975	159,415
Thailand	66,721	81,315	88,918
United Kingdom	334,858	347,894	367,550
USA	289,459	304,875	316,881
Total (incl. others)	3,358,708	3,725,826	4,164,825

* Visitors intending to stay for less than one year.

Receipts from tourism (million $A): 11,159 in 1994; 13,105 in 1995; 16,101 in 1996.

Source: Australian Tourist Commission, Sydney.

Communications Media

('000 at 30 June)

	1992	1993	1994
Telephone services in operation	8,257	8,540	8,850
Telefax stations in use	400	425	450
Mobile telephones (subscribers)	497	760	1,250

Source: UN, *Statistical Yearbook*.

Radio receivers (1994): 23,050,000 in use.

Television receivers (1994): 8,730,000 in use.

Book production (1994): 10,835 titles.

Newspapers (1994): 69 dailies (estimated combined circulation 4,600,000); (1988, estimates): 460 non-dailies (circulation 17,204,000).

Source: mainly UNESCO, *Statistical Yearbook*.

Education

(1995)

	Institutions	Teaching staff	Students
Government schools	7,366	143,787	2,207,853*
Non-government schools	2,499	58,614	901,484†
Higher educational institutions	44‡	48,772§	604,177

* Comprising 1,361,287 primary and 846,566 secondary students.

† Comprising 472,394 primary and 429,090 secondary students.

‡ 1991 figure.

§ Teaching and/or research staff (excluding casual staff); 1991 figure.

Directory

The Constitution

The Federal Constitution was adopted on 9 July 1900 and came into force on 1 January 1901. Its main provisions are summarized below:

PARLIAMENT

The legislative power of the Commonwealth of Australia is vested in a Federal Parliament, consisting of HM the Queen (represented by the Governor-General), a Senate, and a House of Representatives. The Governor-General may appoint such times for holding the sessions of the Parliament as he or she thinks fit, and may also from time to time, by proclamation or otherwise, prorogue the Parliament, and may in like manner dissolve the House of Representatives. By convention, these powers are exercised on the advice of the Prime Minister. After any general election Parliament must be summoned to meet not later than 30 days after the day appointed for the return of the writs.

THE SENATE

The Senate is composed of 12 senators from each state, two senators representing the Australian Capital Territory and two representing the Northern Territory. The senators are directly chosen by the people of the state or territory, voting in each case as one electorate, and are elected by proportional representation. Senators representing a state have a six-year term and retire by rotation, one-half from each state on 30 June of each third year. The term of a senator representing a territory is limited to three years. In the case of a state, if a senator vacates his or her seat before the expiration of the term of service, the houses of parliament of the state for which the senator was chosen shall, in joint session, choose a person to hold the place until the expiration of the term or until the election of a successor. If the state parliament is not in session, the Governor of the state, acting on the advice of the state's executive council, may appoint a senator to hold office until parliament reassembles, or until a new senator is elected.

The Senate may proceed to the dispatch of business notwithstanding the failure of any state to provide for its representation in the Senate.

THE HOUSE OF REPRESENTATIVES

In accordance with the Australian Constitution, the total number of members of the House of Representatives must be as nearly as practicable double that of the Senate. The number in each state is in proportion to population, but under the Constitution must be at least five. The House of Representatives is composed of 148 members, including two members for the Australian Capital Territory and one member for the Northern Territory.

Members are elected by universal adult suffrage and voting is compulsory. Only Australian citizens are eligible to vote in Australian elections. British subjects, if they are not Australian citizens or already on the rolls, have to take out Australian citizenship before thay can enrol and before they can vote.

Members are chosen by the electors of their respective electorates by the preferential voting system.

The duration of the Parliament is limited to three years.

To be nominated for election to the House of Representatives, a candidate must be 18 years of age or over, an Australian citizen, and entitled to vote at the election or qualified to become an elector.

THE EXECUTIVE GOVERNMENT

The executive power of the Federal Government is vested in the Queen, and is exercisable by the Governor-General, advised by an Executive Council of Ministers of State, known as the Federal Executive Council. These ministers are, or must become within three months, members of the Federal Parliament.

The Australian Constitution is construed as subject to the principles of responsible government and the Governor-General acts on the advice of the ministers in relation to most matters.

THE JUDICIAL POWER

See Judicial System, p. 463.

THE STATES

The Australian Constitution safeguards the Constitution of each state by providing that it shall continue as at the establishment of the Commonwealth, except as altered in accordance with its own provisions. The legislative power of the Federal Parliament is limited in the main to those matters that are listed in section 51 of the Constitution, while the states possess, as well as concurrent powers in those matters, residual legislative powers enabling them to legislate in any way for 'the peace, order and good Government' of their respective territories. When a state law is inconsistent with a law of the Commonwealth, the latter prevails, and the former is invalid to the extent of the inconsistency.

The states may not, without the consent of the Commonwealth, raise or maintain naval or military forces, or impose taxes on any property belonging to the Commonwealth of Australia, nor may the Commonwealth tax state property. The states may not coin money.

The Federal Parliament may not enact any law for establishing any religion or for prohibiting the exercise of any religion, and no religious test may be imposed as a qualification for any office under the Commonwealth.

The Commonwealth of Australia is charged with protecting every state against invasion, and, on the application of a state executive government, against domestic violence.

Provision is made under the Constitution for the admission of new states and for the establishment of new states within the Commonwealth of Australia.

ALTERATION OF THE CONSTITUTION

Proposed laws for the amendment of the Constitution must be passed by an absolute majority in both Houses of the Federal Parliament, and not less than two or more than six months after its passage through both Houses the proposed law must be submitted in each state to the qualified electors.

In the event of one House twice refusing to pass a proposed amendment that has already received an absolute majority in the other House, the Governor-General may, notwithstanding such refusal, submit the proposed amendment to the electors. By convention, the Governor-General acts on the advice of the Prime Minister. If in a majority of the states a majority of the electors voting approve the proposed law and if a majority of all the electors voting also approve, it shall be presented to the Governor-General for Royal Assent.

No alteration diminishing the proportionate representation of any state in either House of the Federal Parliament, or the minimum number of representatives of a state in the House of Representatives, or increasing, diminishing or altering the limits of the state, or in any way affecting the provisions of the Constitution in relation thereto, shall become law unless the majority of the electors voting in that state approve the proposed law.

STATES AND TERRITORIES

New South Wales

The state's executive power is vested in the Governor, appointed by the Crown, who is assisted by an Executive Council composed of cabinet ministers.

The state's legislative power is vested in a bicameral Parliament, composed of the Legislative Council and the Legislative Assembly. The Legislative Council consists of 42 members directly elected for the duration of two parliaments (i.e. eight years), 21 members retiring every four years. The Legislative Assembly consists of 99 members and sits for four years.

Victoria

The state's legislative power is vested in a bicameral Parliament: the Upper House, or Legislative Council, of 44 members, elected for two terms of the Legislative Assembly; and the Lower House, or Legislative Assembly, of 88 members, elected for a minimum of three and maximum of four years. One-half of the members of the Council retires every three–four years.

In the exercise of the executive power the Governor is assisted by a cabinet of responsible ministers. Not more than five members of the Council and not more than 13 members of the Assembly may occupy salaried office at any one time.

The state has 88 electoral districts, each returning one member, and 22 electoral provinces, each returning two Council members.

Queensland

The state's legislative power is vested in a unicameral Parliament composed of 89 members who are elected from 89 districts for a term of three years.

South Australia

The state's Constitution vests the legislative power in a Parliament elected by the people and consisting of a Legislative Council and a House of Assembly. The Council is composed of 22 members, one-half of whom retires every three years. Their places are filled by new members elected under a system of proportional representation, with the whole state as a single electorate. The executive has no authority to dissolve this body, except in circumstances warranting a double dissolution.

The 47 members of the House of Assembly are elected for three years from 47 electoral districts.

The executive power is vested in a Governor, appointed by the Crown, and an Executive Council consisting of 13 responsible ministers.

Western Australia

The state's administration is vested in the Governor, a Legislative Council and a Legislative Assembly.

The Legislative Council consists of 34 members, two of the six electoral regions returning seven members on a proportional representation basis, and four regions returning five members. Election is for a term of four years.

The Legislative Assembly consists of 57 members, elected for four years, each representing one electorate.

Tasmania

The state's executive authority is vested in a Governor, appointed by the Crown, who acts upon the advice of his premier and ministers, who are elected members of either the Legislative Council or the House of Assembly. The Council consists of 19 members who sit for six years, retiring in rotation. The House of Assembly has 35 members elected for four years.

Northern Territory

On 1 July 1978, the Northern Territory was established as a body politic with executive authority for specified functions of government. Most functions of the Federal Government were transferred to the Territory Government in 1978 and 1979, major exceptions being Aboriginal affairs and uranium mining.

The Territory Parliament consists of a single house, the Legislative Assembly, with 25 members. The first Parliament stayed in office for three years. As from the election held in August 1980, members are elected for a term of four years.

The office of Administrator continues. The Northern Territory (Self-Government) Act provides for the appointment of an Administrator by the Governor-General charged with the duty of administering the Territory. In respect of matters transferred to the Territory Government, the Administrator acts with the advice of the Territory Executive Council; in respect of matters retained by the Commonwealth, the Administrator acts on Commonwealth advice.

Australian Capital Territory

On 29 November 1988 the Australian Capital Territory (ACT) was established as a body politic. The ACT Government has executive authority for specified functions, although a number of these were to be retained by the Federal Government for a brief period during which transfer arrangements were to be finalized.

The ACT Parliament consists of a single house, the Legislative Assembly, with 17 members. The first election was held in March 1989. Members are elected for a term of four years.

The Federal Government retains control of some of the land in the ACT for the purpose of maintaining the Seat of Government and the national capital plan.

Jervis Bay Territory

Following the attainment of self-government by the ACT (see above), the Jervis Bay Territory, which had formed part of the ACT since 1915, remained a separate Commonwealth Territory, administered by the then Department of the Arts, Sport, the Environment and Territories. The area is governed in accordance with the Jervis Bay Territory Administration Ordinance, issued by the Governor-General on 17 December 1990.

The Government

Head of State: HM Queen ELIZABETH II (succeeded to the throne 6 February 1952).

Governor-General: Sir WILLIAM DEANE (took office 16 February 1996).

THE MINISTRY
(December 1997)

Cabinet Ministers

Prime Minister: JOHN HOWARD.

Deputy Prime Minister and Minister for Trade: TIM FISCHER.

Treasurer: PETER COSTELLO.

Minister for Primary Industries and Energy: JOHN ANDERSON.

Minister for the Environment, Leader of the Government in the Senate: Senator ROBERT HILL.

Minister for Communications and the Arts, Deputy Leader of the Government in the Senate: Senator RICHARD ALSTON.

Minister for Workplace Relations and Small Business, Leader of the House: PETER REITH.

Minister for Social Security and Minister Assisting the Prime Minister for the Status of Women: Senator JOCELYN NEWMAN.

Minister for Foreign Affairs: ALEXANDER DOWNER.

Minister for Industry, Science and Tourism, Vice-President of the Executive Council: JOHN MOORE.

Minister for Defence: IAN MCLACHLAN.

Minister for Transport and Regional Development: MARK VAILE.

Minister for Health and Family Services: Dr MICHAEL WOOLDRIDGE.

Minister for Finance and Administration: JOHN FAHEY.

Minister for Employment, Education, Training and Youth Affairs: DAVID KEMP.

Attorney-General: DARYL WILLIAMS.

Other Ministers

Minister for Immigration and Multicultural Affairs: PHILLIP RUDDOCK.

Minister for Schools, Vocational Education and Training: Senator CHRIS ELLISON.

Assistant Treasurer: Senator ROD KEMP.

Minister for Resources and Energy: Senator WARWICK PARER.

Minister for Customs and Consumer Affairs: WARREN TRUSS.

Minister for Family Services: WARWICK SMITH.

Minister for Defence Industry, Science and Personnel: BRONWYN BISHOP.

Minister for Justice: Senator AMANDA VANSTONE.

Minister for the Status of Women: JUDI MOYLAN.

Minister for Veterans' Affairs: BRUCE SCOTT.

Minister for Aboriginal and Torres Strait Islander Affairs: Senator JOHN HERRON.

Minister for Regional Development, Territories and Local Government: ALEX SOMLYAY.

Minister for Sport and Tourism: ANDREW THOMSON.

Special Minister of State: NICK MINCHIN.

DEPARTMENTS

Department of the Prime Minister and Cabinet: 3–5 National Circuit, Barton, ACT 2600; tel. (2) 6271-5111; telex 61616; fax (2) 6271-5415.

Aboriginal and Torres Strait Islander Commission: MLC Tower, Woden Town Centre, Phillip, ACT 2606; tel. (2) 6289-1222; telex 862471.

Attorney-General's Department: Robert Garran Offices, Barton, ACT 2600; tel. (2) 6250-6666; telex 62002; fax (2) 6250-5900.

Department of Administrative Services: POB 1920, Canberra City, ACT 2601; tel. (2) 6275-3000; fax (2) 6275-3819.

Department of Defence: Russell Offices, Canberra, ACT 2600; tel. (2) 6265-9111.

Department of Employment, Education, Training and Youth Affairs: GPOB 9880, Canberra, ACT 2601; tel. (2) 6240-8848; fax (2) 6240-7442; e-mail library@deetya.gov.au.

Department of the Environment, Sport and Territories: GPOB 787, Canberra, ACT 2601; tel. (2) 6274-1111; fax (2) 6274-1123.

Department of Finance: Newlands St, Parkes, ACT 2600; tel. (2) 6263-2222; telex 62639; fax (2) 6273-3021.

Department of Foreign Affairs and Trade: Locked Bag 40, QVT, Canberra, ACT 2600; tel. (2) 6261-9111; telex 62007; fax (2) 6261-3111.

Department of Health and Family Services: POB 9848, Canberra, ACT 2601; tel. (2) 6289-1555; telex 61209; fax (2) 6281-6946.

Department of Immigration and Multicultural Affairs: Benjamin Offices, Chan St, Belconnen, ACT 2617; tel. (2) 6264-1111; telex 62037; fax (2) 6264-2670.

Department of Industry, Science and Tourism: 20 Allara St, Canberra, ACT 2601; tel. (2) 6213-6000; fax (2) 6213-7000.

Department of Primary Industries and Energy: GPOB 858, Canberra, ACT 2601; tel. (2) 6272-3933; fax (2) 6272-5161; internet http://www.dpie.gov.au/home.html.

Department of Social Security: Box 7788, Canberra Mail Centre, ACT 2610; tel. (2) 6244-7788; fax (2) 6244-5900.

Department of Transport and Regional Development: GPOB 594, Canberra, ACT 2601; tel. (2) 6274-7111; telex 62018; fax (2) 6257-2505.

Department of the Treasury: Parkes Place, Parkes, ACT 2600; tel. (2) 6263-2111; fax (2) 6273-2614.

Department of Veterans' Affairs: POB 21, Woden, ACT 2606; tel. (2) 6289-1111; fax (2) 6289-6025.

Department of Workplace Relations and Small Business: GPO Box 9879, Canberra, ACT 2601; tel. (2) 6243-7904; fax (2) 6243-7542; e-mail dwrsb@netinfo.com.au.

Legislature

FEDERAL PARLIAMENT

Senate

President: Senator MICHAEL BEAHAN.

Election, 2 March 1996

Party	Seats*
Liberal Party of Australia	31
Australian Labor Party	29
Australian Democrats Party	7
National Party of Australia	6
Independents	2
Greens	1
Total	76

* The election was for 36 of the 72 seats held by state senators and for all four senators representing the Northern Territory and the Australian Capital Territory (the terms of the latter being limited to three years). The figures for seats refer to the totals held after the election.

House of Representatives

Speaker: BOB HALVERSON (Liberal-National)

Election, 2 March 1996

Party	Seats
Liberal Party of Australia	75
Australian Labor Party	49
National Party of Australia	19
Independents	5
Total	148

State and Territory Governments

(November 1997)

NEW SOUTH WALES

Governor: GORDON SAMUELS, Level 3, Chief Secretary's Bldg, 121 Macquarie St, Sydney, NSW 2000; tel. (2) 9242-4200; fax (2) 9242-4200; e-mail ersm1@waratah.www.NSW.gov.au.

Premier: ROBERT (BOB) E. CARR (Labor).

VICTORIA

Governor: Sir JAMES GOBBO, Government House, Melbourne, Vic 3004; tel. (3) 9651-4211; fax (3) 9651-4282.

Premier: JEFFREY KENNETT (Liberal-National).

QUEENSLAND

Governor: Maj.-Gen. PETER ARNISON, Government House, Brisbane, Qld 4000; tel. (7) 3369-7744; fax (7) 3369-9419.

Premier: ROBERT (ROB) E. BORBIDGE (Liberal-National).

SOUTH AUSTRALIA

Governor: Sir ERIC NEAL, Government House, North Terrace, Adelaide, SA 5000; tel. (8) 8223-6166; fax (8) 8223-6049.

Premier: JOHN OLSEN (Liberal-National).

WESTERN AUSTRALIA

Governor: Maj.-Gen. PHILIP MICHAEL JEFFERY, Government House, Perth, WA 6000; tel. (8) 9429-9199; fax (8) 9325-4476; e-mail govhouse@highway1.com.au.

Premier: RICHARD COURT (Liberal-National).

TASMANIA

Governor: Sir GUY GREEN, Government House, Hobart, Tas 7000; tel. (3) 6234-2611; fax (3) 6234-2556.

Premier: ANTHONY RUNDLE (Liberal-National).

NORTHERN TERRITORY

Administrator: Dr NEIL CONN, Government House, The Esplanade, Darwin, NT 0800; tel. (8) 8999-7103; fax (8) 8981-9379.

Chief Minister: SHANE STONE (Liberal-National).

AUSTRALIAN CAPITAL TERRITORY

Chief Minister: A. KATHERINE (KATE) CARNELL (Liberal-National).

Political Organizations

Australian Democrats Party: Victorian Division, G1/Eastbourne House, 62 Wellington Pde, East Melbourne, Vic 3002; tel. (3) 9419-5808; fax (3) 9419-5697; f. 1977; comprises the fmr Liberal Movement and the Australia Party; Leader Senator MEG LEES.

Australian Labor Party (ALP): Centenary House, 19 National Circuit, Barton, ACT 2600; tel. (2) 6273-3133; fax (2) 6273-2031; f. 1891; advocates social democracy; trade unions form part of its structure; Fed. Parl. Leader KIM BEAZLEY; Nat. Pres. BARRY O. JONES; Nat. Sec. GARY GRAY.

Communist Party of Australia: 65 Campbell St, Surry Hills, NSW 2010; tel. (2) 9212-6855; fax (2) 9281-5795; f. 1971; fmrly Socialist Party; advocates public ownership of the means of production, working-class political power; Pres. Dr H. MIDDLETON; Gen. Sec. P. SYMON.

Liberal Party of Australia: Federal Secretariat, Cnr Blackall and Macquarie Sts, Barton, ACT 2600; tel. (2) 6273-2564; fax (2) 6273-1534; e-mail libadm@liberal.org.au; internet http://www.liberal.org.au; f. 1944; advocates private enterprise, social justice, individual liberty and initiative; committed to national development, prosperity and security; Fed. Pres. TONY STALEY; Fed. Parl. Leader JOHN HOWARD.

National Party of Australia: John McEwen House, National Circuit, Barton, ACT 2600; tel. (2) 6273-3822; fax (2) 6273-1745; f. 1916 as the Country Party of Australia; adopted present name in 1982; advocates balanced national development based on free enterprise, with special emphasis on the needs of people outside the major metropolitan areas; Fed. Pres. DON MCDONALD; Fed. Parl. Leader TIMOTHY FISCHER; Fed. Dir CECILE FERGUSON.

One Nation Party: c/o House of Representatives, Canberra; f. 1997; opposes immigration; Leader PAULINE HANSON.

Other political organizations include the Green Party, the Australian Republican Movement (Chair. MALCOLM TURNBULL) and Australians for a Constitutional Monarchy.

Diplomatic Representation

EMBASSIES AND HIGH COMMISSIONS IN AUSTRALIA

Argentina: POB 262, Woden, ACT 2606; tel. (2) 6282-4855; fax (2) 6285-3062; Ambassador: NÉSTOR E. STANCANELLI.

Austria: POB 3375, Manuka, ACT 2603; tel. (2) 6295-1533; telex 62726; fax (2) 6239-6751; Ambassador: Dr STEPHAN TOTH.

Bangladesh: POB 5, Red Hill, ACT 2603; tel. (2) 6295-3328; fax (2) 6295-3351; e-mail bdoot.canberra@cyberone.com.au; High Commissioner: Maj.-Gen. MOINUL HUSSAIN CHOUDHURY.

Belgium: 19 Arkana St, Yarralumla, ACT 2600; tel. (2) 6273-2501; telex 62601; fax (2) 6273-3392; e-mail belgemb@spirit.com.au; Ambassador: RAF VAN HELLEMONT.

Bosnia and Herzegovina: 15 State Circle, Forrest, ACT 2603; tel. (2) 6239-5955; fax (2) 6239-5793; Chargé d'affaires a.i.: FUAD DJIDIĆ.

Brazil: GPOB 1540, Canberra, ACT 2601; tel. (2) 6273-2372; fax (2) 6273-2375; Ambassador: RENATO PRADO GUIMARÃES.

Brunei: 16 Bulwarra Close, O'Malley, ACT 2606; tel. (2) 6290-1801; fax (2) 6290-1832; High Commissioner: Dato' MALAI Haji AHMAD MURAD.

Cambodia: 5 Canterbury Cres., Deakin, ACT 2600; tel. (2) 6273-1259; fax (2) 6273-1053; Ambassador: CHHEANG VUN.

Canada: Commonwealth Ave, Canberra, ACT 2600; tel. (2) 6273-3844; fax (2) 6273-3285; High Commissioner: WILLIAM BRIAN SCHUMACHER.

Chile: POB 69, Monaro Cres., ACT 2603; tel. (2) 6286-2430; telex 62685; fax (2) 6286-1289; Ambassador: JORGE TARUD.

China, People's Republic: 15 Coronation Drive, Yarralumla, ACT 2600; tel. (2) 6273-4780; telex 62489; fax (2) 6273-4235; Ambassador: HUA JUNDUO.

Colombia: GPOB 2892, Canberra, ACT 2601; tel. (2) 6257-2027; fax (2) 6257-1448; Ambassador: LUIS GUILLERMO SORZANO.

Croatia: 14 Jindalee Cres., O'Malley, ACT 2606; tel. (2) 6286-6988; fax (2) 6286-3544; Ambassador: Dr JOZO METER.

Cyprus: 30 Beale Crescent, Deakin, ACT 2600; tel. (2) 6281-0832; fax (2) 6281-0860; High Commissioner: ANDREAS GEORGIADES.

Czech Republic: 38 Culgoa Circuit, O'Malley, ACT 2606; tel. (2) 6290-1386; fax (2) 6290-0006; e-mail canberra@embassy.mzv.cz; Ambassador: Dr JAROSLAV SUCHÁNEK.

Denmark: 15 Hunter St, Yarralumla, ACT 2600; tel. (2) 6273-2195; telex 62661; fax (2) 6273-3864; Ambassador: KRISTIAN LUND-JENSEN.

Egypt: 1 Darwin Ave, Yarralumla, ACT 2600; tel. (2) 6273-4437; telex 62497; fax (2) 6273-4279; Ambassador: MOHAMED ALI EL-SHEREI.

Eritrea: 26 Guilfoyle St, Yarraluma, ACT 2600; tel. (2) 6282-3489; fax (2) 6282-5233; Ambassador: OGBAI HABTEMICHAEL.

Fiji: POB 159, Queen Victoria Terrace, ACT 2600; tel. (2) 6260-5115; fax (2) 6260-5105; High Commissioner: ISIKELI MATAITOGA.

Finland: 10 Darwin Ave, Yarralumla, ACT 2600; tel. (2) 6273-3800; fax (2) 6273-3603; e-mail finland@dynamite.com.au; Ambassador: ESKO HAMILO.

France: 6 Perth Ave, Yarralumla, ACT 2600; tel. (2) 6216-0100; fax (2) 6216-0127; Ambassador: DOMINIQUE GIRARD.

Germany: 119 Empire Circuit, Yarralumla, ACT 2600; tel. (2) 6270-1911; fax (2) 6270-1951; Ambassador: Dr KLAUS ZELLER.

Greece: 9 Turrana St, Yarralumla, ACT 2600; tel. (2) 6273-3011; fax (2) 6273-2620; Ambassador: IOANNIS BEVERATOS.

Holy See: POB 3633, Manuka, ACT 2603 (Apostolic Nunciature); tel. (2) 6295-3876; Apostolic Pro-Nuncio: Most Rev. FRANCO BRAMBILLA, Titular Archbishop of Viminacium.

Hungary: 17 Beale Crescent, Deakin, ACT 2600; tel. (2) 6282-3226; fax (2) 6285-3012; Ambassador: Dr GYÖRGY VARGA.

India: 3–5 Moonah Place, Yarralumla, ACT 2600; tel. (2) 6273-3999; telex 62362; fax (2) 6273-3328; High Commissioner: G. PARTHASARATHY.

Indonesia: 8 Darwin Ave, Yarralumla, ACT 2600; tel. (2) 6273-3222; telex 62525; fax (2) 6250-8600; Ambassador: SASTROHANDOJO WIRYONO.

Iran: POB 3219, Manuka, ACT 2603; tel. (2) 6290-2421; telex 62490; fax (2) 6290-2431; Ambassador: MOHAMMAD ROOHI-SEFAT.

Iraq: 48 Culgoa Circuit, O'Malley, ACT 2606; tel. (2) 6286-1333; fax (2) 6290-1788; Chargé d'affaires: KHALID J. MOHAMMED.

Ireland: 20 Arkana St, Yarralumla, ACT 2600; tel. (2) 6273-3022; fax (2) 6273-3741; Ambassador: RICHARD A. O'BRIEN.

Israel: 6 Turrana St, Yarralumla, ACT 2600; tel. (2) 6273-1309; telex 62224; fax (2) 6273-4273; e-mail IsrEmb.Canberra@u030.aone.net.au; Ambassador: SHMUEL E. MOYAL.

Italy: 12 Grey St, Deakin, ACT 2600; tel. (2) 6273-3333; telex 62028; fax (2) 6273-4223; Ambassador: Dr MARCELLO SPATAFORA.

Japan: 112 Empire Circuit, Yarralumla, ACT 2600; tel. (2) 6273-3244; telex 62034; fax (2) 6273-1848; Ambassador: YUKIO SATOH.

Jordan: 20 Roebuck St, Red Hill, ACT 2603; tel. (2) 6295-9951; telex 62551; fax (2) 6239-7236; Ambassador: HANI BAHJAT TABBARA.

Kenya: GPOB 1990, Canberra, ACT 2601; tel. (2) 6247-4788; telex 61929; fax (2) 6257-6613; High Commissioner: GREEN H. O. JOSIAH.

Korea, Republic: 113 Empire Circuit, Yarralumla, ACT 2600; tel. (2) 6273-3044; fax (2) 6273-4839; Ambassador: DONG SUK MOON.

Laos: 1 Dalman Cres., O'Malley, ACT 2606; tel. (2) 6286-4595; fax (2) 6290-1910; Ambassador: PHANTHONG PHOMMAHAXAY.

Lebanon: 27 Endeavour St, Red Hill, ACT 2603; tel. (2) 6295-7378; fax (2) 6239-7024; Ambassador: LATIF ABUL-HUSN.

Malaysia: 7 Perth Ave, Yarralumla, ACT 2600; tel. (2) 6273-1543; telex 62032; fax (2) 6273-2496; High Commissioner: Dato' ADNAN OTHMAN.

Malta: 261 La Perouse St, Red Hill, ACT 2603; tel. (2) 6295-1586; fax (2) 6239-6084; e-mail maltahc@cs.net.au; High Commissioner: GEORGE N. BUSUTTIL.

Mauritius: 2 Beale Cres., Deakin, ACT 2600; tel. (2) 6281-1203; fax (2) 6282-3235; e-mail Mauritius@caber.net; High Commissioner: (vacant).

Mexico: 14 Perth Ave, Yarralumla, ACT 2600; tel. (2) 6273-3905; fax (2) 6273-1190; Ambassador: RAPHAEL STEGER-CATAÑO.

Myanmar: 22 Arkana St, Yarralumla, ACT 2600; tel. (2) 6273-3811; telex 61376; fax (2) 6273-4357; Ambassador: U MAUNG MAUNG LAY.

Netherlands: 120 Empire Circuit, Yarralumla, ACT 2600; tel. (2) 6273-3111; fax (2) 6273-3206; e-mail nlgovcan@ozemail.com.au; Ambassador: ROELOF R. SMIT.

New Zealand: Commonwealth Ave, Canberra, ACT 2600; tel. (2) 6270-4211; fax (2) 6273-3194; e-mail nzhccba@u030.aone.net.au; High Commissioner: GRAHAM C. FORTUNE.

Nigeria: POB 241, Civic Square, ACT 2608; tel. (2) 6286-1322; fax (2) 6286-5332; High Commissioner: JOHN O. OBOH (acting).

Norway: 17 Hunter St, Yarralumla, ACT 2600; tel. (2) 6273-3444; telex 62569; fax (2) 6273-3669; Ambassador: KJELL-MARTIN FREDERIKSEN.

Pakistan: POB 684, Mawson, ACT 2607; tel. (2) 6290-1676; fax (2) 6290-1073; High Commissioner: G. FARID FARRUKH (acting).

Papua New Guinea: POB E432, Queen Victoria Terrace, Parkes, ACT 2600; tel. (2) 6273-3322; telex 62592; fax (2) 6273-3732; High Commissioner: Brig.-Gen. (retd) KENNETH KORA NOGA.

Peru: POB 106, Red Hill, ACT 2606; tel. (2) 6290-0922; fax (2) 6290-0924; Ambassador: JOSÉ LUIS GARAYCOCHEA.

Philippines: POB 3297, Manuka, ACT 2603; tel. (2) 6273-2535; fax (2) 6273-3984; Ambassador: DELIA DOMINGO-ALBERT.

Poland: 7 Turrana St, Yarralumla, ACT 2600; tel. (2) 6273-1208; telex 62584; fax (2) 6273-3184; e-mail beata@clover.com.au; Chargé d'affaires a.i.: BEATA STOCZYŃSKA.

Portugal: 23 Culgoa Circuit, O'Malley, ACT 2606; tel. (2) 6290-1733; telex 62649; fax (2) 6290-1957; Ambassador: Dr ZÓZIMO JUSTO DA SILVA.

Romania: 4 Dalman Cres., O'Malley, ACT 2606; tel. (2) 6286-2343; fax (2) 6286-2433; Ambassador: Dr IOAN GAF-DEAC.

Russia: 78 Canberra Ave, Griffith, ACT 2603; tel. (2) 6295-9033; telex 61365; fax (2) 6295-1847; Chargé d'affaires: ANDREI TROFIMOV.

Samoa: POB 3274, Manuka, ACT 2603; tel. (2) 6286-5505; fax (2) 6286-5678; e-mail samoahcaussi@netspeed.com.au; High Commissioner: Leiataua Dr KILIFOTI ETEUATI.

Saudi Arabia: POB 63, Garran, ACT 2605; tel. (2) 6286-2099; telex 61454; fax (2) 6290-1835; Ambassador: MOHAMAD I. AL-HEJAILAN.

Singapore: 17 Forster Crescent, Yarralumla, ACT 2600; tel. (2) 6273-3944; telex 62192; fax (2) 6273-3260; e-mail shc.cbr@u30.aone.net.au; High Commissioner: LOW CHOON MING.

Slovakia: 47 Culgoa Circuit, O'Malley, ACT 2606; tel. (2) 6290-1516; fax (2) 6290-1755; Chargé d'affaires: Dr OLGA SIMOROVA.

Slovenia: POB 284, Civic Square, Canberra, ACT 2608; tel. (2) 6243-4830; fax (2) 6243-4827; Chargé d'affaires: ALJAZ GOSNAR.

Solomon Islands: Unit 4, JAA House, 19 Napier Close, Deakin, ACT 2600; tel. (2) 6282-7030; fax (2) 6282-7040; High Commissioner: GEORGE A. HIELE.

South Africa: cnr State Circle and Rhodes Place, Yarralumla, ACT 2600; tel. (2) 6273-2424; fax (2) 6273-3543; High Commissioner: Dr BHADRA G. RANCHOD.

Spain: POB 9076, Deakin, ACT 2600; tel. (2) 6273-3555; fax (2) 6273-3918; Ambassador: EMILIO FERNÁNDEZ CASTAÑO.

Sri Lanka: 35 Empire Circuit, Forrest, ACT 2603; tel. (2) 6239-7041; fax (2) 6239-6166; e-mail slhc@enternet.com.au; High Commissioner: ELMO DE JACOLYN SENEVIRATNE.

Sweden: 5 Turrana St, Yarralumla, ACT 2600; tel. (2) 6270-2700; telex 62303; fax (2) 6270-2755; e-mail sweden@netinfo.com.au; Ambassador: GÖRAN HASSELMARK.

Switzerland: 7 Melbourne Ave, Forrest, ACT 2603; tel. (2) 6273-3977; fax (2) 6273-3428; Ambassador: Dr BERNHARD MARFURT.

Thailand: 111 Empire Circuit, Yarralumla, ACT 2600; tel. (2) 6273-1149; telex 62533; fax (2) 6273-1518; Ambassador: LAXANACHANTORN LAOHAPHAN.

Turkey: 60 Mugga Way, Red Hill, ACT 2603; tel. (2) 6295-0227; telex 62764; fax (2) 6239-6592; e-mail turkembs@ozemail.com.au; Ambassador: BILAL ŞIMŞIR.

United Arab Emirates: 36 Culgoa Circuit, O'Malley, ACT 2606; tel. (2) 6286-8802; fax (2) 6286-8804; Chargé d'affaires: ASIM MIRZA ALRAHMAH.

United Kingdom: Commonwealth Ave, Canberra, ACT 2600; tel. (2) 6270-6666; fax (2) 6273-3236; High Commissioner: ALEX ALLAN.

USA: Moonah Place, Yarralumla, ACT 2600; tel. (2) 6270-5000; fax (2) 6270-5970; Ambassador: GENTA HAWKINS HOLMES.

Uruguay: POB 318, Woden, ACT 2606; tel. (2) 6282-4800; fax (2) 6282-4335; e-mail urucan@interconnect.com.au; Ambassador: PABLO SADER.

Venezuela: POB 37, Woden, ACT 2606; tel. (2) 6282-4828; telex 62110; fax (2) 6281-1969; Ambassador: ANTONIO RODRÍGUEZ YTURBE.

Viet Nam: 6 Timbarra Crescent, O'Malley, ACT 2606; tel. (2) 6286-6059; fax (2) 6286-4534; Ambassador: TRAN VAN TUNG.

Yugoslavia: POB 3161, Manuka, ACT 2603; tel. (2) 6295-1458; telex 62317; fax (2) 6239-6178; Chargé d'affaires a.i.: DUŠAN VUKASINOVIĆ.

Zimbabwe: 11 Culgoa Circuit, O'Malley, ACT 2606; tel. (2) 6286-2700; telex 62211; fax (2) 6290-1680; High Commissioner: Prof. HASU H. PATEL.

Judicial System

The judicial power of the Commonwealth of Australia is vested in the High Court of Australia, in such other Federal Courts as the Federal Parliament creates, and in such other courts as it invests with Federal jurisdiction.

The High Court consists of a Chief Justice and six other Justices, each of whom is appointed by the Governor-General in Council, and has both original and appellate jurisdiction.

The High Court's original jurisdiction extends to all matters arising under any treaty, affecting representatives of other countries, in which the Commonwealth of Australia or its representative is a party, between states or between residents of different states or between a state and a resident of another state, and in which a writ of mandamus, or prohibition, or an injunction is sought against an officer of the Commonwealth of Australia. It also extends to matters arising under the Australian Constitution or involving its interpretation, and to many matters arising under Commonwealth laws.

The High Court's appellate jurisdiction has, since June 1984, been discretionary. Appeals from the Federal Court, the Family Court and the Supreme Courts of the states and of the territories may now be brought only if special leave is granted, in the event of a legal question that is of general public importance being involved, or of there being differences of opinion between intermediate appellate courts as to the state of the law.

Legislation enacted by the Federal Parliament in 1976 substantially changed the exercise of Federal and Territory judicial power, and, by creating the Federal Court of Australia in February 1977, enabled the High Court of Australia to give greater attention to its primary function as interpreter of the Australian Constitution. The Federal Court of Australia has assumed, in two divisions, the jurisdiction previously exercised by the Australian Industrial Court and the Federal Court of Bankruptcy and was additionally given jurisdiction in trade practices and in the developing field of administrative law. In 1987 the Federal Court of Australia acquired jurisdiction in federal taxation matters and certain intellectual property matters. In 1991 the Court's jurisdiction was expanded to include civil proceedings arising under Corporations Law. Jurisdiction has also been conferred on the Federal Court of Australia, subject to a number of exceptions, in matters in which a writ of mandamus, or prohibition, or an injunction is sought against an officer of the Commonwealth of Australia. The Court also hears appeals from the Court constituted by a single Judge, from the Supreme Courts of the territories, and in certain specific matters from State Courts, other than a Full Court of the Supreme Court of a state, exercising Federal jurisdiction.

In March 1986 all remaining categories of appeal from Australian courts to the Queen's Privy Council in the UK were abolished by the Australia Act.

FEDERAL COURTS

High Court of Australia

POB E435, Kingston, Canberra, ACT 2604; tel. (2) 6270-6811; fax (2) 6270-6868.

Chief Justice: Sir GERARD BRENNAN.

Justices: JOHN TOOHEY, MARY GAUDRON, MICHAEL MCHUGH, WILLIAM GUMMOW, MICHAEL DONALD KIRBY, KENNETH MADISON HAYNE.

Federal Court of Australia

Chief Justice: MICHAEL ERIC JOHN BLACK.

There are more than 30 other judges.

Family Court of Australia

Chief Justice: ALISTAIR BOTHWICK NICHOLSON.

There are more than 50 other judges.

NEW SOUTH WALES

Supreme Court

Chief Justice: ANTHONY MURRAY GLEESON.

President: KEITH MASON.

Chief Judge in Equity: DAVID HARGRAVES HODGSON.

Chief Judge of Common Law: DAVID ANTHONY HUNT.

Chief Judge of the Commercial Division: ROGER DAVID GILES.

VICTORIA

Supreme Court

Chief Justice: JOHN HARBER PHILLIPS.

President of the Court of Appeal: JOHN SPENCE WINNEKE.

QUEENSLAND

Supreme Court

Chief Justice: JOHN MURTAGH MACROSSAN.

President of the Court of Appeal: GERALD EDWARD FITZGERALD.

Senior Judge Administrator, Trial Division: MARTIN PATRICK MOYNIHAN.

Central District (Rockhampton)

Resident Judge: ALAN GEORGE DEMACK.

Northern District (Townsville)

Resident Judge: KEIRAN ANTHONY CULLINANE.

SOUTH AUSTRALIA

Supreme Court

Chief Justice: JOHN JEREMY DOYLE.

WESTERN AUSTRALIA

Supreme Court

Chief Justice: DAVID KINGSLEY MALCOLM.

TASMANIA

Supreme Court

Chief Justice: WILLIAM JOHN ELLIS COX.

AUSTRALIAN CAPITAL TERRITORY

Supreme Court

Chief Justice: JEFFREY ALLAN MILES.

NORTHERN TERRITORY

Supreme Court

Chief Justice: BRIAN FRANK MARTIN.

Religion

CHRISTIANITY

According to the population census of August 1996, Christians numbered an estimated 12,582,764.

National Council of Churches in Australia: Private Bag 199, QVB PO, Sydney, NSW 1230; tel. (2) 9299-2215; telex 171715; fax (2) 9262-4514; f. 1946; 13 mem. churches; Pres. Archbishop JOHN BATHERSBY; Gen. Sec. Rev. DAVID GILL.

The Anglican Communion

The constitution of the Church of England in Australia, which rendered the church an autonomous member of the Anglican Communion, came into force in January 1962. The body was renamed the Anglican Church of Australia in August 1981. The Church comprises five provinces (together containing 22 dioceses) and the extra-provincial diocese of Tasmania. At the 1996 population census there were 3.9m. adherents.

National Office of the Anglican Church: General Synod Office, Box Q190, Queen Victoria Bldg PO, Sydney, NSW 1230; tel. (2) 9265-1525; fax (2) 9264-6552; e-mail anglican@ozemail.com.au; Gen. Sec. Rev. Dr B. N. KAYE.

Archbishop of Adelaide and Metropolitan of South Australia: Most Rev. IAN G. C. GEORGE, Bishop's Court, 45 Palmer Place, North Adelaide, South Australia 5006; fax (8) 8211-8748.

Archbishop of Brisbane and Metropolitan of Queensland: Most Rev. PETER J. HOLLINGWORTH, Bishopsbourne, Box 421, GPO, Brisbane, Queensland 4001; fax (7) 3832-5030; e-mail archbishops .office@docnet.org.au.

Archbishop of Melbourne and Metropolitan of Victoria and Primate: Most Rev. KEITH RAYNER, Bishopscourt, 120 Clarendon St, East Melbourne, Victoria 3002.

Archbishop of Perth and Metropolitan of Western Australia: Most Rev. PETER F. CARNLEY, 52 Mount St, Perth, Western Australia 6000; also has jurisdiction over Christmas Island and the Cocos (Keeling) Islands.

Archbishop of Sydney and Metropolitan of New South Wales: Most Rev. R. HARRY GOODHEW, Box Q190, Queen Victoria Bldg PO, Sydney, NSW 1230; fax (2) 9265-1543.

The Roman Catholic Church

Australia comprises seven archdioceses (including two directly responsible to the Holy See) and 25 dioceses (including one each for Catholics of the Maronite, Melkite and Ukrainian rites). At the census of 1996 there were 4.8m. adherents in the country.

Australian Catholic Bishops' Conference: GPO Box 368, Canberra, ACT 2601; tel. (2) 6201-9845; fax (2) 6247-6083; e-mail gensec @catholic.org.au; f. 1979; Pres. Cardinal EDWARD BEDE CLANCY, Archbishop of Sydney; Sec. Very Rev. BRIAN FINNIGAN.

Archbishop of Adelaide: Most Rev. LEONARD A. FAULKNER, GPO Box 1364, Adelaide, South Australia 5001; tel. (8) 8210-8108.

Archbishop of Brisbane: Most Rev. JOHN A. BATHERSBY, Archbishop's House, 790 Brunswick St, New Farm, Brisbane, Queensland 4005; tel. (7) 3224-3364; fax (7) 3358-1357; e-mail archbish@bne .catholic.net.au.

Archbishop of Canberra and Goulburn: Most Rev. FRANCIS P. CARROLL, GPOB 89, Canberra, ACT 2601; tel. (2) 6248-6411; fax (2) 6247-9636.

Archbishop of Hobart: Most Rev. ERIC D'ARCY, GPOB 62A, Hobart, Tasmania 7001; tel. (3) 6225-1920; fax (3) 6225-3865.

Archbishop of Melbourne: Most Rev. GEORGE PELL, GPOB 146, East Melbourne, Vic 3002; tel. (3) 9926-5677; fax (3) 9926-5617.

Archbishop of Perth: Most Rev. BARRY J. HICKEY, St Mary's Cathedral, Victoria Sq., Perth, Western Australia 6000; tel. (8) 9325-9557; fax (8) 9221-1716.

Archbishop of Sydney: Cardinal EDWARD BEDE CLANCY, Archdiocesan Chancery, Polding House, 13th Floor, 276 Pitt St, Sydney, NSW 2000; tel. (2) 9390-5100; fax (2) 9261-8312.

Orthodox Churches

Greek Orthodox Archdiocese: 242 Cleveland St, Redfern, Sydney, NSW 2016; tel. (2) 9698-5066; fax (2) 9698-5368; f. 1924; 700,000 mems; Primate His Eminence Archbishop STYLIANOS.

The Antiochian, Coptic, Romanian, Serbian and Syrian Orthodox Churches are also represented.

Other Christian Churches

Baptist Union of Australia: POB 377, Hawthorn, Vic 3122; tel. (3) 9818-0341; fax (3) 9818-1041; f. 1926; 64,159 mems; 883 churches; Nat. Pres. Rev. J. H. EDMONDSTONE; Nat. Sec. C. K. MOSS.

Churches of Christ in Australia: 34 Oxley St, Crows Nest, NSW 2065; tel. (2) 9437-0992; fax (2) 9437-0993; 35,500 mems; Pres. R. LEANE; Co-ordinator BOB SMITH.

Lutheran Church of Australia: National Office, 197 Archer St, North Adelaide, SA 5006; tel. (8) 8267-7300; fax (8) 8267-7310; f. 1966; 98,191 mems; Pres. Rev. Dr L. G. STEICKE.

Uniting Church in Australia: POB 1235, Sydney South, NSW 1235; tel. (2) 9287-0900; fax (2) 9287-0999; e-mail assysec@nat .uca.org.au; f. 1977 with the union of Methodist, Presbyterian and Congregational Churches; 1.4m. mems; Pres. Rev. JOHN MAVOR; Sec. Rev. GREGOR HENDERSON.

Other active denominations include the Pentecostal Church (174,720 adherents in 1996), the Armenian Apostolic Church, the Assyrian Church of the East and the Society of Friends (Quakers).

JUDAISM

Great Synagogue: 166 Castlereagh St, Sydney, NSW; tel. (2) 9267-2477; fax (2) 9264-8871; f. 1828; 80,000 adherents; Sr Minister Rabbi RAYMOND APPLE.

OTHER FAITHS

According to the provisional results of the August 1996 census, Muslims numbered 200,185, Buddhists 199,812 and Hindus 67,279.

The Press

The total circulation of Australia's daily newspapers is very high, but in the remoter parts of the country weekly papers are even more popular. Most of Australia's newspapers are published in sparsely populated rural areas where the demand for local news is strong. The only newspapers that may fairly claim a national circulation are the dailies *The Australian* and *Australian Financial Review*, and the weekly magazines *The Bulletin, Time Australia* and *Business Review Weekly*, the circulation of most newspapers being almost entirely confined to the state in which each is produced.

The trend in recent years has been towards the concentration of media ownership. The two major groups are News Limited (subsidiaries: The Herald and Weekly Times Ltd and Davies Brothers) and The John Fairfax Holdings Ltd (owners of David Syme & Co Ltd). Economic conditions have been conducive to the expansion of newspaper companies into magazine and book publishing, radio and television, etc. The principal groups are as follows:

ACP Publishing Pty Ltd: 54–58 Park St, Sydney, NSW 2000; tel. (2) 9282-8000; fax (2) 9267-2111; fmrly Australian Consolidated Press Ltd; publishes *Australian Women's Weekly, The Bulletin with Newsweek, Cleo, Cosmopolitan, Woman's Day, Dolly, Belle, Street Machine* and more than 70 other magazines.

John Fairfax Holdings Ltd: POB 506, Sydney, NSW 2001; tel. (2) 9282-2833; fax (2) 9282-3133; f. 1987; Chair. Sir LAURENCE STREET; Chief Exec. ROBERT S. MUSCAT; controls *The Sydney Morning Herald, The Australian Financial Review* and *Sun-Herald* (Sydney), *The Age, The Sunday Age* and BRW Publications (Melbourne), *Illawarra Mercury* (Wollongong), *The Newcastle Herald* (Newcastle).

The Herald and Weekly Times Ltd: 40 City Rd, Southbank, Vic 3006; tel. (3) 9292-1111; fax (3) 9292-2112; acquired by News Ltd in 1987; Chair. JANET CALVERT-JONES; Man. Dir JULIAN CLARKE; publs include *Herald-Sun, Sunday Herald-Sun, The Weekly Times*.

The News Corporation: 2 Holt St, Surry Hills, Sydney, NSW 2010; tel. (2) 9288-3000; Chair. and CEO K. RUPERT MURDOCH; Exec. Chair. and Man. Dir, News Ltd LACHLAN MURDOCH; controls *Daily Telegraph Mirror, Sunday Telegraph* (Sydney), *The Herald Sun* and *Sunday Herald Sun* (Victoria), *Northern Territory News* (Darwin), *Sunday Times* (Perth), *Townsville Bulletin, Courier Mail, Sunday Mail* (Queensland), *The Mercury* (Tasmania), *The Advertiser, Sunday Mail* (South Australia). Assoc. publs: *New Idea* and *TV Week* (National).

Other newspaper publishers include Australian Provincial Newspapers (O'Reilly), Macquarie Publications (Armati), Rural Press (J. B. Fairfax), West Australian Newspapers and Federal Capital Press (K. Stokes).

NEWSPAPERS

Australian Capital Territory

The Canberra Times: 9 Pirie St, Fyshwick, ACT 2609; POB 7155, Canberra Mail Centre, ACT 2610; tel. (2) 6280-2122; fax (2) 6280-2282; f. 1926; daily and Sun.; morning; Editor JACK WATERFORD; circ. 41,147 (Mon.–Fri.), 71,027 (Sat.), 46,216 (Sun.).

New South Wales

Dailies

The Australian: News Ltd, 2 Holt St, Surry Hills, NSW 2010, POB 4245; tel. (2) 9288-3000; fax (2) 9288-2370; f. 1964; edited in Sydney, simultaneous edns in Sydney, Melbourne, Perth, Townsville, Adelaide and Brisbane; Editor-in-Chief PAUL KELLY; Editor MALCOLM SCHMIDTKE; circ. 148,804.

Australian Financial Review: 201 Sussex St, GPOB 506, Sydney, NSW 2000; tel. (2) 9282-2822; fax (2) 9282-3137; f. 1951; Mon.–Fri.; distributed nationally; Editor-in-Chief GREG HYWOOD; Editor DEBORAH LIGHT; circ. 85,000.

Daily Commercial News: GPOB 1552, Sydney, NSW 2001; tel. (2) 9936-8700; fax (2) 9936-8769; e-mail dcrisp@dciv.com.au; f. 1891; Editor DALE CRISP; circ. 6,500.

The Daily Telegraph: 2 Holt St, Surry Hills, NSW 2010; tel. (2) 9288-3000; telex 20124; fax (2) 9288-2300; f. 1879, merged in 1990 with Daily Mirror (f. 1941); 24-hour tabloid; CEO LACHLAN MURDOCH; circ. 442,000.

The Manly Daily: Level 1, 39 East Esplanade, Manly, NSW 2095; tel. (2) 9977-3333; fax (2) 9977-1830; f. 1906; Tue.–Sat.; Editor STEVE STICKNEY; circ. 89,013.

The Newcastle Herald: 28–30 Bolton St, Newcastle, NSW 2300; tel. (2) 4979-5000; fax (2) 4979-5888; f. 1858; morning; 6 a week; Editor-in-Chief JOHN MCCLUSKEY; circ. 45,253.

The Sydney Morning Herald: 201 Sussex St, GPOB 506, Sydney, NSW 2001; tel. (2) 9282-2833; fax (2) 9282-1640; f. 1831; morning; Editor-in-Chief JOHN ALEXANDER; circ. 231,508 (Mon.–Fri.), 400,000 (Sat.).

Weeklies

Bankstown Canterbury Torch: Nabberly House, Cnr Marion St and Airport Ave, Bankstown, NSW 2200; tel. (2) 9795-0000; f. 1920; Wed.; Editor CHARLES ELIAS; circ. 84,421.

Northern District Times: 79 Rowe St, Eastwood, NSW 2122; tel. (2) 9858-1766; fax (2) 9804-6901; f. 1921; Wed.; Editor D. BARTOK; circ. 55,302.

The Parramatta Advertiser: 142 Macquarie St, Parramatta, NSW 2150; tel. (2) 9689-5500; fax (2) 9689-5353; Wed.; Editor LES POBJIE; circ. 96,052.

St George and Sutherland Shire Leader: 182 Forest Rd, Hurstville, NSW 2220; tel. (2) 9598-3999; fax (2) 9598-3985; f. 1960; Tue. and Thur.; Man. STELLA KYRIACOU; Editor CYPRIAN FERNANDES; circ. 140,287.

Sun-Herald: 201 Sussex St, GPOB 506, Sydney, NSW 2001; tel. (2) 9282-2822; fax (2) 9282-2151; f. 1953; Sun.; Editor ALAN REVELL; circ. 548,393.

Sunday Telegraph: 2 Holt St, Surry Hills, NSW 2010; tel. (2) 9288-3000; telex 20124; fax (2) 9288-3311; f. 1938; Editor ROY MILLER; circ. 675,193.

Northern Territory

Daily

Northern Territory News: Printers Place, POB 1300, Darwin 0801; tel. (8) 8944-9900; fax (8) 8981-6045; f. 1952; Mon.–Sat.; Gen. Man. D. KENNEDY; circ. 22,737.

Weekly

Sunday Territorian: Printers Place, GPOB 1300, Darwin 0801; tel. (8) 8944-9900; fax (8) 8981-6045; Sun.; Editor JOHN AMBROSE; circ. 23,940.

Queensland

Daily

Courier-Mail: 41 Campbell St, Bowen Hills, Brisbane 4006; tel. (7) 3252-6011; telex 40101; fax (7) 3252-6696; f. 1933; morning; Editor-in-Chief C. MITCHELL; circ. 219,646 (Mon.–Fri.), 330,005 (Sat.).

Weekly

Sunday Mail: Campbell St, Bowen Hills, Brisbane 4006; tel. (7) 3252-6011; telex 40110; fax (7) 3252-6692; f. 1923; Editor MICHAEL PRAIN; circ. 582,375.

South Australia

Daily

Advertiser: 121 King William St, Adelaide 5001; tel. (8) 8206-2220; fax (8) 8206-3669; f. 1858; morning; Editor STEVE HOWARD; circ. 199,689 (Mon.–Fri.), 264,876 (Sat.).

Weekly

Sunday Mail: 6th Floor, 121 King William St, Adelaide 5000; tel. (8) 8206-2000; fax (8) 8206-3646; f. 1912; Editor KERRY SULLIVAN; circ. 337,615.

Tasmania

Dailies

The Advocate: POB 63, Burnie 7320; tel. (3) 6430-1409; fax (3) 6430-1461; f. 1890; morning; Editor M. D. CHERRY; circ. 25,623.

Examiner: 71–75 Paterson St, POB 99A, Launceston 7250; tel. (3) 6331-5111; fax (3) 6334-7328; e-mail examiner@rpl.com.au; f. 1842; morning; independent; Editor R. J. SCOTT; circ. 38,721.

Mercury: 91–93 Macquarie St, Hobart 7000; tel. (3) 6230-0622; fax (3) 6230-0711; e-mail mercuryedletter@trump.net.au; f. 1854; morning; Man. Dir REX GARDNER; Editor I. MCCAUSLAND; circ. 52,197.

Weeklies

Sunday Examiner: 71–75 Paterson St, Launceston 7250; tel. (3) 6315-111; fax (3) 6347-328; f. 1924; Editor R. J. SCOTT; circ. 42,000.

Sunday Tasmanian: 91–93 Macquarie St, Hobart 7000; tel. (3) 6230-0622; fax (3) 6230-0711; e-mail mercuryedletter@trump.net.au; f. 1984; morning; Man. Dir REX GARDNER; Editor IAN MCCAUSLAND; circ. 53,449.

Victoria

Dailies

The Age: 250 Spencer St (cnr Lonsdale St), Melbourne 3000; tel. (3) 9600-4211; telex 30449; fax (3) 9670-7514; e-mail DPearson@theage.com.au; f. 1854; independent; morning; Publr and Editor-in-Chief STEVE HARRIS; Editor MICHAEL GAWENDA; circ. 237,474.

Herald Sun: HWT Tower, 40 City Rd, Southbank, Vic 3006; tel. (3) 9292-1111; fax (3) 9292-2112; f. 1840 as The Herald, merged with the Sun-News Pictorial (f. 1922) in 1990; 24-hour tabloid; Editor PETER BLUNDEN; circ. 558,500.

Weeklies

Progress Press: 360 Burwood Rd, Hawthorn 3122; tel. (3) 9818-0555; fax (3) 9818-0029; f. 1960; Tue.; News Editor STUART HOWIE; circ. 66,105.

Sunday Age: GPO Box 257C, Melbourne, Vic 3000; tel. (3) 9600-4211; fax (3) 9602-1856; f. 1989; Editor JILL BAKER; circ. 182,172.

Sunday Herald Sun: HWT Tower, 40 City Rd, Southbank, Vic 3006; tel. (3) 9292-2000; fax (3) 9292-2080; f. 1991; Editor ALAN HOWE; circ. 500,000.

Western Australia

Daily

The West Australian: West Australian Newspapers Ltd, 219 St George's Terrace, Perth 6000; POB D162, GPO Perth 6001; tel. (8) 9482-3111; telex 92109; fax (8) 9324-1416; f. 1833; morning; Editor P. R. MURRAY; circ. 229,180 (Mon.-Fri.), 383,392 (Sat.).

Weekly

Sunday Times: 34–42 Stirling St, Perth 6000; tel. (8) 9326-8326; telex 92015; fax (8) 9221-1121; f. 1897; Gen. Man. BILL REPARD; Man. Editor DON SMITH; circ. 352,254.

PRINCIPAL PERIODICALS

Weeklies and Fortnightlies

Australasian Post: 32 Walsh St, West Melbourne, Vic 3003; tel. (3) 9320-7020; fax (3) 9320-7409; f. 1864; factual, general interest, Australiana; Mon.; Editor GRAEME JOHNSTONE; circ. 81,640.

The Bulletin: 54 Park St, Sydney, NSW 2000; tel. (2) 9282-8000; telex 120514; fax (2) 9267-4359; f. 1880; Wed.; Editor-in-Chief Gerald Stone; circ. 100,523.

Business Review Weekly: Level 2, 469 La Trobe St, Melbourne, Vic 3000; tel. (3) 9603-3888; telex 38995; fax (3) 9670-4328; f. 1981; Chair. and Editorial Dir Robert Gottliebsen; Editor Ross Greenwood; circ. 73,205.

The Countryman: 219 St George's Terrace, Perth 6000; GPO Box D162, Perth 6001; tel. (8) 9482-3111; telex 94999; fax (8) 9482-3314; f. 1885; Thur.; farming; Editor John Dare; circ. 15,246.

The Medical Journal of Australia: Private Bag 901, North Sydney, NSW 2059; tel. (2) 9954-8666; fax (2) 9954-8699; e-mail ampco@magna.com.au; f. 1914; fortnightly; Editor Dr Martin van der Weyden; circ. 25,160.

New Idea: 32 Walsh St, Melbourne, Vic 3003; tel. (3) 9320-7000; fax (3) 9320-7439; weekly; women's; Editor Lucy Bulmer; circ. 546,218.

News Weekly: POB 66A, GPO Melbourne, Vic 3001; tel. (3) 9326-5757; fax (3) 9328-2877; f. 1943; publ. by National Civic Council; fortnightly; Sat.; political, social, educational and trade union affairs; Editor Peter Westmore; circ. 12,000.

People: 54 Park St, Sydney, NSW 2000; tel. (2) 9282-8743; fax (2) 9267-4365; weekly; Editor-in-Chief David Naylor; circ. 104,000.

Picture: GPOB 5201, Sydney, NSW 1028; tel. (2) 9282-8367; fax (2) 9267-4372; weekly; men's; Editor Brad Boxall; circ. 171,087.

Queensland Country Life: POB 586, Cleveland, Qld 4163; tel. (7) 3826-8200; fax (7) 3821-1236; f. 1935; Thur.; Editor Chris Griffith; circ. 33,900.

Stock and Land: 200 Rouse St, Port Melbourne, Vic 3207; tel. (3) 9287-0900; fax (3) 9287-0999; e-mail stockland@rpl.com.au; f. 1914; weekly; livestock, beef, wool markets, crops, dairy, regional and national news; Editor Mark Paterson; circ. 15,000.

That's Life!: Level 2, 140 William St, Sydney, NSW 2000; tel. (2) 9295-3300; fax (2) 9295-3483; f. 1994; weekly; features; Editor Bev Hadgraft; circ. 460,737.

Time Australia Magazine: GPOB 3873, Sydney, NSW 2001; tel. (2) 9925-2646; fax (2) 9954-0828; e-mail time.letters@time.com.au; Editor Steve Waterson; circ. 111,000.

TV Week: 32 Walsh St, Melbourne, Vic 3000; tel. (3) 9320-7000; fax (3) 9320-7409; f. 1957; Wed.; colour national; Editor Garry Williams; circ. 442,796.

The Weekly Times: Box 751F, GPO Melbourne, Vic 3001; tel. (3) 9292-2000; fax (3) 9292-2697; f. 1869; farming, regional issues, gardening, country life, sport; Wed.; Editor Hugh Jones; circ. 81,134.

Woman's Day: 54–58 Park St, POB 5245, Sydney, NSW 1028; tel. (2) 9282-8000; telex 120514; fax (2) 9267-4360; e-mail Womansday@publishing.acp.com.au; weekly; circulates throughout Australia and NZ; Editor Bunty Avieson; circ. 962,442.

Monthlies and Others

Architecture Australia: Architecture Media Pty Ltd, 3rd Floor, 4 Princes St, Port Melbourne, Vic 3207; tel. (3) 9646-4760; fax (3) 9646-4918; e-mail carolyn.winton@archmedia.com.au; f. 1904; 6 a year; Editor Davina Jackson; Man. Carolyn Winton; circ. 13,437.

Australian Cricket: POB 764, Darlinghurst, NSW 2010; tel. (2) 9581-9400; fax (2) 9360-5367; e-mail kcricket@netspace.net.au; f. 1968; monthly during summer; Editor-in-Chief Ken Piesse; circ. 15,000.

Australian Hi-Fi: POB 5555, St Leonards, NSW 2065; tel. (2) 9901-6156; fax (2) 9901-6198; f. 1970; monthly; Editor Greg Borrowman; circ. 24,000.

Australian Home Beautiful: 32 Walsh St, West Melbourne, Vic 3003; tel. (2) 9320-7000; telex 30578; fax (3) 9320-7410; f. 1925; monthly; Editor Wayne Buttner; circ. 111,685.

Australian House and Garden: 54 Park St, Sydney, NSW 2000; tel. (2) 9282-8456; telex 20514; fax (2) 9267-4912; f. 1948; monthly; design, decorating, renovating, gardens, food and travel; Editor Anny Friis-Clark; circ. 113,046.

Australian Journal of Mining: POB 1024, Richmond North, Vic 3121; tel. (3) 9429-5599; fax (3) 9427-0332; e-mail ajm@goldgroup.com.au; f. 1986; monthly; mining and exploration throughout Australia and South Pacific; Editor Geoffrey Gold; circ. 7,500.

Australian Journal of Pharmacy: Suite 5, 174–180 Pacific Highway, North Sydney, NSW 2060; tel. (2) 9955-3499; fax (2) 9922-6845; f. 1886; monthly; journal of the associated pharmaceutical orgs; Man. Editor Snezna Kerekovic; circ. 6,443.

Australian Law Journal: 44–50 Waterloo Rd, North Ryde, NSW 2113; tel. (2) 9936-6444; telex 27995; fax (2) 9888-2229; f. 1927; monthly; Editor Justice P. W. Young; circ 5,000.

Australian Photography: POB 606, Sydney, NSW 2001; tel. (2) 9281-2333; telex 121887; fax (2) 9281-2750; monthly; Editor Robin Nicols; circ. 10,323.

Australian Women's Weekly: 54 Park St, Sydney, NSW 2000; tel. (2) 9282-8000; telex 120514; fax (2) 9267-4459; f. 1933; monthly; Editorial Dir Nene King; circ. 880,384.

Belle: 54 Park St, Sydney, NSW 2000; tel. (2) 9282-8000; telex 32796; fax (2) 9267-8037; f. 1975; every 2 months; Editor Michaela Dunworth; circ. 48,800.

Better Homes and Gardens: 16th Floor, 213 Miller St, North Sydney, NSW 2060; tel. (2) 9956-1000; fax (2) 9956-1013; e-mail philippah@mm.com.au; f. 1978; 13 a year; Editor Toni Eatts; circ. 333,635.

Cleo: 54 Park St, Sydney, NSW 2000; POB 4088, Sydney, NSW 2001; tel. (2) 9282-8617; fax (2) 9267-4368; f. 1972; women's monthly; Editor Gina Johnson; circ. 263,353.

Commercial Photography: Box 606, GPO, Sydney, NSW 2001; tel. (2) 9288-2333; telex 121887; fax (2) 9281-2750; every 2 months; journal of the Professional Photographers Asscn of Australia and Photographic Industry Marketing Asscn of Australia; Editor Saima Morel; circ. 3,514.

Cosmopolitan: 54 Park St, Sydney, NSW 1028; tel. (2) 9282-8000; telex 120514; fax (2) 9267-4457; e-mail cosmo@publishing.acp.com.au; f. 1973; monthly; Editor Mia Freedman; circ. 237,579.

Dolly: 54–58 Park St, Sydney, NSW 1028; tel. (2) 9282-8437; fax (2) 9267-4911; f. 1970; monthly; for young women; Editor Susie Pitts; circ. 177,205.

Economic Record: Dept of Economics, University of Melbourne, Vic 3052; tel. (3) 9344-5311; fax (3) 9347-3986; f. 1925; quarterly; journal of Economic Soc. of Australia; Editor Prof. R. Williams; circ. 3,500.

Ecos: CSIRO, POB 1139, Collingwood, Vic 3066; tel. (3) 9662-7500; fax (3) 9662-7555; f. 1974; quarterly; reports of CSIRO environmental research findings for the non-specialist reader; Editor Bryony Bennett; circ. 8,000.

Electronics Australia: POB 199, Alexandria, NSW 2015; tel. (2) 9353-0620; fax (2) 9353-0613; f. 1922; monthly; technical, radio, television, microcomputers, hi-fi and electronics; Man. Editor Jamieson Rowe; circ. 19,675.

Elle: 54 Park St, Sydney, NSW 2000; tel. (2) 9282-8790; fax (2) 9267-4375; f. 1990; monthly; Editor Deborah Thomas; circ. 68,154.

Family Circle: Murdoch Magazines, Level 13, 213 Miller St, North Sydney, NSW 2060; tel. (2) 9956-1000; fax (2) 9956-1020; 14 a year; circ. 300,000.

Gardening Australia: POB 199, Alexandria, NSW 2015; tel. (2) 9353-6666; fax (2) 9353-0935; f. 1991; monthly; Editor Anne Lawton; circ. 72,561.

Houses: Architecture Media Pty Ltd, 3rd Floor, 4 Princes St, Port Melbourne, Vic 3207; tel. (3) 9646-4760; fax (3) 9646-4918; e-mail sue.harris@archmedia.com.au; f. 1989; 2 a year; Editor Sue Harris; circ. 25,133.

HQ: 54 Park St, Sydney, NSW 2000; tel. (2) 9282-8260; fax (2) 9267-3616; f. 1989; every 2 months; Publr Tim Trumper; Editor Kathy Bail; circ. 34,102.

Manufacturer's Monthly: 46 Porter St, Prahran, Vic 3181; tel. (3) 9936-8700; fax (3) 9245-7606; f. 1961; Editor Lisa Cruz; circ. 15,510.

Modern Boating: The Federal Publishing Co Pty Ltd, 180 Bourke Rd, Alexandria, NSW 2015; tel. (2) 9353-6666; fax (2) 9353-0613; f. 1965; every 2 months; Editor Mark Rothfield; circ. 9,007.

Motor: 54 Park St, Sydney, NSW 2000; tel (2) 9282-8467; fax (2) 9267-4373; f. 1954; monthly; Editor Ewen Page; circ. 37,785.

New Woman: Murdoch Magazines, 213 Miller St, North Sydney, NSW 2060; tel. (2) 9956-1000; fax (2) 9956-1088; monthly; Editor Gay Bryant; circ. 117,259.

The Open Road: 151 Clarence St, Sydney, NSW 2000; tel. (2) 9292-9275; fax (2) 9292-9069; f. 1927; every 2 months; journal of National Roads and Motorists' Asscn (NRMA); Editor Jillian McFarlane; circ. 1,528,186.

Personal Investment: Level 2, 469 La Trobe St, Melbourne, Vic 3000; tel. (3) 9603-3888; fax (3) 9670-4328; internet http://www.personalinvestment.com.au; monthly; Editor Robin Bowerman; circ. 65,785.

Reader's Digest: 26–32 Waterloo St, Surry Hills, NSW 2010; tel. (2) 9690-6111; fax (2) 9690-6211; monthly; Editor-in-Chief Bruce Heilbuth; circ. 505,477.

Street Machine: Locked Bag 756, Epping, NSW 2121; tel. (2) 9868-4832; fax (2) 9869-7390; e-mail streetmachine@acp-syme.com.au; Editor Mark Oastler; circ. 55,000.

TV Hits: 140 William St, Sydney, NSW; tel. (2) 9295-3300; fax (2) 9281-5350; f. 1988; monthly; circ. 114,509.

TV Soap: 55 Chandos St, St Leonards, NSW 2065; tel. (2) 9901-6100; fax (2) 9901-6166; f. 1983; monthly; Editor Ben Mitchell; circ. 85,751.

Vogue Australia: 170 Pacific Highway, Greenwich, NSW 2065; tel. (2) 9964-3888; fax (2) 9964-3882; f. 1959; monthly; fashion; Editor MARION HUME; circ. 62,130.

Wildlife Research: CSIRO Publishing, 150 Oxford St, POB 1139, Collingwood, Vic 3066; tel. (3) 9662-7622; fax (3) 9662-7611; e-mail david.morton@publish.csiro.au; f. 1974; 6 a year; Man. Editor D. W. MORTON; circ. 1,000.

Your Garden: 32 Walsh St, West Melbourne, Vic 3003; tel. (3) 9320-7000; fax (3) 9929-0244; monthly; Editor TONY FAWCETT; circ. 66,672.

NEWS AGENCIES

AAP Information Services: Locked Bag 21, Grosvenor Place, Sydney, NSW 2000; tel. (2) 9322-8000; fax (2) 9322-8888; f. 1983; owned by major daily newspapers of Australia; Chair. and CEO C. L. CASEY.

Foreign Bureaux

Agence France-Presse (AFP): 7th Floor, 259 George St, Sydney, NSW 2000; tel. (2) 9251-1544; fax (2) 9251-5230; Bureau Chief RON WALL.

Agenzia Nazionale Stampa Associata (ANSA) (Italy): Suite 4, 2 Grosvenor St, Bondi Junction, NSW 2022; tel. (2) 9369-1427; fax (2) 9369-4351; e-mail ansasyd@ozemail.com.au; Bureau Chief CLAUDIO MARCELLO.

Deutsche Presse-Agentur (dpa) (Germany): 3/73 Darley Rd, Manly, NSW 2095; tel. (2) 9977-0478; Correspondent ALEXANDER HOFMAN.

Informatsionnoye Telegrafnoye Agentstvo Rossii—Telegrafnoye Agentstvo Suverennykh Stran (ITAR—TASS) (Russia): 2 Clyde St, Bandick, Sydney, NSW 2031; tel. (2) 9398-6674; fax (2) 9717-3606; Correspondent SERGEI MSTISLAVOVICH ALMAZOV.

Jiji Press (Australia) Pty Ltd (Japan): Paxton House, 5th Floor, 90 Pitt St, Sydney, NSW 2000; tel. (2) 9221-6148; telex 75974; fax (2) 9221-6204; Bureau Chief MASANORI GURI.

Kyodo News Service (Japan): Level 7, 9 Lang St, Sydney, NSW 2000; tel. (2) 9251-5240; fax (2) 9251-4980; Bureau Chief MASANORI SUZUKI.

Reuters Australia Pty Ltd: Level 30, 60 Margaret St, Sydney, NSW 2000; Bureau Chief TED KERR.

United Press International (UPI) (USA): Suite 901A, 1 Newland St, Bondi Junction, Sydney, NSW 2022; tel. (2) 9369-2393; telex 20578; fax (2) 9387-5609; Bureau Chief BILL PERRY.

Xinhua (New China) News Agency (People's Republic of China): 50 Russell St, Hackett, Canberra, ACT 2602; tel. (2) 6248-6369; fax (2) 6257-4706; Correspondent TAO ZHIPENG.

The Central News Agency (Taiwan) and the New Zealand Press Association are represented in Sydney, and Antara (Indonesia) is represented in Canberra.

PRESS ASSOCIATIONS

Australian Press Council: Suite 303, 149 Castlereagh St, Sydney, NSW 2000; tel. (2) 9261-1930; fax (2) 9267-6826; Chair. Prof. DAVID FLINT.

Australian Suburban Newspapers Association: POB 19, Hawthorn, Vic 3122, tel. (3) 9818-0055; fax (3) 9819-5904; Admin. Sec. LINDA TOCCHET.

Country Press Association of New South Wales Inc: POB Q182, Queen Victoria Bldg, Sydney, NSW 2000; tel. (2) 9299-4658; fax (2) 9299-1892; f. 1900; Exec. Dir D. J. SOMMERLAD; 120 mems.

Country Press Association of SA Incorporated: 198 Greenhill Rd, Eastwood, SA 5063; tel. (8) 8373-6533; fax (8) 8373-6544; f. 1912; represents South Australian country newspapers; Pres. B. PRICE; Exec. Dir M. R. TOWNSEND.

Country Press Australia: POB Q182, Queen Victoria Bldg, Sydney, NSW 2000; tel. (2) 9299-4658; fax (2) 9299-1892; f. 1906; Exec. Dir D. J. SOMMERLAD; 420 mems.

Queensland Country Press Association: POB 103, Paddington, Qld 4064; tel. (7) 3356-0033; Pres. W. CREIGHTON; Sec. N. D. MCLARY.

Regional Dailies of Australia Ltd: 255 Whitehorse Rd, Balwyn, Vic 3103; tel. (3) 9888-4166; f. 1936; Chair. P. E. ZULPO; CEO R. W. SINCLAIR; 34 mems.

Tasmanian Press Association Pty Ltd: 71–75 Paterson St, Launceston, Tas 7250; tel. (3) 6320-255; Sec. P. B. COOPER.

Victorian Country Press Association Ltd: 33 Rathdowne St, Carlton, Vic 3053; tel. (3) 9662-3244; fax (3) 9663-7433; f. 1910; Pres. I. PURDEY; Exec. Dir J. E. RAY; 114 mems.

Publishers

Addison Wesley Longman Australia Pty Ltd: 95 Coventry St, South Melbourne, Vic 3205; tel. (3) 9697-0666; fax (3) 9699-2041; f. 1957; mainly educational, academic, computer, some general; Man. Dir ROBERT W. FISHER.

Allen and Unwin Pty Ltd: 9 Atchison St, St Leonards, NSW 2065; tel. (2) 9901-4088; fax (2) 9906-2218; fiction, trade, educational, children's; Man. Dir PATRICK A. GALLAGHER.

Australasian Medical Publishing Co Ltd: Level 1, 76 Berry St, North Sydney, NSW 2060; tel. (2) 9954-8666; fax (2) 9956-7644; e-mail ampco@magna.com.au; f. 1913; scientific, medical and educational; CEO Dr MARTIN VAN DER WEYDEN.

Butterworths: Tower 2, 475 Victoria Ave, Chatswood, NSW 2067; tel. (2) 9422-2222; fax (2) 9422-2444; f. 1910; div. of Reed International Books Australia Pty Ltd; legal and commercial; Man. Dir MURRAY HAMILTON.

Cambridge University Press (Australia): 10 Stamford Road, Oakleigh, Melbourne, Vic 3166; tel. (3) 9568-0322; fax (3) 9569-9292; e-mail info@cup.edu.au; scholarly and educational; Dir KIM W. HARRIS.

Commonwealth Scientific and Industrial Research Organisation (CSIRO Publishing): 150 Oxford St, POB 1139, Collingwood, Vic 3066; tel. (3) 9662-7500; fax (3) 9662-7555; f. 1926; scientific and technical journals, books, magazines, videos, CD-ROMs; Gen. Man. P. W. REEKIE.

Doubleday Australia Pty Ltd: 91 Mars Rd, Lane Cove, NSW 2066; tel. (2) 9427-0377; fax (2) 9427-6973; educational, trade, non-fiction, Australiana; Man. Dir DAVID HARLEY.

Encyclopaedia Britannica (Australia) Inc: 12 Anella Ave, Castle Hill, NSW 2154; tel. (2) 9680-5666; fax (2) 9899-3231; e-mail ebsales@eba.com.au; reference, education, art, science and commerce; Man. Dir TIM PETHICK.

Gordon and Gotch Ltd: 25–37 Huntingdale Rd, Private Bag 290, Burwood, Vic 3125; tel. (3) 9805-1700; fax (3) 9808-0714; general; Chair. and Man. Dir I. D. GOLDING.

Harcourt Brace and Co Australia Pty Ltd: 30–52 Smidmore St, Marrickville, NSW 2204; tel. (2) 9517-8999; fax (2) 9517-2249; e-mail service@harcourt.com.au; business, science, humanities, social science, engineering, medicine, etc.; Man. Dir BRIAN M. BRENNAN.

Harlequin Enterprises (Australia) Pty Ltd: Units 2 and 3, 3 Gibbes St, Chatswood, NSW 2067; tel. (2) 9417-97333; fax (2) 9417-95232; romantic fiction; Man. Dir NANCY PETERS.

Hodder Headline Australia Pty Ltd: 10–16 South St, Rydalmere, NSW 2116; tel. (2) 9841-2800; fax (2) 9841-2810; fiction, general, educational, technical, children's; Man. Dir MALCOLM EDWARDS.

Hyland House Publishing Pty Ltd: Hyland House, 387–389 Clarendon St, South Melbourne, Vic 3205; tel. (3) 9696-9064; fax (3) 9696-9065; e-mail hyland@peg.apc.org; internet www.peg.apc.org/~hyland; f. 1976; trade, general, Aboriginal, Asian-Pacific and children's; Rep. ANDREW WILKINS.

Jacaranda Wiley Ltd: POB 1226, Milton, Qld 4064; tel. (7) 3859-9755; fax (7) 3859-9715; e-mail headoffice@jacwiley.com.au; f. 1954; educational, reference and trade; Man. Dir PETER DONOUGHUE.

Lansdowne Publishing: Level 1, Argyle Centre, 18 Argyle St, Sydney, NSW 2000; tel. (2) 9240-9222; fax (2) 9241-4818; Australiana, cookery, gardening, health, history, pet care; Chief Exec. MARGARET SEALE.

LBC Information Services: 50 Waterloo Road, North Ryde, NSW 2113; tel. (2) 9936-6444; telex 27995; fax (2) 9888-7240; e-mail lbccustomer@lbc.com.au; legal and professional; Man. Dir E. J. COSTIGAN.

Lothian Books: 11 Munro St, Port Melbourne, Vic 3207; tel. (3) 9645-1544; fax (3) 9646-4882; f. 1888; general, gardening, health, juvenile, craft, business, New Age, self-help; Man. Dir PETER LOTHIAN.

McGraw-Hill Book Publishing Co Australia Pty Ltd: 4 Barcoo St, Roseville, Sydney, NSW 2069; tel. (2) 9417-4288; fax (2) 9417-8872; e-mail books@lothian.com.au; educational and technical; Man. Dir FIRGAL ADAMS.

Maxwell Macmillan Publishing Australia Pty Ltd: 2A Lord St, Botany, NSW 2019; tel. (2) 9316-9444; fax (2) 9316-9485; f. 1949; educational, general, professional; Man. Dirs JERRY MAYER, CHARLES IOSSI.

Melbourne University Press: 268 Drummond St, Carlton South, Vic 3053; tel. (3) 9347-3455; fax (3) 9349-2527; e-mail publish@mup.unimelb.edu.au; f. 1922; academic, educational, Australiana; Chair. Prof. BARRY SHEEHAN; Dir JOHN MECKAN.

Murdoch Books: 11th Floor, 213 Miller St, North Sydney, NSW 2060; tel. (2) 9956-1000; fax (2) 9956-1922; general non-fiction; Publr ANNE WILSON; Man. Dir MATT HANDBURY.

National Library of Australia: Parkes Place, Canberra, ACT 2600; tel. (2) 6262-1111; telex 62100; fax (2) 6257-1703; e-mail ahealy@nla.gov.au; f. 1961; national bibliographical services; Publications Dir Dr PAUL HETHERINGTON.

Nelson ITP: 102 Dodds St, South Melbourne, Vic 3205; tel. (3) 9685-4111; fax (3) 9685-4199; educational; Man. Dir G. J. BROWNE.

Oxford University Press: 253 Normanby Rd, South Melbourne, Vic 3205; tel. (3) 9646-4200; fax (3) 9646-3251; f. 1908; general non-fiction and educational; Man. Dir MAREK PALKA.

Pan Macmillan Australia Pty Ltd: Level 18, St Martin's Tower, 31 Market St, Sydney, NSW 2000; tel. (2) 9261-5611; fax (2) 9261-5047; general, reference, children's, fiction, non-fiction; Chair. R. GIBB.

Pearson Professional (Australia) Pty Ltd: Kings Gardens, 95 Coventry St, South Melbourne, Vic 3205; tel. (3) 9699-5400; fax (3) 9696-5205; f. 1995; incorporates Churchill Livingstone.

Penguin Books Australia Ltd: 487/493 Maroondah Highway, POB 257, Ringwood, Vic 3134; tel. (3) 9871-2400; fax (3) 9870-9618; f. 1946; general; Man. Dir PETER FIELD; Publishing Dir ROBERT SESSIONS.

Random House Australia Pty Ltd: 20 Alfred St, Milsons Point, NSW 2061; tel. (2) 9954-9966; fax (2) 9954-4562; e-mail random@randomhouse.com.au; fiction, non-fiction, general and children's; Man. Dir ERNIE F. MASON.

Reader's Digest (Australia) Pty Ltd: POB 4353, Sydney, NSW 2000; tel. (2) 9690-6111; fax (2) 9699-8165; general; Man. Dir WILLIAM B. TOOHEY.

Reed Books: MDC 5000, Kew, Vic 3101; tel. (3) 9261-5555; fax (3) 9261-5566; general fiction, non-fiction, incl. natural history; Publr BILL TEMPLEMAN.

Reed Books Australia: POB 460, Port Melbourne, Vic 3207; tel. (3) 9646-6688; fax (3) 9646-6925; educational and general; Chair. RICHARD CHARKIN; Man. Dir (Group) SANDY GRANT.

Reed Educational & Professional Publishing: 22 Salmon St, POB 460, Port Melbourne, Vic 3207; tel. (3) 9245-7111; fmrly Rigby Heinemann; primary, secondary and languages educational; Man. Dir JACK MULCAHY.

Scholastic Australia Pty Ltd: Railway Crescent, Lisarow, POB 579, Gosford, NSW 2250; tel. (2) 4328-3555; fax (2) 4323-3827; internet http://www.scholastic.com.au; f. 1968; educational and children's; Man. Dir KEN JOLLY.

Schwartz Publishing (Victoria) Pty Ltd: 45 Flinders Lane, Melbourne, Vic 3000; tel. (3) 9654-2000; telex 30625; fax (3) 9650-5418; fiction, non-fiction; Dir MORRY SCHWARTZ.

Simon and Schuster Australia: 20 Barcoo St, POB 507, East Roseville, NSW 2069; tel. (2) 9417-3255; fax (2) 9417-3188; educational, trade, reference and general; Man. Dir JON ATTENBOROUGH.

Thames and Hudson (Australia) Pty Ltd: 11 Central Boulevard, Portside Business Park, Port Melbourne, Vic 3207; tel. (3) 9646-7788; fax (3) 9646-8790; art, history, archaeology, architecture and photography; Man. Dir RICHARD M. GILMOUR.

D. W. Thorpe: 18 Salmon St, Private Bag 20, Port Melbourne, Vic 3207; tel. (3) 9245-7370; fax (3) 9245-7395; e-mail customer.service@thorpe.com.au; bibliographic, library and book trade reference; Man. Dir M. WEBSTER.

Time Life Australia Pty Ltd: 3 Talavera Rd, North Ryde, NSW 2113; tel. (2) 9856-2212; fax (2) 9856-2255; general and educational; Man. Dir JOHN HALL.

Transworld Publishers (Australia) Pty Ltd: 40 Yeo St, Neutral Bay, NSW 2089; tel. (2) 9908-4366; fax (2) 9953-8563; fiction and non-fiction, romance, politics, humour, health, juvenile, etc.; Man. Dir GEOFFREY S. RUMPF.

University of New South Wales Press Ltd: Sydney, NSW 2052; tel. (2) 9398-8900; fax (2) 9398-3408; e-mail info.press@unsw.edu.au; f. 1961; scholarly, general and tertiary texts; Man. Dir Dr ROBIN DERRICOURT.

University of Queensland Press: POB 42, St Lucia, Qld 4067; tel. (7) 3365-2127; fax (7) 3365-7579; f. 1948; scholarly and general cultural interest, incl. Black Australian writers, adult and children's fiction; Gen. Man. LAURIE MULLER.

University of Western Australia Press: c/o University of Western Australia, Nedlands, WA 6907; tel. (8) 9380-3670; fax (8) 9380-1027; f. 1954; history, environment, economy and culture of WA, children's, biography, autobiography, botanical guides and academic works; Dir Dr JENNY GREGORY.

Government Publishing House

Australian Government Publishing Service: GPOB 84, Canberra, ACT 2601; tel. (2) 6295-4411; fax (2) 6295-4455; f. 1970; Gen. Man. ALAN LAW.

PUBLISHERS' ASSOCIATION

Australian Publishers Association Ltd: Suite 59, Level 3, 89 Jones St, Ultimo, NSW 2007; tel. (2) 9281-9788; fax (2) 9281-1073; f. 1949; c. 150 mems; Pres. PETER DONOUGHUE; Dir SUSAN BLACKWELL.

Broadcasting and Communications

TELECOMMUNICATIONS

Optus Communications Pty Ltd: tel. (2) 9342-7800; fax (2) 9342-7100; general and mobile telecommunication services; Chief Exec. PETER HOWELL-DAVIES.

Telstra Corpn Ltd: Locked Bag 6660, GPO Sydney; tel. (2) 9287-4677; fax (2) 9287-5869; internet http://www.telstra.com.au; general and mobile telecommunication services; Group Man. Dir ZIGGY SWITKOWSKI.

Vodafone Pty Ltd: Tower A, 799 Pacific Highway, Chatswood, NSW 2067; tel. (2) 9878-7000; fax (2) 9878-7788; mobile telecommunication services.

Regulatory Authority

Australian Communications Authority (ACA): POB 7443, St Kilda Rd, Melbourne, Vic 3004; tel. (3) 9828-7300; fax (3) 9820-3021; e-mail webmaster@aca.gov.au; f. 1997 through merger of Australian Telecommunications Authority and Spectrum Management Agency; regulator for telecommunications and radiocommunications; Chair. TONY SHAW.

BROADCASTING

Many programmes are provided by the non-commercial statutory corporation, the Australian Broadcasting Corporation (ABC). Commercial radio and television services are provided by stations operated by companies under licences granted and renewed by the Australian Broadcasting Authority (ABA). They rely for their income on the broadcasting of advertisements. In mid-1993 there were 166 commercial radio stations in operation, and 44 commercial television stations.

In 1994 there were an estimated 23.0m. radio receivers and 8.7m. television receivers in use.

Australian Broadcasting Corporation (ABC): 700 Harris St, Ultimo, POB 9994, Sydney, NSW 2001; tel. (2) 9333-1500 (radio), (2) 9437-8000 (television); telex 176464 (radio), 120432 (television); fax (2) 9333-2603 (radio), (2) 9950-3055 (television); f. 1932 as Australian Broadcasting Commission; one national television network operating on about 600 transmitters and six radio networks operating on more than 6,000 transmitters; Chair. DONALD MCDONALD; Man. Dir BRIAN JOHNS.

Radio Australia: international service broadcast by short wave and satellite in English, French, Indonesian, Standard Chinese, Cantonese, Khmer, Neo-Melanesian, Thai and Vietnamese.

Australia Television: international satellite service; broadcasts to more than 30 countries and territories in Asia and the Pacific.

Radio

Federation of Australian Radio Broadcasters Ltd: POB 299, St Leonards, NSW 2065; tel. (2) 9906-5944; fax (2) 9906-5128; asscn of privately-owned stations; CEO A. M. KING.

Major Commercial Broadcasting Station Licensees

5AD Broadcasting Co Pty Ltd: 201 Tynte St, Nth Adelaide, SA 5006; tel. (8) 8300-1000; fax (8) 8300-1020; also operates Southern State Broadcasters Pty Ltd—5DN; Group Gen. Man. WAYNE CLOUTEN.

Associated Communications Enterprises (ACE) Radio Broadcasters Pty Ltd: POB 7515, Melbourne, Vic 3004; tel. (3) 9645-9877; fax (3) 9645-9886; operates five stations; Man. Dir S. EVERETT.

Austereo Ltd: Ground Level, 180 St Kilda Rd, St Kilda, Vic 3182; tel. (3) 9230-1051; fax (3) 9593-9007; operates 12 stations; Man. Dir PETER HARVIE.

Broadcast Media Group Pty Ltd: POB 1005, Griffith, NSW 2680; tel. (2) 6362-2144; fax (2) 6362-9439; operates 12 radio stations, incl. Radio 2GZ; also one TV station; Man. Dir W. R. GAMBLE.

Broadcast Operations Pty Ltd: POB 493, Griffith, NSW 2680; tel. (2) 6962-4500; fax (2) 6962-6291; operates seven stations; Dir B. CARALIS.

Century Radio: 28 Sharp St, Cooma, NSW 2630; tel. (2) 6451-1521; fax (2) 6452-1006; operates three stations; Man. Dir K. BLYTON.

Grant Broadcasters Pty Ltd: POB 540, Nowra, NSW 2541; tel. (2) 4423-0055; fax (2) 4421-0032; operates seven stations; Man. ROGER SUMMERILL.

Greater Cairns Radio Ltd: Virginia House, Abbott St, Cairns, Qld 4870; tel. (7) 4050-0846; fax (7) 4051-8060; Gen. Man. J. ELLER.

KICK AM 1269: 186 Blues Point Rd, North Sydney, NSW 2060; tel. (2) 9922-1270; fax (2) 9954-3117; f. 1931; fmrly Radio 2SM; CEO TREVOR SMITH.

Macquarie Radio Network Pty Ltd: POB 4290, Sydney, NSW 2001; tel. (2) 9269-0646; fax (2) 9287-2772; operates 2GB and 2CH; CEO GEORGE BUSCHMAN.

Moree Broadcasting and Development Company Ltd: 87–89 Balo St, Moree, NSW 2400; tel. (2) 6752-1155; fax (2) 6752-2601; operates two stations; Man. KEN BIRCH.

Radiowest Kalgoorlie: 89 Egan St, Kalgoorlie, WA; tel. (8) 9021-2666; fax (8) 9091-2209; e-mail radio6KG@gold.net.au; f. 1931; operates two stations; Man. MERRYN VINCENT.

Regional Broadcasters (Australia) Pty: McDowal St, Roma, Qld 4455; tel. (7) 4622-1800; fax (7) 4622-3697; Chair. G. MCVEAN.

Rural Press Ltd: 12 Todman Ave, Kensington, NSW 2033; tel. (2) 9313-8333; fax (2) 9663-2112; operates 22 stations; Gen. Man. PETER HLYWA.

SEA FM Pty Ltd: POB 5910, Gold Coast Mail Centre, Bundall, Qld 4217; tel. (7) 5591-5000; fax (7) 5591-6080; operates six stations; Chair. S. J. WILLMOTT.

Southern Cross Broadcasting (Australia) Ltd: see under Television.

Supernetwork Radio Pty Ltd: POB 97, Coolangatta, Qld 4225; tel. (7) 5524-4497; fax (7) 5554-3970; operates 12 stations; Chair. W. CARALIS.

Tamworth Radio Development Company Pty Ltd: POB 497, Tamworth, NSW 2340; tel. (2) 6765-7055; fax (2) 6765-2762; operates five stations; Man. W. A. MORRISON.

Tasmanian Broadcasting Network (TBN): POB 665G, Launceston, Tas 7250; tel. (3) 6431-2555; fax (3) 6431-3188; operates three stations; Chair. K. FINDLAY.

Wesgo Ltd: POB 234, Seven Hills, NSW 2147; tel. (2) 9831-7611; fax (2) 9831-2001; operates eight stations; CEO G. W. RICE.

Television

Federation of Australian Commercial Television Stations (FACTS): 44 Avenue Rd, Mosman, NSW 2088; tel. (2) 9960-2622; fax (2) 9969-3520; f. 1960; represents all commercial television stations; Chair. GARY RICE; Gen. Man. TONY BRANIGAN.

Commercial Television Station Licensees

Amalgamated Television Services Pty Ltd: Mobbs Lane, Epping, NSW 2121; tel. (2) 9877-7777; telex 20250; fax (2) 9877-7888; f. 1956; originating station for Seven Network TV programming; Man. Dir A. BATEMAN.

Australian Capital Television Pty Ltd (Ten Capital): Private Bag 10, Dickson, ACT 2602; tel. (2) 6242-2400; fax (2) 6241-7230; f. 1962; Gen. Man. TONY FORREST.

Brisbane TV Ltd: GPOB 604, Brisbane, Qld 4001; tel. (7) 3369-7777; fax (7) 3368-2970; f. 1959; operates one station; mem. of Seven Network; Man. Dir L. M. RILEY.

Broken Hill Television Ltd: POB 472, Rocky Hill, Broken Hill, NSW 2880; tel. (8) 8087-6013; fax (8) 8087-8492; f. 1968; operates one station; Chair. PETER STORROCK; Chief Exec. D. WESTON.

General Television Corporation Pty Ltd: 22–46 Bendigo St, POB 100, Richmond, Vic 3121; tel. (3) 9420-3111; telex 30189; fax (3) 9429-1977; f. 1957; operates one station; Man. Dir I. J. JOHNSON.

Golden West Network: Private Mail Bag, Geraldton, WA 6530; tel. (8) 9921-4422; fax (8) 9921-8096.

Golden West Network Pty Ltd: POB 1062, West Perth, WA 6872; tel. (8) 9481-0050; fax (8) 9321-2470; f. 1967; operates three stations (SSW10, VEW and WAW); Gen. Man. W. FENWICK.

HSV Channel 7 Pty Ltd: 119 Wells St, South Melbourne, Vic 3205; tel. (3) 9697-7777; telex 30707; fax (3) 9697-7888; f. 1956; operates one station; Chair. KERRY STOKES; Man. Dir BRIAN MALLON.

Imparja Television Pty Ltd: POB 52, Alice Springs, NT 0870; tel. (8) 8950-1411; fax (8) 8953-0322; e-mail imparja@ozemail.com.au; CEO CORALLIE FERGUSON.

Independent Broadcasters of Australia Pty Ltd: POB 285, Sydney, NSW 2001; tel. (2) 9264-9144; fax (2) 9264-6334; fmrly Regional Television Australia Pty Ltd; Chair. GRAEME J. GILBERTSON; Sec. JEFF EATHER.

Mt Isa Television Pty Ltd: 110 Canooweal St, Mt Isa, Qld 4825; tel. (7) 4743-8888; fax (7) 4743-9803; f. 1971; operates one station; Station Man. LYALL GREY.

MTN Television Pty Ltd: Remembrance Driveway, Griffith, NSW 2680; tel. (2) 6962-4500; fax (2) 6962-7774; Man. Dir R. GAMBLE.

NBN Ltd: Mosbri Crescent, POB 750L, Newcastle, NSW 2300; tel. (2) 4929-2933; fax (2) 4926-2936; f. 1962; operates one station; Man. Dir DENIS LEDBURY.

Network Ten Ltd: GPOB 10, Sydney, NSW 2001; tel. (2) 9650-1010; fax (2) 9650-1170; operates Australian TV network and commercial stations in Sydney, Melbourne, Brisbane, Perth and Adelaide; CEO JOHN MCALPINE.

Nine Network Australia Ltd: POB 27, Willoughby, NSW 2068; tel. (2) 9906-9999; fax (2) 9958-2279; f. 1956; division of Publishing and Broadcasting Ltd; operates three stations: TCN Channel Nine Pty Ltd (Sydney), Queensland Television Ltd (Brisbane) and General Television Corporation Ltd (Melbourne); CEO DAVID LECKIE.

Northern Rivers Television Pty Ltd: Peterson Rd, Locked Bag 1000, Coffs Harbour, NSW 2450; tel. (2) 6652-2777; fax (2) 6652-3034; f. 1965; CEO GARRY DRAFFIN.

NWS Channel 9: 202 Tynte St, North Adelaide 5006; tel. (8) 8267-0111; fax (8) 8267-3996; f. 1959; Man. Dir JOHN W. LAMB.

Prime Television Group: Level 6, 1 Pacific Highway, North Sydney, NSW 2060; tel. (2) 9965-7700; fax (2) 9965-7729; Chair. PAUL RAMSAY; CEO GEORGE BROWN.

Prime Television (Northern) Pty Ltd: POB 2077, Elermore Vale, NSW 2287; tel. (2) 4952-0500; fax (2) 4952-0507; Gen. Man. BRAD JONES.

Prime Television (Southern) Pty Ltd: POB 465, Orange, NSW 2800; tel. (2) 6362-2288; fax (2) 6363-1889; Gen. Man. D. BRIDEKIRK.

Prime Television (Victoria) Pty Ltd: Sunraysia Highway, Ballarat, Vic 3350; tel. (3) 5337-1777; fax (3) 5337-1700; Gen. Man. DOUG EDWARDS.

Queensland Television Ltd: POB 72, GPO Brisbane, Qld 4001; tel. (7) 3214-9999; fax (7) 3369-3512; f. 1959; operates one station; Gen. Man. IAN R. MÜLLER.

Riverland Television Pty Ltd: Murray Bridge Rd, POB 471, Loxton, SA 5333; tel. (8) 8584-6891; telex 80313; fax (8) 8584-5062; f. 1976; operates one station; Exec. Chair. E. H. URLWIN; Gen. Man. W. L. MUDGE.

Seven Network Ltd: 14th Floor, 1 Pacific Highway, North Sydney, NSW 2060; owns Amalgamated Television Services Pty Ltd (Sydney), Brisbane TV Ltd (Brisbane), HSV Channel 7 Pty Ltd (Melbourne), South Australian Telecasters Ltd (Adelaide) and TVW Enterprises Ltd (Perth); Chair. KERRY STOKES; Man. Dir GARY RICE.

Seven Queensland: 140–142 Horton Parade, Maroochydore, Qld 4558; tel. (7) 5430-1777; fax (7) 5479-1714; f. 1965; fmrly Sunshine Television Network Ltd; Man. Dir D. R. ASTLEY.

South Australian Telecasters Ltd: 45–49 Park Terrace, Gilberton, SA 5081; tel. (8) 8342-7777; fax (8) 8342-7717; f. 1965; operates SAS Channel 7; mem. of Seven Network; Man. Dir R. SMITHWICK.

South East Telecasters Ltd: 51 John Watson Drive, POB 821, Mount Gambier, SA 5290; tel. (8) 8721-8888; fax (8) 8721-8811; f. 1966; operates two stations; Chair. A. A. SCOTT; Man. Dir G. J. GILBERTSON.

Southern Cross Broadcasting (Australia) Ltd: 43–49 Bank St, South Melbourne, Vic 3205; tel. (3) 9243-2000; fax (3) 9690-0937; f. 1932; operates three TV and four radio stations; CEO A. E. BELL.

Southern Cross Television (TNT9) Pty Ltd: Watchorn St, Launceston, Tas 7250; tel. (3) 6344-0202; fax (3) 6343-0340; f. 1962; operates one station; Gen. Man. BRUCE ABRAHAM.

Special Broadcasting Service (SBS): 14 Herbert St, Artarmon, NSW 2064; tel. (2) 9430-2828; fax (2) 9430-3700; internet http://www.SBS.com.au; f. 1980; national multi-cultural broadcaster of TV and radio; Man. Dir QUANG LUU (acting).

Spencer Gulf Telecasters Ltd: POB 305, Port Pirie, SA 5540; tel. (8) 8632-2555; fax (8) 8633-0984; e-mail westond@ozemail.com.au; f. 1968; operates two stations; Chair. P. M. STURROCK; Chief Exec. D. WESTON.

Swan Television & Radio Broadcasters Pty Ltd: POB 99, Tuart Hill, WA 6060; tel. (8) 9449-9999; fax (8) 9449-9904; Gen. Man. P. BOWEN.

Telecasters Australia Ltd (Ten Queensland): 12 The Strand, Townsville, Qld 4810; tel. (7) 4721-3377; fax (7) 4721-1705; operates eight stations; Chair. TIM DOWNING; CEO ANDREW WERRO.

Territory Television Pty Ltd: POB 1764, Darwin, NT 0801; tel. (8) 8981-8888; fax (8) 8981-6802; f. 1971; operates one station; Gen. Man. A. G. BRUYN.

TVW Enterprises Ltd: POB 77, Tuart Hill, WA 6060; tel. (8) 9344-0777; fax (8) 9344-0670; f. 1959; Man. Dir K. V. CAMPBELL.

West Coast Telecasters Ltd: POB 1010, Mirrabooka, WA 6061; tel. (8) 9345-1010; fax (8) 9345-2210; Man. Dir W. H. MCKENZIE.

WIN Television Mildura Pty Ltd: 18 Deakin Ave, Mildura, Vic 3500; tel. (3) 5023-0204; telex 55304; fax (3) 5022-1179; f. 1965; Chair. JOHN I. RUSHTON; Man. NOEL W. HISCOCK.

WIN Television NSW Network: Television Ave, Mt St Thomas, Locked Bag 8800, South Coast Mail Centre, NSW 2521; tel. (2) 4223-4199; fax (2) 4227-3682; f. 1962; Man. Dir K. KINGSTON; CEO JOHN RUSHTON.

WIN Television Qld Pty Ltd: POB 568 Rockhampton, Qld 4700; tel. (7) 4930-4499; telex 49008; fax (7) 4930-4490; Station Man. R. HOCKEY.

WIN Television Tas Pty Ltd: 52 New Town Rd, Hobart, Tas 7008; tel. (3) 6228-8999; fax (3) 6228-8995; f. 1959; Gen. Man. DAVID LANGSFORD.

WIN Television Vic Pty Ltd: POB 464, Ballarat, Vic 3353; tel. (3) 5320-1366; fax (3) 5333-1598; f. 1961; operates five stations; Gen. Man. DAVID LANGSFORD.

Satellite and Cable Television

In September 1994 plans for a new cable television network, involving the Nine Network, the Seven Network, an Australian telecommunications company and a US cable operator, were announced. To be called Optus Vision, the venture was to cost $A3,000m. over four years, and services would eventually reach 3m. Australian homes. In December 1994, however, the Seven Network announced its withdrawal from the venture. A second consortium, Foxtel, a joint venture between The News Corporation and Telstra Corpn (the government-owned telecommunications company) was to commence operations on 150 channels in late 1995. Australis, a satellite pay-TV operator, commenced services on nine channels in 1995.

Optus Vision: Tower B, Level 15, 16 Zenith Centre, 821–841 Pacific Highway, Chatswood, NSW 2067; commenced cable services on 11 channels in 1995; CEO GEOFFREY COUSINS.

Regulatory Authority

Australian Broadcasting Authority: POB Q500, QVB Post Office, NSW 1230; tel. (2) 9334-7700; fax (2) 9334-7799; e-mail info@aba.gov.au; regulates radio and TV broadcasting; Chair. Prof. DAVID FLINT.

Finance

Radical reforms of the financial sector, to be introduced from 1998, were announced in September 1997. The banking system was to be opened up to greater competition. The licensing and regulation of deposit-taking institutions was to be supervised by the new Australian Prudential Regulation Authority, while consumer protection was to be the responsibility of the Australian Corporations and Financial Services Commission.

(cap. = capital; p.u. = paid up; res = reserves; dep. = deposits; m. = million; brs = branches; amounts in Australian dollars)

BANKING

Central Bank

Reserve Bank of Australia: GPOB 3947, Sydney, NSW 2001; tel. (2) 9551-8111; telex 121636; fax (2) 9551-8000; f. 1911; bank of issue; cap. and res 7,245.9m., dep. 7,349.0m., total assets 35,997.1m., notes on issue 19,182m. (June 1996); Gov. IAN MACFARLANE.

Development Banks

Commonwealth Development Bank of Australia: GPOB 2719, Sydney, NSW 2001; tel. (2) 9378-2000; telex 120345; fax (2) 9312-9905; f. 1960; cap. and res 295.2m., dep. 550.0m. (June 1996); Gen. Man. R. H. WEAVER.

Primary Industry Bank of Australia Ltd: GPOB 4577, Sydney, NSW 2001; tel. (2) 9234-4200; telex 123495; fax (2) 9221-6218; f. 1978; cap. 123.2m., res 2.5m., dep. 2,136.4m. (Dec. 1996); Chair. H. G. GENTIS; Man. Dir B. H. WALTERS; 24 brs.

Trading Banks

ABN AMRO Australia Ltd: ABN AMRO House, 14th Floor, 10 Spring St, Sydney, NSW 2000; tel. (2) 9321-2121; fax (2) 9223-4310; f. 1983; cap. 70m., res 1.5m. (Dec. 1996); Man. Dir R. JEROME ROWLEY.

ABN AMRO Finance (Aust.) Ltd: Level 40, Governor Phillip Tower, 1 Farrer Place, Sydney, NSW 2000; tel. (2) 9375-5555; fax (2) 9251-1473; f. 1985 as Lloyds Bank NZA Ltd, name changed 1997; cap. 48.1m., res 46.7m., dep. 681.8m. (Dec. 1995); Chair. P. M. MCCAW; CEO DAVID S. WILLIS.

Australia and New Zealand Banking Group Ltd: 100 Queen St, Melbourne, Vic 3000; POB 537 E, Melbourne, Vic 3001; tel. (3) 9273-5555; fax (3) 9273-4909; f. 1835; present name adopted in 1970; cap. and res 6,700m., dep. 85,400m. (Sept. 1995); 1,744 points of representation in Australia, New Zealand and world-wide; Chair. C. B. GOODE; CEO JOHN MCFARLANE.

BA Australia Ltd: 18th Floor, Bank of America Centre, 135 King St, Sydney, NSW 2000; tel. (2) 9931-4200; telex 25041; fax (2) 9221-1023; f. 1964; cap. 149.0m., res 1.3m., dep. 1,099.1m. (Dec. 1995); Chair. BRYCE WAUCHOPE.

Bank of Melbourne Ltd: 52 Collins St, Melbourne, Vic 3000; tel. (3) 9520-0000; telex 35487; fax (3) 9650-6626; f. 1989; cap. 568m., dep. 6,615m. (1995); Chair. CHRIS STEWART; CEO DAVID AIREY; 122 brs.

Bank of Queensland Ltd: 229 Elizabeth St, POB 898, Brisbane, Qld 4001; tel. (7) 3212-3333; telex 41565; fax (7) 3212-3399; f. 1874; cap. 56.8m., res 61.3m., dep. 2,025.6m. (Aug. 1996); Chair. NEIL ROBERTS; Chief Exec. JOHN K. DAWSON; 95 brs.

Bank of Tokyo-Mitsubishi (Australia) Ltd: Level 26, Gateway, 1 Macquarie Place, Sydney, NSW 2000; tel. (2) 9255-1111; fax (2) 9247-4266; f. 1985; Chair. and Man. Dir T. YOSHINO.

Bank of Western Australia Ltd: 108 St George's Terrace, POB E237, Perth, WA 6001; tel. (8) 9449-7000; fax (8) 9449-7050; f. 1895 as Agricultural Bank of Western Australia, 1945 as Rural and Industries Bank of Western Australia; present name adopted in 1994; cap. and res 447.2m., dep. 7,696.5m. (Feb. 1997); Chair. IAN C. R. MACKENZIE; Man. Dir WARWICK G. KENT; 109 brs.

Bankers' Trust Australia Ltd: POB H4, Australia Sq., Sydney, NSW 2000; tel. (2) 9259-3555; telex 121821; fax (2) 9235-2882; f. 1986; cap. 73.3m., dep. 3,670.1m. (Dec. 1995); Chair. DAVID HOARE; 5 brs.

Chase Manhattan Bank Australia Ltd: GPOB 9816, NSW 2001; tel. (2) 9250-4111; telex 176117; fax (2) 9250-4554; Man. Dir W. SCOTT REID.

Colonial State Bank: GPOB 41, Sydney, NSW 2001; tel. (2) 9226-8000; fax (2) 9235-3921; f. 1933; fmrly State Bank of New South Wales; cap. and res 1,541.6m., dep. 7,211m. (1997); Chair. PETER SMEDLEY; Man. Dir STUART JAMES; 350 brs in Australia.

Commonwealth Bank of Australia: GPOB 2719, Sydney, NSW 2001; tel. (2) 9378-7111; telex 120345; fax (2) 9261-5390; f. 1912; cap. 1,981.0m., res 4,415.0m., dep. 72,736.0m. (June 1996); Chair. TIM BESLEY; CEO Dir D. V. MURRAY; more than 1,500 brs world-wide.

Crédit Lyonnais Australia Ltd: Level 18, 9–13 Castlereagh St, GPO Box 4182, Sydney, NSW 2001; tel. (2) 9220-8000; telex 26881; fax (2) 9221-8987; f. 1986; cap. 76.7m., dep. 1,395.5m. (Dec. 1996); Man. Dir JEAN-YVES LE PAULMIER.

Hambros Australia Ltd: 167 Macquarie St, Sydney, NSW 2000; tel. (2) 9373-0300; fax (2) 9233-4302; f. 1978; cap. 21.3m., res 9.6m., dep. 635.2m. (March 1995).

HongkongBank of Australia Ltd: Level 10, 1 O'Connell Street, Sydney, NSW 2000; tel. (2) 9255-2888; telex 24856; fax (2) 9255-2332; f. 1985; CEO CHRIS CROOK; Man. Dir STUART DAVIS; 16 brs.

IBJ Australia Bank Ltd: 21st Level, State Bank Centre, 52 Martin Place, Sydney, NSW 2000; tel. (2) 9377-8888; telex 25454; fax (2) 9377-8884; f. 1985; subsidiary of Industrial Bank of Japan; cap. 104m. (1995); Chair. M. J. PHILLIPS; Man. Dir K. TSUJI.

ING Mercantile Mutual Bank Ltd: Level 1, 347 Kent St, Sydney, NSW 2000; tel. (2) 9234-8444; fax (2) 9290-3683; cap. 60m., res 1.5m., dep. 374.9m. (Sept. 1996).

Macquarie Bank Ltd: Level 22, 20 Bond St, Sydney, NSW 2000; tel. (2) 9237-3333; telex 122246; fax (2) 9237-3350; internet http://wnw.macquarie.com.au; f. 1969 as Hill Samuel Australia Ltd; present name adopted in 1985; cap. 155.4m., res 52.5m., dep. 3,577.7m. (March 1997); Chair. DAVID S. CLARKE; Man. Dir ALLAN E. MOSS; 4 brs.

National Australia Bank Ltd: 500 Bourke St, Melbourne, Vic 3000; tel. (3) 9641-3500; fax (3) 9641-4916; f. 1858; cap. 1,477m., res 5,421m., dep. 110,921m. (Sept. 1996); Chair. W. R. M. IRVINE; Man. and CEO D. R. ARGUS; 2,513 brs.

Rothschild Australia Ltd: 1 O'Connell St, Sydney, NSW 2000; tel. (2) 9323-2000; fax (2) 9323-2323; f. 1967 as International Pacific Corpn, name changed 1983; cap. 75.0m., res 0.3m., dep. 641.3m. (March 1996); Chair. PHILIP BRASS; Man. Dir RICHARD LEE.

Société Générale Australia Ltd: Société Générale House, 350 George St, Sydney, NSW 2000; tel. (2) 9350-7400; telex 71982; fax (2) 9235-3941; f. 1981; cap. 21.5m., res 0.7m., dep. 4,201.6m. (Dec. 1995); Man. Dir and Chair. YANNICK CHAGNON.

St George Bank Ltd: St George House, 4–16 Montgomery St, Kogarah, NSW 2217; tel. (2) 9952-1311; fax (2) 9952-1066; f. 1937 as building society; cap. 232.1m., res 911.8m., dep. 11,989.0m. (Sept. 1996); Chair. F. J. CONROY; Man. Dir A. J. SWEENEY.

Standard Chartered Bank Australia Ltd: 345 George St, Sydney, NSW; tel. (2) 9232-6599; fax (2) 9232-9345; f. 1986; cap. 73.6m., res 152.6m., dep. 697.2m. (Dec. 1995); Chair. Sir BRUCE MACKLIN; CEO THOMAS DUNTON.

Toronto Dominion Australia Ltd: 36th Floor, 385 Bourke St, Melbourne, Vic 3000; tel. (3) 9602-1344; telex 32316; fax (3) 9670-3779; f. 1970; cap. 191.5m., res 6.0m., dep. 2,148.9m. (Oct. 1996); Man. Dir S. H. FRYER.

Westpac Banking Corporation: 60 Martin Place, Sydney, NSW 2000; tel. (2) 9226-3311; fax (2) 9226-4128; f. 1817; incorporated Challenge Bank in 1996; cap. 1,887m., res 4,632m., dep. 68,769m. (Sept. 1996); Chair. JOHN UHRIG; Man. Dir R. L. JOSS.

Savings Bank

Trust Bank: 39 Murray St, Hobart, Tas 7000; tel. (3) 6230-3777; telex 57066; fax (3) 6223-2279; f. 1845; cap. and res 143.3m., dep. 1,557.4m. (Aug. 1996); Chair. G. N. LOUGHRAN; Man. Dir P. W. KEMP; 45 brs.

Foreign Banks

Bank of China (People's Republic of China): 65 York St, cnr of Barrack St, Sydney, NSW 2000; tel. (2) 9267-5188; telex 177033; fax (2) 9262-1794; Gen. Man. Gao Ji Lu.

Bank of New Zealand: 9th Floor, BNZ House, 333–339 George St, Sydney, NSW 2000; tel. (2) 9290-6666; telex 123240; fax (2) 9290-3414; Chief Operating Officer G. Armbruster.

Banque Nationale de Paris (France): 12 Castlereagh St, Sydney, NSW 2000; POB 269, Sydney, NSW 2001; tel. (2) 9232-8733; telex 20132; fax (2) 9221-3026; Gen. Man. Roland Girault; 4 brs.

BOSA Ltd: 15 Castlereagh St, Sydney, NSW 2000; tel. (2) 9235-2022; telex 74295; fax (2) 9221-4360; f. 1986; fmrly Bank of Singapore (Australia); Exec. Dir and CEO Tan Ngiap Joo; 4 brs.

Deutsche Bank AG (Germany): GPOB 7033, Sydney, NSW 2001; tel. (2) 9258-3666; telex 74374; fax (2) 9241-2565; Man. Dir Dr Klaus Albrecht.

NatWest Markets Australia Ltd (UK): Level 16, Grosvenor Place, 225 George St, Sydney, NSW 2000; tel. (2) 9321-4000; telex 177326; fax (2) 9251-2997; f. 1986; subsidiary of National Westminster Bank; Chair. N. F. Greiner; CEO P. B. St George.

STOCK EXCHANGES

Australian Stock Exchange Ltd (ASX): Level 11, 20 Bond St, Sydney, NSW 2000; tel. (2) 9227-0000; fax (2) 9235-0056; f. 1987 by merger of the stock exchanges in Sydney, Adelaide, Brisbane, Hobart, Melbourne and Perth, to replace the fmr Australian Associated Stock Exchanges; 98 mem orgs; Chair. Maurice Newman; Man. Dir Richard Humphry.

Supervisory Body

Australian Securities Commission: POB 4866, Sydney, NSW 2001; tel. (2) 9911-2000; fax (2) 9911-2030; f. 1990; corporations and securities markets regulator; Chair. Alan Cameron.

PRINCIPAL INSURANCE COMPANIES

AMP General Insurance Ltd: 8 Loftus St, Sydney Cove, NSW 2000; tel. (2) 9257-2500; fax (2) 9257-2199; f. 1958; Chair. J. W. Utz; Man. Dir R. R. Lester.

Australian Guarantee Corpn Ltd: 130 Phillip St, Sydney, NSW 2000; tel. (2) 9234-1122; fax (2) 9234-1225; f. 1925; Chair. J. A. Uhrig; Man. Dir R. Thomas.

The Australian Mutual Provident Society: AMP Bldg, 33 Alfred St, Sydney, NSW 2000; tel. (2) 9257-5000; fax (2) 9257-7886; f. 1949; life insurance; Chair. Ian Burgess; Man. Dir George Trumbull.

Australian Unity General Insurance Ltd: 114–124 Albert Rd, South Melbourne, Vic 3205; tel. (3) 9285-0285; fax (3) 9690-5556; f. 1948; Chair. C. S. Vincent; Chief Exec. M. W. Sibree.

Catholic Church Insurances Ltd: 324 St Kilda Rd, Melbourne, Vic 3004; tel. (3) 9934-3000; fax (3) 9934-3460; f. 1911; Chair. Rt Rev. Kevin Manning, Bishop of Parramatta; Gen. Man. Paul Serong.

CE Heath International Holdings Ltd: AMP Centre, 50 Bridge St, Sydney, NSW 2000; tel. (2) 9207-0000; fax (2) 9207-0011; f. 1968; Chair. G. A. Cohen; Man. Dir T. K. Cassidy.

Colonial Ltd: 330 Collins St, Melbourne, Vic 3000; tel. (3) 9200-6111; fax (3) 9200-6294; internet http://www.colonial.com.au; f. 1873; Chair. D. S. Adam; Man. Dir Peter Smedley.

Commercial Union Assurance Co of Australia Ltd: Commercial Union Centre, 485 La Trobe St, Melbourne, Vic 3000; tel. (3) 9601-8222; fax (3) 9601-8366; f. 1960; fire, accident, marine; Chair. A. F. Guy; Man. Dir I. M. Balfe.

The Copenhagen Reinsurance Co Ltd: 60 Margaret St, Sydney, NSW 2000; tel. (2) 9247-7266; fax (2) 9235-3320; reinsurance; Gen. Man. David Lawrence.

FAI Insurances Ltd: FAI Insurance Group, 333 Kent St, Sydney, NSW 2000; tel. (2) 9274-8888; fax (2) 9274-9900; internet http://www.fai.com.au; f. 1956; Chair. John Landerer; CEO Rodney Adler.

Fortis Australia Ltd: 464 St Kilda Rd, Melbourne, Vic 3004; tel. (3) 9869-0300; fax (3) 9820-8537; CEO R. B. Willing..

General and Cologne Reinsurance Australasia Ltd: Level 13, 225 George St, Sydney, NSW 2000; tel. (2) 9336-8100; fax (2) 9251-1665; f. 1961; reinsurance, fire, accident, marine; Chair. F. A. McDonald; Man. Dir G. C. Barnum.

GIO Australia Holdings Ltd: 2 Martin Place, Sydney, NSW 2000; tel. (2) 9228-1000; fax (2) 9235-3909; internet http://www.gio.com.au; f. 1926; Man. Dir W. Jocelyn.

Guild Insurance Ltd: Guild House, 40 Burwood Rd, Hawthorn, Vic 3122; tel. (3) 9810-9820; fax (3) 9819-5670; f. 1963; Man. Dir W. K. Bastian.

Lumley General Insurance Ltd: POB Q338, Queen Victoria Bldg, Postshop, NSW 2000; tel. (2) 9248-1111; fax (2) 9248-1122; e-mail general@lumley.com.au; Dir R. L. Bostock.

Mercantile Mutual Holdings Ltd: 347 Kent St, Sydney, NSW; tel. (2) 9234-8111; fax (2) 9299-3979; f. 1878; Chair. J. B. Studdy; Man. Dir R. J. Atfield.

MLC Insurance Ltd: POB 5577, West Chatswood, NSW 2057; tel. (2) 9957-8000; fax (2) 9414-5782; Chair. A. L. Morokoff; CEO John Messenger.

MMI Ltd: 2 Market St, Sydney, NSW 2000; tel. (2) 9390-6222; fax (2) 9390-6400; f. 1914; workers' compensation; fire, general accident, motor and marine; Chair. C. W. Love; Man. Dir P. Franzen.

Munh Reinsurance Co of Australia Ltd: 143 Macquarie St, Sydney, NSW 2000; tel. (2) 9250-8000; fax (2) 9251-2516; Man. Dir R. Withers.

The National Mutual Life Association of Australasia Ltd: 447 Collins St, Melbourne, Vic 3000; tel. (3) 9616-3911; fax (3) 9614-2240; f. 1869; life insurance, superannuation, income protection; Chair. D. R. Wills; Man. Dir J. A. Killen.

NRMA Insurance Ltd: 151 Clarence St, Sydney, NSW 2000; tel. (2) 9292-9222; telex 22348; fax (2) 9292-8472; f. 1926; CEO Malcolm Jones.

NZI Insurance Australia Ltd: 9th Floor, 10 Spring St, Sydney, NSW 2000; tel. (2) 9551-5000; fax (2) 9551-5865; Man. Dir H. D. Smith.

QBE Insurance Group Ltd: 82 Pitt St, Sydney, NSW 2000; tel. (2) 9235-4444; telex 26914; fax (2) 9235-3166; f. 1886; general insurance; Chair. J. D. O. Burns; Man. Dir E. J. Cloney.

RAC Insurance Pty Ltd: 228 Adelaide Terrace, Perth, WA 6000; tel. (8) 9421-4444; fax (8) 9421-4593; f. 1947; Gen. Man. Tony Carter.

RACQ-GIO Insurance Ltd: POB 4, Springwood, Qld 4127; tel. (7) 3361-2444; fax (7) 3361-2199; f. 1995; CEO R. J. Kent.

RACV Insurance: 550 Princes Highway, Noble Park, Vic 3174; tel. (3) 9790-2211; fax (3) 9790-3091; Gen. Man. D. C. Hurford.

Sun Alliance and Royal Insurance Australia Ltd: 465 Victoria Ave, Chatswood, NSW 2067; tel. (2) 9978-9000; fax (2) 9978-9807; fire, accident and marine insurance; Gen. Man. E. Kulk.

Suncorp Insurance & Finance: Cnr Albert & Turbot Sts, Brisbane, Queensland 4000; tel. (7) 3313-1155; fax (7) 3362-2890; f. *c.* 1916; Char. J. G. A. Tucker; CEO B. C. E. Rowley.

Swiss Re Australia Ltd: 31 Queen St, Melbourne, Vic 3000; tel. (3) 9616-9200; fax (3) 9621-2446; f. 1962; fmrly Australian Reinsurance Co Ltd; reinsurance; Chair. R. H. Syme; Man. Dir R. G. Watts.

Transport Industries Insurance Co Ltd: 310 Queen St, Melbourne, Vic 3000; tel. (3) 9623-3355; fax (3) 9623-2624; f. 1960; Chair. R. H. Y. Syme; Man. Dir R. G. Watts.

Wesfarmers Federation Insurance Ltd: 184 Railway Parade, Bassendean, WA 6054; tel. (9) 9273-5333; fax (9) 9273-5290; Gen. Man. R. J. Buckley.

Westpac Life Ltd: 35 Pitt St, Sydney, NSW 2000; tel. (2) 9220-4768; f. 1986; CEO David White.

World Marine & General Insurances Ltd: 600 Bourke St, Melbourne, Vic 3000; tel. (3) 9609-3333; fax (3) 9609-3634; f. 1961; Chair. G. W. McGregor; Man. Dir A. E. Reynolds.

Zurich Australian Insurance Ltd: 5 Blue St, North Sydney, NSW 2060; tel. (2) 391-1111; fax (2) 9922-4630; Man. Dir A. W. Small.

Insurance Associations

Australian Insurance Association: GPOB 369, Canberra, ACT 2601; tel. (2) 6274-0609; fax (2) 6274-0666; f. 1968; Pres. Raymond Jones; Exec. Sec. P. M. Murphy.

Australian Insurance Institute: Level 17, 31 Queen St, Melbourne, Vic 3000; tel. (3) 9629-4021; fax (3) 9629-4204; e-mail journal@aii.com.au; f. 1919; Pres. John Cloney; CEO Joan Fitzpatrick; 11,984 mems.

Insurance Council of Australia Ltd: Level 14, 275 George St, Sydney, NSW 2000; tel. (2) 9299-7100; fax (2) 9299-8656; internet http://www.ica.com.au; f. 1975; CEO Alan Mason.

Life, Investment and Superannuation Association of Australia Inc (LISA): 24th Floor, 44 Market St, Sydney, NSW 2000; tel. (2) 9299-3022; fax (2) 9299-3198; f. 1996; Chair. Dr P. Jonson; Exec. Dir J. L. Maroney; 36 mems.

Trade and Industry

CHAMBERS OF COMMERCE

International Chamber of Commerce: POB E118, Kingston, Canberra, ACT 2604; tel. (2) 6295-1961; fax (2) 6295-0170; f. 1927; 65 mems; Chair. C. S. Cullen; Sec.-Gen. H. C. Grant.

Australian Chamber of Commerce and Industry (ACCI): POB E14, Queen Victoria Terrace, Canberra, ACT 2600; tel. (2) 6273-2311; fax (2) 6273-3286; Pres. Graeme Samuel; CEO Mark I. Paterson.

Chamber of Commerce and Industry of Western Australia (CCIWA): POB 6209, East Perth, WA 6892; tel. (9) 9365-7555; fax (9) 9481-0980; e-mail whitaker@cciwa.asn.au; internet http://www.cciwa.asn.au; f. 1890; 6,000 mems; Chief Exec. LYNDON ROWE; Pres. DAVID GRAY.

Queensland Chamber of Commerce and Industry: Industry House, 375 Wickham Terrace, Brisbane, Qld 4000; tel. (7) 3842-2222; fax (7) 3832-3195; e-mail cbubb@qcci.com.au; internet http://www.qcci.com.au; f. 1994 through merger; operates World Trade Centre, Brisbane; 3,800 mems; CEO CLIVE BUBB.

South Australian Employers' Chamber of Commerce and Industry Inc: 136 Greenhill Road, Unley, SA 5061; tel. (8) 8300-0000; fax (8) 8300-0001; 4,700 mems; CEO L. M. THOMPSON.

State Chamber of Commerce (New South Wales): Level 12, 83 Clarence St, GPOB 4280, GPO Sydney, NSW 2001; tel. (2) 9350-8100; fax (2) 9350-8199; f. 1825; CEO KATIE LAHEY.

Tasmanian Chamber of Commerce and Industry: GPOB 793H, Hobart, Tas 7001; tel. (3) 6234-5933; fax (3) 6231-1278; CEO TIM ABEY.

Victorian Employers' Chamber of Commerce and Industry: Employers' House, 50 Burwood Rd, Hawthorn, Vic 3122; tel. (3) 9251-4333; fax (3) 9819-3676; f. 1885; CEO D. EDWARDS.

AGRICULTURAL, INDUSTRIAL AND TRADE ASSOCIATIONS

The Agriculture and Resource Management Council of Australia and New Zealand: Dept of Primary Industries and Energy, Barton, Canberra, ACT 2600; tel. (2) 6272-5216; fax (2) 6272-4772; e-mail armcanz.contact@dpie.gov.au; f. 1992 to develop integrated and sustainable agricultural and land and water management policies, strategies and practices; mems comprising the Commonwealth/state/territory and New Zealand ministers responsible for agriculture, soil conservation, water resources and rural adjustment matters; Sec. J. W. GRAHAM.

Standing Committee on Agriculture and Resource Management: f. 1992; an advisory body to the Agriculture and Resource Management Council of Australia and New Zealand; comprises the heads of Commonwealth/state/territory and New Zealand agencies responsible for agriculture, soil conservation and water resources and representatives from CSIRO, Bureau of Meteorology and rural adjustment authorities; Sec. J. W. GRAHAM.

AIDC Ltd: Level 33, AIDC Tower, 201 Kent St, Sydney, NSW 2000; tel. (2) 9235-5155; telex 23107; fax (2) 9235-5195; f. 1989 as listed public investment house to take over the business of the Australian Industry Development Corporation (f. 1970); brs in Sydney, Adelaide, Melbourne, Perth and Brisbane; Chair. Prof. JEREMY DAVIS; CEO CHRIS SKILTON.

Australian Business Ltd: Private Bag 938, North Sydney, NSW 2059; tel. (2) 9927-7500; fax (2) 9923-1166; f. 1885; fmrly Chamber of Manufactures of NSW; CEO P. M. HOLT.

The Australian Chamber of Manufactures (Victoria): 380 St Kilda Rd, Melbourne, Vic 3004, GPOB 1469N, Melbourne, Vic 3001; tel. (3) 9698-4111; fax (3) 9699-1729; f. 1877; 8,000 mems; Nat. CEO ALLAN HANDBERG.

Australian Dairy Corporation: Level 5, IBM Centre, 60 City Rd, Southbank,Vic 3006; tel. (3) 9694-3777; fax (3) 9694-3733; provides export agency and market devt services, and promotes domestic consumption; Chair. KEN P. BAXTER; Man. Dir GRAHAME TONKIN.

Australian Manufacturers' Export Council: POB E14, Queen Victoria Terrace, ACT 2600; tel. (2) 6273-2311; fax (2) 6273-3196; f. 1955; Exec. Dir G. CHALKER.

Australian Meat and Livestock Corporation: 165 Walker St, North Sydney, NSW 2060; tel. 1800-023-100; internet http://www.amlc.com.au; statutory federal govt marketing authority assisting the Australian meat and livestock industries in domestic and international trade; Chair. P. MUSGRAVE.

Australian Trade Policy Advisory Council: c/o Dept of Foreign Affairs and Trade, Canberra, ACT 2600; tel. (2) 6261-2125; fax (2) 6261-2465; f. 1958; advises the Minister for Trade on policy issues; Chair. R. B. VAUGHAN.

Australian Wheat Board: Ceres House, 528 Lonsdale St, Melbourne, Vic 3000; tel. (3) 9209-2000; telex 130196; fax (3) 9670-2782; f. 1939; national and international marketing of grain, financing and marketing of wheat and other grains for growers; 11 mems; Chair. TREVOR FLUGGE; Man. Dir MURRAY ROGERS.

Australian Wool Research & Promotion Organisation: Wool House, 369 Royal Parade, Parkville, Vic 3052; tel. (3) 9341-9111; fax (3) 9341-9273; internet http://www.wool.co.au; f. 1993; operates as IWS International P/L (International Wool Secretariat), responsible for building sustainable demand via research and development, marketing and promotion, Chair. ALEC MORRISON.

Business Council of Australia: POB 7225, Melbourne, Vic 3004; tel. (3) 9274-7777; fax (3) 9274-7744; public policy research and advocacy; governing council comprises chief execs of Australia's major cos; Pres. I. L. SALMON; Exec. Dir P. H. BARRATT.

Department of Primary Industries and Energy: see p. 461.

Wool Council of Australia: POB E10, Kingston, Canberra, ACT 2604; tel. (2) 6273-2531; fax (2) 6273-1120; e-mail woolcouncil@nff.org.au; comprises 20 mems; represents wool-growers in dealings with the Federal Govt and industry; consults with Australian Wool Research and Promotion Organisation/International Wool Secretariat and Wool International; Pres. ROD THIRKELL JOHNSTON.

EMPLOYERS' ORGANIZATIONS

Australian Co-operative Foods Ltd: Level 12, 168 Walker St, North Sydney, NSW 2060; tel. (2) 9903-5222; fax (2) 9957-3530; f. 1900; Man. Dir A. R. TOOTH.

The Master Builders Association of New South Wales: Forest Lodge, 52 Parramatta Rd, NSW 2037; tel. (2) 9660-7188; fax (2) 9660-4437; f. 1873; Exec. Dir SHANE P. GOODWIN; 4,500 mems.

MTIA: 51 Walker St, North Sydney, NSW 2060; tel. (2) 9929-5566; fax (2) 9956-5044; f. 1873; manufacturing, engineering and construction industry asscn.; Nat. Pres. PETER THOMAS; CEO ROBERT N. HERBERT; 6,800 mems.

National Meat Association: 25–27 Albany St, Crows Nest, NSW 2065; POB 1208, Crows Nest, NSW 2065; tel. (2) 9906-7767; fax (2) 9906-8022; f. 1928; Pres. GARY HARDWICK; CEO DAVID ABBA.

NSW Farmers' Association: 1 Bligh St, Sydney, NSW 2001; GPOB 1068, Sydney, NSW 2001; tel. (2) 9251-1700; fax (2) 9221-6913; f. 1978; CEO PETER J. COMENSOLI.

PRINCIPAL TRADE UNIONS

Australian Council of Trade Unions (ACTU): 393–397 Swanston St, Melbourne, Vic 3000; tel. (3) 9663-5266; fax (3) 9663-4051; f. 1927; br. in each state, generally known as a Trades and Labour Council; 47 affiliated trade unions; Pres. JENNIE GEORGE; Sec. WILLIAM J. KELTY.

Association of Professional Engineers, Scientists & Managers, Australia (APESMA): POB 1272L, Melbourne, Vic 3001; tel. (3) 9695-8800; fax (3) 9696-9312; e-mail apesma@ozmail.com.au; internet http://www.apesma.asn.au; Pres. ROB J. ALLEN; Sec. G. F. SUTHERLAND; 22,000 mems.

Australasian Meat Industry Employees' Union (AMIEU): 377 Sussex St, Sydney, NSW 2000; tel. (2) 9264-2279; fax (2) 9261-1970; Fed. Pres. JOHN PYSING; Fed. Sec. T. R. HANNAN; 32,500 mems.

Australian Education Union: POB 1158, South Melbourne, Vic 3205; tel. (3) 9254-1800; fax (3) 9254-1805; e-mail aeu@edunions.labor.net.au; f. 1984; Fed. Pres. SHARAN BURROW; Fed. Sec. ROBERT DURBRIDGE; 157,388 mems.

Australian Manufacturing Workers' Union/AMWU: POB 189, Strawberry Hills, NSW 2012; tel. (2) 9690-1411; fax (2) 9698-7516; internet http://www.amwu2@amwa.asn.au; Nat. Pres. DAVE GOODGER; Nat. Sec. DOUG CAMERON; 185,393 mems.

Australian Services Union (ASU): 2nd Floor, 116-124 Queensberry St, Carlton South, Vic 3053; tel. (3) 9348-1788; fax (3) 9349-1108; e-mail asunatm@asu.asn.au; Nat. Sec. PAUL SLAPE; 165,000 mems.

Australian Workers' Union (AWU): 51–65 Bathurst St, Sydney, NSW 2000; tel. (2) 9264-2877; fax (2) 9261-1701; f. 1886; Nat. Pres. BILL LUDWIG; Nat. Secs STEVE HARRISON, IAN CAMBRIDGE; 170,000 mems.

Communications, Electrical, Electronic, Energy, Information, Postal, Plumbing and Allied Services Union of Australia (CEPU): POB 812, Rockdale, NSW 2216; tel. (2) 9597-4499; fax (2) 9597-6354; Nat. Pres. P. WATSON; Nat. Sec. P. TIGHE; 180,000 mems.

Community and Public Sector Union (CPSU): Level 4, 160 Clarence St, Sydney, NSW 2000; tel. (2) 9299-5655; fax (2) 9299-7181; Nat. Sec. B. JARDINE; 225,000 mems.

Construction, Forestry, Mining and Energy Union (CFMEU): Box Q235, Queen Victoria Bldg PO, Sydney, NSW 2000; tel. (2) 9290-3699; fax (2) 9299-1685; f. 1992 by amalgamation; Jt Nat. Pres J. MAITLAND, T. SMITH; Jt Nat. Secs S. SHARKEY, V. FITZGERALD; 160,000 mems.

Finance Sector Union of Australia (FSU): 341 Queen St, Melbourne, Vic 3000; tel. (3) 9261-5300; fax (3) 9670-2950; e-mail fsuinfo@fsunion.org.au; f. 1991; Nat. Pres. JOY MCSHANE; 105,000 mems.

Health Services Union of Australia (HSUA): 88 Mt Alexander Rd, Flemington, Vic 3031; tel. (3) 9376-8242; fax (3) 9376-8243; e-mail hsuno@c031.aone.net.au; Nat. Pres. MICHAEL WILLIAMSON; Nat. Sec. ROBERT ELLIOTT; 90,000 mems.

Independent Education Union of Australia (IEU): POB 1301, South Melbourne, Vic 3205; tel. (3) 9254-1830; fax (3) 9254-1835; Fed. Sec. LYNNE ROLLEY; 42,000 mems.

Liquor, Hospitality and Miscellaneous Workers Union (LHMU): POB K975, Haymarket, NSW 2000; tel. (2) 9281-9511; fax (2) 9281-4480; f. 1992; Jt Nat. Pres EUGENE FRY, CHRIS RAPER; 210,000 mems.

Maritime Union of Australia (MUA): 365 Sussex St, Sydney, NSW 2000; tel. (2) 9267-9134; fax (2) 9261-3481; f. 1993; Nat. Sec. JOHN COOMBS; 10,058 mems.

Media, Entertainment & Arts Alliance (MEAA): POB 723, Strawberry Hills, NSW 2012; tel. (2) 9333-0999; fax (2) 9333-0933; e-mail meaa@alliance.aust.com; Jt Fed. Secs ANNE BRITTON, CHRISTOPHER WARREN; 30,000 mems.

National Union of Workers (NUW): POB 343, North Melbourne, Vic 3051; tel. (3) 9287-1850; fax (3) 9287-1818; Gen. Sec. GREG SWORD; 110,000 mems.

Public Transport Union (PTU): 83–89 Renwick St, Redfern, NSW 2016; tel. (2) 9310-3966; fax (2) 9319-2096; e-mail publictu@magna.com.au; Nat. Pres. T. AVERY; Nat. Sec. R. G. JOWETT; 46,000 mems.

Shop, Distributive & Allied Employees Association (SDA): 5th Floor, 53 Queen St, Melbourne, Vic 3000; tel. (3) 9629-2299; fax (3) 9629-2646; e-mail sdanat@c031.aone.net.au; f. 1908; Nat. Pres. DON FARRELL; Nat. Sec. JOE DE BRUYN; 230,000 mems.

Textile, Clothing and Footwear Union of Australia (TCFUA): Ground Floor, 28 Anglo Rd, Campsie, NSW 2194; tel. (2) 9789-4188; fax (2) 9789-6510; f.1919; Pres. KEVIN BOYD; 29,900 mems.

Transport Workers' Union of Australia (TWU): Level 2, 18–20 Lincoln Sq., North Carlton, Vic 3053; tel. (3) 9347-0099; fax (3) 9347-2502; e-mail twufed@ozemail.com.au; Fed. Pres. STEVE HUTCHINS; Fed. Sec. JOHN ALLAN; 88,000 mems.

United Firefighters' Union of Australia (UFU of A): POB 289, Torrensville, SA 5031; tel. (8) 8352-7211; fax (8) 8234-1031; Nat. Pres. SIMON FLYNN; Nat. Sec. PAUL CAICA; 11,000 mems.

Transport

Australian Transport Council: POB 594, Canberra, ACT 2601; tel. (2) 6274-7851; fax (2) 6274-7703; f. 1993; mems include: Federal Minister for Transport and Regional Development, State and Territory Ministers responsible for transport, roads and marine and ports; initiates discussion, and reports as necessary, on any matter relating to better co-ordination of transport development, while encouraging modernization and innovation; promotes research; Sec. D. JONES.

State Transit Authority of New South Wales: 100 Miller St, North Sydney, NSW 2060; tel. (2) 9245-5777; fax (2) 9245-5710; internet http://www.sta.nsw.gov.au; operates government buses and ferries in Sydney and Newcastle metropolitan areas; Chair. DAVID HERLIHY; CEO JOHN STOTT.

TransAdelaide (South Australia): GPOB 2351, Adelaide, SA 5001; tel. (8) 8218-2200; fax (8) 8211-7614; e-mail transadl@camtech.net.au; f. 1994; fmrly State Transport Authority; operates metropolitan train, bus, tram and Busway services; Gen. Man. KEVIN BENGER.

RAILWAYS

In 1995 there were 36,026 km of government-operated railways in Australia.

Australian National: 1 Richmond Rd, Keswick, SA 5035; tel. (8) 9217-4111; telex 88445; fax (8) 9231-9936; f. 1975; a federal statutory authority; responsible for intrastate freight services in SA and Tasmania and for interstate passenger services; Chair. JACK SMORGON; Man. Dir ANDREW NEAL (acting).

National Rail Corporation: 85 George St, Parramatta, NSW 2150; tel. (2) 9685-2555; fax (2) 9687-1808; Chair. B. BAIRD.

Public Transport Corporation (Victoria): 15th Floor, 589 Collins St, Melbourne, Vic 3000; tel. (3) 9619-1111; telex 151923; fax (3) 9619-2343; f. 1989; operates 6,127.8 km of track; Chief Exec. IAN R. DOBBS.

Queensland Rail: POB 1429, Brisbane, Qld 4001; tel. (7) 3235-2222; fax (7) 3235-1799; CEO VINCE O'ROURKE.

State Rail Authority of New South Wales: GPOB 29, Sydney, NSW 2001; tel. (2) 9219-8888; fax (2) 9224-4711; f. 1980; administers urban and country passenger services in NSW over a track network of 9,917 km; CEO (vacant).

Western Australian Government Railways (Westrail): Westrail Centre, POB S1422, Perth 6845, WA; tel. (8) 9326-2222; fax (8) 9326-2589; statutory authority competing in the freight, passenger and related transport markets in southern WA; operates over 5,583 main line route-km of track; Commr WAYNE JAMES (acting).

ROADS

In 1996 there were 810,000 km of roads, including 1,000 km of freeways, a further 103 km of toll roads, 45,889 km of highways, 77,045km of arterial and major roads and 30,596 of secondary tourist and other roads. Local roads in urban areas account for 93,677 km of the network and those in rural localities for 537,278 km.

Austroads Inc: POB K659, Haymarket, NSW 2000; tel. (2) 9264-7088; fax (2) 9264-1657; e-mail austroad@ozemail.com.au; f. 1989; asscn of road transport and traffic authorities.

SHIPPING

In December 1996 the Australian merchant fleet comprised 625 vessels, with a total displacement of 2,717,870 grt.

Adsteam Marine Ltd: Level 22, 6–10 O'Connell St, Sydney, NSW 2000; tel. (2) 9232-3955; fax (2) 9232-3988; e-mail info@adsteam.com.au; f. 1875; fmrly Adelaide Steamship Co; Man. Dir DAVID RYAN; Chief Exec. CLAY FREDERICK.

ANL Ltd (Australian National Line): POB 2238T, Melbourne, Vic 3001; tel. (3) 9257-0555; fax (3) 9257-0619; f. 1956; shipping agents; coastal and overseas container shipping and coastal bulk shipping; container management services; overseas container services to Hong Kong, Taiwan, the Philippines, Korea, Singapore, Malaysia, Thailand, Indonesia and Japan; extensive transhipment services; Chair. E. G. ANSON; CEO R. B. PERKINS.

BHP Transport Pty Ltd: 27th Level, 600 Bourke St, POB 86A, Melbourne, Vic 3000; tel. (3) 9609-3333; fax (3) 9609-2400; Chair. JEREMY ELLIS; Man. Dir JOHN B. PRESCOTT.

William Holyman and Sons Pty Ltd: No. 3 Berth, Bell Bay, Tas 7253; tel. (3) 6382-2383; telex 58517; fax (3) 6382-3391; coastal services; Chair. R. J. HOY.

Howard Smith Ltd: POB N364, Grosvenor Place, Sydney, NSW 2000; tel. (2) 9230-1777; fax (2) 9251-1190; harbour towage and other services; Chair. FRANCIS JOHN CONROY; CEO KENNETH JOHN MOSS.

CIVIL AVIATION

In the sparsely-populated areas of central and western Australia, air transport is extremely important, and Australia has pioneered services such as the Flying Doctor Service to overcome the problems of distance. The country is also well served by international airlines.

Ansett Australia (Ansett Australia Holdings Ltd): 501 Swanston St, Melbourne, Vic 3000; tel. (3) 9623-3333; telex 30085; fax (3) 9623-2691; e-mail Emma_Marsh@ansett.com.au; f. 1936; domestic and international passenger and cargo services; Exec. Chair. ROD EDDINGTON.

Eastern Australia Airlines: POB 538, Mascot, Sydney, NSW 2020; tel. (2) 9691-2333; telex 27231; fax (2) 9693-2715; domestic flights; Gen. Man. NEIL SHEA.

Qantas Airways Ltd: Qantas Centre, 203 Coward St, Mascot, NSW 2020; tel. (2) 9691-3636; telex 20113; fax (2) 9691-3277; f. 1920 as Queensland and Northern Territory Aerial Services; Australian Govt became sole owner in 1947; merged with Australian Airlines in Sept. 1992; British Airways purchased 25% in March 1993; remaining 75% transferred to private sector in 1995; services to 29 countries, including destinations in the UK, Europe, the USA, Canada, Japan, Asia, the Pacific, Africa and New Zealand; domestic services throughout Australia; Chair. GARY PEMBERTON; CEO JAMES STRONG.

Sunstate Airlines: POB 256, Hamilton, Qld 4007; tel. (7) 3308-9222; fax (7) 3308-9288; wholly owned by Qantas; operates passenger services within Queensland and to Newcastle (NSW) and Lord Howe Island; Gen. Man. ASHLEY KILROY.

Tourism

The main attractions are the cosmopolitan cities, the Great Barrier Reef, the Blue Mountains, water sports and also winter sports in the Australian Alps, notably the Snowy Mountains. The town of Alice Springs, the Aboriginal culture and the sandstone monolith of Ayers Rock (Uluru) are among the attractions of the desert interior. Much of Australia's wildlife is unique to the country. Australia received 4,164,825 foreign visitors in 1996. The majority of visitors come from Japan (813,113 in 1996) and other Asian countries, New Zealand (671,889 in 1996), Europe and the USA. Receipts totalled $A16,101m. in 1996.

Australian Tourist Commission: GPOB 2721, Sydney, NSW 1006; Level 4, 80 William St, Woolloomooloo, Sydney, NSW 2011; tel. (2) 9360-1111; fax (2) 9331-6469; internet http://www. aussie.net.au; f. 1967 for promotion of tourism; 10 offices, of which nine are overseas; Chair. DON MORRIS; Man. Dir JOHN MORSE.

AUSTRALIAN EXTERNAL TERRITORIES

CHRISTMAS ISLAND

Introduction

Christmas Island lies 360 km south of Java Head (Indonesia) in the Indian Ocean. The nearest point on the Australian coast is North West Cape, 1,408 km to the south-east. Christmas Island has no indigenous population. The population was 1,275 at the 1991 census (compared with 2,871 in 1981), comprising mainly ethnic Chinese (some 72%), but there were large minorities of Malays (about 7%) and Europeans (about 21%). A variety of languages are spoken, but English is the official language. The predominant religious affiliation is Buddhist (55% in 1991). The principal settlement and only anchorage is Flying Fish Cove.

Following annexation by the United Kingdom in 1888, Christmas Island was incorporated for administrative purposes with the Straits Settlements (now Singapore and part of Malaysia) in 1900. Japanese forces occupied the island from March 1942 until the end of the Second World War, and in 1946 Christmas Island became a dependency of Singapore. Administration was transferred to the United Kingdom on 1 January 1958, pending final transfer to Australia, effected on 1 October 1958. The Australian Government appointed Official Representatives to the Territory until 1968, when new legislation provided for an Administrator, appointed by the Governor-General. Responsibility for administration lies with the Minister for Sport, Territories and Local Government. In 1980 an Advisory Council was established for the Administrator to consult. In 1984 the Christmas Island Services Corporation was created to perform those functions which are normally the responsibility of municipal government. This body was placed under the direction of the Christmas Island Assembly, the first elections to which took place on 28 September 1985. Nine members were elected for one-year terms. On 3 November 1987 the Assembly was dissolved, and the Administrator empowered to perform its functions. The Corporation was superseded by the Christmas Island Shire Council in 1992.

In May 1994 an unofficial referendum on the island's status was held concurrently with local government elections. At the poll, sponsored by the Christmas Island Workers' Union, the islanders rejected an option to secede from Australia, but more than 85% of voters favoured increased local government control. The referendum was prompted, in part, by the Australian Government's plans to abolish the island's duty-free status (which had become a considerable source of revenue).

Since 1981 all residents of the island have been eligible to acquire Australian citizenship. In 1984 the Australian Government extended social security, health and education benefits to the island, and enfranchised Australian citizens resident there. Full income-tax liability was introduced in the late 1980s.

The economy has been based on the recovery of phosphates. During the year ending 30 June 1984 about 463,000 metric tons were exported to Australia, 332,000 tons to New Zealand and 341,000 tons to other countries. Reserves were estimated to be sufficient to enable production to be maintained until the mid-1990s. In November 1987 the Australian Government announced the closure of the phosphate mine, owing to industrial unrest and mining activity ceased in December. In 1990, however, the Government allowed the mine to be reopened by private operators, subject to certain conditions such as the preservation of the rain forest. A total of 220,000 metric tons of phosphates were produced in 1995. In that year an estimated 100 people were employed in the phosphate industry (whose activities consisted largely of the removal of stock-piles). Efforts are being made to develop the island's considerable potential for tourism. In 1989, in an attempt to protect the natural environment and many rare species of flora and fauna (including the Abbott's Booby and the Christmas frigate bird), the National Park was extended to cover some 70% of the island. Construction of a hotel and casino complex, covering 47 ha of land, began in 1991, and the resort opened in November 1993. In 1994 revenue from the development, which employed some 400 people in that year, totalled $A500m. A 50-room extension to the complex was constructed in 1995. In early 1997, however, fears for the nascent industry were expressed, following the decision by Ansett Australia to discontinue its twice-weekly air service to the island from September of that year.

The Australian Government announced that in 1992–97 an estimated $A132m. would be invested in the development of Christmas Island's infrastructure. The cost of the island's imports from Australia declined from $A27m. in 1994/95 to $A21m. in 1995/96, when the Territory's exports to that country earned $A2m.

Statistical Survey

AREA AND POPULATION

Area: 135 sq km (52 sq miles).

Population: 2,871 (males 1,918, females 953) at census of 30 June 1981; 1,275 at August 1991 census. *Ethnic Groups* (1981): Chinese 1,587; Malay 693; European 336; Total (incl. others) 2,871. Source: mainly UN, *Demographic Yearbook*.

Density (1991): 9.4 per sq km.

Births and Deaths (1985): Registered live births 36 (birth rate 15.8 per 1,000); Registered deaths 2.

MINING

Natural Phosphates (official estimates, '000 metric tons): 285 in 1994; 220 in 1995.

FINANCE

Currency and Exchange Rates: Australian currency is used (see p. 455).

EXTERNAL TRADE

Principal Trading Partners (phosphate exports, '000 metric tons, year ending 30 June 1984): Australia 463; New Zealand 332; Total (incl. others) 1,136.

1995/96 ($A'000): *Imports:* Australia 21,000. *Exports:* Australia 2,000.

TRANSPORT

International Sea-borne Shipping (estimated freight traffic, '000 metric tons, 1990): Goods loaded 1,290; Goods unloaded 68. Source: UN, *Monthly Bulletin of Statistics*.

EDUCATION

Pre-primary (1992): 53 pupils.
Primary (1992): 253 pupils.
Secondary (1992): 53 pupils.

Source: *The Commonwealth Yearbook*.

Directory

The Government

The Administrator, appointed by the Governor-General of Australia and responsible to the Minister for Sport, Territories and Local Government, is the senior government representative on the island.

Administrator: Graham Nicholls.

Administration Headquarters: POB AAA, Christmas Island 6798, Indian Ocean; tel. 7901; fax 8524.

Christmas Island Shire Council: Govt Offices, POB 863, Christmas Island 6798, Indian Ocean; tel. 8300; fax 8304.

Judicial System

The judicial system comprises the Supreme Court, District Court, Magistrate's Court and Children's Court.

Supreme Court: c/o Govt Offices, Christmas Island 6798, Indian Ocean; tel. 647911; fax 648530; Judges (non-resident): Robert Sheraton French, Malcolm Cameron Lee.

Managing Registrar: Jeffery Low; Govt Offices, Christmas Island 6798, Indian Ocean; tel. 647911; fax 648530.

Religion

According to the census of 1991, of the 1,275 residents of Christmas Island, some 55% were Buddhists, 10% were Muslims, and 15% were Christians. Within the Christian churches, Christmas Island lies in the jurisdiction of both the Anglican and Roman Catholic Archbishops of Perth, in Western Australia.

Radio and Television

There were an estimated 1,000 radio receivers and 600 television receivers in use in 1997.

Christmas Island Community Radio Service: POB AAA, Christmas Island 6798, Indian Ocean; tel. 648316; telex 78002; fax 648304; f. 1967; operated by the Administration since 1991; daily broadcasting service by Radio VLU-2 on 1422 KHz, in English, Malay, Cantonese and Mandarin; Station Man. The Administrator.

Christmas Island Tropical Radio VLU2: POB AAA, Christmas Island 6798, Indian Ocean; tel. 648316; fax 648315; Station Man. The Administrator.

Trade and Industry

Christmas Island Shire Council: Govt Offices, POB 863, Christmas Island 6798, Indian Ocean; tel. 648300; fax 648304; f. 1992 by Territories Law Reform Act to replace Christmas Island Services Corpn; provides local govt services; major wholesaler and retailer; manages tourism and economic development; Pres. ANDREW SMOLDERS; CEO PAUL MABERLY.

Christmas Island Workers' Union: Poon Saan Rd, POB 84, Christmas Island 6798, Indian Ocean; tel. 648471; fax 648470; fmrly represented phosphate workers; Pres. CHAN BOO HWA (acting); Gen. Sec. TONY MOCKERIDGE; 800 mems.

Transport

Railway lines, with a total length of 24 km, exist to serve the island's phosphate mines. There are good roads in the developed areas. Ansett Australia operates a twice-weekly flight from Perth, via the Cocos (Keeling) Islands, and a private Christmas Island-based charter company operates services to Singapore. In early 1997, however, Ansett Australia announced its decision to discontinue its twice-weekly service to the island from September of that year. The Australian National Line (ANL) operates ships to the Australian mainland. Cargo vessels from Perth deliver supplies to the island every six to eight weeks. The Joint Island Supply System, established in 1989, provides a shipping service for Christmas Island and the Cocos Islands. The only anchorage is at Flying Fish Cove.

Tourism

Tourism is a growing sector of the island's economy. Visitors are attracted by the unique flora and fauna, as well as the excellent conditions for scuba-diving and game-fishing. An increasing number of tourists from Indonesia, Malaysia and Singapore visit the island for its gambling facilities.

Christmas Island Resort Pty Ltd: POB 888, Christmas Island 6798, Indian Ocean; tel. 648888; fax 648897; Gen. Man. JOHN FARROW; Dir FRANK WOODMORE.

Christmas Island Tours and Travel: Christmas Island 6798, Indian Ocean; Dir TAN SIM KIAT.

COCOS (KEELING) ISLANDS

Introduction

The Cocos (Keeling) Islands are 27 in number and lie 2,768 km north-west of Perth, in the Indian Ocean. The islands form two low-lying coral atolls, densely covered with coconut palms. The climate is equable, with temperatures varying from 21°C (69°F) to 32°C (88°F), and rainfall of 2,000 mm per year. In 1981 some 58% of the population were of the Cocos Malay community, and 26% were Europeans. The Cocos Malays are descendants of the people brought to the islands by Alexander Hare and of labourers who were subsequently introduced by the Clunies-Ross family (see below). English is the official language, but Cocos Malay and Malay are also widely spoken. Most of the inhabitants are Muslims (56.8% in 1981). Home Island, which had a population of 446 in mid-1992, is where the Cocos Malay community is based. The only other inhabited island is West Island, with a population of 147 in mid-1992, and where most of the European community lives, the administration is based and the airport is located. The total population of the islands was estimated at 670 in 1994.

The islands were uninhabited when discovered by Capt. William Keeling, of the British East India Company, in 1609, and the first settlement was not established until 1826, by Alexander Hare. The islands were declared a British possession in 1857 and came successively under the authority of the Governors of Ceylon (now Sri Lanka), from 1878, and the Straits Settlements (now Singapore and part of Malaysia), from 1886. Also in 1886 the British Crown granted all land on the islands above the high-water mark to John Clunies-Ross and his heirs and successors in perpetuity. In 1946, when the islands became a dependency of the Colony of Singapore, a resident administrator, responsible to the Governor of Singapore, was appointed. Administration of the islands was transferred to the Commonwealth of Australia on 23 November 1955. The agent of the Australian Government was known as the Official Representative until 1975, when an Administrator was appointed. The Minister for Sport, Territories and Local Government is responsible for the governance of the islands. The Territory is part of the Northern Territory Electoral District.

In June 1977 the Australian Government announced new policies concerning the islands, which resulted in its purchase from John Clunies-Ross of the whole of his interests in the islands, with the exception of his residence and associated buildings. The purchase for $A6.5m. took effect on 1 September 1978. An attempt by the Australian Government to acquire Clunies-Ross' remaining property was deemed by the Australian High Court in October 1984 to be unconstitutional.

In July 1979 the Cocos (Keeling) Islands Council was established, with a wide range of functions in the Home Island village area (which the Government transferred to the Council on trust for the benefit of the Cocos Malay community) and, from September 1984, in the greater part of the rest of the Territory.

On 6 April 1984 a referendum to decide the future political status of the islands was held by the Australian Government, with UN observers present. A large majority voted in favour of integration with Australia. As a result, the islanders were to acquire the rights, privileges and obligations of all Australian citizens. In July 1992 the Cocos (Keeling) Islands Council was replaced by the Cocos (Keeling) Islands Shire Council, modelled on the local government and state law of Western Australia.

Following unsuccessful investment in a shipping venture, the Clunies-Ross family was declared bankrupt in mid-1993, and the Australian Government took possession of its property.

Although local fishing is good, some livestock is kept and domestic gardens provide vegetables, bananas and papayas (pawpaws), the islands are not self-sufficient, and other foodstuffs, fuels and consumer items are imported from mainland Australia. A Cocos postal service (including a philatelic bureau) came into operation in September 1979, and revenue from the service is used for the benefit of the community.

Coconuts, grown throughout the islands, are the sole cash crop: total output was an estimated 6,000 metric tons in 1995. Total exports of coconuts in 1984/85 were 202 metric tons. It was hoped that a tourist industry could be developed to provide an additional source of revenue for the islands by the late 1990s.

Primary education is provided at the schools on Home and West Islands. Secondary education is provided to the age of 16 years on West Island. A bursary scheme enables Cocos Malay children to continue their education on the Australian mainland.

Statistical Survey

AREA AND POPULATION

Area: 14.2 sq km (5.5 sq miles).

Population: 555 (males 298, females 257) at census of 30 June 1981; 647 at census of 1991; 593 (Home Island residents 446, West Island residents 147) at mid-1992; 670 (official estimate) in 1994. *Ethnic Groups* (1981): Cocos Malay 320; European 143; Total (incl. others) 555. Source: mainly UN, *Demographic Yearbook*.

Density (1994): 47.2 per sq km.

Births and Deaths (1986): Registered live births 12 (birth rate 19.8 per 1,000); Registered deaths 2.

AGRICULTURE

Production (FAO estimates, metric tons, 1995): Coconuts 6,000; Copra 1,000. Source: FAO, *Production Yearbook*.

FINANCE

Currency and Exchange Rates: Australian currency is used (see p. 455).

EXTERNAL TRADE

Principal Commodities (metric tons, year ending 30 June 1985): *Exports*: Coconuts 202. *Imports*: Most requirements come from Australia. The trade deficit is offset by philatelic sales and Australian federal grants and subsidies.

Directory

The Government

The Administrator, appointed by the Governor-General of Australia and responsible to the Minister for Sport, Territories and Local Government, is the senior government representative in the islands.

Administrator: RON HARVEY.

Administrative Headquarters: West Island, Cocos (Keeling) Islands 6799, Indian Ocean; tel. 626660; fax 626697.

Cocos (Keeling) Islands Shire Council: West Island, Cocos (Keeling) Islands 6799, Indian Ocean; tel. 626649; fax 626668; f. 1992 by Territories Law Reform Act; Pres. YAKIN CAPSTAN; CEO CHRIS JACKSON.

Judicial System

Supreme Court, Cocos (Keeling) Islands: West Island Police Station, Cocos (Keeling) Islands 6799, Indian Ocean; tel. 626660; fax 626601; Judge: ROBERT SHERATON FRENCH; Additional Judge: MALCOLM CAMERON LEE.

Magistrates' Court, Cocos (Keeling) Islands: Special Magistrate: KEN MOORE (non-resident).

Managing Registrar: MAUREEN ELLIS; Cocos (Keeling) Islands 6799, Indian Ocean; tel. 6661; fax 6697.

Religion

According to the census of 1981, of the 555 residents, 314 (some 57%) were Muslims and 124 (22%) Christians. The majority of Muslims live on Home Island, while most Christians are West Island residents. The Cocos Islands lie within both the Anglican and the Roman Catholic archdioceses of Perth (Western Australia).

Radio

There were an estimated 300 radio receivers in use in 1992.

Radio VKW Cocos: POB 33, Cocos (Keeling) Islands 6799, Indian Ocean; tel. 626666; non-commercial; daily broadcasting service in Cocos Malay and English; Station Man. SEAN LAVERY.

A television service, broadcasting Indonesian satellite television programmes and videotapes of Australian television programmes, began operating on an intermittent basis in September 1992.

Industry

Cocos (Keeling) Islands Co-operative Society Ltd: Home Island, Cocos (Keeling) Islands, Indian Ocean; tel. 626702; fax 626764; f. 1979; conducts the business enterprises of the Cocos Islanders; activities include boat construction and repairs, copra and coconut production, sail-making, stevedoring and airport operation; owns and operates a supermarket and tourist accommodation; Chair. MOHAMED SAID BIN CHONGKIN; Gen. Man. RONALD TAYLOR.

Transport

Ansett Australia provides a twice-weekly service from Perth, via Christmas Island, for passengers, supplies and mail to and from the airport on West Island. In early 1997, however, the airline announced its intention to discontinue this service from September of that year. Cargo vessels from Perth deliver supplies, at intervals of six to eight weeks.

NORFOLK ISLAND

Introductory Survey

Location, Climate, Language, Religion, Capital

Norfolk Island lies off the eastern coast of Australia, about 1,400 km east of Brisbane, to the south of New Caledonia and 640 km north of New Zealand. The Territory also comprises uninhabited Phillip Island and Nepean Island, 7 km and 1 km south of the main island respectively. Norfolk Island is hilly and fertile, with a coastline of cliffs and an area of 34.6 sq km (13.3 sq miles). It is about 8 km long and 4.8 km wide. The climate is mild and subtropical, and the average annual rainfall is 1,350 mm, most of which occurs between May and August. The population, which numbered 1,772 in August 1996, consists of 'islanders' (descendants of the mutineers from HMS *Bounty*, evacuated from Pitcairn Island, who numbered 683 in 1996) and 'mainlanders' (originally from Australia, New Zealand or the United Kingdom). English is the official language, but a local Polynesian dialect (related to Pitcairnese) is also spoken. Most of the population (71.5% at the 1991 census) adhere to the Christian religion. The capital of the Territory is Kingston.

Recent History and Economic Affairs

The island was uninhabited when discovered in 1774 by a British expedition, led by Capt. James Cook. Norfolk Island was used as a penal settlement from 1788 to 1814 and again from 1825 to 1855, when it was abandoned. In 1856 it was resettled by 194 emigrants from Pitcairn Island, which had become overpopulated. Norfolk Island was administered as a separate colony until 1897, when it became a dependency of New South Wales. In 1913 control was transferred to the Australian Government. Norfolk Island has a continuing dispute with the Australian Government concerning the island's status as a territory of the Commonwealth of Australia. There have been successive assertions of Norfolk Island's right to self-determination, as a distinct colony.

Under the Norfolk Island Act 1979, Norfolk Island is progressing to responsible legislative and executive government, enabling the Territory to administer its own affairs to the greatest practicable extent. Wide powers are exercised by the nine-member Legislative Assembly and by the Executive Council, comprising the executive members of the Legislative Assembly who have ministerial-type responsibilities. The Act preserves the Australian Government's responsibility for Norfolk Island as a territory under its authority, with the Minister for Sport, Territories and Local Government as the responsible minister. The Act indicated that consideration would be given within five years to an extension of the powers of the Legislative Assembly and the political and administrative institutions of Norfolk Island. In 1985 legislative and executive responsibility was assumed by the Norfolk Island government for public works and services, civil defence, betting and gaming, territorial archives and matters relating to the exercise of executive authority. In 1988 further amendments empowered the Legislative Assembly to select a Norfolk Island government auditor (territorial accounts were previously audited by the Commonwealth Auditor-General). The office of Chief Minister was replaced by that of the President of the Legislative Assembly. David Ernest Buffett was reappointed to this post following the May 1992 general election. A lack of consensus among members of the Executive Council on several major issues prompted early legislative elections in April 1994. The newly-elected seventh Legislative Assembly was remarkable in having three female members. Following elections in April 1997, in which 22 candidates contested the nine seats, George Smith was appointed President of the eighth Legislative Assembly.

In December 1991 the population of Norfolk Island overwhelmingly rejected a proposal, made by the Australian Government, to include the island in the Australian federal electorate. The outcome of the poll led the Australian Government, in June 1992, to announce that it had abandoned the plan. Similarly, in late 1996 a proposal by the Australian Government to combine Norfolk Island's population with that of Canberra for record-keeping purposes was strongly opposed by the islanders.

In late 1997 the Legislative Assembly debated the issue of increased self-determination for the island. Pro-independence supporters argued that the Territory could generate sufficient income by exploiting gas- and oilfields in the island's exclusive economic zone.

Despite the island's natural fertility, agriculture is no longer the principal economic activity. About 400 ha of land are arable. The main crops are Kentia palm seed, cereals, vegetables and fruit. Cattle and pigs are farmed for domestic consumption. Development of a fisheries industry is restricted by the lack of a harbour. Some flowers and plants are grown commercially. The administration is increasing the area devoted to Norfolk Island pine and hardwoods. Seed of the Norfolk Island pine is exported. Potential oil- and gas-bearing sites in the island's waters may provide a possible future source of revenue. A re-export industry has been developed to serve the island's tourist industry.

The authorities receive revenue from customs duties (some $A2.5m., equivalent to 27.0% of total revenue, in 1995/96) and the sale of postage stamps, but tourism is the island's main industry. In 1996 there were 29,787 tourist arrivals on the island. The cessation of scheduled airline operations from Australia by Ansett Australia during 1997, however, resulted in a marked decrease in tourist arrivals in that year. In 1985 and 1986 the Governments of Australia and Norfolk Island jointly established the 465-ha Norfolk Island National Park. This was to protect the remaining native forest, which is the habitat of several unique species of flora (including the largest fern in the world) and fauna (such as the Norfolk Island green parrot, the guavabird and the boobook owl). Conservation efforts include the development of Phillip Island as a nature reserve.

Education

Education is free and compulsory for all children between the ages of six and 15. Pupils attend the government school from infant to secondary level. A total of 329 pupils were enrolled at infant, primary and secondary levels in 1991/92. Students wishing to follow higher education in Australia are eligible for bursaries and scholarships. The budgetary allocation for education was $A1,376,419 in 1995/96.

Weights and Measures

The metric system is in force.

Statistical Survey

Source: The Administration of Norfolk Island, Administration Offices, Kingston, Norfolk Island 2899; tel. 22001; telex 30003; fax 23177.

AREA AND POPULATION

Area: 34.6 sq km (13.3 sq miles).

Population: 2,285 (males 1,111, females 1,174), including 373 visitors, at census of 6 August 1991; 1,896 (resident population) at 30 June 1993; 2,181 (males 1,039, females 1,142), including 409 visitors, at census of 6 August 1996.

Density (resident population, 1996): 51.2 per sq km.

Births, Marriages and Deaths (1996): Live births 15; Marriages 34; Deaths 21.

Economically Active Population (persons aged 10 years and over, 1996 census): 1,273 (males 629, females 644).

FINANCE

Currency and Exchange Rates: Australian currency is used (see p. 455).

Budget (year ending 30 June 1996): Revenue $A9,324,156 (Customs duties $A2,517,768); Expenditure $A8,723,704.

EXTERNAL TRADE

1995/96 (year ending 30 June): *Imports*: $A26,907,000, mainly from Australia and New Zealand. *Exports*: $A4,985,000.

TOURISM

Visitors (year ending 30 June): 27,224 in 1994; 28,501 in 1995; 29,787 in 1996.

COMMUNICATIONS MEDIA

Radio Receivers (1996): 2,500 in use.

Television Receivers (1996): 1,200 in use.

Non-daily Newspaper (1996): 1 (estimated circulation 1,000).

Source: UNESCO, *Statistical Yearbook*.

EDUCATION

Institution (1997): 1 state school incorporating infant, primary and secondary levels.

Teachers (1997): Full-time 21; Part-time 2.

Students (1997): Infants 87; Primary 106; Secondary 135.

Directory

The Constitution

The Norfolk Island Act 1979 constitutes the administration of the Territory as a body politic and provides for a responsible legislative and executive system, enabling it to administer its own affairs to the greatest practicable extent. The preamble of the Act states that it is the intention of the Australian Parliament to consider the further extension of powers.

The Act provides for an Administrator, appointed by the Australian Government, who shall administer the government of Norfolk Island as a territory under the authority of the Commonwealth of Australia. The Administrator is required to act on the advice of the Executive Council or the responsible Commonwealth Minister in those matters specified as within their competence. Every proposed law passed by the Legislative Assembly must be effected by the assent of the Administrator, who may grant or withhold that assent, reserve the proposed law for the Governor-General's pleasure or recommend amendments.

The Act provides for the Legislative Assembly and the Executive Council, comprising the executive members of the Assembly who have ministerial-type responsibilities. Both bodies are led by the President of the Legislative Assembly. The nine members of the Legislative Assembly are elected for a term of not more than three years under a cumulative method of voting: each elector is entitled to as many votes (all of equal value) as there are vacancies, but may not give more than four votes to any one candidate. The nine candidates who receive the most votes are declared elected.

The Government

The Administrator, who is the senior representative of the Commonwealth Government, is appointed by the Governor-General of Australia and is responsible to the Minister for Sport, Territories and Local Government. A form of responsible legislative and executive government was extended to the island in 1979, as outlined above.

Administrator: TONY MESSNER (assumed office on 4 August 1997).

EXECUTIVE COUNCIL

(December 1997)

President of the Legislative Assembly and Minister for Finance and Strategic Planning: GEORGE CHARLES SMITH.

Deputy President: DAVID ERNEST BUFFETT.

Minister for Community and Resource Management: CEDRIC NEWTON ION-ROBINSON.

Minister for Tourism and Commerce: JAMES GARY ROBERTSON.

Minister for Health and Immigration: JOHN T. BROWN.

GOVERNMENT OFFICE

Administration of Norfolk Island: Administration Offices, Kingston, Norfolk Island 2899; tel. 22001; telex 30003; fax 23177; all govt depts; Chief Administrative Officer: IVENS F. BUFFETT (acting).

Legislature

LEGISLATIVE ASSEMBLY

Nine candidates are elected for not more than three years. The most recent general election was held on 30 April 1997.

President: GEORGE CHARLES SMITH.

Members: DAVID ERNEST BUFFETT, JOHN T. BROWN, JAMES GARY ROBERTSON, CEDRIC NEWTON ION-ROBINSON, GEOFFREY R. GARDNER, RONALD C. NOBBS, ROBERT E. ADAMS, BRIAN G. BATES.

Judicial System

Supreme Court of Norfolk Island: Kingston; appeals lie to the Federal Court of Australia.

Judges: BRYAN ALAN BEAUMONT (Chief Justice), MURRAY RUTLEDGE WILCOX.

Religion

The majority of the population professes Christianity (70.4%, according to the census of 1996), with the principal denominations being the Church of England (38%), the Uniting Church (14%) and the Catholic Church (11%).

The Press

Norfolk Island Government Gazette: Kingston, Norfolk Island 2899; tel. 22001; fax 23177; weekly.

Norfolk Islander: Greenways Press, POB 150, Norfolk Island 2899; tel. 22159; fax 22948; f. 1965; weekly; Co-Editors TOM LLOYD, TIM LLOYD; circ. 1,000.

Radio and Television

There were an estimated 2,500 radio receivers and 1,200 television receivers in use in 1997.

Norfolk Island Broadcasting Service: New Cascade Rd, POB 456, Norfolk Island 2899; tel. 22137; fax 23298; govt-owned; non-commercial; relays television programmes from Australia; broadcasts 112 hours per week; Broadcasting Man. MARGARET MEADOWS.

Norfolk Island Television Service: f. 1987; programmes of Australian Broadcasting Corpn and Special Broadcasting Service Corpn, relayed by satellite.

TV Norfolk (TVN): locally-operated service featuring programmes of local events and information for tourists.

Finance

BANKING

Commonwealth Banking Corpn (Australia): Burnt Pine, Norfolk Island 2899; tel. 22144; fax 22805.

Westpac Banking Corpn Savings Bank Ltd (Australia): Burnt Pine, Norfolk Island 2899; tel. 22120; fax 22808.

Trade

Norfolk Island Chamber of Commerce: POB 370, Norfolk Island 2899; tel. 22317; fax 22802; f. 1966; affiliated to the Australian Chamber of Commerce; 60 mems; Pres. BRUCE WALKER; Sec. TOM JACOBSON.

Transport

ROADS

There are about 100 km of roads, including 85 km of sealed road.

SHIPPING

Norfolk Island is served by the three shipping lines, Neptune Shipping, Pacific Direct Line and Roslyndale Shipping Company Pty Ltd. A small tanker from Nouméa (New Caledonia) delivers petroleum products to the island and another from Australia delivers liquid propane gas.

CIVIL AVIATION

Norfolk Island has one airport, with two runways (of 1,900 m and 1,550 m), capable of taking medium jet aircraft. Air New Zealand operates a twice-weekly direct service between Auckland and Norfolk Island. Charter flights from New Caledonia also serve the island. The cessation of scheduled services from Australia by Ansett Australia during 1997 had a negative effect on the island's important tourist industry. As a consequence, Norfolk Jet Express was established to provide a daily service to Australia, and Flight West Airlines began to operate a flight from Brisbane (Australia) to the island.

Tourism

Norfolk Island Visitors Information Centre: Taylors Rd, Burnt Pine, POB 211, Norfolk Island 2899; tel. 22147; fax 23109; e-mail info@nigtb.gov.nf; Gen. Man. ANTHONY KIRCHNER.

OTHER TERRITORIES

Territory of Ashmore and Cartier Islands

The Ashmore Islands (known as West, Middle and East Islands) and Cartier Island are situated in the Timor Sea, about 850 km and 790 km west of Darwin respectively. The Ashmore Islands cover some 93 ha of land and Cartier Island covers 0.4 ha. The islands are small and uninhabited, consisting of sand and coral, surrounded by shoals and reefs. Grass is the main vegetation. Maximum elevation is about 2.5 m above sea-level. The islands abound in birdlife, sea-cucumbers (*bêches-de-mer*) and, seasonally, turtles.

The United Kingdom took formal possession of the Ashmore Islands in 1878, and Cartier Island was annexed in 1909. The islands were placed under the authority of the Commonwealth of Australia in 1931. They were annexed to, and deemed to form part of, the Northern Territory of Australia in 1938. On 1 July 1978 the Australian Government assumed direct responsibility for the administration of the islands, which rests with a parliamentary secretary appointed by the Minister for Sport, Territories and Local Government. Periodic visits are made to the islands by the Royal Australian Navy and aircraft of the Royal Australian Air Force, and the Civil Coastal Surveillance Service makes aerial surveys of the islands and neighbouring waters. The oilfields of Jabiru and Challis are located in waters adjacent to the Territory.

In August 1983 Ashmore Reef was declared a national nature reserve. An agreement between Australia and Indonesia permits Indonesian traditional fishermen to continue fishing in the territorial waters and to land on West Island to obtain supplies of fresh water. In 1985 the Australian Government extended the laws of the Northern Territory to apply in Ashmore and Cartier, and decided to contract a vessel to be stationed at Ashmore Reef during the Indonesian fishing season (March–November) to monitor the fishermen.

Australian Antarctic Territory

The Australian Antarctic Territory was established by Order in Council in February 1933 and proclaimed in August 1936, subsequent to the Australian Antarctic Territory Acceptance Act (1933). It consists of the portion of Antarctica (divided by the French territory of Terre Adélie) lying between 45°E and 136°E, and between 142°E and 160°E. The Antarctic Division of the Department of the Environment, Sport and Territories was established in 1948 as a permanent agency, and to administer and provide support for the Australian National Antarctic Research Expeditions (ANARE), which maintains three permanent scientific stations (Mawson, Davis and Casey) in the Territory. The area of the Territory is estimated to be 5,896,500 sq km (2,276,650 sq miles), and there are no permanent inhabitants, although there is a permanent presence of scientific personnel. In late 1997 the Antarctic Science Advisory Committee suggested closing two of Australia's three research stations (Mawson and Casey), partly as a result of the increasing automation of data-gathering, and the establishment of an airline service and a base for adventure tourism. Environmentalists expressed alarm at the proposal to encourage tourism in the Territory, which, they claimed, could damage the area's sensitive ecology. The Territory is administered by a parliamentary secretary, appointed by the Minister for Sport, Territories and Local Government. Australia is a signatory to the Antarctic Treaty (see p. 398).

Coral Sea Islands Territory

The Coral Sea Islands became a Territory of the Commonwealth of Australia under the Coral Sea Islands Act of 1969. The Territory lies east of Queensland, between the Great Barrier Reef and longitude 156° 06′E, and between latitude 12°S and 24°S, and comprises several islands and reefs. The islands are composed largely of sand and coral, and have no permanent fresh water supply, but some have a cover of grass and scrub. The area has been known as a notorious hazard to shipping since the 19th century, the danger of the reefs being compounded by shifting sand cays and occasional tropical cyclones. The Coral Sea Islands have been acquired by Australia by numerous acts of sovereignty since the early years of the 20th century.

Spread over a sea area of approximately 780,000 sq km (300,000 sq miles), all the islands and reefs in the Territory are very small, totalling only a few sq km of land area. They include Cato Island, Chilcott Islet in the Coringa Group, and the Willis Group. A meteorological station, operated by the Commonwealth Bureau of Meteorology and with a staff of four, has provided a service on one of the Willis Group since 1921. The other islands are uninhabited. There are eight automatic weather stations (on Cato Island, Flinders Reef, Frederick Reef, Holmes Reef, Lihou Reef, Creal Reef, Marion Reef and Gannet Cay) and several navigation aids distributed throughout the Territory.

The Act constituting the Territory did not establish an administration on the islands, but provides means of controlling the activities of those who visit them. The Lihou Reef and Coringa-Herald National Nature Reserves were established in 1982 to provide protection for the wide variety of terrestrial and marine wildlife, which include rare species of birds and sea turtles (one of which is the largest, and among the most endangered, of the world's species of sea turtle). The Australian Government has concluded agreements for the protection of endangered and migratory birds with Japan and the People's Republic of China. The Governor-General of Australia is empowered to make ordinances for the peace, order and good government of the Territory and, by ordinance, the laws of the Australian Capital Territory apply. The Supreme Court and Court of Petty Sessions of Norfolk Island have jurisdiction in the Territory. The Territory is administered by a parliamentary secretary appointed by the Minister for Sport, Territories and Local Government, and the area is visited regularly by the Royal Australian Navy.

Territory of Heard Island and the McDonald Islands

These islands are situated about 4,000 km (2,500 miles) south-west of Perth, Western Australia. The Territory, consisting of Heard Island, Shag Island (8 km north of Heard) and the McDonald Islands, is almost entirely covered in ice and has a total area of 369 sq km (142 sq miles). The Territory has been administered by the Australian Government since December 1947, when it established a scientific research station on Heard Island (which functioned until 1955) and the United Kingdom ceded its claim to sovereignty. There are no permanent inhabitants, but Australian expeditions visit occasionally. The island is of considerable scientific interest, as it is believed to be one of the few Antarctic habitats uncontaminated by introduced organisms. Heard Island is about 44 km long and 20 km wide and possesses an active volcano, named Big Ben. In January 1991 an international team of scientists travelled to Heard Island to conduct research involving the transmission of sound waves, beneath the surface of the ocean, in order to monitor any evidence of the 'greenhouse effect' (melting of polar ice and the rise in sea-level as a consequence of pollution). The pulses of sound, which travel at a speed largely influenced by temperature, were to be received at various places around the world, with international co-operation. Heard Island was chosen for the experiment because of its unique location, from which direct paths to the five principal oceans extend. The McDonald Islands, with an area of about 1 sq km (0.4 sq miles), lie some 42 km west of Heard Island. The islands are administered by the Antarctic Division of the Department of the Environment, Sport and Territories.

AUSTRIA

Introductory Survey

Location, Climate, Language, Religion, Flag, Capital

The Republic of Austria lies in central Europe, bordered by Switzerland and Liechtenstein to the west, by Germany and the Czech Republic to the north, by Hungary and Slovakia to the east, and by Italy and Slovenia to the south. The climate varies sharply, owing to great differences in elevation. The mean annual temperature lies between 7°C and 9°C (45°F and 48°F). The population is 99% German-speaking, with small Croat and Slovene-speaking minorities. The majority of the inhabitants profess Christianity: about 77% are Roman Catholics and about 5% are Protestants. The national flag (proportions 3 by 2) consists of three equal horizontal stripes, of red, white and red. The state flag has, in addition, the coat of arms (a small shield, with horizontal stripes of red separated by a white stripe, superimposed on a black eagle, wearing a golden crown and holding a sickle and a hammer in its feet, with a broken chain between the legs) in the centre. The capital is Vienna (Wien).

Recent History

Austria was formerly the centre of the Austrian (later Austro-Hungarian) Empire, which comprised a large part of central Europe. The Empire, under the Habsburg dynasty, was dissolved in 1918, at the end of the First World War, and Austria proper became a republic. The first post-war Council of Ministers was a coalition led by Dr Karl Renner, who remained Chancellor until 1920, when a new Constitution introduced a federal form of government. Many of Austria's inhabitants favoured union with Germany but this was forbidden by the post-war peace treaties. In March 1938, however, Austria was occupied by Nazi Germany's armed forces and incorporated into the German Reich, led by the Austrian-born Adolf Hitler.

After Hitler's defeat in Austria, a provisional Government, under Dr Renner, was established in April 1945. In July, following Germany's surrender to the Allied forces, Austria was divided into four zones, occupied by forces of the USA, the USSR, the United Kingdom and France. At the first post-war elections to the 165-seat Nationalrat (National Council), held in November 1945, the conservative Österreichische Volkspartei (ÖVP, Austrian People's Party) won 85 seats and the Sozialistische Partei Österreichs (SPÖ, Socialist Party of Austria) secured 76. The two parties formed a coalition Government. In December Dr Renner became the first President of the second Austrian Republic, holding office until his death in December 1950. However, it was not until May 1955 that the four powers signed a State Treaty with Austria, ending the occupation and recognizing Austrian independence, effective from 27 July; occupation forces left in October.

More than 20 years of coalition government came to an end in April 1966 with the formation of a Council of Ministers by the ÖVP alone. Dr Josef Klaus, the Federal Chancellor since April 1964, remained in office. The SPÖ achieved a relative majority in the March 1970 general election and formed a minority Government, with Dr Bruno Kreisky (a former Minister of Foreign Affairs, who had been party leader since 1967) as Chancellor. In April 1971 the incumbent President, Franz Jonas of the SPÖ, was re-elected, defeating the ÖVP candidate, Dr Kurt Waldheim, a former Minister of Foreign Affairs (who subsequently served two five-year terms as UN Secretary-General, beginning in January 1972). The SPÖ won an absolute majority of seats in the Nationalrat at general elections in October 1971 (when the number of seats was increased from 165 to 183) and October 1975. President Jonas died in April 1974, and the subsequent presidential election, held in June, was won by Dr Rudolf Kirchschläger, the Minister of Foreign Affairs since 1970. He was re-elected for a second six-year term in 1980.

In November 1978 the Government's proposal to commission Austria's first nuclear power plant was defeated in a national referendum. Despite expectations that Kreisky would resign, he received full support from the SPÖ and emerged in an apparently even stronger position: at the general election in May 1979 the SPÖ increased its majority in the Nationalrat. The possible use of nuclear power remained a controversial issue, however.

The general election of April 1983 marked the end of the 13-year era of one-party government, when the SPÖ lost its absolute majority in the Nationalrat and Kreisky, unwilling to participate in a coalition, resigned as Chancellor. The reduction in the SPÖ's representation was partly attributed to the emergence of two environmentalist 'Green' parties, both founded in 1982. The two parties together received more than 3% of the total votes, but failed to win any seats. Kreisky's successor, Dr Fred Sinowatz (the former Vice-Chancellor and Minister of Education), took office in May, leading a coalition of the SPÖ and the small right-wing Freiheitliche Partei Österreichs (FPÖ, Freedom Party of Austria). The new Government continued the social welfare policy of its predecessor, in addition to maintaining Austria's foreign policy of 'active neutrality'.

A presidential election was held in May 1986 to choose a successor to Kirchschläger. The SPÖ candidate for the election was Dr Kurt Steyrer (the Minister of Health and Environment), while Dr Waldheim, the former UN Secretary-General, stood as an independent candidate, although with the support of the ÖVP. The campaign was dominated by allegations that Waldheim, a former officer in the army of Nazi Germany, had been implicated in atrocities committed by the Nazis in the Balkans in 1942–45; the resulting controversy divided the country and brought unexpected international attention to the election. Waldheim won a run-off ballot in June, with 54% of the votes. The defeat of the SPÖ presidential candidate led Chancellor Sinowatz and four of his ministers to resign. Dr Franz Vranitzky, hitherto the Minister of Finance, became the new Chancellor. In September the FPÖ elected a new leader, Dr Jörg Haider, who represented the right wing of his party. This precipitated the end of the partnership between the SPÖ and the FPÖ, and the general election for the Nationalrat, scheduled for April 1987, was brought forward to November 1986. No party won an absolute majority: the SPÖ took 80 seats, the ÖVP 77, the FPÖ 18 and the alliance of 'Green' parties eight. Following several weeks of negotiations, a 'grand coalition' of the SPÖ and the ÖVP, with Vranitzky as Chancellor, was formed in January 1987.

Waldheim's election to the presidency was controversial both domestically and internationally, and Austria's relations with Israel and the USA, in particular, were severely strained. In February 1988 a specially-appointed international commission of historians concluded that Waldheim must have been aware of the atrocities that had been committed. Waldheim refused to resign, but in June 1991 he announced that he would not seek a second presidential term.

At the general election held in October 1990 the SPÖ retained its position as the largest single party, securing 43% of the votes and increasing its number of seats in the Nationalrat by one, to 81. The ÖVP, however, suffered a considerable reverse: with 32% of the votes, it obtained 60 seats in the Nationalrat, a loss of 17. The FPÖ received 17% of the votes, increasing its representation in the Nationalrat by 15 seats, to 33. The FPÖ's success was attributed, in large part, to its support of restricted immigration, especially from eastern Europe. The Green Alternative List (GAL), an informal electoral alliance comprising Die Grüne Alternative (The Green Alternative) and the Vereinte Grüne Österreichs (United Green Party of Austria), increased its number of seats by one, to nine. In December, following several weeks of negotiations, the SPÖ and the ÖVP formed a new coalition Government, again led by Vranitzky.

A congress of the SPÖ held in June 1991 voted to revert to the party's original name, the Sozialdemokratische Partei Österreichs (SPÖ, Social-Democratic Party of Austria). Chancellor Vranitzky was re-elected party Chairman by an almost unanimous vote. In the same month the FPÖ leader, Dr Haider, was dismissed as Governor of Carinthia (Kärnten) after publicly praising Hitler's employment policies.

In December 1991 the Nationalrat approved government legislation whereby Austria became the only country in Europe able to reject asylum requests from individuals without identity papers. Following the imprisonment, in January 1992, of a prominent right-wing activist for demanding the restoration of the Nazi party, and the subsequent fire-bombing of a refugee hostel by neo-Nazis in northern Austria, the Nationalrat voted unanimously in February to amend anti-Nazi legislation. The minimum prison sentence for Nazi agitation was reduced from five years to one year (in order to increase the number of successful prosecutions) and the denial of the Nazi holocaust was made a criminal offence.

At the presidential election held in April 1992 the two main candidates were Dr Rudolf Streicher (hitherto the Minister of Public Economy and Transport), for the SPÖ, and Dr Thomas Klestil (a former ambassador to the USA), representing the ÖVP. No candidate achieved the required 50% of the vote at the first ballot, but in the second 'run-off' ballot, held in May, Klestil received almost 57% of the votes; he assumed the presidency in July.

In June 1992 a 32-year-old dispute between Austria and Italy was resolved when Austria formally accepted autonomy proposals for Italy's German-speaking Trentino-Alto Adige (South Tyrol) region. In January 1993 the FPÖ organized a national petition seeking to require the Nationalrat to debate the introduction of legislation that would halt immigration into Austria and impose stricter controls on foreign residents in the country (the estimated number of whom had increased from 350,000 to 600,000 since 1989). Although the petition was signed by 7.4% of the electorate (417,000 signatures, compared with the constitutional requirement of 100,000 to force parliamentary debate), the result was considered disappointing by the FPÖ. The initiative was strongly opposed by a broad coalition of politicians, church leaders and intellectuals. In February 1993 five FPÖ deputies in the Nationalrat left the party, partly in protest at the petition on immigration, and formed a new political organization, the Liberales Forum (LF, Liberal Forum), under the leadership of Dr Heide Schmidt, hitherto the Vice-President of the FPÖ. In December four people, including the Mayor of Vienna, were injured by letter-bombs sent to public figures who supported the rights of immigrant and refugee communities in Austria. Periodic assaults by right-wing extremists on members and supporters of ethnic minorities continued during the mid-1990s, including, in February 1995, a bomb attack which killed four gypsies.

In late 1993 an ongoing debate over Austria's future in Europe intensified when the European Union (EU, see p. 152) set a deadline of 1 March 1994 by which time the conditions of Austria's entry into the Union (pending a national referendum) were to be agreed. Austria strongly defended its right to preserve its neutrality, to uphold higher environmental standards and to impose restrictions on the transit of road-freight traffic through the Austrian Alps. Eventually a number of compromises were reached, including an extension of the existing limit on lorry transit traffic until 2001. At the ensuing national referendum on the terms of Austria's membership of the EU, held in June 1994, some two-thirds of voters (66.4%) supported Austria's entry into the Union. Following the referendum Austria announced plans to sign NATO's Partnership for Peace programme (see p. 206). Austria formally entered the EU on 1 January 1995. Observer status at Western European Union (see p. 240) was subsequently granted.

At the general election held in October 1994 the ruling coalition lost its two-thirds' majority in the Nationalrat. The SPÖ obtained 66 seats (winning 35% of the votes), the ÖVP won 52 seats (with 28% of the votes), and the FPÖ (which had campaigned against Austria's accession to the EU) increased its share of the votes by 6%, to 23%, securing 42 seats. The GAL and the LF also made gains, winning 13 and 10 seats respectively. The success of the FPÖ's populist campaign, which had concentrated on countering corruption and immigration and had advocated referendum- rather than parliamentary-based governance, unsettled the Austrian political establishment after years of consensus. At the end of November, following protracted negotiations, the SPÖ and ÖVP finally agreed to form a new coalition Government, with Vranitzky remaining as Chancellor. A subsequent ministerial reshuffle left the main portfolios largely unaltered.

The new SPÖ-ÖVP coalition was beleaguered by disagreements, mainly concerning differences in approach to the urgent need to reduce the annual budgetary deficit in compliance with Austria's commitment, as a member of the EU, to future economic and monetary union (EMU). In March 1995 four ministers resigned from the Government, including the Minister of Finance, Ferdinand Lacina, whose draft 1995 budget, containing several economic austerity measures, had generated widespread adverse criticism. In April Dr Erhard Busek, the Vice-Chancellor and Minister of Education and Culture, resigned from both posts and was replaced as Chairman of the ÖVP by Dr Wolfgang Schüssel; Busek had been widely blamed for the ruling coalition's poor performance at the October 1994 election. A reorganization of ministerial posts was undertaken at the end of April 1995. In October a deepening rift between the SPÖ and ÖVP regarding the means of curtailing the 1996 budgetary deficit (with the former advocating increased taxation measures and the latter proposing to restrain public expenditure) proved irreconcilable, culminating in the collapse of the coalition. Consequently a new general election was held in December 1995. The SPÖ improved upon its disappointing performance at the previous election, receiving 38.1% of the votes cast and winning 71 of the 183 seats in the Nationalrat. The ÖVP secured 28.3% of the votes (obtaining 53 seats), the Freiheitlichen (as the FPÖ had been renamed in January 1995) 21.9% (40 seats), the LF 5.5% (10 seats) and the GAL 4.8% (nine seats). In early March 1996, following lengthy negotiations, the SPÖ and ÖVP agreed an economic programme and formed a new coalition Government, with Vranitzky remaining as Chancellor. In June the Minister of Economic Affairs, Johannes Ditz of the ÖVP, resigned, reportedly following disagreements within his party over the pace of economic reform. In December tensions arose in the governing coalition regarding the planned sale of Creditanstalt-Bankverein (traditionally aligned with the ÖVP) to Bank Austria AG (controlled by the SPÖ-dominated Vienna city council); an agreement was reached in the following month, whereby the ownership of both banks would be substantially depoliticized.

In mid-January 1997 Vranitzky unexpectedly resigned as Chancellor, citing reasons of age and of length of tenure. Viktor Klima, the Minister of Finance, was appointed as his successor, both as Chancellor and as Chairman of the SPÖ, and the Council of Ministers was reorganized. In July a motion censuring Schüssel, the Vice-Chancellor and Minister of Foreign Affairs, who was alleged to have made derogatory remarks concerning a number of foreign dignitaries, was rejected at a vote in the Nationalrat.

Meanwhile, mounting popular disillusionment with Austria's membership of the EU was reflected in the results of the first national elections to the European Parliament, which took place in mid-October 1996. The Freiheitlichen, which opposed EU membership and had undertaken to petition the Nationalrat for a referendum on EMU, won an unprecedented 27.6% of the votes cast, at the expense of the SPÖ, which registered its worst ever election performance, with 29.1% of the votes. The ÖVP secured 29.6% of the votes. At concurrent elections to the Vienna city administration the SPÖ lost the absolute majority of seats which it had held since the end of the Second World War, while the Freiheitlichen increased their representation. The election results were regarded as a protest against the ruling coalition's alleged misrepresentation, prior to the June referendum, of the immediate effects of admission to the EU; the Government's programme of economic austerity measures was particularly unpopular, while demands by the Union that Austria abolish anonymously-held bank accounts were also resented. In March 1997 concern was expressed in Germany, particularly by members of the Bavarian state legislature, over the efficacy of Austrian border policing, and questions were raised regarding Austria's forthcoming participation in the Schengen agreement on frontier controls (see p. 168); none the less, in July it was agreed that frontier posts between Austria and Germany would be abolished in April 1998.

Government

Austria is a federal republic, divided into nine provinces, each with its own provincial assembly and government. Legislative power is held by the bicameral Federal Assembly. The first chamber, the Nationalrat (National Council), has 183 members, elected by universal adult suffrage for four years (subject to dissolution) on the basis of proportional representation. The second chamber, the Bundesrat (Federal Council), has 64 members, elected for varying terms by the provincial assemblies. The Federal President, elected by popular vote for six years, is the Head of State, and normally acts on the advice of the Council of Ministers, which is led by the Federal Chancellor, and which is responsible to the Nationalrat.

Defence

After the ratification of the State Treaty in 1955, Austria declared its permanent neutrality. To protect its independence, the armed forces were instituted. Military service is compulsory and normally consists of seven months' initial training, followed by a maximum of 30 days' reservist training over 10 years (officers, non-commissioned officers and specialists undergo 60–90 days' reservist training). In August 1997 the total armed forces numbered 45,500 (including 16,600 conscripts), comprising an army of 41,250 (13,200 conscripts) and an air force of 4,250 (3,400 conscripts). Austrian air units are an integral part of the army. Total reserves numbered 100,700, compared with 200,000 in June 1992. The estimated defence budget for 1997 amounted to 20,900m. Schilling.

Economic Affairs

In 1995, according to estimates by the World Bank, Austria's gross national product (GNP), measured at average 1993–95 prices, was US $216,547m., equivalent to $26,890 per head. During 1985–95, it was estimated, GNP per head increased, in real terms, by an average annual rate of 1.9%. Over the same period, the population increased by only 0.6% per year. Austria's gross domestic product (GDP) grew, in real terms, by an annual average of 2.5% in 1985–95. Real GDP grew by 2.1% in 1995 and by 1.6% in 1996.

The contribution of agriculture (including hunting, forestry and fishing) to GDP was 1.5% in 1996. In that year some 7.1% of the economically active population were engaged in the agricultural sector. Austrian farms produce more than 90% of the country's food requirements, and surplus dairy products are exported. The principal crops are wheat, barley, maize and sugar beet. Agricultural production increased by an annual average of 0.5% in 1985–95. Output rose by 1.5% in 1994, but fell by 0.2% in 1995 and by 2.7% in 1996.

Industry (including mining and quarrying, manufacturing, construction and power) contributed 31.6% of GDP in 1996, in which year it engaged 31.3% of the economically active population. Industrial production (not including construction) increased by an annual average of 4.5% during 1991–95, but declined by 3.2% in 1993 before rising by 4.1% in 1994 and by 3.4% in 1995.

In 1996 mining and quarrying contributed 0.4% of GDP and employed 0.3% of the economically active population. The most important indigenous mineral resource is iron ore (2.1m. metric tons, with an iron content of 31%, were mined in 1995). Austria also has deposits of petroleum, lignite, magnesite, lead and some copper.

Manufacturing contributed 20.6% of GDP and engaged 21.3% of the economically active population in 1996. Measured by the value of output, the principal branches of manufacturing in 1994 were machinery (accounting for 22.0% of the total), metals and metal products (13.7%), food products (11.5%), wood and paper products (11.2%) and chemical products (8.4%). The output of the manufacturing sector increased at an average annual rate of 2.8% during 1980–91, but declined by 3.7% in 1993 before rising by 3.7% in 1994 and by 2.7% in 1995.

Power supplies in Austria are provided by petroleum, natural gas, coal and hydroelectric plants. Hydroelectric power resources provide the major domestic source of energy, accounting for 71% of total electricity production in 1986. Austria is heavily dependent on imports of energy, mainly from eastern Europe.

The services sector contributed 66.9% of GDP and employed 61.6% of the economically active population in 1996. Tourism has traditionally been a leading source of revenue, providing receipts of 148,250m. Schilling in 1996.

In 1996 Austria recorded a visible trade deficit of US $4,722m., and the current account of the balance of payments showed a deficit of $4,202m. Much of Austria's trade is conducted with other member countries of the European Union (EU, see p. 152), which accounted for 65.9% of Austria's imports and 62.9% of exports in 1994. In 1996 the principal source of imports (43%) was Germany, which was also the principal market for exports (37%); Italy is another major trading partner. At the end of 1993 Austria accounted for about one-fifth of joint ventures under way between western and eastern European companies and had the highest export ratio within the OECD to eastern Europe.

The federal budget for 1996 produced a deficit of 89,365m. Schilling, equivalent to 3.7% of GDP. The central Government's debt was estimated at 1,400,000m. Schilling in 1996, amounting to about 60% of GDP. The average annual rate of inflation was 2.7% in 1985–95. Consumer prices increased by 3.0% in 1994, by 2.2% in 1995 and by 1.9% in 1996. According to the OECD, consumer prices remained static in the twelve months to August 1997. In July 1997 some 4.5% of the labour force were unemployed.

Austria joined the EU on 1 January 1995, having resigned its membership of the European Free Trade Association at the end of 1994.

From the late 1980s until 1991 the Austrian economy showed strong growth. In 1992, however, depressed export markets, combined with comparatively high domestic production costs, resulted in a slower rate of economic growth and increased unemployment. A subsequent rapid rise in exports to eastern Europe and increase in domestic demand restored the momentum of economic growth. Since the early 1990s there has been a significant decline in earnings from tourism, which has contributed to a succession of balance-of-payments deficits. In November 1993, following a major restructuring of the state sector during the 1980s, the Government announced further wide-ranging privatization measures, with the dual aim of attracting foreign investors and stimulating the domestic capital market. The measures included proposals for the eventual dissolution of the state holding company, Österreichische Industrieholding AG (ÖIAG), and full privatization of the petroleum and chemicals group ÖMV and of two major banks, one of which, Creditanstalt-Bankverein, was acquired by the other, Bank Austria AG, in January 1997, in anticipation of the sale of publicly-held Bank Austria stocks. Upon joining the EU in January 1995 the Government committed itself to compensating certain economic sectors, particularly agriculture, which were likely to be initially adversely affected by alignment with prices in the other EU countries and the removal of protective trade barriers. During the mid-1990s the Government implemented a far-reaching austerity programme, including large reductions in public expenditure, with the aim of reducing the expanding budget deficit and bringing it into conformity with the convergence criteria of the Treaty on European Union. The reduction in the budgetary deficit from 5.0% of GDP in 1995 to only 3.7% of GDP in 1996 represented a considerable success in this objective, but concerns were raised that GDP growth was too slight for this trend to be maintained.

Social Welfare

The social insurance system covers all wage-earners and salaried employees, agricultural and non-agricultural self-employed and dependants, regardless of nationality. The coverage is compulsory and provides earnings-related benefits in the event of old age, invalidity, death, sickness, maternity and injuries at work. About 99% of the population are protected. There are separate programmes which provide unemployment insurance, family allowance, benefits for war victims, etc. In 1995 Austria had 76,634 hospital beds (one for every 105 inhabitants), and in December 1996 there were 32,055 physicians working in the country. Of total expenditure by the central Government in 1994, 123,930m. Schilling (13.5%) was for health services, while a further 424,650m. Schilling (46.4%) was for social security and welfare. In 1996 total expenditure by the central Government on social welfare amounted to some 670,000m. Schilling, of which 170,000m. Schilling was for health services and 394,345m. Schilling for social insurance payments.

Education

The central controlling body is the Federal Ministry of Education and Cultural Affairs. Higher education and research are the responsibility of the Federal Ministry of Science and Transport. Provincial boards (Landesschulräte) supervise school education in each of the nine federal provinces. Expenditure on education by all levels of government in 1992 was 117,519m. Schilling (7.7% of total public spending), decreasing to 115,780m. Schilling in 1993.

Education is free and compulsory between the ages of six and 15 years. All children undergo four years' primary education at a Volksschule, after which they choose between two principal forms of secondary education. This may be a Hauptschule which, after four years, may be followed by one of a variety of schools offering technical, vocational and other specialized training, some of which provide a qualification for university. Alternatively, secondary education may be obtained in an Allgemeinbildende höhere Schule, which provides an eight-year general education covering a wide range of subjects, culminating in the Reifeprüfung or Matura. This gives access to all Austrian universities. In addition, all Austrian citizens over the age of 24, and with professional experience, may attend certain university courses in connection with their professional career or trade.

Opportunities for further education exist at 18 universities as well as 13 colleges of technology, all of which have university status, and schools of art and music. Institutes of adult education (Volkshochschulen) are found in all provinces, as are other centres operated by public authorities, church organizations and the Austrian Trade Union Federation.

Public Holidays

1998: 1 January (New Year's Day), 6 January (Epiphany), 13 April (Easter Monday), 1 May (Labour Day), 21 May (Ascension Day), 1 June (Whit Monday), 11 June (Corpus Christi), 15 August (Assumption), 26 October (National Holiday), 1 November (All Saints' Day), 8 December (Immaculate Conception), 25 December (Christmas Day), 26 December (St Stephen's Day).

1999: 1 January (New Year's Day), 6 January (Epiphany), 5 April (Easter Monday), 1 May (Labour Day), 13 May (Ascension Day), 24 May (Whit Monday), 3 June (Corpus Christi), 15 August (Assumption), 26 October (National Holiday), 1 November (All Saints' Day), 8 December (Immaculate Conception), 25 December (Christmas Day), 26 December (St Stephen's Day).

Weights and Measures

The metric system is in force.

Statistical Survey

Source (unless otherwise stated): Austrian Central Statistical Office, 1033 Vienna, Hintere Zollamtsstr. 2; tel. (1) 711-28; telex 132600; fax (1) 711-28-77-28.

Area and Population

AREA, POPULATION AND DENSITY

Area (sq km)	83,858*
Population (census results)†	
12 May 1981	7,555,338
15 May 1991	
Males	3,753,989
Females	4,041,797
Total	7,795,786
Population (official estimates at mid-year)	
1994	8,031,000
1995	8,054,802
1996	8,067,800
Density (per sq km) at mid-1996	96.2

* 32,378 sq miles.
† Figures include all foreign workers.

PROVINCES (mid-1996)

	Area (sq km)	Population ('000)	Density (per sq km)	Provincial Capital (with 1991* population)
Burgenland	3,965.4	275.8	69.6	Eisenstadt (10,349)
Kärnten (Carinthia)	9,533.0	563.6	59.1	Klagenfurt (89,415)
Niederösterreich (Lower Austria)	19,173.3	1,527.7	79.7	Sankt Pölten (50,026)
Oberösterreich (Upper Austria)	11,979.6	1,378.1	115.0	Linz (203,044)
Salzburg	7,154.2	510.5	71.4	Salzburg (143,978)
Steiermark (Styria)	16,388.1	1,207.1	73.7	Graz (237,810)
Tirol (Tyrol)	12,647.8	661.0	52.3	Innsbruck (118,112)
Vorarlberg	2,601.4	343.7	132.1	Bregenz (27,097)
Wien (Vienna)	415.0	1,600.5	3,856.6	
Total	83,858.1	8,067.8	96.2	

* Census of 15 May 1991.

PRINCIPAL TOWNS
(population at 1991 census)

Vienna (capital)	1,539,848	Klagenfurt	89,415
Graz	237,810	Villach	54,640
Linz	203,044	Wels	52,594
Salzburg	143,978	Sankt Pölten	50,026
Innsbruck	118,112	Dornbirn	40,735

BIRTHS, MARRIAGES AND DEATHS

	Registered live births		Registered marriages		Registered deaths	
	Number	Rate (per 1,000)	Number	Rate (per 1,000)	Number	Rate (per 1,000)
1989	88,759	11.6	42,523	5.6	83,407	10.9
1990	90,454	11.7	45,212	5.9	82,952	10.7
1991	94,629	12.1	44,106	5.6	83,428	10.7
1992	95,302	12.1	45,701	5.8	83,162	10.5
1993	95,227	11.9	45,014	5.6	82,517	10.3
1994	92,415	11.5	43,284	5.4	80,684	10.0
1995	88,669	11.0	42,946	5.3	81,171	10.1
1996	88,809	10.9	42,298	5.2	80,790	9.9

Expectation of life (years at birth, 1996): Males 73.9; females 80.2.

ECONOMICALLY ACTIVE POPULATION*
(ISIC Major Divisions, '000 persons aged 15 years and over)

	1994	1995	1996
Agriculture, hunting, forestry and fishing	273.5	282.9	275.3
Mining and quarrying	9.5	11.8	10.7
Manufacturing	854.8	854.1	824.6
Electricity, gas and water	36.1	38.0	35.3
Construction	373.1	354.7	341.4
Trade, restaurants and hotels	812.0	823.7	825.3
Transport, storage and communications	251.5	244.2	237.5
Financing, insurance, real estate and business services	355.5	366.4	386.3
Community, social and personal services	914.5	926.7	933.8
Total labour force	3,880.4	3,902.5	3,870.2
Males	2,219.4	2,234.2	2,216.9
Females	1,661.0	1,668.3	1,653.3

* Yearly averages, based on the results of quarterly sample surveys. The figures include unemployed persons, totalling (in '000): 138.4 (males 72.6, females 65.7) in 1994.

Agriculture

PRINCIPAL CROPS ('000 metric tons)

	1994	1995	1996
Wheat	1,255.1	1,301.3	1,239.7
Barley	1,184.4	1,065.2	1,082.8
Maize	1,420.6	1,473.7	1,735.6
Rye	318.8	313.8	156.2
Oats	171.7	161.6	152.7
Mixed grain	47.5	35.6	43.9
Potatoes	593.7	724.4	769.0
Sugar beet	2,560.6	2,885.8	3,131.3
Apples	334.3	383.9	367.6
Pears	81.6	123.7	78.2
Plums	46.0	40.6	54.4
Cherries	24.3	28.7	21.6
Currants	16.5	17.8	15.6

Grapes ('000 metric tons): 344 in 1994; 290 in 1995. Source: FAO, *Production Yearbook*.

LIVESTOCK ('000 head at December)

	1994	1995	1996
Horses	66.7	72.5	73.2
Cattle	2,328.5	2,325.8	2,271.9
Pigs	3,729.0	3,706.2	3,663.7
Sheep	342.1	365.3	380.9
Goats	49.7	54.2	54.5
Chickens	13,265.6	13,157.1	12,215.2
Ducks	105.1	99.6	101.6
Geese	26.5	22.1	20.7
Turkeys	781.6	680.5	642.5

LIVESTOCK PRODUCTS ('000 metric tons)

	1994	1995	1996
Milk	3,278.5	3,167.8	3,054.9
Butter	42.5	40.7	41.6
Cheese	85.5	104.7	103.6
Hen eggs*	1,759.1	1,717.7	1,640.1
Beef and veal	235.5	208.4	238.8
Pig meat	473.0	453.7	461.9
Poultry meat	102.0	98.6	98.1

* Millions.

Forestry

ROUNDWOOD REMOVALS ('000 cubic metres, excluding bark)

	1994	1995	1996
Sawlogs, veneer logs and logs for sleepers	8,549	8,081	8,195
Pitprops (mine timber), pulpwood, and other industrial wood	2,552	2,665	3,018
Fuel wood	3,259	3,059	3,797
Total	14,360	13,806	15,010

SAWNWOOD PRODUCTION ('000 cubic metres)

	1993	1994	1995
Coniferous sawnwood*	6,539	6,518	7,363
Broadleaved sawnwood*	225	215	204
Sub-total	6,764	6,733	7,567
Railway sleepers	15	13	11
Total	6,779	6,746	7,578

* Including boxboards.

Fishing

('000 metric tons)

	1994	1995	1996
Total catch	4.5	4.5	4.5

Mining

('000 metric tons, unless otherwise indicated)

	1993	1994	1995
Brown coal (incl. lignite)	1,691	1,369	1,283
Crude petroleum	1,155	1,100	1,035
Iron ore:			
gross weight	1,427	1,644	2,107
metal content	448	515	656
Magnesite (crude)	627	654	785
Salt (unrefined)	712	786	834
Lead ore (metric tons)*	2,047	n.a.	n.a.
Zinc ore (metric tons)*	20,014	n.a.	n.a.
Graphite (natural)	4	12	12
Gypsum (crude)	874	1,012	975
Kaolin	346	467	479
Natural gas (million cu metres)	1,488	1,350	1,480

* Figures refer to the metal content of ores.

Tungsten ore: 104 metric tons (metal content) in 1993 (Source: UN, *Industrial Commodity Statistics Yearbook*, quoting US Bureau of Mines).

Industry

SELECTED PRODUCTS
('000 metric tons, unless otherwise indicated)

	1993	1994	1995
Wheat flour	258	242	240
Raw sugar	518	458	443
Margarine (metric tons)	50,486	47,195	48,536
Wine ('000 hectolitres)	1,865.5	2,646.6	2,228
Beer ('000 hectolitres)	9,789	9,936	9,474
Cigarettes (million)	16,247	16,929	16,298
Cotton yarn—pure and mixed (metric tons)	23,225	22,210	21,961
Woven cotton fabrics—pure and mixed (metric tons)	15,028	16,409	15,129
Wool yarn—pure and mixed (metric tons)	5,361	4,646	3,597
Woven woollen fabrics—pure and mixed (metric tons)	1,591	1,267	1,369
Mechanical wood pulp	375	399	n.a.
Chemical and semi-chemical wood pulp	1,079	1,197	1,231
Newsprint	387	403	n.a.
Other printing and writing paper	1,574	1,728	n.a.
Other paper	971	1,058	n.a.
Paperboard	368	413	n.a.
Nitrogenous fertilizers (metric tons)[1]	210,000	220,000	n.a.
Phosphate fertilizers (metric tons)[1]	76,000	80,000	n.a.
Plastics and resins	955	997	972
Motor spirit (petrol)[2]	2,336	2,420	2,271
Jet fuel	375	376	421
Distillate fuel oils	3,593	3,643	3,373
Residual fuel oils	1,678	1,299	1,502
Petroleum bitumen (asphalt)	257	294	n.a.
Coke	1,402	n.a.	n.a.
Cement	4,941	4,828	3,844
Crude steel	4,149	4,399	4,990
Refined copper—unwrought (metric tons): secondary	46,900	n.a.	n.a.

— *continued*	1993	1994	1995
Refined lead—unwrought (metric tons): secondary	17,857	17,165	21,689
Passenger motor cars (number)	40,777	45,785	59,196
Motorcycles, etc. (number)	94,356	75,888	14,157
Construction: new dwellings completed (number)	43,449	48,851	53,353
Electric energy (million kWh)	50,425	50,987	52,566
Manufactured gas (terajoules)[3]	43,000	29,000	n.a.

* Estimate.

[1] Estimated production during 12 months ending 30 June of the year stated. Figures for nitrogenous fertilizers are in terms of nitrogen, and those for phosphate fertilizers are in terms of phosphoric acid.

[2] Including aviation gasoline.

[3] Production from gasworks and cokeries.

Sources: mainly Austrian Central Statistical Office, Vienna; FAO, *Yearbook of Forest Products*; UN, *Industrial Commodity Statistics Yearbook*; International Road Federation, *World Road Statistics*.

Finance

CURRENCY AND EXCHANGE RATES

Monetary Units

100 Groschen = 1 Schilling.

Sterling and Dollar Equivalents (30 September 1997)

£1 sterling = 20.08 Schilling;
US $1 = 12.43 Schilling;
1,000 Schilling = £49.80 = $80.45.

Average Exchange Rate (Schilling per US $)

1994 11.422
1995 10.081
1996 10.587

FEDERAL BUDGET (million Schilling)*

Revenue	1994	1995	1996
Direct taxes on income and wealth	187,691	212,757	235,141
Social security contributions—unemployment insurance	41,947	44,604	45,300
Indirect taxes	225,115	188,556	204,257
Current transfers	30,292	43,085	61,935
Sales and charges	18,695	16,368	18,777
Interest, shares of profit and other income	35,308	40,889	37,092
Sales of assets	2,632	9,316	10,523
Repayments of loans granted	409	376	634
Capital transfers	488	525	386
Borrowing	225,910	322,743	219,596
Other revenue	14,089	20,000	7,869
Total	782,526	899,219	841,510

Expenditure	1994	1995	1996
Current expenditure on goods and services	149,778	156,171	168,954
Interest on public debt	83,469	93,536	96,974
Current transfers to:			
Regional and local authorities	50,900	52,549	55,381
Other public bodies	101,265	138,606	136,847
Households	128,391	125,693	126,085
Other	54,826	44,646	51,942
Deficits of government enterprises	2,386	2,335	2,429
Gross capital formation	12,537	12,685	12,742
Capital transfers	47,660	46,013	47,590
Acquisition of assets	5,363	6,268	6,073
Loans granted	3,972	3,893	358
Debt redemption	121,092	204,840	130,231
Other expenditure	20,887	11,984	5,904
Total	782,526	899,219	841,510

* Figures refer to federal government units covered by the general budget. The data exclude the operations of social insurance institutions and other units with their own budgets.

NATIONAL BANK RESERVES (US $ million at 31 December)

	1994	1995	1996
Gold*	3,099	2,223	1,805
IMF special drawing rights	283	181	195
Reserve position in IMF	531	682	809
Foreign exchange	16,008	17,867	21,861
Total	19,921	20,953	24,670

* Valued at 60,000 Schilling per kilogram.

Source: IMF, *International Financial Statistics*.

MONEY SUPPLY ('000 million Schilling at 31 December)

	1994	1995	1996
Currency outside banks	133.6	142.7	146.7
Demand deposits at deposit money banks	201.1	244.0	255.2
Total money	334.7	386.7	401.9

Source: IMF, *International Financial Statistics*.

COST OF LIVING (Consumer Price Index; base: 1986 = 100)

	1994	1995	1996
Food and beverages	120.0	119.3	120.3
Rent (incl. maintenance and repairs)	138.5	146.5	152.6
Fuel and light	97.6	98.5	103.8
Clothing	128.5	130.3	129.3
Total (incl. others)	125.6	128.4	130.8

NATIONAL ACCOUNTS ('000 million Schilling at current prices)

National Income and Product

	1994	1995	1996
Compensation of employees	1,189.02	1,230.70	1,244.97
Operating surplus*	462.52	498.81	537.44
Domestic factor incomes	1,651.54	1,729.51	1,782.41
Consumption of fixed capital	288.69	306.78	324.70
Gross domestic product at factor cost	1,940.23	2,036.29	2,107.11
Indirect taxes	356.60	367.34	387.46
Less Subsidies	57.21	69.27	72.95
GDP in purchasers' values	2,239.62	2,334.36	2,421.62
Factor income received from abroad	102.16	115.35	135.69
Less Factor income paid abroad	110.39	122.97	143.30
Gross national product	2,231.39	2,326.74	2,414.01
Less Consumption of fixed capital	288.69	306.78	324.70
National income in market prices	1,942.70	2,019.96	2,089.31
Other current transfers from abroad	23.08	28.65	28.71
Less Other current transfers paid abroad	31.33	33.98	39.99
Subsidies from EU institutions	—	7.18	9.32
Less Indirect taxes to EU institutions	—	25.94	27.27
National disposable income	1,934.45	1,995.87	2,060.08

* Including a statistical discrepancy.

Expenditure on the Gross Domestic Product

	1994	1995	1996
Government final consumption expenditure	454.96	469.32	478.30
Private final consumption expenditure	1,254.60	1,310.25	1,375.41
Increase in stocks	0.83	10.32	4.12
Gross fixed capital formation	533.35	554.07	576.79
Total domestic expenditure	2,343.74	2,343.96	2,434.63
Exports of goods and services	838.84	900.91	988.78
Less Imports of goods and services	842.96	910.50	1,001.79
GDP in purchasers' values	2,339.62	2,334.36	2,421.62
GDP at constant 1983 prices	1,604.25	1,637.26	1,664.05

Gross Domestic Product by Economic Activity

	1994	1995	1996
Agriculture, hunting, forestry and fishing	50.45	35.90	34.69
Mining and quarrying	8.26	8.60	8.75
Manufacturing	455.61	468.49	480.50
Electricity, gas and water	60.75	63.32	67.13
Construction	165.30	169.48	179.85
Wholesale and retail trade	287.13	313.41	323.21
Restaurants and hotels	90.50	92.53	93.12
Transport, storage and communications	148.08	150.68	154.56
Finance and insurance	160.54	170.32	176.15
Real estate and business services*	269.07	297.46	322.83
Public administration and defence	303.57	314.12	318.02
Other community, social and personal services	104.35	114.93	123.03
Private non-profit services	45.52	48.02	49.50
Sub-total	2,149.13	2,247.26	2,331.34
Value-added tax	186.09	191.07	194.97
Import duties	13.90	12.86	14.69
Less Imputed bank service charges	109.49	116.82	119.36
Total	2,239.62	2,334.36	2,421.62

* Including imputed rents of owner-occupied dwellings.

BALANCE OF PAYMENTS (US $ million)

	1994	1995	1996
Exports of goods f.o.b.	44,645	72,718	72,995
Imports of goods f.o.b.	-53,373	-77,821	-77,716
Trade balance	-8,727	-5,103	-4,722
Exports of services	29,132	25,085	24,315
Imports of services	-21,189	-22,252	-22,455
Balance on goods and services	-784	-2,270	-2,862
Other income received	8,825	11,316	12,175
Other income paid	-9,195	-11,671	-12,727
Balance on goods, services and income	-1,154	-2,625	-3,414
Current transfers received	1,443	2,612	4,048
Current transfers paid	-2,498	-4,830	-4,836
Current balance	-2,209	-4,842	-4,202
Capital account (net)	346	84	-40
Direct investment abroad	-1,203	-1,046	-1,368
Direct investment from abroad	1,311	639	3,757
Portfolio investment assets	-4,475	-2,836	-8,097
Portfolio investment liabilities	4,253	12,292	5,954
Other investment assets	-3,568	-10,605	-3,738
Other investment liabilities	6,781	8,066	5,133
Net errors and omissions	-417	-308	3,590
Overall balance	819	1,443	989

Source: IMF, *International Financial Statistics.*

External Trade

Note: Austria's customs territory excludes Mittelberg im Kleinen Walsertal (in Vorarlberg) and Jungholz (in Tyrol). The figures also exclude trade in silver specie and monetary gold.

PRINCIPAL COMMODITIES
(distribution by SITC, million Schilling)

Imports c.i.f.	1994	1995	1996
Food and live animals	30,362.1	35,249.7	38,611.3
Vegetables and fruit	10,929.9	11,167.4	11,763.7
Crude materials (inedible) except fuels	26,568.7	31,041.6	26,791.2
Mineral fuels, lubricants, etc. (incl. electric current)	27,711.1	29,604.0	38,079.5
Petroleum, petroleum products, etc.	17,688.4	17,564.7	23,137.6
Chemicals and related products	65,247.4	71,404.7	73,741.9
Medicinal and pharmaceutical products	15,252.3	17,476.0	19,515.0
Artificial resins, plastic materials, etc.	19,098.3	20,544.4	19,931.2
Basic manufactures	120,322.8	129,145.5	129,508.3
Paper, paperboard and manufactures	13,395.2	14,724.0	14,979.0
Textile yarn, fabrics, etc.	20,523.5	20,593.0	20,067.5
Non-metallic mineral manufactures	13,268.0	13,959.6	14,317.3
Iron and steel	16,397.8	19,460.0	17,367.3
Non-ferrous metals	16,896.7	16,747.0	15,748.3
Other metal manufactures	25,046.5	27,438.8	30,184.4
Machinery and transport equipment	238,949.5	246,254.5	269,884.3
Power-generating machinery and equipment	15,091.5	15,894.6	17,130.9
Machinery specialized for particular industries	21,693.0	22,153.1	23,525.7
General industrial machinery, equipment and parts	36,929.3	38,181.7	40,659.1
Office machines and automatic data-processing equipment	22,508.7	21,316.8	21,496.7
Telecommunications and sound equipment	16,497.2	15,301.0	17,474.8
Other electrical machinery, apparatus, etc.	44,363.1	43,887.3	48,447.2
Road vehicles and parts (excl. tyres, engines and electrical parts)	71,960.1	76,263.0	86,168.9
Miscellaneous manufactured articles	115,787.8	117,168.2	126,791.7
Furniture and parts	13,498.9	14,393.1	16,228.3
Clothing and accessories (excl. footwear)	30,300.7	31,134.1	33,730.4
Professional, scientific and controlling instruments, etc.	12,238.2	12,321.5	13,212.3
Total (incl. others)	628,877.7	668,031.1	712,759.6

Exports f.o.b.	1994	1995	1996
Food and live animals	14,973.5	19,198.3	22,928.1
Crude materials (inedible) except fuels	21,976.8	24,065.6	22,239.7
Cork and wood	11,940.0	12,773.4	11,433.7
Chemicals and related products	46,883.7	53,346.9	57,187.0
Medicinal and pharmaceutical products	11,981.0	13,443.6	14,550.8
Artificial resins, plastic materials, etc.	15,876.0	18,601.1	19,044.9
Basic manufactures	147,945.1	168,899.8	166,295.3
Paper, paperboard and manufactures	29,576.6	36,291.9	34,263.5
Textile yarn, fabrics, etc.	20,951.5	20,741.1	21,220.9
Non-metallic mineral manufactures	14,839.1	16,399.5	16,273.9
Iron and steel	26,983.2	33,093.6	29,443.1
Non-ferrous metals	10,669.1	13,562.5	13,694.7
Other metal manufactures	27,537.4	29,163.7	30,380.6
Machinery and transport equipment	199,671.0	226,317.0	248,833.5
Power-generating machinery and equipment	31,358.8	33,507.3	38,368.7

Exports f.o.b. — *continued*	1994	1995	1996
Machinery specialized for particular industries	30,641.0	33,283.4	34,083.7
General industrial machinery, equipment and parts	31,827.3	37,305.4	39,495.5
Telecommunications and sound equipment	17,616.1	17,215.8	18,681.0
Other electrical machinery, apparatus, etc.	39,230.0	43,360.2	45,941.2
Road vehicles and parts (excl. tyres, engines and electrical parts)	32,585.9	42,205.2	54,156.2
Miscellaneous manufactured articles	70,204.6	77,419.2	81,148.3
Clothing and accessories (excl. footwear)	12,090.7	12,970.2	14,716.6
Total (incl. others)	512,515.2	580,014.3	612,189.8

PRINCIPAL TRADING PARTNERS (million Schilling)*

Imports c.i.f.	1994	1995	1996
Belgium-Luxembourg	18,190.1	17,897.3	16,327.4
China, People's Republic	9,681.3	8,232.9	8,990.3
Czech Republic	11,289.7	12,629.4	14,363.6
France	29,626.3	32,833.6	34,214.7
Germany	251,752.0	291,202.3	305,559.6
Hungary	12,830.3	12,583.2	19,151.6
Italy	55,524.4	58,513.6	62,742.4
Japan	26,915.3	16,457.0	17,211.5
Netherlands	18,969.4	22,937.5	22,889.2
Russia	10,180.4	11,299.1	11,271.9
Spain	8,480.4	8,721.8	10,197.4
Sweden	11,030.1	11,061.1	10,979.4
Switzerland-Liechtenstein	25,629.6	25,562.8	24,890.2
United Kingdom	18,226.4	19,804.4	21,477.5
USA	27,445.4	28,330.7	31,780.3
Total (incl. others)	628,877.7	668,031.0	712,759.6

Exports f.o.b.	1994	1995	1996
Belgium-Luxembourg	9,651.1	10,842.0	11,806.3
Czech Republic	13,426.1	15,880.6	17,751.7
France	23,349.3	25,768.2	26,186.6
Germany	195,307.7	222,474.1	229,041.8
Hungary	20,049.5	21,115.9	24,338.1
Italy	41,583.9	50,952.0	51,313.2
Japan	7,974.8	7,590.4	9,457.7
Netherlands	15,276.7	16,551.9	15,833.9
Poland	6,020.8	7,901.4	9,057.8
Russia	7,472.2	8,494.2	7,946.3
Slovenia	7,999.7	9,815.3	9,864.3
Spain	10,978.2	12,170.2	13,638.1
Sweden	7,145.2	8,257.5	8,082.3
Switzerland-Liechtenstein	32,614.1	31,465.3	30,303.7
United Kingdom	16,223.1	19,159.7	21,649.3
USA	17,841.8	17,205.2	14,487.9
Total (incl. others)	512,515.2	580,014.3	612,189.8

* Imports by country of production; exports by country of consumption.

Transport

RAILWAYS (Federal Railways only)

	1994	1995	1996
Passenger-km (millions)	9,629	9,625	9,689
Freight net ton-km (millions)	13,049.6	13,715.4	13,909.0
Freight tons carried ('000)	66,147.7	68,474.3	69,948.0

ROAD TRAFFIC (motor vehicles in use at 31 December)

	1994	1995	1996
Private cars	3,479,595	3,593,588	3,690,692
Buses and coaches	9,598	9,752	9,740
Goods vehicles	283,157	290,290	293,614
Motorcycles and scooters	154,297	174,907	193,685
Mopeds	378,028	371,505	366,506

SHIPPING

Merchant Fleet (registered at 31 December)

	1994	1995	1996
Number of vessels	31	29	29
Total displacement ('000 grt)	133.7	91.9	94.7

Source: Lloyd's Register of Shipping, *World Fleet Statistics*.

Freight Traffic ('000 metric tons)

	1994	1995	1996
Goods loaded	1,068	1,311	1,352
Goods unloaded	4,901	5,122	5,830

CIVIL AVIATION (Austrian Airlines, '000)

	1994	1995	1996
Kilometres flown	47,222	51,389	57,400
Passenger ton-km	361,149	466,793	523,765
Cargo ton-km	92,726	122,723	124,510
Mail ton-km	5,923	5,538	7,322

Tourism

FOREIGN TOURIST ARRIVALS (by country of origin)

	1994	1995	1996
Belgium-Luxembourg	434,590	427,476	415,844
France-Monaco	618,269	563,897	536,819
Germany	10,409,230	10,013,543	9,877,394
Italy	942,490	820,777	856,354
Netherlands	1,178,245	1,127,939	1,073,008
Switzerland-Liechtenstein	720,874	726,032	746,106
United Kingdom	608,706	537,842	512,578
USA	575,629	539,097	575,178
Total (incl. others)	17,893,824	17,172,968	17,089,973

Communications Media

	1994	1995	1996
Telephones in use	3,681,370	3,749,087	3,779,000
Radio licences issued	2,794,445	2,814,544	2,792,584
Television licences issued	2,627,680	2,653,842	2,641,367
Book titles produced	19,587	22,291	20,653

1996: Daily newspapers 17; Weekly newspapers 153; Other periodicals 2,617.

Telefax stations ('000 in use): 210 in 1993 (Source: UN, *Statistical Yearbook).*

Mobile cellular telephones ('000 subscribers): 220.9 in 1993; 278.2 in 1994 (Source: UN, *Statistical Yearbook*).

Education

(1996/97)

	Institutions	Staff	Students
Primary	3,689	37,914	390,135
General secondary and upper primary	1,856	54,844	476,846
Compulsory vocational	203	4,478	125,039
Technical and vocational	746	19,282	164,204
Teacher training:			
second level	38	1,298	12,565
third level	26	2,388	8,204
Universities	18	15,297	220,345
Tertiary vocational	33	n.a.	3,756

Directory

The Constitution

The Austrian Constitution of 1920, as amended in 1929, was restored on 1 May 1945. Its main provisions, with subsequent amendments, are summarized below:

Austria is a democratic republic, having a President (Bundespräsident), elected directly by the people, and a two-chamber legislature, the Federal Assembly, consisting of the National Council (Nationalrat) and the Federal Council (Bundesrat). The republic is organized on the federal system, comprising the nine provinces (Länder) of Burgenland, Carinthia, Lower Austria, Upper Austria, Salzburg, Styria, Tyrol, Vorarlberg and Vienna. There is universal suffrage for men and women who are more than 19 years of age.

The National Council consists of 183 members, elected by universal direct suffrage, according to a system of proportional representation. It functions for a period of four years.

The Federal Council represents the federal provinces. Lower Austria sends 12 members, Vienna and Upper Austria 11 each, Styria 10, Carinthia and Tyrol 5 each, Salzburg 4, and Burgenland and Vorarlberg 3 each, making 64 in all. The seats are divided between the parties according to the number of seats that they control in the provincial assemblies and are held during the life of the provincial government that they represent. Each province in turn provides the chairman for six months.

For certain matters of special importance the two chambers meet together; this is known as a Bundesversammlung.

The Federal President, elected by popular vote, is the Head of State and holds office for six years. The President is eligible for re-election only once in succession. Although invested with special emergency powers, the President normally acts on the authority of the Government, and it is the Government which is responsible to the National Council for governmental policy.

The Government consists of the Federal Chancellor, the Vice-Chancellor and the other ministers, who may vary in number. The Chancellor is chosen by the President, usually from the party with the strongest representation in the newly-elected National Council, and the other ministers are then chosen by the President on the advice of the Chancellor.

If the National Council adopts an explicit motion expressing 'no confidence' in the Federal Government or individual members thereof, the Federal Government or the Federal Minister concerned shall be removed from office.

All new legislative proposals must be read and submitted to a vote in both chambers of the Federal Assembly. A new draft law is presented first to the National Council, where it usually has three readings, and secondly to the Federal Council, where it can be delayed, but not vetoed.

The Constitution also provides for appeals by the Government to the electorate on specific points by means of referendum. If a petition supported by 100,000 or more electors is presented to the Government, the Government must submit it to the National Council.

The Provincial Assembly (Landtag) exercises the same functions in each province as the National Council does in the State. The members of the Provincial Assembly elect a government (Landesregierung) consisting of a provincial governor (Landeshauptmann) and his or her councillors (Landesräte). They are responsible to the Provincial Assembly.

The spheres of legal and administrative competence of both national and provincial governments are clearly defined. The Constitution distinguishes four groups:

1. Law-making and administration are the responsibility of the State: e.g. foreign affairs, justice and finance.
2. Law-making is the responsibility of the State, administration is the responsibility of the provinces: e.g. elections, population matters and road traffic.
3. The State formulates the rudiments of the law, the provinces enact the law and administer it: e.g. charity, rights of agricultural workers, land reform.
4. Law-making and administration are the responsibility of the provinces in all matters not expressly assigned to the State: e.g. municipal affairs.

The Government

HEAD OF STATE

Federal President: Dr THOMAS KLESTIL (sworn in 8 July 1992).

COUNCIL OF MINISTERS

(January 1998)

A coalition of the Sozialdemokratische Partei Österreichs (SPÖ), the Österreichische Volkspartei (ÖVP) and one independent.

Federal Chancellor: Mag. VIKTOR KLIMA (SPÖ).

Vice-Chancellor and Minister of Foreign Affairs: Dr WOLFGANG SCHÜSSEL (ÖVP).

Minister of the Environment and Family Affairs: MARTIN BARTENSTEIN (ÖVP).

Minister of Economic Affairs: JOHANN FARNLEITNER (ÖVP).

Minister of the Interior: KARL SCHLÖGL (SPÖ).

Minister of Defence: Dr WERNER FASSLABEND (ÖVP).

Minister of Education and Cultural Affairs: Dr ELIZABETH GEHRER (ÖVP).

Minister of Finance: RUDOLPH EDLINGER (SPÖ).

Minister of Women's Issues and Consumer Protection: BARBARA PRAMMER (SPÖ).

Minister of Labour, Health and Social Affairs: LORE HOSTASCH (SPÖ).

Minister of Justice: Dr NIKOLAUS MICHALEK (Independent).

Minister of Agriculture and Forestry: Mag. WILHELM MOLTERER (ÖVP).

Minister of Science and Transport: CASPAR EINEM (SPÖ).

Secretary of State in the Ministry of Foreign Affairs: BENITA FERRERO-WALDNER (ÖVP).

Secretary of State in the Federal Chancellery: PETER WITTMAN (SPÖ).

Secretary of State in the Ministry of Finance: WOLFGANG RUTTENSTORFER (SPÖ).

MINISTRIES

Office of the Federal Chancellor: 1014 Vienna, Ballhausplatz 2; tel. (1) 53-11-50; telex 115585; fax (1) 531-15-28-80.

Ministry of Agriculture and Forestry: 1010 Vienna, Stubenring 1; tel. (1) 71100; telex 11145; fax (1) 713-80-14.

Ministry of Defence: 1030 Vienna, Dampfschiffstr. 2; tel. (1) 51-5-95; telex 112145; fax (1) 515-95-17033.

Ministry of Economic Affairs: 1010 Vienna, Stubenring 1; tel. (1) 711-00-0; fax (1) 713-79-95; e-mail post@bmwa.bmwa.gv.at.

Ministry of Education and Cultural Affairs: 1014 Vienna, Minoritenplatz 5; tel. (1) 531-20; fax (1) 531-20-4499.

Ministry of the Environment and Family Affairs: 1031 Vienna, Radetzkystr. 2; tel. (1) 71-1-58; telex 3221371; fax (1) 711-58-42-21.

Ministry of Finance: 1010 Vienna, Himmelpfortgasse 4-8B; tel. (1) 51-4-33; telex 111688; fax (1) 512-78-69.

Ministry of Foreign Affairs: 1014 Vienna, Ballhausplatz 2; tel. (1) 53-1-15; telex 01371; fax (1) 535-45-30.

Ministry of the Interior: 1014 Vienna, Herrengasse 7; tel. (1) 53126-0; fax (1) 531-26-39-10.

Ministry of Justice: 1016 Vienna, Museumstr. 7; tel. (1) 52-1-52-0; fax (1) 52-1-52-727.

Ministry of Labour, Health and Social Affairs: 1030 Vienna, Radetzkystr. 2; tel. (1) 71172; fax (1) 715-58-30.

Ministry of Science and Transport: 1014 Vienna, Minoritenplatz 5; tel. (1) 53120-0; fax (1) 53120-4499.

Ministry of Social Affairs: 1010 Vienna, Stubenring 1; tel. (1) 71-1-00; fax (1) 713-93-11.

Ministry of Women's Issues and Consumer Protection: 1014 Vienna, Ballhausplatz 1; tel. (1) 536-33-23; fax (1) 536-33-36.

President and Legislature

PRESIDENT

Presidential Election, First Ballot, 26 April 1992

Candidates	Votes	%
Dr Rudolf Streicher (SPÖ)	1,888,599	40.66
Dr Thomas Klestil (ÖVP)	1,728,234	37.20
Dr Heide Schmidt (Freedom Party)	761,390	16.39
Dr Robert Jungk (Die Grünen)	266,954	5.75
Total	4,645,177	100.00

Second Ballot, 24 May 1992

Candidates	Votes	%
Dr Thomas Klestil (ÖVP)	2,528,006	56.89
Dr Rudolf Streicher (SPÖ)	1,915,380	43.11
Total	4,443,386	100.00

FEDERAL ASSEMBLY

Nationalrat
(National Council)

President of the Nationalrat: Dr Heinz Fischer.

General Election, 17 December 1995

	Votes	% of Total	Seats
Social-Democratic Party (SPÖ)	1,843,679	38.06	71
People's Party (ÖVP)	1,370,497	28.29	53
Freedom Party	1,060,175	21.89	40
Liberal Forum (LF)	267,078	5.51	10
Greens (Die Grünen)*	233,232	4.81	9

Other parties together received about 1.4% of the votes but won no seats.

* An informal electoral alliance comprising Die Grüne Alternative (The Green Alternative) and Vereinte Grüne Österreichs (United Green Party of Austria).

Bundesrat
(Federal Council)
(January 1998)

Chairman of the Bundesrat: Ludwig Bieringer (Jan.– June 1998).

Provinces	Total seats	SPÖ	ÖVP	Die Freiheitlichen
Burgenland	3	2	1	—
Carinthia	5	2	1	2
Lower Austria	12	5	6	1
Upper Austria	11	4	5	2
Salzburg	4	1	2	1
Styria	10	4	4	2
Tyrol	5	1	3	1
Vorarlberg	3	—	2	1
Vienna	11	5	2	4
Total	64	24	26	14

Political Organizations

Die Freiheitlichen (Freedom Party): 1010 Vienna, Kärntnerstr. 28; tel. (1) 512-35-35; fax (1) 513-88-58; f. 1955 as Freiheitliche Partei Österreichs, partially succeeding the Verband der Unabhängigen (League of Independents): present name adopted 1995; populist right-wing party advocating the participation of workers in management, stricter immigration controls and opposing Austria's membership of the EU; Chair. Dr Jörg Haider; Gen. Sec. Susi Riess.

Die Grünen–Die Grüne Alternative (The Greens–The Green Alternative): 1070 Vienna, Lindengasse 40; tel. (1) 52-125-0; fax (1) 526-91-10; f. 1986; campaigns for environmental protection, peace and social justice; Chair. Prof. Dr Alexander van der Bellen; Leader of Parliamentary Group Dr Madeline Petrovic.

Kommunistische Partei Österreichs (KPÖ) (Communist Party of Austria): 1020 Vienna, Schönngasse 15–17; tel. (1) 21742; fax (1) 21742-599; f. 1918; strongest in the industrial centres and trade unions; advocates a policy of strict neutrality and opposes Austria's membership of the EU; Chair. Walter Baier.

Liberales Forum (LF) (Liberal Forum): 1010 Vienna, Reichsratstr. 7/10; tel. (1) 402-78-81; fax (1) 402-78-89; e-mail bund@lif.or.at; f. 1993 by fmr mems of Freiheitliche Partei Österreichs (now Die Freiheitlichen); Leader Dr Heide Schmidt.

Österreichische Volkspartei (ÖVP) (Austrian People's Party): 1010 Vienna, Lichtenfelsgasse 7; tel. (1) 401-26; telex 111735; fax (1) 401-26-329; internet http://www.oevp.or.at; f. 1945; Christian-Democratic party; advocates an ecologically-orientated social market economy; 760,000 mems; Chair. Dr Wolfgang Schüssel; Secs-Gen. Othmar Karas, Maria Rauch-Kallat.

Sozialdemokratische Partei Österreichs (SPÖ) (Social-Democratic Party of Austria): 1014 Vienna, Löwelstr. 18; tel. (1) 534-27-0; telex 114198; fax (1) 535-96-83; f. as the Social-Democratic Party in 1889, subsequently renamed the Socialist Party, reverted to its original name in 1991; advocates democratic socialism and Austria's permanent neutrality; 500,000 mems; Chair. Mag. Viktor Klima; Sec. Andreas Rudas.

Vereinte Grüne Österreichs (VGÖ) (United Green Party of Austria): Linz; tel. (732) 66-83-91; fax (732) 650668; f. 1982; ecologist party; Chair. Adi Pinter; Gen. Secs Wolfgang Pelikan, Günter Ofner.

Diplomatic Representation

EMBASSIES IN AUSTRIA

Afghanistan: 1070 Vienna, Kaiserstr. 84/1/3; tel. (1) 524-78-06; fax (1) 524-78-07; Chargé d'affaires: Farid A. Amin.

Albania: 1190 Vienna, Blaasstr. 24; tel. (1) 36-91-229; telex 133248; fax (1) 36-14-83; Ambassador: Albert Iljaz Alickaj.

Algeria: 1190 Vienna, Rudolfinergasse 16–18; tel. (1) 369-88-53; telex 134163; fax (1) 369-88-56; Ambassador: Halim Benattallah.

Argentina: 1010 Vienna, Goldschmiedgasse 2/1; tel. (1) 533-85-77; telex 114512; fax (1) 533-87-97; Ambassador: Andrés Guillermo Pesci Bourel.

Armenia: 1070 Vienna, Neubaugasse 12–14/1/16; tel. (1) 522-74-79; fax (1) 522-74-81; Ambassador: (vacant).

Australia: 1040 Vienna, Mattiellistr. 2–4/III; tel. (1) 512-85-80; fax (1) 504-11-78; Ambassador: Ronald Alfred Walker.

Azerbaijan: 1080 Vienna, Strozzigasse 10; tel. (1) 403-13-22; fax (1) 403-13-23; Ambassador: Vagif Sadykhov.

Belarus: 1220 Vienna, Erzherzog-Karl-Str. 182; tel. (1) 283-58-85; fax (1) 283-58-86; Ambassador: Valyantsin M. Fisenka.

Belgium: 1040 Vienna, Wohllebengasse 6; tel. (1) 50-20-7; telex 113364; fax (1) 502-07-11; Ambassador: LUC CEYSSENS.

Bolivia: 1040 Vienna, Waaggasse 10/4; tel. (1) 587-46-75; telex 135555; fax (1) 586-68-80; Chargé d'affaires a.i.: MARÍA TAMAYO DE ARNAL.

Bosnia and Herzegovina: 1020 Vienna, Tivoligasse 54; tel. (1) 811-85-55; fax (1) 811-85-69; Ambassador: HADŽO EFENDIĆ.

Brazil: 1010 Vienna, Lugeck 1/V/15; tel. (1) 512-06-31; fax (1) 513-83-74; Ambassador: AFFONSO CELSO DE OURO-PRETO.

Bulgaria: 1040 Vienna, Schwindgasse 8; tel. (1) 505-64-44; fax (1) 505-14-23; Chargé d'affaires: GEORGI DIMOV.

Canada: 1010 Vienna, Laurenzerberg 2/111; tel. (1) 535-38-0; fax (1) 531-38-3321; e-mail paul.dubois@vienn01.x400gc.ca; Ambassador: PAUL DUBOIS.

Chile: 1010 Vienna, Lugeck 1/III/10; tel. (1) 512-92-08-0; telex 115952; fax (1) 512-92-08-33; Ambassador: OSVALDO PUCCIO HUIDOBRO.

China, People's Republic: 1030 Vienna, Metternichgasse 4; tel. (1) 714-31-49; telex 135794; fax (1) 713-68-16; Ambassador: WANG YANYI.

Colombia: 1010 Vienna, Stadiongasse 6–8; tel. (1) 406-44-46; telex 116798; fax (1) 408-83-03; Ambassador: CARLOS LEMON SIMMONDS.

Costa Rica: 1120 Vienna, Schlöglgasse 10; tel. (1) 804-05-37; fax (1) 804-90-71; Chargé d'affaires: AVIRAM NEUMAN.

Croatia: 1170 Vienna, Heuberggasse 10; tel. (1) 480-20-83; fax (1) 480-29-42; Ambassador: Dr MILAN RAMLJAK.

Cuba: 1130 Vienna, PF 36, Himmelhofgasse 40 a-c; tel. (1) 877-81-98; telex 131398; fax (1) 877-77-03; Ambassador: ALBERTO VELAZCO SAN JOSÉ.

Cyprus: 1010 Vienna, Parkring 20; tel. (1) 513-06-30; fax (1) 513-06-32; e-mail embassy@cyprus.vienna.at; Ambassador: PETROS MICHAELIDES.

Czech Republic: 1140 Vienna, Penzinger Str. 11–13; tel. (1) 894-21-25; fax (1) 894-12-00; Ambassador: PAVEL JAJTNER.

Denmark: 1015 Vienna, PF 298, Führichgasse 6; tel. (1) 512-79-04-0; telex 113261; fax (1) 513-81-20; Ambassador: JØRGEN BØJER.

Ecuador: 1010 Vienna, Goldschmiedgasse 10/2/24; tel. (1) 535-32-08; telex 134958; fax (1) 535-08-97; Ambassador: JAIME MARCHAN.

Egypt: 1190 Vienna, Kreindlgasse 22; tel. (1) 36-11-34; telex 115623; fax (1) 36-11-34-27; Ambassador: ABDEL HAMID A. ONSY.

Estonia: 1030 Vienna, Marokkanergasse 22/6; tel. and fax (1) 718-07-29; Ambassador: TOIVO TASA.

Ethiopia: 1080 Vienna, Friedrich Schmidtplatz 3/3; tel. (1) 402-84-10; fax (1) 402-84-13; Ambassador: MENBERE ALEMAYEHO.

Finland: 1010 Vienna, Gonzagagasse 16; tel. (1) 53-15-90; telex 135230; fax (1) 535-57-03; Ambassador: EVA-CHRISTINA MÄKELÄINEN.

France: 1040 Vienna, Technikerstr. 2; tel. (1) 505-47-47; telex 131333; fax (1) 505-63-92-68; Ambassador: MARIE-FRANCE DE HARTINGH.

Georgia: 1191 Vienna, Heiligenstädterstr. 40; tel. (1) 368-38-58; fax (1) 368-38-59; Chargé d'affaires a.i.: NODAR K. GIORGADZE.

Germany: 1030 Vienna, Metternichgasse 3; tel. (1) 71-1-54; telex 134261; fax (1) 713-83-66; internet http://www.deubowien.magnet.at; Ambassador: URSULA SEILER-ALBRING.

Greece: 1040 Vienna, Argentinierstr. 14; tel. (1) 505-57-91; telex 133176; fax (1) 505-62-17; Ambassador: PANAYIOTIS TSOUNIS.

Guatemala: 1030 Vienna, Reisnerstr. 20/1/4; tel. (1) 714-35-70; fax (1) 714-36-69; Ambassador: MARIO JUÁREZ TOLEDO.

Holy See: 1040 Vienna, Theresianumgasse 31; tel. (1) 505-13-27; fax (1) 505-61-40; Apostolic Nuncio: Most Rev. DONATO SQUICCIARINI, Titular Archbishop of Tiburnia.

Hungary: 1010 Vienna, Bankgasse 4–6; tel. (1) 533-26-31; telex 135546; fax (1) 535-99-40; Ambassador: Dr SÁNDOR PEISCH.

India: 1015 Vienna, Kärntner Ring 2A; tel. (1) 505-86-66; telex 113721; fax (1) 505-92-19; Ambassador: KIRAN KUMAR DOSHI.

Indonesia: 1180 Vienna, Gustav-Tschermak-Gasse 5–7; tel. (1) 479-05-37; telex 75579; fax (1) 310-99-78; Ambassador: (vacant).

Iran: 1030 Vienna, Jaurèsgasse 9; tel. (1) 712-26-57; telex 131718; fax (1) 713-46-94; e-mail botschaft.d.islam.rep.iran@acv.at; Ambassador: MEHDI MOHTASHAMI.

Iraq: 1010 Vienna, Johannesgasse 26; tel. (1) 713-81-95; telex 135397; fax (1) 713-67-20; Ambassador: (vacant).

Ireland: 1030 Vienna, Hilton Centre, 16th Floor; tel. (1) 715-42-46; fax (1) 713-60-04; Ambassador: THELMA M. DORAN.

Israel: 1180 Vienna, Anton-Frank-Gasse 20; tel. (1) 470-47-41; fax (1) 470-47-46; Ambassador: YOEL SHER.

Italy: 1030 Vienna, Rennweg 27; tel. (1) 712-51-21; telex 132620; fax (1) 713-97-19; Ambassador: Dr JOSEPH NITTI.

Japan: 1040 Vienna, Argentinierstr. 21; tel. (1) 501-71-0; telex 135810; fax (1) 505-45-37; Ambassador: YUSHU TAKASHIMA.

Jordan: 1010 Vienna, Doblhoffgasse 3/2; tel. (1) 405-10-25; fax (1) 405-10-31; Ambassador: Dr MAZEU ARMOUTI.

Korea, Democratic People's Republic: 1140 Vienna, Beckmanngasse 10–12; tel. (1) 89-42-311; fax (1) 89-43-174; Ambassador: KIM KWANG SOP.

Korea, Republic: 1180 Vienna, Gregor-Mendel-Str. 25; tel. (1) 478-19-91; fax (1) 478-10-13; Ambassador: SEUNG KON-LEE.

Kuwait: 1010 Vienna, Universitätsstr. 5; tel. (1) 405-56-46; fax (1) 405-56-46-13; Ambassador: FAISAL R. AL-GHAIS.

Kyrgyzstan: 1010 Vienna, Naglergasse 25/5; tel. (1) 535-03-78; fax (1) 535-03-79-13; Ambassador: KAMIL BAIALINOV.

Latvia: 1090 Vienna, Währinger Str. 3/8; tel. (1) 403-31-12; fax (1) 403-31-12/27; Ambassador: MĀRTIŅŠ VIRSIS.

Lebanon: 1010 Vienna, Oppolzergasse 6/3; tel. (1) 533-88-22; telex 115273; fax (1) 533-49-84; Ambassador: SAMIR NAJIB HOBEICA.

Libya: 1170 Vienna, Dornbacherstr. 27; tel. (1) 45-36-11; telex 116267; fax (1) 45-36-15; Chargé d'affaires a.i.: AHMED A. OWN.

Lithuania: 1010 Vienna, Löwengasse 47; tel. (1) 718-54-67; fax (1) 718-54-69; Chargé d'affaires a.i.: Dr RIMANTAS JUOZAPAS TONKUNAS.

Luxembourg: 1180 Vienna, Sternwartestr. 81; tel. (1) 478-21-42; fax (1) 478-21-44; Ambassador: GEORGES SANTER.

Macedonia, former Yugoslav republic: 1010 Vienna, Walfischgasse 8/20; tel. (1) 512-85-10; fax (1) 512-85-12; Chargé d'affaires: ALEKSANDAR TAVCIOVSKI.

Malaysia: 1040 Vienna, Prinz Eugen-Str. 18; tel. (1) 505-10-42-0; telex 133830; fax (1) 505-79-42; Ambassador: MELANIE LEONG SOOK LEI.

Mexico: 1090 Vienna, Türkenstr. 15; tel. (1) 310-73-83; fax (1) 310-73-87; e-mail embamex@mail.austria.eu.net; Ambassador: ROBERTA LAJOUS

Moldova: 1060 Vienna, Köstlergasse 4/7; tel. (1) 581-83-01; fax (1) 581-83-00; e-mail amda@netway.at; Ambassador: VALENTIN CIUMAC.

Morocco: 1010 Vienna, Opernring 3–5/I/4; tel. (1) 586-66-50; telex 135728; fax (1) 216-79-84; Ambassador: ABDERRAHIM BENMOUSSA.

Netherlands: 1010 Vienna, Opernring 3–5; tel. (1) 589-39-200; fax (1) 589-39-265; e-mail nlgovwen@cso.co.at; Ambassador: JOHAN THEODOOR H. C. VAN EBBENHORST TENGBERGEN.

Nicaragua: 1010 Vienna, Ebendorferstr. 10/3/12; tel. (1) 403-18-38; fax (1) 403-27-52; Ambassador: XAVIER ARGÜELLO HURTADO.

Nigeria: 1030 Vienna, PF 182, Rennweg 25; tel. (1) 712-66-85; telex 131583; fax (1) 714-14-02; Ambassador: SULAIMAN DAHIRU.

Norway: 1030 Vienna, Bayerngasse 3; tel. (1) 715-66-92; telex 132768; fax (1) 712-65-52; Ambassador: ERIK CHRISTIAN SELMER.

Oman: 1090 Vienna, Währingerstr. 2–4/24–25; tel. (1) 310-86-43; telex 116662; fax (1) 310-72-68; Ambassador: MOHAMMED Y. AL-ZARAFY.

Pakistan: 1190 Vienna, Hofzeile 13; tel. (1) 36-73-81; telex 135634; fax (1) 36-73-76; Ambassador: Dr MASUMA HASAN.

Panama: 1010 Vienna, Elisabethstr. 4–5/4/10; tel. (1) 587-23-47; fax (1) 586-30-80; e-mail mail@empanvienna.co.at; Ambassador: Dr JORGE ENRIQUE HALPHEN PÉREZ.

Paraguay: 1030 Vienna, Strohgasse 16/6; tel. (1) 715-56-08; fax (1) 715-56-09; Ambassador: MARIA CHRISTINA ACOSTA-ALVAREZ.

Peru: 1030 Vienna, Gottfried-Keller-Gasse 2/8; tel. (1) 713-43-77; fax (1) 712-77-04; Ambassador: GILBERT CHAUNY DE PORTURAS-HOYLE.

Philippines: 1190 Vienna, Billrothstr. 2/II/21; tel. (1) 318-71-34; telex 132740; fax (1) 318-71-38; Ambassador: JOSÉ A. ZAIDE.

Poland: 1130 Vienna, Hietzinger Hauptstr. 42c; tel. (1) 877-74-44; fax (1) 877-74-44-222; Ambassador: Prof. JAN BARCZ.

Portugal: 1040 Vienna, Operngasse 20B; tel. (1) 586-75-36; telex 113237; fax (1) 587-58-39; Ambassador: ALVARO DE MENDONÇA E MOURA.

Qatar: 1090 Vienna, Strudlhofgasse 10; tel. (1) 31-66-39; telex 131306; fax (1) 319-70-86; Ambassador: JASIM YOUSOF JAMAL.

Romania: 1040 Vienna, Prinz-Eugen-Str. 60; tel. (1) 505-32-27; telex 133335; fax (1) 504-14-62; Ambassador: Prof. Dr PETRU FORNA.

Russia: 1030 Vienna, Reisnerstr. 45–47; tel. (1) 712-12-29; telex 136278; fax (1) 712-33-88; Ambassador: VALERIY N. POPOV.

San Marino: 1010 Vienna, Getreidemarkt 12; tel. (1) 586-21-80; fax (1) 586-22-35; Ambassador: GIOVANNI VITO MARCUCCI.

Saudi Arabia: 1190 Vienna, Formanekgasse 38; tel. (1) 368-23-16; telex 116625; fax (1) 368-25-60; Ambassador: ESSA A. AL-NOWAISER.

Slovakia: 1190 Vienna, Armbrustergasse 24; tel. (1) 318-90-55; fax (1) 318-90-60; Ambassador: Dr JOSEF KLIMKO.

Slovenia: 1010 Vienna, Nibelungengasse 13/3; tel. (1) 586-13-07; fax (1) 586-12-65; Ambassador: Dr KATJA BOH.

South Africa: 1190 Vienna, Sandgasse 33; tel. (1) 32-64-93; telex 116671; fax (1) 32-64-93-51; Ambassador: N. J. MXAKATO-DISEKO.

Spain: 1040 Vienna, Argentinierstr. 34; tel. (1) 505-57-80; telex 131545; fax (1) 504-20-76; Ambassador: Dr MIGUEL ANGEL OCHOA BRUN.

Sri Lanka: 1010 Vienna, Herrengasse 6-8; tel. (1) 533-74-26; fax (1) 533-74-32; e-mail srilanka.embassy.vienna@magnet.at; Ambassador: C. S. POOLOKASINGHAM.

Sudan: 1030 Vienna, Reisnerstr. 29/5; tel. (1) 710-23-43; fax (1) 710-23-46; Ambassador: AHMED ABDEL HALIM MOHAMED.

Sweden: 1025 Vienna, Obere Donaustr. 49–51; tel. (1) 214-77-01; telex 114720; fax (1) 214-50-44; Ambassador: BJÖRN SKALA.

Switzerland: 1030 Vienna, Prinz-Eugen-Str. 7; tel. (1) 795-05; telex 132960; fax (1) 795-05-21; Ambassador: Dr ADOLF G. LACHER.

Syria: 1010 Vienna, Wallnerstr. 8; tel. (1) 533-46-33; fax (1) 533-46-32; Ambassador: Dr RIAD SIAGE.

Tajikistan: 1030 Vienna, Strohgasse 11/13; tel. (1) 718-38-63; fax (1) 712-96-67; Chargé d'affaires a.i.: YUSUPOV DODOSCHON.

Thailand: 1180 Vienna, Weimarer-Str. 68; tel. (1) 310-16-30; fax (1) 310-39-35; e-mail thai.vn@embthai.telecom.at; Ambassador: CHUCHAI KASEMSARN.

Tunisia: 1010 Vienna, Opernring 5/3; tel. (1) 581-52-81; telex 111748; fax (1) 581-55-92; Ambassador: MOHAMED EL FADHEL KHALIL.

Turkey: 1040 Vienna, Prinz-Eugen-Str. 40; tel. (1) 505-73-38-0; telex 131927; fax (1) 505-36-60; Ambassador: FILIZ DINCMEN.

Turkmenistan: Vienna, tel. (1) 503-64-70; Ambassador: BATYR BERDYEV.

Ukraine: 1180 Vienna, Naaffgasse 23; tel. (1) 479-71-72; telex 111-256; fax (1) 479-71-72-47; Ambassador: MYKOLA P. MAKAREVYCH.

United Arab Emirates: 1190 Vienna, Peter-Jordan-Str. 66; tel. (1) 368-14-55; telex 114106; fax (1) 36-23-41; Ambassador: ABDUL REDA ABDULLA MAHMOOD KHOURI.

United Kingdom: 1030 Vienna, Jaurèsgasse 12; tel. (1) 716-13-0; fax (1) 716-13-6900; Ambassador: Sir ANTHONY FIGGIS.

USA: 1090 Vienna, Boltzmanngasse 16; tel. (1) 31-3-39; telex 114634; fax (1) 31-00-682; Ambassador: SWANEE HUNT.

Uruguay: 1010 Vienna, Krugerstr. 3/1/4–6; tel. (1) 513-22-40; telex 112589; fax (1) 513-99-13; Ambassador: ALEJANDRO LORENZO Y LOSADA.

Uzbekistan: Vienna; tel. (1) 405-09-27; fax (1) 405-09-29; Ambassador: ALISHER ERHINOVICH SHAIKHOV.

Venezuela: 1030 Vienna, Marokkanergasse 22; tel. (1) 712-26-38; telex 136219; fax (1) 715-32-19; Ambassador: Prof. Dr DEMETRIO BOERSNER.

Viet Nam: 1190 Vienna, Félix Mottlstr. 20; tel. (1) 310-40-74; fax (1) 310-40-72; Ambassador: NGUYEN THI HOI.

Yemen: 1090 Vienna, Alser Str. 28/1/12; tel. (1) 403-19-69; telex 111246; fax (1) 403-17-97; Ambassador: (vacant).

Yugoslavia: 1030 Vienna, Rennweg 3; tel. (1) 713-25-95; telex 135398; fax (1) 713-25-97; Ambassador: DOBROSAV VEIZOVIĆ.

Zimbabwe: 1080 Vienna, Strozzigasse 10/15; tel. (1) 407-92-36; fax (1) 407-92-38; Ambassador: EVELYN LILLIAN KAWONZA.

Judicial System

The Austrian legal system is based on the principle of a division between legislative, administrative and judicial power. There are three supreme courts (Verfassungsgerichtshof, Verwaltungsgerichtshof and Oberster Gerichtshof). The judicial courts are organized into about 200 local courts (Bezirksgerichte), 17 provincial and district courts (Landes- und Kreisgerichte), and 4 higher provincial courts (Oberlandesgerichte) in Vienna, Graz, Innsbruck and Linz.

SUPREME ADMINISTRATIVE COURTS

Verfassungsgerichtshof (Constitutional Court): 1010 Vienna, Judenplatz 11; fax (1) 531-22-499; e-mail vfgh@ufgh.gv.at; internet http://www.vfgh.gv.at; f. 1919; deals with matters affecting the Constitution, examines the legality of legislation and administration; Pres. Prof. Dr LUDWIG ADAMOVICH; Vice-Pres. Dr KARL PISKA.

Verwaltungsgerichtshof (Administrative Court): 1010 Vienna, Judenplatz 11; deals with matters affecting the legality of administration; Pres. ALFRED KOBZINA; Vice-Pres. Dr GERHARD JABLONER.

SUPREME JUDICIAL COURT

Oberster Gerichtshof: Vienna I, Museumstr. 12; tel. (1) 52-152; fax (1) 52-152-3310; Pres. Prof. Dr HERBERT STEININGER; Vice-Pres Dr KURT HOFMANN, Dr EDGAR REISENLEITNER.

Religion

CHRISTIANITY

Ökumenischer Rat der Kirchen in Österreich (Ecumenical Council of Churches in Austria): 1010 Vienna, Fleischmarkt 13; tel. (1) 533-29-65; fax (1) 533-38-89; f. 1958; 14 mem. Churches, 11 observers; Hon. Pres. Bishop MICHAEL STAIKOS (Greek Orthodox Church); Vice-Pres Dr JOHANNES DANTINE (Protestant Church of the Augsburgian Confession), Mother Superior CHRISTINE GLEIXNER (Roman Catholic Church); Sec. Superintendent HELMUT NAUSNER (United Methodist Church).

The Roman Catholic Church

Austria comprises two archdioceses, seven dioceses and the territorial abbacy of Wettingen-Mehrerau (directly responsible to the Holy See). The Archbishop of Vienna is also the Ordinary for Catholics of the Byzantine rite in Austria (totalling an estimated 4,500 at 31 December 1995). At 31 December 1995 there were an estimated 5,932,590 adherents (about 77% of the population).

Bishops' Conference: Österreichische Bischofskonferenz, 1010 Vienna, Wollzeile 2; tel. (1) 516-11-3820; fax (1) 516-11-3436; f. 1979; Pres. Dr JOHANN WEBER, Bishop of Graz-Seckau; Sec. Mgr Dr MICHAEL WILHELM.

Archbishop of Salzburg: Most Rev. Dr GEORG EDER, 5020 Salzburg, Kapitelplatz 2; 5010 Salzburg, PF 62; tel. (662) 84-25-91; fax (662) 84-25-91-74.

Archbishop of Vienna: Cardinal Dr CHRISTOPH SCHÖNBORN, 1010 Vienna, Wollzeile 2; tel. (1) 515-52-0; fax (1) 515-52-760.

Orthodox Churches

The Armenian Apostolic Church and the Bulgarian, Coptic, Greek, Romanian, Russian, Serbian and Syrian Orthodox Churches are active in Austria.

The Anglican Communion

Within the Church of England, Austria forms part of the diocese of Gibraltar in Europe. The Bishop is resident in London.

Archdeacon of the Eastern Archdeaconry: Ven. JEREMY PEAKE, Christ Church, 1030 Vienna, Jaurèsgasse 17; tel. (1) 720-79-73; fax (1) 720-79-73.

Protestant Churches

Bund der Baptistengemeinden in Österreich (Fed. of Baptist Communities): 1030 Vienna, Krummgasse 7/4; tel. (1) 713-68-28; fax (1) 713-68-284; Pres. Rev. HORST FISCHER.

Evangelische Kirche Augsburgischen Bekenntnisses in Österreich (Protestant Church of the Augsburgian Confession): 1180 Vienna, Severin-Schreiber-Gasse 3; tel. (1) 479-15-23; fax (1) 479-15-23-330; 340,422 mems; Bishop Mag. HERWIG STURM.

Evangelische Kirche HB (Helvetischen Bekenntnisses) (Protestant Church of the Helvetic Confession): 1010 Vienna, Dorotheergasse 16; tel. (1) 513-65-64; fax (1) 512-44-90; 15,863 mems; Landessuperintendent Pfr. PETER KARNER.

Evangelisch-methodistische Kirche (United Methodist Church): 1100 Vienna, Landgutgasse 39/7; tel. (1) 604-53-47; fax (1) 606-67-17; Superintendent HELMUT NAUSNER.

Other Christian Churches

Altkatholische Kirche Österreichs (Old Catholic Church in Austria): 1010 Vienna, Schottenring 17; tel. (1) 317-83-94; fax (1) 317-83-95-9; c. 18,000 mems; Bishop BERNHARD HEITZ.

JUDAISM

There are about 10,000 Jews in Austria.

Israelitische Kultusgemeinde (Jewish Community): 1010 Vienna, Seitenstettengasse 4; tel. (1) 53-104-0; telex 136298; fax (1) 533-15-77; Pres. PAUL GROSZ.

The Press

Austria's first newspaper was published in 1605. The *Wiener Zeitung*, founded in 1703, is the world's oldest daily paper. Restrictions on press freedom are permissible only within the framework of Article 10 (2) of the European Convention of Human Rights.

The Austrian Press Council (Presserat), founded in 1961, supervises the activities of the press. Vienna is the focus of newspaper and periodical publishing, although there is also a strong press in some provinces. The three highest circulation dailies are the *Neue Kronen-Zeitung*, the *Kurier*, and the *Kleine Zeitung* (Graz).

PRINCIPAL DAILIES

Bregenz

Neue Vorarlberger Tageszeitung: 6901 Bregenz, Arlbergstr. 117; tel. (5574) 4090; fax (5574) 409300; f. 1972; morning; independent; Editor (vacant); circ. 20,136.

Vorarlberger Nachrichten: 6901 Bregenz, Kirchstr. 35; tel. (5574) 512-227; telex 57710; fax (5574) 512-230; morning; Editor EUGEN A. RUSS; circ. 74,948.

Graz

Kleine Zeitung: 8011 Graz, Schönaugasse 64; tel. (316) 875-0; fax (316) 875-4034; f. 1904; independent; Chief Editor Dr ERWIN FANKEL; circ. 177,050.

Neue Zeit: 8054 Graz, Ankerstr. 4; tel. (316) 28-08-0; fax (316) 28-08-325; f. 1945; morning; Editor JOSEF RIEDLER.

Innsbruck

Tiroler Tageszeitung: 6020 Innsbruck, Ing.-Etzel-Str. 30; tel. (512) 5354-0; telex 534482; fax (512) 57-59-24; morning; independent; Chief Editor CLAUS REITEN; circ. 103,630.

Klagenfurt

Kärntner Tageszeitung: 9020 Klagenfurt, Viktringer Ring 28; tel. (463) 58-660; fax (463) 5866-321; f. 1946; morning except Monday; Socialist; Chief Editor Dr HELLWIG VALENTIN.

Kleine Zeitung: 9020 Klagenfurt, Funderstr. 1A; tel. (463) 200-58-00; fax (463) 56500; independent; Editor Dr HORST PIRKER; circ. 99,380.

Linz

Neues Volksblatt: 4020 Linz, Hafenstr. 1–3; tel. (732) 78-19-01; fax (732) 77-92-42; f. 1869; Austrian People's Party; Chief Editor KURT HORWITZ.

Oberösterreichische Nachrichten: 4010 Linz, Promenade 23; tel. (732) 78-05-410; fax (732) 78-05-217; f. 1865; morning; independent; Chief Editor Dr HANS KÖPPL; circ. 123,470.

Salzburg

***Salzburger Nachrichten:** 5021 Salzburg, Karolingerstr. 40; tel. (662) 8373-0; fax (662) 8373-399; f. 1945; morning; independent; Editor-in-Chief Dr MAX DASCH; circ. 91,970.

Salzburger Volkszeitung: 5020 Salzburg, Bergstr. 12; tel. (662) 87-94-91; fax (662) 8794-91-13; Austrian People's Party; Editor HELMUT MÖDLHAMMER; circ. weekdays 12,030.

Vienna

***Kurier:** 1072 Vienna, Lindengasse 52; tel. (1) 52100; telex 132631; fax (1) 52100-2263; f. 1954; independent; Chief Editor PETER RABL; circ. weekdays 334,204, Sunday 545,700.

***Neue Kronen-Zeitung:** 1190 Vienna, Muthgasse 2; tel. (1) 3601-0; fax (1) 369-83-85; f. 1900; independent; Editor HANS DICHAND; circ. weekdays 510,226, Sunday 751,296.

***Die Presse:** 1015 Vienna, Parkring 12A; tel. (1) 51-4-14; fax (1) 514-14-400; f. 1848; morning; independent; Editors JULIUS KAINZ, Dr THOMAS CHORHERR; circ. Mon.–Wed. 96,000, Thur.–Fri. 105,000; Sat. 156,000.

***Der Standard:** 1014 Vienna, Herrengasse 19–21; tel. (1) 53-1-70; fax (1) 53170-131; e-mail documentation@derstandard.at; f. 1988; independent; Editors-in-Chief OSCAR BRONNER, Dr GERFRIED SPERL; circ. 104,050.

***Wiener Zeitung:** 1037 Vienna, Rennweg 12A; tel. (1) 79789; fax (1) 79789433; f. 1703; morning; official govt paper; Editor HORST TRAXLER; circ. 20,020.

* National newspapers.

PRINCIPAL WEEKLIES

Blickpunkt: 6020 Innsbruck, Furstenweg 77A; tel. (512) 210; fax (512) 29-44-32; Editor OTTO STEIXNER.

Die Furche: 1010 Vienna, Lobkowitzplatz 1, Singerstr. 7; tel. (1) 512-52-61; fax (1) 512-82-15; f. 1945; Catholic; Editor Dr GOTTFRIED MOIK.

Die ganze Woche: 1210 Vienna, Ignaz-Köck Str. 17; tel. (1) 39-1600; fax (1) 39-1600-64; circ. 582,060.

industrie: 1030 Vienna, Reisnerstr. 40/2; tel. (1) 711-95-0; fax (1) 71195-5299; Editor MILAN FRÜHBAUER; circ. 14,330.

IW-Internationale Wirtschaft: 1051 Vienna, Nikolsdorfer Gasse 7–11; tel. (1) 546-64-346; fax (1) 546-64-342; economics; Editor NIKOLAUS GERSTMAYER; circ. 13,430.

Kärntner Nachrichten: 9010 Klagenfurt, Waagplatz 7; tel. (463) 51-14-17-22; fax (463) 50-41-85; f. 1954; Editor HANS RIEPAN.

Die neue Wirtschaft: 1051 Vienna, Nikolsdorfer Gasse 7–11; tel. (1) 546-64-247; fax (1) 546-64-347; economics; circ. 25,650.

Neue Wochenschau: 7210 Mattersburg, J. N. Bergerstr. 2; tel. and fax (2622) 674-73; f. 1908; Editor HELMUT WALTER; circ. 128,500.

NFZ—Neue Freie Zeitung: 1010 Vienna, Grillparzerstr. 7/7A; tel. (1) 402-3585-0; fax (1) 408-68-38-31; organ of Freedom Party; Chief Editor MICHAEL A. RICHTER; circ. 60,000.

Niederösterreichische Nachrichten: 3100 St Pölten, Gutenbergstr. 12; tel. (2742) 802-0; telex 15512; fax (2742) 802-480; e-mail noen-knabl@apanet.at; Editor HARALD KNABL; circ. 158,500.

Oberösterreichische Rundschau: 4010 Linz, Hafenstr. 1–3; tel. (732) 7616-0; fax (732) 7616-307; Editor-in-Chief RUDOLF CHMELIR; circ. 284,650.

Der Österreichische Bauernbündler: 1014 Vienna, Schenkenstr. 2; tel. (1) 533-16-76-16; fax (1) 533-16-76-45; Editor Prof. PAUL GRUBER; circ. 70,000.

Präsent: 6020 Innsbruck, Exlgasse 20; tel. (512) 22-33; fax (512) 22-33-501; f. 1892; independent Catholic; Chief Editor PAUL MVIGG.

Samstag: 1081 Vienna, Faradaygasse 6; tel. (1) 79594-126; f. 1951; weekly; independent; Chief Editor ANGELIKA STEINWEG-SEELEIB; circ. 41,000.

Tiroler Bauernzeitung: 6021 Innsbruck, Brixner Str. 1; tel. (512) 59-900-0; fax (1) 59-900-31; publ. by Tiroler Bauernbund; Chief Dir GEORG KEUSCHNIGG; circ. 23,000.

Volksstimme: 1070 Vienna, Kaiserstr. 67/1/D6; tel. (1) 52166; fax (1) 5236885; f. 1994; Chief Editor WALTER BAIER.

POPULAR PERIODICALS

Agrar Post: Vienna, 2103 Langenzersdorf, Schulstr. 80; tel. (2244) 4647; f. 1924; monthly; agriculture.

Austria-Ski: 6020 Innsbruck, Olympiastr. 10; tel. (512) 59501; telex 533876; 6 a year; official journal of Austrian Skiing Assen; Editor Mag. JOSEF SCHMID.

auto touring: 3400 Klosterneuburg, Hölzlgasse 66; tel. (2243) 25600; fax (2243) 26671; monthly; official journal of the Austrian Automobile Organizations; Editor-in-Chief OTTO BURGHART; circ. 1,080,000.

Bunte Österreich: 1010 Vienna, Karl Luegel Platz 2; tel. (1) 513-88-33; fax (1) 513-88-38; illustrated weekly.

Frauenblatt: 1032 Vienna, Faradaygasse 6; tel. (1) 795-94-126; women's weekly; Editor GERLINDE KOLANDA; circ. 22,300.

News: 1020 Vienna, Praterstr. 31; tel. (1) 213-120; fax (1) 213-12-300; weekly; illustrated; Editor WOLFGANG FELLNER; circ. 342,244.

Profil: 1010 Vienna, Marc-Aurel-Str. 10–12; tel. (1) 53-4-70-0; fax (1) 535-32-50; e-mail redaktion@profil.at; f. 1970; weekly; political, general; independent; circ. 98,490.

RZ—Wochenschau: Vienna; tel. (1) 523-56-46; fax (1) 523-56-46-22; f. 1936; weekly illustrated; Chief Editor PAUL WEISS.

Sportzeitung: 1080 Vienna, Piaristengasse 16; tel. (1) 405-55-88; fax (1) 405-55--88-27; weekly sports illustrated; Editor HORST HÖTSCH; circ. 28,330.

Trend: 1010 Vienna, Marc-Aurel-Str. 10–12; tel. (1) 53-4-70; monthly; economics.

TV Media: 1020 Vienna, Praterstr. 31; tel. (1) 213-120; weekly; illustrated; Editor WOLFGANG FELLNER; circ. 210,150.

Vídeňské svobodné listy: 1050 Vienna, Margaretenplatz 7/2; tel. (1) 587-83-08; fortnightly for Czech and Slovak communities in Austria; Editor HEINRICH DRAZDIL.

Welt der Frau: 4020 Linz, Lustenauerstr. 21; tel. (732) 77-00-01-11; fax (732) 77-00-01-24; women's monthly magazine; circ. 73,530.

Wiener: 3400 Klosterneuburg, Büropark Donau, Donaustr. 102; tel. (1) 88-600; fax (1) 88600-199; monthly; Chief Editor HANS SCHMID; circ. 130,530.

SPECIALIST PERIODICALS

Eurocity: 1110 Vienna, Leberstr. 122; tel. (1) 74095-0; telex 132312; fax (1) 74095-183; f. 1928; every 2 months; Editor-in-Chief GEORG KARP.

Forum: 1070 Vienna, Museumstr. 5; tel. (1) 93-27-33; fax (1) 93-83-68; f. 1954; every 2 months; international magazine for cultural freedom, political equality and labour solidarity; Editor-in-Chief GERHARD OBERSCHLICK.

itm praktiker: ZB-Verlag, 1125 Vienna, Marochallplatz 23/1/21; tel. (1) 804-04-74; fax (1) 804-44-39; technical hobbies; Chief Editor GERHARD K. BUCHBERGER; circ. 18,800.

Juristische Blätter (mit Beilage 'Wirtschaftsrechtliche Blätter'): Springer Verlag, 1201 Vienna, Sachsenplatz 4; tel. (1) 330-24-15-0; f. 1872; monthly; Editors F. BYDLINSKI, M. BURGSTALLER.

Die Landwirtschaft: 1010 Vienna, Löwelstr. 16; tel. (1) 53441; fax (1) 53441-450; f. 1923; monthly; agriculture and forestry; owned and publ. by Österreichischer Agrarverlag; Editor Gerd Rittenauer.

Liberal Konkret: 1010 Vienna, Reichsratstr. 7/10; tel. (1) 402-78-81; fax (1) 402-78-89; e-mail bund@lif.or.at; 10 a year; organ of Liberal Forum.

Literatur und Kritik: Otto-Müller-Verlag, 5020 Salzburg, Ernest-Thun-Str. 11; tel. (662) 88-19-74; fax (662) 87-23-87; f. 1966; 5 a year; Austrian and European literature and criticism; Editor Karl-Markus Gauss.

Monatshefte für Chemie: 1201 Vienna, Sachsenplatz 4–6; tel. (1) 330-24-15-0; f. 1880; monthly; chemistry; Man. Editor K. Schlögl.

Österreichische Ärztezeitung: 1010 Vienna, Weihburggasse 9; tel. (1) 512-44-86; telex 112701; fax (1) 51-31-92-524; f. 1945; 21 a year; organ of the Austrian Medical Board; Editor Martin Stickler.

Österreichische Ingenieur- und Architekten-Zeitschrift (ÖIAZ): 1010 Vienna, Eschenbachgasse 9; tel. (1) 587-35-36-28; f. 1849; monthly; Editor Dr Georg Widtmann; circ. 4,000.

Österreichische Monatshefte: 1010 Vienna, Lichtenfelsgasse 7; tel. (1) 40126-532; telex 111735; f. 1945; monthly; organ of Austrian People's Party; Editor Gerhard Wilflinger.

Österreichische Musikzeitschrift: 1010 Vienna, Hegelgasse 13; tel. (1) 512-68-69; fax (1) 512-46-29; f. 1946; monthly; Editor Dr M. Diederichs-Lafite; circ. 5,000.

Reichsbund-Aktuell mit SPORT: 1010 Vienna, Ebendorferstr. 6/V; tel. and fax (1) 405-54-06; f. 1917; monthly; Catholic; organ of Reichsbund, Bewegung für christliche Gesellschaftspolitik und Sport; Editor Walter Raming; circ. 12,000.

Welt der Arbeit: A-1230 Vienna, Altmannsdorferstr. 154-156; tel. (1) 661-22/344; socialist industrial journal; Editor Christoph Mandl; circ 64,350.

Wiener klinische Wochenschrift: 1201 Vienna, Sachsenplatz 4–6; tel. (1) 330-24-15; telex 114506; fax (1) 330-24-26; f. 1888; medical bi-weekly; Editors O. Kraupp, H. Sinzinger.

Die Zukunft: A-1014 Vienna, Loewelstr. 18; tel. (1) 53-427-206; fax (1) 535-96-83; monthly; organ of Social-Democratic Party of Austria; Editor Albrecht K. Konecny; circ. 15,000.

NEWS AGENCIES

APA (Austria Presse-Agentur): Internationales Pressezentrum (IPZ), 1199 Vienna, Gunoldstr. 14; tel. (1) 360-60-0; telex 114721; f. 1946; co-operative agency of the Austrian Newspapers and Broadcasting Co (private co); 37 mems; Man. Dir Dr Wolfgang Vyslozil; Chief Editor Josef A. Nowak.

Foreign Bureaux

Agence France-Presse (AFP) (France): IPZ, 1199 Vienna, Gunoldstr. 14; tel. (1) 368-31-87; telex 117833; fax (1) 36-83-188-20; e-mail afpvie@compuserve.com; Bureau Chief Didier Fauqueux.

Agenzia Nazionale Stampa Associata (ANSA) (Italy): IPZ, 1199 Vienna, Gunoldstr. 14; tel. (1) 368-13-00; fax (1) 368-79-35; Bureau Chief Roberto Papi.

Associated Press (AP) (USA): IPZ, 1199 Vienna, Gunoldstr. 14; tel. (1) 36-41-56; telex 115930; fax (1) 36-91-558; Bureau Chief Alison Smale.

Central News Agency (CNA) (Taiwan): 1030 Vienna, Trubelgasse 17-4-40; tel. (1) 799-17-02; fax (1) 798-45-98; Bureau Chief Ou Chun-Lin.

Česká tisková kancelář (ČTK) (Czech Republic): Vienna; tel. and fax (1) 43-92-18; telex 114215.

Deutsche Presse-Agentur (dpa) (Germany): IPZ, 1199 Vienna, Gunoldstr. 14; tel. (1) 368-21-58; fax (1) 369-85-49.

Informatsionnoye Telegrafnoye Agentstvo Rossii—Telegrafnoye Agentstvo Suverennykh Stran (ITAR—TASS) (Russia): 1040 Vienna, Grosse Neugasse 28; tel. (1) 8-10-43-1; telex 113413; fax (1) 56-65-36; Correspondent Aleksandr S. Kuzmin.

Jiji Tsushin-Sha (Japan): IPZ, 1199 Vienna, Gunoldstr. 14; tel. (1) 36-91-797; fax (1) 36-91-052; Bureau Chief Tatsubo Mutsumi.

Kyodo Tsushin (Japan): IPZ, 1199 Vienna, Gunoldstr. 14; tel. (1) 368-18-20; telex 135736; fax (1) 36-92-522; Bureau Chief Toshiya Nakamura.

Magyar Távirati Iroda (MTI) (Hungary): 1130 Vienna, Premreinergasse, tel. and fax (1) 876-69-94; Correspondent Zsófia Fülep.

Novinska Agencija Tanjug (Tanjug) (Yugoslavia): IPZ, 1199 Vienna, Gunoldstr. 14; tel. (1) 37-60-82; fax (1) 368-11-80.

Reuters (UK): 1010 Vienna, Börsegasse 11; tel. (1) 531-12-0; telex 114645; fax (1) 531-12-5; Bureau Chief Giancarlo Orlando.

Xinhua (New China) News Agency (People's Republic of China): 1030 Vienna, Reisnerstr. 15/8; tel. (1) 713-41-40; telex 134384; fax (1) 714-14-57; Chief Correspondent Yang Huanqin.

PRESS ASSOCIATIONS

Österreichischer Zeitschriftenverband (Asscn of Periodical Publrs): 1090 Vienna, Hörlgasse 18/5; tel. (1) 31-97-001; fax (1) 31-97-001; f. 1946; 190 mems; Pres. Dr Rudolf Bohmann.

Verband Österreichischer Zeitungen (Newspaper Asscn of Austria): 1010 Vienna, Renngasse 12; tel. (1) 533-79-79-0; fax (1) 533-79-79-22; f. 1946; all daily and most weekly papers are mems; Pres. Dr Werner Schrotta; Sec.-Gen. Dr Walter Schaffelhofer.

Publishers

Akademische Druck- und Verlagsanstalt: 8010 Graz, Auersperggasse 12, PF 598; tel. (316) 36-44; fax (316) 36-44-24; e-mail adeva@sime.com; internet http://www.adeva.com; f. 1949; scholarly reprints and new works, facsimile editions of Codices; Dir Dr Ursula Struzl.

Betz, Annette, Verlag GmbH: 1091 Vienna, Alser Str. 24; tel. (1) 40-444-0; fax (1) 40-444-5; f. 1962; Man. Dir Johanna Rachinger.

Blackwell Wissenschafts-Verlag GmbH: 1140 Vienna, Zehetnergasse 6; tel. (1) 894-06-90; fax (1) 894-06-90-24; e-mail black@via.at; internet http://www.blackwis.com/austria.htm; f. 1989; medicine, medical journals; Dir Dr Axel Bedürftig.

Böhlau Verlag GmbH & Co KG: 1201 Vienna, Sachsenplatz 4–6; tel. (1) 330-24-27; telex 114506; fax (1) 330-24-32; e-mail dr.rauch@boehlau.at; f. 1947; history, law, philology, the arts, sociology; Dirs Dr Peter Rauch, Rudolf Siegle.

Bohmann Druck und Verlag GmbH & Co KG: 1010 Vienna, Universitätsstr. 11; tel. (1) 407-27-08; fax (1) 407-27-08-88; e-mail buchverlag@bohmann.co.at; internet http://www.bohmann-buch.co.at; f. 1936; trade, technical and educational books and periodicals.

Christian Brandstätter, Verlag und Edition: 1080 Vienna, Wickenburggasse 26; tel. (1) 408-38-14; fax (1) 408-72-00; e-mail books@cbv.co.at; f. 1982; art books; Chair. Dr Christian Brandstätter.

Wilhelm Braumüller, GmbH: 1092 Vienna, Servitengasse 5; tel. (1) 319-14-82; fax (1) 310-28-05; e-mail braumueller@mis.magnet.at; f. 1783; sociology, politics, history, ethnology, linguistics, psychology and philosophy; university publrs; Dir Brigitte Pfeifer.

Franz Deuticke Verlagsgesellschaft mbH: 1010 Vienna, Hegelgasse 21; tel. (1) 514-05-281; fax (1) 514-05-289; f. 1878; culture, literature, travel guides; Dirs Walter Amon, Dr Robert Sedlaczek.

Ludwig Doblinger, KG: 1010 Vienna, Dorotheergasse 10; tel. (1) 515-03-0; fax (1) 515-03-51; e-mail music@doblinger.co.at; f. 1876; music; Dir Helmuth Pany.

Freytag-Berndt und Artaria KG Kartographische Anstalt: 1071 Vienna, Schottenfeldgasse 62; tel. (1) 523-95-01; telex 133526; fax (1) 523-95-01-38; f. 1879 (1770—Artaria); geography, maps and atlases; Chair. Richard Gerin.

Gerold & Co: 1011 Vienna, Graben 31; tel. (1) 533-50-14; fax (1) 512-47-31-29; f. 1867; philology, literature, eastern Europe, sociology and philosophy; Dir Peter Neusser.

Verlag Kerle im Verlag Herder & Co: 1010 Vienna, Wollzeile 33; tel. (1) 512-14-13; fax (1) 512-14-13-42; f. 1886; children's books, juvenile.

Hölder-Pichler-Tempsky Verlag: 1096 Vienna, Frankgasse 4; tel. (1) 401-36-93; fax (1) 401-36-85; f. 1960; school text-books; Man. Dir Gustav Glöckler.

Verlagsbuchhandlung Brüder Hollinek und Co GmbH: 1238 Vienna, Feldgasse 13; tel. (1) 889-36-46; fax (1) 889-36-47-24; f. 1872; science, law and administration, printing, reference works, dictionaries; Dir Richard Hollinek.

Jugend and Volk GmbH: 1016 Vienna,Universitätsstr. 11; tel. (1) 407-27-07; fax (1) 407-27-07-22; f. 1921; pedagogics, art, literature, children's books.

Verlag Kremayr & Scheriau: 1121 Vienna, Niederhofstr. 37; tel. (1) 811-02; telex 31405; fax (1) 811-02-616; f. 1951; non-fiction, history.

Kunstverlag Wolfrum: 1010 Vienna, Augustinerstr. 10; tel. (1) 512-41-78; fax (1) 512-15-57; f. 1919; art; Dir Hubert Wolfrum.

Leykam Verlag: 8011 Graz, Stempfergasse 3; tel. (316) 8076; telex 32209; fax (316) 8076-39; art, literature, academic, law; Dir Dr Klaus Brunner.

Linde Verlag Wien: 1211 Vienna, Scheydgasse; tel. (1) 278-05-26; fax (1) 278-05-26-23; e-mail info.service@linde-verlag.telecom.at; business; Man. Dir Heidelinde Langmayr.

Manz'sche Verlags- und Universitätsbuchhandlung GmbH: 1014 Vienna, Kohlmarkt 16; tel. (1) 53-1610; telex 75310631; fax (1) 531-61-181; e-mail redaktion@manz.co.at; f. 1849; law, political and economic sciences; textbooks and schoolbooks; Man. Dir Dr Wolfgang Pichler.

Wilhelm Maudrich: 1096 Vienna, Spitalgasse 21A; tel. (1) 408-58-92; fax (1) 408-50-80; f. 1909; medical; Man. Dir GERHARD GROIS.

Otto Müller Verlag: 5021 Salzburg, Ernest-Thun-Str. 11; tel. (662) 88-19-74; fax (662) 872-387; f. 1937; general; Man. ARNO KLEIBEL.

R. Oldenbourg: 1030 Vienna, Neulinggasse 26/12; tel. (1) 712-62-580; f. 1959; Dir Dr THOMAS CORNIDES.

Verlag Orac: 1010 Vienna, Graben 17; tel. (1) 534-52; telex 136365; fax (1) 534-52-141; f. 1946; Dir HELMUT HANUSCH.

Österreichischer Gewerbeverlag GmbH: 1014 Vienna, Herrengasse 10; tel. (1) 533-07-68; fax (1) 533-07-68-30; f. 1945; general; Man. F. SCHARETZER.

Pinguin Verlag Pawlowski GmbH: 6021 Innsbruck, Lindenbühelweg 2; tel. (512) 281-1-83; fax (512) 29-32-43; illustrated books; Dirs OLAF PAWLOWSKI, HELLA PFLANZER.

Residenz Verlag GmbH: 5020 Salzburg, Gaisbergstr. 6; tel. (662) 64-19-86; fax (662) 64-35-48; f. 1956; Dir Dr JOCHEN JUNG.

Anton Schroll & Co: 1051 Vienna, Spengergasse 39; tel. (1) 544-56-41; fax (1) 544-56-41-66; f. 1884; also in Munich; art books; Man. F. GEYER.

Springer-Verlag KG: 1201 Vienna, Sachsenplatz 4–6; tel. (1) 330-24-15; telex 114506; fax (1) 330-24-26; f. 1924; medicine, science, technology, law, sociology, economics, periodicals; Man. Dir RUDOLF SIEGLE.

Leopold Stocker Verlag: 8011 Graz, Hofgasse 5; tel. (316) 82-16-36; fax (316) 83-56-12; f. 1917; history, nature, hunting, fiction, agriculture, textbooks; Dir WOLFGANG DVORAK-STOCKER.

Verlag Styria: 8011 Graz, Schönaugasse 64; tel. (316) 8063-0; telex 312387; fax (316) 80-63-7004; e-mail skaiser@styria.co.at; f. 1869; literature, history, theology, philosophy; Chair. Dr REINHARD HABER-FELLNER.

Verlagsanstalt Tyrolia GmbH: 6020 Innsbruck, Exlgasse 20, PF 220; tel. (512) 2233; fax (512) 2233-501; f. 1888; geography, history, science, children's, religion, fiction; Chair. Dr RAIMUND TISCHLER.

Carl Ueberreuter Verlag: 1091 Vienna, Alser Str. 24; tel. (1) 40-444-0; fax (1) 40-444-5; e-mail office@vcu.ueberreuter.com; non-fiction, children's, economics; Dir JOHANNA RACHINGER.

Universal Edition: 1010 Vienna, PF 3, Bösendorferstr. 12; tel. (1) 505-86-95; fax (1) 505-27-20; e-mail uemusic@uemusic.co.at; internet http://www.uemusic.co.at; f. 1901; music; Dir Dr J. JURANEK; Dir. MARION VON HARTLIEB.

Urban & Schwarzenberg GmbH: 1096 Vienna, Frankgasse 4; tel. (1) 405-27-31; fax (1) 405-27-24-41; f. 1866; science, medicine; Dir GUNTER ROYER.

Paul Zsolnay Verlag GmbH: 1041 Vienna, Prinz Eugen-Str. 30; tel. (1) 505-76-61; fax (1) 505-76-61-10; f. 1923; fiction, non-fiction; Dirs MICHAEL KRÜGER, JÜRGEN HORBACH.

Government Publishing Houses

Österreichischer Bundesverlag GmbH (Austrian Federal Publishing House): 1015 Vienna, Schwarzenbergstr. 5; tel. (1) 514-05; fax (1) 514-05-210; f. 1772 by Empress Maria Theresia; school textbooks, education, culture, travel guides, science, children's books; Dirs WALTER AMON, Dr ROBERT SEDLACZEK.

Verlag Österreich (Austrian Publishing House): 1037 Vienna, Rennweg 12A; tel. (1) 79789-419; fax (1) 797-89-104; e-mail verlag-oesterreich@verlag.oesd.co.at; f. 1804; law, CD-ROMs; Gen. Dir GERHARD GEHMAYR.

PUBLISHERS' ASSOCIATION

Hauptverband des österreichischen Buchhandels (Asscn of Austrian Publrs and Booksellers): 1010 Vienna, Grünangergasse 4; tel. (1) 512-15-35; fax (1) 512-84-82; f. 1859; Pres. Dr ANTON C. HILSCHER; 605 mems.

Broadcasting and Communications

TELECOMMUNICATIONS

Austria Post und Telekom AG: 1011 Vienna, Postgasse 8; tel. (1) 515510; Chair. Dr JOSEF SINDELKA.

Connect Austria Gesellschaft für Telekommunikation GmbH: 1010 Vienna, Opernring 1; tel. (1) 58157300; fax (1) 581873010; Chair. FRANZ GEIGER.

max.mobil Telekommunikation Service GmbH: 1030 Vienna; tel. (1) 795850; fax (1) 79585532; Chair. Dr STEPHAN HUXOLD.

RADIO AND TELEVISION

In December 1996 there were 1,757 radio and television transmitters in Austria, broadcasting three national and nine regional radio channels, as well as an overseas service on shortwave. There were also two terrestrial television channels, as well as a satellite station operated in conjunction with German and Swiss companies. Radio and television broadcasting are controlled by the state-owned Österreichischer Rundfunk, although several commercial radio stations are expected to be launched in 1998.

Österreichischer Rundfunk (ORF) (Austrian Broadcasting Company): 1136 Vienna, Würzburggasse 30; tel. (1) 87878-0; telex 133601; fax (1) 87878-22-50; f. 1955; state-owned; controls all radio and television in Austria; Dir-Gen. GERHARD ZEILER; Dirs Dr RUDOLF NAGILLER, KATHRIN ZECHNER (Television), GERHARD WEIS (Radio).

Finance

(cap. = capital; res = reserves; dep. = deposits; m. = million; brs = branches; amounts in Schilling)

BANKS

Banks in Austria, apart from the National Bank, belong to one of five categories. The first category comprises banks that are organized as corporations (i.e. joint-stock and private banks), and special-purpose credit institutions. In December 1993 these numbered, respectively, 56 and 95. The second category comprises savings banks, which numbered 80. The third category comprises co-operative banks. These include rural credit co-operatives (Raiffeisenbanken), which numbered 728 in December 1994, and industrial credit co-operatives (Volksbanken), which numbered 80. The remaining two categories comprise the mortgage banks of the various Austrian 'Länder', which numbered 9 in December 1994, and the building societies, which numbered five. The majority of Austrian banks (with the exception of the building societies) operate on the basis of universal banking, although certain categories have specialized. Banking operations are governed by the Banking Act of 1993 (Bankwesengesetz–BWG).

Central Bank

Oesterreichische Nationalbank (Austrian National Bank): 1090 Vienna, Otto Wagner-Platz 3; tel. (1) 404-20-0; telex 114669; fax (1) 404-20-6699; f. 1922; cap. 150m., res 114,590m., dep. 50,491m. (Dec. 1996); Pres. Dr KLAUS LIEBSCHER; CEO ADOLF WALA; 7 brs.

Commercial Banks

ABN AMRO Bank Österreich AG: 1011 Vienna, Schottenring 35, PF 544; tel (1) 313-06; telex 135606; fax (1) 313-06-4; f. 1988; affiliated to ABN AMRO Bank NV (Netherlands); cap. 293m., res 132m., dep. 8,386m. (Dec. 1995); Chair. Dr RICHARD VORNBERG.

Adria Bank AG: 1011 Vienna, Tegetthoffstr. 1; tel. (1) 514-09; telex 134892; fax (1) 51409-43; f. 1980; cap. 170m., res 232m., dep. 2,671m. (Dec. 1996); Mans CIRIL KRPAC, Dr ALFRED SCHERHAMMER.

Anglo Irish Bank (Austria) AG: 1011 Vienna, Rathausstr. 20, PF 306; tel. (1) 406-61-61; telex 114911; fax (1) 405-81-42; f. 1890; present name adopted 1995; cap. 70m., res 79m., dep. 2,108m. (Dec. 1995); Chair. and CEO TERENCE A. CAROLL.

Bank Austria AG: 1010 Vienna, Am Hof 2; tel. (1) 71191-0; telex 115561; fax (1) 71191-6155; f. 1991 by merger of Österreichische Länderbank and Zentralsparkasse und Kommerzialbank; cap. 8,752m., res 25,563m., dep. 604,960m. (Dec. 1995); Chair. Bd of Man. Dir GERHARD RANDA; 381 brs.

Bank Austria Handelsbank AG: 1010 Vienna, Operngasse 6; tel. (1) 514-40-0; telex 133468; fax (1) 512-66-01; cap. 81m., res 223m., dep. 2,901m. (Dec. 1995); Chair. HELMUT HORVATH.

Bank der Österreichischen Postsparkasse AG: 1015 Vienna, Wipplingerstr. 1; tel. (1) 531-63-0; telex 112268; fax (1) 531-63-222; cap. and res 1,736m., dep. 20,087m. (1994); Chair. and Man. FREIMUT DOBRETSBERGER.

Bank für Arbeit und Wirtschaft AG: 1010 Vienna, Seitzergasse 2–4; tel. (1) 534-53-0; telex 115311; fax (1) 534-53-2840; f. 1947; cap. 6,996m., res 8,601m., dep. 220,239m. (Dec. 1996); Chair. and Gen. Man. HELMUT EWNER; 154 brs.

Bank für Wirtschaft und Freie Berufe AG: 1072 Vienna, Zieglergasse 5; tel. (1) 52107; fax (1) 52107-57; e-mail wifbank@wifbank.-co.at; f. 1914; cap. and res 68.163m., dep. 1,290m. (Dec. 1995); Mans PETER WENINGER, KURT KAPELLER, CLAUS FISCHER-SEE.

Bank Gutmann AG: 1011 Vienna, Schwarzenbergplatz 16; tel. (1) 50220-0; telex 136506; fax (1) 50220-249; f. 1922; cap. and res 92m., dep. 1,762m. (1994); Mans Dr WALTER DAWID, Dr RUDOLF STAHL, Dr ANTON FINK.

Bank Winter & Co AG: 1011 Vienna, Singerstr. 10; tel. (1) 515-04-0; telex 135858; fax (1) 513-48-44; f. 1959; cap. 850m., res 1,154m., dep. 20,742m. (June 1996); Chair. THOMAS MOSKOVICS, 1 br.

Bankhaus Kathrein & Co AG: 1013 Vienna, Wipplingerstr. 25; tel. (1) 53451; telex 14123; fax (1) 53451/384; f. 1924; cap. 151m., res 304m. (Dec. 1994), dep. 4,587m. (Dec. 1995); Gen. Man. Dr WOLFGANG FENKART-FRÖSCHL; Man. Dr GERHARD GRUND.

Bankhaus Schelhammer & Schattera AG: 1010 Vienna, Goldschmiedgasse 3; 1011 Vienna, PF 618; tel. (1) 534-34; telex 113206; fax (1) 53-4-34-64; f. 1832; cap. 259m., res 253m., dep. 3,903m. (Dec. 1995); private bank; Chair. JOSEF MELCHART; Dir JOSEF LÖW; 1 br.

Central Wechsel- und Creditbank AG: 1015 Vienna, Kärntner Str. 43, PF 140; tel. (1) 515-66-0; telex 112387; fax (1) 515-66-9; f. 1918; cap. and res 724m., dep. 10,427m. (1996); Chair. Dr PAUL AUERBACH.

Centro Internationale Handelsbank AG: 1015 Vienna, Tegetthoffstr. 1; tel. (1) 515-20-0; telex 136990; fax (1) 513-43-96; e-mail voelket.centrobank@telecom.at; f. 1973; cap. 350m., res 172m., dep. 6,606m. (Dec. 1995); Exec. Bd Dr GERHARD VOGT (Chair.), JERZY PLUSA, CHRISTIAN SPERK.

Citibank International Plc (Austria): 1015 Vienna, Lothringer str. 7; tel. (1) 717-17-0; telex 112105; fax (1) 713-92-06; f. 1959 as Internationale Investitions- und Finanzierungs Bank AG; present name adopted 1978; wholly-owned subsidiary of Citibank Overseas Investment Corpn; Gen. Man. WALTER HOELLMER.

Constantia Privatbank AG: 1010 Vienna, Opernring 17; tel. (1) 58875-0; fax (1) 58875-90; cap. 436m., dep. 1,669m. (1994); Gen. Man. Dr CHRISTOPH KRAUS.

Crédit Lyonnais Bank (Austria) AG: 1011 Vienna, Wallnerstr. 8, PF 582; Parkring 12A, tel. (1) 53150; telex 112570; fax (1) 53150-50; e-mail clwien-corporate@via.at; internet http://www.creditlyonnais.at; f. 1956 as Österreichische Privat- und Kommerzbank AG; present name adopted in 1993; cap. 160m., res 109m., dep. 2,984m. (Dec. 1995); Gen. Man. PASCAL GRUNDRICH.

Creditanstalt-Bankverein: 1010 Vienna, Schottengasse 6; tel. (1) 531-31-0; telex 133030; fax (1) 531-31-7566; f. 1855; acquired by Bank Austria AG in January 1997; cap. 8,262m., res 20,837m., dep. 595,057m. (Dec. 1996); Chair. Dr GUIDO SCHMIDT-CHIARI; 194 brs.

Deutsche Bank (Austria) AG: 1010 Vienna, Hohenstaufengasse 4; tel. (1) 531-810; fax (1) 531-81-14; f. 1989; cap. 250m., res 386m., dep. 10,200m. (Dec. 1994); Mans STEPHAN HANDL, FRANZ-HESSO ZU LEININGEN.

Donau-Bank AG: 1011 Vienna, Parkring 6, PF 1451; tel. (1) 515-35; telex 116473; fax (1) 515-35-297; f. 1974; cap. 1,105m., res 848m., dep. 3,995m. (Dec. 1996); Chair. ANDREI E. CHETYRKIN.

Gara Real- und Personalkreditbank AG: 1061 Vienna, Theobaldgasse 19; tel. (1) 58823-0; fax (1) 58823-224; cap. 106m., dep. 1,193m. (1994); Mans WERNER KRONFELLNER, ARTHUR SCHNEIDER.

Internationale Bank für Aussenhandel AG: 1011 Vienna, Neuer Markt 1; tel. (1) 515-56-0; telex 113564; fax (1) 515-56-50; f. 1970; cap. 75m., res 123m., dep. 5,229m. (Dec. 1994); Mans Dr WALTER BEYER, ILSE SMEYKAL.

Meinl Bank AG: 1015 Vienna, Bauernmarkt 2; tel. (1) 531-88; telex 132256; fax (1) 531-88-44; f. 1922; cap. 328m., res 327m., dep. 4,192m. (Dec. 1996); Chair. Dr ANTON OSOND; 2 brs.

Mercurbank AG: 1015 Vienna, Kärntner Ring 8; tel. (1) 50132-217; fax (1) 50132-341; cap. 768m., dep. 6,677m. (1994); Mans MANFRED KOPRIVA, SCOTT SCHELDLER; 23 brs.

Österreichische Verkehrskreditbank AG: 1081 Vienna, Auerspergstr. 17; tel. (1) 405-76-48-0; telex 115965; fax (1) 405-76-48-18; cap. 151m., dep. 2,496m. (1994); Chair. HERBERT WAGNER.

Pinka Bank AG: 1010 Vienna, Mahlerstr. 14; tel. (1) 514-26; Mans WOLFGANG SCHUPF, NORBERT NAGL.

Sanpaolo Bank (Austria) AG: 1010 Vienna, Trattnerhof 1; tel. (1) 536-61; fax (1) 536-61-106; f. 1984; cap. 82m., res 8m., dep. 2,195m. (Dec. 1995); CEO Dr ALFRED W. MALLMANN.

Schoellerbank AG: 1011 Vienna, Renngasse 1–3; tel. (1) 53471; telex 114219; fax (1) 5334390; e-mail info@schoellerbank.at; f. 1833; acquired by Bayerische Vereinsbank (Germany) 1992; cap. 590m., res 716m., dep. 22,633m. (Dec. 1996); Mans MANFRED MAUTNER MARKHOF, MICHAEL Graf VON MEDEM; 11 brs.

Société Générale (Austria) Bank AG: 1010 Vienna, Schwarzenbergplatz 1; tel. (1) 712-51-03-0; telex 133766; fax (1) 712-51-03/35; f. 1972; wholly-owned subsidiary of Société Générale (France); cap. 131m., res 128m., dep. 8,985m. (Dec. 1995); Gen. Man. DIETER DULIAS.

Westdeutsche Landesbank (Austria) AG: 1060 Vienna, Mariahilferstr. 77-79; 1061 Vienna, PF 258; tel. (1) 58825-0; telex 133608; fax (1) 586-25-02; f. 1984 as Standard Chartered Bank (Austria) AG; present name adopted 1990; cap. 260m., res 89m., dep. 18,950m. (Dec. 1995); Chair. HANS JOSEF SCHWARZ.

Regional Banks

Allgemeine Sparkasse Oberösterreich Bank AG: 4041 Linz, Promenade 11–13, PF 92, tel. (732) 7327-39-10; telex 221393; fax (732) 7844-04; f. 1849; cap. 1,084m., res 2,076m., dep. 52,993m. (Dec. 1996); Gen. Man. MANFRED REITINGER; 117 brs.

Alpenbank AG: 6020 Innsbruck, Kaiserjägerstr. 9; tel. (512) 599-77; telex 534465; fax (512) 56-20-15; f. 1983 as Save Rössler Bank; cap. 70m., res 31m., dep. 978m. (Dec. 1996); Dirs KARL H. MEIER, W. DIETER HESS.

Bank für Kärnten und Steiermark AG: 9010 Klagenfurt, St. Veiter Ring 43; tel. (463) 5858-0; telex 422454; fax (463) 5858-538; f. 1922; cap. 985m., res 1,583m., dep. 30,009m. (Dec. 1996); Dirs Dr HEIMO PENKER, MARKUS ORSINI-ROSENBERG; 37 brs.

Bank für Oberösterreich und Salzburg (Oberbank): 4010 Linz, Hauptplatz 10-11; tel. (732) 2802-23-05; telex 221802; fax (732) 780812; f. 1869; cap. 2,635m., res 3,422m., dep. 76,348m. (Dec. 1996); Chair. Dr HERMANN BELL; 89 brs.

Bank für Tirol und Vorarlberg AG: 6021 Innsbruck, Erlerstr. 5–9; tel. (512) 5333-0; telex 533619; fax (512) 5333-133; f. 1904; cap. 1,186m., res 1,675m., dep. 42,539m. (Dec. 1995); Gen. Man. Dr GERHARD MOSER; Dir PETER GAUGG; 36 brs.

Bankhaus Krentschker & Co AG: 8010 Graz, Am Eisernen Tor 3; tel. (316) 80300; telex 311411; fax (316) 8030-222; f. 1924; cap. 289m., res 246m., dep. 8,300m. (Dec. 1995); Chair. Dr JÖRG BRUCKBAUER; 3 brs.

Bankhaus Carl Spängler & Co AG: 5020 Salzburg, Schwarzstr. 1; 5024 Salzburg, PF 41; tel. (662) 8686-0; fax (662) 8686-89; cap. 114m., res 175m., dep. 4,553m. (Dec. 1995); Chair. Dr HEINRICH WIESMÜLLER; 11 brs.

Kärntner Landes- und Hypothekenbank AG: 9020 Klagenfurt, Domgasse 5, PF 517; tel. (463) 5860; telex 422438; fax (463) 5860-50; f. 1896; cap. 455m., res 644m., dep. 30,451m. (Dec. 1995); Man. Dirs Dr WOLFGANG KULTERER, Dr JÖRG SCHUSTER; 10 brs.

Niederösterreichische Landesbank-Hypothekenbank AG: 1010 Vienna, Wipplingerstr. 2; tel. (1) 531-55-0; telex 134750; fax (1) 531-55-444; f. 1889; cap. 446m., res 739m., dep. 38,211m. (Dec. 1995); Chair. Dr OTTO BERNAU; Gen. Man. EDWIN PIRCHER; 27 brs.

Oberösterreichische Landesbank: 4010 Linz, Landstr. 38; tel. (70) 7639-0; telex 21239; fax (70) 7639-205; f. 1891; cap. 240m., res 1,234m., dep. 31,924m. (Dec. 1996); Chair Dr WOLFGANG STAMPL; Gen. Man. Dr JOSEF KOLMHOFER; 13 brs.

Privatinvest Bank AG: 5020 Salzburg, Griesgasse 11; tel. (662)8048-0; telex 633267; fax (662) 8048-333; f. 1885 as Bankhaus Daghofer & Co; present name adopted 1990; cap. and res 142m., dep. 2,796m. (Dec. 1996); Chair. HANS-WERNER ZESCHKY.

Quelle Bank C. A. Steinhäusser: 4060 Leonding, Kornstr. 4; tel. (732) 6867-0; telex 0133146; fax (732) 6867150; f. 1856; cap. 130m. (1994); Mans BERND SCHADRACK, KARL-HEINZ STOIBER.

Salzburger Kredit- und Wechsel-Bank AG: 5024 Salzburg, Makartplatz 3; tel. (662) 8684-0; telex 633625; fax (662) 8684-21; f. 1922; cap. 150m., res 433m., dep. 7,417m. (Dec. 1996); Dirs UWE BÜTTNER, JÜRGEN DANZMAYR; 8 brs.

Steiermärkische Bank und Sparkassen AG: 8011 Graz, Landhausgasse 16, Sparkassenplatz 4, PF 844; tel. (316) 8033-0; telex 311280; fax (316) 8033-30; f. 1825; cap. 1,291m., res 2,721m., dep. 53,660m. (Dec. 1996); Man. Dir JOSEPH KASSLER; 95 brs.

Tiroler Sparkasse–Bankaktiengesellschaft Innsbruck: 6020 Innsbruck, Sparkassenplatz 1; tel. (512) 5905; telex 534614; fax (512) 5910-500; f. 1975 by merger; cap. and res. 3,277m., dep. 36,627m. (Dec. 1995); Chair. and Gen. Man. Dr E. WUNDERBALDINGER; 65 brs.

Volkskreditbank AG: 4010 Linz, Rudigierstr. 5–7; tel. (732) 7637-0; telex 222282; fax (732) 7637-200; f. 1872; cap. 260m., res 1,046m., dep. 16,681m. (Dec. 1995); Gen. Man. Dr GERNOT KRENNER; 45 brs.

Vorarlberger Landes- und Hypothekenbank AG: 6900 Bregenz, Hypo-Passage 1; tel. (5574) 414; telex 057634; fax (5574) 414-457; f. 1899; cap. 692m., res 1,506m., dep. 34,011m. (Dec. 1994); Chair. Dr RUDOLF MANDL; 22 brs.

Specialized Banks

Oesterreichische Kontrollbank AG: 1010 Vienna, Am Hof 4, PF 70; tel. (1) 531-27-0; telex 132747; fax (1) 531-27-533; f. 1946; export financing, stock exchange clearing, money market operations; cap. 440m., res 2,047m., dep. 8,858m. (Dec. 1995); Mans Dr JOHANNES ATTEMS, GERHARD PRASCHAK.

Österreichische Investitionskredit AG: 1013 Vienna, Renngasse 10; tel. (1) 53135-0; telex 111619; fax (1) 53135-993; cap. 3,007m. (1994); Gen. Man. Dkfm. ALFRED REITER.

Österreichische Kommunalkredit AG: 1092 Vienna, Türkenstr. 9; tel. (1) 31631-0; fax (1) 31631-105; e-mail kommunal@kommunalkredit.at; internet http://www.kommunalkredit.at; f. 1958; cap. 374m., dep. 5,727m. (1994); Mans Dr REINHARD PLATZER, GERHARD GANGL.

Österreichischer Exportfonds GmbH: 1031 Vienna, Neulinggasse 29; tel. (1) 7126151-0; fax (1) 7126151-30; cap. 122m. (1994); Mans HERBERT NIEMETZ, BRIGITTE BRUCK.

Savings Banks

GiroCredit Bank AG der Sparkassen (Central Bank of the Austrian Savings Banks): 1011 Vienna, Schubertring 5; tel. (1) 711-

94-0; telex 132591; fax (1) 713-70-32; f. 1937; central institution of savings banks; 56% owned by Bank Austria AG; cap. 4,100m., res 12,768m., dep. 299,876m. (Dec. 1995); Chair. and CEO FERDINAND LACINA.

Die Erste Österreichische Spar-Casse-Bank (First Austrian Savings Bank): 1010 Vienna, Graben 21, PF 162; tel. (1) 53100; telex 114012; fax (1) 53100-2272; f. 1819; cap. 5,299m., res 6,437m., dep. 196,051m. (Dec. 1995); Chair. HERBERT SCHIMETSCHEK, CEO Dr KONRAD FUCHS; 230 brs.

Österreichische Postsparkasse: 1018 Vienna, Georg-Coch Platz 2; tel. (1) 51-40-00; telex 111663; fax (1) 514-00-17-00; f. 1883; cap. 800m., res 7,588m., dep. 215,855m. (Dec. 1994); Gov. Dr ERICH HEMPEL; Vice-Gov Dr VIKTOR WOLF.

Salzburger Sparkasse Bank AG: 5021 Salzburg, Alter Markt 3, PF 5000; tel. (662) 8040-0; telex 613622320; fax (662) 8040-85; f. 1855; cap. 1,413m., res 1,639m., dep. 39,675m. (Dec. 1995); Gen. Man. GERHARD SCHMID; 83 brs.

Co-operative Banks

Österreichische Volksbanken-AG: 1090 Vienna, Peregringasse 3; tel. (1) 31340; telex 114233; fax (1) 31340-3103; f. 1922; cap. 1,713m., res 1,336m., dep. 63,453m. (Dec. 1995); Chair. and CEO ROBERT MÄDL.

Raiffeisen Zentralbank Österreich AG: 1030 Vienna, Am Stadtpark 9; tel. (1) 71707-0; telex 136989; fax (1) 71707-1715; f. 1927; cap. 4,223m., res 7,004m., dep. 205,922m. (Dec. 1995); central institute of the Austrian Raiffeisen banking group; Chair. Supervisory Bd Dr CHRISTIAN KONRAD; Chair. Bd of Management Dr WALTER ROTHENSTEINER; 2 brs.

Bankers' Organization

Verband österreichischer Banken und Bankiers (Asscn of Austrian Banks and Bankers): 1013 Vienna, Börsegasse 11; tel. (1) 535-17-71; telex 132824; fax (1) 535-17-71/38; f. 1945; Pres. Dr HERMANN BELL; Gen. Sec. FRANZ OVESNY; 55 mems.

STOCK EXCHANGES

Wiener Börse (Vienna Stock Exchange): 1013 Vienna, Wipplingerstr. 34; tel. (1) 53-4-99; fax (1) 535-68-57; f. 1771; two sections: Stock Exchange, Commodity Exchange; Pres. GERHARD REIDLINGER; Gen. Sec. Dr ULRICH KAMP.

Österreichische Termin- und Optionenbörse (Austrian Futures and Options Exchange): 1014 Vienna, PF 192, Strauchgasse 1-3; tel. (1) 531-650; fax (1) 532-9740; f. 1991; by appointment to the Vienna Stock Exchange, provides a fully automated screen-based trading system, the Austrian Traded Index (ATX), and acts as clearing house for options and futures; trades futures on the Austrian Govt Bond (Bond-Futures) and options on six Austrian stocks listed on the Vienna Stock Exchange; CEO Dr CHRISTIAN IMO.

INSURANCE COMPANIES

A selection of companies is given below.

Allianz Elementar Versicherungs-AG: 1130 Vienna, Hietzinger Kai 101–105; tel. (1) 87-807-0; telex 134222; fax (1) 87-807-5390; internet http://www.allianz-elementar.at; f. 1860; all classes except life insurance; Gen. Man. Dr ALEXANDER HOYOS.

Allianz Elementar Lebensversicherung-AG: 1130 Vienna, Hietzinger Kai 101–105; tel. (1) 87-807-0; fax (1) 87-807/2703; life insurance; Gen. Man. Dr ALEXANDER HOYOS.

Anglo-Elementar Versicherungs-AG: 1015 Vienna, Kärntner Ring 12; tel. (1) 501-67-0; telex 132355; fax (1) 505-40-08; Gen. Man. Dr ALEXANDER HOYOS.

Austria-Collegialität Österreichische Versicherungs-AG: 1021 Vienna II, Untere Donaustr. 25; tel. (1) 21-1-75; telex 135308; fax (1) 21175-1999; f. 1936; Gen. Man. HERBERT SCHIMETSCHEK.

Donau Allgemeine Versicherungs-AG: 1010 Vienna, Schottenring 15; tel. (1) 31-311; telex 114588; fax (1) 310-77-51; f. 1867; all classes; Gen. Man. Dr GERHARD PUSCHMANN.

EA-General Aktiengesellschaft: 1011 Vienna, Landskrongasse 1-3; tel. (1) 534-01; telex 114085; fax (1) 534-01/1226; e-mail office—km@ea-generali.com; f. 1882 as Erste Österreichische Allgemeine Unfall-Versicherungs-Gesellschaft; Gen. Man. Dr DIETRICH KARNER.

Grazer Wechselseitige Versicherung: 8011 Graz, Herrengasse 18–20; tel. (316) 8037-0; telex 31414; fax (316) 80-37-414; f. 1828; all classes; Gen. Man. Dr FRIEDRICH FALL.

Interunfall Versicherungs-Aktiengesellschaft: 1011 Vienna, Tegetthoffstr. 7; tel. (1) 51403-0; telex 112111; fax (1) 514-03/560; all classes of insurance (including reinsurance); Man. JOSEPH SUOBODA.

Versicherungsanstalt der österreichischen Bundesländer Versicherungs-AG: 1021 Vienna, Praterstr. 1–7; tel. (1) 21111-0; telex 134800; fax (1) 211-11/552; Gen. Man. HERBERT SCHIMETSCHEK.

Wiener Städtische Allgemeine Versicherung Aktiengesellschaft: 1010 Vienna, Schottenring 30; tel. (1) 531-39-0; telex 135140; fax (1) 535-34-37; f. 1824; all classes; CEO Dr SIEGFRIED SELLITSCH.

Zürich Kosmos Versicherungen AG: 1015 Vienna I, Schwarzenbergplatz 15; tel. (1) 501-25-0; telex 133375; fax (1) 505-04-85; f. 1910; all classes; Gen. Man. FRANZ WIPFLI BEHR.

Insurance Organization

Verband der Versicherungsunternehmen Österreichs (Asscn of Austrian Insurance Cos): 1030 Vienna, Schwarzenbergplatz 7; tel. (1) 711-56-0; fax (1) 711-56/270; e-mail versver@ibm.net; f. 1945; Pres. Dr SIEGFRIED SELLITSCH; Gen. Sec. Dr HERBERT RETTER.

Trade and Industry

GOVERNMENT AGENCY

Österreichische Industrieholding AG (ÖIAG): 1015 Vienna, PF 99, Kantgasse 1; tel. (1) 711140; telex 132047; fax (1) 71114378; f. 1970; Mans. KARL HOLLWEGER, Dr ERICH BECKER.

CHAMBERS OF COMMERCE

All Austrian enterprises must by law be members of the Economic Chambers. The Federal Economic Chamber promotes international contacts and represents the economic interests of trade and industry on a federal level. Its Foreign Trade Organization includes about 90 offices abroad.

Wirtschaftskammer Österreich (Austrian Federal Economic Chamber): 1045 Vienna, Wiedner Hauptstr. 63; tel. (1) 50105; fax (1) 50206-250; e-mail mservice@wkoe.wk.or.at; f. 1946; six depts: Commerce, Industry, Small-scale Production, Banking and Insurance, Transport and Tourism; these divisions are subdivided into branch asscns; Local Economic Chambers with divisions and branch asscns in each of the nine Austrian provinces; Pres. LEOPOLD MADERTHANER; Sec.-Gen. GÜNTER STUMMVOLL; c. 300,000 mems.

INDUSTRIAL AND TRADE ASSOCIATIONS

Wirtschaftskammer Österreich—Bundessektion Industrie: 1045 Vienna, Wiedner Hauptstr. 63; tel. (1) 501-05-3457; fax (1) 502-06-273; e-mail bsi@wkoesk.wk.or.at; f. 1896 as Zentralverband der Industrie Österreichs (Central Fed. of Austrian Industry), merged into present org. 1947; Chair. HEINZ KESSLER; Dir JOACHIM LAMEL; comprises the following industrial feds:

Fachverband der Audiovisions- und Filmindustrie Österreichs (Film): 1045 Vienna, PF 327, Wiedner Hauptstr. 63; tel. (1) 501-05/3010; telex 111871; fax (1) 50206/276; e-mail faf@wk.or.at; Chair. MICHAEL WOLKENSTEIN, Prof. Dr ELMAR A. PETERLUNGER; 1,300 mems.

Fachverband der Bauindustrie (Building): 1040 Vienna, Karlsgasse 5; tel. (1) 504-15-51; fax (1) 504-15-55; Chair. Ing. ERNST NUSSBAUMER; Dir Dr JOHANNES SCHENK; 150 mems.

Fachverband der Bekleidungsindustrie (Clothing): 1030 Vienna, Schwarzenbergplatz 4; tel. (1) 712-12-96; fax (1) 713-92-04; Chair. WILHELM EHRLICH; Dir CHRISTOPH HAIDINGER; 310 mems.

Fachverband der Bergwerke und Eisenerzeugenden Industrie (Mining and Iron Production): 1015 Vienna, PF 300, Goethegasse 3; tel. (1) 512-46-01-0; fax (1) 512-46-01/20; Chair. Pres. Dir HELLMUT LONGIN; Sec. Ing. Mag. HERMANN PRINZ; 112 mems.

Fachverband der Chemischen Industrie (Chemicals): 1045 Vienna, Wiedner Hauptstr. 63; tel. (1) 501-050; fax (1) 502-06-280; e-mail fcio@wkoesk.wk.or.at; Pres. JOSEF FRICK; Gen. Dir Dr WOLFGANG EICKHOFF; 530 mems.

Fachverband der Eisen- und Metallwarenindustrie Österreichs (Iron and Metal Goods): 1045 Vienna, PF 335, Wiedner Hauptstr. 63; tel. (1) 501-05; fax (1) 505-09-28; f. 1908; Chair. REINHARD JORDAN; Gen. Man. Dr WOLFGANG LOCKER; 800 mems.

Fachverband der Elektro- und Elektronikindustrie (Electrical): 1060 Vienna, Mariahilferstr. 37-39; tel. (1) 588390; fax (1) 5866971; Chair. Dr WALTER WOLFSBERGER; Dir Dr HEINZ RASCHKA; 558 mems.

Fachverband der Erdölindustrie (Oil): 1031 Vienna, Erdbergstr. 72; tel. (1) 713-23-48; telex 132138; fax (1) 713-05-10; e-mail fv—erdoel@telenetz.com; f. 1947; Gen. Dirs Dr RICHARD SCHENZ, Dr RUDOLF MERTEN; 27 mems.

Fachverband der Fahrzeugindustrie (Vehicles): 1045 Vienna, Wiedner Hauptstr. 63; tel. (1) 501-05; telex 111871; fax (1) 502-06-289; Pres. Dr RICHARD DAIMER; Gen. Sec. ERIK BAIER; 160 mems.

Fachverband der Gas- und Wärmeversorgungsunternehmungen (Gas and Heating): 1010 Vienna, Schubertring 14; tel. (1) 513-15-88; fax (1) 513-15-88-25; e-mail fvizz@wkoesk.wr.or.at; Gen. Dir Dr KARL SKYBA; Dir ROBERT G. KOCK; 190 mems.

Fachverband der Giessereiindustrie (Foundries): 1045 Vienna, PF 339, Wiedner Hauptstr. 63; tel. (1) 50105-3463; fax (1) 50206-279; Chair. MICHAEL ZIMMERMANN; Dir Dipl. Ing. Dr HANSJÖRG DICHTL; 64 mems.

Fachverband der Glasindustrie (Glass): 1045 Vienna, Wiedner Hauptstr. 63; tel. (1) 501-05/3428; fax (1) 502-06/281; Chair. RUDOLF SCHRAML; Dir Dr PETER SCHOEPF; 65 mems.

Fachverband der Holzverarbeitenden Industrie (Wood Processing): 1037 Vienna, PF 123, Schwarzenbergplatz 4; tel. (1) 712-26-01; fax (1) 713-03-09; f. 1946; Chair. Dr ERICH WIESNER; Dir Dr CLAUDIUS KOLLMANN; 360 mems.

Fachverband der Ledererzeugenden Industrie (Leather Production): 1045 Vienna 4, PF 312, Wiedner Hauptstr. 63; tel. (1) 501-05; fax (1) 502-06/278; f. 1945; Chair. HELMUT SCHMIDT; Dir PETER KOVACS; 7 mems.

Fachverband der Lederverarbeitenden Industrie (Leather Processing): 1045 Vienna, PF 313, Wiedner Hauptstr. 63; tel. (1) 501-05; fax (1) 502-06/278; f. 1945; Chair. Gen. Dir GERHARD WALLNER; Dir PETER KOVACS; 47 mems.

Fachverband der Maschinen- und Stahlbauindustrie (Machinery and Steel Construction): 1045 Vienna, Wiedner Hauptstr. 63; tel. (1) 502-25; telex 111970; fax (1) 505-10-20; Pres. Dr JOSEF BERTSCH; Dir Dr RUDOLF TUPPA; 850 mems.

Fachverband der Metallindustrie (Metals): 1045 Vienna, PF 338, Wiedner Hauptstr. 63; tel. (1) 501-05/3309; fax (1) 501-05-3378; f. 1946; Chair. Dr OTHMAR RANKL; Dir Dr GÜNTER GREIL; 69 mems.

Fachverband der Nahrungs- und Genussmittelindustrie (Provisions): Vienna, Zaunergasse 1-3; tel. (1) 712-21-21; telex 131247; fax (1) 713-18-02; Chair. Dr ERWIN BUNDSCHUH; Dir Dr MICHAEL BLASS; 674 mems.

Fachverband der Papier und Pappe verarbeitenden Industrie (Paper and Board Processing): 1041 Vienna, Brucknerstr. 8; tel. (1) 505-53-82-0; fax (1) 505-90-18; Chair. GUSTAV GLÖCKLER; RUDOLF BERGOLTH; 134 mems.

Fachverband der Papierindustrie (Paper): 1061 Vienna, Gumpendorferstr. 6; tel. (1) 58-886-0; fax (1) 58-886-222; e-mail fvpapier@fvpapier.wk.or.at; Chair. Dr ROBERT LAUNSKY-TIEFFENTHAL; Dir Dr GEROLF OTTAWA; 30 mems.

Fachverband der Sägeindustrie (Sawmills): 1011 Vienna, Uraniastr. 4/1; tel. (1) 712-04-74-0; fax (1) 713-1018; e-mail info@proholz.at; f. 1947; Chair. HANS MICHAEL OFFNER; Dir Dr GERHARD ALTRICHTER; 1,800 mems.

Fachverband der Stein- und keramischen Industrie (Stone and Ceramics): 1045 Vienna, PF 329, Wiedner Hauptstr. 63; tel (1) 501-05-3531; telex 111871; fax (1) 505-62-40; e-mail steine@wkoesk.wk.or.at; f. 1946; Chair. Dr CARL HENNRICH; Pres. Sen. LEOPOLD HELBICH; 440 mems.

Fachverband der Textilindustrie (Textiles): 1013 Vienna, Rudolfsplatz 12; tel. (1) 533-37-26-0; fax (1) 533-37-26-40; Pres. Dr PETER PFNEISL; Dir Dr F. PETER SCHINZEL; 265 mems.

TRADE UNIONS

Österreichischer Gewerkschaftsbund (ÖGB) (Austrian Trade Union Fed.): 1010 Vienna, Hohenstaufengasse 10-12; tel. (1) 534-44; telex 114316; fax (1) 534-44-204; non-party union organization with voluntary membership; f. 1945; org. affiliated with ICFTU and ETUC; Pres. FRIEDRICH VERZETNITSCH; Exec. Secs KARL DROCHTER, HERBERT TUMPEL; 1,616,016 mems (Dec. 1993); comprises the following 15 trade unions:

Gewerkschaft Agrar-Nahrung-Genuss (Food, Beverage and Tobacco Workers): 1080 Vienna, Albertgasse 35; tel. (1) 0222-401-49; fax (1) 0222-401-49-20; Chair. Dr LEOPOLD SIMPERL; 40,113 mems (1989).

Gewerkschaft Bau-Holz (Building Workers and Woodworkers): 1010 Vienna, Ebendorferstr. 7; tel. (1) 401-47; fax (1) 401-47-258; Chair. JOHANN DRIEMER; 177,629 mems (1996).

Gewerkschaft der Chemiearbeiter (Chemical Workers): 1060 Vienna, Stumpergasse 60; tel. (1) 597-15-01; fax (1) 597-21-01-23; Chair. GERHARD LINNER; 51,172 mems (1993).

Gewerkschaft Druck und Papier (Printing and Paper Trade Workers): 1072 Vienna, PF 91, Seidengasse 15–17; tel. (1) 523-82-31; fax (1) 523-35-68-28; f. 1842; Chair. FRANZ BITTNER; 19,287 mems (1997).

Gewerkschaft der Eisenbahner (Railwaymen): 1051 Vienna, Margaretenstr. 166; tel. (1) 54641-500; fax (1) 54641-504; e-mail gde@gde.oegb.or.at; Chair. GERHARD NOWAK; 105,000 mems (1997).

Gewerkschaft der Gemeindebediensteten (Municipal Employees): 1090 Vienna, Maria-Theresien-Str. 11; tel. (1) 31316-83601; fax (1) 31316-7701; Chair. GÜNTER WENINGER; 175,257 mems (1993).

Gewerkschaft Land-Forst-Garten (Agricultural and Forestry Workers): Vienna; tel. (1) 53-444-480; f. 1906; Chair. ERICH DIRNGRABNER; 18,549 mems (1989).

Gewerkschaft Handel, Transport, Verkehr (Workers in Commerce and Transport): 1010 Vienna, Teinfaltstr. 7; tel. (1) 53-4-54; fax (1) 53-4-54-325; f. 1904; Chair. PETER SCHNEIDER; 37,846 mems (1989).

Gewerkschaft Hotel, Gastgewerbe, Persönlicher Dienst (Hotel and Restaurant Workers): 1013 Vienna, Hohenstaufengasse 10; tel. (1) 534-44; fax (1) 534-44-505; e-mail hgpd@hgpd.oegb.or.at; f. 1906; Chair. RUDOLF KASKE; 52,280 mems (1995).

Gewerkschaft Kunst, Medien, freie Berufe (Musicians, Actors, Artists, Journalists, etc.): 1090 Vienna, Maria-Theresien-Str. 11; tel. (1) 313-16; fax (1) 313-16/7700; f. 1945; Chair. Prof. PAUL FURST; Sec.-Gen. FRANZ BECKE; 16,310 mems (1989).

Gewerkschaft Metall-Bergbau-Energie (Metal Workers, Miners and Power Supply Workers): 1041 Vienna, Plösslgasse 15; tel. (1) 501-46; f. 1890; Chair. RUDOLF NÜRNBERGER; 240,185 mems (1989).

Gewerkschaft Öffentlicher Dienst (Public Employees): 1010 Vienna, Teinfaltstr. 7; tel. (1) 53-4-54; fax (1) 53-4-54-207; f. 1945; Chair. SIEGFRIED DOHR; Gen. Secs ERICH BÜRGER, Dr MANFRED MÖGELE, GERHARD NEUGEBAUER; 228,000 mems (1993).

Gewerkschaft der Post- und Fernmeldebediensteten (Postal and Telegraph Workers): 1010 Vienna, PF 343; Biberstr. 5; tel. (1) 512-55-11; fax (1) 512-55-11/52; Chair. HANS-GEORG DÖRFLER; 83,182 mems (1994).

Gewerkschaft der Privatangestellten (Commercial, Clerical and Technical Employees): 1013 Vienna, Deutschmeisterplatz 2; tel. and fax (1) 313-93; Chair. HANS SALLMUTTER; 301,046 mems (1997).

Gewerkschaft Textil, Bekleidung, Leder (Textile, Garment and Leather Workers): 1010 Vienna, Hohenstaufengasse 10; tel. (1) 534-44; fax (1) 534-44-498; f. 1945; Chair. HARALD ETTL; 38,580 mems (1989).

Bundesfraktion Christlicher Gewerkschafter im Österreichischen Gewerkschaftsbund (Christian Trade Unionists' Section of the Austrian Trade Union Fed.): 1010 Vienna, Hohenstaufengasse 12; tel. (1) 534-44; organized in Christian Trade Unionists' Sections of the above 15 trade unions; affiliated with WCL; Sec.-Gen. KARL KLEIN.

UTILITIES

Electricity

Energie-Versorgung-Niederösterreich AG: 2344 Maria Enzersdorf, Johann-Steinboeck-Str. 1; tel. (2742) 8000; fax (2742) 800360; Chair. Dr RUDOLF GRUBER.

Burgenländische Elektrizitätswirtschafts-AG: 7001 Eisenstadt, Kasemenstr. 9; tel. (2682) 6030; fax (2682) 603485; Chair. Dr GÜNTHER OFNER.

Kärntner Elektrizitäts-AG: 9020 Klagenfurt, Arnulfplatz 2; tel. (463) 5250; fax (463) 5251596; Chair. Dr GÜNTHER BRESITZ.

Oberösterreichische Kraftwerke AG: 4020 Linz, Böhmerwaldstr. 3; tel. (732) 65930; fax (732) 65933600; Chair. Dr LEOPOLD WINDTNER.

Österreichische Elektrizitätswirtschafts-AG: 1010 Vienna, Am Hof 6A; tel. (1) 531130; fax (1) 531134191; e-mail info@pol.verbund.co.at; internet http://www.verbund.co.at/verbund; Chair. Dr MICHAEL PISTAUER.

Salzburger AG für Energiewirtschaft: 5021 Salzburg, Bayerhamerstr. 16; tel. (662) 88840; fax (662) 8884170; Chair. Dr JOHANN OBERHAMBERGER.

Steirische Wasserkraft- und Elektrizitäts-AG: 8011 Graz, Leonhardgurtel 10; tel. (316) 3870; fax (316) 387290; Chair. Dr OSWIN KOIS.

Tiroler Wasserkraftwerke AG: 6010 Innsbruck, Landhausplatz; tel. (512) 5060; fax (512) 5062126; Chair. Dr HELMUT MAYR.

Vorarlberger Kraftwerke AG: 6900 Bregenz, Weidachstr. 6; tel. (5574) 6010; fax (5574) 601500; e-mail energie@vkw.vol.at; Chair. Dr OTTO WAIBEL.

Wiener Stadtwerke: 1010 Vienna, Schottenring 30; tel. (1) 531230; fax (1) 5312373999; Chair. Dr KARL SKYBA.

Gas

BEGAS-Burgenländische Erdgasversorgungs-AG: 7000 Eisenstadt, Kasernenstr. 10; tel. (2682) 709; fax (2682) 709174; Chair. HERIBERT ARTINGER.

Oberösterreichische Ferngas-AG: 4030 Linz, Neubauzeile 99; tel. (732) 38830; fax (732) 381421; Chair. MAX DOBRUCKT.

Steirische Ferngas-AG: 8041 Graz, Gaslaternenweg 4; tel. (316) 4760; fax (316) 47630; Chair. ADOLF FEHRINGER.

Transport

RAILWAYS

The Austrian Federal Railways operate more than 90% of all the railway routes in Austria. There are 5,600 km of track and all main lines are electrified.

Österreichische Bundesbahnen (ÖBB) (Austrian Federal Railways): Head Office: 1010 Vienna, Elisabethstr. 9; tel. (1) 5800-0; telex 1377; fax (1) 5800/25001; Gen. Dir Dr HELMUT DRAXLER.

Innsbruck Divisional Management: 6020 Innsbruck, Claudiastr. 2; tel. (512) 503-3000; fax (512) 503-5005; Dir JOHANN LINDENBERGER.

Linz Divisional Management: 4021 Linz, Bahnhofstr. 3; tel. (732) 6909-0; fax (732) 6909-1833; Dir HELMUTH AFLENZER; Vice-Dir KLAUS SEEBACHER.

Vienna Divisional Management: 1020 Vienna, Nordbahnstr. 50; fax (1) 5800-50000; fax (1) 5800-25601; Dir FRANZ POLZER.

Villach Divisional Management: 9500 Villach, 10-Oktober-Str. 20; tel. (4242) 2020-3200; fax (4242) 2020-3229; Dir Dr WILLIBALD SCHICHO.

Other railway companies include: Achenseebahn AG, AG der Wiener Lokalbahnen, Graz-Köflacher Eisenbahn- und Bergbau-Gesellschaft m.b.H., Montafonerbahn AG, Raab-Oedenburg-Ebenfurter Eisenbahn, Salzburger Stadtwerke AG-Verkehrsbetriebe, Lokalbahn, Stern & Hafferl Verkehrsgesellschaft m.b.H., Steiermärkische Lokalbahnen, Zillertaler Verkehrsbetriebe AG.

ROADS

At 31 December 1993 Austria had 106,307 km of classified roads, of which 1,587 km were modern motorways, 293 km expressways, 9,955 km main roads, 23,472 km secondary roads and 71,000 km communal roads.

INLAND WATERWAYS

The Danube (Donau) is Austria's only navigable river. It enters Austria from Germany at Passau and flows into Slovakia near Hainburg. The length of the Austrian section of the river is 351 km. Danube barges carry up to 1,800 tons, but loading depends on the water level, which varies considerably throughout the year. Cargoes are chiefly petroleum and derivatives, coal, coke, iron ore, iron, steel, timber and grain. The Rhine-Main-Danube Canal opened in 1992. A passenger service is maintained on the Upper Danube and between Vienna and the Black Sea. Passenger services are also provided on Bodensee (Lake Constance) and Wolfgangsee by Austrian Federal Railways, and on all the larger Austrian lakes.

Ministry of Science and Transport: 1014 Vienna, Minoritenplatz 5; tel. (1) 53120-0; fax (1) 53120-4499; responsible for the administration of inland waterways.

DDSG-Cargo GmbH: 1021 Vienna, Handelskai 265; tel. (1) 217-10-0; telex 131589; fax (1) 217-10-250.

CIVIL AVIATION

The main international airport, at Schwechat, near Vienna, handled more than 8m. passengers in 1995. There are also international flights from Innsbruck, Salzburg, Graz, Klagenfurt and Linz, and internal flights between these cities.

Principal Airlines

Austrian Airlines (Österreichische Luftverkehrs AG): 1107 Vienna, Fontanastr. 1; tel. (1) 1766; telex 131811; fax (1) 688-55-05; f. 1957; 51.9% state-owned; serves 89 cities in 51 countries in Europe, Africa, Asia and North America; Chair. Dr RUDOLF STREICHER; Pres Dr HERBERT BAMMER, MARIO REHULKA.

Austrian Airtransport (AAT): 1107 Vienna, PF 50, Fontanastr. 1; tel. (1) 688-1691; telex 131792; fax (1) 688-1191; f. 1964; 80% owned by Austrian Airlines, from which it leases most of its aircraft; operates scheduled and charter flights for passengers and cargo, and tour services; Man Dir Dr HERBERT KOSCHIER.

Lauda Air Luftfahrt AG: 1300 Vienna-Schwechat, PF 56, Lauda Air Bldg; tel. (1) 7007-2081; telex 133850; fax (1) 7007-6705; e-mail office@laudaair.com; f. 1979; became a scheduled carrier 1987; operates scheduled passenger services and charter flights to Europe, Australia, the Far East and the USA; Chair. NIKI LAUDA.

Tiroler Luftfahrt AG (Tyrolean Airways): 6026 Innsbruck, PF 98, Fürstenweg 80; tel. (7144) 44-44; fax (7144) 44-44-9005; f. 1958 as Aircraft Innsbruck; adopted present name 1980; operates scheduled services and charter flights within Austria and to other European countries; Pres. and CEO FRITZ FEITL.

Tourism

Tourism plays an important part in the Austrian economy. However, receipts from the sector, estimated at 161,000m. Schilling in 1991, have declined during the 1990s, and stood at 148,250m. Schilling in 1996. In 1996 Austria received 17.1m. foreign visitors (compared with 19.1m. visitors in 1992). The country's mountain scenery attracts visitors in both summer and winter, while Vienna and Salzburg, where internationally-renowned art festivals are held, are important cultural centres.

Österreich Werbung (Austrian National Tourist Office): 1040 Vienna, Margaretenstr. 1; tel. (1) 588-66-0; fax (1) 588-66-20; f. 1955.

AZERBAIJAN

Introductory Survey

Location, Climate, Language, Religion, Flag, Capital

The Azerbaijan Republic (formerly the Azerbaijan Soviet Socialist Republic) is situated in eastern Transcaucasia, on the western coast of the Caspian Sea. To the south it borders Iran, to the west Armenia, to the north-west Georgia, and to the north the Republic of Dagestan, in Russia. The Nakhichevan Autonomous Republic is part of Azerbaijan, although it is separated from the rest of Azerbaijan by Armenian territory. Azerbaijan also includes the Nagorno-Karabakh Autonomous Oblast (Nagornyi Karabakh), which is largely populated by Armenians but does not legally constitute part of Armenia. The Kura plain has a hot, dry, temperate climate with an average July temperature of 27°C (80°F) and an average January temperature of 1°C (34°F). Average annual rainfall on the lowlands is 200 mm–300 mm, but the Lenkoran plain normally receives between 1,000 mm and 1,750 mm. The official language is Azerbaijani (Azeri), one of the South Turkic group of languages; in 1992 the Turkish version of the Latin script replaced the Cyrillic alphabet (which had been in use since 1939). Religious adherence corresponds largely to ethnic origins: almost all ethnic Azerbaijanis are Muslims, some 70% being Shi'ite and 30% Sunni. There are also Christian communities, mainly representatives of the Russian Orthodox and Armenian Apostolic denominations. The national flag (proportions 2 by 1) consists of three equal horizontal stripes, of pale blue, red and green, with a white crescent moon framing a white eight-pointed star on the central red stripe. The capital is Baku.

Recent History

An independent state in ancient times, Azerbaijan was dominated for much of its subsequent history by foreign powers. Under the Treaty of Turkmanchai of 1828, Azerbaijan was divided between Persia (which was granted southern Azerbaijan) and Russia (northern Azerbaijan). During the latter half of the 19th century petroleum was discovered in Azerbaijan, and by 1900 the region had become one of the world's leading petroleum producers. Immigrant Slavs began to dominate Baku and other urban areas.

After the October Revolution of 1917 in Russia, there was a short period of pro-Bolshevik rule in Baku before a nationalist Government took power and established an independent state on 28 May 1918, with Gyanja (formerly Elisavetpol, but renamed Kirovabad in 1935) as the capital. Azerbaijan was occupied by troops of both the Allied and Central Powers during its two years of independence; after their withdrawal, Azerbaijan was invaded by the Red Army in April 1920, and on 28 April a Soviet Republic of Azerbaijan was established. In December 1922 the republic became a member of the Transcaucasian Soviet Federative Socialist Republic (TSFSR), which entered the USSR as a constituent republic on 31 December. The TSFSR was disbanded in 1936, and Azerbaijan became a full union republic, the Azerbaijan Soviet Socialist Republic (SSR).

Following the Soviet seizure of power in 1920, many nationalist and religious leaders and their followers were persecuted or killed. Religious intolerance was particularly severe in the 1930s, and many mosques and religious sites were destroyed. In 1930–31 forced collectivization of agriculture led to peasant uprisings, which were suppressed by Soviet troops. The Stalinist purges of 1937–38 involved the execution or imprisonment of many members of the Communist Party of Azerbaijan (CPA), including Sultan Mejit Efendiyev, the republic's leader, and two republican premiers. In 1945 the Soviet Government attempted to unite the Azerbaijani population of northern Iran with the Azerbaijan SSR, by supporting a local 'puppet' government in Iran with military forces, but Soviet troops were forced to withdraw from northern Iran in the following year by US-British opposition.

The most influential of Azerbaijan's communist leaders in the period following the Second World War was Heydar Aliyev, installed as First Secretary of the CPA in 1969. He greatly increased the all-Union sector of the economy at the expense of republican industry, while retaining popularity with his liberal attitude to local corruption. Attempts to address corruption in the CPA followed the accession to power of Mikhail Gorbachev, who became leader of the USSR in 1985. Aliyev was dismissed in October 1987, but popular dissatisfaction with the poor state of the economy and the party élite became more vocal. Unlike most Soviet republics, Azerbaijan had an annual trade surplus with the rest of the USSR, and yet its income per head was the lowest outside Central Asia. Public grievances over economic mismanagement and the privileges enjoyed by the party leadership were expressed at demonstrations in November 1988. Protesters occupied the main square in Baku, the capital, for 10 days before being dispersed by troops, who arrested the leaders of the demonstrations.

The initial impetus, however, for the demonstrations was the debate on the status of Nagornyi Karabakh (an autonomous region within Azerbaijan) and Nakhichevan (an autonomous republic of Azerbaijan, separated from it by Armenian land). Both territories were claimed by Armenia, on historical grounds, and Nagornyi Karabakh still had an overwhelming majority of (non-Muslim) Armenians in the population. Nakhichevan, despite an apparent surrender of Azerbaijan's claims to the territory in 1920, never became part of Soviet Armenia. The Soviet-Turkish Treaty of March 1921 included a clause guaranteeing Azerbaijani jurisdiction over Nakhichevan. The 45%–50% of the republic's population which had been ethnically Armenian in 1919 was reduced to less than 5% by 1989. Nagornyi Karabakh had been a disputed territory during the period of Armenian and Azerbaijani independence (1918–20), but in June 1921 the Bureau for Caucasian Affairs (the Kavburo) voted to unite Nagornyi Karabakh with Armenia. However, some days after the Kavburo vote, following an intervention by Stalin, the decision was reversed. In 1923 the territory was declared an autonomous oblast (region) within the Azerbaijan SSR. There were attempts to challenge Azerbaijan's jurisdiction over the region, including two petitions by the inhabitants of Nagornyi Karabakh in the 1960s, but they were strongly opposed by the Soviet and Azerbaijani authorities.

Conflict over the territory began again in February 1988, when the Nagornyi Karabakh regional soviet (council) requested the Armenian and Azerbaijani Supreme Soviets to agree to the transfer of the territory to Armenia. The Soviet and Azerbaijani authorities rejected the request, thus provoking huge demonstrations by Armenians, not only in Nagornyi Karabakh, but also in the Armenian capital, Yerevan. Azerbaijanis began leaving Armenia, and rumours that refugees had been attacked led to three days of anti-Armenian violence in the Azerbaijani town of Sumgait. According to official figures, 32 people died, 26 of whom were Armenians. Disturbances over the issue of Nagornyi Karabakh continued throughout 1988, leading to a large-scale exodus of refugees from both Armenia and Azerbaijan.

In January 1989, in an attempt to end the tension, the Soviet Government suspended the activities of the local authorities in Nagornyi Karabakh and established a Special Administration Committee (SAC), responsible to the USSR Council of Ministers. Although it was stressed that the region would formally retain its status as an autonomous oblast within Azerbaijan, the decision was widely viewed by Azerbaijanis as an infringement of Azerbaijan's territorial integrity. This imposition of 'direct rule' from Moscow and the dispatch of some 5,000 troops of the Soviet Ministry of Internal Affairs did little to reduce tensions within Nagornyi Karabakh, where Armenians went on strike in May and did not resume work until September.

In mid-1989 the nationalist Popular Front of Azerbaijan (PFA) was established. Following sporadic strikes and demonstrations throughout August, the PFA organized a national strike in early September and demanded discussion on the issue of sovereignty, the situation in Nagornyi Karabakh, the release of political prisoners and official recognition of the PFA. After a week of the general strike, the Azerbaijan Supreme Soviet agreed to concessions to the PFA, including official recognition. In addition, draft laws on economic and political sovereignty were published, and on 23 September the Supreme Soviet adopted the 'Constitutional Law on the Sovereignty of the Azerbaijan

SSR', effectively a declaration of sovereignty. The conflict with Armenia continued, with the imposition by Azerbaijan of an economic blockade of Armenia.

In November 1989 the Soviet Government transferred control of Nagornyi Karabakh from the SAC to an Organizing Committee, which was dominated by ethnic Azerbaijanis. This decision was denounced by the Armenian Supreme Soviet, which declared Nagornyi Karabakh to be part of a 'unified Armenian republic', prompting further outbreaks of violence in Nagornyi Karabakh and along the Armenian–Azerbaijani border. Growing unrest within Azerbaijan, exacerbated by the return of refugees from Armenia to Baku, was directed both at the local communist regime and at ethnic Armenians.

In January 1990 radical members of the PFA led assaults on CPA and government buildings in Baku and other towns. Border posts were attacked on the Soviet–Iranian border, and nationalist activists seized CPA buildings in Nakhichevan and declared its secession from the USSR. In addition, renewed violence against Armenians, with some 60 people killed in rioting in Baku, led to a hasty evacuation of the remaining non-Azerbaijanis, including ethnic Russians, from the city. On 19 January a state of emergency was declared in Azerbaijan, and Soviet troops were ordered into Baku, where the PFA was in control. According to official reports, 131 people were killed, and some 700 wounded, during the Soviet intervention. The inability of the CPA to ensure stability in the republic led to the dismissal of Abdul Vezirov as First Secretary of the party; he was replaced by Ayaz Mutalibov. Order was restored in Azerbaijan by the end of January, following the arrest of leading members of the PFA, the outlawing of other radical nationalist organizations, and the issuing of decrees banning all strikes, rallies and demonstrations.

The continuing unrest caused the elections to the republic's Supreme Soviet (held in most of the other Soviet republics in February 1990) to be postponed. When the elections did take place, on 30 September 1990 (with a second round on 14 October), the CPA won an overall majority. Its victory was attributed to an increasingly firm stance on the issue of Nagornyi Karabakh, which attracted nationalist support, combined with a willingness to compromise with Moscow to avoid further bloodshed. The opposition Democratic Alliance (which included the PFA), however, questioned the validity of the elections. In addition, the continuing state of emergency, which prohibited large public meetings, severely disrupted campaigning by the opposition. When the new Supreme Soviet convened in February 1991, some 80% of the deputies were members of the CPA. The small group of opposition deputies united as the Democratic Bloc of Azerbaijan.

Unlike the other Caucasian republics (Armenia and Georgia), Azerbaijan declared a willingness to sign a new Union Treaty and participated in the all-Union referendum concerning the preservation of the USSR, which took place in March 1991. Official results of the referendum demonstrated a qualified support for the preservation of the USSR, with 75.1% of eligible voters participating, of whom 93.3% voted for a 'renewed federation'. In Nakhichevan, however, only some 20% of eligible voters approved President Gorbachev's proposal. Opposition politicians also contested the results of the referendum, claiming that only 15%–20% of voters had actually participated.

In August 1991, when the State Committee for the State of Emergency seized power in Moscow, Mutalibov issued a statement which appeared to demonstrate support for the coup. Despite denials that he had supported the coup leaders, large demonstrations took place, demanding his resignation, the declaration of Azerbaijan's independence, the repeal of the state of emergency, and the postponement of the presidential elections, scheduled for 8 September. The opposition was supported by Heydar Aliyev, the former First Secretary of the CPA, and now the Chairman of the Supreme Majlis (legislature) of Nakhichevan, who had become increasingly critical of Mutalibov's leadership. Mutalibov responded by ending the state of emergency and resigning as First Secretary of the CPA; on 30 August the Azerbaijani Supreme Soviet voted to 'restore the independent status of Azerbaijan'.

Despite continued protests from the PFA, the elections to the presidency proceeded, although they were boycotted by the opposition, with the result that Mutalibov was the only candidate. According to official results, he won 84% of the total votes cast. At a congress of the CPA, held later in September, it was agreed to dissolve the party.

Independence was formally restored on 18 October 1991. The Supreme Soviet voted not to sign the treaty to establish an economic community, which was signed by the leaders of eight other Soviet republics on the same day. In a further move towards full independence, the Supreme Soviet adopted legislation allowing for the creation of national armed forces, and Azerbaijani units began to take control of the Soviet Army's military facilities in the republic. However, Azerbaijan did join the Commonwealth of Independent States (CIS, see p. 132), signing the Alma-Ata Declaration on 21 December.

Following the dissolution of the USSR, hostilities intensified in Nagornyi Karabakh in early 1992. In March President Mutalibov resigned, owing to military reverses suffered by Azeri forces. He was replaced, on an interim basis, by Yagub Mamedov, the Chairman of the Milli Majlis, or National Assembly (which had replaced the Supreme Soviet following its suspension in late 1991), pending a presidential election in June. However, further military set-backs prompted the Majlis to reinstate Mutalibov as President in mid-May. His immediate declaration of a state of emergency and the cancellation of the forthcoming presidential election outraged the opposition PFA, which organized a large-scale protest rally in Baku. The demonstrators occupied both the Majlis building and the presidential palace, and succeeded in deposing Mutalibov, who had held office for only one day. (He subsequently took refuge in Russia.) The PFA's effective takeover was consolidated in the following month, when the party's leader, Abulfaz Elchibey, was elected President of Azerbaijan by direct popular vote, defeating four other candidates by a substantial margin.

During 1992 the Government had to contend with a steadily deteriorating economic situation, largely the result of the continuing conflict in Nagornyi Karabakh and the collapse of the former Soviet economic system. Severe shortages of food and fuel were reported throughout the country, and the Government's failure to provide adequate support for an estimated 500,000 refugees from Nagornyi Karabakh and from Armenia prompted a number of protest actions in Baku from mid-1992.

The background of military defeats and continuing economic decline severely undermined the Government and led to divisions within the PFA in early 1993. In June a rebel army, led by Col Surat Husseinov (the former Azerbaijani military commander in Nagornyi Karabakh), seized the city of Gyanja and advanced towards the capital, with the apparent intention of deposing Elchibey. In an attempt to bolster his leadership, Elchibey summoned Heydar Aliyev to Baku. In mid-June Aliyev was elected Chairman of the legislature. Following Elchibey's subsequent flight from the capital, Aliyev announced that he had assumed the powers of the presidency. There ensued what appeared to be a power struggle between Aliyev and Husseinov, following the bloodless capture of Baku by the rebel forces. However, in late June virtually all presidential powers were transferred, on an acting basis, to Aliyev by the legislature (which had voted to impeach Elchibey), while Husseinov was appointed Prime Minister, with control over all security services.

A referendum of confidence in Elchibey (who had taken refuge in Nakhichevan and still laid claim to the presidency) was held in late August 1993; of the 92% of the electorate which participated, 97.5% voted against him. The legislature endorsed the result and announced the holding of a direct presidential election. This took place on 3 October: Aliyev was elected President of Azerbaijan, against two other candidates, with 98.8% of the votes cast. In the months preceding the election there had been an escalation of harassment of opposition members, particularly the PFA. Several leading supporters of Elchibey were arrested, while PFA rallies were violently dispersed. The PFA boycotted the election in protest.

The domestic political situation remained tense during 1994. There was a noticeable increase in organized crime (drugs-trafficking, in particular) as well as political violence; some 19 people were killed, and more than 100 wounded, in two separate bomb explosions on the Baku metro, in March and July. (In May 1996 two members of Sadval, a separatist movement, were sentenced to death in connection with the explosions.) Opponents of President Aliyev and his New Azerbaijan Party (NAP) were subject to increasing harassment, and their media activities were severely restricted. In February 1994 more than 40 members of the PFA were arrested at a regional conference of the party. In the following month police raided the PFA headquarters in Baku, arresting more than 100 people; the PFA, it was claimed, had been planning to overthrow the Government. The signature, in May, of a cease-fire in Nagornyi Karabakh (see below) led to further unrest in Azerbaijan. Nationalist opposition leaders claimed that the cease-fire would result in humiliating concessions by Azerbaijan and would be followed by the deployment of Russian troops as peace-keepers in Azerbaijan. Large-scale, anti-Government demonstrations were organized by the PFA in Baku in May and September. On both occasions many people were reported to have been injured or arrested.

A new political crisis arose in late September 1994 when the Deputy Chairman of the Milli Majlis and Aliyev's security chief were assassinated. Three members of the special militia (known as OPON) attached to the Ministry of Internal Affairs were arrested on suspicion of involvement in the murders. In early October some 100 OPON troops, led by Rovshan Javadov (a Deputy Minister of Internal Affairs), stormed the office of the Procurator-General, taking him and his officials hostage and demanding the release of the three OPON members in custody. These were released, and the OPON militia withdrew to their base. President Aliyev described the incident as an attempted coup and declared a state of emergency in Baku and Gyanja.

In the immediate aftermath of these events, other forces mutinied in Baku and elsewhere in Azerbaijan. In Gyanja, rebel forces, reportedly led by a relative of Surat Husseinov, occupied government and strategic buildings, although troops loyal to Aliyev quickly re-established control. Despite Husseinov's assurances of allegiance to Aliyev, the President dismissed him as Prime Minister, replacing him, on an acting basis, by Fuad Kuliyev. However, Aliyev stated that he himself would head the Government for the immediate future. The President then initiated a series of purges of senior members of the Government and the armed forces. In mid-October 1994 the Milli Majlis voted unanimously to remove Husseinov's parliamentary immunity from prosecution, in order that he could be arrested on charges of treason. However, Husseinov was rumoured to have fled to Russia.

Azerbaijan experienced only a short period of calm before political turmoil occurred again. In March 1995, following a decree by the Government to disband the OPON militia (which had remained under the control of Rovshan Javadov), OPON forces seized government and police buildings in Baku and in north-western Azerbaijan. Many casualties were reported as government forces clashed with the OPON units, but the rebellion was crushed when government troops stormed the OPON headquarters near Baku; Javadov and many of his men were killed, while some 160 rebels were arrested. Aliyev accused former President Elchibey and Surat Husseinov of collusion in the attempted coup. In the aftermath of the unrest the PFA was also accused of involvement, and the party was banned. In early April Aliyev extended the state of emergency in Baku (introduced in October 1994) until June. However, the state of emergency in Gyanja was lifted. In May Fuad Kuliyev was confirmed as Prime Minister.

Political life in the latter half of 1995 was dominated by preparations for Azerbaijan's first post-Soviet legislative election in November. However, unrest continued: in late July a new plot to overthrow Aliyev was allegedly uncovered. This was again linked to Elchibey, Husseinov and other anti-Aliyev forces based in exile in Moscow. The harassment of opposition parties in Azerbaijan intensified, and in August–October a number of parties, as well as independent candidates, were refused permission to participate in the forthcoming election. In response, opposition parties staged protest actions in Baku.

The election of the new 125-member Milli Majlis took place, as scheduled, on 12 November 1995. Of Azerbaijan's 31 officially-registered parties, as few as eight were, in the event, permitted to participate; of these, only two were opposition parties—the PFA (recently relegalized) and the National Independence Party (NIP). Almost 600 independent candidates were barred from participation. The election was held under a mixed system of voting: 25 seats were to be filled by proportional representation of parties and the remaining 100 by majority vote in single-member constituencies. These included the constituencies of Nagornyi Karabakh and of the other Armenian-occupied territories (refugees from those regions voted in areas under Azerbaijani control, in anticipation of the eventual restoration of the country's territorial integrity). The result demonstrated widespread support for President Aliyev and his NAP, which won 19 of the 25 party seats (with the PFA and the NIP receiving three seats each). The NAP and independent candidates supporting Aliyev won an overwhelming majority of single-constituency seats. Of the remaining 28 seats in the Majlis, 27 were filled at 'run-off' elections held in late November 1995 and in February 1996, while one seat remained unfilled. Some international observers monitoring the election declared that it had not been conducted in a free and fair manner: 'serious electoral violations' included the exclusion of parties, the harassment of party leaders and the restriction of media activities. The Round Table bloc (a loose association of 21 opposition parties) claimed that the new legislature was 'illegal' and demanded the holding of fresh elections.

On the same occasion as the election of the Milli Majlis, Azerbaijan's new Constitution was approved by an overwhelming majority of the electorate (91.9%, according to official data) in a national referendum. The Constitution, which replaced the 1978 Soviet version, provided for a secular state, headed by the President, who was accorded wide-ranging executive powers.

In early 1996 supporters of Surat Husseinov and former President Elchibey received lengthy custodial sentences for their involvement in the alleged coup attempts of October 1994 and March 1995. In February 1996 two former members of the Government, Nariman Imranov and Alikram Gumbatov, were sentenced to death on charges of treason, and were executed shortly afterwards. Rahim Gaziyev, a former Minister of Defence, was tried *in absentia* and was also sentenced to death. In late March Muzamil Abdullayev, a former Minister of Agriculture and Produce, was sentenced to death for his involvement in the alleged coup attempt in October 1994. Gaziyev and former President Mutalibov, whom Aliyev had accused of conspiring with Javadov, were arrested in Russia in April 1996. Gaziyev was extradited to Azerbaijan, but Mutalibov remained in Moscow for medical treatment (following a heart attack). The Russian authorities later refused to extradite him on the grounds that there was insufficient evidence against him.

Repressive measures against the opposition continued, with the seizure by the police of the PFA headquarters in April 1996. Several members of the party were later arrested, one for an alleged attempt to assassinate Aliyev in 1993, and the others on charges of establishing illegal armed groups. In July 1996 Aliyev criticized the Cabinet of Ministers for failing to implement economic reform proposals, and dismissed several senior government officials for corruption. Kuliyev resigned from the office of Prime Minister, officially on grounds of ill health, after he was accused by Aliyev of hindering the process of reform; Artur Rasizade, hitherto first Deputy Prime Minister, was appointed acting Prime Minister. (His appointment as Prime Minister was confirmed in November.) This was followed, in September, by the resignation, also allegedly on grounds of ill health, of the Chairman of the Milli Majlis, Rasul Kuliyev, who had been criticized by the NAP. Murtuz Aleskerov, a staunch supporter of Aliyev and erstwhile rector of Baku State University, was elected in his place.

In January 1997 the Azerbaijani authorities released details of an abortive coup in October 1996, which had reportedly been organized by, amongst others, Mutalibov and Surat Husseinov. Charges were subsequently brought against some 40 alleged conspirators; in early 1997 many people, including 31 former members of the Baku police force, received prison sentences for their part in the attempted coups of October 1994 and March 1995. The Chairman of the State Committee for Ecology and Use of Natural Resources, Arif Mansurov, was also arrested, on suspicion of aiding Gaziyev to escape from prison in 1994, and of maintaining contact with Husseinov. The latter was extradited from Russia to Azerbaijan in March 1997, and subsequently charged with abuse of office and theft of state property. No charges concerning the alleged coup attempt in 1994 were brought against Husseinov at this stage. Meanwhile, in February 1997 four leading members of the opposition Islamic Party of Azerbaijan, including its Chairman, Ali Akram Aliyev, went on trial on charges of espionage on behalf of Iran (which denied any involvement). The trial concluded in April, and the four men received lengthy terms of imprisonment.

In April 1997 President Aliyev established a Security Council, the creation of which was stipulated in the 1995 Constitution. The formation in that month of an informal alliance of 10 parties (including the ruling NAP) to support Aliyev's policies, and to unite behind him in the 1998 presidential election, was criticized as unrepresentative by the opposition PFA; nevertheless, in May, following a renewed outbreak of hostilities on the Armenian–Azerbaijani border (see below), many opposition parties issued a statement expressing their intention to support the Government, should war be declared on Armenia. Meanwhile, former President Elchibey was elected Chairman of the Democratic Congress, an opposition alliance.

At the time of the disintegration of the USSR in late 1991, the leadership of Nagornyi Karabakh declared the enclave to be an independent republic. Azerbaijan refused to accept the territory's attempts to secede, and in January 1992 Nagornyi Karabakh was placed under direct presidential rule. International efforts to negotiate a peace settlement foundered, owing to Azerbaijan's insistence that the conflict was a domestic problem. Military successes by the ethnic Armenian forces of Nagornyi Karabakh in early 1992 culminated in the creation, in May, of a 'corridor' through Azerbaijani territory to link Nagornyi Karabakh with Armenia proper. Despite a successful Azerbaijani counter-offensive in late 1992, ethnic Armenian forces were able to open a second 'corridor' in early 1993, following which they extended their operations into Azerbaijan itself, apparently in an attempt to create a secure zone around Nagornyi Karabakh.

By August 1993 some 20% of Azerbaijan's territory had been seized by Armenian units, while all of Nagornyi Karabakh had already come under their control. The Armenian military gains prompted mounting alarm among the Azeri population, and there was a massive new movement of refugees fleeing from Armenian-occupied territory. The Armenian offensive in Azerbaijan continued, despite widespread international condemnation. Although it did not directly accuse Armenia itself of aggression, the UN Security Council adopted a series of resolutions demanding an immediate cease-fire and the withdrawal of all Armenian units from Azerbaijan. There were also strong protests by Turkey and Iran, both of which mobilized troops in regions bordering Armenia and Azerbaijan in September.

In December 1993 Azeri forces launched a new counter-offensive in Nagornyi Karabakh, recapturing some areas that they had lost to Armenian control, although suffering heavy casualties. Meanwhile, international efforts to halt the conflict continued. These were led by the 'Minsk Group', which had been established by the Conference on Security and Co-operation in Europe (CSCE) in 1992 to provide a framework for peace negotiations between the parties. However, all cease-fire agreements that were reached were quickly violated. In early 1994 it was estimated that, since the conflict began in 1988, some 18,000 people had been killed and a further 25,000 had been wounded. The number of Azeri refugees was believed to have exceeded 1m.

However, in early May 1994 a major breakthrough was achieved with Azerbaijan's signature of the so-called Bishkek Protocol, which had been adopted several days previously at a meeting of the CIS Inter-Parliamentary Assembly, with the approval of representatives of both Armenia and Nagornyi Karabakh. The protocol, although not legally binding, was regarded as an expression of willingness by the warring factions to negotiate a lasting peace accord. On 8 May the Nagornyi Karabakh leadership ordered its forces to cease hostilities, in accordance with the protocol. Although isolated violations were subsequently reported, the cease-fire remained in force. In the latter half of the year efforts were made to co-ordinate the separate peace proposals of the CSCE 'Minsk Group' and Russia. However, Azerbaijan refused either to negotiate a peace settlement or to discuss the future status of Nagornyi Karabakh until Armenian forces were withdrawn entirely from occupied Azerbaijani territory and Azerbaijani refugees had returned to their homes. Azerbaijan also insisted that international peace-keeping forces be deployed in Nagornyi Karabakh (as opposed to the Russian- and CIS-led force favoured by Armenia). In December, at a summit meeting of the CSCE (subsequently known as the Organization for Security and Co-operation in Europe—OSCE), delegates agreed in principle to deploy a 3,000-strong multinational peace-keeping force in Nagornyi Karabakh; the agreement had apparently received the approval of the Russian Government, which was to contribute not more than 30% of the peacekeepers.

The cease-fire was maintained in Nagornyi Karabakh throughout 1995, with only minor violations reported. However, no real progress towards a full political settlement was achieved, although negotiations continued to be held under the aegis of the OSCE. Nevertheless, in May the exchange of prisoners of war and other hostages was commenced. In April–June a new 33-seat republican legislature was elected in Nagornyi Karabakh (replacing the former 81-member Supreme Soviet). Robert Kocharian, hitherto Chairman of the State Defence Committee, was appointed to the new office of an executive presidency. In August the new legislature extended martial law in Nagornyi Karabakh until January 1996 (this was subsequently extended until December 1997).

Efforts to reach a political settlement continued throughout 1996, with negotiations being held both under the auspices of the 'Minsk Group', and through direct discussions between the sides. Aliyev, who met President Ter-Petrossian of Armenia on several occasions, continued to affirm his commitment to Azerbaijan's territorial integrity, reiterating that Nagornyi Karabakh could be granted autonomy within Azerbaijan, but not full independence. The cease-fire remained in force and a further exchange of prisoners of war was carried out in May. The forthcoming election to the office of President of Nagornyi Karabakh, scheduled for November, attracted criticism from the OSCE and was condemned by Azerbaijan, which warned that the results of any election would be considered invalid. Nevertheless, the election was held on 24 November, and Kocharian, the incumbent President, was elected with some 89% of votes cast. Azerbaijani refugees from the enclave staged protests in Baku, while Azerbaijan declared that it would not recognize the election results.

In December 1996 Aliyev and Ter-Petrossian attended a summit meeting of the OSCE, in Lisbon, Portugal. Azerbaijan threatened to veto the final statement of the summit on the promotion of security and stability in Europe, unless an additional declaration was issued by the Chairman, concerning the conflict in Nagornyi Karabakh. A statement was therefore released, recommending three principles that would form the basis of a political settlement to the conflict: the territorial integrity of Armenia and Azerbaijan; legal status for Nagornyi Karabakh, which would be granted self-determination within Azerbaijan; and guaranteed security for Nagornyi Karabakh and its population, including mutual obligations to ensure compliance by all parties with the provisions of the settlement. However, Armenia refused to accept the terms of the statement.

Relations between Azerbaijan and Armenia deteriorated in February 1997, when Azerbaijan expressed concern at the provision of weapons to Armenia by several countries, including Russia, and condemned it as a violation of the Conventional Forces in Europe (CFE) Treaty. Armenia retaliated by accusing Azerbaijan of preparing for a military offensive against Nagornyi Karabakh to regain the territory. The admission by the Russian Minister of Defence, Igor Rodionov, that weapons had been delivered to Armenia in 1994–96 without the authorization, or knowledge, of the Russian Government, resulted in a deterioration in relations between Russia and Azerbaijan, particularly since Russia, as a participant in the 'Minsk Group', was expected to act as an impartial mediator. Azerbaijan demanded that the issue be investigated by the signatories to the CFE Treaty. It also criticized the appointment in March 1997 of Robert Kocharian, hitherto President of Nagornyi Karabakh, as Prime Minister of Armenia.

Negotiations under the auspices of the OSCE resumed in Moscow in April 1997, but little progress was made, and later in that month a series of clashes, which left many people killed or wounded, occurred on the Armenian–Azerbaijani border, with each side accusing the other of initiating the hostilities. The suggestion by Aliyev that a pipeline for the export of crude petroleum might be constructed through Armenia in exchange for the return of Armenian-occupied territory to Azerbaijan was rejected by the Armenian authorities.

In late May 1997 a draft peace settlement for the disputed enclave was presented by the 'Minsk Group' to Armenia and Azerbaijan. The proposals were initially rejected by the two parties, but a revised plan, issued in July, received the qualified support of President Aliyev. The proposals provided for a stage-by-stage settlement of the conflict: Nagornyi Karabakh would receive autonomous status within Azerbaijan, and the withdrawal of Armenian forces from the enclave was to be followed by the deployment of OSCE peace-keeping troops, which would guarantee freedom of movement through the Lachin 'corridor' linking Armenia with Nagornyi Karabakh. The proposed presidential elections in Nagornyi Karabakh, scheduled for September, following the appointment of Kocharian as Prime Minister of Armenia, were severely criticized by Aliyev; the Azerbaijani authorities also expressed concern at the conclusion of a partnership treaty between Armenia and Russia, fearing that a strengthening of relations between the two countries was a hindrance to the peace process.

The election of Arkadyi Gukasian to the post of President of Nagornyi Karabakh, on 1 September 1997, was not recognized by the international community and threatened to hamper further progress on reaching a settlement, owing to his outright dismissal of the OSCE proposals; it was reported later in that month, however, that both Azerbaijan and Armenia had accepted the revised plan drawn up by the 'Minsk Group'. In addition, President Ter-Petrossian of Armenia publicly admitted that Nagornyi Karabakh could expect neither to gain full independence, nor to be united with Armenia. Moreover, the Azerbaijani authorities indicated that they would be willing to discuss with the leadership of Nagornyi Karabakh the level of autonomy to be granted to the enclave, providing that the principles of the Lisbon statement were accepted, having previously refused to recognize the Nagornyi Karabakh administration as an equal party in the negotiations. At a meeting in Strasbourg, France, in October, while attending a Council of Europe summit, Presidents Aliyev and Ter-Petrossian reaffirmed their commitment to a peaceful settlement of the conflict.

Although it signed the Alma-Ata Declaration in December 1991, Azerbaijan's subsequent attitude towards its membership of the CIS was equivocal. Indeed, the Milli Majlis failed to ratify the Commonwealth's founding treaty, and in October 1992 it voted overwhelmingly against further participation in the CIS. However, with the overthrow of the nationalist PFA Government and the accession to power of Heydar Aliyev, the country's position regarding the CIS was again reversed, and in September 1993 Azerbaijan was formally admitted to full membership of the body. In late 1994, owing to the conflict in Chechnya, Russia closed its border with Azerbaijan, to prevent illicit trade in armaments. It was reopened in August 1996. Negotiations concerning the repair and reopening of an existing oil pipeline from Azerbaijan, via Chechnya, to Novorossiisk on Russia's Black Sea coast, were the focus of Azerbaijani-Russian relations in 1997. Security guarantees for personnel working on the pipeline were an essential part of the discussions, and Azerbaijan actively pursued the development of alternative, new pipelines, primarily through Georgia and Turkey (see Economic Affairs). Agreements were concluded with a number of Russian companies concerning both the extraction and the transportation of crude petroleum from the offshore oilfields in the Caspian Sea, and in October the first delivery of crude petroleum was consigned to Novorossiisk through the refurbished pipeline. However, a dispute with Turkmenistan concerning ownership of the Kyapaz offshore oilfield (the legal status of the Caspian Sea has yet to be established by the littoral states, following the dissolution of the USSR) appeared to threaten the conclusion of a contract with Russia to develop the area.

The strengthening of relations with Turkey, which had been cultivated by successive leaderships following independence in 1991, continued under Aliyev. Throughout the conflict over Nagornyi Karabakh, Azerbaijan was supported by Turkey, which provided humanitarian and other aid, and reinforced Azerbaijan's economic blockade of Armenia. Proposals were made in 1997 for the construction of an oil pipeline from the Azerbaijani oilfields to the Turkish port of Ceyhan. Concerning relations with neighbouring Iran, it was believed that the large Azeri minority there (numbering an estimated 20m.) might prove to be a potential source of tension. In early 1995 it was reported that ethnic Azeri organizations in northern areas of Iran had established a 'national independence front' in order to achieve unification with Azerbaijan. Nevertheless, official relations between Iran and Azerbaijan remained friendly, and bilateral trade increased significantly in the 1990s, with Iran becoming one of Azerbaijan's largest trading partners by 1997.

Relations with the USA expanded significantly in the mid-1990s, and in July 1997 President Aliyev visited the USA, the first visit by an Azerbaijani Head of State since the country regained its independence. An agreement was signed on military co-operation between the two countries, and four contracts between the Azerbaijani State Oil Company, SOCAR, and US petroleum companies to develop offshore oilfields in the Caspian Sea were also concluded. The USA assumed co-chairmanship of the 'Minsk Group' in early 1997, together with Russia and France.

In March 1992 Azerbaijan was admitted to the UN; it subsequently became a member of the CSCE (now OSCE). In April 1996, together with Georgia and Armenia, Azerbaijan signed a co-operation agreement with the European Union (see p. 152), and in June the Council of Europe (see p. 140) granted Azerbaijan special 'guest status'.

Government

Under the Constitution of November 1995, the President of the Azerbaijan Republic is Head of State and Commander-in-Chief of the armed forces. The President, who is directly elected for a five-year term of office, holds supreme executive authority in conjunction with the Cabinet of Ministers, which is appointed by the President and is headed by the Prime Minister. Supreme legislative power is vested in the 125-member Milli Majlis (National Assembly).

Defence

After gaining independence in 1991, Azerbaijan began the formation of national armed forces. In August 1997 these numbered an estimated 66,700: an army of 53,300, a navy of 2,200 and an air force of 11,200. Military service is for 17 months (but may be extended for ground forces). The Ministry of Internal Affairs controls a militia of an estimated 20,000. As a member of the Commonwealth of Independent States (CIS), Azerbaijan's naval forces operate under CIS (Russian) control. In May 1994 Azerbaijan became the 15th country to join NATO's 'Partnership for Peace' (see p. 206) programme of military co-operation. The 1997 budget allocated an estimated US $120m. to defence.

Economic Affairs

In 1995, according to World Bank estimates, Azerbaijan's gross national product (GNP), measured at average 1993–95 prices, was US $3,601m., equivalent to $480 per head. During 1985–94, it was estimated, GNP per head declined by an annual average of 16.3% in real terms. During 1985–95 the population increased by an annual average of 1.2%. Over the same period, Azerbaijan's gross domestic product (GDP) decreased, in real terms, by an average of 12.1% annually. In 1995, according to estimates by the IMF, GDP declined by 11.0%, but in 1996 GDP was estimated to have increased by 1.0%.

Agriculture (including forestry) contributed 26.7% of GDP in 1995. In that year some 31.3% of the working population were employed in the sector. The principal crops are grain, grapes and other fruit, vegetables and cotton. By late 1996 5,300 farms had passed into private ownership, accounting for some 50% of arable land. More than 80% of the production of vegetables, fruit, livestock and animal products was generated by private farms by the end of that year. In 1994, according to the IMF, agricultural GDP declined by 13.0%, and in 1995 it decreased by 8%.

Industry (including mining, manufacturing, construction and power) contributed 24.3% of GDP in 1995. In that year 19.6% of the working population were employed in industry. Production in the non-petroleum manufacturing sector declined by an estimated 26% in 1995, and in 1996 industrial output decreased by 6.7%.

Azerbaijan is richly endowed with mineral resources, the most important of which is petroleum. The country's known reserves of petroleum were estimated to total 1,300m.–1,500m. metric tons in December 1996, of which more than 95% was located in offshore fields in the Caspian Sea. Production of crude petroleum declined by 1% in 1996 (compared with the previous year), owing mainly to inefficient technology and poor maintenance of the oilfields. In September 1994 an agreement was concluded by Azerbaijan with a consortium of international oil companies, the Azerbaijan International Operating Company (AIOC), to develop these offshore oilfields. By July 1997 six agreements had been signed between the State Oil Company (SOCAR) and international consortia, and negotiations were under way with Russia, Georgia, Turkey and Iran concerning the pipeline routes for the export of the crude petroleum. Production of 'early' oil began in October and was transported to the Russian Black Sea port of Novorossiisk, via Chechnya, and the first shipment of petroleum from AIOC-operated fields was made in November. It was envisaged that production of crude petroleum would exceed 1m. barrels per day when all the fields were developed. Azerbaijan also has substantial reserves of natural gas, most of which are located off shore. Other minerals extracted include gold, silver, iron ore, alunite (alum-stone), iron pyrites, barytes, cobalt and molybdenum.

The manufacturing sector is dominated by heavy industries, such as the metallurgy and chemical industries. Production in the sector has declined significantly since 1991, owing to the collapse of the Soviet internal trading systems and the increasing cost of energy products. However, light industry, such as textiles, is gaining in importance.

In 1992 Azerbaijan's supply of primary energy was provided by natural gas (58%), nuclear power (31%), petroleum and petroleum products (6%) and hydroelectric and other sources (5%). Some 85% of electricity generation was provided by thermal power stations, while the remaining 15% was provided by hydroelectric stations in 1997. In 1994 some 30% of gas used for domestic purposes was imported from Turkmenistan. However, in 1995 imports of gas from Turkmenistan ceased, owing to the increase in gas prices to world market levels.

The services sector has expanded since 1991, with retail trade, restaurants and hotels gaining in importance in the mid-1990s. In 1995 services accounted for 49.1% of employment and provided 49.1% of GDP. According to the World Bank, the real GDP of the services sector declined by 9.8% in 1994 and by 18.5% in 1995.

In 1995 Azerbaijan recorded a visible trade deficit of US $343m., and there was a deficit of $379m. on the current account of the balance of payments. In 1995 the principal source of imports was Turkey (21.0%). Other major sources of imports were Russia, Iran, Turkmenistan and Germany. The main market for exports in that year was Iran (29.8%). Other important purchasers were Russia, the United Kingdom, Georgia and Ukraine. The major exports in 1995 were mineral products (mainly energy materials), textiles and textile articles, and machinery and mechanical appliances. The principal imports in that year were mineral products, foodstuffs, machinery and animal products.

Azerbaijan's overall budget deficit for 1995 was 522,800m. manats. At the end of 1995 the country's total external debt was estimated to be US $321.0m., of which $206.1m. was long-term public debt. The annual rate of inflation averaged 720.6% during 1990–94. Consumer prices increased by an average of 1,664% in 1994 and by 412% in 1995. However, the inflation rate declined to an estimated 19.9% in 1996. In April 1997 some 32,000 people were officially registered as unemployed; however, the number of people without work, but not registered as unemployed, was believed to be significantly greater.

Azerbaijan became a member of the IMF and the World Bank in 1992. It also joined the Islamic Development Bank (see p. 194), the European Bank for Reconstruction and Development (EBRD, see p. 148), the Economic Co-operation Organization (ECO, see p. 260) and the Black Sea Economic Co-operation organization (BSEC, see p. 260).

The dissolution of the USSR in 1991, the conflict in Nagornyi Karabakh and the disruption of trade routes through Georgia and Chechnya caused significant economic problems for Azerbaijan. However, owing to its enormous mineral wealth, Azerbaijan's prospects for eventual economic prosperity are considered to be favourable, although major investment and foreign technological expertise are required for the full potential of the country's unexploited mineral reserves to be realized. The agreements that have been concluded with international consortia to develop these reserves were expected greatly to improve Azerbaijan's economic situation. The Government's stabilization and reform programme, adopted in early 1995, had achieved considerable success by late 1997. The value of the national currency, the manat, had stabilized, there was a significant increase in investment, the budget deficit had been reduced, a low rate of inflation was recorded, and growth in GDP appeared likely for the second successive year. A large-scale privatization programme aimed to transfer some 75% of all state-owned property to private control between 1995 and 1998, and the Government intended to complete the privatization of small and medium-sized businesses by the end of 1997. A scheme of privatization through voucher auctions was launched in March, and in May a denationalization commission was established to prepare state enterprises for their transfer to private ownership. Reform of the banking sector was also under way, with the restructuring of commercial banks and the eventual privatization of state-owned banks envisaged. However, living standards for much of the population (in particular, thousands of refugees displaced by the conflict in Nagornyi Karabakh) remained low, with more than 60% of households classified as 'poor' in late 1996. Unemployment remained extremely prevalent. Pollution of the Caspian Sea, as a result of the exploitation of the oilfields, was becoming a serious problem, as was the rising level of the Sea, which threatened many coastal areas with flooding. Nevertheless, the IMF, the World Bank and other international organizations continued to endorse Azerbaijan's programme of economic restructuring.

Social Welfare

Azerbaijan has a comprehensive social security system, which aims to ensure that no citizen receives less than a subsistence income and that health care and education are freely available to all. However, in the late 1990s Azerbaijan's social welfare system was under enormous strain, owing to the conflict in Nagornyi Karabakh (see Recent History) and the massive influx of refugees into the republic, as well as the effects of comprehensive economic reforms. Among the most important provisions of the system are: old-age, disability, and survivor pensions; birth, child, and family allowances, as well as benefits for sick leave, maternity leave, temporary disability, and burial; unemployment compensation; price subsidies; and tax exemptions for specific social groups. The above social benefits are financed by three extrabudgetary funds, the Social Protection Fund, the Employment Fund and the Disabled Persons' Fund. The Social Protection Fund receives transfers from the republican budget, and the Employment Fund is financed by social insurance contributions from employers. In 1995 government expenditure on health care amounted to 1.2% of GDP. Transfers from the republican budget to the Social Protection Fund in that year totalled 534,200m. manats (22.3% of total budgetary expenditure).

Education

Before 1918 Azerbaijan was an important centre of learning among Muslims of the Russian Empire. Under Soviet rule, a much more extensive education system was introduced. In the early 1990s this was reorganized, as part of overall economic and political reforms. Education is officially compulsory between the ages of six and 17 years. Primary education begins at seven years of age and lasts for three years. Secondary education, beginning at 10, comprises a first cycle of five years and a second cycle of two years. In 1993 total enrolment at primary and secondary schools was equivalent to 97% of the school-age population (males 98%; females 95%). Approximately 85% of secondary schools use Azerbaijani as the medium of instruction, while some 13% use Russian. Since 1992 a Turkic version of the Latin alphabet has been used in Azerbaijani-language schools (replacing the Cyrillic script). There were 17 institutions of higher education in 1992; courses of study for full-time students last between four and five years. Higher education institutes include Baku State University (established in 1919 by the nationalist Government of independent Azerbaijan), which specializes in the sciences, and the State Petroleum Academy, which trains engineers for the petroleum industry. In 1989, according to census results, the rate of adult illiteracy in Azerbaijan was only 2.7% (males 1.1%; females 4.1%). In 1995 it was estimated that the rate of adult illiteracy was 0.4% (males 0.3%; females 0.5%). Government expenditure on education was 91,798m. manats in 1994. Such spending was estimated to total 4% of GDP in 1996.

Public Holidays

1998: 1 January (New Year), 20 January (Day of Sorrow), 8 March (International Women's Day), 28 May (Republic Day), 15 June (Day of Liberation of the Azerbaijani People), 9 October (Day of the Armed Services), 18 October (Day of Statehood), 12 November (Constitution Day), 17 November (Day of National Survival), 31 December (Day of Azerbaijani Solidarity World-wide).

1999: 1 January (New Year), 20 January (Day of Sorrow), 8 March (International Women's Day), 28 May (Republic Day), 15 June (Day of Liberation of the Azerbaijani People), 9 October (Day of the Armed Services), 18 October (Day of Statehood), 12 November (Constitution Day), 17 November (Day of National Survival), 31 December (Day of Azerbaijani Solidarity World-wide).

Weights and Measures

The metric system is in force.

Statistical Survey

Principal sources: IMF, *Azerbaijan: Economic Review, International Financial Statistics: Supplement on Countries of the Former Soviet Union*, and *Azerbaijan Republic—Recent Economic Developments;* World Bank, *Statistical Handbook: States of the Former USSR.*

Area and Population

AREA, POPULATION AND DENSITY

Area (sq km)	86,600*
Population (census results)†	
17 January 1979	6,026,515
12 January 1989	
Males	3,423,793
Females	3,597,385
Total	7,021,178
Population (official estimates)‡	
1994 (1 January)	7,391,000
1995 (1 January)	7,499,000
1996 (1 November)	7,563,000
Density (per sq km) at 1 November 1996	87.3

* 33,400 sq miles.

† Figures refer to *de jure* population. The *de facto* total at the 1989 census was 7,037,867.

‡ Provisional.

POPULATION BY NATIONALITY
(permanent inhabitants, 1989 census)

	%
Azerbaijani	82.7
Russian	5.6
Armenian	5.6
Lezghi	2.4
Others	3.7
Total	100.0

PRINCIPAL TOWNS
(estimated population at 1 January 1990)

Baku (capital) 1,149,000; Gyanja (formerly Kirovabad) 281,000; Sumgait 235,000.

BIRTHS, MARRIAGES AND DEATHS

	Registered live births		Registered marriages		Registered deaths	
	Number	Rate (per 1,000)	Number	Rate (per 1,000)	Number	Rate (per 1,000)
1987	184,585	26.9	68,031	9.9	45,744	6.7
1988	184,350	26.4	68,887	9.9	47,485	6.8
1989	181,631	25.6	71,874	10.1	44,016	6.2

1994: Registered marriages 47,386 (marriage rate 6.4 per 1,000); Registered deaths 54,921 (death rate 7.4 per 1,000).

Source: UN, *Demographic Yearbook*.

Expectation of life (official estimates, years at birth, 1989): 70.6 (males 66.6; females 74.2) (Source: Goskomstat USSR).

EMPLOYMENT (annual average, '000 persons)

	1993	1994	1995
Material sphere	2,092	2,008	2,002
Agriculture	939	895	883
Forestry	5	4	5
Industry*	392	374	370
Construction	212	192	185
Trade and catering†	351	366	367
Transport and communications‡	111	105	116
Other activities	81	73	76
Non-material sphere	825	844	835
Transport and communications‡	85	86	73
Housing and municipal services	86	91	92
Health care, social security, physical culture and sports	178	174	175
Education	380	394	395
Science, research and development	34	37	37
Government	50	49	50
Other activities	13	13	13
Total employed	2,917	2,851	2,837

* Comprising manufacturing (except printing and publishing), mining and quarrying, electricity, gas, water, logging and fishing.

† Including material and technical supply.

‡ Transport and communications servicing material production are included in activities of the material sphere. Other branches of the sector are considered to be non-material services.

Agriculture

PRINCIPAL CROPS ('000 metric tons)

	1994	1995	1996
Wheat	739	598	725*
Barley	262	250	275*
Maize	14	12	24*
Potatoes	150	200	209
Cottonseed*	170	150	165
Cabbages*	40	50	61
Tomatoes*	300	290	325
Cucumbers and gherkins*	10	10	12
Onions (dry)*	15	15	20
Carrots*	12	14	18
Other vegetables	74	71	76
Watermelons† ‡	300	300	300
Grapes	317	340†	330†
Apples*	240	245	238
Pears*	10	10	10
Peaches and nectarines*	25	20	18
Plums*	30	28	35
Citrus fruits*	6	6	5
Apricots*	12	15	16
Tea (made)†	4	4	4
Tobacco (leaves)†	68	68	68
Cotton (lint)	93	83*	91*

* Unofficial figure(s). † FAO estimate(s).

‡ Including melons, pumpkins and squash.

Source: FAO, *Production Yearbook*.

LIVESTOCK ('000 head, year ending September)

	1994	1995	1996
Horses*	30	30	32
Asses*	5	5	5
Cattle	1,621	1,633	1,658
Buffaloes*	10	10	10
Camels*	30	30	30
Pigs	48	33	31
Sheep†	4,357	4,376	4,390
Goats†	182	182	184
Chickens (million)†	16	14	13

* FAO estimates. † Unofficial figures.

Source: FAO, *Production Yearbook*.

LIVESTOCK PRODUCTS ('000 metric tons)

	1994	1995	1996
Beef and veal	43	41	43*
Mutton and lamb	22	23	24*
Pig meat	2	2	2*
Poultry meat	17	13	14*
Cows' milk	784	826	841
Cheese†	43	43	43
Butter†	2	2	2
Hen eggs*	28	25	26
Honey†	4	4	4
Wool:			
greasy†	8	8	8
clean†	5	5	5
Cattle and buffalo hides†	16	16	16

* Unofficial figure(s). † FAO estimates.

Source: FAO, *Production Yearbook*.

Fishing

(FAO estimates, metric tons, live weight)

	1993	1994	1995
Common carp	1,912	1,859	1,960
Azov sea sprat	33,102	32,182	34,020
Other fishes	986	959	1,020
Total catch	36,000	35,000	37,000

Source: FAO, *Yearbook of Fishery Statistics*.

Mining

	1993	1994	1995
Crude petroleum ('000 metric tons)	10,295	9,563	9,200
Natural gas (million cu metres)	6,810	6,379	6,600

Industry

SELECTED PRODUCTS ('000 metric tons, unless otherwise indicated)

	1993	1994	1995
Steel	236	37	20
Cement	643	467	196
Fertilizers	32	5	2
Pesticides	1	1	—
Sulphuric acid	141	56	24
Caustic soda	49	40	36
Sulphanol	23	7	—
Concrete (reinforced, million cu m)	594	250	91
Bricks (million)	764	498	161
Radio receivers ('000)	30	3	1
Bicycles ('000)	51	40	40
Electric motors ('000)	1,355	834	512
Electric energy (million kWh)	19,100	17,600	16,957
Motor spirit (petrol)	1,200	1,300	1,000
Kerosene	541	600	600
Diesel oil	2,700	2,300	2,200
Lubricants	208	230	100
Residual fuel oil (Mazout)	5,104	4,149	4,400

1991 ('000 metric tons): Aviation fuel 58.2; Naphtha 427.0; Bitumen 113.1; Petroleum coke 161.3.

Finance

CURRENCY AND EXCHANGE RATES

Monetary Units

100 gopik = 1 Azerbaijani manat.

Sterling and Dollar Equivalents (30 September 1997)

£1 sterling = 6,348.5 manats;
US $1 = 3,930.0 manats;
10,000 manats = £1.575 = $2.545.

Average exchange rate (Azerbaijani manats per US $)

1994 1,570.2
1995 4,413.5
1996 4,301.3

Note: The Azerbaijani manat was introduced in August 1992, initially to circulate alongside the Russian (formerly Soviet) rouble, with an exchange rate of 1 manat = 10 roubles. Following the dissolution of the USSR in December 1991, Russia and several other former Soviet republics retained the rouble as their monetary unit. The average interbank market rate in 1992 was $1 = 222.1 Russian roubles. In December 1993 Azerbaijan left the rouble zone, and the manat became the country's sole currency.

STATE BUDGET ('000 million manats)

Revenue	1993	1994	1995*
Individual income tax	3.7	27.8	116.9
Enterprise profits tax	13.3	97.5	408.7
Social security contributions	15.0	79.6	250.2
Value-added tax	12.7	62.7	176.1
Excises	6.3	37.0	88.4
Revenues in foreign exchange	7.2	251.6	317.2
Taxes on international trade	1.2	12.8	69.0
Strategic export tax	—	—	187.5
Other receipts	4.3	89.1	258.5
Total	63.7	658.1	1,872.5

Expenditure†	1993	1994	1995*
Wages and salaries	n.a.	86.0	390.1
Purchases of goods and services	16.4	120.0	731.4
Defence	13.3	120.0	197.8
Settlement of refugees	3.1	n.a.	57.9
Other	—	—	475.7
Current transfers to households	26.0	160.4	534.2
Pensions	12.7	73.5	204.3
Price compensations	5.4	62.4	275.0
Other compensations and allowances	7.9	24.5	54.8
Subsidies	7.3	101.9	233.0
National economy	n.a.	n.a.	195.0
Other current expenditure	33.2	480.1	18.6
Capital investment	4.9	16.1	78.9
Employment Fund	—	1.0	5.3
Total	87.8	965.5	2,395.3

* Figures are not fully comparable with those for earlier years, owing to changes in definition.

† Excluding lending minus repayments ('000 million manats): 403.8 in 1995.

MONEY SUPPLY ('000 million manats at 31 December)

	1993	1994	1995
Currency outside banks	43.2	276.1	602.4
Manat deposits*	30.4	154.9	355.2
Foreign currency deposits*	12.8	617.0	342.0
Total money*	86.3	1,048.1	1,299.6

* Including time and savings deposits.

COST OF LIVING (Consumer Price Index; base: 1990 = 100)

	1992	1993	1994
Food	2,132.5	29,547	529,872
All items (incl. others)	2,091.9	25,711	453,423

Source: ILO, *Yearbook of Labour Statistics.*

1995 (base: 1994 = 100): All items 511.8.

NATIONAL ACCOUNTS (million manats at current prices)

Expenditure on the Gross Domestic Product

	1993	1994	1995
Government final consumption expenditure	22,373	283,771	1,334,214
Private final consumption expenditure	128,084	1,588,880	8,162,878
Increase in stocks	1,325	−205,067	782,166
Gross fixed capital formation	32,897	491,957	1,303,166
Total domestic expenditure	184,679	2,159,541	11,582,424
Exports of goods and services	90,216	1,196,712	3,041,751
Less Imports of goods and services	119,364	1,482,866	4,248,376
Sub-total	155,531	1,873,387	10,375,799
Statistical discrepancy*	1,551	−72,583	192,434
GDP in purchasers' values	157,082	1,800,804	10,568,233

* Referring to the difference between the sum of the expenditure components and official estimates of GDP, compiled from the production approach.

Gross Domestic Product by Economic Activity

	1993	1994	1995
Agriculture and forestry	42,562	605,996	2,837,056
Industry*	39,127	309,639	2,306,855
Construction	11,759	138,755	274,172
Trade and catering†	8,451	117,419	735,534
Transport and communications‡	12,532	230,046	2,659,713
Other activities of the material sphere	732	4,371	32,276
Finance and insurance	11,277	104,951	432,693
Housing	1,109	19,416	71,508
General administration and defence	9,415	96,018	392,271
Other community, social and personal services	22,260	228,460	894,859
Private non-profit institutions serving households	220	515	2,400
Sub-total	159,445	1,855,586	10,639,337
Less Imputed bank service charge	10,045	91,383	375,211
GDP at factor cost	149,400	1,764,203	10,264,126
Indirect taxes	20,468	105,223	604,074
Less Subsidies	12,786	68,622	299,967
GDP in purchasers' values	157,082	1,800,804	10,568,233

* Comprising manufacturing (except printing and publishing), mining and quarrying, electricity, gas, water, logging and fishing.

† Including material supply and procurement.

‡ Including road maintenance.

BALANCE OF PAYMENTS (US $ million)

	1994	1995
Exports of goods f.o.b.	682	612
Imports of goods f.o.b.	−845	−955
Trade balance	−163	−343
Exports of services	137	172
Imports of services	−170	−312
Balance on goods and services	−196	−483
Other income (net)	0	−7
Balance on goods, services and income	−196	−490
Current transfers (net)	75	111
Current balance	−121	−379
Capital transfers (net)	—	−2
Direct investment (net)	22	277
Portfolio investment (net)	—	−2
Medium- and long-term capital (net)	54	87
Short-term capital (net)	−22	95
Net errors and omissions	−12	68
Overall balance	−79	145

External Trade

PRINCIPAL COMMODITIES (US $ million)

Imports c.i.f.	1993	1994	1995
Live animals and animal products	8.0	42.2	74.3
Vegetable products	79.5	78.4	51.5
Animal or vegetable fats and oils; prepared edible fats; animal or vegetable waxes	24.3	23.0	54.5
Prepared foodstuffs; beverages, spirits and vinegar; tobacco and manufactured substitutes	29.6	61.4	96.8
Mineral products	108.9	259.3	100.8
Products of chemical or allied industries	20.8	37.8	61.3
Textiles and textile articles	16.0	18.1	11.4
Base metals and articles thereof	30.6	97.4	42.0
Machinery and mechanical appliances; electrical equipment; sound and television apparatus	24.2	78.9	82.9
Vehicles, aircraft, vessels and associated transport equipment	21.3	22.7	36.6
Total (incl. others)	549.9	777.9	667.6

Exports f.o.b.	1993	1994	1995
Vegetable products	14.5	14.5	13.3
Prepared foodstuffs; beverages, spirits and vinegar; tobacco and manufactured substitutes	21.2	48.7	24.4
Mineral products	210.3	217.7	283.3
Products of chemical or allied industries	22.1	22.8	19.6
Textiles and textile articles	71.6	114.4	124.5
Base metals and articles thereof	85.5	105.2	17.5
Machinery and mechanical appliances; electrical equipment; sound and television apparatus	89.3	89.4	39.4
Total (incl. others)	724.6	636.8	547.4

PRINCIPAL TRADING PARTNERS (US $ million)

Imports	1993	1994	1995
Belarus	8.2	7.9	4.7
Belgium	0.1	8.9	8.8
Georgia	18.4	8.0	18.9
Germany	18.8	32.0	43.8
Iran	n.a.	67.0	80.0
Italy	8.7	3.9	2.5
Kazakhstan	35.1	51.9	17.6
Korea, Republic	—	14.2	2.4
Moldova	9.5	13.5	4.4
Russia	127.0	117.5	88.3
Switzerland	9.7	2.4	3.3
Turkey	63.6	76.0	140.5
Turkmenistan	54.6	95.6	51.4
Ukraine	53.6	86.3	33.5
United Kingdom	5.3	6.9	9.3
USA	10.8	10.0	13.3
Total (incl. others)	549.9	777.9	667.6

Exports	1993	1994	1995
Austria	5.6	9.5	3.5
Belarus	14.9	7.6	2.7
Georgia	30.6	16.6	41.5
Iran	n.a.	242.0	163.0
Italy	13.3	0.1	26.5
Kazakhstan	30.5	16.5	16.8
Moldova	13.2	12.6	3.1
Russia	185.2	139.7	98.9
Switzerland	3.2	4.0	28.3
Turkey	60.6	16.5	26.4
Turkmenistan	39.3	17.1	13.2
Ukraine	48.3	58.0	33.4
United Kingdom	2.9	61.7	48.6
Total (incl. others)	724.6	636.8	547.4

Transport

ROAD TRAFFIC (vehicles in use at 31 December)

	1993	1994	1995*
Passenger cars	263,315	276,414	289,000
Buses	13,327	12,827	12,600
Lorries and vans	84,289	81,244	76,200

* Estimates.

Source: International Road Federation, *World Road Statistics*.

SHIPPING

Merchant Fleet (registered at 31 December)

	1994	1995	1996
Number of vessels	269	296	289
Total displacement ('000 grt)	621.4	654.9	636.1

Source: Lloyd's Register of Shipping, *World Fleet Statistics*.

CIVIL AVIATION (traffic on scheduled services)

	1992	1993	1994
Kilometres flown (million)	0	23	23
Passengers carried ('000)	1,455	1,383	1,380
Passenger-km (million)	3,511	1,738	1,731
Total ton-km (million)	339	184	183

Source: UN, *Statistical Yearbook*.

Tourism

	1992	1993	1994
Tourist arrivals ('000)	212	298	321
Tourist receipts (US $ million)	42	60	64

Source: UN, *Statistical Yearbook*.

Communications Media

	1992	1994*
Daily newspapers:		
Titles	6	3
Average circulation ('000 copies)	427	210†
Non-daily newspapers:		
Titles	273	n.a.
Average circulation ('000 copies)	3,476	n.a.
Other periodicals:		
Titles	49	n.a.
Average circulation ('000 copies)	801	n.a.
Book production:		
Titles	599	375
Copies ('000)	8,954	5,557

* 1993 figures not available.
† Provisional.

Source: UNESCO, *Statistical Yearbook*.

Telephones ('000 main lines in use): 657 in 1992; 647 in 1993; 635 in 1994 (Source: UN, *Statistical Yearbook*).

Telefax stations (number in use): 2,500 in 1994 (Source: UN, *Statistical Yearbook*).

Mobile cellular telephones (subscribers): 500 in 1994 (Source: UN, *Statistical Yearbook*).

Education

(1993/94, unless otherwise indicated)

	Institutions	Teachers	Students
Pre-primary	2,115	20,140	124,371
Primary	4,406	n.a.	580,266
Secondary:			
General	n.a.	n.a.	838,546
Teacher-training	n.a.	n.a.	721
Vocational	167*	n.a.	29,778
Higher	17†	18,184	129,469

* 1991. † 1992.

Source: mainly UNESCO, *Statistical Yearbook*.

Directory

The Constitution

The new Constitution was endorsed by 91.9% of the registered electorate in a national referendum, held on 12 November 1995. It replaced the amended Soviet Constitution of 1978. The following is a summary of the 1995 Constitution's main provisions:

The Azerbaijan Republic is a democratic, secular and unitary state. The President, who is directly elected for a term of five years, is Head of State and Commander-in-Chief of the armed forces. Executive power is held by the President, who acts as guarantor of the independence and territorial integrity of the republic. The President appoints the Cabinet of Ministers, headed by the Prime Minister, which is the highest executive body. The President proposes candidates for the Constitutional Court and the Supreme Court, and may call legislative elections. The supreme legislative body is the 125-member Milli Majlis (National Assembly), which is directly elected for a five-year term. Three types of ownership—state, private and municipal—are recognized. The state is committed to a market economic system and to freedom of entrepreneurial activity.

The Government

HEAD OF STATE

President: HEYDAR A. ALIYEV (elected by direct popular vote, 3 October 1993; inaugurated on 10 October 1993).

CABINET OF MINISTERS

(December 1997)

Prime Minister: ARTUR RASIZADE.

First Deputy Prime Minister: ABBAS A. ABBASSOV.

Deputy Prime Ministers: TOFIK M. AZIZOV, ELCHIN I. EFENDIYEV, RAFIG R. KHALAFOV, IZZET A. RUSTAMOV, ABID G. SHARIFOV.

Minister of the Economy: NAMIK N. NASRULLAYEV.

Minister of Health: ALI B. INSANOV.

Minister of Foreign Affairs: HASSAN A. HASSANOV.

Minister of Agriculture and Produce: IRSHAD N. ALIYEV.

Minister of Internal Affairs: RAMIL I. USUBOV.

Minister of Culture: POLAD BYUL-BYUL OGLY.

Minister of Education: AHMED ABDINOV (acting).

Minister of Communications: NADIR AKHMEDOV.

Minister of Trade: FARKHAD ALIYEV (acting).

Minister of Finance: FIKRET G. YUSIFOV.

Minister of Justice: SUDABA D. HASANOVA (acting).

Minister of Labour and Social Protection: ALI NAGIYEV.

Minister of National Security: NAMIG R. ABBASOV.

Minister of Defence: Lt-Gen. SAFAR A. ABIYEV.

Minister of Information and the Press: SIRUS TEBRIZLI.

Minister of Youth and Sport: ABULFAZ M. KARAYEV.

Chairmen of State Committees

Chairman of the State Committee for Inter-ethnic Relations: ABBAS ABBASSOV.

Chairman of the State Property Committee: NADIR NASIBLI.

Chairman of the State Committee for Construction and Architectural Affairs: ABID G. SHARIFOV.

Chairman of the State Committee for Anti-monopoly Policy and Enterprise Support: RAHIB GULIYEV.

Chairman of the State Committee for Statistics: ARIF A. VELIYEV.

Chairman of the State Committee for Geology and Mineral Resources: AKRAM SHEKINSKY.

Chairman of the State Committee for Ecology and Use of Natural Resources: (vacant).

Chairman of the State Committee for Supervision of Safety at Work in Industry and Mining: AHMEDAGA RAHIMOV.

Chairman of the State Committee for Geodesy and Cartography: ADIL SULTANOV.

Chairman of the State Committee for Material Resources: (vacant).

Chairman of the State Committee for Specialized Machinery: (vacant).

Chairman of the State Committee for Science and Technology: AZAD MIRZAJANZADE.

Chairman of the State Land Committee: (vacant).

Chairman of the State Customs Committee: KAMALEDDIN HEYDAROV.

Chairman of the State Committee for Veterinary Affairs: MIRSALEH HUSEYNOV.

Chairman of the State Committee for Hydrometeorology: ZULFUGAR MUSAYEV.

Chairman of the State Committee for the Protection and Refurbishment of Historical and Cultural Monuments: FAKHREDDIN MIRALIYEV.

Chairman of the State Committee for Work with Refugees and Displaced Persons: (vacant).

Chairman of the State Committee for Improvements in the Water Industry: AHMED AHMEDZADE.

MINISTRIES

Ministry of Agriculture and Produce: 370016 Baku, Azadlyg Sq. 1, Government House; tel. (12) 93-53-55.

Ministry of Communications: 370139 Baku, Azerbaijan Ave 33; tel. (12) 93-00-04; telex 142492; fax (12) 98-42-85.

Ministry of Culture: 370016 Baku, Azadlyg Sq. 1, Government House; tel. (12) 93-43-98; fax (12) 93-56-05.

Ministry of Defence: 370139 Baku, Azerbaijan Ave.

Ministry of the Economy: Baku.

Ministry of Education: 370016 Baku, Azadlyg Sq. 1, Government House; tel. (12) 93-72-66.

Ministry of Finance: 370000 Baku, Samed Vurghun St 6; tel. (12) 93-93-98; fax (12) 98-79-69; e-mail piu@ibta.baku.az.

Ministry of Foreign Affairs: 370004 Baku, Ghanjlar meydani 3; tel. (12) 93-30-12.

Ministry of Health: 370014 Baku, Malaya Morskaya St 4; tel. (12) 93-29-77.

Ministry of Information and the Press: 370001 Baku, A. Yarayev St 12; tel. (12) 92-63-57; fax (12) 93-65-36.

Ministry of Internal Affairs: 370005 Baku, Gusi Hajiyev St 7; tel. (12) 92-57-54.

Ministry of Justice: 370601 Baku, Kirov Ave 13; tel. (12) 93-97-85.

Ministry of Labour and Social Protection: 370016 Baku, Azadlyg Sq. 1, Government House; tel. (12) 93-05-42; fax (12) 93-94-72.

Ministry of National Security: 370016 Baku, Azadlyg Sq. 1, Government House; tel. (12) 93-10-00.

Ministry of Trade: 370016 Baku, Azadlyg Sq. 1, Government House; tel. (12) 98-50-74.

Ministry of Youth and Sport: 370072 Baku, Fhataly Chan Choyski Ave 98A; tel. (12) 90-64-62; telex 142171; fax (12) 90-64-38.

President and Legislature

PRESIDENT

A presidential election was held on 3 October 1993. (President ABULFAZ ELCHIBEY, elected on 7 June 1992, was impeached on 25 June 1993. On 29 August, in a referendum of confidence in the President, 97.5% of participants voted in favour of his impeachment. The results of the referendum were endorsed by the Milli Majlis on 1 September.) According to official figures, HEYDAR ALIYEV, acting President of Azerbaijan, won 98.8% of the votes cast. The other two candidates were ZAKIR TAGIYEV and KERRAR ABILOV. HEYDAR ALIYEV was inaugurated as President on 10 October 1993.

MILLI MAJLIS
(National Assembly)

Elections to Azerbaijan's new 125-member Milli Majlis were held on 12 November 1995. The electoral law of August 1995 provided for a mixed system of voting: 25 seats to be filled by proportional representation according to party lists, the remaining 100 deputies to be elected in single-member constituencies. The latter included the constituencies of Armenian-held Nagornyi Karabakh and other occupied territories: refugees from those regions cast their votes in other parts of Azerbaijan (in anticipation of the eventual return of occupied areas to Azerbaijani jurisdiction). All 25 party seats were filled: New Azerbaijan Party (NAP) 19, Popular Front of Azerbaijan (PFA) three, National Independence Party (Istiklal) three. However, only 72 of the 100 constituency seats were filled. Of these, the overwhelming majority were taken by the NAP and by independent candidates supporting the NAP's leader, the President of the Republic, HEYDAR ALIYEV. A further round of voting was held on 26 November in order to elect members for 20 of the 28 vacant seats (the respective seats being contested by the two leading candidates in the first round). However, only 12 of these were filled. On 4 February 1996 a further 14 deputies were elected—12 from the NAP, one from the PFA and one from the Muslim Democratic Party (Musavat)—and on 18 February one more seat was filled. Thus, following all the rounds of voting, only one seat in the Majlis remained vacant (representing the Khankendi-Khojali-Khojavend constituency in Nagornyi Karabakh).

Chairman (Speaker): MURTUZ ALESKEROV.

First Deputy Chairman: A. RAHIMZADE.

Political Organizations

At mid-1995 31 political parties and groups were officially registered. However, only eight of these were permitted to participate in the legislative election of November 1995.

Communist Party of Azerbaijan (CPA): Baku; disbanded Sept. 1991, re-established Nov. 1993; Chair. RAMIZ AHMADOV.

Democratic Party of Azerbaijan: Baku; f. 1994; Leader SARDAR JALALOGLU.

Grey Wolves Party (Boz Gurd): Baku; Leader ISKENDER HAMIDOV.

Independent Azerbaijan Party: Baku; Leader NIZAMI SULEYMANOV.

Independent Democratic Party of Azerbaijan: Baku; Chair. LEYLA YUNUSOVA.

Islamic Party of Azerbaijan: Baku; f. 1992; 50,000 mems (1997); Leader ALI AKRAM ALIYEV (ALIYEV imprisoned 1997 on charges of treason. A temporary supreme council was established to lead the party).

Labour Party of Azerbaijan: Baku; Leader SABUTAY HAJIYEV.

Liberal Party of Azerbaijan: Leader LALA SHOVKAT; Dep. Chair. ZAKIR MAMEDOV.

Motherland Party (Ana Vatan): Baku; Leader FAZAIL AGAMALIYEV.

Muslim Democratic Party (Musavat): Baku, Azerbaijan Ave 37; tel. (12) 98-18-70; fax (12) 98-31-65; f. 1911; in exile from 1920; re-established 1992; Chair. ISA GAMBAR; Gen. Sec. NIYAZI IBRAHIMLI.

National Independence Party (Istiklal): c/o Milli Majlis, Baku; f. 1992; Chair. ETIBAR MAMEDOV.

National Statehood Party: Baku; Chair. HAFIZ AGAYARZADE.

New Azerbaijan Party (NAP) (Yeni Azerbaijan): c/o Milli Majlis, Baku; f. 1992; Chair. HEYDAR ALIYEV.

Party of Equality of the Peoples of Azerbaijan: Leader FAHRADDIN AYDAYEV.

People's Freedom Party (Halg Azadlyg): Baku; Leader PANAH SHAHSEVENLI.

Popular Front of Azerbaijan (PFA): c/o Milli Majlis, Baku; f. 1989; Chair. ABULFAZ ELCHIBEY.

Social Democratic Party: 370014 Baku, 28 May St 3–11; tel. (12) 93-33-78; fax (12) 98-75-55; e-mail asdp@ngonet.baku.az; f. 1989; 2,000 mems (1990); Chair. ARAZ ALIZADEH.

Other political groups include the Alliance for Azerbaijan Party, the Ana Toprag (Native Soil) party, the Azeri Party of Popular Revival, the Democratic Party of Azerbaijan Business People, the Green Party of Azerbaijan, the Modern Turan Party, the National Resistance Movement and the Yurdash (Compatriot) party.

Diplomatic Representation

EMBASSIES IN AZERBAIJAN

China, People's Republic: Baku, Azadlyg Ave 1, Hotel Azerbaijan; tel. (12) 98-00-10; Ambassador: LEI YINCHENG.

Egypt: Baku, Hotel Respublika; tel. (12) 92-55-95; Ambassador: FARUK AMIN AL-HAVARI.

France: Baku, Hotel Respublika; tel. (12) 92-89-77; fax (12) 98-92-53; Ambassador: JEAN-PIERRE GUINHUT.

Georgia: Baku, Azadlyg Ave 1, Hotel Azerbaijan, Rms 1322-1325; tel. (12) 98-17-79; fax (12) 98-94-40; Ambassador: GYORGI CHANTURIA.

Germany: 370000 Baku, Mamedaliyev St 15; tel. (12) 98-78-19; telex 142143; fax (12) 98-54-19; Ambassador: Dr CHRISTIAN SIEBECK.

Greece: 370148 Baku, Hotel Anba; tel. (12) 65-12-94; fax (12) 98-91-13; Ambassador: PANAYOTIS KARAKASSIS.

Iran: Baku, B. Sadarov St 4; tel. (12) 92-64-53; Ambassador: ALIREZA BIGDELI.

Iraq: 370000 Baku, Khagani St 9; tel. (12) 93-72-07; Chargé d'affaires a.i.: FARUQ SALMAN DAVUD.

Israel: Baku, Stroiteley Ave 1; tel. (12) 38-52-82; fax (12) 98-92-83; Chargé d'affaires: ARKADIY MIL-MAN.

Pakistan: Baku, Azadlyg Ave 1, Hotel Azerbaijan, Rms 541 and 534; tel. (12) 98-90-04; telex 142215; fax (12) 98-94-85; Ambassador: PERVEZ KHANZADA.

Russia: Baku, Azadlyg Ave 1, Hotel Azerbaijan; tel. (12) 98-90-04; Ambassador: ALEKSANDR BLOKHIN.

Sudan: Baku, Neftchilar Ave 60; tel. (12) 98-48-97; fax (12) 93-40-47; Ambassador: HASSAN BESHIR ABDELWAHAB.

Turkey: 370000 Baku, Khagani St 27; (12) 98-81-43; Ambassador: OSMAN FRANK LOGOGLU.

United Kingdom: 370065 Baku, Izmir St 2; tel. (12) 97-51-88; fax (12) 92-27-39; e-mail office@britemb.baku.az; Ambassador: ROGER THOMAS.

USA: 370007 Baku, Azadlyg Ave 83; tel. (12) 98-03-35; fax (12) 98-37-55; Ambassador: STANLEY ESCUDERO.

Judicial System

Constitutional Court: comprises a Chairman and eight judges, who are nominated by the President and confirmed in office by the

Milli Majlis for a term of office of 10 years. Only the President, the Milli Majlis, the Cabinet of Ministers, the Procurator-General, the Supreme Court and the legislature of the Autonomous Republic of Nakhichevan are permitted to submit cases to the Constitutional Court.

Chairman of the Supreme Court: KHANLAR HAJIYEV.

Procurator-General: ELDAR HASSANOV.

Religion

ISLAM

The majority (some 70%) of Azerbaijanis are Shi'ite Muslims; most of the remainder are Sunni (Hanafi school). The Muslim Board of Transcaucasia is based in Baku. It has spiritual jurisdiction over the Muslims of Armenia, Georgia and Azerbaijan. The Chairman of the Directorate is normally a Shi'ite, while the Deputy Chairman is usually a Sunni.

Muslim Board of Transcaucasia: Baku; Chair. Sheikh ALLASHUKUR PASHEZADE.

CHRISTIANITY

The Roman Catholic Church

The Apostolic Administrator of the Caucasus is the Holy See's Apostolic Nuncio to Georgia, Armenia and Azerbaijan, who is resident in Tbilisi, Georgia.

The Press

In 1994 there were 430 newspaper titles and 104 periodicals officially registered in Azerbaijan. However, owing to financial and technical difficulties, many publications reportedly suffered a sharp decrease in circulation.

PRINCIPAL NEWSPAPERS

In Azerbaijani, except where otherwise stated.

Adabiyat ve Injisenet: 370146 Baku, Metbuat Ave, Block 529; tel. (12) 39-50-37; organ of the Union of Writers of Azerbaijan.

Azadlyg (Liberty): Baku, Khagani St 33; tel. (12) 98-90-81; f. 1989; weekly; organ of the Popular Front of Azerbaijan; in Azerbaijani and Russian; Editor-in-Chief J. TAHIRLY; circ. 9,034.

Azerbaijan: Baku, Metbuat Ave, Block 529; f. 1991; 5 a week; publ. by the People's Committee for Relief to Karabakh; in Azerbaijani and Russian; Editor-in-Chief A. MUSTAFAYEV; circ. 10,242 (Azerbaijani), 3,040 (Russian).

Azerbaijan Ganjlyari (Youth of Azerbaijan): Baku; f. 1919; 3 a week; Editor YU. A. KERIMOV.

Bakinskii Rabochii (Baku Worker): 370146 Baku, Metbuat Ave, Block 529; tel. (12) 32-11-10; f. 1906; 5 a week; govt newspaper; in Russian; Editor I. VEKILOVA; circ. 4,776.

Hayat (Life): 370146 Baku, Metbuat Ave, Block 529; f. 1991; 5 a week; publ. by the National Assembly of Azerbaijan; Editor-in-Chief A. H. ASKEROV.

Istiklal (Independence): 370014 Baku, 28 May St 3–11; tel. (12) 93-33-78; fax (12) 98-75-55; e-mail istiklal@ngonet.baku.az; 4 a month; organ of the Social Democratic Party; Editor ZARDUSHT ALIZADEH; circ. 5,000.

Khalg Gazeti: Baku; f. 1919; fmrly *Kommunist*; 6 a week; Editor T. T. RUSTAMOV.

Molodezh Azerbaijana (Youth of Azerbaijan): 370146 Baku, Metbuat Ave, Block 529, 8th Floor; tel. (12) 39-00-51; f. 1919; weekly; in Russian; Editor V. EFENDIYEV; circ. 7,000.

Panorama: 370146 Baku, Metbuat Ave, Block 529; f. 1995; 5 a week; organ of the Centre of Strategic and International Investigations; in Azerbaijani and Russian; Editor-in-Chief A. ZEYNALOV; circ. 8,000.

Respublika (Republic): 370146 Baku, Metbuat Ave, Block 529; tel. (12) 38-01-14; fax (12) 92-19-05; f. 1990; weekly; govt newspaper; Editor-in-Chief T. AHMADOV; circ. 4,634.

Veten Sesi (Voice of the Motherland): 370146 Baku, Metbuat Ave, Block 529; f. 1990; weekly; publ. by the Society of Refugees of Azerbaijan; in Azerbaijani and Russian; Editor-in-Chief T. A. AHMEDOV.

Vyshka (Tower): 370146 Baku, Metbuat Ave, Block 529; tel. (12) 39-85-65; fax (12) 39-96-97; f. 1928; 4 a week; independent social-political newspaper; in Russian; Editor H. A. ALIYEV.

Yeni Azerbaijan: Baku, Metbuat Ave, Block 529; f. 1993; weekly; publ. by the Cabinet of Ministers; Editor-in-Chief KH. GOJA; circ. 2,493.

PRINCIPAL PERIODICALS

Azerbaijan: 370001 Baku, Istiglaliyat St 31; tel. (12) 92-59-63; f. 1923; monthly; publ. by the Union of Writers of Azerbaijan; recent works by Azerbaijani authors; Editor-in-Chief YUSIF SAMEDOGLU.

Azerbaijan Gadyny (Woman of Azerbaijan): Baku; f. 1923; monthly; illustrated; Editor H. M. HASILOVA.

Dialog (Dialogue): Baku; f. 1989; fortnightly; in Azerbaijani and Russian; Editor R. A. ALEKPEROV.

Iki Sahil: Baku, Nobel Ave 64; f. 1965; weekly; organ of the New Baku Oil-Refining Plant; Editor-in-Chief V. RAHIMZADEH; circ. 2,815.

Kend Khayaty (Country Life): Baku; f. 1952; monthly; journal of the Ministry of Agriculture and Produce; advanced methods of work in agriculture; in Azerbaijani and Russian; Editor D. A. DAMIRLI.

Kirpi (Hedgehog): Baku; f. 1952; fortnightly; satirical; Editor A. M. AIVAZOV.

Literaturnyi Azerbaijan (Literature of Azerbaijan): 370001 Baku, Istiglaliyat St 31; tel. (12) 92-39-31; f. 1931; monthly; journal of the Union of Writers of Azerbaijan; fiction; in Russian; Editor-in-Chief I. P. TRETYAKOV.

Ulus: 370001 Baku, Istiglaliyat St 31; tel. (12) 92-27-43; monthly; Editor TOFIK DADASHEV.

NEWS AGENCIES

AzerTAJ (State Telegraph Agency of Azerbaijan Republic): 370000 Baku, Bul-Bul Ave 18; tel. (12) 93-59-29; telex 142141; fax (12) 93-62-65; f. 1919; Gen. Dir SHAMIL MAMMAD OGLY SHAHMAMMADOV.

Turan News Agency: Baku, Khagani St 33; tel. (12) 98-42-26; telex 142168; fax (12) 98-38-17; independent news agency.

Publishers

Azerbaijan Ensiklopediyasy (Azerbaijan Encyclopedia): 370004 Baku, Boyuk Gala St 41; tel. (12) 92-87-11; f. 1965; Editor-in-Chief I. O. VELIYEV (acting).

Azerneshr (State Publishing House): Baku, Gusi Hajiyev St 4; tel. (12) 92-50-15; f. 1924; various; Dir NAZIM IBRAHIMOV.

Elm (Azerbaijani Academy of Sciences Publishing House): 370073 Baku, Narimanov Ave 37; scientific books and journals.

Gyanjlik (Youth): 370005 Baku, Gusi Hajiyev St 4; books for children and young people; Dir E. T. ALIYEV.

Ishyg (Light): 370601 Baku, Gogol St 6; posters, illustrated publs; Dir G. N. ISMAILOV.

Maarif (Education): 370122 Baku, Tagizade St 4; educational books.

Madani-maarif Ishi (Education and Culture): 370146 Baku, Metbuat Ave, Block 529; tel. (12) 32-79-17; Editor-in-Chief ALOVSAT ATAMALY OGLY BASHIROV.

Medeniyyat (Publishing House of the 'Culture' Newspaper): 370146 Baku, Metbuat Ave, Block 529; tel. (12) 32-98-38; Dir SHAKMAR AKPER OGLY AKPERZADE.

Shur: 370001 Baku, M. Muchtarov St 6; tel. (12) 92-93-72; f. 1992; Dir GASHAM ISA OGLY ISABEYLI.

Yazychy (Writer): 370005 Baku, Natavan St 1; fiction; Dir F. M. MELIKOV.

Broadcasting and Communications

Radio and Television Company of Azerbaijan: 370011 Baku, Mekhti Hussein St 1; tel. (12) 39-85-85; telex 142214; fax (12) 39-54-52; Dir NIZAMI KHUDIYEV.

Radio Baku: f. 1926; broadcasts in Azerbaijani, Arabic, English and Turkish.

Azerbaijan National Television: f. 1956; programmes in Azerbaijani and Russian (14 hours a day).

BM–TI TV: Baku; f. 1993; first privately-owned TV station in Azerbaijan; broadcasts in Azerbaijani and Russian, five hours a day; Dir MAHMUD MAMMADOV.

Finance

(cap. = capital; res = reserves; dep. = deposits; m. = million; brs = branches; amounts in manats, unless otherwise stated)

BANKING

Central Bank

National Bank of Azerbaijan: 370070 Baku, Bjul-Bjul Ave 19; tel. (12) 93-50-58; telex 142116; fax (12) 93-55-41; f. 1992 as central bank and supervisory authority; Chair. ELMAN ROUSTAMOV.

State-owned Banks

Agroprombank (Agricultural Bank): 370006 Baku, Kadyrly St 125; tel. (12) 38-93-48; telex 335111; fax (12) 38-91-15; f. 1992 from br of USSR Agroprombank; 51% state-owned; cap. 10,000m. (June 1995); Chair. MAMED MUSAYEV; 75 brs.

Amanatbank: 370014 Baku, Fizuli St 71; tel. (12) 93-18-26; fax (12) 98-31-80; f. 1992 to replace br of USSR Sberbank; 361 brs.

International Bank of Azerbaijan: 370005 Baku, Nizami St 67; tel. (12) 93-03-07; telex 142159; fax (12) 93-40-91; f. 1992 to succeed br of USSR Vneshekonombank; carries out all banking services; cap. 20,000m., res 12,160m., dep. 259,892m. (Dec. 1996); Chair. FUAD AKHOUNDOV; 26 brs.

Prominvestbank (Industrial Investment Bank): 370014 Baku, Fizuli St 71; tel. (12) 98-79-46; telex 142389; fax (12) 98-12-66; f. 1992 to succeed br of USSR Prominvestbank.

Other Banks

In December 1996 there were about 160, mainly small, registered commercial banks operating in Azerbaijan, some of the most prominent of which are listed below:

Azakbank: 370070 Baku, Khagani St 25; tel. (12) 93-89-26; telex 142130; fax (12) 93-20-85; f. 1991; joint-stock bank with 100% private ownership; first Azerbaijani bank with foreign shareholders; deals with crediting and settlements carried out in local currency and trade and retail banking involving all major operations in foreign currencies; cap. 1,273.5m., plus US $2.6m. (Nov. 1995).

Azerigazbank: 370073 Baku, Inshaatchylar Ave 3; tel. (12) 97-50-17; telex 142198; joint-stock investment bank; Chair. AZER MOVSUMOV.

Günay Bank: 370095 Baku, Rasul Rza St 4/6; tel. (12) 98-14-29; telex 142185; fax (12) 98-14-39; f. 1992; first privately-owned bank in Azerbaijan; cap. 3,433m., res 477m., dep. 991.7m.; Chair. ALOISAT GODJAEV; 2 brs.

Inpatbank Investment Commercial Bank: 370125 Baku, Istiglaliyat St 9; tel. (12) 98-48-37.

Ruzubank: 370055 Baku, Istiglaliyat St 27; tel. (12) 92-42-58; telex 142337; fax (12) 92-78-12; f. 1992; joint-stock bank; cap. 216m., res 30.4m., dep. 1,834m.; Pres. S. A. ALIYEV; Chair. of Bd V. N. MUSAYEV.

Foreign Banks

In August 1997 there were seven foreign banks licensed to operate in Azerbaijan.

Bank Melli Iran: 370009 Baku, Salatin Askerova 85; tel. (12) 94-63-38; telex 142296; fax (12) 98-04-37; Man. HASSAN BAHADORY.

British Bank of the Middle East: 370000 Baku, Hyatt Regency Towers, POB 132; tel. (12) 90-70-00; fax (12) 90-70-06.

INSURANCE

Günay Anadolu Sigorta JV: Baku, Terlan Aliyarbekov St 3; tel. (12) 98-13-56; fax (12) 98-13-60; f. 1992; serves major international cos operating in Azerbaijan.

Trade and Industry

CHAMBER OF COMMERCE

Chamber of Commerce and Industry: 370601 Baku, Istiglaliyat St 31/33; tel. (12) 92-89-12; telex 142211; fax (12) 98-93-24; e-mail expo@chamber.baku.az; Pres. SULEYMAN BAYRAM OGLY TATLIYEV.

INDUSTRIAL AND TRADE ASSOCIATIONS

Azerbintorg: 370004 Baku, Beyuk Gala St 14; tel. (12) 92-97-61; telex 212189; fax (12) 98-32-92; imports and exports a wide range of goods (90.4% of exports in 1995); Chair. KAMAL R. ABBASOV; Dir SADIKH KAMAL OGLY MAMEDOV.

Azerkontract: 370141 Baku, A. Alekperov St 83/23; tel. (12) 39-42-96; fax (12) 39-91-76; Pres. MIRI AHAD OGLY GAMBAROV.

Azertijaret: 370000 Baku, Genjler Sq. 3; tel (12) 92-66-67; telex 142274; fax (12) 98-07-56; Dir RAFIK SH. ALIYEV.

Improtex: 370000 Baku, Azi Aslanov St 115; tel. (12) 98-91-00; telex 142152; fax (12) 90-92-25; e-mail group@impro.azerbaijan.su; Pres. FIZULI HASAN OGLY ALEKPEROV.

MIT International Trade Co: 370148 Baku, Mehti Guseyn St, Hotel Anba; tel. (12) 98-45-20; telex 142208; fax (12) 98-45-19; f. 1993; food products and consumer goods; Dir TAIR RAMAZAN OGLY ASADOV.

UTILITY

Gas

Azerigaz: 370025 Baku, Yusif Safarov St 23; tel. (12) 67-74-47; fax (12) 67-42-55; f. 1992; Pres. TARIEL ABULFAZ OGLY HUSSEINOV.

MAJOR STATE-OWNED INDUSTRIAL COMPANIES

Bakinsky Rabochy Engineering: 370034 Baku, Proletar St 10; tel. (12) 25-93-75; telex 142445; fax (12) 25-93-82; equipment for the petroleum industry, including pumping units and pipe transporters; Dir MAMED AKPER OGLY VELIYEV; 1,200 employees.

State Oil Company of the Azerbaijan Republic (SOCAR): 370004 Baku, Neftchilar Ave 73; tel. (12) 92-07-45; telex 142114; fax (12) 93-64-92; f. Sept. 1992, following a merger of the two state oil companies, Azerineft and Azneftkhimiya; conducts production and exploration activities, oversees refining and capital construction activities; two separate subsidiaries of Azerineft, Azneft (for onshore areas) and Kasmorneftgaz (for offshore areas), also merged; Pres. NATIK ALIYEV.

TRADE UNIONS

Association of Independent Workers of Azerbaijan: Baku; Chair. NEYMAT PANAKHLI.

Confederation of Azerbaijan Trade Unions: Baku; tel. and fax (12) 92-72-68; Chair. SATTAR MEHBALIYEV.

Free Trade Unions of Oil and Gas Industry Workers: mems are employees of c. 118 enterprises in oil and gas sectors; Chair. MIRMOVSUM MAHMUDOV.

Transport

RAILWAYS

In 1993 there were 2,125 km of railway track, of which 1,278 km were electrified. The overwhelming majority of total freight traffic is carried by the railways (some 78% in 1991). Railways connect Baku with Tbilisi (Georgia), Makhachkala (Dagestan, Russia) and Yerevan (Armenia). In 1997 passenger rail services between Moscow and Baku were resumed, and a service to Kiev (Ukraine) was inaugurated. The rail link with Armenia runs through the Autonomous Republic of Nakhichevan, but is currently disrupted, owing to Azerbaijan's economic blockade of Armenia. From Nakhichevan an international line links Azerbaijan with Tabriz (Iran). In 1991 plans were agreed with the Iranian Government for the construction of a rail line between Azerbaijan and Nakhichevan, which would pass through Iranian territory, thus bypassing Armenia. There is an underground railway in Baku (the Baku Metro); it comprises two lines (total length 28 km) with 18 stations.

Azerbaijani Railways: 370010 Baku, 1 May St 230; tel. (12) 98-44-67; f. 1992, following the dissolution of the former Soviet Railways; Pres. E. ISMAILOV.

ROADS

At 31 December 1995 the total length of roads in Azerbaijan was estimated at 57,770 km (28,900 km main roads, 24,300 km secondary roads and 4,570 km other roads). Some 94% of the total network was hard-surfaced.

SHIPPING

Shipping services on the Caspian Sea link Baku with Astrakhan (Russia), Turkmenbashy (Turkmenistan) and the Iranian ports of Bandar Anzali and Bandar Nowshar. At 31 December 1996 the Azerbaijani merchant fleet comprised 289 vessels, with a combined displacement of 636,112 grt. The total included 41 oil tankers (180,730 grt).

Shipowning Company

Caspian Shipping Company: 370005 Baku, Rasul Zade St 5; tel. (12) 93-20-58; telex 142102; fax (12) 93-53-39; f. 1858; nationalized by the Azerbaijani Govt in 1991; Pres. TEIMUR K. AKHMEDOV.

CIVIL AVIATION

Azerbaijan Airlines (Azerbaijan Hava Yollari): 370000 Baku, Azadlyg Ave 11; tel. (12) 93-84-05; telex 142222; fax (12) 96-52-37; f. 1992; state airline operating scheduled and charter passenger and cargo services to the CIS, Europe and the Middle East; Gen. Dir ALIYEV ADAEAT.

Tourism

Tourism is not widely developed. However, there are resorts on the Caspian Sea, including the Ganjlik international tourist centre, on the Apsheron Peninsula, near Baku, which has four hotels as well as camping facilities.

THE BAHAMAS

Introductory Survey

Location, Climate, Language, Religion, Flag, Capital

The Commonwealth of the Bahamas consists of about 700 islands and more than 2,000 cays and rocks, extending from east of the Florida coast of the USA to just north of Cuba and Haiti, in the West Indies. The main islands are New Providence, Grand Bahama, Andros, Eleuthera and Great Abaco. Almost 70% of the population reside on the island of New Providence. The remaining members of the group are known as the 'Family Islands'. A total of 29 of the islands are inhabited. The climate is mild and sub-tropical, with average temperatures of about 30°C (86°F) in summer and 20°C (68°F) in winter. The average annual rainfall is about 1,000 mm (39 ins). The official language is English. Most of the inhabitants profess Christianity, the largest denominations being the Anglican, Baptist, Roman Catholic and Methodist Churches. The national flag comprises three equal horizontal stripes, of blue, gold and blue, with a black triangle at the hoist, extending across one-half of the width. The capital is Nassau, on the island of New Providence.

Recent History

A former British colonial territory, the Bahamas attained internal self-government in January 1964, although the parliamentary system dates back to 1729. The first elections under universal adult suffrage were held in January 1967 for an enlarged House of Assembly. The Progressive Liberal Party (PLP), supported mainly by Bahamians of African origin and led by Lynden (later Sir Lynden) Pindling, won 18 of the 38 seats, as did the ruling United Bahamian Party (UBP), dominated by those of European origin. With the support of another member, the PLP formed a Government and Pindling became Premier. At the next elections, in April 1968, the PLP won 29 seats and the UBP only seven.

Following a constitutional conference in September 1968, the Bahamas Government was given increased responsibility for internal security, external affairs and defence in May 1969. In the elections of September 1972, which were dominated by the issue of independence, the PLP maintained its majority. Following a constitutional conference in December 1972, the Bahamas became an independent nation, within the Commonwealth, on 10 July 1973. Pindling remained Prime Minister. The PLP increased its majority in the elections of July 1977 and was again returned to power in the June 1982 elections, with 32 of the 43 seats in the House of Assembly. The remaining 11 seats were won by the Free National Movement (FNM), which had reunited for the elections after splitting into several factions over the previous five years.

Trading in illicit drugs, mainly for the US market, has become a major problem for the country, since many of the small islands and cays are used by drugs-traffickers in their smuggling activities. According to estimates by the US Department of Justice's Drug Enforcement Administration, some 70% of cocaine and 50% of marijuana entering the USA between the early 1970s and the early 1990s passed through the Bahamas. In 1983 allegations were made of widespread corruption, and the abuse of Bahamian bank secrecy laws by drugs-traffickers and US tax evaders. These claims were denied by Pindling, who announced, in November 1983, the appointment of a Royal Commission to investigate thoroughly all aspects of the drug trade in the Bahamas. The Commission's hearings revealed the extent to which money deriving from the drug trade had permeated Bahamian social and economic affairs. By November 1985 a total of 51 suspects had been indicted, including the assistant police commissioner. In October 1984 two cabinet ministers, implicated by the evidence presented to the Commission, resigned. The Commission also revealed that Pindling had received several million dollars in gifts and loans from business executives, although the Commission stated that there was no evidence that the payments were related to trade in narcotics. After unsuccessfully demanding Pindling's resignation, the Deputy Prime Minister, Arthur Hanna, resigned, and two other ministers, Perry Christie and Hubert Ingraham, were dismissed.

An early general election was held in June 1987. The issue of the illegal drugs trade and of drugs-related corruption within the Government dominated the campaign, but the PLP was returned to power for a fifth consecutive term, winning 31 of the 49 seats in the enlarged House of Assembly. The FNM won 16 seats, while the remaining two seats were secured by Christie and Ingraham as independents. The opposition later claimed that the election had been fraudulent, and in December the courts agreed to examine the allegations in nearly one-half of the constituencies.

Statistics relating to crime in 1987 indicated unprecedented levels of violent and drugs-related offences, and in February 1988 new claims of official corruption were made at the trial in Florida, USA, of a leading Colombian drugs-trafficker. Pindling and the Deputy Prime Minister were alleged to have accepted bribes, but this was vehemently denied.

In March 1990 the Minister of Agriculture, Trade and Industry, Ervin Knowles, resigned, following allegations of nepotism and the misuse of public funds. He was replaced by Christie, who rejoined the PLP. The other independent member, Ingraham, subsequently joined the FNM and became its leader in May, upon the death of Sir Cecil Wallace-Whitfield.

In mid-1992 Parliament was dissolved in preparation for a general election. The ensuing election campaign was disrupted by industrial unrest in the country's telephone and electricity companies, and by the continuing problems of the state airline, Bahamasair. Despite predictions of a PLP victory, the FNM won the general election on 19 August, securing 33 seats, while Pindling's party won the remaining 16. Ingraham replaced Pindling as Prime Minister, and, at the opening session of the House of Assembly, he announced a programme of measures aimed at increasing the accountability of government ministers, combating corruption and revitalizing the economy.

In late August 1992 the Bahamas were struck by Hurricane Andrew, which resulted in the deaths of four people and left more than 1,700 islanders homeless. The cost of the damage resulting from the storm was estimated at B $250m.

Acknowledging responsibility for his party's defeat in the 1992 general election, Pindling resigned as leader of the PLP, but, at the party's annual convention in January 1993, agreed to continue in office. In that month the electoral court ruled that slight irregularities had occurred in one seat secured by the PLP and, as a result, the FNM candidate took office, thus increasing the party's representation in the House of Assembly to 34.

The resignation of Orville Turnquest, the Deputy Prime Minister, Minister of Foreign Affairs and Attorney-General, in January 1995, in order to assume the post of Governor-General, prompted an extensive cabinet reorganization.

In March 1995 a marked increase in violent crime in parts of New Providence led the Government to announce the creation of a special police unit to tackle the problem. The outbreak of murders, violent assaults and vandalism, as well as an increase in the illegal possession of firearms, gave rise to widespread concern regarding the state of law and order in the country.

Meanwhile, the trade in illegal drugs remained widely evident in the country, and in late 1995 several local business executives, as well as close relatives of a member of Parliament, were arrested in connection with a large seizure of cocaine. In October of that year the Prime Minister introduced further legislation that aimed to prevent the abuse of Bahamian banks by drugs-traffickers, and thus improve the reputation of the country's financial sector, particularly in the USA.

The decision in March 1996 to hang a man convicted of murder in early 1991 was controversial, owing to the fact that the period spent awaiting execution had exceeded five years. In recognition of a prisoner's suffering in anticipation of execution, previous cases had held five years to constitute the maximum term after which the case should be subject to review with a possible commutation to life imprisonment. However, in October the Judicial Committee of the Privy Council ruled that to await execution for more than three and a half years would amount to inhuman punishment, and that all such cases should be commuted. The ruling was believed to affect 22 of the 39 prisoners under sentence of death in the Bahamas at that time.

At a general election held on 14 March 1997, in which 91.7% of the electorate participated, the FNM won 34 of the 40 seats in a reduced House of Assembly, and the PLP six. The FNM's overwhelming victory in the election, which was held five months earlier than necessary, was due both to the Prime Minister's success in reversing the decline in the economy and the involvement of the PLP in various financial scandals. Most notably, Pindling was implicated in February in the findings of a public inquiry (instituted in 1993) to investigate alleged corruption and misappropriation of funds in the three principal state corporations. Following the election, a cabinet reorganization was implemented. Pindling, who had retained his seat in the House of Assembly, resigned as leader of the PLP and was replaced by Christie. In July Pindling announced his retirement from parliamentary politics, and his seat was won by the FNM at a by-election in September.

The Bahamas' traditionally close relationship with the USA has been strained by the increasingly aggressive attitude of the US Government towards the bank secrecy laws and the drugs-smuggling in the islands. Nevertheless, the USA and the Bahamas have collaborated in a series of operations to intercept drugs-traffickers. Bilateral relations were adversely affected by a warning to US citizens, issued in July 1997 by the US State Department, against visiting the Bahamas, owing to the threat of unspecified violence against US interests in the Bahamas. In August an incendiary device exploded at a travel agency in Nassau commonly used by US tourists.

Relations with the Bahamas' other neighbours, Haiti and Cuba, have been strained by the influx of large numbers of illegal immigrants from both countries. In 1994 the Government announced that it would increase its efforts to deport approximately 40,000 Haitian immigrants residing illegally in the islands. During 1996 more than 400 Haitian and some 100 Cuban immigrants were deported. Between January and June 1997 414 Haitians were deported. However, despite the Government's rigorous deportation policy, the number of Haitian immigrants reportedly increased during August and September, when more than 500 immigrants were detained over a five week period.

In May 1997 the Bahamas agreed to establish diplomatic relations with the People's Republic of China, thus withdrawing diplomatic recognition from the Republic of China (Taiwan). Despite this decision (which was influenced by economic considerations, including the return of Hong Kong to the People's Republic of China in July), the Bahamas hoped to maintain economic links with Taiwan.

Government

Legislative power is vested in the bicameral Parliament. The Senate has 16 members, of whom nine are appointed by the Governor-General on the advice of the Prime Minister, four by the Leader of the Opposition and three after consultation with the Prime Minister. The House of Assembly has 40 members, elected for five years (subject to dissolution) by universal adult suffrage. Executive power is vested in the British monarch, represented by a Governor-General, who is appointed on the Prime Minister's recommendation and who acts, in almost all matters, on the advice of the Cabinet. The Governor-General appoints the Prime Minister and, on the latter's recommendation, selects the other ministers. The Cabinet is responsible to the House of Assembly.

Defence

The Royal Bahamian Defence Force, a paramilitary coastguard, is the only security force in the Bahamas, and numbered 860 (including 70 women) in August 1997. Expenditure on defence totalled B $19m. in 1996.

Economic Affairs

In 1995, according to estimates by the World Bank, the Bahamas' gross national product (GNP), measured at average 1993–95 prices, was US $3,297m., equivalent to US $11,940 per head (the highest level among Caribbean countries). During 1985–95, it was estimated, GNP per head decreased, in real terms, at an average rate of 1.0% per year. The population increased by an annual average of 1.7% over the same period. During 1985–94, according to UN estimates, gross domestic product (GDP) increased, in real terms, by 2.2% per year. In 1995 real GDP rose by an estimated 0.3% to total US $3,504m. at current prices.

Agriculture, hunting, forestry and fishing, which together accounted for only 3.4% of GDP in 1992 and engaged an estimated 5.4% of the employed labour force in 1994, have been developed by the Government in an attempt to reduce dependence on imports (80% of food supplies were imported in the 1980s). In 1996, however, agricultural production accounted for only 1.0% of total land area. The increase in agricultural output has resulted in the export of certain crops, particularly of cucumbers, tomatoes, pineapples, papayas, avocados, mangoes, limes and other citrus fruits. The development of commercial fishing has concentrated on conchs and crustaceans. In 1995 exports of Caribbean spiny lobster (crawfish) provided 60.6% of total domestic export earnings. There is also some exploitation of pine forests in the northern Bahamas.

Industry (comprising mining, manufacturing, construction and utilities) employed 12.9% of the working population in 1994 (construction accounted for 7.1%) and provided 10.9% of GDP in 1992.

Mining and manufacturing together contributed only 4.0% of GDP in 1992. Mining provided 0.2% of employment, and manufacturing 4.1%, in 1994. The islands' principal mineral resources are salt (which provided 14.5% of domestic export earnings in 1995) and aragonite.

The manufacturing sector contributed some 10% of GDP in 1982, since when it has declined, owing to the reduced activity and subsequent closure, in 1985, of the country's petroleum refinery. In 1992 the principal branches of manufacturing, based on the value of output, were beverages (accounting for 44.7% of the total), chemicals (16.2%) and printing and publishing. Exports of rum provided 27.5% of domestic export earnings in 1991, but the proportion declined to only 3.1% in 1995. Construction of a polystyrene factory in Freeport began in late 1995 at a cost of US $70m. Petroleum transhipment on Grand Bahama remains an important activity (crude petroleum accounted for some 53% of total trade in 1990, and petroleum products for about 11% in 1988). The construction sector has, since 1986, experienced much activity, owing to hotel-building and harbour developments.

Most of the energy requirements of the Bahamas are fulfilled by the petroleum that Venezuela and, particularly, Mexico provide under the San José Agreement (originally negotiated in 1980), which commits both the petroleum-producers to selling subsidized supplies, on favourable terms, to the developing countries of the region. Excluding transhipments of petroleum, imports of mineral fuels accounted for 12.6% of total imports in 1995.

Service industries constitute the principal sectors of the economy, providing 85.7% of GDP in 1992 and 81.1% of total employment in 1994. The Bahamas established its own shipping registry in 1976, and by 1983 had one of the largest 'open-registry' fleets in the world. At the end of 1996 a total of 1,186 vessels were registered under the Bahamian flag. With a combined displacement of 24.4m. grt, the fleet was the fourth largest in the world. In 1996 the country was ranked as the 12th largest 'offshore' financial centre in the world. Banking is the second most important economic activity in the Bahamas. Tourism is the predominant sector of the economy, directly accounting for about 27% of GDP in 1992, and employing some 30% of the working population in 1994. About 82% of tourists are from North America, although attempts are being made further to attract other countries. In 1996 the Central Bank announced a significant increase of tourists from non-traditional markets such as Latin America and Japan. Tourist arrivals increased steadily during the 1980s, and by 1991 amounted to some 3.7m. However, figures declined somewhat during the 1990s, as a result of recession in the important US market, an increase in the incidence of crime in the islands and competition from alternative destinations). Total arrivals were expected to increase to 4m.–5m. per year by 2000. Receipts from tourism declined to some B $880m. in 1991, but by 1996 totalled B $1,450m.

In 1996 the Bahamas recorded a visible trade deficit (excluding figures for petroleum and petroleum products not for domestic consumption) of US $990.0m., and there was a deficit of US $186.6m. on the current account of the balance of payments. The USA is the principal trading partner of the Bahamas, providing 92.8% of non-petroleum imports and taking 81.1% of total exports in 1995. Excluding the trade in petroleum and its products, the principal exports (including re-exports) in 1995 were food and live animals (36.8% of the total), machinery and transport equipment (26.1%) and inedible crude materials. In that year the principal imports were machinery and transport equipment (24.8% of the total), food and live animals, miscellaneous manufactured articles and basic manufactures.

In the year ending 30 June 1996 there was a budgetary deficit of B $44.7m. The deficit was projected to increase to B $51.5m. in 1996/97 and to B $190m. in 1997/98. At 31 December 1996 the external debt of the central Government was B $77.1m. The annual rate of inflation averaged 4.4% during 1985–95, but fell to 1.4% in 1996. Consumer prices increased by only 0.7% in the year to June 1997. The rate of unemployment declined from 13.3% of the labour force in April 1994 to an estimated at 11.1% in 1995.

The Bahamas is a member of the Caribbean Community and Common Market (CARICOM, see p. 119) and the Organization of American States (OAS, see p. 219), the Association of Caribbean States (see p. 259) and is a signatory of the Lomé Conventions with the EU (see p. 178).

Despite increasing competition, the Bahamas continues to be the principal tourist destination of the Caribbean. However, the tourism sector was severely affected by world recession in the early 1990s and, as a result, many hotels and casinos were closed, leading to some 1,500 redundancies in the industry. In 1995 legislation was approved which aimed to encourage tourism by reducing import duties on certain luxury goods. By 1996 the tourist industry was reportedly recovering: receipts from tourism increased by 7.7%, and visitor arrivals by 5.5%, in that year. Meanwhile, economic expansion through foreign investment continued to be restricted by fears of widespread corruption and instability, caused by the activities of illegal drugs-trafficking networks in the islands. In May 1993 the Government announced a programme of privatization of state enterprises. In 1995 further measures were introduced in an attempt to combat corruption in the financial sector and thus improve the reputation of the country's economic institutions. By 1997 almost all state-owned hotels had been privatized, with a number of foreign companies investing in various projects. The extent of the Government's commitment to increase foreign investment in the islands was demonstrated in 1996 when the Prime Minister led investment promotion missions to Canada, Argentina, Brazil and Chile.

Social Welfare

The health service is centralized in Nassau at the government general hospital, which has 457 beds. There is also a mental hospital (with 289 beds), a geriatric hospital (with 158 beds) and two private clinics on New Providence. There is a 74-bed hospital on Grand Bahama, and in the Family Islands several cottage hospitals and medical centres operate. A Flying Doctor Service supplies medical attention to islands that lack resident personnel. Flying Dental Services and nursing personnel from the Community Nursing Service are also provided. In 1993 there was one physician for every 692 inhabitants, and one hospital bed for every 258. A National Insurance Scheme, established in 1972, provides a wide range of benefits, including sickness, maternity, retirement and widows' pensions as well as social assistance payments. The scheme is administered by the National Insurance Board (NIB), which is funded mainly by contributions and investment income. Total expenditure by the NIB in 1994 was B $74.9m., including B $56.4m. in benefit payments. In 1990 the Government proposed a national health insurance scheme, financed by compulsory contributions from earnings. An Industrial Injuries Scheme has been established. In addition to payments by the NIB, there is some government expenditure on social welfare from the General Budget: in 1995/96 this included B $33.1m. on health (4.9% of total expenditure) and B $14.3m. on social services (2.1%).

Education

Education is compulsory between the ages of five and 14 years, and is provided free of charge in government schools. There are several private and denominational schools. Primary education begins at five years of age and lasts for six years. In 1993 enrolment at primary level included 95% of children in the relevant age-group. Secondary education, beginning at the age of 11, also lasts for six years and is divided into two equal cycles. In 1993 enrolment at secondary level included 87% of children in the relevant age-group. The University of the West Indies has an extra-mural department in Nassau, offering degree courses in hotel management and tourism. A training college for the tourist and hotel industry was established in 1992. Technical, teacher-training and professional qualifications can be obtained at the two campuses of the College of the Bahamas.

In 1995, according to UNESCO estimates, the average rate of adult illiteracy was 1.8% (males 1.5%; females 2.0%). Government expenditure on education in 1995/96 was B $125.0m. (or 18.4% of total spending from the General Budget).

Public Holidays

1998: 1 January (New Year's Day), 10 April (Good Friday), 13 April (Easter Monday), 1 June (Whit Monday), 5 June (Labour Day), 10 July (Independence Day), 4 August (Emancipation Day), 12 October (Discovery Day/Columbus Day), 25–26 December (Christmas).

1999: 1 January (New Year's Day), 2 April (Good Friday), 5 April (Easter Monday), 24 May (Whit Monday), 4 June (Labour Day), 10 July (Independence Day), 4 August (Emancipation Day), 12 October (Discovery Day/Columbus Day), 25–26 December (Christmas).

Weights and Measures

The imperial system is used.

Statistical Survey

Source (unless otherwise stated): Central Bank of the Bahamas, Frederick St, POB N-4868, Nassau; tel. 322-2193; telex 20115; fax 322-4321.

AREA AND POPULATION

Area: 13,939 sq km (5,382 sq miles).

Population: 209,505 at census of 12 May 1980; 254,685 (males 123,507, females 131,178) at census of 2 May 1990; 284,000 (official estimate) at mid-1996. *By island* (1990): New Providence 172,196 (including the capital, Nassau); Grand Bahama 40,898; Andros 8,187; Eleuthera 10,586.

Density (mid-1996): 20.4 per sq km.

Principal Town: Nassau (capital), population 171,542 (1990).

Births, Marriages and Deaths (1995): Registered live births 6,253 (birth rate 22.5 per 1,000); Registered marriages (1994) 2,537 (marriage rate 9.3 per 1,000); Registered deaths 1,638 (death rate 5.9 per 1,000). Source: UN, *Demographic Yearbook* and *Population and Vital Statistics Report*.

Expectation of Life (UN estimates, years at birth, 1990–95): 73.1 (males 68.7; females 77.9). Source: UN, *World Population Prospects: The 1994 Revision*.

Economically Active Population (sample survey, persons aged 15 years and over, excl. armed forces, April 1994): Agriculture, hunting and forestry 4,375; Fishing 2,130; Mining and quarrying 285; Manufacturing 4,980; Electricity, gas and water supply 1,690; Construction 8,515; Wholesale and retail trade; repair of motor vehicles, motorcycles and personal and household goods 20,415; Hotels and restaurants 18,215; Transport, storage and communications 10,650; Financial intermediation 6,090; Real estate, renting and business activities 5,660; Public administration and defence; compulsory social security 10,685; Education 6,265; Health and social work 5,260; Other community, social and personal service activities 6,625; Private households with employed persons 7,735; Activities not adequately defined 725; *Total employed* 120,300 (males 63,710, females 56,590); Unemployed 18,400 (males 9,150, females 9,250). *Total labour force* 138,700 (males 72,860, females 65,840). Source: ILO, *Yearbook of Labour Statistics*.

AGRICULTURE, ETC.

Principal Crops (FAO estimates, '000 metric tons, 1996): Roots and tubers 1; Sugar cane 55; Tomatoes 3; Onions (dry) 1; Other vegetables 18; Lemons and limes 3; Grapefruit and pomelos 13; Bananas 3; Other fruits 4. Source: FAO, *Production Yearbook*.

Livestock ('000 head, year ending September 1996): Cattle 1; Pigs 5; Sheep 6; Goats 16; Poultry (million) 3 (FAO estimate). Source: FAO, *Production Yearbook*.

Livestock Products ('000 metric tons, 1996): Poultry meat 9; Cows' milk 1*; Goats' milk 1*; Hen eggs 1* (*FAO estimates). Source: FAO, *Production Yearbook*.

Forestry (FAO estimates, '000 cu m, 1994): Roundwood removals: Sawlogs and veneer logs 17; Pulpwood 100; Total 117; Sawnwood production: Coniferous (softwood) 1. Source: FAO, *Yearbook of Forest Products*.

Fishing (metric tons, live weight): Total catch 10,081 in 1993; 9,707 in 1994; 9,638 (Caribbean spiny lobster 7,750) in 1995. Source: FAO, *Yearbook of Fishery Statistics*.

MINING AND INDUSTRY

Production (estimates, '000 metric tons, unless otherwise indicated): Unrefined salt 698* in 1991; Sulphur 48* in 1990; Electric energy 985m. kWh in 1994. *Data from the US Bureau of Mines. Source: UN, *Industrial Commodity Statistics Yearbook*.

FINANCE

Currency and Exchange Rates: 100 cents = 1 Bahamian dollar (B $). *Sterling and US Dollar equivalents* (30 September 1997): £1 sterling = B $1.6154; US $1 = B $1.0000; B $100 = £61.90 = US $100.00. *Exchange rate:* Since February 1970 the official exchange rate, applicable to most transactions, has been US $1 = B $1, i.e. the Bahamian dollar has been at par with the US dollar. There is also an investment currency rate, applicable to certain capital transactions between residents and non-residents and to direct investments outside the Bahamas. Since 1987 this exchange rate has been fixed at US $1 = B $1.225.

General Budget (estimates, B $ million, year ending 30 June 1996): *Revenue:* Total 633.0. *Expenditure:* Education 125.0; Uniformed services 71.6; Health 33.1; Finance and treasury 18.7; Tourism 48.5; Public works 56.3; Social services 14.3; Public debt interest 84.9; Total (incl. other) 677.7 (current 610.6; capital 67.1).

1996/97 (estimates, B $ million): Recurrent revenue 714.9; Recurrent expenditure 658.9; Capital expenditure 107.5.

1997/98 (estimates, B $ million): Recurrent revenue 778; Recurrent expenditure 846; Capital expenditure 122.

International Reserves (US $ million at 31 December 1996): Reserve position in IMF 9.0; Foreign exchange 162.4; Total 171.4. Source: IMF, *International Financial Statistics*.

Money Supply (B $ million at 31 December 1996): Currency outside banks 97.1; Demand deposits at deposit money banks 347.8; Total money 444.9. Source: IMF, *International Financial Statistics*.

Cost of Living (consumer price index; base: 1990 = 100): 118.0 in 1994; 120.4 in 1995; 122.1 in 1996. Source: IMF, *International Financial Statistics*.

Gross Domestic Product (B $ million at current prices): 3,323 in 1993; 3,425 in 1994; 3,504 in 1995. Source: IMF, *The Bahamas—Recent Economic Developments* (November 1996).

Expenditure on the Gross Domestic Product (B $ million at current prices, 1992): Government final consumption expenditure 448; Private final consumption expenditure 2,269; Gross capital formation 639; *Total domestic expenditure* 3,356; Exports of goods and services 1,405; *Less* Imports of goods and services 1,689; Statistical discrepancy -13; *GDP in purchasers' values* 3,059. Source: UN, *National Accounts Statistics*.

Gross Domestic Product by Economic Activity (B $ million at current prices, 1992): Agriculture, hunting, forestry and fishing 89; Manufacturing (incl. mining and quarrying) 105; Electricity, gas and water 88; Construction 91; Trade, restaurants and hotels 705; Transport, storage and communications 227; Finance, insurance, real estate and business services 610; Government services 336; Other community, social and personal services 310; Other services 55; Statistical discrepancy 13; *Sub-total* 2,629; Import duties 268; Other indirect taxes 162; *GDP in purchasers' values* 3,059. Source: UN, *National Accounts Statistics*.

Balance of Payments* (US $ million, 1996): Exports of goods f.o.b. 273.3; Imports of goods f.o.b. -1,263.3; *Trade balance* -990.0; Exports of services 1,616.4; Imports of services -710.7; *Balance on goods and services* -84.3; Other income received 77.3; Other income paid -196.6; *Balance on goods, services and income* -203.6; Current transfers received 25.7; Current transfers paid -8.7; *Current balance* -186.6; Capital account (net) -21.8; Direct investment from abroad 62.1; Other investment assets 13.9; Other investment liabilities 45.1; Net errors and omissions 79.7; *Overall balance* -7.6. Source: IMF, *International Financial Statistics*.

* The figures for merchandise imports and exports exclude petroleum and petroleum products, except imports for local consumption.

EXTERNAL TRADE*

Principal Commodities (US $ million, 1995): *Imports c.i.f.:* Food and live animals 209.0; Crude materials (inedible) except fuels 26.2; Mineral fuels, lubricants etc. 156.4; Chemicals 100.7; Basic manufactures 194.0; Machinery and transport equipment 308.6; Miscellaneous manufactured articles 202.9; Total (incl. others) 1,243.1. *Exports f.o.b.:* Food and live animals 64.8; Beverages and tobacco 3.5; Crude materials (inedible) except fuels 31.2; Chemicals 16.8; Basic manufactures 7.4; Machinery and transport equipment 46.0; Miscellaneous manufactured articles 6.0; Total (incl. others) 175.9.

1996 (US $ million): Total imports c.i.f. 1,262; Total exports f.o.b. 202. (Source: IMF, *International Financial Statistics*).

Principal Trading Partners (US $ million, 1991): *Imports c.i.f.:* Aruba 52.2; Canada 21.2; Denmark 23.7; France 20.8; Nigeria 23.9; USA 866.0; Total (incl. others) 1,091.2. *Exports f.o.b.:* Canada 6.7; France 14.5; Germany 6.2; Mexico 4.0; United Kingdom 27.2; USA 142.5; Total (incl. others) 225.1. Source: UN, *International Trade Statistics Yearbook*.

1995 (US $ million): *Imports c.i.f.* (excl. mineral fuels): Canada 11.3; USA 1,008.7; Total (incl. others) 1,086.7. *Exports f.o.b.:* Canada 3.4; United Kingdom 4.0; USA 142.6; Total (incl. others) 175.9.

* The data exclude imports and exports of crude petroleum and residual fuel oils that are brought into the Bahamas for storage on behalf of foreign companies abroad. Also excluded is trade in certain chemical products. In 1991 total imports were valued at US $1,801.2m. and total exports at US $1,517.1m.

TRANSPORT

Road Traffic (vehicles in use, 1993): 46,100 passenger cars; 11,900 commercial vehicles. Source: UN, *Statistical Yearbook*.

Shipping: *Merchant fleet* (displacement, '000 grt at 31 December): 22,915 in 1994; 23,603 in 1995; 24,409 in 1996 (Source: Lloyd's Register of Shipping, *World Fleet Statistics*). *International sea-borne freight traffic* (estimates, '000 metric tons, 1990): Goods loaded 5,920; Goods unloaded 5,705. Source: UN, *Monthly Bulletin of Statistics*.

Civil Aviation (1994): Kilometres flown (million) 4; Passengers carried ('000) 862; Passenger-km (million) 191; Total ton-km (million) 18. Source: UN, *Statistical Yearbook*.

TOURISM

Tourist Arrivals: 3,446,376 in 1994; 3,239,155 in 1995; 3,415,858 (1,368,038 by air, 2,047,820 by sea) in 1996.

Tourist Receipts (estimates, B $ million): 1,333 in 1994; 1,346 in 1995; 1,450 in 1996.

COMMUNICATIONS MEDIA

Radio Receivers (1994): 200,000 in use.

Television Receivers (1994): 61,000 in use.

Telephones (1993): 76,000 main lines in use.

Telefax Stations (1993): 550 in use.

Mobile Cellular Telephones (1993): 2,400 subscribers.

Daily Newspapers (1994): 3 titles (total circulation 35,000 copies).

Sources: UN, *Statistical Yearbook*; UNESCO, *Statistical Yearbook*.

EDUCATION

Pre-Primary (1993): 7 schools; 325 pupils.

Primary (1993): 115 schools; 33,343 students.

Secondary (1993): 37 junior/senior high schools (1990); 1,775 teachers; 28,532 students.

Tertiary (1987): 249 teachers; 5,305 students.

In 1993 there were 3,201 students registered at the College of the Bahamas.

Source: mainly UNESCO, *Statistical Yearbook*.

Directory

The Constitution

A representative House of Assembly was first established in 1729, although universal adult suffrage was not introduced until 1962. A new Constitution for the Commonwealth of the Bahamas came into force at independence, on 10 July 1973. The main provisions of the Constitution are summarized below:

Parliament consists of a Governor-General (representing the British monarch, who is Head of State), a nominated Senate and an elected House of Assembly. The Governor-General appoints the Prime Minister and, on the latter's recommendation, the remainder of the Cabinet. Apart from the Prime Minister, the Cabinet has no fewer than eight other ministers, of whom one is the Attorney-General. The Governor-General also appoints a Leader of the Opposition.

The Senate (upper house) consists of 16 members, of whom nine are appointed by the Governor-General on the advice of the Prime Minister, four on the advice of the Leader of the Opposition and three on the Prime Minister's advice after consultation with the Leader of the Opposition. The House of Assembly (lower house) has 40 members. A Constituencies Commission reviews numbers and boundaries at intervals of not more than five years and can recommend alterations for approval of the House. The life of Parliament is limited to a maximum of five years.

The Constitution provides for a Supreme Court and a Court of Appeal.

The Government

Head of State: HM Queen ELIZABETH II (succeeded to the throne 6 February 1952).

Governor-General: Sir ORVILLE TURNQUEST (appointed 22 February 1995).

THE CABINET
(December 1997)

Prime Minister: HUBERT ALEXANDER INGRAHAM.

Deputy Prime Minister and Minister of National Security with responsibility for the Public Service and Public Utilities: FRANK HOWARD WATSON.

Minister of Foreign Affairs: JANET G. BOSTWICK.

Minister of Tourism: CORNELIUS ALVIN SMITH.

Minister of Finance and Planning: WILLIAM C. ALLEN.

Minister of Education: Dame IVY LEONA DUMONT.

Attorney-General and Minister of Justice: TENNYSON ROSCOE GABRIEL WELLS.

Minister of Labour, Immigration and Training: THERESA MOXEY-INGRAHAM.

Minister of Social Development and Housing: ALGERNON SIDNEY PATRICK BENEDICT ALLEN.

Minister of Consumer Welfare and Aviation: PIERRE V. DUPUCH.

Minister of Public Works: TOMMY TURNQUEST.

Minister of Transport: JAMES F. KNOWLES.

Minister of Agriculture and Fisheries: EARL DEVEAUX.

Minister of Health and the Environment: Dr. RONALD KNOWLES.

MINISTRIES

Attorney-General's Office and Ministry of Justice: East Hill, POB N-3007, Nassau; tel. 322-1141; fax 356-4179.

Office of the Prime Minister: Cecil V. Wallace-Whitfield Centre, POB N-7147, Nassau; tel. 322-2805; fax 328-8294.

Office of the Deputy Prime Minister: POB N-3217, Nassau; tel. 356-6792; fax 356-6087.

Ministry of Agriculture and Fisheries: East Bay St, POB N-3028, Nassau; tel. 325-7502; fax 322-1767.

Ministry of Education: Shirley St, POB N-3913, Nassau; tel. 322-8140; fax 322-8491.

Ministry of Finance and Planning: Rawson Sq., POB N-3017, Nassau; tel. 327-1530; telex 20255; fax 327-1618.

Ministry of Foreign Affairs: East Hill St, POB N-3746, Nassau; tel. 322-7624; telex 20264; fax 328-8212.

Ministry of Health and the Environment: Royal Victoria Gardens, East Hill St, POB N-3730, Nassau; tel. 322-7425; telex 20516; fax 322-7788.

Ministry of Public Safety and Immigration: East Hill St, POB N-4891, Nassau; tel. 322-6250; fax 322-6546.

Ministry of Public Works: Rawson Sq., POB N-8156, Nassau; tel. 322-4831; telex 20255; fax 326-7344.

Ministry of Social Development and Housing: Frederick House, Frederick St, POB N–275, Nassau; tel. 323-3333; fax 323-3737.

Ministry of Tourism: Bay St, POB N-3701, Nassau; tel. 322-7500; fax 328-0945.

Ministry of Transport: Post Office Bldg, East Hill St, POB N-3008, Nassau; tel. 394-5095; telex 20263; fax 322-1767.

Ministry of Youth and Culture: Centerville House, POB N-10114, Nassau; tel. 322-3140; fax 324-4941.

Legislature

PARLIAMENT

Houses of Parliament: Parliament Sq., Nassau.

Senate

President: J. HENRY BOSTWICK.

There are 16 nominated members.

House of Assembly

Speaker: ITALIA JOHNSON.

The House has 40 members.

General Election, 14 March 1997

Party	Seats*
Free National Movement (FNM)	34
Progressive Liberal Party (PLP)	6
Total	40

* In September 1997 an FNM member replaced the former PLP leader, Sir Lynden Pindling, who announced his retirement from parliamentary politics in July.

Political Organizations

Free National Movement (FNM): POB N-10713, Nassau; tel. 393-7863; fax 393-7914; f. 1972; Leader HUBERT A. INGRAHAM.

People's Democratic Force (PDF): Nassau; f. 1989; Leader FRED MITCHELL.

Progressive Liberal Party (PLP): Nassau; tel. 325-2900; f. 1953; centrist party; Leader PERRY CHRISTIE; Chair. OBIE WILCHCOMBE.

Vanguard Party: Nassau; socialist; Leader Dr JOHN MCCARTNEY.

Diplomatic Representation

EMBASSY AND HIGH COMMISSION IN THE BAHAMAS

United Kingdom: Ansbacher Bldg, 3rd Floor, East St, POB N-7516, Nassau; tel. 325-7471; fax 323-3871; e-mail jlloyd@mail.bahamas.net.bs; High Commissioner: PETER YOUNG.

USA: Mosmar Bldg, Queen St, POB N-8197, Nassau; tel. 322-1181; telex 20138; fax 328-7838; Ambassador: SIDNEY WILLIAMS.

Judicial System

The Judicial Committee of the Privy Council (based in the United Kingdom), the Bahamas Court of Appeal, the Supreme Court and the Magistrates' Courts are the main courts of the Bahamian judicial system.

All courts have both a criminal and civil jurisdiction. The Magistrates' Courts are presided over by professionally qualified Stipendiary and Circuit Magistrates in New Providence and Grand Bahama, and by Commissioners sitting as Magistrates in the other Family Islands.

Whereas all magistrates are empowered to try offences which may be tried summarily, a Stipendiary and Circuit Magistrate may, with the consent of the accused, also try certain less serious indictable offences. The jurisdiction of magistrates is, however, limited by law.

The Supreme Court consists of the Chief Justice, a Senior Justice and five Judges. The Supreme Court also sits in Freeport, with one Judge.

Appeals in almost all matters lie from the Supreme Court to the Court of Appeal, with further appeal in certain instances to the Judicial Committee of the Privy Council.

Supreme Court of the Bahamas: Parliament Sq., POB N-8167, Nassau; tel. 322-3315; fax 323-6895; Chief Justice JOAN SAWYER.

Court of Appeal: POB N-8167, Nassau; Pres. KENNETH C. HENRY.

Magistrates' Courts: POB N-421, Nassau; 14 magistrates and a circuit magistrate.

Registrar of the Supreme Court: NATHANIEL M. DEAN; POB N-167, Nassau.

Attorney-General: TENNYSON ROSCOE GABRIEL WELLS.

Office of the Attorney-General: East Hill, POB N-3007, Nassau; tel. 322-1141; fax 322-2255; Dir of Legal Affairs MICHAEL F. HAMILTON; Dir of Public Prosecutions VELMA HYLTON.

Religion

Most of the population profess Christianity, but there are also small communities of Jews and Muslims. Traditional beliefs in witchcraft and 'bush medicine' persist in some areas; these practices are known as voodoo or obeah.

CHRISTIANITY

According to the census of 1990, there were 79,465 Baptists (31.2% of the population), 40,894 Roman Catholics (16.0%) and 40,881 Anglicans (16.0%). Other important denominations include the Pentecostal Church (5.5%), the Church of Christ (5.0%) and the Methodists (4.8%).

Bahamas Christian Council: POB SS-5863, Nassau; tel. 393-2710; f. 1948; 10 mem. churches; Sec. Rt Rev. HARCOURT PINDER.

The Roman Catholic Church

The Bahamas comprises the single diocese of Nassau, suffragan to the archdiocese of Kingston in Jamaica. At 31 December 1995 there were an estimated 45,237 adherents in the Bahamas. The Bishop participates in the Antilles Episcopal Conference (whose Secretariat is based in Port of Spain, Trinidad). The Turks and Caicos Islands are also under the jurisdiction of the Bishop of Nassau.

Bishop of Nassau: Rt Rev. LAWRENCE A. BURKE, The Hermitage, West St, POB N-8187, Nassau; tel. 322-28919; fax 322-2599.

The Anglican Communion

Anglicans in the Bahamas are adherents of the Church in the Province of the West Indies (the metropolitan is based in St John's, Antigua and Barbuda). The diocese of Nassau and the Bahamas also includes the Turks and Caicos Islands.

Bishop of Nassau and the Bahamas: Rt Rev. DREXEL GOMEZ, Bishop's Lodge, POB N-7107, Nassau; tel. 322-3015; fax 322-7943.

Other Churches

Bahamas Conference of Seventh-day Adventists: Shirley St, POB N-356, Nassau; tel. 322-3032; fax 325-7248.

Bahamas Evangelical Church Association: Carmichael Rd, POB N-1224, Nassau; tel. 362-1024.

Greek Orthodox Church: Church of the Annunciation, West St, POB N-823, Nassau; tel. 322-4382; f. 1928; part of the Archdiocese of North and South America, based in New York (USA); Priest Rev. THEOPHANIS KULYVAS.

Methodist Church in the Bahamas: POB N-3702, Nassau; Gen. Superintendent Rev. Dr KENNETH HUGGINS; Pres. Rev. CHARLES SWEETING.

Other denominations include the Assemblies of Brethren, the Jehovah's Witnesses, the Salvation Army, Pentecostal, Presbyterian, Lutheran and Assembly of God churches.

BAHÁ'Í FAITH

Bahá'í National Spiritual Assembly: Shirley St, POB N-7105, Nassau; tel. 326-0607.

OTHER RELIGIONS

Islam: there is a small community of Muslims in the Bahamas.

Judaism: most of the Bahamian Jewish community are based on Grand Bahama. There were 126 Jews, according to the 1990 census.

The Press

NEWSPAPERS

Freeport News: Cedar St, POB F-7, Freeport; tel. 352-8321; fax 352-8324; f. 1961; daily; Gen. Man. DEBRA S. DAMES; Editor OSWALD BROWN; circ. 4,000.

Nassau Daily Tribune: Shirley St, POB N-3207, Nassau; tel. 322-1986; fax 328-2398; f. 1903; Publr and Editor EILEEN DUPUCH CARRON; circ. 12,000.

Nassau Guardian: 4 Carter St, Oakes Field, POB N-3011, Nassau; tel. 323-5654; telex 20100; fax 325-3379; f. 1844; daily; Publr and Gen. Man. KENNETH N. FRANCIS; Editor OSWALD BROWN; circ. 14,100.

The Punch: Nassau; Editor IVAN JOHNSON.

PERIODICALS

The Bahamas Financial Digest: Miramar House, Bay and Christie Sts, POB N-4271, Nassau; tel. 356-2981; fax 356-7118; e-mail michael.symonette@batelnet.bs; f. 1973; 4 a year; business and investment; Publr and Editor MICHAEL A. SYMONETTE.

Bahamas Tourist News: Bayparl Bldg, Parliament St, POB N-4855, Nassau; tel. 322-3724; monthly; Editor BOBBY BOWER; circ. 360,000 (annually).

Bahamian Review Magazine: Collins Ave, POB N-494, Nassau; tel. 322-8922; f. 1952; monthly; banking, finance, tourism; Editor WILLIAM CARTWRIGHT; circ. 55,000.

Nassau: Miramar House, Bay and Christie Sts, POB N-4846, Nassau; tel. 356-2981; fax 356-7118; f. 1984; literature, current affairs, reviews; 4 a year; Publr MICHAEL A. SYMONETTE.

Nassau City Magazine: Miramar House, Bay and Christie Sts, POB N-4846, Nassau; tel. 356-2981; fax 356-7118.

Official Gazette: c/o Cabinet Office, POB N-7147, Nassau; tel. 322-2805; weekly; publ. by the Cabinet Office.

Publishers

Bahama Publishers Ltd: N-3011, Nassau; tel. 323-5654; fax 328-8943; Gen. Man. KENNETH N. FRANCIS.

Bahamas Free Press Ltd: POB N-8195, Nassau; tel. 323-8961.

Bahamas International Publishing Co Ltd: Miramar House, Bay and Christie Sts, POB N-4846, Nassau; tel. 356-2981; fax 356-7118; e-mail michael.symonette@batelnet.bs.

Commonwealth Publications Ltd: POB N-4826, Nassau; tel. 322-1038; telex 20275; f. 1979; publishes *Bahamas Business Guide* (a guide to doing business in the Bahamas and the Government's economic and financial policies) and *An Economic History of the Bahamas*.

Etienne Dupuch Jr Publications Ltd: Oakes Field, POB N-7513, Nassau; tel. 323-5665; fax 323-5728; publishes *Bahamas Handbook*, *Trailblazer* maps, *What To Do* magazines, *Welcome Bahamas*, *Tadpole* (educational colouring book) series and *Dining and Entertainment Guide*; Dirs ETIENNE DUPUCH, Jr, S. P. DUPUCH.

Firth Publications: POB N-8350, Cable Beach, New Providence; tel. 327-7748.

Island Publishing Co: Musgrove Chippingham, POB N-7937, Nassau; tel. 325-2698.

Broadcasting and Communications

TELECOMMUNICATIONS

Bahamas Telecommunications Co (Batelco): POB N-3048, JFK Dr, Nassau; tel. 323-4911; fax 393-4798; state-owned; scheduled for privatization in late 1998.

RADIO

Broadcasting Corporation of the Bahamas: POB N-1347, Centreville, New Providence; tel. 322-4623; telex 20253; fax 322-3924; f. 1936; govt-owned; commercial; Chair. MICHAEL D. SMITH; Gen. Man. SANDRA J. KNOWLES.

Radio Bahamas: f. 1936; broadcasts 24 hours per day on four stations: the main Radio Bahamas (ZNS1), Radio New Providence (ZNS2), which are both based in Nassau, Radio Power 104.5 FM, and the Northern Service (ZNS3—Freeport; f. 1973; Station Man. EDWIN LIGHTBOURN); Programme Man. CARL BETHEL.

TELEVISION

Broadcasting Corporation of the Bahamas: (see Radio).

Bahamas Television: f. 1977; broadcasts for Nassau, New Providence and the Central Bahamas; transmitting power of 50,000 watts; full colour; Programme Man. DEBBIE BARTLETT.

US television programmes and some satellite programmes can be received. Freeport, the second city, has a cable television network which broadcasts four hours per day.

Finance

In recent years the Bahamas has developed into one of the world's foremost financial centres (there are no corporation, income, capital gains or withholding taxes or estate duty), and finance has become a significant feature of the economy. At mid-1997 there were 425 banks and trust companies operating in the Bahamas, of which 180 had a physical presence in the islands.

BANKING

(cap. = capital; dep. = deposits; res = reserves; m. = million; brs = branches)

Central Bank

The Central Bank of the Bahamas: Frederick St, POB N-4868, Nassau; tel. 322-2193; telex 20115; fax 322-4321; f. 1973; bank of issue; cap. B $3.0m., res B $73.8m., dep. B $11.8m. (Dec. 1996); Gov. JULIAN FRANCIS.

Development Bank

The Bahamas Development Bank: Cable Beach, West Bay St, POB N-3034, Nassau; tel. 327-5780; telex 20297; fax 327-5047; f. 1978 to fund approved projects and channel funds into appropriate investments; Chair. LARRY GIBSON.

Principal Bahamian-based Banks

Bahama Bank Ltd: POB N-272, Nassau; f. 1964.

Bank of the Bahamas Ltd: 50 Shirley St, POB N-7118, Nassau; tel. 326-2560; fax 325-2762; f. 1970, name changed 1988, when Bank of Montreal Bahamas Ltd became jointly owned by Govt and European Canadian Bank; 80% owned by Govt in 1995; cap. B $10.0m., res B $0.2m., dep. B $149.3m. (June 1996); Chair. J. O. KENNING; Man. Dir P. M. ALLEN-DEAN; 6 brs.

Commonwealth Bank Ltd: 610 Bay St, POB SS-5541, Nassau; tel. 394-7373; f. 1960; Pres. JAMES D. COCKWELL; 8 brs.

Deltec Banking Corporation Ltd: Deltec House, Lyford Cay, POB N-3229, Nassau; tel. 362-4549; fax 362-4623; f. 1961; cap. US $7.2m., res US $38.9m., dep. US $34.3m. (Aug. 1996); Pres. MATTHEW F. GIBBONS; Chair. PETER STORMONTH DARLING.

Eni International Bank Ltd: IBM Bldg, East Bay St, POB SS-6377, Nassau; tel. 322-1928; fax 323-8600; f. 1971 as Tradinvest Bank and Trust Co of Nassau Ltd, name changed 1985; cap. US $200.0m., res US $60.0m., dep. US $2,105.8m. (Dec. 1995); Pres. and Chair. FRANCO LUGLI.

Eurobanco Bank Ltd: Bolan House, King and George Sts, Nassau; tel. 356-5454; fax 356-9432; f. 1992; cap. US $3.0m., dep. US $136.3m. (Dec. 1994); Pres. CHRISTOPHER GEOFFREY DOUGLAS HOOPER.

Fidenas International Bank Ltd: Bolam House, George St, POB N-4816, Nassau; tel. 325-6052; telex 20278; fax 325-2592; f. 1979; cap. US $10.0m., dep. US $50.3m. (Dec. 1992); Chair. GEOFFREY P. JURICK; Pres. COLIN G. HONESS.

Finance Corporation of the Bahamas Ltd (FinCo): Charlotte and Shirley Sts, POB N-3038, Nassau; tel. 322-4822; fax 326-3031; f. 1953; Man. Dir PETER THOMPSON; 4 brs.

Guaranty Trust Bank Ltd: Charlotte House, Charlotte St, POB N-10051, Nassau; tel. 323-7441; fax 326-8489; f. 1962; cap. US $18.0m., dep. US $22.9m. (Jan. 1995); Chair. Sir GERALD CASH; Man. Dir ROBERT McLEAN BEASE.

HSBC Equator Bank Ltd: 2nd Floor, Claughton House, Shirley and Charlotte Sts, Nassau; tel. 322-2754; telex 20409; fax 326-5706; f. 1975 as Equator Bank Ltd, name changed in 1996; cap. US $1.0m., res US $12.7m., dep. US $121.4m. (Dec. 1994); CEO FRANKLIN H. KENNEDY.

W & P Bank and Trust Co Ltd: Cumberland House, 27 Cumberland St, POB N-3918, Nassau; tel. 326-0282; fax 326-5213; f. 1984 as Demanchy Worms and Co International, renamed in 1996; cap. US $3.0m., res US $2.1m., dep. US $205.1m. (Dec. 1995); Chair. JEAN SEVAUX; Gen. Man. PATRICK DE BRAQUILANGES.

Principal Foreign Banks

Banco Internacional de Costa Rica Ltd (Costa Rica): Bank Lane, Nassau; tel. 374-0855; fax 381-6971; f. 1989; Chair. ORLANDO GUERRERO; CEO JORGE SÁNCHEZ.

Bank Leu Ltd (Switzerland): Norfolk House, Frederick St, POB N-3926, Nassau; tel. 326-5054; fax 323-8828; subsidiary of Bank Leu AG, Zurich.

Bank of Nova Scotia (Canada): Scotiabank Bldg, Rawson Sq., POB N-7518, Nassau; tel. 322-1071; telex 20187; fax 322-7989; Man. A. C. ALLEN; 13 brs.

Barclays Bank PLC (United Kingdom): Charlotte House, Shirley St, POB N-3221, Nassau; tel. 325-7384; telex 20149; fax 322-8267; Man. MARK TEVERSHAM.

BSI Overseas (Bahamas) Ltd (Italy): Norfolk House, Frederick St, POB N-7130, Nassau; tel. 394-9200; telex 20197; fax 394-9220; f. 1990; wholly-owned subsid. of Banca della Svizzera Italiana; cap. US $10.0m., res US $32.0m., dep. US $1,317.2m. (Dec. 1995); Chair. Dr A. GYSI; Man. IVOR J. HERRINGTON.

Canadian Imperial Bank of Commerce (Canada): 308 East Bay St, POB N-8329, Nassau; tel. 393-4710; fax 393-4280; Area Man. TERRY HILTS; 9 brs.

Citibank NA (USA): Citibank Bldg, Thompson Blvd, Oakes Field, POB N-8158, Nassau; tel. 322-4240; telex 20153; fax 323-3088; Gen. Man. PAUL D. MAJOR; 2 brs.

Credit Suisse (Bahamas) Ltd (Switzerland): Rawson Sq., POB N-4928, Nassau; tel. 322-8345; subsidiary of Credit Suisse Zurich; portfolio and asset management, offshore company management, trustee services; Man. Dir GREGORY BETHEL.

Handelsfinanz-CCF Bank International Ltd (Switzerland): Maritime House, Frederick St, POB N-10441, Nassau; tel. 328-8644; fax 328-8600; f. 1971; cap. US $5.0m., res US $1.9m., dep. US $670.4m. (Dec. 1995); Pres. and Gen. Man. FERDINANDO M. MENCONI.

Lloyds Bank International (Bahamas) Ltd (United Kingdom): Bolam House, King and George Sts, POB N-1262, Nassau; tel. 322-8711; telex 20107; fax 322-8719; f. 1977; cap. US $25.0m., res US $27.5m., dep. US $325.4 (Dec. 1994); Gen. Man. R. C. SEAMER; Asst Man. J. R. BROWN; 1 br.

Overseas Union Bank and Trust (Bahamas) Ltd (Switzerland): 250 Bay St, POB N-8184, Nassau; tel. 322-2476; fax 323-8771; f. 1980; cap. US $5.0m., res US $3.1m., dep. US $133.7m. (Dec. 1995); Chair. Dr CARLO SGANZINI.

Pictet Bank and Trust Ltd (Switzerland): Charlotte House, Charlotte St, POB N-4837, Nassau; tel. 322-3938; telex 20308; f. 1978; cap. US $1.0m., res US $10.0m., dep. US $126.2m. (Dec. 1995); Chair. CLAUDE DEMOLE.

The Royal Bank of Canada Ltd (Canada): 323 Bay St, POB N-7537, Nassau; tel. 322-8700; telex 20182; fax 323-6381; internet http://www.royalbank.com; Man. Dir G. B. GREENSLAND; Vice-Pres. D. C. GALE; 16 brs.

The Royal Bank of Scotland (Nassau) Ltd (United Kingdom): Shirley and Charlotte Sts, POB N-3045, Nassau; tel. 322-4643; fax 326-7559; f. 1951 as E. D. Sassoon Bank and Trust Ltd, name changed 1978, 1986 and 1989; cap. US $2.0m., res US $1.0m., dep. US $67.9m. (Sept. 1995); Chair. C. G. PEARSON; CEO T. A. CAPELL.

Swiss Bank Corpn (Overseas) Ltd (Switzerland): Swiss Bank House, East Bay St, POB N-7757, Nassau; tel. 322-7570; telex 20348; fax 323-8953; f. 1968; cap. US $4.0m., dep. US $393.9m. (Dec. 1995); Chair. ERNST BALSIGER; Exec. Dir PHILIP WHITE.

Principal Bahamian Trust Companies

Ansbacher (Bahamas) Ltd: Bitco Bldg, Bank Lane, POB N-7768, Nassau; tel. 322-1161; telex 20143; fax 326-5020; incorporated 1957 as Bahamas International Trust Co Ltd, name changed 1994; cap. B $1.0m., res B $10.5m., dep. B $70.3m. (Sept. 1994); Chair. PETER N. SCAIFE; Man. Dir DAVID L. E. FAWKES.

Chase Manhattan Trust Corpn: Shirley and Charlotte Sts, POB N-3708, Nassau; tel. 322-8792; telex 20140; Gen. Man. KEN BROWN; 4 brs.

Coutts and Co (Bahamas) Ltd: West Bay St, POB N-7788, Nassau; tel. 326-0404; telex 20111; fax 326-6709; f. 1936; Swiss-registered subsid. of National Westminster Bank (United Kingdom); cap. US $2.0m., dep. US $652.9m. (Nov. 1993); Chair. PETER G. STRADLING; Man. Dir WILLIAM H. JENNINGS.

Euro-Dutch Trust Co (Bahamas) Ltd: Charlotte House, POB N-9204, Nassau; f. 1975; tel. 325-1033; telex 20303.

Leadenhall Trust Co Ltd: Cumberland Court, 1 Cumberland St, POB N-1965, Nassau; tel. 325-5508; fax 328-7030; f. 1976; Man. Dir DAVID J. ROUNCE.

MeesPierson Trust: Windermere House, 404 East Bay St, Nassau; tel. 393-8777; fax 393-9021; subsidiary of MeesPierson International AG of Zug, Switzerland; Chair. IAN FAIR.

Rawson Trust Co Ltd: Euro Canadian Centre, POB N-8327, Nassau; tel. 322-7461; telex 20172; fax 326-6177; f. 1969.

Winterbotham Trust Co Ltd: Bolam House, King and George Sts, POB N-3026, Nassau; tel. 356-5454; fax 356-9432; e-mail winterbm@bahamas.net.bs.

Bankers' Organizations

Association of International Banks and Trust Companies in the Bahamas: POB N-7880, Nassau; tel. 394-6755.

Bahamas Institute of Bankers: The Plaza, Mackey St, POB N-3202, Nassau; tel. 393-0456; fax 393-0456.

INSURANCE

The leading British and a number of US and Canadian companies have agents in Nassau and Freeport. Local insurance companies include the following:

Bahamas First General Insurance Co Ltd: Third Terrace and Collins Ave, POB N-1216, Nassau; tel. 326-5439; fax 326-5472.

Bahamas International Assurance Co: Palmdale Ave, POB SS-6201, Nassau; tel. 322-3196.

Bahamas Pioneer Insurance Co Ltd: East Shirley St and Kemp Rd, POB SS-6207, Nassau; tel. 325-7468.

Trade and Industry

DEVELOPMENT ORGANIZATIONS

Bahamas Agricultural and Industrial Corpn (BAIC): BAIC Bldg, East Bay St, POB N-4940, Nassau; tel. 322-3740; fax 322-2123; f. 1981 to amalgamate Bahamas Development Corpn and Bahamas Agricultural Corpn for the promotion of greater co-operation between tourism and other sectors of the economy through the development of small- and medium-sized enterprises; Exec. Chair. BERKLEY EVANS.

Bahamas Investment Authority: Cecil V. Wallace-Whitfield Centre, POB CB-10980, Nassau; tel. 327-5970; fax 327-5907; Exec. Dir BASIL H. ALBURY.

Nassau Paradise Island Promotion Board: Dean's Lane, Fort Charlotte, POB N-7799, Nassau; tel. 322-8381; fax 325-8998; f. 1970; Chair. GEORGE R. MYERS; Sec. MICHAEL C. RECKLEY; 30 mems.

CHAMBER OF COMMERCE

Bahamas Chamber of Commerce: Shirley St, POB N-665, Nassau; tel. 322-2145; fax 322-4649; f. 1935 to promote, foster and protect trade, industry and commerce; Pres. D. NEIL MCKINNEY; Exec. Dir RUBY L. SWEETING; 450 mems.

EMPLOYERS' ASSOCIATIONS

Bahamas Association of Architects: Shirley St, POB N-1207, Nassau; tel. 325-6115; Pres. WINSTON JONES.

Bahamas Association of Land Surveyors: POB N-10147, Nassau; tel. 322-4569; Pres. DONALD THOMPSON; Vice-Pres. GODFREY HUMES; 30 mems.

Bahamas Association of Shipping Agents: POB N-1451, Nassau.

Bahamas Boatmen's Association: POB ES-5212, Nassau; f. 1974; Pres. and Sec. FREDERICK GOMEZ.

Bahamas Contractors' Association: POB N-8049, Nassau; Pres. BRENDON C. WATSON; Sec. EMMANUEL ALEXIOU.

Bahamas Employers' Confederation: POB N-166, Nassau; tel. 393-5613; fax 322-4649; f. 1963; Pres. DOROTHY BAIN.

Bahamas Hotel Employers' Association: Dean's Lane, Fort Charlotte, POB N-7799, Nassau; tel. 322-2262; telex 20392; fax 326-5346; f. 1958; Pres. J. BARRIE FARRINGTON; Exec. Dir MICHAEL C. RECKLEY; 26 mems.

Bahamas Institute of Chartered Accountants: Shirley St and Elizabeth Ave, POB N-7037, Nassau; tel. 325-0272; fax 325-0272; f. 1971; Pres. L. EDGAR MOXEY.

Bahamas Institute of Commerce: Robinson Rd, POB N-7917, New Providence; tel. 323-6117.

Bahamas Institute of Professional Engineers: Nassau; tel. 322-3356; fax 323-8503; Pres. IVERN DAVIES.

Bahamas Motor Dealers' Association: POB N-4824, Nassau; tel. 322-1149; fax 328-1922; Pres. RICK LOWE.

Bahamas Petroleum Retailers' Association: Nassau; tel. 325-1141; fax 325-3936.

Bahamas Real Estate Association: Bahamas Chamber Bldg, POB N-8860, Nassau; tel. 325-4942; fax 322-4649; Pres. BARBARA BROOKS.

Nassau Association of Shipping Agents: Nassau.

Soft Drink Bottlers' Association: POB N-272, Nassau.

UTILITIES

Electricity

The Bahamas Electricity Corpn (BEC): POB N-7509, Pond and Tucker Rd, Nassau; tel. 325-4101; fax 323-6852; state-owned; scheduled for privatization in 1999; provides 70% of the islands' power-generating capacity.

Freeport Power Co Ltd: POB F-888, Mercantile Bldg, Cedar St, Freeport; tel. 352-6611.

Gas

Bahamas Gas Ltd: Nassau; tel. 325-6401.

Water

The Bahamas Water and Sewerage Corpn: Nassau.

TRADE UNIONS

Commonwealth of the Bahamas Trade Union Congress (CBTUC): Nassau; all Bahamian unions are mems of the CBTUC; affiliated to the Caribbean Congress of Labour; Pres. ARLINGTON MILLER; 11,000 mems.

The main unions are as follows:

Bahamas Airport, Service and Industrial Workers' Union: Workers House, Balfour Ave, POB N-3364, Nassau; tel. 323-5030; f. 1958; Pres. HENRY DEAN; Gen. Sec. RAMON NEWBALL; 532 mems.

Bahamas Brewery, Distillers and Allied Workers' Union: POB N-299, Nassau; f. 1968; Pres. BRADICK CLEARE; Gen. Sec. DAVID KEMP; 140 mems.

Bahamas Communication and Public Officers' Union: East St, POB N-3190, Nassau; tel. 322-1537; fax 323-8719; f. 1973; Pres. KEITH E. ARCHER; Sec.-Gen. AUDLEY G. WILLIAMS; 1,611 mems.

Bahamas Doctors' Union: Nassau; Pres. Dr EUGENE NEWERY; Gen. Sec. GEORGE SHERMAN.

Bahamas Electrical Workers' Union: East West Highway, POB GT-2535, Nassau; tel. 323-1838; telex 2535; Pres. SAMUEL MITCHELL; Gen. Sec. JONATHAN CAMBRIDGE.

Bahamas Hotel Catering and Allied Workers' Union: POB GT-2514, Nassau; tel. 323-5933; fax 325-6546; f. 1958; Pres. THOMAS BASTIAN; Gen. Sec. LEONARD WILSON; 5,500 mems.

Bahamas Housekeepers' Union: POB 898, Nassau; f. 1973; Pres. MERLENE DECOSTA; Gen. Sec. MILLICENT MUNROE.

Bahamas Maritime Port and Allied Workers' Union: POB SS-6501, Nassau; tel. 328-7502; Pres. ANTHONY WILLIAMS; Sec.-Gen. FREDERICK N. RODGERS.

Bahamas Musicians' and Entertainers' Union: Horseshoe Drive, POB N-880, Nassau; tel. 322-3734; fax 323-3537; f. 1958; Pres. LEROY (DUKE) HANNA; Sec. RONALD SIMMS; 410 mems.

Bahamas Oil and Fuel Services Workers' Union: POB 10597, Nassau; f. 1956; Pres. VINCENT MUNROE.

Bahamas Public Services Union: Wulff Rd, POB N-4692, Nassau; tel. 325-0038; fax 323-5287; f. 1959; Pres. WILLIAM MCDONALD; Sec.-Gen. HUGH M. BOWLEG; 4,247 mems.

Bahamas Taxi-Cab Union: POB N-1077, Nassau; tel. 323-5952; telex 20480; Pres. OSWALD NIXON; Gen. Sec. ROSCOE WEECH.

Bahamas Transport, Agricultural, Distributive and Allied Workers' Trade Union: Wulff Rd, Nassau; tel. 323-4538; f. 1959; Pres. RANDOLF FAWKES; Gen. Sec. MAXWELL N. TAYLOR; 1,362 mems.

Bahamas Union of Teachers: 104 Bethel Ave, Stapledon Gardens, POB N-3482, Nassau; tel. 323-7085; fax 323-7124; f. 1945; Pres. DONALD SYMONETTE; Gen. Sec. LESLIE DEAN; 1,985 mems.

Bahamas Utilities Services and Allied Workers' Union: POB GT-2515, Nassau; Pres. DREXEL DEAN; Gen. Sec. HERMAN ROKER.

Bahamas Workers' Council International: POB MS-5337, Nassau; f. 1969; Chair. DUDLEY WILLIAMS.

Commonwealth Cement and Construction Workers' Union: POB N-8680, Nassau; Pres. AUDLEY HANNA; Gen. Sec. ERMA MUNROE.

Commonwealth Electrical Workers' Union: POB F-1983, Grand Bahama; Pres. OBED PINDER, Jr; Gen. Sec. CHRISTOPHER COOPER.

Commonwealth Transport Union: POB F-1983, Freeport; Pres. LEO DOUGLAS; Gen. Sec. KENITH CHRISTIE.

Commonwealth Union of Hotel Services and Allied Workers: White House of Labour, Cedar St, POB F-1983, Freeport; tel. 352-9361; Pres. HURIE BODIE.

Commonwealth Wholesale, Retail and Allied Workers' Union: POB F-1983, Freeport; tel. 352-9361; Pres. MERLENE THOMAS; Gen. Sec. KIM SMITH.

Eastside Stevedores' Union: POB N-1176, Nassau; f. 1972; Pres. SALATHIEL MACKEY; Gen. Sec. CURTIS TURNQUEST.

Grand Bahama Commercial, Clerical and Allied Workers' Union: 33A Kipling Bldg, POB F-839, Freeport; tel. 352-7438; Pres. NEVILLE SIMMONS; Gen. Sec. LIVINGSTONE STUART.

Grand Bahama Construction, Refinery and Maintenance Workers' Union: 33A Kipling Bldg, POB F-839, Freeport; tel. 352-7438; f. 1971; Pres. JAMES TAYLOR; Gen. Sec. EPHRAIM BLACK.

Grand Bahama Entertainers' Union: POB F-2672, Freeport; Pres. CHARLES SMITH; Gen. Sec. IRMA THOMPSON.

Grand Bahama Telephone and Communications Union: POB F-2478, Freeport; Pres. NAAMAN ELLIS; Gen. Sec. DOROTHY CLARKE.

United Brotherhood of Longshoremen's Union: Wulff Rd, POB N-7317, Nassau; f. 1959; Pres. J. MCKINNEY; Gen. Sec. W. SWANN; 157 mems.

Transport

ROADS

There are about 966 km (600 miles) of roads in New Providence and 1,368 km (850 miles) in the Family Islands, mainly on Grand Bahama, Cat Island, Eleuthera, Exuma and Long Island.

SHIPPING

The principal seaport is at Nassau, on New Providence, which can accommodate the very largest cruise ships. The other main ports are at Freeport (Grand Bahama) and Matthew Town (Inagua). There are also modern berthing facilities for cruise ships at Potters Cay (New Providence), Governor's Harbour (Eleuthera), Morgan's Bluff (North Andros) and George Town (Exuma).

The Bahamas converted to free-flag status in 1976, and by 1983 possessed the world's third largest open-registry fleet. The fleet's displacement was 24,408,787 grt in December 1996 (the fourth largest national fleet in the world).

There is a weekly mail and passenger service to all the Family Islands.

Bahamas Maritime Authority: Nassau; f. 1995; promotes ship registration and co-ordinates maritime administration.

Freeport Harbour Co Ltd: POB F-42465, Freeport; tel. 352-9651; telex 30020; fax 352-6888; e-mail fhcol@batelnet.bs; Gen. Man. MICHAEL J. POWER.

Grand Bahama Port Authority: National Insurance Bldg, POB F-2044, Freeport; tel. 352-9169; telex 30020.

Nassau Port Authority: Prince George Wharf, POB N-8175, Nassau; tel. 356-7354; fax 322-5545; regulates principal port of the Bahamas; Port Dir HARVEY SWEETING.

Principal Shipping Companies

Archipelago Shipping Co Ltd: POB N-3018, Nassau.

Bahamas Ranger Ltd: POB N-3709, Nassau.

Cavalier Shipping: Arawak Cay, POB N-8170, New Providence; tel. 328-3035.

Dockendale Shipping Co Ltd: Bitco Bldg, Bank Lane, POB N-10455, Nassau; tel. 325-0448; telex 20219; fax 328-1542; f. 1973; ship management; Technical Mans K. VALLURI; P. R. C. DATT; Gen. Man. L. J. FERNANDES.

Dorick Navigation: POB N-351, Nassau.

R. R. Farrington & Sons: Union Dock, POB N-93, Nassau; tel. 322-2203; telex 20123.

Paramount Shipmanagement Ltd: 83 Shirley St, POB N-3247, Nassau; four vessels.

Pioneer Shipping Ltd: Union Dock Bay, POB N-3044, Nassau; tel. 325-7889; telex 20350.

Romo Shipping Co: 5 Atlantic Ave, POB F-2544, Freeport; Pres. and Man. Dir ROBERT CORDES.

Sea Link Bahamas Ltd: POB N-3709-601, Nassau; tel. 322-7982.

Teekay Shipping Ltd: Scotiabank Bldg, 1st Floor, Bay St, POB SS-6293, Nassau; tel. 683-3529; fax 844-6619; Pres. and CEO Capt. J. N. HOOD.

United Shipping Co Ltd: POB F-42552, Freeport; tel. 352-9315; telex 30048; fax 352-4034.

CIVIL AVIATION

Nassau International Airport (15 km (9 miles) outside the capital) and Freeport International Airport (5 km (3 miles) outside the city, on Grand Bahama) are the main terminals for international and internal services. There are also important airports at West End (Grand Bahama) and Rock Sound (Eleuthera) and some 50 smaller airports and landing strips throughout the islands.

Bahamasair: Windsor Field, POB N-4881, Nassau; tel. 327-8228; telex 20239; fax 327-7409; f. 1973; scheduled services between Nassau, Freeport, destinations within the USA and 20 locations within the Family Islands; Chair. ANTHONY MILLER; Gen. Man. BILL CURTIS.

Tourism

The mild climate and beautiful beaches attract many tourists. In 1996 tourist arrivals increased by 5.5%, to 3,415,858 (including 2,047,820 cruise-ship passengers), following several years of decline. The majority of arrivals (82% in 1996) were from the USA. Receipts from the tourist industry increased by 7.7% in 1996, to B $1,450m. In 1995 there were 208 hotels in the country, with a total of 13,943 rooms.

Ministry of Tourism: Bay St, POB N-3701, Nassau; tel. 322-7500; fax 328-0945; Dir-Gen. VINCENT VANDERPOOL-WALLACE.

Bahamas Hotel Association: Dean's Lane, Fort Charlotte, POB N-7799, Nassau; tel. 322-8381; fax 326-5346.

Hotel Corporation of the Bahamas: POB N-9520, Nassau; tel. 327-8395; fax 327-6978.

BAHRAIN

Introductory Survey

Location, Climate, Language, Religion, Flag, Capital

The State of Bahrain consists of a group of about 35 islands, situated midway along the Persian (Arabian) Gulf, approximately 24 km (15 miles) from the east coast of Saudi Arabia (to which it is linked by a causeway), and 28 km (17 miles) from the west coast of Qatar. There are six principal islands in the archipelago, and the largest of these is Bahrain itself, which is about 50 km (30 miles) long and between 13 km and 25 km (8 to 15 miles) wide. To the north-east of Bahrain island, and linked to it by a causeway and motor-road, lies Muharraq island, which is approximately 6 km (4 miles) long. Another causeway links Bahrain with Sitra island. The climate is temperate from December to the end of March, with temperatures ranging between 19°C (66°F) and 25°C (77°F), but becomes very hot and humid during the summer months. In August and September temperatures can rise to 40°C (104°F). The official language is Arabic, but English is also widely spoken. Almost all Bahraini citizens are Muslims, divided into two sects: Shi'ites (almost 60%) and Sunnis (more than 40%). Non-Bahrainis comprised 36.4% of the total population at the 1991 census. The national flag (proportions 5 by 3) is red, with a vertical white stripe at the hoist, the two colours being separated by a straight or (more frequently) serrated line. The capital is Manama.

Recent History

Bahrain, a traditional Arab monarchy, became a British Protected State in the 19th century. Under this arrangement, government was shared between the ruling sheikh and his British adviser. Following a series of territorial disputes in the 19th century, Persia (now Iran) made renewed claims to Bahrain in 1928. This disagreement remained unresolved until May 1970, when Iran accepted the findings of a report, commissioned by the UN, which showed that the inhabitants of Bahrain overwhelmingly favoured complete independence, rather than union with Iran.

During the reign of Sheikh Sulman bin Hamad al-Khalifa, who became ruler of Bahrain in 1942, social services and public works were considerably expanded. Sheikh Sulman died in November 1961 and was succeeded by his eldest son, Sheikh Isa bin Sulman al-Khalifa. Extensive administrative and political reforms were implemented in January 1970, when a supreme executive authority, the 12-member Council of State, was established, representing the first formal derogation of the ruler's powers. Sheikh Khalifa bin Sulman al-Khalifa, the ruler's eldest brother, was appointed President of the Council.

Meanwhile, in January 1968 the United Kingdom had announced its intention to withdraw British military forces from the area by 1971. In March 1968 Bahrain joined the nearby territories of Qatar and the Trucial States (now the United Arab Emirates), which were also under British protection, in the Federation of Arab Emirates. It was intended that the Federation should become fully independent, but the interests of Bahrain and Qatar proved to be incompatible with those of the smaller sheikhdoms, and both seceded from the Federation. Bahrain thus became a separate independent state on 15 August 1971, when a new treaty of friendship was signed with the United Kingdom. Sheikh Isa took the title of Amir, while the Council of State became the Cabinet, with Sheikh Khalifa as Prime Minister. A Constituent Assembly, convened in December 1972, formulated a new Constitution providing for a National Assembly to be comprised of 14 cabinet ministers and 30 elected members. On 6 December 1973 the Constitution came into force, and on the following day elections to the new Assembly were conducted. In the absence of political parties, candidates sought election in an individual capacity. In August 1975 the Prime Minister submitted his resignation, complaining that the National Assembly was obstructing the Government's initiatives for new legislation, particularly regarding national security. However, Sheikh Khalifa was reappointed and, at his request, the Assembly was dissolved by Amiri decree. New elections were to be conducted following minor changes to the Constitution and to the electoral law, but there were few subsequent signs that the National Assembly would be reconvened.

With no elected legislative body, the ruling family exercises near-absolute power. In late 1992 plans were announced for the establishment of a 30-member Consultative Council, to be appointed by the ruling authorities. As in other Gulf states, the Council would act in a purely advisory capacity, with no legislative powers. The Council—which comprised a large number of businessmen and some members of the old National Assembly—held its inaugural meeting on 16 January 1993, at which issues of employment and training were debated.

Although major international territorial claims were brought to an end by the 1970 agreement with Iran, the Iranian revolution of 1979 led to uncertainty about possible future claims to Bahrain. There has also been evidence of tension between Shi'ite Muslims, who form a slender majority in Bahrain (and many of whom are of Iranian descent), and the dominant Sunni Muslims, the sect to which the ruling family belongs. In December 1981 more than 70 people, mainly Bahrainis, were arrested when a plot to overthrow the Government, organized with alleged support from Iran, was thwarted. Allegations of external support for attempts to destabilize the country were renewed following the reported discovery of a weapons cache in a Bahraini village in February 1984, and the arrest in the United Kingdom, in June 1985, of eight men (including six Bahrainis) who were implicated in a further plot to overthrow the Government. In early 1988 three Bahrainis were arrested in connection with a plot, uncovered in late 1987, to sabotage Bahrain's petroleum installations. Allegations of Iranian support for the plot were, again, widely reported. In December 1993 the human rights organization Amnesty International published a report criticizing the Bahraini Government's treatment of Shi'ite Muslims, some of whom had been forcibly exiled. In March 1994, apparently in response to this criticism, the Amir issued a decree pardoning 64 Bahrainis who had been in exile since the 1980s and permitting them to return to Bahrain. In December Sheikh Ali Salman Ahmad Salman, a Muslim cleric, was arrested following his criticism of the government of the country, and his public appeal for reform, particularly the restoration of the National Assembly. Widespread rioting ensued throughout Bahrain, especially in Shi'ite districts, and large-scale demonstrations were held in Manama in support of Sheikh Salman's demands and to petition for his release. Civil unrest ensued despite the Amir's pledge, in mid-December, to extend the powers of the Consultative Council; some 2,500 demonstrators were arrested and as many as 12 people were killed during clashes with the security forces in December and early January 1995. Sheikh Salman sought asylum in the United Kingdom, following his deportation in January. The unprecedented scale of the disturbances was widely attributed to a marked deterioration in socio-economic conditions in Bahrain, and in particular to a high level of unemployment.

Anti-Government demonstrations erupted in Shi'ite districts in late March 1995, and again in April, following a police search of the property of an influential Shi'ite clergyman, Sheikh Abd al-Amir al-Jamri, who was subsequently placed under house arrest and later imprisoned. In mid-April, after Bahrain convened a meeting of Ministers of the Interior of member states of the Gulf Co-operation Council (GCC—see below), the Governments of the GCC countries issued a statement supporting the measures adopted by Bahrain to quell civil disturbances. In May and July several people were sentenced to terms of imprisonment, ranging from one year to life imprisonment, for damaging public installations, and one Bahraini was sentenced to death for the murder of a police officer in March. In late June, in an apparent attempt to appease Shi'ite opposition leaders, the Prime Minister announced the first major cabinet reshuffle for 20 years. However, the important posts of the Interior, Defence, Finance and National Economy, and Foreign Affairs remained unchanged.

In mid-August 1995 the Government initiated talks with Shi'ite opposition leaders in an effort to foster reconciliation. In the same month the Amir issued a decree pardoning 150 people detained since the disturbances. A report issued by Amnesty International in September indicated that as many as 1,500 demonstrators remained in detention in Bahrain, and that two prisoners (including a 16-year-old student) had died in police custody following torture. In mid-September talks between the Government and opposition leaders collapsed. None the less, more than 40 political prisoners were released from detention later in the month, including Sheikh al-Jamri. In late October al-Jamri and six other opposition figures began a hunger strike in protest at the Government's refusal to concede to their demands, which included the release of all political prisoners and the restoration of the National Assembly. In early November, following a large demonstration to mark the end of the hunger strike, the Government announced that it would take 'necessary action' to prevent future 'illegal' gatherings. In December the Amir declared an amnesty for nearly 150 prisoners, mostly people arrested during the disturbances earlier in the year. Large-scale demonstrations were staged in late December and in early January 1996, in protest at the heavy deployment of security forces in Shi'ite districts and at the closure of two mosques. Opposition figures strongly criticized the use of tear-gas and plastic bullets to disperse protesters. It was also suggested that some 4,000 Saudi security officers had been dispatched to reinforce the Bahrain police, while subsequent reports indicated that large numbers of riot police had also been seconded from India. In mid-January eight opposition leaders, including Sheikh al-Jamri, were arrested and accused of inciting unrest. The Government threatened to impose martial law, following a spate of rioting and arson attacks, including a bomb explosion in a Manama hotel. By the end of January some 500 opposition activists had been detained. In early February Ahmad ash-Shamlan, a noted lawyer and writer, became the first prominent Sunni to be arrested in connection with the disturbances, following his distribution of a statement criticizing the authoritarian actions of the Government. However, civil unrest continued. A number of car-bomb and fire-bomb explosions in February and early March culminated in an arson attack on a restaurant in Sitra, which resulted in the deaths of seven Bangladeshi workers. Also in March, jurisdiction with regard to a number of criminal offences was transferred from ordinary courts to the High Court of Appeal, acting in the capacity of State Security Court. This move effectively accelerated court proceedings, while removing the right of appeal and limiting the role of the defence. In late March Isa Ahmad Hassan Qambar was executed by firing squad, having been condemned to death for killing a policeman during clashes with security forces in March 1995 (see above). The execution was the first to be performed in Bahrain since 1977, and provoked massive popular protest and condemnation by international human rights organizations, which challenged the validity (by international standards) of Qambar's confession and trial. Civil disturbances continued during the first half of 1996, and tensions were exacerbated by the Government's announcement, in April, of the creation of a Higher Council of Islamic Affairs (to be appointed by the Prime Minister and headed by the Minister of Justice and Islamic Affairs), to supervise all religious activity (including that of the Shi'ite community) in the country. In July 1996 the State Security Court imposed the death sentence on three of the eight young Bahrainis convicted of the arson attack in Sitra. Another four men were sentenced to life imprisonment. The death sentences provoked widespread domestic protests and international criticism. In response the Government agreed to allow an appeal against the ruling. In October the Court of Cassation ruled that it had no jurisdiction to overturn the verdict, and the fate of the three men seemed likely to be decided by the Amir. There were more anti-Government demonstrations in July and August, and towards the end of the year government plans to close a number of Shi'ite mosques resulted in further unrest. Demonstrators who had gathered at the Ras Roman mosque in central Manama became involved in a violent confrontation with the security forces during which police fired tear-gas at worshippers. The continuing unrest in December and in early 1997 prompted rumours of division within the ruling family concerning the use of force in response to the crisis. In January 1997 a National Guard was created, to provide support for the Bahraini Defence Force and the security forces of the Ministry of the Interior. The Amir's son, Hamad, was appointed to command the new force, prompting speculation that its primary duty would be to protect the ruling family. In March a week of anti-Government protests marked the first anniversary of the execution of Isa Ahmad Hassan Qambar. It was reported that since the outbreak of civil unrest at the end of 1994, some 28 people had been killed and 220 imprisoned in connection with the disturbances. In July and August 1997 two human rights groups produced reports criticizing the Bahraini police for allegedly making arbitrary arrests, using torture, and arresting children as young as seven years of age. The Government rejected these reports, claiming that they were based on dishonest sources.

Relations with Iran continued to deteriorate during 1996. While there was sufficient evidence to suggest largely domestic motivation for the recent increase in popular disaffection, the Bahraini authorities continued to imply that the disturbances were the result of the efforts of Iranian-backed Shi'a fundamentalist terrorists to destabilize the country. These allegations were frequently dismissed by the Iranian press. In early June, following a meeting convened in Riyadh, Saudi Arabia, the Ministers of Foreign Affairs of the GCC member nations issued a statement condemning alleged Iranian interference in Bahrain's affairs. On the following day the Bahraini Government announced that it had uncovered details of a carefully-planned terrorist campaign, initiated in 1993 with support from fundamentalist Shi'a groups in Iran, which sought to oust the Government and ruling family in Bahrain and replace them with a pro-Iranian administration. It was claimed that a previously unknown Shi'a terrorist group, Hezbollah Bahrain, had been established and financed by Iran's Revolutionary Guard. Young Bahraini Shi'ites were alleged to have received military training in the Iranian city of Qom and at guerrilla bases in the Beka'a valley in Lebanon, in preparation for a terrorist offensive in Bahrain, which had culminated in the disturbances of the previous 18 months. Within days of the Government's announcement more than 50 Bahrainis had been arrested in connection with the plot. Many of the detained persons admitted membership of Hezbollah Bahrain, including six prisoners who made confessions on national television. The Iranian authorities denied any involvement in the planned insurrection, but bilateral relations were severely undermined by the unprecedented directness of the Bahraini Government's accusations, and diplomatic relations between the two countries were downgraded in early June. While the national press congratulated the Government and the security services for discovering the conspiracy, independent observers were again sceptical of the validity of confessions obtained during detention with no legal representation, and further doubts were expressed that the inexpert execution of recent terrorist acts in Bahrain was inconsistent with the involvement of an established movement such as Hezbollah. During June more than 30 Bahrainis received prison sentences of between one and 13 years—for offences connected to the disturbances—from the State Security Court (and were therefore denied the right of appeal). In March 1997 59 Bahraini Shi'ites accused of belonging to Hezbollah Bahrain were brought to trial. The State Security Court sentenced 37 of the defendants to terms of imprisonment ranging from three to 15 years, and acquitted the others. In November the State Security Court sentenced eight prominent exiled opposition leaders (including Sheikh Ali Salman Ahmad Salman) in absentia, to between five and 15 years in prison, for their alleged membership of Hezbollah Bahrain and various other anti-Government activities.

Meanwhile, in early June 1996, the Amir had sought to appease the demands of opposition reformers by announcing the future expansion of the Consultative Council from 30 to 40 members. A new 40-member Council was appointed by the Amir in late September.

In March 1981 Bahrain was one of the six founder-members of the Co-operation Council for the Arab States of the Gulf (more generally known as the Gulf Co-operation Council—GCC, see p. 136), which was established in order to co-ordinate defence strategy and to promote freer trading and co-operative economic protection among Gulf states. In 1986 the King Fahd Causeway between Bahrain and Saudi Arabia was opened, indicating Bahrain's commitment to closer links with other Gulf states.

In common with other Gulf states, Bahrain consistently expressed support for Iraq at the time of the Iran–Iraq war (1980–88). However, following the Iraqi invasion of Kuwait in August 1990, Bahrain firmly supported the implementation of UN economic sanctions against Iraq and permitted the stationing of US troops and combat aircraft in Bahrain. (Military co-operation with the USA had been close for many years.) British armed forces, participating in the multinational force for the defence of Saudi Arabia and the liberation of Kuwait, were also stationed in Bahrain in 1990–91. In June 1991 it was confirmed that Bahrain would remain a regional support base for the USA, and later in the year the two countries signed a defence co-operation agreement. In January 1994 Bahrain signed further accords of military co-operation with the USA and the United Kingdom. In March 1995 William Perry, the US Secretary of Defense, visited Bahrain and held talks with the Amir on Gulf security issues. In late 1995 Bahrain agreed to the temporary deployment on its territory of US fighter aircraft in order to deter any possible military threat from Iraq.

During the early 1990s Bahrain allowed a tentative *rapprochement* with Iran. Relations were upgraded to ambassadorial level in late 1990, and the two countries signed an important protocol for industrial co-operation in early 1992. By mid-1996, relations between the two countries had deteriorated again and diplomatic relations were downgraded, following accusations, made by the Bahraini Government, that extremist Shi'a groups in Iran had encouraged and supported widespread civil unrest which occurred in Bahrain during 1994–97 (see above). Following talks in December 1997, it was announced that relations at ambassadorial level were to be re-established between Bahrain and Iran. Relations with Iraq remained strained following the liberation of Kuwait in February 1991; in mid-1992, none the less, Sheikh Isa expressed the hope that his country's relations with Iraq would improve, in the context of wider regional harmony, and that both Iran and Iraq might eventually be incorporated into the GCC. However, such hopes receded in October 1994, when Iraqi forces were again deployed in the Iraq–Kuwait border area, in an apparent threat to Kuwait's sovereignty. In response, Bahrain deployed combat aircraft and naval units to join GCC and US forces in the defence of Kuwait. In mid-October the Ministers of Foreign Affairs of Egypt, Syria and the GCC member states issued a statement condemning Iraqi threats against Kuwait and affirming their full support for Kuwait's sovereignty.

In April 1986 Qatari military forces raided the island of Fasht ad-Dibal, which had been artificially constructed on a coral reef (submerged at high tide), situated midway between Bahrain and Qatar; both countries claimed sovereignty over the island. During the raid Qatar seized 29 foreign workers who were constructing a Bahraini coastguard station on the island. Officials of the GCC met representatives from both states in an attempt to reconcile them and to avoid a split within the Council, and in May the workers were released and the two Governments agreed to destroy the island. Other areas of dispute between the two countries are Zubara (which was part of Bahraini territory until the early 20th century), in mainland Qatar, and the region of the Hawar islands, which is believed to contain potentially valuable reserves of petroleum and natural gas. In July 1991 Qatar instituted proceedings at the International Court of Justice (ICJ) regarding the issue of the Hawar islands (in 1939 a British judgment had awarded sovereignty of the islands to Bahrain), the shoals of Dibal and Qit'at Jaradah (over which the British had recognized Bahrain's 'sovereign rights' in 1947), together with the delimitation of the maritime border between Qatar and Bahrain. The question of sovereignty was further confused in April 1992, when the Government of Qatar issued a decree redefining its maritime borders to include territorial waters claimed by Bahrain, and tensions were exacerbated by Qatar's persistent rejection of Bahrain's insistence that the two countries should seek joint recourse to the ICJ. Moreover, it was reported that Bahrain had attempted to widen the issue to include its claim to the Zubara region. In February 1994 the ICJ began to examine whether it had jurisdiction over the territorial dispute, as Qatar had applied unilaterally to the Court. In February 1995 the ICJ ruled that it would have authority to adjudicate in the dispute. Bahrain maintained that a bilateral solution should be sought and welcomed a Saudi Arabian offer to mediate in the dispute. Relations between Bahrain and Qatar deteriorated in September, following the Bahraini Government's decision to construct a tourist resort on the Hawar islands, and remained tense subsequently, with the Bahraini Government advocating a regional solution to the dispute in preference to ICJ jurisdiction. In December 1996 Bahrain boycotted the GCC annual summit convened in Doha, Qatar, at which it was decided to establish a quadripartite committee (comprising those GCC members not involved in the dispute) to facilitate a solution. The committee reportedly made some progress towards resolving the territorial dispute, and following meetings between prominent government ministers from Bahrain and Qatar in London, United Kingdom, and Manama in February and March 1997, it was announced that diplomatic relations at ambassadorial level were to be established between the two countries.

In November 1993 Bahrain removed sanctions against South Africa, and the two countries established diplomatic relations. The South African embassy, which was subsequently opened in Manama, was the first to be established in the Arab world. The first official Israeli delegation to visit Bahrain arrived in September 1994, and the following month the Bahraini Minister of Foreign Affairs met the Israeli Minister of the Environment during multilateral talks on Middle Eastern environmental issues, held in Manama. However, in March 1997, in protest at Israel's decision to construct a Jewish settlement in a disputed area of East Jerusalem, the League of Arab States (or Arab League, of which Bahrain is a member) voted to suspend negotiations to establish diplomatic links with Israel, close Israeli missions, restore the economic boycott and withdraw from multilateral peace talks. Relations between Bahrain and Jordan became strained following the Gulf crisis in 1990–91. An improvement in relations was perceived in September 1995, when Bahrain appointed an ambassador to Jordan, and in November the two countries issued a joint statement rejecting terrorism and extremism and pledging their commitment to increasing bilateral co-operation, particularly in economic, cultural and security matters.

Government

Bahrain is ruled by an Amir through an appointed Cabinet.

Defence

Military service is voluntary. In August 1997 the Bahraini Defence Force consisted of some 11,000 men (8,500 army, 1,000 navy, 1,500 air force). In January 1997 a National Guard was established to provide support for the Bahraini Defence Force and the security forces of the Ministry of the Interior. The defence budget for 1997 was estimated at BD 109m.

Economic Affairs

In 1995, according to estimates by the World Bank, Bahrain's gross national product (GNP), measured at average 1993–95 prices, was US $4,525m., equivalent to $7,840 per head. During 1985–95, it was estimated, GNP per head increased, in real terms, at an average rate of 0.6% per year, while the population increased by an annual average of 3.4%. Over the same period, the country's gross domestic product (GDP) increased, in real terms, by an average of 4.4% per year.

Agriculture and fishing engaged 2.4% of the employed labour force in 1991, and contributed 1.0% of GDP in 1995. The principal crops are dates, tomatoes and melons. Total production of vegetables was sufficient to fulfil 75% of Bahrain's needs in 1988. Poultry production is also important. At mid-1989 about 75% of the country's potential fish resources remained unexploited. Agricultural GDP was estimated to have increased, in real terms, by an annual average of 1.4% during 1985–92.

Industry (comprising mining, manufacturing, construction and utilities) engaged 28.2% of the employed labour force in 1991, and provided 44.0% of GDP in 1995. Industrial GDP was estimated to have increased, in real terms, by an annual average of 1.4% during 1985–92.

Mining and quarrying engaged 1.7% of the employed labour force in 1991, and contributed 15.8% of GDP in 1995. The major mining activities are the exploitation of petroleum and natural gas. Petroleum production and processing are estimated to provide some 60% of state revenues and around 30% of GDP. At 1994 levels of production (105,000 barrels per day), Bahrain's known reserves of crude petroleum will have been exhausted by 2000. There are sufficient reserves of natural gas to maintain the 1996 output level (7,200m. cu m) for 20.4 years.

In 1991 manufacturing engaged 12.6% of the employed labour force; the sector provided 20.5% of GDP in 1995. Important industries include the petroleum refinery at Sitra, aluminium (Bahrain is the region's largest producer) and aluminium-related enterprises, shipbuilding, iron and steel and chemicals. Since the mid-1980s the Government has encouraged the development of light industry. Manufacturing GDP was estimated to have increased by an annual average of 8.6% during 1985–92.

Industrial expansion resulted in energy demands which threatened to exceed the country's 984-MW total installed generating capacity. In 1994, however, a 200-km link between the national grid and Aluminium Bahrain's newly-installed 800-MW power-station provided the Government with access to an additional 250 MW for a 10-year period. The Government is also seeking to attract private investment in the energy sector.

Banking is a major source of Bahrain's prosperity. Since the mid-1970s the Government has licensed 'offshore' banking units

(OBUs). Largely owing to regional instability, by 1996 the number of OBUs had declined to 48, compared with 56 prior to the Iraqi invasion and occupation of Kuwait in 1990–91, and 74 in mid-1985. According to the World Bank, the GDP of the services sector increased, in real terms, by an annual average of 5.7% during 1985–92. The sector contributed 54.9% of GDP in 1995. A stock exchange was inaugurated in Bahrain in 1989. It has since been linked to the Oman and Jordan Stock Exchanges (with each other's shares listed under reciprocal agreements), and in September 1997 plans were announced to link it to the Kuwait Stock Exchange.

In 1995 Bahrain recorded a visible trade surplus of US $768.6m. and there was a surplus of $557.0m. on the current account of the balance of payments. In 1995 the principal sources of non-petroleum imports were the USA (accounting for 13.0% of the total), the United Kingdom, Australia, Japan and Germany, while Saudi Arabia provided most of Bahrain's petroleum imports (and accounted for 50.8% of all imports in 1990). Saudi Arabia was the principal customer for Bahrain's non-petroleum exports (15.3% of the total) in 1995; other important markets were the Republic of Korea, Japan, the USA and India. The principal exports are petroleum, petroleum products and aluminium. Sales of petroleum and petroleum products provided 60.0% of total export earnings in 1995. The principal import is crude petroleum (for domestic refining), accounting for 38.1% of total imports in 1995. The main category of non-petroleum imports (some 26% in 1995) is machinery and transport equipment.

In the financial year ending 31 December 1995 there was a budgetary deficit of BD 65.2m. (equivalent to 3.4% of GDP). The average annual rate of inflation was 0.4% in 1985–95; consumer prices increased by an annual average of 0.4% in 1994 and 3.2% in 1995. About 60% of the labour force were expatriates in 1994. The official rate of unemployment among the national labour force was 1.8% in late 1995; however, Western diplomats estimated the level of unemployment to have reached 25%–30%.

Bahrain is a member of the Gulf Co-operation Council (GCC, see p. 136), which seeks to co-ordinate defence strategy and to promote freer trading and co-operative economic protection among Gulf states. The country is also a member of the Organization of Arab Petroleum Exporting Countries (OAPEC, see p. 223), the Arab Monetary Fund (see p. 259) and the Islamic Development Bank (see p. 194).

The opening of the King Fahd Causeway, linking Bahrain with Saudi Arabia, in 1986 and the cease-fire in the Iran–Iraq War in 1988 generated an economic recovery in the late 1980s. However, Bahrain suffered immediate losses totalling an estimated US $2,000m. as a result of the 1990–91 Gulf crisis. In recognition of the fact that Bahrain's reserves of petroleum and natural gas are nearing exhaustion, the Government has sought both to diversify the country's industrial base and to attract wider foreign investment. In mid-1991 the establishment of wholly foreign-owned companies in Bahrain was permitted. In the early 1990s the Government continued to encourage the greater participation of the private sector in economic development and indicated that it would adopt a gradual approach to the privatization of state enterprises (excluding the petroleum sector), and would prioritize employment opportunities for Bahraini nationals. Increased petroleum revenues were expected to bolster the economy during 1996, following Saudi Arabia's decision to allocate its share of the 1996 annual output of petroleum from the Abu Saafa oilfield to Bahrain. By early 1997 the Government had announced a three-year development programme, which included the proposed creation of a port and free-trade zone at Hidd on Muharraq island, a new power-station and desalination plant, and the renovation of Bahrain's international airport.

Social Welfare

The state-administered medical service provides comprehensive treatment for all residents, including expatriates. There are also physicians, dentists and opticians in private practice. In 1988 Bahrain had 1,445 hospital beds. In that year there were seven hospitals, 19 government health centres and seven government maternity centres. A social security law covers pensions, industrial accidents, sickness, unemployment, maternity and family allowances. In 1985 there were 518 physicians (12.4 per 10,000 inhabitants), 19 dentists and 1,148 nursing personnel (including midwifery personnel) working in the country. Of total expenditure by the central Government in 1995, BD 55.0m. (9.3%) was for health, and a further BD 25.0m. (4.2%) for social security and welfare.

Education

Education is compulsory between the ages of six and 17 and is available free of charge. Private and religious education are also available. The education system is composed of three different stages: primary schooling (for children aged six to 11 years), intermediate (12–14 years) and secondary—general, industrial or commercial—(15–17 years). An alternative structure for post-primary schooling provides for eight years, divided into two four-year stages. The University of Bahrain, the establishment of which was proclaimed by Amiri decree in 1986, comprises five colleges: the College of Engineering, the College of Arts, the College of Science, the College of Education and the College of Business and Management. About 6,760 students were enrolled at the University in 1995. Higher education is also provided by the College of Health Sciences (528 students) and the Hotel and Catering Training Centre. The first phase in the construction of the Arabian Gulf University (AGU) was completed in 1982, but lack of funding from the seven Arab Governments sponsoring the project has delayed its completion, which is scheduled for 2006. Some 368 students were enrolled at the AGU in 1993. In 1994 enrolment at primary and secondary (including intermediate) levels included 100% and 85% (84% of boys; 87% of girls), respectively, in the relevant age-groups. Expenditure on education by the central Government in 1995 was BD 79.9m. (13.4% of total expenditure). According to UNESCO estimates, the average rate of adult illiteracy in 1995 was 14.8% (males 10.9%; females 20.6%).

Public Holidays

1998: 1 January (New Year's Day), 30 January* (Id al-Fitr, end of Ramadan), 8 April* (Id al-Adha, Feast of the Sacrifice), 28 April* (Muharram, Islamic New Year), 7 May* (Ashoura), 7 July* (Mouloud, Birth of the Prophet), 16 December (National Day).

1999: 1 January (New Year's Day), 19 January* (Id al-Fitr, end of Ramadan), 28 March* (Id al-Adha, Feast of the Sacrifice), 17 April* (Muharram, Islamic New Year), 26 April* (Ashoura), 26 June* (Mouloud, Birth of the Prophet), 16 December (National Day).

* These holidays are dependent on the Islamic lunar calendar and may vary by one or two days from the dates given.

Weights and Measures

The metric system is being introduced.

Statistical Survey

Source (unless otherwise stated): Central Statistics Organization, POB 5835, Manama; tel. 725725; telex 8853; fax 728989.

AREA AND POPULATION

Area (1995): 707.3 sq km (273.1 sq miles).

Population: 350,798 (males 204,793, females 146,005) at census of 5 April 1981; 508,037 (males 294,346, females 213,691), comprising 323,305 Bahrainis (males 163,453, females 159,852) and 184,732 non-Bahraini nationals (males 130,893, females 53,839), at census of 16 November 1991; 598,625 (official estimate) at mid-1996.

Density (mid-1996): 846.4 per sq km.

Principal Towns (population in 1991): Manama (capital) 136,999; Muharraq Town 74,245. *Mid-1992:* Manama 140,401.

Births, Marriages and Deaths (1995): Registered live births 13,481 (birth rate 23.3 per 1,000); Registered marriages 3,321 (marriage rate 5.7 per 1,000); Registered deaths 1,910 (death rate 3.3 per 1,000).

Expectation of Life (UN estimates, years at birth, 1990–95): 71.6 (males 69.8; females 74.1). Source: UN, *World Population Prospects: The 1994 Revision*.

Economically Active Population (persons aged 15 years and over, 1991 census): Agriculture, hunting, forestry and fishing 5,108; Mining and quarrying 3,638; Manufacturing 26,618; Electricity, gas and water 2,898; Construction 26,738; Trade, restaurants and hotels 29,961; Transport, storage and communications 13,789; Financing, insurance, real estate and business services 17,256; Community, social and personal services 83,201; Activities not adequately defined 2,863; *Total employed* 212,070 (males 177,154; females 34,916); Unemployed 14,378 (males 9,703; females 4,675); *Total labour force* 226,448 (males 186,857; females 39,591), comprising 90,662 Bahrainis (males 73,118, females 17,544) and 135,786 non-Bahraini nationals (males 113,739, females 22,047).

AGRICULTURE, ETC.

Principal Crops (FAO estimates, '000 metric tons, 1996): Tomatoes 9; Other vegetables 7; Dates 20; other fruits 5. Source: FAO, *Production Yearbook*.

Livestock (FAO estimates, '000 head, year ending September 1996): Cattle 17; Camels 1; Sheep 29; Goats 18. Source: FAO, *Production Yearbook*.

Livestock Products (FAO estimates, '000 metric tons, 1996): Mutton and lamb 6; Goat meat 2; Poultry meat 5; Milk 20; Poultry eggs 4. Source: FAO, *Production Yearbook*.

Fishing ('000 metric tons, live weight): Total catch 9.0 in 1993; 7.6 in 1994; 9.4 in 1995. Source: FAO, *Yearbook of Fishery Statistics*.

MINING

Production (1995): Crude petroleum 14,459,000 barrels; Natural gas 7,701.7 million cubic metres.

INDUSTRY

Production ('000 barrels, unless otherwise indicated, 1995): Liquefied petroleum gas 365; Naphtha 12,772; Motor spirit (Gasoline) 7,766; Kerosene 11,327; Jet fuel 6,219; Fuel oil 20,807; Diesel oil and Gas oil 31,024; Petroleum bitumen (asphalt) 1,399; Electric energy 4,611.9 million kWh; Aluminium (unwrought) 461,245 metric tons (1996).

FINANCE

Currency and Exchange Rates: 1,000 fils = 1 Bahraini dinar (BD). *Sterling and Dollar Equivalents* (30 September 1997): £1 sterling = 607.4 fils; US \$1 = 376.0 fils; 100 Bahraini dinars = £164.65 = \$265.96. *Exchange Rate:* Fixed at US \$1 = 376.0 fils (BD 1 = \$2.6596) since November 1980.

Budget (BD million, 1995): *Revenue:* Taxation 168.4 (Taxes on income and profits 23.3, Social security contributions 62.9, Domestic taxes on goods and services 27.4, Import duties 47.6); Entrepreneurial and property income 325.7; Other current revenue 31.1; Capital revenue 1.4; Total 526.6, excl. grants from abroad (37.6). *Expenditure:* General public services 169.2; Defence 102.5; Education 79.9; Health 55.0; Social security and welfare 25.0; Housing and community amenities 8.8; Recreational, cultural and religious affairs and services 9.7; Economic affairs and services 119.4 (Fuel and energy 57.1, Transport and communications 53.2); Other purposes 24.6 (Interest payments 20.5); Total 594.1 (Current 492.1, Capital 102.0), excl. lending minus repayments (96.7). Source: IMF, *Government Finance Statistics Yearbook*. **1995** (revised figures, BD million): Petroleum revenue 318.6; Non-petroleum revenue 204.6; Grants 37.6; *Total revenue* 560.8; Recurrent expenditure 521.3; Capital expenditure 104.7; *Total expenditure* 626.0. **1996** (estimates, BD million): Revenue 530; Expenditure 644. **1997** (estimates, BD million): Revenue 615; Expenditure 690.

International Reserves (US \$ million at 31 December 1996): Gold (valued at cost of acquisition) 6.6; IMF special drawing rights 16.8; Reserve position in IMF 64.8; Foreign exchange 1,236.8; Total 1,325.0. Source: IMF, *International Financial Statistics*.

Money Supply (BD million at 31 December 1996): Currency outside banks 102.86; Demand deposits at commercial banks 188.02; Total money 290.88. Source: IMF, *International Financial Statistics*.

Cost of Living (Consumer Price Index for Bahraini nationals; base: 1990 = 100): 104.0 in 1994; 106.8 in 1995; 106.5 in 1996. Source: IMF, *International Financial Statistics*.

Expenditure on the Gross Domestic Product (BD million, 1995): Government final consumption expenditure 455.6; Private final consumption expenditure 486.4; Increase in stocks 17.0; Gross fixed capital formation 532.5; *Total domestic expenditure* 1,491.7; Exports of goods and services 1,922.1; *Less* Imports of goods and services 1,513.6; *GDP in purchasers' values* 1,900.2. Source: IMF, *International Financial Statistics*.

Gross Domestic Product by Economic Activity (BD million at current prices, 1995): Agriculture, hunting, forestry and fishing 20.5; Mining and quarrying 316.6; Manufacturing 412.1; Electricity, gas and water 58.4; Construction 97.9; Trade, restaurants and hotels 151.0; Transport, storage and communications 158.2; Finance, insurance, real estate and business services 328.0; Government services 369.5; Other community, social and personal services 97.2; *Sub-total* 2,009.4; *Less* Imputed bank service charge 170.7; *GDP at factor cost* 1,838.7; Indirect taxes (net) 61.6; *GDP in purchasers' values* 1,900.2.

Balance of Payments (US \$ million, 1995): Exports of goods f.o.b. 4,112.8; Imports of goods f.o.b. –3,344.1; *Trade balance* 768.6; Exports of services 1,325.5; Imports of services –861.4; *Balance on goods and services* 1,232.8; Other income received 343.1; Other income paid –796.5; *Balance on goods, services and income* 779.4; Current transfers received 156.6; Current transfers paid –379.0; *Current balance* 557.0; Direct investment from abroad –27.1; Portfolio investment assets –18.4; Other investment assets 278.5; Other investment liabilities –316.0; Net errors and omissions –375.9; *Overall balance* 98.2. Source: IMF, *International Financial Statistics*.

EXTERNAL TRADE

Total Trade (BD million): *Imports c.i.f.:* 1,409.2 in 1994; 1,397.1 in 1995; 1,538.8 in 1996. *Exports:* 1,359.9 in 1994, 1,546.4 in 1995; 1,730.5 in 1996. Source: IMF, *International Financial Statistics*.

Principal Commodities (US \$ million, 1995): *Imports c.i.f.:* Food and live animals 320.0; Mineral fuels, lubricants, etc. 1,382.2 (Crude petroleum 1,330.1); Chemicals and related products 316.2; Basic manufactures 557.5; Machinery and transport equipment 588.3; Miscellaneous manufactured articles 279.8; Total (incl. others) 3,624.8. *Exports f.o.b.:* Mineral fuels, lubricants, etc. 2,455.6 (Crude petroleum 2,454.5); Chemicals and related products 206.4; Basic manufactures 1,153.7; Miscellaneous manufactured articles 125.5; Total (incl. others) 4,092.1. Source: UN, *International Trade Statistics Yearbook*.

Principal Trading Partners (US \$ million, 1995): *Imports c.i.f.:* Australia 172.6; Brazil 72.9; People's Republic of China 51.5; France 84.7; Germany 145.2; India 89.3; Italy 79.2; Japan 147.9; Republic of Korea 39.9; Malaysia 41.1; Netherlands 52.4; Saudi Arabia 178.9; Switzerland 45.1; United Arab Emirates 96.1; United Kingdom 212.6; USA 298.2; Total (incl. others) 3,624.8. *Exports f.o.b.:* India 103.6; Iran 46.6; Japan 142.2; Jordan 41.4; Republic of Korea 157.5; Kuwait 58.3; Malaysia 42.3; Netherlands 46.9; Saudi Arabia 250.7; Singapore 79.0; United Arab Emirates 74.1; USA 130.7; Total (incl. others) 4,092.1. Note: Except for totals, figures exclude trade in petroleum (US \$ million): Imports 1,330.1; Exports 2,454.5. Source: UN. *International Trade Statistics Yearbook*.

TRANSPORT

Road Traffic (registered motor vehicles, 31 December 1995): Passenger cars 141,901; Buses and coaches 4,157; Lorries and vans 25,427; Motorcycles 1,759. Source: IRF, *World Road Statistics*.

Shipping (international sea-borne freight traffic, '000 metric tons, 1990): *Goods loaded:* Dry cargo 1,145; Petroleum products 12,140.

Goods unloaded: Dry cargo 3,380; Petroleum products 132. Source: UN, *Monthly Bulletin of Statistics*. *Merchant Fleet* (31 December 1996): Registered vessels 83; Total displacement 164,258 grt. Source: Lloyd's Register of Shipping, *World Fleet Statistics*.

Civil Aviation (1994): Kilometres flown (million) 21; Passengers carried ('000) 1,151; Passenger-km (million) 2,439; Total ton-km (million) 354. Figures include an apportionment (equivalent to one-quarter) of the traffic of Gulf Air, a multinational airline with its headquarters in Bahrain. Source: UN, *Statistical Yearbook*.

TOURISM

Tourist Arrivals (1994): 2,270,000.

Tourist Receipts (1994): US $302 million.

COMMUNICATIONS MEDIA

Radio Receivers (1994): 305,000 in use.

Television Receivers (1994): 236,000 in use.

Telephones (1994): 136,000 main lines in use.

Telefax Stations (telephone subscriptions, 1994): 5,390.

Mobile Cellular Telephones (subscribers, 1994): 17,620.

Book Production (1989, estimate): 150 titles.

Daily Newspapers (1994): 3 (estimated circulation 70,000 copies).

Non-daily Newspapers (1993): 5 (circulation 17,000 copies).

Other Periodicals (1993): 26 (circulation 73,000 copies).

Sources: UNESCO, *Statistical Yearbook*; UN, *Statistical Yearbook*.

EDUCATION

Government Institutions (1994/95): *Primary:* 59,378 pupils. *Intermediate:* 26,851 pupils. *Secondary* (general): 15,210 pupils; (commercial): 3,194 pupils; (industrial): 3,560 pupils. *Total:* 108,606 pupils; 6,661 teachers; 174 schools; 4,116 classes. *Higher:* 2 universities and 5 institutes.

Directory

The Constitution

A 108-article Constitution was ratified in June 1973. It states that 'all citizens shall be equal before the law' and guarantees freedom of speech, of the press, of conscience and religious beliefs. Other provisions include the outlawing of the compulsory repatriation of political refugees. The Constitution also states that the country's financial comptroller should be responsible to the legislature and not to the Government, and allows for national trade unions 'for legally justified causes and on peaceful lines'. Compulsory free primary education and free medical care are also laid down in the Constitution. The Constitution, which came into force on 6 December 1973, also provided for a National Assembly, composed of 14 members of the Cabinet and 30 members elected by popular vote, although this was dissolved in August 1975.

The Government

HEAD OF STATE

Amir: Sheikh Isa bin Sulman al-Khalifa (succeeded to the throne on 2 November 1961; took the title of Amir on 16 August 1971).

Crown Prince and Commander-in-Chief of Bahraini Defence Force and National Guard: Sheikh Hamad bin Isa al-Khalifa.

CABINET
(December 1997)

Prime Minister: Sheikh Khalifa bin Sulman al-Khalifa.

Minister of Justice and Islamic Affairs: Sheikh Abdullah bin Khalifa al-Khalifa.

Minister of Foreign Affairs: Sheikh Muhammad bin Mubarak bin Hamad al-Khalifa.

Minister of the Interior: Sheikh Muhammad bin Khalifa bin Hamad al-Khalifa.

Minister of Transport and Civil Aviation: Sheikh Ali bin Khalifa bin Salman al-Khalifa.

Minister of State: Jawad Salim al-Arrayedh.

Minister of Housing, Municipalities and Environment: Sheikh Khalid bin Abdullah bin Khalid al-Khalifa.

Minister of Public Works and Agriculture: Majid Jawad al-Jishi.

Minister of Finance and National Economy: Ibrahim Abd al-Karim Muhammad.

Minister of Defence: Maj.-Gen. Sheikh Khalifa bin Ahmad al-Khalifa.

Minister of Cabinet Affairs and Information: Muhammad Ibrahim al-Mutawa.

Minister of Oil and Industry: Sheikh Isa bin Ali al-Khalifa.

Minister of Commerce: Ali Saleh Abdullah as-Saleh.

Minister of Education: Brig.-Gen. Abd al-Aziz bin Muhammad al-Fadhil.

Minister of Health: Dr Faisal Radhi al-Mousawi.

Minister of Power and Water: Abdullah Muhammad Juma.

Minister of Labour and Social Affairs: Abd an-Nabi ash-Shula.

Minister of Amiri Court Affairs: Sheikh Ali bin Isa bin Sulman al-Khalifa.

MINISTRIES

Amiri Court: POB 555, Riffa Palace, Manama; tel. 666666; telex 8666.

Office of the Prime Minister: POB 1000, Government House, Government Rd, Manama; tel. 225522; telex 9336; fax 229022.

Ministry of Cabinet Affairs and Information: POB 26613, Government House, Government Rd, Manama; tel. 223366; telex 7424; fax 225202.

Ministry of Commerce: POB 5479, Diplomatic Area, Manama; tel. 531531; fax 530455.

Ministry of Defence: POB 245, West Rifa'a; tel. 665599; telex 8429; fax 662854.

Ministry of Education: POB 43, Isa Town; tel. 685558; telex 9094; fax 680161.

Ministry of Finance and National Economy: POB 333, Diplomatic Area, Manama; tel. 530800; telex 8933; fax 532853.

Ministry of Foreign Affairs: POB 547, Government House, Government Rd, Manama; tel. 227555; fax 212603.

Ministry of Health: POB 12, Sheikh Sulman Rd, Manama; tel. 255555; fax 254459.

Ministry of Housing, Municipalities and Environment: POB 11802, Diplomatic Area, Manama; tel. 533000; fax 534115.

Ministry of the Interior: POB 13, Police Fort Compound, Manama; tel. 272111; telex 9572; fax 262169.

Ministry of Justice and Islamic Affairs: POB 450, Diplomatic Area, Manama; tel. 531333; fax 532984.

Ministry of Labour and Social Affairs: POB 32333, Isa Town; tel. 687800; fax 686954.

Ministry of Oil and Industry: POB 1435, Manama; tel. 291511; telex 9199; fax 293007.

Ministry of Power and Water: POB 2, Manama; tel. 533133; telex 8515; fax 537151.

Ministry of Public Works and Agriculture: POB 5, Muharraq Causeway Rd, Manama; tel. 535222; telex 8515; fax 533095.

Ministry of Transport and Civil Aviation: POB 10325, Diplomatic Area, Manama; tel. 534534; telex 8989; fax 537537.

CONSULTATIVE COUNCIL

The Consultative Council is an advisory body of 40 members appointed by the ruling authorities for a four-year term, which is empowered to advise the Government but has no legislative powers. The Council held its inaugural session on 16 January 1993.

President: Ibrahim Muhammad Humaidan.

Legislature

NATIONAL ASSEMBLY

In accordance with the 1973 Constitution, elections to a National Assembly took place in December 1973. About 30,000 electors elected

30 members for a four-year term. Since political parties are not allowed, all 114 candidates stood as independents but, in practice, the National Assembly was divided almost equally between conservative, moderate and more radical members. In addition to the 30 elected members, the National Assembly contained 14 members of the Cabinet. In August 1975 the Prime Minister resigned because, he complained, the National Assembly was preventing the Government from carrying out its functions. The Amir invited the Prime Minister to form a new Cabinet, and two days later the National Assembly was dissolved by Amiri decree. It has not been revived.

Diplomatic Representation

EMBASSIES IN BAHRAIN

Algeria: POB 26402, Villa 579, Rd 3622, Adliya, Manama; tel. 713669; telex 7775; Ambassador: LAHSSAN BOUFARES.

Bangladesh: POB 26718, House 159, Rd 2004, Area 320, Hoora; tel. 293373; telex 7029; fax 291272; Chargé d'affaires: MUHAMMAD ABD AL-HYE.

China, People's Republic: POB 3150, Bldg 158, Road 382, Juffair Ave, Block 341, Manama; tel. 723800; fax 727304; Ambassador: WANG XIAOZHUANG.

Egypt: POB 818, Adliya; tel. 720005; telex 8248; Ambassador: MAHMOUD SAMI ESMAT.

Finland: POB 5794, Manama; tel. 530995; telex 8211; fax 536631.

France: POB 11134, Road 1901, Building 51, Block 319, Diplomatic Area, Manama; tel. 291734; telex 8323; fax 293655; Ambassador: GEORGES DUQUIN.

Germany: POB 10306, Al-Hasan Bldg, Sheikh Hamad Causeway, Manama; tel. 530210; telex 7128; fax 536282; Ambassador: NORBERT HEINZE.

India: POB 26106, Bldg 182, Rd 2608, Area 326, Adliya, Manama; tel. 712785; telex 9047; fax 715527; e-mail Indemb@batelco.com.bh; Ambassador: RAJANIKANTA VERMA.

Iran: POB 26365, Entrance 1034, Rd 3221, Area 332, Mahooz, Manama; tel. 722400; telex 8238; fax 722101; Chargé d'affaires: SAYEED MUHAMMAD AHMADI.

Iraq: POB 26477, Ar-Raqib Bldg, No 17, Rd 2001, Comp 320, King Faysal Ave, Manama; tel. 721213; telex 8325; fax 722482; Chargé d'affaires: AHMAD TAYES ABDULLAH.

Japan: 55 Salmaniya Ave, Manama Tower 327, Manama; tel. 716565; telex 7002; fax 712950; Ambassador: TOSHIAKI TANABE.

Jordan: POB 5242, Villa 43, Rd 915, Area 309, Hoora; tel. 291109; telex 7650; fax 291980; Dr SHAKER ARABIAT.

Korea, Republic: POB 11700, Bldg 69, Rd 1901, Block 319, Hoora; tel. 291629; fax 291628; Ambassador: LEE SOO-WHAN.

Kuwait: POB 786, Rd 1703, Diplomatic Area, Rd 1703, Manama; tel. 534040; telex 8830; fax 533579; Ambassador: ABD AL-WAHAB Y. AL-ADSANI.

Norway: POB 10580, Manama; tel. 531480; telex 9714; fax 530158.

Oman: POB 26414, Diplomatic Area, Bldg 37, Rd 1901, Manama; tel. 293663; telex 9332; fax 293540; Ambassador: RASHID BIN OBAID AL-GHARAIBI.

Pakistan: POB 563, Bldg 261, Rd 2807, Block 328, Segeiya, Manama; tel. 244113; fax 255960; Ambassador: MUHAMMAD NASSER MIAN.

Philippines: POB 26681, Bldg 81, Rd 3902, Block 339, Umm Al-Hassan; tel. 710200; fax 710300; Ambassador: AKMAD ATLAH SAKKAM.

Russia: POB 26612, House 877, Rd 3119, Block 331, Zinj, Manama; tel. 725222; telex 7006; fax 725921; Ambassador: ALEKSANDR NOVOZHILOV.

Saudi Arabia: POB 1085, Bldg 1450, Rd 4043, Area 340, Juffair, Manama; tel. 537722; telex 8061; fax 533261; Ambassador: ABDULLAH BIN ABD AR-RAHMAN ASH-SHEIKH.

Tunisia: POB 26911, House 54, Rd 3601, Area 336, Manama; tel. 714149; telex 7136; fax 715702; Ambassador: MOHSEN FRINI.

Turkey: POB 10821, Flat 10, Bldg 81, Rd 1702, Area 317, Manama; tel. 533448; telex 7049; fax 536557; e-mail tcbahrbe@batelco.com.bh; Ambassador: AYDEMIR ERMAN.

United Kingdom: POB 114, 21 Government Ave, Area 306, Manama; tel. 534404; telex 8213; fax 531273; e-mail britemb@batelco.com.bh; Ambassador: DAVID IAN LEWTY.

USA: POB 26431, Bldg 979, Rd 3119, Block 331, Zinj, Manama; tel. 273300; fax 272594; Ambassador: DAVID RANSOM.

Yemen: POB 26193, House 1048, Rd 1730, Area 517, Saar; tel. 277072; telex 8370; fax 262358; Ambassador: NASSER M.Y. ALGAADANI.

Judicial System

Since the termination of British legal jurisdiction in 1971, intensive work has been undertaken on the legislative requirements of Bahrain. The Criminal Law is at present contained in various Codes, Ordinances and Regulations. All nationalities are subject to the jurisdiction of the Bahraini courts which guarantee equality before the law irrespective of nationality or creed.

Directorate of Courts: POB 450, Government House, Government Rd, Manama; tel. 531333.

Religion

At the November 1991 census the population was 508,037, distributed as follows: Muslims 415,427; Christians 43,237; Others 49,373.

ISLAM

Muslims are divided between the Sunni and Shi'ite sects. The ruling family is Sunni, although the majority of the Muslim population (estimated at almost 60%) are Shi'ite.

CHRISTIANITY

The Anglican Communion

Within the Episcopal Church in Jerusalem and the Middle East, Bahrain forms part of the diocese of Cyprus and the Gulf. There are two Anglican churches in Bahrain, St Christopher's Cathedral in Manama and the Community Church in Awali, and the congregations are entirely expatriate. The Bishop and Archdeacon in Cyprus and the Gulf are both resident in Cyprus.

Provost: Very Rev. KEITH W. T. W. JOHNSON, St Christopher's Cathedral, POB 36, Al-Mutanabi Ave, Manama; tel. 253866; fax 246436; e-mail provost@batelco.com.bh.

Roman Catholic Church

A small number of adherents, mainly expatriates, form part of the Apostolic Vicariate of Arabia. The Vicar Apostolic is resident in the United Arab Emirates.

The Press

DAILIES

Akhbar al-Khalij (Gulf News): POB 5300, Manama; tel. 620111; telex 8565; fax 621566; f. 1976; Arabic; Chair. IBRAHIM AL-MOAYED; Man. Dir and Editor-in-Chief Dr HILAL ASH-SHAIJI; circ. 25,000.

Al-Ayam (The Days): POB 3232, Manama; tel. 727111; fax 729009; f. 1989; publ. by Al-Ayam Establishment for Press and Publications; Chair. and Editor-in-Chief NABIL YAQUB AL-HAMER; circ. 37,000.

Gulf Daily News: POB 5300, Manama; tel. 620222; telex 8565; fax 622141; e-mail gdn1@batelco.com.bh; f. 1978; English; Editor-in-Chief GEORGE WILLIAMS; Deputy Editor LES HORTON; circ. 50,000.

Khaleej Times: POB 26707, City Centre Bldg, Suite 403, 4th Floor, Government Ave, Manama; tel. 213911; telex 8973; fax 211819; f. 1978; English; circ. 79,000.

WEEKLIES

Al-Adhwaa' (Lights): POB 250, Old Exhibition Rd, Manama; tel. 291226; telex 8564; fax 293166; f. 1965; Arabic; publ. by Arab Printing and Publishing House; Chair. RAID MAHMOUD AL-MARDI; Editor-in-Chief MUHAMMAD QASSIM SHIRAWI; circ. 7,000.

Akhbar BAPCO (BAPCO News): Bahrain Petroleum Co BSC, POB 25149, Awali; tel. 755055; telex 8214; fax 755047; f. 1981; formerly known as *an-Najma al-Usbou'* (The Weekly Star); Arabic; house journal; Editor KHALID F. MEHMAS; circ. 3,000.

Al-Bahrain ath-Thaqfya: POB 26613, Manama; tel. 290210; fax 292678; Arabic; publ. by the Ministry of Cabinet Affairs and Information; Editor ABDULLAH YATIM.

BAPCO Weekly News: Refinery, Bahrain; tel. 755049; telex 8214; fax 755047; English; publ. by the Bahrain Petroleum Co BSC; Editor KATHLEEN CROES; circ. 600.

Huna al-Bahrain: POB 26005, Isa Town; tel. 731888; fax 681292; Arabic; publ. by the Ministry of Cabinet Affairs and Information; Editor HAMAD AL-MANNAI.

Al-Mawakif (Attitudes): POB 1083, Manama; tel. 231231; fax 271720; f. 1973; Arabic; general interest; Editor-in-Chief MANSOOR M. RADHI; circ. 6,000.

Oil and Gas News: POB 224, Bldg 149, Exhibition Ave, Manama; tel. 293131; telex 8981; fax 293400; English; publ. by Al-Hilal Publishing and Marketing Co; Editor GURDIP SINGH.

Sada al-Usbou' (Weekly Echo): POB 549, Bahrain; tel. 291239; telex 8880; fax 290507; f. 1969; Arabic; Owner and Editor-in-Chief ALI SAYYAR; circ. 40,000 (in various Gulf states).

OTHER PERIODICALS

Arab Agriculture: POB 10131, Manama; tel. 213900; fax 211765; annually; English and Arabic; publ. by Fanar Publishing WLL; Editor-in-Chief ABDUL WAHED AL-ALWANI; Gen. Man. FAYEK ALARAYED.

Arab World Agribusiness: POB 10131, Manama; tel. 213900; fax 211765; nine per year; English and Arabic; publ. by Fanar Publishing WLL; Editor-in-Chief ABDUL WAHED AL-ALWANI; Gen. Man. FAYEK ALARAYED.

Discover Bahrain: POB 10704, Manama; f. 1988; publ. by G. and B. Media Ltd; Publr and Editor ROBERT GRAHAM.

Gulf Construction: POB 224, Exhibition Ave, Manama; tel. 293131; telex 8981; fax 293400; e-mail hilalpmg@batelco.com.bh; monthly; English; publ. by Al-Hilal Publishing and Marketing Group; Editor BINA PRABHU GOVEAS; circ. 10,200.

Gulf Economic Monitor: POB 224, Exhibition Ave, Manama; tel. 293131; fax 293400; e-mail hilalpmg@batelco.com.bh; weekly; English; published by Al-Hilal Publishing and Marketing Group; Man. Dir RONNIE MIDDLETON.

The Gulf Tourism Directory: POB 33770, Manama; tel. 244613; fax 731067; f. 1990; English; Publr RASHID BIN MUHAMMAD AL-KHALIFA.

Al-Hayat at-Tijariya (Commerce Review): POB 248, Manama; tel. 229555; telex 8691; fax 224985/212937; e-mail bahcci@batelco.com.bh; monthly; English and Arabic; publ. by Bahrain Chamber of Commerce and Industry; Editor KHALIL YOUSUF; circ. 6,500.

Al-Hidayah (Guidance): POB 450, Manama; tel. 522384; fax 534626; f. 1978; monthly; Arabic; publ. by Ministry of Justice and Islamic Affairs; Editor-in-Chief ABD AR-RAHMAN BIN MUHAMMAD RASHID AL-KHALIFA; circ. 5,000.

Al-Mohandis (The Engineer): POB 835, Manama; f. 1972; quarterly; Arabic and English; publ. by Bahrain Association of Engineers; Editor KHALID AL-MOHANADI.

Al-Murshid (The Guide): POB 553, Manama; fax 293145; monthly; English and Arabic; includes 'What's on in Bahrain'; publ. by Arab Printing and Publishing House; Editor M. SOLIMAN.

Al-Musafir al-Arabi (Arab Traveller): POB 10131, Manama; tel. 213900; fax 211765; f. 1984; six per year; Arabic; publ. by Fanar Publishing WLL; Editor-in-Chief ABDUL WAHED AL-ALWANI; Gen. Man. FAYEK ALARAYED.

Panorama: POB 3232, Manama; tel. 727111; fax 729009; monthly; Editor IBRAHIM BASHMI; circ. 15,000.

Profile: POB 10243, Manama; tel. 291110; fax 294655; f. 1992; monthly; English; publ. by Bahrain Market Promotions; Editor ISA KHALIFA AL-KHALIFA.

Al-Quwwa (The Force): POB 245, Manama; tel. 291331; fax 659596; f. 1977; monthly; Arabic; publ. by Bahrain Defence Force; Editor-in-Chief Maj. AHMAD MAHMOUD AS-SUWAIDI.

Shipping and Transport News International: POB 224, Exhibition Ave, Manama; tel. 293131; telex 8981; fax 293400; six per year; English; publ. by Al-Hilal Publishing and Marketing Group; Editor FREDERICK ROCQUE; circ. 5,500.

Travel and Tourism News Middle East: POB 224, Exhibition Ave, Manama; tel. 293131; telex 8981; fax 293400; e-mail hilalpmg@batelco.com.bh; f. 1983; monthly; English; travel trade; publ. by Al-Hilal Publishing and Marketing Group; Editorial Research MARIA D'SOUZA; circ. 6,050.

NEWS AGENCIES

Agence France-Presse (AFP): POB 5890, Kanoo Tower, Phase 3, Tijaar Ave, Manama; tel. 259115; telex 8987; fax 277438; Dir JEAN-PIERRE PERRIN.

Associated Press (AP) (USA): POB 26940, Mannai Bldg, Manama; tel. 273238; telex 9470; fax 530249.

Deutsche Presse-Agentur (dpa) (Germany): POB 26995, Rd 2772, Villa 2788, Adliya 327, Manama; tel. 716655; telex 9542; fax 714119; Correspondent UTE MEINEL.

Gulf News Agency: POB 301, Manama; tel. 687272; telex 9030; fax 687008; Editor-in-Chief KHALID ZAYANI.

Inter Press Service (IPS) (Italy): c/o Gulf News Agency, POB 301, Manama; tel. 532235; fax 687008.

Press Trust of India: POB 2546, Manama; tel. 713431; telex 8482; Chief of Bureau SHAKIL AHMAD.

Reuters (United Kingdom): POB 1030, UGB Bldg, 6th Floor, Diplomatic Area, Manama; tel. 536111; telex 8301; fax 536192; Bureau Man. KENNETH WEST.

Publishers

Arab Communicators: POB 551, Manama; tel. 534664; telex 8263; fax 531837; publrs of annual Bahrain Business Directory; Dirs AHMAD A. FAKHRI, HAMAD A. ABUL.

Falcon Publishing WLL: POB 5028, Manama; tel. 253162; telex 8917; fax 259695; business magazines and directories; Chair. ABD AL-NABI ASH-SHOALA.

Gulf Advertising: POB 5518, Manama; tel. 226262; telex 8494; fax 228660; e-mail gulfad@batelco.com.bh; f. 1974; advertising and marketing communications.

Al-Hilal Publishing and Marketing Group: POB 224, Exhibition Ave, Manama; tel. 293131; fax 293400; e-mail hilalpmg@batelco.com.bh; f. 1977; specialist magazines and newspapers of commercial interest; Chair. A. M. ABD AR-RAHMAN; Man. Dir R. MIDDLETON.

Manama Publishing Co WLL: POB 1013, Manama; tel. 213223; telex 9246; fax 211548.

Al-Masirah Journalism, Printing and Publishing House: POB 5981, Manama; tel. 258882; telex 7421; fax 276178.

Tele-Gulf Directory Publications, WLL: POB 2738, 3rd Floor, Bahrain Tower, Manama; tel. 213301; fax 210503; e-mail telegulf@batelco.com.bh; publrs of annual *Gulf Directory* and *Arab Banking and Finance*; Chair. ABD AN-NABI ASH-SHO'ALA.

Government Publishing House

Directorate of Publications: POB 26005, Manama; tel. 689077; Dir MUHAMMAD AL-KHOZAI.

Broadcasting and Communications

TELECOMMUNICATIONS

AT & T Communications Middle East: POB 2603, Manama; tel. 233233; telex 7999; fax 230222; telecommunications systems.

Bahrain Telecommunications Co BSC (BATELCO): POB 14, Manama; tel. 881881; telex 8201; fax 883451; f. 1981; operates all telecommunications services; cap. BD 100m.; 80% owned by Government of Bahrain, financial institutions and public of Bahrain, 20% by Cable and Wireless PLC (United Kingdom); Chair. Sheikh ALI BIN KHALIFA BIN SALMAN AL-KHALIFA; CEO ANDREW HEARN.

Cabletron Systems: POB 3282, Manama; tel. 214642; fax 214645; telecommunication systems.

Intercol Telecom Systems: POB 584, Manama; tel. 727177; fax 727228.

Manama Telecom: POB 20211, Manama; tel. 404242; fax 404088; communications.

Satlink WLL: POB 3300, Manama; tel. 213333; telex 8172; fax 536666; satellite and telecommunication services.

Société Internationale de Télécom: POB 45, Manama; tel. 254081; telex 8252; fax 246093; telecommunication services.

BROADCASTING

English language television programmes, broadcast by the Arabian-American Oil Co (Aramco), can be received in Bahrain.

Bahrain Radio and Television Corpn: POB 1075, Manama; tel. 781888; telex 8311; fax 681544; commenced colour broadcasting in 1973; broadcasts on five channels, of which the main Arabic and the main English channel accept advertising, and three radio frequencies; covers Bahrain, eastern Saudi Arabia, Qatar and the UAE; an Amiri decree in early 1993 established the independence of the Corpn, which was to be controlled by a committee; CEO KHALIL ATH-THAWADI.

Radio

English language radio programmes, broadcast from Saudi Arabia by the US Air Force in Dhahran and by the Arabian-American Oil Co (Aramco), can be received in Bahrain.

Bahrain Broadcasting Station: POB 194, Manama; tel. 781888; telex 9259; f. 1955; state-owned and -operated enterprise; two 10-kW transmitters; programmes are in Arabic and English, and include news, plays and talks; Head of Station ABD AR-RAHMAN ABDULLAH.

Radio Bahrain: POB 702, Manama; tel. 781888; telex 8311; fax 780911; f. 1977; commercial radio station in English language; Head of Station AHMAD M. SULAIMAN.

Finance

(cap. = capital; p.u. = paid up; res = reserves; dep. = deposits; m. = millions; brs = branches; amounts in Bahraini dinars unless otherwise stated)

BANKING

Central Bank

Bahrain Monetary Agency (BMA): POB 27, Manama; tel. 535535; telex 8295; fax 534170; f. 1973, in operation from January 1975; controls issue of currency, regulates exchange control and credit policy, organization and control of banking system and bank credit; cap. 200m., res 47.3m., dep. 91.2m., total assets 455.7m. (Dec. 1996);

Governor ABDULLAH HASSAN SAIF; Chair. Sheikh KHALIFA BIN SULMAN AL-KHALIFA.

Locally-incorporated Commercial Banks

Al-Ahli Commercial Bank BSC: POB 5941, Bahrain Car Park Bldg, Government Rd, Manama; tel. 244333; telex 9130; fax 224322; f. 1977; full commercial bank; cap. 13.2m., res 26.0m., dep. 191.7m., total assets 236.8m. (Dec. 1996); Chair. MUHAMMAD Y. JALAL; CEO MICHAEL J. FULLER; 9 brs.

Arlabank International EC: POB 5070, Manama Centre, Manama; tel. 232124; telex 9345; fax 246239; f. 1977; wholly-owned subsidiaries: Arab-Latin American Bank (Banco Arabe Latino-americano) in Peru, Alpha Lambda Investment and Securities Corpn in the British Virgin Islands; cap. p.u. US $90.3m., dep. US $585.8m., total assets US $620.7m. (Dec. 1991); Chair. ABD AL-WAHAB A. AT-TAMMAR.

Bahrain Middle East Bank EC: POB 797, Manama; tel. 532345; telex 9706; fax 530987; f. 1982; owned by Burgan Bank (28%) and GCC nationals (72%); cap. US $84.0m., res US $22.8m., dep. US $531.0m., total assets US $646.0m. (Dec. 1996); Chair. ABD AR-RAHMAN SALEM AL-ATEEQI; CEO ALBERT I. KITTANEH; 1 br overseas and 1 rep. office.

Bahraini Saudi Bank BSC (BSB): POB 1159, Government Rd, Manama; tel. 211010; telex 7010; fax 210989; f. 1983; commenced operations in early 1985; licensed as a full commercial bank; cap. 20.0m., res 4.7m., dep. 95.3m., total assets 125.8m. (Dec. 1995); Chair. Sheikh IBRAHIM BIN HAMAD AL-KHALIFA; Gen. Man. MANSOOR AS-SAYED ALI; 4 brs.

Bank of Bahrain and Kuwait BSC (BBK): POB 597, Manama; tel. 223388; telex 8919; fax 229822; f. 1971; cap. 56.9m., res 16.6m., dep. 661.7m., total assets 758.8m. (Dec. 1996); Chair. RASHID ABD AR-RAHMAN AZ-ZAYANI; Gen. Man. and CEO MURAD ALI MURAD; 22 local brs, 2 brs overseas.

Faysal Islamic Bank of Bahrain EC: Chamber of Commerce Bldg, POB 20492, King Faysal Rd, Manama; tel. 275040; telex 9411; fax 210118; f. 1982 as Massraf Faysal Al-Islami of Bahrain EC; renamed as above in 1987; cap. US $70.0m., res US $30.8m., dep. US $180.8m., total assets US $368.1m. (Dec. 1995); Pres. and CEO NABIL ABD AL-ILLAH NASEER; 1 local br. and 7 brs overseas.

Grindlays Bahrain Bank BSC: POB 793, Manama; tel. 225999; telex 8335; fax 224482; f. 1984; commercial bank owned by Bahraini shareholders (60%) and ANZ Grindlays Bank PLC, London (40%); cap. 6.0m., res 4.0m., dep. 64.6m., total assets 76.7m. (Dec. 1996); Chair. MUHAMMAD ABDULLAH AZ-ZAMIL; Gen. Man. PETER TOMKINS; 3 brs.

Gulf International Bank BSC (GIB): POB 1017, Al-Dowali Bldg, 3 Palace Ave, Manama; tel. 534000; telex 8802; fax 522633; e-mail gibmktg@batelco.com.bh; internet http://www.gibonline.com; f. 1975; owned by the Gulf Investment Corpn; cap. US $450.0m., res US $202.5m., dep. US $7,673.6m., total assets US $8,982.9m. (Dec. 1996); Gen. Man. Dr ABDULLAH I. AL-KUWAIZ; 2 brs overseas and 3 rep. offices.

Gulf Riyad Bank EC: POB 20220, Manama Centre Bldg (Central Wing), Manama; tel. 232030; telex 9088; fax 250102; f. 1978; joint stock bank; 60% owned by Riyad Bank (Saudi Arabia), 40% by Crédit Lyonnais (France); cap US $50.0m., res US $26.1m., dep. US $120.0m., total assets US $196.8m. (Dec. 1994); Chair. TALAL AL-QUDAIBI; Gen. Man. PIERRE OUTIN.

National Bank of Bahrain BSC (NBB): POB 106, Government Ave, Manama; tel. 228800; telex 8242; fax 263876; f. 1957; 49% govt-owned; cap. 40.0m., res 45.0m., dep. 741.5m., total assets 857.4m. (Dec. 1996); Gen. Man. ABD AR-RAZAK A. HASSAN; CEO HUSSAN ALI JUMA; 25 brs.

Foreign Commercial Banks

ABN AMRO Bank NV (Netherlands): POB 350, Manama; tel. 255420; telex 8356; fax 262241; Man. C. A. A. VAN DER HAM; 1 br.

Arab Bank PLC (Jordan): POB 395, Government Rd, Manama; tel. 212255; telex 8232; fax 210443; internet http://www.arabbank.com; Chair. ABD AL-MAJEED SHOMAN; 4 brs.

Bank Melli Iran: POB 785, Government Rd, Manama; tel. 259910; telex 8266; fax 270768; Gen. Man. ALI ASGHAR KAMALI ROUSTA; 1 br.

Bank of Tokyo-Mitsubishi Ltd (Japan): Standard Chartered Bank Bldg, Government Ave, Manama; tel. 227518; fax 225013.

Bank Saderat Iran: POB 825, Government Rd, Manama; tel. 210003; telex 8363; fax 210398; Man. MUHAMMAD JAVAD NASSIRI; 2 brs.

Bankers' Trust Co (USA): First Floor, West Wing, Manama Centre, Manama; 1 br.

Banque de Commerce et de Placements (Switzerland): POB 11720, Bahrain Development Bank Bldg, Diplomatic Area, Manama; tel. 530500; telex 7900; fax 532400.

Banque du Caire (Egypt): POB 815, Manama; tel. 254454; telex 8298; fax 213704; Man. ES-SAYED MOUSTAFA EL-DOKMAWEY.

Banque Française de l'Orient (France): POB 5820, Zina Complex, Tijar Rd, Manama; tel. 257319; telex 8969; fax 261685; Man. HERMAN DOM.

Banque Nationale de Paris (France): POB 5253, BKIC House, Building No. 168, Road No. 1703, Diplomatic Area, Manama; tel. 531152; telex 8595; fax 531237.

Banque Paribas FCB (France): POB 5241, Manama; tel. 225275; telex 8458; fax 224697; Gen. Man. M. APTHORPE.

British Bank of the Middle East (BBME): POB 57, Al-Khalifa Rd, Manama; tel. 242555; telex 8230; fax 256822; CEO ROGER J. JORDAN; 4 brs.

Chase Manhattan Bank NA (USA): POB 368, Manama; tel. 535388; telex 8286; fax 535135; Vice-Pres. and Man. STEVEN J. FULLENKAMP.

Citibank NA (USA): POB 548, Government Rd, Manama; tel. 223344; telex 8225; fax 211323; Gen. Man. MUHAMMAD ASH-SHROOGI; 1 br.

Habib Bank Ltd (Pakistan): POB 566, Manama Centre, Manama; tel. 254889; telex 8240; fax 276685; f. 1941; Exec. Vice-Pres. and Gen. Man. ASHRAF BIDIWALA; 5 brs.

Hanil Bank (Republic of Korea): POB 1151, Manama Centre Bldg, Entrance 1, 4th Floor, Government Rd, Manama; tel. 243503; telex 7048; fax 271812; Gen. Man. MOO LEE.

Korea Exchange Bank (Republic of Korea): POB 5767, 4th Floor, Yateem Centre Bldg, Manama; tel. 258282; telex 8846; fax 243269; Gen. Man. JIN-HOE YOON.

National Bank of Kuwait: POB 5290, BMB Centre, Diplomatic Area, Manama; tel. 532225; telex 9024; fax 530658; Gen. Man. ALI Y. FARDAN.

Rafidain Bank (Iraq): POB 607, Manama; tel. 275796; telex 8332; fax 255656; f. 1969; Man. IBTISAM NAJEM ABOUD; 1 br.

Saudi National Commercial Bank: POB 10363, Manama; tel. 531182; telex 9298; fax 530657; Gen. Man. SALEH HUSSAIN.

Standard Chartered Bank (United Kingdom): POB 29, Government Rd, Manama; tel. 255946; telex 8229; fax 230503; f. in Bahrain 1920; Man. PETER RAWLINGS; 5 brs.

State Bank of India: POB 5466, 9th Floor, Bahrain Towers, Government Ave, Manama; tel. 245256; telex 8804; fax 263045; CEO S. C. BHAVE.

United Bank Ltd (Pakistan): POB 546, Government Rd, Manama; tel. 224032; telex 8247; fax 224099; Gen. Man. ZAFAR AL-HAQ MEMON; 3 brs.

Yapı ve Kredi Bankası AŞ (Turkey): POB 1104, Bahrain Development Bank Bldg, 2nd Floor, Diplomatic Area, Manama; tel. 530312; telex 9931; fax 530311.

Development Bank

Bahrain Development Bank (BDB): POB 20501, Manama; tel. 537007; telex 7022; fax 534005; f. 1992; invests in manufacturing, agribusiness and services; cap. and res 10.0m., dep. 0.1m., total assets 20.3m. (Dec. 1995); Chair. Sheikh EBRAHIM BIN KHALIFA AL-KHALIFA.

Specialized Financial Institutions

Arab Banking Corpn BSC: POB 5698, ABC Tower, Diplomatic Area, Manama; tel. 532235; telex 9432; fax 533163; internet http://www.arabbanking.com; f. 1980 by Amiri decree; jointly owned by Kuwait Ministry of Finance, Central Bank of Libya, Abu Dhabi Investment Authority and private investors; offers full range of commercial, merchant and investment banking services; cap. and res US $1,657m., total assets $22,988m. (Dec. 1996); Chair. ABD AL-YOUSEF AL-HUNAIF; 7 brs.

Bahrain Housing Bank: POB 5370, Diplomatic Area, Manama; tel. 534443; telex 8599; fax 533437; f. 1979; provides housing loans for Bahraini citizens and finances construction of commercial properties. Chair. Sheikh KHALID BIN ABDULLAH BIN KHALID AL-KHALIFA; Gen. Man. ISA SULTAN ADH-DHAWADI.

Bahrain Islamic Bank BSC: POB 5240, Government Rd, Manama; tel. 223402; telex 9388; fax 223956; f. 1979; cap. and res 14m., dep. 130.2m., total assets 147.9m. (May 1997); Chair. Sheikh ABD AR-RAHMAN AL-KHALIFA; Gen. Man. ABD AL-LATIF ABD AR-RAHIM JANAHI; 4 brs.

'Offshore' Banking Units

Bahrain has been encouraging the establishment of 'offshore' banking units (OBUs) since 1975. An OBU is not permitted to provide local banking services, but is allowed to accept deposits from governments and large financial organizations in the area and make medium-term loans for local and regional capital projects. Prior to the Iraqi invasion of Kuwait in August 1990, there were 56 OBUs in operation in Bahrain. By 1996, however, the number of OBUs had declined to 48.

Representative Offices

In late 1994 a total of 31 banks maintained representative offices in Bahrain.

Investment Banks

Al-Baraka Islamic Investment Bank BSC (EC): POB 1882, 1 Al-Hedaya Bldg, Government Rd, Manama; tel. 274488; telex 8220; fax 274499; f. 1984; cap. and res US $54.5m., dep. US $91.2m., total assets US $155.6m. (Dec. 1996); Chair. Sheikh SALEH ABDULLAH KAMEL.

Citi Islamic Investment Bank (CIIB): f. 1996; subsidiary of Citibank NA; cap. US $20m.; Chair. MUHAMMAD E. ASH-SHROOGI.

INVESTCORP Bank EC: POB 5340, Diplomatic Area, Manama; tel. 532000; telex 9664; fax 530816; f. 1982 as Arabian Investment Banking Corpn (INVESTCORP) EC, current name adopted in 1990; cap. and res US $179.1m., dep. US $548.2m., total assets US $1,742.8m. (Dec. 1996); Pres. and CEO NEMIR A. KIRDAR.

TAIB Bank EC: POB 20485, Sehl Centre, Diplomatic Area, Manama; tel. 533334; telex 8598; fax 533174; f. 1979 as Trans-Arabian Investment Bank EC; current name adopted in 1994; cap. and res US $99.5m., dep. US $202.9m., total assets US $306.9m. (Dec. 1995); Chair. ABD AR-RAHMAN AL-JERAISY; Vice-Chair. and CEO IQBAL G. MAMDANI.

Other investment banks operating in Bahrain include the following: Arab Financial Services Co EC, Arab Multinational Investment Co (AMICO), Bahrain International Investment Centre (BIIC), Bahrain Investment Bank EC, Bahrain Islamic Investment Co BSC, Bahraini Kuwaiti Investment Group (BKIG), Citicorp Investment Bank (CIB), Elders IXL, Gulf Investments Co, EF Hutton International Inc., InvestBank EC, Islamic Investment Company of the Gulf (Bahrain) EC, Merrill Lynch Int. Inc., National Bank of Pakistan, Nikko Investment Banking (Middle East) EC, Nomura Investment Banking (Middle East) EC, Okasan Int. (Middle East) EC, Robert Fleming Holdings Ltd, Sumitomo Finance (Middle East) EC, United Gulf Investment Co, Yamaichi International (Middle East) EC, Az-Zayani Investments Ltd.

STOCK EXCHANGE

Bahrain Stock Exchange: POB 3203, Manama; tel. 259690; telex 7937; fax 276181; f. 1989; nine mems; linked to Muscat Securities Market (Oman) in March 1995, and to Amman Financial Market (Jordan) in March 1996; Dir-Gen. Sheikh AHMAD BIN MUHAMMAD AL-KHALIFA.

INSURANCE

Abdullah Yousuf Fakhro Corpn: POB 39, Government Ave, Manama; tel. 275000; telex 8867; fax 256999; general.

Al-Ahlia Insurance Co BSC: POB 5282, Manama; tel. 258860; telex 8761; fax 245597; f. 1976; Chair. QASSIM AHMAD FAKHRO.

Arab Insurance Group BSC (ARIG): POB 26992, Arig House, Diplomatic Area, Manama; tel. 544444; telex 9395; fax 531155; f. 1980; owned by Governments of Kuwait, Libya and the UAE; reinsurance and insurance; Chair. and CEO ABD AL-WAHAB A. AT-TAMMAR.

Arab International Insurance Co EC (AIIC): POB 10135, Manama; tel. 530087; telex 9226; fax 530122; f. 1981; non-life reinsurance; Chair. and Man. Dir Sheikh KHALID J. AS-SABAH.

Bahrain Insurance Co BSC (BIC): POB 843, Suite 310, City Centre, Government Ave, Manama; tel. 227800; telex 8463; fax 224385; f. 1969; all classes including life insurance; 80% Bahraini-owned, 19% Iraqi-owned; Gen. Man. PATRICK N. V. IRWIN; 3 brs.

Bahrain Kuwait Insurance Co BSC: POB 10166, Diplomatic Area, Manama; tel. 532323; telex 8672; fax 530799; f. 1975; Gen. Man. HAMEED AL-NASSER.

Moustafa bin Abd al-Latif: POB 18, Bab al-Bahrain Rd, Manama; tel. 253417; telex 8558; fax 291423; Dir Sheikh MUHAMMAD YOUSUF NAJEEBI.

National Insurance Co BSC (NIC): POB 1818, Unitag House, Government Rd, Manama; tel. 228877; telex 8908; fax 228870; f. 1982; all classes of general insurance; Chair. J. A. WAFA; Gen. Man. SAMIR AL-WAZZAN.

Trade and Industry

CHAMBER OF COMMERCE

Bahrain Chamber of Commerce and Industry: POB 248, New Chamber of Commerce Bldgs, King Faysal Rd, Manama; tel. 229555; telex 8691; fax 224985; e-mail bahcci@batelco.com.bh; internet http://www.bahchamber.com; f. 1939; 6,500 mems (1996); Pres. ALI BIN YOUSEF FAKHROO; Sec.-Gen. JASSIM MUHAMMAD ASH-SHATTI.

UTILITIES

Gas

Bahrain Gas: POB 254, Manama; tel. 531111; telex 8988; fax 532112; gas supplies.

Nader Gas Co WLL: POB 507, Manama; tel. 404535; telex 8757; fax 404140; gas manufacturers and suppliers.

MAJOR STATE ENTERPRISES

(cap. = capital; p.u. = paid up)

Aluminium Bahrain BSC (ALBA): POB 570, Manama; tel. 830000; telex 8253; fax 830083; f. 1971; operates a smelter owned by the Government of Bahrain (77%) and the Saudi Public Investment Fund (20%), the remainder being held by Breton Investments; capacity now stands at 500,000 metric tons per year; Chair. Sheikh ISA BIN ALI AL KHALIFA.

Bahrain Atomizers International: POB 5328, Manama; tel. 830880; fax 830025; f. 1973; produces 7,000 metric tons of atomized aluminium powder per year; owned by the Government of Bahrain (51%) and Breton Investments (49%); Chair. Y. SHIRAWI.

Bahrain National Gas Co BSC (BANAGAS): POB 29099, Rifa'a; tel. 756222; telex 9317; fax 756991; f. 1979; responsible for extraction, processing and sale of hydrocarbon liquids from associated gas derived from onshore Bahraini fields; ownership is 75% Government of Bahrain, 12.5% Caltex and 12.5% Arab Petroleum Investments Corpn (APICORP); produced 202,955 metric tons of LPG and 189,803 tons of naphtha in 1996; Chair. Sheikh HAMAD BIN IBRAHIM AL-KHALIFA; Gen. Man. Dr. Sheikh MUHAMMAD BIN KHALIFA AL-KHALIFA.

Bahrain National Oil Co (BANOCO): POB 25504, Awali; tel. 754666; telex 8670; fax 753203; f. 1976; responsible for exploration, production, processing, transportation and storage of petroleum and petroleum products; distribution and sales of petroleum products (including natural gas), international marketing of crude petroleum and petroleum products, supply and sales of aviation fuels; produced an average of 40,000 barrels per day in 1994; Man. Dir MUHAMMAD SALEH SHEIKH ALI; Gen. Man. Dr FAYEZ HASHIM AS-SADAH.

Bahrain Petroleum Co BSC (BAPCO): POB 25504, Manama; tel. 754444; telex 8214; fax 752924; f. 1980; a refining company wholly owned by the Government of Bahrain; refined 95m. barrels of crude petroleum in 1996; Chair. Minister of Oil and Industry; Chief Exec. BRIAN WAYWELL.

Bahrain-Saudi Aluminium Marketing Co (BALCO): POB 20079, Manama; tel. 532626; telex 9110; fax 532727; f. 1976; to market ALBA products; owned by the Government of Bahrain (74.33%) and Saudi Basic Industries Corpn (25.67%); Gen. Man. HASSAN ALI FALAH.

Gulf Aluminium Rolling Mill Co (GARMCO): POB 20725, Manama; tel. 731000; telex 9786; fax 730542; f. 1980 as a joint venture between the Governments of Bahrain, Saudi Arabia, Kuwait, Iraq, Oman and Qatar; produced 60,000 tons of rolled aluminium in 1991; Chair. and Man. Dir Sheikh IBRAHIM BIN KHALIFA AL-KHALIFA; Gen. Man. JOHN PATERSON.

Gulf Petrochemical Industries Co BSC (GPIC): POB 26730, Sitra; tel. 731777; telex 9897; fax 731047; f. 1979 as a joint venture between the Governments of Bahrain, Kuwait and Saudi Arabia, each with one-third equity participation; cap. p.u. BD 60m.; a petrochemical complex at Sitra, inaugurated in 1981; produces 1,200 tons of both methanol and ammonia per day (1990); Chair. Sheikh ISA BIN ALI AL-KHALIFA; Gen. Man. MUSTAFA AS-SAYED.

TRADE UNIONS

There are no trade unions in Bahrain.

Transport

RAILWAYS

There are no railways in Bahrain.

ROADS

At 31 December 1996 Bahrain had 2,938 km of roads, of which 75% were hard-surfaced. Most inhabited areas of Bahrain are linked by bitumen-surfaced roads. In early 1997 the number of private cars in Bahrain totalled 132,750. Public transport consists of taxis and privately-owned bus services. A national bus company provides public services throughout the country. A modern network of dual highways is being developed, and a 25-km causeway link with Saudi Arabia was opened in 1986. A three-lane dual carriageway links the causeway to Manama. A joint Bahraini-Saudi bus company was formed in 1986, with capital of US $266,600, to operate along the causeway. Other causeways link Bahrain with Muharraq island and with Sitra island. In March 1997 the Government approved the construction of a US $80m.-causeway linking Hidd on Muharraq island with the port of Mina Salman; the new causeway was scheduled to be completed in 2001. A second 2.5-km Manama-to-Muharraq causeway was opened in early 1997.

Directorate of Roads: POB 5, Sheikh Hamad Causeway, Manama; tel. 535222; telex 7129; fax 532565; responsible for traffic engineering, safety, planning, road maintenance and construction; Dir ISAM A. KHALAF.

SHIPPING

Numerous shipping services link Bahrain and the Gulf with Europe, the USA, Pakistan, India, the Far East and Australia. In 1988 a total of 14,316 vessels called at Bahraini ports.

The deep-water harbour of Mina Salman was opened in 1962; it has 14 conventional berths, two container terminals and a roll-on/roll-off berth. Two nearby slipways can accommodate vessels of up to 1,016 tons and 73m in length, and services are available for ship repairs afloat. The second container terminal, which has a 400-m quay (permitting two 180-m container ships to be handled simultaneously), was opened in 1979. Further development of Mina Salman, to allow handling of larger quantities of container cargo, was completed in 1985. During 1992 Mina Salman handled about 90,000 TEUs (20-ft equivalent units).

Plans to build a new port and industrial zone at Hidd, on Muharraq island, were approved by the Cabinet in March 1997. At an estimated total cost of US $330m., the proposed port would have an annual handling capacity of 234,000 TEUs and would include a general cargo berth and two container berths with roll-on/roll-off facilities. The project was expected to be put out to tender in 1998.

Directorate of Customs and Ports: POB 15, Manama; tel. 725555; telex 8642; fax 725534; responsible for customs activities and acts as port authority; Pres. of Customs and Ports EID ABDULLAH YOUSUF; Dir-Gen. of Ports Capt. M. Y. ALMAHMOOD; Dir-Gen. of Customs JASSIM JAMSHEER.

Arab Shipbuilding and Repair Yard Co (ASRY): POB 50110, Hidd; tel. 671111; telex 8455; fax 670236; e-mail Asryco@batelco.com.bh; f. 1974 by OAPEC members; 500,000-ton dry dock opened 1977; two floating dry docks in operation since 1992; repaired 131 ships in 1996; Chair. Sheikh DAIJ BIN KHALIFA AL-KHALIFA; CEO MUHAMMAD M. AL-KHATEEB.

Principal Shipping Agents

Gray Mackenzie & Co Ltd: POB 210, Manama; tel. 712750; telex 7068; fax 712749; Dir A. A. MACASKILL.

The Gulf Agency Co (Bahrain) Ltd: POB 412, Manama; tel. 254228; telex 8211; fax 530063; Man. Dir SKJALM BANG.

International Agencies Co Ltd: POB 584, Manama; tel. 727114; telex 8273, fax 727509; Dir SADIQ M. AL-BAHARNA.

Al-Jazeera Shipping Co WLL: POB 302, Manama; tel. 728837; telex 7891; fax 728217.

Al-Sharif Shipping Agency: POB 1322, Manama; tel. 530535; telex 8341; fax 537637; e-mail alsharif@batelco.com.bh; Dir ABD AL-HUSSAIN AL-SHARIF.

Yusuf bin Ahmad Kanoo: POB 45, Al-Khalifa Rd, Manama; tel. 254081; telex 8215; fax 246093; air and shipping cargo services; Dir AHMAD KANOO.

CIVIL AVIATION

Bahrain International Airport has a first-class runway, capable of taking the largest aircraft in use. In 1996 there were 56,751 flights to and from the airport, carrying a total of 3.4m. passengers. Extension work to the airport's main terminal building was completed in mid-1992. Further extension work was due to be carried out in 1995, in order to increase the airport's cargo-handling facilities.

Department of Civil Aviation Affairs: POB 586, Bahrain International Airport, Muharraq; tel. 321095; telex 9186; fax 321139; Under-Sec. IBRAHIM ABDULLAH AL-HAMER.

Gulf Air Co GSC (Gulf Air): POB 138, Gulf Air Tower, Muharraq; tel. 322200; telex 8255; fax 338033; f. 1950; jointly owned by Govts of Bahrain, Oman, Qatar and Abu Dhabi (part of the United Arab Emirates) since 1974; services to the Middle East, South-East Asia, Africa and Europe; Chair. Sheikh AHMAD BIN NASSER BIN FALEH ATH-THANI (Qatar); Pres. and Chief Exec. Sheikh AHMAD BIN SAIF AN-NAHYAN (Abu Dhabi).

Tourism

There are several archaeological sites of importance. Bahrain is the site of the ancient trading civilization of Dilmun. There is a wide selection of hotels and restaurants, and a new national museum opened in 1989. In 1994 some 2.3m. tourists visited Bahrain, and income from tourism totalled more than US $300m.

Bahrain Tourism Co (BTC): POB 5831, Manama; tel. 530530; telex 8929; fax 530867; e-mail Bahtours@batelco.com.bh; Chair. MUHAMMAD YOUSUF JALAL.

Directorate of Tourism and Archaeology: POB 26613, Manama; tel. 201200; telex 8311; fax 210969; Dir Dr KADHIM RAJAB.

BANGLADESH

Introductory Survey

Location, Climate, Language, Religion, Flag, Capital

The People's Republic of Bangladesh lies in southern Asia, surrounded by Indian territory except for a short south-eastern frontier with Myanmar (formerly Burma) and a southern coast fronting the Bay of Bengal. The country has a tropical monsoon climate and suffers from periodic cyclones. The average temperature is 19°C (67°F) from October to March, rising to 29°C (84°F) between May and September. The average annual rainfall in Dhaka is 188 cm (74 ins), of which about three-quarters occurs between June and September. About 95% of the population speak Bengali, the state language, while the remainder mostly use tribal dialects. More than 85% of the people are Muslims, Islam being the state religion, and there are small minorities of Hindus, Buddhists and Christians. The national flag (proportions 5 by 3) is dark green, with a red disc slightly off-centre towards the hoist. The capital is Dhaka (Dacca).

Recent History

Present-day Bangladesh was formerly East Pakistan, one of the five provinces into which Pakistan was divided at its initial creation, when Britain's former Indian Empire was partitioned in August 1947. East Pakistan and the four western provinces were separated by about 1,000 miles (1,600 km) of Indian territory. East Pakistan was formed from the former Indian province of East Bengal and the Sylhet district of Assam. Although the East was more populous, government was based in West Pakistan. Dissatisfaction in East Pakistan at its dependence on a remote central Government flared up in 1952, when Urdu was declared Pakistan's official language. Bengali, the main language of East Pakistan, was finally admitted as the joint official language in 1954, and in 1955 Pakistan was reorganized into two wings, east and west, with equal representation in the central legislative assembly. However, discontent continued in the eastern wing, particularly as the region was under-represented in the administration and armed forces, and received a disproportionately small share of Pakistan's development expenditure. The leading political party in East Pakistan was the Awami League (AL), led by Sheikh Mujibur (Mujib) Rahman, who demanded autonomy for the East. General elections in December 1970 gave the AL an overwhelming victory in the East, and thus a majority in Pakistan's National Assembly; Sheikh Mujib should have become Prime Minister, but Pakistan's President, Gen. Yahya Khan, would not accept this, and negotiations on a possible constitutional compromise broke down. The convening of the new National Assembly was postponed indefinitely in March 1971, leading to violent protests in East Pakistan. The AL decided that the province should unilaterally secede from Pakistan, and on 26 March Mujib proclaimed the independence of the People's Republic of Bangladesh ('Bengal Nation').

Civil war immediately broke out. President Yahya Khan outlawed the AL and arrested its leaders. By April 1971 the Pakistan army dominated the eastern province. In August Sheikh Mujib was secretly put on trial in West Pakistan. Resistance continued, however, from the Liberation Army of East Bengal (the Mukhti Bahini), a group of irregular fighters who launched a major offensive in November. As a result of the fighting, an estimated 9.5m. refugees crossed into India. On 4 December India declared war on Pakistan, with Indian forces intervening in support of the Mukhti Bahini. Pakistan surrendered on 16 December and Bangladesh's independence became a reality. Pakistan was thus confined to its former western wing. In January 1972 Sheikh Mujib was freed by Pakistan's new President, Zulfiqar Ali Bhutto, and became Prime Minister of Bangladesh. Under a provisional Constitution, Bangladesh was declared to be a secular state and a parliamentary democracy. The new nation quickly achieved international recognition, causing Pakistan to withdraw from the Commonwealth in January 1972. Bangladesh joined the Commonwealth in April. The members who had been elected from the former East Pakistan for the Pakistan National Assembly and the Provincial Assembly in December 1970 formed the Bangladesh Constituent Assembly. A new Constitution was approved by this Assembly in November 1972 and came into effect in December. A general election for the country's first Jatiya Sangsad (Parliament) was held in March 1973. The AL received 73% of the total votes and won 292 of the 300 directly-elective seats in the legislature. Bangladesh was finally recognized by Pakistan in February 1974. Internal stability, however, was threatened by opposition groups which resorted to terrorism and included both political extremes. In December a state of emergency was declared and constitutional rights were suspended. In January 1975 parliamentary government was replaced by a presidential form of government. Sheikh Mujib became President, assuming absolute power, and created the Bangladesh Peasants' and Workers' Awami League. In February Bangladesh became a one-party state.

In August 1975 Sheikh Mujib and his family were assassinated in a right-wing coup, led by a group of Islamic army majors. Khandakar Mushtaq Ahmed, the former Minister of Commerce, was installed as President, declared martial law and banned political parties. A counter-coup on 3 November brought to power Brig. Khalid Musharaf, the pro-Indian commander of the Dhaka garrison, who was appointed Chief of Army Staff; on 7 November a third coup overthrew Brig. Musharaf's four-day-old regime and power was assumed by the three service chiefs jointly, under a non-political President, Abusadet Mohammed Sayem, the Chief Justice of the Supreme Court. A neutral non-party Government was formed, in which the reinstated Chief of Army Staff, Major-Gen. Ziaur Rahman (Gen. Zia), took precedence over his colleagues. Political parties were legalized again in July 1976.

An early return to representative government was promised, but in November 1976 elections were postponed indefinitely and, in a major shift of power, Gen. Zia took over the powers of Chief Martial Law Administrator from President Sayem, assuming the presidency also in April 1977. He amended the Constitution, making Islam, instead of secularism, its first basic principle. In a national referendum in May 99% of voters affirmed their confidence in President Zia's policies, and in June 1978 the country's first direct presidential election resulted in a clear victory for Zia, who formed a Council of Ministers to replace his Council of Advisers. Parliamentary elections followed in February 1979 and, in an attempt to persuade opposition parties to participate in the elections, President Zia met some of their demands by repealing 'all undemocratic provisions' of the 1974 constitutional amendment, releasing political prisoners and withdrawing press censorship. Consequently, 29 parties contested the elections, in which President Zia's Bangladesh Nationalist Party (BNP) received 49% of the total votes and won 207 of the 300 directly-elective seats in the Jatiya Sangsad. In April 1979 a new Prime Minister was appointed, and martial law was repealed. The state of emergency was revoked in November.

Political instability recurred, however, when Gen. Zia was assassinated on 30 May 1981 during an attempted military coup, allegedly led by Maj.-Gen. Mohammad Abdul Manzur, an army divisional commander who was himself later killed in confused circumstances. The elderly Vice-President, Justice Abdus Sattar, assumed the role of acting President but was confronted by strikes and demonstrations in protest against the execution of several officers who had been involved in the coup, and pressure from opposition parties to have the date of the presidential election moved. As the only person acceptable to the different groups within the BNP, Sattar was nominated as the party's presidential candidate, gaining an overwhelming victory at the November election. President Sattar announced his intention of continuing the policies of the late Gen. Zia. He found it increasingly difficult, however, to retain civilian control over the country, and in January 1982 he formed a National Security Council, which included military personnel, led by the Chief of Army Staff, Lt-Gen. Hossain Mohammad Ershad. On 24 March Gen. Ershad seized power in a bloodless coup, claiming that political corruption and economic mismanagement had become intolerable. The country was placed under martial law, with Ershad as Chief Martial Law Administrator (in October his title was changed to Prime Minister), aided by a mainly military Council of Advisers; a retired judge, Justice Abul Chowdhury, was nominated as President by Ershad. Political activities were banned. Later in the year, several former ministers were tried and imprisoned on charges of corruption.

Although the Government's economic policies achieved some success and gained a measure of popular support for Ershad, there were increasing demands in 1983 for a return to democratic government. The two principal opposition groups that emerged were an eight-party alliance, headed by the AL under Sheikh Hasina Wajed (daughter of the late Sheikh Mujib), and a seven-party group which was led by the BNP under the former President Sattar (who died in October 1985) and Begum Khaleda Zia (widow of Gen. Zia). In September 1983 the two groups formed an alliance, the Movement for the Restoration of Democracy (MRD), and jointly issued demands for an end to martial law, for the release of political prisoners and for the holding of parliamentary elections before any others. In November permission was given for the resumption of political activity, and it was announced that a series of local elections between December 1983 and March 1984 were to precede a presidential election and parliamentary elections later in the year. A new political party, the Jana Dal (People's Party), was formed in November 1983 to support Ershad as a presidential candidate. Following demonstrations demanding civilian government, the ban on political activity was reimposed at the beginning of December, only two weeks after it had been rescinded, and leading political figures were detained. On 11 December Ershad declared himself President.

Bangladesh remained disturbed in 1984, with frequent strikes and political demonstrations. Local elections to *upazilla* (sub-district) councils, due to take place in March, were postponed, as the opposition objected to their being held before the presidential and parliamentary elections, on the grounds that Ershad was trying to strengthen his power-base. The presidential and parliamentary elections, scheduled for May, were also postponed, until December, because of persistent opposition demands for the repeal of martial law and for the formation of an interim neutral government to oversee a fair election. In October Ershad agreed to repeal martial law in three stages in November and December if the opposition would participate in the elections. They responded with an appeal for a campaign of civil disobedience, which led to the announcement in October that the elections were to be indefinitely postponed.

In January 1985 it was announced that parliamentary elections would be held in April, to be preceded by a relaxation of martial law in certain respects: the Constitution was to be fully restored after the elections. The announcement was followed by the formation of a new Council of Ministers, composed entirely of military officers and excluding all members of the Jana Dal, in response to demands by the opposition parties for a neutral government during the pre-election period. Once more, the opposition threatened to boycott the elections, as President Ershad would not relinquish power to an interim government, and in March the elections were abandoned and political activity was again banned. This was immediately followed by a referendum, held in support of the presidency, in which Ershad received 94% of the total votes. Local elections for *upazilla* councils in rural areas were held in May, without the participation of the opposition, and Ershad claimed that 85% of the elected council chairmen were his supporters, although not necessarily of his party. In September a new five-party political alliance, the National Front (comprising the Jana Dal, the United People's Party, the Gonotantrik Party, the Bangladesh Muslim League and a breakaway section of the BNP), was established to promote government policies.

In January 1986 the 10-month ban on political activity was ended. The five components of the National Front formally became a single pro-Government entity, named the Jatiya Dal (National Party). In March President Ershad announced that parliamentary elections were to be held (under martial law) at the end of April. He relaxed martial law, however, by removing all army commanders from important civil posts and by abolishing more than 150 military courts and the martial law offices. These concessions fulfilled some of the opposition's demands and, as a result, candidates from the AL alliance (including Sheikh Hasina Wajed herself), the Jamaat-e-Islami Bangladesh and other smaller opposition parties participated in the parliamentary elections on 7 May (postponed from 26 April). However, the BNP alliance, led by Begum Khaleda Zia, boycotted the polls. The elections were characterized by allegations of extensive fraud, violence and intimidation. The Jatiya Dal won 153 of the 300 directly-elective seats in the Jatiya Sangsad. In addition, the 30 seats reserved for women in the legislature were filled by nominees of the Jatiya Dal. In July a mainly civilian Council of Ministers was sworn in. Mizanur Rahman Chowdhury, former General-Secretary of the Jatiya Dal, was appointed Prime Minister.

In order to be eligible to stand as a candidate in the presidential election in October 1986, Ershad retired as Chief of Army Staff in August, while remaining as Chief Martial Law Administrator and Commander-in-Chief of the Armed Forces. In early September Ershad joined the Jatiya Dal, being elected as Chairman of the party and nominated as its presidential candidate. At the presidential election in mid-October, which was boycotted by both the BNP and the AL, Ershad won an overwhelming victory over his 11 opponents.

In November 1986 the Jatiya Sangsad approved indemnity legislation, legalizing the military regime's actions since March 1982. Ershad repealed martial law and restored the 1972 Constitution. The opposition alliances criticized the indemnity law, stating that they would continue to campaign for the dissolution of the Jatiya Sangsad and the overthrow of the Ershad Government. In December 1986, in an attempt to curb increasing dissension, President Ershad formed a new Council of Ministers, including four MPs from the AL. The Justice Minister, Justice A. K. M. Nurul Islam, was appointed Vice-President.

In 1987 the opposition groups continued to hold anti-Government strikes and demonstrations, often with the support of the trade unions and student groups. In July the Jatiya Sangsad approved the Zilla Parishad (District Council) Amendment Bill, enabling army representatives to participate in the district councils, along with the elected representatives. The adoption of this controversial legislation led to widespread and often violent strikes and demonstrations, organized by the opposition groups, who claimed that the bill represented an attempt by the President to secure an entrenched military involvement in the governing of the country, despite the ending of martial law in November 1986. Owing to the intensity of public opposition, President Ershad was forced to withdraw the bill in August 1987 and return it to the Jatiya Sangsad for reconsideration. Political events were overshadowed in August and September, however, when the most severe floods in the region for 40 years resulted in widespread devastation. In a renewed effort to oust President Ershad, the opposition groups combined forces and organized further protests in November. Thousands of activists were detained, but demonstrations, strikes and opposition rallies continued, leading to numerous clashes between police units and protesters. The unrest caused considerable economic dislocation, and the Government claimed that the country was losing US $50m. per day. As a result of this, and in an attempt to forestall another general strike being planned by opposition groups, President Ershad declared a nationwide state of emergency on 27 November, suspending political activity and civil rights, and banning all anti-Government protests, initially for 120 days. In spite of the imposition of curfews on the main towns, reports of disturbances continued, as the opposition maintained its campaign to force Ershad's resignation. In early December, when about 6,000 people were being detained in prison as a result of the unrest, opposition parties in the Jatiya Sangsad announced that their representatives intended to resign their seats. On 6 December, after 12 opposition members had resigned and the 73 AL members had agreed to do likewise, President Ershad dissolved the Jatiya Sangsad. In January 1988 the President announced that parliamentary elections would be held on 28 February, but leaders of the main opposition parties declared their intention to boycott the proposed poll while Ershad remained in office. Local elections to the Union Parishads, which were held throughout Bangladesh in February and which were not boycotted by the opposition, were marred by serious outbreaks of violence. The parliamentary elections (postponed until 3 March) were also characterized by widespread violence, as well as by alleged fraud and malpractice. The opposition's boycott campaign proved to be highly successful and the actual level of participation by the electorate appeared to have been considerably lower than the Government's estimate of 50%. As expected, the Jatiya Dal won a large majority of the seats.

In late March 1988 a radical reshuffle of the Council of Ministers included the appointment of a new Prime Minister, Moudud Ahmed, a long-time political ally of Ershad and hitherto the Minister of Industry and a Deputy Prime Minister, in place of Mizanur Rahman Chowdhury. Owing to an abatement in the opposition's anti-Government campaign, Ershad repealed the state of emergency in April. Despite strong condemnation by the opposition and sections of the public, legislation to amend the Constitution, establishing Islam as Bangladesh's state religion, was approved by an overall majority in the Jatiya Sangsad in June. By early September, however, political events had been completely overshadowed by a new wave of disastrous monsoon floods, which began in August and proved to be the most severe in the area's recorded history. Bangladesh suffered further flooding in December 1988 and January 1989, following a severe cyclone in late November. The resultant economic problems undoubtedly compounded the political unrest in Bangladesh. In late 1988 the Government established a national Disaster Prevention Council and urged the use of regional co-operation to evolve a comprehensive solution to the problem of flooding.

The Government claimed that it was reinforcing constitutionality and democracy when, in July 1989, the Jatiya Sangsad approved legislation limiting the tenure of the presidency to two electoral terms of five years each and creating the post of a directly-elected Vice-President (previously appointed by the President). In August Ershad appointed Moudud Ahmed, hitherto the Prime Minister, as Vice-President, to replace Justice A.K.M. Nurul Islam, who was dismissed following charges of inefficiency. Kazi Zafar Ahmed, formerly the Minister of Information and a Deputy Prime Minister, was promoted to the post of Prime Minister. Local elections were held in March 1990. These elections were officially boycotted by the opposition parties, but, in fact, many of their members participated on an individual basis. In April Ershad announced that he would present himself as a candidate in the presidential election, which was scheduled to be held in mid-1991.

In late 1990 the opposition groups, with the support of thousands of students, worked more closely together and increased the intensity of their anti-Government campaign of strikes and demonstrations. In October at least eight demonstrators were shot dead by riot police, more than 500 people were arrested and Ershad announced the closure of Dhaka University and other educational institutions. Violent incidents also occurred in Chittagong and in several other towns in southern and central Bangladesh. On 27 November President Ershad proclaimed a nationwide state of emergency for the second time in three years, suspending civil rights, imposing strict press censorship and enforcing an indefinite curfew throughout the country. On the following day, however, army units were summoned to impose order in the capital when crowds of thousands defied the curfew and attacked police in protest at the imposition of the state of emergency. The death toll in resultant clashes between the troops and demonstrators was variously estimated at between 20 and 70. Under intensifying pressure from the opposition groups, President Ershad resigned on 4 December and declared that parliamentary elections would be held before the presidential election. At the same time, the state of emergency was revoked, and the Jatiya Sangsad was dissolved. Following his nomination by the opposition, Justice Shahabuddin Ahmed, the Chief Justice of the Supreme Court, was appointed Vice-President. He assumed the responsibilities of acting President and was placed at the head of a neutral caretaker Government, pending fresh parliamentary elections. Shahabuddin Ahmed dismissed heads of financial institutions, purged local government and ordered a massive reshuffle in the civil service to remove persons appointed by Ershad from important posts. The opposition parties welcomed all these dramatic political developments and abandoned their protest campaigns, while appealing for calm. They also demanded that Ershad should be tried for alleged corruption and abuse of power. In the week following his resignation, Ershad was put under house arrest and detained for 120 days, in accordance with a law that permits arrest without charges (he was later sentenced to 20 years' imprisonment for illegal possession of firearms and other offences).

Fresh parliamentary elections were held on 27 February 1991. The BNP alliance won an overall majority and, following discussions with the Jamaat-e-Islami, as a result of which the BNP was ensured a small working majority in the Jatiya Sangsad, Begum Khaleda Zia assumed office as Prime Minister. In May the new Government was faced with the immense problems caused by a devastating cyclone which killed up to 250,000 people and wrought massive economic damage. In August the Jatiya Sangsad approved a constitutional amendment ending 16 years of presidential rule and restoring the Prime Minister as executive leader (under the previous system, both the Prime Minister and the Council of Ministers had been answerable to the President). The amendment, which was formally enforced when it was approved by national referendum in the following month, reduced the role of the President, who was now to be elected by the Jatiya Sangsad for a five-year term, to that of a titular Head of State. Accordingly, a new President was elected by the Jatiya Sangsad on 8 October. The successful candidate was the BNP nominee, the erstwhile Speaker of the Jatiya Sangsad, Abdur Rahman Biswas. In September the BNP had gained an absolute majority in the Jatiya Sangsad, following the party's victory in five of the 11 by-elections. In late November, despite strong protest from the opposition parties, the Government abolished the *upazilla* (sub-district) system of rural administration, introduced by Ershad in 1982. Henceforth, all public functions at *upazilla* level were to be performed through executive orders of the central Government, pending the introduction of a new system of rural administration. To this end, the Government established a special committee, headed by the Minister of Information, to review all aspects of local government.

In early 1992 measures to transfer public-sector industries to private ownership and to curb endemic labour unrest, introduced as part of the process of economic restructuring undertaken by the Government in conjunction with aid donors, led to strong political resistance from the opposition. In April, in an apparent attempt to destabilize the Government, accusations were made against the leader of the Jamaat-e-Islami, Golam Azam, of complicity in Pakistani war crimes in 1971 and of having remained a Pakistani citizen while participating in Bangladesh politics. The AL MPs boycotted the Jatiya Sangsad over the issue and demanded that Azam be put on trial immediately before a special tribunal. Eventually a compromise was reached in late June 1992, whereby charges were to be brought against him, but only through the highly dilatory regular courts. In mid-August the Government survived a parliamentary motion of no confidence, introduced by the AL, by 168 votes to 122. The opposition accused the Government of failing to curb the increasing lawlessness in the country, notably amongst university students. The stringent anti-terrorism measures introduced by the Government in November, however, were widely criticized as being excessively harsh and undemocratic. Subsequently, the opposition parties sank their differences in pursuit of a common demand that the general election due in 1996 be held under the auspices of a neutral, caretaker government. From late 1993 and into the first half of 1994 large-scale anti-Government demonstrations were organized by the Jatiya Dal and the AL, with the co-operation of the Jamaat-e-Islami. A boycott of parliamentary proceedings was initiated by the opposition in February 1994. In January the AL won the mayoralties of Dhaka and Chittagong, the country's two largest cities, but a by-election success in March revealed the continuing strength of the BNP elsewhere.

In 1993–94 the apparently increasing influence and popularity of Islamic fundamentalism in Bangladesh was reflected in the high-profile campaign against the feminist author, Taslima Nasreen, who angered certain traditionalist sectors of the population with her allegedly anti-Islamic public stance and statements. Despite her claim that she had been misquoted in the national press, there were demands from Islamic bodies, often expressed at large demonstrations, that Nasreen should be executed. The Government issued a warrant for the author's arrest on blasphemy-related charges, although she had gone into hiding before it could be implemented. In August 1994, with the apparent complicity of government officials, Nasreen secretly fled Bangladesh and was granted refuge in Sweden.

The number of strikes and violent protests staged by the opposition increased in the latter half of 1994. Despite concerted efforts to resolve the situation through negotiations between the two sides, under the auspices of Commonwealth officials, the anti-Government actions culminated in the resignation of all the opposition members from the Jatiya Sangsad *en masse* on 28 December. A few days later the opposition rejected the Prime Minister's offer of standing down 30 days before the next general election to meet demands for the establishment of a caretaker administration to oversee the polls. In spite of the political chaos, compounded by the holding of further general strikes by the opposition, the Prime Minister, with her party's parliamentary majority, pledged to maintain constitutional government.

In June 1995 former President Ershad was acquitted of illegally possessing arms; his sentence was thus reduced to 10 years. In the following month, however, Ershad was sentenced to a further three years' imprisonment for criminal misconduct.

The opposition caused more general disruption in September–October 1995 by organizing nation-wide strikes, which were, at times, marked by outbreaks of violence between police and demonstrators. In response to the intensification of the anti-Government campaign and in an attempt to break the political impasse (the opposition were refusing to take part in the coming by-elections), the Jatiya Sangsad was dissolved on 24 November at the request of the Prime Minister, pending the holding of a general election in early 1996. Despite opposition demands for a neutral interim government to oversee the election, Begum Khaleda Zia's administration was requested to continue in office in an acting capacity. In December 1995 the date for the general election was moved from 18 January 1996 to 7 February in an attempt to encourage all parties to take part. Strikes and demonstrations aimed at obstructing the electoral process were organized by the opposition, however, throughout December 1995 and into January 1996. In early January the election date was postponed again, to 15 February. In the event, all of the main opposition parties boycotted the election and independent monitors estimated the turn-out at only about 10%–15% of the electorate. Of the 207 legislative seats declared by the end of February, the BNP had won 205 (a partial repoll had been ordered in most of the 93 remaining constituencies where violence had disrupted the electoral process). The opposition refused to recognize the legitimacy of the polls and announced the launch of a 'non-co-operation' movement against the Government. Renewed street protest made the country virtually ungovernable and, finally, pressure from the army and other sources forced Begum Khaleda Zia to agree to the holding of fresh elections under neutral auspices, as the opposition had demanded all along. The Prime Minister and her Government duly resigned from their posts on 30 March and the Jatiya Sangsad was dissolved. President Biswas appointed the former Chief Justice, Muhammad Habibur Rahman, as acting Prime Minister and requested that a fresh general election be held, under the auspices of an interim neutral government, within three months. In the general election, which was held on 12 June, the AL won 146 of the 300 elective seats in the Jatiya Sangsad, the BNP 116, the Jatiya Dal 32 and the Jamaat-e-Islami three. An understanding was rapidly reached between the AL and the Jatiya Dal, whose major interest was the release of Ershad, who had gained a legislative seat from within prison. (The former President was released on bail in January 1997.) Sheikh Hasina Wajed was sworn in as the new Prime Minister on 23 June 1996. Her Council of Ministers incorporated one member from the Jatiya Dal; it also included a number of retired officials and army officers.

During the electoral campaign an unsuccessful military coup attempt was carried out (on 20 May 1996), which indicated the continuing fragility of the country's institutions. The Chief of Army Staff, Lt-Gen. Abu Saleh Mohammed Nasim, who had objected to the action of the President (who retained direct control of the armed forces during the caretaker period prior to the general election) in dismissing some senior officers for political activity, endeavoured to seize power, but was unable to mobilize sufficient support to achieve his aim. Lt-Gen. Nasim was immediately dismissed, and a new Chief of Army Staff was appointed.

On 23 July 1996 the AL's presidential nominee, retired Chief Justice and former acting President, Shahabuddin Ahmed, was elected unopposed (the opposition did not present any candidates) as Bangladesh's new Head of State. In early September the AL won eight of the 15 seats contested in by-elections; this result gave the AL, which was also allocated 27 of the 30 nominated women's parliamentary seats in July, an absolute majority in the Jatiya Sangsad.

On assuming power, Sheikh Hasina Wajed had vowed to bring to justice those responsible for the assassination of her father, Sheikh Mujibur Rahman, in 1975. In November 1996 the Jatiya Sangsad voted unanimously to repeal the indemnity law that had been enacted in 1975 to protect the perpetrators of the military coup in that year; the BNP and the Jamaat-e-Islami Bangladesh, however, boycotted the vote. The trial of 20 people accused of direct involvement in Sheikh Mujib's assassination began in March 1997, with 14 of the defendants being tried *in absentia*.

Agitational politics continued throughout 1997; in March the opposition launched a campaign to protest against the Government's agreement with India with regard to the sharing of the Ganges waters (see below), and during an anti-Government strike held at the end of the month one person was killed and many were injured. The opposition organized further disruptive general strikes in July and August in protest at the Government's imposition of higher taxes as part of the annual budget and at the increase in fuel prices, respectively. Despite a subsequent government ban on street rallies and processions, a series of strikes and demonstrations, organized by the BNP in conjunction with Islamic and right-wing groups, ensued. In addition to the disruption caused by such actions (which frequently involved violent clashes between demonstrators and police), the efficacy of the Jatiya Sangsad was limited by several boycotts of parliamentary proceedings organized by BNP deputies throughout the year.

In foreign affairs Bangladesh has traditionally maintained a policy of non-alignment. Relations with Pakistan improved in 1976: ambassadors were exchanged, and trade, postal and telecommunication links were resumed. In September 1991 Pakistan finally agreed to initiate a process of phased repatriation and rehabilitation of some 250,000 Bihari Muslims (who supported Pakistan in Bangladesh's war of liberation in 1971) still remaining in refugee camps in Bangladesh. The first group of Bihari refugees returned to Pakistan from Bangladesh in January 1993, but the implementation of the repatriation process has since been very slow. Relations with India have been strained over the questions of cross-border terrorism (especially around the area of the Chittagong Hill Tracts, where Buddhist tribal rebels, the Shanti Bahini, have been waging guerrilla warfare against the Bangladeshi police and the Bengali settlers for several years) and of the Farrakka barrage, which was constructed by India on the Ganga (Ganges) river in 1975, so depriving Bangladesh of water for irrigation and river transport during the dry season. In December 1996, however, Indo-Bangladesh relations were given a major boost following the signing of an historic 30-year water-sharing agreement. The agreement also allowed for India to have transit rights over Bangladesh territory in order to reach parts of its remote north-eastern states more easily. In January 1997 the Indian Prime Minister, H. D. Deve Gowda, paid an official visit to Bangladesh, the first Indian Premier to do so for 20 years. In August 1985 Bangladesh and Burma (now Myanmar) completed work on the demarcation of their common border, in accordance with a May 1979 agreement. During 1991 more than 50,000 Rohingya Muslims, a Myanma ethnic minority, crossed into Bangladesh to escape political persecution in Myanmar. Despite the signing of an agreement by the Ministers of Foreign Affairs of Bangladesh and Myanmar in April 1992 regarding the repatriation of the Rohingyas, the influx of refugees continued unabated (by the end of June the number of Rohingya refugees in Bangladesh had increased to about 270,000). By early September 1994 about 65,000 refugees had reportedly been voluntarily repatriated. Meanwhile, in December 1993 Bangladesh and Myanmar had signed an agreement to instigate border trade between the two countries. By the end of May 1995, according to government figures, more than 216,000 Rohingyas had been repatriated. In August 1997, however, about 28,000 Rohingya refugees remained in camps in Bangladesh, despite the expiry of the official deadline for their repatriation in that month.

In 1989 the Government attempted to suppress the continuing insurgency being waged by the Shanti Bahini in the Chittagong Hill Tracts, by introducing concessions providing limited autonomy to the region in the form of three new semi-autonomous hill districts. In June voting to elect councils for the districts took place reasonably peacefully, despite attempts at disruption by the Shanti Bahini, who continued to demand total autonomy for the Chakma tribals. The powers vested in the councils were designed to give the tribals sufficient authority to regulate any further influx of Bengali settlers to the districts (the chief complaint of the tribals since Bengalis were settled in the Chittagong Hill Tracts, as plantation workers and clerks, by the British administration in the 19th century). Despite these concessions, the violence continued unabated in the latter half of 1989 and in 1990–92, and refugees continued to flee across the border into India (the number of refugees living in camps in Tripura reached about 56,000). In May 1992 the Governments of Bangladesh and India negotiated an agreement which was intended to facilitate the refugees' return. However, the refugees, fearing persecution by the Bangladesh security forces, proved reluctant to move. Following the conclusion of a successful round of negotiations between representatives of the Indian Government, the Bangladesh Government and the Chakma refugees in early 1994, the process of repatriation, which was to be carried out in phases, commenced in mid-February. By August, however, only about 2,000 refugees had returned. In December 1997 the Bangladesh Government signed a peace agreement with the political wing of the Shanti Bahini ending the insurgency in the Chittagong Hill Tracts. The treaty offered the rebels a general amnesty in return for the surrender of their arms and gave the tribal people greater powers of self-governance through the establishment of a new regional council (the chairman of which was to enjoy the rank of a state minister). The peace agreement, which was strongly criticized by the opposition for representing a 'sell-out' of the area to India and a threat to Bangladesh's sovereignty, was expected to accelerate the process of repatriating the remaining refugees from Tripura (who totalled about 31,000 at the end of December).

In late June 1992 the Indian Government, under the provisions of an accord signed with Bangladesh in 1974, formally leased the Tin Bigha Corridor (a small strip of land covering an area of only 1.5 ha) to Bangladesh for 999 years. India maintains sovereignty over the corridor, but the lease gives Bangladesh access to its enclaves of Dahagram and Angarpota. In September 1997 India granted Nepal a transit route through a 60-km corridor in the Indian territory joining Nepal and Bangladesh, thus facilitating trade between the latter two countries.

Bangladesh is a member of the South Asian Association for Regional Co-operation (SAARC, see p. 263), formally constituted in December 1985, with Bhutan, India, Maldives, Nepal, Pakistan and Sri Lanka. Included in SAARC's newly-drafted charter were pledges of non-interference by members in each other's internal affairs and a joint effort to avoid 'contentious' issues whenever the association meets.

Government

The role of the President, who is elected by the Jatiya Sangsad (Parliament) for a five-year term, is essentially that of a titular Head of State. Executive power is held by the Prime Minister, who heads the Council of Ministers. The President appoints the Prime Minister and, on the latter's recommendation, other ministers. Three hundred of the 330-member Jatiya Sangsad are elected by universal suffrage. An additional 30 women members are appointed by the other members. The Jatiya Sangsad serves a five-year term, subject to dissolution.

Defence

Military service is voluntary. In August 1997 the armed forces numbered 121,000: an army of 101,000, a navy of 10,500 and an air force of 9,500. The paramilitary forces totalled 49,700, and included the Bangladesh Rifles (border guard) of 30,000. Budget expenditure on defence was estimated at 24,600m. taka for 1997.

Economic Affairs

In 1995, according to estimates by the World Bank, Bangladesh's gross national product (GNP), measured at average 1993–95 prices, was US $28,599m., equivalent to $240 per head. During 1985–95, it was estimated, GNP per head increased, in real terms, at an average annual rate of 2.1%. Over the same period, the population increased by an annual average of 2.0%. Bangladesh's gross domestic product (GDP) increased by an annual average of 4.1% in 1985–95; GDP grew by 4.4% in 1994/95, by 5.3% in 1995/96 and by 5.7% in 1996/97.

Agriculture (including hunting, forestry and fishing) contributed about 32% of total GDP in 1996/97. About 61% of the economically active population were employed in agriculture in 1996. The principal sources of revenue in the agricultural sector are jute (which accounted for an estimated 10.3% of total export earnings in 1996/97), fish and tea. In 1990–95 agricultural GDP rose by an annual average of 1.1%. Partly owing to a bumper rice crop and high tea production, agricultural output rose by 6.0% in 1996/97, compared with 3.7% in 1995/96.

Industry (including mining, manufacturing, power and construction) employed 13.0% of the working population in 1990, and contributed an estimated 17.5% of total GDP in 1995/96. During 1990–95 industrial GDP increased by an annual average of 7.3%; industrial output grew by 5.3% in 1995/96 and by 3.6% in 1996/97.

Manufacturing contributed an estimated 9.6% of total GDP in 1995/96, and employed 11.8% of the working population in 1990. Based on a census of establishments engaged in manufacturing (excluding hand-loom weaving), the principal branches of the sector, measured by value of output, in 1991/92 were textiles (accounting for 23.8% of the total), food products (20.4%), wearing apparel (excluding footwear) (13.6%) and chemicals (11.4%). During 1980–93 manufacturing GDP increased by an annual average of 3.4%. Manufacturing output grew by 5.3% in 1995/96 and by 3.3% in 1996/97.

Mineral resources in Bangladesh are few. There are, however, large but underdeveloped reserves of natural gas and smaller deposits of coal (estimated at more than 1,000m. metric tons) and petroleum.

Energy is derived principally from natural gas and petroleum. In 1997 Bangladesh's 17 gas fields were estimated to hold reserves of about 350,000m. cu metres and an annual average of about 2,300m. cu metres (with the fields operating at full capacity) of natural gas was being produced. In late 1997 it was announced that two British companies would start natural gas production in Bangladesh's first offshore gasfield in 1998. Imports of petroleum products and crude petroleum comprised an estimated 7.1% of the cost of total imports in 1996/97.

In 1996, according to the IMF, Bangladesh recorded a visible trade deficit of US $2,254.9m., and there was a deficit of $1,250.9m. on the current account of the balance of payments. In 1996/97 the principal source of imports was India, while Western Europe was the principal market for exports. Other major trading partners were the USA, Japan, the People's Republic of China and Hong Kong. The principal exports in 1996/97 were ready-made garments (accounting for an estimated 49.1% of export revenue), knitwear and hosiery products, raw jute and jute goods, and frozen shrimp and frogs' legs. The principal imports were capital goods, textiles, yarn and petroleum products.

In 1997/98 there was a projected overall budgetary deficit of 74,940m. taka. Bangladesh's total external debt, according to the World Bank, was US $16,370m. at the end of 1995, of which $15,543m. was long-term public debt. In that year the cost of debt-servicing was equivalent to 13.3% of the total revenue from exports of goods and services. The annual rate of inflation averaged 3.9% in 1990–96; consumer prices increased by an estimated 4.0% in 1996/97. About 1.9% of the total labour force were unemployed in 1990. Remittances from Bangladeshis working abroad, which are of crucial importance to the Bangladeshi economy, rose by about 23.3% in 1996/97, compared with the previous year, to an estimated $1,500m.

Bangladesh is a member of the South Asian Association for Regional Co-operation (SAARC, see p. 263), which seeks to improve regional co-operation, particularly in economic development.

The problems of developing Bangladesh are manifold, in view of the widespread poverty, malnutrition and underemployment superimposed on an increasing population and a poor resource base. There are grounds, however, for cautious optimism. Despite the frequency of natural disasters, food production has improved somewhat in recent years, the birth rate has decreased considerably, owing to a successful nation-wide birth control campaign, and quite remarkable achievements have been made in the field of export-promotion, especially in non-traditional items (notably cotton garments). Bangladesh remains, however, heavily dependent on large amounts of foreign aid. The World Bank-led Paris aid group, which co-ordinates annual aid flows to Bangladesh, commits about US $2,000m. in aid every year, of which around $1,700m.–$1,800m. is actually disbursed. In 1994 Bangladesh's economy showed clear signs of stabilization as a result of the Government's reform and liberalization programme, which was introduced in 1991. In 1995–97, however, the social and political unrest (including frequent general strikes) had a negative impact on the level of foreign investment. By March 1997 foreign exchange reserves had decreased to $1,765m. (sufficient to fund only about 10 weeks of imports of goods and services). The Awami League Government, which came to power in June 1996, has emphasized its commitment to rehabilitating the weak banking sector and, despite resistance from trade unionists, to accelerating the process of privatizing the country's chronically infirm state-owned enterprises. In mid-1997 it was estimated that Bangladesh's public-sector companies were collectively making losses of about $500m. annually. In 1996 legislation was passed allowing the creation of private export-processing zones (EPZs), in addition to the two existing state-owned EPZs. In October a South Korean company won official approval to establish a new EPZ near Chittagong; the zone was expected to become operational in 1998. Bangladesh's vital garments industry suffered a severe set-back in September 1997 when, under pressure from the European Commission, the Government was forced to withdraw almost 7,000 fraudulent export licences to the EU. The Government claimed that up to 1m. jobs were thus placed in jeopardy and that there would be a 'drastic' reduction in export earnings.

Social Welfare

Basic health services remain relatively undeveloped. Health programmes give particular priority to the popularization of birth control (an estimated 4.2% of public-sector development expenditure was allocated to family planning in 1997/98. In 1981 Bangladesh had 504 hospital establishments, with a total of only 19,727 beds, equivalent to one for every 4,545 inhabitants: one of the lowest levels of health-care provision in the world. In 1985 there were 14,944 physicians (1.5 per 10,000 inhabitants), 5,533 nursing personnel and 5,664 midwifery personnel working in the country. The Government's projected expenditure on health totalled 5,900m. taka in 1997/98 (equivalent to 4.6% of total public-sector development expenditure). In late 1996 about 20m. children were inoculated against polio as part of a mass campaign by the Bangladeshi authorities to eradicate the disease.

Education

The Government provides free schooling for children of both sexes for eight years. Primary education, which is compulsory, begins at six years of age and lasts for five years. Secondary education, beginning at the age of 11, lasts for up to seven years, comprising a first cycle of five years and a second cycle of two further years. In 1990 an estimated 70% of children (74% of boys; 66% of girls) in the relevant age-group attended primary schools, while the enrolment ratio at secondary schools was equivalent to 18% of children (23% of boys; 13% of girls) in the relevant age-group. Secondary schools and colleges in the private sector vastly outnumber government institutions. There are seven state universities, including one for agriculture, one for Islamic studies and one for engineering. The Government launched an Open University Project in 1992 at an estimated cost of US $34.3m. In 1990 the Government initiated the Primary Education Sector Project, which aimed to help to achieve universal primary education and the eradication of illiteracy by the year 2000. In 1995, according to UNESCO estimates, the rate of adult illiteracy was 61.9% (males 50.6%; females 73.9%). Government expenditure on education was set at 16,900m. taka for 1997/98 (equivalent to 13.2% of total development expenditure).

Public Holidays

1998: 1 January (New Year's Day), 30 January* (Id al-Fitr, end of Ramadan), 21 February (National Mourning Day), 26 March (Independence Day), 8 April* (Id al-Adha, Feast of the Sacrifice), 10 April (Good Friday), 13 April (Easter Monday), 28 April* (Muharram, Islamic New Year), May* (Buddha Purinama), 1 May (May Day), July* (Jamat Wida), 7 July* (Birth of the Prophet), August/September (Janmashtami), September* (Shab-i-Bharat), September/October* (Durga Puja), 7 November (National Revolution Day), 16 December (National Day), 25 December (Christmas), 26 December (Boxing Day).

1999: 1 January (New Year's Day), 19 January* (Id al-Fitr, end of Ramadan), 21 February (National Mourning Day), 26 March (Independence Day), 28 March* (Id al-Adha, Feast of the Sacrifice), 2 April (Good Friday), 5 April (Easter Monday), 17 April* (Muharram, Islamic New Year), May* (Buddha Purinama), 1 May (May Day), 26 June* (Birth of the Prophet), July* (Jamat Wida), August/September (Janmashtami), September* (Shab-i-Bharat), September/October* (Durga Puja), 7 November (National Revolution Day), 16 December (National Day), 25 December (Christmas), 26 December (Boxing Day).

* Dates of certain religious holidays are subject to the sighting of the moon, and there are also optional holidays for different religious groups.

Weights and Measures

The imperial system of measures is in force, pending the introduction of the metric system. The following local units of weight are also used:

1 maund = 82.28 lb (37.29 kg).
1 seer = 2.057 lb (932 grams).
1 tola = 180 grains (11.66 grams).

Statistical Survey

Source (unless otherwise stated): Bangladesh Bureau of Statistics, Industry, Trade, Labour Statistics and National Income Wing, 14/2 Topkhana Rd, Dhaka 1000; tel. (2) 409871.

Area and Population

AREA, POPULATION AND DENSITY

Area (sq km)	147,570*
Population (census results)	
6 March 1981	89,912,000†
11 March 1991‡	
Males	56,499,785
Females	53,377,192
Total	109,876,977
Population (UN estimates at mid-year)§	
1993	115,203,000
1994	117,787,000
1995	120,433,000
Density (per sq km) at mid-1995	816.1

* 56,977 sq miles.

† Including adjustment for net underenumeration, estimated to have been 3.2%. The enumerated total was 87,119,965 (males 44,919,191, females 42,200,774).

‡ Including adjustment for net underenumeration, estimated to have been 4.9%. The enumerated total was 104,766,143 (males 53,918,319, females 50,847,824).

§ Source: UN, *World Population Prospects: The 1994 Revision*.

POPULATION BY DIVISIONS*

	1981 Census	1991 Census
Chittagong	23,322,000	28,811,446
Dhaka	27,091,000	33,593,103
Khulna	17,695,000	20,804,515
Rajshahi	21,804,000	26,667,913
Total	89,912,000	109,876,977

* Including adjustments for net underenumeration (3.2% in 1981, 4.9% in 1991).

PRINCIPAL TOWNS (population at 1991 census)

Dhaka (capital)	3,637,892*	Barisal	180,014
Chittagong	1,566,070	Jessore	176,398
Khulna	601,051	Comilla	164,509
Rajshahi	324,532	Sylhet	114,284
Rangpur	220,849	Saidpur	110,494

* Including Narayanganj (population 270,680 in 1974).

BIRTHS AND DEATHS*

	Registered live births	Registered deaths
	Rate (per 1,000)	Rate (per 1,000)
1987	33.3	11.5
1988	33.2	11.3
1989	33.0	11.3
1990	32.8	11.4
1991	31.6	11.2
1992	30.8	11.0
1993†	28.4	9.2

* Registration is incomplete. According to UN estimates, the average annual rates per 1,000 were: Births 39.1 in 1985–90, 36.1 in 1990–95; Deaths 15.2 in 1985–90, 11.7 in 1990–95. Source: UN, *World Population Prospects: The 1994 Revision*.

† Provisional.

Expectation of life (UN estimates, years at birth, 1990–95): 55.6 (males 55.6; females 55.6). Source: UN, *World Population Prospects: The 1994 Revision*.

ECONOMICALLY ACTIVE POPULATION
(sample survey, '000 persons aged 10 years and over, 1990)

	Males	Females	Total
Agriculture, hunting, forestry and fishing	16,560	16,743	33,303
Mining and quarrying	15	–	15
Manufacturing	4,240	1,685	5,925
Electricity, gas and water	39	1	40
Construction	485	41	526
Trade, restaurants and hotels	4,162	123	4,285
Transport, storage and communications	1,600	11	1,611
Financing, insurance, real estate and business services	284	12	296
Community, social and personal services	1,647	262	1,909
Household sector	1,411	838	2,249
Total employed	30,443	19,716	50,159
Unemployed	616	380	996
Total labour force	31,059	20,096	51,155

Agriculture

PRINCIPAL CROPS
(million metric tons, unless otherwise indicated, year ending 30 June)

	1993/94	1994/95	1995/96
Rice (milled)	18.0	16.8	17.7
Wheat	1.1	1.3	1.4
Jute (million bales*)	4.5	5.3	4.1
Tea ('000 metric tons)	51.4	51.7	47.7
Cotton ('000 bales†)	57.2	69.8	75.9
Oilseed	0.5	0.5	0.5
Pulses	0.5	0.5	0.5
Potatoes	1.7	1.9	1.9
Other vegetables	1.2	1.3	1.2
Tobacco ('000 metric tons)	37.8	37.8	39.4
Sugar cane	7.1	7.5	7.2
Fruit	1.1	1.6	1.6

* Each of 400 lb (181.4 kg).

† Each of 500 lb (226.8 kg) gross or 480 lb (217.7 kg) net.

LIVESTOCK ('000 head, year ending September)

	1994*	1995*	1996†
Cattle	24,130	24,340	24,340
Buffaloes	874	882	882
Sheep	1,070	1,155	1,155
Goats	28,050	30,330	30,330
Chickens	116,000	123,000	123,000
Ducks	15,000	16,000	16,000

* Unofficial figures. † FAO estimates.

Source: FAO, *Production Yearbook*.

LIVESTOCK PRODUCTS ('000 metric tons)

	1994	1995	1996
Beef and veal	147	148	148*
Buffalo meat*	3	3	3
Mutton and lamb*	2	2	2
Goat meat*	98	105	105
Poultry meat	99	106	106*
Cows' milk*	774	782	782
Buffalo milk*	24	24	24
Sheeps' milk*	19	21	21
Goats' milk*	1,075	1,152	1,152
Butter and ghee*	15	16	15
Cheese*	1	1	1
Hen eggs*	77	82	82
Other poultry eggs*	27	28	28
Wool:			
greasy*	1	1	1
clean*	1	1	1
Cattle and buffalo hides*	32	33	33
Sheepskins*	462	500	500
Goatskins*	31	34	34

* FAO estimate(s).

Source: FAO, *Production Yearbook*.

Forestry

ROUNDWOOD REMOVALS
(FAO estimates, '000 cubic metres, excl. bark)

	1992	1993	1994
Sawlogs, veneer logs and logs for sleepers	304	304	304
Pulpwood*	69	69	69
Other industrial wood	338	345	353
Fuel wood	29,300	29,950	30,620
Total	30,011	30,668	31,346

* Assumed to be unchanged since 1986.

Source: FAO, *Yearbook of Forest Products*.

SAWNWOOD PRODUCTION ('000 cubic metres, incl. railway sleepers)

	1984	1985	1986
Total	154*	99	79

* FAO estimate.

1987–94: Annual production as in 1986 (FAO estimates).

Source: FAO, *Yearbook of Forest Products*.

Fishing

('000 metric tons, live weight)

	1993	1994	1995
Freshwater fishes	579.2	686.5	724.3
Toli shad	227.2	192.5	204.8
Other marine fishes	161.9	110.4	111.7
Crustaceans and molluscs	78.2	100.5	128.7
Frogs	0.7	0.7	0.8
Total	1,047.2	1,090.6	1,170.4

Source: FAO, *Yearbook of Fishery Statistics.*

Mining

(million cu ft, year ending 30 June)

	1991/92	1992/93	1993/94*
Natural gas	188,474	210,975	223,828

* Estimate.

Industry

SELECTED PRODUCTS ('000 metric tons, unless otherwise indicated; public sector only, year ending 30 June)

	1992/93	1993/94	1994/95
Jute textiles	283	271	275
Hessian	79	85	89
Sacking	161	146	144
Carpet backing	38	35	35
Others	5	5	7
Cotton cloth (million yards)	49	35	19
Cotton yarn (million lb)	134	128	108
Newsprint	46	47	43
Other paper	43	44	40
Cement	207	324	316
Steel ingots	7	6	25
Re-rolled steel products	11	10	10
Petroleum products	1,321	1,195	1,371
Urea fertilizer	1,997	2,182	1,981
Ammonium sulphate	5	6	5
Chemicals	22	21	20
Refined sugar	187	221	270
Wine and spirits ('000 litres)	2,233	3,225	3,650
Tea (million lb)	108	113	104
Edible oil and vegetable ghee	10	15	13
Cigarettes ('000 million)	12	13	17
Electric energy (million kWh)	9,206	9,784	10,806

Finance

CURRENCY AND EXCHANGE RATES

Monetary Units

100 poisha = 1 taka.

Sterling and Dollar Equivalents (30 September 1997)

£1 sterling = 71.97 taka;
US $1 = 44.55 taka;
1,000 taka = £13.90 = $22.45.

Average Exchange Rate (taka per US $)

1994 40.212
1995 40.278
1996 41.794

BUDGET (estimates, million taka, year ending 30 June)

Revenue	1995/96	1996/97	1997/98
Taxation	120,040	139,090	158,730
Customs duties	37,710	42,520	49,100
Income and profit taxes	15,020	17,350	19,500
Excise duties	1,830	2,070	2,300
Value-added tax	56,780	66,130	75,600
Non-tax	30,240	32,760	37,360
Profits from non-financial enterprises	2,010	2,160	2,840
Profits from financial institutions	5,190	4,500	5,300
Interest receipts	4,700	5,300	5,500
Registration fees	1,240	1,650	1,800
Services	7,050	8,880	9,360
Bangladesh Telephone and Telegraph Board	5,660	6,300	7,500
Total	150,280	171,850	196,090

Expenditure	1995/96	1996/97	1997/98
Goods and services	71,730	75,970	84,960
Pay and allowances	42,080	43,920	50,670
Operations and maintenance	8,280	8,370	8,540
Works	2,000	2,100	2,300
Interest payments	17,280	17,560	19,650
Domestic	11,050	10,800	12,400
Foreign	6,240	6,760	7,250
Subsidies and current transfers	26,700	31,860	35,000
Local government transfers	710	710	730
Grants in aid	14,130	16,300	17,540
Pensions and gratuities	6,480	7,100	7,500
Targeted food distribution	3,500	4,710	4,850
Subsidies for fertilizer	—	1,620	2,120
Subsidies for agricultural credit	—	—	1,000
Operational deficits	1,760	1,150	850
Unallocated	50	270	5,530
Gross current expenditure	115,760	125,660	145,140
Less Recoveries	2,690	2,100	2,100
Net current expenditure	113,070	123,560	143,030

Source: IMF, *Bangladesh — Statistical Appendix* (October 1997).

PUBLIC-SECTOR DEVELOPMENT EXPENDITURE
(estimates, million taka, year ending 30 June)

	1995/96	1996/97	1997/98
Agriculture	4,500	6,400	6,200
Rural development	6,800	10,300	9,900
Water and flood control	5,600	10,600	10,600
Industry	1,500	1,900	1,500
Power, scientific research and natural resources	18,000	19,300	20,600
Transport*	20,100	23,300	22,700
Communications	3,100	2,700	3,400
Physical planning and housing	4,600	6,800	8,700
Education	13,000	15,800	16,900
Health	2,800	5,800	5,900
Family planning	4,100	4,900	5,400
Social welfare†	900	1,900	1,700
Other sectoral	1,500	100	300
Total sectoral allocations	86,500	109,800	113,700
Block allocations	2,600	2,400	9,400
Food for Work	—	—	5,500
Technical assistance	3,400	3,200	3,200
Self-financing	0	1,600	1,800
Domestic	4,100	1,600	1,800
Foreign	–4,100	—	—
Total development expenditure	92,500	117,000	128,000

* Includes Jamuna Bridge.
† Includes employment.

Source: Ministry of Planning (Implementation, Monitoring and Evaluation Division).

INTERNATIONAL RESERVES (US $ million at 31 December)

	1994	1995	1996
Gold*	27.2	26.9	28.0
IMF special drawing rights	36.0	159.5	109.6
Reserve position in IMF	0.1	0.1	0.2
Foreign exchange	3,102.6	2,180.1	1,724.9
Total	3,165.9	2,366.6	1,862.7

* Valued at market-related prices.

Source: IMF, *International Financial Statistics.*

MONEY SUPPLY (million taka at 31 December)

	1994	1995	1996
Currency outside banks	57,248	64,523	68,195
Demand deposits at deposit money banks*	58,717	70,819	73,481
Total money	115,965	135,342	141,676

* Comprises the scheduled banks plus the agricultural and industrial development banks.

Source: IMF, *International Financial Statistics.*

COST OF LIVING (Consumer Price Index for middle-class families in Dhaka, year ending 30 June; base: 1973/74 = 100)

	1993/94	1994/95	1995/96
Food	679	732	774
Fuel and lighting	1,061	1,014	1,030
Housing and household requisites	1,019	1,040	1,047
Clothing and footwear	431	439	439
Miscellaneous	805	860	883
All items	747	786	818

NATIONAL ACCOUNTS (year ending 30 June)

Expenditure on the Gross Domestic Product
('000 million taka at current prices)

	1994/95	1995/96*	1996/97†
Government final consumption expenditure	160.8	177.7	195.6
Private final consumption expenditure	1,007.6	1,136.8	1,193.1
Gross fixed capital formation	194.7	221.2	243.7
Total domestic expenditure	1,363.1	1,535.6	1,632.3
Exports of goods and services	165.7	184.4	213.3
Less Imports of goods and services	263.1	310.9	329.3
GDP in purchasers' values	1,265.6	1,409.1	1,516.3

* Estimates. † Preliminary estimates.

Source: IMF, *Bangladesh — Statistical Appendix* (October 1997).

Gross Domestic Product by Economic Activity
(million taka at current prices)

	1993/94	1994/95	1995/96*
Agriculture and hunting	223,744	265,512	293,405
Forestry and logging	33,739	38,943	43,059
Fishing	48,405	56,912	63,407
Mining and quarrying	190	209	255
Manufacturing	101,463	112,739	124,548
Electricity, gas and water	20,534	23,646	27,057
Construction	60,395	69,209	75,226
Wholesale and retail trade	86,156	100,548	116,904
Transport, storage and communications	129,221	139,049	145,995
Owner-occupied dwellings	97,314	106,869	123,892
Finance, insurance and business services	21,500	23,127	24,654
Public administration and defence	55,040	62,308	71,331
Other services	152,664	171,190	191,443
Total	1,030,365	1,170,261	1,301,176

* Provisional figures.

BALANCE OF PAYMENTS (US $ million)

	1994	1995	1996
Exports of goods f.o.b.	2,934.4	3,733.3	4,009.3
Imports of goods f.o.b.	–4,350.5	–6,057.4	–6,264.2
Trade balance	–1,416.1	–2,324.1	–2,254.9
Exports of services	589.8	698.2	604.8
Imports of services	–1,025.0	–1,531.2	–1,152.7
Balance on goods and services	–1,851.3	–3,157.1	–2,802.8
Other income received	150.5	270.1	129.5
Other income paid	–188.7	–201.8	–194.1
Balance on goods, services and income	–1,889.6	–3,088.8	–2,867.3
Current transfers received	2,091.4	2,266.7	1,620.4
Current transfers paid	–2.2	–1.8	–4.0
Current balance	199.6	–823.9	–1,250.9
Direct investment from abroad	11.1	1.9	1.8
Portfolio investment liabilities	105.9	–15.2	–117.0
Other investment assets	–1.6	–243.9	–387.7
Other investment liabilities	633.4	436.1	–294.3
Net errors and omissions	–257.1	133.3	–17.2
Overall balance	691.3	–511.7	–1,694.2

Source: IMF, *International Financial Statistics.*

FOREIGN AID DISBURSEMENTS (US $ million, year ending 30 June)

	1994/95	1995/96	1996/97*
Bilateral donors	915.8	756.9	615.7
Canada	47.1	24.8	21.1
Denmark	30.8	13.6	20.0
France	30.3	9.7	16.8
Germany	111.7	64.1	41.8
Japan	356.5	331.1	299.5
Netherlands	17.9	32.9	35.0
Norway	34.1	29.8	15.0
Saudi Arabia	18.7	30.8	14.5
United Kingdom	53.4	33.3	20.0
USA	114.6	51.3	32.0
Multilateral donors	823.2	686.9	834.4
Asian Development Bank	336.8	279.0	298.0
International Development Association	286.0	225.6	335.3
Total aid disbursements	1,739.0	1,443.8	1,450.1

Source: Ministry of Finance (Economic Relations Division).

External Trade

PRINCIPAL COMMODITIES (US $ million, year ending 30 June)

Imports	1994/95	1995/96	1996/97*
Rice	220	358	39
Wheat	256	228	178
Edible oil	220	179	190
Petroleum products	206	290	315
Crude petroleum	177	166	197
Cotton	135	185	200
Yarn	200	296	345
Fertilizer	142	97	110
Cement	116	171	180
Textiles	1,025	1,043	1,200
Capital goods	1,688	1,918	2,000
Total (incl. others)	5,834	6,881	7,170

Exports	1994/95	1995/96	1996/97*
Raw jute	79.0	90.7	110.0
Jute goods	310.0	324.8	340.0
Leather and leather products	202.0	211.7	185.0
Frozen shrimp and frogs' legs	306.0	313.7	353.0
Ready-made garments	1,839.0	1,948.8	2,150.0
Knitwear and hosiery products	393.0	598.3	780.0
Chemical fertilizers	91.0	94.7	85.0
Total (incl. others)	3,473.0	3,882.4	4,380.0

* Estimates.

Source: Bangladesh Bank.

PRINCIPAL TRADING PARTNERS (%, year ending 30 June)

Imports c.i.f.	1994/95	1995/96	1996/97*
Australia	2.0	1.0	1.0
Canada	3.0	1.0	1.0
China, People's Republic	7.0	10.0	9.0
Eastern Europe	2.0	1.0	1.0
Hong Kong	7.0	6.0	7.0
India	10.0	16.0	16.0
Indonesia	2.0	1.0	1.0
Japan	13.0	9.0	7.0
Korea, Republic	5.0	5.0	6.0
Malaysia	1.0	1.0	2.0
Pakistan	2.0	2.0	1.0
Saudi Arabia	2.0	1.0	1.0
Singapore	6.0	5.0	6.0
Thailand	1.0	1.0	1.0
USA	5.0	5.0	3.0
Western Europe	15.0	11.0	15.0
Total (incl. others)	100.0	100.0	100.0

Exports f.o.b.	1994/95	1995/96	1996/97*
Canada	2.0	2.0	2.0
China, People's Republic	—	1.0	0.4
Eastern Europe	1.0	1.0	1.0
Hong Kong	4.0	4.0	2.4
India	1.0	1.0	1.0
Iran	1.0	1.0	1.0
Japan	3.0	4.0	2.7
Pakistan	1.0	1.0	1.1
Singapore	1.0	1.0	1.0
USA	34.0	30.0	33.0
Western Europe	42.0	49.0	49.0
Total (incl. others)	100.0	100.0	100.0

* Estimates.

Source: Bangladesh Bank.

Transport

RAILWAYS (traffic, year ending 30 June)

	1993/94	1994/95	1995/96
Passenger-kilometres (million)	4,570	4,037	3,333
Freight ton-kilometres (million)	641	760	689

Source: Bangladesh Railway.

ROAD TRAFFIC (motor vehicles in use at 31 December)

	1994	1995	1996
Passenger cars	48,373	51,114	55,764
Buses and coaches	27,165	29,573	31,778
Lorries and vans	32,886	34,936	37,534
Road tractors	2,657	2,702	2,806
Motor cycles and mopeds	128,047	134,303	142,596
Total	239,128	252,628	270,478

Source: IRF, *World Road Statistics*.

SHIPPING

Merchant Fleet (registered at 31 December)

	1994	1995	1996
Number of vessels	287	279	317
Total displacement ('000 grt)	379.7	379.1	435.7

Source: Lloyd's Register of Shipping, *World Fleet Statistics*.

International Sea-borne Freight Traffic
('000 long tons, year ending 30 June)

	1992/93	1993/94	1994/95
Mongla			
Goods loaded	621	468	725
Goods unloaded	1,758	1,463	2,322
Chittagong			
Goods loaded	1,117	1,189	1,417
Goods unloaded	6,497	6,729	8,638
Total goods loaded	1,738	1,657	2,142
Total goods unloaded	8,255	8,192	10,960

Tourism

	1993	1994	1995
Tourist arrivals	126,785	140,122	156,231
Tourist receipts (US $ million)	15	19	24

Communications Media

	1993	1994	1995
Radio receivers ('000 licensed)*	340	308	323
Television receivers ('000 in use)	513	549	613
Telephones ('000 in use)	246	296	315

* The estimated number of radio receivers in use was 5,189,000 in 1992, 5,360,000 in 1993 and 5,500,000 in 1994. Source: UNESCO, *Statistical Yearbook*.

Book titles published: 1,643 in 1990.

Daily newspapers: 51 in 1994 (estimated total average circulation 710,000). Source: UNESCO, *Statistical Yearbook*.

Telefax stations: 2,000 in use in 1993/94.

Mobile cellular telephones: 1,100 subscribers in 1993/94. Source: UN, *Statistical Yearbook*.

Education

(1993/94)

	Institutions	Students
Primary schools	95,886	16,713,000
Secondary schools	11,488	4,534,802
Universities (government)	11	117,359

Technical colleges and institutes (government, 1990/91)*: 141 institutions, 23,722 students.

* In addition to government-owned and managed institutes, there are many privately-administered vocational training centres.

Directory

The Constitution

The members who were returned from East Pakistan (now Bangladesh) for the Pakistan National Assembly and the Provincial Assembly in the December 1970 elections formed the Bangladesh Constituent Assembly. A new Constitution for the People's Republic of Bangladesh was approved by this Assembly on 4 November 1972 and came into effect on 16 December 1972. Following the military coup of 24 March 1982, the Constitution was suspended, and the country was placed under martial law. On 10 November 1986 martial law was repealed and the suspended Constitution was revived. The main provisions of the Constitution, including amendments, are listed below.

SUMMARY

Fundamental Principles of State Policy

The Constitution was initially based on the fundamental principles of nationalism, socialism, democracy and secularism, but in 1977 an amendment replaced secularism with Islam. The amendment states that the country shall be guided by 'the principles of absolute trust and faith in the Almighty Allah, nationalism, democracy and socialism'. A further amendment in 1988 established Islam as the state religion. The Constitution aims to establish a society free from exploitation in which the rule of law, fundamental human rights and freedoms, justice and equality are to be secured for all citizens. A socialist economic system is to be established to ensure the attainment of a just and egalitarian society through state and co-operative ownership as well as private ownership within limits prescribed by law. A universal, free and compulsory system of education shall be established. In foreign policy the State shall endeavour to consolidate, preserve, and strengthen fraternal relations among Muslim countries based on Islamic solidarity.

Fundamental Rights

All citizens are equal before the law and have a right to its protection. Arbitrary arrest or detention, discrimination based on race, age, sex, birth, caste or religion, and forced labour are prohibited. Subject to law, public order and morality, every citizen has freedom of movement, of assembly and of association. Freedom of conscience, of speech, of the press and of religious worship are guaranteed.

GOVERNMENT

The President

The President is the constitutional Head of State and is elected by Parliament (Jatiya Sangsad) for a term of five years. He is eligible for re-election. The supreme control of the armed forces is vested in the President. He appoints the Prime Minister and other Ministers as well as the Chief Justice and other judges.

The Executive

Executive authority shall rest in the Prime Minister and shall be exercised by him either directly or through officers subordinate to him in accordance with the Constitution.

There shall be a Council of Ministers to aid and advise the Prime Minister.

The Legislature

Parliament (Jatiya Sangsad) is a unicameral legislature. It comprises 300 members and an additional 30 women members elected by the other members. Members of Parliament, other than the 30 women members, are directly elected on the basis of universal adult franchise from single territorial constituencies. Persons aged 18 and over are entitled to vote. The parliamentary term lasts for five years. War can be declared only with the assent of Parliament. In the case of actual or imminent invasion, the President may take whatever action he may consider appropriate.

THE JUDICIARY

The Judiciary comprises a Supreme Court with High Court and an Appellate Division. The Supreme Court consists of a Chief Justice and such other judges as may be appointed by the President. The High Court division has such original appellate and other jurisdiction and powers as are conferred on it by the Constitution and by other law. The Appellate Division has jurisdiction to determine appeals from decisions of the High Court division. Subordinate courts, in addition to the Supreme Court, have been established by law.

ELECTIONS

An Election Commission supervises elections, delimits constituencies and prepares electoral rolls. It consists of a Chief Election Commissioner and other Commissioners as may be appointed by the President. The Election Commission is independent in the exercise of its functions. Subject to the Constitution, Parliament may make provision as to elections where necessary.

The Government

HEAD OF STATE

President: SHAHABUDDIN AHMED (elected 23 July 1996; took office 9 October 1996).

COUNCIL OF MINISTERS
(January 1998)

All ministers were members of the Awami League, with the exception of the two specified.

Prime Minister and Minister of the Armed Forces Division, of the Cabinet Division, of Special Affairs, of Defence, and of the Establishment: Sheikh HASINA WAJED.

Minister of Foreign Affairs: ABDUS SAMAD AZAD.

Minister of Local Government, Rural Development and Co-operatives: MOHAMMAD ZILLUR RAHMAN.

Minister of Finance: S. A. M. S. KIBRIA.

Minister of Education, of the Primary and Mass Education Division, and of Science and Technology: A. S. H. K. SADEQUE.

Minister of Water Resources: ABDUR RAZZAK.

Minister of Commerce and Industry: TOFAEL AHMED.

Minister of Power, Energy and Mineral Resources: Lt-Gen. (retd) NOORUDDIN KHAN.

Minister of Home Affairs: Maj.-Gen. (retd) RAFIQUL ISLAM BIR UTTAM.

Minister of Posts and Telecommunications: MOHAMMAD NASIM.

Minister of Agriculture and of Food: MATIA CHOUDHRY.

Minister of Law, Justice and Parliamentary Affairs: ABDUL MATIN KHASRU.

Minister of Communications: ANWAR HUSSAIN MANJU (Jatiya Dal).

Minister of Health and Family Welfare: SALAHUDDIN YOUSUF.

Minister of the Environment and Forests: Syeda SAJEDA CHOWDHURY.

Minister of Shipping: A. S. M. ABDUR RAB (Jatiya Samajtantrik Dal—Rab).

Minister of State for Planning, Civil Aviation and Tourism: MOHIUDDIN KHAN ALAMGIR.

Minister of State for Women's and Children's Affairs: MOZAMMEL HOSSAIN.

Minister of State for Youth and Sports and Cultural Affairs: OBAIDUL KADER.

Minister of State for Fisheries and Livestock: SATISH CHANDRA RAY.

Minister of State for Religious Affairs: MOHAMMAD NURUL ISLAM.

Minister of State for Women's Affairs: Begum SARWARI RAHMAN.

Minister of State for Industry: LUTFUR RAHMAN KHAN.

Minister of State for Disaster Management and Relief: FALUKDER M.A. KHALEQUE.

MINISTRIES

All ministries are situated in Dhaka.

Ministry of Agriculture: Bangladesh Secretariat, Bhaban 4, 2nd Storey, Dhaka.

Ministry of Commerce: Shilpa Bhaban, Motijheel C/A, Dhaka; telex 642201.

Ministry of Communications: Bangladesh Secretariat, Bhaban 7, 1st 9-Storey Bldg, 8th Floor, Dhaka; telex 65712.

Ministry of Defence: Old High Court Bldg, Dhaka; tel. (2) 259082.

Ministry of Education: Bangladesh Secretariat, Bhaban 7, 2nd 9-Storey Bldg, 6th Floor, Dhaka.

Ministry of Energy and Mineral Resources: Bangladesh Secretariat, Bhaban 6, New Bldg, 2nd Floor, Dhaka.

Ministry of Finance and Planning: Bangladesh Secretariat, Bhaban 7, 1st 9-Storey Bldg, 3rd Floor, Dhaka; telex 65886.

Ministry of Food: Bangladesh Secretariat, Bhaban 4, 2nd 9-Storey Bldg, 3rd Floor, Dhaka; telex 65671.

Ministry of Foreign Affairs: Topkhana Rd, Dhaka: tel. (2) 236020; telex 642200; fax (2) 411281.

Ministry of Health and Family Welfare: Bangladesh Secretariat, Main Bldg, 3rd Floor, Dhaka.

Ministry of Home Affairs: School Bldg, 2nd and 3rd Floors, Bangladesh Secretariat, Dhaka.

Ministry of Industry: Shilpa Bhaban, 91 Motijheel C/A, Dhaka 1000; telex 672830.

Ministry of Information: Bangladesh Secretariat, 2nd 9-Storey Bldg, 8th Floor, Dhaka; tel. (2) 235111.

Ministry of Labour and Manpower: Bangladesh Secretariat, 1st 9-Storey Bldg, 4th Floor, Dhaka.

Ministry of Land: Bangladesh Secretariat, Bhaban 4, 2nd 9-Storey Bldg, 3rd Floor, Dhaka.

Ministry of Local Government, Rural Development and Co-operatives: Bangladesh Secretariat, Bhaban 7, 1st 9-Storey Bldg, 6th Floor, Dhaka.

Ministry of Posts and Telecommunications: Bangladesh Secretariat, Ramna, Dhaka 1000; fax (2) 865775.

Ministry of Public Works: Bangladesh Secretariat, Main Extension Bldg, 2nd Floor, Dhaka.

Ministry of Shipping: Dhaka; tel. (2) 404345.

Ministry of Social Welfare and Women's Affairs: Bangladesh Secretariat, Bhaban 6, New Bldg, Dhaka.

President and Legislature

PRESIDENT

On 23 July 1996 the Awami League's presidential candidate, SHAHABUDDIN AHMED, was elected unopposed as Bangladesh's new Head of State by the Jatiya Sangsad.

JATIYA SANGSAD
(Parliament)

Speaker: HUMAYUN RASHID CHOWDHURY.

General Election, 12 June 1996

	Seats
Awami League (AL)	146
Bangladesh Jatiyatabadi Dal (Bangladesh Nationalist Party—BNP)	116
Jatiya Dal	32
Jamaat-e-Islami Bangladesh	3
Jatiya Samajtantrik Dal (Rab)	1
Islami Oikya Jote	1
Independent	1
Total	300

In addition to the 300 directly-elected members, a further 30 seats are reserved for women members.

Political Organizations

Awami League (AL): 23 Bangabandhu Ave, Dhaka; f. 1949; supports parliamentary democracy; advocates socialist economy, but with a private sector, and a secular state; pro-Indian; 28-member central executive committee, 15-member central advisory committee and a 13-member presidium; Pres. Sheikh HASINA WAJED; Gen.-Sec. ZILLUR RAHMAN; c. 1,025,000 mems.

Bangladesh Jatiya League: 500A Dhanmandi R/A, Rd 7, Dhaka; f. 1970 as Pakistan National League, renamed in 1972; supports parliamentary democracy; Leader ATAUR RAHMAN KHAN; c. 50,000 mems.

Bangladesh Jatiyatabadi Dal (Bangladesh Nationalist Party—BNP): c/o Jatiya Sangsad, Dhaka; f. 1978 by merger of groups supporting Ziaur Rahman, including Jatiyatabadi Gonotantrik Dal (Jagodal—Nationalist Democratic Party); right of centre; favours muiltiparty democracy and parliamentary system of govt; Chair. Begum KHALEDA ZIA; Sec.-Gen. ABDUL MANNAN BHUIYAN.

Bangladesh Khilafat Andolon: 314/2 Jagannath Saha Rd, Lalbagh Killar mor, Dhaka; tel. (2) 250500.

Bangladesh Krishak Sramik Party (Peasants' and Workers' Party): Sonargaon Bhavan, 99 South Kamalapur, Dhaka 1217; tel. (2) 834512; f. 1914, renamed 1953; supports parliamentary democracy, non-aligned foreign policy, welfare state, guarantee of fundamental rights for all religions and races, free market economy and non-proliferation of nuclear weapons; 15-mem. exec. council; Pres. A. S. M. SULAIMAN; Sec.-Gen. RASHEED KHAN MEMON; c. 125,000 mems.

Bangladesh Muslim League: Dhaka; Sec.-Gen. Alhaj MOHAMMAD ZAMIR ALI.

Bangladesh People's League: Dhaka; f. 1976; supports parliamentary democracy; c. 75,000 mems.

The Five-Party Alliance: Dhaka; comprises five Marxist-Leninist parties; Leaders RASHID KHAN MENON, HASANUL HUQ INU, MAHBUBUL HAQUE.

Islamic Solidarity Movement: 84 East Tejturi Bazar, Tejgaon, Dhaka 1215; tel. (2) 325886; fmrly known as Islamic Democratic League; renamed as above in 1984; Chair. HAFIZ MUHAMMAD HABIBUR RAHMAN.

Jamaat-e-Islami Bangladesh: 505 Elephant Rd, Bara Maghbazar, Dhaka 1217; tel. (2) 401581; f. 1941; Islamic fundamentalist; Chair. Prof. GHULAM AZAM; Sec.-Gen. Maulana MATIUR RAHMAN NIZAMI.

Jatiya Dal (National Party): c/o Jatiya Sangsad, Dhaka; f. 1983 as Jana Dal; reorg. 1986, when the National Front (f. 1985), a five-party alliance of the Jana Dal, the United People's Party, the Gonotantrik Dal, the Bangladesh Muslim League and a breakaway section of the Bangladesh Nationalist Party, formally converted itself into a single pro-Ershad grouping; advocates nationalism, democracy, Islamic ideals and progress; Chair. MIZANUR RAHMAN CHOWDHURY (acting); Sec.-Gen. ANWAR HOSSAIN MANJU; in June 1997 a group of dissidents, led by Kazi ZAFAR AHMED and SHAH MOAZZEM HOSSAIN, formed a rival faction.

Jatiya Samajtantrik Dal (Rab): breakaway faction of JSD; Sec.-Gen. A. S. M. ABDUR RAB.

Jatiya Samajtantrik Dal (JSD—(S)) (National Socialist Party): 23 DIT Ave, Malibagh Choudhury Para, Dhaka; f. 1972; left-wing; Leader SHAJAHAN SIRAJ; c. 5,000 mems.

Jatiyo Janata Party: Janata Bhaban, 47A Toyenbee Circular Rd, Dhaka 1203; tel. 9567315; f. 1976; social democratic; Chair. NURUL ISLAM KHAN; Gen. Sec. MUJIBUR RAHMAN HIRO; c. 30,000 mems.

National Awami Party—Bhashani (NAP): Dhaka; f. 1957; Maoist; Pres. ABU NASSER KHAN BHASHANI; Gen.-Sec. ABDUS SUBHANI.

National Democratic Alliance: Dhaka; f. 1993 as an alliance of 10 small parties; advocates consolidating Bangladesh's sovereignty and establishing Islamic principles; Exec. Chair. Lt-Col (retd) KHANDAKAR ABDUR RASHID; Sec.-Gen. SHAFIQUR RAHMAN.

Democratic League: 68 Jigatola, Dhaka 9; tel. (2) 507994; f. 1976; conservative.

Freedom Party: f. 1987; Islamic; Co-Chair. Lt-Col (retd) SAID FARUQ RAHMAN, Lt-Col (retd) KHANDAKAR ABDUR RASHID.

Parbattya Chattagram Jana Sanghati Samity: f. 1972; political wing of the Shanti Bahini; represents interests of Buddhist tribals in Chittagong Hill Tracts; Leader JATINDRA BODDHIPRIYA ('SHANTU') LARMA.

Patriotic Democratic Front: Dhaka; f. 1991 as an informal alliance comprising the following four left-wing parties:

Communist Party of Bangladesh: 21/1 Purana Paltan, Dhaka 1000; tel. (2) 9558612; fax (2) 837464; e-mail manzur@bangla.net; f. 1948; Pres. SHAHIDULLAH CHOWDHURY; Gen. Sec. MUJAHIDUL ISLAM SELIM; c. 22,000 mems.

Gonoazadi League: 30 Banagran Lane, Dhaka.

National Awami Party—Muzaffar (NAP—M): 21 Dhanmandi Hawkers' Market, 1st Floor, Dhaka 5; f. 1957, reorg. 1967; c. 500,000 mems; Pres. MUZAFFAR AHMED; Sec.-Gen. PANKAJ BHATTACHARYA.

Samyabadi Dal: Dhaka; Maoist; Leader MOHAMMAD TOAHA.

Zaker Party: f. 1989; supports sovereignty and the introduction of an Islamic state system; Leader SYED HASMATULLAH; Mem. of the Presidium MUSTAFA AMIR FAISAL.

Diplomatic Representation

EMBASSIES AND HIGH COMMISSIONS IN BANGLADESH

Afghanistan: House CWN(C)-2A Gulshan Ave, Gulshan Model Town, Dhaka 12; tel. (2) 603232; Chargé d'affaires a.i.: ABDUL AHAD WOLASI.

Australia: 184 Gulshan Ave, Gulshan Model Town, Dhaka 12; tel. (2) 873101; fax (2) 871125; High Commissioner: CHARLES STUART.

Belgium: House 40, Rd 21, Block B, Banani, Dhaka; tel. (2) 600138; telex 642304; Ambassador: Baron OLIVIER GILLES.

Bhutan: House No. F5 (SE), Gulshan Ave, Dhaka 1212; tel. (2) 545018; Ambassador: D. K. CHHETRI.

Brazil: House CEN(D)-14, Rd 101, Gulshan Model Town, POB 6064, Dhaka 1212; tel. (2) 606911; telex 642334; fax (2) 883330; e-mail chanc@bdmail.net; Chargé d'affaires a.i.: MÁRIO CÉSAR DE MORÃES PITÃO.

Canada: House 16A, Rd 48, Gulshan Model Town, POB 569, Dhaka 12; tel. (2) 607071; telex 642328; fax (2) 883043; High Commissioner: JON SCOTT.

China, People's Republic: Plot NE(L)6, Rd 83, Gulshan Model Town, Dhaka 12; tel. (2) 884862; Ambassador: ZHANG XUJIANG.

Czech Republic: House 3A NE(O), Rd 90, Gulshan Model Town, Dhaka 12; tel. (2) 601673; telex 65730.

Denmark: House NW(H)1, Rd 51, Gulshan Model Town, POB 2056, Dhaka 12; tel. (2) 881799; telex 642320; fax (2) 883638; e-mail dandhaka@mail.citecho.net; Chargé d'affaires a.i.: FINN THILSTED.

Egypt: House NE(N)-9, Rd 90, Gulshan Model Town, Dhaka 12; tel. (2) 882766; telex 632308; fax (2) 884883; Ambassador: OSSAMA MOHAMED TAWFIK.

France: POB 22, House 18, Rd 108, Gulshan Model Town, Dhaka 12; tel. (2) 607083; Ambassador: RENÉE VEYRET.

Germany: 178 Gulshan Ave, Gulshan Model Town, POB 108, Dhaka 1212; tel. (2) 884735; telex 642331; fax (2) 883141; Ambassador: BRUNO WEBER.

Holy See: UN Rd 2, Diplomatic Enclave, Baridhara, Gulshan, POB 6003, Dhaka 1212; tel. (2) 882018; fax (2) 883574; Apostolic Nuncio: Most Rev. EDWARD J. ADAMS, Titular Archbishop of Scala.

Hungary: House 14, Rd 68, Gulshan Model Town, POB 6012, Dhaka 1212; tel. (2) 608101; telex 642314; fax (2) 883117; Chargé d'affaires a.i.: I. B. BUDAY.

India: House 120, Rd 2, Dhanmandi R/A, Dhaka 1205; tel. (2) 503606; telex 642336; fax (2) 863662; High Commissioner: DEV MUKHERJEE.

Indonesia: CWS (A)-10, 75 Gulshan Ave, Gulshan Model Town, Dhaka 1212; tel. (2) 600131; telex 632309; fax (2) 885391; Ambassador: HADI A. WAYARABI ALHADAR.

Iran: CWN(A)-12 Kamal Ataturk Ave, Gulshan Model Town, Dhaka 12; tel. (2) 601432; telex 65714; Ambassador: MUHAMMAD GANJIDOOST.

Iraq: 112 Gulshan Ave, Gulshan Model Town, Dhaka 12; tel. (2) 600298; telex 642307; Ambassador: ZUHAIR MUHAMMAD ALOMAR.

Italy: Plot No. 2 & 3, Rd 74/79, Gulshan Model Town, Dhaka 1212; tel. (2) 600152; telex 642313; fax (2) 882578; Ambassador: Dr RAFFAELE MINIERO.

Japan: 5 & 7, Dutabash Rd, Baridhara, Dhaka; tel. (2) 870087; telex 642330; fax (2) 886737; Ambassador: TAKEO IGUCHI.

Korea, Democratic People's Republic: House 6, Rd 7, Baridhara Model Town, Dhaka; tel. (2) 601250; Ambassador: KIM KI DUK.

Korea, Republic: House NW(E)17, Rd 55, Gulshan Model Town, Dhaka 12; tel. (2) 604921; Ambassador: MAN SOON CHANG.

Kuwait: Plot 39, Rd 23, Block J, Banani, Dhaka 13; tel. (2) 600233; telex 65600; Ambassador: AHMAD MURSHED AL-SULIMAN.

Libya: NE(D), 3A, Gulshan Ave (N), Gulshan Model Town, Dhaka 12; tel. (2) 600141; Secretary of People's Committee: MUSBAH ALI A. MAIMOON (acting).

Malaysia: House 4, Rd 118, Gulshan Model Town, Dhaka 1212; tel. (2) 887759; telex 642309; fax (2) 883115; High Commissioner: Dato' ZULKIFLY IBRAHIM BIN ABDUR RAHMAN.

Myanmar: 89(B), Rd 4, Banani, Dhaka; tel. (2) 601915; Ambassador: U TINT LWIN.

Nepal: United Nations Rd 2, Baridhara Model Town, Dhaka; tel. (2) 601790; telex 65643; Ambassador: Dr MOHAN PRASAD LOHANI.

Netherlands: House 49, Rd 90, Gulshan Model Town, POB 166, Dhaka 12; tel. (2) 882715; fax (2) 883326; e-mail nlgovdha@bangla.net; Ambassador: D.C.B. DEN HAAS.

Pakistan: House NEC-2, Rd 71, Gulshan Model Town, Dhaka 12; tel. (2) 885388; High Commissioner: KARAM ELAHI.

Philippines: House NE(L) 5, Rd 83, Gulshan Model Town, Dhaka 1212; tel. (2) 605945; Ambassador: CESAR C. PASTORES.

Poland: House 111, Rd 4, Banani, POB 6089, Dhaka 1200; tel. (2) 608503; telex 632301; fax (2) 871458; Chargé d'affaires a.i.: JERZY SADOWSKI.

Qatar: House 23, Rd 108, Gulshan Model Town, Dhaka 12; tel. (2) 604477; Chargé d'affaires a.i.: ABDULLAH AL-MUTAWA.

Romania: House 33, Rd 74, Gulshan Model Town, Dhaka 12; tel. (2) 601467; telex 65739; Chargé d'affaires a.i.: ALEXANDRU VOINEA.

Russia: NE(J) 9, Rd 79, Gulshan Model Town, Dhaka 1212; tel. (2) 888147; telex 632310; fax (2) 883735; Ambassador: YEVGENII P. IVANOV.

Saudi Arabia: House 12, Rd 92, Gulshan (North), Dhaka 1212; tel. (2) 889124; fax (2) 883616; Ambassador: ABDULLAH OMAR BARRY.

Sri Lanka: House 15, Rd 50, Gulshan 2, Dhaka; tel. (2) 882790; telex 642321; fax (2) 883971; High Commissioner: S. B. ATUGODA.

Sweden: House 1, Rd 51, Gulshan, Dhaka 1212; tel. (2) 884761; telex 642303; fax (2) 883948; Ambassador: ANDERS JOHNSON.

Thailand: House NW (E) 12, Rd 59, Gulshan Model Town, Dhaka; tel. (2) 601475; Ambassador: CHAIYA CHINDAWONGSE.

Turkey: House 7, Rd 62, Gulshan Model Town, Dhaka 12; tel. (2) 882198; fax (2) 883873; Ambassador: K. OZCAN DAVAZ.

United Arab Emirates: House CEN(H) 41, Rd 113, Gulshan Model Town, Dhaka 1212; tel. (2) 604775; telex 642301; Chargé d'affaires a.i.: ABDUL RAZAK HADI.

United Kingdom: United Nations Rd, Baridhara, Dhaka 1212; tel. (2) 882705; fax (2) 883437; e-mail combhcbd@citechco.net; High Commissioner: DAVID C. WALKER.

USA: Diplomatic Enclave, Madani Ave, Baridhara Model Town, POB 323, Dhaka 1212; tel. (2) 884700; telex 642319; fax (2) 883744; Ambassador: JOHN HOLZMAN.

Judicial System

A judiciary, comprising a Supreme Court with High Court and Appellate Divisions, is in operation (see under Constitution).

Chief Justice: ABU TAHER MOHAMMED AFZAL.

Attorney-General: M. NURULLAH.

Religion

Preliminary results of the 1981 census classified 86.6% of the population as Muslims, 12.1% as caste Hindus and scheduled castes, and the remainder as Buddhists, Christians and tribals.

Freedom of religious worship is guaranteed under the Constitution but, under the 1977 amendment to the Constitution, Islam was declared to be one of the nation's guiding principles and, under the 1988 amendment, Islam was established as the state religion.

BUDDHISM

World Federation of Buddhists Regional Centre: Buddhist Monastery, Kamalapur, Dhaka 14; Leader Ven. VISUDDHANANDA MAHATHERO.

CHRISTIANITY

Jatiyo Church Parishad (National Council of Churches): 395 New Eskaton Rd, Moghbazar, Dhaka 2; tel. (2) 402869; f. 1949 as East Pakistan Christian Council; four mem. churches; Pres. Dr SAJAL DEWAN; Gen. Sec. M. R. BISWAS.

Church of Bangladesh—United Church

After Bangladesh achieved independence, the Diocese of Dacca (Dhaka) of the Church of Pakistan (f. 1970 by the union of Anglicans, Methodists, Presbyterians and Lutherans) became the autonomous Church of Bangladesh. In 1986 the Church had an estimated 12,000 members. In 1990 a second diocese, the Diocese of Kushtia, was established.

Bishop of Dhaka: Rt Rev. BARNABAS DWIJEN MONDAL, St Thomas's Church, 54 Johnson Rd, Dhaka 1100; tel. (2) 236546; fax (2) 238218.

Bishop of Kushtia: Rt Rev. MICHAEL BAROI, Church of Bangladesh, 94 N.S. Rd, Thanapara, Kushtia; tel. (71) 3603.

The Roman Catholic Church

For ecclesiastical purposes, Bangladesh comprises one archdiocese and five dioceses. At 31 December 1995 there were an estimated 231,083 adherents in the country.

Catholic Bishops' Conference: Archbishop's House, 1 Kakrail Rd, POB 3, Dhaka 1000; tel. (2) 408879; fax (2) 834993; f. 1978; Pres. Most Rev. MICHAEL ROZARIO, Archbishop of Dhaka.

Archbishop of Dhaka: Most Rev. MICHAEL ROZARIO, Archbishop's House, 1 Kakrail Rd, POB 3, Dhaka 1000; tel. (2) 408879.

Other Christian Churches

Bangladesh Baptist Sangha: 33 Senpara, Parbatta, Mirpur 10, POB 8018, Dhaka 1216; tel. (2) 802967; telex 632469; fax (2) 803556; f. 1922; 26,500 mems (1985); Pres. M. S. ADHIKARI; Gen. Sec. Rev. MARTIN ADHIKARY.

Among other denominations active in Bangladesh are the Bogra Christian Church, the Evangelical Christian Church, the Garo Baptist Union, the Reformed Church of Bangladesh and the Sylhet Presbyterian Synod.

The Press

PRINCIPAL DAILIES

Bengali

Anandapatra: 188 Motijheel Circular Rd, Dhaka 1000; tel. (2) 408898; fax (2) 863060; Editor MUSTAFA JABBAR.

Azadi: 9 C.D.A. C/A, Momin Rd, Chittagong; tel. (31) 224341; f. 1960; Editor Prof. MOHAMMAD KHALED; circ. 13,000.

Banglar Bani: 81 Motijheel C/A, Dhaka 1000; tel. (2) 237548; f. 1972; Editor Sheikh FAZLUL KARIM SALIM; circ. 20,000.

Dainik Bangla: 1 Rajuk Ave, Dhaka 1000; tel. (2) 864748; f. 1964; Editor AHMED HUMAYUN; circ. 65,000.

Dainik Bhorer Kagoj: 8 Link Rd, Banglamotor, Dhaka; tel (2) 868802; fax (2) 868801; Editor MATIUR RAHMAN; circ. 50,000.

Dainik Birol: 26/F R. K. Mission Rd, Dhaka 1203; tel. (2) 9567152; fax (2) 9567153; Chair. ABDULLAH AL-NASER.

Dainik Inquilab: 2/1 Ramkrishna Mission Rd, Dhaka 1203; tel. (2) 9563162; fax (2) 9552881; e-mail inquilab1@bangla.net; Editor A. M. M. BAHAUDDIN; circ. 180,025.

Dainik Ittefaq: 1 Ramkrishna Rd, Dhaka 1203; tel. (2) 256075; f. 1953; Propr/Editor ANWAR HUSSAIN MANJU; circ. 200,000.

Dainik Jahan: 3/B Shehra Rd, Mymensingh; tel. (91) 5677; f. 1980; Editor MUHAMMAD HABIBUR RAHMAN SHEIKH; circ. 4,000.

Dainik Janakantha (Daily People's Voice): Dhaka; f. 1993; Man. Editor TOAB KHAN; Exec. Editor BORHAN AHMED; circ. 100,000.

Dainik Janata: 24 Aminbagh, Shanti Nagar, Dhaka 1217; tel. (2) 400498; Editor Dr M. ASADUR RAHMAN.

Dainik Janmobhumi: 110/1 Islampur Rd, Khulna; tel. (41) 21280; fax (41) 20413; f. 1982; Editor HUMAYUN KABIR; circ. 25,000.

Dainik Karatoa: Chalkjadu Rd, Bogra; tel. (51) 3660; fax (51) 5898; f. 1976; Editor MOZAMMEL HAQUE LALU; circ. 40,000.

Dainik Khabar: 137 Shanti Nagar, Dhaka 1217; tel. (2) 406601; f. 1985; Editor MIZANUR RAHMAN MIZAN; circ. 18,000.

Dainik Millat: Dhaka; tel. (2) 242351; Editor CHOWDHURY MOHAMMAD FAROOQ.

Dainik Nava Avijan: Lalkuthi, North Brook Hall Rd, Dhaka; tel. (2) 257516; Editor A. S. M. REZAUL HAQUE; circ. 15,000.

Dainik Patrika: 85 Elephant Rd, Maghbazar, Dhaka 1217; tel. (2) 415057; fax (2) 841575; e-mail patrika@citechco.net; Publr and Chief Editor MIA MUSA HOSSAIN; Editor M. FAISAL HASSAN (acting).

Dainik Purbanchal: 38 Iqbal Nagar Mosque Lane, Khulna 9100; tel. (41) 22251; fax (41) 21432; f. 1974; Editor LIAQUAT ALI; circ. 42,000.

Dainik Rupashi Bangla: Abdur Rashid Rd, Natun Chowdhury Para, Bagicha Gaon, Comilla 3500; tel. (81) 6689; f. 1972 (a weekly until 1979); Editor Prof. ABDUL WAHAB; circ. 8,000.

Dainik Sangram: 423 Elephant Rd, Baramaghbazar, Dhaka 1217; tel. (2) 9330579; fax (2) 831250; f. 1970; Chair. MOHAMMAD YOUNUS; Editor ABUL ASAD; circ. 45,000.

Dainik Shakti: Dhaka; tel. (2) 405535; Editor A. Q. M. ZAIN-UL-ABEDIN; circ. 4,000.

Dainik Sphulinga: Amin Villa, P-5 Housing Estate, Jessore 7401; tel. (421) 6433; f. 1971; Editor Mian ABDUS SATTAR; circ. 14,000.

Dainik Uttara: Bahadur Bazar, Dinajpur Town, Dinajpur; tel. (531) 4326; f. 1974; Editor Prof. MUHAMMAD MOHSIN; circ. 8,500.

Ganakantha: 24C Tipu Sultan Rd, Dhaka 1203; tel. (2) 606784; telex 642696; f. 1979; morning; publication suspended in 1989; Editor JAHANGIR KABIR CHOWDHURY; Exec. Editor SAIYED RABIUL KARIM; circ. 15,000.

Jaijaidin Protidin: 3/4 Purana Paltan, Dhaka 1000; Editor SHAFIK REHMAN.

Janabarta: 5 Babu Khan Rd, Khulna; tel. (41) 21075; f. 1974; Editor SYED SOHRAB ALI; circ. 4,000.

Jugabheri: Rasheedistan, Rai Hussain, Amberkhana, Sylhet; tel. (821) 5461; f. 1931; Editor FAHMEEDA RASHEED CHOUDHURY; circ. 6,000.

Naya Bangla: 101 Momin Rd, Chittagong; tel. (31) 206247; f. 1978; Editor ABDULLAH AL-SAGIR; circ. 12,000.

Probaho: 2 Raipara Cross Rd, Khulna; tel. (41) 23650; f. 1977; Editor ASHRAFUL HOQUE; circ. 3,000.

Protidin: Ganeshtola, Dinajpur; tel. (531) 4555; f. 1980; Editor KHAIRUL ANAM; circ. 3,000.

Runner: Pyari Mohan Das Rd, Bejpara, Jessore; tel. (421) 6943; f. 1980; Editor R. M. SAIFUL ALAM MUKUL; circ. 2,000.

Sangbad: 36 Purana Paltan, Dhaka 1000; tel. (2) 9558147; telex 642454; fax (2) 9562882; e-mail sangbad@bangla.net; f. 1952; Editor AHMADUL KABIR; circ. 71,050.

Swadhinata: 99A Zamal Khan Lane, Chittagong; tel. (31) 209644; f. 1972; Editor ABDULLAH-AL-HARUN; circ. 4,000.

English

Bangladesh Observer: Observer House, 33 Toyenbee Circular Rd, Motijheel C/A, Dhaka 1000; tel. (2) 235105; f. 1949; morning; Editor S. M. ALI; circ. 43,000.

The Bangladesh Times: 1 Rajuk Ave, Dhaka 1000; tel. (2) 233195; f. 1975; morning; Editor MAHBUB ANAM; circ. 35,000.

Daily Evening News: 26 R. K. Mission Rd, Dhaka 1203; tel. (2) 9567152; fax (2) 9567153; Chair. ABDULLAH AL-NASER.

Daily Star: House 11, Rd 3, Dhanmandi R/A, Dhaka 1205; tel.(2) 500092; fax (2) 863035; f. 1991; circ. 30,000; Editor MAHFUZ ANAM.

Daily Tribune: 38 Iqbal Nagar Mosque Lane, Khulna 9100; tel. (41) 21944; fax (41) 22251; f. 1978; morning; Editor FERDOUSI ALI; circ. 22,000.

Financial Express: Dhaka; f. 1994.

The Independent: Rahman Mansion, 3rd Floor, 161 Motijheel C/A, Dhaka 1000; tel. (2) 9564638; fax (2) 9564637; e-mail bexml@enigma,kaifnet.com.; f. 1995; Editor MAHBUBUL ALAM.

New Nation: 1 Ramkrishna Mission Rd, Dhaka 1203; tel. (2) 245011; fax (2) 245536; f. 1981; Editor ALAMGIR MOHIUDDIN; circ. 15,000.

People's View: 102 Siraj-ud-Daulla Rd, Chittagong; tel. (31) 227403; f. 1969; Editor SABBIR ISLAM; circ. 3,000.

PERIODICALS

Bengali

Aachal: 100B Malibagh Chowdhury Para, Dhaka 1219; tel. (2) 414043; weekly; Editor FERDOUSI BEGUM.

Adhuna: 1/3 Block F, Lalmatia, Dhaka 1207; tel. (2) 812353; telex 642940; fax (2) 813095; f. 1974; quarterly; publ. by the Assen of Devt Agencies in Bangladesh (ADAB); Exec. Editor MINAR MONSUR; circ. 5,000.

Ahmadi: 4 Bakshi Bazar Rd, Dhaka 1211; f. 1925; fortnightly; Editor MOQBUL AHMAD KHAN.

Alokpat: 166 Arambagh, Dhaka 1000; tel. (2) 413361; fax (2) 863060; fortnightly; Editor RABBANI JABBAR.

Amod: Chowdhury Para, Comilla 3500; tel. (81) 5193; f. 1955; weekly; Editor SHAMSUN NAHAR RABBI; circ. 6,000.

Ananda Bichitra: 1 DIT Ave, Dhaka; tel. (2) 241639; f. 1986; fortnightly; Editor SHAHADAT CHOWDHURY; circ. 32,000.

Begum: 66 Loyal St, Dhaka 1; tel. (2) 233789; f. 1947; women's illustrated weekly; Editor NURJAHAN BEGUM; circ. 25,000.

Bichitra: Dainik Bangla Bhaban, 1 DIT Ave, Dhaka 1000; tel. (2) 232086; f. 1972; weekly; Editor SHAHADAT CHOWDHURY; circ. 42,000.

Chakra: 242A Nakhalpara, POB 2682, Dhaka 1215; tel. (2) 604568; social welfare weekly; Editor HUSNEARA AZIZ.

Chitra Desh: 24 Ramkrishna Mission Rd, Dhaka 1203; weekly; Editor HENA AKHTAR CHOWDHURY.

Chitrakalpa: 12 Folder St, Dhaka 3; Editor ASIRUDDIN AHMED.

Chitrali: Observer House, 33 Toyenbee Circular Rd, Motijheel C/A, Dhaka 1000; tel. (2) 9550938; fax (2) 9562243; f. 1953; film weekly; Editor PRODIP KUMAR DEY; circ. 25,000.

Dhakar Chithi: 188 Motijheel Circular Rd, Dhaka 1000; tel. (2) 408898; fax (2) 863060; weekly; Editor MUSTAFA JABBAR.

Ekota: 15 Larmini St, Wari, Dhaka; tel. (2) 257854; f. 1970; weekly; Editor MATIUR RAHMAN; circ. 25,000.

Fashal: 28J Toyenbee Circular Rd, Motijheel C/A, Dhaka 1000; tel. (2) 233099; f. 1965; agricultural weekly; Chief Editor ERSHAD MAZUMDAR; circ. 8,000.

Ispat: Majampur, Kushtia; tel. (71) 3676; f. 1976; weekly; Editor WALIUR BARI CHOUDHURY; circ. 3,000.

Jahan-e-Nau: 13 Karkun Bari Lane, Dhaka; tel. (2) 252205; f. 1960; weekly; Editor MD HABIBIUR RAHMAN; circ. 9,000.

Jaijaidin: 3/4 Purana Paltan, Dhaka 1000; weekly; Editor SHAFIK REHMAN.

Jhorna: 4/13 Block A, Lalmatia, Dhaka; tel. (2) 415239; Editor MUHAMMAD JAMIR ALI.

Kalantar: 87 Khanjahan Ali Rd, Khulna; tel. (41) 61424; f. 1971; weekly; Editor NOOR MOHAMMAD; circ. 12,000.

Kankan: Nawab Bari Rd, Bogra; tel. (51) 6424; f. 1974; weekly; Editor Mrs SUFIA KHATUN; circ. 6,000.

Kirajagat: National Sports Control Board, 62/63 Purana Paltan, Dhaka; f. 1977; weekly; Editor ALI MUZZAMAN CHOWDHURY; circ. 7,000.

Kishore Bangla: Observer House, Motijheel C/A, Dhaka 1000; juvenile weekly; f. 1976; Editor RAFIQUL HAQUE; circ. 5,000.

Lekhak Pathak: 188 Motijheel Circular Rd, Dhaka 1000; tel. (2) 408898; fax (2) 863060; monthly; Editor ROKSHANA SULTANA.

Moha Nagar: 4 Dilkusha C/A, Dhaka 1000; tel. (2) 255282; Editor SYED MOTIUR RAHMAN.

Moshal: 4 Dilkusha C/A, Dhaka 1000; tel. (2) 231092; Editor MUHAMMAD ABUL HASNAT; circ. 3,000

Muktibani: Toyenbee Circular Rd, Motijheel C/A, Dhaka 1000; tel. (2) 253712; telex 642474; f. 1972; weekly; Editor NIZAM UDDIN AHMED; circ. 35,000.

Natun Bangla: 44/2 Free School St Bylane, Hatirpool, Dhaka 1205; tel. (2) 866121; fax (2) 863794; f. 1971; weekly; Editor MUJIBUR RAHMAN.

Natun Katha: 31E Topkhana Rd, Dhaka; weekly; Editor HAJERA SULTANA; circ. 4,000.

Nipun: 520 Peyarabag, Magbazar, Dhaka 11007; tel. (2) 312156; monthly; Editor SHAJAHAN CHOWDHURY.

Parikrama: 65 Shanti Nagar, Dhaka; tel. (2) 415640; Editor MOMTAZ SULTANA.

Prohar: 35 Siddeswari Rd, Dhaka 1217; tel. (2) 404206; Editor MUJIBUL HUQ.

Protirodh: Dept of Answar and V.D.P. Khilgoan, Ministry of Home Affairs, School Bldg, 2nd and 3rd Floors, Bangladesh Secretariat, Dhaka; tel. (2) 405971; f. 1977; fortnightly; Editor ZAHANGIR HABIBULLAH; circ. 20,000.

Purbani: 1 Ramkrishna Mission Rd, Dhaka 1203; tel. (2) 256503; f. 1951; film weekly; Editor KHONDKER SHAHADAT HOSSAIN; circ. 22,000.

Robbar: 1 Ramkrishna Mission Rd, Dhaka; tel. (2) 256071; f. 1978; weekly; Editor ABDUL HAFIZ; circ. 20,000.

Rokshena: 13B Avoy Das Lane, Tiktuli, Dhaka; tel. (2) 255117; Editor SYEDA AFSANA.

Sachitra Bangladesh: 112 Circuit House Rd, Dhaka 1000; tel. (2) 402129; f. 1979; fortnightly; Editor A. B. M. ABDUL MATIN; circ. 8,000.

Sachitra Sandhani: 68/2 Purana Paltan, Dhaka; tel. (2) 409680; f. 1978; weekly; Editor GAZI SHAHABUDDIN MAHMUD; circ. 13,000.

Sandip: 28/A/3 Toyenbee Circular Rd, Dhaka; tel. (2) 235542; weekly; Editor MOHSEN ARA RAHMAN.

Shishu: Bangladesh Shishu Academy, Old High Court Compound, Dhaka 1000; tel. (2) 230317; f. 1977; children's monthly; Editor GOLAM KIBRIA; circ. 5,000.

Sonar Bangla: 423 Elephant Rd, Mogh Bazar, Dhaka 1217; tel. (2) 400637; f. 1961; Editor MUHAMMED QAMARUZZAMAN; circ. 25,000.

Swadesh: 19 B.B. Ave, Dhaka; tel. (2) 256946; weekly; Editor ZAKIUDDIN AHMED; circ. 8,000.

Tarokalok: 8/3 Neelkhet, Babupura, Dhaka 1205; tel. (2) 507952; weekly; Editor SAJJAD KADIR.

Tide: 56/57 Motijheel C/A, Dhaka 1000; tel. (2) 259421; Editor ENAYET KARIM.

Tilotwoma: 14 Bangla Bazar, Dhaka; Editor ABDUL MANNAN.

English

ADAB News: 1/3, Block F, Lalmatia, Dhaka 1207; tel. (2) 327424; telex 642940; f. 1974; 6 a year; publ. by the Assn of Devt Agencies in Bangladesh (ADAB); Editor-in-Chief AZFAR HUSSAIN; circ. 10,000.

Bangladesh: 112 Circuit House Rd, Dhaka 1000; tel. (2) 402013; fortnightly; Editor A. B. M. ABDUL MATIN.

Bangladesh Gazette: Bangladesh Government Press, Tejgaon, Dhaka; f. 1947, name changed 1972; weekly; official notices; Editor M. HUDA.

Bangladesh Illustrated Weekly: 31A Rankin St, Wari, Dhaka; tel. (2) 23358; Editor ATIQUZZAMAN KHAN; circ. 3,000.

Cinema: 81 Motijheel C/A, Dhaka 1000; Editor SHEIKH FAZLUR RAHMAN MARUF; circ. 11,000.

Detective: Polwell Bhaban, Naya Paltan, Dhaka 2; tel. (2) 402757; f. 1960; weekly; also publ. in Bengali; Editor SYED AMJAD HOSSAIN; circ. 3,000.

Dhaka Courier: Cosmos Centre, 69/1 New Circular Rd, Malibagh, Dhaka 1217; tel. (2) 408420; telex 642499; fax (2) 831942; weekly; Editor ENAYETULLAH KHAN; circ. 18,000.

Herald: 87 Bijoy Nagar, Dhaka; tel. (2) 231533; f. 1981; weekly; Editor JAQADUL KARIM; circ. 4,000.

Holiday: Holiday Bldg, 30 Tejgaon Industrial Area, Dhaka 1208; tel. (2) 329163; telex 675632; fax (2) 833113; f. 1959; weekly; independent; Editor-in-Chief ENAYETULLAH KHAN; circ. 18,000.

Motherland: Khanjahan Ali Rd, Khulna; tel. (41) 61685; f. 1974; weekly; Editor M. N. KHAN.

Tide: 56/57 Motijheel C/A, Dhaka; tel. (2) 259421; Editor ENAYET KARIM.

Voice From the North: Dinajpur Town, Dinajpur; tel. (531) 3256; f. 1981; weekly; Editor Prof. MUHAMMAD MOHSIN; circ. 5,000.

NEWS AGENCIES

Bangladesh Sangbad Sangstha (BSS) (Bangladesh News Agency): 68/2 Purana Paltan, Dhaka 1000; tel. (2) 235036; telex 642202; Man. Dir and Chief Editor MAHBUBUL ALAM; Gen. Man. D. P. BARUA.

Eastern News Agency (ENA): 3/3C Purana Paltan, Dhaka 1000; tel. (2) 234206; telex 642410; f. 1970; Man. Dir and Chief Editor GOLAM RASUL MALLICK.

Foreign Bureaux

Agence France-Presse (AFP): Shilpa Bank Bldg, 5th Floor, 8 DIT Ave, nr Dhaka Stadium, Dhaka 1000; tel. (2) 242234; telex 5526; Bureau Chief GOLAM TAHABOOR.

Associated Press (AP) (USA): 69/1 New Circular Rd, Dhaka 1217; tel. (2) 833717; telex 642967; Representative HASAN SAEED FARID HOSSAIN.

Inter Press Service (IPS) (Italy): c/o Bangladesh Sangbad Sangstha, 68/2 Purana Paltan, Dhaka 1000; tel. (2) 235036; Correspondent A. K. M. TABIBUL ISLAM.

Reuters Ltd (UK): POB 3993, Dhaka; tel. (2) 864088; telex 632420; fax (2) 832976; Bureau Chief ATIQUL ALAM.

South Asian News Agency (SANA): Dhaka.

United Press International (UPI) (USA): Dhaka; tel. (2) 233132; telex 642817.

PRESS ASSOCIATIONS

Bangladesh Council of Newspapers and News Agencies: Dhaka; tel. (2) 413256; Pres. Kazi SHAHED AHMED; Sec.-Gen. HABIBUL BASHAR.

Bangladesh Federal Union of Journalists: National Press Club Bldg, 18 Topkhana Rd, Dhaka 1000; tel. (2) 254777; f. 1973; Pres. REAZUDDIN AHMED; Sec.-Gen. SYED ZAFAR AHMED.

Bangladesh Sangbadpatra Karmachari Federation (Newspaper Employees' Fed.): 47/3 Toyenbee Circular Rd, Bikrampur House, Dhaka 1000; tel. (2) 235065; f. 1972; Pres. RAFIQUL ISLAM; Sec.-Gen. MIR MOZAMMEL HOSSAIN.

Bangladesh Sangbadpatra Press Sramik Federation (Newspaper Press Workers' Federation): 1 Ramkrishna Mission Rd, Dhaka 1203; f. 1960; Pres. M. ABDUL KARIM; Sec.-Gen. BOZLUR RAHMAN MILON.

Dhaka Union of Journalists: National Press Club, Dhaka; f. 1947; Pres. ABEL KHAIR; Gen.-Sec. ABDUL KALAM AZAD.

Overseas Correspondents' Association of Bangladesh (OCAB): 18 Topkhana Rd, Dhaka 1000; f. 1979; Pres. ZAHIDUZZAMAN FAROOQ; Gen. Sec. TAHMINA SAYEED; 51 mems.

Publishers

Adeyle Brothers: 60 Patuatuly, Dhaka 1.

Ahmed Publishing House: 7 Zindabahar 1st Lane, Dhaka 1; tel. (2) 36492; f. 1942; literature, history, science, religion, children's, maps and charts; Man. Dir KAMALUDDIN AHMED; Man. MESBAHUDDIN AHMED.

Ashrafia Library: 4 Hakim Habibur Rahman Rd, Chawk Bazar, Dhaka 1000; Islamic religious books, texts, and reference works of Islamic institutions.

Asiatic Society of Bangladesh: 5 Old Secretariat Rd, Ramna, Dhaka; tel. (2) 9560500; f. 1952; periodicals on science, Bangla and humanities; Pres. Prof. WAKIL AHMED; Admin. Officer MD. ABDUL AWAL MIAH.

Bangla Academy (National Academy of Arts and Letters): Burdwan House, 3 Kazi Nazrul Islam Ave, Dhaka 1000; tel. (2) 869577; f. 1955; higher education textbooks in Bengali, research works in language, literature and culture, language planning, popular science, drama, encyclopaedias, translations of world classics, dictionaries; Dir-Gen. Prof. MONSUR MUSA.

Bangladesh Book Corporation: 73/74 Patuatuly, Dhaka.

Bangladesh Publishers: 45 Patuatully, Dhaka 1100; tel. (2) 233135; f. 1952; textbooks for schools, colleges and universities, cultural books, journals, etc.; Dir MAYA RANI GHOSAL.

Bangladesh Books International Ltd: Ittefaq Bhaban, 1 Ramkrishna Mission Rd, POB 377, Dhaka 3; tel. (2) 256071; f. 1975; reference, academic, research, literary, children's in Bengali and English; Chair. MOINUL HOSSEIN; Man. Dir ABDUL HAFIZ.

Barnamala Prakashani: 30 Bangla Bazar, Dhaka.

Boi Prakashani: 38A Bangla Bazar, Dhaka.

Boighar: 149 Government New Market, Dhaka.

Book Society: 38 Bangla Bazar, Dhaka.

Emdadia Library: Chawk Bazar, Dhaka.

Habibia Library: Chawk Bazar, Dhaka.

Islamic Foundation: Baitul Mukarram, Dhaka.

Jatiya Sahitya Prakashani: 51 Purana Paltan, Dhaka 1000; f. 1970; Prin. Officer MOFIDUL HOQUE.

Khan Brothers & Co: 67 Pyari Das Rd, Dhaka.

Liaquat Publications: 34 North Brook Hall Rd, Dhaka.

Model Publishing House: 34 Bangla Bazar, Dhaka.

Mofiz Book House: 37 Bangla Bazar, Dhaka.

Muktadhara: 74 Farashganj, Dhaka 1100; tel. (2) 231374; f. 1971; educational, literary and general; Bengali and English; Man. Dir C. R. Saha.

Mullick Brothers: 3/1 Bangla Bazar, Dhaka 1100; tel. (2) 232088; telex 642037; fax (2) 833983; educational.

Osmania Book Depot: 30/32 North Brook Hall Rd, Dhaka 1100.

Puthighar Ltd: 74 Farashganj, Dhaka 1100; tel. (2) 231374; f. 1951; educational; Bengali and English; Man. Dir C. R. Saha; Chief Editor S. P. Lahiry.

Puthipatra: 1/6 Shirish Das Lane, Banglabazar, Dhaka 1; f. 1952.

Rahman Brothers: 5/1 Gopinath Datta, Kabiraj St, Babu Bazar, Dhaka; tel. (2) 282633; educational.

Royal Library: Ispahani Bldg, 31/32 P. K. Roy Rd, Banglabazar, Dhaka 1; tel. (2) 250863.

Sahitya Kutir: Bogra.

Sahityika: 6 Bangla Bazar, Dhaka.

Student Ways: 9 Bangla Bazar, Dhaka.

University Press Ltd: Red Crescent Bldg, 114 Motijheel C/A, POB 2611, Dhaka 1000; tel. (2) 9565441; telex 642460; fax (2) 867547; f. 1975; educational, academic and general; Man. Dir Mohiuddin Ahmed; Editor Abdar Rahman.

Government Publishing Houses

Bangladesh Bureau of Statistics: Bldg 8, Room 14, Bangladesh Secretariat, Dhaka 1000; tel. (2) 832274; f. 1971; statistical year book and pocket book, censuses, surveys, agricultural year book and special reports; Jt Dir S. M. Tajul Islam; Sec. Dr Tawfiq-e-Elahi Chowdhury Bir Bikram.

Bangladesh Government Press: Tejgaon, Dhaka; tel. (2) 603897; f. 1972.

Department of Films and Publications: 112 Circuit House Rd, Dhaka 1000; tel. (2) 402263.

Press Information Department: Bhaban 6, Bangladesh Secretariat, Dhaka 1000; tel. (2) 400958; telex 65619.

PUBLISHERS' ASSOCIATIONS

Bangladesh Publishers' and Booksellers' Association: 3rd Floor, 3 Liaquat Ave, Dhaka 1; f. 1972; Pres. Janab Jahangir Mohammed Adel; 2,500 mems.

National Book Centre of Bangladesh: 67A Purana Paltan, Dhaka 1000; f. 1963 to promote the cause of 'more, better and cheaper books'; organizes book fairs, publs a monthly journal; Dir Fazle Rabbi.

Broadcasting and Communications

TELECOMMUNICATIONS

Bangladesh Telegraph and Telephone Board: Central Office, Telejogajog Bhaban, 37/E Eskaton Garden, Dhaka 1000; tel. (2) 831500; telex 642030; fax (2) 832577; Chair. M.A. Mannan Chowdhury; Dir (International) Md Hassanuzzaman.

BROADCASTING

National Broadcasting Authority (NBA): NBA House, 121 Kazi Nazrul Islam Ave, Dhaka 1000; tel. (2) 500143; telex 642228; f. 1984 by merger of Radio Bangladesh and Bangladesh Television; Chair. Janab Saiful Bari.

Radio

Bangladesh Betar: NBA House, 121 Kazi Nazrul Islam Ave, Shahabag, Dhaka 1000; tel. (2) 865294; telex 642228; fax (2) 862021; e-mail dgradio@drik.bgd.toolnet.org; f. 1971; govt-controlled; regional stations at Dhaka, Chittagong, Khulna, Rajshahi, Rangpur, Sylhet and Thakurgaon broadcast a total of approximately 160 hours daily; transmitting centres at Lalmai and Rangamati; external service broadcasts 8 transmissions daily in Arabic, Bengali, English, Hindi, Nepalese and Urdu; Dir-Gen. M.I. Chowdhury.

Television

Bangladesh Television (BTV): NBA House, Shahabag Mymensingh Rd, Rampura, Dhaka 1000; tel. (2) 866606; telex 675624; fax (2) 832927; f. 1971; govt-controlled; daily broadcasts on one channel from Dhaka station for 10 hours; transmissions also from relay stations at Chittagong, Khulna, Mymensingh, Natore, Noakhali, Rangpur, Satkhira, Sylhet, Cox's Bazar and Rangamati; Dir-Gen. Shahryar Z. R. Iqbal; Gen. Man. and Dir (Programmes and Planning) Mustafizur Rahman.

Finance

(cap. = capital; res = reserves; dep. = deposits; m. = million; brs = branches; amounts in taka)

BANKING

Central Bank

Bangladesh Bank: Motijheel C/A, POB 325, Dhaka 1000; tel. (2) 9555000; telex 632226; fax (2) 9566212; f. 1971; cap. 30m., res 30m., dep. 81,043.3m. (June 1995); Gov. Lutfor Rahman Sarkar; 9 brs.

Nationalized Commercial Banks

Agrani Bank: 9D Dilkusha C/A, Motijheel, POB 531, Dhaka 1000; tel. (2) 9569562; telex 642757; fax (2) 867643; f. 1972; 100% state-owned; cap. 2,484.2m., res 299m., dep. 65,172m. (June 1996); Chair. H. T. Imam; Man. Dir Khondaker Ibrahim Khaled; 903 brs.

Janata Bank: 110 Motijheel C/A, Motijheel, POB 468, Dhaka 1000; tel. (2) 9560027; telex 675840; fax (2) 9564644; f. 1972; 100% state-owned; cap. 2,594m., res 124m., dep. 69,115m. (June 1996); Chair. Dr Mohammad Harun-or-Rashid; Man. Dir Golam Mostafa; 897 brs in Bangladesh, 4 brs in the UAE.

Rupali Bank Ltd: 34 Dilkusha C/A, POB 719, Dhaka 1000; tel. (2) 9551624; telex 675635; fax (2) 867536; f. 1972; 94.55% state-owned, 5.45% by public; cap. 1,250m., res 76.1m., dep. 29,585m. (June 1996); Chair. M. Abu Syeed; Man. Dir Rafiqul Karim Chowdhury; 518 brs in Bangladesh, 1 br. in Pakistan.

Sonali Bank: 35–44 Motijheel C/A, POB 3130, Dhaka 1000; tel. (2) 9550426; telex 642644; fax (2) 9561410; f. 1972; 100% state-owned; cap. 3,272.2m., res 893.2m., dep. 110,232.5m. (May 1996); Chair. Mohammad Asafuddowlah; Man. Dir A. Q. Siddiqui; 1,313 brs.

Private Commercial Banks

Al-Arafah Islami Bank Ltd: Rahman Mansion, 161 Motijheel C/A, Dhaka; tel. (2) 9560198; telex 632409; f. 1995; 100% owned by 23 sponsors; cap. 101.2m., res 10m., dep. 534.4m. (Aug. 1996); Chair. A. Z. M. Shamsul Alam; Man. Dir M. M. Nurul Haque.

Al-Baraka Bank Bangladesh Ltd: Kashfia Plaza, 35C Naya Paltan (VIP Rd), POB 3467, Dhaka 1000; tel. (2) 410050; telex 632118; fax (2) 834943; f. 1987 on Islamic banking principles; 34.68% owned by Al-Baraka Group, Saudi Arabia, 5.78% by Islamic Development Bank, Jeddah, 45.91% by local sponsors, 5.75% by Bangladesh Govt., 7.8% by general public; cap. 259.6m., res 14.9m., dep. 4,898.1m. (June 1996); Chair. Dr Saleh J. Malaikah; Man. Dir Anowar Ahmed; 33 brs.

Arab Bangladesh Bank Ltd: BCIC Bhaban, 30–31 Dilkusha C/A, POB 3522, Dhaka 1000; tel. (2) 9560312; telex 642520; fax (2) 642944; f. 1982; 95% owned by Bangladesh nationals and 5% by Bangladesh Govt; cap. p.u. 282.3m., res 284.5m., dep. 9,383.9m. (July 1996); Chair. M. Morshed Khan; Man. Dir A. Rahim Chowdhury; 54 brs.

City Bank Ltd: Jiban Bima Tower, 10 Dilkusha C/A, POB 3381, Dhaka 1000; tel. (2) 9565925; telex 642581; fax (2) 632241; f. 1983; 50% owned by sponsors, 45% by general public and 5% by Govt; cap. p.u. 160.0m., res 125m., dep. 7,050m. (June 1996); Chair. Ibrahim Mia; Man. Dir Md Taheruddin; 75 brs.

Dhaka Bank Ltd: Adamjee Court, 115–120 Motijheel C/A, Dhaka 1000; tel. (2) 9556587; fax (2) 9556584; f. 1995; cap. p.u. 100m., res 3m., dep. 1,260m. (July 1996); Chair. Abdul Hai Sarkar; Man. Dir Ashfaque U. Chowdhury; 3 brs.

Eastern Bank Ltd: Jiban Bima Bhaban, 10 Dilkusha C/A, POB 896, Dhaka 1000; tel. (2) 9558390; telex 642482; fax (2) 9562364; f. 1992; appropriated assets and liabilities of fmr Bank of Credit and Commerce International (Overseas) Ltd; 20% govt.-owned; cap. 600m., res 212.8m., dep. 7,487.5m. (Dec. 1996); Chair. Nurul Hossain Khan; Man. Dir A. I. M. Iftikhar Rahman; 11 brs.

International Finance Investment and Commerce Bank Ltd (IFICB): BSB Bldg, 17th–19th Floors, 8 Rajuk Ave, POB 2229, Dhaka 1000; tel. (2) 9563020; telex 632404; fax (2) 9562015; f. 1983; 40% state-owned; cap. 279.4m., res 226.4m., dep. 15,917.1m. (Dec. 1996); Chair. A.S.F. Rahman; Man. Dir Abbas Uddin Ahmed; 52 brs in Bangladesh, 2 brs in Pakistan.

Islami Bank Bangladesh Ltd (IBB): Head Office, 71 Dilkusha C/A, POB 233, Dhaka 1000; tel. (2) 9563040; telex 642525; fax (2) 9564532; f. 1983 on Islamic banking principles; cap. p.u. 315.7m., res 759.4m., dep. 14,027m. (Dec. 1996); Chair. Cdre (retd) Mohammad Ataur Rahman; Exec. Pres. and CEO M. Kamaluddin Chowdhury; 100 brs.

National Bank Ltd: 18 Dilkusha C/A, POB 3424, Dhaka 1000; tel. (2) 9563081; telex 642791; fax (2) 9563953; e-mail nblho@citech-co.net; f. 1983; 50% owned by sponsors, 45% by general public and 5% by Govt; cap. p.u. 391.2m., res 469.3m., dep. 15,619.9m. (Dec. 1996); Chair. Abdul Awal; Man. Dir Kazi Abdul Mazid; 63 brs.

National Credit and Commerce Bank Ltd: 7–8 Motijheel C/A, POB 2920, Dhaka 1000; tel. (2) 9561902; telex 642821; fax (2) 9566290; f. 1993; 50% owned by sponsors, 45% by general public and 5% by Govt; cap. p.u. 195m., res 4m., dep. 3,968m. (June 1996); Chair. MD ABDUL AWAL; Man. Dir CHOWDHURY ABDUL QUAYUM; 25 brs.

Prime Bank Ltd: Adamjee Court Annex Bldg, 119–20, Motijheel C/A, Dhaka 1000; tel. (2) 9567265; telex 671543; fax (2) 9567230; e-mail primebnk@bangla.net; f. 1995; cap. 100m., res 175.2m., dep. 3,125.5m. (Dec. 1996); Chair. Dr R. A. GHANI; Man. Dir and Chief Exec. Kazi ABDUL MAZID; 11 brs.

Pubali Bank Ltd: Pubali Bank Bhaban, 26 Dilkusha C/A, POB 853, Dhaka 1000; tel. (2) 9551614; telex 675844; fax (2) 863246; f. 1959 as Eastern Mercantile Bank Ltd; name changed to Pubali Bank in 1972; 95% privately-owned, 5% state-owned; cap. p.u. 160.0m., res 271m., dep. 19,777m. (June 1996); Chair. EMADUDDIN AHMED CHAUDHURY; Man. Dir MOHAMMAD QAMRUL HUDA; 354 brs.

Social Investment Bank: 15 Dilkusha C/A, Dhaka 1000; tel. (2) 881654; telex 671557; fax (2) 881654; f. 1995; cap. p.u. 118.4m., dep. 322.4m. (July 1996); Chair. Dr M. A. MANNAN; Man. Dir M. AZIZUL HUQ; 5 brs.

Southeast Bank Ltd: 1 Dilkusha C/A, Dhaka 1000; tel. (2) 9550081; telex 632425; fax (2) 9550093; e-mail seastbk@citechco.net; f. 1995; cap. 100m., dep. 3,000m. (Dec. 1996); Chair. M. A. KASHEM; CEO SYED ANISUL HUQ; 10 brs.

United Commercial Bank Ltd: Federation Bhaban, 60 Motijheel C/A, POB 2653, Dhaka 1000; tel. (2) 9568690; telex 642733; fax (2) 29560587; f. 1983; cap. p.u. 194.6m., res 131m., dep. 7,707.8m. (Dec. 1995); Chair. M. A. SABUR; Man. Dir M. A. YUSSOUF KHAN; 77 brs.

Uttara Bank Ltd: 90 Motijheel C/A, POB 818, Dhaka 1000; tel. (2) 9566067; telex 642915; fax (2) 863529; f. 1965 as Eastern Banking Corpn Ltd; name changed to Uttara Bank in 1972 and to Uttara Bank Ltd in 1983; cap. p.u. 99.8m., res 153.7m., dep. 14,207.8m. (June 1996); Chair. A. M. ANISUZZAMAN; Man. Dir M. AMINUZAMMAN; 198 brs.

Foreign Commercial Banks

American Express Bank Ltd (USA): ALICO Bldg, 18–20 Motijheel C/A, POB 420, Dhaka 1000; tel. (2) 9561496; telex 632305; fax (2) 863808; res 537.5m., dep. 6,236.5m. (Dec. 1995); Chair. JOHN A. WARD III; Gen. Man. STEVEN R. BRITTAINS; 2 brs.

ANZ Grindlays Bank PLC (UK): 2 Dilkusha C/A, POB 502, Dhaka 1000; tel. (2) 9550181; telex 642597; fax (2) 9562332; res 6.5m., dep. 7,067.4m. (Dec. 1995); Gen. Man. FRANKLIN JOHN GAMBLE; 9 brs.

Banque Indosuez (France): 47 Motijheel C/A, POB 3490, Dhaka 1000; tel. (2) 9566566; telex 642438; fax (2) 863137; res 221m., dep. 3,397m. (Dec. 1995); Chair. GÉRARD MESTRALLET; 2 brs.

Citibank, NA (USA): 122-124 Motijheel C/A, POB 1000, Dhaka 1000; tel. (2) 9550060; fax (2) 642611; f. 1995; cap. p.u. 209.5m., res 5.5m., dep. 648.8m. (July 1996); Chair. JOHN S. REED; Man. Dir S. SRIDHAR; 1 br.

Habib Bank Ltd (Pakistan): 53 Motijheel C/A, POB 201, Dhaka 1000; tel. (2) 9555091; telex 632572; fax (2) 9561784; cap. 80.5m., res 14.3m., dep. 578.6m. (Dec. 1996); Man. Dir J. A. SHAHID; 2 brs.

The Hongkong and Shanghai Banking Corpn Ltd (Hong Kong): Dhaka; CEO for Bangladesh DAVID HUMPHREYS.

Muslim Commercial Bank Ltd (Pakistan): 4 Dilkusha C/A, POB 7213, Dhaka 1000; tel. (2) 9568871; telex 642167; fax (2) 860671; cap. p.u. 100m., res 4m., dep. 650.3m. (July 1996); Man. Dir HADI ALI KHAN; 2 brs.

Standard Chartered Bank (UK): ALICO Bldg, 18–20 Motijheel C/A, POB 420, Dhaka 1000; tel. (2) 9561465; telex 675859; fax (2) 9561758; cap. p.u. 215m., dep. 5,850m. (Dec. 1995); Chief Exec. (Bangladesh) GEOFF WILLIAMS; 3 brs.

State Bank of India: 24–25 Dilkusha C/A, POB 981, Dhaka 1000; tel. (2) 9559935; telex 642431; fax (2) 9563992; e-mail sbibd@bangla.net; cap. 190.4m., dep. 557.1m. (March 1997); CEO K. K. CHATTOPADHYAY; 1 br.

Development Finance Organizations

Bangladesh House Building Finance Corpn (BHBFC): HBFC Bldg, 22 Purana Paltan, POB 2167, Dhaka 1000; tel. (2) 9562767; f. 1952; provides low-interest credit for residential house-building; 100% state-owned; cap. p.u. 972.9m., res 2,937.8m. (June 1996); Chair. AMINUL ISLAM; Man. Dir MD HELAL UDDIN; 9 zonal offices, 12 regional offices and 6 camp offices.

Bangladesh Krishi Bank (BKB): 83–85 Motijheel C/A, POB 357, Dhaka 2; tel. (2) 9560031; telex 642526; fax (2) 236903; f. 1971; provides credit for agricultural and rural devt; 100% state-owned; cap. p.u. 1,000m., res 820.5m., dep. 17,360m. (June 1996); Chair. Dr MIRZA JALIL; Man. Dir MOSHARAF HOSSAIN; 836 brs.

Bangladesh Samabaya Bank Ltd (BSBL): 'Samabaya Sadan', 9D Motijheel C/A, POB 505, Dhaka 1000; tel. (2) 9564628; f. 1948; provides credit for agricultural co-operatives; cap. p.u. 31.6m., res 558m., dep. 22m. (June 1996); Chair. Dr ABDUL MOYEEN KHAN; Gen. Man. MD ABDUL WAHED.

Bangladesh Shilpa Bank (BSB) (Industrial Development Bank): 8 D.I.T. Ave, POB 975, Dhaka; tel. (2) 9555151; telex 642950; fax (2) 9562061; f. 1972; fmrly Industrial Devt Bank; provides long- and short-term financing for industrial devt in the private and public sectors; also provides underwriting facilities and equity support; 66% state-owned; cap. p.u. 1,320.0m., res 644m., dep. 2,439m. (June 1996); Chair. Dr JAMILUR REZA CHOWDHURY; Man. Dir MAHMUD-UL-KARIM (acting); 15 brs.

Bangladesh Shilpa Rin Sangstha (BSRS) (Industrial Loan Agency): BIWTA Bhaban, 5th Floor, 141-143 Motijheel C/A, POB 473, Dhaka 1000; tel. (2) 9565046; fax (2) 956705; f. 1972; 100% state-owned; cap. p.u. 700m., res 462.8m. (June 1996); Chair. Dr M. FARASHUDDIN; Man. Dir AL-AMEEN CHAUDHURY; 4 brs.

Bank of Small Industries and Commerce Bangladesh Ltd (BASIC): Suite 601/602, Sena Kalyan Bhaban, 6th Floor, 195 Motijheel C/A, Dhaka 1000; tel. (2) 956430; telex 632185; fax (2) 9564829; f. 1988; 100% state-owned; cap. p.u. 80m., res 106m., dep. 2,738m. (Dec. 1995); Chair. A. M. AKHTER; Man. Dir ALAUDDIN A. MAJID; 19 brs.

Delta BRAC Housing Finance Corpn: Dhaka; f. 1996; Bangladesh's first privately-owned housing finance co.; cap. 500m. (1996); CEO ABUL MAL ABDUL MUHITH.

Grameen Bank: Head Office, Mirpur-2, POB 1216, Dhaka 1216; tel. (2) 801138; fax (2) 803559; f. 1976; provides credit for the landless rural poor; 10% owned by Govt; cap. p.u. 227m., res 70m., dep. 3,809m. (Dec. 1995); Chair. REHMAN SOBHAN; Man. Dir Dr MUHAMMAD YUNUS; 1,056 brs.

Investment Corpn of Bangladesh (ICB): BSB Bldg, 12th–14th Floor, 8 Rajuk Ave, POB 2058, Dhaka 1000; tel. (2) 9563455; fax (2) 865684; f. 1976; provides devt financing; 27% owned by Govt; cap. p.u. 200.0m., res 315.2m. (June 1996); Chair. HEDAYAT AHMED; Man. Dir KHAIRUL HUDA; 5 brs.

Rajshahi Krishi Unnayan Bank: Sadharan Bima Bhaban, Kazihata, Greater Rd, Rajshahi 6000; tel. (721) 5543; fax (721) 5947; f. 1987; 100% state-owned; cap. p.u. 980m., res 208.4m., dep. 2,622.7m. (June 1996); Chair. TAJUL ISLAM MOHAMMAD FARUQUE; Man. Dir A. K. M. SAJEDUR RAHMAN; 300 brs.

STOCK EXCHANGES

Chittagong Stock Exchange: Kashfia Plaza, 923/A, Sk Mujib Rd, Agrabad, Chittagong; tel. (31) 714632; fax (31) 714101.

Dhaka Stock Exchange Ltd: 9F Motijheel C/A, Dhaka 1000; tel. (2) 9559118; fax (2) 9564727; f. 1960; 186 listed cos; Chair. ABDUL HUQ HOWLADAR.

Regulatory Authority

Bangladesh Securities and Exchange Commission: Dhaka; CEO M. ABU SAYEED.

INSURANCE

Bangladesh Insurance Association: Dhaka; Chair. MAYEEDUL ISLAM.

In 1973 the two corporations below were formed, one for life insurance and the other for general insurance:

Jiban Bima Corpn: 24 Motijheel C/A, POB 346, Dhaka 1000; tel. (2) 256876; telex 642704; fax (2) 868112; state-owned; comprises 37 national life insurance cos; life insurance; Man. Dir A. K. M. MOSTAFIZUR RAHMAN.

Sadharan Bima Corpn: 33 Dilkusha C/A, POB 607, Dhaka 1000; tel. (2) 9552070; state-owned; general insurance; Man. Dir M. LUTFAR RAHMAN.

Trade and Industry

GOVERNMENT AGENCIES

Board of Investment: Prime Minister's Office, Shilpa Bhaban, 91 Motijheel C/A, Dhaka 1000; tel. (2) 9561430; telex 642212; fax (2) 9562312; e-mail ec@boi.bdmail.net; Exec. Chair. TAUFIK ELAHI CHOWDHURY; Dep. Dir LUTFUR RAHMAN BHUIYA.

Export Promotion Bureau: 122–124 Motijheel C/A, Dhaka 1000; tel. (2) 9552245; telex 642204; fax (2) 9568000; e-mail epb.tic@pradeshta.net; f. 1972; attached to Ministry of Commerce; regional offices in Chittagong, Khulna and Rajshahi; brs in Comilla, Sylhet, Barisal and Bogra; Dir-Gen. MAZHARUL HAQUE; Vice-Chair. FAISAL AHMED CHOUDHURY.

Planning Commission: Planning Commission Secretariat, G.O. Hostel, Sher-e-Bangla Nagar, Dhaka; f. 1972; govt agency responsible for all aspects of economic planning and development including the preparation of the five-year plans and annual development programmes (in conjunction with appropriate govt ministries), promotion of savings and investment, compilation of statistics and evaluation of development schemes and projects.

Privatization Board: Dhaka; Chair. KAZI ZAFRULLAH.

DEVELOPMENT ORGANIZATIONS

Bangladesh Chemical Industries Corpn: BCIC Bhaban, 30–31 Dilkusha C/A, Dhaka; tel. (2) 259852; telex 65847; Chair. A. K. M. MOSHARRAF HOSSAIN.

Bangladesh Export Processing Zones Authority: 222 New Eskaton Rd, Dhaka 1000; tel. (2) 832553; fax (2) 834967; f. 1983 to plan, develop, operate and manage export processing zones in Bangladesh; Exec. Chair. M. MOAZZEM HOSSAIN KHAN.

Bangladesh Fisheries Development Corpn: 24/25 Dilkusha C/A, Motijheel, Dhaka 1000; tel. (2) 9552689; telex 632154; fax (2) 9563990; f. 1964; under the Ministry of Fisheries and Livestock; development and commercial activities; Chair. M. MUZAFFAR HUSSAIN; Sec. D. M. YASIN.

Bangladesh Forest Industries Development Corpn: 186 Circular Rd, Motijheel C/A, Dhaka 1000; Chair. M. ATIKULLAH.

Bangladesh Jute Mills Corpn: Adamjee Court (Annexe), 115–120 Motijheel C/A, Dhaka 1000; tel. (2) 861980; telex 675662; fax (2) 863329; f. 1972; operates 35 jute mills, incl. 2 carpet mills; world's largest manufacturer and exporter of jute goods; bags, carpet backing cloth, yarn, twine, tape, felt, floor covering, etc.; Chair. MANIRUDDIN AHMAD; Man. (Marketing) MD JAHIRUL ISLAM.

Bangladesh Mineral Exploration and Development Corpn: HBFC Bldg, 8th–9th Floors, 22 Purana Paltan, Dhaka 1000; telex 65737; Chair. M. W. ALI.

Bangladesh Small and Cottage Industries Corpn (BSCIC): 137/138 Motijheel C/A, Dhaka 1000; tel. (2) 233202; f. 1957; Chair. MUHAMMAD SIRAJUDDIN.

Bangladesh Steel and Engineering Corpn (BSEC): BSEC Bhaban, 102 Kazi Nazrul Islam Ave, Dhaka 1215; tel. (2) 814616; telex 642225; fax (2) 812846; 16 industrial units; sales US $83m. (1994); cap. US $52m.; Chair. A. I. M. NAZMUL ALAM; Gen. Man. (Marketing) ASHRAFUL HAQ; 8,015 employees.

Bangladesh Sugar and Food Industries Corpn: Shilpa Bhaban, Motijheel C/A, Dhaka 1000; tel. (2) 258084; telex 642210; f. 1972; Chair. M. NEFAUR RAHMAN.

Bangladesh Textile Mills Corpn: Shadharan Bima Bhaban, 33 Dilkusha C/A, Dhaka 1000; tel. (2) 252504; telex 65703; f. 1972; Chair. M. NURUNNABI CHOWDHURY.

Trading Corpn of Bangladesh: Kawranbazar, Dhaka; tel. (2) 811516; telex 642217; fax (2) 813582; f. 1972; Chair. SHOAIB AHMED; Sec. NIRMAL CHANDRA SARKER.

CHAMBERS OF COMMERCE

Federation of Bangladesh Chambers of Commerce and Industry (FBCCI): Federation Bhaban, 60 Motijheel C/A, 4th Floor, POB 2079, Dhaka 1000; tel. (2) 250566; telex 642733; f. 1973; comprises 135 trade asscns and 58 chambers of commerce and industry; Pres. SALMAN F. RAHMAN.

Barisal Chamber of Commerce and Industry: Asad Mansion, 1st Floor, Sadar Rd, Barisal; tel. (431) 3984; Pres. Qazi ISRAIL HOSSAIN.

Bogra Chamber of Commerce and Industry: Chamber Bhaban, 2nd Floor, Kabi Nazrul Islam Rd, Jhautola, Bogra 5800; tel. (51) 6257; fax (51) 4138; f. 1963; Pres. TAHER UDDIN CHOWDHURY; Sr Vice-Pres. MOMTAZ UDDIN.

Chittagong Chamber of Commerce and Industry: Chamber House, Agrabad C/A, POB 481, Chittagong; tel. (31) 713366; telex 66472; fax (31) 710183; f. 1959; 4,000 mems; Pres. SARWAR JAMAL NIZAM: Sec. M. H. CHOWDHURY.

Comilla Chamber of Commerce and Industry: Rammala Rd, Ranir Bazar, Comilla; tel. (81) 5444; Pres. AFZAL KHAN.

Dhaka Chamber of Commerce and Industry: Dhaka Chamber Bldg, 1st Floor, 56–66 Motijheel C/A, POB 2641, Dhaka 1000; tel. (2) 9552808; telex 632475; fax (2) 9560830; f. 1958; 5,000 mems; Pres. A. S. M. QUASEM; Sr Vice-Pres. ASHRAF IBN NOOR.

Dinajpur Chamber of Commerce and Industry: Jail Rd, Dinajpur; tel. (531) 3189; Pres. KHAIRUL ANAM.

Faridpur Chamber of Commerce and Industry: Chamber House, Niltuly, Faridpur; tel. 3530; Pres. KHANDOKER MOHSIN ALI.

Foreign Investors' Chamber of Commerce and Industry: 'Mahbub Castle', 4th Floor, 35-1 Purana Paltan Line, Inner Circular Rd, GPO Box 4086, Dhaka 1000; tel. (2) 412877; fax (2) 839449; e-mail ficci@fastnet.bangla.net; f. 1963 as Agrabad Chamber of Commerce and Industry, name changed as above in 1987; Pres. A.K.M. SHAMSUDDIN; Sec. JAHANGIR BIN ALAM.

Khulna Chamber of Commerce and Industry: 6 Lower Jessore Rd, Khulna; tel. (41) 24135; f. 1934; Pres. S. K. ZAHOIUL ISLAM.

Khustia Chamber of Commerce and Industry: 15, NS Rd, Kushtia; tel. (71) 3448; Pres. DIN MOHAMMAD.

Metropolitan Chamber of Commerce and Industry: Chamber Bldg, 4th Floor, 122–124 Motijheel C/A, Dhaka 1000; tel. (2) 9565208; telex 642413; fax (2) 9565212; e-mail sg@citechco.net; f. 1904; 262 mems; Sec.-Gen. C. K. HYDER.

Noakhali Chamber of Commerce and Industry: Noakhali Pourshara Bhaban, 2nd Floor, Maiydee Court, Noakhali; tel. 5229; Pres. MOHAMMAD NAZIBUR RAHMAN.

Rajshahi Chamber of Commerce and Industry: Chamber Bhaban, Station Rd, P.O. Ghoramara, Rajshahi 6100; tel. (721) 772115; fax (721) 2412; f. 1960; 800 mems; Pres. MOHAMMAD ALI SARKER.

Sylhet Chamber of Commerce and Industry: Chamber Bldg, Jail Rd, POB 97, Sylhet 3100; tel. (821) 4403; telex 633235; Pres. M. A. SALAM CHOUDHURY.

INDUSTRIAL AND TRADE ASSOCIATIONS

Bangladesh Garment Manufacturers and Exporters Association: Dhaka; Pres. REZWAN AHMAD.

Bangladesh Jute Association: BJA Bldg, 77 Motijheel C/A, Dhaka; tel. (2) 256558; Chair. M.A. MANNAN; Sec. S. H. PRODHAN.

Bangladesh Jute Goods Association: 3rd Floor, 150 Motijheel C/A, Dhaka 1000; tel. (2) 253640; f. 1979; 17 mems; Chair. M. A. KASHEM, Haji MOHAMMAD ALI.

Bangladesh Jute Mills Association: Adamjee Court, 4th Floor, 115–120 Motijheel C/A, Dhaka 1000; tel. (2) 9560071; telex 671430; fax (2) 9566472; Chair. A. M. ZAHIRUDDIN KHAN.

Bangladesh Jute Spinners Association: 55 Purana Paltan, 3rd Floor, Dhaka 1000; tel. (2) 9551317; telex 642456; fax (2) 9562772; f. 1979; 34 mems; Chair. SHABBIR YUSUF; Sec. SHAHIDUL KARIM.

Bangladesh Tea Board: 171-172 Baizid Bostami Rd, Nasirabad, Chittagong; tel. (31) 210491; telex 66304; fax (2) 863237; Chair. MUSIB UDDIN CHOWDHURY; Sec. M. ALI AHMED.

Bangladeshiyo Cha Sangsad (Tea Association of Bangladesh): 'Dar-e-Shahidi', 3rd Floor, 69 Agrabad C/A, POB 287, Chittagong 4100; tel. (31) 501009; f. 1952; Chair. LAILA RAHMAN KABIR; Sec. G. S. DHAR.

UTILITIES

Electricity

Bangladesh Atomic Energy Commission (BAEC): 4 Kazi Nazrul Islam Ave, POB 158, Dhaka 1000; tel. (2) 502600; telex 632203; fax (2) 863051; f. 1964 as Atomic Energy Centre of the fmr Pakistan Atomic Energy Comm. in East Pakistan; reorg. 1973; operates an atomic energy research establishment and a 3-MW research nuclear reactor (inaugurated in January 1987) at Savar, an atomic energy centre at Dhaka, one nuclear medicine institute at IPGMR, Dhaka, nine nuclear medicine centres, and a beach-sand exploitation centre at Cox's Bazar; nuclear mineral project involving the exploitation of uranium and thorium; gamma radiation sources for food preservation and industrial radiography; Chair. M. A. QUAIYUM; Sec. RAFIQUL ALAM.

TRADE UNIONS

In 1986 only about 3% of the total labour force was unionized. There were 2,614 registered unions, organized mainly on a sectoral or occupational basis. There were about 17 national trade unions to represent workers at the national level.

Transport

RAILWAYS

Bangladesh Railway: Rail Bhaban, Abdul Ghani Rd, Dhaka 1000; tel. (2) 9561200; fax (2) 9563413; e-mail systcan@citechco.net; f. 1862; supervised by the Railway and Road Transport Division of the Ministry of Communications; divided into East and West zones, with HQ at Chittagong (tel. (31) 711294; telex 66200) and Rajshahi (tel. (721) 761576; fax (721) 761982); total length of 2,706 route km (June 1997); 489 stations; Dir-Gen. M. A. MANAF; Gen. Man. (East Zone) M. FARHAD REZA; Gen. Man. (West Zone) A.T.M. NURUL ISLAM.

ROADS

In 1995 the total length of roads in use was 223,391 km (16,070 km of highways, 22,780 km of secondary roads and 184,541 km of other roads), of which 7.2% were paved. In early 1992 the World Bank approved Bangladesh's US $700m. Jamuna Bridge Project. The construction of the 4.8-km bridge, which will, for the first time, link the east and the west of the country with a railway and road network, was begun in early 1994.

Bangladesh Road Transport Corpn: Dhaka.

INLAND WATERWAYS

In Bangladesh there are some 8,433 km of navigable waterways, which transport 70% of total domestic and foreign cargo traffic and on which are located the main river ports of Dhaka, Narayanganj, Chandpur, Barisal and Khulna. A river steamer service connects these ports several times a week. Vessels of up to 175-m overall length can be navigated on the Karnaphuli river.

Bangladesh Inland Water Transport Corpn: 5 Dilkusha C/A, Dhaka 1000; tel. (2) 257092; f. 1972; 273 vessels (1986).

SHIPPING

The chief ports are Chittagong, where the construction of a second dry-dock is planned, and Chalna. A modern seaport is being developed at Mongla.

Atlas Shipping Lines Ltd: 7 Sk. Mujib Rd, Agrabad, Chittagong 2; tel. (31) 504287; telex 66213; fax (31) 225520; Man. Dir S. U. Chowdhury; Gen. Man. M. Kamal Hayat.

Bangladesh Shipping Corpn: BSC Bhaban, Saltgola Rd, POB 641, Chittagong 4100; tel. (31) 505062; telex 676277; fax (31) 710506; f. 1972; maritime shipping; 16 vessels, 239,693 dwt capacity (1997); Chair. Janab A.S.M. Abdur Rob; Man. Dir Janab Zulfikar Haider Chowdhury.

Bengal Shipping Line Ltd: Palm View, 100A Agrabad C/A, Chittagong 4100; tel. (31) 714800; telex 633288; fax (31) 710362; Chair. Mohammed Abdul Awwal; Man. Dir Mohammed Abdul Malek.

Blue Ocean Lines Ltd: 1st Floor, H.B.F.C. Bldg, 1D AgrabadC/A, Agrabad, Chittagong; tel. (31) 501567; telex 66488; fax (31) 225415.

Broadway Shipping Line: Hafiz Estate, 65 Shiddeswari Rd, Dhaka; tel. (2) 404598; telex 642976; fax (2) 412254.

Chittagong Port Authority: POB 2013, Chittagong 4100; tel. (31) 505041; telex 66264; f. 1887; provides bunkering, ship repair, towage and lighterage facilities as well as provisions and drinking water supplies; Chair. Md Shahadat Hussain.

Continental Liner Agencies: 3rd Floor, Facy Bldg, 87 Agrabad C/A, Chittagong; tel. (31) 721572; telex 633083; fax (31) 710965; Man. Saiful Ahmed; Dir (Technical and Operations) Capt. Mahfuzul Islam.

United Trading Corpn: Gulshan House, POB 775, Dhaka 2.

CIVIL AVIATION

There is an international airport at Dhaka (Zia International Airport) situated at Kurmitola, with the capacity to handle 5m. passengers annually. There are also airports at all major towns.

Biman Bangladesh Airlines: Biman Bhaban, 100 Motijheel C/A, Dhaka 1000; tel. (2) 9560151; telex 642649; fax (2) 863005; f. 1972; 100% state-owned; internal services to eight major towns; international services to the Middle East, the Far East, Europe, and North America; Chair. Minister of State for Civil Aviation and Tourism; Man. Dir Al-Ameen Chaudhury.

Aero Bengal Airline: Dhaka; f. 1995; Bangladesh's first privately-owned carrier.

Tourism

Tourist attractions include the cities of Dhaka and Chittagong, Cox's Bazar—which has the world's longest beach (120 km)—on the Bay of Bengal, and Teknaf, at the southernmost point of Bangladesh. Tourist arrivals totalled 156,231 in 1995 and earnings from tourism reached about US $24m. The majority of visitors are from India, Pakistan, Japan, the United Kingdom and the USA.

Bangladesh Parjatan Corpn (National Tourism Organization): 233 Airport Rd, Tejgaon, Dhaka 1215; tel. (2) 817855; telex 642206; fax (2) 817235; there are four tourist information centres in Dhaka, and one each in Bogra, Chittagong, Cox's Bazar, Khulna, Rangpur, Rajshahi and Rangamati; Chair. Col (retd) Bazlul Ghani Patwary; Man. (Public Relations Division) Mohammad Ahsan Ullah.

BARBADOS

Introductory Survey

Location, Climate, Language, Religion, Flag, Capital

Barbados is the most easterly of the Caribbean islands, lying about 320 km (200 miles) north-east of Trinidad. The island has a total area of 430 sq km (166 sq miles). There is a rainy season from July to November and the climate is tropical, tempered by constant sea winds, during the rest of the year. The mean annual temperature is about 26°C (78°F). Average annual rainfall varies from 1,250 mm on the coast to 1,875 mm in the interior. The language is English. Almost all of the inhabitants profess Christianity, but there are small groups of Hindus, Muslims and Jews. The largest denomination is the Anglican church, but about 90 other Christian sects are represented. The national flag (proportions 3 by 2) has three equal vertical stripes, of blue, gold and blue; superimposed on the centre of the gold band is the head of a black trident. The capital is Bridgetown.

Recent History

Barbados was formerly a British colony. The Barbados Labour Party (BLP) won a general election in 1951, when universal adult suffrage was introduced, and held office until 1961. Although the parliamentary system dates from 1639, ministerial government was not established until 1954, when the BLP's leader, Sir Grantley Adams, became the island's first Premier. He was subsequently Prime Minister of the West Indies Federation from January 1958 until its dissolution in May 1962.

Barbados achieved full internal self-government in October 1961. An election in December 1961 was won by the Democratic Labour Party (DLP), formed in 1955 by dissident members of the BLP. The DLP's leader, Errol Barrow, became Premier, succeeding Dr Hugh Cummins of the BLP. When Barbados achieved independence on 30 November 1966, Barrow became the island's first Prime Minister, having won another election earlier in the month.

The DLP retained power in 1971, but in the general election of September 1976 the BLP, led by J. M. G. M. ('Tom') Adams (Sir Grantley's son), ended Barrow's 15-year rule. The BLP successfully campaigned against alleged government corruption, winning a large majority over the DLP. Both parties were committed to retaining a system of free enterprise and alignment with the USA. At a general election in June 1981 the BLP was returned to office with 17 of the 27 seats in the newly-enlarged House of Assembly. The DLP won the remainder of the seats. Adams died suddenly in March 1985 and was succeeded as Prime Minister by his deputy, Bernard St John, a former leader of the BLP.

At a general election in May 1986 the DLP won a decisive victory, receiving 59.4% of the total votes and winning 24 seats in the House of Assembly. Bernard St John and all except one of his cabinet ministers lost their seats, and Errol Barrow returned as Prime Minister after 10 years in opposition. In June it was announced that Barrow was to review Barbados' participation in the US-supported Regional Security System (RSS), the defence force that had been established soon after the US invasion of Grenada in October 1983. Barbados, under Adams, was one of the countries whose troops supported the invasion. In November 1986 Barrow announced a halt in recruitment to the Barbados Defence Force. In June 1987 Barrow died suddenly. He was succeeded by L. Erskine Sandiford (hitherto the Deputy Prime Minister), who pledged to continue Barrow's economic and social policies.

In September 1987, however, the Minister of Finance, Dr Richard (Richie) Haynes, resigned, accusing Sandiford of failing to consult him over financial appointments. Sandiford assumed the finance portfolio, but acrimony over government policy continued to trouble the DLP. In February 1989 Haynes and three other members of Parliament resigned from the DLP and announced the formation of the National Democratic Party (NDP). Haynes was subsequently appointed as leader of the parliamentary opposition. This was in recognition of the NDP's total of four seats in the House of Assembly, compared with the three of the BLP.

At a general election in January 1991 the DLP won 18 of the 28 seats in the enlarged House of Assembly, while the BLP secured the remaining 10. However, only 62% of the electorate participated in the poll (compared with 76% in 1986). The creation of a Ministry of Justice and Public Safety by the new Government, shortly after its election, and the reintroduction of flogging for convicted criminals, reflected widespread concern over increased levels of violent crime on the island. As a result of serious economic problems, legislation providing for the introduction of a series of austerity measures was narrowly approved by Parliament in September. However, the proposals attracted severe criticism, and in October large demonstrations, protesting against the measures, took place in Bridgetown. Strikes and protests continued in 1992, as large numbers of civil servants and agricultural workers were made redundant under the austerity programme. The increasing unpopularity of Sandiford's leadership provoked continued demands for his resignation during 1993, and at the annual convention of the DLP in August of that year a challenge to his position as leader of the party was mounted. However, Sandiford remained in office, and shortly after the convention he announced a major reallocation of cabinet portfolios. Moreover, a controversial reorganization of the Barbados Tourist Authority (in which Sandiford dismissed almost all the members of the board and assumed the tourism portfolio) prompted the resignation of three cabinet ministers in early 1994. Increasing dissatisfaction with the Prime Minister culminated in his defeat, by 14 votes to 12, in a parliamentary motion of confidence in June. Despite intense speculation that he would resign, Sandiford remained in office, but announced the dissolution of Parliament in preparation for a general election, which was to take place in September. At the DLP annual conference in August, David Thompson defeated Brandford Taitt in an election to the leadership of the party.

A general election took place on 6 September 1994, at which the BLP won a decisive victory, securing 19 of the 28 seats in the House of Assembly (and 48.3% of the total votes), compared with the DLP's eight seats and the NDP's one. Owen Arthur was subsequently appointed as Prime Minister. He identified his Government's priorities as encouraging economic growth and international competitiveness in order to reduce the high levels of unemployment in the country.

In May 1995 the Prime Minister announced the formation of a 10-member commission to advise the Government on possible reforms of the country's Constitution and political institutions. Moreover, in July 1996 the commission was asked to consider, in particular, the continuing role of the British monarch as Head of State in Barbados.

In December 1996 the DLP retained a seat in a by-election. The result reinforced the pressure for the reunification of the DLP and the NDP, which together secured more votes than the BLP in the general election. In mid-1997 two prominent members of the NDP (including the influential General Secretary of the National Union of Public Workers, Joseph Goddard) rejoined the DLP. The NDP lost a further electoral candidate to the ruling BLP in November. In September two candidates (one of whom subsequently joined the DLP) resigned from the BLP, citing the Prime Minister's lack of control over the party.

Relations with Trinidad and Tobago were strained between 1982 and 1985 by publicly-stated differences over the intervention in Grenada, and by Trinidad and Tobago's imposition of import restrictions (a compromise on this was reached in August 1986). In November 1990 the two Governments signed a bilateral fishing agreement. In late 1996 Barbados signed an agreement with the USA to co-operate with a regional initiative to combat the illegal drugs trade.

Government

Executive power is vested in the British monarch, represented by a Governor-General, who acts on the advice of the Cabinet. The Governor-General appoints the Prime Minister and, on the latter's recommendation, other members of the Cabinet. Legislative power is vested in the bicameral Parliament, comprising a Senate of 21 members, appointed by the Governor-

General, and a House of Assembly with 28 members, elected by universal adult suffrage for five years (subject to dissolution) from single-member constituencies. The Cabinet is responsible to Parliament. In 1969 elected local government bodies were abolished in favour of a division into 11 parishes, all of which are administered by the central Government.

Defence

The Barbados Defence Force was established in April 1978. The total strength of the Barbados armed forces in August 1997 was estimated at 610; the army consisted of 500 members and the navy (coastguard) 110. There was also a reserve force of 430. Government spending on defence in 1996 was an estimated Bds $27m.

Economic Affairs

In 1995, according to estimates by the World Bank, the island's gross national product (GNP), measured at average 1993–95 prices, was US $1,745m., equivalent to US $6,560 per head. Between 1985 and 1995, it was estimated, GNP per head decreased, in real terms, at an average annual rate of 0.2%. Over the same period, the population increased by 0.3% per year. Barbados' gross domestic product (GDP), at factor cost, increased, in real terms, at an average rate of 3.8% per year during 1985–90, but declined by 1.0% per year during 1990–94. Real GDP increased by 4.7% in 1994, by 2.3% in 1995 and by 5.2% in 1996.

Agriculture (including forestry and fishing) contributed 6.4% of GDP and engaged 4.6% of the employed labour force in 1995. Sugar remains the main commodity export, earning Bds $427.1m. in 1996. In 1996 raw sugar production increased by 55% to 59,100 metric tons, following a decline of 26% in 1995 to 38,500 tons, owing to a drought. Sea-island cotton, once the island's main export crop, was revived in the mid-1980s. The other principal crops, primarily for local consumption, are sweet potatoes, carrots, yams and other vegetables and fruit. Fishing was also developed in the 1980s, and in 1988 there was a fleet of about 750 fishing vessels. Agricultural GDP declined, in real terms, at an average rate of 4.5% per year during 1985–93. According to the FAO, agricultural production decreased by 6.5% in 1994 but rose by 10.4% in 1995 and by 21.2% in 1996.

Industry accounted for an estimated 15.6% of GDP in 1995 and 19.5% of the working population were employed in all industrial activities (manufacturing, construction, quarrying and utilities) in 1995. In real terms, industrial GDP in 1992 was at the same level as in 1985. It increased at an average rate of 4.3% per year during 1985–89, but fell by an average of 3.9% annually in 1989–93. Industrial production rose by 5.5% in 1994, by 7.7% in 1995 and by 1.4% in 1996.

Owing to fluctuations in international prices, the production of crude petroleum declined substantially from its peak in 1985, to 454,424 barrels in 1990, or 31% of Barbados' requirements. In late 1996 the Barbados National Oil Company signed a five-year agreement with a US company to intensify exploration activity, with the aim of increasing petroleum production from 1,000 barrels per day (b/d) to 10,000 b/d by 2001. Production of natural gas was 29.3m. cu m in 1995. Mining and construction contributed 5.3% to GDP in 1995 and employed 8.0% of the working population.

Manufacturing contributed an estimated 6.8% of GDP in 1995, and employed 10.6% of the working population. Excluding sugar factories and refineries, the principal branches of manufacturing, measured by the value of output, in 1993 were chemical, petroleum, rubber and plastic products (accounting for 28.7% of the total), food products (27.3%), and beverages and tobacco (15.6%). Manufacturing GDP declined, in real terms, at an average rate of 4.5% per year during 1989–93. However, output from the sector increased by 6.7% in 1995.

Service industries are the main sector of the economy, accounting for an estimated 78.0% of GDP in 1995 and 75.8% of employment. The combined GDP of the service sectors declined, in real terms, at an average rate of 3.1% per year during 1989–93. Finance, insurance, real estate and business services contributed an estimated 15.9% of GDP in 1995. The Government has encouraged the growth of 'offshore' financial facilities, particularly through the negotiation of double taxation agreements with other countries. At the end of 1995 there were 1,834 international business companies and 1,501 foreign sales corporations operating in the country. It was estimated that the 'offshore' sector contributed almost US $150m. in foreign earnings in 1995. In the following year the Government announced a series of proposals which aimed to expand the industry.

Tourism made a direct contribution of 14.7% to GDP in 1995. Tourism employed 10.8% of the working population in that year. Receipts from the tourist industry almost doubled between 1980 and 1988, and in 1996 totalled some Bds $1,450m. Stop-over tourist arrivals increased by 1.4% in 1996 compared with the previous year, to 447,083, while cruise-ship passenger arrivals increased by 5.2%, to 509,975. In 1995 almost 28% of stop-over arrivals were from the USA and more than 31% were from the United Kingdom.

In 1995 Barbados recorded a visible trade deficit of US $440.0m., but receipts of US $903.7m. from services helped to result in a surplus of US $87.7m. on the current account of the balance of payments. In 1995 the principal source of imports (40%) was the USA, which also received 16% of exports. The principal single market for exports (16.4%) in 1995 was the United Kingdom, which also imported 9.5% of goods. Other major trading partners included Trinidad and Tobago (11% of imports, 9% of exports). The principal commodity exports were provided by the sugar industry (sugar, molasses, syrup and rum), which together accounted for some 28% of total receipts from exports in 1991. The principal imports were machinery, transport equipment and basic manufactures.

For the financial year ending 31 March 1998 there was a projected total budgetary deficit of Bds $363.4m. At December 1995 the total external debt of Barbados was US $597.0m., of which US $369.6m. was long-term public debt. In 1993 the cost of foreign debt-servicing was equivalent to 12.8% of the value of exports of goods and services. The average annual rate of inflation was 3.0% in 1990–95, and stood at 2.4% in 1996. In early 1997 an estimated 15.9% of the labour force were unemployed.

Barbados is a member of the Caribbean Community and Common Market (CARICOM, see p. 119), of the Inter-American Development Bank (IDB, see p. 183), of the Latin American Economic System (SELA, see p. 261) and of the Association of Caribbean States (see p. 259).

Political stability and consensus have contributed to the economic strengths of Barbados. Tourism dominates the economy but 'offshore' banking and sugar production are also important. In September 1997 the Prime Minister presented the 1997/98 budget, which represented the second year of relaxation of fiscal policy, owing to buoyant growth of the economy and improved methods of taxation. The value-added tax (VAT) of 15%, which was introduced in January to replace 11 other indirect taxes on sales and consumption, was unexpectedly successful (although causing a temporary increase in inflation), enabling the Government to remove VAT from 50 basic food items in September. Measures introduced to stimulate the economy included the establishment of two institutions to provide loans to small businesses and the relaxation of exchange controls to encourage trade. The 'offshore' business sector continued to expand, reducing the country's dependence on tourism. The current account surplus was expected to strengthen as inflows of private capital and tourist receipts offset a widening of the trade deficit. The stagnation of the manufacturing sector was likely to continue in 1998, as a result of increased competition arising from trade liberalization.

Social Welfare

A social security scheme was established in 1967, and a National Drug Plan was introduced in 1980. Old-age pensions and unemployment insurance are available. The Government has also created a building scheme of group housing for lower-income families. In 1993 Barbados had one hospital bed for every 119 citizens, and one physician for every 1,100 inhabitants on the island. Of total expenditure by the central Government in the 1989/90 financial year, Bds $135.6m. (11.9%) was for health services and Bds $245.7m. (21.6%) was for social security and welfare.

Education

Education is compulsory for 12 years, between five and 16 years of age. Primary education begins at the age of five and lasts for seven years. Secondary education, beginning at 12 years of age, lasts for six years. Enrolment of children in the primary age-group was 78% in 1991 (males 78%; females 78%). Enrolment at secondary level included 75% of children in the relevant age-group in 1989 (males 78%; females 72%). Enrolment at tertiary level was equivalent to 28.1% of the relevant age-group in 1994 (males 22.2%; females 34.2%). Degree courses in arts, law, education, natural sciences and social sciences are offered at the Barbados branch of the University of the West Indies. The faculty of medicine administers the East Caribbean Medical Scheme, while an in-service training programme for graduate teachers in secondary schools is provided by the School of Education.

In 1995, according to UNESCO estimates, adult illiteracy in Barbados was 2.6% (males 2.0%; females 3.2%).

Current expenditure on education by the central Government in 1995/6 was Bds $224.6m. (equivalent to 21.2% of total current spending).

Public Holidays

1998: 1 January (New Year's Day), 19 January (for Errol Barrow Day), 10 April (Good Friday), 13 April (Easter Monday), 4 May (for Labour Day), 8 June (Whit Monday), 3 August (Kadooment Day), 5 October (United Nations Day), 30 November (Independence Day), 25–26 December (Christmas).

1999: 1 January (New Year's Day), 18 January (for Errol Barrow Day), 2 April (Good Friday), 5 April (Easter Monday), 3 May (for Labour Day), 24 May (Whit Monday), 2 August (Kadooment Day), 1 October (United Nations Day), 30 November (Independence Day), 25–26 December (Christmas).

Weights and Measures

The metric system is used.

Statistical Survey

Sources (unless otherwise stated): Barbados Statistical Service, National Insurance Bldg, Fairchild St, Bridgetown; tel. 427-7841; Central Bank of Barbados, POB 1016, Bridgetown; tel. 436-6870; fax 427-9559.

AREA AND POPULATION

Area: 430 sq km (166 sq miles).

Population: 252,029 (males 119,665, females 132,364) at census of 12 May 1980; 257,082 (provisional) at census of 2 May 1990; 264,400 (official estimate) at 31 December 1995.

Density (31 December 1995): 614.9 per sq km.

Ethnic Groups (*de jure* population, excl. persons resident in institutions, 1990 census): Black 228,683; White 8,022; Mixed race 5,886; Total (incl. others) 247,288..

Principal Town: Bridgetown (capital), population 7,466 at 1980 census. Source: UN, *Demographic Yearbook*.

Births, Marriages and Deaths (provisional registrations, 1996): Live births 3,519 (birth rate 13.3 per 1,000); Marriages (1994) 2,963 (marriage rate 11.2 per 1,000); Deaths 2,400 (death rate 9.1 per 1,000). Source: UN, mainly *Population and Vital Statistics Report*.

Expectation of Life (UN estimates, years at birth, 1990–95): 75.6 (males 72.9; females 77.3). Source: UN, *World Population Prospects: The 1994 Revision*.

Economically Active Population (labour force sample survey, '000 persons aged 15 years and over, excl. armed forces, 1995): Agriculture, forestry and fishing 5.1; Manufacturing 11.7; Electricity, gas and water 1.0; Construction and quarrying 8.8; Wholesale and retail trade 16.6; Tourism 11.9; Transport, storage and communications 5.1; Financing, insurance, real estate and business services 7.6; Community, social and personal services 42.2; Total employed 109.9 (males 57.7, females 52.1); Unemployed 26.9 (males 11.4, females 15.5); Total labour force 136.8 (males 69.1, females 67.6). Source: mainly ILO, *Yearbook of Labour Statistics*.

AGRICULTURE, ETC.

Principal Crops ('000 metric tons, 1996): Maize 2*; Sweet potatoes 5; Cassava 1*; Yams 3*; Pulses 1*; Coconuts 2*; Cabbages 1; Tomatoes 1; Pumpkins 1*; Cucumbers 1*; Peppers 1*; Onions (dry) 1*; Carrots 2; Other vegetables 9; Sugar cane 535; Bananas 1*; Other fruits 2* (* FAO estimate). Source: FAO, *Production Yearbook*.

Livestock (FAO estimates, '000 head, year ending September 1996): Horses 1; Mules 2; Asses 2; Cattle 28; Pigs 30; Sheep 41; Goats 5; Poultry (million) 4. Source: FAO, *Production Yearbook*.

Livestock Products ('000 metric tons, 1996): Beef and veal 1; Pig meat 4 (FAO estimate); Poultry meat 12; Cows' milk 8; Hen eggs 1. Source: FAO, *Production Yearbook*.

Forestry (FAO estimates, '000 cubic metres): Roundwood removals 1 in 1992; 5 in 1993; 5 in 1994. Source: FAO, *Yearbook of Forest Products*.

Fishing (metric tons, live weight): Total catch 2,852 in 1993; 2,585 in 1994; 3,284 (Flying fishes 1,766, Common dolphinfish 758) in 1995. Source: FAO, *Yearbook of Fishery Statistics*.

MINING

Production (1995): Natural gas 29.3 million cu m; Crude petroleum 460,300 barrels.

INDUSTRY

Selected Products (1995): Raw sugar 38,500 metric tons; Rum 8,004,000 litres; Beer 7,429,000 litres; Cigarettes 65 metric tons; Batteries 28,612; Electric energy 613m. kWh. **1996:** Raw sugar 59,100 metric tons.

FINANCE

Currency and Exchange Rates: 100 cents = 1 Barbados dollar (Bds $). *Sterling and US Dollar equivalents* (30 September 1997): £1 sterling = Bds $3.249; US $1 = Bds $2.011; Bds $100 = £30.78 = US $49.72. *Exchange Rate*: Fixed at US $1 = Bds $2.0113 since August 1977.

Budget (Bds $ million, year ending 31 March 1996): *Revenue*: Tax revenue 1,081.5 (Taxes on income and profits 376.5, Taxes on property 69.7, Consumption Tax 309.0, Other domestic taxes on goods and services 129.1, Import duties 93.1, Stamp duties 90.7); Other current revenue 84.3 (Government departments 45.7, Property income 28.8); Total 1,165.8. *Expenditure:* Current expenditure 1,058.4 (General public services 181.8, Defence 29.2, Education 224.6, Health 153.3, Social security and welfare 96.5, Housing and community amenities 41.7, Transport 52.8, Other economic services 73.7, Debt charges 189.9); Capital expenditure 135.5; Total 1,193.9, excluding net lending (0.6).

1996/97 (Bds $ million): Total revenue 1,231.1; Total expenditure 1,354.3, excluding net lending (4.8). Source: IMF, *International Financial Statistics*.

1997/98 (projections, Bds $ million) Total revenue 1,298; Current expenditure 1,398; Capital expenditure 263.4.

Note: Budgetary data refer to current and capital budgets only and exclude operations of the National Insurance Fund and other central government units with their own budgets.

International Reserves (US $ million at 31 December 1996): IMF special drawing rights 0.03; Reserve position in IMF 0.04; Foreign exchange 289.62; Total 289.69. Source: IMF, *International Financial Statistics*.

Money Supply (Bds $ million at 31 December 1996): Currency outside banks 220.1; Demand deposits at commercial banks 370.0; Total money (incl. others) 626.7. Source: IMF, *International Financial Statistics*.

Cost of Living (Index of Retail Prices; base: 1990 = 100): 114.1 in 1994; 116.2 in 1995; 119.0 in 1996. Source: IMF, *International Financial Statistics*.

Gross Domestic Product (Bds $ million in current purchasers' values): 3,301.1 in 1993; 3,473.9 in 1994; 3,765.2 in 1995.

Gross Domestic Product by Economic Activity (Bds $ million at current prices, 1995): Agriculture, hunting, forestry and fishing 203.1; Mining and quarrying 18.0; Manufacturing 216.5; Electricity, gas and water 108.6; Construction 150.5; Wholesale and retail trade 542.8; Tourism 466.1; Transport, storage and communications 291.4; Finance, insurance, real estate and business services 505.9; Government services 538.7; Other community, social and personal services 131.8; *GDP at factor cost* 3,173.4; Indirect taxes, *less* subsidies 591.8; *GDP in purchasers' values* 3,765.2.

Balance of Payments (US $ million, 1995): Exports of goods f.o.b. 244.1; Imports of goods f.o.b. –684.0; *Trade balance* –440.0; Exports of services 903.7; Imports of services –361.1; *Balance on goods and services* 102.7; Other income received 48.1; Other income paid –95.6; *Balance on goods, services and income* 55.2; Current transfers received 55.8; Current transfers paid -23.4; *Current balance* 87.7; Direct investment abroad -3.3; Direct investment from abroad 11.7; Portfolio investment assets -3.0; Portfolio investment liabilities 40.2; Other investment assets -166.1; Other investment liabilities 59.0; Net errors and omissions 14.3; *Overall balance* 40.4. Source: IMF, *International Financial Statistics*.

EXTERNAL TRADE*

Principal Commodities (US $ '000, 1995): *Imports:* Food and live animals 112,459; Beverages and tobacco 14,715; Crude materials (inedible) except fuels 29,517; Mineral fuels, lubricants, etc. 65,134; Animal and vegetable oils and fats 4,536; Chemicals 90,342; Basic manufactures 132,105; Machinery and transport equipment 204,911; Miscellaneous manufactured articles 110,240; Goods not classified by kind 2,076; Total 766,034. *Exports:* Food and live animals 54,005 (Sugar 28,619); Beverages and tobacco 14,141; Petroleum and products 34,141; Chemicals 32,004; Basic manufactures 33,820; Machinery and transport equipment 46,918; Miscellaneous manufactured articles 15,698; Total (incl. others) 237,538.

Principal Trading Partners (US $ '000, 1995): *Imports:* Canada 38,639; Japan 51,572; Trinidad and Tobago 82,746; United Kingdom 73,127; USA 311,988; Total (incl. others) 766,021. *Exports:* Canada 12,603; Jamaica 17,454; Saint Lucia 11,946; Trinidad and Tobago 21,672; United Kingdom 38,916; USA 38,099; Total (incl. others) 237,538.

* Source: UN, *International Trade Statistics Yearbook*. Note: Figures for imports exclude crude petroleum.

TRANSPORT

Road Traffic (motor vehicles in use, 1995): Private cars 43,711; Taxis 1,405; Buses and minibuses 390; Lorries 2,215; Vans and pick-ups 3,967; Total 55,665..

Shipping (estimated freight traffic, '000 metric tons, 1990): Goods loaded 206; Goods unloaded 538. Source: UN, *Monthly Bulletin of Statistics*. *Merchant Fleet* (vessels registered at 31 December 1996): Number of vessels 74; Total displacement 496,959 grt. Source: Lloyd's Register of Shipping, *World Fleet Statistics*.

Civil Aviation (1994): Aircraft movements 36,100; Freight loaded 5,052.3 metric tons; Freight unloaded 8,548.3 metric tons.

TOURISM

Tourist Arrivals: *Stop-overs:* 425,632 in 1994; 442,632 in 1995; 447,083 in 1996. *Cruise-ship passengers*: 459,502 in 1994; 484,670 in 1995; 509,975 in 1996.

COMMUNICATIONS MEDIA

Radio Receivers (1994): 229,000 in use.

Television Receivers (1994): 73,000 in use.

Telephones (1996): 127,495 in use.

Book Production (1983): 87 titles (18 books, 69 pamphlets).

Newspapers: *Daily* (1994): 2 (circulation 41,000). *Non-daily* (1990): 4 (circulation 95,000).

Source: mainly UNESCO, *Statistical Yearbook*.

EDUCATION

Pre-primary (1995/96): 84 schools; 529 teachers; 4,689 pupils.

Primary (1995/96): 79 schools; 944 teachers; 18,513 pupils.

Secondary (1995/96): 21 schools; 1,263 teachers; 21,455 pupils.

Tertiary (1995/96): 4 schools; 544 teachers (1984); 6,622 students.

Directory

The Constitution

The parliamentary system has been established since the 17th century, when the first Assembly sat, in 1639, and the Charter of Barbados was granted, in 1652. A new Constitution came into force on 30 November 1966, when Barbados became independent. Under its terms, protection is afforded to individuals from slavery and forced labour, from inhuman treatment, deprivation of property, arbitrary search and entry, and racial discrimination; freedom of conscience, of expression, assembly, and movement are guaranteed.

Executive power is nominally vested in the British monarch, as Head of State, represented in Barbados by a Governor-General, who appoints the Prime Minister and, on the advice of the Prime Minister, appoints other ministers and some senators.

The Cabinet consists of the Prime Minister, appointed by the Governor-General as being the person best able to command a majority in the House of Assembly, and not fewer than five other ministers. Provision is also made for a Privy Council, presided over by the Governor-General.

Parliament consists of the Governor-General and a bicameral legislature, comprising the Senate and the House of Assembly. The Senate has 21 members: 12 appointed by the Governor-General on the advice of the Prime Minister, two on the advice of the Leader of the Opposition and seven as representatives of such interests as the Governor-General considers appropriate. The House of Assembly has (since January 1991) 28 members, elected by universal adult suffrage for a term of five years (subject to dissolution). The minimum voting age is 18 years.

The Constitution also provides for the establishment of Service Commissions for the Judicial and Legal Service, the Public Service, the Police Service and the Statutory Boards Service. These Commissions are exempt from legal investigation; they have executive powers relating to appointments, dismissals and disciplinary control of the services for which they are responsible.

The Government

Head of State: HM Queen ELIZABETH II (succeeded to the throne 6 February 1952).

Governor-General: Sir CLIFFORD HUSBANDS (appointed 1 June 1996).

THE CABINET
(December 1997)

Prime Minister and Minister of Finance and Economic Affairs, of Defence and Security and for the Civil Service: OWEN S. ARTHUR.

Deputy Prime Minister and Minister of Foreign Affairs, Tourism and International Transport: BILLIE A. MILLER.

Attorney-General and Minister of Home Affairs: DAVID A. C. SIMMONS.

Minister of Public Works, Transport and Housing: GEORGE PAYNE.

Minister of Agriculture and Rural Development: RAWLE EASTMOND.

Minister of Labour, Community Development and Sports: RUDOLPH N. GREENIDGE.

Minister of Health and the Environment: H. ELIZABETH THOMPSON.

Minister of Education, Youth Affairs and Culture: MIA A. MOTTLEY.

Minister of Industry, Commerce and Business Development: Sen. REGINALD FARLEY.

Minister of Foreign Trade and International Business: PHILLIP R. GODDARD.

Minister of State in the Office of the Prime Minister and the Ministry for the Civil Service (with responsibility for Information): GLYNE S. H. MURRAY.

MINISTRIES

Office of the Prime Minister: Government Headquarters, Bay St, St Michael; tel. 436-3179; fax 436-9280.

Ministry of Agriculture and Rural Development: Graeme Hall, POB 505, Christ Church; tel. 428-4061; fax 420-8444.

Ministry for the Civil Service: Government Headquarters, Bay St, St Michael; tel. 436-6435, fax 436-9280.

Ministry of Defence and Security: Government Headquarters, Bay St, St Michael; tel. 436-6435.

Ministry of Education, Youth Affairs and Culture: Jemmott's Lane, St Michael; tel. 426-5416; fax 426-5570.

Ministry of Finance and Economic Affairs: Government Headquarters, Bay St, St Michael; tel. 426-2814; fax 429-4032.

Ministry of Foreign Affairs, Tourism and International Transport: Herbert House, Reef Rd, Fontabelle, St Michael; tel. 429-4839; fax 431-0121.

Ministry of Health and the Environment: Jemmott's Lane, St Michael; tel. 426-5080; fax 426-5570.

Ministry of Home Affairs: General Post Office Bldg, Level 5, Cheapside, Bridgetown; tel. 228-8950; fax 437-3794.

Ministry of Industry, Commerce and Business Development: Reef Rd, Fontabelle, St Michael; tel. 426-4452; fax 431-0056.

Ministry of Foreign Trade and International Business: 1 Culloden Rd, St Michael; tel. 427-0427; fax 429-6652.

Ministry of Justice: Marine House, Hastings, Christ Church; tel. 427-0622.

Ministry of Labour, Community Development and Sports: National Insurance Bldg, 5th Floor, Fairchild St, Bridgetown; tel. 427-2326; fax 426-8959.

Ministry of Public Works, Transport and Housing: The Pine, St Michael; tel. 429-3495; fax 437-8133.

Legislature

PARLIAMENT

Senate

President: FRED GOLLOP.

There are 21 members.

House of Assembly

Speaker: ISHMAEL ROETT.

Clerk of Parliament: GEORGE BRANCKER.

General Election, 6 September 1994

Party	Votes	%	Seats
Barbados Labour Party (BLP)	60,540	48.3	19
Democratic Labour Party (DLP)	48,108	38.4	8
National Democratic Party (NDP)	15,909	12.7	1
Others	684	0.5	—
Total	125,241	100.0	28

Political Organizations

Barbados Labour Party: Grantley Adams House, 111 Roebuck St, Bridgetown; tel. 426-2274; f. 1938; moderate social democrat; Leader OWEN ARTHUR; Chair. DAVID SIMMONS; Gen. Sec. GEORGE PAYNE.

Democratic Labour Party: George St, Belleville, St Michael; tel. 429-3104; f. 1955; Leader DAVID THOMPSON.

National Democratic Party: 'Sueños', 3 Sixth Ave, Belleville; tel. 429-6882; f. 1989 by split from Democratic Labour Party; Leader Dr RICHARD (RICHIE) HAYNES.

People's Pressures Movement: Bridgetown; f. 1979; Leader ERIC SEALY.

Workers' Party of Barbados: Bridgetown; tel. 425-1620; f. 1985; small left-wing organization; Gen. Sec. Dr GEORGE BELLE.

Diplomatic Representation

EMBASSIES AND HIGH COMMISSIONS IN BARBADOS

Brazil: Sunjet House, Fairchild St, Bridgetown; tel. 427-1735; fax 427-1744; Ambassador: CARLOS ALFREDO PINTO DA SILVA.

Canada: Bishops Court Hill, POB 404, St Michael; tel. 429-3550; fax 429-3780; High Commissioner: COLLEEN SWORDS.

China, People's Republic: 17 Golf View Terrace, Rockley, Christ Church; tel. 435-6890; fax 435-8300; Ambassador: JIANG CHENZONG.

Colombia: 'Rosemary', Dayrells Rd, Rockley, POB 37W, Christ Church; tel. 429-6821; telex 2499; fax 429-6830; Ambassador: NICOLÁS CURI VERGARA.

Costa Rica: Golden Anchorage House, Sunset Crest, St James; tel. 432-0194; fax 432-5566; Ambassador: JOSÉ DE J. CONEJO.

United Kingdom: Lower Collymore Rock, POB 676, St Michael; tel. 436-6694; fax 436-5398; High Commissioner: RICHARD THOMAS.

USA: Canadian Imperial Bank of Commerce Bldg, Broad St, POB 302, Bridgetown; tel. 436-4950; telex 2259; fax 429-5246; Ambassador: G. PHILLIP HUGHES.

Venezuela: Hastings, Main Rd, Christ Church; tel. 435-7619; fax 435-7830; Ambassador: ANGEL BRITO VILLARROEL.

Judicial System

Justice is administered by the Supreme Court of Judicature, which consists of a High Court and a Court of Appeal. Final appeal lies with the Judicial Committee of the Privy Council, in the United Kingdom. There are Magistrates' Courts for lesser offences, with appeal to the Court of Appeal.

Supreme Court: Judiciary Office, Bridgetown; tel. 426-3461.

Chief Justice: Sir DENYS WILLIAMS.

Justices of Appeal: Sir FREDERICK SMITH, G. C. R. MOE.

Judges of the High Court: ELLIOTT F. BELGRAVE, ERROL DACOSTA CHASE, F. A. WATERMAN, F. DEC. KING.

Registrar of the Supreme Court: MARIE A. MACCORMACK.

Office of the Attorney-General: Sir Frank Walcott Bldg, Culloden Rd, St Michael; tel. 431-7750; fax 435-9533.

Chief Magistrate: SANDRA MASON.

Religion

More than 90 religious denominations and sects are represented in Barbados, but the vast majority of the population profess Christianity. According to the 1980 census, there were 96,894 Anglicans (or some 40% of the total population), while the Pentecostal (8%) and Methodist (7%) churches were next in importance. The regional Caribbean Conference of Churches is based in Barbados. There are also small groups of Hindus, Muslims and Jews.

CHRISTIANITY

The Anglican Communion

Anglicans in Barbados are adherents of the Church in the Province of the West Indies, comprising eight dioceses. The Archbishop of the Province is the Bishop of the North Eastern Caribbean and Aruba, resident at St John's, Antigua. In Barbados there is a Provincial Office (St George's Church, St George) and an Anglican Theological College (Codrington College, St John).

Bishop of Barbados: Rt Rev. RUFUS BROME, Diocesan Office, Mandeville House, Bridgetown; tel. 426-2761; fax 427-5867.

The Roman Catholic Church

Barbados comprises a single diocese (formed in January 1990, when the diocese of Bridgetown-Kingstown was divided), which is suffragan to the archdiocese of Port of Spain (Trinidad and Tobago). At 31 December 1995 there were an estimated 10,000 adherents in the diocese. The Bishop participates in the Antilles Episcopal Conference (currently based in Port of Spain, Trinidad and Tobago).

Bishop of Bridgetown: Rt Rev. MALCOLM GALT, St Patrick's Presbytery, Jemmott's Lane, POB 1223, Bridgetown; tel. 426-3510; fax 429-6198.

Protestant Churches

Baptist Churches of Barbados: National Baptist Convention, President Kennedy Dr., Bridgetown; tel. 429-2697.

Church of God (Caribbean Atlantic Assembly): St Michael's Plaza, St Michael's Row, POB 1, Bridgetown; tel. 427-5770; Pres. Rev. VICTOR BABB.

Church of Jesus Christ of Latter-day Saints (Mormons)—West Indies Mission: West Indies Mission, 15 Golf View Terrace, Rockley, Christ Church, Bridgetown; tel. 435-8595; fax 435-8278.

Church of the Nazarene: District Office, Eagle Hall, Bridgetown; tel. 425-1067.

Methodist Church: Bethel Church Office, Bay St, Bridgetown; tel. 426-2223.

Moravian Church: Roebuck St, Bridgetown; tel. 426-2337; Superintendent Rev. RUDOLPH HOLDER.

Seventh-day Adventists (East Caribbean Conference): Brydens Ave, Brittons Hill, POB 223, St Michael; tel. 429-7234; fax 429-8055.

Wesleyan Holiness Church: General Headquarters, Bank Hall; tel. 429-4864.

Other denominations include the Apostolic Church, the Assemblies of Brethren, the Salvation Army, Presbyterian congregations, the African Methodist Episcopal Church, the Mt Olive United Holy Church of America and Jehovah's Witnesses.

ISLAM

In 1996 there were an estimated 2,000 Muslims in Barbados.

Islamic Teaching Centre: Harts Gap, Hastings; tel. 427-0120.

JUDAISM

Jewish Community: Nidhe Israel and Shaara Tzedek Synagogue, Rockley New Rd, POB 651, Bridgetown; tel. 437-1290; fax 437-1303; there were 60 Jews in Barbados in 1997; Pres. RACHELLE ALTMAN; Sec. SHARON ORAN.

Caribbean Jewish Congress: POB 1331, Bridgetown; tel. 436-8163; f. 1994; aims to foster closer relations between Jewish communities in the region and to promote greater understanding of the Jewish faith; Sec.-Gen. MICHAEL DAVIS; Chair. BENNY GILBERT; Exec. Dir WINSTON BEN ZEBEDEE.

HINDUISM

Hindu Community: Bridgetown; there were 411 Hindus at the census of 1980.

The Press

Barbados Advocate: Fontabelle, POB 230, St Michael; tel. 426-1210; telex 2613; fax 429-7045; f. 1895; daily; Man. Dir and Publr PATRICK HOYOS; Man. Editor ROBERT BEST; circ. 11,413.

The Beacon: 111 Roebuck St, Bridgetown; organ of the Barbados Labour Party; weekly; circ. 15,000.

Caribbean Week: Lefferts Place, River Rd, St Michael; tel. 436-1902; fax 436-1904; e-mail cweek@sunbeach.net; f. 1989; fortnightly; Editor-in-Chief JOHN E. LOVELL; Publr TIMOTHY C. FORSYTHE; circ. 60,000.

EC News (East Caribbean News): Nation House, Fontabelle, St Michael; tel. 436-6240; telex 2310; fax 427-6968; daily.

The Nation: Nation House, Fontabelle, St Michael; tel. 436-6240; telex 2310; fax 427-6968; f. 1973; daily; Man. Dir HAROLD HOYTE; circ. 23,470 (weekday), 33,084 (weekend).

The New Bajan: Nation House, Fontabelle, St Michael; tel. 436-6240; fax 427-6968; f. 1953; fmrly *The Bajan and South Caribbean*; monthly; illustrated magazine; Man. Editor GLYNE MURRAY; circ. 9,000.

Official Gazette: Government Printing Office, Bay St, St Michael; tel. 436-6776; Mon. and Thur.

Sunday Advocate: Fontabelle, POB 230, St Michael; tel. 426-1210; fax 429-7045; f. 1895; CEO COLIN MURRAY; Man. Editor DENZIL AGARD; circ. 17,490.

The Sunday Sun: Fontabelle, St Michael; tel. 436-6240; telex 2310; fax 427-6968; e-mail subs@sunbeach.net; f. 1977; Dir HAROLD HOYTE; circ. 42,286.

Weekend Investigator: Fontabelle, POB 230, St Michael; tel. 426-1210; circ. 14,305.

NEWS AGENCIES

Caribbean News Agency (CANA): Culloden View, Beckles Rd, St Michael; tel. 429-2903; telex 2228; fax 429-4355; f. 1976; public and private shareholders from English-speaking Caribbean; Chair. COLIN D. MURRAY; Gen. Man. TREVOR SIMPSON.

Foreign Bureaux

Agencia EFE (Spain): 48 Gladioli Dr., Husbanos, St James; tel. 425-1542; Rep. YUSSUFF HANIFF.

Inter Press Service (IPS) (Italy): POB 697, Bridgetown; tel. 426-4474; Correspondent MARVA COSSY.

United Press International (UPI) (USA): Bridgetown; tel. 436-0465; Correspondent RICKEY SINGH.

Xinhua (New China) News Agency (People's Republic of China): 29 Newton Terrace, POB 22A, Christ Church; telex 2458; Chief Correspondent DING BAOZHONG.

Agence France-Presse (AFP) is also represented.

Publishers

Caribbean Publishing Co Ltd: Barbados Hotel, Assn Bldg, 4th Ave Belleville, Bridgetown; tel. and fax 436-5889.

Nation Publishing Co Ltd: Nation House, Fontabelle, St Michael; tel. 436-6240; telex 2310; fax 427-6968.

Broadcasting and Communications

TELECOMMUNICATIONS

Barbados External Telecommunications Ltd (BET): Wildey, St Michael, Bridgetown; tel. 427-5200; fax 427-5808; provides international telecommunications services; subsidiary of Cable and Wireless.

Barbados Telephone Co Ltd (Bartel): The Windsor Lodge, Government Hill; tel. 429-5050; fax 436-5036; provides domestic telecommunications services; subsidiary of Cable and Wireless.

RADIO

Barbados Broadcasting Service Ltd: Astoria St George, Bridgetown; tel. 437-9550; fax 437-9554; f. 1981; FM station.

Barbados Rediffusion Service Ltd: River Rd, Bridgetown; tel. 430-7300; fax 429-8093; f. 1935; public company; Gen. Man. VIC FERNANDES.

Rediffusion Star Radio, at River Rd, Bridgetown, is a commercial wired service with island-wide coverage.

Voice of Barbados, at River Rd, Bridgetown (f. 1981), is a commercial station covering Barbados and the eastern Caribbean.

YESS Ten-Four FM, at River Rd, Bridgetown (f. 1988), is a commercial station.

Caribbean Broadcasting Corporation (CBC): The Pine, POB 900, Bridgetown; tel. 429-2041; fax 429-4795; f. 1963; Chair. Dr C. HOPE.

CBC Radio: POB 900, Bridgetown; tel. 429-2041; telex 2560; fax 429-4795; e-mail CBC.@.CaribNet.Net; f. 1963; commercial; Gen. Man. MELBA SMITH; Programme Man. W. CALLENDER.

CBC Radio 900, f. 1963, broadcasts 21 hours daily.

Radio Liberty FM, f. 1984, broadcasts 24 hours daily.

TELEVISION

CBC TV: POB 900, Bridgetown; tel. 429-2041; fax 429-4795; f. 1964; Channel Eight is the main national service, broadcasting 24 hours daily; four cabled subscription channels are available; Gen. Man. T. CUMMING; Programme Man. O. CUMBERBATCH.

Finance

At the end of 1995 a total of 1,834 international business companies, 1,501 foreign sales corporations, 34 offshore banks licensees and 230 captive insurance companies were registered in Barbados.

BANKING

(cap. = capital; auth. = authorized; dep. = deposits; res = reserves; brs = branches; m. = million; amounts in Barbados dollars)

Central Bank

Central Bank of Barbados: Church Village, POB 1016, Bridgetown; tel. 436-6870; telex 2251; fax 427-9559; f. 1972; bank of issue; cap. 2.0m., res 10.0m., dep. 400.4m. (Dec. 1996); Gov. WINSTON COX.

Commercial Bank

Caribbean Commercial Bank Ltd: Broad St, POB 1007C, Bridgetown; tel. 431-2500; telex 2289; fax 431-2530; f. 1984; cap. 25.0m., res 1.6m., dep. 96.1m. (Dec. 1993); Pres. and CEO MARIANO R. BROWNE; 4 brs.

Regional Development Bank

Caribbean Development Bank: Wildey, POB 408, St Michael; tel. 431-1600; telex 2287; fax 426-7269; f. 1970; cap. 143.4m., res 5.8m. (Dec. 1995); Pres. Sir NEVILLE NICHOLLS; 2 brs.

National Bank

Barbados National Bank: 1 Broad St, POB 1002, Bridgetown; tel. 431-5700; telex 2271; fax 429-2606; f. 1978 by merger; cap 12.5m., res 10.8m., dep. 562.8m., total assets 625.3m. (Dec. 1995); identified for privatization; Chair. GRENVILLE PHILLIPS; Man. Dir LOUIS GREENIDGE; 6 brs.

Foreign Banks

Bank of Nova Scotia (Canada): Broad St, POB 202, Bridgetown; tel. 431-3000; telex 2223; fax 426-0969; Man. Y. L. LESSARD; 7 brs.

Barclays Bank PLC (United Kingdom): Broad Street, POB 301, Bridgetown; tel. 431-5262; telex 2211; fax 429-4785; f. 1837; Man. P. A. WEATHERHEAD; 12 brs.

Canadian Imperial Bank of Commerce: Broad St, POB 405, Bridgetown; tel. 426-0571; telex 2230; Man. T. MULLOY; 3 brs.

Royal Bank of Canada: Trident House, Broad St, POB 68, Bridgetown; tel. 431-6580; fax 426-4139; f. 1911; Man. C. D. MALONEY; 7 brs.

Trust Companies

Bank of Commerce Trust Company Barbados Ltd: POB 503, Bridgetown; tel. 426-2740.

Bank of Nova Scotia Trust Co (Caribbean) Ltd: Bank of Nova Scotia Bldg, Broad St, POB 1003B, Bridgetown; tel. 431-3120; telex 2223; fax 426-0969.

Barbados International Bank and Trust Co Ltd: Price Waterhouse Centre, POB 634C, Collymore Rock, St Michael; tel. 436-7000.

Barclays Bank Trust Co: Roebuck St, POB 180, Bridgetown; tel. 426-1608.

Caribbean Commercial Trust Co Ltd: White Park Rd, Bridgetown; tel. 431-4719; fax 431-2530.

Royal Bank of Canada Financial Corporation: Royal Bank House, Bush Hill, Garrison, POB 48B, St Michael; tel. 431-6580; fax 426-4139; Man. N. L. SMITH.

STOCK EXCHANGE

Securities Exchange of Barbados (SEB): Central Bank Bldg, 5th Floor, Church Village, Bridgetown; tel. 436-9871; fax 429-8942; e-mail sebd@caribsurf.com; f. 1987; in 1989 the Govts of Barbados, Trinidad and Tobago and Jamaica agreed to combine their national exchanges into a regional stock exchange; cross-trading began in April 1991; Gen. Man. VIRGINIA MAPP.

INSURANCE

The leading British and a number of US and Canadian companies have agents in Barbados. Local insurance companies include the following:

Barbados Fire & Commercial Insurance Co: Beckwith Place, Broad St, POB 150, Bridgetown; tel. 426-4291; fax 426-0752; f. 1996, following merger of Barbados Commercial Insurance Co. Ltd and Barbados Fire and General Insurance Co (f. 1880).

Barbados Mutual Life Assurance Society: Collymore Rock, St Michael; tel. 431-7000; fax 436-8829; f. 1840; Chair. COLIN G. GODDARD; Pres. J. ARTHUR L. BETHELL.

Insurance Corporation of Barbados: Roebuck St, Bridgetown; tel. 427-5590; telex 2317; fax 426-3393; f. 1978; cap. Bds $3m.; Man. Dir WISMAR GREAVES; Gen. Man. MONICA SKINNER.

Life of Barbados Ltd: Wildey, POB 69, St Michael; tel. 426-1060; fax 436-8835; f. 1971; Pres. CECIL F. DE CAIRES.

United Insurance Co Ltd: Cavan House, Lower Broad St, POB 1215, Bridgetown; tel. 436-1991; fax 436-7573; f. 1976; Man. Dir G. M. CHALLENOR.

Insurance Association

Insurance Association of the Caribbean: IAC Bldg, St Michael; Collymore Rock, St Michael; tel. 427-5608; fax 427-7277; regional asscn.

Trade and Industry

GOVERNMENT AGENCIES

Barbados Agricultural Management Co Ltd: Warrens, POB 719c, St Michael; tel. 425-0010; fax 425-3505; Exec. Chair. Dr ATTLEE BRATHWAITE; Gen. Man. E. M. JOHNSON.

Barbados Sugar Industry Ltd: POB 719C, Warrens, St Thomas; tel. 422-8725; fax 422-5357; Lt-Col STEPHEN F. CAVE.

DEVELOPMENT ORGANIZATIONS

Agricultural Venture Trust: 'Hillcarr', Worthing, Christ Church; tel. 435-8990; fax 435-8895; f. 1987; US-financial regional development org.; develops agriculture and agro-industries.

Barbados Agriculture Development and Marketing Corpn: Fairy Valley, Christ Church; tel. 428-0250; fax 428-0152; f. 1993 by merger of Barbados Agricultural Development and Marketing Corpns; programme of diversification and land reforms; Chair. TYRONE POWER; CEO E. LEROY ROACH.

Barbados Investment and Development Corpn: Pelican House, Princess Alice Highway, Bridgetown; tel. 427-5350; telex 2295; fax 426-7802; f. 1992 by merger of Barbados Export Promotion Corpn and Barbados Industrial Development Corpn; facilitates the devt of the industrial sector, especially in the areas of manufacturing and data-processing; offers free consultancy to investors; provides factory space; administers the Fiscal Incentives Legislation; Chair. TREVOR CLARKE; CEO Dr LAWSON NURSE.

British Development Division in the Caribbean: Collymore Rock, POB 167, St Michael; tel. 436-9873; fax 426-2194; Head BRIAN THOMSON.

CHAMBER OF COMMERCE

Barbados Chamber of Commerce Inc: Nemwil House, 1st Floor, Lower Collymore Rock, POB 189, St Michael; tel. 426-2056; fax 429-2907; f. 1825; 176 mem. firms, 276 reps; Pres. G. ANTHONY KING; Exec. Dir ROLPH JORDAN.

INDUSTRIAL AND TRADE ASSOCIATIONS

Barbados Agricultural Society: The Grotto, Beckles Rd, St Michael; tel. 436-6680; Pres. KEITH LAURIE.

Barbados Association of Medical Practitioners: BAMP Complex, Spring Garden, St Michael; tel. 429-7569; fax 435-2328; e-mail bamp@sunbeach.net; Pres. Dr MALCOLM HOWITT.

Barbados Association of Professional Engineers: POB 666, Bridgetown; tel. 425-6105; fax 425-6673; f. 1964; Pres. GLYNE BARKER; Sec. PATRICK CLARKE.

Barbados Builders' Association: Bridgetown; Pres. KEITH CODRINGTON.

Barbados Hotel and Tourism Association: Fourth Ave, Belleville, St Michael; tel. 426-5041; telex 2314; fax 429-2845; Pres. ALLAN BANFIELD; Exec. Vice-Pres. NOEL LYNCH.

Barbados Manufacturers' Association: Bldg 1, Pelican Industrial Park, St Michael; tel. 426-4474; fax 436-5182; f. 1964; Pres. RAM MIRCHANDANI; 100 mem. firms.

West Indian Sea Island Cotton Association (Inc): c/o Barbados Agriculture Development and Marketing Corpn, Fairy Valley, Christ Church; tel. 428-0250; Pres. E. LEROY WARD; Sec. MICHAEL I. EDGHILL; 8 mem. asscns.

EMPLOYERS' ORGANIZATION

Barbados Employers' Confederation: Nemwil House, 1st Floor, Lower Collymore Rock, St Michael; tel. 426-1574; fax 429-2907; f. 1956; Pres. DEIGHTON MARSHALL; Exec. Dir EDWARD BUSHELL; 254 mems (incl. associate mems).

UTILITIES

Electricity

The Barbados Light and Power Co. (BL & P): POB 142, Garrison Hill, St Michael; tel. 436-1800; fax 436-9933; electricity generator and distributor; operates two stations with a combined capacity of 152,500 kW.

Public Utilities Board: Bridgetown; electricity regulator.

Water

Barbados Water Authority: Bridgetown.

TRADE UNIONS

Principal unions include:

Barbados Industrial and General Workers' Union: Bridgetown; f. 1981; Leader ROBERT CLARKE; Gen. Sec. DAVID DENNY; c. 2,000 mems.

Barbados Secondary Teachers' Union: Ryeburn, Eighth Ave, Belleville, St Michael; tel. 429-7676; f. 1948; Pres. WAYNE WILLCOCK; Sec. PATRICK FROST; 384 mems.

Barbados Union of Teachers: Welches, POB 58, St Michael; tel. 436-6139; f. 1974; Pres. RONALD DAC. JONES; Gen. Sec. HARRY HUSBANDS; 2,000 mems.

Barbados Workers' Union: Solidarity House, Harmony Hall, POB 172, St Michael; tel. 426-3492; telex 2527; fax 436-6496; f. 1941; operates a Labour College; Sec.-Gen. LEROY TROTMAN; 20,000 mems.

Caribbean Association of Media Workers (Camwork): Bridgetown; f. 1986; regional; Pres. RICKEY SINGH.

National Union of Public Workers: Dalkeith Rd, POB 174, Bridgetown; tel. 426-1764; fax 436-1795; f. 1944; Pres. MILLICENT M. B SMALL; Gen. Sec. JOSEPH E. GODDARD; 6,000 mems.

National Union of Seamen: 34 Tudor St, Bridgetown; tel. 436-6137; Pres. LORENZO COWARD.

Transport

ROADS

Ministry of Public Works, Transport and Housing: Marine House, Hastings, Christ Church; tel. 427-5420; maintains a network of 1,573 km (977 miles) of roads, of which 1,496 km (930 miles) are paved; Chief Tech. Officer C. H. ARCHER.

SHIPPING

Inter-island traffic is catered for by a fortnightly service of one vessel of the West Indies Shipping Corpn (WISCO, the regional shipping company, based in Trinidad and Tobago, in which the Barbados Government is a shareholder) operating from Trinidad as far north as Jamaica. The CAROL container service consortium connects Bridgetown with western European ports and several foreign shipping lines call at the port. Bridgetown harbour has berths for eight ships and simultaneous bunkering facilities for five. A four-year project to extend the harbour, providing increased capacity for cruise ships, was due to begin in 1997 at a cost of Bds $120m.

Barbados Port Authority: University Row, Bridgetown Harbour; tel. 436-6883; telex 2367; fax 429-5348; Gen. Man. P. B. PARKER; Port Dir Capt. H. L. VAN SLUYTMAN.

Barbados Shipping and Trading Co Ltd: Musson Bldg, Hincks St, POB 1227C, Bridgetown; tel. 426-3844; fax 427-4719; f. 1920; Chair. and Man. Dir C. D. BYNOE; Sec. A. R. S. MARSHALL.

Booth Steamship Company (Barbados) Ltd: Cockspur House, 1st Floor, Nile St, POB 263, Bridgetown; tel. 427-5131; fax 426-0484.

DaCosta Mannings Ltd: Carlisle House, Hincks St, POB 103, Bridgetown; tel. 431-8700; telex 2328; fax 431-0051; shipping company.

Hassell, Eric and Son Ltd: Carlisle House, Hincks St, Bridgetown; tel. 436-6102; fax 429-3416; shipping agent, stevedoring contractor and cargo fowarder.

Shipping Association of Barbados: Trident House, 2nd Floor, Broad St, Bridgetown; tel. 427-9860; fax 426-8392.

Tore Torsteinson: Fairfield House, St Philip; tel. 423-6125; fax 423-4664; f. 1970; shipping company.

Windward Lines Ltd: Fairfield House, St Philip.

CIVIL AVIATION

The principal airport is Grantley Adams International Airport, at Seawell, 18 km (11 miles) from Bridgetown.

Tourism

The natural attractions of the island consist chiefly of the warm climate and varied scenery. In addition, there are many facilities for outdoor sports of all kinds. Revenue from tourism increased from Bds $13m. in 1960 to some Bds $1,400m. in 1996. The number of stop-over tourist arrivals increased by 1.1% compared with the previous year, to 447,083 in 1996, while the number of visiting cruise-ship passengers increased by 5.2%, to 509,975. There were some 5,911 hotel rooms on the island in 1996.

Barbados Tourism Authority: Harbour Rd, POB 242, Bridgetown; tel. 427-2623; telex 2420; fax 426-4080; f. 1993 to replace Barbados Board of Tourism; offices in London, New York, Montreal, Miami, Toronto, California and Frankfurt; Chair. Maj. ALLAN BATSON; Pres. and CEO EARLYN SHUFFLER.

BELARUS

Introductory Survey

Location, Climate, Language, Religion, Flag, Capital

The Republic of Belarus (formerly the Belarusian Soviet Socialist Republic—BSSR) is a land-locked state in north-eastern Europe. Historically, the country has also been known as White Russia or White Ruthenia. It is bounded by Lithuania and Latvia to the north-west, by Ukraine to the south, by the Russian Federation to the east, and by Poland to the west. The climate is of a continental type, with an average January temperature, in Minsk, of −5°C (23°F) and an average for July of 19°C (67°F). Average annual precipitation is between 560 mm and 660 mm. The official languages of the republic are Belarusian and Russian. The major religion is Christianity—the Roman Catholic Church and the Eastern Orthodox Church being the largest denominations. There are also small Muslim and Jewish communities. The national flag (proportions 2 by 1) consists of two unequal horizontal stripes, of red over light green, with a red-outlined white vertical stripe at the hoist, bearing in red a traditional embroidery pattern. The capital is Minsk (Miensk).

Recent History

Following periods of Lithuanian and Polish rule, Belarus became a part of the Russian Empire in the late 18th century. During the 19th century there was a growth of national consciousness in Belarus and, as a result of industrialization, a significant movement of people from rural areas to the towns. After the February Revolution of 1917 in Russia, Belarusian nationalists and socialists formed a rada (council), which sought a degree of autonomy from the Provisional Government in Petrograd (St Petersburg). In November, after the Bolsheviks had seized power in Petrograd, Red Army troops were dispatched to Minsk, and the rada was dissolved. However, the Bolsheviks were forced to withdraw by the invasion of the German army. The Treaty of Brest-Litovsk, signed in March 1918, assigned most of Belarus to the Germans. On 25 March Belarusian nationalists convened to proclaim a Belarusian National Republic, but it achieved only limited autonomy. After the Germans had withdrawn, the Bolsheviks easily reoccupied Minsk, and the Belarusian Soviet Socialist Republic (BSSR) was declared on 1 January 1919.

In February 1919 the BSSR was merged with neighbouring Lithuania in a Lithuanian-Belarusian Soviet Republic (known as 'Litbel'). In April, however, Polish armed forces entered Lithuania and Belarus, and both were declared part of Poland. In July 1920 the Bolsheviks recaptured Minsk, and in August the BSSR was re-established; Lithuania became an independent state. However, the BSSR comprised only the eastern half of the lands populated by Belarusians. Western Belarus was granted to Poland by the Treaty of Riga, signed on 18 March 1921. The Treaty also assigned Belarus's easternmost regions to the Russian Federation, but they were returned to the BSSR in 1924 and 1926. Meanwhile, the BSSR, with Ukraine and Transcaucasia, had joined with the Russian Federation to form the Union of Soviet Socialist Republics (USSR), established in December 1922.

The Soviet leadership's New Economic Policy of 1921–28, which permitted some liberalization of the economy, brought a measure of prosperity, and there was significant cultural and linguistic development, with the use of the Belarusian language officially encouraged. This period ended in 1929 with the emergence of Iosif Stalin as the dominant figure in the USSR. In that year Stalin began a campaign to collectivize agriculture, which was strongly resisted by the peasantry. In Belarus, as in other parts of the USSR, there were frequent riots and rebellions in rural areas, and many peasants were deported or imprisoned. The purges of the early 1930s were initially targeted against Belarusian nationalists and intellectuals, but by 1936–38 they had widened to include all sectors of the population.

After the invasion of Poland by German and Soviet forces in September 1939, the BSSR was enlarged by the inclusion of the lands that it had lost to Poland and Lithuania in 1921. Between 1941 and 1944 the BSSR was occupied by Nazi German forces; an estimated 2.2m. people died during this period, including most of the republic's large Jewish population. At the Yalta conference, in February 1945, the Allies agreed to recognize the 'Curzon line' as the western border of the BSSR, thus endorsing the unification of western and eastern Belarus. As a result of the Soviet demand for more voting strength in the UN, the Western powers permitted the BSSR to become a member of the UN in its own right.

The immediate post-war period was dominated by the need to rehabilitate the republic's infrastructure. The reconstruction programme's requirements and the local labour shortage led to an increase in Russian immigration into the republic, thus discouraging use of the Belarusian language. During the 1960s and 1970s the process of 'russification' continued; there was a decrease in the use of Belarusian in schools, and in publishing and other media. The republic was, however, one of the most prosperous in the USSR, with a wider variety of consumer goods available than in other republics.

This relative prosperity was one reason why the ruling Communist Party of Belarus (CPB) was initially able to resist implementing the economic and political reforms that were proposed by the Soviet leader, Mikhail Gorbachev, from 1985 onwards. By 1987, however, the CPB was being criticized in the press for its stance on cultural and ecological issues. Intellectuals and writers campaigned for the greater use of Belarusian in education, indicating that there were no Belarusian-language schools operating in any urban areas in the republic. Campaigners also demanded more information about the consequences of the explosion at the Chernobyl nuclear power station, in Ukraine, in April 1986, which had affected large areas of southern Belarus. Not surprisingly, the two most important unofficial groups that emerged in the late 1980s were the Belarusian Language Association and the Belarusian Ecological Union.

There was, however, little opportunity for overt political opposition. A Belarusian Popular Front (BPF) was established in October 1988, but the CPB did not permit the republican media to report its activities, and refused to allow rallies or public meetings to take place. At the end of the month riot police were used to disperse a pro-BPF demonstration in Minsk, commemorating the victims of mass executions under Stalin. The BPF did have some success in the elections to the all-Union Congress of People's Deputies, which took place in March 1989, persuading voters to reject several leading officials of the CPB. However, the inaugural congress of the BPF took place in Vilnius (Lithuania), in June, the Front having been refused permission to meet in Minsk.

In early 1990, in anticipation of the elections to the republican Supreme Soviet, or Supreme Council (legislature), the CPB did adopt some of the BPF's policies regarding the Belarusian language. On 26 January the authorities approved a law declaring Belarusian to be the state language, effective from 1 September. However, Russian was reinstated as a second state language, following the adoption of a new Constitution in November 1996.

The BPF was not officially permitted to participate in the elections to the Belarusian Supreme Council, which took place on 4 March 1990. Instead, its members joined other pro-reform groups in a coalition known as the Belarusian Democratic Bloc (BDB). The BDB won about one-quarter of the 310 seats that were decided by popular election; most of the remainder were won by CPB members loyal to the republican leadership. The opposition won most seats in the large cities, notably Gomel (Homiel) and Minsk, where Zyanon Paznyak, the leader of the BPF, was elected.

When the new Supreme Council first convened, on 15 May 1990, the deputies belonging to the BDB immediately demanded the adoption of a declaration of sovereignty. The CPB initially opposed such a move, but on 27 July, apparently after consultations with the leadership of the Communist Party of the Soviet Union in Moscow, a Declaration of State Sovereignty of the BSSR was adopted unanimously by the Supreme Council. The declaration asserted the republic's right to maintain armed forces, to establish a national currency and to exercise full control over its domestic and foreign policies. On the insistence of the opposition, the declaration included a clause stating the right of the republic to compensation for the damage caused by the accident at the Chernobyl nuclear power station.

The issue of the Chernobyl accident united both communist and opposition deputies. The Belarusian Government appealed to the all-Union Government for a minimum of 17,000m. roubles to address the consequences of the disaster, but was offered only 3,000m. roubles in compensation. Moreover, in June 1990 Gorbachev, then the Soviet President, declined an invitation to visit Minsk to discuss the problem, an action that was unfavourably received in the republic. He eventually visited the BSSR in February 1991, but promised little further assistance.

The 31st Congress of the CPB, which took place in November 1990, was notable for delegates' criticisms of Gorbachev's reforms, in particular his foreign policy towards Eastern Europe. Yefrem Sakalau, who had led the CPB since 1987, did not seek re-election as First Secretary. He was replaced by Anatol Malafeyeu, who only narrowly defeated an outspoken critic of Gorbachev, Uladzimir Brovikou.

The Belarusian Government took part in the negotiation of a new Treaty of Union and signed the protocol to the draft treaty on 3 March 1991. The all-Union referendum on the preservation of the USSR took place in the BSSR on 17 March; of the 83% of the electorate who participated, 83% voted in favour of Gorbachev's proposals for a 'renewed federation of equal sovereign republics'. Members of the BPF conducted a campaign advocating rejection of Gorbachev's proposals, but complained that they were denied the opportunity to present their views to the general public.

The BSSR's reputation as the most stable of the European Soviet republics was challenged in April 1991 by a series of strikes that threatened the continued power of the CPB. Demonstrators demanded higher wages and the cancellation of the 5% sales tax (introduced in January), but also announced political demands, including the resignation of the Belarusian Government and the depoliticization of republican institutions. On 10 April a general strike took place, and an estimated 100,000 people attended a demonstration in Minsk. The Government finally agreed to certain economic concessions, including high wage increases, but the strikers' political demands were rejected. Some 200,000 workers were estimated to have taken part in a second general strike on 23 April, in protest at the legislature's refusal to reconvene.

The Supreme Council, which was still dominated by members of the CPB, was eventually convened in May 1991. Although it rejected the workers' political demands, the power of the conservative CPB was threatened by increased dissent within the party. In June 33 deputies joined the opposition as a 'Communists for Democracy' faction, led by Alyaksandr Lukashenka.

The Belarusian leadership did not strongly oppose the attempted coup in Moscow in August 1991. The Presidium of the Supreme Council released a neutral statement on the last day of the coup, but the Central Committee of the CPB issued a declaration unequivocally supporting the coup. Following the failure of the coup attempt, an extraordinary session of the Supreme Council was convened. Mikalay Dzemyantsei, the Chairman of the Supreme Council (republican head of state), was forced to resign. He was replaced by Stanislau Shushkevich, a respected centrist politician, pending an election to the office. In addition, the Supreme Council agreed to nationalize all CPB property, to prohibit the party's activities in law-enforcement agencies, and to suspend the CPB, pending an investigation into its role in the coup. On 25 August the legislature voted to grant constitutional status to the July 1990 Declaration of State Sovereignty, and declared the political and economic independence of Belarus.

On 19 September 1991 the Supreme Council voted to rename the BSSR the Republic of Belarus. The Council also elected Shushkevich as its Chairman. Shushkevich demonstrated his strong support for the continuation of some form of union by signing, in October, a treaty to establish an economic community and by agreeing, in November, to the first draft of the Treaty on the Union of Sovereign States. On 8 December Shushkevich, with the Russian and Ukrainian Presidents, signed the Minsk Agreement establishing a new Commonwealth of Independent States (CIS—see p. 132). On 21 December the leaders of 11 former Soviet republics confirmed this decision by the Alma-Ata Declaration. The proposal that the headquarters of the CIS should be in Minsk was widely welcomed in Belarus as a means of attracting foreign political and economic interest in the republic.

By comparison with other former Soviet republics, Belarus experienced relative stability in domestic affairs during 1992, which was attributed to the country's more favourable social and economic policies, as well as to the comparatively homogenous nature of the population. In governmental affairs, the opposition BPF censured the continued dominance of the communists in both the Supreme Council and the Cabinet of Ministers, notwithstanding the temporary suspension of the CPB itself. (In February 1993, however, the suspension was lifted and the CPB was permitted to re-establish itself.) In addition, the BPF campaigned insistently for the holding of a referendum to assess the electorate's confidence in the Supreme Council and the Government. In June 1992, having collected the required number of signatures, the BPF accused the Supreme Council of seeking to obstruct such a referendum. In October the Council voted against the holding of a referendum, owing to alleged irregularities in the collection of signatures.

Divisions between the various branches of government in Belarus became more pronounced during 1993. A major source of controversy was the drafting of Belarus's new Constitution, three separate versions of which were submitted to the Supreme Council in 1991–93. Shushkevich and the BPF strongly opposed the establishment of Belarus as a presidential republic; nevertheless, the new Constitution, which provided for a presidential system, was adopted in March 1994. A further point of dispute was the question of whether Belarus should adopt closer economic, military and other relations with the Russian Federation and the CIS (as advocated by the Supreme Council). Shushkevich and the BPF were opposed to Belarus's signing the Treaty on Collective Security (which had been concluded by six other CIS states in May 1992), on the grounds that this would contravene the Declaration of State Sovereignty which defines Belarus as a neutral state, and would also lead to renewed Russian domination. None the less, in April the Supreme Council voted to sign the Treaty. Three months later the legislature passed a vote of 'no confidence' in Shushkevich, in response to his continued opposition to the Treaty; he remained in office, however, as the Council had been inquorate at the time of the vote. A second vote of confidence in Shushkevich was held in January 1994; this time the Council voted overwhelmingly to dismiss him, on charges of corruption. He was replaced by Mechislau Gryb, formerly a senior police official. The premier, Vyacheslau Kebich, survived a similar vote of confidence.

Support for the CPB increased substantially during 1993: the party's popularity was attributed in large part to nostalgia for the relative prosperity enjoyed under communist rule, as well as regret for the demise of the USSR. In March the CPB formed, with 17 other parties and groups opposed to Belarusian independence, a loose coalition, the Popular Movement of Belarus.

Renewed allegations of corruption against Kebich and leading members of the Cabinet of Ministers, coupled with the worsening economic situation, culminated in a BPF-led general strike in Minsk in February 1994. Protesters returned to work only when Gryb announced that the presidential election would be brought forward to mid-1994. Six candidates collected the requisite number of signatures, including Kebich, Shushkevich, Paznyak and Lukashenka, who, as head of the Supreme Council's anti-corruption committee, had been responsible for bringing the corruption charges against Shushkevich. In the first ballot, held in late June, no candidate gained an overall majority, although Lukashenka, with 47% of the valid votes, led by a considerable margin. In the second ballot, between Lukashenka and Kebich (held in early July), Lukashenka received 85% of the votes, and he was inaugurated as the first President of Belarus on 20 July. Mikhail Chigir, an economic reformist, replaced Kebich as Chairman of a new Cabinet of Ministers. In December one of the Deputy Chairmen of the Cabinet of Ministers, Viktar Ganchar, tendered his resignation in protest at what he perceived as the President's disregard for the Cabinet. This was followed later in the month by a report to the Supreme Council by a BPF deputy, alleging widespread corruption in the presidential administration.

In early 1995 there were repeated confrontations between President Lukashenka and the Supreme Council over constitutional issues. In late January the Council voted for a second time to adopt legislation whereby the President could be removed by a two-thirds vote of the Council. In March Lukashenka announced that, simultaneously with the legislative elections scheduled to take place in May, a referendum would be held on four policy questions. In early April, following the Council's rejection of all but one of the proposed questions (on closer integration with Russia), Lukashenka threatened to dissolve the legislature. A number of opposition deputies (including Paznyak) were forcibly evicted from the Supreme Council building, where they had declared a hunger strike in protest at the referendum. Shortly after this action, deputies voted in favour of the inclusion in the referendum of the remaining three questions: to give the Russian language equal status with Belarusian as an official language; to abandon the state insignia and flag of independent Belarus in favour of a modified version of those used in the republic during the Soviet era; and to amend the Constitution in order to empower the President to suspend the Supreme Council in the event of unconstitutional acts. Some 65% of the electorate participated in the referendum, which was held, as scheduled, on 14 May. All four questions received overwhelming popular support.

On the same occasion as the referendum, Belarus's first post-Soviet legislative elections were held. However, owing to the stringent electoral regulations, only 18 of the total 260 seats in the Supreme Council were filled. At 'run-off' elections, held on 28 May 1995, a further 101 deputies were elected, but the two rounds of voting failed to produce the necessary two-thirds quorum, and a further round was scheduled for November. In the mean time, the confrontation between Lukashenka and the existing Supreme Council intensified. Lukashenka insisted that the Council's mandate had expired in March (five years after its election in 1990); the Council's Chairman, Mechislau Gryb, countered that the body was legitimate until the election of a new legislature had been completed. Gryb also requested the Constitutional Court to examine the legality of a number of decrees issued by Lukashenka, five of which were subsequently found to be unconstitutional.

A quorum was finally achieved in the Supreme Council at two further rounds of voting, held on 29 November and 10 December 1995. Seventy-nine new deputies were elected to the Council, bringing the total to 198. The CPB emerged with the largest number of seats in the new legislature (42), followed by the Agrarian Party (AP) (33), the United Civic Party of Belarus (nine) and the Party of People's Accord (eight). Independent candidates accounted for 95 seats. The BPF failed to win representation in the Council. No announcements were made concerning elections to fill the 62 seats remaining vacant. The Supreme Council held its inaugural session in early January 1996. Syamyon Sharetski, the leader of the AP, was appointed Chairman of the Council, replacing Gryb. With the realignment of independent candidates and parties into parliamentary factions, five major groupings emerged: Accord (59 deputies), Agrarians (47), Communists (44), People's Unity (17) and Social Democrats 'Belarus' (15).

Relations between the Constitutional Court and President Lukashenka deteriorated in early 1996, with the Court declaring the observance of constitutional law in 1995 to have been unsatisfactory. Lukashenka extended his authority over the security services and over the state-owned media, giving control of editorial appointments to the Cabinet of Ministers. In March 1996 many thousands of people gathered in central Minsk to protest against government proposals to sign a new union treaty with Russia. Despite the strength of the opposition, the Treaty on the Formation of a Community of Sovereign Republics was signed by President Lukashenka and President Yeltsin in Moscow on 2 April 1996. Although not actually establishing a single state, the treaty included extensive provisions covering military, economic and political co-operation between the two component parts of the new Community of Sovereign Republics (CSR). Following the endorsement of this important document, confrontation between Lukashenka and the opposition parties increased. A warrant was issued in April for the arrest of Paznyak, who was accused of organizing the anti-union treaty demonstrations. The offices of the BPF were searched, but Paznyak fled the country and later applied for political asylum in the USA. Several activists were arrested, and riot police clashed with demonstrators demanding their release. (They were later released on health grounds after staging a hunger strike.) Unauthorized rallies, organized by the opposition movement, were held in Minsk at the end of the month to commemorate the 10th anniversary of the disaster at the Chernobyl nuclear power station. The demonstrators used the opportunity to express publicly their dissatisfaction with the Government and, in particular, with the formation of the CSR. It was reported that the rallies were brutally dispersed by the police, and about 200 people were arrested.

In May 1996 the committee for human rights at the Supreme Council launched an investigation into alleged violations of human rights, particularly with regard to the laws concerning the media, and in June a conference on human rights concluded that there had been systematic abuse in Belarus since March. The conflict between the Supreme Council and Lukashenka escalated in July, when Sharetski asked the Constitutional Court to review the legality of several presidential decrees. In early August the President, seeking to enhance his powers further, scheduled a national referendum for early November, which was to contain, amongst other questions, proposed amendments to the 1994 Constitution. If approved, the amendments would give the President the power to appoint members of the judiciary and other senior officials, and to issue decrees that would carry legal force; the Supreme Council would be transformed into a bicameral National Assembly. In September demands for the impeachment of the President became more insistent, and protesters carrying the red and white flag of independent Belarus appealed for the Supreme Council to begin proceedings to remove Lukashenka. The Presidium of the Supreme Council proposed three further questions for the referendum, seeking to curtail the President's powers. Despite disagreement between Lukashenka and the Supreme Council over the date of the referendum, it was eventually scheduled for 24 November (with polling stations to be open from 9 November for those unable to vote on the later date). Elections for the remaining vacant seats in the Supreme Council were also due to be held on 24 November. Relations between Lukashenka and the Constitutional Court deteriorated in November, following a ruling by the Court that the results of the referendum questions concerning amendments to the Constitution could be used only for consultative purposes and would not be legally binding. Lukashenka's revocation of this decision by presidential decree provoked fierce criticism.

The referendum ballot papers contained seven questions, four of which were proposed by Lukashenka: whether amendments should be made to the 1994 Constitution to extend the President's term of office from 1999 to 2001, and to grant him extensive powers of appointment; whether the Belarusian Independence Day should be moved from 27 July (the anniversary of the Declaration of State Sovereignty) to 3 July (the anniversary of the liberation from the Nazis); whether there should be an unrestricted right to purchase and sell land; and whether the death penalty should be abolished. The remaining three questions were submitted by the Supreme Council and proposed that there be a significant reduction in the powers of the President (in effect, virtually abolishing the presidency); that the Supreme Council should be allowed to elect heads of local administration (currently appointed by the President); and that state institutions should be funded from the budget instead of from a non-budgetary fund controlled by the President.

Despite the inclusion of questions concerning proposed constitutional changes, copies of the draft Constitution were not available to the public by the time that voting began on 9 November 1996. The Chairman of the Central Electoral Commission, Viktar Ganchar, stated that he would not approve the results of the voting, owing to this and other electoral violations; he was shortly afterwards dismissed by President Lukashenka. The crisis worsened in mid-November, when the Chairman of the Council of Ministers, Mikhail Chigir, resigned, urging that the referendum be cancelled; he was replaced, in an acting capacity, by Syargey Ling. Some 10,000 people attended an anti-Government rally in Minsk, protesting at the restrictions on their freedom of expression. Independent radio stations were closed down, and as many as 200,000 issues of *Nasha Niva*, an independent newspaper containing criticisms of Lukashenka, were confiscated at the Lithuanian border. Widespread violations of the law were reported by parliamentary electoral observers—in particular, no record was kept of those who had voted early. The Organization for Security and Co-operation in Europe (OSCE, see p. 212) refused to send observers to monitor the referendum, and the Council of Europe declared that the presidential draft of the amended Constitution did not comply with European standards. Meanwhile, 75 deputies in the Supreme Council submitted a motion to the Constitutional Court to begin impeachment proceedings against the President. The Court had already found 17 decrees issued by Lukashenka to be unconstitutional. An apparent compromise was reached on 22 November, when an agreement, mediated by the Russian Prime

Minister, was signed by Lukashenka, Sharetski and Valery Tsikhinya, the Chairman of the Constitutional Court. Its basic provisions were that the results of the referendum would be of a recommendatory, rather than obligatory, nature, that the impeachment proceedings against the President would be halted, and that a constitutional assembly, consisting of presidential appointees and elected representatives, would draw up a new version of the Constitution within three months of the referendum. However, a large number of deputies in the Supreme Council refused to support the agreement, which consequently collapsed on 23 November. Lukashenka announced that the referendum would be legally binding after all, and Sharetski declared that the impeachment process against the President would be reactivated.

The outcome of the voting revealed considerable support for the President, although the reported widespread electoral violations meant that the accuracy of this result was disputed by opposition movements and electoral observers. According to official figures, some 84% of the electorate took part, 70.5% of whom voted for the President's constitutional amendments, while only 7.9% voted for those of the Supreme Council. More than 88% of those who participated voted to transfer the Belarusian Independence Day to 3 July, while the remaining motions were all rejected. The Constitutional Court was forced to abandon the impeachment proceedings against the President, as deputies withdrew their signatures from the motion. The amended Constitution was published on 27 November 1996 and came into immediate effect.

Following the referendum, the Supreme Council divided into two factions. More than 100 deputies declared their support for Lukashenka, and adopted legislation abolishing the Supreme Council and establishing a 110-member House of Representatives, the lower chamber of the new National Assembly. Some 50 other deputies denounced the referendum as invalid and declared themselves to be the legitimate legislature. The House of Representatives convened shortly afterwards and elected Anatol Malafeyeu as its Chairman. Deputies were granted a four-year mandate, while the term of office of those opposed to the new legislature was curtailed to two months. Deputies elected in the by-elections held simultaneously with the referendum were denied registration. Legislation governing the formation of the upper house of the National Assembly, the 64-member Council of the Republic, was approved by Lukashenka in early December 1996: eight members were appointed by the President, while the remaining 56 were elected by regional councils. In the event, no deputies from the former Supreme Council participated in the Council of the Republic, which convened for the first time in mid-January 1997, and elected Pavel Shypuk as its Chairman. Meanwhile, in protest at the constitutional amendments introduced through the referendum, Tsikhinya and several other judges announced their resignation from the Constitutional Court. Tsikhinya was replaced in early January by a presidential appointee, Ryhor Vasilevich. Also in that month, the Chairwoman of the National Bank, Tamara Vinnikava, was arrested on charges of corruption. She was replaced by Genadz Aleynikaw.

Continued opposition to the provisions of the referendum from deputies of the former legislature resulted in the formation in early January 1997 of the Public Coalition Government–National Economic Council, a form of 'shadow' cabinet, chaired by Genadz Karpenka. Structural changes to the Belarusian Government were implemented by Lukashenka, with the Chairmen of State Committees henceforth to be included in the Council of Ministers; the President also made several ministerial and judicial appointments. Doubts about the legitimacy of the referendum were expressed by international organizations, including the Council of Europe, which suspended Belarus's 'guest status', citing the lack of democracy in the new political structures, and the Permanent Council of the Parliamentary Assembly of the OSCE, which recognized the right of a delegation from the former Supreme Council, rather than members of the new House of Representatives, officially to represent Belarus at that organization. Delegates from these international bodies visited Belarus in late January to investigate reports of electoral violations, and to rule on the validity of the referendum results. In February Syargey Ling was confirmed as Prime Minister by the legislature.

Repression against opponents of the new Constitution was maintained throughout early 1997, despite the conclusion by the international observers that the referendum and subsequent legislative elections could not be deemed legal, and that the provisions of the 1994 Constitution should be restored. Several opposition members were brought to trial for organizing unauthorized rallies, and in early March 1997 a presidential decree restricted further the right to demonstrate. Moves towards greater integration with Russia (see below) continued to provoke protest from opposition parties, led, in particular, by the BPF, and in late March an anti-Lukashenka demonstration, which attracted some 10,000 participants, was violently dispersed by police. Many people were detained, including a US diplomat, who was subsequently requested to leave the country. The USA responded by expelling a Belarusian embassy official from Washington. In addition, a Russian television journalist lost his accreditation, following the transmission to Russia of video material from the demonstration. Concern at human rights violations by the authorities was expressed by the Belarusian Congress of Democratic Trade Unions, which had earlier been denied registration.

The signing with Russia of the Treaty of Union, and initialling of the Charter of the Union, on 2 April 1997, by Presidents Lukashenka and Yeltsin (see below) prompted a further anti-Union demonstration in Minsk, which was violently suppressed by the police, and which resulted in many arrests. Charges of violating the presidential decree on demonstrations were subsequently brought against opposition members, including Mikalay Statkevich, leader of the Belarusian Social Democratic Party. Nevertheless, support for the union treaty appeared widespread, with some 15,000 people participating in a pro-Union rally in Minsk in mid-May. The treaty was ratified shortly afterwards by the respective legislatures, and came into effect in mid-June, following the exchange of documents of ratification.

Negotiations mediated by the Council of Europe and the European Union (EU) to end the confrontation between the deputies of the former Supreme Council and the new legislature were held in June 1997. A second round of talks collapsed in July, following disagreement over which constitution was to form the basis of the discussions. Disputes over the composition of the government delegation resulted in the indefinite suspension of the negotiations.

Harassment of the independent media became more persistent in mid-1997. In late July legislation was approved requiring all foreign journalists in Belarus to renew their accreditation by mid-September. The arrest of several journalists, employed by the Russian state television company, ORT, for allegedly violating the border, prompted condemnation from President Yeltsin and precipitated opposition protests. Lukashenka had already criticized the Russian media for spreading disinformation about Belarus. A proposed visit by Lukashenka to the Russian region of Kaliningrad was subsequently cancelled, at the request of the Governor of the area. The arrest of a second Russian television crew in mid-August led to a further deterioration in relations between the two countries, and requests for the journalists to be released immediately were met with anger by Lukashenka. By early September six of the seven journalists had been released. The remaining reporter, Pavel Sheremet, was released in October, but was forbidden to leave the country. Meanwhile, it was reported that many journalists had failed to have their accreditation renewed before the expiry of the deadline.

International concern at Belarus's failure to observe human rights was expressed in August 1997 in the report of one organization, Human Rights Watch, which declared that Lukashenka had reversed most of the progress achieved during the *perestroika* (restructuring) period. In November the UN Commission on Human Rights echoed this concern. Opposition to the Belarusian authorities took a more violent direction in September, when responsibility for an explosion at the Minsk District Court was claimed by the Belarusian Liberation Army, which subsequently issued a statement demanding the restoration of the 1994 Constitution and the cessation of harassment of the opposition. Despite a statement by the EU that it was willing to assist Belarus in redrafting the new Constitution, while still recognizing the 1994 version as legitimate, negotiations between the deputies of the former and current legislatures, scheduled to recommence in September, were postponed indefinitely following a severe breakdown in relations betwen the EU and the Belarusian authorities.

Following the dissolution of the USSR in 1991, Belarus's closest relations continued to be with member states of the CIS, in particular the neighbouring Russian Federation. In April 1993 Belarus signed the CIS Treaty on Collective Security (see above), and accords on closer economic co-operation with CIS member states followed. In April 1994 Belarus and Russia concluded an agreement on an eventual monetary union. In March 1996 Belarus, Kazakhstan, Kyrgyzstan and Russia signed the Quadripartite Treaty, which envisaged a common market and a customs union between the four countries, as well as joint transport, energy and communications systems. In the following month Belarus and Russia concluded the far-reaching and controversial Treaty on the Formation of a Community of Sovereign Republics (see above), providing for closer economic, political and military integration between the two countries.

Relations between Belarus and Russia in 1996–97 were dominated by preparations for further integration. In March 1997 the Russian-Belarusian Parliamentary Assembly, provision for which had been made in the 1996 Treaty, elected the Chairman of the Russian State Duma, Gennadii Seleznev, as its Chairman, with Anatol Malafeyeu as his deputy. On 2 April 1997 a further Treaty of Union was signed by Yeltsin and Lukashenka in Moscow, and a Charter of the Union, detailing the process of integration, was also initialled. The stated aim of the Union was for the 'voluntary unification of the member states', and was to include the development of a common infrastructure, a single currency and a joint defence policy. The Union's ruling body was to be a Supreme Council, chaired alternately by the Presidents of the member states, and comprising the Heads of State and Government, the leaders of the legislatures and the Chairman of the Executive Committee. The Executive Committee was to be appointed by the Supreme Council. The Parliamentary Assembly (which had already convened) comprised 36 members from the legislature of each country. The Charter was submitted for nation-wide discussion in both countries, before being signed in Moscow on 23 May. Ratification of the documents by the respective legislatures took place in June, and the first official session of the Parliamentary Assembly followed shortly afterwards, with the Assembly adopting the anthem of the former Soviet Union as its national anthem. Progress towards further integration, however, appeared threatened by the arrest of two Russian television crews in mid-1997 (see above), which led to strong exchanges of opinion between the two Presidents, and the subsequent cancellation of two visits by Lukashenka to Russia, the second of these visits being prevented by orders from Yeltsin's administration to deny landing permission to Lukashenka's plane.

Belarus's relations with the USA were severely hampered in 1997 by its apparent disregard for the democratic process and for the observance of human rights. In February the US State Department issued a highly critical report on the violation of human rights in Belarus, emphasizing, in particular, the monopoly control by the executive of the security forces and the media. In late 1997 international organizations, including the OSCE, continued to recognize the former Supreme Council as the legitimate legislature.

With the dissolution of the USSR, Belarus effectively became a nuclear power, with approximately 80 SS-25 intercontinental ballistic missiles stationed on its territory. However, the Government of independent Belarus has consistently stressed that, under the Declaration of State Sovereignty of July 1990, Belarus is a neutral and non-nuclear state. Accordingly, in May 1992 Belarus signed the Lisbon Protocol to the Treaty on the Non-Proliferation of Nuclear Weapons (see under International Atomic Energy Agency, p. 65), under which it pledged to transfer all nuclear missiles to the Russian Federation by 1999. In February 1993 the Supreme Council ratified the first Strategic Arms Reduction Treaty (START 1—for further details, see chapter on the USA). Substantial amounts of financial and technical aid were pledged by the USA to help Belarus dismantle its nuclear arsenal. The last remaining nuclear warhead was removed from Belarus and transported to Russia in late November 1996.

Government

Under the Constitution of March 1994, which was amended in November 1996, legislative power is vested in the bicameral National Assembly. The lower chamber, the 110-member House of Representatives, is elected by universal adult suffrage for a term of four years. The upper chamber, the Council of the Republic, comprises 64 members: 56 members elected by organs of local administration, and eight members appointed by the President. The President is the Head of State, and is elected by popular vote for five years. Executive authority is exercised by the Cabinet of Ministers, which is led by the Chairman (Prime Minister) and which is responsible to the National Assembly. For administrative purposes, Belarus is divided into six regions (*oblasts*) and the capital city of Minsk; the regions are divided into districts (*rayons*).

Defence

In August 1997 the total strength of Belarus's armed forces was an estimated 81,800, comprising an army of 50,500, an air force of 22,000 (including air defence of 10,000), as well as an estimated 4,700 in centrally controlled units, 3,400 women and 1,200 Ministry of Defence staff. There is also a border guard numbering 8,000, which is controlled by the Ministry of Internal Affairs. Military service is compulsory and lasts for 18 months. In May 1996 it was reported that the term of military service would be reduced to 12 months from the year 2000. In October 1994 it was announced that two Russian non-nuclear military installations were to remain in Belarus. The defence budget for 1997 was projected at 2,700,000m. new roubles. In January 1995 Belarus joined NATO's 'Partnership for Peace' programme of military co-operation.

Economic Affairs

In 1995, according to estimates by the World Bank, Belarus's gross national product (GNP), measured at average 1993–95 prices, was US $21,356m., equivalent to $2,070 per head. During 1985–94, it was estimated, GNP per head declined by an annual average of 5.2%. Over the period 1985–95 the population increased by an annual average of 0.4%. During the same period Belarus's gross domestic product (GDP) declined, in real terms, by an average of 3.2% annually. The World Bank estimated a decline in GDP of 10.2%, in real terms, in 1995. However, in 1996 it was estimated that GDP increased by 2.6%.

Agriculture and forestry contributed 15.8% of GDP in 1996, and 21.2% of the labour force were employed in the sector (including fishing and hunting) in 1994. The principal crops are potatoes, grain and sugar beet. The livestock sector accounted for some 37% of agricultural output in 1995. Large areas of arable land (some 1.6m. ha) are still unused after being contaminated in 1986, following the accident at the Chernobyl nuclear power station in Ukraine. The Belarusian authorities have largely opposed private farming, and in 1995 collective and state farms still accounted for some 80% of agricultural land. However, more than 50% of total crop output was produced by private farms in that year. During 1985–95, according to the World Bank, agricultural GDP decreased by an annual average of 5.1%. In 1995 agricultural production decreased by an estimated 7.3%, compared with 1994.

Industry (comprising mining, manufacturing, construction and power) provided 39.5% of GDP in 1996, and employed 34.9% of the labour force in 1994. According to the World Bank, industrial GDP increased by an annual average of 3.2% during 1985–95. However, industrial GDP decreased by an estimated 13.0%, in real terms, in 1995. It was estimated that industrial output increased by 3.2% in 1996.

According to the World Bank, the manufacturing sector contributed an estimated 21.1% of GDP in 1995, and employed 26.5% of the labour force in 1994. Machine-building, power generation and chemicals are the principal branches of the sector. In 1995 oil refineries and petrochemical companies increased production by 8% and 10%, respectively, compared with 1994. During 1985–95, according to the World Bank, manufacturing GDP increased by 3.8%. However, in 1995 the GDP of the sector decreased by an estimated 10.6%.

Belarus has relatively few mineral resources, although there are small deposits of petroleum and natural gas, and important peat reserves. Peat extraction, however, was severely affected by the disaster at Chernobyl, since contaminated peat could not be burned. Belarus produced 50% of the Soviet Union's output of potash. However, production of potash has declined in recent years. In 1994 only 0.6% of the labour force were engaged in mining and quarrying.

In 1990 Belarus's supply of primary energy was provided by petroleum and petroleum products (60%), natural gas (29%), coal and lignite (3%) and other sources (8%). The country imports some 90% of its energy requirements, the principal supplier (approximately 85%) being Russia. Imports of energy products comprised 40.2% of the total value of imports in 1995. There are two large petroleum refineries, at Novopolotsk and Mozyr.

Services accounted for 40.1% of total employment in 1994, and provided 44.7% of GDP in 1996. As in other sectors of the economy, activity has declined in recent years. The volume of retail trade fell by 22% in 1994 and by a further 26% in 1995. During 1985–95 the GDP of the service sector increased by an annual average of 0.5%. However, the GDP of the sector declined by an estimated 9.3% in 1995.

In 1995 Belarus recorded a visible trade deficit of US $529m., and there was a deficit of $254m. on the current account of the balance of payments. Since the dissolution of the USSR in December 1991, Belarus has endeavoured to promote economic links with non-traditional trading partners. In 1996 these partners accounted for some 34% of Belarus's total trade, the remaining 66% being conducted with former Soviet republics. Belarus's principal trading partners in the former USSR in 1996 were Russia (which accounted for 77% of total imports and 80% of exports in 1996), Ukraine and Kazakhstan; outside the former USSR the most important trading partners are Germany, Poland and the USA. In 1996 the principal exports were machinery, chemicals and petrochemicals, processed food and light industrial goods. The principal imports were petroleum and natural gas, machinery, chemicals, ferrous metals and processed foods.

The 1996 state budget registered a deficit of 3,645,963m. new roubles. Belarus's total external debt was US $1,648m. at the end of 1995, of which $1,255m. was long-term public debt. In that year the cost of debt-servicing was equivalent to 3.6% of the value of exports of goods and services. During 1990–94 consumer prices increased at an average rate of 788% per year. In 1995 the average annual rate of inflation was 709%, compared with 2,221% in 1994. In 1996 the annual rate of inflation decreased to 52.7%. In late August 1997 some 140,200 people were officially registered as unemployed (approximately 3.1% of the economically-active population).

Belarus joined the IMF and the World Bank in 1992. It also became a member of the European Bank for Reconstruction and Development (EBRD, see p. 148).

Prior to 1991, Belarus was widely considered to have the most stable republican economy of the Soviet Union, supported largely by a comparatively advanced engineering sector. Following the dissolution of the USSR, however, Belarus experienced serious economic problems comparable to those prevalent in other former Soviet republics, and suffered a severe contraction in output in all sectors. A programme of strict economic measures was adopted in October 1994, which, by mid-1995, had achieved moderate success, most notably with a significant reduction in the rate of inflation. However, the inconclusive nature of the 1995 elections to the Supreme Council severely disrupted the introduction of economic legislation and structural reforms. Increased government intervention and the imposition of administrative controls further slowed the introduction of market economic principles. Despite the adoption of privatization legislation in the early 1990s, the transfer of enterprises to private ownership remained extremely limited. Legislation introduced in late 1995 required all enterprises to be re-registered, with only profit-making, or strategically-important, concerns granted new licences. The suspension of the registration programme in early 1996 effectively halted the privatization process. Despite positive signs of growth in 1996—an increase in GDP and in some branches of industrial production was reported—the deterioration of political stability in 1997 had serious implications for Belarus's economy. The World Bank and the IMF reported that there had been no structural changes in the Belarusian economy since 1995, and that there had been no significant achievements in the process of privatization and the introduction of market reforms. The IMF subsequently decided not to allocate credit to Belarus in the next financial year. In September 1997 the Soros Fund, which had already contributed US $13m. to medical, cultural, scientific and economic programmes, closed its office in Belarus, following the seizure of money from its bank account by the Government, ostensibly to cover tax violations. Foreign investment continued to be minimal, accounting for less than 7% of the total volume of investment in 1996. Proposals to increase this to 15% within two years appeared threatened by the weakening of internal democracy in 1997. The direction of Belarus's economic policy will largely be influenced by progress towards closer integration with Russia, as envisaged in a number of treaties and agreements signed in the mid- to late 1990s. These include an agreement with Russia to form a customs union in 1995 (subsequently signed by Kazakhstan and Kyrgyzstan) and the Treaty on the Formation of a Community of Sovereign Republics, signed in April 1996. In February Russia agreed to the cancellation of Belarus's debt for gas supplies, in exchange for the cost of maintaining Russian military units in Belarus. However, by 1997 gas arrears had increased substantially. The Treaty and Charter of the Union, signed with Russia in April 1997, (see Introductory Survey), provide for a programme of common economic and social policies, leading to the eventual unification of the two countries' monetary, taxation and budgetary systems.

Social Welfare

Since 1993 the social security system has been financed by two principal funds: the Social Protection Fund (covering family allowances, pensions and sickness and disability benefits), and the Employment Fund (directing employment schemes, retraining projects and unemployment benefits). More than 2.5m. people were receiving pensions in 1995. A variety of benefits, financed through the Chernobyl tax, are paid to victims of the accident at the Chernobyl power station, in April 1986. In 1995 expenditure on social security from the Social Protection Fund was 9,023,352.4m. new roubles (some 7.6% of GDP), and expenditure on health from the state budget was 5,500,000m. new roubles (4.6% of GDP). In 1995 there were 41.2 physicians and 117.1 hospital beds per 10,000 inhabitants.

Education

Education is officially compulsory for 11 years from six to 17 years of age. Primary education generally begins at six years of age and lasts for four years (Grades 1–4). Secondary education, beginning at the age of 10, lasts for a further seven years (Grades 5–11), comprising a first cycle of five years and a second of two years. In the early 1990s, in response to public demand, the Government began to introduce greater provision for education in the Belarusian language and more emphasis on Belarusian, rather than Soviet or Russian, history and literature. In 1994/95 34.8% of all pupils were taught in Belarusian, and 65.2% were taught in Russian. Higher education institutions include 11 general and seven specialized universities, as well as eight academies. Research is co-ordinated by the Belarusian Academy of Sciences. Expenditure on education by all levels of government was about 582,000m. old roubles (10.4% of total government expenditure) in 1993 and a projected 2,024,000m. old roubles (also 10.4%) in 1994. In 1989, according to census results, the average rate of adult illiteracy was 2.1% (males 0.6%; females 3.4%).

Public Holidays

1998: 1 January (New Year's Day), 7 January (Orthodox Christmas), 8 March (International Women's Day), 15 March (Constitution Day), 13 April (Catholic Easter), 20 April (Orthodox Easter), 28 April (Memorial Day), 1 May (Labour Day), 9 May (Victory Day), 3 July (Anniversary of Liberation from the Nazis), 2 November (Day of Commemoration), 7 November (October Revolution Day), 25 December (Catholic Christmas).

1999: 1 January (New Year's Day), 7 January (Orthodox Christmas), 8 March (International Women's Day), 15 March (Constitution Day), 5 April (Catholic Easter), 12 April (Orthodox Easter), 28 April (Memorial Day), 1 May (Labour Day), 9 May (Victory Day), 3 July (Anniversary of Liberation from the Nazis), 2 November (Day of Commemoration), 7 November (October Revolution Day), 25 December (Catholic Christmas).

Weights and Measures

The metric system is in force.

Statistical Survey

Source: mainly Ministry of Statistics and Analysis, 220070 Minsk, pr. Partizanski 12; tel. (172) 49-52-00; fax (172) 49-22-04.

Area and Population

AREA, POPULATION AND DENSITY

Area (sq km)	207,595*
Population (census results)†	
17 January 1979	9,532,516
12 January 1989	
Males	4,749,324
Females	5,402,482
Total	10,151,806
Population (official estimates at 1 January)	
1995	10,297,225
1996	10,264,388
1997	10,236,127
Density (per sq km) at 1 January 1997	49.3

* 80,153 sq miles.

† Figures refer to the *de jure* population. The *de facto* total was 9,560,543 in 1979 and 10,199,709 in 1989.

POPULATION BY NATIONALITY (1989 census)

	%
Belarusian	77.9
Russian	13.2
Polish	4.1
Ukrainian	2.9
Others	1.9
Total	100.0

PRINCIPAL TOWNS*
(estimated population at 1 January 1997)

Minsk (Miensk, capital)	1,679,500	Baranovichi (Baranavichy)	172,200
Gomel (Homiel)	501,000	Borisov (Barysau)	153,400
Mogilev (Mahilou)	367,700	Pinsk	131,100
Vitebsk (Viciebsk)	355,800	Orsha (Vorsha)	124,300
Grodno (Horadnia)	303,600	Mozyr (Mazyr)	108,500
Brest (Bierascie)†	294,600	Soligorsk	101,300
Bobruysk (Babrujsk)	226,600	Lida	100,800

* The Belarusian names of towns, in Latin transliteration, are given in parentheses after the more widely used Russian names.

† Formerly Brest-Litovsk.

BIRTHS, MARRIAGES AND DEATHS

	Registered live births		Registered marriages		Registered deaths	
	Number	Rate (per 1,000)	Number	Rate (per 1,000)	Number	Rate (per 1,000)
1989	153,449	15.0	97,929	9.6	103,479	10.1
1990	142,167	13.9	99,229	9.7	109,582	10.7
1991	132,045	12.9	94,760	9.2	114,650	11.2
1992	127,971	12.4	79,813	7.7	116,674	11.3
1993	117,384	11.3	82,326	7.9	128,544	12.4
1994	110,599	10.7	75,540	7.3	130,003	12.6
1995	101,144	9.8	77,027	7.5	133,775	13.0
1996	95,798	9.3	63,677	6.2	133,422	13.0

Expectation of life (official estimates, years at birth, 1996): 68.6 (males 63.0, females 74.3).

EMPLOYMENT (annual averages, '000 persons)

	1992	1993	1994
Agriculture, hunting, forestry and fishing	1,089.7	1,048.8	995.7
Mining and quarrying	24.5	29.6	27.2
Manufacturing	1,329.1	1,311.8	1,245.6
Electricity, gas and water	34.7	38.1	38.7
Construction	418.8	369.1	328.9
Trade, restaurants and hotels	340.8	405.3	422.3
Transport, storage and communications	350.9	328.9	318.0
Financing, insurance, real estate and business services	31.0	33.6	40.9
Community, social and personal services	1,069.6	1,075.6	1,099.7
Activities not adequately defined	198.3	182.9	179.0
Total	4,887.4	4,823.7	4,696.0
Males	2,389.9	2,363.6	2,272.9
Females	2,497.5	2,460.1	2,423.1

Economically Active Population (persons aged 15 years and over, 1989 census, provisional): Total 5,327,000 (males 2,718,000; females 2,609,000).

1995 ('000 persons): Total employed 4,405.1 (males 2,101.2; females 2,303.9).

1996 ('000 persons): Total employed 4,360.3 (males 2,123.5; females 2,236.8).

Agriculture

PRINCIPAL CROPS ('000 metric tons)

	1994	1995	1996
Wheat	230	439	600
Barley	3,013	1,965	2,194
Maize	1	3	5
Rye	1,864	2,143	1,794
Oats	760	638	707
Other cereals	4	14	20
Potatoes	8,241	9,504	10,677
Dry beans	155	187	310
Dry peas	104	112	181
Lentils*	20	24	24
Other pulses	65	68	68
Rapeseed	19	26	19
Linseed*	20	25	20
Cabbages†	422	430	490
Tomatoes†	93	96	106
Cucumbers and gherkins†	124	122	130
Onions (dry)†	51	53	60
Carrots	46	61	54
Other vegetables	293	304	336
Sugar beet	1,078	1,172	1,012
Apples†	255	240	230
Pears†	23	18	15
Plums†	48	60	54
Other fruits and berries†	70	65	56
Walnuts*	10	10	10
Tobacco (leaves)*	2	2	2
Flax fibre*	50	50	50

* FAO estimates. † Unofficial figures.

Source: FAO, *Production Yearbook*.

LIVESTOCK ('000 head at 1 January)

	1994	1995	1996
Horses	215	220	229
Cattle	5,851	5,403	5,054
Pigs	4,181	4,004	3,895
Sheep	271	230	204
Goats	51	54	54
Chickens	47,308	45,265	n.a.

LIVESTOCK PRODUCTS ('000 metric tons)

	1994	1995	1996
Beef and veal	384	316	298
Mutton and lamb	5	4	3
Pig meat	252	263	248
Poultry meat	97	69	65
Cows' milk	5,510	5,070	4,950
Cheese	89	79	83
Butter	74	65	61
Hen eggs	190	189	192
Honey†	4	4	4
Cattle and buffalo hides*	45	45	45

* FAO estimates.

Source: FAO, *Production Yearbook*.

Forestry

ROUNDWOOD REMOVALS ('000 cubic metres, excl. bark)

	1992	1993	1994*
Sawlogs, veneer logs and logs for sleepers	3,940	3,920	3,920
Other industrial wood	6,643	5,286	5,286
Fuel wood	813	825	809
Total	11,396	10,031	10,015

* FAO estimates.

Source: FAO, *Yearbook of Forest Products*.

SAWNWOOD PRODUCTION ('000 cubic metres, incl. railway sleepers)

	1992	1993	1994*
Coniferous (softwood)	1,031	938	938
Broadleaved (hardwood)	662	607	607
Total	1,693	1,545	1,545

* FAO estimates.

Source: FAO, *Yearbook of Forest Products*.

Fishing

(FAO estimates, metric tons, live weight)

	1993	1994	1995
Common carp	13,277	13,700	14,200
Roaches	349	362	380
Other fishes	374	388	420
Total catch	14,000	14,450	15,000

Source: FAO, *Yearbook of Fishery Statistics*.

Mining

('000 metric tons, unless otherwise indicated)

	1994	1995	1996
Crude petroleum	2,000	1,932	1,860
Natural gas (million cu metres)	294	266	249
Chalk	68	97	64
Gypsum (crude)	20	16	21
Peat: for fuel	3,482	3,145	2,793
for agriculture	2,190	961	528

Industry

SELECTED PRODUCTS ('000 metric tons, unless otherwise indicated)

	1994	1995	1996
Refined sugar	144	140	226
Margarine	19.2	17.0	25.3
Wheat flour	1,698	1,417	1,393
Ethyl alcohol ('000 hectolitres)	827	985	1,025
Wine ('000 hectolitres)	57.4	33.5	97.8
Beer ('000 hectolitres)	1,488.5	1,518.1	2,012.5
Mineral water ('000 hectolitres)	236.4	175.0	288.2
Soft drinks ('000 hectolitres)	786.4	1,264.2	1,650.9
Cigarettes (million)	7,378	6,228	6,267
Cotton yarn (pure and mixed)	13.0	9.7	11.4
Flax yarn	15.1	16.1	16.1
Wool yarn (pure and mixed)	22.0	11.8	12.8
Woven cotton fabrics (million sq metres)	45.3	33.2	42.8
Woven woollen fabrics (million sq metres)	19.1	7.3	7.0
Linen fabrics (million sq metres)	40.7	41.5	43.1
Woven fabrics of cellulosic fibres (million sq metres)	79.8	35.1	39.5
Carpets ('000 sq metres)	8,892	4,170	5,612
Footwear (excluding rubber, '000 pairs)	26,358	13,004	11,381
Plywood ('000 cu metres)	104	94	103
Paper	22	27	30
Paperboard	109	106	112
Benzene (Benzol)	39.8	55.0	34.7
Ethylene (Ethene)	80.3	111.3	78.9
Propylene (Propene)	50.3	72.4	55.1
Xylenes (Xylol)	25.4	21.5	7.6
Sulphuric acid (100%)	291	437	549
Nitrogenous fertilizers (a)[1]	424	502	565
Phosphate fertilizers (b)[1]	42	52	100
Potash fertilizers (c)[1]	2,515	2,796	2,717
Non-cellulosic continuous fibres	41.2	43.5	46.6
Cellulosic continuous filaments	8.1	9.5	10.7
Soap	19.2	18.1	29.7
Rubber tyres ('000)[2]	1,205	1,292	1,916
Rubber footwear ('000 pairs)	3,035	2,180	3,054
Quicklime	589	453	450
Cement	1,488	1,235	1,467
Concrete blocks ('000 cu metres)	2,680	1,719	1,372
Crude steel	880	744	886
Tractors ('000)	42.9	28.0	26.8
Refrigerators ('000)	742	746	754
Domestic washing machines ('000)	76.9	36.9	58.7
Television receivers ('000)	473	250	307
Radio receivers ('000)	545	277	138
Lorries (number)	21,264	12,902	10,403
Motorcycles ('000)	54.6	41.8	30.1
Bicycles ('000)	385	271	280
Cameras ('000)	128	34	35
Watches ('000)	14,311	6,603	4,809
Electric energy (million kWh)	31,397	24,918	23,726

[1] Production in terms of (a) nitrogen; (b) phosphoric acid; or (c) potassium oxide.

[2] For lorries and farm vehicles.

Finance

CURRENCY AND EXCHANGE RATES

Monetary Units:

100 kopeks = 1 new Belarusian rouble (rubel).

Sterling and Dollar Equivalents (31 August 1997)

£1 sterling = 44,486 new roubles;
US $1 = 27,430 new roubles;
100,000 new Belarusian roubles = £2.248 = $3.646.

Average exchange rate (new Belarusian roubles per US $)

1994 776.7
1995 5,697.4

Note: The Belarusian rouble was introduced in May 1992, initially as a coupon currency, to circulate alongside (and at par with) the Russian (formerly Soviet) rouble. Based on the official rate of exchange, the average value of Soviet currency (roubles per US dollar) was: 0.6274 in 1989; 0.5856 in 1990; 0.5819 in 1991. However, a multiple exchange rate system was in operation, with separate non-commercial and tourist rates. A commercial exchange rate was introduced on 1 November 1990, replacing the official rate for most transactions. The commercial rate (roubles per US dollar) was: 1.692 at 31 December 1990; 1.671 at 31 December 1991. Between November 1989 and April 1991 the tourist exchange rate valued the rouble at one-tenth of the official rate. In April 1991 this rate, renamed the 'special rate', was set at $1 = 27.6 roubles. It was subsequently adjusted. The average market exchange rate in 1991 was $1 = 31.2 roubles. Following the dissolution of the USSR in December 1991, Russia and several other former Soviet republics retained the rouble as their monetary unit. The parity between Belarusian and Russian currencies was subsequently ended, and the Belarusian rouble was devalued. At 30 September 1993 the exchange rate was 1 Russian rouble = 2 Belarusian roubles. The rate per Russian rouble was adjusted to 3 Belarusian roubles in October 1993, and to 4 Belarusian roubles in November. In April 1994 Belarus and Russia signed a treaty providing for the eventual union of their monetary systems. However, it was subsequently recognized that, under the prevailing economic conditions, such a union was not practicable. In August a new Belarusian rouble, equivalent to 10 old roubles, was introduced. On 1 January 1995 the Belarusian rouble became the sole national currency, while the circulation of Russian roubles ceased.

STATE BUDGET (million roubles)*

Revenue	1994	1995	1996
Tax revenue	5,485,199	31,242,141	43,486,194
Income taxes	473,160	3,300,136	5,297,023
Value-added tax	1,779,856	9,933,853	14,273,982
Excises	687,980	2,805,967	6,335,907
Fuel tax	145,144	596,828	252,465
Chernobyl tax†	318,807	2,752,609	3,821,430
Other taxes	2,080,252	11,852,748	13,505,387
Non-tax revenue	1,007,366	4,225,808	7,182,437
Grants	13,000	—	—
Total	6,505,565	35,467,949	50,668,631

Expenditure	1994	1995	1996
National economy	1,957,644	8,504,623	10,815,565
Socio-cultural activities	2,556,169	16,600,419	26,430,607
Administration, law and order	394,249	3,902,614	5,755,691
Chernobyl fund†	491,537	3,002,297	4,164,652
Total (incl. others)	7,109,663	38,816,631	54,314,594

* Excluding the operations of social funds and extrabudgetary accounts. The consolidated totals of government transactions (in '000 million new roubles) were: Revenue and grants 8,463 in 1994, 51,203 in 1995; Expenditure and net lending 8,916 in 1994, 53,440 in 1995 (Source: IMF Staff Country Report, September 1996).

† Relating to measures to relieve the effects of the accident at the Chernobyl nuclear power station, in northern Ukraine, in April 1986.

INTERNATIONAL RESERVES (US $ million at 31 December)

	1994	1995	1996
IMF special drawing rights	0.01	4.54	0.14
Reserve position in IMF	0.03	0.03	0.03
Foreign exchange	100.95	372.45	468.98
Total	100.99	377.02	469.15

Source: IMF, *International Financial Statistics*.

MONEY SUPPLY (million new roubles at 31 December)

	1994	1995	1996
Currency outside banks	736,000	3,779,000	6,199,400
Demand deposits at deposit money banks	1,877,300	6,131,700	9,240,100
Total money (incl. others)	2,686,700	10,026,600	15,708,400

Source: IMF, *International Financial Statistics*.

COST OF LIVING (Consumer price index; base: 1992 = 100)

	1993	1994	1995
Food (incl. beverages)	1,515.1	37,477	285,492
Fuel and light	1,883.3	45,636	807,659
Clothing (incl. footwear)	899.6	17,746	133,547
Rent	2,131.1	17,509	n.a.
All items (incl. others)	1,290.2	29,946	242,349

Source: ILO, *Yearbook of Labour Statistics*.

1996: Food 427,096; All items 370,067 (Source: Ministry of Statistics and Analysis).

NATIONAL ACCOUNTS ('000 million new roubles at current prices)

Expenditure on the Gross Domestic Product

	1994	1995	1996*
Government final consumption expenditure	3,582	23,157	34,689
Private final consumption expenditure	10,717	72,356	116,059
Increase in stocks	-58	63	3,791
Gross fixed capital formation	5,918	29,984	40,479
Total domestic expenditure	20,159	125,560	195,018
Exports of goods and services	12,644	59,890	82,153
Less Imports of goods and services	14,988	-65,637	-97,351
GDP in purchasers' values	17,814	119,813	179,820

* Figures are preliminary.

Source: partly IMF, *International Financial Statistics*.

Gross Domestic Product by Economic Activity

	1994	1995	1996*
Agriculture	2,324.4	18,259.5	24,578.8
Forestry	93.4	844.1	1,233.2
Industry†	4,974.9	33,921.5	54,540.9
Construction	992.5	6,562.8	9,973.5
Transport	1,914.3	12,500.8	16,591.7
Communications	202.5	2,366.5	3,855.8
Trade and catering	1,798.1	9,191.1	14,058.5
Material supply	743.8	3,271.5	2,967.1
Procurement	87.1	442.4	542.8
Housing	296.4	2,323.3	3,217.4
Public utilities	437.3	2,377.7	3,264.8
Health care	507.7	3,583.8	5,547.0
Education	613.9	4,272.3	7,663.1
Culture and science	213.2	1,435.5	1,923.8
Banks and insurance	1,339.9	4,993.1	3,992.9
Public administration and defence	616.4	4,236.8	6,856.3
Other services	178.3	1,582.2	2,660.4
Sub-total	17,194.0	112,164.9	163,468.0
Less Imputed bank service charge	1,196.1	4,128.3	3,112.5
GDP at factor cost	15,987.3	108,036.6	160,355.5
Indirect taxes, *less* subsidies	1,674.0	11,776.5	19,464.1
GDP in purchasers' values	17,661.3	119,813.1	179,819.6

* Figures are preliminary.

† Principally mining, manufacturing, electricity, gas and water.

BALANCE OF PAYMENTS (US $ million)

	1993	1994	1995
Exports of goods f.o.b.	2,812	2,641	4,621
Imports of goods f.o.b.	−3,863	−3,351	−5,149
Trade balance	−1,051	−710	−529
Exports of services } Imports of services }	−119	94	262
Balance on goods and services	−1,170	−616	−267
Other income received } Other income paid }	−12	−33	−66
Balance on goods, services and income	−1,182	−649	−333
Current transfers (net)	69	50	79
Current balance	−1,113	−599	−254
Capital transfers	n.a.	n.a.	7
Direct investment (net)	18	10	7
Other long-term capital (net)	320	193	79
Short-term capital (net)	212	586	−10
Net errors and omissions	381	−452	−41
Overall balance	−182	−261	−212

Source: IMF Staff Country Report, September 1996.

External Trade

PRINCIPAL COMMODITIES (million roubles at domestic prices)

Imports	1994	1995*	1996*
Industrial products	13,064,530	61,973,336	88,240,289
Electric energy	191,688	1,413,048	2,414,738
Petroleum and gas	5,500,688	20,077,080	24,656,946
Iron and steel	761,307	4,422,713	8,897,745
Non-ferrous metallurgy	225,307	750,603	1,891,725
Chemical and petroleum products	2,068,181	9,986,341	15,293,645
Machinery and metalworking	2,500,104	13,641,080	17,554,312
Wood and paper products	248,515	1,417,537	2,389,820
Light industry	590,435	2,188,130	3,934,900
Food and beverages	486,468	6,108,864	8,179,958
Agricultural products (unprocessed)	398,788	1,180,077	4,610,398
Total (incl. others)	13,492,447	63,752,635	92,850,698
USSR (former)†	9,730,311	42,105,783	61,430,171
Other countries	3,762,136	21,646,852	31,420,527

Exports	1994	1995*	1996*
Industrial products	10,177,031	53,503,552	71,069,320
Petroleum and gas	1,522,164	6,272,076	8,802,010
Iron and steel	510,229	2,415,472	4,582,615
Non-ferrous metallurgy	224,109	194,832	575,095
Chemical and petroleum products	2,062,510	14,352,906	15,524,385
Machinery and metalworking	3,650,876	17,728,338	23,271,904
Wood and paper products	451,422	2,998,971	4,218,808
Construction materials	267,081	1,395,122	1,717,107
Light industry	977,388	3,805,935	6,040,811
Food and beverages	366,585	3,884,202	5,237,490
Agricultural products (unprocessed)	32,833	501,661	1,504,402
Total (incl. others)	10,219,163	54,035,811	72,573,792
USSR (former)†	6,878,015	33,558,880	48,185,480
Other countries	3,341,148	20,476,931	24,388,312

* Figures are calculated on the basis of customs declarations.
† Excluding trade with Estonia, Latvia and Lithuania.

PRINCIPAL TRADING PARTNERS

Trade with the former USSR (excluding trade with Estonia, Latvia and Lithuania; million roubles at domestic prices)

Imports f.o.b.	1994	1995*	1996*
Kazakhstan	159,115	645,564	762,711
Moldova	42,180	403,397	649,962
Russia	8,716,730	33,908,300	47,142,914
Ukraine	702,483	6,552,982	12,174,038
Uzbekistan	51,371	422,231	493,672
Total (incl. others)	9,730,311	42,105,783	61,430,171

Exports f.o.b.	1994	1995*	1996*
Kazakhstan	116,491	880,941	1,103,172
Moldova	130,407	816,762	920,260
Russia	5,385,069	23,854,800	38,364,786
Ukraine	1,142,342	7,010,394	6,378,435
Uzbekistan	49,250	691,244	1,020,625
Total (incl. others)	6,878,015	33,558,880	48,185,480

* Figures are calculated on the basis of customs declarations.

Trade with Other Countries (US $ million)

Imports	1993	1995*†	1996†
Europe	603	1,494	1,947
Austria	46	45	54
Germany	179	413	601
Poland	22	197	195
Switzerland	59	17	38
USA	87	97	152
Total (incl. others)	996	1,887	2,369

Exports	1993	1995*†	1996†
Europe	390	1,378	1,398
Austria	27	18	15
Germany	100	275	198
Italy	25	61	57
Poland	106	271	325
Switzerland	27	8	20
Turkey	31	34	30
USA	39	58	61
Total (incl. others)	838	1,776	1,816

* Figures for 1994 are unavailable.
† Figures are calculated on the basis of customs declarations.

Transport

RAILWAYS (traffic)

	1994	1995	1996
Passenger-km (million)	16,063	12,505	11,657
Freight ton-km (million)	27,963	25,510	26,018

ROAD TRAFFIC (motor vehicles in use at 31 December)

	1994	1995	1996
Passenger cars	875,612	939,595	1,048,015
Buses and coaches	9,782	9,289	8,922

CIVIL AVIATION (traffic on scheduled services)

	1994	1995	1996
Passengers carried ('000)	423	387	362
Passenger-km (million)	1,390	1,228	1,085
Total ton-km (million)	68	60	123

Communications Media

	1994	1995	1996
Book production*:			
titles	3,346	3,205	3,809
copies ('000)	80,606	62,859	59,073
Daily newspapers:			
number	11	10	12
average circulation ('000)	2,007	1,480	1,261
Non-daily newspapers:			
number	413	484	500
average circulation ('000)	7,057	7,024	7,825
Other periodicals:			
number	215	225	269
average circulation ('000)	2,443	1,421	1,424

* Including pamphlets (1,016 titles and 16,918,000 copies in 1994; 817 titles and 16,577,000 copies in 1995; 1,015 titles and 16,789,000 copies in 1996).

Telephones ('000 main lines in use): 1,892 in 1994; 1,968 in 1995; 2,128 in 1996.

Telefax stations (number in use): 1,514 in 1992; 3,160 in 1993.

Mobile cellular telephones (subscribers): 324 in 1993.

Radio receivers ('000 in use): 3,138 in 1994; 3,031 in 1995; 3,021 in 1996.

Television receivers ('000 in use): 3,337 in 1994; 3,139 in 1995; 3,040 in 1996.

Education

(1995/96)

	Institutions	Teachers	Students
Pre-primary	4,576	54,749	458,000
Primary (Grades 1–4) Secondary (Grades 5–11)	4,921	141,495	1,561,100
Vocational and technical	252	14,100	130,100
Specialized secondary	146	8,410	121,600
Higher	39	15,100	174,200
Institutions offering post-graduate studies	94	1,964	3,082

Source: Ministry of Education and Science, Minsk.

Directory

The Constitution

A new Constitution came into effect on 30 March 1994. An amended version of the 1994 Constitution became effective on 27 November 1996, following a referendum held on 24 November. The following is a summary of its main provisions:

PRINCIPLES OF THE CONSTITUTIONAL SYSTEM

The Republic of Belarus is a unitary, democratic, social state based on the rule of law. The people are the sole source of state power and the repository of sovereignty in the Republic of Belarus. The people shall exercise their power directly through representative and other bodies in the forms and within the bounds specified by the Constitution. Democracy in the Republic of Belarus is exercised on the basis of diversity of political institutions, ideologies and opinions. State power in the Republic of Belarus is exercised on the principle of division of powers between the legislature, executive and judiciary, which are independent of one another. The Republic of Belarus is bound by the principle of supremacy of law; it recognizes the supremacy of the universally acknowledged principles of international law and ensures that its laws comply with such principles. Property may be the ownership of the State or private. The mineral wealth, waters and forests are the sole and exclusive property of the State. Land for agricultural use is the property of the State. All religions and creeds are equal before the law. The official languages of the Republic of Belarus are Belarusian and Russian. The Republic of Belarus aims to make its territory a neutral, nuclear-free state. The capital is Minsk.

THE INDIVIDUAL, SOCIETY AND THE STATE

All persons are equal before the law and entitled without discrimination to equal protection of their rights and legitimate interests. Every person has the right to life. Until its abolition, the death penalty may be applied in accordance with the verdict of a court of law as an exceptional penalty for especially grave crimes. The State ensures the freedom, inviolability and dignity of the individual. No person may be subjected to torture or cruel, inhuman or humiliating treatment or punishment. Freedom of movement is guaranteed. Every person is guaranteed freedom of opinion and beliefs and their free expression. The right to assemble publicly is guaranteed, as is the right to form public associations, including trade unions. Citizens of the Republic of Belarus have the right to participate in the solution of state matters, both directly and through freely elected representatives; the right to vote freely and to be elected to state bodies on the basis of universal, equal, direct or indirect suffrage by secret ballot. The State shall create the conditions necessary for full employment. The right to health care is guaranteed, as is the right to social security in old age, in the event of illness, disability and in other instances. Each person has the right to housing and to education. Everyone has the right to preserve his or her ethnic affiliation, to use his or her native language and to choose the language of communication. Payment of statutory taxes and other levies is obligatory. Every person is guaranteed the protection of his or her rights and freedom by a competent, independent and impartial court of law, and every person has the right to legal assistance.

THE ELECTORAL SYSTEM AND REFERENDUMS

Elections and referendums are conducted by means of universal, free, equal and secret ballot. Citizens of the Republic of Belarus who have reached the age of 18 years are eligible to vote. Deputies are elected by direct ballot. Referendums may be held to resolve the most important issues of the State and society. National referendums may be called by the President of the Republic of Belarus, by the National Assembly or by no fewer than 450,000 citizens eligible to vote. Local referendums may be called by local representative bodies or on the recommendation of no less than 10% of the citizens who are eligible to vote and resident in the area concerned. Decisions adopted by referendum may be reversed or amended only by means of another referendum.

THE PRESIDENT

The President of the Republic of Belarus is Head of State, the guarantor of the Constitution of the Republic of Belarus, and of the rights and freedoms of its citizens. The President is elected for a term of five years by universal, free, equal, direct and secret ballot for no more than two terms.

The President calls national referendums; calls elections to the National Assembly and local representative bodies; dissolves the chambers of the National Assembly, as determined by the Constitution; appoints six members to the Central Electoral Commission; forms, dissolves and reorganizes the Administration of the President, as well as other bodies of state administration; appoints the Chairman of the Cabinet of Ministers (Prime Minister) of the Republic of Belarus with the consent of the House of Representatives; determines the structure of the Government, appoints and dismisses Ministers and other members of the Government, and considers the resignation of the Government; appoints, with the consent of the Council of the Republic, the Chairman of the Constitutional, Supreme and Economic Courts, the judges of the Supreme and Economic Courts, the Chairman of the Central Electoral Commission, the Procurator General, the Chairman and members of the board of the National Bank, and dismisses the aforementioned, having notified the Council of the Republic; appoints six members of the Constitutional Court, and other judges of the Republic of Belarus; appoints and dismisses the Chairman of the State Supervisory Committee; reports to the people of the Republic of Belarus on the state of the nation and on domestic and foreign policy; may chair meetings of the Government of the Republic of Belarus; conducts negotiations and signs international treaties, appoints and recalls diplomatic representatives of the Republic of Belarus; in the event of a natural disaster, a catastrophe, or unrest involving violence or the threat of violence that may endanger people's lives or jeopardize the territorial integrity of the State, declares a state of emergency; has the right to abolish acts of the Government and to suspend decisions of local councils of deputies; forms and heads the Security Council of the Republic of Belarus, and appoints and dismisses the Supreme State Secretary of the Security Council; is the Commander-in-Chief of the Armed Forces and appoints and dismisses the Supreme Command of the Armed Forces; imposes, in the event of military threat or attack, martial law in the Republic of Belarus; issues decrees and orders which are mandatory in the Republic of Belarus. In instances determined by the Constitution, the President may issue decrees which have the force of law. The President may be removed from office for acts of state treason and other grave crimes, by a decision of the National Assembly.

THE NATIONAL ASSEMBLY

The National Assembly is a representative and legislative body of the Republic of Belarus, consisting of two chambers: the House of Representatives and the Council of the Republic. The term of the National Assembly is four years. The House of Representatives comprises 110 deputies. Deputies are elected by universal, equal, free, direct suffrage and by secret ballot. The Council of the Republic is a chamber of territorial representation, consisting of eight deputies from every region and from Minsk, elected by deputies of local councils. Eight members of the Council of the Republic are appointed by the President. Any citizen who has reached the age of 21 years may become a deputy of the House of Representatives. Any citizen who has reached the age of 30 years, and who has been resident in the corresponding region for no less than five years, may become a member of the Council of the Republic. The chambers of the National Assembly elect their Chairmen.

The House of Representatives considers draft laws concerning amendments and alterations to the Constitution; domestic and foreign policy; the military doctrine; ratification and denunciation of international treaties; the approval of the republican budget; the introduction of national taxes and levies; local self-government; the administration of justice; the declaration of war and the conclusion of peace; martial law and a state of emergency; and the interpretation of laws. The House of Representatives calls elections for the presidency; grants consent to the President concerning the appointment of the Chairman of the Cabinet of Ministers; accepts the resignation of the President; together with the Council of the Republic, takes the decision to remove the President from office.

The Council of the Republic approves or rejects draft laws adopted by the House of Representatives; consents to appointments made by the President; elects six judges of the Constitutional Court and six members of the Central Electoral Commission; considers charges of treason against the President; takes the decision to remove the President from office; considers presidential decrees on the introduction of a state of emergency, martial law, and general or partial mobilization.

Any proposed legislation is considered initially in the House of Representatives and then in the Council of the Republic. On the proposal of the President, the House of Representatives and the Council of the Republic may adopt a law, delegating to him legislative powers to issue decrees which have the power of a law.

THE GOVERNMENT

Executive power in the Republic of Belarus is exercised by the Cabinet of Ministers. The Government is accountable to the President and responsible to the National Assembly. The Chairman of the Cabinet of Ministers is appointed by the President with the consent of the House of Representatives. The Government of the Republic of Belarus formulates and implements domestic and foreign policy; submits the draft national budget to the President; and issues acts that have binding force.

THE JUDICIARY

Judicial authority in the Republic of Belarus is exercised by the courts. Justice is administered on the basis of adversarial proceedings and equality of the parties involved in the trial. Supervision of the constitutionality of enforceable enactments of the State is exercised by the Constitutional Court, which comprises 12 judges (six of whom are appointed by the President and six are elected by the Council of the Republic).

LOCAL GOVERNMENT AND SELF-GOVERNMENT

Citizens exercise local and self-government through local councils of deputies, executive and administrative bodies and other forms of direct participation in state and public affairs. Local councils of deputies are elected by citizens for a four-year term, and the heads of local executive and administrative bodies are appointed and dismissed by the President of the Republic of Belarus.

THE PROCURATOR'S OFFICE AND THE STATE SUPERVISORY COMMITTEE

The Procurator's office exercises supervision over the implementation of the law. The Procurator General is appointed by the President with the consent of the Council of the Republic, and is accountable to the President. The Supervisory Authority monitors the implementation of the national budget and the use of public property. The State Supervisory Committee is formed by the President, who appoints the Chairman.

APPLICATION OF THE CONSTITUTION AND THE PROCEDURE FOR AMENDING THE CONSTITUTION

The Constitution has supreme legal force. Amendments and supplements to the Constitution are considered by the chambers of the National Assembly on the initiative of the President, or of no fewer than 150,000 citizens of the Republic of Belarus who are eligible to vote. The Constitution may be amended or supplemented via a referendum.

The Government

HEAD OF STATE

President: ALYAKSANDR R. LUKASHENKA (took office 20 July 1994).

CABINET OF MINISTERS

(December 1997)

Chairman: SYARGEY LING.

First Deputy Chairman: PYOTR PRAKAPOVICH.

Deputy Chairmen: VASIL DALGALYOU, ULADZIMIR G. GARKUN, ULADZIMIR ZAMYATALIN, ULADZIMIR I. KOKARAU, GENADZ NAVITSKY.

Minister of Agriculture and Food: IVAN SHAKOLA.

Minister of Architecture and Construction: VIKTAR VYATROU.

Minister for CIS Affairs: VALYANTSIN VYALICHKA.

Minister of Culture: ALYAKSANDR U. SASNOUSKI.

Minister of Defence: Lt-Gen. ALYAKSANDR CHUMAKOU.

Minister of the Economy: ULADZIMIR SHYMAU.

Minister of Education: VASIL I. STRAZHAU.

Minister for Emergency Situations: IVAN A. KENIK.

Minister of Entrepreneurship and Investments: ALYAKSANDR YU. SASONAU.

Minister of Finance: MIKALAI P. KORBUT.

Minister of Foreign Affairs: IVAN ANTANOVICH.

Minister of Foreign Economic Relations: MIKHAIL A. MARYNICH.

Minister of Forestry: VALYANTSIN P. ZORYN.

Minister of Fuel and Energy: VALYANTSIN V. GERASIMAU.

Minister of Health Care: IGAR ZELYANKEVICH.

Minister of Housing and Municipal Services: BARYS V. BATURA.

Minister of Industry: ANATOL KHARLAP.

Minister of Internal Affairs: Maj.-Gen. VALYANTSIN S. AGALETS.

Minister of Justice: GENADZ VARANTSOU.

Minister of Labour: IVAN LYAKH.

Minister for Natural Resources and Environmental Protection: MIKHAIL I. RUSY.

Minister of Post and Telecommunications: ULADZIMIR I. GANCHARENKA.

Minister for Social Protection: VOLGA B. DARGEL.

Minister of Sports and Tourism: ULADZIMIR MAKEYCHYK.

Minister of State Property Management and Privatization: VASIL A. NOVAK.

Minister of Statistics and Analysis: ULADZIMIR N. NICHYPAROVICH.

Minister of Trade: PYOTR A. KAZLOU.

Minister of Transport and Communications: ALYAKSANDR LUKASHOU.

Head of the Presidential Administration: MIKHAIL MYASNIKOVICH.

Chairman of the National Bank: GENADZ ALEYNIKAW.

Chairmen of State Committees

Chairman of the State Security Committee: ULADZIMIR MATSKEVICH.

Chairman of the State Committee for the Press: ZINOVI PRYGODZICH (acting).

Chairman of the State Committee for Aviation: RYGOR FYODARAW.

Chairman of the State Committee for Youth Affairs: ALYAKSANDR PAZNYAK.

Chairman of the State Customs Committee: VIKENTSI MAKAREVICH (acting).

Chairman of the State Taxation Committee: MIKALAY DZYAMCHUK.

Chairman of the State Committee for Border Troops: ALYAKSANDR PAWLOUWKI.

Chairman of the State Committee for Land Resources, Geodesy and Cartography: GEORGIY KUZNYATSOW.

Chairman of the State Committee for Energy and Energy Supervision: LEW DUBOVIK.

Chairman of the State Committee for Archives and Records: ALYAKSANDR MIKHALCHANKA.

Chairman of the State Patents Committee: VALERY KUDASHOW.

Chairman of the State Committee for Standardization, Metrology and Certification: VALERY KARASHKOW.

Chairman of the State Committee for Hydrometeorology: YURY PAKUMEYKA.

Chairman of the State Higher Appraisal Committee: ANATOL DASTANKA.

Chairman of the State Committee for Science and Technology: VIKTAR GAYSYONAK.

Chairman of the State Committee for Religious and Ethnic Affairs: ALYAKSANDR BELYK.

Chairman of the State Control Committee: MIKALAY DAMASHKEVICH.

Chairman of the State Committee for Material Resources: ULADZIMIR I. YARMOLIK.

MINISTRIES AND STATE COMMITTEES

Ministries

Cabinet of Ministers of the Republic of Belarus: 220010 Minsk, pl. Nezalezhnasti, Dom Urada; tel. (172) 22-69-05; fax (172) 22-66-65.

Ministry of Agriculture and Food: 220050 Minsk, vul. Kirava 15; tel. (172) 27-37-51; fax (172) 27-43-88.

Ministry of Architecture and Construction: 220079 Minsk, vul. Myasnikova 39; tel. (172) 27-26-42; fax (172) 20-74-24.

Ministry for CIS Affairs: 220010 Minsk, pl. Nezalezhnasti, Dom Urada; tel. (172) 22-63-37; fax (172) 22-66-65.

Ministry of Culture: 220004 Minsk, pr. Masherava 11; tel. (172) 23-75-74; fax (172) 23-58-25.

Ministry of Defence: 220001 Minsk, vul. Kamunistychnaya 1; tel. (172) 39-23-79; fax (172) 27-35-64.

Ministry of the Economy: 220050 Minsk, vul. Stankevicha 14; tel. (172) 22-60-48; fax (172) 22-63-35.

Ministry of Education: 220010 Minsk, vul. Savetskaya 9; tel. (172) 27-47-36; fax (172) 20-80-57.

Ministry for Emergency Situations: 220004 Minsk, pr. Masherava 23; tel. (172) 27-58-63; fax (172) 29-34-39.

Ministry of Entrepreneurship and Investments: 220050 Minsk, vul. Myasnikova 39; tel. (172) 20-16-23; fax (172) 27-22-40.

Ministry of Finance: 220048 Minsk, vul. Savetskaya 7; tel. (172) 22-61-37; telex 252622; fax (172) 20-21-72; e-mail mofb@office.un.minsk.by.

Ministry of Foreign Affairs: 220030 Minsk, vul. Lenina 19; tel. (172) 27-29-22; fax (172) 27-45-21.

Ministry of Foreign Economic Relations: 220050 Minsk, vul. Myasnikova 29; tel. (172) 20-26-35; fax (172) 27-39-24.

Ministry of Forestry: 220039 Minsk, vul. Chkalova 6; tel. (172) 24-47-05; fax (172) 24-41-83.

Ministry of Fuel and Energy: 220050 Minsk, vul. K. Marksa 14; tel. (172) 29-83-59; fax (172) 29-84-68.

Ministry of Health Care: 220096 Minsk, vul. Myasnikova 39; tel. (172) 22-60-33; fax (172) 22-62-97.

Ministry of Housing and Municipal Services: 220050 Minsk, vul. Bersana 16; tel. (172) 20-15-45; telex 252121; fax (172) 20-38-94.

Ministry of Industry: 220033 Minsk, pr. Partizanski 2-4; tel. (172) 24-95-95; fax (172) 24-87-84.

Ministry of Internal Affairs: 220050 Minsk, Gorodskoy Val 4; tel. (172) 29-78-08; fax (172) 23-99-18.

Ministry of Justice: 220048 Minsk, vul. Kalektarnaya 10; tel. and fax (172) 20-97-55.

Ministry of Labour: 220004 Minsk, pr. Masherava 23; tel. (172) 23-11-71; fax (172) 23-45-21.

Ministry for Natural Resources and Environmental Protection: 220048 Minsk, vul. Kalektarnaya 10; tel. (172) 20-66-91; fax (172) 20-55-83; e-mail minproos@minproos.belpak.minsk.by.

Ministry of Post and Telecommunications: 220050 Minsk, pr. F. Skaryny 10; tel. (172) 27-38-61; fax (172) 26-08-48.

Ministry for Social Protection: 220010 Minsk, vul. Savetskaya 9; tel. (172) 22-62-55; fax (172) 22-69-90.

Ministry of Sports and Tourism: 220600 Minsk, vul. Kirava 8-2; tel. (172) 27-72-37; fax (172) 27-76-22.

Ministry of State Property Management and Privatization: 220050 Minsk, vul. Myasnikova 39; tel. (172) 76-81-78; fax (172) 20-65-47.

Ministry of Statistics and Analysis: 220070 Minsk, pr. Partizanski 12; tel. (172) 49-52-00; fax (172) 49-22-04; e-mail svet@domhos.belpak.minsk.by.

Ministry of Trade: 220050 Minsk, vul. Kirava 8, kor. 1; tel. (172) 27-08-97; fax (172) 27-24-80.

Ministry of Transport and Communications: 220000 Minsk, vul. Chicherina 21; tel. (172) 34-11-52; fax (172) 32-83-91.

State Committees

All State Committees are in Minsk.

State Customs Committee: 220029 Minsk, vul. Kamunistychnaya 11; tel. (172) 33-23-16; fax (172) 34-68-93.

State Security Committee: 220050 Minsk, pr. F. Skaryny 17; tel. (172) 29-94-01; fax (172) 26-00-38.

State Committee for Religious and Ethnic Affairs: 220050 Minsk, vul. Bersana 1A; tel. and fax (172) 22-69-50.

President and Legislature

PRESIDENT

Presidential Election, First Ballot, 23 June 1994

Candidates	Votes	%
ALYAKSANDR LUKASHENKA	2,646,140	47.10
VYACHESLAU KEBICH	1,023,174	18.21
ZYANON PAZNYAK	757,195	13.48
STANISLAU SHUSHKEVICH	585,143	10.42
ALYAKSANDR DUBKO	353,119	6.29
VASIL NOVIKAU	253,009	4.50
Total	5,617,780	100.00

Second Ballot, 10 July 1994 (preliminary result)

Candidates	Votes	%
ALYAKSANDR LUKASHENKA	4,219,991	84.95
VYACHESLAU KEBICH	747,793	15.05
Total	4,967,784	100.00

NATIONAL ASSEMBLY*

Council of the Republic

Chairman: PAVEL SHYPUK.

Deputy Chairman: TAMARA DUDKO.

The Council of the Republic is the upper chamber of the legislature and comprises 64 deputies. Of the total, 56 deputies are elected by regional councils and eight deputies are appointed by the President.

House of Representatives

Chairman: ANATOL MALAFEYEU.

Deputy Chairman: ULADZIMIR KANAPLYOW.

The House of Representatives is the lower chamber of the legislature and comprises 110 deputies elected by universal, equal, free, direct electoral suffrage and by secret ballot.

* The National Assembly was formed following a referendum held on 24 November 1996. Deputies who had been elected to the Supreme Council at the general election held in late 1995 were invited to participate in the new legislative body. However, many deputies regarded the new National Assembly as unconstitutional and declared themselves to be the legitimate legislature. A form of 'shadow' cabinet, the Public Coalition Government–National Economic Council, chaired by Genadz Karpenka, was established in January 1997 by opposition deputies. International organizations

continued to urge President Lukashenka to recognize the legitimacy of the Supreme Council.

Political Organizations

In October 1997 there were 35 political parties officially registered with the Ministry of Justice.

Agrarian Party (AP) (Agrarnaya Partya): 220050 Minsk, vul. Myasnikova 32; tel. (172) 20-38-29; fax (172) 49-50-18; f. 1992; Leaders SYAMYON SHARETSKI, ANATOL YUNTSEVICH.

All-Belarusian Party of Popular Unity and Accord (Vsebelaruskaya Partya Narodnaga Adzinstva i Zgody): Minsk, pr. F. Skaryny 74A; tel. (172) 29-36-60; f. 1994; Leader DZMITRY BULAKHAU.

Belarusian Christian-Democratic Party (Belaruskaya Khrystsiyanska-Demakratychnaya Partya): Minsk, vul. Bagdanovicha 7A; f. 1994; Leader MIKALAY KRUKOUSKI.

Belarusian Christian-Democratic Union (Belaruskaya Khrystsiyanska-Demakratychnaya Zluchnasts): 220065 Minsk, vul. Avakyana 38-59; tel. and fax (172) 29-67-56; f. 1991; nationalist, reformist; Leader PETR SILKO.

Belarusian Ecological Party (Belaruskaya Ekalagichnaya Partya): 220068 Minsk, vul. Asipenki 19-51; tel. (172) 37-29-41; fax (172) 56-82-72; f. 1993; Leaders LYUDMILA ELIZARAVA, MIKALAY FRADLYAND.

Belarusian Greenpeace Party (Belaruskaya Partya Zyaleny Mir): 246012 Gomel, vul. Kosareva 41-36; tel. (232) 47-96-96; fax (232) 53-84-73; f. 1994; Leader ALEG GRAMYKA.

Belarusian National Party (Belaruskaya Natsiyanalnaya Partya): 220094 Minsk, vul. Plekhanava 32-198; tel. (172) 27-43-76; f. 1994; Leader ANATOL ASTAPENKA.

Belarusian Party 'For Social Justice' (Belaruskaya Partya 'Za Satsiyalnuyu Spravyadlivasts'): 220050 Minsk, vul. Internatsiyanalnaya 13A; tel. (172) 23-37-10; f. 1996; Leader IGAR KLYUEU.

Belarusian Party of Labour (Belaruskaya Partya Pratsy): Minsk, vul. Kazintsa 21-3; tel. (172) 23-82-04; fax (172) 23-97-92; f. 1993; Leader ALYAKSANDR BUKHVOSTAU.

Belarusian Party of Women 'Hope' (Belaruskaya Partya Zhanchyn 'Nadzeya'): 220099 Minsk, vul. Kazintsa 21-3; f. 1994; Leader VALENTINA PALEVIKOVA.

Belarusian Patriotic Party (Belaruskaya Patryatychnaya Partya): 220050 Minsk, vul. Myasnikova 38; tel. (172) 20-27-57; f. 1994; Leader ANATOL BARANKEVICH.

Belarusian Peasant Party (Belaruskaya Syalyanskaya Partya): 220068 Minsk, vul. Gaya 38-1; tel. (172) 77-19-05; fax (172) 77-96-51; f. 1991; advocates agricultural reforms; 7,000 mems; Leader YAUGEN M. LUGIN.

Belarusian Popular Party (Belaruskaya Narodnaya Partya): 220050 Minsk, vul. K. Marksa 18; tel. (172) 27-89-52; f. 1994; Leader VIKTAR TERESCHENKO.

Belarusian Republican Party (Belaruskaya Respublikanskaya Partya): 220100 Minsk, vul. Kulman 13-71; tel. (172) 34-07-49; f. 1994; Leaders VALERY ARTYSHEUSKI, ULADZIMIR RAMANAU.

Belarusian United Sports Party (Belaruskaya Abyadnanaya Spartyunaya Partya): 220088 Minsk, vul. Salomennaya 23; tel. (172) 76-89-85; f. 1994; Leader IGAR RAZHNOUSKI.

Belarusian Scientific Production Congress (Belaruski Navukova-Vytvorchy Kangres): 220007 Minsk, vul. Magileuskaya 39-308; tel. (172) 29-82-63; fax (172) 27-15-49; f. 1992; Leader ALYAKSANDR SANCHUKOUSKI.

Belarusian Social Democratic Party (National Assembly) (Belaruskaya Satsyal-demakratychnaya Partya (Narodnaya Hramada): 220026 Minsk, pr. Partizanski 83, room 53; tel. (172) 46-46-91; fax (172) 45-78-52; f. 1903, re-established 1991; merged with Party of People's Accord (f. 1992) in 1996; centrist; Leader MIKALAI STATKEVICH; c. 2,500 mems.

Belarusian Socialist Party (Belaruskaya Satsyalistychnaya Partya): Minsk, pr. F. Skaryny 25; tel. (172) 29-37-38; f. 1994; aims for a civilized society, where rights and freedoms are guaranteed for all; Leader VYACHESLAU KUZNYATSOU.

Belarusian Social-Sports Party (Belaruskaya Satsyalna-Spartyunaya Partya): 220000 Minsk, pr. Partizanski 89A; tel. (172) 26-93-15; f. 1994; Leader ULADZIMIR ALYAKSANDROVICH.

Christian-Democratic Choice (Khrystsiyanska-Demakratychny Vybar): 220050 Minsk, vul. Leningradskaya 3-1; tel. (172) 20-17-67; f. 1995; Leader VALERY SAROKA.

Communist Party of Belarus (CPB) (Kamunistychnaya Partya Belarusi): 220007 Minsk, vul. Varanyanskaga 52; tel. (172) 26-64-22; fax (172) 32-31-23; Leader VIKTAR CHYKIN.

Green Party of Belarus (Belaruskaya Partya Zyalenykh): 246027 Gomel, vul. Zakhodnaya 33; tel. (232) 55-42-37; fax (232) 57-73-59; f. 1992; Leader MIKALAY KARAVAYCHYK.

Liberal Democratic Party of Belarus (Liberalna-Demakratychnaya Partya Belarusi): 220056 Minsk, vul. Sadovaya 6A-34; tel. (172) 69-59-09; fax (172) 47-72-57; f. 1994; advocates economic and political union with Russia; Leader SYARGEY GAYDUKEVICH; 3,000 mems.

National Democratic Party of Belarus (Natsyanalna-Demakratychnaya Partya Belarusi): 220116 Minsk, pr. Partizanski 83-59; tel. (172) 71-95-16; fax (172) 36-99-72; f. 1990; Leader VIKTAR NAVUMENKA.

Party of Beer Lovers (Partya Lyubiteley Piva): Minsk, vul. Kaltsova 12-3-29; tel. (172) 52-29-76; f. 1993; Leader ANDREY RAMASHEYSKI.

Party of Belarusian Popular Front (BPF) (Partya Belaruskaga Narodnaga Frontu): 220005 Minsk, vul. Varvasheni 8; tel. (172) 31-48-93; fax (172) 39-58-69; f. 1988; anti-communist movement campaigning for democracy, genuine independence for Belarus and national and cultural revival; Chair. ZYANON PAZNYAK; Acting Chair. LYAVON BARSHCHEWSKI; Sec. VYACHESLAU SIWCHYK.

Party 'Cleansing' (Partya 'Achyschenne'): 230023 Grodna, vul. Savetskaya 31-7; f. 1995; Leader BARYS BARYKIN.

Party of Common Sense (Partya Zdarovaga Sensu): 220094 Minsk, pr. Rakasouskaga 37-40; tel. (172) 47-08-68; f. 1994; Leader IVAN KARAVAYCHYK.

Party of Communists of Belarus (Partya Kamunistau Belaruskaya): 220123 Minsk, vul. V. Haruzhay 24-2-17; tel. (172) 32-31-23; f. 1991; Leader SERGEY KALYAKIN.

Popular Party 'Revival' (Narodnaya Partya 'Adradzhenne'): 212009 Mogilev, vul. Budaunikou 14A; tel. (172) 26-30-59; f. 1995; Leader VALENTIN JEZHULA.

Republican Party (Respublikanskaya Partya): 220000 Minsk, vul. Pershamayskaya 18; tel. (172) 36-50-71; fax (172) 36-32-14; f. 1994; aims to build a neutral, independent Belarus; Leader ULADZIMIR BELAZOR.

Republican Party of Labour and Justice (Respublikanskaya Partya Pratsy i Spravyadlivasti): 220004 Minsk, vul. Amuratarskaya 7; tel. (172) 23-93-21; fax (172) 23-86-41; f. 1993; Leader ANATOL NYATYLKIN.

Slavonic Council 'Belaya Rus' (Slavyanski Sabor 'Belaya Rus'): 220088 Minsk, vul. Pershamayskaya 24-1-80; tel. (172) 39-52-32; fax (172) 70-09-28; f. 1992; Leader MIKALAY SYARGEEU.

Social-Democratic Party of Popular Accord (Satsiyal-Demakratychnaya Partya Narodnay Zgody): 220050 Minsk, vul. K. Marksa 10; tel. (172) 48-02-21; f. 1997; Leader LEANID SECHKA.

United Civic Party of Belarus (Abyadnanaya Hramadzyanskaya Partya Belarusi): 220033 Minsk, vul. Sudmalisa 10-4; tel. (172) 29-08-34; fax (172) 27-29-12; e-mail ucp@ucp.minsk.by; f. 1990; liberal-conservative; Chair. STANISLAU A. BAHDANKEVICH; Dep. Chair. ALYAKSANDR A. DABRAVOLSKI, VASILY SHLYNDZIKAV, ANATOL U. LIABEDZKA.

Diplomatic Representation

EMBASSIES IN BELARUS

Armenia: 220020 Minsk, vul. Drozdy; tel. (172) 27-51-53; fax (172) 27-23-39; Chargé d'affaires a.i.: SPARTAK KOSTANIAN.

Bulgaria: 220034 Minsk, Branyavy per. 5; tel. (172) 27-55-02; fax (172) 36-56-61; Ambassador: MARKO GANCHEV.

China, People's Republic: 220071 Minsk, vul. Berestyanskaya 22; tel. (172) 22-44-95; fax (172) 22-44-96; Ambassador: ZHAO XIDI.

Czech Republic: 220034 Minsk, Branyavy per. 5A; tel. (172) 36-42-44; fax (172) 36-74-35; Chargé d'affaires a.i.: DUŠAN DOSKOČIL.

Estonia: 220029 Minsk, vul. Varvasheni 17; tel. (172) 34-59-65; fax (172) 10-12-60.

France: 220030 Minsk, pl. Svabody 11; tel. (172) 10-28-68; fax (172) 10-25-48; Ambassador: BERNARD FASSIER.

Germany: 220034 Minsk, vul. Zakharava 26B; tel. (172) 33-07-52; fax (172) 36-85-52; Ambassador: GOTTFRIED ALBRECHT.

Greece: 220030 Minsk, vul. Engelsa 13; tel. (172) 27-27-60; fax (172) 26-08-05.

Holy See: Minsk, vul. Volodarsky 6, 3rd Floor; tel. (172) 76-85-84; fax (172) 76-85-17; Apostolic Nuncio: Most Rev. HRUŠOVSKÝ DOMINIK, Titular Archbishop of Tubia.

India: 220090 Minsk, vul. Kaltsova 4, kor. 5; tel. (172) 62-93-99; telex 252510; fax (172) 62-97-99; Ambassador: RAMESH CHANDRA SHUKLA.

Israel: 220033 Minsk, pr. Partizanski 6A; tel. (172) 30-44-44; fax (172) 10-52-70; Ambassador: ELIAHU VALK.

Italy: 220030 Minsk, vul. K. Marska 37, Hotel Belarus; tel. (172) 29-29-69; fax (172) 34-30-46; Ambassador: GIOVANNI CERUTI.

Japan: 220030 Minsk, vul. Engelsa 13, Hotel Oktyabrskaya, Room 303; tel. (172) 27-47-18; fax (172) 27-43-19; Chargé d'affaires a.i.: SHIGEO NATSUI.

Kazakhstan: 220088 Minsk, vul. Kuibysheva 12; tel. (172) 34-99-37; fax (172) 34-96-50; Ambassador: VALERY TEMIRBAYEV.

Kyrgyzstan: 220052 Minsk, vul. Staravilenskaya 57; tel. (172) 34-91-17; fax (172) 34-16-02; e-mail manas@nsys.minsk.by; Ambassador: ESENGUL OMURALIEV.

Latvia: 220029 Minsk, vul. Starazhouskaya 15; tel. (172) 39-16-31; fax (172) 50-67-84; Chargé d'affaires a.i.: INGRĪDA LEVRENCE.

Lithuania: 220029 Minsk, vul. Varvasheni 17; tel. (172) 34-72-00; fax (172) 76-94-71; Ambassador: VIKTORAS BAUBLYS.

Moldova: 220020 Minsk, vul. Drozdy 32; tel. (172) 50-39-53; fax (172) 50-65-73.

Poland: 220034 Minsk, vul. Rumyantsava 6; tel. (172) 13-43-13; fax (172) 36-49-92; Ambassador: EWA SPYCHALSKA.

Romania: 220035 Minsk, per. Moskvina 4; tel. (172) 23-77-26; fax (172) 10-40-85; Ambassador: NICOLAE STANEA.

Russia: 220002 Minsk, vul. Staravilenskaya 48; tel. (172) 50-36-66; fax (172) 50-36-64; Ambassador: VALERII LOSHCHININ.

Slovakia: 220092 Minsk, pr. Pushkina 39; tel. (172) 57-78-52; fax (172) 57-78-50.

Tajikistan: 220000 Minsk, vul. Kirava 17; tel. (172) 27-37-98; fax (172) 27-76-13.

Turkey: 220000 Minsk, vul. Volodarsky 6, 4th Floor; tel. (172) 27-13-83; fax (172) 27-27-46; Ambassador: TANSU OKANDAN.

Turkmenistan: 220000 Minsk, vul. Kirava 17; tel. (172) 22-34-27; fax (172) 22-33-67.

Ukraine: 220000 Minsk, vul. Kirava 17; tel. and fax (172) 27-28-61; Ambassador: VOLODYMYR I. ZHELIBA.

United Kingdom: 220030 Minsk, vul. K. Marksa 37; tel. (172) 29-23-03; fax (172) 29-23-06; e-mail pia@bepost.belpak.minsk.by; Ambassador: JESSICA PEARCE.

USA: 220002 Minsk, vul. Staravilenskaya 46; tel. (172) 31-50-00; fax (172) 34-78-53; Ambassador: DANIEL SPECKHARD.

Yugoslavia: 220000 Minsk, vul. Surganova 28A; tel. (172) 39-90-90; fax (172) 32-51-54.

Judicial System

Supreme Court: 220030 Minsk, vul. Lenina 28; tel. (172) 26-12-06; Chair. VALYANTSIN SUKALA.

Supreme Economic Court: Minsk; Chair ULADZIMIR BOYKA.

Procuracy: 220050 Minsk, vul. Internatsionalnaya 22; tel. (172) 26-41-66; Procurator General ALEG BAZHELKA.

Constitutional Court: Minsk; 12 mem. judges; Chair. RYHOR VASILEVICH: Dep. Chair. ALYAKSANDR MARYSKIN.

Religion

State Committee for Religious and Ethnic Affairs: see section on The Government.

CHRISTIANITY

The major denomination is the Eastern Orthodox Church, but there are also an estimated 1.2m. adherents of the Roman Catholic Church. Of these, some 25% are ethnic Poles and there is a significant number of Uniates or 'Greek Catholics'. There is also a growing number of Baptist churches.

The Eastern Orthodox Church

In 1990 Belarus was designated an exarchate of the Russian Orthodox Church, thus creating the Belarusian Orthodox Church.

Belarusian Orthodox Church: 220004 Minsk, vul. Osvobozhdeniya 10; tel. (172) 23-44-95; Patriarch and Exarch of All Belarus FILARET.

The Roman Catholic Church

Although five Roman Catholic dioceses, embracing 455 parishes, had officially existed since the Second World War, none of them had a bishop. In 1989 a major reorganization of the structure of the Roman Catholic Church in Belarus took place. The dioceses of Minsk and Mogilev (Mahilou) were merged, to create an archdiocese, and two new dioceses were formed, in Grodno (Horadnia) and Pinsk. The Eastern-rite, or Uniate, Church was abolished in Belarus in 1839, but was re-established in the early 1990s. At 31 December 1995 the Roman Catholic Church had an estimated 1.2m. adherents in Belarus.

Latin Rite

Archdiocese of Minsk and Mogilev: 225710 Pinsk, vul. Shevtshenki 12-1; tel. and fax 23-970; Archbishop: Cardinal KAZIMIERZ SWIATEK.

Byzantine Rite

Belarusian Greek Catholic (Uniate) Church: 220030 Minsk, vul. Hertsena 1.

Protestant Churches

Union of Evangelical Christian Baptists of Belarus: 220093 Minsk, POB 108; tel. (172) 53-92-67; fax (172) 53-82-49.

ISLAM

There are small communities of ethnic Tatars, who are adherents of Islam. In January 1994 the supreme administration of Muslims in Belarus, which had been abolished in 1939, was reconstituted.

Muslim Society: 220004 Minsk, vul. Zaslavskaya 11, kor. 1, kv. 113; tel. (172) 26-86-43; f. 1991; Chair. ALI HALIMBERK.

JUDAISM

Before Belarus was occupied by Nazi German forces, in 1941–44, there was a large Jewish community, notably in Minsk. There were some 142,000 Jews at the census of 1989, but many have since emigrated.

Jewish Religious Society: 220030 Minsk, pr. F. Skaryny 44A.

The Press

In October 1996 there were a total of 736 registered periodicals in Belarus, of which 107 were in Belarusian and 198 in Russian, and 315 were in both Belarusian and Russian. Most daily newspapers are government-owned, and there is only one Belarusian-language daily, *Zvyazda*.

PRINCIPAL DAILIES

In Russian, except where otherwise stated.

Belorusskaya Niva (Belarusian Cornfield): 220013 Minsk, vul. B. Hmyalnitskaga 10A; tel. (172) 32-39-62; fax (172) 68-26-43; f. 1921; 5 a week; organ of the Cabinet of Ministers; in Belarusian and Russian; Editor V. LEHANKOV; circ. 139,000 (1994).

Narodnaya Hazeta (The People's Newspaper): 220013 Minsk, vul. B. Hmyalnitskaga 10A; tel. (172) 68-28-75; fax (172) 68-26-24; f. 1990; 5–6 a week; in Belarusian and Russian; Editor-in-Chief M. SHIMANSKIY; circ. 300,000 (1995).

Respublika (Republic): 220013 Minsk, vul. B. Hmyalnitskaga 10A; tel. (172) 68-26-12; fax (172) 68-26-15; organ of the Cabinet of Ministers; 5 a week; in Belarusian and Russian; Editor SERGEY DUBOVIK; circ. 143,000 (1994).

Sovetskaya Belorossiya (Soviet Belorussia): 220013, Minsk, vul. B. Hmyalnitskaga 10A; tel. (172) 32-14-32; fax (172) 32-14-51; 5 a week; organ of the Cabinet of Ministers; Editor-in-Chief PAVEL YAKUBOVICH; circ. 306,000 (1994).

Vechernii Minsk (Evening Minsk): 220805 Minsk, pr. F. Skaryny 44; tel. (172) 13-47-32; fax (172) 76-80-05; e-mail omp@nsys.minsk.by; internet http://www.belarus.net/minsk-evl; Editor S. SVERKUNOU; circ. 115,000 (1997).

Znamya Yunosti (Banner of Youth): 220013 Minsk, vul. B. Hmyalnitskaga 10A; tel. (172) 68-26-84; fax (172) 32-24-96; f. 1938; 5 a week; organ of the Cabinet of Ministers; Editor-in-Chief IGOR GUKOVSKI; circ. 130,000 (1994).

Zvyazda (Star): 220013 Minsk, vul. B. Hmyalnitskaga 10A; tel. (172) 32-38-92; fax (172) 68-27-83; f. 1917 as *Zvezda*; 5 a week; organ of the Cabinet of Ministers; in Belarusian; Chair. ALYAKSANDR R. LUKASHENKA; Editor ULADZIMIR B. NARKEVICH; circ. 173,000 (1994).

PRINCIPAL PERIODICALS

In Belarusian, except where otherwise stated.

Advertisements Weekly; 220805 Minsk, pr. F. Skaryny 44; tel. and fax (172) 13-45-25; e-mail omp@bm.belpak.minsk.by; Editor T. ANANENKO; circ. 21,500 (1997).

Alesya: 220013 Minsk, pr. F. Skaryny 77; tel. (172) 32-20-51; f. 1924; monthly; Editor MARYA KARPENKA; circ. 96,000.

Belarus: 220005 Minsk, vul. Zakharava 19, tel. (172) 33-20-01; f. 1930; monthly; publ. by the State Publishing House; journal of the Union of Writers of Belarus 'Press House' and the Belarusian Society of Friendship and Cultural Links with Foreign Countries; fiction and political essays; in Belarusian and Russian; Editor-in-Chief A. A. SHABALIN.

Belaruskaya Krinitsa: 220065 Minsk, vul. Avakyana 38-59; tel. and fax (172) 29-67-56; f. 1991; monthly; journal of the Belarusian Christian-Democratic Union; Editor-in-Chief NIKOLAY SVIDERSKY; circ. 10,000.

Byarozka (Birch Tree): 220013 Minsk, pr. F. Skaryny 77; tel. (172) 32-94-66; f. 1924; monthly; fiction; illustrated; for 10–15-year-olds; Editor-in-Chief V. V. ADAMCHIK.

Chyrvonaya Zmena (Red Rising Generation): 220013 Minsk, vul. B. Hmyalnitskaga 10A; tel. and fax (172) 32-21-03; f. 1921; weekly; Editor A. SALAMAHA.

Gramadzyanin: 220033 Minsk, vul. Sudmalisa 10; tel. (172) 29-08-34; fax (172) 72-95-05; publ. by the United Civic Party of Belarus; circ. 20,000.

Holas Radzimy (Voice of the Motherland): 220005 Minsk, pr. F. Skaryny 44; tel. (172) 33-01-97; f. 1955; weekly; articles of interest to Belarusians in other countries; Editor-in-Chief VATSLAU G. MATSKEVICH.

Krynitsa (Spring): 220807 Minsk, vul. Kiseleva 11; tel. (172) 36-60-71; f. 1988; monthly; political and literary; in Belarusian and Russian; Editor V. P. NEKLYAEV.

Litaratura i Mastatstva (Literature and Art): 220600 Minsk, vul. Zakharava 19; tel. (172) 33-24-61; f. 1932; weekly; publ. by the Ministry of Culture and the Union of Writers of Belarus; Editor MIKOLA S. GIL; circ. 18,000 (1992).

Maladosts (Youth): 220016 Minsk, vul. B. Hmyalnitskaga 10A; tel. (172) 23-95-68; f. 1953; monthly; journal of the Union of Writers of Belarus; novels, short stories, essays, translations, etc., for young people; Editor-in-Chief G. DALIDOVICH.

Mastatstva (Art): 220029 Minsk, vul. Chicherina 1; tel. (172) 76-94-67; fax (172) 36-69-82; monthly; illustrated; Editor-in-Chief ALYAKSEY DUDARAU.

Nabat: 220002 Minsk, vul. Krapotkina 44; tel. (172) 34-22-41; f. 1990; publ. by the Belarusian Socio-Ecological Union 'Chernobyl'; Editor VASIL YAKAVENKA.

Narodnaya Asveta (People's Education): 220023 Minsk, vul. Makaenka 12; tel. (172) 64-62-68; f. 1924; publ. by the Ministry of Education; Editor-in-Chief N. I. KALESNIK.

Neman (The River Nieman): 220005 Minsk, pr. F. Skaryny 39; tel. (172) 33-10-72; f. 1945; monthly; publ. by the Polymya (Flame) Publishing House; journal of the Union of Writers of Belarus; fiction; in Russian; Editor-in-Chief A. P. KUDRAVETS.

Polymya (Flame): 220005 Minsk, vul. Zakharava 19; tel. (172) 33-20-12; f. 1922; monthly; publ. by the Polymya (Flame) Publishing House; journal of the Union of Writers of Belarus; fiction; Editor-in-Chief S. I. ZAKONNIKOU.

Vozhyk (Hedgehog): 220013 Minsk, pr. F. Skaryny 77; tel. (172) 32-41-92; f. 1941; fortnightly; satirical; Editor-in-Chief VALYANTSIN V. BOLTACH; circ. 50,000.

Vyaselka (Rainbow): 220004 Minsk, vul. Kalektarnaya 10; tel. (172) 20-92-61; f. 1957; monthly; popular, for 5–10-year-olds; Editor-in-Chief V. S. LIPSKI; circ. 115,000.

PRESS ASSOCIATIONS

Belarusian Journalists' Association: Minsk; tel. (172) 27-05-58; f. 1995; Pres. ZHANNA LITVINA.

Belarusian Union of Journalists: 220005 Minsk, vul. Rumyantsava 3; tel. and fax (172) 36-51-95; 3,000 mems; Pres. L. EKEL.

NEWS AGENCY

BelTa (Belarusian News Agency): 220600 Minsk, vul. Kirava 26; tel. (172) 27-19-92; fax (172) 27-13-46; Dir YAKAU ALAKSEYCHYK.

Publishers

In 1994 there were 3,346 titles (books and pamphlets) published in Belarus (81m. copies).

Belarus: 220600 Minsk, pr. F. Skaryny 79; tel. (172) 23-87-42; fax (172) 23-87-31; f. 1921; social, political, technical, medical and musical literature, fiction, children's, reference books, art reproductions, etc.; Dir MIKALAY KAVALEVSKI.

Belaruskaya Entsiklopediya (Belarusian Encyclopaedia): 220072 Minsk, pr. F. Skaryny 15A; tel. (172) 68-47-67; fax (172) 39-31-44; f. 1967; encyclopaedias, dictionaries, directories and scientific books; Editor-in-Chief G. P. PASHKOV.

Belaruski Dom Druku (Belarusian House of Printing): 220013 Minsk, pr. F. Skaryny 79; tel. (172) 68-27-03; telex 252182; fax (172) 31-67-74; f. 1917; social, political, children's and fiction in Belarusian, Russian and other European languages; Dir BARYS KUTAVY.

Belblankovyd: 220600 Minsk, vul. Kamsamolskaya 11; tel. (172) 26-71-22; reference books in Belarusian and Russian; Dir VALENTINA MILOVANOVA.

Mastatskaya Litaratura (Art Publishing House): 220600 Minsk, pr. Masherava 11; tel. (172) 23-48-09; f. 1972; fiction in Belarusian and Russian; Dir SERAFIM ANDRAYUK.

Mizhvydavetski Fotatsentr (Publishers' Photo Centre): 220600 Minsk, vul. Karzhaneuskaya 20; tel. (172) 78-08-31; reference, scientific, popular, children's, fiction and art and photograph materials; Dir ULADZIMIR KAZLOUT.

Narodnaya Asveta (People's Education Publishing House): 220600 Minsk, pr. Masherava 11; tel. and fax (172) 23-61-84; f. 1951; scientific, educational, reference literature and fiction in Belarusian, Russian and other European languages; Dir IGAR N. LAPTSYONAK.

Navuka i Tekhnika (Science and Technology Publishing House): 220067 Minsk, vul. Zhodinskaya 18; tel. (172) 63-76-18; f. 1924; scientific, technical, reference books, educational literature and fiction in Belarusian and Russian; Dir FADZEY I. SAVITSKI.

Polymya (Flame Publishing House): 220600 Minsk, pr. Masherava 11; tel. and fax (172) 23-52-85; f. 1950; social, political, scientific, technical, religious, children's and fiction; Dir MIKHAIL A. IVANOVICH.

Universitetskae (University Publishing House): 220048 Minsk, pr. Masherava 11; tel. and fax (172) 23-58-51; f. 1967; scientific, educational, art and fiction; Dir ULADZIMIR K. KASKO.

Uradzhay (Harvest Publishing House): 220600 Minsk, pr. Masherava 11; tel. (172) 23-64-94; f. 1961; scientific, technical, educational, books and booklets on agriculture; in Belarusian and Russian; Dir BARYS ULYANKA.

Vysheyshaya Shkola (Higher School Publishing House): 220048 Minsk, pr. Masherava 11; tel. and fax (172) 23-54-15; f. 1954; textbooks and science books for higher educational institutions; in Belarusian, Russian and other European languages; Dir ANATOL A. ZHADAN; Editor-in-Chief T. K. MAIBORODA.

Yunatstva (Youth Publishing House): 220600 Minsk, pr. Masherava 11; tel. (172) 23-24-30; fax (172) 23-31-16; f. 1981; fiction and children's books; Dir VALYANTSIN A. LUKSHA.

Broadcasting and Communications

BROADCASTING

National State Television and Radio Company of Belarus: 220807 Minsk, vul. A. Makayenka 9; tel. (172) 64-75-05; telex 252267; fax (172) 64-81-82; Chair. RYGOR KISEL.

Belarusian Television: 220807 Minsk, vul. A. Makayenka 9; tel. (172) 33-45-01; telex 152267; fax (172) 64-81-82; f. 1956; Chair. VIKTOR DUDKO.

Belarusian Radio: 220807 Minsk, vul. Chyrvonaya 4; tel. (172) 33-39-22; fax (172) 36-66-43; Gen. Dir V. YADRENTSEV.

Television

Minsk Television Company: Minsk; private; broadcasts to CIS, western Europe and North America.

A second national television channel, BT-2, was due to be established in 1997. It was to use networks currently used by Russian Public Television (ORT) and was expected to commence broadcasting within two years.

Finance

(cap. = capital; dep. = deposits; res = reserves; m. = million; brs = branches; amounts in new Belarusian roubles)

BANKING

After Belarus gained its independence, the Soviet-style banking system was restructured and a two-tier system was introduced. In October 1997 there were 30 universal commercial banks operating in Belarus.

Central Bank

National Bank of Belarus: 220008 Minsk, pr. F. Skaryny 20; tel. (172) 27-09-46; telex 252449; fax (172) 27-48-79; f. 1990; cap. 90,000m., res 42,000m. (Oct. 1996); Chair. GENADZ ALEYNIKAW; 6 brs.

Commercial Banks

Absolutbank: 220023 Minsk, POB 9, pr. F. Skaryny 115; tel. (172) 64-24-43; fax (172) 64-60-43; f. 1993; cap. 35,824.8m. (Dec. 1996); Chair. DANIIL P. SVIRID; 3 brs.

Andrey Klimov Bank: 220050 Minsk, vul. Chapaeva 5; tel. and fax (172) 36-79-43; f. 1994; cap. 450m. (Dec. 1996); Chair. ALYAKSANDR M. SAVICH.

Bank for Foreign Economic Affairs (Belvneshekonombank—BVEB): 220050 Minsk, vul. Myasnikova 32; tel. (172) 26-59-09; telex 252426; fax (172) 26-48-09; f. 1991; cap. 93,027.5m. (Dec. 1996), res 168,650m., dep. 1,920,925m. (Dec. 1995); Chair. GEORGIY YEGOROV; 23 brs.

Bank OLIMP: 220121 Minsk, vul. Pritytskiy 60/2; tel. (172) 59-40-24; telex 252104; fax (172) 59-45-25; e-mail telecom@olimp2.belpak.minsk.by; f. 1990; cap. 159,083m. (Dec. 1996), res 12,434m., dep. 497,411m. (Oct. 1997); Chair. VALERY V. SELYAVKO; 6 brs.

Bank Poisk: 220009 Minsk, vul. Gamarnika 4/9; tel. (172) 28-32-48; telex 252455; fax (172) 38-38-28; f. 1974 (as a regional branch of Gosbank of the USSR); renamed Housing and Communal Bank (Zhilsotsbank) in 1989; present name adopted in 1992; cap. 69,342.4m. (Dec. 1996), res 37,649m., dep. 621,975m. (Dec. 1995); Chair. VALENTINA P. SURINA; 26 brs.

Belarusbank: 220050 Minsk, vul. Myasnikova 32; tel. (172) 20-18-31; telex 252488; fax (172) 26-47-50; f. 1995 following merger with Sberbank (Savings Bank; f. 1926); cap. 268,018.2m. (Dec. 1996), res 221,916m., dep. 3,717,886m. (Dec. 1995); Chair. NADEZHDA A. YERMAKOVA; 186 brs.

Belaruski Bank Razvitiya: 220004 Minsk, vul. Melnikaite 2; tel. and fax (172) 23-93-96; telex 252690; f. 1993; cap. 78,120m. (Dec. 1996); Chair. NATALYA A. ALEKSEYEVA; 5 brs.

Belaruski Birzhevoy Bank: 220012 Minsk, vul. Surganova 6; tel. (172) 69-10-86; fax (172) 32-67-00; e-mail beb@exchbank.belpak.minsk.by; f. 1992; cap. 37,146m. (Oct. 1997); Chair. PAVEL V. DIK; 7 brs.

Belaruski Narodnyi Bank: 220004 Minsk, vul. Tankovaya 1; tel. and fax (172) 23-84-57; telex 64114418; f. 1992; cap. 43,021.3m. (Dec. 1996); Chair. ANDREY S. TARATUKHIN; 1 br.

Belbaltia: 220050 Minsk, Privokzalnaya pl., Express Hotel, 8th Floor; tel. (172) 26-58-88; telex 252115; fax (172) 26-49-18; f. 1994; cap. 32,821.2m. (Dec. 1996); Chair. DMITRIY V. OMELYANOVICH; 1 br.

Belkombank: 220007 Minsk, vul. Mogilevskaya 43; tel. (172) 29-25-28; telex 253214; fax (172) 29-21-94; f. 1991; cap. 78,265.5m. (Dec. 1996); Chair. ALYAKSANDR E. KIRNOZHITSKY; 22 brs.

Belkoopbank: 220121 Minsk, vul. Masherava 17; tel. (172) 26-96-96; telex 252216; fax (172) 26-97-93; f. 1992; cap. 44,710m. (Dec. 1996); Chair. LIDIYA A. NIKITENKO; 16 brs.

Djembank: 220023 Minsk, vul. Surganava 28; tel. (172) 68-81-82; telex 252219; fax (172) 68-81-26; f. 1995; cap. 39,459.3m. (Dec. 1996); Chair. MIKHAIL B. DOUBSON.

Infobank: 220035 Minsk, vul. Ignatenka 11; tel. (172) 50-43-96; telex 252183; fax (172) 53-43-88; e-mail infobk.belpak.minsk.by; f. 1994; cap. 30,140m. (Dec. 1996); Chair. ALYAKSANDR D. OSMOLOVSKIY; 3 brs.

Joint-Stock Commercial Agricultural and Industrial Bank (Belagroprombank): 220073 Minsk, vul. Olshevskaga 24; tel. (172) 28-55-13; telex 252514; fax (172) 28-53-19; f. 1991; cap. 36,000m., res 721,530m. (Jan. 1997); Chair. ALYAKSANDR GAVRUSHEV; 131 brs.

Joint-Stock Commercial Bank for Industry and Construction (Belpromstroibank): 220678 Minsk, pr. Lunacharskaga 6; tel. (172) 33-21-10; telex 252410; fax (172) 31-44-76; f. 1991; provides credit to enterprises undergoing privatization and conversion to civil production; cap. 49,943m., res. 577,816m., dep. 5,214,452m. (Dec. 1996); Chair. MIKALAY YA. RAKOU; 59 brs.

Joint-Stock Commercial Bank for Reconstruction and Development (Belbiznesbank): 220002 Minsk, vul. Varvasheni 81; tel. (172) 76-95-42; telex 252421; fax (172) 76-95-40; f. 1992; cap. 40,334m., res 9,249m., dep. 670,123m. (Oct. 1997); Chair. KAZIMIR V. TURUTO; First Vice-Chair. NIKOLAY F. PRIMA; 49 brs.

Korpobank: 220050 Minsk, pr. Masherava 7; tel. and fax (172) 32-11-81; f. 1994; cap. 51m. (Dec. 1996); Chair. YEVGENII V. BHZNETZ.

MinskComplexbank (Joint Byelorusian-Russian Bank): 220050 Minsk, vul. Myasnikova 40; tel. (172) 28-20-50; fax (172) 28-20-60; e-mail administrator@complex.nsys.minsk.by; f. 1992; cap. 16,703.6m. (Dec. 1996); Chair. YEVGENII I. KRAVTSOV; 6 brs.

Minski Tranzitnyi Bank: 220033 Minsk, pr. Partizanski 6A; tel. (172) 29-81-48; telex 252157; fax (172) 13-29-03; f. 1994; cap. 36,001.9m. (Dec. 1996); Chair. ANNA G. GRINKEVICH; 5 brs.

Novokom: 220141 Minsk, vul. Russiyanov 8; tel. (172) 66-16-37; fax (172) 66-37-31; f. 1994; cap. 32,405.8m. (Dec. 1996); Chair. SERGEY V. KOSTEREV; 2 brs.

Obyedinyonnyi Capital: 220019 Minsk, vul. Chicherina 21; tel. (172) 33-71-97; f. 1995; cap. 2,587.5m. (Dec. 1996); Chair. TATIANA G. KOZLOVA.

Priorbank: 220002 Minsk, vul. V. Khoruzhey 31A; tel. (172) 34-01-35; telex 252696; fax (172) 34-15-54; f. 1989, present name since 1992; cap. 117,742m. (Dec. 1996), res 28,745m., dep. 2,688,573m. (Dec. 1995); Pres. MIKHAIL F. LAVRINOVICH; Chair. SYARGEY A. KOSTYUCHENKA; 33 brs.

Profbank: 220126 Minsk, vul. Melnikaite 8; tel. (172) 23-95-28; telex 242485; fax (172) 22-26-15; f. 1991; cap. 36,122.8m. (Dec. 1996); Chair. MIKHAIL P. SLESAREV; 6 brs.

Rassvet: 213944 Mogilev Region, Kirov District, Myshkovichi, vul. Tsentralnaya 24; tel. 4-65-77; fax 4-62-57; f. 1994; cap. 2,875.1m. (Dec. 1996); Chair. NATALIA V. KOVALCHUK.

RRB-Bank: 220037 Minsk, vul. Avangardnaya 61; tel. (172) 35-66-33; telex 252628; fax (172) 35-30-00; f. 1994; cap. 32,842.1m. (Dec. 1996); Chair. IRINA A. VERETELNIKOVA.

Slavneftebank: 220007 Minsk, vul. Fabritsius 8; tel. (172) 22-07-09; telex 252670; fax (172) 22-07-52; e-mail snb@snbank.belpak.minsk.by; f. 1996; cap. 82,200m. (Dec. 1996); Chair. VLADIMIR V. IVANOV.

Tchistinvestbank: 220086 Minsk, vul. Antonovskaya 2; tel. (172) 23-67-10; fax (172) 23-75-80; f. 1994; cap. 27,674.7m. (Dec. 1996); Chair. ANNA A. BARMASH; 6 brs.

Tekhnobank: 220002 Minsk, vul. Krapotkina 44; tel. and fax (172) 34-17-12; f. 1994; cap. 30,518.2m. (Dec. 1996); Chair. VITALIY A. KAZBANOV; 6 brs.

Zolotoy Taler: 220035 Minsk, vul. Vileiskaya 3; tel. (172) 23-67-26; telex 252106; fax (172) 10-55-32; e-mail vsh@mnsk.tsi.ru; f. 1994; cap. and res 34,479.5m., dep. 6,341.2m. (July 1997); Chair. ALYAKSANDR A. ZHILINSKIY.

BANKING ASSOCIATION

Association of Belarusian Banks: Minsk; Pres. MIKHAIL KAVALYOW (acting).

COMMODITY AND STOCK EXCHANGES

Belagroprambirzha (Belarusian Agro-Industrial Trade and Stock Exchange): 220108 Minsk, vul. Kazintsa 86, kor. 2; tel. (172) 77-07-26; telex 252296; fax (172) 77-01-37; f. 1991; trade in agricultural products, industrial goods, shares; 900 mems; Pres. ANATOL TIBOGANOU; Chair. of Bd ALYAKSANDR P. DECHTYAR.

Belarusian Stock Exchange: 220012 Minsk, vul. Surganava 6; tel. (172) 68-56-02; fax (172) 66-37-31; f. 1991.

Belarusian Universal Exchange (BUE): 220099 Minsk, vul. Kazintsa 4; tel. (172) 78-11-21; fax (172) 78-85-16; f. 1991; Pres. ULADZIMIR SHEPEL.

Gomel Regional Commodity and Raw Materials Exchange (GCME): 246000 Gomel, vul. Savetskaya 16; tel. (232) 55-73-28; fax (232) 55-70-07; f. 1991; Gen. Man. ANATOL KUZILEVICH.

Minsk Stock Exchange: 220034 Minsk, vul. Byaduli 12; tel. (172) 39-06-68; fax (172) 39-69-48.

INSURANCE

Belarusian Insurance Co: 220141 Minsk, vul. Zhodinskaya 1-4; tel. and fax (172) 63-38-57; f. 1992; Pres. E. V. ERDKHOVETS.

Belgosstrakh (State Insurance Co): 220029 Minsk, vul. Kalektarnaya 10; tel. (172) 20-62-97.

Belingosstrakh: 220078 Minsk, pr. Masherava 19; tel. (172) 23-58-78; fax (172) 26-98-04; f. 1977; non-life, property, vehicle and cargo insurance.

GARIS: 220600 Minsk, vul. Myasnikova 32; tel. (172) 20-37-01.

Polis: 220050 Minsk, pr. F. Skaryny 11; tel. (172) 20-03-80.

SNAMI: 220040 Minsk, vul. Nekrasova 40A; tel. and fax (172) 31-63-86; f. 1991; Dir S. N. SHABALA.

Trade and Industry

CHAMBER OF COMMERCE

Belarusian Chamber of Commerce and Industry: 220035 Minsk, pr. Masherava 14; tel. (172) 26-91-27; fax (172) 26-98-60; f. 1953; brs in Brest, Gomel, Grodno, Mogilev and Vitebsk; Pres. ULADZIMIR K. LESUN.

EMPLOYERS' ORGANIZATION

Confederation of Industrialists and Entrepreneurs: 220004 Minsk vul. Kalvaryskaya 1-410; tel. (172) 22-47-91; fax (172) 22-47-91; e-mail belka@belpak.minsk.by; f. 1990; Pres. MAX KUNYAVSKI.

UTILITIES

Electricity

Institute of Nuclear Energy: 223061 Minsk, Sosny Settlement; tel. (172) 46-77-12.

Gas

Belnaftagaz: Minsk; tel. (172) 33-06-75.

Beltopgaz: distributes natural gas to end-users.

Beltransgaz: imports natural gas; acts as holding co for regional transmission and storage enterprises.

TRADE UNIONS

Belarusian Congress of Democratic Trade Unions: 220030 Minsk, pl. Svabody 23; tel. (172) 27-04-54; fax (172) 27-13-16; f. 1993; Chair. ALYAKSANDR LYSENKA; 25,000 mems.

Free Trade Union of Belarus: 220030 Minsk, pl. Svabody 23; tel. (172) 27-57-78; fax (172) 27-13-16; f. 1992; Chair. GENADZ BYKAU; Vice-Chair. SYARGEY IVCHIN; 13,000 mems.

Independent Trade Union of Belarus: 223710 Soligorsk, vul. Zhyeleznodorozhnaya 12; tel. (1710) 20-622; fax (1710) 20-059; f. 1991; Chair. VIKTAR BABAYED; Sec. NIKOLAY ZIMIN; 12,000 mems.

Belarusian Peasants' Union (Syalanski Sayuz): 220199 Minsk, vul. Brestskaya 64-327; tel. (172) 77-99-93; Chair. KASTUS YARMOLENKA.

Federation of Trade Unions of Belarus: Minsk; Chair. ULADZIMIR GANCHARYK.

Independent Association of Industrial Trade Unions of Belarus: 220013 Minsk, vul. Kulman 4; tel. (172) 23-80-74; fax (172) 23-97-92; f. 1992; Chairs A. I. BUKHVOSTOU, G. F. FEDYNICH; 600,000 mems.

Union of Motor Car and Agricultural Machinery Construction Workers: Minsk; 200,000 mems.

Union of Small Ventures: 220010 Minsk, vul. Sukhaya 7; tel. (172) 20-23-41; fax (172) 20-93-41; f. 1990; legal, business; Gen. Dir VIKTAR F. DROZD.

Transport

RAILWAYS

In 1993 the total length of railway lines in use was 5,488 km. Minsk is a major railway junction, situated on the east-west line between Moscow and Warsaw, and north-south lines linking the Baltic countries and Ukraine. There is an underground railway in Minsk, the Minsk Metro, which has two lines (total length 20 km), with 17 stations.

Belarusian State Railways: 220745 Minsk, vul. Lenina 17; tel. (172) 96-44-63; fax (172) 27-56-48; f. 1992, following the dissolution of the former Soviet Railways; Pres. YAVHEN VALODKA; First Vice-Pres. V. BORISUK.

ROADS

At 31 December 1995 the total length of roads in Belarus was 51,547 km (15,433 km main roads and 36,114 km secondary roads). Some 98.6% of the total network was hard-surfaced.

CIVIL AVIATION

Minsk has two airports, one largely for international flights and one for domestic connections.

Belair Belorussian Airlines: 222039 Minsk, vul. Korotkevicha 5; tel. (172) 25-07-02; fax (172) 25-30-45; f. 1991; operates regional and domestic charter services.

Belavia: 220004 Minsk, vul. Nemiga 14; tel. (172) 29-23-61; fax (172) 29-23-83; f. 1993 from former Aeroflot division of the USSR; operates services in Europe and selected destinations in Asia; Gen. Dir A. GUSAROV.

Gomel Air Detachment: 246011 Gomel, Gomel Airport; tel. (232) 51-14-07; fax (232) 53-14-15; telex 110110; f. 1944; CEO VALERY N. KULAKOUSKI.

Tourism

Belintourist: 220078 Minsk, pr. Masherava 19; tel. (172) 26-98-40; telex 252270; fax (172) 23-11-43; e-mail belintrst@nttcmk.belpak.minsk.by; f. 1992; leading tourist org. in Belarus; Dir-Gen. VYACHESLAV V. IVANOV (acting).

Ministry of Sports and Tourism: see section on The Government.

BELGIUM

Introductory Survey

Location, Climate, Language, Religion, Flag, Capital

The Kingdom of Belgium lies in north-western Europe, bounded to the north by the Netherlands, to the east by Luxembourg and Germany, to the south by France, and to the west by the North Sea. The climate is temperate. Temperatures in Brussels are generally between 0°C (32°F) and 23°C (73°F). Flemish (closely related to Dutch), spoken in the north (Flanders), and French, spoken in the south (Wallonia), are the two main official languages. The capital, Brussels (which is situated in Flanders), has bilingual status. Nearly 60% of the population are Flemish-speaking, about 40% are French-speaking and less than 1% speak German. The majority of the inhabitants profess Christianity, and about four-fifths are Roman Catholics. The national flag (proportions 15 by 13) consists of three equal vertical stripes, of black, yellow and red.

Recent History

Since the Second World War, Belgium has become recognized as a leader of international co-operation in Europe. It is a founder member of many important international organizations, including the North Atlantic Treaty Organization (NATO, see p. 204), the Council of Europe (see p. 140), the European Union (EU, see p. 152) and the Benelux Economic Union (see p. 259).

In the post-war period linguistic divisions have been exacerbated by the political and economic polarization of Flemish-speaking Flanders in the north and francophone Wallonia in the south. The faster-growing and relatively prosperous population of Flanders has traditionally supported the conservative Flemish Christelijke Volkspartij (CVP—Christian Social Party) and the nationalist Volksunie (VU—People's Union), while Wallonia has traditionally been a stronghold of socialist political sympathies. Most major parties have both French and Flemish sections, as a result of a trend away from centralized administration towards greater regional control. Moderate constitutional reforms, introduced in 1971, were the first steps towards regional autonomy; in the following year further concessions were made, with the German-speaking community being represented in the Cabinet for the first time, and in 1973 linguistic parity was assured in central government. Provisional legislation, adopted in 1974, established separate Regional Councils and Ministerial Committees. The administrative status of Brussels remained contentious: 85% of the city's inhabitants are francophone but the Flemish parties were, until the late 1980s, unwilling to grant the capital equal status with the other two regional bodies (see below).

In June 1977 the Prime Minister, Leo Tindemans, formed a coalition composed of the Christian Social parties, the Socialists, the Front Démocratique des Francophones (FDF—French-speaking Democratic Front) and the VU. The Cabinet, in what became known as the Egmont Pact, proposed the abolition of the virtually defunct nine-province administration, and devolution of power from the central Government to create a federal Belgium, comprising three political and economic regions (Flanders, Wallonia and Brussels), and two linguistic communities. However, these proposals were not implemented. Tindemans resigned in October 1978 and the Minister of Defence, Paul Vanden Boeynants, was appointed Prime Minister in a transitional Government. Legislative elections in December caused little change to the distribution of seats in the Chamber of Representatives. Four successive Prime Ministers-designate failed to form a new government, the main obstacle being the future status of Brussels. The six-month crisis was finally resolved when a new coalition Government was formed in April 1979 under Dr Wilfried Martens, the President of the CVP.

During 1980 the linguistic conflict worsened, sometimes involving violent incidents. Legislation was formulated, under the terms of which Flanders and Wallonia were to be administered by regional assemblies, with control of cultural matters, public health, roads, urban projects and 10% of the national budget, while Brussels was to retain its three-member executive.

Belgium suffered severe economic difficulties during the late 1970s and early 1980s, and internal disagreement over Martens' proposals for their resolution resulted in the formation of four successive coalition Governments between April 1979 and October 1980. Proposed austerity measures, including a 'freeze' on wages and reductions in public expenditure at a time of high unemployment, provoked demonstrations and lost Martens the support of the Socialist parties. Martens also encountered widespread criticism over plans to install NATO nuclear missiles in Belgium. In April 1981 a new Government was formed, comprising a coalition of the Christian Social parties and the Socialist parties and led by Mark Eyskens (CVP), hitherto Minister of Finance. However, lack of parliamentary support for his policies led to Eyskens' resignation in September. In December Martens formed a new centre-right Government, comprising the two Christian Social parties and the two Liberal parties. In 1982 Parliament granted special powers for the implementation of economic austerity measures; these were effective until 1984, and similar powers were approved in March 1986. Opposition to reductions in public spending was vigorous, with public-sector unions undertaking damaging strike action throughout the 1980s.

In November 1983 the Chamber of Representatives debated the controversial proposed installation of 48 US 'cruise' nuclear missiles on Belgian territory, deferring a final decision on the issue until 1985. A series of bombings, directed against NATO-connected targets, occurred during 1984. Responsibility for the attacks was claimed by an extreme left-wing organization. In March 1985 the Chamber finally adopted a majority vote in favour of the cruise sitings, and 16 missiles were installed at Florennes. Further terrorist attacks against NATO targets were perpetrated in 1985, before a number of arrests were made. The missiles were removed in December 1988, under the terms of the Intermediate-range Nuclear Forces treaty concluded by the USA and the USSR in December 1987.

In May 1985 a riot at a football match between English and Italian clubs at the Heysel Stadium in Brussels, which resulted in 39 deaths, precipitated demands for the resignation of the Minister of the Interior, Charles-Ferdinand Nothomb, over accusations of inefficient policing. In July the resignation, in connection with the issue, of six Liberal cabinet members (including the Deputy Prime Minister, Jean Gol) led to the collapse of the coalition. Martens offered the resignation of his Government, but this was 'suspended' by King Baudouin pending a general election, which was called for October. Meanwhile, however, controversy regarding educational reform provoked a dispute between the two main linguistic groups and caused the final dissolution of Parliament in September. The general election returned the Christian Social-Liberal alliance to power, and in November Martens formed his sixth Cabinet.

The Government collapsed in October 1987, as a result of continuing division between the French- and Flemish-speaking parties of the coalition. At the ensuing general election in December, the CVP sustained significant losses in Flanders, while the French-speaking Parti Socialiste (PS—Socialist Party) gained seats in Wallonia, and the Socialists became the largest overall grouping in the Chamber of Representatives. No party, however, had a clear mandate for power, and the ensuing negotiations for a new coalition lasted 146 days. During this time, Martens assumed a caretaker role, pending the formation of a new government, and a series of mediators, appointed by King Baudouin, attempted to reach a compromise. In May 1988 Martens was sworn in at the head of his eighth administration, after agreement was finally reached by the French- and Flemish-speaking wings of both the Christian Social and Socialist parties and by the VU.

The five-party coalition agreement committed the new Government to a programme of further austerity measures, together with tax reforms and increased federalization. In August 1988 Parliament approved the first phase of the federalization plan, intended ultimately to lead to a constitutional amendment, whereby increased autonomy would be granted to the country's Communities and Regions in several areas of jurisdiction, including education and socio-economic policy. It was also agreed that Brussels would have its own Regional Council, with an executive responsible to it, giving the city equal status with Flanders and Wallonia.

In January 1989 Parliament approved the second phase of the federalization programme, allocating the public funds necessary to give effect to the regional autonomy that had been approved in principle in August 1988, providing for the creation of a regional authority for Brussels, and establishing a body whose purpose was to consider conflicts of a constitutional nature that might arise during the period of transition to a federal system of government. The federal Constitution formally came into effect in July 1989.

A brief constitutional crisis in 1990 provoked widespread demands for a review of the powers of the Monarch, as defined by the Constitution. In March proposals for the legalization of abortion (in strictly-controlled circumstances) completed their passage through Parliament. However, King Baudouin had previously stated that his religious convictions would render him unable to give royal assent to any such legislation. A compromise solution was reached in early April, whereby Article 82 of the Constitution, which makes provision for the Monarch's 'incapacity to rule', was invoked. Baudouin thus abdicated for 36 hours, during which time the new legislation was promulgated. A joint session of Parliament was then convened to declare the resumption of Baudouin's reign. However, the incident prompted considerable alarm within Belgium: it was widely perceived as setting a dangerous precedent for the reinterpretation of the Constitution.

The Government was weakened by the resignation of both VU Ministers in September 1991 and by the resultant loss of its two-thirds parliamentary majority, necessary for the implementation of the third stage of the federalization programme. Further linguistic conflict between the remaining coalition partners led to Martens' resignation as Prime Minister in October and the subsequent collapse of the Government. However, King Baudouin rejected the resignations of Martens and the Cabinet. The Government was to remain in office until the next general election, scheduled for late November 1991. The results of the election reflected a significant decline in popular support for all five parties represented in the outgoing Government. The Socialist parties remained the largest overall grouping in the Chamber of Representatives, although they sustained the highest combined loss of seats (nine). The Christian Social parties and the Liberal parties remained, respectively, the second and third largest groupings, while the two ecologist parties (Agalev and Ecolo) increased their representation in the Chamber to become the fourth strongest grouping. The Vlaams Blok (Flemish Bloc), an extreme right-wing party advocating Flemish separatism and the repatriation of immigrants, obtained 12 seats, recording the highest increase (10 seats) of any party.

Following the November 1991 general election, the political parties conducted protracted negotiations, during which Martens' interim Cabinet continued in office. In early March 1992 the four parties that had composed the previous Government, the CVP, the francophone Parti Social Chrétien (PSC—Christian Social Party), the Socialistische Partij (SP) and the PS (which together controlled 120 seats in the 212-member Chamber of Representatives), agreed to form a new administration; a leading member of the CVP, Jean-Luc Dehaene, was appointed Prime Minister. The new Government committed itself to the completion of the constitutional reforms that had been initiated under Martens' premiership. For several months, however, the coalition partners repeatedly failed to reach agreement, both on proposals for the implementation of the third stage of the federalization programme and on amendments to the 1993 budget. A compromise on both issues was eventually reached at the end of September 1992.

In July 1992 the Chamber of Representatives voted, by 146 to 33, in favour of ratifying the Treaty on European Union, agreed by the heads of government of member states of the European Community (now EU) at Maastricht, in the Netherlands, in December 1991. The Senate approved ratification in November 1992.

In February 1993 (in accordance with the constitutional reforms agreed in September 1992) Parliament voted to amend the Constitution to create a federal state of Belgium, comprising the largely autonomous regions of Flanders, Wallonia and (bilingual) Brussels. The three regions, and the country's three linguistic groups, were to be represented by the following directly-elected assemblies: a combined assembly for Flanders and the Flemish-speaking community, regional assemblies for Wallonia and Brussels, and separate assemblies for French- and German-speakers. The regional administrations were to assume sole responsibility for the environment, housing, transport and public works, while the language community administrations were to supervise education policy and culture. Legislation to implement the reforms was enacted in July 1993.

In March 1993 Dehaene offered to resign as Prime Minister, owing to continuing failure by the ruling coalition to agree measures to reduce the level of the budget deficit. At the end of that month, however, a solution was achieved; Dehaene remained in his post and, in early April, Parliament adopted a vote of confidence in his Government.

In July 1993 King Baudouin died; Baudouin was succeeded by his brother, hitherto Prince Albert of Liège, in August.

From mid-November 1993 trade union movements united to organize several one-day strikes, including a general strike in late November, in protest at the Dehaene administration's intention to implement a series of severe economic austerity measures and at the relatively high rate of unemployment; the strike action was suspended in mid-December, when the Government agreed to negotiate with the unions.

In January 1994 three government ministers who were members of the PS (including a Deputy Prime Minister, Guy Coëme) resigned from their posts, following allegations that they had been involved in a bribery scandal concerning the apparently illegal receipt by the SP (the Flemish section of the party) of a substantial sum of money in connection with the award, in 1988, of a defence contract to an Italian helicopter company. The PS (the Walloon section of the party) was subsequently implicated in a similar scandal involving a French aviation company. In April 1996 Coëme and seven others were found guilty of fraud and abuse of public office; Coëme, who received a two-year suspended prison sentence, subsequently resigned from the Chamber of Representatives.

At elections to the European Parliament in June 1994 all four parties of the governing coalition registered a decline in support, while the Liberal parties increased their number of seats. Extreme right-wing parties also performed well: the Vlaams Blok and the Wallonia-based Front National (FN—National Front) together gained more than 10% of the total votes.

The investigation into the PS/SP bribery scandal (see above) intensified during 1995. Although the SP party treasurer maintained that he had accepted the funds unilaterally, without the knowledge of any colleagues, increasing numbers of people became implicated. In early March a retired Chief of Staff of the Air Force, who had been in office at the time of the illegal financial transaction, committed suicide, having been arrested and questioned in connection with the inquiry. In the same month Frank Vandenbroucke, a Deputy Prime Minister and the Minister of Foreign Affairs, and a member of the SP, resigned from the Cabinet, claiming that he had participated unwittingly in the affair. Meanwhile, Willy Claes, a prominent SP official and former Deputy Prime Minister and Minister of Foreign Affairs, who had been elected Secretary-General of NATO in 1994, came under increasing pressure to resign from his post, owing to (strenuously refuted) allegations of his involvement in the scandal. In May 1995 Claes was questioned about the affair by the Supreme Court, and in October, following the withdrawal by Parliament of his immunity from prosecution (held by all serving and retired government ministers under Belgian law), Claes was committed to trial on charges of corruption, fraud and forgery. Immediately afterwards Claes resigned as Secretary-General of NATO.

At a general election held in mid-May 1995, the ruling centre-left coalition retained significant support, securing a total of 82 seats in the Chamber of Representatives (membership of which had been reduced from 208 to 150), despite the ongoing investigation into allegedly illegal activities by officials of the two Socialist parties. The performance of the extreme right-wing Vlaams Blok was not as strong as had been anticipated: although the party won nearly 28% of the votes cast in Antwerp, Belgium's second largest city, it received only 12% of the votes overall in Flanders. Elections to the regional assemblies took place concurrently with the national legislative elections. Following an unusually short period of negotiations the CVP-PSC-PS-SP coalition was reformed and in mid-June a new Cabinet was appointed, with Dehaene remaining as Prime Minister. The Government, which continued to be strongly committed to meeting the economic targets for future European economic and monetary union, introduced several strict economic austerity measures in late 1995; public-sector unions responded by organizing protest strike action. In April 1996 the Government, employers and trade unions agreed a package of measures which aimed to reduce the high level of unemployment. The agreement was, however, short-lived, owing to the subsequent withdrawal of one of the main trade unions, on the grounds that the proposals for job creation were not sufficiently detailed. In the following month Parliament granted the Dehaene administration special emergency powers to implement economic austerity measures by decree.

The latter half of 1996 was dominated by extreme public concern over allegations of endemic official corruption, following the discovery, in August, of an international paedophile network based in Belgium, and subsequent widespread speculation (fuelled by the arrests in early September of several police officers) that this had received protection from the police force and from senior figures in the judicial and political establishment, who were allegedly implicated in the activities of organized crime syndicates. During September King Albert promised a thorough investigation of the network and, in an unprecedented gesture, demanded a review of the judicial system. In October, however, allegations of a judicial and political conspiracy to impede the progress of the investigation were prompted by the removal from the case of Jean-Marc Connerotte, a widely-respected senior investigating judge. The prevailing mood of national crisis was heightened by the arrests, during September, of Alain van der Biest of the PS (a former federal Minister of Pensions) and four others, on charges connected with the assassination in 1991 of a former Deputy Prime Minister, André Cools. It was alleged that Cools' murder had been ordered by PS colleagues, in order to prevent him from disclosing corruption within the party. In November 1996 Elio di Rupo, a Deputy Prime Minister, was accused of participating in paedophile activities; he was, however, subsequently cleared of the charges by a parliamentary committee.

During 1997 the sense of national malaise was exacerbated by industrial unrest. In February demonstrations in protest at the closure of a Wallonian steelworks, Forges de Clabecq (which had employed some 1,800 people), received much popular support. At the end of the same month the French automobile manufacturer Renault announced the impending closure of its Belgian factory, with the loss of more than 3,000 jobs in a town in which it was the principal employer. Strikes and widely-attended demonstrations ensued, while the Belgian Government mounted an ultimately unsuccessful legal challenge to Renault's action. Concerns were raised that the cost to employers of Belgian social welfare contributions was prompting businesses to relocate elsewhere within the EU. The incident strained regional relations, with the French Government, the principal shareholder in Renault, refusing to overturn the company executive's decision. By mid-1997, however, the Belgian authorities and Renault employees appeared resigned to the eventual closure of the factory (provisionally scheduled for the end of the year).

Meanwhile, in March 1997 Guy Spitaels (a former Deputy Prime Minister and an erstwhile President of the PS), having resigned in the previous month as President of the Walloon regional assembly, was indicted on bribery charges relating to the political scandals of 1994–95 (see above). In April 1997 a parliamentary committee, which had been established in October 1996 to investigate allegations of official corruption and mismanagement, issued a report which claimed that rivalry between the country's various police and judicial divisions often prevented their effective co-operation; it recommended the establishment of a single integrated national police force. However, the committee found little evidence that paedophile networks had received official protection. In October 1997 the Government announced plans to integrate the gendarmerie and the judicial police; local police forces, however, were to remain autonomous.

From late 1988 Belgium's hitherto cordial relations with its former colonies underwent considerable strain. Proposals that Prime Minister Martens made in November 1988 regarding the relief of public and commercial debts owed to Belgium by Zaire (formerly the Belgian Congo) were opposed by the Socialist parties and provoked allegations, in certain Belgian newspapers, of corruption within the Zairean Government and of the misappropriation of development aid to the former colony. President Mobutu Sese Seko of Zaire responded by ordering the withdrawal of all Zairean state-owned businesses from Belgium and by demanding that all Zairean nationals resident in Belgium remove their assets from, and leave, their host country. In July 1989 the situation was apparently resolved following meetings between Martens and Mobutu, at which a new debt-servicing agreement was signed. However, relations again deteriorated when, in May 1990, the Mobutu regime refused to accede to demands for an international inquiry into the alleged massacre of as many as 150 students by the Zairean security forces. Mobutu accused Belgium of interfering in his country's internal affairs, and ordered the expulsion from Zaire of some 700 Belgian technical workers, together with the closure of three of Belgium's four consular offices. Following violent rioting by Zairean soldiers in many parts of Zaire in September 1991, and the ensuing collapse of public order, the Belgian Government dispatched 1,000 troops to Zaire for the protection of the estimated 11,000 Belgian nationals resident there. By the end of 1991 all the troops had been withdrawn and about 8,000 Belgian nationals had been evacuated from Zaire. Prospects for the normalization of relations improved following the establishment of a transitional Government in Zaire in July 1992 and the removal of Zairean sanctions against Belgium. Relations deteriorated again, however, in January 1993, when, in response to rioting by troops loyal to President Mobutu, Belgium dispatched 520 troops to evacuate the remaining 3,000 Belgian nationals in Zaire. In October 1994 the Belgian Government pledged to resume humanitarian aid to Zaire, although it stated that the restoration of normal relations would depend on the Zairean Government's commitment to democratization, the respect of human rights and the implementation of economic reforms. In May 1997, following the deposition of Mobutu's regime, the Belgian Government granted *de facto* recognition to the newly-established administration of Laurent-Désiré Kabila in the Democratic Republic of the Congo (DRC—as Zaire was now renamed), and in August it was announced that normal relations between the two countries were gradually to be restored.

In October 1990 the Martens Government dispatched 600 troops to protect the interests of some 1,600 Belgian nationals resident in Rwanda (part of the former Belgian territory of Ruanda-Urundi), when that country was invaded by opponents of the incumbent regime who had been living in exile. The Belgian Government insisted that the deployment was a purely humanitarian action, and stated that it would not agree to a request from the Rwandan Government for military assistance in repelling the opposition forces, citing unacceptable violations of human rights by the Rwandan authorities. In late October a cease-fire agreement came into force; Belgian forces were withdrawn from Rwanda in early November. Nevertheless, the conflict in Rwanda continued during 1991–94. Following a peace accord signed by the Rwandan Government and the opposition Front patriotique rwandais in August 1993, some 420 Belgian troops were redeployed as part of a 2,500-strong UN peace-keeping force; this was, however, unable to prevent an outbreak of extreme violence, beginning in April 1994, which resulted in the deaths of many hundreds of thousands of people. Following the execution of 10 Belgian troops in April, the Belgian Government withdrew its peace-keeping contingent. It also dispatched some 800 paratroopers to Rwanda to co-ordinate the evacuation of the estimated 1,500 Belgian expatriates remaining in the country, as well as other foreign nationals.

Government

Belgium is a constitutional and hereditary monarchy, consisting of a federation of the largely autonomous regions of Brussels, Flanders and Wallonia and of the Flemish-, French- and German-speaking language communities. The central legislature consists of a bicameral Parliament (the Chamber of Representatives and the Senate). The Chamber has 150 members, all directly elected by universal adult suffrage, on the basis of proportional representation. The Senate has 72 members, of whom 40 are directly elected, also by universal suffrage on the basis of proportional representation, and 21 are appointed by the legislative assemblies of the three language communities (see below), 10 are co-opted by the elected members and one is a representative of the royal family. Members of both Houses serve for up to four years. Executive power, nominally vested in the King, is exercised by the Cabinet. The King appoints the Prime Minister and, on the latter's advice, other Ministers. The Cabinet is responsible to the Chamber of Representatives. The three regions and three linguistic communities are represented by directly-elected legislative assemblies. The regional administrations have sole responsibility for the environment, housing, transport and public works, while the language community administrations supervise education policy and culture.

Defence

Belgium is a member of NATO. In August 1997 the total strength of the armed forces was 44,450, including an army of 28,500, a navy of 2,700 and an air force of 12,000. The defence budget for 1997 was estimated at 98,900m. Belgian francs. Compulsory military service was abolished in 1995. A reduction in the size of the country's armed forces to 40,000 was expected to be completed during the late 1990s. In 1996 the Belgian and Netherlands navies came under a joint operational command, based at Den Helder, the Netherlands.

Economic Affairs

In 1995, according to estimates by the World Bank, Belgium's gross national product (GNP), measured at average 1993–95 prices, was US $250,710m., equivalent to $24,710 per head. During 1985–95, it was estimated, GNP per head increased by 2.2% per year in real terms. Over the same period, the population increased at an average rate of 0.3% per year. The country's gross domestic product (GDP) increased, in real terms, by an annual average of 0.9% in 1990–94. In 1994 GDP growth improved to 2.2%, following a decline of 1.6% in 1993; growth of 1.9% was recorded in 1995.

Agriculture (including forestry and fishing) contributed 1.7% of GDP in 1994. An estimated 2.5% of the employed labour force were engaged in the sector in 1992. The principal agricultural products are sugar beet, cereals and potatoes. Pig meat, beef and dairy products are also important. Exports of food, livestock and livestock products accounted for 9.1% of the total export revenue of the Belgo–Luxembourg Economic Union (BLEU) in 1994. Agricultural GDP increased, in real terms, at an average annual rate of 4.0% in 1990–94. It declined by 6.3% in 1994, but increased by an estimated 2.7% in 1995.

Industry (including mining and quarrying, manufacturing, power and construction) contributed 31.0% of GDP in 1994. An estimated 27.5% of the employed labour force were engaged in industry in 1992. Industrial production (excluding construction) increased by 1.8% in 1994, by 3.4% in 1995 and by 1.1% in 1996.

Belgium has few mineral resources, and the country's last coal-mine closed in 1992. In 1994 extractive activities accounted for only 0.2% of GDP. An estimated 0.2% of the employed labour force worked in the sector in 1992.

Manufacturing contributed 22.9% of GDP in 1994. The sector accounted for an estimated 20.0% of the employed labour force in 1992. In 1990 the main branches of manufacturing, in terms of value added, were fabricated metal products, machinery and equipment (accounting for 29.2% of the total); chemical, petroleum, coal, rubber and plastic products (23.8%); and food, beverages and tobacco (13.8%). During 1980–92 manufacturing production increased by an annual average of 1.7%, but in 1993 it fell by 1.0%, before recovering by 2.0% in 1994 and by a further 4% in 1995; in 1996 manufacturing production remained unchanged.

Belgium's seven nuclear reactors accounted for 59% of total electricity generation in 1993 (one of the highest levels in the world). The country's dependence on imported petroleum and natural gas began to increase, following the announcement by the Government in 1988 of the indefinite suspension of its nuclear programme and of the construction of a gas-powered generator. Imports of mineral fuels comprised 6.9% of the value of the BLEU's total imports in 1994.

The services sector contributed 67.3% of GDP in 1994, and engaged an estimated 70.0% of the employed labour force in 1992. The presence in Belgium of the offices of many international organizations and businesses is a significant source of revenue.

In 1996 the BLEU recorded a visible trade surplus of US $9,146m., while there was a surplus of $14,387m. on the current account of the balance of payments. In 1994 Belgium's three major trading partners (Germany, the Netherlands and France) together accounted for 54.2% of the BLEU's total imports and 53.4% of exports. The principal exports in 1993 were basic manufactures (including gem diamonds and iron and steel), machinery and transport equipment, chemicals and related products, food and live animals and miscellaneous manufactured articles. The principal imports in that year were machinery and transport equipment, basic manufactures, chemicals and related products, miscellaneous manufactured articles and food and live animals.

In 1994 there was a budget deficit of BF 329,772m., equivalent to 4.3% of GDP. The annual rate of inflation averaged 2.3% in 1985–95. Consumer prices increased by an annual average of 2.4% in 1994, by 1.5% in 1995 and by 2.1% in 1996. In the 12 months to August 1997 the rate of inflation was 1.9%. An estimated 9.6% of the labour force were unemployed in June 1997, compared with 12.8% in mid-1996.

Belgium is a member of the European Union (EU—see p. 152), including the European Monetary System (EMS, see p. 172), and of the Benelux Economic Union (see p. 259). The dual exchange rate that had been operated by the single customs region of the BLEU was abolished in March 1990, in compliance with plans to remove all capital controls within the European Community (now EU).

Following strong and sustained economic growth during the late 1980s, the Belgian economy entered recession in 1991: GDP growth decelerated, registering a decline in 1993, and unemployment mounted rapidly. By the end of 1994, however, economic growth appeared to have regained momentum, with a higher-than-expected increase in exports and an improvement in GDP growth to 2.2%. Nevertheless, the improved economic performance appeared to be at the expense of continued high unemployment. Severe structural weaknesses remained, notably the chronic public-sector debt, which was equivalent to 133.8% of GDP in 1995. The future of the social security system was another cause for concern, with the increasing pensionable proportion of the population representing a growing burden on public finances, and with a markedly low labour force participation rate (at about 65%), compared with other industrialized nations. Moreover, in the mid-1990s the Government was concerned to reduce the level of employers' social security contributions, in the belief that unemployment was being exacerbated by the decision of companies to relocate where their unemployment costs would be lower. Together with an already low level of public expenditure per caput on health (compared with other EU nations), these factors left little leeway for reductions in spending to help to reduce the budget deficit to 2.9% of GDP by the end of 1997, in order to qualify for the final stage of EU economic and monetary union. Austerity measures, aimed at keeping the budget deficit under control, have been in force since 1992. In May 1996 the Government assumed special emergency powers to implement economic austerity measures by decree.

A four-year programme to transfer certain state-owned enterprises to private-sector ownership commenced in October 1993.

Social Welfare

Social welfare is administered mainly by the National Office for Social Security. Contributions are paid by employers and employees towards family allowances, health insurance, unemployment benefit and pensions. Self-employed people's contributions cover only family allowances, pensions and a more limited level of health insurance. Most allowances and pensions are periodically adjusted in accordance with changes to the consumer price index. Workers and employees are entitled to four weeks' holiday for every 12-month period of work. They are insured against accidents occurring on the work premises or on the way to and from work. Unemployment benefit is paid by trade unions to their affiliates on behalf of the National Employment Office; unemployed people without trade union affiliation are paid from a public fund. A higher rate of medical reimbursement applies to widows, pensioners, orphans and the disabled, if they fall within a designated income bracket. Ordinary and supplementary family allowances are the entitlement of all families. Social welfare is also administered at a local level by Public Assistance Commissions which have been set up in every municipality. In 1982 Belgium had 531 hospital establishments, with a total of 92,686 beds (one for every 106 inhabitants), and in 1985 there were 29,776 physicians (30.2 per 10,000 inhabitants) working in the country. Current legislation restricts the number of hospital beds and establishments to the 1982 level. Of total expenditure by the central Government in 1988, about 48,800m. francs (1.7%) was allocated to health, and 1,183,800m. francs (41.6%) to social security and welfare. Government expenditure on social security, health benefits, family allowances and pensions has been curtailed during the 1990s, and the social welfare system is expected to be radically restructured by 2000.

Education

Legislation granting responsibility for the formulation of education policy to the administrations of the Flemish-, French- and German-speaking communities came into effect in 1993. Education may be provided by the Communities, by public authorities or by private interests. All educational establishments, whether official or 'free' (privately-organized), receive most of their funding from the Communities. Roman Catholic schools constitute the greatest number of 'free' establishments.

Full-time education in Belgium is compulsory from the ages of six to 16 years. Thereafter, pupils must remain in part-time education for a further two-year period. About 90% of infants attend state-financed nursery schools. Elementary education begins at six years of age and consists of three courses of two years each. Secondary education, beginning at the age of 12, lasts for six years and is divided into three two-year cycles or, in a few cases, two three-year cycles.

The requirement for university entrance is a pass in the 'examination of maturity', taken after the completion of secondary studies. Courses are divided into 2–3 years of general preparation followed by 2–3 years of specialization. The French Community controls four universities, while the Flemish Community controls three such institutions; in addition, there are 11 university centres or faculties (six French, five Flemish). In 1992/93 a total of 123,320 students were enrolled in university-level establishments. Non-university institutions of higher education provide arts education, technical training and teacher training. A national study fund provides grants where necessary and almost 20% of students receive scholarships.

Expenditure on education by the central Government was 409,254m. francs in 1993 (equivalent to 9.9% of total government spending).

Public Holidays

1998: 1 January (New Year's Day), 13 April (Easter Monday), 1 May (Labour Day), 21 May (Ascension Day), 1 June (Whit Monday), 21 July (National Day), 15 August (Assumption), 1 November (All Saints' Day), 11 November (Armistice Day), 25 December (Christmas Day).

1999: 1 January (New Year's Day), 5 April (Easter Monday), 1 May (Labour Day), 13 May (Ascension Day), 24 May (Whit Monday), 21 July (National Day), 15 August (Assumption), 1 November (All Saints' Day), 11 November (Armistice Day), 25 December (Christmas Day).

Weights and Measures

The metric system is in force.

Statistical Survey

Source: mainly Institut National de Statistique, 44 rue de Louvain, 1000 Brussels; tel. (2) 548-62-11; fax (2) 548-63-67.

Area and Population

AREA, POPULATION AND DENSITY

Area (sq km)	30,528*
Population (census results)†	
1 March 1981	9,848,647
1 March 1991	
Males	4,875,982
Females	5,102,699
Total	9,978,681
Population (official estimates at 31 December)†	
1993	10,100,631
1994	10,130,574
1995	10,143,047
Density (per sq km) at 31 December 1995	332.3

* 11,787 sq miles. † Population is *de jure*.

PROVINCES (population at 31 December 1995, excluding Brussels)

	Population	Capital (with population)
Antwerp	1,631,243	Antwerp (455,852*)
Brabant (Flemish)	999,186	Leuven (87,132)
Brabant (Walloon)	339,062	Wavre (29,906)
Flanders (East)	1,351,777	Ghent (226,464)
Flanders (West)	1,122,849	Brugge (115,815)
Hainaut	1,284,761	Mons (92,260)
Liège	1,013,729	Liège (190,525)
Limburg	775,302	Hasselt (67,456)
Luxembourg	241,339	Arlon (24,417)
Namur	435,677	Namur (105,059)

* Including suburbs.

PRINCIPAL TOWNS (population at 31 December 1995)

Bruxelles (Brussel, Brussels)	948,122*
Antwerpen (Anvers, Antwerp)	455,852†
Gent (Gand, Ghent)	226,464
Charleroi	205,591
Liège (Luik)	190,525
Brugge (Bruges)	115,815
Namur (Namen)	105,059
Mons (Bergen)	92,260
Leuven (Louvain)	87,132
Kortrijk (Courtrai)	75,951
Mechelen (Malines)	75,294
Oostende (Ostend)	68,635
Hasselt	67,456

* Including Schaerbeek, Anderlecht and other suburbs.

† Including Deurne and other suburbs.

BIRTHS, MARRIAGES AND DEATHS

	Registered live births		Registered marriages*		Registered deaths†	
	Number	Rate (per 1,000)	Number	Rate (per 1,000)	Number	Rate (per 1,000)
1988	119,456	12.1	59,093	6.0	104,552	10.6
1989	121,117	12.2	63,528	6.4	106,949	10.8
1990	123,726	12.4	64,658	6.5	104,818	10.5
1991	126,068	12.6	60,740	6.1	105,150	10.5
1992	125,075	12.4	58,156	5.8	105,717	10.5
1993	119,828	11.9	54,112	5.4	106,601	10.6
1994	115,361	11.4	51,962	5.1	103,566	10.3
1995	114,226	11.3	51,402	5.1	104,590	10.3

* Including marriages among Belgian armed forces stationed outside the country and alien armed forces in Belgium, unless performed by local foreign authority.

† Including Belgian armed forces stationed outside the country but excluding alien armed forces stationed in Belgium.

ECONOMICALLY ACTIVE POPULATION
(ISIC Major Divisions, estimates, '000 persons aged 15 years and over, at 30 June each year)

	1990	1991	1992
Agriculture, forestry and fishing	100.0	98.4	94.9
Mining and quarrying	8.1	7.3	6.6
Manufacturing	782.3	771.0	751.7
Electricity, gas and water	30.0	29.5	29.2
Construction	235.7	242.6	245.2
Trade, restaurants and hotels	634.4	637.3	634.2
Transport, storage and communications	257.1	259.4	257.1
Finance, insurance, real estate and business services	327.6	335.8	341.6
Community, social and personal services	1,389.0	1,388.5	1,392.6
Total in home employment	3,764.1	3,769.8	3,753.1
Persons working abroad	50.4	49.6	48.4
Total in employment	3,814.5	3,819.4	3,801.5
Unemployed	364.7	391.1	435.7
Total labour force	4,179.2	4,210.5	4,237.2
Males	2,440.3	2,447.0	2,444.1
Females	1,738.9	1,763.4	1,793.1

Source: ILO, *Yearbook of Labour Statistics*.

Agriculture

PRINCIPAL CROPS ('000 metric tons)

	1992	1993	1994
Wheat	1,328.9	1,392.1	1,346.8
Spelt	35.5	35.4	39.9
Barley	449.6	390.6	346.2
Maize	89.1	163.9	58.5
Rye	10.0	10.3	11.7
Oats	35.7	54.2	42.4
Potatoes	2,428.6	2,155.1	1,820.3
Linseed	5.4	7.5	9.0
Flax fibre	5.4	7.4	9.0
Sugar beet	5,958.6	6,264.2	5,393.7

LIVESTOCK ('000 head at 1 December)

	1992	1993	1994
Horses	20.8	21.8	22.6
Cattle	3,099.5	3,084.2	3,161.1
Pigs	6,902.8	6,876.1	6,984.1
Sheep	129.2	127.3	119.1
Goats	9.0	7.5	8.3
Chickens	26,412.5	29,166.6	31,389.1
Ducks	88.6	76.7	78.4
Turkeys	174.0	204.5	180.7

LIVESTOCK PRODUCTS ('000 metric tons)

	1992	1993	1994
Beef and veal	352	367	349
Pig meat	944	993	1,012
Milk	3,514	3,329	3,344
Butter	73	70	70
Cheese	69	69	70
Hen eggs	201	210	245

Fishing*

('000 metric tons)

	1992	1993	1994
Marine fishes	23.8	22.1	18.8
Crustaceans and molluscs	2.4	2.3	1.8
Total catch	26.1	24.4	20.7

* Figures refer to marketable quantities landed in Belgium, which may be less than the live weight of the catch. The total catch (in '000 metric tons) was: 38.0 in 1992; 36.9 in 1993; 35.1 in 1994; 36.4 in 1995 (Source: FAO, *Yearbook of Fishery Statistics*).

Mining

('000 metric tons, unless otherwise indicated)

	1991	1992	1993
Hard coal*	634	218	—
Lignite	1,473	979	862
Uranium (metric tons)	38	36	34
Kaolin	188	171	139
Chalk	378	6,159	5,409

* Mining of hard coal ceased in 1992.

1994: Lignite ('000 metric tons) 753; Uranium (metric tons) 40.

Source: UN, *Industrial Commodity Statistics Yearbook*.

Industry

SELECTED PRODUCTS
('000 metric tons, unless otherwise indicated)

	1993	1994	1995
Wheat flour[1]	795	1,097*	1,200*
Raw sugar[2]	1,118	1,005	1,049
Margarine	216.9	283.5*	297.0*
Beer ('000 hectolitres)	n.a.	148,870*	150,204*
Cigarettes (million)	27,480.9	22,130.6*	20,857.3*
Cotton yarn—pure and mixed (metric tons)	43,766	4,371.1†	15,314.7*
Woven cotton fabrics—pure and mixed (metric tons)[3]	51,913	26,867†	32,911*
Flax yarn (metric tons)[4]	5,163	n.a.	3,153*
Jute yarn (metric tons)	4,252	n.a.	n.a.
Other vegetable textile yarns (metric tons)	8,913	1,647*	1,588*
Wool yarn—pure and mixed (metric tons)	70,542	11,505†	11,824†
Woven woollen fabrics—pure and mixed (metric tons)[2]	28,289	350†	461†
Rayon continuous filaments (metric tons)	6,802	n.a.	n.a.
Woven rayon and acetate fabrics—pure and mixed (metric tons)[5]	34,238	13,710*	14,647*
Mechanical wood pulp[2]	203	210	n.a.
Chemical and semi-chemical wood pulp[2]	107	168	n.a.
Newsprint	120.6	n.a.	n.a.
Other paper and paperboard	1,127.8	1,217.6*	1,295.6*
Ethyl alcohol—Ethanol ('000 hectolitres)	29.2	n.a.	n.a.
Sulphuric acid (100%)	1,593.3	n.a.	n.a.
Nitric acid (100%)	1,320.1	n.a.	n.a.
Nitrogenous fertilizers[6]	755	n.a.	n.a.
Phosphate fertilizers[7]	340	n.a.	n.a.
Liquefied petroleum gas	409	501	458
Naphtha	820	906	696
Motor spirit (petrol)	5,614	5,686	5,259
Kerosene	14	84	88
White spirit	271.9	288.2	245.0
Jet fuel	1,514.4	1,617.9	1,268.3
Distillate fuel oils	10,706.6	11,438.0	10,992.6
Residual fuel oil	6,611.3	5,392.4	4,945.7

— continued	1993	1994	1995
Petroleum bitumen (asphalt)	805.1	817.3	893.1
Coke-oven coke	3,909	3,736	3,696
Cement	7,569	9,449*	10,398*
Pig-iron	8,178.9	8,979.4	9,198.8
Crude steel	10,118.8	11,265.2*	11,539.9*
Refined copper—unwrought (metric tons)[8]	455,235	558,405†	544,237†
Refined lead—unwrought (metric tons)[9]	131,117	148,703†	133,054†
Tin: secondary (metric tons)[10]	5,000	5,000	5,000
Zinc—unwrought (metric tons)[11]	399,567	n.a.	n.a.
Radio receivers ('000)[12]	408	n.a.	n.a.
Television receivers ('000)[12]	559	n.a.	n.a.
Merchant vessels launched ('000 gross reg. tons)[13]	25	45	n.a.
Passenger motor cars ('000)[14]	1,091.3	1,212.8*	1,177.9*
Commercial motor vehicles ('000)[14]	56.4	77.4*	90.4*
Electric energy (million kWh)	68,131.2	69,366.8	71,539.2
Manufactured gas (million cu metres)	1,678	1,556	1,541

* Figure for delivery from source, not production.

† Provisional figure for delivery from source.

1 Industrial production only.

2 Including production in Luxembourg. Source: FAO, *Production Yearbook*.

3 Including blankets and carpets.

4 Including yarn made from tow.

5 Including fabrics of natural silk and blankets and carpets of cellulosic fibres.

6 Estimated production in Belgium and Luxembourg during 12 months ending 30 June of the year stated. Figures are in terms of nitrogen. Source: FAO, *Quarterly Bulletin of Statistics*.

7 Estimated production in Belgium and Luxembourg during 12 months ending 30 April of the year stated. Figures are in terms of phosphoric acid. Source: FAO, *Quarterly Bulletin of Statistics*.

8 Including alloys and the processing of refined copper imported from the Democratic Republic of the Congo.

9 Primary and secondary production, including alloys and remelted lead.

10 Estimated production. Source: US Geological Survey.

11 Including alloys and remelted zinc.

12 Factory shipments.

13 Source: Lloyd's Register of Shipping.

14 Assembled wholly or mainly from imported parts.

Finance

CURRENCY AND EXCHANGE RATES

Monetary Units

100 centimes (centiemen) = 1 franc belge (frank) or Belgian franc (BF).

Sterling and Dollar Equivalents (30 September 1997)

£1 sterling = 58.87 francs;
US $1 = 36.44 francs;
1,000 Belgian francs = £16.99 = $27.44.

Average Exchange Rate (francs per US $)

1994 33.456
1995 29.480
1996 30.962

BUDGET (million Belgian francs)

Revenue	1992	1993	1994
National Government			
Direct taxation	732,534	741,602	790,473
Customs and excise	165,832	172,478	175,014
VAT, stamp, registration and similar duties	203,739	219,252	228,009
Other current revenue	127,590	132,881	171,602
Capital revenues	4,607	2,237	10,712
Regions and Communities	754,371	821,981	886,533
Total	1,988,673	2,090,431	2,262,343

Expenditure	1992	1993	1994
National Government			
Government departments	634,940	598,7201	615,566
Public debt	677,994	693,333	660,707
Pensions	250,149	259,924	269,958
Defence	97,877	95,772	97,666
Other expenditure	11,231	10,696	11,159
Regions and Communities	815,958	874,141	937,059
Total	2,488,149	2,532,586	2,592,115

NATIONAL BANK RESERVES (US $ million at 31 December)

	1994	1995	1996
Gold*†	8,482	7,306	n.a.
IMF special drawing rights	180	492	498
Reserve position in IMF	812	1,005	1,075
Foreign exchange†	12,884	14,680	15,380
Total	22,358	23,483	n.a.

* Valued at market-related prices.

† Figures for gold and foreign exchange refer to the monetary association between Belgium and Luxembourg and exclude deposits made with the European Monetary Institute.

Source: IMF, *International Financial Statistics*.

MONEY SUPPLY ('000 million Belgian francs at 31 December)

	1994	1995	1996
Currency outside banks	396.3	428.0	240.4
Demand deposits at commercial banks	1,111.3	1,152.7	1,198.8
Total money	1,507.6	1,580.7	1,439.2

Source: IMF, *International Financial Statistics*.

COST OF LIVING (Consumer Price Index; base: 1990 = 100)

	1993	1994	1995
Food	101.0	102.9	104.1
Fuel and light	103.4	103.6	103.0
Clothing	109.1	111.1	112.7
Rent	114.8	120.0	123.5
All items (incl. others)	108.6	111.2	112.8

Source: ILO, *Yearbook of Labour Statistics*.

1996: All items 115.2 (Source: IMF, *International Financial Statistics*).

NATIONAL ACCOUNTS

('000 million Belgian francs at current prices)

National Income and Product

	1992	1993	1994
Compensation of employees	3,849.3	3,912.1	4,065.8
Operating surplus	1,901.2	1,955.2	2,058.9
Domestic factor incomes	5,750.5	5,867.3	6,124.7
Consumption of fixed capital	692.6	702.6	720.2
Gross domestic product (GDP) at factor cost	6,443.1	6,569.9	6,844.9
Indirect taxes	865.0	908.0	985.8
Less Subsidies	209.7	209.3	204.7
GDP in purchasers' values	7,098.4	7,268.6	7,626.0
Factor income from abroad	1,664.3	1,678.6	1,784.9
Less Factor income paid abroad	1,716.2	1,656.4	1,750.8
Gross national product (GNP)	7,046.5	7,290.8	7,660.1
Less Consumption of fixed capital	692.6	702.6	720.2
National income in market prices	6,353.9	6,588.2	6,939.9
Other current transfers from abroad	179.5	182.3	185.0
Less Other current transfers paid abroad	253.2	266.9	288.3
National disposable income	6,280.2	6,503.5	6,838.5

Expenditure on the Gross Domestic Product

	1993	1994	1995
Government final consumption expenditure	1,081	1,129	1,173
Private final consumption expenditure	4,602	4,810	4,947
Increase in stocks	−4	17	25
Gross fixed capital formation	1,299	1,332	1,396
Total domestic expenditure*	6,978	7,295	7,549
Exports of goods and services	5,012	5,491	5,764
Less Imports of goods and services	−4,674	−5,108	−5,377
GDP in purchasers' values	7,317	7,678	7,936
GDP at constant 1990 prices	6,630	6,777	n.a.

* Including statistical discrepancy.

Source: IMF, *International Financial Statistics.*

Gross Domestic Product by Economic Activity

	1992	1993	1994
Agriculture and livestock	116.2	110.5	117.2
Forestry and logging	7.2	7.2	7.2
Fishing	2.2	2.2	2.2
Mining and quarrying	17.6	15.6	18.1
Manufacturing[1]	1,568.1	1,562.0	1,656.3
Electricity, gas and water	174.5	178.9	185.8
Construction	375.7	366.2	384.9
Wholesale and retail trade	712.5	748.1	771.7
Distribution of petroleum products	189.7	199.2	211.8
Transport, storage and communications	539.0	549.7	593.6
Finance and insurance	397.0	401.0	419.1
Real estate	436.9	471.8	506.5
Business services	416.8	430.0	466.7
Public administration and defence	493.8	515.1	545.5
Education	375.3	401.4	417.8
Health services	207.2	214.0	218.4
Other community, social and personal services[2]	592.1	621.9	664.9
Domestic service of households	57.3	58.9	60.0
Sub-total	6,679.0	6,853.7	7,247.7
Imputed bank service charge	−180.4	−185.1	−186.7
Value-added tax and import duties	553.0	559.5	606.6
Statistical discrepancy[3]	46.8	40.5	−41.5
Total	7,098.4	7,268.6	7,626.0

[1] Including garages.

[2] Including restaurants and hotels.

[3] Including a correction to compensate for the exclusion of certain own-account capital investments ('000 million francs): 13.2 in 1992; 10.5 in 1993; 10.4 in 1994.

BALANCE OF PAYMENTS (US $ million)*

	1994	1995	1996
Exports of goods f.o.b.	122,795	154,692	154,407
Imports of goods f.o.b.	−115,895	−144,662	−145,260
Trade balance	6,901	10,031	9,146
Exports of services	40,440	35,759	36,325
Imports of services	−36,500	−33,595	−33,811
Balance on goods and services	10,841	12,195	11,660
Other income received	89,403	73,102	61,007
Other income paid	−84,166	−66,265	−54,063
Balance on goods, services and income	16,078	19,032	18,604
Current transfers received	4,501	7,737	7,190
Current transfers paid	−8,009	−12,073	−11,408
Current balance	12,571	14,696	14,387
Capital account (net)	—	378	254
Direct investment abroad	−1,371	−11,753	−8,781
Direct investment from abroad	8,514	10,450	14,688
Portfolio investment assets	−40,963	−20,137	−37,809
Portfolio investment liabilities	17,445	−2,298	27,130
Other investment assets	11,269	−33,900	−6,154
Other investment liabilities	−5,076	45,264	−2,307
Net errors and omissions	−2,169	−2,191	−1,329
Overall balance	219	509	80

* Data refer to the Belgium-Luxembourg Economic Union and exclude transactions between the two countries.

Source: IMF, *International Financial Statistics.*

External Trade of Belgium and Luxembourg

Note: Figures exclude trade in monetary gold, non-commercial military goods and silver specie.

Exports include stores and bunkers for foreign ships and aircraft.

PRINCIPAL COMMODITIES
(distribution by SITC, million Belgian francs)

Imports c.i.f.	1992	1993	1994
Food and live animals	349,395	337,205	373,605
Dairy products and birds' eggs	63,207	69,599	68,778
Vegetables and fruit	69,020	62,539	74,995
Beverages and tobacco	49,690	54,264	54,486
Crude materials (inedible) except fuels[1]	201,317	174,554	215,492
Metalliferous ores and metal scrap[1]	69,565	58,018	75,322
Mineral fuels, lubricants, etc. (incl. electric current)	305,020	285,193	290,409
Petroleum, petroleum products, etc.	217,045	194,147	201,801
Crude petroleum oils, etc.	124,868	106,705	104,609
Refined petroleum products	88,492	81,786	91,395
Animal and vegetable oils, fats and waxes	14,705	15,052	20,704
Chemicals and related products[2]	479,203	481,279	554,734
Organic chemicals[2]	142,024	137,281	166,718
Basic manufactures[1,2]	875,861	851,617	947,990
Paper, paperboard and manufactures[2]	91,628	87,739	98,584
Paper and paperboard (not cut to size or shape)[2]	60,555	57,162	65,590
Textile yarn, fabrics, etc.	114,887	105,588	120,763
Non-metallic mineral manufactures	302,674	342,960	360,121
Pearls, precious and semi-precious stones	238,829	287,246	300,154
Non-industrial diamonds (unset)	237,042	194,899	298,863
Sorted diamonds (rough or simply worked)	122,367	79,639	223,589
Cut diamonds (unmounted)	91,342	101,159	133,360
Iron and steel	109,773	97,457	121,045
Non-ferrous metals[1,2]	88,988	76,272	89,314
Other metal manufactures	106,581	82,903	92,853
Machinery and transport equipment	1,029,899	947,877	1,074,515
Power-generating machinery and equipment	64,773	55,016	71,294
Machinery specialized for particular industries	99,486	73,506	87,209
General industrial machinery, equipment and parts	143,273	116,123	132,295
Office machines and automatic data-processing equipment	83,410	72,758	84,092
Electrical machinery, apparatus, etc.	196,269	201,596	227,571
Road vehicles and parts[3]	373,959	361,046	426,411
Passenger motor cars (excl. buses)	201,283	190,866	227,222
Parts and accessories for cars, buses, lorries, etc.	111,837	121,439	145,065
Miscellaneous manufactured articles	464,093	434,293	454,304
Clothing and accessories (excl. footwear)[2]	133,720	132,641	128,304
Other commodities and transactions	254,109	210,541	220,176
Confidential transactions	40,726	26,767	30,213
Total	4,023,293	3,791,874	4,206,414

[1] Copper matte, usually classified with metal ores and concentrates (under 'crude materials'), is included in non-ferrous metals (under 'basic manufactures').

[2] Figures exclude the value of certain confidential transactions, included in the last item of the table.

[3] Excluding tyres, engines and electrical parts.

Exports f.o.b.	1992	1993	1994
Food and live animals[1]	384,644	393,218	418,649
Meat and meat preparations	89,031	86,381	85,036
Fresh, chilled or frozen meat	68,473	69,764	64,734
Dairy products and birds' eggs	69,133	71,787	76,564
Vegetables and fruit	63,230	67,673	47,057
Beverages and tobacco	28,138	36,860	41,058
Crude materials (inedible) except fuels[1,2]	89,614	91,447	106,660
Mineral fuels, lubricants, etc. (incl. electric current)	137,596	140,444	138,726
Petroleum, petroleum products, etc.	128,525	128,357	126,299
Refined petroleum products	121,805	118,660	115,905
Animal and vegetable oils, fats and waxes	15,581	13,941	18,074
Chemicals and related products[1]	583,134	638,924	778,369
Organic chemicals[1]	107,756	137,270	176,684
Artificial resins, plastic materials, etc.	201,536	208,507	244,449
Products of polymerization, etc.[1]	88,509	90,996	108,763
Basic manufactures[1]	1,122,518	1,141,037	1,246,023
Paper, paperboard and manufactures	66,698	66,789	73,792
Textile yarn, fabrics, etc.[1]	207,509	212,992	226,960
Floor coverings, etc.[1]	75,435	77,742	80,622
Carpets, carpeting, rugs, mats, etc.	74,404	77,313	79,983
Non-metallic mineral manufactures[1]	337,540	385,742	412,208
Pearls, precious and semi-precious stones	247,819	294,028	312,330
Non-industrial diamonds (unset)	246,422	292,411	311,134
Sorted diamonds (rough or simply worked)	132,831	156,886	164,034
Cut diamonds (unmounted)	124,248	113,583	147,091
Iron and steel[1]	250,973	231,602	269,024
Bars, rods, angles, shapes, etc.	83,961	74,448	85,553
Non-ferrous metals[1,2]	106,905	102,783	114,946
Other metal manufactures	87,050	78,221	80,418
Machinery and transport equipment[1]	1,072,995	1,140,703	1,292,685
Machinery specialized for particular industries[1]	87,841	90,360	111,932
General industrial machinery, equipment and parts[1]	88,715	96,061	107,349
Telecommunications and sound equipment	64,362	88,730	96,671
Other electrical machinery, apparatus, etc.	101,486	112,783	128,118
Road vehicles and parts[1,3]	610,270	625,061	725,950
Passenger motor cars (excl. buses)	454,901	492,342	566,320
Parts and accessories for cars, buses, lorries, etc.[3]	66,070	57,980	68,164
Miscellaneous manufactured articles[1]	359,662	377,298	384,676
Clothing and accessories (excl. footwear)	75,869	73,947	72,189
Other commodities and transactions	175,928	184,510	163,233
Confidential transactions	163,261	169,884	146,672
Total	3,969,811	4,158,382	4,588,184

[1] Figures exclude the value of certain confidential transactions, included in the last item of the table.

[2] Copper matte, usually classified with metal ores and concentrates (under 'crude materials'), is included in non-ferrous metals (under 'basic manufactures').

[3] Excluding tyres, engines and electrical parts.

PRINCIPAL TRADING PARTNERS* (million Belgian francs)

Imports c.i.f.	1992	1993	1994
France	662,581	611,962	677,516
Germany	961,639	816,115	849,271
Italy	180,757	166,399	180,176
Japan	89,847	97,194	112,873
Netherlands	704,661	677,855	745,683
Spain (excl. Canary Is.)	64,532	63,401	70,266
Sweden	80,716	71,978	95,889
Switzerland	69,811	75,644	66,990
United Kingdom	309,693	354,834	395,330
USA	176,980	206,212	227,085
All countries (incl. others)	4,020,135	3,785,290	4,196,502
Not distributed	3,158	6,584	9,912
Total	4,023,293	3,791,874	4,206,414

Exports f.o.b.	1992	1993	1994
Austria	52,482	48,260	47,779
France	764,018	789,953	871,529
Germany	906,902	871,463	962,776
India	45,344	63,667	62,144
Israel	73,846	81,096	88,204
Italy	233,749	226,169	237,300
Japan	41,038	47,082	60,138
Netherlands	544,161	543,697	604,090
Spain (excl. Canary Is.)	108,901	115,959	136,107
Sweden	55,233	52,246	60,797
Switzerland	87,693	88,141	94,919
United Kingdom	311,430	350,758	388,527
USA	153,037	197,505	229,458
All countries (incl. others)	3,942,605	4,138,233	4,566,604
Not distributed	27,206	20,149	21,580
Total	3,969,811	4,158,382	4,588,184

* Imports by country of production; exports by country of last consignment.

Transport

RAILWAYS (traffic)

	1993	1994	1995
Passenger-km (million)	6,695	6,638	6,757
Freight ton-km (million)	7,568	8,081	7,287

ROAD TRAFFIC (motor vehicles in use at 1 August)

	1994	1995	1996
Private cars	4,210,197	4,273,451	4,339,230
Buses and coaches	14,880	14,667	14,660
Goods vehicles	390,591	402,389	416,710
Tractors (non-agricultural)	38,888	40,074	40,440
Motorcycles and mopeds*	185,270	198,470	n.a.

* Source: IRF, *World Road Statistics*.

SHIPPING

Fleet (at 30 June)

	1994	1995	1996
Merchant shipping:			
Steamships:			
number	1	1	1
displacement*	81.8	81.8	81.8
Motor vessels:			
number	67	65	51
displacement*	1,544	1,284	865
Inland waterways:			
Powered craft:			
number	1,235	1,213	1,159
displacement*	880	882	866
Non-powered craft:			
number	164	160	159
displacement*	395	398	398

* '000 gross registered tons.

Freight Traffic ('000 metric tons)

	1992	1993	1994
Sea-borne shipping:			
Goods loaded	58,074	55,550	33,783
Goods unloaded	91,129	77,503	65,534
Inland waterways:			
Goods loaded	42,776	48,646	n.a.
Goods unloaded	62,478	63,127	n.a.

CIVIL AVIATION (traffic)

	1993	1994	1995
Kilometres flown ('000)	80,894	89,725	89,691
Passenger-km ('000)	6,485,298	7,496,971	8,619,821
Ton-km ('000)	583,687	674,729	775,784
Mail ton-km ('000)	18,982	19,282	19,589

Figures refer to SABENA.

Tourism

	1993	1994	1995
Number of tourist nights*	13,073,911	13,179,971	13,877,662
Number of tourist arrivals*	5,119,883	5,308,776	5,559,875

* Foreign visitors only.

Communications Media

	1992	1993	1994
Telephones ('000 main lines in use)	4,264	4,396	4,526
Telefax stations ('000 in use)	150	165	n.a.
Mobile cellular telephones ('000 subscribers)	61.5	66.9	126.9
Radio receivers ('000 in use)	7,690	7,745	7,800
Television receivers ('000 in use)	4,530	4,550	4,565

Sources: UN, *Statistical Yearbook*; UNESCO, *Statistical Yearbook*.

Newspapers (1994): 28 general interest dailies (combined circulation 1,962,422 copies per issue).

Book production (titles): 6,822 in 1989; 12,157 in 1990; 13,913 in 1991.

Source: partly UNESCO, *Statistical Yearbook*, and Association Belge des Editeurs de Journaux.

Education

(1993/94)

	Institutions		Students	
	French and German	Flemish*	French and German	Flemish*
Pre-primary	1,933	2,190	168,751	255,703
Primary	2,030	2,405	316,670	413,022
Secondary	759	1,099	347,745	450,973
Non-university higher education	155	107	66,544	91,231
University level	11	10	62,466	66,686

* Figures for 1995/96.

Teachers: Pre-primary and Primary 72,589 in 1991/92; Secondary 110,599 in 1991/92; Non-university higher education 17,008 in 1990/91; University level 11,050 in 1990/91. (Source: UNESCO, *Statistical Yearbook*.)

Directory

The Constitution

The Belgian Constitution has been considerably modified by amendments since its origin in 1831. Belgium is a constitutional monarchy. The central legislature consists of a bicameral Parliament (the Chamber of Representatives and Senate). In July 1993 the Constitution was amended to provide for a federation of the largely autonomous regions of Brussels, Flanders and Wallonia and of the Flemish-French- and German-speaking language communities. Article 1 of the Constitution states 'Belgium is a federal state which consists of communities and regions'. The three regions and three linguistic groups are represented by the following directly-elected legislative assemblies: a combined assembly for Flanders and the Flemish-speaking community, regional assemblies for Wallonia and Brussels, and separate assemblies for French- and German-speakers. Each assembly is elected for a term of four years. The regional administrations have sole responsibility for the local economy, the environment, housing, transport and public works, while the language community administrations supervise education policy and culture.

ELECTORAL SYSTEM

Members of Parliament must be 25 years of age, and they are elected by secret ballot according to a system of proportional representation. Suffrage is universal for citizens of 18 years or over, and voting is compulsory.

The Chamber of Representatives consists of 150 members, who are elected for four years unless the Chamber is dissolved before that time has elapsed. The Senate comprises 72 members, of whom 40 are directly elected, normally at intervals of four years, 21 are appointed by the legislative assemblies of the three language communities (10 each from the Flemish- and French-speaking communities and one from the German-speaking community), 10 are co-opted by the elected members and one is a representative of the royal family.

THE CROWN

The King has the right to veto legislation, but, in practice, he does not exercise it. The King is nominally the supreme head of the executive, but, in fact, he exercises his control through the Cabinet, which is responsible for all acts of government to the Chamber of Representatives. According to the Constitution, the King appoints his own ministers, but in practice, since they are responsible to the Chamber of Representatives and need its confidence, they are generally the choice of the Representatives. Similarly, the royal initiative is in the control of the ministry.

LEGISLATION

Legislation is introduced either by the federal Government or the members in the two Houses, and as the party complexion of both Houses is generally almost the same, measures passed by the Chamber of Representatives are usually passed by the Senate. Each House elects its own President at the beginning of the session, who acts as an impartial Speaker, although he is a party nominee. The Houses elect their own committees, through which all legislation passes. They are so well organized that through them the Legislature has considerable power of control over the Cabinet. Nevertheless, according to the Constitution (Article 68), certain treaties must be communicated to the Chamber only as soon as the 'interest and safety of the State permit'. Further, the Government possesses an important power of dissolution which it uses; a most unusual feature is that it may be applied to either House separately or to both together (Article 71).

Revision of the Constitution is to be first settled by an ordinary majority vote of both Houses, specifying the article to be amended. The Houses are then automatically dissolved. The new Chambers thereupon determine the amendments to be made, with the provision that in each House the presence of two-thirds of the members is necessary for a quorum, and a two-thirds majority of those voting is required.

The Government

HEAD OF STATE

King of the Belgians: HM King ALBERT II (took the oath 9 August 1993).

THE CABINET

(January 1998)

A coalition of the Parti Social Chrétien (PSC)/Christelijke Volkspartij (CVP), the Parti Socialiste (PS) and the Socialistische Partij (SP).

Prime Minister: JEAN-LUC DEHAENE (CVP).

Deputy Prime Minister, Minister of the Budget: HERMAN VAN ROMPUY (VP).

Deputy Prime Minister, Minister of Economic Affairs and Telecommunications: ELIO DI RUPO (PS).

Deputy Prime Minister, Minister of Finance and Foreign Trade: PHILIPPE MAYSTADT (PSC).

Deputy Prime Minister, Minister of the Interior: JOHAN VANDE LANOTTE (SP).

Minister of Foreign Affairs: ERIC DERYCKE (SP).

Minister of National Defence: JEAN-POL PONCELET (PSC).

Minister of Justice: STEFAAN DE CLERCK (CVP).

Minister of Employment, Labour and Equal Opportunities: MIET SMIET (CVP).

Minister of Agriculture and Small- and Medium-sized Enterprises: KAREL PINXTEN (CVP).

Minister of Social Affairs: MAGDA DE GALAN (PS).

Minister of Transport: MICHEL DAERDEN (PS).

Minister of Scientific Policy: YVAN YLIEFF (PS).

Minister of the Civil Service: ANDRÉ FLAHAUT (PS).

Minister of Pensions and Public Health: MARCEL COLLA (SP).

Secretary of State for Development Co-operation: RÉGINALD MOREELS (CVP).

Secretary of State for Security, Social Integration and the Environment: JAN PEETERS (SP).

MINISTRIES

Office of the Prime Minister: 16 rue de la Loi, 1000 Brussels; tel. (2) 501-02-11; fax (2) 512-69-53.

Department of Development Co-operation: 6 rue Brederode, 1000 Brussels; tel. (2) 500-62-11; fax (2) 500-65-85.

Department of Security, Social Integration and the Environment: 5 ave Galilée, 1210 Brussels; tel. (2) 210-19-11; fax (2) 217-33-28.

Ministry of Agriculture and Small- and Medium-sized Enterprises: 1 rue Marie-Thérèse, 1040 Brussels; tel. (2) 211-06-11; fax (2) 219-61-30.

Ministry of the Budget: 7 place Quetelet, 1030 Brussels; tel. (2) 219-01-19; fax (2) 219-09-14.

Ministry of the Civil Service: Résidence Palais, 155/16 rue de la Loi, 1040 Brussels; tel. (2) 233-05-11; fax (2) 233-05-90.

Ministry of Economic Affairs and Telecommunications: 23 square de Meeûs, 1040 Brussels; tel. (2) 506-51-11; telex 61932; fax (2) 514-46-83.

Ministry of Employment, Labour and Equal Opportunities: 51 rue Belliard, 1040 Brussels; tel. (2) 233-41-11; fax (2) 233-44-88; e-mail info@meta.fgov.be.

Ministry of Finance: 12 rue de la Loi, 1000 Brussels; tel. (2) 233-81-11; fax (2) 233-80-03.

Ministry of Foreign Affairs: 19 rue des Petits Carmes, 1000 Brussels; tel. (2) 501-81-11; telex 23979; fax (2) 514-30-67.

Ministry of Foreign Trade: 19 rue des Petits Carmes, 1000 Brussels; tel. (2) 516-83-11; fax (2) 512-72-11.

Ministry of the Interior: 60 rue Royale, 1000 Brussels; tel. (2) 504-85-11; fax (2) 504-85-00.

Ministry of Justice: 115 blvd de Waterloo, 1000 Brussels; tel. (2) 542-65-11; telex 62440; fax (2) 542-70-01.

Ministry of National Defence: 6–8 rue Lambermont, 1000 Brussels; tel. (2) 550-28-11; fax (2) 550-28-49.

Ministry of Pensions and Public Health: 33 blvd Bischoffsheim, 1000 Brussels; tel. (2) 220-20-11; fax (2) 220-20-67.

Ministry of Scientific Policy: 66 rue de la Loi, 1040 Brussels; tel. (2) 238-28-11; telex 63477; fax (2) 230-8-62; e-mail cabspo@belspo.be.

Ministry of Social Affairs: 66 rue de la Loi, 1040 Brussels; tel. (2) 238-28-11; fax (2) 230-38-95.

Ministry of Transport: 65 rue de la Loi, 1040 Brussels; tel. (2) 237-67-11; telex 25183; fax (2) 231-19-12.

Legislature

CHAMBRE DES REPRÉSENTANTS/KAMER VAN VOLKSVERTEGENWOORDIGERS

(Chamber of Representatives)

General Election, 21 May 1995

	Seats
CVP	29
VLD	21
PS	21
SP	20
PRL-FDF	18
PSC	12
Vlaams Blok	11
Ecolo	6
Agalev	5
VU	5
FN	2
Others	0
Total	150

SÉNAT/SENAAT

General Election, 21 May 1995

	Seats
CVP	7
SP	6
VLD	6
PRL-FDF	5
PS	5
PSC	3
Vlaams Blok	3
Ecolo	2
VU	2
Agalev	1
Others	0
Total	40

In addition, the Senate has 21 members appointed by the legislative assemblies of the three language communities, 10 members co-opted by the elected members and one member representing the royal family.

Political Organizations

Anders Gaan Leven (Agalev) (Ecologist Party—Flemish-speaking): 78 Tweekerkenstraat, 1040 Brussels; tel. (2) 230-66-66; fax (2) 230-47-86; e-mail agalev@agalev.be; f. 1982; Pres. WILFRED BERVOETS.

Ecolo (Ecologist Party—French-speaking): 12 rue Charles VI, 1030 Brussels; tel. (2) 218-30-35; fax (2) 217-52-90; Fed. Secs ISABELLE DURANT, DANY JOSSE, JACKY MORAEL.

Front Démocratique des Francophones (FDF) (French-speaking Democratic Front): 127 chaussée de Charleroi, 1060 Brussels; tel. (2) 538-83-20; fax (2) 539-36-50; f. 1964; aims to preserve the French character of Brussels and the establishment of a federal state; Pres. OLIVIER MAINGAIN; Sec.-Gen. SERGE DE PATOUL.

Front National (FN): Clos du Parnasse 12, 1040 Brussels; tel. (2) 512-05-75; f. 1988; extreme right-wing nationalist party; Leader Dr FERET.

Partei der Deutschsprachigen Belgier (PDB) (German-speaking Party): 6 Kaperberg, 4700 Eupen; tel. (87) 55-59-87; fax (87) 55-59-84; f. 1971; promotes equality for the German-speaking minority; Pres. GUIDO BREVER.

Parti Communiste (PC) (Communist Party): 4 rue Rouppe, 1000 Brussels; tel. (2) 548-02-90; fax (2) 548-02-95; f. 1921 as Parti Communiste de Belgique–Kommunistische Partij van België, name changed 1990; Pres. PIERRE BEAUVOIS; 5,000 mems.

Parti de la Liberté du Citoyen/Parti Libéral Chretien/Partij der Liberale Christenen (PLC): 46 ave de Scheut, 1070 Brussels; tel. (2) 524-39-66; telex 63903; fax (2) 521-60-71; Pres. LUC EYKERMAN, PAUL MOORS.

Parti Féministe Humaniste: 35 ave des Phalènes, BP 14, 1050 Brussels; tel. (2) 648-87-38; f. 1972 as Parti Féministe Unifié, name changed 1990; aims to create a humanistic and egalitarian republic where the fundamental rights of the individual and of society are respected.

Parti Réformateur Libéral (PRL) (Liberal Party—French-speaking wing): rue de Naples, 41-1050 Brussels; tel. (2) 500-35-11; fax (2) 500-35-00; e-mail prl@prl.be; f. 1846 as Parti Libéral; Pres. LOUIS MICHEL; 50,000 mems.

Parti Social Chrétien (PSC)/Christelijke Volkspartij (CVP) (Christian Social Party): 45 rue des Deux-Eglises, 1040 Brussels; tel. (2) 238-01-11; fax (2) 238-01-29 (PSC); 89 Wetstraat, 1040 Brussels; tel. (2) 238-38-11; fax (2) 230-43-60 (CVP); e-mail inform@cvp.be; Internet http://www.cvp.be; f. 1945; Pres. (PSC) GÉRARD DEPREZ; Pres. (CVP) MARC VAN PEEL; 186,000 mems.

Parti Socialiste (PS) (Socialist Party—French-speaking wing): Maison du PS, 13 blvd de l'Empereur, 1000 Brussels; tel. (2) 548-32-11; fax (2) 548-33-80; e-mail amheletellier@infoboard; f. in 1885 as the Parti Ouvrier Belge; split from the Flemish wing in 1979; Pres. PHILIPPE BUSQUIN; Sec. JEAN-POL BARAS.

Parti Wallon (PW) (Walloon Party): 14 rue du Faubourg, 1430 Quenast; f. 1985 by amalgamation of the Rassemblement Wallon (f. 1968), the Rassemblement Populaire Wallon and the Front Indépendantiste Wallon; left-wing socialist party advocating an independent Walloon state; Pres. JEAN-CLAUDE PICCIN.

Partij van de Arbeid van België (PvdA)/Parti du Travail de Belgique (PTB) (Belgian Labour Party): f. 1979; Marxist-Leninist; Leader LUDO MARTENS.

ROSSEM: Brussels; 'ultra-liberal' Flemish party advocating the privatization of the social security system, the abolition of the monarchy and of marriage; Leader JEAN-PIERRE VAN ROSSEM.

Socialistische Partij (SP) (Socialist Party—Flemish wing): 13 blvd de l'Empereur, 1000 Brussels; tel. (2) 548-32-11; fax (2) 548-35-90; f. 1885; Pres. LOUIS TOBBACK; Sec. LINDA BLOMME.

Vlaams Blok (Flemish Bloc): 8 Madouplein, bus 9, 1210 Brussels; tel. (2) 219-60-09; fax (2) 217-52-75; e-mail vlblok@vlaams-blok.be; f. 1979; advocates Flemish separatism; Chair. FRANK VANHECKE; Chief Officer ROELAND RAES.

Vlaamse Liberalen en Demokraten—Partij van de Burger (VLD) (Flemish Liberals and Democrats—Citizens' Party: Liberal Party—Flemish-speaking wing): 34 Melsensstraat, 1000 Brussels; tel. (2) 549-00-20; fax (2) 512-60-25; f. 1961 as Partij voor Vrijheid en Vooruitgang; Pres. GUY VERHOFSTADT.

Volksunie (VU) (People's Union): 12 Barrikadenplein, 1000 Brussels; tel. (2) 219-49-30; fax (2) 217-35-10; e-mail secretariaat@vu.be; f. 1954; 30,000 mems; Flemish nationalist party supporting national and European federalism; Pres. BERT ANCIAUX; Sec. LAURENS APPELTANS.

Diplomatic Representation

EMBASSIES IN BELGIUM

Albania: 335 ave Louise, 1050 Brussels; tel. (2) 640-14-22; fax (2) 640-28-58; Ambassador: BASHKIM SELIM TRENOVA

Algeria: 209 ave Molière, 1050 Brussels; tel. (2) 343-50-78; fax (2) 343-51-68; Ambassador: MISSOUM SBIH.

Andorra: 10 rue de la Montagne, 1000 Brussels; tel. (2) 513-28-06; fax (2) 513-39-34; Ambassador: ALBERT PINTAT SANTOLARIA.

Angola: 182 rue Franz Merjay, 1180 Brussels; tel. (2) 346-18-72; fax (2) 344-08-94; Ambassador: JOSÉ GUERREIRO ALVES PRIMO.

Argentina: 225 ave Louise, BP 3, 1050 Brussels; tel. (2) 647-78-12; fax (2) 647-93-19; Ambassador: MARIO CÁMPORA.

Armenia: 157 rue Franz Merjay, 1050 Brussels; tel. and fax (2) 346-56-67; Chargé d'affaires a.i.: ARMEN SARKISSIAN.

Australia: 6–8 rue Guimard, 1040 Brussels; tel. (2) 231-05-00; fax (2) 230-68-02; Ambassador: DONALD KENYON.

Austria: 5 place du Champs de Mars, 1050 Brussels; tel. (2) 289-07-00; telex 22463; fax (2) 513-66-41; Ambassador: WINFRIED LANG.

Azerbaijan: 464 ave Molière, 1060 Brussels; tel. (2) 345-26-60; fax (2) 345-91-58; Ambassador: MIR-HAMZA EFENDIEV.

Bangladesh: 29–31 rue Jacques Jordaens, 1000 Brussels; tel. (2) 640-55-00; fax (2) 646-59-98; Ambassador: SYED SHAH MOHAMMED ALI.

Barbados: 78 ave Général Lartigue, 1200 Brussels; tel. (2) 732-17-37; fax (2) 732-32-66; Ambassador: MICHAEL IAN KING.

Belarus: 192 ave Molière, 1050 Brussels; tel. (2) 340-02-70; fax (2) 340-02-87; Ambassador: ULADZIMIR A. LABUNOU.

Benin: 5 ave de l'Observatoire, 1180 Brussels; tel. (2) 374-91-92; fax (2) 375-83-26; Chargé d'affaires: ALBERT AGOSSOU.

Bolivia: 176 ave Louise, BP 6, 1050 Brussels; tel. (2) 627-00-10; fax (2) 647-47-82; Chargé d'affaires a.i.: HORACIO BAZOBERRY.

Bosnia and Herzegovina: 9 rue Paul Lauters, 1000 Brussels; tel. (2) 644-20-08; fax (2) 644-16-98; Chargé d'affaires a.i.: HARIS LUKOVAC.

Botswana: 169 ave de Tervueren, 1150 Brussels; tel. (2) 735-20-70; fax (2) 735-63-18; Ambassador: SASARA CHASALA GEORGE.

Brazil: 350 ave Louise, BP 5, 1050 Brussels; tel. (2) 640-20-15; fax (2) 640-81-34; Ambassador: BERNARDO PERICAS NETO.

Brunei: 238 ave F. D. Roosevelt, 1050 Brussels; tel. (2) 675-08-78; fax (2) 672-93-58; Chargé d'affaires a.i.: MOHAMED NOR Haji JELUDIN.

Bulgaria: 58 ave Hamoir, 1180 Brussels; tel. (2) 374-59-63; fax (2) 375-84-94; Ambassador: BOYKO NOEV.

Burkina Faso: 16 place Guy d'Arezzo, 1180 Brussels; tel. (2) 345-99-12; telex 22252; fax (2) 345-06-12; Ambassador: YOUSSOUF OUÉDRAOGO.

Burundi: 46 square Marie-Louise, 1000 Brussels; tel. (2) 230-45-35; telex 23572; fax (2) 230-78-83; Ambassador: LÉONIDAS NDORICIMPA.

Cameroon: 131 ave Brugmann, 1190 Brussels; tel. (2) 345-18-70; telex 24117; fax (2) 344-57-35; Ambassador: ISABELLE BASSONG.

Canada: 2 ave de Tervueren, 1040 Brussels; tel. (2) 741-06-11; fax (2) 741-06-09; Ambassador: JEAN-PAUL HUBERT.

Cape Verde: 30 rue Antoine Labarre, 1050 Brussels; tel. (2) 646-90-25; fax (2) 646-33-85; Ambassador: JOSÉ LUIS ROCHA.

Central African Republic: 416 blvd Lambermont, 1030 Brussels; tel. (2) 242-28-80; fax (2) 242-30-81; Chargé d'affaires a.i.: JEAN-PIERRE MBAZOA.

Chad: 52 blvd Lambermont, 1030 Brussels; tel. (2) 215-19-75; fax (2) 216-35-26; Ambassador: RAMADANE BARMA.

Chile: 40 rue Montoyer, 1000 Brussels; tel. (2) 280-16-20; fax (2) 280-14-81; Ambassador: HUGO CUBILLOS BRAVO.

China, People's Republic: 443 ave de Tervueren, 1150 Brussels; tel. (2) 771-33-09; fax (2) 772-37-45; Ambassador: DING YUANHONG.

Colombia: 96A ave F. D. Roosevelt, 1050 Brussels; tel. (2) 649-56-79; fax (2) 646-54-91; Ambassador: CARLOS ARTURO MARULANDA RAMÍREZ.

Congo, Democratic Republic: 30 rue Marie de Bourgogne, 1000 Brussels; tel. (2) 513-66-10; telex 21983; fax (2) 514-04-03; Ambassador: JUSTINE MPOYO KASAVUBU.

Congo, Republic: 16-18 ave F. D. Roosevelt, 1050 Brussels; tel. (2) 648-38-56; telex 23677; fax (2) 648-42-13; Ambassador: PAUL ALEXANDRE MAPINGOU.

Costa Rica: 489 ave Louise, (Ae étage), 1050 Brussels; tel. (2) 640-55-41; fax (2) 648-31-92; Ambassador: MARIO CARVAJAL.

Côte d'Ivoire: 234 ave F. D. Roosevelt, 1050 Brussels; tel. (2) 672-23-57; telex 21993; fax (2) 672-04-91; Ambassador: ANET N'ZI NANAN KOLIABO.

Croatia: 50 ave des Arts, 1000 Brussels; tel. (2) 512-24-41; fax (2) 512-03-38; Ambassador: ŽELJKO MATIÉ.

Cuba: 77 rue Roberts-Jones, 1180 Brussels; tel. (2) 343-00-20; fax (2) 344-96-91; Ambassador: RENÉ JUAN MUJICA CANTELAR.

Cyprus: 2 square Ambiorix, 1000 Brussels; tel. (2) 735-35-10; fax (2) 735-45-52; e-mail ambassade.chypre.bruxelles@infoboard.be; Ambassador: MICHALIS ATTALIDES.

Czech Republic: 555 rue Engeland, 1080 Brussels; tel. (2) 374-12-03; fax (2) 375-92-72; Ambassador: KATEŘINA LUKEŠOVÁ (designate).

Denmark: 221 ave Louise, BP 7, 1050 Brussels; tel. (2) 626-07-70; fax (2) 647-07-09; Ambassador: OLE PHILIPSON.

Dominican Republic: 106A ave Louise, 1050 Brussels; tel. (2) 646-08-40; fax (2) 640-95-61; Ambassador: CLARA QUIÑONES RODRÍGUEZ.

Ecuador: 363 ave Louise, 1050 Brussels; tel. (2) 644-30-50; fax (2) 644-28-13; Ambassador: MENTO P. VILLAGOMEZ MERINO.

Egypt: 44 ave Léo Errera, 1180 Brussels; tel. (2) 345-52-53; telex 23716; fax (2) 343-65-33; Ambassador: C. MUHAMMAD CHABANE.

El Salvador: 171 ave de Tervueren, 1150 Brussels; tel. (2) 733-04-85; fax (2) 735-02-11; Ambassador: JOAQUÍN RODEZNO MUNGUIA.

Equatorial Guinea: 295 ave Brugman, 1180 Brussels; tel. (2) 346-25-09; fax (2) 346-33-09; Ambassador: AURELIO MBA OLO.

Eritrea: 382 ave Louise, 1050 Brussels; tel. (2) 644-24-01; fax (2) 644-23-99; Ambassador: ANDEBRHAN WELDEGIORGIS.

Estonia: 1 ave Isidore Gérard, 1160 Brussels; tel. (2) 779-07-55; fax 779-28-17; e-mail saatkond@estemb.be; Ambassador: JÜRI LUIK.

Ethiopia: 231 ave de Tervueren, 1150 Brussels; tel. (2) 771-32-94; fax (2) 771-49-14; Ambassador: Dr PETER GABRIEL ROBLEH.

Fiji: 66 ave de Cortenberg, 1000 Brussels; tel. (2) 736-90-50; fax (2) 736-14-58; Ambassador: KALIOPATE TAVOLA.

Finland: 58 ave des Arts, 1000 Brussels; tel. (2) 287-12-12; fax (2) 287-12-00; Ambassador: LEIF BLOMQVIST.

France: 65 rue Ducale, 1000 Brussels; tel. (2) 548-87-11; telex 21478; fax (2) 513-68-71; Ambassador: JACQUES BERNIERE.

Gabon: 112 ave Winston Churchill, 1180 Brussels; tel. (2) 343-00-55; telex 23383; fax (2) 346-46-69; Ambassador: JEAN ROBERT GOULONGANA.

Gambia: 126 ave F. D. Roosevelt, 1050 Brussels; tel. (2) 640-10-49; telex 24344; fax (2) 646-32-77; Ambassador: ISMAILA BRIAMA CEESAY.

Georgia: 15 rue Vergote, 1030 Brussels; tel. (2) 732-85-50; fax (2) 732-85-47; Ambassador: ZURAB ABACHIDZE.

Germany: 190 ave de Tervueren, 1150 Brussels; tel. (2) 774-19-11; telex 21382; fax (2) 772-36-92; Ambassador: ROLF HOFSTETTER.

Ghana: blvd Général Wahis, 1030 Brussels; tel. (2) 705-82-20; fax (2) 705-66-53; Ambassador: ALEX NTIM ABANKWA.

Greece: 2 ave F. D. Roosevelt, 1050 Brussels; tel. (2) 648-17-30; telex 25521; fax (2) 647-45-25; Ambassador: ANASTASE SIDERIS.

Grenada: 24 ave de la Toison d'Or (5e étage), 1050 Brussels; tel. (2) 514-12-42; fax (2) 513-87-24; Chargé d'affaires a.i.: JOAN-MARIE COUTAIN.

Guatemala: 53 blvd Général Wahis, 1030 Brussels; tel. (2) 705-39-40; fax (2) 705-78-89; Ambassador: CLAUDIO RIEDEL TELGE.

Guinea: 75 ave Roger Vandendriessche, 1150 Brussels; tel. (2) 771-01-26; telex 64731; fax (2) 762-60-32; Ambassador: NABY MOUSSA SOUMAH.

Guinea-Bissau: 70 ave F. D. Roosevelt, 1050 Brussels; tel. (2) 647-13-51; fax (2) 640-43-12; Chargé d'affaires: JOSÉ FONSECA.

Guyana: 12 ave du Brésil, 1000 Brussels; tel. (2) 675-62-16; fax (2) 675-63-31; Ambassador: SAMUEL MANN.

Haiti: 160A ave Louise, BP 25, 1050 Brussels; tel. (2) 649-73-81; fax (2) 640-60-80; Ambassador: YOLETTE AZOR-CHARLES .

Holy See: 9 ave des Franciscains, 1150 Brussels (Apostolic Nunciature); tel. (2) 762-20-05; fax (2) 762-20-32; Apostolic Nuncio: Most Rev. GIOVANNI MORETTI, Titular Archbishop of Vartana.

Honduras: 3 ave des Gaulois (5e étage), 1040 Brussels; tel. (2) 734-00-00; fax (2) 735-26-26; Ambassador: IVAN ROMERO MARTÍNEZ.

Hungary: 41 rue Edmond Picard, 1050 Brussels; tel. (2) 343-67-90; fax (2) 347-60-28; Ambassador: S. E. M. TIBOR KISS.

Iceland: 74 rue de Trèves, 1040 Brussels; tel. (2) 286-17-00; telex 29459; fax (2) 286-17-70; Ambassador: GUNNAR SNORRI GUNNARSSON.

India: 217 chaussée de Vleurgat, 1050 Brussels; tel. (2) 640-91-40; telex 22510; fax (2) 648-96-38; e-mail eoibru@mail.interpac.be; Ambassador: CHANDRASHEKHARA DASGUPTA.

Indonesia: 294 ave de Tervueren, 1150 Brussels; tel. (2) 771-20-14; fax (2) 771-22-91; Ambassador: H. SABANA KARTASASMITA.

Iran: 415 ave de Tervueren, 1150 Brussels; tel. (2) 762-37-45; telex 24083; fax (2) 762-39-15; Ambassador: HAMID ABOUTALÉBI.

Iraq: 23 ave des Aubépines, 1180 Brussels; tel. (2) 374-59-92; telex 26414; fax (2) 374-76-15; Chargé d'affaires a.i.: TARIK M. YAHYA.

Ireland: 89 rue Froissard, 1040 Brussels; tel. (2) 230-53-37; fax (2) 286-17-70; Ambassador: PADRAIC CRADOCK.

Israel: 40 ave de l'Observatoire, 1180 Brussels; tel. (2) 373-55-00; fax (2) 373-56-17; Ambassador: SENNY OMER.

Italy: 28 rue Emile Claus, 1050 Brussels; tel. (2) 649-97-00; telex 23950; fax (2) 648-54-85; Ambassador: FRANCESCO CORRIAS.

Jamaica: 2 ave Palmerston, 1000 Brussels; tel. (2) 230-11-70; fax (2) 230-37-09; e-mail emb.jam.brussels@skynet.be; Ambassador: DOUGLAS SAUNDERS.

Japan: 58 ave des Arts, BP 17/18, 1000 Brussels; tel. (2) 513-23-40; telex 22174; fax (2) 513-15-56; Ambassador: Junichi Nakamura.

Jordan: 104 ave F. D. Roosevelt, 1050 Brussels; tel. (2) 640-77-55; fax (2) 640-27-96; Ambassador: Dr Umayya Toukan.

Kazakhstan: 30 ave Van Bever, 1180 Brussels; tel. (2) 374-95-62; fax (2) 374-50-91; Ambassador: Aoueskhan M. Kyrbassov.

Kenya: 1–5 ave de la Joyeuse Entrée, 1040 Brussels; tel. (2) 340-10-40; fax (2) 340-10-50; Ambassador: Dr P. M. Mwanzia.

Korea, Republic: 3 ave Hamoir, 1180 Brussels; tel. (2) 375-39-80; telex 26256; fax (2) 374-53-95; Ambassador: Moon Chang-Hwa.

Kuwait: 43 ave F. D. Roosevelt, 1050 Brussels; tel. (2) 647-79-50; telex 62904; fax (2) 646-12-98; Ambassador: Ahmad A. K. al-Ebrahim.

Kyrgyzstan: 133 rue Tenbosch, 1050 Brussels; tel. (2) 534-63-99; fax (2) 534-23-25; Ambassador: Chingiz Torekulovitch Aitmatov.

Latvia: 158 ave Molière, 1050 Brussels; tel. (2) 344-16-82; fax (2) 344-74-78; Ambassador: Imants Liegis.

Lebanon: 2 rue Guillaume Stocq, 1050 Brussels; tel. (2) 649-94-60; telex 22547; fax (2) 649-90-02; Ambassador: Jihad Mortada.

Lesotho: 45 blvd Général Wahis, 1030 Brussels; tel. (2) 705-36-39; fax (2) 705-67-79; Ambassador: R. V. Lechesa.

Liberia: 50 ave du Château, 1081 Brussels; tel. (2) 411-09-12; fax (2) 411-01-12; Ambassador: Youngor Telewoda.

Libya: 28 ave Victoria, 1000 Brussels; tel. (2) 647-37-37; fax (2) 640-90-76; Sec. of People's Bureau: Hamed Ahmed Elhouderi.

Liechtenstein: 1 place du Congrès, 1000 Brussels; tel. (2) 229-39-00; fax (2) 219-35-45; Ambassador: Prince Nikolaus von Liechtenstein.

Lithuania: 48 rue Maurice Liétart, 1150 Brussels; tel. (2) 772-27-50; fax (2) 772-17-01; Ambassador: Dalius Čekuolis.

Luxembourg: 75 ave de Cortenbergh, 1000 Brussels; tel. (2) 737-57-00; fax (2) 737-57-00; Ambassador: Paul Schuller.

Macedonia, former Yugoslav republic: 276 ave de Tervueren, 1150 Brussels; tel. (2) 732-91-08; fax (2) 732-91-11; Ambassador: Jovan Tegovski.

Madagascar: 276 ave de Tervueren, 1150 Brussels; tel. (2) 770-17-26; telex 61197; fax (2) 772-37-31; Ambassador: Jean Omer Beriziky.

Malawi: 15 rue de la Loi, 1040 Brussels; tel. (2) 231-09-80; telex 24128; fax (2) 231-10-66; Ambassador: Julie Nanyoni Mphande.

Malaysia: 414A ave de Tervueren, 1150 Brussels; tel. (2) 762-67-67; telex 26396; fax (2) 762-50-49; Ambassador: Dato Martyn M. Sathiah.

Mali: 487 ave Molière, 1060 Brussels; tel. (2) 345-74-32; fax (2) 344-57-00; Ambassador: Ntji Laïco Traoré.

Malta: 44 rue Jules Lejeune, 1050 Brussels; tel. (2) 343-01-95; fax (2) 343-01-06; e-mail victor.camilleri@magnet.mt; Ambassador: Victor Camilleri.

Mauritania: 6 ave de la Colombie, 1000 Brussels; tel. (2) 672-47-47; fax (2) 672-20-51; Ambassador: Boullah Ould Mogueye.

Mauritius: 68 rue des Bollandistes, 1040 Brussels; tel. (2) 733-99-88; telex 23114; fax (2) 734-40-21; Ambassador: Parrwiz Cassim Hossen.

Mexico: 94 ave F. D. Roosevelt, 1050 Brussels; tel. (2) 629-07-77; fax (2) 646-87-68; e-mail embamexbel@pophost.eunet.be; Ambassador: Carlos A. de Icaza.

Moldova: 175 ave Emile Max, 1030 Brussels; tel. (2) 732-96-59; fax (2) 732-96-60; Ambassador: Anatol Arapu.

Monaco: 17 place Guy d'Arezzo, BP 7, 1180 Brussels; tel. (2) 347-49-87; fax (2) 343-49-20; Ambassador: Jean André Gréther.

Mongolia: 18 ave Besme, 1190 Brussels; tel. (2) 344-69-74; fax (2) 344-32-15; Ambassador: Jagvaralyn Hanibal.

Morocco: 29 blvd St-Michel, 1040 Brussels; tel. (2) 736-11-00; telex 21233; fax (2) 734-64-68; Ambassador: Rachad Bouhlal.

Mozambique: 97 blvd St-Michel, 1040 Brussels; tel. (2) 736-25-64; telex 65478; fax (2) 735-62-07; Ambassador: Alvaro O. da Silva.

Namibia: 454 ave de Tervueren, 1150 Brussels; tel. (2) 771-14-10; fax (2) 771-96-89; Ambassador: Dr Zedekia J. Ngavirue.

Nepal: F. D. Roosevelt, 1050 Brussels; tel. (2) 649-40-48; fax (2) 649-84-54; Ambassador: Dr Durgesh Man Singh.

Netherlands: 48 ave Debroux, 1160 Brussels; tel. (2) 679-17-11; fax (2) 679-17-71; Ambassador: E. Röell.

New Zealand: 47–48 blvd du Régent, 1000 Brussels; tel. (2) 512-10-40; fax (2) 513-48-56; Ambassador: Derek William Leask.

Nicaragua: 55 ave de Wolvendael, 1180 Brussels; tel. (2) 375-65-00; fax (2) 375-71-88; Ambassador: Roger Quant Pallavicini.

Niger: 78 ave F. D. Roosevelt, 1050 Brussels; tel. (2) 648-61-40; telex 22857; fax (2) 648-27-84; Ambassador: Housseini Abdou-Saleye.

Nigeria: 288 ave de Tervueren, 1150 Brussels; tel. (2) 762-52-00; telex 22435; fax (2) 762-37-63; Ambassador: Prof. Alaba Ogunsanwo.

Norway: 130A ave Louise (6e étage), 1050 Brussels; tel. (2) 646-07-80; telex 62563; fax (2) 646-28-82; Ambassador: Tor B. Naess.

Pakistan: 57 ave Delleur, 1170 Brussels; tel. (2) 673-80-07; telex 61816; fax (2) 675-31-37; Ambassador: Riaz Mohammad Khan.

Panama: 8 blvd Brand Whitlock, 1150 Brussels; tel. (2) 733-90-89; fax (2) 733-77-79; e-mail epb@netropolis.be; Ambassador: Vilma E. Ramírez.

Papua New Guinea: 430 ave de Tervueren, 1150 Brussels; tel. (2) 779-08-26; fax (2) 772-70-88; Ambassador: Gabriel Koiba Pepson.

Paraguay: 522 ave Louise (3e étage), 1050 Brussels; tel. (2) 649-90-55; fax (2) 647-42-48; Ambassador: Manuel M. Cáceres.

Peru: 179 ave de Tervueren, 1150 Brussels; tel. (2) 733-33-19; fax (2) 733-48-19; e-mail embassy.of.peru@unicall.be; Ambassador: José Antonio Arrospide del Busto.

Philippines: 85 rue Washington, 1050 Brussels; tel. (2) 533-18-11; fax (2) 538-35-40; Ambassador: Pacifico A. Castro.

Poland: 29 ave des Gaulois, 1040 Brussels; tel. (2) 735-72-12; telex 21562; fax (2) 736-18-81; e-mail 106032.2752@compuserve.com; Ambassador: Andrzej Krzeczunowicz.

Portugal: 55 ave de la Toison d'Or, 1060 Brussels; tel. (2) 539-35-21; telex 24570; fax (2) 539-07-73; Ambassador: João da Rocha-Páris.

Qatar: 71 ave F. D. Roosevelt, 1050 Brussels; tel. (2) 640-29-00; telex 63754; fax (2) 648-40-78; e-mail qatar@infonie.be; Chargé d'affaires: Mohamed al-Haiyki.

Romania: 105 rue Gabrielle, 1180 Brussels; tel. (2) 345-26-80; telex 21859; fax (2) 346-23-45; Ambassador: Virgil N. Constantinescu.

Russia: 66 ave de Fré, 1180 Brussels; tel. (2) 374-34-00; telex 65272; fax (2) 374-26-13; Ambassador: Vitalii Churkin.

Rwanda: 1 ave des Fleurs, 1150 Brussels; tel. (2) 763-07-05; fax (2) 763-07-53; Ambassador: Manzi Bakuramutza.

Saint Lucia: 100 rue des Aduatiques, 1040 Brussels; tel. (2) 733-43-28; fax (2) 735-72-37; e-mail ecs.embassies@skynet.be; Ambassador: Edwin Pontien Joseph Larent.

Saint Vincent and the Grenadines: 100 rue des Aduatiques, 1040 Brussels; tel. (2) 733-43-28; fax (2) 735-72-37; e-mail ecs.embassies@skynet.be; Ambassador: Edwin Pontien Joseph Laurent.

Samoa: 123 ave F. D. Roosevelt, bte 14, 1050 Brussels; tel. (2) 660-84-54; fax (2) 675-03-36; Ambassador: Afamasaga Fa'amatala Toleafoa.

San Marino: 62 ave F. D. Roosevelt, 1050 Brussels; tel. (2) 644-22-24; fax (2) 644-20-57; Ambassador: Savina Zafferani.

São Tomé and Príncipe: 175 ave de Tervueren, 1150 Brussels; tel. (2) 734-88-15; fax (2) 734-88-15; Chargé d'affaires a.i.: António de Lima Viegas.

Saudi Arabia: 45 ave F. D. Roosevelt, 1050 Brussels; tel. (2) 649-57-25; telex 64626; fax (2) 647-24-92; Ambassador: Nasser Assaf Hussein al-Assaf.

Senegal: 196 ave F. D. Roosevelt, 1050 Brussels; tel. (2) 673-00-97; telex 21644; fax (2) 675-04-60; Ambassador: Saloum Kande.

Seychelles: 157 blvd du Jubilé, 1080 Brussels; tel. (2) 425-62-36; fax (2) 426-06-29; Ambassador: Sylvestre L. Radegonde.

Sierra Leone: 410 ave de Tervueren, 1150 Brussels; tel. (2) 771-00-53; telex 63624; fax (2) 771-11-80; Chargé d'affaires a.i. James Goodwill.

Singapore: 198 ave F. Roosevelt, 1050 Brussels; tel. (2) 660-29-79; telex 26731; fax (2) 660-86-85; e-mail amb.eu@singembbru.be; Ambassador: Pang Eng Fong.

Slovakia: 195 ave Molière, 1050 Brussels; tel. (2) 346-40-45; fax (2) 346-63-85; Ambassador: Julius Hauser.

Slovenia: 179 ave Louise, 1050 Brussels; tel. (2) 646-90-99; fax (2) 646-36-67; Ambassador: Jaša Zlobec-Lukič.

Solomon Islands: ave de l'Yser, 13, BP 3, 1040 Brussels; tel. (2) 732-70-85; fax (2) 732-68-85; Ambassador: Robert Sisilo.

South Africa: 26 rue de la Loi, BP 7/8, 1040 Brussels; tel. (2) 285-44-00; fax (2) 285-44-02; Ambassador: Annette de Kock Joubert.

Spain: 19 rue de la Science, 1040 Brussels; tel. (2) 230-03-40; telex 22092; fax (2) 230-93-80; Ambassador: Manuel Benavides.

Sri Lanka: 27 rue Jules Lejeune, 1050 Brussels; tel. (2) 344-53-94; fax (2) 344-67-37; Ambassador: Christopher Daneshan Casie Chetty.

Sudan: 124 ave F. D. Roosevelt, 1050 Brussels; tel. (2) 647-94-94; telex 24370; fax (2) 648-34-99; Ambassador: Abdelrahim Ahmed Khalil.

Suriname: 379 ave Louise, 1050 Brussels; tel. (2) 640-11-72; telex 62680; fax (2) 646-39-62; Ambassador: Ewald C. Leeflang.

Swaziland: 188 ave Winston Churchill, 1180 Brussels; tel. (2) 347-47-71; fax (2) 347-46-23; Ambassador: Dr Thembayena Annastasia Dlamini.

Sweden: 148 ave Louise, 1050 Brussels; tel. (2) 289-57-60; telex 21148; fax (2) 289-57-90; Ambassador: Göran Berg.

Switzerland: 26 rue de la Loi, BP 9, 1040 Brussels; tel. (2) 285-43-50; telex 63711; fax (2) 230-37-81; Ambassador: PIERRE-YVES SIMONIN.

Syria: 3 ave F. D. Roosevelt, 1050 Brussels; tel. (2) 648-01-35; telex 26669; fax (2) 646-40-18; Chargé d'affaires a.i.: SAMI SALAMEH.

Tanzania: 363 ave Louise (7e étage), 1050 Brussels; tel. (2) 640-65-00; telex 63616; fax (2) 640-80-26; Ambassador: ALI ABEID KARUME.

Thailand: 2 square du Val de la Cambre, 1050 Brussels; tel. (2) 640-68-10; telex 63510; fax (2) 648-30-66; Ambassador: Dr SOMKIATI ARIYAPRUCHYA.

Togo: 264 ave de Tervueren, 1150 Brussels; tel. (2) 770-17-91; telex 25093; fax (2) 771-50-75; Ambassador: KATI KORGA.

Trinidad and Tobago: 14 ave de la Faisanderie, 1150 Brussels; tel. (2) 762-94-00; fax (2) 772-27-83; Ambassador: LINGSTON LLOYD CUMBERBATCH.

Tunisia: 278 ave de Tervueren, 1150 Brussels; tel. (2) 771-73-95; telex 22078; fax (2) 771-94-33; Ambassador: TAHAR SIOUD.

Turkey: 4 rue Montoyer, 1000 Brussels; tel. (2) 513-40-95; telex 24677; fax (2) 514-07-48; e-mail turkdelegeu@euronet.be; Ambassador: GÜNER ÖZTEK.

Uganda: 317 ave de Tervueren, 1150 Brussels; tel. (2) 762-58-25; fax (2) 763-04-38; Ambassador: KAKIMA NTAMBI.

Ukraine: 99–101 ave Louis Lepoutre, 1050 Brussels; tel. (2) 344-40-20; fax (2) 344-44-66; Ambassador: BORYS TARASYUK.

United Arab Emirates: 73 ave F. D. Roosevelt, 1050 Brussels; tel. (2) 640-60-00; telex 26559; fax (2) 646-24-73; Ambassador: ABDEL HADI ABDEL WAHID AL-KHAJA (designate).

United Kingdom: 85 rue d'Arlon, 1040 Brussels; tel. (2) 287-62-11; fax (2) 287-63-55; Ambassador: DAVID HUGH COLVIN.

USA: 27 blvd du Régent, 1000 Brussels; tel. (2) 508-21-11; fax (2) 511-27-25; Ambassador: ALAN J. BLINKEN.

Uruguay: 22 ave F. D. Roosevelt, 1050 Brussels; tel. (2) 640-11-69; fax (2) 648-29-09; e-mail uruemb@infoboard.be; Ambassador: GUILLERMO E. VALLES GALMES.

Uzbekistan: 99 ave F. D. Roosevelt, 1050 Brussels; tel. (2) 672-88-44; fax (2) 672-39-46; Ambassador: ALISHER FAIZULLAEV.

Venezuela: 10 ave F. D. Roosevelt, 1050 Brussels; tel. (2) 639-03-40; fax (2) 647-88-20; Ambassador: LUIS XAVIER GRISANTI.

Viet Nam: 130 ave de la Floride, 1180 Brussels; tel. (2) 374-91-33; fax (2) 374-93-76; Ambassador: HUYNH ANH DZUNG.

Yemen: 44 rue Van Eyck, 1000 Brussels; tel. (2) 646-52-90; fax (2) 646-29-11; Ambassador: A. K. AL-AGHBARI.

Yugoslavia: 11 ave Emile de Mot, 1000 Brussels; tel. (2) 647-57-81; telex 26156; fax (2) 647-29-41; Chargé d'affaires a.i.: DRAGAN MOMCILOVIĆ.

Zambia: 469 ave Molière, 1050 Brussels; tel. (2) 343-56-49; fax (2) 347-43-33; Ambassador: ISAIAH ZIMBA CHABALA.

Zimbabwe: 11 square Joséphine Charlotte, 1200 Brussels; tel. (2) 762-58-08; telex 24133; fax (2) 762-96-05; Ambassador: SIMBARASHE S. MUMBENGEGWI.

Judicial System

The independence of the judiciary is based on the constitutional division of power between the legislative, executive and judicial bodies, each of which acts independently. Judges are appointed by the crown for life, and cannot be removed except by judicial sentence. The judiciary is organized on four levels, from the judicial canton to the district, regional and national courts. The lowest courts are those of the Justices of the Peace and the Police Tribunals. Each district has one of each type of district court, including the Tribunals of the First Instance, Tribunals of Commerce, and Labour Tribunals, and there is a Court of Assizes in each province. There are Courts of Appeal and Labour Courts in each region. The highest courts are the national civil and criminal Courts of Appeal, Labour Courts and the Supreme Court of Justice. The Military Court of Appeal is in Brussels.

COUR DE CASSATION/HOF VAN CASSATIE (SUPREME COURT OF JUSTICE)

First President: P. ANARCHAL.

President: J. D'HAENENS.

Counsellors: D. HOLSTERS, P. GHISLAIN, M. CHARLIER, M. LAHOUSSE, Y. BELLE-JEANMART, T. VERHEYDEN, I. VEROUGSTRAETE, E. FORRIER, F. FISCHER, C. PARMENTIER, R. BOES, M. D'HONT, E. WAÛTERS, G. DHAEYER, G. SUETENS-BOURGEOIS, L. HUYBRECHTS, E. GOETHALS, J.-P. FRÈRE, P. ECHEMENT, CHR. STORCK, J. DE CODT, F. CLOSE, G. LONDERS.

Attorney-General: E. LIEKENDAEL.

First Advocate-General: J. DU JARDIN.

Advocates-General: J.-M. PIRET, J.-F. LECLERQ, P. GOEMINNE, M. DE SWAEF, G. BRESSELEERS, A. DE RAEVE, G. DUBRULLE, X. DE RIEMAECKER, J. SPREUTELS.

COURS D'APPEL/HOVEN VAN BEROEP (CIVIL AND CRIMINAL HIGH COURTS)

Antwerp: First Pres. L. JANSSENS; Attorney-Gen. Mme CHR. DEKKERS.

Brussels: First Pres. Mme J. CLOSSET-COPPIN; Attorney-Gen. A. VAN OUDENHOVE.

Ghent: First Pres. E. DEGRAEVE; Attorney-Gen. F. SCHINS.

Liège: First Pres. M. MOUREAU; Attorney-Gen. Mme A. THILY.

Mons: First Pres. CHR. JASSOGNE; Attorney-Gen. O. LADRIERE.

COURS DU TRAVAIL/ARBEIDSHOVEN (LABOUR COURTS)

Antwerp: First Pres. J. BEULS.

Brussels: First Pres. P. TAELMAN.

Ghent: First Pres. A. OPSTAELE.

Liège: First Pres. J. HUBIN.

Mons: First Pres. J. GILLAIN.

Religion

CHRISTIANITY

The Roman Catholic Church

Belgium comprises one archdiocese and seven dioceses. At 31 December 1995 there were an estimated 8,099,853 adherents (about 81% of the total population).

Bishops' Conference: Bisschoppenconferentie van België/Conférence Episcopale de Belgique, 1 rue Guimard, 1040 Brussels; tel. (2) 509-96-93; fax (2) 509-96-95; f. 1981; Pres. Cardinal GODFRIED DANNEELS, Archbishop of Mechelen-Brussels.

Archbishop of Mechelen-Brussels: Cardinal GODFRIED DANNEELS, Aartsbisdom, 15 Wollemarkt, 2800 Mechelen; tel. (15) 21-65-01; fax (15) 20-94-85; e-mail aartsbisdom@kerknet.be.

Protestant Churches

Belgian Evangelical Lutheran Church: Brussels; tel. (2) 511-92-47; f. 1950; 425 mems; Pres C. J. HOBUS.

Church of England: 29 rue Capitaine Crespel, 1050 Brussels; tel. (2) 511-71-83; fax (2) 511-10-28; Rev. Canon NIGEL WALKER, Chaplain and Chancellor of the Pro-Cathedral of the Holy Trinity, Brussels.

Eglise Protestante Unie de Belgique: 5 rue du Champ de Mars, 1050 Brussels; tel. (2) 511-44-71; fax (2) 511-28-90; 35,000 mems; Pres. Rev. DANIEL VANESCOTE; Sec. Mrs B. SMETRYNS-BAETENS.

Mission Evangélique Belge: 158 blvd Lambermont, 1030 Brussels; tel. (2) 241-30-15; fax (2) 245-79-65; e-mail 100307.2377@compuserve.com; f. 1918; about 3,000 mems.

Union of Baptists in Belgium (UBB): 85 A. Liebaertstraat, 8400 Ostend; tel. (59) 32-46-10; fax (41) 32-46-10; e-mail 106466.3510@compuserve.com; f. 1922 as Union of Evangelical Baptist Churches; Pres. SAMUEL VERHAEGHE; Sec. PATRICK DENEUT.

ISLAM

There are some 250,000 Muslims in Belgium.

Leader of the Islamic Community: Imam Prof. SALMAN AL-RAHDI.

JUDAISM

There are about 35,000 Jews in Belgium.

Consistoire Central Israélite de Belgique (Central Council of the Jewish Communities of Belgium): 2 rue Joseph Dupont, 1000 Brussels; tel. (2) 512-21-90; fax (2) 512-35-78; f. 1808; Chair. M. GEORGES SCHNEK; Sec. MICHEL LAUB.

The Press

Article 25 of the Belgian Constitution states: 'The Press is free; no form of censorship may ever be instituted; no cautionary deposit may be demanded from writers, publishers or printers. When the author is known and is resident in Belgium, the publisher, printer or distributor may not be prosecuted.'

There are 28 general information dailies (16 French-language, 10 Flemish, one with Flemish and French editions and one German). In 1995 the combined circulation of all daily newspapers averaged 1,962,422 copies per issue.

There is a trend towards concentration. The 'Le Soir' group consists of five dailies. Other significant groupings are the 'De Standaard' and 'Vers l'Avenir' groups. The former consists of four Catholic newspapers, while the latter links five titles. The most widely-circulating dailies in French in 1995 were: *Le Soir* (182,520), *L'Avenir de Luxembourg / Vers l'Avenir* (139,960) and *La Lanterne, La Meuse, La Wallouie* (129,840). The corresponding figures for Flemish-language dailies were: *De Standaard / Nieuwsblad / De Gentenaar* (372,410) and, *Het Laatste Nieuws / De Nieuwe Gazet* (306,240), The major weeklies include *De Bond, Flair, Humo* and *Télémoustique*. Some periodicals are printed in French and in Flemish.

PRINCIPAL DAILIES

Antwerp

De Financieel Economische Tijd: Franklin Bldg, 3 Posthoflei, PB 9, 2600 Berchem; tel. (3) 286-02-11; fax (3) 286-02-10; f. 1968; economic and financial; Gen. Man. PAUL HUYBRECHTS; Chief Editor HANS MAERTENS; circ. 42,110.

Gazet van Antwerpen: 2 Katwilgweg, 2050 Antwerp; tel. (3) 210-02-10; fax (3) 219-40-41; e-mail webmaster@gva.be; Internet http://www.gva.be; f. 1891; Christian Democrat; Gen. Man. P. BAERT; Editor LUC VAN LOON; circ. 163,068 (with *Gazet van Mechelen*).

De Lloyd/Le Lloyd: 23 Eiermarkt, 2000 Antwerp; tel. (3) 234-05-50; telex 31446; fax (3) 234-25-93; f. 1858/1979; Flemish and French edns, with supplements in English; shipping, commerce, industry, finance; Dir GUY DUBOIS; Editor BERNARD VAN DEN BOSSCHE; circ. 10,600.

De Nieuwe Gazet: 5 Posthhoflei, 2600 Berchem; tel. (3) 286-89-30; fax (3) 286-89-40; f. 1897; Liberal; Chief Editor MARCEL WILMET; circ. 306,240 (with *Het Laatste Nieuws*).

Arlon

L'Avenir du Luxembourg: 38 rue des Déportés, 6700 Arlon; tel. (63) 22-03-49; fax (63) 22-05-16; f. 1897; Catholic; Chief Editor JEAN-LUC HENQUINET; circ. 139,960 (with *Vers l'Avenir*).

Brussels

La Dernière Heure/Les Sports: 127 blvd Emile Jacqmain, 1000 Brussels; tel. (2) 211-28-88; fax (2) 211-28-70; f. 1906; independent Liberal; Dir FRANÇOIS LE HODEY; Chief Editor DANIEL VAN WYLICK; circ. 73,130.

L'Echo: 131 rue de Birmingham, 1070 Brussels; tel. (2) 526-55-11; telex 23396; fax (2) 526-55-26; f. 1881; economic and financial; Dir R. WATSON; Editor F. MELAET; circ. 22,230.

Het Laatste Nieuws: 347 Brusselsesteenweg, 1730 Asse-Kobbegem; tel. (2) 454-22-11; fax (2) 454-28-22; f. 1888; Flemish; independent; Dir-Gen. E. CLAEYS; Editor MARCEL WILMET; circ. 306,240 (with *De Nieuwe Gazet*).

La Lanterne: 134 rue Royale, 1000 Brussels; tel. (2) 225-56-00; fax (2) 225-59-13; f. 1944; independent; Dir-Gen. M. FROMONT; Chief Editor GUY DEBISSCHOP; circ. 129,840 (with *La Meuse* and *La Wallonie*).

La Libre Belgique: 127 blvd Emile Jacqmain, 1000 Brussels; tel. (2) 211-27-77; fax (2) 211-28-32; f. 1884; Catholic; independent; Chief Editor JEAN-PAUL DUCHATEAU; circ. 80,000 (with *La Libre Belgique*—Liège).

De Morgen; 54 Brogniezstraat, 1070 Brussels; tel. (2) 556-68-11; fax (2) 520-35-15; Dir-Gen. KOEN CLEMENT; Editor YVES DESMET; circ. 35,000.

Het Nieuwsblad: 28 Gossetlaan, 1702 Groot Bijgaarden; tel. (2) 467-22-11; telex 23039; fax (2) 466-30-93; f. 1923; Dir-Gen. GUIDO VERDEYEN; Chief Editor POL VAN DEN DRIESSCHE; circ. 372,410 (with *De Standaard* and *De Gentenaar*).

Le Soir: 21 place de Louvain, 1000 Brussels; tel. (2) 225-54-32; telex 21312; fax (2) 225-59-14; f. 1887; independent; Chief Editor GUY DUPLAT; circ. 182,520.

De Standaard: 28 Gossetlaan, 1702 Groot Bijgaarden; tel. (2) 467-22-11; telex 23039; fax (2) 466-30-93; f. 1914; Dir-Gen. GUIDO VERDEYEN; Chief Editor DIRK ACHTEN; circ. 372,410 (with *Het Nieuwsblad* and *De Gentenaar*).

Charleroi

Le Journal de Charleroi/Le Peuple: 18 rue du Collège, 6000 Charleroi; tel. (71) 31-01-90; fax (71) 33-16-50; f. 1837; Gen. Man. CHRISTIAN RENARD; Chief Editor JEAN GUY; circ. 94,610 (with *La Nouvelle Gazette; La Province*).

La Nouvelle Gazette (Charleroi, La Louvière, Philippeville, Namur, Nivelles); La Province (Mons): 2 quai de Flandre, 6000 Charleroi; tel. (71) 27-64-11; fax (71) 27-66-09; f. 1878; Man. Dir PATRICK HURBAIN; Editor M. FROHONT; circ. 94,610 (with *Le Journal de Charleroi / Le Peuple*).

Le Rappel: 24 rue de Montigny, 6000 Charleroi; tel. (71) 31-22-80; fax (71) 31-43-61; f. 1900; Dir-Gen. JACQUES DE THYSEBAERT; Chief Editor CARL VAN DOORNE.

Eupen

Grenz-Echo: 8 Marktplatz, 4700 Eupen; tel. (87) 59-13-00; fax (87) 74-38-20; f. 1927; German; independent Catholic; Dir A. KÜCHENBERG; Chief Editor HEINZ WARNY; circ. 12,040.

Ghent

De Gentenaar: 102 Lousbergskaai, 9000 Ghent; tel. (9) 265-68-51; fax (9) 265-68-50; e-mail gentenaar@vum.be; f. 1879; Catholic; Dir-Gen. GUIDO VERDEYEN; Chief Editor POL VAN DRIESSCHE; circ. 372,410 (with *Het Nieuwsblad* and *De Standaard*).

Het Volk: 22 Forelstraat, 9000 Ghent; tel. (9) 265-61-11; telex 11228; fax (9) 225-35-27; f. 1891; Dir-Gen. GUIDO VERDEYEN; Catholic; Man. Editor JAKI LOUAGE; circ. 143,330.

Hasselt

Het Belang van Limburg: 10 Herckenrodesingel, 3500 Hasselt; tel. (11) 87-81-11; fax (11) 87-84-97; f. 1879; Dir MARC LEYNEN; Editors MARC PLATEL, R. SWARTENBROEKX; circ. 100,980.

Liège

La Libre Belgique—Gazette de Liège: 26–28 blvd d'Avroy, 4000 Liège; tel. (4) 223-19-33; fax (4) 222-41-26; f. 1840; Dir-Gen. F. LE HODEY; Editor LOUIS MARAITE; circ. 80,140 (with *La Libre Belgique*—Brussels).

La Meuse: 8-12 blvd de la Sauvenière, 4000 Liège; tel. (4) 220-08-01; telex 41521; fax (4) 220-08-40; f. 1855; independent; Gen. Man. M. FROMONT; Editor-in-Chief W. MEURENS; circ. 129,840 (with *La Lanterne* and *La Wallonie*).

La Wallonie: 55 rue de la Régence, 4000 Liège; tel. (4) 220-18-11; telex 41143; fax (4) 223-31-17; f. 1919; progressive; Dir RENÉ PIRON; Editor FABRICE JACQUEMART; circ. 129,840 (with *La Lanterne* and *La Meuse*).

Mons

La Province: 29 rue des Capucins, 7000 Mons; tel. (65) 31-71-51; fax (65) 33-84-77; Internet http://charline.be/gazette; Dir PHILIPPE DAUTEZ; Chief Editor BENOIT DEGARDIN.

Namur

Vers l'Avenir: 12 blvd Ernest Mélot, 5000 Namur; tel. (81) 24-88-11; telex 59121; fax (81) 22-60-24; f. 1918; Editor JO MOTTET; circ. 139,960 (with *L'Avenir du Luxembourg*).

Tournai

Le Courrier de l'Escaut: 24 rue du Curé Notre-Dame, 7500 Tournai; tel. (69) 88-96-20; fax (69) 88-96-61; f. 1829; Chief Editor WILLY THOMAS.

Verviers

Le Jour/Le Courrier: 14 rue du Brou, 4800 Verviers; tel. (87) 32-20-90; fax (87) 31-67-40; f. 1894; independent; Dir JACQUES DE THYSEBAERT; Chief Editor THIERRY DEGIVES.

WEEKLIES

La Cité: 26 rue St Laurent, 1000 Brussels; tel. (2) 217-23-90; fax (2) 217-69-95; f. 1950 as daily, weekly 1988; Christian Democrat; Editor JOS SCHOONBROODT; circ. 20,000.

De Boer en de Tuinder: 8 Minderbroedersstraat, 3000 Leuven; tel. (16) 24-21-60; telex 24166; fax (16) 24-21-68; f. 1891; agriculture and horticulture; circ. 38,000.

De Bond: 170 Langestraat, 1150 Brussels; tel. (2) 779-00-00; fax (2) 779-16-16; f. 1921; general interest; circ. 332,520.

Brugsch Handelsblad: 4 Eekhoutstraat, 8000 Brugge; tel. (50) 33-06-61; telex 81222; fax (50) 33-46-33; f. 1906; local, national and international news; Dirs RIK DE NOLF, LEO CLAEYS; Editor J. HERREBOUDT; circ. 40,000.

European Voice: 17–19 rue Montoyer, 1000 Brussels; tel. (2) 540-90-90; fax (2) 540-90-87; e-mail europeanvoice@compuserve.com; f. 1995; EU news; Editor JACKI DAVIS; circ 15,000.

Femmes d'Aujourd'hui: 109 rue Neewald, 1200 Brussels; tel. (2) 776-28-50; fax (2) 776-28-58; f. 1933; women's magazine; Chief Editor ROBERT MALIES; circ. 160,000.

Flair: 7 Jan Blockxstraat, 2018 Antwerp; tel. (3) 247-45-11; telex 32979; fax (3) 237-95-19; Flemish and French; women's magazine; Dir C. VON WACKERBARTH; Chief Editor A. BROUCKMANS; circ. (in Belgium) 239,858.

Foot Magazine: 97 blvd Louis Schmidtlaan 97, 1040 Brussels; tel. (2) 737-72-22; fax (2) 737-72-24; circ. 50,000.

Humo: 109 Neerveldstraat, 1200 Brussels; tel. (2) 776-24-20; fax (2) 776-23-24; general weekly and TV and radio guide in Flemish; Chief Editor GUY MORTIER; circ. 278,350.

L'Instant: Brussels; f. 1990; current affairs; circ. 55,000.

Joepie TV Plus: 2 Brandekensweg, 2627 Schelle; tel. (3) 880-84-65; fax (3) 844-61-52; f. 1973; teenagers' interest; Chief Editor GUIDO VAN LIEFFERINGE; circ. 144,841.

Kerk en Leven: 92 Halewijnlaan, 2050 Antwerp; tel. (3) 210-09-40; fax (3) 210-09-36; f. 1942; religious; circ. 800,000.

Knack: 153 Tervurenlaan, 1150 Brussels; tel. (2) 736-60-40; fax (2) 735-68-57; independent news magazine; Dir FRANS VERLEYEN; Chief Editors HUBERT VAN HUMBEECK, FRANK DE MOOR; circ. 140,000.

Kwik: Brusselsesteenweg 347, 1730 Kobbegem; tel. (2) 454-25-01; fax (2) 454-28-28; f. 1962; men's interest; Dir CHRISTIAN VAN THILLO; Editor FRANK SCHRAETS; circ. 55,000.

Landbouwleven/Le Sillon Belge: 92 ave Léon Grosjean, 1140 Brussels; tel. (2) 730-33-00; fax (2) 726-91-34; e-mail erulu@euronet.be; f. 1952; agriculture; Gen. Dir P. CALLEBAUT; Editorial Man. ANDRÉ DE MOL; circ. 38,194.

Libelle: 7 Jan Blockxstraat, 2018 Antwerp; tel. (3) 247-45-11; fax (3) 247-46-88; f. 1945; Flemish; women's interest; Dir JAN VANDENWYNGAERDEN; Chief Editor LILIANE SENEPERT; circ. 255,000.

Het Rijk der Vrouw: Brussels; tel. (2) 526-84-11; telex 25104; fax (2) 526-85-60; f. 1932; women's interest; Dir L. HIERGENS; Chief Editor Y. MIGNOLET; circ. 187,571.

Le Soir Illustré: 21 place de Louvain, 1000 Brussels; tel. (2) 225-55-55; fax (2) 225-59-11; f. 1928; independent illustrated; Dir A. PARON; circ. 107,500.

Spirou/Robbedoes: rue Jules Deserée 52, 6001 Marcinelle; tel. (71) 60-05-00; children's interest; circ. 80,000.

TeVe-Blad: Antwerp; tel. (3) 231-47-90; telex 33134; fax (3) 234-34-66; f. 1981; illustrated; Dir W. MERCKX; Chief Editor ROB JANS; circ. 230,000.

Télémoustique: Brussels; tel. (2) 537-08-00; telex 23291; fax (2) 537-45-63; f. 1924; radio and TV; Dir LOUIS CROONEN; Editor ALAIN DE KUYSSCHE; circ. 226,982.

TV Ekspres: Antwerp; tel. (3) 231-47-90; telex 33134; fax (3) 234-34-66; Dir WIM MERCKX; Chief Editor STEF DURNEZ; circ. 160,000.

TV Story: 7 Jan Blockxstraat, 2018 Antwerp; tel. (3) 247-45-11; fax (3) 216-17-67; f. 1975; Flemish; women's interest; Dir J. VANDENWYNGAERDEN; Chief Editor L. VAN RAAK; circ. 175,111.

TV Strip: Antwerp; tel. (3) 231-47-90; telex 33134; fax (3) 234-34-66; circ. 227,208 (with *TV Ekpress, ZIE Magazine*).

Le Vif/L'Express: 33 place Jamblinne de Meux, 1030 Brussels; tel. (2) 736-65-11; fax (2) 734-30-40; Dir Gen. PATRICK DE BORCHGRAVE; Chief Editor JACQUES GEVERS.

Het Wekelijks Nieuws: 5 Nijverheidslaan, 8970 Poperinge; tel. (57) 33-67-21; fax (57) 33-40-18; Christian news magazine; Dir WIM WAUTERS; Editor HERMAN SANSEN; circ. 56,000.

ZIE-Magazine: Antwerp; tel. (3) 231-47-90; telex 33134; fax (3) 234-34-66; f. 1930; illustrated; Dir JAN MERCKX; Chief Editor ROB JANS; circ. 227,208 (with *TV Ekpress, TV Strip*).

Zondag Nieuws: 2 Brandekensweg, 2627 Schelle; tel. (2) 220-22-11; telex 21495; fax (2) 217-98-46; f. 1958; general interest; Dir RIK DUYCK; Chief Editor LUC VANDRIESSCHE; circ. 113,567.

Zondagsblad: 22 Forelstraat, 9000 Ghent; tel. (9) 265-68-02; fax (9) 223-16-77; f. 1949; Gen. Man. WIM SCHAAP; Editor JEF NIJS; circ. 75,000.

SELECTED OTHER PERIODICALS

Belge: Brussels; f. 1990; satirical; Editor JAN BUCQUOY.

Belgian Business Magazine: 42 ave du Houx, 1170 Brussels; tel. (2) 673-81-70; telex 23830; fax (2) 660-36-00; monthly; management; circ. 31,500.

Het Beste uit Reader's Digest: 29 Henegouwenkaai, 1080 Brussels; tel. (2) 412-11-11; fax (2) 412-11-38; monthly; general; Dir-Gen. EMILE VERMEULEN; circ. 90,000.

Eigen Aard: 170 Langestraat, 1150 Brussels; tel. (2) 799-00-00; fax (2) 799-16-16; f. 1911; monthly; women's interest; circ. 154,870.

International Engineering News: 216 rue verte, 1210 Brussels; tel. (2) 242-29-92; telex 25828; fax (2) 242-71-11; f. 1975; 9 a year; Man. Dir H. BRIELS; circ. 50,026.

Jet Limburg: 10 Heckenrodesingel, 3500 Hasselt; tel. (11) 87-84-85; fax (11) 87-84-84; fortnightly; general interest; circ. 242,000.

Marie Claire: 68 ave Winston Churchill, 1180 Brussels; tel. (2) 349-00-90; fax (2) 344-28-27; monthly; women's interest; circ. 80,000.

Le Moniteur de l'Automobile: Brussels; tel. (2) 660-19-20; telex 26379; fortnightly; motoring; Editor ÉTIENNE VISART; circ. 85,000.

The Office: Brusssels; tel. (2) 640-69-80; telex 64028; fax (2) 648-39-77; f. 1935; English; monthly; Editor WILLIAM R. SCHULHOF; circ. 160,000.

Santé: Drogenbos; tel. (2) 331-06-13; fax (2) 331-23-33; monthly; popular medicine, diet, fitness; circ. 200,000.

Sélection du Reader's Digest: 29 quai du Hainaut, 1080 Brussels; tel. (2) 412-11-11; fax (2) 412-11-38; monthly; general; Dir-Gen. EMILE VERMEULEN; circ. 90,000.

Sphere: Brussels; 6 a year; travel; circ. 77,000.

Vie Féminine: 170 Langestraat, 1150 Brussels; tel. (2) 799-00-00; fax (2) 799-16-16; f. 1917; monthly; women's interest; circ. 68,600.

Vrouw & Wereld: 170 Langestraat, 1150 Brussels; tel. (2) 799-00-00; fax (2) 799-16-16; f. 1920; monthly; women's interest; circ. 263,560.

NEWS AGENCIES

Agence Belga (Agence Télégraphique Belge de Presse SA)—Agentschap Belga (Belgisch Pers-telegraafagentschap NV): 8B rue F. Pelletier, 1030 Brussels; tel. (2) 743-13-11; fax (2) 735-18-74; f. 1920; largely owned by daily newspapers; Chair. L. NEELS; Gen. Man. R. DE CEUSTER.

Agence Europe SA: 10 blvd St Lazare, 1210 Brussels; tel. (2) 219-02-56; telex 21108; fax (2) 217-65-97; f. 1952; daily bulletin on EU activities.

Centre d'Information de Presse (CIP): 199 blvd du Souverain, 1160 Brussels; tel. (2) 675-25-79; f. 1946; Dir T. SCHOLTES.

Foreign Bureaux

Agence France-Presse (AFP): Brussels; tel. (2) 230-83-94; telex 24889; fax (2) 230-23-04; Dir CHARLES SCHIFFMANN.

Agencia EFE (Spain): 1 blvd Charlemagne, BP 20, 1041 Brussels; tel. (2) 230-45-68; telex 23185; Dir RAMÓN CASTILLO MESEGUER.

Agenzia Nazionale Stampa Associata (ANSA) (Italy): 1 blvd Charlemagne, BP 7, 1040 Brussels; tel. (2) 230-81-92; telex 63717; fax (2) 230-60-82; Dir FABIO CANNILLO.

Algemeen Nederlands Persbureau (ANP) (Netherlands): 1 blvd Charlemagne, BP 6, 1041 Brussels; tel. (2) 230-11-88; fax (2) 231-18-04; Correspondents TON VAN LIEROP, KEES PIJNAPPELS, WILMA VAN MELEREN.

Allgemeiner Deutscher Nachrichtendienst (ADN) (Germany): 47 ave des Cattleyas, 1150 Brussels; tel. (2) 734-59-57; telex 23731; fax (2) 736-27-11; Correspondents BARBARA SCHUR, ULLRICH SCHUR.

Associated Press (AP) (USA): 1 blvd Charlemagne, BP 49, 1041 Brussels; tel. (2) 230-52-49; telex 21741; Dir ROBERT WIELAARD.

Central News Agency (CNA) (Taiwan): Brussels; tel. (2) 762-51-05; fax (2) 762-51-05; Bureau Chief TZOU MING-JHI.

Česká tisková kancelář (ČTK) (Czech Republic): 2 rue des Egyptiens, BP 6, 1050 Brussels; tel. (2) 648-01-33; fax (2) 640-31-91; Correspondent M. BARTAK.

Deutsche Presse-Agentur (dpa) (Germany): 1 blvd Charlemagne, BP 17, 1041 Brussels; tel. (2) 230-36-91; telex 22356; fax (2) 230-98-96; Dir HEINZ-PETER DIETRICH.

Informatsionnoye Telegrafnoye Agentstvo Rossii-Telegrafnoye Agentstvo Suverennykh Stran (ITAR-TASS) (Russia): 103 rue Général Lotz, BP 10, 1180 Brussels; tel. (2) 343-86-70; fax (2) 344-83-76; e-mail mineev@arcadis.be; Correspondent ALEKSANDR I. MINEYEV.

Inter Press Service (IPS) (Italy): 21 Inquisitiestraat, 1040 Brussels; tel. (2) 736-18-31; fax (2) 736-82-00; Dir DIRK PEETERS.

Jiji Tsushin (Japan): 1 blvd Charlemagne, BP 26, 1041 Brussels; tel. (2) 285-09-48; fax (02) 230-14-50; Dir HITOSHI SUGIMOTO.

Kyodo News Service (Japan): 1 blvd Charlemagne, Bte 37, 1041 Brussels; tel. (2) 285-09-10; fax (02) 230-53-34; Dir MASARU IWATA.

Magyar Távirati Iroda (MTI) (Hungary): 41 rue Jean Chapelie, 1060 Brussels; tel. and fax (2) 343-75-35; telex 24455; Dir Dr GYÖRGY FÓRIS.

Reuters (UK): 61 rue de Trèves, 1040 Brussels; tel. (2) 287-66-11; fax (2) 230-55-40; Man. Dir PETER KAYER.

Rossiyskoye Informatsionnoye Agentstvo—Novosti (RIA—Novosti) (Russia): 74 rue du Merlot, 1180 Brussels; tel. (2) 332-17-29; Dir IGOR RUZHENSTEV.

Tlačová agentúra Slovenskej republiky (TASR) (Slovakia): BP 16, 1170 Brussels; tel. and fax (2) 675-40-52; Correspondent ROBERT HAJŠEL.

United Press International (UPI) (USA): 1 blvd Charlemagne, BP 64, 1041 Brussels; tel. (2) 230-43-30; fax (2) 230-43-81; Bureau Chief BILL LAMP.

Xinhua (New China) News Agency (People's Republic of China): 32 square Ambiorix, Résidence le Pavois, BP 4, 1040 Brussels; tel. (2) 230-32-54; telex 26555; Chief Correspondent LE ZUDE.

Novinska Agencija Tanjug (Yugoslavia) also has a bureau in Brussels.

PRESS ASSOCIATIONS

Association belge des Editeurs de Journaux/Belgische Vereniging van de Dagbladuitgevers: 22 blvd Paepsem, BP 7, 1070

Brussels; tel. (2) 522-96-60; fax (2) 522-60-04; e-mail abes.bvdu@club.innet.be; f. 1964; 17 mems; Pres JAN SCHEERLINK; Gen. Secs ALEX FORDYN (Flemish), MARGARET BORIBON (French).

Association générale des Journalistes professionnels de Belgique/Algemene Vereniging van de Beroepsjournalisten in België: 9B Quai à la Houille, 1000 Brussels; tel. (2) 229-14-60; fax (2) 223-02-72 f. 1978 on merger of Association Générale de la Presse Belge (f. 1885) and Union Professionnelle de la Presse Belge (f. 1914); 4,000 mems; affiliated to IFJ (International Federation of Journalists); Pres. PHILIPPE LERUTH; Vice-Pres. GERRIT LUTS.

Fédération de la Presse Périodique de Belgique/Federatie van de periodieke pers van België (FPPB): 54 rue Charles Martel, 1000 Brussels; tel. (2) 230-09-99; fax (2) 231-14-59; f. 1891; Pres. P. VAN SINT JAN; Sec.-Gen. JOHAN VAN CLEEMPUT.

Fédération nationale des hebdomadaires d'Information/ Nationale Federatie der Informatieweekbladen: 22 blvd Paepsemlaan, BP 8, 1070 Brussels; tel. (2) 522-57-91; fax (2) 522-85-27; Pres. LOUIS CROONEN.

Principal Publishers

Acco CV: 134-136 Tiensestraat, 3000 Louvain; tel. (16) 29-11-00; fax (16) 20-73-89; f. 1960; general reference, scientific books, periodicals; Dir ROB BERREVOETS.

Uitgeverij Altiora Averbode NV (Publishing Dept): 1 Abdijstraat, BP 54, 3271 Averbode; tel. (13) 78-01-02; fax (13) 78-01-79; e-mail averbode.publ.@verbode.be; f. 1993; children's fiction and non-fiction, religious; Man. Dir R. BIEMANS.

Atlen NV: 4 G. Rodenbachstraat, 1030 Brussels; tel. (2) 242-39-00; telex 63698; f. 1978; reference; Dir J. THURMAN.

De Boeck & Larcier SA: 39 rue des Minimes, 1000 Brussels; tel. (10) 48-25-11; fax (10) 48-26-50; f. 1795; school, technical and university textbooks, youth, nature, legal publs and documentaries; Dirs CHR. DE BOECK, G. HOYOS.

Brepols NV: 68 Steenweg op Tielen, 2300 Turnhout; tel. (14) 40-25-00; fax (14) 42-89-19; e-mail postmaster@brepols.com; f. 1796; humanities, diaries; Dir PAUL VANGERVEN.

Casterman SA: 28 rue des Soeurs Noires, 7500 Tournai; tel. (69) 25-42-11; telex 57328; fax (69) 25-42-29; f. 1780; fiction, encyclopaedias, education, history, comic books and children's books; Man. Dir J. SIMON.

Davidsfonds vzw: 79 Blijde Inkomststraat, 3000 Louvain; tel. (16) 31-06-00; fax (16) 31-06-08; f. 1875; general, reference, textbooks; Dir J. RENS.

Didier Hatier SA: 18 rue Antoine Labarre, 1050 Brussels; tel. (2) 649-99-45; fax (2) 646-06-48; f. 1979; school books, general literature; Dir M. SÉNAT.

Editions Dupuis SA: 52 rue Jules Destrée, 6001 Marcinelle; tel. (71) 60-50-00; fax (71) 60-05-99; f. 1898; children's fiction, periodicals and comic books for children and adults, multimedia and audio-visual; Dir JEAN DENEUMOSTIER.

Etablissements Emile Bruylant: 67 rue de la Régence, 1000 Brussels; tel. (2) 512-98-45; fax (2) 511-72-02; e-mail bruylant@pophost.eunet.be; Internet http://www.bruylant.be; f. 1838; law; Chief Man. Dir J. VANDEVELD.

Hadewijch NV: 33 Vrijheidstraat, 2000 Antwerp; tel. (3) 238-12-96; fax (3) 238-80-41; f. 1983; Dir L. DE HAES.

Halewijn NV: 92 Halewijnlaan, 2050 Antwerp; tel. (3) 210-09-11; fax (3) 210-09-36; f. 1953; general, periodicals; Dir-Gen. J. CORNILLE.

Editions Hemma SA: 106 rue de Chevron, 4987 Chevron; tel. (86) 43-01-01; telex 41507; fax (86) 43-36-40; f. 1956; juveniles, educational books and materials; Dir A. HEMMERLIN.

Die Keure NV: 108 Oude Gentweg, 8000 Brugge; tel. (50) 33-12-35; telex 81411; fax (50) 34-37-68; e-mail die.keure@pophost.eunet.be; f. 1948; textbooks, law, political and social sciences; Dirs J. P. STEEVENS (textbooks), R. CARTON (law, political and social sciences).

Kritak NV: 249 Diestsestraat, 3000 Louvain; tel. (16) 23-12-64; fax (16) 22-33-10; f. 1976; art, law, social sciences, education, humanities, literature, periodicals; Dir ANDRÉ VAN HALEWIJCK.

Editions Labor: 156-158 chaussée de Haecht, 1030 Brussels; tel. (2) 240-05-70; fax (2) 216-34-47; f. 1925; general; *L'Ecole 2000* (periodical); Gen. Man. MARIE-PAULE ESKÉNAZI.

Lannoo Uitgeverij NV: 97 Kasteelstraat, 8700 Tielt; tel. (51) 42-42-11; fax (51) 40-11-52; e-mail lannoo@lannoo.be; f. 1909; general, reference; Dirs GODFRIED LANNOO, MATTHIAS LANNOO, LUC DEMEESTER.

Editions du Lombard SA: 1–11 ave Paul-Henri Spaak, 1070 Brussels; tel. (2) 526-68-11; telex 23097; f. 1946; juveniles, games, education, geography, history, religion; Man. Dir ROB HARREU.

Imprimerie Robert Louis Editions: 35–43 rue Borrens, 1050 Brussels; tel. (2) 640-10-40; fax (2) 640-07-39; f. 1952; science and technical; Man. PIERRE LOUIS.

Manteau NV: 76 Isabellalei, 2018 Antwerp; tel. (3) 230-12-64; fax (3) 230-12-25; f. 1932; literature, periodicals; Dir W. VERHEIJE.

Mercatorfonds: 85 Meir, 2000 Antwerp; tel. (3) 202-72-60; fax (3) 231-13-19; f. 1965; art, ethnography, literature, music, geography and history; Dir JAN MARTENS.

Nouvelles Editions Marabout SA: 30 ave de l'Energie, 4432 Alleur; tel. (41) 46-38-63; telex 42072; fax (41) 63-88-63; f. 1977; paperbacks; Man. Dir J. FIRMIN; Dir JEAN-PAUL MICHAUD.

Peeters pvba: 153 Bondgenotenlaan, 3000 Louvain; tel. (16) 23-51-70; fax (16) 22-85-00; f. 1970; general, reference; Dir M. PEETERS-LISMOND.

Uitgeverij Pelckmans NV: 222 Kapelsestraat, 2950 Kapellen; tel. (3) 664-53-20; fax (3) 655-02-63; f. 1893 as De Nederlandsche Boekhandel, name changed 1988; school books, scientific, general; Dirs J. and R. PELCKMANS.

Reader's Digest SA: 29 quai du Hainaut, 1080 Brussels; tel. (2) 412-11-11; telex 21876; fax (2) 412-11-38; f. 1967; education, sport, games, geography, history, travel, periodicals; Dir-Gen. EMILE VERMEULEN.

Roularta NV: Antwerp; f. 1954; Man. Dirs P. VAN DEN HEUVEL, R. DE NOLF.

De Sikkel: 8 Nijverheidsstraat, 2390 Malle; tel. (3) 309-13-30; fax (3) 311-77-39; e-mail sikkel@club.innet.be; f. 1919; educational books and magazines; Dir K. DE BOCK.

Snoeck-Ducaju en Zoon NV: 464 Begijnhoflaan, 9000 Ghent; tel. (9) 23-48-97; fax (9) 23-68-30; f. 1948; art books, travel guides; Pres. SERGE SNOECK.

Société Belgo-Française de Presse et de Promotion (SBPP) SA: 68 ave Winston Churchill, 1180 Brussels; tel. (2) 349-00-90; fax (2) 344-28-27; periodicals; Dir CLAUDE CUVELIER.

Standaard Uitgeverij NV: 147A Belgiëlei, 2018 Antwerp; tel. (3) 239-59-00; fax (3) 230-85-50; f. 1924; general, comics, dictionaries; Dir (vacant).

Wolters Plantyn: 21-23 Santvoortbeeklaan, 2100 Deurne; tel. (3) 360-03-37; fax (3) 360-03-30; e-mail wolters.plantyn@wpeu.wkb.be; f. 1959; education; Dir JACQUES GERMONPREZ.

Wolters Kluwer Belgie NV: Kovterveldstraat 14, 1831 Diegem; tel. (2) 723-11-11; fax (2) 725-13-06; law, business, school books, scientific; Dir C. BREEKWEG.

Zuidnederlandse Uitgeverij NV: 7 Vluchtenburgstraat, 2630 Aartselaar; tel. (3) 887-14-64; fax (3) 877-21-15; f. 1956; general fiction and non-fiction, children's books; Dir J. VANDE VELDEN.

PUBLISHERS' ASSOCIATIONS

Association des Editeurs Belges (ADEB): 140 blvd Lambermont, 1030 Brussels; tel. (2) 241-65-80; fax (2) 216-71-31; f. 1922; asscn of French-language book publrs; Dir BERNARD GÉRARD.

Cercle Belge de la Librairie: 35 rue de la Chasse Royale, 1160 Brussels; tel. (2) 640-52-41; f. 1883; asscn of Belgian booksellers and publrs; 205 mems; Pres. M. DESTREBECQ.

Vlaamse Uitgevers Vereniging: Antwerp; tel. (3) 230-89-23; fax (3) 281-22-40; asscn of Flemish-language book publrs; Sec. WIM DE MONT.

Broadcasting and Communications

TELECOMMUNICATIONS

Belgacom: 177 blvd E. Jacqmain, 1030 Brussels; tel. (2) 202-81-11; fax (2) 203-54-93; internet http://www.belgacom.be.

STATE BROADCASTING ORGANIZATIONS

Flemish

De Nederlandse Radio- en TV-uitzendingen in België, Omroep de Vlaamse Gemeenschap (Belgische Radio en Televisie—BRTN): 52 Auguste Reyerslaan, 1043 Brussels; tel. (2) 741-31-11; fax (2) 734-93-51; e-mail info@brtn.be; Chair. Prof. B. DE SCHUTTER; Man. Dir B. DE GRAEVE; Dir of Radio Programmes C. CLEEREN; Dir of Television Programmes P. VAN ROE.

French

Radio-Télévision Belge de la Communauté Française (RTBF): 52 blvd Auguste Reyers, 1044 Brussels; tel. (2) 737-21-11; Chair. EDOUARD DESCAMPE; Admin-Gen. JEAN-LOUIS STALPORT; Dir of Radio Programmes ETIENNE SEVRIN; Dir of Television Programmes GERARD LOVERIUS; Dir of Information Service (Radio and Television) JEAN-PIERRE GALLET.

German

Belgisches Rundfunk- und Fernsehzentrum der Deutschsprachigen Gemeinschaft (BRF): 11 Kehrweg, 4700 Eupen; tel. (87) 59-11-11; fax (87) 59-11-99; Dir H. ENGELS.

COMMERCIAL, CABLE AND PRIVATE BROADCASTING

Numerous private radio stations operate in Belgium. Television broadcasts, including foreign transmissions, are received either directly or via cable. Belgium's first subscription-funded channel, Canal Plus Belgique, came into operation in 1989.

Canal Plus Belgique: 656 chaussée de Louvain, 1030 Brussels; fax (2) 732-18-48; f. 1989; 42% owned by Canal Plus France, 25% by RTBF, 25% by DEFICOM; broadcasts to Brussels region and Wallonia.

Télévision Indépendante (TVI): 1 ave Ariane, 1201 Brussels; tel. (2) 778-68-11; telex 64330; fax (2) 778-68-12; commercial station; broadcasts in French.

Vlaamse Televisie Maatschappij: 1 Medialaan, 1800 Vilvoorde; tel. (2) 255-32-11; fax (2) 252-37-87; commercial station; broadcasts in Flemish; Gen. Man. Eric Claeys.

Finance

(cap. = capital; m. = million; res = reserves; dep. = deposits; brs = branches; amounts in Belgian francs)

BANKING

Commission bancaire et financière/Commissie voor het Bank- en Financiewezen: 99 ave Louise, 1050 Brussels; tel. (2) 535-22-11; fax (2) 535-23-23; f. 1935 to supervise the application of legislation relating to the legal status of credit institutions and to the public issue of securities; Chair. Jean-Louis Duplat; CEOs M. Cardon, J. le Brun, C. Lempereur, M. Maes.

Central Bank

Banque Nationale de Belgique: 14 blvd de Berlaimont, 1000 Brussels; tel. (2) 221-21-11; telex 21355; fax (2) 221-31-01; f. 1850; bank of issue; cap. 400m., res 1,134m., dep. 240,611m. (Dec. 1996); Gov. Alfons Verplaetse; Vice-Gov. William Fraeys; Exec. Dirs J.-P. Pauwels, G. Quaden, J.-J. Rey, R. Reynders; 2 brs.

Development Banks

Institut de Réescompte et de Garantie (IRG)/Herdiscontering- en Waarborginstituut (HWI): 78 rue du Commerce, 1040 Brussels; tel. (2) 511-73-30; fax (2) 514-34-50; f. 1935; deals with banks, public credit institutions, private savings banks and other financial intermediaries (money-market dealer and administrator of a deposit protection scheme); cap. and res 2,674m.; Chair. William Fraeys; Gen. Man. Fernand Vanbever.

Investeringsmaatschappij voor Vlaanderen (IMV): 37 Karel Oomsstraat, 2018 Antwerp; tel. (3) 248-23-21; fax (3) 238-41-93; f. 1980; promotes creation, restructuring and expansion of private cos; cap. 15,932,000m.; Chair. R. van Outryve d'Ydewalle; Pres. and CEO G. van Acker.

Société Régionale d'Investissement de Wallonie: 13 ave Destenay, 4000 Liège; tel. (41) 21-98-11; fax (41) 21-99-99; f. 1979; shareholding co; promotion of creation, restructuring and extension of private enterprises; stimulation of the industrial policy of the Walloon region; cap. 12,940m.; Pres. Jean-Claude Dehovre.

Major State-owned Banks

Caisse Nationale de Crédit Professionnel S.A./Nationale Kas voor Beroepskrediet N.V.: 16 blvd de Waterloo, 1000 Brussels; tel. (2) 289-89-89; telex 22026; fax (2) 289-89-90; f. 1929; cap. and res 5,496m., dep. 142,900m. Gen. Man. Thierry Faut.

Crédit à l'Industrie/Krediet aan de Nijverheid: 14 ave de l'Astronomie, 1210 Brussels; tel. (2) 214-12-11; telex 64635; fax (2) 218-04-78; f. 1919; share capital 98% owned by private interests; cap. 4,500m., res 7,5554m., dep. 511,133m. (Dec. 1995); Chair. Wim Coumans; 4 brs.

Agricole SA/NV Landbouwkrediet: 56 rue Joseph II, 1000 Brussels; tel. (2) 287-71-11; telex 26527; fax (2) 230-66-49; f. 1937; agricultural credits; credits granted to agricultural asscns; financing of agricultural products and foodstuffs; cap. 7,634m., res. 2,409m., dep. 140,616m. (Dec. 1996); Pres. Jacques Rousseaux.

Major Commercial Banks

ABN AMRO Bank (België) NV: 53 Regentlaan, 1000 Brussels; tel. (2) 546-04-60; telex 27040; fax (2) 546-04-00; Internet http://www.abnamro.be; affiliated to ABN AMRO Bank (Netherlands); cap. 1,050m., res 1,887m., dep. 106,649m. (Dec. 1996); Chairs J. Koopman; Dir J. J. W. Zweegers; 7 brs.

Antwerpse Diamantbank NV/Banque Diamantaire Anversoise SA: 54 Pelikaanstraat, 2018 Antwerp; tel. (3) 204-72-04; telex 31673; fax (3) 233-90-95; f. 1934; cap. 1,386m., res 2,064m., dep. 27,044m. (Dec. 1996); Chair. André Dirckx; Man. Dir and Chair. of Exec. Cttee Paul C. Goris.

Antwerpse Hypotheekkas/Caisse Hypothécaire Anversoise (AN–HYP): 214 Grotesteenweg, 2600 Antwerp; tel. (3) 286-22-11; telex 33100; fax (3) 286-24-07; e-mail info@anyhp.be; Internet http://www.anhyp.be; f. 1881; savings bank; cap. 1,000m., res 13,159m., dep. 253,976m. (Oct. 1997); Chair. Reynald Moretus; Gen. Man. Baron Carl Holsters; 12 brs.

ASLK—CGER Bank (Algemene Spaar- en Lijfrentekas/Caisse Générale d'Epargne et de Retraite): 48 Wolvengracht, 1000 Brussels; tel. (2) 228-61-11; fax (2) 228-71-99; f. 1865; cap. 43,668m., res 4,820m., dep. 1,789,746m. (Dec. 1995); Chair. of Exec. Cttee Herman Verwilst; Chair. of Board of Dirs Valère Croes; 1,206 brs.

BACOB Bank SC: 25 Trierstraat, 1040 Brussels; tel. (2) 285-20-20; fax (2) 230-71-78; e-mail bacob@bacob.be; f. 1924 as BACOB Savings Bank SC; cap. 10,500m., res 16,590m., dep. 1,329,654m. (Dec. 1996); Chair. D. Bruneel; 666 brs.

Banca Monte Paschi Belgio SA/NV: 24 rue Joseph II, 1000 Brussels; tel. (2) 220-72-11; fax (2) 218-83-91; f. 1947; cap. 1,050m., res 449.7m., dep. 59.9m. (Dec. 1995); Chair. of Exec. Cttee and Gen. Man. Carlo Fiabane; 5 brs.

Bank J. van Breda & Co GCV: 295 Plantin & Moretuslei, 2140 Antwerp; tel. (3) 217-51-11; telex 31788; fax (3) 217-07-08; f. 1930; cap. 650m., res 1,208m., dep. 46,107m. (Dec. 1995); Mans Mark Leysen, Paul van Antwerpen; 30 brs.

Bank Brussels Lambert: 24 ave Marnix, 1000 Brussels; tel. (2) 547-21-11; telex 21421; fax (2) 547-38-44; f. 1975 by merger; cap. 33,091m., res 46,592m., dep. 2,664,838m. (Dec. 1995); Chair. Moulaert; CEO Michel Tilmant; 950 brs.

Bank of Tokyo—Mitsubishi (Belgium) SA: 58 ave des Arts, 1000 Brussels; tel. (2) 551-44-11; telex 20120; fax (2) 551-45-99; f. 1974 as Mitsubishi Bank (Europe); present name adopted 1996; cap. 2,405m., res 126m., dep. 57,174m. (Dec. 1994); Chair. Kazuo Ibuki; Man. Dirs K. Hara, S. Oki.

Bank of Yokohama (Europe) SA: 287 ave Louise, BP 1, 1050 Brussels; tel. (2) 648-82-85; telex 21709; fax (2) 648-31-48; f. 1983; cap. 875m., res 89m., dep. 14,163m. (Dec. 1995); Chair. Mikio Noda; Man. Dir and Gen. Man. Hidetsueu Mihara.

Bank van Roeselare NV: 38 Noordstraat, 8800 Roeselare; tel. (51) 23-52-11; telex 81734; fax (51) 21-00-06; f. 1924, present name adopted 1986; commercial savings bank; cap. 3,000m., res 1,457m., dep. 85,426m. (Dec. 1995); Chair. Gerard Tyvaert; Man. Dirs Aimé Decat, Frans Sercu; 75 brs.

Banque Belgolaise SA: 1 Cantersteen, BP 807, 1000 Brussels; tel. (2) 551-72-11; telex 21375; fax (2) 551-75-15; f. 1960 as Banque Belgo-Congolaise SA, present name adopted 1991; cap. 1,000m., res 2,819m., dep. 67,845m. (Dec. 1995); Chair. Michel Isralson; Exec. Dir Marc Yves Blanpain; 1 br.

Banque Européenne pour l'Amérique Latine (BEAL) SA: 59 rue de l'Association, 1000 Brussels; tel. (2) 229-20-20; telex 22431; fax (2) 229-20-35; f. 1974; cap. 3,200m., res 2,987m., dep. 59,076m. (Dec. 1996); Chair. Jürgen Sengera; Man. Dirs Horst R. Magiera.

Banque Indosuez Belgique SA: 9 Grote Markt, 2000 Antwerp; tel. (3) 505-91-11; telex 23406; fax (3) 511-63-51; f. 1954, present name adopted 1986; cap. 1,500m., res 2,213m., dep. 201,094m. (Dec. 1995); Chair. Jo Holvoet; 5 brs.

Banque Nagelmackers 1747 SA: 5 ave Galilée, bte 16, 1210 Brussels; tel. (2) 229-76-00; telex 21612; fax (2) 229-77-21; f. 1747; cap. 1,849m., res 2,194m., dep. 94,798m. (Dec. 1996); Exec. Cttee Jean-Louis Luyckx, Peter de Proft, Aymon Detroch, Juan de Callatay, Luc Ronsmans; 77 brs.

Banque Paribas Belgique SA/Paribas Bank België NV: 162 blvd Emile Jacqmain, 1000 Brussels; tel. (2) 220-41-11; telex 21349; fax (2) 203-20-14; f. 1968; cap. 4,600m., res 12,589m., dep. 662,749m. (Dec. 1995); Chair. Philippe Romagnoli; 49 brs.

CERA Bank: 100 Brusselsesteenweg, 3000 Leuven; tel. (16) 30-31-11; telex 24166; fax (16) 30-31-99; e-mail info@cera.be; Internet http://www.cera.be; f. 1935 as Centrale Raiffeisenkas CV/Centrale des Caisses Rurales; central org. of co-operative banks; cap. 16,084m., res 44,903m., dep. 1,213,436m. (Dec. 1996); Chair. of Board of Dirs R. Donckels; Chair. of Exec. Cttee W. Breesch; 939 brs.

Central Hispano Benelux SA/NV: 227 rue de la Loi, 1040 Brussels; tel. (2) 286-54-11; telex 21219; fax (2) 230-09-40; f. 1914, present name adopted 1992; cap. 1,000m., res 580m., dep. 87,503m. (Dec. 1996); Pres. Leopoldo Calvo Sotelo y Bustelo; Man. Dir Miguel Sánchez Tovar

Crédit Communal SA/Gemeentekrediet NV: 44 blvd Pachéco, 1000 Brussels; tel. (2) 222-11-11; telex 26354; fax (2) 222-55-04; f. 1860; cap. 15,000m., res 44,375m., dep. 2,420,999m. (Dec. 1995); Chair. G. Mottard; Man. Dir François Narmon; 970 brs.

Crédit Général SA de Banque: 5 Grand-Place, 1000 Brussels; tel. (2) 547-12-11; fax (2) 547-11-00; f. 1958; cap. 3,000m., res 16,101m., dep. 231,310m. (Dec. 1995); Chair. Jan Huyghebaert; 78 brs.

Crédit Lyonnais Belgium SA: 17 ave Marnix, 1000 Brussels; tel. (2) 516-05-11; telex 20227; fax (2) 511-24-58; f. 1893 as Banque de Commerce SA (Handelsbank NV), present name adopted 1989; cap. 6,558m., res 3,501m., dep. 422,539m. (Dec. 1994); Chair. ALFRED BOUCKAERT; Chief Exec. PHILIPPE CLOËS; 35 brs.

Generale Bank NV/Générale de Banque SA: 3 Montagne du Parc, 1000 Brussels; tel. (2) 565-11-11; telex 21283; fax (2) 565-42-22; f. 1965 as Société Générale de Banque SA/Generale Bankmaatschappij NV, name changed 1985; cap. 34,496m., res 40,897m., dep. 4,997,242m. (Dec. 1996); Chair. of Exec. Cttee FERDINAND CHAFFART; Chair. of Board of Dirs Baron PAUL-EMMANUEL JANSSEN; 1,109 brs.

Générale de Banque Belge pour l'Etranger: 3 Montagne du Parc, 1000 Brussels; tel. (2) 565-11-11; f. 1935, present name adopted 1985; cap. 1,100m., res 3,099m., dep. 104,540m. (Dec. 1995); Chair. MARC YVES BLANPAIN.

ING Bank (Belgium) SA/NV: 1 rue de Ligne, 1000 Brussels; tel. (2) 229-87-11; telex 21780; fax (2) 229-88-10; f. 1934, present name adopted 1995; wholly-owned subsidiary of ING Bank (Netherlands); cap. 540m., res 1,560m., dep. 43,452m. (Dec. 1996); Chair. P. VAN ZANTEN; Man. Dir P. C. M. VAN DER VOORT VAN ZIJP.

Ippa Bank NV/SA: 23 blvd du Souverain, 1170 Brussels; tel. (2) 676-12-11; telex 26594; fax (2) 676-12-14; f. 1969; cap. 3,620m., res 844m., dep. 264,429m. (Dec. 1996); Pres. J. P. GÉRARD; Man. Dir ALBERT VAN HOUTTE; 36 brs.

Kredietbank NV: 7 Arenbergstraat, 1000 Brussels; tel. (2) 546-41-11; telex 21207; fax (2) 422-81-31; e-mail u20615@kb.be; f. 1935; cap. 13,734m., res 66,611m., dep. 3,246,100m. (Dec. 1996); Chair. MARCEL COCKAERTS; Man. Dirs JAN VANHEVEL, REMI VERMEIREN, LUC PHILIPS, RUDY BROECKAERT, HERMAN AGNEESSENS; 742 brs.

Metropolitan Bank NV: 191–197 blvd du Souverain, 1160 Brussels; tel. (2) 673-80-01; telex 24036; fax (2) 673-75-19; f. 1935, present name adopted 1966; cap. 2,533m., res 53m., dep. 31,836m. (Dec. 1994); Chair. GEORGES VALKENAERE; Pres. of Exec. Cttee J. HÖNEN; 6 brs.

Mitsubishi Trust and Banking Corporation (Europe) SA: 40 blvd du Régent, 1000 Brussels; tel. (2) 511-22-00; telex 62091; fax (2) 511-26-13; f. 1976; cap. 600m., res 1,573m., dep. 27,470m. (Dec. 1996); Chair. T. SUZUKI; Man. Dir S. SEKIJIMA.

Mitsui Trust Bank (Europe) SA: 287 ave Louise, bte 5, 1050 Brussels; tel. (2) 640-88-50; telex 64720; fax (2) 640-73-29; f. 1980; cap. 1,561m., res 1,310m., dep. 14,344m. (Dec. 1996); Chair. KEN TAKAHASHI; Man. Dir MASAYOSHI TAKAHASHI.

Parfibank SA: 40 blvd du Régent, 1000 Brussels; tel. (2) 513-90-20; telex 61393; fax (2) 512-73-20; f. 1976 as Nippon European Bank SA, present name adopted 1996; cap. 1,850m., res 673m., dep. 20,698m. (Sept. 1996); Chair. RENAUD GREINDL; Man. Dir ROLAND DERAS.

Takugin International Bank (Europe) SA: 40 rue Montoyer, 1040 Brussels; tel. (2) 230-07-14; telex 23568; fax (2) 231-18-99; f. 1981; cap. 740m., res 61.393m., dep. 14,712.7m. (Dec. 1994); Chair. SHIGETOSHI INADA; Man. Dir S. SATO.

Banking Association

Association Belge des Banques/Belgische Vereniging van Banken: 36 rue Ravenstein, BP 5, 1000 Brussels; tel. (2) 507-68-11; fax (2) 512-58-61; e-mail abb.bvb@abb-bvb.be; f. 1936; 137 mems; affiliated to Fédération des Entreprises de Belgique and Fédération Bancaire de l'UE; Pres. WILLY BREESCH; Dir-Gen. GUIDO RAVOET.

STOCK EXCHANGE

Société de la Bourse de Valeurs Mobilières de Bruxelles SC (SBVM) (Stock Exchange): 2 rue Henri Maus, 1000 Brussels; tel. (2) 509-12-11; telex 21186; fax (2) 509-12-12; Pres. O. LEFEBVRE; Dir E. COOREMANS.

There is also a stock exchange in Antwerp.

HOLDING COMPANY

Société Générale de Belgique: 30 rue Royale, 1000 Brussels; tel. (2) 507-02-11; fax 512-18-95; f. 1822; investment and holding co with substantial interests in banking and finance, industry, mining and energy; CEO PHILIPPE LIOTIER.

INSURANCE COMPANIES

Assurances Groupe Josi SA: 135 rue Colonel Bourg, 1140 Brussels; tel. (2) 730-12-11; fax (2) 730-16-00; f. 1955; accident, fire, marine, general, life; Pres. and Dir-Gen. J. P. LAURENT JOSI.

Aviabel, Compagnie Belge d'Assurances Aviation, SA: 10 ave Brugmann, 1060 Brussels; tel. (2) 349-12-11; telex 21928; fax (2) 349-12-99; f. 1935; aviation, insurance, reinsurance; Chair. P. GERVY; Gen. Man. J. VERWILGHEN.

Belgamar, Compagnie Belge d'Assurances Maritimes SA: 66 Mechelsesteenweg, 2018 Antwerp; tel. (3) 247-36-11; telex 33411; fax (3) 247-35-90; f. 1945; marine insurance; Chair. P. H. SAVERYS; Man. Dir A. THIÈRY.

Compagnie d'Assurance de l'Escaut: 10 rue de la Bourse, Antwerp; f. 1821; fire, accident, life, burglary, reinsurance; Man E. DIERCXSENS.

Compagnie Belge d'Assurance-Crédit SA (COBAC): 15 rue Montoyer, 1040 Brussels; tel. (2) 289-31-11; fax (2) 289-44-89; f. 1929; Chair. F. AURILLAC; Man. Dir M. DE BROQUEVILLE.

Compagnie de Bruxelles 1821 SA d'Assurances: Brussels; tel. (2) 237-12-11; telex 24443; fax (2) 237-12-16; f. 1821; fire, life, general; Pres. C. BASECQ.

Fortis AG: 53 blvd Emile Jacqmain, 1000 Brussels; tel. (2) 220-81-11; fax (2) 220-81-50; Internet http://www.fortis.com; f. 1990; asscn between Fortis AG (Belgium) and Fortis AMEV (Netherlands); Chair. and Man. Dir MAURICE LIPPENS; Deputy Chair. ETIENNE DAVIGNON.

Generali Belgium SA: 149 ave Louise, 1050 Brussels; tel. (2) 533-81-11; fax (2) 533-88-99; fire, accident, marine, life, reinsurance; Pres. G. BECKERS; Dir-Gen. R. GRANDI.

Les Patrons Réunis SA: Brussels; tel. (2) 535-96-11; fax (2) 535-98-80; f. 1887; fire, life, accident; Chair. H. LIEKENS; Gen. Man. R. NICOLAS.

Royale Belge: 25 blvd du Souverain, 1170 Brussels; tel. (2) 678-61-11; telex 23000; fax (2) 678-93-40; f. 1853; life, accident, fire, theft, reinsurance, and all other risks; Pres. Comte J. P. DE LAUNOIT; Vice-Pres JACQUES FRIEDMANN, ALBERT FRERE; Man. Dirs JEAN-PIERRE GERARD, PIERRE LABADIE, Comte J. P. DE LAUNOIT.

Société Mutuelle des Administrations Publiques: 24 rue des Croisiers, 4000 Liège; tel. (41) 220-31-11; telex 41216; institutions, civil service employees, public administration and enterprises.

Victoire, Société Anonyme Belge d'Assurances: 80 rue de la Loi, 1040 Brussels; tel. (2) 286-24-11; telex 21819; fax (2) 230-94-73; life and non-life; Chair. M. P. DE COURCEL; Gen. Man. G. DUPIN.

Insurance Associations

Fédération des Producteurs d'Assurances de Belgique (FEPRABEL): 40 ave Albert-Elisabeth, 1200 Brussels; tel (2) 743-25-60; fax (2) 735-44-58; f. 1934; Pres. ALAIN DE MIOMANDRE; 500 mems.

Union Professionnelle des Entreprises d'Assurances Belges et Etrangères Opérant en Belgique—Beroepsvereniging der Belgische en in België werkzame Buitenlandse Verzekeringsondernemingen: 29 square de Meeûs, 1040 Brussels; tel. (2) 547-56-11; telex 63652; fax (2) 547-56-01; f. 1921; affiliated to Fédération des Entreprises de Belgique; Pres. JEAN-PIERRE GÉRARD; Man. Dir MICHEL BAECKER; 137 mems.

Trade and Industry

GOVERNMENT AGENCIES

Investeren in Vlaanderen: Leuvenseplein 4, 1000 Brussels; tel. (2) 507-38-52; fax (2) 507-38-51; f. 1988; promotes investment in Flanders; Dir JOSEE MERCKEN.

Société Développement Régionale de Bruxelles (SDRB): 6 rue Gabrielle Petit, 1210 Brussels; tel. (2) 422-51-12; fax (2) 422-51-12; f. 1974; promotes economic development in the capital; Chair. A. M. HERMANUS.

Société Régionale d'Investissement de Wallonie: 13 ave Destenay, 4000 Liège; tel. (41) 21-98-11; fax (41) 21-99-99; f. 1979; promotes private enterprise in Wallonia; Pres. JEAN-CLAUDE DEHOVRE.

PRINCIPAL CHAMBERS OF COMMERCE

There are chambers of commerce and industry in all major towns and industrial areas.

Kamer van Koophandel en Nijverheid van Antwerpen: 12 Markgravestraat, 2000 Antwerp; tel. (3) 232-22-19; fax (3) 233-64-42; f. 1969; Pres. LUC MEURRENS; Gen. Man. L. LUWEL.

Chambre de Commerce et d'Industrie de Bruxelles: 500 ave Louise, 1050 Brussels; tel. (2) 648-50-02; telex 22082; fax (2) 640-93-28; f. 1875; Pres. JACQUES-ISAAC CASTIAU.

Chambre de Commerce et d'Industrie de Liège: Palais de Congrès, 2 Esplanade de l'Europe, 4020 Liège; tel. (43) 43-92-92; fax (43) 43-92-67; Pres. JACQUES ARNOLIS.

INDUSTRIAL AND TRADE ASSOCIATIONS

Fédération des Entreprises de Belgique (Federation of Belgian Companies): 4 rue Ravenstein, 1000 Brussels; tel. (2) 515-08-11; telex 26576; fax (2) 515-09-99; e-mail red@vbo-feb.be; f. 1895; federates all the main industrial and non-industrial asscns; Pres. KAREL BOONE; Man. Dir TONY VANDEPUTTE; 35 full mems.

Association Belge des Banques (ABB): (see above).

Association des Exploitants de Carrières de Porphyre (Porphyry): 64 rue de Belle-Vue, 1000 Brussels; tel. (2) 648-68-60; f. 1967; Pres. GEORGES HANSEN.

Association des Fabricants de Pâtes, Papiers et Cartons de Belgique (COBELPA) (Paper): Brussels; tel. (2) 646-64-50; fax (2) 646-82-97; f. 1940; Pres. FRANS WALTERS.

Confédération des Brasseries de Belgique (CBB) (Breweries): Maison des Brasseurs, 10 Grand' Place, 1000 Brussels; tel. (2) 511-49-87; fax (2) 511-32-59; f. 1971; Pres. PAUL DE KEERSMAEKER.

Confédération Nationale de la Construction (CNC) (Civil Engineering, Road and Building Contractors and Auxiliary Trades): 34–42 rue du Lombard, 1000 Brussels; tel. (2) 545-56-00; fax (2) 545-59-00; f. 1946; Pres. ROB LENAERS.

Confédération Professionnelle du Sucre et de ses Dérivés (Sugar): 182 ave de Tervueren, 1150 Brussels; tel. (2) 775-80-69; fax (2) 775-80-75; f. 1938; mems 10 groups, 66 firms; Pres. E. KESSELS; Dir-Gen. M. ROSIERS.

Fédération Belge des Dragueurs de Gravier et de Sable (BELBAG-DRAGBEL) (Quarries): 3500 Hasselt; tel. (89) 56-73-45; fax (89) 56-45-42; f. 1967; Pres. CHARLES LECLUYSE.

Fédération Belge des Entreprises de la Transformation du Bois (FEBELBOIS) (Wood): 109–111 rue Royale, 1000 Brussels; tel. (2) 217-63-65; fax (2) 217-59-04; Pres. GUSTAAF NEYT.

Fédération Belge des Industries Graphiques (FEBELGRA) (Graphic Industries): 20 rue Belliard, BP 16, 1040 Brussels; tel. (2) 512-36-38; fax (2) 513-56-76; f. 1978; Pres. FRANCIS MAES.

Fédération Belge des Industries de l'Habillement (Clothing): 24 rue Montoyer, 1040 Brussels; tel. (2) 238-10-11; telex 61055; fax (2) 230-47-00; f. 1946; Pres. BERNARD SIAN.

Fédération Belgo-Luxembourgeoise des Industries du Tabac (FEDETAB) (Tobacco): 7 ave Lloyd George, 1050 Brussels; tel. (2) 646-04-20; fax (2) 646-22-13; f. 1947; Pres. FRANCIS DE VROEY; Gen. Dir NORBERT VITS.

Fédération Charbonnière de Belgique (Coal): Brussels; tel. (2) 230-37-40; fax (2) 230-88-50; f. 1909; Pres. YVES SLEUWAEGEN; Dir JOS VAN DEN BROECK.

Fédération des Carrières de Petit Granit (Limestone): 245 rue de Cognebeau, 7060 Soignies; tel. (67) 34-78-00; fax (67) 33-00-59; f. 1948; Pres. J.-F. ABRAHAM.

Fédération des Entreprises de l'Industrie des Fabrications Métalliques, Mécaniques, Electriques, Electroniques et de la Transformation des Matières Plastiques (FABRIMETAL) (Metalwork, Engineering, Electrics, Electronics and Plastic Processing): 21 rue des Drapiers, 1050 Brussels; tel. (2) 510-23-11; fax (2) 510-23-01; e-mail info@fabrimetal.be; Internet http://www.fabrimetal.be; f. 1946; Pres. JULIEN DE WILDE.

Fédération de l'Industrie Alimentaire/Federatie Voedingsindustrie (Food and Agriculture): 172 Kortenberglaan, BP 7, 1000 Brussels; tel. (2) 743-08-00; fax (2) 733-94-26; f. 1937; Pres. PAUL DE KEERSMAEKER; Dir-Gen. PAUL VERHAEGHE.

Fédération de l'Industrie du Béton (FeBe) (Precast Concrete): 207–209 blvd August Reyers, 1030 Brussels; tel. (2) 735-80-15; fax (2) 734-77-95; f. 1936; Pres. P. DECLERCK; Dir WILLY SIMONS.

Fédération des Industries Chimiques de Belgique (FIC): (Chemical Industries): 49 square Marie-Louise, 1000 Brussels; tel. (2) 238-97-11; fax (2) 231-13-01; e-mail webmaster@fic-fcn.be; f. 1919; Pres. RENÉ PEETERS; Man. Dir PAUL-F. SMETS.

Fédération de l'Industrie Cimentière Belge (Cement): 46 rue César Franck, 1050 Brussels; tel. (2) 645-52-11; fax (2) 640-06-70; e-mail febelcem@infoboard.be; f. 1949; Pres. PAUL VANFRACHEM; Dir-Gen. JEAN-PIERRE JACOBS.

Fédération des Industries Extractives et Transformatrices de Roches non Combustibles (FEDIEX) (Extraction and processing of non-fuel rocks): 61 rue du Trône, 1050 Brussels; tel. (2) 511-61-73; fax (2) 511-12-84; f. 1942 as Union des Producteurs Belges de Chaux, Calcaires, Dolomies et Produits Connexes, name changed 1990; co-operative society; Pres. GILLES PLAQUET.

Fédération de l'Industrie du Gaz (FIGAZ) (Gas): 4 ave Palmerston, 1000 Brussels; tel. (2) 237-11-11; fax (2) 230-44-80; f. 1946; Pres. JEAN-PIERRE DEPAEMELAERE.

Fédération de l'Industrie Textile Belge (FEBELTEX) (Textiles): 24 rue Montoyer, 1000 Brussels; tel. (2) 287-08-11; fax (2) 230-65-85; f. 1945; Pres. BENOÎT-VALÈRE DEVOS; Dir-Gen. JEAN-FRANÇOIS QUIX; 500 mems.

Fédération des Industries Transformatrices de Papier et Carton (FETRA) (Paper and Cardboard): 715 chaussée de Waterloo, BP 25, 1180 Brussels; tel. (2) 344-19-62; fax (2) 344-86-61; f. 1947; Pres. ISIDOOR THIJS.

Fédération de l'Industrie du Verre (Glass): 89 ave Louise, 1050 Brussels; tel. (2) 509-15-20; fax (2) 514-23-45; f. 1947; Pres. R. BUEKENHOUT; Man. Dir ROLAND DERIDDER.

Fédération Patronale des Ports Belges (Port Employers): 33 Brouwersvliet, bus 7, 2000 Antwerp; tel. (3) 221-99-85; fax (3) 226-83-71; f. 1937; Pres. FRANÇOIS VAN GEEL; Secs FRANS GIELEN, GUY VANKRUNKELSVEN.

Fédération Pétrolière Belge (Petroleum): 4 rue de la Science, 1000 Brussels; tel. (2) 512-30-03; fax (2) 511-05-91; f. 1926; Pres. PAUL VAN DE WALLE; Sec.-Gen. G. VAN DE WERVE.

Groupement National de l'Industrie de la Terre Cuite (Bricks): 13 rue des Poissonniers, BP 22, 1000 Brussels; tel. (2) 511-25-81; fax (2) 513-26-40; f. 1947; Pres. GILBERT DE BAERE.

Groupement Patronal des Bureaux Commerciaux et Maritimes (Employers' Association of Trade and Shipping Offices): 33 Brouwersvliet, bus 7, 2000 Antwerp; tel. (3) 221-99-90; fax (3) 226-83-71; f. 1937; Pres. FRANÇOIS VAN GEEL; Sec. FRANS GIELEN.

Groupement des Sablières (Sand and Gravel): 49 Quellinstraat, 2018 Antwerp; tel. (3) 223-66-83; fax (3) 223-66-47; f. 1937; Pres. ALFRED PAULUS; Sec. PAUL DE NIE.

Groupement de la Sidérurgie (Iron and Steel): 47 rue Montoyer, 1000 Brussels; tel. (2) 509-14-11; fax (2) 509-14-00; f. 1953; Pres. PAUL MATTHYS.

Union des Armateurs Belges (Shipowners): 9 Lijnwaadmarkt, 2000 Antwerp; tel. (3) 232-72-31; fax (3) 225-28-36; Chair. NICOLAS SAVERYS; Man. C. BETRAINS.

Union des Carrières et Scieries de Marbres de Belgique (UCSMB) (Marble): 8 Heideveld, 1654 Huizingen; tel. (2) 361-36-81; fax (2) 361-31-55; Pres. P. STONE.

Union des Exploitations Electriques et Gazières en Belgique (UEGB) (Electricity and Gas): 8 blvd du Régent, 1000 Brussels; tel. (2) 518-67-07; fax (2) 518-64-58; f. 1911; Pres. ANDRÉ MARCHAL.

Industrie des Huiles Minérales de Belgique (IHMB—IMOB) (Mineral Oils): 49 square Marie-Louise, 1000 Brussels; tel. (2) 238-97-11; fax (2) 230-03-89; f. 1921; Pres. J. VERCHEVAL; Sec. D. DE HEMPTINNE; 65 mems.

Union Professionnelle des Producteurs de Fibres-Ciment (Fibre-Cement): 361 ave de Tervueren, 1150 Brussels; tel. (2) 778-12-11; fax (2) 778-12-12; f. 1941; Pres. JEAN BEECKMAN; Sec. ANNIE NAUS.

Union de la Tannerie et de la Mégisserie Belges (UNITAN) (Tanning and Tawing): c/o 140 rue des Tanneurs, 7730 Estaimbourg; tel. (69) 36-23-23; fax (69) 36-23-10; f. 1962; Pres. ALBERT CAPPELLE; Sec. ANNE VANDEPUTTE; 8 mems.

UTILITIES

Electricity

Electrabel: 8 Regentlaan, 1000 Brussels; tel. (2) 518-61-11; fax (2) 518-64-00; http://www.electrabel.be.

Gas

Distrigas: 31 Kunstlaan, 1040 Brussels; tel. (2) 282-72-11; fax (2) 230-02-39.

Water

Société Wallonne des Distributions d'Eau: 41 rue de la Concorde, 4800 Verviers; tel. (87) 34-28-11; fax (87) 34-28-00.

Vlaamse Maatschappij voor Watervoorziening: 73 Belliardstraat, 1040 Brussels; tel. (2) 238-94-11; fax (2) 230-97-98.

TRADE UNIONS

Fédération Générale du Travail de Belgique (FGTB)/Algemeen Belgisch Vakverbond (ABVV): 42 rue Haute, 1000 Brussels; tel. (2) 506-82-11; fax (2) 513-47-21; f. 1899; affiliated to ICFTU; Pres. MICHEL NOLLET; Gen. Sec. MIA DE VITS; has eight affiliated unions with an estimated total membership of 1,176,701 (1995). Affiliated unions:

Belgische Transportarbeidersbond/Union Belge des Ouvriers du Transport (Belgian Transport Workers' Union): 66 Paardenmarkt, 2000 Antwerp: tel. (3) 224-34-11; fax (3) 234-01-49; f. 1913; Pres. ALFONS GEERAERTS; 24,000 mems (1990).

La Centrale Générale/De Algemene Centrale (Central Union, building, timber, glass, paper, chemicals and petroleum industries): 26–28 rue Haute, 1000 Brussels; tel. (2) 549-05-49; fax (2) 514-16-91; Pres. HANS RAES; Sec. Gen. MAURICE CORBISIER; Nat. Secs DAN PLAUM, PAUL LOOTENS, FERDY DE WOLF, JACQUES MICHIELS; 300,000 mems (1995).

Centrale Générale des Services Publics/Algemene Centrale der Openbare Diensten (Public Service Workers): Maison des Huit Heures, 9–11 place Fontainas, 1000 Brussels; tel. (2) 508-58-11; telex 22563; fax (2) 508-59-02; f. 1945; Pres. J. LOREZ; Vice-Pres. F. FERMON; Gen. Secs J. DUCHESNE, A. MORDANT, K. STESSENS, T. BERGS.

Centrale de l'Industrie du Livre et du Papier/Centrale der Boek- en Papiernijverheid (Graphical and Paper Workers): Brussels; tel. (2) 512-13-90; fax (2) 512-57-85; f. 1945; Sec.-Gen. ROGER SAGON; Nat. Sec. JEAN-MICHEL CAPPOEN; 12,000 mems (1995).

Centrale de l'Industrie du Métal de Belgique/Centrale der Metaalindustrie van België (Metal Workers): 17 rue Jacques Jordaens, 1000 Brussels; tel. (2) 627-74-11; fax (2) 627-74-90; f. 1887; Pres. JACQUES FONTAINE; 185,570 mems (1993).

Centrale Syndicale des Travailleurs des Mines de Belgique/Belgische Mijnwerkerscentrale (Miners): 8 J. Stevensstraat, bus 4, 1000 Brussels; tel. (2) 511-96-45; f. 1889; Pres. J. OLYSLAEGERS.

Centrale Alimentation-Horeca-Services/Voedingscentrale-Horeca-Diensten (Catering and Hotel Workers): 18 rue des Alexiens, 1000 Brussels; tel. (2) 512-97-00; fax (2) 512-53-68; f. 1912; Pres. ARTHUR LADRILLE; Nat. Sec. RONNY DESMET.

FGTB—Textile, Vêtement, et Diamant/ABVV—Textiel, Kleding - Diamant (Textile, Clothing and Diamond Workers): 143 Opvoedingstraat, 9000 Ghent; tel. (9) 242-86-86; fax (9) 242-86-96; f. 1994; Pres. DONALD WITTEVRONGEL; 60,000 mems (1994).

Syndicat des Employés, Techniciens et Cadres de Belgique/Bond der Bedienden, Technici en Kaders van België (Employees, Technicians and Administrative Workers): 42 rue Haute, 1000 Brussels; tel. (2) 512-52-50; fax (2) 511-05-08; f. 1891; Pres. CHRISTIAN ROLAND; Gen. Sec. ROBERT WITTEBROUCK.

Les Cadets, an organization for students and school pupils, is also affiliated to the FGTB/ABVV.

Confédération des Syndicats Chrétiens (CSC): 121 rue de la Loi, 1040 Brussels; tel. (2) 237-31-11; fax (2) 237-33-00; Pres. WILLY PEIRENS; has 18 affiliated unions with an estimated total membership of 1,546,360 (1993). Affiliated unions:

Centrale Chrétienne de l'Alimentation et des Services (Food and Service Industries): Brussels; tel. (2) 218-21-71; f. 1919; Pres. W. VIJVERMAN; Sec.-Gen. F. BOCKLANDT.

Centrale Chrétienne des Métallurgistes de Belgique (Metal Workers): 127 rue de Heembeek, 1120 Brussels; tel. (2) 244-99-11; fax (2) 241-48-27; Pres. T. JANSSEN.

Centrale Chrétienne des Mines, de l'Energie, de la Chimie et du Cuir (CCMECC) (Mines, Power, Chemical and Leather Workers): 26 ave d'Auderghem, 1040 Brussels; tel. (2) 238-73-32; f. 1912; Pres. A. VAN GENECHTEN; Gen. Sec. M. ANDRÉ; Nat. Sec. A. CUYVERS; 63,155 mems (1993).

Centrale Chrétienne des Ouvriers du Textile et du Vêtement de Belgique (Textile and Clothing Workers): 27 Koning Albertlaan, 9000 Ghent; tel. (91) 22-57-01; fax (91) 20-45-59; f. 1886; Pres. A. DUQUET; Gen. Sec. L. MEULEMAN.

Centrale Chrétienne des Ouvriers du Transport et des Ouvriers du Diamant (Transport and Diamond Workers): 12 Entrepotplaats, 2000 Antwerp; tel. (3) 232-99-29; fax (3) 231-47-81; Pres. JOHN JANSSENS.

Centrale Chrétienne du Personnel de l'Enseignement Moyen et Normal Libre (Lay Teachers in Secondary and Teacher-Training Institutions): 26–32 ave d'Auderghem, 1040 Brussels; tel. and fax (2) 238-72-33; f. 1924; f. 1950; Pres. WILLEM MILLER.

Centrale Chrétienne du Personnel de l'Enseignement Technique (Teachers in Technical Education): 16 rue de la Victoire, 1060 Brussels; tel. (2) 5420900; fax (2) 5420908; Sec.-Gen. PROSPER BOULANGE; 8,000 mems (1993).

Centrale Chrétienne des Services Publics—Christelijke Centrale van de Openbare Diensten (Public Service Workers): 26-32 ave d'Auderghem, 1040 Brussels; tel. (2) 231-00-90; f. 1921; Pres. FILIP WIEERS; Sec.-Gen. GUY RASNEUR.

Centrale Chrétienne des Travailleurs du Bois et du Bâtiment (Wood and Building Workers): 31 rue de Trèves, 1040 Brussels; tel. (2) 285-02-11; fax (2) 230-74-43; Pres. J. JACKERS; Sec.-Gen. RAYMOND JONGEN; 174,620 mems (1992).

Christelijke Centrale van Diverse Industrieen (Miscellaneous): Oudergemselaan 26–32, 1040 Brussels; tel. (2) 238-72-11; fax (2) 238-73-12; Pres. LEO DUSOLEIL; Nat. Secs FRANÇOIS LICATA, LEON VAN HAUDT.

Christelijk Onderwijzersverbond van België (School teachers): 203 Koningsstraat, 1210 Brussels; tel. (2) 227-41-11; fax (2) 219-47-61; f. 1893; Pres. G. BOURDEAUD'HUI; Sec.-Gen. L. VAN BENEDEN; 41,000 mems (1993).

Fédération des Instituteurs Chrétiens (Schoolteachers): 16 rue de la Victoire, 1060 Brussels; tel. (2) 539-00-01; fax (2) 534-13-36; f. 1893; publishes twice monthly periodical 'L'éducateur'; Sec.-Gen. R. DOHOGNE; 16,000 mems (1996).

Service Syndical Sports (Sport): 121 rue de la Loi, 1040 Brussels; tel. (2) 237-34-64; fax (2) 237-36-00; Nat. Sec. M. VAN MOL; Sec. M. LIPPENS.

Syndicat Chrétien des Communications et de la Culture (Christian Trade Unions of Railway, Post and Telecommunications, Shipping, Civil Aviation, Radio, TV and Cultural Workers): Galerie Agora, 105 rue du Marché aux Herbes, BP 38/40, 1000 Brussels; tel. (2) 549-07-62; fax (2) 512-85-91; f. 1919; Pres. M. BOVY; Vice-Pres. P. BERTIN.

Union Chrétienne des Membres du Personnel de l'Enseignement Officiel: 16 rue de la Victoire, 1060 Brussels; tel. (2) 5420900; fax (2) 5420908; Pres. G. BULTOT; Sec. Gen. P. BOULANGE.

Centrale Générale des Syndicats Libéraux de Belgique (CGSLB) (General Federation of Liberal Trade Unions of Belgium): 72-74 blvd Poincaré, 1070 Brussels; tel. (2) 558-51-50; fax (2) 558-51-51; f. 1891; Nat. Pres. GUY HAAZE; 220,000 mems.

Fédération Nationale des Unions Professionnelles Agricoles de Belgique: 47 chaussée de Namur, 5030 Gembloux; tel. (81) 60-00-60; Pres. H. TILMANT; Sec.-Gen. J. P. CHAMPAGNE.

Landelijke Bedienden Centrale-Nationaal Verbond voor Kader-personeel (Employees): 1 Beggaardenstraat, 2000 Antwerp; tel. (3) 220-87-11; fax (2) 231-66-64; f. 1912; Sec-Gen. L. STRAGIER; 236,000 mems (1996).

Nationale Unie der Openbare Diensten (NUOD)/Union Nationale des Services Publics (UNSP): 25 rue de la Sablonnière, 1000 Brussels; tel. and fax (2) 219-88-02; f. 1983; Pres. GÉRALD VAN ACKER; Sec.-Gen. FRANCIS SACRE.

Transport

RAILWAYS

The Belgian railway network is one of the densest in the world. The main lines are operated by the Société Nationale des Chemins de Fer Belges (SNCB) under lease from the State Transport Administration. Construction of the Belgian section of a high-speed railway network for northern Europe, that will eventually link Belgium, France, the Netherlands, the United Kingdom and Germany, is expected to be completed by 2005.

Société Nationale des Chemins de Fer Belges (SNCB)/Nationale Maatschappij der Belgische Spoorwegen (NMBS): 85 rue de France, 1060 Brussels; tel. (2) 525-21-11; telex 20424; fax (2) 525-40-45; f. 1926; 144m. passengers were carried in 1995; 3,368 km of lines, of which 2,371 km are electrified; board of 18 members; Chair. MICHEL DAMAR; Man. Dir ETIENNE SCHOUPPE.

ROADS

At 31 December 1995 there were 1,666 km of motorways, 12,750 km of other main or national roads and 1,347 km of secondary or regional roads. In addition there were about 126,800 km of minor roads.

Société Régionale Wallonne du Transport (Light railways, buses and trams): 96 ave Gouverneur Bovesse, 5100 Namur; tel. (81) 32-27-11; fax (81) 32-27-10; f. 1991; Dir-Gen. JEAN-CLAUDE PHLYPO.

VVM-De Lijn: 1 Hendrik Consciencestraat, 2800 Mechelen; tel. (15) 44-07-11; fax (15) 44-07-09; f. 1991; public transport; Dir-Gen. HUGO VAN WESEMAEL.

INLAND WATERWAYS

There are over 1,520 km of inland waterways in Belgium, of which 660 km are navigable rivers and 860 km are canals. In 1991 an estimated 94.8m. metric tons of cargo were carried on the inland waterways.

In 1989 waterways administration was divided between the Flemish region (1,055 km), the Walloon region (450 km) and the Brussels region (15 km):

Flemish region:

Departement Leefmilieu en Infrastructuur Administratie Waterwegen en Zeewezen: Graaf de Ferraris-Gebouw, 156 ave Emile Jacqmain, BP 5, 1000 Brussels; tel. (2) 553-77-11; fax (2) 553-77-05; e-mail janej.strubbe@lin.vlaanderen.be; Dir-Gen. JAN STRUBBE.

Walloon region:

Direction Générale des Voies Hydrauliques: W. T. C. Tour 3, 30 blvd S. Bolivar, 1210 Brussels; tel. (2) 208-41-36; fax (2) 208-41-41; Dir-Gen. B. FAES.

Brussels region:

Haven van Brussel: 6 place des Armateurs, 1210 Brussels; tel. (2) 425-10-00; fax (2) 425-18-74; f. 1993; Gen. Man. STEVEN VANACKERE; Admin. Dir CHARLES HUYGENS.

SHIPPING

The modernized port of Antwerp is the second biggest in Europe and handles 80% of Belgian foreign trade by sea and inland waterways. It is also the largest railway port and has one of the largest petroleum refining complexes in Europe. It has 98 km of quayside and 17 dry docks, and is currently accessible to vessels of up to 75,000 tons:

extensions are being carried out which will increase this limit to 125,000 tons. Other ports include Zeebrugge, Ostend, Ghent, Liège and Brussels.

Ahlers Shipping NV: 139 Noorderlaan, 2030 Antwerp; tel. (3) 543-72-11; telex 72154; fax (3) 541-23-09; services to Finland, Poland, Latvia, Morocco; Chair. C. Leysen; Man. Dir H. Knoche.

Belfranline NV: Antwerp 1; tel. (3) 233-08-89; telex 34115; fax (3) 234-22-04; f. 1957; liner services to and from Venezuela and northern Europe; Man. Dir E. J. Sasse.

De Keyser Thornton: 38 Huidevettersstraat, 2000 Antwerp; tel. (3) 205-31-00; telex 72511; fax (3) 234-27-86; e-mail info@multimod-al.be; f. 1853; shipping agency, forwarding and warehousing services; Man. Dir M. P. Ingham.

ESSO Belgium: Antwerp; tel. (3) 543-31-11; telex 35600; fax (3) 543-34-95; refining and marketing of petroleum products; Pres. S. R. McGill.

North Sea Ferries (Belgium) NV: Leopold II Dam, 13, 8380 Zeebrugge; tel. (50) 54-34-11; telex 81469; fax (50) 54-68-35; operated in conjunction with North Sea Ferries Ltd, UK; roll-on/roll-off ferry services between Zeebrugge and Hull and Middlesbrough; Dirs P. V. D. Bromdhof, R. B. Lough.

Northern Shipping Service NV: 54 St Katelijnevest, 2000 Antwerp; tel. (3) 204-78-78; telex 32315; fax (3) 231-30-51; forwarding, customs clearance, liner and tramp agencies, chartering, Rhine and inland barging, multi-purpose bulk/bags fertilizer terminal; Pres. and Man. Dir Bernard Montaldier.

Petrofina SA: 52 rue de l'Industrie, 1040 Brussels; tel. (2) 233-91-11; telex 21556; fax (2) 288-34-45; integrated petroleum co active in exploration and production, transportation and petroleum refining, petrochemicals, etc., marketing of petroleum products and research; Vice-Chair. and Man. Dir François Cornelis.

CIVIL AVIATION

The main international airport is at Brussels, with a direct train service from the air terminal. A major programme of expansion, more than doubling the airport's passenger-handling capacity, was completed in 1994. Further expansion work was to include the construction of a new concourse by 2000. There are also international airports at Antwerp, Liège, Charleroi and Ostend.

SABENA Belgian Airlines (Société anonyme belge d'exploitation de la navigation aérienne): 2 ave E. Mounierlaan, 1200 Brussels; tel. (2) 723-31-11; telex 21322; fax (2) 723-80-99; f. 1923; 49.5% owned by Swissair; services to most parts of the world; Chair. and CEO Paul Reutlinger.

Delta Air Transport (DAT) NV: Antwerp Airport, BP 4, 2100 Deurne (Antwerp); tel. (3) 285-18-11; telex 32602; fax (3) 218-76-15; f. 1966; 79% owned by SABENA; scheduled and charter services from Antwerp and Brussels to many European destinations; Pres. Bernadette Franzi; Gen. Dir Walter Vermeiren.

Sobelair (Société Belge de Transports par Air) NV: 117a Airport Bldg, 1820 Melsbroek; tel. (2) 754-12-11; telex 22095; fax (2) 754-12-88; f. 1946; subsidiary of SABENA, operating charter and inclusive-tour flights; Pres. P. Reutlinger; Gen. Man. L. Cloetens.

Virgin Express: Airport Bldg 116, 1820 Melsbroek; tel. (2) 752-05-11; telex 21886; fax (2) 752-05-06; f. 1991 as EuroBelgium Airlines, name changed as above 1996; 90% owned by Virgin Group (UK), scheduled and charter services to European destinations; Man. Dir Jonathan Ornstein.

Tourism

Belgium has several towns of rich historic and cultural interest, such as Brussels, Brugge (Bruges), Ghent, Antwerp, Liège, Tournai, Namur and Durbuy. The country's seaside towns attract many visitors. The forest-covered Ardennes region is renowned for hill-walking and gastronomy.

Office de Promotion du Tourisme Wallonie–Bruxelles: 61 rue Marché-aux-Herbes, 1000 Brussels; tel. (2) 504-02-00; fax (2) 513-69-50; f. 1981; promotion of tourism in French-speaking Belgium; Dir Viviane Jacobs.

Tourist Information Brussels (TIB): Hôtel de Ville, Grand-Place, 1000 Brussels; tel. (2) 513-89-40; fax (2) 514-45-38; Dirs E. Puttaert, G. Renders, A. Vrydagh.

Tourist Office for Flanders: 61 Grasmarkt, 1000 Brussels; tel. (2) 504-03-00; fax (2) 504-03-77; f. 1985; official promotion and policy body for tourism in Flemish part of Belgium; Gen. Commissioner Urbain Claeys.

BELIZE

Introductory Survey

Location, Climate, Language, Religion, Flag, Capital

Belize lies on the Caribbean coast of Central America, with Mexico to the north-west and Guatemala to the south-west. The climate is sub-tropical, tempered by trade winds. The temperature averages 24°C (75°F) from November to January, and 27°C (81°F) from May to September. Annual rainfall ranges from 1,290 mm (51 ins) in the north to 4,450 mm (175 ins) in the south. The average annual rainfall in Belize City is 1,650 mm (65 ins). Belize is ethnically diverse, the population (according to the 1991 census) consisting of 44% Mestizos (Maya-Spanish), 30% Creoles (those of predominantly African descent), 11% Amerindian (mainly Maya), 7% Garifuna ('Black Caribs', descendants of those deported from the island of Saint Vincent in 1797) and communities of Asians, Portuguese, German Mennonites and others of European descent. English is the official language and an English Creole is widely understood. Spanish is the mother-tongue of some 15% of the population but is spoken by many others. There are also speakers of Garifuna (Carib), Maya and Ketchi, while the Mennonites speak a German dialect. Most of the population profess Christianity, with about 58% being Roman Catholics in 1995. The national flag (proportions usually 5 by 3) is dark blue, with narrow horizontal red stripes at the upper and lower edges; at the centre is a white disc containing the state coat of arms, bordered by an olive wreath. The capital is Belmopan.

Recent History

Belize, known as British Honduras until June 1973, was first colonized by British settlers (the 'Baymen') in the 17th century, but was not recognized as a British colony until 1862. In 1954 a new Constitution granted universal adult suffrage and provided for the creation of a legislative assembly. The territory's first general election, in April 1954, was won by the only party then organized, the People's United Party (PUP), led by George Price. The PUP won all subsequent elections until 1984. In 1961 Price was appointed First Minister under a new ministerial system of government. The colony was granted internal self-government in 1964, with the United Kingdom retaining responsibility for defence, external affairs and internal security. Following an election in 1965, Price became Premier and a bicameral legislature was introduced. In 1970 the capital of the territory was moved from Belize City to the newly-built town of Belmopan.

Much of the recent history of Belize has been dominated by the territorial dispute with Guatemala, particularly in the years prior to Belize's independence (see below). This was achieved on 21 September 1981, within the Commonwealth, and with Price becoming Prime Minister. However, the failure of the 1981 draft treaty with Guatemala, and the clash of opposing wings within the ruling party, undermined the dominance of the PUP. Internal disputes within the PUP intensified during 1983, although Price succeeded in keeping the factions together. However, at the general election held in December 1984 the PUP's 30 years of rule ended when the United Democratic Party (UDP) received 53% of the total votes and won 21 of the 28 seats in the enlarged House of Representatives. The remaining seven seats were won by the PUP, with 44% of the votes, but Price and several of his ministers lost their seats. The UDP's leader, Manuel Esquivel, was appointed Prime Minister. The new Government pledged itself to reviving Belize's economy through increased foreign investment.

A general election was held in September 1989. The UDP underwent a damaging selection process for candidates to contest the election, and encountered criticism that its economic successes had benefited only foreign investors and a limited number of Belizeans. The PUP campaigned for a more liberal broadcasting policy, including the establishment of a broadcasting corporation independent of direct government control, and against the sale of citizenship, of which many Hong Kong Chinese had taken advantage. At the election the PUP obtained almost 51% of the total valid votes cast, and won 15 seats in the 28-member House of Representatives. The UDP received 49% of the votes and retained 13 seats, although one of their members subsequently joined the PUP. Price was again appointed Prime Minister, and his new Government immediately began moves to end the issue of citizenship bonds.

A general election was held in June 1993. The UDP formed an alliance with the National Alliance for Belizean Rights (NABR) to contest the election, and their campaign concentrated on concern about the security situation in the light of the imminent withdrawal of British troops and the prevailing political crisis in neighbouring Guatemala (see below). The PUP had called the election 15 months before it was constitutionally due, following recent successes at local and by-elections. However, at the election the PUP secured only 13 seats in the House of Representatives, despite obtaining more than 51% of the votes. The UDP/NABR alliance received 48.7% of the votes but secured 16 seats (the total number of seats having been increased from 28 to 29). The leader of the UDP, Manuel Esquivel, was sworn in as Prime Minister on 2 July. In November, at Esquivel's request, Dame Minita Gordon, who had been the Governor-General since independence, resigned from her position. She was replaced by Dr (later Sir) Colville Young, formerly President of the University College of Belize. In the same month the Chairman of the PUP and former Minister of Foreign Affairs, Said Musa, was among five members of the PUP who were arrested for allegedly attempting to bribe two government ministers to transfer parliamentary allegiance to the PUP. Musa was acquitted in July 1994.

In April 1994 the Public Service Union organized an indefinite strike in support of demands for the payment of salary increases ranging between 10% and 12.5% for the 1994/95 financial year. The increases, which would have constituted the third consecutive annual increment under an agreement with the previous administration, had been reduced by the new Government to 5%. The strike was suspended in May to allow for renewed negotiations. A settlement was finally reached in November 1996, when a contract was also signed determining the salary increases for 1996–99.

In June 1994 the sale of citizenship was officially ended, following criticism that the system was open to corruption. However, a revised economic citizenship programme, including mechanisms to prevent corruption, received government approval in early 1995. In January of that year Esquivel conducted a redistribution of cabinet portfolios. The changes included the replacement of the Ministry of Defence with a new portfolio, of National Security, with responsibility for defence and the police. In addition, the Ministry of Energy and Communications was restyled the Ministry of Science, Technology and Transportation. In June the Minister of Human Resources, Community and Youth Development, Culture and Women's Affairs, Philip S. W. Goldson, was relieved of responsibility for immigration and nationality affairs, following allegations implicating him in the sale of false residence and visitor permits to nationals of the People's Republic of China and the Republic of China (Taiwan). Reportedly some 5,000 such permits had been issued over the previous 12-month period, and the recipients then smuggled into the USA. In August the Judicial Committee of the Privy Council in the United Kingdom (the final court of appeal for Belize) issued stays of execution for two convicted murderers. The ruling, which came amid growing concern at rising crime in Belize, prompted widespread criticism of the British court, which was considered to be undermining the authority of the Belizean judiciary, and demands for a revision of the appeals system.

In July 1996 Belize issued an official protest to the US Government following a statement by a US diplomat criticizing Belize's effectiveness in combating drugs-trafficking and the channelling of illegal immigrants to the USA. Popular discontent at economic austerity measures implemented by the Government was reflected at local elections conducted in March 1997, when the opposition PUP recorded a resounding victory over the ruling alliance. In April Esquivel conducted a reorganization of the Cabinet and created a new ministry, of National Co-ordination and Mobilisation.

The frontier with Guatemala was agreed by a convention in 1859 but this was declared invalid by Guatemala in 1940. Guatemalan claims to sovereignty of Belize date back to the middle of the 19th century and were written into Guatemala's Constitution in 1945. In November 1975 and July 1977 British troops and aircraft were sent to protect Belize from the threat of Guatemalan invasion, and a battalion of troops and a detachment of fighter aircraft remained in the territory. Negotiations between the United Kingdom and Guatemala began in 1977. In 1980 the United Kingdom warned that it might unilaterally grant independence to Belize if no settlement with Guatemala were forthcoming, and later that year the British Government finally excluded the possibility of any cession of land to Guatemala, although offering economic and financial concessions. In November the UN General Assembly overwhelmingly approved a resolution urging that Belize be granted independence (similar resolutions having been adopted in 1978 and 1979), and the United Kingdom decided to proceed with a schedule for independence. A tripartite conference in March 1981 appeared to produce a sound basis for a final settlement, with Guatemala accepting Belizean independence in exchange for access to the Caribbean Sea through Belize and the use of certain offshore cayes and their surrounding waters. A constitutional conference began in April. Further tripartite talks in May and July collapsed, however, as a result of renewed claims by Guatemala to Belizean land. With Belizean independence imminent, Guatemala made an unsuccessful appeal to the UN Security Council to intervene, severing diplomatic relations with the United Kingdom and sealing its border with Belize on 7 September. However, on 21 September, as scheduled, Belize achieved independence. Guatemala alone refused to recognize Belize's new status, and during 1982 requested the reopening of negotiations with the United Kingdom, alleging that Belize was not legally independent. Tripartite talks in January 1983 collapsed when Belize rejected Guatemala's proposal that Belize should cede the southern part of the country. This claim was subsequently suspended. Belize is a member of the Caribbean Community and Common Market (CARICOM—see p. 119), whose summit conferences have consistently expressed support for Belize's territorial integrity against claims by Guatemala.

At independence the United Kingdom had agreed to leave troops as protection and for training of the Belize Defence Force 'for an appropriate time'. In 1984 Prime Minister Esquivel was given renewed assurances from the British Government as regards its commitment to keep British troops in Belize until the resolution of the territorial dispute with Guatemala. Discussions with Guatemala resumed in February 1985, with greater optimism shown by all three parties. In July the new draft Guatemalan Constitution omitted the previous unconditional claim to Belize, while Esquivel had previously acknowledged Guatemala's right of access to the Caribbean Sea, but no settlement was forthcoming. In January 1986 Dr Marco Vinicio Cerezo was inaugurated as the elected President of Guatemala, representing a change from military to civilian government. In August the United Kingdom and Guatemala renewed diplomatic relations at consular level, and in December the restoration of full diplomatic relations was announced. In March 1987 the first Guatemalan trade delegation since independence visited Belize, and in April renewed discussions were held between Guatemala, the United Kingdom and Belize (although Belize was still regarded by Guatemala as being only an observer at the meetings). Tripartite negotiations continued, and in May 1988 the formation of a permanent joint commission (which, in effect, entailed a recognition of the Belizean state by Guatemala) was announced.

In the latter half of 1991 relations between Belize and Guatemala showed considerable signs of improvement, and in September the two countries signed an accord under the terms of which Belize pledged to legislate to reduce its maritime boundaries and to allow Guatemala access to the Caribbean Sea and use of its port facilities. In return, President Jorge Serrano Elías of Guatemala officially announced his country's recognition of Belize as an independent state and established diplomatic relations. The Maritime Areas Bill was approved in January 1992 by 16 votes to 12 in the Belizean House of Representatives. The legislation, however, had caused serious divisions within the UDP, leading to the formation, in December 1991, of the Patriotic Alliance for Territorial Integrity (PATI) by certain members of the party to co-ordinate opposition to the Bill. Further disagreement between PATI activists and the leaders of the UDP resulted in the expulsion or resignation of five UDP members (including two members of Parliament) in January 1992. In February these members formed a new organization, the NABR, led by the former UDP Deputy Leader and Minister of Transport, Derek Aikman. In November 1992 the Guatemalan legislature voted to ratify Serrano's decision to recognize Belize. Serrano, however, indicated that the accord was not definitive and that Guatemala maintained its territorial claim over Belize.

In April 1993 Belize and Guatemala signed a non-aggression pact, affirming their intent to refrain from the threat or use of force against each other, and preventing either country from being used as a base for aggression against the other. Relations between the two countries were jeopardized when, in June, President Serrano was ousted following an attempt to suspend certain articles of the Constitution and dissolve Congress. However, in late June the new Guatemalan President, Ramiro de León Carpio, announced that Guatemala would continue to respect Belize's independence. In July the Belizean Prime Minister, Manuel Esquivel, reportedly suspended the September 1991 accord, which had been signed by the previous administration and had still not been formally ratified, stating that it involved too many concessions on the part of Belize and that the issue should be put to a referendum.

In May 1993 the British Government announced that the British troops stationed in Belize were to be withdrawn. In September it was announced that responsibility for the defence of Belize would be transferred to the Belize Defence Force on 1 January 1994, and that all British troops would be withdrawn by October 1994, with the exception of some 100 troops, who would remain to organize training for jungle warfare.

In March 1994, in a letter to the UN Secretary-General, Guatemala formally reaffirmed its territorial claim to Belize, prompting the Belizean Minister of Foreign Affairs to seek talks with the British Government regarding assistance with national defence. Concern was also expressed by the Standing Committee of CARICOM Ministers of Foreign Affairs, which reaffirmed its support for Belizean sovereignty. In mid-1994 Esquivel accused Guatemala of employing destabilizing tactics against Belize by encouraging Guatemalans to occupy and settle in areas of Belizean forest. In September 1996 the Ministers of Foreign Affairs of Belize and Guatemala conducted preliminary talks in New York, USA, concerning a resumption of negotiations on the territorial dispute. Further such discussions, involving representatives of the Governments and armed forces of both countries, were conducted in Miami, USA, in February 1997.

Government

Belize is a constitutional monarchy, with the British sovereign as Head of State. Executive authority is vested in the sovereign and is exercised by the Governor-General, who is appointed on the advice of the Prime Minister, must be of Belizean nationality, and acts, in almost all matters, on the advice of the Cabinet. The Governor-General is also advised by an appointed Belize Advisory Council. Legislative power is vested in the bicameral National Assembly, comprising a Senate (eight members appointed by the Governor-General) and a House of Representatives (29 members elected by universal adult suffrage for five years, subject to dissolution). The Governor-General appoints the Prime Minister and, on the latter's recommendation, other ministers. The Cabinet is responsible to the House of Representatives.

Defence

The Belize Defence Force was formed in 1978 and was based on a combination of the existing Police Special Force and the Belize Volunteer Guard. Military service is voluntary. Provision has been made for the establishment of National Service if necessary to supplement normal recruitment. In August 1997 the regular armed forces totalled 1,050 (including 50 in the maritime wing and 15 in the air wing), with some 700 militia reserves. In September 1993 the British Government announced that all except about 100 of the contingent of approximately 600 British troops stationed in Belize would be withdrawn by October 1994. The remaining troops were to organize jungle warfare training. The defence budget for 1997 was an estimated BZ $20m.

Economic Affairs

In 1995, according to estimates by the World Bank, the country's gross national product (GNP), measured at average 1993–95 prices, was US $568m., equivalent to US $2,630 per head. During 1985–95, it was estimated, GNP per head increased, in real terms, by 4.4% per year. Over this period, Belize's population grew by 2.6% per year. Belize's gross domestic product (GDP) increased, in real terms, by an average of 7.0% per year in 1985–95, and by an estimated 3.0% in 1996.

Although 40% of the country is considered suitable for agriculture, only an estimated 3.7% of total land area was used for agricultural purposes in 1995. Nevertheless, agriculture, forestry and fishing employed 29.9% of the working population in 1997, and contributed 20.3% of GDP in 1996. The principal cash crops are sugar cane (sugar and molasses accounted for an estimated 33.6% of total domestic exports in 1996), citrus fruits (citrus products accounted for an estimated 19.6%) and bananas (an estimated 19.4%). Maize, red kidney beans and rice are the principal domestic food crops, and the development of other crops, such as cocoa, coconuts and soybeans (soya beans), is being encouraged. The country is largely self-sufficient in fresh meat and eggs. Belize has considerable timber reserves, particularly of tropical hardwoods, and the forestry sector is being developed. In 1996 fishing provided export earnings of an estimated BZ $25m. (8.2% of total domestic export revenue). According to World Bank estimates, the GDP of the agricultural sector increased at an average rate of 6.9% per year during 1985–95, although it declined by 1.3% in 1995.

Industry (including mining, manufacturing, construction, water and electricity) employed 18.2% of the working population in 1997, and contributed 22.6% of GDP in 1996. Manufacturing alone, particularly of clothing, accounted for 13.0% of GDP in 1996 and employed 11.3% of the working population in 1997. The processing of agricultural products is important, particularly sugar cane (for sugar and rum). According to World Bank estimates, industrial GDP increased at an average annual rate of 8.1% during 1985–95. It rose by an estimated 2.9% in 1995, following a decline of 0.5% in 1994. Manufacturing GDP increased by an annual average of 5.6% during 1985–95, and by 4.1% per year in 1994 and 1995. Mining accounted for 0.6% of GDP in 1996 and only 0.1% of employment in 1997.

Belize has no indigenous energy resources other than wood. Exploration for petroleum in the interior of Belize continued in the 1990s, despite increasing concern for the impact of such activity on the environment. Imports of mineral fuels and lubricants accounted for 11.3% of total import costs in 1996. Hydroelectric power was to be developed in the 1990s.

The services sector employed 51.8% of the working population in 1997, and contributed 57.1% of GDP in 1996. Tourist development is concentrated on promoting 'eco-tourism', based on the attraction of Belize's natural environment, particularly its rain forests and the barrier reef, the second largest in the world. Tourist arrivals totalled 349,277 in 1996, which represented an increase of 6.2% compared with the previous year.

In 1996 Belize recorded a visible trade deficit of US $95.9m., and a deficit of US $16.9m. on the current account of the balance of payments. In that year the principal source of imports was the USA (54.9%), while the principal market for exports was the United Kingdom (45.7%). Other important trading partners are Mexico and Canada. The principal exports in 1996 were agricultural products (85.8%, including forestry and fish products). The principal imports in that year were machinery and transport equipment, basic manufactures, food and live animals and miscellaneous manufactured articles.

For the financial year ending 31 March 1997 there was a budgetary deficit of BZ $28.8m. (equivalent to 2.2% of GDP). Budget proposals for the financial year ending 31 March 1998 envisaged a deficit of BZ $62m. Belize's total external debt was US $260.5m. at the end of 1995, of which US $220.3m. was long-term public debt. In that year the cost of debt-servicing was equivalent to 12.4% of the value of exports of goods and services. The annual rate of inflation averaged 2.3% in 1985–95. Consumer prices increased by an average of 6.4% in 1996. In 1996 an estimated 13.8% of the labour force were unemployed. Many Belizeans, however, work abroad, and remittances to the country from such workers are an important source of income. Emigration, mainly to the USA, is offset by the number of immigrants and refugees from other Central American countries, particularly El Salvador.

Belize is a member of the Caribbean Community and Common Market (CARICOM, see p. 119), and in 1991 acceded to the Organization of American States (OAS, see p. 219). In September 1992 Belize was granted membership of the Inter-American Development Bank (IDB, see p. 183).

Agriculture is the dominant sector of the Belizean economy. As a member of the Commonwealth, Belize enjoys low tariffs on its exports to the European Union (EU) under the Lomé Convention, and tariff-free access to the USA under the Caribbean Basin Initiative. The development of tourism and the availability of foreign investment have been hindered by the uncertainties arising from the territorial dispute with Guatemala. The Government is attempting to develop service industries, and established an international shipping register in 1989 and introduced legislation on 'offshore' financial services in 1990. The withdrawal of British troops from Belize in 1994 had serious economic repercussions, with the loss of an estimated BZ $60m. annually to the economy. In late 1995 some 870 civil service employees (equivalent to 9% of the total central government work-force) were made redundant as the initial phase of a structural adjustment programme, introduced to address the country's serious budget deficit. As part of a reform of the tax system, value-added tax (VAT), at a basic rate of 15%, was introduced with effect from April 1996. In June 1997 an IMF economic evaluation mission identified as a priority the further strengthening of Belize's fiscal consolidation efforts. It recommended the implementation of additional fiscal measures, including a broadening of the tax base, the curtailment of tax exemptions and improved customs valuation procedures. A more prudent wage policy for the public sector was also advised.

Social Welfare

There were nine urban and 26 rural health centres in Belize in 1996; pre-natal and child welfare clinics are sponsored by the Ministry of Health and Sport. In that year there were 554 hospital beds and 142 registered physicians. The infant mortality rate declined from 51 per 1,000 live births in 1970 to 18.2 per 1,000 in 1995. Of total estimated budgetary expenditure by the central Government in the financial year 1994/95, BZ $66.7m. (15.9%) was for health.

Education

Education is compulsory for all children for a period of 10 years between the ages of five and 14 years. Primary education, beginning at five years of age and lasting for eight years, is provided free of charge, principally through subsidized denominational schools under government control. There were 52,955 pupils enrolled at 245 primary schools in 1995/96. Secondary education, beginning at the age of 13, lasts for four years. There were 10,648 students enrolled in 31 general secondary schools in 1995/96. In 1994 primary enrolment included an estimated 97% of children in the relevant age-group (males 97%; females 96%), while secondary enrolment in that year was 36% (males 33%; females 39%).

In 1995/96 there were 2,434 students enrolled in 11 other educational institutions, which included technical, vocational and teacher-training colleges. The University College of Belize was established in 1986 and there is also an extra-mural branch of the University of the West Indies in Belize. Budgetary expenditure on education in the financial year 1995/96 was projected at BZ $72.8m., representing 20.3% of total spending by the central Government. In 1991 the average rate of adult illiteracy was 29.7% (males 29.7%; females 29.7%).

Public Holidays

1998: 1 January (New Year's Day), 9 March (Baron Bliss Day), 10–13 April (Easter), 1 May (Labour Day), 24 May (Commonwealth Day), 10 September (St George's Caye Day), 21 September (Independence Day), 12 October (Columbus Day, anniversary of the discovery of America), 19 November (Garifuna Settlement Day), 25–26 December (Christmas).

1999: 1 January (New Year's Day), 9 March (Baron Bliss Day), 2–5 April (Easter), 3 May (for Labour Day), 24 May (Commonwealth Day), 10 September (St George's Caye Day), 21 September (Independence Day), 12 October (Columbus Day, anniversary of the discovery of America), 19 November (Garifuna Settlement Day), 25–26 December (Christmas).

Weights and Measures

Imperial weights and measures are used, but petrol and paraffin are measured in terms of the US gallon (3.785 litres).

Statistical Survey

Source (unless otherwise stated): Central Statistical Office, Ministry of Finance, Belmopan; tel. (8) 22207; fax (8) 23206; e-mail csogob@blt.net .

AREA AND POPULATION

Area: 22,965 sq km (8,867 sq miles).

Population: 144,857 at census of 12 May 1980; 189,774 (males 96,289, females 93,485) at census of 12 May 1991; 228,695 at April 1997 (official estimate).

Density (April 1997): 10.0 per sq km.

Principal Towns (estimated population, April 1997): Belmopan (capital) 6,785; Belize City (former capital) 53,915; Orange Walk 15,035; San Ignacio/Santa Elena 11,375; Corozal 7,715; Dangriga (formerly Stann Creek) 7,110; Benque Viejo 5,995; Punta Gorda 4,770.

Births, Marriages and Deaths (1995, provisional figures): Registered live births 5,454 (birth rate 25.2 per 1,000); Registered marriages 1,347 (marriage rate 6.2 per 1,000); Registered deaths 931 (death rate 4.3 per 1,000).

Expectation of Life (years at birth, 1991): males 69.95; females 74.07. Source: UN, *Demographic Yearbook*.

Economically Active Population (sample survey, April 1997): Agriculture, hunting, forestry and fishing 21,140; Mining and quarrying 95; Manufacturing 7,980; Electricity, gas and water 985; Construction 3,835; Trade, restaurants and hotels 15,155; Transport, storage and communications 3,655; Financing, insurance, real estate and business services 2,360; Community, social and personal services 12,225; Private households 2,915; Other 335; Total employed 70,680.

AGRICULTURE, ETC.

Principal Crops (estimates, '000 metric tons unless otherwise stated, 1996): Sugar cane 1,091; Red kidney beans (million lb) 5.4 (provisional figure); Maize 28; Rice (paddy) 10; Roots and tubers 4; Pulses (dry beans) 3; Coconuts 3; Vegetables and melons 5; Oranges 128; Grapefruit and pomelo 44; Bananas 67; Other fruit 4. Source: mainly FAO, *Production Yearbook*.

Livestock (FAO estimates, '000 head, year ending September 1996): Horses 5; Mules 4; Cattle 60; Pigs 22; Sheep 3; Goats 1; Chickens 1. Source: FAO, *Production Yearbook*.

Livestock Products (FAO estimates, '000 metric tons, 1996): Meat 10; Cows' milk 7; Hen eggs 1. Source: FAO, *Production Yearbook*.

Forestry ('000 cu m): *Roundwood removals* (1987): Industrial wood (Sawlogs) 62, Fuel wood 126 (FAO estimate), Total 188 (FAO estimated annual production in 1988–94 as in 1987). *Sawnwood* (1986): 14 (FAO estimated annual production in 1987–94 as in 1986). Source: FAO, *Yearbook of Forest Products*.

Fishing (metric tons, live weight): Total catch: 2,129 in 1993; 2,034 in 1994; 2,094 in 1995. Source: FAO, *Yearbook of Fishery Statistics*.

INDUSTRY

Production (1995): Raw sugar 105,344 long tons; Molasses 45,814 long tons; Cigarettes 94 million; Beer 1,086,000 gallons; Batteries 11,097; Flour 25,400,000 lb; Fertilizers 26,606 metric tons; Garments 1,974,000 items; Citrus concentrate 3,335,000 gallons; Soft drinks 1,724,000 cases.

FINANCE

Currency and Exchange Rates: 100 cents = 1 Belizean dollar (BZ $). *Sterling and US Dollar equivalents* (30 September 1997): £1 sterling = BZ $3.231; US $1 = BZ $2.000; BZ $100 = £30.95 = US $50.00. *Exchange rate:* Fixed at US $1 = BZ $2.000 since May 1976.

Budget (BZ $ million, year ending 31 March): **1995/96** (projections): *Revenue:* Taxation 245.1 (Import duties 126.3); Other current revenue 20.8; Capital revenue 1.3; Total 267.1. *Expenditure:* General public services 44.1; Law, order and defence 41.8; Community and social services 154.8 (Education 72.8; Health 32.0; Housing, community development, water and sanitation 25.7; Other social services 24.4); Economic services 88.8 (Agriculture, lands, forestry and fisheries 17.9; Energy and resources development 1.4; Transport and communications 51.4; Other economic services 18.1); Interest payments 26.8; Other expenditure 3.3; Total 359.5. Source: IMF, *Government Finance Statistics Yearbook*.

1996/97 (estimates): Total revenue 287.6, excl. grants received (10.1); Total expenditure and net lending 326.5. Source: IMF, *Belize—Statistical Appendix,* July 1997. **1997/98** (proposals): Total revenue 300.8, excl. grants received (36.1); Total expenditure 398.9. Source: *Caribbean Insight.*

International Reserves (US $ million at 31 December 1996): IMF special drawing rights 0.88; Reserve position in the IMF 4.19; Foreign exchange 53.34; Total 58.40. Source: IMF, *International Financial Statistics*.

Money Supply (BZ $ million at 31 December 1996): Currency outside banks 63.61; Demand deposits at commercial banks 99.12; Total money (incl. others) 164.02. Source: IMF, *International Financial Statistics*.

Cost of Living (Consumer Price Index; base: 1990 = 100): 109.0 in 1994; 112.1 in 1995; 119.3 in 1996. Source: IMF, *International Financial Statistics*.

Expenditure on the Gross Domestic Product (BZ $ million at current prices, 1996): Government final consumption expenditure 194.4; Private final consumption expenditure 773.1; Increase in stocks 5.8; Gross fixed capital formation 260.5; *Total domestic expenditure* 1,233.8; Exports of goods and service 611.0; *Less* Imports of goods and services 627.6; *GDP in purchasers' values* 1,217.3. Source: IMF, *International Financial Statistics*.

Gross Domestic Product by Economic Activity (BZ $ million at current prices, 1996): Agriculture 176.4; Forestry and logging 18.3; Fishing 21.6; Mining 6.6; Manufacturing 138.9; Electricity and water 33.8; Construction 61.8; Trade, restaurants and hotels 176.3; Transport and communications 104.5; Finance, insurance, real estate and business services 136.0; Public administration 127.1; Other services 65.3; *Sub-total* 1,066.5; *Less* Imputed bank service charges 41.9; *GDP at factor cost* 1,024.6.

Balance of Payments (US $ million, 1996): Exports of goods f.o.b. 166.3; Imports of goods c.i.f. –262.2; *Trade balance* –95.9; Exports of services 124.0; Imports of services –51.3; *Balance on goods and services* –23.2; Other income received 8.5; Other income paid –35.7; *Balance on goods, services and income* –50.4; Current transfers received 38.0; Current transfers paid –4.5; *Current balance* –16.9; Official borrowing (net) 32.5; Other official capital flows (net) –0.6; Direct investment (net) 12.4; Portfolio investment (net) –4.2; Commercial banks (net) –5.9; Other private capital (net) 3.0; Net errors and omissions 1.0; *Overall balance* 21.1. Source: IMF, *Belize—Statistical Appendix*.

EXTERNAL TRADE

Principal Commodities (provisional figures, BZ $ million, 1996): *Imports c.i.f.:* Food and live animals 86.0; Beverages and tobacco 13.9; Mineral fuels, lubricants, etc. 58.0; Chemicals 58.9; Basic manufactures 92.9; Machinery and transport equipment 128.3; Miscellaneous manufactured articles 63.8; Total (incl. others) 511.1. *Exports f.o.b.:* Food and live animals 263.4; Miscellaneous manufactured articles 36.1; Total (incl. others) 307.1. Note: Data for exports exclude re-exports. The value of total exports in 1996 was BZ $335.3 million. Source: IMF, *International Financial Statistics*.

Principal Trading Partners (provisional figures, BZ $ million, 1996): *Imports c.i.f.:* Canada 7.9; Mexico 62.5; United Kingdom 23.8; USA 280.7; Total (incl. others) 511.1. *Exports f.o.b.* (excl. re-exports): Canada 8.4; Mexico 4.5; United Kingdom 140.2; USA 124.9; Total (incl. others) 307.1.

TRANSPORT

Road Traffic (motor vehicles licensed, 1996): 24,585.

Shipping (sea-borne freight traffic, '000 short tons, 1996): Goods loaded 281.5; Goods unloaded 305.4. *Merchant Fleet* (vessels registered at 31 December 1996): Number of vessels 640; Total displacement 1,015,838 grt. Source: Lloyd's Register of Shipping, *World Fleet Statistics*.

Civil Aviation (1996): Passenger movements 328,011.

TOURISM

Tourist Arrivals: 328,073 in 1994; 328,760 in 1995; 349,277 in 1996.

Tourist Receipts (1996): BZ $167.1m.

Hotels (1996): 360.

COMMUNICATIONS MEDIA

Radio Receivers (1994): 122,000 in use*.

Television Receivers (1994): 35,000 in use*.

Telephones (1996): 29,439 main lines in use.

Book Production (1993): 70 titles*

Newspapers (1990): There are no daily newspapers, but seven newspapers are published weekly (estimated circulation 37,000 copies per issue)*.

* Source: UNESCO, *Statistical Yearbook*.

EDUCATION

Pre-primary* (1994/95): 90 schools, 190 teachers, 3,533 students.

Primary (1995/96): 245 schools, 1,966 teachers, 52,955 students.

Secondary (1995/96): 31 schools, 697 teachers, 10,648 students.

Higher (1995/96): 11 institutions, 254 teachers, 2,434 students.

* Source: UNESCO, *Statistical Yearbook*.

Directory

The Constitution

The Constitution came into effect at the independence of Belize on 21 September 1981. Its main provisions are summarized below:

FUNDAMENTAL RIGHTS AND FREEDOMS

Regardless of race, place of origin, political opinions, colour, creed or sex, but subject to respect for the rights and freedoms of others and for the public interest, every person in Belize is entitled to the rights of life, liberty, security of the person, and the protection of the law. Freedom of movement, of conscience, of expression, of assembly and association and the right to work are guaranteed and the inviolability of family life, personal privacy, home and other property and of human dignity is upheld. Protection is afforded from discrimination on the grounds of race, sex, etc, and from slavery, forced labour and inhuman treatment.

CITIZENSHIP

All persons born in Belize before independence who, immediately prior to independence, were citizens of the United Kingdom and Colonies automatically become citizens of Belize. All persons born outside the country having a husband, parent or grandparent in possession of Belizean citizenship automatically acquire citizenship, as do those born in the country after independence. Provision is made which permits persons who do not automatically become citizens of Belize to be registered as such. (Belizean citizenship was also offered, under the Belize Loans Act 1986, in exchange for interest-free loans of US $25,000 with a 10-year maturity. The scheme was officially ended in June 1994, following sustained criticism of alleged corruption on the part of officials. However, a revised economic citizenship programme, offering citizenship in return for a minimum investment of US $75,000, received government approval in early 1995.)

THE GOVERNOR-GENERAL

The British monarch, as Head of State, is represented in Belize by a Governor-General, a Belizean national.

Belize Advisory Council

The Council consists of not less than six people 'of integrity and high national standing', appointed by the Governor-General for up to 10 years upon the advice of the Prime Minister. The Leader of the Opposition must concur with the appointment of two members and be consulted about the remainder. The Council exists to advise the Governor-General, particularly in the exercise of the prerogative of mercy, and to convene as a tribunal to consider the removal from office of certain senior public servants and judges.

THE EXECUTIVE

Executive authority is vested in the British monarch and exercised by the Governor-General. The Governor-General appoints as Prime Minister that member of the House of Representatives who, in the Governor-General's view, is best able to command the support of the majority of the members of the House, and appoints a Deputy Prime Minister and other Ministers on the advice of the Prime Minister. The Governor-General may remove the Prime Minister from office if a resolution of 'no confidence' is passed by the House and the Prime Minister does not, within seven days, either resign or advise the Governor-General to dissolve the National Assembly. The Cabinet consists of the Prime Minister and other Ministers.

The Leader of the Opposition is appointed by the Governor-General as that member of the House who, in the Governor-General's view, is best able to command the support of a majority of the members of the House who do not support the Government.

THE LEGISLATURE

The Legislature consists of a National Assembly comprising two chambers: the Senate, with eight nominated members; and the House of Representatives, with 29 elected members. The Assembly's normal term is five years. Senators are appointed by the Governor-General: five on the advice of the Prime Minister; two on the advice of the Leader of the Opposition or on the advice of persons selected by the Governor-General; and one after consultation with the Belize Advisory Council. If any person who is not a Senator is elected to be President of the Senate, he or she shall be an ex-officio Senator in addition to the eight nominees.

Each constituency returns one Representative to the House, who is directly elected in accordance with the Constitution.

If a person who is not a member of the House is elected to be Speaker of the House, he or she shall be an ex-officio member in addition to the 29 members directly elected. Every citizen older than 18 years is eligible to vote. The National Assembly may alter any of the provisions of the Constitution.

The Government

Head of State: HM Queen ELIZABETH II (succeeded to the throne 6 February 1952).

Governor-General: Sir COLVILLE YOUNG (appointed 17 November 1993).

THE CABINET
(November 1997)

Prime Minister and Minister of Finance and Economic Development: MANUEL ESQUIVEL.

Deputy Prime Minister, Attorney General and Minister of Foreign Affairs and National Security: DEAN O. BARROW.

Minister of Trade and Industry: ALFREDO MARTINEZ.

Minister of Natural Resources: EDUARDO JUAN.

Minister of Agriculture and Fisheries: RUSSELL GARCIA.

Minister of Human Resources, Community and Youth Development, Culture and Women's Affairs: PHILIP S. W. GOLDSON.

Minister of Works: MELVIN HULSE, Jr.

Minister of Education and Public Service: ELODIO ARAGON.

Minister of Tourism and Environment: HENRY YOUNG.

Minister of Health and Sport: SALVADOR FERNANDEZ.

Minister of Housing, Urban Development and Co-operatives: (vacant).

Minister of Home Affairs, Labour and Local Government: HUBERT ELRINGTON.

Minister of Science, Technology and Transportation: JOSEPH CAYETANO.

Minister of National Co-ordination and Mobilisation: RUBEN CAMPOS.

There were, in addition, three Ministers of State.

MINISTRIES

Office of the Prime Minister: New Administrative Bldg, Belmopan; tel. (8) 22346; fax (8) 20071.

Ministry of Agriculture and Fisheries: Belmopan; tel. (8) 22332; fax (8) 22409.

Ministry of the Attorney-General: Belmopan; tel. (8) 22504; fax (8) 23390.

Ministry of Education and Public Service: Belmopan; tel. (8) 22067; fax (8) 22206.

Ministry of Finance and Economic Development: New Administrative Bldg, Belmopan; tel. (8) 22169; fax (8) 22886.

Ministry of Foreign Affairs and National Security: New Administrative Bldg, POB 174, Belmopan; tel. (8) 22167; fax (8) 22854.

Ministry of Health and Sport: Belmopan; tel. (8) 23325; fax (8) 22942.

Ministry of Home Affairs, Labour and Local Government: Belmopan; tel. (8) 22336; fax (8) 22016.

Ministry of Housing, Urban Development and Co-operatives: Belmopan; tel. (1) 23338; fax (8) 23298.

Ministry of Human Resources, Community and Youth Development, Culture and Women's Affairs: Belmopan; tel. (8) 22248; fax (8) 23175.

Ministry of National Co-ordination and Mobilisation: Belmopan.

Ministry of Natural Resources: Cayo District, Belmopan; tel. (8) 23286; fax (8) 22333.

Ministry of Science, Technology and Transportation: Belmopan; tel. (8) 22435; fax (8) 23317.

Ministry of Tourism and Environment: Belmopan; tel. (8) 23393; fax (8) 23815.

Ministry of Trade and Industry: Belmopan; tel. (8) 22321; fax (8) 22923.

Ministry of Works: Belmopan; tel. (8) 22136; fax (8) 23282.

Legislature

NATIONAL ASSEMBLY

The Senate

President: EDWARD FLOWERS.

Vice-President: LELIZ CARBALLO.

There are eight nominated members.

House of Representatives

Speaker: BERNARD Q. PITTS.

Deputy Speaker: FAITH BABB.

Clerk: JESUS KEN.

General Election, 30 June 1993

	Votes cast	% of total	Seats
People's United Party (PUP)	36,082	51.23	13
United Democratic Party (UDP)/National Alliance for Belizean Rights (NABR)	34,306	48.71	16
Independent	43	0.06	—
Total	70,431	100.00	29

Political Organizations

National Alliance for Belizean Rights (NABR): Belize City; f. 1992 by UDP members opposed to compromise over territorial dispute with Guatemala; Chair. (vacant); Co-ordinator PHILIP S. W. GOLDSON.

People's United Party (PUP): Belize City; tel. (2) 45886; fax (2) 31940; f. 1950; based on organized labour; merged with Christian Democratic Party in 1988; Leader SAID MUSA; Chair. JORGE ESPAT.

United Democratic Party (UDP): 19 King St, POB 1143, Belize City; tel. (2) 72576; fax (2) 31004; f. 1974 by merger of People's Development Movement, Liberal Party and National Independence Party; conservative; Leader MANUEL ESQUIVEL; Chair. ELODIO ARAGON.

Diplomatic Representation

EMBASSIES AND HIGH COMMISSION IN BELIZE

Belgium: Belize City; Ambassador: WILLY VERRIEST.

China (Taiwan): 3rd Floor, Blake's Bldg, cnr Hutson and Eyre Sts, POB 1020, Belize City; tel. (2) 78744; fax (2) 31890; Ambassador: SHU-CHI CHANG.

Colombia: Belmopan; Ambassador: KENT FRANCIS JAMES.

Costa Rica: 11 Roseapple St, Belmopan; tel. (8) 23801; fax (8) 23805; Ambassador: ROBERTO FRANCISCO ANGLEDA SOLER.

Germany: Belize City; Ambassador: Dr NILS GRÜBER.

Guatemala: 8 'A' St, Belize City; tel. (2) 33150; fax (2) 35140; e-mail guatemb.bz@btl.net; Ambassador: ANTONIO CASTELLANOS LÓPEZ.

Honduras: 91 North Front St, POB 285, Belize City; tel. (2) 45889; fax (2) 30562; Chargé d'affaires: CARLOS AUGUSTO MATUTÉ RIVERA.

Mexico: 20 North Park St, Belize City; tel. (2) 30193; fax (2) 78742; Ambassador: FEDERICO URUCHUA.

Panama: POB 1692, Belize City; tel. (2) 44991; fax (2) 30654; Chargé d'affaires: JOSÉ DE LA CRUZ PAREDES.

United Kingdom: Embassy Sq., POB 91, Belmopan; tel. (8) 22146; fax (8) 22761; High Commissioner: GORDON M. BAKER.

USA: 29 Gabourel Lane, POB 286, Belize City; tel. (2) 77161; telex 213; fax (2) 30802; Ambassador: GEORGE C. BRUNO.

Venezuela: 18–20 Unity Blvd, POB 49, Belmopan; tel. (8) 22384; fax (8) 22022; Ambassador: CHRISTIAAN VAN DER REE.

Judicial System

Summary Jurisdiction Courts (criminal jurisdiction) and District Courts (civil jurisdiction), presided over by magistrates, are established in each of the six judicial districts. Summary Jurisdiction Courts have a wide jurisdiction in summary offences and a limited jurisdiction in indictable matters. Appeals lie to the Supreme Court, which has jurisdiction corresponding to the English High Court of Justice and where a jury system is in operation. From the Supreme Court further appeals lie to a Court of Appeal, established in 1967, which holds an average of four sessions per year. Final appeals are made to the Judicial Committee of the Privy Council in the United Kingdom.

Court of Appeal: Prof. PHILIP TELFORD GEORGES, HORACE WALWYN YOUNG, Dr NICHOLAS LIVERPOOL.

Chief Justice: Sir GEORGE N. BROWN.

Supreme Court: Supreme Court Bldg, Belize City; tel. (2) 77256; fax (2) 70181; e-mail ww.supremecourt.com; Registrar RAYMOND A. USHER.

Chief Magistrate: ADOLPH LUCAS, Paslow Bldg, Belize City; tel. (2) 77164.

Religion

CHRISTIANITY

Most of the population are Christian, the largest denomination being the Roman Catholic Church (62% of the population, according to the census of 1980). The other main groups were the Anglican (12% in 1980), Methodist (6%), Mennonite (4%), Seventh-day Adventist (3%) and Pentecostal (2%) churches.

Belize Council of Churches: 149 Allenby St, POB 508, Belize City; tel. (2) 77077; f. 1957 as Church World Service Committee, present name adopted 1984; eight mem. Churches, four assoc. bodies; Pres. Maj. ERROL ROBATEAU (Salvation Army); Gen. Sec. SADIE VERNON.

The Roman Catholic Church

Belize comprises the single diocese of Belize City-Belmopan, suffragan to the archdiocese of Kingston in Jamaica. In December 1995 it was estimated that there were 121,918 adherents in the diocese. The Bishop participates in the Antilles Episcopal Conference (whose secretariat is based in Port of Spain, Trinidad and Tobago).

Bishop of Belize City-Belmopan: OSMOND PETER MARTIN, Bishop's House, 144 North Front St, POB 616, Belize City; tel. (2) 72122; fax (2) 31922.

The Anglican Communion

Anglicans in Belize belong to the Church in the Province of the West Indies, comprising eight dioceses. The Archbishop of the Province is the Bishop of the North Eastern Caribbean and Aruba, resident at St John's, Antigua.

Bishop of Belize: Rt Rev. SYLVESTRE DONATO ROMERO-PALMA, Bishopthorpe, Southern Foreshore, POB 535, Belize City; tel. (2) 73029; fax (2) 74645.

Protestant Churches

Methodist Church (Belize/Honduras District Conference): POB 212, Belize City; c. 2,620 mems; District President Rev. Dr LESLEY G. ANDERSON.

Mennonite Congregations in Belize: POB 427, Belize City; tel. (8) 30137; fax (8) 30101; f. 1958; four main Mennonite settlements: at Spanish Lookout, Shipyard, Little Belize and Blue Creek; Bishops J. B. LOEWEN, J. K. BARKMAN, P. THIESSEN, H. R. PENNER, CORNELIUS ENNS.

Other denominations active in the country include the Seventh-day Adventists, Pentecostals, Presbyterians, Baptists, Moravians, Jehovah's Witnesses, the Church of God, the Assemblies of Brethren and the Salvation Army.

OTHER RELIGIONS

There are also small communities of Hindus (106, according to the census of 1980), Muslims (110 in 1980), Jews (92 in 1980) and Bahá'ís.

The Press

Amandala: Amandala Press, 3304 Partridge St, POB 15, Belize City; tel. (2) 24476; fax (2) 24702; f. 1969; weekly; independent; Editor Evan X. Hyde; circ. 45,000.

The Belize Times: 3 Queen St, POB 506, Belize City; tel. (2) 45757; fax (2) 31940; f. 1956; weekly; party political paper of PUP; Editor Amalia Mai; circ. 6,000.

Belize Today: Belize Information Service, East Block, POB 60, Belmopan; tel. (8) 22159; fax (8) 23242; monthly; official; Editor Miguel H. Hernández, Jr; circ. 17,000.

Government Gazette: Government Printery, Power Lane, Belmopan; tel. (8) 22127; official; weekly.

People's Pulse: 7 Tanoomah St, POB 1104, Belize City; tel. (2) 77035; fax (2) 76012; f. 1988; weekly; organ of UDP; Editor Richard Stuart; circ. 5,000.

The Reporter: 147 cnr Allenby and West Sts, POB 707, Belize City; tel. (2) 72503; f. 1968; weekly; Editor Harry Lawrence; circ. 6,500.

NEWS AGENCY

Agencia EFE (Spain): c/o POB 506, Belize City; tel. (2) 45757; Correspondent Amalia Mai.

Broadcasting and Communications

TELECOMMUNICATIONS

Belize Telecommunications Ltd: Esquivel Telecom Centre, St Thomas St, Belize City; tel. (2) 7708; Gen. Man. Edberto Tesecum.

RADIO

Broadcasting Corporation of Belize (BCB): Albert Cattouse Bldg, Regent St, POB 89, Belize City; tel. (2) 77246; telex 157; fax (2) 75040; e-mail rbgold@btl.net; f. 1937; govt-operated semi-commercial service; broadcasts in English (75%) and Spanish; also transmits programmes in Garifuna and Maya; Gen. Man. (vacant).

Radio Belize Gold broadcasts for about 168 hours per week on FM. Friends FM broadcasts for about 133 hours per week on FM.

Radio Krem Ltd: 3304 Partridge St, POB 15, Belize City; tel. (2) 75929; fax (2) 74079; commercial; Man. Eva S. Hyde.

There are a further three private radio stations broadcasting in Belize.

TELEVISION

In August 1986 the Belize Broadcasting Authority issued licences to eight television operators for 14 channels, which mainly retransmit US satellite programmes, thus placing television in Belize on a fully legal basis for the first time.

BCB Teleproductions: POB 89, Belize City; govt-owned; video production unit; local programmes for broadcasting.

CTV (Channel 9): 27 Dayman Ave, Belize City; tel. (2) 44400; commercial; Man. Marie Hoare.

Tropical Vision (Channels 7 and 11): 73 Albert St, Belize City; tel. (2) 73988; fax (2) 78583; commercial; Man. Nestor Vasquez.

Finance

(cap. = capital; res = reserves; dep. = deposits; brs = branches)

BANKING

Central Bank

Central Bank of Belize: Treasury Lane, POB 852, Belize City; tel. (2) 77216; telex 225; fax (2) 73116; f. 1982; cap. BZ $10m., res 9.3m., dep. 49.5m. (1995); Gov. Sir Keith A. Arnold.

Development Bank

Development Finance Corporation: Bliss Parade, Belmopan; tel. (8) 22350; telex 248; fax (8) 23096; issued cap. BZ $10m.; Chair. Joy Grant; Gen. Man. Douglas Singh; 5 brs.

Other Banks

Bank of Nova Scotia (Canada): Albert St, POB 708, Belize City; tel. (2) 77027; telex 218; fax 77416; Man. C. E. Marcel; 4 brs.

Barclays Bank PLC (United Kingdom): 21 Albert St, POB 363, Belize City; tel. (2) 77211; telex 217; fax (2) 78572; Man. Tilvan King; 3 brs.

Belize Bank Ltd: 60 Market Sq., POB 364, Belize City; tel. (2) 77132; telex 158; fax (2) 72712; cap. BZ $4.3m., res BZ $16.6m., dep. BZ $269.7m. (April 1996); Chair. Sir Edney Cain; Senior Vice-Pres. and Gen. Man. Louis Anthony Swasey; 10 brs.

There is also a government savings bank.

INSURANCE

General insurance is provided by local companies, and British, US and Jamaican companies are also represented.

Trade and Industry

STATUTORY BODIES

Banana Control Board: c/o Dept of Agriculture, West Block, Belmopan; management of banana industry; in 1989 it was decided to make it responsible to growers, not an independent executive; Head Lalo Garcia.

Belize Beef Corporation: c/o Dept of Agriculture, West Block, Belmopan; f. 1978; semi-governmental organization to aid development of cattle-rearing industry; Dir Deedie Runkel.

Belize Sugar Board: 7, 2nd St South, Corozal Town; tel. (4) 22005; fax (4) 22672; f. 1960 to control the sugar industry and cane production; includes representatives of the Government, sugar manufacturers, cane farmers and the public sector; Chair. Orlando Puga; Exec. Sec. Maria Puerto.

Citrus Control Board: c/o Dept of Agriculture, West Block, Belmopan; tel. (8) 22199; f. 1966; determines basic quota for each producer, fixes annual price of citrus; Chair. C. Sosa.

Marketing Board: POB 479, Belize City; tel. (2) 77402; fax (2) 77656; f. 1948 to encourage the growing of staple food crops; purchases crops at guaranteed prices, supervises processing, storing and marketing intelligence; Chair. Silas C. Cayetano.

DEVELOPMENT ORGANIZATIONS

Belize Export and Investment Promotion Unit: 63 Regent St, POB 291, Belize City; tel. (2) 70668; fax (2) 74984; f. 1986 as a joint government and private-sector institution to encourage export and investment; Gen. Man. Hugh Fuller.

Belize Reconstruction and Development Corporation: 36 Trinity Blvd, POB 1, Belmopan; tel. (8) 22271; fax (8) 23992; Chair. John Saldivar; Gen. Man. Philip Brackett.

Department of Economic Development: Ministry of Foreign Affairs and Economic Development, POB 42, Belmopan; tel. (8) 22526; fax (8) 23111; administration of public and private sector investment and planning; statistics agency; Head Humberto Paredes.

CHAMBER OF COMMERCE

Belize Chamber of Commerce and Industry: 63 Regent St, POB 291, Belize City; tel. (2) 73148; fax (2) 74984; f. 1920; Pres. Godwin Hulse; Gen. Man. Merilyn Young (acting); 626 mems.

EMPLOYERS' ASSOCIATIONS

Cane Farmers' Association: San Antonio Rd, Orange Walk; tel. (3) 22005; f. 1959 to assist cane farmers and negotiate with the Sugar Board and manufacturers on their behalf; Chair. Pablo Tun; 16 district brs.

Citrus Growers' Association: POB 7, Dangriga; tel. (5) 22442; f. 1966; citrus crop farmers' asscn; Chair. Leroy Diaz; Gen. Man. Clinton Hernandez.

Livestock Producers' Association: National Agricultural and Trade Show Grounds, POB 183, Belmopan; tel. (8) 23202; Chair. John Carr.

UTILITIES

Electricity

Office of Electricity Supply: Mahogany St, POB 1846, Belize City; tel. (2) 24995; fax (2) 24994; f. 1992; Dir-Gen. Gregory Gill.

Belize Electricity Co Ltd (BECOL): 115 Barrack Rd, POB 327, Belize City; tel. (2) 77141; fax (2) 33757; CEO Luis Lue.

TRADE UNIONS

National Trades Union Congress of Belize (NTUCB): POB 2359, Belize City; tel. (2) 71596; fax (2) 72864; Pres. Ray Davis; Gen. Sec. Dorene Quiros.

Principal Unions

United General Workers' Union: 1259 Lakeland City, Dangriga; tel. (5) 22105; f. 1979 by amalgamation of the Belize General Development Workers' Union and the Southern Christian Union; three branch unions affiliated to the central body; affiliated to ICFTU; Pres. Francis Sabal; Gen. Sec. Conrad Sambula.

Belize National Teachers' Union: POB 382, Belize City; tel. (2) 72857; Pres. Helen Stuart; Sec. Miguel Wong; 1,000 mems.

Christian Workers' Union: 107B Cemetery Rd, Belize City; tel. (2) 72150; f. 1962; general; Pres. JAMES MCFOY; Gen. Sec. ANTONIO GONZALEZ; 1,000 mems.

Democratic Independent Union: Belize City; Pres. CYRIL DAVIS; 1,250 mems.

Public Service Union of Belize: 81 Almara Avenue, POB 45, Belize City; tel. (2) 72318; fax (2) 70029; f. 1922; public workers; Pres. HUBERT ENRIQUEZ; Sec.-Gen. PATRICIA BENNETT; 1,236 mems.

United Banners Banana Workers' Union: Dangriga; f. 1995; Pres. MARCIANA FUNEZ.

Transport

RAILWAYS

There are no railways in Belize.

ROADS

There are 1,419 km (882 miles) of all-weather main and feeder roads and 651 km (405 miles) of cart roads and bush trails. About 805 km (500 miles) of logging and forest tracks are usable by heavy-duty vehicles in the dry season.

SHIPPING

There is a deep-water port at Belize City and a second port at Commerce Bight, near Dangriga (formerly Stann Creek), to the south of Belize City. There is a port for the export of bananas at Big Creek. Nine major shipping lines operate vessels calling at Belize City, including the Carol Line (consisting of Harrison, Hapag-Lloyd, Nedlloyd and CGM).

Belize Port Authority: Caesar Ridge Rd, POB 633, Belize City; tel. (2) 72439; fax (2) 73571; f. 1980; Chair. WILLIAM LONGSWORTH; Ports Commr ALFRED B. COYE.

Belize Lines Ltd: 37 Regent St, Belize City.

CIVIL AVIATION

Philip S. W. Goldson International Airport, 14 km (9 miles) from Belize City, can accommodate medium-sized jet-engined aircraft. A new terminal was completed in 1990. There are airstrips for light aircraft on internal flights near the major towns and offshore islands.

Maya Island Air: Municipal Airport, POB 458, Belize City; tel. (2) 35795; telex 280; fax (2) 30584; e-mail mayair@btl.net; f. 1997 as merger between Maya Airways Ltd and Island Air; operated by Belize Air Group; internal services, centred on Belize City, and charter flights to neighbouring countries; Gen. Man. PABLO ESPAT.

Tropical Air Services (Tropic Air): San Pedro, Ambergris Caye; tel. (2) 62012; fax (2) 62338; f. 1979; operates internal services and services to Mexico and Guatemala; Chair. CELI MCCORKLE; Man. Dir JOHN GREIF.

Tourism

The main tourist attractions are the beaches and the barrier reef, diving, fishing and the Mayan archaeological sites. There are nine major wildlife reserves (including the world's only reserves for the jaguar and for the red-footed booby), and government policy is to develop 'eco-tourism', based on the attractions of an unspoilt environment and Belize's natural history. The country's wildlife also includes howler monkeys and 500 species of birds, and its barrier reef is the second largest in the world. There were 360 hotels in Belize and 349,277 tourist arrivals in 1996. Tourist receipts totalled BZ $167.1m. in that year. In February 1996 the Mundo Maya Agreement was ratified, according to which Belize, El Salvador, Guatemala, Honduras and Mexico would co-operate in the management of Mayan archaeological remains.

Belize Tourist Board: 83 North Front St, POB 325, Belize City; tel. (2) 77213; fax (2) 77490; e-mail btbb@btl.net; f. 1964; fmrly Belize Tourist Bureau; eight mems; Chair. SANTINO J. CASTILLO; Dir KEVIN GONZALEZ.

Belize Tourism Industry Association: 99 Albert St, Belize City; Pres. WADE BEVIER (acting).

BENIN

Introductory Survey

Location, Climate, Language, Religion, Flag, Capital

The Republic of Benin (known as the People's Republic of Benin between 1975 and 1990) is a narrow stretch of territory in West Africa. The country has an Atlantic coastline of about 100 km (60 miles), flanked by Nigeria to the east and Togo to the west; its northern borders are with Burkina Faso and Niger. Benin's climate is tropical, and is divided into three zones: the north has a rainy season between July and September, with a hot, dry season in October–April; the central region has periods of abundant rain in May–June and in October, while there is year-round precipitation in the south, the heaviest rains being in May–October. Average annual rainfall in Cotonou is 1,300 mm. French is the official language, but each of the indigenous ethnic groups has its own language. Bariba and Fulani are the major languages in the north, while Fon and Yoruba are widely spoken in the south. The majority of the people (about 60%) follow traditional beliefs and customs; more than 20% are Christians, mainly Roman Catholics, and the remainder are Muslims. The national flag (proportions 3 by 2) has a vertical green stripe at the hoist, with equal horizontal stripes of yellow over red in the fly. The administrative capital is Porto-Novo, but most government offices and other state bodies are presently in the economic capital, Cotonou.

Recent History

Benin, called Dahomey until 1975, was formerly part of French West Africa. It became a self-governing republic within the French Community in December 1958, and an independent state on 1 August 1960. The country's history from independence until 1972 was marked by chronic political instability, with five successful coups involving the army, and by periodic regional unrest, fuelled by long-standing rivalries between north and south.

Elections in December 1960 were won by the Parti dahoméen de l'unité, whose leader, Hubert Maga (a northerner), became the country's first President. In October 1963, following riots by workers and students, Maga was deposed by a military coup, led by Col (later Gen.) Christophe Soglo, Chief of Staff of the Army. Soglo served as interim Head of State until January 1964, when Sourou-Migan Apithy, a southerner who had been Vice-President under Maga, was elected President. Another southerner, Justin Ahomadegbé, became Prime Minister. In November 1965, following a series of political crises, Gen. Soglo forced Apithy and Ahomadegbé to resign. A provisional Government was formed, but the army intervened again in December, and Soglo assumed power at the head of a military regime. In December 1967 industrial unrest, following a ban on trade union activity, provoked another coup, led by Maj. (later Lt-Col) Maurice Kouandété. Lt-Col Alphonse Alley, hitherto Chief of Staff, became interim Head of State, and Kouandété Prime Minister.

A return to civilian rule was attempted in 1968. A referendum in March approved a new Constitution, and a presidential election took place in May. Leading politicians, including all former Heads of State, were banned from contesting the presidency, and urged their supporters to boycott the election. As a result, only about 26% of the electorate voted, with the abstention rate reaching 99% in the north. The election was declared void, and in June the military regime nominated Dr Emile-Derlin Zinsou, a former Minister of Foreign Affairs, as President; he was confirmed in office by referendum in the following month. In December 1969 Zinsou was deposed by Lt-Col Kouandété, then Commander-in-Chief of the Army, and a three-member military Directoire assumed power.

In March 1970 a presidential election was held amid violent incidents and widespread claims of irregularities. The poll was abandoned when counting revealed roughly equal support for the three main candidates—Ahomadegbé, Apithy and Maga—to whom the Directoire ceded power in May: it was intended that each member of this Presidential Council would act as Head of State, in rotation, for a two-year period. As a concession to the north, Maga was the first to hold this office, being succeeded in May 1972 by Ahomadegbé. In October, however, the civilian leadership was deposed by Maj. (later Brig.-Gen.) Mathieu Kérékou, Deputy Chief of Staff of the armed forces. Kérékou, a northerner, asserted that his military regime would be based on equal representation between northern, central and southern regions. In September 1973 a Conseil national révolutionnaire (CNR), comprising representatives from each of these regions, was established.

Kérékou pursued a Marxist-based policy of 'scientific socialism'. Banks, the distribution of petroleum products and other strategic sectors were acquired by the State. Between 1974 and 1978 a decentralized local administration was established, the education system was placed under government control, and the legal system was revised. A restructuring of the armed forces followed an unsuccessful coup attempt, in January 1975, led by the Minister of Public Administration and Labour and elements of the paramilitary forces. A further plot to depose Kérékou, allegedly initiated by the exiled Zinsou, was disclosed in October. In November the Parti de la révolution populaire du Bénin (PRPB) was established as the 'highest expression of the political will of the people of Benin', and the country's name was changed from Dahomey to the People's Republic of Benin.

In January 1977 an airborne mercenary attack on Cotonou, led by a French national, Col Robert Denard, was repelled by the armed forces. In August the CNR adopted a *Loi fondamentale* decreeing new structures in government. Accordingly, elections to a new 'supreme authority', the Assemblée nationale révolutionnaire (ANR), took place in November 1979: a single list of 336 candidates was approved by 97.5% of voters. At the same time a Comité exécutif national (CEN) was established to replace the CNR. The PRPB designated Kérékou as the sole candidate for President of the Republic, and in February 1980 he was unanimously elected to this office by the ANR. In April 1981 it was announced that Ahomadegbé, Apithy and Maga, imprisoned following the coup of 1972, had been released from house arrest. A gradual moderation in Benin's domestic policies followed, and subsequent ministerial changes reflected a government campaign against corruption and inefficiency. Members of the extreme left lost influence, as did the army, whose officers were, for the first time, outnumbered by civilians in the Government.

In February 1984 the ANR amended the *Loi fondamentale*, increasing the mandates of assembly members (People's Commissioners) and of the President from three years to five, while reducing the number of People's Commissioners to 196. At legislative elections in June 97.96% of voters approved the single list of candidates for the ANR, and in July the ANR re-elected Kérékou, again the sole candidate, as President. Kérékou subsequently consolidated his position, reducing the membership of the CEN and effectively depriving southern communities of influence in government. Student unrest in April–May 1985 prompted several arrests, and in November there was a purge of suspected members of the banned Parti communiste dahoméen.

In January 1987 Kérékou resigned from the army to become a civilian Head of State. Concern among army officers at perceived corruption within Kérékou's civilian Government, together with opposition to the proposed establishment of a Court of State Security, were the apparent catalysts for a coup attempt in March 1988: almost 150 officers, including members of the Presidential Guard, were reportedly arrested. There were reports of a further attempt to overthrow the Government in June, while Kérékou had been attending a regional conference in Togo.

Elections to the ANR took place in June 1989. A comparative decline in support for the single PRPB list (which was approved by 89.6% of voters) was attributed to popular dissatisfaction with the country's chronic economic difficulties—which had been exacerbated by the closure, between 1984 and 1986, of the border with Nigeria. In August 1989 the ANR re-elected Kérékou (the sole candidate) to the presidency. An ensuing reorganization of the CEN included the appointment of several known proponents of political reform.

In 1986 negotiations were begun with the IMF and the World Bank, in an effort to facilitate a rescheduling of Benin's external debt and the granting of new credits. In early 1989 public-sector employees staged strikes in protest against delays in the payment of salaries, while students, who were demanding the disbursement of outstanding grants and scholarships, boycotted classes. Although the payment of salaries was subsequently authorized, arrears again accumulated, and in March proposals for substantial reductions in remuneration provoked further industrial action. In June economic adjustment measures were agreed with the IMF and the World Bank. Unrest escalated in July: civil servants at several government ministries withdrew their labour, teaching staff were suspended, and the 1988/89 academic year was declared invalid in all institutions where strikes had taken place. In September the Government promised partial payment to teachers of outstanding salaries, following pledges of financial assistance from overseas creditors. In the following month the Union nationale des syndicats de travailleurs du Bénin (UNSTB), the sole officially-recognized trade union, announced that it was to sever its ties with the PRPB. In December further disruption was precipitated by the Kérékou administration's failure to fulfil its earlier commitments to public-sector employees. The Government then yielded to domestic pressure and to demands made by France and other external creditors, instituting radical political changes. It was announced that Marxism-Leninism would no longer be the official ideology of the State, and a national conference was promised, at which the drafting of a new constitution was to be initiated. Foreign donors subsequently agreed to contribute towards the payment of outstanding salaries.

The national conference of what were termed the 'active forces of the nation' was convened in Cotonou in February 1990. The sessions were attended by 488 representatives of more than 50 political organizations. Delegates voted to abolish the 1977 *Loi fondamentale* and its institutions: all resolutions adopted by the conference were incorporated in a 'national charter' that was to form the basis of a new constitution. An Haut conseil de la République (HCR) was appointed to assume the functions of the ANR pending the appointment of a new legislature. Among the members of the HCR were former Presidents Ahomadegbé, Maga and Zinsou, all of whom had recently returned to Benin as the leaders of opposition parties. Presidential and legislative elections (to be held on the basis of universal suffrage, in the context of a multi-party political system) were scheduled for early 1991. A former official of the World Bank (who had briefly been Minister of Finance and Economic Affairs in the mid-1960s), Nicéphore Soglo, was designated interim Prime Minister, and Kérékou, who reluctantly acceded to the conference's decisions, subsequently relinquished the defence portfolio to the new premier. Delegates also voted to change the country's name to the Republic of Benin.

In March 1990 an amnesty was announced for all political dissidents. The HCR was inaugurated, and Soglo appointed a transitional, civilian Government; of the previous administration, only Kérékou remained in office. Soglo pledged to honour all financial commitments to public-sector employees and students, and all those detained during the unrest of late 1989 were released. In May 1990 civilian administrators were appointed to Benin's six provinces, which had hitherto been governed by military prefects. In June the Government undertook an extensive restructuring of the armed forces. Legislation permitting the registration of political parties was promulgated in August (the PRPB had itself been succeeded by a new party, the Union des forces du progrès, in May).

After considerable delay, a national referendum on the draft Constitution was conducted on 2 December 1990. Voters were asked to choose between two proposed documents, one of which incorporated a clause stipulating upper and lower age-limits for presidential candidates (and would therefore exclude Ahomadegbé, Maga and Zinsou from contesting the presidency). It was reported that 95.8% of those who voted gave their approval to one or other of the versions, with 79.7% of voters favouring the Constitution in its entirety.

As many as 24 political parties (many of which had formed electoral alliances) contested the legislative election, which took place on 17 February 1991. No party or group of parties won an overall majority in the 64-member Assemblée nationale, the greatest number of seats (12) being secured by an alliance of three parties that were known to support the policies of Nicéphore Soglo.

Thirteen candidates, including Kérékou and Soglo, contested the first round of the presidential election on 10 March 1991. The distribution of votes largely reflected ethnic divisions: of the leading candidates, Soglo, who took 36.2% of the total votes cast, received his greatest support in the south of the country, while Kérékou, who received 27.3% of the overall vote, was reported to have secured the support of more than 80% of voters in the north. Soglo and Kérékou proceeded to a second round of voting, which was conducted two weeks later amid violence and allegations of electoral malpractice. Despite strong support for Kérékou in the north, Soglo was elected President, obtaining 67.7% of the total votes cast. In late March, prior to its own dissolution, the HCR granted Kérékou immunity from any legal proceedings connected with actions committed since the *coup d'état* of October 1972.

Soglo was inaugurated as President on 4 April 1991. Shortly afterwards he relinquished the defence portfolio to Désiré Vieyra (his brother-in-law), who was designated Minister of State. In July the Assemblée nationale elected Adrien Houngbédji, the leader of the Parti du renouveau démocratique (PRD) and himself a presidential candidate, as its Speaker. In the same month the defence portfolio was transferred to Florentin Feliho, while Vieyra took the post of Senior Minister, Secretary-General at the Office of the President of the Republic.

As President, Soglo furthered attempts that had been initiated by his transitional administration to address Benin's economic problems and to recover state funds allegedly embezzled by former members of the Kérékou regime. None the less, the new administration's inability immediately to pay public-sector salary arrears which had accumulated during the late 1980s precipitated renewed labour unrest in the second half of 1991. There was further disruption in the education sector in early 1992, when security forces were deployed on campus at the University of Benin, in response to a students' boycott of classes. There was, moreover, considerable opposition in the Assemblée nationale to elements of the Government's programme of economic reform: many deputies opposed the sale of former state-owned enterprises to foreign interests, and during the first six months of 1992 the legislature refused to ratify budget proposals for that financial year. Tensions between the executive and legislature were temporarily resolved following the formation, in June, of a 34-member pro-Soglo grouping, known as Le Renouveau, in the Assemblée nationale. However, the Soglo administration's pursuit of economic reforms, while favourably received by the international financial community, continued to be a source of domestic disquiet, and in February 1993 government proposals for a 10% reduction in civil servants' salaries provoked renewed industrial unrest.

In May 1992, meanwhile, several disaffected army officers were arrested following an incident outside the presidential palace in Cotonou. In August it was reported that some of the detainees, including their leader, Capt. Pascal Tawes (formerly deputy commander of the now-disbanded Presidential Guard), had escaped from custody and that Tawes was leading a mutiny at an army camp in the northern town of Natitingou. The rebellion was quickly suppressed by forces loyal to Soglo, and about 45 mutineers were detained, although Tawes was among those who evaded arrest. In March 1993 more than 100 prisoners, including several soldiers who were implicated in the previous year's disturbances, escaped from detention in the south-western town of Ouidah. The dismissal, shortly afterwards, of the Chief of Staff of the armed forces and of other senior members of the security forces prompted Feliho to resign the defence portfolio, protesting that Soglo had acted unconstitutionally by making new appointments to the military command without consulting him. Following a reorganization of the Council of Ministers in September, Vieyra, now Minister of State, in charge of National Defence, remained the most senior member of the Government. Controversy arose when the Assemblée nationale delayed the official publication of the new government list for several days, reportedly because deputies believed that Soglo had been discourteous in leaving Benin for a visit to Europe without first having presented the list to parliament. In the following month 15 assembly members withdrew from Le Renouveau, alleging that Soglo was consistently excluding the legislature from the decision-making process. In July Soglo, who had previously asserted his political neutrality, had made public his membership of the (Parti de la) Renaissance du Bénin (RB), an organization formed by his wife in the previous year. President Soglo was appointed leader of the RB in July 1994.

Social tensions re-emerged following the 50% devaluation of the CFA franc in January 1994. In late January the deployment of security forces in Cotonou to disperse an unauthorized demonstration by union activists (who were demanding 30% salary increases) prompted workers' representatives to withdraw contacts with the authorities, and in early February a 3,000-strong demonstration took place in Cotonou in support of the unions' demands. In February and March students' protests were ended by force. Workers' organizations (excluding the UNSTB) organized a three-day general strike in early March and a five-day strike later in the month, causing widespread disruption. In May the Government announced salary increases of 10% for all state employees, as well as the reintroduction of housing allowances (abolished in 1986) and an end to the eight-year freeze on promotions within the civil service. In July, however, the Assemblée nationale approved amendments to the Government's draft budget whereby wages would rise by 15% and student grants by 20% (the latter compared with an increase of 15% that had been budgeted by the Government). Stating that the imbalanced budget arising from the legislature's amendments was unconstitutional, and would, moreover, result in the loss of funding and debt-relief already agreed with external creditors, Soglo announced in August that he was to impose the Government's draft budget by decree. The Assemblée nationale referred the matter to the Constitutional Court for adjudication. The Court ruled that the presidential ordinances relating to the budget were invalid, but that presidential recourse to the relevant article of the Constitution was discretionary, and could not therefore be subject to legal control. The Government confirmed that its draft budget would be implemented, in the interests of fulfilling Benin's commitments to the international financial community. The payment of salary arrears from 1983–91 began in November 1994.

In September 1994 Tawes and 15 others were sentenced *in absentia* to life imprisonment with hard labour, after having been convicted of plotting to overthrow the Government in May 1992; eight of those who were present at the trial received lesser custodial sentences, while three defendants were acquitted.

Preparations for elections to the Assemblée nationale, which were originally scheduled for early February 1995, were the cause of further friction between the executive and legislature. In November 1994 parliament voted to establish an independent commission to oversee the elections: the creation of the Commission électorale nationale autonome (CENA) was subsequently approved by the Constitutional Court. Soglo, who was known to have opposed such a body, had also objected to the planned increase in the number of parliamentary deputies from 64 to 83. Organizational difficulties twice necessitated the postponement of the elections, which finally took place on 28 March 1995. Some 31 political organizations had been authorized to participate, and a total of 5,580 candidates contested seats in the enlarged assembly. Although observers concluded that the elections had generally been conducted fairly, irregularities were apparent in several constituencies in Atlantique province, in the south, where the CENA accused polling agents of sabotage, and in Bourgou province in the north. Provisional results indicated that the RB had won the largest number of seats in the Assemblée nationale, but that opposition parties were likely, in alliance, to outnumber the President's supporters. Of the opposition parties, Houngbédji's PRD emerged as the strongest, while supporters of ex-President Kérékou, mainly representing the Front d'action pour le renouveau et le développement—Alafia (FARD—Alafia), enjoyed particular success in the north, although Kérékou himself had not actively campaigned in the elections. The final composition of the new parliament remained uncertain, owing to the annulment by the Constitutional Court of the results of voting for nine seats in Cotonou (part of Atlantique province) and for four seats in Bourgou. Among those who were obliged to seek re-election were the President's wife, Rosine Vieyra Soglo, who had (controversially) headed the RB list of candidates. By-elections for the 13 invalidated seats took place on 28 May. Representatives of the RB (among them Rosine Vieyra Soglo) were elected to five of the seats being contested in Cotonou. (One of the newly elected RB deputies was, however, immediately disqualified by the Constitutional Court, on the grounds that he had failed to fulfil the necessary residency criteria.) In June, in response to a letter in which the President of the Constitutional Court, Elisabeth Kayissan Pognon, had criticized the RB for organizing a demonstration in Cotonou to protest against the annulment of the by-election result, Soglo accused Pognon of incitement to riot and rebellion.

Following the elections, the RB thus held 20 seats in the Assemblée nationale, and other supporters of Soglo a total of 13. Opposition parties held, in all, 49 seats, the most prominent organizations being the PRD, with 19 seats, and FARD—Alafia, with 10. In June 1995 Bruno Amoussou, the leader of the opposition Parti social-démocrate, was elected Speaker of the legislature: Soglo's supporters had voted for Amoussou in preference to Houngbédji, who was expected to present a strong challenge to Soglo at the 1996 presidential election. A new Government was formed later in June, dominated by the RB.

From late October 1995 rumours circulated of a coup plot and of attempts to sabotage a conference of Heads of State and Government of the Conseil permanent de la francophonie, which was due to take place in Cotonou, under the chairmanship of ex-President Zinsou, in December. The Government denied allegations that a destabilization plot had been discovered, attributing such rumours (together with reports that Soglo was in poor health and that Algerian fundamentalist organizations had threatened to disrupt the francophone conference) to those wishing to discredit the Soglo regime in advance of the summit and the presidential election. None the less, it was confirmed that members of the military had been among several people arrested in security operations. Tensions escalated in mid-November, following a rocket attack on the newly-built conference centre at which the francophone summit was to take place. Although the authorities dismissed the attack as a minor act of sabotage, it was announced shortly afterwards that one person had been killed and seven arrested, and that munitions stolen during a raid on the Ouidah barracks in early 1994 had been recovered, as part of operations to apprehend the perpetrators of the rocket attack. Later in November 1995 Soulé Dankoro, a former government minister under Kérékou, was arrested, together with a business executive who had earlier served a prison sentence in connection with violence in northern Benin at the time of the 1991 presidential elections, accused of assisting in the preparation of the rocket attack.

Despite Kérékou's effective withdrawal from active politics following his defeat in 1991, the success of his supporters at the 1995 parliamentary elections prompted speculation that he might again contest the presidency in 1996. While Soglo's economic policies had earned his regime the respect of the international financial community, there was disquiet within Benin that strong growth had been achieved at the expense of social concerns; moreover, criticism was increasingly levelled at what was termed the regime's 'authoritarian drift' and at the undue influence in political life of members of Soglo's family. Tribute was paid, meanwhile, to what was regarded as Kérékou's dignified acceptance of the decisions of the 1990 national conference and of his 1991 electoral defeat. By the time Kérékou officially announced, at the end of January 1996, that he was again to contest the presidency, promising greater emphasis on social issues, it was widely accepted that his would be the most powerful challenge to Soglo. In mid-February Soglo formally announced that he would seek a second mandate, asserting that the economic successes now attained would henceforth permit his administration to concentrate on addressing unemployment and other social problems exacerbated by the adjustment policies of the first half of the decade.

Renewed institutional conflict followed the Assemblée nationale's decision, in December 1995, to delay ratification of the third phase of the country's structural adjustment programme, a particularly contentious element of which was the planned restructuring of the state company responsible for the distribution of petroleum products. Deputies rejected ratification of a modified programme twice during January 1996, and also rejected the Government's draft budget for that year, prompting Soglo, citing the national interest, to implement the budget and adjustment programme by decree.

The first round of the presidential election, on 3 March 1996, was contested by seven candidates. As had been expected, Soglo and Kérékou emerged as the leading candidates, although Soglo's supporters alleged widespread vote-rigging. Some 22.8% of the votes cast were subsequently invalidated by the Constitutional Court prior to the announcement, five days after the poll, of the official results. Soglo secured 35.7% of the valid votes and Kérékou 33.9%, followed by Houngbédji (19.7%) and Amoussou (7.8%). The rate of participation by voters was high, at 86.9%. Most of the defeated candidates quickly expressed their support for Kérékou, among them Houngbédji (who had in 1975 been sentenced *in absentia* to death for his part in a plot to overthrow Kérékou's military regime), who stated that the first-round result clearly indicated the desire of the electorate for a change of regime. A government decision to delay the second round of voting by four days, to 21 March (owing to the late proclamation of the results of the first poll), was overturned by the Constitutional Court following an appeal by Kérékou's supporters, and the vote was reset for 18 March.

Soglo's supporters asserted that indications of a clear victory for Kérékou at the second round of voting were based on incomplete results and attributable to 'massive fraud', and Soglo himself spoke of an international plot to end democracy in Benin. Kérékou's supporters denounced delays in the publication of the official results: although collated by the national statistical service, it appeared that the results of voting had not been transmitted to the CENA, while a senior official of the statistical service was arrested on suspicion of 'issuing false documents and incitement to rebellion'. International monitors, for their part, stated that any irregularities in the conduct of voting in no way affected the overall credibility of the result. Prior to the official announcement of the second-round results, a gun attack was reported on the home of a member of the Constitutional Court. (Members of the court had also received intimidatory letters, signed by 'southerners in rebellion', accusing them of plotting against democracy.) Soglo meanwhile dismissed Vieyra and the presidential chief of staff. Finally, on 24 March 1996 the Constitutional Court announced that Kérékou had received the support of 52.5% of voters. Some 78.1% of those eligible had voted, and less than 3% of the votes had been invalidated. Kérékou had won the support of a majority of voters in four of the country's six provinces, and had secured more than 90% of the votes in his home province of Atakora; Soglo had won some 80% of the votes in his native Zou province, in central Benin, and (despite a high rate of unemployment) had also performed strongly in Atlantique province. On 1 April the Court announced that it had rejected all appeals against the outcome of the election, and accordingly confirmed Kérékou's victory. Soglo conceded defeat the following day, formally congratulating the new President; he left the country shortly afterwards, failing to attend the incoming President's inauguration.

Having sought authorization by the Constitutional Court for the appointment of a Prime Minister (provision for such a post is not stipulated in the Constitution), Kérékou named Houngbédji as premier in a Government mostly composed of representatives of those parties that had supported his presidential campaign; a former associate of Soglo, Moïse Mensah, was named Minister of Finance. Kérékou assumed personal responsibility for defence. The Government's stated priorities were to be to strengthen the rule of law, and to promote economic revival and social development. It was announced that a national economic conference would be organized to identify, and ensure consensus regarding, economic aims. Despite campaign pledges by Kérékou to halt the privatization programme, a new funding arrangement was approved by the IMF in late August 1996.

Soglo returned to Benin in early August 1996, having spent the previous four months in the USA and France. Speaking in Washington, DC, in mid-June, he had expressed his desire to lead Benin's opposition. He subsequently indicated, in an article written for a US newspaper, recognition of the legitimacy of Kérékou's election. Meanwhile, Zinsou was named as an adviser to the President in late August; Ahomadegbé was among other erstwhile opponents of the military regime who had by now come to support Kérékou.

Seven of those detained in late 1995, including Soulé Dankoro, were released on bail in late April 1996. The authorities stated, none the less, that no political pressure had been exerted to secure their release, and it was emphasized that applications for bail made by five other defendants had been rejected. In September three defendants were sentenced to five years' enforced labour, and one to a year's imprisonment, having been convicted of involvement in the rocket attack; a fifth defendant was sentenced *in absentia* to 15 years' imprisonment. In early September 1997 the Assemblée nationale approved an amnesty benefiting, most notably, members of the military and civilians implicated in the events of late 1995. The amnesty, embracing all acts seeking to undermine state security, election and media crimes committed between January 1990 and June 1996, provoked protests by the RB, which warned that the measure would exacerbate ethnic and regional divisions, as well as tensions and indiscipline within the army.

The national economic conference took place in mid-December 1996. The six-day meeting was attended by some 500 delegates from all sectors, including representatives of commerce, industry, trade unions and political organizations, together with observers from the IMF and World Bank. Addressing the conference, Kérékou expressed his belief that the maintenance of democracy was vital to Benin's future prosperity. He also recognized the need for the further development of the private sector, and, in particular, emphasized the need to combat corruption in all areas of public and economic life.

The Government's draft budget for 1997 was amended in late December 1996, to include a 5% salary increase for civil servants, in place of an intended increase in the level of family benefit payments. Civil servants had been threatening a general strike if the Assemblée nationale approved a draft budget that made no provision for their pay demands. In early 1997 measures permitting the private ownership of radio and television stations received parliamentary approval; however, the legislation stipulated new, stringent penalties for libel. In early August a new law on territorial administration was endorsed by the Assemblée nationale, whereby Benin was henceforth to be divided into 12 administrative departments.

Under the Soglo administration extensive efforts were made to foster harmonious trading and diplomatic relations with external creditors. Relations with France (Benin's principal trading partner and supplier of aid, and a prominent advocate of Benin's transition to multi-party democracy) were generally cordial, as were links with the USA and other creditors. Funding of some 30m. French francs was provided by the French Government for the construction of the new conference centre at which the December 1995 summit meeting of francophone leaders took place. Following Kérékou's election to the presidency in March 1996, there was some initial uncertainty regarding his Government's likely conduct of external political and economic relations, particularly with the IMF (which stipulated continued spending restraint as a precondition for assistance) and thus with other creditors. However, Kérékou swiftly demonstrated a pragmatic approach to international economic relations. Kérékou made an official visit to France in October 1996, during which he was received by President Jacques Chirac and by other senior state officials. During the visit, Kérékou asked for French assistance in transferring the economic capital from Cotonou to the administrative capital, Porto-Novo. Houngbédji visited France in December.

Kérékou led a government delegation to Togo in September 1996; he and the Togolese President, Gnassingbe Eyadéma, discussed issues of mutual concern, including efforts to combat the proliferation of organized crime and banditry in the sub-region. Benin, Burkina Faso and Togo conducted joint military exercises in March 1997. As part of its stated policy of countering violent crime in Benin, the Kérékou administration expelled some 700 foreign nationals in mid-October 1996. In August the Governments of Benin and Nigeria had agreed to review the demarcation of disputed areas of their joint border.

Recognition of the 'Sahrawi Arab Democratic Republic' accorded by the military regime in 1976, was withdrawn in March 1997. The new Kérékou administration appeared at this time to be developing close relations with Morocco.

Government

The Constitution of the Republic of Benin, which was approved in a national referendum on 2 December 1990, provides for a civilian, multi-party political system. Executive power is vested in the President of the Republic, who is elected by direct universal adult suffrage with a five-year mandate, renewable only once. The legislature is the 64-member Assemblée nationale, which is similarly elected, for a period of four years, by universal suffrage. The President of the Republic appoints the Council of Ministers, subject to formal parliamentary approval.

For the purposes of local administration, Benin is divided into 12 departments, each administered by a civilian prefect.

Defence

In August 1997 the Beninois Armed Forces numbered an estimated 4,800 in active service (land army 4,500, navy about 150, air force 150). Paramilitary forces comprised a 2,500-strong gendarmerie. Military service is by selective conscription, and lasts for 18 months. The estimated defence budget for 1997 was 16,000m. francs CFA.

Economic Affairs

In 1995, according to estimates by the World Bank, Benin's gross national product (GNP), measured at average 1993–95 prices, was US $2,034m., equivalent to $370 per head. During 1985–95, it was estimated, GNP per head declined by an annual average of 0.4% in real terms. Over the same period the population was estimated to have increased by an annual average of 3.0%. Benin's gross domestic product (GDP) increased, in real terms, by an average of 2.6% annually during 1980–90, and of 4.1% per year in 1990–95. GDP growth was 6.3% in 1995, and was projected by the IMF at 5.8% in 1996.

Agriculture (including forestry and fishing) contributed an estimated 36.0% of GDP in 1995. About 59% of the labour force were employed in the sector in 1996. The principal cash crops are cotton (exports of which accounted for an estimated 81.1% of domestic exports and 47.0% of total exports in 1995) and oil palm. Benin is self-sufficient in basic foods; the main subsistence crops are yams, cassava and maize. During 1985–95, according to the World Bank, agricultural GDP increased by an annual average of 4.6%. The IMF estimated growth in agricultural GDP at 0.6% in 1995.

Industry (including mining, manufacturing, construction and power) contributed an estimated 15.1% of GDP in 1995, and engaged 10.4% of the employed labour force at the time of the 1992 census. According to the World Bank, industrial GDP increased by an annual average of 1.2% in 1985–95. The IMF estimated growth in industrial GDP at 5.9% in 1995.

Mining contributed only an estimated 0.7% of GDP in 1995, and engaged less than 0.1% of the employed labour force in 1992. Petroleum, marble and limestone are exploited commercially. There are also deposits of gold, phosphates, natural gas, iron ore, silica sand and chromium. The GDP of the mining sector was estimated to have declined by an average of 5.6% per year in 1990–95; the IMF estimated a decline of 14.3% in 1995.

The manufacturing sector, which contributed an estimated 8.6% of GDP in 1995, engaged 7.8% of the employed labour force in 1992. The sector is based largely on the processing of primary products (such as cotton-ginning and oil-palm processing). Construction materials and some simple consumer goods are also produced for the domestic market. According to the World Bank, manufacturing GDP increased by an annual average of 5.3% in 1985–95. Growth in manufacturing GDP was estimated by the IMF at 5.3% in 1995.

Benin is at present highly dependent on imports of electricity from Ghana (which supplied almost 90% of total available production in 1995). It is envisaged that a hydroelectric installation on the Mono river, constructed and operated jointly with Togo, will reduce Benin's dependence on imported electricity, and there are plans for a second such installation. An agreement was signed in 1995 regarding the construction of a pipeline to supply natural gas from Nigeria to Benin, Togo and Ghana. Imports of energy products comprised 14.4% of the value of merchandise imports in 1990.

The services sector contributed an estimated 48.9% of GDP in 1995, and engaged 31.8% of the employed labour force in 1992. Benin's status as an entrepôt for regional trade was enhanced in the early 1990s as a consequence of political upheaval in Togo, from where significant amounts of transit trade were diverted. Re-exports comprised an estimated 42.0% of the value of total exports in 1995. According to the World Bank, the GDP of the services sector increased by an average of 1.7% per year in 1985–95. The IMF estimated growth in the sector at 6.5% in 1995.

In 1994 Benin recorded a visible trade deficit of US $64.8m., while there was a surplus of $36.4m. on the current account of the balance of payments. In 1989 the principal source of imports (18.7%) was France; other major sources were the Netherlands, the USA, Ghana, Thailand and Côte d'Ivoire. The principal market for exports in that year was the USA (21.3%); other important purchasers were Portugal, the People's Republic of China, Nigeria and Italy. The principal exports in 1990 were ginned cotton, fuels and palm products. The main imports in that year were miscellaneous manufactured articles (most notably cotton yarn and fabrics), foodstuffs (particularly cereals), fuels, machinery and transport equipment, chemical products and beverages and tobacco.

Benin's overall budget deficit for 1995 was estimated at 89,700m. francs CFA (equivalent to 8.7% of GDP). A deficit of 115,560m. francs CFA was forecast for 1997. The country's total external debt at the end of 1995 was US $1,646m., of which $1,514m. was long-term public debt. In that year the cost of debt-servicing was equivalent to 8.5% of the value of exports of goods and services. The annual rate of inflation, which had been negligible prior to the 50% devaluation of the CFA franc in January 1994 (averaging 0.5% in 1993), increased to 38.5% in 1994, but slowed to 14.5% in 1995 and to 4.8% in 1996. About one-third of the urban labour force was estimated to be unemployed or underemployed in the early 1990s.

Benin is a member of the Economic Community of West African States (ECOWAS, see p. 145), of the West African organs of the Franc Zone (see p. 181), of the African Petroleum Producers' Association (APPA, see p. 256), of the Conseil de l'Entente (see p. 260) and of the Niger Basin Authority (see p. 262).

Benin has experienced considerable economic growth since the beginning of the 1990s, as the country's transition to political pluralism has attracted official development assistance and private investment. Economic liberalization measures undertaken by the Kérékou administration in the second half of the 1980s were extended by the Soglo administration, and considerable success was achieved in strengthening public finances, improving the external balance-of-payments position and in reforming the financial sector. The competitiveness of cotton and other agricultural exports was, moreover, among the principal benefits to the economy of the devaluation of the CFA franc in 1994. At his election to the presidency in March 1996 Kérékou undertook to address unemployment and other socio-economic problems arising from the rigorous adjustment measures implemented by his predecessor. The new President also emphasized the need to eliminate corruption in public and economic life, identified as a major obstacle to sustained growth. A new three-year (1996–99) Enhanced Structural Adjustment Facility (ESAF) was agreed with the IMF in August 1996. Annual growth averaging almost 6% was envisaged for the remainder of the 1990s, and it was aimed to reduce dependence on external financial assistance and to maintain Benin's external competitiveness. Despite Kérékou's campaign pledges to halt privatizations, the continuation of the divestment programme was a prerequisite for the new ESAF, although the Government intended that future sales should be of minority stakes only in state-owned enterprises. The renewal of co-operation with the IMF ensured new debt relief, notably along concessionary terms by the 'Paris Club' of official creditors. In addition, a new programme to develop transport infrastructure aimed to enhance regional transport links and also improve the internal market. Meanwhile, sustained growth is to an extent impeded by the narrow manufacturing base, and Benin's economy remains vulnerable to political and economic developments in neighbouring Nigeria.

Social Welfare

In 1994 Benin had 318 physicians, 1,247 nurses and 409 midwives. In mid-1995 the International Development Association approved funding of US $27.8m., in support of a health and population project—costing $33.4m.—a principal aim of which was to be the establishment of a nation-wide family planning programme. Moreover, a particular emphasis of economic policy for the second half of the 1990s was to be the improvement of health care and social services provisions for the poorest sectors of the population. There is a minimum wage for workers (which stood at 21,924 francs CFA per month in 1997). Budget estimates for 1990 allocated 6,484m. francs CFA to social security and welfare (representing 5.6% of total expenditure). The health budget for 1994 was 3,738.7 francs CFA (representing 4.1% of total national budgetary expenditure).

Education

Education in Benin is public, secular and provided free of charge. Primary education, which is officially compulsory, begins at six years of age and lasts for six years. Secondary education, beginning at 12 years of age, lasts for up to seven years, comprising a first cycle of four years and a second of three years. Primary enrolment in 1991 included only 53% of children in the appropriate age-group (males 71%; females 35%). Enrolment at secondary schools in the same year was equivalent to only 12% (17% of boys; 7% of girls). The Government's economic adjustment programme for the second half of the 1990s was to include, with assistance both from multilateral and bilateral donors, schemes to extend the provision of primary and vocational education facilities. The University of Benin, at Cotonou, was founded in 1970. In 1993/94 9,964 students were enrolled at tertiary institutions. Adult illiteracy at the time of the 1992 census was 72.5% (males 59.9%; females 83.2%). In 1995, according to UNESCO estimates, the average rate of adult illiteracy was 63.0% (males 51.3%; females 74.2%).

Consolidated budget estimates for 1990 allocated 14,839m. francs CFA to the education sector (12.8% of total expenditure by the central Government).

Public Holidays

1998: 1 January (New Year's Day), 10 January (*Vodoun* national holiday), 16 January (Martyrs' Day, anniversary of mercenary attack on Cotonou), 30 January* (Id al-Fitr, end of Ramadan), 1 April (Youth Day), 8 April* (Id al-Adha, Feast of the Sacrifice), 10 April (Good Friday), 13 April (Easter Monday), 1 May (Workers' Day), 21 May (Ascension Day), 1 June (Whit Monday), 1 August (Independence Day), 15 August (Assumption), 26 October (Armed Forces Day), 1 November (All Saints' Day), 30 November (National Day), 25 December (Christmas Day), 31 December (Harvest Day).

1999: 1 January (New Year's Day), 10 January (*Vodoun* national holiday), 16 January (Martyrs' Day, anniversary of mercenary attack on Cotonou), 19 January* (Id al-Fitr, end of Ramadan), 28 March* (Id al-Adha, Feast of the Sacrifice), 1 April (Youth Day), 2 April (Good Friday), 5 April (Easter Monday), 1 May (Workers' Day), 13 May (Ascension Day), 24 May (Whit Monday), 1 August (Independence Day), 15 August (Assumption), 26 October (Armed Forces Day), 1 November (All Saints' Day), 30 November (National Day), 25 December (Christmas Day), 31 December (Harvest Day).

* These holidays are dependent on the Islamic lunar calendar and may vary by one or two days from the dates given.

Weights and Measures

The metric system is in force.

Statistical Survey

Source (unless otherwise stated): Institut National de la Statistique et de l'Analyse Economique, BP 323, Cotonou; tel. 31-40-81.

Area and Population

AREA, POPULATION AND DENSITY

Area (sq km)	112,622*
Population (census results)	
20–30 March 1979	
Total	3,331,210
15–29 February 1992	
Males	2,390,336
Females	2,525,219
Total	4,915,555
Population (official estimates at mid-year)	
1993	5,215,000
1994	5,387,000
1995	5,561,000
Density (per sq km) at mid-1995	49.4

* 43,484 sq miles.

ETHNIC GROUPS

1979 census (percentages): Fon 39.2; Yoruba 11.9; Adja 11.0; Bariba 8.5; Houeda 8.5; Peulh 5.6; Djougou 3.0; Dendi 2.1; Non-Africans 6.5; Others 1.2; Unknown 2.4.

POPULATION BY PROVINCE (1992 census)

Atakora	649,308
Atlantique	1,066,373
Borgou	827,925
Mono	676,377
Ouémé	876,574
Zou	818,998
Total	4,915,555

Note: Legislation was approved in August 1997 whereby Benin was reorganized into 12 administrative departments.

PRINCIPAL TOWNS (population at 1992 census)

Cotonou	536,827	Djougou	134,099
Porto-Novo (capital)	179,138	Parakou	103,577

BIRTHS AND DEATHS (UN estimates, annual averages)

	1980–85	1985–90	1990–95
Birth rate (per 1,000)	49.3	49.0	48.7
Death rate (per 1,000)	20.8	19.1	17.8

Expectation of life (UN estimates, years at birth, 1990–95): 47.6 (males 45.9; females 49.3).

Source: UN, *World Population Prospects: The 1994 Revision.*

1994 (official estimates): Death rate (per 1,000) 14.3; Expectation of life (years at birth) 54.3

ECONOMICALLY ACTIVE POPULATION
(persons aged 10 years and over, 1992 census)

	Males	Females	Total
Agriculture, hunting, forestry and fishing	780,469	367,277	1,147,746
Mining and quarrying	609	52	661
Manufacturing	93,157	67,249	160,406
Electricity, gas and water	1,152	24	1,176
Construction	50,959	696	51,655
Trade, restaurants and hotels	36,672	395,829	432,501
Transport, storage and communications	52,228	609	52,837
Finance, insurance, real estate and business services	2,705	401	3,106
Community, social and personal services	126,122	38,422	164,544
Activities not adequately defined	25,579	12,917	38,496
Total employed	1,169,652	883,476	2,053,128
Unemployed	26,475	5,843	32,318
Total labour force	1,196,127	889,319	2,085,446

Source: ILO, *Yearbook of Labour Statistics.*

Mid-1996 (estimates in '000): Agriculture, etc. 1,481; Total 2,511 (Source: FAO, *Production Yearbook*).

Agriculture

PRINCIPAL CROPS ('000 metric tons)

	1994	1995	1996
Rice (paddy)	14	19	22
Maize	492	597	504
Millet	25	22	29
Sorghum	113	108*	112
Sweet potatoes	50	61	68
Cassava (Manioc)	1,146	1,343	1,343†
Yams	1,250	1,259	1,259†
Taro (Coco yam)	4	3	3†
Dry beans	63	63	59
Groundnuts (in shell)	78	103	84
Cottonseed	132	185†	252
Cotton (lint)	103	150†	166
Coconuts	20†	20†	20*
Palm kernels†	13	14	14
Tomatoes	93	109	72
Green peppers†	12	12	12
Oranges†	12	12	12
Mangoes†	12	12	12
Bananas	13†	13†	13*
Pineapples†	3	3	3

* Unofficial figure. † FAO estimate(s).

Source: FAO, *Production Yearbook*.

LIVESTOCK ('000 head, year ending September)

	1994	1995*	1996
Horses*	6	6	6
Asses*	1	1	1
Cattle	1,223	1,250	1,350
Pigs	555	610	584
Sheep	960	965	601
Goats	1,190*	1,200	1,013

Poultry (million): 20 in 1994; 22* in 1995; 25† in 1996.

* FAO estimate(s). † Unofficial figure.

Source: FAO, *Production Yearbook*.

LIVESTOCK PRODUCTS (FAO estimates, '000 metric tons)

	1994	1995	1996
Beef and veal	17	18	18
Mutton and lamb	3	3	3
Goat meat	4	4	4
Pig meat	6	7	8
Poultry meat	22	25	28
Other meat	7	5	6
Cows' milk	19	19	19
Goats' milk	6	6	6
Poultry eggs	14	16	18

Source: FAO, *Production Yearbook*.

Forestry

ROUNDWOOD REMOVALS
(FAO estimates, '000 cubic metres, excl. bark)

	1992	1993	1994
Sawlogs, veneer logs and logs for sleepers	50	50	50
Other industrial wood	247	254	262
Fuel wood	5,087	5,246	5,414
Total	5,384	5,550	5,726

Source: FAO, *Yearbook of Forest Products*.

SAWNWOOD PRODUCTION
('000 cubic metres, incl. railway sleepers)

	1992	1993	1994
Total	24	24*	24*

* FAO estimate.

Source: FAO, *Yearbook of Forest Products*.

Fishing

(FAO estimates, '000 metric tons, live weight)

	1993	1994	1995*
Tilapias	10.2*	10.2	9.4
Black catfishes	1.1*	1.1	1.1
Torpedo-shaped catfishes	1.6*	1.4	1.3
Freshwater gobies	1.1*	1.3	1.2
Other freshwater fishes	8.1*	7.9	7.2
Groupers and seabasses*	1.3	1.5	1.4
Mullets	0.6*	0.8	0.7
Threadfins and tasselfishes*	0.9	1.0	1.0
Sardinellas*	1.2	1.4	1.3
Bonga shad	2.1*	2.1	1.9
Other marine fishes*	3.3	3.6	3.5
Total fish*	31.5	32.2	29.9
Freshwater crustaceans	3.9*	3.9	3.6
Marine crustaceans*	3.8	3.8	3.5
Total catch	39.2	39.9	37.0

* FAO estimates.

Note: Figures exclude catches by Beninois canoes operating from outside the country.

Source: FAO, *Yearbook of Fishery Statistics*.

Mining

(provisional or estimated figures, '000 metric tons)

	1992	1993	1994
Crude petroleum	298	302	310

Source: UN, *Industrial Commodity Statistics Yearbook*.

Industry

SELECTED PRODUCTS ('000 metric tons, unless otherwise indicated)

	1992	1993	1994
Salted, dried or smoked fish*	2.0	n.a.	n.a.
Cement†	370	380	380
Electric energy (million kWh)‡	5	5	6

* Data from the FAO.
† Data from the US Bureau of Mines.
‡ Provisional or estimated figures.

Source: UN, *Industrial Commodity Statistics Yearbook*.

Palm oil and palm kernel oil ('000 metric tons): 9.9 in 1992; 10.8 in 1993; 10.3 in 1994; 5.4 in 1995 (Source: IMF, *Benin—Recent Economic Developments,* October 1996).

Finance

CURRENCY AND EXCHANGE RATES

Monetary Units

100 centimes = 1 franc de la Communauté financière africaine (CFA).

French Franc, Sterling and Dollar Equivalents (30 September 1997)

1 French franc = 100 francs CFA;
£1 sterling = 958.3 francs CFA;
US $1 = 593.2 francs CFA;
1,000 francs CFA = £1.044 = $1.686.

Average Exchange Rate (francs CFA per US $)

1994	555.20
1995	499.15
1996	511.55

Note: An exchange rate of 1 French franc = 50 francs CFA, established in 1948, remained in force until January 1994, when the CFA franc was devalued by 50%, with the exchange rate adjusted to 1 French franc = 100 francs CFA.

BUDGET ('000 million francs CFA)

Revenue	1993	1994	1995*
Tax revenue	65.8	91.6†	123.0
Taxes on income and profits	18.1	30.5	40.2
Individual	6.3	7.1	8.8
Corporate	8.5	20.7	25.9
Domestic taxes on goods and services	12.8	15.6	19.2
Turnover taxes	7.8	11.4	10.4
Excises	3.4	2.0	1.8
Arrears of taxes on goods and services	0.6	0.6	5.2
Taxes on international trade and transactions	32.7	42.1	60.3
Import duties	30.0	38.5	56.4
Non-tax revenue	11.8	14.5	26.1
From non-financial public enterprises	2.3	3.1	10.7
Contribution to government employees' pension fund	5.0	5.5	7.3
Repayment on on-lending	2.5	4.2	4.8
Total	77.7	106.2	149.1

Expenditure‡	1993	1994	1995*
Primary expenditure§	64.7	88.3	126.0
Salaries	37.7	45.7	53.9
Pensions and scholarships	8.9	10.4	11.5
Other current expenditure (incl. current transfers)	15.2	27.9	47.5
Budgetary contribution to investment	3.0	4.3	13.2
Interest due	15.9	26.2	27.9
Domestic debt	4.6	3.7	2.7
External debt	11.3	22.5	25.2
Investment expenditure (financed from abroad)	25.5	49.9	65.0
Total	106.1	164.4	218.9

* Estimates.
† Including adjustment.
‡ Excluding net lending ('000 million francs CFA): 3.0 (estimate) in 1995.
§ Excluding foreign-financed investment.

Note: Excluding official grants, the overall budget deficit on a commitment basis (in '000 million francs CFA) was: 28.4 in 1993; 58.3 in 1994; 72.7 (estimate) in 1995. After adjusting for changes in domestic arrears, the deficit on a cash basis (in '000 million francs CFA) was: 37.9 in 1993; 68.9 in 1994; 89.7 (estimate) in 1995.

Source: IMF, *Benin—Recent Economic Developments* (October 1996).

1996 (draft budget, '000 million francs CFA): Revenue 168.7; Expenditure 251.9.

1997 (draft budget, '000 million francs CFA): Revenue 184.0; Expenditure 295.5.

INTERNATIONAL RESERVES (US $ million at 31 December)

	1994	1995	1996
Gold*	4.1	4.3	4.2
IMF special drawing rights	—	0.1	0.3
Reserve position in IMF	3.1	3.2	3.1
Foreign exchange	255.1	194.7	258.4
Total	262.3	202.2	266.0

* Valued at market-related prices.

Source: IMF, *International Financial Statistics.*

MONEY SUPPLY ('000 million francs CFA at 31 December)

	1994	1995	1996
Currency outside banks	77.34	50.65	69.02
Demand deposit at deposit money banks	106.32	107.80	114.75
Checking deposits at post office	2.04	2.84	5.29
Total money (incl. others)	186.22	161.73	189.65

Source: IMF, *International Financial Statistics.*

COST OF LIVING

(Consumer price index; base: December 1991 = 100)

	1994	1995	1996
All items	144.7	165.7	173.7

Source: IMF, *International Financial Statistics.*

NATIONAL ACCOUNTS

('000 million francs CFA at current prices)

Expenditure on the Gross Domestic Product

	1993	1994	1995*
Government final consumption expenditure	71.2	91.1	107.5
Private final consumption expenditure	501.2	674.1	832.2
Increase in stocks	2.3	2.0	24.0
Gross fixed capital formation	87.4	131.5	172.6
Total domestic expenditure	662.1	898.7	1,136.3
Exports of goods and services	135.5	228.3	265.0
Less Imports of goods and services	195.8	279.3	365.5
GDP in purchasers' values	601.7	847.7	1,035.8
GDP at constant 1992 prices	592.0	617.7	647.2

* Estimates.

Gross Domestic Product by Economic Activity

	1993	1994*	1995*
Agriculture, livestock, forestry and fishing	215.3	292.2	351.5
Mining and petroleum	3.7	6.6	7.2
Manufacturing and handicrafts	47.1	64.5	83.7
Water, gas and electricity	5.3	6.1	6.8
Construction and public works	21.3	37.6	49.6
Trade	103.6	164.4	215.6
Transport and other marketable services	47.8	67.6	78.0
Public administration	55.1	72.4	79.8
Other non-marketable services	72.9	93.6	103.6
GDP at factor cost	572.1	804.9	975.8
Indirect taxes, *less* subsidies	29.7	42.8	60.0
GDP in purchasers' values	601.7	847.7	1,035.8

* Estimates.

Source: IMF, *Benin—Recent Economic Developments* (October 1996).

BALANCE OF PAYMENTS (US $ million)

	1992	1993	1994
Exports of goods f.o.b.	371.4	341.1	301.0
Imports of goods f.o.b.	−560.6	−538.9	−365.8
Trade balance	−189.2	−197.8	−64.8
Exports of services	142.8	137.4	103.9
Imports of services	−158.7	−152.6	−111.1
Balance on goods and services	−205.1	−213.0	−72.0
Other income paid	−61.6	−39.9	−40.5
Balance on goods, services and income	−266.7	−252.9	−112.6
Current transfers received	244.1	257.8	159.6
Current transfers paid	−16.6	−19.1	−10.6
Current balance	−39.2	−14.1	36.4
Investment assets	−21.9	−4.9	−70.8
Investment liabilities	−18.0	35.4	36.4
Net errors and omissions	1.6	−56.4	54.0
Overall balance	−77.5	−40.1	56.0

Source: IMF, *International Financial Statistics.*

External Trade

Source: Banque centrale des états de l'Afrique de l'ouest.

PRINCIPAL COMMODITIES (million francs CFA)

Imports c.i.f.*	1988	1989	1990
Food products	25,743	12,814	17,863
Food products of animal origin	2,856	2,040	1,300
Food products of plant origin	19,655	8,579	15,020
Rice	13,523	4,753	9,110
Wheat	2,170	1,769	3,562
Processed foodstuffs	3,222	2,195	1,543
Beverages and tobacco	4,643	4,688	5,268
Alcoholic beverages	1,863	1,199	2,241
Manufactured tobacco products	2,760	3,482	2,983
Energy products	13,343	10,113	10,393
Refined petroleum products	9,355	5,795	6,158
Other raw materials (inedible)	4,500	2,449	2,410
Machinery and transport equipment	13,302	9,593	7,860
Non-electrical machinery	5,478	3,486	n.a.
Electrical machinery	4,239	2,251	n.a.
Road transport equipment	3,454	3,812	n.a.
Other industrial products	34,774	25,036	28,026
Chemical products	7,726	4,710	7,235
Fertilizers	866	3	1,533
Miscellaneous manufactured articles	27,048	20,326	20,791
Cotton yarn and fabrics	14,988	11,160	7,715
Total (incl. others)	97,257	66,132	72,192

Exports f.o.b.†	1988	1989	1990
Food products	517	228	266
Energy products	6,388	6,636	7,765
Crude petroleum	6,314	6,636	7,765
Other raw materials (inedible)	8,772	20,007	18,734
Cottonseed	717	1,119	68
Cotton (ginned)	7,725	18,681	16,792
Oils and fats	2,243	1,951	1,191
Palm and palm-kernel oil	1,586	1,437	1,181
Machinery and transport equipment	1,278	613	460
Other industrial products	1,756	1,505	4,833
Miscellaneous manufactured articles	1,337	1,378	4,704
Cotton yarn and fabrics	189	1,008	4,021
Total (incl. others)	20,995	31,090	33,254

* Excluding imports for re-export.
† Excluding re-exports.

PRINCIPAL TRADING PARTNERS (million francs CFA)

Domestic imports	1987	1988	1989
Belgium-Luxembourg	2,002	1,345	856
Brazil	798	1,066	481
China, People's Repub.	4,253	3,667	2,498
Côte d'Ivoire	2,481	4,487	3,814
Czechoslovakia	809	1,240	1,401
France	18,493	18,786	12,357
German Democratic Repub.	226	1,183	165
Germany, Fed. Repub.	3,924	2,739	2,507
Ghana	3,449	4,245	4,390
Ireland	188	66	1,526
Italy	3,707	2,198	8
Japan	5,894	2,265	1,806
Netherlands	7,427	5,223	5,895
Nigeria	1,851	4,296	3,181
Senegal	1,013	1,517	692
Spain	1,372	1,138	801
Thailand	14,766	11,649	3,958
Togo	1,375	2,688	2,359
USSR	526	2,352	181
United Kingdom	4,897	4,012	2,902
USA	4,124	5,117	4,804
Total (incl. others)	104,980	97,257	66,132

Domestic exports	1987	1988	1989
Belgium-Luxembourg	364	131	551
China, People's Repub.	1,983	36	3,581
France	1,298	1,536	453
Germany, Fed. Repub.	1,044	356	278
Italy	4,742	443	1,785
Morocco	298	105	668
Netherlands	480	159	720
Niger	207	315	460
Nigeria	2,505	2,692	1,928
Portugal	7,189	2,889	3,800
Spain	864	289	367
Switzerland	260	337	368
Taiwan	1,910	—	878
Togo	212	1,048	684
United Kingdom	1,080	991	469
USA	5,742	6,328	6,636
Total (incl. others)	34,266	20,995	31,090

Transport

RAILWAYS (traffic)

	1993*	1994	1995
Passenger-km (million)	75.8	107.0	116.0
Freight ton-km (million)	225.3	253.0	206.5

* Estimates.

ROAD TRAFFIC (estimates, '000 motor vehicles in use)

	1993	1994	1995
Passenger cars	32.1	33.6	35.6
Lorries and vans	16.8	18.8	19.3

Source: IRF, *World Road Statistics.*

SHIPPING

Merchant Fleet (registered at 31 December)

	1994	1995	1996
Number of vessels	7	7	7
Total displacement ('000 grt)	1	1	1

Source: Lloyd's Register of Shipping, *World Fleet Statistics.*

International Sea-borne Freight Traffic
(at Cotonou, including goods in transit, '000 metric tons)

	1993*	1994	1995
Goods loaded	236.9	373.5	338.5
Goods unloaded	1,680.3	1,611.2	1,738.4

* Estimates.

Source: IMF, *Benin—Recent Economic Developments* (October 1996).

CIVIL AVIATION (traffic on scheduled services)*

	1992	1993	1994
Kilometres flown (million)	2	2	2
Passengers carried ('000)	66	68	69
Passenger-km (million)	201	207	215
Total ton-km (million)	33	33	33

* Including an apportionment of the traffic of Air Afrique.

Source: UN, *Statistical Yearbook.*

Tourism

	1992	1993	1994
Tourist arrivals ('000)	130	140	142
Tourist receipts (US $ million)	32	38	55

Source: UN, *Statistical Yearbook.*

Communications Media

	1992	1993	1994
Radio receivers ('000 in use)	442	461	480
Television receivers ('000 in use)	25	28	29
Telephones ('000 main lines in use)	16	20	24
Telefax stations (number in use)	300	500	600
Daily newspapers			
Number	1	n.a.	1
Average circulation ('000 copies)	12	n.a.	12
Book production*			
Titles	647†	n.a.	84
Copies ('000)	874†	n.a.	42

* First editions. † Excluding pamphlets.

Sources: UNESCO, *Statistical Yearbook*; UN, *Statistical Yearbook*.

Education

(1993/94)

	Institu- tions	Teach- ers	Students		
			Males	Females	Total
Pre-primary	282	n.a.	7,528	6,299	13,827
Primary	2,889	12,343	392,748	209,321	602,069
Secondary					
General	145	2,384	70,831	27,649	97,480
Vocational	14	283	3,553	1,320	4,873
Higher	16	602	8,330	1,634	9,964

Source: Ministère de l'Education Nationale, Cotonou.

Directory

The Constitution

A new Constitution was approved in a national referendum on 2 December 1990.

The Constitution of the Republic of Benin guarantees the basic rights and freedoms of citizens. The functions of the principal organs of state are delineated therein.

The President of the Republic, who is Head of State and Head of Government, is directly elected, by universal adult suffrage, for a period of five years, renewable only once. The executive is responsible to the legislature—the 83-member Assemblée nationale—which is elected, also by direct universal suffrage, for a period of four years.

The Constitution upholds the principle of an independent judiciary, and provides for the creation of a Constitutional Court, an Economic and Social Council and an authority regulating the media, all of which are intended to counterbalance executive authority.

The Government

HEAD OF STATE

President: Gen. (retd) MATHIEU KÉRÉKOU (took office 4 April 1996).

COUNCIL OF MINISTERS
(December 1997)

President and Minister of Defence: Gen. (retd) MATHIEU KÉRÉKOU.

Prime Minister: ADRIEN HOUNGBÉDJI.

Minister-delegate, responsible for Defence: SÉVÉRIN ADJOVI.

Minister of Foreign Affairs and Co-operation: PIERRE OTCHO.

Minister of Justice: ISMAEL DJANI-CERPOS.

Minister of Finance: MOÏSE MENSAH.

Minister of the Interior: THÉOPHILE NDA.

Minister of Planning, Economic Restructuring and Employment Promotion: ALBERT TÉVOÉDJRÉ.

Minister of Rural Development: JÉRÔME-DÉSIRÉ SAKASSINA.

Minister of Industry, Tourism and Handicrafts: DELPHIN HOUNGBÉDJI.

Minister of Energy and Water Resources: EMMANUEL GOLOU.

Minister of Public Works and Transport: OUMAROU FASSASSI.

Minister of the Environment and Housing: SAHIDOU DANGO-NADEY.

Minister of the Civil Service: YACOUBOU ASSOUMA.

Minister of National Education: DJIDJOFON LÉONARD KPADONOU.

Minister of Health: MARINA D'ALMEIDA.

Minister of Communications, Culture and Information: TIMOTHÉE ZANOU.

Minister of Youth and Sports: ZINSOU DAMIEN ALAHATA.

MINISTRIES

Office of the President: BP 1288, Cotonou; tel. 30-02-28; telex 5222.

Ministry of the Civil Service : BP 907, Cotonou; tel. 31-26-18.

Ministry of Communications, Culture and Information: BP 120, Cotonou; tel. 31-59-31; telex 5266.

Ministry of Defence: BP 2493, Cotonou; tel. 30-08-90.

Ministry of Energy and Water Resources: BP 363, Cotonou; tel. 31-45-20; fax 31-08-90.

Ministry of the Environment and Housing: 01 BP 3621, Cotonou; tel. 31-55-96; fax 31-50-81.

Ministry of Finance: BP 342, Cotonou; tel. 30-10-20; fax 30-18-51.

Ministry of Foreign Affairs and Co-operation: BP 318, Cotonou; tel. 30-04-00; telex 5200.

Ministry of Health: BP 882, Cotonou; tel. 33-08-70.

Ministry of Industry, Tourism and Handicrafts: BP 363, Cotonou; tel. 30-16-46; telex 5252.

Ministry of the Interior: BP 925, Cotonou; tel. 30-10-06; telex 5065.

Ministry of Justice: BP 967, Cotonou; tel. 31-31-46.

Ministry of National Education: BP 348, Cotonou; tel. 30-06-81; fax 30-18-48.

Ministry of Planning, Economic Restructuring and Employment Promotion: BP 342, Cotonou; tel. 30-05-41; telex 5118.

Ministry of Public Works and Transport: BP 351, Cotonou; tel. 31-56-96; telex 5289.

Ministry of Rural Development: 03 BP 2900, Cotonou; tel. 30-19-55; fax 30-03-26.

Ministry of Youth and Sports: BP 03-2103, Cotonou; tel. 31-46-00; telex 5036.

President and Legislature

PRESIDENT

Presidential Election, First Ballot, 3 March 1996

Candidate	% of votes
Nicéphore Soglo	35.69
Mathieu Kérékou	33.94
Adrien Houngbédji	19.71
Bruno Amoussou	7.76
Pascal Fantondji	1.08
Léandre Djagoue	0.92
Jacques Lionel Agbo	0.90
Total	100.00

Second Ballot, 18 March 1996

Candidate	Votes	% of votes
Mathieu Kérékou	999,453	52.49
Nicéphore Soglo	904,626	47.51
Total	1,904,079	100.00

ASSEMBLÉE NATIONALE

Speaker: Bruno Amoussou (PSD).

Elections, 28 March and 28 May 1995*

Party	Seats
RB	20
PRD	19
FARD—Alafia	10
PSD	8
UDS	5
IPD	3
NCC	3
RDL—Vivoten	3
NG	2
AC	1
ADD	1
ADP	1
ASD	1
MNDD†	1
PCB	1
RAP	1
RDP	1
UNDP	1
Total	82

* The results of voting for 13 seats at the March 1995 general election were subsequently annulled by the Constitutional Court, and by-elections for these seats were held on 28 May. The result of one by-election was itself invalidated by the Court, and the seat was to remain vacant: the electoral code stipulates that supplementary elections may not be organized unless the number of vacant seats in the Assemblée nationale is equivalent to one-fifth of the overall membership.

† The Mouvement national pour la démocratie et le développement subsequently merged with the RB.

Advisory Councils

Cour Constitutionnelle: BP 2050, Cotonou; tel. 31-59-92; fax 31-37-12; f. 1990, inaug. 1993; seven mems (four appointed by the Assemblée nationale, three by the President of the Republic); determines the constitutionality of legislation, oversees national elections and referendums, responsible for protection of individual and public rights and obligations, charged with regulating functions of organs of state and authorities; Pres. Elisabeth Kayissan Pognon; Sec.-Gen. Jean-Baptiste Monsi.

Conseil Economique et Social (ECOSOC): Cotonou; f. 1994; 30 mems, representing the executive, legislature and 'all sections of the nation'; competent to advise on proposed economic and social legislation, as well as to recommend economic and social reforms; Pres. Valentin Agbo.

Haute Autorité de l'Audiovisuel et de la Communication (HAAC): Cotonou; f. in accordance with the 1990 Constitution to act as the highest authority for the media; Pres. René M. Dossa.

Political Organizations

The registration of political parties commenced in August 1990. Of the 88 parties holding legal status, 31 contested the 1995 legislative elections. The following secured seats in the Assemblée nationale:

The **Alliance caméléon (AC)**; the **Alliance pour la démocratie et le développement (ADD):** Leader Karim Dramane; the **Alliance pour la démocratie et le progrès (ADP):** Leader Adekpedjou S. Akindes; the **Alliance pour la social-démocratie (ASD):** Leader Robert Dossou; The **Front d'action pour le renouveau et le développement—Alafia (FARD—Alafia):** Leader Saka Kina; **Impulsion au progrès et à la démocratie (IPD);** Leader Bertin Borna; **Notre cause commune (NCC):** Leader François Odjo Tankpinon; **Nouvelle génération pour la République (NGR):** Leader Paul Dossou; the **Parti communiste du Bénin (PCB):** Leader Pascal Fantondji; the **Parti du renouveau démocratique (PRD):** Leader Adrien Houngbédji; the **Parti social-démocrate (PSD):** Leader Bruno Amoussou; the **Rassemblement africain pour le progrès et la solidarité (RAP)**; the **Rassemblement des démocrates libéraux pour la reconstruction nationale—Vivoten (RDL—Vivoten):** Leader Sévérin Adjovi; the **Rassemblement pour la démocratie et le progrès (RDP)**; the **(Parti de la) Renaissance du Bénin (RB):** Leader Nicéphore Soglo; the **Union pour la démocratie et la solidarité nationale (UDS):** Leader Adamou N'Diaye Mama; the **Union nationale pour la démocratie et le progrès (UNDP):** Leader Dr Emile Derlin Zinsou; the **Union nationale pour la solidarité et le progrès (UNSP):** Leader Wallis M. Zoumarou.

Diplomatic Representation

EMBASSIES IN BENIN

Chad: BP 080359, Cotonou; tel. 33-08-51; Chargé d'affaires a.i.: Darkou Ahmat Kalabassou.

China, People's Republic: BP 196, Cotonou; tel. 30-12-92; Ambassador: Zhao Huimin.

Congo, Democratic Republic: BP 130, Cotonou; Ambassador: Tatu Longwa.

Cuba: BP 948, Cotonou; tel. 31-52-97; telex 5277; Ambassador: Evangelio Montero Hernández.

Denmark: 04 BP 1223, Cotonou; tel. 30-38-62; telex 5078; fax 30-38-60; Chargé d'affaires a.i.: Flemming Nichols.

Egypt: BP 1215, Cotonou; tel. 30-08-42; telex 5274; Ambassador: Mohamed Mahmoud Aguib.

France: route de l'Aviation, BP 966, Cotonou; tel. 30-08-24; telex 5209; Ambassador: Cathérine Boivineau.

Germany: 7 ave Jean-Paul II, BP 504, Recette Principale, Cotonou; tel. 31-29-67; telex 5224; fax 31-29-62; Ambassador: Volker Seitz.

Ghana: Les Cocotiers, BP 488, Cotonou; tel. 30-07-46; Ambassador: Christian T. K. Quarshie.

Korea, Democratic People's Republic: Cotonou; tel. 30-10-97; Ambassador: Pak Song Il.

Libya: Les Cocotiers, BP 405, Cotonou; tel. 30-04-52; telex 5254; People's Bureau Representative: Sanoussi Awad Abdallah.

Niger: derrière Hôtel de la Plage, BP 352, Cotonou; tel. 31-56-65; Ambassador: Mahamaje Bashir Gada.

Nigeria: blvd de France Marina, BP 2019, Cotonou; tel. 30-11-42; telex 5247; Chargé d'affaires a.i.: Abdul Kader Ibrahim.

Russia: BP 2013, Cotonou; tel. 31-28-34; telex 9725008; fax 31-28-35; Ambassador: Yurii Tchepik.

USA: rue Caporal Anani Bernard, BP 2012, Cotonou; tel. 30-06-50; fax 30-14-39; e-mail usis.cotonou@bow.intnet.bj; Ambassador: John M. Yates.

Judicial System

The Constitution of December 1990 establishes the judiciary as an organ of state whose authority acts as a counterbalance to that of the executive and of the legislature. There is provision for a Constitutional Court (see Advisory Councils, above), a High Court of Justice and a Supreme Court.

President of the Supreme Court: ABRAHAM ZINZINDOHOUE.

Attorney-General: LUCIEN DEGENO.

Religion

Some 60% of the population hold animist beliefs; more than 20% are Christians (mainly Roman Catholics) and the remainder mostly Muslims. Religious and spiritual cults, which were discouraged under Kérékou's military regime, re-emerged as a prominent force in Beninois society during the early 1990s.

CHRISTIANITY

The Roman Catholic Church

Benin comprises one archdiocese and eight dioceses. At 31 December 1995 there were an estimated 1.2m. Roman Catholics (about 20.4% of the population), mainly in the south of the country.

Bishops' Conference: Conférence Episcopale du Bénin, Archevêché, BP 491, Cotonou; tel. 31-31-45; fax 30-07-07; Pres. Rt Rev. LUCIEN MONSI-AGBOKA, Bishop of Abomey.

Archbishop of Cotonou: Most Rev. ISIDORE DE SOUZA, Archevêché, BP 491, Cotonou; tel. 30-01-45; fax 30-07-07.

Protestant Church

There are 257 Protestant mission centres, with a personnel of about 120.

Eglise protestante méthodiste en République du Bénin: 54 ave Mgr Steinmetz, BP 34, Cotonou; tel. 31-11-42; fax 31-25-20; f. 1843; Pres. Rev. Dr MOÏSE SAGBOHAN; Sec. Rev. MATHIEU D. OLODO; 95,827 mems (1996).

VODOUN

The origins of the traditional *vodoun* religion can be traced to the 14th century. Its influence is particularly notable in spiritual religions of Latin America and the Caribbean, owing to the shipment of slaves from the West African region to the Americas in the 18th and 19th centuries.

Grand conseil de la réligion vodoun du Bénin: Ouidah; Supreme Chief DAAGBO HOUNON HOUNA.

The Press

In the mid-1990s some 50 newspapers and magazines were being published in Benin.

La Croix du Bénin: BP 105, Cotonou; tel. and fax 32-11-19; f. 1946; fortnightly; Roman Catholic; Dir BARTHÉLEMY ASSOGBA CAKPO.

FLASH-HEBDO: BP 120, Cotonou; tel. 30-18-57; weekly; Dir PASCAL ADISSODA.

Le Forum de la Semaine: BP 04-0391, Cotonou; tel. 30-03-40; weekly; Dir BRUNO SODEHOU.

La Gazette du Golfe: Carré 961 'J' Etoile Rouge, 03 BP 1624, Cotonou; tel. 31-35-58; telex 5053; fax 30-01-99; f. 1987; weekly; Dir ISMAËL Y. SOUMANOU; Editor KARIM OKANLA; circ. 18,000 (nat. edn), 5,000 (international edn).

Initiatives: BP 2093, Cotonou; tel. 31-44-47; six a year; Dir THÉOPHILE CAPO-CHICHI.

Journal Officiel de la République du Bénin: BP 59, Porto-Novo; tel. 21-39-77; f. 1890; official govt bulletin; fortnightly; Dir AFIZE D. ADAMON.

La Lumière de l'Islam: BP 08-0430, Cotonou; tel. 31-34-59; fortnightly; Dir MOHAMED BACHIR SOUMANOU.

Le Matin: Cotonou; f. 1994; daily; Dir SAID SAHNOUN.

La Nation: BP 1210, Cotonou; tel. 30-08-75; f. 1990; official newspaper; daily; Dir AKUETE ASSCOI.

L'Observateur: Cotonou; fortnightly; Dir FRANÇOIS COMLAN.

Le Patriote: BP 2093, Cotonou; tel. 31-44-47; monthly; Dir CALIXTE DA SILVA.

Le Pays: 06 BP 2170, Cotonou; tel. 33-10-09; fortnightly; Dir ENOCK YAKA.

La Récade: 08 BP 0086, Cotonou; tel. 33-11-15; monthly; Dir TITOMAS MEGNASSAN.

La Sentinelle: BP 34, Cotonou; tel. 31-25-20; monthly; Dir MICHÉE D. AHOUANDJINOU.

Le Soleil: Cotonou; tel. 30-14-90; fortnightly; Dir EDGARD KAHO.

Tam-Tam-Express: BP 2302, Cotonou; tel. 30-12-05; fax 30-39-75; f. 1988; fortnightly; Dir DENIS HODONOU; circ. 8,000.

L'Union: Cotonou; tel. 31-55-05; fortnightly; Dir PAUL HERVÉ D'ALMEIDA.

NEWS AGENCIES

Agence Bénin-Presse (ABP): BP 72, Cotonou; tel. 31-26-55; telex 5208; fax 31-12-26; e-mail abpben@bow.intnet.bj; f. 1961; national news agency; section of the Ministry of Communications, Culture and Information; Dir YAOVI R. HOUNKPONOU.

Foreign Bureaux

Agence France-Presse (AFP): 06 BP 1382, Cotonou; tel. 33-24-02; Correspondent VIRGILE C. AHISSOU.

Reuters (UK) and Associated Press (USA) are also represented in Benin.

Publishers

Les Editions du Flamboyant: 08 BP 271, Cotonou; tel. and fax 31-02-20; f. 1985.

Government Publishing House

Office National d'Edition, de Presse et d'Imprimerie (ONEPI): BP 1210, Cotonou; tel. 30-08-75; f. 1975; Dir-Gen. BONI ZIMÉ MAKO.

Broadcasting and Communications

Legislation was approved by the Assemblée nationale in early 1997 permitting the private ownership of radio and television stations. Broadcasting licences were to be issued by the Haute Autorité de l'Audiovisuel et de la Communication (see Advisory Councils, above).

Office de Radiodiffusion et de Télévision du Bénin: BP 366, Cotonou; tel. 30-10-96; telex 5132; state-owned; radio programmes broadcast from Cotonou and Parakou in French, English and 18 local languages; TV transmissions 25 hours weekly; Dir-Gen. JACQUES PHILIPPE DA MATHA; Dir of Radio PELU DIOGO; Dir of TV CLÉMENT HOUENONTIN.

Radio Parakou: BP 128, Parakou; tel. 61-07-73; Dir DIEUDONNÉ METOZOUNVÉ.

Finance

(cap. = capital; res = reserves; m. = million; br. = branch; amounts in francs CFA)

BANKING

Central Bank

Banque Centrale des Etats de l'Afrique de l'Ouest (BCEAO): ave d'Ornano, route Inter-Etat no 11, Zone portuaire, BP 325, Cotonou; tel. 31-24-66; telex 5211; fax 31-24-65; headquarters in Dakar, Senegal; f. 1962; bank of issue for the member states of the Union économique et monétaire ouest-africaine (UEMOA); cap. and res 657,592m. (Dec. 1995); Gov. CHARLES KONAN BANNY; Dir in Benin PAULIN COSSI; br. at Parakou.

Commercial Banks

Bank of Africa—Bénin: ave Jean-Paul II, 08 BP 0879, Cotonou; tel. 31-32-28; telex 5079; fax 31-31-17; e-mail boa-benin@elodia.intnet.bj; f. 1990; 27% owned by African Financial Holding; cap. and res 7,200m. (Dec. 1995); Pres. FRANÇOIS TANKPINOU; Man. Dir PAUL DERREUMAUX.

Banque Internationale du Bénin (BIBE): carrefour des Trois Banques, ave Giran, 03 BP 2098, Jericho, Cotonou; tel. 31-55-49; telex 5075; fax 31-23-65; f. 1989; 49% owned by Nigerian commercial banks; cap. and res 1,978m. (Dec. 1995); Pres. Chief JOSEPH OLADÉLÉ SANUSI; Man. Dir RANSOME OLADÉLÉ ADEBOLU; 4 brs.

Continental Bank–Bénin: ave Jean-Paul II, carrefour des Trois Banques, 01 BP 2020, Cotonou 01; tel. 31-24-24; telex 5151; fax 31-51-77; f. 1995 to assume activities of Crédit Lyonnais Bénin; cap. 3,600m.; Pres. EMMANUEL KOUTON; Man. Dir MOUSSIBAOU ADJIBI.

Ecobank—Bénin SA: rue du Gouverneur Bayol, BP 1280, Cotonou; tel. 31-40-33; telex 5394; fax 31-33-85; f. 1989; 72% owned by Ecobank Transnational Inc (operating under the auspices of the Economic Community of West African States); cap. and res 2,441.8m. (Dec. 1995); Pres. ISSA DIOP; Man. Dir RIZWAN HAIDER; 1 br.

Financial Bank: Immeuble Adjibi, rue du Commandant Decoeur, 01 BP 2700 RP, Cotonou; tel. 31-31-00; telex 5280; fax 31-31-02; f. 1988; 93.7% owned by Financial BC (Switzerland); cap. 1,578m. (Dec. 1996); Pres. RÉMY BAYSSET; Man. Dir THOMAS WIELEZYNSKI; 8 brs.

Financial Institution

Caisse Autonome d'Amortissement du Bénin: BP 59, Cotonou; tel. 31-47-81; telex 5289; fax 31-53-56; manages state funds; Man. Dir IBRAHIM PEDRO BONI.

STOCK EXCHANGE

Côte d'Ivoire's Bourse des Valeurs d'Abidjan was scheduled to become a regional stock exchange, serving the member states of the UEMOA, in January 1998.

INSURANCE

Union Béninoise d'Assurance-Vie: Cotonou; f. 1994 as Benin's first private insurance co; cap. 400m.; 51% owned by Union Africaine Vie (Côte d'Ivoire).

Trade and Industry

GOVERNMENT AGENCIES AND UTILITIES

Office National du Bois (ONAB): BP 1238, Recette Principale, Cotonou; tel. 33-16-32; fax 33-19-56; f. 1983; forest development and management, manufacture and marketing of wood products; cap. 300m. francs CFA; transfer of industrial activities to private ownership pending; Man. Dir PASCAL PATINVOH.

Société Béninoise d'Electricité et d'Eau (SBEE): BP 123, Cotonou; tel. 31-21-45; fax 31-50-28; f. 1973; cap. 10,000m. francs CFA; state-owned; production and distribution of electricity and water; Man. Dir GODEFROY CHEKETE.

Société Nationale pour l'Industrie des Corps Gras (SONICOG): BP 312, Cotonou; tel. 33-07-01; telex 5205; fax 33-15-20; f. 1962; cap. 2,555m. francs CFA; state-owned; processes shea-nuts (karité nuts), palm kernels and cottonseed; Man. Dir JOSEPH GABIN DOSSOU.

Société Nationale pour la Promotion Agricole (SONAPRA): BP 933, Cotonou; tel. 33-08-20; telex 5248; fax 33-19-48; f. 1983; cap. 500m. francs CFA; state-owned; manages five cotton-ginning plants and one fertilizer plant; distributes fertilizers and markets agricultural products; Pres. IMOROU SALLEY; Man. Dir MICHEL DASSI.

DEVELOPMENT ORGANIZATIONS

Caisse Française de Développement (CFD): blvd Jean-Paul II, BP 38, Cotonou; tel. 31-35-80; telex 5082; fax 31-20-18; fmrly Caisse Centrale de Coopération Economique; Dir HENRI PHILIPPE DE CLERCQ.

Mission de Coopération et d'Action Culturelle (Mission Française d'Aide et de Coopération): BP 476, Cotonou; tel. 30-08-24; telex 5209; administers bilateral aid from France according to the co-operation agreement of 1975; Dir BERNARD HADJADJ.

CHAMBER OF COMMERCE

Chambre de Commerce, d'Agriculture et d'Industrie de la République du Bénin (CCIB): ave du Général de Gaulle, BP 31, Cotonou; tel. 31-32-99; Pres. WASSI MOUFTATOU; Sec.-Gen. N. A. VIADENOU.

EMPLOYERS' ORGANIZATIONS

Association des Syndicats du Bénin (ASYNBA): Cotonou; Pres. PIERRE FOURN.

Conseil Nationale des Chargeurs du Bénin (CNCB): carré no 114, Zone Industrielle d'Akpakpa PK3, 06 BP 2528, Cotonou; tel. 33-13-71; telex 5023; fax 33-18-49; Pres. FIDELIA AZODOGBEHOU.

Groupement Interprofessionnel des Entreprises du Bénin (GIBA): BP 6, Cotonou; Pres. A. JEUKENS.

Syndicat des Commerçants Importateurs et Exportateurs du Bénin: BP 6, Cotonou; Pres. M. BENCHIMOL.

Syndicat Interprofessionnel des Entreprises Industrielles du Bénin: Cotonou; Pres. M. DOUCET.

Syndicat National des Commerçants et Industriels Africains du Bénin (SYNACIB): BP 367, Cotonou; Pres. URBAIN DA SILVA.

Syndicat des Transporteurs Routiers du Bénin: Cotonou; Pres. PASCAL ZENON.

TRADE UNIONS

Confédération Générale du Travail (CGT): Leader: PASCAL TODJENOU.

Confédération des Syndicats Autonomes du Bénin (CSAB): Cotonou; First Sec. ALBERT GOUGAN.

Union Nationale des Syndicats de Travailleurs du Bénin (UNSTB): 1 blvd Saint-Michel, BP 69, Cotonou; tel. and fax 30-36-13; sole officially-recognized trade union 1974–90; Sec.-Gen. AMIDOU LAWANI.

Other autonomous labour organizations include the **Collectif des Syndicats Indépendants**, the **Confédération Générale des Travailleurs du Bénin** and the **Confédération des Syndicats des Travailleurs du Bénin**.

Transport

In October 1996 the World Bank approved a credit of US $40m., to be issued through the International Development Association, in support of a major programme of investment in Benin's transport network. The integrated programme aimed to enhance Benin's status as an entrepôt for regional trade, and also to boost domestic employment and, by improving the infrastructure and reducing transport costs, agricultural and manufacturing output.

RAILWAYS

In 1995 the network handled 388,000 metric tons of goods. Plans for a 650-km extension, linking Parakou to Niamey (Niger), via Gaya, were postponed in the late 1980s, owing to lack of finance.

Organisation Commune Bénin-Niger des Chemins de Fer et des Transports (OCBN): BP 16, Cotonou; tel. 31-33-80; telex 5210; fax 31-41-50; f. 1959; 50% owned by Govt of Benin, 50% by Govt of Niger; total of 579 track-km; main line runs for 438 km from Cotonou to Parakou in the interior; br. line runs westward via Ouidah to Segboroué (34 km); also line of 107 km from Cotonou via Porto-Novo to Pobé (near the Nigerian border); Man. Dir ISAAC ENIDÉ KILANYOSSI.

ROADS

In 1995 there were an estimated 8,460 km of roads, including 3,440 km of main roads and 2,640 km of secondary roads. About 2,700 km of the network were paved. Road construction or rehabilitation projects in progress at this time were intended primarily to enhance Benin's regional trading links.

Compagnie de Transit et de Consignation du Bénin (CTCB Express): route de l'Aéroport, BP 7079, Cotonou; f. 1986; Pres. SOULÉMAN KOURA ZOUMAROU.

SHIPPING

The main port is at Cotonou. In 1995 the port handled some 2,076,900 metric tons of goods, of which 210,100 tons were in transit. The rehabilitation and expansion of facilities at the port of Cotonou is in progress, with financial assistance from the Netherlands.

Port Autonome de Cotonou: BP 927, Cotonou; tel. 31-28-90; telex 5004; fax 31-28-91; f. 1965; state-owned port authority; Man. Dir ISSA BADAROU-SOULÉ.

Association pour la Défense des Intérêts du Port de Cotonou (AIPC) (Communauté Portuaire du Bénin): BP 927, Cotonou; tel. 31-17-26; telex 5004; fax 31-28-91; f. 1993; promotes, develops and co-ordinates of port activities at Cotonou; Pres. ISSA BADAROU-SOULÉ; Sec.-Gen. CAMILLE MÉDÉGAN.

Association des Professionnels Agréés en Douanes du Bénin (APRAD): BP 2141, Cotonou; tel. 31-55-05; telex 5355; Chair. GATIEN HOUNGBÉDJI.

Cie Béninoise de Navigation Maritime (COBENAM): 01 BP 2032, Recette Principale, Cotonou; tel. 31-32-87; telex 5225; fax 31-09-78; f. 1974; 51% state-owned, 49% by Govt of Algeria; Pres. ABDEL KADER ALLAL; Man. Dir COCOU THÉOPHILE HOUNKPONOU.

SDV Bénin: route du Collège de l'Union, BP 433, Cotonou; tel. 33-11-78; fax 33-06-11; f. 1986; fmrly Delmas–Bénin; Pres. J. F. MIGNONNEAU; Dir F. LEBRAT.

Société Béninoise des Manutentions Portuaires (SOBEMAP): place des Martyrs, BP 35, Cotonou; tel. 31-39-83; telex 5135; state-owned; Pres. GEORGES SEKLOKA; Man. Dir THÉODORE AHOUMÉNOU AHOUASSOU.

CIVIL AVIATION

The international airport at Cotonou (Cotonou-Cadjehoun) has a 2.4-km runway, and there are secondary airports at Parakou, Natitingou, Kandi and Abomey.

Air Afrique: ave du Gouverneur Ballot, BP 200, Cotonou; tel. 31-21-07; fax 31-53-41; see under Côte d'Ivoire; Dir in Benin JOSEPH KANZA.

Bénin Inter-Régional: Cotonou; f. 1991 as a jt venture by private Beninois interests and Aeroflot (then the state airline of the USSR); operates domestic and regional flights.

Tourism

Benin's national parks and game reserves are its principal tourist attractions. About 142,000 tourists visited Benin in 1994, when receipts from tourism were estimated at US $55m.

Conseil National du Tourisme: Cotonou; f. 1993.

BHUTAN

Introductory Survey

Location, Climate, Language, Religion, Flag, Capital

The Kingdom of Bhutan lies in the Himalaya range of mountains, with Tibet (the Xizang Autonomous Region), in China, to the north and India to the south. Average monthly temperature ranges from 4.4°C (40°F) in January to 17°C (62°F) in July. Rainfall is heavy, ranging from 150 cm (60 ins) to 300 cm (120 ins) per year. The official language is Dzongkha, spoken mainly in western Bhutan. Written Dzongkha is based on the Tibetan script. The state religion is Mahayana Buddhism, mainly the Drukpa school of the Kagyupa sect, although Nepali settlers, who comprise about one-quarter of the country's total population, practise Hinduism. The Nepali-speaking Hindus dominate southern Bhutan and are referred to as southern Bhutanese. The national flag (proportions 3 by 2) is divided diagonally from the lower hoist to the upper fly, so forming two triangles, one orange and the other maroon, with a white dragon superimposed in the centre. The capital is Thimphu.

Recent History

The first hereditary King of Bhutan was installed on 17 December 1907. An Anglo-Bhutanese Treaty, signed in 1910, placed Bhutan's foreign relations under the supervision of the Government of British India. After India became independent, that treaty was replaced in August 1949 by the Indo-Bhutan Treaty of Friendship, whereby Bhutan agrees to seek the advice of the Government of India with regard to its foreign relations, but remains free to decide whether or not to accept such advice. King Jigme Dorji Wangchuck, installed in 1952, established the National Assembly (Tshogdu) in 1953 and a Royal Advisory Council in 1965. He formed the country's first Council of Ministers in May 1968. He died in July 1972 and was succeeded by the Western-educated 16-year-old Crown Prince, Jigme Singye Wangchuck. The new King stated his wish to maintain the Indo-Bhutan Treaty and further to strengthen friendship with India. In 1979, however, during the Non-Aligned Conference and later at the UN General Assembly, Bhutan voted in opposition to India, in favour of Chinese policy. In December 1983 India and Bhutan signed a new trade agreement concerning overland trade with Bangladesh and Nepal. India raised no objection to Bhutan's decision to negotiate directly with the People's Republic of China over the Bhutan-China border, and discussions were begun in April 1984 (see below).

When Chinese authority was established in Tibet (Xizang) in 1959, Bhutan granted asylum to more than 6,000 Tibetan refugees. As a result of the discovery that many refugees were engaged in spying and subversive activities, the Bhutan Government decided in 1976 to disperse them in small groups, introducing a number of Bhutanese families into each settlement. In June 1979 the National Assembly approved a directive establishing the end of the year as a time-limit for the refugees to decide whether to acquire Bhutanese citizenship or accept repatriation to Tibet. By September 1985 most of the Tibetans had chosen Bhutanese citizenship, and the remainder were to be accepted by India. A revised Citizenship Act, adopted by the National Assembly in 1985, confirmed residence in Bhutan in 1958 as a fundamental basis for automatic citizenship (as provided for by the 1958 Nationality Act), but this was to be flexibly interpreted. Provision was also made for citizenship by registration for Nepalese immigrants who had resided in the country for at least 20 years (15 years if employed by the Government) and who could meet linguistic and other tests of commitment to the Bhutanese community.

The violent ethnic Nepalese agitation in India for a 'Gurkha homeland' in the Darjeeling-Kalimpong region during the late 1980s and the populist movement in Nepal in 1988–90 (see chapters on India and Nepal respectively) spread into Bhutan in 1990. Ethnic unrest became apparent in that year when a campaign of intimidation and violence, directed by militant Nepalese against the authority of the Government in Thimphu, was initiated. In September thousands of southern Bhutanese villagers, and Nepalese who entered Bhutan from across the Indian border, organized demonstrations in at least nine border towns in southern Bhutan to protest against domination by the indigenous Buddhist Drukpa. The 'anti-nationals', as they are called by the Bhutanese authorities, demand a greater role in the country's political and economic life and are bitterly opposed to official attempts to strengthen the Bhutanese sense of national identity through an increased emphasis on Tibetan-derived, rather than Nepalese, culture and religion (including a formal dress code, Dzongkha as the sole official language, etc.). Bhutanese officials, on the other hand, view the southerners as recent arrivals who abuse the hospitality of their hosts through acts of violence and the destruction of development infrastructure.

Most southern villagers are relatively recent arrivals from Nepal and many of them have made substantial contributions to the development of the southern hills. The provision of free education and health care by the Bhutan Government acted for many years as a magnet for Nepalese who were struggling to survive in their own country and who came to settle illegally in Bhutan. This population movement was largely ignored by local administrative officials, many of whom accepted incentives to disregard the illegal nature of the influx. The Government's policy of encouraging a sense of national identity, together with rigorous new procedures (introduced in February–March 1988) to check citizenship registration, revealed thousands of illegal residents in southern Bhutan, many of whom had lived there for a decade or more, married local people and raised families. During the ethnic unrest in September 1990, the majority of southern villagers were coerced into participating in the demonstrations by groups of armed and uniformed young men (including many of Nepalese origin who were born in Bhutan). Many of these dissidents, including a large number of secondary school students and former members of the Royal Bhutan Army and of the police force, had fled Bhutan in 1989 and early 1990. In 1988–90 a large number of the dissidents resided in the tea gardens and villages adjoining southern Bhutan. Following the demonstrations that took place in Bhutan in September–October 1990, other ethnic Nepalese left Bhutan. In January 1991 some 234 persons, who claimed to be Bhutanese refugees, reportedly arrived in Maidhar and Tinmai in the Jhapa district of eastern Nepal. In September, at the request of the Nepalese Government, the United Nations High Commissioner for Refugees (UNHCR) inaugurated a relief programme providing food and shelter for more than 300 people in the *ad hoc* camps. By December the number of people staying in the camps had risen to about 6,000. The sizes of these camps have been substantially augmented by landless and unemployed Nepalese, who have been expelled from Assam and other eastern states of India. The small and faction-ridden ethnic Nepalese Bhutan People's Party (BPP), which was founded in Kathmandu in 1990 (as a successor to the People's Forum on Democratic Rights, an organization established in 1989), purports to lead the agitation for 'democracy', but has, as yet, presented no clear or convincing set of objectives and has attracted no significant support from within Bhutan itself. Schools and bridges became principal targets for arson and looting during 1990–92, and families known to be loyal to the Bhutan Government were robbed of their valuables. Most of the schools in southern Bhutan were closed indefinitely from the end of September 1990, in response to threats to the lives of teachers and students' families, but the majority of pupils affected by these closures were provided with temporary places in schools in northern Bhutan. By mid-1995, despite the continuing security problems, some 74 schools and 89 health facilities had been reopened in the five southern districts.

Since 1988 King Jigme, as head of government, has personally authorized the release of 1,685 militants captured by the authorities. He has stated that, while he has an open mind regarding the question of the pace and extent of political reform (including a willingness to hold discussions with any minority group that has grievances), his Government cannot tolerate pressures for change that are based on intimidation and violence. Although several important leaders of the dissident movement remain in custody, the King has said that they will be released when conditions of law and order return to normal. Some leaders of the BPP have stated that they have no quarrel with the King, but with 'corrupt officials'; on the other hand, certain militants strongly condemn the King as their 'main enemy'. A number of southern Bhutanese officials (including the Director-General of Power, Bhim Subba, and the Managing Director of the State Trading Corporation, R. B. Basnet) absconded in June 1991 (on the eve of the publication of departmental audits) and went directly to Nepal, where they reportedly sought political asylum on the grounds of repression and atrocities against southern Bhutanese. These accusations were refuted in detail by the Government in Thimphu. The former Secretary-General of the BPP, D. K. Rai, was tried by the High Court in Thimphu in May 1992 and was sentenced to life imprisonment for terrorist acts; a further 35 defendants received lesser sentences. The alleged master-mind behind the ethnic unrest, Teknath Rizal, came to trial, and was sentenced to life imprisonment in November 1993 after having been found guilty on four of nine charges of offences against the Tsawa Sum ('the country, the King, and the people). King Jigme subsequently decreed that Rizal would be released from prison 'once the Governments of Bhutan and Nepal resolve the problems of the people living in the refugee camps in eastern Nepal'. About 130 detainees, who were accused of criminal and terrorist acts, were tried during 1995.

Violence continued in the disturbed areas of Samtse, Chhukha, Tsirang, Sarpang and Gelephu throughout 1991–97, and companies of trained militia volunteers were posted to these areas to relieve the forces of the regular army. The state government of West Bengal in India, whose territory abuts much of southern Bhutan, reaffirmed in 1991 and 1992 that its land would not be used as a base for any agitation against Bhutan.

In late 1991 and throughout 1992 several thousand legally-settled villagers left southern Bhutan for the newly-established refugee camps in eastern Nepal. The Bhutan Government alleged that the villagers were being enticed or threatened to leave their homes by militants based outside Bhutan, in order to augment the population of the camps and gain international attention; the dissidents, on the other hand, claimed that the Bhutan Government was forcing the villagers to leave. The formation of the Bhutan National Democratic Party (BNDP), including members drawn from supporters of the BPP and with the leading dissident R. B. Basnet as its President, was announced in Kathmandu in February 1992. Incidents of ethnic violence, almost all of which involved infiltration from across the border by ethnic Nepalese who had been trained and dispatched from the camps in Nepal, reportedly diminished substantially in the first half of 1993 as talks continued between Bhutanese and Nepalese government officials regarding proposals to resolve the issues at stake. The Nepalese Government steadfastly refused to consider any solution that did not include the resettlement in Bhutan of all ethnic Nepalese 'refugees' living in the camps (by November 1993 the number of alleged ethnic Nepalese refugees from Bhutan totalled about 85,000). This proposal was rejected by the Bhutan Government, which maintained that the majority of the camp population merely claimed to be from Bhutan, had absconded from Bhutan (and thus forfeited their citizenship, according to Bhutan's citizenship laws), or had voluntarily departed after selling their properties and surrendering their citizenship papers and rights. The apparent deadlock was broken, however, when a joint statement was signed by the Ministers of Home Affairs of Bhutan and Nepal in July, which committed each side to establishing a 'high-level committee' to work towards a settlement and, in particular, to fulfilling the following mandate prior to undertaking any other related activity: to determine the different categories of people claiming to have come from Bhutan in the refugee camps in eastern Nepal (which now numbered eight); and to specify the positions of the two Governments on each of these categories, which would provide the basis for the resolution of the problem. The two countries held their first ministerial-level meeting regarding the issue in Kathmandu in October, at which it was agreed that four categories would be established among the people in the refugee camps — '(i) bona fide Bhutanese who have been evicted forcefully; (ii) Bhutanese who emigrated; (iii) non-Bhutanese; and (iv) Bhutanese who have committed criminal acts.' Further meetings were held in February, April and June 1994. The joint press communiqué from the June meeting recorded that there had been 'an extensive exchange of views in a warm and cordial atmosphere'. Following the election of a new Government in Nepal in November, however, little progress was made at joint ministerial meetings held in the first half of 1995. Nepal's communist Government demanded that all persons in the camps be accepted by Bhutan; the Bhutanese authorities, on the other hand, were prepared to accept only the unconditional return of any bona fide Bhutanese citizens who had left the country involuntarily. The Nepalese Government seemed reluctant to inquire too closely into the national status of the ethnic Nepalis in the camps. Nevertheless, diplomatic exchanges continued in the latter half of the year, despite serious political instability in Nepal.

In January 1996 the new Napalese Prime Minister, Sher Bahadur Deuba, proposed a resumption of intergovernmental talks, this time at foreign minister level. King Jigme welcomed the proposal, but the seventh round of talks, which was held in early April, resulted in demands by Nepal that went beyond the mandate drawn up by the joint ministerial committee in mid-1993. It was widely understood that the Nepalese Government had again reverted to a requisition that all persons in the camps be accepted by Bhutan, regardless of status. This demand remained unacceptable to Bhutanese Government, which stated that the problem of the people in the camps would not have arisen in the first place, if conditions (such as prospects of free food, shelter, health and education, and 'moral support' by the Nepalese authorities for all persons claiming to be Bhutanese refugees) had not been created when there were only 234 persons in Jhapa making such claims. In addition, the Bhutanese Government stated that even with such conditions attracting people to the refugee camps, a well-organized screening process would have prevented the sheer scale of ethnic Nepalese claiming to be Bhutanese refugees. (Until June 1993 no screening of claimants to refugees status had been enforced on the Indo-Nepalese border). In August 1996 a UNHCR delegation visited Bhutan at the invitation of the authorities and received detailed information from the Bhutan Government regarding the issue of the camps. Talks at ministerial level were held in March and July 1997, without any public communiqué.

From December 1995 terrorist incidents in Bhutan were fewer, coinciding with the adoption of the 'peace march' tactic by persons claiming to be Bhutanese and seeking to travel from Nepal into Bhutan. These marches contined throughout 1996; a small group of marchers actually reached Phuentsholing in mid-August and again in December before being forced to return to India. The Bhutanese Minister of Home Affairs asserted that those participating in the marches were not Bhutanese, but were non-nationals and emigrants who were attempting to enter the country illegally.

In 1991 'Rongthong' Kinley Dorji, a former Bhutanese businessman accused of unpaid loans and of acts against the State, had absconded to Nepal and joined the anti-Government movement. In 1992 he established and became President of a 'Druk National Congress' claiming human-rights violations in Bhutan. The Bhutan Goverment's 74th Assembly held in July 1996 discussed Kinley Dorji's case at length, and unanimously demanded his extradition from Nepal in conjunction with the Bhutan-Nepal talks. Following the signing of an extradition treaty between India and Bhutan in December, Kinley was arrested by the Indian authorities during a visit to Delhi in April 1997, and remained in detention while his case was being examined by the Indian courts. The extradition treaty was read to the 75th Assembly in July, when Kinley Dorji's case was again discussed at length and demands for his return to Bhutan for trial were unanimously supported. At the same time the Assembly resolved that all relatives of 'ngolops' (anti-national militants) in government service should be 'compulsorily retired with post-service benefits', and that the Royal Civil Service Commission should implement this decision 'without undue delay'. The 75th Assembly also discussed the intrusions into Bhutan's south-eastern border forests by Bodo and Maoist extremists from the neighbouring Indian state of Assam. In September a group of Bodo militants attacked a Bhutanese police station in the south-eastern district of Samdrup Jongkhar, killing four policemen and looting large quantities of arms and ammunition.

Following the relaxation of many policies in the People's Republic of China since 1978, and looking forward to improved relations between India and China, Bhutan has moved cautiously to assert positions on regional and world affairs that take account of those of India but are not necessarily identical to them. Discussions with China for the formal delineation and demarcation of the northern border were begun in April 1984, and substantive negotiations began in April 1986. The 10th round of talks, held in Beijing in May 1995, were described as 'useful and constructive'. Demarcation of the southern border has been agreed with India, except for small sectors in the middle zone (between Sarpang and Gelephu) and in the eastern zone of Arunachal Pradesh and the *de facto* Sino-Indian border.

Bhutan has asserted itself as a fully sovereign, independent state, becoming a member of the UN in 1971 and of the Non-aligned Movement in 1973. By 1993 Bhutan had established diplomatic relations with 17 countries and with the EU, and maintained diplomatic missions at the UN in New York and Geneva, in New Delhi, Dhaka and Kuwait; it is also represented by several honorary consulates.

In 1983 Bhutan was an enthusiastic founder-member of the South Asian Regional Co-operation (SARC) organization, with Bangladesh, India, Maldives, Nepal, Pakistan and Sri Lanka. In May 1985 Bhutan was host to the first meeting of ministers of foreign affairs from SARC member countries, which agreed to give their grouping the formal title of South Asian Association for Regional Co-operation (SAARC, see p. 263).

Government

Bhutan is an absolute monarchy, without a written constitution. The system of government is unusual in that power is shared by the monarchy (assisted by the Royal Advisory Council), the Council of Ministers, the National Assembly (Tshogdu) and the Head Abbot (Je Khempo) of Bhutan's 3,000–4,000 Buddhist monks. The National Assembly, which serves a three-year term, has 151 members, including 106 directly elected by adult suffrage. Ten seats in the Assembly are reserved for religious bodies, while the remainder are occupied by officials, ministers and members of the Royal Advisory Council.

Defence

The strength of the Royal Bhutanese Army, which is under the direct command of the King, is just over 5,000. Army training facilities are provided by an Indian military training team. Although India is not directly responsible for the country's defence, the Indian Government has indicated that any act of aggression against Bhutan would be regarded as an act of aggression against India. Part-time militia training for senior school pupils and government officials was instituted in 1989.

Economic Affairs

In 1995, according to estimates by the World Bank, the kingdom's gross national product (GNP), measured at average 1993–95 prices, was US $295m., equivalent to $420 per head. In 1985–95 GNP per head increased, in real terms, at an average annual rate of 4.0%. During 1985–95 the population increased by an annual average of 2.6%. Bhutan's gross domestic product (GDP) increased, in real terms by an annual average of 7.5% in 1980–90. GDP grew by 7.5% in 1995 and by an estimated 6.4% in 1996.

Agriculture (including livestock and forestry) contributed an estimated 38.2% of GDP in 1996. About 94% of the economically active population were employed in agriculture in that year. The principal sources of revenue in the agricultural sector in 1994 were apples, oranges and cardamom. Timber production is also important; about 60% of the total land area is covered by forest.

Industry (including mining, manufacturing, electricity and construction) employed only about 1% of the labour force in 1981/82, but contributed an estimated 34.0% of GDP in 1996. The production of low-cost electricity by the Chhukha hydroelectric project (see below) helped to stimulate growth in the industrial sector in the 1990s.

Mining and quarrying contributed an estimated 2.2% of GDP in 1996. Calcium carbide was the major mineral export in 1995. Gypsum, coal, limestone, slate and dolomite are also mined.

Manufacturing contributed an estimated 11.6% of GDP in 1996. The most important sector is cement production. Commercial production began at a calcium carbide plant and a ferro-alloy plant at Pasakha, near Phuentsholing, in 1988 and 1995, respectively. Bhutan also has some small-scale manufacturers, producing, for example, textiles, soap, matches, candles and carpets.

Energy is derived principally from hydroelectric power. The Chhukha hydroelectric project, with a generating capacity of about 338 MW, began production in 1986 and was formally inaugurated in 1988. The project provides about 40% of Bhutan's national revenue. In 1994 the cost of imports of diesel oil and petroleum increased by 31.6%, compared with the previous year, to reach Nu 200m.

In the financial year ending 30 June 1996 Bhutan recorded a visible trade deficit of an estimated Nu 453.2m., and there was a deficit of an estimated Nu 1,272.5m. on the current account of the balance of payments. In 1995/96 the principal source of imports (73.4%) was India, which was also the principal market for exports (91.9%). The principal exports in 1995 were electricity, calcium carbide and particle board. Exports of electric energy to India commenced in 1988, with the inauguration of the Chhukha hydroelectric project. The principal imports in 1995 were rice, industrial machinery and diesel oil.

The 1996/97 budget envisaged a deficit of Nu 556m. Bhutan's total external debt amounted to US $87.2m. at the end of 1995, of which $86.6m. was long-term public debt. For 1997/98, grants from the Government of India provided an estimated 28.9% of total budgetary revenue, and grants from the UN and other international agencies amounted to 21.9%. The average annual rate of inflation was 11.6% in 1990–94; consumer prices rose by 10.7% in 1995 and by 8.3% in 1996.

Bhutan is a member of the South Asian Association for Regional Co-operation (SAARC, see p. 263), which seeks to improve regional co-operation, particularly in economic development.

The Seventh Plan (1992–97) asserted seven main objectives: self-reliance, with emphasis on internal resource mobilization; sustainability, with emphasis on environmental protection; private-sector development; decentralization and popular participation; human resources' development; balanced development in all districts; and national security. In September 1996 King Jigme announced a number of new measures aimed at stimulating the economy through further liberalization, including a reduction in interest rates, the simplification of the loans system and a comprehensive new customs tariff structure for third-country imports. The Eighth Plan (1997–2002) further refined the seven objectives of the Seventh Plan and explicitly added another: 'the preservation and promotion of cultural and traditional values'. During these five years, GDP was expected to grow at an average annual rate of 6.7%, while the population growth rate was projected to decline to 2.56%. Revenue, which was forecast to reach Nu 15,912m. during the plan, was to cover 53% of the total plan outlay of Nu 30,000m. The agriculture sector was projected to grow by 2.5% per year over the Plan period through productivity gains and horticultural development. Exports to India and third countries were expected to increase by 15% and 10%, respectively, by 2002. The guiding goal was declared as the establishment of sustainability in development, while balancing achievements with the popular sense of contentment. Core areas were to be the further development of hydro-power (long-term potential was assessed at 20,000 MW) and further industrialization. The Plan also provided for further development of the infrastructure (18.6% of outlay) and social services (22%), human resource development (10.7%), and renewable natural resources. Development partners meeting in Geneva in January 1997 pledged US $450m. (about 50% of the projected Plan outlay).

Social Welfare

In December 1996 there were 27 hospitals (including five leprosy hospitals, providing general health services also), with a total of 970 beds (one for every 688 inhabitants, on the basis of the 1990 official population figure), and there were 100 doctors (one for every 6,000 inhabitants) and 1,058 village health workers in the country. Because of a shortage of medical personnel and a lack of funds, local dispensaries are being converted into basic health units (of which there were 97 by the end of 1996), providing basic medical services. In 1990 the World Health Organization declared that universal child immunization had been achieved in Bhutan. Malaria and tuberculosis are, however, still widespread. The budget for the financial year 1996/97 allocated an estimated Nu 626m. (11.1% of total projected expenditure) to health.

Education

Education is not compulsory. Pre-primary education usually lasts for one year. Primary education begins at six years of age and lasts for seven years. Secondary education, beginning at the age of 13, lasts for a further four years, comprising two cycles of two years each. Virtually free education is available (nominal fees are demanded), but there are insufficient facilities to accommodate all school-age children. In order to accommodate additional children, community schools (established in 1989 as 'extended classrooms'—ECRs, but renamed, as above, in 1991) were set up as essentially one-teacher schools for basic primary classes, whence children were to be 'streamed' to other schools. In 1988 the total enrolment at primary schools was equivalent to an estimated 26% of children in the relevant age-group (31% of boys; 20% of girls), while the comparable ratio for secondary schools was only 5% (boys 7%; girls 2%). All schools are co-educational. English is the language of instruction and Dzongkha is a compulsory subject. Bhutan has no mission schools. Since 1988 seven privately-operated schools have been established (the majority in Thimphu); these schools are under the supervision of the Department of Education. Owing to a shortage of qualified staff, many Indian teachers are employed. In April 1997 the total number of enrolled pupils was 92,267, and the total number of teachers was 2,715. In 1996 there were about 300 educational institutions under the supervision of the Department of Education, including 150 primary schools, 107 community schools, 25 junior high schools, 13 high schools, two teacher-training institutes (TTIs), two Sanskrit Pathsalas, and five post-secondary institutions (excluding TTIs). Some Bhutanese students were receiving higher education abroad. The 1996/97 budget allocated an estimated Nu 482m. (8.5% of total projected expenditure) to education. In 1995, according to UNESCO estimates, the rate of adult illiteracy in Bhutan averaged 57.8% (males 43.8%; females 71.9%).

Public Holidays

1998 and 1999: The usual Buddhist holidays are observed, as well as the Birthday of HM Jigme Singye Wangchuck (11 November), the movable Hindu feast of Dussehra and the National Day of Bhutan (17 December).

Weights and Measures

The metric system is in operation.

Statistical Survey

Source (unless otherwise stated): Royal Government of Bhutan, Thimphu.

Area and Population

AREA, POPULATION AND DENSITY

Area (sq km)	46,500*
Population (official estimates)†	
1995	582,000
1996	600,042
1997	618,643
Density (per sq km) in 1997	13.3

* 17,954 sq miles.

† These figures are much lower than former estimates. It was previously reported that a census in 1969 enumerated a population of 931,514, and a 1980 census recorded a total of 1,165,000. On the basis of the latter figure, a mid-1988 population of 1,375,400 was projected. Other figures in this Survey are derived from the earlier, higher estimates of Bhutan's population.

Capital: Thimphu (estimated population 27,000 at 1 July 1990).

POPULATION OF DISTRICTS* (mid-1985 estimates, based on 1980 census)

Bumthang	23,842
Dagana	28,352
Gasa†	16,907
Gelephu	111,283
Ha	16,715
Lhuentse	39,635
Mongar	73,239
Paro	46,615
Pemagatshel	37,141
Punakha†	16,700
Samdrup Jongkhar	73,044
Samtse	172,109
Zhemgang	44,516
Thimphu	58,660
Trashigang	177,718
Trongsa	26,017
Tsirang	108,807
Wangdue Phodrang	47,152
Total rural population	1,119,452
Total urban population	167,823
Total	1,286,275

* The above figures are approximate, and predate the creation of a new district, Chhukha, in 1987. Chhukha has an estimated total population of about 13,372 (based on the figure of 3,343 households, with an estimated average of four persons per household), who were formerly included in Samtse, Paro or Thimphu districts. The above figures also predate the creation of a further two new districts, Laya (previously within Punakha) and Trashi Yangtse (previously within Trashigang), in 1992.

† Gasa and Punakha were merged into a single district, which was to be known as Punakha, in 1987.

BIRTHS AND DEATHS (UN estimates, annual averages)

	1980–85	1985–90	1990–95
Birth rate (per 1,000)	40.3	39.9	39.6
Death rate (per 1,000)	19.1	16.9	15.3

Source: UN, *World Population Prospects: The 1994 Revision*.

Infant mortality rate (1994): 70.7 per 1,000 live births.

LIFE EXPECTANCY (UN estimates, years at birth)

50.7 (males 49.1; females 52.4) in 1990–95. Source: UN, *World Population Prospects: The 1994 Revision*.

ECONOMICALLY ACTIVE POPULATION (estimates, '000 persons, 1981/82)

Agriculture, etc.	613
Industry	6
Trade	9
Public services	22
Total	650

1984 (estimates, '000 persons): Agriculture, hunting, forestry and fishing 629; Total 721 (Source: UN, *Statistical Yearbook for Asia and the Pacific*).

Agriculture

PRINCIPAL CROPS (FAO estimates, '000 metric tons)

	1994	1995	1996
Rice (paddy)	45	50	50
Wheat	5	5	5
Barley	4	4	4
Maize	39	39	39
Millet	7	7	7
Other cereals	7	7	7
Potatoes	34	34	34
Other roots and tubers	22	22	22
Pulses	2	2	2
Vegetables and melons	10	10	10
Oranges	58	58	58
Other fruits (excl. melons)	6	6	6

Source: FAO, *Production Yearbook*.

LIVESTOCK (FAO estimates, '000 head, year ending September)

	1994	1995	1996
Horses	30	30	30
Mules	10	10	10
Asses	18	18	18
Cattle	435	435	435
Buffaloes	4	4	4
Pigs	75	75	75
Sheep	59	59	59
Goats	42	42	42

Source: FAO, *Production Yearbook*.

Yaks ('000 head): 35 in 1993; 39* in 1994; 40† in 1995.
Poultry ('000 head): 170 in 1993; 166* in 1994; 171† in 1995.

* Provisional. † Estimate.
Source: IMF, *Bhutan—Selected Issues* (February 1997).

LIVESTOCK PRODUCTS (FAO estimates, '000 metric tons)

	1994	1995	1996
Beef and veal	6	6	6
Pigmeat	1	1	1
Other meat	1	1	1
Cows' milk	29	29	29
Buffaloes' milk	3	3	3
Cheese	2	2	2
Butter and ghee	0.5	0.5	n.a.
Hen eggs	0.4	0.4	n.a.
Cattle and buffalo hides	1.2	1.2	1.0

Source: FAO, *Production Yearbook*.

Forestry

ROUNDWOOD REMOVALS
('000 cubic metres, excl. bark)

	1992	1993	1994
Sawlogs, veneer logs and logs for sleepers*	41	26	26*
Other industrial wood*	38	38	38
Fuel wood*	1,308	1,320	1,334
Total	1,387	1,384	1,398

Sawnwood production ('000 cubic metres, incl. railway sleepers): 21 in 1992; 18 in 1993; 18* in 1994.

* FAO estimate(s).

Source: FAO, *Yearbook of Forest Products*.

Fishing

Total estimated catch 340 metric tons of freshwater fishes per year in 1994–95. Source: FAO, *Yearbook of Fishery Statistics*.

Mining

(metric tons, unless otherwise indicated, year ending 30 June)

	1994/95	1995/96
Dolomite	211,716	258,597
Limestone	231,598	304,770
Gypsum	43,002	67,450
Coal	75,852	61,970
Marble (sq ft)	26,173	47,405
Slate (sq ft)	11,089	92,857
Quartzite	29,205	87,973
Talc	1,574	9,158
Iron ore	546	5,516
Pink shale/quartzite	103	5,112

Source: Geology and Mines Division, Ministry of Trade and Industry.

Industry

SELECTED PRODUCTS (year ending 31 March)

	1981/82	1982/83	1983/84
Minerals (metric tons)	136,010	33,188	37,988
Cement (metric tons)	99,008	88,688	169,624
Electric energy (million kWh)	22	24	26

Source: Department of Industries and Mines, Royal Government of Bhutan.

Revenue from the Chhukha Hydroelectric Project (million ngultrum): 567.8 (Internal consumption 48.8, Exports 519.0) in 1994; 826.7 (Internal consumption 105.6, Exports 721.1) in 1995; 857.6 (Internal consumption 110.0, Exports 747.6) in 1996.

Source: Department of Power, Royal Government of Bhutan.

Finance

CURRENCY AND EXCHANGE RATES

Monetary Units
100 chetrum (Ch) = 1 ngultrum (Nu).

Sterling and Dollar Equivalents (30 September 1997)
£1 sterling = 58.43 ngultrum;
US $1 = 36.17 ngultrum;
1,000 ngultrum = £17.11 = $27.65.

Average Exchange Rate (ngultrum per US $)
1994 31.374
1995 32.427
1996 35.433

Note: The ngultrum is at par with the Indian rupee, which also circulates freely within Bhutan. The foregoing figures relate to the official rate of exchange, which is applicable to government-related transactions alone. Since April 1992 there has also been a market rate of exchange, which values foreign currencies approximately 20% higher than the official rate of exchange.

BUDGET (estimates, million ngultrum, year ending 30 June)

Revenue	1994/95	1995/96*	1996/97
Domestic revenue	1,860	2,159	1,980
Tax	650	847	833
Non-tax	1,210	1,312	1,148
Grants from Government of India	453	1,958	1,413
Grants from UN and other international agencies	806		1,713
Total	3,118	4,117	5,107

* Revised estimates.

Expenditure	1994/95	1995/96*	1996/97
General public services	997	1,521	2,138
Economic services	1,510	1,810	2,388
Agriculture and irrigation	413	344	278
Animal husbandry	178	127	132
Forestry	125	97	122
Industries, mining, trade and commerce	23	73	95
Public works, roads and housing	473	373	723
Transport and communication	116	120	432
Power	188	677	607
Social services	602	719	1,120
Education	378	381	482
Health	211	329	626
Urban development and municipal corporations	13	9	12
Net lending	38	7	17
Total expenditure and net lending	3,148	4,058	5,663

* Revised estimates.

Source: IMF, *Bhutan—Selected Issues* (February 1997).

1997/98 (estimates, million ngultrum): *Revenue:* Domestic receipts 2,931.5, Government of India programme grants 800.0, Government of India project grants 1,128.2, Grants from UN and other international agencies 1,460.8, Borrowings from other external sources 353.9; **Total revenue** 6,674.3. *Expenditure:* Current expenditure 2,562.7, Capital expenditure 3,662.1, Net lending 66.6, Repayments 382.9; **Total expenditure** 6,674.3 (Source: Ministry of Finance, Royal Government of Bhutan).

FOREIGN EXCHANGE RESERVES (year ending 30 June)

	1993/94	1994/95	1995/96
Indian rupee reserves (million Indian rupees).	125.3	71.0	150.4
Royal Monetary Authority	33.5	33.4	34.0
Bank of Bhutan	91.8	37.6	116.6
Convertible currency reserves (US $ million)	102.9	118.7	140.8
Royal Monetary Authority*	98.7	114.4	135.5
Bank of Bhutan	4.2	4.3	5.3

* Includes tranche position in the International Monetary Fund.

Source: Royal Monetary Authority of Bhutan.

MONEY SUPPLY (million ngultrum at 31 December)

	1994	1995	1996
Currency outside banks*	347.5	432.4	422.5
Demand deposits at the Bank of Bhutan	696.5	889.9	1,651.6
Total money	1,044.0	1,322.3	2,074.1

* Including an estimate for Indian rupees.

Source: Royal Monetary Authority of Bhutan.

COST OF LIVING
(Consumer Price Index at 31 December; base: 1979 = 100)

	1994	1995	1996
All items (excl. rent)	395.3	437.7	474.1

Source: Central Statistical Office of the Planning Commission.

NATIONAL ACCOUNTS (million ngultrum at current prices)

Expenditure on the Gross Domestic Product

	1993	1994	1995
Government final consumption expenditure	1,901.2	2,065.1	2,116.5
Private final consumption expenditure	3,044.3	3,201.0	3,904.7
Increase in stocks	−93.7	—	5,131.7
Gross fixed capital formation	3,245.4	4,312.3	
Total domestic expenditure	8,097.2	9,578.4	11,152.9
Exports of goods and services	2,367.0	2,522.0	2,685.9
Less Imports of goods and services	3,272.0	3,783.0	4,426.1
GDP in purchasers' values	7,192.2	8,317.4	9,412.7

Source: UN, *Statistical Yearbook for Asia and the Pacific*.

Gross Domestic Product by Economic Activity

	1994	1995	1996*
Agriculture, forestry and livestock	3,154.4	3,897.7	4,383.6
Mining and quarrying	118.7	193.1	249.1
Manufacturing	831.6	1,088.8	1,328.3
Electricity	553.5	1,058.7	1,238.7
Construction	989.0	930.7	1,088.9
Trade, restaurants and hotels	647.2	730.7	833.0
Transport, storage and communications	614.3	687.6	825.1
Finance, insurance and real estate	477.4	503.0	603.6
Community, social and personal services	715.3	751.4	939.3
Sub-total	8,101.5	9,841.7	11,489.6
Less Imputed bank service charges	89.0	231.0	268.0
GDP in purchasers' values	8,012.5	9,610.7	11,221.6
GDP at constant 1980 factor cost	2,716.1	2,920.1	3,105.6

* Projected figures.

Source: Royal Monetary Authority of Bhutan.

BALANCE OF PAYMENTS
(revised estimates, million ngultrum, year ending 30 June)

	1993/94	1994/95	1995/96
Merchandise exports f.o.b.	1,990.3	2,196.7	3,349.1
Merchandise imports c.i.f.	−2,914.2	−3,053.2	−3,802.3
Trade balance	−923.9	−856.5	−453.2
Services and transfers:			
Receipts	845.4	886.5	995.7
Payments	−1,177.1	−1,101.5	−1,814.9
Current balance	−1,253.6*	−1,071.5	−1,272.5
Foreign aid	1,780.6	1,692.7	2,396.5
Other loans	158.8	−71.0	−77.5
Net errors and omissions	−293.0	−109.3	−190.8
Total (net monetary movements)	392.7	440.9	855.9

* Including adjustment (2 million ngultrum).

Source: Royal Monetary Authority of Bhutan.

OFFICIAL DEVELOPMENT ASSISTANCE (US $ million)

	1992	1993	1994
Bilateral donors	32.6	43.5	57.3
Multilateral donors	23.6	22.3	19.2
Total	56.2	65.8	76.5
Grants	54.3	62.0	72.0
Loans	1.9	3.8	4.5
Per caput assistance (US $)	35.6	41.2	47.4

Source: UN, *Statistical Yearbook for Asia and the Pacific*.

SELECTED COMMODITIES (million ngultrum)

Imports c.i.f.	1994	1995
Diesel oil	101	136
Petroleum	51	64
Rice	192	217
Wheat	45.0	39.4
Vegetable oil	98.0	135.7
Cotton fabric	36	42
Industrial machinery	350	142
Tyres for buses and trucks	36.0	37.5
Steel	87	115
Galvanized iron	25.0	30.5
Total (incl. others)	2,900	3,600

Exports f.o.b.	1994	1995
Electricity	519	721
Calcium carbide	415	498
Cement	270.0	278.3
Particle board	81.0	330.4
Block board	19	19
Sawn logs (hard)	52.0	71.8
Sawn timber (soft)	10.0	60.7
Cardamom	68.0	73.7
Atta and maida	10.0	23.8
Mixed fruit/vegetable juice	74.0	119.5

PRINCIPAL TRADING PARTNERS
(estimates, US $ million, year ending 30 June)

Imports c.i.f.	1993/94	1994/95	1995/96
India	65.8	70.9	81.4
Other countries	27.0	26.3	29.5
Total	92.8	97.2	110.9

Exports f.o.b.	1993/94	1994/95	1995/96
India	56.9	65.6	89.8
Other countries	6.5	4.4	7.9
Total	63.4	70.0	97.7

Source: Royal Monetary Authority of Bhutan.

Transport

ROAD TRAFFIC

In 1995 there were 9,506 registered, roadworthy vehicles, including 3,316 light four-wheeled vehicles, 4,300 two-wheeled vehicles (motor cycles and scooters), 1,512 heavy vehicles (trucks, buses, bulldozers, etc.) and 340 taxis. Source: Central Statistical Office, Ministry of Planning.

CIVIL AVIATION (traffic, year ending 30 June)

	1985	1986	1987
Kilometres flown ('000)	152	201	n.a.
Passengers	5,928	7,776	8,700
Passenger-km ('000)	3,349	4,381	n.a.

Paying passengers: 19,608 in 1993, 21,115 in 1994, 22,286 in 1995.
Revenue (million ngultrum, year ending 30 June): 241.5 in 1992/93, 188.3 in 1993/94, 210.0 in 1994/95.

Source: Central Statistical Office, Ministry of Planning.

Tourism

FOREIGN VISITORS BY COUNTRY OF ORIGIN*

	1993	1994	1995†
Australia	63	—	142
France	129	219	338
Germany	368	566	500
Italy	127	202	202
Japan	645	1,029	1,192
USA	709	689	865
Total (incl. others)	2,997	3,968	4,795

Government hotel rooms: 414 in 1993; 414 in 1994; 510† in 1995.
* Figures relate to tourists paying in convertible currency.
† Provisional.

Source: IMF, *Bhutan—Selected Issues* (February 1997).

Receipts (US $ million): 3.00 in 1994; 5.83 in 1995; 6.45 in 1996.

Arrivals: 5,133 in 1996.

Source: Tourism Authority of Bhutan.

Communications Media

In 1985 there were 200 television receivers. In 1994 there were 9,126 telephones and 300 telefax stations in use. There were 27,000 radio receivers in 1993. There are no television transmission stations in Bhutan, but broadcasts from Bangladesh and India can be received in Phuentsholing.

Education

(at 30 April 1997)

Community schools	107
Primary schools	150
Junior high schools	25
High schools	13
Teacher-training institutes (TTIs)	2
Sanskrit Pathsalas	2
Private schools	7
Post-secondary institutions (excl. TTIs)	5
Total pupils	92,267
Total teachers	2,715

Source: Department of Education, Royal Government of Bhutan.

Directory

The Constitution

The Kingdom of Bhutan has no formal constitution. However, the state system is a modified form of constitutional monarchy. Written rules, which are changed periodically, govern procedures for the election of members of the Royal Advisory Council and the Legislature, and define the duties and powers of those bodies.

The Government

Head of State: HM Druk Gyalpo ('Dragon King') Jigme Singye Wangchuck (succeeded to the throne in July 1972).

LODOI TSOKDE
(Royal Advisory Council)
(February 1998)

The Royal Advisory Council (Lodoi Tsokde), established in 1965, comprises nine members: two monks representing the Central and District Monastic Bodies (Rabdeys), six people's representatives and a Chairman (Kalyon), nominated by the King. Each gewog (group of villages, known also as a block) within a dzongkhag (district) selects one representative, from whom the respective Dzongkhag Yargye Tshogchungs (DYTs—District Development Committees) each agree on one nomination to be forwarded to the Tshogdu (National Assembly). From these 20 nominees, the Tshogdu, in turn, elects six persons to serve on the Royal Advisory Council as people's representatives for the whole country. The Council's principal task is to advise the King, as head of government, and to supervise all aspects of administration. The Council is in permanent session, virtually as a government department, and acts, on a daily basis, as the *de facto* Standing Committee of the Tshogdu. Representatives of the monastic bodies serve for one year, representatives of the people for three years, and the duration of the Chairman's term of office is at the discretion of the King. Representatives may be re-elected, but not for consecutive terms; they are all full members of the Council of Ministers.

Chairman: Dasho Karma Letho.

Councillors: Tenzin, Lungten Tshering, Bap Yeshey Dorji, Gembo Dorji, Tikaram Giri, Yam Bahadur Gurung, Lopen Bokto, Lopen Kezang.

LHENGYE SHUNGTSOG
(Council of Ministers)
(February 1998)

Chairman: HM Druk Gyalpo JIGME SINGYE WANGCHUCK.

Minister of Finance: Lyonpo DORJI TSHERING.

Representative of His Majesty in the Ministry of Agriculture: HRH Ashi (Princess) SONAM CHHODEN WANGCHUCK.

Representative of His Majesty in the Ministry of Communications: HRH Ashi (Princess) DECHAN WANGMO WANGCHUCK DORJI.

Representative of His Majesty in the Ministry of Health and Education: HRH Prince NAMGYAL WANGCHUCK.

Minister of Trade and Industry: Lyonpo OM PRADHAN.

Minister of Home Affairs: Lyonpo DAGO TSHERING.

Minister of Planning: Lyonpo CHENKYAB DORJI.

Minister of Foreign Affairs and Secretary of the Council of Ministers: Lyonpo DAWA TSERING.

Minister of Health and Education: (vacant).

Minister of Communications: (vacant).

Chief of Operations of the Royal Bhutan Army and Deputy Minister of Defence: Lt-Gen. LAM DORJI.

The following are also members of the Council of Ministers: deputy ministers, all members of the Royal Advisory Council, the Speaker of the National Assembly and departmental secretaries.

MINISTRIES

All Ministries are in Thimphu.

Ministry of Agriculture: POB 252, Thimphu; tel. 22129; telex 890221; fax 23153.

Ministry of Communications: Tashichhodzong, POB 278, Thimphu; tel. 22567; telex 890233; fax 22184.

Ministry of Finance: Tashichhodzong, POB 117, Thimphu; tel. 22223; telex 890201; fax 23154.

Ministry of Foreign Affairs: Convention Centre, POB 103, Thimphu; tel. 24111; telex 890214; fax 23240.

Ministry of Health and Education: Tashichhodzong, POB 726, Thimphu; tel. 22912; telex 890203; fax 22719.

Ministry of Home Affairs: Tashichhodzong, POB 133, Thimphu; tel. 22301; fax 22214.

Ministry of Planning: POB 127, Thimphu; tel. 22304; fax 23069.

Ministry of Trade and Industry: Tashichhodzong, POB 141, Thimphu; tel. 22159; telex 890215; fax 223507.

Office of the Royal Advisory Council: POB 200, Tashichhodzong, Thimphu; tel. 22816.

Legislature

TSHOGDU

A National Assembly (Tshogdu) was established in 1953. The Assembly has a three-year term and meets at least once a year, in spring (May–June) and/or autumn (October–November), although in recent years the Assembly has met for a longer session once a year only. The size of the membership is based, in part, on the population of the districts; although the size is, in principle, subject to periodic revision, in practice the popular representation has remained unchanged since 1953. In 1997 the Assembly had 150 members, of whom 105 were elected by direct popular consensus (formal voting is used, however, in the event of a deadlock). Ten seats were reserved for religious bodies, one was reserved for a representative of industry (elected by the Bhutan Chamber of Commerce and Industry), and the remainder were occupied by officials nominated by the Government (including the Dzongdas). Not all of the 105 public members are elected simultaneously; there are, therefore, overlaps in tenure. The Assembly elects its own Speaker from among its members. It enacts laws, advises on constitutional and political matters and debates all important issues. There is provision for a secret ballot on controversial issues, but, in practice, decisions are reached by consensus. Both the Royal Advisory Council and the Council of Ministers are responsible to the Assembly.

Speaker: Dasho KUNZANG DORJI.

LOCAL ADMINISTRATION

There are 20 districts (dzongkhags), each headed by a Dzongda (district officer) (in charge of administration and law and order) and a Thrimpon (magistrate) (in charge of judicial matters). Dzongdas were previously appointed by the King, but are now appointed by the Royal Civil Service Commission, established in 1982. The Dzongdas are responsible to the Royal Civil Service Commission and the Ministry of Home Affairs, while the Thrimpons are responsible to the High Court. The principal officers under the Dzongda are the Dzongda Wongma and the Dzongrab, responsible for locally administered development projects and fiscal matters respectively. Seven of the districts are further sub-divided into sub-districts (dungkhags), and the lowest administrative unit in all districts is the block (gewog) of several villages.

In July 1991 Gewog Yargye Tshogchungs (GYTs—Gewog Development Committees) were established in each of the gewogs in Bhutan (of which there were 197 in 1994). Membership of these committees consists of between five and 13 members (gewog yargye tshogpas), depending on the size of the block. Members are directly elected, on the basis of merit, by the villagers. Each GYT also elects a representative to the Dzongkhag Yargye Tshogchungs (DYTs—District Development Committees).

In 1987 Gasa and Punakha were amalgamated into a single district, and a new district, named Chhukha, was created from portions of three existing districts in western Bhutan. Two new districts, Gasa and Trashi Yangtse, were created in 1992. There are two municipal corporations (in Thimphu and Phuentsholing), each of which is headed by a Thrompon (mayor) and is composed of government officials from the Department of Works and Housing in the Ministry of Social Services.

Political Organizations

Political parties are banned in Bhutan, in accordance with long-standing legislation. There are, however, a small number of anti-Government organizations, composed principally of Nepali-speaking former residents of Bhutan, which are based in Kathmandu, Nepal.

Bhutan National Democratic Party (BNDP): POB 3334, Kathmandu, Nepal; tel. 525682; f. 1992; also has offices in Delhi and Varanasi, India, and in Thapa, Nepal; Pres. R. B. BASNET; Gen. Secs HARI P. ADHIKARI, Dr D. N. S. DHAKAL.

Bhutan People's Party (BPP): f. 1990 as a successor to the People's Forum on Democratic Rights (f. 1989); advocates unconditional release of all political prisoners, change from absolute monarchy to constitutional monarchy, judicial reform, freedom of religious practices, linguistic freedom, freedom of press, speech and expression, and equal rights for all ethnic groups; Pres. R. K. BUDATHOKI; Gen. Sec. R. K. CHETTRI.

Druk National Congress (DNC): Maharagunj, Chakrapath, POB 9409, Kathmandu, Nepal; f. 1992; claims to represent 'all the oppressed people of Bhutan'; Pres. 'RONGTHONG' KINLEY DORJI.

Human Rights Organization of Bhutan (HUROB): POB 172, Patan Dhoka, Lalitpur, Kathmandu, Nepal; tel. 525046; fax 526038; f. 1991; documents alleged human rights violations in Bhutan and co-ordinates welfare activities in eight refugee camps in Nepal for ethnic Nepalese claiming to be from Bhutan; Chair. S. B. SUBBA; Gen. Sec. OM DHUNGEL.

United Liberation People's Front: f. 1990; Leader BALARAM POUDYAL.

Diplomatic Representation

EMBASSIES IN BHUTAN

Bangladesh: POB 178, Upper Choubachu, Thimphu; tel. 22362; fax 22629; Ambassador: MAHMUDA HAQUE CHOWDARY.

India: India House, Lungtenzampa, Thimphu; tel. 22100; telex 890211; fax 23195; Ambassador: DALIP MEHTA.

Judicial System

Bhutan has Civil and Criminal Codes, which are based on those laid down by the Shabdrung Ngawang Namgyal in the 17th century. An independent judicial authority was established in 1961, but law was mostly administered at the district level until 1968, when the High Court was set up. Existing laws were consolidated in 1982, although annual or biennial conferences of Thrimpons are held to keep abreast of changing circumstances and to recommend (in the first instance, to the King) amendments to existing laws. Most legislation is sent by the Council of Ministers to the National Assembly for approval and enactment. During 1995–97 substantial revisions to the civil and criminal codes were being drafted.

Appeal Court: The Supreme Court of Appeal is the King.

High Court (Thrimkhang Gongma): Thimphu; tel. 22344; fax 22921; established 1968 to review appeals from Lower Courts, although some cases are heard at the first instance. The Full Bench is presided over by the Chief Justice. There are normally seven other judges, who are appointed by the King on the recommendation of the Chief Justice and who serve until their superannuation. Three judges form a quorum. The judges are assisted by senior rabjams (judges in training). Assistance to defendants is available through jabmis (certificated pleaders). The operation of the legal system and proposed amendments are considered by regular meetings of all the judges and thrimpons (usually annually, or at least once every two years). Proposed amendments are transmitted in the first instance to the King as Head of Government.

Chief Justice: Dasho SONAM TOBGYE.

Judges of the High Court: Dasho THINLEY YOEZER, Dasho PASANG TOBGYE, Dasho KARMA D. SHERPA, Dasho D. N. KATWAL*, Dasho K. B. GHALEY*, Dasho GAGEY LHAM.

* Originally nominated as public representative.

Magistrates' Courts (Dzongkhag Thrimkhang): Each district has a court, headed by the thrimpon (magistrate) and aided by a junior rabjam, which tries most cases. Appeals are made to the High Court, and less serious civil disputes may be settled by a gup or mandal (village headman) through written undertakings by the parties concerned.

All citizens have the right to make informal appeal for redress of grievances directly to the King, through the office of the gyalpoi zimpon (court chamberlain).

Religion

The state religion is Mahayana Buddhism, but the southern Bhutanese are predominantly followers of Hinduism. Buddhism was introduced into Bhutan in the eighth century AD by the Indian saint Padmasambhava, known in Bhutan as Guru Rimpoche. In the 13th century Phajo Drugom Shigpo made the Drukpa school of Kagyupa Buddhism pre-eminent in Bhutan, and this sect is still supported by the dominant ethnic group, the Drukpas. The main monastic group, the Central Monastic Body (comprising 1,160 monks), is led by an elected Head Abbot (Je Khenpo), is directly supported by the State and spends six months of the year at Tashichhodzong and at Punakha respectively. A further 2,120 monks, who are members of the District Monastic Bodies, are sustained by the lay population. The Council for Ecclesiastical Affairs oversees all religious bodies. Monasteries (Gompas) and shrines (Lhakhangs) are numerous. Religious proselytizing, in any form, is illegal.

Council for Ecclesiastical Affairs (Dratshang Lhentshog): POB 254, Thimphu; tel. 22754; f. 1984, replacing the Central Board for Monastic Studies, to oversee all Buddhist meditational centres and schools of Buddhist studies, as well as the Central and District Monastic Bodies; daily affairs of the Council are run by the Central Monastic Secretariat; Chair. His Holiness the Je Khenpo JIGME CHOEDRA; Sec. SANGAY WANGCHUK; Dep. Sec. SANGAY TENZIN.

The Press

The Bhutan Review: POB 172, Patan Dhoka, Lalitpur, Kathmandu, Nepal; tel. 525046; fax 523819; f. 1993; monthly organ of the Human Rights Organization of Bhutan (HUROB); opposed to existing government policies.

Kuensel: POB 204, Thimphu; tel. 23043; telex 890212; fax 22975; f. 1965 as a weekly govt bulletin; reorg. as a national weekly newspaper in 1986; became autonomous corporation in 1992 (previously under Dept of Information), incorporating former Royal Government Press; in English, Dzongkha and Nepali; Editor-in-Chief KINLEY DORJI; Editors R. N. MISHRA (Nepali), TASHI PHUNTSHO (English), GOEMBO DORJI (Dzongkha); circ. 331 (Nepali), 8,102 (English), 2,729 (Dzongkha).

Broadcasting and Communications

TELECOMMUNICATIONS

Ministry of Communications (Telecommunications Division): Thimphu; tel. 22678; telex 890200; fax 23041; Dir SANGEY TENZING.

RADIO

In 1994 there were 52 radio stations for administrative communications. Of these, 34 were for internal communications (to which the public had access), and three were external stations serving Bhutan House at Kalimpong and the Bhutanese diplomatic missions in India and Bangladesh. A further 11 stations are for hydrological and meteorological purposes.

BBS Corporation (Bhutan Broadcasting Service): POB 101, Thimphu; tel. 23070; f. 1973 as Radio National Youth Association of Bhutan (NYAB); became autonomous corporation in 1992 (previously under Dept of Information); short-wave radio station broadcasting 30 hours per week in Dzongkha, Sharchopkha, Nepali (Lhotsamkha) and English; a daily FM programme (for Thimphu only) began in 1987; Chair. Dasho YESHEY ZIMBA; Exec. Dir SONAM TSHONG.

Finance

(cap. = capital; auth. = authorized; p.u. = paid up; res = reserves; dep. = deposits; m. = million; brs = branches; amounts in ngultrum)

BANKING

Central Bank

Royal Monetary Authority (RMA): POB 154, Thimphu; tel. 22540; telex 890206; fax 22847; f. 1982; bank of issue; frames and implements official monetary policy, co-ordinates the activities of financial institutions and holds foreign-exchange deposits on behalf of the Govt; cap. 1.5m.; Chair. Lyonpo DORJI TSHERING; Man. Dir SONAM WANGCHUCK.

Commercial Banks

Bank of Bhutan: POB 75, Phuentsholing; tel. 2225; telex 890304; fax 2641; f. 1968; 20%-owned by the State Bank of India and 80% by the Govt of Bhutan; wholly managed by Govt of Bhutan from 1997; auth. cap. 100m., cap. p.u. 50m., res 292.9m., dep. 3,575.8m. (Dec. 1996); Dirs nominated by the Bhutan Govt: Chair. Lyonpo DORJI TSHERING; Dirs Dasho YESHEY ZIMBA, KUNZANG WANGDI, SONAM WANGCHUK, Gup UGEN DORJI; Dirs nominated by the State Bank of India: P. P. R. UPADHYAYA, S. K. MUKHOPADHYAY; Man. Dir TSHERING DORJI; 26 brs and 3 extension counters.

Bhutan National Bank: POB 439, Thimphu; tel. 22767; fax 23601; f. as Unit Trust of Bhutan (a savings institution); reorganized, as Bhutan's second commercial bank, in 1996; auth. cap. 50m., cap. p.u. 42.5m.; Chair. Lyonpo DORJI TSHERING; Gen. Man. KIPCHU TSHERING; 4 brs.

Development Bank

Bhutan Development Finance Corporation (BDFC): POB 256, Thimphu; tel. 22579; telex 890223; f. 1988; provides industrial loans and short- and medium-term agricultural loans; auth. cap. 200m., cap. p.u. 100m. (1995), loans 148m. (1996); Chair. Lyonpo D. TSHERING; Man. Dir KARMA RANGDOL.

STOCK EXCHANGE

Royal Securities Exchange of Bhutan Ltd: POB 72, Thimphu; tel. 23995; fax 23849; f. 1993; under temporary management of the Royal Monetary Authority.

INSURANCE

Royal Insurance Corporation of Bhutan: POB 77, Phuentsholing; tel. 2453; telex 890305; fax 2640; f. 1975; cap. and free res 62.2m., total investments 769.9m. (1996); Chair. Lyonpo D. TSHERING; Man. Dir SANGAY KHANDU; 10 brs and development centres.

Trade and Industry

GOVERNMENT AGENCIES

Food Corporation of Bhutan (FCB): POB 80, Phuentsholing; tel. 2241; fax 2289; f. 1974; activities include procurement and distribution of food grains and other essential commodities through appointed Fair Price Shop Agents; marketing of surplus agricultural and horticultural produce through FCB-regulated market outlets; logistics concerning World Food Programme food aid; accumulation of buffer stocks to offset any emergency food shortages; maintenance of SAARC Food Security Reserve Stock; Man. Dir KINLEY TSHERING.

National Commission for Trade and Industry: Thimphu; tel. 22403; fmrly Industrial Development Corpn; regulates the type, quality and quantity of proposed industrial projects; Chair. HM Druk Gyalpo JIGME SINGYE WANGCHUCK.

Planning Commission: Tashichhodzong, Thimphu; tel. 22493; fax 23069; headed by the King until 1991; consists of 15 high-level officials, the majority of whom are members of the Council of Ministers; issues broad policy directives; approves, supervises and co-ordinates assistance for, and implementation of, all development programmes; responsible for preparation of five-year plans and supervision of their implementation; Chair. Lyonpo CHENKYAB DORJI; Sec. (vacant).

State Trading Corpn of Bhutan Ltd (STCB): POB 76, Phuentsholing; tel. 2286; telex 890301; fax 2619; manages imports and exports on behalf of the Govt; Man. Dir TSHERING WANGDI; Jt Man. Dirs L. B. RAI (Admin.), SONAM GYAMTSHO; brs in Thimphu (POB 272; tel. 22953; fax 23781) and Calcutta, India.

Export Development Corporation: Industrial Estate, Phuentsholing; tel. 2530; telex 890312.

CHAMBER OF COMMERCE

Bhutan Chamber of Commerce and Industry: POB 147, Thimphu; tel. 22742; telex 890229; fax 23936; f. 1980; reorg. 1988;

promotion of trade and industry, information dissemination, private-sector human resource development, trade and industrial consultancy services; 434 registered mems; 12-mem. technical advisory committee; 25-mem. executive committee; 20 liaison offices; Pres. Gup UGEN DORJI; Vice-Pres M. T. NADIK, TSHERING DORJI.

Utilities

ELECTRICITY

Chhukha Hydropower Corporation: Phuentsholing; fax 2582; f. 1991; Chair. Lyonpo OM PRADHAN; Man. Dir Padmashiri G. N. RAO.

TRADE UNIONS

Under long-standing legislation, trade union activity is illegal in Bhutan.

Transport

ROADS AND TRACKS

In December 1996 there were 3,285 km of roads in Bhutan, of which 60.7% were paved. Surfaced roads link the important border towns of Phuentsholing, Gelephu, Sarpang and Samdrup Jongkhar in southern Bhutan to towns in West Bengal and Assam in India. There is a shortage of road transport. Yaks, ponies and mules are still the chief means of transport on the rough mountain tracks. By April 1990 most of the previously government-operated transport facilities on major and subsidiary routes had been transferred to private operators on the basis of seven-year contracts.

Surface Transport Authority: Phuentsholing; manages former Bhutan Government Transport Service (f. 1962); operates fleet of buses and minibuses.

Transport Corpn of Bhutan: POB 7, Phuentsholing; tel. 2476; telex 890305; f. 1982; subsidiary of Royal Insurance Corpn of Bhutan; operates direct coach service between Phuentsholing and Calcutta via Siliguri.

Other operators are Barma Travels (f. 1990), Dawa Transport (Propr SHERUB WANGCHUCK), Dhendup Travel Service (Phuentsholing; tel. 2437), Gyamtsho Transport, Gurung Transport Service, Namgay Transport, Nima Travels (Phuentsholing; tel. 2384), and Rimpung Travels (Phuentsholing; tel. 2354).

Lorries for transporting goods are operated by the private sector.

CIVIL AVIATION

There is an international airport at Paro. There are also numerous helicopter landing pads, which are used, by arrangement with the Indian military and aviation authorities, solely by government officials.

Druk-Air Corpn Ltd (Royal Bhutan Airlines): POB 209, Old Bhutan Hotel, Thimphu; tel. 22825; telex 890219; fax 22775; national airline; f. 1981; became fully operational in 1983; services from Paro to India, Nepal, Thailand, Myanmar and Bangladesh; charter services also undertaken; Chair. Lyonpo LEKI DORJI; Man. Dir SONAM TSHERING.

Tourism

Bhutan was opened to tourism in 1975. In 1996 the total number of foreign visitors was 5,133 and receipts from tourism totalled US $6.45m. Tourists travel in organized 'package' or trekking tours, or individually, accompanied by government-appointed guides. Hotels have been constructed at Phuentsholing, Paro, Bumthang and Thimphu, with lodges at Trongsa, Trashigang and Mongar. In addition, there are many small privately-operated hotels and guest-houses. The Government exercises close control over the development of tourism. In 1987 the National Assembly resolved that all monasteries, mountains and other holy places should be inaccessible to tourists from 1988 (this resolution is flexibly interpreted, however—e.g. Japanese Buddhist tour groups are permitted to visit 'closed' monasteries). In 1991 the Government began transferring the tourism industry to the private sector and licences were issued to new private tourism operators. New rules were introduced in 1995, asserting more stringent controls over private operators, through the Tourism Authority of Bhutan.

Bhutan Hotels and Travels (BHT): f. 1991; consortium of eight cos; majority shareholder in BTCL (see below); Chair. Gup UGEN DORJI.

Bhutan Mandala Tours and Treks: POB 397, Thimphu; tel. 24842; fax 23675; Man. Dir DOMINIC SITLING.

Bhutan Tourism Corpn Ltd (BTCL): POB 159, Thimphu; tel. 24045; telex 890217; fax 22479; transferred to private ownership in mid-1991; Bhutan Hotels and Travels (BHT), a consortium of eight cos, purchased 51% of the shares in 1991; operates three hotels for tourists and govt and state guests; also operates three tourist lodges and many tourist rest houses throughout the kingdom; conducts tours and treks throughout Bhutan; Man. Dir YESHEY NORBU; Gen. Man. ROBIN WANGDI.

Bhutan Yod Sel Tours and Treks: POB 574, Thimphu; tel. 23912; fax 23589; f. 1991; conducts small group and special interest tours and trekking expeditions throughout Bhutan; operates own fleet of transport and traditional farmhouse lodges in Paro and Thimphu; Man. Dir DAWA PENJORE; Exec. Gen. Man. TASHI YANGZOME.

Etho Metho Tours and Treks Ltd: POB 360, Thimphu; tel. 23162; fax 22884; travel, trekking and car rental; Man. Dir DAGO BEDA.

Gangri Tours and Trekking Co Ltd: POB 607, Thimphu; tel. 23556; fax 23322; Man. Dir KINLEY GYELTSHEN.

Kinga Tours and Treks: POB 635, Thimphu; tel. 23468; telex 8902340; fax 22088; Gen. Man. CHEWANG DORJI.

Takin Travels and Trekking Co: Gatoen Lam, POB 454, Thimphu; tel. 23129; telex 890224; fax 23130; f. 1991; eco-related and activity tours and treks; Man. Dir WANGDI GYALTSHEN; Gen. Man. UGYEN DHENDUP DORJI.

Yangphel Tours and Travels: POB 236, Thimphu; tel. 23293; fax 22897; Man. Dir UGYEN RINZIN.

TOURISM AUTHORITY

Tourism Authority of Bhutan: POB 126, Thimphu; tel. 25225; fax 23695; f. 1991; under control of Ministry of Communications; exercises overall authority over tourism policy, pricing, hotel, restaurant and travel agency licensing, visa approvals, etc.; Man. Dir THUJI D. NADIK.

BOLIVIA

Introductory Survey

Location, Climate, Language, Religion, Flag, Capital

The Republic of Bolivia is a land-locked state in South America, bordered by Chile and Peru to the west, by Brazil to the north and east, and by Paraguay and Argentina to the south. The climate varies, according to altitude, from humid tropical conditions in the northern and eastern lowlands, which are less than 500 m (1,640 ft) above sea-level, to the cool and cold zones at altitudes of more than 3,500 m (about 11,500 ft) in the Andes mountains. The official languages are Spanish, Quechua and Aymará. Almost all of the inhabitants profess Christianity, and the great majority are adherents of the Roman Catholic Church. The national flag (proportions 3 by 2) has three equal horizontal stripes, of red, yellow and green. The state flag has, in addition, the national emblem (an oval cartouche enclosing a representation of Mount Potosí, an alpaca, a breadfruit tree and a sheaf of grain, all surmounted by a condor and superimposed on crossed cannons, rifles and national banners) in the centre of the yellow stripe. The legal capital is Sucre. The administrative capital and seat of government is La Paz.

Recent History

The Incas of Bolivia were conquered by Spain in 1538 and, although there were many revolts against Spanish rule, independence was not achieved until 1825. Bolivian history has been characterized by recurrent internal strife, resulting in a succession of presidents, and frequent territorial disputes with its neighbours, including the 1879–83 War of the Pacific between Bolivia, Peru and Chile, and the Chaco Wars of 1928–30 and 1932–35 against Paraguay.

At a presidential election in May 1951 the largest share of the vote was won by Dr Víctor Paz Estenssoro, the candidate of the Movimiento Nacionalista Revolucionario (MNR), who had been living in Argentina since 1946. He was denied permission to return to Bolivia and contested the election *in absentia*. However, he failed to gain an absolute majority, and the incumbent President transferred power to a junta of army officers. This regime was itself overthrown in April 1952, when a popular uprising, supported by the MNR and a section of the armed forces, enabled Dr Paz Estenssoro to return from exile and assume the presidency. His Government, a coalition of the MNR and the Labour Party, committed itself to profound social revolution. It nationalized the tin mines and introduced universal suffrage (the franchise had previously been limited to literate adults) and land reform. Dr Hernán Siles Zuazo, a leading figure in the 1952 revolution, was elected President for the 1956–60 term, and Dr Paz Estenssoro was again elected President in 1960. However, the powerful trade unions came into conflict with the Government, and in November 1964, following widespread strikes and disorder, President Paz Estenssoro was overthrown by the Vice-President, Gen. René Barrientos Ortuño, who was supported by the army. After serving with Gen. Alfredo Ovando Candía as Co-President under a military junta, Gen. Barrientos resigned in January 1966 to campaign for the presidency. He was elected in July 1966.

President Barrientos met strong opposition from left-wing groups, including mineworkers' unions. There was also a guerrilla uprising in south-eastern Bolivia, led by Dr Ernesto ('Che') Guevara, the Argentine-born revolutionary who had played a leading role in the Castro regime in Cuba. However, the insurgency was suppressed by government troops, with the help of US advisers, and guerrilla warfare ended in October 1967, when Guevara was captured and killed. In April 1969 President Barrientos was killed in an air crash and Dr Luis Adolfo Siles Salinas, the Vice-President, succeeded to the presidency. In September 1969, however, President Siles Salinas was deposed by the armed forces, who installed Gen. Ovando in power again. He was forced to resign in October 1970, when, after a power struggle between right-wing and left-wing army officers, Gen. Juan José Torres González, who had support from leftists, emerged as President, pledging support for agrarian reform and worker participation in management. A 'People's Assembly', formed by Marxist politicians, radical students and leaders of trade unions, was allowed to meet and demanded the introduction of extreme socialist measures, causing disquiet in right-wing circles. President Torres was deposed in August 1971 by Col (later Gen.) Hugo Bánzer Suárez, who drew support from the right-wing Falange Socialista Boliviana and a section of the MNR, as well as from the army. In June 1973 President Bánzer announced an imminent return to constitutional government, but elections were later postponed to June 1974. The MNR withdrew its support and entered into active opposition.

Following an attempted military coup in June 1974, all portfolios within the Cabinet were assigned to military personnel. After an attempt to overthrow him in November 1974, President Bánzer declared that elections had been postponed indefinitely and that his military regime would retain power until at least 1980. All political and union activity was banned. Political and industrial unrest in 1976, however, led President Bánzer to announce that elections would be held in July 1978. Allegations of fraud rendered the elections void, but Gen. Juan Pereda Asbún, the armed forces candidate in the elections, staged a successful military coup. In November 1978 his right-wing Government was overthrown in another coup, led by Gen. David Padilla Aranciba, Commander-in-Chief of the Army, with the support of national left-wing elements.

Presidential and congressional elections were held in July 1979. The presidential poll resulted in almost equal support for two ex-Presidents, Dr Siles Zuazo (with 36.0% of the vote) and Dr Paz Estenssoro (with 35.9%), who were now leading rival factions of the MNR. Congress, which was convened in August to resolve the issue, failed to give a majority to either candidate. An interim Government was formed under Walter Guevara Arce, President of the Senate (the upper house of Congress), but this administration was overthrown on 1 November by a right-wing army officer, Col Alberto Natusch Busch. He withdrew 15 days later after failing to gain the support of Congress, which elected Dra Lidia Gueiler Tejada, President of the Chamber of Deputies (the lower house of Congress), as interim Head of State pending presidential and legislative elections scheduled for June 1980.

The 1980 presidential election also yielded no clear winner, and in July, before Congress could meet to decide between the two main contenders (again Siles Zuazo and Paz Estenssoro), a military junta led by the army commander, Gen. Luis García Meza, staged a coup—the 189th in Bolivia's 154 years of independence. In August 1981 a military uprising forced Gen. García to resign. In September the junta transferred power to the army commander, Gen. Celso Torrelio Villa, who declared his intention to fight official corruption and to return the country to democracy within three years. Labour unrest, provoked by Bolivia's severe economic crisis, was appeased by restitution of trade union and political rights, and a mainly civilian Cabinet was appointed in April 1982. Elections were scheduled for April 1983. The political liberalization disturbed the armed forces, who attempted to create a climate of violence, and President Torrelio resigned in July 1982, amid rumours of an impending coup. The junta installed the less moderate Gen. Guido Vildoso Calderón, the Army Chief of Staff, as President. Unable to resolve the worsening economic crisis or to control a general strike, the military regime announced in September 1982 that power would be handed over in October to the Congress that had originally been elected in 1980. Dr Siles Zuazo, who had obtained most votes in both 1979 and 1980, was duly elected President by Congress, and was sworn in for a four-year term in October 1982.

President Siles Zuazo appointed a coalition Cabinet consisting of members of his own party, the Movimiento Nacionalista Revolucionario de Izquierda (MNRI), the Movimiento de la Izquierda Revolucionaria (MIR) and the Partido Comunista de Bolivia (PCB). Economic aid from the USA and Europe was resumed but the Government found itself unable to fulfil the expectations that had been created by the return to democratic rule. The entire Cabinet resigned in August 1983, and the President appointed a Cabinet in which the number of portfolios that were held by the right-wing of the MNRI, the Partido Demócrata Cristiano (PDC) and independents was increased.

The MIR joined forces with the MNR and with business interests in rejecting the Government's policy of complying with IMF conditions for assistance, which involved harsh economic measures. The Government lost its majority in Congress and was confronted by strikes and mass labour demonstrations. In November the opposition-dominated Senate approved an increase of 100% in the minimum wage, in defiance of the Government's austerity measures. Following a 48-hour general strike, the whole Cabinet resigned once again in December, in anticipation of an opposition motion of censure; the ministers accused the Senate of planning a 'constitutional coup' and urged the formation of a government of 'national unity'. In January 1984 President Siles Zuazo appointed a new coalition Cabinet, including 13 members of the previous Government.

The new Cabinet's main priority was to reverse Bolivia's grave economic decline. However, constant industrial agitation by the trade union confederation, the Central Obrera Boliviana (COB), coupled with rumours of an imminent coup, seriously undermined public confidence in the President. In June 1984 the country was again thrown into turmoil by the temporary abduction of President Siles Zuazo. Two former cabinet ministers and some 100 right-wing army officers were arrested in connection with the kidnapping, which was believed to have been supported by leading figures in the illicit drugs trade.

In September 1984 another crisis faced the Government following the discovery of a plot by extreme right-wing groups to overthrow the President. The disclosure that Congress had ordered an enquiry into suspected links between the Government and cocaine-dealers prompted President Siles Zuazo to undertake a five-day hunger strike in a bid to secure national unity and stability. In January 1985 a new Cabinet was formed, comprising only members of the MNRI and independents. In the same month it was announced that an attempted coup by former military officers had been thwarted.

At elections in July 1985, amid reports of electoral malpractice and poor organization, the right-wing Acción Democrática Nacionalista (ADN), whose presidential candidate was Gen. Hugo Bánzer Suárez (the former dictator), received 28.6% of the votes cast, and the MNR obtained 26.4%, while the MIR was the leading left-wing party. At a further round of voting in Congress in August, an alliance between the MNR and the leading left-wing groups, including the MIR, enabled Dr Víctor Paz Estenssoro of the MNR to secure the presidency (which he had previously held in 1952–56 and 1960–64). The armed forces pledged their support for the new Government.

On taking office in August 1985, the new Government immediately introduced a very strict economic programme, designed to reduce inflation, which was estimated to have reached 14,173% in the year to August. The COB rejected the programme and called an indefinite general strike in September. The Government responded by declaring the strike illegal and by ordering a 90-day state of siege throughout Bolivia. Leading trade unionists were detained or banished, and thousands of strikers were arrested. The strike was called off in October, when union leaders agreed to hold talks with the Government. The conclusion of the strike was regarded as a considerable success for the new administration which, in spite of having achieved office with the assistance of left-wing parties, had subsequently found a greater ally in the right-wing ADN. The alliance between the MNR and the ADN was consolidated by the signing of a 'pacto por la democracia' in October. The collapse of the world tin market in late 1985 had a catastrophic impact on the Bolivian economy.

In July 1986 the Government was strongly criticized by opposition groups and trade unions when 160 US soldiers arrived in Bolivia to participate in a joint campaign with the Bolivian armed forces to eradicate illegal coca plantations. The Government was accused of having contravened the Constitution and of compromising national sovereignty. The allocation of US aid, however, was to be conditional upon the elimination of Bolivia's illegal cocaine trade. In October the US administration agreed to provide more than US $100m. in aid to continue the coca-eradication campaign, and US troops were withdrawn, so that the Bolivian authorities could assume responsibility for the campaign. However, within a few months of the troops' withdrawal, cocaine production was once again flourishing.

Throughout 1986 demonstrations and strikes were held by the COB in protest at the Government's austerity measures. Following a general strike in August, the Government imposed a state of siege for 90 days. Social discontent persisted in 1987 and extensive unrest continued in 1988 (following a further increase in the price of petrol in February of that year), which culminated in April with a national hunger strike, called by the COB, to protest against the continuing austerity measures. These problems led to the resignation of the Cabinet in August, although all except four ministers were reappointed.

Presidential and congressional elections took place in May 1989. Of the votes cast in the presidential election, Gonzalo Sánchez de Lozada of the MNR (and hitherto Minister of Planning) obtained 23.1%, Gen. Hugo Bánzer Suárez of the ADN 22.7%, and Jaime Paz Zamora of the MIR 19.6%. As no candidate had gained the requisite absolute majority, responsibility for the choice of President passed to the newly-elected Congress, which was to convene in August. Political uncertainty prevailed in the interim, and this led, in turn, to economic stagnation. Initially, a power-sharing agreement between the MNR and the MIR appeared to be the most likely outcome, as animosity between Sánchez and Bánzer precluded a renewal of the MNR-ADN pact. However, shortly before the second stage of the election, Bánzer withdrew his candidacy in order to support his former adversary, Paz Zamora. The 46 ADN and 41 MIR seats in Congress were sufficient to assure a majority vote for Paz Zamora, who assumed the presidency. A coalition Government of 'national unity', the Acuerdo Patriótico, was then formed. At the same time, a joint political council (with undefined powers), headed by Gen. Bánzer, was established. In his inaugural speech, President Paz Zamora gave assurances that fiscal discipline would be maintained. A state of siege, banning strikes, was imposed in November, since, according to the Government, teachers striking over the issue of bonuses presented a threat to the anti-inflation austerity policy.

Meanwhile, further measures to reduce the production of coca were taken during 1988. An anti-narcotics department was established in April. The drug control troops, Unidad Móvil de Patrullaje Rural (UMOPAR), were provided with greater resources and were further supported by a coca limitation law, restricting the area of land allowed for coca production (the leaves to be used for 'traditional' purposes only). In the same month, Roberto Suárez, Bolivia's leading cocaine-trafficker, was arrested and imprisoned for trading in illicit drugs. Suárez's arrest led to the exposure of drugs-trading involving leading members of the ADN, and was linked to a bomb attack on US Secretary of State George Shultz's motorcade in La Paz in August, during a visit to show support for the campaign against coca production.

By mid-1989, however, the Government had failed to attain the targets of its coca eradication programme, having encountered staunch opposition from the powerful coca-growers' organizations. Clashes between UMOPAR and drugs-traffickers had become increasingly violent, especially in the coca-processing region of northern Beni. Paz Zamora was critical of the militaristic approach of the USA to coca eradication and emphasized the need for economic and social support. In May 1990, however, he accepted US $35m. in military aid from the USA. In late 1990 reaction to US involvement in Bolivia became increasingly violent. The left-wing Nestor Paz Zamora guerrilla group claimed responsibility for several bomb attacks, declaring that its actions were in response to the violation of Bolivia's political and territorial sovereignty by the USA.

In December 1989 a serious institutional conflict arose when the Government allowed a former Minister of the Interior, Migration and Justice, Col Luis Arce Gómez, to be taken to Miami, Florida, to be tried on drugs-trafficking charges, despite the absence of a formal extradition treaty between Bolivia and the USA. Arce Gómez had been on trial in Bolivia since 1986, accused of violating human rights. His extradition, therefore, constituted a contravention of Bolivian law, which states that a Bolivian cannot be extradited while undergoing trial in Bolivia. Following an acrimonious conflict between the Government and the judiciary, Congress temporarily suspended eight of the 12 supreme court judges in late 1990. In retaliation, the court threatened to annul the 1989 elections. The conflict came to an end in early 1991 with the signing by the country's five main political parties of a pact affirming the independence of the Supreme Court. In January 1991 a federal jury in Miami found Arce Gómez guilty on two charges of drugs-trafficking, and in March he was sentenced to 30 years' imprisonment. (In July 1997 the Bolivian Government officially requested his extradition to Bolivia.)

In March 1991 the reputation of the Government was seriously undermined when three of its senior officials were forced to resign amid allegations of corruption. Moreover, the appointment in February of Col. Faustino Rico Toro as the new head of Bolivia's Special Force for the Fight Against Drugs-Trafficking (FELCN) had provoked widespread outrage. In addition to his alleged connections with illegal drugs-traffickers, Rico was accused of having committed human rights abuses during his tenure as chief of army intelligence under the regime of Gen. Luis García Meza (1980–81). On 4 March, after considerable pressure from the USA (including the suspension of all military and economic aid), Rico resigned from his new position. On 13 March, following accusations by the USA linking them with illegal drugs-traffickers, the Minister of the Interior, Migration and Justice, Guillermo Capobianco, and the Chief of Police, Felipe Carvajal, resigned from their posts, although both maintained their innocence. In July the Government announced a decree granting a period of amnesty, lasting 120 days, for drugs-traffickers to surrender voluntarily. A condition of the amnesty was that those giving themselves up confess their crimes and contribute effectively to the apprehension of other such criminals. In return, they were offered minimum prison sentences and the guarantee that they would not risk extradition to the USA. In the months that followed, as many as seven of the country's most powerful drugs-traffickers were reported to have taken advantage of the amnesty.

A series of strikes in December 1991 by workers protesting at government plans to privatize state-owned enterprises, including the state mining corporation, COMIBOL, culminated, in January 1992, in a national strike, organized by the COB. Later that month a pact between the Government and the COB, allowing the unions consultative rights over planned privatizations in the mining sector, was signed, putting an end to the dispute. However, in July the COB called a further general strike. In October, in what was regarded as a major reversal for the Government and a considerable victory for the mining union, Federación Sindical de Trabajadores Mineros de Bolivia (FSTMB), the Government suspended its programme of joint ventures between COMIBOL and private companies. The decision followed industrial action by the FSTMB involving the occupation of COMIBOL mines. Continued social unrest led to violent confrontation between protesters and troops throughout the country in early 1993, and the military occupation of La Paz in March of that year.

In April 1993 the Supreme Court found the former military dictator, Gen. Luis García Meza, guilty on 49 charges of murder, human rights abuses, corruption and fraud, and sentenced him, *in absentia*, to 30 years' imprisonment. Similar sentences were imposed on 14 of García Meza's collaborators.

Presidential and congressional elections were held in June 1993. Gonzalo Sánchez de Lozada was presented as the MNR's presidential candidate, while Gen. Hugo Bánzer Suárez (who had made several previous attempts at gaining the presidency by democratic means) was supported by both the ADN and the MIR, owing to the fact that Paz Zamora was ineligible for re-election. Of the votes cast in the presidential election, Sánchez received 33.8%, while Bánzer secured 20.0%. The other principal candidates, Max Fernández Rojas, an industrialist and leader of the populist Unión Cívica Solidaridad (UCS), Carlos Palenque Aviles, a popular television presenter and leader of Conciencia de Patria (Condepa), and Antonio Araníbar Quiroga, President of the Movimiento Bolivia Libre (MBL), received 13.1%, 13.6% and 5.1%, respectively, of the total votes. Since no candidate had secured the requisite absolute majority, a congressional vote was scheduled to take place in August. However, Bánzer withdrew from the contest, thereby leaving Sánchez de Lozada's candidacy unopposed. At legislative elections, conducted simultaneously, the MNR secured 69 of the 157 seats in the bicameral Congress, while the ruling Acuerdo Patriótico coalition won only 43. The MNR subsequently concluded a pact with the UCS and the MBL, thus securing a congressional majority. Sánchez de Lozada was sworn in as President on 6 August.

In March 1994 the leader of the opposition MIR, former President Jaime Paz Zamora, announced his retirement from political life. His statement followed the presentation of a report by the FELCN to Congress alleging his co-operation with drugs-traffickers. The report, which also implicated several of Paz Zamora's political allies and family members, was largely based on information provided by one of the country's most notorious drugs-traffickers, Carmelo 'Meco' Domínguez, and his former associate, Isaac 'Oso' Chavarría, who had been a paramilitary leader during Gen. García Meza's military regime in 1980–81 and was arrested in January 1994.

The former military dictator, Gen. Luis García Meza (sentenced to 30 years' imprisonment *in absentia* in April 1993), was arrested in Brazil in March 1994. In October the Brazilian Supreme Court approved his extradition to Bolivia, and in March 1995 he began his prison sentence.

Despite the new Government's stated intention to combat corruption in Bolivia's political and public life, evidence of fraudulent practice continued to feature widely in the country's affairs. In June 1994 the President of the Supreme Court and its third judge were found guilty of bribery by the Senate and were dismissed and banned from holding public office for 10 years. In the same month it was revealed that a large proportion of the US $20m. seized from drugs-traffickers between 1988 and 1993 had disappeared. Members of the FELCN, trustees from the Attorney-General's office and local government officials were implicated in the affair.

Meanwhile, the US-funded coca-eradication programme (see above) continued to cause serious unrest during 1994, particularly in the Chapare valley of Cochabamba, where UMOPAR forces were occupying the area. Large-scale demonstrations throughout the year culminated in August and September in protests across the country by teachers, students and COB members, as well as coca producers. The unrest subsided in late September, when the Government pledged to cease forcible eradication of coca and to withdraw its forces gradually from Chapare.

In January 1995 Jaime Paz Zamora announced that he was to return to political life, contrary to his statement in March 1994 (see above). He denied the allegations against him in the FELCN report, while admitting certain errors of judgement during his period in office.

In early 1995 some 80,000 teachers across the country undertook a campaign of industrial action in opposition to a proposed programme of education reforms, which advocated the privatization of much of the education system and the restriction of teachers' rights to union membership. In March the COB called an indefinite strike after a demonstration by 3,000 teachers in La Paz was violently disrupted by police and army personnel. In response to the strike, and in an attempt to quell several weeks of civil unrest, the Government declared a state of siege for 90 days. Military units were deployed throughout the country, and 370 union leaders (including the Secretary-General of the COB, Oscar Salas) were arrested and banished to remote areas. However, protests continued nation-wide, and some 70,000 teachers remained on strike. In April COB leaders agreed to sign a memorandum of understanding with the Government to end the strike in return for the release of trade union officials and the initiation of negotiations. Despite these developments, the state of siege was extended by a further 90 days in July, owing to continued civil unrest, which had become particularly intense in the Chapare valley, where, in spite of the introduction of a voluntary coca-eradication programme, UMOPAR forces had begun to occupy villages and to destroy coca plantations. Violent clashes between peasant farmers and UMOPAR personnel between July and September resulted in the deaths of several peasants, the injury of many more and the arrest of almost 1,000 coca-growers. Human rights organizations expressed alarm at the force with which UMOPAR was conducting its operations and at the number of peasants killed and injured in the campaign. In mid-October the state of siege was revoked, and negotiations between the Government and the coca-growers were undertaken. By the following month, however, the talks had broken down, and further violent clashes between security forces and some 5,000 peasants were reported. Despite sustained resistance by coca-growers throughout 1995, a total of 5,520 ha of the crop were destroyed during the year (some 120 ha more than the target set by the US Government in its eradication programme).

Meanwhile, allegations implicating senior public officials in the illegal drugs trade continued to emerge in 1995. Four members of the FELCN, including the organization's second-in-command, Col Fernando Tarifa, were dismissed in September, following an investigation into their links with drugs-traffickers. A further 100 FELCN members were detained in November on drugs-related charges. Also in September 13 police officers and 10 civilians were arrested in connection with a large haul of cocaine seized from a Bolivian aircraft in Peru. Moreover, a serious political scandal erupted in October, following allegations that Guillermo Bedregal, the President of the Senate and a deputy leader of the MNR, had co-operated with leading drugs-traffickers.

In November 1995 Max Fernández, the leader of the UCS, was killed in an air crash. He was replaced as UCS candidate for Santa Cruz in the municipal elections by his son Johnny, who won the seat in December. The MNR suffered serious losses in the elections, winning control in only one of the 10 principal cities.

In December 1995 a team of experts from Argentina began a search for the body of the guerrilla leader and revolutionary, Ernesto ('Che') Guevara, at the request of Sánchez de Lozada, following revelations by a retired general concerning the whereabouts of his remains. The Government of Cuba had long sought to recover Guevara's remains. The search was abandoned in mid-1996, but was resumed in the following year. In July 1997 Guevara's remains, together with those of three of his comrades, were located and returned to Cuba.

The issue of fraudulent practice in political and public life re-emerged in early 1996, when allegations concerning the abuse of the personal expenses system resulted in the resignation of 10 MNR members of Congress and the suspension of 12 others on criminal charges. Moreover, a supreme court judge who had presided over numerous cases involving drugs-related offences was arrested by the FELCN in March after having been filmed accepting a cash sum of US $3,000 from a defendant's relative in a public restaurant in Santa Cruz.

Continued opposition to the Government's capitalization programme led to further industrial unrest in early 1996. Strikes by rural teachers and later by doctors in March culminated in a general strike at the end of the month. In April more than 100,000 transport workers undertook a series of strikes and demonstrations in protest at the sale of the Eastern Railway to a Chilean company. Riots in La Paz resulted in damage to Chilean-owned railway property, which prompted threats from the Chilean Government to withdraw its investment from Bolivia. During violent clashes with the police several protesters were injured and one was killed. The dispute ended later in the month, when the COB signed an agreement with the Government which provided for modest public-sector wage increases, but which made no concessions in the Government's plans to continue implementation of its capitalization policies.

The proposed introduction of an agrarian reform law proved highly controversial and led to a series of protests in September and October 1996 by indigenous and peasant groups who feared that their land rights would be undermined by measures contained in the proposed legislation. In early October the leaders of several peasant farmers' groups began a hunger strike, while the COB called an indefinite general strike. Shortly afterwards Sánchez de Lozada agreed to hold discussions with representatives of some of the indigenous and peasant groups (although not with the COB) and subsequently secured their support for the law by making a number of significant concessions. The most important of these was the modification of the proposed role of the Agrarian Superintendency, such that it would not be authorized to rule on issues of land ownership. The law was approved by Congress later that month.

Dissatisfaction with the continued privatization of major industrial companies in Bolivia, particularly in the mining sector, resulted in further unrest in late 1996. In mid-December a group of miners occupied a pit at Amayapampa in northern Potosí to protest at the mine's Canadian operators, who, they alleged, had failed to pay local taxes and had caused damage to the environment. When troops arrived at the site to remove the miners 10 protesters were killed and 50 others injured in ensuing violent clashes. The incident provoked outrage throughout the country and was the subject of an investigation by the Organization of American States' Inter-American Human Rights Commission in early 1997. A similar occupation by miners opposed to private development of the Cerro Rico site in Potosí took place in January 1997.

A total of 10 presidential candidates were presented to contest the elections scheduled for June 1997. The MNR confirmed Juan Carlos Durán as its candidate (owing to the fact that Sánchez de Lozada was ineligible for re-election), the MIR presented Jaime Paz Zamora, while Gen. (retd) Hugo Bánzer Suárez stated his intention to make a fourth attempt to gain the presidency by democratic means, on behalf of the ADN. The sudden death in March 1997 of Carlos Palenque Aviles, founder, leader and presidential candidate of Condepa, was viewed as representing a significant reversal for Bolivia's populist parties and their efforts to challenge the domination of the country's traditional political organizations. He was replaced by Remedios Loza, an established figure in the party, who enjoyed particular support among the largely indigenous population of El Alto. An often acrimonious election campaign was characterized by expressions of increasing discontent with the Government's radical economic reform programme and repeated criticism of Bánzer, who was held responsible for numerous human rights abuses during his dictatorship in the 1970s.

At the election on 1 June 1997 Bánzer secured 22.3% of the total votes, Durán won 17.7%, Paz Zamora received 16.7% and Ivo Kuljis (of the UCS) and Remedios Loza won 15.9% and 15.8% respectively. At legislative elections held concurrently the ADN won a total of 46 congressional seats, the MIR won 31, the MNR secured 29 and the UCS and Condepa secured 23 and 20 seats respectively. The ADN subsequently concluded a pact with the MIR, the UCS and Condepa to form a congressional majority. The inclusion of the MIR in the coalition prompted concern among some observers, as it was feared that previous allegations of corruption and of involvement in the illegal drugs trade against the party and, in particular, against Paz Zamora (see above) would jeopardize the country's ability to attract international aid and investment. However, the grouping remained, and on 5 August Bánzer was elected President for a newly-extended term of five years with 118 congressional votes. The new administration pledged to consolidate the free-market reforms introduced by the previous Government and sought to assure the USA that the alliance with the MIR would not compromise its commitment to combating the illegal drugs trade.

In late August 1997 the newly-elected Government signed a financial co-operation agreement with the USA for continued action to combat the illegal drugs trade. The agreement, which provided finance for the implementation of eradication programmes, was criticized for its emphasis on the suppression of coca cultivation rather than on the development of alternative crops. On a visit to the Cochabamba region in October to assess the progress of the coca eradication programme, the head of the US anti-narcotics policy, Gen. Barry McCaffrey, was declared *persona non grata* by five coca growers' federations. The previous Government's commitment to destroy 7,000 ha of coca plantations during 1997 in order to keep Bolivia's 'certification' status led to concern that violence might erupt if the new Government felt under pressure to implement an aggressive eradication programme in order to meet this target (particularly as only 3,600 ha had been destroyed by September of that year). Moreover, many observers believed the policy to be ineffective, as, despite the provision of US finance worth US $500m. since 1990 to eradicate the crop, there had been no net reduction in coca production in Bolivia. There was also evidence that compensation payments given to coca growers for the destruction of their crops had been used to replant coca in more remote areas.

In September 1990, following the completion of a 32-day, 650-km march of protest by 700 indigenous Indians from the town of Trinidad, in Beni, to the capital, La Paz, the Government issued four decrees in an unprecedented act of recognition of Indian land rights. Besides acknowledging as Indian territory more than 1.6m. ha of tropical rainforest in northern Bolivia, a multi-party commission, comprising government and indigenous Indian representatives, was to be established in order to draft a new Law for Indigenous Indians of the East and Amazonia.

Bolivia's relations with its neighbours Peru and Chile, in particular, have been dominated by the long-standing issue of possible Bolivian access to the Pacific Ocean. An agreement with Peru, completed in 1993, granted Bolivia free access from the border town of Desaguadero, Bolivia, to the Pacific port of Ilo, Peru, until 2091. Bolivia's desire to regain sovereign access to the sea, however, continued to impair relations with Chile in 1997, when the Bolivian Government repeatedly requested that discussions on the subject take place and sought Peru's assistance as a mediator in the dispute. In February Bolivia's Minister of Foreign Affairs directly accused Gen. Augusto Pinochet Ugarte, the Commander-in-Chief of the Chilean Army, of being the main obstacle in Bolivia's quest for access to the sea. Moreover, talks which aimed to improve trade arrangements between the two countries were suspended in March and again in May following failure to reach agreement. Relations deteriorated further in late 1997 when the Bolivian Government filed an official protest note to Chile regarding its failure to remove land-mines along the common border (planted during the 1970s). Bolivia's decision to raise the issue at a UN meeting provoked strong criticism from the Chilean Government, which argued that it was a matter for the two countries alone and, as such, should be discussed at a bilateral level.

In November 1994 an agreement to provide a waterway linking Bolivia with the Atlantic coast in Uruguay was concluded. The project was expected to take three years to complete at a cost of some US $7,000m.

Government

Legislative power is held by the bicameral Congress, comprising a Senate (27 members) and a Chamber of Deputies (130 members). Both houses are elected for a four-year term by universal adult suffrage. Executive power is vested in the President and the Cabinet, which is appointed by the President. The President is also directly elected for five years (extended from four years in 1997). If no candidate gains an absolute majority of votes, the President is chosen by Congress. The country is divided, for administrative purposes, into nine departments, each of which is governed by a prefect, appointed by the President.

Defence

Military service, for one year, is selective. In August 1997 the armed forces numbered 33,500 men, of whom the army had 25,000 (including 18,000 conscripts), the air force 4,000, and the navy 4,500. Expenditure on defence by the central Government in 1995 was 572.9m. bolivianos, equivalent to 8.4% of total spending.

Economic Affairs

In 1995, according to World Bank estimates, Bolivia's gross national product (GNP), measured at average 1993–95 prices, totalled US $5,905m., equivalent to about $800 per head. In the period 1985–95 real GNP per head grew by an average of 1.7% per year. During the same period the population increased by an annual average of 2.3%. Bolivia's gross domestic product (GDP) increased, in real terms, by an annual average of 3.8% in 1990–95, by 3.9% in 1995 and by an estimated 4.0% in 1996.

Agriculture (including forestry and fishing) contributed 17.3% of GDP in 1994. In 1996 an estimated 44.1% of the economically active population were employed in agriculture. Wood accounted for 5.6% of export earnings in 1995. The principal cash crops are soybeans, sugar, chestnuts and coffee. Beef and hides are also important exports. In the period 1980–92 agricultural GDP increased at an average annual rate of 1.8%; output from the sector increased by some 4.5% in 1994.

Industry (including mining, manufacturing, construction and power) provided 31.1% of GDP in 1994. In 1990 12.8% of the working population were employed in industry. During the period 1980–92 industrial GDP declined at an average annual rate of 0.8%.

Mining (including petroleum exploration) contributed 10.4% of GDP in 1994 and employed about 1% of the working population in that year. Investment in mineral exploitation increased 10-fold between 1991 and 1996; private interests invested a total of US $45m. in exploration activity in 1996. Zinc, tin, silver, gold, lead and antimony are the major mineral exports. Tungsten and copper continue to be mined. Exports of zinc and tin earned US $151m. and US $90m., respectively, in 1995. Minerals accounted for some 40% of legal exports in 1993–95.

In 1994 manufacturing accounted for 14.6% of GDP. In 1990 7.1% of the working population were employed in manufacturing. The GDP of this sector declined during 1980–92 at an average annual rate of 0.1%. Measured by the value of output, the principal branches of manufacturing in 1994 were food products (providing 31.8% of the total), petroleum refineries (23.2%), beverages (8.7%) and jewellery and related articles (6.8%).

Energy is derived principally from petroleum and natural gas. In 1994 production of crude petroleum increased by 15% to 9.4m. barrels. Petroleum reserves at mid-1986 were estimated to be 151m. barrels. Earnings from exports of petroleum and petroleum products accounted for 5.1% of the total in 1995, compared with 1.3% in the previous year. Exports of natural gas accounted for 26.1% of total export earnings in 1991, but only 7.8% in 1995. Reserves of natural gas were estimated at 4,500,000m. cu ft at the end of 1995, in which year exports of the commodity earned US $150m. Energy production increased during the period 1980–92 at an average annual rate of 0.1%.

The services sector accounted for 51.6% of GDP in 1994. During the period 1980–92 the GDP of this sector increased at an average annual rate of 0.2%.

In 1995 Bolivia recorded a visible trade deficit of US $182.3m., and there was a deficit of $328.4m. on the current account of the balance of payments. In that year the main sources of imports were the USA (21.9%), Brazil (12.6%), Japan (12.4%) and Argentina (8.5%). The USA, Argentina, Peru and the United Kingdom were the major recipients of Bolivian exports in 1995 (31.5%, 13.6%, 13.7% and 11.0% respectively). The principal imports in that year included industrial materials and machinery, transport equipment and consumer goods. The principal legal exports were metallic minerals, natural gas, soybeans and wood. In 1990 government sources estimated that around US $600m. (almost equivalent to annual earnings from official exports) were absorbed annually into the economy as a result of the illegal trade in coca and its derivatives (mainly cocaine).

In 1996 Bolivia's budget deficit amounted to 857m. bolivianos. Bolivia's total external debt at the end of 1995 was US $5,266m., of which $4,452m. was long-term public debt. The cost of debt-servicing in that year was equivalent to 28.9% of the total value of exports of goods and services. In 1985–93 the average annual rate of inflation was 33.3%. Consumer prices increased by an average of 7.9% in 1994, by 10.2% in 1995 and by 12.4% in 1996. In 1993 an estimated 6% of the labour force were unemployed.

In 1990 the Government announced plans to undertake a major programme of privatization, whereby 100 of the country's 157 state-owned companies would be sold to private interests, over a period of five years, in an attempt to give a much-required stimulus to the economy. However, government plans encountered strong resistance from opposition parties and from trade unions, which were opposed to overseas ownership of major sectors of the economy, particularly the mining industry. By the end of 1993 only 15 enterprises had been transferred to the private sector, earning US $4.5m. A public-sector capitalization programme, which aimed to attract more private-sector involvement in the country's principal industries by selling a 50% controlling share in several state-owned companies to private investors, began in early 1995.

In 1992 Bolivia signed a preliminary agreement with Brazil for the construction of a 3,000-km pipeline to carry natural gas from Bolivia to southern Brazil. The project, which was expected to cost US $1,800m. and was the largest of its kind in South America, was finalized, following considerable delay, in mid-1996. The pipeline was expected to be completed in December 1998. Furthermore, the continued success of exploratory missions in locating new sources of petroleum and natural gas, in particular, resulted in a series of projects in 1996 (including schemes to export electricity to southern and western areas of Brazil and an agreement to supply natural gas to Paraguay), which aimed to develop Bolivia's potential as one of the region's most important energy-producing countries. A fresh round of leases for natural gas exploration were offered in mid-1997.

Official development assistance was equivalent to some 10% of GNP annually in the mid-1990s. Negotiations in late 1994 with a group of industrialized countries resulted in the provision of aid and credit of some US $1,000m. for Bolivia over four years. International donors, similarly, pledged US $650m. to support Bolivia's economic reform programme in early 1997. The country's severe debt burden is widely acknowledged to be a major factor in inhibiting economic growth, and in recognition of this the World Bank and the IMF approved a debt-relief package worth US $579m. (under its Highly-Indebted Poor Countries' Initiative), which was to be released in mid-1998.

In May 1991 Bolivia was one of five Andean Pact countries to sign the Caracas Declaration providing the foundation for a common market. In October 1992 Bolivia officially joined the Andean free-trade area, removing tariff barriers to imports from Colombia, Ecuador and Venezuela. Bolivia also agreed to sign a free-trade accord with Mexico in September 1994. In late 1996 Bolivia concluded a free-trade agreement with Mercosur (see p. 239), equivalent to associate membership of the organization, with effect from January 1997.

Bolivia is a member of the Andean Community (see p. 106), and in 1989 the Andean Social Development Fund was established. The country is also a member of the Organization of American States (OAS, see p. 219), and of the Latin American Integration Association (ALADI, see p. 261). Bolivia became the 97th contracting party to GATT (which was superseded by the World Trade Organization, WTO, in 1995—see p. 244) in 1989.

Social Welfare

There are benefits for unemployment, accident, sickness, old age and death. In 1987 there was one physician per 2,124 inhabitants and one hospital bed for every 686 inhabitants. A privately-managed national pension scheme was established in

1995, as a result of the Government's capitalization programme, in which a 50% share in several state-owned industries was sold to private-sector investors while the remaining 50% was invested in a pension fund for all Bolivian citizens. In May 1997 some 300,000 Bolivians over the age of 65 years began to receive a bonus payment (bono solidaridad) of US $248 from the pension fund. Of total expenditure by the central Government in 1995, 420.6m. bolivianos (6.2%) was for health, and a further 1,085.3m. bolivianos (16.0%) for social security and welfare.

Education

Primary education, beginning at six years of age and lasting for eight years, is officially compulsory and is available free of charge. Secondary education, which is not compulsory, begins at 14 years of age and lasts for up to four years. In 1990 the total enrolment at primary and secondary schools was equivalent to 77% of the school-age population (81% of boys; 73% of girls). In that year enrolment at primary schools included an estimated 95% of children in the relevant age-group (99% of boys; 90% of girls), while the comparable ratio for secondary enrolment was only 37% (40% of boys; 34% of girls). There are eight state universities and two private universities. At the 1992 census the average rate of adult illiteracy was 19.9% (males 11.8%; females 27.5%). Expenditure on education by the central Government in 1995 was 1,313.3m. bolivianos, representing 19.3% of total spending.

Public Holidays

1998: 1 January (New Year), 10 February (Oruro only), 10 April (Good Friday), 15 April (Tarija only), 1 May (Labour Day), 25 May (Sucre only), 11 June (Corpus Christi), 16 July (La Paz only), 6 August (Independence), 14 September (Cochabamba only), 24 September (Santa Cruz only), 1 October (Pando only), 12 October (Columbus Day), 1 November (All Saints' Day and Potosí), 10 November (Oruro only), 18 November (Beni only), 25 December (Christmas).

1999: 1 January (New Year), 10 February (Oruro only), 2 April (Good Friday), 15 April (Tarija only), 1 May (Labour Day), 25 May (Sucre only), 3 June (Corpus Christi), 16 July (La Paz only), 6 August (Independence), 14 September (Cochabamba only), 24 September (Santa Cruz only), 1 October (Pando only), 11 October (Columbus Day), 1 November (All Saints' Day and Potosí), 10 November (Oruro only), 18 November (Beni only), 25 December (Christmas).

Weights and Measures

The metric system is officially in force, but various old Spanish measures are also used.

Statistical Survey

Sources (unless otherwise indicated): Instituto Nacional de Estadística, Plaza Mario Guzmán Aspiazu No. 1, Casilla 6129, La Paz; tel. (2) 36-7443; Banco Central de Bolivia, Ayacucho esq. Mercado, Casilla 3118, La Paz; tel. (2) 37-4151; telex 2286; fax (2) 39-2398.

Area and Population

AREA, POPULATION AND DENSITY

Area (sq km)	
Land	1,084,391
Inland water	14,190
Total	1,098,581*
Population (census results)†	
29 September 1976	4,613,486
3 June 1992	
Males	3,171,265
Females	3,249,527
Total	6,420,792
Population (official estimates at mid-year)	
1994	7,237,000
1995	7,413,834
1996	7,588,000
Density (per sq km) at mid-1996	6.9

* 424,164 sq miles.

† Figures exclude adjustment for underenumeration. This was estimated at 6.99% in 1976 and at 6.92% in 1992.

DEPARTMENTS (1992 census)*

	Area (sq km)	Population	Density (per sq km)	Capital
Beni	213,564	276,174	1.3	Trinidad
Chuquisaca	51,524	453,756	8.8	Sucre
Cochabamba	55,631	1,110,205	20.0	Cochabamba
La Paz	133,985	1,900,786	14.2	La Paz
Oruro	53,588	340,114	6.3	Oruro
Pando	63,827	38,072	0.6	Cobija
Potosí	118,218	645,889	5.5	Potosí
Santa Cruz	370,621	1,364,389	3.7	Santa Cruz de la Sierra
Tarija	37,623	291,407	7.7	Tarija
Total	1,098,581	6,420,792	5.8	

* Excluding adjustment for underenumeration.

PRINCIPAL TOWNS (estimated population at mid-1993)

La Paz (administrative capital)	784,976
Santa Cruz de la Sierra	767,260
Cochabamba	448,756
El Alto	446,189
Oruro	201,831
Sucre (legal capital)	144,994
Potosí	123,327

Source: UN, *Demographic Yearbook.*

BIRTHS AND DEATHS (UN estimates, annual averages)

	1980–85	1985–90	1990–95
Birth rate (per 1,000)	38.2	36.6	35.7
Death rate (per 1,000)	13.5	11.5	10.2

Expectation of life (UN estimates, years at birth, 1990–95): 59.4 (males 57.7, females 61.0).

Source: UN, *World Population Prospects: The 1994 Revision.*

ECONOMICALLY ACTIVE POPULATION
(mid-year estimates, '000 persons aged 10 years and over)

	1988	1989	1990
Agriculture, hunting, forestry and fishing	838.3	787.5	873.4
Mining and quarrying	45.6	42.9	47.6
Manufacturing	125.1	117.5	130.3
Electricity, gas and water	8.7	8.1	9.0
Construction	47.8	44.9	49.8
Trade, restaurants and hotels	144.2	135.4	150.2
Transport, storage and communications	130.0	122.2	135.5
Financing, insurance, real estate and business services	15.0	14.1	15.7
Community, social and personal services	414.6	389.4	431.9
Total employed	1,769.4	1,662.0	1,843.4
Unemployed	388.4	443.2	433.4
Total labour force	2,157.8	2,105.2	2,276.8
Males	1,647.5	1.615.6	1,741.8
Females	510.3	489.6	535.1

1992 census (persons aged 7 years and over): Total labour force 2,530,409 (males 1,544,105; females 986,304).

Source: ILO, *Yearbook of Labour Statistics*.

Agriculture

PRINCIPAL CROPS ('000 metric tons)

	1994	1995	1996
Wheat	85	125	92
Rice (paddy)	247	263	296
Barley	64	59	64
Maize	537	521	581
Sorghum	50	104	105
Potatoes	632	642	725
Cassava (Manioc)	293	296	296*
Other roots and tubers	103	103	102
Soya beans	710	887	858
Groundnuts (in shell)	11	10	12
Sunflower seeds	28	58	33
Cottonseed	16	17	27
Cotton (lint)	11	17	13
Sugar cane	3,450	3,697	3,807
Oranges	94	92	93
Lemons and limes	59	60	61
Other citrus fruits	73	75	77
Papayas	20	20*	20*
Apricots	23	22	19*
Peaches and nectarines	36	35	35*
Grapes	22	20	21
Watermelons	19	19*	19*
Bananas†	279	273	279
Plantains†	150	150	150
Coffee (green)	19	20	23
Natural rubber	9	10	10

* FAO estimate. † Unofficial figures.

Source: FAO, *Production Yearbook*.

LIVESTOCK ('000 head, year ending September)

	1994	1995	1996
Horses*	322	322	322
Mules*	81	81	81
Asses*	631	631	631
Cattle	5,912	5,996	6,118
Pigs	2,331	2,405	2,482
Sheep	7,686	7,884	8,039
Goats	1,479	1,496	1,496*
Poultry (million)	51	56	56*

* FAO estimate(s).

Source: FAO, *Production Yearbook*.

LIVESTOCK PRODUCTS ('000 metric tons)

	1994	1995	1996
Beef and veal	136	140	143
Mutton and lamb	14	14	14
Goat meat*	5	6	6
Pig meat*	60	62	62
Poultry meat	89	96	98
Cows' milk	139	142	142*
Sheep's milk*	29	29	29
Goats' milk*	11	11	11
Cheese*	7	7	7
Hen eggs	61*	68†	68*
Wool: greasy*	8	8	8
scoured*	4	4	4
Cattle hides (fresh)*	16	16	17
Sheepskins (fresh)*	5	5	5

* FAO estimate(s). † Unofficial figure.

Source: FAO, *Production Yearbook*.

Forestry

ROUNDWOOD REMOVALS ('000 cubic metres, excl. bark)

	1992	1993	1994
Sawlogs, veneer logs and logs for sleepers	305	443*	443*
Pulpwood	364	370	444
Other industrial wood	2	8	18
Fuel wood*	1,263	1,292	1,322
Total	1,934	2,113	2,227

* FAO estimate(s).

Source: FAO, *Yearbook of Forest Products*.

SAWNWOOD PRODUCTION ('000 cubic metres, incl. railway sleepers)

	1992	1993	1994
Coniferous (softwood)*	10	10	10
Broadleaved (hardwood)	220	258	350
Total	230	268	360

* FAO estimates.

Source: FAO, *Yearbook of Forest Products*.

Fishing

('000 metric tons, live weight)

	1993	1994	1995
Total catch	6.2	6.0	6.3

Source: FAO, *Yearbook of Fishery Statistics*.

Mining*

(metric tons, unless otherwise indicated)

	1992	1993	1994
Tin	16,516	18,634	16,027
Lead	20,002	21,220	19,678
Zinc	143,936	122,638	100,751
Copper	101	94	79
Tungsten (Wolfram)	1,073	330	583
Antimony	6,022	4,155	7,050
Silver	282	333	352
Gold	4.7	16.4	12.8

Petroleum ('000 metric tons): 1,029 in 1991; 1,029 in 1992; 969 in 1993.
Natural gas (petajoules): 100 in 1991; 108 in 1992; 107 in 1993.

(Source: UN, *Industrial Commodity Statistics Yearbook*).

* Figures for metallic minerals refer to the metal content of ores.

Industry

SELECTED PRODUCTS (metric tons, unless otherwise indicated)

	1990	1991*	1992*
Flour	124,846	143,395	172,000
Cement	560,446	588,468	63,000
Refined sugar	257,724	218,831	n.a.
Coffee	23,979	24,601	n.a.
Beer ('000 hectolitres)	1,031	1,278	1,333
Alcohol ('000 litres)	19,185	19,500	n.a.
Electric energy (million kWh)	2,126	2,131	2,412

* Provisional.

Tin (primary metal, metric tons): 14,507 in 1991; 13,051 in 1992; 18,551 in 1993; 19,469 in 1994 (Source: UNCTAD, *International Tin Statistics*).

Finance

CURRENCY AND EXCHANGE RATES

Monetary Units

100 centavos = 1 boliviano (B).

Sterling and Dollar Equivalents (30 September 1997)

£1 sterling = 8.537 bolivianos;
US $1 = 5.285 bolivianos;
100 bolivianos = £11.71 = $18.92.

Average Exchange Rate (bolivianos per US $)

1994 4.6205
1995 4.8003
1996 5.0746

BUDGET (million bolivianos)*

Revenue†	1993	1994	1995
Taxation	2,613.9	2,960.2	3,476.9
Taxes on income, profits and capital gains	205.7	137.0	132.1
Social security contributions	286.3	279.2	342.9
Taxes on property	332.5	374.2	536.5
Sales taxes	1,110.1	1,426.9	1,552.7
Excises	398.5	405.9	514.2
Import duties	244.5	301.5	349.8
Entrepreneurial and property income	1,008.3	1,129.6	1,293.6
Administrative fees, charges, etc.	206.1	237.5	303.9
Other current revenue	134.7	34.2	78.8
Capital revenue	29.6	84.4	102.9
Total	3,992.6	4,445.9	5,256.1

Expenditure‡	1993	1994	1995
General public services	833.2	797.3	950.6
Defence	482.0	527.0	572.9
Public order and safety	347.9	392.5	549.1
Education	1,000.3	1,181.2	1,313.3
Health	386.0	454.0	420.6
Social security and welfare	879.9	935.4	1,085.3
Housing and community amenities	118.5	41.0	54.1
Recreational, cultural and religious affairs and services	25.2	27.9	33.4
Economic services	1,200.4	1,157.5	1,094.6
Fuel and energy	86.5	27.9	5.7
Agriculture, forestry and fishing	101.1	65.2	70.1
Mining and mineral resources, manufacturing and construction	38.2	19.6	27.9
Transport and communications	768.9	859.2	835.0
Other purposes	603.1	886.2	727.7
Total	5,876.5	6,400.0	6,801.6
Current§	4,554.0	5,023.9	5,498.6
Capital	1,322.5	1,376.1	1,303.1

* Figures refer to the transactions of central government units covered by the General Budget, plus the operations of other units (government agencies and social security institutions) with their own budgets.

† Excluding grants received (million bolivianos): 1,236.7 in 1993; 871.7 in 1994; 646.8 in 1995.

‡ Excluding lending minus repayments (million bolivianos): –170.1 in 1993; –176.5 in 1994; 149.7 in 1995.

§ Including interest payments (million bolivianos): 450.3 in 1993; 610.3 in 1994; 727.7 in 1995.

Source: IMF, *Government Finance Statistics Yearbook.*

INTERNATIONAL RESERVES (US $ million at 31 December)*

	1994	1995	1996
IMF special drawing rights	24.8	40.0	38.5
Reserve position in IMF	13.0	13.2	12.8
Foreign exchange	413.2	606.8	903.7
Total	451.0	660.0	955.0

* Excluding gold reserves ($39.6 million at 31 December 1993).

Source: IMF, *International Financial Statistics.*

MONEY SUPPLY (million bolivianos at 31 December)

	1994	1995	1996
Currency outside banks	1,406	1,694	1,802
Demand deposits at commercial banks	1,826	2,219	2,957
Total money	3,232	3,913	4,759

Source: IMF, *International Financial Statistics.*

COST OF LIVING

(Consumer Price Index for urban areas; base: 1991 = 100)

	1992	1993	1994
Food	114.5	122.2	133.2
Fuel and light	107.5	121.0	132.4
Clothing	111.8	120.4	127.9
Rent	105.8	111.1	115.3
All items (incl. others)	113.0	122.6	132.2

Source: ILO, *Yearbook of Labour Statistics.*

1995: Food 149.2; All items 145.7 (Source: UN, *Monthly Bulletin of Statistics*).

NATIONAL ACCOUNTS

Expenditure on the Gross Domestic Product
(million bolivianos at current prices)

	1993	1994	1995
Government final consumption expenditure	3,490	4,076	4,497
Private final consumption expenditure	19,676	21,852	24,504
Increase in stocks	–1	6	52
Gross fixed capital formation	4,504	4,796	6,469
Total domestic expenditure	27,669	30,730	35,522
Exports of goods and services	5,326	6,557	7,246
Less Imports of goods and services	7,357	8,183	9,297
GDP in purchasers' values	25,637	29,104	33,470
GDP at constant 1990 prices	17,295	18,158	18,824

Source: IMF, *International Financial Statistics.*

Gross Domestic Product by Economic Activity
(estimates, '000 bolivianos at constant 1990 prices)

	1992	1993	1994
Agriculture, hunting, forestry and fishing	2,957,453	3,057,709	3,205,503
Mining and quarrying	1,698,855	1,813,731	1,928,325
Manufacturing	2,476,884	2,585,874	2,711,699
Electricity, gas and water	290,389	314,059	354,245
Construction	719,035	747,725	760,585
Trade	1,929,848	1,996,057	2,058,622
Restaurants and hotels	513,474	531,970	554,111
Transport, storage and communications	1,963,423	2,077,747	2,167,303
Finance, insurance, real estate and business services	1,975,770	2,067,893	2,133,445
Government services	1,660,303	1,693,929	1,738,010
Other community, social and personal services	769,578	789,886	804,506
Other producers	96,339	98,268	100,379
Sub-total	17,051,351	17,774,846	18,516,734
Import duties	1,375,828	1,409,437	1,492,101
Less Imputed bank service charge	352,167	394,122	421,989
Total	18,075,012	18,790,161	19,586,846

BALANCE OF PAYMENTS (US $ million)

	1993	1994	1995
Exports of goods f.o.b.	715.5	985.1	1,041.4
Imports of goods f.o.b.	–1,111.7	–1,121.9	–1,223.7
Trade balance	–396.2	–136.8	–182.3
Exports of services	181.4	230.7	198.0
Imports of services	–321.7	–338.2	–349.8
Balance on goods and services	–536.5	–244.3	–334.1
Other income received	9.2	10.3	28.3
Other income paid	–215.1	–209.6	–254.4
Balance on goods, services and income	–742.4	–443.6	–560.2
Current transfers received	241.0	230.4	235.6
Current transfers paid	–4.1	–5.2	–3.8
Current balance	–505.5	–218.4	–328.4
Capital account (net)	1.0	1.2	2.0
Direct investment abroad	2.0	2.2	–2.0
Direct investment from abroad	145.2	145.0	392.6
Other investment liabilities	41.6	67.9	80.7
Net errors and omissions	221.7	–90.4	–69.5
Overall balance	–94.0	–92.5	75.4

Source: IMF, *International Financial Statistics.*

External Trade

PRINCIPAL COMMODITIES (distribution by SITC, US $ '000)

Imports c.i.f.	1993	1994	1995
Food and live animals	99,030	112,395	124,577
Cereals and cereal preparations	58,076	63,858	70,205
Wheat (including spelt) and meslin, unmilled	32,244	42,385	42,928
Durum wheat, unmilled	30,314	32,769	26,132
Crude materials (inedible) except fuels	40,011	43,499	51,175
Mineral fuels, lubricants, etc.	57,355	60,441	63,768
Petroleum, petroleum products, etc.	56,642	59,915	63,728
Refined petroleum products	52,595	56,989	58,306
Gas oils (distillate fuels)	24,898	30,053	36,081
Chemicals and related products	127,225	152,714	185,488
Essential oils, perfume materials and cleansing preparations	19,412	28,503	23,678
Artificial resins, plastic materials, etc.	24,551	29,590	41,513
Products of polymerization, etc.	20,928	24,598	33,665
Basic manufactures	187,221	203,221	216,809
Paper, paperboard, etc.	23,109	26,387	38,696
Textile yarn, fabrics, etc.	21,991	28,392	28,753
Iron and steel	58,871	59,703	60,990
Tubes, pipes and fittings	26,244	24,155	15,110
Machinery and transport equipment	553,479	515,972	645,499
Power-generating machinery and equipment	32,715	18,787	50,284
Machinery specialized for particular industries	87,009	90,731	107,377
Civil engineering and contractors' plant and equipment	30,016	28,557	43,876
General industrial machinery, equipment and parts	59,872	62,556	64,803
Telecommunications and sound equipment	42,721	26,852	43,645
Other electrical machinery, apparatus, etc.	46,534	36,091	50,841
Road vehicles and parts*	183,432	249,390	234,190
Passenger motor cars (excl. buses)	80,511	109,709	100,072
Motor vehicles for the transport of goods, etc.	57,477	82,734	82,263
Goods vehicles	52,736	78,854	75,875
Other road motor vehicles	23,861	31,275	26,210
Other transport equipment and parts*	77,747	11,054	69,821
Aircraft, associated equipment and parts*	77,374	8,628	68,421
Miscellaneous manufactured articles	84,361	83,425	92,451
Total (incl. others)	1,176,941	1,196,345	1,396,260

* Excluding tyres, engines and electrical parts.

Exports f.o.b.	1993	1994	1995
Food and live animals	95,542	157,690	113,616
Cereals and cereal preparations	29,273	28,769	4,757
Vegetables and fruit	18,922	28,847	29,879
Sugar, sugar preparations and honey	15,781	45,506	16,968
Sugar and honey	15,727	45,486	16,766
Refined sugars (solid)	15,727	45,430	16,545
Feeding-stuff for animals	24,958	31,046	39,346
Oil-cake and other residues from the extraction of vegetable oils	23,837	30,998	39,241
Oil-cake and residues from soya beans	23,537	30,882	38,507
Crude materials (inedible) except fuels	277,058	329,889	415,289
Oil seeds and oleaginous fruit	18,889	44,244	69,509
Soya beans	18,182	43,174	46,716
Cork and wood	49,711	78,548	66,115
Simply worked wood and railway sleepers	49,649	78,548	66,057
Metalliferous ores and metal scrap	189,559	180,852	240,199
Base metal ores and concentrates	141,058	132,709	182,758
Zinc ores and concentrates	119,508	105,334	151,346
Precious metal ores and concentrates	47,759	48,011	57,374
Mineral fuels, lubricants etc.	103,045	107,047	152,875
Petroleum, petroleum products, etc.	12,167	15,144	60,176
Gas (natural and manufactured)	90,621	91,621	92,407
Petroleum gases and other gaseous hydrocarbons	90,203	91,621	92,407
Animal and vegetable oils, fats and waxes	5,858	21,613	35,559
Fixed vegetable oils and fats	5,858	21,561	35,476
Soya bean oil	5,658	20,451	34,679
Basic manufactures	136,822	157,891	154,103
Non-ferrous metals	115,422	133,171	128,022
Tin and tin alloys	96,004	110,032	112,926
Machinery and transport equipment	16,266	28,714	38,134
Miscellaneous manufactured articles	94,337	190,360	117,879
Jewellery, goldsmiths' and silversmiths' wares, etc.	72,879	164,314	90,927
Non-monetary gold (excl. ores and concentrates)	71,612	119,088	130,802
Total (incl. others)	808,939	1,124,232	1,181,213

Source: UN, *International Trade Statistics Yearbook*.

PRINCIPAL TRADING PARTNERS (US $ '000)*

Imports c.i.f.	1993	1994	1995
Argentina	114,731	117,483	117,416
Belgium-Luxembourg	4,632	6,677	54,727
Brazil	149,914	178,613	174,202
Canada	6,679	10,591	22,418
Chile	88,545	93,962	104,786
Colombia	15,764	22,729	22,947
France	15,860	9,679	13,453
Germany	66,441	59,259	69,937
Italy	23,241	16,297	36,606
Japan	128,865	181,826	171,699
Korea, Republic	8,971	14,453	18,069
Mexico	12,820	16,657	19,457
Panama	11,872	10,923	6,379
Peru	54,104	64,801	73,042
Spain	36,605	16,869	19,314
Sweden	26,589	32,380	38,752
United Kingdom	67,240	13,053	26,253
USA	248,335	222,291	303,920
Venezuela	6,034	12,621	10,930
Total (incl. others)	1,159,340	1,182,407	1,387,221

Exports f.o.b.	1993	1994	1995
Argentina	126,793	160,110	142,657
Belgium-Luxembourg	48,750	26,592	40,392
Brazil	22,208	35,369	23,441
Chile	14,857	19,202	25,834
Colombia	36,910	63,940	64,368
Ecuador	6,874	14,562	7,346
Germany	11,901	19,242	23,154
Peru	79,206	122,916	144,377
Switzerland	2,831	14,497	59,641
United Kingdom	114,115	102,072	115,915
USA	214,372	360,544	330,523
Total (incl. others)	737,326	1,005,144	1,050,411

* Imports by country of provenance; exports by country of last consignment. Figures exclude trade in gold.

Source: UN, *International Trade Statistics Yearbook*.

Transport

RAILWAYS (traffic)

	1992	1993	1994
Passenger-kilometres (million)	334	288	276
Freight ton-kilometres (million)	710	692	782

Source: UN, *Statistical Yearbook*.

ROAD TRAFFIC (motor vehicles in use at 31 December)

	1994	1995	1996
Passenger cars	198,734	213,666	223,829
Buses	18,884	19,627	20,322
Lorries and vans	108,214	114,357	118,214
Tractors	9	9	10
Motorcycles	62,725	64,936	66,113

Source: IRF, *World Road Statistics*.

CIVIL AVIATION (traffic on scheduled services)

	1992	1993	1994
Kilometres flown (million)	11	11	14
Passengers carried ('000)	1,214	1,117	1,175
Passenger-km (million)	1,069	1,092	1,139
Freight ton-km (million)	107	120	151

Source: UN, *Statistical Yearbook*.

Tourism

	1992	1993	1994
Arrivals at hotels	244,583	268,968	319,578
Receipts (US $ million)	107	115	135

Source: UN, *Statistical Yearbook*.

Communications Media

	1992	1993	1994
Radio receivers ('000 in use)	4,610	4,725	4,850
Television receivers ('000 in use)	775	800	820
Telephones ('000 main lines in use)	193	234	n.a.
Mobile cellular telephones (subscribers)	1,556	2,651	4,060

Daily newspapers (1992): 16.

Sources: UNESCO, *Statistical Yearbook*; UN, *Statistical Yearbook*.

Education

(1990)

	Institutions	Teachers	Students
Pre-primary	2,294*	2,895	121,132
Primary	12,639†	51,763	1,278,775
Secondary	n.a.	12,434	219,232
Higher	n.a.	4,261‡	140,890§

* 1988. † 1987. ‡ 1991 (universities and equivalent institutions). § 1989

Source: UNESCO, *Statistical Yearbook*.

Directory

The Constitution

Bolivia became an independent republic in 1825 and received its first Constitution in November 1826. Since that date a number of new Constitutions have been promulgated. Following the *coup d'état* of November 1964, the Constitution of 1947 was revived. Under its provisions, executive power is vested in the President, who chairs the Cabinet. According to the revised Constitution, the President is elected by direct suffrage for a five-year term (extended from four years in 1997) and is not eligible for immediate re-election. In the event of the President's death or failure to assume office, the Vice-President or, failing the Vice-President, the President of the Senate becomes interim Head of State.

The President has power to appoint members of the Cabinet, diplomatic representatives and archbishops and bishops from a panel proposed by the Senate. The President is responsible for the conduct of foreign affairs and is also empowered to issue decrees, and initiate legislation by special messages to Congress.

Congress consists of a Senate (27 members) and a Chamber of Deputies (130 members). Congress meets annually and its ordinary sessions last only 90 working days, which may be extended to 120. Each of the nine departments (La Paz, Chuquisaca, Oruro, Beni, Santa Cruz, Potosí, Tarija, Cochabamba and Pando), into which the country is divided for administrative purposes, elects three senators. Members of both houses are elected for four years.

The supreme administrative, political and military authority in each department is vested in a prefect appointed by the President. The sub-divisions of each department, known as provinces, are administered by sub-prefects. The provinces are further divided into cantons. There are 94 provinces and some 1,000 cantons. The capital of each department has its autonomous municipal council and controls its own revenue and expenditure.

Public order, education and roads are under national control.

A decree issued, in July 1952, conferred the franchise on all persons who had reached the age of 21 years, whether literate or illiterate. Previously the franchise had been restricted to literate persons. (The voting age for married persons was lowered to 18 years at the 1989 elections.)

The death penalty was restored, in October 1971, for terrorism, kidnapping and crimes against government and security personnel. In 1981 its scope was extended to drugs trafficking.

The Government

HEAD OF STATE

President: HUGO BÁNZER SUÁREZ (ADN) (took office 6 August 1997).

Vice-President: JORGE FERNANDO QUIROGA RAMÍREZ (ADN).

THE CABINET
(December 1997)

A coalition comprising members of the Acción Democrática Nacionalista (ADN), the Nueva Fuerza Republicana (NFR), the Movimiento de la Izquierda Revolucionaria (MIR), Conciencia de Patria (Condepa), the Unión Cívica Solidaridad (UCS) and an Independent (Ind.).

Minister of Foreign Affairs and Worship: JAVIER MURILLO DE LA ROCHA (ADN).

Minister of the Interior: GUIDO NAYAR PARADA (ADN).

Minister of National Defence: FERNANDO KIEFFER GUZMÁN (ADN).

Minister of the Presidency: CARLOS ITURRALDE BALLIVIÁN (ADN).

Minister of Sustainable Development and Environment: ERICK REYES VILLA (NFR).

Minister of Justice: ANA MARÍA CORTÉS DE SORIANO (ADN).

Minister of Finance: EDGAR MILLARES ARDAYA (Ind.).

Minister of Health and Human Development: TONCI MARINKOVIC (MIR).

Minister of Labour: LEOPOLDO LÓPEZ COSSIO (MIR).

Minister of Education, Culture and Sports: TITO HOZ DE VILA (ADN).

Minister of Agriculture: ODIN BAUER (Condepa).

Minister of External Trade: JORGE CRESPO (MIR).

Minister without Portfolio, responsible for economic development: IVO KULJIS (UCS).

Minister without Portfolio, responsible for housing and utilities: JAVIER ESCOBAR (Condepa).

MINISTRIES

Office of the President: Palacio de Gobierno, Plaza Murillo, La Paz; tel. (2) 37-1317; telex 5242.

Ministry of Economic Development: Edif. Palacio de Comunicaciones, Avda Mariscal Santa Cruz, La Paz; tel. (2) 37-7234; fax (2) 35-9955.

Ministry of Finance Development: Edif. Palacio de Comunicaciones, Avda Mariscal Santa Cruz, La Paz; tel. (2) 37-7234; fax (2) 35-9955.

Ministry of Foreign Affairs and Worship: Plaza Murillo, La Paz; tel. (2) 37-1150; telex 5242; fax (2) 37-1155.

Ministry of Health and Human Development: Plaza del Estudiante, La Paz; tel. (2) 37-1373; telex 5242; fax (2) 39-1590.

Ministry of the Interior: Avda Arce, esq. Belisario Salinas, La Paz; tel. (2) 37-0460; telex 5437; fax (2) 37-1334.

Ministry of Justice: Casilla 6966, La Paz; tel. (2) 36-1083; fax (2) 36-530.

Ministry of Labour: Calle Yanacocha esq. Mercado, La Paz; tel. (2) 36-4164; telex 5242; fax (2) 37-1387.

Ministry of National Defence: Plaza Avaroa, esq. 20 de Octubre, La Paz; tel. (2) 37-7130; fax (2) 35-3156.

Ministry of the Presidency: Plaza Murillo, La Paz; tel. (2) 35-9956; fax (2) 37-1388.

Ministry of Sustainable Development and Environment: Casilla 3116, La Paz; tel. (2) 35-9820; fax (2) 39-2892.

President and Legislature

PRESIDENT

At the presidential election that took place on 1 June 1997 the majority of votes were spread between five of the 10 candidates. Gen. (retd) Hugo Bánzer Suárez of the Acción Democrática Nacionalista (ADN) obtained 22.3% of the votes cast, Juan Carlos Durán of the Movimiento Nacionalista Revolucionario (MNR) won 17.7%, Jaime Paz Zamora of the Movimiento de la Izquierda Revolucionaria (MIR) won 16.7%, Ivo Kuljis of the Unión Cívica Solidaridad (UCS) secured

15.9% and Remedios Loza of Conciencia de Patria (Condepa) won 15.8%. As no candidate obtained the requisite absolute majority, responsibility for the selection of the President passed to the new National Congress. As a result of the formation of a coalition between the ADN, the MIR, the UCS, the NFR, Condepa and an Independent, Bánzer was elected President with 118 votes on 5 August and took office the following day.

CONGRESO NACIONAL

President of the Senate: WALTER GUITERAS.

President of the Chamber of Deputies: HORMANDO VALADIEZ.

General election, 1 June 1997

Party	Seats: Chamber of Deputies	Seats: Senate
Acción Democrática Nacionalista (ADN)	33	13
Movimiento Nacionalista Revolucionario (Histórico) (MNR)	26	3
Movimiento de la Izquierda Revolucionaria (MIR)	25	6
Unión Cívica Solidaridad (UCS)	21	2
Conciencia de Patria (Condepa)	17	3
Movimiento Bolivia Libre (MBL)	4	—
Izquierda Unida	4	—
Total	130	27

Political Organizations

Acción Democrática Nacionalista (ADN): La Paz; f. 1979; right-wing; Leader MARCELO OSTRIA TRIGO; Nat. Exec. Sec. JORGE FERNANDO QUIROGA RAMÍREZ.

Bolivia Insurgente: La Paz; f. 1996; populist party; Leader MÓNICA MEDINA.

Conciencia de Patria (Condepa): La Paz; f. 1988; populist party; Leader REMEDIOS LOZA.

Condepa Movimiento Patriótico (CMP): La Paz; f. 1993 as a breakaway faction of Condepa; Leader JORGE ESCOBAR CUSICANQUI.

Frente Revolucionario de Izquierda (FRI): La Paz; left-wing; Leader Dr MANUEL MORALES DÁVILA.

Izquierda Unida: La Paz; left-wing.

Movimiento Bolivia Libre (MBL): Edif. Camiri, Of. 601, Calle Comercio 972 esq. Yanacocha, Casilla 10382, La Paz; tel. (2) 34-0257; fax (2) 39-2242; f. 1985; left-wing; breakaway faction of MIR; Pres. MIGUEL URIOSTE.

Movimiento de la Izquierda Nacional (MIN): La Paz; left-wing; Leader Dr LUIS SANDOVAL MORÓN.

Movimiento de la Izquierda Revolucionaria (MIR): Avda América 119, 2°, La Paz; telex 3210; f. 1971; split into several factions in 1985; left-wing; Sec.-Gen. OSCAR EID FRANCO.

Movimiento Nacionalista Revolucionario (Histórico)—MNR: Genaro Sanjines 541, Pasaje Kuljis, La Paz; formerly part of the Movimiento Nacionalista Revolucionario (MNR, f. 1942); centre-right; Leader GONZALO SÁNCHEZ DE LOZADA; Sec.-Gen. JUAN CARLOS DURÁN; 700,000 mems.

Movimiento Nacionalista Revolucionario de Izquierda (MNRI): La Paz; f. 1979; formerly part of the Movimiento Nacionalista Revolucionario (MNR, f. 1942); left of centre; Leader Dr HERNÁN SILES ZUAZO; Sec.-Gen. FEDERICO ALVAREZ PLATA.

Movimiento Revolucionario Túpac Katarí de Liberación (MRTKL): Avda Baptista 939, Casilla 9133, La Paz; tel. 35-4784; f. 1978; peasant party; Leader VÍCTOR HUGO CÁRDENAS CONDE; Sec.-Gen. NORBERTO PÉREZ HIDALGO; 80,000 mems.

Nueva Fuerza Republicana (NFR): Cochabamba; Leader MANFRED REYES VILLA.

Partido Comunista de Bolivia (PCB): La Paz; f. 1950; First Sec. SIMÓN REYES RIVERA.

Partido Demócrata Cristiano (PDC): Casilla 4345, La Paz; telex 2532; f. 1954; Pres. Dr JORGE AGREDA VALDERRAMA; Sec. ANTONIO CANELAS-GALATOIRE; 50,000 mems.

Partido Indio: La Paz; represents native Indian (Amerindian) interests.

Partido Obrero Revolucionario (POR): Correo Central, La Paz; f. 1935; Trotskyist; Leader GUILLERMO LORA.

Partido Revolucionario de la Izquierda Nacionalista (PRIN): Calle Colón 693, La Paz; f. 1964; left-wing; Leader JUAN LECHIN OQUENDO.

Partido Socialista-Uno (PS-1): La Paz; Leader ROGER CÓRTEZ.

Partido Socialista-Uno—Marcelo Quiroga: La Paz; Leader JOSÉ MARÍA PALACIOS.

Partido de Vanguardia Obrera: Plaza Venezuela 1452, La Paz; Leader FILEMÓN ESCOBAR.

Unión Cívica Solidaridad (UCS): Calle Mercado 1064, 6°, La Paz; tel. (2) 36-0297; fax (2) 37-2200; f. 1989; populist; Leader JOHNNY FERNÁNDEZ.

Vanguardia Revolucionaria 9 de Abril: Avda 6 de Agosto 2170, Casilla 5810, La Paz; tel. (2) 32-0311; fax 39-1439; Leader Dr CARLOS SERRATE REICH.

Other parties include the Alianza de Renovación Boliviana, the Alianza Democrática Socialista and the Eje Patriótica.

Diplomatic Representation

EMBASSIES IN BOLIVIA

Argentina: Calle Aspiazu 497, La Paz; tel. (2) 32-2102; telex 3334; fax (2) 39-1083; Ambassador: MARÍA DEL CARMEN ECHEVERRÍA.

Belgium: Avda Hernando Siles 5290, Casilla 2433, La Paz; tel. (2) 78-4925; telex 3274; fax (2) 78-6764; Ambassador: CHRISTINE STEVENS.

Brazil: Edif. Foncomin, 9°, Avda 20 de Octubre 2038, Casilla 429, La Paz; tel. (2) 35-0718; telex 2494; fax (2) 39-1258; Ambassador: LUIZ ORLANDO C. GELIO.

China, People's Republic: La Paz; telex 5558; Ambassador: TANG MINGXIN.

Colombia: Calle 20 de Octubre 2427, Casilla 1418, La Paz; tel. (2) 35-9658; telex 3593; Ambassador: CARLOS EDUARDO LOZANO TOVAR.

Costa Rica: Avda 14 de Septiembre 4850, Casilla 2780, La Paz; tel. and fax (2) 78-6751; Ambassador: JUAN RAMÓN GUTIÉRREZ ARAYA.

Cuba: Avda Arequipa 8037, Calacoto, La Paz; tel. (2) 79-2616; telex 2447; Ambassador: GUSTAVO BRUGUÉS-PÉREZ.

Denmark: Avda 6 de Agosto 2577, Casilla 9860, La Paz; tel. (2) 43-0046; fax (2) 43-0064; Chargé d'affaires: MICHAEL HJORTSØ.

Ecuador: Edif. Herrman, 14°, Plaza Venezuela, Casilla 406, La Paz; tel. (2) 32-1208; telex 3388; Ambassador: OLMEDO MONTEVERDE PAZ.

Egypt: Avda Ballivián 599, Casilla 2956, La Paz; tel. (2) 78-6511; telex 2612; Ambassador: Dr GABER SABRA.

France: Avda Hernando Silés 5390, esq. Calle 8, Obrajes, Casilla 717, La Paz; tel. (2) 78-6114; telex 2484; fax (2) 78-6746; Ambassador: JEAN-MICHEL MARLAUD.

Germany: Avda Arce 2395, Casilla 5265, La Paz; tel. (2) 39-0850; telex 3303; fax (2) 39-1297; Ambassador: Dr HERMANN SAUMWEBER.

Holy See: Avda Arce 2990, Casilla 136, La Paz; tel. (2) 43-1007; fax (2) 43-2120; Apostolic Nuncio: Most Rev. RINO PASSIGATO, Titular Archbishop of Nova Caesaris.

Israel: Edif. Esperanza, 10°, Avda Mariscal Santa Cruz, Casilla 1309, La Paz; tel. (2) 37-4239; fax 39-1712; Ambassador: VAIR RECANATI.

Italy: Avda 6 de Agosto 2575, Casilla 626, La Paz; tel. (2) 36-1129; telex 2654; Ambassador: Dr ENRIC ANGIOLO FERRONI CARLI.

Japan: Calle Rosendo Gutiérrez 497, Casilla 2725, La Paz; tel. (2) 37-3152; telex 2548; Ambassador: HIROSHI IKEDA.

Korea, Democratic People's Republic: La Paz; Ambassador: KIM CHAN SIK.

Korea, Republic: Avda 6 de Agosto 2592, Casilla 1559, La Paz; tel. (2) 36-4485; telex 3262; Ambassador: CHO KAB-DONG.

Mexico: Avda 6 de Agosto 2652, Casilla 430, La Paz; tel. (2) 32-9505; telex 3316; Ambassador: Lic. MARCELO VARGAS CAMPOS.

Panama: Calle Potosí 1270, Casilla 678, La Paz; tel. (2) 37-1277; telex 2314; Chargé d'affaires a.i.: Lic. JOSÉ RODRIGO DE LA ROSA.

Paraguay: Edif. Venus, Avda Arce esq. Montevideo, Casilla 882, La Paz; tel. (2) 32-2018; Ambassador: Gen. RAMÓN DUARTE VERA.

Peru: Calle F. Guachalla, Casilla 668, La Paz; tel. (2) 35-3550; fax (2) 36-7640; e-mail embbol@wara.bolnet.bo; Ambassador: Dr HARRY BELEVAN MCBRIDE.

Romania: Avda Ecuador 2286, Sopocachi, Casilla 12280, La Paz; tel. (2) 37-7265; telex 3260; Ambassador: VASILE LUCA.

Russia: Avda Arequipa 8128, Casilla 5494, La Paz; tel. (2) 79-2048; telex 2480; Ambassador: TAKHIR BYASHIMOVICH DURDIYEV.

South Africa: Calle 22, Calacoto 7810, Casilla 6018, La Paz; tel. (2) 79-2101; telex 3279; Chargé d'affaires a.i.: J. S. ALDRICH.

Spain: Avda 6 de Agosto 2860, Casilla 282, La Paz; tel. (2) 43-3518; fax (2) 43-2752; Ambassador: MANUEL VITURRO DE LA TORRE.

Switzerland: Edif. Petrolero, Avda 16 de Julio 1616, Casilla 657, La Paz; tel. (2) 35-3091; telex 2325; Chargé d'affaires a.i.: FERMO GEROSA.

United Kingdom: Avda Arce 2732–2754, Casilla 694, La Paz; tel. (2) 43-3424; fax (2) 43-1073; Ambassador: DAVID RIDGWAY.

USA: Avda Arce 2780, Casilla 425, La Paz; tel. (2) 43-0251; fax (2) 43-3900; Ambassador: DONNA J. HRINAK.

Uruguay: Avda 6 de Agosto 2577, Casilla 441, La Paz; tel. (2) 43-0080; telex 2378; fax 43-0087; Ambassador: HOMAR MURDOCH SCARONI.

Venezuela: Edif. Illimani, 4°, Avda Arce esq. Campos, Casilla 960, La Paz; tel. (2) 43-1365; telex 2383; Ambassador: OTTO R. VEITIA MATOS.

Judicial System

SUPREME COURT

Corte Suprema: Calle Pilinco 352, Sucre; tel. (64) 21883; telex 6916; fax (64) 32696.

Judicial power is vested in the Supreme Court. There are 12 members, appointed by Congress for a term of 10 years. The court is divided into four chambers of three justices each. Two chambers deal with civil cases, the third deals with criminal cases and the fourth deals with administrative, social and mining cases. The President of the Supreme Court presides over joint sessions of the courts and attends the joint sessions for cassation cases.

President of the Supreme Court: Dr HUGO ROSALES LIGERÓN.

DISTRICT COURTS

There is a District Court sitting in each Department, and additional provincial and local courts to try minor cases.

ATTORNEY-GENERAL

In addition to the Attorney-General at Sucre (appointed by the President on the proposal of the Senate), there is a District Attorney in each Department as well as circuit judges.

Attorney-General: OSCAR CRESPO.

Religion

The majority of the population are Roman Catholics; there were an estimated 6.5m. adherents at 31 December 1995, equivalent to 87.6% of the population. Religious freedom is guaranteed. There is a small Jewish community, as well as various Protestant denominations, in Bolivia.

CHRISTIANITY

The Roman Catholic Church

Bolivia comprises four archdioceses, six dioceses, two Territorial Prelatures and five Apostolic Vicariates.

Bishops' Conference: Conferencia Episcopal de Bolivia, Calle Potosí 814, Casilla 2309, La Paz; tel. (2) 32-4535; fax (2) 34-0604; e-mail comceb@ceibo.entelnet.bo; f. 1972; Pres. Most Rev. JULIO TERRAZAS SANDOVAL, Archbishop of Santa Cruz de la Sierra.

Archbishop of Cochabamba: Most Rev. RENÉ FERNÁNDEZ APAZA, Calle Calama E. 0169, Casilla 129, Cochabamba; tel. (42) 56562; fax (42) 50522.

Archbishop of La Paz: Most Rev. EDMUNDO LUIS FLAVIO ABASTOFLOR MONTERO, Calle Ballivián 1277, Casilla 259, La Paz; tel. (2) 34-1920; fax (2) 39-1244.

Archbishop of Santa Cruz de la Sierra: Most Rev. JULIO TERRAZAS SANDOVAL, Calle Ingavi 49, Casilla 25, Santa Cruz; tel. (3) 324416; fax (3) 330181.

Archbishop of Sucre: Most Rev. JESÚS GERVASIO PÉREZ RODRÍGUEZ, Calle Bolívar 702, Casilla 205, Sucre; tel. (64) 51587; fax (64) 60336.

The Anglican Communion

Within the Iglesia Anglicana del Cono Sur de América (Anglican Church of the Southern Cone of America), Bolivia forms part of the diocese of Peru. The Bishop is resident in Lima, Peru.

Protestant Churches

Baptist Union of Bolivia: Casilla 1408, La Paz; Pres. Rev. AUGUSTO CHUIJO.

Convención Bautista Boliviana (Baptist Convention of Bolivia): Casilla 3147, Santa Cruz; tel. (3) 340717; fax (3) 340717; f. 1947; Pres. EIRA SORUCO DE FLORES.

Iglesia Evangélica Metodista en Bolivia (Evangelical Methodist Church in Bolivia): Casillas 356 y 8347, La Paz; tel. (2) 34-2702; fax (2) 32-1560; autonomous since 1969; 10,000 mems; Bishop Pbro. ZACARÍS MAMANI HUACOTA.

BAHÁ'Í FAITH

National Spiritual Assembly of the Bahá'ís of Bolivia: Casilla 1613, La Paz; tel. (2) 78-5058; fax (2) 78-2387; e-mail aebahais@caoba.entelnet.bo; mems resident in 6,195 localities.

The Press

DAILY NEWSPAPERS

Cochabamba

Los Tiempos: Plaza Quintanilla-Norte, Casilla 525, Cochabamba; tel. (42) 41870; f. 1943; morning; independent; Dir CARLOS CANELAS; circ. 18,000.

La Paz

El Diario: Calle Loayza 118, Casilla 5, La Paz; tel. (2) 39-0900; telex 3250; fax (2) 36-3846; f. 1904; morning; conservative; Dir JORGE CARRASCO JAHNSEN; circ. 55,000.

Hoy: Avda 6 de Agosto 2170, Casilla 477, La Paz; tel. (2) 32-6683; telex 2613; fax (2) 37-0564; f. 1968; morning and midday editions; independent; Dir Dr CARLOS SERRATE REICH; circ. 45,000.

Jornada: Junín 608, Casilla 1628, La Paz; tel. (2) 35-3844; f. 1964; evening; independent; Dir JAIME RÍOS CHACÓN; circ. 11,500.

Presencia: Avda Mariscal Santa Cruz 2150, Casilla 3276, La Paz; tel. (2) 37-2344; telex 2659; fax (2) 39-1040; e-mail prsencia@caoba.entelnet.bo; f. 1952; morning and evening; Catholic; Dir Lic. JUAN CRISTÓBAL SORUCO; Man. Lic. MARÍA LUISA URDAY; circ. 50,000.

Ultima Hora: Avda Camacho 1372, Casilla 5920, La Paz; tel. (2) 39-2115; fax (2) 39-2139; f. 1939; evening; independent; Dir MARIANO BAPTISTA GUMUCIO; Editor JORGE CANELAS; circ. 35,000.

Oruro

El Expreso: Potosí 319 esq. Oblitas, Oruro; f. 1973; morning; independent; right-wing; Dir GENARO FRONTANILLA VISTAS; circ. 1,000.

La Patria: Avda Camacho 1892, Casilla 48, Oruro; tel. (52) 50761; fax (52) 50781; f. 1919; morning; independent; Dir ENRIQUE MIRALLES; circ. 5,000.

Potosí

El Siglo: Calle Linares 99, Casilla 389, Potosí; f. 1975; morning; Dir WILSON MENDIETA PACHECO; circ. 1,500.

Santa Cruz

La Crónica: Calle Junia 222, Santa Cruz; daily.

El Deber: Avda El Trompillo 1144, Casilla 2144, Santa Cruz; tel. (3) 53-8000; f. 1955; morning; independent; Dir PEDRO RIVERO MERCADO; circ. 35,000.

El Mundo: Parque Industrial PI-7, Casilla 1984, Santa Cruz; tel. (3) 364646; telex 4296; fax (3) 365057; f. 1979; morning; owned by Santa Cruz Industrialists' Association; Dir HUGO PAZ MÉNDEZ; circ. 20,000.

Tarija

La Verdad: Tarija; weekly; Dir JOSÉ LANZA; circ. 3,000.

Trinidad

La Razón: Avda Bolívar 295, Casilla 166, Trinidad; tel. (2) 1377; f. 1972; Dir CARLOS VÉLEZ.

PERIODICALS

Actualidad Boliviana Confidencial (ABC): Fernando Guachalla 969, Casilla 648, La Paz; f. 1966; weekly; Dir HUGO GONZÁLEZ RIOJA; circ. 6,000.

Aquí: Casilla 10937, La Paz; tel. (2) 34-3524; fax (2) 35-2455; f. 1979; weekly; circ. 10,000.

Bolivia Libre: Edif. Esperanza, 5°, Avda Mariscal Santa Cruz 2150, Casilla 6500, La Paz; fortnightly; publ. by the Ministry of Information.

Carta Cruceña de Integración: Casilla 3531, Santa Cruz de la Sierra; weekly; Dirs HERNÁN LLANOVARCED A., JOHNNY LAZARTE J.

Comentarios Económicos de Actualidad (CEA): Casilla 312097, La Paz; tel. (2) 35-4520; fax (2) 43-2554; e-mail veceba@utama.bolnet.bo; f. 1983; fortnightly; articles and economic analyses.

Información Política y Económica (IPE): Calle Comercio, Casilla 2484, La Paz; weekly; Dir GONZALO LÓPEZ MUÑOZ.

Informe R: La Paz; weekly; Editor SARA MONROY.

Notas: Casilla 5782, La Paz; tel. (2) 37-3773; telex 3236; fax (2) 36-5153; weekly; political and economic analysis; Editor JOSÉ GRAMUNT DE MORAGAS.

El Noticiero: Sucre; weekly; Dir DAVID CABEZAS; circ. 1,500.

Prensa Libre: Sucre; tel. (64) 41293; fax (64) 32768; f. 1989; weekly; Dir JORGE ENCERAS DIAZ.

Servicio de Información Confidencial (SIC): Elías Sagárnaga 274, Casilla 5035, La Paz; weekly; publ. by Asociación Nacional de Prensa; Dir JOSÉ CARRANZA.

Siglo XXI: La Paz; weekly.

Unión: Sucre; weekly; Dir JAIME MERILES.

Visión Boliviana: Calle Loayza 420, Casilla 2870, La Paz; 6 a year.

PRESS ASSOCIATIONS

Asociación Nacional de la Prensa: Avda 6 de Agosto 2170, Casilla 477, La Paz; tel. (2) 36-9916; Pres. Dr CARLOS SERRATE REICH.

Asociación de Periodistas de La Paz: Avda 6 de Agosto 2170, Casilla 477, La Paz; tel. (2) 36-9916; fax (2) 32-3701; f. 1929; Pres. MARIO MALDONADO VISCARRA; Vice-Pres. MARÍA EUGENIA VERASTEGUI A.

NEWS AGENCIES

Agencia de Noticias Fides (ANF): Edif. Mariscal de Ayacucho, 5°, Of. 501, Calle Loayza, Casilla 5782, La Paz; tel. (2) 36-5152; telex 3236; fax (2) 36-5153; owned by Roman Catholic Church; Dir JOSÉ GRAMUNT DE MORAGAS.

Foreign Bureaux

Agencia EFE (Spain): Edif. Esperanza, Avda Mariscal Santa Cruz 2150, Casilla 7403, La Paz; tel. (2) 36-7205; fax (2) 39-1441; e-mail fvv@caoba.entelnet.bo; Bureau Chief FERNANDO DE VALENZUELA.

Agenzia Nazionale Stampa Associata (ANSA) (Italy): La Paz; tel. (2) 35-5521; telex 3410; fax (2) 36-8221; Correspondent RAÚL PENARANDA UNDURRAGA.

Associated Press (AP) (USA): Edif. Mariscal de Ayacucho, Of. 1209, Calle Loayza, Casilla 9569, La Paz; tel. (2) 37-0128; telex 3283; Correspondent PETER J. MCFARREN.

Deutsche Presse-Agentur (dpa) (Germany): Edif. Esperanza, 9°, Of. 3, Av. Mariscal Santa Cruz 2150, Casilla 13885, La Paz; tel. (2) 35-2684; telex 2601; fax (2) 39-2488; Correspondent ROBERT BROCKMANN.

Informatsionnoye Telegrafnoye Agentstvo Rossii-Telegrafnoye Agentstvo Suverennykh Stran (ITAR-TASS) (Russia): Casilla 6839, San Miguel, Bloque 0–33, Casa 958, La Paz; tel. (2) 79-2108; Correspondent ELDAR ABDULLAEV.

Inter Press Service (IPS) (Italy): Edif. Esperanza, 6°, Of. 6, Casilla 4313, La Paz; tel. (2) 36-1227; Correspondent RONALD GREBE LÓPEZ.

Prensa Latina (Cuba): Edif. Mariscal de Ayacucho, 9°, Of. 905, Calle Loayza, La Paz; tel. (2) 32-3479; telex 2525; Correspondent MANUEL ROBLES SOSA.

Reuters (United Kingdom): Edif. Loayza, 3°, Of. 301, Calle Loayza 349, Casilla 4057, La Paz; tel. (2) 35-1106; fax (2) 39-1366; Correspondent RENÉ VILLEGAS MONJE.

Rossiyskoye Informatsionnoye Agentstvo—Novosti (RIA—Novosti) (Russia): Edif. Mariscal Ballivián, Of. 401, Calle Mercado, La Paz; tel. (2) 37-3857; telex 3285; Correspondent VLADIMIR RAMÍREZ.

United Press International (UPI) (USA): Plaza Venezuela 1479, 7°, Of. 702, Casilla 1219, La Paz; tel. (2) 37-1278; fax (2) 39-1051; Correspondent ALBERTO ZUAZO NATHES.

Agence France-Presse and Telam (Argentina) are also represented.

Publishers

Editora Khana Cruz SRL: Avda Camacho 1372, Casilla 5920, La Paz; tel. (2) 37-0263; Dir GLADIS ANDRADE.

Editora Lux: Edif. Esperanza, Avda Mariscal Santa Cruz, Casilla 1566, La Paz; tel. (2) 32-9102; fax (2) 34-3968; f. 1952; Dir FELICISIMO TARILONTE PÉREZ.

Editorial los Amigos del Libro: Avda Heroínas E-0311, Casilla 450, Cochabamba; tel. (42) 51140; fax (41) 15128; e-mail amigol@amigol.bo.net; f. 1945; general; Man. Dir WERNER GUTTENTAG.

Editorial Bruño: Calle Mercado esq. Loayza, Casilla 4809, La Paz; tel. (2) 32-0198; f. 1964; Dir IRINEO LOMAS.

Editorial Don Bosco: Calle Tiahuanaçu 116, Casilla 4458, La Paz; tel. (2) 37-1757; fax (2) 36-2822; f. 1896; social sciences and literature; Dir GIAMPAOLO MARIO MAZZON.

Editorial Icthus: Avda 16 de Julio 1800, Casilla 8353, La Paz; tel. (2) 35-4007; f. 1967; general and textbooks; Man. Dir DANIEL AQUIZE.

Editorial y Librería Juventud: Plaza Murillo 519, Casilla 1489, La Paz; tel. (2) 34-1694; f. 1946; textbooks and general; Dirs RAFAEL URQUIZO, GUSTAVO URQUIZO.

Editorial Popular: Plaza Pérez Velasco 787, Casilla 4171, La Paz; tel. (2) 35-0701; f. 1935; textbooks, postcards, tourist guides, etc; Man. Dir GERMÁN VILLAMOR.

Editorial Puerta del Sol: Edif. Litoral Sub Suelo, Avda Mariscal Santa Cruz, La Paz; tel. (2) 36-0746; f. 1965; Man. Dir OSCAR CRESPO.

Empresa Editora Proinsa: Avda Saavedra 2055, Casilla 7181, La Paz; tel. (2) 22-7781; fax (2) 22-6671; f. 1974; school books; Dirs FLOREN SANABRIA G., CARLOS SANABRIA C.

Gisbert y Cía, SA: Calle Comercio 1270, Casilla 195, La Paz; tel. (2) 39-0056; fax (2) 39-1522; f. 1907; textbooks, history, law and general; Pres. JAVIER GISBERT; Dirs CARMEN G. DE SCHULCZEWSKI, ANTONIO SCHULCZEWSKI.

Ivar American: Calle Potosí 1375, Casilla 6016, La Paz; tel. (2) 36-1519; Man. Dir HÉCTOR IBÁÑEZ.

Librería El Ateneo SRL: Calle Ballivián 1275, Casilla 7917, La Paz; tel. (2) 36-9925; fax (2) 39-1513; Dirs JUAN CHIRVECHES D., MIRIAN C. DE CHIRVECHES.

Librería Dismo Ltda: Calle Comercio 806, Casilla 988, La Paz; tel. (2) 35-3119; fax (2) 31-6545; Dir TERESA GONZÁLEZ DE ALVAREZ.

Librería La Paz: Calle Colón 618, Casilla 539, La Paz; tel. (2) 35-3323; fax (2) 39-1513; f. 1900; Dirs CARLOS BURGOS R., CARLOS BURGOS M.

Librería La Universal SRL: Calle Genaro Sanjines 538, Casilla 2888, La Paz; tel. (2) 34-2961; f. 1958; Man. Dir ROLANDO CONDORI.

Librería San Pablo: Calle Colón 627, Casilla 3152, La Paz; tel. (2) 32-6084; f. 1967; Man. Dir MARÍA DE JESÚS VALERIANO.

PUBLISHERS' ASSOCIATION

Cámara Boliviana del Libro: Calle Capitán Ravelo 2116, Casilla 682, La Paz; tel. (2) 32-7039; fax (2) 32-7039; f. 1947; Pres. FREDDY CARRASCO JARA; Vice-Pres. ANDRÉS CARDÓ SORIA.

Broadcasting and Communications

TELECOMMUNICATIONS

Cámara Nacional de Medios de Comunicación: Casilla 2431, La Paz.

Empresa Nacional de Telecomunicaciones (ENTEL): Edif. Palacio de Comunicaciones, Avda Mariscal Santa Cruz esq. Oruro, Casilla 4450, La Paz; tel. (2) 35-5908; telex 3202; fax (2) 39-1789; f. 1965; privatized under the Govt's capitalization programme in 1995; Exec. Pres. GERMÁN MEDRANO KREIDLER.

Superintendencia de Telecomunicaciones: Edif. Cosmos, 6°, Avda 16 de Julio 1800, Casilla 6692, La Paz; tel. (2) 36-9674; fax (2) 11-2760; f. 1995; govt-controlled broadcasting authority; Dir-Gen. Ing. JAIME REQUENA G.

RADIO

There were 145 radio stations, in 1990, the majority of which were commercial. Broadcasts are in Spanish, Aymará and Quechua.

Asociación Boliviana de Radiodifusoras (ASBORA): Avda Sánchez Lima 2278, Casilla 5324, La Paz; tel. (2) 36-5154; fax (2) 36-3069; broadcasting authority; Pres. TERESA SANJINÉS L.; Vice-Pres. LUIS ANTONIO SERRANO.

Educación Radiofónica de Bolivia (ERBOL): Calle Ballivian 1323, 4°, Casilla 5946, La Paz; tel. (2) 35-4142; fax (2) 39-1985; asscn of 28 educational radio stations in Bolivia; Gen. Sec. RONALD GREBE LÓPEZ.

TELEVISION

Empresa Nacional de Televisión Boliviana–Canal 7: Edif. La Urbana, 6° y 7°, Avda Camacho 1486, Casilla 900, La Paz; tel. (2) 37-6356; telex 2312; fax (2) 35-9753; f. 1969; govt network operating stations in La Paz, Oruro, Cochabamba, Potosí, Chuquisaca, Pando, Beni, Tarija and Santa Cruz; Gen. Man. MIGUEL N. MONTERO VACA.

Televisión Boliviano–Canal 2: Casilla 4837, La Paz.

Televisión Universitaria–Canal 13: Edif. 'Hoy', 12°–13°, Avda 6 de Agosto 2170, La Paz; tel. (2) 35-9297; telex 3438; fax (2) 35-9491; f. 1980; educational programmes; stations in Oruro, Cochabamba, Potosí, Sucre, Tarija, Beni and Santa Cruz; Dir MIGUEL ANGEL MARTÍNEZ PORTOCARRERO.

Finance

(cap. = capital; p.u. = paid up; res = reserves; dep. = deposits; m. = million; brs = branches; amounts are in bolivianos unless otherwise stated)

BANKING

Supervisory Authority

Superintendencia de Bancos y Entidades Financieras: Plaza Isabel la Católica 2507, Casilla 447, La Paz; tel. (2) 43-1919; fax (2) 43-0028; f. 1928; Supt Lic. JACQUES TRIGO LOUBIÈRE.

State Banks

Banco Central de Bolivia: Avda Ayacucho esq. Mercado, Casilla 3118, La Paz; tel. (2) 37-4151; telex 2286; fax (2) 39-2398; e-mail vmarquez@mail.bcb.gov.bo; f. 1911 as Banco de la Nación Boliviana, name changed as above 1928; bank of issue; cap. 96.6m., res 215.6m.

(Dec. 1996); Pres. Dr JUAN ANTONIO MORALES ANAYA; Gen. Man. Lic. JAIME VALENCIA VALENCIA.

Banco del Estado: Calle Colón esq. Mercado, Casilla 1401, La Paz; tel. (2) 35-2868; telex 3267; fax (2) 39-1682; f. 1970; state bank incorporating banking department of Banco Central de Bolivia; cap. and res 51.1m., dep. 92.5m. (June 1990); Pres. Lic. RAMÓN RADA VELASCO; Gen. Man. JUAN LUIS PACHECO RAMÍREZ; 55 brs.

Banco Agrícola de Bolivia: Avda Mariscal Santa Cruz esq. Almirante Grau, Casilla 1179, La Paz; tel. (2) 36-5876; telex 3278; fax (2) 35-5940; f. 1942; cap. and res 100.4m. (June 1990); Pres. Lic. WALTER NÚÑEZ R.; Gen. Man. Lic. JUAN CARLOS PEREDO P.

Banco Minero de Bolivia: Calle Comercio 1290, Casilla 1410, La Paz; tel. (2) 35-2168; telex 2568; fax (2) 36-8870; f. 1936; finances private mining industry; cap. and res 44.6m. (June 1990); Pres. Ing. JAIME ASCARRUNZ E.; Gen. Man. Ing. RENÉ SANZ M.

Banco de la Vivienda: Avda Camacho 1336, Casilla 8155, La Paz; tel. (2) 34-3510; telex 2295; f. 1964; to encourage and finance housing developments; 51% state participation; initial cap. 100m. Bolivian pesos; Pres. (vacant); Gen. Man. Lic. JOSÉ RAMÍREZ MONTALVA.

Commercial Banks

Banco Boliviano Americano: Avda Camacho esq. Loayza, Casilla 478, La Paz; tel. (2) 31-4111; telex 2279; fax (2) 35-3984; f. 1957; cap. and res US $13.4m., dep. US $186m. (June 1997); Pres. DAVID BLANCO; Gen. Man. RICARDO VARGAS; 5 brs.

Banco de Cochabamba, SA: Warnes 40, Casilla 4107, Santa Cruz; tel. (3) 351036; telex 4265; fax (3) 340871; f. 1962; cap. 7.8m., dep. 112.0m. (July 1994); Exec. Pres. GUILLERMO GUTIÉRREZ SOSA; Gen. Man. MARÍA ELENA BLANCO DE ESTENSSORO; 5 brs.

Banco de Crédito de Bolivia, SA: Calle Colón esq. Mercado 1308, Casilla 6014, La Paz; tel. (2) 36-0025; telex 2404; fax (2) 39-1044; f. 1993 as Banco Popular, SA, name changed as above 1994; 69% owned by Banco de Crédito del Perú; cap. 65.4m., res 6.0m., dep. 1,001.5m. (Dec. 1995); Chair. DIONISIO ROMERO SEMINARIO; Gen. Man. RUBÉN LOAIZA NEGREIROS; 6 brs.

Banco de Financiamiento Industrial, SA: Plaza 10 de Febrero acera Adolfo Mier esq. La Plata, Casilla 51, Oruro; tel. (52) 53759; telex 2234; f. 1974 to encourage and finance industrial development; cap. p.u. 2.6m. Bolivian pesos, dep. 1.1m. Bolivian pesos; Pres. Lic. HUGO CAMPOS; Man. FRANCISCO BERMÚDEZ.

Banco Industrial, SA: Avda 16 de Julio 1628, 12°, Casilla 1290, La Paz; tel. (2) 31-7272; fax (2) 39-2013; f. 1963; industrial credit bank; cap. and res 36.7m., dep. 248.2m. (June 1996); Pres. JULIO LEÓN PRADO; CEO JUAN OTERO; 4 brs.

Banco Industrial y Ganadero del Beni, SA: Edif. Bigbeni, Avda 6 de Agosto, Casilla 54, Trinidad; tel. (46) 21476; telex 6320; cap. and res 22.4m., dep. 121.8m. (June 1990); Pres. Dr ISAAC SHIRIQUI V.; 11 brs.

Banco Internacional de Desarrollo, SA: Calle Nuflo de Chávez 150, Santa Cruz; tel. (3) 361555; telex 4423; fax (3) 338485; f. 1991; cap. 13.5m., res 11.8m., dep. 545.2m. (Dec. 1993); Pres. CARLOS LANDIVAR GIL; Gen. Man. Lic. ROBERTO LANDIVAR ROCA; 2 brs.

Banco de Inversión Boliviano, SA: Avda 16 de Julio 1571, Casilla 8639, La Paz; tel. (2) 35-4233; telex 2465; fax (2) 32-6536; f. 1977; cap. and res 11.2m., dep. 126.8m. (June 1991); Pres. JAIME GUTIÉRREZ MOSCOSO; Exec. Vice-Pres. MAURICIO URQUIDI URQUIDI.

Banco de La Paz, SA: Avda 16 de Julio 1473, Casilla 6826, La Paz; tel. (2) 36-4142; telex 2423; fax (2) 32-6536; f. 1975; cap. 53.1m., res 8.4m., dep. 767.5m. (Dec. 1995); Exec. Pres. Lic. GUIDO E. HINOJOSA CARDOSO; First Vice-Pres. Dr JORGE RENGEL SILLERICO; 11 brs.

Banco Mercantil, SA: Avda Ayacucho 277, Casilla 423, La Paz; tel. (2) 31-5131; fax (2) 39-1472; e-mail bercant@wara.bolnet.bo; f. 1905; cap. and res 38.5m., dep. 379m. (Sept. 1997); Pres. EDUARDO QUINTANILLA; Exec. Vice-Pres. EMILIO UNZUETA ZEGARRA; 6 brs.

Banco Nacional de Bolivia: Avda Camacho esq. Colón, Casilla 360, La Paz; tel. (2) 35-4616; telex 2583; fax (2) 35-9146; f. 1872; cap. 58.3m., res 7.2m., dep. 1,610.6m. (Dec. 1994); Pres. FERNANDO BEDOYA B.; Gen. Man. EDUARDO ALVAREZ LEMAITRE; 10 brs.

Banco de Santa Cruz de la Sierra, SA: Calle Junín esq. 21 de Mayo, Casilla 865, Santa Cruz; tel. (3) 339911; telex 5611; fax (3) 350114; f. 1966; cap. and res 44.2m., dep. 315.4m. (June 1990); Pres. Ing. LÍDERS PAREJA EGUEZ; Gen. Man. Ing. LUIS FERNANDO SAAVEDRA BRUNO; 18 brs.

Banco de la Unión, SA: Calle Libertad 156, Casilla 4057, Santa Cruz; tel. (3) 366869; telex 4285; fax (3) 340684; f. 1982; cap. 48.8m., res 7.6m., dep. 1,056.5m. (Dec. 1994); Pres. JORGE ARIAS LAZCANO; Chair. JUAN ABUAWAD CHAHUAN; 2 brs.

BHN Multibanco, SA: Avda 16 de Julio 1630, Casilla 4824, La Paz; tel. (2) 35-9351; telex 2290; fax (2) 39-1358; f. 1890; fmrly known as Banco Hipotecario Nacional, named changed 1989; cap. 72.6m., res 12.5m., dep. 1,386.0m. (Dec. 1994); Chair. FERNANDO ROMERO MORENO; Exec. Vice-Pres. Lic. CARLOS H. FERNÁNDEZ M.; 4 brs.

Caja Central de Ahorros y Préstamos para la Vivienda: Avda Mariscal Santa Cruz 1364, 20°, Casilla 4808, La Paz; tel. (2) 37-1280; telex 5611; fax (2) 36-1346; f. 1967; assets US $51m. (1993); Gen. Man. EDUARDO FRIAS T.

Foreign Banks

Banco do Brasil, SA: Avda Camacho 1448, Casilla 1650, La Paz; tel. (2) 37-7272; telex 2316; fax (2) 39-1036; f. 1960; Man. MARIO JOSÉ SOARES ESTEVES; 3 brs.

Banco de la Nación Argentina: Avda 16 de Julio 1486, Casilla 4312, La Paz; tel. (2) 35-9211; telex 2282; fax (2) 39-1392; Man. ROBERTO FERNÁNDEZ; 2 brs.

Banco Popular del Perú: Calle Mercado esq. Colón, Casilla 907, La Paz; tel. (2) 35-5023; telex 2404; fax (2) 35-5023; f. 1942; Gen. Man. MANUEL BARRETO BOGGIO; 6 brs.

Banco Real, SA: Avda 16 de Julio 1642, Casilla 10008, La Paz; tel. (2) 36-6603; telex 2396; fax (2) 39-1413; Gen. Man. LAFAIETE ANTONIO MARQUES, Jr.

Citibank NA (USA): Plaza Venezuela 1434, Casilla 260, La Paz; tel. (2) 35-5755; telex 2546; fax (2) 35-4645; Vice-Pres. FERNANDO ANKER.

Deutsch-Südamerikanische Bank AG (Banco Germánico de la América del Sud) and Dresdner Bank AG (Germany): Joint representation: Edif. Hansa, 4°, Avda Mariscal Santa Cruz, esq. Yanacocha, Casilla 1077, La Paz; tel. (2) 37-4450; telex 2311; fax (2) 39-1060; Rep. WOLFGANG LEANDER.

Banking Association

Asociación de Bancos Privados de Bolivia (ASOBAN): Edif. Cámara Nacional de Comercio, 15°, Avda Mariscal Santa Cruz esq. Colombia 1392, Casilla 5822, La Paz; tel. (2) 36-1308; fax (2) 39-1093; f. 1957; Pres. JAVIER ZUAZO CH.; Exec. Sec. CARLOS ITURRALDE B.; 18 mems.

STOCK EXCHANGE

Bolsa Boliviana de Valores SA: Edif. Mutual La Paz, 3°, Avda 16 de Julio XL1525, Casilla 12521, La Paz; tel (2) 39-2911; fax (2) 35-2308; e-mail bbvsalp@caoba.entelnet.bo; f. 1989; Pres. Ing. GERARDO GARRETT MENDIETA; Gen. Man. Dr FERNANDO CAMPERO PAZ.

INSURANCE

Supervisory Authority

Superintendencia Nacional de Seguros y Reaseguros: Edif. María Cristina, Plaza España esq. Gregorio Reynolds 612, Casilla 6118, La Paz; tel. (2) 41-0108; fax (2) 41-1819; f. 1975; Superintendent Lic. FERNANDO MOSCOSO SALMÓN; Man. DAVID ALCOREZA MARCHETTI.

National Companies

Alianza, Cía de Seguros y Reaseguros, SA: Avda 20 de Octubre 2680, esq. Campos Zona San Jorge, Casilla 11873, La Paz; tel. (2) 43-2121; fax (2) 43-2713; Gen. Man. CÉSAR EYZAGUIRRE ANGELES.

Bisa Seguros y Reaseguros, SA: Edif. San Pablo, 13°, Avda 16 de Julio 1479, Casilla 3669, La Paz; tel. (2) 35-2123; fax (2) 39-2500; Pres. JULIO LEÓN PRADO; Gen. Man. SUSANA PEÑARANDA B.

Bolívar SA de Seguros Generales: Edif. Bolívar, Avda Mariscal, Santa Cruz 1287, Casilla 1459, La Paz; tel. (2) 36-3688; fax (2) 39-1248; f. 1952; all classes; Pres. Lic. FREDDY OPORTO MÉNDEZ; Gen. Man. MARIO OPORTO MÉNDEZ.

Cía Santa Cruz de Seguros y Reaseguros, SA: Edif. CIA CRUZ, Calle Parí 28, Casilla 2223, Santa Cruz; tel. (33) 42319; telex 4257; fax (33) 91143; f. 1980; all classes; Pres. LYDERS PAREJA EGUEZ; Gen. Man. ANTONIO OLEA BAUDOIN.

Cooperativa de Seguros Cruceña Ltda: Calle Junín 363, Casilla 287, Santa Cruz; tel. (3) 343254; telex 4326; Pres. ADALBERTO TERCEROS BANZER; Man. MARTHA O. LUCCA.

Credinform International SA de Seguros: Edif. Credinform, Calle Potosí esq. Ayacucho 1220, Casilla 1724, La Paz; tel. (2) 35-6931; telex 2304; fax (2) 39-1225; f. 1954; all classes; Pres. Dr ROBÍN BARRAGÁN PELÁEZ; Gen. Man. MIGUEL ANGEL BARRAGÁN IBARGUEN.

Delta Insurance Co, SA: Avda 25 de Mayo, Casilla 920, Cochabamba; tel. (42) 26006; f. 1965; all classes except life; Pres. JUAN JOSÉ GALINDO B.; Gen. Man. CARLOS CHRISTIE J.

La Boliviana Ciacruz de Seguros y Reaseguros, SA: Calle Colón 288, Casilla 288, La Paz; tel. (2) 37-9438; fax (2) 39-1309; e-mail bolseg@wara.bolnet.bo; f. 1946; all classes; Pres. GONZALO BEDOYA HERRERA; Exec. Vice-Pres. ALFONSO IBÁÑEZ MONTES.

Nacional de Seguros y Reaseguros, SA: Edif. Aspiazu, Avda 20 de Octubre 2095, Casilla 14, La Paz; tel. (2) 35-3566; telex 3235; fax (2) 36-0566; f. 1977; fmrly known as Condor, SA de Seguros y Reaseguros; Pres. Ing. JUSTO YÉPEZ KAKUDA; Gen. Man. Dr HERNÁN OSUNA ARANO.

Seguros Illimani, SA: Edif. Mariscal de Ayacucho, 10°, Calle Loayza, Casilla 133, La Paz; tel. (2) 37-1090; telex 3261; fax (2) 39-

1149; f. 1979; all classes; Pres. FERNANDO ARCE GRANDCHANT; Gen. Man. RAÚL UGARTE.

Unicruz Cía de Seguros y Reaseguros, SA: Avda El Trompillo 632, Casilla 1232, Santa Cruz; tel. (3) 341777; fax (3) 339549; Man. FRANCISCO NALDA MUJICA.

Unión de Seguros, SA: Edif. El Cóndor, 16°, Calle Batallón Colorados, Casilla 2922, La Paz; tel. (2) 35-8155; telex 2315; fax (2) 39-2049; all classes; Pres. DR JORGE RENGEL SILLERICO; Man. VÍCTOR ROSAS.

There are also three foreign-owned insurance companies operating in Bolivia: American Life Insurance Co, American Home Assurance Co and United States Fire Insurance Co.

Insurance Association

Asociación Boliviana de Aseguradores: Edif. Castilla, 5°, Of. 506, Calle Loayza esq. Mercado 250, Casilla 4804, La Paz; tel. (2) 32-8804; fax (2) 37-9154; f. 1962; Pres. MIGUEL ANGEL BARRAGÁN I.; Exec. Sec. BLANCA M. DE OTERMIN.

Trade and Industry

GOVERNMENT AGENCIES

Cámara Nacional de Exportadores: Avda Arce 2017, esq. Goitia, Casilla 12145, La Paz; tel. (2) 34-1220; telex 2471; fax (2) 36-1491; f. 1970; Pres. LUIS NEMTALA YAMIN; Gen. Man. JORGE ADRIAZOLA REIMERS.

Instituto Nacional de Inversiones (INI): Edif. Cristal, 10°, Calle Yanacocha, Casilla 4393, La Paz; tel. (2) 37-5730; fax (2) 36-7297; f. 1971; state institution for the promotion of new investments and the application of the Investment Law; Exec. Dir Ing. JOSÉ MARIO FERNÁNDEZ IRAHOLA.

Instituto Nacional de Promoción de Exportaciones (INPEX): Calle Federico Zuazo esq. Reyes Ortiz, Casilla 10871, La Paz; tel. (2) 37-8000; fax (2) 39-1226.

DEVELOPMENT ORGANIZATIONS

Consejo Nacional de Acreditación y Medición de la Calidad Educativa (CONAMED): La Paz; f. 1994; education quality board.

Consejo Nacional de Planificación (CONEPLAN): Edif. Banco Central de Bolivia, 26°, La Paz; tel. (2) 37-7115; f. 1985.

Corporación de las Fuerzas Armadas para el Desarrollo Nacional (COFADENA): Avda 6 de Agosto 2649, Casilla 1015, La Paz; tel. (2) 37-7305; telex 3286; fax (2) 36-0900; f. 1972; industrial, agricultural and mining holding company and development organization owned by the Bolivian armed forces; Gen. Man. EDGAR AMPUERO ANGULO.

Corporación Regional de Desarrollo de La Paz (CORDEPAZ): Calle Comercio 1200 esq. Ayacucho, Casilla 6102, La Paz; tel. (2) 37-1524; fax (2) 39-2283; f. 1972; decentralized government institution to foster the development of the La Paz area; Pres. Lic. RICARDO PAZ BALLIVIÁN; Gen. Man. Ing. JUAN G. CARRASCO R.

CHAMBERS OF COMMERCE

Cámara Nacional de Comercio: Edif. Cámara Nacional de Comercio, Avda Mariscal Santa Cruz 1392, 1°, Casilla 7, La Paz; tel. (2) 35-0042; fax (2) 39-1004; f. 1890; 30 brs and special brs; Pres. GUILLERMO MORALES F.; Exec. Sec. FERNANDO CÁCERES PACHECO.

Cámara de Comercio de Oruro: Pasaje Guachalla s/n, Casilla 148, Oruro; tel. and fax (52) 50606; f. 1895; Pres. ALVARO CORNEJO GAZCÓN; Gen. Man. LUIS CAMACHO VARGAS.

Cámara Departamental de Industria y Comercio de Santa Cruz: Calle Suárez de Figueroa 127, 3°, Casilla 180, Santa Cruz; tel. (3) 334555; fax (3) 342353; e-mail eurobol@bibosi.scz.entelnet.bo; f. 1915; Pres. Lic. LUIS FERNANDO TERRAZAS SALAS; Gen. Man. Ing. GORAN MATKOVIC VRANJICAN.

Cámara Departamental de Comercio de Cochabamba: Calle Sucre E-0336, Casilla 493, Cochabamba; tel. (42) 57715; fax (42) 57717; f. 1922; Pres. RAQUEL ALEN DE SABA; Gen. Man. Lic. JUAN CARLOS AVILA S.

Cámara Departamental de Comercio e Industria de Potosí: Casilla 149, Potosí; tel. (62) 22641; telex 2266; fax (62) 22641; Pres. OSCAR VARGAS IPORRE; Gen. Man. WALTER ZABALA AYLLON.

Cámara Departamental de Industria y Comercio de Chuquisaca: Casilla 33, Sucre; tel. (64) 51194; fax (64) 51850; Pres. MARCELO TORRICOS MEYER; Gen. Man. Lic. ALFREDO YÁÑEZ MERCADO.

Cámara Departamental de Comercio e Industria de Cobija—Pando: Cobija; tel. 2153; telex 2152; fax 2291; Pres. DULFREDO CÁRDENAS BERRIOS.

Cámara Departamental de Industria y Comercio de Tarija: Avda Bolívar 0413, 1°, Casilla 74, Tarija; tel. (66) 22737; telex 2264; fax (66) 24053; Pres. MILTON CASTELLANOS; Gen. Man. VÍCTOR ARAMAYO.

Cámara Departamental de Comercio de Trinidad—Beni: Casilla 96, Trinidad; tel. (46) 22365; telex 2102; fax (46) 21400; Pres. ALCIDES ALPIRE DURÁN.

INDUSTRIAL AND TRADE ASSOCIATIONS

Cámara Agropecuaria del Oriente: 3 anillo interno entre Pirai y Roca Coronado, Casilla 116, Santa Cruz; tel. (3) 323164; telex 4438; fax (3) 322621; f. 1964; agriculture and livestock association for eastern Bolivia; Pres. Ing. OSMAN LANDÍVAR; Gen. Man. Ing. JUAN CARLOS VELARDE.

Cámara Agropecuaria de La Paz: Calle Santa Cruz 266, Casilla 6297, La Paz; tel. (2) 35-3942; fax (2) 35-3942; Pres. FERNANDO PALACIOS; Gen. Man. HARLEY RODRÍGUEZ.

Cámara Forestal de Bolivia: Calle Manuel Ignacio Salvatierra 1055, Casilla 346, Santa Cruz; tel. (3) 332699; fax (3) 331456; e-mail camaraforestal@index.org; f. 1971; represents the interests of the Bolivian timber industry; Pres. Dr TIENANDO AUTILO GIL; Gen. Man. Lic. ARTURO BOWLES OLHAGARAY.

Cámara Nacional de Industrias: Edif. Cámara Nacional de Comercio, 14°, Avda Mariscal Santa Cruz 1392, Casilla 611, La Paz; tel. (2) 37-4476; fax (2) 35-0620; f. 1931; Pres. GARY LACUNZA V.; Man. Dr ALFREDO ARANA RUCK.

Cámara Nacional de Minería: Pasaje Bernardo Trigo 429, Casilla 2022, La Paz; tel. (2) 35-0623; f. 1953; mining institute; Pres. Ing. LUIS PRADO BARRIENTOS; Sec.-Gen. GERMÁN GORDILLO S.

Comité Boliviano de Productores de Antimonio: Pasaje Bernardo Trigo 429, Casilla 14451, La Paz; tel. (2) 32-5140; fax (2) 37-9653; f. 1978; controls the marketing, pricing and promotion policies of the antimony industry; Pres. ALBERTO BARRIOS MORALES; Sec.-Gen. Dr ALCIDES RODRÍGUEZ J.

Comité Boliviano del Café (COBOLCA): Avda Villazón 1970, Casilla 9770, La Paz; tel. (2) 36-2561; telex 3504; controls the export, marketing and growing policies of the coffee industry; Gen. Man. JUAN CARLOS CONCHA URQUIZO.

Corporación Minera de Bolivia (COMIBOL): Avda Camacho 1396, Casilla 349, La Paz; tel. (2) 35-7979; telex 2420; fax (2) 34-3385; f. 1952; state mining corporation; taken over by FSTMB (miners' union) in April 1983; owns both mines and processing plants; Pres. Dr ALBERTO ALANDIA BARRÓN.

Instituto Boliviano de Ciencia y Tecnología Nuclear (IBTEN): Avda 6 de Agosto 2905, Casilla 4821, La Paz; tel. (2) 35-6877; telex 2220; f. 1983; main activities include: nuclear engineering, agricultural and industrial application of radio-isotopes, radio-chemical analysis, neutron generating, nuclear physics and dosimetry; Exec. Dir Ing. JUAN CARLOS MÉNDEZ FERRY (acting).

Yacimientos Petrolíferos Fiscales Bolivianos (YPFB): Calle Bueno 185, Casilla 401, La Paz; tel. (2) 35-6540; telex 2376; fax (2) 39-1048; f. 1936; state petroleum enterprise; privatized under the Govt's capitalization programme in 1996; Pres. Ing. RAFAEL PEÑA PARADA; Vice-Pres. for Operations Ing. MARIO ARENAS VISCARRA.

EMPLOYERS' ASSOCIATIONS

Asociación Nacional de Mineros Medianos: Calle Pedro Salazar 600 esq. Presbítero Medina, Casilla 6190, La Paz; tel. (2) 41-2232; fax (2) 41-4123; f. 1939; association of the 14 private medium-sized mining companies; Pres. RAÚL ESPAÑA-SMITH; Sec.-Gen. ROLANDO JORDÁN.

Confederación de Empresarios Privados de Bolivia (CEPB): Edif. Cámara Nacional de Comercio, 7°, Avda Mariscal Santa Cruz 1392, Casilla 20439, La Paz; tel. (2) 35-6831; telex 2305; largest national employers' organization; Pres. Lic. CARLOS CALVO GALINDO; Exec. Sec. Lic. JOHNNY NOGALES VIRUEZ.

There are also employers' federations in Santa Cruz, Cochabamba, Oruro, Potosí, Beni and Tarija.

UTILITIES

Electricity

Compañía Boliviana de Energía Eléctrica, SA (COBEE): Plaza Venezuela 1401, Casilla 353, La Paz; tel. (2) 37-1208; telex 2482; fax (2) 39-1536; f. 1925; principal private producer and distributor of electricity serving the areas of La Paz and Oruro; in 1994 the company generated 36% of all electricity produced in Bolivia; Chair. D. H. BUSWELL.

Empresa Nacional de Electricidad, SA (ENDE): Colombia 655, esq. Falsuri, Casilla 565, Cochabamba; tel. (42) 46322; telex 6251; fax (42) 42700; f. 1962; former state electricity company; privatized under the Govt's capitalization programme in 1995; Pres. Ing. CLAUDE BESSE ARZE; Gen. Man. Ing. JOHNNY COSCIO MALDONADO.

CO-OPERATIVES

Instituto Nacional de Co-operativas: La Paz.

TRADE UNIONS

Central Obrera Boliviana (COB): Edif. COB, Calle Pisagua 618, Casilla 6552, La Paz; tel. (2) 35-2426; telex 3594; fax (2) 32-4740; f. 1952; main union confederation; 800,000 mems; Exec. Sec. EDGAR RAMÍREZ SANTIESTÉBAN; Sec.-Gen. OSCAR SALAS MOYA.

Affiliated unions:

Central Obrera Departamental de La Paz: Estación Central 284, La Paz; tel. (2) 35-2898; Exec. Sec. FLAVIO CLAVIJO.

Confederación Sindical Unica de los Trabajadores Campesinos de Bolivia (CSUTCB): Calle Sucre, esq. Yanacocha, La Paz; tel. (2) 36-9433; f. 1979; peasant farmers' union; Exec. Sec. JUAN DE LA CRUZ VILLCA.

Federación de Empleados de Industria Fabril: Edif. Fabril, 5°, Plaza de San Francisco, La Paz; tel. (2) 37-2759; Exec. Sec. CARLOS SOLARI.

Federación Sindical de Trabajadores Mineros de Bolivia (FSTMB): Plaza Venezuela 1470, Casilla 14565, La Paz; tel. (2) 35-9656; f. 1944; mineworkers' union; Exec. Sec. VÍCTOR LÓPEZ ARIAS; Gen. Sec. EDGAR RAMÍREZ SANTIESTÉBAN; 27,000 mems.

Federación Sindical de Trabajadores Petroleros de Bolivia: Calle México 1504, La Paz; tel. (2) 35-1748; Exec. Sec. NEFTALYMENDOZA DURÁN.

Confederación General de Trabajadores Fabriles de Bolivia (CGTFB): Avda Armentia 452, Casilla 21590, La Paz; tel. (2) 37-1603; fax (2) 32-4302; e-mail dirabc@bo.net; f. 1951; manufacturing workers' union; Exec. Sec. ANGEL ASTURIZAGA; Gen. Sec. ROBERTO ENCINAS.

Transport

RAILWAYS

Empresa Nacional de Ferrocarriles (ENFE): Estación Central de Ferrocarriles, Plaza Zalles, Casilla 428, La Paz; tel. (2) 32-7401; telex 2405; fax (2) 39-2677; f. 1964; administers most of the railways in Bolivia; privatized under the Government's capitalization programme in 1995. Total networks: 3,697 km (1994); Western network: 2,274 km; Eastern network: 1,423 km; Pres. J. L. LANDIVAR B.

A former private railway, Machacamarca–Uncia, owned by Corporación Minera de Bolivia (105 km), merged with the Western network of ENFE, in February 1987. There are plans to construct a railway line with Brazilian assistance, to link Cochabamba and Santa Cruz.

ROADS

In 1995 Bolivia had 52,216 km of roads, of which 2,872 km were paved. Almost the entire road network is concentrated in the altiplano region and the Andes valleys. A 560 km highway runs from Santa Cruz to Cochabamba, serving a colonization scheme on virgin lands around Santa Cruz. The Pan-American highway, linking Argentina and Peru, crosses Bolivia from south to north-west. In 1990 plans were announced for the construction of a US $90.9m. highway linking Patacamaya, south of La Paz, to the existing highway, which links Tambo Quemado, with Arica, on the Pacific coast of Chile. The project was to be financed jointly by Japan and the Inter-American Development Bank (IDB).

INLAND WATERWAYS

By agreement with Paraguay in 1938 (confirmed in 1939), Bolivia has an outlet on the River Paraguay. This arrangement, together with navigation rights on the Paraná, gives Bolivia access to the River Plate and the sea. The River Paraguay is navigable for vessels of 12-ft draught for 288 km beyond Asunción, in Paraguay, and for smaller boats another 960 km to Corumbá in Brazil. In late 1994 plans were finalized to widen and deepen the River Paraguay, providing a waterway from Bolivia to the Atlantic coast in Uruguay.

In 1974 Bolivia was granted free duty access to the Brazilian coastal ports of Belém and Santos and the inland ports of Corumbá and Port Velho. In 1976 Argentina granted Bolivia free port facilities at Rosario on the River Paraná. In 1992 an agreement was signed with Peru, granting Bolivia access to (and the use, without customs formalities, of) the Pacific port of Ilo. Most of Bolivia's foreign trade is handled through the ports of Matarani (Peru), Antofagasta and Arica (Chile), Rosario and Buenos Aires (Argentina) and Santos (Brazil). An agreement signed between Bolivia and Chile in mid-1995 to reform Bolivia's access arrangements to the port of Arica came into effect in January 1996.

Bolivia has over 14,000 km of navigable rivers, which connect most of Bolivia with the Amazon basin.

Bolivian River Navigation Company: f. 1958; services from Puerto Suárez to Buenos Aires (Argentina).

OCEAN SHIPPING

Líneas Navieras Bolivianas (LINABOL): Edif. Hansa, 16°, Avda Mariscal Santa Cruz, Apdo 11160, La Paz; tel. (2) 37-9459; telex 2411; fax (2) 39-1079; Pres. Vice-Adm. LUIS AZURDUY ZAMBRANA; Vice-Pres. WOLFGANG APT.

CIVIL AVIATION

Bolivia has 30 airports including the two international airports at La Paz (El Alto) and Santa Cruz (Viru-Viru).

Dirección General de Aeronaútica Civil: La Paz.

Lloyd Aéreo Boliviano, SAM (LAB): Casilla 132, Aeropuerto 'Jorge Wilstermann', Cochabamba; tel. (42) 50750; telex 6290; fax (42) 50744; e-mail líder@labairlines.bo.net; internet http://www.labairlines.bo.net; f. 1925; privatized under the Government's capitalization programme in 1995; owned by Bolivian Govt (48.3%), VASP-Brazil (49%), private interests (2.7%); operates a network of scheduled services to 12 cities within Bolivia and to 17 international destinations in South America, Central America and the USA; Pres. ULISSES CANHEDO AZEVEDO; CEO ANTONIO SPAGNUOLO SÁNCHEZ.

Transportes Aéreos Bolivianos: Casilla 132, Cochabamba; tel. (42) 50743; fax (42) 50766; f. 1977; regional scheduled and charter cargo services; Gen. Man. LUIS GUERECA PADILLA.

Transportes Aéreos Militares: Avda Panamericana Alto, La Paz; tel. (2) 38-9433; internal passenger and cargo services; Dir-Gen. Col. J. M. COQUIS.

Tourism

Bolivia's tourist attractions include Lake Titicaca, at 3,810 m (12,500 ft) above sea-level, pre-Incan ruins at Tiwanaku, Chacaltaya in the Andes mountains, which has the highest ski-run in the world, and the UNESCO World Cultural Heritage Sites of Potosí and Sucre. In 1994 319,578 foreign visitors arrived at Bolivian hotels and similar establishments. In that year receipts from tourism totalled US $135m. Tourists come mainly from South American countries, the USA and Europe.

Asociación Boliviana de Agencias de Viajes y Turismo: Edif. Litoral, Avda Mariscal Santa Cruz 1351, Casilla 3967, La Paz; f. 1984; Pres. EUGENIO MONROY VÉLEZ.

Secretaría Nacional de Turismo: Calle Mercado 1328, Casilla 1868, La Paz; tel. (2) 36-7463; telex 2534; fax (2) 37-4630; f. 1977; Dir Lic. RICARDO ROJAS HARRISON.

BOSNIA AND HERZEGOVINA

Introductory Survey

Location, Climate, Language, Religion, Flag, Capital

Bosnia and Herzegovina (formerly the Socialist Republic of Bosnia and Herzegovina, a constituent republic of the Socialist Federal Republic of Yugoslavia) is situated in south-eastern Europe. It is bounded by Croatia to the north and west, by Serbia to the east and by Montenegro to the south-east, and has a short (20 km—12 miles) western coastline on the Adriatic Sea. It is a largely mountainous territory with a continental climate and steady rainfall throughout the year; in areas nearer the coast, however, the climate is more Mediterranean. The principal language is Serbo-Croat. Although it is a single spoken language, Serbo-Croat has two written forms: the Muslims (Bosniaks) and Croats use the Roman alphabet, while the Serbs use Cyrillic script. The Muslims (the majority of whom belong to the Sunni sect) are the largest religious grouping in Bosnia and Herzegovina, comprising 43.7% of the population in 1991. Religious affiliation is roughly equated with ethnicity, the Serbs (31.4% of the population) belonging to the Serbian Orthodox Church and the Croats (17.3%) being members of the Roman Catholic Church. The national flag (proportions 2 by 1) consists of two unequal sections of blue, separated by a yellow triangle, which is bordered on the left by a diagonal line of nine white five-pointed stars. The capital is Sarajevo.

Recent History

The provinces of Bosnia and Herzegovina formed part of the Turkish (Ottoman) Empire for almost 400 years before annexation to the Austro-Hungarian Empire in 1878. The population of the provinces was composed of an ethnic mixture of Orthodox Serbs, Roman Catholic Croats and Muslims (mainly Bosnian Slavs who had converted to Islam). Serbian expansionist aims troubled the area from the beginning of the 20th century, and Austria-Hungary attempted to end the perceived Serbian threat in 1914 by declaring war on Serbia; this conflict was to escalate into the First World War. On 4 December 1918 the Kingdom of Serbs, Croats and Slovenes was proclaimed when the Serbs and Croats agreed with other ethnic groups to establish a common state under the Serbian monarchy. The provinces of Bosnia and Herzegovina formed part of the new kingdom. Bitter disputes ensued between Serbs and Croats, however, and in January 1929 King Alexander imposed a dictatorship, changing the name of the country to Yugoslavia later the same year.

Though officially banned in 1921, the Communist Party of Yugoslavia (CPY) operated clandestinely, and in 1937 Josip Broz (alias Tito) became the General Secretary of the CPY. During the Second World War, Tito's Partisans, who were from a variety of ethnic groups, dominated most of Bosnia and Herzegovina, simultaneously waging war against invading German and Italian troops, the 'Ustaša' regime in Croatia and the Serb-dominated 'Chetniks'. On Tito's victory, after the War, Bosnia and Herzegovina became one of the six constituent republics of the Yugoslav federation (despite Serbian pressure to limit the region to provincial status, as with Kosovo and the Vojvodina). In the 1960s Tito established Muslim power in Bosnia and Herzegovina in an effort to counter the growing ethnic tension between the Serbs and Croats of the republic. The federal authorities were attempting to create a Muslim power-base independent of, but equal to, the Serbs and Croats. To this end, Slav Muslims were granted a distinct ethnic status, as a nation of Yugoslavia, for the 1971 census, and a collective state presidency was established in that year, with a regular rotation of posts. The politicians of Bosnia and Herzegovina became adept at coalition politics, most remaining committed to the institution of a collective presidency even throughout the changes of 1990.

Increasing ethnic tension in Bosnia and Herzegovina, potentially the most dangerous in the mosaic of ethnic groups of Yugoslavia, became evident in September 1990. Followers of the Party of Democratic Action (PDA), the principal Muslim party of the republic, demonstrated in the neighbouring Sandjak area of Serbia in support of Muslim rights in the Novi Pazar district, clashing with Serb nationalists. Later in the year, ethnic affiliation proved to be a decisive factor in the republican elections in November and December. The ruling League of Communists of Bosnia and Herzegovina was ousted, and the three main parties to emerge were all nationalist: the Muslim (Bosniak) PDA, with 86 seats; the Serbian Democratic Party (SDP), with 72 seats; and the Croatian Democratic Union of Bosnia and Herzegovina (CDU—BH), an affiliate of the ruling CDU party of Croatia, with 44 seats. The three nationalist parties also took all seven seats on the directly elected collective Presidency and formed a coalition administration for the republic. On 20 December they announced that Dr Alija Izetbegović of the PDA was to be President of the Presidency, Jure Pelivan of the CDU—BH was to be President of the Executive Council (Prime Minister) and Momčilo Krajišnik of the SDP was to be President of the Assembly.

In 1991 the politics of Bosnia and Herzegovina were increasingly dominated by the Serb–Croat conflict. Following the declarations of independence by Slovenia and Croatia in June, Serb-dominated territories in Bosnia and Herzegovina declared their intent to remain within the Yugoslav federation (or in a 'Greater Serbia'). On 27 June the self-proclaimed Serb 'Municipal Community of Bosanska Krajina', in Bosnia, announced its unification with the 'Serbian Autonomous Region (SAR) of Krajina', in Croatia. An SAR of Bosanska Krajina was proclaimed on 16 September. The republican Government rejected these moves and declared the inviolability of the internal boundaries of Yugoslavia. Armed incidents contributed to the rising tension throughout mid-1991 and many Serb areas announced the formation of other 'Autonomous Regions'. Other ethnic groups accused the Serbs of planning a 'Greater Serbia', with the support of the Jugoslavenska Narodna Armija (JNA, Yugoslav People's Army). In October the JNA assumed effective control of Mostar, to the north-west of the Serb 'Old' Herzegovina, and began a siege of the Croatian city of Dubrovnik.

A federation dominated by Serbia was not an attractive proposition to the Muslims and Croats of Bosnia and Herzegovina. In October 1991 both the republican Presidency (with the dissenting votes of the Serb members) and the PDA proposed to the Assembly that the republic declare its independence (Macedonia had already done so in September). The proposals did favour a renewed federation, but only one in which the republic had equal relations with both Serbia and Croatia. On 14 October, during the debate in the Assembly, the Serbs (mainly the SDP) rejected any such declaration as a move towards secession, claiming that all Serbs should live in one state. No compromise was reached, and Krajišnik, the President of the Assembly and a member of the SDP, declared the debate to be concluded and ordered the session to be closed; the Serb representatives, mainly the SDP, then withdrew from the chamber. However, the other deputies, dominated by the members of the PDA and the CDU—BH, continued the session; on 15 October the remaining members of the Assembly approved a resolution declaring that the Republic of Bosnia and Herzegovina was a sovereign state within its existing borders.

The deputies of the three main parties continued to negotiate, but the PDA condemned what it described as the threats of the SDP leader, Dr Radovan Karadžić. The 'Autonomous Regions' of the Serbs rejected the republican Assembly's resolution and declared that only the federal laws and Constitution would apply on their territory. On 24 October 1991 the Serb deputies of the Bosnia and Herzegovina Assembly constituted an 'Assembly of the Serb Nation' (Serb Assembly). This body then resolved to hold a referendum on whether the Serbs of Bosnia and Herzegovina should stay in a common Yugoslav state or not. In early November another SAR was proclaimed, consisting of the Serbs of Northern Bosnia, with an Assembly based in Doboj (an area without a Serb majority). On 9–10 November the referendum of Bosnia and Herzegovina's Serbs overwhelmingly supported their remaining in a Yugoslav or Serb state. However, in another referendum held on 29 February and 1 March 1992, which was open to all ethnic groups but was boycotted by the Serbs, 99.4% of the 63% of the electorate who participated were in favour of full independence. President Izetbegović immediately declared the republic's independence and omitted the word 'socialist' from the new state's official title.

Following the declaration of independence, there was renewed Serb-Muslim tension, leading to clashes in Sarajevo, the republican capital, and elsewhere. On 18 March 1992, following mediation by the European Community (EC, now European Union—EU—see p. 152), the leaders of the Serb, Croat and Muslim communities of Bosnia and Herzegovina signed an agreement providing for the division of the republic into three autonomous units. One week later, however, Izetbegović stated that he had signed the agreement only because it was a precondition to gaining diplomatic recognition. The EC and the USA recognized Bosnia and Herzegovina's independence on 7 April. On 27 March the Serbs announced the formation of a 'Serbian Republic of Bosnia and Herzegovina', which comprised Serbian-held areas of the republic (about 65% of the total area), including the SARs, and which was to be headed by Karadžić. The Bosnian Government immediately declared this breakaway republic, the headquarters of which were based in Banja Luka, to be illegal. In April fighting between the Serbian-dominated JNA in Bosnia and Herzegovina and Muslim and Croatian forces intensified; several cities, including Sarajevo, were besieged by Serbian troops. In early May, however, the newly-established Federal Republic of Yugoslavia (FRY—composed solely of the republics of Serbia and Montenegro), in an apparent attempt to disclaim any responsibility for Bosnia and Herzegovina's internal strife, ordered all of its citizens in the JNA to withdraw from the republic within 15 days. Early EC and UN efforts at mediation proved unsuccessful, and their respective peace monitors were withdrawn from Sarajevo in mid-May after a state of emergency had been declared and successive cease-fires had failed to take effect. Izetbegović requested foreign military intervention, but the UN, while deploying 14,000 troops (the United Nations Protection Force—UNPROFOR, see p. 52) in Croatia and demanding a halt to the fighting and the withdrawal of Yugoslav and Croat troops from Bosnia and Herzegovina, decided against the deployment of a peace-keeping force in the republic under prevailing conditions. On 20 May the Government of Bosnia and Herzegovina declared the JNA to be an 'occupying force' and announced the formation of a republican army. Two days later Bosnia and Herzegovina was accepted as a member of the UN. On 30 May the UN imposed economic sanctions against the FRY for its continuing involvement in the Bosnian conflict. In early June, in an apparent effort to placate the UN, Serb leaders in Belgrade (the FRY capital) ordered the Bosnian Serbs to end the siege of Sarajevo and to surrender Sarajevo airport to UN control. In the same month the UN Security Council decided to redeploy 1,000 of the UNPROFOR troops in Croatia to protect Sarajevo airport. An additional 500 troops were dispatched to Sarajevo in mid-July.

On 7 July 1992 there was a major development in the Bosnian conflict, when a breakaway Croat state, 'The Croatian Union of Herzeg-Bosna', was declared. The new state covered about 30% of the territory of Bosnia and Herzegovina and was headed by Mate Boban. Izetbegović's Government promptly declared it illegal, while Karadžić proposed that Serbs and Croats partition Bosnia and Herzegovina among themselves. Despite their political differences, Izetbegović and President Franjo Tudjman of Croatia (who supported the establishment of 'The Croatian Union of Herzeg-Bosna'), signed a treaty of friendship and co-operation in late July.

At the end of July 1992, as the number of people being killed in the Bosnian conflict rapidly increased, Izetbegović protested to the UN Security Council that the arms embargo that had been imposed on the former Yugoslavia in September 1991 favoured the Serbs, since it denied Bosnia and Herzegovina the opportunity to provide for its own defence. When the UN failed to react positively to this protest, the Government of Bosnia and Herzegovina decided to seek help from the Muslim world, and in early August the Bosnian Minister of Foreign Affairs, Haris Silajdžić, visited a number of Muslim countries in an attempt to win support for the afflicted population of Bosnia and Herzegovina.

Revelations concerning the predominantly Serb policy of 'ethnic cleansing' (involving the expulsion by one ethnic group of other ethnic groups in an attempt to create a homogenous population) and the discovery of a number of detention camps in Bosnia and Herzegovina led to the unanimous adoption by the UN Security Council, in early August 1992, of a resolution condemning the camps and those responsible for abuses of human rights. A further UN Security Council resolution, adopted in mid-August, demanded unimpeded access to the detention camps for the International Committee of the Red Cross (ICRC), authorized 'all measures necessary' to ensure the delivery of humanitarian aid, and reiterated that those abusing human rights in the former Yugoslavia would be held personally responsible. The ICRC was consequently given permission to inspect the camps and, having done so, accused all three ethnic communities in Bosnia and Herzegovina of using 'systematic brutality'.

In an annex to the agreement signed in July 1992, the Governments of Croatia and of Bosnia and Herzegovina formed a Joint Defence Committee in late September, and repeated demands that the UN remove its arms embargo on Croatia and Bosnia and Herzegovina. Within Bosnia and Herzegovina itself, however, hostilities erupted between Bosnian Croats and Muslims in mid-October, and the towns of Mostar, Novi Travnik and Vitez were captured by the Croats. Mostar was subsequently proclaimed the capital of 'The Croatian Union of Herzeg-Bosna'. In early November the Croat Jure Pelivan resigned as Prime Minister of Bosnia and Herzegovina, and was replaced by Mile Akmadžić. In mid-November the Croatian Government admitted for the first time that Croatian regular army units had been deployed in Bosnia and Herzegovina, and agreed to withdraw them. In accordance with this official admission, Croatia became a signatory to the latest cease-fire agreement in Bosnia and Herzegovina.

In early December 1992 the UN Human Rights Commission, echoing a statement made by the ICRC in October, declared that the Serbs were largely responsible for violations of human rights in Bosnia and Herzegovina. Following allegations of the organized rape of more than 20,000 Muslim women by Serb forces, the UN Security Council unanimously adopted, in mid-December, a resolution condemning these 'acts of unspeakable brutality' and demanding access to all Serb detention camps. The US Secretary of Defense, Richard Cheney, subsequently threatened the Serbs with air strikes if the ban on military flights (issued by the UN Security Council in October) was not respected, and appeared to be in favour of removing the arms embargo on Bosnia and Herzegovina.

Meanwhile, in mid-December 1992 the Serbian enclave in Bosnia and Herzegovina, now calling itself the 'Serbian Republic', unilaterally declared that the conflict was at an end and that the Serbs had won their own 'independent and sovereign state'. However, by late December Muslim forces appeared to be regaining territory. In early January 1993 the co-Chairmen of the Geneva Peace Conference (a permanent forum for talks on the conflict, established in 1992), Lord Owen (a former British Secretary of State for Foreign and Commonwealth Affairs) and Cyrus Vance (the UN mediator and a former US Secretary of State), visited Belgrade for talks with the newly re-elected President of Serbia, Slobodan Milošević. Their aim was to persuade him to convince the Bosnian Serbs to agree to a division of Bosnia and Herzegovina into 10 provinces (with three provinces allocated to each faction and Sarajevo as a province with special status). The peace plan was approved by the leader of the Bosnian Croats, Mate Boban, and, in part, by Izetbegović, but was rejected by the Bosnian Serb leader, Karadžić, who insisted on the establishment of a Serbian state within the territory of Bosnia and Herzegovina.

There appeared to be an improvement in the general situation in mid-January 1993, when Milošević attended the peace talks in Geneva for the first time. Karadžić, under pressure from Milošević and President Dobrica Cosić of the FRY, agreed to the constitutional proposals included in the plan and subsequently to the military arrangements. On 19–20 January the Bosnian Serb Assembly, meeting at its seat in Pale, voted to accept the general outline of the Vance-Owen plan. Hostilities between Croats and Muslims intensified, however, in central Bosnia.

In February 1993 the UN Security Council adopted a resolution providing for the establishment of an international court to try alleged war criminals for acts committed since 1991 in the former Yugoslav republics. (The court, which held its opening session in December, was the first of its kind since the Nuremberg trials of 1946.) In the following month the UN Security Council adopted a resolution to allow aircraft under the command of NATO to fire on any aircraft violating the 'no-fly zone' imposed on Bosnian airspace in October 1992.

During March 1993, at a new round of peace talks, Izetbegović agreed to both the military arrangements and the proposed territorial divisions included in the Vance-Owen plan, leaving the Bosnian Serbs as the only party not to have signed the section on the division of Bosnia and Herzegovina. In April the Bosnian Serb Assembly rejected the territorial arrangements, incurring international disapproval (including that of Serbia, which had endorsed the plan under pressure from UN and EC sanctions). In early May Karadžić signed the Vance-Owen plan in Geneva, but two days later it was decisively rejected by the Serb Assembly at Pale, since under the terms of the plan the Bosnian Serbs would be forced to surrender some territory that they had seized during the fighting. In late May the USA, France, Russia, Spain and the United Kingdom signed a communiqué declaring that the arms embargo on the former Yugoslavia would continue and that international armed forces would not intervene in the conflict on behalf of the Muslims; they proposed instead the creation of six UN 'safe areas' (Sarajevo, Bihać, Tuzla, Goražde, Srebreniča and Zepa) to protect the Muslim population from Serb attack, to take effect from 22 July. UN-negotiated cease-fires collapsed in May, as both the Bosnian Serbs and Croats initiated offensives to expand and consolidate their territorial holdings. In mid-June new peace proposals were announced in Geneva by Lord Owen and Thorvald Stoltenberg (formerly Norwegian Minister of Foreign Affairs, who had replaced Vance as the UN mediator in May), under which Bosnia and Herzegovina would become a confederation of three states divided on ethnic grounds. The Owen-Stoltenberg plan was welcomed by the Serb and Croat leaderships, since Milošević of Serbia and Tudjman of Croatia had initially conceived the plan, but the Bosnian State Presidency was divided. Izetbegović refused to discuss the tripartite division of Bosnia and boycotted the remainder of the Geneva talks, although other members of the Presidency continued discussions.

In early June 1993 the UN adopted a resolution to allow UNPROFOR to use force, including air power, in response to attacks against 'safe areas', but later that month failed to approve a resolution, supported by the USA, on the exemption of the Bosnian Muslims from the UN arms embargo. Muslims and Croats were, by this time, very clearly no longer allies in the war; in late June a joint Serb-Croat offensive began against the northern Muslim town of Maglaj, and in the following month Muslims and Croats began a fierce battle for control of the city of Mostar. Meanwhile, Izetbegović refused to attend the Geneva peace talks until Bosnian Serb forces withdrew from the strategic Mount Igman, overlooking Sarajevo. On 30 July the three warring factions reached a constitutional agreement in Geneva on the reconstruction of Bosnia and Herzegovina into a confederation of three ethnically-based states, styled the 'Union of Republics of Bosnia and Herzegovina', under a central government with powers limited to foreign policy and foreign trade. Under this agreement, Sarajevo, except for the municipality of Pale, would be placed under UN administration during a two-year transitional period. Despite this agreement and numerous negotiated cease-fires, fighting continued, and in early August the three Croat members of the Bosnian State Presidency (including Mile Akmadžić, the Prime Minister of Bosnia and Herzegovina) left the Bosnian Geneva delegation in protest at Muslim attacks on Croat populations and joined the Croatian negotiating team. On 27 August Akmadžić was dismissed from the premiership. On the following day the 'Croatian Republic of Herzeg-Bosna' was proclaimed by a Croat 'House of Representatives of the Assembly of the Croatian Republic of Herzeg-Bosna' (Croat Assembly) in Grude, which proceeded to accept the Owen-Stoltenberg plan on condition that the Serbs and Muslims also accepted it. On the same day the Serb Assembly in Pale also voted in favour of the plan. On 31 August, however, a session of the Assembly of Bosnia and Herzegovina rejected the Geneva plan in its existing form, while agreeing to use it as a basis for further peace negotiations.

On 10 September 1993 Fikret Abdić, a Muslim member of the Bosnian State Presidency and a rival of President Izetbegović, announced the creation of an 'Autonomous Province of Western Bosnia' in the Muslim region around Bihać, which was to form part of the 'Union of Republics of Bosnia and Herzegovina'. On 27 September, in Velika Kladusa, the province was declared to have been established and Abdić was elected President by a 'Constituent Assembly'. Abdić was subsequently dismissed from the Bosnian State Presidency, Izetbegović imposed martial law on the area, and fighting erupted between Abdić's followers and government forces. The Muslim Democratic Party was founded in Bihać, with Abdić as Chairman.

In late September 1993 the Croat and Serb Assemblies announced their intention to withdraw concessions offered during negotiations earlier that month: the Croats had allowed Bosnian access to the sea; the Serbs had agreed to accept a territorial division awarding them 52% of Bosnia's territory compared with the 70% they currently controlled. During September Izetbegović had agreed, in a significant concession, that after two years the Serb and Croat republics in a future confederation would be permitted to hold a referendum on whether to remain in the 'Union' or to join Serbia and Croatia respectively.

On 23 October 1993 Fikret Abdić and the Bosnian Croat leader, Mate Boban, officially declared their intent to establish peace in Western Bosnia; two days later Abdić and the Bosnian Serb leader, Karadžić, announced their commitment to peace between their two 'republics'. Later in the month two Croats and one Muslim were elected to the three vacant positions in the Bosnian State Presidency, while Dr Haris Silajdžić, formerly the Minister of Foreign Affairs, was appointed Prime Minister of the Bosnian Government, replacing Akmadžić. Silajdžić's Government took office on 30 October.

At further talks in late December 1993 the Bosnian Serbs refused to accept the establishment of a UN administration in Sarajevo and the reopening of Tuzla airport (which was surrounded by Serb positions) to accelerate the passage of aid. The Bosnians demanded access through Croatian territory to the Adriatic (thus interrupting continuous Croatian control of the coast) and, although they accepted the proposed division of the country (whereby Bosnian Muslims were to receive 33.3% of the territory, Croats 17.5% and Serbs 49.2%), they remained opposed to the specific areas allocated to Bosnian Muslims. In January 1994 NATO renewed its threat of tactical bombing against the Bosnian Serbs in retaliation for their continued siege of Sarajevo.

The massacre, in early February 1994, of 68 civilians in a Sarajevo market place by a single mortar round, fired (it was believed) by the Bosnian Serbs, prompted the EU and the USA to draft a joint French-US proposal that NATO set a deadline for Serb forces to cease their bombardment or risk being subjected to air attacks. Following a Russian initiative, the Bosnian Serbs withdrew most of their heavy weaponry, and Russian peace-keeping troops were deployed in the 'exclusion zone' around Sarajevo. However, the city remained effectively blockaded. In late February NATO aircraft shot down four Serb light attack aircraft near Banja Luka, which had violated the UN 'no-fly zone' over Bosnia and Herzegovina. The incident represented the first aggressive military action taken by NATO since its establishment. There was continuous Serb shelling of the Maglaj area in northern Bosnia throughout March, while Goražde, Bihać and other UN-designated 'safe areas' were also shelled. In the same month UNHCR officials accused the Serbs of the 'ethnic cleansing' of Banja Luka's Muslim population.

Following a cease-fire signed by the Bosnian Government and the Bosnian Croats in late February 1994, a major breakthrough was achieved: on 18 March, in Washington (USA), Prime Minister Silajdžić and Kresimir Zubak (who had replaced Mate Boban as the leader of the Bosnian Croats) signed an agreement on the creation of a Federation of Bosnia and Herzegovina, with power shared equally between Muslims and Croats. Under the federal Constitution (which had been finalized earlier in the month), a federal government was to be responsible for defence, foreign affairs and the economy. Greater executive power was to be vested in the prime ministerial post than in the presidency; the offices were to rotate annually between the two ethnic groups. Until the full implementation of the Federation and the holding of elections, Izetbegović was to remain President of the collective Presidency of Bosnia and Herzegovina; the emerging federal institutions were to operate in parallel during the interim period. At the same ceremony, a second, 'preliminary' agreement was signed by Presidents Izetbegović and Tudjman, which provided for the eventual creation of a loose confederation of the Federation and Croatia. As well as the establishment of a 'Confederative Council', closer economic ties between the two states were to be introduced, with the eventual aim of establishing a common market and monetary union. In late March the accords were approved by the Bosnian Croat Assembly, while the new Constitution was ratified by the Bosnian Assembly. However, the Bosnian Serb Assembly in Pale vetoed Serb participation in the agreements.

In April 1994, in response to the continued shelling of the 'safe area' of Goražde by Bosnian Serb forces, UN-sanctioned air strikes were launched by NATO aircraft on Serb ground positions. However, these did not prevent the Serb capture of Goražde later in the month, after intense fighting. This development prompted strong criticism from Russia, which hitherto had been perceived as sympathetic towards the Serbs, and on 24 April the Russian Minister of Foreign Affairs, Andrey Kozyrev, indicated that his Government would not oppose the use of force against the Bosnian Serbs. Following Kozyrev's intervention and faced with the threat of further NATO air strikes, Bosnian Serb forces withdrew from Goražde in late April. On 26 April a new negotiating forum was established in London, United Kingdom, following an appeal by President Yeltsin of Russia for an international summit to bring peace to Bosnia and Herzegovina. The 'Contact Group' comprised representatives from Russia, the USA, France, Germany and the United Kingdom.

In late May 1994 the Constituent Assembly of the Federation of Bosnia and Herzegovina held its inaugural meeting, at which it elected Kresimir Zubak to the largely ceremonial post of President of the Federation. Ejup Ganić, a Muslim, was elected Vice-President of the Federation (he was concurrently Vice-President of the collective Presidency of Bosnia and Herzegovina), while Silajdžić was appointed Prime Minister of the Federation. A joint Government of the Republic of Bosnia and Herzegovina and the Federation, led by Silajdžić, was appointed in late June. Earlier in the month it was announced that the existing Bosnian Assembly would act additionally as the interim legislature of the Federation.

Following peace negotiations in Geneva in early June 1994, a one-month cease-fire was declared throughout Bosnia and Herzegovina. Repeated violations were reported by the end of the month, however, by which time Bosnian government forces had captured Serb-held areas of central Bosnia in an attempt to link the region with the Adriatic coast. Fighting also escalated in the Bihać enclave between the Bosnian army and rebel forces led by Fikret Abdić.

The Contact Group presented new peace proposals in early July 1994, after its members had reached agreement on a territorial division of Bosnia and Herzegovina in late June. According to the new plan, the Federation of Bosnia and Herzegovina would be granted 51% of the territory of Bosnia and Herzegovina, while the Bosnian Serbs would yield approximately one-third of the territory they currently controlled. Key sensitive areas, including Sarajevo, Srebreniča, Goražde and Brčko, would be placed under UN and EU administration. In an indication of the international community's increasing impatience with the warring factions, the Contact Group warned of various measures that would be taken in the event of the parties' refusal of the plan. These included the relaxation of economic sanctions against Serbia and Montenegro if the Bosnian Government rejected the proposal, and the lifting of the arms embargo against Bosnia and Herzegovina in the event of Bosnian Serb refusal.

On 17 July 1994 Izetbegović and Tudjman endorsed the Contact Group plan, which was also approved by the Bosnian Assembly. However, the proposed territorial division was rejected by the Bosnian Serb Assembly at Pale. The Serbs' refusal to accept the plan centred on the question of Serb access to the Adriatic Sea, the status of Sarajevo and the right of the Bosnian Serbs to enter a confederation with the FRY. President Milošević of Serbia subsequently criticized the Bosnian Serbs for rejecting the plan, and in early August the FRY announced the closure of its border with Serb-occupied Bosnia and Herzegovina, blocking transits into the area with the exception of humanitarian aid convoys. On 5 August further NATO air strikes (the first since April) were launched against Bosnian Serb targets, following Serb attacks against UN forces and the renewed shelling of Sarajevo. In late August the Bosnian Serbs held a referendum in which 96% of participants voted to reject the Contact Group plan; the result was unanimously approved by the Bosnian Serb Assembly on 1 September. Meanwhile, on 21 August, the Bihać enclave, held by Abdić's forces, fell to the Bosnian government army.

In August and September 1994 tensions emerged between Muslims and Croats over the establishment of the Federation of Bosnia and Herzegovina. Contentious issues were addressed at a meeting between Izetbegović and Tudjman in Zagreb (Croatia) in mid-September, when it was agreed that interim municipal governments should be established by 30 September and cantonal authorities by 31 October. It was also agreed that a joint command of the Bosnian government army and the Bosnian Croat army should be instituted as soon as possible.

In early October 1994 Bosnian government troops infiltrated the demilitarized zone of Mount Igman, near Sarajevo, and attacked Serb forces there, to be repelled shortly afterwards by UNPROFOR troops. Later in the month government forces took control of tracts of Serb-held land around the Bihać enclave. In early November government forces, supported by Bosnian Croat troops, launched offensives on three fronts: in central Bosnia, in the Bihać area and around Sarajevo. The fall of the strategic Serb-held town of Kupres on 3 November represented the first significant military gain for the Muslim-Croat alliance (and the first decisive victory for government forces since the beginning of the conflict). By late November, however, the Serbs had regained most of the Bihać territory. Meanwhile, in early November, the USA announced that its warships in the Adriatic Sea would no longer police the international arms embargo.

On 30 November 1994 an attempt by the UN Secretary-General, Dr Boutros Boutros-Ghali, to protect the Bihać 'safe area' from further Bosnian Serb attack and to salvage the UN peace-keeping operation in Bosnia and Herzegovina met with failure when Karadžić refused to meet him at Sarajevo airport. (Karadžić boycotted the proposed discussions owing to the UN's refusal to recognize the 'Serbian Republic'.) In early December the Contact Group issued a text based on the July peace plan (dividing Bosnia between the Federation and the Bosnian Serbs), which indicated the possibility of confederal links between the Bosnian Serbs and the FRY. President Milošević supported the proposals. In mid-December the former US President, Jimmy Carter (acting in a non-official capacity), visited Bosnia and Herzegovina with the aim of persuading the Bosnian Serb leadership to accept the Contact Group plan. On 19 December Carter won the promise of a four-month cease-fire from the Bosnian Serbs and the Bosnian Government, to take effect from 1 January 1995. Both sides expressed their readiness to resume peace negotiations based on the revised Contact Group plan; there were also agreements on the exchange of prisoners. The cease-fire agreement was formally signed by both parties on 31 December.

The cease-fire was generally observed throughout Bosnia and Herzegovina during January 1995. However, intense fighting continued in the Bihać enclave between government forces and troops loyal to Abdić, supported by troops from the self-proclaimed 'Republic of Serbian Krajina' (RSK) in Croatia (adjoining the Bihać enclave). There were renewed disagreements between Muslims and Croats over the implementation of the new Federation, the most controversial issues being the co-ordination of a joint military command, the division of power, and territorial reorganization. In mid-January members of the Muslim PDA demanded Zubak's resignation as President of the Federation. In early February, however, Zubak and Silajdžić were signatories to an accord allowing grievances concerning the implementation of the Federation of Bosnia and Herzegovina to be submitted to some form of (as yet unspecified) international arbitration. In the same month the USA refused to continue negotiations with Karadžić until the Bosnian Serbs accepted the Contact Group plan. In mid-February the War Crimes Tribunal for the Former Yugoslavia (established by the UN Security Council in 1993, with its seat in The Hague, the Netherlands) charged 21 Serbs with crimes against humanity (including one charge of genocide), allegedly committed at the Omarska concentration camp in north-western Bosnia and Herzegovina in 1992.

In early 1995 hostilities continued in the Bihać enclave, where Bosnian Serb and Bosnian government troops had resumed fighting around Bosanska Krupa, with the 'safe area' of Bihać town being directly targeted by the Serbs. In mid-February the UN announced that Serb and rebel Muslim attacks on humanitarian aid convoys into the Bihać enclave were resulting in the starvation of Muslim civilians within the 'safe area'. On 20 February, a military pact was signed between the Bosnian Serbs and the Croatian Serbs, guaranteeing mutual assistance in the event of attack and providing for the establishment of a joint Supreme Defence Council to be led by Karadžić and the Croatian Serb leader, Milan Martić. In late February the Bosnian Government introduced new restrictions on the movements of peace-keepers within its borders, preventing UN observers from monitoring front lines. In early March, following talks in Zagreb, Croatia, a formal military alliance was announced between the armies of Croatia, the Bosnian Croats and the Bosnian Government, whose commander criticized the cease-fire, claiming that it was serving only to consolidate the Serbs' territorial gains.

In late March 1995 the UN threatened to order NATO air strikes against Serb targets unless the Bosnian Serbs halted their shelling of the UN 'safe areas' of Sarajevo, Tuzla, Bihać and Goražde. The Contact Group appealed to the warring factions to respect and work towards the extension of the four-month cease-fire, while Russia presented a fresh peace plan to the US Secretary of State, Warren Christopher, in Geneva. The plan, involving Serbian recognition of Bosnia and Herzegovina in exchange for the simultaneous lifting of UN sanctions against the FRY, had reportedly been drafted by President Milošević and the Russian Minister of Foreign Affairs, Andrey Kozyrev.

Attacks by government forces against the Serbs in the Majevica mountains, near Tuzla, continued in April 1995. Government troops also seized control of a strategic telecommunications centre on Mount Vlasić in central Bosnia following fierce clashes in early April, while Bosnian Croat forces regained high ground from the Serbs near the border with Croatia. Intense fighting also persisted in the Bihać enclave, where government forces came under attack from rebel Muslims and their Serb allies. Four consecutive days of Serb artillery attacks on the designated 'safe area' of Bihać in early April prompted the UN to request reconnaissance flights by NATO to identify the location of Serb weaponry. Repeated calls made by the UNPROFOR commander in Bosnia and Herzegovina, Lt-Gen. Rupert Smith, for a meeting with the Bosnian Serb commander, Gen. Ratko Mladić, were ignored. In addition, persistent Serb sniper attacks in Sarajevo blatantly violated the foundering cease-fire accord, and by 6 April fighting around the capital had spread to the western suburb of Hrasniča. On 11 April NATO aircraft flew over Goražde following a Serb artillery attack on the town. In mid-April there were also outbreaks of hostilities in and around the central Bosnian towns of Tesanj, Zepce, Maglaj and Kladanj.

The Serbs intensified their besiegement of Sarajevo in mid-April 1995, attacking the only land route out of the capital and forcing the closure of the airport through their refusal to guarantee the safe passage of aircraft. At this point in time, the possibility of all-out war in Bosnia and Herzegovina seemed ever more likely, since the cease-fire was due to expire on 30 April. On 12 April Contact Group officials travelled to Belgrade to offer the FRY a partial lifting of sanctions in exchange for the latter's recognition of Bosnia and Herzegovina and Croatia. The proposal was rejected by President Milošević, however, and the negotiators were unable to hold discussions with the Bosnian Government, since the Bosnian Serbs refused to guarantee their safe passage into Sarajevo. Subsequent negotiations in Zagreb with President Tudjman proved unsuccessful.

On 8 April 1995 an agreement was signed between President Zubak of the Federation and Ejup Ganić, Vice-President of both the Federation and of Bosnia and Herzegovina, aimed at accelerating the establishment of federal institutions. The inaugural session of the Federation's Constituent Assembly duly took place in Novi Travnik on 4 May, during which the Bonn Agreement on the implementation of federal principles was unanimously adopted.

Serb attacks on Sarajevo continued in early May 1995. On 7 May shells fired into the Butmir suburb resulted in the deaths of 11 civilians and soldiers; Lt-Gen. Smith ordered punitive air strikes the following day. Controversy arose, however, when the British commander's order was countermanded by the UN Special Envoy, who cited the potential risk of Serb reprisals against UNPROFOR personnel should such an order be carried out. In mid-May heavy fighting was reported around the Serb-held corridor near Brčko, while hostilities intensified around Sarajevo, with Bosnian government forces regaining territory to the south-east of the capital. In a move reflecting increasing UN impatience at the situation, Lt-Gen. Smith issued a formal ultimatum to both the Bosnian Serbs and the Bosnian Government on 24 May, which threatened NATO air strikes unless all heavy weapons were removed from the 20-km 'exclusion zone' around Sarajevo (or surrendered to peace-keepers) by midday on 26 May. On 25 May, however, NATO aircraft carried out strikes on Serb ammunition depots near Pale, a move which was openly criticized by Russia. Within hours of the NATO air strikes, Serb forces responded by shelling five of the six UN 'safe areas' and, following further NATO air strikes against Serb positions on 26 May, retaliated with a massive bombardment of Tuzla, which resulted in at least 70 deaths. Over the next few days, in an attempt to deter more NATO attacks, Serb troops disarmed and took hostage 222 UNPROFOR personnel. On 28 May the Bosnian Minister of Foreign Affairs, Irfan Ljubijankić, was killed when the helicopter in which he was travelling to Bihać was shot down by Croatian Serbs.

In early June 1995 the UN and NATO were unable to take retaliatory action against fighting in the Goražde 'safe area' due to the Serbs' holding of UNPROFOR hostages in the region. While the Organization for Security and Co-operation in Europe (OSCE) demanded the unconditional release of the peace-keepers and President Clinton of the USA offered a suspension of sanctions against the FRY in exchange for a denunciation of hostage-taking by President Milošević, the UN rejected the Serbs' offer of conditional negotiations on the release of the hostages. In the mean time, on 3 June defence ministers from NATO and some other European states agreed on the creation of a 10,000-strong 'rapid reaction force', which was to operate in Bosnia and Herzegovina under UN command from mid-July and the mandate of which was to provide 'enhanced protection' to UNPROFOR. The ongoing hostage crisis, led, however, to a withdrawal of UNPROFOR troops from Bosnian Serb territory around Sarajevo in mid-June and the consequent collapse of the 20-km 'exclusion zone'. Although the UN denied that any deal had been struck with the Bosnian Serbs, the release of the remaining hostages roughly coincided with the withdrawal of UNPROFOR from around the capital. The Bosnian Prime Minister, Haris Silajdžić, subsequently claimed that Serb aircraft were circulating freely in the 'no-fly' zone over Bosnia and Herzegovina.

On 11 July 1995 the 'safe area' of Srebreniča in south-eastern Bosnia was captured by the Bosnian Serbs after Dutch peace-keeping troops based in the town were taken hostage, prompting NATO air strikes on Serb tanks approaching the town. (A third air strike was halted when Serb troops threatened to kill a number of the Dutch hostages; the hostages were eventually released on 21 July.) The fall of Srebreniča was followed by the capture of the nearby 'safe area' of Zepa on 25 July. On the following day the Bosnian Prime Minister demanded that the UN employ force, if so required, to evacuate civilians from Zepa (in Srebreniča draft-age Muslim men had been detained by the Bosnian Serb command and transported to camps in Bosnian Serb territory to be investigated for involvement in 'war crimes'). Another 'safe area', Bihać, was attacked on 20 July; the assault involved a concerted effort by Bosnian Serbs, Croatian Serbs and rebel Bosnian Muslims led by Fikret Abdić. The situation in Bihać prompted the signature of a military co-operation agreement between Bosnian President Alija Izetbegović and Croatian President Franjo Tudjman in Split, Croatia, on 22 July. Five days later, Croatian government troops massed in western Bosnia in an attempt to relieve the crisis in Bihać. Croatian and Bosnian Croat troops launched attacks on Serb positions around Bihać, as a result of which Serb supply routes into the Krajina enclave were blocked.

Croatian government forces invaded Serb-held Krajina on 4 August 1995; by 9 August the whole of the enclave had been recaptured by Croatia, resulting in a massive exodus of Serb civilians from the region into Serb-held areas of Bosnia and Herzegovina and into Serbia itself. On 6–7 August the siege of Bihać was effectively broken by Bosnian government and Croatian troops. On 9 August a fresh peace initiative, known as the 'Holbrooke initiative' after its architect, Richard Holbrooke, the US Assistant Secretary of State for European and Canadian Affairs, was unveiled by the US Government; the proposals, which were based on the Contact Group plan of 1994, allowed the Bosnian Serbs to retain control of Srebreniča and Zepa.

On 28 August 1995 a suspected Serb mortar attack near a market place in central Sarajevo resulted in 37 deaths, prompting Bosnian Prime Minister Silajdžić to demand a clarification of the UN peace-keeping role in the 'safe area' of Sarajevo. NATO responded to the mortar attack by launching a series of air strikes on Serb positions across Bosnia and Herzegovina on 30 August. The devastating strikes (codenamed 'Operation Deliberate Force') were criticized by the Russian President, who described them as a 'cruel bombardment'. NATO air strikes were resumed on 5 September, however, following the collapse of cease-fire negotiations between UNPROFOR and the Bosnian Serbs.

On 8 September 1995 major progress in the peace process was achieved when, at a meeting in Geneva, Switzerland, chaired by the Contact Group, the Ministers of Foreign Affairs of Bosnia and Herzegovina, Croatia and the FRY (the latter acting on behalf of the Bosnian Serbs), signed an agreement determining basic principles for a peace accord. These principles incorporated the territorial division of Bosnia and Herzegovina as earlier proposed by the Contact Group, with 51% apportioned to the

Federation and 49% to the Bosnian Serbs. They also included the continuing existence of Bosnia and Herzegovina within its present borders, but the country was to be composed of two entities, namely the Federation of Bosnia and Herzegovina (as stated in the Washington Agreements of 1994) and a Serb Republic, with each entity existing under its present Constitution. In mid-September 'Operation Deliberate Force' was suspended, following the withdrawal of Bosnian Serb weaponry from the 'exclusion zone' around Sarajevo. Agreement on further basic principles for a peace accord was reached by the foreign ministers of Bosnia and Herzegovina, Croatia and the FRY, meeting in New York on 26 September. These included a one-third share in the republican parliamentary seats for the Serb Republic, while the Federation would control two-thirds of the seats (legislative decisions would only be implemented, however, with the approval of at least one-third of the deputies of each entity). A collective presidency would also be organized according to the one-third Serb/two-thirds Muslim-Croat proportional division, with all decisions being taken by majority vote. It was decided, furthermore, that free elections, under international auspices, would be held in Bosnia and Herzegovina at the earliest opportunity.

On 5 October 1995 a 60-day cease-fire was announced by President Clinton in Washington, DC, USA, which came into effect in Bosnia and Herzegovina on 12 October. The UN simultaneously announced its intention to reduce the number of peace-keeping troops in the area. Sporadic fighting continued in northern Bosnia and Herzegovina in early October, however, as the warring factions made final attempts to seize land before further negotiations. In late October, at a summit meeting between Presidents Yeltsin and Clinton, it was agreed that Russian peace implementation troops would co-operate with, but work independently of, the NATO Peace Implementation Force, which was to be deployed in the country following the signature of a formal peace accord.

On 1 November 1995 peace negotiations between the three warring parties in the Bosnian conflict began in Dayton, Ohio, USA, and were attended by Presidents Izetbegović, Tudjman and Milošević (the latter representing both the FRY and the Bosnian Serbs) and representatives of the Contact Group and the EU. On 10 November Izetbegović and Tudjman signed an accord aimed at reinforcing the 1994 federation agreement, which included a provision for the unification of the divided city of Mostar as the federal capital and seat of the federal presidency. This significant Muslim-Croat agreement was followed two days later by the signature of an accord between Croatia and the Croatian Serbs of Eastern Slavonia, which provided for the eventual reintegration of Serb-held Eastern Slavonia into Croatia. The most comprehensive peace agreement was achieved on 21 November, however, when Izetbegović, Tudjman and Milošević initialled a definitive accord dividing Bosnia and Herzegovina between the Federation, with 51% of the territory, and a Serb Republic, which would control 49% of the area; it was stressed, however, that any relations with neighbouring countries should honour the sovereignty and territorial integrity of Bosnia and Herzegovina. The Dayton agreement, which was based on the agreements on basic principles signed in Geneva and New York in September, included provisions for a central government with a democratically elected collective presidency and a parliament, based in Sarajevo; and provisions for a single monetary system and central bank, and other institutions for the economic reconstruction of Bosnia and Herzegovina. It also stipulated the right of all refugees and displaced persons to return to their homes and to have seized property returned to them, or else receive fair compensation. A central feature of the agreement was the special status of Sarajevo as a united city within the Federation, while it was also envisaged that each of the warring factions would relinquish some of the territory under its control at the time of the October cease-fire. Serb-held suburbs of Sarajevo were to be transferred to the administration of the Federation, while Bosnian Serbs were to retain control of Srebreniča and Zepa; Goražde was to remain under the control of the Federation and was to be linked to Sarajevo via a Federation-administered land corridor. No agreement was reached, however, regarding the width of the strategically vital Posavina corridor connecting the northern sector of the Serb Republic with the southern sector and control of the town of Brčko which is located at this point; the three sides agreed to place the issue under international arbitration. Under the Dayton agreement, UNPROFOR troops were to be replaced by an international NATO-commanded 60,000-strong 'Implementation Force' (IFOR, see p. 206). The agreement provided IFOR with broad authority: its mandate included overseeing the withdrawal of the warring parties from zones of separation and monitoring the agreed exchanges of territory; it also encompassed resolving boundary disputes, creating 'secure conditions' for the holding of free elections and responding to violence against civilians. Under the agreement, IFOR had the right to 'complete and unimpeded freedom of movement by ground, air and water'. Following the initialling of the Dayton peace agreement, on 22 November the UN voted to suspend the remaining economic sanctions against the FRY and to phase out gradually the arms embargo imposed on all of the former Yugoslav republics in September 1991. On 30 November 1995 the deadline of 31 January 1996 was set by the UN Security Council for the withdrawal of UNPROFOR troops from Bosnia and Herzegovina. Foreign ministers and officials from more than 50 countries and international organizations attended a conference held in London in early December 1995 on the implementation of the Dayton peace agreement. During this Peace Implementation Conference it was agreed that an OSCE mission would organize and oversee parliamentary elections in Bosnia and Herzegovina and that the Contact Group would be replaced by a Peace Implementation Council (notably including no UN representatives) based in Brussels, Belgium. The former Swedish Prime Minister and EU envoy to the Bosnian peace talks, Carl Bildt, was appointed High Representative of the International Community in Bosnia and Herzegovina, with responsibility for the implementation of the civilian aspects of the Dayton agreement. On 14 December the Dayton peace agreement was formally signed by Izetbegović, Tudjman and Milošević and by President Clinton and a number of European political leaders in Paris, France. The formal transfer of power from UNPROFOR to IFOR took place on 20 December.

In mid-December 1995 the People's Assembly of the Serb Republic elected a new Government, headed by Rajko Kasagić. On 30 January 1996 Hasan Muratović was elected by the republican Assembly as Prime Minister of the Republic of Bosnia and Herzegovina, following the resignation from the premiership of Haris Silajdžić; a new central Government was appointed on the same day. Silajdžić was reportedly rejecting the increasing Bosniak nationalism of the ruling PDA. On 31 January the Constituent Assembly of the Federation appointed a new federal Government, with Izudin Kapetanović as Prime Minister.

In mid-February 1996, in response to unrest in the city of Mostar and isolated attacks elsewhere, the USA demanded the holding of an emergency summit. A three-day meeting subsequently took place in Rome, Italy, on 16–18 February, during which Izetbegović, Tudjman and Milošević reaffirmed their adherence to the Dayton agreement. A joint Croat-Muslim police patrol, accompanied by officers from the UN International Police Task Force (IPTF) and Western European Union (WEU) subsequently began operating in Mostar.

By the end of April 1996 substantial progress had been made in the implementation of the military aspects of the Dayton agreement. The former warring parties completed staged withdrawals from the IFOR-controlled zone of separation; agreement was reached, under the auspices of the OSCE in Vienna, on the exchange of information on weaponry and the submission of arsenals to OSCE inspection; and the majority of prisoners of war were released, albeit with some delays. However, the exchange of territory between the two Bosnian 'entities' did not proceed as envisaged in the peace agreement. From mid-January there was a mass exodus from the Serb-held suburbs of Sarajevo that were passing to the control of the Bosnian Federation. This was accompanied by the destruction of homes and public buildings that were being vacated on a large scale. The Serb authorities in Pale were criticized for using intimidation to coerce the Serb inhabitants of these districts into leaving and to resettle in towns in the Serb Republic from which Muslims had been driven during the war. The Bosnian Government was also criticized for failing adequately to reassure the Serbs on Bosnian Federation territory that their interests would be protected. By late March only about 10% of the previous Serb population in the Sarajevo area remained.

In early April 1996 Muslim and Croat leaders agreed on a customs union linking the two parts of the Bosnian Federation. They also agreed on a single state budget and a unitary banking system. In mid-May further agreement was reached betwen the two sides, meeting in Washington, on the merger of their armed forces and the return of refugees. The agreement on a unified federation army was the principal precondition for the implementation of the controversial US programme to train and equip the Federation's army in order to place it on an equal military footing with that of the Serb Republic. Also in mid-May Karadžić dismissed Kasagić as Serb Prime Minister and appointed Gojko Klicković, a former Serb Minister for Health, in his place; Klicković's appointment was endorsed by the Bosnian Serb People's Assembly. Kasagić, who was considered a moderate among Serbs, had been co-operating to a large extent with the international community, and high-level diplomatic efforts were undertaken both to effect Kasagić's reinstatement and to oust Karadžić from the presidency. Karadžić had been indicted by the International Criminal Tribunal on the Former Yugoslavia for his part in the siege of Sarajevo and the alleged massacre at Srebreniča in July 1995. His continued position as President—as well as that of Gen. Ratko Mladić, also indicted for war crimes, as head of the armed forces—was in breach of the Dayton agreement, which prohibited indicted war criminals from holding public office. In response to international pressure, Karadžić announced the delegation of some of his powers to his deputy, Dr Biljana Plavšić. In early June 1996 the USA threatened Milošević with renewed sanctions against the FRY unless he effect the removal from office of Karadžić and Mladić and their extradiction to the Netherlands to stand trial. At the Peace Implementation Conference on Bosnia and Herzegovina held in Florence, Italy, in mid-June, the holding of all-Bosnia elections in September was approved. Later in the same month the Chairman-in-Office of the OSCE, which was given responsibility under the Dayton accord for the organization and supervision of the Bosnian elections, formally announced that these would proceed on 14 September.

In early May 1996 the first trial at the International Criminal Tribunal for the Former Yugoslavia opened: a Bosnian Serb, Dušan Tadić, faced prosecution for multiple charges relating to atrocities committed at the Omarska concentration camp during the Serb campaign of 'ethnic cleansing' that began in 1992. In mid-June Bosnian Croats in Mostar announced a new government of Herzeg-Bosna, in defiance of agreements that the separate Croat state would be dissolved; Pero Marković was named as prime minister of the new government. Municipal elections in Mostar were held on 30 June: the PDA-dominated List for a United Mostar gained 21 of the council seats, while the CDU secured 16 seats. At a summit meeting of the Presidents of Bosnia and Herzegovina, Croatia and Serbia, which was convened by the USA in Geneva in mid-August, Tudjman and Izetbegović agreed on the full establishment of the Bosnian Federation by the end of the month. Tudjman vouched for the dismantling of Herzeg-Bosna, while Izetbegović agreed that the functions of the current Bosnian Government that would not pass to the tripartite Presidency would revert to the Federation. The three Presidents signed a fresh declaration committing themselves to the Dayton agreement.

In late June 1996 Western European countries issued an ultimatum to Karadžić to resign, on penalty of the reimposition of sanctions against the Serb Republic (suspended in April, following the Serb withdrawal behind IFOR's line of separation). In defiance of this, the SDP re-elected Karadžić as their party leader. At the end of June Karadžić sent a letter to Bildt announcing his temporary resignation and the appointment of Plavšić as the acting Serb President. It was then confirmed that Karadžić would not stand in the election to the Serb presidency in September, and Plavšić was nominated as the SDP candidate. None the less, it was deemed unacceptable that Karadžić should retain the powerful position of party leader, and Robert Frowick, the head of the OSCE Bosnian mission, declared that the SDP would be excluded from the elections if Karadžić retained any office in the party. In mid-July the International Criminal Tribunal issued arrest warrants for Karadžić and Mladić; however, IFOR's mandate was not changed, and NATO remained cautious regarding pursuit of the indicted men. A few days later the USA dispatched former Assistant Secretary of State, Richard Holbrooke, to the former Yugoslavia in an attempt to engineer Karadžić's removal. Following intensive negotiations with Milošević and Bosnian Serb leaders, Holbrooke secured Karadžić's resignation on 19 July both from the presidency and as head of the SDP. Plavšić remained acting President, while Aleksa Buha succeeded Karadžić as leader of the SDP. Both politicians were considered to be as uncompromisingly nationalist as Karadžić himself.

Following Karadžić's resignation, the OSCE announced that campaigning for the September 1996 election could begin. Reports of harassment and violence perpetrated by the PDA and its supporters against members of the opposition increased during August. Opposition candidates in the Serb Republic were also subjected to intimidation, amid complaints from many international observers, as well as opposition activists themselves, that the conditions for the holding of free and fair elections did not exist. Absence of freedom of movement and freedom of the media (overwhelmingly controlled by the three nationalist parties) and manipulation of voter registration were cited as major obstacles to the democratic process. In late August the OSCE announced that the Bosnian municipal elections, which were to have been held concurrently with the other elections, were to be postponed. This was in response to evidence that the Serb authorities were forcibly registering displaced Serbs in formerly Muslim-dominated localities. This arose from the provision included in the Dayton agreement permitting refugees and displaced persons to vote either in their former homes or in the place where they chose to settle. National elections were held on 14 September for the republican Presidency and legislature, the presidency and legislature of the Serb Republic, and the legislature and cantonal authorities of the Bosnian Federation. The elections were monitored by about 1,200 OSCE observers, while IFOR and the IPTF were responsible for maintaining a secure environment. They provided, in particular, protection to displaced Muslims who travelled to vote in their towns of origin in the Serb Republic. Of the total electorate, about 850,000 (or nearly one-third) were internally-displaced or refugees living abroad. As expected, the three principal nationalist parties secured the largest portion of the votes cast. In the elections for the republican Presidency Izetbegović won 80% of the Bosniak vote; Kresimir Zubak (CDU) 88% of the Croat vote; and Momčilo Krajišnik (SDP), the former Speaker of the Serb Assembly, 67% of the Serb vote. Having received the largest number of votes of the three winning presidential candidates, Izetbegović became Chairman of the Presidency. The Federation section of the republican House of Representatives and the Federation's own House of Representatives were dominated by the PDA and the CDU. None the less, the Joint List of Bosnia and Herzegovina, comprising an alliance of social-democrat Bosniak and Croat parties, and the Party for Bosnia and Herzegovina (established earlier that year by the former Prime Minister, Haris Silajdžić) won a significant number of votes in the elections to both the republican and federation Houses. Although the SDP secured a majority of votes in both the Serb section of the House of Representatives and in the Serb National Assembly, the PDA polled about one-sixth of the votes cast on the territory of the Serb Republic. The People's Alliance for Peace and Progress also gained a significant share of the Serb vote in the elections to the House of Representatives and the Serb National Assembly. Plavšić was elected President of the Serb Republic and Dragolub Mirjanić her Vice-President, securing some 59% of the votes cast. The validity of the election results was questioned by the International Crisis Group, comprising senior Western European politicians, who had calculated the rate of participation by Muslim voters at 103.9% (the OSCE had estimated an overall turnout of 82%); they suggested that a large number of voting papers had been fraudulently added to the ballot boxes. The OSCE subsequently revised its estimate of the Bosnian electorate from 2.92m. to 3.2m. and refused to order a recount of the ballot papers. On 30 September the three members of the Presidency met for the first time at a session hosted by Bildt in the outskirts of Sarajevo. Following the OSCE certification of the election results, the UN Security Council decided on 1 October to remove definitively the sanctions regime against the FRY and the Serb Republic. A few days later Izetbegović and Milošević, meeting in Paris, agreed to establish full diplomatic relations. Their agreement included a commitment from Milošević to respect the territorial integrity of Bosnia and Herzegovina, while Izetbegović consented to recognize the FRY as the successor state to Yugoslavia. The inaugural session of the Presidency was held on 5 October; however, Krajišnik failed to attend, claiming that his personal safety might be threatened in Sarajevo (where the ceremony was held). The inaugural session of the republican Assembly was to have been held on the same day, but was boycotted by the Serb deputies. The new National Assembly of the Serb Republic held its inaugural session on 19 October; the inaugural session of the federation House of Representatives was held on 6 November.

In mid-October 1996 the OSCE changed the regulations regarding voting in the delayed municipal elections, ruling that people could only vote in their places of residence prior to 1992. The municipal elections were to have taken place in November 1996, but were postponed again until April or May 1997. In early November 1996 Plavšić announced that she had dismissed Gen. Mladić as commander of the Serb armed forces, replacing him with a little-known officer, Maj.-Gen. Pero Colić. A large number of the members of Mladić's general staff were also replaced, but Mladić and the other officers refused to accept their dismissal. After a power struggle, during which the Minister of Defence of the Serb Republic was taken captive for a short time by Mladić's supporters, Mladić agreed to surrender his position at the end of November.

In mid-November 1996 there was a series of clashes between Muslims and Serbs along the inter-entity boundary near the Serb-held village of Gajevi, to which the Muslims were attempting to return. One Muslim was killed and two were injured by grenades fired by the Serbs. This was one of many incidents in which Muslims attempting to return home on Serb-held territory were forcibly repulsed. In many parts of the country hostility between the ethnic groups continued, with minority elements being intimidated and often driven out from their homes. At a conference on Bosnia and Herzegovina hosted by the French Government in mid-November, it was agreed that the post of High Representative of the International Community would be maintained for a further two years, and that Bildt's powers would be increased to make him the final arbiter in the interpretation of the civilian provisions of the Dayton agreement. A Bosnian Peace Implementation Conference was held in London in early December, at which the NATO Secretary-General announced the readiness of the Alliance to provide a successor to IFOR, to be known as the Stabilization Force (SFOR). SFOR was to be about one-half the size of IFOR and was to have a mandate of 18 months, with six-monthly reviews. SFOR took over from IFOR on 20 December. In mid-December, after some delay, the Presidency appointed the two Co-Prime Ministers of the republican Council of Ministers: Haris Silajdžić of the Party for Bosnia and Herzegovina and Boro Bosić of the SDP. One week later the federal House of Representatives elected Edhem Bicackić as the federal Prime Minister, replacing Izudin Kapetanović. (On the previous day the Bosnian Croats had announced that 'Herzeg-Bosna' had ceased to exist.) The republican Council of Ministers was appointed by the Co-Prime Ministers and approved by the inaugural session of the Bosnian Assembly, which was finally held on 3 January 1997. The Council of Ministers comprised Ministers for Foreign Affairs, for Foreign Trade and Economic Relations, and for Communications and Civilian Affairs. Each post had two Deputy Ministers, with each of the Bosnian ethnic groups holding an equal number of offices. In February a ruling on the future status of the disputed town of Brčko was postponed until March 1998 by an international arbitration commission, and in the following month Robert Farrand, a US diplomat, was appointed to act as supervisor of the town in the interim period. In March 1997 Vladimir Soljić was elected to replace Kresimir Zubak as President of the Federation. (Soljić, in turn, was succeeded by Vice-President, Dr Ejup Ganić, in December.)

On 28 February 1997 Krajišnik signed, on behalf of the Serb Republic, an agreement with the FRY to foster mutual economic co-operation and to collaborate on regional security. The accord was ratified by the National Assembly of the Serb Republic in March, despite opposition voiced by President Plavšić and by a number of Bosnian Muslim and Bosnian Croat leaders. In June Plavšić suspended Dragan Kilac as Minister of Internal Affairs, following the alleged failure of Kilac to consult Plavšić on important decisions. The suspension was opposed by the National Assembly, which contested the constitutional legality of the decision. On her return to the Serb Republic from the UK on 29 June, Plavšić was briefly detained by FRY interior ministry officials at Belgrade airport and questioned. Plavšić responded by accusing Karadžić of corruption and of orchestrating the opposition to her in the Bosnian Serb legislature. In the following month Plavšić announced the dissolution of the National Assembly and scheduled parliamentary elections to be held at the beginning of September. Although this action was supported by both the UN and the OSCE, it was sharply criticized by Gojko Klicković, the Prime Minister of the Serb Republic, and a number of resolutions designed to undermine Plavšić were approved at a session of the National Assembly held in Pale immediately following the dissolution announcement. In mid-August the Constitutional Court ruled that Plavšić's decision to dissolve the legislature had been illegal: the Assembly proceeded to vote to disregard future decrees by Plavšić. (It subsequently emerged that one of the Constitutional Court judges had been subject to physical intimidation, allegedly by supporters of Karadžić, prior to the judgment). Plavšić's position was strengthened in August following a decision by the Serb Republic's Vice-President, Dragolub Mirjanić, to abandon the Assembly in Pale and join the presidential team in Banja Luka. Later in the month Plavšić appointed Mark Pavić to replace Kilac as Minister of Internal Affairs; however the appointment was rejected by the Assembly, which subsquently promoted Kilac to the post of Deputy Prime Minister and appointed an alternative to Pavić to head the interior ministry. In late September a constitutional crisis was averted following a meeting in Belgrade hosted by President Milošević and attended by Plavšić and Krajišnik. A joint statement was issued detailing an agreement which provided for elections to the National Assembly to be held in November under the aegis of the OSCE (see below), and for presidential elections for both the Serb Republic and the Bosnian collective presidency to be held on 7 December. (Early presidential elections were discounted, however, by Plavšić in October.) The agreement also stated that radio and television would be broadcast on alternate days from the studios in Pale and Banja Luka. A sharp difference in editorial policy between the two stations, which supported, respectively, the National Assembly and President Plavšić, had arisen in August. On 1 October troops from SFOR seized four television transmitters allegedly being used for propaganda purposes by supporters of Karadžić—the action was immediately condemned as unlawful by Krajišnik and other prominent members of the Serb National Assembly. Later in the month Carlos Westendorp, who had replaced Bildt as High Representative in June, announced his intention to reorganize the Bosnian Serb television service and to demand the resignation of the management board, including Krajišnik.

At a further Bosnian Peace Implementation Conference, held in Sintra, Portugal, in May 1997, NATO stipulated deadlines for the approval by the entities of a number of laws on property, passports and citizenship. In addition a new list of ambassadors was demanded better to reflect the ethnic diversity of the country. Following the expiry on 1 August of the deadline for the submission of the new diplomatic list, the USA and the EU suspended recognition of Bosnia and Herzegovina's ambassadors. (An agreement was reached later in the month whereby the posts were to be distributed evenly between the three communities.) In July, at a conference of international donors, the Serb Republic was warned that the supply of economic aid might be disrupted if suspected war criminals were not extradited to the International Criminal Tribunal for the former Yugoslavia, based in the Hague (Netherlands). Earlier in the month the EU had announced the suspension of aid to the republic for its failure to comply with this requirement. In late November the collective Presidency accepted a Croatian proposal for the creation of a joint committee to improve co-operation between the two countries; a Croatian proposal to establish special relations with the Federation, which included a customs and monetary union, had been rejected earlier in the month by Izetbegović, who deemed that the authority of the collective Presidency would be undermined. On 17 December the Bosnian Assembly approved the law on passports within the deadline established by the international community, but failed to ratify the law on citizenship; the following day Westendorp announced that the citizenship law would be imposed on Bosnian territory from 1 January 1998. (An agreement had been signed earlier in the month by Krajišnik and the FRY Government, which accorded Bosnian Serbs citizenship of both Bosnia and Herzegovina and the FRY.) In late December it was announced that NATO had agreed to extend indefinitely the mandate of the peace-keeping forces; in November Westendorp had warned that renewed hostilities might ensue, following the scheduled withdrawal of SFOR troops at the expiry of their mandate in June 1998. In February 1998 NATO formally approved the establishment of a new peace-keeping force for Bosnia and Herzegovina, which was to be deployed in the country following the expiry of SFOR's mandate; the force was to comprise 35,000 troops, but was to be reduced to number 20,000-25,000 after republican presidential and legislative elections in September of that year.

Municipal elections for both entities, which had initially been postponed in August 1996 owing to alleged iregularities in voter registration and which had again been rescheduled in March 1997, were finally held in September 1997 under the aegis of the OSCE. Voters were permitted to register either in the districts in which they had been resident in 1991 or in those where they had been living since 1996. Although some 91 parties contested the elections (in which voter participation was estimated at about 60%) the three main nationalist parties, the PDA, the CDU and the SDP, received the vast majority of the votes cast. Parliamentary elections to the National Assembly of the Serb Republic were held during 22–23 November, under the supervision of the OSCE. Participating parties included the Serb National Alliance (SNS), which had been established by Plavšić in September, following her expulsion from the SDP in July. In the elections the SDP received a much-reduced number of seats (24, compared with 45 in 1996), but still remained the largest party in the Assembly. A newly-formed electoral alliance, the Coalition for a Single and Democratic Bosnia, which included the PDA and the Party for Bosnia and Herzegovina, secured 16 seats, while the SNS and the Serb Radical Party each achieved 15 seats. At the inaugural session of the new Assembly on 27 December, Plavšić nominated as prime minister-designate Mladen Ivanić, an economist with no political affiliation. The nomination was immediately challenged by the leadership of the SDP, which considered that as the largest party in the new Assembly it should have the first opportunity to propose a new prime minister and government; accordingly, the SDP proposed Klicković, the outgoing Prime Minister, and Aleksa Buha, the acting Chairman of the party. Ivanić declared, however, that he would continue negotiating with all the parties represented in the new Assembly to try to form an interim government of 'national unity', which would hold power until new elections scheduled for September 1998. On 18 January 1998, however, following the failure of Ivanić's inter-party talks, Milorad Dodik, who was considered to be a proponent of moderate rather than extremist policies, secured sufficient parliamentary support to form a new government. Following the announcement of the new administration, which contained a large number of Bosnian Muslims, Dodik assured the international community of his determination to govern according to the terms of the Dayton peace agreement. His appointment was condemned, however, by Krajišnik who warned that it would lead to the destabilization of the Serb Republic. At the end of January Dodik announced that government bodies were to be transferred from Pale to Banja Luka.

A number of accused war criminals were put on trial in the Hague in 1997. In March the first trial was held of Muslims and Croats accused of committing offences against Serbs and in May Dušan Tadić, who had been indicted in 1996 for organizing 'ethnic cleansing' in Omarska concentration camp (see above), was convicted of torturing Bosnian Muslims and sentenced to 20 years' imprisonment. In July an indicted Serbian war criminal, Simo Drljaca, was killed following an exchange of fire with soldiers of SFOR, who had sought to arrest him. For many observers the operation demonstrated an increased determination on the part of the international community, and in particular Westendorp, to enforce indictments issued by the International Criminal Tribunal; to this end it had been decided not to publish the identity of accused war criminals (the policy was entitled 'sealed indictments') to facilitate their apprehension. The shooting of Drljaca was condemned as murder, however, by President Plavšić and other Bosnian Serb leaders, and the actions of SFOR were strongly criticized by Russia, which claimed that SFOR had exceeded its mandate. In mid-December a further operation by SFOR resulted in the arrest of two Bosnian Croats suspected of war crimes.

Government

The Constitution of the former Socialist Republic of Bosnia and Herzegovina (which was part of the Socialist Federal Republic of Yugoslavia) provided for a legislative, bicameral Assembly, composed of a 130-member Chamber of Citizens and a 110-member Chamber of Communes; a seven-member, collective State Presidency; and an executive body of ministers (presided over by a Prime Minister). Following the declaration of independence of Bosnia and Herzegovina by the Bosniak and Croat constituencies of the Assembly in October 1991, the Serb deputies withdrew and formed the Assembly of the Serb Nation in Pale. In March 1992 the Serb deputies proclaimed an autonomous Serb Republic, while in July Bosnian Croats declared a breakaway Croat state, the 'Croatian Union of Herzeg-Bosna'. Thenceforth, the republican Government was dominated by the Bosniaks, while the Serb- and Croat-held territories were administered by separate governments.

In March 1994 a Federation of Bosnia and Herzegovina was created, following an agreement in Washington (USA) between representatives of the Bosnian Government, the Bosnian Croats and Croatia. The Federation was to consist of cantons ruled by a strong federal Government, with the offices of President and Prime Minister rotated annually between members of the Muslim and Croat ethnic groups. The inaugural meeting of a Constituent Assembly took place in May (the election of the Assembly, due by 30 September, was subsequently postponed). Until the full implementation of the provisions of the new federal Constitution, the existing bicameral Assembly was to exercise a dual capacity as the Bosnian legislature and the interim legislature of the Federation. A joint Government of the Republic of Bosnia and Herzegovina and the Federation took office in June.

The General Framework Agreement for Peace in Bosnia and Herzegovina, which was signed in December 1995, provided for the creation of a central republican government and a republican bicameral Assembly in Bosnia and Herzegovina (comprising a House of Peoples and a House of Representatives). Two-thirds of the seats in both chambers would be allocated to representatives of the Federation and one-third to deputies of the Serb Republic. Legislative decisions would only be implemented, however, with the approval of at least one-third of the deputies of each entity. A collective presidency would also function on the basis of two-thirds representation for the Federation and one-third for the Serb Republic, with all decisions to be taken by a majority vote. The existing Constitutions and political bodies of the Federation and the Serb Republic were to remain in force, with amendments to allow for the implementation of the principles of the peace agreement. Following the all-Bosnia elections that were held on 14 September 1996, the newly-elected three-member republican Presidency took office and appointed a Council of Ministers. On 3 January 1997 the inaugural sessions of both houses of the Assembly were held. Further republican presidential and legislative elections were scheduled to be held in 1998.

On 19 October 1996 the new (renamed) National Assembly of the Serb Republic was inaugurated, and on 6 November the inaugural session of the Federation's newly-elected House of Representatives was held. In mid-December the functions of the former republican Government that had not been assumed by the new Presidency were transferred to the Federation, while the Bosnian Croats announced that the administrative functions and powers of 'Herzeg-Bosna' would simultaneously be subsumed within those of the Federation.

Defence

In late 1995 it was estimated that government forces in Bosnia and Herzegovina numbered about 40,000 (with some 100,000 reserves), the army of the 'Serbian Republic of Bosnia and Herzegovina' totalled more than 30,000 and Croatian forces (comprising the Croatian Defence Council—HVO) around 16,000. In May 1996 agreement was reached on the merger of the Bosniak and Croat armed forces, to form a Federation army. In October 1997 it was reported that the merger had been completed, and that the armed forces numbered some 45,000.

From 1992 the United Nations Protection Force (UNPROFOR) was deployed in Bosnia and Herzegovina for aid distribution and the protection of 'safe areas'. On 20 December 1995, following the signing of the Dayton peace agreement (see Recent History), UNPROFOR formally transferred power to an international NATO-commanded 60,000-strong 'Implementation Force' (IFOR), which was granted wide-ranging authority to oversee the implementation of the peace accord. A follow-on Stabilization Force (SFOR), comprising about 33,000 troops, took over from IFOR on 20 December 1996. Government expenditure on defence in 1996 was estimated at US $250m.

Economic Affairs

Bosnia and Herzegovina was one of the least economically developed republics of the former Yugoslav federation. The major agricultural products were tobacco and fruit, and the livestock sector was of economic importance. Timber reserves were also exploited. Bosnia and Herzegovina possesses extensive mineral resources, the republic being a major producer of copper, lead, zinc and gold before the outbreak of the civil war. There are also reserves of iron ore and lignite. Federal government policy favoured the development of Bosnia and Herzegovina and the other poorer regions of the former Yugoslavia, but industrialization did not become a significant feature of the local economy. There were, however, some light industries, and during the 1970s and 1980s the Sava Valley (along the northern border of the republic) became a favoured development area for heavy industries. There were iron and steel plants at Zenica, and the armaments-manufacturing industry was also important. In 1990 heavy and light industries accounted for some 43% of gross domestic product (GDP).

Bosnia and Herzegovina's economy was severely affected by the civil war, which began in June 1991. The naval blockade of the Croatian ports, through which Bosnia and Herzegovina's petroleum supplies were delivered, added to the republic's economic difficulties. By late 1991 the total of unemployed persons had reached 320,000, the highest number since shortly after the Second World War, and the annual rate of inflation had reportedly reached almost 120%. By mid-1992 Bosnia and Herzegovina had suffered extensive material damage, and gross national product (GNP) in government-controlled areas was estimated to have declined, in real terms, by 40%, while the total external debt was more than US $2,000m. In 1995 revenue from exports totalled US $150m., compared with $2,000m. in 1990.

The official reconstruction of Bosnia and Herzegovina's economy was initiated in late 1995, following the signing of the Dayton peace agreement in December, which included provisions for the establishment of a new central bank. On 20 December Bosnia and Herzegovina became a member of the IMF (see p. 80) and an emergency credit of US $45m. was immediately approved. The World Bank estimated that GDP increased, in real terms, by 50% in 1996, to reach the equivalent of 33% of 1990 GDP, largely as a result of an assistance programme financed by international donors. In 1996 an estimated trade deficit of $1,546m. was recorded, while there was a deficit of $1,620m. (excluding interest and transfers) on the current account of the balance of payments. According to the World Bank, the overall budget deficit (excluding unpaid interest) was DM 6m. in that year. Total external debt was estimated at $3,518m. at the end of 1995, of which arrears accounted for $1,979m. In 1996 the ratio of debt-servicing to export earnings was estimated at 66% (compared with 135% in 1995). International donors pledged $1,100m. in financial aid to Bosnia and Herzegovina in 1996, of which the majority was allocated to the Bosnian Federation, while the Serb Republic received only $7m.

Bosnia and Herzegovina was admitted as a member of the International Bank for Reconstruction and Development (the World Bank) on 1 April 1996 and immediately secured loans totalling US $269m. for emergency reconstruction projects. During 1996 and 1997 NATO's Implementation Force (IFOR) and Stabilization Force (SFOR), which included a team of military engineers, together with other international agencies, restored many roads and bridges to use, reopened rail and air services and rehabilitated power stations. With the advent of peace, industrial activity recommenced, and the Bosnian Federation Government estimated that industrial production had increased by 87% in 1996, while the Government of the Serb Republic estimated that industrial activity had grown by 58% in the Serb entity. Independent analysts predicted that the Bosnian economy might grow by 30%-35% in 1997, and might reach the equivalent of 66% of pre-war GDP by 2000. According to World Bank analysts, economic priorities for 1997–98 included the introduction of a stable and convertible currency (for which the new republican central bank was to act as the sole authority), a continuation in the reconstruction of infrastructure and in the restoration of public services, and an acceleration in the transfer to the private sector of state-owned enterprises, the legal framework for which had been established in both entities in 1996. Emphasis was also placed on the creation of employment opportunities (the rate of unemployment was estimated at 45% of the labour force in December 1996) and on the stimulation of exports (the average annual trade deficit was projected to total some 30% of GDP during 1996–2000). In April 1997 the Bosnian Government undertook to introduce a new currency in all parts of the country, the exchange rate for which was to be fixed at 1 Bosnian convertible mark to 1 Deutsche mark. The 1997 budget envisaged expenditure and revenue of DM 136m., with some DM 45m. provided by the two entities (two-thirds by the Federation and one-third by the Serb Republic, according to the terms of the Dayton peace agreement) and some DM 91m. supplied by international donors.

Social Welfare

There is a state-administered health service, which is open to all. Before the civil war the number of doctors in Bosnia and Herzegovina was equivalent to approximately one for every 636 inhabitants. The health service was greatly disrupted by the war. During the conflict basic humanitarian welfare became increasingly dependent on international relief organizations. Following the end of hostilities, budgetary funds allocated to the health service were used principally for emergency relief and humanitarian aid.

Education

Elementary education is free and compulsory for all children between the ages of seven and 15 years, when children attend the 'eight-year school'. Various types of secondary education are available to all who qualify, but the vocational and technical schools are the most popular. Alternatively, children may attend a general secondary school (gymnasium), where they follow a four-year course to prepare them for university entrance. At the secondary level there are also a number of art schools, apprentice schools and teacher-training schools. There are four universities, situated in Sarajevo, Banja Luka, Mostar and Tuzla, with a combined total of about 40,000 students. The educational system in Bosnia and Herzegovina was severely disrupted by the civil war.

Public Holidays

1998: 1–2 January (New Year), 1 March (Independence Day) 1–2 May (Labour Days), 27 July, 25 November.

1999: 1–2 January (New Year), 1 March (Independence Day) 1–2 May (Labour Days), 27 July, 25 November.

Weights and Measures

The metric system is in force.

Statistical Survey

Source (unless otherwise stated): *Yugoslav Survey*, Belgrade, POB 677, Moše Pijade 8/I; tel. (11) 333610; fax (11) 332295.

Area and Population

AREA, POPULATION AND DENSITY

Area (sq km)	51,129*
Population (census results)	
31 March 1981	4,124,008
31 March 1991	
Males	2,183,795
Females	2,193,238
Total	4,377,033
Population (official estimates at mid-year)†	
1994	4,459,000
1995	4,484,000
1996	4,510,000
Density (per sq km) at mid-1996	88.2

* 19,741 sq miles.

† Figures include refugees outside the country. The number of people living in the country was estimated to be 3,250,000 in early 1996.

Source: mainly UN, *Demographic Yearbook* and *Population and Vital Statistics Report*.

PRINCIPAL ETHNIC GROUPS (1991 census, provisional)

	Number	% of total population
Muslims	1,905,829	43.7
Serbs	1,369,258	31.4
Croats	755,892	17.3
'Yugoslavs'	239,845	5.5
Total (incl. others)	4,364,574	100.0

PRINCIPAL TOWNS (population at 1991 census): Sarajevo (capital) 415,631; Banja Luka 142,644 (Source: *Statistički godišnjak Jugoslavije*—Statistical Yearbook of Yugoslavia).

Sarajevo (estimated population in 1993): 383,000.

BIRTHS, MARRIAGES AND DEATHS

1989: Registered live births 66,809 (birth rate 14.9 per 1,000); Registered deaths 30,383 (death rate 6.8 per 1,000).

1990: Registered live births 66,952; Registered marriages 29,990; Registered deaths 29,093.

1990-95 (UN estimates, annual averages): Birth rate 13.4 per 1,000; Death rate 7.0 per 1,000 (Source: UN, *World Population Prospects: The 1994 Revision*).

Expectation of life (UN estimates, years at birth, 1990–95): 72.4 (males 69.5; females 75.1) (Source: UN, *World Population Prospects: The 1994 Revision*).

EMPLOYMENT (Bosniak-majority area, average for December)

	1994	1995
Activities of the material sphere	113,701	172,085
Non-material services	30,251	48,311
Total	143,952	220,396

Source: IMF, *Bosnia and Herzegovina—Recent Economic Developments* (October 1996).

1996: Total formal employment 506,000: Bosniak-majority area 255,000 (excluding Ministry of Defence and Interior) in September; Croat-majority area 52,000 (including 19,000 soldiers and police) in April; Republika Srpska 199,000 (Source: World Bank, *Bosnia and Herzegovina: From Recovery to Sustainable Growth,* May 1997).

Agriculture

PRINCIPAL CROPS ('000 metric tons)

	1994	1995	1996
Wheat	330†	281†	166
Barley	45†	45*	47
Maize	694†	372	589
Rye	6†	7	5
Oats	11*	11	36
Potatoes	180†	377	347
Dry beans	13*	14	13
Soybeans (Soya beans)	4*	3	4
Rapeseed	2*	1	2
Cabbages	60*	88	66
Tomatoes	16*	20	29
Green chillies and peppers	4	4	4
Onions (dry)	19*	22	27
Garlic*	2	2	2
Beans (green)*	2	2	2
Carrots	9*	6	8
Watermelons*	3	3	3
Grapes	12*	9	17
Sugar beets	40*	42	1
Apples	17*	18	18
Pears*	10	10	10
Peaches and nectarines*	2	2	2
Plums	35*	35	35
Strawberries*	5	5	5
Tobacco (leaves)	3*	2	4

† FAO estimate(s). * Unofficial figure.

Source: FAO, *Production Yearbook*.

LIVESTOCK ('000 head, unless otherwise indicated, year ending September)

	1994	1995	1996
Horses*	50	50	50
Cattle	390*	273	314
Pigs	223*	147	165
Sheep	300*	260*	276
Chickens (million)	4*	3	4

* FAO estimate(s).

Source: FAO, *Production Yearbook*.

LIVESTOCK PRODUCTS ('000 metric tons)

	1994	1995	1996
Beef and veal	30*	16	18
Mutton and lamb	2*	3	3
Pig meat	20*	16*	16
Poultry meat	13*	15*	11
Cows' milk	240*	239*	292
Sheep's milk	7*	3	3
Cheese*	14	14	14
Eggs	17	7	7
Cattle and buffalo hides*	6	3	3

* FAO estimate(s).

Source: FAO, *Production Yearbook*.

Fishing

(FAO estimates, '000 metric tons, live weight)

	1993	1994	1995
Total catch (freshwater fish)	2.5	2.4	2.5

Source: FAO, *Yearbook of Fishery Statistics.*

Mining

('000 metric tons)

	1992	1993	1994
Lignite	2,000*	1,500*	1,400
Barytes	10	n.a.	n.a.
Gypsum (crude)	150	n.a.	n.a.

* Estimated production.

Source: UN, *Industrial Commodity Statistics Yearbook.*

Industry

SELECTED PRODUCTS ('000 metric tons, unless otherwise indicated)

	1990
Electric energy (million kWh)	14,632
Crude steel	1,421
Aluminium	89
Machines	16
Tractors (number)	34,000
Lorries (number)	16,000
Motor cars (number)	38,000
Cement	797
Paper and paperboard	281
Television receivers (number)	21,000

Electric energy (million kWh): 5,000 in 1992; 3,500 (estimate) in 1993; 1,921 in 1994 (source: UN, *Industrial Commodity Statistics Yearbook*).

Finance

CURRENCY AND EXCHANGE RATES

Monetary Units

100 para = 1 new Bosnia and Herzegovina dinar (BHD).

Sterling and Dollar Equivalents (30 September 1997)

£1 sterling = 285.31 BHD;
US $1 = 176.62 BHD;
1,000 BHD = £3.505 = $5.662.

Average Exchange Rate (new BHD per US $)

1995 143.31
1996 150.48

Note: The new dinar was introduced in August 1994, with an official value fixed at 100 BHD = 1 Deutsche Mark (DM). The DM, the Croatian kuna and the Yugoslav dinar also circulate within Bosnia and Herzegovina. In January 1998 the Government inaugurated a new currency, the convertible mark, the exchange rate for which was to be fixed at 1 convertible mark = 1 DM. The currency was to circulate for an interim period, beginning in April.

BUDGET (million Deutsche Marks)*

Revenue	1994	1995	1996
Tax revenue	366.9	573.7	1,398
Sales tax and excise taxes	255.1	318.4	766
Enterprise tax	2.7	20.2	297
Wage tax and tax for reconstruction	44.7	82.1	
Customs duties	63.1	111.4	314
Social security contributions	141.4	244.3	519
Other revenue	27.4	56.3	122
Grants	76.0	168.5	
Total	611.7	1,042.8	2,040

Expenditure†	1994	1995	1996
Wages and contributions	59.5	87.0	222
Goods and services	441.2	580.3	280
Military‡	335.4	461.9	189
Education	38.5	69.6	n.a.
Interest payments§	—	0.8	12
Social Fund expenditure	137.2	217.3	524
Transfers to households (incl. subsidies)	30.5	166.0	428
Other expenditure (incl. unallocated)‖			581
Total	668.4	1,051.4	2,046

* Figures represent a consolidation of the budgetary accounts of authorities in the Bosniak-majority area (excluding, in 1994, isolated regions and regions under occupation), the Croat-majority area and the Serb Republic. The data for 1994 and 1995 exclude the operations of local and district administrations. Owing to lack of data, some military expenditure and associated external grant financing are excluded. Sources: (1994 and 1995) IMF, *Bosnia and Herzegovina—Recent Economic Developments* (October 1996); (1996) World Bank, *Bosnia and Herzegovina: From Recovery to Sustainable Growth* (May 1997).

† Figures are on a cash basis.

‡ Military expenditure includes only reported cash payments.

§ Unpaid arrears of external interest totalled 287 million DM in 1994 and 258 million DM in 1995.

‖ Figure for 1996 includes expenditure by district, canton and municipal authorities, for which sufficient data are not available to allocate to other categories.

MONEY SUPPLY (million Deutsche Marks at 31 December)

	1994	1995
Currency outside banks:		
Federation	3.0	20.6
Serb Republic	0.0	7.7
Demand deposits at banks:		
Federation	160.1	216.0
Serb Republic	52.2	33.6
Total money	215.4	277.8

Source: IMF, *Bosnia and Herzegovina—Recent Economic Developments* (October 1996).

NATIONAL ACCOUNTS
(estimates, US $ million at current prices)

	1994	1995	1996
Gross domestic product	1,538	2,105	3,260

Source: World Bank, *Bosnia and Herzegovina: From Recovery to Sustainable Growth* (May 1997).

BALANCE OF PAYMENTS (estimates, US $ million).

	1994	1995
Exports of goods f.o.b.	91	152
Imports of goods f.o.b.	–894	–1,082
Trade balance	–803	–930
Exports of services	103	229
Imports of services	–191	–252
Balance on goods and services	–891	–953
Other income (net)	–177	–183
Balance on goods, services and income	–1,068	–1,136
Unrequited transfers received	888	1,073
Unrequited transfers paid	–9	–71
Current balance	–189	–134
Capital account (net)	–248	–257
Net errors and omissions	–1	106
Overall balance	–438	–285

Source: IMF, *Bosnia and Herzegovina—Recent Economic Developments* (October 1996).

1996 (US $ million): Exports of goods 336; Imports of goods –1,882 (Source: World Bank, *Bosnia and Herzegovina: From Recovery to Sustainable Growth*, May 1997).

Communications Media

	1992	1993	1994
Telephones ('000 main lines in use)	600	600	250
Radio receivers ('000 in use)	n.a.	n.a.	800
Daily newspapers*:			
Number	2	n.a.	n.a.
Average circulation ('000 copies)	518	n.a.	n.a.
Non-daily newspapers			
Number	22	n.a.	n.a.
Average circulation ('000 copies)	2,508	n.a.	n.a.

* Figures refer to government-controlled areas only.

1995: Radio receivers ('000 in use) 840; Daily newspapers (estimates) 2 (average circulation 520,000 copies).

Sources: UN, *Statistical Yearbook*; UNESCO, *Statistical Yearbook*.

Directory

The Constitution

The Constitution of Bosnia and Herzegovina was Annexe 4 to the General Framework Agreement for Peace in Bosnia and Herzegovina, signed in Paris (France) on 14 December 1995. These peace accords were negotiated at Dayton, Ohio (USA), in November and became the Elysée or Paris Treaty in December. Annexe 4 took effect as a constitutional act upon signature, superseding and amending the Constitution of the Republic of Bosnia and Herzegovina.

The previous organic law, an amended version of the 1974 Constitution of the then Socialist Republic of Bosnia and Herzegovina (part of the Socialist Federal Republic of Yugoslavia—the name was changed to the Republic of Bosnia and Herzegovina upon the declaration of independence following a referendum on 29 February–1 March 1992), provided for a collective State Presidency, a Government headed by a Prime Minister and a bicameral Assembly.

The institutions of the Republic continued to function until the firm establishment of the bodies provided for by the Federation of Bosnia and Herzegovina, which was formed on 31 March 1994. This was an association of the Muslim- or Bosniak-led Republic and the Croat Republic of Herzeg-Bosna. The federal Constitution provided for a balance of powers between Bosniak and Croat elements in a Federation divided into cantons. The federal Government was to be responsible for defence, foreign and economic affairs, and its head, the Prime Minister, was to have a greater executive role than the President. These two posts were to rotate between the two ethnic groups.

According to the General Framework Agreement, the Federation was one of the two constituent 'entities' of the new union of Bosnia and Herzegovina, together with the Serb Republic of Bosnia and Herzegovina. The Serb Republic was proclaimed by the Serb deputies of the old Bosnian Assembly on 27 March 1992. Its Constitution provided for an executive President (with two Vice-Presidents), a Government headed by a Prime Minister and a unicameral National Assembly. Under the terms of the General Framework Agreement, known as the Dayton accords (after Dayton, Ohio, the US town where the treaty was negotiated in November 1995), the two Entities were to exist under their current Constitutions, which were to be amended to conform with the peace agreement.

The Dayton accords included 12 annexes on: the military aspects of the peace settlement (including the establishment of an international Implementation Force—IFOR); regional stabilization; inter-entity boundaries; elections; arbitration; human rights; refugees and displaced persons; a Commission to Preserve National Monuments; Bosnia and Herzegovina public corporations (specifically a Transportation Corporation); civilian implementation (including the office of a High Representative of the International Community); and an international police task force. One of the annexes was the Constitution of Bosnia and Herzegovina, summarized below, and it was signed by representatives of the Republic, the Federation and the Serb Republic.

CONSTITUTION OF BOSNIA AND HERZEGOVINA

The Preamble declares the basic, democratic principles of the country and its conformity with the principles of international law. The Bosniaks, Croats and Serbs are declared to be the constituent peoples (along with Others) of Bosnia and Herzegovina.

Article I affirms the continuation of Bosnia and Herzegovina with the Republic of Bosnia and Herzegovina, within its existing international boundaries, but with its internal structure modified. Bosnia and Herzegovina is a democratic state, consisting of two Entities, the Federation of Bosnia and Herzegovina and the Serb Republic. The capital of the country is Sarajevo and the symbols are to be determined by the legislature. Citizenship is to exist both for Bosnia and Herzegovina and for the Entities.

Article II guarantees human rights and fundamental freedoms, and makes specific mention of the Human Rights Commission to be established under Annexe 6 of the General Framework Agreement. The provisions of a number of international agreements are assured and co-operation and access for the international war-crimes tribunal specified. The provisions of this Article, according to Article X, are incapable of diminution or elimination by any amendment to the Constitution.

The responsibilities of and relations between the Entities and the institutions of Bosnia and Herzegovina are dealt with in Article III. The institutions of Bosnia and Herzegovina are responsible for foreign policy (including trade and customs), overall financial policy, immigration and refugee issues, international and inter-entity law enforcement, common and international communications facilities, inter-entity transportation and air-traffic control. Any governmental functions or powers not reserved to the institutions of Bosnia and Herzegovina by this Constitution are reserved to the Entities, unless additional responsibilities are agreed between the Entities or as provided for in the General Framework Agreement (Annexes 5–8). The Entities may establish special, parallel relations with neighbouring states, provided this is consistent with the sovereignty and territorial integrity of Bosnia and Herzegovina. The Constitution of Bosnia and Herzegovina has primacy over any inconsistent constitutional or legal provisions of the Entities.

The Parliamentary Assembly

Bosnia and Herzegovina is to have a bicameral legislature, known as the Parliamentary Assembly. It is to consist of a House of Peoples and a House of Representatives. The House of Peoples is to comprise 15 members, five each from the Bosniaks, the Croats and the Serbs. The Bosniak and Croat Delegates are to be selected by, respectively, the Bosniak and Croat Delegates to the House of Representatives of the Federation, and the Serb Delegates by the National Assembly of the Serb Republic. The first House of the Peoples selected under the Constitution is protected from an early dissolution.

The House of Representatives is to consist of 42 Members, two-thirds to be directly elected from the territory of the Federation and one-third from the territory of the Serb Republic. The first general election is to be conducted in accordance with Annexe 3 of the General Framework Agreement, which provides for a Permanent Election Commission then to be appointed.

The Parliamentary Assembly is to convene in Sarajevo and each chamber is to rotate its chair between three members, one from each of the constituent peoples. The Parliamentary Assembly is responsible for: necessary legislation under the Constitution or to implement Presidency decisions; determining a budget for the institutions of Bosnia and Herzegovina; and deciding whether to ratify treaties.

The Presidency

Article V concerns the state Presidency of Bosnia and Herzegovina. The head of state is to consist of three Members: one Bosniak and one Croat, each directly elected from the Federation; and one Serb, directly elected from the Serb Republic. Elections will be in accordance with legislation of the Parliamentary Assembly, but the first elections are to be as agreed in Annexe 3 of the General Framework Agreement. The first elected Members will have a term of two years, but, thereafter, a Member's term shall be for four years. The Chair for the first term of the Presidency will be the Member to receive the largest number of votes, thereafter the method of selection must be determined by parliamentary legislation. A Presidency decision, if declared to be destructive of a vital interest of an Entity, can be vetoed by a two-thirds majority in the relevant body: the National Assembly of the Serb Republic if the declaration was made by the Serb Member; or by the Bosniak or Croat Delegates in the Federation House of Peoples if the declaration was made by, respectively, the Bosniak or Croat Members of the Presidency. The Presidency is responsible for the foreign policy and international relations of Bosnia and Herzegovina. It is required to execute the decisions of the Parliamentary Assembly and to propose an annual central budget to that body, upon the recommendation of the Council of Ministers.

The Chair of the Council of Ministers is nominated by the Presidency and confirmed in office by the House of Representatives. Other Ministers, including, specifically, a foreign minister and a foreign-trade minister, are nominated by the Chair of the Council of Ministers, and also approved by the House of Representatives. The Council of Ministers is responsible for carrying out the policies and decisions of Bosnia and Herzegovina and reporting to the Parliamentary Assembly. There are also guarantees that no more than two-thirds of Ministers be from the territory of the Federation, and Deputy Ministers are to be from a different constituent people to their Minister.

Each Member of the Presidency has, *ex officio*, civilian command authority over armed forces. Each Member is to be a member of a Standing Committee on Military Matters, appointed by the Presidency and responsible for co-ordinating the activities of armed forces in the country. The inviolability of each Entity to any armed force of the other is assured.

Other Institutions and Provisions

Article VI is on the Constitutional Court, which is to have nine members, four selected by the House of Representatives of the Federation and two by the National Assembly of the Serb Republic. The three remaining judges, at least initially, are to be selected by the President of the European Court of Human Rights. The first judges will have a term of office of five years; thereafter judges will usually serve until they are 70 years of age (unless they retire or are removed by the consensus of the other judges). The Constitutional Court of Bosnia and Herzegovina is to uphold the Constitution, to resolve the jurisdictions of the institutions of Bosnia and Herzegovina and the Entities, to ensure consistency with the Constitution and to guarantee the legal sovereignty and territorial integrity of the country. Its decisions are final and binding.

The Central Bank of Bosnia and Herzegovina is the sole authority for issuing currency and for monetary policy in Bosnia and Herzegovina. For the first six years of the Constitution, however, it is not authorized to extend credit by creating money; moreover, during this period the first Governing Body will consist of a Governor, appointed by the International Monetary Fund, and three members appointed by the Presidency (a Bosniak and a Croat, sharing one vote, from the Federation, and one from the Serb Republic). The Governor, who may not be a citizen of Bosnia and Herzegovina or any neighbouring state, will have a deciding vote. Thereafter, the Governing Body shall consist of five members, appointed by the Presidency for a term of six years, with a Governor selected by them from among their number.

Article VIII concerns the finances of Bosnia and Herzegovina and its institutions. Article IX concerns general provisions, notably forbidding anyone convicted or indicted by the International Tribunal on war crimes in the former Yugoslavia from standing for or holding public office in Bosnia and Herzegovina. These provisions also guarantee the need for all public appointments to be generally representative of the peoples of Bosnia and Herzegovina. Amendments to the Constitution need a two-thirds majority of those present and voting in the House of Representatives.

The penultimate Article XI is on transitional arrangements provided for in an annexe to the Constitution. This is mainly concerned to legitimize the parallel competence of existing authorities and legislation until such time as the institutions of Bosnia and Herzegovina are properly established. A Joint Interim Commission is to co-ordinate the implementation of the Constitution of Bosnia and Herzegovina and of the General Framework Agreement and its Annexes. It is to be composed of four members from the Federation, three from the Serb Republic and one representative of Bosnia and Herzegovina. Meetings of the Commission are to be chaired by the High Representative of the International Community.

The Government

(February 1998)

HIGH REPRESENTATIVE OF THE INTERNATIONAL COMMUNITY IN BOSNIA AND HERZEGOVINA

Under the terms of the treaty and annexes of the General Framework Agreement for Peace in Bosnia and Herzegovina, signed in December 1995, the international community, as authorized by the UN Security Council, was to designate a civilian representative to oversee the implementation of the peace accords and the establishment of the institutions of the new order in Bosnia and Herzegovina. The first High Representative, Carl Bildt, was appointed in December 1995.

High Representative: CARLOS WESTENDORP (appointed 30 May 1997); 71000 Sarajevo, trg Djece Sarajeva bb; tel. (71) 447275; fax (71) 447420.

BOSNIA AND HERZEGOVINA

Presidency

The Dayton peace agreement, which was signed in December 1995, provides for a three-member Presidency, comprising one Bosniak (Muslim), one Croat and one Serb. The Presidency has responsibility for governing Bosnia and Herzegovina at republican level (see below for the Governments of the two Bosnian entities, the Federation of Bosnia and Herzegovina and the Serb Republic). The members of the Presidency were elected by their respective constituencies in the Bosnian elections that were held on 14 September 1996. The Presidency assumed authority for Bosnia and Herzegovina on 29 September when the election results were certified by the OSCE, and held its inaugural session on 5 October. The Presidency appointed two co-Prime Ministers who in turn appointed the republican Council of Ministers in December; these appointments were endorsed by the Assembly of Bosnia and Herzegovina on 3 January 1997.

President and Chairman of the Presidency: Dr ALIJA IZETBEGOVIĆ (PDA).

Co-Presidents: MOMČILO KRAJIŠNIK (SDP), KRESIMIR ZUBAK (CDU).

Council of Ministers

Co-Prime Ministers: Dr HARIS SILAJDŽIĆ (Party for Bosnia and Herzegovina), BORO BOSIĆ (SDP).

Deputy Prime Minister: NEVEN TOMIĆ (CDU).

Minister for Foreign Affairs: Dr JADRANKO PRLIĆ (CDU).

Deputy Ministers for Foreign Affairs: HUSEIN ZIVALJ (PDA), DRAGAN BOZANIĆ (SDP).

Minister for Foreign Trade and Economic Relations: MIRSAD KURTOVIĆ.

Deputy Ministers for Foreign Trade and Economic Relations: Dr NIKOLA GRABOVAC (CDU), GAVRO BOGIĆ (SDP).

Minister for Communications and Civilian Affairs: SPASOJE ALBIJANIĆ (SDP).

Deputy Ministers for Communications and Civilian Affairs: NUDZEIM RECICA (PDA), MILAN KRIZANOVIĆ (CDU).

THE FEDERATION OF BOSNIA AND HERZEGOVINA

Following an agreement reached in Washington, DC (USA), by representatives of the Republic of Bosnia and Herzegovina and the 'Croat Republic of Herzeg-Bosna' (declared on 28 August 1993), the Federation of Bosnia and Herzegovina was formed on 31 March 1994. The President and Vice-President of the Federation were elected in May 1994. The Federation was reorganized as one of the two constituent entities of Bosnia and Herzegovina in the peace agreements of 1995.

President: Dr EJUP GANIC (PDA).

Vice-President: VLADIMIR SOLJIĆ (CDU).

Government

Prime Minister: EDHEM BICAKCIĆ.

Deputy Prime Minister and Minister of Finance: DRAGO BILANDŽIJA.

Minister of Internal Affairs: MEHMED ZILIĆ.

Minister of Defence: ANTE JELAVIĆ.

Minister of Justice: MATE TADIĆ.

Minister of Industry, Energy and Mining: (vacant).

Minister of Transport and Communications: Dr RASIM GAČANOVIĆ.

Minister for Social Welfare, Displaced Persons and Refugees: RASIM KADIĆ.

Minister of Health: Dr BOZO LJUBIĆ.

Minister of Education, Science, Culture and Sport: Dr FAHRUDIN RIZVANBEGOVIĆ.

Minister of Trade: ILE KREZO.

Minister of the Environment: IBRAHIM MORANKIĆ.

Minister of Agriculture, Water Management and Forestry: Dr AHMED SMAJIĆ.

Ministers without Portfolio: NIKOLA ANTUNOVIĆ, NEDELJKO DESPOTOVIĆ.

Ministries

Office of the Prime Minister: 71000 Sarajevo, Zmaja od Bosne 3; tel. (71) 213777; fax (71) 272877.

Ministry of Agriculture, Water Management and Forestry: 71000 Sarajevo.

Ministry of Defence: 71000 Sarajevo, Zmaja od Bosne 3A; tel. (71) 35427; fax (71) 653592.

Ministry of Education, Science, Culture and Sport: 71000 Sarajevo, Zmaja od Bosne 3; tel. (71) 213777; fax (71) 653592.

Ministry of Energy, Mining and Industry: 71000 Sarajevo.

Ministry of the Environment: 71000 Sarajevo.

Ministry of Finance: 71000 Sarajevo, Zmaja od Bosne 3; tel. (71) 213777; fax (71) 653592.

Ministry of Foreign Affairs: 71000 Sarajevo, Zmaja od Bosne 3; tel. (71) 213777; fax (71) 653592.

Ministry of Health: 71000 Sarajevo, Zmaja od Bosne 3; tel. (71) 213777; fax (71) 653592.

Ministry of Information: 71000 Sarajevo, Zmaja od Bosne 3; tel. (71) 213777; fax (71) 213350.

Ministry of Internal Affairs: 71000 Sarajevo, Boriše Kovačevića 7; tel. (71) 512877; fax (71) 653592.

Ministry of Justice: 71000 Sarajevo, Zmaja od Bosne 3; tel. (71) 213777; fax (71) 653592.

Ministry for Social Welfare, Displaced Persons and Refugees: 71000 Sarajevo, Alipašina 41 II; tel. (71) 213777; fax (71) 653592.

Ministry of Trade: 71000 Sarajevo.

Ministry of Transport and Communications: 71000 Sarajevo.

Note: Despite the formation of the Federation, the institutions of the 'Croat Republic of Herzeg-Bosna' continued to function until December 1996, when the dissolution of Herzeg-Bosna and the transfer of former Bosnian Government powers to the Federation was announced.

SERB REPUBLIC OF BOSNIA AND HERZEGOVINA

On 27 March 1992 a 'Serb Republic of Bosnia and Herzegovina' was proclaimed. It was immediately declared illegal by the President of the State Presidency. The Republic comprised Serb-held areas of Bosnia and Herzegovina, including the 'Serb Autonomous Regions' of Eastern and Old Herzegovina, Bosanska Krajina, Romanija and Northern Bosnia. Its headquarters were in Banja Luka. Its parliament, originally constituted as the 'Assembly of the Serb Nation', on 24 October 1991 by Serb deputies of the Assembly of Bosnia and Herzegovina, was based in Pale. According to the peace treaty of December 1995, the Serb Republic was to constitute one of the two territorial entities comprising Bosnia and Herzegovina, with 49% of the country's area. It was to retain its own executive presidency, government and parliament (now known as the National Assembly—see below).

President: Dr BILJANA PLAVŠIĆ.

Vice-President: DRAGOLUB MIRJANIĆ.

Government

Prime Minister: MILORAD DODIK.

Deputy Prime Minister and Minister of Industry and Technology: DJURADJ BANJAC.

Deputy Prime Minister and Minister of Administration and Local Government: OSTOJA KRMANOVIĆ.

Deputy Prime Minister and Minister of Foreign Trade Relations: SAVO LONCAR.

Deputy Prime Minister and Minister for War Veterans and War and Labour Victims: TIHOMIR GLIGORIĆ.

Minister of Defence: Col-Gen. (retd) MANOJLO MILOVANOVIĆ.

Minister of Internal Affairs: MILOVAN STANKOVIĆ.

Minister of Justice: PETKO CANCAR.

Minister of Finance: NOVAK KONDIĆ.

Minister of Trade and Tourism: NIKOLA KRAGULJ.

Minister of Energy and Mining: VLADIMIR DOKIĆ.

Minister of Transport and Communications: MARKO PAVIĆ.

Minister of Agriculture, Waterways and Forestry: MILENKO SAVIĆ.

Minister of Urban Planning, Construction, Housing, Public Services and the Environment: JOVO BASIĆ.

Minister of Education: NENAD SUZIĆ.

Minister of Refugees and Displaced Persons: MILADIN DRAGICEVIĆ.

Minister of Health and Social Welfare: ZELJKO RODIĆ.

Minister of Science and Culture: ZIVOJIN ERIĆ.

Minister of Information: RAJKO VASIĆ.

Minister of Sport and Youth: MILORAD KARALIĆ.

Minister of Religion: JOVO TURANJANIN.

Presidency and Legislature

PRESIDENCY OF BOSNIA AND HERZEGOVINA

Election, 14 September 1996

	Votes
Bosniak Candidates	
ALIJA IZETBEGOVIĆ (Party for Democratic Action)	730,592
Dr HARIS SILAJDŽIĆ (Party for Bosnia and Herzegovina)	124,396
FIKRET ABDIĆ (Democratic People's Union)	25,584
SEAD AVDIĆ (Joint List for Bosnia and Herzegovina*)	21,254
Croat Candidates	
KRESIMIR ZUBAK (Croatian Democratic Union)	330,477
IVO KOMISIĆ (Joint List for Bosnia and Herzegovina)	37,684
Serb Candidates	
MOMČILO KRAJIŠNIK (Serb Democratic Party)	690,646
MLADEN IVANIĆ (People's Alliance for Peace and Progress†)	307,461
MILIVOJE ZARIĆ (Serb Patriotic Party)	15,407
BRANKO LATINOVIĆ (Serb Party of Krajina)	12,643

* Comprised the Union of Social Democrats of Bosnia and Herzegovina (UBSD), the Social Democratic Party, the HSS and the Muslim Bosniak Organization (MBO).

† Comprised the Socialist Party of Serbia for the Bosnian Serb Republic, the Independent Social Democrats of the Serb Republic, the Social Liberal Party, the Yugoslav United Left and the New Radical Party.

ASSEMBLY OF BOSNIA AND HERZEGOVINA

The Dayton peace agreement, signed in December 1995, provided for an Assembly of Bosnia and Herzegovina, comprising two chambers, the House of Peoples and the House of Representatives. In both houses two-thirds of the deputies were to be drawn from the Federation of Bosnia and Herzegovina, while one-third were to come from the Serb Republic. Deputies to the House of Representatives were elected in national polls held on 14 September 1996. The inaugural session of the two constituent houses of the Assembly were held on 3 January 1997. The Speakers of each house were to rotate, according to ethnic origin, every seven months, until fresh legislative elections, scheduled to be held in 1998.

House of Peoples

There are 15 deputies in the House of Peoples, who are not directly elected but are appointed by the relevant constituency in the House of Representatives.

Speakers of the House of Peoples: MOMIR TOSIĆ (SDP), AVDO CAMPARA (PDA), PETAR MAJIĆ (CDU).

House of Representatives

There are 42 deputies in the House of Representatives.

Election, 14 September 1996

Party	Votes	Seats
Federation of Bosnia and Herzegovina		
Party of Democratic Action	725,417	16
Croatian Democratic Union	338,440	8
Joint List of Bosnia and Herzegovina*	105,918	2
Party for Bosnia and Herzegovina	93,816	2
Democratic People's Union	25,562	—
Croatian Rights Party	14,879	—
Serb Republic		
Serb Democratic Party	578,723	9
Party for Democratic Action	184,553	3
People's Alliance for Peace and Progress†	136,077	2
Serb Radical Party of the Serb Republic	62,409	—
Joint List of Bosnia and Herzegovina*	30,285	—
Serb Patriotic Party	14,146	—
People's Party of the Serb Republic	13,285	—

* Comprised the Union of Social Democrats of Bosnia and Hezegovina (UBSD), the Social Democratic Party, the HSS and the Muslim Bosniak Organization (MBO).

† Comprised the Socialist Party of Serbia for the Bosnian Serb Republic, the Independent Social Democrats of the Serb Republic, the Social Liberal Party, the Yugoslav United Left and the New Radical Party.

Speakers of the House of Representatives: Ivo Lozancić (CDU), Slobodan Bijelić (SDP), Dr Halid Genjac (PDA).

HOUSE OF REPRESENTATIVES OF THE FEDERATION

There are 140 deputies in the House of Representatives.

Election, 14 September 1996

Party	Votes	Seats
Party of Democratic Action	725,810	78
Croatian Democratic Union	337,794	36
Joint List of Bosnia and Herzegovina*	105,879	11
Party for Bosnia and Herzegovina	98,207	10
Democratic People's Union	23,660	3
Croatian Rights Party	16,344	2

* Comprised the Union of Social Democrats of Bosnia and Herzegovina (UBSD), the Social Democratic Party, the HSS and the Muslim Bosniak Organization (MBO).

Speaker of the Federation House of Representatives: Enver Kreso.

Deputy Speaker: Stjepan Mitić (CDU).

PRESIDENCY OF THE SERB REPUBLIC

Election, 14 September 1996

Candidate	Votes
Dr Biljana Plavšić (Serb Democratic Party)	636,654
Adib Jozić (Party of Democratic Action)	197,389
Zivko Radisić (People's Alliance for Peace and Progress*)	168,024
Predrag Radić (Democratic Patriotic Block of the Serb Republic)	44,755
Slavko Lisica (Serb Patriotic Party)	20,050

* An electoral coalition comprising the Socialist Party of Serbia for the Bosnian Serb Republic, the Independent Social Democrats of the Serb Republic, the Social Liberal Party, the Yugoslav United Left and the New Radical Party.

NATIONAL ASSEMBLY OF THE SERB REPUBLIC

Election, 22–23 November 1997

Party	Seats
Serb Democratic Party	24
Coalition for a Single and Democratic Bosnia*	16
Serb Radical Party	15
Serb National Alliance	15
Socialist Party of the Bosnian Serb Republic	9
Party of Independent Social Democrats	2
Social Democratic Party	2

* Comprised the Civil Democratic Party, the Liberal Party, the Party for Bosnia and Herzegovina and the Party of Democratic Action.

Speaker of the National Assembly: Dr Dragan Kalinić.

Deputy Speaker: Nikola Poplasen (SRS).

Provisional Election Commission: Sarajevo; tel. (71) 444444; f. under terms of Dayton accords to organize for local elections, and for national and entity elections scheduled for 14 September 1996; mandate extended in order to permit supervision of the local elections that were held in September 1997; under aegis of Organization for Security and Co-operation in Europe (OSCE); Chair. Robert Frowick, Head of the OSCE Mission; mems Mirko Bosković (Federation), Slobodan Kovačević (Serb Republic).

Political Organizations

Association of the Democratic Initiative of Sarajevo Serbs (Udruženje demokratske inicijative Srba iz Sarajeva): Sarajevo; f. 1996 to affirm and protect the rights of Serbs in Muslim-held Sarajevo; Chair. Maksim Stanisić.

Bosnian Party (Bosanska Stranka): Chair. Mirnes Ajanović.

Civic Democratic Party (Gradjanska Demokratska Stranka): member of the Coalition for a Single and Democratic Bosnia electoral alliance; Chair. Ibrahim Spahić.

Croat National Council of Bosnia and Herzegovina: Sarajevo; f. 1993; established by Bosnian Croats opposed to Croatia's official policy towards Bosnia and Herzegovina as well as to radical Bosnian Muslims; Chair. Ivo Komsić, Ivan Lovrenović.

Croatian Democratic Union of Bosnia and Herzegovina (CDU—BH) (Hrvatska Demokratska Zajednica Bosne i Hercegovine—HDZ BiH): 71000 Sarajevo; f. 1990; affiliate of the CDU in Croatia; Croat nationalist party; Pres. Bozo Rajić; Vice-Pres. Ivić Pasalić; Sec.-Gen. Pero Marković.

Croatian Peasants' Party (Hrvatska Seljacka Stranka): affiliated to Croatian Peasants' Party in Croatia; member of the Joint List of Bosnia and Herzegovina electoral alliance.

Croatian Rights Party (Hrvatska Stranka Prava): contested 1996 elections; nationalist; Pres. Stanko Slisković.

Democratic Party for Banja Luka and Krajina: Banja Luka; f. 1997, by fmr mems of Serb Radical Party (q.v.); Chair. Nikola Spirić.

Democratic Patriotic Bloc of the Serb Republic (Demokratski Patriotski Blok Republike Srpske): contested 1996 elections; Chair. Predrag Radić.

Democratic People's Union (Narodna Demokratska Zajednica—NDZ): f. 1996; Chair. Fikret Abdić; Vice-Chair. Zlatko Jusić.

Eastern Bosnian Muslim Party (Istocnobosanska Muslimanska Stranka): Sarajevo; f. 1997; Chair. Ibran Mustafić.

Homeland Party: Banja Luka; f. 1996 by fmr members of Serb Democratic Union—Homeland Front; nationalist; Chair. Predrag Rasić.

Liberal Bosniak Organization (LBO) (Liberalna Bosnjacka Organizacija): 71000 Sarajevo; f. 1992; secular Muslim party; Pres. Muhamed Filipović; Vice-Pres. Salih Foco.

Liberal Party (Liberalna Stranka): member of the Coalition for a Single and Democratic Bosnia electoral alliance; Pres. Rasim Kadić.

Muslim Bosniak Organization (MBO): Sarajevo; f. 1990; member of the Joint List of Bosnia and Herzegovina electoral alliance; Chair. Zulfik Ardasić; Deputy Chair. Mujo Kafedzić.

Muslim Democratic Alliance (Muslimanski Demokratski Savez—MDS): Bihać; f. 1994; seeks to promote equality between the ethnic groups of Bosnia and Herzegovina.

New Radical Party: member of the People's Alliance for Peace and Progress electoral coalition.

Party for Bosnia and Herzegovina: Sarajevo; f. 1996; integrationist; member of the Joint List of Bosnia and Herzegovina and of the Coalition for a Single and Democratic Bosnia electoral alliances; Pres. Dr Haris Silajdžić; Sec. Safet Redzepagić.

Party of Democratic Action (PDA) (Stranka Demokratske Akcije—SDA): c/o 71000 Sarajevo, trg Dure Pucara bb; leading Muslim nationalist party; has brs in Yugoslavia; member of the Coalition for a Single and Democratic Bosnia electoral alliance; Chair. Dr Alija Izetbegović; Deputy Chair. Edhem Bicakcić, Dr Halid Genjac, Dr Ejup Ganić; Sec. Gen. Mirsad Ceman.

Party of Economic Prosperity (Stranka Privednog Prosperita—SPP): Zenica; f. 1996; joined the Joint List of Bosnia and Herzegovina electoral alliance in April 1997; Chair. Pane Skrbić; Sec.-Gen. Safet Redzepagić.

Party of Independent Social Democrats of the Serb Republic: Banja Luka; member of the People's Alliance for Peace and Progress electoral coalition; Chair. MILORAD DODIK; Deputy Chair. NENAD BASTINAĆ.

Party of Serb Unity (Stranka Srpskog Jedinstva): Bijeljina; extreme nationalist; Chair. ZELKO RAZNJATOVIĆ ('Arkan').

People's Party of the Serb Republic (Narodna Stranka Republicka Srpska): Leaders RADOSLAV BRDJANIN, MILAN TRBOJEVIĆ.

Republican Party: Sarajevo; integrationist; member of the Joint List of Bosnia and Herzegovina electoral alliance; Chair. STJEPAN KLJUIĆ.

Serb Civic Council: Sarajevo; anti-nationalist; org. of Serbs in the Federation of Bosnia and Herzegovina; Chair. Dr MIRKO PEJANOVIĆ.

Serb Democratic Party of Bosnia and Herzegovina (SDP) (Srpska Demokratska Stranka Bosne i Hercegovine—SDS BiH): c/o Pale, National Assembly of the Serb Republic; f. 1990; allied to SDP of Croatia; Serb nationalist party; Pres. ALEKSA BUHA (acting); First Vice-Pres. MOMČILO KRAJIŠNIK; Sec. of Presidency VLADO VRKES.

Serb Democratic Union—Homeland Front: nationalist; Pres. BOŽIDAR BOJANIĆ.

Serb National Alliance (Srpski Narodni Savez): Banja Luka; f. 1997; Chair. Dr. BILJANA PLAVŠIĆ; Vice-Chair. OSTOJA KNEZEVIĆ.

Serb Patriotic Party (Srpska Patriotska Stranka): contested 1996 elections; Chair. STOJAN ZUPLJANIN; Vice-Chair. PETAR DJAKOVIĆ.

Serb Party of Krajina (Srpska Stranka Krajina—SSK): Banja Luka; f. 1996; regional party in favour of the creation of clear borders between nations; Pres. PREDRAG LAZAREVIĆ; Chair. of Exec. Cttee DJORDJE UMICEVIĆ.

Serb Radical Party of the Serb Republic (Srpska Radikalna Stranka Srpske Republike—SRS SR): branch of SRS in Serbia; Chair. Dr NIKOLA POPLASEN; Vice-Chair. PANTELIJA DAMJANOVIĆ; Gen. Sec. MILODRAG RAKIĆ.

Social Alliance: c/o 71000 Sarajevo, trg Dure Pucara bb; fmr communist mass organization; allies of Social Democratic Party; left-wing.

Social Democratic Party (Social demokratska Partija): 71000 Sarajevo, Dure Dakovića 41; tel. (71) 216644; fax (71) 218168; registered 1990; fmrly the ruling League of Communists of Bosnia and Herzegovina; withdrew from the Joint List of Bosnia and Herzegovina electoral alliance in April 1997; Chair. ZLATKO LAGUMDZIJA; Sec.-Gen. KARLO FILIPOVIĆ.

Social Liberal Party: Banja Luka; reintegrationist; member of the People's Alliance for Peace and Progress electoral coalition; Chair. MIODRAG ZIVANOVIĆ; Gen. Sec. MILAN TUKIĆ.

Socialist Party of the Bosnian Serb Republic (Socijalistička partija Srbije za Republiku Srpsku—SPS za RS): Banja Luka; f. 1993; branch of the Socialist Party of Serbia; organized the electoral alliance, the People's Alliance for Peace and Progress, for the 1996 elections; Chair. ZIVKO RADISIĆ; Vice-Chair. DRAGUTIN ILIĆ; 40,000 mems.

Union of Social Democrats of Bosnia and Herzegovina: Sarajevo; member of the Joint List of Bosnia and Herzegovina electoral alliance; Chair. SELIM BESLAGIĆ.

Yugoslav Left of the Serb Republic: Bijeljina; f. 1996; branch of pro-communist party based in Belgrade (Yugoslavia); member of the People's Alliance for Peace and Progress electoral coalition; Pres. MILORAD IVOSEVIĆ.

Note: The following parties and electoral blocs were also registered in the elections of 14 September 1996: Serb Peasant Party (Srpska Seljacka Stranka); Patriotic Party of Bosnia and Herzegovina (Patriotska Stranka BiH); Democratic Popular Union (Demokratska Narodna Zajednica); Democratic Party of Federalists (Demokratska Stranka Federalista); Party of Women of Bosnia and Herzegovina (Stranka Žena BiH); Serbian Renaissance Party.

Diplomatic Representation

EMBASSIES IN BOSNIA AND HERZEGOVINA

Bangladesh: 71000 Sarajevo; Ambassador: KHURSID HAMID.

Canada: 71000 Sarajevo; Ambassador: SERGE MARCOUX.

Croatia: 71000 Sarajevo, Boriše Kovačevida 20; tel. and fax (71) 444428; Ambassador: DARINKO BAGO.

Denmark: 71000 Sarajevo; Ambassador: JØRGEN BØJER.

Finland: 71000 Sarajevo; Ambassador: HAJKI KOPONEN.

France: 71000 Sarajevo; Ambassador: YVES GAUDEUL.

Germany: 71000 Sarajevo; Ambassador: Graf VON HENNECKE BASSEWITZ.

Holy See: 71000 Sarajevo; Apostolic Nuncio: Mgr FRANCESCO MONTERISI.

Iran: 71000 Sarajevo, Obala Maka Dizdara 6; tel. (71) 650210; fax (71) 663910; Ambassador: MOHAMMAD EBRAHIM TAHERIAN.

Italy: 71000 Sarajevo; Ambassador: VITTORIO PENNAROLA.

Malaysia: 71000 Sarajevo; Ambassador: RASTAM MOHD ISA.

Morocco: 71000 Sarajevo; Ambassador: Mr ROLIK.

Slovenia: 71000 Sarajevo; Ambassador: DRAGO MIROSIĆ.

Turkey: 71000 Sarajevo; Ambassador: SUKRU TUFAN.

United Kingdom: 71000 Sarajevo, Tina Vjevica 8; tel. (71) 444429; fax (71) 666131; Ambassador: CHARLES CRAWFORD.

USA: 71000 Sarajevo; Ambassador: RICHARD KAUZLARICH.

Judicial System

The courts in Bosnia and Herzegovina are supervised by the Ministry of Justice. The Constitutional Court has competence regarding constitutional matters in both Bosnian 'entities', but there are separate judicial systems in the Bosnian Federation and the Serb Republic. In March 1997 Marko Arsović and Vitomir Popović were appointed judges of the Supreme Court of the Serb Republic.

Constitutional Court of the Republic of Bosnia and Herzegovina: 71000 Sarajevo, Save Kovačevića 6; tel. (71) 214555; nine mems; mems elected for four-year term; Pres. Dr KASIM TRNKA: Vice-Pres. VITOMIR POPOVIĆ.

Constitutional Court of the Serb Republic: Pale; eight mems; Pres. GASO MIJANOVIĆ; Sec. MIODRAG SIMOVIĆ.

Supreme Court of the Federation of Bosnia and Herzegovina: 71000 Sarajevo, Valtera Perića 11; tel. (71) 213577; Pres. HATIDŽA HADŽIOSMANOVIĆ.

Office of the Federal Prosecutor: 71000 Sarajevo, Valtera Perića 11; tel. (71) 214990; Federal Prosecutor SULJO BABIĆ.

Religion

Bosnia and Herzegovina has a diversity of religious allegiances. Just over one-half of the inhabitants are nominally Christian, but these are divided between the Serbian Orthodox Church and the Roman Catholic Church. The dominant single religion is Islam. The Reis-ul-ulema, the head of the Muslims in the territory comprising the former Yugoslavia, is resident in Sarajevo. Most of the Muslims are ethnic Muslims or Bosniaks (Slavs who converted to Islam under the Ottomans). There are, however, some ethnic Albanian and Turkish Muslims. Virtually all are adherents of the Sunni sect. There is a small Jewish community; since 1966, however, there has been no rabbi in the community. In June 1997 an agreement to establish an interreligious council was signed by the leaders of the Roman Catholic, Serbian Orthodox, Jewish and Islamic communities.

ISLAM

Islamic Community of the Sarajevo Region: 71000 Sarajevo, Save Kovačevića 2; Pres. of Massahat SALIH EFENDIJA COLAKOVIĆ; Mufti of Bosnia and Herzegovina Hadži MUSTAFA TIRIĆ; Reis-ul-ulema MUSTAFA EFENDI CERIĆ.

CHRISTIANITY

The Serbian Orthodox Church

Metropolitan of Dabrobosna: NICOLAJ; (c/o Serbian Patriarchate, 11001 Belgrade, Kralja Petra 5, POB 182; Yugoslavia).

The Roman Catholic Church

For ecclesiastical purposes, Bosnia and Herzegovina comprises one archdiocese and three dioceses. At 31 December 1993 there were an estimated 786,000 adherents in the country.

Bishops' Conference: Biskupska Konferencija Bosne i Hercegovine, Nadbiskupski Ordinarijat, 71000 Sarajevo, Kaptol 7; tel. and fax (71) 472178; f. 1995; Pres. Cardinal VINKO PULJIĆ, Archbishop of Vrhbosna-Sarajevo; Vice-Pres. Rt Rev. FRANJO KOMARICA, Bishop of Banja Luka.

Archbishop of Vrhbosna-Sarajevo: Cardinal VINKO PULJIĆ, Nadbiskupski Ordinarijat Vrhbosanski, 71000 Sarajevo, Kaptol 7; tel. (71) 663512; fax (71) 472429.

JUDAISM

Jewish Community of the Sarajevo Region: 71000 Sarajevo, Hamdije Kreševljekoviće 59; tel. (71) 663472; fax (71) 663473; Pres. JAKOB FINCI.

The Press

The majority of publications were obliged to cease production as a result of the civil war in 1992–95, although the daily newspaper,

Oslobodjenje, continued to circulate throughout the siege of Sarajevo.

PRINCIPAL DAILIES

Dnevni Avaz: 71000 Sarajevo.

Glas Srpski: Banja Luka; Serb Republic government newspaper; Editor-in-Chief NENAD NOVAKOVIC (acting).

Horizont: Mostar; f. 1996; Croat independent.

Oslobodjenje (Liberation): 71000 Sarajevo, Džemala Bijedića 185; tel. (71) 454144; telex 41136; fax (71) 460982; f. 1943; morning; Editor KEMAL KURSPAHIĆ; circ. 56,000.

Večernje novine: 71000 Sarajevo, Pruščakova St 13; tel. (71) 664874; fax (71) 664875; f. 1964; special edition published daily in Serb Republic; Editor and Dir SEAD DEMIROVIĆ; Exec. Editor BERIN EKMEČIĆ; circ. 15,000.

WEEKLY NEWSPAPERS

Hratska Rijec: 71000 Sarajevo; Croat weekly.

Ljiljan: 71000 Sarajevo; official newspaper of the PDA; Editor-in-Chief ZEHRUDIN ISAKOVIĆ.

Nezavisne novine (The Independent): Banja Luka; f. 1995; Editor-in-Chief ZELJKO KOPANJA.

PERIODICALS

Alternativa: Doboj; f. 1996; fortnightly; Editor-in-Chief PAVLE STANISIĆ; Deputy Editor-in-Chief ZIVKO SAVKOVIĆ; Dir SLOBODAN BABIĆ; circ. 5,000.

Dani: 71000 Sarajevo; independent; monthly; Editor-in-Chief SENAD PECANIN.

Novi prelom: Banja Luka; monthly.

Slobodna Bosna: 71000 Sarajevo, Muhameda Kantardžića 3; tel. (71) 444041; fax (71) 444895; e-mail slobo-bosna@zamir-sa.ztn.atc.-org; fortnightly; Editor SENAD AVDIĆ.

Svijet: Sarajevo; illustrated; weekly; Editor-in-Chief JELA JEVREMOVIĆ; circ. 115,000.

Zadrugar: Sarajevo, Omladinska 1; f. 1945; weekly; journal for farmers; Editor-in-Chief FADIL ADEMOVIĆ; circ. 34,000.

NEWS AGENCIES

HABENA: Mostar; Bosnian Croat nationalist news agency.

BH Press: Sarajevo; state news agency.

ONASA (Oslobodjenje News Agency): Sarajevo; tel. (71) 521175; fax (71) 444237.

SNRA: Banja Luka; Bosnian Serb news agency.

Publishers

Novi Glas: 78000 Banja Luka, Borisa Kidriča 1; tel. (78) 12766; fax (78) 12758; general literature; Dir MIODRAG ŽIVANOVIĆ.

Svjetlost: 71000 Sarajevo, Petra Preradovića 3; tel. (71) 212144; telex 41326; fax (71) 272352; f. 1945; textbooks and literature; Dir SAVO ZIROJEVIĆ.

Veselin Masleša: 71000 Sarajevo, Obala 4; tel. (71) 214633; telex 41154; fax (71) 272369; f. 1950; school and university textbooks, general literature; Dir RADOSLAV MIJATOVIĆ.

Broadcasting and Communications

TELECOMMUNICATIONS

Director of Telecommunications: Musala 2, 71000 Sarajevo; tel. (71) 472657; fax (71) 441248; Dir EMIN SKOPLJAK.

BROADCASTING

In 1997 broadcasting in Bosnia and Herzegovina was largely controlled by the three nationalist parties: the Party of Democratic Action (PDA); the Croatian Democratic Union in Bosnia and Herzegovina (CDU-BH); and the Serb Democratic Party (SDP). There were, however, a number of locally based independent radio and television stations. In May 1996 two such organizations, Sarajevo-based Hajat and Zenica-based Zetel (both television companies), had created, with the Mostar and Tuzla branches of Radio-Televizija Bosne i Hercegovine, the TVIN-TV International Network. This was to be open to media and correspondents from the Muslim–Croat Federation and the Serb Republic, in accordance with the aims of the Dayton agreement. In 1997 Serb Radio and Television (SRT) was divided, following a sharp difference in editorial policy between the studio in Pale, including the management board, which opposed President Plavšić, and a rival station in Banja Luka, which supported the President. In October the international community requested the resignation of the management board of the SRT.

Radio-Televizija (RTV) Bosne i Hercegovine: 71000 Sarajevo, VI Proleterske brigade 4; tel. (71) 455107; telex 41124; fax (71) 455166 (Radio); tel. (71) 652333; telex 41122; fax (71) 461569 (TV); f. 1945 (Radio), 1969 (TV); 4 radio and 2 TV programmes; broadcasts in Serbo-Croat; Dir-Gen. AHMED HADŽIJAMAKOVIĆ; Dir of Radio NADJA PAŠIĆ; Dir of TV AMILA OMERSOFTIĆ (acting); Editor-in-Chief ESAD CEROVIĆ.

Serb Radio and Television (SRT): Pale; Dir-Gen. MIROSLAV TOHOLJ; Chair. of Man. Bd MOMČILO KRAJIŠNIK; Editor-in-Chief DRAGO VUKOVIĆ.

Radio

Croat Radio Herzeg-Bosna: Mostar; Dir TOMISLAV MAZALO; Editor-in-Chief IVAN KRISTIĆ.

Serb Radio Banja Luka: Banja Luka; f. 1997 as independent radio station following breakaway from Serb Radio and Television (q.v.); eight-mem. editorial council; Chair. RADOMIR NESKOVIĆ.

Finance

(d.d. = dioničko društvo (joint-stock company); cap. = capital; res = reserves; dep. = deposits; m. = million; amounts in Yugoslav dinars unless otherwise stated; brs = branches)

BANKING

The Yugoslav National Bank refused to supply Bosnia and Herzegovina with Yugoslav dinars in June 1992. A new currency, the Bosnia and Herzegovina dinar, was introduced on 14 October 1994, while the Croatian kuna remained in use in Bosnian Croat-populated areas of Bosnia and Herzegovina. The Dayton peace agreement, which was signed in December 1995, included provisions for the establishment of a new central bank in Bosnia and Herzegovina (see below). In 1996 there were 23 state-owned banks and 30 private banks, of which 42 operated in the Federation and 11 in the Serb Republic. Total assets in the banking system, excluding non-performing assets, were estimated at US $728m. in June 1996.

Central Bank

Central Bank of Bosnia and Herzegovina: 71000 Sarajevo; f. under the provisions of the Dayton peace agreement to be sole authority for monetary policy and the issuing of domestic currency. The Bank was to act as a currency board for a minimum of six years. During this period the Bank's Governor was to be a foreign national appointed by the IMF. The first appointment was made in October 1996. Gov. PETER NICHOLL (New Zealand); Deputy Gov. DRAGAN KOVACEVIC; Mems of Governing Bd KASIM OMICEVIĆ, JURE PELIVAN, MANOJILO CORIĆ.

National Banks

National Bank of the Republic of Bosnia and Herzegovina: 71000 Sarajevo, Maršala Tita 25; tel. (71) 33326; Gov. KASIM OMICEVIĆ.

National Bank of the Serb Republic: Banja Luka; f. 1996; performs regulatory and supervisory functions; Gov. MANOJILO CORIĆ.

Selected Banks

Export Banka a.d., Bijeljina: ul. Svetog Save br. 46, Bijeljina; tel. (76) 401409; fax (76) 401410; f. 1992; Pres. JOVO STANKIĆ; Chair. SLAVKO ROGULJIĆ; Man. Dir MILADIN VIDIĆ.

Investiciono-Komercijalna Banka d.d., Zenica: 72000 Zenica, trg Samoupravljača 1; tel. (72) 21804; telex 43117; fax (72) 417022; f. 1990; cap. 15,006.1m., res 39,182.1m., dep. 62,969.3m. (Dec. 1995); Gen. Man. ALIJA ALIHODŽIĆ.

Micro Enterprise Bank (MEB): Sarajevo; f. 1997; owned by World Bank, European Bank for Reconstruction and Development, and German, Bosnian and Dutch financial institutions; cap. DM 3.5m.; Man. RALF NIPEL; 2 brs.

Privredna Banka Brčko d.d.: Kralja Petra I Oslobodioca broj 1, Brčko; tel. (76) 204222; fax (76) 204055; f. 1993; Pres. JOVICA SOPIĆ; Chair. MILAN KARANOVIĆ; Gen. Man. STOJAN MAJSTOROVIĆ.

Privredna Banka Gradiška d.d.: Vidovdanska bb, Gradiška; tel. (78) 813333; telex 45108; fax (78) 813205; f. 1953, registered as independent bank since 1992; Pres. MICO RISTIĆ; Chair. BORISLAV CVJETKOVIĆ.

Privredna Banka Sarajevo a.d.: ul. Srpskih Ratnika br. 14, Pale; tel. (71) 786806; fax (71) 786805; f. 1970 by merger of five banks; Man. Dir. MOMČILO MANDIĆ.

Privredna Banka Sarajevo d.d., Sarajevo: 71000 Sarajevo, Vojvode Stepe Obala 19, POB 160; tel. (71) 213144; telex 41289; fax (71) 218511; f. 1971; cap. 3,713.1m., res 1,131.1m., dep. 35,471.6m. (Dec. 1990); Pres. and Gen. Man. DJORDJE ZARIĆ; 14 brs.

Semberska Banka d.d., Bijeljina: Karadjordjeva 3, Bijeljina; tel. (76) 471588; fax (76) 472247; Pres. MILAN MIHAJLOVIĆ; Chair. ARSEN TEŠIĆ; Man. Dir CVIJETIN NIKIĆ.

Srpska Državna Banka a.d.: Magistralni Put 1A, Pale; tel. (71) 783357; fax (71) 783412; f. 1996; Pres. VELIBOR OSTOJIĆ; Chair. GOJKO LIČKOVIĆ; Man. Dir GOJKO DURSUN.

Banking Agency

Agency for Banking (Agencija za Bankarstvo): 71000 Sarajevo; f. 1996; Dir ZLATKO BAROS.

Trade and Industry

CHAMBERS OF COMMERCE

Chamber of Economy of Bosnia and Herzegovina: 71000 Sarajevo, Mis Irbina 13; tel. (71) 663631; fax (71) 663632; Pres. ANTE DOMAZET.

Chamber of Commerce of the Serb Republic: Banja Luka; Pres. BOZO ANTIĆ.

TRADE UNIONS

Independent Trade Union Association of Bosnia and Herzegovina: Sarajevo; Pres. SULEJMAN HRLE.

Serb Republic Trade Union Federation: Banja Luka; legalized 1996; Chair. CEDO GOLAS.

Transport

RAILWAYS

At the beginning of the 1990s the railway system consisted of some 1,030 km of track, of which 75% was electrified. Much of the system was damaged or destroyed during the civil wars, but in July 1996 the Sarajevo–Mostar service was restored and in 1997 the Tuzla–Doboj and Tuzla–Brčko services were reopened. Following the outbreak of hostilities, the state railway company was divided into three regional state-owned companies: the **Bosnia and Herzegovina Railway Company (ZBH),** based in Sarajevo; the **Herzeg-Bosnia Railway Company (ZHB),** based in the Croat-majority part of the Federation; and the **Serb Republic Railway and Transport Company (ZTP),** based in Banja Luka.

ROADS

The transport infrastructure in Bosnia and Herzegovina was badly damaged during the civil war of 1992–95. Some 35% of the country's roads and 40% of its bridges were affected by the conflict. A new Transportation Corporation was to be established (with its headquarters in Sarajevo), under the terms of the Dayton accords, which would organize and operate roads, ports and railways on the territory of the two entities. The agreement also provided for the construction of a new road linking the Goražde enclave, in the east of Bosnia and Herzegovina, with the rest of the Federation.

Transportation Corporation: Sarajevo; public corporation.

CIVIL AVIATION

The country has an international airport at Sarajevo, and three smaller civil airports, at Tuzla, Banja Luka and Mostar. Civil aviation was severely disrupted by the 1992–95 civil wars. Commercial flights resumed to Sarajevo in August 1996 and to Banja Luka in November 1997; negotiations to reopen the airports in Tuzla and Mostar proved unsuccessful throughout 1997. In March 1997 a new airline (RS Airlines) was founded in the Serb Republic, and in June it was announced that a new airport at Dubrave, near Tuzla, was to be built.

Air Bosna: 71000 Sarajevo; regular services to Croatia, Germany, Slovenia, Sweden and Turkey; Gen. Man. OMER KULIĆ.

Air Commerce: charter flights from Sarajevo to Turkey and Egypt, and scheduled service to Switzerland; Dir MOHAMED ABADŽIĆ.

RS Airlines: Pale; f. 1997; flights from Banja Luka airport to Yugoslavia, Greece, Hungary, Romania, Bulgaria and Russia; Dir JOVAN TINTOR.

BOTSWANA

Introductory Survey

Location, Climate, Language, Religion, Flag, Capital

The Republic of Botswana is a land-locked country in southern Africa, with South Africa to the south and east, Zimbabwe to the north-east and Namibia to the west and north. A short section of the northern frontier adjoins Zambia. The climate is generally sub-tropical, with hot summers. Annual rainfall averages about 457 mm (18 ins), varying from 635 mm (25 ins) in the north to 228 mm (9 ins) or less in the western Kalahari desert. The country is largely near-desert, and most of its inhabitants live along the eastern border, close to the main railway line. English is the official language, and Setswana the national language. Most of the population follow traditional animist beliefs, but several Christian churches are also represented. The national flag (proportions 3 by 2) consists of a central horizontal stripe of black, edged with white, between two blue stripes. The capital is Gaborone.

Recent History

Botswana was formerly Bechuanaland, which became a British protectorate, at the request of the local rulers, in 1885. It was administered as one of the High Commission Territories in southern Africa, the others being the colony of Basutoland (now Lesotho) and the protectorate of Swaziland. The British Act of Parliament that established the Union of South Africa in 1910 also allowed for the inclusion in South Africa of the three High Commission Territories, on condition that the local inhabitants were consulted. Until 1960 successive South African Governments asked for the transfer of the three territories, but the native chiefs always objected to such a scheme.

Within Bechuanaland, gradual progress was made towards self-government, mainly through nominated advisory bodies. A new Constitution was introduced in December 1960, and a Legislative Council (partly elected, partly appointed) first met in June 1961. Bechuanaland was made independent of High Commission rule in September 1963, and the office of High Commissioner was abolished in August 1964. The seat of government was transferred from Mafeking (now Mafikeng), in South Africa, to Gaberones (now Gaborone) in February 1965. On 1 March 1965 internal self-government was achieved, and the territory's first direct election, for a Legislative Assembly, was held on the basis of universal adult suffrage. Of the Assembly's 31 seats, 28 were won by the Bechuanaland Democratic Party (BDP or Domkrag), founded in 1962. The leader of the BDP, Seretse Khama, was sworn in as the territory's first Prime Minister. Bechuanaland became the independent Republic of Botswana, within the Commonwealth, on 30 September 1966, with Sir Seretse Khama (as he had become) taking office as the country's first President. The BDP, restyled the Botswana Democratic Party at independence, won elections to the National Assembly, with little opposition, in 1969, 1974 and 1979.

Khama died in July 1980, and was succeeded as President by Dr Quett Masire (later Sir Ketumile Masire), hitherto Vice-President and Minister of Finance. Following elections to the National Assembly in September 1984, at which the BDP again achieved a decisive victory, Masire was re-elected President by the legislature. However, the BDP fared badly in local government elections which were held simultaneously with the parliamentary elections, apparently reflecting discontent at the country's high level of unemployment. An unprecedented outbreak of rioting, in March 1987, was similarly attributed by observers to popular dissatisfaction with the Government as a result of increasing unemployment; the Government accused the principal opposition party, the Botswana National Front (BNF), of fomenting the unrest. At a referendum in September a large majority endorsed amendments to the electoral system, as defined by the Constitution, although the BNF boycotted the vote.

During 1989 there was widespread labour unrest involving bank employees, mineworkers and schoolteachers. Nevertheless, in October the BDP received 65% of the votes cast at a general election to the National Assembly, winning 27 of the 30 elective seats (the remaining three seats were won by the BNF), and the new legislature re-elected Masire for a third term as President. In November 1991 the Government dismissed some 12,000 members of public-service trade unions who had been campaigning for wage increases.

In March 1992 the Vice-President and Chairman of the BDP, Peter Mmusi, resigned as Vice-President and Minister of Local Government and Lands, while the party's Secretary-General, Daniel Kwelagobe, resigned as Minister of Agriculture, having been accused of corruption involving the illegal transfer of land. Festus Mogae, the Minister of Finance and Development Planning, was appointed as the new Vice-President. In June Mmusi and Kwelagobe were suspended from the Central Committee of the BDP; both were, however, re-elected to their former positions within the party at the BDP congress in July 1993. In early 1993 the Deputy Minister of Finance and Development Planning was forced to resign, apparently implicated in allegations of improper financial transactions involving the Botswana Housing Corporation. In the same year it was revealed that seven government ministers were among the debtors of the National Development Bank, which was reported to be in financial difficulties.

For the general election of 15 October 1994 the number of directly-elective seats in the National Assembly was increased to 40. The BDP, which received 53.1% of the votes cast, won 26 seats (three government ministers failed to secure re-election, and several members were returned with considerably reduced majorities), while the BNF, which obtained 37.7% of the votes, increased its representation to 13 seats. More than 70% of registered voters participated in the election. In general, the BDP retained its dominance in rural areas, while the BNF received strong support in urban constituencies. The National Assembly re-elected Masire to the presidency on 17 October. One week later the Assembly elected four additional parliamentary members. The new Cabinet, the composition of which was announced on the same day, included two of these, as well as Kwelagobe, who had been acquitted by the High Court in connection with the 1992 allegations.

Rioting, which had begun in January 1995 in Mochudi (to the north of Gaborone) following the release without charge of three people who had been detained on suspicion of involvement in a ritual murder, spread to the capital in February. One person was killed during three days of violent confrontations; shops were looted and government vehicles damaged. The BNF denied government assertions that it had incited the unrest, countering that the demonstrations reflected frustrations at the high level of unemployment and other social problems. Masire later defended the actions of the security forces, in response to allegations that their use of force in suppressing the demonstrations had been excessive.

In June 1995 the Governor of the central Bank of Botswana stated that the country's economic strategies must be revised if growth were to be restored and social unrest and political instability avoided. In the following month a BNF motion expressing 'no confidence' in the Government—prompted by the alleged involvement of members of the Masire administration in the National Development Bank scandal and in other questionable financial affairs, as well as by the Government's apparent failure to address social concerns—was defeated in the National Assembly. Also in July the Minister of Presidential Affairs and Public Administration, Ponatshego Kedikilwe, was elected Chairman of the BDP (the post had remained vacant since the death of Mmusi prior to the 1994 elections).

A number of amendments to the Constitution, which had been proposed during 1995–96, were adopted in August and September 1997. On 6 August the National Assembly formally approved revisions restricting the presidential mandate to two terms of office and providing for the automatic succession to the presidency of the Vice-President, in the event of the death or resignation of the President. Further amendments approved by the National Assembly, reforming aspects of the electoral system, were endorsed in a national referendum on 5 September. The reforms reduced the age of eligibility to vote from 21 to 18 years and provided for the introduction of votes for Batswana resident abroad, and for the establishment of an independent electoral commission; opposition parties had hitherto been critical of the prevailing system, whereby the election supervisor was an appointee of the President's office. According to official figures, only 16.7% of the electorate participated in the referendum; the low turnout was attributed to a certain degree of apathy among voters, given the consensus of all the political parties on the need for reform, and to the requirement that votes be cast in the constituencies at which voters had registered for the 1994 general election.

Masire effected a minor cabinet reshuffle in September 1997, replacing the Minister of Local Government, Lands and Housing and the Minister of Agriculture, Roy Blackbeard, who had resigned amid allegations of corruption regarding his ministry's handling of a severe outbreak of cattle lung disease. In early November Masire formally announced his intention to retire from politics in March 1998; in accordance with the constitutional amendment adopted three months earlier, Vice-President Mogae was temporarily to assume the presidency pending the holding of elections in 1999.

The Government's attempts to relocate Bushmen from their homeland within the Central Kalahari Game Reserve to a new settlement outside the reserve provoked international concern during 1996–97; it was claimed that officials had forced many Bushmen to move by cutting off water supplies and threatening military intervention.

Although, as one of the 'front-line' states, Botswana did not have diplomatic links with the apartheid regime in South Africa, it was (and remains) heavily dependent on its neighbour for trade and communications. Botswana is a member of the Southern African Development Community (SADC—see p. 236), which superseded the Southern African Development Co-ordination Conference (SADCC), in 1992. The SADC, of which South Africa became a member in 1994, has its headquarters in Gaborone.

From independence, it was the Botswana Government's stated policy not to permit any guerrilla groups to operate from Botswanan territory. Relations with South Africa deteriorated in May 1984, when Masire accused the South African Government of exerting pressure on Botswana to sign a non-aggression pact, aimed at preventing the alleged use of Botswana's territory by guerrilla forces of the (then outlawed) African National Congress of South Africa (ANC). In the second half of the 1980s South African forces launched a number of raids on alleged ANC bases in Botswana, causing several deaths. Owing to Botswana's vulnerable position, however, the Government did not commit itself to the imposition of economic sanctions against South Africa when this was recommended by the SADCC in August 1986. In 1988–89 Botswana took action against the extension onto its territory of hostilities between South African government and anti-apartheid forces. Two South African commandos, who had allegedly opened fire on Botswana security forces while engaged in a raid, were sentenced to 10 years' imprisonment; nine South Africans were expelled for 'security reasons', and five ANC members were convicted on firearms charges. It was reported in August 1989 that the South African army had erected an electrified fence along a 24-km section of the South Africa–Botswana border, in order to halt the reputed threat of guerrilla infiltration into South Africa via Botswana.

With the dismantling of apartheid in the first half of the 1990s, Botswana's relations with South Africa improved markedly and full diplomatic relations were established in June 1994. President Nelson Mandela of South Africa visited Botswana in September 1995; the need for the two countries to co-operate in combating crime was identified as a priority during discussions on issues of mutual concern. Meanwhile, in August 1994 it was announced that the 'front-line' states were to form a political and security wing within the SADC.

In 1983, following allegations that armed dissidents from Zimbabwe were being harboured among Zimbabwean refugees encamped in Botswana, the Botswana Government agreed to impose stricter restrictions on the refugees. In May Botswana and Zimbabwe established full diplomatic relations. The first meeting of the Botswana-Zimbabwe joint commission for co-operation was held in October 1984. A new influx of refugees, following the Zimbabwe general election in July 1985, threatened to strain relations between the two countries. In May 1988, however, Masire expressed confidence that the Zimbabwean refugees would return to their country as a result of an apparent improvement in the political climate in Zimbabwe. Nevertheless, in April 1989 about 600 Zimbabwean refugees remained in Botswana; at the end of that month the Botswana Government announced that refugee status for Zimbabwean nationals was to be revoked; by September almost all former Zimbabwean refugees had reportedly left Botswana. In the mid-1990s, however, the Government expressed concern at the growing number of illegal immigrants in the country, the majority of whom were from Zimbabwe; of more than 40,000 illegal immigrants repatriated during 1995, more than 14,000 were Zimbabwean.

Following Namibian independence, in July 1990 it was announced that a commission for bilateral co-operation was to be established by Botswana and Namibia. In 1992, however, a border dispute developed between the two countries regarding their rival territorial claims over a small island (Sedudu-Kasikili) in the Chobe river. In early 1995 the two states agreed to present the issue of the demarcation of their joint border for arbitration at the International Court of Justice, and in February 1996 the two countries signed an agreement committing themselves in advance to the Court's eventual judgment. Meanwhile, Namibia appealed to Botswana to remove its troops—stated by the Botswana authorities to be anti-poaching patrols—and national flag from the island. In the following month the two countries agreed joint measures aimed at deterring smuggling and illegal border crossings. None the less, what were perceived as attempts by Botswana to extend the role and capabilities of its armed forces (most notably the completion of a new air base in 1995 and efforts during 1996–97 to procure military tanks) remained a source of friction between the two countries, although Botswana emphasized that a principal aim of such expansion was to enable its military to fulfil a wider regional and international peace-keeping role. Namibia's decision to construct a pipeline to take water from the Okavango river caused some concern in Botswana in 1996–97. (The river feeds the Okavango delta, which is an important habitat for Botswana's varied wildlife, and therefore of great importance to the tourist industry.) In early 1997 it was reported that Namibia had been angered by Botswana's erection of a fence along Namibia's Caprivi Strip, which separates the two countries to the north; Botswana insisted, however, that the fence was simply a measure to control the spread of livestock diseases.

Government

Legislative power is vested in Parliament, consisting of the President and the National Assembly. The National Assembly is elected for a term of five years and comprises 40 members directly elected by universal adult suffrage, together with four members who are elected by the National Assembly from a list of candidates submitted by the President; the President and the Attorney-General are also *ex-officio* members of the Assembly. Executive power is vested in the President, elected by the Assembly for its duration. (The President is to be restricted to two terms of office, with effect from the 1999 elections.) He appoints and leads a Cabinet, which is responsible to the Assembly. The President has powers to delay implementation of legislation for six months, and certain matters also have to be referred to the 15-member House of Chiefs for approval, although this body has no power of veto. Local government is effected through nine district councils and four town councils.

Defence

Military service is voluntary. In August 1997 the total strength of the Botswana Defence Force was some 7,500, comprising an army of 7,000 and an air force of 500. In addition, there was a paramilitary police force of 1,000. There are plans to enlarge the strength of the army to 10,000 men. Budgeted expenditure on defence by the central Government in the financial year 1996/97 was forecast at P445.2m.

Economic Affairs

In 1995, according to estimates by the World Bank, Botswana's gross national product (GNP), measured at average 1993–95 prices, was US $4,381m., equivalent to $3,020 per head. During 1985–95, it was estimated, GNP per head increased, in real terms, by an annual average of 6.0%. Over the same period the population increased by an average of 3.0% per year. Botswana's gross domestic product (GDP) increased, in real terms, by an annual average of 10.3% during 1980–90 (one of the highest growth rates in the world), and by an average of 4.2% yearly in 1990–95. Real GDP growth in the year to June 1996 was 7.0%, according to provisional figures.

Agriculture (including hunting, forestry and fishing) contributed 3.7% of GDP in 1995/96, according to provisional figures, and engaged some 38.1% of the total labour force in 1996. The principal agricultural activity is cattle-raising (principally beef production), which supports about one-half of the population and contributes more than 80% of agricultural GDP. The main subsistence crops are sorghum, vegetables and pulses. Botswana, which is not self-sufficient in basic foods, imported some 133,000 metric tons of cereals in 1993. According to the World Bank, agricultural GDP increased by an annual average of 2.2% in 1980–90, and by 0.7% in 1990–95. The GDP of the sector declined by 4.6% in 1994/95, and, according to provisional figures, by 0.4% in 1995/96.

Industry (including mining, manufacturing, construction and power) engaged 27.7% of the employed labour force in 1991 and, according to provisional figures, provided 44.5% of GDP in 1995/96. According to the World Bank, industrial GDP increased by an annual average of 11.4% during 1980–90, but the rate of growth declined to an average of 1.4% per year in 1990–95. Growth in the sector was negligible in 1994/95, but industrial GDP increased by 8.0% in 1995/96, according to provisional figures.

Mining contributed 32.4% of GDP in 1995/96, according to provisional figures, although the sector engaged only 3.5% of the employed labour force in 1991. In terms of value, Botswana is the world's largest producer of diamonds (which accounted for 67.2% of export earnings in 1995, according to provisional figures); copper-nickel matte and soda ash are also exported. In addition, coal, gold, cobalt and salt are mined, and there are known reserves of plutonium, asbestos, chromite, fluorspar, iron, manganese, potash, silver, talc and uranium. The GDP of the mining sector increased, in real terms, at an average rate of 11.1% per year between 1980/81 and 1990/91. The average rate of increase slowed to 0.1% in 1990/91–1994/95 (largely reflecting a decline of 4.6% in 1992/93); however, according to provisional figures, there was an increase of 9.9% in 1995/96.

Manufacturing engaged 7.3% of the employed labour force in 1991 and provided 4.6% of GDP in 1995/96, according to provisional figures. Based on the gross value of output, the principal branches of manufacturing in the year to June 1993 were food products (accounting for 38.6% of the total), beverages (13.2%) and textiles and clothing (10.9%). The GDP of the manufacturing sector increased at an average rate of 10.0% per year between 1985/86 and 1994/95; according to provisional figures, growth of 6.5% was recorded in 1995/96.

The services sector contributed 51.8% of GDP in 1995/96, according to provisional figures, and engaged 43.9% of the employed labour force in 1991. Within the sector, tourism is of considerable importance, and the tourist industry is the third largest source of total foreign exchange. According to the World Bank, the GDP of the services sector increased by an annual average of 11.0% in 1980–90, and by an average of 7.7% in 1990–95. Growth was 6.4% in 1995/96, according to provisional figures.

Energy is derived principally from fuel wood and coal. According to provisional figures, imports of fuels accounted for 5.1% of the value of total imports in 1995.

In 1995 Botswana recorded a visible trade surplus of US $585.7m., and there was a surplus of $342.1m. on the current account of the balance of payments. In that year countries of the Southern African Customs Union (SACU—see below) provided 73.9% of imports; other major sources were the Republic of Korea and Zimbabwe. European countries took 73.6% of exports in 1995; other important purchasers were the countries of SACU. The principal exports in that year were diamonds, vehicles and copper-nickel matte. The principal imports were vehicles and transport equipment, food, beverages and tobacco, machinery and electrical equipment, chemicals and rubber products, metals and metal products, wood and paper products, textiles and footwear, and fuels.

In the financial year to 31 March 1996 the central Government recorded a budgetary surplus of P269.9m. Botswana's external debt totalled US $698.9m. at the end of 1995, of which $682.1m. was long-term public debt. In that year the cost of debt-servicing was equivalent to 3.2% of the value of exports of goods and services. The average annual rate of inflation was 11.4% in 1985–95; consumer prices increased by an annual average of 10.5% in 1995 and by 10.1% in 1996. In the year to August 1997 the inflation rate was 8.5%. About 21% of the labour force were unemployed in mid-1997.

Botswana is a member of the Southern African Development Community (see p. 236) and (with Lesotho, Namibia, South Africa and Swaziland) of SACU.

Botswana's high rate of growth during the 1980s was based predominantly on the successful exploitation of diamonds and other minerals. However, domestic factors, such as a vulnerability to drought, in conjunction with the world-wide economic recession of the early 1990s, depressed Botswana's economy and exemplified the need to reduce dependence on diamond-mining, to diversify agricultural production and to broaden the manufacturing base. By the mid-1990s, a return to growth had enabled the resumption of both public and private construction projects, and major schemes such as the North–South Water Carrier Project were expected to generate much-needed employment opportunities. The Government initiated measures to attract both domestic and foreign private investment in all sectors, in accordance with its aim of stimulating growth by means of economic liberalization. Increased capacity at the Jwaneng diamond mine contributed to the strong performance of the economy in 1995/96, and further optimism regarding prospects for the mining sector was afforded by a major project, announced in mid-1996, for the expansion of the Orapa diamond mine. None the less, the development of non-mining activities remains a government priority. The introduction of reforms aimed at encouraging private-sector growth, particularly in the manufacturing sector, was a key element of Botswana's eighth National Development Plan (1997/98–2002/03), which was presented in 1997 with the theme 'sustainable economic diversification'.

Social Welfare

Compared with those of many other countries of the region, Botswana's health services are well-developed. In 1997 there were 14 primary hospitals, six district hospitals, three mission hospitals, three mine hospitals, two national referral hospitals, one private hospital and one mental hospital. In addition, there were 209 clinics, 314 health posts and 687 mobile health stops. There were 94 registered medical specialists, 292 medical officers, 34 dentists and 3,866 nurses. Medical treatment for children under 12 years of age is provided free of charge. Old-age pensions for all persons over 65 years of age were introduced in October 1996. Budget forecasts for 1996/97 allocated P303.6m. to health (equivalent to 5.0% of total projected expenditure by the central Government) and P50.5m. (0.8%) to the food and social welfare programme.

Education

Although education is not compulsory in Botswana, enrolment ratios are high. Primary education, which is provided free of charge, begins at seven years of age and lasts for up to seven years. Secondary education, beginning at the age of 14, lasts for a further five years, comprising a first cycle of two years and a second of three years. As a proportion of the school-age population, the total enrolment at primary and secondary schools increased from 52% in 1975 to the equivalent of 92% (boys 91%; girls 93%) in 1994. Enrolment at primary schools in 1993 included 96% of children in the relevant age-group (boys 93%; girls 99%), while the comparable ratio for secondary enrolment was 45% (boys 42%; girls 49%). The Government aims to provide universal access to nine years of basic education by the late 1990s. Botswana has the highest teacher-pupil ratio in Africa, but continues to rely heavily on expatriate secondary school teachers.

A National Literacy Programme was initiated in 1980, and 9,473 people were enrolled under the programme in 1991. According to estimates by UNESCO, the average rate of adult illiteracy in 1995 was 30.2% (males 19.5%; females 40.1%). Education was allocated some 10% of total projected expenditure under the National Development Plan for 1991–97. Budget estimates for 1996/97 allocated P1,545.5m. to education (representing 25.5% of total forecast expenditure by the central Government).

Public Holidays

1998: 1–2 January (New Year), 10–13 April (Easter), 1 May (Labour Day), 21 May (Ascension Day), 1 July (Sir Seretse Khama Day), 15–16 July (for President's Day), 30 September (Botswana Day), 25–26 December (Christmas).

1999: 1–2 January (New Year), 2–5 April (Easter), 1 May (Labour Day), 13 May (Ascension Day), 1 July (Sir Seretse Khama Day), 15–16 July (for President's Day), 30 September (Botswana Day), 25–26 December (Christmas).

Weights and Measures

The metric system is in use.

Statistical Survey

Source (unless otherwise stated): Central Statistics Office, Private Bag 0024, Gaborone; tel. 352200; fax 352201.

Area and Population

AREA, POPULATION AND DENSITY

Area (sq km)	581,730*
Population (census results)	
16 August 1981	941,027†
21 August 1991	
Males	634,400
Females	692,396
Total	1,326,796
Population (official estimates at 19 August)	
1994	1,423,000
1995	1,456,000
1996	1,490,000
Density (per sq km) at August 1996	2.6

* 224,607 sq miles.

† Excluding 42,069 citizens absent from the country during enumeration.

POPULATION BY CENSUS DISTRICT (August 1991 census)

Barolong	18,400	Kweneng	170,437
Central	412,970	Lobatse	26,052
Chobe	14,126	Ngamiland	94,534
Francistown	65,244	Ngwaketse	128,989
Gaborone	133,468	North-East	43,354
Ghanzi	24,719	Orapa	8,827
Jwaneng	11,188	Selebi-Phikwe	39,772
Kgalagadi	31,134	South-East	43,584
Kgatleng	57,770	Sowa	2,228

PRINCIPAL TOWNS (August 1988 estimates)

Gaborone (capital)	110,973	Kanye	26,300
Francistown	49,396	Mahalapye	26,239
Selebi-Phikwe	46,490	Lobatse	25,689
Molepolole	29,212	Maun	18,470
Serowe	28,267	Ramotswa	17,961
Mochudi	26,320		

August 1991 (census results): Gaborone 133,468; Francistown 65,244; Selebi-Phikwe 39,772; Lobatse 26,052.

BIRTHS AND DEATHS (UN estimates, annual averages)

	1980–85	1985–90	1990–95
Birth rate (per 1,000)	42.8	39.4	37.1
Death rate (per 1,000)	9.4	7.7	6.6

Expectation of life (UN estimates, years at birth, 1990–95): 64.9 (males 63.0; females 66.7).

Source: UN, *World Population Prospects: The 1994 Revision*.

ECONOMICALLY ACTIVE POPULATION
(persons aged 12 years and over, 1991 census*)

	Males	Females	Total
Agriculture, hunting, forestry and fishing	70,439	27,187	97,626
Mining and quarrying	12,556	779	13,335
Manufacturing	13,751	13,797	27,548
Electricity, gas and water	5,637	778	6,415
Construction	50,347	7,701	58,048
Trade, restaurants and hotels	13,802	21,392	35,194
Transport, storage and communications	9,651	1,844	11,495
Financing, insurance, real estate and business services	8,743	4,624	13,367
Community, social and personal services	48,616	58,046	106,662
Activities not adequately defined	6,031	4,217	10,248
Total employed	239,573	140,365	379,938
Unemployed	31,852	29,413	61,265
Total labour force	271,425	169,778	441,203

* Excluding members of the armed forces.

Source: ILO, *Yearbook of Labour Statistics*.

Mid-1996 (estimates, '000 persons): Agriculture, etc. 251; Total labour force 658. (Source: FAO, *Production Yearbook*).

Agriculture

PRINCIPAL CROPS ('000 metric tons)

	1994	1995	1996
Wheat*	1	1	1
Maize	11	5	23†
Millet	2	2	4*
Sorghum	37	38	55*
Roots and tubers*	9	9	9
Pulses*	16	12	14
Cottonseed*	2	2	2
Cotton (lint)*	1	1	1
Vegetables*	16	13	16
Fruit*	11	10	11

* FAO estimate(s). † Unofficial figure.

Source: FAO, *Production Yearbook*.

LIVESTOCK ('000 head, year ending September)

	1994	1995*	1996*
Cattle*	1,820	1,900	1,950
Horses	31	32	32
Asses	231	235	235
Sheep	238	250	250
Goats	1,850	1,900	1,900
Pigs*	5	6	7

* FAO estimates.

Poultry (FAO estimates, million): 2 in 1994; 2 in 1995; 2 in 1996.

Source: FAO, *Production Yearbook*.

LIVESTOCK PRODUCTS (FAO estimates, '000 metric tons)

	1994	1995	1996
Beef and veal	35	41	49
Goat meat	5	5	5
Poultry meat	4	4	4
Other meat	8	9	9
Cows' milk	79	81	82
Goats' milk	3	3	3
Cheese	2	2	2
Butter and ghee	1	1	1
Hen eggs	2	2	2
Cattle hides	5	5	7

Source: FAO, *Production Yearbook*.

Forestry

ROUNDWOOD REMOVALS (FAO estimates, '000 cubic metres)

	1992	1993	1994
Industrial wood	89	92	95
Fuel wood	1,358	1,400	1,443
Total	1,447	1,492	1,538

Source: FAO, *Yearbook of Forest Products*.

Fishing

(FAO estimates, metric tons, live weight)

	1993	1994	1995
Total catch (freshwater fishes)	2,000	2,000	2,000

Source: FAO, *Yearbook of Fishery Statistics*.

Mining

(metric tons, unless otherwise indicated)

	1993	1994	1995
Coal	890,497	900,298	816,724
Copper ore*	21,621	22,780	21,029
Nickel ore*	20,132	19,041	18,672
Cobalt ore*	205	200†	n.a.
Gold ore (kilograms)*	192	n.a.	n.a.
Diamonds ('000 carats)	14,731	15,540	16,674
Soda ash	126,000	174,222	201,641
Salt	98,000	185,986	392,258

* Figures refer to the metal content of ores.

† Data from the US Bureau of Mines.

Sources: Central Statistics Office, Gaborone, and UN, *Industrial Commodity Statistics Yearbook*.

Industry

SELECTED PRODUCTS

	1991	1992	1993
Beer ('000 hectolitres)	1,283	1,290	1,374
Soft drinks ('000 hectolitres)	274	317	276
Electric energy (million kWh)*	910	910	910

Electric energy (million kWh): 1,011* in 1994.

* Provisional or estimated figure(s).

Source: UN, *Industrial Commodity Statistics Yearbook*.

Finance

CURRENCY AND EXCHANGE RATES

Monetary Units

100 thebe = 1 pula (P).

Sterling and Dollar Equivalents (30 September 1997)

£1 sterling = 5.974 pula;
US $1 = 3.698 pula;
100 pula = £16.74 = $27.04.

Average Exchange Rate (pula per US $)

1994 2.6846
1995 2.7722
1996 3.3241

BUDGET (million pula, year ending 31 March)

Revenue*	1994/95	1995/96	1996/97†
Taxation	3,632.7	4,019.9	4,017.6
Mineral revenues	2,349.4	2,591.4	2,568.9
Customs pool revenues	711.8	829.4	897.3
Non-mineral income tax	386.9	356.9	330.0
General sales tax	169.2	219.4	192.9
Other current revenue	764.1	1,407.4	1,335.1
Interest	200.5	231.6	248.2
Other property income	452.5	1,063.5	965.0
Fees, charges, etc.	92.7	99.0	103.7
Sales of fixed assets and land	18.4	13.3	18.3
Total	4,396.8	5,427.3	5,352.7

* Excluding grants received (million pula): 75.7 in 1994/95; 37.1 in 1995/96; 68.6 in 1996/97.

† Forecasts.

Expenditure*	1994/95	1995/96	1996/97†
General administration	659.2	1,439.0	907.0
Public order and safety	161.7		234.7
Defence	452		445.2
Education	937.5	1,167.2	1,545.5
Health	227.5	256.6	303.6
Food and social welfare programme	47.6	127.9	50.5
Housing, urban and regional development	416.3	406.3	501.1
Other community and social services	68.2	82.7	109.8
Economic services	826.4	1,149.3	1,346.6
Agriculture, forestry and fishing	252.9	284.4	292.1
Mining	89.4	246.7	66.6
Electricity and water supply	124.4	252.2	469.0
Roads	211.3	215.4	288.5
Promotion of commerce and industry	73.3	n.a.	116.8
Interest on public debt	84.5	91.6	112.2
Deficit grants to local authorities	359.2	403.3	462.1
Other grants	36.2	72.0	40.0
Total	4,276.8	5,195.7	6,057.3

* Figures refer to recurrent and development expenditure, including net lending (million pula): −112.2 in 1994/95; 14.2 in 1995/96; 30.0 in 1996/97.

† Forecasts.

Source: Bank of Botswana, Gaborone, and Central Statistics Office, Gaborone.

INTERNATIONAL RESERVES (US $ million at 31 December)

	1994	1995	1996
IMF special drawing rights	37.07	40.22	41.28
Reserve position in IMF	23.86	28.66	28.63
Foreign exchange	4,401.47	4,695.48	5,027.66
Total	4,462.40	4,764.36	5,097.57

Source: IMF, *International Financial Statistics*.

MONEY SUPPLY (million pula at 31 December)

	1994	1995	1996
Currency outside banks	195	223	247
Demand deposits at commercial banks	579	607	704
Total money	774	829	951

Source: IMF, *International Financial Statistics*.

COST OF LIVING (Consumer Price Index; base: 1990 = 100)

	1993	1994	1995
Food	150.9	165.0	182.9
Clothing	157.4	179.1	198.0
All items (incl. others)	148.5	164.2	181.4

Source: ILO, *Yearbook of Labour Statistics*.

1996: Food 207.0; All items 199.8 (Source: UN, *Monthly Bulletin of Statistics*).

NATIONAL ACCOUNTS
(million pula at current prices, year ending 30 June)

National Income and Product

	1985/86	1986/87	1987/88
Compensation of employees	700.7	849.6	1,051.6
Operating surplus	1,216.7	1,312.3	1,936.3
Domestic factor incomes	1,917.4	2,161.9	2,987.9
Consumption of fixed capital	349.8	432.4	575.6
Gross domestic product (GDP) at factor cost	2,267.2	2,594.3	3,563.5
Indirect taxes	160.4	226.2	251.2
Less Subsidies	7.0	10.7	19.1
GDP in purchasers' values	2,420.6	2,809.8	3,795.6
Factor income received from abroad	173.0	225.9	308.7
Less Factor income paid abroad	495.8	477.9	773.8
Gross national product	2,097.8	2,557.8	3,330.5
Less Consumption of fixed capital	349.8	432.4	575.6
National income in market prices	1,748.0	2,125.4	2,754.9
Other current transfers from abroad	141.5	123.2	115.1
Less Other current transfers paid abroad	68.5	78.6	233.3
National disposable income	1,821.0	2,169.9	2,636.7

Source: UN, *National Accounts Statistics*.

Expenditure on the Gross Domestic Product

	1993/94	1994/95	1995/96*
Government final consumption expenditure	3,186.8	3,618.5	4,233.6
Private final consumption expenditure	3,637.1	4,130.0	4,155.6
Gross capital formation	2,731.0	3,053.4	3,522.8
Total domestic expenditure	9,554.9	10,801.9	11,912.0
Exports of goods and services	5,413.6	5,980.1	7,486.7
Less Imports of goods and services	3,853.5	4,251.6	4,767.7
GDP in purchasers' values	11,115.0	12,530.3	14,631.0
GDP at constant 1985/86 prices	4,700.5	4,847.5	5,184.8

* Provisional figures.

Source: Bank of Botswana, Gaborone, and Central Statistics Office, Gaborone.

Gross Domestic Product by Economic Activity

	1993/94	1994/95	1995/96*
Agriculture, hunting, forestry and fishing	495.2	520.6	563.1
Mining and quarrying	3,932.3	4,086.3	4,859.0
Manufacturing	499.5	593.9	693.2
Water and electricity	239.4	269.5	270.6
Construction	694.5	757.1	858.4
Trade, restaurants and hotels	1,706.7	2,093.7	2,489.1
Transport	363.1	437.4	504.2
Finance, insurance and business services	1,148.6	1,397.8	1,613.3
Government services	1,846.7	2,159.0	2,544.5
Social and personal services	479.3	550.9	622.3
Sub-total	11,405.3	12,866.2	15,017.7
Less Imputed bank service charge	290.3	335.9	386.7
GDP in purchasers' values	11,115.0	12,530.3	14,631.0

* Provisional figures.

Source: Bank of Botswana, Gaborone, and Central Statistics Office, Gaborone.

BALANCE OF PAYMENTS (US $ million)

	1993	1994	1995
Exports of goods f.o.b.	1,722.2	1,878.4	2,164.4
Imports of goods f.o.b.	−1,455.4	−1,350.0	−1,578.7
Trade balance	266.8	528.4	585.7
Exports of services	191.3	186.1	260.4
Imports of services	−325.6	−322.0	−444.2
Balance on goods and services	132.5	392.6	401.8
Other income received	554.5	230.8	483.2
Other income paid	−260.9	−455.0	−515.6
Balance on goods, services and income	426.1	168.4	369.4
Current transfers received	352.3	370.0	342.3
Current transfers paid	−275.1	−295.1	−369.5
Current balance	503.3	243.3	342.1
Capital account (net)	8.5	6.0	2.9
Direct investment abroad	−9.5	−9.5	−40.9
Direct investment from abroad	−286.9	−14.3	70.4
Portfolio investment assets	—	—	−36.4
Portfolio investment liabilities	0.2	−0.1	5.8
Other investment assets	63.4	15.8	−88.7
Other investment liabilities	192.5	49.2	55.9
Net errors and omissions	−74.5	−151.1	−104.6
Overall balance	397.0	139.3	206.6

Source: IMF, *International Financial Statistics*.

External Trade

PRINCIPAL COMMODITIES (million pula)

Imports c.i.f.	1993	1994	1995*
Food, beverages and tobacco	764.1	775.0	844.0
Fuels	273.2	262.6	270.6
Chemicals and rubber products	394.6	425.7	490.6
Wood and paper products	233.7	256.1	401.8
Textiles and footwear	309.0	391.0	399.8
Metals and metal products	434.6	411.6	461.0
Machinery and electrical equipment	743.2	774.0	831.4
Vehicles and transport equipment	568.3	528.4	988.7
Total (incl. others)	4,285.0	4,407.3	5,304.8

Exports f.o.b.	1993	1994	1995*
Meat and meat products	160.6	181.8	179.2
Diamonds	3,340.2	3,717.8	3,983.7
Copper-nickel matte	219.8	258.8	319.2
Textiles	95.0	177.4	146.3
Vehicles and parts	91.0	300.6	957.2
Total (incl. others)	4,312.1	4,965.0	5,931.5

* Provisional figures.

1996 (million pula): Total imports c.i.f. 5,728.8; Total exports f.o.b. 10,739.5. (Source: IMF, *International Financial Statistics*).

PRINCIPAL TRADING PARTNERS (million pula)

Imports c.i.f.	1993	1994	1995*
SACU†	3,541.0	3,437.4	3,922.7
Zimbabwe	196.2	258.9	293.0
United Kingdom	112.1	109.9	134.7
Other Europe	192.3	259.9	319.3
Korea, Republic	—	91.7	377.5
USA	140.8	82.9	107.4
Total (incl. others)	4,285.0	4,407.3	5,304.8

Exports f.o.b.	1993	1994	1995*
SACU†	379.5	691.4	1,277.6
Zimbabwe	135.2	134.1	176.4
Other Africa	57.4	49.1	49.3
United Kingdom	639.4	1,245.4	2,223.0
Other Europe	3,082.9	2,800.6	2,143.1
USA	14.3	34.8	51.6
Total (incl. others)	4,312.1	4,965.0	5,931.5

* Provisional figures.

† Southern African Customs Union, of which Botswana is a member; also including Lesotho, Namibia, South Africa and Swaziland.

Transport

RAILWAYS

	1994/95	1995/96	1996/97
Number of passengers ('000)	525	722	574
Passenger-km (million)	86	95	96
Freight ('000 metric tons)	1,759	1,745	1,967
Freight net ton-km (million)	626	672	795

Source: Botswana Railways.

ROAD TRAFFIC (vehicles registered at 31 December)

	1993	1994	1995
Passenger cars	26,320	27,058	30,517
Lorries and vans	51,352	57,235	59,710
Others	16,938	17,153	17,448
Total	94,610	101,446	107,675

CIVIL AVIATION (traffic on scheduled services)

	1992	1993	1994
Kilometres flown (million)	3	3	2
Passengers carried ('000)	111	123	101
Passenger-km (million)	76	75	58
Total ton-km (million)	8	8	6

Source: UN, *Statistical Yearbook*.

Tourism

FOREIGN TOURIST ARRIVALS (incl. same-day visitors)

Country of origin	1993	1994*	1995*
South Africa and Namibia	498,574	513,687	529,238
United Kingdom and Ireland	38,651	39,823	41,029
Zambia	31,978	32,947	33,944
Zimbabwe	308,018	317,355	326,962
Total (incl. others)	961,844	991,000	1,021,000

* Estimated figures.

Receipts from tourism (US $million): 24 in 1992; 31 in 1993; 35 in 1994 (Source: UN, *Statistical Yearbook*).

Communications Media

	1990	1991	1992
Radio receivers ('000 in use)	150	155	160
Television receivers ('000 in use)	20	21	22
Book production: titles*	n.a.	158	n.a.
Daily newspapers:			
Number	1	n.a.	1
Average circulation ('000 copies)	18	n.a.	40
Non-daily newspapers:			
Number	n.a.	n.a.	4
Average circulation ('000 copies)	n.a.	n.a.	61
Other periodicals:			
Number	n.a.	n.a.	14
Average circulation ('000 copies)	n.a.	n.a.	177

* Figures refer to first editions only and include pamphlets (61 titles in 1991).

Radio receivers ('000 in use): 167 in 1993; 180 in 1994.

Television receivers ('000 in use): 23 in 1993; 24 in 1994.

Daily newspapers: 1 in 1994 (average circulation 35,000 copies).

Source: UNESCO, *Statistical Yearbook*.

Telephones ('000 main lines in use, year ending 31 March): 36 in 1992/93; 43 in 1993/94; 50 in 1994/95 (Source: UN, *Statistical Yearbook*).

Telefax stations (number in use, year ending 31 March): 235 in 1992/93; 250 in 1993/94; 220 in 1994/95 (Source: UN, *Statistical Yearbook*).

Education

(1994)

	Institutions	Teachers	Students
Primary	670	11,731	310,128
Secondary	188	4,712	86,684
Brigades*	19	218	2,118
Teacher training	6	295	2,363
Technical education	7	544	3,544
University	1	507	5,062

* Semi-autonomous units providing craft and practical training.

Directory

The Constitution

The Constitution of the Republic of Botswana took effect at independence on 30 September 1966; it was amended in August and September 1997.

EXECUTIVE

President

Executive power lies with the President of Botswana, who is also Commander-in-Chief of the armed forces. Election for the office of President is linked with the election of members of the National Assembly. The President is to be restricted to two terms of office, with effect from the 1999 elections. Presidential candidates must be over 30 years of age and receive at least 1,000 nominations. If there is more than one candidate for the Presidency, each candidate for office in the Assembly must declare support for a presidential candidate. The candidate for President who commands the votes of more than one-half of the elected members of the Assembly will be declared President. In the event of the death or resignation of the President, the Vice-President will automatically assume the Presidency. The President, who is an *ex-officio* member of the National Assembly, holds office for the duration of Parliament. The President chooses four members of the National Assembly.

Cabinet

There is also a Vice-President, whose office is ministerial. The Vice-President is appointed by the President and deputizes in the absence of the President. The Cabinet consists of the President, the Vice-President and 14 other Ministers, including four Assistant Ministers, appointed by the President. The Cabinet is responsible to the National Assembly.

LEGISLATURE

Legislative power is vested in Parliament, consisting of the President and the National Assembly, acting after consultation in certain cases with the House of Chiefs. The President may withhold assent to a Bill passed by the National Assembly. If the same Bill is again presented after six months, the President is required to assent to it or to dissolve Parliament within 21 days.

House of Chiefs

The House of Chiefs comprises the Chiefs of the eight principal tribes of Botswana as *ex-officio* members, four members elected by sub-chiefs from their own number, and three members elected by the other 12 members of the House. Bills and motions relating to chieftaincy matters and alterations of the Constitution must be referred to the House, which may also deliberate and make representations on any matter.

National Assembly

The National Assembly consists of 40 members directly elected by universal adult suffrage, together with four members who are elected by the National Assembly from a list of candidates submitted by the President; the President and the Attorney-General are also *ex-officio* members of the Assembly. The life of the Assembly is five years.

The Constitution contains a code of human rights, enforceable by the High Court.

The Government

HEAD OF STATE

President: Sir KETUMILE MASIRE (took office as Acting President 29 June 1980; elected President 18 July 1980; re-elected 10 September 1984, 10 October 1989 and 17 October 1994).

CABINET
(November 1997)

President: Sir KETUMILE MASIRE.

Vice-President and Minister of Finance and Development Planning: FESTUS G. MOGAE.

Minister of Health: CHAPSON BUTALE.

Minister of Agriculture: RONALD SEBEGO.

Minister of Foreign Affairs: Lt-Gen. MOMPATI MERAFHE.

Minister of Mineral Resources and Water Affairs: DAVID MAGANG.

Minister of Commerce and Industry: GEORGE KGOROBA.

Minister of Local Government, Lands and Housing: MARGARET NASHA.

Minister of Works, Transport and Communications: DANIEL KWELAGOBE.

Minister of Presidential Affairs and Public Administration: PONATSHEGO KEDIKILWE.

Minister of Education: GAOSITWE CHIEPE.

Minister of Labour and Home Affairs: BAHITI TEMANE.

There are also four assistant ministers.

MINISTRIES

Office of the President: Private Bag 001, Gaborone; tel. 350800; telex 2414.

Ministry of Agriculture: Private Bag 003, Gaborone; tel. 350581; telex 2543; fax 356027.

Ministry of Commerce and Industry: Private Bag 004, Gaborone; tel. 3601200; telex 2674; fax 371539.

Ministry of Education: Private Bag 005, Gaborone; tel. 3600400; fax 3600458.

Ministry of Finance and Development Planning: Private Bag 008, Gaborone; tel. 350100; telex 2401; fax 356086.

Ministry of Foreign Affairs: Private Bag 00368, Gaborone; tel. 3600700; telex 2414; fax 313366.

Ministry of Health: Private Bag 0038, Gaborone; tel. 352000; telex 2959.

Ministry of Labour and Home Affairs: Private Bag 002, Gaborone; tel. 3601000.

Ministry of Local Government, Lands and Housing: Private Bag 006, Gaborone; tel. 354100.

Ministry of Mineral Resources and Water Affairs: Private Bag 0018, Gaborone; tel. 352454; telex 2503; fax 372738.

Ministry of Works, Transport and Communications: Private Bag 007, Gaborone; tel. 358500; telex 2743; fax 358500.

Legislature

HOUSE OF CHIEFS

The House has a total of 15 members.

Chairman: Chief SEEPAPITSO IV.

NATIONAL ASSEMBLY

Speaker: M. P. K. NWAKO.

General Election, 15 October 1994

Party	Votes	%	Seats
Botswana Democratic Party	138,826	53.1	26
Botswana National Front	98,427	37.7	13
Botswana People's Party	12,052	4.6	—
Independence Freedom Party	7,685	2.9	—
Botswana Progressive Union	3,016	1.2	—
Others	1,225	0.5	—
Total	261,231	100.0	39*

* Polling in one constituency was delayed, owing to the death of a candidate. Four additional members were subsequently elected by the National Assembly. The President and the Attorney-General are also *ex-officio* members of the National Assembly.

Political Organizations

Botswana Democratic Party (BDP): Gaborone; f. 1962; Pres. Sir KETUMILE MASIRE; Chair. PONATSHEGO KEDIKILWE; Sec.-Gen. DANIEL K. KWELAGOBE.

Botswana Labour Party: f. 1989; Pres. LENYELETSE KOMA.

Botswana Liberal Party (BLP): Gaborone.

Botswana National Front (BNF): POB 42, Mahalapye; f. 1967; Pres. Dr KENNETH KOMA; Sec.-Gen. JAMES PILANE.

Botswana People's Party (BPP): POB 159, Francistown; f. 1960; Pres. Dr KNIGHT MARIPE; Chair. KENNETH MKHWA; Sec.-Gen. MATLHOMOLA MODISE.

Botswana Progressive Union (BPU): POB 10229, Francistown; f. 1982; Pres. TABULAWA MOKGETHI; Sec.-Gen. R. K. MONYATSIWA.

Botswana Workers' Front (BWF): Gaborone.

Independence Freedom Party (IFP): POB 3, Maun; f. by merger of Botswana Freedom Party and Botswana Independence Party; Pres. MOTSAMAI K. MPHO.

Lesedi La Botswana (LLB): Gaborone.

Social Democratic Party (SDP): Gaborone.

United Action Party (UAP): Gaborone; f. 1997; Leader LEPETU SETSHWEALO.

United Socialist Party (USP): Gaborone.

Diplomatic Representation

EMBASSIES AND HIGH COMMISSIONS IN BOTSWANA

Angola: Private Bag 111, Phala Crescent, Gaborone; tel. 300204; telex 2361; fax 375089; Ambassador: PEDRO F. MAVUNZA.

China, People's Republic: POB 1031, Gaborone; tel. 352209; telex 2428; fax 300156; Ambassador: ZHANG SHIHUA.

Germany: Professional House, Broadhurst, Segodithsane Way, POB 315, Gaborone; tel. 353143; telex 2225; fax 353038; Ambassador: ALBERT JOSEF GISY.

India: Private Bag 249, 4th Floor, Tirelo House, The Mall, Gaborone; tel. 372676; telex 2622; fax 374636; e-mail hicomind@global.bw; High Commissioner: CHERRY GEORGE.

Libya: POB 180, Gaborone; tel. 352481; telex 2501; Ambassador: TAHER ETTOUMI.

Namibia: POB 987, Gaborone; tel. 302181; fax 302248; High Commissioner: Dr JOSEPH HOEBEB.

Nigeria: POB 274, Gaborone; tel. 313561; telex 2415; fax 313738; High Commissioner: ALABA OGUNSANWO.

Russia: POB 81, Gaborone; tel. 353389; telex 22595; Ambassador: VLADIMIR UKHIN.

South Africa: Private Bag 00402, Kopanyo House, Plot 5131, Nelson Mandela Rd, Gaborone; tel. 304800; fax 305502; High Commissioner: O. R. W. MOKOU.

Sweden: Private Bag 0017, Gaborone; tel. 353912; telex 2421; fax 353942; Ambassador: CHRISTINA REHLEN.

United Kingdom: Private Bag 0023, Gaborone; tel. 352841; fax 356105; High Commissioner: DAVID C. B. BEAUMONT.

USA: POB 90, Gaborone; tel. 353982; telex 2554; fax 356947; Ambassador: ROBERT C. KRUEGER.

Zambia: POB 362, Gaborone; tel. 351951; telex 2416; fax 353952; High Commissioner: J. PHIRI.

Zimbabwe: POB 1232, Gaborone; tel. 314495; telex 2701; High Commissioner: LUCIA MUVINGI.

Judicial System

There is a High Court at Lobatse and a branch at Francistown, and Magistrates' Courts in each district. Appeals lie to the Court of Appeal of Botswana.

High Court: Private Bag 1, Lobatse; tel. 330396; telex 2758; fax 332317.

Chief Justice: JULIAN NGANUNU.

President of the Court of Appeal: A. N. E. AMISSAH.

Justices of Appeal: T. A. AGUDA, W. H. R. SCHREINER, J. STEYN, P. H. TEBBUTT, W. COWIE, G. G. HOEXTER, W. ALLANBRIDGE.

Puisne Judges: I. R. ABOAGYE, J. B. GITTINGS, M. DIBOTELO, M. GAEFELE, J. Z. MASOJANE, I. K. B. LESETEDI (acting).

Registrar and Master: W. G. GRANTE.

Attorney-General: PHANDU SKELEMANI.

Religion

The majority of the population hold animist beliefs; an estimated 30% are thought to be Christians. There are Islamic mosques in Gaborone and Lobatse. The Bahá'í Faith is also represented.

CHRISTIANITY

Lekgotla la Sekeresete la Botswana (Botswana Christian Council): POB 355, Gaborone; tel. 351981; f. 1966; comprises 34 churches and organizations; Pres. Rev. K. F. MOKOBIJ; Gen. Sec. DAVID J. MODIEGA.

The Anglican Communion

Anglicans are adherents of the Church of the Province of Central Africa, comprising 12 dioceses and covering Botswana, Malawi, Zambia and Zimbabwe. The Province was established in 1955, and the diocese of Botswana was formed in 1972.

Archbishop of the Province of Central Africa and Bishop of Botswana: Most Rev. WALTER PAUL KHOTSO MAKHULU, POB 769, Gaborone; fax 313015.

Protestant Churches

African Methodist Episcopal Church: POB 141, Lobatse; Rev. L. M. MBULAWA.

Evangelical Lutheran Church in Botswana: POB 1976, Gaborone; tel. 352227; fax 313966; Bishop Rev. PHILIP ROBINSON; 16,305 mems.

Evangelical Lutheran Church in Southern Africa (Botswana Diocese): POB 400, Gaborone; tel. 353976; Bishop Rev. M. NTUPING.

Methodist Church in Botswana: POB 260, Gaborone; Dist. Supt Rev. Z. S. M. MOSAI.

United Congregational Church of Southern Africa (Synod of Botswana): POB 1263, Gaborone; tel. 352491; Synod status since 1980; Chair. Rev. D. T. MAPITSE; Sec. Rev. M. P. P. DIBEELA; 24,000 mems.

Other denominations active in Botswana include the Church of God in Christ, the Dutch Reformed Church, the United Methodist Church and the Seventh-day Adventists.

The Roman Catholic Church

Botswana comprises a single diocese. The metropolitan see is Bloemfontein, South Africa. The church was established in Botswana in 1928, and had an estimated 54,854 adherents in the country at 31 December 1995. The Bishop participates in the Southern African Catholic Bishops' Conference, currently based in Pretoria, South Africa.

Bishop of Gaborone: Rt Rev. BONIFACE TSHOSA SETLALEKGOSI, POB 218, Bishop's House, Gaborone; tel. 312958; fax 356970.

The Press

DAILY NEWSPAPER

Dikgang tsa Gompieno (Daily News): Private Bag 0060, Gaborone; tel. 352541; telex 2409; f. 1964; publ. by Dept of Information and Broadcasting; Setswana and English; Mon.–Fri.; Editor L. LESHAGA; circ. 50,000.

PERIODICALS

Agrinews: Private Bag 003, Gaborone; f. 1971; monthly; agriculture and rural development; circ. 6,000.

Botswana Advertiser: POB 130, 5647 Nakedi Rd, Broadhurst, Gaborone; tel. 312844; telex 2351; weekly.

The Botswana Gazette: POB 1605, Gaborone; tel. 312833; fax 312833; weekly; circ. 16,000.

Botswana Guardian: POB 1641, Gaborone; tel. 314937; telex 2692; fax 374381; f. 1982; weekly; Editor KETO SEGWAI; circ. 18,700.

Government Gazette: Private Bag 0081, Gaborone; tel. 314441; fax 312001.

Kutlwano: Private Bag 0060, Gaborone; tel. 352541; telex 2409; monthly; Setswana and English; publ. by Dept of Information and Broadcasting; circ. 24,000.

The Midweek Sun: Private Bag 00153, Gaborone; tel. 352085; fax 374381; f. 1989; weekly; circ. 16,445.

Mmegi/The Reporter: Private Bag BR50, Gaborone; tel. 374784; fax 305508; f. 1984; weekly; Setswana and English; publ. by Dikgang Publishing Co; circ. 22,000.

Northern Advertiser: POB 402, Francistown; tel. 212265; fax 213769; f. 1985; weekly; advertisements, local interest, sport; Editor GRACE FISH; circ. 5,500.

The Zebra's Voice: Private Bag 00114, Gaborone; f. 1982; quarterly; cultural affairs; circ. 7,000.

NEWS AGENCIES

Botswana Press Agency (BOPA): Private Bag 0060, Gaborone; tel. 313601; telex 2284; f. 1981.

Foreign Bureaux

Deutsche Presse-Agentur (Germany) and **Reuters** (UK) are represented in Botswana.

Publishers

A.C. Braby (Botswana) (Pty) Ltd: POB 1549, Gaborone; tel. 371444; fax 373462; telephone directories.

Department of Information and Broadcasting: Private Bag 0060, Gaborone; tel. 352541; telex 2409; fax 357138.

Heinemann Educational Boleswa (Pty) Ltd: Plot 10223, Mokolwane Rd, Gaborone; tel. 372305; telex 2378; fax 371832.

Longman Botswana (Pty) Ltd: POB 1083, Gaborone; tel. 322969; fax 322682; f. 1981; educational; Man. Dir J. K. CHALASHIKA.

Macmillan Botswana Publishing Co (Pty) Ltd: POB 1155, Gaborone; tel. 314379; telex 2841; fax 374326.

Magnum Press (Pty) Ltd: Gaborone; tel. 372852; fax 374558.

Printing and Publishing Co (Botswana) (Pty) Ltd: POB 130, 5647 Nakedi Rd, Broadhurst, Gaborone; tel. 312844; telex 2351.

Government Publishing House

Department of Government Printing and Publishing Services: Private Bag 0081, Gaborone; tel. 314441; fax 312001.

Broadcasting and Communications

TELECOMMUNICATIONS

Botswana Posts and Telecommunications Corporation: POB 700, Gaborone; tel. 358000; f. 1980; CEO M. T. CURRY.

RADIO

Radio Botswana: Private Bag 0060, Gaborone; tel. 352541; telex 2633; fax 357138; broadcasts in Setswana and English; f. 1965; Dir TED MAKGEKENENE.

Radio Botswana II: Private Bag 0060, Gaborone; tel. 352541; telex 2409; f. 1992; commercial radio network.

TELEVISION

Gaborone Television Corporation: Private Bag 0060, Gaborone; tel. 352541; fax 357138; limited service; Dep. Dir BATATU TAFA.

TV Association of Botswana: Gaborone; relays SABC-TV and BOP-TV programmes from South Africa; plans for a national TV service are under consideration.

Finance

(cap. = capital; res = reserves; dep. = deposits; m. = million; brs = branches; amounts in pula)

BANKING

Central Bank

Bank of Botswana: Private Bag 154, Plot 1863, Khama Crescent, Gaborone; tel. 3606000; telex 2448; fax 372984; f. 1975; bank of issue; cap. 3.6m., res 3,316.2m., dep. 8,558.8m. (Dec. 1995); Gov. H. C. L. HERMANS.

Commercial Banks

Barclays Bank of Botswana Ltd: POB 478, Barclays House, Plot 8842, Khama Crescent, Gaborone; tel. 352041; telex 2417; fax 313672; f. 1975; 74.9% owned by Barclays Bank PLC (UK); cap. 8.5m., res 107.6m., dep. 985.0m. (Dec. 1995); Chair. B. GAOLATHE; Man. Dir C. J. MIDDLETON; 48 brs, etc.

First National Bank of Botswana: POB 1552, Finance House, 5th Floor, Plot 8843, Khama Crescent, Gaborone; tel. 311669; telex 2520; fax 306130; f. 1991; 70% owned by First National Bank Holdings Botswana Ltd; cap. 25.4m., res 75.2m., dep. 755.7m. (Dec. 1996); Chair. P. C. H. THOMPSON; Man. Dir J. K. MACASKILL; 13 brs.

Stanbic Bank Botswana Ltd: Private Bag 00168, Travaglini House, Old Lobatse Rd, Gaborone; tel. 301600; telex 2562; fax 300171; f. 1992, following the merger of ANZ Grindlays PLC and UnionBank Botswana; subsidiary of Standard Bank Investment Corpn Africa Holdings Ltd; cap. 23.1m., res 9.4m., dep 250.6m. (Sept. 1996); Chair. G. C. BELL; Man. Dir J. N. MCLEMAN; 5 brs.

Standard Chartered Bank Botswana Ltd: POB 496, Standard House, 5th Floor, The Mall, Gaborone; tel. 353111; telex 2422; fax 372933; f. 1975; 75% owned by Standard Chartered Bank Africa PLC, London; cap. 28.8m., res 52.6m., dep. 881.7m. (Dec. 1995); Chair. P. L. STEENKAMP; Man. Dir L. S. GIBSON; 15 brs.

Other Banks

Botswana Savings Bank: POB 1150, Tshomarelo House, Gaborone; tel. 312555; telex 2401; fax 352608; Chair. F. MODISE; Man. Dir E. B. MATHE.

National Development Bank: POB 225, Development House, The Mall, Gaborone; tel. 352801; telex 2553; fax 374446; f. 1964; cap. 77.7m., res 11.5m., dep 20.5m. (March 1995); priority given to agricultural credit for Botswana farmers, and co-operative credit and loans for local business ventures; Chair. F. MODISE; Gen. Man. J. HOWELL; 6 brs.

STOCK EXCHANGE

Botswana Stock Exchange: Private Bag 00417, Barclays House, Ground Floor, Khama Crescent, Gaborone; tel. 357900; fax 357901; e-mail bse@info.bw; f. 1989 as Stockbrokers Botswana; formally inaugurated as a stock exchange in Nov. 1995; CEO ALAN D. NORRIE.

INSURANCE

Botswana Co-operative Insurance Co Ltd: POB 199, Gaborone; tel. 313654; fax 313654.

Botswana Eagle Insurance Co Ltd: POB 1221, 501 Botsalano House, Gaborone; tel. 212392; telex 2259; fax 213745; Gen. Man. JOHN MAIN.

Botswana Insurance Co (Pty) Ltd: POB 336, BIC House, Gaborone; tel. 351791; telex 2359; fax 313290; Gen. Man. P. B. SUMMER.

Sedgwick James Insurance Brokers (Pty) Ltd: POB 103, Plot 730, The Mall, Botswana Rd, Gaborone; tel. 314241; fax 373120.

Tshireletso Insurance Brokers: POB 1967, Gaborone; tel. 357064; telex 2916; fax 371558.

Trade and Industry

GOVERNMENT AGENCY

Botswana Housing Corporation: POB 412, Gaborone; tel. 353341; telex 2729; fax 352070; f. 1971; provides housing for central govt and local authority needs and assists with private-sector housing schemes; Chair. Z. P. PITSO; Gen. Man. (vacant); 900 employees.

DEVELOPMENT ORGANIZATIONS

Botswana Development Corporation Ltd: Private Bag 160, Moedi, Plot 50380, Gaborone International Showgrounds, Off Machel Drive, Gaborone; tel. 351811; telex 2251; fax 303105; f. 1970; Chair. O. K. MATAMBO; Man. Dir M. O. MOLEFANE.

Botswana Livestock Development Corporation (Pty) Ltd: POB 455, Gaborone; tel. 351949; fax 357251; f.1977; Chair. M. M. MANNATHOKO; Gen. Man. S. M. R. BURNETT.

Department of Trade and Investment Promotion (TIPA), Ministry of Commerce and Industry: Private Bag 00367, Gaborone; tel. 351790; telex 2674; fax 305375; promotes industrial and commercial investment, diversification and expansion; offers consultancy, liaison and information services; participates in int. trade fairs and trade and investment missions; Dir D. TSHEKO.

Financial Services Co of Botswana (Pty) Ltd: POB 1129, Finance House, Khama Crescent, Gaborone; tel. 351363; telex 2207; fax 357815; f. 1974; hire purchase, mortgages, industrial leasing and debt factoring; Chair. M. E. HOPKINS; Man. Dir R. A. PAWSON.

Integrated Field Services: Private Bag 004, Ministry of Commerce and Industry, Gaborone; tel. 353024; telex 2674; fax 371539; promotes industrialization and rural development; Dir B. T. TIBONE.

CHAMBER OF COMMERCE

Botswana National Chamber of Commerce and Industry: POB 20344, Gaborone; tel. 52677.

INDUSTRIAL AND TRADE ASSOCIATIONS

Botswana Agricultural Marketing Board (BAMB): Private Bag 0053, 1227 Haile Selassie Rd, Gaborone; tel. 351341; fax 352926; Chair. the Perm. Sec., Ministry of Agriculture; Gen. Man. S. B. TAUKOBONG.

Botswana Meat Commission (BMC): Private Bag 4, Lobatse; tel. 330321; telex 2420; fax 330530; f. 1966; slaughter of livestock, export of hides and skins, carcasses, frozen and chilled boneless beef; operates tannery and beef products cannery; Exec. Chair. Dr MARTIN M. MANNATHOKO.

EMPLOYERS' ORGANIZATION

Botswana Confederation of Commerce, Industry and Manpower (BOCCIM): POB 432, BOCCIM House, Gaborone; f. 1971; Chair. D. N. MOROKA; Dir MODIRI J. MBAAKANYI; 1,478 affiliated mems.

UTILITIES

Electricity

Botswana Power Corporation: POB 48, Motlakase House, Macheng Way, Gaborone; tel. 352211; telex 2431; fax 373563; f. 1971; operates power stations at Selebi-Phikwe and Moropule, with capacity of 65 MW and 132 MW respectively; Chair. the Dep. Perm. Sec., Ministry of Mineral Resources and Water Affairs; CEO K. SITHOLE.

Water

Water Utilities Corporation: Private Bag 00276, Gaborone; tel. 360400; telex 2545; fax 373852; f. 1970; public water supply undertaking for principal townships; Chair. the Perm. Sec., Ministry of Mineral Resources and Water Affairs; CEO B. MPHO.

CO-OPERATIVES

Department of Co-operative Development: POB 86, Gaborone; f. 1964; promotes marketing and supply, consumer, dairy, horticultural and fisheries co-operatives, thrift and loan societies, credit societies, a co-operative union and a co-operative bank.

Botswana Co-operative Union: Gaborone; telex 2298; f. 1970; Dir AARON RAMOSAKO.

TRADE UNIONS

Botswana Federation of Trade Unions: POB 440, Gaborone; tel. and fax 352534; f. 1977; Gen. Sec. MARANYANE KEBITSANG.

Affiliated Unions

Air Botswana Employees' Union: POB 92, Gaborone; Gen. Sec. DANIEL MOTSUMI.

Barclays Management Staff Union: POB 478, Gaborone; Gen. Sec. TEFO LIONJANGA.

BCL Senior Staff Union: POB 383, Selebi-Phikwe; Gen. Sec. KABELO MATTHEWS.

Botswana Agricultural Marketing Board Workers' Union: Private Bag 0053, Gaborone; Gen. Sec. M. E. SEMATHANE.

Botswana Bank Employees' Union: POB 111, Gaborone; Gen. Sec. KEOLOPILE GABORONE.

Botswana Beverages and Allied Workers' Union: POB 41358, Gaborone; Gen. Sec. S. SENWELO.

Botswana Brigade Teachers' Union: Private Bag 007, Molepolole; Gen. Sec. SADIKE KGOKONG.

Botswana Commercial and General Workers' Union: POB 62, Gaborone; Gen. Sec. KEDIRETSE MPETANG.

Botswana Construction Workers' Union: POB 1508, Gaborone; Gen. Sec. JOSHUA KESIILWE.

Botswana Diamond Sorters-Valuators' Union: POB 1186, Gaborone; Gen. Sec. FELIX T. LESETEDI.

Botswana Housing Corporation Staff Union: POB 412, Gaborone; Gen. Sec. GORATA DINGALO.

Botswana Meat Industry Workers' Union: POB 181, Lobatse; Gen. Sec. JOHNSON BOJOSI.

Botswana Mining Workers' Union: Gaborone; Gen. Sec. BALEKAMANG S. GANASIANE.

Botswana Postal Services Workers' Union: POB 87, Gaborone; Gen. Sec. AARON MOSWEU.

Botswana Power Corporation Workers' Union: Private Bag 0053, Gaborone; Gen. Sec. MOLEFE MODISE.

Botswana Railways and Artisan Employees' Union: POB 1486, Gaborone; Gen. Sec. PATRICK MAGOWE.

Botswana Railways Senior Staff Union: POB 449, Mahalapye; Gen. Sec. LENTSWE LETSWELETSE.

Botswana Railways Workers' Union: POB 181, Gaborone; Gen. Sec. ERNEST T. G. MOHUTSIWA.

Botswana Telecommunications Employees' Union: Gaborone; Gen. Sec. SEDIBANA ROBERT.

Botswana Vaccine Institute Staff Union: Private Bag 0031, Gaborone; Gen. Sec. ELLIOT MODISE.

Central Bank Union: POB 712, Gaborone; Gen. Sec. GODFREY NGIDI.

National Amalgamated Local and Central Government, Parastatal, Statutory Body and Manual Workers' Union: POB 374, Gaborone; Gen. Sec. DICKSON KELATLHEGETSWE.

National Development Bank Employees' Union: POB 225, Gaborone; Sec.-Gen. MATSHEDISO FOLOGANG.

Non-Academic Staff Union: Private Bag 0022, Gaborone; Gen. Sec. ISAAC THOTHE.

Transport

RAILWAYS

The 960-km railway line from Mafikeng, South Africa, to Bulawayo, Zimbabwe, passes through Botswana and has been operated by Botswana Railways (BR) since 1987. In 1997 there were 888 km of 1,067-mm-gauge track within Botswana, including three branches serving the Selebi-Phikwe mining complex (56 km), the Morupule colliery (16 km) and the Sua Pan soda ash deposits (175 km). BR derives 85%–90% of its earnings from freight traffic, although passenger services do operate between Gaborone and Francistown, and Lobatse and Bulawayo. Through its links with Spoornet, which operates the South African railways system and the National Railways of Zimbabwe, BR provides connections with Namibia and Swaziland to the south, and an unbroken rail link to Zambia, the Democratic Republic of the Congo, Angola, Mozambique, Tanzania and Malawi to the north.

Botswana Railways (BR): Private Bag 0052, Mahalapye; tel. 411375; telex 2980; fax 411385; Gen. Man. A. RAMJI.

ROADS

In 1995 there were an estimated 11,800 km of roads, of which some 14.2% were bituminized (including a main road from Gaborone, via Francistown, to Kazungula, where the borders of Botswana, Namibia, Zambia and Zimbabwe meet). The construction of a 340-km road between Nata and Maun is currently under way. Construction of the Trans-Kalahari road, from Jwaneng to the port of Walvis Bay on the Namibian coast, commenced in 1990 and was scheduled for completion in 1998. A car-ferry service operates from Kazungula across the Zambezi river into Zambia.

CIVIL AVIATION

The main international airport is at Gaborone. A second major airport, at Kasane in the Chobe area of northern Botswana, opened in 1992. There are airfields at Francistown, Maun and at other population centres, and there are numerous airstrips throughout the country. Scheduled services of Air Botswana are supplemented by an active charter and business sector.

Air Botswana: POB 92, Head Office Bldg, Sir Seretse Khama Airport, Gaborone; tel. 352812; telex 2413; fax 375408; f. 1972; govt-owned; domestic services and regional services to most countries in eastern and southern Africa; Chair. A. V. LIONJANGA; Gen. Man. J. B. GALEFOROLWE.

Tourism

There are five game reserves and three national parks, including Chobe, near Victoria Falls, on the Zambia–Zimbabwe border. Efforts to expand the tourist industry include plans for the construction of new hotels and the rehabilitation of existing hotel facilities. In 1995 tourist arrivals (including same-day visitors) totalled an estimated 1,021,000, and in 1994 receipts from tourism amounted to US $35m.

Department of Tourism: Ministry of Commerce and Industry, Private Bag 0047, Koh-I-Noor House, Main Mall, Gaborone; tel. 353024; telex 2674; fax 308675; Dir GAYLARD KOMBANI.

Department of Wildlife and National Parks: POB 131, Gaborone; tel. 371405; Dir. G. SEELETSO.

BRAZIL

Introductory Survey

Location, Climate, Language, Religion, Flag, Capital

The Federative Republic of Brazil, the fifth largest country in the world, lies in central and north-eastern South America. To the north are Venezuela, Colombia, Guyana, Suriname and French Guiana, to the west Peru and Bolivia, and to the south Paraguay, Argentina and Uruguay. Brazil has a very long coastline on the Atlantic Ocean. Climatic conditions vary from hot and wet in the tropical rain forest of the Amazon basin to temperate in the savannah grasslands of the central and southern uplands, which have warm summers and mild winters. In Rio de Janeiro temperatures are generally between 17°C (63°F) and 29°C (85°F). The official language is Portuguese. Almost all of the inhabitants profess Christianity, and about 90% are adherents of the Roman Catholic Church. The national flag (proportions 10 by 7) is green, bearing, at the centre, a yellow diamond containing a blue celestial globe with 26 white five-pointed stars (one for each of Brazil's states), arranged in the pattern of the southern firmament, below an equatorial scroll with the motto 'Ordem e Progresso' ('Order and Progress'), and a single star above the scroll. The capital is Brasília.

Recent History

Formerly a Portuguese possession, Brazil became an independent monarchy in 1822, and a republic in 1889. A federal constitution for the United States of Brazil was adopted in 1891. Following social unrest in the 1920s, the economic crisis of 1930 resulted in a major revolt, led by Dr Getúlio Vargas, who was installed as President. He governed the country as a benevolent dictator until forced to resign by the armed forces in December 1945. During Vargas's populist rule, Brazil enjoyed internal stability and steady economic progress. He established a strongly authoritarian corporate state, similar to fascist regimes in Europe, but in 1942 Brazil entered the Second World War on the side of the Allies.

A succession of ineffectual presidential terms (including another by Vargas, who was re-elected in 1950) failed to establish stable government in the late 1940s and early 1950s. President Jânio Quadros, elected in 1960, resigned after only seven months in office, and in September 1961 the Vice-President, João Goulart, was sworn in as President. Military leaders suspected Goulart, the leader of the Partido Trabalhista Brasileiro (PTB), of communist sympathies, and they were reluctant to let him succeed to the presidency. As a compromise, the Constitution was amended to restrict the powers of the President and to provide for a Prime Minister. However, following the appointment of three successive premiers during a 16-month period of mounting political crisis, the system was rejected when a referendum, conducted in January 1963, approved a return to the presidential system of government, whereupon President Goulart formed his own Cabinet.

Following a period of economic crisis, exacerbated by allegations of official corruption, the left-wing regime of President Goulart was overthrown in April 1964 by a bloodless right-wing military coup led by Gen. (later Marshal) Humberto Castelo Branco, the Army Chief of Staff, who was promptly elected President by the Congresso Nacional (National Congress). In October 1965 President Castelo Branco assumed dictatorial powers, and all 13 existing political parties were banned. In December, however, two artificially-created parties, the pro-Government Aliança Renovadora Nacional (ARENA) and the opposition Movimento Democrático Brasileiro (MDB), were granted official recognition. President Castelo Branco nominated as his successor the Minister of War, Marshal Artur da Costa e Silva, who was elected in October 1966 and took office in March 1967 as President of the redesignated Federative Republic of Brazil (a new Constitution was introduced simultaneously). The ailing President da Costa e Silva was forced to resign in September 1969 and was replaced by a triumvirate of military leaders.

The military regime granted the President wide-ranging powers to rule by decree. In October 1969 the ruling junta introduced a revised Constitution, vesting executive authority in an indirectly-elected President. The Congresso, suspended since December 1968, was recalled and elected Gen. Emílio Garrastazú Médici as President. Médici was succeeded as President by Gen. Ernesto Geisel and Gen. João Baptista de Figueiredo respectively. Despite the attempts of both Presidents to pursue a policy of *abertura*, or opening to democratization (legislation to end the controlled two-party system was approved in 1979), opposition to military rule intensified throughout the 1970s and early 1980s. In November 1982 the government-sponsored Partido Democrático Social (PDS) suffered significant losses at elections to the Câmara dos Deputados (Chamber of Deputies), state governorships and municipal councils. However, the PDS secured a majority of seats in the Senado Federal (Federal Senate) and, owing to pre-election legislation, seemed likely to enjoy a guaranteed majority in the electoral college, scheduled to choose a successor to Gen. Figueiredo in 1985.

However, in July 1984 Vice-President Chaves de Mendonça and the influential Marco de Oliveira Maciel, a former Governor of Pernambuco State, announced the formation of an alliance of liberal PDS members with members of the Partido do Movimento Democrático Brasileiro (PMDB). This offered the opposition a genuine opportunity to defeat the PDS in the electoral college. In August Senator Tancredo Neves, the Governor of Minas Gerais State (who had been Prime Minister in 1961–62), was named presidential candidate for the liberal alliance, while the former President of the PDS, José Sarney, was declared vice-presidential candidate. In December the liberal alliance formed an official political party, the Partido Frente Liberal (PFL). At the presidential election, conducted in January 1985, Neves was elected as Brazil's first civilian President for 21 years, winning 480 of the 686 votes in the electoral college. Prior to the inauguration ceremony in March 1985, however, Neves was taken ill, and in April, following a series of operations, he died. José Sarney, who had assumed the role of Acting President in Neves' absence, took office as President in April. President Sarney made no alterations to the Cabinet selected by Neves, and he affirmed his commitment to fulfilling the objectives of the late President-designate. In May the Congresso approved a constitutional amendment restoring direct elections by universal suffrage. The right to vote was also extended to illiterate adults. The first direct elections, to municipal councils in 31 cities, took place in November.

The introduction in February 1986 of an anti-inflation programme, the Cruzado Plan, proved, initially, to be successful and boosted the popularity of President Sarney. Support for the Government was further demonstrated in November 1986 at elections to the Congresso, which was to operate as a Constitutional Assembly. The Constitutional Assembly was installed in February 1987, and the constitutional debate was dominated by the issue of the length of the presidential mandate. In June 1988 the Constitutional Assembly finally approved a presidential mandate of five years. The first round of voting for the presidential election was provisionally set for 15 November 1989, thereby enabling Sarney to remain in office until March 1990. This *de facto* victory for the President precipitated a series of resignations from the PMDB by some of its leading members, who subsequently formed a new centre-left party, the Partido da Social Democracia Brasileira (PSDB). The Constitution was approved by the Congresso on 22 September 1988, and was promulgated on 5 October. Among its 245 articles were provisions transferring many hitherto presidential powers to the legislature. In addition, censorship was abolished; the National Security Law, whereby many political dissidents had been detained, was abolished; the minimum voting age was lowered to 16 years; and the principle of habeas corpus was recognized. However, the Constitution offered no guarantees of land reform, and was thought by many to be nationalistic and protectionist.

In April 1988 the Government revealed its commitment to drastic reductions in planned public-sector expenditure, primarily based on a 'freeze' on salary increases for state employees. The combination of industrial unrest and social tension which resulted was thought to have been a decisive factor in the PMDB's poor results at municipal elections held on 15 November, when the centre-left Partido Democrático Trabalhista

(PDT) and the left-wing Partido dos Trabalhadores (PT) made important gains at the expense of the ruling party. In early 1989 further attempts to resolve the continuing economic crisis failed to contain the threat of hyperinflation and provoked increased industrial unrest.

The murder of Francisco (Chico) Mendes, the leader of the rubber-tappers' union and a pioneering ecologist, in December 1988 brought Brazil's environmental problems to international attention. Widespread concern was expressed that large-scale development projects, together with the 'slash-and-burn' farming techniques of cattle ranchers, peasant smallholders and loggers, and the release of large amounts of mercury into the environment by an estimated 60,000 gold prospectors (or *garimpeiros*) in the Amazon region, presented a serious threat to the survival of both the indigenous Indians and the rain forest.

Brazil's first presidential election by direct voting since 1960 took place on 15 November 1989. The main contenders were a young conservative, Fernando Collor de Mello of the newly-formed Partido de Reconstrução Nacional (PRN), Luiz Inácio (Lula) da Silva of the PT and Leonel Brizola of the PDT. Since no candidate received the required overall majority, a second round of voting was held on 17 December, contested by Collor de Mello and da Silva, who were first and second, respectively, in the November poll. Collor de Mello was declared the winner, with 53% of the votes cast. Following his inauguration as President on 15 March 1990, Collor de Mello announced an ambitious programme of economic reform, with the principal aim of reducing inflation, which had reached a monthly rate of more than 80%. Among the extraordinary provisions of the programme entitled 'New Brazil' (or, more commonly, the 'Collor Plan') was the immediate sequestration of an estimated US $115,000m. in personal savings and corporate assets for an 18-month period. A new currency, the cruzeiro (to replace, at par, the novo cruzado) was also introduced, together with a comprehensive divestment and rationalization programme. The decision to rationalize the public sector, and the large number of redundancies implicit in such a measure, encountered almost immediate opposition from trade union organizations, giving rise to widespread labour unrest.

The results of elections to 31 senatorial seats, 503 seats in the Câmara dos Deputados and 27 state governorships, conducted in October 1990, were interpreted as a rejection of extreme left- and right-wing parties in favour of familiar candidates from small, centre-right parties. Although the President would be forced to maintain a more delicate balance of political alliances in the Congresso as a result, Collor de Mello was confident of securing sufficient support to continue to pursue a programme of radical economic reform. However, the results of a second round of voting to elect governors in those states where candidates had received less than the required 50% of the votes on 3 October, which was conducted on 25 November, represented a serious reversal for the Government. Few candidates associated with or supported by the Government were successful, and particularly damaging defeats were suffered by government-favoured candidates in the crucial states of São Paulo, Rio Grande do Sul, Rio de Janeiro and Espírito Santo.

The Government's dramatic loss of popularity was largely attributed to the severity and apparent failure of its economic austerity programme. A second economic plan, announced by the Minister of the Economy, Zélia Cardoso de Mello, and presented as a simple intensification of the first 'Collor Plan', had been implemented in February 1991. In March Collor de Mello announced a new Plan for National Reconstruction, which envisaged further deregulation and rationalization of many state-controlled areas, including the ports, and the communications and fuel sectors. By May 1991, despite a considerable decrease in the monthly rate of inflation, Cardoso de Mello's political popularity had been undermined by her confrontational style of negotiation, and she was forced to resign.

Collor de Mello's position became increasingly precarious towards the end of 1991, after allegations of mismanagement of federal funds were made against his wife and against several associates in the President's home state of Alagoas. In September 1991 the President embarked upon a series of informal multi-party negotiations in an attempt to achieve greater congressional consensus and to reinforce his own mandate. Following lengthy discussions at a specially-convened meeting of the emergency Council of the Republic in the same month, Collor de Mello presented a comprehensive series of proposals for constitutional amendment, popularly known as the 'emendão', before the Congresso.

Allegations of high-level corruption persisted into 1992 and despite attempts, in January and April, to restore public confidence in the integrity of the Government with the implementation of comprehensive cabinet changes, the President failed to dispel suspicions sufficiently to attract the wider political participation in government which was considered necessary to facilitate the passage of legislation through an increasingly ineffectual Congresso. In May, moreover, the President became the focus of further allegations, following a series of disclosures made by Collor de Mello's younger brother, Pedro, which appeared to implicate the President in a number of corrupt practices (including the misappropriation of federal funds) orchestrated by Paulo César Farias, Collor de Mello's 1989 election campaign treasurer. While the President dismissed the allegations as false, in late May the Congresso approved the creation of a special commission of inquiry to investigate the affair. In early September, acting upon the report of the special commission of inquiry, and bolstered by massive popular support, a 49-member congressional committee authorized the initiation of impeachment proceedings against the President, within the Câmara dos Deputados. On 29 September 1992 the Câmara voted to proceed with the impeachment of the President for abuses of authority and position, prompting the immediate resignation of the Cabinet. On 2 October Collor de Mello surrendered authority to Vice-President Itamar Franco for a six-month period, pending the final pronouncement regarding his future in office, to be decided by the Senado. Following lengthy negotiations, Franco announced the composition of a new Cabinet in October, representing a broad political base. A final round of municipal elections, conducted in November, revealed a significant resurgence of support for left-wing parties. In December the Minister of the Economy, Gustavo Krause, resigned, following Franco's unilateral decision to suspend, by presidential decree, the Government's privatization programme for a three-month period.

Meanwhile, in early December 1992, the Senado had voted overwhelmingly to proceed with Collor de Mello's impeachment and to indict the President for 'crimes of responsibility'. Within minutes of the opening of the impeachment trial on 29 December, however, Collor de Mello announced his resignation from the presidency. Itamar Franco was immediately sworn in as President (to serve the remainder of Collor de Mello's term) at a specially convened session of the Congresso. On the following day the Senado, which had agreed to continue with proceedings against Collor de Mello (despite his resignation), announced that the former President's political rights (including immunity from prosecution and the holding of public office for an eight-year period) were to be removed. In January 1993 Collor de Mello was notified by the Supreme Court that he was to stand trial, as an ordinary citizen, on charges of 'passive corruption and criminal association'. Proceedings against Collor de Mello were initiated in June, and in December the Supreme Federal Tribunal endorsed the Senado's eight-year ban on his holding public office. In December 1994, however, the Tribunal voted to acquit Collor de Mello of the charges, owing to insufficient evidence against him. In January 1998 the former President was cleared of charges of illegal enrichment.

At a referendum conducted in April 1993 voters overwhelmingly rejected the introduction of a parliamentary system of government or the restoration of the monarchy, opting instead to retain the presidential system.

In late 1992 and early 1993 several unsuccessful attempts, by three successive economic teams, to address the crucial economic problems of burgeoning inflation and massive budget deficit largely failed to inspire confidence in the business sector or in international finance organizations. In June 1993 the new Minister of the Economy, Fernando Henrique Cardoso, announced the terms of the Government's latest economic programme, the 'plano de verdade' (real plan), including an acceleration of the reactivated privatization programme. A new currency, the cruzeiro real, was introduced in August. A programme for economic stability, announced in December 1993, sought to control inflation and to reduce public spending (reinforcing the austere provisions of the 1994 budget, presented in November) by regulating the flow of federal resources to states and municipalities. A new transitional index, the Unidade Real de Valor (URV), was to be introduced to monitor inflation more efficiently, and would eventually become a new unit of currency. Further measures to increase tax revenue were also endorsed. Congressional approval for the establishment of a Social Emergency Fund (providing for further centralization of control over the expenditures and revenue of states and government agencies) prompted the activation of the URV, linked to the dollar, on 1 March 1994. On 1 July the new currency, the real, was introduced, at par with the dollar.

During 1993 the stability and credibility of the Government were significantly undermined by frequent changes to the Cabinet and by the political manoeuvring of member parties of the ruling coalition in preparation for presidential elections, scheduled for 1994. In April 1993 the PDT leader, Leonel Brizola, announced the party's withdrawal from the ruling coalition, following Franco's decision to proceed with the privatization of the prestigious National Steel Company (Companhia Siderúrgica Nacional—CSN). Minister of Justice and PDT member Maurício Corrêa Lima subsequently resigned from the party rather than relinquish the justice portfolio. In August the Partido Socialista Brasileiro (PSB) withdrew from the coalition, and in September the PMDB national council narrowly defeated a motion to end its association with the Government. The fragility of the Government was exacerbated by the emergence of a new corruption scandal in October, in which 22 deputies, four senators, two incumbent ministers, two former ministers and three governors were seemingly implicated in a fraudulent scheme in which political influence was allegedly exercised in order to secure state projects for individual construction companies, in exchange for bribes. A 44-member congressional committee of inquiry was established in October, and in January 1994 recommended the expulsion of 18 federal deputies, and the further investigation of 12 deputies, three governors and one senator. In mid-April the Câmara voted to expel three of the 18 named deputies and to continue investigations into four deputies who had recently resigned, in order to prevent their participation in the October elections. In May, Ibsen Pinheiro, a prominent deputy who had been leader of the Câmara when impeachment proceedings were initiated against Collor de Mello, was similarly expelled from the Congresso.

In October 1993, as stipulated in the 1988 Constitution, a congressional review of the Constitution was initiated, despite the opposition of left-wing parties who feared the possible erosion of existing guarantees of civil and social rights. In May 1994 the Congresso concluded its review of the Constitution, having adopted just six amendments, including a reduction in the length of the presidential term from five to four years.

A number of ministerial changes were made in late 1993 and early 1994, largely to enable ministers to seek election in the forthcoming polls. In March 1994 Cardoso resigned from the finance portfolio in order to meet the 2 April deadline for registration as presidential candidate of the PSDB. The election was expected to be closely contested between Cardoso and 'Lula' da Silva, who was formally endorsed as presidential candidate of the PT-led Frente Popular (FP) on 1 May. Political events in the months preceding the election were dominated by numerous allegations of corruption and misconduct, which forced the replacement of the vice-presidential running mates of both Cardoso and da Silva, the withdrawal from the contest of the presidential candidate of the PL, Flávio Rocha, and the resignation of the Ministers of Finance and Mines and Energy, following two separate incidents in September 1994 in which they were accused of having abused their position.

Presidential, gubernatorial and legislative elections were conducted on 3 October 1994. Cardoso, whose candidacy was supported by the PFL, the PTB, the PL and the business community, won the presidential contest in the first round, with an overall majority of 54.3% of the votes, following a campaign that had focused largely on the success of his economic initiatives. The PT candidate, da Silva, with the support of the PSB, was second with 27.0% of the votes cast. The elections were notable for the high rate of voter abstention and for the large number of blank and spoiled ballots (almost 16% of total votes cast). The discovery of large-scale, organized electoral fraud in the State of Rio de Janeiro forced the annulment of elections for state and federal deputies there, which were reorganized (with a large military presence) to coincide with the 15 November run-off elections for governorships in states where no overall majority had been achieved in the October poll. PSDB candidates were also successful in the gubernatorial contests, securing six of the 27 state governorships, including the crucial industrial centres of São Paulo, Minas Gerais and Rio de Janeiro. While the PMDB increased its number of state governorships from seven to nine, and continued to boast the largest single-party representation in the Congresso, the party's presidential candidate, Orestes Quércia, had attracted only 4.4% of the votes cast. The multi-party composition of Cardoso's Cabinet (with portfolios allocated not only to those parties that had supported his candidacy, but also to the PT and the PMDB), announced in late December 1994, demonstrated the new President's need to maintain a broad base of congressional support in order to secure prompt endorsement for proposed constitutional reform of the taxation and social security systems.

Cardoso was inaugurated as President on 1 January 1995 and a new Cabinet was installed on the following day. Cardoso immediately made clear his intention to continue the programme of economic reform in order to control public expenditure and reduce inflation. In February Cardoso employed the presidential veto to reject a draft congressional proposal to increase the minimum monthly wage. At the same time he announced a temporary reduction in ministerial salaries, pending a more comprehensive adjustment to the minimum wage. In March, in response to economic difficulties arising from the instability of the exchange rate, the currency was devalued. In the same month the privatization programme, suspended by Franco during 1994, was reactivated (with the announcement of the future sale of the State's controlling interest in the Companhia Vale do Rio Doce—CVRD—mining concern), interest rates and tariffs on consumer durables were raised and the increase in the minimum wage, previously vetoed by the President, was approved. However, opposition to the programme of economic stabilization and to renewed efforts by the Government to introduce constitutional amendments, including those that would end state monopolies in the telecommunications and petroleum sectors, resulted in the organization, by the Central Unica dos Trabalhadores (CUT) trade union confederation, of a general strike in May 1995, which interrupted a number of public services, and widespread industrial action at oil refineries. The President's decision to order military intervention in a number of crucial refineries was widely interpreted as evidence of the Government's intent to undermine the concerted action of the political opposition and the trade unions. By early June, however, employees in the petroleum sector had begun to return to work, and on 20 June (despite vociferous congressional opposition) the Câmara approved the proposal to open the sector to private participation. (The amendment relating to the petroleum sector was subsequently approved by the Senado in November; constitutional amendments providing for an end to state control of telecommunications, natural gas distribution and a number of shipping routes, were formally promulgated by the Congresso in mid-August.)

Meanwhile, the Government's attempts to secure congressional approval for reforms to the tax and social security systems, and for the extension of the existence of the Social Emergency Fund had proved less successful. In September, however, following presidential assurances that the reforms would not result in a reduction in state government revenues and that state debts to the Federal Government might be rescheduled, Cardoso's proposals for further constitutional reform attracted the support of the majority of state governors. In October the Congresso approved the extension of the Social Emergency Fund for 18 months. In late May the Government had announced further economic adjustment, including plans to end the use of monetary correction indices in a broad rage of financial calculations and negotiations. This 'de-indexation' of the economy was formally implemented on 1 July.

In September 1995 three existing right-wing parties, the Partido Progressista Reformador, the Partido Progressista and the Partido Republicano Progressista, merged to create the Partido Progressista Brasileiro (PPB). The new party's congressional representation would be the third-largest in the country and its expression of cautious support for the Government seemed likely to consolidate Cardoso's position in late 1995. By mid-December, however, Cardoso's political integrity had been seriously compromised by the alleged involvement of a number of his political associates in irregular financial transactions organized by the Banco Econômico in support of recent electoral campaigns, and by an influence-peddling scandal arising from the award to a US company, Raytheon, of the contract for development of an Amazon Regional Surveillance System (Sivam), which resulted in the resignation, in November, of the Minister of the Air Force. A congressional inquiry into the Sivam affair was initiated during November 1995. In February 1996 a special committee of the Senado made a recommendation, supported by Cardoso, that the Government should negotiate a substantial foreign loan to honour the Sivam contract with

Raytheon, and by October 1996, controversy surrounding the project had dissipated sufficiently for the President to endorse the agreement.

Meanwhile, investigation of the so-called 'pink folder' of politicians, recovered from the ailing Banco Econômico, continued during 1996, as the banking sector was plunged into further crisis. In March it was revealed that the Government had withheld recently uncovered details of a US $5,000m.-fraud perpetrated at the Banco Nacional some 10 years earlier, in order to avert further loss of confidence in the finance sector. Moreover, it emerged that the Government had extended a recent credit facility of US $5,800m. to the bank in order to facilitate its merger with UNIBANCO in November 1995. Also in March the Government announced emergency financing for the Banco do Brasil, which, in common with many Brazilian banks, had suffered huge losses during 1995 as a result of the sudden decline in the rate of inflation and in interest rates. Earlier in the month the Government had opposed proposals made by the Senado to establish a commission of inquiry to investigate the banking system. In December 1996 the President of the Central Bank announced that during the previous two years the Government had invested US $14,000m. in struggling banks, in an attempt to stabilize the sector.

During 1996 renewed attempts by the Government to secure congressional approval for constitutional reforms relating to taxation, public administration and social security were repeatedly obstructed, delayed or defeated in the Congresso, despite the adoption of a number of concessionary clauses, and the successful negotiation of a compromise agreement on social security with trade union organizations in January. In February Cardoso publicly criticized the predominance within the legislature of deputies who were preoccupied with the special interest groups (often motivated by economic considerations).

A minor reorganization of the Cabinet was implemented in April 1996 in order to accommodate the introduction of the new Ministry of Political Co-ordination. In May José Serra resigned from the Planning, Budget and Co-ordination portfolio in order to contest the mayorship of São Paulo at municipal elections scheduled for October. Serra was replaced by Antônio Kandir, also a member of the PSDB. In August the Minister of Transport, Odacir Klein, resigned following his son's arraignment on charges relating to the death of a building worker as a result of a motor accident, and in November the Minister of Health, Abid Jatene, resigned in protest at inadequate levels of state funding for the health sector. Also in November the Government revealed a national defence plan.

The results of municipal elections conducted on 3 October 1996 revealed a reduction in support for the PSDB; Serra was third in the contest for the São Paulo mayorship, with only 15.6% of the votes. Celso Pitta of the PPB was finally elected to the post at a second round of voting conducted on 15 November. The results of other run-off elections, conducted concurrently, also demonstrated a significant level of support for the PPB. The elections represented a disappointment for many veteran parties. The PPB, the PFL and the PSB, however, all made significant gains. None the less, Cardoso's own popularity continued to benefit from the success of the Government's attempts to control inflation, and in late January 1997 a legislative document, sponsored by the President, which sought to amend the Constitution in order to allow the incumbent head of state, state governors and mayors to seek re-election, received tentative endorsement from the Câmara, despite vociferous opposition from the PMDB.

In mid-1996 the moderate Força Sindical trade union organization joined the CUT in urging workers to observe Brazil's first general strike in five years, to be organized on 21 June. Despite the Government's announcement, in April, of a job-creation programme (Proempleo) to provide employment for 3m. Brazilians, the unions were dissatisfied with the Government's failure to halt rising levels of unemployment. However, the strike was only partially observed, and on the same day the Government announced details of the next phase of its massive divestment programme. Several companies in the power sector, 31 ports (including Santos and Rio de Janeiro) and the prestigious CVRD were among those state concerns to be offered for sale to the private sector. In July the Government announced that the divestment programme was to be accelerated, and that the state telecommunications company, TELEBRÁS, together with large sections of the rail and power networks, would be privatized by the end of 1998. Further reductions in public spending were announced in August 1996. A new programme of economic measures designed to further reduce the fiscal deficit in 1997 was introduced, by executive decree, in October 1996. The long-term effectiveness of the proposals, which included 100,000 redundancies in the public sector, the ending of special privileges for certain occupations, improved mechanisms for the collection of taxes and the reform of the pensions system, would be dependent on the successful adoption of administrative reform legislation currently under consideration in the Congresso. The Social Emergency Fund was again extended, to the end of 1999.

In February 1997 the Câmara confirmed its approval of a constitutional amendment to permit the President to stand for re-election in 1998, Cardoso's position having been strengthened by the election of two of his supporters to the presidencies of both chambers of the Congresso Nacional. Following the Senado's vote in favour of the legislation in May (despite allegations of bribery relating to the passage through the Câmara), the constitutional amendment received the upper house's final approval in June. The legislation was swiftly ratified by President Cardoso.

In March 1997, meanwhile, controversial legislation to end the long-standing monopoly of PETROBRÁS over the petroleum industry was approved by the Câmara, which in the following month voted narrowly in favour of proposals to reform the civil service (thus to prepare for the dismissal of surplus employees). The Senado's rejection of the latter item of legislation in June, however, was a major set-back to the Government's programme of economic reform and in particular to its attempts to reduce the budget deficit. Nevertheless, a series of compromises enabled the Government to renew its plans for reform of the civil service, and in July an opposition amendment to the proposed legislation was narrowly defeated in the Câmara. In November the lower house gave its final approval to the legislation. In early 1998, as the Government attempted to proceed with its reform programme, scrutiny of proposed legislation relating to amendments to the social security system continued.

As public confidence in the integrity of the country's police force continued to diminish, in mid-1997 thousands of troops were deployed in response to a strike by police officers protesting against low rates of pay. President Cardoso denounced as an 'uprising' the illegal strikes, which in some areas resulted in a complete breakdown of law and order and to a notable increase in the murder rate.

In June 1997 the PT ordered an inquiry into allegations of corruption on the part of its presidential candidate, Lula da Silva. Although da Silva was exonerated by the investigation (thus permitting him to renew his candidacy for the 1998 election), other financial irregularities were uncovered, leading to a sharp decline in the PT's popularity. As the 1998 presidential election approached, various potential candidates announced changes in their party affiliation. In August 1997 Ciro Gomes, a former Minister of Finance, defected from the PSDB to the smaller Partido Popular Socialista (PPS), thereby exacerbating the internal crisis within the PSDB. (In the same month the Minister of Communications, Sérgio Vieira da Motta, announced his resignation from the party.) Former President Itamar Franco, meanwhile, declared his affiliation to the PMDB. In October 1997 the incumbent President Cardoso's candidacy was endorsed by the PMDB, and in November Lula da Silva officially declared his intention to stand as the PT's candidate.

In July 1997, meanwhile, an investigation by the Senado into a financial scandal arising from fraudulent bond issues concluded that 20 prominent politicians and senior officials (including three state governors and the mayor of São Paulo, Celso Pitta, along with his predecessor, Paulo Maluf), had been involved in a criminal operation. A total of 161 financial institutions, including Banco Bradesco, Brazil's largest private bank, were implicated in the scandal. In January 1998 Celso Pitta was found guilty of fraud, but remained in office pending an appeal.

In late February 1995, having announced an initiative to improve the quality of primary education earlier in the month, Cardoso launched a social improvement programme, Comunidade Solidária, with a consultative council comprising representatives of 10 ministries and headed by the President's wife, Ruth Cardoso, and with a budget of US $3,000m. In September the President announced a new programme for the defence of human rights and later in the month a government-sponsored bill was approved by the Câmara, whereby responsibility for the deaths of more than 100 left-wing politicians and activists during the military regimes of the 1960s and 1970s was assumed by the State, which also approved financial compensation for the relatives of the victims. A National Plan for Human Rights, introduced in May 1996, contained 168 recommendations, including proposals to increase protection for the rights of children and workers. However, the absence of a financial or procedural framework for adoption of the plan prompted a cautious response to the document from human rights organizations. During 1995 the Government suffered from repeated criticism of its failure to address burgeoning urban crime (particularly in Rio de Janeiro) and the demands of the Landless Peasant Movement, the Movimento dos Sem-Terra (MST), which organized a number of illegal occupations of disputed land during the year in support of demands for an acceleration of the Government's programme of expropriation of uncultivated land for distribution to landless rural families.

Tensions arising from land ownership and reallocation disputes persisted. In January 1996 protests and land occupations were renewed following the enactment, by presidential decree, of a new law regulating the demarcation of Indian lands, which many indigenous groups interpreted as a serious erosion of the previously-existing land rights of the Indian population. Meanwhile, landless peasant groups challenged government claims that 100,000 itinerant families had been resettled during 1995 and 1996, and described the Government's reallocation programme as inadequate. (Official estimates of the number of landless families in Brazil are considerably lower than the figure of 4.8m. quoted by the MST.) Rapidly deteriorating relations between the authorities and the MST were further exacerbated in April 1996 by the violent intervention of the local military police in a demonstration, organized by the MST and supported by some 1,500 protesters at Eldorado de Carajás in the State of Pará, which resulted in the deaths of some 23 demonstrators. (It was subsequently alleged that a number of those killed had been summarily executed.) Widespread public outrage prompted Cardoso to request immediate congressional priority for legislation relating to land expropriation, and to afford full cabinet status to the former agriculture ministry department responsible for executing the agrarian reform programme. Raúl Jungman of the PPS was appointed to the new post of Minister for Land Policy. José Eduardo de Andrade Vieira, who had attributed responsibility for the April massacre to the increasingly confrontational operations of the MST, was replaced as Minister of Agriculture and Supplies by Arlindo Porto of the PTB. However, Cardoso's attempts to propel land reform legislation through the Congresso were promptly obstructed, and the emergence of a number of reports detailing the creation of close associations between local military police units and powerful rural landowners seemed likely to undermine efforts to bring to justice those responsible for the Eldorado de Carajás atrocity. Despite Jungman's stated intention to facilitate dialogue amongst opposing groups in the dispute through the creation of a discussion council, by late 1996 the MST-sponsored campaign of illegal land seizures and occupations of federal and state government buildings had intensified, particularly in the States of São Paulo and Santa Catarina.

In April 1997, in response to the growing unrest and the arrival in Brasília of 1,500 MST members at the conclusion of a two-month march, the Government announced new measures to accelerate the process of land reform. At the end of April landless peasants threatened to occupy land belonging to the CVRD, in protest at the company's forthcoming transfer to the private sector. In May, however, despite various legal challenges, the sale of assets in this major producer of iron ore proceeded. In the following month José Rainha Júnior, an MST leader, was sentenced to more than 26 years' imprisonment for his involvement in the murder in 1989 of a landowner and of a police officer. In August 1997 a clash between riot police and illegal occupants of public land in Brasília resulted in 49 arrests and 20 persons injured. In the same month some 200 landless families seized two ranches in the state of São Paulo.

Despite the appointment in March 1990 of internationally-acclaimed ecologist José Lutzemberger as Minister of the Environment, and the implementation of a number of initiatives to curb unauthorized gold prospecting in the Amazon region, international criticism of the Government's poor response to the threat to the environment persisted throughout the early 1990s. Of particular concern to many international observers was the plight of the Yanomami Indian tribe in Roraima. It was estimated that, since the arrival of the *garimpeiros* in the region, some 10%–15% of the Yanomami's total population had been exterminated as a result of pollution and disease, introduced to the area by the gold prospectors. The National Indian Foundation (FUNAI) was heavily criticized for its role in the affair and was accused of failing to provide effective protection and support for Brazil's Indian population. In March 1992 Lutzemberger was dismissed following his repeated criticism of institutionalized opposition to his environmental programme. In June 1992, however, national prestige was heightened when Brazil successfully hosted the UN Conference on Environment and Development or 'Earth Summit'. In August 1993 international attention was again focused on the region, following the slaughter of 73 members of the Yanomami tribe by *garimpeiros*, in the context of the ongoing territorial dispute prompted by the miners' attempts to exploit the rich mineral deposits of the Yanomami land. A new cabinet post of Minister with Special Responsibility for the Brazilian Amazon was subsequently created. In March 1996 a US $5,700m.-rain forest protection-programme (to be funded by the Brazilian Government, the European Union and the G-7 group of industrialized countries over a five-year period) was concluded between President Cardoso and the Secretary-General of the United Nations, Dr Boutros Boutros-Ghali. At a meeting in Manaus in October 1997, the G-7 group pledged an additional US $68m. In July 1997 Júlio Gaiger, the head of FUNAI, resigned, claiming that the Government had failed to honour its commitment to assist indigenous people.

In 1990 a series of bilateral trade agreements were signed with Argentina, in a development widely believed to signify the first stage in a process leading to the eventual establishment of a Southern Cone Common Market (Mercado Comum do Sul—Mercosul), also to include Paraguay and Uruguay. In March 1991, in Paraguay, the four nations signed the Asunción treaty whereby they reaffirmed their commitment to the creation of such a market by the end of 1994. Mercosul duly came into effect on 1 January 1995, following the signing, by the Presidents of the four member nations, of the Ouro Prêto Protocol, in Brazil, in December 1994. While a complete common external tariff was not expected until 2006, customs barriers on 80%–85% of mutually exchanged goods were removed immediately.

In May 1994 Brazil declared its full adherence to the 1967 Tlatelolco Treaty for the non-proliferation of nuclear weapons in Latin America and the Caribbean. The Treaty was promulgated by presidential decree in September 1994. Brazil signed the international Treaty on the Non-Proliferation of Nuclear Weapons in June 1997.

Government

Under the 1988 Constitution, the country is a federal republic comprising 26 States and a Federal District (Brasília). Legislative power is exercised by the bicameral Congresso Nacional (National Congress), comprising the Câmara dos Deputados (Chamber of Deputies—members elected by a system of proportional representation for four years) and the Senado Federal (Federal Senate—members elected by the majority principle in rotation for eight years). The number of deputies is based on the size of the population. Election is by universal adult suffrage. Executive power is exercised by the President, elected by direct ballot for four years. The President appoints and leads the Cabinet. Each State has a directly elected Governor and an elected legislature. For the purposes of local government, the States are divided into municipalities.

Defence

Military service, lasting 12 months, is compulsory for men between 18 and 45 years of age. In August 1997 the armed forces comprised 314,700 men (including 132,000 conscripts): army 200,000 (125,000 conscripts), navy 64,700 and air force 50,000. Public security forces number about 385,600 men. Defence expenditure for 1997 was budgeted at R$15,900m.

Economic Affairs

In 1995, according to estimates by the World Bank, Brazil's gross national product (GNP), measured at average 1993–95 prices, was US $579,787m., equivalent to $3,640 per head. During 1985–95, it was estimated, GNP per head decreased, in real terms, by 0.7% per year. Over the same period, the population increased by an annual average of 1.6%. Brazil's gross domestic product (GDP) increased, in real terms, by an annual average of 1.5% in 1985–95. GDP increased by 3.0% in 1996.

Agriculture (including hunting, forestry and fishing) engaged 24.5% of the employed labour force in 1996 and contributed 11.4% of GDP in 1995. The principal cash crops are soya beans (soya products accounted for some 9.5% of export earnings in 1994), coffee (4.8% of export revenue in 1996), tobacco, sugar cane and cocoa beans. Subsistence crops include wheat, maize, rice, potatoes, beans, cassava and sorghum. Beef and poultry production are also important, as is fishing (particularly cod, crab, lobster and shrimp). During 1985–95 agricultural GDP increased by an annual average of 2.3% (agricultural GDP increased by 5.9% in 1995).

Industry (including mining, manufacturing, construction and power) employed 19.9% of the working population in 1996 and provided 31.4% of GDP in 1995. During 1985–95 industrial GDP declined by an annual average of 0.5%. However growth of 7.1% and 2.0% was recorded in the sector in 1994 and 1995, respectively.

Mining contributed less than 1.0% of GDP in 1995. The major mineral exports are iron ore (haematite—in terms of iron content, Brazil is the largest producer in the world), tin and aluminium (Brazil is the world's fourth largest producer of bauxite). Gold, phosphates, platinum, uranium, manganese, copper and coal are also mined. In 1990 deposits of niobium, thought to be the world's largest, were discovered in the state of Amazonas. Brazil's reserves of petroleum were estimated at 4,120m. barrels in 1995. Brazil's largest state-run company, PETROBRÁS, is one of the world's leading oil-producing companies.

Manufacturing contributed 20.6% of GDP in 1995. The sector employed 12.4% of the total employed population in 1996. There is considerable state involvement in a broad range of manufacturing activity. While traditionally-dominant areas, including textiles and clothing and food- and beverage-processing, continue to contribute a large share to the sector (orange juice accounted for 2.3% of total export earnings in 1994), more recent developments in the sector have resulted in the emergence of machinery and transport equipment (including road vehicles and components, passenger jet aircraft and specialist machinery for the petroleum industry), construction materials (especially iron and steel), wood and sugar cane derivatives, and chemicals and petrochemicals as the significant new manufacturing activities. According to the World Bank, manufacturing GDP declined by an average of 0.9% per year in 1985–95. However, growth in the sector's GDP was estimated at 5.5% in 1994 and 1.6% in 1995.

In the mid-1980s some 32% of total energy was derived from electricity (90% of which was hydroelectric), 30% from petroleum, 18% from wood and charcoal and 12% from fuel alcohol. Other energy sources, including coal and natural gas, accounted for some 8%. Attempts to exploit further the country's vast hydroelectric potential (estimated at 213,000 MW) were encouraged by the successful completion of preliminary stages of development of ambitious dam projects at Itaipú, on the border with Paraguay, and at Tucuruí, on the Tocantins river. The 12,600-MW Itaipú project is expected to produce as much as 35% of Brazil's total electricity requirements when fully operational. Plans to construct a 17,000-MW hydroelectric plant on the Xingu river, in the Amazon region, are also under consideration. By 1993 the share of electricity produced by hydroelectric sources had increased to 93.3%. The Angra I nuclear power plant, inaugurated in 1985, has subsequently operated only intermittently, while financial constraints have hindered the completion of the Angra II plant and have prevented further development of the country's nuclear programme. Imports of fuel and energy comprised 10.3% of the value of total merchandise imports in 1995.

The services sector contributed an estimated 57.2% of GDP in 1995 and engaged 55.7% of the employed labour force in 1996. According to the World Bank, the GDP of the services sector increased by 3.0% per year in 1985–95. Growth in the sector's GDP was estimated at 4.4% in 1994 and 5.7% in 1995.

In 1997 Brazil recorded a visible trade deficit of US $8,520m. There was a deficit of US $24,802m. on the current account of the balance of payments. In 1996 the principal source of imports (25.0%) was the USA, which was also the principal market for exports (19.5%). Other major trading partners were Germany, Japan, Italy, the Netherlands and Argentina. The principal exports in 1994 were food and food-processing products (notably coffee, soya beans and orange juice), iron ore and concentrates, iron and steel, and road vehicles and parts. The principal imports were mineral fuels, machinery and mechanical appliances, road vehicles and parts, and chemical products.

Although the Government had projected a balanced budget in 1997, a deficit equivalent to 4% of GDP was predicted, compared with 4.7% in 1996. The 1998 budget envisaged expenditure of R$437,000m. Brazil's external debt was US $159,130m. at the end of 1995, of which $96,609m. was long-term public debt. In that year the cost of debt-servicing was equivalent to 37.9% of revenue from exports of goods and services. The annual rate of inflation averaged 500% in 1990–96. In 1997 consumer prices rose by only 7.4%. Official figures indicated an unemployment rate of 6.9% of the labour force in 1996, while other sources suggested that the figure was higher. (Unemployment in São Paulo was estimated at a record 16.3% in September 1997.)

Brazil is a member of ALADI (see. p. 261) and Mercosul (see p. 239). Brazil also joined the Comunidade dos Países de Língua Portuguesa (CPLP, see p. 269), founded in 1996.

The 'economic miracle' of the 1960s and early 1970s in Brazil (with GDP expanding, in real terms, by an annual average of 11.3% between 1967 and 1974) gradually subsided in the 1980s, when economic affairs were dominated by Brazil's position as the developing world's largest debtor. The International Coffee Organization's suspension of export quotas from July 1989 had a detrimental effect on Brazilian exports. Prospects for future negotiations on debt-rescheduling improved greatly as a result of the success of an economic stabilization programme (implemented during 1994 with the aim of balancing the budget and controlling inflation), which was bolstered by the success of a new currency (the real), introduced on 1 July 1994, and by the reactivation of the privatization programme in early 1995. In November 1997, following the temporary doubling of interest rates to 43% amid concern that the real had become overvalued, the Government announced numerous fiscal adjustment measures. These included 33,000 immediate redundancies in the civil service, reductions in budgetary expenditures, and increases in personal income tax, import duties and various other taxes. Furthermore, an acceleration of the privatization programme was expected to raise revenue of almost US $54,000m. during the two years 1998–99 (compared with US $18,600m. in 1997). As a result of the Government's measures, GDP growth in 1998 was projected at only 2%, compared with an estimated 4% in 1997.

Social Welfare

The social security system, in existence since 1923, was rationalized in 1960, and the Instituto Nacional de Previdência Social (INPS) was formed in 1966. All social welfare programmes were consolidated in 1977 under the National System of Social Insurance and Assistance (SINPAS). The INPS administers benefits to urban and rural employees and their dependants. Benefits include sickness benefit, invalidity, old age, length of service and widows' pensions, maternity and family allowances and grants. There are three government agencies: the Instituto de Administração Financeira da Previdência e Assistência Social collects contributions and revenue and supplies funds, the Instituto Nacional de Assistência Médica da Previdência Social is responsible for medical care, and CEME (Central Medicines) supplies medicines at a low price. According to official sources, the state social security budget for 1997 was projected at R $52,322m. In the early 1990s privatization of pension fund management, based on the Chilean model, was being implemented. By early 1997 it was estimated that some US $70,000m. were being managed by pension funds in Brazil (including US $17,600m. controlled by Previ—the pension fund for the Banco do Brasil, and US $7,000m. controlled by the 260 members of the private funds association—the Associaçao Brasileira das Entidades Fechadas de Previdência Privada). Total assets controlled by pension funds were expected to exceed US $400,000m. by 2010.

In 1984 there were 122,818 physicians working in Brazil; in the same year the country had 12,175 hospital establishments, with a total of 538,721 beds. The private medical sector controls 90% of Brazil's hospitals. Budget forecasts for 1997 envisaged expenditure on health services of R $20,234m. (equivalent to 4.7% of the national treasury's forecast total expenditure).

The welfare of the dwindling population of indigenous American Indians is the responsibility of the Fundação Nacional do Indio (FUNAI), which was formed to assign homelands to the Indians, most of whom are landless and threatened by the exploitation of the Amazon forest.

Education

Education is free in official pre-primary schools and is compulsory between the ages of seven and 14 years. Primary education begins at seven years of age and lasts for eight years. Secondary education, beginning at 15 years of age, lasts for three years and is also free in official schools. In 1994 some 91% of children in the relevant age-group were enrolled at primary schools, but only 20% of those aged 15 to 17 were enrolled at secondary schools. The Federal Government is responsible for higher education, and in 1994 there were 127 universities, of which 68 were state-administered. Numerous private institutions exist at all levels of education. Expenditure on education and sport by the central Government was forecast at R $10,376m. for 1997, representing 2.4% of total expenditure.

Despite an anti-illiteracy campaign, initiated in 1971, according to official estimates published in 1995, the adult illiteracy rate was 17.2%.

Public Holidays

1998: 1 January (New Year's Day—Universal Confraternization Day), 23–24 February (Carnival), 10 April (Good Friday), 21 April (Tiradentes Day—Discovery of Brazil), 1 May (Labour Day), 11 June (Corpus Christi), 7 September (Independence Day), 12 October (Our Lady Aparecida, Patron Saint of Brazil), 2 November (All Souls' Day), 15 November (Proclamation of the Republic), 25 December (Christmas Day).

1999: 1 January (New Year's Day—Universal Confraternization Day), 15–16 February (Carnival), 2 April (Good Friday), 21 April (Tiradentes Day—Discovery of Brazil) 1 May (Labour Day), 13 May (Ascension Day), 3 June (Corpus Christi), 7 September (Independence Day), 12 October (Our Lady Aparecida, Patron Saint of Brazil), 2 November (All Souls' Day), 15 November (Proclamation of the Republic), 25 December (Christmas Day).

Other local holidays include 20 January (Foundation of Rio de Janeiro) and 25 January (Foundation of São Paulo).

Weights and Measures

The metric system is in force.

Statistical Survey

Sources (unless otherwise stated): Economic Research Department, Banco Central do Brasil, Brasília, DF; tel. (61) 414-1074; telex 1702; fax (61) 414-2036; e-mail depec.copec.@bcb.gov.br; internet http://www.bcb.gov.br; Fundação Instituto Brasileiro de Geografia e Estatística (IBGE), Centro de Documentação e Disseminação de Informações (CDDI), Rua Gen. Canabarro 706, 2° andar, 20271-201 Maracanã, Rio de Janeiro, RJ; tel. (21) 569-3424; telex 34128; fax (21) 284-1959; internet http://www.ibge.gov.br.

Area and Population

AREA, POPULATION AND DENSITY

Area (sq km)	8,547,403.5*
Population (census results)†	
1 September 1980	119,002,706
1 September 1991	
Males	72,485,122
Females	74,340,353
Total	146,825,475
1 August 1996	157,079,573
Population (official estimates at mid-year)†	
1993	151,571,727
1994	153,725,670
1995	155,822,440
Density (per sq km) at 1 August 1996	18.4

* 3,300,170.9 sq miles.

† Excluding Indian jungle population, numbering 45,429 in 1950.

ADMINISTRATIVE DIVISIONS
(population at census of 1 August 1996)

State	Population	Capital
Acre (AC)	483,726	Rio Branco
Alagoas (AL)	2,633,339	Maceió
Amapá (AP)	379,459	Macapá
Amazonas (AM)	2,389,279	Manaus
Bahia (BA)	12,541,745	Salvador
Ceará (CE)	6,809,794	Fortaleza
Espírito Santo (ES)	2,802,707	Vitória
Goiás (GO)	4,515,868	Goiânia
Maranhão (MA)	5,222,565	São Luís
Mato Grosso (MT)	2,235,832	Cuiabá
Mato Grosso do Sul (MS)	1,927,834	Campo Grande
Minas Gerais (MG)	16,673,097	Belo Horizonte
Pará (PA)	5,510,849	Belém
Paraíba (PB)	3,305,616	João Pessoa
Paraná (PR)	9,003,804	Curitiba
Pernambuco (PE)	7,399,131	Recife
Piauí (PI)	2,673,176	Teresina
Rio de Janeiro (RJ)	13,406,379	Rio de Janeiro
Rio Grande do Norte (RN)	2,558,660	Natal
Rio Grande do Sul (RS)	9,637,682	Porto Alegre
Rondônia (RO)	1,231,007	Porto Velho
Roraima (RR)	247,131	Boa Vista
Santa Catarina (SC)	4,875,244	Florianópolis
São Paulo (SP)	34,120,886	São Paulo
Sergipe (SE)	1,624,175	Aracaju
Tocantins (TO)	1,048,642	Palmas
Distrito Federal (DF)	1,821,946	Brasília
Total	157,079,573	—

PRINCIPAL TOWNS* (population estimates at census of 1 August 1996)

Brasília (capital)	1,821,946	Campo Grande	600,069
São Paulo	9,839,436	João Pessoa	549,363
Rio de Janeiro	5,551,538	Jaboatão	529,966
Salvador	2,211,539	Contagem	492,350
Belo Horizonte	2,091,448	São José dos Campos	486,467
Fortaleza	1,965,513	Ribeirão Preto	456,252
Curitiba	1,476,253	Feira de Santana	450,487
Recife	1,346,045	Niterói	450,364
Porto Alegre	1,288,879	São João de Meriti	434,323
Manaus	1,157,357	Cuiabá	433,355
Belém	1,144,312	Sorocaba	431,561
Goiânia	1,004,098	Aracaju	428,194
Guarulhos	972,384	Juíz de Fora	424,479
Campinas	908,906	Londrina	421,343
São Gonçalo	833,379	Uberlândia	438,986
Nova Iguaçu	826,188	Santos	412,243
São Luis	780,833	Joinville	397,951
Maceió	723,230	Campos dos Goytacazes	389,547
Duque de Caxias	715,089	Olinda	349,380
São Bernardo do Campo	660,396	Diadema	323,116
Natal	656,037	Jundiai	293,373
Teresina	655,473		
Santo André	625,564		
Osasco	622,912		

* Figures refer to *municípios,* which may contain rural districts.

BIRTHS AND DEATHS (official estimates)

	Birth rate (per 1,000)	Death rate (per 1,000)
1989	24.53	7.28
1990	23.64	7.19
1991	22.89	7.11
1992	22.09	7.04
1993	21.37	6.98
1994	20.75	6.92
1995	20.14	6.87
1996	19.69	6.82

Expectation of life (official estimates, years at birth, mid-1996): 67.32 (males 64.12; females 70.64).

ECONOMICALLY ACTIVE POPULATION (household surveys, September each year, '000 persons aged 10 years and over)*

	1995	1996
Agriculture, hunting, forestry and fishing	18,154.2	16,647.0
Manufacturing	8,548.4	8,407.1
Mining and quarrying; Electricity, gas and water	862.8	770.5
Construction	4,229.2	4,335.6
Wholesale and retail trade	9,116.6	9,079.3
Transport and communications	2,542.8	2,554.9
Community, social and personal services (incl. restaurants and hotels)	24,840.6	24,940.2
Financing, insurance, real estate and business services; Activities not adequately defined	1,334.0	1,305.6
Total employed	69,628.6	68,040.2
Unemployed	4,509.8	5,079.9
Total labour force	74,138.4	73,120.1
Males	44,191.2	43,824.8
Females	29,947.2	29,295.3

* Figures exclude aborigines, non-resident foreigners and the rural population of the northern region. Also excluded are members of the armed forces in barracks.

Agriculture

PRINCIPAL CROPS ('000 metric tons)

	1994	1995	1996
Wheat	2,092	1,534	3,302
Rice (paddy)	10,499	11,226	10,035
Barley	91	105	219
Maize	32,488	36,275	31,975
Oats	257	177	197
Sorghum	292	243	313
Potatoes	2,480	2,677	2,699
Sweet potatoes	656	655*	655*
Cassava (Manioc)	24,464	25,316	24,587
Yams*	215	215	215
Dry beans	3,368	2,946	2,837
Soybeans (Soya beans)	24,912	25,651	23,211
Groundnuts (in shell)	159	169	154
Castor beans	53	32	46
Cottonseed	850†	915†	650*
Coconuts	902	949	998
Babassu kernels*	185	185	185
Tomatoes	2,678	2,700	2,639
Onions (dry)	1,019	931	943
Other vegetables†	2,134	2,109	2,108
Water-melons	448	420*	420*
Sugar cane	292,070	303,557	324,435
Grapes	807	825	731
Apples	700	664	653
Peaches and nectarines	136	135*	135*
Oranges	17,418	19,613	21,811
Tangerines, mandarins, clementines and satsumas	760	760*	760*
Lemons and limes	491	495*	495*
Avocados	103	110*	110*
Mangoes	432	435*	435*
Pineapples	974	914	1,048
Bananas	5,722	5,680	5,692
Papayas	2,342	2,350*	2,350*
Other fruits and berries†	1,705	1,708	1,708
Cashew nuts	126	164	165
Coffee beans (green)‡	1,306	929	1,290
Cocoa beans	330	296	256
Tobacco (leaves)	519	455	471
Jute and allied fibres	19	12	12
Sisal	131	118	133
Cotton (lint)	501	510*	360*
Other fibre crops*	84	85*	85*
Natural rubber	45	44	44*

* FAO estimate(s).

† Unofficial figure(s).

‡ Official figures, reported in terms of dry cherries, have been converted into green coffee beans at 50%.

Source: FAO, *Production Yearbook*.

LIVESTOCK ('000 head, year ending September)

	1994	1995	1996*
Cattle	158,243	162,000*	165,000
Buffaloes	1,571	1,650*	1,700
Horses	6,356	6,300*	6,300
Asses	1,313	1,300*	1,300
Mules	1,987	1,950*	1,950
Pigs	35,142	35,350*	36,600
Sheep	18,436	18,000†	18,000
Goats	10,879	10,500*	10,500

Chickens (million): 681 in 1994; 800* in 1995; 900* in 1996.
Ducks (FAO estimates, million): 9 in 1994–96.
Turkeys (FAO estimates, million): 6 in 1994–96.

* FAO estimate(s). † Unofficial figure.

Source: FAO, *Production Yearbook*.

LIVESTOCK PRODUCTS ('000 metric tons)

	1994	1995	1996
Beef and veal*	4,475	4,750	4,960
Mutton and lamb	84*	84†	84†
Goat meat†	31	30	30
Pig meat*	1,300	1,450	1,520
Horse meat	18	18†	18†
Poultry meat	3,508	3,752	4,350
Edible offals†	973	996	1,042
Cows' milk	20,068	21,800†	23,600†
Goats' milk†	143	141	141
Butter	70*	85*	85†
Cheese†	60	60	60
Dried milk	175*	200*	200†
Hen eggs	1,385	1,400†	1,400†
Other poultry eggs†	24	24	24
Honey	18	18†	18†
Wool:			
greasy	26	25†	25†
scoured†	16	16	16
Cattle hides (fresh)*	448	475	496

* Unofficial figure(s). † FAO estimate(s).

Source: FAO, mainly *Production Yearbook*.

Forestry

ROUNDWOOD REMOVALS
(FAO estimates, '000 cubic metres, excluding bark)

	1992	1993	1994
Sawlogs, veneer logs and logs for sleepers	41,171	41,171	41,171
Pulpwood	30,701	30,701	30,701
Other industrial wood	5,829	5,930	6,031
Fuel wood	190,800	194,100	197,400
Total	268,501	271,902	275,303

Source: FAO, *Yearbook of Forest Products*.

SAWNWOOD PRODUCTION
(FAO estimates, '000 cubic metres, incl. railway sleepers)

	1989	1990	1991
Coniferous (softwood)	8,384	7,923	8,591
Broadleaved (hardwood)	9,795	9,256	10,037
Total	18,179	17,179	18,628

1992–94: Annual production as in 1991 (FAO estimates).

Source: FAO, *Yearbook of Forest Products*.

Fishing

(FAO estimates, metric tons, live weight)

	1993	1994	1995
Inland waters	215,000	220,000	210,000
Atlantic Ocean	565,600	600,000	590,000
Total catch	780,000	820,000	800,000

Source: FAO, *Yearbook of Fishery Statistics*.

Mining

('000 metric tons, unless otherwise indicated)

	1992	1993	1994
Hard coal	4,731	4,595	5,194
Crude petroleum	31,569	32,252	33,494
Natural gas (petajoules)	159	173	179
Iron	98,309	100,344	109,000‡
Copper	39.8	42.2	45.0‡
Nickel†	14.7	15.2	16.5
Bauxite†	9,366	9,669	8,673
Lead†	4.2	4.0	4.0
Zinc†	115.2	138.0	140.0
Tin†	21.7	25.9	19.6
Manganese‡	777.0	716.0	897.0
Chromium*‡	135	92	108
Tungsten (metric tons)‡	205	245	250
Silver (metric tons)	50	n.a.	n.a.
Gold (kg)‡	85,900	74,200	76,000
Limestone	58,779§	n.a.	n.a.
Sea salt	5,261§	6,180§	n.a.
Diamonds (industrial, '000 carats)‡	665	900	900
Crude gypsum	998*	n.a.	n.a.
Asbestos fibres	170§	185§	n.a.
Mica	5.0‡	n.a.	n.a.
Talc	480	n.a.	n.a.
Diamonds (gem, '000 carats)‡	653	600	600*

Figures for metals refer to metal content of ores and concentrates; figures for gold refer to gold refined from domestic ores only.

* Estimate.

† Source: *World Metal Statistics* (London).

‡ Source: US Bureau of Mines.

§ Source: Ministério de Minas e Energia.

Source: UN, *Industrial Commodity Statistics Yearbook*.

Industry

SELECTED PRODUCTS ('000 metric tons, unless otherwise indicated)

	1993	1994	1995
Asphalt	1,092	1,298	1,252
Electric power (million kWh)	265,888	278,089	296,268
Coke*	8,162	8,166	n.a.
Pig-iron	23,899	25,092	25,021
Crude steel	25,207	25,747	25,076
Cement†	24,843	25,230	28,256
Tyres ('000 units)*	31,795	33,820	n.a.
Synthetic rubber	192	209	221
Passenger cars ('000 units)	1,100	1,249	1,297
Commercial vehicles (units)	291,098	332,616	331,541
Tractors (units)	25,734	42,899	22,919
Newsprint	276	264	295

* Source: UN, *Industrial Commodity Statistics Yearbook*.

† Portland cement only.

Finance

CURRENCY AND EXCHANGE RATES

Monetary Units

100 centavos = 1 real (plural: reais).

Sterling and Dollar Equivalents (30 September 1997)

£1 sterling = 1.770 reais;
US $1 = 1.096 reais;
100 reais = £56.50 = $91.27.

Average Exchange Rates (reais per US $1,000)

1994	639
1995	918
1996	1,005

Note: In March 1986 the cruzeiro (CR $) was replaced by a new currency unit, the cruzado (CZ $), equivalent to 1,000 cruzeiros. In January 1989 the cruzado was, in turn, replaced by the new cruzado (NCZ $), equivalent to CZ $1,000 and initially at par with the US dollar (US $). In March 1990 the new cruzado was replaced by the cruzeiro (CR $), at an exchange rate of one new cruzado for one cruzeiro. In August 1993 the cruzeiro was replaced by the cruzeiro real, equivalent to CR $1,000. On 1 March 1994, in preparation for the introduction of a new currency, a transitional accounting unit, the Unidade Real de Valor (at par with the US $), came into operation, alongside the cruzeiro real. On 1 July 1994 the cruzeiro real was replaced by the real (R $), also at par with the US $ and thus equivalent to 2,750 cruzeiros reais.

GENERAL BUDGET (estimates, R $ million)

Revenue	1995	1996	1997*
Taxes	50,468	53,558	62,626
Patrimonial revenue	5,849	3,577	2,554
Industrial revenue	77	106	44
Service revenue	7,125	8,386	9,234
Capital revenue	121,632	142,058	247,655
Currency transfers	67,590	212	21
Miscellaneous	57,236	79,388	98,526
Other revenue	8,220	11,642	3,378
National Treasury total	318,197	298,926	424,037
Indirect administration funds	n.a.	n.a.	7,556
General total	n.a.	n.a.	431,593

Expenditure	1995	1996	1997*
Legislative and auxiliary	1,544	1,797	1,642
Judiciary	3,682	4,396	5,168
Executive	236,043	283,543	422,054
Presidency	2,014	1,777	4,085
Air	3,494	3,584	3,986
Agriculture	4,232	6,305	3,736
Communications	383	448	571
Culture	152	173	263
Education and sport	10,483	10,884	10,376
Army	6,015	6,671	7,445
Finance	138,505	168,564	288,456
Industry and commerce	641	962	1,034
Interior	267	n.a.	n.a.
Justice	1,191	1,485	1,848
Marine	3,625	3,757	4,346
Environment	1,243	1,169	1,885
Social security	37,857	47,418	52,322
Mines and power	378	636	331
Health	14,919	14,727	20,234
Foreign affairs	429	427	472
Labour	5,818	7,150	10,607
Social welfare	135	n.a.	n.a.
Transport	2,932	2,934	5,530
Science and technology	940	1,051	1,264
Others	390	3,421†	3,264†
Contingency reserves	—	—	2,729
National Treasury total	241,269	289,736	431,593

* Projected figures.

† Figure includes Interior.

CENTRAL BANK RESERVES (US $ million at 31 December)

	1994	1995	1996
Gold*	1,418	1,767	1,381
IMF special drawing rights	0	1	1
Foreign exchange	37,069	49,707	58,322
Total	38,488	51,475	59,704

* Valued at market-related prices.

Source: IMF, *International Financial Statistics.*

MONEY SUPPLY (R $ million at 31 December)

	1994	1995	1996
Currency outside banks	8,892	12,517	15,484
Demand deposits at deposit money banks	12,711	14,034	12,195
Total money (incl. others)	24,464	32,094	39,591

Source: IMF, *International Financial Statistics.*

COST OF LIVING (Consumer Price Index; annual averages of 11 main cities; base: August 1994 = 100)

	1994	1995	1996
Food and beverages	73.34	114.10	121.83
Clothing	73.75	115.07	112.76
Housing	76.76	158.15	232.03
Household articles	73.67	121.71	125.33
Transport and communications	71.31	113.26	140.38
All items (incl. others)	73.52	122.01	140.94

NATIONAL ACCOUNTS (R $ '000 at current prices)

Composition of the Gross National Product

	1993	1994	1995
Gross domestic product (GDP) at factor cost	12,328,246	308,675,847	561,780,515
Indirect taxes	1,944,060	56,173,326	102,740,592
Less Subsidies	156,136	3,929,811	6,379,870
GDP in purchasers' values	14,116,170	360,919,362	658,141,237
Factor income received from abroad	65,032	2,195,202	5,074,640
Less Factor income paid abroad	458,401	8,960,205	16,266,328
Gross national product	13,722,800	354,154,359	646,949,549

Expenditure on the Gross Domestic Product

	1993	1994	1995
Government final consumption expenditure	2,295,957	57,665,930	110,482,528
Private final consumption expenditure } Increase in stocks }	8,791,670	228,362,408	429,753,134
Gross fixed capital formation	2,714,429	70,877,024	126,643,575
Total domestic expenditure	13,802,056	356,905,362	666,879,237
Exports of goods and services	1,377,985	30,087,000	46,311,000
Less Imports of goods and services	1,063,872	26,073,000	55,049,000
GDP in purchasers' values	14,116,170	360,919,362	658,141,237
GDP at constant 1995 prices	595,689,313	631,371,102	658,141,237

Gross Domestic Product by Economic Activity (at factor cost)

	1993	1994	1995
Agriculture, hunting, forestry and fishing	1,531,596	43,977,425	68,290,207
Mining and quarrying	210,641	3,488,501	5,866,642
Manufacturing	3,098,228	73,141,758	123,820,889
Electricity, gas and water	378,373	9,085,619	14,198,321
Construction	984,516	25,635,521	45,123,644
Trade, restaurants and hotels	936,665	22,302,101	38,036,958
Transport, storage and communications	756,766	17,466,372	30,701,567
Finance, insurance, real estate and business services	2,009,252	40,158,974	42,824,317
Government services	1,273,963	33,470,861	70,153,657
Other community, social and personal services	3,171,462	79,365,007	162,096,966
Sub-total	14,351,463	348,092,139	601,113,168
Less Imputed bank service charge	2,023,217	39,416,292	39,332,653
Total	12,328,246	308,675,847	561,780,515

BALANCE OF PAYMENTS (US $ million)

	1993	1994	1995
Exports of goods f.o.b.	39,630	44,102	46,506
Imports of goods f.o.b.	–25,301	–33,241	–49,663
Trade balance	14,329	10,861	–3,157
Exports of services	3,965	4,908	6,135
Imports of services	–9,555	–10,254	–13,630
Balance on goods and services	8,739	5,515	–10,652
Other income received	1,308	2,202	3,457
Other income paid	–11,630	–11,293	–14,562
Balance on goods, services and income	–1,583	–3,576	–21,757
Current transfers received	1,704	2,577	3,861
Current transfers paid	–101	–154	–240
Current balance	20	–1,153	–18,136
Capital account (net)	81	173	352
Direct investment abroad	–491	–1,037	–1,384
Direct investment from abroad	1,292	3,072	4,859
Portfolio investment assets	–606	–3,052	–936
Portfolio investment liabilities	12,928	47,784	10,171
Other investment assets	–2,696	–4,368	–1,783
Other investment liabilities	–2,823	–34,434	18,383
Net errors and omissions	–815	–442	1,447
Overall balance	6,890	6,543	12,973

Source: IMF, *International Financial Statistics.*

External Trade

PRINCIPAL COMMODITIES
(distribution by SITC, US $ '000, excl. military goods)

Imports c.i.f.	1992	1993	1994
Food and live animals	1,801,203	2,323,302	3,197,994
Cereals and cereal preparations	1,040,888	1,400,877	1,604,421
Cereal preparations, etc.	372,942	959,347	995,046
Prepared breakfast foods	231,944	833,000	859,015
Crude materials (inedible) except fuels	1,313,392	1,785,149	2,003,628
Textile fibres (excl. wool tops) and waste	278,632	779,576	696,589
Cotton	219,877	689,131	593,022
Raw cotton (excl. linters)	218,482	686,545	584,944
Metalliferous ores and metal scrap	466,973	433,760	491,568
Mineral fuels, lubricants, etc.	5,531,230	5,672,156	5,294,709
Coal, coke and briquettes	810,164	761,257	783,594
Coal, lignite and peat	669,226	648,479	618,640
Coal other than anthracite (not agglomerated)	642,899	632,454	576,494
Petroleum, petroleum products, etc.	4,404,607	4,642,586	4,250,817
Crude petroleum oils, etc.	3,491,956	2,414,492	2,562,669
Refined petroleum products	471,989	2,158,508	1,616,394
Motor spirit (gasoline) and other light oils	1,197	1,116,693	783,851
Gas oils (distillate fuels)	348,544	631,699	432,146
Residual petroleum products, etc.	440,661	69,587	71,754
Chemicals and related products	3,478,321	4,359,696	5,803,891
Organic chemicals	1,331,310	1,695,360	2,409,863
Nitrogen-function compounds	448,674	549,473	645,186
Medicinal and pharmaceutical products	381,827	494,356	734,601
Manufactured fertilizers	510,996	583,148	711,461
Artificial resins, plastic materials, etc.	402,442	574,573	672,325
Basic manufactures	1,946,551	2,408,870	3,176,037
Machinery and transport equipment	6,858,879	8,986,426	13,516,584
Power-generating machinery and equipment	564,576	648,131	1,186,729
Machinery specialized for particular industries	1,008,038	1,090,697	1,729,388
General industrial machinery, equipment and parts	1,033,579	1,189,644	1,608,999
Office machines and automatic data-processing equipment	747,742	941,294	1,234,372
Automatic data-processing machines and units	383,547	540,012	743,255
Telecommunications and sound equipment	555,019	884,786	1,360,565
Other electrical machinery, apparatus, etc.	1,344,979	1,737,560	2,449,735
Thermionic valves, tubes, etc.	380,608	561,095	807,600
Road vehicles and parts*	941,110	1,889,336	3,294,962
Passenger motor cars (excl. buses)	281,351	710,203	1,524,002
Parts and accessories for cars, buses, lorries, etc.*	539,126	828,827	1,166,295
Miscellaneous manufactured articles	1,190,907	1,455,658	2,023,041
Professional, scientific and controlling instruments, etc.	558,135	565,783	700,583
Total (incl. others)	22,346,268	27,300,226	35,510,426

* Excluding tyres, engines and electrical parts.

Source: UN, *International Trade Statistics Yearbook.*

Exports f.o.b.	1994*	1995†	1996†
Food and live animals	9,203,566	9,985,208	10,756,576
Meat and meat preparations	1,332,997	1,295,121	1,502,828
Fresh, chilled or frozen meat	1,008,660	n.a.	n.a.
Vegetables and fruit	1,366,679	1,488,487	1,826,410
Preserved fruit and fruit preparations	1,070,708	n.a.	n.a.
Fruit juices and vegetable juices	1,019,382	1,131,880	1,453,664
Orange juice	987,734	n.a.	n.a.
Sugar, sugar preparations and honey	1,067,645	n.a.	n.a.
Sugar and honey	996,923	n.a.	n.a.
Coffee, tea, cocoa and spices	3,018,866	2,749,033	2,461,526
Coffee and coffee substitutes	2,585,417	2,462,395	2,135,136
Coffee (incl. husks and skins) and substitutes containing coffee	2,220,338	1,969,870	1,718,593
Unroasted coffee, husks and skins	2,218,689	1,969,847	1,718,593
Feeding-stuff for animals	2,152,135	2,184,080	2,930,074
Oil-cake and other vegetable oil residues	2,029,387	n.a.	n.a.
Oil-cake, etc., of soya beans	1,982,716	n.a.	n.a.

Exports f.o.b. — *continued*	1994*	1995†	1996†
Beverages and tobacco	1,123,863	1,263,855	1,618,455
Tobacco and tobacco manufactures	1,030,708	768,571	917,958
Tobacco, unmanufactured; tobacco refuse	693,896	666,120	917,958
Crude materials (inedible) except fuels	5,447,309	6,118,562	5,953,144
Oil seeds and oleaginous fruit	1,320,889	775,467	1,020,111
Oil seeds, etc., for 'soft' fixed vegetable oils	1,320,199	774,022	1,019,577
Soya beans	1,315,979	770,425	1,017,918
Pulp and waste paper	851,333	1,475,408	999,464
Soda or sulphate wood pulp	839,729	n.a.	n.a.
Bleached or semi-bleached pulp	833,473	n.a.	n.a.
Metalliferous ores and metal scrap	2,544,283	2,793,600	3,017,615
Iron ore and concentrates	2,293,992	2,547,781	2,695,207
Iron ore and concentrates (not agglomerated)	1,532,504	1,701,388	1,740,771
Animal and vegetable oils, fats and waxes	957,031	1,234,394	880,892
Fixed vegetable oils and fats	882,254	1,107,743	749,081
Chemicals and related products	2,543,153	3,060,453	3,160,357
Organic chemicals	892,919	1,078,648	1,064,645
Basic manufactures	10,751,692	11,612,290	11,164,159
Paper, paperboard and manufactures	1,040,402	1,228,342	933,329
Paper and paperboard (not cut to size or shape)	968,945	900,174	672,183
Textile yarn, fabrics, etc.	1,006,743	998,549	1,006,807
Iron and steel	4,119,744	4,296,643	4,195,650
Ingots and other primary forms	1,566,927	1,395,567	1,329,757
Blooms, billets, slabs and sheet bars	1,102,908	n.a.	n.a.
Universals, plates and sheets	934,215	333,538	322,866
Non-ferrous metals	1,536,069	1,853,970	1,636,735
Aluminium and aluminium alloys	1,189,743	1,461,653	1,296,370
Unwrought aluminium and alloys	1,024,900	1,255,744	1,102,817
Machinery and transport equipment	8,973,851	8,846,590	9,522,233
Power-generating machinery and equipment	1,278,624	1,305,249	1,403,226
Internal combustion piston engines, and parts thereof	853,972	922,872	1,029,351
Machinery specialized for particular industries	976,437	922,383	1,049,471
General industrial machinery, equipment and parts	1,369,246	1,569,774	1,521,686
Electrical machinery, apparatus, etc.	1,284,353	949,984	969,011
Road vehicles and parts‡	2,992,723	2,663,378	2,929,363
Passenger motor cars (excl. buses)	533,979	455,540	619,248
Parts and accessories for cars, buses, lorries, etc.‡	1,423,802	1,470,854	1,562,343
Miscellaneous manufactured articles	3,111,067	2,993,696	3,049,354
Footwear	1,537,203	1,498,811	1,650,112
Leather footwear	1,488,963	n.a.	n.a.
Total (incl. others)	43,557,977	43,445,830	44,586,372

* Source: UN, *International Trade Statistics Yearbook*.

† Source: Ministério da Indústria, do Comércio e do Turismo, Brasília, DF.

‡ Excluding tyres, engines and electrical parts.

PRINCIPAL TRADING PARTNERS (US $ million)*

Imports c.i.f.	1994	1995	1996
Algeria	279	253	659
Argentina	3,829	5,758	6,787
Belgium-Luxembourg	515	774	668
Canada	895	1,220	1,284
Chile	635	1,183	1,010
France	932	1,411	1,354
Germany	3,614	5,496	5,378
Hong Kong	459	908	841
Italy	2,067	2,881	2,931
Japan	1,938	2,727	2,181
Korea, Republic	588	1,294	1,078
Mexico	360	842	930
Netherlands	571	828	798
Paraguay	375	532	572
Saudi Arabia	1,416	1,267	1,223
Singapore	312	595	573
Spain	326	819	901
Sweden	390	600	687
Switzerland	757	1,086	1,295
Taiwan	387	673	678
United Kingdom	781	991	1,274
USA	8,069	12,712	14,212
Uruguay	697	1,000	1,477
Venezuela	581	911	1,044
Total (incl. others)	35,512	53,828	56,749

Exports f.o.b.	1994	1995	1996
Argentina	4,136	4,041	5,170
Belgium-Luxembourg	1,355	1,610	1,432
Canada	501	461	506
Chile	999	1,210	1,055
China, People's Republic	822	1,204	1,114
France	901	1,038	912
Germany	2,049	2,158	2,083
Italy	1,647	1,713	1,531
Japan	2,574	3,102	3,047
Korea, Republic	634	827	838
Mexico	1,050	496	679
Netherlands	3,077	2,918	3,549
Paraguay	1,054	1,301	1,325
Spain	709	877	937
United Kingdom	1,229	1,326	1,324
USA	8,951	8,798	9,312
Uruguay	732	812	811
Total (incl. others)	43,545	46,506	47,747

* Imports by country of purchase; exports by country of last consignment.

Source: Economic Research Department, Banco Central do Brasil, Brasília, DF.

Transport

RAILWAYS

	1994	1995	1996
Passengers (million)	1,290	1,265	1,257
Passenger-km (million)	15,758	14,506	13,999
Freight ('000 metric tons)	256,368	260,248	248,224
Freight ton-km (million)	133,690	136,437	128,917

Source: Empresa Brasileira de Planejamento de Transportes (GEIPOT), Brasília, DF.

ROAD TRAFFIC (motor vehicles in use at 31 December)

	1994	1995	1996
Passenger cars	16,487,234	17,874,423	19,354,083
Buses and coaches	265,791	292,210	331,796
Light goods vehicles	4,044,727 (incl. heavy goods vehicles)	2,588,410	4,694,483 (incl. heavy goods vehicles)
Heavy goods vehicles		1,620,882	
Motorcycles and mopeds	2,479,491	2,725,956	2,924,227

Source: Empresa Brasileira de Planejamento de Transportes (GEIPOT), Brasília, DF.

SHIPPING

Merchant Fleet (registered at 31 December)

	1994	1995	1996
Number of vessels	565	551	539
Total displacement ('000 grt)	5,283	5,077	4,530

Source: Lloyd's Register of Shipping, *World Fleet Statistics.*

International Sea-borne Freight Traffic ('000 metric tons)

	1988	1989	1990
Goods loaded	160,640	166,956	168,026
Goods unloaded	53,280	58,550	52,570

Source: UN, *Monthly Bulletin of Statistics.*

CIVIL AVIATION (embarked passengers, mail and cargo)

	1994	1995	1996
Number of passengers ('000)	18,005	21,422	26,898
Freight ('000 metric tons)	568,417	564,353	618,605
Freight ton-km ('000)*	1,793,519	1,949,011	1,936,624

* Including mail.

Source: Empresa Brasileira de Planejamento de Transportes (GEIPOT), Brasília, DF.

Tourism

	1993	1994	1995
Tourist arrivals ('000)	1,641	1,853	1,991
Tourist receipts (US $ million)	1,091	1,925	2,097

Source: Instituto Brasileiro de Turismo—EMBRATUR, Brasília, DF.

Communications Media

	1992	1993	1994
Radio receivers ('000 in use)*	59,500	61,000	62,500
Television receivers ('000 in use)*	32,000	32,000	33,200
Daily newspapers: number†	n.a.	323	285
Telephones in use ('000 main lines)‡	n.a.	11,567	13,055
Telefax stations ('000)§	160	200	n.a.
Mobile cellular telephones (subscribers)§	30,729	180,220	574,000

Daily newspapers (number)†: 352 in 1995; 380 in 1996.

Telephones in use ('000 main lines)‡: 14,875 in 1995.

* Source: UNESCO, *Statistical Yearbook.*

† Source: Associação Nacional de Jornais (ANJ).

‡ Source: Fundação Instituto Brasileiro de Geografia e Estatística (IBGE).

§ Source: UN, *Statistical Yearbook.*

Education

(1996)

	Institutions	Teachers	Students
Pre-primary	77,740	219,517	4,270,376
Literacy classes (Classe de Alfabetização)	55,548	75,549	1,443,927
Primary	195,767	1,388,247	33,131,270
Secondary	15,213	326,827	5,739,077
Higher*	851	141,482	1,661,034

* 1994 figures.

Source: Ministério da Educação e do Desporto, Brasília, DF.

Directory

The Constitution

A new Constitution was promulgated on 5 October 1988. The following is a summary of the main provisions:

The Federative Republic of Brazil, formed by the indissoluble union of the States, the Municipalities and the Federal District, is constituted as a democratic state. All power emanates from the people. The Federative Republic of Brazil seeks the economic, political, social and cultural integration of the peoples of Latin America.

All are equal before the law. The inviolability of the right to life, freedom, equality, security and property is guaranteed. No one shall be subjected to torture. Freedom of thought, conscience, religious belief and expression are guaranteed, as is privacy. The principles of habeas corpus and 'habeas data' (the latter giving citizens access to personal information held in government data banks) are granted. There is freedom of association, and the right to strike is guaranteed.

There is universal suffrage by direct secret ballot. Voting is compulsory for literate persons between 18 and 69 years of age, and optional for those who are illiterate, those over 70 years of age and those aged 16 and 17.

Brasília is the federal capital. The Union's competence includes maintaining relations with foreign states, and taking part in international organizations; declaring war and making peace; guaranteeing national defence; decreeing a state of siege; issuing currency; supervising credits, etc.; formulating and implementing plans for economic and social development; maintaining national services, including communications, energy, the judiciary and the police; legislating on civil, commercial, penal, procedural, electoral, agrarian, maritime, aeronautical, spatial and labour law, etc. The Union, States, Federal District and Municipalities must protect the Constitution, laws and democratic institutions, and preserve national heritage.

The States are responsible for electing their Governors by universal suffrage and direct secret ballot for a four-year term. The organization of the Municipalities, the Federal District and the Territories is regulated by law.

The Union may intervene in the States and in the Federal District only in certain circumstances, such as a threat to national security or public order, and then only after reference to the National Congress.

LEGISLATIVE POWER

The legislative power is exercised by the Congresso Nacional (National Congress), which is composed of the Câmara dos Deputados (Chamber of Deputies) and the Senado Federal (Federal Senate). Elections for deputies and senators take place simultaneously throughout the country; candidates for the Congresso must be Brazilian by birth and have full exercise of their political rights. They must be at least 21 years of age in the case of deputies and at least 35 years of age in the case of senators. The Congresso meets twice a year in ordinary sessions, and extraordinary sessions may be convened by the President of the Republic, the Presidents of the Câmara and the Senado, or at the request of the majority of the members of either house.

The Câmara is made up of representatives of the people, elected by a system of proportional representation in each State, Territory and the Federal District for a period of four years. The total number of deputies representing the States and the Federal District will be established in proportion to the population; each Territory will elect four deputies.

The Senado is composed of representatives of the States and the Federal District, elected according to the principle of majority. Each State and the Federal District will elect three senators with a mandate of eight years, with elections after four years for one-third of the members and after another four years for the remaining two-thirds. Each Senator is elected with two substitutes. The Senado approves, by secret ballot, the choice of Magistrates, when required by the Constitution; of the Attorney-General of the Republic, of the Ministers of the Accounts Tribunal, of the Territorial Governors, of the president and directors of the central bank and of the permanent heads of diplomatic missions.

The Congresso is responsible for deciding on all matters within the competence of the Union, especially fiscal and budgetary arrangements, national, regional and local plans and programmes, the strength of the armed forces and territorial limits. It is also responsible for making definitive resolutions on international treaties, and for authorizing the President to declare war.

The powers of the Câmara include authorizing the instigation of legal proceedings against the President and Vice-President of the Republic and Ministers of State. The Senado may indict and impose sentence on the President and Vice-President of the Republic and Ministers of State.

Constitutional amendments may be proposed by at least one-third of the members of either house, by the President or by more than one-half of the legislative assemblies of the units of the Federation. Amendments must be ratified by three-fifths of the members of each house. The Constitution may not be amended during times of national emergency, such as a state of siege.

EXECUTIVE POWER

Executive power is exercised by the President of the Republic, aided by the Ministers of State. Candidates for the Presidency and Vice-Presidency must be Brazilian-born, be in full exercise of their political rights and be over 35 years of age. The candidate who obtains an absolute majority of votes will be elected President. If no candidate attains an absolute majority, the two candidates who have received the most votes proceed to a second round of voting, at which the candidate obtaining the majority of valid votes will be elected President. The President holds office for a term of four years and (under an amendment adopted in 1997) is eligible for re-election.

The Ministers of State are chosen by the President and their duties include countersigning acts and decrees signed by the President, expediting instructions for the enactment of laws, decrees and regulations, and presentation to the President of an annual report of their activities.

The Council of the Republic is the higher consultative organ of the President of the Republic. It comprises the Vice-President of the Republic, the Presidents of the Câmara and Senado, the leaders of the majority and of the minority in each house, the Minister of Justice, two members appointed by the President of the Republic, two elected by the Senado and two elected by the Câmara, the latter six having a mandate of three years.

The National Defence Council advises the President on matters relating to national sovereignty and defence. It comprises the Vice-President of the Republic, the Presidents of the Câmara and Senado, the Minister of Justice, military Ministers and the Ministers of Foreign Affairs and of Planning.

JUDICIAL POWER

Judicial power in the Union is exercised by the Supreme Federal Tribunal; the Higher Tribunal of Justice; the Regional Federal Tribunals and federal judges; Labour Tribunals and judges; Electoral Tribunals and judges; Military Tribunals and judges; and the States' Tribunals and judges. Judges are appointed for life; they may not undertake any other employment. The Tribunals elect their own controlling organs and organize their own internal structure.

The Supreme Federal Tribunal, situated in the Union capital, has jurisdiction over the whole national territory and is composed of 11 ministers. The ministers are nominated by the President after approval by the Senado, from Brazilian-born citizens, between the ages of 35 and 65 years, of proved judicial knowledge and experience.

The Government

HEAD OF STATE

President: FERNANDO HENRIQUE CARDOSO (took office 1 January 1995).

Vice-President: MARCO MACIEL.

THE CABINET
(January 1998)

Minister of Foreign Affairs: LUIZ FELIPE PALMEIRA LAMPREIA.

Minister of Justice: IRIS REZENDE MACHADO.

Minister of the Economy: PEDRO SAMPAIO MALAN.

Minister of Agriculture and Supplies: ARLINDO PORTO NETO.

Minister of Labour: PAULO DE TARSO ALMEIDA PAIVA.

Minister of Administration: LUIZ CARLOS BRESSER GONÇALVES PEREIRA.

Minister of Education: PAULO RENATO DE SOUZA.

Minister of Health: CARLOS CÉSAR DE ALBUQUERQUE.

Minister of Social Welfare: REINHOLD STEPHANES.

Minister of Communications: SÉRGIO ROBERTO VIEIRA DA MOTTA.

Minister of Transport: ELISEU PADILHA.

Minister of Planning, the Budget and Co-ordination: ANTÔNIO KANDIR.

Minister of Mining and Energy: RAIMUNDO MENDES DE BRITO.

Minister of Culture: FRANCISCO CORREA WEFFORT.

Minister of the Environment, Water Resources and Amazonia: GUSTAVO KRAUSE GONÇALVES SOBRINHO.

Minister of Science and Technology: JOSÉ ISRAEL VARGAS.

Minister of Industry, Trade and Tourism: FRANCISCO OSWALDO NEVES DORNELLES.

Minister of the Navy: Adm. MAURO CÉSAR RODRÍGUES PEREIRA.

Minister of the Army: Gen. ZENILDO GONZAGA ZOROASTRO DE LUCENA.

Minister of the Air Force: Air Chief Marshal LÉLIO VIANA LOBO.

Minister (Extraordinary) for Sport: PELÉ (EDSON ARANTES DO NASCIMENTO).

Minister (Extraordinary) for Land Policy: RAÚL BELENS JUNGMAN PINTO.

Secretariat

Secretary of Communication of the Presidency: SÉRGIO SILVA DO AMARAL.

Secretary of Strategic Affairs: RONALDO MOTTA SARDENBERG.

MINISTRIES

Office of the President: Palácio do Planalto, Praça dos Três Poderes, 70150 Brasília, DF; tel. (61) 211-1221; telex 1451; fax (61) 226-7566.

Ministry of Administration: Esplanada dos Ministérios, Bloco C, 8° andar, Brasília, DF; tel. (61) 226-6432; telex 1158; fax (61) 226-3577.

Ministry of Agriculture and Supplies: Esplanada dos Ministérios, Bloco D, 8° andar, 70043 Brasília, DF; tel. (61) 226-5161; telex 1930; fax (61) 218-2586.

Ministry of the Air Force: Esplanada dos Ministérios, Bloco M, 8° andar, 70045-900 Brasília, DF; tel. (61) 223-3018; telex 1152; fax (61) 223-2592.

Ministry of the Army: Setor Militar Urbano, QG do Exercito, 70630 Brasília, DF; tel. (61) 223-3169; telex 3453; fax (61) 223-7019.

Ministry of Communications: Esplanada dos Ministérios, Bloco R, 8° andar, 70.000 Brasília, DF; tel. (61) 225-9446; fax (61) 226-3980.

Ministry of Culture: Esplanada dos Ministérios, Bloco B, 3° andar, 70068-900 Brasília, DF; tel. (61) 224-6114; telex 1066; fax (61) 225-9162.

Ministry of the Economy: Esplanada dos Ministérios, Bloco P, 5° andar, 70048 Brasília, DF; tel. (61) 314-2000; telex 1142; fax (61) 223-5239.

Ministry of Education and Sport: Esplanada dos Ministérios, Bloco L, 8° andar, 70047-900 Brasília, DF; tel. (61) 225-6515; telex 1068; fax (61) 223-0564.

Ministry of the Environment and Water Resources: SAIN, Av. L4 Norte, Edif. Sede Terreo, 70800 Brasília, DF; tel. (61) 226-8221; telex 2120; fax (61) 322-1058.

Ministry of Foreign Affairs: Palácio do Itamaraty, Esplanada dos Ministérios, 70170 Brasília, DF; tel. (61) 224-2773; telex 1148; fax (61) 226-1762.

Ministry of Health: Esplanada dos Ministérios, Bloco G, 5° andar, 70058 Brasília, DF; tel. (61) 223-3169; telex 4721; fax (61) 224-8747.

Ministry of Industry, Trade and Tourism: Esplanada dos Ministérios, Bloco J, 7° andar, sala 700, 70056-900 Brasília, DF; tel. (61) 325-2056; fax (61) 325-2063.

Ministry of Justice: Esplanada dos Ministérios, Bloco T, 4° andar, 70064-900 Brasília, DF; tel. (61) 226-4404; telex 1088; fax (61) 322-6817.

Ministry of Labour: Esplanada dos Ministérios, Bloco C, 8° andar, Brasília, DF; tel. (61) 226-6432; telex 1158; fax (61) 226-3577.

Ministry for Land Policy: Brasília, DF; tel. (61) 223-8852; fax (61) 226-3855.

Ministry of Mining and Energy: Esplanada dos Ministérios, Bloco U, 7° andar, 70000 Brasília, DF; tel. (61) 225-8106; telex 1147; fax (61) 225-5407.

Ministry of the Navy: Esplanada dos Ministérios, Bloco N, 2° andar, 70055-900 Brasília, DF; tel. (61) 223-6058; telex 1166; fax (61) 312-1202.

Ministry of Planning, the Budget and Co-ordination: Esplanada dos Ministérios, Bloco K, 70040-602 Brasília, DF; tel. (61) 215-4100; fax (61) 321-5292.

Ministry of Science and Technology: Esplanada dos Ministérios, Bloco E, 4° andar, 70062-900 Brasília, DF; tel. (61) 224-4364; telex 2882; fax (61) 225-7496.

Ministry of Social Welfare: Esplanada dos Ministérios, Bloco A, 6° andar, 70054-900 Brasília, DF; tel. (61) 224-7300; telex 1015; fax (61) 226-3861.

Ministry of Transport: Esplanada dos Ministérios, Bloco R, 70000 Brasília, DF; tel. (61) 218-6335; fax (61) 218-6315.

Secretariats

Secretariat of Communication of the Presidency: Brasília, DF; tel. (61) 315-1705; fax (61) 226-3861.

Secretariat of Strategic Affairs: Palácio do Planalto, Esplanada dos Ministérios, 70150 Brasília, DF; tel. (61) 226-6772; telex 1451; fax (61) 321-2466.

President and Legislature

PRESIDENT

Election, 3 October 1994

Candidate	Valid votes cast	% valid votes cast
Fernando Henrique Cardoso (PSDB)	34,377,055	54.28
Luiz Inácio 'Lula' da Silva (PT)	17,126,232	27.04
Enéas Ferreira Carneiro (Prona)	4,671,991	7.38
Orestes Quércia (PMDB)	2,773,784	4.38
Leonel Brizola (PDT)	2,016,335	3.18
Esperidão Amin (PPR)	1,740,203	2.75
Carlo Gomes (PRN)	387,923	0.61
Hernani Fortuna (PSC)	238,322	0.38
Total	63,331,845	100.00

CONGRESSO NACIONAL
(National Congress)

Câmara dos Deputados
(Chamber of Deputies)

President: Michel Temer (PMDB).

The Chamber has 513 members who hold office for a four-year term.

General Election, 3 October 1994

Party	Seats
Partido do Movimento Democrático Brasileiro (PMDB)	107
Partido da Frente Liberal (PFL)	89
Partido da Social Democracia Brasileira (PSDB)	64
Partido Progressista Reformador (PPR)	52
Partido dos Trabalhadores (PT)	49
Partido Progressista (PP)	35
Partido Democrático Trabalhista (PDT)	33
Partido Trabalhista Brasileiro (PTB)	31
Partido Liberal (PL)	14
Partido Socialista Brasileiro (PSB)	14
Partido Comunista do Brasil (PC do B)	10
Partido da Mobilização Nacional (PMN)	4
Partido Social-Democrático (PSD)	3
Partido Social Cristão (PSC)	3
Partido Popular Socialista (PPS)	2
Partido de Reconstrução Nacional (PRN)	1
Partido Verde (PV)	1
Partido Republicano Progressista (PRP)	1
Total	513

Senado Federal
(Federal Senate)

President: Antônio Carlos Magalhães (PFL).

The 81 members of the Senate are elected by the 26 States and the Federal District (three Senators for each) according to the principle of majority. The Senate's term of office is eight years, with elections after four years for one-third of the members and after another four years for the remaining two-thirds.

Following the elections of 3 October 1994, the PMDB were represented by 22 senators, the PFL by 19 and the PSDB by 10. The PT, the PPR, the PP, the PDT, the PTB, the PSB, the PL, the PPS and the PRN were also represented.

Governors

STATES

Acre: Orleir Cameli (PPR).

Alagoas: Divaldo Suruagy (PMDB).

Amapá: João Capiberibe (PSB).

Amazonas: Amazonino Mendes (PPR).

Bahia: Paulo Souto (PFL).

Ceará: Tasso Jereissati (PSDB).

Espírito Santo: Victor Buaiz (PT).

Goias: Maguito Vilela (PMDB).

Maranhão: Roseana Sarney (PFL).

Mato Grosso: Dante de Oliveira (PDT).

Mato Grosso do Sul: Wilson Martins (PMDB).

Minas Gerais: Eduardo Azeredo (PSDB).

Pará: Almir Gabriel (PSDB).

Paraíba: Antônio Mariz.

Paraná: Jaime Lerner (fmrly PDT).

Pernambuco: Miguel Arraes (PSB).

Piauí: Francisco Souza (PMDB).

Rio de Janeiro: Marcello Alencar (PSDB).

Rio Grande do Norte: Garibaldi Alves, Filho (PMDB).

Rio Grande do Sul: Antônio Brito (PMDB).

Rondônia: Valdir Raupp (PMDB).

Roraima: Neudo Campos (PMDB).

Santa Catarina: Paulo Afonso Vieira (PMDB).

São Paulo: Mário Covas (PSDB).

Sergipe: Albano Franco (PSDB).

Tocantins: Siquiera Campos (PPR).

FEDERAL DISTRICT

Brasília: Cristovão Buarque (PT).

Political Organizations

In May 1985 the National Congress approved a constitutional amendment providing for the free formation of political parties. The following parties are represented in Congress:

Partido Comunista do Brasil (PC do B): São Paulo, SP; tel. (11) 232-1622; fax (11) 606-4104; f. 1922; Leader Aldo Rebelo ; Sec.-Gen. João Amazonas; 185,000 mems.

Partido Democrático Trabalhista (PDT): Rua 7 de Setembro 141, 4°, 20050 Rio de Janeiro, RJ; f. 1980; formerly the PTB (Partido Trabalhista Brasileiro), renamed 1980 when that name was awarded to a dissident group following controversial judicial proceedings; member of Socialist International; Pres. Leonel Brizola; Gen. Sec. Vivaldo Barbosa.

Partido da Frente Liberal (PFL): Brasília, DF; f. 1984 by moderate members of the PDS and PMDB; Pres. Ricardo Fiuza; Gen. Sec. Saulo Queiroz.

Partido Liberal (PL): Brasília, DF; Pres. Alvaro Valle; Leader Valdemar Costa Neto.

Partido do Movimento Democrático Brasileiro (PMDB): f. 1980; moderate elements of former MDB; merged with Partido Popular February 1982; Pres. Antônio Paes de Andrade; Gen.-Sec. Tarcísio Delgado; factions include: the **Históricos** and the **Movimento da Unidade Progressiva (MUP).**

Partido Popular Socialista (PPS): Rua Coronel Lisboa 260, Vila Mariana, 04020-040, São Paulo, SP; tel. (11) 570-2182; fax (11) 549-9841; f. 1922; Pres. Roberto Freire.

Partido Progressista Brasileiro (PPB): Brasília, DF; f. 1995 by merger of Partido Progressista Reformador (PPR), Partido Progressista (PP) and the Partido Republicano Progressista (PRP); right-wing; Pres. Espiridião Amin.

Partido de Reconstrução Nacional (PRN): Brasília, DF; f. 1988; right-wing; Leader Fernando Collor de Mello.

Partido da Social Democracia Brasileira (PSDB): Brasília, DF; f. 1988; centre-left; formed by dissident members of the PMDB (incl. Históricos), PFL, PDS, PDT, PSB and PTB; Leader Artur de Tavola.

Partido Socialista Brasileiro (PSB): Brasília, DF; tel. (61) 318-6951; fax (61) 318-2104; f. 1947; Pres. Miguel Arraes; Sec.-Gen. Renato Soares.

Partido dos Trabalhadores (PT): Congresso Nacional, 70160, Brasília, DF; tel. (61) 224-1699; f. 1980; first independent labour party; associated with the *autêntico* branch of the trade union movement; 350,000 mems; Pres. José Dirceu de Oliveira e Silva; Vice-Pres. Jacó Bittar.

Partido Trabalhista Brasileiro (PTB): Brasília, DF; f. 1980; Pres. Luís Gonzaga de Paiva Muniz; Gen. Sec. José Correia Pedroso, Filho.

Other political parties represented in the Congresso Nacional include the Partido Social Cristão (PSC), the Partido Social-Democrático (PSD), the Partido Verde (PV) and the Partido da Mobilização Nacional (PMN).

Diplomatic Representation

EMBASSIES IN BRAZIL

Algeria: SHIS, QI 09, Conj. 13, Casa 01, Lago Sul, 71625-010 Brasília, DF; tel. (61) 248-4039; telex 1278; fax (61) 248-4691; Ambassador: HOCINE MEGHALOUI.

Angola: SHIS, QI 07, Conj. 11, Casa 9, Brasília, DF; tel. (61) 248-4489; fax (61) 248-1567; telex 4971; Ambassador: OSWALD DE JESÚS VAN-DÚNEM.

Argentina: SHIS, QL 02, Conj. 1, Casa 19, Lago Sul, 70442-900 Brasília, DF; tel. (61) 356-3000; fax (61) 365-2109; Ambassador: JORGE HUGO HERRERA VEGAS.

Australia: SHIS, QI 09, Conj. 16, Casa 01, Lago Sul, 70469 Brasília, DF; tel. (61) 248-5569; fax (61) 248-1066; e-mail embaustr@nutecnet .com.br; Ambassador: HAMILTON CHARLES MOTT.

Austria: SES, Quadra 811, Av. das Nações, Lote 40, CP 07-1215, 70426-900 Brasília, DF; tel. (61) 243-3111; telex 1202; fax (61) 443-5233; Ambassador: Dr MANFRED ORTNER.

Bangladesh: SHIS, QL 10, Conj. 1, Casa 17, 70468-900 Brasília, DF; tel. (61) 248-4830; fax (61) 248-4609; e-mail bdoot.bzl@persocom .com.br; Ambassador: AMSA AMIN.

Belgium: SES, Av. das Nações, Lote 32, 70422-900 Brasília, DF; tel. (61) 243-1133; telex 1261; fax (61) 243-1219; Ambassador: FRANZ MICHILS.

Bolivia: SHIS, QL 04, Bloco E, 70470-900 Brasília, DF; tel. (61) 322-4227; telex 1946; fax (61) 322-4148; Ambassador: GONZALO MONTENEGRO IRIGOYEN.

Bulgaria: SEN, Av. das Nações, Lote 8, 70432-900 Brasília, DF; tel. (61) 223-6193; telex 1305; fax (61) 226-7239; Ambassador: TCHAVDAR MLADENOV NIKOLOV.

Cameroon: SHIS, QI 09, Conj. 07, Casa 01, Lago Sul, 71625-070 Brasília, DF; tel. (61) 248-4433; telex 2235; Ambassador: MARTIN NGUELE MBARGA.

Canada: SES, Av. das Nações, Lote 16, 70410-900 Brasília, DF; CP 00961, 70359-970 Brasília, DF; tel. (61) 321-2171; telex 1296; fax (61) 321-4529; Ambassador: NANCY M. STILES.

Cape Verde: SHIS, QL 6, Conj. 4, Casa 15, 71260-045 Brasília, DF; tel. (61) 365-3190; fax (61) 365-3191; e-mail chelu@rudah.com.br; Ambassador: JOSÉ EDUARDO BARBOSA.

Chile: SES, Av. das Nações, Lote 11, 70407 Brasília, DF; tel. (61) 226-5762; telex 1075; fax (61) 225-5478; Ambassador: HERALDO MUÑOZ.

China, People's Republic: SES, Av. das Nações, Lote 51, 70443-900 Brasília, DF; tel. (61) 346-4436; fax (61) 346-3299; telex 1300; Ambassador: LI GUOXIN.

Colombia: SES, Av. das Nações, Lote 10, 70444-900 Brasília, DF; tel. (61) 226-8997; telex 1458; fax (61) 224-4732; Ambassador: MARIO GALOFRE CANO.

Congo, Democratic Republic: SHIS, QI 09, Conj. 8, Casa 20, Lago Sul, CP 07-0041, 71600 Brasília, DF; tel. (61) 248-3348; telex 1435; Chargé d'affaires: BOIDOMBE MANZIJI.

Costa Rica: SHIS, QL 10, Conj. 4, Casa 03, Lago Sul, 71630-045 Brasília, DF; tel. (61) 248-7656; telex 1690; fax (61) 248-6234; e-mail embrica@solar.com.br; Ambassador: JAVIER SANCHO BONILLA.

Côte d'Ivoire: SEN, Av. das Nações, Lote 9, 70473-900 Brasília, DF; tel. (61) 321-4656; telex 1095; fax (61) 321-1306; Ambassador: DJIBO FELICIEN ABDOULAYE.

Croatia: SHIS QI 9, Conj. 11, Casa 3, 71625-110 Brasília, DF; tel. (61) 248-0610; fax (61) 248-1708; Ambassador: LUKA MESTROVIĆ.

Cuba: SHIS, QI 05, Conj. 18, Casa 01, Lago Sul, 70481-900 Brasília, DF; tel. (61) 248-4710; fax (61) 248-6778; Ambassador: RAMÓN SÁNCHEZ-PAROD.

Czech Republic: Via L-3/Sul, Q-805, Lote 21, 70414, CP 70414-900 Brasília, DF; tel. (61) 242-7785; fax 242-7833; Ambassador: LADISLAV SKERIK.

Denmark: SES, Av. das Nações, Lote 26, 70416-900 Brasília, DF; tel. (61) 242-8188; telex 1494; fax (61) 244-5245; Ambassador: ANITA HUGAU.

Dominican Republic: SHIS, QL 8, Conj. 5, Casa 14, Lago Sul, 71620-255 Brasília, DF; tel. (61) 248-1405; fax (61) 248-1405; Ambassador: CIRO AMAURY DARGAM CRUZ.

Ecuador: SHIS, QI 11, Conj. 9, Casa 24, 71625-290 Brasília, DF; tel. (61) 248-5560; telex 1290; fax (61) 248-1290; e-mail embec@solar .com.br; Ambassador: CÉSAR VALDIVIESO CHIRIBOGA.

Egypt: SEN, Av. das Nações, Lote 12, 70435-900 Brasília, DF; tel. (61) 225-8517; telex 1387; fax (61) 223-5812; e-mail embegypt@brnet .com.br; Ambassador: EL SAYED RAMZI EZEDIM RAMZI.

El Salvador: SHIS, QI 07, Conj. 6, Casa 14, 71615-260 Brasília, DF; tel. (61) 248-3788; fax (61) 248-5636; Ambassador: GUILLERMO IRAHETA BASIL.

Finland: SES, Av. das Nações, Lote 27, 70417-900 Brasília, DF; tel. (61) 248-0017; telex 1155; fax (61) 364-2251; e-mail suomi@ tba.com.br; Ambassador: ASKO NUMMINEN.

France: SES, Av. das Nações, Lote 4, 70404-900 Brasília, DF; tel. (61) 312-9100; telex 1078; fax (61) 312-9108; Ambassador: PHILIPPE LECOURTIER.

Gabon: SHIS QI 9, Conji. 11, Casa 24, 71615-300, Brasília, DF; tel. (61) 248-3536; fax (61) 248-2241; Ambassador: MARCEL ODONGUI-BONNARD.

Germany: SES, Av. das Nações, Lote 25, 70415-900 Brasília, DF; tel. (61) 244-7273; telex 1198; fax (61) 244-6063; Ambassador: CLAUS J. DUISBERG.

Ghana: SHIS, QL 10, Conj. 8, Casa 2, CP 07-0456, 70466-900 Brasília, DF; tel. (61) 248-6047; telex 1024; fax (61) 248-7913; Ambassador: (vacant).

Greece: SHIS, QL 04, Conj. 1, Casa 18, 70461-900 Brasília, DF; tel. (61) 365-3090; telex 611843; fax (61) 3653093; e-mail joul@ ssopnutecnet.com.br; internet http://www.emb.gzecik.org; Ambassador: EMMANUEL WLANDIS.

Guatemala: SHIS, QL 08, Conj. 5, Casa 11, 70460-900 Brasília, DF; tel. (61) 248-3318; fax (61) 248-4383; Ambassador: MARIO MARROQUÍN NAJERA.

Guyana: SBN, Quadra 2, Bloco J, Edif. Paulo Maurício, 13° andar, salas 1310–1315, 70438-900 Brasília, DF; tel. (61) 224-9229; fax (61) 220-3022; Ambassador: IVAN B. EVELYN, Sr.

Haiti: SHIS, QI 17, Conj. 4, Casa 19, Lago Sul, 70465-900 Brasília, DF; tel. (61) 248-6860; fax (61) 248-7472; Chargé d'affaires: JEAN-BAPTISTE HARVEL.

Holy See: SES, Av. das Nações, Lote 1, CP 07-0153, 70359-970 Brasília, DF (Apostolic Nunciature); tel. (61) 223-0794; telex 2125; fax (61) 224-9365; e-mail nunapost@ucb.br; Apostolic Nuncio: Most Rev. ALFIO RAPISARDA, Titular Archbishop of Cannae.

Honduras: SHIS, QI 05, Conj. 13, Casa 1, 70464-900 Brasília, DF; tel. (61) 248-1200; telex 3736; fax (61) 248-1425; Ambassador: CARLOS MARTÍNEZ CASTILLO.

Hungary: SES, Av. das Nações, Lote 19, 70413-900 Brasília, DF; tel. (61) 243-0822; telex 1285; fax (61) 244-3426; e-mail embhung@ uninet.com.br; Ambassador: GÁBOR TÓTH.

India: SHIS, QI 9, Conj. 9, Casa 7, 71625-090 Brasília, DF; tel. (61) 248-4006; telex 1245; fax (61) 248-7849; Ambassador: ISHRAT AZIZ.

Indonesia: SES, Av. das Nações, Lote 20, Q. 805, 70200 Brasília, DF; tel. (61) 243-0233; telex 2541; fax (61) 243-1713; Ambassador: ADIAN SILALAHI.

Iran: SES, Av. das Nações, Lote 31, 70421 Brasília, DF; tel. (61) 242-5733; telex 1347; fax (61) 244-9640; Ambassador: BAHMAN TAHERIAN MOBAREKAH.

Iraq: SES, Av. das Nações, Lote 64, Brasília, DF; tel. (61) 346-2822; telex 1331; fax (61) 346-7034; Ambassador: OAIS TAWFIG ALMUKHFAR.

Israel: SES, Av. das Nações, Lote 38, 70424-900 Brasília, DF; tel. (61) 244-7675; telex 1093; fax (61) 244-6129; e-mail embisrae@solar .com.br; Ambassador: YAACOV KEINAN.

Italy: SES, Av. das Nações, Lote 30, 70420 Brasília, DF; tel. (61) 244-0044; telex 1488; fax (61) 244-0034; e-mail itu.org.br/itembassy/ busit.html; Ambassador: MICHELANGELO JACOBUCCI.

Japan: SES, Av. das Nações, Lote 39, 70425-900 Brasília, DF; tel. (61) 242-6866; telex 1376; fax (61) 242-0738; Ambassador: CHIHIRO TSUKADA.

Jordan: SHIS, QI 9, Conj. 18, Casa 14, 70483-900 Brasília, DF; tel. (61) 248-5407; fax (61) 248-1698; Ambassador: AZMI ABBAS MIRZA.

Korea, Republic: SEN, Av. das Nações, Lote 14, 70436-900 Brasília, DF; tel. (61) 321-2500; fax (61) 321-2508; Ambassador: SAM HOON KIM.

Kuwait: SHIS, QI 05, Chácara 30, 71600-750 Brasília, DF; tel. (61) 248-1633; telex 1367; fax (61) 248-09691; Ambassador: ABDUL AZIZ AL DU'AIJ.

Lebanon: SES, Av. das Nações, Q- 805, Lote 17, 70411-900 Brasília, DF; tel. (61) 242-4801; telex 1295; fax (61) 242-2327; Ambassador: GAZI CHIDIAC.

Libya: SHIS, QI 15, Chácara 26, CP 3505, 70462-900 Brasília, DF; tel. (61) 248-6710; telex 1099; fax (61) 248-0598; Head of People's Bureau: ALI SULEIMAN AL-AUJALI.

Malaysia: SHIS, QI 05, Chácara 62, Lago Sul, 70477-900 Brasília, DF; tel. (61) 248-5008; telex 3666; fax (61) 248-6307; Ambassador: ZAINAL ABIDIN BIN MOHD ZAIN.

Mexico: SES, Av. das Nações, Lote 18, 70412-900 Brasília, DF; tel. (61) 244-1011; fax (61) 443-6275; Ambassador: EUGENIO ANGUIANO ROCH.

Morocco: Av. das Nacões, Lote 2, 70432-900 Brasília, DF; tel. (61) 321-4487; fax (61) 321-0745; internet http://www.mincom.gov.ma; Ambassador: LARBI REFFOUH.

Mozambique: SHIS, QL 12, Conj. 7, Casa 9, 71630-275 Brasília, DF; tel. (61) 248-4222; fax (61) 248-3917; Ambassador: Felizarda Isaura Monteiro.

Myanmar: SHIS, QL 8, Conj. 4, Casa 5, 71620-245 Brasília, DF; tel. (61) 248-3747; fax (61) 248-1922; e-mail mebrsl@brnet.com.br; Ambassador: Kyar Nyo Chit Pe.

Netherlands: SES, Av. das Nações, Quadra 801, Lote 5, CP 07-0098, 70359-970 Brasília, DF; tel. (61) 321-4769; telex 1492; fax (61) 321-1518; Ambassador: Franciscus B. A. M. van Haren.

Nicaragua: SHIS, QI 15, Conj. 07, Casa 14, Lago Sul, 70365-270 Brasília, DF; tel. (61) 248-5366; fax (61) 248-3148; telex 2495; Ambassador: Domingos Salinas Alvarado.

Nigeria: SEN, Av. das Nações, Lote 05, CP 11-1190, 70432 Brasília, DF; tel. (61) 226-1717; telex 1315; fax (61) 224-9830; Ambassador: Dr Patrick Dele Cole.

Norway: SES, Av. das Nações, Lote 28, CP 07-0670, 70359-970 Brasília, DF; tel. (61) 243-8720; telex 1265; fax (61) 242-7989; Ambassador: Liv A. Kerr.

Pakistan: SHIS, QI 05, Conj. 14, Casa 21, 71615-140 Brasília, DF; tel. (61) 364-1632; telex 2252; fax (61) 248-3484; Ambassador: Samuel Thomas Joshua.

Panama: SHIS, QI 11, Conj. 6, Casa 6, 71625-260 Brasília, DF; tel. (61) 248-7309; fax (61) 248-2834; e-mail empanama@nettur.com.br; Ambassador: Oswaldo Fernández Echeverria.

Paraguay: SES, Av. das Nações, Lote 42, CP 14-2314, 70427-900 Brasília, DF; tel. (61) 242-3742; telex 1845; fax (61) 242-4605; Ambassador: Dido Florentín Bogado.

Peru: SES, Av. das Nações, Lote 43, 70428-900 Brasília, DF; tel. (61) 242-9933; fax (61) 244-9344; e-mail emb-peru@nutecnet.com.br; Ambassador: Alfonso Rivero Monsalve.

Philippines: SEN, Av. das Nações, Lote 1, 70431 Brasília, DF; tel. (61) 223-5143; telex 2733; fax (61) 226-7411; e-mail pr@pop.persocom.com.br; Ambassador: Francisco L. Benedicto.

Poland: SES, Av. das Nações, Lote 33, 70423-900 Brasília, DF; tel. (61) 243-3438; telex 1165; fax (61) 242-8543; Ambassador: Bogusław Zakrzewski.

Portugal: SES, Av. das Nações, Lote 2, 70402-900 Brasília, DF; tel. (61) 321-3434; telex 1033; fax (61) 225-5296; Ambassador: Pedro Ribeiro de Menezes.

Romania: SEN, Av. das Nações, Lote 6, 70456 Brasília, DF; tel. (61) 226-0746; fax (61) 226-6629; Ambassador: Ioan Bar.

Russia: SES, Av. das Nações, Quadra 801, Lote A, 70476-900 Brasília, DF; tel. (61) 223-3094; telex 1273; fax (61) 223-5094; e-mail brnet.com.br/pages/embrus; Ambassador: Iosif N. Podrazhanets.

Saudi Arabia: SHIS, QL 10, Conj. 9, Casa 20, 70471 Brasília, DF; tel. (61) 248-3523; telex 1656; fax (61) 284-2905; Ambassador: Yahya Ahmed al Yahya.

Slovakia: A/C, W/3 Sul 508, CP 880, 70359-970 Brasília, DF; tel. (61) 243-1263; fax (61) 243-1267; Ambassador: Branislav Hitka.

South Africa: SES, Av. das Nações, Lote 6, CP 11-1170, 70406 Brasília, DF; tel. (61) 223-4873; telex 1683; fax (61) 322-8491; Ambassador: C. J. B. Wessels.

Spain: SES, Av. das Nações, Lote 44, 70429-900 Brasília, DF; tel. (61) 244-2121; telex 1313; fax (61) 242-1781; Ambassador: César Alba y Fuster.

Suriname: SHIS, QI 09, Conj. 8, Casa 24, 70457-900 Brasília, DF; tel. (61) 248-6706; telex 1414; fax (61) 248-3791; Ambassador: Rupert L. Christopher.

Sweden: SES, Av. das Nações, Lote 29, 70419-900 Brasília, DF; tel. (61) 243-1444; telex 1225; fax (61) 243-1187; e-mail swebra@tba.com.br; Ambassador: Christer Manhusen.

Switzerland: SES, Av. das Nações, Lote 41, 70448 Brasília, DF; CP 08671, 70312-970 Brasília, DF; tel. (61) 244-5500; fax (61) 244-5711; e-mail swissembra@brasilia.com.br; Ambassador: Oscar Knapp.

Syria: SEN, Av. das Nações, Lote 11, 70434-900 Brasília, DF; tel. (61) 226-0970; telex 1721; fax (61) 223-2595; Ambassador: Muhammad Taufik Juhani.

Thailand: SEN, Av. das Nações Norte, Lote 10, 70433-900 Brasília, DF; tel. (61) 224-6943; telex 3763; fax (61) 321-2994; Ambassador: Saksit Srisorn.

Togo: SHIS, QI 11, Conj. 9, Casa 10, 70478-900 Brasília, DF; tel. (61) 248-4209; telex 1837; fax (61) 248-4752; Ambassador: Lambana Tchaou.

Trinidad and Tobago: SHIS, QL 08, Conj. 4, Casa 05, 71600 Brasília, DF; tel. (61) 365-1132; telex 1844; fax (61) 365-1733; e-mail trinbago@tba.com.br; Ambassador: Robert Torry.

Tunisia: SHIS, QI 19, Conj. 16, Casa 20, 71625-160 Brasília, DF; tel. (61) 248-3725; fax (61) 248-7355; Ambassador: Abbes Mohsen.

Turkey: SES, Av. das Nações, Lote 23, 70452-900 Brasília, DF; tel. (61) 242-1850; telex 611663; fax (61) 242-1448; e-mail emb.turquia@nrp.com.br; Ambassador: Dogan Alpan.

Ukraine: SHIS, QL 6, Conj. 2, Casa 17, 71620-025 Brasília, DF; tel. (61) 365-3898; fax (61) 365-3898; e-mail brucemb@brnet.com.br; Ambassador: Oleksandr Nikonenko.

United Arab Emirates: SHIS, QI 5, Chácara 18, 70486-901 Brasília, DF; tel. (61) 248-0717; fax (61) 248-7543; Ambassador: Ali Mubarak Ahmed al-Mansoori.

United Kingdom: SES, Quadra 801, Conj. K, Lote 8, CP 07-0586, 70408-900 Brasília, DF; tel. (61) 225-2710; telex 1360; fax (61) 225-1777; Ambassador: Keith Haskell.

USA: SES, Av. das Nações, Lote 3, 70403-900 Brasília, DF; tel. (61) 321-7272; telex 41167; fax (61) 225-9136; Ambassador: Melvyn Levitsky.

Uruguay: SES, Av. das Nações, Lote 14, 70450-900 Brasília, DF; tel. (61) 322-1200; fax (61) 322-6534; e-mail urubras@tba.com.br; Ambassador: Mario C. Fernández.

Venezuela: SES, Av. das Nações, Lote 13, Q-803, 70451-900 Brasília, DF; tel. (61) 223-9325; telex 1325; fax (61) 226-5633; e-mail embvenbr@nutecnet.com.br; Ambassador: Milos Alcalay.

Yugoslavia: SES, Av. das Nações, Q-803, Lote 15, 70409-900 Brasília, DF; CP 1240, 70000 Brasília, DF; tel. (61) 223-7272; telex 2053; fax (61) 223-8462; e-mail embiugos@nutecnet.com.br; Ambassador: David Dasić.

Judicial System

The judiciary powers of the State are held by the following: the Supreme Federal Tribunal, the Higher Tribunal of Justice, the five Regional Federal Tribunals and Federal Judges, the Higher Labour Tribunal, the 24 Regional Labour Tribunals, the Conciliation and Judgment Councils and Labour Judges, the Higher Electoral Tribunal, the 27 Regional Electoral Tribunals, the Electoral Judges and Electoral Councils, the Higher Military Tribunal, the Military Tribunals and Military Judges, the Tribunals of the States and Judges of the States, the Tribunal of the Federal District and of the Territories and Judges of the Federal District and of the Territories.

The Supreme Federal Tribunal comprises 11 ministers, nominated by the President and approved by the Senado. Its most important role is to rule on the final interpretation of the Constitution. The Supreme Federal Tribunal has the power to declare an act of Congress void if it is unconstitutional. It judges offences committed by persons such as the President, the Vice-President, members of the Congresso Nacional, Ministers of State, its own members, the Attorney General, judges of other higher courts, and heads of permanent diplomatic missions. It also judges cases of litigation between the Union and the States, between the States, or between foreign nations and the Union or the States; disputes as to jurisdiction between higher Tribunals, or between the latter and any other court, in cases involving the extradition of criminals, and others related to the writs of habeas corpus and habeas data, and in other cases.

The Higher Tribunal of Justice comprises at least 33 members, appointed by the President and approved by the Senado. Its jurisdiction includes the judgment of offences committed by State Governors. The Regional Federal Tribunals comprise at least seven judges, recruited when possible in the respective region and appointed by the President of the Republic. The Higher Labour Tribunal comprises 27 members, appointed by the President and approved by the Senado. The judges of the Regional Labour Tribunals are also appointed by the President. The Higher Electoral Tribunal comprises at least seven members: three judges from among those of the Supreme Federal Tribunal, two from the Higher Tribunal of Justice (elected by secret ballot) and two lawyers appointed by the President. The Regional Electoral Tribunals are also composed of seven members. The Higher Military Tribunal comprises 15 life members, appointed by the President and approved by the Senate; three from the navy, four from the army, three from the air force and five civilian members. The States are responsible for the administration of their own justice, according to the principles established by the Constitution.

THE SUPREME FEDERAL TRIBUNAL

Supreme Federal Tribunal: Praça dos Três Poderes, 70175-900 Brasília, DF; tel. (61) 316-5000; telex 1125; fax (61) 316-5483.

President: José Celso de Mello, Filho.

Vice-President: Carlos Mário da Silva Velloso.

Justices: José Carlos Moreira Alves, José Néri da Silveira, Ilmar Nascimento Galvão, Maurício José Corrêa, Sydney Sanches, Marco Aurélio Mendes de Farias Mello, Luiz Octavio Pires e Albuquerque Gallotti, José Paulo Sepúlveda Pertence, Nelson de Azevedo Jobim.

Procurator-General: Geraldo Brindeiro.

Director-General (Secretariat): MARLENE FREITAS RODRIGUES ALVES.

Religion

CHRISTIANITY

Conselho Nacional de Igrejas Cristãs do Brasil—CONIC (National Council of Christian Churches in Brazil): Rua Senhor dos Passos 202, CP 2876, 90020-180 Porto Alegre, RS; tel. (51) 224-5724; fax (51) 228-8829; f. 1982; seven mem. churches; Pres. GLAUCO SOARES DE LIMA; Exec. Sec. P. ERVINO SCHMIDT.

The Roman Catholic Church

Brazil comprises 38 archdioceses, 201 dioceses (including one each for Catholics of the Maronite, Melkite and Ukrainian Rites), 13 territorial prelatures and two territorial abbacies. The Archbishop of São Sebastião do Rio de Janeiro is also the Ordinary for Catholics of other Oriental Rites in Brazil (estimated at 10,000 in 1994). The great majority of Brazil's population are adherents of the Roman Catholic Church (around 106m. at the time of the 1980 census), although a report published by the Brazilian weekly, *Veja*, in July 1989 concluded that since 1950 the membership of non-Catholic Christian Churches had risen from 3% to 6% of the total population, while membership of the Roman Catholic Church had fallen from 93% to 89% of Brazilians.

Bishops' Conference: Conferência Nacional dos Bispos do Brasil, SE/Sul Q 801, Conj. B, CP 02067, 70259-970 Brasília, DF; tel. (61) 225-2955; fax (61) 225-4361; e-mail cnbb@embratel.net.br; f. 1980 (statutes approved 1986); Pres. Cardinal LUCAS MOREIRA NEVES, Archbishop of São Salvador da Bahia, BA; Sec.-Gen. RAYMUNDO DAMASCENO ASSIS.

Latin Rite

Archbishop of São Salvador da Bahia, BA: Cardinal LUCAS MOREIRA NEVES, Primate of Brazil, Palácio da Sé, Praça da Sé 1, 40020-210 Salvador, BA; tel. (71) 247-4346; fax (71) 336-4039.

Archbishop of Aparecida, SP: Cardinal ALOÍSIO LORSCHEIDER.

Archbishop of Aracajú, SE: LUCIANO JOSÉ CABRAL DUARTE.

Archbishop of Belém do Pará, PA: VICENTE JOAQUIM ZICO.

Archbishop of Belo Horizonte, MG: Cardinal SERAFIM FERNANDES DE ARAÚJO.

Archbishop of Botucatú, SP: ANTÔNIO MARIA MUCCIOLO.

Archbishop of Brasília, DF: Cardinal JOSÉ FREIRE FALCÃO.

Archbishop of Campinas, SP: GILBERTO PEREIRA LOPES.

Archbishop of Campo Grande, MS: VITÓRIO PAVANELLO.

Archbishop of Cascavel, PR: LÚCIO IGNÁCIO BAUMGAERTNER.

Archbishop of Cuiabá, MT: BONIFÁCIO PICCININI.

Archbishop of Curitiba, PR: PEDRO ANTÔNIO MARCHETTI FEDALTO.

Archbishop of Diamantina, MG: GERALDO MAJELA REIS.

Archbishop of Florianópolis, SC: EUSÉBIO OSCAR SCHEID.

Archbishop of Fortaleza, CE: CLÁUDIO HUMMES.

Archbishop of Goiânia, GO: ANTÔNIO RIBEIRO DE OLIVEIRA.

Archbishop of Juiz de Fora, MG: CLÓVIS FRAINER.

Archbishop of Londrina, PR: ALBANO BORTOLETTO CAVALLIN.

Archbishop of Maceió, AL: EDVALDO GONÇALVES AMARAL.

Archbishop of Manaus, AM: LUIZ SOARES VIEIRA.

Archbishop of Mariana, MG: LUCIANO P. MENDES DE ALMEIDA.

Archbishop of Maringá, PR: JAIME LUIZ COELHO.

Archbishop of Natal, RN: HEITOR DE ARAÚJO SALES.

Archbishop of Niterói, RJ: CARLOS ALBERTO ETCHANDY GIMENO NAVARRO.

Archbishop of Olinda e Recife, PE: JOSÉ CARDOSO SOBRINHO.

Archbishop of Palmas, PR: ALBERTO TAVEIRA CORRÊA.

Archbishop of Paraíba, PB: MARCELO PINTO CARVALHEIRA.

Archbishop of Porto Alegre, RS: ALTAMIRO ROSSATO.

Archbishop of Porto Velho, RO: JOSÉ MARTINS DA SILVA.

Archbishop of Pouso Alegre, MG: RICARDO PEDRO PINTO, Filho.

Archbishop of Ribeirão Prêto, SP: ARNALDO RIBEIRO.

Archbishop of São Luís do Maranhão, MA: PAULO EDUARDO DE ANDRADE PONTE.

Archbishop of São Paulo, SP: Cardinal PAULO EVARISTO ARNS.

Archbishop of São Sebastião do Rio de Janeiro, RJ: Cardinal EUGÊNIO DE ARAÚJO SALES.

Archbishop of Sorocaba, SP: JOSÉ LAMBERT.

Archbishop of Teresina, PI: MIGUEL FENELON CÂMARA, Filho.

Archbishop of Uberaba, MG: ALOISIO ROQUE OPPERMANN.

Archbishop of Vitória, ES: SILVESTRE LUÍS SCANDIAN.

Maronite Rite

Bishop of Nossa Senhora do Líbano em São Paulo, SP: JOSEPH MAHFOUZ.

Melkite Rite

Bishop of Nossa Senhora do Paraíso em São Paulo, SP: PIERRE MOUALLEM.

Ukrainian Rite

Bishop of São João Batista em Curitiba, PR: EFRAIM BASÍLIO KREVEY.

The Anglican Communion

Anglicans form the Episcopal Anglican Church of Brazil (Igreja Episcopal Anglicana do Brasil), comprising seven dioceses.

Igreja Episcopal Anglicana do Brasil: CP 11-510, 90841-970 Porto Alegre, RS; tel. (51) 336-0651; fax (51) 336-5087; f. 1890; 95,000 mems (1994); Primate Most Rev. GLAUCO SOARES DE LIMA, Bishop of São Paulo-Brazil; Gen. Sec. Rev. MAURICIO J. A. DE ANDRADE.

Protestant Churches

Igreja Cristã Reformada do Brasil: CP 2808, 01000 São Paulo, SP; Pres. Rev. JANOS APOSTOL.

Igreja Evangélica de Confissão Luterana no Brasil (IECLB): Rua Senhor dos Passos 202, 2° andar, CP 2876, 90020-180 Porto Alegre, RS; tel. (51) 221-3433; fax (51) 225-7244; f. 1949; 870,000 mems; Pres. Pastor HUBERTO KIRCHHEIM.

Igreja Evangélica Congregacional do Brasil: CP 414, 98700 Ijuí, RS; tel. (55) 332-4656; f. 1942; 41,000 mems, 310 congregations; Pres. Rev. H. HARTMUT W. HACHTMANN.

Igreja Evangélica Luterana do Brasil: Rua Cel. Lucas de Oliveira 894, CP 1076, 90001-970 Porto Alegre, RS; tel. (51) 332-2111; fax (51) 332-8145; e-mail ielb@luther.ulbra.tche.br; f. 1904; 207,000 mems; Pres. LEOPOLDO HEIMANN.

Igreja Metodista do Brasil: General Communication Secretariat, Rua Artur Azevedo 1192, Apdo 81, Pinheiros, 05404 São Paulo, SP; Exec. Sec. Dr ONÉSIMO DE OLIVEIRA CARDOSO.

Igreja Presbiteriana Unida do Brasil (IPU): CP 01-212, 29001-970 Vitória, ES; tel. (27) 222-8024; f. 1978; Sec. PAULO RÜCKERT.

BAHÁ'Í FAITH

Bahá'í Community of Brazil: SHIS, QL 08, Conj. 2, Casa 15, 71620-285, Brasília, DF; CP 7035, 71619-970 Brasília, DF; tel. (61) 364-3597; fax (61) 364-3470; e-mail bahai@ax.apc.org; f. 1921; Sec. GUITTY M. MILANI.

BUDDHISM

Federação das Seitas Budistas do Brasil: Av. Paulo Ferreira 1133, 02915-100, São Paulo, SP; tel. (11) 876-5771; fax (11) 877-8687.

Sociedade Budista do Brasil (Rio Buddhist Vihara): Dom Joaquim Mamede 45, Lagoinha, Santa Tereza, 20241-390 Rio de Janeiro, RJ; tel. (21) 205-4400; f. 1972; Principal Dr PUHULWELLE VIPASSI.

The Press

The most striking feature of the Brazilian press is the relatively small circulation of newspapers in comparison with the size of the population. The newspapers with the largest circulations are *O Día* (250,000), *O Globo* (350,000), *Fôlha de São Paulo* (560,000), and *O Estado de São Paulo* (242,000). The low circulation is mainly owing to high costs resulting from distribution difficulties. In consequence there are no national newspapers. In 1996 a total of 380 daily newspaper titles were published in Brazil.

DAILY NEWSPAPERS

Belém, PA

O Liberal: Rua Gaspar Viana 253, 66020 Belém, PA; tel. (91) 222-3000; telex 1825; fax (91) 224-1906; f. 1946; Pres. LUCIDEA MAIORANA; circ. 20,000.

Belo Horizonte, MG

Diário da Tarde: Rua Goiás 36, 30190 Belo Horizonte, MG; tel. (31) 273-2322; telex 3770; fax (31) 273-4400; f. 1931; evening; Dir-Gen. PAULO C. DE ARAÚJO; total circ. 150,000.

Diário de Minas: Rua Francisco Salles 540, 30150-220 Belo Horizonte, MG; tel. (31) 222-5622; telex 1264; f. 1949; Pres. MARCO AURÍLIO F. CARONE; circ. 50,000.

Diário do Comércio: Av. Américo Vespúcio 1660; 31.230 Belo Horizonte, MG; tel. (31) 469-1011; telex 2126; fax (31) 469-1080; f. 1932; Pres. JOSÉ COSTA.

Estado de Minas: Rua Goiás 36, 30190 Belo Horizonte, MG; tel. (31) 273-2322; telex 3770; fax (31) 273-4400; f. 1928; morning; independent; Pres. PAULO C. DE ARAÚJO; circ. 65,000.

Blumenau, SC

Jornal de Santa Catarina: Rua São Paulo 1120, 89010 Blumenau, SC; tel. (473) 26-6411; telex 1343; f. 1971; Dir PAULO A. MALBU, Filho; circ. 25,000.

Brasília, DF

Correio Brasiliense: SIG, Q2, Lotes 300/340, 70610-901 Brasília, DF; tel. (61) 321-1314; telex 1727; fax (61) 321-2856; f. 1960; Dir-Gen. PAULO C. DE ARAÚJO; circ. 30,000.

Jornal de Brasília: SIG, Trecho 1, Lotes 585/645, 70610-400 Brasília, DF; tel. (61) 225-2515; telex 1208; f. 1972; Dir-Gen. FERNANDO CÔMA; circ. 25,000.

Campinas, SP

Correio Popular: Rua Conceição 124, 13010-902 Campinas, SP; tel (192) 32-8588; telex 7694; fax (192) 31-8152; f. 1927; Pres. SYLVINO DE GODOY NETO; circ. 40,000.

Curitiba, PR

O Estado do Paraná: Rua João Tschannerl 800, 80820-000 Curitiba, PR; tel. (41) 335-8811; telex 5291; fax (41) 335-2838; f. 1951; Pres. PAULO CRUZ PIMENTEL; circ. 15,000.

Gazeta do Povo: Praça Carlos Gomes 4, 80010 Curitiba, PR; tel. (41) 224-0522; telex 6520; fax (41) 225-6848; f. 1919; Pres. FRANCISCO CUNHA PEREIRA; circ. 40,000.

Tribuna do Paraná: Rua João Tschannerl 800, 80820-010 Curitiba PR; tel. (41) 335-8811; telex 5388; fax (41) 335-2838; f. 1956; Pres. PAULO CRUZ PIMENTEL; circ. 15,000.

Florianópolis, SC

O Estado: Rodovia SC-401, Km 3, 88030 Florianópolis, SC; tel. (482) 388-8888; telex 177; fax (482) 380-0711; f. 1915; Pres. JOSÉ MATUSALÉM COMELLI; circ. 20,000.

Fortaleza, CE

Jornal O Povo: Av. Aguanambi 282, 60055 Fortaleza, CE; tel. (85) 211-9666; telex 1107; fax (85) 231-5792; f. 1928; evening; Pres. DEMÓCRITO ROCHA DUMMAR; circ. 20,000.

Tribuna do Ceará: Av. Desemb. Moreira 2900, 60170 Fortaleza, CE; tel. (85) 247-3066; telex 1207; fax (85) 272-2799; f. 1957; Dir JOSÉ A. SANCHO; circ. 12,000.

Goiânia, GO

Diário da Manhã: Av. Anhanguera 2833, Setor Leste Universitário, 74000 Goiânia, GO; tel. (62) 261-7371; telex 1055; f. 1980; Pres. JULIO NASSER CUSTÓDIO DOS SANTOS; circ. 16,000.

Jornal O Popular: Rua Thómas Edson Q7, Setor Serrinha, 74835-130 Goiânia, GO; tel. (62) 250-1000; telex 2110; fax (62) 241-1018; f. 1938; Pres. JAIME CÂMARA JÚNIOR; circ. 65,000.

Londrina, PR

Fôlha de Londrina: Rua Piauí 241, 86010 Londrina, PR; tel. (432) 24-2020; telex 2123; fax (432) 21-1051; f. 1948; Pres. JOÃO MILANEZ; circ. 40,000.

Manaus, AM

A Crítica: Av. André Araújo, Km 3, 69060 Manaus; tel. (92) 642-2000; telex 2103; fax (92) 642-1501; f. 1949; Dir UMBERTO CADERARO; circ. 19,000.

Niterói, RJ

O Fluminense: Rua Visconde de Itaboraí 184, 24030 Niterói, RJ; tel. (21) 719-3311; telex 37054; fax (21) 719-6344; f. 1978; Dir ALBERTO FRANCISCO TORRES; circ. 80,000.

A Tribuna: Rua Barão do Amazonas 31, 24210 Niterói, RJ; tel. (21) 719-1886; f. 1926; Dir-Gen. JOURDAN AMÓRA; circ. 18,000.

Porto Alegre, RS

Zero Hora: Av. Ipiranga 1075, 90160-093 Porto Alegre, RS; tel. (51) 223-4400; telex 4100; fax (51) 229-5848; f. 1964; Pres. JAYME SIROTSKY; circ. 110,000 (Mon.), 115,000 weekdays, 250,000 Sunday.

Recife, PE

Diário de Pernambuco: Praça da Independência 12, 2° andar, 50010-300 Recife, PE; tel. (81) 424-3666; telex 1057; fax (81) 424-2527; f. 1825; morning; independent; Pres. ANTÔNIO C. DA COSTA; circ. 31,000.

Ribeirão Preto, SP

Diário da Manhã: Rua Duque de Caxias 179, 14015 Ribeirão Preto, SP; tel. (16) 634-0909; f. 1898; Dir PAULO M. SANT'ANNA; circ. 17,000.

Rio de Janeiro, RJ

O Dia: Rua Riachuelo 359, 20235 Rio de Janeiro, RJ; tel. (21) 272-8000; telex 22385; fax (21) 507-1038; f. 1951; morning; centrist labour; Pres. ANTÔNIO ARY DE CARVALHO; circ. 250,000 weekdays, 500,000 Sundays.

O Globo: Rua Irineu Marinho 35, CP 1090, 20233-900 Rio de Janeiro, RJ; tel. (21) 534-5000; telex 22595; fax (21) 534-5510; f. 1925; morning; Dir FRANCISCO GRAELL; circ. 350,000 weekdays, 600,000 Sundays.

Jornal do Brasil: Av. Brasil 500, 6° andar, São Cristovão, 20949-900 Rio de Janeiro, RJ; tel. (21) 585-4422; telex 23262; f. 1891; morning; Catholic, liberal; Pres. M. F. DO NASCIMENTO BRITO; circ. 200,000 weekdays, 325,000 Sundays.

Jornal do Comércio: Rua do Livramento 189, 20221 Rio de Janeiro, RJ; tel. (21) 253-6675; telex 22165; f. 1827; morning; Pres. AUSTREGÉSILO DE ATHAYDE; circ. 31,000 weekdays.

Jornal dos Sports: Rua Tenente Possolo 15/25, Cruz Vermelha, 20230 Rio de Janeiro, RJ; tel. (21) 232-8010; telex 39567; f. 1931; morning; sporting daily; Dir VENÂNCIO P. VELLOSO; circ. 38,000.

Ultima Hora: Rua Equador 702, 20220 Rio de Janeiro, RJ; tel. (21) 223-2444; telex 22551; fax (21) 223-2444; f. 1951; evening; Dir K. NUNES; circ. 56,000.

Salvador, BA

Jornal da Bahia: Rua Peruvia Carneiro 220, 41100 Salvador, BA; tel. (71) 384-2919; telex 1296; fax (71) 384-5726; f. 1958; Pres. MÁRIO KERTÉSZ; circ. 20,000.

Jornal Correio da Bahia: Av. Luis Viana Filho s/n, 41100 Salvador, BA; tel. (71) 371-2811; telex 1594; fax (71) 231-3944; f. 1979; Pres. ARMANDO GONÇALVES.

Jornal da Tarde: Av. Tancredo Neves 1092, 41820-020 Salvador, BA; tel. (71) 231-9683; telex 2638; fax (71) 231-1064; f. 1912; evening; Pres. REGINA SIMÕES DE MELLO LEITÃO; circ. 54,000.

Santo André, SP

Diário do Grande ABC: Rua Catequese 562, 09090-900 Santo André, SP; tel. (11) 715-8000; fax (11) 440-3087; f. 1958; Pres. MAURY DE CAMPOS DOTTO; circ. 98,000.

Santos, SP

A Tribuna: Rua General Câmara 90/94, 11010-903 Santos, SP; tel. (132) 32-7711; telex 1058; fax (132) 33-6971; f. 1984; Dir ROBERTO M. SANTINI; circ. 35,000.

São Luís, MA

O Imparcial: Rua Afonso Pena 46, 65000 São Luís, MA; tel. (98) 222-5120; telex 2106; fax (98) 222-5120; f. 1926; Dir-Gen. PEDRO BATISTA FREIRE.

São Paulo, SP

Diário Comércio e Indústria: Rua Alvaro de Carvalho 354, 01050-020 São Paulo, SP; tel. (11) 256-5011; telex 21936; fax (11) 258-1989; f. 1933; morning; Pres. HAMILTON LUCAS DE OLIVEIRA; circ. 50,000.

Diário Popular: Rua Major Quedinho 28, 1°-6° andares, 01050 São Paulo, SP; tel. (11) 258-2133; telex 21213; fax (11) 256-1627; f. 1884; evening; independent; Dir RICARDO GURAL DE SABEYA; circ. 90,000.

O Estado de São Paulo: Av. Eng. Caetano Álvares 55, 02550 São Paulo, SP; tel. (11) 856-2122; telex 24013; fax (11) 266-2206; f. 1875; morning; independent; Dir FRANCISCO MESQUITA NETO; circ. 242,000 weekdays, 460,000 Sundays.

Fôlha de São Paulo: Alameda Barão de Limeira 425, Campos Elíseos, 01202-900 São Paulo, SP; tel. (11) 224-3222; telex 22930; fax (11) 223-1644; f. 1921; morning; Editorial Dir OCTAVIO FRIAS, Filho; circ. 557,650 weekdays, 1,401,178 Sundays.

Gazeta Mercantil: Rua Major Quedinho 90, 5° andar, 01050 São Paulo, SP; tel. (11) 256-3133; telex 25407; fax (11) 258-5864; f. 1920; business paper; Pres. LUIZ FERREIRA LEVY; circ. 80,000.

Jornal da Tarde: Rua Peixoto Gomidi 671, 01409 São Paulo, SP; tel. (11) 284-1944; telex 33430; fax (11) 289-3548; f. 1966; evening; independent; Dir R. MESQUITA; circ. 120,000, 180,000 Mondays.

Notícias Populares: Alameda Barão de Limeira 425, 01202 São Paulo, SP; tel. (11) 874-2222; telex 22930; fax (11) 223-1644; f. 1963; Dir RENATO CASTANHARI; circ. 150,000.

Vitória, ES

A Gazeta: Rua Charic Murad 902, 29050 Vitória, ES; tel. (27) 222-8333; telex 2138; fax (27) 223-1525; f. 1928; Pres. MARIO LINDENBERG; circ. 19,000.

PERIODICALS

Rio de Janeiro, RJ

Amiga: Rua do Russel 766/804, 22214 Rio de Janeiro, RJ; tel. (21) 285-0033; telex 21525; fax (21) 205-9998; weekly; women's interest; Pres. ADOLPHO BLOCH; circ. 83,000.

Antena-Eletrônica Popular: Av. Marechal Floriano 143, CP 1131, 20080-005 Rio de Janeiro, RJ; tel. (21) 223-2442; fax (21) 263-8840; f. 1926; monthly; telecommunications and electronics, radio, TV, hi-fi, amateur and CB radio; Dir (vacant); circ. 24,000.

Carinho: Rua do Russel 766/804, 22214 Rio de Janeiro, RJ; tel. (21) 285-0033; telex 21525; fax (21) 205-9998; monthly; women's interest; Pres. ADOLPHO BLOCH; circ. 65,000.

Conjuntura Econômica: Praia de Botafogo 190, Sala 923, 22253-900 Rio de Janeiro, RJ; tel. (21) 536-9267; fax (21) 551-2799; f. 1947; monthly; economics and finance; published by Fundação Getúlio Vargas; Pres. JORGE OSCAR DE MELLO FLÔRES; Editor LAURO VIEIRA DE FARIA; circ. 20,000.

Desfile: Rua do Russel 766/804, 22214 Rio de Janeiro, RJ; tel. (21) 285-0033; telex 21525; fax (21) 205-9998; f. 1969; monthly; women's interest; Dir ADOLPHO BLOCH; circ. 120,000.

Ele Ela: Rua do Russel 766/804, 22214 Rio de Janeiro RJ; tel. (21) 285-0033; telex 21525; fax (21) 205-9998; f. 1969; monthly; men's interest; Dir ADOLPHO BLOCH; circ. 150,000.

Manchete: Rua do Russel 766/804, 20214 Rio de Janeiro, RJ; tel. (21) 285-0033; telex 22214; fax (21) 205-9998; f. 1952; weekly; general; Dir ADOLPHO BLOCH; circ. 110,000.

São Paulo, SP

Capricho: Rua Geraldo Flausino Gomes 61, 6°, 04573-900 São Paulo, SP; tel. (11) 534-5231; telex 57359; monthly; youth interest; Dir ROBERTO CIVITA; circ. 250,000.

Carícia: Av. Nações Unidas 5777, 05479-900 São Paulo, SP; tel. (11) 211-7866; telex 83178; fax (11) 813-9115; monthly; women's interest; Dir ANGELO ROSSI; circ. 210,000.

Casa e Jardim: B. Machado 82, 01230-010 São Paulo, SP; telex 30812; fax (11) 824-9079; f. 1953; monthly; homes and gardens, illustrated; Pres. LUCIANA JALONETSKY; circ. 120,000.

Claudia: Rua Geraldo Flausino Gomes 61, CP 2371, 04573-900 São Paulo, SP; tel. (11) 534-5130; telex 54563; fax (11) 534-5638; f. 1962; monthly; women's magazine; Dir ROBERTO CIVITA; circ. 460,000.

Criativa: Rua do Centúria 655, 05065-001, São Paulo, SP; tel. (11) 874-6003; telex 81754; fax (11) 864-0271; monthly; women's interest; Dir-Gen. RICARDO A. SÁNCHEZ; circ. 121,000.

Digesto Econômico: Associação Comercial de São Paulo, Rua Boa Vista 51, 01014-911 São Paulo, SP; tel. (11) 234-3322; telex 23355; fax (11) 239-0067; every 2 months; Pres. ELVIO ALIPRANDI; Chief Editor JOÃO DE SCANTIMBURGO.

Dirigente Rural: Rua Alvaro de Carvalho 354, 01050 São Paulo, SP; tel. (11) 256-5011; fax (11) 258-1919; monthly; agriculture; Dir HAMILTON LUCAS DE OLIVEIRA; Editor ORIOVALDO BONAS; circ. 64,577.

Disney Especial: Av. das Nações Unidas 7221, 05477-000 São Paulo, SP; tel. (11) 3037-2000; fax (11) 3037-4124; every 2 months; children's magazine; Dir ROBERTO CIVITA; circ. 211,600.

Exame: Av. Octaviano Alves de Lima, 4400, 02909-900 São Paulo, SP; tel. (11) 877-1421; fax (11) 877-1437; e-mail publicidade.exame@email.abril.com.br; two a week; business; Dir JOSÉ ROBERTO GUZZO; circ. 168,300.

Iris, A Revista da Imagem: Rua Brito Peixoto 322, Brooklin, 04582-020 São Paulo, SP; tel. (11) 531-1299; fax (11) 531-1627; e-mail irisfoto@totalnet.com.br; f. 1947; monthly; photography and general pictures; Dirs BEATRIZ AZEVEDO MARQUES, HÉLIO M. VALENTONI; circ. 50,000.

Manequim: Rua Geraldo Flausino Gomes 61, 04573-900 São Paulo, SP; tel. (11) 534-5668; telex 15463; fax (11) 534-5632; monthly; fashion; Dir ROBERTO CIVITA; circ. 300,000.

Máquinas e Metais: Alameda Olga 315, 01155-900, São Paulo, SP; tel. (11) 826-4511; fax (11) 3666-9585; e-mail aranda@nutecnet.com.br; f. 1964; monthly; machine and metal industries; Editor JOSÉ ROBERTO GONÇALVES; circ. 15,000.

Mickey: Av. das Nações Unidas 7221, 05477-000 São Paulo, SP; tel. (11) 3037-2000; fax (11) 3037-4124; monthly; children's magazine; Dir ROBERTO CIVITA; circ. 76,000.

Micromundo-Computerworld do Brasil: Rua Caçapava 79, 01408 São Paulo, SP; tel. (11) 289-1767; telex 32017; monthly; computers; Gen. Dir ERIC HIPPEAU; circ. 38,000.

Nova: Rua Geraldo Flausino Gomes 61, 04573-900 São Paulo, SP; tel. (11) 534-5712; telex 57359; fax (11) 534-5187; f. 1973; monthly; women's interest; Dir ROBERTO CIVITA; circ. 300,000.

Pato Donald: Av. das Nações Unidas 7221, 05477-000 São Paulo, SP; tel. (11) 3037-2000; fax (11) 3037-4124; every 2 weeks; children's magazine; Dir ROBERTO CIVITA; circ. 120,000.

Placar: Av. das Nações Unidas 7221, 14° andar, 05477-000 São Paulo, SP; tel. (11) 3037-5816; fax (11) 3037-5597; e-mail placar.leitor@email.abril.com.br; f. 1970; monthly; soccer magazine; Dir MARCELO DURATE; circ. 127,000.

Quatro Rodas: Rua Geraldo Flausino Gomes 61, Brooklin, 04573-900 São Paulo, SP; tel. (11) 534-5491; telex 24134; fax (11) 530-8549; f. 1960; monthly; motoring; Pres. ROBERTO CIVITA; circ. 250,000.

Revista O Carreteiro: Rua Palacete das Aguias 239, 04035-021 São Paulo, SP; tel. (11) 542-9311; monthly; transport; Dirs JOÃO ALBERTO ANTUNES DE FIGUEIREDO, EDSON PEREIRA COELHO; circ. 80,000.

Saúde: Av. Nações Unidas 5777, 05479-900 São Paulo, SP; tel. (11) 211-7675; telex 83178; fax (11) 813-9115; monthly; health; Dir ANGELO ROSSI; circ. 180,000.

Veja: Rua do Copturno 571, 6°, São Paulo, SP; tel. (11) 877-1322; telex 22115; fax (11) 877-1640; f. 1968; news weekly; Dirs JOSÉ ROBERTO GUZZO, TALES ALVARENGA, MÁRIO SERGIO CONTI; circ. 800,000.

Visão: São Paulo, SP; tel. (11) 549-4344; telex 23552; f. 1952; weekly; news magazine; Editor HENRY MAKSOUD; circ. 148,822.

NEWS AGENCIES

Editora Abril, SA: Av. Otaviano Alves de Lima 4400, CP 2372, 02909-970 São Paulo, SP; tel. (11) 877-1322; telex 22115; fax (11) 877-1640; f. 1950; Pres. ROBERTO CIVITA.

Agência ANDA: Edif. Correio Brasiliense, Setor das Indústrias Gráficas 300/350, Brasília, DF; Dir EDILSON VARELA.

Agência o Estado de São Paulo: Av. Eng. Caetano Alvares 55, 02588-900 São Paulo, SP; tel. (11) 856-2122; telex 23511; Rep. SAMUEL DIRCEU F. BUENO.

Agência Fôlha de São Paulo: Alameda Barão de Limeira 425, 4° andar, 01290-900 São Paulo; tel. (11) 224-3790; fax (11) 221-0675; Dir MARION STRECKER.

Agência Globo: Rua Irineu Marinho 35, 2° andar, Centro, 20233-900 Rio de Janeiro, RJ; tel. (21) 292-2000; telex 31614; fax (21) 292-2000; Dir CARLOS LEMOS.

Agência Jornal do Brasil: Av. Brasil 500, 6° andar, São Cristóvão, 20949-900 Rio de Janeiro, RJ; tel. (21) 585-4453; telex 21160; fax (21) 580-9944; f. 1966; Exec. Dir. EDGAR LISBOA.

Foreign Bureaux

Agence France-Presse (AFP) (France): CP 2575-ZC-00, Rua México 21, 7° andar, 20031-144 Rio de Janeiro, RJ; tel. (21) 533-4555; fax (21) 262-7933; e-mail afprio@unisys.com.br; Bureau Chief (Brazil) ALAIN BOEBION.

Agencia EFE (Spain): Praia de Botafogo 228, Bloco B, Gr. 1106, 22359-900 Rio de Janeiro, RJ; tel. (21) 553-6355; fax (21) 553-4494; Bureau Chief ZOILO G. MARTÍNEZ DE LA VEGA.

Agenzia Nazionale Stampa Associata (ANSA) (Italy): Rio de Janeiro, RJ; tel. (21) 220-5528; telex 22296; Bureau Chief MANUEL HORACIO PALLAVIDINI; Av. São Luís 258, 23° andar, Of. 1302, São Paulo, SP; tel. (11) 256-5835; telex 21421; Bureau Chief RICCARDO CARUCCI; c/o Correio Brasiliense 300/350, 70610 Brasília, DF; tel. (61) 226-1755; telex 2211; Bureau Chief HUMBERTO ANTONIO GIANNINI; Rua Barão do Rio Branco 556, Curitiba, PA; tel. (41) 24-5000; Bureau Chief ELOIR DANTÉ ALBERTI.

Associated Press (AP) (USA): Av. Brasil 500, sala 847, CP 72-ZC-00, 20001 Rio de Janeiro, RJ; tel. (21) 580-4422; telex 21888; Bureau Chief BRUCE HANDLER; Rua Major Quedinho Sala 707, CP 3815, 01050 São Paulo, SP; tel. (11) 256-0520; telex 21595; fax (11) 256-4135; Correspondent STAN LEHMAN; a/c Sucursal Folha de São Paulo, CLS 104 Bloco C Loja 41, CP 14-2260, 70343 Brasília, DF; tel. (61) 223-9492; telex 1454; Correspondent JORGE MEDEROS.

Deutsche Presse-Agentur (dpa) (Germany): Rua Abade Ramos 65, 22461-90 Rio de Janeiro, RJ; tel. (21) 266-5937; fax (21) 537-8273; Bureau Chief ESTEBAN ENGEL.

Informatsionnoye Telegrafnoye Agentstvo Rossii—Telegrafnoye Agentstvo Sovetskovo Soyuza (ITAR—TASS) (Russia): Rua General Barbosa 34, Apto 802, Rio de Janeiro, RJ; Correspondent ALEKSANDR MAKSIMOV; Av. das Naçoes, Lote A, 70000 Brasília, DF; Correspondent YURII BESPALCO.

Inter Press Service (IPS) (Italy): Rua Vicente de Souza 29, 2° andar, 22251-070 Rio de Janeiro; tel. (21) 286-5605; fax (21) 286-5324; Correspondent MARIO CHIZUO OSAVA.

Jiji Tsushin-Sha (Jiji Press) (Japan): Av. Paulista 854, 13° andar, Conj. 133, Bela Vista, 01310-913 São Paulo, SP; tel. (11) 285-0025; fax (11) 285-3816; f. 1958; Chief Correspondent NOBORU OKAMOTO.

Kyodo Tsushin (Japan): Praia do Flamengo 168-701, Flamengo, 22210 Rio de Janeiro, RJ; tel. (21) 285-2412; telex 33653; fax (21) 285-2270; Bureau Chief TAKAYOSHI MAKITA.

Prensa Latina (Cuba): Marechal Mascarenhas de Moraís 121, Apto 602, Copacabana, 22030-040 Rio de Janeiro, RJ; tel. and fax (21) 237-1766; telex 36510; Correspondent FRANCISCO FORTEZA.

Reuters (United Kingdom): SCS, Edif. Oscar Niemeyer 3, 1° andar, sala 101, 70316-900 Brasília, DF; tel. (61) 223-0358; fax (61) 223-5918; Rua Boa Vista 254, 4° andar, salas 401-410, 01014-100 São Paulo, SP; tel. (11) 232-4411; fax (11) 604-6538;Rua Sete de Setembro 99, 4° andar, sala 401, 20050-005 Rio de Janeiro, RJ; tel. (21) 507-4151; fax (21) 507-2120; Bureau Chief (News and Television): ADRIAN DICKSON.

United Press International (UPI) (USA): Rua Uruguaina 94, 18°, Centro, 20050 Rio de Janeiro, RJ; tel. (21) 224-4194; telex 22680; fax (21) 232-8293; Rua Sete de Abril 230, Bloco A, 816/817, 01044 São Paulo, SP; tel. (11) 258-6869; telex 22235; Edif. Gilberto Salamão, Sala 805/806, 70305 Brasília, DF; tel. (61) 224-6413; telex 1507; Gen. Man. ANTÔNIO PRAXEDES; Chief Correspondent H. E. COYA HONORES.

Xinhua (New China) News Agency (People's Republic of China): SHIS QI 15, Conj. 16, Casa 14, CP 7089; 71.600 Brasília, DF; tel. (61) 248-5489; telex 2788; Chief Correspondent WANG ZHIGEN.

Central News Agency (Taiwan) and Rossiyskoye Informatsionnoye Agentstvo—Novosti (Russia) are also represented in Brazil.

PRESS ASSOCIATIONS

Associação Brasileira de Imprensa: Rua Araújo Pôrto Alegre 71, Castelo, 20030 Rio de Janeiro, RJ; f. 1908; 4,000 mems; Pres. BARBOSA LIMA SOBRINHO; Sec. JOSUÉ ALMEIDA.

Federação Nacional dos Jornalistas—FENAJ: CRS 502, Bloco A, Entrada 51, 1°–2°, 70330-510 Brasília, DF; tel. (61) 223-7002; telex 1792; fax (61) 321-8640; f. 1946; represents 31 regional unions.

Publishers

Rio de Janeiro, RJ

Ao Livro Técnico Indústria e Comércio Ltda: Rua Sá Freire 36/40, São Cristovão, 20930-430 Rio de Janeiro, RJ; tel. (21) 580-1168; telex 30472; fax (21) 580-9955; f. 1933; textbooks, children's and teenagers' fiction and non-fiction, art books, dictionaries; Man. Dir REYNALDO MAX PAUL BLUHM.

Bloch Editores, SA: Rua do Russell 766/804, Glória, 22214 Rio de Janeiro, RJ; tel. (21) 265-2012; telex 21525; fax (21) 205-9998; f. 1966; general; Pres. ADOLPHO BLOCH.

Distribuidora Record de Serviços de Imprensa, SA: Rua Argentina 171, São Cristóvão, CP 884, 20921 Rio de Janeiro, RJ; tel. (21) 585-2000; telex 30501; fax (21) 580-4911; f. 1941; general fiction and non-fiction, education, textbooks, fine arts; Pres. SERGIO MACHADO.

Ebid-Editora Páginas Amarelas Ltda: Av. Liberdade 956, 5° andar, 01502-001 São Paulo, SP; tel. (11) 278-6622; fax (11) 278-7229; f. 1947; commercial directories.

Ediouro Publicações, SA: Rua Nova Jerusalém 345, CP 1880, Bonsucesso, 21042-230 Rio de Janeiro, RJ; tel. (21) 260-6122; fax (21) 280-2438; f. 1939; general.

Editora Artenova, SA: Rua Pref. Olímpio de Mello 1774, Benfica, 20000 Rio de Janeiro, RJ; tel. (21) 264-9198; f. 1971; sociology, psychology, occultism, cinema, literature, politics and history; Man. Dir ALVARO PACHECO.

Editora Brasil-América (EBAL), SA: Rua Gen. Almério de Moura 302/320, São Cristóvão, 20921-060 Rio de Janeiro, RJ; tel. (21) 580-0303; fax (21) 580-1637; f. 1945; children's books; Dir PAULO ADOLFO AIZEN.

Editora Delta, SA: Av. Almirante Barroso 63, 26° andar, CP 2226, 20031 Rio de Janeiro, RJ; tel. (21) 240-0072; f. 1958; reference books.

Editora Expressão e Cultura—Exped Ltda: Rua Desembargador Vinato 2, Sala 106, 20030-090 Rio de Janeiro, RJ; tel. (21) 533-3168; telex 33280; fax (21) 220-0432; f. 1967; textbooks, literature, reference; Gen. Man. RICARDO AUGUSTO PAMPLONA VAZ.

Editora e Gráfica Miguel Couto, SA: Rua da Passagem 78, Loja A, Botafogo, 22290-030 Rio de Janeiro, RJ; tel. (21) 541-5145; f. 1969; engineering; Dir PAULO KOBLER PINTO LOPES SAMPAIO.

Editora Nova Fronteira, SA: Rua Bambina 25, Botafogo, 22251-050 Rio de Janeiro, RJ; tel. (21) 537-8770; telex 34695; fax (21) 286-6755; e-mail novafr2@embratel.net.br; f. 1965; fiction, psychology, history, politics, science fiction, poetry, leisure, reference; Pres. CARLOS AUGUSTO LACERDA.

Editora Vecchi, SA: Rua do Rezende 144, Esplanada do Senado, 20231 Rio de Janeiro, RJ; tel. (21) 221-0822; telex 32756; f. 1913; general literature, juvenile, reference, cookery, magazines; Dir DELMAN BONATTO.

Editora Vozes, Ltda: Rua Frei Luís 100, CP 90023, 25689-900 Petrópolis, RJ; tel. (242) 43-5112; fax (242) 31-4676; e-mail editorial@vozes.com.br; f. 1901; Catholic publishers; management, theology, anthropology, fine arts, history, linguistics, science, fiction, education, data processing, etc.; Dir Dr GILBERTO M. S. PISCITELLI.

Fundação de Assistência ao Estudante (FAE): SAS, Q01, Bloco A, 10° andar, 70729-900 Brasíla, DF; tel. (61) 212-4177; telex 2119; fax (61) 226-0625; f. 1967; education; Man. Dir RUBENS JOSÉ DE CASTRO.

Gráfica Editora Primor, Ltda: Rodv. Pres. Dutra 2611, 21530 Rio de Janeiro, RJ; tel. (21) 371-6622; telex 22150; f. 1968.

Livraria Francisco Alves Editora, SA: Rua Uruguaiana 94/13°, 20050-002 Rio de Janeiro, RJ; tel. (21) 221-3198; fax (21) 242-3438; f. 1854; textbooks, fiction, non-fiction; Pres. CARLOS LEAL.

Livraria José Olympio Editora, SA: Rua da Glória 344, 4° andar, Glória, 20241-180 Rio de Janeiro, RJ; tel. (21) 221-6939; fax (21) 242-0802; f. 1931; juvenile, science, history, philosophy, psychology, sociology, fiction; Dir MANOEL ROBERTO DOMINGUES.

Otto Pierre Editores, Ltda: Rua Dr Nunes 1225, Olaria, 21021 Rio de Janeiro, RJ.

Tesla Publicações, Ltda: Rua da Quitanda 49, 1° andar, salas 110/12, 20011 Rio de Janeiro, RJ; tel. (21) 242-0135; f. 1960; children's books.

São Paulo, SP

Atual Editora, Ltda: Av. Gen. Valdomiro de Lima 833, Pq. Jabaquara, 04344-070 São Paulo, SP; tel. (11) 5071-2288; fax (11) 5071-3099; e-mail www.atualeditora.com.br; f. 1973; school and children's books, literature; Dirs GELSON IEZZI, OSVALDO DOLCE.

Cedibra Editora Brasileiro, Ltda: São Paulo, SP; tel. (11) 829-3433; fax (11) 820-3503; literature and children's books; Man. Dir JAN RAIS.

Cia Editora Nacional: Rua Joli 294, Brás, CP 5312, 03016 São Paulo, SP; tel. (11) 291-2355; fax (11) 291-8614; f. 1925; textbooks, history, science, social sciences, philosophy, fiction, juvenile; Dirs JORGE YUNES, PAULO C. MARTI.

Cia Melhoramento de São Paulo: Rua Tito 479, 05051-000 São Paulo, SP; tel. (11) 873-2200; telex 83151; fax (11) 872-0556; f. 1890; general non-fiction; Gen. Man. INGO PLÖGER.

Editora Abril, SA: Av. Octaviano Alves de Lima 4400, 02909-900 São Paulo, SP; tel. (11) 877-1322; telex 22115; fax (11) 877-1640; f. 1950; Pres. ROBERTO CIVITA.

Editora Atica, SA: Rua Barão de Iguape 110, 01507-900 São Paulo, SP; tel. (11) 278-9322; telex 32969; fax (11) 279-2185; f. 1965; textbooks, Brazilian and African literature; Pres. ANDERSON FERNANDES DIAS.

Editora Atlas, SA: Rua Conselheiro Nébias 1384, Campos Elíseos, 01203-904 São Paulo, SP; tel. 221-9144; fax (11) 220-7830; f. 1944; business administration, data-processing, economics, accounting, law, education, social sciences; Pres. LUIZ HERRMANN.

Editora Brasiliense, SA: Rua Atucuri 318, 03646 São Paulo, SP; tel. (11) 6942-0545; fax (11) 6942-0813; e-mail brasilse@uol.com.br; f. 1943; education, racism, gender studies, human rights, ecology, history, literature, social sciences; Man. YOLANDA C. DA SILVA PRADO.

Editora do Brasil, SA: Rua Conselheiro Nébias 887, Campos Elíseos, CP 4986, 01203-001 São Paulo, SP; tel. (11) 222-0211; fax (11) 222-5583; f. 1943; commerce, education, history, psychology and sociology.

Editora Caminho Suave, Ltda: Rua Fagundes 157, Liberdade, 01508 São Paulo, SP; tel. (11) 278-5840; f. 1965; textbooks.

Editora F.T.D., SA: Rua do Lavapés 1023, CP 30402, 01519 São Paulo, SP; tel. (11) 278-8264; f. 1897; textbooks; Pres. JOÃO TISSI.

Editora Globo, SA: Rua do Curtume 665, Lapa de Baixo, 05065-001 São Paolo, SP; tel. (11) 874-6000; telex 81574; fax (11) 861-2064; f. 1957; general; Gen. Man. RICARDO A. FISCHER.

Editora Luzeiro Ltda: Rua Almirante Barroso 730, Brás, 03025-001 São Paulo, SP; tel. (11) 292-3188; f. 1973; folklore and literature.

Editora Michalany Ltda: Rua Biobedas 321, Saúde, CP 12933, 04302-010 São Paulo, SP; tel. (11) 585-2012; fax (11) 276-4138; f. 1965; biographies, economics, textbooks, geography, history, religion, maps; Dir DOUGLAS MICHALANY.

Editora Moderna, Ltda: Rua Padre Adelino 758, Belenzinho, 03303-904, São Paulo, SP; tel. (11) 291-4811; fax (11) 693-7453; e-mail valentim@moderna.com.br; internet http://www.moderna.com.br.

Editora Pioneira: Praça Dirceu de Lima 313, Casa Verde, 02515-050 São Paulo, SP; tel. (11) 858-3199; fax (11) 858-0443; e-mail pioneira@virtual-net.com.br; f. 1960; architecture, computers, political and social sciences, business studies, languages, children's books; Dirs ROBERTO GUAZZELLI, LILIANA GUAZZELLI.

Editora Revista dos Tribunais Ltda: Rua Conde do Pinhal 78, CP 8153, 01501 São Paulo, SP; tel. (11) 37-8689; f. 1955; law and jurisprudence, administration, economics and social sciences; Man. Dir NELSON PALMA TRAVASSOS.

Editora Rideel Ltda: Alameda Afonso Schmidt 879, Santa Terezinha, 02450-001 São Paulo, SP; tel. (11) 267-8344; fax (11) 290-7415; e-mail rideel@virtual-net.com.br; f. 1971; general; Dir ITALO AMADIO.

Editora Scipione Ltda: Praça Carlos Gomes 46, 01501-040 São Paulo, SP; tel. (11) 239-2255; fax (11) 607-8511; e-mail scipionebr

.homeshopping.com.br; f. 1983; school-books, literature, reference; Dirs Maurício Fernandes Dias, Luiz Esteves Sallum.

Encyclopaedia Britannica do Brasil Publicações Ltda: Rua Rego Freitas 192, Vila Buarque, CP 8094, 01220-907 São Paulo, SP; tel. (11) 224-8211; telex 21460; fax (11) 221-8747;f. 1951; reference books.

Instituto Brasileiro de Edições Pedagógicas, Ltda: Rua Joli 294, Brás, CP 5321, 03016 São Paulo, SP; tel. (11) 291-2355; fax (11) 264-5338; f. 1972; textbooks, foreign languages, reference books and chemistry.

Lex Editora, SA: Rua Machado de Assis 47/57, Vila Mariana, CP 12888, 04106-900 São Paulo, SP; tel. (11) 549-0122; fax (11) 575-9138; f. 1937; legislation and jurisprudence; Dir Affonso Vitale Sobrinho.

Saraiva SA Livreiros Editores: Av. Marquês de São Vicente 1697, CP 2362, 01139-904 São Paulo, SP; tel. (11) 861-3344; telex 26789; fax (11) 861-3308; f. 1914; education, textbooks, law, economics; Pres. Jorge Eduardo Saraiva.

Belo Horizonte, MG

Editora Lê, SA: Av. D. Pedro II, 4550 Jardin Montanhês, CP 2585, 30730 Belo Horizonte, MG; tel. (31) 462-6262; telex 3340; f. 1967; textbooks.

Editora Lemi, SA: Av. Nossa Senhora de Fátima 1945, CP 1890, 30000 Belo Horizonte, MG; tel. (31) 201-8044; f. 1967; administration, accounting, law, ecology, economics, textbooks, children's books and reference books.

Editora Vigília, Ltda: Rua Felipe dos Santos 508, Bairro de Lourdes, CP 1068, 30180-160 Belo Horizonte, MG; e-mail lerg@planetarium.com.br; tel. (31) 337-2744; fax (31) 337-2834; f. 1960; general.

Curitiba, PR

Editora Educacional Brasileira, SA: Rua XV de Novembro 178, salas 101/04, CP 7498, 80000 Curitiba, PR; tel. (41) 223-5012; f. 1963; biology, textbooks and reference books.

PUBLISHERS' ASSOCIATIONS

Associação Brasileira do Livro: Av. 13 de Maio 23, 16°, 20031 Rio de Janeiro, RJ; tel. (21) 240-9115; Pres. Ernesto Zahar.

Câmara Brasileira do Livro: Av. Ipiranga 1267, 10° andar, 01039-907 São Paulo, SP; tel. (11) 225-8277; fax (11) 229-7463; f. 1946; Pres. Altair Ferreira Brasil.

Sindicato Nacional dos Editores de Livros: Av. Rio Branco 37, 1503/6 and 1510/12, 20090-003 Rio de Janeiro, RJ; tel. (21) 233-6481; fax (21) 253-8502; 200 mems; Pres. Sergio Abreu da Cruz Machado; Man. Nilson Lopes da Silva.

There are also regional publishers' associations.

Broadcasting and Communications

TELECOMMUNICATIONS

Legislation providing for the transfer of Telebrás, the state telecommunications holding company, to the private sector was under consideration in 1997. A new national telecommunications agency, Anatel, was to assume many of the responsibilities of the Ministry of Communications.

Empresa Brasileira de Telecomunicações, SA (EMBRATEL): Av. Pres. Vargas 1012, CP 2586, 20179-900 Rio de Janeiro, RJ; tel. (21) 519-8182; telex 30522; f. 1965; operates national and international telecommunications system; Pres. Dilio Sergio Penedo.

Empresa Brasileira de Comunicação, SA (Radiobrás) (Brazilian Communications Company): CP 04-0340, 70710 Brasília, DF; tel. (61) 321-3949; telex 1682; fax (61) 321-7602; f. 1988 following merger of Empresa Brasileira de Radiodifusão and Empresa Brasileira de Notícias; Pres. Marcelo Amorim Netto.

RADIO

In April 1992 there were 2,917 radio stations in Brazil, including 20 in Brasília, 38 in Rio de Janeiro, 32 in São Paulo, 24 in Curitiba, 24 in Porto Alegre and 23 in Belo Horizonte.

The main broadcasting stations in Rio de Janeiro are: Rádio Nacional, Rádio Globo, Rádio Eldorado, Rádio Jornal do Brasil, Rádio Tupi and Rádio Mundial. In São Paulo the main stations are Rádio Bandeirantes, Rádio Mulher, Rádio Eldorado, Rádio Gazeta and Rádio Excelsior; and in Brasília: Rádio Nacional, Rádio Alvorada, Rádio Planalto and Rádio Capital.

TELEVISION

In April 1992 there were 256 television stations in Brazil, of which 118 were in the state capitals and six in Brasília. PAL-M colour television was adopted in 1972 and the Brazilian system is connected with the rest of the world by satellite.

The main television networks are:

TV Bandeirantes—Canal 13: Rádio e Televisão Bandeirantes Ltda, Rua Radiantes 13, 05699 São Paulo, SP; tel. (11) 842-3011; telex 56375; fax (11) 842-3067; 65 TV stations and repeaters throughout Brazil; Pres. João Jorge Saad.

RBS TV-TV Gaúcha, SA: Rua Rádio y TV Gaúcha 189, 90850-080 Porto Alegre, RS; tel. (51) 218-5002; fax (51) 218-5005; Vice-Pres Walmor Bergesch.

TV Globo—Canal 4: Rua Lopes Quintas 303, Jardim Botanico, 22460-010 Rio de Janeiro, RJ; tel. (21) 529-2000; telex 22795; fax (21) 294-2042; f. 1965; 8 stations; national network; Dir A. Pontes Malta.

TV Manchete-Canal 6: Rua do Russel 766, 20000 Rio de Janeiro, RJ; tel. (21) 265-2012; telex 21525; Dir-Gen. R. Furtado.

TV Record—Rede Record de Televisão—Radio Record, SA: Rua de Várzea 240, Barra Funda, 01140-080 São Paulo, SP; tel. (11) 824-7000; Pres. João Batista R. Silva; Exec. Vice-Pres. H. Gonçalves.

TVSBT—Canal 4 de São Paulo, SA: Rua Dona Santa Veloso 535, Vila Guilherme, 02050 São Paulo, SP; tel. (11) 292-9044; telex 22126; fax (11) 264-6004; Vice-Pres. Guilherme Stoliar.

BROADCASTING ASSOCIATIONS

Associação Brasileira de Emissoras de Rádio e Televisão (ABERT): Centro Empresarial Varig, SCN Quadra 04, Bloco B, Conjunto 501, Pétala A, 70710-500 Brasília, DF; tel. (61) 327-4600; fax (61) 327-3660; e-mail abert@nutecnet.com.br; f. 1962; mems: 32 shortwave, 1,275 FM, 1,574 medium-wave and 80 tropical-wave radio stations and 258 television stations (1997); Pres. Joaquim Mendonça; Exec. Dir Edgar Falcão.

There are regional associations for Bahia, Ceará, Goiás, Minas Gerais, Paraná, Pernambuco, Rio de Janeiro and Espírito Santo (combined), Rio Grande do Sul, Santa Catarina, São Paulo, Amazonas, Distrito Federal, Mato Grosso and Mato Grosso do Sul (combined) and Sergipe.

Finance

(cap. = capital; dep. = deposits; res = reserves; m. = million; brs = branches; amounts in reais, unless otherwise stated)

BANKING

Conselho Monetário Nacional: SBS, Q.03, Bloco B, Edif. Sede do Banco do Brasil, 21° andar, 70074-900 Brasília, DF; tel. (61) 414-1945; fax (61) 414-2528; f. 1964 to formulate monetary policy and to supervise the banking system; Pres. Minister of the Economy.

Central Bank

Banco Central do Brasil: SBS, Q 03, Bloco B, CP 04-0170, 70074-900 Brasília, DF; tel. (61) 414-1000; telex 1211; fax (61) 223-1033; f. 1965 to execute the decisions of the Conselho Monetário Nacional; bank of issue; Pres. Gustavo Franco; 10 brs.

State Commercial Banks

Banco do Brasil, SA: Eixo Rodoviário Sul, SBS, Bloco A, CP 562, 70073-900 Brasília, DF; tel. (61) 310-3400; fax (61) 310-2499; f. 1808; cap. 17,392.8m., res –11,551.5m., dep. 54,121.6m. (Dec. 1996); Chair. Paulo César Ximenes; 4,781 brs.

Banco do Estado do Paraná, SA: Rua Máximo João Kopp 274, Santa Cândida, 82630-900 Curitiba, PR; tel. (41) 351-8122; telex 30004; fax (41) 351-7252; f. 1928; cap. 182.2m., res 130.7m., dep. 2,170.5m. (Dec. 1995); Pres. Domingos Tarso Murta Ramalho; 393 brs.

Banco do Estado do Rio Grande do Sul, SA: Rua Capitão Montanha 177, CP 505, 90010-040 Porto Alegre, RS; tel. (51) 221-5023; telex 518171; fax (51) 228-6473; f. 1928; cap. 227.2m., res 213.1m., dep. 6,503.1 (Dec. 1995); Pres. Ricardo Russowsky; 303 brs.

Banco do Estado de São Paulo, SA (Banespa): Praça Antônio Prado 6, 01062-900 São Paulo, SP; tel. (11) 249-1033; telex 18647; f. 1926; cap. US $620.1m., res US $718.6m., dep. US $15,405.7m. (Dec. 1993); to be transferred to private sector in 1998; Chair. Antônio Carlos Feitosa; 1,702 brs.

Banco do Nordeste do Brasil, SA: Praça Murilo Borges 1, Edif. Raul Barbosa, CP 628, 60035-210 Fortaleza, CE; tel. (85) 231-4777; telex 1141; fax (85) 255-4685; f. 1954; cap. 26.4m., res 300.3m., dep. 1,002.6m. (Dec. 1994); Pres. João Alves de Melo; 180 brs.

Private Banks

Banco da Amazônia, SA: Av. Presidente Vargas 800, 66017-000 Belém, PA; tel. (91) 216-3252; telex 1191; fax (91) 223-5403; f. 1942; cap. 5,494.3m., res 234,345.2m., dep. 2,456,847.5m. (cruzeiros, Dec. 1992); Pres. Anivaldo Juvenil Vale; 109 brs.

Banco América do Sul, SA: Av. Brig. Luiz Antônio 2020, CP 8075, 01318-911 São Paulo, SP; tel. (11) 281-1504; telex 21892; fax (11) 253-1955; f. 1940; cap. 229.4m., res 136.5m., dep. 2,634.2m. (Dec. 1996); Pres. KOHEI DENDA; 132 brs.

Banco BBA-Creditanstalt, SA: Av. Paulista 37, 18°-20°, 01311-902 São Paulo, SP; tel. (11) 281-8000; telex 31637; fax (11) 284-2158; f. 1988; cap. 95.2m., res 333.8m., dep. 2,428.4m. (Dec. 1996); Pres. FERNÃO CARLOS BOTELHO BRACHER; 4 brs.

Banco BCN BARCLAYS, SA: Av. Paulista 1842, Edif. Cetenco Plaza, Torre Norte 24°–25° andares, 01310-200 São Paulo, SP; tel. (11) 284-0077; telex 30930; fax (11) 283-3168; f. 1967; cap. 96.0m., res 30.2m., dep. 322.1m. (Dec. 1996); multiple services; Pres. ADEMAR LINS DE ALBUQUERQUE.

Banco BMC, SA: Av. Paulista 306, 01310-100 São Paulo, SP; tel. (11) 283-7807; telex 33831; fax (11) 284-1257; f. 1939, adopted current name in 1990; cap. 61.3m., res 145.6m., dep. 743.7m. (Dec. 1995); Chair. FRANCISCO JAIME NOGUEIRA PINHEIRO; 13 brs.

Banco BMG, SA: Av. Alvares Cabral 1707, Santo Agostinho, 30170-001 Belo Horizonte, MG; tel. (31) 290-3000; telex 33400; fax (31) 290-3315; f. 1988; cap. 89.8m., res 50.9m., dep. 305.0m. (Dec. 1996); Pres. FLÁVIO PENTAGNA GUIMARÃES; 2 brs.

Banco Bandeirantes, SA: Rua Boa Vista 150, 01014-902 São Paulo, SP; tel. (11) 233-7155; fax (11) 233-7329; f. 1944; cap. 185.8m., res 152.3m., dep. 3,706.4m. (Dec. 1996); assumed control of Banorte in Dec. 1995; Pres. Dr GILBERTO DE ANDRADE FARIA; 122 brs.

Banco Bozano, Simonsen, SA: Av. Rio Branco 138-Centro, 20057-900 Rio de Janeiro, RJ; tel. (21) 508-4000; telex 22921; fax (21) 508-4053; e-mail info@bozano.com.br; f. 1967; cap. 248.2m., res 89.9m., dep. 355.5m. (June 1997); Pres. PAULO VEIGA FERRAZ PEREIRA; 1 br.

Banco Bradesco, SA: Av. Ipiranga 282, 10° andar, 01046-920 São Paulo, SP; tel. (11) 235-9566; telex 36460; fax (11) 256-8742; internet http://www.bradesco.com.br; f. 1943; fmrly Banco Brasileiro de Descontos; cap. and res US $5,316m., dep. US $16,346m. (June 1997); Chair. LÁZARO DE MELLO BRANDÃO; Vice-Chair. DURVAL SILVÉRIO; 1,930 brs.

Banco Chase Manhattan, SA: Rua Verbo Divino, 1400 São Paulo, SP; tel. (11) 546-4433; telex 53643; fax (11) 546-4624; f. 1925; fmrly Banco Lar Brasileiro, SA; cap. 1,076.7m., res 32,850.2m., dep. 52,290.2m. (cruzeiros reais, Dec. 1993); Pres. PETER J. T. G. ANDERSON.

Banco Cidade, SA: Praça Dom José Gaspar 106, 01047-001 São Paulo, SP; tel. (11) 259-6811; telex 22198; fax (11) 255-4176; f. 1965; cap. 72.3m., res 71.8m., dep. 1,479.9m. (Dec. 1995); Pres. EDMUNDO SAFDIÉ.

Banco Credibanco, SA: Av Paulista 1294, 21° andar, 01310-915 São Paulo, SP; tel. (11) 281-4775; telex 37925; fax (11) 285-3431; f. 1967; cap. 110.2m., res 40.1m., dep. 393.8m. (Dec. 1995); Pres. LORENZO ROSSIGNOLI; 8 brs.

Banco de Crédito Nacional, SA (BCN): Av. Andrõmeda s/n°, Alphaville, Barueri, 06473-900, São Paulo, SP; tel. (11) 726-7122; telex 21284; fax (11) 726-7225; f. 1924; acquired by Banco Bradesco in 1997; cap. 385.0m., res 549.8m., dep. 3,142.7m. (Dec. 1996); Pres. PEDRO CONDE; 108 brs.

Banco de Crédito Real de Minas Gerais, SA: Rua Espírito Santo 495, 3° andar, CP 90, 30160-030 Belo Horizonte, MG; tel. (31) 239-3935; telex 1351; fax (31) 224-1281; f. 1889; cap. 121.0m., res –25.4m., dep. 760.9m. (Dec. 1994); Pres. JOÃO HERALDO LIMA; 86 brs.

Banco Dibens, SA: Alameda Santos 200, Cerqueira Cesar, 01418-000 São Paulo, SP; tel. (11) 253-2177; fax (11) 284-4141; f. 1989; cap. 81.7m., res 84.0m., dep. 760.9m. (Dec. 1996); Pres. MAURO SADDI; 23 brs.

Banco do Estado de Minas Gerais, SA: Rua Rio de Janeiro 471, Centro Belo Horizonte, 30160-910 Belo Horizonte, MG; tel. (31) 239-1211; telex 2134; fax (31) 239-1859; f. 1967; acquired by Banco de Crédito Nacional in 1997; cap. 234.3m., res 12.3m., dep. 1,885.7m. (Dec. 1995); Pres. JOSÉ AFONSO B. BELTRÃO DA SILVA; 755 brs.

Banco do Estado do Rio de Janeiro, SA (Banerj): Av. Nilo Peçanha 175, 17° andar, CP 21090, 20020-100 Rio de Janeiro, RJ; tel. (21) 212-3244; telex 23290; fax (21) 220-4900; f. 1976; cap. 32,854.8m., res 80.9m., dep. 443,501.6m. (cruzeiros reais, Dec. 1993); Federal Government intervened in operations in Jan. 1995; acquired by Banco Itaú in 1997; 232 brs.

Banco Excel Econômico, SA: Rua Augusta 1638, 01304-903 São Paulo SP; tel. (11) 251-4155; telex 23173; fax (11) 289-5531; f. 1996 as a result of merger of Excel Banco and Banco Econômico; Pres. RAHMO NASSER SHAYO; 282 brs.

Banco Francês e Brasileiro, SA: Av. Paulista 1294, 01310-915 São Paulo, SP; tel. (11) 238-8273; telex 23340; fax (11) 251-2195; f. 1948; affiliated with Crédit Lyonnais; cap. 646.1m., res –163.9m., dep. 781.9m. (Dec. 1996); Pres. ROBERTO EGYDIO SETUBAL; 57 brs.

Banco HSBC Bamerindus do Brasil, SA: Travessa Oliveira Belo 11-B, 5° andar Centro, 80020-030 Curitiba, PR; tel. (41) 321-6161; fax (41) 321-6081; f. 1952; cap. 652.8m., res 684.3m., dep. 9,381.0m. (Dec. 1995); Chair. MAURICIO SCHULMAN; 1,214 brs.

Banco Industrial e Comercial, SA: Rua Boa Vista 192 andar, 01014-030 São Paulo, SP; tel. (11) 237-6800; telex 1344; fax (11) 607-3204; f. 1938; cap. 150.0m., res 53.4m., dep. 2,876.0m. (Dec. 1996); Pres. FRANCISCO HUMBERTO BEZERRA; 38 brs.

Banco Itaú, SA: Rua Boa Vista 176, CP 30341, 01092-900 São Paulo, SP; tel. (11) 237-3000; telex 22131; fax (11) 277-1044; internet http://www.itau.com.br; f. 1944; cap. US $1,922m., res US $466m., dep. US $11,118m. (Dec. 1996); Chair. OLAVO EGYDIO SETUBAL; Pres. and CEO ROBERTO EGYDIO SETUBAL; 1,772 brs.

Banco Meridional do Brasil, SA: Rua 7 de Setembro 1028, 3° andar, 90010-230 Porto Alegre, RS; tel. (51) 225-6088; telex 3250; fax (51) 221-5033; f. 1985, formerly Banco Sulbrasileiro, SA; taken over by the Government in Aug. 1985; acquired by Banco Bozano, Simonsen in 1997; cap. 430.4m., res –104.2m., dep. 1,615.8m. (Dec. 1996); Pres. FRANCISCO BARBOSA QUEIROZ; 256 brs.

Banco Multiplic, SA: Av. Jurubatuba 73, Edif. Morumbi Plaza, 04583 São Paulo, SP; tel. (11) 534-6855; telex 52535; fax (11) 534-6946; f. 1978; cap. 1,440.0m., res 53,177.9m., dep. 127,950.2m. (cruzeiros reais, Dec. 1993); Pres. ANTÔNIO JOSÉ DE ALMEIDA CARNEIRO; 8 brs.

Banco Noroeste, SA: Rua Alvares Penteado 216, CP 8119, 01012-900 São Paulo, SP; tel. (11) 605-1674; telex 23600; fax (11) 605-4845; f. 1923; acquired by Banco Santander in 1997; cap. 183.7m., res 196.7m., dep. 1,687.9m. (Dec. 1995); Pres. LÉO WALLACE COCHRANE; 90 brs.

Banco Pontual, SA: Rua Haddock Lobo 684, 01414-000 São Paulo, SP; tel. (11) 306-7381; telex 38271; fax (11) 853-1779; f. 1941; cap. 136.9m., res 24.2m., dep. 1,078.5m. (Dec. 1996); Pres. JOSÉ BAIA SOBRINHO; 11 brs.

Banco Real, SA: Av. Paulista 1374, 3° andar, CP 5766, 01310-916 São Paulo, SP; tel. (11) 251-9045; fax (11) 251-9145; f. 1925; cap. 317.6m., res 480.0m., dep. 8,289.0m. (Dec. 1996); Chair. Dr ALOYSIO DE ANDRADE FARIA; 535 brs.

Banco Safra, SA: Av. Paulista 2100, 16° andar, 01310-930 São Paulo, SP; tel. (11) 251-7575; telex 37742; fax (11) 251-7413; f. 1940; cap. 277.9m., res 293.0m., dep. 3,869.1m. (Dec. 1995); Pres. CARLOS ALBERTO VIEIRA; 65 brs.

Banco Sogeral, SA: Rua Verbo Divino 1207, 28° andar, CP 8785, 04719-002 São Paulo, SP; tel. (11) 281-5148; telex 22924; fax (11) 283-1449; f. 1981; cap. 60.0m., res 24.7m., dep. 863.6m. (Dec. 1995); Pres. BERNARD SONNTAC; 11 brs.

Banco Sudameris Brasil, SA: Av. Paulista 1000, 2°, 10°–16° andares, 01310-100 São Paulo, SP; tel. (11) 283-9633; telex 30397; fax (11) 289-1239; f. 1910; cap. 267.9m., res 123.1m., dep. 2,622.2m. (Dec. 1995); Exec. Dir MILTON BARDINI; 97 brs.

UNIBANCO—União de Bancos Brasileiros, SA: Avda Eusébio Matoso 891, 22° andar, CP 8185, 05423-901 São Paulo, SP; tel. (11) 867-4461; telex 26511; fax (11) 814-0528; f. 1924; cap. 1,100.0m., res 1,053.8m., dep. 10,359.0m. (Dec. 1996); absorbed Banco Nacional in Nov. 1995; Pres. TOMAS ZINNER; 692 brs.

Development Banks

Banco de Desenvolvimento de Minas Gerais, SA—BDMG: Rua da Bahia 1600, CP 1026, Belo Horizonte, MG; tel. (31) 222-5008; telex 1343; fax (31) 273-5084; f. 1962; long-term credit operations; cap. 250.5m., res –111.4m., dep. 229.7m. (Dec. 1996); Pres. MARCOS RAYMUNDO PESSÔA DUARTE.

Banco de Desenvolvimento do Espírito Santo, SA: Av. Princesa Isabel 54, Edif. Caparão, 12° andar, CP 1168, 29010-906 Vitoria, ES; tel. (27) 223-8333; telex 2131; fax (27) 223-6307; total assets US $12.5m. (Dec. 1993); Pres. SERGIO MANOEL NADER BORGES.

Banco de Desenvolvimento do Estado do Rio Grande do Sul, SA (BADESUL): Rua 7 de Setembro 666, 1° andar, CP 10151, 90010 Porto Alegre, RS; tel. (51) 21-2655; telex 1159; fax (51) 227-2221; f. 1975; cap. 154.8m. (cruzeiros, July 1990); Pres. PAULO LAERCIO SOARES MADEIRA.

Banco Nacional de Crédito Cooperativo, SA: Brasília, DF; tel. (61) 224-5575; telex 1370; established in association with the Ministry of Agriculture and guaranteed by the Federal Government to provide co-operative credit; cap. 4.7m. (cruzeiros, July 1990); Pres. ESUPÉRIO S. DE CAMPOS AGUILAR (acting); 41 brs.

Banco Nacional do Desenvolvimento Econômico e Social (BNDES): Av. República do Chile 100, 20031 Rio de Janeiro, RJ; tel. (21) 291-4442; telex 22466; fax (21) 220-9786; f. 1952 to act as main instrument for financing of development schemes sponsored by the Government and to support programmes for the development of the national economy; charged with supervision of privatization programme of early 1990s; cap. 3.3m. (cruzeiros, July 1990); Pres. LUIZ CARLOS MENDONÇA DE BARROS; 2 brs.

Banco Regional de Desenvolvimento do Extremo Sul (BRDE): Rua Uruguai 155, 3°–4° andares, CP 139, 90010-140 Porto Alegre,

RS; tel. (51) 121-9200; telex 1229; f. 1961; cap. 15m. (Dec. 1993); development bank for the states of Paraná, Rio Grande do Sul and Santa Catarina; finances small- and medium-sized enterprises; Dir-Pres. NELSON WEDEKIN; 3 brs.

Investment Bank

Banco de Investimentos Garantia, SA: Rua Jorge Coelho 16, 14° andar, 01451-020 São Paulo, SP; tel. (11) 821-6000; telex 22805; fax (11) 821-6900; f. 1969; cap. 956.6m., res 51,633.1m., dep. 207,831.8m. (cruzeiros reais, Dec. 1993); Dir CLAUDIO LUIZ DA SILVA HADDED; 3 brs.

State-owned Savings Bank

Caixa Econômica Federal: SBS, Q 04, Lote 3/4, Edif. Sede de Caixa Econômica, 70070-000 Brasília, DF; tel. (61) 321-9209; fax (61) 225-0215; f. 1860; cap. 60,247,000m. (cruzeiros, May 1993); dep. 796,113,000m. (April 1993); Pres. SERGIO CUTOLO DOS SANTOS; 1,752 brs.

Foreign Banks

ABN AMRO Bank NV (Netherlands): Rua Verbo Divino 1711, 4° andar, 04719-002 São Paulo, SP; tel. (11) 525-6000; fax (11) 525-6387.

Banco Bilbao Vizcaya (Spain): Edif. Olivetti, andar 13°, Av. Paulista 453, 1311-907 São Paulo, SP; tel. (11) 284-9348; fax (11) 289-6469.

Banco de la Nación Argentina: Av. Paulista 2319, Sobreloja, 01310 São Paulo, SP; tel. (11) 883-1555; telex 32591; fax (11) 881-4630; e-mail bnaspbb@dialdata.com.br; f. 1891; Dir-Gen. GERARDO LUIS PONCE; 2 brs.

Banco Santander (Spain): Av. Paulista 810, 3° andar, 01310-100 São Paulo, SP; tel. (11) 253-4362.

Banco Unión (Venezuela): Av. Paulista 1708, 01310 São Paulo, SP; tel. (11) 283-3722; telex 30476; fax (11) 283-2434; f.1892; Dir-Gen. DONALDISON MARQUES DA SILVA.

BankBoston NA (USA): Rua Líbero Badaró 487, 01009-900 São Paulo, SP; tel. (11) 249-5622; telex 46205; fax (11) 249-5529; Pres. CARLOS LOPES CRAIDE; 31 brs.

The Chase Manhattan Bank (USA): Rua Verbo Divino 1400, São Paulo, SP; tel. (11) 546-4433; fax (11) 546-44624.

Citibank NA (USA): Av. Nilo Pecanha 50, 22° andar, Rio de Janeiro, RJ; tel. (21) 296-1222; telex 22907; fax (21) 276-3287; f. 1812; Dir ARNOLDO SOUZA DE OLIVEIRA; 21 brs.

Dresdner Bank Lateinamerika AG (Germany): Rua Verbo Divino 1488, Centro Empresarial Transatlântico, CP 3641, 01064-970 São Paulo, SP; fmrly Deutsch-Sudamerikanische Bank; tel. (11) 547-6700; telex 53207; fax (11) 524-7709; f. 1969; Man. JÜRGEN BORN MANFRED HAMBURGER; 3 brs.

Lloyds Bank PLC (United Kingdom): Av. Jurubatuba 73, 4°–10° andares, 04583-900 São Paulo, SP; tel. (11) 534-6983; fax (11) 534-6373; e-mail lloyds.dmkt@lloyds.com.br; Gen. Man. DAVID V. THOMAS; 11 brs.

Banking Associations

Federação Brasileira das Associações de Bancos: Rua Líbero Badaró 425, 17° andar, 01069-900 São Paulo, SP; tel. (11) 239-3000; telex 26195; fax (11) 607-8486; f. 1966; Pres. MAURÍCIO SCHULMAN; Vice-Pres ROBERTO EGYDIO SETÚBAL, JOSÉ AFONSO SANCHO.

Sindicato dos Bancos dos Estados do Rio de Janeiro e Espírito Santo: Av. Rio Branco 81, 19° andar, Rio de Janeiro, RJ; Pres. THEÓPHILO DE AZEREDO SANTOS; Vice-Pres. Dr NELSON MUFARREJ.

Sindicato dos Bancos dos Estados de São Paulo, Paraná, Mato Grosso e Mato Grosso do Sul: Rua Líbero Badaró 293, 13° andar, 01905 São Paulo, SP; f. 1924; Pres. PAULO DE QUEIROZ.

There are other banking associations in Maceió, Salvador, Fortaleza, Belo Horizonte, João Pessoa, Recife and Porto Alegre.

STOCK EXCHANGES

Comissão de Valores Mobiliários CVM: Rua Sete de Setembro 111, 32° andar, 20159-900 Rio de Janeiro, RJ; tel. (21) 212-0200; fax (21) 212-0524; e-mail pte@cvm.gov.br; f. 1977 to supervise the operations of the stock exchanges and develop the Brazilian securities market; Chair. FRANCISCO AUGUSTO DA COSTA E SILVA.

Bolsa de Valores do Rio de Janeiro: Praça XV de Novembro 20, 20010-010 Rio de Janeiro, RJ; tel. (21) 271-1001; fax (21) 221-2151; f. 1845; 585 companies listed in 1997; Chair. FERNANDO OPITZ.

Bolsa de Valores de São Paulo (BOVESPA): Rua XV de Novembro 275, 01013-001 São Paulo, SP; tel. (11) 233-2000; telex 21116; fax (11) 233-2099; e-mail bovespa@bovespa.com.br; f. 1890; 550 companies listed in 1997; CEO GILBERTO MIFANO.

There are commodity exchanges at Porto Alegre, Vitória, Recife, Santos and São Paulo.

INSURANCE

Supervisory Authorities

Superintendência de Seguros Privados (SUSEP): Rua Buenos Aires 256, 4° andar, 20061-000 Rio de Janeiro, RJ; tel. (21) 297-4415; fax (21) 221-6664; f. 1966; within Ministry of the Economy; Superintendent HELIO PORTOCARRERO.

Conselho Nacional de Seguros Privados (CNSP): Rua Buenos Aires 256, 20061-000 Rio de Janeiro, RJ; tel. (21) 221-6954; fax (21) 221-6664; f. 1966; Sec. ANDRE LUIZ ALVES BARCELLOS.

Federação Nacional dos Corretores de Seguros e de Capitalização (FENACOR): Av. Rio Branco 147, 6° andar, 20040-006 Rio de Janeiro, RJ; tel. (21) 507-0033; fax (21) 507-0041; e-mail fenacor@IBM.net; Pres. LEÔNCIO DE ARRUDA.

Federação Nacional das Empresas de Seguros Privados e de Capitalização (FENASEG): Rua Senador Dantas 74, 20031-200 Rio de Janeiro, RJ; tel. (21) 210-1204; telex 34505; fax (21) 220-0046; e-mail fenaseg@fenaseg.org.br; Pres. JOÃO ELISIO FERRAZ DE CAMPOS.

IRB—Brasil Resseguros: Av. Marechal Câmara 171, 20023-900 Rio de Janeiro, RJ; tel. (21) 272-0200; telex 21237; fax (21) 240-6261; e-mail irb.info@ibm.net; f. 1939; fmrly Instituto de Resseguros do Brasil; reinsurance; Pres. DEMÓSTHENES MADUREIRA DE PINHO, Filho.

Principal National Companies

The following is a list of the principal national insurance companies, selected on the basis of premium income.

Brasília, DF

Sasse, Cia Nacional de Seguros Gerais: SCN Qd. 1 Lt. A, 15° andar, Ed. Number One, 70710-500 Brasília, DF; tel. (61) 329-2400; f. 1967; general; Pres. PEDRO PEREIRA DE FREITAS.

Rio de Janeiro, RJ

Bradesco Seguros, SA: Rua Barão de Itapagipe 225, 20269-900 Rio de Janeiro, RJ; tel. (21) 563-1199; telex 22721; fax (21) 503-1343; f. 1935; general; Pres. ARARINO SALLUM DE OLIVEIRA.

Generali do Brasil, Cia Nacional de Seguros: Av. Rio Branco 128, 7° andar, 20040-002 Rio de Janeiro, RJ; tel. (21) 292-0144; telex 22846; fax (21) 224-9836; f. 1945; general; Pres. CLÁUDIO BIETOLINI LOTTI.

Golden Cross Seguradora, SA: Rua Moraes e Silva 40, 10° andar, 20271-030; Rio de Janeiro, RJ; tel. (21) 264-7802; telex 82345; fax (21) 264-2112; Pres. PAULO CARVALHO D. S. AFONSO.

Sul América, Cia Nacional de Seguros: Rua da Quitanda 86, 20091-000 Rio de Janeiro, RJ; tel. (21) 296-5112; telex 30677; fax (21) 276-8801; f. 1895; life and risk; Pres. RONY CASTRO DE OLIVEIRA LYRIO.

São Paulo, SP

Cia Paulista de Seguros: Rua Líbero Badaró 158, 1°–10° andares, 01008-000 São Paulo, SP; tel. (11) 229-0811; fax (11) 605-3426; f. 1906; general; Pres. ROBERTO PEREIRA DE ALMEIDA, Filho.

Cia Real Brasileira de Seguros: Av. Paulista 1374, 6° andar, 01310-916 São Paulo, SP; tel. (11) 251-9431; telex 261002; fax (11) 251-5342; f. 1965; Chair. ALOYSIO DE ANDRADE FARIA.

Cia de Seguros do Estado de São Paulo: Rua Pamplona 227, 01405-000 São Paulo, SP; tel. (11) 284-4888; telex 21999; fax (11) 251-1441; f. 1967; life and risk; Pres. JOÃO LEITE NETO.

Itaú Seguros, SA: Praça Alfredo Egydio de Souza Aranha 100, Bloco A, 04344-920 São Paulo, SP; tel. (11) 5582-3322; telex 56212; fax (11) 577-6058; f. 1921; all classes; Pres. LUIZ DE CAMPOS SALLES.

Marítima Seguros, SA: Rua Cel Xavier Toledo 114, 9°–10° andares, 01048-902 São Paulo, SP; tel. (11) 214-1444; telex 35866; fax (11) 239-5848; Pres. FRANCISCO CALUBY VIDIGAL.

Porto Seguro Companhia de Seguros Gerais: Av. Rio Branco 1489, 01205-001 São Paulo, SP; tel. (11) 222-8833; telex 32613; fax (11) 222-7544; f. 1945; life and risk; Pres. ROSA GARFINKEL.

Unibanco Seguros: Av. Paulista 1106, 13° andar, 01310-100 São Paulo, SP; fax (11) 287-8665; f. 1946; life and risk; Pres. JOSÉ CASTRO ARAÚJO RUDGE.

Vera Cruz Seguradora, SA: Av. Maria Coelho Aguiar 215, Bloco D, 2° andar, 05805-000 São Paulo, SP; tel. (11) 545-4944; telex 25642; fax (11) 545-6435; f. 1955; general; Pres. ALFREDO FERNANDES DE L. ORTIZ DE ZARATE.

Provincial Companies

The following is a list of the principal provincial insurance companies, selected on the basis of premium income.

Cia de Seguros Aliança da Bahia: Rua Pinto Martins 11, 9° andar, 40015-020 Salvador, BA; tel. (71) 242-1065; telex 1890; fax (71) 242-6980; f. 1870; general; Pres. PAULO SERGIO FREIRE DE CARVALHO GONÇALVES TOURINHO.

Cia de Seguros Minas-Brasil: Rua dos Caetés 745, 30120-080 Belo Horizonte, MG; tel. (31) 201-5799; telex 1506; fax (31) 219-3820; f. 1938; life and risk; Pres. JOSÉ CARNEIRO DE ARAÚJO.

Cia União de Seguros Gerais: Av. Borges de Medeiros 261, 12° andar, 90020-021 Porto Alegre, RS; tel. (51) 226-7933; telex 2530; fax (51) 226-5330; f. 1891; Pres. NEY MICHELUCCI RODRIGUES.

HSBC Bamerindus Seguros, SA: Rua Marechal Floriano Peixoto 5500, Bloco 01, V. Hauer, 81630-000 Curitiba, PR; tel. (41) 321-6044; fax (41) 321-6078; f. 1938; all classes; Pres. SIMON LLOYD BRETT.

Trade and Industry

GOVERNMENT AGENCIES

Comissão de Fusão e Incorporação de Empresa (COFIE): Ministério da Fazenda, Edif. Sede, Ala B, 1° andar, Esplanada dos Ministérios, Brasília, DF; tel. (61) 225-3405; telex 1539; mergers commission; Pres. SEBASTIÃO MARCOS VITAL; Exec. Sec. EDGAR BEZERRA LEITE, Filho.

Conselho de Desenvolvimento Comercial (CDC): Bloco R, Esplanada dos Ministérios, 70044 Brasília, DF; tel. (61) 223-0308; telex 2537; commercial development council; Exec. Sec. Dr RUY COUTINHO DO NASCIMENTO.

Conselho de Desenvolvimento Econômico (CDE): Bloco K, 7° andar, Esplanada dos Ministérios, 70063 Brasília, DF; tel. (61) 215-4100; f. 1974; economic development council; Gen. Sec. JOÃO BATISTA DE ABREU.

Conselho de Desenvolvimento Social (CDS): Bloco K, 3° andar, 382, Esplanada dos Ministérios, 70063 Brasília, DF; tel. (61) 215-4477; social development council; Exec. Sec. JOÃO A. TELES.

Conselho Nacional do Comércio Exterior (CONCEX): Fazenda, 5° andar, Gabinete do Ministro, Bloco 6, Esplanada dos Ministérios, 70048 Brasília, DF; tel. (61) 223-4856; telex 1142; f. 1966; responsible for foreign exchange and trade policies and for the control of export activities; Exec. Sec. NAMIR SALEK.

Conselho Nacional de Desenvolvimento Científico e Tecnológico (CNPq): Brasília, DF; tel. (61) 348-9401; telex 1089; fax (61) 273-2955; f. 1951; scientific and technological development council; Pres. JOSÉ GALIZIA TUNDISI.

Conselho Nacional de Desenvolvimento Pecuário (CONDEPE): to promote livestock development.

Conselho de Não-Ferrosos e de Siderurgia (CONSIDER): Ministério da Indústria, Comércio e Turismo, Esplanada dos Ministérios, Bloco 7, 7° andar, 70056-900 Brasília, DF; tel. (61) 224-6039; telex 1012; f. 1973; exercises a supervisory role over development policy in the non-ferrous and iron and steel industries; Exec. Sec. WILLIAM ROCHA CANTAL.

Fundação Instituto Brasileiro de Geografia e Estatística (IBGE): Centro de Documentação e Disseminação de Informações (CDDI), Rua Gen. Canabarro 706, 2° andar, Maracanã, 20271-201 Rio de Janeiro, RJ; tel. (21) 569-5997; fax (21) 569-1103; e-mail webmaster@ibge.gov.br; internet http://www.ibge.gov.br; f. 1936; produces and analyses statistical, geographical, cartographic, geodetic, demographic and socio-economic information; Pres. (IBGE) SIMON SCHWARTZMAN; Superintendent (CDDI) DAVID WU TAI.

Instituto Nacional de Metrologia, Normalização e Qualidade Industrial (INMETRO): Rua Santa Alexandrina 416, Rio Comprido, 20261-232 Rio de Janeiro, RJ; tel. (21) 273-9002; telex 34599; fax (21) 293-0954; in 1981 INMETRO absorbed the Instituto Nacional de Pesos e Medidas (INPM), the weights and measures institute; Pres. Dr ARNALDO PEREIRA RIBEIRO.

Instituto de Planejamento Econômico e Social (IPEA): SBS, Edif. BNDE, 6° andar, 70076 Brasília, DF; tel. (61) 225-4350; telex 01979; planning institute; Pres. RICARDO SANTIAGO.

Secretaria Especial de Desenvolvimento Industrial: Brasília, DF; tel. (61) 225-7556; telex 2225; fax (61) 224-5629; f. 1969; industrial development council; offers fiscal incentives for selected industries and for producers of manufactured goods under the Special Export Programme; Exec. Sec. Dr ERNESTO CARRARA.

REGIONAL DEVELOPMENT ORGANIZATIONS

Companhia de Desenvolvimento do Vale do São Francisco (CODEVASF): SGAN, Q 601, Lote 1, Edif. Sede, 70830 Brasília, DF; tel. (61) 223-2797; telex 1057; fax (61) 226-2468; f. 1974; Pres. ELISEU ROBERTO DE ANDRADE ALVES.

Superintendência do Desenvolvimento da Amazônia (SUDAM): Av. Almirante Barroso 426, Bairro do Marco, 66000 Belém, PA; tel. (91) 226-0044; telex 1117; f. 1966 to develop the Amazon regions of Brazil; supervises industrial, cattle breeding and basic services projects; Superintendent Eng. HENRY CHECRALLA KAYATH.

Superintendência do Desenvolvimento do Nordeste (SUDENE): Edif. SUDENE s/n, Praça Ministro João Gonçalves de Souza, Cidade Universitária, 50670-900 Recife, PE; tel. (81) 416-2880; fax (81) 453-1277; f. 1959; attached to the Ministry of Planning, Budget and Co-ordination; assists development of north-east Brazil; Superintendent NILTON MOREIRA RODRIGUES.

Superintendência do Desenvolvimento da Região Centro Oeste (SUDECO): SAS, Quadra 1, Bloco A, Lotes 9/10, 70070 Brasília, DF; tel. (61) 225-6111; telex 1616; f. 1967 to co-ordinate development projects in the states of Goiás, Mato Grosso, Mato Grosso do Sul, Rondônia and Distrito Federal; Superintendent RAMEZ TEBET.

Superintendência da Zona Franca de Manaus (SUFRAMA): Rua Ministro João Gonçalves de Souza s/n, Distrito Industrial, 69075-770 Manaus, AM; tel. (92) 237-1691; fax (92) 237-6549; e-mail 15dinf@internet.com.br; to assist in the development of the Manaus Free Zone; Superintendent MAURO RICARDO MACHADO COSTA.

Other regional development organizations include Poloamazônia (agricultural and agro-mineral nuclei in the Amazon Region), Polocentro (woodland savannah in Central Brazil), Poloeste (agricultural and agro-mineral nuclei in the Centre-West), Polonordeste (integrated areas in the North-East), Procacau (expansion of cocoa industry), Prodoeste (development of the Centre-South), Proterra (land distribution and promotion of agricultural industries in the North and North-East), Provale (development of the São Francisco basin).

AGRICULTURAL, INDUSTRIAL AND TRADE ORGANIZATIONS

ABRASSUCOS: São Paulo, SP; association of orange juice industry; Pres. MÁRIO BRANCO PERES.

Associação do Comércio Exterior do Brasil (AEB): Av. General Justo 335, 4° andar, Rio de Janeiro, RJ; tel. (21) 240-5048; telex 22211; fax (21) 240-5463; e-mail aebbras@embratel.net.br; internet http://www.probrazil.com/aeb.html; exporters' association; Pres. MARCUS VINICIUS PRATINI DE MORAES.

Companhia de Pesquisa de Recursos Minerales (CPRM): Esplanada dos Ministérios, Bloco U, 7° andar, 70055-900 Brasília, DF; mining research, attached to the Ministry of Mining and Energy; Pres. CARLOS BERBERT.

Confederação das Associações Comerciais do Brasil: Brasília, DF; confederation of chambers of commerce in each state; Pres. AMAURY TENPORAL.

Confederação Nacional da Agricultura (CNA): Brasília, DF; tel. (61) 225-3150; national agricultural confederation; Pres. ALYSSON PAULINELLI.

Confederação Nacional do Comércio (CNC): SCS, Edif. Presidente Dutra, 4° andar, Quadra 11, 70327 Brasília, DF; tel. (61) 223-0578; national confederation comprising 35 affiliated federations of commerce; Pres. ANTÔNIO JOSÉ DOMINGUES DE OLIVEIRA SANTOS.

Confederação Nacional da Indústria (CNI): Av. Nilo Peçanha 50, 34° andar, 20044 Rio de Janeiro, RJ; tel. (21) 292-7766; telex 22634; fax (21) 262-1495; f. 1938; national confederation of industry comprising 26 state industrial federations; Pres. Dr ALBANO DO PRADO FRANCO; Vice-Pres. MÁRIO AMATO.

Departamento Nacional da Produção Mineral (DNPM): SAN, Quadra 1, Bloco B, 3° andar, 70040-200 Brasília, DF; tel. (61) 224-2670; telex 1116; fax (61) 225-8274; f. 1934; responsible for geological studies and control of exploration of mineral resources; Dir-Gen. MIGUEL NAVARRETE FERNANDEZ, Filho.

Empresa Brasileira de Pesquisa Agropecuária (EMBRAPA): SAIN, Parque Rural, W/3 Norte, CP 040315, 70770-901 Brasília, DF; tel. (61) 348-4433; telex 2074; fax (61) 347-1041; f. 1973; attached to the Ministry of Agriculture, Supplies and Land Reform; agricultural research; Pres. ALBERTO DUQUE PORTUGAL.

Federação Brasileira dos Exportadores do Café: Brasília, DF, coffee exporters federation; Pres. OSVALDO ARANGA.

Federação das Indústrias do Estado de São Paulo (FIESP): Av. Paulista 1313, 01311-923 São Paulo, SP; tel. (11) 252-4200; telex 22130; fax (11) 284-3611; regional manufacturers' association; Pres. CARLOS EDUARDO MOREIRA FERREIRA.

Instituto Brasileiro do Meio Ambiente e Recursos Naturais Renováveis (IBAMA): Ed. Sede IBAMA, Av. SAIN, L4 Norte, Bloco C, Subsolo, 70800-200 Brasília, DF; tel. (61) 316-1205; fax (61) 226-5094; e-mail cnia@sede.ibama.gov.br; internet http://www.ibama.gov.br; f. 1967; responsible for the annual formulation of national environmental plans; merged with SEMA (National Environmental Agency) in 1988 and replaced the IBDF in 1989; Pres. EDUARDO MAILIUS.

Instituto Brasileiro do Mineração (IBRAM): Brasília, DF; Pres. JOÃO SÉRGIO MARINHO NUNES.

Instituto Nacional da Propriedade Industrial (INPI): Praça Mauá 7, 18° andar, 20081-240 Rio de Janeiro, RJ; tel. (21) 223-4182; fax (21) 263-2539; f. 1970; intellectual property, etc.; Pres. AMÉRICO PUPPIN.

Instituto Nacional de Tecnologia (INT): Av. Venezuela 82, 8° andar, 20081 Rio de Janeiro, RJ; tel. (21) 223-1320; telex 30056; f.

1921; co-operates in national industrial development; Dir PAULO ROBERTO KRAHE.

União Democrática Ruralista (UDR): f. 1986; landowners' organization; Pres. RONALDO CAIADO.

UTILITIES

Electricity

Centrais Elétricas Brasileiras, SA (ELETROBRÁS): Av. Pres. Vargas 642, 10° andar, 20079-900 Rio de Janeiro, RJ; tel. (21) 203-3137; telex 22395; fax (21) 233-3248; f. 1961; government holding company responsible for planning, financing and managing Brazil's electrical energy programme; scheduled for privatization; 1,148 employees (1993); Pres. FIRMINO SAMPAIO.

Centrais Elétricas do Norte do Brasil, SA (ELETRONORTE): SCN, Quadra 6, Conj. A, Blocos B E C, sala 602, Super Center Venâncio 3000, 70718-900 Brasília, DF; tel. (61) 212-6101; telex 1279; fax (61) 321-7798; f. 1973; Pres. RICARDO PINTO PINHEIRO.

Centrais Elétricas do Sul do Brasil, SA (ELETROSUL): Rua Deputado Antônio Edu Vieira 353, Pantanal, 88040-901 Florianópolis, SC; tel. (482) 31-7010; telex 482164; fax (81) 34-5678; f. 1969; Pres. CLÁUDIO AVILA DA SILVA.

Companhia Hidro Elétrica do São Francisco (CHESF): 333 Edif. André Falcão, Bloco A, sala 313 Bongi, Rua Delmiro Golveia, 50761-901 Recife, PE; tel. (81) 228-3160; telex 1350; fax (81) 227-4970; e-mail chesf@cr.pe.rnp.br; f. 1945; Pres. JÚLIO SÉRGIO DE MAYA PEDROSA MOREIRA.

Furnas Centrais Elétricas, SA: Rua Real Grandeza 219, Bloco A, 16° andar, Botafogo, 22281-031 Rio de Janeiro, RJ; tel. (21) 536-3112; telex 21166; fax (21) 286-2249; f. 1957; Pres. RONALDO A. C. FABRICIO.

Associated companies included:

Espírito Santo Centrais Elétricas, SA (ESCELSA): Rua Sete de Setembro 362, Centro, CP 01-0452, 29015-000 Vitória, ES; tel. (27) 322-0155; telex 272159; fax (27) 222-8650; f. 1968; Pres. HENRIQUE MELLO DE MORÃES.

Nuclebrás Engenharia, SA (NUCLEN): Rua Visconde de Ouro Preto 5, 12° andar, Botafogo, 22250-180 Rio de Janeiro, RJ; tel. (21) 552-2345; telex 22709; fax (21) 552-1745; f. 1975; nuclear-power generation and distribution; Pres. EVALDO CÉSARI DE OLIVEIRA.

Comissão Nacional de Energia Nuclear (CNEN): Rua General Severiano 90, Botafogo, 22294 Rio de Janeiro, RJ; tel. (21) 295-9596; telex 21280; fax (21) 546-2442; f. 1956; controlling organization for: Centro de Desenvolvimento da Tecnologia Nuclear—CDTN (nuclear research); Instituto de Engenharia Nuclear—IEN (nuclear engineering); Instituto de Radioproteção e Dosimetria—IRD (radiation protection and dosimetry) and Instituto de Pesquisas Energéticas e Nucleares—IPEN (energetics and nuclear research); in 1988 assumed responsibility for management of nuclear power programme; Pres. JOSÉ MAURO ESTEVES DOS SANTOS.

Itaipú Binacional: Rua Comendador Araújo 551, 11° andar, 80420-000 Curitiba, PR; tel. (41) 223-2389; telex 5163; fax (41) 321-4474; f. 1974; 1,841 employees (Itaipú Brasil—1993); Dir-Gen. (Brazil) FRANCISCO LUIZ SIBUT GOMIDE.

LIGHT Serviços de Eletricidade, SA: Av. Pres. Vargas 642, 19° andar, 20071-001 Rio de Janeiro, RJ; tel. (21) 211-2552; telex 21179; fax (21) 233-6823; f. 1899; electricity generation and distribution in Rio de Janeiro; formerly state-owned, in May 1996 it was sold to a Brazilian-French-US consortium; Pres. JOAQUIM ALFONSO MACDOWELL LEITE DE CASTRO.

Gas

Companhia Estadual de Gás do Rio de Janeiro: Av. Pres. Vargas 2610, 20210 Rio de Janeiro, RJ; tel. (21) 351-8852; gas distribution in the Rio de Janeiro region.

Companhia de Gás de São Paulo (COMGÁS): Rua Augusta 1600, 01304 São Paulo, SP; tel. (11) 289-0344; distribution in São Paulo of gas.

TRADE UNIONS

Central Unica dos Trabalhadores (CUT): Rua São Bento 405, Edif. Martinelli, 7° andar, 01011 São Paulo, SP; tel. (11) 255-7500; telex 21524; fax (11) 37-5626; f. 1983; central union confederation; left-wing; Pres. VINCENTE PAULO DA SILVA; Gen. Sec. GILMAR CARNEIRO.

Confederação General dos Trabalhadores (CGT): São Paulo, SP; f. 1986; fmrly Coordenação Nacional das Classes Trabalhadoras; represents 1,258 labour organizations linked to PMDB; Pres. LUÍS ANTÔNIO MEDEIROS.

Confederação Nacional dos Metalúrgicos (Metal Workers): f. 1985; Pres. JOAQUIM DOS SANTOS ANDRADE.

Confederação Nacional das Profissões Liberais (CNPL) (Liberal Professions): SAU/SUL, Edif. Belvedere Gr. 202, 70070-000 Brasília, DF; tel. (61) 223-1683; fax (61) 223-1944; e-mail cnpliber@nutecnet.com.br; internet http://www.bsb.nutecut.com.br/web/cnpl; f. 1953; confederation of liberal professions; Pres. LUÍS EDUARDO GAUTÉRIO GALLO; Exec. Sec. JOSÉ ANTÔNIO BRITO ANDRADE.

Confederação Nacional dos Trabalhadores na Indústria (CNTI) (Industrial Workers): Av. W/3 Norte, Quadra 505, Lote 01, 70730-517 Brasília, DF; tel. (61) 274-4150; telex 4230; fax (61) 274-7001; f. 1946; Pres. JOSÉ CALIXTO RAMOS.

Confederação Nacional dos Trabalhadores no Comércio (CNTC) (Commercial Workers): Av. W/5 Sul, Quadra 902, Bloco C, 70390 Brasília, DF; tel. (61) 224-3511; f. 1946; Pres. ANTÔNIO DE OLIVEIRA SANTOS.

Confederação Nacional dos Trabalhadores em Transportes Marítimos, Fluviais e Aéreos (CONTTMAF) (Maritime, River and Air Transport Workers): Av. Pres. Vargas 446, gr. 2205, 20071 Rio de Janeiro, RJ; tel. (21) 233-8329; f. 1957; Pres. MAURÍCIO MONTEIRO SANT'ANNA.

Confederação Nacional dos Trabalhadores em Comunicações e Publicidade (CONTCOP) (Communications and Advertising Workers): SCS, Edif. Serra Dourada, 7° andar, gr. 705/709, Q 11, 70315 Brasília, DF; tel. (61) 224-7926; telex 3056; fax (61) 224-5686; f. 1964; 350,000 mems; Pres. ANTÔNIO MARIA THAUMATURGO CORTIZO.

Confederação Nacional dos Trabalhadores nas Empresas de Crédito (CONTEC) (Workers in Credit Institutions): SEP-SUL, Av. W4, EQ 707/907 Lote E, 70351 Brasília, DF; tel. (61) 244-5833; telex 2745; f. 1958; 814,532 mems (1988); Pres. LOURENÇO FERREIRA DO PRADO.

Confederação Nacional dos Trabalhadores em Estabelecimentos de Educação e Cultura (CNTEEC) (Workers in Education and Culture): SAS, Quadra 4, Bloco B, 70302 Brasília, DF; tel. (61) 226-2988; f. 1967; Pres. MIGUEL ABRAHÃO.

Confederação Nacional dos Trabalhadores na Agricultura (CONTAG) (Agricultural Workers): SDS Ed Venâncio VI, 1° andar, 70393-900 Brasília, DF; tel. (61) 321-2288; fax (61) 321-3229; f. 1964; Pres. FRANCISCO URBANO ARAÚJO, Filho.

Força Sindical (FS): São Paulo, SP; f. 1991; 6m. mems (1991); Pres. LUÍS ANTÔNIO MEDEIROS.

Transport

Ministério dos Transportes (MT): Esplanada dos Ministérios, Bloco R, 70044-900 Brasília, DF; tel. (61) 224-0185; telex 1096; fax (61) 225-0915; f. 1990 to study, co-ordinate and execute government transport policy and reorganize railway, road and ports and waterways councils; Exec. Sec. JOSÉ LUIZ PORTELLA PEREIRA.

Empresa Brasileira de Planejamento de Transportes (GEIPOT): SAN, Quadra 3, Blocos N/O, Edif. Núcleo dos Transportes, 70040-902 Brasília, DF; tel. (61) 315-4890; telex 1316; fax (61) 315-4895; internet http://www.geipot.gov.br; f. 1973; agency for the promotion of an integrated modern transport system; advises the Minister of Transport on transport policy; Pres. CARLOS ALBERTO WANDERLEY NÓBREGA.

RAILWAYS

Rede Ferroviária Federal, SA (RFFSA) (Federal Railway Corporation): Praça Procópio Ferreira 86, 20224-900 Rio de Janeiro, RJ; tel. (21) 291-2185; telex 21372; fax (21) 263-0420; f.1957; holding company for 18 railways grouped into regional networks, with total track length of 21,371 km in 1995; privatization of federal railways was completed in 1997; freight services predominate but some long-distance passenger services are also provided; Pres. ISAAC POPOUTCHI.

Companhia Brasileira de Trens Urbanos (CBTU): Estrada Velha da Tijuca 77, Usina, 20531-080 Rio de Janeiro, RJ; tel. (21) 575-3399; telex 36286; fax (21) 571-6149; fmrly responsible for surburban networks and metro systems throughout Brazil; the transfer of each city network to its respective local government is currently under way; Pres. JOSÉ ANTÔNIO ESPOSITO.

Belo Horizonte Metro (CBTU/STU/BH-Demetrô): Av. Afonso Pena 1500, 11° andar, 30130-921 Belo Horizonte, MG; tel. (31) 250-4002; fax (31) 250-4004; e-mail metrobh@gold.horizontes.com.br; f. 1986; 21.2 km open in 1997; Gen. Man. M. L. L. SIQUEIRA.

Trem Metropolitano do Recife: Rua José Natário 478, Areias, 50900-000 Recife, PE; tel. (81) 455-4655; telex 4390; fax (81) 455-4422; f.1985; 53 km open in 1996; Supt FERNANDO ANTÔNIO C. DUEIRE.

Trem Urbano do Recife-Linha Sul: Av. Sul s/n São José, Estação Cinco Pontas, 50020 Recife, PE; tel. (81) 224-3024; telex 1734; fax (81) 251-4844; 31 km open in 1991; Gen. Man. R. P. BARREIRAS GONÇALVES.

There are also railways owned by state governments and several privately-owned railways:.

Companhia Fluminense de Trens Urbanos (Flumitrens): Praça Cristiano Otoni, sala 445, 20221 Rio de Janeiro, RJ; tel. (21) 233-8594; fax (21) 253-3089; f. 1975 as operating division of RFFSA, current name adopted following takeover by state government in 1994; suburban services in Rio de Janeiro and its environs; 264 km open in 1996; Supt P. MUNCK MACHADO.

Companhia do Metropolitano do Rio de Janeiro: Av. Nossa Senhora de Copacabana 493, 22021-031 Rio de Janeiro, RJ; tel. (21) 235-4041; telex 21094; fax (21) 235-4546; 2-line metro system, 26 km open in 1996; Pres. ALVARO SANTO.

Companhia do Metropolitano de São Paulo: Rua Augusta 1626, 03310-200 São Paulo, SP; tel. (11) 283-4933; telex 38104; fax (11) 283-5228; f. 1974; 3-line metro system, 44 km open in 1996; Pres. PAULO CLARINDO GOLDSCHMIDT.

Companhia Paulista de Trens Metropolitanos (CPTM): Av. Paulista 402, 5° andar, 01310-903 São Paulo, SP; tel. (11) 281-6101; fax (11) 288-2224; f. 1993 to incorporate suburban lines fmrly operated by the CBTU and FEPASA; 270 km; Pres. JOSÉ ROBERTO MEDEIROS DA ROSA.

Departamento Metropolitano de Transportes Urbanos: Anexo Palacio do Buriti, 70075 Brasília, DF; tel. (61) 226-9546; the first section of the Brasília metro, linking the capital with the western suburb of Samambaia, was inaugurated in 1994; 38.5 km open in 1997.

Empresa de Trens Urbanos de Porto Alegre, SA: Av. Ernesto Neugebauer 1985, 90250-140 Porto Alegre, RS; tel. (51) 337-3533; telex 5168; fax (51) 337-4173; f. 1985; 28 km open in 1996; Pres. ADÃO DORNELLES FARACO.

Estrada de Ferro do Amapá: Praia de Botafogo 300, 11° andar, ala A, 22250-050 Rio de Janeiro, RJ; tell. (21) 552-4422; f. 1957; operated by Indústria e Comércio de Minérios, SA; 194 km open in 1996; Pres. OSVALDO LUIZ SENRA PESSOA.

Estrada de Ferro Campos do Jordão: Rua Martin Cabral 87, CP 11, 12400-000 Pindamonhangaba, SP; tel. (22) 242-4233; fax (22) 242-2499; operated by the Tourism Secretariat of the State of São Paulo; 47 km open in 1996; Dir ARTHUR FERREIRA DOS SANTOS.

Estrada de Ferro Carajás: Av. dos Portugueses s/n, 65085-580 São Luís, MA; tel. (98) 218-4000; telex 4554; fax (98) 218-4530; f. 1985 for movement of minerals from the Serra do Carajás to the new port at Ponta da Madeira; operated by the Companhia Vale do Rio Doce; 1,089 km open in 1996; Supt LAURO JOSE VAREJÃO FASSARELLA.

Estrada de Ferro do Jari: Monte Dourado, 68230-000 Pará, PA; tel. (91) 735-1155; fax (91) 735-1475; transportation of timber and bauxite; 68 km open; Dir ARMINDO LUIZ BARETTA.

Estrada de Ferro Mineração Rio do Norte, SA: Praia do Flamengo 200, 5° e 6° andares, 22210-030 Rio de Janeiro, RJ; tel. (21) 205-9112; fax (21) 545-5717; 35 km open in 1996; Pres. ANTÔNIO JOÃO TORRES.

Estrada de Ferro Paraná-Oeste, SA (Ferroeste): Rua Desemb. Costa Carvalho 178, 80440-210 Curitiba, PR; tel. (41) 243-5758; fax (41) 243-5482; f. 1988 to serve the grain-producing regions in Paraná and Mato Grosso do Sul; 248 km inaugurated in 1995; privatized in late 1996, South African company, Comazar, appointed as administrator; Pres. MARTIN ROEDER.

Estrada de Ferro Vitória-Minas: Rod BR-262, km 1, Jardim América, 29140-900 Porto Velho, ES; tel. (27) 226-0762; telex 2161; fax (27) 226-0093; f. 1942; operated by Companhia Vale de Rio Doce; transport of iron ore, general cargo and passengers; 898 km open in 1996; Supt ALCIO FERREIRA PASSOS.

Estrada de Ferro Votorantim: Praça Brasil 16, 18110-100 Votorantim, SP; tel. (15) 243-2484; fax (15) 243-3911; 20 km open in 1996; Supt PAULO ROBERTO MANSUR DA SILVA.

Ferrovia Paulista, SA (FEPASA): Rua Mauá 51, 01018-900 São Paulo, SP; tel. (11) 222-3392; fax (11) 220-8852; f. 1971 by merger of five railways operated by São Paulo State; 4,625 km open in 1996; Supt RENATO CASALI PAVAN.

Association

Associação Brasileira de Preservação Ferroviaria (ABPF) (Brazilian Railway Preservation Society): CP 6501, 01064-970 São Paulo, SP; maintains and operates railways with tourist interest; Pres. H. GAZETTA, Filho.

Estrada de Ferro Campinas a Jaguariuna: CP 6501, 01064-970 São Paulo, SP; tel. (192) 53-6067; 25 steam and two diesel locomotives; 24 km open; Man. V.A. SILVA.

Estrada de Ferro Vale do Bom Jesús: CP 6051, 01064-970 São Paulo, SP; tel. (16) 771-1624; four steam locomotives; 36 km open; Man. B.M.L. GRASSI.

ROADS

In 1996 there were an estimated 1,980,000 km of roads in Brazil, of which 3,630 km were main roads. Brasília has been a focal point for inter-regional development, and paved roads link the capital with every region of Brazil. The building of completely new roads has taken place predominantly in the north. Roads are the principal mode of transport, accounting for 60% of freight and 95% of passenger traffic, including long-distance bus services, in 1993. Major projects include the 5,000-km Trans-Amazonian Highway, running from Recife and Cabedelo to the Peruvian border, the 4,138-km Cuibá–Santarém highway, which will run in a north–south direction, and the 3,555-km Trans-Brasiliana project, which will link Marabá, on the Trans-Amazonian highway, with Aceguá, on the Uruguayan frontier. In 1990 the Government announced plans to privatize many of Brazil's major roads and transfer others from federal to state jurisdiction. In a two-phase programme, some 800 km of federal highways have been offered for operation concessions, with successful private operators committed to initial improvement projects to be implemented at an estimated cost of US $1,250m., in return for toll revenues during a 25-year period. The second phase, in which the operation of more than 15,000 km of federal highways will be offered to private concerns, is expected to attract initial investment of some $6,800m. A 20-year plan to construct a highway linking São Paulo with the Argentine and Chilean capitals was endorsed in 1992 within the context of the development of the Southern Cone Common Market (Mercosul).

Departamento Nacional de Estradas de Rodagem (DNER) (National Roads Development): SAN, Quadra 3, Blocos N/O, 4° andar, Edif. Núcleo dos Transportes, 70040-902 Brasília, DF; tel. (61) 315-4100; telex 1354; fax (61) 315-4050; f. 1945 to plan and execute federal road policy and to supervise state and municipal roads with the aim of integrating them into the national network; Dir MAURICO H. BORGES.

INLAND WATERWAYS

River transport plays only a minor part in the movement of goods, although total freight carried increased from 4.7m. tons in 1980 to 7.7m. tons in 1988. There are three major river systems, the Amazon, Paraná and the São Francisco. The Amazon is navigable for 3,680 km, as far as Iquitos in Peru, and ocean-going ships can reach Manaus, 1,600 km upstream. Plans have been drawn up to improve the inland waterway system and one plan is to link the Amazon and Upper Paraná to provide a navigable waterway across the centre of the country. In October 1993 the member governments of Mercosul, together with Bolivia, reaffirmed their commitment to a 10-year development programme (initiated in 1992) for the extension of the Tietê Paraná river network along the Paraguay and Paraná Rivers as far as Buenos Aires, improving access to Atlantic ports and creating a 3,442 km waterway system, navigable throughout the year.

Secretaria de Transportes Aquavirários: Departamento de Portos, Ministerio dos Transportes, SAN, Q.3, Blocos N/O, 70040-902 Brasília, DF; Sec. JORGE FRANCISCO MEDAUAR.

Administração da Hidrovia do Paraguai (AHIPAR): Rua Treze de Junho 960, Corumbá, MS; tel. (67) 231-2841; telex 7015; fax (67) 231-2661; Supt. PAULO CÉSAR C. GOMES DA SILVA.

Administração da Hidrovia do Paraná (AHRANA): Rua Vinte e Quatro de Maio 55, 9° andar, Conj. B, 01041-001 São Paulo, SP; tel. (11) 221-3230; telex 23535; fax (11) 220-8689; Supt LUIZ EDUARDO GARCIA.

Administração da Hidrovia do São Francisco (AHSFRA): Praça do Porto 70, Distrito Industrial, 39270-000 Pirapora, MG; tel. (38) 741-2555; telex 7092; fax (38) 741-2510; Supt JOSÉ H. BORATO JABUR JÚNIOR.

Administração das Hidrovias do Sul (AHSUL): Praça Oswaldo Cruz 15, 3° andar, 90030-160 Porto Alegre, RS; tel. (51) 228-3677; telex 3313; fax (51) 226-9068; Supt JOSÉ LUIZ F. DE AZAMBUJA.

Empresa de Navegação da Amazônia, SA (ENASA): Av. Pres. Vargas 41, 66000-000 Belém, PA; tel. (91) 223-3878; telex 2064; fax (91) 224-0528; f. 1967; cargo and passenger services on the Amazon river and its principal tributaries, connecting the port of Belém with all major river ports; Pres. ANTÔNIO DE SOUZA MENDONÇA; 48 vessels.

SHIPPING

There are more than 40 deep-water ports in Brazil, all but two of which (Luis Correia and Imbituba) are directly or indirectly administered by the Government. The majority of ports are operated by eight state-owned concerns (Cia Docas do Pará, Maranhão, Ceará, Rio Grande do Norte, Bahia, Espírito Santo, Rio de Janeiro and Estado de São Paulo), while a smaller number (including Suape, Cabedelo, Barra dos Coqueiros, São Sebastião, Paranaguá, Antonina, São Francisco do Sul, Porto Alegre, Pelotas and Rio Grande do Sul) are administered by state governments. In late 1996 the Government announced plans to privatize 31 ports (including Santos and Rio de Janeiro).

The largest handlers of general cargo are the ports of Santos, Rio de Janeiro, Angra dos Reis, Praia Mole, Vitória and Rio Grande. Other ports specialize in bulk cargo, such as Tubarão and Ponta da Madeira (iron ore), Santana (manganese), Sepetiba (coal), Paranaguá, Rio Grande, Santos and São Francisco do Sul (soya beans and derivatives), Recife and Maceió (sugar), Ilhéus (cocoa), and Areia Branca (salt). The principal petroleum-handling terminals include São Sebastião, Madre de Deus and Angra dos Reis.

The ports of Santos, Rio de Janeiro and Rio Grande have specialized container terminals handling more than 700,000 TEUs (20-ft equivalent units of containerized cargo) per year. Santos is the major container port in Brazil, accounting for 500,000 TEUs annually. The ports of Paranaguá, Itajaí, São Francisco do Sul, Salvador, Vitória and Imbituba cater for containerized cargo to a lesser extent and total container movement at Brazilian ports in 1992 involved around 1m. TEUs.

Total cargo handled by Brazilian ports in 1994 amounted to 360.4m. tons, of which 204.6m. was bulk cargo, 117.7m. was liquid cargo and 38.1m. was general cargo. Some 43,000 vessels used Brazil's ports in 1992.

In Latin America, Brazil's merchant fleet is second in size only to that of Panama, comprising 539 vessels (amounting to 4,530,039 grt) in December 1996.

Departamento de Marinha Mercante: Coordenação Geral de Transporte Maritimo, Av. Rio Branco 103, 6° e 8° andar, 20040-004 Rio de Janeiro, RJ; tel. (21) 221-4014; fax (21) 221-5929; Dir PAULO OCTÁVIO DE PAIVA ALMEIDA.

Port Authorities

Paranaguá: Administração dos Portos de Paranaguá e Antonina (APPA), BR-277, km 0, 83206-380 Paranaguá, PR; tel. (41) 422-0955; telex 4182; fax (41) 422-5324; Port Admin. MARIO MARCONDES LOBO.

Recife: Administração do Porto do Recife, Praça Artur Oscar, 50030-370 Recife, PE; tel. (81) 424-4044; telex 1018; fax (81) 224-2848; Port Dir CARLOS DO REGO VILAR.

Rio de Janeiro: Companhia Docas do Rio de Janeiro (CDRJ), Rua do Acre 21, 20081-000 Rio de Janeiro, RJ; tel. (21) 296-5151; telex 22163; fax (21) 233-2064; CDRJ also administers the ports of Forno, Niterói, Sepetiba and Angra dos Reis; Pres. MAURO OROFINO CAMPO.

Rio Grande: Administração do Porto de Rio Grande, Av. Honório Bicalho, CP 198, 96201-020 Rio Grande do Sul, RS; tel. (532) 31-1996; telex 2423; fax (532) 31-1857; Port Admin. DANTEUSLENGHI DAPUZZO.

Santos: Companhia Docas do Estado de São Paulo (CODESP), Av. Conselheiro Rodrigues Alves s/n, 11015-900 Santos, SP; tel. (13) 233-6565; fax (13) 233-3080; CODESP also administers the ports of Charqueadas, Estrela, Cáceres, Corumbá/Ladário, and the waterways of Paraná (AHRANA), Paraguai (AHIPAR) and the South (AHSUL); Pres. PEDRO BATOURI.

São Francisco do Sul: Administração do Porto de São Francisco do Sul, Av. Eng. Leite Ribeiro 782, CP 71, 89240-000 São Francisco do Sul, SC; tel. (474) 44-0200; telex 4348; fax (474) 44-0115; Dir-Gen. ARNALDO S. THIAGO.

Tubarão: Companhia Vale do Rio Doce, Porto de Tubarão, Vitória, ES; tel. (27) 335-5727; telex 2517; fax (27) 228-0612; Port Dir CANDIDO COTTA PACHECO.

Vitória: Companhia Docas do Espírito Santo (CODESA), Av. Getúlio Vargas 560, Centro, 29020-030 Vitória, ES; tel. (27) 321-1311; telex 2118; fax (27) 222-7360; f. 1983; Chair. WILSON CALMON ALVES.

Other ports are served by the following state-owned companies:

Companhia Docas do Estado de Bahia: Av. da França 1551, 40010-000 Salvador, BA; tel. (71) 243-5066; telex 1110; fax (71) 241-6712; administers the ports of Aracaju, Salvador, Aratu, Ilhéus and Pirapora, and the São Francisco waterway (AHSFRA); Pres. JORGE FRANCISCO MEDAUAR.

Companhia Docas do Estado de Ceará (CDC): Praça Amigos da Marinha s/n, 60182-640 Fortaleza, CE; tel. (85) 263-1551; telex 1113; fax (85) 263-2433; administers the port of Fortaleza; Dir MARCELO MOTA TEIXEIRA.

Companhia Docas de Maranhão (CODOMAR): Porto do Itaquí, Rua de Paz 561, 65085-370 São Luís, MA; tel. (98) 222-2412; telex 1042; fax (98) 221-1394; administers ports of Itaquí and Manaus, and the waterways of the Western Amazon (AHIMOC) and the North-East (AHINOR); Dir WASHINGTON DE OLIVEIRA VIEGAS.

Companhia Docas do Pará (CDP): Av. Pres. Vargas 41, 2° andar, 66010-000 Belém, PA; tel. (91) 216-2011; telex 912320; fax (91) 241-1741; f. 1967; administers the ports of Belém, Macapá, Porto Velho, Santarém and Vila do Conde, and the waterways of the Eastern Amazon (AHIMOR) and Tocantins and Araguaia (AHITAR); Dir-Pres. CARLOS ACATAUSSÚ NUNES.

Companhia Docas do Estado do Rio Grande do Norte (CODERN): Av. Hildebrando de Góis 2220, Ribeira, 59010-700 Natal, RN; tel. (84) 211-5311; telex 2114; fax (84) 221-6072; administers the ports of Areia Branca, Natal, Recife and Maceió; Dir EMILSON MEDEIROS DOS SANTOS.

Other State-owned Companies

Companhia de Navegação Lloyd Brasileiro: Rua do Rosário 1, 10° andar, CP 1501, 20041-000 Rio de Janeiro, RJ; tel. (21) 291-0077; telex 23364; fax (21) 253-4867; f. 1890; partly government-owned; operates between Brazil, the USA, Northern Europe, Scandinavia, the Mediterranean, East and West Africa, the Far East, the Arabian Gulf, Japan, Australia and New Zealand, and around the South American coast through the associated company Lloyd-Libra. Operates with palletized, containerized and frozen cargoes, as well as with general and bulk cargoes; Pres. JORGE SILVEIRA MELLO NETTO.

Companhia de Navegação do Estado de Rio de Janeiro: Praça 15 de Novembro 21, 20010-010 Rio de Janeiro, RJ; tel (21) 231-0398; telex 38251; fax (21) 252-0524; Pres. JOSÉ CARLOS DELGADO SÉLVICO.

Frota Nacional de Petroleiros—Fronape: Rua Carlos Seidl 188, CP 51015, 20931, Rio de Janeiro, RJ; tel. (21) 580-9773; telex 22286; fleet of tankers operated by the state petroleum company, PETROBRÁS, and the Ministry of Transport; Chair. ALBANO DE SOUZA GONÇALVES.

Private Companies

Companhia Docas de Imbituba (CDI): Porto de Imbituba, Av. Presidente Vargas s/n, 88780-000 Imbituba, SC; tel. (482) 55-0080; telex 2421; fax (482) 55-0701; administers the port of Imbituba; Exec. Dir. MANUEL ALVES DO VALE.

Companhia de Navegação do Norte (CONAN): Av. Rio Branco 23, 25° andar, 20090-003 Rio de Janeiro, RJ; tel. (21) 223-4155; telex 22713; fax (21) 253-7128; f. 1965; services to Brazil, Argentina, Uruguay and inland waterways; Chair. J. R. RIBEIRO SALOMÃO.

Empresa de Navegação Aliança, SA: Av. Pasteur 110, Botafogo, 22290-240 Rio de Janeiro, RJ; tel. (21) 546-1112; telex 23778; fax (21) 546-1161; f. 1950; cargo services to Argentina, Uruguay, Europe, Baltic, Atlantic and North Sea ports; Pres. CARLOS G. E. FISCHER.

Companhia de Navegação do São Francisco: Av. São Francisco 1517, 39270-000 Pirapora, MG; tel. (38) 741-1444; fax (38) 741-1164; Pres. JOSÉ HUMBERTO BARATA JABUR.

Frota Oceânica Brasileira, SA: Av. Venezuela 110, CP 21-020, 20081-310 Rio de Janeiro, RJ; tel. (21) 291-5153; telex 23564; fax (21) 263-1439; f. 1947; Pres. JOSÉ CARLOS FRAGOSO PIRES; Vice-Pres. LUIZ J. C. ALHANATI.

Serviço de Navegação Bacia Prata: Av. 14 de Março 1700, 79370-000 Ladário, MS; tel. (67) 231-2561; Dir LUIZ CARLOS DA SILVA ALEXANDRE.

Vale do Rio Doce Navegação, SA (DOCENAVE): Rua Voluntários da Pátria 143, Botafogo, 22279-900 Rio de Janeiro, RJ; tel. (21) 536-8002; telex 22142; fax (21) 536-8276; bulk carrier to Japan, Arabian Gulf, Europe, North America and Argentina; Pres. HENRIQUE SABÓIA.

CIVIL AVIATION

There are about 1,500 airports and airstrips. Of the 62 principal airports 22 are international, although most international traffic is handled by the two airports at Rio de Janeiro and two at São Paulo.

Empresa Brasileira de Infra-Estrutura Aeroportuária (INFRAERO): Edif. Chams, Q 04, Bloco A, 6° andar, 70300-500 Brasília, DF; tel. (61) 312-3222; telex 1028; fax (61) 321-0512; Pres. ADYR DA SILVA.

Principal Airlines

Brasil Central Linha Aérea Regional: Rua Monsenhor Antônio Pepe 94, Jardim Aeroporto, 04355-040 São Paulo, SP; tel. (11) 5582-8811; fax (11) 578-5946; Pres. Capt. ROLIM ADOLFO AMARO.

Lider Taxi Aéreo, SA: Av. Santa Rosa 123, 31270 Belo Horizonte, MG; tel. (31) 448-4700; fax (31) 443-4179; Pres. JOSÉ AFONSO ASSUMPÇÃO.

Nordeste Linhas Aéreas Regionais: Av. Tancredo Neves 1672, Edif. Catabas Empresarial, 1° andar, Pituba, 41820-020 Salvador, BA; tel. (71) 341-7533; fax (71) 341-0393; e-mail nordeste@provider.com.br; f. 1976; services to 26 destinations in north-east Brasil; Pres. PERCY LOURENÇO RODRIGUES.

Pantanal Taxi Aéreo (Pantanal Linhas Aéreas Sul-Matogrossenses, SA): Av. Nações Unidas 10989, 8° andar, São Paulo, SP; tel. (11) 3040-3900; fax (11) 866-3424; e-mail pantanal@uninet.com.br; f. 1993; regional services; Pres. MARCOS FERREIRA SAMPAIO.

Rio-Sul Serviços Aéreos Regionais, SA: Av. Rio Branco 85, 11° andar, 20040-004 Rio de Janeiro, RJ; tel. (21) 263-4282; telex 31429; fax (21) 253-2044; f. 1976; subsidiary of VARIG; domestic passenger services to cities in southern Brazil; Pres. PAULO ENRIQUE MORÃES COCO.

Transbrasil SA Linhas Aéreas: Rua Gen. Pantaleão Teles 40, Hangar Transbrasil, Aeroporto de Congonhas, 04355-900 São Paulo, SP; tel. (11) 533-5367; telex 21386; fax (11) 543-8048; f. 1955 as Sadia, renamed 1972; scheduled passenger and cargo services to major Brazilian cities and Orlando; cargo charter flights to the USA; Pres. Dr Omar Fontana.

Transportes Aéreos Regionais (TAM): Rua Monsenhor Antônio Pepe 09, Jardim Aeroporto, 04342-001 São Paulo, SP; tel. (11) 5582-8811; telex 34240; fax (11) 578-5946; f. 1976; scheduled passenger and cargo services from São Paulo to destinations throughout Brazil; Chair. Capt. Rolim Adolfo Amaro.

Transportes Aéreos Regionais da Bacia Amazônica (TABA): Rua João Balb 202, Nazaré, 66055-260 Belém, PA; tel. (91) 242-6300; telex 1314; fax (91) 222-0471; f. 1976; domestic passenger services throughout north-west Brazil; Chair. Marcílio Jacques Gibson.

VARIG, SA (Viação Aérea Rio Grandense): Av. Almirante Sílvio de Noronha 365, Bloco A, sala 45, 20021-010 Rio de Janeiro, RJ; tel. (21) 272-5000; telex 22363; fax (21) 272-5700; f. 1927; international services throughout North, Central and South America, Africa, Western Europe and Japan; domestic services to major Brazilian cities; cargo services; Chair. and Pres. Fernando Pinto.

VASP, SA (Viação Aérea São Paulo): Praça Comte-Lineu Gomes s/n, Aeroporto Congonhas, 04626-910 São Paulo, SP; tel. (11) 533-7011; telex 56575; fax (11) 542-0880; f. 1933; privatized in Sept. 1990; domestic services throughout Brazil; international services to Argentina, Belgium, the Caribbean, South Korea and the USA; Pres. Wagner Canhedo.

Tourism

In 1997 some 2.8m tourists visited Brazil. Receipts from tourism totalled US $972m. in 1995. Rio de Janeiro, with its famous beaches, is the centre of the tourist trade. Like Salvador, Recife and other towns, it has excellent examples of Portuguese colonial and modern architecture. The modern capital, Brasília, incorporates a new concept of city planning and is the nation's show-piece. Other attractions are the Iguaçu Falls, the seventh largest (by volume) in the world, the tropical forests of the Amazon basin and the wildlife of the Pantanal.

Divisão de Feiras e Turismo/Departamento de Promoção Comercial: Ministério das Relações Exteriores, Esplanada dos Ministérios, 5° andar, 70170-900 Brasília, DF; tel. (61) 211-6394; f 1977; organizes Brazil's participation in trade fairs and commercial exhibitions abroad; Principal Officer João Alberto Dourado Quintães.

Instituto Brasileiro de Turismo—EMBRATUR: SCN, Q 02, Bloco G, 3° andar, 70710-500 Brasília, DF; tel. (61) 224-9100; telex 1335; fax (61) 223-9889; f. 1966; Pres. Caio Luiz de Carvalho.

BRUNEI

Introductory Survey

Location, Climate, Language, Religion, Flag, Capital

The Sultanate of Brunei (Negara Brunei Darussalam) lies in South-East Asia, on the north-west coast of the island of Borneo (most of which is comprised of the Indonesian territory of Kalimantan). It is surrounded and bisected on the landward side by Sarawak, one of the two eastern states of Malaysia. The country has a tropical climate, characterized by consistent temperature and humidity. Annual rainfall averages about 2,540 mm (100 ins) in coastal areas and about 3,300 mm (130 ins) in the interior. Temperatures are high, with average daily temperatures ranging from 24°C (75°F) to 32°C (90°F). The principal language is Malay, although Chinese is also spoken and English is widely used. The Malay population (an estimated 66.9% of the total in 1996) are mainly Sunni Muslims. Most of the Chinese in Brunei (15.2% of the population) are Buddhists, and some are adherents of Confucianism and Daoism. Europeans and Eurasians are predominantly Christians, and the majority of indigenous tribespeople (Iban, Dayak and Kelabit—5.9% of the population) adhere to various animist beliefs. The flag (proportions 2 by 1) is yellow, with two diagonal stripes, of white and black, running from the upper hoist to the lower fly; superimposed in the centre is the state emblem (in red, with yellow Arabic inscriptions). The capital is Bandar Seri Begawan (formerly called Brunei Town).

Recent History

Brunei, a traditional Islamic monarchy, formerly included most of the coastal regions of North Borneo (now Sabah) and Sarawak, which later became states of Malaysia. During the 19th century the rulers of Brunei ceded large parts of their territory to the United Kingdom, reducing the sultanate to its present size. In 1888, when North Borneo became a British Protectorate, Brunei became a British Protected State. In accordance with an agreement made in 1906, a British Resident was appointed to the court of the ruling Sultan as an adviser on administration. Under this arrangement, a form of government that included an advisory body, the State Council, emerged.

Brunei was invaded by Japanese forces in December 1941, but reverted to its former status in 1945, when the Second World War ended. The British-appointed Governor of Sarawak was High Commissioner for Brunei from 1948 until the territory's first written Constitution was promulgated in September 1959, when a further agreement was made between the Sultan and the British Government. The United Kingdom continued to be responsible for Brunei's defence and external affairs until the Sultanate's declaration of independence in 1984.

In December 1962 a large-scale revolt broke out in Brunei and in parts of Sarawak and North Borneo. The rebellion was undertaken by the 'North Borneo Liberation Army', an organization linked with the Parti Rakyat Brunei (PRB—Brunei People's Party), led by Sheikh Ahmad Azahari, which was strongly opposed to the planned entry of Brunei into the Federation of Malaysia. The rebels proclaimed the 'revolutionary State of North Kalimantan', but the revolt was suppressed, after 10 days' fighting, with the aid of British forces from Singapore. A state of emergency was declared, the PRB was banned, and Azahari was given asylum in Malaya. In the event, the Sultan of Brunei, Sir Omar Ali Saifuddin III, decided in 1963 against joining the Federation. From 1962 he ruled by decree, and the state of emergency remained in force. In October 1967 Saifuddin, who had been Sultan since 1950, abdicated in favour of his son, Hassanal Bolkiah, who was then 21 years of age. Under an agreement signed in November 1971, Brunei was granted full internal self-government.

In December 1975 the UN General Assembly adopted a resolution advocating British withdrawal from Brunei, the return of political exiles and the holding of a general election. Negotiations in 1978, following assurances by Malaysia and Indonesia that they would respect Brunei's sovereignty, resulted in an agreement (signed in January 1979) that Brunei would become fully independent within five years. Independence was duly proclaimed on 1 January 1984, and the Sultan took office as Prime Minister and Minister of Finance and of Home Affairs, presiding over a Cabinet of six other ministers (including two of the Sultan's brothers and his father, the former Sultan).

The future of the Chinese population, who controlled much of Brunei's private commercial sector but had become stateless since independence, appeared threatened in 1985, when the Sultan indicated that Brunei would become an Islamic state in which the indigenous, mainly Malay, inhabitants, known as *bumiputras* ('sons of the soil'), would receive preferential treatment. Several Hong Kong and Taiwan Chinese, who were not permanent Brunei residents, were repatriated.

In May 1985 a new political party, the Parti Kebangsaan Demokratik Brunei (PKDB—Brunei National Democratic Party), was formed. The new party, which comprised business executives loyal to the Sultan, based its policies on Islam and a form of liberal nationalism. However, the Sultan forbade employees of the Government (about 40% of the country's working population) to join the party. Persons belonging to the Chinese community were also excluded from membership. Divisions within the new party led to the formation of a second group, the Parti Perpaduan Kebangsaan Brunei (PPKB—Brunei National Solidarity Party), in February 1986. This party, which also received the Sultan's official approval, placed greater emphasis on co-operation with the Government, and was open to both Muslim and non-Muslim ethnic groups.

Although the Sultan was not expected to allow any relaxation of restrictions on radical political activities, it became clear during 1985 and 1986 that a more progressive style of government was being adopted. The death of Sir Omar Ali Saifuddin, the Sultan's father, in September 1986 was expected to hasten modernization. In October the Cabinet was enlarged to 11 members, and commoners and aristocrats were assigned portfolios that had previously been given to members of the royal family. In February 1988, however, the PKDB was dissolved by the authorities after it had demanded the resignation of the Sultan as Head of Government (although not as Head of State), an end to the 26-year state of emergency and the holding of democratic elections. The official reason for the dissolution of the party was its connections with a foreign organization, the Pacific Democratic Union. The leaders of the PKDB, Abdul Latif Hamid and Abdul Latif Chuchu, were arrested, under provisions of the Internal Security Act, and detained until March 1990. Abdul Latif Hamid died in May. In January of that year the Government ordered the release of six political prisoners, who had been detained soon after the revolt in 1962.

In 1990 the Government encouraged the population to embrace *Melayu Islam Beraja* (Malay Islamic Monarchy) as the state ideology. This affirmation of traditional Bruneian values for Malay Muslims was widely believed to be a response to an increase in social problems, including the abuse of alcohol and mild narcotics. Muslims were encouraged to adhere more closely to the tenets of Islam, greater emphasis was laid on Islamic holiday celebrations, and the distribution of alcohol was discouraged. In January 1991 the import of alcohol to Brunei was banned, and in December the public celebration of the Christian festival, Christmas, was forbidden. In 1992 the Sultan made his third pilgrimage to Mecca, Saudi Arabia, and delivered the sermon on the occasion of the holiday, *Hari Raya Puasa* (the end of Ramadan), at the Grand Mosque. In January 1993 the International Bank of Brunei was renamed the Islamic Bank of Brunei and adopted Islamic banking practices.

In 1992 there was a 15-day celebration leading to the 25th anniversary of the Sultan's accession to the throne in early October. Contrary to rumours that the Sultan intended to announce the creation of a consultative assembly in his anniversary address, he instead emphasized the munificence of the monarchy and endorsed the existing system. However, extremely moderate progress towards reform was apparent in subsequent years. In 1994 a constitutional committee, appointed by the Government and chaired by the Minister of Foreign Affairs, Prince Mohamad Bolkiah, submitted a recommendation that the Constitution be amended to provide for an elected legislature. In February 1995 the PPKB was given permission to convene a general assembly, at which Abdul Latif Chuchu, the former Secretary-General of the PKDB, was elected President. In July 1996 the Sultan released a well-known political prisoner, Zaini Ahmad, who had been detained since the revolt in 1962.

In February 1997 the Sultan replaced his brother, Prince Jefri Bolkiah, as Minister of Finance. It was rumoured that the Sultan's assumption of the finance portfolio was due to alleged financial disagreements rather than Prince Jefri's frequently criticized extravagant lifestyle. In March the Sultan denied accusations of misconduct made by a former winner of a US beauty contest. A US court granted the Sultan immunity from legal action in August, owing to his status as a foreign head of state.

Relations with the United Kingdom had become strained during 1983, following the Brunei Government's decision, in August, to transfer the management of its investment portfolio from the British Crown Agents to the newly-created Brunei Investment Agency. However, normal relations were restored in September, when the British Government agreed that a battalion of Gurkha troops, stationed in Brunei since 1971, should remain in Brunei after independence, at the Sultanate's expense, specifically to guard the oil and gas fields.

Brunei has developed close relations with the members of the Association of South East Asian Nations (ASEAN—see p. 113), in particular Singapore, and became a full member of the organization immediately after independence. Royal visits were made to Thailand and Indonesia in 1984, and diplomatic relations with Japan were established in the same year. Brunei also joined the UN, the Commonwealth (see p. 125) and the Organization of the Islamic Conference (see p. 224) in 1984. In September 1991 Brunei applied for membership of the Non-aligned Movement (see p. 271), and was formally admitted to the organization in September 1992. In late 1991 Brunei established diplomatic relations with the People's Republic of China at ambassadorial level. As a member of ASEAN, Brunei's relations with Viet Nam improved during 1991 (following Viet Nam's withdrawal from Cambodia in September 1989). In February 1992 diplomatic relations were formally established with Viet Nam during a visit to Brunei of the Vietnamese Premier. In July 1990, in response to the uncertainty over the future of US bases in the Philippines (see chapter on the Philippines, Vol. II), Brunei joined Singapore in offering the USA the option of operating its forces from Brunei. A bilateral memorandum of understanding was subsequently signed, providing for up to three visits a year to Brunei by US warships. Under the memorandum, Brunei forces were to train with US personnel. In August 1993 the Malaysian Prime Minister led a delegation to Brunei, and the two countries agreed to seek to resolve all outstanding border disputes through negotiations. In January 1994 a joint commission was established to strengthen economic and cultural relations between Brunei and Malaysia. In October 1993 the Brunei Government announced the establishment of diplomatic relations at ambassadorial level with Myanmar.

Conflicting claims (from Brunei, Viet Nam, the People's Republic of China, the Philippines, Malaysia and Taiwan) to all, or some, of the uninhabited Spratly Islands, situated in the South China Sea, remained a source of tension in the region. Brunei is the only claimant not to have stationed troops on the islands, which are both strategically important and possess potentially large reserves of petroleum. Attempts through the 1990s to restore the dispute through a negotiated settlement have resulted in little progress, and military activity in the area has increased.

Government

The 1959 Constitution confers supreme executive authority on the Sultan. He is assisted and advised by four Constitutional Councils: the Religious Council, the Privy Council, the Council of Cabinet Ministers and the Council of Succession. Since the rebellion of 1962, certain provisions of the Constitution have been suspended, and the Sultan has ruled by decree.

Defence

At 1 August 1997 the Royal Brunei Malay Regiment numbered 5,000 (including 600 women): army 3,900; navy 700; air force 400. Military service is voluntary, but only Malays are eligible for service. Paramilitary forces comprised 1,750 Royal Brunei Police. Defence expenditure in 1996 was an estimated B $490m. A Gurkha battalion of the British army, comprising more than 2,300 men, has been stationed in Brunei since 1971. There are also about 500 troops from Singapore, operating a training school in Brunei.

Economic Affairs

In 1994, according to estimates by the World Bank, Brunei's gross national product (GNP), measured at average 1992–94 prices, was US $3,975m., equivalent to US $14,240 per head. During 1985–94, it was estimated, GNP per head declined, in real terms, at an average rate of 1.5% per year. In 1985–95 the population increased by an average of 2.5% annually. Brunei's gross domestic product (GDP) increased at an average annual rate of 1.0% during 1985–95.

Agriculture (including forestry and fishing) employed an estimated 1.8% of the working population in 1996 and provided an estimated 2.5% of GDP in that year. In 1995 an estimated 1.3% of the total land area was cultivated; the principal crops include rice, cassava, bananas and pineapples. In the 1990s Brunei imported about 80% of its total food requirements. During 1985–95 agricultural GDP increased, in real terms, by an annual average of 3.5%.

Industry (comprising mining, manufacturing, construction and utilities) employed 24.1% of the working population in 1991 and contributed an estimated 41.5% of GDP in 1996. Industrial GDP declined by an annual average of 1.6% in 1985–95.

Brunei's economy depends almost entirely on its petroleum and natural gas resources. Mining and quarrying employed only 5.0% of the working population in 1991, but the petroleum sector provided an estimated 37.8% of GDP in 1991. Production of crude petroleum from the eight offshore and two onshore fields averaged 172,000 barrels per day in 1996. In that year output of natural gas totalled 11,097m. cu m. In the early 1990s there were significant further discoveries of both petroleum and natural gas reserves. Crude petroleum and natural gas together accounted for 89.6% of total export earnings in 1995. In 1991 reserves of petroleum were sufficient to enable production to be maintained at current levels until the year 2025. At the end of 1992 proven recoverable reserves of natural gas were estimated at 400,000m. cu m. In 1993 3.0% of petroleum production was used for domestic energy requirements. The GDP of the mining sector declined at an average rate of 5.3% per year in 1985–89, but rose by 1.4% in 1990 and by 10.0% in 1991.

Manufacturing is dominated by petroleum refining. The sector employed 3.8% of the working population in 1991 and contributed an estimated 8.1% of GDP in 1991. Since the mid-1980s Brunei has attempted to expand its manufacturing base. In the mid-1990s the textile industry provided the largest non-oil and -gas revenue; other industries included cement, mineral water, canned food, dairy products, publishing and printing. Manufacturing GDP increased by an annual average of 4.8% in 1985–89 and by 5.3% in 1990, but fell by 22.6% in 1991.

Services employed 73.7% of the working population in 1991 and provided an estimated 56.0% of GDP in 1996. In 1995 the sector comprising wholesale and retail trade, restaurants and hotels contributed 9.5% of GDP, and the finance sector 5.2%. During 1985–96 the combined GDP of the service sectors increased, in real terms, at an average rate of 5.5% per year.

In 1994 Brunei recorded a visible trade surplus of US $653m., while, as a result of high investment income from abroad, there was a surplus of US $2,999m. on the current account of the balance of payments. In 1995 the principal source of imports (31.7%) was Singapore; other major suppliers were countries of the European Union (EU—see p. 152), Malaysia, the USA and Japan. The principal market for exports in that year was Japan, which accounted for 55.6% of total exports (mainly natural gas on a long-term contract); other significant purchasers were the Republic of Korea, Thailand and Singapore. Principal imports comprised machinery and transport equipment, basic manufactures, food and live animals and chemicals; principal exports were crude petroleum and natural gas.

In 1995 government revenue, excluding investment income (unofficially estimated at between US $1,500m. and US $2,500m. in 1987), totalled B $4,407.3m., and expenditure B $3,656.4m., resulting in a budgetary surplus of B $750.9m. Brunei has no external public debt. International reserves totalled an estimated US $35,000m. in 1992. Consumer prices increased at an average rate of 3.1% per year in 1990–95 and by 2.0% in 1996. Foreign workers, principally from Malaysia and the Philippines, have helped to ease the labour shortage resulting from the small size of the population, and comprised about 41% of the labour force in 1995. However, at the 1991 census the rate of unemployment was 4.7%, reflecting a shortage of non-manual jobs for the well-educated Bruneians.

Brunei is a member of the Association of South East Asian Nations (ASEAN—see p. 113). In October 1991 the member states formally announced the establishment of the ASEAN Free Trade Area, which was to be implemented over 15 years (later reduced to 10), and, as a member of ASEAN, Brunei endorsed Malaysia's plan for an East Asia Economic Caucus. Brunei is also a member of the UN Economic and Social Commission for Asia and the Pacific (see p. 27), which aims to accelerate economic progress in the region. In 1994 the East ASEAN Growth Area (EAGA) was established, encompassing Mindanao, in the Philippines, Sarawak and Sabah, in Malaysia, Kalimantan and Sulawesi in Indonesia, and Brunei. The EAGA was modelled on the Singapore-Johore-Riau 'growth triangle'. In October 1995 Brunei joined the International Monetary Fund (IMF—see p. 80) and the World Bank.

The seventh (1996–2000) Plan continued the emphasis of the fifth (1986–1990) and sixth (1991–95) Plans on diversification of the economy to reduce the country's dependence on income from petroleum and natural gas. In 1996 the Government announced plans to develop Brunei as a 'Service Hub for Trade and Tourism', following earlier plans for the development of the private sector and the conversion of Brunei into a regional centre for banking and finance. Certain government functions and activities were to be considered for corporatization or privatization, and private-sector workers were given greater financial security through a government pension scheme. To stimulate tourism, the year 2000 was designated 'Visit Brunei Year', a new tourism unit was established and visa requirements were relaxed. The improvement of infrastructure for industrial development remained a priority that was addressed primarily through the creation of industrial parks. In 1996 the Brunei Industrial Development Authority was established to allocate sites on existing parks and to provide further industrial complexes. Foreign investment, which was essential to provide the necessary technology and marketing expertise, was encouraged through investment incentives and the creation of an investment agency. Brunei's entry into the IMF also qualified the country for technical assistance and consultative advice on diversification. However, progress towards the broadening of Brunei's economic base has been extremely slow, owing to the constraints of high labour costs, the small domestic market and a lack of entrepreneurial skills and motivation in the indigenous population.

Social Welfare

Free medical services are provided by the Government. In 1996 there were 281 physicians working in the country and 961 hospital beds. The main central referral hospital is in Bandar Seri Begawan, but there are three other hospitals (in Kuala Belait, Tutong and Temburong), as well as private facilities provided by Brunei Shell in Seria. For medical care not available in Brunei, citizens are sent abroad at the Government's expense. There is a 'flying doctor' service, as well as various clinics, travelling dispensaries and dental clinics. A non-contributory state pensions scheme for elderly and disabled persons came into operation in 1955. The State also provides financial assistance to the poor, the destitute and widows. Of total ordinary expenditure by the Government in 1994, B $148m. (6.6%) was for the Ministry of Health.

Education

Education is free and is compulsory for 12 years from the age of five years. Islamic studies form an integral part of the school curriculum. Pupils who are Brunei citizens and reside more than 8 km (5 miles) from their schools are entitled to free accommodation in hostels, free transport or a subsistence allowance. Schools are classified according to the language of instruction, i.e. Malay, English or Chinese (Mandarin). In 1994 enrolment at pre-primary level was equivalent to 54% of children in the relevant age-group (males 55%; females 54%). Primary education lasts for six years from the age of six years. Secondary education, usually beginning at 12 years of age, lasts for seven years, comprising a first cycle of five years and a second of two years. In 1994 enrolment in primary schools included 90% of children in the relevant age-group (males 90%; females 89%), while the comparable enrolment ratio at secondary level was 61% (males 58%; females 65%). In 1996 there was one teacher-training college, five colleges for vocational and technical education, three institutes of higher education and one university. The University of Brunei Darussalam was formally established in 1985, but many students continue to attend universities abroad, at government expense. In 1992 enrolment at tertiary level was equivalent to 6.0% of the relevant age-group (males 5.1%; females 6.9%). In 1995, according to UNESCO estimates, the adult illiteracy rate averaged 11.8% (males 7.4%; females 16.6%). Of total ordinary expenditure by the Government in 1994, B $301m. (13.5%) was for the Ministry of Education.

Public Holidays

1998: 1 January (New Year's Day), 18 January† (Memperingati Nuzul Al-Quran, Anniversary of the Revelation of the Koran), 28–30 January* (Chinese New Year), 30 January† (Hari Raya Puasa, end of Ramadan), 23 February (National Day), 8 April† (Hari Raya Haji, Feast of the Sacrifice), 28 April† (Hizrah, Islamic New Year), 1 June (Royal Brunei Armed Forces Day), 7 July† (Hari Mouloud, Birth of the Prophet), 15 July (Sultan's Birthday), 17 November† (Isra Meraj, Ascension of the Prophet Muhammad), 20 December† (Beginning of Ramadan), 25 December (Christmas).

1999: 1 January (New Year's Day), 7 January† (Memperingati Nuzul Al-Quran, Anniversary of the Revelation of the Koran), 19 January† (Hari Raya Puasa, end of Ramadan), 16–18 February* (Chinese New Year), 23 February (National Day), 28 March† (Hari Raya Haji, Feast of the Sacrifice), 17 April† (Hizrah, Islamic New Year), 1 June (Royal Brunei Armed Forces Day), 26 June† (Hari Mouloud, Birth of the Prophet), 15 July (Sultan's Birthday), 6 November† (Isra Meraj, Ascension of the Prophet Muhammad), 9 December† (Beginning of Ramadan), 25 December (Christmas).

* From the first to the third day of the first moon of the lunar calendar.

† These holidays are dependent on the Islamic lunar calendar and may vary by one or two days from the dates given.

Weights and Measures

The imperial system is in operation but local measures of weight and capacity are used. These include the gantang (1 gallon), the tahil (1⅓ oz) and the kati (1⅓ lb).

Statistical Survey

Source (unless otherwise stated): Department of Economic Planning and Development, Ministry of Finance, Bandar Seri Begawan 2012; tel. (2) 241991; telex 2676; fax (2) 226132.

AREA AND POPULATION

Area: 5,765 sq km (2,226 sq miles); *by district:* Brunei/Muara 570 sq km (220 sq miles), Seria/Belait 2,725 sq km (1,052 sq miles), Tutong 1,165 sq km (450 sq miles), Temburong 1,305 sq km (504 sq miles).

Population (excluding transients afloat): 192,832 (males 102,942, females 89,890) at census of 25 August 1981; 260,482 (males 137,616, females 122,866) at census of 7 August 1991; 296,000 (males 156,600, females 139,400) at mid-1995 (official estimates). *By district* (official estimates at mid-1996): Brunei/Muara 201,100; Seria/Belait 61,800; Tutong 33,500; Temburong 8,700; Total 305,100.

Density (mid-1996): 52.9 per sq km.

Ethnic Groups (1991 census): Malay 174,317, Chinese 40,621, Other indigenous 15,665, Others 29,879, Total 260,482; (official estimates at mid-1996): Malay 204,000, Chinese 46,300, Other indigenous 18,100, Others 36,700, Total 305,100.

Principal Town: Bandar Seri Begawan (capital), population 45,867 at 1991 census, 50,000 in 1995 (estimate).

Births, Marriages and Deaths (registrations, 1996): Live births 7,633 (birth rate 25.0 per 1,000), Deaths 1,002 (death rate 3.3 per 1,000); (1994): Marriages 1,925 (marriage rate 6.8 per 1,000).

Expectation of Life (years at birth, 1991): Males 72.1; Females 76.5.

Economically Active Population (1991 census): Agriculture, hunting, forestry and fishing 2,162; Mining and quarrying 5,327; Manufacturing 4,070; Electricity, gas and water 2,223; Construction 14,145; Trade, restaurants and hotels 15,404; Transport, storage and communications 5,392; Financing, insurance, real estate and business services 5,807; Community, social and personal services 52,121; Activities not adequately defined 95; *Total employed* 106,746 (males 72,338; females 34,408); Unemployed 5,209 (males 2,745; females 2,464); *Total labour force* 111,955 (males 75,083; females 36,872).

AGRICULTURE, ETC.

Principal Crops (FAO estimates, '000 metric tons, 1996): Rice (paddy) 1, Cassava (Manioc) 2, Vegetables (incl. melons) 9, Fruit 5 (Pineapples 1, Bananas 1). Source: FAO, *Production Yearbook*.

Livestock ('000 head, year ending September 1996): Cattle 2.0, Buffaloes 4.0, Goats 3.1, Poultry 3,109.

Livestock Products (1996): Poultry meat 4,663 metric tons; Hen eggs ('000) 75,100.

Forestry ('000 cu m, 1996): *Roundwood removals:* Sawlogs, veneer logs and logs for sleepers 203.5; Other industrial wood 158.8; Fuel wood 60.8; Total 423.1.
Sawnwood production: Total (incl. railway sleepers) 90 (FAO estimate) in 1994 (Source: FAO, *Yearbook of Forest Products*).

Fishing (metric tons, live weight, 1996): Inland waters 14.7 (Freshwater fishes 0.7, Giant river prawn 14.0); Pacific Ocean 1,424.0 (Marine fishes 1,100.3, Crustaceans and molluscs 323.7); Total catch 1,438.7.

MINING

Production (1996): Crude petroleum ('000 cu m) 8,767; Natural gas (million cu m) 11,097.

INDUSTRY

Production ('000 metric tons, unless otherwise indicated, 1996): Motor spirit (petrol) 191.6; Distillate fuel oils 127.8; Kerosene 62.8; Electric energy (million kWh, 1995) 1,555.8.

FINANCE

Currency and Exchange Rates: 100 sen (cents) = 1 Brunei dollar (B $). *Sterling and US Dollar Equivalents* (30 September 1997): £1 sterling = B $2.472; US $1 = B $1.530; B $100 = £40.46 = US $65.36. *Average Exchange Rate* (Brunei dollars per US $): 1.5274 in 1994; 1.4174 in 1995; 1.4100 in 1996. Note: The Brunei dollar is at par with the Singapore dollar.

Budget (B $ million, 1994): *Revenue:* Tax revenue 1,092 (Import duty 101, Corporate income tax 989); Non-tax revenue 3,226 (Commercial receipts 259, Property income 880, Transfers from Brunei Investment Agency 2,072); Total 4,318. *Expenditure:* Ordinary expenditure 2,235 (Prime Minister's Office 162, Defence 400, Foreign Affairs 90, Finance 425, Home Affairs 88, Education 301, Religious Affairs 96, Development 350, Health 148); Other current expenditure 92; Capital expenditure 1,057; Investment in public enterprises by Brunei Investment Agency 901; Total 4,285. Source: IMF, *Brunei Darussalam—Recent Economic Developments* (June 1996).

(B $ million, 1995): *Revenue:* 4,407.3; *Expenditure:* 3,656.4 (excl. investment by Brunei Investment Agency).

Money Supply (B $ million, 1996): Currency in circulation 601.1; Demand deposits of private sector 2,689.7; Total money 3,290.8.

Cost of Living (Consumer Price Index; base: 1990 = 100): All items 109.9 in 1994; 116.5 in 1995; 118.8 in 1996 (Food 113.4; Clothing and footwear 111.2; Rent, fuel and power 110.7).

Gross Domestic Product by Economic Activity (B $ million in current prices, 1996, provisional): Agriculture, hunting, forestry and fishing 201.0; Mining, quarrying and manufacturing 2,737.0; Electricity, gas and water 79.0; Construction 454.7; Trade, restaurants and hotels 937.8; Transport, storage and communications 376.4; Finance, insurance, real estate and business services 603.3; Community, social and personal services 2,497.1; *Sub-total* 7,886.3; *Less* Imputed bank service charge 201.5; *GDP in purchasers' values* 7,684.8.

Gross Domestic Product (B $ million in current purchasers' values, 1996, provisional): Petroleum sector 2,832.2; Non-petroleum government sector 2,260.2; Non-petroleum private sector 2,592.4; Total 7,684.8.

Balance of Payments (US $ million, 1994): Exports of goods 2,215; Imports of goods −1,562; *Trade balance* 653; Exports of services 53; Imports of services −171; *Balance on goods and services* 534; Other income received 2,622; Other income paid −151; *Balance on goods, services and income* 3,005; Current transfers received 1; Current transfers paid −7; *Current balance* 2,999; Foreign investment (net) 670; Long-term capital (net) −4,452; Short-term capital (net) 820; *Overall balance* 37. Source: IMF, *Brunei Darussalam—Recent Economic Developments* (June 1996).

EXTERNAL TRADE

Principal Commodities (B $ million, 1995): *Imports:* Food and live animals 324.3, Chemicals 166.1, Basic manufactures 908.9, Machinery and transport equipment 1,033.5, Miscellaneous manufactured articles 303.0; Total (incl. others) 2,953.7. *Exports*: Crude and partly-refined petroleum 1,475.8; Natural gas 1,561.4; Total (incl. others) 3,388.0.

Principal Trading Partners (B $ million, 1995, provisional): *Imports:* Hong Kong 81.2; Japan 260.5; Malaysia 406.0; Singapore 937.2; Thailand 76.5; USA 261.5; Western Europe 506.8; Total (incl. others) 2,953.7. *Exports:* Australia 23.6; Japan 1,882.8; Republic of Korea 530.6; Philippines 21.2; Singapore 312.6; Thailand 372.1; USA 66.9; Western Europe 26.5; Total (incl. others) 3,388.0.

TRANSPORT

Road Traffic (registered vehicles, 1996): Private cars 149,738, Goods vehicles 15,797, Motor-cycles and scooters 5,833, Buses and taxis 1,865, Others 4,368.

Merchant Fleet (displacement, '000 grt at 31 December): 365.8 in 1994; 366.3 in 1995; 368.9 in 1996. Source: Lloyd's Register of Shipping, *World Fleet Statistics*.

International Sea-borne Shipping (freight traffic, '000 metric tons): Goods loaded (1990) 13,554*; Goods unloaded (1995) 2,148.2; Registered boats (1996) 212.
* Source: UN, *Monthly Bulletin of Statistics*.

Civil Aviation (1996): Passenger arrivals 529,800, Passenger departures 522,600; freight loaded 4,913 metric tons, freight unloaded 18,775 metric tons; mail loaded 81.7 metric tons, mail unloaded 311.8 metric tons.

TOURISM

Visitor Arrivals: 622,354 in 1994; 497,961 in 1995; 837,156 in 1996.

Tourist Receipts (US $ million): 35 in 1992; 36 in 1993; 36 in 1994 (Source: UN, *Statistical Yearbook*).

COMMUNICATIONS MEDIA

Radio Receivers (1996): 310,105 in use.

Television Receivers (1996, estimate): 190,300 in use.

Telephones (1996): 76,000 direct exchange lines in use.

Telefax Stations (1994): 1,500 in use (Source: UN, *Statistical Yearbook*).

Mobile Cellular Telephones (1994): 15,620 subscribers (Source: UN, *Statistical Yearbook*).

Book Production (1990): 25 titles; 56,000 copies.

Daily Newspaper (1996): 1 (estimated circulation 10,000 copies per issue).

Non-daily Newspapers (1996): 2 (estimated combined circulation 66,200 copies per issue).

Other Periodicals (1996): 15 (estimated combined circulation 132,000 copies per issue).

EDUCATION

(1996)

Pre-primary and Primary: 172 schools; 3,596 teachers; 55,561 pupils (29,074 males; 26,487 females).

General Secondary: 38 schools; 2,403 teachers; 28,162 pupils (13,505 males; 14,657 females).

Teacher Training: 1 college; 43 teachers; 529 pupils (235 males; 294 females).

Vocational: 5 colleges; 421 teachers; 2,018 pupils (1,203 males; 815 females).

Higher Education: 4 institutes (incl. 1 university); 400 teachers; 2,012 students.

Directory

The Constitution

Note: Certain sections of the Constitution have been in abeyance since 1962.

A new Constitution was promulgated on 29 September 1959. Under its provisions, sovereign authority is vested in the Sultan and Yang Di-Pertuan, who is assisted and advised by four Councils:

THE RELIGIOUS COUNCIL

In his capacity as head of the Islamic faith in Brunei, the Sultan and Yang Di-Pertuan is advised on all Islamic matters by the Religious Council, whose members are appointed by the Sultan and Yang Di-Pertuan.

THE PRIVY COUNCIL

This Council, presided over by the Sultan and Yang Di-Pertuan, is to advise the Sultan on matters concerning the Royal prerogative of mercy, the amendment of the Constitution and the conferment of ranks, titles and honours.

THE COUNCIL OF CABINET MINISTERS

Presided over by the Sultan and Yang Di-Pertuan, the Council of Cabinet Ministers considers all executive matters.

THE COUNCIL OF SUCCESSION

Subject to the Constitution, this Council is to determine the succession to the throne, should the need arise.

The State is divided into four administrative districts, in each of which is a District Officer responsible to the Prime Minister and Minister of Home Affairs.

The Government

HEAD OF STATE

Sultan and Yang Di-Pertuan: HM Sultan Haji HASSANAL BOLKIAH (succeeded 4 October 1967; crowned 1 August 1968).

COUNCIL OF CABINET MINISTERS

(December 1997)

Prime Minister, Minister of Defence and of Finance: HM Sultan Haji HASSANAL BOLKIAH.

Minister of Foreign Affairs: HRH Prince MOHAMAD BOLKIAH.

Minister of Home Affairs and Special Adviser to the Prime Minister: Pehin Dato' Haji ISA BIN Pehin Haji IBRAHIM.

Minister of Education: Pehin Dato' Haji ABDUL AZIZ BIN Pehin Haji UMAR.

Minister of Law: Pengiran Haji BAHRIN BIN Pengiran Haji ABBAS.

Minister of Industry and Primary Resources: Pehin Dato' Haji ABDUL RAHMAN BIN Dato' Setia Haji MOHAMAD TAIB.

Minister of Religious Affairs: Pehin Dato' Dr Haji MOHAMAD ZAIN BIN Haji SERUDIN.

Minister of Development: Pengiran Dato' Dr Haji ISMAIL BIN Haji DAMIT.

Minister of Culture, Youth and Sports: Pehin Dato' Haji HUSSEIN BIN Pehin Haji MOHAMAD YOSOF.

Minister of Health: Dato' Dr Haji JOHAR BIN Dato Haji NOORDIN.

Minister of Communications: Pehin Dato' Haji ZAKARIA BIN Haji SULEIMAN.

There are, in addition, eight deputy ministers.

MINISTRIES

Office of the Prime Minister: Istana Nurul Iman, Bandar Seri Begawan 1100; tel. (2) 229988; telex 2727; fax (2) 241717.

Ministry of Communications: Old Airport, Berakas, Bandar Seri Begawan 1150; tel. (2) 383838; telex 2682; fax (2) 380127.

Ministry of Culture, Youth and Sports: Jalan Residency, Bandar Seri Begawan 1200; tel. (2) 240585; telex 2642; fax (2) 241620.

Ministry of Defence: Bolkiah Garrison, Bandar Seri Begawan 1110; tel. (2) 230130; telex 2840; fax (2) 230110.

Ministry of Development: Old Airport, Berakas, Bandar Seri Begawan 1190; tel. (2) 241911; telex 2722.

Ministry of Education: Old Airport, Berakas, Bandar Seri Begawan 1170; tel. (2) 244233; telex 2602; fax (2) 240250.

Ministry of Finance: Bandar Seri Begawan 1130; tel. (2) 241991; telex 2674; fax (2) 226132.

Ministry of Foreign Affairs: Jalan Subok, Bandar Seri Begawan 1120; tel. (2) 261177; telex 2292.

Ministry of Health: Old Airport, Berakas, Bandar Seri Begawan 1210; tel. (2) 226640; telex 2421; fax (2) 240980.

Ministry of Home Affairs: Bandar Seri Begawan 1140; tel. (2) 223225.

Ministry of Industry and Primary Resources: Old Airport, Berakas, Bandar Seri Begawan 1220; tel. (2) 382822; fax (2) 383811.

Ministry of Law: Bandar Seri Begawan 1160; tel. (2) 244872.

Ministry of Religious Affairs: Bandar Seri Begawan 1180; tel. (2) 242565.

Political Organizations

Parti Perpaduan Kebangsaan Brunei—PPKB (Brunei National Solidarity Party—BNSP): Bandar Seri Begawan; f. 1986, after split in PKDB (see below); ceased political activity in 1988, but re-emerged in 1995; Pres. ABDUL LATIF CHUCHU.

Former political organizations included: **Parti Rakyat Brunei—PRB** (Brunei People's Party), banned in 1962, leaders are all in exile; **Barisan Kemerdeka'an Rakyat—BAKER** (People's Independence Front), f. 1966 but no longer active; **Parti Perpaduan Kebangsaan Rakyat Brunei—PERKARA** (Brunei People's National United Party), f. 1968 but no longer active, and **Parti Kebangsaan Demokratik Brunei—PKDB** (Brunei National Democratic Party—BNDP), f. 1985 and dissolved by government order in 1988.

Diplomatic Representation

EMBASSIES AND HIGH COMMISSIONS IN BRUNEI

Australia: Teck Guan Plaza, 4th Floor, Jalan Sultan, Bandar Seri Begawan 2085; tel. (2) 229435; fax (2) 221652; High Commissioner: NEAL DAVIS.

China, People's Republic: Lot 23966, Simpang 612, Kampong Salambigar, Jalan Muara, Bandar Seri Begawan 3895; tel. (2) 334164; Ambassador: LIU XINSHENG.

France: Units 301–306, 3rd Floor, Jalan Sultan Complex, Jalan Sultan, Bandar Seri Begawan 2085; tel. (2) 220960; telex 2743; fax (2) 243373; Ambassador: LOUIS BARDOLLET.

Germany: Wisma Raya, 6th Floor, 49–50 Jalan Sultan, Bandar Seri Begawan 1930; tel. (2) 225547; telex 2742; fax (2) 225583; Ambassador: INGMAR BRENTLE.

India: Simpang 337, Lot 14034, Kampong Manggis, Jalan Muara, Bandar Seri Begawan; tel. (2) 339947; fax (2) 339783; e-mail hicomind@pso.brunei.bn; High Commissioner: DINESH K. JAIN.

Indonesia: Simpang 528, Jalan Sungai Hanching Baru, off Jalan Muara, Bandar Seri Begawan 3890; tel. (2) 330180; telex 2654; fax (2) 330646; Ambassador: KOESNADI POEDJIWINARTO.

Iran: Bandar Seri Begawan; Ambassador: JAVAD ANSARI.

Japan: Kampong Mabohai, 1–3 Jalan Jawatan Dalam, Bandar Seri Begawan 2092; tel. (2) 229265; fax (2) 229481; Ambassador: SHIGENOBI YOSHIDA.

Korea, Republic: No. 9, Lot 21652, Kampong Beribi, Jalan Gadong, Bandar Seri Begawan 3188; POB 2169, Bandar Seri Begawan 1921; tel. (2) 650471; fax (2) 650299; Ambassador: SA BOO-SUNG.

Malaysia: 473 Kampong Pelambayan, Jalan Kota Batu, Bandar Seri Begawan 2282; tel. (2) 228410; telex 2401; fax (2) 228412; High Commissioner: SALIM HASHIM.

Oman: 35, Simpang 100, Kampong Pengkalan, Jalan Tungku Link, Gadong, Bandar Seri Begawan; tel. (2) 446953; fax (2) 449646; Ambassador: AHMAD BIN MOHAMMED AL-RIYAMI.

Pakistan: No. 5, Simpang 396/128, Kampong Sungai Akar, Jalan Kebangsaan, POB 3026, Bandar Seri Begawan; tel. (2) 339797; fax (2) 334990; High Commissioner: Maj.-Gen. (retd) IRSHAD ULLAH TARAR.

Philippines: Badiah Bldg, 4th–5th Floors, Mile 1, Jalan Tutong, Bandar Seri Begawan 1930; tel. (2) 241465; telex 2673; fax (2) 237707; Ambassador: RAMON TIROL.

Singapore: RBA Plaza, 5th Floor, Jalan Sultan, Bandar Seri Begawan 2085; tel. (2) 227583; telex 2385; fax (2) 220957; High Commissioner: ANTHONY CH'NG CHYE TONG.

Thailand: No. 13, Simpang 29, Kampong Kiarong, Jalan Elia Fatimah, Bandar Seri Begawan 3186; tel. (2) 429653; telex 2607; fax (2) 421775; Ambassador: PRASART MANSUWAN.

United Kingdom: Block D, Bangunan Yayasan Sultan Haji Hassanal Bolkiah, 2nd Floor, Jalan Pretty, POB 2197, Bandar Seri Begawan 1921; tel. (2) 222231; fax (2) 226002; High Commissioner: IVAN CALLAN.

USA: Teck Guan Plaza, 3rd Floor, Jalan Sultan, Bandar Seri Begawan 2085; tel. (2) 229670; telex 2609; fax (2) 225293; Ambassador: GLEN ROBERT RASE.

Viet Nam: Lot 13489, Jalan Manggis Dua, off Jalan Muara, Bandar Seri Begawan; tel. (2) 343167; fax (2) 343169; Ambassador: NGUYEN NGOC DIEN.

Judicial System

SUPREME COURT

The Supreme Court consists of the Court of Appeal and the High Court.

Supreme Court: Km 1½, Jalan Tutong, Bandar Seri Begawan 2056; tel. (2) 225853; fax (2) 241984.

Chief Registrar: KIFRAWI BIN Dato' Paduka Haji KIFLI.

The Court of Appeal: composed of the President and two Commissioners appointed by the Sultan. The Court of Appeal considers criminal and civil appeals against the decisions of the High Court.

President: KUTLU TEKIN FUAD.

The High Court: composed of the Chief Justice and judges sworn in by the Sultan as Judicial Commissioners of the High Court. In its appellate jurisdiction, the High Court considers appeals in criminal and civil matters against the decisions of the Subordinate Courts. The High Court has unlimited original jurisdiction in criminal and civil matters.

Chief Justice: Dato' Seri Paduka Sir DENYS TUDOR EMIL ROBERTS.

OTHER COURTS

Intermediate Courts: have jurisdiction to try all offences other than those punishable by the death sentence and civil jurisdiction to try all actions and suits of a civil nature where the amount in dispute or value of the subject/matter does not exceed B $60,000.

The Subordinate Courts: presided over by the Chief Magistrate and magistrates, with limited original jurisdiction in civil and criminal matters and civil jurisdiction to try all actions and suits of civil nature where the amount in dispute does not exceed B $30,000 (for Chief Magistrate) and B $20,000 (for magistrates).

Chief Magistrate: STEVEN CHONG WAN OON.

The Courts of Kathis: deal solely with questions concerning Islamic religion, marriage and divorce. Appeals lie from these courts to the Sultan in the Religious Council.

Chief Kathi: Dato' Seri Setia Haji SALIM BIN Haji BESAR.

Attorney-General: Minister of Law.

Religion

The official religion of Brunei is Islam, and the Sultan is head of the Islamic community. The majority of the Malay population are Muslims of the Sunni sect; at the 1991 census Muslims accounted for 67.2% of the total population. The Chinese population is either Buddhist (accounting for 12.8% of the total population at the 1991 census), Confucianist, Daoist or Christian. Large numbers of the indigenous ethnic groups practise traditional animist forms of religion. The remainder of the population are mostly Christians, generally Roman Catholics, Anglicans or members of the American Methodist Church of Southern Asia. At the 1991 census Christians accounted for 10.0% of the total population.

ISLAM

Supreme Head of Islam: Sultan and Yang Di-Pertuan.

CHRISTIANITY

The Anglican Communion

Brunei is within the jurisdiction of the Anglican diocese of Kuching (Malaysia).

The Roman Catholic Church

Brunei is within the jurisdiction of the Roman Catholic archdiocese of Kuching (Malaysia).

The Press

NEWSPAPERS

Borneo Bulletin: Locked Bag No. 2, MPC (Old Airport Rd, Berakas), Bandar Seri Begawan 3799; tel. (2) 451468; fax (2) 451461; f. 1953; daily; English; independent; Editor CHARLES REX DE SILVA; circ. 25,000.

Brunei Darussalam Newsletter: Dept of Information, Prime Minister's Office, Istana Nurul Iman, Bandar Seri Begawan 1100; tel. (2) 229988; monthly; English; circ. 14,000.

Pelita Brunei: Dept of Information, Prime Minister's Office, Istana Nurul Iman, Bandar Seri Begawan 1100; tel. (2) 229988; fax (2) 225942; f. 1956; weekly (Wed.); Malay; govt newspaper; distributed free; Editor TIMBANG BIN BAKAR; circ. 45,000.

Salam: c/o Brunei Shell Petroleum Co Sdn Bhd, Seria 7082; tel. (3) 4184; fax (3) 4189; f. 1953; monthly; Malay and English; distributed free to employees of the Brunei Shell Petroleum Co Sdn Bhd; circ. 9,200.

Publishers

Borneo Printers & Trading Sdn Bhd: POB 2211, Bandar Seri Begawan 1922; tel. (2) 224856; fax (2) 243407.

Brunei Press Sdn Bhd: Lots 8 and 11, Perindustrian Beribi II, Gadong, Bandar Seri Begawan; tel. (2) 451468; fax (2) 451460; f. 1953; Gen. Man. REGGIE SEE.

Capital Trading & Printing Pte Ltd: POB 1089, Bandar Seri Begawan; tel. (2) 244541.

Leong Bros: 52 Jalan Bunga Kuning, POB 164, Seria; tel. (3) 22381.

Offset Printing House: POB 1111, Bandar Seri Begawan; tel. (2) 224477.

The Star Press: Bandar Seri Begawan; f. 1963; Man. F. W. ZIMMERMAN.

Government Publishing House

Government Printer: Government Printing Department, Ministry of Law, Bandar Seri Begawan 2017; tel. (2) 382541; fax (2) 381141.

Broadcasting and Communications

RADIO

Radio Television Brunei (RTB): Jalan Elizabeth II, Bandar Seri Begawan 2042; tel. (2) 243111; telex 2720; fax (2) 227204; f. 1957; five radio networks: four broadcasting in Malay, the other in English, Chinese (Mandarin) and Gurkhali; Dir Pengiran Dato' Paduka Haji BADARUDDIN BIN Pengiran Haji GHANI.

DST Communications: private television and radio satellite transmission service.

The British Forces Broadcasting Service (Military) broadcasts a 24-hour radio service to a limited area.

TELEVISION

Radio Television Brunei (RTB): Jalan Elizabeth II, Bandar Seri Begawan 2042; tel. (2) 243111; telex 2720; fax (2) 227204; f. 1957; programmes in Malay and English; a satellite service relays RTB television programmes to the South-East Asian region for nine hours per day; Dir Pengiran Dato' Paduka Haji BADARUDDIN BIN Pengiran Haji GHANI.

Finance

BANKING

The Department of Financial Services (Treasury), the Brunei Currency Board and the Brunei Investment Agency, under the Ministry of Finance, perform most of the functions of a central bank.

Commercial Banks

Baiduri Bank Bhd: 145 Jalan Pemancha, POB 2220, Bandar Seri Begawan 1922; tel (2) 233233; telex 2433; fax (2) 237575; Gen. Man. LUC ROUSSELET; 2 brs.

Development Bank of Brunei Bhd: RBA Plaza, 1st Floor, Jalan Sultan, Bandar Seri Begawan 2085; POB 3080, Bandar Seri Begawan 1930; tel. (2) 233430; fax (2) 233429; Man. Dir Datuk Hajah URAI Pengiran ALI; 1 br.

Islamic Bank of Brunei Bhd: Lot 159, Bangunan IBB, Jalan Pemancha POB 2725, Bandar Seri Begawan 1927; tel. (2) 235686; telex 2320; fax (2) 235722; f. 1981 as Island Development Bank; name changed from International Bank of Brunei Bhd to present name in January 1993; practises Islamic banking principles; Chair. Yam Pengiran LAILA KANUN DIRAJA Pengiran Haji BAHRIN Pengiran Haji ABAS; Man. Dir Haji ZAINASALLEHEN BIN Haji MOHAMED TAHIR; 10 brs.

Foreign Banks

Citibank NA (USA): Darussalam Complex 12–15, Jalan Sultan, Bandar Seri Begawan 2085; tel. (2) 243983; telex 2224; fax (2) 237344; Vice-Pres. and Country Corporate Man. PAGE STOCKWELL; 1 br.

The Hongkong and Shanghai Banking Corpn Ltd (Hong Kong): POB 59, Bandar Seri Begawan 1900; tel. (2) 242305; telex 2273; fax (2) 241316; f. 1947; acquired assets of National Bank of Brunei in 1986; CEO STUART R. BANNISTER; 9 brs.

Malayan Banking Bhd (Malaysia): 148 Jalan Pemancha, Bandar Seri Begawan 2085; tel. (2) 242494; telex 2316; fax (2) 226101; f. 1960; Chief Man. SAMSURI Haji ITAM; 1 br.

Overseas Union Bank Ltd (Singapore): Unit G5, RBA Plaza, Jalan Sultan, POB 2218, Bandar Seri Begawan 2085; tel. (2) 225477; telex 2256; fax (2) 240972; f. 1973; Vice-Pres. and Man. SAN BENG; 1 br.

Sime Bank Bhd (Malaysia): Unit G02, Block D, Bangunan Yayasan Sultan Haji Hassanal Bolkiah, Ground Floor, Jalan Pretty, Bandar Seri Begawan 2085; tel. (2) 222515; telex 2207; fax (2) 237487; fmrly United Malayan Banking Corpn Bhd; Gen. Man. SHAFIK YUSSOF; 1 br.

Standard Chartered Bank (United Kingdom): 51–55 Jalan Sultan, POB 186, Bandar Seri Begawan 1901; tel. (2) 242386; telex 2223; fax (2) 242390; f. 1958; CEO WILLIAM BRUCE; 10 brs.

INSURANCE

In 1997 there were 19 general, three life and two composite (takaful) insurance companies operating in Brunei, including:

General Companies

AGF Insurance (S) Pte Ltd: c/o A&S Associates Sdn Bhd, Bangunan Gadong Properties, 03-01, Jalan Gadong, Bandar Seri Begawan 3180; tel. (2) 420766; fax (2) 440279; Man. SEBASTIAN TAN.

The Asia Insurance Co Ltd: 04A, Bangunan Gadong Properties, 1st Floor, Jalan Gadong, Bandar Seri Begawan 3180; tel. (2) 443663; fax (2) 443664; Man. DAVID WONG KOK MING.

BALGI Insurance (B) Sdn Bhd: Unit 13, Kompleks Haji Tahir II, 1st Floor, Jalan Gadong, Bandar Seri Begawan 3180; tel. (2) 422736; fax (2) 445204; Man. Dir PATRICK SIM SONG JUAY.

Borneo Insurance Sdn Bhd: Unit 103, Bangunan Kambang Pasang, Km 2, Jalan Gadong, Bandar Seri Begawan 3180; tel. (2) 420550; fax (2) 428550; Man. LIM TECK LEE.

Citystate Insurance Pte Ltd: c/o Dominic Choong & Sons, No 311, Bangunan Guru-Guru Melayu Brunei, 2nd Floor, Jalan Kianggeh, Bandar Seri Begawan 1913; tel. (2) 223822; fax (2) 223469; Man. BETTY CHOONG.

Commercial Union Assurance (M) Sdn Bhd: c/o Jasra Harrisons Sdn Bhd, Jalan McArthur/Jalan Kianggeh, Bandar Seri Begawan 2085; tel. (2) 242361; fax (2) 226203; Man. WHITTY LIM.

Cosmic Insurance Corpn Sdn Bhd: Abd Razak Complex, Block J, Unit 11, 1st Floor, Jalan Gadong, Bandar Seri Begawan 3180; tel. (2) 427112-3; fax (2) 427114; Man. RONNIE WONG.

General Accident Fire & Life Assurance Corpn Ltd: c/o Vincent & Associates Sdn Bhd, 4th Floor, Suite 46, Brittania House, Jalan Cator, Bandar Seri Begawan 2085; tel. (2) 224517; fax (2) 241048; Man. LEE TEE SENG.

GRE Insurance (B) Sdn Bhd: Unit 608, 6th Floor, Jalan Sultan Complex, 51-55 Jalan Sultan, Bandar Seri Begawan 2085; tel. (2) 266138; fax (2) 243474; Man. MOK HAI TONG.

ING General Insurance International NV: Shop Lot 86, 2nd Floor, Jalan Bunga Raya, Kuala Belait; tel. (3) 335338; fax (3) 335338; Man. SHERRY SOON PECK ENG.

MBA Insurance Sdn Bhd: 7 Bangunan Hasbullah I, 1st Floor, Mile 2½, Jalan Gadong, Bandar Seri Begawan 3180; tel. (2) 441535; fax (2) 441534; Man. CHAN LEK WEI.

Motor and General Insurance Sdn Bhd: 6 Bangunan Hasbullah II, Mile 2½, Jalan Gadong, Bandar Seri Begawan 3180; tel. (2) 440797; fax (2) 420336; Man. Dir Haji ABD AZIZ BIN ABD LATIF.

National Insurance Co Bhd: Unit 604-606, Jalan Sultan Complex, 6th Floor, 51-55 Jalan Sultan, Bandar Seri Begawan 2085; tel. (2) 227493; fax (2) 227495; Man. Dir TIMOTHY ONG.

New Zealand Insurance Co Ltd: Unit 311, Mohamad Yussof Complex, 3rd Floor, Mile 1½, Jalan Tutong, Bandar Seri Begawan 2682; tel. (2) 223632; fax (2) 220965.

The Royal Insurance (Global) Ltd: c/o H C Lau & Sons, Khoon Foh Building, 2nd Floor, Lot 308, Bangunan Maju, Jalan Bunga Raya, Kuala Belait 6000; tel. (3) 334599; fax (3) 334671; Gen. Man. TOMMY LEONG TONG KAW.

Sime AXA Assurance Bhd: No 9, Abd Razak Complex, 1st Floor, Jalan Gadong, Bandar Seri Begawan 3180; tel. (2) 443393; fax (2) 427451; Man. ROBERT LAI CHIN YIN.

South East Asia Insurance (B) Sdn Bhd: Unit 2, Block A, Abd Razak Complex, 1st Floor, Jalan Gadong, Bandar Seri Begawan 3180; tel. (2) 443842; fax (2) 420860; Man. BILLINGS TEO.

Standard Insurance (B) Sdn Bhd: 11 Bangunan Hasbullah II, Ground Floor, Bandar Seri Begawan 3702; tel. and fax (2) 445348; Man. PAUL KONG.

Winterthur Insurance (Far East) Pte Ltd: c/o Borneo Co (B) Sdn Bhd, Lot 9771, Km 3½, Jalan Gadong, Bandar Seri Begawan 1924; tel. (2) 422561; fax (2) 424352; Man. HII CHANG WOO.

Life Companies

American International Assurance Co Ltd: Unit 509A, Wisma Jaya Building, 5th Floor, No 85/94, Jalan Pemancha, Bandar Seri Begawan 2085; tel. (2) 239112; fax (2) 221667; Man. FEBIAN NG.

The Asia Life Assurance Society Ltd: 04A, Bangunan Gadong Properties, 1st Floor, Jalan Gadong, Bandar Seri Begawan 1924; tel. (2) 443663; fax (2) 443664; Man. DAVID WONG KOK MING.

The Great Eastern Life Assurance Co Ltd: Suite 1, Badi'ah Complex, 2nd Floor, Jalan Tutong, Bandar Seri Begawan 2604; tel. (2) 243792; fax (2) 225754; Man. HELEN YEO.

Takaful (Composite Insurance) Companies

Takaful IBB Bhd: Unit 5, Block A, Kiarong Complex, Lebuhraya Sultan Hassanal Bolkiah, Bandar Seri Begawan 3186; tel. (2) 451803-5; fax (2) 451808; Man. Dir Haji ABD HAMID BIN Haji JANUDIN.

Takaful TAIB Sdn Bhd: Bangunan Pusat Komersil dan Perdagangan Bumiputera, Ground Floor, Jalan Cator, Bandar Seri Begawan 2085; tel. (2) 237724; fax (2) 237729; Man. Dir Haji MOHAMED ROSELAN BIN Haji MOHAMED DAUD.

Trade and Industry

Trade in Brunei is largely conducted by Malay and Chinese agency houses and merchants.

GOVERNMENT AGENCY

Brunei Oil and Gas Authority: Bandar Seri Begawan; f. 1993 to oversee the hydrocarbons sector; Chair. Minister of Finance.

DEVELOPMENT ORGANIZATIONS

Brunei Industrial Development Authority (BINA): Ministry of Industry and Primary Resources, 4th Floor, Jalan Menteri Besar 2069, Bandar Seri Begawan; tel. (2) 382822; fax (2) 382838; f. 1996.

Brunei Islamic Trust Fund (Tabung Amanah Islam Brunei): Bandar Seri Begawan; f. 1991; promotes trade and industry.

CHAMBERS OF COMMERCE

Brunei Darussalam International Chamber of Commerce and Industry: POB 2246, Bandar Seri Begawan 1922; tel. (2) 236601;

telex 2214; fax (2) 228389; Chair. SULAIMAN Haji AHAI; Sec. Haji SHAZALI BIN Dato' Haji SULAIMAN; 108 mems.

Brunei Malay Chamber of Commerce and Industry: Bangunan Guru-Guru Melayu Brunei, Suite 301, 2nd Floor, Jalan Kianggeh, Bandar Seri Begawan 1910; tel. (2) 227297; telex 2445; fax (2) 227298; f. 1964; Pres. Dato' A. A. HAPIDZ ; 160 mems.

Chinese Chamber of Commerce: 9 Jalan Pretty, POB 281, Bandar Seri Begawan; tel. (2) 224374; Chair. LIM ENG MING.

Indian Chamber of Commerce: Bandar Seri Begawan; tel. (2) 223886; fax (2) 229271; Pres. BIKRAMJIT BHALLA.

TRADE UNIONS

Brunei Government Junior Officers' Union: Bandar Seri Begawan; tel. (2) 241911; Pres. Haji ALI BIN Haji NASAR; Gen. Sec. Haji OMARALI BIN Haji MOHIDDIN.

Brunei Government Medical and Health Workers' Union: Bandar Seri Begawan; Pres. Pengiran Haji MOHIDDIN BIN Pengiran TAJUDDIN; Gen. Sec. HANAFI BIN ANAI.

Brunei Oilfield Workers' Union: XDR/11, BSP Co Sdn Bhd, Seria 7082; f. 1961; 500 mems; Pres. SUHAINI Haji OTHMAN; Sec.-Gen. ABU TALIB BIN Haji MOHAMAD.

Royal Brunei Custom Department Staff Union: Badan Sukan dan Kebajikan Kastam, Royal Brunei Customs and Excise, Kuala Belait 6045; tel. (3) 334248; fax (3) 334626; Chair. Haji MOHD DELI BAKAR; Sec. HAMZAH Haji ABD. HAMID.

Transport

RAILWAYS

There are no public railways in Brunei. The Brunei Shell Petroleum Co Sdn Bhd maintains a 19.3-km section of light railway between Seria and Badas.

ROADS

In 1995 there were an estimated 2,469.6 km of roads in Brunei, comprising 1,678.7 km with a bituminous or concrete surface, 593.8 km surfaced with gravel and 197.1 km passable only in dry conditions. The main highway connects Bandar Seri Begawan, Tutong and Kuala Belait. A 59-km coastal road links Muara and Tutong.

Land Transport Department: Ministry of Communications, Km 4, Jalan Gadong, Bandar Seri Begawan; tel. (2) 424833; fax (2) 424775; Dir Haji HAMIDON BIN Haji MOHD TAHIR.

SHIPPING

Most sea traffic is handled by a deep-water port at Muara, 28 km from the capital, which has a 611-m wharf and a draught of 8 m. The port has a container terminal, warehousing, freezer facilities and cement silos. The original, smaller port at Bandar Seri Begawan itself is mainly used for local river-going vessels, for vessels to Malaysian ports in Sabah and Sarawak and for vessels under 30 m in length. There is a port at Kuala Belait, which takes shallow-draught vessels and serves mainly the Shell petroleum field and Seria. Owing to the shallow waters at Seria, tankers are unable to come up to the shore to load, and crude petroleum from the oil terminal is pumped through an underwater loading line to a single buoy mooring, to which the tankers are moored. At Lumut there is a 4.5-km jetty for liquefied natural gas (LNG) carriers.

Four main rivers, with numerous tributaries, are the principal means of communication in the interior, and boats or water taxis the main form of transport for most residents of the water villages. Larger water taxis operate daily to the Temburong district.

Bee Seng Shipping Co: Mile 1½, Jalan Tutong, POB 92, Bandar Seri Begawan; tel. (2) 220033; telex 2219; fax (2) 224495.

Brunei Shell Tankers Sdn Bhd: Seria 7082; tel. (3) 373999; telex 3313; f. 1986; vessels operated by Shell Tankers (UK) Ltd; Man. Dir R. V. D. BERG.

Harper Wira Sdn Bhd: Muara Port; tel. (2) 448529; fax (2) 448529.

Inchcape Borneo: Muara Port; tel. (2) 422396; fax (2) 424352.

New Island Shipping: Muara Port; tel. (2) 243059; fax (2) 243058.

Pansar Co Sdn Bhd: Muara Port; tel. (2) 445246; fax (2) 445247.

Seatrade Shipping Co: Muara Port; tel. (2) 421457; fax (2) 421453.

Silver Line (B) Sdn Bhd: Muara Port; tel. (2) 445069; fax (2) 430276.

Wei Tat Shipping and Trading Co: Mile 4½, Jalan Tutung, POB 103, Bandar Seri Begawan; tel. 65215.

CIVIL AVIATION

There is an international airport near Bandar Seri Begawan, which can handle up to 1.5m. passengers and 50,000 metric tons of cargo a year. The Brunei Shell Petroleum Co Sdn Bhd operates a private airfield at Anduki for helicopter services.

Department of Civil Aviation: Brunei International Airport, Bandar Seri Begawan 2015; tel. (2) 330142; telex 2267; fax (2) 331706; Dir Pengiran Haji ABDUL RAHMAN BIN PSI Pengiran Haji ISMAIL (acting).

Royal Brunei Airlines Ltd: RBA Plaza, POB 737, Bandar Seri Begawan 1907; tel. (2) 240500; telex 2737; fax (2) 244737; f. 1974; operates services within the Far East and to the Middle East, Australasia and Europe; Chair. Minister of Law; Man. Dir Haji BRAHIM Haji ISMAIL.

Tourism

There were 837,156 foreign visitor arrivals (including same-day visitors) in 1996. In 1994 international tourist receipts totalled US $36m.

Tourism Development Division: c/o Ministry of Industries and Primary Resources, Jalan Menteri Besar, Bandar Seri Begawan 1220; tel. (2) 382822; fax (2) 383811; Man. Sheikh JAMALUDDIN BIN Sheikh MOHAMED.

BULGARIA

Introductory Survey

Location, Climate, Language, Religion, Flag, Capital

The Republic of Bulgaria lies in the eastern Balkans, in south-eastern Europe. It is bounded by Romania to the north, by Turkey and Greece to the south, by Yugoslavia (Serbia) to the west and by the former Yugoslav republic of Macedonia to the south-west. The country has an eastern coastline on the Black Sea. The climate is one of fairly sharp contrasts between winter and summer. Temperatures in Sofia are generally between –5°C (23°F) and 28°C (82°F). The official language is Bulgarian, a member of the Slavonic group, written in the Cyrillic alphabet. Minority languages include Turkish and Macedonian. The majority of the population are Christian, most of whom adhere to the Bulgarian Orthodox Church, while there is a substantial minority of Muslims. The national flag (proportions 3 by 2) has three equal horizontal stripes, of white, green and red. The capital is Sofia.

Recent History

After almost 500 years of Ottoman rule, Bulgaria declared itself an independent kingdom in 1908. In both the First and Second World Wars Bulgaria allied itself with Germany, and in 1941 joined in the occupation of Yugoslavia. Soviet troops occupied Bulgaria in 1944. In September of that year the Fatherland Front, a left-wing alliance formed in 1942, seized power, with help from the USSR, and installed a Government, led by Kimon Georgiev. In September 1946 the monarchy was abolished, following a popular referendum, and a republic was proclaimed. The first post-war election was held in October, when the Fatherland Front received 70.8% of the votes and won 364 seats, of which 277 were held by the Bulgarian Communist Party (BCP), in the 465-member National Assembly. In November Georgi Dimitrov, the First Secretary of the BCP and a veteran international revolutionary, became Chairman of the Council of Ministers (Prime Minister) in a Government that comprised members of the Fatherland Front. All opposition parties were abolished, and a new Constitution, based on the Soviet model, was adopted in December 1947, when Bulgaria was designated a People's Republic. Dimitrov was replaced as Prime Minister by Vasil Kolarov in March 1949, but remained leader of the BCP until his death in July. His successor as party leader, Vulko Chervenkov, became Prime Minister in February 1950.

Todor Zhivkov succeeded Chervenkov as leader of the BCP in March 1954, although the latter remained Prime Minister until April 1956, when he was replaced by Anton Yugov. Following an ideological struggle within the BCP, Zhivkov became Prime Minister in November 1962. In March 1965 a conspiracy to overthrow the Government was discovered by Soviet intelligence agents. In May 1971 a new Constitution was adopted, and in July Zhivkov relinquished his position as Prime Minister to become the first President of the newly-formed State Council. He was re-elected in 1976, 1981 and 1986. In September 1978 a purge of BCP members commenced. At the twelfth BCP Congress, held in March and April 1981, the party's leader was restyled General Secretary. In June, following elections to the National Assembly, a new Government was formed, headed by Grisha Filipov, a member of the BCP's Political Bureau, succeeding Stanko Todorov, who had been Prime Minister since 1971. In March 1986 Filipov was replaced in this post by Georgi Atanasov, a former Vice-President of the State Council.

In local elections, held in March 1988, the nomination of candidates other than those endorsed by the BCP was permitted for the first time. Candidates presented by independent public organizations and workers' collectives obtained about one-quarter of the total votes cast. At a plenum of the BCP, held in July 1988, several prominent proponents of the Soviet-style programme of reform were dismissed from office.

On 10 November 1989 Zhivkov was unexpectedly removed from his post of General Secretary of the BCP (which he had held for 35 years) and from the Political Bureau. He was replaced as General Secretary by Petur Mladenov, who had been the Minister of Foreign Affairs since 1971 and a member of the BCP's Political Bureau since 1977. Mladenov also replaced Zhivkov as President of the State Council (while resigning as Minister of Foreign Affairs). In mid-November 1989 the National Assembly voted for the abolition of part of the penal code prohibiting 'anti-State propaganda', and for the granting of an amnesty to persons who had been convicted under the code's provisions. Zhivkov was subsequently denounced by the BCP and divested of his party membership, and an investigation into the extent of corruption during his tenure of power was initiated. In 1990 Zhivkov was arrested on charges of embezzlement of state funds.

In early December 1989 Angel Dimitrov became the new leader of the Bulgarian Agrarian People's Union (BAPU, the sole legal political party apart from the BCP, with which it was originally allied); the BAPU was subsequently reconstituted as an independent opposition party. In mid-December the BCP proposed amendments to the Constitution and the adoption of a new electoral law that would permit free and democratic elections to be held in the second quarter of 1990. In January 1990 the National Assembly voted overwhelmingly to remove from the Constitution the article guaranteeing the BCP's dominant role in society. It also approved legislation permitting citizens to form independent groups and to stage demonstrations.

A series of discussions regarding political and economic reforms was initiated in early January 1990 between the BCP, the BAPU and the Union of Democratic Forces (UDF), a co-ordinating organization (established in December 1989) which comprised several dissident and independent groups, including Ecoglasnost and the Podkrepa (Support) Trade Union Confederation. In early February the BCP adopted a new manifesto, pledging the party's commitment to extensive political and economic reforms, the separation of party and state, and the introduction of a multi-party system. It was stressed, however, that the BCP would retain its Marxist orientation. The party's Central Committee was replaced by a Supreme Council, chaired by Aleksandur Lilov, who was formerly head of the BCP's ideology department and who had been expelled from the party in 1983 for criticism of Zhivkov. The Political Bureau and Secretariat of the Central Committee were replaced by the Presidium of the Supreme Council, also with Lilov as Chairman. Mladenov (who remained as President of the State Council) proposed the formation of an interim coalition government, pending elections to the National Assembly (which were subsequently scheduled for June 1990). The UDF and the BAPU, however, rejected Mladenov's invitation to participate in such a coalition. Accordingly, the new Council of Ministers, which was appointed on 8 February 1990, was composed solely of BCP members, chaired by Andrei Lukanov, the former Minister of Foreign Economic Relations, who was regarded as an advocate of reform.

There was further unrest in mid-February 1990, when an estimated 200,000 supporters of the UDF gathered in Sofia to demand the end of BCP rule. Following discussions on reform in late March, with the participation of the BAPU and other political and public organizations, it was finally agreed that Mladenov was to be re-elected as President, pending elections to the National Assembly in June and the subsequent approval of a new constitution. The participants in the talks also decided to dissolve the State Council. In early April the National Assembly adopted an electoral law, together with legislation that provided for political pluralism, and guaranteed the right to form political parties. Also in early April the BCP voted overwhelmingly to rename itself the Bulgarian Socialist Party (BSP) and expressed support for an accelerated, but state-controlled, transition to a market economy.

Following an electoral campaign which was marred by acts of intimidation and violence, elections to the 400-seat Grand National Assembly were held in two rounds, on 10 and 17 June 1990. The BSP won 211 seats, but failed to gain the two-thirds majority of seats in the legislature necessary to secure support for the approval of constitutional and economic reforms. The UDF, which won the majority of votes in urban areas, obtained 144 seats in the Assembly. The Movement for Rights and Freedoms (MRF), which had been established earlier in 1990 to represent the country's Muslim minority, won a large percentage of the votes in areas populated by ethnic Turks, and secured 23 seats. The BAPU won 16 seats in the legislature, considerably fewer than had been expected. The UDF, after initial protests against alleged electoral fraud, accepted the validity of the result, although it again rejected the BSP's invitation to join a coalition government.

In July 1990 Mladenov announced his resignation as President, following a campaign of protests and strikes, led by students. Zhelyu Zhelev, the Chairman of the UDF, was elected to replace him in early August. Zhelev was succeeded as Chairman of the UDF by Petur Beron, hitherto the Union's Secretary, and, following Beron's resignation in December, by Filip Dimitrov, a lawyer and the Vice-President of the Green Party.

Anti-Government demonstrations continued in late 1990, prompted, in particular, by the severe deterioration in the economy, which had resulted in widespread shortages of food and fuel. In October Lukanov proposed that the Grand National Assembly approve a programme of extensive economic reforms, and threatened to resign if the programme did not receive the requisite support of two-thirds of the members of the Assembly. The UDF (which held more than one-third of the seats in the legislature) refused to support the reforms, although it agreed to join a coalition government, on condition that its representatives form the majority in the Council of Ministers and that the post of Chairman be occupied by a UDF member. The UDF proceeded to organize rallies in many parts of Bulgaria to demand the resignation of Lukanov's Government.

In mid-November 1990 the Grand National Assembly voted to rename the country the Republic of Bulgaria, and voted to remove from the national flag the state emblem, which included communist symbols.

Increasing division between conservative and reformist elements within the BSP became manifest in early November 1990, when 16 BSP delegates to the Grand National Assembly announced their decision to form a separate parliamentary group, as a result of which the party no longer held an absolute majority in the legislature. A motion expressing no confidence in the Government, proposed by the UDF in late November, was defeated by 201 votes to 159. However, following a four-day general strike organized by the Podkrepa Trade Union Confederation (in which, according to claims by Podkrepa, about 830,000 workers participated), Lukanov and his Government resigned at the end of the month. Subsequent discussions between representatives of all the political forces in the Grand National Assembly resulted in the formation of a new 'government of national consensus' in mid-December, comprising members of the BSP, the UDF, the BAPU and four independents. Dimitur Popov, a lawyer with no party affiliation, had been elected in early December to chair the new Council of Ministers.

As part of its programme of reform to create a market economy, the newly-elected Government abolished price controls in early February 1991, in fulfilment of conditions determined by the IMF (which Bulgaria had joined in September 1990). Sharp increases in the prices of many commodities ensued, thereby exacerbating public resentment at the already widespread shortages of food and fuel. In June 1991 the International Atomic Energy Agency declared the nuclear power plant at Kozlodui, north of Sofia, to be unsafe and recommended its closure; by November of that year two of the plant's six reactors had been taken out of operation.

The new Constitution was adopted by the Grand National Assembly in mid-July 1991. The document stipulated, *inter alia,* a five-year residency qualification for presidential candidates, effectively disqualifying the candidacy of Simeon II, the pretender to the Bulgarian throne, who had lived in exile since 1946. Following its approval of the Constitution, the Grand National Assembly voted to dissolve itself, although it continued sessions in an interim capacity pending legislative elections. In the months preceding the elections, internal divisions occurred in many of the major parties, and in the UDF two splinter groups emerged (Liberals and Centre). Nevertheless, at the elections to the new 240-seat National Assembly, which were held on 13 October, the majority UDF obtained the largest share of the vote (34.4%), defeating the BSP (which contested the election in alliance with a number of smaller parties) by a narrow margin of just over 1% of votes cast. The UDF won a total of 110 seats in the legislature, while the BSP obtained 106 seats. The ethnic Turkish MRF became the third strongest political force, securing a total of 24 seats and thus holding the balance of power in the National Assembly. No other party or alliance gained the 4% of the votes required for representation in the legislature. The new Council of Ministers, composed of UDF members and six independents, was announced in early November. Filip Dimitrov, the leader of the UDF, was elected Chairman of the new Government.

A direct presidential election was held in January 1992. Following an inconclusive first round, a second ballot, involving the two leading candidates—the incumbent President Zhelev and Velko Valkanov, an independent supported by the BSP—took place. Zhelev was re-elected for a five-year term with 53% of the votes cast.

Throughout 1992 labour unrest was endemic. A miners' strike in late March exacerbated severe energy shortages, which had resulted from the closure in February of another reactor at the Kozlodui nuclear power station and the erratic nature of petroleum supplies from Russia. In April the Government's programme of price liberalization caused further trade union disaffection, and the main trade union federations, the Confederation of Independent Trade Unions in Bulgaria (CITUB) and Podkrepa, abandoned talks with the Government.

In March 1992 attempts by the Government to introduce legislation that would further reduce the power of former communists was opposed by the BSP with the support of President Zhelev, who maintained that the apparent restriction of political freedom could undermine Bulgaria's application for membership of the Council of Europe (see p. 140). In the same month a compromise solution was agreed by the Minister of Foreign Affairs, Stoyan Ganev, and President Zhelev, whereby the National Intelligence Service was eventually to be placed under the jurisdiction of the Government rather than the Office of the Presidency. Ganev also announced that he would dismiss 200 diplomats with connections to the former State Security and the BCP.

In early April 1992, despite BSP opposition, the Government adopted legislation restoring ownership of land and property that had been transferred to the state sector during 1947–62. This was followed in the same month by legislation approving the privatization of state-owned companies.

In May 1992 Dimitrov threatened to resign as Prime Minister unless the Minister of Defence, Dimitur Ludzhev, relinquished his post. This was widely believed to be indicative of a broader struggle for control of the increasingly factional UDF. Ludzhev resigned later that month, and Dimitrov implemented an extensive reorganization of the Council of Ministers. In July the former BCP Prime Minister, Lukanov (now a BSP deputy of the National Assembly), was arrested, prompting the BSP deputies to withdraw from a meeting of the National Assembly in protest. Later in the month the BSP proposed a motion expressing no confidence in the Government, which was, however, defeated by the UDF with the support of the MRF. Legal proceedings were initiated against Lukanov and a further 60 senior officials (including two other former Prime Ministers, Grisha Filipov and Georgi Atanasov) on charges of misappropriating state funds. (Atanasov was officially pardoned by President Zhelev in August 1994 on the grounds of ill health.)

In mid-July 1992 there were further strikes, and miners were joined by other public-sector employees. Despite the Government's offer of a 26% pay increase for all government employees, Podkrepa continued to support the strike and to condemn the Government's economic policies. In early August the Chairman of Podkrepa, Konstantin Trenchev, was arrested with 37 others, and charged with incitement to destroy public property in 1990.

Relations between President Zhelev and the UDF became increasingly strained. In late August 1992 Zhelev publicly criticized Dimitrov's Government and received support for his position from both the MRF and the CITUB. In September the UDF convened a national conference and agreed to initiate discussions with the President and the MRF, but reaffirmed its support for Dimitrov. In late September the MRF declared a lack of confidence in Dimitrov's leadership. Strikes by teachers and munitions workers during October were followed by allegations that Konstantin Mishev, a prime ministerial adviser, had attempted to sell arms to the former Yugoslav republic of Macedonia. At the end of October MRF and BSP deputies in the National Assembly defeated the Government by 121 votes to 111 in a motion of confidence, requested by Dimitrov. The Government subsequently resigned.

In November 1992 President Zhelev invited Dimitrov (as the nominee of the party with the largest representation in the National Assembly) to form a new government. The MRF, however, declined to form a coalition with the UDF, and Dimitrov's nomination was thus defeated in the National Assembly. The BSP was then assigned a mandate to nominate a candidate for the premiership. President Zhelev, however, rejected the candidacy of the BSP nominee, Petur Boyadzhiev, on the grounds that he held dual nationality (Bulgarian and French) and his candidacy was thus disallowed under the terms of the Constitution. Following the failure of the UDF and the MRF to reach agreement for a coalition under the MRF mandate, in December the MRF nominated an academic, Prof. Lyuben Berov, hitherto an economic adviser to President Zhelev, to the office of Prime Minister. The UDF accused Berov of collaborating with the former communist regime and organized a large rally to protest against his candidacy, while threatening to expel members who voted in his favour in the National Assembly. In the event, the majority of UDF deputies abstained but Berov was approved as Prime Minister on 30 December by 124 votes to 25 in a secret ballot. Berov's proposed Council of Ministers, principally composed of 'experts' without party political allegiances, was also accepted by the National Assembly. On the same day, the BSP and the MRF voted in the National Assembly to discharge Lukanov from custody. It was widely speculated that BSP support for Berov's Government had been, in part, conditional on Lukanov's release.

In March 1993 internal divisions within the UDF became more apparent when a breakaway faction of the party formed a new organization, known as the New Union for Democracy (NUD). The UDF, in response to the formation of the pro-Berov NUD, intensified its campaign of opposition, claiming, in particular, that the Government was planning to reintroduce socialism. In May the former Speaker of the National Assembly, Stefan Savov, was injured by a policeman during a demonstration, organized by the UDF, outside the parliamentary building in Sofia; the UDF claimed that he had been attacked on government orders. In early June a UDF deputy, Edvin Sugarev, began a hunger strike to demand President Zhelev's resignation. In the same month large demonstrations were staged by the UDF in Sofia and several other cities to denounce Zhelev for allegedly attempting the restoration of communism and to demand immediate elections. The situation improved slightly later that month, when Sugarev ended his hunger strike. On 29 June, however, the Vice-President, Blaga Dimitrova, resigned from her post, claiming that she had been insufficiently consulted while in office. The crisis finally subsided when two votes expressing no confidence in Berov's Government, which were proposed by the UDF in the National Assembly, proved unsuccessful. Political unrest continued, however, and in November the Berov administration survived another motion of no confidence, proposed by the UDF. In the same month Berov's National Security Adviser was dismissed from his post, and in December further allegations of government corruption were presented to the Chief Prosecutor.

In August 1993 the former Prime Minister, Andrei Lukanov, and 21 other ex-BCP officials were arrested on charges of misappropriation of funds. In January 1994 the former communist dictator, Todor Zhivkov, was sentenced to seven years in prison for embezzlement of government funds. (In February 1996, however, the Supreme Court upheld his subsequent appeal against the sentence.)

In mid-January 1994 the Minister of the Interior, Viktor Mihailov, resigned, following the accidental shooting of two policemen by their colleagues. In the following month the Berov Government survived a fifth motion of no confidence, proposed by the UDF in protest against the Government's apparent inability to control the dramatic increase in the crime rate. Political unrest intensified in mid-March, following an announcement by President Zhelev that he was in favour of calling an early general election, which prompted the UDF to reiterate its own demands for early elections. On 2 April Zhelev announced that he could no longer give his political support to Berov's administration, citing its failure to achieve certain objectives, such as the imposition of an accelerated privatization programme. On 5 April, following the controversial introduction of value-added tax (VAT), unpopular rises in fuel prices and the dramatic fall of the lev, thousands of demonstrators protested in Sofia against government policies. In mid-May a proposal by Berov for the appointment of a new Council of Ministers was rejected by the National Assembly; it was claimed by certain political groups that Berov wished to install a BSP-dominated administration. Later that month Berov's Government survived a further vote of no confidence, again proposed by the UDF. In late May the Government narrowly won a vote of confidence presented in the National Assembly. The UDF deputies subsequently boycotted National Assembly sessions throughout June.

In late June 1994 the Government finally launched the delayed May privatization programme, whereby each Bulgarian citizen was offered a 500-leva voucher which could be invested either directly into state enterprises or into private investment funds. In early September, however, Berov's Government submitted its resignation, following increasing criticism of the poor organization of the privatization programme. Both the BSP and the UDF refused presidential mandates to form a new Government. In October President Zhelev dissolved the National Assembly and announced that a general election would take place on 18 December. Later in October Zhelev appointed an interim neutral Government, headed by Reneta Indzhova.

At the general election, which was held as scheduled on 18 December 1994, the BSP (in alliance, as the Democratic Left, with two small parties, the Aleksandur Stamboliyski Bulgarian Agrarian People's Union and the Ecoglasnost Political Club—the political wing of the Ecoglasnost National Movement) obtained an outright majority in the National Assembly, with 125 seats (43.5% of the total votes cast), while the UDF won 69 seats (24.2%). Other groups that gained more than the 4% of votes required for representation in the legislature were: the People's Union (an alliance of BAPU and the Democratic Party), the MRF and the Bulgarian Business Bloc (BBB). A new Government, headed by the Chairman of the BSP, Zhan Videnov, was appointed at the end of January 1995; the majority of the ministers were members of the BSP.

In February 1995 the National Assembly passed a bill that amended the 1992 property restitution law (see above), extending for a further three years the deadline by which certain properties had to be restored to their rightful owners. In March the National Assembly abolished a law, adopted by the UDF Government in 1992, prohibiting former communists from senior academic positions. In the same month the Government drafted a programme for mass privatization in 1995, which envisaged payment through a combination of cash, debt bonds and investment vouchers (the vouchers were made available from early January 1996). Mass demonstrations took place throughout March 1995, however, reflecting widespread dissatisfaction with government amendments to the Agricultural Land Tenure Act, on the grounds that they would restrict landowners' rights to dispose of their property and would encourage the restoration of communist-style collective farms. In late April President Zhelev exercised his right of veto against the highly unpopular amendments, which had been adopted by the National Assembly in mid-April; the President claimed that the amendments contravened the constitutional right of Bulgarian citizens to own private property. The case was subsequently examined by the Constitutional Court, which in June 1995 rejected the amendments as unconstitutional.

In late June 1995 the Government removed the heads of the state television and radio services and the Director-General of the national news agency; the opposition alleged that the dismissals represented an attempt by the BSP to control the state media. In August the Government also dismissed the Director of the Centre for Mass Privatization, Yosif Iliev, following a series of delays to the privatization process. In late August President Zhelev refused to implement the appointments of three BSP nominees to senior military positions, claiming that the appointments were politically biased.

In late September 1995 the Government survived a motion of no confidence (by 130 votes to 102), which was introduced by the opposition in the National Assembly, in protest at the continued failure of Videnov's administration to control the rapid increase in levels of crime. In early October the Bulgarian energy sector again became the subject of media attention when the Government authorized the reopening of one of the reactors at the Kozlodui nuclear power station, despite warnings from the international community that the reactor was unsafe.

At municipal elections, which took place in late October and early November 1995, the ruling coalition won 195 of a total of 255 mayoralties, although the UDF secured the mayoralties in the country's three main cities. In mid-November President Zhelev announced that he would seek re-election in 1997.

On 10 January 1996 a further motion of no confidence in the Videnov administration was proposed by the opposition, in protest at a severe shortage of grain, which had resulted from the Government's repeal of a ban on grain exports in July 1995. The motion was defeated, but the situation prompted the resignation of the Deputy Prime Minister and a further two ministers. In Febuary 1996 the MRF staged a demonstration in Sofia in protest at the annulment, owing to alleged irregularities, of the result of the municipal elections in the south-eastern town of Kurdzhali (where the MRF had narrowly secured a victory). In April, however, the Supreme Court upheld the election result. In the same month protests were staged in Sofia, following a proposal by Russia that Bulgaria be included in an association of former Soviet states; the Government denied accusations by Zhelev that it had engaged in clandestine discussions with Russia prior to the offer. A demonstration was subsequently staged by opponents of Bulgaria's possible entry into NATO (which was favoured by Zhelev). In May the Minister of the Interior resigned, following an incident in which three members of the security forces were killed by criminals. Meanwhile, a sharp devaluation of the lev (see Economic Affairs) resulted in further economic hardship, exacerbated by continuing shortages of grain. In June the UDF proposed a motion expressing no confidence in the Government's management of the economy, which was, however, defeated by a large majority in the National Assembly.

In primary elections for a UDF presidential candidate, which were conducted in early June 1996, Petar Stoyanov, a lawyer and senior member of the opposition alliance, secured 66% of votes cast, defeating Zhelev. Zhelev subsequently announced that he would support Stoyanov's candidature for the presidency. In July the National Assembly scheduled the presidential election for 27 October. In the same month the Constitutional Court ruled that Georgi Pirinski, the candidate who had been nominated in June to contest the election on behalf of the BSP, was ineligible, on the grounds that he was not a Bulgarian citizen by birth, as stipulated in the Constitution. Pirinski (who had been considered to be the most popular of the nominated candidates) declared that political bias had influenced the decision, and initially insisted that he would contest the election. In September, following a ruling by the Supreme Court that confirmed the invalidity of Pirinski's candidature, the BSP selected the Minister of Culture, Ivan Marazov, as its presidential candidate; Marazov was to represent a newly-formed electoral alliance, known as Together for Bulgaria, which comprised the parties in the Democratic Left parliamentary coalition (the BSP, Aleksandur Stamboliyski and the Ecoglasnost Political Club). Also in September the National Assembly voted narrowly in favour of a presidential veto on the proposed new national emblem, which Zhelev had criticized on the grounds that it resembled the BSP party badge. Acrimony between Zhelev and the Videnov administration was further exacerbated by Zhelev's refusal to accede to a government request that Bulgaria's Permanent Representative at the UN, Slavi Pashovski, be withdrawn; Pashovski had publicly accused the Government of employing repressive measures against political dissidents.

In early October 1996 the former Prime Minister, Andrei Lukanov (who had remained an influential member of the BSP), was assassinated. Ensuing speculation regarding the motive for the killing focused, in particular, on Lukanov's critical stance towards the Videnov administration's slow implementation of economic reforms. Later that month CITUB and Podkrepa organized a demonstration in Sofia to demand the resignation of the Government. In the first round of the presidential election, which was contested by 14 political groups on 27 October (as scheduled), Stoyanov secured 44.1% of votes cast; Marazov received only 27.0% of the votes, while the candidate of the BBB, Georgi Ganchev, won 21.9%. Only 61% of the electorate voted in the second round of the presidential election, which took place on 3 November, reflecting increasing public disaffection with the Government's management of the critical economic situation. Stoyanov was elected to the presidency, with 59.7% of votes cast. Stoyanov (who was believed to favour Bulgaria's entry into NATO) subsequently announced that he was to establish a Council of National Salvation, which would devise measures to improve financial stability.

Following the election of Stoyanov, the political council of the UDF agreed to initiate a campaign to demand that parliamentary elections be conducted later that year (earlier than scheduled). The electoral defeat of the BSP in the presidential election aggravated existing divisions within the organization; in early November 1996 several senior members of the BSP accused Videnov of causing the party's unpopularity and demanded the resignation of the Government. However, a joint convention of the BSP and its allied parties subsequently rejected a motion of no confidence in the Government. Later in November Pirinski, who was a leading opponent of Videnov within the BSP, submitted his resignation from the post of Minister of Foreign Affairs, on the grounds that the Government no longer commanded public support and that the party vote had failed to indicate sufficient confidence in Videnov. Meanwhile, continuing dissent between Zhelev and the Government represented an impediment to the adoption of urgent measures, which were recommended by the IMF in response to a further deterioration in the economy.

In December 1996 the UDF staged a series of demonstrations to demand early legislative elections and the resignation of the Government. On 21 December, at an extraordinary congress of the BSP, Videnov unexpectedly tendered his resignation from the office of Prime Minister and the post of party leader. (The incumbent Council of Ministers was to remain in office, pending the formation of a new administration.) Georgi Purvanov, who was a supporter of Videnov, subsequently replaced him as Chairman of the BSP. At the end of December the National Assembly voted by a large majority to accept the resignation of Videnov's Government. In January 1997 the BSP designated the Minister of the Interior, Nikolai Dobrev, to replace Videnov as Prime Minister. The UDF, however, intensified its campaign of demonstrations; in early January an attempt by protesters to seize the parliamentary building was suppressed by security forces. Zhelev subsequently announced that he would not invite Dobrev to form a new government as expected. Later that month the UDF, with the support of Podkrepa, organized a series of one-hour strikes to demand early parliamentary elections. On 19 January Stoyanov was inaugurated as President. However, the establishment of a new administration continued to be impeded by the UDF, which threatened to organize a general strike if a new BSP Council of Ministers was formed, while refusing to participate in a coalition government during the tenure of the incumbent National Assembly. Following the failure of parliamentary deputies to reach an agreement on early elections, it was reported that the BSP and the UDF were negotiating a compromise arrangement, whereby an interim coalition government, which would be authorized to implement IMF-approved economic reforms, would be installed, prior to legislative elections later that year. At the end of January the BSP accepted a proposal by Stoyanov that the party form a new government, pending legislative elections, which were expected to take place in the second half of 1997. In early February the BSP announced the appointment of a new Council of Ministers; following continued protests and strikes, however, Dobrev agreed to relinquish the party's mandate to form a new government (owing to increasing concern that the disorder might escalate into civil conflict). The Consultative National Security Council adopted recommendations (which were approved by the National Assembly) that, in the absence of agreement between the political parties represented in the legislature on the formation of a government, the President should appoint an interim council of ministers, dissolve the incumbent National Assembly and schedule new legislative elections. Stoyanov subsequently nominated the mayor of Sofia, Stefan Sofianski, to the office of Prime Minister, and formed an interim Council of Ministers, pending elections, which were scheduled to be held on 19 April; the National Assembly was dissolved on 19 February. Following the resumption of negotiations between the new Government and the IMF, agreement was reached in March regarding the establishment of a currency control board (see Economic Affairs), as a prerequisite to economic and financial stability. Later in March the interim Government announced that Videnov was to be charged with criminal negligence as a result of government policies that had caused the severe shortage of grain in 1995–96; the Minister of Agriculture in the Videnov administration and three of his deputies were also prosecuted.

At the elections to the National Assembly, which took place as scheduled on 19 April 1997, the UDF secured 137 seats, while the BSP (which again contested the elections in the Democratic Left alliance) obtained only 58 seats; the Alliance for National Salvation (a coalition comprising the MRF and other monarchist and centrist groups) won 19 seats, a newly-established left-wing organization, known as Euro-Left, gained 14 seats and the BBB 12 seats. Later in April the UDF formally nominated the party Chairman, Ivan Kostov, to the office of Prime Minister (subject to the approval of the National Assembly). At the first session of the new National Assembly, which was convened in early May, deputies adopted a seven-point declaration of national consensus, which had been proposed by the UDF; the stated policies included the implementation of economic reforms which had been agreed with the IMF, the acceleration of measures to restore agricultural land to rightful ownership, and support for Bulgaria's accession to the EU and NATO. (However, a number of the issues, particularly the proposed introduction of the currency control board in agreement with the IMF, were opposed by some groups in the National Assembly.) Later in May the National Assembly elected Kostov to the office of Prime Minister; only deputies belonging to the Democratic Left alliance opposed his nomination. The new Council of Ministers, which had been formed by Kostov, included five members of the outgoing interim administration.

Following its installation, the new Government replaced the President of the State Savings Bank. In June 1997 the National Assembly adopted legislation providing for the establishment of a currency control board as stipulated by the IMF; the new monetary board, which fixed the exchange rate of the lev to that of the Deutsche Mark, was installed at the beginning of July. In a further effort to impose fiscal discipline, the Government replaced the senior officials of the Bulgarian National Bank; Svetoslav Gavriyski, who had served as Minister of Finance in the interim Council of Ministers, was appointed Governor. At the end of July the National Assembly voted in favour of declassifying security files on politicians and public officials, and adopted legislation to expedite the restoration of land to rightful ownership. In early September two parliamentary representatives of the BBB were expelled from the party after criticizing the leadership of Ganchev, who, they claimed, intended to establish links with the BSP; another deputy resigned in protest at their removal. The BBB was consequently obliged to dissolve its parliamentary group, which had been reduced to below the required minimum of 10 representatives. In October a government commission announced that 23 prominent public officials, including 14 members of the National Assembly, had been members of the security services of former communist governments. In early November, following protests from deputies belonging to the Democratic Left, the Constitutional Court ruled that the appointment of directors of the national radio and television stations by the National Assembly (rather than by an independent media council) was in contravention of the Constitution. In January 1998 the National Assembly rejected a motion expressing 'no confidence' in the Government, which had been proposed by Democratic Left deputies in protest at the Council of Ministers' policy on health care.

Bulgaria maintained close links with other Eastern European countries through its membership of the Warsaw Pact and of the Council for Mutual Economic Assistance (CMEA). Following the political upheavals which took place in Eastern Europe in 1989 and 1990, both the Warsaw Pact and the CMEA were dissolved in mid-1991. Diplomatic relations with several Western nations were re-established in 1990 and 1991, and in mid-1992 Bulgaria became a member of the Council of Europe (see p. 140). In May 1994 Bulgaria was granted associate partnership status by the Western European Union (WEU—see p. 240). In June 1992 Bulgaria, together with 10 other countries (including six of the former Soviet republics), signed a pact to establish the Black Sea Economic Co-operation Group (see p. 260), which envisaged the creation of a Black Sea economic zone that would complement the European Community (now European Union—EU, see p. 152). In 1996 Bulgaria submitted an official application for membership of the EU. In October of that year Bulgaria joined the World Trade Organization (see p. 244).

Bulgaria's establishment of formal relations with the former Yugoslav republic of Macedonia (FYRM) in January 1992 prompted harsh criticism from the Greek Government. Relations with Greece appeared to improve, however, after the visit of the Bulgarian Minister of Foreign Affairs to Athens in May 1992. In November 1993 the FYRM expressed its desire to establish full diplomatic relations with Bulgaria. In the following month Bulgaria announced that it was to open an embassy in the FYRM and relax border procedures between the two states.

Relations between Bulgaria and Russia improved in 1992, following the signing of co-operation agreements, and the visit of the Russian President, Boris Yeltsin, to Sofia in August of that year. Reciprocal visits by the premiers of Bulgaria and Russia in 1995 further improved relations between the two countries. In late 1996 a Russian parliamentary delegation visited Sofia to meet Bulgarian deputies; it was agreed that joint Bulgarian-Russian debates would be conducted on significant issues of mutual concern.

Relations with neighbouring Turkey have been intermittently strained since the mid-1980s, when the Zhivkov regime began a campaign of forced assimilation of Bulgaria's ethnic Turkish minority (which constitutes an estimated 10% of the total population). The ethnic Turks were forced to adopt Slavic names prior to the December 1985 census, and were banned from practising Islamic religious rites. In 1986 the Bulgarian Government continued to refute allegations by a prominent human rights organization, Amnesty International, that more than 250 ethnic Turks had been arrested or imprisoned for refusing to accept new identity cards, and that many more had been forced to resettle away from their homes, in other regions of the country. In February 1988, on the eve of a conference of Ministers of Foreign Affairs of the six Balkan nations, Bulgaria and Turkey signed a protocol to further bilateral economic and social relations. However, the situation deteriorated in May 1989, when Bulgarian militia units violently suppressed demonstrations by an estimated 30,000 ethnic Turks in eastern Bulgaria against the continued assimilation campaign. In June more than 80,000 ethnic Turks were expelled from Bulgaria, although the Bulgarian authorities claimed that the Turks had chosen to settle in Turkey, following a relaxation in passport regulations to ease foreign travel. Furthermore, the Ministry of the Interior stated that it had received 250,000 applications for permission to travel to Turkey. In response, the Turkish Government opened the border and declared its commitment to accepting all the ethnic Turks as refugees from Bulgaria. By mid-August an estimated 310,000 Bulgarian Turks had crossed into Turkey. In late August the Turkish Government, alarmed by the continued influx of refugees, closed the border. In the following month a substantial number of the Bulgarian Turks, disillusioned with conditions in Turkey, began to return to Bulgaria (more than 100,000 had returned by February 1990).

The Turkish Government repeatedly proposed that discussions with the Bulgarian Government be held, under the auspices of the UN High Commissioner for Refugees, to establish the rights of the Bulgarian Turks and to formulate a clear immigration policy. Finally, Bulgaria agreed to negotiations, and friendly relations between Bulgaria and Turkey had apparently been restored by late 1991. In March 1992 a bilateral defence agreement was signed. In May Prime Minister Dimitrov visited Turkey, and the two countries signed a treaty of friendship and co-operation.

Meanwhile, in December 1989, some 6,000 Pomaks (ethnic Bulgarian Muslims who form a community of about 300,000 people) held demonstrations to demand religious and cultural freedoms, as well as an official inquiry into alleged atrocities against Pomaks during Zhivkov's tenure of office. In January 1990 anti-Turkish demonstrations were held in the Kurdzhali district of southern Bulgaria, in protest at the Government's declared intention to restore civil and religious rights to the ethnic Turkish minority. Despite continuing demonstrations by Bulgarian nationalist protesters, in March the National Assembly approved legislation that permitted ethnic Turks and Pomaks to use their original Islamic names. This development was welcomed by the Turkish Government. Nevertheless, inter-ethnic disturbances continued, particulary in the Kurdzhali region, during 1990. Proposals in early 1991 to introduce the teaching of Turkish in schools in predominantly Turkish regions led to renewed inter-ethnic conflict. In November of that year the Government finally decreed that Turkish be taught as an optional subject four times weekly in the regions concerned, following which the MRF ended a boycott on school attendance, which it had imposed in mid-1991. By 1993 ethnic tensions had generally been contained in Bulgaria, although there were reports of some disturbances between ethnic Turks and ethnic Bulgarian Muslims in the south of the country in September. In July 1995 a visit by President Demirel of Turkey to Bulgaria, during which regional security and economic relations between the two countries were discussed, indicated a significant improvement in Bulgarian-Turkish relations.

Government

Legislative power is held by the unicameral National Assembly, comprising 240 members, who are elected for four years by universal adult suffrage. The President of the Republic (Head of State) is elected directly by the voters for a period of five years, and is also Supreme Commander-in-Chief of the Armed Forces. The Council of Ministers, the highest organ of state administration, is elected by the National Assembly. For local administration, Bulgaria comprises nine regions (divided into a total of 273 municipalities). The territorial administration of Bulgaria was partially reorganized in 1994.

Defence

Military service is compulsory and lasts for 18 months. The total strength of the armed forces in August 1997 was 101,500 (including 49,300 conscripts), comprising an army of 50,400, an air force of 19,300, a navy of an estimated 6,100, 22,300 centrally-controlled staff and 3,400 Ministry of Defence staff. Paramilitary forces include an estimated 12,000 border guards, 18,000 railway and construction troops and 4,000 security police. Defence expenditure for 1995 was estimated at 24,000m. leva. The 1995 state budget allocated 22,763m. leva to defence (representing 6.3% of total expenditure by the central Government). Bulgaria joined NATO's 'partnership for peace' programme of military co-operation (see p. 206) in February 1994.

Economic Affairs

In 1995, according to estimates by the World Bank, Bulgaria's gross national product (GNP), measured at average 1993–95 prices, was US $11,225m., equivalent to $1,330 per head. During 1985–95, it was estimated, GNP per head decreased, in real terms, at an average annual rate of 2.2%. Over the same period the population decreased at an average rate of 0.6% per year. According to the World Bank, Bulgaria's gross domestic product (GDP) declined, in real terms, by an average of 3.0% annually during 1985–95. According to official estimates, real GDP increased by 2.1% in 1995, but declined by 10.9% in 1996.

Agriculture (including forestry and fishing) contributed 11.7% of GDP in 1996. In 1995 the sector engaged 24.2% of all employees. In 1990 private farming was legalized, and farmland was restituted, in its former physical boundaries, to former owners and their heirs. In 1996 privately-owned farms supplied 75.4% of total agricultural production. The principal crops are wheat, maize, barley, sunflower seeds, grapes, potatoes and tobacco. Viticulture has been developed extensively in recent years; in 1989 Bulgaria was the world's fourth largest exporter of wine. There is a large exportable surplus of processed agricultural products. During 1985–95, according to the World Bank, the real GDP of the agricultural sector declined by an annual average of 1.3%. According to official estimates, agricultural GDP increased by 14.5% in 1995, but declined by 18.1% in 1996.

Industry (including mining, manufacturing, construction and utilities) provided 32.6% of GDP in 1996, and engaged 33.8% of all employees in 1995. According to the World Bank, industrial GDP declined, in real terms, by an annual average of 4.9% in 1985–95. Industrial GDP declined, according to official estimates, by 5.4% in 1995 and by 8.3% in 1996.

In 1992 mining and quarrying engaged 2.5% of the employed labour force. Coal, iron ore, copper, manganese, lead and zinc are mined, while petroleum is extracted on the Black Sea coast. Bulgaria's annual output of coal (including brown coal) increased from 30.8m. metric tons in 1995 to 31.3m. tons in 1996. In 1986 the construction of a gas pipeline, linking Bulgaria to the USSR, was completed. Under an agreement, which was signed in that year, Russia supplies Bulgaria with 3,340m. cu m of gas annually.

The manufacturing sector engaged 29.6% of the employed labour force in 1992. Based on the value of output, the main branches of manufacturing (excluding publishing) in 1994 were petroleum and coal products (accounting for 15.4% of the total), food products (13.5%), metals (10.8%), chemical products (9.7%), beverages and tobacco (8.9%) and non-electrical machinery (4.8%). The output of the manufacturing sector increased at an average rate of 4.5% per year during 1980–88, but declined in subsequent years. Output fell by about 17% in 1990 and by a further 23% in 1991.

Bulgaria's production of primary energy in 1992 was equivalent to 44% of gross consumption. Coal and nuclear power are the main domestic sources of energy. The country's sole nuclear power station, at Kozlodui, provided some 40% of electric energy in 1990. In 1996 two of the station's reactors were closed for repairs, exacerbating existing energy shortages; the reactors were scheduled to resume operating by early 1997. Imports of mineral fuels comprised 27% of the value of the merchandise imports in 1994.

The services sector contributed an estimated 55.6% of GDP in 1996, and engaged 42.0% of all employees in 1995. Trade represented an estimated 11.2% of GDP in 1996. According to the World Bank, the average annual GDP of the services sector showed no significant change in 1985–95. The sector's GDP declined, according to official estimates, by 0.7% in 1995 and by 6.5% in 1996.

In 1995 Bulgaria recorded a visible trade surplus of US$121.0m., but there was a deficit of $25.6m. on the current account of the balance of payments. In 1996 there was a trade deficit of $543m. In that year the principal source of imports was the Russian Federation, which provided 37.2% of the total; Germany and Italy were also major suppliers. The main market for exports was Italy (taking 9.6% of the total) in 1996; the Russian Federation, Germany and Greece were also significant purchasers. The principal exports in 1993 were basic manufactures, machinery and transport equipment, and chemicals and related products. The principal imports in that year were mineral fuels and lubricants (particularly petroleum and petroleum products), machinery and transport equipment and miscellaneous manufactured articles.

Bulgaria's overall budget deficit for 1995 was 46,168m. leva. Bulgaria's total external debt at the end of 1995 was US $10,887m., of which $9,574m. was long-term public debt. In that year the cost of debt-servicing was equivalent to 18.8% of revenue from exports of goods and services. The annual rate of inflation averaged 106.1% in 1990–95. Consumer prices increased by 62.1% in 1995 and by 123.0% in 1996. An estimated 12.5% of the labour force were unemployed at the end of 1996.

Bulgaria is a member of the International Bank for Economic Co-operation (see p. 261), the UN Economic Commission for Europe (see p. 26) and the Black Sea Economic Co-operation Group (see p. 260). In September 1990 Bulgaria became a member of the IMF and the World Bank. In 1996 Bulgaria made a formal application for membership of the European Union (EU, see p. 152). Bulgaria is a founding member of the European Bank for Reconstruction and Development (EBRD, established in May 1990, see p. 148).

In the late 1980s the Bulgarian economy entered a severe decline. Output in most sectors was considerably reduced, and there was a sharp rise in the rates of unemployment and inflation. Bulgaria's economy was further affected by UN sanctions against Iraq, Libya and Yugoslavia in the early 1990s. In an effort to prevent total economic collapse, the Government introduced an extensive programme of privatization and restructuring of the banking system, under a planned transition to a market economy, and in 1991 adopted austerity measures in fulfilment of conditions stipulated by the IMF. The implementation of structural reforms was, however, subsequently impeded by political dissension. In May 1996 the Government initiated emergency measures in response to a collapse in the value of the lev (which had been precipitated by declining foreign-exchange reserves). Widespread hardship was exacerbated by shortages of grain and energy. In September, however, the IMF suspended the disbursement of funds, pending progress in the implementation of planned reforms of the banking system and of the privatization programme, and the closure of unprofitable companies. In the same month the Government again increased central interest rates, to 300%, in an attempt to prevent a further devaluation of the lev (after public concern prompted depositors to withdraw large amounts of national currency from bank accounts). Nevertheless, the value of the lev declined sharply in November. Following the resumption of negotiations between a new interim administration (see Recent History) and the IMF, agreement was reached in March 1997 regarding the adoption of structural reforms, which included the establishment of a currency control board, the acceleration of the privatization programme, the liberalization of trade and price controls, and the rationalization of state-sector employees in an effort to reduce government expenditure on loss-making companies. In April the IMF approved financial credit to support the government programme. At the beginning of July, in an effort to impose fiscal discipline, the Government established a currency control board which fixed the exchange rate of the lev to that of the Deutsche Mark. Legislation providing for the trading of mass privatization shares was adopted, and it was announced that some 80% of state-owned enterprises were to be transferred to the private sector by the end of 1998. In September 1997 the majority of restrictions on foreign investors were removed. The operations of the currency control board achieved some success, owing in part to a rapid decline in the rate of inflation which favoured foreign investment, and in late 1997 international financial institutions approved further loans in continued support of the Government's programme of economic reform.

Social Welfare

The Bulgarian health service is administered by the Ministry of Health, with the assistance of local government and the Bulgarian Red Cross; medical care is provided free of charge. The development of the private health sector is also encouraged (private medical and dentistry practices were banned between 1972 and November 1989). In 1996 there were 29,529 doctors and 5,467 dentists. In the same year there were 289 hospital establishments, with 86,160 hospital beds, and 53,335 beds in sanatoriums and other institutions. State provision is made for social benefits, including sickness and unemployment allowances, maternity leave payments and pensions. The retirement age is 60 years for men and 55 years for women; many employees are entitled to early retirement.

State social insurance is directed by the Department of Public Insurance and the Directorate of Pensions. Of total government expenditure in 1995, 12,094m. leva (3.4%) was for health, and a further 91,320m. leva (25.3%) for social security and welfare.

Education

Education is free and compulsory between the ages of six and 16 years. Children between the ages of three and six years may attend kindergartens (in 1994 57% of pre-school age children attended). Primary education, beginning at six years of age, lasts for eight years. Education at secondary level is continued at gymnasiums, which provide a general academic course, or vocational and technical schools, which offer specialized training; in addition, there are 16 art schools. In 1994 primary enrolment included 83% of children in the relevant age-group (boys 84%; girls 82%), while the comparable ratio for secondary education was 58% (boys 57%; girls 58%). In 1996/97 there were a total of 42 higher educational institutions, with a total enrolment of 235,701 students, and an additional 46 semi-higher institutions.

In 1994 enrolment in higher education courses was equivalent to 34.3% of those in the relevant age-group (males 26.5%; females 42.5%). The 1995 state budget allocated 14,301m. leva to education (representing 4.0% of total expenditure by the central Government). In 1995, according to UNESCO estimates, 1.7% of the adult population were illiterate (males 1.1%; females 2.3%).

Public Holidays

1998: 1 January (New Year), 3 March (National Day), 13 April (Easter Monday), 1 May (Labour Day), 6 May (St George's Day), 24 May (Education Day), 1 November (Commemoration of the Leaders of the Bulgarian National Revival), 24–25 December (Christmas).

1999: 1 January (New Year), 3 March (National Day), 5 April (Easter Monday), 1 May (Labour Day), 6 May (St George's Day), 24 May (Education Day), 1 November (Commemoration of the Leaders of the Bulgarian National Revival), 24–25 December (Christmas).

Weights and Measures

The metric system is in force.

Statistical Survey

Source (unless otherwise stated): National Statistical Institute, 1000 Sofia, ul. Shesti Septemvri 10; tel. (2) 54-31-54; telex 22001; fax (2) 81-63-04.

Area and Population

AREA, POPULATION AND DENSITY

Area (sq km)*	110,994†
Population (census results)	
4 December 1985	8,948,649
4 December 1992	
Males	4,170,622
Females	4,316,695
Total	8,487,317
Population (official estimates at 31 December)	
1994	8,427,418
1995	8,384,715
1996	8,339,847
Density (per sq km) at 31 December 1996	75.1

* Including territorial waters of frontier rivers (261.4 sq km).
† 42,855 sq miles.

ETHNIC GROUPS (1992 census)

	Number	%
Bulgarian	7,271,185	85.67
Turkish	800,052	9.43
Gypsy	313,396	3.69
Armenian	13,677	0.16
Others	80,526	0.95
Unknown	8,481	0.10
Total	8,487,317	100.00

ADMINISTRATIVE REGIONS (31 December 1993)

	Area (sq km)	Estimated population*	Density (per sq km)
Sofia (town)†	1,310.8	1,188,556	906.7
Burgas	14,724.3	850,003	57.7
Khaskovo	13,824.1	903,928	65.4
Lovech	15,150.0	1,009,196	66.6
Montana‡	10,606.8	626,205	59.0
Plovdiv	13,585.4	1,221,449	89.9
Ruse	10,842.5	765,719	70.6
Sofia (region)†	19,021.1	980,588	51.6
Varna	11,928.6	914,079	76.6
Total	110,993.6	8,459,723	76.2

* Figures are provisional. The revised total is 8,459,763.
† The city of Sofia, the national capital, has separate regional status. The area and population of the capital region are not included in the neighbouring Sofia region.
‡ Formerly Mikhailovgrad.

PRINCIPAL TOWNS
(estimated population at 31 December 1992)

Sofia (capital)	1,114,476	Sliven	106,225
Plovdiv	341,374	Dobrich*	104,485
Varna	308,601	Shumen	93,292
Burgas (Bourgas)	195,986	Yambol	91,561
Ruse (Roussé)	170,203	Pernik	90,586
Stara Zagora	150,451	Pazardzhik	82,619
Pleven	130,747	Khaskovo	80,773

* Dobrich was renamed Tolbukhin in 1949, but its former name was restored in 1990.

BIRTHS, MARRIAGES AND DEATHS

	Registered live births		Registered marriages*		Registered deaths	
	Number	Rate (per 1,000)	Number	Rate (per 1,000)	Number	Rate (per 1,000)
1989	112,289	12.5	63,263	7.0	106,902	11.9
1990	105,180	12.1	59,874	6.9	108,608	12.5
1991	95,910	11.1	48,820	5.6	110,423	12.8
1992	89,134	10.4	44,806	5.2	107,998	12.6
1993	84,987	10.0	40,022	4.7	109,540	12.9
1994	79,934	9.4	37,910	4.5	111,787	13.2
1995	72,428	8.6	n.a.	4.4	114,670	13.6
1996	72,743	8.6	n.a.	4.3	117,056	14.0

* Including marriages of Bulgarian nationals outside the country but excluding those of aliens in Bulgaria.

Expectation of Life (years at birth, 1991–93): Males 67.7; Females 74.7.

ECONOMICALLY ACTIVE POPULATION (1992 census)*

	Males	Females	Total
Agriculture, hunting, forestry and fishing	266,929	204,359	471,288
Mining and quarrying	61,897	19,898	81,795
Manufacturing	484,594	489,310	973,904
Electricity, gas and water	31,495	11,822	43,317
Construction	164,754	41,847	206,601
Trade, restaurants and hotels	182,688	218,269	400,957
Transport, storage and communications	178,483	69,814	248,297
Financing, insurance, real estate and business services	8,872	29,387	38,259
Community, social and personal services	326,987	494,489	821,476
Activities not adequately defined	479	282	761
Total employed	1,707,178	1,579,477	3,286,655
Unemployed	323,015	322,798	645,813
Total labour force	2,030,193	1,902,275	3,932,468

* Figures refer to employed persons aged 14 years and over and to unemployed persons aged 15 to 59 years.

Source: ILO, *Yearbook of Labour Statistics*.

November 1996 ('000 persons): Total employed 3,085.4 (males 1,637.0, females 1,448.4); Unemployed 490.8 (males 258.2, females 232.6); Total labour force 3,576.2 (males 1,895.2, females 1,681.0).

EMPLOYMENT

(annual averages, excluding armed forces)

	1993	1994	1995*
Agriculture, hunting, forestry and fishing†	712,600	751,500	801,600
Mining and quarrying Manufacturing Electricity, gas and water	978,700	942,900	932,400
Construction	200,000	185,400	186,100
Trade, restaurants and hotels	352,300	394,000	391,200
Transport and communications	241,000	232,600	233,300
Financing, insurance, real estate and business services	66,800	61,300	58,700
Community, social and personal services	670,400	673,900	707,600
Total employees	3,221,800	3,241,600	3,310,900

* Figures are provisional. The revised total is 3,282,183.

† Including veterinary services.

Source: mainly ILO, *Yearbook of Labour Statistics*.

1996 (annual average): Total employees 3,279,482.

Agriculture

PRINCIPAL CROPS ('000 metric tons)

	1994	1995	1996
Wheat	3,754	3,438	1,788*
Rice (paddy)	3	5	8*
Barley	1,143	1,171	459*
Maize	1,384	1,792	1,198*
Rye	22	20	13*
Oats	85	47	14*
Potatoes	497	649	302*
Dry beans	30	51	17*
Dry peas	11	11	8†
Soybeans	9	14	18*
Sunflower seed	602	767	530
Seed cotton	7	14	10*
Cabbages	75	102	102†
Tomatoes	477	530	330*
Pumpkins, squash and gourds	26	46	46†
Cucumbers and gherkins	99	158	125*
Green peppers	223	263	263†
Dry onions	81	180	150†
Green beans	15	20	20†
Green peas	2	3	3†
Melons and watermelons	357	422	422†
Grapes	516	699	350*
Apples	76	149	170*
Pears	34	22	21*
Plums	79	100	100†
Peaches and nectarines	57	72	72†
Apricots	21	5	5†
Strawberries	6	8	8†
Sugar beets	112	158	102*
Tobacco (leaves)	33	19	40*

* Unofficial figure. † FAO estimate.

Source: FAO, *Production Yearbook*.

LIVESTOCK ('000 head at 1 January each year)

	1994	1995	1996
Horses	113	133	133*
Asses	297	276	276*
Cattle	750	638	632
Pigs	2,071	1,986	2,140
Sheep	3,763	3,398	3,383
Goats	676	795	757†
Buffaloes	17	14	14
Poultry	18,211	19,126	18,609

* FAO estimate. † Unofficial figure.

Source: partly FAO, *Production Yearbook*.

LIVESTOCK PRODUCTS ('000 metric tons)

	1994	1995	1996
Beef and veal†	87	69	49
Buffalo meat	2	2*	2*
Mutton and lamb†	40	40	30
Goat meat	7	5†	3†
Pigmeat	218	257†	150†
Poultry meat	82	97†	81†
Cow milk	1,135	1,129†	1,050†
Buffalo milk	14	12†	12*
Sheep milk	134	124†	124*
Goats' milk	79	98*	98*
Butter	4	3	2
Cheese (all kinds)	88	85	75
Hen eggs	96	110†	97†
Other poultry eggs	2	2*	2*
Honey	4	4*	4*
Wool:			
greasy	12	9†	10*
scoured	6	4†	5*
Cattle and buffalo hides*	14	11	11
Sheepskins*	16	16	12

* FAO estimate(s). † Unofficial figure(s).

Source: FAO, *Production Yearbook*.

Forestry

ROUNDWOOD REMOVALS ('000 cubic metres, excl. bark)

	1992	1993	1994*
Sawlogs, veneer logs and logs for sleepers	778	802	802
Pulpwood	618	679	679
Other industrial wood	279	356	356
Fuel wood	1,888	1,728	1,728
Total	3,563	3,565	3,565

* FAO estimates.

Source: FAO, *Yearbook of Forest Products.*

SAWNWOOD PRODUCTION ('000 cubic metres, incl. sleepers)

	1992	1993	1994*
Coniferous (softwood)	214	186	186
Broadleaved (hardwood)	110	67	67
Total	324	253	253

* FAO estimates.

Source: FAO, *Yearbook of Forest Products.*

Fishing

('000 metric tons, live weight)

	1993	1994*	1995*
Freshwater bream	6.2	6.3	6.5
Common carp	1.0	1.0	1.1
Southern blue whiting	3.1	3.0	3.3
Beaked redfish	3.2	3.6	3.8
European sprat	2.2	2.2	2.3
Atlantic mackerel	1.9	2.1	2.3
Other fishes (incl. unspecified)	3.0	2.8	3.0
Total fish	20.5	21.0	22.2
Argentine shortfin squid	1.1	1.0	1.2
Total catch	21.6	22.0	23.4
Inland waters	9.6	9.7	10.1
Mediterranean and Black Seas	2.3	2.3	2.5
Atlantic Ocean	9.7	10.0	10.8

* FAO estimates.

Source: FAO, *Yearbook of Fishery Statistics.*

Mining

('000 metric tons, unless otherwise indicated)

	1994	1995	1996
Anthracite	29	24	19
Other hard coal	144	170	117
Lignite	25,429	27,449	28,104
Other brown coal	3,155	3,187	3,057
Iron ore*	268	270	282
Copper ore*	75.5†	n.a.	n.a.
Lead ore*	32.0†	n.a.	n.a.
Zinc ore*	25.1†	n.a.	n.a.
Manganese ore*	–	5.6	13.1
Crude petroleum	36	43	32
Natural gas (million cu metres)	7.6	22.5	18.8

* Figures relate to the metal content of ores. Data for copper, lead and zinc are from *World Metal Statistics* (London).

† Source: UN, *Industrial Commodity Statistics Yearbook.*

Industry

SELECTED PRODUCTS

('000 metric tons, unless otherwise indicated)

	1994	1995	1996
Flour	988	977	861
Refined sugar	274	237	210
Wine ('000 hectolitres)	1,647	2,481	2,217
Beer ('000 hectolitres)	4,792	4,331	4,509
Cigarettes and cigars (metric tons)	53,700	74,600	57,300
Cotton yarn (metric tons)[1]	23,700	27,600	25,600
Woven cotton fabrics ('000 metres)[2]	69,900	76,600	69,200
Flax and hemp yarn (metric tons)	800	800	800
Wool yarn (metric tons)[1]	14,100	14,000	12,600
Woven woollen fabrics ('000 metres)[2]	14,000	13,200	12,000
Woven fabrics of man-made fibres ('000 metres)[3]	16,700	19,200	18,900
Leather footwear ('000 pairs)	9,700	11,000	8,000
Rubber footwear ('000 pairs)	1,700	1,300	1,000
Chemical wood pulp	93.7	105.6	84.6
Paper	143.2	194.9	174.4
Paperboard	20.9	31.3	26.9
Rubber tyres ('000)[4]	553	642	532
Sulphuric acid (100%)	428.0	453.8	517.8
Caustic soda (96%)	70.8	70.4	80.8
Soda ash (98%)	451.0	796.0	866.1
Nitrogenous fertilizers[5]	322.8	459.2	468.2
Phosphate fertilizers[5]	50.6	53.1	90.4
Coke (gas and coke-oven)	1,116	1,240	1,157
Unworked glass—rectangles ('000 sq metres)	11,000	12,000	12,300
Clay building bricks (million)	666	668	566
Cement	1,910	2,070	2,132
Pig-iron and ferro-alloys	1,475	1,614	1,513
Crude steel	2,491	2,724	2,457
Refined copper—unwrought (metric tons)	26,500	25,500	22,300
Refined lead—unwrought (metric tons)	64,000	60,100	74,700
Zinc—unwrought (metric tons)	64,000	68,800	68,000
Metal-working lathes (number)	1,979	2,496	2,507
Fork-lift trucks (number)[6]	5,700	11,700	3,600
Refrigerators—household (number)	69,300	53,800	36,200
Washing machines—household (number)	41,300	26,500	23,700
Radio receivers (number)	2,000	1,800	300
Television receivers (number)	19,000	9,700	10,000
Merchant vessels launched ('000 gross reg. tons	47	n.a.	n.a.
Buses (number)[7]	59	83	93
Lorries (number)[7]	321	253	60
Construction: dwellings completed (number)[8]	8,669	6,815	8,099
Electric energy (million kWh)	38,113	41,790	42,710

[1] Pure and mixed yarn. Figures for wool include yarn of man-made staple.

[2] Pure and mixed fabrics, after undergoing finishing processes.

[3] Finished fabrics, including fabrics of natural silk.

[4] Tyres for road motor vehicles (passenger cars and commercial vehicles).

[5] Figures for nitrogenous fertilizers are in terms of nitrogen, and for phosphate fertilizers in terms of phosphoric acid. Data for nitrogenous fertilizers include urea.

[6] Including hoisting gears.

[7] Including vehicles assembled from imported parts.

[8] Including restorations and conversions.

Finance

CURRENCY AND EXCHANGE RATES

Monetary Units

100 stotinki (singular: stotinka) = 1 lev (plural: leva).

Sterling and Dollar Equivalents (30 September 1997)

£1 sterling = 2,879.6 leva;
US $1 = 1,782.6 leva;
10,000 leva = £3.473 = $5.610.

Average Exchange Rate (leva per US$)

1994 54.25
1995 67.17
1996 175.82

STATE BUDGET (million leva)*

Revenue†	1993	1994	1995
Taxation	75,154	157,045	243,018
Taxes on income, profits, etc.	12,613	29,605	52,668
Social security contributions	29,680	45,413	66,848
From employers	27,378	39,253	58,645
Taxes on payroll or work-force	4,299	6,376	9,400
Domestic taxes on goods and services	18,238	57,707	86,978
Sales or turnover taxes	6,911	39,305	62,887
Excises	11,322	18,395	24,086
Taxes on international trade and transactions	9,108	16,157	25,646
Import duties	7,746	12,438	19,486
Other current revenue	24,468	47,752	69,649
Entrepreneurial and property income	15,222	30,509	34,309
Administrative fees and charges, non-industrial and incidental sales	6,545	10,493	23,934
Capital revenue	253	4,524	1,957
Total revenue	99,875	209,321	314,624

Expenditure‡	1993	1994	1995
General public services	5,481	9,159	13,185
Defence	8,475	14,275	22,763
Public order and safety	5,247	9,127	15,613
Education	4,534	7,893	14,301
Health	4,481	6,560	12,094
Social security and welfare	44,200	66,020	91,320
Housing and community amenities	1,522	4,428	3,942
Recreational, cultural and religious affairs and services	1,437	2,510	4,090
Economic affairs and services	13,701	16,964	25,572
Fuel and energy	3,954	2,898	3,519
Agriculture, forestry, fishing and hunting	2,264	5,287	6,954
Mining, manufacturing and construction	1,732	2,397	2,305
Transport and communications	4,650	5,103	10,282
Other purposes	44,799	98,969	157,727
Total expenditure	133,877	235,905	360,607
Current§	130,570	229,767	347,049
Capital	3,307	6,138	13,558

* Figures refer to the consolidated accounts of the central Government (including social security funds and other extrabudgetary units).

† Excluding grants received (million leva): 92 in 1993; 117 in 1994; 920 in 1995.

‡ Excluding lending minus repayments (million leva): 2,240 in 1993; −2,080 in 1994; 1,105 in 1995.

§ Including interest payments (million leva): 29,172 in 1993; 76,411 in 1994; 128,708 in 1995.

Source: IMF, *Government Finance Statistics Yearbook*.

MONEY SUPPLY (million leva at 31 December)

	1994	1995	1996
Currency outside banks	38,498	61,615	126,461
Demand deposits at banks	36,633	46,271	110,167
Total money	75,131	107,886	236,628

COST OF LIVING

(Consumer Price Index; base: 1990=100)

	1993	1994	1995
Food	1,296.3	2,483.6	3,968.3
Fuel and light	1,540.5	2,632.8	4,026.1
Clothing	1,045.8	1,883.7	3,251.8
Rent	1,548.1	2,559.3	4,391.3
All items (incl. others)	1,227.5	2,296.3	3,722.0

Source: ILO, *Yearbook of Labour Statistics*.

1996: All items 8,300.2.

NATIONAL ACCOUNTS (million leva at current prices)

Expenditure on the Gross Domestic Product (excl. holding gains or losses)

	1994	1995	1996
Government final consumption expenditure	90,347	134,408	206,635
Private final consumption expenditure	389,130	610,150	1,283,924
Increase in stocks	−22,967	1,538	−33,000
Gross fixed capital formation	72,327	123,588	224,000
Total domestic expenditure	528,837	869,684	1,681,559
Exports of goods and services	236,770	387,710	865,415
Less Imports of goods and services	240,055	389,703	893,472
GDP in purchasers' values	525,552	867,691	1,660,237*

* Including adjustment (6,735 million leva).

Gross Domestic Product by Economic Activity (excl. holding gains or losses)

	1994	1995	1996
Agriculture	59,014	108,913	183,732
Forestry	1,370	2,503	5,101
Industry*	157,355	270,168	524,615
Trade	52,934	88,258	180,739
Transport	25,248	37,522	69,075
Communications	8,786	12,160	30,050
Other services	185,408	283,716	614,646
Sub-total	490,115	803,240	1,607,958
Turnover tax and excises	26,935	25,320	61,993
Import duties and value-added tax / *Less* Imputed bank service charge	8,502	39,131	−9,714
GDP in purchasers' values	525,552	867,691	1,660,237

* Comprising mining and quarrying, manufacturing, construction, and electricity, gas and water.

BALANCE OF PAYMENTS (US $ million)

	1994	1995
Exports of goods f.o.b.	3,935.1	5,345.0
Imports of goods f.o.b.	−3,952.0	−5,224.0
Trade balance	−16.9	121.0
Services (net)	10.8	153.4
Balance on goods and services	−6.1	274.4
Other income (net)	−192.5	−432.0
Balance on goods, services and income	−198.6	−157.6
Current transfers (net)	166.7	132.0
Current balance	−31.9	−25.6
Capital account (net)	763.3	—
Direct investment abroad	−0.0	8.0
Direct investment from abroad	105.5	90.4
Portfolio investment (net)	−231.8	−65.8
Other investment assets	−209.2	404.2
Other investment liabilities	−159.2	−316.9
Net errors and omissions	107.1	139.4
Overall balance	343.7	233.7

External Trade

PRINCIPAL COMMODITIES (US $ million)

Imports c.i.f.	1993	1994	1995
Food and live animals	295.0	n.a.	n.a.
Sugar, sugar preparations and honey	72.3	112.4	112.5
Sugar and honey	n.a.	98.9	105.4
Beverages and tobacco	117.8	n.a.	n.a.
Tobacco and tobacco manufactures	103.3	46.6	21.0
Crude materials (inedible) except fuels	203.8	n.a.	n.a.
Textile fibres and wastes	55.8	n.a.	n.a.
Cotton	n.a.	91.0	100.5
Synthetic fibres	n.a.	135.6	148.9
Mineral fuels, lubricants, etc.	1,743.2	1,242.7	1,350.2
Petroleum, petroleum products, etc.	1,249.0	n.a.	n.a.
Crude petroleum oils, etc.	994.7	636.9	720.0
Gas (natural and manufactured)	358.8	n.a.	n.a.
Chemicals and related products	454.8	n.a.	n.a.
Organic chemicals	64.3	121.4	133.2
Inorganic chemicals	114.0	28.1	103.5
Artificial resins, plastic materials, etc.	45.0	117.7	138.5
Basic manufactures	614.0	n.a.	n.a.
Paper, paperboard, etc.	76.1	111.7	175.3
Textile yarn, fabrics, etc.	173.7	n.a.	n.a.
Iron and steel	176.2	147.6	130.6
Machinery and transport equipment	934.6	n.a.	n.a.
Power-generating machinery and equipment	37.5	460.0	483.5
Machinery specialized for particular industries	170.6	n.a.	n.a.
General industrial machinery, equipment and parts	128.8	n.a.	n.a.
Electrical machinery, apparatus, etc. (excl. telecommunications and sound equipment)	126.3	218.4	250.5
Road vehicles and parts (excl. tyres, engines and electrical parts)	289.0	243.6	226.8
Passenger motor cars (excl. buses)	171.2	121.5	99.3
Miscellaneous manufactured articles	290.4	n.a.	n.a.
Total (incl. others)	4,962.3	4,593.0	5,125.0

Exports f.o.b.	1993	1994	1995
Food and live animals	598.7	300.5	n.a.
Cereals and cereal preparations	17.9	n.a.	n.a.
Wheat and meslin (unmilled)	5.0	1.4	100.7
Vegetables and fruit	89.7	n.a.	n.a.
Beverages and tobacco	331.6	n.a.	n.a.
Beverages	111.5	160.3	186.1
Wine, etc.	75.3	100.5	122.6
Tobacco and tobacco manufactures	220.1	241.1	301.3
Manufactured tobacco	167.0	n.a.	n.a.
Cigarettes	166.7	189.8	238.4
Crude materials (inedible) except fuels	199.7	n.a.	n.a.
Mineral fuels, lubricants, etc.	304.1	302.7	318.1
Petroleum, petroleum products, etc.	281.1	302.7	318.1
Chemicals and related products	510.4	n.a.	n.a.
Organic chemicals	68.0	148.4	185.1
Medicinal and pharmaceutical products	171.1	93.1	89.1
Manufactured fertilizers	92.6	140.6	236.0
Artificial resins, plastic materials, etc.	56.7	120.0	150.3
Basic manufactures	879.2	n.a.	n.a.
Textile yarn, fabrics, etc.	106.9	n.a.	n.a.
Iron and steel	340.9	479.2	528.5
Universals, plates and sheets	123.8	223.0	266.6
Non-ferrous metals	220.7	n.a.	n.a.
Copper	137.8	177.9	270.1
Machinery and transport equipment	603.4	n.a.	n.a.
Power-generating machinery and equipment	41.4	255.8	288.0
General industrial machinery, equipment and parts	250.2	n.a.	n.a.
Electrical machinery, apparatus, etc. (excl. telecommunications and sound equipment)	133.9	205.0	182.5
Miscellaneous manufactured articles	342.1	n.a.	n.a.
Clothing and accessories (excl. footwear)	166.5	195.0	230.5
Footwear	73.7	98.2	94.3
Total (incl. others)	3,500.4	4,446.7	5,184.4

Source: UN, *International Trade Statistics Yearbook*.

1996 (US $ million): Imports c.i.f. 5,356; Exports f.o.b. 4,813 (Source: UN, *Monthly Bulletin of Statistics*).

PRINCIPAL TRADING PARTNERS (million leva)*

Imports c.i.f.	1994	1995	1996
Algeria	2,230.7	5,126.0	1,383.3
Austria	6,601.7	10,570.3	20,199.9
Belgium	2,592.8	5,013.0	9,478.6
Czech Republic	3,028.1	5,105.0	10,901.1
France	6,081.5	10,596.4	27,516.0
Germany	29,034.4	46,983.5	98,417.8
Greece	10,884.0	16,729.9	30,792.7
Italy	12,195.7	22,018.6	53,352.5
Macedonia, former Yugoslav republic	6,988.2	11,826.0	5,295.2
Netherlands	4,427.0	7,471.3	14,985.7
Poland	2,448.5	2,068.5	5,515.8
Romania	4,327.0	4,101.1	13,483.8
Russia†	59,891.2	106,658.4	337,120.6
Switzerland	2,969.0	6,676.7	13,527.6
Ukraine	9,479.8	12,668.1	21,922.3
United Kingdom	6,238.6	9,960.2	16,877.6
USA	6,733.7	8,020.1	18,320.0
Total (incl. others)	227,010.3	380,012.1	905,612.9

Exports f.o.b.	1994	1995	1996
Austria	2,957.3	3,089.9	8,664.2
Belgium	4,493.5	5,526.7	10,830.2
China, People's Republic	3,297.4	1,325.7	7,849.1
France	5,948.1	10,295.9	20,360.9
Germany	19,253.6	30,795.4	74,721.9
Greece	16,828.4	24,760.0	61,383.7
Italy	16,497.3	29,279.4	78,951.4
Macedonia, former Yugoslav republic	22,294.7	29,257.7	24,651.6
Netherlands	5,035.7	6,891.3	12,430.2
Romania	3,430.1	6,391.8	12,290.0
Russia†	29,203.6	36,110.0	76,398.2
Syria	3,585.2	4,760.1	13,396.5
Ukraine	7,003.9	12,869.5	29,295.5
United Kingdom	5,777.1	11,307.3	24,492.1
USA	11,188.4	10,939.0	21,369.3
Yugoslavia‡	7,874.2	5,786.7	35,420.6
Total (incl. others)	216,194.4	359,663.6	818,315.0

* Imports by country of purchase; exports by country of sale.
† Including Azerbaijan, Kazakhstan, Kyrgyzstan, Tajikistan, Turkmenistan and Uzbekistan.
‡ Serbia and Montenegro.

Transport

RAILWAYS (traffic)

	1994	1995	1996
Passengers carried ('000)	65,730	58,940	66,097
Passenger-kilometres (million)	5,059	4,693	5,065
Freight carried ('000 metric tons)	30,274	32,916	30,118
Freight net ton-kilometres (million)	7,774	8,595	7,549

ROAD TRAFFIC (motor vehicles in use at 31 December)

	1994	1995	1996
Passenger cars	1,587,873	1,647,571	1,707,023
Buses and coaches	40,610	41,019	40,835
Lorries and vans	195,786	203,257	207,258
Motorcycles and mopeds	516,957	519,266	521,710

Source: International Road Federation, *World Road Statistics*.

INLAND WATERWAYS (traffic)

	1994	1995	1996
Passengers carried ('000)	10	10	11
Passenger-kilometres (million)	6	10	12
Freight carried ('000 metric tons)	608	1,121	999
Freight ton-kilometres (million)	360	733	627

SHIPPING

Merchant Fleet (registered at 31 December)

	1994	1995	1996
Number of vessels	211	202	192
Total displacement ('000 grt)	1,294.9	1,166.1	1,149.7

Source: Lloyd's Register of Shipping, *World Fleet Statistics*.

Sea-borne Traffic (international and coastal)

	1994	1995	1996
Passengers carried ('000)	51	18	20
Freight ('000 metric tons)	17,087	18,089	17,070

CIVIL AVIATION (traffic)

	1994	1995	1996
Passengers carried ('000)	1,542	1,297	1,216
Passenger-kilometres (million)	3,604	3,133	2,840
Freight carried ('000 metric tons)	17	14	10
Freight ton-kilometres (million)	47	46	35

Tourism

ARRIVALS OF FOREIGN VISITORS

Country of origin	1994	1995	1996
Czech Republic*	47,239	74,901	74,139
Slovakia*			55,035
Germany	157,221	202,401	124,592
Greece	357,345	230,767	156,392
Poland*	39,014	37,324	83,084
Romania*	1,873,818	1,509,601	1,280,431
Turkey*	2,005,513	1,825,061	1,185,826
USSR (former)	1,828,894	1,216,463	1,418,722
United Kingdom	60,167	51,063	41,581
Yugoslavia (former)	3,152,580	2,346,382	1,815,382
Total (incl. others)	10,068,181	8,004,584	6,810,688

* Mainly visitors in transit, totalling 6,172,437 in 1994, 4,538,713 in 1995 and 4,015,493 in 1996.

Communications Media

	1992	1993	1994
Telephone subscribers (at 31 December)	2,838,836	2,886,200	2,955,500
Telefax stations (number in use)	7,500	10,000	n.a.
Mobile cellular telephones (subscribers)	n.a.	1,000	n.a.
Radio licences (at 31 December)	1,780,335	1,677,600	1,570,300
Television licences (at 31 December)	1,550,063	1,494,100	1,482,600
Book production:			
Titles*	4,773	5,771	5,925
Copies ('000)*	53,677	55,356	42,746
Daily newspapers:			
Titles	46	54	n.a.§
Copies ('000)†	1,464	n.a.	1,843
Non-daily newspapers‡:			
Titles	871	874	n.a.§
Copies ('000)†	8,992	8,280	n.a.
Other periodicals:			
Titles	745	n.a.	n.a.
Copies ('000)†	3,097	n.a.	n.a.

* Figures include pamphlets (728 titles and 6,303,000 copies in 1992; 974 titles and 7,978,000 copies in 1993; 898 titles and 8,469,000 copies in 1994).
† Average circulation.
‡ Including regional editions.
§ The combined total of daily and non-daily newspapers was 1,059 in 1994.

Sources: partly UNESCO, *Statistical Yearbook*, and UN, *Statistical Yearbook*.

1995: Telephone subscribers (at 31 December) 3,030,300; Radio licences (at 31 December) 1,448,000; television licences (at 31 December) 1,479,100; Book production 5,400 titles, 32.1 million copies; Daily and non-daily newspapers 1,058.

1996: Telephone subscribers (at 31 December) 3,107,400; Radio licences (at 31 December) 1,389,800; Television licences (at 31 December) 1,470,700; Book production 5,100 titles, 22.9 million copies; Daily and non-daily newspapers 1,053.

Education

(1996/97)

	Institutions	Teachers	Students
Kindergartens	3,713	23,353	247,000
General schools	3,286	71,431	944,733
Special	129	2,336	13,849
Vocational technical	7	125	3,384
Secondary vocational	203	5,113	77,299
Technical colleges and schools of arts	337	13,943	125,887
Semi-higher institutes*	46	3,018	24,981
Higher educational	42	23,285	235,701

* Including technical, teacher-training, communications and librarians' institutes.

Directory

The Constitution

The Constitution of the Republic of Bulgaria, summarized below, took effect upon its promulgation, on 13 July 1991, following its enactment on the previous day.

FUNDAMENTAL PRINCIPLES

Chapter One declares that the Republic of Bulgaria is to have a parliamentary form of government, with all state power derived from the people. The rule of law and the life, dignity and freedom of the individual are guaranteed. The Constitution is the supreme law; the power of the State is shared between the legislature, the executive and the judiciary. The Constitution upholds principles such as political and religious freedom (no party may be formed on separatist, ethnic or religious lines, however), free economic initiative and respect for international law.

FUNDAMENTAL RIGHTS AND OBLIGATIONS OF CITIZENS

Chapter Two establishes the basic provisions for Bulgarian citizenship and fundamental human rights, such as the rights of privacy and movement, the freedoms of expression, assembly and association, and the enfranchisement of Bulgarian citizens aged over 18 years. The Constitution commits the State to the provision of basic social welfare and education and to the encouragement of culture, science and the health of the population. The study and use of the Bulgarian language is required. Other obligations of the citizenry include military service and the payment of taxes.

THE NATIONAL ASSEMBLY

The National Assembly is the legislature of Bulgaria and exercises parliamentary control over the country. It consists of 240 members, elected for a four-year term. Only Bulgarian citizens aged over 21 years (who do not hold a state post or another citizenship and are not under judicial interdiction or in prison) are eligible for election to parliament. A member of the National Assembly ceases to serve as a deputy while holding ministerial office. The National Assembly is a permanently-acting body, which is free to determine its own recesses and elects its own Chairman and Deputy Chairmen. The Chairman represents and convenes the National Assembly, organizes its proceedings, attests its enactments and promulgates its resolutions.

The National Assembly may function when more than one-half of its members are present, and may pass legislation and other acts by a majority of more than one-half of the present members, except where a qualified majority is required by the Constitution. Ministers are free to, and can be obliged to, attend parliamentary sessions. The most important functions of the legislature are: the enactment of laws; the approval of the state budget; the scheduling of presidential elections; the election and dismissal of the Chairman of the Council of Ministers (Prime Minister) and of other members of the Council of Ministers; the declaration of war or conclusion of peace; the foreign deployment of troops; and the ratification of any fundamental international instruments to which the Republic of Bulgaria has agreed. The laws and resolutions of the National Assembly are binding on all state bodies and citizens. All enactments must be promulgated in the official gazette, *Durzhaven Vestnik*, within 15 days of their passage through the legislature.

THE PRESIDENT OF THE REPUBLIC

Chapter Four concerns the Head of State, the President of the Republic of Bulgaria, who is assisted by a Vice-President. The President and Vice-President are elected jointly, directly by the voters, for a period of five years. A candidate must be eligible for election to the National Assembly, but also aged over 40 years and a resident of the country for the five years previous to the election. To be elected, a candidate must receive more than one-half of the valid votes cast, in an election in which more than one-half of the eligible electorate participated. If necessary, a second ballot must then be conducted, contested by the two candidates who received the most votes. The one who receives more votes becomes President. The President and Vice-President may hold the same office for only two terms and, during this time, may not engage in any unsuitable or potentially compromising activities. If the President resigns, is incapacitated, impeached or dies, the Vice-President carries out the presidential duties. If neither official can perform their duties, the Chairman of the National Assembly assumes the prerogatives of the Presidency, until new elections take place.

The President's main responsibilities include the scheduling of elections and referendums, the conclusion of international treaties and the promulgation of laws. The President is responsible for appointing a Prime Minister-designate (priority must be given to the leaders of the two largest parties represented in the National Assembly), who must then attempt to form a government.

The President is Supreme Commander-in-Chief of the Armed Forces of the Republic of Bulgaria and presides over the Consultative National Security Council. The President has certain emergency powers, usually subject to the later approval of the National Assembly. Many of the President's actions must be approved by the Chairman of the Council of Ministers. The President may return legislation to the National Assembly for further consideration, but can be over-ruled.

THE COUNCIL OF MINISTERS

The principal organ of executive government is the Council of Ministers, which supervises the implementation of state policy and the state budget, the administration of the country and the Armed Forces, and the maintenance of law and order. The Council of Ministers is headed and co-ordinated by the Chairman (Prime Minister), who is responsible for the overall policy of government. The Council of Ministers, which also includes Deputy Chairmen and Ministers, must resign upon the death of the Chairman or if the National Assembly votes in favour of a motion of no confidence in the Council or in the Chairman.

JUDICIAL POWER

The judicial branch of government is independent. All judicial power is exercised in the name of the people. Individuals and legal entities are guaranteed basic rights, such as the right to contest administrative acts or the right to legal counsel. One of the principal organs is the Supreme Court of Cassation, which exercises supreme judicial responsibility for the precise and equal application of the law by all courts. The Supreme Administrative Court rules on all challenges to the legality of acts of any organ of government. The Chief Prosecutor supervises all other prosecutors and ensures that the law is observed, by initiating court actions and ensuring the enforcement of penalties, etc.

The Supreme Judicial Council is responsible for appointments within the ranks of the justices, prosecutors and investigating magistrates, and recommends to the President of the Republic the appointment or dismissal of the Chairmen of the two Supreme Courts and of the Chief Prosecutor (they are each appointed for a single, seven-year term). These last three officials are, *ex officio*, members of the Supreme Judicial Council, together with 22 others, who must be practising lawyers of high integrity and at least 15 years of professional experience. These members are elected for a term of five years, 11 of them by the National Assembly and 11 by bodies of the judiciary. The Supreme Judicial Council is chaired by the Minister of Justice, who is not entitled to vote.

LOCAL SELF-GOVERNMENT AND LOCAL ADMINISTRATION

Chapter Seven provides for the division of Bulgaria into regions and municipalities. Municipalities are the basic administrative territorial unit at which local self-government is practised; their principal organ is the municipal council, which is elected directly by the population for a term of four years. The council elects the mayor, who is the principal organ of executive power. Bulgaria is also divided into regions (nine in 1993, including the capital). Regional government, which is entrusted to regional governors (appointed by the Council of Ministers) and administrations, is responsible for regional policy, the implementation of state policy at a local level and the harmonization of local and national interests.

THE CONSTITUTIONAL COURT

The Constitutional Court consists of 12 justices, four of whom are elected by the National Assembly, four appointed by the President of the Republic and four elected by the justices of the two Supreme Courts. Candidates must have the same eligibility as for membership of the Supreme Judicial Council. They serve a single term of nine years, but a part of the membership changes every three years. A chairman is elected by a secret ballot of the members.

The Constitutional Court provides binding interpretations of the Constitution. It rules on the constitutionality of: laws and decrees; competence suits between organs of government; international agreements; national and presidential elections; and impeachments. A ruling of the Court requires a majority of more than one-half of the votes of all the justices.

CONSTITUTIONAL AMENDMENTS AND THE ADOPTION OF A NEW CONSTITUTION

Chapter Nine provides for constitutional changes. Except for those provisions reserved to the competence of a Grand National Assembly (see below), the National Assembly is empowered to amend the Constitution with a majority of three-quarters of all its Members, in three ballots on three different days. Amendments must be proposed by one-quarter of the parliamentary membership or by the President. In some cases, a majority of two-thirds of all the Members of the National Assembly will suffice.

Grand National Assembly

A Grand National Assembly consists of 400 members, elected by the generally-established procedure. It alone is empowered to adopt a new constitution, to sanction territorial changes to the Republic of Bulgaria, to resolve on any changes in the form of state structure or form of government, and to enact amendments to certain parts of the existing Constitution (concerning the direct application of the Constitution, the domestic application of international agreements, the irrevocable nature of fundamental civil rights and of certain basic individual rights even in times of emergency or war, and amendments to Chapter Nine itself).

Any bill requiring the convening of a Grand National Assembly must be introduced by the President of the Republic or by one-third of the members of the National Assembly. A decision to hold elections for a Grand National Assembly must be supported by two-thirds of the members of the National Assembly. Enactments of the Grand National Assembly require a majority of two-thirds of the votes of all the members, in three ballots on three different days. A Grand National Assembly may resolve only on the proposals for which it was elected, whereupon its prerogatives normally expire.

The Government

(January 1998)

HEAD OF STATE

President: PETAR STOYANOV (elected 3 November 1996; took office 19 January 1997).

COUNCIL OF MINISTERS

Prime Minister: IVAN KOSTOV.

Deputy Prime Minister and Minister of Industry: ALEKSANDER BOZHKOV.

Deputy Prime Minister and Minister of Regional and Urban Development: EVGENII BAKURDZHIEV.

Deputy Prime Minister and Minister of Education and Science: VESSELIN METODIEV.

Minister of Foreign Affairs: NADEZHDA MIHAILOVA.

Minister of the Interior: BOGOMIL BONEV.

Minister of Defence: GEORGI ANANIEV.

Minister of Culture: EMMA MOSKOVA.

Minister of the Environment and Waters: EVDOKIA MANEVA.

Minister of Labour and Social Policy: IVAN NEIKOV.

Minister of State Administration and Secretary-General of the Council of Ministers: MARIO TAGARINSKI.

Minister of Finance: MOURAVEI RADEV.

Minister of Health: PETAR BOYADZHIEV.

Minister of Trade and Tourism: VALENTIN VASSILEV.

Minister of Justice and Legal Euro-integration: VASSIL GOTSEV.

Minister of Agriculture, Forestry and Land Reform: VENTSISLAV VURBANOV.

Minister of Transport: WILHELM KRAUS.

MINISTRIES

Council of Ministers: 1000 Sofia, Blvd Knjaz Dondukov 1; tel. (2) 85-01; fax (2) 87-08-78.

Ministry of Agriculture, Forestry and Land Reform: 1040 Sofia, Blvd Botev 55; tel. (2) 85-31; fax (2) 88-55-57.

Ministry of Culture: 1040 Sofia, A Stamboliiski Blvd 17; tel. (2) 861-11; telex 22384; fax (2) 981-81-45.

Ministry of Defence: 1000 Sofia, Aksakov St 1; tel. (2) 54-60-01; fax (2) 87-57-32.

Ministry of Education and Science: 1000 Sofia, Blvd Knjaz Dondukov 2A; tel. (2) 84-81; telex 23255; fax (2) 886-00.

Ministry of the Environment and Waters: 1000 Sofia, ul. William Gladstone 67; tel. (2) 81-42-69; telex 22145; fax (2) 52-16-34.

Ministry of Finance: 1000 Sofia, Rakovski St 102; tel. (2) 87-06-22; fax (2) 80-11-48.

Ministry of Foreign Affairs: 1000 Sofia, Al. Zhendov St 2; tel. (2) 71-431; telex 22530; fax (2) 70-05-36.

Ministry of Health: 1000 Sofia, pl. Sveta Nedelya 5; tel. (2) 86-31; fax (2) 80-00-31.

Ministry of Industry: 1406 Sofia, Slavyanska St 8; tel. (2) 87-07-41; telex 23490; fax (2) 89-76-05.

Ministry of the Interior: 1000 Sofia, ul. Shesti Septemvri 29; tel. (2) 88-33-28.

Ministry of Justice and Legal Euro-integration: 1000 Sofia, Blvd Knjaz Dondukov 2; tel. (2) 86-01; telex 23822; fax (2) 767-32-26.

Ministry of Labour and Social Policy: 1000 Sofia, Triaditza St 2; tel. and fax (2) 980-85-30.

Ministry of Regional and Urban Development: Sofia, Kirili Metodi 17–19; tel. (2) 83-841; fax (2) 87-25-17.

Ministry of State Administration: 1000 Sofia.

Ministry of Trade and Tourism: 1000 Sofia, Kujaz A. Batemberg St; tel. (2) 88-20-41.

Ministry of Transport: 1080 Sofia, Levski St 9; tel. (2) 88-12-30; telex 23200; fax (2) 88-50-94.

President and Legislature

PRESIDENT

Presidential Election, First Ballot, 27 October 1996

Candidates	% of votes
PETAR STOYANOV (Union of Democratic Forces)	44.07
IVAN MARAZOV (Together for Bulgaria)*	27.01
GEORGI GANCHEV (Bulgaria Business Bloc)	21.87
Others	7.05
Total	100.0

Second Ballot, 3 November 1996

Candidates	% of votes
PETAR STOYANOV	59.73
IVAN MARAZOV	40.27
Total	100.0

* An electoral alliance, comprising the Bulgarian Socialist Party, the Aleksandur Stamboliyski Bulgarian Agrarian People's Union and the Ecoglasnost Political Club.

NARODNO SOBRANIYE

(National Assembly)

Chairman: YORDAN SOKOLOV.

General Election, 19 April 1997

Parties	% of votes	Seats
Union of Democratic Forces	52.57	137
Bulgarian Socialist Party*	22.08	58
Alliance for National Salvation†	7.60	19
Euro-Left	5.50	14
Bulgarian Business Bloc	4.93	12
Others	7.32	—
Total	100.00	240

* The BSP contested the election in alliance (as the Democratic Left) with the Aleksandur Stamboliyski Bulgarian Agrarian People's Union and the Ecoglasnost Political Club.

† An alliance comprising the Movement for Rights and Freedoms and other groups.

Political Organizations

There are over 80 registered political parties in Bulgaria, many of them incorporated into electoral alliances. The most significant political forces are listed below:

Aleksandur Stamboliyski Bulgarian Agrarian People's Union (Bulgarski Zemedelski Naroden Sayuz 'Aleksandur Stamboliyski'): c/o National Assembly, 1000 Sofia, pl. Narodno Sobraniye 3; contested 1994 general election and 1996 presidential election in alliance with the Bulgarian Socialist Party and the Ecoglasnost Political Club.

Alliance for National Salvation (ONS): c/o National Assembly, 1000 Sofia, pl. Narodno Sobraniye 3; f. 1997; electoral coalition of

Movement for Rights and Freedoms and other monarchist and centrist groups; Leader AHMED DOGAN.

Bulgarian Business Bloc—BBB: c/o National Assembly, 1000 Sofia, pl. Narodno Sobraniye 3; Leader GEORGI GANCHEV.

Bulgarian Communist Party (Bulgarska Komunisticheska Partiya): 1404 Sofia, Mladeshki Prokhod Blvd 5B; tel. (2) 59-16-73; f. 1990 by conservative mems of the former, ruling Bulgarian Communist Party (now the Bulgarian Socialist Party); First Sec. of the Central Cttee VLADIMIR SPASSOV.

Bulgarian Socialist Party—BSP (Bulgarska Sotsialisticheska Partiya): Sofia, 20 Positano St; POB 382; tel. (2) 980-12-91; telex 22268; fax (2) 980-52-91; e-mail BSP@mail.bol.bg; f. 1891 as the Bulgarian Social Democratic Party (BSDP); renamed the Bulgarian Communist Party (BCP) in 1919; renamed as above in 1990; 320,000 mems (Jan. 1996); Chair. GEORGI PURVANOV.

Christian Republican Party: 1606 Sofia, POB 113; tel. (2) 52-24-06; f. 1989; Chair. KONSTANTIN ADZHAROV.

Confederation—Kingdom Bulgaria (Tsarstvo Bulgaria): 7000 Ruse, Vassil Kolarov 45; tel. (82) 299-64; f. 1990; advocates the restoration of the former King, Simeon II; Chair. GEORGI BAKARDZHIEV.

Democratic Alternative for the Republic—DAR: c/o National Assembly, Sofia; left-of-centre coalition.

Democratic Party of Justice: Sofia; f. 1994 as ethnic Turkish group that split from the Movement for Rights and Freedoms; Chair. NEDIM GENDZHEV.

Ecoglasnost Political Club: 1000 Sofia, Blvd Knjaz Dondukov 9, 4th Floor, Rm 45; tel. (2) 80-23-23; political wing of the Ecoglasnost National Movement (f. 1989); contested 1994 general election and 1996 presidential election in alliance with the Bulgarian Socialist Party and Aleksandur Stamboliyski; represented in more than 140 clubs and organizations in Bulgaria; Chair. EDWIN SUGAREV; Sec. LUCHEZAR TOSHEV.

Euro-Left: c/o National Assembly, 1000 Sofia, pl. Narodno Sobraniye 3; f. 1997 by the Civic Union of the Republic, the Movement for Social Humanism, and former mems of the Bulgarian Socialist Party; Leader ALEKSANDUR TOMOV.

Fatherland Party of Labour: 1000 Sofia, Slavyanska St 3, Hotel Slavyanska Beseda; tel. (2) 65-83-10; nationalist; Chair. RUMEN POPOV.

Fatherland Union: Sofia, Blvd Vitosha 18; tel. (2) 88-12-21; telex 22783; f. 1942 as the Fatherland Front (a mass organization unifying the BAPU, the BCP (now the BSP) and social organizations); named as above when restructured in 1990; a socio-political organization of independents and individuals belonging to different political parties; Chair. GINYO GANEV.

Liberal Congress Party: 1000 Sofia, Blvd Knjaz Dondukov 39; tel. and fax (2) 39-00-18; f. 1989 as the Bulgarian Socialist Party, renamed Bulgarian Social Democratic Party (non-Marxist) in 1990 and as above in 1991; membership of UDF suspended 1993; c. 20,000 mems; Chair. YANKO N. YANKOV.

Liberal Democratic Alternative: f. 1997; Leader/Pres. ZHELYU ZHELEV.

Movement for Rights and Freedoms—MRF (Dvizhenie za Prava i Svobodi—DPS): 1408 Sofia, Ivan Vazov, Tzarigradsko Shosse 47/1; tel. (2) 88-18-23; f. 1990; represents the Muslim minority in Bulgaria; 95,000 mems (1991); Pres. AHMED DOGAN.

New Choice: f. 1994 by a former faction of the UDF; Co-Chair. DIMITUR LUDZHEV, IVAN PUSHKAROV.

New Union for Democracy—NUD: Sofia; f. 1993; fmrly section of UDF.

Party of Democratic Change: Sofia; f. 1994 by a group from the mainly ethnic Turkish Movement for Rights and Freedoms; Chair. MUKADDES NALBANT.

Party of Free Democrats (Centre): 6000 Stara Zagora; tel. (42) 2-70-42; f. 1989; Chair. Asst Prof. KHRISTO SANTULOV.

Union of Democratic Forces—UDF (Sayuz na Demokratichni Sili—SDS): 1000 Sofia, Blvd Rakovski 134; tel. (2) 88-25-01; f. 1989; Chair. IVAN KOSTOV; alliance of the following parties, organizations and movements:

Bulgarian Agrarian People's Union—'Nikola Petkov' (Bulgarski Zemedelski Naroden Sayuz—'Nikola Petkov'): 1000 Sofia, 1 Vrabtcha St; tel. (2) 87-80-81; fax (2) 981-09-49; f. 1899; in govt coalition since April 1997; Leader GEORGI PINCHEV.

Bulgarian Democratic Forum: 1505 Sofia, Rakovski St 82; tel. (2) 89-022-85; Chair. VASSIL ZLATAREV.

Bulgarian Social Democratic Party (United—BSDP): 1504 Sofia, Ekzarkh Yosif St 37; tel. (2) 80-15-84; fax (2) 39-00-86; f. 1891; re-established 1989; Pres. IVAN KURTEV.

Christian Democratic Union: Sofia; Chair. JULIUS PAVLOV.

Christian 'Salvation' Union: Sofia; Chair. Bishop KHRISTOFOR SAHEV.

Citizens' Initiative Movement: 1000 Sofia, Blvd Knjaz Dondukov 39; tel. (2) 39-01-93; Chair. TODOR GAGALOV.

Conservative Ecological Party: Sofia; Chair. KHRISTO BISSEROV.

Democratic Party 1896: f. 1994 by a former faction of the Democratic Party; Chair. STEFAN RAYCHEVSKI.

Federation of Democracy Clubs: 1000 Sofia, Blvd Knjaz Dondukov 39; tel. (2) 39-01-89; f. 1988 as Club for the Support of Glasnost and Perestroika; merged with other groups, as above, 1990; Chair. YORDAN VASSILEV.

Federation of Independent Student Committees: Sofia; Leader ANDREI NENOV.

New Social Democratic Party: 1504 Sofia, POB 14; tel. (2) 44-99-47; f. 1990; membership of UDF suspended 1991, resumed 1993; Chair. Dr VASSIL MIKHAILOV.

New United Labour Bloc: f. 1997; Chair. KRUSTYU PETKOV.

People's Union: c/o National Assembly, 1000 Sofia, pl. Narodno Sobraniye 3; f. 1994 as an electoral alliance between the following:

Bulgarian Agrarian People's Union (BAPU) (Bulgarski Zemedelski Naroden Sayuz—BZNS): 1000 Sofia, Yanko Zabunov St 1; tel. (2) 88-19-51; telex 23302; fax (2) 80-09-91; f. 1899; in ruling coalition 1946–89; Leader ANASTASIA MOSER.

Democratic Party: 1000 Sofia, Blvd Knjaz Dondukov 34; tel. (2) 80-01-87; re-formed 1990; Chair. STEFAN SAVOV.

Radical Democratic Party: 1000 Sofia, Blvd Knjaz Dondukov 8, 3rd Floor, Rms 6–8; tel. (2) 980-54-91; fax (2) 980-34-85; Chair. Dr KYRIL BOYADZHIEV.

Real Reform Movement (DESIR): f. 1997; Leader RENATA INDZHOVA.

Republican Party: Sofia; Chair. LENKO RUSSANOV.

United Christian Democratic Centre: 1000 Sofia, Blvd Knjaz Dondukov 34; tel. (2) 80-04-09; Chair. STEFAN SOFIANSKI.

The Independent Association for Human Rights in Bulgaria (Leader STEFAN VALKOV), the Union of Victims of Repression (Leader IVAN NEVROKOPSKY) and the Union of Non-Party Members (Leader BOYAN VELKOV) all enjoy observer status in the UDF.

Diplomatic Representation

EMBASSIES IN BULGARIA

Afghanistan: 1618 Sofia, Bl. 216A, Boryana St 61; tel. (2) 56-71-55; fax (2) 55-61-35; Chargé d'affaires: FAZEL SAIFI.

Albania: Sofia, Dimitur Polyanov St 10; tel. (2) 44-33-81; Ambassador: KOCO KOTE.

Algeria: Sofia, Slavyanska St 16; tel. (2) 87-56-83; telex 22519; Ambassador: ZINE EL-ABIDINE HACHICHI.

Argentina: Sofia, Dragan Tsankov 36, 2nd Floor, POB 635; tel. (2) 971-25-39; fax (2) 71-46-30-28; Ambassador: NELLY MARIA FREYERE PENABAD.

Austria: 1000 Sofia, Shipka St 4; tel. (2) 80-35-72; fax (2) 87-22-60; Ambassador: Dr ERICH KRISTEN.

Belarus: 1421 Sofia, ul. Kokitche 20; tel. (2) 65-28-43; fax (2) 963-40-23; Ambassador: ALYAKSANDR GERASIMENKA.

Belgium: Sofia, ul. Velchova Zavera 1; tel. (2) 963-36-22; telex 22455; fax (2) 963-36-22; Ambassador: KOENRAAD ROUVROY.

Brazil: Sofia, Blvd Ruski 27; tel. (2) 44-36-55; telex 22099; Ambassador: GUY BRANDÃO.

Cambodia: Sofia, Mladost 1, Blvd S. Allende, Res. 2; tel. (2) 75-71-35; fax (2) 75-40-09 Ambassador: BO RASSI.

China, People's Republic: Sofia, Blvd Ruski 18; tel. (2) 87-87-24; telex 22545; Ambassador: BAI SHOUMIAN.

Colombia: 1113 Sofia, Aleksandur Zhendov St 1, POB 562; tel. (2) 971-31-03; fax (2) 72-76-60; e-mail emcolsof@mbox.digsys.bg; Ambassador: (vacant).

Congo: Sofia, Blvd Klement Gottwald 54; tel. (2) 44-65-18; telex 23828; Ambassador: JEAN NONO.

Cuba: 1113 Sofia, Mladezhka St 1; tel. (2) 72-09-96; telex 22428; fax (2) 72-07-94; Ambassador: LUIS FELIPE VÁZQUEZ.

Czech Republic: 1000 Sofia, ul Panajot Volov; tel. (2) 946-11-10; fax (2) 946-18-00; Ambassador: PETR POSPÍCHAL.

Denmark: 1000 Sofia, Blvd Tsar Osvoboditel 10, POB 1393; tel. (2) 88-04-55; telex 22099; fax (2) 65-01-84; Ambassador: PREBEN STEEN SEIERSEN.

Egypt: 1000 Sofia, ul. Shesti Septemvri 5; tel. (2) 87-02-15; telex 22270; fax (2) 980-12-63; Ambassador: MAY ABOUL-DAHAB.

Ethiopia: Sofia, Vasil Kolarov St 28; tel. (2) 88-39-24; Chargé d'affaires a.i.: AYELLE MAKONEN.

Finland: 1126 Sofia, Simeonovsko 57, Res. 3; tel. (2) 68-33-26; telex 23148; fax (2) 68-93-22; Ambassador: PEKKA ARTTURI OINONEN.

France: 1505 Sofia, Oborishte St 29; tel. (2) 44-11-71; telex 22336; Ambassador: MARCEL TREMEAU.

Germany: 1113 Sofia, ul. Henri Barbusse 7; POB 869; tel. (2) 72-21-27; telex 22590; fax (2) 71-80-41; Ambassador: CHRISTEL STEFFLER.

Ghana: Sofia; tel. (2) 70-65-09; telex 23118; Chargé d'affaires a.i.: HENRY ANDREW ANUM AMAH.

Greece: Sofia, Blvd Klement Gottwald 68; tel. (2) 44-37-70; telex 22458; Ambassador: ANASTASIOS SIDHERIS.

Hungary: Sofia, ul. Shesti Septemvri 57; tel. (2) 963-04-60; telex 22459; fax (2) 963-21-10; Ambassador: IOAN TALPES.

India: Sofia, Blvd Patriiarkh Evtimii 31; tel. (2) 981-17-02; telex 22954; fax 981-41-24; e-mail india@inet.bg; Ambassador: NIRUPAM SEN.

Indonesia: 1126 Sofia, Simeonovsko Shosse 53; tel. (2) 962-52-40; telex 22358; fax (2) 962-58-42; Ambassador: R. SUHARJONO.

Iran: Sofia, Blvd Vassil Levski 77; tel. (2) 44-10-13; telex 22303; Ambassador: MOHAMMAD ALI KORMI-NOURI.

Iraq: Sofia, Anton Chekhov St 21; tel. (2) 87-00-13; telex 22307; Ambassador: MUHAMMAD AMIN MUHAMMAD AHMAD.

Italy: Sofia, Shipka St 2; tel. (2) 88-17-06; telex 22173; Ambassador: AGOSTINO MATHIS.

Japan: Sofia, ul. Lyulyakova Gradina 14; tel. (2) 72-39-84; telex 22397; fax (2) 49-210-95; Ambassador: YOSHIHIRO JIBIKI.

Korea, Democratic People's Republic: Sofia, Mladost 1, Blvd S. Allende, Res. 4; tel. (2) 77-53-48; Ambassador: PAK YONG GOL.

Korea, Republic: 1414 Sofia, Bulgaria Sq. 1, National Palace of Culture; tel. (2) 650-162; Ambassador: PILL-JOO SUNG.

Kuwait: Sofia, Blvd Klement Gottwald 47; tel. (2) 44-19-92; telex 23586; Ambassador: TALIB JALAL AD-DIN AN-NAQIB.

Laos: Sofia, Ovcha Kupel, Buket St 80; tel. (2) 56-55-08; Ambassador: SOMSAVAT LENGSAVAD.

Lebanon: 1113 Sofia, ul. Frédéric Joliot-Curie 19; tel. (2) 72-04-31; telex 23140; fax (2) 973-32-56; Ambassador: HUSSEIN MOUSSAWI.

Libya: Sofia, Oborishte St 10; tel. (2) 44-19-21; telex 22180; Secretary of People's Bureau: MOHAMAD GAMUDI.

Moldova: Sofia; Ambassador: MIHAI COSCODAN.

Morocco: Sofia, Blvd Klement Gottwald 44; tel. (2) 44-27-94; telex 23515; Ambassador: BENASER KEYTONI.

Mozambique: Sofia; Ambassador: GONÇALVES RAFAEL SENGO.

Netherlands: 1126 Sofia, Galichitsa St 38; tel. (2) 962-57-90; telex 22686; fax (2) 962-59-88; e-mail nlgovsof@mbox.digsys.bg; Ambassador: W. SIX.

Nicaragua: Sofia, Mladost 1, Blvd Allende, Res. 1; tel. (2) 75-41-57; Ambassador: UMBERTO CARIÓN.

Peru: Sofia, Volokolamsko Shose 11; tel. (2) 68-32-43; telex 23182; Chargé d'affaires: JULIO VEGA ERAUSQUÍN.

Poland: Sofia, Khan Krum St 46; tel. (2) 88-51-66; telex 22595; Ambassador: Prof. TADEUSZ WASILEWSKI.

Portugal: 1124 Sofia, Ivatz Voivoda St 6; tel. (2) 46-86-83; telex 22082; fax (2) 46-40-70; Ambassador: HEITOR MAIA E SILVA.

Romania: Sofia, Sitnyakovo St 4; tel. (2) 70-70-47; telex 22321; Ambassador: ALEXANDRU PETRESCU.

Russia: Sofia, Blvd Dragan Tsankov 28; tel. (2) 963-44-88; fax (2) 963-41-03; Ambassador: LEONID KERESTEDZHIYANTS.

Slovakia: Sofia, Blvd Janko Sakazov 9; tel. (2) 943-32-81; fax (2) 943-38-37; e-mail svkemba@mbox.ttm.bg; Ambassador: JOZEF DRAVECKY.

Spain: Sofia, Sheinovo 27; tel. (2) 943-30-32; fax (2) 946-12-01; Ambassador: JOSÉ CORDERCH.

Sweden: Sofia, Alfred Nobel Str. 4; tel. (2) 971-24-31; telex 23956; fax (2) 973-37-95; Ambassador: BERTIL LUND.

Switzerland: 1504 Sofia, Shipka St 33; tel. (2) 946-01-97; telex 22792; fax (2) 946-11-86; Ambassador: GAUDENZ RUF.

Syria: Sofia, Khristo Georgiev 10; tel. (2) 44-15-85; telex 23464; Chargé d'affaires: SADDIK SADDIKNI.

Turkey: Sofia, Blvd Tolbukhin 23; tel. (2) 87-23-06; telex 22199; Ambassador: MEHMED ALI IRTEMCELIK.

Ukraine: Sofia; Ambassador: OLEKSANDR VOROBYOV.

United Kingdom: Sofia, Blvd Vassil Levski 38; tel. (2) 88-53-61; telex 22363; fax (2) 49-20-345; Ambassador: ROGER SHORT.

USA: Sofia, Suborna St 1; tel. (2) 980-52-41; fax (2) 981-89-77; Ambassador: AVIS T. BOHLEN.

Uruguay: Sofia, Tsar Ivan Asen II St 91; POB 213; tel. (2) 44-19-57; telex 23087; Ambassador: GUIDO M. YERLAS.

Venezuela: 1504 Sofia, ul. Tulovo 1; tel. (2) 44-32-82; telex 22087; fax (2) 46-52-05; Ambassador: GERARDO E. WILLS.

Viet Nam: Sofia, Ilya Petrov St 1; tel. (2) 65-83-34; telex 22717; Ambassador: NGUYEN TIEN THONG.

Yemen: Sofia, Blvd S. Allende, Res. 3; tel. (2) 75-61-63; Ambassador: ALI MUNASSAR MUHAMMAD.

Yugoslavia: Sofia, Veliko Turnovo St 3; tel. (2) 44-32-37; telex 23537; Ambassador: MILENKO STEFANOVIĆ.

Judicial System

The 1991 Constitution provided for justice to be administered by the Supreme Court of Cassation, the Supreme Administrative Court, courts of appeal, courts of assizes, military courts and district courts. The main legal officials are the justices, or judges, of the higher courts, the prosecutors and investigating magistrates. The Chief Prosecutor is responsible for the precise and equal application of the law. The judicial system is independent, most appointments being made or recommended by the Supreme Judicial Council. The Ministry of Justice co-ordinates the administration of the judicial system and the prisons. There is also the Constitutional Court, which is the final arbiter of constitutional issues. Under transitional arrangements attached to the Constitution, until the new system was enacted and established, the existing Supreme Court of Bulgaria was to exercise the prerogatives of the two new Supreme Courts.

Supreme Court of Cassation: 1000 Sofia, Blvd Vitosha 2; tel. (2) 987-76-98; fax (2) 88-39-85; Chair. RUMEN YANKOV.

Constitutional Court: 1000 Sofia; Chair. ASSEN DIMITROV MANOV.

Office of the Chief Prosecutor: 1000 Sofia, Blvd Vitosha 2; tel. (2) 85-71; fax (2) 80-13-27; Chief Prosecutor IVAN TATARCHEV; Military Prosecutor MILKO YOTSOV.

Ministry of Justice: see The Government (Ministries).

Religion

Most of the population profess Christianity, the main denomination being the Bulgarian Orthodox Church (over 80% of the population). The 1991 Constitution guarantees freedom of religion, although Eastern Orthodox Christianity is declared to be the 'traditional religion in Bulgaria'. In accordance with the 1949 Bulgarian Law on Religious Faith, however, all new religious denominations must be registered by a governmental board before being allowed to operate freely. There is a significant Muslim minority (some 9% of the population), most of whom are ethnic Turks, although there are some ethnic Bulgarian Muslims, known as Pomaks. There is a small Jewish community.

Directorate of Religious Affairs: 1000 Sofia, Blvd Dondukov 1; tel. and fax (2) 88-04-88; a dept of the Council of Ministers; conducts relations between govt and religious organizations; Chair. Dr KHRISTO MATANOV.

CHRISTIANITY

In 1992 a schism occurred in the Bulgarian Orthodox Church when two Metropolitans, one of whom was Bishop Pimen, established a separate synod in opposition to Bulgarian Patriarch Maksim. In July 1996 the convention of clergy and laity called by the alternative synod elected Pimen as its patriarch.

Bulgarian Orthodox Church: 1090 Sofia, Oborishte St 4, Synod Palace; tel. (2) 87-56-11; fax (2) 89-76-00; f. 865; autocephalous Exarchate 1870 (recognized 1945); administered by the Bulgarian Patriarchy; there are 11 dioceses in Bulgaria and two dioceses abroad (Diocese of North and South America and Australia, and Diocese of West Europe), each under a Metropolitan; Chair. of the Bulgarian Patriarchy His Holiness Patriarch MAKSIM.

Armenian Apostolic Orthodox Church: Sofia 1080, Nishka St 31; tel. (2) 88-02-08; some 20,000 adherents (1996); administered by Bishop DIRAYR MARDIKIYAN (resident in Bucharest, Romania); Chair. of the Diocesan Council in Bulgaria OWANES KIRAZIAN.

The Roman Catholic Church

Bulgarian Catholics may be adherents of either the Latin (Western) Rite, which is organized in two dioceses, or the Byzantine-Slav (Eastern) Rite (one diocese). All three dioceses are directly responsible to the Holy See.

Western Rite

Bishop of Nikopol: PETKO CHRISTOV, 7000 Ruse, Rostislav Blaskov St 14; tel. (82) 22-81-88; some 25,000 adherents (1994).

Diocese of Sofia and Plovdiv: GEORGI IVANOV YOVCHEV (Apostolic Administrator), 4000 Plovdiv, Nezavisimost St 3; tel. and fax (32) 22-84-30; some 35,000 adherents (1994).

Eastern Rite

Apostolic Exarch of Sofia: METODI DIMITROV STRATIYEV (Titular Bishop of Diocletianopolis in Thrace), 1606 Sofia, ul. Bratya Pashovi 10B; tel. (2) 52-02-97; some 30,000 adherents (1993).

The Protestant Churches

Bulgarian Church of God: Sofia 1408, Petko Karavelov St 1; tel. (2) 65-75-52; fax 51-91-31; 30,000 adherents (1992); Head Pastor PAVEL IGNATOV.

Bulgarian Evangelical Church of God: Plovdiv, Velbudge St 71; tel. (32) 43-72-92; 300 adherents (1992); Head Pastor BLAGOI ISEV.

Bulgarian Evangelical Methodist Episcopal Church: 1000 Sofia, 86 Rakovski St; tel. and fax (2) 981-37-83; 1,000 adherents (1994); Gen. Superintendent Rev. BEDREA ALTUNIAN.

Church of Jesus Christ of Latter-day Saints in Bulgaria: Sofia, Drugba estate, Bl. 82/B/6, Flat 54; tel. (2) 74-08-06; f. 1991; 64 adherents (1992); Pres. VENTSESLAV LAZAROV.

Open Biblical Confraternity: 1404 Sofia, Strelbiste estate, Bl. 1A/A/1, Flat 2; f. 1991; Head Pastor MARIA MINDEVA.

Union of the Churches of the Seventh-day Adventists: Sofia, Solunska St 10; tel. (2) 88-12-18; fax (2) 980-17-09; e-mail sda.bg@sbline.net; 6,700 adherents (1997); Head Pastor AGOP TACHMISSJAN.

Union of Evangelical Baptist Churches: 1303 Sofia, Ossogovo St 63; tel. and fax (2) 31-60-87; 2,500 adherents (1993); Pres. Dr TEODOR ANGELOV.

Union of Evangelical Congregational Churches: Sofia, Solunska St 49; tel. (2) 88-05-93; 4,000 adherents (1992); Head Pastor KHRISTO KULISHEV.

Union of Evangelical Pentecostal Churches: 1557 Sofia, Bacho Kiro St 21; tel. (2) 83-51-69; f. 1928; 30,000 adherents (1991); Head Pastor VIKTOR VIRCHEV.

Universal White Fraternity: 1612 Sofia, Balshik St 8/B, Flat 27; tel. (2) 54-69-43; f. 1900; unifies the principles of Christianity with the arts and sciences; more than 6,000 adherents (1994); Chair. Dr ILIYAN STRATEV.

ISLAM

Supreme Muslim Theological Council: Sofia, Bratya Miladinovi St 27; tel. (2) 87-73-20; fax (2) 39-00-23; adherents estimated at 9% of the actively religious population, with an estimated 708 acting regional imams; Chair. Hadzhi NEDIM GENDZHEV; Chief Mufti of the Muslims in Bulgaria HADZHIBASRI HADZHISHARIF.

JUDAISM

Central Jewish Theological Council: 1000 Sofia, Eksarkh Yosif St 16; tel. 83-12-73; fax (2) 83-50-85; some 5,000 adherents (1992); Head YOSSIF LEVI.

The Press

In 1990 the press laws were liberalized, and many publications, hitherto banned, became freely available. A large number of independent publications were subsequently established.

PRINCIPAL DAILIES

24 Chasa (24 Hours): 1000 Sofia, Blvd Tsarigradsko shosse 47; tel. (2) 44-19-45; fax (2) 43-39-339; f. 1991; privately-owned; Editor-in-Chief VALERI NAIDENOV; circ. 330,000.

Bulgarska Armiya (Bulgarian Army): 1080 Sofia, Ivan Vasov St 12, POB 629; tel. (2) 87-47-93; telex 22651; fax (2) 987-91-26; f. 1944 as Narodna Armiya, name changed 1991; organ of the Ministry of Defence; Editor-in-Chief Col VLADI VLADKOV; circ. 30,000.

Chernomorsky Far (Black Sea Lighthouse): 8000 Burgas, Milin Kamak St 9; tel. and fax (56) 423-96; f. 1950; independent regional since 1988; Editor-in-Chief GALENTIN VLAHOV; circ. 37,000.

Debati (Debates): 1000 Sofia, Blvd Kniyas Korsakov 2; tel. (2) 887-25-04; fax 80-05-10; f. 1990; parliamentary issues, on politics and diplomacy; independent; Editor-in-Chief GEORGI INGILIROV; circ. 50,000.

Demokratsiya (Democracy): 1000 Sofia, Rakovski St 134; tel. (2) 981-29-79; fax (2) 980-73-42; f. 1990; newspaper of the Union of Democratic Forces; Editor-in-Chief NEVEN KOPANDANOVA; circ. 45,000.

Duma (Word): 1000 Sofia, Blvd Tzarigradsko Shosse 47; tel. (2) 43-431; telex 22547; fax (2) 87-50-73; f. 1927; fmrly *Rabotnichesko Delo*; organ of the Bulgarian Socialist Party; Editor-in-Chief STEFAN PRODEV; circ. 130,000.

Glas (Voice): 4000 Plovdiv, Lev Tolstoy St 2; tel. (32) 22-67-40; fax (32) 22-82-23; f. 1943; fmrly *Otechestven Glas*, an official organ; now independent regional newspaper for district of Plovdiv; 6 a week; Editor-in-Chief BOJKO VATER; circ. 90,000.

Isik/Svetlina (Light): 1000 Sofia, Blvd Tzarigradsko Shosse 47; tel. (2) 44-21-07; telex 22197; f. 1945; formerly *'Eni Isik' Nova Svetlina*; independent newspaper in Turkish and Bulgarian; Editor-in-Chief IVAN BADZHEV; circ. 30,000.

Kontinent: 1000 Sofia, Blvd Tzarigradsko Shosse 47-A; tel. (2) 943-44-46; fax (2) 44-19-04; e-mail kont@bgnet.bg; f. 1992; independent; Editor-in-Chief BOIKO PANGELOV; circ. 12,000.

Maritza: 4000 Plovdiv, Bogomil St 59; POB 27 and 348; tel. (32) 26-84-34; fax (32) 27-47-60; f. 1991; Editor-in-Chief SPASS VASSILEV; circ. 40,000.

Narodno Delo (People's Cause): 9000 Varna, Blvd Khristo Botev 3; tel. (52) 23-10-71; fax (52) 23-90-67; f. 1944; regional independent; business, politics and sport; 6 days a week; Editor-in-Chief DIMITUR KRASIMIROV; circ. 56,000.

Noshten Trud (Night Labour): 1000 Sofia, Blvd Kniyas Dondukov 52; tel. and fax (2) 87-70-63; telex 22427; f. 1992; 5 a week; Editor-in-Chief PLAMEN KAMENOV; circ. 332,000.

Nov Glas (New Voice): 5500 Lovech, G. Dimitrov St 24, 3rd Floor; tel. (68) 2-22-42; telex 37429; f. 1988; regional independent; Editor-in-Chief VENETSII GEORGIEV; circ. 50,000.

Otechestven Vestnik (Fatherland Newspaper): 1504 Sofia, Blvd Tzarigradsko Shosse 47; tel. (2) 43-431; telex 22555; fax (2) 46-31-08; f. 1942 as *Otechestven Front*; published by the journalists' co-operative 'Okchestvo'; Editor-in-Chief KONSTANCE ANSCHVA; total circ. 16,000.

Pari (Money): 1504 Sofia, Blvd Tzarigradsko Shosse 47; POB 46; tel. (2) 44-65-73; telex 22555; fax (2) 46-35-32; f. 1991; financial and economic news; Editor-in-Chief EVGENII PETROV; circ. 13,500.

Pirinsko Delo (Pirin's Cause): 2700 Blagoevgrad, Assen Khristove St 19; tel. 2-37-36; telex 26300; fax 2-31-06; f. 1945; independent regional daily since 1989; Editor-in-Chief KATYA Z. CATKOVA; circ. 20,000.

Podkrepa (Support): 1000 Sofia, Ekzarkh Yosif St 37; tel. (2) 83-12-27; fax (2) 46-73-74; f. 1991; organ of the Podkrepa (Support) Trade Union Confederation; Editor-in-Chief (vacant); circ. 18,000.

Shipka: 6300 Khaskovo, Georgi Dimitrov St 14; tel. (38) 12-52-52; telex 43470; fax (38) 3-76-28; f. 1988; independent regional newspaper; Editor-in-Chief DIMITUR DOBREV; circ. 25,000.

Sport: 1000 Sofia, National Stadium 'Vassil Levski', Sektor V; POB 88; tel. (2) 88-03-43; telex 22594; fax (2) 81-49-70; f. 1927; Editor-in-Chief IVAN NANKOV; circ. 80,000.

Standart News Daily: Sofia, Blvd Tzarigradsko Shosse 113A; tel. (2) 675-36-88; fax (2) 76-28-77; e-mail standart@mobiltel.bg; f. 1992; Editor-in-Chief YULY MOSKOV; circ. 110,000.

Telegraf: 1113 Sofia, Blvd Tzarigradsko Shosse 72; POB 135; tel. (2) 75-11-22; fax (2) 77-04-11; f. 1990; privately-owned independent newspaper; Editor-in-Chief PLAMEN DIMITROV; circ. 30,000.

Trud (Labour): 1000 Sofia, Kniyas Dondukov 52; tel. (2) 987-98-05; fax (2) 80-11-40; f. 1923; organ of the Confederation of Independent Trade Unions in Bulgaria; Editor-in-Chief TOSHO TOSHEV; circ. 200,000.

Vecherni Novini (Evening News): 1000 Sofia, Blvd Tzarigradsko Shosse 47; tel. (2) 44-14-69; telex 22324; fax (2) 46-73-65; f. 1951; independent newspaper; centre-left; publ. by the Vest Publishing House; Dir GEORGI GANCHEV; Editor-in-Chief LYUBOMIR KOLAROV; circ. 35,000.

Vselena (Universe): 34000 Montana, pl. Geravitza; tel. (96) 2-25-06; fmrly *Delo*; Editor-in-Chief BOYAN MLADENOV.

Zemedelsko Zname (Agrarian Banner); Sofia, Yanko Zabunov St 23; tel. (2) 87-38-51; telex 23303; fax (2) 87-45-35; f. 1902; organ of the Bulgarian Agrarian People's Union; circ. 178,000.

Zemya (Earth): Sofia, 11 August St 18; tel. (2) 88-50-33; telex 23174; fax (2) 83-52-27; f. 1951 as *Kooperativno Selo*; renamed 1990; fmrly an organ of the Ministry of Agriculture, BSP daily; Editor-in-Chief KOSTA ANDREEV; circ. 53,000.

PRINCIPAL PERIODICALS

168 Chasa (168 Hours): 1504 Sofia, Blvd Tzarigradsko Shosse 47; tel. (2) 43-39-288; fax (2) 43-39-315; f. 1990; weekly; business, politics, entertainments; Editor-in-Chief VASELKA VALILEVA; circ. 93,000.

166 Politzeiski Vesti (166 Police News): 1680 Sofia, J.K. Belite Brezi, Solun St bl. 25 and 26, Ground Floor; tel. (2) 82-30-30; fax 82-30-28; f. 1945; fmrly *Naroden Strazh*; weekly; criminology and public security; Editor-in-Chief PETUR VITANOV; circ. 22,000.

Anteni (Antennae): 1000 Sofia, Han Krum St 12; tel. (2) 87-48-95, 89-31-57; fax (2) 87-30-60; f. 1971; weekly; politics and culture; Editor-in-Chief GEORGI CHATALBASHEV; circ. 72,000.

Anti: 1000 Sofia, Blvd Dondukov 9; tel. and fax (2) 80-43-03; f. 1991; weekly; Editor-in-Chief VASIL STANILOV; circ. 7,000.

Avto-moto Svyat (Automobile World): 1000 Sofia, Sveta Sofia St 6; POB 1348; tel. and fax (2) 88-08-08; f. 1957; monthly; illustrated publication on cars and motor sports; Editor-in-Chief ILJA SELIKTAR; circ. 33,600.

Az Buki (Alphabet): 1113 Sofia, Blvd Tzarigradsko Shosse 125; tel. (2) 71-65-73; f. 1991; weekly; education, and culture; for schools;

sponsored by the Ministry of Education and Science; Editor-in-Chief MILENA STRAKOVA; circ. 11,800.

Bulgarski Biznes (Bulgarian Business): 1505 Sofia, Oborishte St 44; POB 15; tel. (2) 46-70-23; telex 22105; fax (2) 44-63-61; weekly; organ of National Union of Employers; Editor-in-Chief DETELIN SERTOV; circ. 10,000–15,000.

Bulgarski Fermer (Bulgarian Farmer): 1797 Sofia, Blvd Dr G. M. Dimitrov 89; tel. (2) 71-04-48; fax (2) 73-10-08; f. 1990; weekly; Editor-in-Chief VASSIL ASPARUHOV; circ. 20,000.

Businessman: 1527 Sofia, Blvd Tzarigradsko Shosse 23; tel. and fax (2) 44-52-80; f. 1991; Editor-in-Chief GRIGOR SCHERNER.

Computer World: 1421 Sofia, Blvd Hr. Smirnenski 1, Block B, Flat 11; tel. (2) 81-42-70; fax (2) 80-26-52; f. 1990; weekly; US-Bulgarian joint venture; information technologies; Editor-in-Chief SNEZHINA BADZHEVA; circ. 15,000.

Domashen Maistor (Household Manager): 1000 Sofia, Blvd Tolbukhin 51A; tel. (2) 87-09-14; f. 1991; monthly; magazine for household repairs; Editor-in-Chief GEORGI BALANSKI; circ. 12,000.

Durzhaven Vestnik (State Gazette): 1169 Sofia; tel. (2) 80-01-27; official organ of the National Assembly; 2 a week; bulletin of parliamentary proceedings and the publication in which all legislation is promulgated; Editor-in-Chief PLAMEN MLADENOV; circ. 73,000.

Edinstvo (Unity): 1000 Sofia, Blvd Khristo Botev 48; tel. (2) 84-101 Ext. 218; f. 1991; weekly; Editor-in-Chief GENCHO BUCHVAROV.

Ekho (Echo): 1000 Sofia, Serdika St 2; tel. (2) 87-28-42; f. 1957; weekly; tourism publication; organ of the Bulgarian Tourist Union; Editor-in-Chief LUBOMIR GLIGOROV; circ. 7,000.

Emigrant: Sofia; tel. (2) 87-23-08; fax (2) 87-46-17; f. 1991 (to replace *Kontakti*); weekly; magazine for Bulgarians living abroad; Editor-in-Chief MANOL MANOV; circ. 20,000.

Futbol (Football): 1000 Sofia, Bulgaria Blvd 1, Vassil Levski Stadium; tel. (2) 87-19-51; fax (2) 65-72-57; f. 1988; weekly; independent soccer publication; Editor-in-Chief IVAN CHOMAKOV; circ. 132,500.

Ikonomicheski Zhivot (Economic Life): 1000 Sofia, Alabin St 33; tel. (2) 87-95-06; fax (2) 87-65-60; f. 1970; weekly; independent; marketing and advertising; Editor-in-Chief VASIL ALEKSIEV; circ. 21,000.

Kompyutar (Computer): 1000 Sofia, Blvd Tolbukhin 51A; tel. (2) 87-50-45; f. 1985; monthly; hardware and software; Editor-in-Chief GEORGI BALANSKI; circ. 14,000.

Komunistichesko Delo (Communist Cause): 1000 Sofia, Central Post Office; POB 183; tel. (2) 598-16-73; organ of the Bulgarian Communist Party; Editor-in-Chief VLADIMIR SPASSOV; circ. 15,000–20,000.

Krile (Wings): 1184 Sofia, Blvd Tzarigradsko Shosse 111; tel. (2) 70-45-73; f. 1911; fmrly *Kam Nebeto*, renamed 1991; monthly; civil and military aviation; official organ; Editor-in-Chief TODOR ANDREEV; circ. 20,000.

Kultura (Culture): 1040 Sofia, Kniyas Alexander Battenberg St 4; tel. (2) 83-33-22; fax (2) 87-40-27; f. 1957; weekly; newspaper on arts, publicity and cultural affairs; issue of the Ministry of Culture; Editor-in-Chief KOPRINKA CHERVENKOVA; circ. 3,300.

Kurier 5 (Courier 5): 1000 Sofia, Blvd Tzarigradsko Shosse 47; tel. (2) 46-30-26; f. 1991; weekdays; advertising newspaper; Editor-in-Chief STEPAN ERAMIAN; circ. 30,000.

Liberalen Kongres (Liberal Congress): 1000 Sofia, Blvd Dondukov 9; tel. (2) 39-00-18; fax (2) 68-77-14; f. 1990; weekly; organ of the Liberal Congress Party; Editor-in-Chief ROSSEN ELEZOV; circ. 12,000.

LIK: Sofia, Blvd Tzarigradsko Shosse 49; weekly publication of the Bulgarian Telegraph Agency; literature, art and culture; Editor-in-Chief SIRMA VELEVA; circ. 19,000.

Literaturen Forum (Literary Forum): 1000 Sofia, Alexander Battenberg Ave 4; tel. (2) 88-10-69; fax (2) 88-10-69; f. 1990; weekly; independent; Editor-in-Chief ATANAS SVILENOV; circ. 5,300.

Makedonia (Macedonia): 1301 Sofia, Pirotska St 5; tel. (2) 80-05-32; fax 87-46-64; e-mail mpress@virbus.bg; f. 1990; weekly; organ of the Inner Macedonian Revolutionary Organization (IMRO)—Union of Macedonian Societies; Editor-in-Chief DINKO DRAGANOV; circ. 22,000.

Missul (Thought): 1000 Sofia, Pozitano St 20; POB 382; tel. (2) 85-141; f. 1990; weekly; politics, culture; organ of the Marxist Alternative Movement; Editor-in-Chief GEORGI SVEZHIN; circ. 15,000.

Napravi Sam (Do It Yourself): 1000 Sofia, Blvd Levski 51A; tel. 87-50-45; f. 1981; monthly; Editor-in-Chief GEORGI BALANSKI; circ. 45,000.

Nie Zhenite (We the Women): 1000 Sofia, Patriarch Evtimii Blvd 84; tel. (2) 52-31-98; f. 1990; weekly; organ of the Democratic Union of Women; Editor-in-Chief EVGINIA KIRANOVA; circ. 176,600.

Nov Den (New Day): 1000 Sofia, Blvd Vassil Levski 65, 3rd Floor; tel. (2) 80-02-05; f. 1990; weekly; organ of the Union of Free Democrats; Editor-in-Chief IVAN KALCHEV; circ. 25,000.

Orbita: 1000 Sofia, Tsar Kaloyan St 8; tel. (2) 88-51-68; f. 1969; weekly; science and technology for youth; Editor-in-Chief NIKOLAI KATRANDZHIEV; circ. 10,200.

Paraleli: Sofia, Blvd Tzarigradsko Shosse 49; tel. (2) 87-40-35; f. 1964; weekly; illustrated publication of the Bulgarian Telegraph Agency; Editor-in-Chief KRASSIMIR DRUMEV; circ. 50,000.

Pardon: 1000 Sofia, Blvd Tzarigradsko Shosse 47; tel. (2) 43-431; f. 1991; weekly; satirical publication; Editor-in-Chief CHAVDAR SHINOV; circ. 8,560.

Pogled (Review): 1090 Sofia, pl. Slaveikov 11; tel. (2) 87-70-97; fax (2) 65-80-23; f. 1930; weekly; organ of the Union of Bulgarian Journalists; Editor-in-Chief EVGENII STANCHEV; circ. 47,300.

Prava i Svobodi (Rights and Freedoms): 1504 Sofia, Blvd Tzarigradsko Shosse 47-A, Alley 1; POB 208; tel. (2) 46-72-12; fax 46-73-35; f. 1990; weekly; politics, culture; organ of the Movement for Rights and Freedoms; Editor-in-Chief (vacant); circ. 7,500.

Progres (Progress): 1000 Sofia, Gurko St 16; tel. (2) 89-06-24; fax (2) 89-59-98; f. 1894; fmrly *Tekhnichesko Delo*; weekly; organ of the Federation of Scientific and Technical Societies in Bulgaria; Editor-in-Chief PETKO TOMOV; circ. 35,000.

Reporter 7: 1124 Sofia, Evlogi Georgiev St 54; tel. (2) 44-04-05; fax (2) 46-52-76; f. 1990; weekly; private independent newspaper; Editor-in-Chief BINKA PEEVA; circ. 60,000.

Start: 1000 Sofia, Vassil Levski Stadium; POB 797; tel. (2) 980-25-17; telex 22736; fax (2) 981-29-42; f. 1971; weekly; sports, illustrated; Editor-in-Chief NIKOLAY RANGELOV; circ. 21,300.

Studentska Tribuna (Students' Tribune): 1000 Sofia, Aksakov St 13; tel. (2) 88-33-02; f. 1927; weekly; student magazine; independent; Editor-in-Chief ATANAS TODOROV; circ. 20,000.

Sturshel (Hornet): 1504 Sofia, Blvd Tzarigradsko Shosse 47; tel. (2) 44-35-50; fax 443-550; f. 1946; weekly; humour and satire; Editor-in-Chief YORDAN POPOV; circ. 45,200.

Svoboden Narod (Free People): 1000 Sofia, Ekzarch Yosif St 37, 8th Floor; f. 1990; weekly; organ of the Bulgarian Social Democratic Party; Editor-in-Chief TEODOR DETCHEV; circ. 10,000.

Televiziya i Radio (Television and Radio): 1000 Sofia, Bulgarian National Television, San Stefano St 29; tel. (2) 44-32-94; f. 1964; weekly; broadcast listings; Editor-in-Chief LUBOMIR YANKOV; circ. 70,300.

Tsarkoven Vestnik (Church Newspaper): 1000 Sofia, Oborishte St 4; tel. (2) 87-56-11; f. 1900; weekly; organ of the Bulgarian Orthodox Church; Editor-in-Chief DIMITUR KIROV; circ. 4,000.

Uchitelsko Delo (Teachers' Cause): 1113 Sofia, Blvd Tzarigradsko Shosse 125, Studentski Obshtezhitiya, Blok 5; tel. (2) 70-00-12; f. 1905; weekly; organ of the Union of Bulgarian Teachers; Editor-in-Chief YORDAN YORDANOV; circ. 12,700.

Vek 21 (21st Century): 1000 Sofia, Kaloyan St 10; tel. (2) 46-54-23; fax (2) 46-61-23; f. 1990; liberal weekly; politics and culture; organ of the Radical Democratic Party; Editor-in-Chief ALEKSANDUR YORDANOV; circ. 5,900.

Zdrave (Health): 1527 Sofia, Byalo More St 8; tel. (2) 44-30-26; fax (2) 44-17-59; f. 1936; monthly; published by Bulgarian Red Cross; Editor-in-Chief YAKOV YANAKIEV; circ. 55,000.

Zhenata Dnes (Women Today): 1000 Sofia, pl. Narodno Sobraniye 12; tel. (2) 89-16-00; f. 1946; monthly organ of Zhenata Dnes Ltd. Editor-in-Chief BOTIO ANGELOV; circ. 50,000.

Zname (Banner): 1184 Sofia, Blvd Kniyas Korsakov 34; tel. (2) 80-01-83; f. 1894, publ. until 1934 and 1945–49; resumed publishing 1990; weekly; Editor-in-Chief BOGDAN MORFOV; circ. 20,000.

Zora (Dawn): 1000 Sofia, Blvd Tzarigradsko Shosse 77; tel. (2) 71-41-826; f. 1990; independent weekly; Editor-in-Chief MINCHO MINCHEV; circ. 20,000.

NEWS AGENCIES

Bulgarska Telegrafna Agentsia—BTA (Bulgarian Telegraph Agency): 1040 Sofia, Blvd Tzarigradsko Shosse 49; tel. (2) 84-61; telex 22821; f. 1898; official news agency; publishes weekly surveys of science and technology, international affairs, literature and art; Dir-Gen. MILEN VULKOV.

Bulnet: 1000 Sofia, Rakovski St 127; tel. and fax (2) 81-34-42; f. 1994; provides on-line access, internet services, communications software and hardware and consultancy; photo service; Exec. Dir. R. MILEVA.

Sofia-Press Agency: 1040 Sofia, Slavyanska St 29; tel. (2) 88-58-31; telex 22622; fax (2) 88-34-55; f. 1967 by the Union of Bulgarian Writers, the Union of Bulgarian Journalists, the Union of Bulgarian Artists and the Union of Bulgarian Composers; publishes socio-political and scientific literature, fiction, children's and tourist literature, publications on the arts, a newspaper, magazines and bulletins in foreign languages; also operates **Sofia-Press Info** (tel. (2) 87-66-80; Pres. ALEKSANDUR NIKOLOV), which provides up-to-date information on Bulgaria, in print and for broadcast; Dir-Gen. KOLIO GEORGIEV.

Foreign Bureaux

Agence France-Presse (AFP): 1000 Sofia, Blvd Tolbukhin 16; tel. (2) 71-91-71; telex 22572; Correspondent VESSELA SERGEVA-PETROVA.

Agencia EFE (Spain): Sofia; tel. (2) 87-29-63; Correspondent SAMUEL FRANCES.

Allgemeiner Deutscher Nachrichtendienst (ADN) (Germany): 1000 Sofia, Moskovska 27A; tel. (2) 87-82-73; telex 22050; fax (2) 87-53-16; Correspondent HANS-PETKO TEUCHERT.

Česká tisková kancelář (ČTK) (Czech Republic): 1113 Sofia, Bl. 154A, Apt 19, ul. Gagarin; tel. (2) 70-91-36; telex 22537; Correspondent VĚRA IVANOVIČOVÁ.

Deutsche Presse Agentur (dpa) (Germany): Sofia; tel. (2) 72-02-02; Correspondent ELENA LALOVA.

Informatsionnoye Telegrafnoye Agentstvo Rossii—Telegrafnoye Agentstvo Suverennykh Stran (ITAR—TASS) (Russia): 1000 Sofia, ul. A. Gendov 1, Apt 29; tel. (2) 87-38-03; Correspondent ALEKSANDR STEPANENKO.

Magyar Távirati Iroda (MTI) (Hungary): Sofia, ul. Frédéric Joliot-Curie 15, blok 156/3, Apt 28; tel. (2) 70-18-12; telex 22549; Correspondent TIVADAR KELLER.

Novinska Agencija Tanjug (Yugoslavia): 1000 Sofia, L. Koshut St 33; tel. (2) 71-90-57; Correspondent PERO RAKOSEVIĆ.

Polska Agencja Prasowa (PAP) (Poland): Sofia; tel. (2) 44-14-39; Correspondent BOGDAN KORNEJUCK.

Prensa Latina (Cuba): 1113 Sofia, ul. Yuri Gagarin 22, Bl. 154B, Apt 22; tel. (2) 71-91-90; telex 22407; Correspondent SUSANA UGARTE SOLER.

Reuters (United Kingdom): 1000 Sofia, Ivan Vazov St 16; tel. (2) 911-88; fax (2) 980-91-31; e-mail sofia.newsroom@reuters.com; Correspondent THALIA GRIFFITHS.

Rossiyskoye Informatsionnoye Agentstvo—Novosti (RIA—Novosti) (Russia): Sofia, San Stefano St 6; tel. and fax (2) 943-48-47; Bureau Man. YEVGENII VOROBYOV.

United Press International (UPI) (USA): Sofia; tel. (2) 62-24-65; Correspondent GUILLERMO ANGELOV.

Xinhua (New China) News Agency (People's Republic of China): Sofia; tel. (2) 88-49-41; telex 22539; Correspondent U. SIZIUN.

The following agencies are also represented: SANA (Syria) and Associated Press (USA).

PRESS ASSOCIATIONS

Union of Bulgarian Journalists: 1000 Sofia, Graf Ignatiev St 4; tel. (2) 87-27-73; telex 22635; fax (2) 88-30-47; f. 1955; Pres. (vacant); Gen.-Sec. ALEKSANDUR ANGELOV; 5,600 mems.

Union of Journalists in Bulgaria: 1000 Sofia, Exzarh Yossif St 37; tel. (2) 83-19-95; fax (2) 83-54-84; Chair. CHAVDAR TONCHEV.

Publishers

Darzhavno Izdatelstvo 'Khristo G. Danov' ('Khristo G. Danov' State Publishing House): 4005 Plovdiv, Stoyan Chalakov St 1; tel. (32) 23-12-01; fax (32) 26-05-60; f. 1855; fiction, poetry, literary criticism; Dir NACHO HRISTOSKOV.

Darzhavno Izdatelstvo 'Meditsina i Fizkultura': 1080 Sofia, pl. Slaveikov 11; tel. (2) 87-13-08; f. 1948; medicine, physical culture and tourism; Dir PETUR GOGOV.

Darzhavno Izdatelstvo 'Nauka i Izkustvo': 1080 Sofia, Blvd Ruski 6; tel. (2) 87-57-01; f. 1948; general publishers; Dir ANELIA VASSILEVA.

Darzhavno Izdatelstvo 'Prosveta': 1184 Sofia, Tsarugradsko Shosse Blvd 117; tel. (2) 76-06-51; fax (2) 76-44-51; f. 1948; educational publishing house; Man. Dir RUMEN EVTIMOV.

Darzhavno Izdatelstvo 'Tekhnika': 1000 Sofia, pl. Slaveikov 1; tel. (2) 87-12-83; fax (2) 87-49-06; f. 1958; textbooks for technical and higher education and technical literature; Dir NINA DENEVA.

Darzhavno Izdatelstvo 'Zemizdat': 1504 Sofia, Blvd Tzarigradsko Shosse 47; tel. (2) 44-18-29; f. 1949; specializes in works on agriculture, shooting, fishing, forestry, livestock-breeding, veterinary medicine and popular scientific literature and textbooks; Dir PETUR ANGELOV.

Galaktika: 9000 Varna, pl. Nezavissimost 6; tel. (52) 24-11-56; fax (52) 23-47-50; f. 1960; science fiction, economics, Bulgarian and foreign literature; Dir ASSYA KADREVA.

Izdatelstvo na Bulgarskata Akademiya na Naukite 'Marin Drinov': 1113 Sofia, Acad. Georgi Bonchev St, blok 6; tel. (2) 72-09-22; telex 23132; fax (2) 70-40-54; f. 1869; scientific works and periodicals of the Bulgarian Academy of Sciences; Dir TODOR RANGELOV.

Izdatelstvo 'Bulgarski Houdozhnik': 1504 Sofia, Shipka St 6; tel. and fax (2) 46-72-85; f. 1952; art books, children's books; Dir BOUYAN FILCHEV.

Izdatelstvo 'Bulgarsky Pisatel': Sofia, ul. Shesti Septemvri 35; publishing house of the Union of Bulgarian Writers; Bulgarian fiction and poetry, criticism; Dir SIMEON SULTANOV.

Izdatelstvo 'Khristo Botev': 1504 Sofia, Blvd Tzarigradsko Shosse 47; tel. (2) 43-431; f. 1944; fmrly the Publishing House of the Bulgarian Communist Party; renamed as above 1990; Dir IVAN GRANITSKY.

Izdatelstvo na Ministerstvo na Otbranta (Ministry of Defence Publishing House): 1000 Sofia, ul. Ivan Vazov 12; tel. (2) 88-44-31; fax (2) 88-15-68; Head Maj. BOYAN SULTANOV.

Izdatelstvo Mladezh, (Youth Publishing House): 1000 Sofia, ul. Tsar Kaloyan 10; tel (2) 88-21-37; fax (2) 87-61-35; art, history, original and translated fiction and original and translated poetry for children; Gen. Dir STANIMIR ILCHEV.

Izdatelstvo 'Profizdat' (Publishing House of the Central Council of Bulgarian Trade Unions): Sofia, Blvd Dondukov 82; specialized literature and fiction; Dir STOYAN POPOV.

Knigoizdatelstvo 'Galaktika': 9000 Varna, pl. Deveti Septemvri 6; tel. (2) 22-50-77; fax (2) 22-50-77; f. 1960; popular science, science fiction, economics, Bulgarian and foreign literature; Dir PANKO ANCHEV.

'Narodna Kultura' Publishers: 1000 Sofia, Angel Kanchev St 1, tel. (2) 987-80-63; f. 1944; general; Dir PETAR MANOLOV.

Sinodalno Izdatelstvo: Sofia; religious publishing house; Dir KIRIL BOINOV.

STATE ORGANIZATION

Jusautor: 1463 Sofia, Ernst Thälmann Ave 17; tel. (2) 87-28-71; telex 23042; fax (2) 87-37-40; state organization of the Council of Ministers; Bulgarian copyright agency; represents Bulgarian authors of literary, scientific, dramatic and musical works, and deals with all formalities connected with the grant of options, authorization for translations, drawing up of contracts for the use of their works by foreign publishers and producers; negotiates for the use of foreign works in Bulgaria; controls the application of copyright legislation; Dir-Gen. YANA MARKOVA.

PUBLISHERS' ASSOCIATION

Union of Publishers in Bulgaria: 1000 Sofia, pl. Slaveikov 11; Chair. VERA GYOREVA.

WRITERS' UNION

Union of Bulgarian Writers: Sofia, Angel Kanchev 5; tel. (2) 88-00-31; fax (2) 87-47-57; f. 1913; Chair. NIKOLAI HAITOV; 480 mems.

Broadcasting and Communications

TELECOMMUNICATIONS

Bulgarian Telecommunications Company: Sofia; privatization pending in Aug. 1997; Pres. MARIN DRAGOSTINOV.

BROADCASTING

National Radio and Television Council: 1504 Sofia, ul. San Stefano 29, tel. (2) 46-81; telex 22581; Chair. (vacant).

Radio

About nine private local radio stations were broadcasting in 1995.

Bulgarsko Radio: 1040 Sofia, Blvd Dragan Tsankov 4; tel. (2) 85-41; telex 22557; fax (2) 66-22-15; f. 1929; there are two Home Service programmes and local stations at Blagoevgrad, Plovdiv, Shumen, Stara Zagora and Varna. The Foreign Service broadcasts in Bulgarian, Turkish, Greek, Serbo-Croat, French, Italian, German, English, Portuguese, Spanish, Albanian and Arabic; Dir-Gen. MARTIN MINKOV (acting).

Radio Alma Mater: 1000 Sofia, Moscowska St 49; tel. (2) 80-12-10; fax (2) 80-14-34; f. 1993; cable radio service introduced by Sofia Univ.; culture and science programmes; almost 100,000 subscribers.

Television

Bulgarska Televiziya: 1504 Sofia, ul. San Stefano 29; tel. (2) 65-28-70; fax (2) 87-18-71; f. 1959; programmes are transmitted daily; there are two channels, Channel 1 and Efir 2; Dir.-Gen. ANDREY DIMITROV (acting).

Nova Televiziya: 1000 Sofia, pl. Sveta Nedela 16; tel. (2) 80-50-25; fax (2) 87-02-98; f. 1994; first private television channel in Bulgaria; commercial news and entertainment.

Finance

(cap. = capital; dep. = deposits; res = reserves;
m. = million; amounts in leva, unless otherwise indicated)

BANKING

In 1996 the Bulgarian banking system was undergoing a process of restructuring as part of a comprehensive reform of the entire economic system to establish a market economy. By late 1991 the banking sector had already accomplished its transition to a two-tier structure. In September 1992, apart from the Bulgarian National Bank and the State Savings Bank, almost 80 commercial banks were organized as self-managing joint-stock companies. However, only 16 of these had been licensed for cross-border foreign exchange operations, while most of the remainder were less important in terms of size and activities. In late 1992 21 commercial banks merged to form the United Bulgarian Bank, which opened in 1993. In early 1993 two more new banks emerged as a result of the further consolidation of commercial banks. These were Commercial Bank Expressbank (a merger of 12 banks) and Hebrosbank (a merger of eight banks). At May 1996 the total number of banks stood at 47.

Central Bank

Bulgarska Narodna Banka (Bulgarian National Bank): 1000 Sofia, 1 Aleksandur Battenberg Sq.; tel. (2) 85-51; telex 24090; fax (2) 980-24-25; f. 1879; bank of issue; cap. 20,000m., res 871,743m., dep. 3,909,048m. (July 1997); Gov. SVETOSLAV GAVRIYSKI; 6 brs.

State Savings Bank

State Savings Bank: 1040 Sofia, Moskovska St 19; tel. (2) 88-10-41; telex 22719; fax (2) 54-13-55; f. 1951; provides general retail banking services throughout the country; cap. 217m. (1993); Pres. SPAS DIMITROV; 481 brs.

Commercial Banks Licensed for Cross-border Foreign Exchange Operations

BNP-Ak-Dresdner Bank: 1000 Sofia, Narodno Sobraniye 1, POB 11; tel. (2) 980-12-37; telex 22295; fax (2) 981-69-91; f. 1994; Gen. Man. XAVIER DE BAUSSE.

Bulbank (Bulgarian Foreign Trade Bank): 1000 Sofia, Sveta Nedelya Sq. 7; tel. (2) 84-91; telex 22031; fax (2) 88-46-36; f. 1964; cap. 15,125m., res 54,127m., dep. 1,060,265m. (1996); Chair. and Chief Exec. CHAVDAR KANTCHEV.

Bulgarian Post Bank: 1414 Sofia, Bulgaria Sq. 1; tel. (2) 963-21-04; telex 22290; fax (2) 963-04-82; f. 1991; cap. 10,458.4m., res 571.8m., dep. 82,569.5m. (Dec. 1996); Chair. VLADIMIR VLADIMIROV; 30 brs.

Bulgarian-Russian Investment Bank plc: 1000 Sofia, Saborna St 11A; tel. (2) 860-72-40; fax (2) 981-25-26; cap. 5,010.6m., res 482.8m., dep. 15,243.3m. (1996). Chair. EMIL KYULEV.

Central Co-operative Bank Ltd: 1000 Sofia, G. S. Rakovsky St 103; tel. (2) 98-44-32-37; telex 24066; fax (2) 987-19-48; f. 1991; cap. 2,008m., dep. 15,220m. (1996); Chair. STOYAN ALEXANDROV.

Commercial Bank Biochim: 1040 Sofia, Ivan Vazov St 1; tel. (2) 86-16-9; telex 24757; fax (2) 981-93-60; f. 1987; cap. 16,757.2m., res 65,593.0m., dep. 100,983.3m. (1996); Chair. EVGENI CHACHEV.

Commercial Bank Expressbank AD: 9000 Varna, Blvd Varnenchik 92; tel. (52) 66-00; telex 77303; fax (52) 60-16-81; f. 1993 through the merger of 12 banks; cap. 3,566m. (Dec. 1996); Chair. and CEO IVAN KONSTANTINOV; 26 brs.

Corporate Commercial Bank: 1000 Sofia, Ekzarh Yosif St 65, POB 632; tel. (2) 980-93-62; telex 23593; fax (2) 980-89-48; f. 1989; cap. 862.1m., res 1,736.3m., dep. 1,271.9m. (1996); Chair. VENTZISLAV ANTONOV.

Credit Bank plc: Sofia, Angel Kantchev St 3; tel. (2) 980-00-74; fax (2) 981-63-98; cap. 10,000m., res 3.8m., dep. 32,735.7m. (1996); Chair. ILIA PAVLOV.

Elektronika Bank: 1000 Sofia, Blvd Vitosha 6; tel. (2) 87-85-41; telex 23789; fax (2) 88-54-67; f. 1987; cap. 70m. (1993); Pres. VESSELIN KARADZHOV; 4 brs.

First East International Bank: 1000 Sofia, Legue St 10, POB 256; tel. (2) 80-39-57; telex 23319; fax (2) 80-12-21; cap. 3,000.0m., res 1,574.7m., dep. 26,003.1m. (1996); Pres. ANNA SABEVA.

First Private Bank: 1000 Sofia, Ivan Vazov St 16; tel. (2) 980-50-10; telex 24540; fax (2) 980-51-01; f. 1990; placed under supervision of the Bulgarian National Bank in May 1996; cap. 2,015.7m., res 36,444.7m., dep. 129,426.9m. (1996); Pres. VENTSISLAV YOSIFOV; 76 brs.

Hebrosbank: 4018 Plovdiv, Blvd Vazrazhdane 37; tel. (32) 56-26-68; telex 44650; fax (2) 22-39-64; f. 1993 as merger of eight banks; cap. 10,401.1m., res 137.2m., dep. 58,328.7 (1996); Chair. JULLI POPOV.

Hemus Commercial Bank: 1505 Sofia, Yanko Sakuzov Blvd 25; tel. (2) 433-21; telex 22409; fax (2) 43-01-22; f. 1990; cap. 50m., dep. 806m. (Dec. 1992); Pres. MARA KOTEVA; 8 brs.

International Bank for Trade and Development: Sofia, ul. Kaloyan 6; tel. (2) 87-15-16; telex 25100; fax (2) 80-33-83; cap. 50m. (1993).

International Orthodox Bank 'St. Nikola': 1000 Sofia, Rakovsky St 155; tel. (2) 981-77-55; telex 25706; fax (2) 980-77-22; f. 1994; cap. 32,200m., dep. 30,000m.; CEO TZVETAN NACHEV.

Raiffeisenbank (Bulgaria): 1000 Sofia, Serdika St 14; tel. (2) 286-08-11; telex 22006; fax (2) 980-74-79; f. 1994; cap. 800m., dep. 11,985.9m. (Dec. 1996); Exec. Gen. Mans JOHN W. PALMROTH, DOUGLAS G. DRYDEN.

Teximbank: 1202 Sofia, Blvd Maria Luisa 107, Sredetz Municipality; tel. (2) 33-32-40; telex 25104; fax (2) 931-12-07; f. 1992; cap. 1,142.0m., res 35.0m., dep. 3,497.2m. (1995); Pres GEORGI NAYDENOV, MARIA VIDOLOVA.

Unionbank Ltd: 1606 Sofia, Damyan Gruev St 10-12; tel. (2) 988-46-39; telex 23571; fax (2) 980-20-04; f. 1992; cap. 956.6m., res 4,266.6m., dep. 10,183.7m. (Dec. 1996); Exec. Dirs IVAN TOTEV RADEV, EMANUIL YANKOV MANOLOV, EMIL IVANOV IVANOV.

United Bulgarian Bank Inc.: 1000 Sofia, Blvd Maria Luisa 70; tel. (2) 31-81-92; telex 25298; fax (2) 931-04-46; f. 1992 as a merger of 22 commercial banks; universal commercial bank; cap. 1,208m. (1995); Exec. Dirs RADKA TONCHEVA, OLEG NEDYALKOV, STILIAN VATEV.

Vuzrazhdane Commercial Bank: 1303 Sofia, Blvd A. Stamboliiski 50; tel. (2) 87-74-31; telex 23659; fax (2) 80-20-85; f. 1990; cap. 42m., dep. 660m., res 15m. (1991); Pres. MARINA KOZOVSKA.

STOCK EXCHANGE

Bulgarian Stock Exchange: 1040 Sofia, 1 pl. Makedonia; tel. (2) 81-57-11; fax (2) 87-55-66; f. 1991; Exec. Dir VIKTOR PAPAZOV.

INSURANCE

State Insurance Institute (DZI): 1000 Sofia, Blvd Tzar Osvoboditel 6; tel. (2) 87-93-41, 87-01-02; telex 24209; fax (2) 87-69-82; f. 1946; all insurance firms were nationalized during 1947, and were reorganized into one single state insurance company; in 1989 private insurance companies reappeared; the State Insurance Institute was to be transformed into a holding company in 1996; all areas of insurance; Chair. MAXIM SIRAKOV; 110 brs.

Bulstrad Insurance and Reinsurance: 1000 Sofia, Dunav St 5; POB 627; tel. (2) 8-51-91; telex 22564; fax (2) 981-34-07; f. 1961; deals with all classes of insurance and reinsurance; Chair. RUMEN YANCHEV.

Trade and Industry

INTERNATIONAL FREE ZONES

Bourgas Free Trade Zone: 8000 Burgas, Trapezitza St 5; POB 154; tel. (56) 64-77-64; telex 83345; fax (56) 64-20-47; Gen. Mans S. KORADOV, V. SKRIPKA.

Dobrotitza Free Trade Zone: 4649 Kranevo, Dobrich District.

Dragoman Free Trade Zone: 2210 Dragoman; tel. (9971) 72-20-14.

Plovdiv Free Trade Zone: 4003 Plovdiv, V. Turnovo St 25; tel. (32) 65-02-85; fax (32) 65-08-33; f. 1990; CEO NEDELTCHO DRAGANOV.

Rousse International Free Trade Zone: 7000 Ruse, Knyazheska St 5; POB 107; tel. (82) 27-22-47; telex 62285; fax (82) 27-00-84; f. 1987; 45 employees; assets 748m. leva (mid-1996); Gen. Man. YORDAN KAZAKOV.

Svilengrad Free Trade Zone: 6500 Svilengrad; tel. (379) 73-44; telex 43360; fax (379) 75-41; f. 1990; Gen. Dir DIMITUR MITEV.

Vidin Free Trade Zone: 3700 Vidin; tel. (94) 228-37; fax (94) 309-47; f. 1988; Gen. Man. K. MARINOV.

CHAMBER OF COMMERCE

Bulgarian Chamber of Commerce and Industry: 1040 Sofia, Suborna St 11A; tel. (2) 87-26-31; telex 22374; fax (2) 87-32-09; f. 1895; promotes economic relations and business contacts between Bulgarian and foreign cos and orgs; organizes participation in international fairs and exhibitions; publishes economic publs in Bulgarian and foreign languages; organizes foreign trade advertising and publicity; provides legal and economic consultations, etc.; registers all Bulgarian cos trading internationally (more than 67,000 at mid-1994); Pres. BOJIDAR BOJINOV.

EMPLOYERS' ASSOCIATIONS

Bulgarian Industrial Association (BISA): 1000 Sofia, Alabin St 16-20; tel. (2) 980-99-14; telex 23523; fax (2) 87-26-04; e-mail office@bia.bol.bg; f. 1980; assists Bulgarian economic enterprises with promotion and foreign contacts; analyses economic situation; assists development of small-and medium-sized firms; Chair. BOJIDAR DANEV.

National Union of Employers: 1505 Sofia, Oborishte St 44; POB 15; f. 1989; federation of businessmen in Bulgaria.

Union of Private Owners in Bulgaria: 1000 Sofia, Graf Ignatiev St 2; f. 1990; Chair. DIMITUR TODOROV.

Vuzrazhdane Union of Bulgarian Private Manufacturers: 1618 Sofia, Todor Kableshkov Blvd 2; tel. (2) 55-00-16; Chair. DRAGOMIR GUSHTEROV.

UTILITIES

Electricity

Central Laboratory of Solar Energy and New Energy Sources: 1784 Sofia, Carigradsko shosse 72; tel. and fax (2) 75-40-16; research into alternative energy production; Dir Prof. STEFAN KANEV.

National Electricity Company: 1040 Sofia, Triaditsa St 8; tel. (2) 8-61-99; fax (2) 87-58-26; responsible for all thermal, nuclear and hydroelectric electricity production.

Gas

Bulgargaz: Sofia; tel. (2) 25-90-74; Chair. KRASIMIR NIKOLOV.

Topenergy Joint-Stock Co: Sofia; f. 1995; owned by Gazprom of Russia (50%) and Bulgargaz (25%); responsible for supply of Russian natural gas to Bulgaria; Chair. ILIYA PAVLOV; Dir SERGEI PASHIN.

MAJOR COMPANIES

Until 1989 foreign trade was a state monopoly in Bulgaria, and was conducted through foreign trade organizations and various state enterprises and corporations. However, in 1989 legislation was enacted whereby the *firma* (company) was introduced as a basic structural unit of the economy. The Bulgarian economy was subsequently opened to foreign investment. In 1991 the introduction of further legislation provided for the transfer of state enterprises to the private sector. Following the acceleration of the privatization programme in 1997, the Government aimed to transfer some 80% of state-owned enterprises to the private sector by the end of 1998.

Balkancarpodem; Sofia, Kliment Ohridsky St 18; tel. (2) 85-301; fax (2) 77-13-96; electric hoists and equipment.

Balkantourist: see section on Tourism below.

Bulgarski Morski Flot Co: see section on Transport (Shipping and Inland Waterways) below.

Bulgartabac: 1000 Sofia, Graf Ignatiev St 62; tel. (2) 987-52-11; telex 23288; fax (2) 987-88-20; covers manufacture, import and export of raw and manufactured tobacco; Chair. and CEO BOIKO KISHKOV.

Chimco: Vratsa; tel. (92) 2-40-81; state-owned chemical producer.

Chimimport: 1000 Sofia, St Karadja St 2; tel. (2) 980-16-11; telex 22521; fax (2) 981-61-91; f. 1947; import and export of pharmaceuticals, chemicals, petrochemicals, fertilizers, etc.; Dir-Gen. BELO BELOV.

Electroimpex: 1000 Sofia, G. Washington 17; tel. (2) 86-181; telex 22959; fax (2) 980-02-72; e-mail elimpex@mb.bia-bg.com; f. 1960; engineering and import and export of electrical tools and equipment; Exec. Dir ALEXANDAR VAKLINOV.

Eltos: 5500 Lovech, Kubrat St 9; tel. (68) 2-35-50; fax (68) 2-00-69; production of electrical tools; f. 1989; Dir-Gen. D. KOVATCHEV.

Hemus: 1000 Sofia, Benkovsky St 14; tel. (2) 80-03-65; telex 22267; fax (2) 981-33-41; import and export of books, periodicals, numismatic items, art products, musical instruments, gramophone records and CDs, cinematographic equipment, film and photo consumables and souvenirs; consigned paper warehouse; Exec. Dir ASEN PEYNERDZIEV.

Incoms-Telecom Holding: 1309 Sofia, Kiril Ptchelinski St 1; tel. (2) 2-13-41; export and import of radioelectronic equipment and technology for the communications industry; Dir-Gen. LYUBOMIR BUTURANOV.

Interinvest Engineering Ltd: 1113 Sofia, Zhendov St 6; tel. (2) 71-00-33; fax (2) 71-00-38; engineering, trade and investment services; Dir-Gen. EMIL ALADZHEM.

Karaminchev PLC: 7005 Rousse, Blvd Lipnik 73; tel. (82) 45-93-36; telex 62511; fax (82) 44-86-09; e-mail pkar@mbox.digsys.bg; manufacture of floorings, synthetic leather, PVC goods, etc.; Man. Dir GUEORGUI BAYRAKOV.

Koraboimpex Co Ltd: 9000 Varna, Blvd Osmi Primorski Polk 128; tel. (52) 88-20-91; telex 77448; fax (2) 82-33-86; holding company of Koraboimpex group of companies; imports and exports ships, marine and port equipment; Exec. Dir. NIKOLAI PRASHKEVOV.

Kremikovitzi Co: 1770 Sofia, Botunetz; tel. (2) 45-45-12; telex 22478; fax (2) 87-98-96; ferrous metals; Dir-Gen. L. VATCHKOV.

Kvartz Co: 8800 Sliven; tel. (44) 2-32-63; fax (44) 8-06-91; glassware.

Machinoexport: 1000 Sofia, Aksakov St 5; tel. (2) 88-53-21; telex 23425; fax (2) 87-56-75; export of metal-cutting and wood-working machines, industrial robots, hydraulic and pneumatic products and other equipment, tools and spare parts; Gen. Dir E. MANEVA.

Mladost: 1000 Sofia, Blvd Hristo Botev 48; tel. (2) 87-61-36; telex 22168; fax (2) 87-27-97; trade in footwear, sportswear, ready-made dresses and toys; Dir-Gen. BOJIDAR VASILEV.

Neftochim: 8104 Burgas, Industrial Zone; tel. (56) 4-59-84; petroleum products, synthetic fabrics, plastics; Dir-Gen. (vacant).

Plama: 5800 Pleven, Industrial Zone; tel. (64) 2-81-11; fax (64) 3-35-76; petroleum products.

Plovdiska Conserva Ltd: 4000 Plovdiv, D. Stambolov St 2; tel. (32) 55-31-72; fax (32) 55-37-71; e-mail villy@mail.techno-link.com; f. 1947; fruit and vegetable processing; Dir BORIS KALIBATZEV; 1,200 employees.

Raznoiznos: 1040 Sofia, Tsar Assen St 1; tel. (2) 88-02-11; telex 23244, 23880; fax (2) 31-70-12; export and import of industrial and craftsmen's products, timber products, paper products, glassware, kitchen utensils, furniture, carpets, toys, sports equipment, musical instruments, etc.; Dir-Gen. MAXIM SCHWARZ.

Rudmetal: 1000 Sofia, Dobrudzha St 1; tel. (2) 88-12-71; telex 22027; fax (2) 980-45-04; f. 1952; export and import of ferrous and non-ferrous metals and products, lead zinc, copper, pure lead, coal, etc.; Dir-Gen. EMIL DELIRADEV.

Sofarma Co.: 1220 Sofia, Iliensko Shosse St 16; (2) 38-55-31; fax (2) 38-30-21; trade in chemical and pharmaceutical products, perfumery and cosmetics.

Stomana Co.: 2300 Pernik, Kv. Iztok; tel. (76) 87-20-70; telex 28501; steel products.

Technoimpex: 1000 Sofia, Tsar Kaloyan St 8; POB 932; tel. (2) 88-15-71; telex 22950; fax (2) 88-34-15; scientific and technological assistance abroad in the fields of industry, architecture, construction, transport and communications and education; representation of foreign companies, barter, import-export, re-export, specific commercial operations, leasing, etc.; Dir-Gen. SPAS PANCHEV.

Technoimportexport plc: Sofia, Fr. J. Curie St 20; tel. (2) 63-991; telex 22193; fax (2) 65-81-47; engineering and import and export of power generating equipment, etc.

Transimpex JSC Co: 1606 Sofia, Blvd Skobelev 65; tel. (2) 54-91-61; telex 22123; fax (2) 52-23-25; e-mail trimp@transimpex.bg; f. 1967; 5 divs; general trading; ship suppliers; manning of sea-going vessels; duty-free operations; hotels and restaurants; import and export of railway equipment, wagons, locomotives, boats and shipping parts; Chair. KALCHO HINOV; Man. Dir BORIS HALACHEV; 640 employees.

Zarno Co.: 1000 Sofia, Blvd Vitosha 15; tel. (2) 88-23-81; telex 23441; fax (2) 83-23-38; processing and trade in grains and pulses.

ZMM Inc.: 1220 Sofia, Iliensko Shosse St 8; tel. (2) 3-85-41; telex 22174; manufacture of machines for metal-and woodwork.

CO-OPERATIVES

Central Union of Workers' Productive Co-operatives: 1000 Sofia, Blvd Dondukov 11; POB 55; tel. (2) 80-39-38; telex 23229; fax (2) 87-03-20; f. 1988; umbrella organization of 164 workers' productive co-operatives; Pres. STILIAN BALASSOPOULOV; 60,000 mems.

TRADE UNIONS

Confederation of Independent Trade Unions in Bulgaria (CITUB): Sofia, pl. D. Blagoev 1; tel. (2) 86-61; telex 22446; fax (2) 87-17-87; f. 1904; changed name from Bulgarian Professional Union and declared independence from all parties and state structures in 1990; still the main trade union organization; at mid-1991 there were 75 mem. federations and four associate mems (principal mems listed below); Chair. Prof. Dr KRUSTYU PETKOV; Sec. MILADIN STOYNOV; total mems 3,064,000 (mid-1991).

Edinstvo (Unity) People's Trade Union: 1000 Sofia, Moskovska St 5; tel. (2) 87-96-40; f. 1990; co-operative federation of Clubs, based on professional interests, grouped into Asscns and Regional Asscns; there are 84 asscns and 2 prof. asscns, in 14 regional groups; Chair. OGNYAN BONEV; 384,000 mems (mid-1991).

Podkrepa (Support) Trade Union Confederation: 1000 Sofia, Angel Kanchev St 2; tel. (2) 988-78-39; fax (2) 988-87-38; e-mail fciw@mail.techno-link.com; f. 1990 as an oppostion trade union (affiliated to the Union of Democratic Forces); organized into territorial (31 regions) and professional asscns (33 syndicates); Pres. Dr KONSTANTIN TRENCHEV; Gen. Sec. PETUR GANCHEV; 15,000 mems (1997).

Principal CITUB Trade Unions

Federation of Independent Agricultural Trade Unions: 1606 Sofia, ul. Dimo Hadzhidimov 29; tel. (2) 52-15-40; Pres. LYUBEN KHARALAMPIEV; 44,600 mems (mid-1994).

Federation of Independent Trade Unions of Construction Workers: 1000 Sofia, pl. Sveta Nedelya 4; tel. (2) 80-16-003; Chair. NIKOLAI RASHKOV; 220,000 mems (mid-1991).

Federation of the Independent Trade Unions of Employees of the State and Social Organizations: 1000 Sofia, ul. Alabin 52; tel. (2) 87-98-52; Chair. PETUR SUCHKOV; 144,900 mems (mid-1991).

Federation of Independent Mining Trade Unions: 1000 Sofia, 6 September St 4; tel. (2) 87-72-54; fax (2) 88-45-66; f. 1909; Pres. PENCHO TOKMAKCHIEV; 42,000 mems.

Federation of Light Industry Trade Unions: 1040 Sofia, pl. Makedonia 1; tel. (2) 88-15-70; fax (2) 88-15-20; Chair. IORDAN VASSILEV IVANOV; 64,320 mems (1997).

Federation of Metallurgical Trade Unions: 1000 Sofia, 6 September St 4; tel. (2) 88-48-21; fax (2) 88-27-10; f. 1992; Pres. VASSIL YANACHKOV; 20,000 mems.

Federation of Trade Unions in the Chemical Industry: 1040 Sofia, pl. Makedonia 1; tel. (2) 87-39-07; Pres. LYUBEN MAKOV; 60,000 mems (mid-1993).

Federation of Trade Union Organizations in the Forestry and Woodworking Industries: 1606 Sofia, ul. Vladayska 29; tel. (2) 52-21-31; fax (2) 51-73-97; Pres. BOUDEN TODOROV; 29,600 mems (mid-1996).

Federation of Trade Unions of Health Services: 1202 Sofia, Blvd Maria Louisa 45; tel. (2) 88-20-97; fax (2) 83-18-14; f. 1990; Pres. Dr IVAN KOKALOV; 60,500 mems (mid-1994).

Independent Trade Union Federation of the Co-operatives: 1000 Sofia, ul. Rakovski 99; tel. (2) 87-36-74; Chair. NIKOLAI NIKOLOV; 96,000 mems (mid-1991).

Independent Trade Union Federation for Trade, Co-operatives, Services and Tourism: 1000 Sofia, 6 September St 4; tel. (2) 88-02-51; Chair. PETUR TSEKOV; 212,221 mems (mid-1991).

Independent Trade Union of Food Industry Workers: 1606 Sofia, ul. Dimo Hadzhidimov 29; tel. (2) 52-30-72; fax (2) 52-16-70; Pres. SLAVCHO PETROV; 53,000 mems (mid-1994).

'Metal-electro' National Trade Union Federation: 1040 Sofia, pl. Makedonia 1; POB 543; tel. (2) 87-48-06; fax (2) 87-75-38; Pres. ASSEN ASSENOV; 80,000 mems (1995).

National Federation of Energy Workers: 1040 Sofia, pl. Makedonia 1; tel. (2) 88-48-22; f. 1927; Pres. BOJIL PETROV; 15,000 mems.

Union of Bulgarian Teachers: 1000 Sofia, pl. Sveta Nedelya 4; tel. (2) 87-78-18; f. 1905; Chair. IVAN YORDANOV; 186,153 mems (mid-1991).

Union of Transport Workers: 1233 Sofia, Blvd Princess Maria Luiza 106; tel. (2) 31-51-24; fax (2) 31-71-24; f. 1911; Pres. ATANAS STANEV; 70,000 mems (mid-1991).

Other Principal Trade Unions

Bulgarian Military Legion 'G. S. Rakovski': 1000 Sofia, Blvd Ruski 9; tel. (2) 87-72-96; Chair. DOICHIN BOYADZHIEV.

Inner Macedonian Revolutionary Organization–Union of Macedonian Associations: 1361 Sofia, Pirotska St 5; tel. 87-64-60; fax 87-84-88; Chairs KRASIMIR KARAKACHANOV, EVGENI EKOV, RAINA DRANGOVA.

Podkrepa Construction and Design Industry Workers' Federation: 1000 Sofia, Uzundjovska St 12; Pres. IOANIS PARTHENIOTIS; 15,000 mems (1995).

Podkrepa Professional Trade Union for Chemistry, Geology and Metallurgy Workers: 1000 Sofia, Angel Kanchev St 2; Chair. LACHEZAR MINKOV (acting); 15,000 mems (mid-1991).

Podkrepa Professional Trade Union for Doctors and Medical Personnel: 1000 Sofia, Angel Kanchev St 2; Chair. Dr K. KRASTEV; 20,000 mems (mid-1991).

Union of Bulgarian Architects: 1504 Sofia, Krakra St 11; tel. (2) 44-26-73; telex 23569; fax (2) 946-08-00; f. 1893; Chair. EVLOGI TSVETKOV.

Union of Bulgarian Lawyers: 1000 Sofia, Treti April St 7; tel. (2) 87-58-59; Chair. PETUR KORNAZHEV.

Transport

Ministry of Transport: 1000 Sofia, Levski St 9–11; tel. (2) 87-10-81; telex 23200; fax (2) 88-50-94; directs the state rail, road, water and air transport organizations.

Despred International Freight Forwarders Ltd: 1080 Sofia, Slavyanska St 2; tel. (2) 87-60-16; telex 23306; fax (2) 981-33-40; Exec. Dir DIMITAR NESTOROV.

RAILWAYS

In 1996 there were 4,293 km of track in Bulgaria, of which 2,708 km were electrified. The international and domestic rail networks are centred on Sofia. In 1995 a US $45m. loan from the European Bank for Reconstruction and Development was granted to Bulgarian State Railways. Construction of a 52-km underground railway system for Sofia commenced in 1979; the first section, comprising 6.1 km, was opened in January 1998.

Bulgarian State Railways (BDZ): 1080 Sofia, Ivan Vazov St 3; tel. (2) 87-30-45; telex 22423; fax (2) 980-25-64; e-mail bdzboev @bg400.bg; owns and controls all railway transport; Dir-Gen. YORDAN MIRTCHEV.

ROADS

There were 36,720 km of roads in Bulgaria in 1996, of which 3,075 km were principal roads and 10,055 km were secondary roads; 91.9% of the network was paved. Two important international motorways traverse the country and a major motorway runs from Sofia to the coast.

General Road Administration: 1606 Sofia, Blvd Makedonia 3; tel. and fax (2) 951-50-92; f. 1952; Dir-Gen. DIMITAR DIMOV.

SHIPPING AND INLAND WATERWAYS

The Danube River is the main waterway, the two main ports being Ruse and Lom. In 1990 external services linked Black Sea ports (the largest being Varna and Burgas) to the former USSR, the Mediterranean and western Europe. The port of Tsarevo was opened to international shipping in 1995.

Bulgarian River Shipping Company: 7000 Ruse, pl. Otets Paisi 2; tel. (82) 700-93; telex 62403; fax (82) 701-61; f. 1935; shipment of cargo and passengers on the Danube; storage, handling and forwarding of cargo; Dir-Gen. DIMITUR STANCHEV.

Bulgarski Morski Flot Co.: 9000 Varna, Panaguirishte St 17; tel. (52) 22-63-16; telex 77524; fax (52) 22-53-94; organization of sea and river transport; carriage of goods and passengers on waterways; controls all aspects of shipping and shipbuilding, also engages in research, design and personnel training; Dir-Gen. ATANAS YONKOV.

Navigation Maritime Bulgare Ltd: 9000 Varna, Primorski 1; tel. (52) 22-24-74; telex 77351; fax (52) 22-24-91; f. 1892; major enterprise in Bulgaria employed in sea transport; owns 103 tankers, bulk carriers and container, ferry, cargo and passenger vessels with a capacity of 1,817,169 dwt (1995); Dir-Gen. Capt. IVAN BORISSOV.

CIVIL AVIATION

There are three international airports in Bulgaria, at Sofia, Varna and Bourgas, and seven other airports for domestic services. In mid-1995 construction work began on the modernization of Sofia Airport.

Balkan Bulgarian Airlines: 1540 Sofia, Sofia Airport; tel. (2) 88-18-00; telex 23097; fax (2) 79-12-06; f. 1947; restructured and split in 1991; designated national carrier; services to 52 international destinations; also operates domestic routes; Man. Dir VALERI DOGANOV.

Heli Air Services: 1540 Sofia, Sofia Airport North; tel. and fax (2) 795036; telex 22342; f. 1991; Man. Dir GEORGI SPASSOV.

Hemus Airlines: 1540 Sofia, Sofia Airport; tel. (2) 70-20-76; telex 22342; fax (2) 79-63-80; f. 1991; Dir-Gen. ZDRAVKO VELICHKOV.

Jes Air: 1540 Sofia, Sofia Airport; f. 1991; Exec. Dir TATIANA STOICHKOVA.

Via Air: 1540 Sofia, Sofia Airport; f. 1990; private airline.

Tourism

Bulgaria's tourist attractions include the resorts on the Black Sea coast, mountain scenery and historic centres. In 1996 there were 6,810,688 foreign visitor arrivals (including 4,015,493 visitors in transit).

Bulgarian Tourist Chamber: Sofia, Triaditza St 5; tel. (2) 87-40-59; some 350 firms are mems, incl. state enterprises, which are in the process of privatization; Chair. TSVETAN TONCHEV.

Balkantourist: 1040 Sofia, Blvd Vitosha 1; tel. (2) 4-33-31; telex 22583; fax (2) 80-01-34; f. 1948; Bulgaria's first privatized travel company; leading tour operator and travel agent; Man. Dir ALEXANDER SPASSOV.

BURKINA FASO

Introductory Survey

Location, Climate, Language, Religion, Flag, Capital

Burkina Faso (formerly the Republic of Upper Volta) is a land-locked state in West Africa, bordered by Mali to the west and north, by Niger to the east, and by Benin, Togo, Ghana and Côte d'Ivoire to the south. The climate is hot and mainly dry, with an average temperature of 27°C (81°F) in the dry season December–May). A rainy season occurs between June and October. Levels of rainfall are generally higher in the south than in the north; average annual rainfall in Ouagadougou is 894 mm (35 ins). The official language is French, and there are numerous indigenous languages (principally Mossi), with many dialects. The majority of the population follow animist beliefs; about 30% are Muslims and some 10% Christians, mainly Roman Catholics. The national flag (proportions 3 by 2) has two equal horizontal stripes, of red and green, with a five-pointed gold star in the centre. The capital is Ouagadougou.

Recent History

Burkina Faso (Upper Volta until August 1984) was formerly a province of French West Africa. It became a self-governing republic within the French Community in December 1958 and achieved full independence on 5 August 1960, with Maurice Yaméogo as President. In January 1966 Yaméogo was deposed in a military coup, led by Lt-Col (later Gen.) Sangoulé Lamizana, the Chief of Staff of the army, who took office as President and Prime Minister. The new regime dissolved the legislature, suspended the Constitution and established a Conseil suprême des forces armées. Political activities were suspended between September 1966 and November 1969. A new Constitution, approved by popular referendum in June 1970, provided for a return to civilian rule after a four-year transitional regime of joint military and civilian administration. Elections for an Assemblée nationale took place in December, at which the Union démocratique voltaïque (UDV) won 37 of the 57 seats. In early 1971 Lamizana appointed the UDV leader, Gérard Ouédraogo, as Prime Minister at the head of a mixed civilian and military Council of Ministers.

A series of conflicts between the Government and the legislature prompted Lamizana, in February 1974, to announce that the army had again assumed power. Ouédraogo was dismissed, the legislature was dissolved, and the Constitution and all political activity were suspended. The Assemblée was replaced in July by a Conseil national consultatif pour le renouveau, with 65 members nominated by the President. Political parties were allowed to resume their activities from October 1977. A referendum in November of that year approved a draft Constitution providing for a return to civilian rule. Seven parties contested elections for a new Assemblée nationale in April 1978. The UDV won 28 of the 57 seats, while the Union nationale pour la défense de la démocratie (UNDD), led by Herman Yaméogo, the son of the former President, secured 13 seats. The seven parties grouped themselves into three alliances in the legislature, as required by the Constitution, with the main opposition front being formed by the UNDD and the Union progressiste voltaïque. In May Lamizana was elected President, and in July the Assemblée elected the President's nominee, Dr Joseph Conombo, to be Prime Minister.

In November 1980, following protracted industrial unrest, Lamizana was overthrown in a bloodless coup, led by Col Saye Zerbo, who had been Minister of Foreign Affairs during the previous period of military rule. A 31-member Comité militaire de redressement pour le progrès national (CMRPN) was established, and in December the regime formed a new Government, comprising both army officers and civilians. The Constitution was suspended, the legislature was dissolved, and political parties were banned. Opposition to the Zerbo regime, most notably to its attempts to suppress trade union activity, soon emerged, and in November 1982 Zerbo was deposed by a group of non-commissioned army officers. Maj. Jean-Baptiste Ouédraogo, President of the Conseil de salut du peuple (CSP), emerged as leader of the new regime. The CMRPN was dissolved, and a predominantly civilian Government was formed. In February 1983 several arrests were made, following the discovery of an alleged plot to reinstate the Zerbo regime. A power struggle within the CSP became apparent with the arrest, in May, of radical left-wing elements within the Government, including the recently-appointed Prime Minister, Capt. Thomas Sankara. Ouédraogo announced the withdrawal of the armed forces from political life, and disbanded the CSP. Sankara and his supporters were released following a rebellion by pro-Sankara commandos at Pô, near the border with Ghana, under the leadership of Capt. Blaise Compaoré.

In August 1983 Sankara seized power in a violent coup. A Conseil national révolutionnaire (CNR) was established, and Maj. Ouédraogo and other perceived opponents of the new administration were placed under house arrest. Compaoré, as Minister of State at the Presidency, became the regime's second-in-command. In September ex-President Zerbo was formally arrested after his supporters attempted to overthrow the new Government. Administrative, judicial and military reforms were announced, and Tribunaux populaires révolutionnaires (TPRs) were inaugurated to consider cases of alleged corruption. Several former politicians, including Zerbo, appeared before these tribunals and were subsequently imprisoned. Meanwhile, citizens were urged to join Comités pour la défense de la révolution (CDRs), which, by imposing government policies and organizing local affairs, played an important role in consolidating Sankara's position.

In June 1984 seven army officers were executed, convicted of plotting to overthrow the Government. Sankara accused an outlawed left-wing political group, the Front progressiste voltaïque, of complicity in the plot, alleging that it had been supported by France and other foreign powers: the French Government vigorously denied any involvement, and relations between the two countries underwent some strain. In August the country was renamed Burkina Faso ('Land of the Incorruptible Men'). In response to indications of growing factionalism within the CNR, Sankara made efforts to reduce the influence of Marxist elements which had begun to oppose Sankara's populist rhetoric.

In December 1985 a long-standing border dispute with Mali erupted into a six-day war which left some 50 people dead. The conflict centred on a reputedly mineral-rich area known as the Agacher strip. Following the cease-fire, arranged by the regional defence grouping, Accord de non-agression et d'assistance en matière de défense, and as a result of an interim decision on the dispute delivered by the International Court of Justice (ICJ) in January 1986, troops were withdrawn from the Agacher area. Ambassadors were exchanged in June, and both countries accepted the ICJ's ruling, made in December, that the territory be divided equally between the two.

Amnesty measures for Sankara's political opponents were gradually effected. However, tensions between the Government and trade unions were apparent, exacerbated by policies aimed at developing the rural economy and by the introduction, from 1985, of austerity measures. In May 1987 several prominent trade union activists were detained on charges of 'counter-revolutionary' activities, and at the same time a major tax-recovery operation reportedly led to the closure of many small businesses. There was, moreover, evidence of growing disharmony within the CNR (in part engendered by Sankara's suppression of the trade unions), and in August two members of a leading communist faction were dismissed from the Government. On 15 October a self-styled Front populaire (FP), led by Compaoré, took power in a violent coup, in which Sankara and 13 of his close associates were killed. The CNR was dissolved, and Sankara denounced. The new regime pledged a continuation of the revolutionary process begun under Sankara, but emphasized the need for a 'rectification process', principally in the area of economic policy. A new, predominantly civilian Council of Ministers was named at the end of October, including seven members of the previous administration. Compaoré became Head of State, with the title of Chairman of the FP. Many of Sankara's close associates, among them members of his family and former ministers, were arrested and detained without trial in the months following the coup; most had been released by mid-1988.

Among institutional reforms instigated in the aftermath of the coup, the CDRs were disarmed and replaced by Comités révolutionnaires (which had only limited success in recruiting members), and the powers of the TPRs were curtailed. Civilian government members, meanwhile, had considerable influence in the implementation of the FP's economic programme. In April 1989 a new political grouping, the Organisation pour la démocratie populaire/Mouvement du travail (ODP/MT), was established, under the leadership of Clément Oumarou Ouédraogo. The swift dismissal of government members who had declined to join the new party was an apparent indication that the ODP/MT was intended to assume a prominent role in Compaoré's regime. At the same time Ouédraogo was appointed to the newly-created position of Minister-Delegate to the Co-ordinating Committee of the FP.

In August 1989 an amnesty was proclaimed for all political prisoners. In the following month it was announced that the Commander-in-Chief of the Armed Forces and Minister of Popular Defence and Security, Maj. Jean-Baptiste Boukary Lingani, and the Minister of Economic Promotion, Capt. Henri Zongo (both of whom had been prominent at the time of the 1983 and 1987 coups), had been executed, together with two others, following the discovery of a plot to overthrow Compaoré. It was widely believed that Boukary Lingani and Zongo had been opposed to aspects of the 'rectification' process, notably the promotion of private enterprise and the principle of negotiations, which had begun in 1988, with the IMF and the World Bank. Compaoré subsequently assumed personal responsibility for defence. In December 1989 it was announced that a further attempt to overthrow the Government had been thwarted. In November 1990 it was stated that 19 people (including a former Minister of Justice under Sankara) were awaiting trial in connection with the alleged plot.

The first congress of the FP, in March 1990, was attended by delegates from seven political tendencies. The congress sanctioned the establishment of a commission to draft a new constitution that would define a process of 'democratization'. Herman Yaméogo, widely regarded as a political moderate, was appointed to the Executive Committee of the FP. (Three months later, however, Yaméogo and his supporters were expelled from the organization.) In April Clément Oumarou Ouédraogo was dismissed from prominent posts within the FP, the ODP/MT and the Council of Ministers. He was replaced as Secretary for Political Affairs of the FP and as Secretary-General of the ODP/MT by Roch Marc Christian Kaboré, hitherto Minister of Transport and Communications and, unlike Ouédraogo, a known supporter of Compaoré's ideals. In September Kaboré was appointed Minister of State within the Government.

The draft Constitution, which was presented to Compaoré in October 1990, included a clause denying legitimacy to any regime that might take power as the result of a *coup d'état*. In December a constituent assembly of some 2,400 delegates was convened to review the document. The final draft delineated the division of power between the executive, legislature and judiciary, in a 'revolutionary, democratic, unitary and secular state'. Multi-party elections, by universal suffrage, would take place for a President and legislative Assemblée des députés populaires (ADP), while provision was made for the establishment of a second, consultative chamber of the legislature, to be composed of the 'active forces of the nation'.

In March 1991 the first congress of the ODP/MT adopted Compaoré as the party's presidential candidate. The party also renounced its Marxist-Leninist ideology, embracing instead policies of free enterprise. In the following month an amnesty was proclaimed for the alleged perpetrators of the November 1989 coup attempt. In May 1991 a congress was convened to restructure the FP and to provide for the separation, upon the adoption of the new Constitution, of the functions of the FP and the organs of state. Compaoré, redesignated Secretary-General of the FP, was confirmed in office as Head of State pending the presidential election. Delegates also approved the rehabilitation of Maurice Yaméogo, and an appeal was made to all political exiles to return to Burkina. In June plans were announced for the construction of a memorial honouring Sankara.

About 49% of the registered electorate voted in the constitutional referendum, which took place on 2 June 1991: of these, 93% were reported to have endorsed the Constitution of what was to be designated the Fourth Republic. The new document took effect on 11 June, whereupon the Council of Ministers was dissolved. A transitional Government was subsequently appointed, its most senior member being Kaboré (as Minister of State, with responsibility for the Co-ordination of Government Action). The dominant role of the ODP/MT was widely criticized, and several nominated government members declined their posts. In July Herman Yaméogo, now leader of the Alliance pour la démocratie et la fédération (ADF), and several other representatives of parties outside the FP were appointed to the Government. In August, however, Yaméogo (who had announced his intention to contest the presidency) was one of three government members who resigned in protest against proposed electoral procedures. Seven further opposition members resigned from the transitional administration in September, when Compaoré failed to accede to demands for a national conference. The Head of State's persistent assertion that to convene a sovereign national conference in advance of the forthcoming presidential and legislative elections would not be compatible with the spirit of the new Constitution caused considerable disquiet among opposition groups. Opposition parties, grouped in a Coordination des forces démocratiques (CFD), organized rallies and demonstrations in support of the campaign for a national conference, and violent incidents at one such gathering prompted the Government to impose a temporary ban on political processions. Attempts to achieve a compromise failed, and in October five CFD candidates withdrew from the presidential contest.

The presidential election proceeded on 1 December 1991, whereupon Compaoré (who had resigned from the army to contest the presidency as a civilian) was elected, unopposed, with the support of 90.4% of those who voted. An abstention rate of 74.7% was said by the CFD to reflect the success of its appeal for a boycott of the poll. Compaoré emphasized the need for national reconciliation, but shortly after the election Clément Oumarou Ouédraogo was assassinated while leaving a CFD meeting, and attacks on other opposition members were also reported. Although the Government condemned the violence, the CFD held Compaoré responsible for the incidents, and further disturbances followed Ouédraogo's funeral. Apparently in response, the Government announced the indefinite postponement of the legislative elections, which had been scheduled for January 1992: the CFD had for some weeks been advocating a boycott of the elections, and few political parties had registered their intention to contest the poll.

Compaoré was officially inaugurated as President of the Fourth Republic on 24 December 1991, and in the following month it was announced that some 4,000 people who had been convicted in connection with political or trade union activities since the time of Sankara's accession to power were to be rehabilitated. By contrast, Compaoré was seen to impose restrictions on the remit of an impending 'national reconciliation forum', which was intended to embrace the country's diverse political and social groups, and to overrule several recommendations made by its preparatory committee. The forum, which was convened in February 1992 and attended by some 380 delegates, was suspended by the Government within two weeks, following disagreements regarding the broadcasting of debates by the state-owned media. None the less, four opposition members, among them Herman Yaméogo (as Minister of State), were appointed to the Government later in the month.

The legislative election finally took place on 24 May 1992, contested by 27 political parties. According to official results, the ODP/MT won 78 of the ADP's 107 seats. Nine other parties secured representation: of these, the most successful was Pierre Tapsoba's Convention nationale des patriotes progressistes—Parti social-démocrate (CNPP—PSD), which took 12 seats, while Herman Yaméogo's ADF won four seats. The rate of participation by voters was reported to have been little more than 35%. The ADP was inaugurated on 15 June. Shortly afterwards Compaoré appointed Youssouf Ouédraogo, hitherto President of the country's Economic and Social Council, as Prime Minister. His Council of Ministers included representatives of seven political parties, although the ODP/MT was allocated most strategic posts—among them the finance and planning portfolio, which was assigned to Kaboré. A 'freeze' in public-sector salaries, in force since 1987, was ended in January 1993, although trade union leaders deemed a newly-imposed salary structure to be unfavourable in real terms. In September Kaboré was redesignated Minister of State, with responsibility for Relations with the Organs of State.

Following the 50% devaluation of the CFA franc, in January 1994, trade unions denounced emergency measures adopted by the Government in an attempt to offset the immediate adverse effects of the currency's depreciation as inadequate, and began a campaign for salary increases of 40%–50%. Negotiations between the Government and workers' representatives failed to reach a compromise, and in March Ouédraogo resigned. He was replaced as Prime Minister by Kaboré, whose ODP/MT dominated Government included a new Minister of the Economy, Finance and Planning, Zéphirin Diabré (hitherto Minister of Industry, Trade and Mines). The new administration's proposals for salary increases of 6%–10%, as well as other concessions designed to mitigate the consequences of the ending of temporary price controls, failed to avert a three-day general strike, in April, by members of the Confédération générale du travail burkinabè.

Municipal elections took place in February 1995, at which the ODP/MT won control of 24 of the country's 33 major towns. However, fewer than 10% of those eligible were reported to have registered to vote. Several opposition parties had, moreover, refused to present candidates, in protest at what they claimed were inadequate preparations for the elections. In August Ernest Nongma Ouédraogo, the Secretary-General of the Bloc socialiste burkinabè (BSB), was convicted of insulting the Head of State and sentenced to six months' imprisonment, having alleged in an article published in an independent newspaper that Compaoré had amassed a personal fortune by fraudulent means.

In early February 1996 Kaboré was replaced as Prime Minister by Kadré Désiré Ouédraogo, hitherto Deputy Governor of the Banque centrale des états de l'Afrique de l'ouest. Kaboré was himself named Special Adviser to the Presidency, and also First Vice-President of a new, pro-Compaoré political party, the Congrès pour la démocratie et le progrès (CDP). The CDP, termed a social-democratic party, grouped the ODP/MT and some 10 other parties (including the CNPP—PSD). Named as its President was a long-time ally of Compaoré, Arsène Bognessan Yè, the President of the legislature and the former head of the OPD/MT. Most of the members of the outgoing administration were reappointed to Ouédraogo's first Council of Ministers. The new premier, who claimed to have no party political affiliation, stated that his Government's priority would be to strengthen and revitalize economic development, with particular emphasis on the agro-pastoral sector, employment, the stable management of public finances and on environmental protection. Ouédraogo assumed personal responsibility for the economy and finance in a government reshuffle in early September 1996; Diabré subsequently became President of the Economic and Social Council. Meanwhile, in late March the Parti pour la démocratie et le progrés (PDP), led by a veteran politician, Joseph Ki-Zerbo, was enlarged to include three other organizations. At the same time the establishment was announced of a Front démocratique burkinabè—an alliance of the PDP, the BSB and the Union des verts pour le développement du Burkina.

In early October 1996 the Government confirmed newspaper reports of the arrest of several members of the presidential security services. It emerged that those detained (numbering about 25) were close associates of Chief Warrant Officer Hyacinthe Kafando, hitherto responsible for the Head of State's security, who had been ordered to return from a period of training in Morocco but who was reportedly seeking asylum at the French embassy in Abidjan, Côte d'Ivoire. Rumours circulated, in particular, of animosity between Kafando and Capt. Gilbert Diendéré, Compaoré's personal Chief of Staff. It was reported that the recent closure of the élite commando training centre from which members of the presidential guard were recruited had been a source of dissatisfaction within the service, and Compaoré's sudden cancellation, in late September, of an official visit to Libya had been attributed to what were termed security difficulties by some observers. Other sources, meanwhile, asserted that the arrests reflected the authorities' desire to restore discipline within the guard prior to the Franco-African summit meeting that was to take place in Ouagadougou in December. The Government denied press speculation that a coup attempt had been foiled, emphasizing that there was no 'political connotation' to the arrests. Representatives of the national human rights organization, the Mouvement burkinabè des droits de l'homme et du peuple (MBDHP), visited the detainees, and subsequently confirmed that two relations of Kafando (one a civilian) were among those arrested. The MBDHP was, meanwhile, informed by Diendéré that Kafando had left the French embassy in Abidjan, and that his whereabouts were unknown.

Constitutional amendments and a new electoral code were approved by the ADP in January 1997: among the changes were an increase in the number of provinces from 30 to 45, the removal of restrictions on the renewal of the Head of State's mandate (hitherto renewable only once), as well as an increase (with effect from the forthcoming elections) in the number of parliamentary seats to 111. The national motto, 'fatherland or death, we shall conquer', was changed to 'unity, progress, justice', and parts of the text of the national anthem were modified. In February the ADP approved proposals for a national commission for the organization of elections. The Government's original proposals, adopted in November 1996, had been severely criticized by the opposition, which objected, in particular, to the fact that the processes of compiling and revising voters' lists remained under the control of the Ministry of Territorial Administration and Security. The new commission was denounced by the opposition as non-independent.

Legislative elections took place on 11 May 1997, at which some 569 candidates from 13 parties contested seats in the enlarged ADP. As expected, the CDP won a resounding victory. The results of voting for four seats, all of which had been won by the CDP, were subsequently annulled by the Supreme Court: these were regained by the party at re-run elections in mid-June. The CDP thus held 101 seats in the ADP. The opposition was represented by the PDP, with six seats, and the Rassemblement démocratique africain, with two. Herman Yaméogo's ADF held two seats. A new Government, under Ouédraogo, was appointed in mid-June. Yaméogo left the Council of Ministers, while Arsène Bognessan Yè was named Minister of State at the Presidency of the Republic. Maurice Mélégué Traoré, hitherto Minister of Secondary and Higher Education and Scientific Research, had been elected President of the ADP earlier in the month. The appointment of a new minister responsible for higher education followed a period of unrest at the University of Ouagadougou in recent months.

In late October 1997 the ADP adopted legislation regarding rights of assembly and public procession. The new law had provoked considerable controversy prior to its adoption, and was denounced by opposition parties and trade unions as a severe curtailment of public freedoms.

Compaoré has, in recent years, gained wide recognition for his efforts as a regional mediator and as a proponent of inter-African conflict-resolution initiatives. In the early 1990s, however, relations with some members of the Economic Community of West African States (ECOWAS) suffered a reverse, owing to the Compaoré Government's apparent support for Charles Taylor's rebel National Patriotic Front of Liberia (NPFL) and Burkina's initial refusal to participate in the military intervention by ECOWAS in Liberia (ECOMOG, see p. 146). In September 1991 Compaoré admitted that some 700 Burkinabè troops had been dispatched to Liberia to assist the NPFL in the overthrow of Samuel Doe's regime in mid-1990. However, his assertion that the country's involvement in Liberia had ended contrasted with reports that Burkina was continuing to assist the NPFL with arms and training facilities. Compaoré's insistence that Burkina would not contribute troops to ECOMOG until that force ceased to play an active part in efforts to suppress the NPFL contributed to a marked deterioration in external relations during the second half of 1992. In November of that year the US Government recalled its ambassador to Burkina, and announced that the recently-appointed Burkinabè ambassador to the USA would not be welcome in Washington, DC, owing to Burkina's alleged role in transporting arms from Libya to the NPFL. Shortly afterwards, however, Compaoré expressed willingness in principle to contribute a military contingent to the ECOWAS force, on condition that ECOMOG be confined to the role of a neutral peace-keeping body. Allegations of Burkinabè support for, and collusion with, the NPFL persisted, but in September 1995 the Compaoré administration, stating that it regarded the peace agreement that had been signed in Abuja, Nigeria, in the previous month as more 'credible' than earlier peace settlements for Liberia, announced that Burkina would contribute troops to ECOMOG. In early February 1997 the ADP approved legislation authorizing the participation of Burkinabè military personnel in the cease-fire monitoring group, in preparation for the forthcoming elections in Liberia.

Burkina's relations with Mali and Niger have, since 1990, to a large extent been dominated by the repercussions for Burkina—principally the inflow of refugees and border insecurity—of the Tuareg rebellions in these two countries. During 1994 Compaoré hosted negotiations between the Nigerien Government and Tuareg leaders, in an attempt to achieve a lasting peace in Niger. In July 1994 the Burkinabè and Malian Governments, in co-operation with the office of the UN High Commissioner for Refugees, reached agreement regarding the repatriation of refugees from Burkina to Mali; however, a subsequent escalation of violence in Mali prompted a new influx of refugees, with the result that at mid-1995 some 50,000 Malian refugees were estimated to be sheltering in Burkina, although the return of peace in Mali was expected to facilitate the repatriation of refugees from Burkina.

Compaoré visited France in June 1993 (his first official visit to that country) and in April 1994, and attended the Franco-African summit meeting in Biarritz, France, in November 1994. Burkina swiftly established close relations with Jacques Chirac following his election to the French presidency in May 1995. Compaoré travelled to meet President Chirac in Yamoussoukro, Côte d'Ivoire, in July of that year, and visited France in November 1995 and June 1996. The 1996 summit meeting of Franco-African Heads of State took place in Ouagadougou in December. Compaoré subsequently participated in a regional mediation effort, conceived at the meeting, to resolve the political crisis in the Central African Republic (CAR). The ADP authorized the dispatch of a Burkinabè military contingent to the surveillance mission for the CAR in February 1997. In October of that year, following the seizure of power by forces of Denis Sassou-Nguesso in the Republic of the Congo, the deposed President Pascal Lissouba was granted asylum in Ouagadougou.

Diplomatic relations with Israel (which had been severed in 1973) were restored in October 1993. Following the re-establishment of diplomatic links with Taiwan (also ended in 1973), in February 1994, that country announced a comprehensive programme of assistance for Burkina. The People's Republic of China severed relations with Burkina shortly afterwards. Recognition of the 'Sahrawi Arab Democratic Republic', accorded by the Sankara regime in 1984, was withdrawn in June 1996.

Government

Under the terms of the Constitution of June 1991, executive power is vested in the President and in the Government, and is counterbalanced by a multi-party legislature, the Assemblée des députés populaires (ADP), and by an independent judiciary. Presidential and legislative elections are conducted by universal adult suffrage, with the President being elected for a seven-year term, renewable only once (see Recent History), and delegates to the ADP being elected for a five-year term. The President is empowered to appoint a Prime Minister; however, the ADP has the right to veto any such appointment. Both the Government and the ADP are competent to initiate legislation. The Constitution also provides for the establishment of a second, consultative chamber—the Chambre des représentants—whose 120 members are to be nominated to serve a three-year term of office.

Burkina is divided into 45 provinces, each of which is administered by a civilian governor.

Defence

National service is voluntary, and lasts for two years on a part-time basis. In August 1997 the active armed forces numbered 10,000 (army 5,600, air force 200, gendarmerie 4,200). Other units include a 'security company' of 250 and a part-time people's militia of 45,000. Defence expenditure for 1997 was budgeted at 39,000m. francs CFA.

Economic Affairs

In 1995, according to estimates by the World Bank, Burkina Faso's gross national product (GNP), measured at average 1993–95 prices, was US $2,417m., equivalent to $230 per head. During 1985–95, it was estimated, GNP per head declined, in real terms, at an average annual rate of 0.1%. Over the same period the population increased by an average of 2.8% per year. During 1985–95 Burkina's gross domestic product (GDP) increased, in real terms, by an annual average of 2.7%. GDP increased by 3.8% in 1995, and by an estimated 6.2% in 1996; the IMF projected growth at 6.6% in 1997.

According to IMF estimates, agriculture (including livestock-rearing, forestry and fishing) contributed 33.2% of GDP in 1995. About 92.4% of the labour force were employed in agriculture in 1996. The principal cash crop is cotton (exports of which, according to IMF calculations, accounted for an estimated 42.2% of the value of total exports in 1995). Smaller amounts of other crops, including shea-nuts (karité nuts) and sesame seed, are also exported. The principal subsistence crops are millet, sorghum and maize. Burkina is almost self-sufficient in basic foodstuffs in non-drought years; a surplus of about 69,000 metric tons of cereals was recorded in 1996/97, although problems of transport and storage were expected to result in deficits in some areas. Livestock-rearing is of considerable significance, contributing 29.3% of export revenue, according to IMF estimates, in 1995. During 1985–95, according to the World Bank, agricultural GDP increased by an annual average of 3.5%. The IMF estimated that agricultural GDP declined by 0.2% in 1994, and by 0.9% in 1995.

Industry (including mining, manufacturing, construction and power) contributed 27.6% of GDP, according to IMF estimates, in 1995, and engaged only 1.5% of the employed labour force in 1991. During 1985–95, according to the World Bank, industrial GDP increased by an annual average of 1.3%. The IMF estimated growth in industrial GDP at 5.8% in 1995.

Although Burkina has considerable mineral resources, extractive activities accounted for 0.6% of GDP in 1992, and engaged only 0.6% of the employed labour force in 1991. However, the development of reserves of gold (exports of which were estimated by the IMF to have contributed 12.1% of the value of total exports in 1995) has since brought about an increase in the sector's economic importance, while there is considerable potential for the exploitation of zinc, manganese and limestone. Antimony and marble are also extracted, and other known mineral reserves include phosphates, silver, lead and nickel. Exploration for diamonds and petroleum is also envisaged.

The manufacturing sector engaged only 1.1% of the employed labour force in 1991, and—together with mining—contributed 21.0% of GDP in 1995, according to IMF estimates. The sector is dominated by the processing of primary products: major activities are cotton-ginning, the production of textiles, food-processing (including milling and sugar-refining), brewing and the processing of hides and skins. Motorcycles and bicycles are also manufactured. Manufacturing GDP declined by an annual average of 5.8% in 1985–95; however, the IMF estimated growth of 6.4% in 1995.

Two hydroelectric stations supplied about one-third of Burkina's electricity output in 1994; the remainder was derived from thermal power stations (using imported fuel). A third hydroelectric scheme is envisaged. There are, moreover, plans to link the Burkinabè electricity network with those of Côte d'Ivoire and Ghana. Imports of fuel and energy comprised an estimated 9.4% of the value of merchandise imports in 1995, according to the World Bank.

The services sector contributed 39.2% of GDP in 1995, according to IMF estimates, and engaged 5.4% of the employed labour force in 1991. During 1985–95, according to World Bank figures, the GDP of the services sector increased by an annual average of 2.9%. The IMF estimated growth in services GDP of 6.2% in 1995.

In 1994 Burkina recorded a visible trade deficit of US $128.7m., while there was a surplus of $14.9m. on the current account of the balance of payments. In 1991 the principal sources of imports were France (24.4%) and Côte d'Ivoire (19.4%). The principal markets for exports in that year were Switzerland (20.3%) and France (13.4%); other important purchasers were Côte d'Ivoire, Italy, Portugal, Thailand and Taiwan. The principal exports in 1991 were ginned cotton, livestock and livestock products (including hides and skins) and unworked gold. In the same year the principal imports were miscellaneous manufactured articles, machinery and transport equipment, food products (notably cereals), chemicals and refined petroleum products.

In 1995 Burkina recorded an overall budget deficit of 41,200m. francs CFA, equivalent to an estimated 3.5% of GDP. Burkina's total external debt was US $1,267m. at the end of 1995, of which $1,136m. was long-term public debt. In that year the cost of debt-servicing was equivalent to 13.2% of the value of exports of goods and services. Consumer prices declined by an annual average of 0.2% in 1985–93. Inflation averaged 24.6% in 1994, following the devaluation of the CFA franc, but the rate slowed to 7.9% in 1995 and to 6.1% in 1996. Some 26,600 people were registered as unemployed in 1994.

Burkina is a member of numerous regional organizations, including the Economic Community of West African States (ECOWAS, see p. 145), the West African organs of the Franc Zone (see p. 181), the Conseil de l'Entente (see p. 260) and the Liptako–Gourma Integrated Development Authority (see p. 262).

The 50% devaluation, in January 1994, of the CFA franc was of immediate benefit to the 'traditional' sectors of Burkina's economy (above all stimulating exports of cotton and of livestock and livestock products), while increased revenue from sales of gold offset a decline in actual output. Unfavourable weather restricted economic expansion in 1994, but strong growth in overall GDP was achieved in 1995–97. Objectives for 1997–98, agreed under the terms of the Enhanced Structural Adjustment Facility granted by the IMF in mid-1996, include average annual growth of some 6% and the containment of annual inflation at 3%. Small primary budget surpluses (projected at the equivalent of 1.9% of GDP in 1997) are to be achieved by means of fiscal reforms (including reductions in exemptions and an increase, from September 1996, in the rate of value-added tax from 15% to 18%), in conjunction with continued restraint on public spending. There was to be a continuation of the liberalization measures that have characterized Burkina's economic orientation under Compaoré, with particular emphasis on accelerated privatization, the elimination of monopolies and the fostering of foreign investment, notably (in large part through a new mining code adopted in mid-1997) in the industrial mining sector. Pressure on the balance of payments was relieved by a series of debt-relief measures by external creditors, and in mid-1997 Burkina was deemed by the IMF and the World Bank to be eligible for special measures of debt reduction under the new Heavily Indebted Poor Countries initiative. Moreover, the elimination of all external and most internal debt arrears after 1995 allowed the use of funds from the state budget for investment purposes. A priority for the late 1990s was to be to address serious inadequacies in the provision of basic education, health care and social welfare, and to arrest the decline in GDP per head. Furthermore, the country's land-locked position, poor infrastructure and narrow manufacturing base may continue to present considerable obstacles to sustained growth.

Social Welfare

The Government provides hospitals and rural medical services. In 1990 there were 314 physicians, 325 midwives, 19 dentists and 112 pharmacists; there were 2,003 nurses in 1988. In 1987 there were 11 hospitals and 59 health centres. Old-age and veterans' pensions are provided by the State, and workers' insurance schemes are also in operation. Of total planned budgetary expenditure by the central Government in 1990, 7,963m. francs CFA (7.2%) was for health, and a further 130m. francs CFA (0.1%) was for social security and welfare. Further payments (3,168m. francs CFA in 1985) are made from social security funds.

Education

Education is provided free of charge, and is officially compulsory for six years between the ages of seven and 14. Primary education begins at seven years of age and lasts for six years. Secondary education, beginning at the age of 13, lasts for a further seven years, comprising a first cycle of four years and a second of three years. In 1993 primary enrolment included only 32% of children in the relevant age-group (males 39%; females 25%). Secondary education in that year included only 7% of children in the appropriate age-group (males 10%; females 5%). The Government aimed to increase the overall rate of school enrolment to 60% by 2005, compared with 25% in 1993. There is a university in Ouagadougou; the number of students enrolled at university-level institutions in 1992/93 was 8,276, compared with 1,520 in 1980/81. Private education has increased in importance since the late 1980s, and in mid-1992 a government department was established with responsibility for this sector. In 1995, according to UNESCO estimates, adult illiteracy averaged 80.8% (males 70.5%; females 90.8%). Expenditure on education by the central Government in 1994 totalled 36,315m. francs CFA, representing 11.1% of total government spending in that year.

Public Holidays

1998: 1 January (New Year's Day), 30 January* (Aid es Segheir, end of Ramadan), 8 March (International Women's Day), 8 April* (Aid el Kebir—Tabaski, Feast of the Sacrifice), 13 April (Easter Monday), 1 May (Labour Day), 21 May (Ascension Day), 7 July* (Mouloud, Birth of the Prophet), 3 August (for National Day), 15 August (Assumption), 15 October (Anniversary of the 1987 *coup d'état*), 1 November (All Saints' Day), 11 December (Proclamation of the Republic), 25 December (Christmas).

1999: 1 January (New Year's Day), 19 January* (Aid es Segheir, end of Ramadan), 8 March (International Women's Day), 28 March* (Aid el Kebir—Tabaski, Feast of the Sacrifice), 5 April (Easter Monday), 1 May (Labour Day), 13 May (Ascension Day), 26 June* (Mouloud, Birth of the Prophet), 4 August (National Day), 15 August (Assumption), 15 October (Anniversary of the 1987 *coup d'état*), 1 November (All Saints' Day), 11 December (Proclamation of the Republic), 25 December (Christmas).

* These holidays are dependent on the Islamic lunar calendar and may vary by one or two days from the dates given.

Weights and Measures

The metric system is in force.

Statistical Survey

Source (except where otherwise stated): Institut National de la Statistique et de la Démographie, BP 374, Ouagadougou; tel. 33-55-37.

Area and Population

AREA, POPULATION AND DENSITY

Area (sq km)	274,200*
Population (census results)	
1–7 December 1975	5,638,203
10–20 December 1985	
Males	3,833,237
Females	4,131,468
Total	7,964,705
Population (official estimates at mid-year)	
1992	9,433,428
1993	9,682,470
1995†	10,200,453
Density (per sq km) at mid-1995	37.2

* 105,870 sq miles.

† An official estimate for mid-1994 is not available.

POPULATION BY PROVINCE (at 1985 census)

Province	Population	Capital
Bam	162,575	Kongoussi
Bazèga	303,941	Kombissiri
Bougouriba	220,895	Diébougou
Boulougou	402,236	Tenkodogo
Boulkiemdé	365,223	Koudougou
Comoé	249,967	Banfora
Ganzourgou	195,452	Zorgo
Gnagna	229,152	Bogandé
Gourma	294,235	Fada-Ngourma
Houet	581,722	Bobo-Dioulasso
Kadiogo	459,826	Ouagadougou
Kénédougou	139,973	Orodara
Kossi	332,960	Nounga
Kouritenga	198,486	Koupéla
Mouhoun	288,735	Dédougou
Nahouri	105,509	Pô
Namentenga	198,890	Boulsa
Oubritenga	304,265	Ziniaré
Oudalan	106,194	Gorom-Gorom

Province	Population	Capital
Passoré	223,830	Yako
Poni	235,480	Gaoua
Sangouié	217,277	Réo
Sanmatenga	367,724	Kaya
Séno	228,875	Dori
Sissili	244,919	Léo
Soum	186,812	Djibo
Sourou	268,108	Tougan
Tapoa	158,859	Diapaga
Yatenga	536,578	Ouahigouya
Zoundwéogo	156,007	Manga
Total	7,964,705	

Sources: UN, *Demographic Yearbook*; Secrétariat du Comité de la Zone Franc *La Zone Franc—Rapport 1994*.

Note: In early 1997 the number of provinces was increased from 30 to 45.

PRINCIPAL TOWNS (population at 1985 census)

Ouagadougou (capital)	441,514	Ouahigouya	38,902
Bobo-Dioulasso	228,668	Banfora	35,319
Koudougou	51,926	Kaya	25,814

1991 (official estimates at mid-year): Ouagadougou 634,479; Bobo-Dioulasso 268,926.

BIRTHS AND DEATHS (UN estimates, annual averages)

	1980–85	1985–90	1990–95
Birth rate (per 1,000)	47.2	47.1	46.8
Death rate (per 1,000)	19.8	18.6	18.2

Expectation of life (UN estimates, years at birth, 1990–95): 47.4 (males 45.8; females 49.0).

Source: UN, *World Population Prospects: The 1994 Revision*.

ECONOMICALLY ACTIVE POPULATION
(sample survey, persons aged 10 years and over, 1991)

	Males	Females	Total
Agriculture, hunting, forestry and fishing	2,162,759	2,131,025	4,293,784
Mining and quarrying	2,286	304	2,590
Manufacturing	26,996	24,698	51,694
Electricity, gas and water	3,038	806	3,844
Construction	10,988	28	11,016
Trade, restaurants and hotels	48,117	72,197	120,314
Transport, storage and communications	14,620	421	15,041
Finance, insurance, real estate and business services	1,650	425	2,075
Community, social and personal services	84,136	27,420	111,556
Activities not adequately defined	8,355	9,105	17,460
Total employed	2,362,945	2,266,429	4,629,374
Unemployed	38,515	11,304	49,819
Total labour force	2,401,460	2,277,733	4,679,193

Source: ILO, *Yearbook of Labour Statistics*.

Mid-1995 (estimates in '000): Agriculture, etc. 5,197; Total 5,622 (Source: FAO, *Production Yearbook*).

Agriculture

PRINCIPAL CROPS ('000 metric tons)

	1994	1995	1996
Maize	350	212	222*
Millet	831	734	785*
Sorghum	1,232	1,266	1,514*
Rice (paddy)	61	84	124†
Sweet potatoes	11	20†	20†
Yams	38	40†	40†
Other roots and tubers	10	10†	10†
Vegetables†	254	254	254
Fruit†	73	73	73
Pulses	72	62†	62†
Groundnuts (in shell)	203	213*	213†
Cottonseed†	110	105	105
Cotton (lint)	67	70†	70†
Sesame seed	2	6†	6†
Tobacco (leaves)†	1	1	1
Sugar cane†	400	400	400

* Unofficial figure. † FAO estimate(s).

Source: FAO, *Production Yearbook*.

LIVESTOCK ('000 head, year ending September)

	1994	1995*	1996*
Cattle	4,261	4,350	4,350
Sheep	5,686	5,800	5,800
Goats	7,242†	7,300	7,300
Pigs	551	560	560
Horses	23†	23	23
Asses	445†	455	455
Camels*	13†	12	12

Poultry (million): 19 in 1994; 19* in 1995; 19 in 1996.

* FAO estimate(s). † Unofficial figure.

Source: FAO, *Production Yearbook*.

LIVESTOCK PRODUCTS (FAO estimates, '000 metric tons)

	1994	1995	1996
Beef and veal	40	40	40
Mutton and lamb	11	11	11
Goat meat	19	20	20
Pig meat	6	6	6
Poultry meat	20	21	21
Other meat	9	9	9
Cows' milk	121	121	121
Goats' milk	21	21	21
Butter	1	1	1
Hen eggs	17	17	17
Cattle hides	6	7	7
Sheepskins	3	3	3
Goatskins	5	5	5

Source: FAO, *Production Yearbook*.

Forestry

ROUNDWOOD REMOVALS
(FAO estimates, '000 cubic metres, excluding bark)

	1992	1993	1994
Sawlogs, veneer logs and logs for sleepers*	1	1	1
Other industrial wood	417	428	440
Fuel wood	8,823	9,075	9,330
Total	9,241	9,504	9,771

* Estimated to be unchanged since 1985.

Source: FAO, *Yearbook of Forest Products*.

Fishing

('000 metric tons, live weight)

	1993	1994	1995
Total catch	7.0	8.0	8.0

Source: FAO, *Yearbook of Fishery Statistics*.

Mining

(mineral content of ore, metric tons)

	1994	1995	1996
Gold	3.0	2.7	2.5

Source: Gold Fields Mineral Services Ltd, *Gold 1997*.

Industry

SELECTED PRODUCTS

	1993	1994	1995
Edible oils (metric tons)	8,906	6,412	4,286
Shea (karité) butter (metric tons)	1,758	574	296
Flour (metric tons)	27,555	26,235	31,046
Pasta (metric tons)	1,175	633	788
Sugar (metric tons)	34,955	54,824	47,107
Beer ('000 hl)	334	287	172
Soft drinks ('000 hl)	106	86	115
Cigarettes (million packets)	47	44	47
Printed fabric ('000 sq metres)	4,618	5,957	5,297
Soap (metric tons)	14,056	6,526	5,787
Matches (cartons)	14,587	n.a.	n.a.
Bicycles (units)	24,464	18,321	11,150
Mopeds (units)	12,857	5,423	8,673
Tyres ('000)	294	23	1,738
Inner tubes ('000)	1,924	165	2,660
Electric energy ('000 kWh)	215,517	216,006	n.a.

Source: IMF, *Burkina Faso—Statistical Tables* (March 1997).

Finance

CURRENCY AND EXCHANGE RATES

Monetary Units

100 centimes = 1 franc de la Communauté financière africaine (CFA).

French Franc, Sterling and Dollar Equivalents (30 September 1997)

1 French franc = 100 francs CFA;
£1 sterling = 958.3 francs CFA;
US $1 = 593.2 francs CFA;
1,000 francs CFA = £1.044 = $1.686

Average Exchange Rate (francs CFA per US $)

1994 555.20
1995 499.15
1996 511.55

Note: An exchange rate of 1 French franc = 50 francs CFA, established in 1948, remained in force until January 1994, when the CFA franc was devalued by 50%, with the exchange rate adjusted to 1 French franc = 100 francs CFA.

BUDGET ('000 million francs CFA)

Revenue	1993	1994	1995
Current revenue	99.4	113.3	138.5
Tax revenue	72.6	104.0	127.8
Income and profits	18.9	21.2	29.7
Domestic goods and services	14.8	19.4	23.3
International trade	36.4	61.2	71.9
Other tax revenue	2.5	2.1	2.9
Other current revenue	26.8	9.4	10.7
Capital revenue	0.6	—	—
Total	100.0	113.3	138.5

Expenditure and net lending	1993	1994	1995
Domestic expenditure and net lending	124.6	137.2	140.6
Wages and salaries	52.2	58.2	61.6
Goods and services	19.3	26.6	24.8
Interest payments	12.4	15.0	16.4
Current transfers	34.3	31.2	29.1
Other current expenditure	—	—	9.7
Budgetary contribution to investment	8.8	9.2	11.6
Net lending*	−2.5	−3.0	−3.0
Foreign-financed government investment	54.6	62.5	97.5
On-lending	0.9	—	—
Restructuring operations	2.2	27.3	7.6
Total	182.4	227.0	245.8

* Including proceeds from privatization, which are excluded from revenue and are treated as a deduction from expenditure.

Source: IMF, *Burkina Faso—Statistical Tables* (March 1997).

INTERNATIONAL RESERVES (US $ million at 31 December)

	1994	1995	1996
Gold*	4.1	4.3	4.2
IMF special drawing rights	8.1	8.2	2.6
Reserve position in IMF	10.5	10.7	10.4
Foreign exchange	218.6	328.4	325.6
Total	241.3	351.7	342.8

* Valued at market-related prices.

Source: IMF, *International Financial Statistics*.

MONEY SUPPLY ('000 million francs CFA at 31 December)

	1994	1995	1996
Currency outside banks	94.90	123.49	139.65
Demand deposits at deposit money banks*	69.84	81.54	80.24
Checking deposits at post office	2.37	2.68	2.71
Total money (incl. others)	170.32	213.70	228.73

* Excluding the deposits of public establishments of an administrative or social nature.

Source: IMF, *International Financial Statistics*.

COST OF LIVING (Consumer Price Index for African households in Ouagadougou; base: 1990 = 100)

	1994	1995	1996
Food	112.6	125.9	145.3
All items	126.0	135.9	144.2

Source: UN, *Monthly Bulletin of Statistics*.

NATIONAL ACCOUNTS
(estimates, '000 million francs CFA at current prices)

Expenditure on the Gross Domestic Product

	1993	1994	1995
Government final consumption expenditure	121.0	160.2	165.1
Private final consumption expenditure	635.2	806.0	916.4
Increase in stocks	8.4	–18.3	–20.6
Gross fixed capital formation	149.0	216.5	279.1
Total domestic expenditure	913.7	1,164.5	1,340.0
Exports of goods and services	92.2	135.6	155.6
Less Imports of goods and services	209.8	270.7	332.6
GDP in purchasers' values	796.1	1,029.4	1,163.0
GDP at constant 1985 prices	814.7	824.5	856.4

Gross Domestic Product by Economic Activity

	1993	1994	1995
Agriculture, livestock, forestry and fishing	270.2	335.0	367.1
Mining and manufacturing	120.2	198.3	232.3
Electricity, gas and water	7.4	9.0	10.6
Construction and public works	42.4	55.7	62.4
Trade	102.8	122.7	140.4
Transport	33.5	39.0	44.7
Non-marketable services	93.1	102.7	112.1
Other services	102.6	119.0	136.1
Sub-total	774.0*	981.5	1,105.8
Import taxes and duties	32.9	58.7	68.0
Less Imputed bank service charge	–10.8	–10.8	–10.8
GDP in purchasers' values	796.1	1,029.4	1,163.0

* Including adjustment.

Source: IMF, *Burkina Faso—Statistical Tables* (March 1997).

BALANCE OF PAYMENTS (US $ million)

	1992	1993	1994
Exports of goods f.o.b.	237.2	226.1	215.6
Imports of goods f.o.b.	–458.9	–469.1	–344.3
Trade balance	–221.7	–243.0	–128.7
Exports of services	64.5	64.6	56.3
Imports of services	–207.7	–209.0	–138.3
Balance on goods and services	–364.9	–387.4	–210.7
Other income received	21.7	21.5	8.7
Other income paid	–19.1	–28.6	–38.1
Balance on goods, services and income	–362.3	–394.5	–240.1
Current transfers received	419.2	389.6	308.0
Current transfers paid	–79.9	–66.3	–53.0
Current balance	–23.0	–71.1	14.9
Investment assets	–45.2	24.2	–139.2
Investment liabilities	79.9	44.9	125.3
Net errors and omissions	8.3	4.6	–8.3
Overall balance	20.0	2.5	–7.3

Source: IMF, *International Financial Statistics*.

External Trade

Source: Banque centrale des états de l'Afrique de l'ouest.

PRINCIPAL COMMODITIES (million francs CFA)

Imports c.i.f.	1989	1990	1991
Food products	29,222	26,522	29,186
Food products of animal origin	4,810	5,928	6,218
Dairy products	3,326	4,743	5,155
Food products of plant origin	20,402	15,534	18,730
Cereals	15,413	9,375	10,832
Processed foodstuffs	4,010	5,060	4,238
Beverages and tobacco	2,775	2,911	3,251
Refined petroleum products	10,801	16,344	17,383
Other raw materials (inedible)	2,744	3,104	2,841
Oils and fats	1,253	2,115	3,199
Machinery and transport equipment	32,178	35,166	31,321
Non-electrical machinery	13,569	13,220	12,506
Electrical machinery	6,653	9,017	7,972
Road transport equipment	11,549	12,554	10,799
Other industrial products	46,379	59,671	63,073
Chemical products	15,252	20,912	27,779
Miscellaneous manufactured articles	31,127	38,759	35,294
Hydraulic cement	5,877	7,461	6,560
Total (incl. others)	125,352	145,833	150,255

Exports f.o.b.	1989	1990	1991
Food products	3,072	3,766	3,826
Food products of animal origin	1,681	2,738	2,993
Cattle, beef and veal	1,142	1,938	2,147
Food products of plant origin	812	855	667
Vegetables	519	654	519
Other raw materials (inedible)	17,727	27,437	20,792
Shea-nuts (karité nuts)	111	630	158
Hides and skins	2,809	3,071	1,449
Cotton (ginned)	14,356	23,415	18,754
Machinery and transport equipment	1,048	325	286
Other industrial products	8,301	9,586	4,487
Miscellaneous manufactured articles	8,236	9,539	4,455
Unworked gold	6,893	8,104	2,452
Total (incl. others)	30,269	41,282	29,892

PRINCIPAL TRADING PARTNERS (million francs CFA)

Imports	1989	1990	1991
Belgium-Luxembourg	1,969	2,728	3,305
Cameroon	416	1,392	931
Canada	968	1,975	1,405
Denmark	747	1,449	1,236
China, People's Repub.	1,482	1,320	2,298
Côte d'Ivoire	18,209	23,971	29,130
France	36,145	40,099	36,644
Germany, Fed. Repub.	5,933	6,949	6,020
Italy	5,312	5,057	3,970
Japan	5,931	6,181	6,334
Netherlands	4,314	4,949	4,100
Nigeria	1,839	3,252	4,157
Senegal	1,445	3,172	2,444
Spain	2,273	1,729	1,987
Taiwan	1,414	1,575	3,823
Thailand	11,595	2,561	3,455
Togo	3,611	4,816	3,943
United Kingdom	2,929	2,652	2,584
USA	5,649	9,198	7,395
Total (incl. others)	125,352	145,833	150,255

Exports	1989	1990	1991
Belgium-Luxembourg	1,555	623	115
China, People's Repub.	342	3,218	808
Côte d'Ivoire	3,797	4,676	3,351
Denmark	351	246	150
France	8,848	9,535	4,107
Germany, Fed. Repub.	671	19	173
Italy	1,783	3,136	3,007
Japan	483	542	551
Mali	235	232	366
Nigeria	5	391	425
Portugal	836	1,624	2,793
Spain	986	1,008	455
Switzerland	161	4,392	6,067
Taiwan	5,112	3,113	1,845
Thailand	—	1,891	2,495
Togo	1,846	1,283	853
Tunisia	87	1,986	—
United Kingdom	375	935	104
Total (incl. others)	30,269	41,282	29,892

Transport

RAILWAYS (traffic)

	1991	1992	1993
Passenger-km (million)	340	360	403
Freight ton-km (million)	177	184	180

Source: UN Economic Commission for Africa, *African Statistical Yearbook*.

ROAD TRAFFIC (motor vehicles in use)

	1993	1994	1995
Passenger cars	29,855	32,224	35,460
Buses and coaches	1,760	1,939	2,237
Lorries and vans	13,945	14,439	14,985
Road tractors	1,977	2,087	2,251
Motor cycles and mopeds	93,150	97,900	100,591

Source: IRF, *World Road Statistics*.

CIVIL AVIATION (traffic on scheduled services)*

	1992	1993	1994
Kilometres flown (million)	3	3	3
Passengers carried ('000)	127	128	130
Passenger-km (million)	233	239	247
Total ton-km (million)	37	37	37

* Including an apportionment of the traffic of Air Afrique.

Source: UN, *Statistical Yearbook*.

Tourism

	1991	1992	1993
Tourist arrivals	110,327	128,107	154,937
Tourist receipts (million francs CFA)	6,208	8,650	8,895

Source: Direction de l'Administration Touristique et Hôtelière, Ouagadougou.

Communications Media

	1992	1993	1994
Radio receivers ('000 in use)	255	265	280
Television receivers ('000 in use)	50	54	55
Telephones ('000 main lines in use)	20	22	26
Daily newspapers			
Number	1	n.a.	1
Average circulation ('000 copies)	3	n.a.	3

Non-daily newspapers (1990): 10; average circulation 14,000 copies.

Book production (1985): 9 titles.

Sources: UNESCO, *Statistical Yearbook*; UN, *Statistical Yearbook*.

Education

(1993/94, unless otherwise indicated)

	Institutions	Teachers	Students: Males	Students: Females	Students: Total
Pre-primary*	95	259†	3,744	3,911	7,655
Primary	2,971	10,300	366,226	233,806	600,032
Secondary					
General	n.a.	3,346	76,482	39,551	116,033
Vocational	n.a.	639	4,473	4,335	8,808
Teacher training‡	n.a.	n.a.	220	130	350
Tertiary	n.a.	571	6,684	2,131	8,815

* 1989/90 figures.

† State education only.

‡ 1992/93 estimates.

Source: UNESCO, *Statistical Yearbook*.

Directory

The Constitution

The present Constitution was approved in a national referendum on 2 June 1991, and was formally adopted on 11 June. The following are its main provisions:

The Constitution of the 'revolutionary, democratic, unitary and secular' Fourth Republic of Burkina Faso guarantees the collective and individual political and social rights of Burkinabè citizens, and delineates the powers of the executive, legislature and judiciary.

Executive power is vested in the President, who is Head of State, and in the Government, which is appointed by the President upon the recommendation of the Prime Minister. The President is elected, by universal suffrage, for a seven-year term; as amended in January 1997, there are no restrictions on the renewal of the presidential mandate.

Legislative power is exercised by the multi-party Assemblée des députés populaires (ADP). Delegates to the ADP are elected, by universal suffrage, for a five-year term. An increase in the number of deputies, from 107 to 111, was provided for by constitutional amendment in January 1997. The President is empowered to appoint a Prime Minister; however, the ADP has the right to veto any such appointment. Provision is also made for the creation of a second, consultative chamber: the Chambre des représentants is to comprise 120 members, nominated for a three-year term of office.

Both the Government and the ADP may initiate legislation.

The judiciary is independent. Judges are to be accountable to a Higher Council, under the chairmanship of the Head of State.

The Constitution denies legitimacy to any regime that might take power as the result of a *coup d'état*.

The Government

HEAD OF STATE

President: BLAISE COMPAORÉ (assumed power as Chairman of the Front populaire 15 October 1987; elected President 1 December 1991).

COUNCIL OF MINISTERS
(December 1997)

President: BLAISE COMPAORÉ.

Prime Minister and Minister of the Economy and Finance: KADRÉ DÉSIRÉ OUÉDRAOGO.

Minister of State, with responsibility for the Environment and Water Resources: SALIF DIALLO.

Minister of State at the Presidency of the Republic: ARSÈNE BOGESSAN YÈ.

Minister of the Economy and Finance, Spokesperson for the Government: TERTIUS ZONGO.

Minister of External Relations: ABLASSE OUÉDRAOGO.

Minister of Defence: ALBERT D. MILOGO.

Minister of Justice and Keeper of the Seals: YARGA LARBA.

Minister of Territorial Administration and Security: YERO BOLI.

Minister of Trade, Industry and Crafts: IDRISSA ZAMPALIGRÉ KAFANDO.

Minister of Energy and Mines: ELIE OUÉDRAOGO.

Minister of Secondary and Higher Education and Scientific Research: CHRISTOPHE DABIRÉ.

Minister of Primary Education and Mass Literacy: SEYDOU BAWORO SANOU.

Minister of Public Works, Housing and Town Planning: JOSEPH KABORÉ.

Minister of the Civil Service and Administrative Modernization: JULIETTE BONKOUNGOU.

Minister of Employment, Labour and Social Security: ELIE SARE.

Minister of Agriculture: MICHEL KOUTABA.

Minister of Regional Integration: VIVIANE YOLANDE COMPAORÉ.

Minister with responsibility for Relations with Parliament: CYRIL GOUNGOUNGA.

Minister of Communications and Culture: MAHAMADOU OUÉDRAOGO.

Minister of Health: LUDOVIC ALAN TOU.

Minister of Youth and Sports: JOSEPH ANDRÉ TIENDRÉBÉOGO.

Minister of Transport and Tourism: BEDOUMA ALAIN YODA.

Minister of Social Welfare and the Family: BANA OUANDAOGO.

Minister of Animal Resources: ALASSANE SERE.

Minister of Women's Promotion: ALICE TIENDRÉBÉOGO.

There are, in addition, ministers-delegate responsible for the Budget, Finance, Water Resources, Housing and Town Planning and Employment Promotion.

MINISTRIES

Office of the President: Ouagadougou.

Office of the Prime Minister: Ouagadougou.

Ministry of Agriculture and Animal Resources: BP 7005, Ouagadougou.

Ministry of the Civil Service and Administrative Modernization: Ouagadougou.

Ministry of Communications and Culture: 01 BP 2507, Ouagadougou 01; tel. 30-70-52; telex 5237; fax 30-70-56.

Ministry of Defence: BP 496, Ouagadougou; telex 5297.

Ministry of the Economy and Finance: 01 BP 6444, Ouagadougou 01; tel. 30-67-21; fax 31-23-04.

Ministry of Employment, Labour and Social Security: BP 7006, Ouagadougou.

Ministry of Energy and Mines: Ouagadougou.

Ministry of the Environment and Water Resources: BP 7044, Ouagadougou; tel. 33-41-65; telex 5555.

Ministry of External Relations: BP 7038, Ouagadougou; telex 5222.

Ministry of Health: Ouagadougou; tel. 33-28-68; telex 5555.

Ministry of Justice: BP 526, Ouagadougou.

Ministry of Primary Education and Mass Literacy: 01 BP 1179, Ouagadougou 01; tel. 30-12-94.

Ministry of Public Works, Housing and Town Planning: Ouagadougou; tel. 31-53-84; fax 31-53-83.

Ministry of Regional Integration: Ouagadougou.

Ministry of Secondary and Higher Education and Scientific Research: 03 BP 7130, Ouagadougou 03; tel. 31-29-11; telex 5555; fax 31-41-41.

Ministry of Social Welfare and the Family: c/o World Bank Resident Mission, BP 622, Ouagadougou; tel. 30-62-37; telex 5265; fax 30-86-49.

Ministry of Territorial Administration and Security: BP 7034, Ouagadougou.

Ministry of Trade, Industry and Crafts: BP 365, Ouagadougou.

Ministry of Transport and Tourism: BP 177, Ouagadougou.

Ministry of Women's Promotion: Ouagadougou.

Ministry of Youth and Sports: BP 7035, Ouagadougou.

Legislature

ASSEMBLÉE DES DÉPUTÉS POPULAIRES

President: MAURICE MÉLÉGUÉ TRAORÉ.

General Election, 11 May 1997

Party	Seats
Congrès pour la démocratie et le progrès	97
Parti pour la démocratie et le progrès	6
Alliance pour la démocratie et la fédération	2
Rassemblement démocratique africain	2
Total	107*

* Results of voting in four constituencies were cancelled by the Supreme Court. All four seats were won by the CDP at a further round of voting on 18 June.

CHAMBRE DES REPRÉSENTANTS

The 1991 Constitution provides for the establishment of a second chamber, with advisory functions, whose 120 members are to be nominated for a three-year term.

Advisory Council

Conseil Economique et Social: 01 BP 6162, Ouagadougou 01; tel. 32-40-90; fax 31-06-54; f. 1985 as Conseil Révolutionnaire Economique et Social, present name adopted in 1992; 90 mems; Pres. ZÉPHIRIN DIABRÉ.

Political Organizations

The 1997 legislative elections were contested by 13 of the country's 46 registered political organizations. The following parties secured parliamentary representation:

Alliance pour la démocratie et la fédération (ADF): 01 BP 2061 Ouagadougou 01; tel. 31-15-15; f. 1990; mem. of presidential 'group'; Leader HERMAN YAMÉOGO.

Congrès pour la démocratie et le progrès (CDP): f. 1996, by merger of more than 10 parties, to succeed the Organisation pour la démocratie populaire/Mouvement du travail as the prin. political org. supporting Pres. Compaoré; social-democratic; Pres. Dr ARSÈNE BOGNESSAN YÈ; First Vice-Pres. ROCH MARC CHRISTIAN KABORÉ.

Parti pour la démocratie et le progrès (PDP): f. 1993, expanded in 1996 to include three other parties; Pres. JOSEPH KI-ZERBO.

Rassemblement démocratique africain (RDA): pre-independence party; Leader GÉRARD KANGO OUÉDRAOGO.

Diplomatic Representation

EMBASSIES IN BURKINA FASO

Algeria: BP 3893, Ouagadougou; telex 5359.

China (Taiwan): 01 BP 5563, Ouagadougou 01; tel. 31-61-95.

Cuba: BP 3422, Ouagadougou; telex 5360; Ambassador: REME REMIGIO RUIZ.

Denmark: rue Agostino Neto, 01 BP 1760, Ouagadougou 01; tel. 31-31-92; telex 5230; fax 31-31-89; Chargé d'affaires: HANS HENRIK LILJEBORG.

Egypt: Ouagadougou; telex 5289; Ambassador: Dr MOHAMAD ALEY EL-KORDY.

France: 902 ave de l'Indépendance, 01 BP 504, Ouagadougou 01; tel. 30-67-70; telex 5211; Ambassador: FRANÇOIS COUSIN.

Germany: 01 BP 600, Ouagadougou 01; tel. 30-67-31; telex 5217; fax 31-39-91; Ambassador: DORETTA LOSCHELDER.

Ghana: 01 BP 212, Ouagadougou 01; tel. 30-76-35; Ambassador: (vacant).

Libya: BP 1601, Ouagadougou; telex 5311; Secretary of People's Bureau: (vacant).

Netherlands: 415 ave du Dr Kwamé N'Krumah, 01 BP 1302, Ouagadougou 01; tel. 30-61-34; telex 5303; fax 30-76-95; Ambassador: BEATRIX E. A. AMBAGS.

Nigeria: BP 132, Ouagadougou; tel. 33-42-41; telex 5236; Chargé d'affaires a.i.: A. K. ALLI ASSAYOUTI.

USA: 01 BP 35, Ouagadougou 01; tel. 30-67-23; telex 5290; fax 31-23-68; Ambassador: SHARON P. WILKINSON.

Judicial System

The Constitution of 2 June 1991 provides for the independence of the judiciary. Judges are to be accountable to a Higher Council, under the chairmanship of the President of the Republic.

Religion

More than 50% of the population follow animist beliefs.

ISLAM

At 31 December 1986 there were an estimated 2,514,261 Muslims in Burkina Faso.

CHRISTIANITY

The Roman Catholic Church

Burkina comprises one archdiocese and eight dioceses. At 31 December 1995 there were an estimated 1,053,000 adherents.

Bishops' Conference: Conférence des Evêques de Burkina Faso et du Niger, BP 1195, Ouagadougou; tel. 30-60-26; f. 1966, legally recognized 1978; Pres. Rt Rev. JEAN-NAPTISTE SOMÉ, Bishop of Diébougou.

Archbishop of Ouagadougou: Most Rev. JEAN-MARIE UNTAANI COMPAORÉ, 01 BP 1472, Ouagadougou 01; tel. 30-67-04; fax 30-72-75.

Protestant Churches

At 31 December 1986 there were an estimated 106,467 adherents.

The Press

Direction de la presse écrite: Ouagadougou; govt body responsible for press direction.

DAILIES

Le Journal du Soir: Ouagadougou; Dir ISSA TAPSOBA.

Observateur Paalga (New Observer): 01 BP 584, Ouagadougou 01; tel. 33-27-05; fax 31-45-79; f. 1974; Dir EDOUARD OUÉDRAOGO; circ. 8,000.

Le Pays: 01 BP 4577, Ouagadougou 01; tel. 31-35-46; fax 31-45-50; f. 1991; Dir SIGUÉ JÉRÉMIE BOUREIMA; circ. 4,000.

Sidwaya (Truth): 5 rue du Marché, 01 BP 507, Ouagadougou 01; tel. and fax 31-03-62; f. 1984; state-owned; Mossi; Editor-in-Chief ISSAKA SOURWEMA; circ. 3,000.

PERIODICALS

Bendré: Ouagadougou; weekly; Dir CHERIFF SY.

Le Berger: Zone commerciale, ave Binger, BP 2581, Bobo-Dioulasso; f. 1992; weekly; Dir KOULIGA BLAISE YAMÉOGO.

Bulletin de l'Agence d'Information du Burkina: 01 BP 2507, Ouagadougou 01; tel. 30-70-52; telex 5327; fax 30-70-56; 2 a week; Editor-in-Chief JAMES DABIRÉ; circ. 200.

La Clef: 01 BP 6113, Ouagadougou 01; tel. 31-38-27; f. 1992; weekly; Dir KY SATURNIN; circ. 3,000.

L'Indépendant: Ouagadougou; weekly; Dir NORBERT ZONGO.

L'Intrus: 01 BP 2009, Ouagadougou 01; f. 1985; weekly; satirical; Dir JEAN HUBERT BAZIÉ; circ. 3,000.

Le Journal du Jeudi: 01 BP 3654, Ouagadougou 01; tel. 31-41-08; fax 31-17-12; f. 1991; weekly; Dir BOUBACAR DIALLO; circ. 8,000.

Le Matin: Bobo-Dioulasso; tel. 97-16-93; f. 1992; weekly; Dir DOFINITA FLAURENT BONZI.

Nekr Wagati: Ouagadougou; six a year; Dir SIMON COMPAORÉ.

La Nouvelle Tribune: Ouagadougou; weekly; Dir KYALBABOUÉ BAYILI.

L'Ouragan: Ouagadougou; weekly; Dir LOHÉ ISSA KONATÉ.

Regard: Ouagadougou; weekly; Dir CHRIS VALÉA.

Sidwaya Magazine: 5 rue du Marché, 01 BP 507, Ouagadougou 01; state-owned; Mossi; monthly; Editor-in-Chief BONIFACE COULIBALY; circ. 2,500.

Yeelen (Light): Ouagadougou; monthly; pro-Govt.

NEWS AGENCIES

Agence d'Information du Burkina (AIB): 01 BP 2507, Ouagadougou 01; tel. 30-70-52; telex 5327; fax 30-70-56; f. 1963; fmrly Agence Burkinabè de Presse; state-controlled; Dir JAMES DABIRÉ.

Foreign Bureaux

Agence France-Presse (AFP): BP 391, Ouagadougou; tel. 33-56-56; telex 5204; Bureau Chief KIDA TAPSOBA.

Reuters (UK) is also represented in Burkina Faso.

Publishers

Presses Africaines SA: BP 1471, Ouagadougou; tel. 33-43-07; telex 5344; general fiction, religion, primary and secondary textbooks; Man. Dir A. WININGA.

Société Nationale d'Edition et de Presse (SONEPRESS): BP 810, Ouagadougou; f. 1972; general, periodicals; Pres. MARTIAL OUÉDRAOGO.

Government Publishing House

Imprimerie Nationale du Burkina Faso (INBF): route de l'Hôpital Yalgado, BP 7040, Ouagadougou; tel. 33-52-92; f. 1963; Dir LATY SOULEYMANE TRAORÉ.

Broadcasting and Communications

TELECOMMUNICATIONS

Office National des Télécommunications (ONATEL): 01 BP 10000, Ouagadougou 01; tel. 33-40-01; telex 5200; fax 31-03-31; Dir-Gen. JUSTIN T. THIOMBIANO.

RADIO

Radiodiffusion Nationale du Burkina: 03 BP 7029, Ouagadougou 03; tel. 32-40-55; fax 31-04-41; f. 1959; state radio service; Dir RODRIGUE BARRY.

Radio Bobo-Dioulasso: BP 392, Bobo-Dioulasso; tel. 97-14-13; daily programmes in French and vernacular languages; Dir of Programmes SITA KAM.

Radio Horizon FM: 01 BP 2714, Ouagadougou 01; tel. 31-28-58; fax 31-39-34; private commercial station; broadcasts in French, English and eight vernacular languages; Dir MOUSTAPHA LAABLI THIOMBIANO.

TELEVISION

Télévision Nationale du Burkina: 29 blvd de la Révolution, 01 BP 2530, Ouagadougou 01; tel. 31-01-35; telex 5327; f. 1963; Dir AINÉE KOALA.

Finance

(cap. = capital; res = reserves; m. = million; brs = branches; amounts in francs CFA)

BANKING

Central Bank

Banque Centrale des Etats de l'Afrique de l'Ouest (BCEAO): ave Gamal-Abdel-Nasser, BP 356, Ouagadougou; tel. 30-60-15; telex 5205; fax 31-01-22; headquarters in Dakar, Senegal; f. 1962; bank of issue for the member states of the Union économique et monétaire ouest-africaine (UEMOA); cap. and res 657,592m. (Dec. 1995); Gov. CHARLES KONAN BANNY; Dir in Burkina Faso MOUSSA KONÉ; br. in Bobo-Dioulasso.

Other Banks

Banque Commerciale du Burkina (BCB): ave Nelson Mandela, 01 BP 1336, Ouagadougou 01; tel. 30-78-78; telex 5501; fax 31-06-28; f. 1987 as Banque Arabe-Libyenne-Burkinabè pour le Commerce et le Développement; 50% state-owned, 50% owned by Libyan Arab Foreign Bank; cap. and res 881m. (Dec. 1995); Pres. GUÉBRILA OUÉDRAOGO; Man. Dir IBRAHIM K. HELLAWI.

Banque Internationale du Burkina: rue de la Chance, angle rue Patrice Lumumba, 01 BP 362, Ouagadougou 01; tel. 30-61-69; telex 5210; fax 31-00-94; f. 1974; 25% owned by Banque Belgolaise SA (Belgium), 23% state-owned; cap. and res 4,834m. (Dec. 1995); Pres. and Man. Dir GASPARD OUÉDRAOGO; 14 brs.

Banque Internationale pour le Commerce, l'Industrie et l'Agriculture du Burkina (BICIA—B): ave Dr Kwamé N'Krumah, 01 BP 8, Ouagadougou 01; tel. 30-62-26; telex 5203; fax 31-19-55; e-mail biciadg@fasonet.bf; f. 1973; 25% state-owned; cap. and res 5,774m. (Dec. 1995), res 919m. (Dec. 1996); Pres. AMADOU TRAORÉ; Man. Dir HAMADÉ OUÉDRAOGO; 11 brs.

Caisse Nationale de Crédit Agricole du Burkina (CNCAB): 2 ave Gamal-Abdel-Nasser, 01 BP 1644, Ouagadougou 01; tel. 30-24-88; telex 5443; fax 31-43-52; f. 1979; 26% state-owned; cap. and res 5,868m. (Dec. 1995); Pres. TIBILA KABORÉ; Man. Dir NOËL KABORÉ; 4 brs.

Ecobank—Burkina SA: 633 rue Maurice Bishop, 01 BP 145, Ouagadougou 01; operations commenced 1997; 80% owned by Ecobank Transnational Inc (operating under the auspices of the Economic Community of West African States); cap. 1,250m.; Man. Dir OLAYEMI AKAPO.

Groupe BFCIB-UREBA-CAI: 01 BP 585, Ouagadougou 01; tel. 30-60-35; telex 5269; fax 31-05-61; est. in progress, entailing merger of Banque pour le Financement du Commerce et des Investissements du Burkina (BFCIB), Union Révolutionnaire de Banques (UREBA) and Caisse Autonome d'Investissements (CAI); proposed cap. 1,600m.; Dir DER AUGUSTIN SOMDA (provisional).

STOCK EXCHANGE

Côte d'Ivoire's Bourse des Valeurs d'Abidjan was scheduled to become a regional stock exchange, serving the member states of the UEMOA, in January 1998.

INSURANCE

Fonci-Assurances (FONCIAS): ave Léo Frobénius, 01 BP 398, Ouagadougou 01; tel. 30-62-04; telex 5323; fax 31-01-53; f. 1978; 51% owned by Athena Afrique (France), 20% state-owned; cap. 140m.; Pres. El Hadj OUMAROU KANAZOE; Man. Dir GÉRARD G. MANTOUX.

Société Nationale d'Assurances et de Réassurances (SONAR): 01 BP 406, Ouagadougou 01; tel. 33-46-66; telex 5294; fax 30-89-75; f. 1973; 25% state-owned; cap. 240m.; Man. Dir ANDRÉ BAYALA.

Union des Assurances du Burkina (UAB): 08 BP 11041, Ouagadougou 08; tel. 31-26-15; fax 31-26-20; f. 1991; 20% owned by l'Union Africaine—IARD (Côte d'Ivoire); cap. 270m.; Man. Dir J. V. ALFRED YARÉOGO.

Trade and Industry

GOVERNMENT AGENCIES

Bureau des Mines et de la Géologie du Burkina (BUMIGEB): 01 BP 601, Ouagadougou 01; tel. 30-01-94; fax 30-01-87; f. 1978; research into geological and mineral resources; Pres. MODESTE DABIRA; Man. Dir JEAN-LÉONARD COMPAORÉ.

Caisse de Stabilisation des Prix des Produits Agricoles du Burkina (CSPPAB): 01 BP 1453, Ouagadougou 01; tel. 30-62-17; telex 5202; fax 31-06-14; f. 1964; responsible for purchase and marketing of shea-nuts (karité nuts), sesame seeds, cashew nuts and groundnuts; transfer pending to private ownership; Admin. DIANGO CHARLY HEBIE (acting); br. at Bobo-Dioulasso, representation at Boromo, Fada N'Gourma and Gaoua.

Comptoir Burkinabè des Métaux Précieux (CBMP): Ouagadougou; currently responsible for purchase of all gold production; restructuring pending.

Office National d'Aménagement des Terroirs (ONAT): 01 BP 524, Ouagadougou 01; tel. 30-61-10; fax 30-61-12; f. 1974; fmrly Autorité des Aménagements des Vallées des Voltas; integrated rural development, including economic and social planning; Man. Dir ZACHARIE OUÉDRAOGO.

Office National du Commerce Exterieur (ONAC): ave Léo Frobénius, 01 BP 389, Ouagadougou 01; tel. 31-13-00; telex 5258; fax 31-14-69; f. 1974; promotes and supervises external trade; Man. Dir SÉRIBA OUATTARA (acting).

DEVELOPMENT ORGANIZATIONS

Caisse Française de Développement (CFD): ave Binger, BP 529, Ouagadougou; tel. 30-68-26; telex 5271; fmrly Caisse Centrale de Coopération Economique, named changed 1992; Dir M. GLEIZES.

Mission Française de Coopération: 01 BP 510, Ouagadougou 01; tel. 30-67-71; telex 5211; fax 30-89-00; centre for administering bilateral aid from France under co-operation agreements signed in 1961; Dir PIERRE JACQUEMOT.

CHAMBER OF COMMERCE

Chambre de Commerce, d'Industrie et d'Artisanat du Burkina: 180/220 rue 3-119, 01 BP 502, Ouagadougou 01; tel. 30-61-14; telex 5268; fax 30-61-16; f. 1948; Pres. El Hadj OUMAROU KANAZOÉ; Dir.-Gen. SALIF LAMOUSSA KABORÉ; br. in Bobo-Dioulasso.

EMPLOYERS' ORGANIZATIONS

Association Professionnelle des Banques et Établissements Financiers (APBEF): Ouagadougou; Pres. HAMADÉ OUÉDRAOGO.

Conseil National du Patronat Burkinabè: Ouagadougou; Pres. BRUNO ILBOUDO.

Groupement Professionnel des Industriels: BP 810, Ouagadougou; tel. 30-28-19; f. 1974; Pres. MARTIAL OUÉDRAOGO.

Syndicat des Commerçants Importateurs et Exportateurs (SCIMPEX): 01 BP 552, Ouagadougou 01; tel. 31-18-70; fax 31-30-36; Pres. PATRICK LEYDET.

UTILITIES

Office National de l'Eau et de l'Assainissement (ONEA): 01 BP 170, Ouagadougou 01; tel. 30-60-73; fax 30-33-60; f. 1977; storage, purification and distribution of water; Dir ALY CONGO.

Société Nationale Burkinabè d'Electricité (SONABEL): ave Nelson Mandela, BP 54, Ouagadougou; tel. 33-62-05; telex 5208; f. 1968; cap. 963m. francs CFA; production and distribution of electricity; Dir-Gen. M. BARRO.

CO-OPERATIVES

Société de Commercialisation du Burkina 'Faso Yaar': ave du Loudun, BP 531, Ouagadougou; tel. 30-61-28; telex 5274; f. 1967; 99% state-owned; transfer to private ownership pending; import-export and domestic trade; Pres. Minister of Trade, Industry and Crafts.

Union des Coopératives Agricoles et Maraîchères du Burkina (UCOBAM): 01 BP 277, Ouagadougou 01; tel. 30-65-27; telex 5287; f. 1968; comprises 8 regional co-operative unions (20,000 mems); production and marketing of fruit and vegetables.

TRADE UNIONS

There are more than 20 autonomous trade unions. The five trade union syndicates are:

Confédération Générale du Travail Burkinabè (CGTB): Ouagadougou; f. 1988; confed. of several autonomous trade unions; Sec.-Gen. TOLE SAGNON.

Confédération Nationale des Travailleurs Burkinabè (CNTB): BP 445, Ouagadougou; f. 1972; Leader of Governing Directorate ABDOULAYE BÂ.

Confédération Syndicale Burkinabè (CSB): BP 299, Ouagadougou; f. 1974; mainly public service unions; Sec.-Gen. YACINTHE OUÉDRAOGO.

Organisation Nationale des Syndicats Libres (ONSL): BP 99, Ouagadougou; f. 1960; 6,000 mems (1983).

Union Syndicale des Travailleurs Burkinabè (USTB): BP 381, Ouagadougou; f. 1958; Sec.-Gen. BONIFACE SOMDAH; 35,000 mems in 45 affiliated orgs.

Transport

RAILWAY

At the end of 1991 there were some 622 km of track in Burkina Faso. A 105-km extension from Donsin to Ouagadougou was inaugurated in December of that year. Plans exist for the construction of an extension to the manganese deposits at Tambao: in 1989 the cost of the project was estimated at 12,000m. francs CFA. Responsibility for operations on the railway line linking Abidjan (Côte d'Ivoire) and Kaya, via Ouagadougou, was transferred to SITARAIL (a consortium of French, Belgian, Ivorian and Burkinabè interests) in May 1995.

Société des Chemins de Fer du Burkina (SCFB): 01 BP 192, Ouagadougou 01; tel. 30-60-50; telex 5433; fax 30-77-49; f. 1989 to operate the Burkinabè railway network that was fmrly managed by the Régie du Chemin de Fer Abidjan–Niger; services privatized in May 1995 (see above); Pres. SIDIKI SIDIBE; Man. Dir ANDRÉ EMMANUEL YAMÉOGO.

ROADS

In 1995 there were 12,506 km of roads, including 5,610 km of main roads and 2,982 km of secondary roads; about 16% of the road network was paved. A major aim of current projects for the construction or upgrading of roads, as part of the Government's 1991–96 infrastructure development programme (funded by the Arab Bank for Economic Development in Africa, the Islamic Development Bank, the OPEC Fund for International Development and the Governments of Kuwait and Saudi Arabia), was to improve transport links with other countries of the region.

Régie X9: 01 BP 2991, Ouagadougou 01; tel. 30-42-96; telex 5313; f. 1984; urban, national and international public transport co; Dir FRANÇOIS KONSEIBO.

CIVIL AVIATION

There are international airports at Ouagadougou and Bobo-Dioulasso, 49 small airfields and 13 private airstrips. Ouagadougou airport handled 193,773 passengers and 7,986 metric tons of freight in 1991. In late 1995 France agreed funding of 13,500m. francs CFA for improvements to the airport infrastructure at Ouagadougou.

Air Afrique: BP 141, Ouagadougou; tel. 30-60-20; telex 5292; see under Côte d'Ivoire.

Air Burkina: ave Loudun, 01 BP 1459, Ouagadougou 01; tel. 30-76-76; fax 31-48-80; f. 1967 as Air Volta, name changed 1984; 25% state-owned; operates domestic and regional services; Man. Dir MATHIEU BOUDA.

Air Inter-Burkina: Ouagadougou; f. 1994; operates domestic passenger and postal services.

Tourism

Among the principal tourist activities is big game hunting in the east and south-west, and along the banks of the Mouhoun (Black Volta) river. There is a wide variety of wild animals in the game reserves. Important cultural events, notably the pan-African film festival held bienially in Ouagadougou, attract many visitors. In 1993 there were 154,937 tourist arrivals, and receipts from tourism totalled 8,895m. francs CFA.

Direction de l'Administration Touristique et Hôtelière: 01 BP 624, Ouagadougou 01; tel. 30-63-96; telex 5555; Dir-Gen. MOUSSA DIALLO.

Office National du Tourisme Burkinabè: BP 1318, Ouagadougou; tel. 3-19-59; telex 5202; fax 31-44-34; Dir-Gen. ABDOULAYE SANKARA.

BURUNDI

Introductory Survey

Location, Climate, Language, Religion, Flag, Capital

The Republic of Burundi is a land-locked country lying on the eastern shore of Lake Tanganyika, in central Africa, a little south of the Equator. It is bordered by Rwanda to the north, by Tanzania to the south and east, and by the Democratic Republic of the Congo to the west. The climate is tropical (hot and humid) in the lowlands, and cool in the highlands, with an irregular rainfall. The population is composed of three ethnic groups: the Hutu (85%), the Tutsi (14%) and the Twa (1%). The official languages are French and Kirundi, while Swahili is used, in addition to French, in commercial circles. More than 65% of the inhabitants profess Christianity, with the great majority of the Christians being Roman Catholics. A large minority still adhere to traditional animist beliefs. The national flag (proportions 5 by 3) consists of a white diagonal cross on a background of red (above and below) and green (hoist and fly), with a white circle, containing three green-edged red stars, in the centre. The capital is Bujumbura.

Recent History

Burundi (formerly Urundi) became part of German East Africa in 1899. In 1916, during the First World War, the territory was occupied by Belgian forces from the Congo (now the Democratic Republic of the Congo). Subsequently, as part of Ruanda-Urundi, it was administered by Belgium under a League of Nations mandate and later as a UN Trust Territory. Elections in September 1961, conducted under UN supervision, were won by the Union pour le progrès national (UPRONA), which had been formed in 1958 by Ganwa (Prince) Louis Rwagasore, son of the reigning Mwami (King), Mwambutsa IV. As leader of UPRONA, Prince Rwagasore became Prime Minister later in the month, but was assassinated after only two weeks in office. He was succeeded by his brother-in-law, André Muhirwa. Internal self-government was granted in January 1962 and full independence on 1 July, when the two parts of the Trust Territory became separate states, as Burundi and Rwanda. Tensions between Burundi's two main ethnic groups, the Tutsi (traditionally the dominant tribe, despite representing a minority of the overall population) and the Hutu, escalated during 1965. Following an unsuccessful attempt by the Hutu to overthrow the Tutsi-dominated Government in October 1965, virtually the entire Hutu political élite was executed, eliminating any significant participation by the Hutu in Burundi's political life until the late 1980s (see below). In July 1966 the Mwami was deposed, after a reign of more than 50 years, by his son Charles, and the Constitution was suspended. In November 1966 Charles, now Mwami Ntare V, was himself deposed by his Prime Minister, Capt. (later Lt-Gen.) Michel Micombero, who declared Burundi a republic.

Several alleged plots against the Government in 1969 and 1971 were followed, in 1972, by an abortive coup during which Ntare V was killed. Hutu activists were held responsible for the attempted coup, and this served as a pretext for the Tutsi to conduct a series of large-scale massacres of the rival tribe, with the final death-toll being estimated at around 100,000. Large numbers of the Hutu fled to neighbouring countries.

In 1972 Micombero began a prolonged restructuring of the executive, which resulted in 1973 in an appointed seven-member Presidential Bureau, with Micombero as President and Prime Minister. In July 1974 the Government introduced a new republican Constitution which vested sovereignty in UPRONA, the sole legal political party. Micombero was elected Secretary-General of the party and re-elected for a seven-year presidential term.

On 1 November 1976 an army coup deposed Micombero, who died in exile in July 1983. The leader of the coup, Lt-Col (later Col) Jean-Baptiste Bagaza, was appointed President by the Supreme Revolutionary Council (composed of army officers), and a new Council of Ministers was formed. In October 1978 Bagaza announced a ministerial reshuffle in which he abolished the post of Prime Minister. The first national congress of UPRONA was held in December 1979, and a party Central Committee, headed by Bagaza, was elected to take over the functions of the Supreme Revolutionary Council in January 1980. A new Constitution, adopted by national referendum in November 1981, provided for the establishment of a national assembly, to be elected by universal adult suffrage. The first legislative elections were held in October 1982. Having been re-elected President of UPRONA at the party's second national congress in July 1984, Bagaza, the sole candidate, was elected President of Burundi by direct suffrage in August, winning 99.63% of the votes cast.

On 3 September 1987 a military coup deposed Bagaza while he was attending a conference in Canada. The coup was led by Maj. Pierre Buyoya, who accused Bagaza of corruption and immediately formed a Military Committee for National Salvation (CMSN) to administer the country, pending the appointment of a new President. The Constitution was suspended, and the National Assembly was dissolved. On 2 October Buyoya was sworn in as President of the Third Republic. His Council of Ministers included mostly civilians, retaining no minister from the previous regime.

In August 1988 tribal tensions erupted into violence in the north of the country when groups of Hutus, claiming Tutsi provocation, slaughtered hundreds of Tutsis in the towns of Ntega and Marangara. The Tutsi-dominated army was immediately dispatched to the region to restore order, and large-scale tribal massacres, similar to those of 1972, occurred. In October Buyoya announced changes to the Council of Ministers, including the appointment of a Hutu, Adrien Sibomana, to the newly-restored post of Prime Minister. For the first time the Council included a majority of Hutu representatives. Buyoya subsequently established a Committee for National Unity (comprising an equal number of Tutsis and Hutus) to investigate the massacres and make recommendations for national reconciliation. Following the publication of the Committee's report, Buyoya announced plans to combat all forms of discrimination against the Hutu and to introduce new regulations to ensure equal opportunities in education, employment and in the armed forces. Notwithstanding Buyoya's efforts to achieve ethnic reconciliation, political tension remained at a high level in 1989.

In May 1990, in response to a new draft charter on national unity, Buyoya announced plans to introduce a 'democratic constitution under a one-party government' in place of military rule. A charter designed to reconcile the Tutsi and the Hutu was to be the subject of a referendum. During mid-1990, however, anti-Government literature was reportedly disseminated in Bujumbura by the Parti de libération du peuple hutu (PALIPEHUTU), a small, outlawed Hutu opposition group was based in Tanzania, and in August three Burundian soldiers were killed by Hutu guerrillas. Later in that month the Government announced an amnesty for all political prisoners. In December, at an extraordinary national congress of UPRONA, the CMSN was abolished and its functions transferred to an 80-member Central Committee, with Buyoya as Chairman and with a Hutu, Nicolas Mayugi, as Secretary-General. At a referendum conducted in February 1991 the draft charter on national unity was overwhelmingly approved, despite vociferous criticism from PALIPEHUTU and other opposition groups. Later in the month a ministerial reshuffle, whereby Hutus were appointed to 12 of the 23 government portfolios, was viewed with scepticism by political opponents. In March a commission was established to prepare a report on the democratization of national institutions and political structures, in preparation for the drafting of a new constitution. In September Buyoya presented the report of the constitutional commission on 'national democratization'. Among its recommendations were the establishment of a parliamentary system to operate in conjunction with a presidential system of government, a renewable five-year presidential mandate, the introduction of proportional representation, freedom of the press, the compilation of a declaration of human rights and a system of 'controlled multipartyism' whereby political groupings seeking legal recognition would be forced to fulfil specific requirements, including subscription to the Charter of Unity (adopted in February). The state Security Court was abolished in October.

In February 1992 the Government announced that a referendum was to be held on 9 March to ascertain support for the constitutional reform proposals. It was stated that electoral endorsement of the draft Constitution would be followed by legislative elections and a presidential poll. A coup attempt only days before the referendum was swiftly suppressed and failed to disrupt the proceedings: the proposals received the support of more than 90% of voters. The new Constitution was promulgated on 13 March 1992. In an extensive ministerial reshuffle in April, seven ministers left the Government, Buyoya relinquished the defence portfolio, and Hutus were appointed to 15 of the 25 portfolios. In the same month Buyoya approved legislation relating to the creation of new political parties in accordance with the provisions of the new Constitution. New political parties were to be obliged to demonstrate impartiality with regard to ethnic or regional origin, gender and religion, and were to refrain from militarization. In October Buyoya announced the creation of the National Electoral Preparatory Commission (NEPC), a 33-member body comprising representatives of the eight recognized political parties, together with administrative, judicial, religious and military officials. The NEPC was convened for the first time at the end of November. By early December Buyoya had appointed a new 12-member technical commission, charged with drafting an electoral code and a communal law.

In February 1993 Buyoya announced that presidential and legislative elections would take place in June, and that elections for local government officials would be held in November. The presidential poll, conducted on 1 June, was won, with 64.8% of the votes cast, by Melchior Ndadaye, the candidate of the Front pour la démocratie au Burundi (FRODEBU), with the support of the Rassemblement du peuple burundien (RPB), the Parti du peuple and the Parti libéral; Buyoya received 32.4% of the vote as the UPRONA candidate, with support from the Rassemblement pour la démocratie et le développement économique et social (RADDES) and the Parti social démocrate. Legislative elections for 81 seats in the National Assembly were conducted on 29 June. Once again, FRODEBU emerged as the most successful party, with 71% of the votes and 65 of the seats in the new legislature. UPRONA, with 21.4% of the votes, secured the remaining 16 seats. None of the other four parties contesting the elections secured the minimum 5% of votes needed for representation in the legislature. Although the presidential and legislative elections had been conducted without major disturbance, an attempted coup in early July was promptly contained, and resulted in the arrest of four army officers. Ndadaye, Burundi's first Hutu Head of State, assumed the presidency on 10 July. A new Council of Ministers was subsequently announced. The new Prime Minister, Sylvie Kinigi, was one of seven newly-appointed Tutsi ministers.

On 21 October 1993 more than 100 army paratroopers, supported by armoured vehicles, swiftly overwhelmed supporters of the Government and occupied the presidential palace and the headquarters of the national broadcasting company. Ndadaye and several other prominent Hutu politicians and officials were detained and subsequently killed by the insurgents, who later proclaimed François Ngeze, one of the few Hutu members of UPRONA and a minister in the Government of former President Buyoya, as head of a National Committee for Public Salvation (CPSN). While members of the Government sought refuge abroad and in the offices of foreign diplomatic missions in Bujumbura, the armed forces declared a state of emergency, closing national borders and the capital's airport. However, immediate and unanimous international condemnation of the coup, together with the scale and ferocity of renewed tribal violence (fuelled by reports of Tutsi-dominated army units seeking out and eliminating Hutu intellectuals), undermined support for the insurgents from within the armed forces, and precipitated the collapse of the CPSN, which was disbanded on 25 October. Prime Minister Kinigi announced an end to the curfew, but remained in hiding and urged the international community to deploy an international force in Burundi to protect the civilian Government. Communications were restored on 27 October, and on the following day the UN confirmed that the Government had reassumed control of the country. Ngeze and 10 coup leaders were arrested, while some 40 other insurgents were thought to have fled to Zaire (now the Democratic Republic of the Congo). Although the coup was widely interpreted as an attempt by the Tutsi military élite to check the political advancement of Hutus, there was some speculation that supporters of former President Bagaza were responsible for the uprising, which may have been precipitated by suggestions that Ndadaye was attempting to establish an alternative, Hutu-dominated presidential gendarmerie. In December a 27-member commission of judicial inquiry was created to investigate the insurgency.

Meanwhile, in early November 1993 several members of the Government, including the Prime Minister, had left the French Embassy (where they had remained throughout the uprising) with a small escort of French troops, and on 8 November Kinigi met with 15 of the 17 surviving ministers in an attempt to address the humanitarian crisis arising from the massacre and displacement of hundreds of thousands of Burundians following the failed coup. On the same day the Constitutional Court officially recognized the presidential vacancy resulting from the murder of both Ndadaye and his constitutional successor, Giles Bimazubute, the Speaker of the National Assembly, and stated that presidential power should be exercised by the Council of Ministers, acting in a collegiate capacity, pending a presidential election which was to be conducted within three months. However, the Minister of External Relations and Co-operation, Sylvestre Ntibantunganya (who succeeded Ndadaye as leader of FRODEBU), suggested that no electoral timetable should be considered before the resolution of internal security difficulties and the initiation of a comprehensive programme for the repatriation of refugees. In December Ntibantunganya was elected Speaker of the National Assembly. The foreign affairs portfolio was assumed by Jean-Marie Ngendahayo, previously Minister of Communications and Government Spokesman.

Meanwhile, in mid-November 1993, following repeated requests by the Government for an international contribution to the protection of government ministers in Burundi, the OAU agreed to the deployment of a 200-strong protection force (MIPROBU), to be composed of civilian and military personnel, for a period of six months. In December opposition parties, including UPRONA and the RADDES, organized demonstrations in protest at the arrival of the 180-strong military contingent, scheduled for January 1994, claiming that Burundi's sovereignty and territorial integrity were being infringed. As a compromise, in mid-March the Government secured a significant reduction in the size of the force. The mandate of the mission (comprising a military contingent of 47 and 20 civilian observers) was subsequently extended at three-monthly intervals.

In early January 1994 FRODEBU deputies in the National Assembly approved a draft amendment to the Constitution, allowing a President of the Republic to be elected by the National Assembly, in the event of the Constitutional Court's recognition of a presidential vacancy. UPRONA deputies, who had boycotted the vote, challenged the constitutionality of the amendment, and expressed concern that such a procedure represented election by indirect suffrage, in direct contravention of the terms of the Constitution. The continued boycott of the National Assembly by UPRONA deputies, together with procedural impediments to the immediate ratification of the amendment, forced the postponement on 10 January of an attempt by FRODEBU deputies to elect their presidential candidate, the Minister of Agriculture and Livestock, Cyprien Ntaryamira. Three days later, none the less, following the successful negotiation of a political truce with opposition parties, Ntaryamira was elected President by the National Assembly (with 78 of the 79 votes cast). He assumed the post on 5 February; Tutsi Prime Minister, Anatole Kanyenkiko, was appointed two days later, while the composition of a new multi-party Council of Ministers was finally agreed in mid-February.

During February 1994 ethnic tension was renewed as armed Hutu and Tutsi extremist factions attempted to establish territorial strongholds. In March, the Minister of State for Interior and Public Security, Léonard Nyangoma, was accused of having deliberately attempted to provoke a large-scale civil confrontation by exaggerating reports of a security crisis in Bujumbura, arising from the violent response of some sections of the armed forces to the President's insistence that several senior army personnel should be replaced for having failed to address the threat to security posed by armed rebel groups.

On 6 April 1994, returning from a regional summit meeting in Dar es Salaam, Tanzania, Ntaryamira was killed (together with the Ministers of Development, Planning and Reconstruction and of Communications) when the aircraft of Rwandan President Juvénal Habyarimana, in which he was travelling at Habyarimana's invitation, was the target of a rocket attack above Kigali airport, and crashed on landing. Habyarimana was also killed in the crash, and was widely acknowledged to have been the intended victim of the attack. In contrast to the violent political and tribal chaos that erupted in Rwanda (q.v.) in the aftermath of the death of Habyarimana, Burundians responded positively to appeals for calm issued by Ntibantunganya, the Speaker of the National Assembly, who, on 8 April, was confirmed (in accordance with the Constitution) as interim President for a three-month period. However, violent exchanges between Hutu extremist rebels and factions of the armed forces continued in April, claiming numerous victims. The failure of the warring militias to respond to an ultimatum, issued by interim President Ntibantunganya in late April, to surrender all illegal arms by 1 May, resulted in the military bombardment of several rebel strongholds, forcing the withdrawal and surrender of a number of insurgents. Relations between the Government and the armed forces subsequently improved, and were further cemented by the Prime Minister's announcement, in early May, that Nyangoma had forfeited his position in the Council of Ministers, having failed to return from official business abroad.

Having discounted the possibility of organizing a general election, owing to security considerations, in June 1994 all major political parties joined lengthy negotiations to establish a procedure for the restoration of the presidency. The mandate of the interim President was extended for three months by the Constitutional Court in July, and by the end of August it had been decided that a new President would be elected by a broadly representative commission, with a composition yet to be decided. A new agreement on power-sharing was announced on 10 September. This Convention of Government, which detailed the terms of government for a four-year transitional period (including the allocation of 45% of cabinet posts to opposition parties), was incorporated into the Constitution on 22 September. The Convention also provided for the creation of a National Security Council (Conseil de sécurité nationale, CSN), which was formally inaugurated on 10 October to address the national security crisis. On 30 September the Convention elected Ntibantunganya to the presidency from a list of six candidates including Charles Mukasi, the UPRONA leader. Ntibantunganya's appointment was endorsed by the National Assembly, and he was formally inaugurated on 1 October. Anatole Kanyenkiko was reappointed as Prime Minister, and a coalition Government was announced with a composition reflecting the terms of the September Convention. In December, however, UPRONA announced its intention to withdraw from the Government and from the legislature, following the election, in early December, of Jean Minani (a prominent FRODEBU member) to the post of Speaker of the National Assembly. UPRONA members accused Minani of having incited Hutu attacks against Tutsis in the aftermath of the October 1993 attempted coup. In January 1995 the political crisis was averted by agreement on a compromise FRODEBU candidate, Léonce Ngendakumana. Minani subsequently assumed the FRODEBU party leadership. UPRONA subsequently declared its willingness to rejoin the Government, but later in January Kanyenkiko resisted attempts by the UPRONA leadership to expel him from the party for having failed to comply with party demands for the withdrawal from the Government of all party members over the Minani affair. Two UPRONA ministers were subsequently dismissed from the Council of Ministers, in apparent retaliation, prompting Mukasi, in mid-February, to demand the resignation of the Prime Minister and to declare an indefinite general strike in support of this demand. Increased political opposition to Kanyenkiko forced the Prime Minister to acknowledge that he no longer commanded the necessary mandate to continue in office, and on 22 February Antoine Nduwayo, a UPRONA candidate selected in consultation with other opposition parties, was appointed Prime Minister by presidential decree. A new coalition Council of Ministers was announced on 1 March, but political stability was undermined immediately by the murder, in early March, of the Hutu Minister of Energy and Mines, Ernest Kabushemeye. (Another member of the RPB, Emmanuel Sindayigaya, was subsequently appointed to the post.)

Ethnic tension persisted in the second half of 1994, exacerbated by the scale and proximity of the violence in Rwanda and by the presence in Burundi of an estimated 200,000 Rwandan Hutu refugees. Ethnically-motivated atrocities became a daily occurrence in parts of the country (several prominent politicians and government officials were murdered), resulting in the imposition of a partial curfew in the capital in December. Fears that the security crisis in Burundi would develop into civil war were agitated, in late 1994, by reports that the 30,000-strong Force pour la défense de la démocratie (FDD), the armed wing of Nyangoma's extremist Conseil national pour la défense de la démocratie (CNDD), were making preparations for an armed struggle against the armed forces in Burundi. In early November the CSN had urged all political and civilian groups to dissociate themselves from Nyangoma, who was believed to be co-ordinating party activities from Zaire.

An escalation in the scale and frequency of incidents of politically- and ethnically-motivated violence during 1995 prompted renewed concern that the security crisis would precipitate a large-scale campaign of ethnic massacres similar to that in Rwanda during 1994. Government-sponsored military initiatives were concentrated in Hutu-dominated suburbs of Bujumbura (particularly Kamenge) and in the north-east, where an aggressive campaign was waged against the alleged insurgent activities of PALIPEHUTU members, resulting in the deaths of hundreds of Hutu civilians. The Government accused Hutu extremist militias of conducting an intimidating and violent programme of recruitment of Hutu males in the region. In May 1995 humanitarian organizations suspended their activities in Burundi for one week, in an attempt to draw international attention to the deteriorating security situation and the increasingly dangerous position of relief workers in the area. Anti-insurgency operations were intensified in June in several suburbs of the capital, where an estimated 2,000 heavily-armed troops sought to apprehend members of the FDD. It was reported that as many as 130 civilians were killed (many of them women and children) in the ensuing hostilities, which also forced thousands of Hutus to flee into the surrounding countryside. (In October the armed forces claimed to have destroyed the FDD headquarters.) Also in June a report published by the human rights organization, Amnesty International, claimed that national security forces in Burundi had collaborated with extremist Tutsi factions in the murder of thousands of Hutus since 1993. Increased security measures announced by Ntibantunganya in the same month included restrictions on a number of civil liberties (a curfew was imposed, demonstrations were proscribed and the media and the movement of civilians in urban areas were to be strictly regulated) and the regrouping of many communes into administrative sectors to be administered jointly by civilian and military personnel. A request by the President that he be granted the power to rule by decree until the next legislative session, scheduled for October 1995, was subsequently rejected by the National Assembly which considered such a move to be incompatible with the spirit of the Convention of Government. Notwithstanding the latest security initiative, in late June the Minister of State in charge of External Relations and Co-operation, Jean-Marie Ngendahayo, announced his resignation, expressing dissatisfaction at the Government's inability to guarantee the safety and basic rights of the population. Later in the month a meeting of the OAU, convened in Addis Ababa, Ethiopia, concluded that some degree of military intervention in Burundi would be necessary should ethnic violence continue to escalate. (In April the Burundian Government had declined an OAU offer of military intervention in favour of increasing the number of MIPROBU personnel to 67.) In early July Paul Munyembari was appointed to the external relations portfolio. Vedaste Ngendanganya was appointed Minister of Posts and Telecommunications in early September, in place of Innocent Nimpagariste, who had resigned from the post in August following a number of unsuccessful assassination attempts against him. Further changes to the Council of Ministers were announced in October, after a division arose within the governing coalition in response to outspoken comments made by the US ambassador to Burundi with regard to the country's security situation. Among seven ministers replaced was Gabriel Sinarinzi, the UPRONA Minister of the Interior, who had led criticism of the ambassador's remarks.

By early 1996 reports of atrocities perpetrated against both Hutu and Tutsi civilians by rogue elements of the Tutsi-led armed forces (including militias known as the *Sans Echecs*), and by extremist Hutu rebel groups had become almost commonplace in rural areas. It was believed that the capital had been effectively 'cleansed' of any significant Hutu presence by the end of 1995. In late December the UN Secretary-General had petitioned the Security Council to sanction some form of international military intervention in Burundi to address the crisis, and in February 1996 these efforts were renewed after the UN Special Rapporteur on Human Rights which concluded that no discernible improvement had been made in the protection of human rights since mid-1995 and that a state of near civil war existed in many areas of the country. However, the Burundian

Government (and the weight of political opinion in Burundi) remained vehemently opposed to a foreign military presence, claiming that reports of the severity of the security crisis had been exaggerated, and persuading the UN Security Council that a negotiated settlement to the conflict was still attainable. In early April representatives of the US Agency for International Development and the Humanitarian Office of the European Union (EU) visited Burundi. Their findings—which were severely critical of the administration's failure to reconcile the country's various ethnic and political interests within government, and expressed doubts that effective power-sharing could be achieved within the terms of the 1994 Convention of Government and under the leadership of a Tutsi premier with considerable executive power—prompted the USA and the EU to announce the immediate suspension of aid to Burundi.

Despite an undertaking by Ntibantunganya in late April 1996 that a human rights commission was to be established and a comprehensive reform of the security forces and the judiciary was to be undertaken, violence continued to escalate, prompting the suspension of French military co-operation with Burundi at the end of May. (Aid workers reported a number of atrocities perpetrated by units of the armed forces against Hutu civilians—including separate incidents in which some 235 villagers in Buhoro and an estimated 375 villagers in Kivyuka were massacred—during May.) In early June the International Committee of the Red Cross (ICRC) suspended all activities in Burundi, following the murder of three ICRC workers in the north-west of the country; other aid agencies announced that future operations would be restricted to the capital.

In November 1995 the Presidents of Burundi, Rwanda, Uganda and Zaire, together with a Tanzanian Presidential envoy, met in Cairo, Egypt, to discus the crises in Burundi and Rwanda. The Great Lakes' representatives announced a sub-regional peace initiative for Burundi, to be led by the former President of Tanzania, Julius Nyerere. Nyerere's role as principal mediator in the conflict was endorsed at a meeting of representatives of more than 20 African states and European and UN diplomats in Addis Ababa at the end of February 1996. A further Great Lakes summit took place in the Tunisian capital in mid-March 1996, at which Ntibantunganya reiterated his commitment to the restoration of internal security and the organization of democratic, multi-party elections in 1998. Representatives of some 13 political parties (including FRODEBU and UPRONA) participated in inter-party discussions conducted in Mwanza, Tanzania, in April. A second round of discussions, scheduled for May, was subsequently postponed: although a reluctance further to interrupt the work of the current legislative session in Burundi was ostensibly the reason for the stalling of negotiations, unofficial reports indicated that UPRONA representatives had objected to the possible participation of the CNDD. Talks resumed in Mwanza in early June, but political polarization appeared to have been intensified by the negotiating process. UPRONA leader Charles Mukasi, with support from an informal coalition of seven smaller, predominantly Tutsi parties (the Rassemblement unitaire), accused FRODEBU deputies of seeking to abrogate the Convention of Government, a charge which was strenuously denied by FRODEBU spokesmen following the talks. At a conference of regional powers in Arusha, Tanzania, in late June, it was reported that Ntibantunganya and Nduwayo had requested foreign intervention to protect politicians, civil servants and strategic installations. By early July a regional technical commission to examine the request for 'security assistance' (comprising regional defence ministers, but not representatives of the Burundian armed forces) had convened in Arusha and had reached preliminary agreement, with the support of the UN, for an intervention force to be composed of units of the Ugandan and Tanzanian armed forces and police-officers from Kenya. Meanwhile, significant differences of interpretation with regard to the purpose and mandate of such a force had emerged between Ntibantunganya and Nduwayo (who suggested that the President was attempting to neutralize the country's military capability). At a mass rally in Bujumbura of Tutsi-dominated opposition parties, the Prime Minister joined Mukasi and other anti-Government figures in rejecting foreign military intervention and condemning what they regarded as Ntibantunganya's encouragement of external interference in domestic affairs. Some days later, however, full endorsement of the Arusha proposal for intervention was recorded by member nations of the OAU at a summit meeting convened in Yaoundé, Cameroon.

Political and ethnic enmities intensified still further when reports of a massacre of more than 300 Tutsi civilians at Bugendana, allegedly committed by Hutu extremists including heavily-armed Rwandan Hutu refugees, emerged just hours after the UN accused the Burundian authorities of collaborating with the Rwandan administration in a new initiative of (largely enforced) repatriation of Rwandan refugees in Burundi. While FRODEBU members made an urgent appeal for foreign military intervention to contain the increasingly violent civil and military reaction to these events, ex-President Bagaza urged civil resistance to foreign intervention; his appeal for a general strike in Bujumbura was partially observed. Meanwhile, students (with the support of the political opposition) began a second week of protests against regional military intervention, and demonstrated in support of demands for the removal of the country's leadership. On 23 July 1996 Ntibantunganya was forced to abandon an attempt to attend the funeral of the victims of the Bugendana massacre when mourners stoned the presidential helicopter. The following day, amid strong indications that UPRONA intended to join a number of smaller opposition parties that had already withdrawn from the Convention of Government, it was reported that Ntibantunganya had sought refuge in the US embassy building. Several government Ministers and the Speaker of the National Assembly similarly sought refuge within the German embassy compound, while the FRODEBU Chairman, Jean Minani, fled the country. On 25 July, in a bloodless military coup, the armed forces were extensively deployed in the capital. A statement made by the Minister of National Defence, Lt-Col Firmin Sinzoyiheba, criticized the failure of the administration to safeguard national security and announced the suspension of the National Assembly and all political activity, the imposition of a nationwide curfew and the closure of national borders and the airport at Bujumbura. Former President Buyoya was declared as interim President of a transitional republic. In an address to the nation, delivered on the same day, Buyoya defined his immediate aim as the restoration of peace and national security, and sought to reassure former ministers and government officials that their safety would be guaranteed by the new regime. Ntibantunganya conveyed his refusal to relinquish office, but Nduwayo immediately resigned, attributing his failure to effect national reconciliation principally to Ntibantunganya's ineffective leadership. In response to widespread external condemnation of the coup, Buyoya announced that a largely civilian, broadly-based government of national unity would be promptly installed, and that future negotiations with all Hutu groups would be considered. The forced repatriation of Rwandan Hutu refugees was halted with immediate effect.

Despite the appointment, at the end of July 1996, of Pascal-Firmin Ndimira, a Hutu member of UPRONA, as Prime Minister, and an urgent attempt by Buyoya to obtain regional support, the leaders of Ethiopia, Kenya, Rwanda, Tanzania, Uganda and Zaire met in Arusha, under OAU auspices, the same day, and declared their intention to impose stringent economic sanctions against the new regime unless constitutional government was restored immediately. In early August the composition of a new 23-member, multi-ethnic Cabinet was announced. In mid-August Buyoya announced that an expanded transitional national assembly, incorporating existing elected deputies, would be inaugurated during September for a three-year period. A consultative council of elders was also to be established to oversee a period of broad political debate, during which time formal political activity would remain proscribed. Buyoya was formally inaugurated as President on 27 September.

Despite some evidence of violations, the regional sanctions that were imposed in early August 1996 (Zambia joined the embargo later in the month) resulted in the suspension of all significant trade and in Burundi's virtual economic isolation. However, the threat of a humanitarian crisis, particularly among children and the Rwandan refugee population, prompted the sanctions co-ordinating committee, meeting in Arusha in September, to authorize a relaxation of the embargo to facilitate the distribution of food and medical aid. An attempt, later in the month, by Buyoya to secure the repeal of all sanctions, by announcing an end to the ban on political parties and the restoration of the National Assembly, was dismissed by opponents as a purely cosmetic exercise, given the continued suspension of the Constitution and Buyoya's refusal to address preconditions to the ending of sanctions that required the organization of unconditional peace negotiations. In early October

Buyoya agreed to enter into negotiations with the CNDD, but a subsequent meeting, in Arusha, of regional leaders decided that sanctions should be maintained until evidence emerged of constructive progress in the negotiations. This prompted the Burundian Government to denounce the actions and motives of the group, and to withdraw the offer of unconditional dialogue with the CNDD as long as sanctions remained in place. Meanwhile, in early October 1996, some 37 deputies had attended the formal reopening of the National Assembly, which was boycotted by the majority of FRODEBU legislators. According to the Speaker, Léonce Ngendakumana, who had been sheltering in the German embassy since the military coup that had returned Buyoya to power, 22 of the Assembly's original 81 deputies had been murdered during the recent hostilities, and a large number remained in exile or in hiding.

From late July 1996 details began to emerge of the findings of a UN-sponsored inquiry, commissioned in September 1995 to investigate events in Burundi prior to the overthrow of the Ndadaye regime in 1993. It was widely believed that the final report, which appeared to implicate members of the incumbent military high command, including Buyoya, in the attempted coup, was being withheld by the UN in the interests of preventing the further exacerbation of political and ethnic hostilities. The dismissal, in August 1996, of three senior members of the armed and security forces, among them the Chief of Staff of the Army, Col Jean Bikomagu, was stated by the Government to be in no way connected with the attempted coup.

Reports emerged that the armed forces were targeting attacks against Hutus (thousands were estimated to have been killed since the coup), in an attempt to safeguard rural and border regions for Tutsi communities, to which the CNDD and other Hutu militia retaliated with attacks against military installations near Bujumbura as well as against Tutsi civilians. A UN report on the causes of the 1993 coup, published in mid-August, implicated two of Buyoya military leaders who were subsequently dismissed. By late 1996 the military action in eastern Zaire had led to the repatriation of 30,000 Burundians and had severely weakend FDD fighting capacity although some activists continued the fight from Tanzania. In September 1996 the country's most prominent Roman Catholic cleric, the Archbishop of Gitega, was murdered in the Hutu-controlled town of Bugendana. The CNDD strenuously denied responsibility for the killing. A report issued by the UN High Commissioner for Refugees (UNHCR) in December estimated that more than 1,100 individuals (predominantly Hutu refugees) had been killed by the armed forces during October and November alone. Also in December Amnesty International denounced what it termed a 'policy of systematic extermination of a section of population' on the part of the armed forces, alleging that the army had massacred as many as 500 Hutu civilians in Butaganza, in the north-west, earlier in the month. Such reports were denied by the Burundian Government. In January 1997 UNHCR reported that the army had, over a period of seven weeks, massed more than 100,000 (mainly Hutu) civilians in camps—in a 'regroupment' scheme stated by the authorities to protect villagers in areas of rebel activity—and that some 1,000 civilians had been killed by the armed forces. The security situation was, meanwhile, further troubled by the return of CNDD fighters among large numbers of Hutu refugees effectively expelled by the Tutsi-led rebellion in eastern Zaire, as well as by the enforced repatriation of refugees from Tanzania. In mid-January Buyoya condemned the kiling of some 120 Hutu refugees who had apparently been expelled fron Tanzania, accused of fomenting unrest in camps there. Several soldiers were arrested, and it was stated that they would be tried by a military court.

Ex-President Bagaza was placed under house arrest in January 1997, on suspicion of seeking to cause insecurity. In the following month the Secretary-General of FRODEBU, Augustin Nzojibwami, was detained, accused of attempting to undermine efforts to restore peace in Burundi and of 'setting the population against the public authorities and institutions'. However, the Supreme Court subsequently refused to endorse pre-trial custody for Nzojibwami, who was also due to be tried on charges of distributing weapons to the public while Governor of Burari province in 1994, and of having ordered supporters to fire inside a military camp in 1995. At least eight people were arrested in mid-March 1997, following what was officially stated to have been an attempt to assassinate Buyoya, linked to a series of explosions caused by anti-tank mines in Bujumbura. Among those detained were two senior members of Bagaza's Parti pour le redressement national and two serving members of the military.

The trial began in mid-May 1997 of some 79 military officers accused of involvement in the October 1993 coup attempt—an earlier hearing, scheduled for March, having been postponed. (Of those charged, 22 were reportedly at large, while four of the accused had died.) The indicted officers included Bikomagu and Lt-Col Charles Ntakije, who had been Minister of National Defence prior to Ndadaye's assassination. It was reported in early July 1997 that, at a Supreme Court hearing, they and two other senior members of the military had denied charges of plotting a coup, but had entered no formal plea. At the end of the month it was reported that six people convicted of involvement in acts of genocide perpetrated in 1993 had been executed. In all during July–August 1997, the Burundian courts issued 30 death sentences in relation to such crimes; 10 defendants were sentenced to life imprisonment, and 19 to 20 years' custody. Earlier in July the Government had denounced the decision of the UN that conditions in Burundi were not yet suitable for the establishment of an international penal tribunal to examine alleged acts of genocide after 1993.

Six ministers were replaced in a reorganization of Ndimira's Government in early May 1997, and in August it was reported that Buyoya had appointed 10 members of the CSN. In mid-August Ambroise Niyonsaba was allocated the new post of Minister of the Peace Process. Meanwhile, the introduction of a new law regulating the press was denounced by opposition groups, human rights activists and journalists' representatives as seeking to curb the freedom of the media.

The military regime's policy of 'regrouping' civilians into controlled areas continued to be a focus of considerable international concern during the first half of 1997. Although the authorities asserted that the programme was voluntary, and that members of all ethnic groups were seeking the protection of the camps, it was widely believed that Hutu civilians were being coerced into regroupment centres by the armed forces, under threat that they would be treated as guerrillas should they fail to comply. Furthermore, the policy was frequently interpreted as a means of isolating rebel militia from their support base within the civilian population. By mid-1997, according to government figures, some 200,000 civilians had been 'regrouped' in about 50 camps, while non-governmental organizations variously estimated the number of civilians affected at 350,000–500,000. Concern was expressed regarding poor living conditions in the camps, but, despite clear evidence of disease and malnutrition, the reluctance of humanitarian organizations to intervene apparently reflected concerns that to do so might be interpreted as a tacit endorsement of the regroupment policy. In late May UNHCR appealed to bordering countries to cease repatriating Burundian refugees, owing to renewed massacres notably in the regroupment centres. (Confrontations between the army and Hutu fighters had intensified in recent weeks, and there were frequent reports of massacres of civilians as fighting neared the capital.) A further report by Amnesty International, issued in mid-July, denounced extrajudicial executions as a result of regroupment, and appealed to the Buyoya regime to end the policy and ensure the protection of the displaced population. At this time, it was estimated that as many as 250,000 people, mainly civilians, had died since the outbreak of hostilities in 1993.

Meanwhile, little substantive progress was made in regional efforts to bring about direct peace talks between the Buyoya Government and its opponents. Consultations in Arusha in mid-December 1996 were attended by representatives of the Buyoya administration, FRODEBU, the CNDD, PALIPEHUTU and other organizations. However, the Government's stipulation that fighting must be brought to a formal halt prior to any negotiations effectively precluded direct contacts. The first of a series of national seminars on the peace process began in late January 1997, attended by academics, religious leaders, politicians and representatives of civil society. However, prominent political organizations, notably FRODEBU, refused to attend the talks, and the seminars' credibility was undermined when the UN Development Programme, which had initially agreed to finance the negotiations, withdrew its support, on the grounds that all parties were not represented. Buyoya attended the fourth Arusha summit meeting on the Burundi conflict, in mid-April, in his capacity as Head of State. The leaders of the Great Lakes countries agreed to an easing of the economic sanctions, ending restrictions on the supply to Burundi of foodstuffs, agricultural items, medicines, educational and construction materials, in the interests of alleviating conditions for the civilian population. The summit made the full revocation of sanctions dependent on the opening of direct, unconditional peace talks between the Burundian Government and opposition, and, in its final communiqué, urged the Government to dismantle the regroupment camps and to assure the freedom and facilitate the work of the Speaker of the National Assembly. The CNDD pronounced itself 'greatly disappointed' by the outcome of the meeting.

In May 1997 it was disclosed that the Burundian Government and CNDD had been participating in discreet talks in Rome, Italy. The contacts were denounced by elements of UPRONA as a betrayal on the part of the Government, and were apparently a catalyst for student protests in Bujumbura, although Mukasi issued a statement disassociating the 'mainstream' party from condemnation of the Government's actions. A meeting of OAU Heads of State, held in early June in the Zimbabwean capital, Harare, was attended by Buyoya and also by a representative of the CNDD. Also in early June Ntibantunganya left the US embassy for the first time since July 1996, stating that he was prepared to contribute to the peace process. However, initial optimism that planned inter-party talks, scheduled to take place in Arusha in August 1997, would achieve progress in ending the political crisis diminished as the Buyoya Government became increasingly vociferous in its opposition to Nyerere as mediator, denouncing the latter as biased in favour of the opposition. After it became clear that the sanctions would not be revoked immediately upon the opening of negotiations (a decision for which the Burundian authorities appeared to hold Nyerere personally responsible), the Buyoya Government announced that it would not be attending the Arusha talks, stating that it required more time to prepare. The session was effectively abandoned after the Burundian authorities refused to allow an aircraft that had been sent to carry other delegates from Burundi to the meeting to land at Bujumbura. Nyerere openly condemned the stance of the Buyoya regime, announcing that the peace process had reached a stalemate and appealing for wider international assistance in resolving the crisis. A meeting of regional leaders, convened (in Buyoya's absence) in the Tanzanian capital in early September, reaffirmed its support for Nyerere's mediation, castigated the Burundian Government for its intransigence, and resolved to maintain all existing sanctions. It was confirmed that a further round of inter-party talks would take place in Arusha: on the eve of the summit, Buyoya had indicated his administration's willingness to negotiate in a 'neutral African town' outside Tanzania, but his Government subsequently stated that it would attend the next round of talks. The Government was represented at informal discussions between parties involved in the Burundian conflict, organized under UNESCO auspices in Paris, France, in late September; the conference, described as positive by the Government delegation, urged the UNESCO directorate to pursue dialogue between the Government and CNDD.

A new session of the National Assembly was convened in early October 1997. Ngendakumana expressed concern that the Government was impeding the functions of the legislature by refusing to pursue a dialogue with the assembly and by imposing what he termed a political and media embargo on its work.

The cross-border movement of vast numbers of refugees, provoked by regional ethnic and political violence, has dominated recent relations with Rwanda, Tanzania and the Democratic Republic of the Congo (formerly Zaire), and has long been a matter of considerable concern to the international aid community. An estimated 3,000 refugees had fled to Zaire in late 1991, and by early 1992 some 10,000 Burundians were still seeking refuge in Rwanda. In October and November 1993, following the abortive coup by factions of the Tutsi-dominated armed forces (see above), ethnic violence erupted on a massive scale throughout the country, claiming an estimated 150,000 lives and displacing an estimated 800,000 people, including 500,000 who fled into Tanzania, Rwanda and Zaire. Limited relief resources were overburdened in April 1994 by the exodus into Burundi of thousands of Rwandans, and by the repatriation of vast numbers of Burundians from refugee camps in Rwanda, as a result of the political violence and accompanying massacres following the death of President Habyarimana. In July 1995 UNHCR estimated that some 50,000 Rwandan refugees had been repatriated since the beginning of the year.

The uprising by Laurent-Désiré Kabila's Alliance des forces démocratiques pour la libération du Congo-Zaïre (AFDL) in eastern Zaire resulted in the return of large numbers of refugees: an estimated 300,000 returned to Burundi from late 1996, severely undermining the operations from Zaire of large numbers of FDD fighters who were believed to have been massed in refugee camps there. Moreover, the seizure of power in Kinshasa by the AFDL in May 1997 was welcomed by the Buyoya regime, which moved to forge close relations with Kabila's Democratic Republic of the Congo. The Congo remained a party to the continuing regional sanctions against Burundi, although a bilateral trade co-operation agreement was concluded in mid-1997.

Meanwhile, the Buyoya regime's relations with Tanzania were characterized not only by the continued presence of large numbers of Burundian refugees—some 300,000 refugees were registered in Tanzania in July 1997, at which time UNHCR reported that fighting in south-east Burundi was prompting further refugee movements across the border—but also by increasingly vociferous accusations on the part of the Buyoya Government that Tanzania was supporting the Hutu rebellion. Such allegations were strenuously denied by the Tanzanian Government, which stated that it would never allow the use of refugee camps on its territory for military training. Mutual suspicions by Tanzania's refusal to allow a representative of the Buyoya regime to take up the position of chargé d'affaires at the Burundian embassy in Dar es Salaam. In late August Tanzania announced that it had placed its armed forces on alert, stating that Burundian forces were mobilizing near the border in preparation for an invasion of the refugee camps. Meanwhile, the Buyoya Government's assertions that Nyerere was unduly biased in his role as mediator in the Burundian conflict further strained bilateral ties.

Government

Under the Constitution of March 1992, executive power is vested in the President, who is elected directly, by universal adult suffrage, for a five-year term, renewable only once. Statutory power is shared with the Prime Minister, who appoints a Council of Ministers. Legislative power is exercised by the National Assembly, whose members are elected directly, by universal adult suffrage, for a five-year renewable mandate. A Convention of Government, concluded among the major political parties in September 1994, detailed the terms of government for a four-year transitional period, and was incorporated into the Constitution in the same month. Following the *coup d'état* of 25 July 1996, the terms of the Constitution and the Convention of Government were suspended.

For the purposes of local government, Burundi comprises 15 provinces (administered by civilian governors), each of which is divided into districts and further subdivided into communes.

Defence

The army was merged with the police force in 1967. The total strength of the armed forces in August 1997 was estimated at 22,000, comprising an army of 18,500 (including an air wing of 100), and a paramilitary force of 3,500 gendarmes (including a 50-strong marine police force). Defence expenditure for 1997 was budgeted at 21,000m. Burundian francs.

Economic Affairs

In 1995, according to estimates by the World Bank, Burundi's gross national product (GNP), measured at average 1993–95 prices, was US $984m., equivalent to $160 per head. During 1985–95, it was estimated, GNP per head decreased, in real terms, at an average rate of 1.3% per year. Over the same period the population increased by an annual average of 2.8%. Burundi's gross domestic product (GDP) increased, in real terms, by an annual average of 2.2% in 1985–95. GDP increased by 5.0% in 1991 and by 2.7% in 1992; however, political turmoil contributed to a severe economic decline after 1993, with GDP falling by 6.6% in 1994 and 3.7% in 1995.

Agriculture (including forestry and fishing) contributed an estimated 57.8% of GDP in 1995. An estimated 90.8% of the labour force were employed in the sector. The principal cash crops are coffee (which accounted for about 81% of export earnings in 1994 and 1995), tea and cotton. Hides and skins are also exported. The main subsistence crops are cassava and sweet potatoes. Although Burundi is traditionally self-sufficient in food crops, population displacement as a result of the political crisis has resulted in considerable disruption in the sector, while the economic sanctions in force since the 1996 coup have further affected production, owing to a shortage of inputs. Moreover, an army-imposed ban on fishing on Lake Tanganyika has entailed the loss of an important source of food supply. The livestock-rearing sector has also been severely affected by the civil war. During 1985–95 agricultural GDP increased, in real terms, by an annual average of 0.8%. However, the sector's GDP decreased by 10.6% in 1994 and by an estimated 5.2% in 1995. Agricultural output increased by an annual average of 2.5% in 1985–92; during 1992–96, however, production declined by some 3.1% per year.

Industry (comprising mining, manufacturing, construction and utilities) engaged only 2.1% of the employed labour force in 1990, but (excluding handicrafts) contributed an estimated 14.8% of GDP in 1995. Industrial GDP increased, in real terms, by an annual average of 1.9% in 1985–95. Industrial GDP decreased by 9.9% in 1994 and by an estimated 8.2% in 1995.

Mining and power engaged 0.1% of the employed labour force in 1990 and contributed an estimated 0.6% of GDP in 1995. Gold (alluvial), tin, tungsten and columbo-tantalite are mined in small quantities. Burundi has important deposits of vanadium, uranium and also of nickel (estimated at 5% of world reserves). In addition, petroleum deposits have been detected.

Manufacturing engaged 1.2% of the employed labour force in 1990 and contributed an estimated 9.0% of GDP in 1995. The sector consists largely of the processing of agricultural products (coffee, cotton, tea and the extraction of vegetable oils). A number of small enterprises also produce beer, flour, cement, flootwear and textiles. Agricultural processing and food products accounted for an estimated 70.6% of manufacturing GDP in 1995. Manufacturing GDP decreased, in real terms, by an annual average of 5.2% in 1985–93. The sector's GDP declined by 16.8% in 1993, by 11.4% in 1994 and by an estimated 13.0% in 1995. Exports of manufactured products provided 11.8% of the total earnings in 1993, but the proportion was only 4.4% in 1994 and an estimated 6.5% in 1995.

Energy is derived principally from hydroelectric power (45.1% of electricity consumed in 1994 was imported). Peat is also exploited as an additional source of energy. Imports of fuel and energy comprised 32% of the value of merchandise imports in 1995.

The services sector contributed an estimated 27.4% of GDP in 1995 but engaged just 4.4% of the employed labour force in 1990. By 1995 the financial sector was experiencing severe difficulties, with a number of banks relying on financial support from the central bank. According to the World Bank, the GDP of the services sector increased by an average of 3.2% in 1985–95. However, the sector's GDP declined by 0.9% in 1994 and by an estimated 9.0% in 1995.

In 1995 Burundi recorded a visible trade deficit of US $63.1m., and there was a deficit of $6.5m. on the current account of the balance of payments. Countries of the European Union (in particular Belgium, the United Kingdom, France and Germany) accounted for an estimated 42.7% of import costs and 43.2% of export revenues in 1994. Significant trade was also conducted with Kenya and Tanzania prior to the imposition of regional sanctions in 1996. The main imports in 1993 were machinery and transport equipment, basic manufactures, chemicals, mineral fuels and food. The principal exports in 1995 were coffee, tea, cotton and hides and skins.

In 1995 the estimated budgetary deficit was 5,900m. Burundian francs, equivalent to 2.2% of GDP. Burundi's external debt at the end of 1995 was US $1,157m., of which $1,095m. was long-term public debt. In that year the cost of debt-servicing was equivalent to 27.7% of revenue from the export of goods and services. The annual rate of inflation averaged 8.5% in 1985–95. Consumer prices increased by an average of 19.3% in 1995 and by 26.4% in 1996. The inflation rate in the year to June 1997 was 35.4%.

Burundi maintains economic co-operation agreements with its neighbours Rwanda and the Democratic Republic of the Congo (formerly Zaire) through the Economic Community of the Great Lakes Countries (CEPGL, see p. 260). Burundi is also a member of the Common Market for Eastern and Southern Africa (COMESA, see p. 124), and of the International Coffee Organization (see p. 257).

In terms of average income, Burundi is one of the poorest countries in the world, and its economic performance is heavily dependent on world prices for its cash crops, most notably coffee. Burundi is therefore dependent on foreign assistance, not only for capital projects but also for budgetary support. Burundi has experienced a severe economic decline since 1993, largely as a result of the severe political upheaval and accompanying population displacement. Regional economic sanctions, imposed following the *coup d'état* of July 1996, have exacerbated the economic crisis. Despite some evidence of violations, the embargo resulted in fuel shortages, which impeded the distribution of food, and led to a rapid increase in the rate of inflation. A lack of agricultural inputs and supplies to manufacturing impeded these sectors, while the loss of access to traditional export routes obliged the Burundian authorities to seek lengthier and thus more costly means of transporting goods abroad. Meanwhile, acts of sabotage against power and manufacturing installations has caused further disruption, and the 'encampment' programme undertaken by the military (see Recent History) has had severe implications for the agricultural sector, as mainly Hutu farmers have been effectively removed from their areas of activity. An easing of the sanctions regime, on humanitarian grounds, was agreed in April 1997, while international agencies have pledged material and financial assistance to alleviate conditions for the displaced population. However, the normalization of economic activity, and thus the eventual restoration of growth, will greatly depend on the success of efforts to bring about a lasting peace settlement for Burundi.

Social Welfare

Wage-earners are protected by insurance against accidents and occupational diseases, and can draw on a pension fund. Medical facilities are, however, limited. In 1978 there were 22 hospitals, nine maternity units and 100 dispensaries. In 1981 Burundi had one hospital bed for every 286 inhabitants, and in 1984 there were 216 physicians (0.5 per 10,000 inhabitants) and 1,467 nursing personnel working in the country. Of total projected current expenditure (excluding debt-servicing) by the central Government in the budget for 1996, the Ministry of Health was allocated 2,500m. Burundian francs (6.9%).

Education

Education is provided free of charge. Kirundi is the language of instruction in primary schools, while French is used in secondary schools. Primary education, which is officially compulsory, begins at seven years of age and lasts for six years. Secondary education begins at the age of 13 and lasts for up to seven years, comprising a first cycle of four years and a second of three years. In 1992 the total enrolment at primary schools included 51% of children in the relevant age-group (males 56%; females 47%). Enrolment at secondary schools included only 5% of the population in the appropriate age-group (males 6%; females 4%). There is one university, in Bujumbura; some 4,256 students were enrolled at university-level institutions in 1992/93. The average rate of illiteracy among the population aged 15 years and over at the time of the 1990 census was 62.2% (males 51.5%; females 72.0%). Expenditure on education by all levels of government in 1992 was 8,586m. Burundian francs (12.2% of total government expenditure). Of total projected current expenditure (excluding debt-servicing) by the central Government in the budget for 1996, the two education ministries were allocated 10,438m. Burundian francs (28.7%).

Public Holidays

1998: 1 January (New Year's Day), 13 April (Easter Monday), 1 May (Labour Day), 21 May (Ascension Day), 1 July (Independence Day), 15 August (Assumption), 18 September (Victory of UPRONA Party), 1 November (All Saints' Day), 25 December (Christmas).

1999: 1 January (New Year's Day), 5 April (Easter Monday), 1 May (Labour Day), 13 May (Ascension Day), 1 July (Independence Day), 15 August (Assumption), 18 September (Victory of UPRONA Party), 1 November (All Saints' Day), 25 December (Christmas).

Weights and Measures

The metric system is in force.

Statistical Survey

Area and Population

AREA, POPULATION AND DENSITY

Area (sq km)	27,834*
Population (census results)†	
15–16 August 1979	4,028,420
16–30 August 1990	
Males	2,473,599
Females	2,665,474
Total	5,139,073
Population (official estimates at mid-year)	
1994	5,875,000
1995	5,982,000
1996	6,088,000
Density (per sq km) at mid-1996	218.7

* 10,747 sq miles.
† Excluding adjustment for underenumeration.

PRINCIPAL TOWNS

Bujumbura (capital), population 235,440 (census result, August 1990); Gitega 15,943 (1978).

Source: Banque de la République du Burundi.

BIRTHS AND DEATHS (UN estimates, annual averages)

	1980–85	1985–90	1990–95
Birth rate (per 1,000)	46.1	46.6	46.0
Death rate (per 1,000)	17.6	16.7	15.7

Expectation of life (UN estimates, years at birth, 1990–95): 50.2 (males 48.4; females 51.9).

Source: UN, *World Population Prospects: The 1994 Revision.*

ECONOMICALLY ACTIVE POPULATION*
(persons aged 10 years and over, 1990 census)

	Males	Females	Total
Agriculture, hunting, forestry and fishing	1,153,890	1,420,553	2,574,443
Mining and quarrying	1,146	39	1,185
Manufacturing	24,120	9,747	33,867
Electricity, gas and water	1,847	74	1,921
Construction	19,447	290	19,737
Trade, restaurants and hotels	19,667	6,155	25,822
Transport, storage and communications	8,193	311	8,504
Financing, insurance, real estate and business services	1,387	618	2,005
Community, social and personal services	68,905	16,286	85,191
Activities not adequately defined	8,653	4,617	13,270
Total labour force	1,307,255	1,458,690	2,765,945

* Figures exclude persons seeking work for the first time, totalling 13,832 (males 9,608; females 4,224).

Source: UN, *Demographic Yearbook.*

Agriculture

PRINCIPAL CROPS ('000 metric tons)

	1994	1995	1996
Wheat*	8	9	9
Rice (paddy)*	38	27	42
Maize*	123	153	144
Millet*	11	14	11
Sorghum*	45	66	66
Potatoes*	32	42	42
Sweet potatoes*	601	674	670
Cassava (Manioc)*	527	501	549
Yams*	8	8	8
Taro (Coco yam)*	94	102	95
Dry beans*	232	319	288
Dry peas*	24	37	36
Groundnuts (in shell)	10*	13*	10†
Cottonseed	3*	3†	2*
Cotton (lint)	2	2*	1*
Palm kernels†	1	1	1
Vegetables and melons†	210	220	210
Sugar cane	121	138†	148†
Bananas and plantains*	1,487	1,421	1,544
Other fruits (excl. melons)	84	80	80
Coffee (green)	41	26*	25*
Tea (made)	7	5†	5†

* Unofficial figure(s). † FAO estimate(s).

Source: FAO, *Production Yearbook.*

LIVESTOCK (FAO estimates, '000 head, year ending September)

	1994	1995	1996
Cattle	420	400	390
Pigs	80	75	72
Sheep	370	330	320
Goats	930	910	900

Poultry (FAO estimates, million): 4 in 1994; 4 in 1995; 4 in 1996.

Source: FAO, *Production Yearbook.*

LIVESTOCK PRODUCTS (FAO estimates, '000 metric tons)

	1994	1995	1996
Beef and veal	11	11	10
Mutton and lamb	1	1	1
Goat meat	3	3	3
Pig meat	5	5	4
Poultry meat	5	5	5
Cows' milk	32	31	30
Sheep's milk	1	1	1
Goats' milk	7	7	7
Poultry eggs	3	3	3
Cattle hides	2	2	2
Goatskins	1	1	1

Source: FAO, *Production Yearbook.*

Forestry

ROUNDWOOD REMOVALS ('000 cubic metres, excl. bark)

	1992	1993	1994
Sawlogs, veneer logs and logs for sleepers	6*	46	45
Other industrial wood	47*	51	62
Fuel wood*	4,448	4,588	4,724
Total	4,501*	4,685	4,831

* FAO estimate(s).

Source: FAO, *Yearbook of Forest Products*.

SAWNWOOD PRODUCTION ('000 cubic metres, incl. railway sleepers)

	1992*	1993	1994
Coniferous (softwood)	3	11	9
Broadleaved (hardwood)	—	9	12
Total	3	20	21

* FAO estimates.

Source: FAO, *Yearbook of Forest Products*.

Fishing

('000 metric tons, live weight)

	1993	1994*	1995
Dagaas	18.4	18.0	18.2
Freshwater perches	2.5	2.7	2.9
Others	1.2	0.1	0.1
Total catch	22.1	20.7	21.1

* FAO estimates.

Source: FAO, *Yearbook of Fishery Statistics*.

Mining

	1992	1993	1994
Gold (kilograms)*†	32	20	20
Tin ore (metric tons)*†	110	50	50
Kaolin ('000 metric tons)*	10	5†	5†
Peat ('000 metric tons)	12	11	n.a.

* Data from US Bureau of Mines.

† Estimate(s). Figures for gold and tin refer to the metal content of ores.

Source: UN, *Industrial Commodity Statistics Yearbook*.

Industry

SELECTED PRODUCTS ('000 metric tons, unless otherwise indicated)

	1992	1993	1994*
Beer ('000 hectolitres)	1,161.6	1,188.6	1,382.7
Soft drinks ('000 hectolitres)	159.9	179.3	201.4
Cottonseed oil ('000 hectolitres)	3.4	3.3	2.8
Sugar	17.3	13.9	12.3
Cigarettes (million)†	453	517	n.a.
Paint	1.0	0.8	0.6
Insecticides	2.0	2.7	3.9
Soap	3.0	5.2	5.7
Bottles	5.3	3.5	5.1
Blankets ('000)	196.2	242.7	248.4
Footwear ('000 pairs)	450.6	405.2	74.9
Fibro-cement products	0.3	1.9	0.8
Corrugated metal sheets	1.9	1.2	0.6
Steel rods	0.2	0.4	0.3
Batteries ('000 cartons)‡	36.2	35.0	28.9
Electric energy (million kWh)†	107	140*	149

* Estimate(s).

† Source: UN, *Industrial Commodity Statistics Yearbook*.

‡ Cartons of 240 batteries.

Source: Banque de la République du Burundi.

Finance

CURRENCY AND EXCHANGE RATES

Monetary Units

100 centimes = 1 Burundian franc.

Sterling and Dollar Equivalents (30 September 1997)

£1 sterling = 562.6 francs;
US $1 = 348.3 francs;
1,000 Burundian francs = £1.777 = $2.871.

Average Exchange Rate (Burundian francs per US dollar)

1994 252.66
1995 249.76
1996 302.75

Note: In November 1983 the Burundian franc was linked to the IMF's special drawing right (SDR), with the mid-point exchange rate initially fixed at SDR 1 = 122.7 francs. This remained in force until July 1986, after which the rate was frequently adjusted. A rate of SDR 1 = 232.14 francs was established in December 1989. This was in operation until August 1991, when the currency was devalued by about 15%, with the new rate set at SDR 1 = 273.07 francs. This arrangement ended in May 1992, when the Burundian franc was linked to a 'basket' of the currencies of the country's principal trading partners.

BUDGET ('000 million Burundian francs)

Revenue*	1993	1994†	1995†
Tax revenue	34.0	38.9	47.2
Taxes on income and profits	10.6	8.4	9.6
Domestic taxes on goods and services	13.2	17.7	18.8
Transaction tax	6.8	6.7	7.3
Excise tax	6.3	10.7	11.3
Beer	6.1	10.3	10.8
Taxes on international trade	8.3	12.5	18.5
Import duties	7.7	6.9	7.9
Export tax	0.4	5.4	10.4
Coffee	0.3	5.3	10.2
Non-tax revenue	5.8	3.3	2.7
Total	39.8	42.2	49.9

Expenditure‡	1993	1994†	1995†
Current expenditure	39.1	41.9	45.2
Salaries	16.3	17.4	19.0
Military	5.1	5.9	6.4
Goods and services	8.4	10.4	12.7
Military	3.5	4.2	4.1
Transfers and subsidies	5.2	5.8	6.7
Public administrations	3.9	4.3	4.4
International organizations	0.3	0.2	0.3
Households	1.0	1.3	2.0
Interest payments	3.7	3.6	4.4
Foreign	2.9	2.9	3.6
Domestic	0.8	0.7	0.8
Extrabudgetary/exceptional expenditure	5.6	4.7	2.4
Capital expenditure	29.3	19.8	24.7
Domestic resources	5.6	4.1	7.9
Project lending	10.9	11.1	10.8
Capital grants	12.8	4.6	6.0
Sub-total	68.5	61.6	70.0
Adjustment for payments arrears	−2.3	−0.3	−3.5
Total	66.2	61.3	66.5

* Excluding grants received ('000 million Burundian francs): 20.7 in 1993; 5.7† in 1994; 9.7† in 1995.

† Estimate(s).

‡ Excluding lending minus payments ('000 million Burundian francs): 0.4 in 1993; −2.1† in 1994; −0.9† in 1995.

§ Minus sign indicates an increase in arrears.

Source: IMF, *Burundi—Statistical Annex* (May 1996).

CENTRAL BANK RESERVES (US $ million at 31 December)

	1994	1995	1996
Gold*	6.59	6.66	6.36
IMF special drawing rights	0.21	0.07	0.11
Reserve position in IMF	8.56	8.71	8.43
Foreign exchange	195.94	200.67	131.06
Total	211.30	216.11	145.96

* Valued at market-related prices.

Source: IMF, *International Financial Statistics.*

MONEY SUPPLY (million Burundian francs at 31 December)

	1994	1995	1996
Currency outside banks	19,075	n.a.	23,976
Deposits at central bank	649	577	371
Demand deposits at commercial banks	19,095	18,730	18,038
Demand deposits at other monetary institutions	1,329	n.a.	1,259
Total money	40,147	n.a.	43,644

Source: IMF, *International Financial Statistics.*

COST OF LIVING
(Consumer Price Index for Bujumbura; base: January 1991 = 100)

	1993	1994	1995*
Food	113.5	133.7	159.8
Clothing	135.3	136.0	155.6
Housing, heating and light	105.1	119.2	145.6
Transport	100.5	101.4	102.0
All items (incl. others)	111.7	128.2	152.0

* Provisional.

Source: IMF, *Burundi—Statistical Annex* (May 1996).

1995 (revised): Food 160.4; All items 152.9 (Source: UN, *Monthly Bulletin of Statistics*).

1996 (base: 1995 = 100): All items 126.4 (Source: IMF, *International Financial Statistics*).

NATIONAL ACCOUNTS (million Burundian francs at current prices)

Composition of the Gross National Product

	1994	1995	1996
GDP in purchasers' values	251,760	301,753	311,945
Net factor income from abroad	−2,876	−3,152	−4,246
Gross national product	248,884	298,601	307,699

Source: IMF, *International Financial Statistics.*

Expenditure on the Gross Domestic Product

	1994	1995	1996
Government final consumption expenditure	27,986	28,231	34,647
Private final consumption expenditure	241,748	280,763	279,427
Increase in stocks	53	−199	−481
Gross fixed capital formation	24,536	28,933	26,574
Total domestic expenditure	294,323	337,728	340,167
Exports of goods and services	24,029	32,198	15,209
Less Imports of goods and services	66,592	68,173	43,431
GDP in purchasers' values	251,760	301,753	311,945

Source: IMF, *International Financial Statistics.*

Gross Domestic Product by Economic Activity*

	1993	1994	1995
Agriculture, hunting, forestry and fishing	111,027	116,156	126,664
Mining and quarrying; Electricity, gas and water	1,532	1,374	1,296
Manufacturing	18,346	19,858	19,756
Construction	10,041	10,303	11,436
Trade, restaurants and hotels	9,362	10,368	8,709
Transport, storage and communications	7,709	9,963	8,892
Government services	33,826	37,025	37,866
Other services	4,295	5,529	4,648
GDP at factor cost	196,138	210,575	219,268
Indirect taxes, *less* subsidies	23,235	26,495	37,623
GDP in purchasers' values	219,373	237,070	256,891

* Figures are estimates, and exclude the GDP of the artisan branch (million francs): 8,855 in 1993; 8,291 in 1994; 8,099 in 1995.

Source: IMF, *Burundi—Statistical Annex* (May 1996).

BALANCE OF PAYMENTS (US $ million)

	1993	1994	1995
Exports of goods f.o.b.	73.9	80.7	112.5
Imports of goods f.o.b.	−172.8	−172.6	−175.6
Trade balance	−99.0	−91.9	−63.1
Exports of services	14.2	14.6	16.6
Imports of services	−115.5	−95.0	−101.8
Balance on goods and services	−200.2	−172.3	−148.3
Other income received	11.2	8.1	10.4
Other income paid	−22.2	−19.5	−19.7
Balance on goods, services and income	−211.2	−183.7	−157.6
Current transfers received	183.8	167.0	153.3
Current transfers paid	−1.8	−1.6	−2.1
Current balance	−29.2	−18.3	−6.5
Capital account (net)	−1.2	−0.2	−0.8
Direct investment abroad	−0.1	−0.1	−0.6
Direct investment from abroad	0.5	—	2.0
Other investment assets	−1.5	−1.6	7.3
Other investment liabilities	53.6	32.9	18.3
Net errors and omissions	−6.1	23.0	16.1
Overall balance	16.0	35.7	35.8

Source: IMF, *International Financial Statistics.*

External Trade

PRINCIPAL COMMODITIES (distribution by SITC, US $ '000)

Imports c.i.f.	1991	1992	1993
Food and live animals	22,675	19,706	20,312
Cereals and cereal preparations	14,424	12,520	13,341
Wheat meal and flour of wheat and meslin	6,453	3,904	3,859
Flour of wheat or meslin	6,445	3,835	3,859
Cereal preparations, etc.	6,447	7,116	7,480
Malt (including malt flour)	6,290	6,962	7,365
Crude materials (inedible) except fuels	8,081	4,915	5,478
Mineral fuels, lubricants, etc.	31,183	27,992	25,387
Petroleum, petroleum products, etc.	31,044	27,888	25,346
Refined petroleum products	29,603	27,248	24,538
Motor spirit (gasoline) and other light oils	12,511	10,570	8,630
Gas oils	9,893	8,966	7,993
Chemicals and related products	33,890	32,475	28,807
Medicinal and pharmaceutical products	10,289	11,554	8,523
Manufactured fertilizers	3,228	4,865	4,562
Artificial resins, plastic materials, etc.	4,774	4,721	5,401
Disinfectants, insecticides, fungicides, weed-killers, etc., for retail sale	5,809	3,581	2,785
Insecticides	5,713	3,451	2,635
Basic manufactures	52,433	48,948	42,868
Rubber manufactures	6,641	5,383	7,077
Rubber tyres, tubes, etc.	5,334	4,059	5,215
Paper, paperboard and manufactures	6,062	5,777	5,556
Non-metallic mineral manufactures	13,512	12,898	9,445
Lime, cement, etc.	11,093	10,896	7,145
Cement	10,481	10,226	6,820
Machinery and transport equipment	70,144	63,206	43,603
General industrial machinery, equipment and parts	29,926	23,147	20,484
Electrical machinery, apparatus and appliances	12,351	14,437	3,894
Road vehicles and parts (excl. tyres, engines and electrical parts)	26,388	23,999	18,265
Passenger motor cars (excl. buses)	9,687	8,202	5,350
Motor vehicles for the transport of goods or materials	9,557	7,530	5,984
Parts and accessories for cars, buses, lorries, etc.	4,326	5,543	4,194
Miscellaneous manufactured articles	12,105	16,798	8,188
Photographic apparatus, optical goods, watches and clocks	6,725	10,154	4,182
Special transactions and commodities not classified according to kind	14,291	13,406	19,877
Total (incl. others)	247,087	229,508	204,525

Exports f.o.b.	1991	1992	1993
Food and live animals	82,477	59,065	52,300
Coffee, tea, cocoa and spices	82,477	59,065	51,936
Coffee (incl. husks and skins) and substitutes containing coffee	74,149	49,665	43,262
Tea and maté	8,328	9,400	8,674
Tea	n.a.	9,400	8,674
Beverages and tobacco	60	752	2,097
Tobacco and tobacco manufactures	—	562	1,703
Cigarettes	—	562	1,703
Crude materials (inedible) except fuels	2,384	1,676	4,089
Raw hides, skins and furskins	2,384	1,676	844
Textile fibres and waste	—	—	3,245
Cotton	—	—	3,245
Raw cotton (excl. linters)	—	—	3,245
Basic manufactures	2,464	4,413	4,402
Textile yarn, fabrics, etc.	1,340	1,679	2,442
Woven cotton fabrics (excl. narrow or special fabrics)	1,340	1,679	2,442
Non-metallic mineral manufactures	1,051	2,417	1,909
Glassware	1,002	2,390	1,881
Glass bottles, jars, etc.	1,002	2,390	1,729
Special transactions and commodities not classified according to kind	4,150	8,795	4,826
Total (incl. others)	91,536	74,701	68,703

Source: UN, *International Trade Statistics Yearbook*.

1994 (estimates, US $ million): *Imports c.i.f.*: Capital goods 56.1; Intermediate goods 72.0 (Petroleum products 29.0); Consumption goods 111.2 (Food 54.6); Total 239.3. *Exports f.o.b.*: Coffee 99.7; Tea 8.9; Cotton 5.4; Hides and skins 1.3; Other primary products 2.9; Manufactured products 5.5 Total 123.6.

1995 (estimates, US $ million): *Imports c.i.f.*: Capital goods 61.7; Intermediate goods 79.3 (Petroleum products 31.9); Consumption goods 105.0 (Food 51.4); Total 246.1. *Exports f.o.b.*: Coffee 93.6; Tea 9.1; Cotton 1.8; Hides and skins 1.4; Other primary products 2.7; Manufactured products 7.5; Total 116.0.

Source (for 1994 and 1995): IMF, *Burundi—Statistical Annex* (May 1996).

1996 (US $ million): Total imports c.i.f. 130; Total exports f.o.b. 40 (Source: UN, *Monthly Bulletin of Statistics).*

PRINCIPAL TRADING PARTNERS

Imports c.i.f. (US $ '000)	1991	1992	1993
Belgium-Luxembourg	35,781	34,108	33,809
China, People's Repub.	14,562	8,371	8,176
Cyprus	27,123	—	—
France	24,145	25,493	23,676
Germany	18,695	17,614	13,865
Iran	—	7,520	12,578
Italy	8,773	8,053	9,246
Japan	20,876	18,585	18,754
Kenya	6,999	7,520	6,590
Korea, Republic	2,655	1,828	1,876
Malawi	2,936	95	29
Netherlands	5,728	6,305	6,319
Tanzania	4,024	20,538	11,752
United Arab Emirates	1,553	3,093	2,068
United Kingdom	4,118	5,289	3,459
USA	4,346	9,801	3,638
Zambia	7,676	6,648	5,015
Zimbabwe	4,789	2,151	2,237
Total (incl. others)	247,087	229,508	204,525

Source: UN, *International Trade Statistics Yearbook*.

Exports (million Burundian Francs)	1989	1990	1991
Belgium-Luxembourg	169.9	99.8	238.6
France	790.0	1,246.1	818.6
Germany	1,876.4	1,760.0	2,905.5
Italy	275.0	302.5	164.0
Netherlands	119.6	180.9	561.9
United Kingdom	280.0	808.2	410.3
USA	887.7	1,508.8	3,207.1
Others	7,905.8	6,878.0	8,338.9
Total	12,304.4	12,783.6	16,644.9

1991 (revised figure, million Burundian francs): Total exports f.o.b. 16,698.

Source: Banque de la République du Burundi.

Transport

ROAD TRAFFIC (estimates, '000 motor vehicles in use)

	1992	1993	1994
Passenger cars	17.5	18.5	17.5
Commercial vehicles	11.8	12.3	10.2

Source: UN, *Statistical Yearbook*.

LAKE TRAFFIC (Bujumbura—'000 metric tons)

	1989	1990	1991
Goods:			
Arrivals	150.4	152.9	188.4
Departures	33.0	32.5	35.1

Source: Banque de la République du Burundi.

CIVIL AVIATION (traffic on scheduled services)

	1992	1993	1994
Passengers carried ('000)	9	9	9
Passenger-km (million)	2	2	2

Source: UN, *Statistical Yearbook*.

Tourism

	1992	1993	1994
Tourist arrivals ('000)	86	75	29
Tourist receipts (US $ million)	3	3	3

Source: UN, *Statistical Yearbook*.

Communications Media

	1992	1993	1994
Radio receivers ('000 in use)	360	375	400
Television receivers ('000 in use)	5	9	9
Telephones ('000 main lines in use)	13	16	16
Telefax stations (number in use)	n.a.	80	n.a.
Mobile cellular telephones (subscribers)	n.a.	320	340
Daily newspapers:			
Number	1	n.a.	1
Circulation ('000 copies)	20	n.a.	20

Sources: UNESCO, *Statistical Yearbook*; UN, *Statistical Yearbook*..

Education

(1992/93, unless otherwise indicated)

	Teachers	Pupils
Pre-primary*	49	2,381
Primary	10,400	651,086
Secondary:		
General	2,060	46,381
Teacher-training		2,470
Vocational	502	6,862
Higher	556	4,256

* Figures refer to 1988/89.

Primary schools: 1,418 in 1992/93.

Source: UNESCO, *Statistical Yearbook*.

Directory

The Constitution

The Constitution was promulgated on 13 March 1992 and provided for the establishment of a plural political system. The Constitution seeks to guarantee human rights and basic freedoms for all citizens, together with the freedom of the press. Executive powers are vested in the President, who (under normal circumstances—see below) is elected directly, by universal adult suffrage, for a five-year term, renewable only once. Statutory power is shared with the Prime Minister, who appoints a Council of Ministers. Legislative power is exercised by a National Assembly, whose members are elected directly, by universal adult suffrage, for a five-year renewable mandate. In September 1994 a Convention of Government was agreed among the country's major political parties. The Convention, which defines the terms of government for a four-year transitional period, provides for the establishment of a National Security Council of 10 members, including the President, the Prime Minister and the Ministers of State with responsibility for External Affairs, Interior and Public Security, and National Defence. The Convention was incorporated into the Constitution on 22 September 1994. However, the Convention disintegrated in July 1996, prompting the military coup which returned Maj. Pierre Buyoya to power.

The Government

HEAD OF STATE

President: Maj. PIERRE BUYOYA (assumed power 25 July 1996).

NATIONAL SECURITY COUNCIL

(January 1998)

Maj. PIERRE BUYOYA
PASCAL-FIRMIN NDIMIRA
LUC RUKINGAMA
Lt-Col EPITACE BAYAGANAKANDI
VÉNÉRAND NZOHABONAYO
JEAN-BOSCO BUTASI
Lt-Col MARTIN NKURIKIYE
STANISLAS NTAHOBARI
Col ASCENSION TWAGIRAMUNGU

COUNCIL OF MINISTERS

(January 1998)

Prime Minister: PASCAL-FIRMIN NDIMIRA.

Minister of External Relations and Co-operation: LUC RUKINGAMA.

Minister of the Interior and Public Security: Lt.-Col EPITACE BAYAGANAKANDI.

Minister of Justice: TÉRENCE SINUNGURUZA.

Minister of National Defence: (vacant).

Minister of Development, Planning and Reconstruction: EVARISTE MINANI.

Minister of Communal Development: PIERRE BAMBASI.

Minister of Relocation and Resettlement of Displaced and Repatriated Persons: PASCAL NKURUNZIZA.

Minister of Territorial Development and the Environment: SAMUEL BIGAWA.

Minister of Agriculture and Livestock: DAMAS NYIRANGIWANGIRA.

Minister of Finance: (vacant).

Minister of Commerce, Industry and Tourism: GRÉGOIRE BARANYIZIGIYE.

Minister of Labour, Handicrafts and Professional Training: BARNABÉ MUKERAGIRANWA.

Minister of the Public Service: MONIQUE NDAKOZI.

Minister of Primary Education and Adult Literacy: JOSEPH NDAYISABA.

Minister of Secondary and Higher Education and Scientific Research: LOGATIEN NDORICIMPA.

Minister of Social Action and Women's Affairs: CHRISTINE RUHAZA.

Minister of Culture, Youth and Sport: BONAVENTURE GASUTWA.

Minister of Public Health: JUMA KARIBURIJO.

Minister of Communications: PIERRE-CLAVER NDAYISHARYE.

Minister of Public Works and Equipment: VITAL NZOBONIMPA.

Minister of Transport, Posts and Telecommunications: VÉNÉRAND NZOHABONAYO.

Minister of Energy and Mines: BERNARD BARANDEREKA.

Minister of Human Rights, Institutional Reforms and Relations with the National Assembly: EUGÈNE NINDORERA.

Minister of the Peace Process: AMBROISE NIYONSABA.

There are also two Secretaries of State.

MINISTRIES

Office of the President: Bujumbura; tel. (2) 26063; telex 5049.

Office of the Prime Minister: Bujumbura.

Ministry of Agriculture and Livestock: Bujumbura; tel. (2) 22087.

Ministry of Commerce, Industry and Tourism: Bujumbura; tel. (2) 25330.

Ministry of Communal Development: Bujumbura.

Ministry of Communications: Bujumbura.

Ministry of Culture, Youth and Sport: Bujumbura; tel. (2) 26822.

Ministry of Development, Planning and Reconstruction: BP 1830, Bujumbura; tel. (2) 23988; telex 5135.

Ministry of Energy and Mines: BP 745, Bujumbura; tel. (2) 25909; telex 5182; fax (2) 23337.

Ministry of External Relations and Co-operation: Bujumbura; tel. (2) 22150; telex 5065.

Ministry of Finance: BP 1830, Bujumbura; tel. (2) 25142; telex 5135; fax (2) 23128.

Ministry of Human Rights, Institutional Reforms and Relations with the National Assembly: Bujumbura.

Ministry of the Interior and Public Security: Bujumbura.

Ministry of Justice: Bujumbura; tel. (2) 22148.

Ministry of Labour, Handicrafts and Professional Training: Bujumbura.

Ministry of National Defence: Bujumbura.

Ministry of National Education: Bujumbura.

Ministry of the Peace Process: Bujumbura.

Ministry of Public Security: Bujumbura.

Ministry of the Public Service: BP 1480, Bujumbura; tel. (2) 23514; fax (2) 28715.

Ministry of Public Works and Equipment: BP 1860, Bujumbura; tel. (2) 26841; telex 5048; fax (2) 26840.

Ministry of Relocation and Resettlement of Displaced and Repatriated Persons: Bujumbura.

Ministry of Social Action and Women's Affairs: Bujumbura; tel. (2) 25039.

Ministry of Territorial Development and Environment: Bujumbura.

Ministry of Transport, Posts and Telecommunications: BP 2000, Bujumbura; tel. (2) 22923; telex 5103; fax (2) 26900.

President and Legislature

PRESIDENT

Following the assassination of President Melchior Ndadaye and his constitutional successor in October 1993, a constitutional amendment was adopted whereby a successor was to be elected by the National Assembly. On 13 January 1994 Cyprien Ntaryamira, a member of FRODEBU, was elected President by 78 of the 79 votes cast by the National Assembly. Following Ntaryamira's death in April 1994, the Speaker of the National Assembly, Sylvestre Ntibantunganya, assumed the presidency for an interim, three-month period (subsequently extended for a further three months), in accordance with the Constitution. Ntibantunganya was subsequently appointed to the presidency for a four-year transitional term, by broad consensus in accordance with the Convention of Government adopted in September 1994. In July 1996 Ntibantunganya was deposed by a military coup and replaced by Maj. Pierre Buyoya; the National Assembly was immediately suspended, but was reconvened in October.

NATIONAL ASSEMBLY

Speaker: LÉONCE NGENDAKUMANA (FRODEBU).

Legislative Elections, 29 June 1993

Party	Votes cast	% of votes cast	Seats
FRODEBU	1,532,107	71.04	65
UPRONA	462,324	21.44	16
RPB	35,932	1.67	—
PRP	29,966	1.39	—
RADDES	26,631	1.23	—
PP	24,372	1.13	—
Independents	853	0.04	—
Invalid votes	44,474	2.06	—
Total	2,156,659	100.00	81

PROVINCIAL GOVERNORS
(December 1997)

Bubanza: Lt-Col GÉRARD HABIYO

Bujumbura (Rural): STANISLAS NTAHOBARI.

Bururi: ANDRÉ NDAYIZAMBA.

Cankuzo: HENRI TUZAGI.

Cibitoke: Lt-Col ANTOINE NIMBESHA.

Gitega: Lt-Col LOUIS MURENGERA.

Karuzi: Lt-Col GABRIEL GUNUNGU.

Kayanza: Lt-Col DANIEL MENGERI.

Kirundo: DEOGRATIAS BIZIMANA.

Makamba: JEAN-BAPTISTE GAHIMBARE.

Muramvya: NESTOR NIYUNGEKO.

Muyinga: Col ALEXIS BANUMA.

Ngozi: Col ASCENSION TWAGIRAMUNGU.

Rutana: LÉONIDAS HAKIZIMANA.

Ruyigi: HENRI BUKUMBANYA.

Political Organizations

Although the March 1992 Constitution provided for the establishment of a multi-party system, political parties are required to demonstrate firm commitment to national unity, and impartiality with regard to ethnic or regional origin, gender and religion, in order to receive legal recognition.

The military Government recognized 14 political parties at mid-1997.

Alliance burundaise-africaine pour le salut (ABASA): Bujumbura.

Alliance nationale pour les droits et le développement economique (ANADDE): Bujumbura; f. 1992.

AV-Intware (Alliance of the Brave): Bujumbura.

Front pour la démocratie au Burundi (FRODEBU): Bujumbura; f. 1992; Chair. JEAN MINANI; Sec.-Gen. AUGUSTIN NZOJIBWAMI.

Inkinzo y'Ijambo Ry'abarundi (Inkinzo) (Guarantor of Freedom of Speech in Burundi): Bujumbura; f. 1993; Pres. Dr ALPHONSE RUGAMBARARA.

Parti indépendant des travailleurs (PIT): Bujumbura.

Parti libéral (PL): Bujumbura; f. 1992.

Parti du peuple (PP): Bujumbura; f. 1992; Leader SHADRAK NIYONKURU.

Parti de réconciliation du peuple (PRP): Bujumbura; f. 1992; Leader MATHIAS HITIMANA.

Parti pour le redressement national (PARENA): Bujumbura; f. 1994; Leader JEAN-BAPTISTE BAGAZA.

Parti social démocrate (PSD): Bujumbura; f. 1993.

Rassemblement pour le démocratie et le développement économique et social (RADDES): Bujumbura; f. 1992; Chair. JOSEPH NZENZIMANA.

Rassemblement du peuple burundien (RPB): Bujumbura; f. 1992; Leader PHILIPPE NZOGBO.

Union pour le progrès national (UPRONA): BP 1810, Bujumbura; tel. (2) 25028; telex 5057; f. 1958; following the 1961 elections, the numerous small parties which had been defeated merged with UPRONA, which became the sole legal political party in 1966; party activities were suspended following the coup of Sept. 1987, but resumed in 1989; Leader CHARLES MUKASI.

The constitutional reforms, which exclude political organizations advocating 'tribalism, divisionalism or violence' and require party leaderships to be equally representative of Hutu and Tutsi ethnic groups, have been opposed by some externally-based opposition parties. These include the **Parti de libération du peuple hutu (PALIPEHUTU**, f. 1980 and based in Tanzania), which seeks to advance the interests of the Hutu ethnic group. An armed dissident wing of PALIPEHUTU, known as the **Force nationale de libération (FNL)**, led by KABORA KHOSSAN, is based in southern Rwanda. Another grouping representing the interests of Hutu extremists, the **Conseil national pour la défense de la démocratie (CNDD)** is led by LÉONARD NYANGOMA, who was in exile in Zaire (now the Democratic Republic of the Congo) prior to Tutsi-led rebellion of 1996–97. The CNDD claims a 30,000-strong armed wing, the **Force pour la défence de la démocratie (FDD)**.

Diplomatic Representation

EMBASSIES IN BURUNDI

Belgium: 9 ave de l'Industrie, BP 1920, Bujumbura; tel. (2) 23676; telex 5033; Ambassador: DENIS BANNEEL.

China, People's Republic: BP 2550, Bujumbura; tel. (2) 24307; Ambassador: ZHANG LONGBAO.

Congo, Democratic Republic: 5 ave Olsen, BP 872, Bujumbura; tel. (2) 23492; Ambassador: (vacant).

Egypt: 31 ave de la Liberté, BP 1520, Bujumbura; tel. (2) 23161; telex 5040; Ambassador: MUHAMMAD MOUSA.

France: 60 ave de l'UPRONA, BP 1740, Bujumbura; tel. (2) 26767; fax (2) 27443; Ambassador: JEAN-PIERRE LAJAUNIE.

Germany: 22 rue 18 septembre, BP 480, Bujumbura; tel. (2) 26412; telex 5068; Ambassador: KARL FLITTNER.

Holy See: 46 chaussée Prince Louis-Rwagasore, BP 1068, Bujumbura (Apostolic Nunciature); tel. (2) 22326; fax (2) 23176; Apostolic Nuncio: Most Rev. EMIL PAUL TSCHERRIG, Titular Archbishop of Voli.

Korea, Democratic People's Republic: BP 1620, Bujumbura; tel. (2) 22881; Ambassador: PAE SOK JUN.

Romania: rue Pierre Ngendandumwe, BP 2770, Bujumbura; tel. (2) 24135; Chargé d'affaires a.i.: ALEXANDRA ANDREI.

Russia: 78 blvd de l'UPRONA, BP 1034, Bujumbura; tel. (2) 26098; telex 5164; fax (2) 22984; Ambassador: IGOR S. LIAKIN-FROLOV.

Rwanda: 24 ave du Zaïre, BP 400, Bujumbura; tel. (2) 23140; telex 5032; Ambassador: SYLVESTRE UWIBAJIJE.

Tanzania: BP 1653, Bujumbura; Ambassador: NICHOLAS J. MARO.

USA: ave des Etats-Unis, BP 1720, Bujumbura; tel. (2) 23454; fax (2) 22926; Ambassador: MORRIS N. HUGHES.

Judicial System

The 1981 Constitution prescribed a judicial system wherein the judges were subject to the decisions of UPRONA. Under a programme of legal reform, announced in 1986, provincial courts were to be replaced by a dual system of courts of civil and criminal jurisdiction. A network of mediation and conciliation courts was to be established to arbitrate in minor disputes arising among the rural population. Substantial reforms of the legal system were expected to follow the implementation of the 1992 Constitution.

Supreme Court: BP 1460, Bujumbura; tel. (2) 22571; fax (2) 22148. Court of final instance; four divisions: ordinary, cassation, constitutional and administrative.

Courts of Appeal: Bujumbura, Gitega and Ngozi.

Tribunals of First Instance: There are 17 provincial tribunals and 123 smaller resident tribunals in other areas.

Tribunal of Trade: Bujumbura.

Tribunals of Labour: Bujumbura and Gitega.

Administrative Courts: Bujumbura and Gitega.

Religion

More than 65% of the population are Christians, the majority of whom (an estimated 61%) are Roman Catholics. Anglicans number about 60,000. There are about 200,000 Protestants, of whom some 160,000 are Pentecostalists. Fewer than 40% of the population adhere to traditional beliefs, which include the worship of the God 'Imana'. About 1% of the population are Muslims. The Bahá'í Faith is also active in Burundi.

CHRISTIANITY

Conseil National des Eglises protestantes du Burundi (CNEB): BP 17, Bujumbura; tel. (2) 24216; fax (2) 27941; f. 1970; five mem. churches; Pres. Rt. Rev. JEAN NDUWAYO (Anglican Bishop of Gitega); Gen. Sec. Rev. OSIAS HABINGABWA.

The Anglican Communion

The Church of the Province of Burundi, established in 1992, comprises four dioceses.

Archbishop of Burundi and Bishop of Matana: Most Rev. SAMUEL SINDAMUKA, BP 1300, Bujumbura; tel. (2) 24389; telex 5127; fax (2) 29129.

Provincial Secretary: Rev. BERNARD NTAHOTURI, BP 2098, Bujumbura.

The Roman Catholic Church

Burundi comprises one archdiocese and six dioceses. At 31 December 1995 there were an estimated 3,594,127 adherents.

Bishops' Conference: Conférence des Evêques Catholiques du Burundi, 5 blvd de l'UPRONA, BP 1390, Bujumbura; tel. (2) 23263; fax (2) 23270; f. 1980; Pres. Rt Rev. BERNARD BUDUDIRA, Bishop of Bururi.

Archbishop of Gitega: (vacant), Archevêché, BP 118, Gitega; tel. (40) 2160; fax (40) 2547.

Other Christian Churches

Union of Baptist Churches of Burundi: Rubura, DS 117, Bujumbura 1; Pres. PAUL BARUHENAMWO.

Other denominations active in the country include the Evangelical Christian Brotherhood of Burundi, the Free Methodist Church of Burundi and the United Methodist Church of Burundi.

BAHÁ'Í FAITH

National Spiritual Assembly: BP 1578, Bujumbura.

The Press

NEWSPAPERS

Burundi chrétien: BP 232, Bujumbura; Roman Catholic weekly; French.

Le Renouveau du Burundi: BP 2870, Bujumbura; f. 1978; publ. by UPRONA; daily; French; circ. 20,000; Dir JEAN NZEYIMANA.

Ubumwe: BP 1400, Bujumbura; tel. (2) 23929; f. 1971; weekly; Kirundi; circ. 20,000.

PERIODICALS

Au Coeur de l'Afrique: Association des conférences des ordinaires du Rwanda et Burundi, BP 1390, Bujumbura; bimonthly; education; circ. 1,000.

Bulletin économique et financier: BP 482, Bujumbura; bimonthly.

Bulletin mensuel: Banque de la République du Burundi, Service des études, BP 705, Bujumbura; tel. (2) 25142; telex 5071; monthly.

Bulletin officiel du Burundi: Bujumbura; monthly.

Le Burundi en Images: BP 1400, Bujumbura; f. 1979; monthly.

Culture et Sociétés: BP 1400, Bujumbura; f. 1978; quarterly.

Ndongozi Y'uburundi: Catholic Mission, BP 690, Bujumbura; tel. (2) 22762; fax (2) 28907; fortnightly; Kirundi.

Revue administration et juridique: Association d'études administratives et juridiques du Burundi, BP 1613, Bujumbura; quarterly; French.

PRESS ASSOCIATION

Burundian Association of Journalists (BAJ): Bujumbura; Pres. François Sendazirasa.

NEWS AGENCY

Agence burundaise de Presse (ABP): 6 ave de la Poste, BP 2870, Bujumbura; tel. (2) 25417; telex 5056; publ. daily bulletin.

Publishers

BURSTA: BP 1908, Bujumbura; tel. (2) 31796; fax (2) 32842; f. 1986; Dir Richard Kashirahamwe.

Editions Intore: 7 chaussée Prince Louis-Rwagasore, BP 525, Bujumbura; tel. (2) 20603.

GRAVIMPORT: BP 156, Bujumbura; tel. (2) 22285; fax (2) 26953.

IMPARUDI: BP 3010, Bujumbura.

Imprimerie la Licorne: 29 ave de la Mission, BP 2942, Bujumbura; tel. (2) 23503; fax (2) 27225; f. 1991.

Imprimerie MAHI: BP 673, Bujumbura.

MICROBU: BP 645, Bujumbura.

Imprimerie Moderne: BP 2555, Bujumbura.

Imprimerie du Parti: BP 1810, Bujumbura.

Les Presses Lavigerie: 5 ave de l'UPRONA, BP 1640, Bujumbura; tel. (2) 22368; fax (2) 20318.

Régie de Productions Pédagogiques: BP 3118, Bujumbura.

SASCO: BP 204, Bujumbura.

Government Publishing House

Imprimerie nationale du Burundi (INABU): BP 991, Bujumbura; tel. (2) 24046; fax (2) 25399; f. 1978; Dir Nicolas Nijimbere.

Broadcasting and Communications

TELECOMMUNICATIONS

Office nationale des télécommunications (ONATEL): BP 60, Bujumbura; tel. (2) 23196; telex 5168; fax (2) 26917; Dir-Gen. Lt-Col Nestor Misigaro.

RADIO AND TELEVISION

Radio Hope/Radio Umwizero: Bujumbura; f. 1996; EU-funded, private station promoting national reconciliation and peace; broadcasts four hours daily in Kirundi, Swahili and French; Dir. Hubert Vieille.

Voix de la Révolution/La Radiodiffusion et Télévision Nationale du Burundi (RTNB): BP 1900, Bujumbura; tel. (2) 23742; telex 5119; fax (2) 26547; f. 1960; govt-controlled; television service and daily radio broadcasts in Kirundi, Swahili, French and English; Dir-Gen. Charles Ndayiziga; Dir (Radio) Gérard Mfuranzima; Dir (Television) Bonaventure Barizira.

Finance

(cap. = capital; res = reserves; dep. = deposits; m. = million; brs = branches; amounts in Burundian francs)

BANKING

Central Bank

Banque de la République du Burundi (BRB): BP 705, Bujumbura; tel. (2) 25142; telex 5071; fax (2) 23128; f. 1964 as Banque du Royaume du Burundi; state-owned; bank of issue; cap. and res 9,015.4m., dep. 11,008.5m., total assets 71,641.6m. (Dec. 1994); Gov. Mathias Sinamenye; Vice-Gov. Emmanuel Ndayiragije; 2 brs.

Commercial Banks

Banque Burundaise pour le Commerce et l'Investissement SARL (BBCI): blvd du Peuple Murundi, BP 2320, Bujumbura; tel. (2) 23328; telex 5012; fax (2) 23339; f. 1988; cap. and res 419.7m., total assets 3,311.4m. (Dec. 1995); Pres. Charles Kaburahe; Vice-Pres. Gabriel Baziruwisabiye.

Banque Commerciale du Burundi SARL (BANCOBU): 84 chaussée Prince Louis-Rwagasore, BP 990, Bujumbura; tel. (2) 22317; telex 5051; fax (2) 21018; f. 1988 by merger; cap. and res 1,013.6m., total assets 15,944.8m.(Dec. 1995); Pres. Jacques van Eetvelde; Dir-Gen. Libère Ndabakwaje; 6 brs.

Banque de Crédit de Bujumbura SMei: ave Patrice Emery Lumumba, BP 300, Bujumbura; tel. (2) 22091; telex 5063; fax (2) 23007; f. 1964; cap. and res 2,921.8m., total assets 19,935.4m.(Dec. 1995); Pres. Thacien Nzeyimana; Man. Athanase Gahungu; 7 brs.

Banque Populaire du Burundi (BPB): 10 ave du 18 Septembre, BP 1780; Bujumbura; tel. (2) 21255; telex 5174; fax (2) 21256; cap. 285m.

Interbank Burundi SARL: 15 avenue de l'Industrie, BP 2970, Bujumbura; tel. (2) 20629; telex 5193; fax (2) 20461; cap. and res 864.4m., total assets 9,701.0m. (Dec. 1995); Pres. Georges Coucoulis.

Development Banks

Banque de Gestion et de Financement: Immeuble Ucar II, chaussée du Peuple Murundi, BP 1035, Bujumbura; tel. (2) 21352; fax (2) 21351; f. 1992; cap. and res 229.7m., total assets 1,224.0m. (Dec. 1995); Pres. Didace Nzohabonayo; Dir-Gen. Mathias Ndikumana.

Banque Nationale pour le Développement Economique SARL (BNDE): 3 rue du Marché, BP 1620, Bujumbura; tel. (2) 22888; telex 5091; fax (2) 23775; f. 1966; cap. and res 1,381.5m., total assets 9,948.9m. (Dec. 1995); Pres. and Dir-Gen. Gaspard Sindiyigaya; Gen. Sec. François Barwendere.

Caisse de Mobilisation et de Financement (CAMOFI): chausée Prince Louis-Rwagasore, BP 8, Bujumbura; tel. (2) 25106; telex 5081; fax (2) 29589; f. 1979; 50% state-owned; finances public-sector development projects; scheduled for privatization; cap. and res 218.8m., total assets 4,424.6m. (Dec. 1995); Pres. Minister of Finance; Dir-Gen. Gérard Niyibigira.

Société Burundaise de Financement SARL (SBF): 6 rue de la Science, BP 270, Bujumbura; tel. (2) 22126; telex 5080; fax (2) 25437; f. 1981; cap. and res 765.9m., total assets 6,129.3m. (Dec. 1995); Pres and Dir-Gen. Cyprien Sinzobahamvya.

Co-operative Bank

Banque Coopérative d'Epargne et de Crédit Mutuel (BCM): BP 1340, Bujumbura; operating licence granted in April 1995; Vice-Pres. Julien Musaragany.

INSURANCE

Burundi Insurance Corporation (BICOR): BP 2377, Bujumbura.

Société d'Assurances du Burundi (SOCABU): 14–18 rue de l'Amitié, BP 2440, Bujumbura; tel. (2) 26520; telex 5113; fax (2) 26803; f. 1977; partly state-owned; cap. 180m.; Chair. Egide Ndahibeshe; Man. Séraphine Ruvahafi.

Société Générale d'Assurances et de Réassurance (SOGEAR): BP 2432, Bujumbura; tel. (2) 22345; fax (2) 29338; f. 1991.

Union Commerciale d'Assurances et de Réassurance (UCAR): BP 3012, Bujumbura; tel. (2) 23638; telex 5162; fax (2) 23695; f. 1986; cap. 150m.; Chair. Lt-Col Edouard Nzambimana; Man. Dir Henry Tarmo.

Trade and Industry

GOVERNMENT AGENCIES

Office National du Commerce (ONC): Bujumbura; f. 1973; supervises international commercial operations between the Govt of Burundi and other states or private orgs; also organizes the import of essential materials; subsidiary offices in each province.

DEVELOPMENT ORGANIZATIONS

Compagnie de Gérance du Coton (COGERCO): BP 2571, Bujumbura; tel. (2) 22208; telex 5112; fax (2) 25323; f. 1947; promotion and development of cotton industry; Dir François Kabura.

Institut des Sciences Agronomiques du Burundi (ISABU): BP 795, Bujumbura; tel. (2) 23384; f. 1962 for the scientific development of agriculture and livestock.

Office de la Tourbe du Burundi (ONATOUR): BP 2360, Bujumbura; tel. (2) 26480; telex 48; f. 1977 to promote the exploitation of peat deposits.

Office des Cultures Industrielles du Burundi (Office du Café du Burundi) (OCIBU): BP 450, Bujumbura; tel. (2) 26031; fax (2) 25532; supervises coffee plantations and coffee exports; Dir-Gen. Thomas Minani.

Office du Thé du Burundi (OTB): 52 blvd de l'UPRONA, Bujumbura; tel. (2) 24228; telex 5069; fax (2) 24657; f. 1979 supervises production and marketing of tea; Dir Remy Nibigara.

Office National du Logement (ONL): BP 2480, Bujumbura; tel. (2) 26074; telex 48; f. 1974 to supervise housing construction.

Société d'Exploitation du Quinquina du Burundi (SOKINABU): 16 blvd Mwezi Gisabo, BP 1783, Bujumbura; tel. (2) 23469; telex 81; f. 1975 to develop and exploit cinchona trees, the source of quinine; Dir Raphaël Remezo.

Société Sucrière du Mosso (SOSUMO): BP 835, Bujumbura; tel. (2) 26576; telex 5035; fax (2) 23028; f. 1982 to develop and manage sugar cane plantations.

CHAMBER OF COMMERCE

Chambre de Commerce et de l'Industrie du Burundi: BP 313, Bujumbura; tel. (2) 22280; f. 1923; Chair. DONATIEN BIHUTE; 130 mems.

UTILITIES

Régie de Distribution d'Eau et d'Electricité (REGIDESCO): Bujumbura; state-owned distributor of water and electricity services.

TRADE UNIONS

Confédération des Syndicats du Burundi (COSIBU): Bujumbura; Chair. CHARLES NDAMIRAWE.

Union des Travailleurs du Burundi (UTB): BP 1340, Bujumbura; tel. (2) 23884; telex 57; f. 1967 by merger of all existing unions; closely allied with UPRONA; sole authorized trade union prior to 1994, with 18 affiliated nat. professional feds; Sec.-Gen. MARIUS RURAHENYE.

Transport

RAILWAYS

There are no railways in Burundi. Plans have been under consideration since 1987 for the construction of a line passing through Uganda, Rwanda and Burundi, to connect with the Kigoma–Dar es Salaam line in Tanzania. This rail link would relieve Burundi's isolated trade position.

ROADS

The road network is very dense and in 1996 there was a total of 14,480 km of roads, of which 1,950 km were national highways and 2,530 km secondary roads. A new crossing of the Ruzizi River, the Bridge of Concord (Burundi's longest bridge), was opened in early 1992.

INLAND WATERWAYS

Bujumbura is the principal port for both passenger and freight traffic on Lake Tanganyika, and the greater part of Burundi's external trade is dependent on the shipping services between Bujumbura and lake ports in Tanzania, Zambia and the Democratic Republic of the Congo.

CIVIL AVIATION

There is an international airport at Bujumbura, equipped to take large jet-engined aircraft.

Air Burundi: 40 ave du Commerce, BP 2460, Bujumbura; tel. (2) 24,609; telex 5080; fax (2) 23452; f. 1971 as Société de Transports Aériens du Burundi; state-owned; operates charter and scheduled passenger services to destinations throughout central Africa; Man. Dir Maj. ISAAC GAFURERO.

Tourism

Tourism is relatively undeveloped. Tourist arrivals were estimated at 29,000 in 1994, with receipts amounting to US $3m.

Office National du Tourisme (ONT): 2 ave des Euphorbes, BP 902, Bujumbura; tel. (2) 24208; telex 5081; fax (2) 29390; f. 1972; responsible for the promotion and supervision of tourism; Dir HERMENEGILDE NIMBONA (acting).

CAMBODIA

Introductory Survey

Location, Climate, Language, Religion, Flag, Capital

The Kingdom of Cambodia occupies part of the Indochinese peninsula in South-East Asia. It is bordered by Thailand and Laos to the north, by Viet Nam to the east and by the Gulf of Thailand to the south. The climate is tropical and humid. There is a rainy season from June to November, with the heaviest rainfall in September. The temperature is generally between 20°C and 36°C (68°F to 97°F), with March and April generally the hottest months; and the annual average temperature in Phnom-Penh is 27°C (81°F). The official language is Khmer, which is spoken by everybody except the Vietnamese and Chinese minorities. The state religion is Theravada Buddhism. The national flag (proportions 3 by 2) consists of three horizontal stripes, of dark blue, red (half the depth) and dark blue, with a stylized representation (in white) of the temple of Angkor Wat, with three towers, in the centre. The capital is Phnom-Penh.

Recent History

The Kingdom of Cambodia became a French protectorate in the 19th century and was incorporated into French Indo-China. In April 1941 Norodom Sihanouk, then aged 18, succeeded his grandfather as King. In May 1947 he promulgated a Constitution which provided for a bicameral Parliament, including an elected National Assembly. Cambodia became an Associate State of the French Union in November 1949 and attained independence on 9 November 1953. In order to become a political leader, King Sihanouk abdicated in March 1955 in favour of his father, Norodom Suramarit, and became known as Prince Sihanouk. He founded a mass movement, the Sangkum Reastr Niyum (Popular Socialist Community), which won all the seats in elections to the National Assembly in 1955, 1958, 1962 and 1966. King Suramarit died in April 1960, and in June Parliament elected Prince Sihanouk as Head of State. Prince Sihanouk's Government developed good relations with the People's Republic of China and with North Viet Nam, but it was highly critical of the USA's role in Asia. From 1964, however, the Government was confronted by an underground Marxist insurgency movement, the Khmers Rouges, while it also became increasingly difficult to isolate Cambodia from the war in Viet Nam.

In March 1970 Prince Sihanouk was deposed by a right-wing coup, led by the Prime Minister, Lt-Gen. (later Marshal) Lon Nol. The new Government pledged itself to the removal of foreign communist forces and appealed to the USA for military aid. Sihanouk went into exile and formed the Royal Government of National Union of Cambodia (GRUNC), supported by the Khmers Rouges. Sihanoukists and the Khmers Rouges formed the National United Front of Cambodia (FUNC). Their combined forces, aided by South Viet Nam's National Liberation Front and North Vietnamese troops, posed a serious threat to the new regime, but in October 1970 Marshal Lon Nol proclaimed the Khmer Republic. In June 1972 he was elected the first President. During 1973 several foreign states recognized GRUNC as the rightful government of Cambodia. In 1974 the republican regime's control was limited to a few urban enclaves, besieged by GRUNC forces, mainly Khmers Rouges, who gained control of Phnom-Penh on 17 April 1975. Prince Sihanouk became Head of State again but did not return from exile until September. The country was subjected to a pre-arranged programme of radical social deconstruction immediately after the Khmers Rouges' assumption of power; towns were largely evacuated, and their inhabitants forced to work in rural areas. Many hundreds of thousands died as a result of ill-treatment, hunger and disease.

A new Constitution, promulgated in January 1976, renamed the country Democratic Kampuchea, and established a republican form of government; elections for a 250-member People's Representative Assembly were held in March 1976. In April Prince Sihanouk resigned as Head of State and GRUNC was dissolved. The Assembly elected Khieu Samphan, formerly Deputy Prime Minister, to be President of the State Presidium (Head of State). The little-known Pol Pot (formerly Saloth Sar) became Prime Minister. In September 1977 it was officially disclosed that the ruling organization was the Communist Party of Kampuchea (CPK), with Pol Pot as the Secretary of its Central Committee.

After 1975 close links with the People's Republic of China developed, while relations with Viet Nam deteriorated. In 1978, following a two-year campaign of raids across the Vietnamese border by the Khmers Rouges, the Vietnamese army launched a series of offensives into Kampuchean territory. In December the establishment of the Kampuchean National United Front for National Salvation (KNUFNS, renamed Kampuchean United Front for National Construction and Defence—KUFNCD—in December 1981, and United Front for the Construction and Defence of the Kampuchean Fatherland—UFCDKF—in 1989), a communist-led movement opposed to Pol Pot and supported by Viet Nam, was announced. Later in the month, Viet Nam invaded Kampuchea, supported by the KNUFNS.

On 7 January 1979 Phnom-Penh was captured by Vietnamese forces, and three days later the People's Republic of Kampuchea was proclaimed. A People's Revolutionary Council was established, with Heng Samrin, leader of the KNUFNS, as President. It pledged to restore freedom of movement, freedom of association and of religion, and to restore the family unit. The CPK was replaced as the governing party by the Kampuchean People's Revolutionary Party (KPRP). The Khmer Rouge forces, however, remained active in the western provinces, near the border with Thailand, and conducted sporadic guerrilla activities elsewhere in the country. Several groups opposing both the Khmers Rouges and the Heng Samrin regime were established, including the Khmer People's National Liberation Front (KPNLF), headed by a former Prime Minister, Son Sann. In July, claiming that Pol Pot's regime had been responsible for 3m. deaths, the KPRP administration sentenced Pol Pot and his former Minister of Foreign Affairs, Ieng Sary, to death *in absentia.* In January 1980 Khieu Samphan assumed the premiership of the deposed Khmer Rouge regime, while Pol Pot became Commander-in-Chief of the armed forces. In 1981 the CPK was reportedly dissolved and was replaced by the Party of Democratic Kampuchea (PDK).

During the first few years of the KPRP regime Viet Nam launched regular offensives on the Thai-Kampuchean border against the united armed forces of Democratic Kampuchea, the coalition Government-in-exile of anti-Vietnamese resistance groups formed in June 1982. As a result of the fighting, and the prevalence of starvation and disease, thousands of Kampuchean refugees crossed the border into Thailand; in turn, a large number of Vietnamese citizens subsequently settled on Kampuchean territory. The coalition Government-in-exile, of which Prince Sihanouk became President, Khieu Samphan (PDK) Vice-President and Son Sann (KPLNF) Prime Minister, received the support of the People's Republic of China and of member states of the Association of South East Asian Nations (ASEAN—see p. 113), whilst retaining the Kampuchean seat in the UN General Assembly.

In the mid-1980s an increasingly conciliatory attitude between the USSR and the People's Republic of China led to a number of diplomatic exchanges, aimed at reconciling the coalition Government-in-exile with the Government in Phnom-Penh, led by the General Secretary of the KPRP, Heng Samrin. Largely, however, because of mistrust of the PDK (due to Pol Pot's continuing influence), the Heng Samrin Government rejected peace proposals from ASEAN and the coalition Government-in-exile in 1985 and 1986. In September 1987 the Government of the People's Republic of China stated that it would accept a Kampuchean 'government of national reconciliation' under Prince Sihanouk, but that the presence of Vietnamese troops in Kampuchea remained a major obstacle. In the same month the USSR also declared that it was 'prepared to facilitate a political settlement' in Kampuchea. In October, after having announced its readiness to conduct negotiations with some PDK leaders (but not Pol Pot), the Heng Samrin Government offered Prince Sihanouk a government post and issued a set of peace proposals which included the complete withdrawal of Vietnamese troops, internationally-observed elections and the formation of a coalition government. In December 1987 Prince Sihanouk and Hun Sen, the Chairman of the Council of Ministers in the Heng Samrin Government, met in France for private discussions for the first time since the invasion by Viet Nam. The meeting ended in a joint communiqué, which stated that the conflict in Kampuchea was to be settled politically by negotiations among all the Kampuchean parties, and that any resulting agreement should be guaranteed by an international conference.

Under increasing pressure from the USSR and the People's Republic of China, the four Kampuchean factions participated in a series of 'informal meetings', held in Indonesia, which were also attended by representatives of Viet Nam, Laos and the six ASEAN members. At the first of these meetings, in July 1988, Viet Nam, under pressure from the USSR, advanced its deadline for a complete withdrawal of its troops from Kampuchea to late 1989. In April 1989 the National Assembly in Phnom-Penh ratified several constitutional amendments, which were perceived as a concessionary gesture to Prince Sihanouk. Under the provisions of the amendments, the name of the country was changed to the State of Cambodia, a new national flag, emblem and anthem were introduced, Buddhism was reinstated as the state religion, and the death penalty was abolished. In July 1989 the Paris International Conference on Cambodia (PICC) met for the first time. Its principal achievement was an agreement to send a UN reconnaissance party to Cambodia to study the prospects for a cease-fire and the installation of a peace-keeping force.

The withdrawal of Vietnamese forces, completed on schedule in September 1989, was followed by renewed offensives into Cambodia by the resistance forces, particularly the PDK. In November, following substantial military gains by the PDK, the UN General Assembly adopted a resolution supporting the formation of an interim government in Cambodia which would include members of the PDK, but which retained a clause, introduced in 1988, relating to past atrocities committed by the organization. The resolution also cast doubt on the Vietnamese withdrawal (since it had not been monitored by the UN) and, in reference to the alleged presence of 1m. Vietnamese settlers in Cambodia, condemned 'demographic changes' imposed in the country. An Australian peace initiative, first proposed in November, was unanimously approved by the five permanent members of the UN Security Council in January 1990. At the beginning of February Prince Sihanouk declared that the coalition Government-in-exile would henceforth be known as the National Government of Cambodia.

Following a series of successful offensives by the Phnom-Penh Government in March and April 1990, arbitration by Thailand's Minister of Foreign Affairs led to the signing of a conditional cease-fire agreement in Bangkok between Hun Sen and Prince Sihanouk, who had resumed the presidency of the resistance coalition, which he had resigned in favour of his son, Prince Norodom Ranariddh, in May 1989. Further discussions in Tokyo collapsed, however, when the PDK refused to sign a cease-fire agreement. By July 1990 the position of the Phnom-Penh Government also appeared to have hardened after the arrest or dismissal of several 'reformist' allies of Hun Sen, accused of having attempted to establish a new party, and their replacement by supporters of the more 'conservative' Chairman of the National Assembly, Chea Sim.

In July 1990 the USA withdrew its support for the National Government of Cambodia's occupation of Cambodia's seat at the UN. In late August the UN Security Council endorsed the framework for a comprehensive settlement in Cambodia. The agreement provided for UN supervision of an interim government, military arrangements for the transitional period, free elections and guarantees for the future neutrality of Cambodia. Under the plan, a special representative of the Secretary-General of the UN would control the proposed United Nations Transitional Authority in Cambodia (UNTAC). The UN would also assume control of the Ministries of Foreign Affairs, National Defence, Finance, the Interior and Information, Press and Culture. China and the USSR subsequently pledged to cease supplies of military equipment to their respective allies, the PDK and the Phnom-Penh Government.

At a fourth 'informal meeting' in Jakarta in September 1990 the four Cambodian factions accepted the UN proposals. They also agreed to the formation of the Supreme National Council (SNC), with six representatives from the Phnom-Penh Government and six from the National Government of Cambodia. SNC decisions were to be taken by consensus, effectively allowing each faction the power of veto, and the SNC was to occupy the Cambodian seat at the UN General Assembly. Prior to the 'informal meeting' in September, secret talks had been held between the Chinese and the Vietnamese, following which the Vietnamese endorsed the UN plan. It was widely assumed that the Chinese had promised an improvement in Sino-Vietnamese relations in return for Vietnamese approval of the plan. The 12 members of the SNC met for the first time in mid-September, in Bangkok, Thailand. Discussions were abandoned following the SNC's failure to reach agreement on the election of a chairman. Prince Sihanouk was subsequently elected to the chairmanship of the SNC (a position in which he would have final arbitration if a consensus could not be reached), and resigned as leader of the resistance coalition and as President of the National Government of Cambodia (positions to which Son Sann was appointed). Agreement was also reached on the four factions reducing their armed forces by 70% and the remaining 30% being placed in cantonments under UN supervision; the introduction of a system of multi-party democracy; the Phnom-Penh Government abandoning its demand for references to genocide to be included in a draft plan; and the holding of elections to a constituent assembly which would subsequently become a legislative assembly comprising 120 seats.

Following the release of political prisoners by the Phnom-Penh Government in October 1991, including the former associates of Hun Sen arrested in 1990, a Congress of the KPRP was convened at which the party changed its name to the Cambodian People's Party (CPP), removed the communist insignia from its emblem and replaced Heng Samrin as Chairman of the Central Committee (formerly the Politburo) with Chea Sim and elected Hun Sen as Vice-Chairman.

On 23 October 1991 the four factions signed the UN peace accord in Paris, under the auspices of the PICC. UNTAC was expected to be in place by August 1992, and, as an interim measure, the mainly military UN Advance Mission in Cambodia (UNAMIC), comprising 300 men, was in place by the end of 1991. The peace-keeping operation was expected to be completed in 1993. The agreement also provided for the repatriation, under the supervision of the UN High Commissioner for Refugees, of the estimated 340,000 Cambodian refugees living in camps in Thailand. There were continuing fears that the PDK would, in an attempt to ensure electoral support, endeavour forcibly to repatriate refugees to areas of western Cambodia under their control.

In mid-November 1991 Prince Sihanouk returned to Phnom-Penh, accompanied by Hun Sen. The CPP and the United National Front for an Independent, Neutral, Peaceful and Co-operative Cambodia (FUNCINPEC), led by Prince Sihanouk, subsequently formed an alliance and announced their intention to form a coalition government. (The alliance was abandoned in early December, in response to objections from the KPNLF and the PDK.) On 23 November the four factions endorsed the reinstatement of Prince Sihanouk as the Head of State of Cambodia, pending a presidential election in 1993. Political protest increased towards the end of 1991. An attack by demonstrators on Khieu Samphan on his return to Phnom-Penh in late November led senior PDK officials to flee to Bangkok where the SNC met and agreed that, henceforth, officials of the party would occupy the SNC headquarters in Phnom-Penh with members of UNAMIC. Further demonstrations took place in December and in January 1992 in protest against corruption and in support of human rights, during which the security forces killed several protesters. The authorities closed all schools and colleges in the capital, imposed a curfew and prohibited any unauthorized demonstrations. Later in January, the assassination of an official critical of the CPP and the attempted assassination of a prominent dissident, Oung Phan, further served to intimidate government critics. However, following an agreement with representatives of the UN Security Council, the Phnom-Penh Government released all remaining political prisoners between January and March 1992.

In early January 1992 the Japanese UN Under-Secretary-General for Disarmament Affairs, Yasushi Akashi, was appointed the UN Special Representative to Cambodia in charge of UNTAC. At the same time the UN Security Council expanded UNAMIC's mandate to include mine-clearing operations, and, in late February, authorized the dispatch of a 22,000-member peace-keeping force to Cambodia to establish UNTAC, at an estimated cost of nearly US $2,000m. In mid-March UNAMIC, whose efforts had been impeded by a lack of funds and personnel and the refusal of the PDK to allow free access to the zones it controlled, transferred responsibility for the implementation of the peace agreement to UNTAC.

The refugee repatriation programme which began in March 1992 was threatened by continued cease-fire violations. The fighting, concentrated in the central province of Kompong Thom, was widely believed to be an attempt by the PDK to delay implementation of the peace plan in order to make territorial gains and thereby increase its representation in the proposed National Assembly. In June the continued obduracy of the PDK disrupted the implementation of the second phase of the peace-keeping operation, which comprised the cantonment and disarmament of the four factions' forces. Although by mid-July about 12,000 troops from three of the factions had reported to the designated areas, the PDK intensified its violations of the cease-fire agreement, continued to deny the UN access to its zones, and failed to attend meetings on the implementation of the peace agreement. At the Ministerial Conference on the Rehabilitation and Reconstruction of Cambodia, which was convened in Tokyo in late June, the application of economic sanctions against the PDK was considered. Despite criticism from the People's Republic of China at the meeting, the PDK reiterated its former demands that power be transferred from the Phnom-Penh Government to the SNC and that both the SNC and UNTAC should co-operate in ensuring that all Vietnamese forces had withdrawn from Cambodia. During August Akashi affirmed that the elections would proceed without the participation of the PDK if it continued to refuse to co-operate. In late August, at an SNC meeting in Phnom-Penh, the PDK introduced a new precondition for implementing the peace accords: that Cambodia's border with Viet Nam be redrawn, following the cancellation of all treaties signed with Viet Nam since 1979. Shortly afterwards the PDK announced the resumption of its co-operation with UNTAC. Having approved electoral legislation for Cambodia in August and having announced the registration of parties for the elections to be held in May 1993, the UN set a deadline of 15 November 1992, by which time the PDK would have to comply with UN demands. However, by the end of November no consensus had been reached and the Security Council adopted a resolution condemning PDK obduracy. The Security Council approved an embargo on the supplies of petroleum products to the PDK and endorsed a ban on the export of timber (which constituted a principal source of income for the party) from 31 December 1992. On the day the sanctions were adopted, however, the PDK announced the formation of a subsidiary party to contest the forthcoming elections, the Cambodian National Unity Party, led by Khieu Samphan and Son Sen.

In December 1992 the seizure of six members of the UN peace-keeping forces in PDK-controlled areas reflected a growing distrust of UNTAC by the PDK, which had previously alleged UN bias in favour of the Phnom-Penh Government. The slow progress of the peace initiative, coupled with the poor conduct of UN troops, resulted in widespread disaffection with UNTAC, and in the latter part of 1992 resentment towards ethnic Vietnamese intensified, largely as a result of PDK and, subsequently, KPLNF propaganda.

In January 1993 Prince Sihanouk announced that he would no longer co-operate with UNTAC, owing to the increasing level of violence against FUNCINPEC personnel; these attacks were widely attributed to the Phnom-Penh Government. Prince Sihanouk subsequently resumed co-operation after Akashi signed a directive establishing procedures for indicting and prosecuting alleged violators of human rights independently of the Phnom-Penh Government. The PDK continued to violate the terms of the cease-fire (and abducted further groups of UN troops seeking access to areas under its control), claiming that 2m. Vietnamese remained in Cambodia and that the SNC had not been empowered to administrate the country prior to the elections.

By the final deadline at the end of January 1993 20 parties, excluding the PDK, had registered to contest the elections. The Phnom-Penh Government subsequently launched an offensive against the PDK in northern and western Cambodia, recovering much of the territory gained by the PDK since the signing of the peace agreement in October 1991. In early February 1993 Prince Sihanouk returned to Phnom-Penh from Beijing amidst intensifying politically-motivated violence. There were also continuing attacks by the PDK on ethnic Vietnamese, and, following several rural massacres, thousands of Vietnamese took refuge in Viet Nam. Despite the violence, UNTAC's voter registration campaign, which ended in February, had been extremely successful; 4.7m. Cambodians were registered, constituting about 97% of the estimated eligible electorate. The repatriation programme for refugees on the Thai border was also successfully concluded; 360,000 refugees had been returned to Cambodia on schedule by the end of April.

On 23–28 May 1993 about 90% of the electorate participated in the elections to the Constituent Assembly, which were contested by 20 parties. The PDK, which apparently lacked the capability to disrupt the polls systematically, instead offered support to the FUNCINPEC Party in the hope of securing a role in government following the elections. However, despite Prince Sihanouk's previous commitment to national reconciliation, the massive voter participation in the election prompted him to abandon his proposals for the inclusion of the PDK in a future Government. Early results from the election, indicating a FUNCINPEC victory, prompted CPP allegations of electoral irregularities. UNTAC, however, rejected CPP requests for fresh elections in at least four provinces. In early June, without prior consultation with the UN and disregarding the incomplete election results, Prince Sihanouk announced the formation of a new Government, with himself as Prime Minister and Prince Ranariddh and Hun Sen as joint Deputy Prime Ministers. The coalition was created and renounced within hours, owing to objections from Prince Ranariddh, who had not been consulted, and suggestions by UN officials that it was tantamount to a coup. Two days later the official results of the election were released: the FUNCINPEC Party secured 58 seats with 46% of the votes, the CPP 51 seats with 38% of the votes, the Buddhist Liberal Democratic Party (BLDP, founded by the KPNLF) 10 seats (3%) and a breakaway faction from the FUNCINPEC Party, MOLINAKA (National Liberation Movement of Cambodia), one seat. Despite the UN's endorsement of the election as fair, the CPP refused to dissolve the State of Cambodia Government in Phnom-Penh and announced that certain eastern provinces were threatening to secede unless demands for an independent examination of the results were met. Prince Norodom Chakkrapong (a son of Prince Sihanouk who had been appointed to the Council of Ministers of the Phnom-Penh Government in December 1991) subsequently led a secessionist movement in seven provinces in the east and north-east of the country, which, it was widely believed, was sanctioned by the CPP leadership in an attempt to secure a power-sharing agreement with the FUNCINPEC Party.

On 14 June 1993, at the inaugural session of the Constituent Assembly, Prince Sihanouk was proclaimed Head of State, and 'full and special' powers were conferred on him. The Assembly adopted a resolution declaring null and void the overthrow of Prince Sihanouk 23 years previously and recognizing him retroactively as Head of State of Cambodia during that period. The secessionist movement in the eastern provinces collapsed, and on the following day an agreement was reached on the formation of an interim government, with Hun Sen and Prince Ranariddh as Co-Chairmen of the Provisional National Government of Cambodia, pending the drawing up of a new constitution. Prince Chakkrapong returned to Phnom-Penh, where he was reconciled with Prince Sihanouk. A few days later the CPP officially recognized the results of the election.

The PDK had immediately accepted the results of the election and supported the formation of a coalition government, but continued to engage in military action to support its demands for inclusion in a future government. In July 1993 the PDK offered to incorporate its forces into the newly-formed Cambodian National Armed Forces (later restyled the Khmer Royal Armed Forces), which had been created through the merger of the forces of the other three factions in June. PDK offensives escalated, however, after the party was denied a role in government, largely owing to US threats to withhold economic aid from Cambodia if the PDK were included prior to a renunciation of violence. In late August Cambodia's united armed forces initiated a successful offensive against PDK positions in north-western Cambodia. The Government rejected an appeal for urgent discussions by the PDK after government forces had captured PDK bases, insisting that the party surrender unconditionally the estimated 20% of Cambodian territory under its control. The PDK suffered from defections as disillusioned troops were offered the same rank in the Cambodian National Armed Forces under a government amnesty.

On 21 September 1993 the Constituent Assembly adopted a new Constitution, which provided for an hereditary monarchy. On 24 September Prince Sihanouk promulgated the Constitution, thus terminating the mandate of UNTAC (whose personnel left the country by mid-November). Under the provisions of the peace agreement, the Constituent Assembly became the

National Assembly, and, on the same day, Prince Sihanouk acceded to the throne of the new Kingdom of Cambodia. Chea Sim was re-elected Chairman of the National Assembly. Under the terms of the Constitution, government ministers were to be chosen from parties represented in the National Assembly, thus precluding the involvement of the PDK. In October talks scheduled between the Cambodian Government and the PDK were postponed indefinitely, owing to the ill health of King Sihanouk, who was undergoing medical treatment in Beijing (Chea Sim assumed the position of acting Head of State while the King was out of the country). At the end of October the National Assembly approved the new Royal Government of Cambodia (previously endorsed by King Sihanouk), in which Prince Ranariddh was named First Prime Minister and Hun Sen Second Prime Minister.

Between November 1993 and January 1994 initiatives to incorporate the PDK into the new Government failed, owing to objections from various parties. In February the Government announced the capture of Anlong Veng, the second-most important base for the PDK and the headquarters and supply base for guerrilla operations in north and central Cambodia. In the following month government forces captured Pailin, the headquarters of the PDK and the centre of the organization's commercial logging and gem-mining activities, but lost the town in April in a PDK counter-attack, which was halted only a few kilometres from Battambang, Cambodia's second city. In the same month the first of two kidnappings of foreigners by the PDK took place when three tourists were captured south-west of Phnom-Penh. (The PDK later admitted to having executed the hostages for alleged 'spying' offences. A second group of hostages, who were kidnapped in July, were also killed.) In May King Sihanouk threatened to stop negotiating with the PDK and the Government to end the fighting in the north-west of the country, which had reached a severity not witnessed since 1989, and forced the postponement of proposed peace talks in Pyongyang, the Democratic People's Republic of Korea. Following the failure of peace talks held in May and June, the Government ordered the PDK to leave Phnom-Penh and closed the party's mission in the capital.

In early July 1994 the Government claimed to have suppressed an alleged coup attempt led by Prince Chakkrapong and Gen. Sin Song, a former Minister of National Security under the State of Cambodia. Following a personal appeal from King Sihanouk, Prince Chakkrapong, who protested his innocence, was exiled from Cambodia while Gen. Sin Song was placed under arrest. (Gen. Sin Song escaped from prison in September and was captured by Thai authorities in November.) Hun Sen also suspected his rival, Sar Kheng, a Deputy Prime Minister and Minister of the Interior, of involvement in the alleged revolt. Sar Kheng was, however, protected by his powerful brother-in-law, Chea Sim. The coup attempt was also used by the increasingly divided Government as an excuse to suppress press criticism of the regime. Newspapers were closed, editors fined and imprisoned and in September an editor renowned as an outspoken critic of the Government was killed by unidentified assailants. Hun Sen continued to fear a possible coup attempt from rival CPP members, and in August the armed forces mistakenly opened fire on four tourists at a road block.

In July 1994, despite King Sihanouk's continued advocacy of national reconciliation, legislation providing for the outlawing of the PDK was adopted by the National Assembly (whilst allowing for an immediate six-month amnesty for the lower ranks of the party). The proposed legislation was initially opposed by a group led by the Minister of Finance, Sam Rainsy and the Minister of Foreign Affairs, Prince Norodom Sirivudh, but following the inclusion of guarantees safeguarding civil liberties the bill was approved. It was swiftly signed into law by Chea Sim as acting Head of State. In response, the PDK announced the formation of a Provisional Government of National Unity and National Salvation of Cambodia (PGNUNSC), under the premiership of Khieu Samphan, which was to co-ordinate opposition to the Government in Phnom-Penh from its headquarters in Preah Vihear in the north of the country. The PGNUNSC, however, was not recognized by any foreign Government or organization.

In October 1994 as part of a cabinet reorganization, Sam Rainsy, who was highly regarded by independent foreign observers, was dismissed as Minister of Finance, owing to his efforts to combat high-level corruption. Prince Sirivudh subsequently resigned as Minister of Foreign Affairs in protest at Rainsy's removal, which also demonstrated the decline in King Sihanouk's political influence—Prince Ranariddh and Hun Sen had jointly proposed Rainsy's dismissal in March but King Sihanouk had withheld his consent. Prince Sirivudh also criticized the FUNCINPEC Party, of which he was Secretary-General, for submitting too readily to CPP demands, as it became increasingly apparent that real power lay with the former communists.

In January 1995 the government amnesty for PDK members, which was deemed to have been reasonably successful in weakening the PDK, expired. However, the PDK remained an effective guerrilla force capable of inflicting serious disruption on the country and demonstrated this by launching several attacks on government and civilian targets during January and February.

In May 1995 Rainsy was expelled from the FUNCINPEC Party, following his continued criticism of corruption in the Government. The following month he was expelled from the National Assembly. This caused international disquiet and provoked criticism from human rights groups since there was no provision in the Constitution for such an expulsion. Rainsy, who refused to accept the decision, formed a new party, the Khmer Nation Party (KNP), which was officially launched in November. The Government declared the KNP illegal but said it would not take action to disband it. Rainsy's expulsion from the National Assembly coincided with the adoption of the revised draft of a draconian press law, which imposed substantial fines and prison sentences for reporting issues that affect 'national security' or 'political stability'. Since these terms remained undefined it was widely believed that the law would be used to stifle criticism of the Government. Chea Sim signed the bill into law in August, while King Sihanouk, who was known to be opposed to the legislation, was out of the country. Trials involving editors of national newspapers continued in August and in the same month six people were arrested for distributing pamphlets accusing the coalition Government of being anti-democratic and corrupt. The Government's response to criticism concerning the restraints on freedom of speech was to advocate Asian values, citing Singapore, Indonesia and Malaysia as more appropriate models than Western-style democracies, and emphasizing the importance of discipline above democracy.

In July 1995 Ieng Muli, the Minister of Information and the Press and the Secretary-General of the BLDP, called an extraordinary congress of the BLDP, with the support of the CPP and the FUNCINPEC Party, and was elected Chairman in place of Son Sann, who had remained critical of the principal coalition partners. In August Ieng Muli expelled Son Sann from the BLDP together with three other members of the National Assembly. At the end of September Son Sann convened his own BLDP congress; on the eve of the meeting grenade attacks took place at his office and his temple.

Politically-motivated violence, organized crime and drugs-trafficking have all become serious problems in Cambodia. The situation is exacerbated by the inadequacies of law enforcement, the lack of any specific legislation to deter 'money-laundering' and endemic corruption among senior government officials and the armed forces. The security forces were increasingly accused both of criminal activity and of perpetrating violence against opponents of the Government. The restructuring of the ranks of the national police and the armed forces, which were completed in October and December 1995 respectively, failed to have any significant impact on the situation.

In October 1995 Prince Sirivudh was expelled from the National Assembly (and thus deprived of diplomatic immunity) and charged with conspiring to assassinate Hun Sen. Human rights groups declared that Prince Sirivudh, who protested his innocence, was a political prisoner. Under an agreement reached with King Sihanouk's intervention, Prince Sirivudh was allowed to go into exile in France in December on condition that he refrain from political activity. In January 1996 Prince Sirivudh was convicted and sentenced to 10 years' imprisonment *in absentia* on charges of criminal conspiracy and possession of unlicensed firearms. He denied the charges against him, and in October formally requested permission to return from exile. In December Hun Sen threatened to respond with military action if Prince Sirivudh returned to Cambodia, but subsequently announced that Sirivudh would be entitled to return if he was granted a royal amnesty (which had been requested by Prince Ranariddh).

In January 1996 the Government began to adopt repressive measures against the KNP, raiding the organization's headquarters and detaining some 150 supporters. In March Rainsy nominally merged the KNP with a defunct but still legally-registered party, in an attempt to gain legal status. However, in April the Government ordered all parties without parliamentary representation to close their offices (in an effort to prevent Rainsy from legalizing the KNP); in June KNP requests for permission to open a radio station were refused. Several KNP officials were assassinated in 1996, including, in May, the editor of a newspaper that supported the KNP and had frequently criticized the two Prime Ministers.

In August 1996 the prominent PDK leader, Ieng Sary, together with two military divisions that controlled the significant PDK strongholds of Pailin and Malai, defected from the movement and negotiated a peace agreement with the Government. Ieng Sary subsequently denied responsibility for the atrocities committed during Pol Pot's regime, and was granted a royal amnesty in September, at the request of both Hun Sen and Prince Ranariddh. Following his defection, Ieng Sary formed a new political organization, the Democratic National United Movement (DNUM), while his supporters retained control of Pailin and Malai, despite efforts by troops loyal to the PDK leadership to recapture the region (where lucrative mineral and timber resources were situated). Former PDK troops (numbering about 4,000) were integrated into the national army in November; a number of former senior PDK soliders were later granted the rank of officer. Ieng Sary's departure from the PDK precipitated further major defections, with an estimated 2,500 PDK troops transferring allegiance to the Government in October.

Throughout 1996 heightened tension within the ruling coalition resulted in increasing political instability, while there was widespread speculation regarding a potential successor to King Sihanouk (who was reported to be in poor health). The reinstatement of 7 January as a public holiday in commemoration of the overthrow of the Pol Pot regime by Vietnamese forces in 1979, proposed by Hun Sen in January 1996, was strongly opposed by the FUNCINPEC Party (which had been involved in the resistance against Viet Nam). Although Prince Ranariddh agreed to the public holiday, later in the month he condemned alleged Vietnamese encroachments on Cambodian border territory as an invasion. In March Prince Ranariddh threatened to force early elections by leaving the coalition in protest at the CPP's failure to fulfil a power-sharing agreement at district level (the CPP had refused to allow FUNCINPEC members to assume their positions in local government). Hun Sen retaliated by indicating that armed force might be necessary in order to protect the constitutional order, and in July he publicly insulted Prince Ranariddh for failing to carry out his threat.

In September 1996 the partial dissolution of the PDK heightened tensions within the ruling coalition, as both the CPP and the FUNCINPEC Party attempted to attract former PDK troops to join their party in order to increase their military and political influence. However, as the FUNCINPEC Party appeared more successful than the CPP at recruiting former PDK commanders and cadres, Hun Sen became concerned that the alliance between the royalists and the PDK as former resistance forces would be re-established. In mid-November Hun Sen produced PDK defectors who testified that the FUNCINPEC Party had conspired to conceal clandestine links between the KNP and the PDK leadership. Three days later Hun Sen's brother-in-law, a senior official at the Ministry of the Interior, was killed. The security chief of the KNP was arrested in connection with the killing, which Hun Sen declared to have been an attempt to intimidate further PDK defectors from revealing secret alliances. In February 1997 Prince Ranariddh sent a helicopter to Anlong Veng to negotiate with the central PDK faction. However, PDK members opposed to peace talks ambushed the helicopter, killing the majority of the Prince's emissaries.

In February 1997 a new electoral alliance, the National United Front (NUF), was established by the FUNCINPEC Party and the KNP and was joined by Son Sann's faction of the BLDP. Hun Sen, who rebuked Prince Ranariddh for entering an alliance with an opposition leader, began to establish pacts with other small parties to form a similar united front.

In early 1997 the situation in Cambodia was deteriorating still further. The two Prime Ministers were stockpiling weapons, violations of human and civil rights were increasingly prevalent, corruption was rampant, and labour unrest was widespread, as strikes were organized in both the public sector and the garment industry. In February King Sihanouk announced his concern for the welfare of the country and raised the possibility of his abdication. The potential involvement of the popular monarch in the forthcoming polls provoked a threat from Hun Sen to cancel both the local and national elections and to amend the Constitution to prohibit all members of the royal family from participating in politics, to guarantee the neutrality of the constitutional monarchy.

In March 1997 Rainsy, who had increased his attacks against Hun Sen and the CPP-controlled judicial system and police force, led a demonstration outside the National Assembly. The meeting was attacked by assailants who threw four grenades, killing 19 and injuring more than 100 protesters in a presumed attempt to assassinate Rainsy. Rainsy accused Hun Sen of orchestrating the attack and expressed no confidence in the commission established to investigate the incident.

In April 1997 Ung Phan, a former CPP member who had joined the FUNCINPEC Party in the early 1990s, led a rebellion against the party leadership of Prince Ranariddh, with the support of Hun Sen. The National Assembly, which was due to adopt legislation pertaining to local and national elections scheduled for 1998, was unable to convene, as the FUNCINPEC Party refused to attend until its dissident members were expelled from the Assembly, whereas the CPP insisted on their retention. In June the dissident FUNCINPEC members organized a party congress and formed a rival FUNCINPEC Party, with Toan Chhay, the Governor of Siem Reap, as its chairman. Also in June Prince Sirivudh was prevented from returning to Cambodia, as he was refused permission to board flights to Cambodia in Hong Kong, owing to threats by Hun Sen, who had earlier refused to support a royal pardon for the Prince.

In May 1997, following negotiations with representatives of Prince Ranariddh, Khieu Samphan announced the creation of a new political party, the National Solidarity Party, that would support the NUF at the next election. Prince Ranariddh declared that, if the notorious former leadership of the PDK were excluded, he would welcome such an alliance. Hun Sen, however, deemed the potential alliance to be a threat to the CPP, and later that month, following the seizure of a seven-ton shipment of weapons destined for Prince Ranariddh, he accused the Prince of illegally importing weapons to arm PDK soldiers to create unrest. The PDK was divided over the issue of peace negotiations, with certain factions sympathetic to reconciliation with the FUNCINPEC Party, while others, notably that of Pol Pot, were opposed. In an attempt to regain control of the movement, Pol Pot began a violent purge, ordering the death of Son Sen and also that of Ta Mok. Following the execution of Son Sen and his family, many PDK commanders rallied behind Ta Mok and fighting erupted between the two factions. Pol Pot and his supporters fled into the jungle, with Khieu Samphan as a hostage, but were captured by Ta Mok's forces and returned to Anlong Veng.

In late July 1997 a US journalist, Nate Thayer, was invited by the PDK to Anlong Veng to witness the trial of Pol Pot. He was condemned by a 'people's court' for 'destroying national unity' and for the killing of Son Sen and his family. In October Thayer, who was the first journalist to see Pol Pot for 18 years, was permitted to interview the former leader, who denied that atrocities had occurred under his regime.

In June 1997 Prince Ranariddh announced in Phnom-Penh that Pol Pot was under arrest and that Khieu Samphan would surrender, but the statement was received with widespread scepticism, while Hun Sen condemned Ranariddh for his relations with the PDK. At the beginning of June, following rumours of a meeting between Prince Ranariddh and Khieu Samphan, Hun Sen had demanded that Ranariddh choose between himself and Khieu as a partner in government. Tensions between Prince Ranariddh and Hun Sen increased, as FUNCINPEC military forces were strengthened. Hun Sen continued to warn that PDK defectors were massing in Phnom-Penh and there was crossfire between CPP and FUNCINPEC security units close to Ranariddh's residence. On 3 July, following several attempts by CPP troops to detect the presence of PDK soldiers in FUNCINPEC units, CPP forces disarmed a unit of Prince Ranariddh's bodyguards, on the grounds that they were allegedly PDK troops. On the following day Prince Ranariddh left the country. On 5 July (on which day Hun Sen returned from a holiday in Viet Nam) serious fighting erupted in Phnom-Penh, and on 6 July, the day on which Khieu Samphan had been scheduled to broadcast the PDK's agreement with the FUNCINPEC Party to end its resistance and rejoin the political system, Hun Sen appeared on television to demand Prince Ranariddh's arrest (on charges of negotiating with the PDK, introducing proscribed PDK troops into Phnom-Penh and secretly importing weapons to arm those forces) and to urge FUNCINPEC officials to select another leader. More than 24 hours of pillage then ensued, in which the airport and many shops and factories were raided and looted. In the following week, according to human rights groups, at least 25 military and political associates of Prince Ranariddh were killed in custody, including Ho Sok (an official of the Ministry of the Interior and a close collaborator of Prince Ranariddh), who had been responsible for increasing FUNCINPEC's military presence in Phnom-Penh. Many FUNCINPEC and KNP officials, as well as many FUNCINPEC members of the legislature, fled the country.

King Sihanouk's appeals for both sides to travel to the People's Republic of China to negotiate a settlement were rejected by Hun Sen. Prince Ranariddh announced from Paris that a resistence movement was being organized in western Cambodia. Meanwhile, Hun Sen began negotiations with certain prominent members of the FUNCINPEC Party who remained in Phnom-Penh (the General Secretary, Loy Simchheang, the Co-Minister of the Interior, Yu Hokkri, and the Minister of Defence, Tie Chamrat) in an effort to attain the two-thirds' majority of the National Assembly necessary for the investiture of a new government. By the end of July 1997 the National Assembly had reconvened, with 98 of the 120 deputies present, including 40 of the 58 FUNCINPEC deputies. Hun Sen protested to the international community that his actions did not constitute a *coup d'etat,* as he had not abolished the Constitution or the monarchy and had not dissolved the Government or the National Assembly. He also declared that he was in favour of free elections in 1998. Despite these assurances, aid was temporarily suspended by the USA, Japan, Germany and later Australia. However, the UN refused to condemn Hun Sen by name, although it expressed a 'grave preoccupation' with the situation in Cambodia. King Sihanouk, who had been in the People's Republic of China since February, also insisted on remaining neutral and accepted that Chea Sim should continue to sign royal decrees in his absence.

In early August 1997 the National Assembly voted to remove Ranariddh's legal immunity, and a warrant was subsequently issued for his arrest. At the same session of the National Assembly, Ung Huot, the FUNCINPEC Minister of Foreign Affairs, was formally elected to the post of First Prime Minister. The USA opposed his election as undemocratic, since it had taken place in an atmosphere of alleged political intimidation. However, Japan resumed its aid programme in August, and China also accepted Prince Ranariddh's replacement.

In July 1997 troops loyal to Prince Ranariddh, led by Gen Nhiek Bunchhay (a former military Chief of Staff and a principal negotiator with the PDK), were swiftly forced into the north-west of the country by CPP troops. They regrouped near the Thai border in an effective alliance with PDK troops under Ta Mok. Prolonged fighting took place for control of the town of O'Smach, about 70 km west of Anlong Veng, which was the last base for the resistance coalition led by Prince Ranariddh, the Union of Cambodian Democrats, which comprised members of the NUF. At the end of August the King arrived in Siem Reap on a mission of peace and was welcomed at the airport by Chea Sim, Hun Sen and Ung Huot. Hun Sen rejected another proposal from the King to act as a mediator in peace talks, insisting that Ranariddh had to be tried for his alleged crimes. At the end of October the King left the country, declaring that he would stay abroad indefinitely, but actually returned in early December.

In September 1997 Hun Sen announced a cabinet reorganization that effectively removed remaining supporters of Prince Ranariddh from the Government. However, a few days later the National Assembly failed by 13 votes in a secret ballot to approve the changes by the required two-thirds' majority.

In September 1997 the UN Accreditation Committee decided to leave Cambodia's seat at the UN vacant until a further meeting in February. Hun Sen threatened to withdraw UN supervision of elections in 1998 if the UN continued to leave the seat unoccupied. Hun Sen's relationship with the UN was already strained by UN claims that it had documentary evidence showing that at least 43 people, principally from the royalist army structure, were murdered by forces loyal to Hun Sen after the events of 5–6 July and that CPP security forces failed to act during the grenade attack on Rainsy. Despite assurances by Hun Sen of a full investigation, no one was arrested or charged.

In October 1997 Ieng Sary, who controlled the area around Pailin, gave his support to Hun Sen. In early November Ung Huot visited Pailin to confirm its new status as a town and to appoint local officials, including Ieng Sary's son, Ieng Vut, who was named Deputy Governor. Hun Sen assured the UN that opposition candidates for the 1998 elections, for which the National Assembly was in the process of considering enabling legislation, would be free to campaign. Hun Sen had continued his efforts to encourage the return of all opposition representatives who fled the country in July, except Ranariddh and Gen. Nhiek Bunchhay, and in November Rainsy returned to Cambodia. In the same month Hun Sen announced that he would approve a royal pardon for Prince Ranariddh should he be convicted by the court, thus enabling him to participate in the general election. Later he also agreed to the return of Gen. Nhiek Bunchhay if he were prepared to testify in court against Prince Ranariddh. Following his return, Rainsy organized a peace march through Phnom-Penh that was attended by several thousand supporters. As a gesture of conciliation on both sides, Hun Sen and Rainsy held a cordial meeting in December, at which they agreed to co-operate in the national interest.

In December 1997 Loy Simchheang (who, together with Ung Huot, had been expelled from the FUNCINPEC Party by Prince Ranariddh in August) resigned as the party's General Secretary and formed a new party, the New Society Party, with Yu Hokkri. Ung Huot was reported to have formed the Nationalist Party with the support of Ung Phan. In mid-December the National Assembly voted, for technical reasons, to postpone local and legislative elections from May until 26 July 1998 and to increase the number of seats from 120 to 122, owing to the creation of two new cities in areas formerly controlled by the PDK.

One of the most serious international consequences of the events of 5–6 July 1997 was the decision by ASEAN to postpone indefinitely Cambodia's admission to the grouping. Cambodia had attended an ASEAN meeting in July 1995 with official observer status, had its application for membership accepted in July 1996 and was due to join in late July 1997. Hun Sen was angered by ASEAN's decision and initially rejected the grouping's attempts to negotiate a diplomatic solution to the Cambodian crisis. He also declared that Cambodia would withdraw its application for membership of ASEAN if it continued to be rejected. However, at the end of July Hun Sen invited ASEAN to mediate in the dispute and held talks with the grouping in early August. At the end of August the Prime Minister of Singapore announced, however, that Cambodia would not be considered for admission to ASEAN until after elections had been held.

Relations between Cambodia and the People's Republic of China (which had formerly supported the PDK) had already improved during the mid-1990s. However, following the events of 5–6 July 1997, Hun Sen deliberately aligned himself with China, possibly as a reaction to the disapproval of ASEAN, which considered itself to be a counterbalance to the influence of China in the region. In July, despite Taiwan's considerable economic involvement in Cambodia, Hun Sen closed Taiwan's representative office to gain favour with the People's Republic of China. Two weeks later Taiwan rejected a request from Hun Sen to reopen an office in Phnom-Penh, demanding that he first apologize for his earlier action.

In mid-January 1994 the Thai Prime Minister, Chuan Leekpai, undertook the first-ever official visit to Cambodia by a Thai Prime Minister. Bilateral relations between Cambodia and Thailand, which had been strained (owing to the Thai armed forces' unauthorized links with the PDK, who controlled illicit trade in gems and timber along the Thai border, and by Cambodian allegations of Thai involvement in the July 1994 coup attempt), improved in September 1995, when the two countries signed an agreement to establish a joint border commission. Thailand remained neutral following the events of 5–6 July 1997, but extended humanitarian assistance to the estimated 35,000 refugees who crossed into Thailand to avoid the fighting in the north-west of Cambodia.

In August 1994 the National Assembly adopted an immigration bill which prompted concern that it could be used to enforce the mass expulsion of ethnic Vietnamese from Cambodia given that the bill had no provision for the definition of Cambodian citizenship. In January 1995 Prince Ranariddh held talks in Viet Nam on improving relations between the two countries, following an increase in tension over the issue of ethnic Vietnamese in Cambodia. The Vietnamese President, Gen. Le Duc Anh, made an official state visit to Cambodia in early August. In early 1996 Cambodia accused Viet Nam of encroaching on disputed border territory, but in April discussions in Phnom-Penh between the two countries resulted in an agreement providing for the settlement of all border issues through further negotiations. In August a Vietnamese National Assembly delegation visited Cambodia to promote good relations, and in October both of the Cambodian Prime Ministers expressed a desire to develop closer links with Viet Nam.

In May 1996 Hun Sen approved the restoration of diplomatic relations with the Republic of Korea, despite opposition from King Sihanouk (who favoured Cambodia's long-standing relations with the Democratic People's Republic of Korea). Hun Sen headed a Cambodian delegation which visited the Republic of Korea in July and signed agreements providing for economic and scientific co-operation between the two countries. (Cambodia and the Republic of Korea exchanged diplomatic missions in September.)

In April 1995 Cambodia, Thailand, Viet Nam and Laos signed an agreement providing for the establishment of the Mekong River Commission (see p. 262), which was to co-ordinate the sustainable development of the resources of the Lower Mekong River Basin.

Government

The Kingdom of Cambodia is a constitutional monarchy. The monarch is the Head of State and is selected by the Throne Council from among descendants of three royal lines. Legislative power is vested in the 120-member National Assembly (to be increased to 122 members at the 1998 general election), which is elected for a term of five years by universal adult suffrage. Executive power is held by the Cabinet (the Royal Government of Cambodia), headed by the Prime Minister, who is appointed by the King at the recommendation of the Chairman of the National Assembly from among the representatives of the winning party. In 1993, however, a First and a Second Prime Minister were appointed from the two leading parties.

For local administration the Kingdom of Cambodia is divided into provinces, municipalities, districts, khan, khum and sangkat.

Defence

In August 1997 the total strength of the Kingdom of Cambodia's armed forces was estimated to be 140,500, comprising an army of some 84,000, a navy of 5,000, an air force of 1,500 and provincial forces of about 50,000 (although perhaps only 19,000 of these were capable of combat). A system of conscription was in force, for those aged between 18 and 35, for five years. The total strength of the armed forces of the Party of Democratic Kampuchea (the National Army of Democratic Kampuchea) was unknown, but it was believed to number about 1,500 in January 1998. Prince Norodom Ranariddh's resistance coalition, the Union of Cambodian Democrats, was estimated to have forces numbering 10,000. In 1996 current government expenditure on defence and security was estimated at 392,300m. riels (45.9% of total current expenditure).

Economic Affairs

In 1995, according to estimates by the World Bank, Cambodia's gross national product, estimated at average 1993–95 prices, was US $2,718m., equivalent to about $270 per head. During 1985–95 the population increased at an average rate of 3.0% per year. Cambodia's gross domestic product (GDP) increased, in real terms, by an annual average of 6.4% during 1990–95. The World Bank estimated real GDP growth at 7.6% in 1995.

Agriculture (including forestry and fishing) contributed an estimated 53.1% of GDP in 1995. In 1996 the sector engaged an estimated 72.6% of the economically active population. Production of the staple crop, rice, increased in the late 1980s, but in the 1990s was adversely affected by drought, floods and factional aggression. Other principal crops include maize, sugar cane, cassava and bananas. Timber and rubber are the two principal export commodities. A UN survey indicated, however, that the forested area in Cambodia had declined from 73% of the total land area in 1965 to 39% in 1992. The rapid rate of deforestation resulted in the imposition of a ban on log exports, which took effect from May 1995. However, few measures were taken to enforce either the ban or other forestry regulations imposed in conjunction with the IMF. In 1995 the total fishing catch was reported to be 112,500 tons, including 31,200 tons from the sea. Agricultural GDP increased, in real terms, by an annual average of 2.1% during 1990–95. Growth in agricultural GDP was 6.5% in 1995.

Industry (including mining, manufacturing, construction and power) contributed an estimated 13.9% of GDP in 1995, and employed 6.7% of the labour force in 1980. In real terms, industrial GDP increased by an annual average of 11.3% during 1990–95. Growth in industrial GDP was 9.8% in 1995.

In 1995 mining and quarrying contributed only 0.3% of GDP. Cambodia has limited mineral resources, including phosphates, gem stones, iron ore, bauxite, silicon and manganese ore, of which only phosphates and gem stones are, at present, being exploited. In the early 1990s agreements on petroleum exploration were signed with several foreign enterprises. Cambodia's resources of natural gas were unoffically estimated to be 1,500,000m.–3,500,000m. cu m in 1992 and petroleum reserves were estimated to be between 50m. and 100m. barrels. The GDP of the mining sector increased, in real terms, by an annual average of 8.2% during 1989–94, according to IMF estimates; growth in mining GDP was 8.0% in 1995.

The manufacturing sector, which contributed an estimated 5.1% of GDP in 1995, is dominated by about 1,500 rice mills and 79 factories, which produce, *inter alia*, ready-made garments, household goods, textiles, tyres and pharmaceutical products. By September 1994, according to the Government, 62 of the factories had been sold or rented out to private investors, 13 were operated as joint ventures with foreign partners, and four continued to operate under state management. Thai investment, in particular, has been encouraged in light manufacturing and food-processing. The Royal Government of Cambodia announced that it was to encourage the establishment of agro-industrial enterprises (sugar and vegetable oil refineries and factories producing paper pulp) and promote the production of fertilizers, petroleum and heavy construction and mechanical equipment. The GDP of the manufacturing sector increased, in real terms, at an average annual rate of 4.2% during 1989–94, according to IMF estimates. Growth in manufacturing GDP was 10.0% in 1995.

Energy is derived principally from timber. In the early 1990s a thermo-electric power plant was under development, and a diesel-electric power station was being restored. There are about 30 hydroelectric plants in Cambodia and a power plant in Phnom-Penh with a total generating capacity of 71 MW, although, owing to a lack of spare parts and a shortage of fuel, only 21 MW is generally available. In September 1994 the Government announced a project to construct and place under private management a new 35-MW diesel-electric power station in the capital.

The services sector contributed an estimated 33.0% of GDP in 1995, and engaged about 19% of the economically active population in 1980. The tourism sector was increasingly significant, with arrivals reaching nearly 220,000 in 1995. However, the violent events of July 1997 halted virtually all tourist activity. In real terms, the GDP of the services sector increased by an annual average of 7.3% during 1989–94, according to IMF estimates. Growth in the sector was 7.9% in 1995.

In 1996 Cambodia recorded a visible trade deficit of US $428.4m., while there was a deficit of $297.8m. on the current account of the balance of payments. In 1993 the principal source of imports, according to IMF estimates, was Singapore (24.3%); other major sources were Viet Nam, Japan and Australia. Singapore was also the principal market for exports in that year (65.8%); other important purchasers were Japan, Hong Kong and Thailand. The principal exports in 1996 were sawn timber (accounting for 16.6% of the total), logs and rubber. The principal imports in 1995 were gold, cigarettes, motor spirit (petrol) and diesel oil.

Cambodia's overall budget deficit at the end of 1995 was equivalent to 7.7% of GDP. Cambodia's external debt at the end of 1995 totalled US $2,031m., of which $1,942m. was long-term public debt. In that year the cost of debt-servicing was equivalent to 0.6% of revenue from exports of goods and services. The annual rate of inflation averaged 93.1% during 1989–94; the rate declined to 1.1% in 1995 and 10.1% in 1996.

Cambodia is a member of the Asian Development Bank (see p. 110). Cambodia was scheduled to join the Association of South East Asian Nations (ASEAN, see p. 113) in late July 1997. However, owing to the events of 5–6 July (see Recent History), ASEAN decided to postpone Cambodia's entry to the organization indefinitely.

Following the signing of the UN peace agreement in 1991, international embargoes on aid and trade were removed, and in October 1993 lending to Cambodia was resumed in support of comprehensive macroeconomic and structural reforms. Under the IMF programme, fiscal and monetary restraint resulted in a stable exchange rate and lower inflation. Following the adoption of a new foreign investment law in August 1994, Cambodia was reasonably successful in attracting investors, particularly from Malaysia, Singapore and the People's Republic of China.

In 1996 the IMF and the World Bank suspended scheduled disbursements of aid to Cambodia, owing to the country's failure to enforce agreed forestry policies or to address corruption. Illegal and uncontrolled logging largely served to fund the two Prime Ministers' rival private security forces, although the situation failed to improve after Hun Sen's assumption of power. The events of 5–6 July 1997 (see Recent History), together with the regional economic crisis, adversely affected Cambodia's fragile economic revival, as many foreign enterprises closed their operations, tourism was halted, the value of the riel declined rapidly and inflation increased. Cambodia's most significant problem was the suspension of aid, as almost one-half of its budget was funded by multilateral and bilateral aid. At the beginning of July the donor nations had pledged a further US $450m. to Cambodia, but this was now in jeopardy. Commercial investment was also threatened, and, despite measures to reassure investors (including promises of compensation for losses suffered during the fighting and the simplification and amendment of an already liberal investment code), most new foreign investments were likely to be delayed until after the general election. In order to improve the economy, the Government also urgently needed to halt the diversion of funds into fighting the resistance, to reform the grossly overstaffed and inefficient civil service and to implement taxation reforms to stabilize government finance.

Social Welfare

In 1988 there were 188 hospitals in the country, containing 12,953 beds (equivalent to 1 bed per 612 inhabitants). In the same year there were 425 physicians, 7,271 nurses and 2,332 midwives. Under the 1993 Constitution, a social security system was envisaged for workers and employees. In the 1996 budget the Ministry of Health was allocated 122,100m. riels (8.97% of total expenditure) and the Ministry of Social Affairs was allocated 45,400m. riels (3.3% of total expenditure).

Education

Education is compulsory for six years between the ages of six and 12. Primary education begins at six and lasts for five years. In 1994 enrolment at primary level was equivalent to 118% of children in the relevant age-group. (Males 130%; females 106%). Secondary education comprises two cycles, each lasting three years. In 1994 enrolment at secondary level was equivalent to 25% of the relevant age-group (males 31%; females 18%). In the same year enrolment at tertiary level was equivalent to 1.4% of the relevant age-group (males 2.4%; females 0.5%).

In 1993, according to a sample survey, the average rate of adult illiteracy was 34.7% (males 20.3%; females 46.6%). In the 1996 budget the Ministry of Education was allocated 171,800m. riels (12.5% of total expenditure).

Public Holidays

1998: 1 January (International New Year's Day), 7 January (7 January Day), April (Cambodian New Year), 1 May (Labour Day), 24 September (Constitution Day), 23 October (Anniversary of Paris Peace Agreement on Cambodia), 9 November (Independence Day).

1999: 1 January (International New Year's Day), 7 January (7 January Day), April (Cambodian New Year), 1 May (Labour Day), 24 September (Constitution Day), 23 October (Anniversary of Paris Peace Agreement on Cambodia), 9 November (Independence Day).

Weights and Measures

The metric system is in force.

Statistical Survey

Note: Some of the statistics below represent only sectors of the economy controlled by the Government of the former Khmer Republic. During the years 1970–75 no figures were available for areas controlled by the Khmers Rouges.

Area and Population

AREA, POPULATION AND DENSITY

Area (sq km)	181,035*
Population (census results)	
17 April 1962	5,728,771
Prior to elections of 1 May 1981	6,682,000
Population (official estimates at mid-year)	
1993	9,308,000
1994	9,568,000
1995	9,836,000
Density (per sq km) at mid-1995	54.3

* 69,898 sq miles.

Principal Towns: Phnom-Penh (capital), population 900,000 in 1991 (estimate); Sihanoukville (Kompong-Som), population 75,000 in 1990 (estimate).

BIRTHS AND DEATHS (UN estimates, annual averages)

	1980–85	1985–90	1990–95
Birth rate (per 1,000)	45.6	46.7	43.5
Death rate (per 1,000)	17.6	16.3	14.3

Source: UN, *World Population Prospects: The 1994 Revision*.

Expectation of life (UN estimates, years at birth, 1995): Males 51.0; Females 54.0 (Source: UN, *Statistical Yearbook for Asia and the Pacific*).

ECONOMICALLY ACTIVE POPULATION
(ILO estimates, '000 persons at mid-1980)

	Males	Females	Total
Agriculture, etc.	1,346	1,107	2,454
Industry	130	90	220
Services	439	187	625
Total	1,915	1,384	3,299

Source: ILO, *Economically Active Population Estimates and Projections, 1950–2025*.

Mid-1996 (estimates in '000): Agriculture, etc. 3,732; Total 5,138 (Source: FAO, *Production Yearbook*).

Agriculture

PRINCIPAL CROPS ('000 metric tons)

	1994	1995	1996
Rice (paddy)	2,223	3,300	3,390
Maize	45	55	60
Sweet potatoes	36	39	35*
Cassava (Manioc)	65	82	90
Other roots and tubers	18	18	18
Dry beans	17	20	20
Soybeans (Soya beans)	23	17	18
Groundnuts (in shell)	5	7	7
Sesame seed	4	7*	6
Coconuts*	53	53	53
Copra	9†	10†	10
Sugar cane	219	202	205
Tobacco (leaves)	12	11	10
Natural rubber	42†	35	40
Vegetables and melons*	488	450	455
Oranges	49†	50†	60
Mangoes	26†	27†	30
Pineapples	14	15	15
Bananas	129†	132†	140
Other fruits and berries	51	53	54

* FAO estimate(s). † Unofficial figure.

Source: FAO, *Production Yearbook*.

LIVESTOCK ('000 head, year ending September)

	1994	1995	1996
Horses*	21	21	20
Cattle	2,621	2,778	2,800
Buffaloes	810	765	770
Pigs	2,024	2,039	2,050

* FAO estimates.

Chickens (million): 10 in 1994; 10 in 1995; 10 in 1996.

Ducks (FAO estimates, million): 4 in 1994; 4 in 1995; 4 in 1996.

Source: FAO, *Production Yearbook*.

LIVESTOCK PRODUCTS ('000 metric tons)

	1994	1995	1996
Beef and veal*	21	21	21
Buffalo meat*	12	13	13
Pig meat*	75	75	76
Poultry meat*	21	21	21
Cows' milk*	19	19	19
Hen eggs	10†	10†	10
Other poultry eggs*	3	3	3
Cattle and buffalo hides*	8	8	8

* FAO estimates. † Unofficial figure.

Source: FAO, *Production Yearbook*.

Forestry

ROUNDWOOD REMOVALS ('000 cu m, excl. bark)

	1992	1993	1994
Sawlogs, veneer logs and logs for sleepers	105	65	37
Other industrial wood*	630	630	630
Fuel wood*	6,141	6,326	6,512
Total	6,876	7,021	7,179

* FAO estimates.

Source: FAO, *Yearbook of Forest Products*.

SAWNWOOD PRODUCTION
(FAO estimates, '000 cu m, incl. railway sleepers)

	1992	1993	1994
Coniferous (softwood)	10	5	5
Broadleaved (hardwood)	122	122	122
Total	132	127	127

Source: FAO, *Yearbook of Forest Products*.

Fishing

('000 metric tons, live weight)

	1993	1994	1995
Inland waters	75.3	72.6	81.3
Pacific Ocean	33.6	30.6	31.2
Total catch	108.9	103.2	112.5

Source: FAO, *Yearbook of Fishery Statistics*.

Mining

('000 metric tons)

	1992	1993	1994
Salt (unrefined)*	40	40	40

* Estimates by US Bureau of Mines.

Source: UN, *Industrial Commodity Statistics Yearbook*.

Industry

SELECTED PRODUCTS ('000 metric tons, unless otherwise indicated)

	1971	1972	1973
Distilled alcoholic beverages ('000 hectolitres)	45	55	36
Beer ('000 hectolitres)	26	23	18
Soft drinks ('000 hectolitres)	25	25*	25*
Cigarettes (million)	3,413	2,510	2,622
Cotton yarn—pure and mixed (metric tons)	1,068	1,094	415
Bicycle tyres and tubes ('000)	208	200*	200*
Rubber footwear ('000 pairs)	1,292	1,000*	1,000*
Soap (metric tons)	469	400*	400*
Motor spirit (petrol)	2	—	—
Distillate fuel oils	11	—	—
Residual fuel oils	14	—	—
Cement	44	53	78
Electric energy (million kWh)†	148	166	150

* Estimate. † Production by public utilities only.

Cigarettes (million): 4,175 in 1987; 4,200 annually in 1988–92 (estimates by US Department of Agriculture).

Cement ('000 metric tons): 50 in 1976; 50 in 1977; 10 in 1978 (estimates by US Bureau of Mines).

Electric energy (estimates, million kWh): 173 in 1992; 180 in 1993; 187 in 1994.

(Source: UN, *Industrial Commodity Statistics Yearbook*.)

Finance

CURRENCY AND EXCHANGE RATES

Monetary Units

100 sen = 1 new riel.

Sterling and Dollar Equivalents (30 September 1997)

£1 sterling = 5,156.4 riels;
US $1 = 3,192.0 riels;
10,000 new riels = £1.939 = $3.133.

Average Exchange Rate (new riels per US $)

1994	2,545.3
1995	2,450.8
1996	2,624.1

BUDGET ('000 million riels)

Revenue	1994	1995	1996*
Tax revenue	364.6	445.5	577.3
Direct taxes	8.6	20.9	25.2
Taxes on profits	6.3	17.8	20.1
Private enterprises	5.0	12.0	17.8
Indirect taxes	75.0	103.8	178.2
Turnover tax	8.2	17.1	37.7
Private enterprises	6.7	14.9	34.7
Consumption tax	46.9	60.0	66.4
Excise taxes	2.9	9.0	63.0
Taxes on international trade	280.9	320.8	373.9
Taxes and duties on imports	257.6	300.8	354.4
Taxes on exports	18.2	17.3	16.0
Non-tax revenue	225.8	197.5	220.2
Receipts on public property	147.4	120.5	121.7
Forests	86.0	52.8	22.5
Receipts from public enterprises	42.7	26.7	55.9
Factory leases	4.8	5.9	26.1
Receipts from commercial activity	23.9	3.4	—
Royalties and concessions	4.2	17.0	19.2
Other receipts	78.4	77.0	98.5
Posts and telecommunications	61.0	54.4	80.0
Total	590.4	642.9	797.5

Expenditure†	1994	1995	1996*
Current expenditure	673.8	689.6	853.8
Wages	293.4	325.7	376.0
Civil administration	101.4	110.9	128.7
Defence and security	192.1	214.8	247.4
Other	380.3	363.8	477.8
Operating expenditures	324.3	284.4	329.7
Civil administration	121.9	105.2	184.8
Defence and security	202.3	179.2	144.9
Social transfers	41.3	44.8	79.0
Civil administration	37.5	40.6	71.3
Capital expenditure	335.3	511.1	541.3
Locally financed	78.5	56.9	81.0
Externally financed	256.8	454.2	460.3
Total	1,009.1	1,200.6	1,395.1

* Forecasts.

Source: IMF, *Cambodia—Recent Economic Developments*.

INTERNATIONAL RESERVES (US $ million at 31 December)

	1994	1995	1996
IMF special drawing rights	15.90	15.18	13.68
Foreign exchange	102.60	176.80	251.90
Total	118.50	191.98	265.58

Source: IMF, *International Financial Statistics*.

MONEY SUPPLY (million riels at 31 December)

	1994	1995	1996
Currency outside banks	176,298	250,916	299,837
Demand deposits at deposit money banks	20,940	27,291	29,089
Total money (incl. others)	201,679	278,490	328,926

Source: IMF, *International Financial Statistics*.

COST OF LIVING

(Consumer Price Index; base: July–September 1994 = 100)

	1994	1995	1996
All items	104.2	105.3	115.9

Source: IMF, *International Financial Statistics*.

NATIONAL ACCOUNTS ('000 million riels at current prices)

Expenditure on the Gross Domestic Product

	1992	1993	1994
Government final consumption expenditure	255.0	373.2	605.4
Private final consumption expenditure	2,066.4	4,595.6	4,994.4
Increase in stocks } Gross fixed capital formation }	245.4	789.8	1,162.7
Total domestic expenditure	2,566.8	5,758.6	6,762.5
Exports of goods and services	126.6	719.0	969.9
Less Imports of goods and services	185.4	1,063.6	1,684.4
GDP in purchasers' values	2,508.0	5,414.0	6,048.0
GDP at constant 1989 prices	280.6	292.1	303.7

1995 ('000 million riels): GDP 7,178.0 at current prices, 324.9 at constant 1989 prices.

Source: UN, *Statistical Yearbook for Asia and the Pacific*.

Gross Domestic Product by Economic Activity

	1993	1994	1995
Agriculture, hunting, forestry and fishing	2,742.0	3,139.6	3,826
Mining and quarrying	16.2	17.5	20
Manufacturing	285.5	324.9	367
Electricity and water	38.5	43.5	50
Construction	403.1	467.2	561
Trade, restaurants and hotels	812.0	909.0	983
Transport and communications	173.1	195.4	248
Owner-occupied dwellings	311.6	335.9	330
Government, education and health	216.0	232.2	283
Other services	416.1	465.8	532
GDP in purchasers' values	5,414.0	6,131.0	7,200

Source: IMF, *Cambodia—Statistical Tables*, and *Cambodia—Recent Economic Developments*.

BALANCE OF PAYMENTS (US $ million)

	1994	1995	1996
Exports of goods f.o.b.	489.9	855.2	643.6
Imports of goods f.o.b.	–744.4	–1,186.8	–1,072.0
Trade balance	–254.5	–331.6	–428.4
Exports of services	54.5	114.0	162.8
Imports of services	–139.6	–187.9	–221.8
Balance on goods and services	–339.6	–405.5	–487.4
Other income received	2.1	9.7	12.6
Other income paid	–49.1	–66.9	–57.5
Balance on goods, services and income	–386.6	–462.7	–532.3
Current transfers received	230.0	277.9	236.9
Current transfers paid	—	–0.9	–2.4
Current balance	–156.6	–185.7	–297.8
Capital account (net)	73.2	78.0	87.4
Direct investment from abroad	68.9	150.8	293.6
Other investment assets	–46.8	–103.4	–68.0
Other investment liabilities	31.9	75.0	76.4
Net errors and omissions	65.6	11.5	–19.6
Overall balance	36.2	26.2	72.0

Source: IMF, *International Financial Statistics.*

External Trade

PRINCIPAL COMMODITIES (US $ million)

Imports	1993	1994	1995
Cigarettes	60.0	95.9	192.5
Motor spirit (petrol)	17.7	29.0	58.3
Motorcycles	13.3	29.0	36.0
Diesel oil	18.4	30.4	51.0
Vehicles	18.5	12.0	22.0
Beer	10.0	14.7	14.7
Video cassette recorders	15.8	23.1	14.9
Television receivers	10.3	21.2	17.3
Construction material	24.2	20.8	19.2
Fabric	69.5	36.2	12.6
Food products	2.7	11.6	17.8
Clothing	20.7	11.9	17.2
Gold	28.0	78.4	305.0
Sugar	—	13.8	6.4
Cement	—	12.3	12.3
Total	361.2	553.2	930.0

Source: IMF, *Cambodia—Recent Economic Developments.*

Exports f.o.b.†	1991	1992	1993*
Crude rubber	18.7	12.6	13.9
Logs	24.6	25.1	50.4
Sawn timber	3.7	n.a.	34.0
Soybeans	9.9	2.1	0.4
Maize	2.3	0.6	0.5
Fishery products	1.6	1.4	0.2
Sesame seed	1.2	2.1	0.1
Total (incl. others)	67.3	51.3	102.1

* Estimates.

† Excluding re-exports (US $ million): 145.2 in 1991; 213.2 in 1992; 117.0 (estimate) in 1993.

1994 (estimates, US $ million): *Exports:* Crude rubber 30.0; Logs 124.0; Sawn timber 73.0; Total (incl. others) 462.0.

1995 (estimates, US $ million): *Exports:* Crude rubber 41.2; Logs 111.6; Sawn timber 72.9; Total (incl. others) 808.6.

1996 (estimates, US $ million): *Exports:* Crude rubber 34.5; Logs 72.5; Sawn timber 101.9; Total (incl. others) 615.4.

Source: IMF, *Cambodia, Economic Review, Cambodia—Statistical Tables* and *Cambodia—Recent Economic Developments.*

PRINCIPAL TRADING PARTNERS (US $ million)

Imports f.o.b.	1991*	1992*	1993†
Australia	1.7	11.4	20.4
France	9.9	5.7	12.7
Hong Kong	15.0	20.4	13.4
Indonesia	0.3	17.7	5.6
Japan	4.5	5.8	33.4
Singapore	135.6	176.5	98.2
Thailand	1.8	11.5	7.4
USSR (former)	8.9	2.1	0.4
Viet Nam	28.5	85.4	70.8
Total (incl. others)	213.8	344.5	403.9

Exports f.o.b.‡	1991	1992	1993†
Hong Kong	3.4	3.8	1.9
Indonesia	0.9	1.1	1.4
Japan	4.7	4.7	4.0
Malaysia	3.0	1.2	0.9
Singapore	18.4	16.2	24.8
Taiwan	0.4	2.2	1.7
Thailand	3.9	6.7	1.9
USSR (former)	5.1	—	—
Viet Nam	23.3	10.1	0.5
Total (incl. others)	67.3	51.3	37.7

* Excluding estimates for unrecorded imports.

† Estimates.

‡ Excluding re-exports.

Source: IMF, *Cambodia, Economic Review.*

Transport

RAILWAYS (traffic)

	1971	1972	1973
Passenger-kilometres (million)	91	56	54
Freight ton-kilometres (million)	10	10	10

1981 (million): Passenger-km 54; Freight ton-km 10 (Source: Statistisches Bundesamt, Wiesbaden, Germany).

ROAD TRAFFIC (motor vehicles in use at 31 December)

	1994	1995	1996
Passenger cars	34,228	42,210	46,800
Buses and coaches	430	720	790
Lorries and vans	6,887	8,712	11,000
Road tractors	112	390	463
Motorcycles and mopeds	356,418	378,783	397,300

Source: International Road Federation, *World Road Statistics.*

SHIPPING

Merchant Fleet (registered at 31 December)

	1994	1995	1996
Number of vessels	4	16	43
Displacement ('000 grt)	5.8	60.0	206.2

Source: Lloyd's Register of Shipping, *World Fleet Statistics.*

International Sea-borne Freight Traffic (estimates, '000 metric tons)

	1988	1989	1990
Goods loaded	10	10	11
Goods unloaded	100	100	95

Source: UN, *Monthly Bulletin of Statistics.*

CIVIL AVIATION (traffic on scheduled services)

	1975	1976	1977
Passenger-kilometres (million)	42	42	42
Freight ton-kilometres ('000)	400	400	400

Source: Statistisches Bundesamt, Wiesbaden, Germany.

Tourism

	1992	1993	1994
Tourist arrivals ('000)	88	118	177
Tourist receipts (US $ million)	50	48	70

Source: UN, *Statistical Yearbook*.

Communications Media

	1992	1993	1994
Radio receivers ('000 in use)	985	1,045	1,080
Television receivers ('000 in use)	73	77	80
Telephones ('000 main lines in use)	4	4	5
Telefax stations (number in use)	n.a.	1,170	n.a.
Mobile cellular telephones (subscribers)	n.a.	2,510	6,500

Sources: UNESCO, *Statistical Yearbook*, and UN, *Statistical Yearbook*.

Education

(1990/91)

	Schools	Pupils
Kindergarten	264	51,421
Primary schools	36,665	1,322,100
Junior high schools	402	230,700
Senior high schools	69	48,000
Higher education:		
Colleges	36	6,696
Secondary vocational schools	27	13,236
Primary vocational schools	32	23,370

Source: Ministry of Education, Phnom-Penh.

Pre-primary (1994/95): 219 institutions; 1,954 teachers; 49,542 pupils.
Primary (1994/95): 37,827 teachers; 1,703,316 pupils.
General secondary (1994/95): 16,349 teachers; 297,555 pupils.
Higher education (1994/95): 784 teachers; 11,652 students.

Source: UNESCO, *Statistical Yearbook*.

Directory

The Constitution

The Constitution was promulgated on 21 September 1993. The main provisions are summarized below:

GENERAL PROVISIONS

The Kingdom of Cambodia is a unitary state in which the King abides by the Constitution and multi-party liberal democracy. Cambodian citizens have full right of freedom of belief; Buddhism is the state religion. The Kingdom of Cambodia has a market economy system.

THE KING

The King is Head of State and the Supreme Commander of the Khmer Royal Armed Forces. The monarchist regime is based on a system of selection: within seven days of the King's death the Throne Council (comprising the Chairman of the National Assembly, the Prime Minister, the Supreme Patriarchs of the Mohanikay and Thoammayutikanikay sects and the First and Second Vice-Chairmen of the National Assembly) must select a King. The King must be at least 30 years of age and be a descendant of King Ang Duong, King Norodom or King Sisowath. The King appoints the Prime Minister and the Cabinet. In the absence of the King, the Chairman of the National Assembly assumes the duty of acting Head of State.

THE NATIONAL ASSEMBLY

Legislative power is vested in the National Assembly, which has 120 members who are elected by universal adult suffrage (to be increased to 122 at the general election scheduled for July 1998). A member of the National Assembly must be a Cambodian citizen by birth over the age of 25 years and has a term of office of five years, the term of the National Assembly. The National Assembly may not be dissolved except in the case where the Royal Government (Cabinet) has been dismissed twice in 12 months. The National Assembly may dismiss cabinet members or remove the Royal Government from office by passing a censure motion through a two-thirds majority vote of all the representatives in the National Assembly.

CABINET

The Cabinet is the Royal Government of the Kingdom of Cambodia, which is led by a Prime Minister, assisted by Deputy Prime Ministers, with state ministers, ministers and state secretaries as members. The Prime Minister is designated by the King at the recommendation of the Chairman of the National Assembly from among the representatives of the winning party. The Prime Minister appoints the members of the Cabinet, who must be representatives in the National Assembly or members of parties represented in the National Assembly.

THE CONSTITUTIONAL COUNCIL

The Constitutional Council's competence is to interpret the Constitution and laws passed by the National Assembly. It has the right to examine and settle disputes relating to the election of members of the National Assembly. The Constitutional Council consists of nine members with a nine-year mandate. One-third of the members are replaced every three years. Three members are appointed by the King, three elected by the National Assembly and three appointed by the Supreme Council of the Magistracy.

The Government

HEAD OF STATE

HM King Norodom Sihanouk; acceded to the throne on 24 September 1993; duties frequently discharged by Chea Sim.

ROYAL GOVERNMENT OF CAMBODIA
(January 1998)

A coalition of the FUNCINPEC Party, the Cambodian People's Party (CPP), the Buddhist Liberal Democratic Party (BLDP) and MOLINAKA.

First Prime Minister and Minister of Foreign Affairs and International Co-operation: Ung Huot.

Second Prime Minister: Hun Sen.

Deputy Prime Minister and Co-Minister of the Interior: Sar Kheng.

Deputy Prime Minister and Minister of Public Works and Transport: Ing Kiet.

Minister of Finance and Minister of State, with responsibility for Rehabilitation and Development: Keat Chhon.

Minister of State, with responsibility for Inspection: Ung Phan.

Minister of State, with responsibility for Landscaping and Urbanization: VAN MOLIVAN.

Minister of State and Minister of Justice: CHEM SNGUON.

Minister to Cabinet Office: SOK AN.

Minister to Cabinet Office: NADI TAN.

Minister of Tourism: VENG SEREIVUT*.

Minister of Culture and Fine Arts: NUT NARANG.

Ministers of National Defence: TIE BANH, TIE CHAMRAT.

Co-Minister of the Interior: YU HOKKRI.

Minister of Information and the Press: IENG MULI.

Minister of Agriculture, Forestry and Fisheries: TAU SENGHUO.

Minister of Education, Youth Affairs and Sports: TOL LAH*.

Minister of Environment: MOK MARET.

Minister of Trade: CHAM PRASIT.

Minister of Industry, Minerals and Energy: PU SOTHIRAK.

Minister of Planning: CHEA CHANTO.

Minister of Public Health: CHHEA THANG.

Minister-Delegate responsible for Youth Rehabilitation: NHIM VANDA.

Minister of Rural Development: HONG SUNHUOT*.

Secretary of State for Religious Affairs: HEAN VANNAROT.

Secretary of State for Post and Telecommunications: SO KHUN.

Secretary of State for Social Welfare, Labour and Veteran Affairs: SUY SEM.

Secretary of State for Public Functions: PRAK SOK.

Secretary of State for Women's Affairs: KEAT SAKUN.

Secretary of State for Relations with the National Assembly: (vacant).

* In January 1998 these ministers remained in voluntary exile with Prince Norodom Ranariddh.

MINISTRIES

Ministry of Agriculture, Forestry and Fisheries: 200 blvd Norodom, Phnom-Penh; tel. and fax (23) 427320.

Ministry of Culture and Fine Arts: 274 blvd Monivong, cnr rue Red Cross, Phnom-Penh; tel. (23) 362647.

Ministry of Education, Youth Affairs and Sport: 80 blvd Norodom, Phnom-Penh; tel. (23) 360233; fax (23) 426791.

Ministry of Environment: 48 blvd Sihanouk; tel. (23) 426814; fax (23) 427844.

Ministry of Finance: 60 rue 92, Phnom-Penh; tel. (23) 722863; fax (23) 427798.

Ministry of Foreign Affairs and International Co-operation: Tera Vithei Preah, blvd Sisowath, Phnom-Penh; tel. and fax (23) 426144.

Ministry of Industry, Minerals and Energy: 45 blvd Norodom, Phnom-Penh; tel. (23) 723077; fax (23) 427840.

Ministry of Information and the Press: 62 blvd Monivong, Phnom-Penh; tel. (23) 426235; fax (23) 426059.

Ministry of the Interior: 275 blvd Norodom, Phnom-Penh; tel. (23) 724372; fax (23) 426585.

Ministry of Justice: blvd Sothearos, cnr rue 240, Phnom-Penh; tel. (23) 360421.

Ministry of National Defence: blvd Pochentong, Phnom-Penh; tel. (23) 366170; fax (23) 366169.

Ministry of Planning: 386 blvd Monivong, Phnom-Penh; tel. (23) 362307.

Ministry of Post and Telecommunications: rue 102, cnr rue 13, Phnom-Penh; tel. (23) 722823; fax (23) 426011.

Ministry of Public Health: 128 blvd Kampuchea Krom, Phnom-Penh; tel. and fax (23) 426841.

Ministry of Public Works and Transport: blvd Norodom, cnr rue 106, Phnom-Penh; tel. (23) 725113; fax (23) 427862.

Ministry of Religious Affairs: blvd Sisowath, rue 240, Phnom-Penh; tel. (23) 725699.

Ministry of Rural Development: blvd Czechoslovakia/blvd Pochentong, Phnom-Penh; tel. (23) 722425.

Ministry of Social Welfare, Labour and Veteran Affairs: 68 blvd Norodom, Phnom-Penh; tel. (23) 725191; fax (23) 427322.

Ministry of Tourism: 3 blvd Monivong, Phnom-Penh; tel. (23) 426107; fax (23) 426364.

Ministry of Trade: 20 blvd Norodom, Phnom-Penh; tel. (23) 723775; fax (23) 426396.

Ministry of Women's Affairs: Phnom-Penh; tel. (23) 366412.

Legislature

NATIONAL ASSEMBLY*

National Assembly, blvd Sothearos, cnr rue 240, Phnom-Penh; tel. (23) 722535; fax (23) 427769.

Chairman: CHEA SIM (CPP).

Election, 23–28 May 1993

	Seats
FUNCINPEC Party	58
Cambodian People's Party	51
Buddhist Liberal Democratic Party	10
MOLINAKA	1
Total	120

* Under the terms of the UN peace plan (signed in October 1991), elections to a 120-member Constituent Assembly took place as shown above. The Assembly drafted a new Constitution, and when it was promulgated on 21 September 1993 the Constituent Assembly became a legislative body, the National Assembly.

Political Organizations

Buddhist Liberal Democratic Party (BLDP) (Kanakpak Preacheathippatai Serei Niyum Preah Puthasasna): c/o National Assembly, blvd Sothearos, cnr rue 240, Phnom-Penh; f. 1992 by the Khmer People's National Liberation Front (f. 1979, military wing was the Khmer People's National Liberation Armed Forces) to contest the 1993 elections; Chair. SON SANN.

Buddhist Liberal Party (Kanakpak Serei Niyum Preah Put Sasna): Phnom-Penh; f. 1998; a breakaway faction of the BLDP; Chair. IENG MULI; Gen. Sec. SIENG LAPRESSE.

Cambodian Farmers' Party (CFP): Phnom-Penh; f. 1997; aims to defend the interests of farmers and to eradicate Vietnamese influence in Cambodia; supports the CNUP.

Cambodian People's Party (CPP) (Kanakpak Pracheachon Kampuchea): Chamcarmon, blvd Norodom, Phnom-Penh; tel. (23) 725403; fax (23) 722906; (known as the Kampuchean People's Revolutionary Party 1979–91); 20-mem. Standing Cttee of the Cen. Cttee; Cen. Cttee of 153 full mems; Hon. Chair. of Cen. Cttee HENG SAMRIN; Chair. of Cen. Cttee CHEA SIM; Vice-Chair. HUN SEN.

Democratic National United Movement (DNUM): Pailin; f. 1996 by IENG SARY, following his defection from the PDK.

Free Development Republican Party: Phnom-Penh; Chair. TED NGOY.

FUNCINPEC Party (United National Front for an Independent, Neutral, Peaceful and Co-operative Cambodia Party): 61 rue 214, Phnom-Penh; tel. (23) 426053; FUNCINPEC altered its title to the FUNCINPEC Party when it adopted political status in 1992; the party's military wing was the National Army of Independent Cambodia (fmrly the Armée Nationale Sihanoukiste—ANS); Pres. Prince NORODOM RANARIDDH; Gen. Sec. (vacant).

FUNCINPEC Party: Phnom-Penh; f. June 1997 by rebel mems of above; Chair. TOAN CHHAY; Sec.-Gen. UNG PHAN.

Khmer Citizens' Party (Kanakpak Pulroat Khmer): Phnom-Penh; f. 1996; breakaway faction of Khmer Nation Party; Chair. NGUON SOEUR; Sec.-Gen. IEM RA.

Khmer Nation Party (KNP): Phnom-Penh; f. 1995; 70,000 mems; Pres. SAM RAINSY; Gen. Sec. (vacant).

Khmer Republican Democratic Party (KRDP): Phnom-Penh; f. 1997; supports CPP; Chair. NHUNG SEAP.

Khmers Rouges: see National Solidarity Party.

Liberal Democratic Party: Phnom-Penh; f. 1993; receives support from members of the armed forces; pro-Government; Chair. Gen. CHHIM OM YON.

MOLINAKA (National Liberation Movement of Cambodia): c/o National Assembly, blvd Sothearos, cnr rue 240, Phnom-Penh; a breakaway faction of FUNCINPEC.

National United Front (NUF): Phnom-Penh; f. Feb. 1997 by Prince NORODOM RANARIDDH; comprises FUNCINPEC Party, the Khmer Nation Party and Buddhist Liberal Democratic Party; aimed to address problems such as immigration, sovereignty and corruption.

Nationalist Party (Kanakpak Neak Cheat Niyum): Phnom-Penh; f. 1997 by First Prime Minister Ung Huot with the support of Ung Phan.

New Society Party (Kanakpak Neak Cheat Niyum): Phnom-Penh; f. 1997 by Loy Simchheang, formerly the Gen.-Sec. of FUNCINPEC, and Yu Hokkri, the Co-Minister of the Interior.

Party of Democratic Kampuchea (PDK) (Pheakki Kampuchea Prachea Thipatai): f. 1960, known as the Khmers Rouges; adopted title the Communist Party of Kampuchea in 1977, but reportedly dissolved in 1981; the military wing is the National Army of Democratic Kampuchea (NADK); the PDK was declared illegal in July 1994, whereupon it announced the formation of the Provisional Government of National Unity and National Salvation of Cambodia (PGNUNSC); Chair. KHIEU SAMPHAN.

National Solidarity Party (NSP): f. 1997 to contest the elections in 1998; Pres. KHIEU SAMPHAN.

Union of Cambodian Democrats (UCD): Phnom-Penh; f. July 1997 by SAM RAINSY, Prince NORODOM RANARIDDH and more than 20 temporarily-exiled BLDP and FUNCINPEC legislators; aims to restore Prince Ranariddh to the premiership.

United Front for the Construction and Defence of the Kampuchean Fatherland (UFCDKF): Phnom-Penh; f. 1978 as the Kampuchean National United Front for National Salvation (KNUFNS), renamed Kampuchean United Front for National Construction and Defence (KUFNCD) in 1981, present name adopted in 1989; mass organization supporting policies of the CPP; an 89-mem. Nat. Council and a seven-mem. hon. Presidium; Chair. of Nat. Council CHEA SIM; Sec.-Gen. ROS CHHUN.

Uphold the Cambodian Nation Party: Phnom-Penh; f. 1997 by Pen Sovan, fmr Sec.-Gen. of the Cen. Cttee of the CPP, to contest the 1998 legislative elections; Chair. PEN SOVAN.

Other political parties that contested the 1993 election were: the Reconciliation Republican Party; the Liberal Progressive Republican Party; the Neutral Khmer Party; the Rally for National Unity Party; the Neutral Democratic Cambodia Party; the Democrat Party; (Leader IN TAM); the Free Independent Democratic Cambodia Party; the Liberal National Reconciliation Party; the Reborn Cambodia Party; the Action for Democracy and Development Party; the Khmer Nationalist Party; the Liberal Republican Party; the Liberal Democratic Khmer Farmers' Party (Leader KONG PISET); the Khmer Liberal Republican Party; and the Khmer National Congress Party.

Diplomatic Representation

EMBASSIES IN CAMBODIA

Australia: Villa 11, rue 254, Chartaumuk, Daun Penh, Phnom-Penh; tel. (23) 426000; fax (23) 426003; Ambassador: MALCOLM LEADER.

Brunei: Office 5, Hotel Sofitel Cambodiana, Ground Floor, 313 Sisowath Quay, Phnom-Penh; tel. (23) 363331; fax (23) 363332; Ambassador: Pengiran Haji SALLEHUDDIN.

Bulgaria: 177/227 blvd Norodom, Phnom-Penh; tel. (23) 723181; fax (23) 426491; Chargé d'affaires a.i.: STOYAN DAVIDOV.

Canada: Villa 9, RV Senei Vinnavaut Oum, SK Chaktamouk, Khan Daun Penh, Phnom-Penh; tel. (23) 426001; fax (23) 428029; Ambassador: D. GORDON LONGMUIR.

China, People's Republic: 256 blvd Mao Tse Toung, Phnom-Penh; tel. (15) 911062; fax (23) 426271; Ambassador: YAN TINGAI.

Cuba: 98 route 214, Phnom-Penh; tel. (23) 724181; fax (23) 427428; Ambassador: RUBÉN PÉREZ VALDÉS.

France: 1 blvd Monivong, Phnom-Penh; tel. (23) 430020; fax (23) 430037; Ambassador: GILDAS LE LIDEC.

Germany: 76–78 route 214, BP 60, Phnom-Penh; tel. (23) 216193; fax (23) 427746; Ambassador: Dr HAROLD LOESCHNER.

Hungary: 463 blvd Monivong, Phnom-Penh; tel. (23) 722781; fax (23) 426216; Ambassador: (vacant).

India: Villa 777, blvd Monivong, Phnom-Penh; tel. (23) 725981; fax (23) 426212; Ambassador: JASJIT SINGH RANDHAWA.

Indonesia: 179 rue 51, Phnom-Penh; tel. (23) 426148; fax (23) 427566; Ambassador: HAMID ALHADAD.

Japan: 75 blvd Norodom, Phnom-Penh; tel. (23) 427161; fax (23) 426162; Ambassador: MASAKI SAITO.

Korea, Democratic People's Republic: 39 rue 268, Phnom-Penh; tel. (15) 912567; fax (23) 426230; Ambassador: KIM YOUNG SOP.

Korea, Republic: Phnom-Penh; Ambassador: PARK KYUNG-TAI.

Laos: 15–17 blvd Mao Tse Toung, Phnom-Penh; tel. (23) 426441; fax (23) 427454; Ambassador: CHANPHENG SIHAPHOM.

Malaysia: Villa 161, rue 51, Beng Rang Precinct, Daun Penh, Phnom-Penh; tel. (23) 426176; fax (23) 426004; Ambassador: MOHD KAMAL ISMAUN.

Philippines: 33 rue 294, Phnom-Penh; tel. and fax (23) 428048; Ambassador: THELMO CUNANAN.

Russia: 92 blvd Norodom, Phnom-Penh; tel. (23) 360855; fax (23) 360850; Ambassador: VADIM V. SERAFIMOV.

Singapore: 92 blvd Norodom, Phnom-Penh; tel. (23) 360855; fax (23) 360850; Ambassador: MUSHAHID ALI.

Thailand: 4 blvd Monivong, Sangkat Srass Chork, Khan Daun Penh, Phnom-Penh; tel. (23) 426182; fax (18) 810840; Ambassador: DOMEDEJ BUNNAG.

United Kingdom: 27–29 rue 75, Phnom-Penh; tel. (23) 427124; fax (23) 427125; Ambassador: CHRISTOPHER GEORGE EDGAR.

USA: 27 rue 240, Phnom-Penh; tel. (23) 426436; fax (23) 426437; Ambassador: KENNETH QUINN.

Viet Nam: 436 blvd Monivong, Phnom-Penh; tel. (23) 725481; fax (23) 427385; Ambassador: TRAN HUY CHUONG.

Judicial System

An independent judiciary was established under the 1993 Constitution.

Supreme Court: rue 134, cnr rue 63, Phnom-Penh; tel. (23) 362572; Chair. (vacant).

Religion

BUDDHISM

The principal religion of Cambodia is Theravada Buddhism (Buddhism of the 'Tradition of the Elders'), the sacred language of which is Pali. A ban was imposed on all religious activity in 1975. By a constitutional amendment, which was adopted in April 1989, Buddhism was reinstated as the national religion and was retained as such under the 1993 Constitution. By 1992 2,800 monasteries (of a total of 3,369) had been restored and there were 21,800 Buddhist monks. In 1992 about 90% of the population were Buddhists.

Supreme Patriarchs: Ven. Patriarch MONGKOLTEPEACHA, Ven. Patriarch KHOUSANANDA.

Patriotic Kampuchean Buddhists' Association: Phnom-Penh; mem. of UFCDKF; Pres. LONG SIM.

CHRISTIANITY

The Roman Catholic Church

Cambodia comprises the Apostolic Vicariate of Phnom-Penh and the Apostolic Prefectures of Battambang and Kompong-Cham. In 1994 there were an estimated 20,000 adherents (6,000 Cambodians and 14,000 ethnic Vietnamese) in the country. An Episcopal Conference of Laos and Kampuchea was established in 1971. In 1975 the Government of Democratic Kampuchea banned all religious practice in Cambodia, and the right of Christians to meet to worship was not restored until 1990.

Vicar Apostolic of Phnom-Penh: Rt Rev. YVES-GEORGES-RENÉ RAMOUSSE (Titular Bishop of Pisita), 787 (Rue 93) blvd Monivong, BP 123, Phnom-Penh; tel. and fax (23) 720552.

ISLAM

Islam is practised by a minority in Cambodia. Islamic worship was also banned in 1975, but it was legalized in 1979, following the defeat of the Democratic Kampuchean regime.

The Press

NEWSPAPERS

Newspapers are not widely available outside Phnom-Penh.

Cambodia Daily: Villa 50B, rue 240, Phnom-Penh; tel. (23) 360225; fax (23) 426573; e-mail aafc@pactok.peg.apc.org; in English and Khmer; Mon.-Fri.; Editor-in-Chief JAMES KANTER; Publr BERNARD KRISHER.

Cambodia Times: 252A blvd Monivong, Phnom-Penh; tel. (23) 723405; fax (23) 426647; f. 1992 (in Kuala Lumpur, Malaysia); English-language weekly.

Kampuchea: 158 blvd Norodom, Phnom-Penh; tel. (23) 725559; f. 1979; weekly; Chief Editor KEO PRASAT; circ. 55,000.

Phnom Penh Post: 10A rue 264, Phnom-Penh; tel. and fax (23) 426568; f. 1992; English; fortnightly; Publrs MICHAEL HAYES, KATHLEEN HAYES.

Pracheachon (The People): 101 blvd Preah Norodom, Phnom-Penh; f. 1985; 2 a week; organ of the CPP; Editor-in-Chief SOM KIMSUOR; circ. 50,000.

Reaksmei Kampuchea: 476 blvd Monivong, Phnom-Penh; tel. (23) 724040; fax (23) 427580; daily; local newspaper in northern Cambodia.

NEWS AGENCIES

Agence Khmere de Presse (AKP): 62 blvd Monivong, Phnom-Penh; tel. (23) 723469; f. 1978; Dir-Gen. SUM MEAN.

Foreign Bureaux

Agence France-Presse (AFP) (France): Phnom-Penh; tel. (23) 426227; fax (23) 426226.

Associated Press (AP) (USA): BP 870, Phnom-Penh; tel. (23) 426607; Correspondent SHEILA McNULTY.

Reuters (UK): House 15, Street 246 (Vimol Thoang Thom), Phnom-Penh; tel. and fax (23) 723405; Correspondent KATYA ROBINSON.

United Press International (UPI) (USA): 29 rue 200, Phnom-Penh; tel. (23) 426289; Correspondent TRICIA FITZGERALD.

Xinhua (New China) News Agency (People's Republic of China): 12 rue 264, Phnom-Penh; tel. and fax (23) 426613; Correspondent XANG MING.

ASSOCIATION

Khmer Journalists' Association: 101 blvd Preah Norodom, Phnom-Penh; tel. (23) 725459; f. 1979; mem. of UFCDKF; Pres. PIN SAMKHON.

Broadcasting and Communications

RADIO

Vithyu Cheat Kampuchea (National Radio of Cambodia): rue Preah Kossamak, Phnom-Penh; tel. (23) 723369; fax (23) 427319; f. 1978; fmrly Vithyu Samleng Pracheachon Kampuchea (Voice of the Cambodian People); controlled by the Ministry of Information and the Press; home service in Khmer; daily external services in English, French, Lao, Vietnamese and Thai; Dir-Gen. VANN SENG LY; Dep. Dir Gen. TAN YAN.

In August 1991 the FUNCINPEC Party announced the establishment of Radio FUNCINPEC. In December 1994 the Government announced the establishment of a Khmer Royal Armed Forces radio station.

There are also four local radio stations based in Phnom-Penh, Battambang Province, Sihanoukville, and Stung Treng Province.

The PDK radio service was renamed the Radio of the Provisional Government of National Unity and National Salvation in 1994 and the Voice of the National United Army in October 1997.

TELEVISION

In 1996 there were five television channels broadcasting in Phnom-Penh.

Cambodian TV Channel 5: Phnom-Penh; f. 1993 as the International Broadcasting Corpn; Dir PICHAI CHAN-IEM.

National Television of Cambodia (Channel 7): 19 rue Okhna Pech (242), Phnom-Penh; tel. (23) 722983; fax (23) 426407; opened 1983; broadcasts for 10 hours per day in Khmer; Dir-Gen. (Head of Television) MAO AYUTH.

Finance

BANKING

The National Bank of Cambodia, which was established as the sole authorized bank in 1980 (following the abolition of the monetary system by the Government of Democratic Kampuchea in 1975), is the central bank, and assumed its present name in February 1992. The adoption of a market economy led to the licensing of privately-owned and joint-venture banks from July 1991. At the end of October 1996 there were 32 banks operating in Cambodia, including two state-owned banks, three joint-venture banks, seven branches of foreign banks and 20 locally-incorporated private banks.

Central Bank

National Bank of Cambodia: 22–24 blvd Preah Norodom, BP 25, Phnom-Penh; tel. (23) 428105; fax (23) 426117; f. 1980; cap. 1,550m. riels; Gov. THOR PENG LEATH; Dep. Gov. SUM NIPHA.

State Commercial Banks

Foreign Trade Bank: 24–26 blvd Preah Norodom, Phnom-Penh; tel. (23) 525866; Man. TIM BO PHOL.

Municipal Bank: 18 rue Ang Eng, S.K. Wat Phnom, Khan Daun Penh, Phnom-Penh; tel. (23) 525663; Man. RATH SAVUTH.

Joint-Venture Banks

Cambodian Commercial Bank Ltd: 26 blvd Monivong, Phnom-Penh; tel. (23) 25644; telex 46101; fax (23) 426116; f. 1991; jointly owned by the National Bank of Cambodia and the Bangkok-based Siam Commercial Bank; Man. BHENGBHASANG KRISHMMSA; 4 brs.

Cambodian Public Bank (Campu Bank): Villa 23, rue 114, BP 899, Phnom-Penh; tel. (23) 426067; telex 16149; fax (23) 426068; joint venture between Malaysia's Public Bank and the National Bank of Cambodia; Man. ONG HWEE SOO.

Canadia Bank Ltd: 263 rue 110, Doun Penh Division, Phnom-Penh; tel. (23) 724672; Man. PUNG KHEAV SE; 2 brs.

Private Banks

Advanced Bank of Asia Ltd: 97–99 blvd Norodom, Khan Daun Penh, Phnom-Penh; tel. (23) 202915; Man. SEBASTIEN YOS.

Agriculture and Commercial Bank of Cambodia (ACBC) Ltd: 49 rue 214, Samdach Pann, Phnom-Penh; tel. (23) 722272; fax (23) 426363; Man. PAVARIS KAEWDIT.

The Bank of National Wealth Cambodia Ltd: 15 rue 214, S. K. Boeung Reang, Khan Daun Penh, Phnom-Penh; tel. (23) 810806; Man. HENRY SHI CALLE.

Cambodia Agriculture, Industrial and Merchant Bank: 7 rue 221, Sangkat Takhmau, Srok Takhmau, Kandal Province; tel. 366856; Man. CHHOR SANG.

Cambodia Asia Bank Ltd: 252 blvd Monivong, Phnom-Penh; tel. (23) 426628; Man. WONG TOW FOCK.

Cambodia Farmers Bank: 45 rue Kampuchea Viet Nam, Phnom-Penh; tel. (23) 426183; fax (23) 426801; f. 1992; joint venture by Thai business executives and the National Bank of Cambodia; Man. PHOT PUNYARATABANDHU; Dep. Man. NORODOM ARUNRASMY; 2 brs.

Cambodia International Bank Ltd: 21, rue 128-107 S. Monorom, Khan 7 Makara, Phnom-Penh; tel. (23) 725920; Man. CHIEE YOON CHENG.

Cambodia Mekong Bank: 1 rue Kramuonsar S. Phsar Thmei 1, Khan Daun Penh, Phnom-Penh; tel. (23) 426626; Man. KHOV MENG CHANG.

Chansavangwong Bank Corporation: 20–22 rue 154 S. Phsar Thmei III, Khan Daun Penh, Phnom-Penh; tel. (23) 427464; fax (23) 427461; Man. TAING LI PHENG.

Emperor International Bank Ltd: 230–232 blvd Monivong, Phnom-Penh; tel. (23) 722233; Man. VAN SOU IENG.

First Overseas Bank Ltd: 20-FE-EO & 20HG-EO, rue Kramuonsar (114), Khan Daun Penh, Phnom-Penh; tel. (23) 63888; Man. CHOY FOOK ON; 2 brs.

Global Commercial Bank Ltd: 337 blvd Monivong, Sangkat Orasey 4th, Khan 7 Makara, Phnom-Penh; tel. (23) 364258; fax (23) 426612; Man. WELLSON HSIEH.

Great International Bank Ltd: 320A–320B, blvd Monivong, Khan Daun Penh, Phnom-Penh; tel. (23) 427087; Man. TAK BOUA LAY LY.

Khmer Bank (Thaneakar Khmer): 116 rue Preah Sihanouk, Phnom-Penh; tel. (23) 724853; Man. HÉNG KIM Y.

Pacific Commercial Bank Ltd: 350 rue 217 S. Orassey 2, Khan 7 Makara, Phnom-Penh; tel. (23) 426896; Man. TENG DANNY.

Phnom-Penh City Bank Ltd: 101 blvd Norodom, rue 214, Phnom-Penh; tel. (23) 62885; fax (23) 427353; Man. THEERAYUT SEANG AROON.

Singapore Banking Corporation Ltd: 68 rue 214, Samdach Pann, S. Boeung Reang, Khan Daun Penh, Phnom-Penh; tel. (23) 723366; fax (23) 27277; Man. BOB SEH HIOENG YAP.

Singapore Commercial Bank Ltd: 316 blvd Preah Monivong, S. Chactomok, Khan Daun Penh, BP 1199, Phnom-Penh; tel. and fax (23) 427471; telex 16141; cap. US $5m.; Pres. KONG LOOK SEN; Gen. Man. TEOH SAM MING; 1 br.

Standard Chartered Bank: 95A blvd Preah Samdach Sihanouk, Phnom-Penh; tel. (23) 426685; Man. JOHN JANES.

Union Commercial Bank Ltd: 61 rue 130, S. Phsar Chas, Khan Daun Penh, Phnom-Penh; tel. (23) 427995; Man. PHE HOK CHHUON.

Foreign Banks

Bangkok Bank Ltd (Thailand): 26 blvd Preah Norodom, Phnom-Penh; tel. (23) 426593; Man. NICOM PHONGSOIPETCH.

Banque Indosuez (France): 70 blvd Preah Norodom, Doun Penh Division, Phnom-Penh; tel. (23) 724772; fax (23) 427235; Man. GEORGES LOUBEYRE.

Krung Thai Bank Ltd (Thailand): 149 rue 215 Sivutha, Deipo 1 Market, Tuolkok Division, Phnom-Penh; tel. (23) 426587; Man. XOMNUEK WICHTIR.

Lippo Bank (Indonesia): 273 Preah Andoung, S.K. Wat Phnom, Khan Daun Penh, Phnom-Penh; Man. MARKUS PARMADI.

Maybank Bhd (Malaysia): 2 blvd Preah Norodom, Phnom-Penh; tel. (23) 427590; Man. CHAN KIN CHOY.

Siam City Bank Ltd (Thailand): 79 rue Kampuchea Viet Nam, Makara Division, Phnom-Penh; tel. (23) 427199; Man. TOSACHAI SOPHAKALIN.

Thai Farmers Bank (Thailand): 2 rue 118, S. Phsar Tmei 1, Khan Daun Penh, Phnom-Penh; tel. (23) 724035; Man. PERAWAP SING TONG.

INSURANCE

Commercial Union: 28 rue 47, Phnom-Penh; tel. (23) 426694; fax (23) 427171; general insurance; Gen. Man. PAUL CABLE.

Indochine Insurance Union: 55 rue 178, Phnom-Penh; tel. (23) 368050; fax (23) 426625; Dir PHILIPPE LENAIN.

Trade and Industry

DEVELOPMENT ORGANIZATIONS

Cambodian Investment Board: Phnom-Penh; Sec.-Gen. ITH VICHIT.

Council for the Development of Cambodia (CDC): Government Palace, quai Sisowath, Wat Phnom, Phnom-Penh; tel. (23) 426909; fax (23) 361616; f. 1993; sole body responsible for approving foreign investment in Cambodia, also grants exemptions from customs duties and other taxes, and provides other facilities for investors; Chair. Prince NORODOM RANARIDDH; Sec.-Gen. CHANTHOL SUN.

CHAMBER OF COMMERCE

Cambodian Chamber of Commerce: Phnom-Penh; Pres. THENG BUNMA; Sec.-Gen. PUNG KHEAV SE.

INDUSTRIAL AND TRADE ASSOCIATION

Garment Manufacturers' Association: Phnom-Penh; Pres. VEN SOU IENG.

UTILITIES

Electricity

Electricité du Cambodge: Phnom-Penh.

TRADE UNIONS

Cambodian Federation of Trade Unions (KFTU): Phnom-Penh; f. 1979; affiliated to WFTU; Chair. MEN SAM-AN; Vice-Chair. LAY SAMON.

Transport

RAILWAYS

Chemins de Fer du Cambodge: Moha Vithei Pracheathippatay, Phnom-Penh; tel. (23) 725156; prior to April 1975 the total length of railway track was 1,370 km; lines linked Phnom-Penh with the Thai border, via Battambang, and with Kompong-Som (now Sihanoukville); a new line between Samrong Station and Kompong Speu was constructed in 1978; by November 1979 the 260-km Phnom-Penh–Kompong-Som line, and by February 1980 the Phnom-Penh–Battambang line, had been restored. The rail link between Poipet and Aranyaprathet, in Thailand, was reopened in 1992; in 1995 there were 22 locomotives, which in that year carried 100,000 freight tons and 500,000 passengers; Dir PICH KIMSREANG.

ROADS

In 1996 the total road network was 35,769 km in length, of which 4,165 km were highways and 3,604 km were secondary roads; about 7.5% of the road network was paved.

INLAND WATERWAYS

The major routes are along the Mekong river, and up the Tonlé Sap river into the Tonlé Sap (Great Lake), covering, in all, about 2,400 km. The inland ports of Neak Luong, Kompong Cham and Prek Kdam have been supplied with motor ferries and the ferry crossings have been improved.

SHIPPING

The main port is Sihanoukville (fmrly Kompong-Som), on the Gulf of Thailand, which has 11 berths and can accommodate vessels of 10,000–15,000 tons. Phnom-Penh port lies some distance inland. Steamers of up to 4,000 tons can be accommodated.

CIVIL AVIATION

There is an international airport at Pochentong, near Phnom-Penh. In August 1997 the Government announced the formation of a second state-owned airline, Kampuchea Airlines.

Civil Aviation Authority of Cambodia: 62 blvd Norodom, Phnom-Penh; tel. (23) 724167; fax (23) 426169; Gen. Dir KOE SOPHAL.

Royal Air Cambodge (RAC): 24 ave Kramuonsar, blvd Monivong, Pnom-Penh; tel. (23) 428830; fax (17) 202757; re-established 1994; national airline; joint venture between the Govt (60%) and Malaysian Helicopter Services (40%); operates flights to eight domestic destinations and routes to Malaysia, Singapore, Thailand, Viet Nam and Hong Kong; Chair. and CEO ITH VICHIT.

Tourism

Visitor arrivals reached nearly 220,000 in 1995, compared with a total of 176,617 in 1994. The Government aims to attract as many as 1m. visitors per year by 2000. In 1997, however, tourist activity was virtually halted following the political violence in July. In October 1994 the Government announced that it was investing US$500m., in a tourism complex near Sihanoukville (Kompong Som), on the coast.

General Directorate for Tourism: Phnom-Penh; f. 1988; Dir CHEAM YIEP.

CAMEROON

Introductory Survey

Location, Climate, Language, Religion, Flag, Capital

The Republic of Cameroon lies on the west coast of Africa, with Nigeria to the west, Chad and the Central African Republic to the east, and the Republic of the Congo, Equatorial Guinea and Gabon to the south. The climate is hot and humid in the south and west, with average temperatures of 26°C (80°F). Annual rainfall in Yaoundé averages 4,030 mm (159 ins). The north is drier, with more extreme temperatures. The official languages are French and English; many local languages are also spoken, including Fang, Bamileke and Duala. Approximately 53% of Cameroonians profess Christianity, 25% adhere to traditional religious beliefs, and about 22%, mostly in the north, are Muslims. The national flag (proportions 3 by 2) has three equal vertical stripes, of green, red and yellow, with a five-pointed gold star in the centre of the red stripe. The capital is Yaoundé.

Recent History

In 1884 a German protectorate was established in Cameroon (Kamerun). In 1916, during the First World War, the German administration was overthrown by invading British and French forces. Under an agreement reached between the occupying powers in 1919, Cameroon was divided into two zones: a French-ruled area in the east and south, and a smaller British-administered area in the west. In 1922 both zones became subject to mandates of the League of Nations, with France and the United Kingdom as the administering powers. In 1946 the zones were transformed into UN Trust Territories, with British and French rule continuing in their respective areas.

French Cameroons became an autonomous state within the French Community in 1957. Under the leadership of Ahmadou Ahidjo, a northerner who became Prime Minister in 1958, the territory became independent, as the Republic of Cameroon, on 1 January 1960. The first election for the country's National Assembly, held in April 1960, was won by Ahidjo's party, the Union camerounaise. In May the new National Assembly elected Ahidjo to be the country's first President.

British Cameroons, comprising a northern and a southern region, was attached to neighbouring Nigeria, for administrative purposes, prior to Nigeria's independence in October 1960. Plebiscites were held, under UN auspices, in the two regions of British Cameroons in February 1961. The northern area voted to merge with Nigeria (becoming the province of Sardauna), while the south voted for union with the Republic of Cameroon, which took place on 1 October 1961.

The enlarged country was named the Federal Republic of Cameroon, with French and English as joint official languages. It comprised two states: the former French zone became East Cameroon, while the former British portion became West Cameroon. John Ngu Foncha, the Prime Minister of West Cameroon and leader of the Kamerun National Democratic Party, became Vice-President of the Federal Republic. Under the continuing leadership of Ahidjo, who was re-elected President in May 1965, the two states became increasingly integrated. In September 1966 the two governing parties and several opposition groups combined to form a single party, the Union nationale camerounaise (UNC). The only significant opposition party, the extreme left-wing Union des populations camerounaises (UPC), was suppressed in 1971 (although it was allowed to operate again when multi-party politics was reintroduced in the early 1990s). Meanwhile, Ahidjo was re-elected as President in March 1970, and Solomon Muna (who had replaced Foncha as Prime Minister of West Cameroon in 1968) became Vice-President.

In June 1972, following the approval by referendum of a new Constitution, the federal system was ended and the country was officially renamed the United Republic of Cameroon. The office of Vice-President was abolished. A centralized political and administrative system was rapidly introduced, and in May 1973 a new National Assembly was elected for a five-year term. After the re-election of Ahidjo as President in April 1975, the Constitution was revised, and a Prime Minister, Paul Biya (a bilingual Christian southerner), was appointed in June. In April 1980 Ahidjo was unanimously re-elected for a fifth five-year term of office.

Ahidjo announced his resignation as President in November 1982, and nominated Biya as his successor. In subsequent cabinet reorganizations Biya removed a number of supporters of the former President. In August 1983 Biya announced the discovery of a conspiracy to overthrow his Government, and simultaneously dismissed the Prime Minister and the Minister of the Armed Forces, both northern Muslims. Later in August Ahidjo resigned as President of the UNC and strongly criticized Biya's regime. In September Biya was elected President of the ruling party, and in January 1984 he was re-elected as President of the Republic, reportedly obtaining 99.98% of the votes cast. In a subsequent reorganization of the Cabinet the post of Prime Minister was abolished, and it was announced that the country's name was to revert from the United Republic of Cameroon to the Republic of Cameroon.

In February 1984 Ahidjo and two of his close military advisers were tried (Ahidjo *in absentia*) for their alleged complicity in the coup plot of August 1983, and received death sentences, which were, however, commuted to life imprisonment. On 6 April 1984 rebel elements in the presidential guard, led by Col Saleh Ibrahim (a northerner), attempted to overthrow the Biya Government. After three days of intense fighting, in which hundreds of people were reported to have been killed, the rebellion was suppressed by forces loyal to the President; a total of 51 defendants received death sentences at trials held in May and November 1984. Following extensive changes within the military hierarchy, the UNC Central Committee and the leadership of state-controlled companies, Biya reorganized his Government in July and introduced more stringent press censorship.

In March 1985 the UNC was renamed the Rassemblement démocratique du peuple camerounais (RDPC). In January 1986 members of the exiled UPC movement claimed that 200–300 opponents of the Biya Government (most of whom were anglophones or members of clandestine opposition movements) had been arrested in the preceding months, and that some of those in detention were being subjected to torture. A number of detainees were subsequently released. In July 1987 the National Assembly approved a new electoral code providing for multiple candidacy in public elections, and in October voters in more than 40% of communes had a choice of RDPC-approved candidates in local government elections.

Ostensibly for reasons of economy, the presidential election, originally scheduled for January 1989, was brought forward to coincide with elections to the National Assembly in April 1988. In the presidential poll Biya was re-elected unopposed, securing 98.75% of the votes cast. In the concurrent legislative elections voters were presented with a choice of RDPC-approved candidates; 153 of those elected to the National Assembly were new members. (In accordance with constitutional amendments, agreed in March 1988, the number of members in the National Assembly was increased from 150 to 180.)

In February 1990 11 people, including the former President of the Cameroonian Bar Association, Yondo Black, were arrested in connection with their alleged involvement in an unofficial opposition organization, the Social Democratic Front (SDF). In March the human rights organization Amnesty International appealed for an inquiry into the deaths, in December 1989, of two prisoners who had been held in detention since April 1984. In April Yondo Black was sentenced to three years' imprisonment on charges of 'subversion'. Later in the same month, however, Biya announced that all the prisoners who had been detained in connection with the 1984 coup attempt were to be released. In May 1990 a demonstration organized by the SDF was violently suppressed by security forces, and six deaths were subsequently reported. In the same month the Government suspended the publication of an independent newspaper, the *Cameroon Post*, which had implied support for the SDF. In June the Vice-President of the RDPC, John Ngu Foncha, resigned, alleging corruption and human rights violations on the part of the Government. In the same month the Congress of the RDPC re-elected Biya as President of the party. In response to continued civil unrest, Biya stated that he envisaged the future adoption of a multi-party system and announced a series of reforms, including the abolition of laws governing subversion, the revision of the law on political associations, and the reinforcement of press freedom. In the same month a committee was established to revise legislation on human rights. In August several political prisoners, including Yondo Black, were released.

In September 1990 Biya announced an extensive cabinet reshuffle, in which a new ministry to implement the Government's economic stabilization programme was created. In early December the National Assembly adopted legislation whereby Cameroon officially became a multi-party state. Under the new legislation, the Government was required to provide an official response within three months to any political organization seeking legal recognition. However, the recruitment of party activists on an ethnic or regional basis and the financing of political parties from external sources remained illegal. Legislative elections, which were due in April 1993, were rescheduled to take place by the end of 1991 (but were later postponed).

In January 1991 anti-Government demonstrators protested at Biya's failure (despite previous undertakings) to grant an amnesty to prisoners implicated in the April 1984 coup attempt. In the same month the trial of two journalists, who had printed an article critical of Biya in an independent publication, *Le Messager,* provoked violent rioting. Meanwhile, opposition leaders reiterated demands for Biya's resignation and the convening of a national conference to formulate a timetable for multi-party elections. Biya's continued opposition to the holding of a conference provoked a series of demonstrations, which were violently suppressed by the security forces. In April the principal anti-Government groups created an informal alliance, the National Co-ordination Committee of Opposition Parties (NCCOP), which organized a widely-observed general strike. Later in April, in response to increasing pressure for political reform, the National Assembly approved legislation granting a general amnesty for political prisoners and reintroducing the post of Prime Minister. Biya subsequently appointed Sadou Hayatou, hitherto Secretary-General at the Presidency, to the position. Hayatou named a 32-member transitional Government, principally composed of members of the former Cabinet. The Government's refusal to comply with demands issued by the NCCOP for an unconditional amnesty for all political prisoners (the existing provisions for an amnesty excluded an estimated 400 political prisoners jailed for allegedly non-political crimes) and for the convening of a national conference prompted the alliance to organize a campaign of civil disobedience, culminating in a general strike in June, which halted commercial activity in most towns. The Government subsequently placed seven of Cameroon's 10 provinces under military rule, prohibited opposition gatherings, and later in June, following continued civil disturbances, banned the NCCOP and several opposition parties, alleging that the opposition alliance was responsible for terrorist activities. Although opposition leaders announced that the campaign of civil disobedience would continue, the effect of the general strike declined in subsequent months. In September several opposition leaders were temporarily detained, following renewed violent demonstrations in Douala.

In October 1991 Biya announced that legislative elections were to be held in February 1992, and that a Prime Minister would be appointed from the party that secured a majority in the National Assembly. Tripartite negotiations between the Government, the majority of the authorized opposition parties and independent officials commenced at the end of October; however, progress was impeded by opposition demands that the agenda of the meeting be extended to include a review of the Constitution, and in early November the NCCOP withdrew from the discussions. In mid-November, however, the Government and about 40 opposition parties (including some parties belonging to the NCCOP) signed an agreement providing for the establishment of a committee to draft constitutional reforms. The opposition undertook to suspend the campaign of civil disobedience, while the Government agreed to end the ban on opposition meetings and to release all prisoners who had been arrested during anti-Government demonstrations. However, several principal opposition parties belonging to the NCCOP, including the SDF, subsequently declared the agreement to be invalid, and stated that the campaign of civil disobedience would continue. The Government revoked the ban on opposition gatherings later in November, and in December ended the military rule that had been imposed in seven provinces.

In January 1992 the Government announced that the legislative elections were to be postponed until 1 March (opposition leaders had demanded that the elections take place in May), in order to allow parties sufficient time for preparation. However, several opposition movements, including two of the principal parties, the SDF and the Union démocratique du Cameroun (UDC), refused to contest the elections, on the grounds that the scheduled date was too early and therefore benefited the RDPC. In February more than 100 people were killed in the northern town of Kousseri, following violent clashes between the Kokoto and Arab Choa ethnic groups, which occurred during the registration of voters. In the same month those opposition parties that had not accepted the tripartite agreement in November 1991 formed the Alliance pour le redressement du Cameroun (ARC), and announced that they were to boycott the elections.

The legislative elections, which took place on 1 March 1992, were contested by 32 political parties; the RDPC won 88 of the National Assembly's 180 seats, while the Union nationale pour la démocratie et le progrès (UNDP) obtained 68, the UPC 18, and the Mouvement pour la défense de la République (MDR) six seats. The RDPC subsequently formed an alliance with the MDR, thereby securing an absolute majority in the National Assembly. In early April Biya formed a new 25-member Cabinet, which, however, principally comprised members of the previous Government; Simon Achidi Achu, an anglophone member of the RDPC who had served in the Ahidjo administration, was appointed Prime Minister. Five members of the MDR, including the party leader, Dakolle Daissala, also received ministerial portfolios.

In August 1992 Biya announced that the forthcoming presidential election, which was due to take place in May 1993, was to be brought forward to 11 October 1992. In September Biya promulgated legislation regulating the election of the President which prohibited the formation of electoral alliances. Shortly before the election two of the seven opposition candidates withdrew in favour of the leader of the SDF, John Fru Ndi, who received the support of the ARC alliance.

The presidential election, which took place as scheduled, immediately provoked opposition allegations of malpractice on the part of the Government. In mid-October 1992 John Fru Ndi proclaimed himself President, following unconfirmed reports that he had won the election. Later that month, however, the Government announced that Biya had been re-elected by 39.9% of the votes cast, while Ndi had secured 35.9%, prompting violent demonstrations by opposition supporters in many areas, particularly in the north-west and in Douala. The Supreme Court rejected a subsequent appeal by Ndi that the results of the election be declared invalid. At the end of October, in response to the continued unrest, the Government placed Ndi and several of his supporters under house arrest, and imposed a state of emergency in the North-West Province for a period of three months. Biya was inaugurated as President on 3 November, and pledged to implement further constitutional reforms. Later that month international condemnation of the Government increased, following the death by torture of a detained opposition member; the USA and Germany suspended economic aid to Cameroon, in protest at the continued enforcement of the state of emergency. At the end of November Biya announced the appointment of a new 30-member Cabinet, which, in addition to three members of the MDR, included representatives of the UPC, the UNDP and the Parti national du progrès. In late December the state of emergency was revoked in the North-West Province. In January 1993 the Government granted an amnesty to a number of political prisoners who had been arrested in October 1992.

In March 1993 an informal alliance of opposition parties (led by the SDF), the Union pour le changement, organized a series of demonstrations and a boycott of French consumer goods (in protest at the French Government's involvement with Biya), in support of demands for a new presidential election. The Government accused the alliance of planning to destabilize the country by incitement to civil disorder, and continued efforts to suppress opposition activity. Later in March three people were killed in clashes between members of the armed forces and oppposition supporters in Bamenda, in the North-West Province, while a number of members of a prominent opposition movement, the Union des forces démocratiques du Cameroun, were arrested shortly before a demonstration was due to take place. In response to international pressure, however, the Government announced that a national debate on constitutional reform was to be conducted by the end of May. In early April, following the expiry of the date stipulated by the SDF for the submission of a revised constitution to a national referendum, Ndi (who maintained that he was the legitimately elected President of Cameroon) declared that he was to convene a national conference of the political parties that had contested the presidential election. In the same month a gathering organized by the Cameroon Anglophone Movement (CAM) in Buéa, in the South-West Province, demanded the restoration of a federal system of government, in response to the traditional dominance of the French-speaking section of the population.

Following a meeting with the French President, François Mitterrand, in May 1993, Biya announced that the planned debate on the revision of the Constitution was to take place in early June: a technical commission was to be established to prepare recommendations based on proposals from all sectors of the population. Later in May the Government promulgated draft constitutional amendments which provided for the installation of a democratic political system, with the establishment of new organs of government, including an upper legislative chamber, to be known as the Senate, and restricted the power vested in the President (who was to serve a maximum of two five-year terms of office). The draft legislation retained a unitary state, but, in recognition of demands by supporters of federalism, envisaged a more decentralized system of local government. The constitutional proposals were subsequently to be amended in accordance with the recommendations of the technical commission.

During the second half of 1993 the opposition organized a series of anti-Government strikes and demonstrations; consequently, many opposition activists were either arrested or detained. In December public-sector workers initiated a general strike, with the support of the opposition, after the Government announced substantial reductions in state-sector salaries. In early 1994, however, strike action in protest at the devaluation of the CFA franc subsided, following the imposition of sanctions against striking civil servants.

Meanwhile, in September 1993, a peace agreement was signed between the Kokoto and Arab Choa ethnic groups in Kousseri; however, further clashes were reported later in the year. In February 1994 security forces killed some 50 members of the Arab Choa ethnic group at the village of Karena in northern Cameroon, apparently in retaliation for acts of armed banditry in the region, which were, however, widely attributed to former Chadian rebels. In March some 1,200 citizens took refuge in Chad, in response to continuing clashes between security forces and bandits in northern Cameroon.

In February 1994 six principal opposition parties (excluding the SDF) established a coalition, known as the Front démocratique et patriotique, to contest municipal elections (which were due to take place later that year). In April the authorities banned a conference by supporters of the CAM, which nevertheless took place at Bamenda. In July, in accordance with the Government's aim of promoting economic recovery, a new ministerial department with responsibility for the economy and finance was created as part of an extensive cabinet reorganization. At the end of that month about eight people were killed in clashes between two factions of the UNDP, after the party Chairman, Bello Bouba Maigari, threatened to expel the Vice-Chairman, Hamadou Moustapha, on the grounds that he had remained in the Cabinet following the government reorganization without the party's permission. In September an informal alliance of 16 opposition movements, the Front des alliés pour le changement (FAC), was established, effectively replacing the Union pour le changement; the FAC denounced what it alleged to be human rights violations on the part of the authorities, together with the indefinite postponement of the municipal elections and the transfer of state-owned enterprises to the private sector. Two prominent opposition parties, the UNDP and the UDC refused to join the alliance, however, on the grounds that it was dominated by the SDF. In November Biya announced that discussions on the revision of the Constitution were to resume, following the establishment of a Consultative Constitutional Review Committee, and that municipal elections were to take place in 1995. Constitutional discussions commenced in mid-December, but were boycotted by the opposition, which cited limitations in the agenda of the debate; the UDC (the only opposition movement to attend the discussions) withdrew after two days. In early 1995, however, the Consultative Constitutional Review Committee submitted revised constitutional amendments to Biya for consideration.

In February 1995 the leader of the Mouvement pour la démocratie et le progrès (MDP), Samuel Eboua, was elected President of the FAC, replacing Fru Ndi. In the same month Hamadou Moustapha and another member of the Government were expelled from the UNDP; Moustapha subsequently formed a breakaway faction of the party. In April Biya announced the establishment of a number of new local government districts in preparation for the municipal elections, which were scheduled to take place by the end of that year. Following reports of division within the SDF in May, a breakaway group, known as the Social Democratic Movement, was subsequently formed under the leadership of the former Secretary-General of the SDF, Siga Asanga.

In early July 1995 members of a newly-emerged anglophone organization, the Southern Cameroons National Council (SCNC, which demanded that the former portion of the British Cameroons that had amalgamated with the Republic of Cameroon in 1961 be granted autonomy), staged a demonstration in Bamenda, subsequently clashing with security forces. Later that month English-speaking representatives of the Government criticized the demands for the establishment of an anglophone republic (which would be known as Southern Cameroons); the SCNC apparently intended to proclaim formally the independence of Southern Cameroons on 1 October 1996, following the adoption of a separate constitution for the new republic. Also in July 1995 a number of independently-owned newspapers temporarily suspended publication in protest at alleged increasing press censorship and intimidation of journalists. In early August the SCNC was prohibited from staging a demonstration. In the same month representatives of anglophone movements, including the SCNC and the CAM, officially presented their demands for the establishment of an independent republic of Southern Cameroons at the UN, and urged the international community to assist in resolving the issue in order to avert civil conflict in Cameroon; the organizations claimed that the plebiscite of 1961, whereby the former southern portion of British Cameroons had voted to merge with the Republic of Cameroon on terms of equal status, had been rendered invalid by subsequent francophone domination.

In October 1995 a special congress of the RDPC re-elected Biya as leader of the party for a further term of five years. Meanwhile, Cameroon's pending application for membership of the Commonwealth (which had been accepted, in principle, in 1993, subject to the Government's fulfilment of certain democratic conditions) prompted further controversy; opposition movements urged the Commonwealth to refuse admission to Cameroon on the grounds that no progress had been achieved with regard to human rights and the democratic process, while the SCNC submitted a rival application for membership on behalf of the proposed independent republic of Southern Cameroons. In early November, however, Cameroon was formally admitted to the Commonwealth. In the same month Biya announced that the municipal elections were to take place in January 1996 (although both opposition movements and parties belonging to the government coalition had demanded that the elections be preceded by constitutional reform and the establishment of an independent electoral commission). In December 1995 the National Assembly adopted the revised constitutional amendments, submitted by Biya earlier that month, which increased the presidential mandate from five to seven years (while restricting the maximum tenure of office to two terms). Municipal elections, in which some 38 political parties participated, duly took place in January 1996; the RDPC won the majority of seats in 56% of local councils, and the SDF in 27%, while the UNDP received popular support in the north of the country. In March the SDF and the UNDP urged a campaign of civil disobedience in protest at the Government's appointment by decree of representatives to replace the elected mayors in principal towns (following the municipal elections, the opposition had gained control of 13 towns). At the beginning of that month at least two people were killed in a demonstration which had been organized by the SDF in the south-western town of Limbe as part of the campaign. In April the Government imposed a total ban on all media reports of the SDF and UNDP campaign of civil disobedience.

In May 1996, following increasing division within the UPC apparently resulting from its lack of success in the municipal elections, the Secretary-General of the party, Augustin Frédéric Kodock (who held the ministerial portfolio of agriculture), was dismissed from the party. In the same month a two-day general strike, organized by the SDF and the UNDP, was principally observed in western and northern regions, where the parties received popular support; a further general strike in June was supported only in the west of the country. In August a campaign, launched by the SCNC, urging anglophone voters not to enrol on the electoral register, was condemned as being 'separatist' by Fru Ndi, the leader of the SDF. Following a party congress in September, the UPC remained divided into two main groupings, one led by Kodock (who claimed that his dismissal from the party in May had been illegal), and the other headed by Ndeh Ntumazah, the party Chairman. Also in September Simon Achidi Achu was replaced as Prime Minister by Peter Mafany Musonge, the General Manager of the Cameroon Development Corporation, and a new Cabinet was subsequently appointed. In October the editor of *Le Messager,* Pius Njawe, and another journalist were imprisoned after publishing material critical of Biya; following an appeal, however, the Supreme Court ordered the release of Njawe in November. In December Biya was nominated by an RDPC congress as the party's candidate in the forthcoming presidential election (which was due to take place in October 1997).

At the end of January 1997 the Government announced the postponement of the legislative elections (which had been scheduled to take place in early March) owing to organizational difficulties, following opposition complaints that its supporters had been allowed insufficient time for registration; Biya's subsequent failure to extend the mandate of the incumbent National Assembly (which expired in early March), however, prompted criticism from a number of opposition deputies. Also in January Fru Ndi stated that, in order to avert unrest in the period prior to the elections, the opposition would refrain from staging demonstrations in support of demands that the Government establish an independent electoral commission. At the end of March, however, about 10 people were killed when unidentified armed groups staged attacks against government and security buildings in Bamenda and other towns in the North-West Province; the violence was generally attributed to members of the SCNC. In April the Government announced that the legislative elections were to take place on 17 May.

In mid-May 1997 pre-election violence, in which about five people were killed, prompted the imposition of increased security measures, including the closure of the country's borders. The legislative elections, which were contested on 17 May by 46 political parties, were monitored by a Commonwealth observer mission; the poll was extended in parts of northern Cameroon, where voting had been delayed as a result of logistical difficulties. The announcement later that month of provisional election results (which attributed a large majority of seats to the RDPC) prompted claims from the opposition parties of widespread electoral malpractice; the Commonwealth observer group also expressed general dissatisfaction with the election process. The Supreme Court, however, rejected opposition appeals against RDPC victories. Three people were killed in clashes between RDPC and SDF members in the South-West Province in the second half of May, where the election result was disputed by the two parties. In early June the Supreme Court announced the official election results: the RDPC had secured 109 of the 180 seats in the legislature, while the SDF had obtained 43, the UNDP 13 and the UDC five seats; the Mouvement pour la jeunesse du Cameroun (MLJC), the UPC and the MDR obtained one seat each. The Cabinet remained virtually unchanged from the previous administration and Musonge was retained as Prime Minister. In mid-June the SDF announced that it had reversed its earlier decision to boycott the National Assembly. On 3 August further polls were conducted in seven constituencies, where the results had been annulled, owing to alleged irregularities; the RDPC won all of the seats, thus increasing its level of representation in the National Assembly to 116 seats.

In July 1997 it was reported that the former Minister of Public Health, Titus Edzoa, who in April had resigned from the Cabinet in order to contest the presidential election later that year, had been arrested and charged with embezzlement; his supporters claimed, however, that Edzoa (a leading figure in the RDPC) was being held as a political prisoner at a 'torture centre'. In the same month Samuel Eboua, the leader of the MDP, announced his candidacy in the forthcoming presidential election. It was announced in September that the election would be held on 12 October. Shortly afterwards, the three major opposition parties, the SDF, UNDP and UDC, declared a boycott of all elections, including the imminent presidential election, in protest against the absence of an independent electoral commission; a fourth opposition party, Hubert Kamgang's Union du peuple africain, later joined the boycott. In mid-September Biya was officially elected as the RDPC presidential candidate. On 7 October a meeting planned by the main opposition leaders at which they intended to explain their boycott of the forthcoming election was banned by the authorities in Yaoundé. Early in the same month several supporters of Titus Edzoa were arrested. The presidential election was held, as scheduled, on 12 October and was contested by seven candidates. Biya was re-elected, winning 92.6% of the votes cast; Henri Hogbe Nlend of the UPC and Samuel Eboua secured 2.5% and 2.4% of the vote, respectively. The level of voter participation in the election was much-disputed, with official sources asserting that a record 81.4% of the electorate took part, while opposition leaders rejected this figure, claiming that the abstention rate was higher than 80%, and dismissed the poll on various grounds as an 'electoral masquerade'. Biya, however, was formally inaugurated on 3 November, beginning, in accordance with the revised Constitution, a seven-year term in presidential office. Following talks with various opposition groups in November and December, the RDPC reached an agreement with the UNDP on the creation of a coalition government; Fru Ndi's SDF, however, refused to co-operate with the ruling party. In December, after having reappointed Musonge as Prime Minister, President Biya effected a major cabinet reshuffle. The new Government included representatives from four of the country's many political groups, although the RDPC retained 45 of the 50 ministerial posts. The new appointees to the Government included opposition figures: Bello Bouba Maigari of the UNDP, who was appointed Minister of State for Industrial and Commercial Development, Henri Hogbe Nlend of the UPC, who was named as Minister for Scientific and Technical Research, and Antar Gasagay of the Nouvelle convention (NC), who was appointed Secretary of State for Territorial Administration in charge of Prisons Administration.

The independent foreign policy that was pursued under President Ahidjo was continued by his successor. Relations with France have generally remained close, although Cameroon has sought to resist overdependence: France traditionally accounts for more than one-third of the country's foreign trade transactions. From the late 1980s, however, Cameroon became increasingly anxious to attract investment from other countries.

Relations with Nigeria, which had become strained as a result of a series of border disputes, showed signs of improvement following a state visit by President Babangida of that country in late 1987, when it was announced that joint border controls were to be established. In 1991, however, the Nigerian Government claimed that Cameroon had annexed nine Nigerian fishing settlements, following a long-standing border dispute, based on a 1913 agreement between Germany and the United Kingdom that ceded the Bakassi peninsula in the Gulf of Guinea (a region of strategic significance to both countries) to Cameroon. Subsequent negotiations between the Governments of Nigeria and Cameroon, in an effort to resolve the dispute, achieved little progress. In December 1993 some 500 Nigerian troops were dispatched to the region, in response to a number of incidents in which Nigerian nationals had been killed by Cameroonian security forces. Later that month the two nations agreed to establish a joint patrol in the disputed area, and to investigate the incidents. In February 1994, however, the Cameroonian Government announced that it was to submit the dispute for adjudication by the UN, the Organization of African Unity (OAU—see p. 215) and the International Court of Justice (ICJ), and requested military assistance from France. Subsequent reports of clashes between Cameroonian and Nigerian forces in the region prompted fears of a full-scale conflict between the two nations. In March Cameroon agreed to enter into negotiations with Nigeria (without the involvement of international mediators) to resolve the issue. In the same month the OAU issued a resolution urging the withdrawal of troops from the disputed region. In May two members of the Nigerian armed forces were killed in further clashes in the Bakassi region. Later that month negotiations between the two nations, with mediation by the Togolese Government, resumed in Yaoundé. In September the Cameroonian Government submitted additional claims to territory in north-eastern Nigeria to the ICJ. Later that month it was reported that 10 members of the Cameroonian armed forces had been killed in further clashes. In February 1996 renewed hostilities between Nigerian and Cameroonian forces in the Bakassi region resulted in several casualties. Later that month, however, Cameroon and Nigeria agreed to refrain from further military action, and delegations from the two countries resumed discussions, with mediation by the Togolese President, in an attempt to resolve the dispute. In March the ICJ ruled that Cameroon had failed to provide sufficient evidence to substantiate its contention that Nigeria had instigated the border dispute, and ordered both nations to cease military operations in the region, to withdraw troops to former positions, and to co-operate with a UN investigative mission, which was to be dispatched to the area. In April, however, clashes continued, with each Government accusing the other of initiating the attacks. Claims by Nigeria that the Cameroonian forces were supported by troops from France were denied by the French Government. Diplomatic efforts to avoid further conflict increased. Nevertheless, both nations continued to reinforce their contingents in the region (where some 5,000 Cameroonian and 3,000 Nigerian troops were deployed at the end of May). Further tension arose in July, when Nigeria accused Cameroon of substantially increasing troops and artillery on the Bakassi peninsula. In September both countries assured the UN investigative mission of their commitment to a peaceful settlement of the dispute. In December and again in May 1997, however, the Nigerian authorities claimed that Cameroonian troops had resumed attacks in the region. In May 1997 the UN requested that the Togolese Government continue efforts to mediate in the dispute.

Government

Under the amended 1972 Constitution, the Republic of Cameroon is a multi-party state. Executive power is vested in the President, as Head of State, who is elected by universal adult suffrage for a term of seven years, and may serve a maximum of two terms. Legislative power is held by the National Assembly, which comprises 180 members and is elected for a term of five years. In December 1995 constitutional amendments provided for the establishment of an upper legislative chamber (to be known as the Senate). The Cabinet is appointed by the President. Local administration is based on 10 provinces, each with a governor who is appointed by the President.

Defence

In August 1997 Cameroon's armed forces were estimated to total 22,100 men, including 9,000 in paramilitary forces. The army numbered 11,500, the navy about 1,300 and the air force 300. Cameroon has a bilateral defence agreement with France. The defence budget for 1997 was estimated at US $228m.

Economic Affairs

In 1995, according to estimates by the World Bank, Cameroon's gross national product (GNP), measured at average 1993–95 prices, was US $8,615m., equivalent to $650 per head. During 1985–95, it was estimated, GNP per head declined, in real terms, by an average annual rate of 7.0%. Over the same period the population increased by an annual average of 2.9%. Cameroon's gross domestic product (GDP) declined, in real terms, by an annual average of 4.0% in 1985–95; GDP declined by 3.8% in 1994, but increased by an estimated 3.3% in 1995.

Agriculture (including forestry and fishing) contributed an estimated 39.0% of GDP in 1995. An estimated 67.6% of the labour force were employed in agriculture in 1996. The principal cash crops are cocoa (which accounted for 8.1% of export earnings in 1994), coffee and cotton. The principal subsistence crops are roots and tubers (mainly cassava), maize and sorghum; some 424,000 metric tons of cereals were imported in 1992. In 1994 an estimated 77.1% of the country's land area was covered by forest, but an inadequate transport infrastructure has impeded the development of the forestry sector. Livestock-rearing makes a significant contribution to the food supply. During 1985–95, according to the World Bank, agricultural GDP increased by an annual average of 1.3%; a decline of 3.8% was recorded in 1994, but the World Bank estimated an increase of 4.0% in 1995.

Industry (including mining, manufacturing, construction and power) employed 6.7% of the working population in 1985, and contributed 23.5% of GDP in 1993/94. During 1985–95, according to the World Bank, industrial GDP declined by an annual average of 2.9%. Industrial GDP declined by 3.8% in 1994, but increased by an estimated 1.7% in 1995.

Mining contributed 9.4% of GDP in 1993/94, but employed only 0.05% of Cameroon's working population in 1985. Receipts from the exploitation of the country's petroleum reserves constitute a principal source of government revenue. Deposits of limestone are also quarried. Significant reserves of natural gas, bauxite, iron ore, uranium and tin remain largely undeveloped. According to the IMF, the GDP of the mining sector declined by 7.7% in 1993/94, and by an estimated 10.2% and 12.7% in 1994/95 and 1995/96, respectively.

Manufacturing contributed 9.9% of GDP in 1993/94, and employed an estimated 7% of the working population in 1995. The sector is based on the processing of both indigenous primary products (petroleum-refining, agro-industrial activities) and of imported raw materials (an aluminium-smelter uses alumina imported from Guinea). In the financial year ending June 1994, according to a survey of industrial enterprises in the modern sector, the main branches of manufacturing, based on the value of output, were wood products (accounting for 15.5% of the total), beverages (14.1%), food products (13.9%) and petroleum and coal products (12.2%). Manufacturing GDP declined by an average of 2.8% per year in 1985–95; a decline of 3.8% was recorded in 1994, but the IMF estimated growth of 7.7% in 1995.

In the early 1990s about 95% of Cameroon's energy was derived from hydroelectric power installations. Imports of fuel products accounted for only an estimated 0.6% of the value of total imports in 1995.

Services contributed 36.9% of GDP in 1993/94. During 1985–95, according to the World Bank, the GDP of the services sector declined by an average of 8.4% per year; growth of 0.7% was recorded in 1994, but a decline of 0.5% was estimated in 1995.

In 1993 Cameroon recorded a visible trade surplus of US $502.4m. In the same year, however, there was a deficit of $565.4m. on the current account of the balance of payments. In 1991 the principal source of imports (27.3%) was France; other major suppliers were Germany, the USA and the Belgo-Luxembourg Economic Union. The principal market for exports (24.8%) was the Netherlands; other significant purchasers were France, Italy and Spain. The principal exports in 1991 were petroleum and petroleum products, cocoa and timber and timber products. The principal imports were machinery and transport equipment, basic manufactures, and chemicals and related products.

In the financial year ending June 1995 there was a budget surplus of 8,250m. francs CFA (equivalent to 0.2% of GDP). Cameroon's total external debt at the end of 1995 was US $9,350m., of which $8,061m. was long-term public debt. In that year the cost of debt-servicing was equivalent to 15.3% of revenue from exports of goods and services. The annual rate of inflation averaged 6.0% in 1986–96; consumer prices increased by an average of 35.1% in 1994, by 13.9% in 1995 and by 4.5% in 1996. An estimated 5.8% of the labour force were unemployed in mid-1985.

Cameroon is a member of the Central African organs of the Franc Zone (see p. 181), of the Communauté économique des états de l'Afrique centrale (CEEAC, see p. 260), of the International Cocoa Organization (see p. 257) and of the International Coffee Organization (see p. 257).

The decline, beginning in the mid-1980s, of international prices for Cameroon's major export commodities, in conjunction with the cost of maintaining a cumbersome bureaucracy, undermined the country's hitherto buoyant economy. Extensive economic reforms, which were initiated in 1989 under the terms of an agreement with the World Bank, proved largely unsuccessful, owing, in part, to corruption within the civil service and to an opposition campaign of civil disobedience (see Recent History). In January 1994 the CFA franc was devalued by 50% in relation to the French franc, resulting in an immediate increase in economic hardship. An increase in international prices for Cameroon's major export commodities contributed to an improvement in economic conditions in 1995 and 1996 (which included a strong recovery in real GDP and a deceleration in the rate of inflation), while a number of structural reforms were implemented in compliance with IMF requirements. In September 1995 the IMF approved a stand-by credit in support of the Government's economic reform programme for 1995/96, which laid emphasis on the reduction of the overall fiscal deficit. A debt-rescheduling agreement with the 'Paris Club' of official creditors was reached later that year. At the beginning of 1996 the IMF delayed payments to Cameroon, after the Government failed to attain its targets. In February and March, however, further structural adjustment credit was approved, subject to strict provisos. The Government continued with its programme for public-sector reform and the restructuring of the financial sector throughout 1996, and, while progress was initially slower than had been projected, the pace of structural reform increased in 1996/97. In August 1997 the IMF approved a three-year loan for Cameroon, equivalent to about US $219m., as an Enhanced

Structural Adjustment Facility (ESAF). The 1997/98 programme, supported by the first of the three annual loans, aimed to increase non-petroleum revenue, particularly through improvements in tax administration, as well as through the development of the forestry industry. Cameroon's external debt burden remained a source of concern in 1997 in the context of ongoing attempts to restore external viability. However, progress continued to be made towards achieving sustainable economic growth.

Social Welfare

The Government and Christian missions maintain hospitals and medical centres. In 1986 Cameroon had 26,872 hospital beds in 251 hospitals and health centres and 1,534 dispensaries. There were 790 physicians working in the country. Expenditure on health by the central Government in 1992/93 was 24,270m. francs CFA (4.8% of total spending).

Education

Since independence, Cameroon has achieved one of the highest rates of school attendance in Africa, but provision of educational facilities varies according to region. Education, which is bilingual, is provided by the Government, missionary societies and private concerns. Education in state schools is available free of charge, and the Government provides financial assistance for other schools.

Primary education begins at six years of age. It lasts for six years in Eastern Cameroon (where it is officially compulsory), and for seven years in Western Cameroon. Secondary education, beginning at the age of 12 or 13, lasts for a further seven years, comprising two cycles of four years and three years in Eastern Cameroon and five years and two years in Western Cameroon. In 1994 primary enrolment was equivalent to 89% of children in the appropriate age-group (males 93%; females 84%), while enrolment at secondary schools was equivalent to only 27% (males 32%; females 22%). In 1995, according to estimates by UNESCO, the average rate of adult illiteracy was 36.6% (males 25.0%; females 47.9%). The State University at Yaoundé consists of five regional campuses, each devoted to a different field of study. Expenditure on education by the central Government in 1992/93 was 89,960m. francs CFA (18.0% of total spending).

Public Holidays

1998: 1 January (New Year), 30 January* (Djoulde Soumae, end of Ramadan), 11 February (Youth Day), 8 April* (Festival of Sheep), 10 April (Good Friday), 13 April (Easter Monday), 1 May (Labour Day), 20 May (National Day), 21 May (Ascension Day), 10 December (Reunification Day), 25 December (Christmas).

1999: 1 January (New Year), 19 January* (Djoulde Soumae, end of Ramadan), 11 February (Youth Day), 28 March* (Festival of Sheep), 2 April (Good Friday), 5 April (Easter Monday), 1 May (Labour Day), 13 May (Ascension Day), 20 May (National Day), 10 December (Reunification Day), 25 December (Christmas).

* These holidays are dependent on the Islamic lunar calendar and may vary by one or two days from the dates given.

Weights and Measures

The metric system is in force.

Statistical Survey

Source (unless otherwise stated): Direction de la Statistique et de la Comptabilité Nationale, BP 25, Yaoundé; tel. 22-07-88; telex 8203.

Area and Population

AREA, POPULATION AND DENSITY

Area (sq km)	475,442*
Population (census results)	
9 April 1976†	
Males	3,754,991
Females	3,908,255
Total	7,663,246
April 1987	10,493,655
Population (official estimates at mid-year)	
1987	10,821,746
1989‡	11,540,000
1995‡	13,277,000
Density (per sq km) at mid-1995	27.9

* 183,569 sq miles.

† Including an adjustment for underenumeration, estimated at 7.4%. The enumerated total was 7,090,115 (males 3,472,786; females 3,617,329).

‡ Official mid-year estimates for 1988 and 1990–94 are not available.

PROVINCES (population at 1976 census)

	Urban	Rural	Total
Centre-South	498,290	993,655	1,491,945
Littoral	702,578	232,588	935,166
West	232,315	803,282	1,035,597
South-West	200,322	420,193	620,515
North-West	146,327	834,204	980,531
North	328,925	1,904,332	2,233,257
East	75,458	290,750	366,235
Total	2,184,242	5,479,004	7,663,246

Note: In August 1983 the number of provinces was increased to 10. Centre-South province became two separate provinces, Centre and South. The northern province was split into three: Far North, North and Adamoua.

PRINCIPAL TOWNS (population at 1976 census)

Douala	458,426	Bafoussam	62,239
Yaoundé (capital)	313,706	Bamenda	48,111
Nkongsamba	71,298	Kumba	44,175
Maroua	67,187	Limbe	27,016
Garoua	63,900		

1992 (estimated population, '000): Douala 1,200; Yaoundé 800; Garoua 160; Maroua 140; Bafoussam 120 (Source: *La Zone Franc—Rapport 1992*).

BIRTHS AND DEATHS (UN estimates, annual averages)

	1980–85	1985–90	1990–95
Birth rate (per 1,000)	43.9	42.0	40.7
Death rate (per 1,000)	15.7	13.8	12.2

Expectation of life (UN estimates, years at birth, 1990–95): 56.0 (males 54.5; females 57.5).

Source: UN, *World Population Prospects: The 1994 Revision.*

ECONOMICALLY ACTIVE POPULATION
(official estimates, persons aged six years and over, mid-1985)

	Males	Females	Total
Agriculture, hunting, forestry and fishing	1,574,946	1,325,925	2,900,871
Mining and quarrying	1,693	100	1,793
Manufacturing	137,671	36,827	174,498
Electricity, gas and water	3,373	149	3,522
Construction	65,666	1,018	66,684
Trade, restaurants and hotels	115,269	38,745	154,014
Transport, storage and communications	50,664	1,024	51,688
Financing, insurance, real estate and business services	7,447	562	8,009
Community, social and personal services	255,076	37,846	292,922
Activities not adequately defined	18,515	17,444	35,959
Total in employment	2,230,320	1,459,640	3,689,960
Unemployed	180,016	47,659	227,675
Total labour force	2,410,336	1,507,299	3,917,635

Source: ILO, *Yearbook of Labour Statistics*.

Mid-1996 (estimates in '000): Agriculture, etc. 3,731; Total labour force 5,515 (Source: FAO, *Production Yearbook*).

Agriculture

PRINCIPAL CROPS ('000 metric tons)

	1994	1995	1996
Rice (paddy)	80*	62*	54
Maize	450†	654*	750
Millet	50†	66*	71
Sorghum	350†	460*	439
Potatoes	40*	35*	35
Sweet potatoes†	180	200	180
Cassava (Manioc)†	1,500	1,400	1,300
Yams†	110	110	110
Other roots and tubers†	450	450	450
Dry beans	80†	85†	91
Groundnuts (in shell)	100*	100*	171
Sesame seed†	16	16	16
Cottonseed	90*	100†	105†
Cotton lint	71*	79*	79
Palm kernels	55*	56*	56†
Sugar cane†	1,350	1,350	1,350
Tomatoes	60†	60†	60
Onions (dry)	20†	20†	20
Other vegetables	392	403	413
Avocados†	44	45	45
Pineapples	42†	44†	48
Bananas	950†	980†	986
Plantains†	950	970	1,000
Other fruit	105†	104†	104
Coffee (green)	57*	52*	53
Cocoa beans	108*	130*	126
Tea (made)	4*	4*	4
Tobacco (leaves)	2†	2†	2
Natural rubber	54*	58*	53

* Unofficial figure. † FAO estimate(s).

Source: FAO, *Production Yearbook*.

LIVESTOCK (FAO estimates, '000 head, year ending September)

	1994	1995	1996
Horses	15	15	15
Asses	36	36	36
Cattle	4,870	4,900	4,900
Pigs	1,400	1,410	1,410
Sheep	3,780	3,800	3,800
Goats	3,770	3,800	3,800

Poultry (FAO estimates, million): 20 in 1994; 20 in 1995; 20 in 1996.

Source: FAO, *Production Yearbook*.

LIVESTOCK PRODUCTS (FAO estimates, '000 metric tons)

	1994	1995	1996
Beef and veal	75	75	75
Mutton and lamb	16	16	16
Goat meat	14	14	14
Pig meat	17	18	18
Poultry meat	20	20	20
Other meat	47	47	47
Cows' milk	123	125	125
Sheep's milk	17	17	17
Goats' milk	42	42	42
Poultry eggs	13	13	13
Honey	3	3	3
Cattle hides	11	11	11
Sheepskins	3	3	3
Goatskins	1	1	1

Source: FAO, *Production Yearbook*.

Forestry

ROUNDWOOD REMOVALS ('000 cubic metres, excl. bark)

	1992	1993*	1994*
Sawlogs, veneer logs and logs for sleepers	2,111	2,111	2,111
Other industrial wood*	821	844	867
Fuel wood*	11,472	11,762	12,062
Total	14,404	14,717	15,040

* FAO estimates.

Source: FAO, *Yearbook of Forest Products*.

SAWNWOOD PRODUCTION
(FAO estimates '000 cubic metres, incl. railway sleepers)

	1992	1993	1994
Total (all broadleaved)	489	465	465

Source: FAO, *Yearbook of Forest Products*.

Fishing

('000 metric tons, live weight)

	1993	1994*	1995
Freshwater fishes	23.1	23.0	23.6*
Croakers and drums	3.3	3.7	4.6
Threadfins and tasselfishes	2.2	2.4	1.7
Sardinellas	16.0	16.0	15.0*
Bonga shad	16.0	16.0	15.5*
Other marine fishes (incl. unspecified)	4.3	4.4	3.0*
Total fish	64.8	65.5	63.4*
Crustaceans and molluscs	0.5	0.6	0.6*
Total catch	65.3	66.0	63.9*

* FAO estimate(s).

Source: FAO, *Yearbook of Fishery Statistics*.

Mining

	1992	1993	1994
Crude petroleum ('000 metric tons)	6,790	6,210	5,477
Tin ore (metric tons)*	3	3	3
Gold (kilograms)*	10	10	10

* Estimates of metal content (data from the US Bureau of Mines).

Source: UN, *Industrial Commodity Statistics Yearbook.*

Tin ore (estimated metal content, metric tons): 2 in 1994; 2 in 1995; 1 in 1996 (Source: US Geological Survey, *Tin, Annual Review* 1996).

1995 ('000 metric tons): Crude petroleum 5,040 (Source: UN, *Monthly Bulletin of Statistics*).

Industry

SELECTED PRODUCTS ('000 metric tons, unless otherwise indicated)

	1992	1993	1994
Palm oil*	120	106	125
Raw sugar*	65	57	60
Cigarettes (million)*	5,000	n.a.	n.a.
Veneer sheets ('000 cu metres)*	32	31	31
Plywood ('000 cu metres)*	48	43	43
Paper and paperboard*	5	5	5
Aviation gasoline*	12	14	14
Jet fuels*	9	9	9
Motor spirit (petrol)	294*	294*	296
Kerosene	242*	243*	245
Gas-diesel (distillate fuel) oil	284*	283*	287
Residual fuel oils*	152	150	152
Lubricating oils*	35	37	38
Petroleum bitumen (asphalt)*	7	9	10
Liquefied petroleum gas*	19	21	20
Cement†	620	620*	620*
Aluminium (unwrought)‡	82.5	86.5	81.1
Electric energy (million kWh)*	2,726	2,731	2,740

* Provisional or estimated figure(s).
† Data from the US Bureau of Mines.
‡ Data from *World Metal Statistics* (London).

Source: mainly UN, *Industrial Commodity Statistics Yearbook.*

1995 (unofficial figures, '000 metric tons): Palm oil 130; Raw sugar 62.
1996 ('000 metric tons): Palm oil 161; Raw sugar 62 (unofficial figure).

Source (for 1995 and 1996): FAO, *Production Yearbook.*

Finance

CURRENCY AND EXCHANGE RATES

Monetary Units

100 centimes = 1 franc de la Coopération financière en Afrique central (CFA).

French Franc, Sterling and Dollar Equivalents (30 September 1997)

1 French franc = 100 francs CFA;
£1 sterling = 958.3 francs CFA;
US $1 = 593.2 francs CFA;
1,000 francs CFA = £1.044 = $1.686.

Average Exchange Rate (francs CFA per US $)

1994	555.20
1995	499.15
1996	511.55

Note: An exchange rate of 1 French franc = 50 francs CFA, established in 1948, remained in force until January 1994, when the CFA franc was devalued by 50%, with the exchange rate adjusted to 1 French franc = 100 francs CFA.

BUDGET ('000 million francs CFA, year ending 30 June)

Revenue	1990/91	1991/92*	1992/93*
Taxation	327.46	311.66	300.13
Taxes on income, profits, etc.	87.38	90.50	89.15
General income tax	31.26	37.94	47.20
Corporate tax on profits	56.12	52.56	41.95
Social security contributions	30.01	—	—
Domestic taxes on goods and services	96.66	86.92	89.16
Sales taxes	57.11	49.19	53.43
Excises	39.55	36.98	33.40
Taxes on international trade and transactions	67.71	91.80	87.64
Import duties	64.07	87.77	83.29
Export duties	3.64	4.03	4.35
Other current revenue	190.10	172.30	135.25
Entrepreneurial and property income	163.16	131.73	86.78
Unclassified current revenue	23.05	11.95	12.76
Capital revenue	7.29	2.56	0.27
Total	547.90	498.47	448.41

Expenditure†	1990/91	1991/92*	1992/93*
Current expenditure	545.92	464.80	442.62
Expenditure on goods and services	376.51	346.01	324.79
Wages and salaries	286.48	282.34	274.91
Other purchases of goods and services	90.03	63.67	49.88
Interest payments	43.05	39.40	57.88
Subsidies and other current transfers	126.36	79.39	59.95
Capital expenditure	151.45	101.39	47.53
Acquisition of fixed capital assets	151.45	101.39	47.53
Adjustment to cash basis	22.39	12.24	11.00
Total	719.76	578.43	501.15

* Excluding operations of the Caisse Nationale de Prévoyance Sociale (National Social Security Fund).
† Excluding lending minus repayments ('000 million francs CFA, year ending 30 June): 3.02 in 1990/91; 1.20 in 1991/92; 2.00 in 1992/93.

Source: IMF, *Government Finance Statistics Yearbook.*

1993/94 ('000 million francs CFA): Total revenue 385.90; Total expenditure 483.49, excluding net lending (1.46).
1994/95 ('000 million francs CFA): Total revenue 536.54; Total expenditure 525.27, excluding net lending (3.02).

Source (for 1993/94 and 1994/95): IMF, *International Financial Statistics.*

INTERNATIONAL RESERVES
(US $ million, excluding gold, at 31 December)

	1994	1995	1996
Gold*	11.33	11.56	11.04
IMF special drawing rights	0.05	0.04	0.16
Reserve position in IMF	0.49	0.53	0.53
Foreign exchange	1.72	3.22	2.08
Total	13.59	15.35	13.81

* Valued at market-related prices.

Source: IMF, *International Financial Statistics.*

MONEY SUPPLY ('000 million francs CFA at 31 December)

	1994	1995	1996
Currency outside banks	136.33	102.29	95.32
Demand deposits at deposit money banks	223.09	213.97	213.45
Total money (incl. others)	361.29	319.24	314.14

Source: IMF, *International Financial Statistics.*

COST OF LIVING

(Consumer Price Index for Africans in Yaoundé; base: 1990 = 100)

	1994	1995	1996
All items	130.8	149.0	155.8

Source: IMF, *International Financial Statistics*.

NATIONAL ACCOUNTS

('000 million francs CFA at current prices, year ending 30 June)

National Income and Product

	1986/87	1987/88	1988/89
Compensation of employees	1,142.4	1,091.2	1,055.1
Operating surplus	2,197.7	2,003.0	1,934.5
Domestic factor incomes	3,340.1	3,094.3	2,989.7
Consumption of fixed capital	190.8	232.6	230.4
Gross domestic product (GDP) at factor cost	3,530.9	3,326.9	3,220.1
Indirect taxes	430.2	337.9	299.3
Less Subsidies	39.2	20.2	6.3
GDP in purchasers' values	3,921.9	3,644.5	3,513.0
Factor income received from abroad	5.3	3.4	−121.0
Less Factor income paid abroad	88.1	103.5	
Gross national product	3,839.1	3,544.5	3,392.0
Less Consumption of fixed capital	190.8	232.6	230.4
National income in market prices	3,648.4	3,311.9	3,161.6
Other current transfers received from abroad	13.1	8.9	−60.0
Less Other current transfers paid abroad	57.0	82.8	
National disposable income	3,604.5	3,238.0	3,101.6

Source: UN, *National Accounts Statistics*.

Expenditure on the Gross Domestic Product

	1991/92	1992/93	1993/94
Government final consumption expenditure	409	405	340
Private final consumption expenditure	2,179	2,198	2,464
Increase in stocks	−27	30	—
Gross fixed capital formation	457	493	524
Total domestic expenditure	3,018	3,126	3,328
Exports of goods and services	646	535	754
Less Imports of goods and services	469	505	666
GDP in purchasers' values	3,195	3,155	3,416
GDP at constant 1989/90 prices	3,128	3,029	2,954

Source: IMF, *Cameroon—Selected Issues and Statistical Appendix* (November 1996).

Gross Domestic Product by Economic Activity

	1991/92	1992/93	1993/94
Agriculture, hunting, forestry and fishing	849	861	1,322
Mining and quarrying	219	179	314
Manufacturing	445	420	331
Electricity, gas and water	54	55	58
Construction	84	105	82
Government services	335	541	427
Other services	1,128	922	807
GDP at factor cost	3,114	3,082	3,341
Indirect taxes, *less* subsidies	81	73	75
GDP in purchasers' values	3,195	3,155	3,416

Source: IMF, *Cameroon—Selected Issues and Statistical Appendix* (November 1996).

BALANCE OF PAYMENTS (US $ million)

	1991	1992	1993
Exports of goods f.o.b.	1,957.5	1,934.1	1,507.7
Imports of goods f.o.b.	−1,173.1	−983.3	−1,005.3
Trade balance	784.3	950.8	502.4
Exports of services	406.0	407.5	390.9
Imports of services	−1,122.3	−907.3	−741.1
Balance on goods and services	68.0	450.9	152.2
Other income received	18.3	41.8	17.0
Other income paid	−442.7	−823.9	−669.5
Balance on goods, services and income	−356.4	−331.2	−500.3
Current transfers received	57.0	141.0	65.2
Current transfers paid	−105.4	−148.3	−130.2
Current balance	−404.8	−338.5	−565.4
Capital account (net)	7.9	17.0	6.3
Direct investment abroad	−21.5	−33.1	−22.1
Direct investment from abroad	−14.5	29.2	5.1
Portfolio investment from abroad	−2.2	−46.5	−106.3
Other investment assets	−112.3	16.8	105.5
Other investment liabilities	−210.6	−309.4	−292.2
Net errors and omissions	26.9	−640.7	−16.2
Overall balance	−731.1	−1,305.2	−885.3

Source: IMF, *International Financial Statistics*.

External Trade

PRINCIPAL COMMODITIES (distribution by SITC, US $ million)

Imports c.i.f.	1989	1990	1991
Food and live animals	179.6	269.4	314.3
Fish, crustaceans, molluscs and preparations	46.9	55.2	58.7
Fresh, chilled or frozen fish	41.2	47.8	51.1
Cereals and cereal preparations	76.8	137.9	171.1
Rice	11.7	26.5	47.3
Flour of wheat or meslin	19.4	48.5	53.2
Malt (incl. malt flour)	27.9	38.6	37.3
Crude materials (inedible) except fuels	47.9	65.6	162.6
Metalliferous ores and metal scrap	35.7	49.7	129.7
Alumina (aluminium oxide)	34.7	48.4	128.3
Chemicals and related products	193.9	233.1	339.6
Inorganic chemicals	15.4	21.8	52.5
Medicinal and pharmaceutical products	67.2	88.9	68.8
Medicaments (incl. veterinary medicaments)	62.2	84.3	64.6
Artificial resins, plastic materials, etc.	30.2	30.7	55.4
Basic manufactures	292.8	366.6	554.3
Paper, paperboard and manufactures	36.3	54.1	81.5
Paper and paperboard	26.7	38.4	67.3
Textile yarn, fabrics, etc.	41.0	58.6	80.4
Non-metallic mineral manufactures	49.0	51.5	69.7
Lime, cement, etc.	28.1	24.4	40.8
Iron and steel	41.9	59.3	106.0
Structures and parts of structures, of iron, steel or aluminium	25.2	27.6	68.6
Iron or steel structures, etc.	23.5	21.8	61.1
Machinery and transport equipment	391.9	460.1	625.8
Machinery specialized for particular industries	62.9	57.2	98.5
Civil engineering and contractors' plant and equipment	30.6	25.0	34.4
General industrial machinery, equipment and parts	87.0	81.3	146.5
Telecommunications and sound equipment	13.2	54.6	44.8
Other electrical machinery, apparatus, etc.	34.2	62.6	125.4
Road vehicles and parts*	100.8	121.4	125.8

Imports c.i.f. — *continued*	1989	1990	1991
Passenger motor cars (excl. buses)	43.2	51.2	44.1
Motor vehicles for the transport of goods, etc.	28.4	25.5	39.8
Goods vehicles (lorries and trucks)	25.9	22.0	29.9
Other transport equipment*	57.7	43.3	31.0
Ships, boats and floating structures	38.8	32.3	21.5
Tugs, special purpose vessels and floating structures	30.6	31.1	8.4
Special purpose vessels, etc.	27.1	30.6	7.9
Miscellaneous manufactured articles	109.0	198.8	171.3
Printed matter	30.1	108.4	25.5
Printed books, pamphlets, maps and globes	18.3	94.4	8.7
Printed books, etc.	18.1	94.3	8.6
Total (incl. others)	1,273.3	1,656.2	2,306.2

* Excluding tyres, engines and electrical parts.

Exports f.o.b.	1989	1990	1991
Food and live animals	434.9	400.5	546.9
Coffee, tea, cocoa and spices	412.1	351.1	450.0
Coffee and coffee substitutes	214.7	174.6	86.5
Unroasted coffee and coffee husks and skins	214.1	173.4	86.5
Cocoa	196.2	168.5	361.3
Cocoa beans (raw or roasted)	168.7	142.0	327.2
Cocoa butter and cocoa paste	27.4	25.7	32.9
Crude materials (inedible) except fuels	245.6	301.2	404.3
Cork and wood	141.3	190.2	231.1
Rough or roughly squared wood (excl. fuel wood and pulpwood)	107.1	132.7	156.6
Non-coniferous sawlogs and veneer logs	107.1	132.7	153.3
Simply worked wood and railway sleepers	34.2	57.4	74.6
Shaped non-coniferous wood	32.8	56.2	74.0
Textile fibres and waste	68.7	69.5	110.5
Raw cotton (excl. linters)	68.6	69.5	110.0
Mineral fuels, lubricants, etc.	230.9	1,037.5	1,374.0
Petroleum, petroleum products, etc.	230.9	1,037.5	1,374.0
Crude petroleum oils, etc.	229.6	1,034.8	1,371.9

Exports f.o.b. — *continued*	1989	1990	1991
Basic manufactures	243.5	231.1	237.1
Textile yarn, fabrics, etc.	26.1	15.1	15.5
Non-metallic mineral manufactures	40.3	34.3	33.2
Lime, cement, etc.	36.5	29.9	25.7
Cement	36.5	29.9	25.7
Non-ferrous metals	144.6	139.8	108.7
Aluminium and aluminium alloys	144.5	139.7	108.7
Unwrought aluminium and alloys	126.1	125.6	87.6
Machinery and transport equipment	66.8	47.0	217.3
Machinery specialized for particular industries	11.4	14.4	97.2
Civil engineering and contractors' plant and equipment	6.2	12.4	82.2
Construction and mining machinery	5.1	11.3	77.2
Transport equipment (excl. tyres, engines and electrical parts)	43.0	13.6	63.4
Ships, boats and floating structures	27.6	3.1	34.7
Total (incl. others)	1,281.6	2,080.7	2,892.5

Source: UN, *International Trade Statistics Yearbook*.

1992 (million francs CFA): Total imports c.i.f. 307,790; Total exports f.o.b. 487,130.

1993 (million francs CFA): Total imports c.i.f. 311,960; Total exports f.o.b. 533,250.

1994 (million francs CFA): Total imports c.i.f. 601,499; Total exports f.o.b. 825,200.

1995 (million francs CFA): Total imports c.i.f. 619,399; Total exports f.o.b. 1,018,200.

Source (for 1992–95): UN, *Monthly Bulletin of Statistics*.

PRINCIPAL TRADING PARTNERS (US $ million)

Imports c.i.f.	1989	1990	1991
Austria	8.0	30.0	114.6
Bangladesh	11.0	21.1	4.2
Belgium-Luxembourg	39.9	78.3	117.4
Brazil	25.8	34.8	82.2
Canada	49.0	15.4	36.0
China, People's Repub.	8.7	14.2	37.6
Côte d'Ivoire	5.3	9.2	30.8
France (incl. Monaco)	464.7	624.3	628.8
Germany, Fed. Repub.	71.6	149.8	199.4*
Guinea	34.7	41.5	108.6
Italy	38.5	72.9	106.1
Japan	72.6	77.8	68.0
Netherlands	116.4	52.7	69.5
Panama	5.0	26.4	—
Senegal	15.9	24.8	20.2
Spain	19.9	33.7	87.3
Switzerland-Liechtenstein	17.5	20.6	20.7
United Kingdom	7.0	42.5	77.7
USA	64.3	73.7	151.6
Total (incl. others)	1,273.3	1,656.2	2,306.2

* Including the former German Democratic Republic.

Exports f.o.b.	1989	1990	1991
Belgium-Luxembourg	246.9	30.8	36.0
Canada	3.4	1.5	61.0
Central African Repub.	22.8	29.3	35.8
China, People's Repub.	12.1	35.7	43.4
Congo	17.3	15.6	19.6
Côte d'Ivoire	17.4	3.7	2.6
Equatorial Guinea	35.5	30.2	81.8
France (incl. Monaco)	301.3	844.1	485.1
Gabon	30.1	30.6	100.3
Germany, Fed. Repub.	113.4	61.6	59.7*
Gibraltar	—	—	227.8
Italy	18.0	146.2	230.3
Japan	18.8	6.4	9.9
Korea, Repub.	2.8	36.8	8.3
Morocco	2.9	1.7	146.9
Netherlands	81.5	314.9	717.9
Nigeria	30.3	34.9	66.9
Portugal	16.1	30.2	32.0
Senegal	13.1	4.2	1.3
Spain	64.0	143.8	181.5
Switzerland-Liechtenstein	0.2	27.4	142.8
USA	128.1	156.8	12.5
Total (incl. others)	1,281.6	2,080.7	2,892.5

* Including the former German Democratic Republic.

Source: UN, *International Trade Statistics Yearbook*.

Transport

RAILWAYS (traffic, year ending 30 June)

	1985/86	1986/87	1987/88
Passengers carried ('000)	2,079	2,267	2,413
Passenger-km (million)	412	444	469
Freight carried ('000 tons)	1,791	1,411	1,375
Freight ton-km (million)	871	675	594

Source: the former Ministère des Travaux Publics et des Transports, Yaoundé.

Net ton-km (million): 679 in 1991; 613 in 1992; 653 in 1993.
Passenger-km (million): 530 in 1991; 445 in 1992; 352 in 1993.

Source (for 1991–93): UN, *Statistical Yearbook*.

ROAD TRAFFIC (estimates, motor vehicles in use at 31 December)

	1994	1995	1996
Passenger cars	89,000	93,000	98,000
Goods vehicles	57,000	60,000	64,350

Source: International Road Federation, *World Road Statistics*.

SHIPPING

Merchant Fleet (registered at 31 December)

	1994	1995	1996
Number of vessels	50	50	50
Total displacement ('000 grt)	36.0	37.1	36.7

Source: Lloyd's Register of Shipping.

International Sea-borne Freight Traffic
(estimates, '000 metric tons)

	1988	1989	1990
Goods loaded	9,760	9,565	10,081
Goods unloaded	3,100	3,298	3,396

Source: UN, *Monthly Bulletin of Statistics*.

1995 (freight traffic at Douala, '000 metric tons): Goods loaded 1,841; Goods unloaded 2,317.
1996 (freight traffic at Douala, '000 metric tons): Goods loaded 1,976; Goods unloaded 2,211.

Source (for 1995–96): Banque des états de l'Afrique centrale, *Etudes et Statistiques*.

CIVIL AVIATION (traffic on scheduled services)

	1992	1993	1994
Kilometres flown (million)	5	5	6
Passengers carried ('000)	363	275	295
Passenger-km (million)	477	402	436
Total ton-km (million)	53	58	64

Source: UN, *Statistical Yearbook*.

Tourism

	1992	1993	1994
Tourist arrivals ('000)	62	81	84
Tourist receipts (US $ million)	59	47	49

Source: UN, *African Statistical Yearbook*.

Communications Media

	1992	1993	1994
Radio receivers ('000 in use)	1,775	1,830	1,900
Television receivers ('000 in use)	288	307	309
Telephones ('000 main lines in use)	55	57	n.a.

Daily newspapers (1994): 1 (estimated circulation 50,000 copies).

Non-daily newspapers (1988): 25 (average circulation 315,000 copies).

Sources: UNESCO, *Statistical Yearbook*; UN, *Statistical Yearbook*.

Education

(1994/95, unless otherwise indicated)

	Institutions	Teachers	Students
Pre-primary	1,061	3,778	91,242
Primary	6,801	40,970	1,896,722
Secondary			
General	n.a.	14,917	459,068
Teacher-training	183*	123†	435†
Vocational	n.a.	5,885	91,779
Higher‡	n.a.	1,086	33,177
Universities‡	n.a.	761	31,360

* 1986/87 figure. † 1993/94 figure. ‡ 1990/91 figures.

Source: mainly UNESCO, *Statistical Yearbook*.

Directory

The Constitution*

The Republic of Cameroon is a multi-party state. The main provisions of the 1972 Constitution, as amended, are summarized below:

The Constitution declares that the human being, without distinction as to race, religion, sex or belief, possesses inalienable and sacred rights. It affirms its attachment to the fundamental freedoms embodied in the Universal Declaration of Human Rights and the UN Charter. The State guarantees to all citizens of either sex the rights and freedoms set out in the preamble of the Constitution.

SOVEREIGNTY

1. The Republic of Cameroon shall be one and indivisible, democratic, secular and dedicated to social service. It shall ensure the equality before the law of all its citizens. Provisions that the official languages be French and English, for the motto, flag, national anthem and seal, that the capital be Yaoundé.

2–3. Sovereignty shall be vested in the people who shall exercise it either through the President of the Republic and the members returned by it to the National Assembly or by means of referendum. Elections are by universal suffrage, direct or indirect, by every citizen aged 21 or over in a secret ballot. Political parties or groups may take part in elections subject to the law and the principles of democracy and of national sovereignty and unity.

4. State authority shall be exercised by the President of the Republic and the National Assembly.

THE PRESIDENT OF THE REPUBLIC

5. The President of the Republic, as Head of State and Head of the Government, shall be responsible for the conduct of the affairs of the Republic. He shall define national policy and may charge the members of the Government with the implementation of this policy in certain spheres.

6–7. Candidates for the office of President must hold civic and political rights, be at least 35 years old and have resided in Cameroon for a minimum of 12 consecutive months, and may not hold any other elective office or professional activity. The President is elected for seven years, by a majority of votes cast by the people, and may serve a maximum of two terms. Provisions are made for the continuity of office in the case of the President's resignation.

8–9. The Ministers and Vice-Ministers are appointed by the President to whom they are responsible, and they may hold no other appointment. The President is also head of the armed forces, he negotiates and ratifies treaties, may exercise clemency after consultation with the Higher Judicial Council, promulgates and is responsible for the enforcement of laws, is responsible for internal and external security, makes civil and military appointments, provides for necessary administrative services.

10. The President, by reference to the Supreme Court, ensures that all laws passed are constitutional.

11. Provisions whereby the President may declare a state of emergency or state of siege.

THE NATIONAL ASSEMBLY

12. The National Assembly shall be renewed every five years, though it may at the instance of the President of the Republic legislate to extend or shorten its term of office. It shall be composed of 180 members elected by universal suffrage.

13–14. Laws shall normally be passed by a simple majority of those present, but if a bill is read a second time at the request of the President of the Republic a majority of the National Assembly as a whole is required.

15–16. The National Assembly shall meet twice a year, each session to last not more than 30 days; in one session it shall approve the budget. It may be recalled to an extraordinary session of not more than 15 days.

17–18. Elections and suitability of candidates and sitting members shall be governed by law.

RELATIONS BETWEEN THE EXECUTIVE AND THE LEGISLATURE

19. Bills may be introduced either by the President of the Republic or by any member of the National Assembly.

20. Reserved to the legislature are: the fundamental rights and duties of the citizen; the law of persons and property; the political, administrative and judicial system in respect of elections to the National Assembly, general regulation of national defence, authorization of penalties and criminal and civil procedure etc., and the organization of the local authorities; currency, the budget, dues and taxes, legislation on public property; economic and social policy; the education system.

21. The National Assembly may empower the President of the Republic to legislate by way of ordinance for a limited period and for given purposes.

22–26. Other matters of procedure, including the right of the President of the Republic to address the Assembly and of the Ministers and Vice-Ministers to take part in debates.

27–29. The composition and conduct of the Assembly's programme of business. Provisions whereby the Assembly may inquire into governmental activity. The obligation of the President of the Republic to promulgate laws, which shall be published in both languages of the Republic.

30. Provisions whereby the President of the Republic, after consultation with the National Assembly, may submit to referendum certain reform bills liable to have profound repercussions on the future of the nation and national institutions.

THE JUDICIARY

31. Justice is administered in the name of the people. The President of the Republic shall ensure the independence of the judiciary and shall make appointments with the assistance of the Higher Judicial Council.

THE SUPREME COURT

32–33. The Supreme Court has powers to uphold the Constitution in such cases as the death or incapacity of the President and the admissibility of laws, to give final judgments on appeals on the Judgment of the Court of Appeal and to decide complaints against administrative acts. It may be assisted by experts appointed by the President of the Republic.

IMPEACHMENT

34. There shall be a Court of Impeachment with jurisdiction to try the President of the Republic for high treason and the Ministers and Vice-Ministers for conspiracy against the security of the State.

THE ECONOMIC AND SOCIAL COUNCIL

35. There shall be an Economic and Social Council, regulated by the law.

AMENDMENT OF THE CONSTITUTION

36–37. Bills to amend the Constitution may be introduced either by the President of the Republic or the National Assembly. The President may decide to submit any amendment to the people by way of a referendum. No procedure to amend the Constitution may be accepted if it tends to impair the republican character, unity or territorial integrity of the State, or the democratic principles by which the Republic is governed.

* In December 1995 the National Assembly formally adopted constitutional amendments that provided for a democratic system of government, with the establishment of an upper legislative chamber (to be known as the Senate), a Council of Supreme Judiciary Affairs, a Council of State, and a Civil Service High Authority, and restricted the power vested in the President, who was to serve a maximum of two seven-year terms. The restoration of decentralized local government areas was also envisaged.

The Government

HEAD OF STATE

President: PAUL BIYA (took office 6 November 1982; elected 14 January 1984; re-elected 24 April 1988, 11 October 1992 and 12 October 1997).

CABINET

(January 1998)

A coalition of the Rassemblement démocratique du peuple camerounais (RDPC), the Union nationale pour la démocratie et le progrès (UNDP), the Union des populations camerounaises (UPC), and the Nouvelle convention (NC).

All of the cabinet members belong to the RDPC, with the exception of the five specified.

Prime Minister: PETER MAFANY MUSONGE.

Senior Ministers

Senior Minister, Delegate at the Presidency in charge of Defence: AMADOU ALI.

Senior Minister in charge of Economy and Finance: EDOUARD AKAME MFOUMOU.

Senior Minister in charge of External Relations: AUGUSTIN KONTCHOU KOUEMEGNI.

Senior Minister in charge of Culture: FERDINAND-LÉOPOLD OYONO.

Senior Minister in charge of Industrial and Commercial Development: BELLO BOUBA MAIGARI (UNDP).

Senior Minister in charge of Education: CHARLES ETOUNDI.

Ministers

Minister of Justice, Keeper of the Seals: LAURENT ESSO.

Minister of Territorial Administration: SAMSON ENAME ENAME.

Minister of Scientific and Technical Research: HENRI HOGBE NLEND (UPC).

Minister of Public Health: GODLIEB MONEKOSSO.

Minister of Agriculture: ZACHARIE PEREVET.

Minister of the Environment and Forestry: SYLVESTRE NAAH ONDOUA.

Minister of Animal Breeding, Fisheries and Animal Industries: HAMADJODA ADJOUDJI.

Minister of Town Planning and Housing: PIERRE HELE (UNDP).

Minister of City Affairs: ANTOINE ZANGA.

Minister of Social Affairs: MADELEINE FOUDA.

Minister of Higher Education: JEAN-MARIE ATANGANA MEBARA.

Minister of Public Service and Administrative Reform: SALI DAIROU.

Minister of Communication: RENÉ ZÉ NGUÉLÉ.

Minister of Public Investments and Regional Planning: JUSTIN NDIORO.

Minister of Employment, Labour and Social Welfare: PIUS ONDOUA.

Minister of Mines, Water Resources and Energy: YVES MBELE.

Minister of Transport: JOSEPH TSANGA ABANDA.

Minister of Posts and Telecommunications: MOUNCHIPOU SEIDOU.

Minister of Public Works: JÉRÔME ETAH.

Minister of Tourism: JOSEPH CLAUDE MBAFOU.

Minister of Women's Affairs: YAOU AISSATOU.

Minister of Youth and Sports: JOSEPH OWONA.

Ministers in charge of Special Duties at the Presidency: PETER ABETY, MARTIN OKOUDA, BABA HAMADOU, ELVIS NGOLE NGOLE.

Ministers Delegate

Minister Delegate at the Presidency in charge of State Control: LUCY GWANMESIA.

Minister Delegate at the Presidency in charge of Relations with the Assemblies: GRÉGOIRE OWONA.

Minister Delegate at the Ministry of External Relations in charge of Relations with the Commonwealth: JOSEPH DION NGUTE.

Minister Delegate at the Ministry of External Relations in charge of Relations with the Islamic World: ADOUM GARDOUM.

Minister Delegate at the Ministry of Economy and Finance in charge of the Budget: ROGER MELINGUI.

Minister Delegate at the Ministry of Economy and Finance in charge of the Stabilization Plan: JEAN-MARIE GANKOU.

Secretaries of State

Secretary of State for Territorial Administration in charge of Prisons Administration: ANTAR GASSAGAYE (NC).

Secretary of State for Agriculture: ABOUBAKARY ABDOULAYE.

Secretary of State for Defence in charge of Gendarmerie: EMMANUEL EDOU.

Secretary of State for Industrial and Commercial Development: EDMOND MOAMPEA MBIO.

Secretary of State for National Education: JOSEPH YUNGA TEGHEN.

Secretary of State for Public Investments and Regional Planning: TSALA MESSI.

Secretary of State for Posts and Telecommunications: DENIS OUMAROU.

Secretary of State for Public Health: HAYATOU ALIM.

Secretary of State for Transport: DR NANA ABOUBAKAR DJALLOH (UNDP).

Secretary of State for Public Works: EMMANUEL BONDE.

Secretary of State for Town Planning and Housing in charge of Lands: YEMBE SHEY JOHNES.

Other appointees with the rank of Minister:

Secretary-General of the Presidency: YAYA MARAFA HAMIDOU.

Assistant Secretary-General of the Presidency: EPHRAIM INONI.

Assistant Secretary-General of the Presidency: RENÉ OWONA.

Director of the Cabinet of the President of the Republic: NGO'O MEBE.

MINISTRIES

Correspondence to ministries not holding post boxes should generally be addressed c/o the Central Post Office, Yaoundé.

Office of the President: Yaoundé; tel. 23-40-25; telex 8207.

Office of the Prime Minister: Yaoundé.

Ministry of Agriculture: Yaoundé; tel. 23-40-85; telex 8325.

Ministry of Animal Breeding, Fisheries and Animal Industry: Yaoundé; tel. 22-33-11.

Ministry of City Affairs: Yaoundé.

Ministry of Communication: BP 1588, Yaoundé; tel. 22-31-55; telex 8215.

Ministry of Culture: Yaoundé.

Ministry of Defence: Yaoundé; tel. 23-40-55; telex 8261.

Ministry of Economy and Finance: BP 18, Yaoundé; tel. 23-40-40; telex 8260; fax 23-21-50.

Ministry of Education: Yaoundé; tel. 23-40-50; telex 8551.

Ministry of Employment, Labour and Social Welfare: Yaoundé; tel. 22-01-86; telex 88415; fax 23-18-20.

Ministry of the Environment and Forest: Yaoundé.

Ministry of External Relations: Yaoundé; tel. 22-01-33; telex 8252.

Ministry of Higher Education: Yaoundé; telex 8418.

Ministry of Industrial and Commercial Development: Yaoundé; tel. 23-40-40; telex 8638; fax 22-27-04.

Ministry of Justice: Yaoundé; tel. 22-01-97; telex 8566.

Ministry of Mines, Water Resources and Energy: Yaoundé; tel. 23-34-04; telex 8504.

Ministry of Posts and Telecommunications: Yaoundé; tel. 23-06-15; telex 8582; fax 23-31-59.

Ministry of Public Health: Yaoundé; tel. 22-29-01; telex 8565.

Ministry of Public Investments and Regional Planning: Yaoundé; telex 8268.

Ministry of the Public Service and Administrative Reform: Yaoundé; fax 23-08-00.

Ministry of Public Works: Yaoundé; tel. and fax 22-01-56; telex 8653.

Ministry of Scientific and Technical Research: Yaoundé.

Ministry of Social Affairs and of Women's Affairs: Yaoundé; tel. 22-41-48.

Ministry of Territorial Administration: Yaoundé; tel. 23-40-90; telex 8503.

Ministry of Tourism: BP 266, Yaoundé; tel. 22-44-11; telex 8318; fax 22-12-95.

Ministry of Town Planning and Housing: Yaoundé; tel. 23-22-82; telex 8560.

Ministry of Transport: Yaoundé; tel. 23-22-37; fax 23-45-20.

Ministry of Youth and Sports: Yaoundé; tel. 23-32-57; telex 8568.

President and Legislature

PRESIDENT

Election, 12 October 1997

Candidate	Votes	% of votes
PAUL BIYA (RDPC)	3,167,820	92.57
HENRI HOGBE NLEND (UPC)	85,693	2.50
SAMUEL EBOUA (MDP)	83,506	2.44
ALBERT DZONGANG (PPD)	40,814	1.19
JOACHIM TABI OWONO (AMEC)	15,817	0.46
ANTOINE DEMANNU (RDPF)	15,490	0.45
GUSTAVE ESSAKA (DIC)	12,915	0.38
Total*	3,422,055	100.00

* Excluding invalid votes.

ASSEMBLÉE NATIONALE

President: DJIBRIL CAVAYE YEGUIE.

General Election, 17 May 1997

Party	Seats
Rassemblement démocratique du peuple camerounais	109
Social Democratic Front	43
Union nationale pour la démocratie et le progrès	13
Union démocratique du Cameroun	5
Mouvement pour la défense de la République	1
Mouvement pour la jeunesse du Cameroun	1
Union des populations camerounaises (K)	1
Total*	180

* On 3 August 1997 further elections took place in seven constituencies, where the results had been annulled; all the seats were won by the RDPC.

Political Organizations

The Rassemblement démocratique du peuple camerounais (RDPC) was the sole legal party (initially as the Union nationale camerounaise) between 1972 and December 1990, when the Constitution was amended to permit the formation of other political associations. In January 1997 some 133 political parties were in existence. The most important of these are listed below:

Action for Meritocracy and Equal Opportunity Party (AMEC): Leader JOACHIM TABI OWONO.

Alliance pour la démocratie et le développement (ADD): Sec.-Gen. GARGA HAMAN ADJI.

Alliance démocratique pour le progrès du Cameroun (ADPC): Garoua; f. 1991.

Alliance pour le progrès et l'émancipation des dépossédés (APED): Yaoundé; f. 1991; Leader BOHIN BOHIN.

Alliance pour le redressement du Cameroun (ARC): f. 1992 by a number of opposition movements.

Association social-démocrate du Cameroun (ASDC): Maroua; f. 1991.

Cameroon Anglophone Movement (CAM): advocates a federal system of govt.

Congrès panafricain du Cameroun (CPC): Douala; f. 1991.

Convention libérale (CL): f. 1991; Leader PIERRE-FLAMBEAU NGAYAP.

Démocratie intégrale au Cameroun (DIC): Douala; f. 1991; Leader GUSTAVE ESSAKA.

Front des alliés pour le changement (FAC): Douala; f. 1994; alliance of 16 opposition movements; Leader SAMUEL EBOUA.

Front démocratique et patriotique (FDP): f. 1994; alliance of six opposition parties.

Liberal Democratic Alliance (LDA): Buéa; Pres. HENRI FOSSUNG.

Mouvement pour la démocratie et le progrès (MDP): f. 1992; Leader SAMUEL EBOUA.

Mouvement pour la défense de la République (MDR): f. 1991; Leader DAKOLE DAISSALA.

Mouvement pour la jeunesse du Cameroun (MLJC): Leader MARCEL YONDO.

Mouvement progressif (MP): f. 1991; Leader JEAN-JACQUES EKINDI.

Mouvement social pour la nouvelle démocratie (MSND): Leader YONDO BLACK.

Nouvelle convention (NC).

Parti de l'action du peuple (PAP): Leader VICTOR MUKUELLE NGOH.

Parti de l'alliance libérale (PAL): Leader CÉLÉSTIN BEDZIGUI.

Parti des démocrates camerounais (PDC): Yaoundé; f. 1991; Leader LOUIS-TOBIE MBIDA.

Parti libéral-democrate (PLD): f. 1991; Leader NJOH LITUMBE.

Parti national du progrès (PNP): Leader ANTAR GASSAGAY.

Parti ouvrier unifié du Cameroun (POUC): Leader DIEUDONNÉ BIZOLE.

Parti populaire pour le développement (PPD): f. 1997.

Parti républicain du peuple camerounais (PRPC): Bertoua; f. 1991; Leader ATEBA NGOUA.

Parti socialiste camerounais (PSC): Leader JEAN-PIERRE DEMBELE.

Parti socialiste démocratique (PSD): Douala; f. 1991; Leader ERNEST KOUM BIN BILTIK.

Parti socialiste démocratique du Cameroun (PSDC): Leader JEAN MICHEL TEKAM.

Rassemblement camerounais pour la République (RCR): Leader SAMUEL WOUAFFO.

Rassemblement démocratique du peuple camerounais (RDPC): BP 867, Yaoundé; tel. 23-27-40; telex 8624; f. 1966 as Union nationale camerounaise by merger of the Union camerounaise, the Kamerun National Democratic Party and four opposition parties; adopted present name in 1985; sole legal party 1972–90; Pres. PAUL BIYA; Sec.-Gen. JOSEPH-CHARLES DOUMBA.

Rassemblement démocratique du peuple sans frontières (RDPF): f. 1997.

Rassemblement des forces patriotiques (RFP): Leader EMA OTOU.

Rassemblement pour l'unité nationale (RUN): Yaoundé; f. 1991.

Social Democratic Front (SDF): Bamenda; f. 1990; Leader JOHN FRU NDI.

Social Democratic Movement (SDM): f. 1995; breakaway faction of the Social Democratic Front; Leader SIGA ASANGA.

Southern Cameroons National Council (SCNC): f. 1995; supports the establishment of an independent republic in anglophone Cameroon; Chair. SAM EKONTANG ELAD.

Union démocratique du Cameroun (UDC): f. 1991; Leader ADAMOU NDAM NJOYA.

Union des forces démocratiques du Cameroun (UFDC): Yaoundé; f. 1991; Leader VICTORIN HAMENI BIELEU.

Union nationale pour la démocratie et le progrès (UNDP): f. 1991; split in 1995; Chair. BELLO BOUBA MAIGARI.

Union du peuple africain (UPA): Leader HUBERT KAMGANG.

Union des populations camerounaises (UPC): Douala; f. 1948; divided into two main factions in 1996: UPC (N), led by NDEH NTUMAZAH and UPC (K), led by AUGUSTIN FRÉDÉRIC KODOCK.

Union des républicains du Cameroun (URC): Douala; f. 1991.

Union sociale démocratique (USD): Yaoundé; f. 1991.

Diplomatic Representation

EMBASSIES AND HIGH COMMISSIONS IN CAMEROON

Algeria: Yaoundé; tel. 21-53-51; fax 21-53-54; Ambassador: M'HAMED ACHACHE.

Belgium: BP 816, Yaoundé; tel. 20-67-47; telex 8314; fax 20-05-21; Ambassador: BAUDOUIN VANDERHULST.

Brazil: BP 348, Yaoundé; tel. 21-45-67; telex 8587; fax 21-19-57; Chargé d'affaires: SERGIO COURI ELIAS.

Canada: Immeuble Stamatiades, BP 572, Yaoundé; tel. 23-02-03; telex 8209; fax 22-10-90; High Commissioner: PIERRE GIGUERE.

Central African Republic: BP 396, Yaoundé; tel. and fax 20-51-55; Ambassador: JEAN POLOKO.

Chad: BP 506, Yaoundé; tel. and fax 21-06-24; telex 8352; Ambassador: HOMSALA OUANGMOTCHING.

China, People's Republic: BP 1307, Yaoundé; tel. 21-00-83; fax 21-43-95; Ambassador: ZHU YOUROUNG.

Congo, Democratic Republic: BP 632, Yaoundé; tel. 22-51-03; telex 8317; Ambassador: (vacant).

Congo, Republic: BP 1422, Yaoundé; tel. 21-24-58; telex 8379; Ambassador: MARCEL MAKOME.

Egypt: BP 809, Yaoundé; tel. 20-39-22; telex 8360; fax 20-26-47; Ambassador: NOFAL IBRAHIM EL-SAYED.

Equatorial Guinea: BP 277, Yaoundé; tel. and fax 21-14-04; Ambassador: SANTIAGO ENEME OVONO.

France: Plateau Atémengué, BP 1631, Yaoundé; tel. 23-40-13; telex 8233; fax 23-70-47; Ambassador: PHILIPPE SELZ.

Gabon: BP 4130, Yaoundé; tel. 20-29-66; telex 8265; fax 21-02-24; Ambassador: PÉPIN MONGOCKODJI.

Germany: rue Charles de Gaulle, BP 1160, Yaoundé; tel. 20-05-66; telex 88238; fax 20-73-13; Ambassador: KLAUS HOLDERBAUM.

Greece: BP 82, Yaoundé; tel. and fax 20-39-36; telex 8364; Ambassador: ATHANASSIOS CAMILOS.

Holy See: rue du Vatican, BP 210, Yaoundé (Apostolic Nunciature); tel. 20-04-75; fax 20-75-13; Apostolic Pro-Nuncio: Most Rev. FÉLIX DEL BLANCO PRIETO, Titular Archbishop of Vannida.

Israel: BP 5934, Yaoundé; tel. 20-16-44; telex 8632; fax 20-16-43; Ambassador: (vacant).

Italy: Quartier Bastos, BP 827, Yaoundé; tel. 20-33-76; telex 88305; fax 21-52-50; Ambassador: PIETRO LONARDO.

Japan: Bastos-Ekoudou, Yaoundé; tel. 20-62-02; Ambassador: TAKERU SASAGUCHI.

Korea, Republic: BP 301, Yaoundé; tel. 21-32-23; fax 20-17-25; Ambassador: DAE-TAEK LIM.

Liberia: Ekoudou, Quartier Bastos, BP 1185, Yaoundé; tel. 21-12-96; telex 8227; fax 20-97-81; Ambassador: CARLTON ALEXWYN KARPEH.

Libya: Quartier Bastos, POB 1980, Yaoundé; tel. 22-41-38.

Morocco: BP 1629, Yaoundé; tel. 20-50-92; telex 8347; fax 20-37-93; Ambassador: MOHAMED BENOMAR.

Netherlands: Immeuble Desamp 1067, rue 1750, Nouvelle Route Bastos, BP 310, Yaoundé; tel. 20-05-44; telex 8237; fax 20-47-04; Ambassador: ANNA ELISABETH DE BIJLL NACHENIUS.

Nigeria: BP 448, Yaoundé; tel. 22-34-55; telex 8267; High Commissioner: MAHMUD GEORGE BELLO.

Romania: Quartier Bastos, BP 6212, Yaoundé; tel. and fax 21-39-86; telex 8417; Chargé d'affaires a.i.: ION MOGOS.

Russia: BP 488, Yaoundé; tel. 20-17-14; telex 8859; fax 20-78-91; Ambassador: YEVGENII UTKIN.

Saudi Arabia: BP 1602, Yaoundé; tel. 21-26-75; fax 20-66-89; Ambassador: ABDULAZIZ FAHD AR-REBDI.

Spain: BP 877, Yaoundé; tel. 20-35-43; telex 8287; fax 20-64-91; Chargé d'affaires a.i.: JOSÉ JAVIER NAGORE SAN MARTÍN.

Tunisia: rue de Rotary, BP 6074, Yaoundé; tel. 20-33-68; telex 8370; fax 21-05-07; Chargé d'affaires: MOHAMED AMIRI (acting).

United Kingdom: ave Winston Churchill, BP 547, Yaoundé; tel. 22-05-45; fax 22-01-48; High Commissioner: PETER BOON.

USA: rue Nachtigal, BP 817, Yaoundé; tel. 23-40-14; telex 8223; fax 23-07-53; Ambassador: CHARLES TWINING.

Judicial System

Supreme Court: Yaoundé; consists of a president, nine titular and substitute judges, a procureur général, an avocat général, deputies to the procureur général, a registrar and clerks.

President of the Supreme Court: ALEXANDRE DIPANDA MOUELLE.

High Court of Justice: Yaoundé; consists of 9 titular judges and 6 substitute judges, all elected by the National Assembly.

Attorney-General: RISSOUCK A. MOULONG.

Religion

It is estimated that 53% of the population are Christians (mainly Roman Catholics), 25% adhere to traditional religious beliefs and 22% are Muslims.

CHRISTIANITY

Protestant Churches

There are about 1m. Protestants in Cameroon, with about 3,000 church and mission workers, and four theological schools.

Fédération des Eglises et missions évangéliques du Cameroun (FEMEC): BP 491, Yaoundé; tel. 22-30-78; f. 1968; 10 mem. churches; Pres. Rev. Dr JEAN KOTTO (Evangelical Church of Cameroon); Admin. Sec. Rev. Dr GRÉGOIRE AMBADIANG DE MENDENG (Presbyterian Church of Cameroon).

Eglise évangélique du Cameroun (Evangelical Church of Cameroon): BP 89, Douala; tel. 42-36-11; fax 42-40-11; f. 1957; 500,000 mems (1992); Pres. Rev. CHARLES E. NJIKE; Sec. Rev. HANS EDJENGUELE.

Eglise presbytérienne camerounaise (Presbyterian Church of Cameroon): BP 519, Yaoundé; tel. 32-42-36; independent since 1957; comprises four synods and 16 presbyteries; 200,000 mems (1985); Gen. Sec. Rev. GRÉGOIRE AMBADIANG DE MENDENG.

Eglise protestante africaine (African Protestant Church): BP 26, Lolodorf; f. 1934; 8,400 mems (1985); Dir-Gen. Rev. MARNIA WOUNGLY-MASSAGA.

Presbyterian Church in Cameroon: BP 19, Buéa; tel. 32-23-36; telex 5310; 250,000 mems (1990); 211 ministers; Moderator Rev. HENRY ANYE AWASOM.

Union des Eglises baptistes au Cameroun (Union of Baptist Churches of Cameroon): BP 6007, New Bell, Douala; tel. 42-41-06; autonomous since 1957; 37,000 mems (1985); Gen. Sec. Rev. EMMANUEL MBENDA.

Other Protestant churches active in Cameroon include the Cameroon Baptist Church, the Cameroon Baptist Convention, the Church of the Lutheran Brethren of Cameroon, the Evangelical Lutheran Church of Cameroon, the Presbyterian Church in West Cameroon and the Union of Evangelical Churches of North Cameroon.

The Roman Catholic Church

Cameroon comprises five archdioceses and 17 dioceses. At 31 December 1995 there were an estimated 3,431,074 adherents. There are several active missionary orders, and four major seminaries for African priests.

Bishops' Conference: Conférence Episcopale Nationale du Cameroun, BP 807, Yaoundé; tel. 31-15-92; fax 31-29-77; f. 1981; Pres. Rt Rev. ANDRÉ WOUKING, Bishop of Bafoussam; Sec.-Gen. Fr PATRICK LAFON.

Archbishop of Bamenda: Most Rev. PAUL VERDZEKOV, Archbishop's House, BP 82, Bamenda; tel. 36-12-41; fax 36-34-87.

Archbishop of Bertoua: Most Rev. LAMBERTUS JOHANNES VAN HEYGEN, Archevêché, BP 40, Bertoua; tel. 24-17-48; fax 24-25-85.

Archbishop of Douala: Cardinal CHRISTIAN WIYGHAN TUMI, Archevêché, BP 179, Douala; tel. 42-37-14; fax 42-18-37.

Archbishop of Garoua: Most Rev. ANTOINE NTALOU, Archevêché, BP 272, Garoua; tel. 27-13-53; fax 27-29-42.

Archbishop of Yaoundé: Most Rev. JEAN ZOA, Archevêché, BP 185, Yaoundé; tel. 22-24-89; telex 8681; fax 23-50-58.

BAHÁ'Í FAITH

National Spiritual Assembly: BP 145, Limbe; tel. 33-21-46; mems in 1,744 localities.

The Press

Restrictions on the press have been in force since 1966. In 1993 there were about 40 newspapers and other periodical publications.

DAILY

Cameroon Tribune: BP 1218, Yaoundé; tel. 30-40-12; telex 8311; fax 30-43-62; f. 1974; govt-controlled; French and English; Dir PAUL C. NDEMBIYEMBE; Editor-in-Chief EBOKEM FOMENKY; circ. 20,000.

PERIODICALS

Afrique en Dossiers: BP 1715; Yaoundé; f. 1970; French and English; Dir EBONGUE SOELLE.

Cameroon Outlook: BP 124, Limbe; f. 1969; 3 a week; independent; English; Editor JEROME F. GWELLEM; circ. 20,000.

Cameroon Panorama: BP 46, Buéa; tel. 32-22-40; f. 1962; monthly; English; Roman Catholic; Editor Sister MERCY HORGAN; circ. 1,500.

Cameroon Post: Yaoundé; weekly; English; independent; Publr PADDY MBAWA; Editor JULIUS WAMEY; circ. 50,000.

Cameroon Review: BP 408, Limbe; monthly; Editor-in-Chief JEROME F. GWELLEM; circ. 70,000.

Cameroon Times: BP 408, Limbe; f. 1960; weekly; English; Editor-in-Chief JEROME F. GWELLEM; circ. 12,000.

Challenge Hebdo: BP 1388, Douala; weekly; Editor BENJAMIN ZEBAZE.

Le Combattant: Yaoundé; weekly; independent; Editor BENYIMBE JOSEPH; circ. 21,000.

Courrier Sportif du Bénin: BP 17, Douala; weekly; Dir HENRI JONG.

Dikalo: BP 12656, Douala; independent; weekly; Dir EMMANUEL NOUBISSIE NGANKAM.

La Gazette: BP 5485, Douala; 2 a week; Editor ABODEL KARIMOU; circ. 35,000.

The Herald: BP 3659, Yaoundé; tel. 31-55-22; fax 31-81-61; weekly; English; Dir Dr BONIFACE FORBIN; circ. 8,000.

Al Houda: BP 1638, Yaoundé; quarterly; Islamic cultural review.

Le Jeune Observateur: Yaoundé; f. 1991; Editor JULES KOUM.

Journal Officiel de la République du Cameroun: BP 1603, Yaoundé; tel. 23-12-77; telex 8403; fortnightly; official govt notices; circ. 4,000.

Le Messager: 266 blvd de la Liberté, BP 5925, Douala; tel. 42-04-39; fax 42-02-14; f. 1979; 2 a week; independent; Man. Editor PIUS NJAWE; circ. 24,000.

The Messenger: BP 15043, Douala; English edn of Le Messager; Editor HILARY FOKUM.

Nleb Ensemble: Imprimerie Saint-Paul, BP 763, Yaoundé; tel. 23-97-73; fax 23-50-58; f. 1935; fortnightly; Ewondo; Dir Most Rev. JEAN ZOA; Editor JOSEPH BEFE ATEBA; circ. 6,000.

La Nouvelle Expression: BP 15333, Douala; independent; weekly; banned by Govt in Dec. 1996; Man. Editor SÉVERIN TCHOUNKOU.

Presbyterian Newsletter: BP 19, Buéa; telex 5613; quarterly.

Que Savoir: BP 1986, Douala; monthly; industry, commerce and tourism.

Recherches et Études Camerounaises: BP 193, Yaoundé; monthly; publ. by Office National de Recherches Scientifiques du Cameroun.

Le Serviteur: BP 1405, Yaoundé; monthly; Protestant; Dir Pastor DANIEL AKO'O; circ. 3,000.

Le Travailleur/The Worker: BP 1610, Yaoundé; tel. 22-33-15; f. 1972; monthly; French and English; journal of Organisation Syndicale des Travailleurs du Cameroun/Cameroon Trade Union Congress; Sec.-Gen. LOUIS SOMBES; circ. 10,000.

L'Unité: BP 867, Yaoundé; weekly; French and English.

Weekly Post: Obili, Yaoundé; Publr Chief BISONG ETAHOBEN.

NEWS AGENCIES

CAMNEWS: c/o SOPECAM, BP 1218, Yaoundé; tel. 23-40-12; telex 8311; Dir JEAN NGANDJEU.

Foreign Bureaux

Agence France-Presse (AFP): Villa Kamdem-Kamga, BP 229, Elig-Essono, Yaoundé; telex 8218; Correspondent RENÉ-JACQUES LIGUE.

Xinhua (New China) News Agency (People's Republic of China): ave Joseph Omgba, BP 1583, Yaoundé; tel. 20-25-72; telex 8294; Chief Correspondent SUN XINGWEN.

Reuters (UK) and ITAR—TASS (Russia) are also represented in Cameroon.

Publishers

Cameroon Review Publications: Boyo Bldg, Halfmile, BP 408, Limbe; f. 1983; periodicals, maps, books and pamphlets; Dir and Editor-in-Chief JEROME F. GWELLEM.

Editions Buma Kor: BP 727, Yaoundé; tel. 23-13-30; fax 23-07-68; f. 1977; general, children's, educational and Christian; English and French; Man. Dir B. D. BUMA KOR.

Editions Clé: BP 1501, Yaoundé; tel. 22-35-54; fax 23-27-09; f. 1963; African and Christian literature and studies; school textbooks; medicine and science; general non-fiction; Gen. Man. COMLAN PROSPER DEH.

Editions Le Flambeau: BP 113, Yaoundé; tel. 22-36-72; f. 1977; general; Man. Dir JOSEPH NDZIE.

Editions Semences Africaines: BP 5329, Yaoundé-Nlongkak; tel. 22-40-58; f. 1974; fiction, history, religion, textbooks; Man. Dir PHILIPPE-LOUIS OMBEDE.

Government Publishing Houses

Centre d'Edition et de Production pour l'Enseignement et la Recherche (CEPER): BP 808, Yaoundé; tel. 22-13-23; telex 8338; f. 1977; scheduled for transfer to private ownership; general non-fiction, science and technology, tertiary, secondary and primary textbooks; Man. Dir JEAN CLAUDE FOUTH.

Imprimerie Nationale: BP 1603, Yaoundé; tel. 23-12-77; telex 8403; scheduled for transfer to private ownership; Dir AMADOU VAMOULKE.

Société de Presse et d'Editions du Cameroun (SOPECAM): BP 1218, Yaoundé; tel. 30-40-12; telex 8311; fax 30-43-62; f. 1977; under the supervision of the Ministry of Communications; Dir-Gen. PAUL CÉLESTIN NDEMBIYEMBE; Man. Editor PIERRE ESSAMA ESSOMBA.

Broadcasting and Communications

TELECOMMUNICATIONS

Société des télécommunications internationales du Cameroun (INTELCAM): BP 1571, Yaoundé; tel. 23-40-65; telex 8320; fax 23-03-03; Dir-Gen. EMMANUEL NGUIAMBA NLOUTSIRI; Asst Dir-Gen. HENRI DJOUAKA.

BROADCASTING

Television programmes from France were broadcast by the Office de Radiodiffusion—Télévision Camerounaise from early 1990.

Office de Radiodiffusion-Télévision Camerounaise (CRTV): BP 1634, Yaoundé; tel. 21-40-88; telex 8888; fax 20-43-40; f. 1987 by merger; broadcasts in French and English; Pres. HENRI BANDOLO; Dir-Gen. GERVAIS MENDO ZE.

Radio Buéa: POB 86, Buéa; tel. 32-26-15; programmes in English, French and 15 vernacular languages; Man. PETERSON CHIA YUH; Head of Station GIDEON MULU TAKA.

Radio Douala: BP 986, Douala; tel. 42-60-60; programmes in French, English, Douala, Bassa, Ewondo, Bakoko and Bamiléké; Dir BRUNO DJEM; Head of Station LINUS ONANA MVONDO.

Radio Garoua: BP 103, Garoua; tel. 27-11-67; programmes in French, Hausa, English, Foulfouldé, Arabic and Choa; Dir BELLO MALGANA; Head of Station MOUSSA EPOPA.

There are also provincial radio stations at Abong Mbang, Bafoussam, Bamenda, Bertoua, Ebolowa, Maroua and Ngaoundéré, and a local radio station serving Yaoundé.

Finance

(cap. = capital; res = reserves; dep. = deposits; m. = million; brs = branches; amounts in francs CFA)

BANKING

Central Bank

Banque des Etats de l'Afrique Centrale (BEAC): BP 1917, Yaoundé; tel. 23-40-30; telex 8343; fax 23-33-29; f. 1973 as the central bank of issue for mem. states of the Customs and Economic Union of Central Africa (UDEAC); cap. 45,000m., res 169,492.2m., dep. 341,488.6m. (June 1996); Gov. JEAN-FÉLIX MAMALEPOT; Dir in Cameroon SADOU HAYATOU; 5 brs in Cameroon.

Commercial Banks

Amity Bank Cameroon SA: place Joss, BP 2705, Douala; tel. 43-20-49; telex 5639; fax 43-20-46; f. 1991; cap. and res 1,057m. (June 1996); Pres. LAWRENCE LOWEH TASHA; 3 brs.

Banque Internationale du Cameroun pour l'Epargne et le Commerce (BICEC): ave du Général de Gaulle, BP 4070, Douala; tel. 42-29-65; telex 55046; fax 42-41-16; f. 1962 as the Banque Internationale pour le Commerce et l'Industrie du Cameroun; 54% state-owned; cap. 6,000m. (June 1996); Pres. JEAN BAPTISTE BOKAM; Gen. Man. MICHEL TORIELLI; 34 brs.

Highland Corporation Bank SA: Immeuble Hotel Hilton, blvd du 20 mai, BP 10039, Yaoundé; tel. 23-92-87; telex 8439; fax 23-92-91; f. 1995; cap. 600m. (Dec. 1996); Pres PAUL ATANGA NJI.

Société Commerciale de Banque—Crédit Lyonnais Cameroun (SCB—CLC): 220 ave Monseigneur Vogt, BP 700, Yaoundé; tel. 23-40-05; telex 8213; fax 22-41-32; f. 1989; 35% state-owned; cap. and res 5,815m. (June 1995); Pres. MARTIN OKOUDA; Dir-Gen. MICHEL TRICAUD; 18 brs.

Société Générale de Banques au Cameroun (SGBC): 10 rue Joss, BP 4042, Douala; tel. 42-70-10; telex 5646; fax 42-87-72; f. 1963; 26.7% state-owned; cap. and res 6,000m. (June 1996); Pres. AMADOU MOULIOM NJIFENJOU; Gen. Man. GASTON NGUENTI; 29 brs.

Standard Chartered Bank Cameroon SA: Blvd de la Liberté, BP 1784, Douala; tel. 42-36-12; telex 55858; fax 42-27-89; f. 1980; 34% state-owned; cap. 3,500m. (Oct. 1997); Chair. EPHRAIM INONI; Man. Dir JOHN S. TAYLOR.

Development Banks

Banque de Développement des États de l'Afrique Centrale: (see Franc Zone, p. 182).

Crédit Agricole du Cameroun: ave du Maréchal Foch, BP 11801, Yaoundé; tel. 23-23-60; telex 8332; fax 22-53-74; f. 1987; 41.5% state-owned; cap. and res 3,628m. (June 1994); agricultural development bank; transfer of state-owned shares to private ownership pending in 1997; Chair. GILBERT ANDZE TSOUNGUI; Dir-Gen. HUBERT RAUCH.

Crédit Foncier du Cameroun (CFC): BP 1531, Yaoundé; tel. 23-52-15; telex 8368; fax 23-52-21 f. 1977; 70% state-owned; cap. and res 7,966m. (June 1995); provides financial assistance for low-cost housing; Chair. GEORGES NGANGO; Dir-Gen. SYLVESTRE NAAH ONDOA.

Société Nationale d'Investissement du Cameroun (SNI): place de la Poste, BP 423, Yaoundé; tel. 22-44-22; telex 8205; fax 22-39-64; f. 1964; state-owned investment and credit agency; cap. and res 12,510m. (June 1995); Chair. VICTOR AYISSI MVODO; Dir-Gen. ESTHER BELIB DANG.

Financial Institutions

Caisse Autonome d'Amortissement du Cameroun: BP 7167, Yaoundé; tel. 22-01-87; telex 8858; fax 22-01-29; Dir-Gen. ISAAC NJIEMOUN.

Caisse Commune d'Epargne et d'Investissement (CCEI): place de l'Hôtel de Ville, BP 11834, Yaoundé; tel. 22-58-37; telex 8907; fax 22-17-85; cap. 1,505m. (June 1995); Pres. Dr PAUL KANMOGNE FOKAM; Dir-Gen. JACQUES NZEALE.

Fonds d'Aide et de Garantie des Crédits aux Petites et Moyennes Entreprises (FOGAPE): BP 1591, Yaoundé; tel. 23-38-59; telex 8395; fax 22-32-74; f. 1984; cap. 1,000m. (Oct. 1997); Pres. JOSEPH HENGA; Vice-Pres. ARMAND FIRMIN MVONDO.

INSURANCE

State-owned Companies*

Assurances Mutuelles Agricoles du Cameroun (AMACAM): BP 962, Yaoundé; tel. 22-49-66; telex 8300; f. 1965; cap. 100m.; Pres. SAMUEL NGBWA NGUELE; Dir-Gen. LUC CLAUDE NANFA.

Caisse Nationale de Réassurances (CNR): ave Foch, BP 4180, Yaoundé; tel. 22-37-99; telex 8262; fax 23-36-80; f. 1965; all classes of reinsurance; cap. 1,000m.; Pres. JEAN KEUTCHA; Man. Dir ANTOINE NTSIMI.

Société Camerounaise d'Assurances et de Réassurances (SOCAR): 1450 blvd de la Liberté, BP 280, Douala; tel. 42-55-84; telex 5504; fax 42-13-35; f. 1973; cap. 800m.; Chair. J. YONTA; Man. Dir R. BIOUELE.

*In 1996 the Government announced plans to liquidate AMACAM and SOCAR, and to transfer CNR to the private sector.

Privately-owned Companies

Compagnie Camerounaise d'Assurances et de Réassurances (CCAR): 11 rue Franqueville, BP 4068, Douala; tel. 42-31-59; telex 5341; fax 42-64-53; f. 1974; cap. 499.5m.; Pres. YVETTE CHASSAGNE; Dir Gen. CHRISTIAN LE GOFF.

Compagnie Nationale d'Assurances (CNA): BP 12125, Douala; tel. 42-44-46; telex 5100; fax 42-47-27; f. 1986; all classes of insurance; cap. 600m.; Chair. THÉODORE EBOBO; Man. Dir. PROTAIS AYANGMA AMANG.

General and Equitable Assurance Cameroon Ltd (GEACAM): 56 blvd de la Liberté, BP 426, Douala; tel. 42-59-85; telex 5690; fax 42-71-03; cap. 300m.; Pres. V. A. NGU; Man. Dir J. CHEBAUT.

Société Nouvelle d'Assurances du Cameroun (SNAC): rue Manga Bell, BP 105, Douala; tel. and fax 42-92-03; telex 5745; f. 1974; all classes of insurance; cap. 700m.; Dir-Gen. JEAN CHEBAUT.

Trade and Industry

GOVERNMENT AGENCY

Economic and Social Council: BP 1058, Yaoundé; tel. 23-24-74; telex 8275; advises the Govt on economic and social problems; comprises 150 mems and a perm. secr.; mems serve a five-year term; Pres. LUC AYANG; Sec.-Gen. FRANÇOIS EYOK.

DEVELOPMENT ORGANIZATIONS

Caisse Française de Développement (CFD): BP 46, Yaoundé; tel. 22-23-24; telex 8301; fax 23-57-07; Dir DOMINIQUE DORDAIN.

Cameroon Development Corporation (CAMDEV): Bota, Limbe; tel. 33-22-51; telex 5242; fax 43-17-40; f. 1947, reorg. 1982; cap. 15,626m. francs CFA; state-owned; statutory corpn established to acquire and develop plantations of tropical crops for local and export markets; operates two oil mills, seven banana packing stations, three tea and seven rubber factories; transfer to private ownership pending in 1997; Chair. NERIUS NAMASO MBILE; Gen. Man. PETER MAFANY MUSONGE.

Direction Générale des Grands Travaux du Cameroun (DGTC): BP 6604, Yaoundé; tel. 22-18-03; telex 8952; fax 22-13-00; f. 1988; commissioning, implementation and supervision of public works contracts; Chair. JEAN FOUMAN AKAME; Man. Dir MICHEL KOWALZICK.

Hévéa-Cameroun (HEVECAM): BP 1298, Douala and BP 174, Kribi; tel. 42-75-64; telex 5880; f. 1975; cap. 16,518m. francs CFA; state-owned; development of 15,000 ha rubber plantation; 4,500 employees; transferred to private ownership in 1997; Pres. NYOKWEDI MALONGA; Man. Dir JEAN REMY.

Mission d'Aménagement et d'Equipement des Terrains Urbains et Ruraux (MAETUR): BP 1248, Yaoundé; tel. 22-31-13; telex 8571; f. 1977; Pres. LÉOPOLD FERDINAND OYONO; Dir-Gen. ANDRÉ MAMA FOUDA.

Mission de Développement de la Province du Nord-Ouest (MIDENO): BP 442, Bamenda; telex 5842; Dir ANDREW WAINDIM NDONYI.

Mission Française de Coopération et d'Action Culturelle: BP 1616, Yaoundé; tel. 22-44-43; telex 8392; fax 22-33-96; administers bilateral aid from France; Dir JEAN BOULOGNE.

Office Céréalier dans la Province du Nord: BP 298, Garoua; tel. 27-14-38; telex 7603; f. 1975 to combat effects of drought in northern Cameroon and stabilize cereal prices; Pres. Alhadji MAHAMAT; Dir-Gen. GILBERT GOURLEMOND.

Société de Développement du Cacao (SODECAO): BP 1651, Yaoundé; tel. 30-45-44; fax 30-33-95; f. 1974, reorg. 1980; cap. 425m. francs CFA; development of cocoa, coffee and food crop production in the Littoral, Centre and South provinces; Pres. JOSEPH-CHARLES NDOUMBA; Dir-Gen. JOSEPH INGWAT II.

Société de Développement de l'Elevage (SODEVA): BP 50, Kousseri; cap. 50m. francs CFA; Dir Alhadji OUMAROU BAKARY.

Société de Développement et d'Exploitation des Productions Animales (SODEPA): BP 1410, Yaoundé; tel. 22-24-28; f. 1974; cap. 375m. francs CFA; development of livestock and livestock products; Man. Dir ETIENNE ENGUELEGUELE.

Société de Développement de la Haute-Vallée du Noun (UNVDA): BP 25, N'Dop, North-West Province, f. 1970; cap. 1,380m. francs CFA; rice, maize and soya bean cultivation; Dir-Gen. SAMUEL BAWE CHI WANKI.

Société d'Expansion et de Modernisation de la Riziculture de Yagoua (SEMRY): BP 46, Yagoua; tel. 29-62-13; telex 7655; f. 1971; cap. 4,580m. francs CFA; commercialization of rice products and expansion of rice-growing in areas where irrigation is possible; Pres. ALBERT EKONO; Dir-Gen. LIMANGANA TORI.

Société Immobilière du Cameroun (SIC): BP 387, Yaoundé; tel. 23-34-11; telex 8577; fax 22-51-19; f. 1952; cap. 1,000m. francs CFA; housing construction and development; Pres. ENOCH KWAYEB; Dir-Gen. GILLES-ROGER BELINGA.

CHAMBERS OF COMMERCE

Chambre d'Agriculture, d'Elevage et des Forêts du Cameroun: Parc Repiquet, BP 287, Yaoundé; tel. 23-14-96; telex 8243; f. 1955; 120 mems; Pres. RENÉ GOBÉ; Sec.-Gen. SOLOMON NFOR GWEI; other chambers at Yaoundé, Ebolowa, Bertoua, Douala, Ngaoundéré, Garoua, Maroua, Buéa, Bumenda and Bafoussam.

Chambre de Commerce, d'Industrie et des Mines du Cameroun: BP 4011, Douala; tel. 42-36-90; telex 5948; fax 42-55-96; f. 1963; also at BP 12206, Douala; BP 36, Yaoundé; BP 211, Limbe; BP 59, Garoua; BP 944, Bafoussam; BP 551, Bamenda; 138 mems; Pres. PIERRE TCHANQUÉ; Sec.-Gen. SAÏDOU ABDOULAYE BOBBOY.

EMPLOYERS' ORGANIZATIONS

Groupement des Femmes d'Affaires du Cameroun (GFAC): BP 1940, Douala; tel. 42-4-64; telex 6100; Pres. FRANÇOISE FONING.

Groupement Interpatronal du Cameroun (GICAM): ave Konrad Adenauer, BP 1134, Yaoundé; tel. 20-27-22; fax 20-96-94; also at BP 829, Douala; tel. and fax 42-31-41; f. 1957; Pres. ANDRÉ SIAKA; Sec.-Gen. GÉRARD KOSOSSEY.

Syndicat des Commerçants Importateurs-Exportateurs du Cameroun (SCIEC): 16 rue Quillien, BP 562, Douala; tel. 42-03-04; Sec.-Gen. G. TOSCANO.

Syndicat des Industriels du Cameroun (SYNDUSTRICAM): 17 blvd de Liberté, BP 673, Douala; tel. 42-30-58; fax 42-56-16; f. 1953; Pres. SAMUEL KONDO EBELLÉ.

Syndicat des Producteurs et Exportateurs de Bois du Cameroun: BP 570, Yaoundé; tel. 20-27-22; telex 8998; fax 20-96-94; Pres. CARLO ORIANI.

Syndicat Professionnel des Entreprises du Bâtiment, des Travaux Publics et des Activités Annexes: BP 1134, Yaoundé; also at BP 660, Douala; tel. and fax 20-27-22; Pres. PAUL SOPPO-PRISO.

Syndicats Professionnels Forestiers et Activités connexes du Cameroun: BP 100, Douala.

Union des Syndicats Professionnels du Cameroun (USPC): BP 829, Douala; Pres. MOUKOKO KINGUE.

West Cameroon Employers' Association (WCEA): BP 97, Tiko.

UTILITIES

Electricity

Société Nationale d'Electricité du Cameroun (SONEL): BP 4077, 63 ave de Gaulle, Douala; tel. 42-54-44; telex 5551; fax 42-22-47; f. 1974; 93.1% state owned; Chief Exec. JEAN FOUMAN AKAME; Dir-Gen. MARCEL NIAT NJI-FENJI.

Water

Société Nationale des Eaux du Cameroun (SNEC): BP 157, Douala; tel. 42-87-11; telex 5265; f. 1967; 73% state owned; Pres. AMADOU ALI; Dir-Gen. CLÉMENT OBOUH FEGUE.

PRINCIPAL CO-OPERATIVE ORGANIZATIONS

Centre National de Développement des Entreprises Coopératives (CENADEC): Yaoundé; f. 1970; promotes and organizes the co-operative movement; bureaux at BP 43, Kumba and BP 26, Bamenda; Dir JACQUES SANGUE.

Union Centrale des Coopératives Agricoles de l'Ouest (UCCAO): ave Samuel Wonko, BP 1002, Bafoussam; tel. 44-14-39; telex 7005; fax 44-11-01; f. 1957; marketing of cocoa and coffee; 110,000 mems; Pres. VICTOR GNIMPIEBA; Dir-Gen. PIERRE NZEFA TSACHOUA.

West Cameroon Co-operative Association Ltd: BP 135, Kumba; founded as cen. financing body of the co-operative movement; provides short-term credits and agricultural services to mem. socs; policy-making body for the co-operative movement in West Cameroon; 142 mem. unions and socs with total membership of c. 45,000; Pres. Chief T. E. NJEA; Sec. M. M. QUAN.

TRADE UNION FEDERATION

Confederation of Cameroon Trade Unions (CCTU): BP 1610, Yaoundé; tel. 22-33-15; f. 1985; fmrly the Union National des Travailleurs du Cameroun (UNTC); Pres. EMMANUEL BAKOD; Sec.-Gen. LOUIS SOMBES.

Transport

RAILWAYS

There are some 1,104 km of track, the West Line running from Douala to Nkongsamba (166 km) with a branch line leading south-west from Mbanga to Kumba (29 km), and the Transcameroon railway which runs from Douala to Ngaoundéré (885 km), with a branch line from Ngoumou to Mbalmayo (30 km).

Office du Chemin de Fer Transcamerounais: BP 625, Yaoundé; tel. 22-44-33; telex 8293; supervises the laying of new railway lines and improvements to existing lines, and undertakes relevant research; Dir-Gen. LUC TOWA FOTSO.

Régie Nationale des Chemins de Fer du Cameroun (REGIFERCAM): BP 304, Douala; tel. 40-60-45; telex 5607; fax 42-32-05; f. 1947; scheduled for transfer to private ownership; Chair. SAMUEL EBOUA; Man. Dir SAMUEL MINKO.

ROADS

In 1995 there were an estimated 34,300 km of roads, of which about 4,288 km were paved.

SHIPPING

There are seaports at Kribi and Limbe-Tiko, a river port at Garoua, and an estuary port at Douala-Bonabéri, the principal port and main outlet, which has 2,510 m of quays and a minimum depth of 5.8 m in the channels and 8.5 m at the quays. In 1995 the port handled 4.16m. metric tons of cargo. Total handling capacity is 7m. metric tons annually. Plans are under way to increase the annual capacity of the container terminal.

Office National des Ports/National Ports Authority: Centre des Affaires Maritimes, 18 rue Joffre, BP 4020, Douala; tel. 42-01-33; telex 5270; fax 42-67-97; f. 1971; Chair. JOSEPH TSANGA ABANDA (Minister of Transport); Gen. Man. TCHOUTA MOUSSA.

Cameroon Shipping Lines SA (CAMSHIP): Centre des Affaires Maritimes, 18 rue Joffre, BP 4054, Douala; tel. 42-00-38; telex 5615; fax 42-21-81; f. 1975; transferred to private ownership in 1997; 6 vessels trading with western Europe, USA, Far East and Africa; Chair. FRANÇOIS SENGAT KUO; Man. Dir RENÉ MBAYEN.

Compagnie Maritime Camerounaise SA (CMC): Douala.

Conseil National des Chargeurs du Cameroun (CNCC): BP 1588, Douala; tel. 42-32-06; telex 5669; fax 42-89-01; f. 1986; promotion of the maritime sector; Gen. Man. EMMANUEL EDOU.

Delmas Cameroun: rue Kitchener, BP 263, Douala; tel. 42-47-50; telex 5222; fax 42-88-51; f. 1977; Pres. JEAN-GUY LE FLOCH; Dir-Gen. DANY CHUTAUX.

Société Africaine de Transit et d'Affrètement (SATA): Vallée Tokoto, BP 546, Douala; tel. 42-82-09; telex 5239; f. 1950; Man. Dir RAYMOND PARIZOT.

Société Agence Maritime de l'Ouest Africain Cameroun (SAMOA): 5 blvd de la Liberté, BP 1127, Douala; tel. 42-16-80; telex 5256; f. 1953; shipping agents; Dir JEAN PERRIER.

Société Camerounaise de Manutention et d'Acconage (SOCAMAC): BP 284, Douala; tel. 42-40-51; telex 5537; f. 1976; freight handling; Pres. MOHAMADOU TALBA; Dir-Gen. HARRY J. GHOOS.

Société Camerounaise de Transport et d'Affrètement (SCTA): BP 974, Douala; tel. 42-17-24; telex 6181; f. 1951; Pres. JACQUES VIAULT; Dir-Gen. GONTRAN FRAUCIEL.

Société Ouest-Africaine d'Entreprises Maritimes—Cameroun (SOAEM—Cameroon): 5 blvd de la Liberté, BP 4057, Douala; tel. 42-52-69; telex 5220; fax 42-05-18; f. 1959; Pres. JACQUES COLOMBANI; Man. Dir JEAN-LOUIS GRECIET.

Société de Transports Urbains du Cameroun (SOTUC): BP 1697, Yaoundé; tel. 21-38-07; telex 8330; fax 20-77-84; f. 1973; 58% owned by Société Nationale d'Investissement du Cameroun; operates urban transport services in Yaoundé and Douala; Dir-Gen. MARCEL YONDO; Mans JEAN-VICTOR OUM (Yaoundé), GABRIEL VASSEUR (Douala).

SOCOPAO (Cameroun): BP 215, Douala; tel. 42-64-64; telex 5252; f. 1951; shipping agents; Pres. VINCENT BOLLORE; Man. Dir E. DUPUY.

Transcap Cameroun: BP 4059, Douala; tel. 42-72-14; telex 5247; f. 1960; Pres. RENÉ DUPRAZ; Man. Dir MICHEL BARDOU.

CIVIL AVIATION

There are international airports at Douala, Garoua and Yaoundé.

Air Affaires Afrique: BP 1325, Douala; tel. 42-29-77; fax 42-99-03; f. 1978; regional and domestic charter passenger services; CEO BYRON BYRON-EXARCOS.

Cameroon Airlines (CAM-AIR): 3 ave du Général de Gaulle, BP 4092, Douala; tel. 42-25-25; telex 5345; fax 42-34-59; f. 1971; domestic flights and services to Africa and Europe; scheduled for transfer to private ownership; Chair. JOSEPH BELIBI; CEO SAMUEL MINKO.

Tourism

Tourists are attracted by the cultural diversity of local customs, and by the national parks, game reserves, sandy beaches and dinosaur sites. In 1994 an estimated 84,000 tourists visited Cameroon. In that year receipts from tourism totalled some US $49m.

Ministère du Tourisme: BP 266, Yaoundé; tel. 22-44-11; telex 8318; fax 22-12-95.

CANADA

Introductory Survey

Location, Climate, Language, Religion, Flag, Capital

Canada occupies the northern part of North America (excluding Alaska and Greenland) and is the second largest country in the world, after Russia. It extends from the Atlantic Ocean to the Pacific. Except for the boundary with Alaska in the north-west, Canada's frontier with the USA follows the upper St Lawrence Seaway and the Great Lakes, continuing west along latitude 49°N. The climate is an extreme one, particularly inland. Winter temperatures drop well below freezing but summers are generally hot. Rainfall varies from moderate to light and there are heavy falls of snow. The two official languages are English and French, the mother tongues of 60.5% and 23.8%, respectively, at the general census in 1991. More than 98% of Canadians can speak English or French. About 45% of the population are Roman Catholics. The main Protestant churches are the United Church of Canada and the Anglican Church of Canada. Numerous other religious denominations are represented. The national flag (proportions 2 by 1) consists of a red maple leaf on a white field, flanked by red panels. The capital is Ottawa.

Recent History

The Liberals, led by Pierre Trudeau, were returned to office at general elections in 1968, 1972, 1974, and again in 1980 after a short-lived minority Progressive Conservative (PC) administration. Popular support for the Liberals, however, was undermined by an economic recession, while the PC party gained steadily in popularity after 1983 under the leadership of Brian Mulroney. Trudeau resigned in June 1984 and was succeeded as Liberal leader and Prime Minister by John Turner, a former Minister of Finance. At general elections held in September the PC party obtained a substantial legislative majority.

During 1986 the persistence of high rates of unemployment, together with the resignations in discordant circumstances of five cabinet ministers, led to a fall in the PC Government's popularity. Further cabinet changes followed in 1987 in an effort to retrieve support for the Government, which continued, none the less, to decline amid further ministerial resignations, a controversial incident concerning the operations of the Canadian Security Intelligence Service, and criticism by the Liberals and the New Democratic Party (NDP) of the Government's negotiation of a new US-Canadian trade treaty, which the Liberals and the NDP viewed as overly advantageous to US business interests and potentially damaging to Canada's national identity. The trade agreement was, however, approved in August 1988 by the House of Commons. In October, following indications that the Government was gaining public support in the free trade debate, Mulroney called general elections for November. The PC party was re-elected, although with a reduced majority, and full legislative ratification of the trade agreement followed in December. In February 1990 the Federal Government opened negotiations with Mexico, to achieve a lowering of trade barriers. These discussions were joined by the US Government, and in December 1992, Canada, the USA and Mexico finalized terms for a tripartite North American Free Trade Agreement (NAFTA, see p. 203), with the aim of creating a free trade zone encompassing the whole of North America.

In September 1990 a constitutional debate arose over the conduct of business in the Federal Senate, an appointive body in which the Liberals had long held a majority, and in which there were 15 vacant seats left unfilled pending the eventual implementation of senate reform provisions in the Meech Lake Accord (see below). With the demise of the Accord, however, the Senate's refusal to approve controversial legislation implementing a Goods and Services Tax (GST) prompted Mulroney to fill the existing vacancies with PC appointees, and to invoke a constitutional provision allowing the Government temporarily to enlarge the Senate by creating eight additional seats. The GST, which entered into force in January 1991, led to a sharp decline in public support for the Government.

In the province of Québec, where four-fifths of the population speak French as a first language and which maintains its own cultural identity, the question of political self-determination has long been a sensitive issue. At provincial elections in 1976 the separatist Parti Québécois (PQ) came to power, and in 1977 made French the official language of education, business and government in Québec. During 1977 the PQ reiterated its aim of sovereignty for Québec; however in 1978 the party leadership denied that unilateral separation was contemplated and stated that a 'sovereignty-association', with a monetary and customs union, would be sought. At a Québec provincial referendum held in May 1980, these proposals were rejected by 59.5% to 40.5%. In December 1985 the PQ was replaced by the Liberals as the governing party in Québec. The Liberals retained power at the next provincial elections, held in September 1989, in which the PQ obtained 40% of the popular vote. Formal support for separatist aspirations was extended to the Federal Parliament in May 1990, when seven PC members representing Québec constituencies, led by Lucien Bouchard (a former member of Mulroney's Cabinet), formed an independent Bloc Québécois (BQ) with the object of acting in the interests of a 'sovereign Québec'. The BQ later expanded, with disaffected Liberal support, to nine members.

In 1982 the UK Parliament transferred to Canada authority over all matters contained in British statutes relating to Canada, opening the way for institutional reform and the redistribution of legislative powers between Parliament and the provincial legislatures. Following two years of negotiations between Trudeau and the provincial premiers, all the provinces except Québec had accepted constitutional provisions which included a charter of rights and a formula for constitutional amendments, whereby such amendments would require the support of at least seven provinces representing more than 50% of the population. Québec, however, maintained that its legislature could exercise the right to veto constitutional provisions.

Following the return to power in 1985 of the Liberals in Québec, the Federal Government adopted new initiatives to include Québec in the constitutional arrangements. In April 1987 Mulroney and the provincial premiers met at Meech Lake, Québec, to negotiate a constitutional accommodation for Québec. The resultant agreement, the Meech Lake Accord, was finalized in June. It recognized Québec as a 'distinct society' within the Canadian federation, and granted each of the provinces substantial new powers in the areas of federal parliamentary reform, judicial appointments and the creation of new provinces. The Accord was subject to ratification, not later than June 1990, by the Federal Parliament and all provincial legislatures. By early 1990 the Federal Parliament and each of the 10 provincial legislatures, except for New Brunswick and Manitoba, had approved the Accord.

Opposition to the Meech Lake arrangements, on the grounds that they afforded too much influence to Québec and failed to provide Inuit and Indian minorities with the same measure of protection as francophone groups, began to emerge in March 1990, when the Newfoundland legislature rescinded its earlier endorsement of the Accord. Following a meeting in June between Mulroney and the provincial premiers (at which a number of compromise amendments were adopted), the New Brunswick legislature agreed to accept the Accord, but the provinces of Manitoba and Newfoundland upheld their opposition. The Meech Lake Accord duly lapsed on 23 June, and the Québec Government, which had opposed any changes to the earlier terms of the Accord, responded by refusing to participate in future provincial conferences, and by appointing a commission to examine the province's political choices. In October Mulroney appointed a consultative panel to ascertain public opinion both on constitutional reform and on the wider issue of Canada's national future.

In September 1991 the Federal Government announced a new series of constitutional reform proposals, which, unlike the Meech Lake Accord, would require the assent of only seven provinces representing 50% of the total population. Under the new plan, Québec was to be recognized as a distinct society in terms of its language, culture and legal system, while each province would have full control of its cultural affairs. Native peoples were to receive full self-government within 10 years, inter-provincial trade barriers were to be abolished, and the Federal Senate was to become an elected body with limited powers of legislative veto, except in matters involving natural resources, in which it would have full powers of veto. The reform proposals also included the creation of a Council of Federation to resolve disputes between the provinces and Federal Government. A National Unity Committee, comprising an inter-party group of 30 federal legislators, was formed to ascertain public reaction to the plan, about which the Québec provincial government expressed initial reservations on economic grounds.

In March 1992 an all-party committee of the Federal Parliament recommended new constitutional proposals providing for a system of 'co-operative federalism', which would grant Québec powers of veto over future constitutional changes, together with exclusive jurisdiction over the main areas of its provincial affairs. This plan was rejected as inadequate by the Québec Government, which stated that it intended to hold a provincial referendum on full sovereignty.

Further discussions among the provincial premiers (in which Québec refused to participate) took place in April 1992. Mulroney sought to revive the Meech Lake proposals, but this suggestion was opposed by the western provinces, which sought increased representation in a reformed Senate and were unwilling to concede a constitutional veto to Québec until after these changes were carried out. Mulroney undertook to hold a national referendum if the premiers failed to reach agreement by the end of May; however, no further progress was made and the negotiations were suspended in June.

In late August 1992, following resumed consultations between Mulroney and the provincial premiers, a new programme of constitutional reforms, known as the Charlottetown Agreement, was finalized for submission to a national referendum. The proposals, which were endorsed by all of the provincial premiers as well as the leaders of the three main political parties, provided for an equal and elected Senate, a guarantee in perpetuity to Québec of one-quarter of the seats in the Federal House of Commons (regardless of future movements in population), as well as three of the nine seats on the Supreme Court of Canada. There was also to be recognition of provincial jurisdiction in cultural affairs, and increased provincial powers over certain economic affairs and immigration. The inherent right to self-government of the Indian and Inuit population was also to be recognized.

Despite the apparent political consensus, considerable opposition to the Charlottetown Agreement became evident during the national debate that preceded the referendum, which took place in October 1992. Disagreements emerged on a regional basis, as well as among NDP and Liberal supporters (among whom Pierre Trudeau denounced the Agreement). Aspects of the proposed constitution were opposed by the PQ and the BQ, and by the Reform Party (RP), a conservative-populist movement which led opposition in the western provinces. Nationally, the proposals were defeated by a margin of 54.4% to 44.6%; only four of the provinces (Ontario, New Brunswick, Newfoundland and Prince Edward Island) and the Northwest Territories (NWT) endorsed the Agreement.

The defeat of the Charlottetown Agreement, together with the persistence of adverse economic conditions, led to a rapid erosion in the prestige of the Government, and in Mulroney's personal popularity. A reorganization of Cabinet posts in January 1993 failed to restore public confidence, and in the following month Mulroney announced that he was to relinquish office in June. He was succeeded by the former Minister of Defence and Veterans' Affairs, Kim Campbell, who became Canada's first woman Prime Minister.

The Campbell Government proved unable to restore the Government's political standing, and, faced with the expiry in November 1993 of its five-year parliamentary mandate, the Prime Minister announced in September that general elections would take place in October. The outcome of the elections, which were contested primarily on domestic economic issues, resulted in a decisive victory for the Liberals, led by Jean Chrétien. A significant realignment of political forces was reflected in the new Parliament, in which PC representation was reduced to only two seats. The RP emerged with 52 seats, while the BQ, with 54 seats, became the official opposition party. The BQ, which had captured substantial support from the PC in Québec, announced that it would pursue the achievement of full sovereignty for Québec. Kim Campbell, who lost her seat, resigned as PC leader.

The new Liberal Government set out to implement an economic recovery programme, involving the expenditure of C $6,000m. to create up to 120,000 jobs over a two-year period. Substantial reductions in defence expenditure were announced, and in December 1993, following the renegotiation of certain treaty protocols with the US Government, NAFTA, which had received Canadian legislative ratification in June, was formally promulgated, to take effect from January 1994.

The issue of separatism in Québec was reopened by provincial elections held in September 1994, in which the PQ, led by Jacques Parizeau, defeated the incumbent Liberal administration by a margin of 44.7% to 44.3%. Parizeau, whose campaign had included an undertaking that a new referendum on independence would be held during 1995, was supported at federal level by the BQ, although the Federal Government asserted that considerable uncertainty was felt within Québec over the possible economic consequences of secession. In December 1994 the Québec Legislature approved measures to prepare for the referendum, and Parizeau initiated a programme of public consultation to frame the terms under which the provincial electorate would be asked to approve Québec's withdrawal from the Canadian federation. In June 1995 the PQ and the BQ, together with a smaller provincial nationalist group, the Action Démocratique de Québec, agreed a framework for the province's proposed independence. Following provincial legislative approval for the referendum, it was announced in mid-September that voting would take place on 30 October.

During the six-week referendum campaign, indications of growing support within Québec for secession led to considerable anxiety nationally about the political and economic implications of the independence plan. On the eve of the referendum, Chrétien issued an appeal for national unity, and undertook to reinstate negotiations for a new constitutional accord. The sovereignty proposals were defeated by a margin of only 50,000 votes; in a turnout of 93% of eligible voters, 49.4% were in favour of the sovereignty plan, and 50.6% opposed. Parizeau, who blamed the defeat on economic special interest groups and the non-francophone 'ethnic' vote, announced on the following day that he was to relinquish the provincial premiership. In January 1996 Chrétien carried out an extensive reshuffle of his Cabinet and reaffirmed the Federal Government's commitment to the maintenance of Canadian federation and national unity. In the following month Lucien Bouchard, having resigned from the Federal House of Commons and relinquished the leadership of the BQ, succeeded Parizeau as Premier of Québec and leader of the PQ. Bouchard indicated that his administration viewed the sovereignty issue as less urgent than the resolution of Québec's immediate economic problems. In September 1997 Bouchard refused to attend a conference of provincial premiers and territorial commissioners, at which a seven-point framework on Canadian unity was agreed. The conference, held in Calgary, recognized the 'unique character' of Québec, but asserted that any future change in the constitutional powers of one province should be applicable to all provinces.

The reversal of an undertaking by the Liberals in the 1993 general election to abolish GST led in May 1996 to the resignation, on a point of principle, from the House of Commons of the Deputy Prime Minister and Minister of Canadian Heritage, Sheila Copps, who successfully stood for re-election and resumed her cabinet posts in the following month. In December the Minister of National Defence and Veterans' Affairs left the Government, following his admission of a 'technical breach' of ethical guidelines in the conduct of government business. In the same month, the Chief of Staff of the Armed Forces relinquished his post, following an inquiry into alleged attempts to suppress information concerning the maltreatment of a Somalian civilian by Canadian troops participating in the United Nations peacekeeping mission in Somalia in 1993.

The question of land treaty claims by Canada's indigenous peoples assumed prominence during the early 1990s, when disputes over land rights arose in Ontario, Manitoba and, most notably, Québec, where armed confrontations took place in 1990 between the civil authorities and militant Indian groups. The NWT, which form one-third of Canada's land mass but contain a population of only 58,000 (of which Inuit and Indians comprise about one-half), may eventually secure a new constitutional status. In November 1982 the Federal Government agreed in principle to implement the decision of a territorial referendum held in April, in which 56% of the voters approved a division of the NWT into two parts. Detailed arrangements to divide the NWT into the self-governing units of Nunavut (to the east of a proposed boundary running northwards from the Saskatchewan-Manitoba border) and Denendeh (to the west) were approved by the NWT legislature in January 1987 and were endorsed in May 1992 by a plebiscite among NWT residents. In December 1991 specific terms for the creation of a semi-autonomous Nunavut Territory, covering an area of 2.2m. sq km, were agreed by Inuit representatives and the Federal Government. In September 1988, following 13 years of negotiations, the Federal Government formally transferred to indigenous ownership an area covering 673,000 sq km in the NWT. In the Yukon Territory, an area of 41,000 sq km (representing 8.6% of the Territory's land) was transferred to indigenous control. In April 1991 the Federal Government undertook that all outstanding land treaty claims would be resolved by the year 2000. A formal agreement to this effect was finalized in May 1993, providing for the territory of Nunavut to come into official existence on 1 April 1999. In November 1996 an official inquiry into the social and economic condition of Canada's indigenous peoples recommended the creation of a new chamber of the Federal Parliament to function as a permanent commission to review issues affecting the indigenous groups. It was also recommended that these communities receive increased powers of self-government. In October 1997 the NWT Government recommended that the Federal Government approve the establishment of a 17-seat Legislature for Nunavut, to be located at Iqaluit.

During his period in office, Mulroney sought to re-establish Canada's traditional 'special relationship' with the USA, which had operated until the Trudeau period. There was considerable support in Canada for efforts by the Government to secure effective control by the USA of the emission of gases from industrial plants, which move northwards into Canada to produce environmentally destructive 'acid rain'. In 1986 a joint US-Canadian governmental commission recommended the implementation of a US $5,000m. anti-pollution programme, to be financed jointly by the US Government and the relevant industries. The Canadian Government itself proceeded with a programme costing an estimated C $128,000m. to achieve the reduction by 20% of acid-pollution emissions from domestic sources by the year 2005. These aims were extended by a new environmental programme announced in December 1990, under which the Government was to spend a total of C $3,000m. on a range of environmental improvement measures. These sought to reduce air pollution by 40% over a 10-year period, while stabilizing carbon dioxide emissions at 1990 levels by the end of the century. In addition, work was to be undertaken to eliminate industrial pollution from the Great Lakes and other waterways. Financial provision was also made for contributions to projects seeking to stem global warming. In March 1991 the US and Canadian Governments reached a formal agreement under which US industries were to contribute financially to measures reducing acid rain pollution. In the same year, Canada, with the USA and 23 European countries, signed an international treaty on cross-border pollution control, under which the signatories undertook to prevent, reduce and control environmental degradation caused by industrial activity. In June 1994 Canada joined 25 European countries in signing a UN protocol on the reduction of sulphur emissions, which the Canadian Government undertook to reduce by 30% over a six-year period. A further agreement with the USA on the reduction of industrial pollution was signed in April 1997. Canada assumed a leading role in the establishment, with seven other circumpolar countries, of the Arctic Council, which commenced operation in September 1996. The aims of the Council include the protection of the environment of the polar region, the formation of co-ordinated policies governing its future, and the safeguarding of the interests of its indigenous population groups.

Relations between the USA and Canada came under strain in August and September 1985, when a US coastguard ice-breaker traversed the Northwest Passage without seeking prior permission from Canada, in assertion of long-standing US claims that the channels within this 1.6m. sq km tract of ice-bound islands are international waters. The Canadian Government declared sovereignty of this area as from 1 January 1986, and in January 1988 the USA recognized Canadian jurisdiction over the Arctic islands (but not over their waters) and undertook to notify the Canadian Government in advance of all Arctic passages by US surface vessels. There have also been recurrent disagreements between Canada and France concerning the boundary of disputed waters near the French-controlled islands of St Pierre and Miquelon, off the southern coast of Newfoundland. In June 1992 an international arbitration tribunal presented its report, generally regarded as favourable to Canada, on this dispute. It was reported in December 1994 that the two countries had agreed a 10-year accord on the allocation of fishing rights around the islands.

In December 1992 Canada and the EC (European Community, now European Union—EU) announced the resolution of a seven-year disagreement over the allocation of fishing rights to European commercial fleets in the north-west Atlantic Ocean. In 1994, however, the EU unilaterally awarded itself almost 70% of the internationally agreed quota of Greenland halibut (also sometimes known as turbot) caught in the north-west Atlantic fishing grounds. This action was not recognized by other members of the Northwest Atlantic Fishing Organization (NAFO), and was vigorously contested by the Canadian Government, which declared that it would act to prevent EU fishing trawlers (principally from Spain and Portugal) from overfishing the already seriously depleted stocks of Greenland halibut. It was also announced that Canada was extending its maritime jurisdiction beyond its Exclusive Economic Zone (EEZ), already extending 200 nautical miles (370 km) from the coastline. This action was rejected by the EU as contrary to international law.

In February 1995 the Canadian Government formally notified the EU that its fishing fleets would not be permitted to increase their Greenland halibut catches in the Grand Banks, off the eastern coast of Canada, and warned that force would be used if necessary to ensure that total catches by EU vessels did not exceed 3,400 tons of the NAFO-agreed world Greenland halibut quota of 27,000 tons. On 6 March the Canadian Government declared a 60-day moratorium on all trawling for this fish in the north-west Atlantic, and three days later its enforcement vessels fired on and impounded a Spanish trawler fishing in international waters. The EU responded by suspending all official political contacts with Canada, pending the release of the trawler, and the Spanish Government announced that it was to institute proceedings against Canada in the International Court of Justice. The *impasse* was eased by the release of the trawler on 15 March, when it was agreed to initiate quota allocation negotiations. In late March, however, a further three Spanish vessels were prevented by the Canadian coast guard from fishing in international waters. Divisions began to emerge within the EU when the British Government refused to endorse an EU protest against these interceptions, and declared its support of Canada's desire to conserve north-west Atlantic fishing stocks. The progress of negotiations was impeded by further confrontations in April between Spanish trawlers and Canadian enforcement vessels, and by dissident views expressed within the EU by Britain and Denmark. A resolution was eventually reached in mid-April, under which Canada and EU countries each agreed to accept 41% of the 1996 Greenland halibut quota. Canada undertook to cease further seizures of vessels in international waters, and it was agreed that independent observers would monitor the activities of trawlers in the north-west Atlantic fishing zone. However, during the negotiation of an accord in June 1996 governing bilateral relations between Canada and the EU, the Canadian Government rejected a request by Spain that it suspend the enforcement of its fishing regulations outside Canadian territorial waters.

Canada, which maintains significant economic and commercial links with Cuba and operates a policy of 'constructive engagement' in its relations with that country, has taken a prominent role in international opposition to efforts, initiated by the US Government in March 1996, to penalize investors whose business in any way involves property in Cuba that was confiscated from US citizens following the 1959 revolution. The imposition of these measures, known as the Helms-Burton Act, led in July 1996 to the exclusion from the USA of nine Canadian businessmen involved in nickel-mining operations in Cuba. The Canadian Government responded by introducing legislation prohibiting Canadian companies from compliance with the Helms-Burton Act, and refused to recognize foreign court rulings arising from the Act, or to assist in the enforcement of judgments obtained against Canadian businesses under the Act. With Mexico, which also conducts significant trade with Cuba, Canada co-ordinated a joint challenge to the US Government through NAFTA dispute procedures. In November 1996 Canada actively promoted a resolution by the UN General Assembly condemning the US trade sanctions against Cuba, and in the same month joined the EU in a complaint against the embargo to the World Trade Organization. The dispute remained unresolved in November 1997, when the Canadian Government protested to the USA over its penalization of a Canadian petroleum company with business interests in Iran. Relations with the USA were further undermined during 1997 by disagreements over the demarcation of salmon-fishing rights off the Pacific coast.

Since the mid-1990s, Canada has pursued initiatives to secure an international ban on the manufacture and use of land mines. At a conference held in Ottawa in December 1997, Canada became the first signatory of a treaty agreed by 121 countries undertaking to discontinue the use of these armaments and providing for the destruction of existing stockpiles. However, the USA, Russia and the People's Republic of China were not parties to the agreement.

At general elections held in June 1997, the Liberals obtained a reduced majority in the House of Commons, and the RP replaced the BQ as the main opposition party. The Liberals, who had campaigned on their record of economic management, were widely believed to have lost popular support as a result of reduced levels of government expenditure on social programmes and health care.

Government

Canada is a federal parliamentary state. Under the Constitution Act 1982, executive power is vested in the British monarch, as Head of State, and exercisable by her representative, the Governor-General, whom she appoints on the advice of the Canadian Prime Minister. The Federal Parliament comprises the Head of State, a nominated Senate (a maximum of 112 members, appointed on a regional basis) and a House of Commons (301 members, elected by universal adult suffrage for single-member constituencies). A Parliament may last no longer than five years. The Governor-General appoints the Prime Minister and, on the latter's recommendation, other ministers to form the Cabinet. The Prime Minister should have the confidence of the House of Commons, to which the Cabinet is responsible. Canada comprises 10 provinces (each with a Lieutenant-Governor and a legislature, which may last no longer than five years, from which a Premier is chosen), and two territories constituted by Act of Parliament.

Defence

Canada co-operates with the USA in the defence of North America and is a member of NATO. Military service is voluntary. In August 1997 the armed forces numbered 61,600: army 21,900, navy 9,400, air force 14,600, and 15,700 not identified by service. The Federal Government's defence expenditure for 1995/96 was estimated at C $10,468m.

Economic Affairs

In 1995, according to estimates by the World Bank, Canada's gross national product (GNP), measured at average 1993–95 prices, was US $573,695m., equivalent to US $19,380 per head. Between 1985 and 1995, it was estimated, GNP per head increased, in real terms, at an average rate of 0.4% per year. Over the same period, the population increased by an annual average of 1.3%. Canada's gross domestic product (GDP) increased, in real terms, at an average rate of 2.9% per year in 1990–95; GDP increased by 4.1% in 1994, by 2.3 in 1995 and by 1.5% in 1996.

Agriculture (including forestry and fishing) contributed 2.8% of GDP (in constant 1986 prices) in 1993, and engaged 4.1% of the employed labour force in 1995. The principal crops are wheat, barley and other cereals, which, together with livestock production (chiefly cattle and pigs) and timber, provide an important source of export earnings. In 1990 Canada was the world's largest exporter of forest products. Canada is a leading exporter of fish and seafood, and the production of furs is also important. In real terms, agricultural GDP increased by an annual average of 2.1% in 1980–90, but declined by 3.5% in 1991 and by 5.0% in 1992. It rose, however, by 6.8% in 1993. Agricultural produced increased by 1.4% in 1993, by 4.6% in 1994, by 3.2% in 1995 and by an estimated 3.1% in 1996.

Industry (including mining, manufacturing, construction and power) provided 30.4% of GDP (in constant 1986 prices) in 1993, and employed 22.9% of the working population in 1995. Industrial GDP increased at an average annual rate of 2.1% during 1980–90, but declined by 4.9% in 1991 and by 0.9% in 1992. It rose by 3.1% in 1993. Industrial production (excluding construction) increased by 4.4% in 1993, by 7.0% in 1994, by 4.2% in 1995 and by 0.9% in 1996.

Mining provided 4.2% of GDP (in constant 1986 prices) in 1993, but employed only 1.3% of the working population in 1995. In 1991 Canada was the world's largest producer of zinc and asbestos, and the second largest producer of nickel, potash and uranium. Gold, silver, iron, copper, cobalt and lead are also exploited. There are considerable reserves of petroleum and natural gas in Alberta, off the Atlantic coast and in the Canadian Arctic islands. The GDP of the mining sector increased, in real terms, at an average rate of 1.3% per year during 1980–90, and by 3.5% per year in 1990–93.

Manufacturing contributed 17.9% of GDP (in constant 1986 prices) in 1993, and employed 15.3% of the working population in 1995. The principal branches of manufacturing in 1995, measured by the value of output, were transport equipment (accounting for 22% of the total), food products (11.4%), paper and allied products (9.1%), chemical products (7.3%), electrical and electronic products (7.1%) and primary metal industries (6.7%). Manufacturing GDP increased, in real terms, at an average rate of 2.1% per year in 1980–90, but declined by 6.9% in 1991. It rose by 0.7% in 1992 and by 5.0% in 1993. Manufacturing output increased by an average of 1.9% per year during 1990–96.

Energy is derived principally from hydroelectric power (which provided 67% of the electricity supply in 1985) and from coal-fired and nuclear power stations. Canada is an important source of US energy supplies, accounting in 1989 for 7.0% of the USA's requirements of natural gas and for 5.0% of its petroleum imports.

Services engaged 73.0% of the employed labour force in 1995 and provided 66.7% of GDP (in constant 1986 prices) in 1993. The combined GDP of the service sectors increased, in real terms, at an average rate of 3.1% per year in 1980–90, and by 1.2% per year in 1990–93.

In 1996 Canada recorded a visible trade surplus of US $30,062m.; there was a surplus of US $2,808m. on the current account of the balance of payments. In 1996 the USA accounted for 81.3% of Canada's total exports and 67.5% of total imports; the European Union (EU) and Japan were also important trading partners. The principal exports in that year were motor vehicles and parts and wood pulp and paper. The principal imports were motor vehicle parts, passenger vehicles, computers and foodstuffs. In January 1989 a free trade agreement with the USA entered into force, whereby virtually all remaining trade tariffs imposed between the two countries were to be eliminated over a 10-year period. Negotiations with the USA and Mexico, aimed at the eventual creation of a full North American free trade area, began in 1991 and concluded in December 1992 with the signing of an agreement. Following its formal ratification in December 1993, the North American Free Trade Agreement (NAFTA, see p. 203) entered into operation on 1 January 1994. Since the implementation of NAFTA, however, disagreements have persisted between Canada and the USA over alleged violations of the Agreement by the US Government in relation to bilateral trade in softwood lumber, wheat and other commodities. Since the mid-1990s the Canadian Government has implemented measures aimed at expanding trade in the Far East, notably with the People's Republic of China, the Republic of Korea, Indonesia and Viet Nam. In November 1996 Canada finalized a trade agreement with Chile, which will, with effect from June 1997, phase out most customs duties by 2002.

In the financial year ending 31 March 1996 there was an estimated budget deficit of C $32,250m. The annual rate of inflation averaged 3.3% in 1985–93. It stood at 1.8% in 1993 and declined to 0.2% in 1994. Consumer prices increased by 2.2% in 1995 and by 1.6% in 1996. The rate of unemployment exceeded 10% of the labour force in each of the years between 1991 and 1994, declining to 9.5% in 1995 and rising to 9.7% in 1996.

Many sectors of Canadian industry rely heavily on foreign investment. Following the international recession of the mid-1970s, Canada's economy experienced inflationary pressures and, despite anti-inflationary measures (including the imposition of high interest rates), the average annual rate of inflation remained above 4% throughout the 1980s. Persistent budgetary deficits have been attributable largely to high interest rates, which continued into the early 1990s, to the detriment of a sustained economic recovery. The persistence of substantial budgetary deficits both at federal and provincial level, together with political uncertainties surrounding the future of Québec, necessitated further rises in interest levels during 1994, despite the achievement at mid-year of a negative rate of inflation. The 1995/96 budget, announced in February 1995, aimed to secure a reduction in the deficit from 6% to 3% of GDP over a two-year period. This was to be achieved, in part, by a decrease of 4% in federal government allocations to provincial governments for the provision of social and welfare services. The 1996/97 budget, announced in March 1996, imposed additional restraints on government spending and imposed further reductions on foreign borrowing. The Government's emphasis on fiscal stringency, led in part, in August 1996, to the country's first current-account surplus in the balance of payments since 1984. This recovery was further aided by low rates of domestic inflation and by the beneficial effects of NAFTA on Canadian export sales to the USA. Following the June 1997 general elections, the Government stated its aim of achieving a balanced budget not later than 1998/99. The Canadian economy, however, remains vulnerable to adverse movements in world prices for its major exports of raw materials.

Social Welfare

Almost 37% of the 1995/96 federal budget was allocated to health and social welfare. The Federal Government administers family allowances, unemployment insurance and pensions. Other services are provided by the provinces. A federal medical care insurance programme covers all Canadians against medical expenses, and a federal-provincial hospital insurance programme covers over 99% of the insurable population. In 1994/95 there were 978 hospitals, with a total of 156,547 beds.

Education

Education policy is a provincial responsibility, and the period of compulsory school attendance varies. French-speaking students are entitled by law, in some provinces, to instruction in French. Primary education is from the age of five or six years to 13–14, followed by three to five years at secondary or high school. In 1994 an estimated 95% of children aged six to 11 attended primary schools, while 92% of those aged 12 to 17 were enrolled at secondary schools. In 1996/97 there were 77 universities and 198 other institutions of post-secondary education. Federal government expenditure on education was allocated at C $5,129m. in 1996/97.

Public Holidays*

1998: 1 January (New Year's Day), 10 April (Good Friday), 13 April (Easter Monday), 1 July (Canada Day), 7 September (Labour Day), 25 December (Christmas Day), 26 December (Boxing Day).

1999: 1 January (New Year's Day), 2 April (Good Friday), 5 April (Easter Monday), 1 July (Canada Day), 6 September (Labour Day), 27 December (for Christmas Day), 28 December (for Boxing Day).

*Standard public holidays comprise the listed days, together with any other day so proclaimed by individual provinces.

Weights and Measures

The metric system is in force.

Statistical Survey

Source (unless otherwise stated): Statistics Canada, Ottawa, ON K1A 0T6; tel. (613) 951-8116; fax (613) 951-0581.

Area and Population

AREA, POPULATION AND DENSITY

Area (sq km)	
Land	9,203,210
Inland water	755,109
Total	9,958,319*
Population (census results)	
4 June 1991†	
Males	13,454,580
Females	13,842,280
Total	27,296,860
14 May 1996†	28,846,761
Population (official estimates at 1 July)	
1994	29,255,599
1995	29,615,325
1996	29,963,631
Density (per sq km) at 1 July 1996	3.0

* 3,844,928 sq miles.

† Excluding census data for one or more incompletely enumerated Indian reserves or Indian settlements.

PROVINCES AND TERRITORIES (census results, 14 May 1996)

	Land area (sq km)	Population*	Capital
Provinces:			
Alberta	638,233	2,696,826	Edmonton
British Columbia	892,677	3,724,500	Victoria
Manitoba	547,704	1,113,898	Winnipeg
New Brunswick	71,569	738,133	Fredericton
Newfoundland	371,635	551,792	St John's
Nova Scotia	52,841	909,282	Halifax
Ontario	916,734	10,753,573	Toronto
Prince Edward Island	5,660	134,557	Charlottetown
Québec	1,357,812	7,138,795	Québec
Saskatchewan	570,113	990,237	Regina
Territories:			
Northwest Territories	3,246,389	64,402	Yellowknife
Yukon Territory	531,844	30,766	Whitehorse
Total	9,203,210	28,846,761	—

* Excluding census data for one or more incompletely enumerated Indian reserves or Indian settlements.

PRINCIPAL METROPOLITAN AREAS (census results, 14 May 1996)

Toronto	4,263,757	London	398,616
Montréal*	3,326,510	Kitchener	382,940
Vancouver	1,831,665	St Catharines-Niagara	372,406
Ottawa (capital)	1,010,498†	Halifax	332,518
Edmonton*	862,597	Victoria*	304,287
Calgary*	821,628	Windsor	278,685
Québec	671,889	Oshawa	268,773
Winnipeg	667,209	Saskatoon	219,056
Hamilton	624,360		

* Excluding census data for one or more incompletely enumerated Indian reserves or Indian settlements.

† Including Hull.

BIRTHS, MARRIAGES AND DEATHS

	Registered live births*		Registered marriages		Registered deaths*	
	Number	Rate (per 1,000)	Number	Rate (per 1,000)	Number	Rate (per 1,000)
1988	376,795	14.0	187,728	7.0	190,011	7.4
1989	392,661	14.3	190,640	7.0	190,965	7.2
1990	405,486	14.6	187,737	6.8	191,973	7.0
1991	402,258	14.3	172,251	6.1	195,568	7.0
1992	398,642	14.0	164,573	5.8	196,535	6.8
1993	388,394	13.4	159,316	5.5	204,912	6.9
1994	385,112	13.2	159,959	5.5	207,077	6.8
1995	378,011	12.8	160,256	5.4	210,733	6.7

1996 (provisional): Live births 375,680 (birth rate 12.5 per 1,000); Deaths 215,520 (death rate 7.2 per 1,000).

* Including Canadian residents temporarily in the USA but excluding US residents temporarily in Canada.

IMMIGRATION

Country of Origin	1993	1994	1995*
United Kingdom	7,159	5,971	6,146
USA	8,014	6,234	5,156
Other	240,646	221,670	200,775
Total	255,819	223,875	212,077

* Preliminary.

ECONOMICALLY ACTIVE POPULATION*
(annual averages, '000 persons aged 15 years and over)

	1994	1995	1996
Agriculture, trapping and fishing	497	494	523
Forestry and logging	98	110	93
Mining and quarrying	167	184	182
Manufacturing†	2,097	2,200	2,241
Construction	902	859	841
Transport, communications and other utilities	1,034	1,089	1,073
Trade	2,482	2,463	2,514
Finance, insurance and real estate	821	837	824
Public administration	923	848	861
Other services	5,280	5,360	5,478
Unclassified	532	484	514
Total labour force	14,832	14,928	15,145
Males	8,174	8,198	n.a.
Females	6,658	6,730	n.a.

* Figures exclude military personnel, inmates of institutions, residents of the Yukon and Northwest Territories, and Indian reserves. The data include unemployed persons, totalling (in '000): 1,541 in 1994; 1,422 in 1995; 1,469 in 1996.

† Including repair and installation services.

Agriculture

PRINCIPAL CROPS ('000 metric tons)

	1994	1995	1996
Wheat	23,122.1	25,017.4	30,495.1
Barley	11,690.0	13,034.7	15,911.8
Maize (Corn)*	7,042.9	7,270.9	7,239.4
Rye	396.7	309.6	321.5
Oats	3,637.6	2,857.5	4,374.1
Buckwheat	12.4	21.2	20.1
Mixed grain	n.a.	647.5	555.9
Potatoes	n.a.	3,825.5	3,908.5
Beans (dry)	84.8	115.8	62.1
Peas (dry)	n.a.	1,454.7	1,245.4
Soybeans	2,250.7	2,293.0	2,170.4
Sunflower seed	n.a.	66.2	55.7
Rapeseed (Canola)	7,232.5	6,436.4	5,036.6
Linseed	960.1	1,104.9	842.8
Mustard seed	n.a.	253.5	237.5
Sugar beets	n.a.	1,026.9	1,034.2
Tame hay	31,830.8	27,064.1	27,540.3

* Maize for grain only, excluding fodder maize.

LIVESTOCK ('000 head at 1 July)

	1993	1994	1995
Milch cows	1,243	1,258	1,265
Other cattle	13,410	14,036	14,689
Sheep	883	825	859
Pigs	10,822	11,358	12,047

LIVESTOCK PRODUCTS

	1994	1995	1996*
Beef and veal (metric tons)	899,665	928,524	1,015,000
Mutton and lamb (metric tons)	10,453	10,052	n.a.
Pig meat (metric tons)	1,231,787	1,280,769	1,240,000
Poultry meat (metric tons)	863,000	871,000	886,000
Milk (kilolitres)†	6,927,317	7,105,522	7,262,323
Creamery butter (metric tons)	85,135	90,920	96,441
Cheddar cheese (metric tons)	119,025	114,419	117,994
Ice-cream mix (kilolitres)	173,631	173,025	168,399
Eggs ('000 dozen)	478,011	482,635	490,090

* Preliminary. † Farm sales of milk and cream.

Forestry

ROUNDWOOD REMOVALS (1994, '000 cubic metres)

	Softwoods	Hardwoods	Total
Alberta*	11,893	6,028	17,921
British Columbia	73,130	1,963	75,093
Manitoba	1,596	190	1,786
New Brunswick	7,276	1,993	9,269
Newfoundland	2,290†	155	2,445
Nova Scotia†	4,229	877	5,106
Ontario†	20,765	5,188	25,952
Prince Edward Island	368	151†	519†
Québec	28,995†	9,419	38,414†
Saskatchewan	3,007	1,911	4,918
Total	154,150	28,876	182,025

* Preliminary. † Estimates.

SAWNWOOD PRODUCTION
('000 cubic metres, incl. railway sleepers)

	1992	1993	1994
Coniferous (softwood)	55,512	58,651	60,648
Broadleaved (hardwood)	806	1,123	1,002
Total	56,318	59,774	61,650

Source: FAO, *Yearbook of Forest Products*.

Fur Industry

NUMBER OF PELTS PRODUCED*

	1992/93†	1993/94‡	1994/95§
Newfoundland	17,025	15,661	22,761
Prince Edward Island	24,021[1]	24,863	27,530
Nova Scotia	296,279	258,248	544,113
New Brunswick	55,865	57,988	73,596
Québec	238,478	257,658	364,046
Ontario	629,647	594,446	700,610
Manitoba	119,253	159,360	184,780
Saskatchewan	65,371	93,831	135,719
Alberta	154,886[2]	226,540	188,336
British Columbia	178,881	174,703	338,825
Northwest Territories	26,669[3]	37,080	7,280
Yukon	4,843	5,450	38,212
Total	1,811,263	1,881,693	2,238,964

* Including ranch-raised.
† Includes ranch-raised production based on 1992 calendar year.
‡ Includes ranch-raised production based on 1993 calendar year.
§ Includes ranch-raised production based on 1994 calendar year.
[1] Excludes coyote (prairie wolf) from Newfoundland.
[2] Includes wolverine from Saskatchewan.
[3] Includes fisher from the Yukon.

Fishing

('000 metric tons, live weight)

	1993	1994	1995
Atlantic salmon	22.6	25.4	33.6
Sockeye salmon	42.5	30.7	10.5
Atlantic cod	76.6	22.7	12.3
Pollock	21.6	15.6	10.3
Silver hake	25.6	7.3	15.0
Atlantic redfishes	84.8	50.8	17.8
Capelin	48.6	2.2	0.3
Atlantic herring	197.6	206.8	193.8
Pacific herring	41.3	40.9	27.0
Atlantic mackerel	26.5	20.6	17.5
Queen crab	47.7	60.4	64.5
American lobster	40.7	41.4	40.4
Northern prawn	25.8	29.0	30.1
Pink shrimps	17.1	19.7	24.0
American sea scallop	86.9	89.4	58.6
Clams	28.5	30.5	33.7
Total catch (incl. others)	1,211.6	1,089.3	901.2
Inland waters	41.9	42.2	43.0
Atlantic Ocean	855.4	711.1	630.6
Pacific Ocean	314.3	335.9	227.6

Source: FAO, *Yearbook of Fishery Statistics*.

Mining

('000 metric tons, unless otherwise indicated)

	1994	1995	1996*
Metallic			
Bismuth (metric tons)	129	126	n.a.
Cadmium (metric tons)	1,500	1,686	1,587
Cobalt (metric tons)	1,846	2,148	n.a.
Copper (metric tons)	590,784	700,834	665,891
Gold (kilograms)	146,428	150,867	164,136
Iron ore	36,416	36,628	36,030
Lead (metric tons)	167,584	204,227	246,083
Molybdenum (metric tons)	9,759	8,482	n.a.
Nickel (metric tons)	141,974	172,107	184,548
Platinum group (kilograms)	13,422	15,109	n.a.
Selenium (metric tons)	566	553	n.a.
Silver (metric tons)	740	1,245	1,228
Uranium (metric tons)	11,200	10,238	11,448
Zinc (metric tons)	976,309	1,094,703	1,187,829

— continued	1994	1995	1996*
Non-metallic			
Asbestos	531	516	521
Gypsum	8,587	8,055	8,333
Nepheline syenite	602	616	n.a.
Potash (K_2O)	8,517	8,855	8,165
Salt	12,244	10,957	12,289
Sulphur, in smelter gas	805	829	n.a.
Sulphur, elemental	7,900	7,846	8,131
Fuels			
Coal	72,824	74,920	75,950
Natural gas (million cubic metres)†	138,856	148,203	152,985
Natural gas by-products ('000 cubic metres)†‡	22,666	25,040	25,882
Petroleum, crude ('000 cubic metres)†	110,452	114,372	116,832
Structural materials			
Cement	10,584	10,440	11,050
Sand and gravel§	245,278	225,992	217,898
Stone	92,502	98,578	86,057

* Preliminary.
† Marketable production.
‡ Excludes sulphur.
§ Includes quartz.

Industry

VALUE OF SHIPMENTS (preliminary figures, C $ million)

	1993	1994	1995
Food industries	40,789	42,043	44,428
Beverage industries	6,390	6,672	6,857
Tobacco products industries	2,150	2,256	2,548
Rubber products industries	2,960	3,549	3,660
Plastic products industries	6,107	7,092	7,742
Leather and allied products industries	947	987	1,029
Primary textile industries	2,690	3,076	3,245
Textiles products industries	2,859	3,136	3,287
Clothing industries	6,000	6,060	6,283
Wood industries	18,761	22,179	21,852
Furniture and fixture industries	3,839	4,328	5,079
Paper and allied products industries	21,576	25,425	35,470
Printing, publishing and allied industries	12,839	13,625	14,545
Primary metal industries	20,130	23,805	26,233
Fabricated metal products industries	15,961	17,719	19,519
Machinery industries (excl. electrical machinery)	10,099	12,011	14,334
Transportation equipment industries	62,843	75,521	85,937
Electrical and electronic products industries	20,985	24,386	27,862
Non-metallic mineral products industries	6,180	6,864	6,970
Refined petroleum and coal products industries	16,923	17,774	17,321
Chemical and chemical products industries	22,468	24,802	28,556
Other manufacturing industries	6,353	6,586	7,272
Total	309,852	349,895	390,029

Electric Energy (net production, million kWh): 511,000 (provisional) in 1993; 534,000 (provisional) in 1994; 538,400 (provisional) in 1995.

Finance

CURRENCY AND EXCHANGE RATES

Monetary Units

100 cents = 1 Canadian dollar (C $).

Sterling and US Dollar Equivalents (30 September 1997)

£1 sterling = C $2.234;
US $1 = C $1.383;
C $100 = £44.77 = US $72.32.

Average Exchange Rate (C $ per US $)

1994	1.3656
1995	1.3724
1996	1.3635

FEDERAL BUDGET (estimates, C $ million, year ending 31 March)

Revenue	1994/95	1995/96
Tax revenue	126,389	134,765
Taxes on income and profits	75,002	81,475
Personal income tax	62,008	65,602
Corporation income tax	11,604	14,350
Taxes on goods and services	31,950	33,265
Sales tax and goods and services tax	20,957	22,130
Motive fuel tax	3,820	4,180
Alcoholic beverages and tobacco taxes	2,931	2,892
Custom duties	3,575	3,270
Unemployment insurance contributions	18,928	19,520
Non-tax revenue	10,593	10,688
Sales of goods and services	3,425	3,523
Return on investments	5,024	4,952
Government enterprises	4,625	4,449
Profits remitted	3,641	3,383
Total	136,982	145,453

Expenditure	1994/95	1995/96
General services	7,532	7,633
Administrative	4,382	3,969
Protection of persons and property	14,795	14,642
National defence	10,576	10,468
Transport and communications	3,911	3,258
Health	8,895	8,286
Hospital care	5,938	5,646
Social services	57,050	57,276
Old-age security	20,511	21,255
Unemployment insurance	14,815	13,600
Family allowances	5,381	5,333
Social welfare assistance	8,065	8,428
Education	5,260	5,129
Post-secondary	3,521	3,339
Resources conservation and industrial development	6,994	8,128
Foreign affairs and international assistance	4,942	3,371
General-purpose transfers to other levels of government	10,885	10,606
Debt charges	42,298	47,800
Interest	42,046	47,534
Total (incl. others)	174,216	177,703

INTERNATIONAL RESERVES (US $ million at 31 December)

	1994	1995	1996
Gold*	198	178	155
IMF special drawing rights	1,148	1,177	1,168
Reserve position in IMF	919	1,243	1,226
Foreign exchange	10,219	12,629	18,028
Total	12,484	15,227	20,577

* National valuation.

Source: IMF, *International Financial Statistics*.

MONEY SUPPLY (C $ '000 million at 31 December)

	1994	1995	1996
Currency outside banks	27.30	27.99	28.78
Demand deposits at chartered banks	97.65	109.69	126.88
Total money (incl. others)	125.13	137.87	155.83

Source: IMF, *International Financial Statistics*.

COST OF LIVING (Consumer Price Index; base: 1986 = 100)

	1993	1994	1995
Food	122.8	123.3	126.3
Housing	132.0	132.5	134.0
Household expenses and furnishings	119.0	119.3	121.6
Clothing	130.8	131.8	131.8
Transport	125.7	131.3	138.1
Health and personal care	134.8	136.1	135.9
Recreation, education and reading	133.7	137.6	142.9
Tobacco and alcohol	171.7	125.9	143.5
All items	130.4	130.7	133.5

1996 (base: 1995 = 100): All items 101.6 (Source: IMF, *International Financial Statistics*).

NATIONAL ACCOUNTS

National Income and Product (C $ million at current prices)

	1993	1994	1995*
Compensation of employees	398,163	409,085	422,110
Operating surplus	128,521	143,317	154,216
Domestic factor incomes	526,684	552,402	576,326
Consumption of fixed capital	87,904	92,925	96,234
Gross domestic product at factor cost	614,588	645,327	672,560
Indirect taxes, *less* subsidies	88,731	92,492	95,113
Statistical discrepancy	2,668	2,310	906
GDP at market prices	705,987	740,129	768,580
Factor income from abroad†	10,624	11,516	14,613
Less Factor income paid abroad†	34,615	38,615	41,070
Gross national product	681,996	713,030	742,123
Less Consumption of fixed capital	87,904	92,925	96,234
Statistical discrepancy	−2,668	−2,310	−906
National income at market prices	591,424	617,795	644,983
Other current transfers from abroad‡	2,944	3,081	3,184
Less Other current transfers paid abroad‡	3,836	3,563	3,698
National disposable income	590,532	617,313	644,469

* Preliminary.

† Remitted profits, dividends and interest only.

‡ Transfers to and from persons and governments.

Expenditure on the Gross Domestic Product
(C $ '000 million at current prices)

	1994	1995	1996*
Government final consumption expenditure	150.6	150.8	148.6
Private final consumption expenditure	452.4	466.0	483.0
Increase in stocks	4.0	7.0	1.2
Gross fixed capital formation	138.1	134.3	140.0
Exports of goods and services	250.9	290.3	306.5
Less Imports of goods and services	246.5	271.3	281.4
Statistical discrepancy	−2.3	−0.9	—
GDP at market prices	747.3	776.3	797.8
GDP at constant 1990 prices	704.9	721.3	731.9

* Preliminary.

Source: IMF, *International Financial Statistics*.

Gross Domestic Product by Economic Activity
(C $ million at constant 1986 prices)

	1991	1992	1993
Agriculture, hunting, forestry and fishing	14,317	13,596	14,518
Mining and quarrying	19,936	20,294	21,691
Manufacturing	86,483	87,092	91,434
Electricity, gas and water	15,885	16,073	16,353
Construction	29,864	27,337	26,034
Trade, restaurants and hotels	67,855	70,574	73,569
Transport, storage and communications	37,418	37,972	39,145
Finance, insurance, real estate and business services*	101,244	102,474	105,109
Government services	77,364	78,001	77,918
Other community, social and personal services	30,580	30,613	31,247
Other services	13,586	13,764	13,931
Sub-total	494,532	497,791	510,947
Less Imputed bank service charge	5,774	5,571	5,423
GDP at factor cost	488,758	492,220	505,524

* Including imputed rents of owner-occupied dwellings.
Source: UN, *National Accounts Statistics*.

BALANCE OF PAYMENTS (US $ million)

	1994	1995	1996
Exports of goods f.o.b.	166,788	193,085	205,799
Imports of goods f.o.b.	–152,682	–168,443	–175,737
Trade balance	14,106	24,643	30,062
Exports of services	23,838	26,212	28,512
Imports of services	–32,519	–33,767	–35,772
Balance on goods and services	5,426	17,088	22,802
Other income received	14,976	18,913	19,108
Other income paid	–34,883	–41,293	–39,420
Balance on goods, services and income	–14,481	–5,292	2,490
Current transfers received	2,619	2,781	3,290
Current transfers paid	–2,863	–2,794	–2,972
Current balance	14,725	5,305	2,808
Capital account (net)	7,500	4,953	5,919
Direct investment abroad	–9,127	–11,173	–8,515
Direct investment from abroad	8,476	10,824	6,398
Portfolio investment assets	–6,521	–5,228	–13,551
Portfolio investment liabilities	17,140	17,185	14,709
Other investment assets	–20,531	–8,121	–22,647
Other investment liabilities	16,339	–3,288	18,112
Net errors and omissions	1,057	2,862	2,265
Overall balance	–392	2,710	5,498

Source: IMF, *International Financial Statistics*.

External Trade

PRINCIPAL COMMODITIES (C $ million)

Imports f.o.b.	1994	1995	1996
Agricultural and fishing products	12,576	13,370	14,129
Fruits and vegetables	3,642	3,897	4,006
Other agricultural and fishing products	8,934	9,473	10,123
Energy products	7,146	8,122	10,160
Crude petroleum	4,796	5,719	7,269
Forestry products	1,810	2,038	1,912
Industrial goods and materials	38,734	44,981	45,852
Metal and metal products	9,621	11,489	11,105
Chemicals and plastics	13,734	16,341	17,377
Organic chemicals	3,320	4,002	4,234
Plastic materials	4,519	5,648	6,133
Other chemicals and related products	5,895	6,690	7,010
Other industrial goods and materials	15,379	17,151	17,371
Metal fabricated basic products	4,846	5,323	5,537
Machinery and equipment	65,575	75,623	76,589
Industrial and agricultural machinery	17,931	20,524	19,980
Aircraft and other transportation equipment	5,671	7,538	8,208
Aircraft engines and parts	2,842	3,981	4,921
Office machines and equipment	11,410	12,858	13,373
Other machinery and equipment	30,562	34,703	35,028
Communications and related equipment	n.a.	15,698	15,600
Other equipment and tools	n.a.	19,005	19,428
Automotive products	43,318	50,502	51,465
Passenger automobiles and chassis	13,786	13,256	13,877
Trucks and other motor vehicles	6,231	6,888	7,193
Motor vehicle parts	28,302	30,358	30,395
Other consumer goods	23,519	25,571	25,836
Apparel and footwear	4,681	5,146	4,865
Apparel and accessories	n.a.	4,018	3,808
Miscellaneous consumer goods	18,839	20,425	20,971
Special transactions trade	4,881	5,488	6,994
Total	202,559	225,696	232,937

Exports f.o.b.	1994	1995	1996
Agricultural and fishing products	17,717	19,917	21,034
Energy products	21,312	23,562	27,560
Crude petroleum	7,426	9,755	11,043
Natural gas	6,428	5,649	6,799
Other energy products	7,458	8,157	9,718
Petroleum and coal products	4,008	4,659	6,280
Forestry products	31,161	39,253	36,066
Lumber and sawmill products	14,067	14,053	15,886
Lumber	n.a.	10,965	12,582
Wood pulp and other wood products	6,711	10,936	6,915
Newsprint paper	6,950	9,479	8,836
Other paper and paperboard	3,434	4,785	4,429
Industrial goods and materials	39,549	48,371	49,468
Metal ores	3,693	5,108	5,127
Chemicals, plastics and fertilizers	11,553	14,835	15,019
Synthetic rubber and plastics	3,825	5,417	5,706
Metals and alloys	15,895	18,257	18,374
Aluminium (incl. alloys)	4,726	5,802	5,293
Other industrial goods and materials	8,319	10,172	10,948
Machinery and equipment	43,021	52,297	57,425
Industrial and agricultural machinery	9,765	11,796	12,160
Industrial machinery	8,684	10,503	10,799
Aircraft and other transportation equipment	7,930	9,800	11,527
Aircraft, engines and parts	4,521	5,925	7,161
Other machinery and equipment	25,326	30,700	33,738
Television and telecommunication equipment	6,974	8,517	10,451
Office machines and equipment	6,483	8,344	7,426
Other equipment and tools	8,205	9,227	10,679
Other end products (inedible)	3,664	4,612	5,182
Automotive products	57,919	63,270	63,874
Passenger automobiles and chassis	31,367	35,689	35,577
Trucks and other motor vehicles	12,270	12,818	12,358
Motor vehicle parts	14,282	14,764	15,938
Other consumer goods	5,851	7,111	8,212
Special transactions trade	9,422	10,426	11,217
Total	225,862	264,207	274,855

PRINCIPAL TRADING PARTNERS (C $ million)

Imports f.o.b.	1994	1995	1996
China, People's Repub.	3,853	4,639	4,925
France	2,579	3,122	3,339
Germany	4,385	4,800	4,820
Italy	2,585	3,271	2,718
Japan	11,343	12,096	10,439
Korea, Repub.	2,504	3,204	2,727
Mexico	4,464	5,351	6,012
Norway	1,661	2,314	2,777
Taiwan	2,780	2,791	2,863
United Kingdom	4,491	5,475	5,908
USA	136,624	150,754	157,344
Total (incl. others)	202,020	225,628	232,937

Exports f.o.b.	1994	1995	1996
China, People's Repub.	2,292	3,292	2,706
Germany	2,278	3,166	3,149
Japan	9,652	11,900	10,377
Korea, Repub.	2,191	2,697	2,676
United Kingdom	3,269	3,758	3,808
USA	185,217	196,491	210,071
Total (incl. others)	226,607	248,440	258,418

Transport

RAILWAYS (revenue traffic)*

	1993	1994	1995
Passenger-km (million)	1,357	1,385	1,430
Freight ton-km (million)	250,303	279,510	271,032

* Seven major rail carriers only.

ROAD TRAFFIC ('000 vehicles registered at 31 December)

	1993	1994	1995
Passenger cars (incl. taxis and for car hire)	13,477	13,639	13,182
Trucks and truck tractors (commercial and non-commercial)	3,647	3,697	3,420
Buses (school and other)	64	65	64
Motorcycles	308	305	297
Other (ambulances, fire trucks, etc.)	61	62	60

INLAND WATER TRAFFIC (St Lawrence Seaway, '000 metric tons)

	1993	1994	1995
Montréal—Lake Ontario	31,970	38,422	38,684
Welland Canal	31,815	39,703	39,376

Source: St Lawrence Seaway Authority.

SHIPPING

Merchant Fleet (registered at 31 December)

	1994	1995	1996
Number of vessels	896	886	872
Total displacement ('000 grt)	2,489.5	2,401.0	2,406.2

Source: Lloyd's Register of Shipping, *World Fleet Statistics*.

International Sea-borne Freight Traffic

	1993	1994	1995*
Goods ('000 metric tons)			
Loaded	152,556	170,079	176,667
Unloaded	71,585	76,942	83,287
Vessels (number)			
Arrived	26,213	28,783	28,510
Departed	26,030	28,812	28,145

* Preliminary.

CIVIL AVIATION (Canadian carriers—revenue traffic, '000)*

	1993	1994	1995
Passengers	31,483	32,477	35,043
Passenger-km	60,752,162	65,634,307	72,129,440
Goods ton-km	1,646,108	1,790,842	2,022,594

* Unit toll services.

Tourism

	1994	1995	1996
Travellers from the USA:			
Number ('000)	12,542	13,005	12,909
Expenditure (C $ million)	4,396	4,799	5,150
Travellers from other countries:			
Number ('000)	3,429	3,927	4,377
Expenditure (C $ million)	3,346	4,038	4,520

Communications Media

('000)

	1993	1994	1995
Total households	10,247	10,387	11,243
Homes with radio	10,134	10,270	11,119
Homes with television	10,147	10,286	11,143
Homes with telephone	10,141	10,284	11,077

Daily newspapers in French and English 105 (1996); total circulation 5,200,000.

Education

(1996/97)

	Institutions	Teachers*	Pupils*
Primary and secondary	16,096	306,498	4,969,317
Post-secondary colleges	198	n.a.	388,976
Universities	78	36,035	572,179

* Full-time only.

Directory

The Constitution

Under the Constitution Act 1982, which entered into force on 17 April 1982, executive authority is vested in the Sovereign, and exercised in her name by a Governor-General and Privy Council. Legislative power is exercised by a Parliament of two Houses, the Senate and the House of Commons. The Constitution includes a Charter of Rights and Freedoms, and provisions which recognize the nation's multicultural heritage, affirm the existing rights of native peoples, confirm the principle of equalization of benefits among the provinces and strengthen provincial ownership of natural resources.

THE GOVERNMENT

The national government operates through three main agencies: Parliament (consisting of the Sovereign as represented by the Governor-General, the Senate and the House of Commons), which makes the laws; the Executive (the Cabinet or Ministry), which applies the laws; and the Judiciary, which interprets the laws.

The Prime Minister is appointed by the Governor-General and is habitually the leader of the political party commanding the confidence of the House of Commons. He chooses the members of his Cabinet from members of his party in Parliament, principally from those in the House of Commons. Each Minister or member of the Cabinet is usually responsible for the administration of a department, although there may be Ministers without portfolio whose experience and counsel are drawn upon to strengthen the Cabinet, but who are not at the head of departments. Each Minister of a department is responsible to Parliament for that department, and the Cabinet is collectively responsible before Parliament for government policy and administration generally.

Meetings of the Cabinet are presided over by the Prime Minister. From the Cabinet signed orders and recommendations go to the Governor-General for his or her approval, and the Crown acts only on the advice of its responsible Ministers. The Cabinet takes the responsibility for its advice being in accordance with the support of Parliament and is held strictly accountable.

THE FEDERAL PARLIAMENT

Parliament must meet at least once a year, so that 12 months do not elapse between the last meeting in one session and the first meeting in the next. The duration of Parliament may not be longer than five years from the date of election of a House of Commons. Senators (normally a maximum of 104 in number) are appointed until age 75 by the Governor-General in Council. They must be at least 30 years of age, residents of the province they represent and in possession of C $4,000 of real property over and above their liabilities. Members of the House of Commons are elected by universal adult suffrage for the duration of a Parliament.

Under the Constitution, the Federal Parliament has exclusive legislative authority in all matters relating to public debt and property; regulation of trade and commerce; raising of money by any mode of taxation; borrowing of money on the public credit; postal service, census and statistics; militia, military and naval service and defence; fixing and providing for salaries and allowances of the officers of the Government; beacons, buoys and lighthouses; navigation and shipping; quarantine and the establishment and maintenance of marine hospitals; sea-coast and inland fisheries; ferries on an international or interprovincial frontier; currency and coinage; banking, incorporation of banks, and issue of paper money; savings banks; weights and measures; bills of exchange and promissory notes; interest; legal tender; bankruptcy and insolvency; patents of invention and discovery; copyrights; Indians and lands reserved for Indians; naturalization and aliens; marriage and divorce; the criminal law, except the constitution of courts of criminal jurisdiction but including the procedure in criminal matters; the establishment, maintenance and management of penitentiaries; such classes of subjects as are expressly excepted in the enumeration of the classes of subjects exclusively assigned to the Legislatures of the provinces by the Act. Judicial interpretation and later amendment have, in certain cases, modified or clearly defined the respective powers of the Federal Government and provincial governments.

Both the Parliament of Canada and the legislatures of the provinces may legislate with respect to agriculture and immigration, but provincial legislation shall have effect in and for the provinces as long and as far only as it is not repugnant to any Act of Parliament. Both Parliament and the provincial legislatures may legislate with respect to old age pensions and supplementary benefits, but no federal law shall affect the operation of any present or future law of a province in relation to these matters.

PROVINCIAL AND MUNICIPAL GOVERNMENT

In each of the 10 provinces the Sovereign is represented by a Lieutenant-Governor, appointed by the Governor-General in Council, and acting on the advice of the Ministry or Executive Council, which is responsible to the Legislature and resigns office when it ceases to enjoy the confidence of that body. The Legislatures are unicameral, consisting of an elected Legislative Assembly and the Lieutenant-Governor. The duration of a Legislature may not exceed five years from the date of the election of its members.

The Legislature in each province may exclusively make laws in relation to: amendment of the constitution of the province, except as regards the Lieutenant-Governor; direct taxation within the province; borrowing of money on the credit of the province; establishment and tenure of provincial offices and appointment and payment of provincial officers; the management and sale of public lands belonging to the province and of the timber and wood thereon; the establishment, maintenance and management of public and reformatory prisons in and for the province; the establishment, maintenance and management of hospitals, asylums, charities and charitable institutions in and for the province other than marine hospitals; municipal institutions in the province; shop, saloon, tavern, auctioneer and other licences issued for the raising of provincial or municipal revenue; local works and undertakings other than interprovincial or international lines of ships, railways, canals, telegraphs, etc., or works which, though wholly situtated within the province are declared by the Federal Parliament to be for the general advantage either of Canada or two or more provinces; the incorporation of companies with provincial objects; the solemnization of marriage in the province; property and civil rights in the province; the administration of justice in the province, including the constitution, maintenance and organization of provincial courts both in civil and criminal jurisdiction, and including procedure in civil matters in these courts; the imposition of punishment by fine, penalty or imprisonment for enforcing any law of the province relating to any of the aforesaid subjects; generally all matters of a merely local or private nature in the province. Further, provincial Legislatures may exclusively make laws in relation to education, subject to the protection of religious minorities; and to non-renewable natural resources, forestry resources and electrical energy, including their export from one province to another, and to the right to impose any mode or system of taxation thereon, subject in both cases to such laws not being discriminatory.

Under the Constitution Act, the municipalities are the creations of the provincial governments. Their bases of organization and the extent of their authority vary in different provinces, but almost everywhere they have very considerable powers of local self-government.

The Government

Head of State: HM Queen ELIZABETH II (succeeded to the throne 6 February 1952).

Governor-General: ROMÉO A. LEBLANC (took office 22 November 1995).

FEDERAL MINISTRY
(January 1998)

Prime Minister: JEAN CHRÉTIEN.

Deputy Prime Minister: HERBERT GRAY.

Minister of Foreign Affairs: LLOYD AXWORTHY.

Minister of Transport: DAVID COLLENETTE.

Minister of Fisheries and Oceans: DAVID ANDERSON.

Minister of Natural Resources and Minister responsible for the Canadian Wheat Board: RALPH GOODALE.

Minister of Canadian Heritage: SHEILA COPPS.

Minister for International Trade: SERGIO MARCHI.

Minister of Industry: JOHN MANLEY.

Minister for International Co-operation and Minister responsible for Francophonie: DIANE MARLEAU.

Minister of Finance: PAUL MARTIN.

Minister of National Defence: ARTHUR EGGLETON.

President of the Treasury Board and Minister responsible for Infrastructure: MARCEL MASSÉ.

Minister of Justice and Attorney-General: ANNE MCLELLAN.

Minister of Health: ALLAN ROCK.

Minister of Labour: LAWRENCE MACAULAY.

Minister of the Environment: CHRISTINE STEWART.

Minister of Public Works and Government Services: ALFONSO GAGLIANO.

Minister of Citizenship and Immigration: LUCIENNE ROBILLARD.

Minister for Veterans Affairs and Secretary of State (Atlantic Canada Opportunities Agency): FRED MIFFLIN.

Minister of Indian Affairs and Northern Development: JANE STEWART.

President of the Queen's Privy Council for Canada and Minister of Intergovernmental Affairs: STÉPHANE DION.

Minister of Human Resources Development: PIERRE PETTIGREW.

Leader of the Government in the House of Commons: DON BOUDRIA.

Leader of the Government in the Senate: BERNARD GRAHAM.

Minister of Agriculture and Agri-Food: LYLE VANCLIEF.

Minister of National Revenue: HERB DHALIWAL.

Solicitor General: ANDY SCOTT.

Secretary of State (Children and Youth): ETHEL BLONDIN-ANDREW.

Secretary of State (Asia–Pacific): RAYMOND CHAN.

Secretary of State (Federal Office of Regional Development–Québec): MARTIN CAUCHON.

Secretary of State (Multiculturalism and Status of Women): HEDY FRY.

Secretary of State (Latin America and Africa): DAVID KILGOUR.

Secretary of State (International Financial Institutions): JAMES PETERSON.

Secretary of State (Science, Research and Development, and Western Economic Diversification): RONALD DUHAMEL.

Secretary of State (Parks): ANDREW MITCHELL.

MINISTRIES

Office of the Prime Minister: Langevin Block, 80 Wellington St, Ottawa, ON K1A 0A3; tel. (613) 992-4211; fax (613) 941-6900.

Agriculture and Agri-Food Canada: Sir John Carling Bldg, 930 Carling Ave, Ottawa, ON K1A 0C7; tel. (613) 759-1000; fax (613) 759-7977.

Canadian Heritage: Jules Léger Bldg, 25 rue Eddy, Hull, PQ K1A 1K5; tel. (819) 997-0055; fax (819) 953-5382.

Citizenship and Immigration Canada: Journal Tower South, 365 ave Laurier ouest, Hull, PQ K1A 1L1; tel. (613) 954-9019; fax (613) 954-2221.

Environment Canada: Ottawa, ON K1A 0H3; tel. (819) 997-2800; fax (819) 953-2225; e-mail envirinfo@ec.gc.ca.

Finance Canada: L'Esplanade Laurier, 140 O'Connor St, Ottawa, ON K1A 0G5; tel. (613) 992-1573; fax (613) 996-8404.

Fisheries and Oceans Canada: 200 Kent St, Ottawa, ON K1A 0E6; tel. (613) 993-0999; fax (613) 990-1866; e-mail info@www.ncr.dfo.ca.

Foreign Affairs and International Trade Canada: Lester B. Pearson Bldg, 125 Sussex Drive, Ottawa, ON K1A 0G2; tel. (613) 996-9134; fax (613) 952-3904.

Health Canada: Brooke Claxton Bldg, Tunney's Pasture, Ottawa, ON K1A 0K9; tel. (613) 957-2991; fax (613) 941-5366.

Human Resources Development Canada: 140 promenade du Portage, Hull, PQ K1A 0J9; tel. (819) 994-6013; fax (819) 953-3981.

Indian and Northern Affairs Canada: Les Terrasses de la Chaudière, Bureau 1400, 10 rue Wellington, Hull, PQ K1A 0H4; tel. (819) 997-0811; fax (819) 953-5491; e-mail infopubs@inac.gc.ca.

Industry Canada: C. D. Howe Bldg, 235 Queen St, Ottawa, ON K1A 0H5; tel. (613) 954-2788; fax (613) 954-2303.

Justice Canada: Justice Bldg, 239 Wellington St, Ottawa, ON K1A 0H8; tel. (613) 957-4222; fax (613) 954-0811.

National Defence (Canada): Maj.-Gen. George R. Pearkes Bldg, 101 Colonel By Drive, Ottawa, ON K1A 0K2; tel. (613) 992-4581; fax (613) 992-4241.

Natural Resources Canada: 580 Booth St, Ottawa, ON K1A 0E4; tel. (613) 995-0947; fax (613) 996-9094.

Public Works and Government Services Canada: place du Portage, rue Laurier, Hull, PQ K1A 0S5; tel. (819) 956-3115.

Revenue Canada: Ottawa, ON K1A 0L9; tel. (613) 957-0259; fax (613) 954-5456.

Solicitor-General Canada: Ottawa, ON K1A 0P8; tel. (613) 991-2800; fax (613) 993-7062.

Transport Canada: Transport Canada Bldg, 330 Sparks St, Ottawa, ON K1A 0N5; tel. (613) 990-2309; fax (613) 995-0351.

Treasury Board: East Tower, L'Esplanade Laurier, 140 O'Connor St, Ottawa, ON K1A 0R5; tel. (613) 957-2400; fax (613) 996-2690.

Veterans Affairs Canada: 161 Grafton St, POB 7700, Charlottetown, PE C1A 8M9; tel. (902) 566-8988; fax (902) 566-8508.

Western Economic Diversification Canada: Canada Place, 9700 Jasper Ave, Suite 1500, Edmonton, AB T5J 4H7; tel. (403) 495-4164; fax (403) 495-6876.

Federal Legislature

THE SENATE

Speaker: GILDAS MOLGAT.

Seats at September 1997

Liberal	52
Progressive Conservative	48
Independent	3
Vacant	1
Total	104

HOUSE OF COMMONS

Speaker: GILBERT PARENT.

General Election, 2 June 1997

	% of votes at election	Seats at election	Seats at Sept. 1997
Liberal	38.4	155	154
Reform Party	19.4	60	61
Bloc Québécois	10.7	44	44
New Democratic Party	18.9	21	21
Progressive Conservative	11.0	20	20
Others	1.6	1	1
Total	100.0	301	301

Provincial Legislatures

ALBERTA

Lieutenant-Governor: H. A. (BUD) OLSON.

Premier: RALPH KLEIN.

Election, March 1997

	Seats at election	Seats at Oct. 1997
Progressive Conservative	63	63
Liberal	18	18
New Democratic Party	2	2
Total	83	83

BRITISH COLUMBIA

Lieutenant-Governor: GARDE B. GARDOM.

Premier: GLEN CLARK.

Election, May 1996

	Seats at election	Seats at Nov. 1997
New Democratic Party	39	39
Liberal	33	34
Reform Party	2	—
Progressive Democratic Alliance	1	1
Independent	—	1
Total	75	75

MANITOBA

Lieutenant-Governor: YVON DUMONT.

Premier: GARY FILMON.

Election, April 1995

	Seats at election	Seats at Nov. 1997
Progressive Conservative	31	31
New Democratic Party	23	23
Liberal	1	1
Independent	2	2
Total	57	57

NEW BRUNSWICK

Lieutenant-Governor: MARILYN TRENHOLME COUNSELL.

Premier: J. RAYMOND FRENETTE.

Election, September 1995

	Seats at election	Seats at Oct. 1997
Liberal	48	46
Progressive Conservative	6	6
New Democratic Party	1	1
Vacant	—	2
Total	55	55

NEWFOUNDLAND AND LABRADOR

Lieutenant-Governor: DR A. M. (MAX) HOUSE.

Premier: BRIAN TOBIN.

Election, February 1996

	Seats at election	Seats at Nov. 1997
Liberal	37	36
Progressive Conservative	9	10
New Democratic Party	1	1
Independent	1	1
Total	48	48

NOVA SCOTIA

Lieutenant-Governor: J. JAMES KINLEY.

Premier: JOHN SAVAGE.

Election, May 1993

	Seats at election	Seats at Nov. 1997
Liberal	40	39
Progressive Conservative	9	9
New Democratic Party	3	4
Total	52	52

ONTARIO

Lieutenant-Governor: HILARY WESTON.

Premier: MICHAEL D. HARRIS.

Election, June 1995

	Seats at election	Seats at Nov. 1997
Progressive Conservative	82	82
Liberal	30	31
New Democratic Party	17	16
Independent	1	1
Total	130	130

PRINCE EDWARD ISLAND

Lieutenant-Governor: GILBERT R. CLEMENTS.

Premier: PAT BINNS.

Election, November 1996

	Seats at election	Seats at Dec. 1997
Progressive Conservative	18	18
Liberal	8	8
New Democratic Party	1	1
Total	27	27

QUÉBEC

Lieutenant-Governor: LISE THIBAULT.

Premier: LUCIEN BOUCHARD.

Election, September 1994

	Seats at election	Seats at Oct. 1997
Parti Québécois	77	75
Liberal	47	47
Action Démocratique de Québec	1	1
Independent	—	2
Total	125	125

SASKATCHEWAN

Lieutenant-Governor: JOHN E. WIEBE.

Premier: ROY ROMANOW.

Election, June 1995

	Seats at election	Seats at Dec. 1997
New Democratic Party	42	41
Saskatchewan Party	—	8
Liberal	11	6
Progressive Conservative	5	—
Independent	—	3
Total	58	58

Territorial Legislatures

NORTHWEST TERRITORIES

Commissioner: HELEN MAKSAGAK.

Government Leader and Minister of the Executive Department: DON MORIN.

The Legislative Assembly, elected in October 1995, consists of 24 independent members without formal party affiliation.

YUKON TERRITORY

Commissioner: JUDY GINGELL.

Government Leader and Minister of the Executive Council Office: PIERS MCDONALD.

Election, September 1996

	Seats at election	Seats at Oct. 1997
New Democratic Party	11	11
Yukon Party	3	3
Liberal	3	3
Total	17	17

Political Organizations

Action Démocratique de Québec: c/o Assemblée Nationale, Hôtel du Parlement, Québec, PQ G1A 1A4; provincial nationalist; Leader MARIO DUMONT.

Bloc Québécois: 425 rue de Maisonneuve ouest, Bureau 1475, Montréal, PQ H3A 3G5; tel. (514) 499-3000; fax (514) 499-3638; f. 1990 by group of seven Progressive Conservative MPs representing Québec constituencies in fed. parl.; subsequently attracted Liberal support; main opposition party in House of Commons between 1993–97; seeks negotiated sovereignty for Québec; Leader GILLES DUCEPPE; Dir-Gen. YVES DUFOUR.

British Columbia Social Credit Party: 10700 Cambie Rd, Suite 424, Richmond, BC V6Y 3V3; tel. (604) 270-4040; fax (604) 270-4726; conservative; governing party of British Columbia between 1952–72 and 1975–91; Pres. JANE SORKO; 40,000 mems (1996).

Communist Party of Canada (Marxist-Leninist): 171 Dalhousie St, Ottawa, ON K1N 7C7; tel. (613) 241-7052; e-mail cpc-ml@fox.nstn.ca; f. 1970; Nat. Leader (vacant).

COR (Confederation of Regions) Party of New Brunswick: 172 Main St, York Plaza, Fredericton, NB E3A 1C8; tel. (506) 444-4040; fax (506) 444-4053; e-mail cor@nbnet.nb.ca; f. 1989 to promote populist democratic principles; opposes legislation and govt subsidies relating to linguistic and cultural matters; Leader GREG HARGROVE.

Green Party of Canada: POB 397, London, ON N6A 4W1; tel. (519) and fax 474-3294; f. 1983; environmentalist; Leader JOAN RUSSOW.

Liberal Party of Canada: 200 Laurier Ave West, Suite 200, Ottawa, ON K1P 6M8; tel. (613) 237-0740; fax (613) 235-7208; e-mail info@liberal.ca; supports Canadian autonomy, comprehensive social security, economic growth and a balanced economy; Leader JEAN CHRÉTIEN; Pres. DAN HAYS; Nat. Dir GEORGE YOUNG.

New Democratic Party: 81 Metcalfe St, Suite 900, Ottawa, ON K1P 6K7; tel. (613) 236-3613; fax (613) 230-9950; e-mail ndpadmin@fed.ndp.ca; f. 1961; social democratic; Leader ALEXA MCDONOUGH; Pres. ED TCHORZEWSKI; Sec. JILL MARZETTI; 100,000 mems. (1996).

Parti Québécois: 1200 ave Papineau, Bureau 150, Montréal, PQ H2K 4R5; tel. (514) 526-0200; fax (514) 526-0272; e-mail pqnatio@cam.org; f. 1968; social democratic; seeks political sovereignty for Québec; governing party of Québec between 1976–85 and since Sept. 1994; Pres. LUCIEN BOUCHARD; 160,000 mems (1994).

Progressive Conservative Party of Canada: 275 Slater St, Suite 501, Ottawa, ON K1P 5H9; tel. (613) 238-6111; fax (613) 238-7429; e-mail pcinfo@pcparty.ca; f. 1854; advocates individualism and free enterprise; Leader JEAN CHAREST; Pres. PIERRE W. FORTIER; Nat. Dir MICHAEL ALLEN.

Reform Party of Canada: 833 4th Ave, SW, Suite 600, Calgary, AB T2P 0K5; tel. (403) 269-1990; fax (403) 269-4077; e-mail info@reform.ca; f. 1987; supports decentralization of fed. govt, with provincial jurisdiction over language and culture; advocates fiscal reform; became main opposition party in House of Commons following fed. elections in June 1997; Leader PRESTON MANNING; Exec. Dir GLEN MCMURRAY; 97,000 mems (1997).

Diplomatic Representation

EMBASSIES AND HIGH COMMISSIONS IN CANADA

Algeria: 435 Daly Ave, Ottawa, ON K1N 6H3; tel. (613) 789-8505; telex 053-3625; fax (613) 789-1406; Ambassador: ABDESSELAIM BEDRANE.

Antigua and Barbuda, Dominica, Grenada, Montserrat, Saint Christopher and Nevis, Saint Lucia and Saint Vincent and the Grenadines: Place de Ville, Tower B, 112 Kent St, Suite 1610, Ottawa, ON K1P 5P2; tel. (613) 236-8952; fax (613) 236-3042; e-mail echcc@travel-net.com; High Commissioner: GEORGE R. E. BULLEN.

Argentina: 90 Sparks St, Suite 910, Ottawa, ON K1P 5B4; tel. (613) 236-2351; fax (613) 235-2659; Ambassador: LILLIAN O'CONNELL DE ALURRALDE.

Australia: 50 O'Connor St, Suite 710, Ottawa, ON K1P 6L2; tel. (613) 236-0841; telex 053-3391; fax (613) 236-4376; High Commissioner: F.C. MURRAY.

Austria: 445 Wilbrod St, Ottawa, ON K1N 6M7; tel. (613) 789-1444; fax (613) 789-3431; Ambassador: Dr WALTHER LICHEM.

Bahamas: 50 O'Connor St, Suite 1313, Ottawa, ON K1P 6L2; tel. (613) 232-1724; fax (613) 232-0097; e-mail bahighco@sonetis.com; High Commissioner: A. MISSOURI SHERMAN-PETER.

Bangladesh: 275 Bank St, Suite 302, Ottawa, ON K2P 2L6; tel. (613) 236-0138; fax (613) 567-3213; e-mail bdootcanda@iosphere.net; High Commissioner: ANWAR-UL-ALAM (acting).

Barbados: 130 Albert St, Suite 302, Ottawa, ON K1P 5G4; tel. (613) 236-9517; fax (613) 230-4362; e-mail barhcott@travel-net.com; High Commissioner: JUNE Y. CLARKE.

Belgium: 80 Elgin St, 4th Floor, Ottawa, ON K1P 1B7; tel. (613) 236-7267; telex 053-3568; fax (613) 236-7882; Ambassador: CHRISTIAN FELLENS.

Benin: 58 Glebe Ave, Ottawa, ON K1S 2C3; tel. (613) 233-4429; fax (613) 233-8952; Ambassador: Mme VÉRONIQUE AHOYO.

Bolivia: 130 Albert St, Suite 504, Ottawa, ON K1P 5G4; tel. (613) 236-5730; fax (613) 236-8237; Chargé d'affaires a.i.: Sra MYRIAM PAZ CERRUTO.

Brazil: 450 Wilbrod St, Ottawa, ON K1N 6M8; tel. (613) 237-1090; telex 053-3176; fax (613) 237-6144; Ambassador: CARLOS AUGUSTO R. SANTOS NEVES.

Brunei: 395 Laurier Ave East, Ottawa, ON K1N 6R4; tel. (603) 234-5656; fax (603) 234-4397; High Commissioner: Pengiran ABDUL MOMIN.

Bulgaria: 325 Stewart St, Ottawa, ON K1N 6K5; tel. (613) 789-3215; fax (613) 789-3524; Ambassador: SLAV DANEV.

Burkina Faso: 48 Range Rd, Ottawa, ON K1N 8J4; tel. (613) 238-4796; fax (613) 238-3812; Ambassador: MOUHOUSSINE NACRO.

Burundi: 50 Kaymar St, Rothwell Heights, Gloucester, ON K1J 7C7; tel. (613) 741-8828; fax (613) 741-2424; Ambassador: FRÉDÉRIC NDAYEGAMIYE.

Cameroon: 170 Clemow Ave, Ottawa, ON K1S 2B4; tel. (613) 236-1522; fax (613) 238-3885; High Commissioner: PHILÉMON Y. YANG.

Chile: 151 Slater St, Suite 605, Ottawa, ON K1P 5H3; tel. (613) 235-4402; telex 053-3774; fax (613) 235-1176; Ambassador: FERNANDO URRUTIA.

China, People's Republic: 515 St Patrick St, Ottawa, ON K1N 5H3; tel. (613) 789-3434; fax (613) 789-1911; Ambassador: ZHANG YIJUN.

Colombia: 360 Albert St, Suite 1002, Ottawa, ON K1R 7X7; tel. (613) 230-3760; fax (613) 230-4416; Ambassador: ALFONSO LÓPEZ CABALLERO.

Congo, Democratic Republic: 18 Range Rd, Ottawa, ON K1N 8J3; tel. (613) 236-7103; fax (613) 567-1404; Ambassador: KAWETA MILOMBE SAMPASSA.

Costa Rica: 135 York St, Suite 208, Ottawa, ON K1N 5T4; tel. (613) 562-2855; fax (613) 562-2582; Ambassador: CARLOS MIRANDA.

Côte d'Ivoire: 9 Marlborough Ave, Ottawa, ON K1N 8E6; tel. (613) 236-9919; fax (613) 563-8287; Ambassador: JULIEN KACOU.

Croatia: 130 Albert St, Suite 1700, Ottawa, ON K1P 5G4; tel. (613) 230-7351; fax (613) 230-7388; Ambassador: ZELJKO URBAN.

Cuba: 388 Main St, Ottawa, ON K1S 1E3; tel. (613) 563-0141; fax (613) 563-0068; Ambassador: BIENVENIDO GARCÍA NEGRIN.

Czech Republic: 541 Sussex Drive, Ottawa, ON K1N 6Z6; tel. (613) 562-3875; fax (613) 562-3878; Ambassador: STANISLAV CHÝLEK.

Denmark: 47 Clarence St, Suite 450, Ottawa, ON K1N 9K1; tel. (613) 562-1811; fax (613) 562-1812; Ambassador: JØRGEN M. BEHNKE.

Ecuador: 50 O'Connor St, Suite 1311, Ottawa, ON K1N 6L2; tel. (613) 563-8206; fax (613) 235-5776; e-mail mecucan@inasec.ca; Ambassador: ALFREDO CRESPO CORDERO.

Egypt: 454 Laurier Ave East, Ottawa, ON K1N 6R3; tel. (613) 234-4931; fax (613) 234-9347; Ambassador: Dr MAHMOUD FARGHAL.

El Salvador: 209 Kent St, Ottawa, ON K2P 1Z8; tel. (613) 238-2939; fax (613) 238-6940; e-mail 103234.607@compuserve.com; Ambassador: Dr MAURICIO ROSALES R.

Ethiopia: 151 Slater St, Suite 210, Ottawa, ON K1P 5H3; tel. (613) 235-6637; fax (613) 235-4638; e-mail infoethi@magi.com; Ambassador: Dr FECADU GADAMU.

Finland: 55 Metcalfe St, Suite 850, Ottawa, ON K1P 6L5; tel. (613) 236-2389; fax (613) 238-1474; e-mail finamBott@synapse.net; Ambassador: VEIJO SAMPOVAARA.

France: 42 Sussex Drive, Ottawa, ON K1M 2C9; tel. (613) 789-1795; fax (613) 562-3704; e-mail presse@amba.ottawa.fr; Ambassador: LOÏC HENNEKINNE.

Gabon: 4 Range Rd, Ottawa, ON K1N 8J5; tel. (613) 232-5301; fax (613) 232-6916; Ambassador: ALPHONSE OYABI-GNALA.

Germany: 1 Waverley St, Ottawa, ON K2P 0T8; tel. (613) 232-1101; telex 053-4226; fax (613) 594-9330; e-mail bn555@frenet.carleton.ca; Ambassador: Dr HANS-GÜNTER SULIMMA.

Ghana: 1 Clemow Ave, Ottawa, ON K1S 2A9; tel. (613) 236-0871; fax (613) 236-0874; High Commissioner: ANNAN ARKYIN CATO.

Greece: 76–80 MacLaren St, Ottawa, ON K2P 0K6; tel. (613) 238-6271; fax (613) 238-5676; Ambassador: JOHN THOMOGLOU.

Guatemala: 130 Albert St, Suite 1010, Ottawa, ON K1P 5G4; tel. (613) 233-7237; fax (613) 233-0135; Ambassador: FRANCISCO VILLAGRAN DE LEÓN.

Guinea: 483 Wilbrod St, Ottawa, ON K1N 6N1; tel. (613) 789-8444; telex 053-4304; fax (613) 789-7560; Ambassador: THIERNO DIALLO.

Guyana: 151 Slater St, Suite 309, Ottawa, ON K1P 5H3; tel. (613) 235-7249; fax (613) 235-1447; High Commissioner: BRINDLEY H. BENN.

Haiti: Place de Ville, Tower B, 112 Kent St, Suite 205, Ottawa, ON K1P 5P2; tel. (613) 238-1628; fax (613) 238-2986; e-mail rohio@sympatico.ca; Ambassador: EMMANUEL AMBROISE.

Holy See: Apostolic Nunciature, 724 Manor Ave, Rockcliffe Park, Ottawa, ON K1M 0E3; tel. (613) 746-4914; fax (613) 746-4786; Nuncio: Most Rev. CARLO CURIS, Titular Archbishop of Medeli.

Honduras: 151 Slater St, Suite 908, Ottawa, ON K1P 5H3; tel. (613) 233-8900; fax (613) 232-0193; e-mail scastell@magmacom.com; Ambassador: SALOMÉ CASTELLANOS DELGADO.

Hungary: 299 Waverley St, Ottawa, ON K2P 0V9; tel. (613) 230-2717; fax (613) 230-7560; Chargé d'affaires a.i.: ISTVÁN TORZSA.

India: 10 Springfield Rd, Ottawa, ON K1M 1C9; tel. (613) 744-3751; telex 053-4172; fax (613) 744-0913; High Commissioner: PREM KUMAR BUDHWAR.

Indonesia: 55 Parkdale Ave, Ottawa, ON K1Y 1E5; tel. (613) 724-1100; fax (613) 724-1105; e-mail jupiter@prica.org; Ambassador: BUDIMAN DARMOSUTANTO.

Iran: 245 Metcalfe St, Ottawa, ON K2P 2K2; tel. (613) 235-4726; fax (613) 232-5712; e-mail iranemb@salamiran.org; Ambassador: Dr SEYED MOHAMMAD HOSSEIN.

Iraq: 215 McLeod St, Ottawa, ON K2P 0Z8; tel. (613) 236-9177; fax (613) 567-1101; Chargé d'affaires a.i.: HAITHAM TAUFIQ AL-NAJJAR.

Ireland: 130 Albert St, Suite 1105, Ottawa, ON K1P 5G4; tel. (613) 233-6281; fax (613) 233-5835; Ambassador: PAUL DEMPSEY.

Israel: 50 O'Connor St, Suite 1005, Ottawa, ON K1P 6L2; tel. (613) 567-6450; fax (613) 237-8865; Ambassador: DAVID SULTAN.

Italy: 275 Slater St, 21st Floor, Ottawa, ON K1P 5H9; tel. (613) 232-2401; fax (613) 233-1484; Ambassador: ANDREA NEGROTTO CAMBIASO.

Jamaica: 275 Slater St, Suite 800, Ottawa, ON K1P 5H9; tel. (613) 233-9311; fax (613) 233-0611; High Commissioner: MAXINE ROBERTS.

Japan: 255 Sussex Drive, Ottawa, ON K1N 9E6; tel. (613) 241-8541; fax (613) 241-7415; e-mail infocul@embjapan.can.org; Ambassador: TAKASHI TAJIMA.

Jordan: 100 Bronson Ave, Ottawa, ON K1R 6G8; tel. (613) 238-8090; fax (613) 232-3341; Ambassador: SAMIR KHALIFEH.

Kenya: 415 Laurier Ave East, Ottawa, ON K1N 6R4; tel. (613) 563-1773; fax (613) 233-6599; e-mail kenrep@intranet.ca; High Commissioner: HASSAN BAGHA.

Korea, Republic: 151 Slater St, 5th Floor, Ottawa, ON K1P 5H3; tel. (613) 232-1715; fax (613) 232-0928; Ambassador: KEE BOK SHIN.

Kuwait: 80 Elgin St, Ottawa, ON K1P 1C6; tel. (613) 780-9999; fax (613) 780-9905; Ambassador: ABDULMOHSIN YOUSEF AL-DUAIJ.

Latvia: Place de Ville, Tower B, 112 Kent St, Suite 208, Ottawa, ON K1P 5P2; tel. (613) 238-6868; fax (613) 238-7044; e-mail latvia-embassy@magmacom.com; Ambassador: Dr GEORGS ANDREJEVS.

Lebanon: 640 Lyon St, Ottawa, ON K1S 3Z5; tel. (613) 236-5825; fax (613) 232-1609; Ambassador: Dr ASSEM SALMAN JABER.

Lesotho: 202 Clemow Ave, Ottawa, ON K1S 2B4; tel. (613) 236-9449; fax (613) 238-3341; High Commissioner: Dr GWENDOLINE M. MALAHLEHA.

Madagascar: 649 Blair Rd, Gloucester, ON K1J 7M4; tel. (613) 744-7995; fax (613) 744-2530; Ambassador: RENÉ FIDÈLE RAJAONAH.

Malawi: 7 Clemow Ave, Ottawa, ON K1S 2A9; tel. (613) 236-8931; fax (613) 236-1054; High Commissioner: B. M. MSAKA.

Malaysia: 60 Boteler St, Ottawa, ON K1N 8Y7; tel. (613) 241-5182; telex 053-3520; fax (613) 241-5214; e-mail malott@istar.ca; High Commissioner: Dato' ABDULLAH ZAWAWI BIN Haji MOHAMED.

Mali: 50 Goulburn Ave, Ottawa, ON K1N 8C8; tel. (613) 232-1501; fax (613) 232-7429; Ambassador: DIAKITÉ MANASSA DANIOKO.

Mauritania: 249 McLeod St, Ottawa, ON KZP 1A1; tel. (613) 237-3283; fax (613) 237-3287; Ambassador: SIDI OULD MAJID KAMIL.

Mexico: 45 O'Connor St, Suite 1500, Ottawa, ON K1P 1A4; tel. (613) 233-8988; fax (613) 235-9123; Ambassador: SANDRA FUENTES-BERAIN.

Morocco: 38 Range Rd, Ottawa, ON K1N 8J4; tel. (613) 236-7391; fax (613) 236-6164; Ambassador: TAJEDDINE BADDOU.

Myanmar: 85 Range Rd, Suite 902, Ottawa, ON K1N 8J6; tel. (613) 232-6434; fax (613) 232-6435; Ambassador: Dr KYAW WIN UNG.

Netherlands: 350 Albert St, Suite 2020, Ottawa, ON K1R 1A4; tel. (613) 237-5030; fax (613) 237-6471; Ambassador: JOHANNES H. W. FIETELAARS.

New Zealand: Metropolitan House, 99 Bank St, Suite 727, Ottawa, ON K1P 6G3; tel. (613) 238-5991; fax (613) 238-5707; e-mail nzhcott@istar.ca; High Commissioner: JIM GERARD.

Nicaragua: 130 Albert St, Suite 407, Ottawa, ON K1P 5G4; tel. (613) 234-9361; fax (613) 238-7666; Chargé d'affaires a.i.: SUSAN GRIGSBY DE FONSECA.

Niger: 38 Blackburn Ave, Ottawa, ON K1N 8A2; tel. (613) 232-4291; fax (613) 230-9808; Ambassador: ABOUBACAR ABDOU.

Nigeria: 295 Metcalfe St, Ottawa, ON K2P 1R9; tel. (613) 236-0521; fax (613) 236-0529; High Commissioner: M. A. B. ADEYANJU (acting).

Norway: 90 Sparks St, Suite 532, Ottawa, ON K1P 5B4; tel. (613) 238-6571; fax (613) 238-2765; e-mail nor-emb-ott@intranet.ca; Ambassador: JOHAN L. LOVALD.

Pakistan: 151 Slater St, Suite 608, Ottawa, ON K1P 5H3; tel. (613) 238-7881; fax (613) 238-7296; e-mail hcpak@magi.com; High Commissioner: Dr FAROUK A. RANA.

Paraguay: 151 Slater St, Suite 401, Ottawa, ON K1P 5H3; tel. (613) 567-1283; fax (613) 567-1679; Ambassador: WASHINGTON ASHWELL.

Peru: 130 Albert St, Suite 1901, Ottawa, ON K1P 5G4; tel. (613) 238-1777; fax (613) 232-3062; e-mail emperuca@magi.com; Ambassador: HERNÁN COUTURIER MARIATEGUI.

Philippines: 130 Albert St, Suite 606, Ottawa, ON K1P 5G4; tel. (613) 233-1121; fax (613) 233-4165; Ambassador: RAUL GOCO.

Poland: 443 Daly Ave, Ottawa, ON K1N 6H3; tel. (613) 789-0468; fax (613) 789-1218; e-mail polamb@hookup.net; Ambassador: BOGDAN GRZELONSKI.

Portugal: 645 Island Park Drive, Ottawa, ON K1Y 0B8; tel. (613) 729-0883; fax (613) 729-4236; Ambassador: JOSÉ MANUEL DUARTE DE JESUS.

Romania: 655 Rideau St, Ottawa, ON K1N 6A3; tel. (613) 789-3709; fax (613) 789-4365; Ambassador: TUDOREL POSTOLACHE.

Russia: 285 Charlotte St, Ottawa, ON K1N 8L5; tel. (613) 235-4341; fax (613) 236-6342; Ambassador: ALEKSANDR BELONOGOV.

Rwanda: 121 Sherwood Drive, Ottawa, ON K1Y 3V1; tel. (613) 722-5835; fax (613) 722-4052; Ambassador: VALENS MUNYABAGISHA.

Saudi Arabia: 99 Bank St, Suite 901, Ottawa, ON K1P 6B9; tel. (613) 237-4100; fax (613) 237-0567; ASSAD AL-ZUHAIR.

Senegal: 57 Marlborough Ave, Ottawa, ON K1N 8E8; tel. (613) 238-6392; fax (613) 238-2695; Ambassador: PIERRE DIOUF.

Slovakia: 50 Rideau Terrace, Ottawa, ON K1M 2A1; tel. (613) 749-4442; fax (613) 749-4989; Chargé d'affaires a.i.: STANISLAV OPIELA.

Slovenia: 150 Metcalfe St, Suite 2101, Ottawa, ON K2P 1P1; tel. (613) 565-5781; fax (613) 565-5783; Ambassador: Dr BOŽO CERAR.

South Africa: 15 Sussex Drive, Ottawa, ON K1M 1M8; tel. (613) 744-0330; fax (613) 741-1639; e-mail rsafrica@sympatico.ca; High Commissioner: B. I. L. MODISE.

Spain: 74 Stanley Ave, Ottawa, ON K1M 1P4; tel. (613) 747-2252; fax (613) 744-1224; e-mail spain@ott.hookup.net; Ambassador: FERNANDO MARTÍN VALENZUELA MARZO.

Sri Lanka: 333 Laurier Ave West, Suite 1204, Ottawa, ON K1P 1C1; tel. (613) 233-8449; fax (613) 238-8448; e-mail lankacom@magi.com; High Commissioner: A. C. GOONASEKERA.

Sudan: 85 Range Rd, Suite 507, Ottawa, ON K1N 8J6; tel. (613) 235-4000; fax (613) 235-6880; Chargé d'affaires a.i.: ELFADIL O. M. AHMED.

Swaziland: 130 Albert St, Suite 1204, Ottawa, ON K1P 5G4; tel. (613) 567-1480; telex 053-3185; fax (613) 567-1058; High Commissioner: BREMER M. NXUMALO.

Sweden: Mercury Court, 377 Dalhousie St, Ottawa, ON K1N 9N8; tel. (613) 241-8553; telex 053-3331; fax (613) 241-2277; e-mail sweden@cyberus.ca; Ambassador: JAN STÅHL.

Switzerland: 5 Marlborough Ave, Ottawa, ON K1N 8E6; tel. (613) 235-1837; fax (613) 563-1394; e-mail 106335.3143@compuserve.com; Ambassador: DANIEL DAYER.

Tanzania: 50 Range Rd, Ottawa, ON K1N 8J4; tel. (613) 232-1500; fax (613) 232-5184; High Commissioner: FADHIL D. MBAGA.

Thailand: 180 Island Park Drive, Ottawa, ON K1Y 0A2; tel. (613) 722-4444; fax (613) 722-6624; Ambassador: VIRASAKDI FUTRAKUL.

Togo: 12 Range Rd, Ottawa, ON K1N 8J3; tel. (613) 238-5916; fax (613) 235-6425; Ambassador: FOLLY-GLIDJITO AKAKPO.

Trinidad and Tobago: 75 Albert St, Suite 508, Ottawa, ON K1P 5E7; tel. (613) 232-2418; fax (613) 232-4349; e-mail ottawa@ttmissions.com; High Commissioner: ROBERT SABGA.

Tunisia: 515 O'Connor St, Ottawa, ON K1S 3P8; tel. (613) 237-0330; fax (613) 237-7939; Ambassador: HABIB LAZREG.

Turkey: 197 Wurtemburg St, Ottawa, ON K1N 8L9; tel. (613) 789-4044; fax (613) 789-3442; Ambassador: ÖMER ERSUN.

Uganda: 231 Cobourg St, Ottawa, ON K1N 8J2; tel. (613) 789-7797; fax (613) 789-8909; High Commissioner: WILSON W. WAMIMBI.

Ukraine: 310 Somerset St West, Ottawa, ON K2P 0J9; tel. (613) 230-2961; fax (613) 230-2400; Ambassador: VOLODYMYR FURKALO.

United Kingdom: 80 Elgin St, Ottawa, ON K1P 5K7; tel. (613) 237-1530; fax (613) 237-7980; High Commissioner: Sir ANTHONY GOODENOUGH.

USA: 100 Wellington St, POB 866, Station B, Ottawa, ON K1P 5T1; tel. (613) 238-4470; fax (613) 238-8750; Ambassador: GORDON D. GIFFIN.

Uruguay: 130 Albert St, Suite 1905, Ottawa, ON K1P 5G4; tel. (613) 234-2727; fax (613) 233-4670; e-mail urott@iosphere.net; Ambassador: ELBIO ROSSELLI.

Venezuela: 32 Range Rd, Ottawa, ON K1N 8J4; tel. (613) 235-5151; fax (613) 235-3205; e-mail embavene@travel-net.com; Ambassador: ALBERTO J. POLETTO.

Viet Nam: 25B Davidson Drive, Gloucester, ON K1J 6L7; tel. (613) 744-4963; fax (613) 744-1709; Ambassador: DANG NGHIEM BAI.

Yemen: 350 Sparks St, Suite 1100, Ottawa, ON K1R 7S8; tel. (613) 232-8525; fax (613) 232-8276; Ambassador: Dr MOHAMED SAED ALI.

Yugoslavia: 17 Blackburn Ave, Ottawa, ON K1N 8A2; tel. (613) 233-6289; fax (613) 233-7850; Chargé d'affaires a.i.: A. MITIĆ.

Zambia: 130 Albert St, Suite 1610, Ottawa, ON K1P 5G4; tel. (613) 563-0712; fax (613) 235-0430; High Commissioner: JOSHUA SIYOLWE.

Zimbabwe: 332 Somerset St West, Ottawa, ON K2P 0J9; tel. (613) 237-4388; telex 053-4221; fax (613) 563-8269; High Commissioner: LILLIE CHITAURO.

Judicial System

FEDERAL COURTS

The Supreme Court of Canada: Supreme Court Bldg, Wellington St, Ottawa, ON K1A 0J1; tel. (613) 995-4330; fax (613) 996-3063;

e-mail reception@scc-csc.go.ca; ultimate court of appeal in both civil and criminal cases throughout Canada. The Supreme Court is also required to advise on questions referred to it by the Governor-General in Council. Important questions concerning the interpretation of the Constitution Act, the constitutionality or interpretation of any federal or provincial law, the powers of Parliament or of the provincial legislatures, among other matters, may be referred by the Government to the Supreme Court for consideration.

In civil cases, appeals may be brought from any final judgment of the highest court of last resort in a province, or of the Federal Court of Appeal. The Supreme Court will grant permission to appeal if it is of the opinion that a question of public importance is involved, one that transcends the immediate concerns of the parties to the litigation. In criminal cases, the Court will hear appeals as of right concerning indictable offences where an acquittal has been set aside or where there has been a dissenting judgment on a point of law in a provincial court of appeal. The Supreme Court may, in addition, consent to hear appeals on questions of law concerning both summary conviction and all other indictable offences.

Chief Justice of Canada: Antonio Lamer.

Puisne Judges: Michel Bastarache, Claire L'Heureux-Dubé, John Sopinka, Charles Doherty Gonthier, Peter de Carteret Cory, Beverley McLachlin, Frank Iacobucci, John Major.

The Federal Court of Canada: Supreme Court Bldg, Wellington St, Ottawa, ON K1A 0H9; tel. (613) 992-4238; has jurisdiction in claims against the Crown, claims by the Crown, miscellaneous cases involving the Crown, claims against or concerning crown officers and servants, relief against Federal Boards, Commissions, and other tribunals, interprovincial and federal-provincial disputes, industrial or industrial property matters, admiralty, income tax and estate tax appeals, citizenship appeals, aeronautics, interprovincial works and undertakings, residuary jurisdiction for relief if there is no other Canadian court that has such jurisdiction, jurisdiction in specific matters conferred by federal statutes.

The Federal Court of Appeal: Supreme Court Bldg, Wellington St, Ottawa, ON K1A 0H9; tel. (613) 996-6795; has jurisdiction on appeals from the Trial Division, appeals from Federal Tribunals, review of decisions of Federal Boards and Commissions, appeals from Tribunals and Reviews under Section 28 of the Federal Court Act, and references by Federal Boards and Commissions. The Court has one central registry and consists of the principal office in Ottawa and local offices in major centres throughout Canada.

Chief Justice: Julius Isaac.

Associate Chief Justice: James Jerome.

Court of Appeal Judges: Louis Pratte, Louis Marceau, James Hugessen, Arthur Stone, Barry Strayer, Mark MacGuigan, Alice Desjardins, Robert Décary, Allen Linden, Gilles Létourneau, Joseph Robertson, F. Joseph McDonald.

Trial Division Judges: J.-E. Dubé, Paul Rouleau, Francis Muldoon, Barbara Reed, Pierre Denault, Yvon Pinard, L. Marcel Joyal, Bud Cullen, Max Teitelbaum, William MacKay, Donna McGillis, Marshall Rothstein, Marc Noël, Frederick Gibson, William McKeown, Sandra Simpson, Marc Nadon, Howard Wetston, Danièle Tremblay-Lamer, John Richard, Douglas Campbell, Allan Lutfy.

PROVINCIAL COURTS

Alberta

Court of Appeal

Chief Justice of Alberta: Catherine Fraser.

Court of Queen's Bench

Chief Justice: W. K. Moore.

Associate Chief Justice: A. H. Wachowich.

British Columbia

Court of Appeal

Chief Justice of British Columbia: A. McEachern.

Supreme Court

Chief Justice: B. Williams.

Associate Chief Justice: P. D. Dohm.

Manitoba

Court of Appeal

Chief Justice of Manitoba: R. J. Scott.

Court of Queen's Bench

Chief Justice: B. Hewak.

Associate Chief Justice: J. J. Oliphant.

Associate Chief Justice (Family Division): G. W. Mercier.

New Brunswick

Court of Appeal

Chief Justice of New Brunswick: W. L. Hoyt.

Court of Queen's Bench

Chief Justice: Joseph Z. Daigle.

Newfoundland

Supreme Court—Court of Appeal

Chief Justice: J. R. Gushue.

Trial Division

Chief Justice: T. A. Hickman.

Nova Scotia

Court of Appeal

Chief Justice of Nova Scotia: L. O. Clarke.

Supreme Court

Chief Justice: C. R. Glube.

Associate Chief Justice: J. P. Kennedy.

Ontario

Court of Appeal

Chief Justice of Ontario: R. R. McMurtry.

Associate Chief Justice of Ontario: J. W. Morden.

Court of Justice

Chief Justice: P. J. LeSage.

Associate Chief Justice: H. J. Smith.

Prince Edward Island

Supreme Court—Appeal Division

Chief Justice: N. H. Carruthers.

Supreme Court—Trial Division

Chief Justice: K. R. MacDonald.

Québec

Court of Appeal

Chief Justice of Québec: P. A. Michaud.

Superior Court

Chief Justice: Lyse Lemieux.

Senior Associate Chief Justice: R. W. Dionne.

Associate Chief Justice: A. Deslongchamps.

Saskatchewan

Court of Appeal

Chief Justice of Saskatchewan: E. D. Bayda.

Court of Queen's Bench

Chief Justice: D. K. MacPherson.

Northwest Territories

Supreme Court

Judges of the Supreme Court: J. E. Richard, J. Z. Vertes, V. A. Schuler.

Court of Appeal

Chief Justice: Catherine Fraser (Alberta).

Yukon Territory

Supreme Court

Judges of the Supreme Court: H. C. B. Maddison, R. E. Hudson.

Court of Appeal

Chief Justice: A. McEachern (British Columbia).

Religion

CHRISTIANITY

About 75% of the population belong to the three main Christian churches: Roman Catholic, United and Anglican. Numerous other religious denominations are represented.

Canadian Council of Churches/Conseil canadien des Eglises: 40 St Clair Ave East, Suite 201, Toronto, ON M4T 1M9; tel. (416) 921-7759; fax (416) 921-7478; e-mail ccchurch@web.net; f. 1944; 18 mem. churches, one assoc. mem; Pres. Most Rev. Barry Curtis (Anglican Archbishop of Rupert's Land); Gen. Sec. Janet Somerville.

The Anglican Communion

The Anglican Church of Canada (l'Eglise anglicane du Canada) comprises four ecclesiastical provinces (each with a Metropolitan archbishop), containing a total of 30 dioceses. The Church had 848,256 members in 1,767 parishes in 1995.

General Synod of the Anglican Church of Canada: Church House, 600 Jarvis St, Toronto, ON M4Y 2J6; tel. (416) 924-9192; fax (416) 968-7983; e-mail info@national.anglican.ca; Gen. Sec. Archdeacon JAMES BOYLES.

Primate of the Anglican Church of Canada: Archbishop MICHAEL PEERS.

Archbishop of British Columbia and Yukon: DAVID CRAWLEY, Bishop of Kootenay.

Archbishop of Canada: ARTHUR PETERS, Bishop of Nova Scotia.

Archbishop of Ontario: PERCY O'DRISCOLL, Bishop of Huron.

Archbishop of Rupert's Land: BARRY CURTIS, Bishop of Calgary.

The Orthodox Churches

Greek Orthodox Metropolis of Toronto (Canada): 27 Teddington Park Ave, Toronto, ON M4N 2C4; tel. (416) 322-5055; fax (416) 485-5929; e-mail gocanada@astral.magic.ca; 350,000 mems (1997); Metropolitan Archbishop SOTIRIOS ATHANASSOULAS.

Ukrainian Orthodox Church of Canada: 9 St John's Ave, Winnipeg, MB R2W 1G8; tel. (204) 586-3093; fax (204) 582-5241; f. 1918; 258 parishes, 120,000 mems (1992); Metropolitan of Winnipeg and of all Canada His Beatitude WASYLY (FEDAK).

The Romanian, Serbian, Coptic, Antiochian, Armenian and Belarusian Churches are also represented in Canada.

The Roman Catholic Church

For Catholics of the Latin rite, Canada comprises 18 archdioceses (including one directly responsible to the Holy See), 46 dioceses and one territorial abbacy. There are also one archdiocese and four dioceses of the Ukrainian rite. In addition, the Maronite, Melkite and Slovak rites are each represented by one diocese (all directly responsible to the Holy See). In October 1996 the Roman Catholic Church had about 12.8m. adherents in Canada.

Canadian Conference of Catholic Bishops/Conférence des évêques catholiques du Canada: 90 Parent Ave, Ottawa, ON K1N 7B1; tel. (613) 241-9461; fax (613) 241-8117; e-mail cecc@cccb.ca; Pres. Most Rev. FRANCIS J. SPENCE, Archbishop of Kingston; Vice-Pres. Cardinal JEAN-CLAUDE TURCOTTE, Archbishop of Montréal.

Latin Rite

Archbishop of Edmonton: JOSEPH MACNEIL.

Archbishop of Gatineau-Hull: ROGER ÉBACHER.

Archbishop of Grouard-McLennan: HENRI GOUDREAULT.

Archbishop of Halifax: AUSTIN-EMILE BURKE.

Archbishop of Keewatin-Le Pas: PETER ALFRED SUTTON.

Archbishop of Kingston: FRANCIS J. SPENCE.

Archbishop of Moncton: ERNEST LÉGER.

Archbishop of Montréal: Cardinal JEAN-CLAUDE TURCOTTE.

Archbishop of Ottawa: MARCEL GERVAIS.

Archbishop of Québec: MAURICE COUTURE.

Archbishop of Regina: PETER MALLON.

Archbishop of Rimouski: BERTRAND BLANCHET.

Archbishop of St Boniface: ANTOINE HACAULT.

Archbishop of St John's, Nfld: JAMES MACDONALD.

Archbishop of Sherbrooke: ANDRÉ GAUMOND.

Archbishop of Toronto: Cardinal ALOYSIUS AMBROZIC.

Archbishop of Vancouver: ADAM EXNER.

Archbishop of Winnipeg: LEONARD WALL.

Ukrainian Rite

Ukrainian Catholic Church in Canada: 233 Scotia St, Winnipeg, MB R2V 1V7; tel. (204) 338-7801; fax (204) 339-4006; 133,490 mems (1991 census); Archeparch-Metropolitan of Winnipeg Most Rev. MICHAEL BZDEL; Auxiliary Bishop STEFAN SOROKA, Titular Bishop of Acarasso.

The United Church of Canada

The United Church of Canada (L'Eglise unie du Canada) was founded in 1925 with the union of Methodist, Congregational and Presbyterian churches in Canada. The Evangelical United Brethren of Canada joined in 1968. In 1995 there were 2,413 pastoral charges, 3,909 congregations, 3,965 ministers and 728,134 mems.

Moderator: MARION BEST.

General Secretary: VIRGINIA COLEMAN, 3250 Bloor St West, Etobicoke, ON M8X 2Y4; tel. (416) 231-5931; fax (416) 231-3103.

Other Christian Churches

Canadian Baptist Ministries: 7185 Millcreek Drive, Mississauga, ON L5N 5R4; tel. (905) 821-3533; fax (905) 826-3441; e-mail dphillips@cbmin.org; 1,120 churches; 132,000 mems (1994); Pres. CARMEN MOIR; Gen. Sec. Rev. DAVID PHILLIPS.

Christian Reformed Church in North America (Canadian Council): 3475 Mainway, POB 5070, Burlington, ON L7R 3Y8; tel. (905) 336-2920; fax (905) 336-8344; f. 1857; 244 congregations; 84,000 mems (1995); Exec. Sec. ARIE VAN EEK.

Church of Jesus Christ of Latter-day Saints (Mormon): POB 641, Don Mills, ON M3C 2T6; tel. (416) 424-2485; fax (416) 424-7725; 391 congregations; 130,000 mems (1995); Dir JIM DARDEN.

Evangelical Lutheran Church in Canada: 1512 St James St, Winnipeg, MB R3H 0L2; tel. (204) 786-6707; fax (204) 783-7548; f. 1967; 652 congregations, 200,000 mems (1995); Bishop Rev. TELMOR G. SARTISON.

Lutheran Church—Canada: 3074 Portage Ave, Winnipeg, MB R3K 0Y2; tel. (204) 895-3433; fax (204) 897-4319; e-mail BCS@lutheranchurch-canada.ca; f. 1988; 325 congregations; 80,000 mems (1997); Pres. Rev. RALPH MAYAN.

Mennonite Central Committee—Canada: 134 Plaza Drive, Winnipeg, MB R3T 5K9; tel. (204) 261-6381; fax (204) 269-9875; e-mail mcc@mennonitecc.ca; f. 1963; 120,000 mems in 600 congregations; Exec. Dir MARVIN FREY.

Pentecostal Assemblies of Canada: 6745 Century Ave, Mississauga, ON L5N 6P7; tel. (905) 542-7400; fax (905) 542-7313; 1,068 congregations, 227,000 mems (1995); Gen. Supt Rev. WILLIAM D. MORROW.

Presbyterian Church in Canada: 50 Wynford Drive, North York, ON M3C 1J7; tel. (416) 441-1111; fax (416) 441-2825; f. 1875; 999 congregations; 237,000 mems (1995); Moderator Dr ALAN M. MCPHERSON; Prin. Clerk Rev. THOMAS GEMMELL.

Religious Society of Friends: 91A Fourth Ave, Ottawa, ON K1S 2L1; tel. and fax (613) 235-8553; E-mail cym@ottawa.net; Clerk of Canadian Yearly Meeting GALE WILLS.

Seventh-day Adventists: 1148 King St East, Oshawa, ON L1H 1H8; tel. (905) 433-0011; fax (905) 433-0982; org. 1901; 332 congregations; 45,000 mems (1995); Pres. O. PARCHMENT; Sec. C. SABOT.

BAHÁ'Í FAITH

Bahá'í Community of Canada: 7200 Leslie St, Thornhill, ON L3T 6L8; tel. (905) 889-8168; fax (905) 889-8164; e-mail nsacan@interlog.com; f. 1902; 24,000 mems; Sec. REGINALD NEWKIRK.

BUDDHISM

Buddhist Association of Canada: 1330 Bloor St West, Toronto, ON M6H 1P2; tel. and fax (416) 537-1342; Chair. Dr CLEMENT WONG.

Buddhist Churches of Canada: 4860 Garry St, Richmond, BC V7E 2V2; tel. (604) 272-3330; fax (604) 272-6865; Jodo Shinshu Hongwanji-ha of Mahayana Buddhism; Bishop Dr YOSHIHIDE MATSUBAYASHI.

ISLAM

There are an estimated 350,000 Muslims in Canada.

Ahmadiyya Movement in Islam (Canada): 10610 Jane St, Maple, ON L6A 1S1; tel. (416) 832-2669; fax (416) 832-3220; e-mail info@islam.ahmadiyya.org; Pres. and Missionary-in-Charge NASEEM MAHDI.

Council of Muslim Communities of Canada: 4 Forest Lawn Way, North York, ON M2N 5X8; tel. and fax (416) 512-2106; co-ordinating agency; Pres. HANNY HASSAN.

Federation of Islamic Associations: 73 Patricia Ave, North York, ON M2M 1J1; tel. (416) 222-2794; fax (416) 674-8168; Pres. AYUBE ALLY.

JUDAISM

The Jews of Canada are estimated to number 340,000.

Canadian Jewish Congress: 1590 ave Dr Penfield, Montréal, PQ H3G 1C5; tel. (514) 931-7531; fax (514) 931-0548; e-mail canadianjewishcongress@cjc.ca; f. 1919; regional offices in Halifax, Montréal, Ottawa, Toronto, Winnipeg, Saskatoon, Regina, Edmonton, Calgary and Vancouver; Nat. Exec. Dir JACK SILVERSTONE.

SIKHISM

There are an estimated 250,000 Sikhs in Canada.

Federation of Sikh Societies of Canada: POB 91, Station B, Ottawa, ON K1P 6C3; tel. (613) 737-7296; fax (613) 739-7153; f. 1981; Pres. MOHINDER SINGH GOSAL.

The Press

The daily press in Canada is essentially local in coverage, influence and distribution. Independently-owned daily newspapers accounted for 17.3% of the circulation of Canadian dailies in early 1996. Chain ownership is predominant: 43.7% of daily newspaper circulation is represented by two major groups: Southam Inc (31.4% of daily newspaper circulation) and Thomson Newspapers (12.3%). In 1996 Sun Media accounted for 11.3% of the total circulation, while Hollinger and Québecor each had 9.3%. There are also three smaller groups.

In June 1996 there were 105 daily newspapers with a combined circulation of approximately 5.2m., and about 1,100 weekly and twice-weekly community newspapers reached more than 5.0m. people, mainly in the more remote areas of the country. A significant feature of the Canadian press is the number of newspapers catering for ethnic groups: there are over 80 of these daily and weekly publications appearing in over 20 languages.

There are numerous periodicals for business, trade, professional, recreational and special interest readership, although periodical publishing, particularly, encounters substantial competition from publications originating in the USA.

The following are among the principal newspaper publishing groups:

Québecor Inc: 612 rue St-Jacques, Montréal, PQ H3C 1C8; tel. (514) 877-9777; fax (514) 877-9790; f. 1965; Pres. and CEO Pierre Peladieu.

Southam Inc: 1450 Don Mills Rd, Don Mills, ON M3B 2X7; tel. (416) 445-6641; fax (416) 442-2077; Pres. Don Babick.

Thomson Corpn: POB 24, Toronto-Dominion Centre/Bank Tower, Toronto, ON M5K 1A1; tel. (416) 360-8700; fax (416) 360-8812; Chair. Paul Brett; Co-Pres Richard Harrington, W. Michael Brown.

PRINCIPAL DAILY NEWSPAPERS

(D = all day; E = evening; M = morning; S = Sunday)

Alberta

Calgary Herald: 215 16th St, SE, Calgary, AB T2P 0W8; tel. (403) 235-7100; fax (403) 235-8668; f. 1883; Publr Ken King; Man. Editor Crosbie Cotton; circ. 113,000 (M); 113,000 (S).

Calgary Sun: 2615 12th St, NE, Calgary, AB T2E 7W9; tel. (403) 250-4200; fax (403) 250-4258; f. 1980; Publr Lester Peyette; Editor-in-Chief Chris Nelson; circ. 68,000 (M), 98,000 (S).

Daily Herald–Tribune: 10604 100th St, POB 3000, Grande Prairie, AB T8V 6V4; tel. (403) 532-1110; fax (403) 532-2120; f. 1913; Publr Peter J. Woolsey; Man. Editor Fred Rinne; circ. 8,000 (E).

Edmonton Journal: POB 2421, Edmonton, AB T5J OS1; tel. (403) 429-5400; fax (403) 498-5677; f. 1903; Publr Linda Hughes; Editor-in-Chief Murdoch Davis; circ. 143,000 (M); 138,000 (S).

Edmonton Sun: 4990 92nd Ave, Suite 250, Edmonton, AB T6B 3A1; tel. (403) 468-0100; fax (403) 468-0139; f. 1978; Publr Craig Martin; Editor Paul Stanway; circ. 72,000 (M), 110,000 (S).

Fort McMurray Today: 8550 Franklin Ave, Fort McMurray, AB T9H 3G1; tel. (403) 743-8186; fax (403) 790-1006; e-mail today@ccinet.ab.ca; Publr Tim O'Rourke; Editor Darrell Skidnuk; circ. 5,000 (E).

Lethbridge Herald: 504 Seventh St South, Lethbridge, AB T1J 3Z7; tel. (403) 328-4410; fax (403) 329-8089; f. 1907; Publr Greg Lutes; Man. Editor Bill Whitelaw; circ. 21,000 (E), 19,000 (S).

Medicine Hat News: 3257 Dunmore Rd, SE, POB 10, Medicine Hat, AB T1A 7E6; tel. (403) 527-1101; fax (403) 527-6029; f. 1887; Publr Michael J. Hertz; Man. Editor Gordon Wright; circ. 14,000 (E).

British Columbia

Alaska Highway News: 9916 89th St, Fort St John, BC V1J 3T8; tel. (250) 785-5631; fax (250) 785-3522; Publr Bruce Lantz; Editor Joe Pavin; circ. 3,000 (E).

Daily Bulletin: 335 Spokane St, Kimberley, BC V1A 1Y9; tel. (250) 427-5333; fax (250) 427-5336; e-mail bulletin@cyberlink.bc.ca; f. 1932; Publr Sheen Jorgensen; Editor Chris Douan; circ. 2,000 (E).

Daily Courier: 550 Doyle Ave, Kelowna, BC V1Y 7V1; tel. (604) 762-4445; fax (604) 762-3866; f. 1904; Publr Peter Kapyrka; Man. Editor Gordon Smiley; circ. 17,000 (E); 16,000 (S).

Daily Free Press: 2575 McCullough Rd, Nanaimo, BC V9S 5W5; tel. (250) 758-4917; fax (250) 758-4513; f. 1874; Publr Ron Mitchell; Man. Editor Doyle MacKinnon; circ. 9,000 (E).

Daily Townsman: 822 Cranbrook St North, Cranbrook, BC V1C 3R9; tel. (250) 426-5201; fax (250) 426-5003; Publr Nick Lark; Editor David Sands; circ. 4,000 (E).

Kamloops Daily News: 393 Seymour St, Kamloops, BC V2C 6P6; tel. (604) 372-2331; fax (604) 372-0823; f. 1930; Publr Dale Brin; Editor Mel Rothenburger; circ. 16,000 (E).

Nelson Daily News: 266 Baker St, Nelson, BC V1L 4H3; tel. (604) 352-3552; fax (604) 352-2418; f. 1902; Publr John A. Smith; Editor David Howe; circ. 4,000 (E).

Peace River Block News: 901 100th Ave, Dawson Creek, BC V1G 1W2; tel. (250) 782-4888; fax (250) 782-6770; e-mail prbnews@pris.bc.ca; f. 1930; Publr Margaret Forbes; Editor Jeremy Hainsworth; circ. 3,000 (E), 11,000 (S).

Penticton Herald: 186 Nanaimo Ave West, Penticton, BC V2A 1N4; tel. (250) 492-4002; fax (250) 492-2403; e-mail jhcoady@ok.bc.ca; Publr Jane Howard Coady; Editor Mike Turner; circ. 10,000 (E).

Prince George Citizen: 150 Brunswick St, POB 5700, Prince George, BC V2L 5K9; tel. (250) 562-2441; fax (250) 562-7453; f. 1957; Publr Bob McKenzie; Editor Roy K. Nagel; circ. 17,000 (E).

The Province: 2250 Granville St, Vancouver, BC V6H 3G2; tel. (604) 732-2222; fax (604) 732-2720; e-mail mcooke@pacpress.southam.ca; f. 1898; Publr Donald Babick; Editor-in-Chief Michael Cooke; circ. 149,000 (M), 185,000 (S).

Sing Tao Daily: 8874 Hudson St, Vancouver, BC V6A 2V1; tel. (604) 261-5066; fax (604) 261-7093; Chinese; Editor Paul Tsang; circ. 15,000 (M).

Times–Colonist: 2621 Douglas St, POB 300, Victoria, BC V8W 2N4; tel. (250) 380-5211; fax (250) 380-5255; e-mail timesc@interlink.bc.ca; f. 1858; Publr Peter Baillie; Editor-in-Chief Bob Poole; circ. 75,000 (M), 73,000 (S).

Trail Times: 1163 Cedar Ave, Trail, BC V1R 4B8; tel. (250) 364-1416; fax (250) 368-8550; e-mail konschuk@winc.com; Publr Ray Picco; Editor Tracy Konschuk; circ. 5,000 (E).

The Vancouver Sun: 2250 Granville St, Vancouver, BC V6H 3G2; tel. (604) 732-2111; fax (604) 732-2323; e-mail jcruickshank@pacpress.southam.ca; f. 1886; Publr Donald Babick; Editor-in-Chief John Cruickshank; circ. 176,000 (M), 240,000 (Sat.).

Manitoba

Brandon Sun: 501 Rosser Ave, Brandon, POB 460, MB R7A 5Z6; tel. (204) 727-2451; fax (204) 725-0976; f. 1882; Publr Rob Forbes; Man. Editor Brian D. Marshall; circ. 17,000 (E), 22,000 (S).

Daily Graphic: 1941 Saskatchewan Ave West, POB 130, Portage La Prairie, MB R1N 3B4; tel. (204) 857-3427; fax (204) 239-1270; e-mail pdg@cpnet.net; Publr Tom Tenszen; Editor Ian R. White; circ. 4,300 (E).

Flin Flon Reminder: 10 North Ave, Flin Flon, MB R8A 0T2; tel. (204) 687-3454; fax (204) 687-4473; f. 1946; Publr Randy Daneliuk; Editor Rich Billy; circ. 4,000 (E).

Winnipeg Free Press: 1355 Mountain Ave, Winnipeg, MB R2X 3B6; tel. (204) 697-7000; fax (204) 697-7370; f. 1874; Publr H. R. Redekop; Editor D. McMonagle; circ. 128,000 (E), 149,000 (Sat.).

Winnipeg Sun: 1700 Church Ave, Winnipeg, MB R2X 3A2; tel. (204) 694-2022; fax (204) 632-8709; f. 1980; Publr Richard Boyer; Editor Dave Komosky; circ. 44,000 (M), 61,000 (S).

New Brunswick

L'Acadie Nouvelle: 476 blvd St-Pierre ouest, CP 5536, Caraquet, NB E1W 1B7; tel. (506) 727-4444; fax (506) 727-0530; f. 1984; Publr Gilles Gagné; Editor Nelson Landry; circ. 16,000 (M).

Daily Gleaner: POB 3370, Fredericton, NB E3B 5A2; tel. (506) 452-6671; fax (506) 452-7405; f. 1880; Publr Brian A. Butters; Editor-in-Chief Hal Wood; circ. 29,000 (E).

Telegraph–Journal (M), **John Times–Globe** (E): 210 Crown St, POB 2350, Saint John, NB E2L 3V8; tel. (506) 632-8888; fax (506) 648-2661; Publr Jamie Milne; circ. 24,000 (M), 29,000 (E).

Times–Transcript: 939 Main St, POB 1001, Moncton, NB E1C 8P3; tel. (506) 859-4900; fax (506) 859-4899; f. 1983; Publr Johnathan Franklin; Man. Editor Mike Bembridge; circ. 40,000 (E), 53,000 (Sat.).

Newfoundland

Evening Telegram: Columbus Drive, POB 5970, St John's, NF A1C 5X7; tel. (709) 364-6300; fax (709) 364-9333; f. 1879; Publr Miller H. Ayre; Man. Editor Paul Sparkes; circ. 37,000 (E), 62,000 (Sat.).

Western Star: 106 West St, POB 460, Corner Brook, NF A2H 6E7; tel. (709) 634-4348; fax (709) 634-9824; f. 1900; Publr Ian M. Baird; Editor Richard Williams; circ. 11,000 (M).

Nova Scotia

Amherst Daily News: POB 280, Amherst, NS B4H 3Z2; tel. (902) 667-5102; fax (902) 667-0419; f. 1893; Publr Earl J. Gouchie; Editor John Conrad; circ. 4,000 (M).

Cape Breton Post: 255 George St, POB 1500, Sydney, NS B1P 6K6; tel. (902) 564-5451; fax (902) 562-7077; f. 1900; Publr Milton Ellis; Man. Editor Fred Jackson; circ. 30,000 (M).

Chronicle–Herald (M), **Mail–Star** (E): 1650 Argyle St, POB 610, Halifax, NS B3J 2T2; tel. (902) 426-2811; fax (902) 426-3014; e-mail sarahd@herald.ns.ca; Publr Graham Dennis; Man. Editor Jane Purves; circ. 91,000 (M), 38,000 (E).

Daily News: POB 8330, Station A, Halifax, NS B3K 5M1; tel. (902) 468-1222; fax (902) 468-3609; f. 1974; Publr. Mark Richardson; Editor-in-Chief Douglas MacKay; circ. 28,000 (m), 46,000 (s).

Evening News: 352 East River Rd, POB 159, New Glasgow, NS B2H 5E2; tel. (902) 752-3000; fax (902) 752-1945; f. 1910; Publr (vacant); Man. Editor Doug MacNeil; circ. 9,000 (e).

Truro Daily News: 6 Louise St, POB 220, Truro, NS B2N 5C3; tel. (902) 893-9405; fax (902) 893-0518; f. 1891; Publr Leith Orr; Man. Editor Bill McGuire; circ. 7,000 (e).

Ontario

Barrie Examiner: 16 Bayfield St, Barrie, ON L4M 4T6; tel. (705) 728-2414; fax (705) 726-7706; f. 1864; Publr Ron Laurin; Man. Editor Joanne Kushnier; circ. 10,000 (e).

Beacon–Herald: POB 430, Stratford, ON N5A 6T6; tel. (519) 271-2220; fax (519) 271-1026; f. 1854; Co-Publrs Charles Dingman, Stanford Dingman; Man. Editor Ronald C. Carson; circ. 13,000 (e).

Cambridge Reporter: 26 Ainslie St South, Cambridge, ON N1R 3K1; tel. (519) 621-3810; fax (519) 621-8239; f. 1846; Publr L. R. (Verne) Shaull; Man. Editor Clyde Warrington; circ. 8,000 (e).

Chatham Daily News: 45 Fourth St, POB 2007, Chatham, ON N7M 2G4; tel. (519) 354-2000; fax (519) 436-0949; f. 1862; Publr John Cheek; Man. Editor Jim Blake; circ. 15,000 (e).

Chronicle–Journal: 75 South Cumberland St, Thunder Bay, ON P7B 1A3; tel. (807) 343-6200; fax (807) 345-3582; e-mail cj-editorial@cwconnect.ca; Publr Colin Bruce; Man. Editor Peter Haggert; circ. 32,000 (m).

Cobourg Daily Star: 415 King St West, POB 400, Cobourg, ON K9A 4L1; tel. (905) 372-0131; fax (905) 372-4966; Publr C. Burke; Editorial Dir Jim Grossmith; circ. 6,000 (e).

Daily Observer: 186 Alexander St, Pembroke, ON K8A 4L9; tel. (613) 732-3691; fax (613) 732-2645; e-mail observer@fox.nstn.ca; f. 1855; Publr Steve Gloster; Man. Editor Peter Lapinskie; circ. 7,000 (e).

Daily Press: 187 Cedar St South, Timmins, ON P4N 2G9; tel. (705) 268-5050; fax (705) 268-7373; e-mail tdp@nt.net; f. 1933; Publr Syl Bélisle; Man. Editor Dave McGee; circ. 8,000 (m).

Daily Sentinel–Review: POB 1000, Woodstock, ON N4S 8A5; tel. (519) 537-2341; fax (519) 537-3049; f. 1886; Publr Pat Logan; Man. Editor Alison Downie; circ. 10,000 (e).

Le Droit: 47 rue Clarence, Pièce 222, CP 8860, succursale T, Ottawa, ON K1G 3J9; tel. (613) 562-7747; fax (613) 562-7572; e-mail publicite@ledroit.com; f. 1913; Publr Pierre Bergeron; Man. Editor François Roy; circ. 34,000 (m), 42,000 (Sat.).

The Expositor: 53 Dalhousie St, POB 965, Brantford, ON N3T 5S8; tel. (519) 756-2020; fax (519) 756-4911; f. 1852; Publr Michael Pearce; Editor David Schultz; circ. 24,000 (e).

Financial Post: 333 King St East, Toronto, ON M5A 4N2; tel. (416) 350-6300; telex 062-19547; fax (416) 350-6301; e-mail letters@finpost.com; f. 1907; Publr and CEO William Neill; Editor Diane Francis; circ. 78,000 (Tues.–Fri.), 170,000 (Sat.).

The Globe and Mail: 444 Front St West, Toronto, ON M5V 2S9; tel. (416) 585-5000; fax (416) 585-5085; f. 1844; Publr Roger P. Parkinson; Editor-in-Chief William Thorsell; circ. 319,000 (m).

Guelph Mercury: 8–14 Macdonnell St, POB 3604, Guelph, ON N1H 6P7; tel. (519) 822-4310; fax (519) 767-1681; f. 1854; Publr Stephen Rhodes; Editor Ed Cassavoy; circ. 14,000 (e).

Hamilton Spectator: 44 Frid St, Hamilton, ON L8N 3G3; tel. (905) 526-3333; fax (905) 526-1696; f. 1846; Publr Patrick J. Collins; Editor-in-Chief Kirk Lapointe; circ. 103,000 (e).

Intelligencer: 45 Bridge St East, POB 5600, Belleville, ON K8N 5C7; tel. (613) 962-9171; fax (613) 962-9652; e-mail intel@intranet.on.ca; f. 1870; Publr Peter E. Leichnitz; Man. Editor Nick Palmer; circ. 16,000 (e).

Kingston Whig–Standard: 6 Cataraqui St, POB 2300, Kingston, ON K7L 4Z7; tel. (613) 544-5000; fax (613) 530-4122; f. 1834; Publr Fred Laflamme; Man. Editor Lynn Messerschmidt; circ. 27,000 (d).

Kitchener-Waterloo Record: 225 Fairway Rd, Kitchener, ON N2G 4E5; tel. (519) 894-2231; fax (519) 894-0292; f. 1878; Publr Wayne MacDonald; Editor Carolyne Rittinger; circ. 66,000 (e).

Lindsay Daily Post: 15 William St North, Lindsay, ON K9V 2Y6; tel. (705) 324-2114; fax (705) 324-0174; Publr Jim Ambrose; Editor Stephanie Walsh; circ. 7,000 (e).

London Free Press: 369 York St, POB 2280, London, ON N6A 4G1; tel. (519) 679-1111; fax (519) 667-4523; e-mail letters@lfpress.com; f. 1849; Publr John Paton; Editor Philip McLeod; circ. 100,000 (m); 132,000 (Sat.).

Niagara Falls Review: 4801 Valley Way, POB 270, Niagara Falls, ON L2E 6T6; tel. (905) 358-5711; fax (905) 356-0785; f. 1879; Publr David A. Beattie; Man. Editor Michael Brown; circ. 22,000 (e).

Northern Daily News: 8 Duncan Ave, Kirkland Lake, ON P2N 3L4; tel. (705) 567-5321; fax (705) 567-6162; f. 1922; Publr Syl Belisle; Editor Tom Perry; circ. 6,000 (e).

The Nugget: 259 Worthington St, POB 570, North Bay, ON P1B 8J6; tel. (705) 472-3200; fax (705) 472-1438; f. 1909; Publr Robert Hull; Man. Editor Bruce Cowan; circ. 20,000 (e).

Ottawa Citizen: 1101 Baxter Rd, POB 5020, Ottawa, ON K2C 3M4; tel. (613) 829-9100; fax (613) 726-1198; f. 1845; Publr Russell Mills; Editor Neil Reynolds; circ. 135,000 (m), 192,000 (Sat.).

Ottawa Sun: 380 Hunt Club Rd, Ottawa, ON K1G 5H7; tel. (613) 739-7100; fax (613) 739-8043; Publr Bill Neill; Editor Mark Bonokoski; circ. 50,000 (m), 59,000 (s).

The Packet and Times: 31 Colborne St East, Orillia, ON L3V 1T4; tel. (705) 325-1355; fax (705) 325-7691; f. 1953; Publr Bruce MacIntyre; Man. Editor Jeff Day; circ. 10,000 (e), 9,000 (s).

Peterborough Examiner: 400 Water St, POB 3890, Peterborough K9J 8L4; tel. (705) 745-4641; fax (705) 741-3217; f. 1884; Publr Jim Ambrose; Man. Editor Ed Arnold; circ. 23,000 (e).

Recorder and Times: 23 King St West, Brockville, ON K6V 5T8; tel. (613) 342-4441; fax (613) 342-4456; f. 1821; Co-Publr Hunter Grant; Co-Publr and Editor-in-Chief Mrs Perry Beverley; circ. 15,000 (e).

St Catharines Standard: 17 Queen St, St Catharines, ON L2R 5G5; tel. (905) 684-7251; fax (905) 684-8011; f. 1891; Publr Dan Gaynor; Man. Editor Doug Firby; circ. 36,000 (e).

St Thomas Times–Journal: 16 Hincks St, St Thomas, ON N5R 5Z2; tel. (519) 631-2790; fax (519) 631-5653; e-mail tj—mail@st.thomas.on.ca; f. 1882; Publr Amber Ogilvie; Man. Editor Ross Porter; circ. 8,000 (e).

Sarnia Observer: 140 South Front St, POB 3009, Sarnia, ON N7T 7M8; tel. (519) 344-3641; fax (519) 332-2951; f. 1917; Publr Daryl C. Smith; Man. Editor Terry Shaw; circ. 23,000 (e).

Sault Star: POB 460, Sault Ste Marie, ON P6A 5M5; tel. (705) 759-3030; fax (705) 942-8690; f. 1912; Publr Robert Richardson; Man. Editor John Halucha; circ. 22,000 (e).

Simcoe Reformer: 105 Donly Drive South, POB 370, Simcoe, ON N3Y 4L2; tel. (519) 426-5710; fax (519) 426-9255; f. 1858; Publr Michael Fredericks; Man. Editor Kim Novak; circ. 10,000 (e).

Standard–Freeholder: 44 Pitt St, Cornwall, ON K6J 3P3; tel. (613) 933-3160; fax (613) 933-7521; Publr John A. Farrington; Editor Kevin Gould; circ. 17,000 (e).

Sudbury Star: 33 MacKenzie St, Sudbury, ON P3C 4Y1; tel. (705) 674-5271; fax (705) 674-0624; e-mail ss-publisher@cwconnect.ca; f. 1909; Publr Ken Seguin; Man. Editor Roger Cazabon; circ. 25,000 (e).

Sun Times: 290 9th St East, POB 200, Owen Sound, ON N4K 5P2; tel. (519) 376-2250; fax (519) 376-7190; f. 1853; Publr Clyde Wicks; Editor Jim Merriam; circ. 19,000 (e).

Toronto Star: One Yonge St, Suite 300, Toronto, ON M5E 1E6; tel. (416) 367-2000; fax (416) 869-4328; e-mail newsroom@webramp.net; f. 1892; Publr John Honderich; circ. 461,000 (d), 708,000 (Sat.), 463,000 (s).

Toronto Sun: 333 King St East, Toronto, ON M5A 3X5; tel. (416) 947-2222; fax (416) 947-1664; f. 1971; Publr Hartley Steward; Exec. Editor Peter O'Sullivan; circ. 230,000 (m), 405,000 (s).

Welland-Port Colborne Tribune: 228 East Main St, Welland, ON L3B 5P5; tel. (905) 732-2411; fax (905) 732-4883; e-mail tribune@iaw.on.ca; f. 1863; Publr David Beattie; Editor Gary Manning; circ. 18,000 (m).

Windsor Star: 167 Ferry St, Windsor, ON N9A 4M5; tel. (519) 255-5711; fax (519) 255-5778; f. 1918; Publr Jim McCormack; circ. 75,000 (e).

Prince Edward Island

Guardian: 165 Prince St, POB 760, Charlottetown, PE C1A 4R7; tel. (902) 629-6000; fax (902) 566-3808; f. 1887; Publr Don Brander; Editor G. MacDougall; circ. 22,000 (m).

Journal–Pioneer: 4 Queen St, POB 2480, Summerside, PE C1N 4K5; tel. (902) 436-2121; fax (902) 436-3027; f. 1865; Publr Sandy Rundle; Editor Darlene Shea; circ. 11,000 (e).

Québec

Le Devoir: 2050 rue de Bleury, Montréal, PQ H3A 3M9; tel. (514) 985-3399; fax (514) 985-3390; Publr Lise Bissonnette; circ. 28,000 (m), 36,000 (Sat.).

The Gazette: 250 rue St-Antoine ouest, Montréal, PQ H2Y 3R7; tel. (514) 987-2222; telex 055-61767; fax (514) 987-2323; f. 1778; Publr Michael Goldbloom; Editor-in-Chief Joan Fraser; circ. 142,000 (m), 204,000 (Sat.).

Le Journal de Montréal: 4545 rue Frontenac, Montréal, PQ H2H 2R7; tel. (514) 521-4545; fax (514) 525-5442; f. 1964; Publr Pierre

Francoeur; Editor Jean-Phillipe Décarie; circ. 262,000 (m), 318,000 (Sat.).

Le Journal de Québec: 450 ave Béchard, Vanier, PQ G1M 2E9; tel. (418) 683-1573; fax (418) 683-1027; f. 1967; Publr Jean-Claude L'Abbée; Chief Editor Serge Côté; circ. 96,000 (m), 119,000 (Sat.).

Le Nouvelliste: 1920 rue Bellefeuille, Trois Rivières, G9A 3Y2; tel. (819) 376-2501; fax (819) 376-0946; f. 1920; Publr (vacant); Editor Jean Sisto; circ. 46,000 (m).

La Presse: 7 rue St-Jacques, Montréal, PQ H2Y 1K9; tel. (514) 285-7306; fax (514) 845-8129; f. 1884; Publr and Editor Roger D. Landry; circ. 167,000 (m), 300,000 (Sat.).

Le Quotidien du Saguenay-Lac-St-Jean: 1051 blvd Talbot, Chicoutimi, PQ G7H 5C1; tel. (418) 545-4474; fax (418) 545-8805; f. 1973; Publr and Editor Claude Gagnon; circ. 29,000 (m).

The Record: 2850 rue Delorme, Sherbrooke, PQ J1K 5L6; tel. (819) 569-9511; fax (819) 569-3945; f. 1837; Publr Randy Kinnear; Editor Sharon McCully; circ. 5,000 (m).

Le Soleil: 925 chemin St-Louis, CP 1547, succursale Terminus, Québec, PQ G1K 7J6; tel. (418) 686-3233; fax (418) 686-3260; f. 1896; Publr and Editor Gilbert Lacasse; circ. 90,000 (m), 135,000 (Sat.).

La Tribune: 1950 rue Roy, Sherbrooke, PQ J1K 2X8; tel. (819) 564-5450; fax (819) 564-5455; f. 1910; Publr Raymond Tardif; Editor Jacques Pronovost; circ. 33,000 (m), 48,000 (Sat.).

La Voix de L'Est: 76 rue Dufferin, Granby, PQ J2G 9L4; tel. (514) 375-4555; fax (514) 777-7221; f. 1945; Publr Pierre Gobeil; Man. Editor Dany Doucet; circ. 15,000 (m).

Saskatchewan

Daily Herald: 30 10th St East, Prince Albert, SK S6V 5R9; tel. (306) 764-4276; fax (306) 763-3119; f. 1894; Publr and Gen. Man. R. W. Gibb; Man. Editor Barb Gustafson; circ. 9,000 (m).

Leader–Post: 1964 Park St, Regina, SK S4P 3G4; tel. (306) 565-8211; fax (306) 565-8350; f. 1883; Publr (vacant); Editor Bob Hughes; circ. 56,000 (m).

StarPhoenix: 204 5th Ave North, Saskatoon, SK S7K 2P1; tel. (306) 652-9200; fax (306) 664-8208; e-mail spnews@saskstar.sk.ca; f. 1902; Publr Lyle Sinkewicz; Editor Steve Gibb; circ. 57,000 (m).

Times–Herald: 44 Fairford St West, Moose Jaw, SK S6H 6E4; tel. (306) 692-6441; fax (306) 692-2101; e-mail moose.jaw.times@sasknet.sk.ca; f. 1889; Publr Bob Calvert; Editor Carl DeGurse; circ. 10,000 (e).

Yukon Territory

Whitehorse Star: 2149 2nd Ave, Whitehorse, Yukon, YT Y1A 1C5; tel. (403) 668-2063; fax (403) 668-7130; f. 1985; Publr Robert Erlam; Editor Jim Butler; circ. 2,500 (e).

SELECTED PERIODICALS

(w = weekly; f = fortnightly; m = monthly; q = quarterly)

Alberta

Alberta FarmLIFE: 4850 51st St, Suite 200, Red Deer, AB T2N 2A5; tel. (403) 343-2769; fax (403) 343-2736; Man. Keith Rideout; circ. 70,000; 24 a year.

Ukrainski Visti (Ukrainian News): 12227 107th Ave, Suite 1, Edmonton, AB T5M 1Y9; tel. (403) 488-3693; fax (403) 488-3859; e-mail ukrnews@compusmart.ab.ca; f. 1929; Ukrainian and English; Editor Marco Levytsky; circ. 4,000 (f).

British Columbia

BC Business: 4180 Lougheed Hwy, 4th Floor, Burnaby, BC V5C 6A7; tel. (604) 299-7311; fax (604) 299-9188; f. 1973; Editor Bonnie Irving; circ. 9,000 (m).

BC Outdoors: 780 Beatty St, Suite 300, Vancouver, BC V6B 2M1; tel. (604) 687-1581; fax (604) 687-1925; e-mail oppubl@istar.ca; f. 1945; Editor Karl Bruhn; circ. 32,000; 8 a year.

Pacific Yachting: 780 Beatty St, Suite 300, Vancouver, BC V6B 2M1; tel. (604) 687-1581; fax (604) 687-1925; e-mail oppubl@istar.ca; f. 1968; Editor Duart Snow; circ. 15,000 (m).

Vancouver Magazine: 555 West 12th Ave, SE Tower, Suite 300, Vancouver, BC V5Z 4L4; tel. (604) 877-7732; fax (604) 877-4848; e-mail vanmag.editor@vanmag.com; f. 1957; Editor Jim Sutherland; circ. 6,000; 8 a year.

Western Living: 555 West 12th Ave, SE Tower, Suite 300, Vancouver, BC V5Z 4L4; tel. (604) 877-7732; fax (604) 877-4849; e-mail westernliving@ican.net; f. 1971; Editor Carolann Rule; circ. 253,000 (m).

WestWorld BC: 4180 Lougheed Hwy, 4th Floor, Burnaby, BC V5C 6A7; tel. (604) 299-7311; fax (604) 299-9188; f. 1984; Editor Pat Price; circ. 485,000; (q).

Manitoba

The Beaver: Exploring Canada's History: 167 Lombard Ave, Suite 478, Winnipeg, MB R3B 0T6; tel. (204) 988-9300; fax (204) 988-9309; e-mail beaver@cyberspc.mb.ca; f. 1920; Canadian social history; Editor Christopher Dafoe; circ. 45,000; 6 a year.

Cattlemen: POB 6600, Winnipeg, MB R3C 3A7; tel. (204) 944-5753; fax (204) 942-8463; f. 1938; animal husbandry; Editors Andy Sirski, Gren Winslow; circ. 24,000 (m).

Country Guide: 201 Portage Ave, Suite 205, Winnipeg, MB R3C 3A7; tel. (204) 944-5760; fax (204) 942-8463; f. 1882; agriculture; Editor David Wreford; circ. 50,000; 11 a year.

Grainews: 201 Portage Ave, Suite 2500, POB 6600, Winnipeg, MB R3C 3A7; tel. (204) 944-5587; fax (204) 944-5416; e-mail jham@fbc/unitedgrain.ca; f. 1975; grain and cattle farming; Editor Andy Sirski; circ. 52,000; 16 a year.

Kanada Kurier: 955 Alexander Ave, POB 1054, Winnipeg, MB R3C 2X8; tel. (204) 774-1883; fax (204) 783-5740; f. 1889; German; Editor Renate Achenbach; circ. 25,000 (w).

Kids' World Magazine: 93 Lombard Ave, Suite 108, Winnipeg, MB R3B 3B1; tel. (204) 942-2214; fax (204) 943-8991; Editor Stuart Slayden; circ. 225,000; 6 a year.

The Manitoba Co-operator: 220 Portage Ave, 4th Floor, POB 9800, Winnipeg, MB R3C 3K7; tel. (204) 934-0401; fax (204) 934-0480; e-mail news@co-operator.mb.ca; f. 1925; farming; Editor John W. Morriss; circ. 21,000 (w).

Newfoundland

Newfoundland Sportsman: 803 Water St West, POB 13754, Station A, St John's, NF A1B 4G5; tel. (709) 754-3515; fax (709) 754-2490; f. 1990; Editor Gordon Follet; circ. 15,000; 6 a year.

Northwest Territories

L'Aquilon: POB 1325, Yellowknife, NT X1A 2N9; tel. (403) 873-6603; fax (403) 873-2158; f. 1985; Editor Alain Bessette; circ. 1,000 (w).

The Hub: POB 1250, MacKenzie Hwy, Hay River, NT X0E 0R0; tel. (403) 874-6577; fax (403) 874-2679; f. 1973; Editor Chris Brodeur; circ. 4,000 (w).

News/North: POB 2820, Yellowknife, NT X1A 2R1; tel. (403) 873-8109; f. 1945; Editor J. Sigvaldson; circ. 10,000 (w).

Nunatsiaq News: POB 8, Iqaluit, NT X0A 0H0; tel. (819) 979-5357; fax (819) 979-4763; f. 1972; English and Inuktitut; Publr Steven Roberts; Editor Todd Phillips; circ. 6,000 (w).

Slave River Journal: 207 McDougal Rd, POB 990, Fort Smith, NT X0E 0P0; tel. (403) 872-2784; fax (403) 872-2754; e-mail srj@auroranet.nt.ca; Editor Darren Campbell; circ. 2,000 (w).

Yellowknifer: 5108 50th St, POB 2820, Yellowknife, NT X1A 2R1; tel. (403) 873-4031; fax (403) 873-8507; Editor Jack Sigvaldason; circ. 6,000 (w).

Nova Scotia

Canadian Forum: 5502 Atlantic St, Halifax, NS B3H 1G4; tel. (902) 421-7022; fax (902) 425-0166; f. 1920; political, literary and economic; Editor Duncan Cameron; circ. 9,000; 10 a year.

Dalhousie Review: 1456 Henry St, Halifax, NS B3H 3J5; tel. (902) 494-2541; fax (902) 494-3561; e-mail dalhousie.review@is.dal.ca; f. 1921; literary; Editor Dr Ronald Huebert; 3 a year.

Ontario

Anglican Journal: 600 Jarvis St, Toronto, ON M4Y 2J6; tel. (416) 924-9199; fax (416) 921-4452; f. 1871; official publ. of the Anglican Church of Canada; Editor Rev. David Harris; circ. 250,000; 10 a year.

Books in Canada: 30 St Clair Ave East, 3rd Floor, Toronto, ON M4T 1M9; tel. (416) 924-2777; fax (416) 924-8682; e-mail binc@istar.ca; f. 1971; Editor Gerald Owen; circ. 8,000; 9 a year.

CA magazine: The Canadian Institute of Chartered Accountants, 277 Wellington St West, Toronto, ON M5V 3H2; tel. (416) 977-3222; fax (416) 204-3409; e-mail christian.bellavance@cica.ca; f. 1911; Editor-in-Chief Christian Bellavance; circ. 69,000 (m).

Campus Canada: 287 MacPherson Ave, Toronto, ON M4V 1A4; tel. (416) 928-2909; fax (416) 928-1357; 30 campus edns; Man. Editor Sarah Moore; circ. 121,000 (q).

Canada Gazette: Canada Gazette Division, Public Works and Government Services, 350 Albert St, Ottawa, ON K1A 0S5; tel. (613) 991-1347; fax (613) 991-3540; f. 1867; official bulletin of the Govt of Canada; (w).

Canadian Architect: 1450 Don Mills Rd, Don Mills, ON M3B 2X7; tel. (416) 445-6641; telex 069-66612; fax (416) 442-2077; f. 1955; Man. Editor Bronwen Ledger; circ. 11,000 (m).

Canadian Art: 70 The Esplanade, 2nd Floor, Toronto, ON M5E 1R2; tel. (416) 368-8854; fax (416) 368-6135; Editor Richard Rhodes; circ. 20,000 (q).

Canadian Author: 27 Doxsee Ave North, POB 419, Campbellford, ON K0L 1L0; tel. (519) 438-2011; e-mail douglasbale@netcom.ca; f. 1919; publ. by the Canadian Authors Asscn; Man. Editor DOUGLAS BALE; circ. 3,000 (Q).

Canadian Aviation & Aircraft for Sale: POB 4755, Hamilton, ON L8H 7S7; tel. (909) 544-0560; fax (909) 544-8121; f. 1928; Editor GARTH WALLACE; circ. 10,000 ; 6 a year.

Canadian Banker: Commerce Court West, Box 348, Toronto, ON M5L 1G2; tel. (416) 362-6092; fax (416) 362-5658; f. 1893; Editor SIMON HALLY; circ. 33,000; 6 a year.

Canadian Bar Review: Canadian Bar Asscn, 50 O'Connor St, Suite 902, Ottawa, ON K1P 6L2; tel. (613) 237-2925; fax (613) 237-0185; e-mail CBA:info@cha.org; f. 1923; Editor Prof. EDWARD VEITCH; circ. 36,000 (Q).

Canadian Business: 777 Bay St, 5th Floor, Toronto, ON M5W 1A7; tel. (416) 596-5100; fax (416) 596-5152; f. 1927; Editor ARTHUR JOHNSON; circ. 83,000 (M).

Canadian Chemical News: 130 Slater St, Suite 550, Ottawa, ON K1P 6E2; tel. (613) 232-6252; fax (613) 232-5862; e-mail cic—publ@fox.nstn.ca; f. 1949; Editor NOLA HADDADIAN; circ. 6,000; 10 a year.

Canadian Defence Quarterly: 310 Dupont St, Toronto, ON M5R 1V9; tel. (416) 968-7252; fax (416) 968-2377; e-mail cdq@baxter.net; Editor MARTIN SHADWICK; circ. 6,000.

Canadian Dental Association Journal: 1815 Alta Vista Drive, Ottawa, ON K1G 3Y6; tel. (613) 523-1770; fax (613) 523-7736; e-mail cda–adc.ca; f. 1935; Editor Dr JOHN O'KEEFE; Man. Editor TERENCE DAVIS; (M).

Canadian Electronics: 135 Spy Court, Markham, ON L3R 5H6; tel. (905) 447-3222; fax (905) 477-4320; f. 1986; Editor TIM GOULDSON; circ. 22,000; 6 a year.

Canadian Geographic: 39 McArthur Ave, Vanier, ON K1L 8L7; tel. (613) 745-4629; fax (613) 744-0947; f. 1930; publ. of the Royal Canadian Geographical Soc.; Editor RICK BOYCHUK; circ. 227,000; 6 a year.

Canadian House & Home: 511 King St West, Suite 120, Toronto, ON M5V 2Z4; tel. (416) 593-0204; fax (416) 591-1630; e-mail exec@canhomepub.com; f. 1982; Editor COBI LADNER; circ. 148,000; 9 a year.

Canadian Jewish News: 1500 Don Mills Rd, Suite 205, North York, ON M3B 3KY; tel. (416) 391-1836; fax (416) 391-0829; e-mail TORCJNI@aol.com; Editor MORDECHAI BEN-DAT; circ. 47,000; 50 a year.

Canadian Journal of Economics: c/o University of Toronto Press, 5201 Dufferin St, North York, ON M3H 5T8; tel. (416) 667-7782; fax (416) 667-7881; f. 1968; Editor B. CURTIS EATON; circ. 3,000 (Q).

Canadian Living: 25 Sheppard Ave West, Suite 100, North York, ON M2N 6S7; tel. (416) 733-7600; fax (416) 733-3398; f. 1975; Editor-in-Chief BONNIE COWAN; circ. 569,000 (M).

Canadian Medical Association Journal: 1867 Alta Vista Drive, Ottawa, ON K1G 3Y6; tel. (613) 731-8610; fax (613) 523-0824; f. 1911; Scientific Editor Dr JOHN HOEY; circ. 59,000; 24 a year.

Canadian Musician: 23 Hannover Drive, Suite 7, St Catharines, ON L2W 1A3; tel. (905) 641-1512; fax (905) 641-1648; f. 1979; Man. Editor SHAUNA KENNEDY; circ. 30,000; 6 a year.

Canadian Nurse/L'infirmière canadienne: 50 Driveway, Ottawa, ON K2P 1E2; tel. (613) 237-2133; fax (613) 237-3520; f. 1905; journal of the Canadian Nurses' Asscn; Editor-in-Chief JUDITH HAINES; circ. 112,000; 10 a year.

Canadian Pharmaceutical Journal: c/o C. K. Goodman, Inc, 1382 Hurontario St, Mississauga, ON L5G 3H4; tel. (905) 278-6700; fax (905) 278-4850; f. 1868; Editor ANDREW REINBOLDT; circ. 10,000; 10 a year.

Canadian Public Policy—Analyse de Politiques: School of Policy Studies, Rm 409, Queen's University, Kingston, ON K7L 3N6; tel. (613) 545-6644; fax (613) 545-6960; e-mail cpp@silver .queensu.ca; Editor CHARLES M. BEACH; circ. 2,000 (Q).

Canadian Travel Press Weekly: 310 Dupont St, Toronto, ON M5R 1V9; tel. (416) 968-7252; fax (416) 968-2377; e-mail ctp@baxter.net; Editor EDITH BAXTER; circ. 13,000; 46 a year.

Canadian Workshop: 340 Ferrier St, Markham, ON L3R 2Z5; tel. (905) 475-8440; fax (905) 475-9246; e-mail letters@canadianworkshop.ca; f. 1977; do-it-yourself; Editor DOUG BENNET; circ. 115,000 (M).

ComputerWorld Canada: 501 Oakdale Rd, North York, ON M3N 1W7; tel. (416) 746-7360; fax (416) 746-1421; Editor JOHN PICKETT; circ. 39,000; 25 a year.

Elm Street: 665 Bay St, Suite 1100, Toronto, ON M5G 2K4; tel. (416) 595-9944; fax (416) 595-7217; f. 1996; women's interest; Editor-in-Chief STEVIE CAMERON; circ. 701,000; 6 a year.

Farm and Country: One Yonge St, Suite 1504, Toronto, ON M5E 1E5; tel. (416) 364-5324; fax (416) 364-5857; f. 1936; Man. Editor JOHN MUGGERIDGE; circ. 48,000; 15 a year.

Hockey News: 777 Bay St, Suite 2700, Toronto, ON M5G 2N1; tel. (416) 340-8000; fax (416) 340-2786; e-mail amosb@pathcom.com; f. 1947; Editor-in-Chief STEVE DRYDEN; circ. 205,000; 42 a year.

Holstein Journal: 9120 Leslie St, Unit 105, Richmond Hill, ON L4B 3J9; tel. (905) 886-4222; fax (905) 886-0037; f. 1938; Editor BONNIE COOPER; circ. 10,000 (M).

Legion Magazine: 359 Kent St, Suite 407, Ottawa, ON K2P 0R6; tel. (613) 235-8741; fax (613) 233-7159; f. 1926; Editor MAC JOHNSTON; circ. 434,000; 5 a year.

Magyar Élet (Hungarian Life): 313 Sheppard Ave East, North York, ON M2N 3B3; tel. (416) 221-6195; fax (416) 221-6358; f. 1948; Hungarian; Editor LASZLO BESSENYEI; circ. 8,000 (W).

Northern Miner: 1450 Don Mills Rd, Don Mills, ON M3B 2X7; tel. (416) 442-2164; fax (416) 442-2181; f. 1915; Editor VIVIAN DANIELSON; circ. 23,000 (W).

Ontario Medical Review: 525 University Ave, Suite 300, Toronto, ON M5G 2K7; tel. (416) 599-2580; fax (416) 599-9309; e-mail jeff—henry@oma.org; f. 1922; Editor JEFF HENRY; circ. 23,000 (M).

Ontario Milk Producer: 6780 Campobello Rd, Mississauga, ON L5N 2L8; tel. (905) 821-8970; fax (905) 821-3160; f. 1925; Editor BILL DIMMICK; circ. 12,000.

Oral Health: 1450 Don Mills Rd, Don Mills, ON M3B 2X7; tel. (416) 442-2046; fax (416) 442-2214; e-mail ckeeshan@southam.ca; f. 1911; dentistry; Man. Editor CYNTHIA KEESHAN; circ. 17,000 (M).

Outdoor Canada: 703 Evans Ave, Suite 202, Toronto, ON M9C 5E9; tel. (416) 695-0311; fax (416) 695-0381; f. 1972; Editor JAMES LITTLE; circ. 79,000; 8 a year.

Photo Life: Toronto Dominion Bank Tower, 55 King St West, Suite 2550, POB 77, Toronto, ON M5K 1E7; tel. (800) 905-7468; fax (800) 664-2739; e-mail 76743.3210@compuserve.com; Editor JACQUES THIBAULT; circ. 65,000; 6 a year.

Quill & Quire: 70 The Esplanade, Suite 210, Toronto, ON M5E 1R2; tel. (416) 360-0044; fax (416) 955-0794; e-mail quill@hookup.net; f. 1935; book-publishing industry; Editor SCOTT ANDERSON; circ. 7,000 (M).

Saturday Night: 184 Front St East, Suite 400, Toronto, ON M5A 4N3; tel. (416) 368-7237; fax (416) 368-5112; f. 1887; Editor KENNETH WHYTE; circ. 400,000; 10 a year.

Style: 1448 Lawrence Ave East, Suite 302, Toronto, ON M4A 2V6; tel. (416) 755-5199; fax (416) 755-9123; e-mail style@style.on.ca; f. 1888; Editor DORIS MONTANERA; circ. 9,000 (M).

Style at Home: 25 Sheppard Ave West, Suite 100, North York, ON M2N 6S7; tel. (416) 218-3532; fax (416) 218-3632; e-mail ghabs@styleathome.com; Editor GAIL JOHNSTON HABS; circ. 210,000; 8 a year.

Sympatico Netlife: 25 Sheppard Ave West, Suite 100, North York, ON M2N 6S7; tel. (416) 733-7600; fax (416) 733-8272; e-mail giffen@sympatico.ca; computer technology; Editor PETER GIFFEN; circ. 240,000; 6 a year.

Teviskes Ziburiai (Lights of Homeland): 2185 Stavebank Rd, Mississauga, ON L5C 1T3; tel. (905) 275-4672; fax (905) 275-6755; e-mail tevzib@pathcom.com; f. 1949; Lithuanian; Editor Mgr Dr PR. GAIDA; circ. 4,000 (W).

Toronto Life Magazine: 59 Front St East, 3rd Floor, Toronto, ON M5E 1B3; tel. (416) 364-3333; fax (416) 861-1169; f. 1966; Editor JOHN MACFARLANE; circ. 97,000 (M).

Tribute Magazine: 71 Barber Greene Rd, Don Mills, ON M3C 2A2; tel. (416) 445-0544; fax (416) 445-2894; entertainment; Publr and Editor SANDRA STEWART; circ. 656,000; 8 a year.

TV Guide: 25 Sheppard Ave West, Suite 100, North York, ON M2N 6S7; tel. (416) 733-7600; fax (416) 733-3632; f. 1976; Editor CHRISTOPHER LOUDON; circ. 750,000 (W).

TV Times: 1450 Don Mills Rd, Don Mills, ON M3B 2X7; tel. (416) 442-3444; fax (416) 442-2088; f. 1969; circ. 1,941,000 (W).

The following are all published by Maclean Hunter Ltd, 360 DuPont St, Toronto, ON M5R 1V9; tel. (416) 966-9944; fax (416) 966-9946:

Canadian Grocer: f. 1886; Editor GEORGE CONDON; circ. 20,000 (M).

Chatelaine: f. 1928; women's journal; Editor MILDRED ISTONA; circ. 793,000 (M).

Chatelaine Gardens: f. 1995; Editor ANILA DRAYCOTT; circ. 115,000; 6 a year.

Design Engineering: f. 1955; Editor JAMES BARNES; circ. 19,000 (M).

Flare: f. 1979; Editor SUZANNE BOYD; circ. 173,000 (M).

Heavy Construction News: f. 1956; Editor RUSS NOBLE; circ. 22,000 (M).

Maclean's Canada's Weekly Newsmazagine: f. 1905; Editor ROBERT LEWIS; circ. 504,000 (W).

Marketing: f. 1908; Editor STAN SUTTER; circ. 11,000 (W).

Medical Post: f. 1965; Editor PAT RICH; circ. 41,000; 44 a year.

Québec

L'Actualité: 1001 blvd de Maisonneuve ouest, Montréal, PQ H3A 3E1; tel. (514) 845-2543; fax (514) 845-7503; f. 1976; current affairs; Editor JEAN PARÉ; circ. 222,000 (M).

Affaires Plus: 1100 blvd René-Lévesque ouest, 24e étage, Montréal, PQ H3B 4X9; tel. (514) 392-9000; fax (514) 392-4726; f. 1978; Editor-in-Chief MARIE-AGNÈS THELLIER; circ. 95,000 (M).

Le Bulletin des Agriculteurs: 1001 blvd de Maisonneuve ouest, Montréal, PQ H3A 3E1; tel. (514) 845-5141; fax (514) 845-6261; f. 1918; Editor MARC-ALAIN SOUCY; circ. 36,000 (M).

Canadian Forest Industries: 1 rue Pacifique, Ste-Anne-de-Bellevue, PQ H9X 1C5; tel. (514) 457-2211; fax (514) 457-2558; e-mail JCFT@AEI.CA; f. 1880; Editor SCOTT JAMIESON; circ. 12,000; 8 a year.

Châtelaine: 1001 blvd de Maisonneuve ouest, 11e étage, Montréal, PQ H3A 3E1; tel. (514) 843-2504; fax (514) 845-4302; f. 1960; Editor CATHERINE ELIE; circ. 186,000 (M).

CIM Bulletin: 3400 blvd de Maisonneuve ouest, Bureau 1210, Montréal, PQ H3Z 3B8; tel. (514) 939-2710; fax (514) 939-2714; publ. by the Canadian Inst. of Mining, Metallurgy and Petroleum; Editor PERLA GANTZ; circ. 9,000 (M).

Il Cittadino Canadese: 6020 Jean-Talon est, Bureau 600, Montréal, PQ H1S 3B1; tel. (514) 253-2332; fax (514) 253-6574; f. 1941; Italian; Editor BASILIO GIORDANO; circ. 48,000 (W).

Clin d'Oeil: 7 chemin Bates, Outremont, PQ H2V 1A6; tel. (514) 270-1100; fax (514) 270-7079; Editorial Dir SANDRA CLICHE; circ. 70,000 (M).

Coup de Pouce: 2001 rue Université, Bureau 900, Montréal, PQ H3A 2A6; tel. (514) 499-0561; fax (514) 499-1844; f. 1984; Publr MICHELE CYR; circ. 146,000 (M).

Décormag: 5148 blvd St-Laurent, Montréal, PQ H2T 1R8; tel. (514) 273-9773; fax (514) 273-9034; f. 1973; Editor MICHÈLE DUBREUIL; circ. 33,000; 10 a year.

Equinox: 450 blvd Albert-Hudon, Bureau 1450, Montréal-Nord, PQ H1G 3J9; tel. (514) 327-4464; fax (514) 327-0514; f. 1982; Editor ALAN MORANTZ; circ. 120,000; 6 a year.

Femme d' Aujourd'hui: 2020 rue Université, Bureau 2000, Montréal, PQ H3A 2A5; tel. (514) 848-7000; fax (514) 9854; f. 1995; Publr CLAUDE J. CHARON; circ. 103,000 (M).

Le Lundi: 2020 rue Université, Bureau 2000, Montréal, PQ H5A 2A5; tel. (514) 848-7000; fax (514) 848-9854; f. 1976; Editor MICHÈLE LEMIEUX; circ. 66,000 (W).

Photo Sélection: 185 rue St-Paul, Québec, PQ G1K 3W2; tel. (418) 692-2110; fax (418) 692-3392; f. 1980; Editor JACQUES THIBAULT; circ. 17,000; 6 a year.

Le Producteur de Lait Québécois: 555 blvd Roland-Thérrien, Longueuil, PQ J4H 3Y9; tel. (514) 679-0530; fax (514) 670-4788; e-mail rioiseau@tcn.upa.qc.ca; f. 1980; dairy farming; Editor-in-Chief JEAN VIGNEAULT; circ. 14,000 (M).

Progrès-Dimanche: 1051 blvd Talbot, Chicoutimi, PQ G7H 5C1; tel. (418) 545-4474; fax (418) 690-8805; f. 1964; Pres. and Editor CLAUDE GAGNON; circ. 44,000 (W).

Québec Science: 425 rue de La Gauchetière est, Montréal, PQ H2L 2M7; tel. (514) 843-6888; fax (514) 843-4897; f. 1969; Editor-in-Chief RAYMOND LEMIEUX; circ. 17,000; 10 a year.

Rénovation Bricolage: 7 chemin Bates, Outremont, PQ H2V 1A6; tel. (514) 270-1100; fax (514) 270-6900; f. 1976; Editorial Dir CLAUDE LECLERC; circ. 36,000; 9 a year.

Revue Commerce: 1100 blvd René-Lévesque ouest, 24e étage, Montréal, PQ H3B 4X9; tel. (514) 392-9000; fax (514) 392-4726; f. 1898; Editor-in-Chief PIERRE DUHAMEL; circ. 38,000 (M).

Sélection du Reader's Digest: 215 ave Redfern, Westmount, PQ H3Z 2V9; tel. (514) 934-0751; fax (514) 932-3637; f. 1947; Editor-in-Chief LISE VERSCHELDEN; circ. 321,000 (M).

La Terre de Chez Nous: 555 blvd Roland-Thérrien, Longueuil, PQ J4H 3Y9; tel. (514) 679-0530; fax (514) 679-5436; e-mail rioiseau@tcn.upa.qc.ca; f. 1929; agriculture and forestry; Editor-in-Chief FRANCE GROULX; circ. 40,000 (W).

TV Hebdo: 2020 rue Université, Bureau 20 e étage, Montréal, PQ H3A 2A5; tel. (514) 848-7000; fax (514) 848-0835; f. 1960; Editor-in-Chief JEAN-LOUIS PODLESAK; circ. 234,000 (W).

Saskatchewan

Agworld: 204 5th Ave North, Saskatoon, SK S7K 2P1; tel. (306) 664-8340; fax (306) 664-8208; f. 1996; farming; Editor JOHN CHEMESKI; circ. 68,000 (M).

Farm Light & Power: 2352 Smith St, Regina, SK S4P 2P6; tel. (306) 525-3305; fax (306) 757-1810; f. 1959; Editor PAT REDIGER; circ. 72,000 (M).

Western Producer: 2310 Millar Ave, POB 2500, Saskatoon, SK S7K 2C4; tel. (306) 665-3500; fax (306) 653-8750; f. 1923; world and agricultural news; Editor GARRY FAIRBAIRN; circ. 96,000 (W).

Western Sportsman: 140 Ave F North, Saskatoon, SK S7L 1V8; tel. (306) 665-6302; fax (306) 244-8859; e-mail copi@sk.sympatico.ca; f. 1968; Editor GEORGE GRUENEFELD; circ. 22,000; 6 a year.

Yukon Territory

L'Aurore Boréale: POB 5025, Whitehorse, YT Y1A 4Z1; tel. (403) 667-2931; fax (403) 668-3511; French; circ. 1,000 (M).

Yukon News: 211 Wood St, Whitehorse, YT Y1A 2E4; tel. (403) 667-6285; fax (403) 668-3755; f. 1960; Editor PETER LESNIAK; circ. 7,000; 2 a week.

NEWS AGENCIES

The Canadian Press: 36 King St East, Toronto, ON M5C 2L9; tel. (416) 364-0321; fax (416) 364-0207; f. 1917; national news co-operative; 88 daily newspaper mems; Chair. MICHAEL G. SIFTON; Pres. JIM POLING.

Foreign Bureaux

Agence France-Presse (AFP): 231 rue St-Jacques, Bureau 1201, Montréal, PQ H2Y 1M6; tel. (514) 875-8877; fax (514) 393-1815; Bureau Chief HERVÉ GUILBAUD; also office in Ottawa.

Agencia EFE (Spain): 165 Sparks St, Ottawa, ON K1P 5B9; tel. (613) 230-2282.

Agenzia Nazionale Stampa Associata (ANSA) (Italy): 150 Wellington St, Press Gallery, Room 703, Ottawa, ON K1P 5A4; tel. (613) 235-4248; telex 053-4392; fax (613) 235-4248; Representative ELIO COPPOLA.

Associated Press (USA): 36 King St East, Toronto, ON M5C 2L9; tel. (416) 368-1388.

Deutsche Presse-Agentur (dpa) (Germany): 702 National Press Bldg, 150 Wellington St, Ottawa, ON K1P 5A4; tel. (613) 234-6024; telex 0253-4812; Correspondent BARBARA HALSIG.

Informatsionnoye Telegrafnoye Agentstvo Rossii—Telegrafnoye Agentstvo Sovetskovo Soyuza (ITAR–TASS) (Russia): 200 Rideau Terrace, Suite 1305, Ottawa, ON K1M OZ3; tel. (613) 745-4310; fax (613) 745-5581; Correspondent NIKOLAI SETOUNSKI.

Inter-Press Service (IPS) (Italy): 1262 Kingston Ave, Ottawa, ON K1Z 8K6; tel. (613) 992-4517; also office in Montréal.

Jiji Tsushin-Sha (Japan): 372 Bay St, Suite 605, Toronto, ON M5H 2W9; tel. (416) 368-8037; fax (416) 368-2905; Bureau Chief KENZO TANIAI; also office in Ottawa.

Prensa Latina (Cuba): 221 rue du St-Sacrement, Bureau 40, Montréal, PQ H2Y 1X1; tel. (514) 844-2975; Correspondent R. RAMOS.

Reuters (UK): 2020 rue Université, Bureau 1020, Montréal, PQ H3A 2A5; tel. (514) 282-0744; fax (514) 844-2327; also office in Vancouver.

United Press International (USA): 27 Carlton St, Suite 405, Toronto, ON M5H 1L2; tel. (416) 340-7276; also office in Ottawa.

Xinhua (New China) News Agency (People's Republic of China): 406 Daly Ave, Ottawa, ON K1N 6H2; tel. (613) 234-8424.

PRESS ASSOCIATIONS

Canadian Business Press: 40 Shields Court, Suite 201, Markham, ON L3R 0M5; tel. (905) 946-8889; fax (905) 479-1711; e-mail JJCBP@passport.ca; Chair. TERRY MALDEN; Pres. JUDY JOHNSON; 125 mems.

Canadian Community Newspapers Association: 90 Eglinton Ave East, Suite 206, Toronto, ON M4P 2Y3; tel. (416) 482-1090; fax (416) 482-1908; e-mail info@ccna.ca; f. 1919; Exec. Dir MICHAEL ANDERSON; 692 mems.

Canadian Newspaper Association: 890 Yonge St, Suite 1100, Toronto, ON M4W 3P4; tel. (416) 923-3567; fax (416) 923-7206; e-mail bcantley@fox.nstn.ca; f. 1919; Chair. KEVIN B. PETERSON; Pres. and CEO RICHARD DICERNI; 85 mems.

Canadian Magazine Publishers Association: 130 Spadina Ave, Suite 202, Toronto, ON M5V 2L4; tel. (416) 504-0274; fax (416) 504-0437; f. 1973; Pres. CATHERINE KEACHIE.

Magazines Canada (The Magazine Asscn of Canada): 777 Bay St, 7th Floor, Toronto, ON M5W 1A7; tel. (416) 596-5382; fax (416) 596-6043; e-mail magscan@hookup.net; Chair. BRIAN SEGAL.

Publishers

Addison-Wesley Publishers Ltd: 26 Prince Andrew Place, POB 580, Don Mills, ON M3C 2T8; tel. (416) 447-5101; telex 069-86743; fax (416) 443-0948; f. 1966; educational; CEO ANTHONY VANDER WOUDE.

Annick Press Ltd: 15 Patricia Ave, Willowdale, ON M2M 1H9; tel. (416) 221-4802; fax (416) 221-8400; e-mail annickpress@pw.ca; f. 1976; children's; Co-Dirs RICK WILKS, ANNE MILLYARD.

Arsenal Pulp Press: 1014 Homer St, Suite 103, Vancouver, BC V6B 2W9; tel. (604) 687-4233; fax (604) 669-8250; e-mail arsenal@pinc.com; f. 1982; literary, native, cultural studies; Publr BRIAN LAM.

Bantam Books Canada Inc/Doubleday Canada Inc: 105 Bond St, Toronto, ON M5B 1Y3; tel. (416) 340-0777; fax (416) 977-8488; originals and reprints; Pres. and CEO JOHN NEALE.

Black Rose Books: CP 1258, succursale place du Parc, Montréal, PQ H2W 1Y5; tel. (514) 844-4076; fax (514) 849-1956; e-mail blackrose@web.net; f. 1969; social studies; Pres. JACQUES ROUX.

Blizzard Publishing: 73 Furnaby St, Winnipeg, MB R3C 2A2; tel. (204) 775-2923; fax (204) 77-2947; drama and criticism; Man. Editor PETER ATWOOD.

Borealis Press/Tecumseh Presses: 9 Ashburn Drive, Ottawa, ON K2E 6N4; tel. (613) 224-6837; fax (613) 829-7783; e-mail borealis@istar.ca; f. 1972; Canadian fiction and non-fiction, drama, juveniles, poetry; Pres. FRANK TIERNEY.

Breakwater Books/Softwares Ltd: 100 Water St, POB 2188, St John's, NF A1C 6E6; tel. (709) 722-6680; fax (709) 753-0708; e-mail breakwater@nfld.com; f. 1973; fiction, non-fiction, children's, educational, folklore; Pres. CLYDE ROSE.

Brick Books: 431 Boler Rd, Box 20081, London, ON N6K 4G6; tel. and fax (519) 657-8579; Canadian poetry; Man. KITTY LEWIS.

Canada Law Book Inc: 240 Edward St, Aurora, ON L4G 3S9; tel. (905) 841-6472; fax (905) 841-5085; f. 1855; law reports, law journals, legal textbooks, etc.; Pres. S. G. CORBETT.

Carswell-Thomson Professional Publishing Canada: 2075 Kennedy Rd, Scarborough, ON M1T 3V4; tel. (416) 609-8000; fax (416) 298-5094; f. 1864; Pres. and CEO ROSS M. INKPEN.

Chenelière/McGraw-Hill: 7001 blvd St-Laurent, Montréal, PQ H2S 3E3; tel. (514) 273-1066; fax (514) 276-0324; e-mail chene@dlcmcgrawhill.ca; textbooks; Pres. MICHEL DE CHENELIÈRE.

Coach House Press: 760 Bathurst St, 2nd Floor, Toronto, ON M5S 2R6; tel. (416) 588-8999; fax (416) 588-3615; f. 1965; fiction, poetry, drama; Pres. DAVID YOUNG.

Copp Clark Professional: 200 Adelaide St West, 3rd Floor, Toronto, ON M5H 1W7; tel. (416) 597-1616; fax (416) 597-1617; e-mail info@mail.canadainfo.com; f. 1841; directory, financial and professional material; Pres. (vacant).

Crabtree Publishing Co Ltd: 360 York Rd, RR 4, Niagara-on-the-Lake, ON L0S 1J0; tel. (905) 682-5221; fax (905) 682-7166; f. 1978; children's; Pres. PETER CRABTREE.

Doubleday Canada Ltd: 105 Bond St, Toronto, ON M5B 1Y3; tel. (416) 340-0777; fax (416) 977-8488; f. 1944; general, trade, textbooks, mass market; Pres. JOHN NEALE.

Douglas and McIntyre Ltd: 1615 Venables St, Vancouver, BC V5L 2H1; tel. (604) 254-7191; fax (604) 254-9099; e-mail dm@douglas-mcintyre.com; f. 1964; fiction, general non-fiction, juvenile; Pres. SCOTT MCINTYRE.

The Dundurn Group: 8 Market St, Suite 200, Toronto, ON M5E 1M6; tel. (416) 214-5544; fax (416) 214-5556; e-mail info@dundurn.com; f. 1972; drama and performing arts, reference, fiction and non-fiction; Pres. KIRK HOWARD.

Editions Bellarmin: 165 rue Deslauriers, Ville St-Laurent, PQ H4N 2S4; tel. (514) 745-4290; fax (514) 745-4299; f. 1891; religious, educational, politics, sociology, ethnography, history, sport, leisure; Dir-Gen. ANTOINE DEL BUSSO.

Les Editions CEC Inc: 8101 blvd Métropolitain est, Anjou, Montréal, PQ H1J 1J9; tel. (514) 351-6010; fax (514) 351-3534; f. 1956; textbooks; Pres. and Dir-Gen. JACQUES ROCHEFORT.

Les Editions du Boréal: 4447 rue St-Denis, Montréal, PQ H2J 2L2; tel. (514) 287-7401; fax (514) 287-7664; f. 1963; history, biography, fiction, politics, economics, educational, children's; Exec. Dir PASCAL ASSATHIANY.

Editions Fides: 165 rue Deslauriers, Ville St-Laurent, PQ H4N 2S4; tel. (514) 745-4290; fax (514) 745-4299; f. 1937; juvenile, history, theology, textbooks and literature; Dir-Gen. ANTOINE DEL BUSSO.

Editions Héritage: 300 ave Arran, St-Lambert, PQ J4R 1K5; tel. (514) 672-6710; fax (514) 672-1481; f. 1968; history, biography, sport, juveniles; Pres. JACQUES PAYETTE.

Editions de l'Hexagone: 1010 rue de La Gauchetière est, Montréal, PQ H2L 2N5; tel (514) 523-1182; fax (514) 282-7530; f. 1953; literature; Editorial Dir JEAN ROYER.

Editions du Renouveau Pédagogique Inc: 5757 rue Cyphiot, St-Laurent, PQ H4S 1R3; tel. (514) 334-2690; fax (514) 334-4720; f. 1965; textbooks; Pres. NORMAND CLÉROUX.

Editions du Septentrion: 1300 ave Maguire, Sillery, PQ G1T 1Z3; tel. (418) 688-3556; fax (418) 527-4978; f. 1988; history, essays, general; Man. DENIS VAUGEOIS.

Fenn Publishing Co Ltd: 34 Nixon Rd, Bolton, ON L7E 1W2; e-mail fenn@interhop.net; fiction and non-fiction; Publr C. JORDAN FENN.

Fifth House Publishers Ltd: 165 Third Ave South, Suite 201, Saskatoon, SK S7K 1L8; tel. (306) 242-4936; fax (306) 242-7667; f. 1982; native, literary and non-fiction; Publr FRASER SEELY.

Fitzhenry & Whiteside Ltd: 195 Allstate Pkwy, Markham, ON L3R 4T8; tel. (416) 477-9700; fax (416) 477-9179; f. 1966; textbooks, trade, educational; Pres. SHARON FITZHENRY.

Gage Educational Publishing Co: 164 Commander Blvd, Agincourt, ON M1S 3C7; tel. (416) 293-8141; fax (416) 293-9009; e-mail chris@gage.canpub.ca; f. 1844; Pres. CHRIS BESSE.

General Publishing Co Ltd: 30 Lesmill Rd, North York, ON M3B 2T6; tel. (416) 445-3333; fax (416) 445-5991; fiction and non-fiction; Pres. NELSON DOUCET.

Grolier Ltd: 12 Banigan Drive, Toronto, ON M4H 1A6; tel. (416) 425-1924; fax (416) 425-4015; f. 1912; reference, children's; Gen. Man. R. A. FURLONGER.

Harcourt Brace & Co Canada: 55 Horner Ave, Toronto, ON M8Z 4X6; tel. (416) 255-4491; fax (416) 255-4046; f. 1922; medical, educational, scholarly; Pres. JEAN-GUY BLANCHETTE.

Harlequin Books: 225 Duncan Mill Rd, Don Mills, ON M3B 3K9; tel. (416) 445-5860; fax (416) 445-8655; f. 1949; fiction, paperbacks; Pres. and CEO BRIAN HICKEY.

HarperCollins Canada Ltd: Hazleton Lanes, 55 Avenue Rd, Suite 2900, Toronto, ON M5R 3L2; tel. (416) 975-9334; fax (416) 975-9884; f. 1932; trade, bibles, dictionaries, juvenile, paperbacks; Pres. ED CARSON.

Hyperion Press: 300 Wales Ave, Winnipeg, MB R2M 2S9; tel. (204) 256-9204; fax (204) 255-7845; children's illustrated; Pres. MARVIS TUTIAH.

Institut de Recherches psychologiques, inc/Institute of Psychological Research, Inc: 34 rue Fleury ouest, Montréal, PQ H3L 1S9; tel. (514) 382-3000; fax (514) 382-3007; f. 1964; educational and psychological tests; Pres. DR JEAN-MARC CHEVRIER.

IPI Publishing Ltd: 50 Prince Arthur Ave, Suite 708, Toronto, ON M5R 1B5; tel. (416) 944-1141; fax (416) 944-1143; family studies, psychology, law; Pres. DANIEL J. BAUM.

Irwin Publishing: 1800 Steeles Ave West, Concord, ON L4K 2P3; tel. (905) 660-0611; fax (905) 660-0676; e-mail irwin@irwinpub.com; f. 1945; educational; Pres. BRIAN O'DONNELL.

ITP Nelson: 1120 Birchmount Rd, Scarborough, ON M1K 5G4; tel. (416) 752-9100; telex 069-63813; fax (416) 752-9646; f. 1914; retailing, consumer affairs, textbooks; Pres. (vacant).

Jesperson Press Ltd: 39 James Lane, St John's, NF A1E 3H3; tel. (709) 753-5700; fax (709) 753-5507; f. 1974; educational and trade; Pres. and Publr JOHN SYMONDS.

Key Porter Books: 70 The Esplanade, 3rd Floor, Toronto, ON M5E 1R2; tel. (416) 862-7777; fax (416) 862-2304; e-mail srenouf@KeyPorter.com; f. 1980; general trade; Pres. SUSAN RENOUF.

Lancelot Press Ltd: POB 425, Hantsport, NS BOP 1P0; tel. (902) 684-9129; fax (902) 684-3685; e-mail lancelot@atcon.com; f. 1966; non-fiction, regional; Pres. WILLIAM POPE.

Leméac Editeur: 1124 Marie-Anne est, Montréal, PQ H2J 2B7; tel. (514) 524-5558; fax (514) 524-3145; f. 1957; literary, academic, general; Pres. JULES BRILLANT.

Lidec Inc: 4350 ave de l'Hôtel-de-Ville, Montréal, PQ H2W 2H5; tel. (514) 843-5991; fax (514) 843-5252; f. 1965; educational, textbooks; Pres. MARC-AIME GUÉRIN.

James Lorimer & Co Ltd: 35 Britain St, Toronto, ON M5A 1R7; tel. (416) 362-4762; fax (416) 362-3939; f. 1971; urban and labour studies, children's, general non-fiction; Pres. JAMES LORIMER.

McClelland and Stewart Inc: 481 University Ave, Suite 900, Toronto, ON M5G 2E9; tel. (416) 598-1114; fax (416) 598-7764; f. 1906; trade, illustrated and educational; Chair. AVIE BENNETT.

McGill-Queen's University Press: 3430 rue McTavish, Montréal, PQ H3A 1X9; tel. (514) 398-3750; fax (514) 398-4333; e-mail mqup@printing.lan.mcgill.ca; f. 1960; scholarly and general interest; Pres. DAVID TURPIN.

McGraw-Hill Ryerson Ltd: 300 Water St, Whitby, ON L1N 9B6; tel. (416) 430-5000; fax (416) 430-5020; f. 1944; educational and general; Pres. and CEO JOHN DILL.

Macmillan Canada Inc: 29 Birch Ave, Toronto, ON M4V 1E2; tel. (416) 963-8830; fax (416) 923-4821; f. 1958; trade, reference; Pres. MICHAEL G. RICHARDSON.

Oberon Press: 350 Sparks St, Suite 400, Ottawa, ON K1R 7S8; tel. and fax (613) 238-3275; f. 1966; poetry, children's, fiction and general non-fiction; Pres. MICHAEL MACKLEM.

Orca Book Publishers Ltd: POB 5626, Station B, Vancouver, BC V8R 6S4; tel. (250) 380-1229; fax (250) 380-1892; f. 1984; juvenile, regional history, guides; Pres. R. J. TYRRELL.

Oxford University Press Canada: 70 Wynford Drive, Don Mills, ON M3C 1J9; tel. (416) 441-2941; fax (416) 444-0427; e-mail custserv@

oupcan.com; f. 1904; general, education, religious, Canadiana; Man. Dir SUSAN FROUD.

Penguin Books Canada Ltd: 10 Alcorn Ave, Suite 300, Toronto, ON M4V 3B2; tel. (416) 925-2249; fax (416) 925-0068; f. 1974; Pres. STEVEN PARR.

Pippin Publishing Corpn: 85 Ellesmere Rd, Suite 232, Scarborough, ON M1R 4B9; tel. (416) 510-2918; fax (416) 510-3359; f. 1990; educational; Pres. JONATHAN LOVAT DICKSON.

Pontifical Institute of Mediaeval Studies: 59 Queen's Park Crescent East, Toronto, ON M5S 2C4; tel. (416) 926-7144; fax (416) 926-7258; e-mail pontifex@chass.utoronto.ca; f. 1939; scholarly publs concerning the Middle Ages; Dir of Publs RON B. THOMSON.

Prentice Hall Canada Inc: 1870 Birchmount Rd, Scarborough, ON M1P 2J7; tel. (416) 293-3621; fax (416) 299-2529; f. 1960; trade, textbooks; Pres. BRIAN HEER.

Les Presses de l'Université Laval: Cité Universitaire, Ste-Foy, PQ G1K 7P4; tel. (418) 656-7381; fax (418) 656-3305; f. 1950; scholarly; Publr DENIS VAUGEOIS.

Les Presses de l'Université de Montréal: CP 6128, succursale Centre Ville, Montréal, PQ H3C 3J7; tel. (514) 343-6929; fax (514) 343-2232; e-mail pumedit@brise.ere.montreal.ca; f. 1962; scholarly and general; Gen. Man. MARIE-CLAIRE BORGO.

Les Presses de l'Université du Québec: 2875 blvd Laurier, Ste-Foy, PQ G1V 2M3; tel. (418) 657-4399; fax (418) 657-2096; e-mail admin@puq.uquebec.ca; f. 1969; scholarly and general; Dir-Gen. ANGÈLE TREMBLAY.

Random House of Canada Ltd: 1265 Aerowood Drive, Mississauga, ON L4W 1B9; tel. (905) 624-0672; fax (905) 624-6217; f. 1944; Pres. DAVID KENT.

The Reader's Digest Association (Canada) Ltd: 215 ave Redfern, Westmount, PQ H3Z 2V9; tel. (514) 934-0751; fax (514) 935-4463; Pres. and CEO BERNARD POIRIER.

Scholastic Canada Ltd: 123 Newkirk Rd, Richmond Hill, ON L4C 3G5; tel. (905) 883-5300; fax (905) 883-4113; Pres. F. C. L. MULLER.

Sogides Ltée: 955 rue Amherst, Montréal, PQ H2L 3K4; tel. (514) 523-1182; fax (514) 597-0370; f. 1958; general interest, fiction, psychology, biography; Pres. PIERRE LESPÉRANCE.

Stoddart Publishing Co Ltd: 34 Lesmill Rd, North York, ON M3B 2T6; tel. (416) 445-3333; fax (416) 445-5967; f. 1984; general fiction and non-fiction, textbooks, children's; Pres. JACK STODDART.

Thompson Educational Publishing Inc: 14 Ripley Ave, Suite 104, Toronto, ON M6S 3N9; tel. (416) 766-2763; fax (416) 766-0398; e-mail thompson@canadabooks.ingenia.com; f. 1989; textbooks; Pres. KEITH THOMPSON.

University of Alberta Press: 141 Athabasca Hall, Edmonton, AB T6G 2E8; tel. (403) 492-3662; fax (403) 492-0719; e-mail uap@gpu.srv.ualberta.ca; f. 1969; scholarly, general non-fiction; Dir GLENN ROLLANS.

University of British Columbia Press: 6344 Memorial Rd, Vancouver, BC V6T 1Z2; tel. (604) 822-3259; fax (604) 822-6083; f. 1971; humanities, science, social science; Dir R. PETER MILROY.

University of Manitoba Press: 15 Gillson St, Suite 244, Winnipeg, MB R3T 5V6; tel. (204) 474-9495; fax (204) 275-2270; f. 1967; regional history, native, Icelandic and women's studies; Dir DAVID CARR.

University of Ottawa Press/Presses de l'Université d'Ottawa: 542 ave King Edward, Ottawa, ON K1N 6N5; tel. (613) 562-5246; fax (613) 562-5247; e-mail press@uottawa.ca; f. 1936; university texts, scholarly works in English and French; general; Editor-in-Chief VICKI BENNETT.

University of Toronto Press Inc: 100 Queen's Park, Toronto, ON M5S 2C6; tel. (416) 586-5581; fax (416) 586-5827; f. 1901; scholarly books and journals; Pres. and Publr GEORGE MEADOWS.

Weigl Educational Publishers: 1902 11th St, SE, Calgary, AB T2G 3G2; tel. (403) 233-7747; fax (403) 33-7769; e-mail weigl@mail.telusplanet.net; f. 1979; textbooks; Publr LINDA WEIGL.

John Wiley and Sons Canada Ltd: 22 Worcester Rd, Etobicoke, ON M9W 1L1; tel. (416) 236-4433; fax (416) 236-8743; e-mail canada@wiley.com; f. 1968; Pres. DIANE WOOD.

Government Publishing House

Canada Communication Group–Publishing: Ottawa, ON K1A 0S9; tel. (819) 956-4800; fax (819) 994-1498; f. 1876; books and periodicals on numerous subjects, incl. agriculture, economics, environment, geology, history and sociology; Dir LESLIE-ANN SCOTT.

ORGANIZATIONS AND ASSOCIATIONS

Association of Canadian Publishers: 110 Eglinton Ave West, Suite 401, Toronto, ON M4R 1A3; tel. (416) 487-6116; fax (416) 487-8815; f. 1976; trade asscn of Canadian-owned English-language book publrs; represents Canadian publishing internationally; 136 mems; Exec. Dir PAUL DAVIDSON.

Canadian Publishers' Council: 250 Merton St, Suite 203, Toronto, ON M4S 1B1; tel. (416) 322-7011; fax (416) 322-6999; e-mail pubadmin@pubcouncil.ca; f. 1910; trade asscn of Canadian-owned publrs and Canadian-incorp. subsidiaries of UK and USA publrs; 27 mems; Pres. ED CARSON.

Broadcasting and Communications

The 1968 Broadcasting Act established the Canadian Broadcasting Corporation (CBC) as the national, publicly-owned, broadcasting service and created the Canadian Radio-Television and Telecommunications Commission (CRTC) as the agency regulating radio, television and cable television. The CRTC's telecommunications authority is currently derived from the 1985 Canadian Radio-television and Telecommunications Act. Subsequent Broadcasting Acts, introduced in 1991 and 1993, reconfirmed the CRTC's regulatory powers.

Many privately-owned television and radio stations have affiliation agreements with the CBC and help to distribute the national services. A number of the major private television networks (see below) also have affiliates.

Canadian Broadcasting Corporation/Société Radio Canada (CBC/SRC): 1500 Bronson Ave, POB 8478, Ottawa, ON K1G 3J5; tel. (613) 724-1200; f. 1936; financed mainly by public funds, with supplementary revenue from commercial advertising on CBC television; services in French, English, Dene and Inuktitut languages; Chair. Mme GUYLAINE SAUCIER; Pres. and CEO PERRIN BEATTY.

Canadian Radio-Television and Telecommunications Commission (CRTC): Ottawa, ON K1A 0N2; tel. (819) 997-0313 (Information); fax (819) 994-0218; e-mail info@crtc.x400.gc.ca; f. 1968; offices in Montréal, Halifax, Winnipeg and Vancouver; Chair. FRANÇOISE BERTRAND; Vice-Chair. DAVID COLVILLE (Telecommunications), CHARLES BÉLANGER (Broadcasting); Sec.-Gen. LAURA M. TALBOT-ALLAN.

RADIO

The CBC operates two AM and two FM networks, one each in English and French. The CBC's Northern Service provides both national network programming in English and French, and special local and short-wave programmes, some of which are broadcast in the eight principal languages of the Indian and Inuit peoples. In March 1996 there were 576 outlets for AM radio and 1,229 outlets for FM radio, including private affiliates and rebroadcasters). The CBC radio service, which is virtually free of commercial advertising, is within reach of 99.5% of the population. Radio Canada International, the CBC's overseas short-wave service, broadcasts daily in 11 languages and distributes recorded programmes for use world-wide.

TELEVISION

The CBC operates two television networks, one in English and one in French. CBC's Northern Service provides both radio and television service to 98% of the 90,000 inhabitants of northern Québec, the Northwest Territories and the Yukon. Almost 41% of these inhabitants are native Canadians, and programming is provided in Dene and Inuktitut languages as well as English and French. As of March 1996, CBC television was carried on 881 outlets (22 CBC-owned stations, 613 CBC-owned rebroadcasters, 160 community-owned rebroadcasters, 25 private affiliates and 61 private affiliated rebroadcasters). CBC television is available to approximately 99% of the English- and French-speaking population.

Canadian Satellite Communication Inc (Cancom) of Toronto has been licensed since 1981 by the CRTC to conduct a multi-channel television and radio broadcasting operation via satellite for the distribution of CTV programme output, Réseau de Télévision (TVA) and independent television and radio programmes to remote and under-served communities. Cancom also distributes by satellite the programme output of five US television networks.

In March 1996 there were 2,038 licensed cable operators. There are four educational services: TV-Ontario in Ontario and Radio-Québec in Québec operate their own television stations and networks; the Learning and Skills Television of Alberta provides educational programming in that province; the Saskatchewan Communications Network Corporation distributes educational programming in Saskatchewan; and the Open Learning Agency (OLA) provides child and adult education by television in British Columbia.

In 1996 the CRTC granted approval to a further 22 speciality television services, and to one new service providing sports and special events to fee-paying viewers.

Canadian pay television has been in operation since 1983. These services include general interest, sports, music, children's and youth programming, religious broadcasts and news.

Canadian Satellite Communications Inc (Cancom): 50 Burnhamthorpe Rd West, Suite 1000, Mississauga, ON L5B 3C2; tel. (905) 272-4960; fax (905) 272-3399; e-mail pdumas@cancom.ca; Chair. D. M. HOLTBY; Pres. and CEO ALAIN GOURD.

CTV Television Network: 250 Yonge St, Suite 1800, Toronto, ON M5B 2N8; tel. (416) 595-4100; fax (416) 595-5998; 25 privately-owned affiliated stations from coast to coast, with 247 rebroadcasters; covers 99% of Canadian TV households; Pres. and CEO JOHN CASSADAY.

Global Television Network: 81 Barber Greene Rd, Don Mills, ON M3C 2A2; tel. (416) 446-5311; telex 069-66767; fax (416) 446-5371; one station and eight rebroadcasters serving southern Ontario; Pres. DAVID MINTZ.

Réseau de Télévision (TVA): 1600 blvd de Maisonneuve est, CP 368, succursale C, Montréal, PQ H2L 4P2; tel. (514) 526-0476; fax (514) 526-4285; f. 1971; French-language network, with 10 stations in Québec and 19 rebroadcasters serving 98% of the province, together with francophone communities in Ontario and New Brunswick; Pres. and CEO JEAN GOUEPY.

Réseau de Télévision Quatre-Saisons (TQS): 405 ave Ogilvy, Montréal, PQ H3N 2Y4; tel. (514) 271-3535; fax (514) 495-6826; f. 1986; French-language; 2 stations, 6 rebroadcasters and 2 retransmitters serving 98% of the province of Québec.

Telesat Canada: 1601 Telesat Court, Gloucester, ON K1B 5P4; tel. (613) 748-0123; fax (613) 748-8712; e-mail info@telesat.ca; f. 1969; Chair. J. V. R. CYR; Pres. L. J. BOISVERT.

ASSOCIATIONS

Canadian Association of Broadcasters: 350 Sparks St, Suite 306, Ottawa, ON K1R 7S2; tel. (613) 233-4035; fax (613) 233-6961; e-mail cab@cab-acr.ca; f. 1926; Pres. and CEO MICHAEL MCCABE; 500 individual mems.

Canadian Cable Television Association: 360 Albert St, Suite 1010, Ottawa, ON K1R 7X7; tel. (613) 232-2631; fax (613) 232-2137; Pres. RICHARD STURSBERG; 801 mems.

Radio Advisory Board of Canada: 880 Lady Ellen Place, Suite 201, Ottawa, ON K1Z 5L9; tel. (613) 728-8692; fax (613) 728-3278; f. 1944; Gen. Man. (vacant); 27 mems.

Television Bureau of Canada, Inc: 890 Yonge St, Suite 700, Toronto, ON M4W 3P4; tel. (416) 923-8813; fax (416) 923-8739; f. 1962; Pres. REG WATTS (acting); 86 mems.

Finance

(cap. = capital; auth. = authorized; res = reserves; dep. = deposits; m. = million; brs = branches; amounts in Canadian dollars)

BANKING

The first Canadian commercial bank was founded in 1817. A further 34 banks were established over the next 50 years, and, following Confederation in 1867, the Federal Government assumed exclusive jurisdiction over banking operations throughout Canada.

The Bank Act of 1980 created two categories of banking institution: 'Schedule I' banks, which are widely-held, and in which no one interest is allowed to own more than 10% of the shares; and 'Schedule II' banks, which are either subsidiaries of foreign financial institutions, or are banks controlled by Canadian non-bank financial institutions. In February 1998 there were eight 'Schedule I' banks and 43 'Schedule II' banks.

At the end of July 1996 there were more than 8,000 bank branches in Canada, holding deposits totalling more than C $700,000m. The banks' combined assets amounted to nearly C $969,000m., of which approximately 32% were foreign currency assets.

Major revisions to the Bank Act, the federal Trust and Loans Companies Act, the federal Insurance Companies Act and the Co-operative Credit Associations Act came into force in June 1992. This legislation permits federal financial institutions, with some restrictions, to diversify into each other's markets through subsidiaries. By 1 January 1995, following ratification of the North American Free Trade Agreement (NAFTA) and the enactment of the World Trade Organization Implementation Act, the domestic asset limitations on foreign-owned 'Schedule II' banks in the Canadian market were removed.

In the past, the Bank Act was generally reviewed once every 10 years. As a result of extensive revisions to the federal financial institutions legislation in 1992, a re-examination of the Bank Act is currently proceeding, with a view to a legislative revision in 1997. In addition, the Federal Government has also formed a Task Force on the Future of the Canadian Financial Services Sector to review the legislative framework of the financial services sector. Further legislative changes are anticipated by 2002, following the Task Force's report, which is expected in 1998.

Trust and loan companies, which were originally formed to provide mortgage finance and private customer loans, now occupy an important place in the financial system, offering current account facilities and providing access to money transfer services.

Central Bank

Bank of Canada: 234 Wellington St, Ottawa, ON K1A 0G9; tel. (613) 782-8111; telex 053-4241; fax (613) 782-8655; f. 1934; bank of issue; cap. and res 30m., dep. 1,318.9m. (Dec. 1996); Gov. GORDON THIESSEN.

Principal Commercial Banks

'Schedule I' Banks

Bank of Montréal: 129 rue St-Jacques ouest, Montréal, PQ H2Y 1L6; tel. (514) 877-7110; telex 052-67661; f. 1817; cap. and res 8,329m., dep. 109,605m. (Oct. 1995); Chair. and CEO MATTHEW BARRETT; Pres. and Chief Operating Officer ANTHONY F. COMPER; 1,163 brs.

Bank of Nova Scotia (Scotiabank): Scotia Plaza, 44 King St West, Toronto, ON M5H 1H1; tel. (416) 866-6161; fax (416) 866-4988; f. 1832; cap. and res 7,749m., dep. 117,894m. (Oct. 1996); Chair. and CEO PETER C. GODSOE; 1,137 brs.

Canadian Imperial Bank of Commerce: Commerce Court, Toronto, ON M5L 1A2; tel. (416) 980-2211; telex 065-24116; f. 1867; cap. and res 8,738m., dep. 127,421m. (Oct. 1996); Chair., Pres. and CEO ALVIN L. FLOOD; 1,453 brs.

Canadian Western Bank: 10303 Jasper Ave, Suite 2300, Edmonton, AB T5J 3X6; tel. (403) 423-8888; telex 037-43148; fax (403) 423-8897; e-mail graham@planet.eon.net; f. 1988; cap. and res 150m., dep. 1,600m. (Jan. 1997); Chair. JACK C. DONALD; Pres. and CEO LARRY M. POLLOCK; 8 brs.

Laurentian Bank of Canada: 1981 ave Collège McGill, Montréal, PQ H3A 3K3; tel. (514) 284-3931; telex 052-4217; fax (514) 284-7519; f. 1846; total assets 10,153.1m. (1996); Chair. H. SANTOS; Pres. and CEO H. P. ROUSSEAU.

National Bank of Canada: 600 rue de La Gauchetière ouest, Montréal, PQ H3B 4L2; tel. (514) 394-4000; telex 052-5181; fax (514) 394-6258; f. 1979; cap. and res 2,499m., dep. 40,125m. (Oct. 1996); Chair. ANDRÉ BÉRARD; Pres. and CEO LÉON COURVILLE; 641 brs.

Royal Bank of Canada: 1 place Ville Marie, CP 6001, Montréal, PQ H3C 3A9; tel. (514) 874-2110; telex 055-61086; f. 1869; cap. and res 9,414m., dep. 161,817m. (Oct. 1996); Chair. and CEO JOHN E. CLEGHORN; 1,513 brs.

Toronto-Dominion Bank: Toronto-Dominion Centre, POB 1, Toronto, ON M5K 1A2; tel. (416) 982-8222; telex 065-24267; fax (416) 982-5671; f. 1855; cap. and res 6,679m., dep. 87,563m. (Oct. 1996); Chair. and CEO RICHARD M. THOMSON; Pres. A. CHARLES BAILLIE; 966 brs.

'Schedule II' Banks

ABN AMRO Bank (Canada): Toronto-Dominion Centre, POB 114, Toronto, ON M5K 1G8; tel. (416) 367-0850; fax (416) 363-1312; f. 1981; total assets 2,708m. (1996); Pres. and CEO THEO BARK.

Banque Nationale de Paris (Canada): BNP Tower, 1981 ave Collège McGill, Montréal, PQ H3A 2W8; tel. (514) 285-6000; fax (514) 285-2906; total assets 2,076.7m. (1996); Pres. and CEO ANDRÉ CHAFFRINGEON.

Citibank Canada: Citibank Place, 123 Front St West, Suite 1900, Toronto, ON M5J 2M3; tel. (416) 947-5500; telex 062-3626; fax (416) 947-5813; f. 1981; total assets 7,868.1m. (1996); Pres. and CEO PAUL LABBÉ.

Hongkong Bank of Canada: 885 West Georgia St, Suite 300, Vancouver, BC V6C 3E9; tel. (604) 685-1000; fax (604) 641-1849; f. 1981; total assets 20,477.7m. (1996); Chair. JOHN BOND; Pres. and CEO WILLIAM DALTON.

Swiss Bank Corporation (Canada): 207 Queen's Quay West, Suite 780, POB 103, Toronto, ON M5J 1A7; tel. (416) 203-2180; fax (416) 203-4303; cap. and res 58m., dep. 747m. (Dec. 1995); Chair. J. DUGAN; Pres. and CEO J. H. WRIGHT.

Development Bank

Business Development Bank of Canada: Immeuble BDC, 5 place Ville Marie, Bureau 400, Montréal, PQ H3B 5E7; tel. (514) 283-5904; fax (514) 283-0617; f. 1975; wholly owned by fed. govt; auth. cap. 1,500m. (1995); Pres. and CEO FRANÇOIS BEAUDOIN.

Principal Trust and Loan Companies

Canada Trustco Mortgage Co: Canada Trust Tower, 275 Dundas St, London, ON N6A 4S4; tel. (519) 663-1500; fax (519) 663-5114; f. 1855; total assets 46,000m. (1997); Pres. and CEO W. EDMUND CLARK; 414 brs.

Montréal Trustco Inc: Scotia Plaza, 44 King St West, Toronto, ON M5H 1H1; tel. (416) 866-3675; fax (416) 866-5090; f. 1889; subsidiary of Scotiabank; total assets 18,044.3m. (1994); Chair. and CEO ROBERT W. CHISHOLM.

National Trust Co Ltd: 1 Adelaide St East, Toronto, ON M5C 2W8; tel. (416) 361-3611; fax (416) 361-4037; f. 1898; subsidiary of

Scotiabank; cap. and res 253.7m., dep. 13,849.1m. (Oct. 1996); Chair. and CEO ROBERT W. CHISHOLM.

Royal Trust Corporation of Canada: Royal Trust Tower, POB 7500, Station A, Toronto, ON M5W 1P9; tel. (416) 974-1400; fax (416) 861-9658; f. 1899; total assets 11,500m. (July 1997); Pres. ANTHONY A. WEBB.

Trust Général du Canada Inc: 1100 rue Université, 12e étage, Montréal, PQ H3B 2G7; tel. (514) 871-7200; fax (514) 871-8525; f. 1928; cap. and res 94m., total assets 3,038m. (1985); Pres. and CEO MICHEL PETIT.

Savings Institutions with Provincial Charters

Alberta Treasury Branches: 1200 ATB Plaza, 9925 109 St, POB 1440, Edmonton, AB T5J 2J8; tel. (403) 493-7309; fax (403) 422-4178; f. 1938; assets 8,466m. (March 1997); Pres. and CEO PAUL G. HAGGIS; 147 brs.

Province of Ontario Savings Office: 33 King St West, 2nd Floor, Oshawa, ON L1H 8H5; tel. (905) 433-5788; fax (905) 433-6519; f. 1921; assets 2,200m. (1994); Dir D. BRAND; 23 brs.

Bankers' Organizations

Canadian Bankers Association: Commerce Court West, Box 348, Suite 3000, Toronto, ON M5L 1G2; tel. (416) 362-6092; fax (416) 362-7705; f. 1891; Pres. RAYMOND PROTTI; 8 regional brs, 52 mems.

Trust Companies Association of Canada Inc: One Financial Place, 1 Adelaide St East, Suite 1002, Box 137, Toronto, ON M5C 2V9; tel. (416) 866-8842; fax (416) 866-2122; Chair. J. CHRISTOPHER BARRON; 14 mems.

STOCK EXCHANGES

Alberta Stock Exchange: 300 Fifth Ave SW, 10th Floor, Calgary, AB T2P 3C4; tel. (403) 974-7400; fax (403) 237-0450; e-mail info@ase.ca; f. 1914; 54 mems; Pres. T. A. CUMMING.

Bourse de Montréal/Montréal Exchange: Tour de la Bourse, 800 square Victoria, CP 61, Montréal, PQ H4Z 1A9; tel. (514) 871-2424; fax (514) 871-3553; e-mail info@me.org; f. 1874; 77 mems; Pres. and CEO GÉRALD A. LACOSTE.

Toronto Stock Exchange: The Exchange Tower, 2 First Canadian Place, Toronto, ON M5X 1J2; tel. (416) 947-4700; fax (416) 947-4662; e-mail info@tse.com; f. 1852; 102 mems; Pres. and CEO ROWLAND W. FLEMING.

Vancouver Stock Exchange: Stock Exchange Tower, 609 Granville St, POB 10333, Vancouver, BC V7Y 1H1; tel. (604) 689-3334; fax (604) 688-6051; e-mail llast@vse.ca; f. 1907; 57 mems; Pres. MICHAEL E. JOHNSON.

Winnipeg Stock Exchange: One Lombard Place, Suite 620, Winnipeg, MB R3B 0X3; tel. (204) 987-7070; fax (204) 987-7079; e-mail info@wse.ca; 26 mems; Pres. KEN COOPER.

INSURANCE

Principal Companies

Abbey Life Insurance Co of Canada: 3027 Harvester Rd, Burlington, ON L7N 3G9; tel. (905) 639-6200; fax (905) 827-6773; Pres. MARK SYLVIA.

Aetna Canada: 79 Wellington St West, POB 120, Toronto, ON M5K 1N9; tel. (416) 864-8000; fax (416) 864-8189; Pres. and CEO NICK VILLANI.

Allianz Canada: 425 Bloor St East, Suite 500, Toronto, ON M4W 3R5; tel. (416) 961-5015; fax (416) 961-8874; f. 1928; Pres. R. E. MAYNARD.

Assurance vie Desjardins–Laurentienne: 200 ave des Commandeurs, Lévis, PQ G6V 6R2; tel. (418) 838-7701; fax (418) 835-9171; f. 1994; Pres. FRANÇOIS JOLY.

Blue Cross Life Insurance Co of Canada: POB 220, Moncton, NB E1C 8L3; tel. (506) 853-1811; telex 014-2233; fax (506) 853-4651; Chair. Dr F. W. DU VAL.

Boréal Assurances Inc: 1100 blvd René-Lévesque ouest, 25e étage, Montréal, PQ H3B 4P4; tel. (514) 392-6366; fax (514) 392-6080; Pres. and CEO YVON LAMONTAGNE.

Canada Life Assurance Co: 330 University Ave, Toronto, ON M5G 1R8; tel. (416) 597-1456; fax (416) 597-1940; e-mail info@canadalife.com; f. 1847; Pres. DAVID NIELD.

Canadian General Insurance Co: 2206 Eglinton Ave East, Suite 500, Scarborough, ON M1L 4S8; tel. (416) 288-1800; fax (416) 288-9756; f. 1907; Pres. R. L. DUNN.

The Canadian Surety Co: 2200 Yonge St, Suite 1200, Toronto, ON M4S 2C6; tel. (416) 487-7195; fax (416) 482-6176; e-mail sglickma@cscw.com; Pres. and CEO BARBARA ADDIE.

Groupe Coopérants, inc, et Les Coopérants, société mutuelle d'assurance-vie: Maison des Coopérants, 600 blvd de Maisonneuve ouest, Montréal, PQ H3A 3J9; tel. (514) 287-6600; fax (514) 287-6514; f. 1876; Pres. PAUL DOLAN; CEO PIERRE SHOONER.

Crown Life Insurance Co: 1901 Scarth St, POB 827, Regina, SK S4P 3B1; tel. (306) 751-6000; fax (306) 751-6150; f. 1900; Pres. and CEO R. F. RICHARDSON.

Dominion of Canada General Insurance Co: 165 University Ave, Toronto, ON M5H 3B9; tel. (416) 362-7231; fax (416) 362-9918; f. 1887; Pres. and CEO GEORGE COOKE.

Federation Insurance Co of Canada: 1000 rue de La Gauchetière ouest, Bureau 500, Montréal, PQ H3B 4W5; tel. (514) 875-5790; fax (514) 875-9769; f. 1947; Pres. WILLIAM GREEN.

General Accident Assurance Co of Canada: 2 First Canadian Place, Suite 2600, POB 410, Toronto, ON M5X 1J1; tel. (416) 364-7336; fax (416) 364-9939; f. 1906; Pres. LEONARD LATHAM.

Gerling Global General Insurance Co: 480 University Ave, Suite 1600, Toronto, ON M5G 1V6; tel. (416) 598-4651; fax (416) 598-5478; f. 1955; Pres. A. H. HENKE.

Gore Mutual Insurance Co: 252 Dundas St, Cambridge, ON N1R 5T3; tel. (519) 623-1910; fax (519) 623-8348; f. 1839; Chair. and CEO ROBERT J. COLLINS-WRIGHT.

Guardian Insurance Co of Canada: POB 4096, Station A, Toronto, ON M5W 1N1; tel. (416) 941-5050; fax (416) 941-9791; f. 1911; Pres. ROBERT SHATFORD.

Halifax Insurance Co: 75 Eglinton Ave East, Toronto, ON M4P 3A4; tel. (416) 440-1000; fax (416) 440-0799; f. 1809; Pres. and CEO DONALD LOUGH.

Imperial Life Assurance Co of Canada: 95 St Clair Ave West, Toronto, ON M4V 1N7; tel. (416) 926-2600; fax (416) 923-1599; f. 1896; Pres. and CEO MARCEL PEPIN.

ING Canada: 2450 rue Girouard ouest, St-Hyacinthe, PQ J2S 3B3; tel. (514) 773-9701; fax (514) 773-3515; Pres. and CEO YVES BROUILLETTE.

Kings Mutual Insurance Co: POB 10, Berwick, NS B0P 1E0; tel. (902) 538-3187; fax (902) 538-7271; f. 1904; Pres. B. SAUNDERS.

London Life Insurance Co: 255 Dufferin Ave, London, ON N6A 4K1; tel. (519) 432-5281; fax (519) 679-3518; f. 1874; Pres. and CEO FRED TOMCZYK.

Manufacturers Life Insurance Co (Manulife): 200 Bloor St East, Toronto, ON M4W 1E5; tel. (416) 926-5223; fax (416) 926-5454; f. 1887; Pres. and CEO DOMINIC D'ALESSANDRO.

Mercantile and General Reinsurance Co of Canada: 161 Bay St, Suite 3000, Toronto, ON M5J 2T6; tel. (416) 947-3800; fax (416) 947-1386; f. 1951; Pres. PETER PATTERSON.

Metropolitan Life Insurance Co of Canada: 99 Bank St, Ottawa, ON K1P 5A3; tel. (613) 560-7893; fax (613) 560-7907; Pres. and CEO WILLIAM R. PRUETER.

Mutual Life Assurance Co of Canada: 227 King St South, Waterloo, ON N2J 4C5; tel. (519) 888-3900; fax (519) 888-2990; f. 1870; Pres. and CEO ROBERT ASTLEY.

The National Life Assurance Co of Canada: 522 University Ave, Toronto, ON M5G 1Y7; tel. (416) 598-2122; fax (416) 598-4948; f. 1897; Pres. VINCENT TONNA.

Portage La Prairie Mutual Insurance Co: 749 Saskatchewan Ave East, Portage La Prairie, MB R1N 3B8; tel. (204) 857-3415; fax (204) 239-6655; f. 1884; Pres. H. G. OWENS.

Royal Insurance Co of Canada: 10 Wellington St East, Toronto, ON M5E 1L5; tel. (416) 366-7511; telex 065-24124; fax (416) 367-9869; f. 1851; Pres. and CEO ROBERT GUNN.

Seaboard Life Insurance Co: 2165 Broadway West, POB 5900, Vancouver, BC V6B 5H6; tel. (604) 734-1667; fax (604) 734-8221; f. 1953; Pres. and CEO ROBERT SMITH.

Société Nationale d'Assurance Inc: 425 blvd de Maisonneuve ouest, Bureau 1500, Montréal, PQ H3A 3G5; tel. (514) 288-8711; fax (514) 288-8269; f. 1940; Pres. YVON TRÉPANIER.

Sun Life Assurance Co of Canada: POB 4150, Station A, Toronto, ON M5W 2C9; tel. (416) 979-9966; fax (416) 585-9546; f. 1871; Chair. and CEO JOHN D. MCNEIL.

Toronto Mutual Life Insurance Co: 112 St Clair Ave West, Toronto, ON M4V 2Y3; tel. (416) 960-3463; fax (416) 960-0531; Pres. and CEO JOHN ENGLISH.

Wawanesa Mutual Insurance Co: 191 Broadway, Winnipeg, MB R3C 3P1; tel. (204) 985-3811; fax (204) 947-5192; f. 1896; Pres. and CEO G. J. HANSON.

Western Assurance Co: 230 Westney Rd South, 7th Floor, Ajax, ON L1S 7J5; tel. (416) 366-7511; fax (416) 367-9869; f. 1851; Pres. and CEO ROBERT J. GUNN.

Zurich Life of Canada: 2225 Sheppard Ave East, Willowdale, ON M2J 5C4; tel. (416) 502-3600; fax (416) 502-3488; Pres. and CEO MICHAEL P. STRAMAGLIA.

Insurance Organizations

Canadian Life and Health Insurance Association: 1 Queen St East, Suite 1700, Toronto, ON M5C 2X9; tel. (416) 777-2221; fax (416) 777-1895; e-mail clhia@inforamp.net; f. 1894; Pres. MARK DANIELS.

Insurance Brokers Association of Canada: 181 University Ave, Suite 1902, Toronto, ON M5H 3M7; tel. (416) 367-1831; fax (416) 367-3681; e-mail jbrown@sympatico.ca; f. 1921; Exec. Dir JOANNE BROWN; 12 mem. asscns.

Insurance Bureau of Canada: 181 University Ave, 13th Floor, Toronto, ON M5H 3M7; tel. (416) 362-2031; fax (416) 361-5952; f. 1964; Pres. and CEO GEORGE ANDERSON; 110 corporate mems.

Insurance Institute of Canada: 18 King St East, 6th Floor, Toronto, ON M5C 1C4; tel. (416) 362-8586; fax (416) 362-4239; f. 1952; Pres. J. CHRIS RHIND; 31,000 mems.

Insurers' Advisory Organization Inc: 180 Dundas St West, Suite 2600, Toronto, ON M5G 1G9; tel. (416) 597-1200; fax (416) 597-2180; f. 1989; Pres. and CEO G. A. CHELLEW.

Life Insurance Institute of Canada: 1 Queen St East, Suite 1600, Toronto, ON M5C 2X9; tel. (416) 359-2020; fax (416) 359-9173; e-mail mlem@istar.ca; f. 1935; Exec. Dir DEBBIE COLE-GAUER; 57 mem. asscns.

Life Underwriters' Association of Canada: 41 Lesmill Rd, North York, ON M3B 2T3; tel. (416) 444-5251; fax (416) 444-8031; f. 1906; Pres. DAVID J. THIBAUDEAU; 18,000 mems.

Trade and Industry

CHAMBER OF COMMERCE

The Canadian Chamber of Commerce: 55 Metcalfe St, Suite 1160, Ottawa, ON K1P 6N4; tel. (613) 238-4000; fax (613) 238-7643; f. 1925; mems: 500 community chambers of commerce and boards of trade, 80 nat. trade asscns and 2,500 business corpns; Pres. TIMOTHY E. REID.

INDUSTRIAL AND TRADE ASSOCIATIONS

Alliance of Manufacturers and Exporters of Canada: 75 International Blvd, 4th Floor, Toronto, ON M9W 6L9; tel. (416) 798-8000; fax (416) 798-8050; f. 1871; the nat. org. of mfrs and exporters of Canada; Pres. STEPHEN VAN HOUTEN; 3,500 mems.

Agriculture and Horticulture

Alberta Wheat Pool: 505 2nd St, SW, POB 2700, Calgary, AB T2P 2P5; tel. (403) 290-4910; fax (403) 290-5528; Pres. T. A. GRAHAM; 57,400 mems.

Canada Grains Council: 360 Main St, Suite 330, Winnipeg, MB R3C 3Z3; tel. (204) 942-2254; fax (204) 947-0992; e-mail dmutch@canadagrainscouncil.ca; f. 1969; Exec. Dir and CEO A. DOUGLAS MUTCH; 36 mems.

Canadian Federation of Agriculture: 75 Albert St, Suite 1101, Ottawa, ON K1P 5E7; tel. (613) 236-3633; fax (613) 236-5749; f. 1935; Exec. Dir SALLY RUTHERFORD; 18 mems.

Canadian Horticultural Council: 1101 Prince of Wales Drive, Suite 310, Ottawa, ON K2C 3W7; tel. (613) 226-4187; fax (613) 226-2984; f. 1922; Exec. Vice-Pres. DAN DEMPSTER.

Canadian Nursery Trades Association: 7856 Fifth Lane South, RR 4, Stn Main, Milton, ON L9T 2X8; tel. (905) 875-1399; fax (905) 875-1840; e-mail cntalc@spectranet.ca; Exec. Dir CHRIS ANDREWS; 1,428 mems.

Canadian Seed Growers' Association: POB 8455, Ottawa, ON K1G 3T1; tel. (613) 236-0497; fax (613) 563-7855; f. 1904; Exec. Dir W. K. ROBERTSON; 4,700 mems.

Dairy Farmers of Canada: 75 Albert St, Suite 1101, Ottawa, ON K1P 5E7; tel. (613) 236-9997; fax (613) 236-0905; f. 1942; Exec. Dir RICHARD DOYLE; 11 mem asscns, 29,400 individual mems.

National Dairy Council of Canada: 221 Laurier Ave East, Ottawa, ON K1N 6P1; tel. (613) 238-4116; fax (613) 238-6247; e-mail info@ndcc.ca; f. 1918; Pres. KEMPTON MATTE; 69 mem asscns, 250 individual mems.

National Farmers Union (NFU): 250C 2nd Ave South, Saskatoon, SK S7K 2M1; tel. (306) 652-9465; fax (306) 664-6226; e-mail nfu@sk.sympatico.ca; f. 1969; Pres. NETTIE WIEBE; 10,000 mems.

L'Union des producteurs agricoles: 555 blvd Roland-Therrien, Longueuil, PQ J4H 3Y9; tel. (514) 679-0530; fax (514) 679-4943; e-mail upa@upa.qc.ca; f. 1924; Pres. LAURENT PELLERIN; 27 institutional mems, 42,100 individual mems, 42,200 assoc. mems.

Building and Construction

Canadian Concrete Masonry Producers' Association: 1013 Wilson Ave, Suite 101, Downsview, ON M3K 1G1; tel. (416) 635-7175; fax (416) 630-1916; f. 1949; Exec. Dir MARK PATAMIA; 39 mems.

Canadian Construction Association: 85 Albert St, 10th Floor, Ottawa, ON K1P 6A4; tel. (613) 236-9455; fax (613) 236-9526; f. 1918; Pres. MICHAEL ATKINSON; over 20,000 mems.

Canadian Institute of Steel Construction: 201 Consumers Rd, Suite 300, Willowdale, ON M2J 4G8; tel. (416) 491-4552; fax (416) 491-6461; e-mail ciscmikegilmor@compuserve.com; f. 1930; Pres. HUGH A. KRENTZ; 245 mems.

Canadian Paint and Coatings Association: 9900 blvd Cavendish, Bureau 103, St-Laurent, PQ H4M 2V2; tel. (514) 745-2611; fax (514) 745-2031; e-mail cpca@cam.org; f. 1913; Pres. RICHARD MURRY; 132 mems.

Canadian Prestressed Concrete Institute: 196 Bronson Ave, Suite 100, Ottawa, ON K1R 6H4; tel. (613) 232-2619; fax (613) 232-5129; e-mail cpci@fox.nstn.ca; Pres. JOHN FOWLER; 300 mems.

Ontario Painting Contractors Association: 211 Consumers Rd, Suite 305, Willowdale, ON M2J 4G8; tel. (416) 498-1897; fax (416) 498-6757; f. 1967; Exec. Dir MAUREEN MARQUARDT; 100 mems.

Clothing and Textiles

Canadian Apparel Federation: 130 Slater St, Suite 1050, Ottawa, ON K1P 6E2; tel. (613) 231-3220; fax (613) 231-2305; e-mail 76470.3143@compuserve.com; f. 1977; Exec. Dir STEPHEN BEATTY.

Canadian Carpet Institute: 130 Slater St, Suite 1050, Ottawa, ON K1P 6E2; tel. (613) 232-7183; fax (613) 232-3072; e-mail carpet@maji.com; f. 1961; Exec. Dir MICHAEL KRONICK; 17 mems.

Canadian Textiles Institute: 66 Slater St, Suite 1720, Ottawa, ON K1P 5H1; tel. (613) 232-7195; fax (613) 232-8722; f. 1935; Pres. ERIC BARRY; 60 mems.

Men's Clothing Manufacturers Association: POB 127, Station R, Toronto, ON M4G 3C3; tel. (416) 429-7184; fax (416) 429-0158; f. 1961; Exec. Dir DAVID BALINSKY; 67 mems.

Textile Federation of Canada: c/o CTT, 3000 rue Boullé, St-Hyacinthe, PQ J2S 1H9; tel. (514) 457-2347; fax (514) 457-2147; Exec. Sec. LUMINA FILLION; 1,950 mems.

Electrical and Electronics

Canadian Electricity Association: 1155 rue Metcalfe, Bureau 1120, Montréal, PQ H3Z 2P9; tel. (514) 866-6121; fax (514) 866-1880; e-mail info@canelect.ca; f. 1891; Pres. and CEO HANS R. KONOW; 2,700 mems.

Canadian Electrical Distributors Assocation Inc: 1st Pickering Place, Suite 217, 1550 Kingston Rd, Pickering, ON L1V 1C3; tel. (416) 831-2454; fax (416) 831-4919; Pres. STANLEY G. WILD.

Electrical and Electronic Manufacturers Association of Canada: 10 Carlson Court, Suite 500, Rexdale, ON M9W 6L2; tel. (905) 674-7410; fax (905) 674-7412; f. 1976; Pres. NORMAN ASPIN; 175 mems.

Fisheries

Canadian Association of Fish Exporters: 1770 Woodward Drive, Suite 212, Ottawa, ON K2C 0P8; tel. (613) 228-9220; fax (613) 228-9223; e-mail jbarnett@seafood.ca; f. 1978; Pres. Dr JANE BARNETT.

Fisheries Council of Canada: 38 Antares Drive, Suite 110, Nepean, ON K2E 7V2; tel. (613) 727-7450; fax (613) 727-7453; f. 1945; Pres. R. W. BULMER; 200 mems.

Food and Beverages

Baking Association of Canada: 885 Don Mills Rd, Suite 301, Don Mills, ON M3C 1V9; tel. (416) 510-8041; fax (416) 510-8043; f. 1947; Pres. and CEO PAUL HETHERINGTON; 1,400 institutional mems, 200 assoc. mems.

Brewers Association of Canada: 155 Queen St, Suite 1200, Ottawa, ON K1P 6L1; tel. (613) 232-9601; fax (613) 232-2283; e-mail office@brewers.ca; f. 1943; Pres. and CEO R. A. MORRISON; 26 mems.

Canadian Council of Grocery Distributors: CP 1082, succursale place-du-Parc, Montréal, PQ H2W 2P4; tel. (514) 982-0267; fax (514) 849-3021; f. 1919; Pres. and CEO JOHN F. GECI; 69 institutional mems, 115 assoc. mems.

Canadian Food Brokers Association: 58 Meadowbrook Ave, Suite 100, Unionville, ON L3R 2N9; tel. (905) 477-4644; fax (905) 477-9580; e-mail kbray@idirect.com; f. 1942; Pres. KEITH BRAY; 70 mems, 60 assoc mems.

Canadian Meat Council: 875 Carling Ave, Suite 410, Ottawa, ON K1S 5P1; tel. (613) 729-3911; fax (613) 729-4997; f. 1919; Gen. Man. ROBERT WEAVER; 87 mems.

Canadian National Millers' Association: 90 Sparks St, Suite 1127, Ottawa, ON K1P 5B4; tel. (613) 238-2293; fax (613) 235-5866; f. 1920; Exec. Dir PHIL DE KAMP; 17 mems.

Canadian Pork Council: 75 Albert St, Suite 1101, Ottawa, ON K1P 5E7; tel. (613) 236-9239; fax (613) 236-6658; e-mail cpc@fox.nstn.ca; Exec. Dir. MARTIN RICE; 8 mems.

Confectionery Manufacturers Association of Canada: 885 Don Mills Rd, Suite 301, Don Mills, ON M3C 1V9; tel. (416) 510-8034; fax (416) 510-8044; e-mail cavolin@fcpmc.com; f. 1919; Pres. CAROL HOCHU; 81 corporate mems.

Food and Consumer Products Manufacturers of Canada: 885 Don Mills Rd, Suite 301, Don Mills, ON M3C 1V9; tel. (416) 510-8024; fax (416) 510-8043; e-mail info@cpmc.com; Pres. GEORGE FLEISCHMANN; 180 corporate mems.

Food Institute of Canada: 1600 Scott St, Suite 415, Ottawa, ON K1Y 4N7; tel. (613) 722-1000; fax (613) 722-1404; e-mail fic@foodnet.fic.ca; f. 1989; Pres. JEAN GATTUSO; 200 mems.

Forestry, Lumber and Allied Industries

Canadian Lumbermen's Association: 27 Goulburn Ave, Ottawa, ON K1N 8C7; tel. (613) 233-6205; fax (613) 233-1929; f. 1907; Exec. Dir ROBERT RIVARD; 200 mems.

Canadian Pulp and Paper Association: Sun Life Bldg, 1155 rue Metcalfe, Bureau 1900, Montréal, PQ H3B 4T6; tel. (514) 866-6621; fax (514) 866-3035; f. 1913; Pres. LISE LACHAPELLE; 60 mems.

Canadian Wood Council: 1730 St-Laurent Blvd, Suite 350, Ottawa, ON K1G 5L1; tel. (613) 247-7077; fax (613) 247-7856; f. 1959; Pres. K. MCCLOSKEY.

Ontario Forest Industries Association: 130 Adelaide St West, Suite 1700, Toronto, ON M5H 3P5; tel. (416) 368-6188; fax (416) 368-5445; e-mail ofia@interlog.com; f. 1943; Pres. R. MARIE RAUTER; 20 corporate mems.

Hotels and Catering

Canadian Restaurant and Foodservices Association: 316 Bloor St West, Toronto, ON M5S 1W5; tel. (416) 923-8416; fax (416) 923-1450; f. 1944; Pres. DOUGLAS NEEDHAM; 11,500 mems.

Hotel Association of Canada Inc: 130 Albert St, Suite 1016, Ottawa, ON K1P 5G4; tel. (613) 237-7149; fax (613) 238-3878; e-mail hac@hotels.ca; f. 1929; Pres. ANTHONY POLLARD.

Mining

Canadian Association of Petroleum Producers: 350 7th Ave, SW, Suite 2100, Calgary, AB T2P 3N9; tel. (403) 267-1100; fax (403) 261-4622; f. 1952; Pres. DAVID MANNING; 200 institututional mems, 120 assoc. mems.

Canadian Gas Association: 243 Consumers Rd, Suite 1200, North York, ON M2S 5E3; tel. (416) 498-1994; fax (416) 498-7465; e-mail ecartwright@cga.ca; f. 1907; Pres. and CEO GERALD DOUCET; 270 corporate mems.

Canadian Petroleum Association: 150 6th Ave, SW, Suite 3800, Calgary, AB T2P 3Y7; tel. (403) 269-6721; fax (403) 261-4622; Pres. IAN R. SMYTH.

Mining Association of Canada: 350 Sparks St, Suite 1105, Ottawa, ON K1R 7S8; tel. (613) 233-9391; fax (613) 233-8897; f. 1935; Pres. GORDON PEELING; 75 mems.

Northwest Territories Chamber of Mines: POB 2818, Yellowknife, NT X1A 2R1; tel. (403) 873-5281; fax (403) 920-2145; e-mail nwtmines@ssimicro.com; f. 1967; Gen. Man. MIKE VAYDIK; 380 mems.

Ontario Mining Association: 110 Yonge St, 15th Floor, Toronto, ON M5C 1T4; tel. (416) 364-9301; fax (416) 364-5986; f. 1920; Pres. PATRICK REID; 47 mems.

Yukon Chamber of Mines: POB 4427, Whitehorse, YT Y1A 3T5; tel. (403) 667-2090; fax (403) 668-7127; e-mail ycmines@polarcom.com; f. 1956; Man. Dir DAVE AUSTIN; 400 mems.

Pharmaceutical

Canadian Drug Manufacturers Association: 4120 Yonge St, Suite 409, Toronto, ON M2P 2B8; tel. (416) 223-2333; fax (416) 223-2425; e-mail info@cdma-acfpp.org; Pres. BRENDA DRINKWALTER; 14 mems.

Pharmaceutical Manufacturers Association of Canada: 1111 Prince of Wales Drive, Suite 302, Ottawa, ON K2C 3T2; tel. (613) 727-1380; fax (613) 727-1407; e-mail info@pmac-acim; f. 1914; Pres. JUDY EROLA; 65 mems.

Retailing

Retail Council of Canada: 121 Bloor St, Suite 1210, Toronto, ON M4W 3M5; tel. (416) 922-6678; fax (416) 922-8011; f. 1963; Pres. and CEO DIANE J. BRISEBOIS; 6,000 mems.

Retail Merchants' Association of Canada Inc: 1780 Birchmount Rd, Scarborough, ON M1P 2H8; tel. (416) 291-7903; fax (416) 291-5635; f. 1896; Pres. SEAN MCMAHON; 3,000 mems.

Transport

Air Transport Association of Canada: see Transport—Civil Aviation.

Canadian Institute of Traffic and Transportation: 33 Yonge St, Suite 710, Toronto, ON M5E 1G4; tel. (416) 363-5696; fax (416) 363-5698; e-mail citt@enigma.net; f. 1958; Gen. Man. PATRICK CULLEN; 800 mems.

Canadian Shippers' Council: see Transport—Shipping.

Canadian Trucking Association: National Bldg, 130 Slater St, Suite 1025, Ottawa, ON K1P 6E2; tel. (613) 236-9426; fax (613) 563-2701; e-mail cta@magi.com; f. 1937; Pres. GILLES BÉLANGER.

Canadian Vehicle Manufacturers' Association: 25 Adelaide St East, Suite 1602, Toronto, ON M5C 3A1; tel. (416) 364-9331; fax (416) 367-3221; e-mail cuma@tor.hookup.net; f. 1926; Pres. MARK A. NANTAIS; 6 mems.

Railway Association of Canada: see Transport—Railways.

Shipping Federation of Canada: see Transport—Shipping.

Miscellaneous

Canadian Importers Association, Inc: 438 University Ave, Suite 1618, Box 60, Toronto, ON M5G 2K8; tel. (416) 595-5333; fax (416) 595-8226; f. 1932; Pres. BOB ARMSTRONG; 650 mems.

Canadian Printing Industries Association: 75 Albert St, Suite 906, Ottawa, ON K1P 5E7; tel. (613) 236-7208; fax (613) 236-8169; Pres. MICHAEL MAKIN; 600 institutional mems.

Canadian Tobacco Manufacturers' Council: 99 Bank St, Suite 701, Ottawa, ON K1P 6B9; tel. (613) 238-2799; fax (613) 238-4463; f. 1963; Pres. ROBERT PARKER.

Shipbuilding Association of Canada: 222 Queen St, Suite 1502, Ottawa, ON K1P 5V9; tel. (613) 232-7127; fax (613) 238-5519; f. 1995; Pres. PETER CAIRNS; 20 mems.

TRADE UNIONS

At the beginning of 1997 there were 4,074,000 union members in Canada, representing 26.9% of the civilian labour force. Of these, 29.6% belonged to unions with headquarters in the USA.

In 1997 unions affiliated to the Canadian Labour Congress represented 65.6% of total union membership.

Canadian Labour Congress: 2841 Riverside Drive, Ottawa, ON K1V 8X7; tel. (613) 521-3400; fax (613) 521-4655; f. 1956; Pres. ROBERT WHITE; Sec.-Treas. DICK MARTIN; 2,200,000 mems (1997).

Affiliated unions with more than 15,000 members:

Amalgamated Transit Union: 15 Gervais Drive, Suite 603, Don Mills, ON M3C 1Y8; tel. (416) 445-6204; fax (416) 445-6208; Gen. Canadian Dir KEN FOSTER; 28,000 mems (1997).

American Federation of Musicians of the United States and Canada: 75 The Donway West, Suite 1010, Don Mills, ON M3C 2E9; tel. (416) 391-5161; fax (416) 391-5165; Vice-Pres. from Canada DAVID J. JANDRISCH; 16,000 mems (1997).

British Columbia Nurses' Union: 4259 Canada Way, Suite 100, Burnaby, BC V5G 1H1; tel. (604) 433-2268; fax (604) 433-7945; Pres. IVORY WARNER; 23,000 mems (1997).

Canadian Union of Postal Workers: 337 Bank St, Ottawa, ON K2P 1Y3; tel. (613) 236-7238; fax (613) 563-7861; f. 1965; Nat. Pres. D. W. TINGLEY; 51,000 mems (1997).

Canadian Union of Public Employees: 21 Florence St, Ottawa, ON K2P 0W6; tel. (613) 237-1590; fax (613) 237-5508; Nat. Pres. JUDY DARCY; 452,000 mems (1997).

Communications, Energy and Paperworkers Union of Canada: 350 Albert St, 19th Floor, Ottawa, ON K1R 1A4; tel. (613) 230-5200; fax (613) 230-5801; Pres. FRED W. POMEROY; 167,000 mems (1997).

Graphic Communications International Union: 21 St Clair Ave East, Suite 901, Toronto, ON M4T 1L9; tel. (416) 961-0267; f. 1882; Int. Vice-Pres. JAMES COWAN; 15,000 mems (1997).

Hospital Employees Union: 2006 West 10th Ave, Vancouver, BC V6J 4P5; tel. (604) 734-3431; fax (604) 734-5854; Prov. Pres. FRED MUZIN; 44,000 mems (1997).

Hotel Employees and Restaurant Employees International Union: 1140 blvd de Maisonneuve ouest, Bureau 1150, Montréal, PQ H3A 1M8; tel. (514) 844-4167; fax (514) 844-1536; Vice-Pres JAMES STAMOS (Montréal), NICK WORHAUG (Vancouver); 35,000 mems (1997).

International Association of Machinists and Aerospace Workers: 100 Metcalfe St, Suite 300, Ottawa, ON K1P 5M1; tel. (613) 236-9761; fax (613) 563-7830; Gen. Vice-Pres. in Canada DAVE L. RITCHIE; 53,000 mems (1996).

International Brotherhood of Electrical Workers: 45 Sheppard Ave East, Suite 401, Willowdale, ON M2N 5Y1; tel. (416) 226-5155; fax (416) 226-1492; Int.Vice-Pres. DON LOUNDS; 67,000 mems (1997).

IWA Canada (Industrial Wood and Allied Workers of Canada): 1285 Pender St, Suite 500, Vancouver, BC V6E 4B2; tel. (604) 683-1117; fax (604) 688-6416; f. 1937; Pres. DAVE HAGGARD; 50,000 mems (1997).

Labourers' International Union of North America: 44 Hughson St South, Hamilton, ON L8N 2A7; tel. (905) 522-7177; fax (905) 522-9310; Canadian Dir and Vice-Pres. ENRICO H. MANCINELLI; 55,000 mems (1997).

National Automobile, Aerospace Transportation and General Workers Union of Canada (CAW—Canada): 205 Placer Court, North York, Willowdale, ON M2H 3H9; tel. (416) 497-4110; fax (416) 495-6559; f. 1985; Nat. Pres. BASIL HARGROVE; 205,000 mems (1996).

National Union of Public and General Employees: 15 Auriga Drive, Nepean, Ottawa, ON K2E 1B7; tel. (613) 228-9800; fax (613) 228-9801; e-mail national@nupge.ca; Nat. Pres. JAMES CLANCY; 320,000 mems (1997).

Office and Professional Employees' International Union: 1200 ave Papineau, Bureau 250, Montréal, PQ H2K 4S6; tel. (514) 522-6511; fax (514) 522-9000; Canadian Dir and Int. Vice-Pres. MICHEL LAJEUNESSE; 30,000 mems (1997).

Ontario English Catholic Teachers' Association: 65 St Clair Ave East, Suite 400, Toronto, ON M4T 2Y8; tel. (416) 925-2493; fax (416) 925-7764; Pres. MARSHALL JARVIS; 35,000 mems (1997).

Ontario Public Service Employees' Union: 100 Lesmill Rd, North York, ON M3B 3P8; tel. (416) 443-8888; fax (416) 443-9670; Pres. LEAH CASSELMAN; 111,000 mems (1997).

Public Service Alliance of Canada: 233 Gilmour St, Ottawa, ON K2P 0P1; tel. (613) 560-4200; fax (613) 563-3492; f. 1966; Nat. Pres. DARYL BEAN; 168,000 mems (1997).

Service Employees International Union: 75 The Donway West, Suite 810, North York, ON M3C 2E9; tel. (416) 447-2311; fax (416) 447-2428; Vice-Pres. in Canada KENNETH BROWN; 80,000 mems (1997).

Teamsters Canada: 2540 Daniel-Johnson, Bureau 804, Laval, PQ H7T 2S3; tel. (514) 682-5521; fax (514) 681-2244; Canadian Pres. LOUIS LACROIX; 95,000 mems (1997).

Union of Needletrades, Industrial and Textile Employees: 15 Gervais Drive, Suite 700, Toronto, ON M3C 1Y8; tel. (416) 441-1806; fax (416) 441-9680; Canadian Dirs JOHN ALLERUZZO, GERALD ROY; 33,000 mems (1997).

United Brotherhood of Carpenters and Joiners of America: 5799 Young St, Suite 807, Willowdale, ON M2M 3V3; tel. (416) 225-8885; fax (416) 225-5390; Gen. Exec. Bd Mem. JAMES E. SMITH; 56,000 mems (1997).

United Food and Commercial Workers International Union: 61 International Blvd, Suite 300, Rexdale, ON M9W 6K4; tel. (416) 675-1104; fax (416) 675-6919; f. 1979; Canadian Dir THOMAS KUKOVICA; 200,000 mems (1997).

United Steelworkers of America: 234 Eglinton Ave East, 7th Floor, Toronto, ON M4P 1K7; tel. (416) 487-1571; fax (416) 482-5548; Nat. Dir in Canada LAWRENCE MCBREARTY; 200,000 mems (1997).

Other Central Congresses

Canadian Federation of Labour: 107 Sparks St, Suite 300, Ottawa, ONK1P 5B5; tel. (613) 234-4141; fax (613) 234-5188; f. 1982; Pres. JAMES MCCAMBLY; 10 affiliated unions.

Affiliated unions with over 15,000 members:

International Union of Operating Engineers: 38 Aberdeen St, Kemptville, NS B4N 3X9; tel. (902) 678-9950; fax (902) 678-1838; Canadian Regional Dir EDGAR DOULL; 36,000 mems (1997).

United Association of Journeymen and Apprentices of the Plumbing and Pipe Fitting Industry of the United States and Canada: 1959 152nd St, Suite 316, Surrey, BC V4A 9E3; tel. (604) 531-0516; fax (604) 531-0547; Vice-Pres. and Canadian Dir GEORGE MESERVIER; 38,000 mems (1997).

Centrale de l'enseignement du Québec: 9405 rue Sherbrooke est, Montréal, PQ H1L 6P3; tel. (514) 356-8888; fax (514) 356-9999; Pres. LORRAINE PAGÉ; 14 affiliated unions.

Affiliated union with over 15,000 members:

Fédération des enseignantes et des enseignants de commissions scolaires: 1170 blvd Lebourgneuf, Bureau 300, Québec, PQ G2K 2G1; tel. (418) 627-8888; fax (418) 627-9999; Pres. LUC SAVARD; 78,000 mems (1997).

Centrale des syndicats démocratiques: 801 4e rue Québec, PQ G1J 2T7; tel. (418) 529-2956; fax (418) 529-6323; f. 1972; Pres. FRANÇOIS VAUDREUIL; 2 federated and 392 affiliated unions.

Confederation of Canadian Unions: POB 1159, Gold River, BC V0P 1G0; tel. (604) 283-7111; fax (604) 283-2451; e-mail ccu@goldrur.island.net; f. 1969; Pres. JIM STREB GIFFORD; 10 affiliated unions representing 21,000 mems (1996).

Confédération des syndicats nationaux: 1601 ave de Lorimier, Montréal, PQ H2K 4M5; tel. (514) 598-2121; fax (514) 598-2052; e-mail intcsn@total.net; f. 1921; Pres. GÉRALD LAROSE; 9 federated unions.

Federated unions with over 15,000 members:

Fédération CSN—Construction: 1594 ave de Lorimier, Montréal, PQ H2K 3W5; tel. (514) 598-2044; fax (514) 598-2040; Pres. ANDRÉ PAQUIN; 23,000 mems (1997).

Fédération des employées et employés de services publics inc: 1601 ave de Lorimier, Montréal, PQ H2K 4M5; tel. (514) 598-2231; fax (514) 598-2398; Pres. GINETTE GUÉRIN; 36,000 mems (1997).

Fédération des affaires sociales inc: 1601 ave de Lorimier, Montréal, PQ H2K 4M5; tel. (514) 598-2210; fax (514) 598-2223; Pres. LOUIS ROY; 97,000 mems (1997).

Fédération du commerce inc: 1601 ave de Lorimier, Bureau 122, Montréal, PQ H2K 4M5; tel. (514) 598-2353; fax (514) 598-2304; Pres. LISE POULIN; 31,000 mems (1997).

Fédération de la métallurgie: 2100 blvd de Maisonneuve est, Bureau 204, Montréal, PQ H2K 4S1; tel. (514) 529-4937; fax (514) 529-4935; Pres. ALAIN LAMPRON; 20,000 mems (1997).

Fédération nationale des enseignantes et des enseignants du Québec: 1601 ave de Lorimier, Montréal, PQ H2K 4M5; tel. (514) 598-2241; fax (514) 598-2190; Pres. OLIVIA BOUCHARD; 20,000 mems (1997).

The American Federation of Labor and Congress of Industrial Organizations (AFL–CIO), with headquarters in Washington, DC, USA, represented 0.4% of the total union membership in Canada, at the beginning of 1997.

Principal affiliated union:

International Association of Bridge, Structural and Ornamental Iron Workers: 1350 L'Heritage Drive, Sarnia, ON N7S 6H8; tel. (519) 542-1413; fax (519) 542-3790; Gen. Vice-Pres. JAMES PHAIR; 15,000 mems (1997).

Principal Unaffiliated Unions

Alberta Teachers' Association: 11010 142nd St, Edmonton, AB T5N 2R1; tel. (403) 447-9400; fax (403) 455-6481; Exec. Sec. JULIUS S. BUSKI; 34,000 mems (1997).

British Columbia Teachers' Federation: 550 West 6th Ave, Suite 100, Vancouver, BC V5Z 4P2; tel. (604) 871-2283; fax (604) 871-2294; Pres. ALICE MCQUADE; 42,000 mems (1997).

Canadian Telephone Employees' Association: place du Canada, Bureau 360; Montréal, PQ H3B 2N2; tel. (514) 861-9963; Pres. JUDITH KING; 22,000 mems (1997).

Christian Labour Association of Canada: 5920 Atlantic Drive, Mississauga, ON L4W 1N6; tel. (905) 670-7383; fax (905) 670-8416; Pres. STAN BAKER; 17,000 mems (1997).

Fédération des infirmières et d'infirmiers du Québec: 2050 rue de Bleury, 4e étage, Montréal, PQ H3A 2J5; tel. (514) 987-1141; fax (514) 987-7273; Pres. JENNIE SKENE; 45,000 mems (1997).

Federation of Women Teachers' Associations of Ontario: 1260 Bay St, Toronto, ON M5R 2B8; tel. (416) 964-1232; fax (416) 964-0512; Pres. MARET SÁDEM-THOMPSON; 41,000 mems (1997).

Ontario Nurses' Association: 85 Grenville St, Suite 400, Toronto, ON M5S 3A2; tel. (416) 964-8833; fax (416) 964-8864; Pres. BARB WAHL; 42,000 mems (1997).

Ontario Public School Teachers' Federation: 5160 Orbitor Drive, Mississauga, ON L4W 5H2; tel. (905) 238-0200; fax (905) 238-0201; Pres. J. F. HOLMES; 30,000 mems (1997).

Ontario Secondary School Teachers Federation: 60 Mobile Drive, Toronto, ON M4A 2P3; tel. (416) 751-8300; fax (416) 751-3394; Pres. EARL MANNERS; 51,000 mems (1997).

Professional Institute of the Public Service of Canada: 53 Auriga Drive, Nepean, ON K2E 8C3; tel. (613) 228-6310; fax (613) 228-9048; Pres. STEVE HINDLE; 33,000 mems (1997).

Syndicat de la fonction publique Québec: 5100 blvd des Gradins, Québec, PQ G2J 1N4; tel. (418) 623-2424; fax (418) 623-6109; Gen. Pres. SERGE ROY; 48,000 mems (1997).

Transport

Owing to the size of the country, Canada's economy is particularly dependent upon an efficient system of transport. The St Lawrence Seaway allows ocean-going ships to reach the Great Lakes. In addition to an extensive railway network, the country's transport infrastructure is being increasingly augmented by roads, air services and petroleum pipelines. The Trans-Canada Highway is one of the main features of a network of more than 900,000 km of roads and highways.

Canadian Transportation Agency (CTA): Ottawa, ON K1A 0N9; tel. (819) 997-0344; fax (819) 953-8353; f. 1996; to oversee the economic regulation of transport; Chair. MARIAN L. ROBSON.

RAILWAYS

BC Rail: POB 8770, Vancouver, BC V6B 4X6; tel. (604) 986-2012; fax (604) 984-5004; f. 1912; publicly-owned; 2,314 km of track; Chair. E. PRICE; Pres. and CEO P. J. MCELLIGOTT.

Canadian Pacific Railway: Gulf Canada Sq., 401 9th Ave, SW, Calgary, AB T2P 4Z4; tel. (403) 218-7000; fax (403) 218-7567; f. 1881; 24,000 km of track; Pres. and CEO R. J. RITCHIE.

CN Rail: 935 rue de La Gauchetière ouest, CP 8100, Montréal, PQ H3C 3N4; tel. (514) 399-5430; telex 055-61497; fax (514) 399-5479; f. 1919; investor-owned; 32,500 km of track; Pres. and CEO PAUL TELLIER.

Ontario Northland Transportation Commission: 555 Oak St East, North Bay, ON P1B 8L3; tel. (705) 472-4500; fax (705) 476-5598; an agency of the Govt of Ontario; operates rail services over 1,211 km of track; Chair. M. K. RUKAVINA; Pres. and CEO K. J. WALLACE.

VIA Rail Canada Inc: 2 place Ville-Marie, Bureau 4000, Montréal, PQ H3B 2G6; tel. (514) 871-6000; fax (514) 871-6658; f. 1977; federal govt corpn; operates passenger services over existing rail routes covering 13,822 km of track throughout Canada; Chair. MARC LEFRANÇOIS; Pres. and CEO T. IVANY.

Association

Railway Association of Canada: 800 blvd René-Lévesque ouest, Bureau 1105, Montréal, PQ H3B 1X9; tel. (514) 879-8555; fax (514) 879-1522; e-mail rac@railcan.ca; f. 1917; Pres. R. H. BALLANTYNE; 41 mems.

ROADS

Provincial governments are responsible for roads within their boundaries. The Federal Government is responsible for major roads in the Yukon and Northwest Territories and in National Parks. In 1995 there were an estimated 912,200 km of roads (including 15,000 km of federal roads and highways).

The Trans-Canada Highway extends from St John's, Newfoundland, to Victoria, British Columbia.

INLAND WATERWAYS

The St Lawrence River and the Great Lakes provide Canada and the USA with a system of inland waterways extending from the Atlantic Ocean to the western end of Lake Superior, a distance of 3,769 km (2,342 miles). There is a 10.7-m (35-foot) navigation channel from Montréal to the sea and an 8.25-m (27-foot) channel from Montréal to Lake Erie. The St Lawrence Seaway (see below), which was opened in 1959, was initiated partly to provide a deep waterway and partly to satisfy the increasing demand for electric power. Power development has been undertaken by the provinces of Québec and Ontario, and by New York State. In 1992 cargo traffic through the Seaway totalled 42.3m. metric tons. The navigation facilities and conditions are within the jurisdiction of the federal governments of the USA and Canada.

St Lawrence River and Great Lakes Shipping

St Lawrence Seaway Authority (SLSA): 360 Albert St, Suite 1400, Ottawa, ON K1R 7X7; tel. (613) 598-4600; fax (613) 598-4620; e-mail marketing@seaways.ca; fed. govt agency responsible for supervision of marine traffic through Canadian section of St Lawrence Seaway, which is operated jtly with the USA; Pres. and CEO GLENDON STEWART.

Algoma Central Corpn: 289 Bay St, POB 7000, Sault Ste Marie, ON P6A 5P6; tel. (705) 949-2113; fax (705) 946-7302; f. 1899; Pres. and CEO L. N. SAVOIE; 24 bulk cargo vessels.

Canada Steamship Lines Inc (CSL): 759 square Victoria, CP 100, Montréal, PQ H2Y 2K3; tel. (514) 288-0231; fax (514) 982-3802; f. 1913; Pres. and CEO RAYMOND JOHNSTON; 30 vessels; 750,000 grt.

Paterson, N. M., and Sons Ltd: POB 664, Station F, Thunder Bay, ON P7C 4W6; tel. (807) 577-8421; fax (807) 475-3493; f. 1908; bulk carriers; Pres. and CEO R. J. PATERSON; 7 vessels; 95,536 grt.

Upper Lakes Shipping Ltd: 2100 Bankers Hall, 855 2nd St, SW, Calgary, AB T2P 4J9; tel. (403) 237-4813; fax (403) 237-4814; Chair. J. D. LEITCH; Pres. and CEO S. C. ABRAHAM; 23 vessels.

SHIPPING

British Columbia Ferry Corporation: 1112 Fort St, Victoria, BC V8V 4V2; tel. (250) 699-1211; fax (250) 381-5452; passenger and vehicle ferries; Pres. and CEO FRANK RHODES; 40 vessels.

Fednav Ltd: 1000 rue de La Gauchetière ouest, Bureau 3500, Montréal, PQ H3B 4W5; tel. (514) 878-6500; telex 055-60637; fax (514) 878-6642; f. 1944; shipowners, operators, contractors, terminal operators; Pres. L. G. PATHY; owned and chartered fleet of 68 vessels.

Groupe Desagnés Inc: 21 rue du Marché-Champlain, Bureau 100, Québec, PQ G1K 8Z8; tel. (418) 692-1000; fax (418) 692-6044; Chair. and CEO LOUIS-MARIE BEAULIEU; 10 vessels.

Marine Atlantic Inc: 100 Cameron St, Moncton, NB E1C 5Y6; tel. (506) 851-3600; fax (506) 851-3791; e-mail bstreet@marine-atlantic.ca; Pres. and CEO ROD MORRISON; serves Newfoundland and Labrador; 5 vessels, incl. passenger, roll-on/roll-off and freight ferries.

Soconav Inc: 1801 ave McGill Collège, Bureau 1470, Montréal, PQ H3A 2N4; tel. (514) 284-9535; telex 5267671; fax (514) 845-2175; Great Lakes, St Lawrence River and Gulf, Atlantic Coast, Arctic and NWT; Chair. and Pres. MICHEL GAUCHER; 13 tankers, 76,476 grt.

Associations

Canadian Shipowners Association: 350 Sparks St, Suite 705, Ottawa, ON K1R 7S8; tel. (613) 232-3539; fax (613) 232-6211; e-mail csa@shipowners.ca; f. 1953; Pres. T. NORMAN HALL; 14 mems.

Canadian Shippers' Council: 48 Balsam Drive, Baie d'Urfé, PQ H9X 3K5; tel. (514) 457-7268; fax (514) 457-7269; Sec. W. MUELLER; 12 institutional mems, 2 assoc. mems.

Shipping Federation of Canada: 300 rue St-Sacrement, Bureau 326, Montréal, PQ H2Y 1X4; tel. (514) 849-2325; fax (514) 849-6992; f. 1903; Pres. Capt. FRANCIS C. NICOL; 75 mems.

CIVIL AVIATION

Principal Scheduled Companies

Air Canada: CP 14000, succursale St-Laurent, Montréal, PQ H4Y 1H4; tel. (514) 422-5772; telex 062-17537; fax (514) 422-5798; f. 1937; investor-owned; Pres. and CEO LAMAR DURRETT; operates services throughout Canada and to the USA; also to Europe, the Far East and the Caribbean.

Canadian Airlines International: Scotia Centre, Suite 2800, 700 2nd St, SW, Calgary, AB T2P 2W2; f. 1988 by merger; Pres. and CEO KEVIN BENSON; domestic and international passenger and cargo charters and scheduled services.

Association

Air Transport Association of Canada: 255 Albert St, Suite 1100, Ottawa, ON K1P 6A9; tel. (613) 233-7727; fax (613) 230-8648; e-mail atac@atac.ca; f. 1934; Pres. JOHN CRICHTON; 260 mems.

Tourism

Most tourist visitors (12.9m. of a total 17.3m. in 1996) are from the USA. Expenditure by tourists in 1996 amounted to C $9,670m.

Canadian Tourism Commission: 235 Queen St, 4th Floor East, Ottawa, ON K1A 0H6; tel. (613) 954-3943; fax (613) 954-3945.

Tourism Industry Association of Canada: 130 Albert St, Suite 1016, Ottawa, ON K1P 5G4; tel. (613) 238-3883; fax (613) 238-3878; f. 1931; private-sector asscn; encourages travel to and within Canada; promotes development of travel services and facilities; Pres. DEBRA WARD.

CAPE VERDE

Introductory Survey

Location, Climate, Language, Religion, Flag, Capital

The Republic of Cape Verde is an archipelago of 10 islands and five islets in the North Atlantic Ocean, about 500 km (300 miles) west of Dakar, Senegal. The country lies in a semi-arid belt, with little rain and an average annual temperature of 24°C (76°F). The official language is Portuguese, of which the locally spoken form is Creole (Crioulo). Virtually all of the inhabitants profess Christianity, and more than 95% are Roman Catholics. The national flag, adopted in September 1992 (proportions 5 by 3), comprises five horizontal stripes: blue (half the depth) at the top, white, red, white (each one-twelfth) and blue. Superimposed, to the left of centre, is a circle of 10 five-pointed gold stars (four on the white stripes and three each on the blue stripes above and below). The capital is Cidade de Praia.

Recent History

The Cape Verde Islands were colonized by the Portuguese in the 15th century. From the 1950s, liberation movements in Portugal's African colonies were campaigning for independence, and, in this context, the archipelago was linked with the mainland territory of Portuguese Guinea (now Guinea-Bissau) under one nationalist movement, the Partido Africano da Independência do Guiné e Cabo Verde (PAIGC). The independence of Guinea-Bissau was recognized by Portugal in September 1974, but the PAIGC leadership in the Cape Verde Islands decided to pursue its independence claims separately, rather than enter into an immediate federation with Guinea-Bissau. In December 1974 a transitional Government, comprising representatives of the Portuguese Government and the PAIGC, was formed; members of other political parties were excluded. On 30 June 1975 elections for a legislative body, the Assembléia Nacional Popular (ANP—National People's Assembly) were held, in which only PAIGC candidates were allowed to participate. Independence was granted to the Republic of Cape Verde on 5 July 1975, with Aristides Pereira, Secretary-General of the PAIGC, becoming the country's first President. Cape Verde's first Constitution was approved in September 1980.

Although Cape Verde and Guinea-Bissau remained constitutionally separate, the PAIGC supervised the activities of both states. Progress towards the ultimate goal of unification was halted by the November 1980 coup in Guinea-Bissau (during which the President, Luiz Cabral, who was himself a Cape Verdean, was placed under house arrest). The Cape Verde Government condemned the coup, and in January 1981 the Cape Verde wing of the PAIGC was renamed the Partido Africano da Independência de Cabo Verde (PAICV). In February Pereira was re-elected as President by the ANP, and all articles concerning an eventual union with Guinea-Bissau were removed from the Constitution. Discussions concerning reconciliation were held in June 1982, however, after the release of Luiz Cabral, and diplomatic relations between the two countries were subsequently normalized.

Elections to the ANP took place in December 1985. The 83 candidates on the PAICV-approved list, not all of whom were members of the PAICV, obtained 94.5% of the votes cast. In January 1986 Pereira was re-elected for a further five-year term as President by the ANP. In July 1987 Lisbon radio reported disturbances in Mindelo, São Vicente, after the ANP approved legislation decriminalizing abortion, as part of a policy to promote birth control during the course of the second Development Plan, covering 1986–90. Further demonstrations against abortion and in favour of greater political freedom were held in January 1988, but Pereira dismissed them as insignificant and not indicative of any general discontent.

At the PAICV Congress in November 1988, Pereira and the Prime Minister, Gen. Pedro Verona Rodgrigues Pires, were re-elected Secretary-General and Deputy Secretary-General, respectively, of the party. In September 1989 the Government declared three days' mourning, following the murder of the Secretary of State for Public Administration, Dr Renato de Silas Cardoso. A government communiqué stated that the killing was a common law crime, unconnected with Cardoso's position in the Government. In November two political commissions were established, to regulate legislative elections and to consider proposals for constitutional changes. In the same month it was announced that, although elections to the ANP were to be held (as scheduled) in 1990, local elections were to be deferred until 1991. The postponement was criticized by the opposition Catholic newspaper, *Terra Nova*, which accused the Government of perpetuating its monopoly of power. In February 1990, in an apparent response to increasing pressure from church and academic circles, the PAICV announced the convening of an emergency congress to discuss the possible abolition of Article 4 of the Constitution, which guaranteed the supremacy of the PAICV. In April a newly-formed political organization, the Movimento para a Democracia (MPD), issued a manifesto in Paris, France, which advocated the immediate introduction of a multi-party system. Pereira subsequently announced that the next presidential election, which was planned for December 1990, would be held, for the first time, on the basis of universal suffrage.

In July 1990 Pires implemented an extensive ministerial reshuffle, in which seven new state secretariats were created. In the same month a special congress of the PAICV reviewed proposals for new party statutes and the abolition of Article 4 of the Constitution. Pereira also announced his resignation as Secretary-General of the PAICV, and was later replaced by Pires. On 28 September the ANP approved a constitutional amendment abolishing the PAICV's monopoly of power and permitting a multi-party system. The legislative elections were rescheduled for January 1991. The MPD subsequently received official recognition as a political party. In late November 1990 the MPD announced its support for an independent candidate, António Mascarenhas Monteiro (a former judge), in the presidential election, which had been postponed until February 1991. On 13 January 1991 the legislative elections, the first multi-party elections to take place in lusophone Africa, resulted in a decisive victory for the MPD, which secured 56 of the 79 seats in the ANP. On 26 January Dr Carlos Alberto Wahnon de Carvalho Veiga, the leader of the MPD, was sworn in as Prime Minister at the head of an interim Government, mostly comprising members of the MPD, pending the result of the presidential election. This was duly held on 17 February, and resulted in victory for Mascarenhas, who secured 73.5% of the votes cast. The new President was inaugurated on 22 March. The Government was officially inaugurated on 4 April. The first multi-party local elections, held in December, resulted in another decisive victory for the MPD, which secured control of 10 of the 14 local councils.

In January 1992 Veiga reorganized the Council of Ministers and created three new ministries (Infrastructure and Transport, Culture and Communication, and Tourism, Industry and Commerce) in an attempt to improve government efficiency. In addition, a ministry for Public Administration and Parliamentary Affairs was created, in accordance with Veiga's announcement of a strengthening of the role of the ANP, which was to convene more frequently and for longer periods in order to reduce legislative delays.

On 25 September 1992 a new Constitution came into force, enshrining the principles of multi-party democracy. Under the new Constitution of the Republic of Cape Verde (also referred to as the 'Second Republic'), a new national flag and emblem were adopted, and the ANP became the Assembléia Nacional (AN). In the same month legislation providing for the sale of state enterprises was adopted.

In March 1993 the Council of Ministers was reorganized. The Ministry of Finance and Planning became solely the Ministry of Finance, while a new ministry, of Economic Co-ordination, was created. The posts of Secretary of State for Finance, for Fisheries, and for Tourism, Industry and Commerce were abolished, while the position of Secretary of State for Internal Administration was upgraded to the status of minister. In August the opposition PAICV elected Aristides Lima to the post of Secretary-General of the party, replacing Pires, who was appointed party Chairman. In December the Minister of Justice and Labour, Dr Eurico Correia Monteiro, was dismissed, following his announcement that he would be contesting the leadership of the MPD at an extraordinary national convention of the party, called by Veiga to take place in February 1994. At the convention, Carlos Veiga was re-elected President of the MPD. However, increasing conflict within the party resulted in some 30 party delegates, led by Eurico Monteiro and former Minister of Foreign Affairs, Jorge Carlos Almeida Fonseca, boycotting the convention and holding a convention of their own. That month Monteiro announced the formal establishment of a new political party, the Partido da Convergência Democrática (PCD), which would oppose the MPD at the 1996 elections.

In March 1994 Veiga announced a further reorganization of the Council of Ministers. The Ministry of Internal Administration was restyled the Ministry of Cabinet Affairs. In addition, José António Mendes dos Reis was appointed minister of a newly created ministry, of Employment, Youth and Social Promotion. In May 1994, following the split within the ruling MPD, a motion of confidence in the Government was debated by the legislature. The motion was carried in the Government's favour by a narrow margin of 41 votes to 38.

In December 1994 Veiga implemented an extensive reorganization of the Council of Ministers. The Ministry of Tourism, Industry and Commerce was dissolved, and its functions transferred to the Ministry of Economic Co-ordination. Also discontinued were the Ministries of Culture and Communication, Cabinet Affairs, and Public Administration and Parliamentary Affairs. The Ministry of Fisheries, Agriculture and Rural Activity was divided into two separate ministries, of Agriculture and of the Sea. In October 1995 the Centro de Promoção do Investimento Externo e das Exportações (PROMEX) assumed the functions of the Instituto Nacional do Turismo to become the Centro de Promoção Turística, do Investimento Externo e das Exportações, retaining the original acronym.

At legislative elections conducted on 17 December 1995 the MPD secured an outright majority with 50 of the total 72 seats in the AN (reduced from 79 seats under electoral legislation approved in 1994). The PAICV won 21 seats, while the remaining seat was obtained by the PCD. At a presidential election conducted on 18 February 1996 António Mascarenhas Monteiro, the sole candidate and incumbent President, was re-elected. However, despite appeals for the electorate to demonstrate its support for Mascarenhas' second term of office, the turn-out was low, at only 45%. Veiga, meanwhile, expressed his intention to continue the policies of liberal economic and social reform that had been pursued in his previous term in office, and to introduce further constitutional amendments in 1997.

In March 1996 Veiga announced a further reorganization of the Council of Ministers. The Ministry of Employment, Youth and Social Promotion, headed by José António Reis, was disbanded, and Reis was appointed Assistant Minister to the Prime Minister, with responsibility for Public Administration, Labour, Employment and Training, Social Communication, Youth and Sports. In June 1997, in addition to his existing portfolios, Reis resumed responsibility for Social Promotion. In September Pedro Pires was elected leader of the PAICV.

Cape Verde has traditionally professed a non-aligned stance in foreign affairs and maintains relations with virtually all the power blocs. Cape Verde's reputation for political independence led to its selection as the venue for several important international conferences. In July 1988 the military commanders of Angola, Cuba and South Africa met in Cape Verde to pursue peace negotiations, under the auspices of the USA. In August the South African Deputy Minister of Foreign Affairs conferred with the Cape Verdean Minister of Foreign Affairs in Praia. Cape Verde's relations with Guinea-Bissau showed signs of improvement in 1988, when the two countries signed an agreement on bilateral co-operation. In the same year Mozambique and Cape Verde pledged solidarity with each other, during a visit to the islands by the Mozambican Prime Minister, Mário Machungo.

Since taking office in 1991, the MPD Government has successfully sought to extend Cape Verde's range of international contacts, with special emphasis on potential new sources of development aid: substantial assistance has been received from both Israel and the Gulf states. The MPD Government has enlarged the scope of Cape Verde's diplomatic contacts, establishing embassies in South Africa and Sweden, as well as diplomatic presences in Hong Kong, Spain, Singapore, the United Kingdom and the USA. In January 1997 the Government announced that it was to open an embassy in the People's Republic of China. The country has continued to maintain particularly close relations with Portugal and Brazil, and with other lusophone African former colonies—Angola, Guinea–Bissau, Mozambique and São Tomé and Príncipe, known collectively, with Cape Verde, as the Países Africanos da Língua Oficial Portuguesa (PALOP). Cape Verde is regularly represented at meetings of PALOP, whose principal aid donors include the EU, the IMF, the World Bank and the African Development Bank. In July 1996 a 'lusophone commonwealth', known as the Comunidade dos Países de Língua Portuguesa (CPLP), comprising the five PALOP countries together with Portugal and Brazil, was formed with the intention of benefiting each member state through joint co-operation on technical, cultural and social matters. In December 1996 Cape Verde became a full member of the Sommet francophone, a francophone commonwealth comprising all the French-speaking nations of the world, and benefits in turn from membership of this body's Agence de coopération culturelle et technique, an agency which promotes cultural and technical co-operation among francophone countries. Although a lusophone nation, Cape Verde had been an observer at annual meetings of the Sommet francophone since 1977. In January 1992 Cape Verde became a non-permanent member (for a period of two years) of the United Nations Security Council (see p. 20). In February 1993 Cape Verde and Senegal signed a treaty settling the demarcation of the countries' common maritime border.

Government

Under the 1992 Constitution, Cape Verde is a multi-party state, although the formation of parties on a religious or geographical basis is prohibited. Legislative power is vested in the Assembléia Nacional (AN—National Assembly), which comprises 72 deputies, elected by universal adult suffrage for a five-year term. The Head of State is the President of the Republic, who is elected by universal suffrage for a five-year term. Executive power is vested in the Prime Minister, who is nominated by the deputies of the AN, appointed by the President and governs with the assistance of a Council of Ministers.

Defence

The armed forces, initially formed from ex-combatants in the liberation wars, totalled about 1,100 (army 1,000, air force less than 100) in August 1997. There is also a police force, the Police for Public Order, which is organized by the local municipal councils. National service is by selective conscription. Government defence expenditure in 1997 was budgeted at an estimated 350m. escudos (US $4m.).

Economic Affairs

In 1995, according to estimates from the World Bank, Cape Verde's gross national product (GNP), measured at average 1993–95 prices, was US $366m., equivalent to $960 per head. During 1985–95, it was estimated, GNP per head increased, in real terms, by 2.1% per year. Over the same period, the population increased by an annual average of 2.0%. During 1985–95, according to estimates, Cape Verde's gross domestic product (GDP) increased, in real terms, at an average rate of 4.2% per year. Real GDP increased by 4.7% in 1995 and by 4.1% in 1996.

Agriculture (including forestry and fishing) contributed 20.7% of GDP in 1993, and employed an estimated 26.8% of the economically active population in 1996. The staple crops are maize and beans; potatoes, cassava, coconuts, dates, sugar cane and bananas are also cultivated. Fish, crustaceans and molluscs provided almost one-half of total export earnings in 1994. Lobster and tuna are among the most important exports. However, the total catch declined from 14,730 metric tons in 1981 to 7,081 tons in 1995. In 1994 a five-year project was announced for the redevelopment of the fishing industry with investment of US $28m., largely funded by international development agencies. During 1985–93 the GDP of the agricultural sector increased, in real terms, at an average rate of 3.5% per year.

Industry (including mining, manufacturing, construction and power) contributed 30.1% of GDP in 1993. Industry employed 24.5% of the labour force in 1990. During 1985–93 industrial GDP increased, in real terms, at an average rate of 6.2% per year.

Mining employed 0.3% of the labour force in 1990 and contributed an estimated 0.3% of GDP in 1993. Salt and pozzolana, a volcanic ash used in cement manufacture, are the main non-fuel minerals produced.

Manufacturing contributed 6.4% of GDP in 1993, and employed 4.6% of the labour force in 1990. The most important branches, other than fish-processing, are machinery and electrical equipment, transport equipment, chemicals and textiles. During 1985–93 the GDP of the manufacturing sector increased, in real terms, at an average rate of 5.9% per year.

There are about 700,000 Cape Verdeans living outside the country, principally in the USA, the Netherlands, Portugal, Italy and Angola. In 1993 remittances from emigrants provided an estimated 10,000m. escudos. The Government has attempted to attract emigrants' capital into the light industry and fishing sectors in Cape Verde by offering favourable tax conditions to investors.

Energy is derived principally from hydroelectric power and gas. Imports of mineral fuels comprised 3.6% of the value of total imports in 1994.

Services accounted for 49.3% of GDP in 1993. During 1985–93 the combined GDP of the service sectors increased, in real terms, at an average rate of 4.3% per year. Tourism has been identified as the area with the most potential for economic development. Legislation introduced since 1991 has aimed to provide increased incentives and guarantees to investors. Several new hotel developments began operating in 1996. The construction of a new international airport at Praia, due for completion in 1999, was expected to give considerable impetus to the development of the tourism sector.

In 1995 Cape Verde recorded a trade deficit of US $223.84m., and there was a deficit of $38.77m. on the current account of the balance of payments. In 1994 the principal source of imports was Portugal (34.5%); other major suppliers were France, the Netherlands and Japan. Portugal was also the principal market for exports (58.8%) in that year; other major recipients were the United Kingdom and Spain. The principal exports in 1994 were fish, crustaceans and molluscs (providing 48% of the total) and leather footwear (25.1%). Large-scale exports of bananas, interrupted in 1994 owing to quality restrictions imposed by the EU, were expected to resume in 1998. The major imports in 1994 were machinery and transport equipment (36.0%), food and live animals (23.3%) and basic manufactures (15.6%).

In 1995 there was an estimated budgetary deficit of 10,724m. escudos. Cape Verde's total external debt at the end of 1995 was US $216.3m., of which $185.2m. was long-term public debt. In 1995 the cost of debt-servicing was equivalent to 3.2% of the value of exports of goods and services. The annual rate of inflation averaged 6.7% in 1985–95. Consumer prices increased by an average of 8.3% in 1995. An estimated 25.8% of the labour force were unemployed in 1990.

Cape Verde is a member of the Economic Community of West African States (ECOWAS—see p. 145), which promotes trade and co-operation in West Africa, and is a signatory to the Lomé Convention (see p. 178).

Cape Verde's agricultural economy is highly vulnerable to severe periodic drought, making self-sufficiency in food production impossible; approximately 85% of the country's total food requirements are imported. The country benefits from considerable external assistance (which totalled US $111.5m. in 1995) and substantial remittances from emigrants, whose number is approximately twice that of Cape Verdeans living on the islands; annual remittances averaged some 20% of GDP during 1992–95.

Plans to establish Cape Verde as an international centre of trade, based on transhipping and 'offshore' banking and financial services, were initiated in 1990. In 1992 the MPD Government introduced a national development plan, which included measures to rationalize the public sector and promote the development of private-sector activity. However, a sustained increase in public expenditure was not matched by growth in domestic revenue and external grants, and resulted in a widening public deficit, necessitating substantial domestic and external borrowing. A further national development plan was adopted in 1997, the key aim of which was to alleviate poverty, which was estimated to affect some 40% of the population. The plan aimed to create jobs and wealth by developing the private sector, in particular the light-manufacturing and service-sector industries. It was envisaged that export earnings from the service sector would increase significantly in the near future, particularly from tourism, fishing, maritime services (including transhipping) and the servicing of foreign airliners.

Social Welfare

Medical facilities are limited and there is a severe shortage of staff and buildings, although plans for a national health service are being implemented. In 1980 Cape Verde had 21 hospital establishments, with a total of 632 beds, and in 1984 there were 60 physicians and 186 nursing personnel working in the country. Development plans include the construction of more than 300 small local health units. According to provisional figures, the Ministry of Health received 8.9% of the central Government's total current expenditure in 1995, compared with 10.6% in 1994.

Education

Primary education, beginning at seven years of age and lasting for six years, comprises a first cycle of four years, which is compulsory, and a second cycle of two years. Secondary education, beginning at 13 years of age, is also divided into two cycles, the first comprising a three-year general course, the second a three-year pre-university course. There are three teacher-training units and two industrial and commercial schools of further education. In 1993 the total enrolment at primary and secondary schools was equivalent to 83% of all school-age children (males 85%; females 81%). In 1993/94 78,173 pupils attended primary schools, and 11,808 attended general secondary schools. Primary enrolment in 1993 included 100% of children in the relevant age-group. In that year secondary enrolment was equivalent to 22% of children in the relevant age-group. In 1996/97 there were 1,660 Cape Verdean students studying at overseas universities. A university was to be established in Praia in 1998 with assistance from Portugal. In 1995, according to estimates by UNESCO, the average rate of illiteracy among the population aged 15 years and over was 28.4% (males 18.6%; females 36.2%). According to provisional figures, the Ministry of Education received 21.0% of the central Government's total current expenditure in 1995, compared with 22.1% in 1994.

Public Holidays

1998: 1 January (New Year), 20 January (National Heroes' Day), 1 May (Labour Day), 5 July (Independence Day), 15 August (Assumption), 1 November (All Saints' Day), 25 December (Christmas Day).

1999: 1 January (New Year), 20 January (National Heroes' Day), 1 May (Labour Day), 5 July (Independence Day), 15 August (Assumption), 1 November (All Saints' Day), 25 December (Christmas Day).

Weights and Measures

The metric system is in force.

Statistical Survey

Source (unless otherwise stated): Statistical Service, Banco de Cabo Verde, Av. Amílcar Cabral, Santiago; tel. 61-31-53; telex 99350.

AREA AND POPULATION

Area: 4,033 sq km (1,557 sq miles).

Population: 272,571 at census of 15 December 1970; 295,703 (males 135,695; females 160,008) at census of 2 June 1980; 341,491 (males 161,494; females 179,997) at census of 23 June 1990; 396,000 at mid-1996 (UN estimate). *By island* (1990 census, figures rounded to nearest '00): Boa Vista 3,500, Brava 7,000, Fogo 34,000, Maio 5,000, Sal 7,700, Santo Antão 44,000, São Nicolau 14,000, Santiago 175,000, São Vicente 51,000.

Density (mid-1996): 98.2 per sq. km.

Principal Town: Cidade de Praia (capital), population 61,644 at 1990 census.

Births, Marriages and Deaths (1992): Registered live births 9,671 (birth rate 26.9 per 1,000); Registered marriages 1,360 (marriage rate 3.8 per 1,000); Registered deaths 2,843 (death rate 7.9 per 1,000). Source: UN, *Demographic Yearbook*.

Expectation of Life (years at birth, 1990): males 63.53; females 71.33. Source: UN, *Demographic Yearbook*.

Economically Active Population (persons aged 10 years and over, 1990 census): Agriculture, hunting, forestry and fishing 29,876; Mining and quarrying 410; Manufacturing 5,520; Electricity, gas and water 883; Construction 22,722; Trade, restaurants and hotels 12,747; Transport, storage and communications 6,138; Financing, insurance, real estate and business services 821; Community, social and personal services 17,358; Activities not adequately defined 24,090; Total labour force 120,565 (males 75,786; females 44,779), including 31,049 unemployed persons (males 19,712; females 11,337). Source: International Labour Office, *Yearbook of Labour Statistics*.

AGRICULTURE, ETC.

Principal Crops (FAO estimates, '000 metric tons, 1996): Maize 9; Potatoes 2; Cassava 4; Coconuts 5; Tomatoes 2; Onions (dry) 2; Other vegetables 4; Sugar cane 18; Bananas 6; Other fruits 9. Source: FAO, *Production Yearbook*.

Livestock (FAO estimates,'000 head, year ending September 1996): Cattle 19; Pigs 450; Sheep 4; Goats 132; Asses 14. Source: FAO, *Production Yearbook*.

Livestock Products (FAO estimates, '000 metric tons, 1996): Pig meat 8; Other meat 2; Cows' milk 2; Goats' milk 4. Source: FAO, *Production Yearbook*.

Fishing ('000 metric tons, live weight): Total catch 7.2 in 1993; 7.2 in 1994; 7.1 in 1995. Source: FAO, *Yearbook of Fishery Statistics*.

MINING

Production (metric tons): Salt (unrefined) 4,000 (1994 estimate, Source: US Bureau of Mines—Washington D.C.); Pozzolana 10,000 (1990, Source: UN Economic Commission for Africa, *African Statistical Yearbook*).

INDUSTRY

Production (metric tons, unless otherwise indicated, 1994): Biscuits 348 (1990 figure); Bread 3,926 (1991 figure); Canned fish 273; Frozen fish 2,700 (1992 FAO estimate); Manufactured tobacco 94 (1992 figure); Beer 4,162,033 litres; Soft drinks 932,154 litres; Paint 492; Shoes 120,524 pairs; Electric energy 63.6m. kWh. Sources: UN, *Industrial Commodity Statistics Yearbook;* IMF, *Cape Verde—Recent Economic Developments* (October 1996).

FINANCE

Currency and Exchange Rates: 100 centavos = 1 Cape Verde escudo; 1,000 escudos are known as a conto. *Sterling and Dollar Equivalents* (31 August 1997): £1 sterling = 156.382 escudos; US $1 = 96.425 escudos; 1,000 Cape Verde escudos = £6.395 = $10.371. *Average Exchange Rate* (escudos per US dollar): 81.891 in 1994; 76.853 in 1995; 82.591 in 1996.

Budget (preliminary, million escudos, 1995): *Revenue:* Taxation 6,407 (Taxes on income and profits 2,131, Municipal taxes 103, Taxes on international trade 3,757, Stamp tax 416); Other revenue 1,997 (Licences and miscellaneous fees 256, Property income 487, Transfers 425, Reimbursement of debt principal by public enterprises 101, Sales of fixed assets and services 190, Autonomous revenue 530); Total 8,404, excl. external grants (5,303) and domestic capital participation (761). *Expenditure:* Recurrent 9,284; Capital 9,844; Total 19,128. Source: IMF, *Cape Verde—Recent Economic Developments* (October 1996).

International Reserves (US $ million at 31 December 1996): IMF special drawing rights 0.06; Foreign exchange 51.69; Total 51.76. Source: IMF, *International Financial Statistics*.

Money Supply (million escudos at 31 December 1996): Currency outside banks 4,513.0; Demand deposits at commercial banks 8,488.4; Total money 13,001.4. Source: IMF, *International Financial Statistics*.

Cost of Living (Consumer Price Index for Praia; base: 1989 = 100): 141 in 1994; 153 in 1995; 162 in 1996. Source: UN, *Monthly Bulletin of Statistics*.

Expenditure on the Gross Domestic Product (million escudos at current purchasers' values, 1993): Government final consumption expenditure 5,099; Private final consumption expenditure 22,199; Increase in stocks 811; Gross fixed capital formation 9,404; *Total domestic expenditure* 37,513; Exports of goods and services 3,981; *Less* Imports of goods and services 14,343; *GDP in purchasers' values* 27,151. Source: UN Economic Commission for Africa, *African Statistical Yearbook*.

Gross Domestic Product by Economic Activity (million escudos at current prices, 1993): Agriculture, forestry and fishing 4,878; Mining and quarrying 67; Manufacturing 1,515; Electricity, gas and water 698; Construction 4,814; Trade, restaurants and hotels 5,634; Transport and communications 2,898; Finance, insurance, real estate and business services 939; Government services 1,936; Other community, social and personal services 221; *GDP at factor cost* 23,600; Indirect taxes, *less* Subsidies 3,551; *GDP in purchasers' values* 27,151. Source: UN, Economic Commission for Africa, *African Statistical Yearbook*.

Balance of Payments (US $ million, 1995): Exports of goods f.o.b. 8.41; Imports of goods f.o.b. –232.25; *Trade balance* –223.84; Exports of services 74.90; Imports of services –55.72; *Balance on goods and services* –204.66; Other income received 3.45; Other income paid –6.15; *Balance on goods, services and income* –207.36; Current transfers received 176.84; Current transfers paid –8.26; *Current balance* –38.77; Direct investment from abroad 9.73; Other investment liabilities 14.56; Net errors and omissions 0.71; *Overall balance* –13.77. Source: IMF, *International Financial Statistics*.

EXTERNAL TRADE

Principal Commodities (US $ '000, 1994): *Imports c.i.f.:* Food and live animals 48,981 (Dairy products and birds' eggs 7,346, Cereals and cereal preparations 14,521, Vegetables and fruit 8,341, Sugar, sugar preparations and honey 5,765); Beverages and tobacco 6,712 (Beverages 5,913); Crude materials (inedible) except fuels 4,274; Mineral fuels, lubricants, etc. 7,536 (Refined petroleum products 5,964); Animal and vegetable oils, fats and waxes 8,964 (Fixed vegetable oils and fats 8,369); Chemicals and related products 10,813; Basic manufactures 32,729 (Lime, cement and fabricated construction materials 8,977); Machinery and transport equipment 75,677 (Power-generating machinery and equipment 7,601, General industrial machinery, equipment and parts 9,016, Road vehicles and parts 15,846, Other transport equipment 25,258); Miscellaneous manufactured articles 14,435; Total (incl. others) 210,128. *Exports f.o.b.*: Food and live animals 2,458 (Fish, crustaceans and molluscs 2,406); Basic manufactures 1,062 (Leather, leather manufactures and dressed furskins 1,055); Machinery and transport equipment 108; Miscellaneous manufactured articles 1,267 (Leather footwear 1,260); Total (incl. others) 5,011. Source: UN, *International Trade Statistics Yearbook*.

Principal Trading Partners (US $ '000, 1994): *Imports c.i.f.*: Belgium and Luxembourg 6,553; Brazil 7,236; Côte d'Ivoire 2,236; Denmark 8,126; France 28,972; Germany 8,474; Italy 2,247; Japan 10,444; Netherlands 16,800; Portugal 72,559; Russia 3,617; Sweden 8,778; United Kingdom 2,933; USA 4,834; Total (incl. others) 210,128. *Exports f.o.b.:* France 254; Germany 113; Netherlands 104; Portugal 2,944; Spain 724; United Kingdom 739; Total (incl. others) 5,011. Source: UN, *International Trade Statistics Yearbook*.

TRANSPORT

Road Traffic (motor vehicles in use, estimates, December, 1995): Passenger cars 2,860; Lorries and vans 870. Source: IRF, *World Road Statistics*.

Shipping: Merchant fleet (registered at 31 December 1996): Number of vessels 27, total displacement ('000 grt) 14.9 (Source: Lloyd's Register of Shipping, *World Fleet Statistics*); International freight traffic (estimates, '000 metric tons, 1993): Goods loaded 144, goods unloaded 299 (Source: UN, Economic Commission for Africa, *African Statistical Yearbook*).

Civil Aviation (traffic on scheduled services, 1994): Kilometres flown 3,000,000; passengers carried 118,000; passenger-km 173,000,000; total ton-km 17,000,000. Source: UN, *Statistical Yearbook*.

TOURISM

Tourist Arrivals (1996): 37,000.

Tourist Receipts (1996): US $11m.

COMMUNICATIONS MEDIA

Radio Receivers (1994): 67,000 in use (estimate). Source: UNESCO, *Statistical Yearbook*.

Television Receivers (1994): 1,000 in use (estimate). Source: UNESCO, *Statistical Yearbook*.

Telephones (1995): 21,500 in use. Source: Cabo Verde Telecom.

Telefax stations (1991): 300 in use. Source: UN, *Statistical Yearbook*.

Newspapers (1995): 2 titles (average circulation 5,000 copies).

Periodicals (1995): 7 titles.

Book Production (1989): 10 titles. Source: UNESCO, *Statistical Yearbook*.

EDUCATION

Pre-primary (1986/87): 58 schools; 136 teachers; 4,523 pupils.

Primary (1993/94): 370 schools (1990/91); 2,657 teachers; 78,173 pupils.

Total Secondary: 268 teachers (1987/88); 14,097 pupils (1993/94).

General Secondary (1993/94): 438 teachers; 11,808 pupils.

Teacher Training: 25 teachers (1987/88); 889 pupils (1993/94).

Vocational Schools (1993/94): 94 teachers; 1,400 pupils.

Source: UNESCO, *Statistical Yearbook*.

Directory

The Constitution

A new Constitution of the Republic of Cape Verde ('the Second Republic') came into force on 25 September 1992. The Constitution defines Cape Verde as a sovereign, unitary and democratic republic, guaranteeing respect for human dignity and recognizing the inviolable and inalienable rights of man as a fundament of humanity, peace and justice. It recognizes the equality of all citizens before the law, without distinction of social origin, social condition, economic status, race, sex, religion, political convictions or ideologies and promises transparency for all citizens in the practising of fundamental liberties. The Constitution gives assent to popular will, and has a fundamental objective in the realization of economic, political, social and cultural democracy and the construction of a society which is free, just and in solidarity. The Republic of Cape Verde will create, progressively, the necessary conditions for the removal of all obstacles which impede the development of mankind and limit the equality of citizens and their effective participation in the political, economic, social and cultural organizations of the State and of Cape Verdean society.

The Head of State is the President of the Republic, who is elected by universal adult suffrage and must obtain two-thirds of the votes cast to win in the first round of the election. If no candidate secures the requisite majority, a new election is held within 21 days and contested by the two candidates who received the highest number of votes in the first round. Voting is conducted by secret ballot. Legislative power is vested in the Assembléia Nacional, which is also elected by universal adult suffrage. The Prime Minister is nominated by the Assembléia Nacional, to which he is responsible. On the recommendation of the Prime Minister, the President appoints the Council of Ministers, whose members must be elected deputies of the Assembléia Nacional. There are 17 local government councils, elected by universal suffrage for a period of five years.

The Government

HEAD OF STATE

President: ANTÓNIO MANUEL MASCARENHAS GOMES MONTEIRO (took office 22 March 1991; re-elected 18 February 1996).

COUNCIL OF MINISTERS
(November 1997)

Prime Minister: Dr CARLOS ALBERTO WAHNON DE CARVALHO VEIGA.

Assistant Minister to the Prime Minister, with responsibility for Public Administration, Labour, Employment and Training, Social Communication, Youth and Sports and Social Promotion: Dr JOSÉ ANTÓNIO MENDES DOS REIS.

Minister of Foreign Affairs and Communities: Dr AMÍLCAR SPENCER LOPES.

Minister of Economic Co-ordination: Dr ANTÓNIO GUALBERTO DO ROSÁRIO.

Minister in the Office of the President of the Council of Ministers and of Defence: Dr ULPIO NAPOLEÃO FERNANDES.

Minister of Agriculture, Food and the Environment: Dr JOSÉ ANTÓNIO PINTO MONTEIRO.

Minister of the Sea: Dra HELENA NOBRE DE MORAIS SEMEDO.

Minister of Education, Science and Culture: Eng. JOSÉ LUÍS LIVRAMENTO.

Minister of Justice and Internal Administration: Dr SIMÃO MONTEIRO RODRIGUES.

Minister of Health: Dr JOÃO BAPTISTA MEDINA.

Minister of Infrastructure and Transport: Eng. ARMINDO FERREIRA.

Secretary of State for Finance: Dr JOSÉ ULISSES DE PINA CORREIA E SILVA.

Secretary of State for Foreign Affairs and Co-operation: Dr JOSÉ LUÍS JESUS.

Secretary of State for Sports and Youth: Dr VICTOR OSÓRIO.

Secretary of State for Culture: ANTÓNIO JOSÉ DELGADO.

Secretary of State for Public Administration: Dra PAULA ALMEIDA.

Secretary of State for Decentralization: Dr CÉSAR ALMEIDA.

Secretary of State for the Fight Against Poverty: Dra MANUELA SILVA.

Secretary of State for Tourism, Industry and Commerce: Dr ALEXANDRE MONTEIRO.

MINISTRIES

Office of the President: Presidência da República, Praia, Santiago; tel. 61-26-69; telex 6051.

Office of the Prime Minister: Palácio do Governo, Várzea CP 16, Praia, Santiago; tel. 61-04-05; telex 6054; fax 61-30-99.

Ministry of Agriculture, Food and the Environment: Ponta Belém, Praia, Santiago; tel. 61-57-17; telex 6072; fax 61-40-54.

Ministry of Decentralization: Praia, Santiago.

Ministry of Economic Co-ordination: 107 Avda Amílcar Cabral, CP 30, Praia, Santiago; tel. 61-58-46; telex 6058; fax 61-38-97.

Ministry of Education, Science and Culture: Palácio do Governo, Várzea, Praia, Santiago; tel. 61-05-07; telex 6057.

Ministry of the Fight Against Poverty: Praia, Santiago.

Ministry of Foreign Affairs and Communities: Praça Dr Lorena, Praia, Santiago; tel. 61-57-27; telex 6070; fax 61-39-52.

Ministry of Health: Palácio do Governo, Várzea, Praia, Santiago; tel. 61-05-01; telex 6059.

Ministry of Infrastructure and Transport: Ponta Belém, Praia, Santiago; tel. 61-57-09; telex 6060; fax 61-56-99.

Ministry of Justice and Internal Administration: Rua Serpa Pinto, Praia, Santiago; tel. 61-56-91; telex 6025; fax 61-56-78.

Ministry of National Defence: Palácio do Governo, Várzea, Praia, Santiago; tel. 61-35-91; telex 6077; fax 61-30-99.

Ministry of Public Administration, Labour, Employment and Training, Social Communication, Youth and Sports and Social Promotion: Praia, Santiago.

Ministry of the Sea: Ponta Belém, Praia, Santiago; tel. 61-57-17; telex 6072; fax 61-40-54.

Ministry of Tourism, Industry and Commerce: Praia, Santiago.

President and Legislature

PRESIDENT

At a presidential election conducted on 18 February 1996 the incumbent President, ANTÓNIO MANUEL MASCARENHAS GOMES MONTEIRO, was the sole candidate and was duly re-elected.

ASSEMBLÉIA NACIONAL (AN)

Legislative Election, 17 December 1995

Party	Votes	% of votes	Seats
Movimento para a Democracia (MPD)	93,249	61.3	50
Partido Africano da Independência de Cabo Verde (PAICV)	45,263	29.8	21
Partido da Convergência Democrática (PCD)	10,211	6.7	1
Other parties	3,399	2.2	—
Total	152,122	100.0	72

Political Organizations

Movimento para a Democracia (MPD): Achada Santo António, CP 90A, Praia, Santiago; tel. 61-40-82; fax 61-41-22; f. 1990; advocates administrative decentralization; governing party since Jan. 1991; Chair. Dr CARLOS ALBERTO WAHNON DE CARVALHO VEIGA.

Partido Africano da Independência de Cabo Verde (PAICV): CP 22, Praia, Santiago; telex 6022; fax 61-16-09; f. 1956 as the Partido Africano da Independência do Guiné e Cabo Verde (PAIGC); name changed in 1981, following the 1980 coup in Guinea-Bissau; sole authorized political party 1975–90; Leader Gen. PEDRO VERONA RODRIGUES PIRES; Sec.-Gen. ARISTIDES LIMA.

Partido da Convergência Democrática (PCD): Praia, Santiago; f. 1994 by fmr mems of the MPD; Pres. Dr EURICO CORREIA MONTEIRO.

Partido Socialista Democrático (PSD): Praia, Santiago; f. 1992; Sec.-Gen. JOÃO ALÉM.

União Caboverdiana Independente e Democrática (UCID): Praia, Santiago; f. 1974 by emigrants opposed to the PAICV; obtained legal recognition in 1991; Pres. CELSO CELESTINO.

Diplomatic Representation

EMBASSIES IN CAPE VERDE

Brazil: Chã de Areia, CP 93, Praia, Santiago; tel. 61-56-07; telex 6075; fax 61-56-09; Ambassador: ROMEO ZERO.

China, People's Republic: Achada de Santo António, Praia, Santiago; tel. 61-55-86; Ambassador: YANG YUANDE THIANG.

Cuba: Prainha, Praia, Santiago; tel. 61-55-97; telex 6087; fax 61-55-90; Ambassador: PABLO REYES.

France: CP 192, Praia, Santiago; tel. 61-55-89; telex 6064; fax 61-55-90; Ambassador: ANDRÉ BARBE.

Portugal: Achada de Santo António, CP 160, Praia, Santiago; tel. 61-56-02; telex 6055; fax 61-40-58; Ambassador: EUGÉNIO ANACORETA CORREIA.

Russia: Achada de Santo António, CP 31, Praia, Santiago; tel. 62-27-39; telex 6016; fax 62-27-38; Ambassador: VLADIMIR E. PETUKHOV.

Senegal: Prainha, Praia, Santiago; tel. 61-56-21; Ambassador: AMADOU MOUSTAPHA DIOP.

USA: Rua Hoji Ya Yenna 81, CP 201, Praia, Santiago; tel. 61-56-16; telex 6068; fax 61-13-55; Ambassador: LAWRENCE NEAL BENEDICT.

Judicial System

Supremo Tribunal da Justiça: Praça Alexandre de Albuquerque, Platô, Praia, Santiago; tel. 61-58-10; telex 6025; fax 61-17-51; established 1975; the highest court.

President: Dr OSCAR GOMES.

Attorney-General: Dr HENRIQUE MONTEIRO.

Religion

CHRISTIANITY

At 31 December 1995 there were an estimated 389,680 adherents of the Roman Catholic Church, representing 96.3% of the total population. Protestant churches, among which the Church of the Nazarene is prominent, represent about 1% of the population.

The Roman Catholic Church

Cape Verde comprises the single diocese of Santiago de Cabo Verde, directly responsible to the Holy See. The Bishop participates in the Episcopal Conference of Senegal, Mauritania, Cape Verde and Guinea-Bissau, currently based in Senegal.

Bishop of Santiago de Cabo Verde: Rt Rev. PAULINO DO LIVRAMENTO EVORA, Avda Amílcar Cabral, Largo 5 de Outubro, CP 46, Praia, Santiago; tel. 61-11-19; fax 61-45-99.

The Anglican Communion

Cape Verde forms part of the diocese of The Gambia, within the Church of the Province of West Africa. The Bishop is resident in Banjul, The Gambia.

The Press

Agaviva: Mindelo, São Vicente; tel. 31-21-21; f. 1991; monthly; Editor GERMANO ALMEIDA; circ. 4,000.

Boletim Informativo: CP 126, Praia, Santiago; f. 1976; weekly; publ. by the Ministry of Foreign Affairs; circ. 1,500.

Boletim Oficial da República de Cabo Verde: Imprensa Nacional, CP 113, Praia, Santiago; tel. 61-41-50; weekly; official.

Contacto: CP 89C, Praia, Santiago; tel. 61-57-52; fax 61-14-42; f. 1993; quarterly; economic bulletin produced by Centro de Promoção Turística, do Investimento Externo e das Exportações (PROMEX); circ. 1,500.

Novo Jornal Cabo Verde: Largo do Hospital Dr Agostinho Neto, CP 118, Praia, Santiago; tel. 61-39-89; fax 61-38-29; f. 1993; two a week; Editor LÚCIA DIAS; circ. 5,000.

Perspectiva: Achada de Santo António, CP 89C, Praia, Santiago; tel. 62-27-41; fax 62-27-37; f. 1995; annual; economic bulletin produced by Centro de Promoção Turística, do Investimento Externo e das Exportações; Editor Dr AGUINALDO MARÇAL; circ. 5,000.

Raízes: CP 98, Praia, Santiago; tel. 319; f. 1977; quarterly; cultural review; Editor ARNALDO FRANÇA; circ. 1,500.

A Semana: CP 36C, Avda Cidade de Lisboa, Praia, Santiago; tel. 61-39-50; fax 63-22-71; e-mail asemana@mail.cvtelecom.cv; weekly; independent; Editor FILOMENA SILVA; circ. 5,000.

Terra Nova: CP 166, São Vicente; tel. 32-24-42; fax 32-14-75; f. 1975; monthly; Roman Catholic; Editor P. FIDALGO BARROS; circ. 3,000.

NEWS AGENCIES

Cabopress: Achada de Santo António, CP 40/A, Praia, Santiago; tel. 62-30-21; telex 6044; fax 62-30-23; f. 1988.

Foreign Bureaux

Agence France-Presse (AFP): CP 26/118 Praia, Santiago; tel. 61-38-89; telex 52; Rep. FÁTIMA AZEVEDO.

Agência Portuguesa de Notícias (LUSA): Prainha, Praia, Santiago; tel. 61-35-19.

Inter Press Service (IPS) (Italy): CP 14, Mindelo, São Vicente; tel. 31-45-50; Rep. JUAN A. COLOMA.

Publisher

Government Publishing House

Imprensa Nacional: CP 113, Praia, Santiago; tel. 61-42-09; Admin. JOÃO DE PINA.

Broadcasting and Communications

Rádio Televisão de Cabo Verde (RTC): Praça Albuquerque, CP 26, Praia, Santiago; tel. 61-57-55; fax 61-57-54; govt-controlled; five radio transmitters and five solar relay radio transmitters; FM transmission only; radio broadcasts in Portuguese and Creole for 18 hours daily; one television transmitter and seven relay television transmitters; television broadcasts in Portuguese and Creole for eight hours daily with co-operation of RTPI (Portugal); Dir MANUELA FONSECA SOARES.

Rádio Educativa de Cabo Verde: Achada de Santo António, Praia, Santiago; tel. 61-11-61.

Voz de São Vicente: CP 29, Mindelo, São Vicente; fax 31-10-06; f. 1974; govt-controlled; Dir JOSÉ FONSECA SOARES.

Finance

(cap. = capital; res = reserves; m. = million; dep. = deposits; brs = branches; amounts in Cape Verde escudos)

BANKING

Central Bank

Banco de Cabo Verde (BCV): 117 Avda Amílcar Cabral, CP 101, Praia, Santiago; tel. 61-31-53; telex 99350; fax 61-44-47; f. 1976; bank of issue; cap. and res 1,796.2m., dep. 3,790.4m. (1984); Gov. OSWALDO MIGUEL SEQUEIRA.

Other Banks

Banco Comercial do Atlântico (BCA): 117 Avda Amílcar Cabral, Praia, Santiago; tel. 61-55-29; telex 99350; f. 1993; commercial and development bank; Gov. AMÉLIA FIGUEIREDO; 17 brs.

Banco Totta e Açores (BTA) (Portugal): 1 Rua Justinho Lopes, CP 593, Praia, Santiago; tel. 61-26-65; fax 63-18-46; Cape Verde branch f. 1995; Gen. Man. ANTÃO LOPES DA LUZ.

Caixa de Crédito Rural: Praia, Santiago; f. 1995; rural credit bank.

Caixa Económica de Cabo Verde (CECV): Avda Cidade de Lisboa, CP 199, Praia, Santiago; tel. 61-55-61; telex 6097; fax 61-55-60; f. 1928; commercial and development bank; cap. 348m. (Aug. 1993).

The **Fundo de Solidariedade Nacional** is the main savings institution; the **Fundo de Desenvolvimento Nacional** channels public investment resources; and the **Instituto Caboverdiano** administers international aid.

STOCK EXCHANGE

Plans were announced in 1996 for the establishment of a stock exchange at Praia.

INSURANCE

Companhia Caboverdiana de Seguros (IMPAR): Avda Amílcar Cabral, CP 469, Praia, Santiago; tel. 61-14-05; fax 61-37-65; f. 1991; Pres. Dr CORSINO FORTES.

Garantia Companhia de Seguros: CP 138, Praia, Santiago; tel. 61-35-32; fax 61-25-55; f. 1991.

Trade and Industry

GOVERNMENT AGENCY

Centro de Promoção Turística, do Investimento Externo e das Exportações (PROMEX): CP 89c, Achada de Santo António, Praia, Santiago; tel. 62-27-41; fax 62-27-37; f. 1990; promotes tourism, foreign investment and exports; Pres. Dr JOSÉ LUIS SÁ NOGUEIRA.

CHAMBERS OF COMMERCE

Associação Comercial Industrial e Agrícola de Barlavento (ACIAB): CP 62, Mindelo, São Vicente; tel. 31-32-81; fax 32-36-58; f. 1918.

Associação Comercial de Sotavento (ACAS): Rua Serpa Pinto 23, 1°, CP 78, Praia, Santiago; tel. 61-29-91; telex 6005; fax 61-29-64.

STATE INDUSTRIAL ENTERPRISES

Correios de Cabo Verde, SARL: Direcção-Geral, Praia, Santiago; tel. 61-10-49; telex 6087; fax 63-16-48.

Empresa de Comercialização de Produtos do Mar—INTERBASE, EP: CP 59, Mindelo, São Vicente; tel. 31-46-68; fax 31-39-40; supervises marketing of seafood; shipping agency and ship chandler.

Empresa Nacional de Administração dos Portos, EP (ENAPOR): Avda Marginal, CP 82, Mindelo, São Vicente; tel. 31-44-14; telex 3049; fax 31-46-61.

Empresa Nacional de Aeroportos e Segurança Aérea, EP (ASA): Aeroporto Amílcar Cabral, CP 58, Ilha do Sal; tel. 41-13-94; telex 4036; fax 41-15-70; airports and aircraft security.

Empresa Nacional de Avicultura, EP (ENAVI): CP 135, Praia, Santiago; tel. 61-56-51; telex 6072; fax 61-12-92; f. 1979; poultry farming.

Empresa Nacional de Conservação e Reparação de Equipamentos (SONACOR): Praia, Santiago; tel. 61-25-57; telex 6080.

Empresa Nacional de Produtos Farmacêuticos (EMPROFAC): CP 59, Praia, Santiago; tel. 61-56-36; telex 6024; fax 61-58-72; f. 1979; state monopoly of pharmaceuticals and medical imports.

Empresa Pública de Abastecimento (EMPA): CP 107, Praia, Santiago; tel. 63-39-69; telex 6054; fax 63-39-22; f. 1975; state provisioning enterprise, supervising imports, exports and domestic distribution; Dir-Gen. NASOLINO SILVA DOS SANTOS.

UTILITIES

Electricity and Water

Empresa Pública de Electricidade e Agua (ELECTRA): 10 Avda Unidade Africana, CP 137, Mindelo, São Vicente; tel. 32-44-48; telex 3045; fax 32-44-46; e-mail electra@milton.cvtelecom.cv; f. 1982.

CO-OPERATIVES

Instituto Nacional das Cooperativas: Fazenda, CP 218, Praia, Santiago; tel. 61-41-12; fax 61-39-59; central co-operative organization.

TRADE UNIONS

Confederação Cabo-Verdiana dos Sindicatos Livres (CCSL): Rua Dr Júlio Abreau, Praia, Santiago; tel. 61-63-41.

Sindicato da Indústria, Agricultura e Pesca (SIAP): Plateau, Praia, Santiago; tel. 61-63-19.

Sindicato dos Transportes, Comunicações e Turismo (STCT): Praia, Santiago; tel. 61-63-38.

União Nacional dos Trabalhadores de Cabo Verde—Central Sindical (UNTC—CS): Estrada do Aeroporto, Praia, Santiago; tel. 61-43-05; fax 61-36-29; f. 1978; Chair. JULIO ASCENSÃO SILVA.

Transport

ROADS

In 1995 there were an estimated 1,100 km of roads, of which 858 km were paved.

SHIPPING

Cargo-passenger ships call regularly at Porto Grande, Mindelo, on São Vicente, and Praia, on Santiago. In 1993 plans were announced for the upgrading of Porto Grande, at a cost of US $13.2m., and for the re-establishment of the port of Vale dos Cavaleiros, on Fogo island, at a cost of $10.6m. There are small ports on the other islands.

Comissão de Gestão dos Transportes Marítimos de Cabo Verde: CP 153, São Vicente; tel. 31-49-79; fax 31-20-55; telex 3031.

Companhia Cabo-Verdiana de Transportes Marítimos: CP 150, Praia, Santiago; tel. 61-22-84; fax 61-60-95.

Companhia Nacional de Navegação Arca Verde: Rua 5 de Julho, CP 41, Praia, Santiago; tel. 61-10-60; telex 6067; fax 61-54-96; f. 1975.

Companhia de Navegação Estrela Negra: Avda 5 de Julho 17, CP 91, São Vicente; tel. 31-54-23; telex 3030; fax 31-53-82.

Companhia Nacional de Navegação Portuguesa: Agent in Santiago: João Benoliel de Carvalho, Lda, CP 56, Praia, Santiago.

Companhia Portuguesa de Transportes Marítimos: Agent in Santiago: João Benoliel de Carvalho, Lda, CP 56, Praia, Santiago.

CS Line: Praia, Santiago.

Linhas Marítimas (LINMAC): Dr João Battista Ferreira Medina, Praia, Santiago; tel. 61-40-99.

Mare Verde: Mindelo, São Vicente.

Seage Agência de Navegação de Cabo Verde: Avda Cidade de Lisboa, CP 232, Praia, Santiago; tel. 61-57-58; telex 6033; fax 61-25-24; Chair. CÉSAR MANUEL SEMEDO LOPES.

CIVIL AVIATION

The Amílcar Cabral international airport is at Espargos, on Sal Island, with capacity for aircraft of up to 50 tons and 1m. passengers per year. Expansion of the airport's facilities began in 1987, with EC and Italian aid. There is also a small airport on each of the other inhabited islands. A second international airport, under construction on Santiago, was due for completion in late 1999. The new airport was to be capable of accommodating Airbus 310 aircraft.

CABOVIMO: 32 Avda Unidade Guiné-Cabo Verde, Praia, Santiago; tel. 61-33-14; fax 61-55-59; f. 1992; internal flights; Gen. Man. JORGE DANIEL SPENCER LIMA.

Transportes Aéreos de Cabo Verde (TACV): Avda Amílcar Cabral, CP 1, Praia, Santiago; tel. 61-58-13; telex 6065; fax 61-35-85; f. 1958; internal services connecting the nine inhabited islands; also operates regional services to Senegal, Guinea, the Gambia and Guinea-Bissau, and long-distance services to Europe and the USA; Dir ALFREDO CARVALHO.

Tourism

The islands of Santiago, Santo Antão, Fogo and Brava offer attractive mountain scenery, and Santiago combines this with white sandy beaches. There are also extensive beaches on the islands of Sal, Boa Vista and Maio. There are four hotels on Sal, one on Boa Vista, one on São Vicente, and three in Praia. Some 37,000 tourists visited Cape Verde during 1996, mainly from Portugal (35%), France (12%), Germany (11%), the Netherlands (8%), Italy, Belgium and Spain. In that year tourism receipts totalled US $11m. In 1993 a 15-year National Tourism Development Plan was adopted providing for a projected increase in tourist arrivals to some 400,000 annually by 2008.

Centro de Promocão Turística, do Investimento Externo e das Exportações (PROMEX): CP 89c, Achada de Santo António, Praia, Santiago; tel. 62-27-41; fax 62-27-37; f. 1990; promotes tourism, foreign investment and exports; Dir of Tourism AIDA DUARTE SILVA.

THE CENTRAL AFRICAN REPUBLIC

Introductory Survey

Location, Climate, Language, Religion, Flag, Capital

The Central African Republic is a land-locked country in the heart of equatorial Africa. It is bordered by Chad to the north, by Sudan to the east, by the Democratic Republic of the Congo and the Republic of the Congo to the south and by Cameroon to the west. The climate is tropical, with an average annual temperature of 26°C (79°F) and heavy rainfall in the south-western forest areas. The national language is Sango, but French is the official language. Many of the population hold animist beliefs, but about one-third are Christians and an estimated 5% are Muslims. The national flag (proportions 5 by 3) has four horizontal stripes, of blue, white, green and yellow, divided vertically by a central red stripe, with a five-pointed yellow star in the upper hoist. The capital is Bangui.

Recent History

The former territory of Ubangi-Shari (Oubangui-Chari), within French Equatorial Africa, became the Central African Republic (CAR) on achieving self-government in December 1958. Barthélemy Boganda, the first Prime Minister, died in March 1959. He was succeeded by his nephew, David Dacko, who led the country to full independence, and became the first President, on 13 August 1960. In 1962 a one-party state was established, with the ruling Mouvement d'évolution sociale de l'Afrique noire (MESAN) as the sole authorized party. President Dacko was overthrown on 31 December 1965 by a military coup which brought to power his cousin, Col (later Marshal) Jean-Bédel Bokassa, Commander-in-Chief of the armed forces.

In January 1966 Bokassa formed a new Government, rescinded the Constitution and dissolved the National Assembly. Bokassa, who became Life President in March 1972 and Marshal of the Republic in May 1974, forestalled several alleged coup attempts and employed increasingly repressive measures against dissidents. From January 1975 to April 1976 Elisabeth Domitien, the Vice-President of MESAN, was Prime Minister; she was the first woman to hold this position in any African country.

In September 1976 the Council of Ministers was replaced by the Council for the Central African Revolution, and ex-President Dacko was appointed personal adviser to the President. In December the Republic was renamed the Central African Empire (CAE), and a new Constitution was instituted. Bokassa was proclaimed the first Emperor, and Dacko became his Personal Counsellor. The Imperial Constitution provided for the establishment of a national assembly, but no elections were held.

The elaborate preparations for Bokassa's coronation in December 1977 were estimated to have consumed about one-quarter of the country's income. In May 1978 Bokassa reorganized the army leadership and strengthened its powers. In July he appointed a new Council of Ministers, headed by a former Deputy Prime Minister, Henri Maidou. In January 1979 violent protests, led by students, were suppressed, reportedly with the help of Zairean troops. Following a protest by schoolchildren against compulsory school uniforms (made by a company that was owned by the Bokassa family), many children were arrested in April. About 100 of them were killed in prison, and Bokassa himself allegedly participated in the massacre. On 20 September 1979, while Bokassa was in Libya, David Dacko deposed him in a bloodless coup, which received considerable support from France. The country was again designated a republic, with Dacko as its President and Henri Maidou as Vice-President.

President Dacko's principal concern was to establish order and economic stability in the CAR, but his Government encountered opposition, particularly from students who objected to the continuation in office of CAE ministers. In August 1980 Dacko accepted demands for the dismissal of both Maidou and the Prime Minister, Bernard Christian Ayandho. Bokassa, at that time in exile in Côte d'Ivoire (and subsequently in Paris), was sentenced to death *in absentia* in December 1980.

In February 1981 a new Constitution, providing for a multi-party system, was approved by referendum and promulgated by President Dacko. He won a presidential election in March, amid allegations of electoral malpractice, and was sworn in for a six-year term in April. Political tension intensified in subsequent months, and on 1 September the Chief of Staff of the armed forces, Gen. André Kolingba, deposed President Dacko in a bloodless coup. Kolingba was declared President, and a ruling Comité militaire pour le redressement national (CMRN) and an all-military Government were formed. All political activity was suspended.

In March 1982 the exiled leader of the banned Mouvement pour la libération du peuple centrafricain (MLPC), Ange-Félix Patassé, returned to Bangui and was implicated in an unsuccessful coup attempt. Patassé, who had been the Prime Minister under Bokassa in 1976–78 and who had contested the March 1981 presidential election, sought asylum in the French embassy in Bangui, from where he was transported to exile in Togo. A visit by President Mitterrand of France to the CAR in October 1982 normalized bilateral relations, which had been strained by French support for Patassé.

Opposition to Kolingba's regime continued, despite the suspension of all political activity in September 1981. In August 1983 elements of the three main opposition parties formed a united front. In September 1984 Kolingba announced an amnesty for the leaders of banned political parties, who had been under house arrest since January, and reduced the sentences of two former ministers, Gaston Ouédane and Jérôme Allan, who had been imprisoned in August for involvement in the 1982 coup attempt. Shortly afterwards, in December 1984 President Mitterrand paid a further visit to the country. A total of 89 political prisoners were released in December 1985. In September 1986 Ouédane and Allan were released from prison, along with a further, unspecified number of political prisoners.

In September 1985 the CMRN was dissolved and, for the first time since Kolingba's assumption of power, civilians were appointed to the Council of Ministers. In early 1986 a specially-convened commission drafted a new Constitution, which provided for the creation of a sole legal political party, the Rassemblement démocratique centrafricain (RDC), and conferred extensive executive powers on the President, while defining a predominantly advisory role for the legislature. At a referendum in November some 91.17% of voters approved the draft Constitution and granted Kolingba a mandate to serve a further six-year term as President. The Council of Ministers was reorganized in December to include a majority of civilians. The RDC was officially established in February 1987, with Kolingba as founding President, and elections to the new National Assembly took place in July, at which 142 candidates, all nominated by the RDC, contested the 52 seats.

In October 1986 Bokassa returned unexpectedly to the CAR and was immediately arrested. His new trial, on a total of 14 charges, opened in November and continued until June 1987, when the former Emperor was sentenced to death, after having been convicted on charges of murder, conspiracy to murder, the illegal detention of prisoners and embezzlement. An appeal for a retrial was rejected by the Supreme Court in November. In February 1988, however, President Kolingba commuted the sentence to one of life imprisonment with hard labour.

The appointment during 1988 of former associates of Bokassa, Dacko and Patassé to prominent public offices appeared to represent an attempt by Kolingba to consolidate national unity. In August 1989, however, 12 opponents of the Kolingba regime, including members of the Front patriotique oubanguien-Parti du travail (FPO-PT) and the leader of the Rassemblement populaire pour la reconstruction de la Centrafrique, Brig.-Gen. (later Gen.) François Bozize, were arrested in Benin, where they had been living in exile, and were swiftly extradited to the CAR. Bozize was subsequently found guilty of complicity in the 1982 coup attempt.

During 1990 demands for higher salaries, improved working conditions and the payment of salary arrears owed to workers in the public sector resulted in unrest among certain sectors of the labour force, which escalated into a general strike in November. The Government's continued failure to pay public-sector salary arrears resulted in further labour unrest during the early and mid-1990s.

Throughout 1990 opposition movements exerted pressure on the Government to introduce a plural political system, and in October violent demonstrations by anti-Government protesters were suppressed by the security forces. In December the Executive Council of the RDC recommended a review of the Constitution and the re-establishment of the premiership. Accordingly, in March 1991 Edouard Franck, a former Minister of State at the Presidency, was appointed Prime Minister, and in July the National Assembly approved legislation to revise the Constitution to allow for the establishment of a multi-party political system. President Kolingba announced his resignation from the presidency of the RDC in the following month, in order to remain 'above parties'. In October the Kolingba administration agreed to convene a national debate on the country's political future, comprising representatives of opposition movements as well as of the Government. In December Kolingba pardoned Brig.-Gen. Bozize for his involvement in the attempted coup of March 1982.

The Grand National Debate took place in August 1992. It was, however, boycotted by the influential Concertation des forces démocratiques (CFD), an alliance of opposition groupings, which announced that it would only participate in a multi-party national conference with sovereign powers. At the end of August the National Assembly approved legislation in accordance with decisions taken by the Grand National Debate: constitutional amendments provided for the strict separation of executive, legislative and judicial powers and President Kolingba was granted temporary powers to rule by decree until the election of a new multi-party legislature. Concurrent legislative and presidential elections commenced in October, but were suspended by decree of the President and subsequently annulled by order of the Supreme Court, owing to alleged sabotage of the electoral process. In December Franck resigned as Prime Minister and was replaced by Gen. Timothée Malendoma, the leader of the Forum civique.

In February 1993 Malendoma, who had accused Kolingba of curtailing his powers, was dismissed from the premiership and replaced by Enoch Derant Lakoué, the leader of the Parti social-démocrate. In June, in response to mounting pressure from both the opposition and the French Government, Kolingba announced that elections would commence in August. Accordingly, two rounds of concurrent legislative and presidential elections were held in late August and mid-September. At the legislative elections the MLPC won 34 of the 85 seats in the National Assembly, while the RDC, in second place, secured 13 seats. Patassé, the MLPC leader and former Prime Minister, was elected President, winning 52.47% of the votes cast at the second round of presidential elections. The seven other presidential candidates included Kolingba, Prof. Abel Goumba (the leader of the CFD) and former President Dacko. In late August Kolingba, who had been defeated at the first round of presidential elections, attempted to delay the publication of the election results by issuing two decrees which modified the electoral code and altered the composition of the Supreme Court; however, the decrees were revoked, after the French Government threatened to suspend all co-operation with the CAR in protest at Kolingba's action.

In September 1993 Bokassa was released from prison under a general amnesty for convicts; however, the former Emperor was banned for life from participating in elections and demoted from the military rank of marshal. He died in November 1996.

In October 1993 Patassé was inaugurated as President. Soon afterwards he appointed Jean-Luc Mandaba, Vice-President of the MLPC, as Prime Minister; Mandaba formed a coalition Government, which comprised members of the MLPC, the RDC, the Parti libéral-démocrate (PLD), the Alliance pour la démocratie et le progrès (ADP) and a group headed by David Dacko (later entitled the Mouvement pour la démocratie et le développement—MDD). The coalition thus had a working majority of 53 seats in the National Assembly. In December the Government announced the establishment of a commission of inquiry into the conduct of Kolingba during his 12-year presidency, which was to include an audit of government finances during this period. In March 1994, following the arrest of two senior members of the RDC on charges of provoking popular discontent, Kolingba was stripped of his army rank.

In December 1994 a draft Constitution was approved by 82% of voters in a national referendum. The new Constitution, which was duly adopted in January 1995, included provisions empowering the President to nominate senior military, civil service and judicial officials, and requiring the Prime Minister to implement policies decided by the President. In addition, provision was made for the creation of directly-elected regional assemblies and for the establishment of an advisory State Council, which was to deliberate on administrative issues. Several groups in the governing coalition (notably the MDD) expressed concern at the powers afforded to the President.

In April 1995 Mandaba resigned as Prime Minister, pre-empting a threatened vote of 'no confidence' in his administration (initiated by his own party, the MLPC), following accusations against the Government of corruption and incompetence. Immediately afterwards Patassé appointed Gabriel Koyambounou, formerly a civil servant, as the new Prime Minister. Koyambounou subsequently nominated a new Council of Ministers, with an enlarged membership. In August supporters of the RDC staged a peaceful demonstration in protest at perceived abuses of power by the Government, such as the imposition of a two-year term of imprisonment on the editor of the RDC newspaper, who had been found guilty of treason following the publication of an article critical of Patassé. In December several opposition movements (including the ADP and MDD, but excluding the RDC) united to form the Conseil démocratique des partis politiques de l'opposition (CODEPO), which aimed to campaign against alleged corruption and political and economic mismanagement by the Patassé regime.

In the mid-1990s the Government repeatedly failed to pay the salaries of public-sector employees and members of the security forces, prompting frequent strikes and mounting political unrest. In mid-April 1996 CODEPO staged an anti-Government rally in Bangui. Shortly afterwards part of the national army mutinied in the capital and demanded the immediate settlement of all salary arrears. Patassé promised that part of the overdue salaries would be paid and that the mutineers would not be subject to prosecution. The presence of French troops (the Elements français d'assistance opérationelle—EFAO) in Bangui, with a mandate to secure the safety of foreign nationals and (in accordance with a bilateral military accord) to protect the presidential palace and other key installations, contributed to the swift collapse of the rebellion. About nine people, including civilians, were reported to have died in the uprising. In late April Patassé appointed a new Chief of Staff of the Armed Forces, Col Maurice Regonessa, and banned all public demonstrations. In mid-May, however, discontent again resurfaced and CODEPO organized another rally in Bangui, at which it demanded the resignation of the Government. Patassé defended the record of his administration by blaming the country's economic crisis on his predecessors. Soon afterwards, in an attempt to tighten his hold on power, the President ordered that control of the national armoury should be transferred from the regular army to the traditionally loyal presidential guard. However, adverse reaction to this move within the ranks of the armed forces rapidly escalated into a second, more determined insurrection. Once again EFAO troops were deployed to protect the Patassé administration; some 500 reinforcements were brought in from Chad and Gabon to consolidate the resident French military presence (numbering 1,400). Five hostages were taken by the mutineers, including Col Regonessa, together with a government minister and the President of the National Assembly. After five days of fierce fighting between dissident and loyalist troops, the French forces intervened to suppress the rebellion. France's military action (which allegedly resulted in civilian deaths) prompted intense scrutiny of the role of the former colonial power, and precipitated large pro- and anti-French demonstrations in Bangui. In all, 11 soldiers and 32 civilians were reported to have been killed in the second army mutiny. Following extended negotiations between the mutineers and government representatives, the two sides eventually signed an accord, providing for an amnesty for the rebels (who were to return to barracks under EFAO guard), the immediate release of hostages (upon Col Regonessa's release he was promoted to the rank of general), and the installation of a new Government of National Unity. The political opposition now became active in the debate, rejecting the proposed Government of National Unity and demanding instead a transitional government leading to fresh legislative and presidential elections. The opposition also requested a revision of the Constitution to remove some executive powers from the President and enhance the role of the Prime Minister.

In early June 1996 the Government and the opposition signed a protocol providing for the establishment of a Government of National Unity under the leadership of a civilian Prime Minister with no official party ties. Although the Constitution was not to be amended to alter the balance of power between the President and the Prime Minister, Patassé agreed to permit 'some room for manoeuvre'. Meanwhile, France agreed to assist the CAR authorities with the payment of salary arrears still owed to public-sector employees and members of the security forces. Following the publication of the protocol, Koyambounou's Government resigned. Jean-Paul Ngoupandé, hitherto Ambassador to France and with no official political affiliation (although he had been Secretary-General of the RDC in the late 1980s), was appointed as the new Prime Minister. Ngoupandé immediately nominated a new Council of Ministers. National co-operation, however, remained elusive, as CODEPO, dissatisfied with the level of its ministerial representation, immediately withdrew from the Government of National Unity. Moreover, a growing animosity was reported between Patassé and Ngoupandé, with the former refusing to transfer any effective power to the latter.

At a conference on national defence held in late August and early September 1996, several resolutions were adopted regarding restructuring and improving conditions within the army. In late October, however, it was reported that troops who had been involved in the insurrections of April and May were refusing to be transferred from their barracks in the capital to a more remote location; Patassé insisted that their departure would take place none the less. However, in mid-November a further mutiny erupted among these troops, shortly after the withdrawal from CODEPO of four opposition parties, including the ADP and the MDD. A substantial part of Bangui was occupied by the rebels, and a number of hostages were taken. The latest uprising appeared to have a strong tribal and political motivation: the mutineers, who were demanding the resignation of Patassé, belonged to the Yakoma ethnic group of Kolingba. EFAO troops were deployed once again, ostensibly to maintain order and protect foreign residents; however, by guarding key installations and government buildings they also effectively prevented the overthrow of the Patassé administration. More than 100 people were killed in the unrest during late November and early December, including a former (Yakoma) cabinet Minister under Kolingba, who was abducted and murdered, allegedly by troops loyal to the Government.

In December 1996 the Presidents of Burkina Faso, Chad, Gabon and Mali negotiated a 15-day truce, which was supervised by the former transitional President of Mali, Brig.-Gen. Amadou Toumani Touré; a one-month extension to the cease-fire was subsequently agreed. In January 1997, following the killing of two French soldiers in Bangui (reportedly by mutineers), EFAO troops retaliated by killing at least 10 members of the rebel forces; French military involvement in the CAR was condemned by prominent opposition parties, including the ADP, the MDD and the RDC, which also sought (without success) to initiate a parliamentary vote to bring impeachment proceedings against Patassé. Subsequent to the renewal of violence, Touré again came to Bangui as mediator and assisted in the establishment of a cross-party Committee of Consultation and Dialogue. The 'Bangui accords', drawn up by this committee, were signed towards the end of January; these, as well as offering an amnesty to the mutineers, agreed upon the formation of a new Government of National Unity and on the replacement of the EFAO troops patrolling Bangui by peace-keeping forces from African nations. The opposition at first threatened to boycott the new Government, voicing its discontent with the appointment at the end of January of Michel Gbezera-Bria (a close associate of Patassé and hitherto the Minister of Foreign Affairs) as Prime Minister. However, with the creation of new ministerial posts for opposition politicians, a 'Government of Action' (which did not include Ngoupandé) was formed on 18 February; soon afterwards, Gen. Bozize replaced Gen. Regonessa as Chief of Staff of the Armed Forces.

Meanwhile, in early February 1997 responsibility for peace-keeping operations had been transferred from the EFAO to forces of the newly-formed Mission interafricaine de surveillance des accords de Bangui (MISAB), comprising some 700 soldiers from Burkina Faso, Chad, Gabon, Mali, Senegal and Togo (with logistical support from 50 French military personnel). MISAB soldiers were also to assist in disarming the former mutineers; however, when in late March they attempted to do so, fighting broke out in which some 20 MISAB soldiers were killed. A spokesman for the rebels, Capt. Anicet Saulet, claimed that the lack of representation of the former mutineers in the new Government constituted a breach of the 'Bangui accords'; following a meeting between Saulet and Patassé in early April, the Council of Ministers was expanded to include two military officers as representatives of the rebels. Later that month several hundred of the former mutineers attended a ceremony marking their reintegration into the regular armed forces.

In mid-April 1997 a dusk-to-dawn curfew was imposed on Bangui, owing to a serious escalation in violent crime, much of which was allegedly perpetrated by groups of former mutineers. In early May, following the deaths in police custody of three former rebels suspected of criminal activities, nine Ministers representing the G11 (a grouping of 11 opposition parties, including the ADP, the FPP, the MDD and the RDC), as well as the two representatives of the former mutineers, suspended participation in the Government.

In late June 1997 violent clashes erupted once again between MISAB forces and former mutineers. In response to several attacks on the French embassy by the rebels, several hundred EFAO troops were redeployed on the streets of Bangui, and MISAB forces launched a major offensive in the capital, capturing most of the rebel-controlled districts. This assault led to the arrest of more than 80 former mutineers, but also to some 100 deaths, both of soldiers and of civilians, while numerous homes and business premises were destroyed. Soon afterwards some 500 demonstrators gathered outside the French embassy to protest against alleged abuses of human rights by MISAB troops; MISAB officials claimed that criminals were impersonating their soldiers in order to perpetrate atrocities. On the same day Touré arrived once again in Bangui in his capacity as Chairman of MISAB, and negotiated a four-day truce, which took effect at the end of June, followed by a 10-day cease-fire agreement, signed at the beginning of July; all of the former mutineers were to be reintegrated into the regular armed forces, and their safety and that of the people living in the districts under their control was guaranteed; the rebels, for their part, were to relinquish their weaponry.

Towards the end of July 1997 many of the people who had been held in custody in relation to the previous month's violence were released by the authorities, and the curfew in Bangui was eased, while it was reported that almost all of the former mutineers had rejoined the regular armed forces. In early September the nine representatives of opposition parties in the Council of Ministers resumed their vacant posts. Shortly afterwards students who held a demonstration in Bangui in protest at the alleged non-payment of their grants were dispersed by the security forces. In October an amnesty for the return of weapons was extended, as several thousand firearms had apparently not yet been relinquished.

Meanwhile, at the end of July 1997 the French authorities announced the impending gradual withdrawal of their troops from the CAR; the first contingent of French soldiers left the country in October. The planned departure of the French represented a substantial loss of employment and foreign currency for the CAR, as well as a loss of military support for Patassé and his administration.

France, the former colonial power, remains the country's principal source of budgetary and bilateral development aid. French military forces stationed in the CAR, as well as intervening to suppress insurrections within the country, were also used in support operations for the Government of Chad during that country's conflict with Libya (see chapter on Chad).

In early 1994 the CAR Government denied suggestions that it had been assisting the Sudanese Government in its campaign against the banned Sudan People's Liberation Army. In February the Patassé administration sponsored peace negotiations in Bangui between the Government of Chad and southern opposition factions. At the end of 1994 the CAR and Chad agreed to establish a bilateral security structure to ensure mutual border security.

In May 1997 it was reported that considerable numbers of Rwandan Hutus (many of whom had previously served in that country's army when it was implicated in acts of genocide) were seeking asylum in the CAR. Later that month the CAR recognized the administration of President Laurent Kabila in the Democratic Republic of the Congo (formerly Zaire). However, during mid-1997 armed soldiers of what had been the Zairean army were reported to be fleeing troops loyal to Kabila and crossing the Oubangui river into the CAR.

In 1994 the CAR became the fifth member of the Lake Chad Basin Commission (see p. 261).

Government

Executive power is vested in the President of the Republic, and legislative power in the Congress. The Congress consists of an 85-seat National Assembly, sessions of which are held at the summons of the President, an advisory Economic and Regional

Council, one-half of the members of which are elected by the Assembly and one-half appointed by the President, and an advisory State Council, which deliberates on matters that are referred to it by the President of the National Assembly. Both the President and the Assembly are elected by direct universal suffrage, the former for a six-year term and the latter for a five-year term. The Prime Minister, who presides over a Council of Ministers, is appointed by the President.

For administrative purposes, the country is divided into 16 prefectures, 67 sub-prefectures and two postes de contrôle administratif. At community level there are 65 communes urbaines, 102 communes rurales and seven communes d'élevage. The Constitution that was adopted in January 1995 provided for the election of new regional assemblies by universal suffrage.

Defence

In August 1997 the armed forces numbered about 2,650 men (army 2,500; air force 150), with a further 2,300 men in paramilitary forces. Military service is selective and lasts for two years. In August 1997 about 1,750 French troops and military advisers were based in the CAR, some 1,400 in Bangui and about 350 at Bouar; however, the base at Bouar was scheduled to be closed by the end of 1997, and all French military presence in the CAR was gradually to cease. In the same month the Mission interafricaine de surveillance des accords de Bangui (MISAB) maintained a force of about 750 in Bangui, comprising troops from Burkina Faso, Chad, Gabon, Mali, Senegal and Togo, with French logistical support. Government expenditure on defence in 1996 was estimated at 15,000m. francs CFA.

Economic Affairs

In 1995, according to estimates by the World Bank, the CAR's gross national product (GNP), measured at average 1993–95 prices, was US $1,123m., equivalent to $340 per head. During 1985–95, it was estimated, GNP per head declined, in real terms, at an average rate of 2.0% per year. Over the same period, the population increased by an annual average of 2.3%. The country's gross domestic product (GDP) increased, in real terms, by an annual average of 1.0% in 1990–95. Real GDP declined by 2.5% in 1992 and by an estimated 2.3% in 1993, but estimated rises of 7.7% and 2.4% were achieved in 1994 and 1995, respectively.

Agriculture (including forestry and fishing) contributed 53.4% of GDP in 1995. About 77.9% of the economically active population were employed in the sector in 1996. The principal cash crops are coffee (which accounted for 28.7% of export earnings in 1989 and an estimated 19.0% in 1995) and cotton. Livestock and tobacco are also exported. The major subsistence crops are cassava (manioc) and yams. The Government is encouraging the cultivation of horticultural produce for export. The exploitation of the country's large forest resources represents a significant source of export revenue (wood exports accounting for an estimated 15.8% of the total in 1995); however, the full potential of this sector has yet to be realized, owing to the inadequacy of the transport infrastructure. Rare butterflies are also exported. During 1985–95 agricultural GDP increased by an annual average of 1.4%. Agricultural production increased by 6.4% in 1994, but declined by 2.5% in 1995.

Industry (including mining, manufacturing, construction and power) engaged 3.3% of the employed labour force in 1988 and provided 20.5% of GDP in 1995. During 1980–93 industrial GDP increased by an annual average of 2.4%. Industrial production (excluding construction) increased at an average rate of 1.6% per year during 1985–94, but declined by 9.7% in 1995.

Mining and quarrying engaged 1.1% of the employed labour force in 1988 and contributed 6.2% of GDP in 1995. The principal activity is the extraction of predominantly gem diamonds (exports of diamonds provided an estimated 43.6% of total export revenue in 1995). The introduction of gem-cutting facilities and the eradication of widespread 'black market' smuggling operations would substantially increase revenue from diamond-mining. Deposits of gold are also exploited. The development of uranium resources may proceed. Reserves of iron ore, copper and manganese have also been located. The output of the mining sector increased at an average rate of 4.6% per year during 1985–94, but declined by 8.6% in 1995.

The manufacturing sector engaged 1.6% of the employed labour force in 1988. Manufacturing, which contributed 8.8% of GDP in 1995, is based upon the processing of primary products. In 1990 the major activities, measured by gross value of output, were the processing of foods, beverages and tobacco, furniture, fixtures and paper and textiles. In real terms, the GDP of the manufacturing sector increased by an annual average of 1.9% during 1980–89, but declined in each of the four years 1990–93. According to IMF estimates, it increased by 5.7% in 1994, but fell by 5.0% in 1995.

About 80% of electrical energy generated within the CAR is derived from the country's two hydroelectric power installations. Imports of fuel products comprised 7% of the cost of merchandise imports in 1992.

Services engaged 15.5% of the employed labour force in 1988 and provided 26.1% of GDP in 1995. In real terms, the GDP of the services sector declined during 1990–93, but increased by an estimated 14.4% in 1994 and by 2.2% in 1995.

In 1994 the CAR recorded a visible trade surplus of US $15.3m., but there was a deficit of $24.7m. on the current account of the balance of payments. In 1989 the principal source of imports (42.5%) was France, while the principal market for exports (50.9%) was the Belgo-Luxembourg Economic Union. Other major trading partners in that year were Cameroon, the Federal Republic of Germany, Japan and Switzerland. The principal exports in 1995 were diamonds, coffee, wood products and cotton. The principal imports in 1989 were machinery, basic manufactures, road vehicles and parts, food and chemical products.

In 1995 there was an estimated budget deficit of 37,900m. francs CFA. At the end of 1995 the CAR's external debt was US $943.9m., of which $852.0m. was long-term public debt. In that year the cost of debt-servicing was equivalent to 6.8% of revenue from exports of goods and services. The annual rate of inflation averaged 2.5% in 1986–95. Average consumer prices declined by 1.4% in 1992 and by 2.9% in 1993, but rose by 24.5% in 1994, following the devaluation of the currency (see below); an increase of 19.2% was recorded in 1995. At the December 1988 census 7.5% of the labour force were unemployed.

The CAR is a member of the Central African organs of the Franc Zone (see p. 181) and of the Communauté economique des etats de l'Afrique centrale (CEEAC, see p. 260).

The CAR's land-locked position, the inadequacy of the transport infrastructure and the country's vulnerability to adverse climatic conditions and to fluctuations in international prices for its main agricultural exports have impeded sustained economic growth. From the mid-1980s adjustment efforts, implemented with financial assistance from the IMF and the World Bank, sought to promote growth and diversification in the agricultural sector. During the early 1990s a slump in international prices for coffee and cotton and a sharp increase in illicit trade resulted in a decline in foreign currency earnings and tax and customs revenue; economic growth was severely disrupted and widespread unrest arose as the Government had inadequate resources for expenditure on social services and the payment of salaries to the public-sector labour force. During the mid-1990s the CAR experienced the economic effects of the January 1994 devaluation of the CFA franc (by 50%) in relation to the French franc; these included initial precipitous increases in consumer prices and a boost to export competitiveness. Economic growth was restored in 1994 and 1995, partly reflecting an improvement in international prices for the CAR's agricultural exports. By late 1995, however, the Government, unable to control a mounting budgetary deficit, failed once again to pay the salaries of public-sector employees, as well as those of the armed forces, thereby precipitating serious political instability during 1996–97 (see Recent History). This, in turn, badly disrupted economic activity. In June 1996 France (the CAR's principal bilateral creditor) agreed to assist with the payment of salary arrears. In November the Government signed a letter of intent with the IMF and World Bank: it was hoped that funding would be made available to support the introduction of a programme for economic rehabilitation and development, under which government finances were to be stabilized, public enterprises and the civil service restructured, and the regulatory framework for investment liberalized in order to stimulate private-sector activity. However, the IMF postponed discussions, pending an end to the political and social unrest of the mid-1990s. The gradual withdrawal of French troops from the CAR, announced in July 1997, was likely to have an adverse effect on the economy, in terms of loss of employment and foreign currency.

Social Welfare

The Government's commitments to the social welfare and health sectors have been neglected during the 1990s, owing to a severe lack of funds. The provision of health care facilities in rural areas is minimal. In 1984 there were 7,023 hospital beds in the

CAR (one per 371 inhabitants), but only 112 physicians were working in the country.

Education

Education is officially compulsory for eight years between six and 14 years of age. Primary education begins at the age of six and lasts for six years. Secondary education begins at the age of 12 and lasts for up to seven years, comprising a first cycle of four years and a second of three years. In 1989 an estimated 58% of children in the relevant age-group (71% of boys; 46% of girls) attended primary schools, while secondary enrolment was equivalent to only 12% (boys 17%; girls 6%). According to estimates by UNESCO, the adult illiteracy rate in 1995 averaged 40% (males 31.5%; females 47.6%). Government expenditure on education in 1990 totalled 9,862m. francs CFA, equivalent to 2.8% of GNP. The provision of state-funded education has been severely disrupted during the 1990s, owing to the inadequacy of the Government's resources.

Public Holidays

1998: 1 January (New Year), 29 March (Anniversary of death of Barthélemy Boganda), 13 April (Easter Monday), 1 May (May Day), 21 May (Ascension Day), 1 June (Whit Monday), 30 June (National Day of Prayer), 13 August (Independence Day), 15 August (Assumption), 1 November (All Saints' Day), 1 December (National Day), 25 December (Christmas).

1999: 1 January (New Year), 29 March (Anniversary of death of Barthélemy Boganda), 5 April (Easter Monday), 1 May (May Day), 13 May (Ascension Day), 24 May (Whit Monday), 30 June (National Day of Prayer), 13 August (Independence Day), 15 August (Assumption), 1 November (All Saints' Day), 1 December (National Day), 25 December (Christmas).

Weights and Measures

The metric system is officially in force.

Statistical Survey

Source (unless otherwise stated): Division des Statistiques et des Etudes Economiques, Ministère de l'Economie, du Plan et de la Coopération Internationale, Bangui.

Area and Population

AREA, POPULATION AND DENSITY

Area (sq km)	622,984*
Population (census results)	
8 December 1975	2,054,610
8 December 1988	
Males	1,210,735
Females	1,252,881
Total	2,463,616
Density (per sq km) at 8 December 1988	4.0

* 240,535 sq miles.

PRINCIPAL TOWNS (population, 1988 census)

Bangui (capital)	451,690	Bambari	38,633
Berbérati	41,891	Bossangoa	31,502
Bouar	39,676	Carnot	31,324

BIRTHS AND DEATHS (UN estimates, annual averages)

	1980–85	1985–90	1990–95
Birth rate (per 1,000)	41.5	41.4	41.5
Death rate (per 1,000)	18.6	17.4	16.7

Source: UN, *World Population Prospects: The 1994 Revision*.

1994: Registered live births 124,707 (birth rate 41.6 per 1,000); Registered deaths 50,063 (death rate 16.7 per 1,000) (Source: UN, *Population and Vital Statistics Report*).

Expectation of life (UN estimates, years at birth, 1990–95): 49.4 (males 46.9; females 51.9) (Source: UN, *World Population Prospects: The 1994 Revision*).

ECONOMICALLY ACTIVE POPULATION
(persons aged 6 years and over, 1988 census)

	Males	Females	Total
Agriculture, hunting, forestry and fishing	417,630	463,007	880,637
Mining and quarrying	11,823	586	12,409
Manufacturing	16,096	1,250	17,346
Electricity, gas and water	751	58	809
Construction	5,583	49	5,632
Trade, restaurants and hotels	37,435	54,563	91,998
Transport, storage and communications	6,601	150	6,751
Financing, insurance, real estate and business services	505	147	652
Community, social and personal services	61,764	8,537	70,301
Activities not adequately defined	7,042	4,627	11,669
Total employed	565,230	532,974	1,098,204
Unemployed	66,624	22,144	88,768
Total labour force	631,854	555,118	1,186,972

Source: International Labour Office, *Yearbook of Labour Statistics*.

Mid-1996 (estimates in '000): Agriculture, etc. 1,255; Total labour force 1,611 (Source: FAO, *Production Yearbook*).

Agriculture

PRINCIPAL CROPS ('000 metric tons)

	1994	1995	1996
Rice (paddy)	8	9	9*
Maize	63	71	65*
Millet	9†	10†	10*
Sorghum	21†	23†	25*
Cassava (Manioc)	518	402	400*
Yams*	280	320	320
Taro (Coco yam)*	70	90	80
Groundnuts (in shell)	84	86	85*
Sesame seed	27	29	27†
Cottonseed	16†	19†	20*
Palm kernels*	5	5	5
Pumpkins, squash and gourds	15	16	16*
Other vegetables (incl. melons)	52	55	55*
Oranges*	18	20	20
Mangoes*	9	9	9
Bananas*	98	100	100
Plantains*	76	78	78
Coffee (green)	15	9	10†
Cotton (lint)†	12	13	14

* FAO estimate(s). † Unofficial figure(s).

Source: FAO, *Production Yearbook*.

LIVESTOCK ('000 head, year ending September)

	1994	1995	1996*
Cattle	2,735	2,797	2,800
Goats*	1,340	1,350	1,350
Sheep	164	172	170
Pigs	524	547	550

Poultry (million): 3 in 1994; 3 in 1995; 4* in 1996.

* FAO estimate(s).

Source: FAO, *Production Yearbook*.

LIVESTOCK PRODUCTS (FAO estimates, '000 metric tons)

	1994	1995	1996
Beef and veal	45	45	45
Mutton and lamb	1	1	1
Goat meat	5	6	6
Pig meat	9	9	9
Poultry meat	3	3	3
Other meat	7	7	7
Cows' milk	50	50	50
Cattle hides (fresh)	7	7	7
Hen eggs	1	1	1
Honey	10	11	11

Source: FAO, *Production Yearbook*.

Forestry

ROUNDWOOD REMOVALS ('000 cubic metres, excluding bark)

	1992	1993	1994
Sawlogs, veneer logs and logs for sleepers	217	168	231
Other industrial wood*	267	274	281
Fuel wood	3,250	3,250	3,250*
Total	3,734	3,692	3,762

* FAO estimate(s).

Source: FAO, *Yearbook of Forest Products*.

SAWNWOOD PRODUCTION ('000 cubic metres, including railway sleepers)

	1992	1993	1994
Total (all broadleaved)	68	60*	73

* FAO estimate.

Source: FAO, *Yearbook of Forest Products*.

Fishing

(FAO estimates, '000 metric tons, live weight)

	1993	1994	1995
Total catch (freshwater fish)	13.5	13.0	13.3

Source: FAO, *Yearbook of Fishery Statistics*.

Mining

	1992	1993	1994
Gold (kg, metal content of ore)	154.7	170.6	138.2
Gem diamonds ('000 carats)	328.9	390.1	436.0
Industrial diamonds ('000 carats)	85.4	104.8	96.0

1995: Gold (kg) 97.9; Diamonds ('000 carats, uncut) 484.3 (Source: IMF, *Central African Republic—Recent Economic Developments,* April 1997).

Industry

SELECTED PRODUCTS

	1993	1994	1995*
Beer ('000 hectolitres)	123.8	249.6	268.9
Soft drinks and syrups ('000 hectolitres)	20.9	39.4	58.8
Cigarettes (million packets)	11.5	20.7	29.7
Sugar ('000 metric tons)	10.8	15.1	n.a.
Palm oil ('000 metric tons)	2.8	3.6	3.3
Plywood ('000 cubic metres)	1.5	1.9	2.4
Motor cycles (number)	413	914	412
Bicycles (number)	388	477	647
Electric energy (million kWh)	94.8	98.0	102.8

* Estimates.

Source: IMF, *Central African Republic—Recent Economic Developments* (April 1997).

Finance

CURRENCY AND EXCHANGE RATES

Monetary Units

100 centimes = 1 franc de la Coopération financière en Afrique centrale (CFA).

French Franc, Sterling and Dollar Equivalents (30 September 1997)

1 French franc = 100 francs CFA;
£1 sterling = 958.3 francs CFA;
US $1 = 593.2 francs CFA;
1,000 francs CFA = £1.044 = $1.686.

Average Exchange Rate (francs CFA per US $)

1994	555.20
1995	499.15
1996	511.55

Note: The exchange rate of 1 French franc = 50 francs CFA, established in 1948, remained in force until January 1994, when the CFA franc was devalued by 50%, with the exchange rate adjusted to 1 French franc = 100 francs CFA.

BUDGET (million francs CFA)

Revenue	1993	1994	1995*
Tax revenue	26,500	32,100	49,300
Taxes on income and profits	6,500	8,600	10,600
Domestic taxes on goods and services	10,600	12,000	16,800
Taxes on international trade	9,400	11,500	21,900
Import duties and taxes	8,100	8,500	17,900
Other receipts	1,900	3,200	2,200
Total	28,400	35,400	51,500

Expenditure	1993	1994	1995*
Current expenditure	46,000	57,400	57,700
Wages and salaries	23,000	25,700	26,000
Other goods and services	9,000	12,800	11,500
Transfers and subsidies	3,500	4,000	6,200
Interest payments	7,700	11,500	13,100
Capital expenditure	32,000	48,800	57,900
Sub-total	78,100	106,200	115,600
Adjustment for payments arrears†	−44,400	11,900	−26,300
Total	33,700	118,100	89,300

* Estimates.

† Minus sign indicates an increase in arrears.

Source: IMF, *CAR—Recent Economic Developments* (April 1997).

INTERNATIONAL RESERVES (US $ million at 31 December)

	1994	1995	1996
Gold*	4.21	4.29	4.10
IMF special drawing rights	0.01	0.02	0.01
Reserve position in IMF	0.14	0.14	0.14
Foreign exchange	209.86	233.48	232.09
Total	214.22	237.93	236.34

* National valuation.

Source: IMF, *International Financial Statistics.*

MONEY SUPPLY ('000 million francs CFA at 31 December)

	1994	1995	1996
Currency outside banks	88.53	98.97	104.00
Demand deposits at commercial and development banks	14.86	12.27	12.64
Total money	103.40	111.24	116.64

Source: IMF, *International Financial Statistics.*

COST OF LIVING
(Consumer Price Index for Bangui; base: 1981 = 100)

	1993	1994	1995
Food	117.5	146.3	179.9
Fuel and light	136.0	147.6	151.5
Clothing	153.7	217.2	238.7
All items (incl. others)*	126.3	157.3	187.5

* Excluding rent.

Source: IMF, *CAR—Recent Economic Developments* (April 1997).

NATIONAL ACCOUNTS
(IMF estimates, million francs CFA at current prices)

Expenditure on the Gross Domestic Product

	1993	1994	1995
Government final consumption expenditure	42,300	72,600	66,900
Private final consumption expenditure	302,900	380,800	462,100
Increase in stocks	1,800	4,000	5,300
Gross fixed capital formation	39,900	61,900	76,300
Total domestic expenditure	386,900	519,300	610,600
Exports of goods and services	51,400	112,100	116,800
Less Imports of goods and services	81,800	132,800	159,000
GDP in purchasers' values	356,600	498,600	568,500
GDP at constant 1985 prices	368,900	397,300	406,900

Source: IMF, *CAR—Recent Economic Developments* (April 1997).

Gross Domestic Product by Economic Activity

	1993	1994	1995
Agriculture, hunting, forestry and fishing	166,400	237,800	282,900
Mining and quarrying	17,400	36,500	32,700
Manufacturing	36,000	43,800	46,600
Electricity, gas and water	3,100	3,800	4,300
Construction	14,900	21,700	25,000
Trade, restaurants and hotels	44,400	50,400	56,600
Transport, storage and communications	11,300	13,100	15,600
Other private services	19,800	22,400	25,200
Government services	23,300	45,700	41,000
GDP at factor cost	336,600	475,100	529,800
Indirect taxes	20,000	23,500	38,700
GDP in purchasers' values	356,600	498,600	568,500

Source: IMF, *CAR—Recent Economic Developments* (April 1997).

BALANCE OF PAYMENTS (US $ million)

	1992	1993	1994
Exports of goods	115.9	132.5	145.9
Imports of goods	−189.0	−158.1	−130.6
Trade balance	−73.2	−25.7	15.3
Exports of services	45.1	49.3	33.1
Imports of services	−152.7	−131.9	−113.8
Balance on goods and services	−180.7	−108.3	−65.4
Other income received	6.4	4.5	—
Other income paid	−22.2	−23.2	−22.7
Balance on goods, services and income	−196.5	−127.1	−88.1
Current transfers received	−151.0	152.4	92.6
Current transfers paid	−37.6	−38.3	−29.2
Current balance	−83.1	−13.0	−24.7
Direct investment abroad	−5.9	−5.3	−7.2
Direct investment from abroad	−10.7	−10.0	3.6
Other investment assets	−33.2	−18.2	8.1
Investment liabilities	68.4	34.8	48.3
Net errors and omissions	26.2	6.3	−15.0
Overall balance	−38.2	−5.3	13.1

Source: IMF, *International Financial Statistics.*

External Trade

PRINCIPAL COMMODITIES (distribution by SITC, US $'000)

Imports c.i.f.	1989
Food and live animals	22,768
Cereals and cereal preparations	8,192
Wheat flour	4,320
Sugar, sugar preparations and honey	6,232
Sugar and honey	5,959
Refined sugars	5,945
Beverages and tobacco	5,706
Tobacco and tobacco manufactures	3,715
Mineral fuels, lubricants, etc	10,658
Petroleum and petroleum products	10,390
Refined petroleum products	10,273
Gas oils (distillate fuels)	3,358
Chemicals and related products	22,239
Medicinal and pharmaceutical products	10,333
Medicaments	6,705
Essential oils, perfume materials and cleansing preparations	3,009
Pesticides, disinfectants, etc.	3,104
Basic manufactures	28,364
Paper, paperboard and manufactures	3,325
Textile yarn, fabrics, etc.	5,737
Non-metallic mineral manufactures	6,780
Lime, cement, etc.	5,288
Cement	5,244
Machinery and transport equipment	52,876
Machinery specialized for particular industries	7,605
Civil engineering and contractors' plant and equipment	3,094
General industrial machinery, equipment and parts	7,712
Electrical machinery, apparatus, etc.	8,061
Road vehicles and parts (excl. tyres, engines and electrical parts)	23,638
Passenger motor cars (excl. buses)	5,510
Motor vehicles for goods transport and special purposes	7,395
Goods vehicles (lorries and trucks)	4,969
Parts and accessories for motor vehicles	6,625
Miscellaneous manufactured articles	11,722
Total (incl. others)	159,124

Source: UN, *International Trade Statistics Yearbook.*

Total imports (c.i.f., million francs CFA): 42,050 in 1990; 50,400 in 1991; 43,211 in 1992; 35,559 in 1993; 73,263 in 1994; 86,900 in 1995 (Sources: IMF, *International Financial Statistics*; Ministry of the Economy, Planning and International Co-operation).

Exports f.o.b.	1989
Food and live animals	40,341
Coffee, tea, cocoa and spices	40,204
Coffee (green and roasted)	40,204
Crude materials (inedible) except fuels	34,999
Cork and wood	18,204
Sawlogs and veneer logs	12,712
Sawn lumber	5,102
Textile fibres and waste	12,608
Cotton	12,608
Basic manufactures	59,232
Non-metallic mineral manufactures	58,972
Diamonds (non-industrial)	58,970
Total (incl. others)	140,287

Source: UN, *International Trade Statistics Yearbook.*

Total exports (million francs CFA): 32,770 in 1990; 35,440 in 1991; 28,328 in 1992; 31,073 in 1993; 79,541 in 1994; 85,300 in 1995 (Sources: IMF, *International Financial Statistics*; Ministry of the Economy, Planning and International Co-operation).

PRINCIPAL TRADING PARTNERS (US $'000)

Imports c.i.f.	1989
Belgium/Luxembourg	4,032
Cameroon	14,514
Chad	1,701
China	4,211
Congo	5,111
France	67,631
Gabon	2,469
Italy	2,681
Japan	12,043
Netherlands	3,338
United Kingdom	1,988
USA	2,037
Zaire	5,715
Total (incl. others)	159,124

Exports f.o.b.*	1989
Belgium/Luxembourg	71,353
France	48,242
Spain	2,482
Sudan	3,320
Switzerland	6,967
Total (incl. others)	137,903

* Excluding exports of gold (US $'000): 2,384 in 1989.

Source: UN, *International Trade Statistics Yearbook.*

Transport

ROAD TRAFFIC (motor vehicles in use)

	1992	1993	1994
Passenger cars	8,000	10,400	11,900
Commercial vehicles	1,700	2,400	2,800

Source: UN, *Statistical Yearbook.*

INLAND WATERWAYS TRAFFIC—INTERNATIONAL SHIPPING (metric tons)

	1986	1987	1988
Freight unloaded at Bangui	152,000	113,300	126,300
Freight loaded at Bangui	75,500	57,200	53,100
Total	227,500	170,500	179,400

CIVIL AVIATION (traffic on scheduled services)*

	1992	1993	1994
Kilometres flown (million)	3	3	3
Passengers carried ('000)	120	122	122
Passenger-km (million)	213	219	219
Total ton-km (million)	35	35	35

*Including an apportionment of the traffic of Air Afrique.

Source: UN, *Statistical Yearbook.*

Tourism

	1992	1993	1994
Tourist arrivals ('000)	6	6	6
Tourist receipts (US $ million)	3	6	6

Source: UN, *Statistical Yearbook.*

Communications Media

	1992	1993	1994
Radio receivers ('000 in use)	220	227	235
Television receivers ('000 in use)	14	15	16
Telephones('000mainlinesinuse)	6	7	7
Telefax stations (number in use)	50	30	30

Daily newspapers: 1 (estimated circulation 2,000 copies) in 1994.

Sources: UNESCO, *Statistical Yearbook;* UN, *Statistical Yearbook.*

Education

(1990/91, unless otherwise indicated)

	Schools	Teachers	Pupils
Pre-primary*	173	572	11,677
Primary	930	4,004	308,409
Secondary			
General	46†	1,005	46,989
Vocational	n.a.		1,862
Higher	n.a.	136	2,823

* 1987/88 figures (Source: UNESCO, *Statistical Yearbook*).

† State-funded general secondary schools..

Directory

The Constitution

A new Constitution was adopted on 7 January 1995, following approval by a national referendum held on 28 December 1994. It replaced the 1986 Constitution and all subsequent amendments. The new Constitution provided for decentralization, through the election of regional assemblies by direct universal adult suffrage, and the establishment of a Constitutional Court (whose officials were to be appointed by the President), and it redefined the separation of sovereign and executive powers between the President and the Prime Minister.

THE PRESIDENCY

The President of the Republic is Head of State and Commander-in-Chief of the national armed forces. The President is elected for a six-year term by direct universal suffrage and may serve for a maximum of two consecutive terms*. Election of the President is determined by an absolute majority of votes cast. If such is not obtained at the first ballot, a second ballot is to take place, contested by the two candidates gaining the largest number of votes in the first ballot. The election of the new President is to take place not less than 20 days and not more than 40 days before the expiration of the mandate of the President in office. However, the President may choose to hold a referendum to determine whether or not his mandate is to be renewed. Should the electorate reject the proposal, the President is to resign and a new presidential election is to be held two weeks after the publication of the results of the referendum. The Presidency is to become vacant only in the event of the President's death, resignation, condemnation by the High Court of Justice or permanent physical incapacitation, as certified by a Special Committee comprising the presidents of the National Assembly, the Economic and Regional Council and the Supreme Court (see below). The election of a new President must take place not less than 20 days and not more than 40 days following the occurrence of a vacancy, during which time the president of the National Assembly is to act as interim President, with limited powers.

The President appoints the Prime Minister, who presides over the Council of Ministers. The President promulgates laws adopted by the National Assembly or by the Congress and has the power to dissolve the National Assembly, in which event legislative elections must take place not less than 20 and not more than 40 days following its dissolution.

PARLIAMENT

This is composed of the National Assembly, the Economic and Regional Council and the State Council, which, when sitting together, are to be known as the Congress. The primary function of the Congress is to pass organic laws in implementation of the Constitution, whenever these are not submitted to a referendum.

The National Assembly

The National Assembly is composed of 85 deputies elected by direct universal suffrage for a five-year term. Its president is designated by, and from within, its bureau. Legislation may be introduced either by the President of the Republic or by a consensus of one-third of the members of the Assembly. Provisions are made for the rendering inadmissible of any law providing for the execution of projects carrying a financial cost to the State which exceeds their potential value. The National Assembly holds two ordinary sessions per year of 60 days each, at the summons of the President of the Republic, who may also summon it to hold extraordinary sessions with a pre-determined agenda. Sessions of the National Assembly are opened and closed by presidential decree.

The Economic and Regional Council

The Economic and Regional Council is composed of representatives from the principal sectors of economic and social activity. One-half of its members are appointed by the President, and the remaining half are elected by the National Assembly on the nomination of that body's president. It acts as an advisory body in all legislative proposals of an economic and social nature.

The State Council

The State Council is an advisory body which deliberates on administrative matters that are referred to it by the president of the National Assembly.

The Congress

The Congress has the same president and bureau as the National Assembly. An absolute majority of its members is needed to pass organic laws, as well as laws pertaining to the amendment of the Constitution which have not been submitted to a referendum. It defines development priorities and may meet, at the summons of the President, to ratify treaties or to declare a state of war.

* A special clause was incorporated in the 1995 Constitution, whereby the incumbent President, Ange-Félix Patassé, was to be permitted to remain in office, if re-elected, for three consecutive terms.

The Government

HEAD OF STATE

President: Ange-Félix Patassé (inaugurated 22 October 1993).

COUNCIL OF MINISTERS

(January 1998)

A coalition 'Government of Action' incorporating the Mouvement pour la libération du peuple centrafricain (MLPC), the Convention nationale (CN), the Parti libéral-démocrate (PLD), the Mouvement d'évolution sociale de l'Afrique noire (MESAN), the Rassemblement démocratique centrafricain (RDC), the Front patriotique pour le progrès (FPP), the Mouvement pour la démocratie et le développement (MDD), the Mouvement démocratique pour la renaissance et l'évolution de la République Centrafricaine (MDRERC), the Alliance pour la démocratie et le progrès (ADP), the Parti social-démocrate (PSD) and three independents.

Prime Minister: Michel Gbezera-Bria (Independent).

Minister of Foreign Affairs: Jean Mette-Yapende (MLPC).

Minister of National Defence, War Veterans and War Victims: Dr Pascal Kado (MLPC).

Minister of Territorial Administration and Public Security: Gen. N'Djdder François Bedaya (MLPC).

Minister of Justice: Marcel Metefara (MLPC).

Minister of Finance and the Budget: Anicet Georges Dologuele (MLPC).

Minister of the Economy, Planning and International Co-operation: Christophe Mbremaidou (CN).

Minister of Public Works and Road Infrastructure: Jacquesson Mazette (MLPC).

Minister of Human Rights and Promotion of Democratic Culture: LAURENT GOMINA-PAMPALI (RDC).

Minister of National Education: ALBERT MBERYO (MLPC).

Minister of Higher Education, Scientific and Technological Research: THÉOPHILE TOUBA (RDC).

Minister of Public Health and Population: Dr FERNANDE DJENGBO (Independent).

Minister of Civil Service, Labour and Professional Training: JEAN-CLAUDE GOUANDJA (FPP).

Minister of Mines and Energy: JOSEPH AGBO (MLPC).

Minister of Transport and Civil Aviation: ANDRÉ GOMBAKO (FPP).

Minister of Commerce, Industry, Small and Medium-Scale Enterprises, and Small and Medium-Scale Industries: SIMOM BONGOLAPKE (MDD).

Minister of Communications: THIERRY VAN DEN BOSS YONIFOLO (PLD).

Minister of Tourism, Arts and Culture: GASTON BEINA NGABANDI (MLPC).

Minister of Family Promotion, Social Welfare and National Solidarity: ÉLIANE MOKODOKPO (MESAN).

Minister of Environment, Water, Forest Resources, Hunting and Fishery: JOSEPH GNOMBA (MDRERC).

Minister of Housing and Town Planning: CLÉMENT BELIBANGA (ADP).

Minister of Posts and Telecommunications: MECHEL BINDO (RDC).

Minister of Youth and Sports Promotion: BEERTIN BEYA (MDD).

Minister of Relations with Parliament: CHARLES ARMEL DOUBANE (ADP).

Secretary of State for Territorial Administration: GILBERT MOUSSA LABE (Independent).

Secretary of State for National Solidarity: ALBERTINE BISSA (PSD).

There are, in addition, two Ministers-Delegate responsible for security and civilian disarmament, and the reorganization of the army.

MINISTRIES

Office of the President: Palais de la Renaissance, Bangui; tel. 61-03-23; telex 5253.

Ministry of the Civil Service, Labour and Professional Training: Bangui; tel. 61-01-44.

Ministry of Communications: BP 1290, Bangui; telex 5301.

Ministry of Finance and the Budget: BP 734, Bangui; tel. 61-44-88; telex 5280; fax 61-21-82.

Ministry of Foreign Affairs: Bangui; tel. 61-15-74; telex 5213.

Ministry of Justice: Bangui; tel. 61-16-44.

Ministry of Mines and Energy: Bangui; telex 5243; fax 61-6076.

Ministry of National Defence, War Veterans and War Victims: Bangui; tel. 61-46-11; telex 5298.

Ministry of National Education: BP 791, Bangui; telex 5333.

Ministry of Public Health and Population: Bangui; tel. 61-29-01.

Ministry of Transport and Civil Aviation: BP 941, Bangui; tel. 61-23-07; telex 5335; fax 61-15-52.

President and Legislature

PRESIDENT

Presidential election, First Ballot, 22 August 1993

Candidate	Votes	% of votes
ANGE-FÉLIX PATASSÉ (MLPC)	302,004	37.31
Prof. ABEL GOUMBA (CFD)	175,467	21.68
DAVID DACKO (Independent)	162,721	20.10
Gen. ANDRÉ KOLINGBA (RDC)	97,942	12.10
ENOCH DERANT LAKOUÉ (PSD)	19,368	2.39
Gen. TIMOTHÉE MALENDOMA (FC)	16,400	2.03
Brig.-Gen. FRANÇOIS BOZIZE (RPRC)	12,169	1.50
RUTH ROLLAND JEANNE MARIE (PRC)	8,068	1.00
Invalid votes	15,317	1.89
Total	809,456	100.00

Second Ballot, 19 September 1993

Candidate	% of votes
ANGE-FÉLIX PATASSÉ (MLPC)	52.47
Prof. ABEL GOUMBA (CFD)	45.62
Invalid votes	1.91
Total	100.00

ASSEMBLÉE NATIONALE

Legislative power is vested in the Congress, which comprises the National Assembly and the advisory Economic and Regional Council and State Council.

President: HUGUES DOBOZENDI.

General election, 27 August and 19 September 1993

	Seats
MLPC	34
RDC	13
FPP	7
PLD	7
ADP	6
Supporters of David Dacko*	6
CN	3
PSD	3
MESAN	1
FC	1
PRC	1
MDRERC	1
Independents	2
Total	85

* Formed the Mouvement pour la démocratie et le développement in December 1993.

Political Organizations

Alliance pour la démocratie et le progrès (ADP): Bangui; f. 1991; Leader FRANÇOIS PEHOUA; Nat. Sec. TCHAPKA BRÉDÉ.

Conseil démocratique des partis politiques de l'opposition (CODEPO): Bangui; f. 1995; political alliance led by AUGUSTE BOUKANGA; comprises the following parties:

Mouvement démocratique pour la renaissance et l'évolution de la République Centrafricaine (MDRERC): Bangui; Chair. JOSEPH BENDOUNGA; Sec.-Gen. LÉON SEBOU.

Parti républicain centrafricain (PRC): Bangui.

Convention nationale (CN): Bangui; f. 1991; Leader DAVID GALIAMBO.

Forum civique (FC): Bangui; Leader Gen. TIMOTHÉE MALENDOMA.

Front patriotique pour le progrès (FPP): BP 259, Bangui; tel. 61-52-23; fax 61-10-93; f. 1972; aims to promote political education and debate; Prof. ABEL GOUMBA.

Front pour la libération centrafricaine: based in Brazzaville, Republic of the Congo; f. 1996 to combat French military and political intervention; Leaders Dr JEAN PAUL MANDAKOUZOU, Maj. LÉOPOLD ADETO.

G11: Bangui; f. 1997; alliance of 11 opposition parties led by Prof. ABEL GOUMBA; prin. mems: ADP, FPP, MDD and RDC.

Mouvement centrafricain pour la libération nationale (MCLN): Lagos, Nigeria; Leader Dr IDDI LALA.

Mouvement d'évolution sociale de l'Afrique noire (MESAN): f. 1949; now comprises two factions, led respectively by PROSPER LAVODRAMA and JOSEPH NGBANGADIBO.

Mouvement pour la démocratie et le développement (MDD): Bangui; f. 1993; aims to safeguard national unity and the equitable distribution of national wealth; Leader DAVID DACKO.

Mouvement pour la libération du peuple centrafricain (MLPC): f. 1979; Pres. ANGE-FÉLIX PATASSÉ; Vice-Pres. JEAN-LUC MANDABA.

Mouvement pour la libération de la République Centrafricaine: Bangui; Leader HUGUES DOBOZENDI.

Mouvement socialiste centrafricaine: Bangui.

Parti libéral-démocrate (PLD): Bangui; Leader NESTOR KOMBO-NAGUEMON.

Parti social-démocrate (PSD): Bangui; Leader ENOCH DERANT LAKOUÉ.

Rassemblement démocratique centrafricain (RDC): BP 503, Bangui; tel. 61-53-75; f. 1987; sole legal political party 1987–91; Sec.-Gen. PIERRE LAKOUTINI.

Rassemblement populaire pour la reconstruction de la Centrafrique (RPRC): Leader Gen. FRANÇOIS BOZIZE.

Union populaire pour le développement économique et social: Bangui; Leader HUBERT KATOSSI SIMANI.

Diplomatic Representation

EMBASSIES IN THE CENTRAL AFRICAN REPUBLIC

Cameroon: BP 935, Bangui; telex 5249; fax 61-18-57; Chargé d'affaires a.i.: GILBERT NOULA.

Chad: BP 461, Bangui; telex 5220; Ambassador: El Hadj MOULI SEID.

China (Taiwan): BP 1058, Bangui; tel. 61-36-28; Ambassador: LIU HSIANG-PU.

Congo, Democratic Republic: BP 989, Bangui; telex 5232; Ambassador: EMBE ISEA MBAMBE.

Congo, Republic: BP 1414, Bangui; telex 5292; Chargé d'affaires a.i.: ANTOINE DELICA.

Egypt: BP 1422, Bangui; telex 5284; Ambassador: SAMEH SAMY DARWICHE.

France: blvd du Général de Gaulle, BP 884, Bangui; tel. 61-30-00; telex 5218; fax 61-74-04; Ambassador: JEAN-MARC SIMON.

Gabon: BP 1570, Bangui; tel. 61-29-97; telex 5234; Ambassador: FRANÇOIS DE PAULE MOULENGUI.

Germany: ave G. A. Nasser, BP 901, Bangui; tel. 61-47-65; telex 5219; fax 61-19-89; Ambassador: REINHARD BUCHHOLZ.

Holy See: ave Boganda, BP 1447, Bangui; tel. 61-26-54; fax 61-03-71; Apostolic Nuncio: Most Rev. DIEGO CAUSERO, Titular Archbishop of Meta.

Iraq: Bangui; telex 5287; Chargé d'affaires a.i.: ABDUL KARIM ASWAD.

Japan: ave Barthélemy Boganda, BP 1367, Bangui; tel. 61-06-68; telex 5204; fax 61-16-10; Ambassador: YOICHI HAYASHI.

Libya: Bangui; telex 5317; Head of Mission: EL-SENUSE ABDALLAH.

Nigeria: ave des Martyrs, BP 1010, Bangui; tel. 61-40-97; telex 5269; fax 61-12-79; Chargé d'affaires: AYODELE J. BAKARE.

Russia: rue Fourreau-lamy, BP1405, Bangui; tel. 61-03-11; Ambassador: BORIS KRASNIKOV.

Sudan: ave de l'Indépendance, BP 1351, Bangui; tel. 61-50-11; Ambassador: TIJANI SALIH FADAYL.

USA: blvd David Dacko, BP 924, Bangui; tel. 61-02-00; fax 61-44-94; Ambassador: MOSINA H. JORDAN.

Judicial System

Supreme Court: BP 926, Bangui; tel. 61-41-33; highest judicial organ; acts as a Court of Cassation in civil and penal cases and as Court of Appeal in administrative cases; comprises four chambers: constitutional, judicial, administrative and financial.

President of the Supreme Court: EDOUARD FRANCK.

There is also a Court of Appeal, a Criminal Court, 16 tribunaux de grande instance, 37 tribunaux d'instance, six labour tribunals and a permanent military tribunal. A High Court of Justice was established under the 1986 Constitution, with jurisdiction in all cases of crimes against state security, including high treason by the President of the Republic.

In August 1992 constitutional amendments were introduced which provided for the strict separation of executive, legislative and judicial powers.

The 1995 Constitution provides for the establishment of a Constitutional Court, the judges of which were to be appointed by the President.

Religion

An estimated 60% of the population hold animist beliefs, 35% are Christians and 5% are Muslims; Roman Catholics comprise about 17% of the total population.

CHRISTIANITY

The Roman Catholic Church

The Central African Republic comprises one archdiocese and six dioceses. There were an estimated 621,571 adherents at 31 December 1995.

Bishops' Conference: Conférence Episcopale Centrafricaine, BP 798, Bangui; tel. 61-31-48; fax 61-46-92; f. 1982; Pres. Most Rev. JOACHIM N'DAYEN, Archbishop of Bangui.

Archbishop of Bangui: Most Rev. JOACHIM N'DAYEN, Archevêché, BP 1518, Bangui; tel. 61-31-48; fax 61-46-92.

Protestant Church

Eglise Protestante de Bangui: Bangui.

The Press

DAILIES

E Le Songo: Bangui; Sango; circ. 2,000.

Le Novateur: BP 913, Bangui; tel. 61-48-84; fax 61-87-03; e-mail ccea-ln@intnet.cf; independent; Publr MARCEL MOKWAPI; circ. 750.

PERIODICALS

Bangui Match: Bangui; monthly.

Le Courrier Rural: BP 850, Bangui; publ. by Chambre d'Agriculture.

Le Delit d'Opinion: Bangui; independent.

Journal Officiel de la République Centrafricaine: BP 739, Bangui; f. 1974; fortnightly; economic data; Dir-Gen. GABRIEL AGBA.

Le Rassemblement: Bangui; organ of the RDC; Editor-in-Chief MATHIAS GONEVO REAPOGO.

Renouveau Centrafricain: Bangui; weekly.

Ta Tene (The Truth): BP 1290, Bangui; monthly.

Terre Africaine: BP 373, Bangui; weekly.

NEWS AGENCIES

Agence Centrafricaine de Presse (ACAP): BP 40, Bangui; tel. 61-10-88; telex 5299; f. 1974; Gen. Man. VICTOR DETO TETEYA.

Informatsionnoye Telegrafnoye Agentstvo Rossii—Telegrafnoye Agentstvo Suverennykh Stran (ITAR—TASS) (Russia) and Agence France-Presse are the only foreign press agencies represented in the CAR.

Publisher

Government Publishing House

Imprimerie Centrafricaine: BP 329, Bangui; tel. 61-00-33; f. 1974; Dir-Gen. PIERRE SALAMATE-KOILET.

Broadcasting and Communications

TELECOMMUNICATIONS

Société Centrafricaine de Télécoms: BP 939, Bangui; tel. 61-42-68; telex 5217; fax 61-35-61; parastatal company.

BROADCASTING

Radiodiffusion-Télévision Centrafrique: BP 940, Bangui; tel. 61-25-88; telex 2355; f. 1958 as Radiodiffusion Nationale Centrafricaine; govt-controlled; broadcasts in French and Sango; Man. Dir PAUL SERVICE.

Finance

(cap. = capital; res = reserves; dep. = deposits; m. = million; amounts in francs CFA)

BANKING

Central Bank

Banque des Etats de l'Afrique Centrale (BEAC): BP 851, Bangui; tel. 61-24-00; telex 5636; fax 61-19-95; headquarters in Yaoundé, Cameroon; f. 1973 as the central bank of issue for mem. states of the Customs and Economic Union of Central Africa (UDEAC), comprising Cameroon, the Central African Republic, Chad, the Republic of the Congo, Equatorial Guinea and Gabon; cap. 45,000m., res 169,492m. (June 1996); Gov. JEAN-FÉLIX MAMALEPOT; Dir in CAR AUGUSTE TENÉ-KOYZOA.

Commercial Banks

Banque de Crédit Agricole et de Développement (BCAD): 1 place de la République, BP 801, Bangui; tel. 61-32-00; telex 5207; f. 1984; 50% owned by BPP Holding (Luxembourg), 33.33% state-owned, 8.33% owned by Caisse Nationale de Crédit Agricole and 8.33% owned by Pacfinancial Consultants Ltd; Pres. MICHEL M. CHAUTARD; Gen. Man. RENÉ JAULIN.

Banque Internationale pour le Centrafrique: place de la République, BP 910, Bangui; tel. 61-36-33; telex 5233; fax 61-61-36; f. 1980; present name adopted 1996; 50.1% owned by Banque Belgolaise, 9%

state-owned; cap. 700m., dep. 17,318m. (Dec. 1994); Pres. RAOUL KONTCHOU; Gen. Man. TADI WANTWADI; 1 br.

Banque Populaire Maroco-Centrafricaine (BPMC): rue Guerillot, BP 844, Bangui; tel. 61-12-90; telex 5244; fax 61-62-30; f. 1991; 50% owned by Banque Centrale Populaire (Morocco), 12.5% owned by Banque Marocaine du Commerce Extérieur and 37.5% state-owned; cap. 842m., total assets 4,520m. (Dec. 1995); Pres. ABDELLATIF LARAKI; Gen. Man. AHMED IRAQI HOUSSAINI.

Union Bancaire en Afrique Centrale: rue de Brazza, BP 59, Bangui; tel. 61-29-90; telex 5225; fax 61-34-54; f. 1962; 85% state-owned and 15% owned by Crédit Lyonnais (France); cap. 1,000m., res 834.8m., dep. 17,539m. (Dec. 1995); Pres. JEAN-SERGE WAFIO; Gen. Man. ETIENNE DJIMARIM; 1 br.

Development Bank

Banque de Developpement des Etats de l'Afrique Centrale: (see Franc Zone, p. 182).

Investment Bank

Banque Centrafricaine d'Investissement (BCI): BP 933, Bangui; tel. 61-00-64; telex 5317; f. 1976; 34.8% state-owned; cap. 1,000m.; Pres. ALPHONSE KONGOLO; Man. Dir GÉRARD SAMBO.

Financial Institutions

Caisse Autonome d'Amortissement des Dettes de la République Centrafricaine: Bangui; fax 61-21-82; management of state funds; Dir-Gen. JOSEPH PINGAMA.

Caisse Nationale d'Epargne (CNE): Bangui; tel. 61-22-96; telex 5202; fax 61-78-80; Pres. JUSTIN SALAMATE: Dir-Gen. ANDRÉ NDOMONDJI.

Development Agencies

Caisse Française de Développement: BP 817, Bangui; tel. 61-36-34; telex 5291; Dir NILS ROBIN.

Mission Française de Coopération et d'Action Culturelle: BP 934, Bangui; tel. 61-63-34; fax 61-28-24; administers bilateral aid from France; Dir HERVÉ CRONEL.

INSURANCE

Agence Centrafricaine d'Assurances (ACA): BP 512, Bangui; tel. 61-06-23; f. 1956; Dir Mme R. CERBELLAUD.

Assureurs Conseils Centrafricains Faugère et Jutheau: rue de la Kouanga, BP 743, Bangui; tel. 61-19-33; telex 5331; fax 61-44-70; f. 1968; Dir JEAN CLAUDE ROY.

Entreprise d'Etat d'Assurances et de Réassurances (SIRIRI): Bangui; tel. 61-36-55; telex 5306; f. 1972; Pres. EMMANUEL DOKOUNA; Dir-Gen. JEAN-MARIE YOLLOT.

Legendre, A. & Cie: rue de la Victoire, BP 896, Bangui; Pres. and Dir-Gen. ANDRÉ LEGENDRE.

Trade and Industry

DEVELOPMENT ORGANIZATIONS

Agence de Développement de la Zone Caféière (ADECAF): BP 1935, Bangui; tel. 61-47-30; coffee producers' asscn; assists coffee marketing co-operatives; Dir-Gen. J. J. NIMIZIAMBI.

Caisse de Stabilisation et de Péréquation des Produits Agricoles (CAISTAB): BP 76, Bangui; tel. 61-08-00; telex 5278; supervises pricing and marketing of agricultural products; Dir-Gen. M. BOUNANDELE-KOUMBA.

Comptoir National du Diamant (CND): blvd B. Boganda, BP 1011, Bangui; tel. 61-07-02; telex 5262; f. 1964; 50% state-owned, 50% owned by Diamond Distributors (USA): mining and marketing of diamonds; Dir-Gen. M. VASSOS.

Office National des Forêts (ONF): BP 915, Bangui; tel. 61-38-27; f. 1969; reafforestation, development of forest resources; Dir-Gen. C. D. SONGUET.

Société Centrafricaine de Développement Agricole (SOCADA): ave David Dacko, BP 997, Bangui; tel. 61-30-33; telex 5212; f. 1964; reorg. 1980; 75% state-owned, 25% Cie Française pour le Développement des Fibres Textiles (France); purchasing, transport and marketing of cotton, cotton-ginning, production of cottonseed oil and groundnut oil; Pres. MAURICE METHOT.

Société Centrafricaine des Palmiers (CENTRAPALM): BP 1355, Bangui; tel. 61-49-40; fax 61-38-75; f. 1975; state-owned; production and marketing of palm oil; operates the Bossongo agro-industrial complex; Pres. MATHIEU-FRANCIS NGANAWARA; Gen. Man. Dr JOËL BEASSEM.

Société Petrolière de Centrafrique (PETROCA): BP 724, Bangui; tel. 61-41-06; telex 5316; state-owned; privatization pending; import and marketing of petroleum products; Dir-Gen. DOGONE JIBE.

CHAMBERS OF COMMERCE

Chambre d'Agriculture, d'Elevage, des Eaux, Forêts, Chasses, Pêches et Tourisme: BP 850, Bangui; tel. 61-09-33; f. 1964; Pres. FRANÇOIS T. BEYÉLÉ; Sec.-Gen. MOÏSE DENISSIO.

Chambre de Commerce, d'Industrie, des Mines et de l'Artisanat (CCIMA): BP 813, Bangui; tel. 61-16-68; telex 5261; Pres. RIGOBERT YOMBO; Sec. GERTRUDE ZOUTA-YAMANDJA.

EMPLOYERS' ORGANIZATION

Union Nationale du Patronat Centrafricain (UNPC): Bangui; Pres. RIGOBERT YOMBO.

UTILITIES

Electricity

Société Energie de Centrafrique (ENERCA): ave de l'Indépendance, BP 880, Bangui; tel. 61-20-22; telex 5241; f. 1967; fmrly Energie Centrafricaine; state-owned company, scheduled for privatization; production and distribution of electric energy.

Water

Société Nationale des Eaux (SNE): BP 1838, Bangui; tel. 61-20-28; telex 5306; f. 1975; state-owned company; supply, treatment and distribution of water; Dir.-Gen. FRANÇOIS FARRA-FROND.

TRADE UNION

Union Syndicale des Travailleurs de la Centrafrique (USTC): Bangui; Sec.-Gen. THÉOPHILE SONNY KOLLE.

Transport

RAILWAYS

There are no railways at present. There are long-term plans to connect Bangui to the Transcameroon railway. A line linking Sudan's Darfur region with the CAR's Vakaga province is also planned.

ROADS

In 1996 there were an estimated 24,000 km of roads, including 4,280 km of main roads and 3,910 km of secondary roads. Only about 1.8% of the total network is paved. Eight main routes serve Bangui, and those that are surfaced are toll roads. Both the total road length and the condition of the roads are inadequate for current requirements. A major project of road rehabilitation and construction is being assisted by France, the European Union and Japan. The CAR is linked with Cameroon by the Transafrican Lagos–Mombasa highway.

Bureau d'Affrètement Routier Centrafricain (BARC): BP 523, Bangui; tel. 61-20-55; telex 5336; Dir-Gen. J. M. LAGUEREMA-YADINGUIN.

Compagnie Nationale des Transports Routiers (CNTR): Bangui; tel. 61-46-44; state-owned; Dir-Gen. GEORGES YABADA.

Compagnie de Transports Routiers de l'Oubangui Degrain & Cie (CTRO): Bangui; f. 1940; Man. NICOLE DEGRAIN.

INLAND WATERWAYS

There are some 2,800 km of navigable waterways along two main water courses. The first, formed by the Congo river and its tributary the Oubangui, can accommodate convoys of barges (of up to 800 metric tons load) between Bangui and Brazzaville and Pointe-Noire in the Republic of the Congo, except during the dry season, when the route is impassable. The second is the river Sangha, also a tributary of the Congo, on which traffic is again seasonal. There are two ports, at Bangui and Salo, on the rivers Oubangui and Sangha respectively. Efforts are being made to develop the Sangha upstream from Salo to increase the transportation of timber from this area, and to develop Nola as a timber port.

Agence Centrafricaine des Communications Fluviales (ACCF): BP 822, Bangui; tel. 61-02-11; telex 5256; f. 1969; state-owned; development of inland waterways transport system; Man. Dir JUSTIN NDJAPOU.

Société Centrafricaine de Transports Fluviaux (SOCATRAF): BP 1445, Bangui; tel. and fax 61-43-15; telex 5256; f. 1980; 51%-owned by ACCF; Man. Dir FRANÇOIS TOUSSAINT.

CIVIL AVIATION

The international airport is at Bangui-M'Poko. There are also 37 small airports for internal services.

Air Afrique: BP 875, Bangui; tel. 61-46-60; telex 5281; see under Côte d'Ivoire; Dir in Bangui ALBERT BAGNERES.

Tourism

The main tourist attractions are the waterfalls, forests and wildlife. There are excellent hunting and fishing opportunities. There were an estimated 1,599 tourist arrivals in 1990.

Office National Centrafricain du Tourisme (OCATOUR): BP 655, Bangui; tel. 61-45-66.

CHAD

Introductory Survey

Location, Climate, Language, Religion, Flag, Capital

The Republic of Chad is a land-locked country in north central Africa, bordered to the north by Libya, to the south by the Central African Republic, to the west by Niger, Nigeria and Cameroon, and to the east by Sudan. The climate is hot and arid in the northern desert regions of the Sahara but very wet (annual rainfall 500 cm) in the south. The official languages are French and Arabic, and various African languages are also widely spoken. Almost one-half of the population are Muslims, living in the north. About 30% of the population are Christians. Most of the remainder follow animistic beliefs. The national flag (proportions 3 by 2) has three equal vertical stripes, of blue, yellow and red. The capital is N'Djamena.

Recent History

Formerly a province of French Equatorial Africa, Chad became an autonomous state within the French Community in November 1958, and achieved full independence on 11 August 1960. Its first President was François (later Ngarta) Tombalbaye, a southerner and leader of the Parti progressiste tchadien (PPT). In 1962 the PPT was declared the sole political party. In 1965 a full-scale insurgency began, concentrated mainly in the north. The Muslims of northern Chad have traditionally been in conflict with their black southern compatriots, who are mainly Christians or animists. The banned Front de libération nationale du Tchad (FROLINAT, founded in Sudan in 1966) assumed leadership of the revolt. The rebellion was partially quelled in 1968, following French military intervention.

In 1973 several prominent figures in the regime, including Gen. Félix Malloum, the Army Chief of Staff, were imprisoned on charges of conspiracy. In August of the same year the PPT was reconstituted as the Mouvement national pour la révolution culturelle et sociale (MNRCS). Also in 1973, Libyan troops occupied the so-called 'Aozou strip', a region of some 114,000 sq km (44,000 sq miles) in northern Chad, which is believed to contain significant deposits of uranium and other minerals. The Libyan claim to sovereignty over the region was based on an unratified treaty signed by France and Italy in 1935.

In April 1975 Tombalbaye was killed in a military coup. Malloum was released and appointed President, at the head of a Supreme Military Council, and the MNRCS was dissolved. FROLINAT remained in opposition, receiving clandestine military assistance from Libya. In early 1978 FROLINAT seized control of a large area of the north before its advance was halted by French military intervention. In August, after negotiations with President Malloum, Hissène Habré, a former leader of FROLINAT, was appointed Prime Minister. However, disagreements developed between Habré (a Muslim from the north) and Malloum over the status of Muslims in Chad.

In February 1979 armed conflict broke out between Habré's Forces armées du nord (FAN) and the government armed forces, the Forces armées tchadiennes (FAT). FAN gained control of the capital, and in March Malloum resigned and fled the country. In April a provisional Government was formed, comprising representatives of several groups, including FROLINAT, FAN and FAT, but sporadic fighting continued between rival political factions and between Muslims and non-Muslims. In August a Gouvernement d'union nationale de transition (GUNT) was formed by 11 Chadian factions, with Goukouni Oueddei, the leader of FROLINAT, as President, and Lt-Col (later Gen.) Wadel Abdelkader Kamougue as Vice-President.

Goukouni's authority was undermined by continual disagreements with Habré, and in March 1980 fighting resumed. In October, after numerous attempts at reconciliation had failed, Libyan forces intervened directly in the hostilities, in support of Goukouni. By December Habré had been defeated, and a Libyan force of some 15,000 men was established in the country. In November 1981 Libyan troops were withdrawn, and a peace-keeping force was installed under the auspices of the Organization of African Unity (OAU—see p. 215). The conflict intensified, however, and in June 1982 Habré's forces captured N'Djamena, the capital. Habré was formally inaugurated as President in October, and in the same month Goukouni formed a rival government in Bardai.

In January 1983 some members of FAT joined the ranks of Habré's FAN to form the Forces armées nationales tchadiennes (FANT). In August, after protracted fighting, Goukouni's rebel forces, with Libyan support, captured the northern administrative centre of Faya-Largeau. A further 3,000 French troops were dispatched to Chad, and an 'interdiction line' was imposed by France to separate the warring factions. In mid-September it was announced that fighting had ceased.

In June 1984, in an attempt to consolidate his political support in the south of the country, Habré dissolved the FROLINAT-FAN movement and replaced it with a new political party, the Union nationale pour l'indépendance et la révolution (UNIR). In July a new, more broadly-based Government was formed, with greater participation by politicians from the south. The opposition, meanwhile, was becoming increasingly fragmented, following the defection of several groups from Goukouni's GUNT. In August, however, the *commandos rouges* (or *codos*), rebel movements based in the south, resumed their guerrilla insurgency. As a result of the violent measures taken to suppress the uprising, the Government lost considerable political support. In September Libya and France agreed to a simultaneous withdrawal of their troops from Chad. By mid-November all French troops had left the country; however, it was reported that some 3,000 Libyan troops remained in Chad, in contravention of the agreement.

In August 1985 a GUNT conference was held to establish a new anti-Government coalition, the Conseil suprême de la révolution (CSR), comprising members of seven leading opposition groupings. Later that year, however, a number of other opposition factions declared their support for the Habré regime. By the end of 1985 the *codos* rebellion had collapsed and hostilities in southern Chad had ceased.

In February 1986, however, GUNT forces, with support from Libya, attacked government positions south of the French 'interdiction line'. Habré appealed for French military assistance, and France agreed to establish a defensive air-strike force in the capital. The USA also provided additional military aid. In mid-March hostilities ceased temporarily, following the capture by government forces of a rebel base at Chicha.

During 1986 Habré continued to consolidate his regime by attracting support from former opponents, including erstwhile *codos* rebels. In March of that year several former opponents of the regime were given government posts. The GUNT, meanwhile, began to disintegrate. In June Kamougue resigned as Vice-President of the GUNT, and in February 1987 declared his support for Habré. In August 1986 Acheikh Ibn Oumar's Conseil démocratique révolutionnaire (CDR) also withdrew support from Goukouni, leaving him politically isolated. In October, following armed clashes between the CDR (with Libyan support) and his own Forces armées populaires (FAP), Goukouni declared himself willing to seek a reconciliation with Habré.

In December 1986 clashes began in the Tibesti region between Libyan forces and the now pro-Habré FAP. Habré's FANT troops moved into northern Chad, and, with increased logistical support from France and the USA, forced Libya to withdraw from Faya-Largeau. In May 1987 Libyan troops retreated to the disputed 'Aozou strip'. In early August FANT troops attacked and occupied Aozou, the administrative centre of the area, but Libyan forces recaptured the town three weeks later. The attempt to gain control of Aozou was followed, in early September, by an incursion into southern Libya by FANT. Hostilities were ended by a cease-fire, proposed by the OAU, which took effect on 11 September. However, sporadic fighting continued and the Chadian Government claimed that Libyan aircraft were repeatedly violating Chadian airspace.

In May 1988 Col Qaddafi, the Libyan leader, failed to attend a scheduled meeting with Habré, to discuss the dispute between the two countries. However, he subsequently declared his willingness to recognize the Habré regime, and invited Habré and Goukouni to hold reconciliation talks in Libya. Despite an initially cautious response to these proposals, Habré announced that Chad was willing to resume diplomatic relations with Libya, which had been severed in 1982. Following negotiations between the Ministers of Foreign Affairs of the two countries, held in Gabon, in July 1988, agreement was reached, in principle, to restore diplomatic relations; a number of other issues, notably the sovereignty of the Aozou region, the fate of Libyan prisoners of war in Chad, and the security of common borders, remained unresolved. In October diplomatic relations were resumed and the September 1987 cease-fire agreement was reaffirmed, although Chad continued to accuse Libya of violating the conditions of the agreement.

The cohesion of the GUNT was undermined in 1988 by a dispute between Goukouni and Acheikh Ibn Oumar regarding the leadership of the movement. Several former opposition groups transferred their support to Habré, while the GUNT was reconstituted under Goukouni's leadership. In November, following negotiations with UNIR, Acheikh Ibn Oumar and his supporters returned to Chad. The inclusion of former opponents of Habré in the Government led to a period of apparent political unity in Chad, exemplified by the appointment of Acheikh Ibn Oumar as Minister of Foreign Affairs in March 1989. In early April, however, Mahamat Itno, the Minister of the Interior and Territorial Administration, was arrested following the discovery of an alleged plot to overthrow Habré. Idriss Deby, a former Commander-in-Chief of the Armed Forces, who was also implicated in the attempted coup, fled to Sudan, where he established a new opposition group.

Relations between Chad and Libya deteriorated further in June 1989, when the Chadian Government accused Libya of planning a military offensive against Chad, with the complicity of Sudan. In July, however, Qaddafi and Habré met for the first time, in Mali. The negotiations between the two leaders were inconclusive, but on 31 August Acheikh Ibn Oumar, the Minister of Foreign Affairs, met his Libyan counterpart in Algiers, where they signed an outline peace accord (*accord cadre*). This accord envisaged a peaceful resolution of the dispute over the sovereignty of the Aozou region; if such a negotiated settlement were not achieved within one year, the issue was to be submitted to the International Court of Justice (ICJ) for adjudication. Provision was made for the withdrawal of all armed forces from the Aozou region and the release of all prisoners of war. The accord also reaffirmed the principles of the September 1987 cease-fire agreement.

Despite the agreement, military engagements between FANT troops and pro-Libyan forces were reported in October and November 1989, and attempts to achieve a resolution to the dispute were undermined by mutual recriminations regarding each side's commitment to the negotiation process. In August 1990, shortly before the expiry of the stipulated deadline for a negotiated settlement, discussions between Qaddafi and Habré were held in Morocco. No agreement was reached; however, both Governments agreed to refer the territorial dispute to adjudication by the ICJ.

In December 1989 a new Constitution, which granted greater powers to the President, was approved by a referendum (reportedly receiving the support of 99.94% of those who voted). In endorsing the Constitution, the electorate also approved Habré in the office of President for a further seven-year term. The new Constitution confirmed the UNIR as the sole legal party, and provided for the establishment of a National Assembly, which was to be elected, with a five-year mandate, by universal suffrage. Elections to this 123-seat legislature took place in July 1990.

In late March 1990 Idriss Deby and his supporters, the Forces patriotiques du salut (subsequently known as the Mouvement patriotique du salut—MPS), invaded Chad from Sudan and occupied or destroyed many villages in the east of the country. Although this attack was successfully countered by government forces, the MPS launched a second invasion in November, during which a number of FANT troops transferred allegiance to Deby, while France again affirmed its policy of non-interference in Chad's internal affairs. The MPS subsequently advanced rapidly towards N'Djamena, and on 30 November Habré, together with members of his Government, fled to Cameroon. Deby arrived in N'Djamena two days later. In early December the National Assembly was dissolved and the Constitution suspended. Deby declared his intention to introduce a multi-party political system, and stated that new legislative and presidential elections were to be held at a future date. A provisional Council of State subsequently assumed power, and Deby became interim Head of State; bringing a number of members of the former Habré regime, including Acheikh Ibn Oumar, into the new Government.

Following Deby's accession to power, many political organizations that had opposed Habré announced their support for the MPS. Goukouni indicated his willingness to negotiate with Deby, and denied persistent reports that he was massing forces in northern Chad. Deby announced that FANT was to be restructured to form a smaller national army, known as the Armée nationale tchadienne (ANT). The French Government responded favourably to the new administration, and the Libyan and Sudanese Governments, in declaring their support for the MPS, undertook not to allow forces hostile to Deby to operate on their territory. Deby, however, informed Libya that Chad maintained its claim to the sovereignty of the Aozou region, which remained under consideration by the ICJ.

In March 1991 the Government promulgated a National Charter to operate for a 30-month transitional period, at the end of which a constitutional referendum was to take place. The National Charter confirmed Deby's appointment as President, Head of State and Chairman of the MPS, and replaced the provisional Council of State by a Council of Ministers and a 31-member legislative body, the Council of the Republic. In early May an informal alliance of five principal opposition movements, under the leadership of Goukouni, demanded that the registration of political groups be authorized and that a national conference be convened. Later that month, Deby announced that a National Conference, scheduled for May 1992, was to prepare a new Constitution to provide for the introduction of a multi-party system. Constitutional amendments permitting registration of political parties would enter into force in January 1992. In October 1991 the Council of Ministers announced the requirements for such registration, which included the prohibition of parties formed on an ethnic or regional basis. In the same month the Government suppressed an attempted military coup.

Troops loyal to Habré remained in opposition to the new regime; in September 1991 pro-Habré rebels attacked military garrisons in northern Chad. In December some 3,000 troops loyal to Habré attacked towns in the region of Lake Chad, in the west of the country. These operations were ascribed to the Mouvement pour la démocratie et le développement (MDD), an opposition group based in Libya, led by Goukouni Guët, a former supporter of Habré. In early January, however, the Government reported that the rebels had been defeated. Several prominent members of opposition groups were subsequently arrested on suspicion of complicity in the rebellion, and a number of these were reported to have been summarily executed. The French Government subsequently condemned the violation of human rights, and indicated that its continued support for Deby was dependent on the implementation of political reforms. The Deby regime responded by reiterating its commitment to the democratic process and declaring a general amnesty for political prisoners.

In late February 1992 a *coup d'état* was attempted by disaffected members of the armed forces, who attacked a police station in N'Djamena. However, opposition groups claimed that the incident had been fabricated by the Government, in an attempt to divert attention from the violence perpetrated by troops in the capital. In early April, following the expulsion from Chad of four French citizens suspected of involvement in the coup attempt, the French Government announced that it was to reduce its military support, although some 750 troops were to remain in the country to assist in the planned restructuring of ANT. This change in policy was widely interpreted as a warning to Deby to end the human rights violations perpetrated against opponents of the Government, and to continue the democratic process. In the same month the MDD claimed that more than 40 of its members, including Goukouni Guët, had been arrested in Nigeria, extradited to Chad, and subsequently imprisoned or executed.

In May 1992 the Government announced that the National Conference was to be postponed until September, on the grounds that the work of the preparatory commission had not been completed. Later in May a number of amendments to the National Charter were adopted, and in the same month Joseph Yodoyman, a member of an opposition movement, the Alliance nationale pour la démocratie et le développement (ANDD), was appointed as Prime Minister. Shortly afterwards, a new Council of Ministers was formed, which included, for the first time, members of a number of opposition parties and human rights organizations.

In late May 1992 rebels affiliated to the MDD launched a new offensive in the region of Lake Chad, which was reportedly led by a former minister in the GUNT, Moussa Medella Mahamat. In mid-June an agreement between the Government and the Comité de sursaut national pour la paix et la démocratie (CSNPD), the dissident faction of the armed forces which had staged the abortive coup attempt in February, provided for the release of detained members of the CSNPD, and their reintegration into the ANT. Later that month the Government announced that it had forestalled a coup attempt by an insurgent group known as the Conseil national de redressement du Tchad (CNRT). Subsequent guerrilla attacks by the CNRT in the region of Lake Chad were subdued by government forces during June. At the end of that month an agreement, which was signed in Libreville, Gabon, provided for a cessation of hostilities between government forces and the MDD. In early July a number of members of the MDD in detention were released under the terms of the agreement, although later that month MDD troops were reported again to be active in the region of Lake Chad.

In July 1992 members of the trade union federation, the Union syndicats du Tchad (UST), began a series of strikes, following an announcement by the Government of a planned reduction in salaries. Later in July Yodoyman was expelled from the ANDD for allegedly failing to support the democratic process. The Minister of Civil Service and Labour, Nabia Ndali, who was also a member of the ANDD, subsequently left the Government. A reorganization of the Council of Ministers took place in August, after three representatives of human rights organizations in the Government, including a member of the Ligue tchadienne des droits des Hommes (LTDH), resigned in protest at the continued violence perpetrated against civilians, after six people were killed by security forces in N'Djamena. In the same month clashes between members of the CSNPD and government forces were reported in Doba, in the south. In early September an agreement was reached by the Government and an opposition group based in Sudan, the Front national du Tchad (FNT), which granted the FNT the status of a political party. Later that month the Government signed further peace agreements with the MDD, and the CSNPD.

In October 1992 public-sector workers organized a one-month general strike, orchestrated by the UST, in support of demands for higher salaries and the convening of a national conference to determine the country's political future. Two representatives of former opposition parties in the Government resigned their ministerial portfolios in protest at the Government's subsequent suspension of the activities of the UST. Shortly afterwards, a minor reorganization of the Council of Ministers was effected. In mid-October the Government announced that the National Conference, which had been postponed since May, was to take place in January 1993. Later in October 1992 the MDD was reported to have initiated a renewed offensive against government forces at Bagassola, near Lake Chad; at the end of that month the MDD officially declared the peace agreement, signed in September, to be invalid, on the grounds that the Government had received armaments from Libya and was preparing to resume hostilities. In early November the UST extended the general strike for a further month; a number of prominent members of the UST were subsequently arrested. Later that month, however, the Government ended the ban that had been imposed on the UST in September. In December further clashes between government forces and members of the MDD were reported in the region of Lake Chad. In early January 1993 the Government withdrew sanctions that had been imposed on a number of civil servants, and the general strike ended.

In-mid January 1993 the National Conference (comprising representatives of the organs of state, political organizations, trade unions and professional organizations) was convened to prepare for the establishment of a democratic system of government. (Proceedings were subsequently delayed, however, as a result of various disagreements) In the same month, members of the CSNPD attacked government forces at Goré, in the south. Later in January an abortive coup attempt was staged by troops loyal to Habré; several of the rebels were subsequently arrested. In February government troops, who were engaged in conflict with the MDD in the region of Lake Chad, clashed with members of the Nigerien armed forces, after attacking rebel bases in Niger. In the same month, following renewed military engagements between government troops and CSNPD forces in southern Chad, opposition groups claimed that the Republican Guard (a special unit of the ANT, under the direct supervision of Deby) had massacred civilians in the region of Goré, in retaliation for local support for the CSNPD; by March some 15,000 people had fled to the Central African Republic (CAR), in response to the atrocities committed by government forces.

In early April 1993 the National Conference, which had received sovereign status, adopted a Transitional Charter, elected Dr Fidèle Moungar, hitherto the Minister of National and Higher Education, as Prime Minister, and established a 57-member interim legislature, the Conseil supérieur de la transition (CST). The leader of the Rassemblement pour la démocratie et le progrès (RDP), Lol Mahamat Choua (a former President), was elected Chairman of the CST. Under the terms of the Transitional Charter, Deby was to remain in office as Head of State and Commander-in-Chief of the Armed Forces for a period of one year (with provision for one extension), while a Transitional Government, under the supervision of the CST, was to implement economic, political and social programmes, which had been drafted by the conference; multi-party elections were to take place at the end of this period. Later in April Moungar announced the appointment of a Transitional Government, which included representatives of a number of opposition parties.

In early May 1993, following a report by a commission of inquiry, the Government confirmed that its forces had carried out massacres of civilians in southern Chad earlier that year, apparently in reprisal for hostilities initiated by the CSNPD. Moungar announced that members of the armed forces who were implicated in the violence had been arrested, that military units in the region were to be replaced, and that a judicial investigation was to be instituted. Meanwhile, the CSNPD refuted claims by the Government that it had initiated further attacks against members of the armed forces in the region of Goré. Also in May 1993 a human rights organization, Chad Non-Violence, withdrew its representative from the CST, in protest at the alleged failure of the Government to comply with the decisions of the National Conference. In June the CST refused to ratify the co-operation agreement that had been signed with Libya in November 1992, in view of the unresolved dispute over the sovereignty of the Aozou region. In late June Moungar reshuffled the Transitional Government. In the same month the Government introduced a number of new security measures, and subsequently announced that the ANT and other security forces were to be reorganized, in response to widespread public concern at the increasing incidence of violent crime in the country.

In early August 1993 armed men killed some 82 civilians in the region of Chokoyam, in the southern prefecture of Ouaddaï. Shortly afterwards, it was reported that some 41 people had been killed when a demonstration, staged by residents of N'Djamena originating from Ouaddaï (in protest at the massacre), was violently suppressed by the Republican Guard. The CST subsequently accused the Government of exceeding its powers by deploying the Republican Guard to disperse the demonstration, and by imposing a national curfew in response to the unrest. In mid-August the leader of the CNRT, Abbas Koti, returned to Chad, following an agreement with Deby, mediated by the Governments of Sudan and Libya. In October Koti agreed to the integration of CNRT forces into the ANT. Shortly afterwards, however, Koti was killed by security forces while allegedly resisting arrest on charges of implication in a conspiracy to overthrow the Government. Koti's brother, Eugène, subsequently assumed leadership of the CNRT.

In September 1993 disagreement between Deby and Moungar concerning the Government's economic policy intensified. In October a motion expressing 'no confidence' in the Moungar administration, apparently initiated by supporters of Deby, was approved in the CST. Moungar subsequently resigned and dissolved the Council of Ministers, but protested that the motion of 'no confidence' had contravened normal parliamentary procedure. In early November the CST elected Kassire Delwa Koumakoye, hitherto the Minister of Justice and Keeper of the Seals, as Prime Minister. Later that month a 16-member Transitional Government, which included 10 members of the former administration, was appointed.

In December 1993 a 17-member Institutional Committee, comprising representatives of the transitional organs and a number of political parties, was established to prepare a draft Constitution, an electoral code and legislation governing the registration of political parties. In the same month industrial action by public-sector workers (particularly by teachers), in protest at the Government's failure to pay arrears in salaries, resumed, and in January 1994 the Government threatened to implement sanctions against striking civil servants. Later in January the Transitional Government was reorganized. Meanwhile, opposition activity continued: the MDD and another dissident faction, the Union nationale pour la démocratie et le socialisme, announced that they were to operate jointly against government forces, while members of the FNT (who were to have been integrated into the ANT following the peace agreement with the Government) attacked a military garrison at Abéché. In February negotiations between the Chadian authorities and the CSNPD, which were mediated by the Government of the CAR, resulted in the drafting of a cease-fire agreement. The discussions subsequently ended in failure, however, and further clashes between government and CSNPD forces took place in southern Chad at the end of March. (However, the Government of the CAR prohibited the CSNPD from conducting military operations from CAR territory.)

In February 1994 the ICJ ruled in favour of Chad in the dispute over the sovereignty of the Aozou region (which had been submitted to that organization in 1990), thereby upholding a treaty that had been signed in 1955 by the Governments of France and Libya. Discussions held in March 1994 between Chad and Libya to formulate a timetable for the withdrawal of Libyan troops from the region made little progress, apparently owing to Libyan insistence on adherence to the provisions of the agreement that had been reached in 1989, which included the repatriation of Libyan prisoners of war. In April, however, Libya agreed to commence the withdrawal of troops from the region, in an operation that was monitored by UN observers and officials from both countries. At the end of May the Governments of Chad and Libya issued a joint statement, confirming that the withdrawal of Libyan troops had been completed as scheduled. In June a co-operation agreement consolidated relations between the two nations; however, France announced that its military support force (which then numbered some 800 troops) was to remain in Chad, despite demands from the Libyan Government for its withdrawal.

In March 1994 the Institutional Committee submitted constitutional recommendations, which included provisions for the election of a President for a term of five years, the installation of a bicameral legislature and a Constitutional Court, and the establishment of a decentralized administrative structure. In April, in accordance with demands by the opposition, the CST extended the transitional period for one year, on the grounds that the Government had achieved little progress in the preparation for democratic elections. A new electoral timetable was adopted, whereby the Government was obliged to provide funds for the organization of the elections, reach an agreement with the UST in order to end industrial unrest, and implement further preparatory measures by June, including the adoption of an electoral code, the establishment of a National Reconciliation Council (which was to negotiate a peace settlement with the rebel movements), and the appointment of electoral and human rights commissions; it was expected that the constitutional recommendations would be submitted for approval at a national referendum in December, and that democratic elections would take place in early 1995.

Government efforts to negotiate a settlement with the UST, in accordance with the new electoral timetable, were impeded by further strike action, which was initiated by public-sector workers at the end of April 1994, in support of demands for an increase in salaries to compensate for the effects of the devaluation of the CFA franc in January (see Economic Affairs). Despite the promulgation, at the beginning of May, of a presidential decree declaring the strike to be illegal, industrial action continued throughout that month. Also in May the Government established a 12-member National Reconciliation Council, which was to initiate negotiations with insurgent opposition groups. Later that month Deby extensively reshuffled the Council of Ministers. In early July the Government and the UST reached a negotiated settlement, which provided for a limited increase in salaries and the payment of arrears.

In August 1994, following the resumption of negotiations between the Chadian authorities and the CSNPD (with mediation by the Government of the Central African Republic), the two sides signed a cease-fire agreement, which provided for the recognition of the CSNPD as a legal political organization, and the integration of its forces into the ANT; the implementation of the agreement was to be supervised by a committee, comprising representatives of the UN and the Governments of the Central African Republic, France and Gabon. Later that month, however, it was reported that government troops had killed some 26 civilians in southern Chad, in reprisal for attacks by members of another rebel faction, known as the Forces armées pour la République fédérale (FARF). In mid-August the Government convened a four-day National Conference to allow the proposal of amendments to the draft Constitution; dissent was reported between government and opposition participants in the debate, particularly concerning the extent of the executive powers vested in the constitutional President.

In September 1994, following discussions between Koumakoye and the Sudanese Head of State regarding the occupation (in August) of Chadian villages near the border with Sudan by Sudanese troops, Chad and Sudan signed a co-operation agreement providing for a new demarcation of the frontier between the two countries. Also in September it was reported that the Minister of Mines and Energy, Lt-Col Mahamat Garfa (who had apparently resented his dismissal from the post of Chief of Army Staff), had fled N'Djamena with substantial government funds, and, together with some 600 members of the ANT, had joined CNRT forces in eastern Chad. In October Choua (who had previously been re-elected twice as Chairman of the CST) was replaced by a member of the MPS, Mahamat Bachar Ghadaia. Choua subsequently accused the Government of committing human rights violations, including the assassination of two prominent members of the RDP. Also in October the Government and the FNT negotiated a peace agreement, which was, however, subsequently repudiated by the leader of the FNT. In November a number of former members of the CSNPD, including the leader of the movement, Lt Moïse Nodji Kette, were integrated into the ANT in accordance with the agreement signed by the CSNPD and the Government in August. Later in November Deby officially announced that the process of democratic transition would conclude on 9 April 1995, following presidential and legislative elections. (A number of opposition alliances had been formed in preparation for the forthcoming elections, including a coalition led by Moungar, the Collectif des partis pour le changement, which demanded the establishment of an independent electoral commission.)

In early December 1994 Deby declared a general amnesty for political prisoners and opposition members in exile (excluding Habré); a number of political detainees were subsequently released. Nevertheless, the LTDH continued to allege violations of human rights by the ANT in its suppression of rebel activity. Later in December a minor reorganization of the Transitional Government took place. In the same month an Independent National Electoral Commission was established. In January 1995 the CST adopted a new electoral code, after the French Government expressed concern at delays in the preparation for democratic elections. Later that month the CST approved the draft Constitution, which had been amended in accordance with recommendations reached by consensus at the National Conference in August; the Constitution was to be submitted for ratification at a national referendum. In February an informal grouping of the opposition movements, known as the Concertation des partis politiques (CPP), demanded that the transitional organs of government be dissolved and a new administration installed by the stipulated date in April.

In February 1995 the Government carried out a population census prior to revising the electoral register; following reports of widespread irregularities, however, opposition parties accused the MPS of attempted electoral malpractice and demanded that a new census be held. On 30 March the CST extended the transitional period for a further year and amended the National Charter to debar the incumbent Prime Minister from contesting the forthcoming presidential election or from belonging to a political party. These measures attracted strong criticism from opposition parties, which subsequently instituted a legal challenge to the extension of the transitional period at the Court of Appeal. In early April the CST, which had criticized the Government's lack of progress in the organization of democratic elections, voted in favour of Koumakoye's removal from the office of Prime Minister. (Koumakoye opposed his dismissal, which he declared to be unconstitutional.) On 8 April the CST elected Djimasta Koibla, a prominent member of the Union pour la démocratie et la République, as Prime Minister. A new Transitional Government was subsequently formed, in which Kette received a ministerial portfolio. In the same month the results of the population census were annulled by the Court of Appeal, on the grounds of procedural irregularities.

In May 1995 Amnesty International and the LTDH claimed that members of the ANT had perpetrated violations of human rights against civilians in retaliation for rebel attacks. In June members of the armed forces raided the premises of an independent newspaper, *N'Djamena-Hebdo*, which had published an article criticizing the activities of the ANT. Deby subsequently announced an inquiry into the incident, in response to ensuing protests. Later that month the authorities prohibited a demonstration which had been planned by the opposition in protest at the Government's continued failure to improve democratic conditions. In July a unilateral government declaration of a national cease-fire was received with caution by the rebel movements. Later that month Koumakoye announced that he was to contest the forthcoming presidential election. Also in July the Chadian Government claimed that Nigerian troops had occupied a number of islands in the region of Lake Chad (which were under the sovereignty of Chad).

In August 1995 the Chairman and other members of the Executive Bureau of the CST resigned, following accusations regarding the misappropriation of funds; a new Chairman was subsequently elected. At the end of that month security forces raided the private residence of Saleh Kebzabo, the leader of an opposition movement, the Union nationale pour le développement et le renouveau (UNDR). The CPP subsequently announced that its member organizations were to suspend participation in the CST and the National Reconcilation Council, in protest at the raid, and demanded the resignation of the head of security forces. In September, however, Kebzabo was arrested and charged with endangering state security by associating with rebel groups, prompting further protests from the CPP, urging his release. (Kebzabo was released on bail later that month.) In early November Deby announced that Gabon was to act as a mediator in reconciliation discussions between the Government and political organizations and armed opposition groups, which were to be convened in December. However, a number of rebel movements subsequently presented preconditions to participation in the negotiations, including the dissolution of the national security agency. Later that month the Government and the MDD agreed to a cease-fire (to take effect at the end of November), an exchange of prisoners and the integration of a number of MDD troops into the ANT. Also in November the Independent National Electoral Commission promulgated a further timetable whereby a constitutional referendum was to take place at the end of March 1996, followed by a presidential election in early June and legislative elections later that year. A new population census commenced in December 1995. In the same month a minor reorganization of the Transitional Government took place. The reconciliation discussions between the Government and rebel movements were convened in Franceville, Gabon, in early January 1996. In March the Government and 13 opposition parties signed an agreement providing for a cease-fire and the establishment of a special security force to maintain order during the electoral period; it was reported, however, that the majority of the armed movements had rejected the agreement.

The conclusion of the Franceville agreement allowed the electoral timetable to proceed as scheduled. A number of opposition parties, particularly the southern-based organizations that supported the adoption of a federal system of government, urged their members to reject the draft Constitution (which enshrined a unitary state) at the national referendum; despite this opposition, the new Constitution was adopted by 63.5% of votes cast at the referendum, which took place on 31 March 1996. It was subsequently announced that the multi-party presidential election was to take place in June, as planned. By April 15 presidential candidates, including Deby, had emerged; a further five prospective candidates (including Moungar) had been rejected on the grounds that they failed to meet electoral regulations concerning residency in the country. In the same month a minor government reorganization was effected, after two ministers who had announced their candidature in the forthcoming election resigned their portfolios. Meanwhile, Koumakoye, who in March had been jailed for three months for the illegal possession of arms, was released shortly before the election. The first round of voting took place on 2 June: Deby secured 43.8% of votes cast, while Kamougue, who had contested the election on behalf of the Union pour le renouveau et la démocratie (URD), obtained the second-highest number of votes, with 12.4%. Opposition parties subsequently claimed that the French Government had supported efforts by the Chadian authorities to perpetrate electoral fraud, while the majority of the candidates who had been eliminated urged a boycott of the second round. Following the first round of voting, Kebzabo, who had contested the first round on behalf of the UNDR and had obtained the third-highest number of votes, agreed to transfer support to Deby. In early July the Government suspended the activities of the UST, after it attempted to organize a boycott of the election; the suspension was withdrawn at the end of that month.

The second round of the presidential election took place on 3 July 1996: according to official results, Deby was elected by 69.1% of votes cast (while Kamougue secured 30.9% of votes). Deby was inaugurated as President on 8 August, and subsequently reappointed Koibla to the office of Prime Minister. Later that month Koibla announced the formation of an interim Council of Ministers, which included several opposition members, notably Kebzabo (who, in exchange for his support for Deby in the second round, received the portfolio of foreign affairs). Kamougue, however, refused to join the Government until the legislative elections had taken place.

In early August 1996 the CNRT merged with another dissident faction, the Front d'action pour l'installation de la démocratie au Tchad (FAIDT), to form the Congrès pour le renouveau et la démocratie. Later that month the Government and elements of the FARF signed a peace agreement, which provided for the imposition of a cease-fire and an amnesty for members of the faction, which was to be reconstituted as a legal political organization, to be known as the Front patriotique pour la démocratie. In mid-September a further rebel movement, the Front national du Tchad renové (FNTR), threatened to abandon plans for peace negotiations with the Chadian authorities, after claiming that government forces had launched attacks against FNTR positions in eastern Chad. The Government and the MDD signed a peace agreement in Niger at the end of September, which provided for a cease-fire and an amnesty for all members of the movement. In the following month Deby announced that he had dispatched an adviser to meet representatives of other dissident factions, in an attempt to initiate peace negotiations.

In early October 1996 Amnesty International published a report accusing France of complicity in alleged violations of human rights in Chad; the allegations were denied by the French Government. While the Deby Government appeared to concede that problems existed (and, in particular, that further training of the security forces might be necessary), it asserted that French training of Chadian troops had, in effect, improved the observance of human rights. In the same month the French Minister of Defence announced that, as a result of Chad's improved relations with neighbouring states, the terms of the French military presence were to be redefined, but with no reduction in the number of troops deployed. In mid-October the CST ratified a number of agreements with Libya concerning co-operation between the two countries in areas such as culture and trade. Legislative elections, which had already been postponed in October, were delayed further in November.

In early January 1997 the International Federation of Human Rights Leagues (FIDH) expressed its concern over a number of summary executions of individuals suspected of theft that had been carried out by the security forces in Chad over the preceding weeks, and accused the Government of responsibility for the killings. The Government did not dispute reports that many such executions had taken place, and openly admitted having authorized them; however, in early March, following the adoption by the European Parliament of a resolution condemning Chad for serious violations of human rights, the Government suspended the executions.

Legislative elections, postponed in October and November of 1996, eventually took place in two rounds on 5 January and 23 February 1997. Preliminary results were announced in early March, but were challenged by both the MPS and opposition parties (who claimed that there had been serious irregularities in the second round of voting). Later that month the Court of Appeal announced the final election results, in which a further eight seats were allocated to the MPS. The MPS thus ultimately secured an absolute majority with a final total of 65 seats, while the URD obtained 29 seats, the UNDR 15, the Union pour la démocratie et la république four, the Parti pour la liberté et la démocratie and the RDP three each, while a further five opposition groups each secured six seats. The new National Assembly was installed on 4 April.

On 18 April 1997 the Government and the FARF signed a peace agreement providing for the cessation of all hostile military activities between the Chadian National Army and the FARF, a general amnesty for FARF members, the integration of its civil and military members into the state apparatus and the transformation of the armed movement into a legalized political party. In early May tension arose between Chad and Libya over the expulsion by Libya of a number of Chadian nationals. On 9 May Gen. Wadal Abdelkader Kamougue was re-elected President of the National Assembly by a substantial majority, following an accord between his party (the URD), the MPS and the UNDR. On 16 May Prime Minister Djimasta Koibla tendered his resignation and that of his Government; on the same day Nassour Ouaido (hitherto Secretary-General at the President's Office) was appointed to succeed Koibla. Later in May an extensive government reorganization took place, in which 16 new ministers were appointed and a new state ministry was created. The new Council of Ministers included representatives from a range of political parties, although the MPS retained the most senior ministerial portfolios. A further reorganization of the Council of Ministers was announced on 1 January 1998.

On 12 August 1997 Chad re-established diplomatic ties with Taiwan. The People's Republic of China announced a few days later that, in response, it was severing diplomatic relations with Chad with immediate effect. In August the Chadian Government was reported to have negotiated a peace agreement with Goukouni's FROLINAT. On 24 August a new opposition group, the Résistance armée contre les forces antidémocratique (RAFAD), announced its formation in Nigeria, with the stated aim of deposing the Deby Government by force. At the end of August, at a conference in N'Djamena, the leaders of 21 opposition parties denounced the continuing presence of French troops in Chad as a reinforcement of the personal rule of President Deby.

At the beginning of October 1997 a three-day meeting was convened in N'Djamena between representatives of the Government and those of the FNT, the FNTR and the Mouvement pour la justice sociale et la démocratie (MJSD). The purpose of the meeting was to seek conditions for the legalization of the three organizations; the Government offered a general amnesty to members of the groups and also undertook to organize the return of refugees associated with them. Later that month the Government announced that a Force d'intervention rapide (FIR—Rapid Intervention Force) was to be established within the Chadian army, placed under the direct control of the President. On 30 October clashes erupted in Moundou between the army and former FARF rebels, in which two soldiers and about 40 former rebels were reported to have been killed, together with 10 civilians. The clashes provoked concern over the future of the reconciliation process between the Government and the FARF rebels, the foundations for which had been laid in April with the signing of a peace agreement by the two sides. Following the clashes, FARF rebels accused the Government of reneging on promises made earlier in the year; the Government, in response, made a commitment to pursue reconciliation and to expedite the reintegration of rebel forces.

Government

A new Constitution was adopted by national referendum on 31 March 1996. Under the terms of the Constitution, the Republic of Chad is a unitary state with a multi-party political system. Executive power is vested in the President, who is the Head of State and Commander-in-Chief of the Armed Forces. The President is elected by direct universal suffrage for a maximum of two five-year terms of office. The President appoints the Prime Minister, who nominates the Council of Ministers. Legislative power is vested in a bicameral legislature, comprising the 125-member National Assembly, which is elected by direct universal suffrage for a four-year term, and the Senate, which has a six-year mandate (with one-third of the membership renewable every two years). The new National Assembly was installed on 4 April 1997. By early 1998 the Senate had not yet been established.

Defence

In August 1996 the Armée nationale tchadienne (ANT) was estimated to number 30,350 (army approximately 25,000, air force 350, Republican Guard 5,000). In addition, there was a 4,500-strong gendarmerie. In September of that year it was announced that the army was to be restructured and the number of troops reduced, with financial support from the World Bank and the French Government; in April 1997 it was announced that the army had been reduced in size from 30,000 to about 20,000 soldiers, with a total of 9,500 soldiers leaving. Military service is by conscription for three years. Under defence agreements with France, the army receives technical and other aid: in August 1997 the number of troops deployed in Chad by France numbered 800. Defence expenditure in 1997 was budgeted at an estimated 25,000m. francs CFA.

Economic Affairs

In 1995, according to estimates by the World Bank, Chad's gross national product (GNP), measured at average 1993–95 prices, was US $1,144m., equivalent to $180 per head (one of the lowest per caput levels in the world). During 1985–95, it was estimated, GNP per head increased, in real terms, at an average annual rate of 0.5%. Over the same period, the population increased by an annual average of 2.5%. According to the World Bank, Chad's gross domestic product (GDP) increased, in real terms, by an average of 3.2% per year in 1985–95. According to the IMF, GDP increased by 3.7% in 1995 and by 2.7% in 1996.

Agriculture (including forestry and fishing) contributed an estimated 45.5% of GDP in 1996, and an estimated 80.3% of the labour force were employed in the sector in the same year. Most agricultural activity is concentrated in the south of the country. The principal cash crop is cotton. The principal subsistence crops are millet, sorghum and groundnuts. Livestock-rearing makes an important contribution both to the domestic food supply and to export earnings, although illicit trade accounts for a significant proportion of the output. During 1985–95, according to the World Bank, agricultural GDP increased by an annual average of 4.9%. According to the IMF, agricultural GDP declined by 1.7% in 1995 and by 1.6% in 1996.

Industry (including mining, manufacturing, construction and power) contributed an estimated 15.1% of GDP in 1996. About 4.6% of the population were employed in the sector in 1980. During 1985–95, according to the World Bank, industrial GDP increased by an annual average of 1.6%. According to the IMF, industrial GDP increased by 12.0% in 1995 and by 6.0% in 1996.

The mining sector contributed only 0.5% of GDP in 1991: the only significant activity is the extraction of natron. The commercial development of considerable petroleum resources has been impeded by the uncertain political situation. In 1996, however, some progress was made, when the Governments of Chad and Cameroon signed an agreement on the construction of a pipeline to export petroleum from recently-discovered oilfields in southern Chad through Cameroon; the project was widely perceived to have significant economic potential. Deposits of tungsten, cassiterite (tin ore), bauxite, gold, iron ore, titanium, limestone and kaolin have been located, but their exploitation is minimal. The Aozou region, which was returned to Chad in 1994 (following a protracted territorial dispute with Libya), is believed to contain valuable reserves of uranium and other minerals. A new mining law, introduced in 1995, was expected to encourage the development of new mining projects in Chad.

The manufacturing sector, which contributed an estimated 13.4% of GDP in 1996, operates mainly in the south of the country, and is dominated by agro-industrial activities, notably the processing of the cotton crop by the Société Cotonnière du Tchad (COTONTCHAD, the state-owned cotton monopoly). A sugar-refining complex is also in operation. According to the World Bank, manufacturing GDP increased by an annual average of 1.9% in 1985–95. The GDP of the sector rose, according to the IMF, by 13.7% in 1995 and by 5.9% in 1996.

Chad is heavily dependent on imports of mineral fuels (principally from Cameroon and Nigeria) for the generation of electricity. Imports of fuel products comprised an estimated 3.5% of the total value of imports in 1995. The use of wood-based fuel products by most households has contributed to the severe depletion of Chad's forest resources.

Services contributed an estimated 39.3% of GDP in 1996. According to the World Bank, the GDP of the sector increased by an average of 1.9% per year in 1985–95. Services GDP rose, according to the IMF, by 6.5% in 1995 and by 2.5% in 1996.

In 1994 Chad recorded a visible trade deficit of US $76.8m., and there was a deficit of $37.7m. on the current account of the balance of payments. In 1986 Chad's principal source of imports (37%) was France; other major suppliers were Cameroon, the USA and Nigeria. The principal market for exports in that year was Cameroon (which received 50% of Chadian export commodities); France was also a significant purchaser. The principal export is cotton. Exports of raw cotton contributed 80% of total export earnings in 1990; by 1996, however, the contribution of cotton to export earnings had declined to approximately 42%. The principal imports in 1983 were petroleum products, cereals, pharmaceuticals, chemicals, machinery and transport and electrical equipment.

In 1996 Chad recorded an estimated budgetary deficit of 70,545m. francs CFA (equivalent to 11.8% of GDP). Chad's external debt at the end of 1995 totalled US $908.4m., of which $839.6m. was long-term public debt. In that year the cost of debt-servicing was equivalent to about 5.9% of earnings from exports of goods and services (the low ratio reflecting the highly concessionary nature of most of the country's aid inflows). In 1985–95 the average annual rate of inflation was 2.7%. Consumer prices, which declined in 1992 and 1993 prior to the 50% devaluation of the CFA franc, increased dramatically: inflation reached 40.4% in 1994, but slowed to 9.1% in 1995. Average prices increased by about 12% in 1996.

Chad is a member of the Central African organs of the Franc Zone (see p. 181) and of the Communauté économique des etats de l'Afrique centrale (CEEAC, see p. 260).

Sustained economic growth in Chad has been inhibited by a number of factors: the protracted civil conflict; dependence on an agricultural sector lacking in diversification and vulnerable to adverse climatic conditions; the failure to exploit considerable mineral resources; and the inadequacy of the transport infrastructure. From late 1990 the economy deteriorated severely; structural reform programmes ceased, and Chad became increasingly dependent on bilateral and multilateral credit to finance the substantial budgetary deficit. In March 1994 the Government adopted a stand-by programme in agreement with the IMF, but failed to comply with the stipulations of the agreement. In September 1995 the IMF approved a series of loans under a three-year enhanced structural adjustment facility, which was to support an economic programme for 1995–98; the programme laid emphasis on the further expansion of the private sector, and was designed to improve GDP growth and to reduce the current account deficit and the rate of inflation (which had increased dramatically following the devaluation of the CFA franc in January 1994). Economic conditions improved generally throughout 1994, with strong recovery in real GDP and a reduction in imports. Economic growth was sustained in 1995 and 1996; the rate of inflation slowed and a surplus was recorded in the trade balance, while progress was achieved in the privatization programme. The effective cessation of the civil conflict, in late 1995, resulted in an increase in foreign investment, particularly in the field of petroleum exploration. In late 1996 the IMF approved the second in a series of several loans for Chad originally agreed in September 1995; the loan was intended to support the Government's 1996/97 macroeconomic and structural adjustment programme. Also in late 1996 the Exxon Corporation agreed to invest US $3,000m. in the development of large oil reserves in the Doba basin, leading a consortium which also included the petroleum companies Shell and Elf. The venture, which was to be the first commercial petroleum project ever undertaken in Chad, was to entail the construction of a 1,050-km export pipeline, partly financed by the World Bank, running from the south of Chad to the port of Kribi in Cameroon. There was some concern over the environmental and political implications of the planned development; however, the project was expected to provide a tremendous boost to the struggling Chadian economy. In 1997 economic objectives included the further reduction of the rate of inflation and the external current account deficit.

Social Welfare

An Employment Code guarantees a minimum wage and other rights for employees. There are four hospitals, 28 medical centres and several hundred dispensaries. In 1978 there were 3,373 beds in government-administered hospital establishments (one per 1,278 inhabitants), while only 90 physicians were employed in official medical services. In mid-1994 the International Development Association approved loans of US $18.5m. to finance improvements to Chad's health system, including the construction of further medical clinics.

Education

Education is officially compulsory for eight years between six and 14 years of age. Primary education begins at the age of six and lasts for six years. Secondary education, from the age of 12, lasts for seven years, comprising a first cycle of four years and a second of three years. In 1996 primary enrolment was equivalent to 63.9% of children in the relevant age-group (79.6% of boys; 48% of girls), while the comparable ratio for secondary enrolment was only 9.1%. The Université du Tchad was opened at N'Djamena in 1971. In addition, there are several technical colleges. In 1989 the African Development Bank approved a loan of more than 3,500m. francs CFA for the construction of 40 primary schools. Total expenditure on education by the central Government (including foreign-financed investment) in 1996 was 32,196m. francs CFA (21.2% of total government expenditure). In 1995, according to estimates by UNESCO, the average rate of adult illiteracy was 51.9% (males 37.9%; females 65.3%).

Public Holidays

1998: 1 January (New Year), 30 January* (Id al-Fitr, end of Ramadan), 8 April* (Id al-Adha, Feast of the Sacrifice), 13 April (Easter Monday), 1 May (Labour Day), 25 May ('Liberation of Africa', anniversary of the OAU's foundation), 1 June (Whit Monday), 7 July* (Maloud, Birth of the Prophet), 11 August (Independence Day), 15 August (Assumption), 1 November (All Saints' Day), 28 November (Proclamation of the Republic), 25 December (Christmas).

1999: 1 January (New Year), 19 January* (Id al-Fitr, end of Ramadan), 28 March* (Id al-Adha, Feast of the Sacrifice), 5 April (Easter Monday), 1 May (Labour Day), 24 May (Whit Monday), 25 May ('Liberation of Africa', anniversary of the OAU's foundation), 26 June* (Maloud, Birth of the Prophet), 11 August (Independence Day), 15 August (Assumption), 1 November (All Saints' Day), 28 November (Proclamation of the Republic), 25 December (Christmas).

* These holidays are dependent on the Islamic lunar calendar and may vary by one or two days from the dates given.

Weights and Measures

The metric system is officially in force.

Statistical Survey

Source (unless otherwise stated): Direction de la Statistique, des Etudes Economiques et Démographiques, BP 453, N'Djamena.

Area and Population

AREA, POPULATION AND DENSITY

Area (sq km)	
Land	1,259,200
Inland waters	24,800
Total	1,284,000*
Population (sample survey)	
December 1963–August 1964	3,254,000†
Population (census result)	
8 April 1993‡	
Males	2,950,415
Females	3,208,577
Total	6,158,992
Population (official estimate at mid-year)	
1994	6,214,000§
Density (per sq km) at mid-1994	4.9§

* 495,800 sq miles.

† Including areas not covered by the survey.

‡ Figures are provisional. The revised total, including an adjustment for underenumeration (estimated at 1.4%), is 6,279,931.

§ Not revised to take account of the 1993 census result (see above).

PREFECTURES (official estimates, mid-1988)

	Area (sq km)	Population	Density (per sq km)
Batha	88,800	431,000	4.9
Biltine	46,850	216,000	4.6
Borkou-Ennedi-Tibesti (BET)	600,350	109,000	0.2
Chari-Baguirmi	82,910	844,000	10.2
Guera	58,950	254,000	4.3
Kanem	114,520	245,000	2.1
Lac	22,320	165,000	7.4
Logone Occidental	8,695	365,000	42.0
Logone Oriental	28,035	377,000	13.4
Mayo-Kebbi	30,105	852,000	28.3
Moyen Chari	45,180	646,000	14.3
Ouaddaï	76,240	422,000	5.5
Salamat	63,000	131,000	2.1
Tandjilé	18,045	371,000	20.6
Total	1,284,000	5,428,000	4.2

PRINCIPAL TOWNS (officially-estimated population in 1988)

N'Djamena (capital)	594,000	Moundou	102,000
Sarh	113,400	Abéché	83,000

BIRTHS AND DEATHS (UN estimates, annual averages)

	1980–85	1985–90	1990–95
Birth rate (per 1,000)	44.2	43.9	43.7
Death rate (per 1,000)	21.4	19.5	18.0

Expectation of life (UN estimates, years at birth, 1990–95): 47.5 (males 45.9; females 49.1).

Source: UN, *World Population Prospects: The 1994 Revision*.

ECONOMICALLY ACTIVE POPULATION
(ILO estimates, '000 persons at mid-1980)

	Males	Females	Total
Agriculture, etc.	1,043	318	1,361
Industry	72	4	76
Services	154	44	197
Total labour force	1,269	366	1,635

Source: ILO, *Economically Active Population Estimates and Projections, 1950–2025*.

Mid-1988 (official estimates, persons aged 10 years and over): Total labour force 2,032,401 (males 1,547,626; females 484,775) (Source: ILO, *Yearbook of Labour Statistics*).

Mid-1996 (estimates in '000): Agriculture 2,539; Total 3,161 (Source: FAO, *Production Yearbook*).

Agriculture

PRINCIPAL CROPS ('000 metric tons)

	1994	1995	1996
Wheat	2	3	1
Rice (paddy)	91	79	87
Maize	159	63	60
Millet	307	228	239
Sorghum	379	437	453
Other cereals	121	97	91
Potatoes	8	8*	8*
Sweet potatoes	47*	58	58
Cassava (Manioc)	195	195*	195*
Yams*	240	240	240
Taro (Coco yam)	38	38*	38*
Dry beans	12	12*	12*
Other pulses	22	22*	22*
Groundnuts (in shell)	207	305	305*
Sesame seed	13	10	10*
Cottonseed*	75	90	125
Cotton (lint)	45†	61	75*
Dry onions*	14	14	14
Other vegetables*	60	60	60
Dates	18	18*	18*
Mangoes*	32	32	32
Other fruit*	50	50	50
Sugar cane	308	315*	330

* FAO estimate(s). † Unofficial figure.

Source: FAO, *Production Yearbook*.

LIVESTOCK ('000 head, year ending September)

	1994	1995	1996*
Cattle	4,621	4,539	4,539
Goats	3,178	3,271	3,271
Sheep	2,152	2,219	2,219
Pigs	17	18	18
Horses	214	218*	218
Asses	253	252*	252
Camels	593	600*	600

* FAO estimate(s).

Poultry (FAO estimates, million): 4 in 1994; 4 in 1995; 4 in 1996.

Source: FAO, *Production Yearbook*.

LIVESTOCK PRODUCTS (FAO estimates,'000 metric tons)

	1994	1995	1996
Total meat	98	98	98
Beef and veal	68	68	68
Mutton and lamb	10	10	10
Goat meat	11	11	11
Poultry meat	4	4	4
Cows' milk	123	123	123
Sheep's milk	9	9	9
Goats' milk	16	16	16
Hen eggs	4	4	4
Cattle hides	10	10	10
Sheep skins	2	2	2
Goat skins	2	2	2

Source: FAO, *Production Yearbook*.

Forestry

ROUNDWOOD REMOVALS
('000 cubic metres, excluding bark)

	1992	1993	1994
Sawlogs, veneer logs and logs for sleepers	8	14	14*
Other industrial wood*	585	602	619
Fuel wood*	3,568	3,667	3,773
Total	4,161	4,283	4,406*

* FAO estimate(s).

Source: FAO, *Yearbook of Forest Products*.

Fishing

('000 metric tons, live weight)

	1993	1994	1995
Total catch (freshwater fishes)	87.3	80.0	60.0

Source: FAO, *Yearbook of Fishery Statistics*.

Industry

SELECTED PRODUCTS
('000 metric tons, unless otherwise indicated)

	1994	1995	1996
Salted, dried or smoked fish	15.0	n.a.	n.a.
Edible oil ('000 hectolitres)	86.9	117.0	125.5
Sugar	26.7	26.2	32.5
Beer ('000 hectolitres)	107.7	101.3	118.2
Soft drinks ('000 hectolitres)	26	n.a.	n.a.
Cigarettes (million)	508	570	700
Woven cotton fabrics (million metres)	0.2	0.2	0.8
Electric energy (million kWh)	84.7	89.2	92.1

Source: mainly IMF, *Chad—Statistical Annex* (August 1997).

Finance

CURRENCY AND EXCHANGE RATES

Monetary Units

100 centimes = 1 franc de la Coopération financière en Afrique centrale (CFA).

French Franc, Sterling and Dollar Equivalents (30 September 1997)
1 French franc = 100 francs CFA;
£1 sterling = 958.3 francs CFA;
US $1 = 593.2 francs CFA;
1,000 francs CFA = £1.044 = $1.686.

Average Exchange Rate (francs CFA per US $)
1994 555.20
1995 499.15
1996 511.55

Note: The exchange rate of 1 French franc = 50 francs CFA, established in 1948, remained in force until January 1994, when the CFA franc was devalued by 50%, with the exchange rate adjusted to 1 French franc = 100 francs CFA.

BUDGET (million francs CFA)

Revenue*	1994	1995	1996
Tax revenue	25,779	37,436	53,042
Taxes on income and profits	8,695	16,630	21,507
Companies	3,073	8,395	11,919
Individuals	4,614	7,189	8,475
Employers' payroll tax	1,009	1,046	1,113
Taxes on goods and services	8,337	6,578	11,085
Turnover tax	3,080	1,728	6,501
Tax on petroleum products	2,254	2,046	2,860
Single tax	2,519	2,015	350
Taxes on international trade	6,199	12,166	18,557
Import taxes	4,944	9,600	16,987
Export taxes	1,049	1,432	924
Other tax revenues	2,547	2,062	1,893
Other revenue	5,387	7,398	6,511
Property income	350	1,246	427
Total	31,166	44,834	59,553

Expenditure†	1994	1995	1996
Current expenditure	65,481	64,684	77,195
Primary current expenditure	55,980	56,923	64,380
Wages and salaries	25,968	30,109	30,772
Materials and supplies	12,664	11,851	17,064
Transfers	5,015	4,963	3,863
Defence	12,333	10,000	12,681
Salaries	8,996	7,100	10,741
Materials and supplies	3,337	2,900	1,940
Elections	0	0	3,808
Interest	7,634	7,261	8,412
External	6,503	6,301	7,069
Investment expenditure	59,229	65,620	74,599
Foreign-financed	58,030	65,300	74,000
Total	124,710	130,304	151,794

* Excluding grants received (million francs CFA): 61,998 in 1994; 53,668 in 1995; 50,617 in 1996.

† Excluding adjustment for payments arrears.

Note: Figures include the operations of the extrabudgetary Caisse Autonome d'Amortissement.

Source: IMF, *Chad—Statistical Annex* (August 1997).

INTERNATIONAL RESERVES
(US $ million, at 31 December)

	1993	1994	1995
Gold*	4.42	n.a.	n.a.
IMF special drawing rights	0.01	—	0.03
Reserve position in IMF	0.38	0.41	0.42
Foreign exchange	38.54	75.60	142.07
Total	43.36	n.a.	n.a.

* Valued at market-related prices.

1996 (US $ million, at 31 December): IMF special drawing rights 0.24; Reserve position in IMF 0.40; Foreign exchange 163.84.

Source: IMF, *International Financial Statistics*.

MONEY SUPPLY ('000 million francs CFA at 31 December)

	1994	1995	1996
Currency outside banks	39.69	61.98	91.82
Demand deposits at commercial and development banks	18.73	20.68	22.98
Total money (incl. others)	59.79	85.33	114.80

Source: IMF, *International Financial Statistics*.

COST OF LIVING (Consumer Price Index for African households in N'Djamena; base: February 1988 = 100)

	1994	1995	1996
Food	129.5	138.4	158.3
Other commodities	127.6	155.4	167.5
Services	126.8	133.3	147.7
All items	131.1	143.0	159.9

Source: IMF, *Chad—Statistical Annex* (August 1997).

NATIONAL ACCOUNTS

Expenditure on the Gross Domestic Product
('000 million francs CFA at current prices)

	1994	1995	1995
Government final consumption expenditure	71.7	72.4	80.1
Private final consumption expenditure	426.0	445.3	503.3
Gross capital formation	86.1	93.7	116.1
Total domestic expenditure	583.8	611.4	699.6
Exports of goods and services	105.5	156.5	166.5
Less Imports of goods and services	228.5	242.5	266.6
GDP in purchasers' values	460.9	525.4	599.5
GDP at constant 1977 prices	215.1	223.1	229.1

Source: IMF, *Chad—Statistical Annex* (August 1997).

Gross Domestic Product by Economic Activity
(estimates, million francs CFA at constant 1977 prices)

	1994	1995	1996
Agriculture	102,188	100,489	98,931
Mining and quarrying; Electricity, gas and water	1,684	1,736	1,833
Manufacturing	24,172	27,494	29,109
Construction	1,801	1,753	1,909
Wholesale and retail trade, restaurants and hotels; Transport and communications	56,819	61,321	63,176
Other services	21,486	22,052	22,257
GDP at factor cost	208,150	214,845	217,215
Indirect taxes, *less* subsidies	6,970	8,224	11,843
GDP in purchasers' values	215,120	223,069	229,058

Source: IMF, *Chad—Statistical Annex* (August 1997).

BALANCE OF PAYMENTS (US $ million)

	1992	1993	1994
Exports of goods f.o.b.	182.3	151.8	135.3
Imports of goods f.o.b.	−243.0	−215.2	−212.1
Trade balance	−60.7	−63.5	−76.8
Exports of services	26.7	47.1	54.8
Imports of services	−224.1	−235.1	−199.4
Balance on goods and services	−258.1	−251.4	−221.4
Other income received	17.5	4.3	5.0
Other income paid	−14.9	−15.7	−12.4
Balance on goods, services and income	−255.5	−262.9	−228.7
Current transfers received	222.3	192.4	209.4
Current transfers paid	−52.5	−46.2	−18.4
Current balance	−85.7	−116.6	−37.7
Direct investment abroad	−13.8	−10.9	−0.6
Direct investment from abroad	2.0	15.2	27.1
Other investment assets	3.9	42.1	0.6
Other investment liabilities	41.6	22.5	49.2
Net errors and omissions	9.2	−0.1	−33.0
Overall balance	−42.8	−47.9	5.5

Source: IMF, *International Financial Statistics*.

External Trade

PRINCIPAL COMMODITIES (million francs CFA)

Imports	1983
Beverages	71.7
Cereal products	2,272.1
Sugar, confectionery, chocolate	292.7
Petroleum products	2,280.5
Textiles, clothing, etc.	392.1
Pharmaceuticals, chemicals	1,561.9
Minerals and metals	311.2
Machinery	843.2
Transport equipment	987.6
Electrical equipment	773.3
Total (incl. others)	13,539.6

Total imports (million francs CFA): 74,708 in 1985; 73,437 in 1986; 67,894 in 1987; 68,000 in 1988; 75,100 in 1989; 77,742 in 1990; 70,500 in 1991; 64,320 in 1992; 56,910 in 1993; 98,310 in 1994; 109,720 in 1995. (Source: Banque des Etats de l'Afrique Centrale).

Exports	1983
Live cattle	49.5
Meat	23.5
Fish	2.0
Oil-cake	8.1
Natron	8.1
Gums and resins	0.4
Hides and skins	16.6
Raw cotton	3,753.7
Total (incl. others)	4,120.0

Total exports (million francs CFA): 27,781 in 1985; 34,145 in 1986; 32,892 in 1987; 42,900 in 1988; 49,570 in 1989; 51,202 in 1990; 54,600 in 1991; 48,250 in 1992; 37,330 in 1993; 82,160 in 1994; 125,600 in 1995. (Source: Banque des Etats de l'Afrique Centrale).

Cotton exports ('000 million francs CFA): 26.8 in 1991; 25.3 in 1992.

PRINCIPAL TRADING PARTNERS (million francs CFA)

Imports	1984	1985	1986
Belgium/Luxembourg	435	520	1,712
Cameroon	3,461	12,371	8,777
China, People's Repub.	n.a.	39	896
Congo	417	519	395
France	22,132	14,439	21,772
Germany, Fed. Repub.	1,322	1,562	2,876
Italy	3,133	2,874	3,263
Netherlands	777	1,950	2,017
Nigeria	4,817	4,368	5,673
USA	4,095	9,247	7,670
Total (incl. others)	45,759	51,520	58,831

Exports	1984	1985	1986
Cameroon	929	1,711	2,661
Central African Repub.	64	1,219	321
France	6,950	1,432	1,774
Nigeria	113	1,981	425
Sudan	8	47	101
Zaire	125	5	n.a.
Total (incl. others)	8,231	6,446	5,374

Transport

ROAD TRAFFIC (motor vehicles in use at 31 December)

	1994	1995*	1996*
Passenger cars	8,720	9,700	10,560
Buses and coaches	708	760	820
Lorries and vans	12,650	13,720	14,550
Tractors	1,413	1,500	1,580
Motorcycles and mopeds	1,855	2,730	3,640

* Estimates.

Source: International Road Federation, *World Road Statistics*.

CIVIL AVIATION (traffic on scheduled services*)

	1992	1993	1994
Kilometres flown (million)	2	2	2
Passengers carried ('000)	83	85	86
Passengers-km (million)	208	214	222
Total ton-km (million)	35	34	35

* Including an apportionment of the traffic of Air Afrique.

Source: UN, *Statistical Yearbook*.

Tourism

	1992	1993	1994
Tourist arrivals ('000)	17*	21*	19
Tourist receipts (US $ million)	21	23	36

* Including same-day visitors.

Source: UN, *Statistical Yearbook*.

Tourist arrivals ('000): 57 in 1995 (Source: Ministère de l'environnement et du tourisme).

Communications Media

	1992	1993	1994
Radio receivers ('000 in use)	1,425	1,470	1,520
Television receivers ('000 in use)	8	8	9
Telephones ('000 main lines in use)	4	5	5
Telefax stations (number in use)	128	170	190

Daily newspapers: 1 in 1994 (average circulation 2,000).

Non-daily newspapers: 1 in 1988 (average circulation 1,000).

Sources: UNESCO, *Statistical Yearbook*, and UN, *Statistical Yearbook*.

Education

1995/96

	Institutions	Teachers	Pupils
Primary	2,660	9,395	591,493
Secondary:			
General	153	2,468	90,100
Teacher training	6	65	806
Vocational	12	151	2,120
Higher	6	288	3,446

Source: Ministry of Education.

Directory

The Constitution

The Constitution of the Republic of Chad, which was adopted by national referendum on 31 March 1996, enshrines a unitary state. The President is elected for a term of five years by direct universal adult suffrage, and is restricted to two terms in office. The Prime Minister, who is appointed by the President, nominates the Council of Ministers. The bicameral legislature includes a 125-member National Assembly, which is elected by direct universal suffrage for a term of four years. A Senate, with a six-year mandate (with one-third of members renewed every two years), had not yet been established in early 1998. The Constitution provides for an independent judicial system, with a High Court of Justice, and the establishment of a Constitutional Court and a High Council for Communication.

The Government

HEAD OF STATE

President and Commander-in-Chief of the Armed Forces: IDRISS DEBY (assumed office 4 December 1990; elected President 3 July 1996).

COUNCIL OF MINISTERS
(January 1998)

Prime Minister: NASSOUR GUELENDOUKSIA OUAIDO.

Minister of Energy and Petroleum: SALEH KEBZABO.

Minister of Planning: AHMAT HAMID.

Minister of Foreign Affairs: MAHAMAT SALEH ANNADIF.

Minister of the Interior and Security: ABDRAMAN SALLAH.

Minister of Justice: LIMANE MAHAMAT.

Minister of Finance and the Economy: BICHARA CHERIF DAOUSSA.

Minister of Education: ABDERAHIM BREME HAMID.

Minister of Communications: HAROUN KABADI.

Minister of Public Works, Transport and Housing: AHMAT LAMINE.

Minister of Defence: OUMAR KADJALAMI.

Minister of Tourism: PASCAL YOUADIMNADJI.

Minister of Agriculture: MOCTAR MOUSSA.

Minister of Public Health: KEDELLAH YOUNOUSS.

Minister of Higher Education: DR ADOUM GOUDJA.

Minister of Livestock: MAHAMAT NOURI.

Minister of Civil Service and Labour: SALIBOU GARBA.

Minister of Industrial Development: DJITANGAR DJIBANGAR.

Minister of Posts and Telecommunications: MAHAMAT AHMAT KARAMBAL.

Minister of the Environment and Water Resources: MARIAM MAHAMAT NOUR.

Minister of Social Affairs: AGNES ALAFI.

Minister of Culture, Youth and Sport: MASSOUNGARAL NASSINGAR.

Secretary-General of the Government: HOUDEINGAR DAVID.

MINISTRIES

Office of the President: N'Djamena; tel. 51-44-37; telex 5201.

Office of the Prime Minister: N'Djamena.

Ministry of Agriculture: N'Djamena.

Ministry of the Civil Service and Labour: BP 437, N'Djamena; tel. and fax 52-21-98.

Ministry of Communications: BP 154, N'Djamena; tel. 51-41-64; telex 5254; fax 51-60-94.

Ministry of Culture, Youth and Sports: N'Djamena.

Ministry of Defence: N'Djamena; tel. 51-58-89.

Ministry of Education: N'Djamena.

Ministry of Energy and Petroleum: N'Djamena; tel. 51-56-03; fax 51-25-65.

Ministry of the Environment and Water Resources: N'Djamena.

Ministry of Finance and the Economy: BP 144, N'Djamena; tel. 52-21-61; telex 5257.

Ministry of Foreign Affairs: N'Djamena; tel. 51-50-82; telex 5238.

Ministry of Higher Education: N'Djamena.

Ministry of the Interior and Security: N'Djamena.

Ministry of Justice: N'Djamena; tel. 51-56-56.

Ministry of Livestock: N'Djamena; tel. 51-59-07.

Ministry of Posts and Telecommunications: N'Djamena.

Ministry of Public Health: N'Djamena; tel. 51-39-60.

Ministry of Public Works, Transport and Housing: BP 436, N'Djamena; tel. 51-20-96.

Ministry of Social Affairs: N'Djamena.

Ministry of Tourism: N'Djamena.

President and Legislature

PRESIDENT

In a first round of voting, which took place on 2 June 1996, none of the 15 candidates secured the requisite 50% of total votes cast. A second round of voting took place on 3 July: the incumbent, President IDRISS DEBY, was elected by 69.1% of the votes, while the other candidate, Gen. WADAL ABDELKADER KAMOUGUE, received 30.9%.

ASSEMBLÉE NATIONALE

President: Gen. WADAL ABDELKADER KAMOUGUE.

General Election, 5 January and 23 February 1997

Party	Seats
Movement patriotique du salut	65
Union pour le renouveau et la démocratie	29
Union nationale pour le développement et le renouveau	15
Union pour la démocratie et la République	4
Parti pour la liberté et le développement	3
Rassemblement pour la démocratie et le progrès	3
Other opposition parties	6
Total	125

Note: By early 1998 the upper house of the legislature, the Senate, had not yet been established.

Political Organizations

Legislation permitting the operation of political associations, subject to official registration, took effect in October 1991. In early 1998 about 60 political organizations were in existence, of which the most important are listed below.

Action pour l'unité et le socialisme (ACTUS): N'Djamena; f. 1992; Leader Dr FIDÈLE MOUNGAR.

Action du peuple pour l'unité et le développement (APUD): N'Djamena; f. 1996; Chair. BESHIR DISCO HAMAT.

Alliance nationale pour la démocratie et le développement (ANDD): BP 4066, N'Djamena; tel. 51-46-72; f. 1992; Leader SALIBOU GARBA.

Alliance nationale pour la démocratie et le renouveau (ANDR): N'Djamena; f. 1993.

Alliance nationale pour le progrès et le développement: N'Djamena; f. 1992.

Alliance nationale pour la solidarité et la démocratie: f. 1998; Chair. MANG IGRI TAIDA.

Alliance des partis politiques pour la démocratie (APD): f. 1994; opposition coalition comprising:

- **Forte alliance démocratique (FAD):** Leader NDJIRAWE FATIKAR-EMON.
- **Parti démocratique tchadien (PDT):** Leader Dr ABDOULAYE DJIDA.
- **Parti pour le renouveau du Tchad (PRT):** Leader MAHAMAT KANASSO AKIM.
- **Parti pour l'unité et la reconstruction (PUR):** Leader MAHAMAT SALEH MATIB.
- **Rassemblement démocratique et culturel pour la paix et le travail (RDCPT):** Leader MONGOUNKOU HARAMA.
- **Rassemblement des forces démocratiques tchadiennes (RFDT):** Leader BERNARD MBANGADOU.
- **Union nationale pour la démocratie et le progrès (UNDP):** Leader ABDELKADER YASSINE BAKIT.
- **Union du peuple tchadien pour la reconstruction nationale (UPTRN):** N'Djamena; f. 1992; Leader ABAKAR MOUSSA.

Collectif des partis pour le changement (COPAC): f. 1994; alliance of eight opposition parties: Leader Dr FIDÈLE MOUNGAR (Leader of ACTUS).

Comité de sursaut national pour la paix et la démocratie (CSNPD): fmr dissident faction; obtained legal recognition in Sept. 1994; Leader Col MOÏSE NODJI KETTE.

Concertation nationale pour la démocratie sociale (CNDS): N'Djamena; Leader ADOUM MOUSSA SEIF.

Concertation des partis politiques (CPP): f. 1995; informal grouping comprising all opposition parties; Chair. ABDERAHMANE DJASNABAYE.

Concertation social-démocrate tchadien (CSDT): N'Djamena; Pres. YOUNOUS IBEDOU.

Convention de l'opposition démocratique (CODE): f. 1996; alliance of 23 opposition parties; Leader KASSIRE DELWA KOUMAKOYE (Pres. of the RNDP).

Front des forces d'action pour la République: Leader YORONGAR LEMOHIBAN.

Front patriotique pour la démocratie (FPD): f. 1996 by elements of a fmr dissident faction; Nat. Co-ordinator MICHEL MBAILAMA.

Front républicain: f. 1996; alliance of 27 parties supporting President Idriss Deby.

Mouvement patriotique du salut (MPS): N'Djamena; f. 1990 as a coalition of several opposition movements, incl. the Action du 1 avril, the Mouvement pour le salut national du Tchad and the Forces armées tchadiennes; other opposition groups joined during the Nov. 1990 offensive against the Govt of Hissène Habré, and following the movement's accession to power in Dec. 1990; Chair. MALDOM BADA ABBAS; Exec. Sec. NADJITA BEASSOUMAL.

Mouvement pour la démocratie et le socialisme du Tchad (MDST): N'Djamena; Leader Dr SALOMON NGARBAYE TOMBALBAYE.

Mouvement pour la démocratie du Tchad (MPDT): N'Djamena; Leader MAHAMAT ABDOULAYE.

Mouvement socialiste pour la démocratie du Tchad (MSTD): N'Djamena; Leader ALBERT MBAINAIDO DJOMIA.

Mouvement pour l'unité et la démocratie du Tchad (MUDT): f. 1992; Leader JULIEN MARABAYE.

Parti africain pour le progrès et la justice sociale (PAPJS): Leader NEATOBEI DIDIER VALENTIN.

Parti pour la liberté et le développement (PLD): N'Djamena; f. 1993; Leader IBN OUMAR MAHAMAT SALEH.

Parti social-démocrate tchadien (PSDT): Moundou; Leader NIABE ROMAIN.

Rassemblement pour la démocratie et le progrès (RDP): N'Djamena; f. 1992; Leader LOL MAHAMAT CHOUA.

Rassemblement démocratique du Tchad (RDT): N'Djamena; f. 1992.

Rassemblement pour le développement et le progrès: f. 1992; Leader MAMADOU BISSO.

Rassemblement national pour la démocratie et le progrès (RNDP): N'Djamena; f. 1992; Pres. KASSIRE DELWA KOUMAKOYE.

Rassemblement des nationalistes tchadiennes (RNT): N'Djamena; f. 1992.

Rassemblement du peuple du Tchad (RPT): N'Djamena; f. 1992; Leader DANGBE LAOBELE DAMAYE.

Union pour la démocratie et la République (UDR): N'Djamena; f. 1992; Leader Dr JEAN ALINGUE BAWOYEU.

Union démocratique pour le progrès du Tchad (UDPT): 17 rue de kélo, Kabalaye, POB 1071, N'Djamena; tel. 51-24-34; f. 1992; Pres. ELIE ROMBA.

Union démocratique tchadienne (UDT): N'Djamena; Leader ABDERAHMANE KOULAMALLAH.

Union des forces démocratiques (UFD): N'Djamena; f. 1992; Sec.-Gen. Dr NAHOR MAHAMOUT.

Union des forces démocratiques—Parti républicain (UFD—PR): f. 1992; Leader GALI GATTA NGOTHE.

Union nationale: f. 1992; Leader ABDOULAYE LAMANA.

Union nationale pour le changement du Tchad (UNCT): N'Djamena; f. 1995; Pres. ADOUM HASSAN ISSA.

Union nationale pour le développement et le renouveau (UNDR): Leader SALEH KEBZABO.

Union pour le renouveau et la démocratie (URD): BP 92, N'Djamena; tel. 51-44-23; fax 51-41-87; f. 1992; Leader Gen. WADAL ABDELKADER KAMOUGUE.

A number of dissident factions (some based abroad) are also active. These include the **Concertation nationale pour l'unité et la paix,** led by Maj. ADOUM YACOUB; the **Congrès pour le renouveau et la démocratie,** f. 1996 by merger of the Conseil national de redressement du Tchad and the Front d'action pour l'installation de la démocratie au Tchad; the **Forces armées pour la République fédérale (FARF)**, led by LAOKEIN BARDE; the **Front de libération nationale du Tchad (FROLINAT)**, led by GOUKOUNI OUEDDEI; the **Front national du Tchad (FNT)**, based in Sudan and led by Dr FARIS BACHAR; **Front national du Tchad renové (FNTR)**, led by Maj. ADAM HAMAT; the **Mouvement pour la démocratie et le développement (MDD)**, led by MOUSSA MEDELLA MAHAMAT; the **Mouvement pour la justice sociale et la démocratie (MJSD)**; the **Résistance armée contre les forces antidémocratique (RAFAD)**, based in northern Nigeria; and the **Union nationale pour la démocratie et le socialisme (UNDS)**, led by YOUSSOU SOUGOUDI.

Diplomatic Representation

EMBASSIES IN CHAD

Algeria: N'Djamena; tel. 51-38-15; telex 5216; Ambassador: MOHAMED CHELLALI KHOURI.

Central African Republic: BP 115, N'Djamena; tel. 51-32-06; Ambassador: DAVID NGUINDO.

Congo, Democratic Republic: ave du 20 août, BP 910, N'Djamena; tel. 51-59-35; telex 5322; Ambassador: (vacant).

Egypt: BP 1094, N'Djamena; tel. 51-36-60; telex 5216; Ambassador: AZIZ M. NOUR EL-DIN.

France: BP 431, N'Djamena; tel. 52-25-75; telex 5202; fax 52-28-55; Ambassador: ALAIN DU BOISPÉAN.

Germany: ave Félix Eboué, BP 893, N'Djamena; tel. 51-62-02; telex 5246; fax 51-48-00; Chargé d'affaires a.i.: DIETER FREUND.

Libya: N'Djamena; Ambassador: IDRIS SANDRIL.

Nigeria: 35 ave Charles de Gaulle, BP 752, N'Djamena; tel. 51-24-98; telex 5242; Chargé d'affaires a.i.: A. M. ALIYU BIU.

Sudan: BP 45, N'Djamena; tel. 51-34-97; telex 5235; Ambassador: TAHA MAKKAWI.

USA: ave Félix Eboué, BP 413, N'Djamena; tel. 51-40-09; telex 5203; fax 51-33-72; Ambassador: LAURENCE POPE.

Judicial System

The highest judicial authority is the Supreme Court, which includes a constitutional chamber. The legal structure also comprises the Court of Appeal, and Magistrate and Criminal Courts. Under the terms of the Constitution that was introduced in 1996, a High Court of Justice was to be established.

Religion

It is estimated that some 50% of the population are Muslims and about 30% Christians. Most of the remainder follow animist beliefs.

ISLAM

Conseil Suprême des Affaires Islamiques: POB 1101, N'Djamena; tel. 51-81-80; telex 5248; fax 52-58-84.

Head of the Islamic Community: Imam MOUSSA IBRAHIM.

CHRISTIANITY

The Roman Catholic Church

Chad comprises one archdiocese and four dioceses. At 31 December 1995 the estimated number of adherents represented about 7.6% of the total population.

Bishops' Conference: Conférence Episcopale du Tchad, BP 456, N'Djamena; tel. 51-74-44; fax 52-28-60; Pres. Most Rev. CHARLES VANDAME, Archbishop of N'Djamena.

Archbishop of N'Djamena: Most Rev. CHARLES VANDAME, Archevêché, BP 456, N'Djamena; tel. 51-74-44; fax 52-28-60.

Protestant Churches

Entente des Eglises et Missions Evangéliques au Tchad: BP 2006, N'Djamena; tel. and fax 51-53-93; an assen of churches and missions working in Chad; includes Assemblées Chrétiennes au Tchad (ACT), Eglise Evangélique des Frères au Tchad (EEFT), Eglise Evangélique au Tchad (EET), Eglise Fraternelle Luthérienne au Tchad (EFLT) and five associate members.

BAHÁ'Í FAITH

National Spiritual Assembly: BP 181, N'Djamena; tel. 51-47-05; mems in 1,125 localities.

The Press

Al-Watan: BP 407, N'Djamena; tel. 51-57-96; weekly; Editor-in-Chief MOUSSA NDORKOÏ.

Bulletin Mensuel de Statistiques du Tchad: BP 453, N'Djamena; monthly.

Comnat: BP 731, N'Djamena; tel. 51-46-75; fax 51-46-71; publ. by Commission Nationale Tchadienne for UNESCO.

Contact: N'Djamena; f. 1989; current affairs; Dir KOULAMALO SOURADJ.

Info-Tchad: BP 670, N'Djamena; tel. 515867; telex 5240; news bulletin issued by Agence Tchadienne de Presse; daily; French.

Informations Economiques: BP 458, N'Djamena; publ. by the Chambre de Commerce, d'Agriculture et d'Industrie; weekly.

NEWS AGENCIES

Agence Tchadienne de Presse (ATP): BP 670, N'Djamena; tel. 51-58-67; telex 5240.

Foreign Bureaux

Agence France-Presse (AFP): N'Djamena; tel. 51-54-71; telex 5248; Correspondent ALDOM NADJI TITO.

Reuters (United Kingdom): BP 206, N'Djamena; tel. 51-56-57; Correspondent ABAKAR ASSIDIC.

Publisher

Government Publishing House: BP 453, N'Djamena.

Broadcasting and Communications

TELECOMMUNICATIONS

Société des Télécommunications Internationales du Tchad (TIT): BP 1132, N'Djamena; tel. 51-57-82; telex 5200; fax 51-50-66; cap 150m. francs CFA; 52% state-owned; study and development of international communications systems; Man. Dir KHALIL D'ABZAC.

RADIO

Radiodiffusion Nationale Tchadienne: BP 892, N'Djamena; tel. 51-60-71; state-controlled; programmes in French, Arabic and eight vernacular languages; there are four transmitters; Dir KHAMIS TOGOÏ.

Radio Abéché: BP 105, Abéché; tel. 69-81-49; Dir SANOUSSI SAÏD.

Radio Moundou: BP 122, Moundou; tel. 69-13-22; daily programmes in French, Sara and Arabic; Dir DIMANANGAR DJAÏNTA.

Radio Sarh: BP 270, Sarh; daily programmes in French, Sara and Arabic; Dir BIANA FOUDA NACTOUANDI.

TELEVISION

Télé-Chad: Commission for Information and Culture, BP 748, N'Djamena; tel. 51-29-23; state-controlled; broadcasts c. 12 hours per week in French and Arabic; Dir IDRISS AMANE MAHAMAT; Programme Man. MACLAOU NDILDOUM.

Finance

(cap. = capital; res = reserves; m. = million; br. = branch; amounts in francs CFA)

BANKING

Central Bank

Banque des Etats de l'Afrique Centrale (BEAC): BP 50, N'Djamena; tel. 52-41-76; telex 5220; fax 52-44-87; HQ in Yaoundé, Cameroon; f. 1973 as central bank of issue for mem. states of the Customs and Economic Union of Central Africa (UDEAC); cap. and res 214,492m. (June 1996); Gov. JEAN-FÉLIX MAMALEPOT; Dir in Chad TAHIR SOULEYMAN HAGGAR; 2 brs.

Other Banks

Banque de Développement du Tchad (BDT): rue Capitaine Ohrel, BP 19, N'Djamena; tel. 52-28-29; telex 5375; fax 52-33-18; f. 1962; 25.9% state-owned; cap. 1,581.9m. (Dec. 1995); Pres. NAGOUM YAMASOUM; Dir-Gen. NADJILENGAR NGARDINGA.

Banque Méridien BIAO Tchad: ave Charles de Gaulle, BP 87, N'Djamena; tel. 52-43-14; telex 5228; fax 52-23-45; f. 1980; 19.7% state-owned; cap. and res 1,495.5m., dep. 16,083.3m. (Dec. 1993); Pres. RAOUL KONTCHOU; Dir-Gen. MICHEL LE BLANC.

Banque Tchadienne de Crédit et de Dépôts (BTCD): 2–6 rue Robert Lévy, BP 461, N'Djamena; tel. 52-41-90; telex 5212; fax 52-17-13; f. 1963; 75% state-owned; cap. 1,100m. (Dec. 1996); Pres. KOUMTOG LAOTEGUELNODJI; Dir-Gen. CHEMI KOGRIMI; br. at Moundou.

Financial Bank Tchad: ave Charles de Gaulle, BP 804; tel. 52-33-89; telex 5380; fax 52-29-05; f. 1992; cap. 1,000m. (Dec. 1995); Pres. RÉMY BAYSSET; Dir-Gen. PATRICK LELONG.

Bankers' Organizations

Association Professionnelle des Banques au Tchad: 2–6 rue Robert Lévy, BP 461, N'Djamena; tel. 52-41-90; telex 5212; fax 52-17-13; Pres. CHEMI KOGRIMI.

Conseil National de Crédit: N'Djamena; f. 1965 to formulate a national credit policy and to organize the banking profession.

INSURANCE

Assureurs Conseils Tchadiens Faugère et Jutheau et Cie: BP 139, N'Djamena; tel. 52-21-15; telex 5235; Dir BILIOU ALI-KEKE.

Société de Représentation d'Assurances et de Réassurances Africaines (SORARAF): N'Djamena; Dir Mme FOURNIER.

Société Tchadienne d'Assurances et de Réassurances (STAR): BP 914, N'Djamena; tel. 51-56-77; telex 5268; Dir PHILIPPE SABIT.

Trade and Industry

DEVELOPMENT ORGANIZATIONS

Caisse Française de Développement: BP 478, N'Djamena; tel. 51-40-71; fax 51-28-31; Dir JACBIE BATHANY.

Mission Française de Coopération et d'Action Culturelle: BP 898, N'Djamena; tel. 52-42-87; telex 5340; fax 52-44-38; administers bilateral aid from France; Dir EDOUARD LAPORTE.

Office National de Développement Rural (ONDR): BP 896, N'Djamena; tel. 51-48-64; f. 1968; Dir MICKAEL DJIBRAEL.

Société pour le Développement de la Région du Lac (SODELAC): BP 782, N'Djamena; tel. 51-35-03; telex 5248; f. 1967; cap. 180m. francs CFA; Pres. CHERIF ABDELWAHAB; Dir-Gen. MAHAMAT MOCTAR ALI.

CHAMBER OF COMMERCE

Chambre Consulaire: BP 458, N'Djamena; tel. 51-52-64; f. 1938; Pres. ELIE ROMBA; Sec.-Gen. SALEH MAHAMAT RAHMA; brs at Sarh, Moundou, Bol and Abéché.

TRADE ASSOCIATIONS

Office National des Céréales (ONC): BP 21, N'Djamena; tel. 51-37-31; f. 1978; production and marketing of cereals; Dir YBRAHIM MAHAMAT TIDEI; 11 regional offices.

Société Nationale de Commercialisation du Tchad (SONACOT): N'Djamena; telex 5227; f. 1965; cap. 150m. francs CFA; 76% state-owned; nat. marketing, distribution and import-export co; Man. Dir MARBROUCK NATROUD.

UTILITIES

Electricity and Water

Société Tchadienne d'Eau et d'Électricité (STEE): 11 rue du Colonel Largeau, BP 44, N'Djamena; tel. 51-28-81; telex 5226; fax 51-21-34; f. 1968; production and distribution of electricity and water; Pres. GOMON MAWATA WAKAG; Dir-Gen. ISMAEL MAHAMAT ADOUM.

TRADE UNION

Union Syndicats du Tchad (UST): BP 1143, N'Djamena; tel. 51-42-75; telex 5248; f. 1988 by merger; Pres. DOMBAL DJIMBAGUE; Sec.-Gen. DJIBRINE ASSALI HAMDALLAH.

Transport

RAILWAYS

There are no railways in Chad. In 1962 the Governments of Chad and Cameroon signed an agreement to extend the Transcameroon railway from N'Gaoundéré to Sarh, a distance of 500 km. Although the Transcameroon reached N'Gaoundéré in 1974, its proposed extension into Chad remains indefinitely postponed.

ROADS

The total length of the road network in 1996 was an estimated 33,400 km, of which 7,880 km were principal roads and 5,380 km were secondary roads. There are also some 20,000 km of tracks suitable for motor traffic during the October–July dry season. The EU is contributing to the construction of a highway connecting N'Djamena with Sarh and Lere, on the Cameroon border.

Coopérative des Transportateurs Tchadiens (CTT): BP 336, N'Djamena; tel. 51-43-55; telex 5225; road haulage; Pres. SALEH KHALIFA; brs at Sarh, Moundou, Bangui (Central African Repub.), Douala and N'Gaoundéré (Cameroon).

INLAND WATERWAYS

The Chari and Logone rivers, which converge a short distance south of N'Djamena, are navigable. These waterways connect Sarh with N'Djamena on the Chari and Bongor and Moundou with N'Djamena on the Logone.

CIVIL AVIATION

The international airport at N'Djamena opened in 1967. There are, in addition, more than 40 smaller airfields.

Air Afrique (Société Aérienne Africaine Multinationale): BP 466, N'Djamena; tel. 51-40-20; see under Côte d'Ivoire.

Air Tchad: 27 ave du Président Tombalbaye, BP 168, N'Djamena; tel. 51-50-90; telex 5345; f. 1966; 98% govt-owned; international charters and domestic passenger, freight and charter services; Pres. DJIBANGAR MADJIREBAYE; Dir-Gen. MAHAMAT NOURI.

Tourism

Chad's potential attractions for tourists include a variety of scenery from the dense forests of the south to the deserts of the north. Receipts from tourism in 1994 totalled an estimated US $36m. According to official estimates, about 57,000 tourists visited Chad in 1995.

Délégation Régionale au Tourisme: tel. 68-13-54; f. 1962; Delegate DJASSINRA NINGADOUM.

Direction du Tourisme et de l'Hôtellerie: BP 86, N'Djamena; tel. 52-23-03; telex 5358; fax 52-43-97 Dir ZAKARIA HOSKI.

CHILE

Introductory Survey

Location, Climate, Language, Religion, Flag, Capital

The Republic of Chile is a long, narrow country lying along the Pacific coast of South America, extending from Peru and Bolivia in the north to Cape Horn in the far south. Isla de Pascua (Rapa Nui or Easter Island), about 3,780 km (2,350 miles) off shore, and several other small islands form part of Chile. To the east, Chile is separated from Argentina by the high Andes mountains. Both the mountains and the cold Humboldt Current influence the climate; between Arica in the north and Punta Arenas in the extreme south, a distance of about 4,000 km (2,500 miles), the average maximum temperature varies by no more than 13°C. Rainfall varies widely between the arid desert in the north and the rainy south. The language is Spanish. There is no state religion but the great majority of the inhabitants profess Christianity, and some 79% are adherents of the Roman Catholic Church. The national flag (proportions 3 by 2) is divided horizontally: the lower half is red, while the upper half has a five-pointed white star on a blue square, at the hoist, with the remainder white. The capital is Santiago.

Recent History

Chile was ruled by Spain from the 16th century until its independence in 1818. For most of the 19th century it was governed by a small oligarchy of land-owners. Chile won the War of the Pacific (1879–83) against Peru and Bolivia. Most of the present century has been characterized by the struggle for power between right- and left-wing forces.

In September 1970 Dr Salvador Allende Gossens, the Marxist candidate of Unidad Popular (a coalition of five left-wing parties, including the Partido Comunista de Chile), was elected to succeed Eduardo Frei Montalva, a Christian Democrat who was President between 1964 and 1970. Allende promised to transform Chilean society by constitutional means, and imposed an extensive programme of nationalization. The Government failed to obtain a congressional majority in the elections of March 1973 and encountered a deteriorating economic situation as well as an intensification of violent opposition to its policies. Accelerated inflation led to food shortages and there were repeated clashes between pro- and anti-Government activists. The armed forces finally intervened in September 1973. President Allende died during the coup. The Congreso (Congress) was subsequently dissolved, all political activity banned and strict censorship introduced. The military Junta dedicated itself to the eradication of Marxism and the reconstruction of Chile, and its leader, Gen. Augusto Pinochet Ugarte, became Supreme Chief of State in June 1974 and President in December. The Junta was widely criticized abroad for its repressive policies and violations of human rights. Critics of the regime were tortured and imprisoned, and several thousand were abducted or 'disappeared'. Some of those who had been imprisoned were released, as a result of international pressure, and sent into exile.

In September 1976 three constitutional acts were promulgated with the aim of creating an 'authoritarian democracy'. All political parties were banned in March 1977, when the state of siege was extended. Following a UN General Assembly resolution adopted in December 1977 which condemned the Government for violating human rights, President Pinochet organized a referendum in January 1978 to seek endorsement of the regime's policies. Since more than 75% of the voters supported the President in his defence of Chile 'in the face of international aggression', the state of siege (in force since 1973) was ended and was replaced by a state of emergency.

At a plebiscite conducted in September 1980, 67% of voters demonstrated support for a new Constitution, drafted by the Government, although dubious electoral practices were allegedly employed. The new Constitution was described as providing a 'transition to democracy' but, although President Pinochet ceased to be head of the armed forces, additional clauses allowed him to maintain his firm hold on power until 1989. Political parties, which were still officially outlawed, began to re-emerge, and in July 1983 five moderate parties formed a coalition, the 'Alianza Democrática', which advocated a return to democratic rule within 18 months. A left-wing coalition was also created.

In February 1984 the Council of State, a government-appointed consultative body, began drafting a law to legalize political parties and to prepare for elections in 1989. In March 1984 President Pinochet confirmed that a plebiscite would be held at an unspecified time to decide on a timetable for the elections. In September, however, President Pinochet firmly rejected any possibility of a return to civilian rule before 1989.

Despite the Government's strenuous attempts to eradicate internal opposition through the introduction of anti-terrorist legislation and extensive security measures, a campaign of explosions and public protests continued throughout 1984 and 1985. A number of protesters were killed in violent clashes with security forces during this period, and many opposition leaders and trade unionists were detained and sent into internal exile.

Throughout 1986 President Pinochet's regime came under increasing attack from the Roman Catholic Church, guerrilla organizations (principally the Frente Patriótico Manuel Rodríguez—FPMR) and international critics, including the US administration, which had previously refrained from condemning the regime's notorious record of violations of human rights. In September the FPMR made an unsuccessful attempt to assassinate President Pinochet. The regime's immediate response was to impose a state of siege throughout Chile, under which leading members of the opposition were detained and strict censorship was introduced. One consequence of the state of siege was the reappearance of right-wing death squads, who were implicated in a series of murders which followed the assassination attempt.

The promulgation, in March 1987, of a law under which non-Marxist political parties were to be permitted to register officially, prompted a sceptical response from many opposition parties. By mid-1987 President Pinochet had clearly indicated his intention to remain in office beyond 1989 by securing the presidential candidacy to be rejected or approved by the same plebiscite which would decide the future electoral timetable; a cabinet reshuffle in July enabled him to appoint staunch supporters of his policies. By mid-1988 several political parties and opposition groups had established the Comando por el No to co-ordinate the campaign for the anti-Government vote at the forthcoming referendum. The hopes of the opposition were encouraged by the high level of popular registration for the plebiscite and by the Government's repeal, in August, of the states of exception, which had prohibited opposition groups from organizing public rallies. Later in the month, Pinochet was named by the Junta as the single candidate at the plebiscite, which was scheduled for 5 October. Despite some reports of electoral malpractice, the plebiscite took place without major incident. The official result recorded 54.7% of the votes cast for the anti-Pinochet campaign,and 43.1% for President Pinochet. Following the plebiscite, the opposition made repeated demands for changes to the Constitution, in order to accelerate the democratic process, and sought to initiate discussions with the armed forces. However, President Pinochet rejected the opposition's proposals, and affirmed his intention to remain in office until March 1990.

In mid-1989 Patricio Aylwin Azócar, a lawyer and former senator who had been a vociferous supporter of the 'no' vote in the October 1988 plebiscite, emerged as the sole presidential candidate for the centre-left Concertación de los Partidos de la Democracia (CPD, formerly the Comando por el No), an alliance of 17 parties, including the Partido Demócrata Cristiano (PDC), of which Aylwin had hitherto been President, and several socialist parties. Throughout 1989 the election campaign was dominated by demands from both the CPD and right-wing parties for constitutional reform, and by the ensuing lengthy negotiations with Carlos Cáceres Contreras, the Minister of the Interior. A draft document, proffered by the Government, was initially rejected by the CPD, on the grounds that it contained inadequate provisions for comprehensive constitutional amendment in the future, for controls over the composition and function of the National Security Council and for greater freedom in the creation and composition of the Congreso. A later proposal, expanded to 54 amendments (including the legalization of Marxist political parties) and ratified by the Junta, was finally accepted by the opposition, with some reservations, and the constitutional reforms (see p. 876) were approved by 85.7% of voters in a national referendum in July 1989.

The electoral campaign was conducted amidst intermittent outbursts of political violence and government intervention. Uncertainty regarding President Pinochet's own intentions concerning the forthcoming elections was finally dispelled in mid-1989, when he dismissed the possibility of his candidacy as unconstitutional, but reiterated his intention to continue as Commander-in-Chief of the Army for at least four years. Opposition leaders interpreted subsequent actions by the Government (including the implementation of a law providing for the autonomy of the Banco Central de Chile, the appointment of directors to state-owned companies with mandates of up to 10 years and curbs on the Government's power to remove state officials from their posts) as an attempt by the President to retain a degree of influence beyond his term of office.

The presidential and congressional elections were conducted on 14 December 1989. Patricio Aylwin Azócar of the centre-left CPD secured 55.2% of the valid votes cast in the presidential election, thus achieving a clear victory over the former Minister of Finance, Hernán Büchi Buc, who was supported by the Government and won 29.4%. In January 1990 President-Elect Aylwin announced the composition of his Cabinet, and asked two members of the outgoing Junta to remain as commanders of the air force and police. The transfer of power took place on 11 March 1990 at the newly-constructed Congreso building in Valparaíso.

Having failed to obtain the support of the two-thirds' majority in the Congreso necessary to amend the 1980 Constitution significantly (owing partly to an electoral system weighted heavily in favour of pro-regime candidates and the power of the outgoing Junta to nominate almost one-fifth of the Senado—Senate), Aylwin's new CPD administration was forced to reconcile attempts to fulfil campaign promises as quickly as possible with the need to adopt a conciliatory approach towards more right-wing parties in the Congreso, whose support was essential for the enactment of new legislation. Agreement was reached almost immediately, however, on a series of modifications to the tax laws, which were expected to generate sufficient surplus revenue for the implementation of several new initiatives for social welfare. Attempts to amend existing articles of law considered repressive by the new administration (including the death penalty and provisions for the censorship of the press) were less successful. In October 1990 military courts were continuing to initiate proceedings against journalists for alleged defamation of the armed forces, and in November a draft law proposing the abolition of the death penalty was finally defeated in the Senado, the sentence being retained for some 30 offences.

In April 1990 the Government created the National Commission for Truth and Reconciliation (Comisión Nacional de Verdad y Reconciliación—CNVR) to document and investigate alleged violations of human rights during the previous administration. Although Pinochet, before leaving office, had provided for the impunity of the former military Junta with regard to abuses of human rights, it was suggested by human rights organizations that such safeguards might be circumvented by indicting known perpetrators of atrocities on charges of 'crimes against humanity', a provision which gained considerable public support following the discovery, during 1990, of a number of mass graves containing the remains of political opponents of the 1973–90 military regime. The army High Command openly condemned the Commission for undermining the prestige of the armed forces and attempting to contravene the terms of a comprehensive amnesty declared in 1978. Although a new accord between military leaders and the Government-Elect had been negotiated in January 1990 (whereby the Junta of Commanders-in-Chief was abolished and the role of the armed forces redefined as essentially subservient to the Ministry of Defence), relations between the new Government and the army High Command remained tense throughout the year. Pinochet, who had warned, in early 1990, that attempted reprisals against members of the armed forces would constitute a serious threat to a peaceful transition to democracy, became the focus for widespread disaffection with the army High Command but resisted repeated demands for his resignation, reiterating his intention to continue as Commander-in-Chief of the Army until 1997.

Throughout 1990 and 1991 escalating public and political antagonism towards the former military leadership was fuelled by further revelations of abuses of human rights and financial corruption, and erupted into widespread popular outrage and renewed political violence following the publication, in March 1991, of the findings of the CNVR The report documented the deaths of 2,279 alleged political opponents of the former regime who were executed, died as a result of torture or disappeared (and were presumed to be dead) in 1973–90. In accordance with President Aylwin's recommendation that the report should foster national reconciliation and fulfil an expositionary rather than judicial function, those responsible for the deaths were identified only by the institutions to which they belonged. However, President Aylwin pledged full government co-operation for families wishing to pursue private prosecutions. The report concluded that the military Government had embarked upon a 'systematic policy of extermination' of its opponents through the illegal activities of the covert military intelligence agency, Dirección de Inteligencia Nacional (Dina), and was also highly critical of the Chilean judiciary for failing to protect the rights of individuals by refusing thousands of petitions for habeas corpus submitted by human rights lawyers. Later in the month, Pinochet publicly denounced the document, claiming that it contained no 'historical or juridical validity', and declared his opposition to plans, previously announced by President Aylwin, to make material reparation to the families of the victims named in the report.

In November 1992, following a prolonged investigation, former Dina officials Gen. Manuel Contreras and Col. Pedro Espinoza were charged with the murder of Orlando Letelier, a former cabinet minister (and Chile's Ambassador to the USA during the government of Salvador Allende in the early 1970s), who was assassinated, together with an associate, by a car bomb in Washington in 1976. (In November 1993 Contreras and Espinoza were awarded prison sentences of seven and six years respectively. An appeal against the sentences was rejected by the Supreme Court in May 1995, although their sentences were reduced by 15 months as a result of a Supreme Court ruling on technicalities.) Hopes that this development might herald an end to the apparent impunity of the former military regime were somewhat frustrated, however, following the decision of the Supreme Court, announced later in the month, to withdraw charges, recently brought against former police chief and Junta member, César Mendoza Durán, of complicity in the kidnap and murder of three members of the Partido Comunista de Chile (PCCh) in 1985. (In March 1994 15 former members of the subsequently-disbanded paramilitary police intelligence unit, Dicomcar, were sentenced to varying terms of imprisonment, having been convicted on charges connected with the murders in July 1993. However, Gen. Rodolfo Stange Oelckers, head of the military police since 1985, refused a request, made by President Frei in April 1994, that he should resign the post, refuting formal allegations made during the hearing, that he had impeded the investigation and was therefore guilty of serious dereliction of duty. In October 1995, however, Stange announced his resignation, denying that his decision had been influenced by continued pressure from the Government, but was rather in protest at Government attempts to undermine the autonomy of the armed forces.)

Notwithstanding increasing frustration at the Government's reluctance or inability to bring to justice the perpetrators of the atrocities documented in the report, the conclusions of the Commission were widely welcomed. However, following the publication of the report, a series of terrorist attacks by left-wing extremists against right-wing opponents threatened to undermine the process of national reconciliation. Fears of an escalation in extremist violence were partially dispelled, however, by the Government's announcement, in April 1991, of the creation of a new Public Security Co-ordinating Office, intended to combat terrorism, under the direction of a civilian from the Ministry of the Interior, and by the announcement, in late May, of the FPMR's intention to renounce its armed struggle and join the political mainstream as the Movimiento Patriótico Manuel Rodríguez.

Throughout 1991 President Aylwin reaffirmed his commitment to dismantling the apparatus of political centralization that was embodied in the 1981 Constitution. In November the Congreso approved constitutional amendments to local government, which provided for the replacement of centrally-appointed local officials with directly-elected representatives. Elections to the 326 municipalities were conducted in June 1992, and the results demonstrated clear public endorsement of the ruling coalition, which received some 53% of the votes, compared with 29% for the right-wing opposition. However, constitutional amendments envisaged by the President (including plans to restore presidential power to remove Commanders-in-Chief of the armed forces, to counter right-wing bias in the electoral system, to balance politically the composition of the constitutional tribunal and to abolish government-appointed senators) continued to encounter considerable right-wing opposition in the Senado during 1992. Four cabinet ministers were replaced in September 1992, in preparation for presidential and congressional elections, to be conducted in the following year.

During 1993 the delicate political balance within the Government and within the Congreso continued to frustrate Aylwin's attempts to enact legislation. Proposals to accelerate the prosecution of military personnel accused of human rights abuses, while safeguarding their anonymity, put forward by the President in August 1993, were rejected by the right as ill-considered and precipitate, while left-wing groups challenged the concessionary nature of the legislation, with regard to the military. In September Aylwin was forced to withdraw the proposals from the Congreso, following a declaration of opposition to the legislation, made by two member parties of the ruling coalition, in response to the petitions of human rights organizations. A government proposal to reduce the presidential mandate to a four-year, non-renewable term, approved in the lower house in October 1993, was stalled by the Senado's insistence that the mandate should be renewable. A compromise proposal, providing for a six-year, non-renewable mandate, was finally approved by both houses in December, but was subject to ratification by a plenary session of the Congreso within 60 days.

A presidential election, conducted on 11 December 1993, was won by the CPD candidate Eduardo Frei Ruiz-Tagle, a PDC senator and the son of a former President, with 58% of the votes cast, ahead of Arturo Alessandri Besa (also the son of a former President), the candidate of the right-wing coalition, the Unión para el Progreso de Chile (UPC), who received 24% of the votes. However, the ruling coalition failed to make significant gains at concurrently conducted congressional elections, attributing the disappointing results to the binomial electoral system, which requires each party to secure two-thirds of the votes in each district for the successful election of its two candidates to the legislature. Frei, whose electoral campaign had identified the need for increased spending on health and education, the consolidation of municipalities, and greater support for small businesses, announced the composition of a new Cabinet in December 1993 and January 1994. In February 1994 formal congressional endorsement was secured for constitutional reform whereby the length of the presidential term would be henceforth fixed at six years.

On 11 March Frei duly assumed the presidency. Some days later he identified the immediate aims of his presidency as the alleviation of poverty, the elimination of corrupt government, and the fostering of significant economic growth. However, the President's affirmation of Pinochet's right to remain in office until 1997, appeared to compromise his pre-election demands for greater powers for the executive to nominate and remove the military High Command. In August 1994 Frei presented several constitutional reform proposals to the Congreso, including the abolition of the nine appointed senators (installed by the former military regime) and the introduction of an electoral system based on proportional representation (to replace the unrepresentative binomial system). However, Frei encountered the same level of opposition to constitutional reform (particularly from the right and from the upper house), that had undermined most attempts at constitutional amendment made by the previous administration. Several changes to the Cabinet were effected in September 1994.

In August 1995 a number of congressional bills, presented by the President as a crucial step towards national reconciliation, sought once again to remove the institutionalized influence of the military High Command (implemented by the outgoing military regime) and to accelerate the prosecution of armed forces personnel implicated in abuses of human rights by the report of the CNVR.

In November 1995 the Government secured the support of the opposition Renovación Nacional (RN) for revised proposals for new legislation relating to human rights and constitutional reform (see above). However, the compromised nature of the agreement provoked considerable disaffection within the RN, and within the opposition UPC alliance in general, which was effectively dissolved following the departure of the Unión Demócrata Independiente (UDI) and the Unión de Centro-Centro (UCC) in protest at the actions of the RN. Concern was also expressed by members of the Partido Socialista (PS—within the ruling coalition) that the legislation relating to human rights had been severely compromised. In January 1996 a constitutional reform proposal providing for the abolition of the posts of nine senators appointed by the former military regime was proposed by the RN and was approved by the Government. However, all attempts at reform were again stalled in the Senado, in April, largely owing to the opposition of seven disaffected RN members. A minor cabinet reshuffle was implemented in September.

At municipal elections conducted in late October 1996 the ruling coalition increased its share of the total votes cast to 56.2%, compared with some 53% of the votes in 1992. Jaime Ravinet, the PDC Mayor of Santiago, was re-elected with an overwhelming majority. However, the UDI and the RN, who in July had announced their intention to contest the municipal elections (and legislative elections scheduled for December) as a right-wing alliance (Unión por Chile), also recorded a significant increase in support.

In May 1997 a group of disaffected PDC deputies announced the formation of a new centrist party, the Partido Popular Cristiano (PPC), to be led by Ramón Elizalde and Samuel Venegas. In July Sergio Henríquez was appointed Minister of Housing and Urban Development, replacing Edmundo Hermosilla, who had resigned as a result of allegations of professional misconduct (following the revelation that he had accepted a horse as a gift from a businessman). In August Sergio Jiménez Moraga was appointed Minister of Mining, following the death, earlier in the year, of Benjamín Teplisky.

During 1997 further attempts by the Government to abolish the designated seats in the Senado, instituted by the Pinochet regime, were fuelled by the former President's stated intention to assume one of the seats on retirement as Commander-in-Chief of the Army in March 1998, and by speculation that Pinochet would seek to exert considerable influence over future legislation by installing close military associates in other such seats. In July the Senado rejected the Government's latest petition for reform to the system of appointments to the Senado.

In October 1997 it was announced that Maj.-Gen. Ricardo Izurieta, previously chief of defence staff, was to succeed Pinochet as Commander-in-Chief of the Army. The announcement was made amid a number of changes in the military High Command, which appeared to confirm earlier predictions that military influence was henceforth to be concentrated in the Senado, where it would bolster the political right wing.

Legislative elections to renew all 120 seats in the Cámara de Diputados and 20 of the elective seats in the Senado were conducted on 11 December 1997. The Government expressed satisfaction with the performance of parties within the governing Concertación, which secured 50.5% of the votes for deputies and retained (with 70 seats) a comfortable majority in the lower house. However, political analysts noted an erosion of support for the centre-left alliance (which had attracted 55.4% of votes for the lower house at the 1993 elections) and observed that the group's disappointing showing at elections to the Senado (where one seat was lost to the UDI) would make future attempts to effect constitutional reform as problematic as those undertaken in the past, particularly given the predominance of right-wing sympathizers among the nine designated senators (three nominated by the Supreme Court, four by the National Security Council—from a list of former chiefs of the armed forces—and two by the President), named later in December, who were scheduled to take their seats, together with the newly-elected senators, in March 1998. The elections were notable for the high level of voter absenteeism and blank and spoiled votes (it was calculated that as much as 40% of the potential electorate failed to cast a valid vote) and for the shifting balance of power within the two major political groupings (support for the UDI, in particular, appeared to have superseded that for the RN within the Unión por Chile). There was also renewed criticism of the country's binomial system of voting, the PCCh having failed to secure congressional representation despite attracting 8.4% and 6.9% of the votes to the upper and lower houses, respectively.

During December 1997 Pinochet continued to indicate that he fully intended to exercise his constitutional right, on retirement, to assume an *ex-officio* seat (for life) in the Senado (in addition to the nine designated senators). Expressing the opinion that to extend such an opportunity to Pinochet, who had headed an administration that had suspended all legislative processes for many years, would be wholly inappropriate, a number of centre-left politicians pledged to obstruct Pinochet's accession to the Senado. During January 1998 separate attempts were made by junior members of the Concertación (despite the declarations of senior members of the Government—anxious to ensure a peaceful exchange of offices in March—that such action was untimely and politically inconvenient) and by the leadership of the PCCh to begin judicial proceedings against Pinochet on charges related to gross abuses of human rights. (Abortive attempts to bring charges against the former President for similar violations had been initiated in courts in Spain and Ecuador in late 1997.) Pinochet responded by announcing that he would not retire as Commander-in-Chief of the Army on 26 January, as previously suggested, but would continue in office until 10 March, thereby preserving the immunity from prosecution provided by the position for as long as possible. Pinochet's announcement and a perceived entrenchment of the divergent interests of the Government and the armed forces prompted the resignation of the Minister of National Defence, Edmundo Pérez Yoma, who was immediately replaced by Raúl Troncoso.

In October 1984 it was announced that total agreement had been reached, following papal mediation, regarding Chile's dispute with Argentina over three small islands in the Beagle Channel, south of Tierra del Fuego. Under the terms of the settlement, Chile was awarded 12 islands and islets to the south of the Beagle Channel, including Lennox, Picton and Nueva. The agreement was formally approved by the ruling Junta in April 1985, and was ratified in May by representatives of the Argentine and Chilean Governments. In August 1991 Argentina and Chile reached a settlement regarding disputed territory in the Antarctic region. Responsibility for the contentious Laguna del Desierto region, however, was to be decided by international arbitration. In October 1994 Argentina's claim to the territory was upheld by a five-member international arbitration panel. In July 1997 it was announced unexpectedly that the two countries were to conduct joint military exercises in 1998, and in September it was agreed to proceed with the creation of a conciliation commission, originally envisaged within the terms of a peace and friendship treaty concluded in 1984.

Prospects for renewed diplomatic relations with Bolivia (which severed relations with Chile in 1978 over the issue of Bolivian access to the Pacific Ocean) were encouraged during 1993 by the successful conclusion of a comprehensive trade agreement in April, by a series of bilateral co-operation treaties, negotiated in July. By 1997, however, relations had deteriorated again. The Bolivian Government made repeated requests during the year for the renewal of discussions on Bolivian access to the sea, and sought Peru's assistance in the dispute. Relations between the two countries deteriorated further in late 1997 when the Bolivian Government made an official protest to Chile regarding its failure to remove land-mines (planted during the 1970s) from the two countries' border.

A free trade agreement, the Acuerdo de Complementación Económica (ACE), concluded with Colombia in December 1993, took effect from 1 January 1994, and was expected to have eliminated tariffs on most goods by the time of its full implementation on 1 January 1999. A free trade agreement was negotiated with Ecuador in late 1994, and came into effect on 1 January 1995. Chile also has bilateral free trade ageements with Mexico and Venezuela, and is currently negotiating similar agreements with Peru and Bolivia. In December 1994 the signatory nations to the North American Free Trade Agreement (NAFTA) issued a formal invitation to Chile to join the group. Formal discussions on Chile's accession to the Agreement by late 1996, began in June 1995. However, despite the removal of contentious clauses relating to labour and the environment, US President Bill Clinton failed to secure US congressional support for 'fast track' authorization for Chile's accession to the Agreement, and Chile seemed unlikely to achieve full member status until 1998. In the context of this delay Chile intensified attempts to negotiate a bilateral free trade agreement with Canada and a formal trade agreement with the Mercado Común del Sur (Mercosur—see p. 239). In November 1996 agreement was reached with Canada on the imminent removal of tariffs on three-quarters of bilateral trade, with the gradual removal of remaining duties over a five-year period. The agreement received formal congressional approval in mid-1997 and came into effect in July of that year. Meanwhile, in June 1996, at a summit meeting of Mercosur member nations in San Luis (Argentina), Chile had secured associate membership of the group following negotiations which established the immediate reduction of tariffs on 90% of Chilean goods, and the subsequent elimination of tariffs on 'sensitive' goods including meat, sugar, edible oils and wheat, over an 18-year period. Chile's associate membership became effective from 1 October.

In January 1994 Chile declared its full adherence to the 1967 Tlatelolco Treaty, which proscribes nuclear weapons in Latin America and the Caribbean.

In April 1995 full diplomatic relations with Cuba, severed as a result of the 1973 military coup in Chile, were restored.

Government

Chile is a republic, divided into 12 regions and a metropolitan area. Under the terms of the Constitution, executive power is vested in the President, who is directly elected for a six-year term. The President is assisted by a cabinet. Legislative power is vested in the bicameral Congreso Nacional (National Congress), comprising the 47-member Senado (Senate) and the 120-member Cámara de Diputados (Chamber of Deputies).

Defence

Military service is for one year (army) or 22 months (navy and air force) and is compulsory for men at 19 years of age. In August 1997 the army had a strength of 51,000, the navy 29,800 and the air force 13,500. Paramilitary security forces numbered about 31,200 carabineros. Defence expenditure for 1997 was budgeted at 1,100,000m. pesos.

Economic Affairs

In 1995, according to estimates by the World Bank, Chile's gross national product (GNP), measured at average 1993–95 prices, was US $59,151m., equivalent to $4,160 per head. During 1985–95, it was estimated, GNP per head increased, in real terms, at an average annual rate of 6.1%. Over the same period, the population increased by an annual average of 1.6%. Chile's gross domestic product (GDP) in purchasers' values increased by an annual average of 4.1% in 1980–90, and 7.3% in 1990–95. Real GDP growth was estimated at 4.2% in 1994, 8.5% in 1995 and 7.2% in 1996.

Agriculture (including forestry and fishing) contributed 8.1% of GDP in 1995. About 15.7% of the employed labour force were engaged in this sector in 1995. Important subsistence crops include wheat, oats, barley, rice, beans, lentils, maize and chick-peas. Industrial crops include sugar beet, sunflower seed and rapeseed. Fruit and vegetables are also important export commodities (together contributing 8.6% of total export revenues in 1995), particularly maize, beans, asparagus, onions, garlic, grapes, citrus fruits, avocados, pears, peaches, plums and nuts. The production and export of wine has increased significantly in recent years. Forestry and fishing, and derivatives from both activities, also make important contributions to the sector. During 1985–95 agricultural GDP increased by an annual average of 6.5%. GDP growth in the agriculture sector was 8.5% in 1994 and 5.6% in 1995.

Industry (including mining, manufacturing, construction and power) contributed 32.9% of GDP in 1995 and accounted for 26.1% of the employed labour force in the same year. During 1985–95 industrial GDP increased by an annual average of 6.7%. GDP growth in the industry sector was 2.8% in 1994 and 6.9% in 1995.

Mining contributed 7.9% of GDP in 1995 and engaged 1.8% of the employed labour force in the same year. Chile is the world's largest producer and exporter of copper. Copper accounted for 87.5% of Chile's total export earnings in 1970, but the proportion had decreased to around 40% by 1995. Gold, silver, iron ore, nitrates, molybdenum, manganese, lead and coal are also mined, and the whole sector contributed some 50% of total export earnings in 1995. Petroleum and natural gas have been located in the south, and plans to exploit significant reserves of lithium are under consideration.

Manufacturing contributed 16.8% of GDP in 1995, and engaged 16.3% of the employed labour force in that year. The most important branches of manufacturing, measured by gross value of output, are food (17.1% of the total) and non-ferrous metals (13.9%). Manufacturing GDP increased by an average of 7.0% per year in 1985–95. The sector's GDP increased by 2.9% in 1994 and by 6.5% in 1995.

Energy is derived principally from petroleum and natural gas (some 55%), hydroelectric power (26%) and coal (18%). Chile produces some 40% of national energy requirements. Plans are under consideration to develop Chile's vast hydroelectric potential (estimated at 18,700 MW—the largest in the world). Meanwhile, Chile imported fuel and energy products equivalent to some 9% of the value of total merchandise imports in 1995.

The services sector contributed an estimated 59.0% of GDP in 1995 and engaged some 58.2% of the employed labour force in that year. The financial sector has continued to expand in the 1990s, fuelled, in part, by the success of private pension funds (AFPs—see section on Social Welfare). At the end of 1994 financial assets were estimated at 80% of GDP.

In 1996 Chile recorded a visible trade deficit of US $1,146m., and there was a deficit of $2,921m. on the current account of the balance of payments. In 1995 the principal source of imports (25.4%) was the USA, while Japan was the principal market for exports (18.3%). Other major trading partners were the Belgo-Luxembourg Economic Union, Brazil, Germany, Argentina and the United Kingdom. The principal exports in 1995 were basic copper manufactures (30.1% of total export revenue), copper ores and concentrates (12.1%), fruit and vegetables (8.6%), pulp and waste paper (8.0%) and fish and related products (6.4%). The principal imports in that year were machinery and transport equipment, and chemical and mineral products.

In 1995 there was a budgetary surplus of 667,610m. pesos (equivalent to 2.5% of GDP). Chile's external debt totalled US $25,562m. at the end of 1995, of which $7,178m. was long-term public debt. Debt-servicing costs in that year were equivalent to some 25.7% of the value of exports of goods and services. The annual rate of inflation averaged 16.6% in 1985–95, and stood at 7.4% in 1996. An average 6.4% of the labour force were unemployed in 1996.

Chile is a member of the Latin American Integration Association (ALADI—see p. 261) and was admitted to the Rio Group (see p. 271) in 1990 and to the Asia-Pacific Economic Co-operation group (APEC—see p. 108) in 1994. Chile is also among the founding members of the World Trade Organization (see p. 244).

Owing to the relaxation of import duties in the early 1980s, Chile's potential in the agricultural and manufacturing sectors was stifled by cheaper imported goods. Exports of fruit, seafoods and wines, however, have expanded considerably, yet Chile remains heavily dependent on exports of copper and on the stability of the world copper market. Chile imports some 85% of its petroleum requirements. The 1990–94 Aylwin administration successfully maintained significant economic growth while reducing inflation from 26% in 1990 to 12.7% in 1993. The draft budget for 1998, presented to the Congreso in October 1997, envisaged an overall increase in expenditure, in real terms, of some 7.2%, based on predictions of economic growth of 7% during that year. In September, forecasts of a current account deficit for 1998 equivalent to some 4% of GDP prompted official assurances that strict monetary policy would be maintained in the forthcoming year. Later in September a report published by the World Trade Organization praised the economic achievements of the previous two decades in liberalizing trade and reducing inflation, but warned that recent preoccupation with the creation of regional trade associations was leading to the perpetuation of serious imbalances in the structure of Chile's trade.

Social Welfare

Employees, including agricultural workers, may receive benefits for sickness, unemployment, accidents at work, maternity and retirement, and there are dependants' allowances, including family allowances. In May 1981 the management of social security was opened to the private sector. By the mid-1990s some 90% of Chile's 5m. pensions contributors were participating in the private pension system operated by Administradoras de Fondo de Pensiones (AFPs), while responsibility for the remainder was assumed by the Instituto de Normalización Previsonal, a transitional state organization. In late 1995 it was estimated that Chile's AFPs were managing some US $25,000m. of funds. However, the Government retains ultimate control of the sector, monitoring the performance of AFP managers and regulating the proportion of assets to be invested at home and abroad. A National Health Service was established in 1952. There were 9,684 physicians and 32,150 nursing personnel in 1984. Chile had 300 hospital establishments, with a total of 37,971 beds, in 1980. Of total expenditure by the central Government in 1995, about 614,680m. pesos (12.0%) was for health services, and a further 1,720,180m. pesos (33.5%) for social security and welfare.

Education

Pre-primary education is widely available for all children from five years of age. Primary education is officially compulsory, and is provided free of charge, for eight years, beginning at six or seven years of age. It is divided into two cycles: the first lasts for four years and provides a general education; the second cycle offers more specialized schooling. Secondary education, beginning at 13 or 14 years of age, is divided into the humanities-science programme (lasting for four years), with the emphasis on general education and possible entrance to university, and the technical-professional programme (lasting for between four and six years), designed to fulfil the requirements of specialist training. In 1994 the total enrolment at primary schools included an estimated 86% of children in the relevant age-group, while the comparable ratio for secondary enrolment was 54%. Higher education is provided by three kinds of institution: universities, professional institutes and centres of technical information. An intensive national literacy campaign, launched in 1980, reduced the rate of adult illiteracy from 11% in 1970 to an estimated 4.8% (males 4.6%; females 5.0%) in 1995. Expenditure on education by all levels of government in 1995 was about 754,390m. pesos (14.7% of total public spending).

Public Holidays

1998: 1 January (New Year's Day), 10–11 April (Good Friday and Easter Saturday), 1 May (Labour Day), 21 May (Battle of Iquique), 15 August (Assumption), 11 September (anniversary of 1973 coup), 18 September (Independence Day), 12 October (Day of the Race, anniversary of the discovery of America), 1 November (All Saints' Day), 8 December (Immaculate Conception), 25 December (Christmas Day).

1999: 1 January (New Year's Day), 2–3 April (Good Friday and Easter Saturday), 1 May (Labour Day), 21 May (Battle of Iquique), 15 August (Assumption), 11 September (anniversary of 1973 coup), 18 September (Independence Day), 12 October (Day of the Race, anniversary of the discovery of America), 1 November (All Saints' Day), 8 December (Immaculate Conception), 25 December (Christmas Day).

Weights and Measures

The metric system is officially in force.

Statistical Survey

Source (unless otherwise stated): Instituto Nacional de Estadísticas, Avda Bulnes 418, Casilla 498-3, Correo 3, Santiago; tel. (2) 699-1441; and Banco Central de Chile, Agustinas 1180, Santiago; tel. (2) 696-2281; telex 240658; fax (2) 698-4847.

Area and Population

AREA, POPULATION AND DENSITY*

Area (sq km)	756,626†
Population (census results)‡	
21 April 1982	11,329,736
22 April 1992	
Males	6,553,254
Females	6,795,147
Total	13,348,401
Population (official estimates at mid-year)	
1994	13,994,355
1995	14,210,429
1996	14,419,000§
Density (per sq km) at mid-1996	19.1

* Excluding Chilean Antarctic Territory.
† 292,135 sq miles.
‡ Excluding adjustment for underenumeration.
§ Provisional.

REGIONS*

		Area (sq km)	Population (30 June 1995)	Capital
I	De Tarapacá	58,698	366,257	Iquique
II	De Antofagasta	126,444	436,744	Antofagasta
III	De Atacama	75,573	250,163	Copiapó
IV	De Coquimbo	40,656	536,216	La Serena
V	De Valparaíso	16,396	1,469,148	Valparaíso
VI	Del Libertador Gen. Bernardo O'Higgins	16,341	737,047	Rancagua
VII	Del Maule	30,325	872,011	Talca
VIII	Del Bío-Bío	36,929	1,830,651	Concepción
IX	De la Araucanía	31,842	826,308	Temuco
X	De Los Lagos	67,013	1,004,929	Puerto Montt
XI	Aisén del Gen. Carlos Ibáñez del Campo	109,025	87,789	Coihaique
XII	De Magallanes y Antártica Chilena	132,034	151,355	Punta Arenas
	Metropolitan Region (Santiago)	15,349	5,641,811	—

* Before 1975 the country was divided into 25 provinces. With the new administrative system, the 13 regions are sub-divided into 51 new provinces and the metropolitan area of Santiago.

PRINCIPAL TOWNS (population at 30 June 1995)

Gran Santiago (capital)	5,076,808	Arica	173,336
Concepción	350,268	Talca	169,448
Viña del Mar	322,220	Chillán	157,083
Puente Alto	318,898	Iquique	152,592
Valparaíso	282,168	Osorno	123,055
Talcahuano	260,915	Puerto Montt	122,399
Temuco	239,340	Valdivia	119,431
Antofagasta	236,730	La Serena	117,983
San Bernardo	206,315	Punta Arenas	117,206
Rancagua	193,755	Quilpué	110,340

BIRTHS, MARRIAGES AND DEATHS

	Registered live births		Registered marriages		Registered deaths	
	Number	Rate (per 1,000)	Number	Rate (per 1,000)	Number	Rate (per 1,000)
1989*	303,798	23.4	103,710	8.0	75,453	5.8
1990	307,522	23.5	98,702	7.5	78,434	6.0
1991	299,456	22.5	91,732	6.9	74,862	5.6
1992	293,787	21.7	89,370	6.6	74,090	5.5
1993	290,438	21.1	92,821	6.7	76,261	5.5
1994	288,175	20.6	91,555	6.5	75,445	5.4
1995	279,928	19.7	n.a.	n.a.	78,531	5.5

* Rates are based on unrevised population estimates.

Expectation of life (official estimates, years at birth, 1995): Males 71.8; Females 77.8.

Source: UN, *Demographic Yearbook*.

ECONOMICALLY ACTIVE POPULATION*
('000 persons aged 15 years and over, October-December)

	1993	1994	1995
Agriculture, hunting, forestry and fishing	825.3	808.9	789.2
Mining and quarrying	92.1	86.3	89.8
Manufacturing	835.3	818.8	817.7
Electricity, gas and water	27.0	33.6	27.4
Construction	403.0	360.9	374.6
Trade, restaurants and hotels	925.6	940.7	932.1
Transport, storage and communications	354.8	371.3	385.3
Financing, insurance, real estate and business services	288.9	298.5	323.7
Community, social and personal services	1,233.3	1,268.5	1,285.2
Activities not adequately defined	0.5	0.7	0.9
Total employed	4,985.7	4,988.3	5,025.8
Unemployed	233.6	311.3	248.1
Total labour force	5,219.3	5,299.6	5,273.9
Males	3,522.8	3,567.4	3,564.5
Females	1,696.5	1,732.2	1,709.5

* Figures are based on sample surveys, covering 36,000 households, and exclude members of the armed forces. Estimates are made independently, so totals are not always the sum of the component parts.

Source: ILO, *Yearbook of Labour Statistics*.

Agriculture

PRINCIPAL CROPS ('000 metric tons)

	1994	1995	1996
Wheat	1,271	1,384	1,227
Rice (paddy)	133	146	154
Barley	100	91	64
Oats	176	202	200
Rye	1	2*	2*
Maize	937	942	932
Dry beans	54	56	66
Dry peas	4	4*	3
Chick-peas	10	11	10
Lentils	9	9	4
Potatoes	900	870	828
Sunflower seed	12	12†	6
Sugar beet	3,547	3,744	2,804
Rapeseed	23	26	37
Tomatoes	1,151	1,264	1,370
Pumpkins, etc.	152	152*	152*
Onions (dry)	305	350	390
Watermelons	100	85*	85*
Melons	77	77*	77*
Grapes	1,449	1,527	1,527*
Apples	810	850	910†
Peaches and nectarines	258	270*	270*

* FAO estimate. † Unofficial figure.

Source: FAO, *Production Yearbook*.

LIVESTOCK ('000 head, year ending September)

	1994	1995	1996
Horses*	450	550	550
Cattle	3,692	3,814	3,858
Pigs	1,407	1,490	1,486
Sheep	4,649	4,625	4,516
Goats*	600	600	600

* FAO estimates.

Source: FAO, *Production Yearbook*.

LIVESTOCK PRODUCTS ('000 metric tons)

	1994	1995	1996
Beef and veal	240	258	266*
Mutton and lamb	12	10	17
Pig meat	161	172	186
Horse meat	7	11	11†
Poultry meat	279	289	327
Cows' milk	1,750	1,873	1,873†
Butter	7	7	7†
Cheese	45	48	48†
Hen eggs	94	95†	95†
Wool:			
greasy	19	19	19†
clean	10	9	9†

* Unofficial figure. † FAO estimate.

Source: FAO, *Production Yearbook*.

Forestry

ROUNDWOOD REMOVALS ('000 cubic metres, excluding bark)

	1992	1993	1994
Sawlogs, veneer logs and logs for sleepers	8,186	8,909	13,799
Pulpwood	10,322	10,744	7,219
Other industrial wood	297	330	382
Total*	18,805	19,983	21,400

* Excluding fuel wood.

Fuel wood ('000 cubic metres): 9,316 in 1992; 9,627 in 1993; 9,972 in 1994 (Source: FAO, *Yearbook of Forest Products*).

SAWNWOOD PRODUCTION ('000 cubic metres)

	1992	1993	1994
Coniferous (softwood)	2,565	2,663	2,927
Broadleaved (hardwood)	455	450	437
Total	3,019	3,113	3,364

Fishing*

('000 metric tons, live weight)

	1993	1994	1995
Patagonian grenadier	82.6	81.3	206.7
Chilean jack mackerel	3,236.2	4,041.4	4,404.2
South American pilchard (sardine)	481.1	194.5	161.6
Araucanian herring	244.1	341.3	126.7
Anchoveta (Peruvian anchovy)	1,472.9	2,720.4	2,086.5
Other marine fishes (incl. unspecified)	346.6	281.3	425.7
Total fish	5,863.6	7,660.2	7,411.4
Crustaceans	26.2	30.8	31.0
Molluscs	109.8	104.8	90.6
Other aquatic animals	35.3	42.7	58.0
Total catch	6,034.9	7,838.5	7,590.9

* Excluding aquatic plants but including quantities landed by foreign fishing craft in Chilean ports.

Mining

('000 metric tons, unless otherwise indicated)

	1992	1993	1994
Copper (metal content)	1,967	2,079	2,234
Coal	2,125	1,798	1,667
Iron ore*	7,224	7,379	8,341
Calcium carbonate	4,890	5,650	6,305
Sodium sulphate—hydrous (metric tons)	1,333	1,433	1,668
Molybdenum—metal content (metric tons)	14,840	14,899	15,949
Manganese (metric tons)†	49,857	62,989	62,870
Gold (kilograms)	34,473	33,638	38,626
Silver (kilograms)	1,024,823	970,068	982,750
Petroleum (cubic metres)	862,233	825,082	714,088
Natural gas ('000 cubic metres)	4,044,183	4,196,151	4,243,956

* Gross weight. The estimated iron content is 61%.

† Gross weight. The estimated metal content is 32%.

1995: Copper (metal content, '000 metric tons) 2,478; Coal ('000 metric tons) 1,334; Gold (kilograms) 44,585; Silver (kilograms) 1,041,097.

1996: Copper (metal content, '000 metric tons) 3,141; Coal ('000 metric tons) 1,376; Iron ore (gross weight, '000 metric tons) 9,081; Gold (kilograms) 53,840.

Source: Servicio Nacional de Geología y Minería.

Industry

SELECTED PRODUCTS ('000 metric tons, unless otherwise indicated)

	1992	1993	1994
Wheat flour	1,105	1,087	n.a.
Oils and fats (of aquatic animal origin)*	153.0	191.2	n.a.
Refined sugar	487	453	463
Beer (million litres)	335	362	330
Soft drinks (million litres)	884	962	936
Cigarettes (million)	11,167	10,793	10,801
Non-rubber footwear ('000 pairs)	9,311	9,270	8,317
Particle board ('000 cu metres)	234	255	299
Fibreboard, compressed ('000 cu metres)	161	255	309
Mattresses ('000)	805	886	948
Sulphuric acid	887	920	1,174
Motor spirit (petrol)	1,480	1,685	1,746
Aviation gasoline	13	10	16
Jet fuels	278	309	360
Kerosene	266	266	266
Distillate fuel oils	2,023	2,227	2,450
Residual fuel oils	1,581	1,554	1,601
Cement	2,660	3,024	3,001
Tyres ('000)	2,002	2,198	2,285
Sanitary ceramic fittings	16.9	19.0	22.6
Glass sheets ('000 sq metres)	6,653	7,069	7,089
Blister copper†‡	1,201.5	1,219.1	1,260.4
Refined copper (unwrought)	1,242.3	1,270.0†	1,280.0†
Electric energy (million kWh)	22,362§	24,004§	25,250

* Source: Food and Agriculture Organization (Rome).
† Source: *World Metal Statistics* (London).
‡ Including some production at refined stage.
§ Estimate.

1995: Cement 3,014,000 metric tons; Tyres 2,331,000; Electric energy 26,740 million KWh.

1996: Cement 3,627,000 metric tons; Tyres 2,269,000; Electric energy 30,099 million KWh. Source: UN, *Monthly Bulletin of Statistics*.

Finance

CURRENCY AND EXCHANGE RATES

Monetary Units

100 centavos = 1 Chilean peso.

Sterling and Dollar Equivalents (30 September 1997)

£1 sterling = 670.7 pesos;
US $1 = 415.2 pesos;
1,000 Chilean pesos = £1.491 = $2.408.

Average Exchange Rate (pesos per US $)

1994	420.18
1995	396.77
1996	412.27

BUDGET ('000 million pesos)

Revenue	1993	1994	1995
Current revenue*	4,161.35	4,810.52	5,738.45
Taxation	3,526.98	4,055.64	4,749.72
Taxes on income, profits and capital gains	759.20	880.98	998.18
Social security contributions	276.35	312.91	349.12
Domestic taxes on goods and services	1,901.10	2,224.68	2,604.81
Sales or turnover taxes	1,558.40	1,831.18	2,128.19
Excises	342.70	393.50	476.62
Taxes on international trade and transactions	413.11	429.27	535.55
Other taxes	177.22	207.80	262.06
Administrative fees and charges, non-industrial and incidental sales	284.60	316.68	399.59
Other current revenue*	349.77	438.20	589.14
Capital revenue	16.15	18.77	15.59
Total revenue	4,177.50	4,829.29	5,754.04

* Including unclassified current revenue ('000 million pesos): 116.41 in 1993; 195.20 in 1994; 261.46 in 1995.

Expenditure†	1993	1994	1995
General public services	155.93	176.52	204.75
Defence	351.12	395.89	439.01
Public order and safety	196.57	228.34	271.03
Education	513.55	623.86	754.39
Health	443.74	545.05	614.68
Social security and welfare	1,295.12	1,493.40	1,720.18
Housing	215.57	253.66	288.61
Economic services	557.96	687.74	780.05
Other expenditures	228.77	210.93	192.36
Sub-total	3,958.33	4,615.39	5,265.06
Less Lending included in expenditure	115.61	133.41	128.01
Total expenditure	3,842.72	4,481.98	5,137.05
Current	3,274.63	3,768.17	4,336.07
Capital	568.09	713.81	800.98

† Excluding lending minus repayments ('000 million pesos): –21.74 in 1993; –14.64 in 1994; –50.62 in 1995.

Source: IMF, *Government Finance Statistics Yearbook*.

CENTRAL BANK RESERVES (US $ million at 31 December)

	1994	1995	1996
Gold*	652.0	642.8	637.4
IMF special drawing rights	0.7	3.1	1.9
Reserve position in IMF	—	—	50.4
Foreign exchange	13,086.9	14,136.7	14,780.9
Total	13,739.6	14,782.6	15,470.6

* National valuation.

Source: IMF, *International Financial Statistics*.

MONEY SUPPLY ('000 million pesos at 31 December)

	1994	1995	1996
Currency outside banks	667.3	784.2	859.5
Demand deposits at commercial banks	1,224.6	1,528.3	1,826.6
Total money (incl. others)	1,892.3	2,312.9	2,686.7

Source: IMF, *International Financial Statistics*.

COST OF LIVING

(Consumer Price Index for Santiago; base: 1990 = 100)

	1993	1994	1995
Food	164.6	180.6	195.6
Rent, fuel and light	157.1	176.2	189.5
Clothing	139.8	156.1	154.2
All items (incl. others)	158.5	176.6	191.1

Source: ILO, *Yearbook of Labour Statistics*.

1996: Food 207.5; All items 205.2 (Source UN, *Monthly Bulletin of Statistics*).

NATIONAL ACCOUNTS

Expenditure on the Gross Domestic Product

('000 million pesos at current prices)

	1994	1995	1996
Government final consumption expenditure	2,041.0	2,338.0	2,752.1
Private final consumption expenditure	13,692.8	16,550.9	19,331.9
Increase in stocks	548.9	1,098.9	943.4
Gross fixed capital formation	5,321.9	6,206.5	7,255.3
Total domestic expenditure	21,604.6	26,194.3	30,282.7
Exports of goods and services	6,180.0	7,812.2	7,776.5
Less Imports of goods and services	5,866.7	7,304.4	8,414.6
GDP in purchasers' values	21,917.9	26,702.1	29,644.5
GDP at constant 1990 prices	12,231.0	13,276.1	14,235.1

Source: IMF, *International Financial Statistics*.

Gross Domestic Product by Economic Activity*
(million pesos at constant 1986 prices)

	1992	1993	1994
Agriculture, forestry and fishing	442,055	448,649	486,595
Mining and quarrying	454,460	458,665	470,974
Manufacturing	928,593	975,604	1,003,765
Electricity, gas and water	147,343	153,614	160,600
Construction	277,927	316,800	322,992
Wholesale and retail trade	880,689	956,597	993,408
Transport, storage and communications	387,800	418,308	454,329
Financial services	665,821	711,367	744,739
Housing	216,000	221,399	227,820
Personal services	369,946	384,779	397,881
Public administration	156,052	158,790	159,952
Sub-total	4,926,686	5,204,572	5,423,055
Value-added tax	420,289	455,162	473,263
Import duties	301,020	340,412	359,430
Less Imputed bank service charges	363,113	383,732	400,737
GDP in purchasers' values	5,284,882	5,616,414	5,855,011

* Figures are provisional.
1995 (preliminary figure, '000 million pesos at constant 1986 prices): GDP in purchasers' values 6,355.3.

BALANCE OF PAYMENTS (US $ million)

	1994	1995	1996
Exports of goods f.o.b.	11,604	16,137	15,353
Imports of goods f.o.b.	-10,880	-14,657	-16,499
Trade balance	724	1,480	-1,146
Exports of services	2,848	3,160	3,356
Imports of services	-2,830	-3,325	-3,587
Balance on goods and services	742	1,315	-1,377
Other income received	498	824	695
Other income paid	-2,241	-2,306	-2,711
Balance on goods, services and income	-1,001	-167	-3,393
Current transfers received	375	348	513
Current transfers paid	-18	-39	-41
Current balance	-644	142	-2,921
Direct investment abroad	-926	-697	-1,080
Direct investment from abroad	1,773	1,668	4,091
Portfolio investment assets	-351	-14	-137
Portfolio investment liabilities	1,259	49	1,240
Other investment assets	-163	-49	-141
Other investment liabilities	2,942	430	2,369
Net errors and omissions	-741	-391	-917
Overall balance	3,149	1,138	2,504

Source: IMF, *International Financial Statistics*.

External Trade

PRINCIPAL COMMODITIES (distribution by SITC, US $ million)

Imports c.i.f.	1993	1994	1995
Food and live animals	516.7	634.8	824.5
Cereals and cereal preparations	154.6	205.1	245.7
Crude materials (inedible) except fuels	243.1	278.1	445.5
Mineral fuels, lubricants, etc.	1,057.2	1,101.8	1,341.0
Petroleum, petroleum products, etc.	926.4	952.9	1,129.3
Crude petroleum oils, etc.	779.7	748.0	905.7
Chemicals and related products	1,173.8	1,309.9	1,763.6
Plastic materials, etc.	278.1	320.2	449.3
Products of polymerization, etc.	205.1	247.5	345.9
Basic manufactures	1,721.5	1,689.2	2,473.8
Paper, paperboard and manufactures	192.5	233.6	401.4
Textile yarn, fabrics, etc.	406.7	373.0	488.0
Iron and steel	355.8	328.2	538.2
Machinery and transport equipment	4,567.8	4,738.3	6,273.9
Power-generating machinery and equipment	256.1	457.5	315.0
Machinery specialized for particular industries	722.8	665.5	1,005.0
General industrial machinery, equipment and parts	976.0	959.7	1,226.0
Office machines and automatic data-processing equipment	303.7	350.9	465.9
Automatic data-processing equipment	199.0	237.1	319.6
Telecommunications and sound recording and reproducing apparatus and equipment	474.3	426.7	585.6
Other electrical machinery, apparatus, etc.	472.1	534.4	695.7
Road vehicles and parts	1,269.3	1,236.2	1,824.4
Passenger motor vehicles (excl. buses)	480.7	442.7	741.9
Lorries and trucks	401.0	423.5	586.8
Miscellaneous manufactured articles	974.8	1,100.0	1,419.2
Total (incl. others)	10,541.9	11,149.1	14,903.1

Exports f.o.b.	1993	1994	1995
Food and live animals	2,365.9	2,729.5	3,471.9
Fish, crustaceans and molluscs, and preparations thereof	738.6	806.0	1,021.7
Fish, fresh (live or dead), chilled or frozen	502.1	571.5	716.0
Fish, frozen (excl. fillets)	246.7	284.6	349.3
Vegetables and fruit	1,042.2	1,170.7	1,374.8
Fruit and nuts (excl. oil nuts), fresh or dried	734.7	819.6	907.5
Grapes, fresh or dried	351.2	386.3	376.1
Grapes, fresh	327.5	350.0	345.3
Feeding-stuff for animals (excl. unmilled cereals)	386.8	472.8	657.2
Flours and meals of fish, crustaceans or mulluscs, unfit for human consumption	367.1	454.1	633.4
Crude materials (inedible) except fuels	2,244.8	2,906.5	4,724.4
Cork and wood	479.4	519.0	704.0
Pulp and waste paper	468.9	720.1	1,274.2
Chemical wood pulp, soda or sulphate	468.4	717.7	1,270.4
Metalliferous ores and metal scrap	1,112.8	1,455.0	2,501.3
Copper ores and concentrates (excl. matte)	861.0	1,130.0	1,920.3
Chemicals and related products	359.8	521.4	541.3
Basic manufactures	3,163.9	3,810.4	5,614.8
Non-ferrous metals	2,733.8	3,281.1	4,928.6
Copper	2,646.1	3,160.5	4,782.8
Copper and copper alloys, refined or not, unwrought	2,559.9	3,041.4	4,611.6
Unrefined copper (incl. blister copper but excl. cement copper)	231.1	418.6	509.8
Refined copper (incl. copper alloys other than master alloys), unwrought	2,328.7	2,622.7	4,101.8
Machinery and transport equipment	247.0	312.2	285.9
Miscellaneous manufactured articles	332.3	345.7	356.9
Total (incl. others)	9,308.3	11,368.7	15,901.1

Source: UN, *International Trade Statistics Yearbook*.

PRINCIPAL TRADING PARTNERS (US $ million)*

Imports c.i.f.	1993	1994	1995
Argentina	580.2	954.7	1,384.5
Belgium-Luxembourg	105.3	115.0	125.5
Brazil	1,059.9	999.8	1,194.6
Canada	203.0	264.8	315.1
China, People's Republic	212.5	280.7	390.3
Colombia	98.2	118.9	149.9
Ecuador	129.4	187.1	209.1
France	345.6	362.5	445.9
Germany	620.0	506.5	789.7
Italy	335.5	350.4	508.7
Japan	882.6	1,007.1	1,012.9
Korea, Republic	343.2	333.4	527.4
Mexico	209.6	263.7	600.6
Nigeria	397.3	134.4	166.6
Spain	278.3	340.8	445.0
Switzerland	107.7	117.1	124.5
United Kingdom	214.7	243.1	247.0
USA	2,477.1	2,637.9	3,792.8
Venezuela	141.6	139.9	226.8
Total (incl. others)	10,541.9	11,149.1	14,903.0

Exports f.o.b.	1993	1994	1995
Argentina	588.5	635.6	584.1
Belgium-Luxembourg	141.2	203.9	370.3
Bolivia	162.2	171.6	196.9
Brazil	422.5	616.7	1,063.9
China, People's Republic	183.3	133.3	287.2
Colombia	71.7	116.8	188.4
France	362.3	394.1	500.9
Germany	438.4	475.3	739.5
Italy	330.5	351.5	596.3
Japan	1,542.9	1,972.1	2,840.2
Korea, Republic	421.4	594.5	891.2
Mexico	124.4	202.9	127.4
Netherlands	227.7	293.4	358.9
Peru	206.2	328.3	432.3
Spain	243.4	219.0	303.7
United Kingdom	481.9	423.0	932.0
USA	1,433.0	1,716.7	1,951.1
Total (incl. others)	9,068.7	11,059.8	15,530.1

* Imports by country of purchase; exports by country of sale. Figures exclude trade in gold.

Source: UN, *International Trade Statistics Yearbook*.

Transport

PRINCIPAL RAILWAYS ('000)

	1992	1993	1994
Passenger journeys	9,518	9,563	10,193
Passenger/km	1,009,976	936,456	814,543
Freight (tons)	19,012	17,529	17,895

Source: Empresa de Ferrocarriles del Estado y Particulares.

ROAD TRAFFIC (motor vehicles in use)

	1994	1995	1996
Passenger cars	837,379	930,438	1,017,052
Buses and coaches	32,516	33,970	34,734
Lorries and vans	453,103	495,843	538,443
Motor cycles and mopeds	27,174	29,189	32,179

SHIPPING

Merchant Fleet (registered at 31 December)

	1994	1995	1996
Number of vessels	439	446	456
Total displacement ('000 grt)	721	761	691

Source: Lloyd's Register of Shipping, *World Fleet Statistics*.

International Sea-borne Shipping (freight traffic, '000 metric tons)

	1991	1992	1993
Goods loaded	20,851	22,579	21,771
Goods unloaded	10,948	12,017	13,514

Source: Dirección General del Territorio Marítimo y de Marina Mercante.

CIVIL AVIATION

	1992	1993	1994
Kilometres flown ('000)	62,033*	69,767	78,689
Passengers (number)	1,754,750	2,197,872	2,798,500
Freight ('000 ton-km)	864,291	1,000,584	1,124,776

* Includes airline taxis.

Source: Junta Aeronáutica Civil.

Tourism

	1992	1993	1994
Tourist arrivals (1000)	1,283	1,412	1,623
Tourist receipts (US $ million)	706	744	833

Source: UN, *Statistical Yearbook*.

Communications Media

	1992	1993	1994
Radio receivers ('000 in use)	4,680	4,765	4,850
Television receivers ('000 in use)	2,850	2,910	2,960
Telephones ('000 main lines in use)	1,283	1,520	1,545
Telefax stations (number in use)	12,457	15,000	n.a.
Mobile cellular telephones (subscribers)	64,438	85,186	100,000
Book production: titles	1,820	n.a.	n.a.
Daily newspapers	45	n.a.	32

* Provisional figure.

Source: mainly UNESCO, *Statistical Yearbook*.

Education

(1994)

	Schools	Teachers	Students
Pre-primary	4,389	9,415	263,337
Primary	8,323	78,813	2,119,737
Secondary	n.a.	50,187	664,498
Higher (incl. universities)	n.a.	n.a.	315,653*

*Provisional figure for 1993 (Source: Ministerio de Educación Pública).

Source: UNESCO, *Statistical Yearbook*.

Directory

The Constitution

The 1981 Constitution, described as a 'transition to democracy', separated the presidency from the Junta and provided for presidential elections and for the re-establishment of the bicameral legislature, consisting of an upper chamber (Senado) of both elected and appointed Senators, who are to serve an eight-year term, and a lower chamber (Cámara de Diputados) of 120 Deputies elected for a four-year term. All former Presidents are to be Senators for life. There is a National Security Council consisting of the President of the Republic, the heads of the armed forces and the police, and the Presidents of the Supreme Court and the Senado.

In July 1989 a national referendum approved 54 reforms to the Constitution, including 47 proposed by the Government and seven by the Military Junta. Among provisions made within the articles were an increase in the number of directly elected senators from 26 to 38, the abolition of the need for the approval of two successive Congresos for constitutional amendments (the support of two-thirds of the Cámara de Diputados and the Senado being sufficient), the reduction in term of office for the President to be elected in 1989 from eight to four years, with no immediate re-election possible, and the redrafting of the provision that outlawed Marxist groups so as to ensure 'true and responsible political pluralism'. The President's right to dismiss the Congreso and sentence to internal exile were eliminated.

In November 1991 the Congreso approved constitutional changes to local government. The amendments provided for the replacement of centrally appointed local officials with directly elected representatives.

In February 1994 an amendment to the Constitution was approved whereby the length of the presidential term was reduced from eight to six years.

The Government

HEAD OF STATE

President: EDUARDO FREI RUIZ-TAGLE (took office 11 March 1994).

THE CABINET
(January 1998)

A coalition of parties represented in the Concertación de los Partidos de la Democracia (CPO), including the Partido Demócrata Cristiano (PDC), the Partido Socialista de Chile (PS) and the Partido Radical (PR).

Minister of Agriculture: CARLOS MLADINIC ALONSO (PDC).

Minister of Finance: EDUARDO ANINAT URETA (PDC).

Minister of Foreign Affairs: JOSÉ MIGUEL INSULZA SALINAS (PS).

Minister of Housing and Urban Development: SERGIO HENRÍQUEZ (PDC).

Minister of the Interior: CARLOS FIGUEROA SERRANO (PDC).

Minister of Justice: MARÍA SOLEDAD ALVEAR VALENZUELA (PDC).

Minister of Labour and Social Security: JORGE ARRATE MACNIVEN (PS).

Minister of Mining: SERGIO JIMÉNEZ MORAGA (PR).

Minister of National Defence: RAÚL TRONCOSO (PDC).

Minister of National Properties: ADRIANA DELPIANO PUELMA (PDC).

Minister of the National Women's Service (Senam): JOSEFINA BILBAO MENDOZA (PDC).

Minister of Planning and Co-operation: ROBERTO PIZARRO HOFER (PS).

Minister of Production Development (Vice-President of CORFO): FELIPE SANDOVAL PRECHT (PDC).

Minister of Public Education: JOSÉ PABLO ARELLANO MARÍN (PDC).

Minister of Public Health: ALEX FIGUEROA (PDC).

Minister of Public Works: RICARDO LAGOS ESCOBAR (PS).

Minister Secretary-General of Government: JOSÉ JOAQUÍN BRUNNER (PPD).

Minister Secretary-General of the Presidency: JUAN VILLARZU ROHDE (PDC).

Minister of Trade and Industry: ALVARO GARCÍA HURTADO (PDC).

Minister of Transport and Telecommunications: CLAUDIO HOBMANN BARRIENTOS (PDC).

President of the National Energy Commission: ALEJANDRO JADRESIC MARINOVIC (PDC).

Comptroller-General of the Republic: OSVALDO ITURRIAGA RUÍZ.

MINISTRIES

Ministry of Agriculture: Teatinos 40, Santiago; tel. (2) 696-3241; telex 240745; fax (2) 671-6500.

Ministry of Finance: Teatinos 120, 12°, Santiago; tel. (2) 671-2771; telex 241334; fax (2) 696-4496.

Ministry of Foreign Affairs: Morandé 441, Casilla 91, Correo 21, Santiago; tel. (2) 698-2501; telex 40595; fax (2) 699-4202.

Ministry of Housing and Urban Development: Avda B. O'Higgins, Santiago; tel. (2) 638-3366; telex 240124; fax (2) 633-3892.

Ministry of the Interior: Palacio de la Moneda, Santiago; tel. (2) 671-7054; telex 240273; fax (2) 696-8740.

Ministry of Justice: Morandé 107, Santiago; tel. (2) 696-8151; telex 241316; fax (2) 696-6952.

Ministry of Labour and Social Security: Huérfanos 1273, 6°, Santiago; tel. (2) 671-6443; telex 242559; fax (2) 698-8473.

Ministry of Mining: Teatinos 120, 9°, Santiago; tel. (2) 696-5872; telex 240948; fax (2) 698-9262.

Ministry of National Defence: Villavicencio 364, 22°, Edif. Diego Portales, Santiago; tel. (2) 222-1202; telex 40537; fax (2) 634-5339.

Ministry of National Properties: Juan Antonio Ríos 6, Santiago; tel. (2) 633-9305; fax (2) 633-9316.

Ministry of the National Women's Service (Senam): Rosa Rodríguez 1375, 6°, Casilla 22, Santiago; tel. (2) 695-3325; fax (2) 697-1082.

Ministry of Planning and Co-operation (MIDEPLAN): Ahumada 48, Casilla 9140, Santiago; tel. (2) 672-2033; telex 341400; fax (2) 672-1879.

Ministry of Production Development (CORFO): Moneda 921, Casilla 3886, Santiago; tel. (2) 638-0521; telex 240421; fax (2) 671-1058.

Ministry of Public Education: Avda B. O'Higgins 1371, Of. 702, Santiago; tel. (2) 698-3351; telex 240567; fax (2) 698-7831.

Ministry of Public Health: Enrique MacIver 541, 3°, Santiago; tel. (2) 639-4001; telex 240136; fax (2) 638-4377.

Ministry of Public Works: Dirección de Vialidad, Morandé 59, 2°, Santiago; tel. (2) 696-4839; telex 240777; fax (2) 698-6622.

Ministry of Trade and Industry: Teatinos 120, 10°, Santiago; tel. (2) 672-5164; telex 240558; fax (2) 696-6305.

Ministry of Transport and Telecommunications: Amunátegui 139, 3°, Santiago; tel. (2) 672-6503; telex 240200; fax (2) 672-2785; e-mail ministerio:mtt@mtt.cl.

Office of the Comptroller-General of the Republic: Teatinos 56, 9°, Santiago; tel. (2) 672-4212; telex 240281; fax (2) 672-5565.

Office of the Minister Secretary-General of Government: Palacio de la Moneda, Santiago; tel. (2) 690-4160; telex 240142; fax (2) 699-1657; e-mail jbrunner@segegob.cl.

Office of the Minister Secretary-General of the Presidency: Palacio de la Moneda, Santiago; tel. (2) 690-4000; fax (2) 698-4656.

President and Legislature

PRESIDENT

Election, 11 December 1993*

	Votes cast	Percentage of votes cast
EDUARDO FREI RUIZ-TAGLE (CPD)	4,008,654	58.01
ARTURO ALESSANDRI BESA (UPC)	1,685,584	24.39
JOSÉ PIÑERA (Independent)	427,286	6.18
MANFRED MAX-NEEF (MAPU/IC)	383,847	5.55
EUGENIO PIZARRO (MIDA)	324,121	4.69
CRISTIÁN REITZE (Alianza Humanista-Verde)	81,095	1.17
Total	6,910,587	100.00

* Figures represent 99.1% of valid votes cast.

CONGRESO NACIONAL

Senado*
(Senate)

President: GABRIEL VALDÉS SUBERCASEAUX (PDC).

General Election, 11 December 1997*

	Valid votes	% of valid votes	Seats
Partido Demócrata Cristiano (PDC)	1,223,495	29.24	10
Unión Demócrata Independiente (UDI)	717,919	17.16	3
Renovación Nacional (RN)	620,799	14.84	2
Partido Socialista de Chile (PS)	609,725	14.57	1
Partido Comunista de Chile (PCCh)	352,327	8.42	4
Independents	293,429	7.02	—
Partido por la Democracia (PPD)	180,468	4.31	—
Partido Humanista (PH)	92,880	2.22	—
Partido Radical Socialdemócrata (PRSD)	75,680	1.81	—
Unión de Centro-Centro Progresista (UCCP)	17,725	0.42	—
Total	4,184,447	100.00	20

In addition, there were 220,945 blank and 632,538 spoiled votes.

* Results of elections to renew 20 of the 39 elective seats in the Senado. In addition, there are nine designated senators (see section on Recent History), and a constitutional provision for former Presidents to assume a seat for life, in an *ex-officio* capacity.

Cámara de Diputados
(Chamber of Deputies)

President: GUTENBERG MARTÍNEZ (PDC).

General Election, 11 December 1997

	Valid votes	% of valid votes	Seats
Partido Demócrata Cristiano (PDC)	1,317,441	22.98	39
Renovación Nacional (RN)	962,247	16.78	23
Unión Demócrata Independiente (UDI)	827,324	14.43	17
Partido por la Democracia (PPD)	719,575	12.55	16
Partido Socialista de Chile (PS)	636,357	11.10	11
Independents	433,210	7.56	8
Partido Comunista de Chile (PCCh)	393,523	6.86	—
Partido Radical Socialdemócrata (PRSD)	179,701	3.13	4
Partido Humanista (PH)	166,569	2.91	—
Unión de Centro-Centro Progresista (UCCP)	68,185	1.19	1
Partido Democracia del Sur (PDS)	20,635	0.36	1
Nueva Alianza Popular (NAP)	8,947	0.16	—
Total	5,733,714	100.00	120

In addition, there were 295,581 blank and 943,235 spoiled votes.

Political Organizations

The most prominent political organizations are:

Acción Pinochetista Unitaria (APU): Santiago; f. 1993; pro-Pinochet; Pres. GONZALO TOWNSEND PINOCHET.

Alianza Humanista-Verde: Santiago; withdrew from CPD in 1993 in order to promote own presidential candidate; Leaders ANDRÉS R. KORYZMA, JOSÉ TOMÁS SÁENZ.

Avanzada Nacional: Santiago; tel. (2) 698-3588; right-wing; Pres. Col (retd) ALVARO CORVALÁN.

Concertación de los Partidos de la Democracia (CPD): (see below).

Intransigencia Democrática: Santiago; tel. (2) 72-4164; f. 1985; centre-left alliance; Pres. MANUEL SANHUEZA CRUZ.

Izquierda Cristiana (IC): Christian left; Sec.-Gen. LUIS MAIRA.

Movimiento de Izquierda Democrática Allendista (MIDA): Santiago; left-wing; 1993 presidential candidate EUGENIO PIZARRO.

Movimiento de Izquierda Revolucionaria (MIR): revolutionary left; Leader ANDRÉS PASCAL ALLENDE.

Movimiento Patriótica Manuel Rodríguez (MPMR): (see Frente Patriótica Manuel Rodríguez).

Movimiento Social Cristiano: Santiago; tel. (2) 696-1961; f. 1984; right-wing party; Pres. JUAN DE DIOS CARMONA; Sec.-Gen. MANUEL RODRÍGUEZ.

Nueva Alianza Popular ((NAP): Santiago; left-wing.

Partido Alianza de Centro (PAC): Santiago; centre; member of CPD; Leader GERMÁN RIESCO.

Partido Comunista de Chile (PCCh): Santiago; tel. (2) 72-4164; achieved legal status in October 1990; Pres. GLADYS MARÍN.

Partido por la Democracia (PPD): Constitución 64, Providencia, Santiago; Pres. JORGE SCHAULSOHN BRODSKY.

Partido Democracia Social: San Antonio 220, Of. 604, Santiago; tel. (2) 39-4244; democratic socialist party; Pres. LUIS ANGEL SANTIBÁÑEZ; Sec.-Gen. JAIME CARMONA DONOSO.

Partido Democracia del Sur (PDS): Santiago.

Partido Demócrata Cristiano (PDC): Carmen 8, 6°, Santiago; tel. (2) 33-8535; telex 242397; f. 1957; factions include guatones (right-wing), chascones (left-wing) and renovadores (centre); member of CPD; Pres. ENRIQUE KRAUSS.

Partido Humanista (PH): Santiago.

Partido Liberal: Santiago; tel. (2) 48-0738; liberal party; Pres. GUILLERMO TORO ALBORNOZ; Vice-Pres. OLGA REYES.

Partido Nacional de Democracia Centrista (PNDC): Santiago; f. 1990, following the merger of the Partido Democracia Radical, the Partido Nacional and the Partido Nacional Vanguardista; centre-right; Pres. JULIO DURÁN.

Partido Popular Cristiano (PPC): Santiago; f. 1997 by disaffected congressional deputies from the PDC; centrist; Leaders RAMÓN ELIZALDE; SAMUEL VENEGAS.

Partido Radical (PR): Avda Santa María 281, Santiago; tel. (2) 77-9903; f. 1863; social democratic; mem. of Socialist International; member of CPD; Pres. CARLOS GONZÁLEZ MÁRQUEZ; Sec.-Gen. RICARDO NAVARRETE.

Partido Radical Socialdemócrata (PRSD): Santiago; centre-left; allied to CPD.

Partido Republicano: Santiago; tel. (2) 698-4167; f. 1983; centre-right party; Pres. (vacant); Sec.-Gen. GABRIEL LEÓN ECHAIZ.

Partido Social Demócrata (PSD): París 815, Casilla 50.220, Correo Central, Santiago; tel. (2) 39-9064; f. 1973; member of CPD; Pres. ARTURO VENEGAS GUTIÉRREZ; Sec.-Gen. LEVIÁN MUÑOZ PELLICER.

Partido Socialista de Chile (PS): Concha y Toro 36, Santiago; tel. (2) 696-6596; fax (2) 695-2444; e-mail pschile@reuna.cl; f. 1933; left-wing; member of Socialist International; Pres. CAMILO ESCALONA; Vice-Pres. ISABEL ALLENDE; Gen. Sec. EDGARDO CONDEZA.

Partido Tercera República (PTR): Santiago; f. 1990; Pres. FRANCISCO JAVIER ITURRIAGA ASTE.

Renovación Nacional (RN): Antonio Varas 454, Providencia, Santiago; tel. (2) 235-1337; fax (2) 235-1338; f. 1987; right-wing; Pres. ANDRÉS ALLAMAND; Sec.-Gen. RODRIGO UBILLA M.; comprises:

Frente Nacional del Trabajo: Dr Barros Borgoño 21, Santiago; tel. (2) 41923; Sec.-Gen. ANGEL FANTUZZI.

Unión Nacional: Ricardo Matte Pérez 0140, Santiago; tel. (2) 744-9915; centre-right party; Pres. ANDRÉS ALLAMAND ZAVALA.

Unión de Centro-Centro Progresista (UCCP): Santiago; f. as Unión de Centro-Centro; right-wing.

Unión Demócrata Independiente (UDI): Suecia 286, Santiago; tel. (2) 233-0037; fax (2) 233-6189; f. 1989; right-wing; Pres. JOVINO NOVOA VÁSQUEZ; Sec.-Gen. JUAN ANTONIO COLOMA CORREA.

Unión para el Progreso de Chile (UPC): (see below).

Unión por Chile (UPC): Santiago; f. 1996; right-wing alliance of the RN and the UDI; formed to contest municipal and legislative elections during 1997.

Unión Socialista Popular: Teatinos 251, Of. 809, Santiago; tel. (2) 698-4269; left-wing party; Sec.-Gen. RAMÓN SILVA ULLOA.

In early 1988 16 political parties and opposition groups united to form the **Comando por el No,** an opposition front to campaign against the government candidate in the plebiscite of 5 October 1988. Following the plebiscite, the Comando por el No assumed the title of **Concertación de los Partidos de la Democracia (CPD)** and presented a single, successful candidate at successive presidential elections, conducted in 1989 and in 1993.

Other alliances include:

Unión para el Progreso de Chile (UPC): Santiago; f. 1993; right-wing alliance including Renovación Nacional (RN) and the Union Demócrata Independiente (UDI); presented a single candidate at 1993 presidential elections.

Guerrilla groups include:

Acción Chilena Anticomunista (ACHA): right-wing; Pres. JUAN SERRANO.

Frente Juventil Lautaro (FJL): extreme left-wing; f. 1983 by dissident faction of Movimiento de Acción Popular Unitaria (MAPU); Leader GUILLERMO OSSANDON (captured June 1994).

Fuerzas Rebeldes y Populares Lautaro (FRPL): military wing of FJL.

Frente Patriótico Manuel Rodríguez (FPMR): f. 1983; Communist; Leader Commdr DANIEL HUERTA. In May 1991 the FPMR announced its intention to renounce its armed struggle and join the political mainstream as the **Movimiento Patriótico Manuel Rodríguez (MPMR).** However, a faction of the FPMR (known since 1987 as the **FPMR—Autónomo**) intended to continue to conduct guerrilla activity.

Frente de Resistencia Nacionalista (FRN): right-wing.

Frente Revolucionario Nacionalista (FREN): left-wing.

Diplomatic Representation

EMBASSIES IN CHILE

Argentina: Miraflores 285, Santiago; tel. (2) 33-1076; telex 240280; Ambassador: JOSÉ MARÍA ALVAREZ DE TOLEDO.

Australia: Gertrudis Echeñique 420, Casilla 33, Correo 10, Las Condes, Santiago; tel. (2) 228-5065; telex 240855; fax (2) 208-1707; Ambassador: K. B. BERRY.

Austria: Barrios Errázuriz 1968, 3°, Casilla 16196, Santiago; tel. (2) 223-4774; telex 240528; fax (2) 204-9382; Ambassador: HORST-DIETER RENNAU.

Belgium: Avda Providencia 2653, 11°, Of. 1104, Santiago; tel. (2) 232-1070; telex 440088; Chargé d'affaires: MICHEL GODFRIND.

Brazil: Alonso Ovalle 1665, Santiago; tel. (2) 698-2486; telex 340350; fax (2) 671-5961; Ambassador: GUILHERME LEITE-RIBEIRO.

Canada: Ahumada 11, 10°, Casilla 427, Santiago; tel. (2) 696-2256; fax (2) 696-2424; Ambassador: MARC LORTIE.

China, People's Republic: Pedro de Valdivia 550, Santiago; tel. (2) 25-0755; telex 240863; Ambassador: ZHU XIANGZHONG.

Colombia: La Gioconda 4317, Santiago; tel. (2) 206-1999; fax (2) 208-7007; Ambassador: ALBERTO VELÁSQUEZ.

Costa Rica: Barcelona 2070, Santiago; tel. (2) 231-9839; fax (2) 231-8915; Ambassador: MARIO GARNIER BORELLA.

Cuba: Santiago; Ambassador: ARAMIS FUENTES.

Denmark: Jacques Cazotte 5531, Casilla 13430, Vitacura, Santiago; tel. (2) 218-5949; fax (2) 218-1736; Ambassador: OLE WØEHLERS OLSEN.

Dominican Republic: Mariscal Petain 125, Santiago; tel. (2) 228-8083; Ambassador: RAFAEL VÁLDEZ HICARIO.

Ecuador: Avda Providencia 1979, 5°, Santiago; tel. (2) 231-2015; telex 240717; fax (2) 232-5822; Ambassador: RODRIGO VÁLDEZ BAQUERO.

Egypt: Roberto del Río 1871, Providencia, Santiago; tel. (2) 274-8881; telex 440156; fax (2) 274-6334; Ambassador: TALAAT SELMY.

El Salvador: Calle Noruega 6595, Las Condes, Santiago; tel. (2) 25-1096; Ambassador: Dr JOSÉ HORACIO TRUJILLO.

Finland: Mons. Sótero Sanz 55, Of. 71, Casilla 16657, Santiago 9; tel. (2) 232-4573; fax (2) 232-0456; Ambassador: RISTO KAUPPI.

France: Avda Condell 65, Casilla 38-D, Santiago; tel. (2) 225-1030; telex 240535; fax (2) 274-1353; e-mail ambafran@iusanet.cl; Ambassador: JEAN-MICHEL GAUSSOT.

Germany: Agustinas 785, 7° y 8°, Casilla 9949, Santiago; tel. (2) 633-5031; telex 240583; fax (2) 633-6119; Ambassador: HORST PALENBERG.

Guatemala: Los Españoles 2155, Pedro de Valdivia Norte, Providencia, Santiago; tel. (2) 231-7367; fax (2) 232-4494; Ambassador: CARLOS ALBERTO PRERA FLORES.

Haiti: Zurich 255, Depto 21, Los Condes, Santiago; tel. (2) 231-8233; fax (2) 231-0967; Ambassador: GUY PIERRE ANDRÉ.

Holy See: Calle Nuncio Sótero Sanz 200, Casilla 16.836, Correo 9, Santiago (Apostolic Nunciature); tel. (2) 231-2020; fax (2) 231-0868; e-mail nunciatu@entelchile.net; Nuncio: Most Rev. PIERO BIGGIO, Titular Archbishop of Otricoli.

Honduras: Avda 11 de Septiembre 2155, Of. 303, Santiago; tel. (2) 231-4161; telex 440456; Ambassador: CARLOS H. REYES.

India: Triana 871, Casilla 10433, Santiago; tel. (2) 235-2005; telex 340046; fax (2) 235-9607; Ambassador: RAM MOHAN.

Indonesia: Hernando de Aguirre 1065, Providencia, Casilla 20-D, Santiago; tel. (2) 231-0186; telex 244068; fax (2) 2319447.

Israel: San Sebastián 2812, 5°, Casilla 1224, Santiago; tel. (2) 246-1570; telex 240627; fax (2) 231-0197; e-mail eisraelfr@tmm.cl; Ambassador: ORI NOY.

Italy: Clemente Fabres 1050, Santiago; tel. (2) 225-9029; telex 440321; Ambassador: EMANUELE COSTA.

Japan: Avda Providencia 2653, 19°, Casilla 2877, Santiago; tel. (2) 232-1807; telex 440132; Ambassador: SHUICHI NOMIYAMA.

Jordan: Los Militares 4280, Las Condes, Casilla 10431, Santiago; tel. (2) 228-8989; Ambassador: ATEF HALASA.

Korea, Republic: Alcántara 74, Casilla 1301, Santiago; tel. (2) 228-4214; telex 340380; Ambassador: SUH KYUNG-SUK.

Lebanon: Avda Alianza 1728, Vitacura, Casilla 19150, Correo 19, Santiago; tel. (2) 218-2835; fax (2) 219-3502; e-mail líbano@netline.cl; Ambassador: IBRAHIM KRAIDY.

Malaysia: Santiago; Ambassador LILY ZACHARIAH.

Netherlands: Las Violetas 2368, Casilla 56-D, Santiago; tel. (2) 223-6825; fax (2) 225-2737; e-mail hollemb@tmm.cl; Ambassador: JOHN C. F. VON MÜHLEN.

New Zealand: Avda Isidora Goyenechea 3516, Casilla 112, Las Condes, Santiago; tel. (2) 231-4204; fax (2) 231-9040; Ambassador: DAVID G. MCKEE.

Norway: San Sebastián 2839, Of. 509, Casilla 2431, Santiago; tel. (2) 234-2888; telex 440150; fax (2) 234-2201; Ambassador: MARTIN TORE BJØRNDAL.

Panama: Bustos 2199, Correo 9892, Santiago; tel. (2) 225-0147; Ambassador: RICARDO MORENO VILLALAZ.

Paraguay: Huérfanos 886, 5°, Ofs 514-515, Santiago; tel. (2) 39-4640; telex 645357; Ambassador: Dr FABIO RIVAS ARAÚJO.

Peru: Avda Andrés Bello 1751, Providencia, Santiago 9, Casilla 16277, Santiago; tel. (2) 235-2356; fax (2) 235-8139; e-mail emperch@ctc-mundo.net; Ambassador: JORGE COLUNGE VILLACORTA.

Philippines: La Gloria 17, esq. Apoquindo, Las Condes, Santiago; tel. (2) 208-1313; Ambassador: HERMENEGILDO C. CRUZ.

Romania: Benjamín 2955, Santiago; tel. (2) 231-1893; telex 440378; Chargé d'affaires a.i.: GHEORGHE PETRE.

Russia: Santiago; Ambassador: VASSILI P. GROMOV.

South Africa: Avda 11 de Septiembre 2353, 16°, Torre San Ramón, Santiago; tel. (2) 231-2860; telex 341522; Ambassador: C. S. C. VENTER.

Spain: Avda Andrés Bello 1895, Casilla 16456, Providencia, Santiago; tel. (2) 235-2755; telex 340253; fax (2) 236-1547; Ambassador: JUAN MANUEL EGEA IBÁÑEZ.

Sweden: Casilla 16639, Santiago 9; tel. (2) 231-2733; telex 440153; fax (2) 232-4188; e-mail ambassaden.santiago-de-chile@foreign.ministry.se; Ambassador: MADELEINE STRÖJE WILKENS.

Switzerland: Avda Providencia 2653, Of. 1602, Casilla 3875, Santiago; tel. (2) 232-2693; telex 340870; fax (2) 232-1872; e-mail swissems@ctc-mundo.net; Ambassador: HANS-PETER ERISMANN.

Syria: Carmencita 111, Casilla 12, Correo 10, Santiago; tel. (2) 232-7471; telex 240095; Ambassador: HISHAM HALLAJ.

Turkey: Calle Nuncio Sótero Sanz 136, Providencia, Santiago; tel. (2) 231-8952; telex 340278; fax (2) 231-7762; Ambassador: SADI CALISLAR.

United Kingdom: Avda el Bosque Norte 0125, Casilla 72 D, Santiago; tel. (2) 231-3737; telex 340483; fax (2) 231-9771; Ambassador: GLYNNE EVANS.

USA: Andrés Bello 2800, Las Condes, Santiago; tel. (2) 232-2600; fax (2) 330-3710; Ambassador: GABRIEL GUERRA-MONDRAGÓN.

Uruguay: Avda Pedro de Valdivia 711, Casilla 2636, Santiago; tel. (2) 74-3569; telex 340371; Ambassador: ALFREDO BIANCHI PALAZZO.

Venezuela: Mar del Plata 2055, Casilla 16577, Santiago; tel. (2) 225-0021; telex 440170; Ambassador: HÉCTOR VARGAS ACOSTA.

Yugoslavia: Exequías Allende 2370, Providencia, Casilla 16597, Santiago 9; tel. (2) 223-0510; fax (2) 233-9890; Chargé d'affaires: SVETISLAV RAJEVIC.

Judicial System

The Supreme Courts consist of 21 members.

There are Courts of Appeal (in the cities or departments of Arica, Iquique, Antofagasta, Copiapó, La Serena, Valparaíso, Santiago, San Miguel, Rancagua, Talca, Chillán, Concepción, Temuco, Valdivia, Puerto Montt, Coyhaique and Punta Arenas) whose members are appointed from a list submitted to the President of the Republic by the Supreme Court. The number of members of each court varies. Judges of the lower courts are appointed in a similar manner from lists submitted by the Court of Appeal of the district in which the vacancy arises. Judges and Ministers of the Supreme Court do not continue in office beyond the age of 75.

In March 1998 a major reform of the judiciary was implemented, including an increase, from 17 to 21, in the number of Ministers of the Supreme Court.

Corte Suprema: Plaza Montt Varas, Santiago; tel. (2) 698-0561.

President of the Supreme Court: ROBERTO DAVILA DÍAZ.

Ministers of the Supreme Court:

SERVANDO JORDÁN LÓPEZ
OSCAR CARRASCO ACUÑA
ELEODORO ORTIZ SEPÚLVEDA
ENRIQUE TAPIA WITTING
ORLANDO ALVAREZ HERNÁNDEZ
LUIS CORREA BULÓ
GUILLERMO NAVAS BUSTAMANTE
ALBERTO CHAIGNEAU DEL CAMPO
ENRIQUE CURY URZUA
JOSÉ LUIS PÉREZ ZAÑARTU
OSVALDO FAÚNDEZ VALLEJOS
ARNALDO TORO LEIVA
RICARDO GÁLVEZ BLANCO
JORGE RODRÍGUEZ ARIZTIA
HERNÁN ALVAREZ GARCÍA
MARIO GARRIDO MONTT
MARCOS LIBEDINSKY TSCHORNE
URBANO MARÍN VALLEJO
JOSÉ CAMHI BENQUIS
(vacant)

Attorney-General: ENRIQUE PAILLAS PEÑA.

Secretary of the Court: CARLOS A. MENESES PIZARRO.

Corporación Nacional de Reparación y Reconciliación: f. 1992 in order to co-ordinate and implement the recommendations of the **Comisión Nacional de Verdad y Reconciliación,** which was established in 1990 to investigate violations of human rights committed during the military dictatorship, and which delivered its report in 1991; Pres. ALEJANDRO GONZÁLEZ POBLETE; Exec. Sec. ANDRÉS DOMÍNGUEZ VIAL.

Religion

Some 77% of the population are Roman Catholics; there were an estimated 11.0m. adherents at 31 December 1995.

CHRISTIANITY

The Roman Catholic Church

Chile comprises five archdioceses, 17 dioceses, two territorial prelatures and two apostolic prefectures.

Bishops' Conference: Conferencia Episcopal de Chile, Cienfuegos 47, Casilla 517-V, Correo 21, Santiago; tel. (2) 671-7733; fax (2) 698-1416; e-mail sge@cechnet.cl; f. 1955; Pres. Cardinal CARLOS OVIEDO CAVADA, Archbishop of Santiago de Chile.

Archbishop of Antofagasta: PATRICIO INFANTE ALFONSO, San Martín 2628, Casilla E, Antofagasta; tel. (83) 26-8856; fax (83) 22-3021.

Archbishop of Concepción: ANTONIO MORENO CASAMITJANA, Calle Barros Arana 544, Casilla 65-C, Concepción; tel. (41) 22-8173; fax (41) 23-2844.

Archbishop of La Serena: FRANCISCO JOSÉ COX HUNEEUS, Los Carrera 450, Casilla 613, La Serena; tel. (51) 21-2325; fax (51) 22-5886.

Archbishop of Puerto Montt: SAVINO M. BERNARDO CAZZARO BERTOLLO, Calle Benavente 385, Casilla 17, Puerto Montt; tel. (65) 25-2215; fax (65) 27-1861.

Archbishop of Santiago de Chile: Cardinal CARLOS OVIEDO CAVADA, Erasmo Escala 1884, Casilla 30-D, Santiago; tel. (2) 696-3275; fax (2) 698-5666.

The Anglican Communion

Anglicans in Chile come within the Diocese of Chile, which forms part of the Anglican Church of the Southern Cone of America, covering Argentina, Bolivia, Chile, Paraguay, Peru and Uruguay.

Bishop of Chile: Rt Rev. COLIN FREDERICK BAZLEY, Iglesia Anglicana, Casilla 50675, Santiago; tel. (2) 639-1509; fax (2) 639-4581.

Other Christian Churches

Baptist Evangelical Convention: Casilla 41-22, Santiago; tel. (2) 222-4085; fax (2) 635-4104; f. 1908; Pres. MOISÉS PINTO; Gen. Sec. VÍCTOR OLIVARES.

Evangelical Lutheran Church: Irarrázaval 2005, Ñuñoa, Casilla 15167, Santiago; tel. (2) 225-0091; fax (2) 205-2193; f. 1937 as German Evangelical Church in Chile; present name adopted in 1959; Pres. MARTIN JUNGE; 2,500 mems.

Methodist Church: Sargento Aldea 1041, Casilla 67, Santiago; tel. (2) 556-6074; fax (2) 554-1763; autonomous since 1969; 7,317 mems; Bishop NEFTALÍ ARAVENA BRAVO.

Pentecostal Church: Calle Pena 1103, Casilla de Correo 2, Curicó; tel. (75) 1035; f. 1945; 90,000 mems; Bishop ENRIQUE CHÁVEZ CAMPOS.

Pentecostal Church Mission: Calle Passy 032, Casilla 238, Santiago; tel. (2) 634-6785; fax (2) 634-6786; f. 1952; Sec. Rev. DANIEL GODOY FERNÁNDEZ; Pres. Rev. ERASMO FARFÁN FIGUEROA; 12,000 mems.

BAHÁ'Í FAITH

National Spiritual Assembly: Casilla 3731, Manuel de Salas 356, Ñuñoa, Santiago; tel. (2) 269-2005; fax (2) 225-8276.

The Press

Most newspapers of nation-wide circulation in Chile are published in Santiago. According to official sources, there are 128 newspapers which appear more than twice a week, with a combined circulation of more than 900,000 copies per issue.

DAILIES

Circulation figures listed below are supplied mainly by the Asociación Nacional de la Prensa. Other sources give much lower figures.

Santiago

Diario Oficial de la República de Chile: Agustinas 1269, Santiago; tel. (2) 698-3969; fax (2) 698-2222; f. 1877; Dir Florencio Ceballos B.; circ. 10,000.

La Epoca: Serrano 240, Santiago Centro; tel. (2) 661-9800; f. 1987; morning; centre; independent; Dir Carlos Aldunate Balestra; circ. 50,000.

Fortín Mapocho: Agustinas 1849; tel. (2) 698-8745; f. 1990; independent; Dir Wladimir Aguilera Díaz.

El Mercurio: Avda Santa María 5542, Casilla 13-D, Santiago; tel. (2) 330-1111; fax (2) 228-7541; f. 1827; morning; conservative; Man. Dir Agustín Edwards; circ. 120,000 (weekdays), 280,000 (Sundays).

La Nación: Agustinas 1269, Santiago; tel. (2) 698-2222; f. 1917 to replace government-subsidized *El Cronista*; morning; financial; Propr Soc. Periodística La Nación; Dir Editor Abraham Santibáñez Martínez; circ. 45,000.

La Segunda: Avda Santa María 5542, Santiago; tel. (2) 228-7048; telex 341635; fax (2) 242-1116; f. 1931; evening; Dir Cristián Zegers Ariztía; circ. 40,000.

La Tercera de la Hora: Vicuña Mackenna 1870, Santiago; tel. (2) 551-7067; fax (2) 556-1017; f. 1950; morning; Dir Héctor Olave Vallejos; circ. 200,000.

Las Ultimas Noticias: Avda Santa María 5542, Santiago; tel. (2) 228-7048; f. 1902; morning; Man. Dir Fernando Díaz P.; owned by the Proprs of *El Mercurio*; circ. 150,000 (except Saturdays and Sundays).

Antofagasta

La Estrella del Norte: Manuel Antonio Matta 2112, Antofagasta; tel. (55) 26-4835; f. 1966; evening; Dir Roberto Retamal Pacheco; circ. 5,000.

El Mercurio: Manuel Antonio Matta 2112, Antofagasta; tel. (55) 26-4787; f. 1906; morning; conservative independent; Proprs Soc. Chilena de Publicaciones; Dir Rodolfo Garcés; circ. 9,000.

Arica

La Estrella de Arica: San Marcos 580, Arica; tel. (80) 23-1834; fax (80) 25-2890; f. 1976; Dir Emilio Bakit Vargas; circ. 10,000.

Calama

La Estrella del Loa: Abaroa 1929, Calama; tel. (82) 21-3525; f. 1979; Propr Soc. Chilena de Publicaciones; Dir Roberto Retamal Pacheco; circ. 4,000 (weekdays), 7,000 (Sundays).

El Mercurio: Abaroa 1929, Calama; tel. (82) 21-1604; f. 1968; Propr Soc. Chilena de Publicaciones; Dir Rodolfo Garcés; circ. 4,500 (weekdays), 7,000 (Sundays).

Chillán

La Discusión de Chillán, SA: Calle 18 de Septiembre 721, Casilla 14-D, Chillán; tel. (42) 21-2650; fax (42) 21-3578; f. 1870; morning; independent; Dir Tito Castillo Peralta; circ. 5,000.

Concepción

El Sur: Calle Freire 799, Casilla 8-C, Concepción; tel. (41) 23-5825; f. 1882; morning; independent; Dir Rafael Maira Lamas; circ. 28,000 (weekdays), 45,000 (Sundays).

Copiapó

Atacama: Manuel Rodríguez 740, Copiapó; tel. (52) 2255; morning; independent; Dir Samuel Salgado; circ. 6,500.

Curicó

La Prensa: Merced 373, Casilla 6-D, Curicó; tel. (75) 31-0453; fax (75) 31-1924; f. 1898; morning; right-wing; Man. Dir Manuel Massa Mautino; circ. 4,000.

Iquique

La Estrella de Iquique: Luis Uribe 452, Iquique; tel. (57) 42-2805; fax (57) 42-7975; f. 1966; evening; Dir Arcadio Castillo Ortíz; circ. 10,000.

La Serena

El Día: Brasil 395, Casilla 13-D, La Serena; tel. (51) 21-1284; f. 1944; morning; Dir Antonio Puga Rodríguez; circ. 10,800.

Los Angeles

La Tribuna: Calle Colo Colo 464, Casilla 15-D, Los Angeles; tel. (43) 31-3315; independent; Dir Cirilo Guzmán de la Fuente; circ. 4,500.

Osorno

El Diario Austral: Avda B. O'Higgins 870, Osorno; tel. (64) 235-1591; telex 373014; fax (64) 23-5192; f. 1982; Dir Carlos Noli A.; circ. 6,500 (weekdays), 7,300 (Sundays).

Diario 24 Horas: Osorno; tel. (642) 2300; Dir Roberto Silva Bajit.

Puerto Montt

El Llanquihue: San Felipe 129, Casilla 1047, Puerto Montt; tel. (65) 25-5115; fax (65) 25-5114; f. 1885; Dir Harold Mesías P.; circ. 4,800 (weekdays), 5,700 (Sundays).

Punta Arenas

La Prensa Austral: Waldo Seguel 636, Casilla 9-D, Punta Arenas; tel. (61) 24-3166; telex 280336; fax (61) 24-7406; e-mail prensa@webcom.com; f. 1941; morning; independent; Dir Manuel González Araya; circ. 10,000, Sunday (*El Magallanes*; f. 1894) 12,000.

Rancagua

El Rancagüino: O'Carroll 518, Rancagua; tel. (72) 23-0345; fax (72) 22-1483; f. 1915; independent; Dirs Héctor González, Alejandro González; circ. 10,000.

Talca

La Mañana de Talca: 1 Norte 911, Casilla 7-D, Talca; tel. (71) 32520; Dir Juan C. Bravo; circ. 5,000.

Temuco

El Diario Austral: Antonio Varas 945, Casilla 1-D, Temuco; tel. (45) 21-2575; fax (45) 23-7765; f. 1916; morning; commercial, industrial and agricultural interests; Dir Marco Antonio Pinto Zepeda; Propr Soc. Periodística Araucanía, SA; circ. 15,100 (weekdays), 23,500 (Sundays).

Tocopilla

La Prensa: Bolívar 1244, Tocopilla; tel. (83) 81-1240; f. 1924; morning; independent; Dir Roberto Retamal; circ. 3,000.

Valdivia

El Correo de Valdivia: Yungay 758, Casilla 15-D, Valdivia; f. 1895; morning; non-party; Dir Patricio Gómez Couchot; circ. 12,000.

El Diario Austral: Yungay 499, Valdivia; tel. (63) 21-3353; fax (63) 21-2236; f. 1982; Dir Gustavo Serrano Cotapos; circ. 4,600.

Valparaíso

La Estrella: Esmeralda 1002, Casilla 57-V, Valparaíso; tel. (32) 25-8011; telex 230531; fax (32) 25-0497; f. 1921; evening; independent; Dir Alfonso Castagneto; owned by the Proprs of *El Mercurio*; circ. 25,000, 30,000 (Saturdays).

El Mercurio: Esmeralda 1002, Casilla 57-V, Valparaíso; tel. (32) 25-8011; telex 330445; fax (32) 25-6438; f. 1827; morning; Dir Enrique Schröder Vicuña; owned by the Proprs of *El Mercurio* in Santiago; circ. 65,000.

Victoria

Las Noticias: Casilla 240, Confederación Suiza 895, Victoria; tel. (45) 84-1543; f. 1910; morning; independent; Dir Tránsito Bustamente Molina; circ. 8,000.

El Pehuén de Curacautín: Casilla 92, Avda Central 895, Victoria; morning; independent; Dir Gino Bustamente Barría; circ. 3,000.

PERIODICALS

Santiago

Análisis: Manuel Montt 425, Santiago; tel. (2) 223-4386; f. 1977; weekly; political, economic and social affairs; published by Emisión Ltda; Dir Juan Pablo Cárdenas; circ. 30,000.

Apsi: Gen. Alberto Reyes 032, Providencia, Casilla 9896, Santiago; tel. (2) 77-5450; f. 1976; fortnightly; Dir Marcelo Contreras Nieto; circ. 30,000.

La Bicicleta: José Fagnano 614, Santiago; tel. (2) 222-3969; satirical; Dir Antonio de la Fuente.

CA (Ciudad/Arquitectura) Revista Oficial del Colegio de Arquitectos de Chile AG: Manuel Montt 515, Santiago; tel. (2) 235-3368; fax (2) 235-8403; f. 1964; 4 a year; architects' magazine; Editor Arq. Jaime Márquez Rojas; circ. 3,500.

Carola: San Francisco 116, Casilla 1858, Santiago; tel. (2) 33-6433; telex 240656; fortnightly; women's magazine; published by Editorial Antártica, SA; Dir Isabel Margarita Aguirre de Maino.

Cauce: Huérfanos 713, Of. 604–60, Santiago; tel. (2) 38-2304; fortnightly; political, economic and cultural affairs; Dir Angel Flisfich; circ. 10,000.

Chile Agrícola: Teresa Vial 1172, Casilla 2, Correo 13, Santiago; tel. and fax (2) 551-6039; f. 1976; 8 per year; farming; Dir Ing. Agr. Raúl González Valenzuela; circ. 10,000.

Chile Forestal: Avda Bulnes 259, Of. 406, Santiago; tel. (2) 671-1850; fax (2) 696-6724; f. 1974; monthly; technical information and features on forestry sector; Dir Mariela Espejo Suazo; circ. 4,000.

Cosas: Almirante Pastene 329, Providencia, Santiago; tel. (2) 364-5100; fax (2) 235-8331; f. 1976; fortnightly; international affairs; Dir Mónica Comandari Kaiser; circ. 40,000.

Creces: Manuel Montt 1922, Santiago; tel. (2) 223-4337; telex 341011; monthly; science and technology; Dir Sergio Prenafeta; circ. 12,000.

Deporte Total: Santiago; tel. (2) 251-6236; telex 341194; fax (2) 204-7420; f. 1981; weekly; sport, illustrated; Dir Juan Ignacio Oto Larios; circ. 25,000.

Economía y Sociedad: MacIver 125, 10°, Santiago; tel. (2) 33-1034; telex 340656; Dir José Piñera; circ. 10,000.

Ercilla: Luis Thayer Ojeda 1626, Providencia, Santiago; tel. (2) 251-6236; f. 1936; weekly; general interest; Dir Joaquín González; circ. 28,000.

Estrategia: Rafael Cañas 114, Casilla 16485, Correo 9, Santiago; tel. (2) 235-6959; telex 34036; fax (2) 236-1114; f. 1978; Mon.–Fri.; business, economic and financial affairs; Dir Víctor Manuel Ojeda Méndez; circ. 42,000.

Gestión: Rafael Cañas 114, Santiago; tel. (2) 236-1313; fax (2) 236-1114; f. 1975; monthly; business matters; Dir Víctor Manuel Ojeda Méndez; circ. 38,000.

Hoy: María Luisa Santander 0436, Clasificador 654, Correo Central, Santiago; tel. (2) 225-9699; fax (2) 225-4669; f. 1977; weekly; general interest; Dir Ascanio Cavallo Castro; circ. 30,000.

Jurídica del Trabajo: Avda Bulnes 180, Of. 80, Casilla 9447, Santiago; tel. (2) 696-7474; fax (2) 672-6320; f. 1930; 10 a year; Editor Iván K. Hernández; circ. 1,000.

Mensaje: Almirante Barroso 24, Casilla 10445, Santiago; tel. and fax (2) 696-0653; e-mail mensaje@interaccess.cl; f. 1951; monthly; national, church and international affairs; Dir Antonio Delfau; circ. 7,000.

Microbyte: Avda Condell 1879, Ñuñoa, Santiago; tel. (2) 341-7507; telex 243259; fax (2) 341-7504; f. 1984; monthly; computer science; Dir José Kaffman; circ. 6,000.

Paula: Avda Santa María 0120, Providencia,, Santiago; tel. (2) 200-0585; fax (2) 200-0490; 1967; monthly; women's interest; Dir Alexandra Edwards; circ. 70,000.

Punto Final: San Diego 31, Of. 606, Casilla 13954, Correo 21, Santiago; tel. (2) 697-0615; e-mail punto@interaccess.cl; f. 1965; fortnightly; politics; left-wing; Dir Manuel Cabieses; circ. 15,000.

¿Qué Pasa?: Vicuña Mackenna 1870, Ñuñoa, Santiago; tel. (2) 551-7067; telex 341029; fax (2) 550-7529; f. 1971; weekly; general interest; Dir Roberto Pulido Espinosa; circ. 30,000.

El Siglo: Santiago; f. 1989; fortnightly; published by the Communist Party (PCCh); Dir Juan Andrés Lagos.

Super Rock: Luis Thayer Ojeda 1626, Casilla 3092, Providencia, Santiago; tel. (2) 74-8231; telex 341194; f. 1985; weekly; Latin and European rock music, illustrated; Dir Darío Rojas Morales; circ. 40,000.

Vea: Luis Thayer Ojeda 1626, Casilla 3092, Providencia, Santiago; tel. (2) 74-9421; telex 341194; f. 1939; weekly; general interest, illustrated; Dir Darío Rojas Morales; circ. 150,000.

PRESS ASSOCIATION

Asociación Nacional de la Prensa: Agustinas 1357, 12°, Santiago; tel. (2) 696-6431; fax (2) 698-7699; Pres. Carlos Paul Lamas; Sec. Fernando Silva Vargas.

NEWS AGENCIES

Orbe Servicios Informativos, SA: Phillips 56, 6°, Of. 66, Santiago; tel. (2) 39-4774; Dir Sebastiano Bertolone Galletti.

Foreign Bureaux

Agence France-Presse (France): Avda B. O'Higgins 1316, 9°, Apt. 92, Santiago; tel. (2) 696-0559; telex 440074; Correspondent Humberto Zumarán Araya.

Agencia EFE (Spain): Coronel Santiago Bueras 188, Santiago; tel. (2) 638-0179; telex 240075; fax (2) 633-6130; f. 1966; Bureau Chief Agustín de Gracia Gómez.

Agenzia Nazionale Stampa Associata (ANSA) (Italy): Moneda 1040, Of. 702, Santiago; tel. (2) 698-5811; fax (2) 698-3447; f. 1945; Bureau Chief Giorgio Bagoni Bettollini.

Associated Press (AP) (USA): Tenderini 85, 10°, Of. 100, Casilla 2653, Santiago; tel. (2) 33-5015; telex 645493; Bureau Chief Kevin Noblet.

Deutsche Presse-Agentur (dpa) (Germany): San Antonio 427, Of. 306, Santiago; tel. (2) 639-3633; Correspondent Carlos Dorat.

Inter Press Service (IPS) (Italy): Santiago; tel. (2) 39-7091; Dir and Correspondent Gustavo González Rodríguez.

Prensa Latina (Cuba): Bombero Ossa 1010, Of. 1104, Santiago; tel. (2) 671-8222; telex 441545; fax (2) 695-8605; Correspondent José Bodes Gómez.

Reuters (United Kingdom): Neuva York 33, 11°, Casilla 4248, Santiago; tel. (2) 672-8800; telex 240584; fax (2) 696-0161; Correspondent Roger Atwood.

United Press International (UPI) (USA): Nataniel 47, 9°, Casilla 71-D, Santiago; tel. (2) 696-0162; telex 240570; fax (2) 698-6605; Bureau Chief Fernando Lepé.

Xinhua (New China) News Agency (People's Republic of China): Biarritz 1981, Providencia, Santiago; tel. (2) 25-5033; telex 94293; Correspondent Sun Kuoguowein.

Association

Asociación de Corresponsales de la Prensa Extranjera en Chile: Casilla 2653, Santiago; tel. (2) 39-1330; telex 645493.

Publishers

Ediciones San Pablo: Vicuña MacKenna 10777, Casilla 3746, Santiago; tel. (2) 288-2025; fax (2) 288-2026; e-mail dgraledi@cnet.net; Catholic texts; Dir-Gen. P. Luis Neira Ramírez.

Ediciones Universitarias de Valparaíso: Universidad Católica de Valparaíso, 12 de Febrero 187, Casilla 1415, Valparaíso; tel. (32) 25-3087; fax (32) 27-3429; also Moneda 673, 8°, Santiago; tel. (2) 633-2230; f. 1970; general literature, social sciences, engineering, education, music, arts, textbooks; Gen. Man. Karlheinz Laage H.

Editora Nacional Gabriel Mistral Ltda: Santiago; tel. (2) 77-9522; literature, history, philosophy, religion, art, education; government-owned; Man. Dir José Harrison de la Barra.

Editorial Andrés Bello/Jurídica de Chile: Avda Ricardo Lyon 946, Casilla 4256, Providencia, Santiago; tel. (2) 204-9900; fax (2) 225-3600; f. 1947; history, arts, literature, politics, economics, textbooks, law and social science; Gen. Man. Julio Serrano Lamas.

Editorial El Sembrador: Sargento Aldea 1041, Casilla 2037, Santiago; tel. (2) 556-9454; Dir Isaías Gutiérrez.

Editorial Nascimento, SA: Chiloé 1433, Casilla 2298, Santiago; tel. (2) 555-0254; f. 1898; general; Man. Dir Carlos George Nascimento Márquez.

Editorial Universitaria, SA: María Luisa Santander 0447, Casilla 10220, Santiago; tel. (2) 223-4555; fax (2) 223-7982; f. 1947; general literature, social science, technical, textbooks; Man. Dir Rodrigo Castro C.

Empresa Editora Zig-Zag SA: Avda Ricardo Lyon 1097, Providencia, Santiago; tel. (2) 274-6521; fax (2) 223-5766; f. 1934; general publishers of literary works, reference books and magazines; Pres. Gonzalo Vial C.; Gen. Man. Francisco Pérez Frugone.

PUBLISHERS' ASSOCIATION

Cámara Chilena del Libro AG: Avda B. O'Higgins 1370, Of. 502, Casilla 13526, Santiago; tel. (2) 698-9519; fax (2) 698-9226; Pres. Eduardo Castillo García; Exec. Sec. Carlos Cuneo Lommatzsch.

Broadcasting and Communications

TELECOMMUNICATIONS

Subsecretaría de Telecomunicaciones (Department of Telecommunications, Ministry of Transport and Telecommunications): Amunátegui 139, Casilla 120, Correo 21, Santiago; tel. (2) 672-6503; telex 341156; fax (2) 699-5138; Under-sec. Roberto Pliscoff Vásquez.

Empresa Nacional de Telecomunicaciones, SA—ENTEL CHILE, SA: Santa Lucía 360, Casilla 4254, Santiago; tel. (2) 690-2121; telex 240683; fax (2) 690-2868; f. 1964; operates the Chilean land satellite stations of Longovilo, Punta Arenas and Coihaique, linked to INTELSAT system; Pres. Richard Büchi B.

RADIO

Asociación de Radiodifusores de Chile (ARCHI): Pasaje Matte 956, Of. 801, Casilla 10476, Santiago; tel. (2) 639-8755; fax (2) 639-

4205; f. 1936; 455 broadcasting stations; Pres. César Molfino Mendoza.

Radio Nacional de Chile: San Antonio 220, 2°, Casilla 244-V, Correo 21, Santiago; tel. (2) 33-9071; government station; domestic service; scheduled for privatization; Dir Eduardo Avila Lizana.

TELEVISION

In November 1988 the Government announced that Televisión Nacional de Chile—Canal 7 was to become a *Sociedad Anónima,* prior to its eventual privatization. Canal 4 and Canal 11 (see below) were also included in the Government's long-term proposals for privatization. In 1989 the National Television Council was established to approve concessions for private television stations and the sale of existing stations.

Televisión Nacional de Chile—Canal 7: Bellavista 0990, Casilla 16104, Correo 9, Santiago; tel. (2) 707-7777; telex 240520; fax (2) 707-7766; government network of 145 stations and an international satellite signal; Chair. Luis Ortiz; Gen. Man. René Cortázar Sanz.

Corporación de Televisión de la Universidad Católica de Chile—Canal 13: Inés Matte Urrejola 0848, Casilla 14600, Santiago; tel. (2) 251-4000; telex 440182; fax (2) 630-2040; f. 1959; noncommercial; Exec. Dir Eleodoro Rodríguez Matte.

Corporación de Televisión de la Universidad Católica de Valparaíso—Canal 4: Agua Santa Alto 2455, Casilla 247; Viña del Mar; tel. (32) 61-0140; fax (32) 61-0505; f. 1957; Dir Jorge Bornscheuer Pérez.

Red Televisa Megavisión: Avda Vicuña Mackenna 1348, Santiago; t el. (2) 555-5400; fax (2) 551-8916; Pres. Ricardo Claro Valdes.

Red de Televisión Chilevisión, SA: Inés Matte Urrejola 0825, Casilla 16547, Correo 9, Providencia, Santiago; tel. (2) 252-5122; fax (2) 252-5123; Public Relations Exec. Carolina Gutiérrez.

Universidad de Chile—Canal 11: Inés Matte Urrejola 0825, Casilla 16457, Correo 9, Providencia, Santiago; tel. (2) 737-2227; telex 340492; fax (2) 737-6675; f. 1960; educational; Exec. Dir Felipe Pozo Ruiz.

Red de Televisión Universidad del Norte, SA: Carrera 1625, Casilla 1045, Antofagasta; tel. (83) 22-6725; telex 325142; f. 1981; operates Canal 11-Arica, Canal 12-Iquique, Canal 4-Antofagasta and Canal 5-La Serena; Gen.-Man. Manuel Enrique Berrios Vera.

Finance

(cap. = capital; p.u. = paid up; dep. = deposits; res = reserves; m. = million; amounts in pesos unless otherwise specified)

BANKING

Supervisory Authority

Superintendencia de Bancos e Instituciones Financieras: Moneda 1123, 6°, Casilla 15-D, Santiago; tel. (2) 699-0072; fax (2) 671-1654; f. 1925; run by Ministry of Finance; Superintendent José Florencio Guzmán.

Central Bank

Banco Central de Chile: Agustinas 1180, Santiago; tel. (2) 670-2000; telex 240461; fax (2) 698-4847; f. 1926; under Ministry of Finance until Dec. 1989, when autonomy was granted; bank of issue; cap. 314,734.6m., total assets 14,302,254.5m. (Dec. 1996); Pres. Carlos Massad; 7 brs.

State Bank

Banco del Estado de Chile: Avda B. O'Higgins 1111, Casilla 240-V, Correo 21, Santiago; tel. (2) 670-7000; telex 441152; fax (2) 670-5478; f. 1953; state bank; cap. 4,000.0m., res 210,641.3m., dep. 3,165,793.8m. (Dec. 1995); Pres. Andrés Sanfuentes Vergara; Exec. Gen. Man. José Mena; 191 brs.

National Banks

Banco de A. Edwards: Huérfanos 740, Santiago; tel. (2) 631-3000; telex 441160; fax (2) 631-4161; f. 1851; cap. 73,649m., res 8,649m., dep. 994,221m. (Dec. 1995); Chair. Sergio de Castro; CEO Gustavo Favre Dominguez; 61 brs.

Banco BHIF: Huérfanos 1234, Casilla 517, Santiago; tel. (2) 679-1000; telex 340269; fax (2) 698-5640; f. 1883; was merged with Banco Nacional in 1989; acquired Banesto Chile Bank in Feb. 1994; cap. 56,138.5m., res 2,444.2m., dep. 926,680.8m. (Dec. 1996); Pres. José Said Saffie; CEO Hugo Lavados Montes; 40 brs.

Banco BICE: Teatinos 220, Santiago; tel. (2) 692-2000; telex 645197; fax (2) 696-5324; f. 1979 as Banco Industrial y de Comercio Exterior; name changed as above in 1988; cap. 19,842.4m., res 28,610.7m., dep. 609,614.8m. (Dec. 1996); Pres. and Chair. Gonzalo Valdés; Gen. Man. Cristian Eyzaguirre; 7 brs.

Banco de Chile: Ahumada 251, Casilla 151-D, Santiago; tel. (2) 637-1111; telex 6240479; fax (2) 637-3434; f. 1894; cap. 182,242.1m., res 68,081.1m., dep. 2,807,193.9m. (Dec. 1996); Chair. Adolfo Rojas Gandulfo; Gen. Man. Segismundo Schulin-Zeuthen Serrano; 102 brs.

Banco de Crédito e Inversiones: Huérfanos 1134, Casilla 136-D, Santiago; tel. (2) 692-8000; telex 340373; fax (2) 695-1197; f. 1937; cap. 38,601.7m., res 46,764.0m., dep. 1,800,478.8m. (Dec. 1996); Pres. Luis Enrique Yarur Rey; Gen. Man. Lionel Olavarria; 112 brs.

Banco del Desarrollo: Avda B. O'Higgins 949, 3°, Casilla 320-V, Correo 21, Santiago; tel. (2) 698-2901; telex 340654; fax (2) 671-5547; f. 1983; cap. 28,618.5m., res 2,614.3m., dep. 483,872.2m. (Dec. 1995); Pres. Domingo Santa María Santa Cruz; CEO Vicente Caruz Middleton; 44 brs.

Banco Exterior, SA: MacIver 225, Casilla 324-V, Santiago; tel. (2) 639-4731; telex 340462; fax (2) 639-6095; cap. 11,913.7m., res 141.4m., dep. 66,209.2m. (Dec. 1994); Pres. Luis Abad González; Gen. Man. José Miguel García-Huidobro Nebel.

Banco Internacional: Moneda 818, Casilla 135-D, Santiago; tel. (2) 695-3623; telex 341066; fax (2) 633-9134; f. 1944; cap. and res 11,279.9m., dep. 122,866.0m. (Dec. 1996); placed under state control Jan. 1983 but returned to the private sector in May 1986; Pres. Alejandro L. Furman Sihman; Gen. Man. Alvaro Achondo González; 11 brs.

Banco Osorno y La Unión: Bandera 140, Casilla 57-D, Santiago; tel. (2) 696-0414; telex 340370; fax (2) 699-7842; f. 1908; cap. 55,694.0m., res 106.0m., dep. 1,096,131.0m. (Dec. 1994); incorporated the Banco del Trabajo in 1989; Pres. Carlos Abumohor Touma; Gen. Man. Juan Carlos Martino González; 112 brs.

Banco Santander-Chile: Agustinas 920, Casilla 76-D, Santiago; tel. (2) 631-2000; telex 441102; fax (2) 696-0622; f. 1926; cap. 56,745.0m., res 11,015.1m., dep. 900,891.9m. (Dec. 1994); subsidiary of Banco de Santander, Spain; Pres. Emilio Botín Sanz de Sautuola y García de los Ríos; Gen. Man. Claudio Skarmeta Magri; 72 brs.

Banco Santiago: Bandera 201, Casilla 51-D, Santiago; tel. (2) 630-4000; telex 441096; fax (2) 698-7948; f. 1997 as a result of a merger of Banco O'Higgins and Banco de Santiago; Pres. Andrónico Luksic Craig; Vice-Pres. Fernando Cañas B.; 64 brs.

Banco Security: Agustinas 621, Santiago; tel. (2) 632-5502; telex 340791; fax (2) 251-5925; f. 1981; fmrly Banco Urquijo de Chile; cap. and res 27,471.1m., dep. 331,013.5m. (Dec. 1994); Pres. Francisco Silva S.; Gen. Man. Renato Peñafiel M; 7 brs.

Banco Sud Americano: Morandé 226, Casilla 90-D, Santiago; tel. (2) 692-6000; telex 240954; fax (2) 698-6008; f. 1944; cap. 51,580.4m., res 23,035.2m., dep. 1,243,240.9m. (Dec. 1996); Pres. José Borda Aretxabala; Gen. Man. Juan Luis Köstner Manríquez; 87 brs.

Corp Banca: Huérfanos 1072, Casilla 80-D, Santiago; tel. (2) 637-8664; telex 240566; fax (2) 696-5763; e-mail fburgos@corpbanca.cl; f. 1871 as Banco Concepción, current name adopted in March 1997; cap. and res 57,646m., dep. 742,502m. (June 1997); Chair. Carlos Abumohor; Gen. Man. Jorge Selume; 143 brs.

Dresdner Banque Nationale de Paris: Huérfanos 1219, Casilla 10492, Santiago; tel. (2) 698-8201; telex 645347; fax (2) 671-3307; f. 1958 as Banco Continental; bought by Crédit Lyonnais in Sept. 1987; current name adopted in 1996; cap. US $48.1m., dep. US $146.9m. (Dec. 1996); Pres. Andrés Bianchi Larre; Gen. Man. Ewald Doerner; 1 br.

ING Bank (Chile), SA: Avda Nueva Tajamar 481, 17°, Of. 1701, Casilla 500-V, Las Condes, Santiago; tel. (2) 330-0600; telex 341244; fax (2) 330-0650; cap. and res 10.1m. (Oct. 1995); Pres. Albert Jacob Staal; Gen. Man. Germán Tagle O'Ryan; 1 br.

Foreign Banks

Foreign banks with branches in Chile include the following:

American Express Bank Ltd (USA), Banco do Brasil, Banco do Estado de São Paulo (Brazil), Banco de la Nación Argentina, Banco Real (Brazil), Bank of America NT & SA (USA), Bank of Tokyo-Mitsubishi Ltd (Japan), Chase Manhattan Bank NA, Citibank NA (USA), Bank of Boston, Republic National Bank of New York (USA).

Finance Corporations

Financiera Atlas, SA: Nueva de Lyon 72, 7°, Santiago; tel. (2) 233-3151; fax (2) 233-3152; Gen. Man. Neil A. Denton Feilmann.

Financiera Condell, SA: Ahumada 179, 9°, Santiago; tel. (2) 672-1222; fax (2) 699-2590; Gen. Man. Antonio S. Undurraga Olivos.

Financiera Conosur: Avda B. O'Higgins 1980, 4°, Santiago; tel. (2) 697-2479; fax (2) 632-4530; Gen. Man. V. Hugo Araneda Schiaffino.

Banking Association

Asociación de Bancos e Instituciones Financieras de Chile AG: Ahumada 179, 12°, Santiago; tel. (2) 699-3977; fax (2) 698-8945; f. 1945; Pres. Hernán Somerville Senn; Gen. Man. Alejandro Alarcón Pérez.

Other Financial Supervisory Bodies

Superintendencia de Administradoras de Fondo de Pensiones (AFPs) (Superintendency of Pensions Fund Administrators): Huérfanos 1273, planta 9, Santiago; tel. (2) 696-1474; fax (2) 698-5305; CEO JULIO BUSTAMANTE JERALDO.

Superintendencia de Previsión Social (Superintendency of Social Security): Huérfanos 1376, planta 5, Santiago; tel. (2) 696-8092; fax (2) 696-4672; CEO LUIS ORLANDINI MOLINA.

STOCK EXCHANGES

Bolsa de Comercio de Santiago: La Bolsa 64, Casilla 123-D, Santiago; tel. (2) 698-2001; fax (2) 672-8046; f. 1893; 44 mems; Pres. PABLO YRARRÁZAVAL VALDÉS; Sec.-Gen. RODRIGO SERRANO BOMBAL.

Bolsa de Corredores—Valores de Valparaíso: Prat 798, Casilla 218-V, Valparaíso; tel. (32) 25-0677; fax (32) 21-2764; f. 1905; Pres. CARLOS F. MARÍN ORREGO; Man. ARIE JOEL GELFENSTEIN FREUNDLICH.

Bolsa Electrónica de Chile: Huérfanos 770, 14°, Santiago; tel. (2) 639-4699; fax (2) 633-4174; Gen. Man. JUAN CARLOS SPENCER OSSA.

INSURANCE

In June 1994 there were 23 general insurance, 28 life insurance and four reinsurance companies operating in Chile.

Supervisory Authority

Superintendencia de Valores y Seguros: Teatinos 120, 6°, Santiago; tel. (2) 549-5900; telex 340260; fax (2) 549-5965; e-mail SVALSEG@ibm.net; f. 1931; under Ministry of Finance; Supt DANIEL YARUR ELSACA.

Principal Companies

Cía de Seguros Generales Aetna Chile, SA: Coyancura 2270, 11°, Santiago; tel. (2) 233-4566; telex 241295; fax (2) 231-0989; f. 1900; general; Pres. SERGIO BAEZA VALDÉS.

Cía de Seguros Generales Consorcio General de Seguros, SA: Hendaya 60, 10°, Santiago; tel. (2) 330-2000; telex 240466; fax (2) 330-2060; f. 1920; general; Pres. JEAN JACQUES BUHANNIC.

Cía de Seguros Generales Cruz del Sur, SA: Ahumada 370, 4°, Casilla 2682, Santiago; tel. (2) 672-7572; telex 340030; fax (2) 698-9126; f. 1974; general; Pres. JOSÉ TOMÁS GUZMÁN DUMAS.

Cía de Seguros Generales Euroamérica, SA: Agustinas 1127, 2°, Santiago; tel. (2) 672-7242; fax (2) 696-4086; f. 1986; general; Pres. BENJAMÍN DAVIS CLARKE.

Cía de Seguros Generales La Chilena Consolidada, SA: Casilla 53-D, Pedro de Valdivia 195, Santiago; tel. (2) 200-7246; fax (2) 274-9868; f. 1905; general; Gen. Man. AGUSTIN EDWARDS EASTMAN.

Aetna Chile Seguros de Vida, SA: Coyancura 2270, 10°, Of. 1020, Santiago; tel. (2) 233-4566; telex 341624; fax (2) 231-0989; f. 1981; life; Pres. SERGIO BAEZA VALDÉS.

Cía de Seguros de Vida Consorcio Nacional de Seguros, SA: Avda El Bosque Sur 180, 3°, Santiago; tel. (2) 230-4000; telex 240947; fax (2) 230-4050; f. 1916; life; Pres. JUAN BILBAO HORMAECHE.

Cía de Seguros de Vida La Construcción, SA: Avda Providencia 1806, 1822, Providencia, Santiago; tel. (2) 340-3000; telex 725881; fax (2) 340-3204; e-mail seguros@laconstruccion.sa.cl; f. 1985; life; Pres. VÍCTOR MANUEL JARPA RIVEROS.

Cía de Seguros de Vida Euroamérica, SA: Agustinas 1127, 3°, Santiago; tel. (2) 671-6053; fax (2) 699-6015; f. 1962; life; Pres. BENJAMIN DAVIS CLARKE.

Cía de Seguros de Vida El Roble, SA: Teatinos 333, 9°, Santiago; tel. (2) 672-4351; telex 242122; fax (2) 695-1980; f. 1981; life; Pres. JOSÉ TOMÁS GUZMÁN DUMAS.

Cía de Seguros de Vida Santander, SA: Agustinas 785, 2°, Santiago; tel. (2) 631-1177; fax (2) 632-1875; f. 1989; life; Pres. FRANCISCO MARTÍN LOPEZ-QUESADA.

Instituto de Seguros del Estado (ISE): Encomenderos 113, Providencia, Santiago; tel. (2) 246-8000; f. 1888; general; Pres. GUSTAVO DUPUIS PINILLOS.

La Interamericana Compañía de Seguros de Vida: Agustinas 640, 17°, Santiago; tel. (2) 633-7663; telex 440295; fax (2) 633-3606; f. 1980; life; Pres. RICARDO PERALTA VALENZUELA.

Renta Nacional Compañía de Seguros de Vida, SA: Amunátegui 178, 1° y 2°, Santiago; tel. (2) 670-0200; telex 241136; fax (2) 670-0399; f. 1982; life; Pres. ALFREDO NEUT BLANCO; Gen. Man. JORGE LALANDE DELLEPIANE.

Reinsurance

American Re-Insurance Company (Chile), SA: Huérfanos 1189, 5°, Santiago; tel. (2) 695-4484; telex 242155; fax (2) 672-3169; f. 1981; general; Pres. MAHMOUD ABDALLAH; Gen. Man. ARTURO FALCÓN.

Caja Reaseguradora de Chile, SA (Generales): Apoquindo 4449, 8°, Santiago; tel. (2) 228-6106; telex 340276; fax (2) 698-9730; f. 1927; general; Pres. ANDRÉS JIMÉNES.

Caja Reaseguradora de Chile, SA: Apoquindo 4449, 8°, Santiago; tel. (2) 228-6106; telex 340276; fax (2) 698-9730; f. 1980; life; Pres. ANDRÉS JIMÉNES.

Cía de Reaseguros de Vida Soince, SA: Agustinas 785, 2°, Santiago; tel. (2) 631-1177; fax (2) 632-1875; f. 1990; life; Pres. FRANCISCO MARTÍN LÓPEZ-QUESADA.

Insurance Association

Asociación de Aseguradores de Chile: Moneda 920, Of. 1002, Casilla 2630, Santiago; tel. (2) 696-7431; fax (2) 698-4820; f. 1931; Pres. FRANCISCO SERQUEIRA ABARCA; Gen. Man. JOAQUÍN ECHENIQUE RIVERA.

Trade and Industry

GOVERNMENT AGENCIES

Corporación de Fomento de la Producción—CORFO: Moneda 921, Casilla 3886, Santiago; tel. (2) 638-0521; telex 240421; fax (2) 671-1058; f. 1939; holding group of principal state enterprises; under Ministry of Production Development; grants loans and guarantees to private sector; responsible for sale of non-strategic state enterprises; Vice-Pres., Minister of Production Devt FELIPE SANDOVAL PRECHT; Gen. Man. EDUARDO BITRÁN COLODRO.

PROCHILE (Dirección General de Relaciones Económicas Internacionales): Avda B. O'Higgins 1315, 2°, Casilla 14087, Correo 21, Santiago; tel. (2) 696-0043; telex 240836; fax (2) 696-0639; f. 1974; bureau of international economic affairs; Dir JEAN-JACQUES DUHART.

Servicio Nacional de Instrucción Profesional y Empleo (National Service of Professional Training and Employment): Huérfanos 1273, planta 11, Santiago; tel. (2) 696-8213; fax (2) 696-5039; attached to Ministry of Labour and Social Security; Dir IGNACIO LARRAECHEA LOESSER.

STATE CORPORATION

Corporación Nacional del Cobre de Chile (CODELCO—Chile): Huérfanos 1270; Casilla 150-D, Santiago; tel. (2) 690-3000; telex 240672; fax (2) 672-1473; f. 1976 as a state-owned enterprise with four copper-producing operational divisions at Chuquicamata, Salvador, Andina and El Teniente; attached to Ministry of Mines; Exec. Pres. MARCOS LIMA ARAVENA; 19,500 employees.

DEVELOPMENT ORGANIZATIONS

Comisión Chilena de Energía Nuclear: Amunátegui 95, Casilla 188-D, Santiago; tel. (2) 699-0070; fax (2) 699-1618; f. 1965; government body to develop peaceful uses of atomic energy; concentrates, regulates and controls all matters related to nuclear energy; Exec. Dir GONZALO TORRES OVIEDO.

Corporación Nacional Forestal—CONAF: Avda Bulnes 285, Of. 501, Santiago; tel. (2) 672-2724; fax (2) 671-5881; f. 1970 to promote forestry activities, to enforce forestry law, to promote afforestation, to administer subsidies for afforestation projects and to increase and preserve forest resources; manages 13.97m. ha designated as National Parks, Natural Monuments and National Reserves; under Ministry of Agriculture; Exec. Dir Ing. JOSÉ ANTONIO PRADO DONOSO.

Empresa Nacional de Minería—ENAMI: MacIver 459, 2°, Casilla 100-D, Santiago; tel. (2) 639-6061; telex 240574; fax (2) 638-4094; promotes the development of the small- and medium-sized mines; attached to Ministry of Mines; Exec. Vice-Pres. CLAUDIO AGOSTINI GONZÁLEZ; 3,225 employees.

CHAMBER OF COMMERCE

Cámara de Comercio de Santiago de Chile, AG: Santa Lucía 302, 3°, Casilla 1297, Santiago; tel. (2) 360-7000; telex 240868; fax (2) 633-3395; f. 1919; 1,300 mems; Pres. PETER T. HILL; Man. CLAUDIO ORTIZ T.

There are chambers of commerce in all major towns.

INDUSTRIAL AND TRADE ASSOCIATIONS

Servicio Agrícola y Ganadero (SAG): Avda Bulnes 140, 8°, Santiago; tel. (2) 698-2244; telex 242745; fax (2) 72-1812; under Ministry of Agriculture; Exec. Dir ALEJANDRO MARCHANT BAEZA.

Sociedad Agrícola y Servicios Isla de Pascua: Alfredo Lecannelier 1940, Providencia, Santiago; tel. (2) 232-7497; fax (2) 232-7497; administers agriculture and public services on Easter Island; Gen. Man. GERARDO VELASCO.

Subsecretaría de Pesca: Bellavista 168, 16-18°, Valparaíso; tel. (32) 21-2187; fax (32) 21-2790; f. 1976; controls and promotes fishing industry; Sub-Sec. PATRICIO BERNAL PONCE.

EMPLOYERS' ORGANIZATIONS

Confederación de la Producción y del Comercio: Monseñor Sótero Sanz 182, Providencia, Santiago; tel. (2) 231-9764; fax (2)

231-9808; f. 1936; Pres. WALTER RIESCO SALVO; Gen. Man. CRISTIÁN PIZARRO ALLARD.

Affiliated organizations:

Asociación de Bancos e Instituciones Financieras de Chile (q.v.).

Cámara Chilena de la Construcción: Marchant Pereira 10, 3°, Providencia, Casilla Clasificador 679, Santiago; tel. (2) 233-1131; fax (2) 232-7600; f. 1951; Pres. VÍCTOR MANUEL JARPA RIVEROS; Gen. Man. BLAS BELLOLIO RODRÍGUEZ; 3,000 mems.

Cámara Nacional de Comercio, Servicios y Turismo de Chile: Merced 230, Santiago; tel. (2) 365-4120; telex 340110; fax (2) 365-4001; f. 1858; Pres. ALFONSO MUJICA; Gen. Sec. JOSÉ MANUEL MELERO ABAROA; 120 mems.

Sociedad de Fomento Fabril, FG: Avda Andrés Bello 2777, 3°, Casilla 37, Correo 35, Tobalaba, Santiago; tel. (2) 203-3100; fax (2) 203-3101; f. 1883; largest employers' organization; Pres. PEDRO LIZANA GREVE; Man. FREDERICO MONTES LIRA; 2,000 mems.

Sociedad Nacional de Agricultura—Federación Gremial (SNA): Tenderini 187, 2°, Casilla 40-D, Santiago; tel. (2) 639-6710; telex 240760; fax (2) 633-7771; f. 1838; landowners' association; controls Radio Stations CB 57 and XQB8 (FM) in Santiago, CB-97 in Valparaíso, CD-120 in Los Angeles, CA-144 in La Serena, CD-127 in Temuco; Pres. RICARDO ARIZTÍA DE CASTRO; Gen. Sec. LUIS QUIROZA ARRAU.

Sociedad Nacional de Minería—SONAMI: Teatinos 20, 3°, Of. 33, Casilla 1807, Santiago; tel. (2) 695-5626; fax (2) 697-1778; f. 1883; Pres. WALTER RIESCO SALVO; Man. MANUEL CERECEDA VIDAL .

Confederación de Asociaciones Gremiales y Federaciones de Agricultores de Chile: Lautaro 218, Los Angeles; registered with Ministry of Economic Affairs in 1981; Pres. DOMINGO DURÁN NEUMANN; Gen. Sec. ADOLFO LARRAÍN V.

Confederación del Comercio Detallista de Chile, AG: Merced 380, 8°, Of. 74, Santiago; tel. (2) 39-5719; fax (2) 38-0338; f. 1938; retail trade; registered with Ministry of Economic Affairs in 1980; Nat. Pres. RAFAEL CUMSILLE ZAPAPA; Sec.-Gen. JAIME PÉREZ RODRÍGUEZ.

Confederación Gremial Nacional Unida de la Mediana y Pequeña Industria, Servicios y Artesanado—CONUPIA: Santiago; registered with Ministry of Economic Affairs in 1980; small- and medium-sized industries and crafts; Pres. FÉLIX LUQUE PORTILLA.

There are many federations of private industrialists, organized by industry and region.

UTILITIES

Comisión Nacional de Energía: Teatinos 120, 7°, Casilla 14, Correo 21, Santiago; tel. (2) 698-1757; telex 240948; fax (2) 695-6404; Pres. ALEJANDRO JADRESIC MARINOVIC.

General

COLBUN: Avda 11 de Septiembre 2353, 9°, Santiago; tel. (2) 231-3414; fax (2) 231-6609; state power utility; scheduled for privatization once anti-monopoly legislation was in place.

Electricity

CHILECTRA, SA: Santo Domingo 789, Casilla 1557, Santiago; tel. (2) 632-2000; telex (2) 40645; fax (2) 639-3280; f. 1921; subsidiary of CORFO holding group; transmission and distribution of electrical energy; Gen. Man. MARCOS ZYLBERBERG KLOS.

Chilgener: San Antonio 580, Santiago; tel. (2) 645-228; electricity generating co.

Compañía Chilena de Distribución Eléctrica V Región SA—CHILECTRA V REGION: General Cruz 222, Casilla 12-V, Valparaíso; tel. (32) 25-0081; fax (32) 21-0723; Gen. Man. RICHARD BÜCHI.

Compañía Chilena de Generación Eléctrica, SA—CHILGENER: Miraflores 222, 4°–7°, Casilla 3514, Santiago; tel. (2) 632-3909; fax (2) 633-4499; Gen. Man. JUAN ANTONIO GUZMÁN MOLINARI.

Compañía General de Electricidad Industrial, SA—CGEI: Teatinos 370, Casilla 102-D, Santiago; tel. (2) 696-4101; fax (2) 698-7840; Gen. Man. GUILLERMO MATTA FUENZALIDA.

Empresa Electric Peuhenche, SA—EEP: Puno Horte 1370, Talca; telex 717201; electricity generating co.

Empresa Eléctrica del Norte (EDELNOR): c/o Ministry of Energy, Teatinos 120, 7°, Casilla 14, Correo 21, Santiago; tel. (2) 698-1757; telex 240948; fax (2) 698-1757; subsidiary of CORFO holding group; northern power utility; 48.5% government-owned and scheduled for privatization; in June 1993 33% of the Government's stake was offered for sale.

Empresa Nacional de Electricidad, SA—ENDESA: Santa Rosa 76, Casilla 1392, Santiago; tel. (2) 222-9080; telex 340291; fax (2) 635-3938; f. 1943; cap. and res 594,107m. pesos; installed capacity 2,428,310 MW; Gen. Man. JAIME BAUZÁ BAUZÁ.

ENERSIS, SA: Santo Domingo 789, Casilla 1557, Correo Central, Santiago; tel. (2) 638-0840; fax (2) 639-3280; electricity producer; Chair. JOSÉ ANTONIO GUZMÁN; CEO PABLO IHNEN; 7,580 employees.

Gas

AGA Chili, SA: Juan Bautista Pstene 2344, Santiago; tel. (2) 232-8711; natural-gas utility.

Compañía de Consumidores de Gas de Santiago—GASCO, SA: Santo Domingo 1061, Casilla 8-D, Santiago; tel. (2) 698-2121; fax (2) 696-6986; natural-gas utility; supplies Santiago and Punta Arenas regions; Gen. Man. AGUSTÍN OSSA BEZANILLA.

Compañía de Gas de Concepción, SA: En Continuidad De Giro, Avda Artura Prat 175, Concepción; tel. (41) 235-133; natural-gas utility.

Water

Empresa Metropolitana de Obras Sanitarias, SA: Avda Bulnes 129, Santiago; tel. (2) 672-4049; fax (2) 696-3462; water supply and sanitation services to Santiago and the surrounding area; Gen. Man. SANTIAGO GONZÁLEZ LARRAÍN.

TRADE UNIONS

There are more than 50 national labour federations and unions. The confederations include:

Agrupación Nacional de Empleados Fiscales (ANEF): Avda B. O'Higgins 1603, Santiago; tel. (2) 696-2957; affiliated to CUT; Pres. MILENKO MIHOVILOVIC; Sec.-Gen. RIGOBERTO MUÑOZ SAZO.

Confederación Bancaria: Agustinas 1185, Of. 92, Santiago; tel. (2) 699-5597; affiliated to CUT; Pres. DIEGO OLIVARES ARAVENA; Sec.-Gen. RAÚL REQUENA MARTÍNEZ.

Confederación de Empleados Particulares de Chile—CEPCH: Teatinos 20, Of. 1, Casilla 1771, Santiago; tel. (2) 72-2093; trade union for workers in private sector; Pres. SERGIO ROJAS VERGARA; Sec.-Gen. ANDRÉS BUSTOS GONZÁLEZ.

Confederación General de Trabajadores (CGT): Santa Lucía 162, Santiago; tel. (2) 38-2354; pro-Govt; Pres. MANUEL CONTRERAS LOYOLA.

Confederación General de Trabajadores del Transporte Terrestre y Afines de Chile (CGTT): Moneda 1778, 2°, Santiago; tel. (2) 695-5736; affiliated to CUT; Pres. LUIS JAQUE SALAMANCA; Sec.-Gen. SERGIO MOYA.

Confederación de Gente de Mar, Marítimos, Portuarios y Pesqueros de Chile (CONGEMAR): Tomás Ramos 172, Casilla 2210, Valparaíso; tel. (32) 25-7580; fax (32) 25-5430; affiliated to CUT; Pres. ARTURO SALDIVIA PINEDA; Sec.-Gen. JUAN GUZMÁN CARRASCO.

Confederación Marítima de Chile—COMACH: Eleuterio Ramírez 476, 8°, Casilla 450, Valparaíso; tel. (32) 25-7656; f. 1985; Leader EDUARDO RÍOS; Sec.-Gen. ENRIQUE MONTES; 5,000 mems.

Confederación Minera de Chile: Príncipe de Gales 88, Casilla 10361, Correo Central, Santiago; tel. (2) 696-6945; Pres. MOISÉS LABRAÑA M.; Sec.-Gen. JOSÉ CARRILLO.

Confederación Nacional Campesina: San Ignacio 387, Santiago; tel. (2) 695-2017; Pres. EUGENIO LEÓN GAJARDO; Sec.-Gen. RENÉ ASTUDILLO ROJAS.

Confederación Nacional de Federaciones y Sindicatos de Interempresas y Empresas de Trabajadores del Transporte Terrestre y Afines de Chile (CONATRACH): Concha y Toro 2A, 2°, Santiago; tel. (2) 698-0810; affiliated to CDT; Pres. PEDRO MONSALVE FUENTES; Sec.-Gen. RAÚL MIRANDA VIDAL.

Confederación Nacional de Federaciones y Sindicatos de Trabajadores del Comercio de Chile (CONATRADECO): Teatinos 727, 3°, Santiago; tel. (2) 698-2532; Pres. CARLOS HERNÁNDEZ BETANCOURT; Sec.-Gen. EDMUNDO LILLO ARAVENA.

Confederación Nacional de Federaciones y Sindicatos de Trabajadores Textiles y Ramos Similares y Conexos de Chile (CONTEXTIL): San Francisco 1080, Santiago; tel. (2) 222-7036; Pres. PATRICIA C. CARRILLO; Sec.-Gen. JUAN SARAVIA.

Confederación Nacional de Sindicatos Agrícolas Forestales, de la Madera y Labores Conexas 'Unidad Obrero Campesina' de Chile (UOC): Serrano 297, Casilla 9664, Correo Central, Santiago; tel. (2) 33-9279; affiliated to CUT and to CNC; Pres. OSCAR VALLADARES GONZÁLEZ; Sec.-Gen. JUAN CORVALÁN HUERTA.

Confederación Nacional de Sindicatos de Trabajadores Agrícolas 'Monseñor Manuel Larraín': Erasmo Escala 2170, Santiago; Pres. LUIS SALAMANCA ALARCÓN; Sec.-Gen. LUIZ LAZCANO MUÑOZ.

Confederación Nacional de Sindicatos y Federaciones de Trabajadores Campesinos, Asalariados, Agrícolas, Frutícolas, Agro-industriales, Vitivinícolas, Avícolas, Pecuarias y Actividades Anexas 'El Surco': Copiapó 720, Casilla 378, Correo 3, Santiago; tel. (2) 222-5752; affiliated to CUT; Pres. HUGO DÍAZ TAPIA; Sec.-Gen. MANUEL ALARCÓN CASTRO.

Confederación Nacional de Sindicatos de Trabajadores de la Construcción, Maderas, Materiales de Edificación y Actividades Conexas: Almirante Latorre 93, Casilla 421-3, Correo 3,

Santiago; tel. (2) 698-1004; fax (2) 697-1321; affiliated to CUT; Pres. ADRIÁN FUENTES HERMOSILLA; Sec.-Gen. LUIS FUENTEALBA REYES.

Confederación Nacional de Sindicatos de Trabajadores del Cuero, Calzado y Ramos Conexos, Organismos Auxiliares de la Industria (EX-FONACC): Arturo Prat 1490, Santiago; tel. (2) 556-9602; affiliated to CUT; Pres. ENRIQUE VERGARA; Sec.-Gen. ANGEL CEPEDA BECERRA.

Confederación Nacional de Sindicatos y Federaciones de Trabajadores Forestales, Industriales de la Madera, Celulosa, Papel y Derivados y Servicios Asociados: Ongolmo 670, Casilla 2717, Concepción; tel. (41) 22-6604; Pres. JOSÉ ABELLO JARA; Sec.-Gen. LUIS CUMSILLE.

Confederación Nacional de Sindicatos de Trabajadores Independientes Suplementeros de Chile: Roberto Pretot 18, Santiago; tel. (2) 699-4390; Pres. IVÁN ENCINA CARO; Sec. RAMÓN GONZÁLEZ.

Confederación Nacional de Sindicatos de Trabajadores de la Industria del Pan, Ramos Conexos y Organismos Auxiliares (CONAPAN): Roberto Pretot 32, 2°, Santiago; tel. (2) 696-8759; affiliated to CUT; Pres. GUILLERMO CORTÉS; Sec. HUGO RAMÍREZ.

Confederación Nacional de Sindicatos de Trabajadores de la Industria del Plástico y Ramos Conexos (CONATRAP): Agustinas 1817, Santiago; tel. (2) 672-1622; affiliated to CDT; Pres. LUIS HERNÁN ALEGRÍA; Sec. LUIS VIVES GALLARDO.

Confederación Nacional de Sindicatos de Trabajadores Textiles de la Confección, Vestuario y Ramos Conexos de Chile (CONTEVECH): Agustinas 2349, Santiago; tel. (2) 699-3442; affiliated to CUT; Pres. MIGUEL VEGA; Sec.-Gen. MIGUEL CABRERA.

Confederación Nacional Sindical Campesina Provincias Agrarias Unidas de Chile: Santo Domingo 1083, Of. 504, Santiago; tel. (2) 696-2797; Pres. RAÚL ORREGO ESCANILLA; Sec.-Gen. MIGUEL ARELLANO TORRES.

Confederación Nacional Unitaria de Trabajadores del Transporte Y Afines de Chile (CONUTT): Almirante Latorre 93, 2°, Santiago; tel. (2) 698-1004; fax (2) 697-1321; Pres. RICARDO I. MALDONADO OLIVARES; Gen. Sec. RAMÓN BECERRA.

Confederación de Sindicatos y Federaciones de Trabajadores Electrometalúrgicos, Mineros, Automotrices y Ramos Conexos (CONSFETEMA): Vicuña Mackenna 3101, Casilla 1803, Correo Central, Santiago; tel. (2) 238-1732; Pres. RAÚL PONCE DE LEÓN; Sec. ARNOLDO MONTOYA.

Confederación de Sindicatos y Federaciones de Trabajadores de la Industria Metalúrgica y Ramos Similares y Conexos (CONSTRAMET): Brasil 43, 2°, Santiago; tel. (2) 672-5803; affiliated to CUT; Pres. JOSÉ ORTIZ; Sec.-Gen. MIGUEL CHÁVEZ SOAZO.

Confederación de Trabajadores del Cobre (CTC): MacIver 283, 5°, Casilla 9094, Santiago; tel. (2) 38-0835; fax (2) 33-1449; comprises 21 unions; Pres. DARWIN BUSTAMENTE; Sec.-Gen. JORGE SEPÚLVEDA SEGOVIA; 20,000 mems.

Confederación de Trabajadores Molineros de Chile: Santiago; tel. (2) 698-6538; Pres. LUIS CORDERO LEIVA; Sec. DANIEL MIRANDA.

Confederación de Trabajadores de Santiago: Miguel León Prado 135, Santiago; tel. (2) 556-7759; Pres. MANUEL OYANEDER CÁRDENAS; Sec.-Gen. LUIS GONZÁLEZ SEPÚLVEDA.

The trade unions include:

Central Democrática de Trabajadores: Erasmo Escala 2170, Santiago; tel. (2) 699-4756; 20 affiliated organizations; Pres. EDUARDO RÍOS ARIAS.

Central Democrática de Trabajadores (CDT): Avda B. O'Higgins 1603, Santiago; tel. (2) 696-2957; nine affiliated organizations; Pres. HERNOL FLORES OPAZO; Sec.-Gen. MILENKO MIHOVILOVICH ETEROVIC.

Central de Trabajadores de Chile (CTCH): Teatinos 20, Of. 75, Santiago; tel. (2) 697-0171; Pres. PEDRO BRICEÑO MOLINA; Sec.-Gen. MARIO DELANNAYS AVALOS.

Central Unitaria de Trabajadores de Chile (CUT—Chile): Avda B. O'Higgins 1346, Santiago; tel. (2) 695-8053; fax (2) 695-8055; f. 1988; two associations, 27 confederations, 49 federations; 36 regional headquarters; Pres. MANUEL BUSTOS HUERTA; Sec.-Gen. GUILLERMO CORTÉS; 411,000 mems.

Comisión Nacional Campesina (CNC): Dieciocho 390, Santiago; tel. (2) 698-8407; fax (2) 695-1093; five affiliated organizations; Pres. OSVALDO VALLADARES.

Consejo Coordinador de Trabajadores de Chile: Sazié 1761, Santiago; tel. (2) 698-7318; fax (2) 695-3388; Pres. HERNÁN BAEZA JARA; Sec.-Gen. SANTIAGO PEREIRA BECERRA.

Frente Nacional de Organizaciones Autónomas—FRENAO: Santa Lucía 162, Santiago; tel. (2) 38-2354; seven affiliated organizations; Pres. MANUEL CONTRERAS LOYOLA; Sec.-Gen. JULIETA PROVOSTE SEPÚLVEDA.

Movimiento Unitario Campesino y Etnias de Chile (MUCECH): Lira 220, Santiago; tel. (2) 222-1677; Pres. FRANCISCO LEÓN TOBAR; Sec.-Gen. RAMÓN VELÁSQUEZ.

Transport

Ministerio de Transportes y Telecomunicaciones: Amunátegui 139, Santiago; tel. (2) 72-6503; telex 240200; fax (2) 699-5138.

In September 1991 the Government announced a four-year plan to improve the country's transport infrastructure at an estimated total cost of US $2,350m. The plan provided for the modernization of the railways, the construction of a third underground railway line for Santiago, the surfacing of some 1,000 km of roads, the undertaking of repair work to earthquake damage inflicted upon the ports of Valparaíso and San Antonio in 1985, and the construction of a new passenger terminal at Santiago's Arturo Merino Benítez airport.

RAILWAYS

The total length of the railway system in 1990 was 8,185 km, of which almost 90% was state-owned. The privately-owned lines are in the north. There are also four international railways, two to Bolivia, one to Argentina and one to Peru.

State Railways

Empresa de los Ferrocarriles del Estado: Avda B. O'Higgins 3322, 3°, Casilla 124-D, Santiago; tel. (2) 779-0707; telex 242290; fax (2) 779-2609; f. 1851; 4,229 km of track (1993); the State Railways are divided between the Ferrocarril Regional de Arica (formerly Ferrocarril Arica–La Paz), Ferrocarriles del Pacífico (cargo division), Metro Regional de Valparaíso (passenger service only) and Ferrovía (formerly the Ferrocarril del Sur); several lines scheduled for privatization by 1999; Pres. S. GONZÁLEZ T.

Parastatal Railways

Ferrocarriles del Pacífico (FEPASA): La Concepción, 331, Providencia, Santiago; tel. (2) 235-1686; fax (2) 235-0920; f. 1993; freight services; scheduled for privatization; Gen. Man. E. VALDATTA.

Metro de Santiago: Empresa de Transporte de Pasajeros Metro, SA, Avda B. O'Higgins 1414, Santiago; tel. (2) 671-3119; fax (2) 699-2475; e-mail metrodfk@rdc.cl; started operations 1975; 37.7 km (1997); 3 lines; Pres. DANIEL FERNÁNDEZ KOPRICH; Gen. Man. RODRIGO AZÓCAR HIDALGO.

Private Railways

Antofagasta (Chile) and Bolivia Railway PLC: Bolívar 255, Casilla S-T, Antofagasta; tel. (55) 20-6200; fax (55) 20-6220; e-mail msepulve@fcab.cl; f. 1888; British-owned; operates an internat. railway to Bolivia and Argentina; cargo forwarding services; total track length 728 km; Chair. ANDRÓNICO LUKSIC ABAROA; Gen. Man. M. V. SEPÚLVEDA.

Empresa de Transporte Ferroviario, SA (Ferronor): Josué Smith Solar 426, Santiago; tel. (2) 233-5117; telex 401067; fax (2) 233-2676; 1,429 km of track (1994); established as a public/private concern, following the transfer of the Ferrocarril Regional del Norte de Chile to the Ministry of Production Development (CORFO) as a *Sociedad Anónima* in 1989; controlling interest purchased by RailAmerica of the USA in 1997; operates cargo services only.

Ferrocarril Codelco-Chile: Barquito, Region III, Atacama; tel. (52) 48-8521; fax (52) 48-8522; Gen. Man. B. BEHN THEUNE.

Diego de Almagro a Potrerillos: transport of forest products, minerals and manufactures; 99 km.

Ferrocarril Rancagua–Teniente: transport of forest products, livestock, minerals and manufactures; 68 km.

Ferrocarril Tocopilla–Toco: Calle Arturo Prat 1060, Casilla 2098, Tocopilla; tel. (55) 81-2139; telex 325601; fax (55) 81-2650; owned by Sociedad Química y Minera de Chile, SA; 116 km; Gen. Man. SEGISFREDO HURTADO GUERRERO.

Association

Chilean Railway Society (ACCPF): Casilla 320, Correo 11, Nuñoa, Santiago; tel. (2) 205-0627; fax (2) 280-0252; Pres. I. THOMSON.

ROADS

The total length of roads in Chile in 1996 was an estimated 79,800 km, of which some 6,350 km were highways and some 16,700 km were secondary roads. The road system includes the completely paved Pan American Highway extending 3,455 km from north to south. Toll gates exist on major motorways. The 1,200 km-Carretera Austral (Southern Highway), linking Puerto Montt and Puerto Yungay, was completed in March 1996, at an estimated total cost of US $200m.

Ministerio de Obras Públicas: Dirección de Vialidad, Morandé 59, 2°, Santiago; tel. (2) 696-4839; telex 240777; fax (2) 698-6622; the authority responsible for roads; Dir Ing. OSCAR FERREL MARTÍNEZ.

SHIPPING

As a consequence of Chile's difficult topography, maritime transport is of particular importance. In 1995 90% of the country's foreign trade was carried by sea (44m. metric tons). The principal ports are Valparaíso, Talcahuano, Antofagasta, San Antonio, Arica, Iquique, Coquimbo, San Vicente, Puerto Montt and Punta Arenas.

Chile's merchant fleet amounted to 1.3m. dwt at December 1995.

Supervisory Authorities

Asociación Nacional de Armadores: Blanco 869, 3°, Valparaíso; tel. (32) 21-2057; fax (32) 21-2017; e-mail armadore@entelchile.net; f. 1931; shipowners' association; Pres. JUAN FERNANDO WAIDELE; Gen. Man. ARTURO SIERRA MERINO.

Cámara Marítima y Portuaria de Chile, AG: Blanco 869, Valparaíso; tel. (32) 25-3443; fax (32) 25-8109; Pres. JAIME BARAHONA VARGAS; Gen. Man. RODOLFO GARCÍA SÁNCHEZ.

Dirección General de Territorio Marítimo y Marina Mercante: Errázuriz 537, 4°, Valparaíso; tel. (32) 25-8061; telex 230662; fax (32) 25-2539; maritime admin. of the coast and national waters, control of the merchant navy; Dir Rear Adm. FERNANDO LAZCANO.

Empresa Portuaria de Chile—Emporchi: Avda Errázuriz 629, 3°, Casilla 25-V, Valparaíso; tel. (32) 25-7167; fax (32) 23-4427; Port Admin. DOMINGO O. GONZÁLEZ; Harbour Master CARLOS RODRÍGUEZ.

Emporchi (Antofagasta): Avda Costanera 1946, Antofagasta; tel. (55) 22-3587; fax (55) 22-3171; Harbour Master RUDY BITTENBERG ROJAS.

Emporchi (Arica): Avda Pedro Lira 389, Casilla 932, Arica; tel. and fax (58) 23-2284; Port Captain GERARDO CONEJEROS AVIANZO; Operations Manager JUAN NÚÑEZ REYES.

Emporchi (Coquimbo): Avda Costanera s/n, Melgarejo, Coquimbo 676; tel. (51) 31-1104; fax (51) 31-2215; Port Capt. CARLOS VERGARA LOBOS.

Emporchi (Iquique): Recinto Portuario, Iquique; tel. (57) 42-3498; telex 223054; Port Man. PEDRO DAVILA PIÑA.

Emporchi (San Antonio): Avda Alan Macowan 245, San Antonio; tel. (35) 21-2159; fax (35) 21-2114.

Emporchi (Talcahuano): Avda Latorre 1590, San Vicente, Talcahuano; tel. (41) 54-1419; fax (41) 54-1807; Port Man. ALBERTO ARISMENDE TORRES; Harbour Master Capt. ALEJANDRO OLIVARES ARANCIBIA.

Principal Shipping Companies

Santiago

Cía Marítima Isla de Pascua, SA (COMAIPA): MacIver 225, Of. 2001, 20°, Santiago; tel. (2) 38-3036; telex 240646; Pres. FEDERICO BARRAZA; Gen. Man. ALEJANDRO BARRAZA BARRY.

Marítima Antares, SA: MacIver 225, Of. 2001, 2°, Santiago; tel. (2) 38-3036; telex 340464; Pres. ALFONSO GARCÍA-MIÑAUR G.; Gen. Man. LUIS BEDRIÑANA RODRÍGUEZ.

Naviera Magallanes, SA (NAVIMAG): Avda El Bosque, Norte 0440, 11°, Of. 1103/1104, Las Condes, Santiago; tel. (2) 203-5180; telex 240224; fax (2) 203-5191; f. 1979; Chair. PEDRO LECAROS MENÉNDEZ; Gen. Man. EDUARDO SALAZAR RETAMALES.

Nisa Navegación, SA: Avda El Bosque Norte 0440, 11°, Casilla 2829, Santiago; tel.(2) 203-5180; telex 240224; fax (2) 203-5190; Chair. PEDRO LECAROS MENÉNDEZ; Gen. Man. FRANCISCO SAHLI CRUZ.

Valparaíso

A. J. Broom y Cía, SAC: Blanco 951, Casilla 910, Valparaíso and MacIver 225, 10°, Casilla 448, Santiago; f. 1920; Pres. Capt. GASTON ANRIQUEZ; Gen. Man. JAMES C. WELLS M.

Cía Chilena de Navegación Interoceánica, SA: Plaza de la Justicia 59, Casilla 1410, Valparaíso; tel. (32) 25-9001; telex 645195; fax (32) 25-5949; f. 1930; regular sailings to Japan, Republic of Korea, Taiwan, Hong Kong, USA, Mexico, South Pacific, South Africa and Europe; bulk and dry cargo services; Pres. ALEJANDRO PINO TORCHE; Man. Dir ANTONIO JABAT ALONSO.

Cía Sud-Americana de Vapores: Plaza Sotomayor 50, Casilla 49-V, Valparaíso; tel. (32) 20-3000; telex 330500; fax (32) 21-8724; also Hendaya 60, 12°, Santiago; tel. (2) 330-7000; telex 240480; fax (2) 330-7700; f. 1872; regular service between South America and US/Canadian ports, US Gulf ports, North European, Mediterranean, Scandinavian and Far East ports; bulk carriers, tramp and reefer services; Pres. RICARDO CLARO VALDÉS; Gen. Man. FRANCISCO SILVA DONOSO.

Empresa Marítima, SA (Empremar Chile): Almirante Gómez Carreño 49, Casilla 105-V, Valparaíso; tel. (32) 25-8061; telex 230382; fax (32) 21-3904; f. 1953; international and coastal services; Chair. MAURICIO VILLASEÑOR G.

Naviera Chilena del Pacífico, SA: Almirante Senoret 70, 6°, Casilla 370, Valparaíso; tel. (32) 25-5123; telex 230357; fax (32) 25-3869; also Serrano 14, Of. 502, Santiago; tel. (2) 639-2069; telex 240457; fax (2) 633-3063; cargo; Pres. ARTURO FERNÁNDEZ ZEGERS; Gen. Man. PABLO SIMIAN ZAMORANO.

Pacific Steam Navigation Co: Blanco 625, 6°, Casilla 24-V, Valparaíso; tel. (32) 21-3191; telex 230384; also Moneda 970, 9°, Casilla 4087, Avda Apoquindo 3721, 8°, Santiago; brs in Antofagasta and San Antonio; Man. DAVID KIMBER SMITH.

Sociedad Anónima de Navegación Petrolera (SONAP): Errázuriz 471, 3°, Casilla 1870, Valparaíso; tel. (32) 25-9476; telex 432023; fax (32) 25-1325; f. 1954; tanker services; Chair. FELIPE VIAL C.; Gen. Man. JOSÉ THOMSEN Q.

Transmares Naviera Chilena Ltda: Moneda 970, 20°, Edif. Eurocentro, Casilla 193-D, Santiago; tel. (2) 630-1000; telex 240440; fax (2) 698-9205; also Cochrane 813, 8°, Casilla 52-V, Valparaíso; tel. (32) 20-2000; telex 230383; fax (32) 25-6607; f. 1969; dry cargo service Chile–Uruguay–Brazil; Chair. WOLF VON APPEN; CEO CARLOS KÜHLENTHAL.

Several foreign shipping companies operate services to Valparaíso.

Ancúd

Sociedad Transporte Marítimo Chiloé-Aysén Ltda: Libertad 669, Casilla 387, Ancúd; tel. (656) 317; Deputy Man. PEDRO HERNÁNDEZ LEHMAN.

Punta Arenas

Cía Marítima de Punta Arenas, SA: Avda Independencia 830, Casilla 337, Punta Arenas; tel. (61) 24-1752; telex 280050; fax (61) 24-7514; also Casilla 2829, Santiago; tel. (2) 203-5180; telex 240208; fax (2) 203-5191; f. 1949; shipping agents and owners operating in the Magellan Straits; Dir ROBERTO IZQUIERDO MENÉNDEZ; Gen. Man. ARTURO STORAKER MOLINA.

San Antonio

Naviera Aysén Ltda: San Antonio; tel. (35) 32578; telex 238603; also Huérfanos 1147, Of. 542, Santiago; tel. (2) 698-8680; telex 240982; Man. RAÚL QUINTANA A.

Naviera Paschold Ltda: Centenario 9, San Antonio; tel. (35) 31654; telex 238603; also Huérfanos 1147, Santiago; tel. (2) 698-8680; telex 240982; Gen. Man. FERNANDO MARTÍNEZ M.

CIVIL AVIATION

There are 325 airfields in the country, of which eight have long runways. Arturo Merino Benítez, 20 km north-east of Santiago, and Chacalluta, 14 km north-east of Arica, are the principal international airports.

Fast Air Carrier: Cargo Terminal, Comodoro A. Merino Benítez International Airport, Santiago; tel. (2) 694-7999; fax (2) 601-9701; f. 1978; operates international, scheduled and cargo charter services to Miami, New York and Montevideo; Chair. and Pres. JUAN CUETO SIERRA.

Línea Aérea Nacional de Chile (LAN-Chile): Estado 10, 21°, Santiago; tel. (2) 639-4411; telex 441061; fax (2) 638-1729; f. 1929; operates scheduled domestic passenger and cargo services, also Santiago–Easter Island; international services to French Polynesia, Spain, and throughout North and South America; under the Govt's privatization programme, 99% of LAN-Chile shares have been sold to private interests since 1989; Pres. JOSÉ LUIS MOURE; Gen. Man. SVENERIC PERSSON.

Línea Aérea del Cobre SA—LADECO: Avda B. O'Higgins 107, Santiago; tel. (2) 639-5053; telex 240116; fax (2) 639-7277; f. 1958; internal passenger and cargo services; international passenger and cargo services to the USA and throughout South America; Chair. JOSÉ LUIS IBÁÑEZ; CEO VICTORIA VÁSQUEZ.

Tourism

Chile has a wide variety of attractions for the tourist, including fine beaches, ski resorts in the Andes, lakes, rivers and desert scenery. There are many opportunities for hunting and fishing in the southern archipelago, where there are plans to make an integrated tourist area with Argentina, requiring investment of US $120m. Isla de Pascua (Easter Island) may also be visited by tourists.

Servicio Nacional de Turismo—SERNATUR: Avda Providencia 1550, Casilla 14082, Santiago; tel. (2) 236-1420; fax (2) 236-1417; f. 1975; Dir CÉSAR GÓMEZ VIVEROS.

Asociación Chilena de Empresas de Turismo—ACHET: Moneda 973, Of. 647, Casilla 3402, Santiago; tel. (2) 696-5677; telex 242114; fax (2) 699-4245; f. 1945; 240 mems; Pres. IVONNE LAHAYE DE MONTES; MARDONES; Man. CARLOS MESCHI MONTALDO.

THE PEOPLE'S REPUBLIC OF CHINA

Introductory Survey

Location, Climate, Language, Religion, Flag, Capital

The People's Republic of China covers a vast area of eastern Asia, with Mongolia and Russia to the north, Tajikistan, Kyrgyzstan and Kazakhstan to the north-west, Afghanistan and Pakistan to the west, and India, Nepal, Bhutan, Myanmar (formerly Burma), Laos and Viet Nam to the south. The country borders the Democratic People's Republic of Korea in the north-east, and has a long coastline on the Pacific Ocean. The climate ranges from subtropical in the far south to an annual average temperature of below 10°C (50°F) in the north, and from the monsoon climate of eastern China to the aridity of the north-west. The principal language is Northern Chinese (Mandarin); in the south and south-east local dialects are spoken. The Xizangzu (Tibetans), Wei Wuer (Uygurs), Menggus (Mongols) and other groups have their own languages. The traditional religions and philosophies of life are Confucianism, Buddhism and Daoism. There are also Muslim and Christian minorities. The national flag (proportions 3 by 2) is plain red, with one large five-pointed gold star and four similar but smaller stars, arranged in an arc, in the upper hoist. The capital is Beijing (Peking).

Recent History

The People's Republic of China was proclaimed on 1 October 1949, following the victory of Communist forces over the Kuomintang Government, which fled to the island province of Taiwan. The new Communist regime received widespread international recognition, but it was not until 1971 that the People's Republic was admitted to the United Nations, in place of the Kuomintang regime, as the representative of China. Most countries now recognize the People's Republic.

With the establishment of the People's Republic, the leading political figure was Mao Zedong, who was Chairman of the Chinese Communist Party (CCP) from 1935 until his death in 1976. Chairman Mao, as he was known, also became Head of State in October 1949, but he relinquished this post in December 1958. His successor was Liu Shaoqi, First Vice-Chairman of the CCP, who was elected Head of State in April 1959. Liu was dismissed in October 1968, during the Cultural Revolution (see below), and died in prison in 1969. The post of Head of State was left vacant, and was formally abolished in January 1975, when a new Constitution was adopted. The first Premier (Head of Government) of the People's Republic was Zhou Enlai, who held this office from October 1949 until his death in 1976. Zhou was also Minister of Foreign Affairs from 1949 to 1958.

The economic progress of the early years of Communist rule enabled China to withstand the effects of the industrialization programmes of the late 1950s (called the 'Great Leap Forward'), the drought of 1960–62 and the withdrawal of Soviet aid in 1960. To prevent the establishment of a ruling class, Chairman Mao launched the Great Proletarian Cultural Revolution in 1966. The ensuing excesses of the Red Guards caused the army to intervene; Liu Shaoqi and Deng Xiaoping, General Secretary of the CCP, were disgraced. In 1971 an attempted coup by the Defence Minister, Marshal Lin Biao, was unsuccessful, and by 1973 it was apparent that Chairman Mao and Premier Zhou Enlai had retained power. In 1975 Deng Xiaoping re-emerged as first Vice-Premier and Chief of the General Staff. Zhou Enlai died in January 1976. Hua Guofeng, hitherto Minister of Public Security, was appointed Premier, and Deng was dismissed. Mao died in September 1976. His widow, Jiang Qing, tried unsuccessfully to seize power, with the help of three radical members of the CCP's Politburo. The 'gang of four' and six associates of Lin Biao were tried in November 1980. All were found guilty and were given lengthy terms of imprisonment. (Jiang Qing committed suicide in May 1991.) The 10th anniversary of Mao's death was marked in September 1986 by an official reassessment of his life; while his accomplishments were praised, it was now acknowledged that he had made mistakes, although most of the criticism was directed at the 'gang of four'.

In October 1976 Hua Guofeng succeeded Mao as Chairman of the CCP and Commander-in-Chief of the People's Liberation Army. The 11th National Congress of the CCP, held in August 1977, restored Deng Xiaoping to his former posts. In September 1980 Hua Guofeng resigned as Premier, but retained his chairmanship of the CCP. The appointment of Zhao Ziyang, a Vice-Premier since April 1980, to succeed Hua as Premier confirmed the dominance of the moderate faction of Deng Xiaoping. In June 1981 Hua Guofeng was replaced as Chairman of the CCP by Hu Yaobang, former Secretary-General of the Politburo, and as Chairman of the party's Central Military Commission by Deng Xiaoping. A sustained campaign by Deng to purge the Politburo of leftist elements led to Hua's demotion to a Vice-Chairman of the CCP and, in September 1982, to his exclusion from the Politburo.

In September 1982 the CCP was reorganized and the post of Party Chairman abolished. Hu Yaobang became, instead, General Secretary of the CCP. A year later a 'rectification' (purge) of the CCP was launched, aimed at expelling 'Maoists', who had risen to power during the Cultural Revolution, and those opposed to the pragmatic policies of Deng. China's new Constitution, adopted in December 1982, restored the office of Head of State, and in June 1983 Li Xiannian, a former Minister of Finance, became President of China.

Following the announcement of a major operation to combat crime in late 1983, thousands of people were reported to have been executed. At the same time a campaign was launched against 'spiritual pollution' and stricter censorship was introduced to limit the effects of Western cultural influences. The reorganization of the CCP and of the Government continued. During 1984–85 a programme of modernization for the armed forces was undertaken. In September 1986 the sixth plenary session of the 12th CCP Central Committee adopted a detailed resolution on the 'guiding principles for building a socialist society', which redefined the general ideology of the CCP, to provide a theoretical basis for the programme of modernization and the 'open door' policy of economic reform.

In January 1986 a high-level 'anti-corruption' campaign was launched, to investigate reports that many officials had exploited the programme of economic reform for their own gain. In the field of culture and the arts there was a significant liberalization in 1986, with a revival of the 'Hundred Flowers' movement of 1956–57, which had encouraged the development of intellectual debate. However, a series of student demonstrations in major cities in late 1986 was regarded by China's leaders as an indication of excessive 'bourgeois liberalization'. In January 1987 Hu Yaobang unexpectedly resigned as CCP General Secretary, being accused of 'mistakes on major issues of political principles'. Zhao Ziyang became acting General Secretary.

The campaign against 'bourgeois liberalization' was widely regarded as part of a broader, ideological struggle between those Chinese leaders who sought to extend Deng's reforms and those, generally elderly, 'conservative' leaders who opposed the reforms and the 'open door' policy. At the 13th National Congress of the CCP, which opened in October 1987, it became clear that the 'reformist' faction within the Chinese leadership had prevailed. Deng Xiaoping retired from the Central Committee, but amendments to the Constitution of the CCP permitted him to retain the influential positions of Chairman of the State and of the CCP Central Military Commissions.

A new Politburo was appointed by the Central Committee in November 1987. The majority of its 18 members were relatively young officials, who supported Deng Xiaoping's policies. The membership of the new Politburo also indicated a decline in military influence in Chinese politics. The newly-appointed Standing Committee of the Politburo was regarded, on balance, as being 'pro-reform'. In late November Li Peng was appointed Acting Premier of the State Council, in place of Zhao Ziyang. At the first session of the Seventh National People's Congress (NPC), held in March–April 1988, Li Peng was confirmed as Premier, and Yang Shangkun (a member of the CCP Politburo) was elected President.

The death of Hu Yaobang in April 1989 led to the most serious student demonstrations ever seen in the People's Republic. The students criticized the alleged prevalence of corruption and nepotism within the Government, and sought a limited degree of Soviet-style *glasnost* in public life. When negotiations between government officials and the students' leaders had failed to satisfy the protesters' demands, workers from various professions joined the demonstrations in Tiananmen Square, Beijing, which had now become the focal point of the protests. At one stage more than 1m. people congregated in the Square, as demonstrations spread to more than 20 other Chinese cities. In mid-May some 3,000 students began a hunger strike in Tiananmen Square, while protesters demanded the resignation of both Deng Xiaoping and Li Peng, and invited President Gorbachev of the USSR, who was visiting Beijing, to address them. The students ended their hunger strike at the request of Zhao Ziyang, who was generally regarded as being sympathetic to the students' demands. On 20 May a state of martial law was declared in Beijing. Within days, some 300,000 troops had assembled. At the end of May the students erected a 30-m high replica of the US Statue of Liberty in the Square.

On 3 June 1989 a further unsuccessful attempt was made to dislodge the demonstrators, but on the following day troops of the People's Liberation Army (PLA) attacked protesters on and around Tiananmen Square, killing an unspecified number of people. Television evidence and eye-witness accounts estimated the total dead at between 1,000 and 5,000. The Government immediately rejected these figures and claimed, furthermore, that the larger part of the casualties had been soldiers and that a counter-revolutionary rebellion had been taking place. Arrests and executions ensued, although some student leaders eluded capture and fled to Hong Kong. Zhao Ziyang was dismissed from all his party posts and replaced as General Secretary of the CCP by Jiang Zemin, hitherto the secretary of the Shanghai municipal party committee. Zhao was accused of participating in a conspiracy to overthrow the CCP and placed under house arrest. In November Deng resigned as Chairman of the CCP Central Military Commission, his sole remaining party position, and was succeeded by Jiang Zemin, who was hailed as the first of China's 'third generation' of communist leaders (Mao being representative of the first, and Deng of the second). In January 1990 martial law was lifted in Beijing, and it was announced that a total of 573 prisoners, detained following the pro-democracy demonstrations, had been freed. Further groups of detainees were released subsequently. In March Deng Xiaoping resigned from his last official post, that of Chairman of the State Central Military Commission, being succeeded by Jiang Zemin. An extensive military reshuffle ensued. In December, at the seventh plenary session of the 13th Central Committee of the CCP, proposals for the Eighth Five-Year Plan (1991–95) and for the 10-year development programme (1991–2000) were approved. The fourth plenary session of the Seventh NPC opened in March 1991. Emphasis was placed on the promotion of political stability in China. In the following month government changes included the appointment of two new Vice-Premiers.

In January 1992 Deng Xiaoping toured the Special Economic Zones (SEZs) of southern China, where he emphasized the importance of reform, thus initiating a period of intense debate between reformists and 'hard-liners' within the CCP. In March, at a session of the NPC, Premier Li Peng affirmed China's commitment to rapid economic reform, but stressed the need for stability. In September government changes included the replacement of the Minister of Finance. At the CCP's 14th National Congress, held in October 1992, a new 319-member Central Committee was elected. The Politburo was expanded and a new Secretariat was chosen by the incoming Central Committee. Many opponents of Deng Xiaoping's support for a 'socialist market economy' were replaced.

At the first session of the Eighth NPC, convened in March 1993, Jiang Zemin was elected as the country's President, remaining CCP General Secretary. Li Peng was reappointed as Premier, and an extensive reorganization of the State Council was announced. The Congress also approved amendments to the 1982 Constitution. Changes included confirmation of the State's practice of a 'socialist market economy'. During 1993, however, the Government became concerned at the growing disparity between urban and rural incomes (exacerbated by the heavy taxes imposed on farmers) and the resultant problems of rural migration, and the decline in support for the CCP in the countryside. In June thousands of peasants took part in demonstrations in Sichuan Province to protest against excessive official levies. In response to the ensuing riots, the central Government banned the imposition of additional local taxes.

In March 1995, at the third session of the Eighth NPC, the appointment of Wu Bangguo and of Jiang Chunyun as Vice-Premiers of the State Council was approved. In an unprecedented display of opposition, however, neither nominee received the NPC's full endorsement; Jiang Chunyun received less than 64% of the delegates' votes. Nevertheless, the position of Jiang Zemin, now regarded by many as the eventual successor to the 'paramount' leadership of the ailing Deng Xiaoping, appeared to have been strengthened. Personnel changes in the military hierarchy later in the year were also viewed as favourable to Jiang Zemin.

At the fourth session of the Eighth NPC in March 1996, deputies endorsed the Ninth Five-Year Plan (1996–2000). In October a plenary session of the 14th Central Committee of the CCP was held. Although the party's commitment to economic development was reiterated, emphasis was placed on the need to combat 'Western ideas, bourgeois ideology, feudal practices and corruption'.

The death of Deng Xiaoping, at the age of 92, on 19 February 1997, opened a period of some uncertainty regarding China's future direction. President Jiang Zemin, however, declared that the economic reforms would continue and this was reiterated in Premier Li Peng's address to the fifth session of the Eighth NPC in March 1997, during which he emphasized the urgent need to restructure state-owned enterprises (SOEs). Delegates at the Congress approved legislation reinforcing the CCP's control over the PLA, and revisions to the criminal code were also promulgated, whereby statutes concerning 'counter-revolutionary' acts (under which many of the pro-democracy demonstrators had been charged in 1989) were removed from the code, but were replaced by 11 crimes of 'endangering state security'. Financial offences, such as money laundering, were also included for the first time, an indication of the rapidly-evolving economic situation. The Procurator-General's annual report to the NPC, detailing the Government's progress in addressing the rising levels of criminal activity, was rejected by some 40% of delegates, in an unprecedented vote of protest.

The 15th National Congress of the CCP convened in mid-September 1997, following a period of intense speculation concerning possible changes in personnel among the party leadership. Emphasis on radical reform of the 370,000 SOEs, outlined in President Jiang Zemin's address to the opening session, formed the central theme of the Congress, with proposals put forward to restructure the majority of SOEs into joint-stock companies, or other forms of public ownership. The State was to retain control over a number of strategic industrial enterprises. Jiang Zemin warned of the inevitability of rising unemployment as a necessary consequence of economic reform. The economic restructuring measures, however, were not matched by any substantial commitment to political reform. Delegates approved amendments to the party Constitution, enshrining the 'Deng Xiaoping Theory' of socialism with Chinese characteristics alongside 'Mao Zedong Thought' as the guiding ideology of the CCP. The Congress elected a new 344-member Central Committee, which re-elected Jiang Zemin as General Secretary of the CCP, and appointed a 22-member Politburo. The composition of the new Politburo appeared to confirm Jiang Zemin's enhanced authority: Qiao Shi, a reformist and Jiang's most influential rival, who was ranked third in the party hierarchy, was excluded, reportedly because of his age, as was Gen. Liu Huaqing, China's most senior military figure. Zhu Rongji, a former mayor of Shanghai, replaced Qiao Shi, and was also widely regarded as the likely successor to Li Peng, on Li's retirement as Premier of the State Council in March 1998. Gen. Liu was replaced by a civilian, Wei Jinxiang, who was responsible for combating corruption within the CCP. The absence of the military from the Politburo, and the composition of the new Central Military Commission, confirmed Jiang's increased authority over the PLA.

The first session of the Ninth NPC, at which a new State Council was to be appointed, was scheduled to commence in early March 1998. A wide-ranging government reorganization was expected, and it was predicted that there would be a significant reduction in the number of ministries and state commissions (see Late Information).

Public disquiet over corruption within the CCP, the state bureaucracy and economic enterprises was acknowledged in August 1993, when the Party initiated an anti-corruption campaign. Hundreds of executions of officials were subsequently reported, and in April 1995, following allegations of corruption, Wang Baosen, a deputy mayor of Beijing, committed suicide. In the same month Chen Xitong, Secretary of the Beijing Municipality Committee, was arrested. An extensive inquiry concluded that Wang Baosen, a protégé of Chen Xitong, had been responsible for serious irregularities, including the embezzlement of the equivalent of millions of US dollars. In September, having been similarly disgraced, Chen Xitong was expelled from the Politburo and from the Central Committee of the CCP. In April 1996 it was announced that proceedings against 18 (unidentified) associates of Wang Baosen were to be instigated. Owing to his implication in the scandal, the mayor of Beijing, Li Qiyan, finally resigned in October 1996. The campaign against corruption intensified in 1997 with the sentencing in August of Chen Xiaotong, son of Chen Xitong, to 12 years' imprisonment for the misappropriation of public funds. Lengthy prison terms were also conferred on two former senior officials in the Beijing administration for accepting bribes. In September Chen Xitong was expelled from the CCP, and was to be prosecuted on charges of corruption. It was reported that between October 1992 and June 1997 121,000 people had been expelled from the CCP for corruption, while 37,500 others had faced criminal charges.

A significant increase in the number of labour disputes was recorded in 1996 and 1997, and by mid-1997 the number of incidents had risen by 59%, compared with the same period in 1996. In March 1997, in the worst unrest since 1949, more than 20,000 workers at a silk factory in Sichuan Province took part in a demonstration to demand payment of substantial wage arrears. Later in that year some 100,000 people took to the streets in protest at their dismissal from another silk factory. In August more than 1,000 farmers clashed with police at a demonstration in Guangdong Province, following allegations of fraud against party officials. A factory workers' demonstration against reductions in wages and benefits in Sichuan Province in October was forcibly dispersed by police.

An extensive operation to counter the sharp increase in crimes such as drugs-trafficking, prostitution and the distribution of pornography continued, resulting in hundreds of executions. In April 1996 the Government initiated 'Strike Hard', a new campaign against crime, executing hundreds of people. On 26 June 1996 alone, the UN's Anti-Drugs Day, more than 230 executions were reported, while almost 800 received sentences of death or life imprisonment. In a highly critical report, issued in August 1997, Amnesty International estimated that 4,367 people had been executed in China in 1996, the highest number since the 1983 anti-crime campaign. However, it was believed that the actual figure may have been much greater. In April 1997, for the seventh consecutive year, China survived a motion of censure at the UN Commission on Human Rights in Geneva.

China's treatment of political dissidents attracted international attention in November 1997, with the release on medical grounds into exile in the USA of Wei Jingsheng. Wei had been imprisoned in 1979, but was released on parole in September 1993 (shortly before the International Olympic Committee was due to vote upon the venue for the 2000 Games, for which Beijing was bidding). He was rearrested, however, in April 1994, and detained incommunicado until December 1995, when he was convicted of conspiring to overthrow the Government. His sentencing to 14 years' imprisonment provoked an international outcry, and he was released shortly after Jiang Zemin's visit to the USA in October 1997 (see below). Bao Ge, a prominent Shanghai dissident and campaigner for compensation for Chinese victims of Japanese war aggression, was released from three years' imprisonment without trial in June. He left for the USA in November.

Meanwhile, in June 1990 Fang Lizhi, the prominent astrophysicist and dissident, was permitted to leave the country for the United Kingdom. In October Wang Ruowang, the eminent writer and dissident, was released from prison after 13 months in detention. In January 1991 the trials of many of those arrested during the pro-democracy protests of 1989 commenced. Most activists received relatively short prison sentences. In July 1992 Bao Tong, a senior aide of Zhao Ziyang, the former General Secretary of the CCP, was found guilty of involvement in the pro-democracy unrest of mid-1989. At the end of his seven-year prison sentence, Bao Tong was released in May 1996 and placed under house arrest. He was freed from house arrest in May 1997, but remained under constant police surveillance.

In September 1992, following his return to China from exile in the USA, Shen Tong, a leader of the pro-democracy movement, was arrested and later deported. In February 1994 Asia Watch, an independent New York-based human rights organization, issued a highly critical report of the situation in China, which detailed the cases of more than 1,700 detainees, imprisoned for their political, ethnic or religious views. In April, shortly before the USA was due to decide upon a renewal of China's favourable trading status, Wang Juntao, imprisoned for his part in the 1989 protests, was unexpectedly released and permitted to travel to the USA for medical treatment. Other releases followed. In July, however, the trial on charges of counter-revolutionary activity of 14 members of a dissident group, in detention since 1992, commenced. In December 1994 nine of the defendants received heavy prison sentences. A university lecturer, Hu Shigen, was sentenced to 20 years' imprisonment.

In February 1993 Wang Dan and Guo Haifeng, leading student activists in the 1989 demonstrations, were freed. In late 1994, however, complaining of police harassment, Wang Dan filed a lawsuit against the authorities. Wang Dan was rearrested in May 1995. The imposition of an 11-year sentence on Wang Dan at the conclusion of his cursory trial on charges of conspiracy, in October 1996, received international condemnation. Appeals for his release on medical grounds in 1997 were rejected. In May 1993, having served 12 years of a 15-year sentence, Xu Wenli was released from prison. He was rearrested in April 1994, but released shortly afterwards. In August 1993 the arrest and expulsion from China of Han Dongfang, a trade union activist who had attempted to return to his homeland after a year in the USA, attracted much international attention.

In June 1995 Liu Gang, a leader of the 1989 uprising, was released from prison, and in May 1996 he was granted temporary asylum in the USA. Two further dissidents, Ren Wanding and Zhang Xianliang, were freed upon completion of their prison terms in June 1996. Having been released in the same month, Wang Xizhe escaped from Guangzhou and was permitted to enter the USA in October. His fellow activist, Liu Xiaobo, was arrested in Beijing, however, and ordered to serve three years in a labour camp. In November, shortly before a visit to China by the US Secretary of State, Chen Zeming, another alleged leader of the 1989 pro-democracy demonstrations, was released on medical parole.

In 1997 there was increasing pressure on the CCP to reconsider its assessment of the 1989 Tiananmen Square pro-democracy demonstrations as a 'counter-revolutionary rebellion'. In June 1997, in an unprecedented decision, a court in Liaoning Province overturned convictions of 'counter-revolution' against four dissidents imprisoned for their role in the 1989 pro-democracy movement. However, an appeal to the CCP National Congress by Zhao Ziyang, who remained under house arrest, to reassess the official verdict, was dismissed. During Jiang's visit to the USA, in October 1997, having first described the brutal treatment of the 1989 demonstrators as a 'necessary measure', a subsequent acknowledgement that mistakes may have been made was not, according to the Chinese authorities, to be regarded as an apology. Amnesty International reported that in mid-1997 some 303 people remained in prison for their part in the pro-democracy movement. Beijing, however, declared that there were no political prisoners in China, classifying as criminals the estimated 2,000 people imprisoned on charges of 'counter-revolution'.

Tibet (Xizang), a semi-independent region of western China, was occupied in October 1950 by Chinese Communist forces. In March 1959 there was an unsuccessful armed uprising by Tibetans opposed to Chinese rule. The Dalai Lama, the head of Tibet's Buddhist clergy and thus the region's spiritual leader, fled with some 100,000 supporters to Dharamsala, northern India, where a government-in-exile was established. The Chinese ended the former dominance of the lamas (Buddhist monks) and destroyed many monasteries. Tibet became an 'Autonomous Region' of China in September 1965, but the majority of Tibetans have continued to regard the Dalai Lama as their 'god-king', and to resent the Chinese presence. In October 1987 violent clashes occurred in Lhasa (the regional capital) between the Chinese authorities and Tibetans seeking independence. Further demonstrations during a religious festival in March 1988 resulted in a riot and several deaths, and a number of Tibetan separatists were arrested and detained without trial. The Dalai Lama, however, renounced demands for complete independence, and in 1988 proposed that Tibet become a self-governing Chinese territory, in all respects except foreign affairs. In December 1988 an offer from the Dalai Lama to meet Chinese representatives in Geneva was rejected, and later that month two more demonstrators were killed by security forces during a march to commemorate the 40th anniversary of the UN General Assembly's adoption of the Universal Declaration of Human Rights.

On 7 March 1989 martial law was imposed in Lhasa for the first time since 1959, after further violent clashes between separatists and the Chinese police, which resulted in the deaths of 16 protesters. In October 1989 the Chinese Government condemned as an interference in its internal affairs the award of the Nobel Peace Prize to the Dalai Lama. In November several Tibetan Buddhist nuns claimed to have been severely tortured for their part in the demonstrations in March of that year. In early May 1990 martial law was lifted in Lhasa. Human rights groups claimed that during the last six months of the period of martial law as many as 2,000 persons had been executed. Furthermore, political and religious repression and torture were reported to be continuing throughout 1990. Renewed anti-Chinese protests were reported in October 1991 and in March 1992. In May a report issued by Amnesty International was critical of the Chinese authorities' violations of the human rights of the monks and nuns of Tibet. A document entitled *Tibet—Its Ownership and Human Rights Situation* was published by the Chinese Government in September, attempting to prove that historically the region is part of China. In May 1993 several thousand Tibetans were reported to have demonstrated in Lhasa against Chinese rule. A number of protesters were believed to have been killed by the security forces. In January 1994 two prominent Tibetan activists were released from detention. In July, however, five secessionists were found guilty of counter-revolutionary acts and received prison sentences of up to 15 years.

In March 1994 the Dalai Lama, who had continued to demand only limited autonomy for Tibet, acknowledged that he had made no progress in his attempts to negotiate with the Chinese authorities and, recognizing the disillusionment of many Tibetans, indicated that his moderate approach might be reviewed. In the following month China condemned the Dalai Lama's meeting with President Clinton during the former's lecture tour of the USA. In September the Dalai Lama warned China that Tibet might resort to armed uprising if oppression continued to worsen. In late 1994 the construction of new monasteries and temples in Tibet was banned. In March 1995 regulations restricting the number of Buddhist monks were announced, and in the same month the Dalai Lama's proposal that a referendum be held on the future of Tibet was dismissed by China. In May the Dalai Lama's nomination of the 11th incarnation of the Panchen Lama (the second position in the spiritual hierarchy, the 10th incumbent having died in 1989) was condemned by the Chinese authorities, which stated that the six-year old boy would not be allowed to travel to Dharamsala. In early September 1995, as the 30th anniversary of the imposition of Chinese rule approached, it was reported that independence activists had carried out two bombings in Lhasa.

In September 1995, during the UN World Conference on Women and the Non-Governmental Organizations' Forum held concurrently in China, a silent protest by a group of female Tibetan exiles attracted much attention. Following an informal meeting between the Dalai Lama and President Clinton in Washington in mid-September, China lodged a strong protest. In November the Chinese Government announced its own nomination of a new Panchen Lama. The boy was enthroned at a ceremony in Lhasa in December, the whereabouts of the Dalai Lama's choice remaining unknown until mid-1996, when China's ambassador to the UN in Geneva admitted that the boy was in detention in Beijing. There were violent confrontations in Tibet in May 1996, following the banning of any public display of images of the Dalai Lama. During a visit to the United Kingdom in July the Dalai Lama urged democratic countries to put pressure on China to improve the human rights situation in his homeland. In September the Dalai Lama's visit to Australia and his reception by the Prime Minister aroused further protests from the Chinese Government. A series of minor explosions during 1996 culminated in late December with the detonation of a powerful bomb outside a government office in Lhasa. The attack, which injured several people and caused extensive damage, was denounced by the Dalai Lama, who warned of the likelihood of an increase in repression by the Chinese authorities. In an unprecedented admission, the Chinese Government acknowledged the existence of a terrorist problem in Tibet.

The Chinese leadership condemned the Dalai Lama's visit to Taiwan in March 1997, despite assurances that he was visiting in his capacity as a spiritual leader. In May it was reported that Chatral Rinpoche, an official in the Tibetan administration, and one of Tibet's most senior monks, had been sentenced to six years' imprisonment for allegedly revealing information to the Dalai Lama about Beijing's search for the new Panchen Lama. The USA's decision in mid-1997 to appoint a special co-ordinator for Tibet was criticized by the Chinese authorities. In October the Dalai Lama appealed to the Chinese Government to reopen negotiations over the status of Tibet, confirming that he did not seek full independence for the region.

Anti-Chinese sentiment in the Xinjiang Uygur Autonomous Region intensified in early 1990, and in April as many as 60 people were reported to have been killed when government troops opened fire on Muslim protesters. A new campaign to repress the Islamic separatist movement was initiated and in October 1993 protests by thousands of Muslims in Qinghai Province were brutally suppressed by the authorities. Suppression against separatism intensified in May 1996, following a number of violent incidents. Later in the month it emerged that nine armed activists had been killed in a gun battle with the police. During rioting in Yining, following a public execution, nine people were killed and 100 wounded, according to official figures. Other sources suggested much higher casualty figures. In late February three bombs planted on buses in Urumqi killed nine people and injured 74. A similar attack in Beijing in March injured 11 people. Hundreds of people were detained for their part in the rioting and the bomb attacks, and many were subsequently executed or given lengthy terms of imprisonment. Reports in late 1997 indicated that there had been a renewal of armed separatist activity, prior to the Chinese national day, in which more than 300 people had been killed.

In September 1984, following protracted negotiations, China reached agreement with the British Government over the terms of Chinese administration of Hong Kong, following its return to Chinese sovereignty on 1 July 1997. In 1985 a Basic Law Drafting Committee (BLDC), including 25 representatives from Hong Kong, was established in Beijing to prepare a new Basic Law (Constitution) for Hong Kong. The Basic Law for Hong Kong was approved by the NPC in April 1990. High-level consultations on the future of Hong Kong were held in 1990 and 1991. In September 1991, during a visit to China by the British Prime Minister, a Memorandum of Understanding on the construction of a new airport in Hong Kong was signed. Relations between China and the United Kingdom were strained in 1992 by the announcement of ambitious plans for democratic reform in Hong Kong prior to 1997. In January 1993 a senior Chinese official warned that Hong Kong would experience 'hardship' if the programme of political reform were pursued. China and the United Kingdom resumed negotiations in April on the future of the territory, thus ending an impasse of several months. By the end of the year, however, no progress had been made, and in December, following Hong Kong's decision to press ahead with electoral reform, China declared that it would regard as null and void any laws enacted by the territory's Legislative Council. In December 1994 Lu Ping, the director of the mainland Hong Kong and Macau Affairs Office, formally confirmed that the Legislative Council of Hong Kong would be disbanded in 1997. A detailed accord on the financing of Hong Kong's new airport was signed in June 1995. In the same month China and the United Kingdom also reached agreement on the contentious issue of the establishment in Hong Kong (in 1997) of the Court of Final Appeal. In early July the Chief Secretary of Hong Kong, Anson Chan, confirmed that she had had clandestine meetings with Chinese officials during a three-day visit to Beijing. The improvement in Sino-British relations was confirmed in October when Qian Qichen, the Chinese Vice-Premier and Minister of Foreign Affairs, visited London for discussions with the British Prime Minister and his Foreign Secretary. In November 1995, however, the Governor of Hong Kong warned the Chinese Government that its repudiation of the territory's Bill of Rights, enacted in June 1991, would be detrimental to international confidence. China's disclosure of a plan to establish a parallel administration six months prior to the transfer of sovereignty aroused further controversy.

In January 1996 the 150-member Preparatory Committee of the Hong Kong Special Administrative Region (SAR) was formally established in Beijing, in succession to the Preliminary Working Committee (PWC), which had been formed in July 1993 to study issues relating to the transfer of sovereignty. Chaired by Qian Qichen and comprising 56 mainland and 94 Hong Kong delegates, including representatives of the territory's business and academic communities, the new body was to appoint a 400-member Selection Committee responsible for the choice of Hong Kong's future Chief Executive. In March 1996 the Preparatory Committee approved a resolution to appoint a provisional body to replace Hong Kong's Legislative Council. In September China and the United Kingdom finally reached agreement on the contentious issue of arrangements for the ceremony to mark the transfer of sovereignty on 30 June 1997. In December 1996 the Selection Committee chose Tung Chee-hwa as the Hong Kong SAR's first Chief Executive and elected the 60 members of the Provisional Legislative Council (PLC). The PLC held its first meeting in January 1997. Objections from the United Kingdom and the USA to Chinese proposals to abolish the Legislative Council, and to repeal human rights legislation, were dismissed by China. In May the PLC approved its first bill, despite previous assurances that no legislation would be passed before the handover. However, following objections from democracy campaigners, it was declared that the legislation would only become effective on 1 July.

The handover of Hong Kong from British to Chinese sovereignty was effected at midnight on 30 June 1997. Shortly afterwards some 4,000 PLA troops were deployed in Hong Kong, joining two smaller contingents that had arrived earlier, following protracted negotiations with the United Kingdom. The Government of the new SAR announced that elections to a new Legislative Council would be held in May 1998. Revisions to the SAR's electoral law, introduced in September 1997, which disfranchised many voters, were widely criticized. (For further information, see chapter on Hong Kong.)

Taiwan has repeatedly rejected China's proposals for reunification, whereby the island would become a 'special administrative region' along the lines of Hong Kong, and has sought reunification under its own terms. China threatened military intervention, should Taiwan declare itself independent of the mainland. Trade and reciprocal visits greatly increased in 1988, as relations improved. Reconciliation initiatives were abruptly halted, however, by the violent suppression of the pro-democracy movement in June 1989.

In May 1990 President Lee of Taiwan suggested the opening of direct dialogue on a government-to-government basis with the People's Republic. Beijing, however, maintained that it would negotiate only on a party-to-party basis with the Kuomintang. In April 1991 a delegation from the Straits Exchange Foundation (SEF) of Taiwan, established in late 1990 to handle bilateral issues, travelled to China for discussions, the first such delegation ever to visit the People's Republic. The Association for Relations across the Taiwan Straits (ARATS) was established in Beijing in December 1991. In May 1992 the People's Republic rejected Taiwan's proposal for a non-aggression pact. Nevertheless, in April 1993 historic talks between the Chairmen of the ARATS and SEF took place in Singapore, where a formal structure for future negotiations on economic and social issues was agreed. In August, however, the People's Republic issued a document entitled *The Taiwan Question and the Reunification of China,* reaffirming its claim to sovereignty over the island. Relations were further strained by a series of aircraft hijackings from the mainland to Taiwan, and they deteriorated sharply in April 1994, when 24 Taiwanese tourists were among those robbed and murdered on board a pleasure boat on Qiandao Lake, Zhejiang Province. In June three men were convicted of the murders and promptly executed. In August Tang Shubei, the Vice-Chairman and Secretary-General of the ARATS, travelled to Taipei for discussions, the most senior CCP official ever to visit the island. In mid-November relations were strained once again when, in an apparent accident during a training exercise, Taiwanese anti-aircraft shells landed on a mainland village, injuring several people. Nevertheless, in late November a further round of ARATS-SEF talks took place in Nanjing, at which agreement in principle on the procedure for the repatriation of hijackers and illegal immigrants was confirmed.

Discussions were resumed in Beijing in January 1995. At the end of that month President Jiang Zemin announced an 'eight-point' policy for Taiwan's peaceful reunification with the mainland. In response, in April, President Lee proposed a 'six-point' programme for cross-Straits relations (see p. 942). Following President Lee's controversial visit to the USA in June, however, the ARATS postponed the forthcoming second session of SEF discussions at senior level. Cross-Straits relations deteriorated further in July upon the People's Republic's announcement that it was to conduct a series of guided missile and artillery-firing tests off the northern coast of Taiwan. In the following month President Jiang Zemin confirmed that the People's Republic would not renounce the use of force against Taiwan, and President Lee reaffirmed the island's commitment to reunification.

In early 1996 unconfirmed reports suggested that 400,000 mainland troops had been mobilized around Fujian Province. A new series of missile tests began in March, arousing international concern. Live artillery exercises were conducted in the Taiwan Strait. Tension subsequently eased, however, and at the end of April the SEF urged that bilateral discussions be resumed. Cross-Straits co-operation was renewed from mid-1996: mainland executives from the transport, petroleum, trade and finance sectors travelled to Taiwan. In November President Lee's renewed offer to visit the mainland was rebuffed. In January 1997, however, as the reversion of the entrepôt of Hong Kong to Chinese sovereignty approached, representatives of the People's Republic and Taiwan reached a preliminary consensus on the issue of direct shipping links. Limited services resumed in April, thus ending a ban of 48 years.

Major military exercises were carried out in Taiwan in June 1997. In August the deputy secretary-general of the ARATS, the highest-ranking Chinese official to visit Taiwan since 1995, held talks with members of the SEF. However, in the following month President Lee's assertion of Taiwan's independence threatened the renewal of negotiations. An invitation for the resumption of more formal talks, on the basis of the 'one China' principle, was made by Jiang Zemin in October. Following the success of the pro-independence Democratic Progressive Party in the Taiwanese mayoral elections in November, divisions within Taiwan over its relationship with the People's Republic were becoming apparent. Support for reunification with China was weakening, although many in the business community were opposed to President Lee's continued ban on direct links with the mainland. Nevertheless, it appeared likely that negotiations would resume in early 1998.

In June 1986 China and Portugal opened formal negotiations for the return of the Portuguese overseas territory of Macau to full Chinese sovereignty. In January 1987 Portugal agreed that withdrawal from Macau should take place in December 1999. The agreement is based upon the 'one country, two systems' principle, which formed the basis of China's negotiated settlement regarding the return of Hong Kong. In March 1993 the final draft of the Basic Law for Macau was approved by the NPC. In May 1995 China proposed the swift establishment of a preparatory working committee to facilitate the transfer of sovereignty. Cordial relations were maintained, and the Portuguese Minister of Foreign Affairs visited Beijing in February 1996. The two sides agreed to accelerate the pace of work of the Sino-Portuguese Joint Liaison Group (JLG). In January 1997 Qian Qichen travelled to Portugal for discussions. Confidence in the future of Macau was reiterated.

In the early years of the People's Republic, China was dependent on the USSR for economic and military aid, and Chinese planning was based on the Soviet model, with highly centralized control. From 1955 onwards, however, Mao Zedong set out to develop a distinctively Chinese form of socialism. As a result, the USSR withdrew all technical aid to China in August 1960. Chinese hostility to the USSR increased, and was aggravated by territorial disputes, and by the Soviet invasion of Afghanistan and the Soviet-supported Vietnamese invasion of Cambodia. Sino-Soviet relations remained strained until 1987, when representatives of the two countries signed a partial agreement concerning the exact demarcation of the disputed Sino-Soviet border at the Amur river. The withdrawal of Soviet troops from Afghanistan (completed in February 1989) and Viet Nam's assurance that it would end its military presence in Cambodia by September 1989 resulted in a further *rapprochement*.

In May 1989 the Soviet President, Mikhail Gorbachev, attended a full summit meeting with Deng Xiaoping in Beijing, at which normal state and party relations between the two countries were formally restored. In April 1990 Li Peng paid an official visit to the USSR, the first by a Chinese Premier for 26 years. Jiang Zemin, CCP General Secretary, visited Moscow in May 1991. In December, upon the dissolution of the USSR, China recognized the newly-independent states of the former union. The President of Russia, Boris Yeltsin, visited China in December 1992. In May 1994, in Beijing, Premier Li Peng and his Russian counterpart signed various co-operation agreements relating to the border issue, trade, agriculture and environmental protection. In September President Jiang Zemin travelled to Moscow, the first visit to Russia by a Chinese head of state since 1957. The two sides reached agreement on the formal demarcation of the western section of the border (the eastern section having been delimited in May 1991), and each pledged not to aim nuclear missiles at the other. In June 1995 the

Chinese Premier paid an official visit to Russia, where several bilateral agreements were signed.

Sino-Russian relations continued to improve, and in April 1996 in Beijing Presidents Jiang and Yeltsin signed a series of agreements, envisaging the development of closer co-operation in areas such as energy, space research, environmental protection, and the combating of organized crime. Together with their counterparts from Kazakhstan, Kyrgyzstan and Tajikistan, the two Presidents also signed a treaty aimed at reducing tension along their respective borders. Progress on the Sino-Russian border question, and also on matters such as trade, was made during the Chinese Premier's visit to Moscow in December 1996.

A further treaty on military co-operation and border demilitarization was signed by the Presidents of China, Russia, Kazakhstan, Kyrgyzstan and Tajikistan in April 1997, during a visit by President Jiang Zemin to Russia. Presidents Jiang and Yeltsin affirmed their commitment to building a strategic, co-operative partnership, and a Sino-Russian committee on friendship, peace and development was established. Measures to increase bilateral trade were the focus of the Russian Prime Minister's visit to Beijing in June. Progress on the Sino-Russian border issue culminated in the signing of an agreement, during President Yeltsin's visit to Beijing in November, which formally ended the territorial dispute. A framework agreement for the construction of a gas pipeline from Siberia to China's Pacific coast was also signed. China's ties with Central Asia were boosted by the signing of an agreement worth US $9,500m. with Kazakhstan, which awarded China the exploitation rights to two of Kazakhstan's largest offshore oilfields, with a pipeline to be constructed from the Caspian Sea to the Chinese border.

During the 1970s there was an improvement in China's relations with the West and Japan. Almost all Western countries had recognized the Government of the People's Republic as the sole legitimate government of China, and had consequently withdrawn recognition from the 'Republic of China', which had been confined to Taiwan since 1949. For many years, however, the USA refused to recognize the People's Republic, regarding the Taiwan administration as the legitimate Chinese government. In February 1972 President Richard Nixon of the USA visited the People's Republic and acknowledged that 'Taiwan is a part of China'. In January 1979 the USA recognized the People's Republic and severed diplomatic relations with Taiwan.

China's relations with the USA improved steadily throughout the 1980s. In 1984 Premier Zhao Ziyang visited Washington, and in the same year President Ronald Reagan visited Beijing, where a bilateral agreement on industrial and technological co-operation was signed. Following the suppression of the pro-democracy movement in 1989, however, all high-level government exchanges were suspended and the export of weapons to China was prohibited. In November Deng accused the USA of being deeply involved in the 'counter-revolutionary rebellion'. In the same month the US Congress approved a proposal to extend the sanctions that President Bush had imposed in June. In December representatives of the US Government conferred with Deng in Beijing, and it was revealed that secret Sino-US negotiations had taken place in July of that year. In November 1990 President Bush received the Chinese Minister of Foreign Affairs in Washington, thereby resuming contact at the most senior level. In August 1993 the USA imposed sanctions on China, in response to the latter's sales of technology for nuclear-capable missiles to Pakistan, in alleged violation of international non-proliferation guidelines. The sanctions remained in force until October 1994. In May 1994, and again in 1995, President Bill Clinton renewed China's Most Favoured Nation (MFN) trading status for a further year, despite having warned in May 1993 that future renewals would be dependent upon an improvement in China's record on human rights.

Reports in late 1994 that Israel was providing the expertise to enable China to develop an advanced fighter aircraft, and in mid-1995 that the Chinese Government was permitting the sale of nuclear technology to Iran and again to Pakistan, aroused much concern in Washington. Sino-US relations were further strained in July 1995, when the USA and Viet Nam restored full diplomatic links. In early August two Hong Kong-based US Air Force officers were expelled from China for allegedly spying in a restricted military zone. Later in the month, as Hillary Clinton considered whether or not to attend the forthcoming UN Conference on Women in Beijing, the USA declared its deep regret in response to China's recent nuclear test. In late August, following his arrest in June, (Harry) Wu Hongda, a Chinese-born US citizen and political activist, was found guilty of espionage, sentenced to 15 years' imprisonment and immediately deported from China. In October Sino-US relations appeared to improve when, at a meeting in New York, Presidents Jiang Zemin and Bill Clinton agreed to resume dialogue on various issues, the USA reaffirming its commitment to a 'one China' policy. In November the two countries reached agreement on the resumption of bilateral military contacts.

In February 1996 Sino-US tension was renewed over the issue of China's exports of nuclear-capable technology to Pakistan. Nevertheless, in May, following clarification of the sales, the USA declared that it would not impose sanctions on China. US intelligence reports in August indicating that China was assisting Pakistan in the construction of a missile factory in Rawalpindi were strenuously denied. In May, meanwhile, President Clinton announced the renewal of China's MFN status for a further year. China's sales of textiles, however, remained problematical (the USA claiming that its import quotas were being circumvented), while disputes over matters such as intellectual property rights and the question of China's membership of the World Trade Organization (WTO) remained unresolved. In July Anthony Lake, the US National Security Advisor, paid a four-day visit to China for discussions. The issue of US weapon sales to Taiwan (see below) and China's record on human rights were among the subjects discussed during a visit to Beijing by the US Secretary of State, Warren Christopher, in November. In December Gen. Chi Haotian, the Chinese Minister of National Defence, was warmly received in the USA. In February 1997, however, at the end of a brief visit to Beijing, Madeleine Albright, the new US Secretary of State, declared that no progress had been made on the issue of human rights.

In addition to the above issues, another obstacle to good relations between China and the USA is the question of Taiwan, and, in particular, the continued sale of US armaments to Taiwan. Sino-US relations deteriorated in September 1992, upon President Bush's announcement of the sale of 150 F-16 fighter aircraft to Taiwan. China condemned the USA's decision, in September 1994, to expand its official links with Taiwan. In June 1995, following President Clinton's highly controversial decision to grant him a visa, President Lee of Taiwan embarked upon an unofficial visit to the USA, where he met members of the US Congress. The visit provoked outrage in Beijing, and led to the withdrawal of the Chinese ambassador to Washington. In March 1996, as China began a new series of missile tests (see above), the USA stationed two naval convoys east of Taiwan, its largest deployment in Asia since 1975. President Clinton's decision to sell anti-aircraft missiles and other defensive weapons to Taiwan was condemned by China.

Relations between the USA and China were complicated in early 1997 by reports that Chinese businessmen connected to the CCP had made substantial illegal donations to the US Democratic Party's presidential election campaign in 1996. The Chinese authorities denied attempting to influence US policy. Negotiations on the issue of human rights, the USA's growing trade deficit with China, and China's proposed entry into the WTO were the focus of Sino-US relations in 1997. The US State Department's annual report on human rights, released in January, was highly critical of China's human rights record, as it had been in previous years, but China condemned the report's findings, and warned of interference in its internal affairs. The US Vice-President, Al Gore, visited Beijing in March, the highest-ranking US official to visit China since 1989, but little progress was made on this issue. In May the USA renewed China's MFN trading status for a further year, although the burgeoning trade deficit remained a cause for concern for the US authorities. China's sales of arms and chemical weaponry to Iran were also a source of tension. China was highly critical of the defence co-operation agreement signed by the USA and Japan in September, fearing interference in Chinese sovereignty over Taiwan.

President Jiang Zemin visited the USA in October 1997, the first such visit by a Chinese head of state since 1985. Discussions centred on trade, human rights and the issue of Chinese exports of nuclear material. Vocal public criticism of China's failure to observe human rights, particularly with regard to Tibet, was widespread in the USA, but the Clinton administration defended its policy of engagement with China, warning of the dangers of isolation. Measures to reduce the trade deficit with China and to hasten China's entry into the WTO were negotiated. In addition, the Chinese Government agreed to control the export of nuclear-related materials, in return for the removal of sanctions on the sale of nuclear-reactor technology to the

People's Republic. Increased military co-operation and the holding of annual summit meetings were also agreed.

China's relations with Japan began to deteriorate in 1982, after China complained that passages in Japanese school textbooks sought to justify the Japanese invasion of China in 1937. In June 1989 the Japanese Government criticized the Chinese Government's suppression of the pro-democracy movement and suspended (until late 1990) a five-year aid programme to China. The Prime Minister of Japan visited Beijing for discussions with his Chinese counterpart in August 1991. In April 1992 Jiang Zemin travelled to Japan, the first visit by the General Secretary of the CCP for nine years. In October Emperor Akihito made the first ever imperial visit to the People's Republic. Japan was one of many countries to criticize China's resumption of underground nuclear testing, at Lop Nor in Xinjiang Province, in October 1993. In March 1994 the Japanese Prime Minister paid a visit to China. Relations were seriously strained in May, however, when the Japanese Minister of Justice referred to the 1937 Nanjing massacre (in which more than 300,000 Chinese citizens were killed by Japanese soldiers) as a 'fabrication', and again in August, when a second Japanese minister was obliged to resign, following further controversial remarks about his country's war record. In May 1995, during a visit to Beijing, the Japanese Prime Minister expressed his deep remorse for the wartime atrocities, but offered no formal apology.

China's continuation of its nuclear-testing programme, in defiance of international opinion, prompted Japan to announce a reduction in financial aid to China. In August 1995, after a further test, Japan suspended most of its grant aid to China. Following China's conduct of its 'final' nuclear test in July 1996, and its declaration of a moratorium, Japan resumed grant aid in March 1997. (China signed the Comprehensive Nuclear Test Ban Treaty in September 1996). In July 1996, however, Sino-Japanese relations were affected by a territorial dispute relating to the Diaoyu (or Senkaku) Islands, a group of uninhabited islets in the East China Sea, to which Taiwan also laid claim. The construction of a lighthouse on one of the islands by a group of Japanese nationalists led to strong protests from the Governments of both the People's Republic and Taiwan. The Japanese Government sought to defuse the tension by withholding recognition of the lighthouse, but did not condemn the right-wing activists responsible. A further incursion in September prompted China to warn of damage to bilateral relations if Japan failed to take action.

At a meeting with President Jiang Zemin during the Asia-Pacific Economic Co-operation (APEC) conference, in November 1996, the Japanese Prime Minister, Ryutaro Hashimoto, apologized for Japanese aggression during the Second World War, and emphasized his desire to resolve the dispute over the Diaoyu Islands. In May 1997, following the landing on one of the Islands by a member of the Japanese Diet, the Japanese Government distanced itself from the incident. The US-Japanese agreement on expanded military co-operation caused further tension in Sino-Japanese relations. Nevertheless, Japan's support for China's entry into the WTO remained firm, while China backed Japanese proposals for a permanent seat on the UN Security Council. Hashimoto visited China in September, when measures to dispose of the thousands of chemical weapons deployed in China by the Japanese troops during the Second World War were discussed. Premier Li Peng visited Japan in November.

The long-standing border dispute with India, which gave rise to a short military conflict in 1962, remained unresolved (see chapter on India). Discussions on the issue were held in 1988 and in 1991, and in September 1993 the two countries signed an agreement to reduce their troops along the frontier and to resolve the dispute by peaceful means. Discussions continued in 1994. In December China and India agreed to hold joint military exercises in mid-1995. In August 1995 it was confirmed that the two countries were to disengage their troops from four border posts in Arunachal Pradesh. Further progress was made at the ninth round of Sino-Indian border discussions, held in October 1996, and during the visit of President Jiang Zemin to India (the first by a Chinese head of state) in November. Negotiations continued in August 1997. The question of China's nuclear co-operation with Pakistan, however, remained a contentious issue.

China condemned Viet Nam's invasion of Kampuchea (now Cambodia) in December 1978, and launched a punitive attack into northern Viet Nam in February 1979. Armed clashes across the border continued, and negotiations between the two countries failed to resolve the dispute. China continued to give sustained financial and military support to Cambodian resistance organizations, notably the communist Khmers Rouges, despite the apparent Vietnamese troop withdrawal (completed in September 1989). However, in November 1990 China announced that it had ceased supplying weapons to the Khmers Rouges. Following the holding of elections in Cambodia in May 1993, China welcomed the establishment of a national government. The restoration of normal relations between China and Viet Nam was announced in late 1991. The Chinese Premier visited Hanoi for discussions in December 1992. In October 1993 China and Viet Nam signed a preliminary agreement to facilitate the settlement of their border dispute by peaceful means. In November the Vietnamese President paid a historic visit to China. During President Jiang Zemin's visit to Viet Nam in November 1994 the two countries confirmed their commitment to an early resolution of the dispute. Discussions continued in 1995–96. Rail links between China and Viet Nam were restored in 1996. The Second Prime Minister of Cambodia, Hun Sen, paid a state visit to China in mid-1996. It was reported that China did not support the coup led by Hun Sen in Cambodia in August 1997.

The question of the sovereignty of the Spratly (Nansha) Islands, situated in the South China Sea and claimed by six countries (including China and Viet Nam), remained unresolved. By 1994 both China and Viet Nam had awarded petroleum exploration concessions to US companies, leading to increased tension among the claimants. In February 1995 it emerged that Chinese forces had occupied a reef to which the Philippines laid claim, resulting in a formal diplomatic protest from Manila. More than 60 Chinese fishermen and several vessels were subsequently detained by the Philippine authorities. Discussions between the two countries, held in Beijing in March, ended without agreement. After two days of consultations in August, however, China and the Philippines declared their intention to resolve peacefully their claims to the Spratly Islands. In January 1996 the Chinese Government denied any involvement in a naval skirmish in Philippine waters, during which a ship flying the Chinese flag and a Philippine patrol boat exchanged gunfire. In March China and the Philippines agreed to co-operate in combating piracy in the region.

Tension in the area resurfaced in March 1997, when China defended its right to undertake exploration for petroleum in waters claimed by both China and Viet Nam. Shortly before bilateral talks to discuss the issue were due to convene, China withdrew the exploratory rig. Despite several disputes in waters jointly claimed by the Philippines and China, the Ministers of Foreign Affairs of both countries, meeting in August, agreed to concentrate on expanding bilateral economic relations, while pursuing the resolution of their territorial dispute by peaceful means.

Diplomatic relations with Indonesia, severed in 1967, were formally restored in August 1990. In April 1995 Indonesia revealed that it still awaited a reply to a request, submitted in July 1994, that China clarify the details of new maps and the apparent inclusion within its territory not only of the Spratly Islands, but also of the seas adjacent to the Indonesian Natuna archipelago, and furthermore of an extensive gas field located well inside Indonesia's 370-km exclusive economic zone. Sino-Indonesian relations were further strained in September 1996, when the Taiwanese Minister of Foreign Affairs was permitted to visit Jakarta.

In 1996 China's application to become a full dialogue partner of the Association of South East Asian Nations' Regional Forum (ARF, see p. 114) was approved. It was hoped that this would facilitate discussions on the question of the Spratly Islands. A similar territorial dispute relating to the Paracel (Xisha) Islands, which had been seized by China from South Vietnamese forces in 1974, also remained unresolved. In May 1996, despite having agreed to abide by the UN Convention on the Law of the Sea, China declared an extension of its maritime boundaries in the South China Sea. Other claimants to the Paracel Islands, in particular Indonesia, the Philippines and Viet Nam, expressed grave concern at China's apparent expansionism.

In October 1990 diplomatic relations between China and Singapore were established. During 1992 China established diplomatic relations with Israel and with the Republic of Korea. During a visit to Beijing in March 1994 President Kim Young-Sam of the Republic of Korea urged China, as the most influential ally of the Democratic People's Republic of Korea, to play a more active role in the increasingly serious international dispute over the latter's nuclear intentions. In late 1994 Premier Li Peng visited Seoul, and was requested to help in ensuring that the Democratic People's Republic of Korea adhered to the nuclear accord signed with the USA in October. During President Jiang Zemin's visit to the Republic of Korea in November 1995, the two Governments were united in their criticism of Japan's failure to offer a full apology for its war record. China remained committed to the achievement of peace on the Korean peninsula, and in June 1996 it was reported that secret discussions between representatives of the Republic and of the Democratic People's Republic of Korea had been held in Beijing. In February 1997, however, China was placed in a difficult position when a senior North Korean official, defecting to Seoul, took temporary refuge in the South Korean embassy in Beijing. In late 1997 China participated in quadripartite negotiations, together with the USA, the Democratic People's Republic of Korea and the Republic of Korea, to resolve the Korean issue. The Republic of Korea remained a major trading partner, and was one of the largest investors in China.

Government

China is a unitary state. Directly under the Central Government there are 22 provinces, five autonomous regions, including Xizang (Tibet), and four municipalities (Beijing, Chongqing, Shanghai and Tianjin). The highest organ of state power is the National People's Congress (NPC). In March 1993 the first session of the Eighth NPC was attended by 2,921 deputies, indirectly elected for five years by the people's congresses of the provinces, autonomous regions, municipalities directly under the Central Government, and the People's Liberation Army. The NPC elects a Standing Committee to be its permanent organ. The current Constitution, adopted by the NPC in December 1982 and amended in 1993, was China's fourth since 1949. It restored the office of Head of State (President of the Republic). Executive power is exercised by the State Council (Cabinet), comprising the Premier, Vice-Premiers and other Ministers heading ministries and commissions. The State Council is appointed by, and accountable to, the NPC.

Political power is held by the Chinese Communist Party (CCP). The CCP's highest authority is the Party Congress, convened every five years. In September 1997 the CCP's 15th National Congress elected a Central Committee of 193 full members and 151 alternate members. To direct policy, the Central Committee elected a 22-member Politburo.

Provincial people's congresses are the local organs of state power. Local revolutionary committees, created during the Cultural Revolution, were abolished in January 1980 and replaced by provincial people's governments.

Defence

China is divided into seven major military units. All armed services are grouped in the People's Liberation Army (PLA). In August 1997, according to Western estimates, the regular forces totalled 2,840,000, of whom 1,275,000 were conscripts: the army numbered 2,090,000, the navy 280,000 (including a naval air force of 27,000), and the air force 470,000 (including 220,000 air defence personnel). Reserves number about 1.2m., and the People's Armed Police comprises an estimated 800,000. Military service is by selective conscription, and lasts for three years in the army and marines, and for four years in the air force and navy. In September 1997 it was announced that the number of forces in the PLA was to be reduced by some 500,000 over the next three years. Defence expenditure for 1997 was budgeted at 80,600m. yuan.

Economic Affairs

In 1995, according to estimates by the World Bank, China's gross national product (GNP), measured at average 1993–95 prices, was US $744,890m., equivalent to some $620 per head. During 1985–95, it was estimated, GNP per head increased, in real terms, at an average annual rate of 8.0%, one of the highest growth rates in the world. Over the same period, the population grew at an average annual rate of 1.3%. China's gross domestic product (GDP) increased, in real terms, by an average annual rate of 9.5% in 1985–95. According to official sources, compared with 1995, GDP increased by 9.7% in 1996 to total 6,859,380m. yuan. GDP was estimated to have increased by 8.8% in 1997.

Agriculture (including forestry and fishing) contributed 20.2% of GDP in 1996, and employed 50.5% of the working population in that year. China's principal crops are rice (production of which accounted for an estimated 33.6% of the total world harvest in 1995), sweet potatoes, wheat, maize, soybeans, sugar cane, tobacco, cotton and jute. The harvest of grain (cereals, pulses, soybeans and tubers in 'grain equivalent') rose from 466.6m. metric tons in 1995 to a record 504.5m. tons in 1996. At 24.4m. metric tons in 1995, the Chinese fish catch was by far the largest in the world. According to the World Bank, agricultural GDP increased by an average annual rate of 4.1%, in real terms, in 1985–95. The IMF estimated growth in agricultural GDP at 5.1% in 1996.

Industry (including mining, manufacturing, construction and power) contributed 49.0% of GDP and engaged 23.5% of the employed labour force in 1996. According to the World Bank, industrial GDP increased at an average annual rate of 12.3%, in real terms, in 1985–95. The IMF estimated growth in industrial GDP at 12.7% in 1996. Industrial output rose by 11.6% in the first six months of 1997.

The mining sector accounted for 1.4% of total employment, and output in the sector accounted for some 6% of total industrial output, in 1996. China has enormous mineral reserves and is the world's largest producer of coal, natural graphite, antimony, tungsten, iron ore and zinc. Other important minerals include molybdenum, tin, lead, mercury, bauxite, phosphate rock, diamonds, gold, manganese, crude petroleum and natural gas.

The manufacturing sector contributed an estimated 37.6% of GDP in 1995, and the sector accounted for 15.5% of total employment in 1996. China is the world's leading producer of cotton cloth and cement, with output in 1996 totalling an estimated 20,910m. m and 491.2m. metric tons, respectively. With output of more than 101m. metric tons in 1996, China also became the world's largest producer of steel. The GDP of the manufacturing sector increased by an annual average of 12.3%, in real terms, during 1985–95. The World Bank estimated growth of 13.0% in the sector in 1995.

Energy is derived principally from coal (74.8% in 1997); other sources are petroleum, hydroelectric power and natural gas. China became a net importer of crude petroleum in 1993. The 18,200-MW Three Gorges hydropower scheme on the Chanjiang (River Yangtze), the world's largest civil engineering project, is scheduled for completion in 2009 and will have a potential annual output of 84,700m. kWh. China's national grid was also scheduled for completion in that year. Imports of energy products comprised 4.0% of the cost of total imports in 1995.

Services contributed 30.8% of GDP in 1996 and engaged 26.0% of the employed labour force in that year. Tourism and retail and wholesale trade are expanding rapidly. During 1985–95, according to the World Bank, the GDP of the services sector increased by an annual average of 9.4%, in real terms. In 1996 the IMF estimated growth in services GDP of 8.0%.

In 1996 China recorded a trade surplus of US $19,535m., and there was a surplus of $7,243m. on the current account of the balance of payments. In 1996 the principal source of imports was Japan (which provided 21.0% of total imports). Other important purchasers were the USA (11.6%), Taiwan (11.6%) and Hong Kong (5.6%). The principal markets for exports in 1996 were Hong Kong (21.8% of total exports), Japan (20.4%) and the USA (17.7%). Most of the goods exported to Hong Kong are subsequently re-exported. The principal imports in 1995 were machinery and transport equipment, basic manufactures, and chemicals and related products. The principal exports in that year were miscellaneous manufactured articles (particularly clothing), basic manufactures, and machinery and transport equipment.

In 1996 China's overall budget deficit was 52,956m. yuan, equivalent to 0.8% of GDP. China's total external debt at the end of 1995 was estimated to be US $118,090m., of which $94,675m. was long-term public debt. In 1995 the cost of debt-servicing was equivalent to 9.9% of the value of exports of goods and services. The annual rate of inflation averaged 11.9% in 1985–94, the increase in retail prices reaching 21.7% in 1994, before declining to 14.7% in 1995 and to 6.1% in 1996. Retail prices increased by only 1.3% in the first nine months of 1997. An estimated 1.2% of the labour force were unemployed in December 1996. The scale of rural surplus labour in May 1997, however, was estimated at 130m., equivalent to 25% of the total rural labour force; unofficial estimates put the total as high as 300m. In August 1997 official figures indicated that the total number of registered unemployed had reached 5.3m.

China joined the Asian Development Bank (ADB, see p. 110) in 1986 and the Asia-Pacific Economic Co-operation forum (APEC, see p. 108) in 1991. In 1994 China became a member of the Association of Tin Producing Countries (ATPC, see p. 256). China failed to become a founder-member of the World Trade

Organization (WTO, see p. 244), which succeeded GATT in January 1995. In July of that year, however, China was granted observer status. Negotiations on full membership continued, with early 1998 envisaged as the probable entry date. China joined the Bank for International Settlements (BIS, see p. 118) in 1996. In the same year the secretariat of the Tumen River Economic Development Area (TREDA) was established in Beijing by the Governments of China, North and South Korea, Mongolia and Russia.

In 1978 Deng Xiaoping introduced the 'open door' reform policy, which aimed to decentralize the economic system and to attract overseas investment to China. The state monopoly on foreign trade was gradually relinquished, commercial links were diversified, and several Special Economic Zones were established, the planned economy being combined with market regulation. A new restructuring plan, adopted in November 1993, involved radical reforms in the banking, taxation, investment and foreign trade sectors. During the Eighth Five-Year Plan (1991–95) GDP increased at an average annual rate of 11.8%, far in excess of the target. The Ninth Five-Year Plan (1996–2000), which envisaged an annual growth rate of 8%, and the 15-year plan, known as the Long-Term Target for the Year 2010, aimed to reduce the growing disparity between the newly-prosperous coastal regions and the underdeveloped hinterland by encouraging foreign investment in more inland cities. However, the significant decline in productivity of the state-owned enterprises (SOEs) in the mid-1990s, and the high levels of under- and unemployment, resulted in a large increase in the incidence of labour unrest (a rise of 73% in 1995, to 33,000 disputes, compared with 1994). In 1996 there were 6,232 bankruptcies in the state sector, and losses reached 52,990m. yuan; it was estimated that some 70% of SOEs were operating at a loss. In addition, around 25% of all bank loans were believed to be non-performing, and banks were instructed to reduce the provision of credit to failing enterprises. Rising inventories of consumer goods, accumulated as a result of excess productivity in the early 1990s, and weakening demand were a further threat to the stability of the SOEs in 1997. Proposals for the urgent reform of the 118,000 industrial SOEs, whereby the SOEs were to be transferred into 'diverse forms of ownership' (such as joint-stock companies), provided the focus of President Jiang Zemin's address to the 15th National Congress of the CCP in September 1997. An ambitious target for the revitalization of the SOEs within three years was subsequently set. The strict financial policy pursued by the Government led to a significant decline in the retail price index in 1997, and in September of that year zero inflation was recorded. Furthermore, owing to the sustained trade surplus and to strong inflows of direct investment from overseas, China's reserves of foreign exchange continued to expand rapidly, reaching more than US $134,000m. by September 1997. Provided that structural reform is pursued, China's economic development appears favourable. A report issued by the World Bank in September predicted that China's economy will surpass that of the USA by 2020.

Social Welfare

In mid-1997 five extrabudgetary funds (pension, unemployment, medical, injury and maternity) financed social welfare provisions in China. Large enterprises also provided social services for their employees. However, a programme of comprehensive social security reforms was being devised, in recognition of the increasing levels of expenditure required to provide for an ageing population (it was estimated that by 2050 the number of people aged over 65 will have reached 300m., compared with 76m. in 1995) and the rising rate of unemployment. The Chinese authorities have implemented a variety of social welfare schemes, in order to determine how best to structure and finance the new social security system. These include a health care programme in several cities, where medical costs are financed by the State, the employer and the employee. A medical insurance system, announced in December 1996, was to cover all urban employees by the year 2000. Western and traditional medical care, for which a fee is charged, is available in the cities and, to a lesser extent, in rural areas. Semi-professional peasant physicians assist with simple cures, treatment and the distribution of contraceptives. In December 1996 there were 1.94m. doctors, 1.16m. nurses and almost 2.87m. hospital beds. In that year there were 188,803 health establishments, including 67,964 hospitals. In 1996 it was announced that a unified, nation-wide pension scheme was to be implemented by the year 2000, to provide pensions to all categories of worker (the current pension system is limited to urban areas and state-owned enterprises). Individual pension accounts, financed by contributions from the State, the employer and the employee, were to be established. The provision of social insurance for the rural population was also to be expanded.

Unemployment-insurance funds, established in cities in 1986, were also undergoing revision. In 1996 3.31m. unemployed people received relief funds.

Education

The education system expanded rapidly after 1949. Fees are charged at all levels. Much importance is attached to kindergartens. Primary education begins for most children at seven years of age and lasts for five years. Secondary education usually begins at 12 years of age and lasts for a further five years, comprising a first cycle of three years and a second cycle of two years. Free higher education was abolished in 1985; instead, college students have to compete for scholarships, which are awarded according to academic ability. As a result of the student disturbances in 1989, college students were required to complete one year's political education, prior to entering college. In November 1989 it was announced that postgraduate students were to be selected on the basis of assessments of moral and physical fitness, as well as academic ability. Since 1979 education has been included as one of the main priorities for modernization. The whole educational system was to be reformed, with the aim of introducing nine-year compulsory education in 85% of the country by the year 2000. The establishment of private schools has been permitted since the early 1980s. As a proportion of the total school-age population, enrolment at primary and secondary schools in 1993 was 88% (boys 92%; girls 84%). In that year 100% of both boys and girls in the relevant age-group were enrolled at primary schools. According to census results, the average rate of adult illiteracy in 1990 was 22.2% (males 13.0%; females 31.9%). In 1995, according to estimates by UNESCO, the average rate of adult illiteracy in China, including Taiwan, was 18.5% (males 10.1%, females 27.3%). In 1996 there were about 136m. pupils enrolled at primary schools and 50.5m. students at junior middle schools. More than 3.0m. students were receiving higher education in 1996. Budgetary expenditure on education by all levels of government was 119,384m. yuan in 1995.

Public Holidays

1998: 1 January (Solar New Year), 27–30 January* (Lunar New Year), 8 March (International Women's Day, women only), 1 May (Labour Day), 1 August (Army Day), 9 September (Teachers' Day), 1–2 October (National Days).

1999: 1 January (Solar New Year), 15–18 February* (Lunar New Year), 8 March (International Women's Day, women only), 1 May (Labour Day), 1 August (Army Day), 9 September (Teachers' Day), 1–2 October (National Days).

* From the first to the fourth day of the first moon of the lunar calendar.

Weights and Measures

The metric system is officially in force, but some traditional Chinese units are still used.

Statistical Survey

Source (unless otherwise stated): State Statistical Bureau, 38 Yuetan Nan Jie, Sanlihe, Beijing 100826; tel. (10) 68515074; fax (10) 68515078.

Note: Wherever possible, figures in this Survey exclude Taiwan. In the case of unofficial estimates for China, it is not always clear if Taiwan is included or excluded. Where a Taiwan component is known, either it has been deducted from the all-China figure or its inclusion is noted. Figures for the Hong Kong Special Administrative Region, incorporated into the People's Republic of China on 1 July 1997, are listed separately (pp. 928–932). Transactions between Hong Kong and the rest of the People's Republic continue to be treated as external transactions.

Area and Population

AREA, POPULATION AND DENSITY

Area (sq km)	9,571,300*
Population (census results)	
1 July 1982	1,008,180,738
1 July 1990	
Males	581,820,407
Females	548,690,231
Total	1,130,510,638
Population (official estimates at 31 December)	
1994	1,198,500,000
1995	1,211,210,000
1996	1,223,890,000
Density (per sq km) at 31 December 1996	127.9

* 3,695,500 sq miles.

PRINCIPAL ETHNIC GROUPS (at census of 1 July 1990)

	Number	%
Han (Chinese)	1,039,187,548	91.92
Zhuang	15,555,820	1.38
Manchu	9,846,776	0.87
Hui	8,612,001	0.76
Miao	7,383,622	0.65
Uygur (Uigur)	7,207,024	0.64
Yi	6,578,524	0.58
Tujia	5,725,049	0.51
Mongolian	4,802,407	0.42
Tibetan	4,593,072	0.41
Bouyei	2,548,294	0.23
Dong	2,508,624	0.22
Yao	2,137,033	0.19
Korean	1,923,361	0.17
Bai	1,598,052	0.14
Hani	1,254,800	0.11
Li	1,112,498	0.10
Kazakh	1,110,758	0.10
Dai	1,025,402	0.09
She	634,700	0.06
Lisu	574,589	0.05
Others	3,838,337	0.34
Unknown	752,347	0.07
Total	1,130,510,638	100.00

BIRTHS AND DEATHS (sample surveys)

	1994	1995	1996
Birth rate (per 1,000)	17.70	17.12	16.98
Death rate (per 1,000)	6.49	6.57	6.56

Marriages (number registered): 9,290,027 in 1994; 9,297,061 in 1995; 9,339,615 in 1996.

LIFE EXPECTANCY (years at birth)

67.1 (males 65.8; females 68.4) in 1985–90; 68.5 (males 66.7; females 70.4) in 1990–95 (UN estimates, including Taiwan).

Source: UN, *World Population Prospects: The 1994 Revision*.

1990 (official figures at census of 1 July): 68.52 (males 66.84; females 70.43).
1996 (official estimates): 70.80 (males 68.71; females 73.04).

ADMINISTRATIVE DIVISIONS (previous or other spelling given in brackets)

	Area ('000 sq km)	Estimated population at 31 December 1996: Total ('000)	Density (per sq km)	Capital of province or region	Estimated population ('000) at 31 Dec. 1990*
Provinces					
Sichuan (Szechwan)†	567	114,300	202	Chengdu (Chengtu)	2,810
Henan (Honan)	167	91,720	549	Zhengzhou (Chengchow)	1,710
Shandong (Shantung)	153	87,380	571	Jinan (Tsinan)	2,320
Jiangsu (Kiangsu)	103	71,100	690	Nanjing (Nanking)	2,500
Guangdong (Kwangtung)	178	69,610	391	Guangzhou (Canton)	3,580
Hebei (Hopei)	188	64,840	345	Shijiazhuang (Shihkiachwang)	1,320
Hunan (Hunan)	210	64,280	306	Changsha (Changsha)	1,330
Anhui (Anhwei)	139	60,700	437	Hefei (Hofei)	1,000
Hubei (Hupeh)	186	58,250	313	Wuhan (Wuhan)	3,750
Zhejiang (Chekiang)	102	43,430	426	Hangzhou (Hangchow)	1,340
Liaoning (Liaoning)	146	41,160	282	Shenyang (Shenyang)	4,540
Jiangxi (Kiangsi)	169	41,050	243	Nanchang (Nanchang)	1,350
Yunnan (Yunnan)	394	40,420	103	Kunming (Kunming)	1,520
Heilongjiang (Heilungkiang)	469	37,280	79	Harbin (Harbin)	2,830
Shaanxi (Shensi)	206	35,430	172	Xian (Sian)	2,760
Guizhou (Kweichow)	176	35,550	202	Guiyang (Kweiyang)	1,530
Fujian (Fukien)	121	32,610‡	270	Fuzhou (Foochow)	1,290
Shanxi (Shansi)	156	31,090	199	Taiyuan (Taiyuan)	1,960
Jilin (Kirin)	187	26,100	140	Changchun (Changchun)	2,110
Gansu (Kansu)	454	24,670	54	Lanzhou (Lanchow)	1,510
Hainan	34	7,340	216	Haikou	—
Qinghai (Tsinghai)	721	4,880	7	Xining (Hsining)	650
Autonomous regions					
Guangxi Zhuang (Kwangsi Chuang)	236	45,890	194	Nanning (Nanning)	1,070
Nei Monggol (Inner Mongolia)	1,183	23,070	20	Hohhot (Huhehot)	890
Xinjiang Uygur (Sinkiang Uighur)	1,600	16,890	11	Urumqi (Urumchi)	1,160
Ningxia Hui (Ninghsia Hui)	66	5,210	79	Yinchuan (Yinchuen)	576§
Tibet (Xizang)	1,228	2,440	2	Lhasa (Lhasa)	105§
Municipalities					
Shanghai (Shanghai)	6	14,190	2,365	—	7,830
Beijing (Peking)	17	12,590	741	—	7,000
Tianjin (Tientsin)	11	9,480	862	—	5,770
Total	9,571	1,212,950‖	127		

* Excluding population in counties under cities' administration.

† In 1997 the city of Chongqing, the province's largest, was raised to the status of a municipality. Also incorporating the cities of Wanxian and Fuling, as well as Qianjiang Prefecture, the new municipality's land area totalled 82,000 sq km, with a population of 30,020,000.

‡ Excluding islands administered by Taiwan, mainly Jinmen (Quemoy) and Mazu (Matsu), with 49,050 inhabitants according to figures released by the Taiwan authorities at the end of March 1990.

§ 1982 figure.

‖ This is the sum of the official estimates provided by the administrative divisions, whereas the estimated national total was 1,223,890,000. The difference of 10,940,000 includes military personnel, excluded from regional population figures.

PRINCIPAL TOWNS

(Wade-Giles or other spellings in brackets)

Population at 31 December 1990 (official estimates in '000)*

Shanghai (Shang-hai)	7,830
Beijing (Pei-ching or Peking, the capital)	7,000
Tianjin (T'ien-chin or Tientsin)	5,770
Shenyang (Shen-yang or Mukden)	4,540
Wuhan (Wu-han or Hankow)	3,750
Guangzhou (Kuang-chou or Canton)	3,580
Chongqing (Ch'ung-ch'ing or Chungking)	2,980
Harbin (Ha-erh-pin)	2,830
Chengdu (Ch'eng-tu)	2,810
Xian (Hsi-an or Sian)	2,760
Nanjing (Nan-ching or Nanking)	2,500
Zibo (Tzu-po or Tzepo)	2,460
Dalian (Ta-lien or Dairen)	2,400
Jinan (Chi-nan or Tsinan)	2,320
Changchun (Ch'ang-ch'un)	2,110
Qingdao (Ch'ing-tao or Tsingtao)	2,060
Taiyuan (T'ai-yüan)	1,960
Zhengzhou (Cheng-chou or Chengchow)	1,710
Guiyang (Kuei-yang or Kweiyang)	1,530
Kunming (K'un-ming)	1,520
Lanzhou (Lan-chou or Lanchow)	1,510
Tangshan (T'ang-shan)	1,500
Anshan (An-shan)	1,390
Qiqihar (Ch'i-ch'i-ha-erh or Tsitsihar)	1,380
Fushun (F'u-shun)	1,350
Nanchang (Nan-ch'ang)	1,350
Hangzhou (Hang-chou or Hangchow)	1,340

Population at 31 December 1990 (official estimates in '000)* —*continued*

Changsha (Chang-sha)	1,330
Shijiazhuang (Shih-chia-chuang or Shihkiachwang)	1,320
Fuzhou (Fu-chou or Foochow)	1,290
Jilin (Chi-lin or Kirin)	1,270
Baotau (Pao-t'ou or Paotow)	1,200
Huainan (Huai-nan or Hwainan)	1,200
Luoyang (Lo-yang)	1,190
Urumqi (Urumchi)	1,160
Datong (Ta-t'ung or Tatung)	1,110
Handan (Han-tan)	1,110
Ningbo (Ning-po)	1,090
Nanning (Nan-ning)	1,070
Hefei (Hofei)	1,000

* Data refer to municipalities, which may include large rural areas as well as an urban centre. The listed towns comprise those with a total population of more than 1,000,000 and a non-agricultural population of more than 500,000.

EMPLOYMENT*
(official estimates, '000 persons at 31 December)

	1994	1995	1996
Agriculture, forestry and fishing	333,860	330,180	329,100
Mining	9,150	9,320	9,020
Manufacturing	96,130	98,030	97,630
Electricity, gas and water	2,460	2,580	2,730
Construction	31,880	33,220	34,080
Transport, storage and communications	18,640	19,420	20,130
Wholesale and retail trade and catering	39,210	42,920	45,110
Banking and insurance	2,640	2,760	2,920
Social services	6,260	7,030	7,470
Health care, sports and social welfare	4,340	4,440	4,580
Education, culture, art, radio, film and television broadcasting	14,360	14,760	15,130
Government agencies, etc.	10,330	10,420	10,930
Others	45,460	48,810	49,590
Total	614,700	623,880	628,400

* In addition to employment statistics, sample surveys of the economically active population are conducted. On the basis of these surveys, the total labour force ('000 persons at 31 December) was: 678,790 in 1994; 687,370 in 1995; 696,650 in 1996. Of these totals, the number of employed persons ('000 at 31 December) was: 671,990 (agriculture, etc. 364,890; industry 152,540; services 154,560) in 1994; 679,470 (agriculture, etc. 354,680; industry 156,280; services 168,510) in 1995; 688,500 (agriculture, etc. 347,690; industry 161,800; services 179,010) in 1996.

Agriculture

PRINCIPAL CROPS
(official figures, unless otherwise indicated; '000 metric tons)

	1994	1995	1996
Wheat	99,297	102,207	110,569
Rice (paddy)	175,933	185,226	195,103
Barley*	4,500	3,800	4,100
Maize	99,275	111,986	127,471
Rye*	1,000	700	700
Oats*	1,000	700	700
Millet	3,696	4,350*	4,500*
Sorghum	6,333	4,756	5,000*
Potatoes	43,780	45,721	46,000*
Sweet potatoes	107,469†	117,410	115,000*
Cassava (Manioc)*	3,500	3,500	3,500
Taro (Coco yam)*‡	1,343	1,354	1,354
Dry beans*‡	1,511	1,411	1,711
Dry broad beans*‡	2,000	1,750	1,900
Dry peas*‡	1,275	1,000	1,150
Soybeans (Soyabeans)	20,956	17,875	17,903
Groundnuts (in shell)	9,682	10,235	10,138
Castor beans†	260	250	260
Sunflower seed	1,367	1,269	1,360†
Rapeseed	7,492	9,777	9,201
Sesame seed	548	583	575
Linseed‡	511	500*	500*
Flax fibre and tow‡	252	262*	262*
Cottonseed	8,682	9,536	7,500
Cotton (lint)	4,341	4,768	4,203
Coconuts*‡	75	77	77
Vegetables and melons‡	189,870	201,825	202,155*
Grapes	1,522	1,742	1,883
Apples	11,129	14,008	17,047
Pears	4,043	4,942	5,807
Citrus fruits	6,805	8,225	8,456
Bananas	2,898	3,125	2,535
Other fruits (excl. melons)	8,601	10,104	10,799
Walnuts	210	231	238
Sugar cane	60,927	65,417	66,876
Sugar beet	12,526	13,984	16,726
Tea (made)	588	589	593
Tobacco (leaves)	2,238	2,314	3,234
Jute and jute substitutes	355	371	365
Natural rubber	374	424	402

* FAO estimate(s). † Unofficial figure(s).
‡ Including Taiwan.

Source: FAO, *Production Yearbook*, and State Statistical Bureau, *China Statistical Yearbook*.

LIVESTOCK ('000 head at 31 December)

	1994	1995	1996
Horses	10,038	10,071	10,193
Mules	5,552	5,389	5,401
Asses	10,923	10,745	10,733
Cattle and buffaloes	123,318	132,060	139,813
Camels	356	351	355
Pigs	414,615	441,692	457,357
Sheep	117,445	127,263	132,690
Goats	123,083	149,593	170,684

Chickens (FAO estimates, million, year ending September): 2,692 in 1994; 2,798 in 1995; 2,802 in 1996. Source: FAO, *Production Yearbook*.
Ducks (FAO estimates, million, year ending September): 443 in 1994; 463 in 1995; 463 in 1996. Source: FAO, *Production Yearbook*.

LIVESTOCK PRODUCTS
(FAO estimates, unless otherwise indicated; '000 metric tons)

	1994	1995	1996
Beef and buffalo meat*	3,270	4,154	4,949
Mutton and goat meat*	1,609	2,015	2,400
Pig meat*	32,048	36,484	40,377
Horse meat†	116	70	70
Poultry meat*	7,552	9,347	10,746
Edible offals†	2,541	2,677	n.a.
Cows' milk*	5,288	5,764	6,294
Buffaloes' milk†	2,100	2,200	2,200
Sheep's milk*	801	964	1,064
Goats' milk†	187	195	195
Butter†	74.3	74.3	75
Cheese†	182.3	165.3	202
Poultry eggs*	14,790	16,767	19,540
Honey*	177	178	184
Raw silk (incl. waste)	84*	80*	80
Wool:			
greasy*	254.7	277.4	298.1
clean	130.0*	133.0	141
Cattle and buffalo hides†	586.0	576.8	739
Sheepskins†	196.0	214.8	250
Goatskins†	141.2	153.1	238

* Official figure(s). † Including Taiwan.

Sources: mainly FAO, *Production Yearbook* and *Quarterly Bulletin of Statistics*, and State Statistical Bureau, *China Statistical Yearbook*.

Forestry

ROUNDWOOD REMOVALS*
('000 cubic metres, excl. bark)

	1992	1993	1994
Sawlogs, veneer logs and logs for sleepers†	47,996	51,769	52,423
Pulpwood	9,079	9,767	10,407
Other industrial wood†	36,909	39,072	39,072
Fuel wood†	196,152	200,060	204,059
Total	290,136	300,668	305,961

* Including Taiwan.
† FAO estimates.

Source: FAO, *Yearbook of Forest Products*.

Timber production (official figures, '000 cubic metres): 61,736 in 1992; 63,900 in 1993; 66,150 in 1994; 67,669 in 1995; 67,103 in 1996.

SAWNWOOD PRODUCTION*
(FAO estimates, '000 cubic metres, incl. railway sleepers)

	1992	1993	1994
Coniferous (softwood)	11,452	15,566	15,501
Broadleaved (hardwood)	7,865	9,702	9,661
Total	19,317	25,268	25,162

* Including Taiwan.

Source: FAO, *Yearbook of Forest Products*.

Fishing

('000 metric tons, live weight)

	1993	1994	1995
Common carp	891.6	1,127.6	1,398.6
Crucian carp	291.5	385.2	533.7
Bighead carp	901.9	1,053.7	1,236.7
Grass carp (White amur)	1,464.9	1,789.6	2,071.0
Silver carp	1,806.6	2,139.4	2,473.3
Other freshwater fishes (incl. unspecified)	1,836.3	2,159.5	2,492.7
Scads	260.8	430.9	515.3
Japanese anchovy	557.2	439.0	489.1
Largehead hairtail	635.3	878.1	1,039.7
Other fishes (incl. unspecified)	4,302.7	4,887.2	5,699.1
Total fish	12,949.0	15,290.3	17,949.2
Crustaceans	1,564.1	1,915.7	2,160.0
Sea mussels	509.6	415.2	415.2
Yesso scallop	728.4	825.6	916.5
Japanese carpet shell	428.8	519.5	502.0
Other molluscs	1,255.4	1,634.7	2,300.9
Other aquatic animals	132.7	117.9	189.5
Total catch	17,567.9	20,718.9	24,433.3
Inland waters	7,501.4	9,049.2	10,780.5
Atlantic Ocean	9.4	15.3	15.3
Pacific Ocean	10,057.1	11,654.5	13,637.5

Aquatic plants ('000 metric tons, wet weight): 4,531.8 in 1993; 4,916.0 in 1994; 4,807.1 in 1995.

Source: FAO, *Yearbook of Fishery Statistics*.

Aquatic products (official figures, '000 metric tons): 18,230.0 (marine 10,760.4, freshwater 7,469.6) in 1993; 21,431.3 (marine 12,415.0, freshwater 9,016.2) in 1994; 25,171.8 (marine 14,391.3, freshwater 10,780.5) in 1995; 32,880.9 (marine 20,128.8, freshwater 12,752.2) in 1996. Figures include aquatic plants on a dry-weight basis ('000 metric tons): 693.9 in 1993; 745.2 in 1994; 749.1 in 1995; 929.1 in 1996.

Mining

('000 metric tons, unless otherwise indicated; unofficial figures)

	1992	1993	1994
Coal*	1,116,369	1,149,745	1,239,902
Crude petroleum*	142,097	145,237	146,082
Iron ore†	96,420	117,366	119,514
Bauxite	6,661	6,468	6,621
Copper ore†	332.6‡	347.0	395.6
Lead ore†	329.9	346.3	461.9
Magnesite‡§	1,510.0	1,500.0	1,500.0
Manganese ore†‡§	1,060.0	1,170.0	1,180.0
Zinc ore†	753.3	729.3	990.3
Salt (unrefined)*	28,377	29,430	29,960
Phosphate rock	23,198	n.a.	n.a.
Potash‡§‖	22	25	25
Sulphur (native)‡§	320	330	330
Natural graphite	508.3	310.0‡	320.0‡
Antimony ore (metric tons)†¶	59,400§	60,000	91,000
Mercury (metric tons)‡§	580	520	500
Molybdenum ore (metric tons)†	37,318	39,208	47,536
Silver (metric tons)†‡§	170	200	210
Tin concentrates (metric tons)†	43,947	46,554	54,076
Tungsten concentrates (metric tons)†‡§	25,000	21,600	16,500
Gold (kg)†‡§	140,000	160,000	160,000
Natural gas (million cu m)*	15,788	16,765	17,559

1995*: Coal ('000 metric tons) 1,360,731; Crude petroleum ('000 metric tons) 150,049; Salt (unrefined, '000 metric tons) 29,777; Natural gas (million cu m) 17,947; Gold (kg) 105,000†.

1996*: Coal ('000 metric tons) 1,397,000; Crude petroleum ('000 metric tons) 157,334; Salt (unrefined, '000 metric tons) 29,036; Natural gas (million cu m) 20,114.

* Official figure(s). Figures for coal include brown coal and waste. Figures for petroleum include oil from shale and coal.

† Figures refer to the metal content of ores and concentrates.

‡ Data from the US Bureau of Mines.

§ Provisional or estimated figure(s).

‖ Potassium oxide (K_2O) content of potash salts mined.

¶ Data from *World Metal Statistics* (London).

Source: mainly UN, *Industrial Commodity Statistics Yearbook*.

Industry

SELECTED PRODUCTS

Unofficial Figures ('000 metric tons, unless otherwise indicated)

	1992	1993	1994
Rayon and acetate continuous filaments*	60.0	61.0	63.0
Rayon and acetate discontinuous fibres*	189.0	212.0	275.0
Non-cellulosic continuous filaments*	645.9	719.7	1,046.0
Plywood ('000 cu m)†‡	2,078	2,638	2,132
Mechanical wood pulp†‡	435	500	575
Chemical wood pulp†‡	1,469	1,635	1,825
Other fibre pulp†‡	13,369	15,307	17,551
Sulphur§‖ (a)	650	700	700
(b)	4,500	5,000	5,000
Kerosene	3,945	3,729	4,072
Residual fuel oil	32,322	32,300¶	30,490
Lubricating oils¶	2,000	2,100	2,150
Paraffin wax¶	610	670	740
Petroleum coke¶	1,220	1,380	1,400
Petroleum bitumen (asphalt)¶	2,550	2,650	2,730
Liquefied petroleum gas	3,501	3,700¶	4,445
Aluminium (unwrought)	1,096.4	1,255.4	1,498.3
Refined copper (unwrought)¶**	659.0	733.0	736.1
Lead (unwrought)	366.0	410.3	467.9
Tin (unwrought)	39.6	51.6	67.8
Zinc (unwrought)	718.9	891.4	1,077.6

* Data from the Fiber Economics Bureau, Inc, USA.

† Data from the FAO.

‡ Including Taiwan.

§ Data from the US Bureau of Mines.

‖ Figures refer to (a) sulphur recovered as a by-product in the purification of coal-gas, in petroleum refineries, gas plants and from copper, lead and zinc sulphide ores; and (b) the sulphur content of iron and copper pyrites, including pyrite concentrates obtained from copper, lead and zinc ores.

¶ Provisional or estimated figure(s).

** Data from *World Metal Statistics* (London).

Source: UN, *Industrial Commodity Statistics Yearbook*.

1995 ('000 metric tons): Kerosene and Jet fuel 4,365; Residual fuel oil 27,596 (Source: UN, *Monthly Bulletin of Statistics*).

1996 ('000 metric tons): Kerosene and Jet fuel 5,385 (Source: UN, *Monthly Bulletin of Statistics*).

Official Figures ('000 metric tons, unless otherwise indicated)

	1994	1995	1996
Edible vegetable oils	7,230	11,445	9,465.4
Raw sugar	5,920.0	5,586.4	6,402
Beer	14,150.0	15,688.2	16,819.1
Cigarettes ('000 cases)	34,320	34,850.2	34,019.2
Cotton yarn (pure and mixed)	4,894.6	5,422.0	5,122.1
Woven cotton fabrics—pure and mixed (million metres)	21,125	26,018	20,910
Woollen fabrics ('000 metres)	419,000.0	653,920	459,536.8
Silk fabrics (metric tons)	106,400	113,400	94,900
Chemical fibres	2,803.3	3,411.7	3,754.5
Paper and paperboard	21,380.8	28,123.0	26,382.0
Rubber tyres ('000)	93,020.0	79,458.4	88,056.7
Ethylene (Ethene)	2,129.3	2,400.5	3,039.6
Sulphuric acid	15,365.0	18,110.0	18,835.7
Caustic soda (Sodium hydroxide)	4,296.0	5,318.2	5,737.8
Soda ash (Sodium carbonate)	5,814.0	5,977.1	6,692.9
Insecticides	289.8	416.5	447.5
Nitrogenous fertilizers (a)*	17,363.0	18,591.8	21,360.5
Phosphate fertilizers (b)*	5,044.0	6,626.4	6,511.7
Potash fertilizers (c)*	321.0	263.2	218.2
Synthetic rubber	443.5	585.6	599.7
Plastics	4,014.0	5,168.7	5,768.6
Motor spirit (gasoline)	28,541	30,515.6	32,806.0
Distillate fuel oil (diesel oil)	34,795	39,726.0	44,192.5
Coke	114,770.0	135,100.5	136,431.0
Cement	421,180	475,605.9	491,189.0
Pig-iron	97,410.0	105,292.7	107,225.0
Crude steel	92,610.0	95,359.9	101,240.6
Internal combustion engines ('000 horse-power)†	121,815.2	158,190.0	221,527.9
Tractors—over 20 horse-power (number)	46,700	63,300	83,700

— continued	1994	1995	1996
Sewing machines ('000)	8,612.1	9,706.1	6,836.9
Railway locomotives (number)	992	974	1,050
Railway freight wagons (number)	37,600	37,300	32,800
Road motor vehicles ('000)	1,366.9	1,452.7	1,475.2
Bicycles ('000)	43,649.0	44,722.5	33,611.8
Watches ('000)	477,768.0	481,912.9	479,756.4
Electric fans ('000)	86,135	129,666.7	102,916.8
Recorders ('000)	83,956	85,813.6	86,328.2
Radio receivers ('000)‡	41,323.0	82,045.5	56,507.2
Television receivers ('000)	32,832.6	34,962.3	35,418.1
Cameras ('000)	28,300.2	33,261.5	41,207.7
Electric energy (million kWh)	928,080	1,007,030	1,081,310

* Production in terms of (a) nitrogen; (b) phosphoric acid; or (c) potassium oxide.
† Sales.
‡ Portable battery sets only.

Finance

CURRENCY AND EXCHANGE RATES

Monetary Units

100 fen (cents) = 10 jiao (chiao) = 1 renminbiao (People's Bank Dollar), usually called a yuan.

Sterling and Dollar Equivalents (30 September 1997)

£1 sterling = 13.384 yuan;
US $1 = 8.285 yuan;
1,000 yuan = £74.72 = $120.70.

Average Exchange Rate (yuan per US $)

1994 8.6187
1995 8.3514
1996 8.3142

Note: Since 1 January 1994 the official rate has been based on the prevailing rate in the interbank market for foreign exchange.

STATE BUDGET (million yuan)*

Revenue	1994	1995	1996
Taxes	512,688	603,804	690,982
Industrial and commercial taxes	391,422	458,968	527,004
Tariffs	27,268	29,183	30,184
Agricultural and animal husbandry taxes	23,149	27,809	36,946
Taxes on income of state-owned enterprises	60,975	75,938	82,233
Taxes on income of collectively-owned enterprises	9,874	11,906	14,615
Other receipts	45,744	53,193	83,557
Sub-total	558,432	656,997	774,539
Less Subsidies for losses by enterprises	36,622	32,777	33,740
Total	521,810	624,220	740,799
Central Government	290,650	325,662	366,107
Local authorities	231,160	298,558	374,692

Expenditure†	1994	1995	1996
Capital construction	63,972	78,922	90,744
Agriculture, forestry and water conservancy	39,970	43,022	51,007
Urban construction and maintenance	23,416	28,580	33,649
Education‡	93,915	108,095	170,425
Culture, science and public health‡	33,903	38,611	
National defence	55,071	63,672	72,006
Armed police	6,325	7,386	n.a.
Administration	72,943	87,268	104,080
Pensions and social welfare	9,514	11,546	12,803
Subsidies to compensate price increases	31,447	36,489	45,391
Development of enterprises	41,513	49,445	52,302
Other purposes	107,273	129,336	161,348
Total	579,262	682,372	793,755
Central Government	175,443	199,539	215,127
Local authorities	403,819	482,833	578,628

* Figures represent a consolidation of the regular (current) and construction (capital) budgets of the central Government and local administrative organs. The data exclude extrabudgetary transactions, totalling (in million yuan): Revenue 186,253 (central 28,332; local 157,921) in 1994, 240,650 (central 31,757; local 208,893) in 1995; Expenditure 171,039 (central 22,502; local 148,537) in 1994, 233,126 (central 35,138; local 197,988) in 1995.
† Excluding payments of debt interest (estimates, million yuan): 16,700 in 1994; 35,600 in 1995; 48,900 (provisional) in 1996.
‡ Current expenditure only.

1997 (forecasts, million yuan): *Revenue:* Total 839,794 (central 415,065; local 424,729). *Expenditure:* Agriculture, forestry and water conservancy 59,200; Education 118,907; National defence 80,570 (central budget only); Total (incl. others) 896,794 (central 241,880; local 654,914).

INTERNATIONAL RESERVES (US $ million at 31 December)

	1994	1995	1996
Gold*	646	660	637
IMF special drawing rights	539	582	614
Reserve position in IMF	755	1,216	1,396
Foreign exchange†	51,620	73,579	105,029
Total†	53,560	76,037	107,676

* Valued at SDR 35 per troy ounce.
† Excluding the Bank of China's holdings of foreign exchange.
Source: IMF, *International Financial Statistics*.

MONEY SUPPLY (million yuan at 31 December)*

	1994	1995	1996
Currency outside banking institutions	728,440	788,240	879,890
Deposits at People's Bank of China	186,560	251,330	309,880
Demand deposits at banking institutions	1,238,990	1,520,160	1,876,490
Total money	2,153,990	2,559,730	3,066,260

* Figures are rounded to the nearest 10 million yuan.
Source: IMF, *International Financial Statistics*.

COST OF LIVING

(General Retail Price Index; base: 1990 = 100)

	1992	1993	1994
Food	113.5	132.2	174.2
Fuel	140.7	164.4	n.a.
Clothing	108.4	113.8	178.2
All items (incl. others)	113.2	132.5	165.6

Source: ILO, *Yearbook of Labour Statistics*.

Consumer Price Index (base: previous year = 100): All items 124.2 in 1994; 116.9 in 1995; 108.3 in 1996 (Source: IMF, *International Financial Statistics*).

NATIONAL ACCOUNTS
(million yuan at current prices)

Expenditure on the Gross Domestic Product*

	1994	1954	1996
Government final consumption expenditure	598,620	669,050	758,300
Private final consumption expenditure	2,123,000	2,783,890	3,258,870
Increase in stocks	240,430	357,650	353,110
Gross fixed capital formation	1,685,630	2,030,050	2,333,610
Total domestic expenditure	4,647,680	5,840,640	6,703,890
Exports of goods and services *Less* Imports of goods and services	63,410	99,850	145,930
Sub-total	4,711,090	5,940,490	6,849,820
Statistical discrepancy†	−35,150	−92,680	9,560
GDP in purchasers' values	4,675,940	5,847,810	6,859,380

* Figures are rounded to the nearest 10 million yuan.
† Referring to the difference between the sum of the expenditure components and official estimates of GDP, compiled from the production approach.

Gross Domestic Product by Economic Activity*

	1994	1995	1996
Agriculture, forestry and fishing	945,720	1,199,300	1,388,420
Industry†	1,935,960	2,471,830	2,908,260
Construction	301,260	381,960	453,030
Transport, storage and communications	268,590	305,470	349,400
Wholesale and retail trade and catering	405,040	493,230	556,030
Other services	819,370	996,020	1,204,240
Total	4,675,940	5,847,810	6,859,380

* Figures are rounded to the nearest 10 million yuan.
† Includes mining, manufacturing, electricity, gas and water.

BALANCE OF PAYMENTS (US $ million)

	1994	1995	1996
Exports of goods f.o.b.	102,561	128,110	151,077
Imports of goods f.o.b.	−95,271	−110,060	−131,542
Trade balance	7,290	18,050	19,535
Exports of services	16,620	19,130	20,601
Imports of services	−16,299	−25,223	−22,585
Balance on goods and services	7,611	11,958	17,551
Other income received	5,737	5,191	7,318
Other income paid	−6,775	−16,965	−19,755
Balance on goods, services and income	6,573	184	5,114
Current transfers received	1,269	1,827	2,368
Current transfers paid	−934	−392	−239
Current balance	6,908	1,618	7,243
Direct investment abroad	−2,000	−2,000	−2,114
Direct investment from abroad	33,787	35,849	40,180
Portfolio investment assets	−380	79	−628
Portfolio investment liabilities	3,923	710	2,372
Other investment assets	−1,189	−1,081	−1,126
Other investment liabilities	−1,496	5,116	1,282
Net errors and omissions	−9,100	−17,823	−15,504
Overall balance	30,453	22,469	31,705

Source: IMF, *International Financial Statistics*.

External Trade

PRINCIPAL COMMODITIES (distribution by SITC, US $ million)

Imports c.i.f.	1993	1994	1995
Food and live animals	2,203.9	3,132.1	6,122.7
Cereals and cereal preparations	1,034.1	1,332.5	3,637.1
Crude materials (inedible) except fuels	5,227.8	7,200.3	9,868.8
Textile fibres (excl. wool-tops) and waste	1,360.9	2,782.8	3,827.9
Metalliferous ores and metal scrap	2,058.7	2,150.7	3,059.6
Mineral fuels, lubricants, etc.	5,856.0	4,080.2	5,172.2
Petroleum, petroleum products, etc.	5,412.9	3,641.4	4,612.9
Crude petroleum oils, etc.	2,323.4	1,573.4	2,356.4
Refined petroleum products	3,023.4	2,001.9	2,110.8
Chemicals and related products	9,610.2	11,967.9	16,849.5
Organic chemicals	1,568.2	1,982.1	3,156.2
Manufactured fertilizers	1,469.7	1,925.5	3,732.0
Artificial resins, plastic materials, etc.	4,310.1	5,402.3	7,111.4
Products of polymerization, etc.	3,607.2	4,527.9	6,007.0
Basic manufactures	29,191.6	28,732.4	29,540.9
Textile yarn, fabrics, etc.	7,789.8	9,524.0	11,176.6
Woven fabrics of man-made fibres*	2,566.6	3,146.4	3,744.7
Iron and steel	12,767.4	9,534.9	6,979.4
Ingots and other primary forms	3,481.4	1,648.8	1,016.3
Bars, rods, angles, shapes, etc.	4,544.0	3,433.0	1,589.3
Universals, plates and sheets	3,315.3	2,684.9	2,948.0
Non-ferrous metals	1,862.3	1,658.8	2,682.6
Machinery and transport equipment	44,468.2	51,384.7	52,504.2
Power-generating machinery and equipment	2,519.7	3,185.2	3,111.7
Machinery specialized for particular industries	13,157.9	12,739.9	13,247.4
Textile and leather machinery	4,475.2	3,352.4	3,181.5
Metalworking machinery	2,498.1	3,002.8	3,341.9
Machine-tools for working metal	2,079.8	2,218.1	2,344.3
General industrial machinery, equipment and parts	4,820.1	6,254.3	7,196.6
Office machines and automatic data-processing equipment	1,593.0	2,072.9	2,857.9
Telecommunications and sound equipment	5,453.7	6,805.4	7,616.4
Other electrical machinery, apparatus, etc.	5,941.9	7,702.3	9,807.8
Thermionic valves, tubes, etc.	2,128.1	2,917.6	3,878.1
Road vehicles (incl. air-cushion vehicles) and parts†	5,285.9	4,774.3	2,685.4
Passenger motor cars (excl. buses)	2,130.7	1,637.6	933.0
Other transport equipment†	3,198.0	4,847.6	2,639.1
Aircraft, associated equipment and parts†	2,269.8	3,397.0	1,361.3
Miscellaneous manufactured articles	5,928.8	6,496.8	7,904.7
Total (incl. others)	103,959.0	115,613.6	132,083.5

* Excluding narrow or special fabrics.
† Excluding tyres, engines and electrical parts.

Exports f.o.b.	1993	1994	1995
Food and live animals	8,380.7	9,993.1	9,924.0
Vegetables and fruit	2,216.5	2,935.8	3,399.4
Crude materials (inedible) except fuels	3,041.2	4,093.4	4,347.9
Mineral fuels, lubricants, etc.	4,112.0	4,072.2	5,335.2
Petroleum, petroleum products, etc.	3,226.1	2,799.8	3,243.6
Crude petroleum oils, etc.	2,408.8	2,000.3	2,236.4
Chemicals and related products	4,576.2	6,176.4	8,945.5
Basic manufactures	16,776.7	23,780.3	32,896.1
Textile yarn, fabrics, etc.	8,807.3	11,942.5	14,059.2
Woven cotton fabrics (excl. narrow or special fabrics)	2,248.5	2,711.3	3,457.4
Non-metallic mineral manufactures	1,559.8	2,523.2	3,425.0
Iron and steel	1,202.8	1,867.1	5,531.5
Machinery and transport equipment	15,220.4	21,830.4	31,336.0
Office machines and automatic data-processing equipment	1,646.7	2,664.4	4,802.7
Telecommunications and sound equipment	4,521.7	6,743.8	8,408.6
Other electrical machinery, apparatus, etc.	4,434.0	6,436.7	9,594.9
Miscellaneous manufactured articles	38,134.8	49,199.4	53,726.1
Clothing and accessories (excl. footwear)	18,479.1	23,793.5	24,123.4
Men's and boys' outer garments of non-knitted textile fabrics	3,857.6	5,464.7	5,168.1
Women's, girls' and infants' outer garments of non-knitted textile fabrics	5,252.5	6,613.2	6,306.1
Undergarments (excl. foundation garments) of non-knitted textile fabrics	2,019.3	2,357.2	2,133.8
Knitted or crocheted outer garments and accessories (excl. gloves, stockings, etc.), non-elastic	3,123.2	3,908.3	3,948.7
Non-textile clothing and accessories, and headgear of all materials	1,905.4	2,452.8	2,840.9
Footwear	5,053.9	5,706.9	6,273.6
Leather footwear	3,267.6	3,637.3	3,812.0
Photographic apparatus, optical goods, watches and clocks	1,979.7	2,455.4	2,929.8
Baby carriages, toys, games and sporting goods	4,050.1	5,093.1	5,861.9
Children's toys, indoor games, etc.	3,590.6	4,519.1	5,116.7
Total (incl. others)	91,744.0	121,006.3	148,779.6

Source: UN, *International Trade Statistics Yearbook*.

PRINCIPAL TRADING PARTNERS (US $ million)*

Imports c.i.f.	1994	1995	1996
Australia	2,451.8	2,584.6	3,433.8
Brazil	1,058.8	1,231.6	1,484.1
Canada	1,848.8	2,681.3	2,569.9
France	1,938.8	2,648.4	2,239.9
Germany	7,137.4	8,037.9	7,324.3
Hong Kong	9,441.7	8,590.7	7,827.7
Indonesia	1,589.0	2,052.2	2,280.4
Italy	3,068.5	3,115.0	3,245.9
Japan	26,326.9	29,004.5	29,183.8
Korea, Republic	7,318.2	10,293.2	12,481.5
Malaysia	1,622.0	2,070.6	2,243.5
Russia	3,495.2	3,798.6	5,153.4
Singapore	2,491.7	3,397.8	3,601.1
Taiwan	14,085.6	14,783.9	16,182.2
Thailand	864.4	1,610.8	1,890.3
United Kingdom	1,769.9	1,972.1	1,881.3
USA	13,893.6	16,118.3	16,155.2
Total (incl. others)	115,613.6	132,083.5	138,837.9

Exports f.o.b.	1994	1995	1996
Australia	1,487.9	1,626.2	1,673.3
Canada	1,397.0	1,532.5	1,616.0
France	1,424.3	1,841.8	1,906.9
Germany	4,761.2	5,671.5	5,844.7
Hong Kong†	32,361.0	35,983.4	32,905.5
Italy	1,590.7	2,067.2	1,837.6
Japan	21,578.6	28,466.7	30,874.5
Korea, Republic	4,402.5	6,687.8	7,511.2
Netherlands	2,267.1	3,232.1	3,538.5
Russia	1,580.8	1,664.7	1,692.8
Singapore	2,558.1	3,500.6	3,749.4
Taiwan	2,242.2	3,098.1	2,802.7
Thailand	1,159.3	1,751.7	1,254.9
United Kingdom	2,413.9	2,797.7	3,200.6
USA	21,461.5	24,713.5	26,685.5
Total (incl. others)	121,006.3	148,779.6	151,065.7

* Imports by country of origin; exports by country of consumption.
† The majority of China's exports to Hong Kong are re-exported.

Transport

	1994	1995	1996
Freight (million ton-km):			
Railways	1,245,750	1,287,025	1,297,046
Roads	448,630	469,490	501,120
Waterways	1,568,660	1,755,220	1,786,250
Air	1,859	2,230	2,493
Passenger-km (million):			
Railways	363,605	354,570	332,537
Roads	422,030	460,310	490,879
Waterways	18,350	17,180	16,057
Air	55,158	68,130	74,784

ROAD TRAFFIC ('000 motor vehicles in use)*

	1994	1995	1996
Passenger cars and buses	3,497.4	4,179.0	4,880.2
Goods vehicles	5,603.3	5,854.3	5,750.3
Total (incl. others)	9,419.5	10,400.0	11,000.8

* Excluding military vehicles.

SHIPPING

Merchant Fleet (registered at 31 December)

	1994	1995	1996
Number of vessels	2,701	2,948	3,121
Total displacement ('000 grt)	15,826.7	16,943.2	16,992.9

Source: Lloyd's Register of Shipping, *World Fleet Statistics*.

Sea-borne Shipping (freight traffic, '000 metric tons)

	1994	1995	1996
Goods loaded and unloaded	743,700	801,660	851,520

Tourism

FOREIGN VISITORS ('000)

Country of origin	1994	1995	1996
Hong Kong and Macau	38,387.2	40,384.0	42,494.7
Taiwan			1,733.9
Australia	109.5	129.4	132.7
Canada	113.2	128.8	156.6
France	111.8	118.5	123.3
Germany	148.8	166.5	179.0
Japan	1,141.2	1,305.2	1,548.8
Korea, Republic	340.3	529.5	693.9
Philippines	184.9	219.7	243.7
Russia	n.a.	n.a.	555.9
Singapore	231.9	261.5	286.3
Thailand	163.7	173.3	193.3
Former USSR/CIS	743.4	489.3	n.a.
United Kingdom	167.0	184.9	205.2
USA	469.8	514.9	576.4
Total (incl. others)	43,684.5	46,386.5	51,127.5

Total tourist receipts: US $7,323m. in 1994; US $8,733m. in 1995; US $10,200m. in 1996.

Communications Media

	1994	1995	1996
Radio receivers ('000 in use)*	222,000	225,500	n.a.
Television receivers ('000 in use)*	227,880	250,000	n.a.
Newspapers (million copies printed)	17,790	17,890	17,950
Magazines (million copies printed)	2,210	2,340	2,310
Books (million copies printed)	6,010	6,322	7,158
Telephones ('000 in use)	28,874	57,623	70,468
Telefax stations ('000 in use)†	200	n.a.	n.a.
Mobile cellular telephones ('000 subscribers)	1,567.8	3,629.4	6,852.7

* Source: UNESCO, *Statistical Yearbook*.

† Source: UN, *Statistical Yearbook*.

Education

(1996)

	Institutions	Full-time Teachers ('000)	Students ('000)
Kindergartens	187,324	889	26,663
Primary schools	645,983	5,736	136,150
General secondary schools	79,967	3,465	57,397
Secondary technical schools	3,206	204	3,348
Teacher training schools	893	63	880
Agricultural and vocational schools	10,049	308	4,733
Special schools	980	19	90
Higher education	1,032	403	3,021

Directory

The Constitution

A new Constitution was adopted on 4 December 1982 by the Fifth Session of the Fifth National People's Congress. Its principal provisions, including amendments made in 1993, are detailed below. The Preamble, which is not included here, states that 'Taiwan is part of the sacred territory of the People's Republic of China'.

GENERAL PRINCIPLES

Article 1: The People's Republic of China is a socialist state under the people's democratic dictatorship led by the working class and based on the alliance of workers and peasants.

The socialist system is the basic system of the People's Republic of China. Sabotage of the socialist system by any organization or individual is prohibited.

Article 2: All power in the People's Republic of China belongs to the people.

The organs through which the people exercise state power are the National People's Congress and the local people's congresses at different levels.

The people administer state affairs and manage economic, cultural and social affairs through various channels and in various ways in accordance with the law.

Article 3: The state organs of the People's Republic of China apply the principle of democratic centralism.

The National People's Congress and the local people's congresses at different levels are instituted through democratic election. They are responsible to the people and subject to their supervision.

All administrative, judicial and procuratorial organs of the State are created by the people's congresses to which they are responsible and under whose supervision they operate.

The division of functions and powers between the central and local state organs is guided by the principle of giving full play to the initiative and enthusiasm of the local authorities under the unified leadership of the central authorities.

Article 4: All nationalities in the People's Republic of China are equal. The State protects the lawful rights and interests of the minority nationalities and upholds and develops the relationship of equality, unity and mutual assistance among all of China's nationalities. Discrimination against and oppression of any nationality are prohibited; any acts that undermine the unity of the nationalities or instigate their secession are prohibited.

The State helps the areas inhabited by minority nationalities speed up their economic and cultural development in accordance with the peculiarities and needs of the different minority nationalities.

Regional autonomy is practised in areas where people of minority nationalities live in compact communities; in these areas organs of self-government are established for the exercise of the right of autonomy. All the national autonomous areas are inalienable parts of the People's Republic of China.

The people of all nationalities have the freedom to use and develop their own spoken and written languages, and to preserve or reform their own ways and customs.

Article 5: The State upholds the uniformity and dignity of the socialist legal system.

No law or administrative or local rules and regulations shall contravene the Constitution.

All state organs, the armed forces, all political parties and public organizations and all enterprises and undertakings must abide by the Constitution and the law. All acts in violation of the Constitution and the law must be looked into.

No organization or individual may enjoy the privilege of being above the Constitution and the law.

Article 6: The basis of the socialist economic system of the People's Republic of China is socialist public ownership of the means of production, namely, ownership by the whole people and collective ownership by the working people.

The system of socialist public ownership supersedes the system of exploitation of man by man; it applies the principle of 'from each according to his ability, to each according to his work.'

Article 7: The state-owned economy, namely the socialist economy under the ownership of the whole people, is the leading force in the national economy. The State ensures the consolidation and growth of the state-owned economy.

Article 8: In the rural areas, the responsibility system with the household contract linking output to payment as the main form and other forms of co-operative economy such as producer, supply and marketing, credit and consumer co-operatives, belong to the sector of the socialist economy under collective ownership of the working people. Working people who are members of rural economic collectives have the right, within the limits prescribed by law, to farm private plots of cropland and hilly land, engage in household sideline production and raise privately-owned livestock.

The various forms of co-operative economy in the cities and towns, such as those in the handicraft, industrial, building, transport, commercial and service trades, all belong to the sector of socialist economy under collective ownership by the working people.

The State protects the lawful rights and interests of the urban and rural economic collectives and encourages, guides and helps the growth of the collective economy.

Article 9: Mineral resources, waters, forests, mountains, grassland, unreclaimed land, beaches and other natural resources are owned by the State, that is, by the whole people, with the exception of the forests, mountains, grassland, unreclaimed land and beaches that are owned by collectives in accordance with the law.

The State ensures the rational use of natural resources and protects rare animals and plants. The appropriation or damage of natural resources by any organization or individual by whatever means is prohibited.

Article 10: Land in the cities is owned by the State.

Land in the rural and suburban areas is owned by collectives except for those portions which belong to the state in accordance with the law; house sites and private plots of cropland and hilly land are also owned by collectives.

The State may in the public interest take over land for its use in accordance with the law.

No organization or individual may appropriate, buy, sell or lease land, or unlawfully transfer land in other ways.

All organizations and individuals who use land must make rational use of the land.

Article 11: The individual economy of urban and rural working people, operated within the limits prescribed by law, is a complement to the socialist public economy. The State protects the lawful rights and interests of the individual economy.

The State guides, helps and supervises the individual economy by exercising administrative control.

Article 12: Socialist public property is sacred and inviolable.

The State protects socialist public property. Appropriation or damage of state or collective property by any organization or individual by whatever means is prohibited.

Article 13: The State protects the right of citizens to own lawfully earned income, savings, houses and other lawful property.

The State protects by law the right of citizens to inherit private property.

Article 14: The State continuously raises labour productivity, improves economic results and develops the productive forces by enhancing the enthusiasm of the working people, raising the level of their technical skill, disseminating advanced science and technology, improving the systems of economic administration and enterprise operation and management, instituting the socialist system of responsibility in various forms and improving organization of work.

The State practises strict economy and combats waste.

The State properly apportions accumulation and consumption, pays attention to the interests of the collective and the individual as well as of the State and, on the basis of expanded production, gradually improves the material and cultural life of the people.

Article 15: The State practises a socialist market economy. The State strengthens economic legislation and perfects macro-control. The State prohibits, according to the law, disturbance of society's economic order by any organization or individual.

Article 16: State-owned enterprises have decision-making power in operations within the limits prescribed by law.

State-owned enterprises practise democratic management through congresses of workers and staff and in other ways in accordance with the law.

Article 17: Collective economic organizations have decision-making power in conducting economic activities on the condition that they abide by the relevant laws. Collective economic organizations practise democratic management, elect and remove managerial personnel, and decide on major issues in accordance with the law.

Article 18: The People's Republic of China permits foreign enterprises, other foreign economic organizations and individual foreigners to invest in China and to enter into various forms of economic co-operation with Chinese enterprises and other economic organizations in accordance with the law of the People's Republic of China.

All foreign enterprises and other foreign economic organizations in China, as well as joint ventures with Chinese and foreign investment located in China, shall abide by the law of the People's Republic of China. Their lawful rights and interests are protected by the law of the People's Republic of China.

Article 19: The State develops socialist educational undertakings and works to raise the scientific and cultural level of the whole nation.

The State runs schools of various types, makes primary education compulsory and universal, develops secondary, vocational and higher education and promotes pre-school education.

The State develops educational facilities of various types in order to wipe out illiteracy and provide political, cultural, scientific, technical and professional education for workers, peasants, state functionaries and other working people. It encourages people to become educated through self-study.

The State encourages the collective economic organizations, state enterprises and undertakings and other social forces to set up educational institutions of various types in accordance with the law.

The State promotes the nation-wide use of Putonghua (common speech based on Beijing pronunciation).

Article 20: The State promotes the development of the natural and social sciences, disseminates scientific and technical knowledge, and commends and rewards achievements in scientific research as well as technological discoveries and inventions.

Article 21: The State develops medical and health services, promotes modern medicine and traditional Chinese medicine, encourages and supports the setting up of various medical and health facilities by the rural economic collectives, state enterprises and undertakings and neighbourhood organizations, and promotes sanitation activities of a mass character, all to protect the people's health.

The State develops physical culture and promotes mass sports activities to build up the people's physique.

Article 22: The State promotes the development of literature and art, the press, broadcasting and television undertakings, publishing and distribution services, libraries, museums, cultural centres and other cultural undertakings, that serve the people and socialism, and sponsors mass cultural activities.

The State protects places of scenic and historical interest, valuable cultural monuments and relics and other important items of China's historical and cultural heritage.

Article 23: The State trains specialized personnel in all fields who serve socialism, increases the number of intellectuals and creates conditions to give full scope to their role in socialist modernization.

Article 24: The State strengthens the building of socialist spiritual civilization through spreading education in high ideals and morality, general education and education in discipline and the legal system, and through promoting the formulation and observance of rules of conduct and common pledges by different sections of the people in urban and rural areas.

The State advocates the civic virtues of love for the motherland, for the people, for labour, for science and for socialism; it educates the people in patriotism, collectivism, internationalism and communism and in dialectical and historical materialism; it combats capitalist, feudalist and other decadent ideas.

Article 25: The State promotes family planning so that population growth may fit the plans for economic and social development.

Article 26: The State protects and improves the living environment and the ecological environment, and prevents and remedies pollution and other public hazards.

The State organizes and encourages afforestation and the protection of forests.

Article 27: All state organs carry out the principle of simple and efficient administration, the system of responsibility for work and the system of training functionaries and appraising their work in order constantly to improve quality of work and efficiency and combat bureaucratism.

All state organs and functionaries must rely on the support of the people, keep in close touch with them, heed their opinions and suggestions, accept their supervision and work hard to serve them.

Article 28: The State maintains public order and suppresses treasonable and other counter-revolutionary activities; it penalizes actions that endanger public security and disrupt the socialist economy and other criminal activities, and punishes and reforms criminals.

Article 29: The armed forces of the People's Republic of China belong to the people. Their tasks are to strengthen national defence, resist aggression, defend the motherland, safeguard the people's peaceful labour, participate in national reconstruction, and work hard to serve the people.

The State strengthens the revolutionization, modernization and regularization of the armed forces in order to increase the national defence capability.

Article 30: The administrative division of the People's Republic of China is as follows:

(1) The country is divided into provinces, autonomous regions and municipalities directly under the central government;

(2) Provinces and autonomous regions are divided into autonomous prefectures, counties, autonomous counties and cities;

(3) Counties and autonomous counties are divided into townships, nationality townships and towns.

Municipalities directly under the central government and other large cities are divided into districts and counties. Autonomous prefectures are divided into counties, autonomous counties, and cities.

All autonomous regions, autonomous prefectures and autonomous counties are national autonomous areas.

Article 31: The State may establish special administrative regions when necessary. The systems to be instituted in special administrative regions shall be prescribed by law enacted by the National People's Congress in the light of the specific conditions.

Article 32: The People's Republic of China protects the lawful rights and interests of foreigners within Chinese territory, and while on Chinese territory foreigners must abide by the law of the People's Republic of China.

The People's Republic of China may grant asylum to foreigners who request it for political reasons.

FUNDAMENTAL RIGHTS AND DUTIES OF CITIZENS

Article 33: All persons holding the nationality of the People's Republic of China are citizens of the People's Republic of China.

All citizens of the People's Republic of China are equal before the law.

Every citizen enjoys the rights and at the same time must perform the duties prescribed by the Constitution and the law.

Article 34: All citizens of the People's Republic of China who have reached the age of 18 have the right to vote and stand for election, regardless of nationality, race, sex, occupation, family background, religious belief, education, property status, or length of residence, except persons deprived of political rights according to law.

Article 35: Citizens of the People's Republic of China enjoy freedom of speech, of the press, of assembly, of association, of procession and of demonstration.

Article 36: Citizens of the People's Republic of China enjoy freedom of religious belief.

No state organ, public organization or individual may compel citizens to believe in, or not to believe in, any religion; nor may they discriminate against citizens who believe in, or do not believe in, any religion.

The State protects normal religious activities. No one may make use of religion to engage in activities that disrupt public order, impair the health of citizens or interfere with the educational system of the state.

Religious bodies and religious affairs are not subject to any foreign domination.

Article 37: The freedom of person of citizens of the People's Republic of China is inviolable.

No citizen may be arrested except with the approval or by decision of a people's procuratorate or by decision of a people's court, and arrests must be made by a public security organ.

Unlawful deprivation or restriction of citizens' freedom of person by detention or other means is prohibited; and unlawful search of the person of citizens is prohibited.

Article 38: The personal dignity of citizens of the People's Republic of China is inviolable. Insult, libel, false charge or frame-up directed against citizens by any means is prohibited.

Article 39: The home of citizens of the People's Republic of China is inviolable. Unlawful search of, or intrusion into, a citizen's home is prohibited.

Article 40: The freedom and privacy of correspondence of citizens of the People's Republic of China are protected by law. No organization or individual may, on any ground, infringe upon the freedom and privacy of citizens' correspondence except in cases where, to meet the needs of state security or of investigation into criminal offences, public security or procuratorial organs are permitted to censor correspondence in accordance with procedures prescribed by law.

Article 41: Citizens of the People's Republic of China have the right to criticize and make suggestions to any state organ or functionary. Citizens have the right to make to relevant state organs complaints and charges against, or exposures of, violation of the law or dereliction of duty by any state organ or functionary; but fabrication or distortion of facts with the intention of libel or frame-up is prohibited.

In case of complaints, charges or exposures made by citizens, the state organ concerned must deal with them in a responsible manner after ascertaining the facts. No one may suppress such complaints, charges and exposures, or retaliate against the citizen making them.

Citizens who have suffered losses through infringement of their civic rights by any state organ or functionary have the right to compensation in accordance with the law.

Article 42: Citizens of the People's Republic of China have the right as well as the duty to work.

Using various channels, the State creates conditions for employment, strengthens labour protection, improves working conditions and, on the basis of expanded production, increases remuneration for work and social benefits.

Work is the glorious duty of every able-bodied citizen. All working people in state-owned enterprises and in urban and rural economic collectives should perform their tasks with an attitude consonant with their status as masters of the country. The State promotes socialist labour emulation, and commends and rewards model and advanced workers. The State encourages citizens to take part in voluntary labour.

The State provides necessary vocational training to citizens before they are employed.

Article 43: Working people in the People's Republic of China have the right to rest.

The State expands facilities for rest and recuperation of working people, and prescribes working hours and vacations for workers and staff.

Article 44: The State prescribes by law the system of retirement for workers and staff in enterprises and undertakings and for functionaries of organs of state. The livelihood of retired personnel is ensured by the State and society.

Article 45: Citizens of the People's Republic of China have the right to material assistance from the State and society when they are old, ill or disabled. The State develops the social insurance, social relief and medical and health services that are required to enable citizens to enjoy this right.

The State and society ensure the livelihood of disabled members of the armed forces, provide pensions to the families of martyrs and give preferential treatment to the families of military personnel.

The State and society help make arrangements for the work, livelihood and education of the blind, deaf-mute and other handicapped citizens.

Article 46: Citizens of the People's Republic of China have the duty as well as the right to receive education.

The State promotes the all-round moral, intellectual and physical development of children and young people.

Article 47: Citizens of the People's Republic of China have the freedom to engage in scientific research, literary and artistic creation and other cultural pursuits. The State encourages and assists creative endeavours conducive to the interests of the people that are made by citizens engaged in education, science, technology, literature, art and other cultural work.

Article 48: Women in the People's Republic of China enjoy equal rights with men in all spheres of life, political, economic, cultural and social, including family life.

The State protects the rights and interests of women, applies the principle of equal pay for equal work for men and women alike and trains and selects cadres from among women.

Article 49: Marriage, the family and mother and child are protected by the State.

Both husband and wife have the duty to practise family planning.

Parents have the duty to rear and educate their minor children, and children who have come of age have the duty to support and assist their parents.

Violation of the freedom of marriage is prohibited. Maltreatment of old people, women and children is prohibited.

Article 50: The People's Republic of China protects the legitimate rights and interests of Chinese nationals residing abroad and protects the lawful rights and interests of returned overseas Chinese and of the family members of Chinese nationals residing abroad.

Article 51: The exercise by citizens of the People's Republic of China of their freedoms and rights may not infringe upon the interests of the State, of society and of the collective, or upon the lawful freedoms and rights of other citizens.

Article 52: It is the duty of citizens of the People's Republic of China to safeguard the unity of the country and the unity of all its nationalities.

Article 53: Citizens of the People's Republic of China must abide by the Constitution and the law, keep state secrets, protect public property and observe labour discipline and public order and respect social ethics.

Article 54: It is the duty of citizens of the People's Republic of China to safeguard the security, honour and interests of the motherland; they must not commit acts detrimental to the security, honour and interests of the motherland.

Article 55: It is the sacred obligation of every citizen of the People's Republic of China to defend the motherland and resist aggression.

It is the honourable duty of citizens of the People's Republic of China to perform military service and join the militia in accordance with the law.

Article 56: It is the duty of citizens of the People's Republic of China to pay taxes in accordance with the law.

STRUCTURE OF THE STATE

The National People's Congress

Article 57: The National People's Congress of the People's Republic of China is the highest organ of state power. Its permanent body is the Standing Committee of the National People's Congress.

Article 58: The National People's Congress and its Standing Committee exercise the legislative power of the state.

Article 59: The National People's Congress is composed of deputies elected by the provinces, autonomous regions and municipalities directly under the Central Government, and by the armed forces. All the minority nationalities are entitled to appropriate representation.

Election of deputies to the National People's Congress is conducted by the Standing Committee of the National People's Congress.

The number of deputies to the National People's Congress and the manner of their election are prescribed by law.

Article 60: The National People's Congress is elected for a term of five years.

Two months before the expiration of the term of office of a National People's Congress, its Standing Committee must ensure that the election of deputies to the succeeding National People's Congress is completed. Should exceptional circumstances prevent such an election, it may be postponed by decision of a majority vote of more than two-thirds of all those on the Standing Committee of the incumbent National People's Congress, and the term of office of the incumbent National People's Congress may be extended. The election of deputies to the succeeding National People's Congress must be completed within one year after the termination of such exceptional circumstances.

Article 61: The National People's Congress meets in session once a year and is convened by its Standing Committee. A session of the National People's Congress may be convened at any time the Standing Committee deems this necessary, or when more than one-fifth of the deputies to the National People's Congress so propose.

When the National People's Congress meets, it elects a presidium to conduct its session.

Article 62: The National People's Congress exercises the following functions and powers:

(1) to amend the Constitution;

(2) to supervise the enforcement of the Constitution;

(3) to enact and amend basic statutes concerning criminal offences, civil affairs, the state organs and other matters;

(4) to elect the President and the Vice-President of the People's Republic of China;

(5) to decide on the choice of the Premier of the State Council upon nomination by the President of the People's Republic of China, and to decide on the choice of the Vice-Premiers, State Councillors, Ministers in charge of Ministries or Commissions and the Auditor-General and the Secretary-General of the State Council upon nomination by the Premier;

(6) to elect the Chairman of the Central Military Commission and, upon his nomination, to decide on the choice of all the others on the Central Military Commission;

(7) to elect the President of the Supreme People's Court;

(8) to elect the Procurator-General of the Supreme People's Procuratorate;

(9) to examine and approve the plan for national economic and social development and the reports on its implementation;

(10) to examine and approve the state budget and the report on its implementation;

(11) to alter or annul inappropriate decisions of the Standing Committee of the National People's Congress;

(12) to approve the establishment of provinces, autonomous regions, and municipalities directly under the Central Government;

(13) to decide on the establishment of special administrative regions and the systems to be instituted there;

(14) to decide on questions of war and peace; and

(15) to exercise such other functions and powers as the highest organ of state power should exercise.

Article 63: The National People's Congress has the power to recall or remove from office the following persons:

(1) the President and the Vice-President of the People's Republic of China;

(2) the Premier, Vice-Premiers, State Councillors, Ministers in charge of Ministries or Commissions and the Auditor-General and the Secretary-General of the State Council;

(3) the Chairman of the Central Military Commission and others on the Commission;

(4) the President of the Supreme People's Court; and

(5) the Procurator-General of the Supreme People's Procuratorate.

Article 64: Amendments to the Constitution are to be proposed by the Standing Committee of the National People's Congress or by more than one-fifth of the deputies to the National People's Congress and adopted by a majority vote of more than two-thirds of all the deputies to the Congress.

Statutes and resolutions are adopted by a majority vote of more than one half of all the deputies to the National People's Congress.

Article 65: The Standing Committee of the National People's Congress is composed of the following:

the Chairman;

the Vice-Chairmen;

the Secretary-General; and

members.

Minority nationalities are entitled to appropriate representation on the Standing Committee of the National People's Congress.

The National People's Congress elects, and has the power to recall, all those on its Standing Committee.

No one on the Standing Committee of the National People's Congress shall hold any post in any of the administrative, judicial or procuratorial organs of the state.

Article 66: The Standing Committee of the National People's Congress is elected for the same term as the National People's Congress; it exercises its functions and powers until a new Standing Committee is elected by the succeeding National People's Congress.

The Chairman and Vice-Chairmen of the Standing Committee shall serve no more than two consecutive terms.

Article 67: The Standing Committee of the National People's Congress exercises the following functions and powers:

(1) to interpret the Constitution and supervise its enforcement;

(2) to enact and amend statutes with the exception of those which should be enacted by the National People's Congress;

(3) to enact, when the National People's Congress is not in session, partial supplements and amendments to statutes enacted by the National People's Congress provided that they do not contravene the basic principles of these statutes;

(4) to interpret statutes;

(5) to examine and approve, when the National People's Congress is not in session, partial adjustments to the plan for national economic and social development and to the state budget that prove necessary in the course of their implementation;

(6) to supervise the work of the State Council, the Central Military Commission, the Supreme People's Court and the Supreme People's Procuratorate;

(7) to annul those administrative rules and regulations, decisions or orders of the State Council that contravene the Constitution or the statutes;

(8) to annul those local regulations or decisions of the organs of state power of provinces, autonomous regions and municipalities directly under the Central Government that contravene the Constitution, the statutes or the administrative rules and regulations;

(9) to decide, when the National People's Congress is not in session, on the choice of Ministers in charge of Ministries or Commissions or the Auditor-General and the Secretary-General of the State Council upon nomination by the Premier of the State Council;

(10) to decide, upon nomination by the Chairman of the Central Military Commission, on the choice of others on the Commission, when the National People's Congress is not in session.

(11) to appoint and remove the Vice-Presidents and judges of the Supreme People's Court, members of its Judicial Committee and the President of the Military Court at the suggestion of the President of the Supreme People's Court;

(12) to appoint and remove the Deputy Procurators-General and Procurators of the Supreme People's Procuratorate, members of its Procuratorial Committee and the Chief Procurator of the Military Procuratorate at the request of the Procurator-General of the Supreme People's Procuratorate, and to approve the appointment and removal of the Chief Procurators of the People's Procuratorates of provinces, autonomous regions and municipalities directly under the Central Government;

(13) to decide on the appointment and recall of plenipotentiary representatives abroad;

(14) to decide on the ratification and abrogation of treaties and important agreements concluded with foreign states;

(15) to institute systems of titles and ranks for military and diplomatic personnel and of other specific titles and ranks;

(16) to institute state medals and titles of honour and decide on their conferment;

(17) to decide on the granting of special pardons;

(18) to decide, when the National People's Congress is not in session, on the proclamation of a state of war in the event of an armed attack on the country or in fulfilment of international treaty obligations concerning common defence against aggression;

(19) to decide on general mobilization or partial mobilization;

(20) to decide on the enforcement of martial law throughout the country or in particular provinces, autonomous regions or municipalities directly under the Central Government; and

(21) to exercise such other functions and powers as the National People's Congress may assign to it.

Article 68: The Chairman of the Standing Committee of the National People's Congress presides over the work of the Standing Committee and convenes its meetings. The Vice-Chairmen and the Secretary-General assist the Chairman in his work.

Chairmanship meetings with the participation of the Chairman, Vice-Chairmen and Secretary-General handle the important day-to-day work of the Standing Committee of the National People's Congress.

Article 69: The Standing Committee of the National People's Congress is responsible to the National People's Congress and reports on its work to the Congress.

Article 70: The National People's Congress establishes a Nationalities Committee, a Law Committee, a Finance and Economic Committee, an Education, Science, Culture and Public Health Committee, a Foreign Affairs Committee, an Overseas Chinese Committee and such other special committees as are necessary. These special committees work under the direction of the Standing Committee of the National People's Congress when the Congress is not in session.

The special committees examine, discuss and draw up relevant bills and draft resolutions under the direction of the National People's Congress and its Standing Committee.

Article 71: The National People's Congress and its Standing Committee may, when they deem it necessary, appoint committees of inquiry into specific questions and adopt relevant resolutions in the light of their reports.

All organs of state, public organizations and citizens concerned are obliged to supply the necessary information to those committees of inquiry when they conduct investigations.

Article 72: Deputies to the National People's Congress and all those on its Standing Committee have the right, in accordance with procedures prescribed by law, to submit bills and proposals within the scope of the respective functions and powers of the National People's Congress and its Standing Committee.

Article 73: Deputies to the National People's Congress during its sessions, and all those on its Standing Committee during its meetings, have the right to address questions, in accordance with procedures prescribed by law, to the State Council or the Ministries and Commissions under the State Council, which must answer the questions in a responsible manner.

Article 74: No deputy to the National People's Congress may be arrested or placed on criminal trial without the consent of the presidium of the current session of the National People's Congress or, when the National People's Congress is not in session, without the consent of its Standing Committee.

Article 75: Deputies to the National People's Congress may not be called to legal account for their speeches or votes at its meetings.

Article 76: Deputies to the National People's Congress must play an exemplary role in abiding by the Constitution and the law and keeping state secrets and, in production and other work and their public activities, assist in the enforcement of the Constitution and the law.

Deputies to the National People's Congress should maintain close contact with the units which elected them and with the people, listen to and convey the opinions and demands of the people and work hard to serve them.

Article 77: Deputies to the National People's Congress are subject to the supervision of the units which elected them. The electoral units have the power, through procedures prescribed by law, to recall the deputies whom they elected.

Article 78: The organization and working procedures of the National People's Congress and its Standing Committee are prescribed by law.

The President of the People's Republic of China

Article 79: The President and Vice-President of the People's Republic of China are elected by the National People's Congress.

Citizens of the People's Republic of China who have the right to vote and to stand for election and who have reached the age of 45 are eligible for election as President or Vice-President of the People's Republic of China.

The term of office of the President and Vice-President of the People's Republic of China is the same as that of the National People's Congress, and they shall serve no more than two consecutive terms.

Article 80: The President of the People's Republic of China, in pursuance of decisions of the National People's Congress and its Standing Committee, promulgates statutes; appoints and removes the Premier, Vice-Premiers, State Councillors, Ministers in charge of Ministries or Commissions, and the Auditor-General and the Secretary-General of the State Council; confers state medals and titles of honour; issues orders of special pardons; proclaims martial law; proclaims a state of war; and issues mobilization orders.

Article 81: The President of the People's Republic of China receives foreign diplomatic representatives on behalf of the People's Republic of China and, in pursuance of decisions of the Standing Committee of the National People's Congress, appoints and recalls plenipotentiary representatives abroad, and ratifies and abrogates treaties and important agreements concluded with foreign states.

Article 82: The Vice-President of the People's Republic of China assists the President in his work.

The Vice-President of the People's Republic of China may exercise such parts of the functions and powers of the President as the President may entrust to him.

Article 83: The President and Vice-President of the People's Republic of China exercise their functions and powers until the new President and Vice-President elected by the succeeding National People's Congress assume office.

Article 84: In case the office of the President of the People's Republic of China falls vacant, the Vice-President succeeds to the office of President.

In case the office of the Vice-President of the People's Republic of China falls vacant, the National People's Congress shall elect a new Vice-President to fill the vacancy.

In the event that the offices of both the President and the Vice-President of the People's Republic of China fall vacant, the National People's Congress shall elect a new President and a new Vice-President. Prior to such election, the Chairman of the Standing Committee of the National People's Congress shall temporarily act as the President of the People's Republic of China.

The State Council

Article 85: The State Council, that is, the Central People's Government, of the People's Republic of China is the executive body of the highest organ of state power; it is the highest organ of state administration.

Article 86: The State Council is composed of the following: the Premier; the Vice-Premiers; the State Councillors; the Ministers in charge of ministries; the Ministers in charge of commissions; the Auditor-General; and the Secretary-General.

The Premier has overall responsibility for the State Council. The Ministers have overall responsibility for the respective ministries or commissions under their charge.

The organization of the State Council is prescribed by law.

Article 87: The term of office of the State Council is the same as that of the National People's Congress.

The Premier, Vice-Premiers and State Councillors shall serve no more than two consecutive terms.

Article 88: The Premier directs the work of the State Council. The Vice-Premiers and State Councillors assist the Premier in his work.

Executive meetings of the State Council are composed of the Premier, the Vice-Premiers, the State Councillors and the Secretary-General of the State Council.

The Premier convenes and presides over the executive meetings and plenary meetings of the State Council.

Article 89: The State Council exercises the following functions and powers:

(1) to adopt administrative measures, enact administrative rules and regulations and issue decisions and orders in accordance with the Constitution and the statutes;

(2) to submit proposals to the National People's Congress or its Standing Committee;

(3) to lay down the tasks and responsibilities of the ministries and commissions of the State Council, to exercise unified leadership over the work of the ministries and commissions and to direct all other administrative work of a national character that does not fall within the jurisdiction of the ministries and commissions;

(4) to exercise unified leadership over the work of local organs of state administration at different levels throughout the country, and to lay down the detailed division of functions and powers between the Central Government and the organs of state administration of provinces, autonomous regions and municipalities directly under the Central Government;

(5) to draw up and implement the plan for national economic and social development and the state budget;

(6) to direct and administer economic work and urban and rural development;

(7) to direct and administer the work concerning education, science, culture, public health, physical culture and family planning;

(8) to direct and administer the work concerning civil affairs, public security, judicial administration, supervision and other related matters;

(9) to conduct foreign affairs and conclude treaties and agreements with foreign states;

(10) to direct and administer the building of national defence;

(11) to direct and administer affairs concerning the nationalities, and to safeguard the equal rights of minority nationalities and the right of autonomy of the national autonomous areas;

(12) to protect the legitimate rights and interests of Chinese nationals residing abroad and protect the lawful rights and interests of returned overseas Chinese and of the family members of Chinese nationals residing abroad;

(13) to alter or annul inappropriate orders, directives and regulations issued by the ministries or commissions;

(14) to alter or annul inappropriate decisions and orders issued by local organs of state administration at different levels;

(15) to approve the geographic division of provinces, autonomous regions and municipalities directly under the Central Government, and to approve the establishment and geographic division of autonomous prefectures, counties, autonomous counties and cities;

(16) to decide on the enforcement of martial law in parts of provinces, autonomous regions and municipalities directly under the Central Government;

(17) to examine and decide on the size of administrative organs and, in accordance with the law, to appoint, remove and train administrative officers, appraise their work and reward or punish them; and

(18) to exercise such other functions and powers as the National People's Congress or its Standing Committee may assign it.

Article 90: The Ministers in charge of ministries or commissions of the State Council are responsible for the work of their respective departments and convene and preside over their ministerial meetings or commission meetings that discuss and decide on major issues in the work of their respective departments.

The ministries and commissions issue orders, directives and regulations within the jurisdiction of their respective departments and in accordance with the statutes and the administrative rules and regulations, decisions and orders issued by the State Council.

Article 91: The State Council establishes an auditing body to supervise through auditing the revenue and expenditure of all departments under the State Council and of the local government at different levels, and those of the state financial and monetary organizations and of enterprises and undertakings.

Under the direction of the Premier of the State Council, the auditing body independently exercises its power to supervise through auditing in accordance with the law, subject to no interference by any other administrative organ or any public organization or individual.

Article 92: The State Council is responsible, and reports on its work, to the National People's Congress or, when the National People's Congress is not in session, to its Standing Committee.

The Central Military Commission

Article 93: The Central Military Commission of the People's Republic of China directs the armed forces of the country.

The Central Military Commission is composed of the following: the Chairman; the Vice-Chairmen; and members.

The Chairman of the Central Military Commission has overall responsibility for the Commission.

The term of office of the Central Military Commission is the same as that of the National People's Congress.

Article 94: The Chairman of the Central Military Commission is responsible to the National People's Congress and its Standing Committee.

(Two further sections, not included here, deal with the Local People's Congresses and Government and with the Organs of Self-Government of National Autonomous Areas respectively.)

The People's Courts and the People's Procuratorates

Article 123: The people's courts in the People's Republic of China are the judicial organs of the state.

Article 124: The People's Republic of China establishes the Supreme People's Court and the local people's courts at different levels, military courts and other special people's courts.

The term of office of the President of the Supreme People's Court is the same as that of the National People's Congress; he shall serve no more than two consecutive terms.

The organization of people's courts is prescribed by law.

Article 125: All cases handled by the people's courts, except for those involving special circumstances as specified by law, shall be heard in public. The accused has the right of defence.

Article 126: The people's courts shall, in accordance with the law, exercise judicial power independently and are not subject to interference by administrative organs, public organizations or individuals.

Article 127: The Supreme People's Court is the highest judicial organ.

The Supreme People's Court supervises the administration of justice by the local people's courts at different levels and by the special people's courts; people's courts at higher levels supervise the administration of justice by those at lower levels.

Article 128: The Supreme People's Court is responsible to the National People's Congress and its Standing Committee. Local people's courts at different levels are responsible to the organs of state power which created them.

Article 129: The people's procuratorates of the People's Republic of China are state organs for legal supervision.

Article 130: The People's Republic of China establishes the Supreme People's Procuratorate and the local people's procuratorates at different levels, military procuratorates and other special people's procuratorates.

The term of office of the Procurator-General of the Supreme People's Procuratorate is the same as that of the National People's Congress; he shall serve no more than two consecutive terms.

The organization of people's procuratorates is prescribed by law.

Article 131: People's procuratorates shall, in accordance with the law, exercise procuratorial power independently and are not subject to interference by administrative organs, public organizations or individuals.

Article 132: The Supreme People's Procuratorate is the highest procuratorial organ.

The Supreme People's Procuratorate directs the work of the local people's procuratorates at different levels and of the special people's procuratorates; people's procuratorates at higher levels direct the work of those at lower levels.

Article 133: The Supreme People's Procuratorate is responsible to the National People's Congress and its Standing Committee. Local people's procuratorates at different levels are responsible to the organs of state power at the corresponding levels which created them and to the people's procuratorates at the higher level.

Article 134: Citizens of all nationalities have the right to use the spoken and written languages of their own nationalities in court proceedings. The people's courts and people's procuratorates should provide translation for any party to the court proceedings who is not familiar with the spoken or written languages in common use in the locality.

In an area where people of a minority nationality live in a compact community or where a number of nationalities live together, hearings should be conducted in the language or languages in common use in the locality; indictments, judgments, notices and other documents should be written, according to actual needs, in the language or languages in common use in the locality.

Article 135: The people's courts, people's procuratorates and public security organs shall, in handling criminal cases, divide their functions, each taking responsibility for its own work, and they shall co-ordinate their efforts and check each other to ensure correct and effective enforcement of law.

THE NATIONAL FLAG, THE NATIONAL EMBLEM AND THE CAPITAL

Article 136: The national flag of the People's Republic of China is a red flag with five stars.

Article 137: The national emblem of the People's Republic of China is the Tiananmen (Gate of Heavenly Peace) in the centre, illuminated by five stars and encircled by ears of grain and a cogwheel.

Article 138: The capital of the People's Republic of China is Beijing (Peking).

The Government

HEAD OF STATE

President: JIANG ZEMIN (elected by the Eighth National People's Congress on 27 March 1993).

Vice-President: RONG YIREN.

STATE COUNCIL

(January 1998)

Premier: LI PENG.

Vice-Premiers: ZHU RONGJI, ZOU JIAHUA, QIAN QICHEN, LI LANQING, WU BANGGUO, JIANG CHUNYUN.

State Councillors:

LI TIEYING
Gen. CHI HAOTIAN
SONG JIAN
LI GUIXIAN
CHEN JUNSHENG
ISMAIL AMAT
PENG PEIYUN
LUO GAN

Secretary-General: LUO GAN.

Minister of Foreign Affairs: QIAN QICHEN.

Minister of National Defence: Gen. CHI HAOTIAN.

Minister of State Economic and Trade Commission: WANG ZHONGYU.

Minister of State Planning Commission: CHEN JINHUA.

Minister of State Commission for Economic Restructuring: LI TIEYING.

Minister of State Education Commission: ZHU KAIXUAN.

Minister of State Science and Technology Commission: SONG JIAN.

Minister of State Commission of Science, Technology and Industry for National Defence: CAO GANGCHUAN.

Minister of State Nationalities Affairs Commission: ISMAIL AMAT.

Minister of Machine-Building Industry: BAO XUDING.

Minister of Public Security: TAO SIJU.

Minister of State Security: JIA CHUNWANG.

Minister of Civil Affairs: DOJE CERING.

Minister of Justice: XIAO YANG.

Minister of Supervision: CAO QINGZE.

Minister of Finance: LIU ZHONGLI.

Minister of Internal Trade: CHEN BANGZHU.

Minister of Foreign Trade and Economic Co-operation: WU YI.

Minister of Agriculture: LIU JIANG.

Minister of Forestry: CHEN YAOBANG.

Minister of Power Industry: SHI DAZHEN.

Minister of Coal Industry: WANG SENHAO.

Minister of Electronics Industry: HU QILI.

Minister of Water Resources: NIU MAOSHENG.

Minister of Construction: HOU JIE.

Minister of Geology and Mineral Resources: SONG RUIXIANG.

Minister of Metallurgical Industry: LIU QI.

Minister of Chemical Industry: GU XIULIAN.

Minister of Railways: HAN ZHUBIN.

Minister of Communications: HUANG ZHENDONG.

Minister of Posts and Telecommunications: WU JICHUAN.

Minister of Personnel: SONG DEFU.

Minister of Labour: LI BOYONG.

Minister of Culture: LIU ZHONGDE.

Minister of Radio, Film and Television: SUN JIAZHENG.

Minister of Public Health: CHEN MINZHANG.

Minister of State Physical Culture and Sports Commission: WU SHAOZU.

Minister of State Family Planning Commission: PENG PEIYUN.

Governor of the People's Bank of China: DAI XIANGLONG.

Auditor-General of Auditing Administration: GUO ZHENQIAN.

MINISTRIES

Ministry of Agriculture: 11 Nongzhanguan Nanli, Chaoyang Qu, Beijing 100026; tel. (10) 64193366; telex 22233; fax (10) 64192468.

Ministry of Chemical Industry: Bldg 16, Section 4, Anhuili, Beijing 100723; tel. (10) 64914455; fax (10) 64215982.

Ministry of Civil Affairs: 147 Beiheyan Dajie, Beijing 100721; tel. (10) 65135544.

Ministry of Coal Industry: 21 Hepinglibei Jie, Dongcheng Qu, Beijing 100713; tel. (10) 64214117; fax (10) 64215627.

Ministry of Communications: 11 Jianguomennei Dajie, Beijing 100736; tel. (10) 65292114; telex 22462; fax (10) 65292345.

Ministry of Construction: Baiwanzhuang, Western Suburb, Beijing 100835; tel. (10) 68394114; telex 222302.

Ministry of Culture: Jia 83, Donganmen Bei Jie, Dongcheng Qu, Beijing 100701; tel. (10) 64012255.

Ministry of Electronics Industry: 27 Wanshou Lu, Beijing 100846; tel. (10) 68212233; telex 22383; fax (10) 68213745.

Ministry of Finance: 3 Nansanxiang, Sanlihe, Xicheng Qu, Beijing 100820; tel. (10) 68526612; telex 222308; fax (10) 68513428.

Ministry of Foreign Affairs: 225 Chaoyangmennei Dajie, Dongsi, Beijing 100701; tel. (10) 65135566; telex 210070.

Ministry of Foreign Trade and Economic Co-operation: 2 Dongchangan Jie, Dongcheng Qu, Beijing 100731; tel. (10) 65198114; telex 22168; fax (10) 65129568.

Ministry of Forestry: 18 Hepingli Dongjie, Dongcheng Qu, Beijing 100714; tel. (10) 64229944; telex 22237.

Ministry of Geology and Mineral Resources: 64 Funei Dajie, Xicheng Qu, Beijing 100812; tel. (10) 66031144; telex 22531; fax (10) 66017791.

Ministry of Internal Trade: 25 Yuetanbei Jie, Xicheng Qu, Beijing 100834; tel. (10) 68392000.

Ministry of Justice: 11 Xiaguangli, Sanyuanqiao, Chaoyang Qu, Beijing 100016; tel. (10) 64677144.

Ministry of Labour: 12 Hepinglizhong Jie, Dongcheng Qu, Beijing 100716; tel. (10) 64213431; fax (10) 64219310.

Ministry of Machine-Building Industry: 46 Sanlihe Lu, Xicheng Qu, Beijing 100823; tel. (10) 68594711; fax (10) 68522644.

Ministry of Metallurgical Industry: 46 Dongsixi Dajie, Dongcheng Qu, Beijing 100020; tel. (10) 65131942; telex 222264.

Ministry of National Defence: Jingshanqian Jie, Beijing; tel. (10) 66370000.

Ministry of Personnel: 12 Hepinglizhong Jie, Dongcheng Qu, Beijing 100716; tel. 64213431.

Ministry of Posts and Telecommunications: 13 Xichangan Jie, Beijing 100804; tel. (10) 66014249; telex 222187; fax (10) 62016362.

Ministry of Power Industry: 137 Fuyou Jie, Xicheng Qu, Beijing 100031; tel. (10) 66054131.

Ministry of Public Health: 44 Houhaibeiyan, Xicheng Qu, Beijing 100725; tel. (10) 64034433; telex 22193.

Ministry of Public Security: 14 Dongchangan Jie, Beijing 100741; tel. (10) 65122831; fax (10) 65136577.

Ministry of Radio, Film and Television: 2 Fu Xing Men Wai Dajie, POB 4501, Beijing 100866; tel. (10) 66093114; telex 22236; fax (10) 68512174.

Ministry of Railways: 10 Fuxing Lu, Haidian Qu, Beijing 100844; tel. (10) 63240114; telex 22483.

Ministry of State Security: 14 Dongchangan Jie, Dongcheng Qu, Beijing 100741; tel. (10) 65244702.

Ministry of Supervision: 4 Zaojunmiao, Haidian Qu, Beijing 100081; tel. (10) 62256677.

Ministry of Water Resources: 1 Baiguang Lu, Ertiao, Xuanwu Qu, Beijing 100761; tel. (10) 63260495; telex 22466; fax (10) 63260365.

STATE COMMISSIONS

State Commission for Economic Restructuring: 22 Xianmen Jie, Beijing 100017; tel. (10) 63096437; telex 222854.

State Commission of Science, Technology and Industry for National Defence: Dongguanfang, Dianmenxi Dajie, Xicheng Qu, Beijing 100035; tel. (10) 66738080.

State Economic and Trade Commission: 26 Xuanwumenxi Dajie, Xuanwumen Qu, Beijing 100053; tel. (10) 63045336.

State Education Commission: 37 Damucang Hutong, Xicheng Qu, Beijing 100816; tel. (10) 66011049; telex 22014.

State Family Planning Commission: 14 Zhichun Lu, Haidian Qu, Beijing 100088; tel. (10) 62046622; telex 222298; fax (10) 62051865.

State Nationalities Affairs Commission: 252 Taipingqiao Dajie, Xicheng Qu, Beijing 100800; tel. (10) 66016611.

State Physical Culture and Sports Commission: 9 Tiyuguan Lu, Chongwen Qu, Beijing 100763; tel. (10) 67012233; telex 22323; fax (10) 67015858.

State Planning Commission: 38 Yuetannan Jie, Xicheng Qu, Beijing 100824; tel. (10) 68501240; fax (10) 68512929.

State Science and Technology Commission: 15B Fuxing Lu, Haidian Qu, Beijing 100015; tel. (10) 68515544; telex 22349; fax (10) 68515004.

Legislature

QUANGUO RENMIN DIABIAO DAHUI

(National People's Congress)

The National People's Congress (NPC) is the highest organ of state power, and is indirectly elected for a five-year term. The first plenary session of the Eighth NPC was convened in Beijing in March 1993, and was attended by 2,921 deputies. The first session of the Eighth National Committee of the Chinese People's Political Consultative Conference (CPPCC, Chair. Li Ruihuan), a revolutionary united front organization led by the Communist Party, took place simultaneously. The CPPCC holds discussions and consultations on the important affairs in the nation's political life. Members of the CPPCC National Committee or of its Standing Committee may be invited to attend the NPC or its Standing Committee as observers. The first sessions of the Ninth NPC and the Ninth National Committee of the CPPCC were scheduled to be held in early March 1998.

Standing Committee

In March 1993 134 members were elected to the Standing Committee, in addition to the following:

Chairman: Qiao Shi.

Vice-Chairmen:

Tian Jiyun
Wang Hanbin
Ni Zhifu
Ms Chen Muhua
Fei Xiaotong
Sun Qimeng
Lei Jieqiong
Qin Jiwei
Li Ximing
Wang Bingqian
Pagbalha Geleg Namgyai
Wang Guangying
Cheng Siyuan
Lu Jiaxi
Buhe
Tomur Dawamat
Wu Jieping

Secretary-General: Cao Zhi.

Provincial People's Congresses

Province	Chairman of Standing Committee of People's Congress
Anhui	Meng Fulin
Fujian	Yuan Qitong
Gansu	Lu Kejian
Guangdong	Zhu Senlin
Guizhou	Liu Fangren
Hainan	Du Qinglin
Hebei	Lu Chuanzan
Heilongjiang	Wang Jiangong
Henan	Ren Keli
Hubei	Guan Guangfu
Hunan	Wang Maolin
Jiangsu	Shen Daren
Jiangxi	Shu Huiguo
Jilin	Zhang Dejiang
Liaoning	Wang Huaiyuan
Qinghai	Tian Chengping
Shaanxi	Zhang Boxing
Shandong	Zhao Zhihao
Shanxi	Lu Gongxun
Sichuan	Xie Shijie
Yunnan	Yin Jun
Zhejiang	Li Zemin
Special Municipalities	
Beijing	Zhang Jianmin
Chongqing	(to be appointed)
Shanghai	Chen Tiedi
Tianjin	Nie Bichu
Autonomous Regions	
Guangxi Zhuang	Zhao Fulin
Nei Monggol	Liu Mingzu
Ningxia Hui	Ma Sizhong
Tibet (Xizang)	Raidi
Xinjiang Uygur	Amudun Niyaz

People's Governments

Province	Governor
Anhui	Hui Liangyu
Fujian	He Guoqiang
Gansu	Sun Ying
Guangdong	Lu Ruihua
Guizhou	Wu Yixia
Hainan	Ruan Chongwu
Hebei	Ye Liansong
Heilongjiang	Tian Fengshan
Henan	Ma Zhongchen
Hubei	Jiang Zhuping
Hunan	Yang Zhengwu
Jiangsu	Zheng Silin
Jiangxi	Shu Shengyou
Jilin	Wang Yunkun
Liaoning	Zhang Guogang
Qinghai	Bai Enpei
Shaanxi	Cheng Andong
Shandong	Li Chuting
Shanxi	Sun Wensheng
Sichuan	Song Baorui
Yunnan	Li Jiating
Zhejiang	Chai Songyue
Special Municipalities	Mayor
Beijing	Jia Qinglin
Chongqing	Pu Haiqing
Shanghai	Xu Kuangdi
Tianjin	Zhang Lichang
Autonomous Regions	Chairman
Guangxi Zhuang	Li Zhaozhuo
Nei Monggol	Yun Bulong
Ningxia Hui	Ma Qizhi (acting)
Tibet (Xizang)	Gyaincain Norbu
Xinjiang Uygur	Abdulahat Abdurixit

Political Organizations

COMMUNIST PARTY

Zhongguo Gongchan Dang (Chinese Communist Party—CCP): Beijing; f. 1921; 58m. mems in 1997; at the 15th Nat. Congress of the CCP, in September 1997, a new Cen. Cttee of 193 full mems and 151 alternate mems was elected; at its first plenary session the 15th Cen. Cttee appointed a new Politburo.

Fifteenth Central Committee

General Secretary: Jiang Zemin.

Politburo

Members of the Standing Committee:

Jiang Zemin
Li Peng
Zhu Rongji
Li Ruihuan
Hu Jintao
Wei Jianxing
Li Lanqing

Other Full Members:

Ding Guangen
Tian Jiyun
Li Changchun
Li Tieying
Wu Bangguo
Wu Guanzheng
Gen. Chi Haotian
Gen. Zhang Wannian
Luo Gan
Jiang Chunyun
Jia Qinglin
Qian Qichen
Huang Ju
Wen Jiaobao
Xie Fei

Alternate Members: Zeng Qinghong, Wu Yi.

Secretariat

Hu Jintao
Wei Jianxing
Ding Guangen
Gen. Zhang Wannian
Luo Gan
Wen Jiabao
Zeng Qinghong

OTHER POLITICAL ORGANIZATIONS

China Association for Promoting Democracy: 98 Xinanli Guloufangzhuangchang, Beijing 100009; tel. (10) 64033452; f. 1945; mems drawn mainly from literary, cultural and educational circles; Chair. Xu Jialu; Sec.-Gen. Chen Yiqun.

China Democratic League: 1 Beixing Dongchang Hutong, Beijing 100006; tel. (10) 65137983; fax (10) 65125090; f. 1941; formed from reorganization of League of Democratic Parties and Organizations of China; 131,300 mems, mainly intellectuals active in education, science and culture; Chair. Ding Shisun; Sec.-Gen. Yu Zeyou.

China National Democratic Construction Association: 21–22/F, Jingxin Bldg, 2A Dongsanhuan Beilu, Beijing 100027; tel. (10) 65136677; telex 22044; f. 1945; 70,000 mems, mainly industrialists and business executives; Chair. CHENG SIWEI.

China Zhi Gong Dang (Party for Public Interests): Beijing; f. 1925; reorg. 1947; mems are mainly returned overseas Chinese; Chair. LUO HAOCAI; Sec.-Gen. WU MINGXI.

Chinese Communist Youth League: 10 Qianmen Dongdajie, Beijing 100051; tel. (10) 67018132; fax (10) 67018131; f. 1922; 63.7m. mems; First Sec. of Cen. Cttee LI KEQIANG.

Chinese Peasants' and Workers' Democratic Party: f. 1930 as the Provisional Action Cttee of the Kuomintang; took present name in 1947; more than 65,000 mems, active mainly in public health and medicine; Chair. JIANG ZHENGHUA; Sec.-Gen. SONG JINSHENG.

Jiu San (3 September) Society: f. 1946; fmrly Democratic and Science Soc.; 68,400 mems, mainly scientists and technologists; Chair. WU JIEPING; Sec.-Gen. LIU RONGHAN.

Revolutionary Committee of the Chinese Kuomintang: tel. (10) 6550388; f. 1948; mainly fmr Kuomintang mems, and those in cultural, educational, health and financial fields; Chair. HE LULI.

Taiwan Democratic Self-Government League: f. 1947; recruits Taiwanese living on the mainland; Chair. ZHANG KEHUI; Sec.-Gen. PAN YUANJING.

Diplomatic Representation

EMBASSIES IN THE PEOPLE'S REPUBLIC OF CHINA

Afghanistan: 8 Dong Zhi Men Wai Dajie, Chao Yang Qu, Beijing; tel. (10) 65321582; fax (10) 65321710; Chargé d'affaires: ABDOLBASIR HOTEK.

Albania: 28 Guang Hua Lu, Beijing; tel. (10) 65321120; telex 211207; fax (10) 65325451; Ambassador: HAJDAR MUNEKA.

Algeria: 2 Dong Zhi Men Wai Dajie, Chao Yang Qu, Beijing; tel. (10) 65321231; fax (10) 65321648; Ambassador: AHMED AMINE KHERBI.

Argentina: Bldg 11, 5 Dong Jie, San Li Tun, Beijing; tel. (10) 65322090; telex 22269; fax (10) 65322319; Ambassador: A. ESTRADA-OYUELA.

Australia: 21 Dong Zhi Men Wai Dajie, San Li Tun, Beijing 100600; tel. (10) 65322331; fax (10) 65324605; Ambassador: RICHARD C. SMITH.

Austria: 5 Xiu Shui Nan Jie, Jian Guo Men Wai, Beijing 100600; tel. (10) 65322061; fax (10) 65321505; e-mail oebpekin@public.bta.net.cn; Ambassador: GERHARD ZIEGLER.

Azerbaijan: 2-10-2 Tayuan Diplomatic Office Bldg, Beijing 100600; tel. (10) 65324614; fax (10) 65324615; Ambassador: TAMERLAN GARAYEV.

Bahrain: 2-10-1 Tayuan Diplomatic Office Bldg, Beijing 100600; tel. (10) 65325025; fax (10) 65325016; Ambassador: MOHAMMED HAMAD AL-MAHMEED.

Bangladesh: 42 Guang Hua Lu, Beijing; tel. (10) 65321819; telex 22143; fax (10) 65324346; Ambassador: MUSTAFIZUR RAHMAN.

Belarus: 2-10-1 Tayuan Office Bldg, Xin Dong Lu, Chao Yang Qu, Beijing 100600; tel. (10) 65326426; fax (10) 65326417; Ambassador: VYACHASLAV NIKOLAEVICH KUZNYATSOV.

Belgium: 6 San Li Tun Lu, Beijing 100600; tel. (10) 65321736; telex 22260; fax (10) 65325097; Ambassador: CLAIRE KIRSCHEN.

Benin: 38 Guang Hua Lu, Beijing 100600; tel. (10) 65322741; telex 22599; fax (10) 65325103; Ambassador: AUGUSTE ALAVO.

Bolivia: 2-3-1 Tayuan Diplomatic Office Bldg, Beijing 100600; tel. (10) 65323074; telex 210415; fax (10) 65324686; e-mail embolch@public3.bta.net.cn; Ambassador: Dr MARIO REYES CHÁVEZ.

Botswana: 1-8-1/2 Tayuan Diplomatic Office Bldg, Beijing 100600; tel. (10) 65325751; fax (10) 65325713; Ambassador: ALFRED UYAPO MAJAYE DUBE.

Brazil: 27 Guang Hua Lu, Beijing; tel. (10) 65322881; telex 22117; fax (10) 65322751; Ambassador: SERGIO DE QUEIROZ DUARTE.

Bulgaria: 4 Xiu Shui Bei Jie, Jian Guo Men Wai, Beijing 100600; tel. (10) 65321946; fax (10) 65324502; Ambassador: STEFAN GABEROV.

Burundi: 25 Guang Hua Lu, Beijing 100600; tel. (10) 65321801; telex 22271; fax (10) 65322381; Ambassador: PROCÈS BIGIRIMANA.

Cambodia: 9 Dong Zhi Men Wai Dajie, Beijing 100600; tel. (10) 65322101; fax (10) 65323507; Ambassador: KHEK SYSODA.

Cameroon: 7 San Li Tun, Dong Wu Jie, Beijing; tel. (10) 65321771; telex 22256; fax (10) 65321761; Ambassador: ELEIH ELLE ETIAN.

Canada: 19 Dong Zhi Men Wai Dajie, Beijing 100600; tel. (10) 65323536; telex 22717; fax (10) 65324311; Ambassador: HOWARD BALLOCH.

Chad: 21 Guang Hua Lu, Jian Guo Men Wai, Beijing; tel. (10) 65321296; telex 22287; fax (10) 65323638; Ambassador: HELENA TCHIOUNA. (Diplomatic relations severed, Aug. 1997.)

Chile: 1 Dong Si Jie, San Li Tun, Beijing; tel. (10) 65321641; telex 22252; fax (10) 65323170; e-mail echilecn@public3.bta.net.cn; Ambassador: OCTAVIO ERRAZURIZ.

Colombia: 34 Guang Hua Lu, Beijing 100600; tel. (10) 65321713; fax (10) 65321969; Ambassador: ALVARO ESCALLÓN.

Congo, Democratic Republic: 6 Dong Wu Jie, San Li Tun, Beijing 100600; tel. (10) 65321995; telex 22273; fax (10) 65321360; Ambassador: LOMBO LO MANGAMANGA.

Congo, Republic: 7 Dong Si Jie, San Li Tun, Beijing; tel. (10) 65321644; telex 20428; Ambassador: VINCENT RAYMOND OMBAKA-EKORI.

Côte d'Ivoire: Beijing; tel. (10) 65321482; telex 22723; fax (10) 65322407; Ambassador: PATRICE KOFFI ANOH.

Croatia: 2-1-31 San Li Tun, Beijing 100600; tel. (10) 65326241; fax (10) 65326257; Ambassador: BRANIMIR STRENJA.

Cuba: 1 Xiu Shui Nan Jie, Jian Guo Men Wai, Beijing; tel. (10) 65321714; telex 22249; fax (10) 65322870; Ambassador: JOSÉ ARMANDO GUERRA MENCHERO.

Cyprus: 2-13-2 Tayuan Diplomatic Office Bldg, Liang Ma He Nan Lu, Chao Yang Qu, Beijing 100600; tel. (10) 65325057; fax (10) 65325060; Ambassador: LAKIS SPANOS.

Czech Republic: Ri Tan Lu, Jian Guo Men Wai, Beijing; tel. (10) 65326903; telex 222553; fax (10) 65325653; Ambassador: ALEXANDR KARYCH.

Denmark: 1 Dong Wu Jie, San Li Tun, Beijing 100600; tel. (10) 65322431; telex 22255; fax (10) 65322439; e-mail ambadan@public.bto.net.cn; Ambassador: CHRISTOPHER BO BRAMSEN.

Ecuador: 2-41 San Li Tun, Beijing; tel. (10) 65322264; telex 22710; fax (10) 65323158; Ambassador: FERNANDO CÓRDOVA BOSSANO.

Egypt: 2 Ri Tan Dong Lu, Beijing; tel. (10) 65322541; telex 22134; fax (10) 65325365; Ambassador: SAMIR BORHAN RAGUEB.

Equatorial Guinea: 2 Dong Si Jie, San Li Tun, Beijing; tel. (10) 65323709; fax (10) 65326459; Ambassador: FLORENCIO MAYA.

Eritrea: Beijing; Ambassador: ERMIAS DEBESSAI HIDAD.

Ethiopia: 3 Xiu Shui Nan Jie, Jian Guo Men Wai, Beijing 100600; tel. (10) 65325258; telex 22306; fax (10) 65325591; Ambassador: ADDIS ALEM BALEMA.

Finland: 1-10-1 Tayuan Diplomatic Office Bldg, Beijing 100600; tel. (10) 65321817; fax (10) 65321884; Ambassador: PASI RUTANEN.

France: 3 Dong San Jie, San Li Tun, Beijing; tel. (10) 65321331; telex 22183; fax (10) 65324841; Ambassador: PIERRE MOREL.

Gabon: 36 Guang Hua Lu, Beijing; tel. (10) 65322810; telex 22110; fax (10) 65322621; Ambassador: M. OBIANG-NDOUDUM.

Germany: 5 Dong Zhi Men Wai Dajie, Beijing 100600; tel. (10) 65322161; telex 22259; fax (10) 65325336; Ambassador: Dr KONRAD SEITZ.

Ghana: 8 San Li Tun Lu, Beijing; tel. (10) 65321319; telex 210462; fax (10) 65323602; Ambassador: KOJO AMOO-GOTTFRIED.

Greece: 19 Guang Hua Lu, Beijing; tel. (10) 65321588; telex 22267; fax (10) 65321277; Ambassador: SPYRIDON DOKIANOS.

Guinea: 2 Xi Liu Jie, San Li Tun, Beijing 100600; tel. (10) 65323649; telex 22706; fax (10) 65324957; Ambassador: MAMADY CONDÉ.

Guyana: 1 Xiu Shui Dong Jie, Jian Guo Men Wai, Beijing 100600; tel. (10) 65321601; telex 22295; fax (10) 65325741; Chargé d'affaires a.i.: JUNE ANGELA PERSAUD.

Hungary: 10 Dong Zhi Men Wai Dajie, Beijing 100600; tel. (10) 65321431; fax (10) 65325053; Ambassador: OTTÓ JUHÁSZ.

Iceland: Unit 1005, Beijing Landmark Bldg, Chao Yang Qu, Beijing 100600; tel. (10) 65927795; fax (10) 65927801; e-mail icemb.beijing@utn.stjr.is; Ambassador: HJÁLMAR W. HANNESSON.

India: 1 Ri Tan Dong Lu, Beijing; tel. (10) 65321927; telex 22126; fax (10) 65324684; Ambassador: VIJAY K. NAMBIAR.

Indonesia: San Li Tun, Diplomatic Office, Bldg B, Beijing 100600; tel. (10) 65325485; telex 2215368; fax (10) 65325368; Ambassador: KUNTARA.

Iran: Dong Liu Ji, San Li Tun, Beijing; tel. (10) 65322040; telex 22253; fax (10) 65321403; Ambassador: HOSSEIN MIRFAKHKHAR.

Iraq: 3 Ri Tan Dong Lu, Chao Yang Qu, Beijing; tel. (10) 65321950; telex 22288; fax (10) 65321596; Ambassador: BASSAM SALIH KUBBA.

Ireland: 3 Ri Tan Dong Lu, Beijing 100600; tel. (10) 65322691; telex 22425; fax (10) 65322168; Ambassador: JOSEPH HAYES.

Israel: 1 Jian Guo Men Wai Dajie, Beijing 100004; tel. (10) 65052970; fax (10) 65050328; e-mail israemb@public.bta.net.cn; Ambassador: ORA NAMIR.

Italy: 2 Dong Er Jie, San Li Tun, Beijing 100600; tel. (10) 65322131; telex 22414; fax (10) 65324676; Ambassador: ALESSANDRO QUARONI.

Japan: 7 Ri Tan Lu, Jian Guo Men Wai, Beijing 100600; tel. (10) 65322361; telex 22275; fax (10) 65324625; Ambassador: YOSHIYASU SATO.

Jordan: 5 Dong Liu Jie, San Li Tun, Beijing 100600; tel. (10) 65323906; fax (10) 65323283; Ambassador: SAMIR NAOURI.

Kazakhstan: 9 Dong 6 Jie, San Li Tun, Beijing 100600; tel. (10) 65326182; telex 22364; fax (10) 65326183; Ambassador: KUANYSH SULTANOVICH SULTANOV.

Kenya: 4 Xi Liu Jie, San Li Tun, Beijing; tel. (10) 65323381; telex 22311; fax (10) 65321770; Ambassador: JAMES SIMANI.

Korea, Democratic People's Republic: Ri Tan Bei Lu, Jian Guo Men Wai, Beijing; tel. (10) 65321186; telex 20448; fax (10) 65326056; Ambassador: CHU CHANG JUN.

Korea, Republic: 3rd–4th Floor, China World Trade Centre, 1 Jian Guo Men Wai Dajie, Beijing; tel. (10) 65053171; fax (10) 65053458; Ambassador: CHUNG CHONG-WOOK.

Kuwait: 23 Guang Hua Lu, Beijing 100600; tel. (10) 65322216; telex 22127; fax (10) 65321607; Ambassador: ABDUL-MUHSEN NASIR A. GEAN.

Kyrgyzstan: 2-4-1 Tayuan Office Bldg, Beijing; tel. (10) 65326458; telex 210757; fax (10) 65326459; Ambassador: M. S. IMANALIEV.

Laos: 11 Dong Si Jie, San Li Tun, Chao Yang Qu, Beijing 100600; tel. (10) 65321244; telex 22144; fax (10) 65326748; e-mail laoemcn@mailhost.cinet.co.cn; Ambassador: SOUKTHAVONE KEOLA.

Lebanon: 51 Dong Liu Jie, San Li Tun, Beijing; tel. and fax (10) 65322770; telex 22113; Ambassador: FARID SAMAHA.

Libya: 3 Dong Liu Jie, San Li Tun, Beijing; tel. (10) 65323666; telex 22340; fax (10) 65323391; Secretary of the People's Bureau: MUFTAH OTMAN MADI.

Lithuania: Beijing; fax (10) 65324421.

Luxembourg: 21 Nei Wu Bu Jie, Beijing 100600; tel. (10) 65135937; telex 22638; fax (10) 65137268; Ambassador: PIERRE-LOUIS LORENZ.

Macedonia, former Yugoslav republic: 5-2-2 Diplomatic Apts, San Li Tun, Beijing 100600; tel. (10) 65326282; fax (10) 65326756; Ambassador: VLADIMIR PETKOVSKI.

Madagascar: 3 Dong Jie, San Li Tun, Beijing; tel. (10) 65321353; telex 22140; fax (10) 65322102; Ambassador: JEAN-JACQUES MAURICE.

Malaysia: 13 Dong Zhi Men Wai Dajie, San Li Tun, Beijing; tel. (10) 65322531; telex 22122; fax (10) 65325032; Ambassador: MAT AMIR JAAFAR.

Mali: 8 Dong Si Jie, San Li Tun, Beijing 100600; tel. (10) 65321704; telex 22257; fax (10) 65321618; Ambassador: KAFOUGOUNA KONE.

Malta: 2-1-22 Tayuan Diplomatic Office Bldg, Beijing 100600; tel. (10) 65323114; fax (10) 65326125; Ambassador: CHARLES VELLA.

Marshall Islands: 2-14-1 Tayuan Diplomatic Office Bldg, Beijing 100600; tel. (10) 65325904; fax (10) 65325778; Ambassador: CARL L. HEINE.

Mauritania: 9 Dong San Jie, San Li Tun, Beijing; tel. (10) 65321346; telex 22514; fax (10) 65321685; Ambassador: CHEIKH SID AHMED OULD BABAMINE.

Mexico: 5 Dong Wu Jie, San Li Tun, Beijing 100600; tel. (10) 65321947; fax (10) 65323744; Ambassador: LUIS WYBO ALFARO.

Mongolia: 2 Xiu Shui Bei Jie, Jian Guo Men Wai, Beijing; tel. (10) 65321203; telex 22262; fax (10) 65325045; Ambassador: L. TSAHILGAAN.

Morocco: 16 San Li Tun Lu, Beijing; tel. (10) 65321489; telex 22268; fax (10) 65321453; Ambassador: ABDERRAHIM BENABDEJLIL.

Mozambique: Tayuan 1-7-2, Beijing; tel. (10) 65323664; telex 22705; fax (10) 65325189; Ambassador: JOSÉ MARIA MORAIS.

Myanmar: 6 Dong Zhi Men Wai Dajie, Chao Yang Qu, Beijing; tel. (10) 65321584; telex 10416; fax (10) 65321344; Ambassador: U SET.

Nepal: 1 Xi Liu Jie, San Li Tun Lu, Beijing; tel. (10) 65322739; telex 210408; fax (10) 65323251; Ambassador: Prof. YUBARAJ SINGH PRADHAN.

Netherlands: 4 Liang Ma He Nan Lu, Beijing 100600; tel. (10) 65321131; telex 210759; fax (10) 65324689; Ambassador: D. J. VAN HOUTEN.

New Zealand: 1 Ri Tan, Dong Er Jie, Chao Yang Qu, Beijing 100600; tel. (10) 65322731; fax (10) 65324317; e-mail nzemb@eastnet.co.cn; Ambassador: PETER ADAMS.

Niger: Beijing. Diplomatic relations re-established August 1996.

Nigeria: 2 Dong Wu Jie, San Li Tun, Beijing; tel. (10) 65323631; telex 22274; fax (10) 65321650; Ambassador: MALAM ZUBAIR MAHMUD KAZAURE.

Norway: 1 Dong Yi Jie, San Li Tun, Beijing 100600; tel. (10) 65322261; telex 22266; fax (10) 65322392; Ambassador: SVERRE BERGH JOHANSEN.

Oman: 6 Liang Ma He Nan Lu, San Li Tun, Beijing; tel. (10) 65323956; fax (10) 65325030; Ambassador: ABDULLAH BIN MOHAMMED BIN ABDULLAH AL-FARISY.

Pakistan: 1 Dong Zhi Men Wai Dajie, Beijing 100600; tel. (10) 65322504; fax (10) 65322715; Ambassador: INAMUL HAQUE.

Peru: 2-82 San Li Tun, Bangonglou, Beijing 100600; tel. (10) 65323477; fax (10) 65322178; Ambassador: LUZMILA ZANABRIA.

Philippines: 23 Xiu Shui Bei Jie, Jian Guo Men Wai, Beijing; tel. (10) 65321872; fax (10) 65323761; Ambassador: ROMUALDO A. ONG.

Poland: 1 Ri Tan Lu, Jian Guo Men Wai, Beijing 100600; tel. (10) 65321235; telex 210288; fax (10) 65321745; Ambassador: ZDZISŁAW GÓRALCZYK.

Portugal: 2-15-1 Tayuan Diplomatic Office Bldg, Beijing 100600; tel. (10) 65323220; telex 22326; fax (10) 65324637; Ambassador: PEDRO CATARINO.

Qatar: 2-9-2 Tayuan Diplomatic Office Bldg, 14 Liang Ma He Nan Lu, Beijing 100600; tel. (10) 65322231; fax (10) 65325274; Ambassador: MOHAMMED ABDUL-GHANI.

Romania: Ri Tan Lu Dong Er Jie, Beijing; tel. (10) 65323442; telex 22250; fax (10) 65325728; Ambassador: VIRGIL CONSTANTINESCU.

Russia: 4 Dong Zhi Men Nei, Bei Zhong Jie, Beijing 100600; tel. (10) 65321291; telex 22247; fax (10) 65324853; Ambassador: IGOR ROGACHEV.

Rwanda: 30 Xiu Shui Bei Jie, Beijing; tel. (10) 65322193; telex 22104; fax (10) 65322006; Ambassador: RUGABA SILAS.

Saudi Arabia: 1 Beixiaojie, San Li Tun, Beijing 100600; tel. (10) 65324825; fax (10) 65325324; Ambassador: Mr YUSEF.

Sierra Leone: 7 Dong Zhi Men Wai Dajie, Beijing; tel. (10) 65321222; telex 22166; fax (10) 65323752; Ambassador: MOHAMED LAMIN KAMARA.

Singapore: 1 Xiu Shui Bei Jie, Jian Guo Men Wai, Beijing 100600; tel. (10) 65323926; fax (10) 65322215; Ambassador: CHIN SIAT YOON.

Slovakia: Ri Tan Lu, Jian Guo Men Wai, Beijing 100600; tel. (10) 65321531; fax (10) 65324814; Ambassador: Prof. VLADIMÍR KLÍMO.

Slovenia: 23 Jian Guo Men Wai Dajie, 3-53 Jian Guo Men Wai Diplomatic Residence, Beijing 100600; tel. (10) 65326356; fax (10) 65326358; Ambassador: IVAN SENICAR.

Somalia: 2 San Li Tun Lu, Beijing; tel. (10) 65321752; telex 22121; Ambassador: MOHAMED HASSAN SAID.

South Africa: 50 Liangmaqiao Lu, 801 Beijing Lufthansa Centre, Office C, Beijing 100016; tel. (10) 64651085; fax (10) 64651949; e-mail safrican@eastnet.co.cn; Ambassador: CHRISTOPHER DLAMINI.

Spain: 9 San Li Tun Lu, Beijing; tel. (10) 65321986; telex 22108; fax (10) 65323401; Ambassador: JUAN B. LEÑA CASAS.

Sri Lanka: 3 Jian Hua Lu, Jian Guo Men Wai, Beijing 100600; tel. (10) 65321861; telex 22136; fax (10) 65325426; Ambassador: R. C. A. VANDERGERT.

Sudan: 1 Dong Er Jie, San Li Tun, Beijing; tel. (10) 65323715; telex 22116; fax (10) 65321280; Ambassador: ALI YOUSUF AHMED.

Sweden: 3 Dong Zhi Men Wai Dajie, San Li Tun, Beijing 100600; tel. (10) 65323331; telex 22261; fax (10) 65325008; Ambassador: KJELL ANNELING.

Switzerland: 3 Dong Wu Jie, San Li Tun, Beijing 100600; tel. (10) 65322736; telex 22251; fax (10) 65324353; Ambassador: Dr ULI SIGG.

Syria: 6 Dong Si Jie, San Li Tun, Beijing 100600; tel. (10) 65321563; telex 22138; fax (10) 65321575; Ambassador: LOUTOF ALLAH HAYDAR.

Tanzania: 53 Dong Liu Jie, San Li Tun, Beijing; tel. (10) 65321408; telex 22749; fax (10) 65324985; Ambassador: SEIF ALI IDDI.

Thailand: 40 Guang Hua Lu, Beijing 100600; tel. (10) 65321903; telex 22145; fax (10) 65321748; Ambassador: SAWANIT KONGSIRI.

Togo: 11 Dong Zhi Men Wai Dajie, Beijing; tel. (10) 65322202; telex 22130; Ambassador: YAO BLOUA AGBO.

Tunisia: 1 Dong Jie, San Li Tun, Beijing; tel. (10) 65322435; telex 22103; fax (10) 6325818; Ambassador: ABDELHAMID BEN MESSAOUDA.

Turkey: 9 Dong Wu Jie, San Li Tun, Beijing 100600; tel. (10) 65322650; fax (10) 65325480; e-mail trkelcn@public.bta.net.cn; Ambassador: ÜNAL ÜNSAL.

Uganda: 5 Dong Jie, San Li Tun, Beijing; tel. (10) 65322370; telex 22272; fax (10) 65322242; Ambassador: F. A. OKECHO.

Ukraine: 11 Dong Wu Jie, San Li Tun, Beijing; tel. (10) 65326369; telex 210082; fax (10) 65326765; Ambassador: ANATOLY PLYUSHKO.

United Arab Emirates: 1-9-1 Tayuan Diplomatic Office Bldg, Beijing 100600; tel. (10) 65322112; fax (10) 65325089; Ambassador: ISMAIL OBAID YOUSEF OBAID.

United Kingdom: 11 Guang Hua Lu, Jian Guo Men Wai, Beijing 100600; tel. (10) 65321961; fax (10) 65321937; Ambassador: ANTHONY GALSWORTHY.

USA: 3 Xiu Shui Bei Jie, Beijing 100600; tel. (10) 65323831; telex 22701; fax (10) 65323178; Ambassador: JAMES R. SASSER.

Uruguay: 2-7-2 Tayuan Bldg, Beijing 100600; tel. (10) 65324445; telex 211237; fax (10) 65324357; e-mail urubei@public.bta.net.cn; Ambassador: ALVARO ALVAREZ.

Venezuela: 14 San Li Tun Lu, Beijing 100600; tel. (10) 65321295; telex 22137; fax (10) 65323817; e-mail embvenez@mailhost.cinet.co.cn; Ambassador: MAGLIO E. MONTIEL.

Viet Nam: 32 Guang Hua Lu, Jian Guo Men Wai, Beijing; tel. (10) 65321155; fax (10) 65325720; Ambassador: DANG NGHIEM HOANH.

Yemen: 5 Dong San Jie, San Li Tun, Beijing 100600; tel. (10) 65321558; telex 210297; fax (10) 65324305; Ambassador: MOHAMMED HADI AWAD.

Yugoslavia: 1 Dong Liu Jie, San Li Tun, Beijing 100600; tel. (10) 65323516; telex 22403; fax (10) 65321207; Ambassador: Dr SLOBODAN UNKOVIĆ.

Zambia: 5 Dong Si Jie, San Li Tun, Beijing 100600; tel. (10) 65321554; telex 22388; fax (10) 65321891; Ambassador: Prof. MOSES MUSONDA.

Zimbabwe: 7 Dong San Jie, San Li Tun, Beijing 100600; tel. (10) 65323795; telex 22671; fax (10) 65325383; Ambassador: BONIFACE GUWA CHIDYAUSIKU.

Judicial System

The general principles of the Chinese judicial system are laid down in Articles 123–135 of the December 1982 Constitution (q.v.).

PEOPLE'S COURTS

Supreme People's Court: 27 Dongjiaomin Xiang, Beijing 100745; tel. (10) 65136195; f. 1949; the highest judicial organ of the state; handles first instance cases of national importance; handles cases of appeals and protests lodged against judgments and orders of higher people's courts and special people's courts, and cases of protests lodged by the Supreme People's Procuratorate in accordance with the procedures of judicial supervision; reviews death sentences meted out by local courts, supervises the administration of justice by local people's courts; interprets issues concerning specific applications of laws in judicial proceedings; its judgments and rulings are final; Pres. REN JIANXIN (five-year term of office coincides with that of National People's Congress, by which the President is elected).

Local People's Courts: comprise higher courts, intermediate courts and basic courts.

Special People's Courts: include military courts, maritime courts and railway transport courts.

PEOPLE'S PROCURATORATES

Supreme People's Procuratorate: 147 Beiheyan Dajie, Beijing 100726; tel. (10) 65126655; acts for the National People's Congress in examining govt depts, civil servants and citizens, to ensure observance of the law; prosecutes in criminal cases. Procurator-Gen. ZHANG SIQING (elected by the National People's Congress for five years).

Local People's Procuratorates: undertake the same duties at the local level. Ensure that the judicial activities of the people's courts, the execution of sentences in criminal cases, and the activities of departments in charge of reform through labour, conform to the law; institute, or intervene in, important civil cases which affect the interest of the state and the people.

Religion

During the 'Cultural Revolution' places of worship were closed. After 1977 the Government adopted a policy of religious tolerance, and the 1982 Constitution states that citizens enjoy freedom of religious belief, and that legitimate religious activities are protected. Many temples, churches and mosques have reopened. Since 1994 all religious organizations have been required to register with the Bureau of Religious Affairs.

Bureau of Religious Affairs: Beijing; tel. (10) 652625; Dir YE XIAOWEN.

ANCESTOR WORSHIP

Ancestor worship is believed to have originated with the deification and worship of all important natural phenomena. The divine and human were not clearly defined; all the dead became gods and were worshipped by their descendants. The practice has no code or dogma and the ritual is limited to sacrifices made during festivals and on birth and death anniversaries.

BUDDHISM

Buddhism was introduced into China from India in AD 67, and flourished during the Sui and Tang dynasties (6th–8th century), when eight sects were established. The Chan and Pure Land sects are the most popular. According to official sources, in 1997 there were 13,000 Buddhist temples in China. There were 100m. believers in 1997.

Buddhist Association of China (BAC): f. 1953; Pres. ZHAO PUCHU; Sec.-Gen. DAO SHUREN.

Tibetan Institute of Lamaism: Pres. BUMI JANGBALUOZHU; Vice-Pres. CEMOLIN DANZENGCHILIE.

14th Dalai Lama: His Holiness the Dalai Lama TENZIN GYATSO, Thekchen Choeling, McLeod Ganj 176219, Dharamsala, Himachal Pradesh, India; tel. (91) 1892-21343; fax (91) 1892-21813; e-mail ohhdl@cta.unv.ernet.ind; spiritual and temporal leader of Tibet; fled to India after failure of Tibetan national uprising in 1959.

CHRISTIANITY

During the 19th century and the first half of the 20th century large numbers of foreign Christian missionaries worked in China. According to official sources, there were 10m. Protestants and 4m. Catholics in China in 1997, although unofficial sources estimate that the Christian total could be as high as 90m. In December 1989 a Catholic church was permitted to reopen in Beijing, bringing the total number of functioning Catholic churches there to five. Beijing had an estimated 40,000 Catholics in late 1989. The Catholic Church in China operates independently of the Vatican.

Three-Self Patriotic Movement Committee of Protestant Churches of China: Chair. DING GUANGXUN.

China Christian Council: 169 Yuan Ming Yuan Lu, Shanghai 200002; tel. (21) 63213396; fax (21) 63232605; e-mail cccnjo@public1.ptt.js.cn; f. 1980; comprises provincial Christian councils; Pres. Dr HAN WENZAO.

The Roman Catholic Church: Catholic Mission, Si-She-Ku, Beijing; Bishop of Beijing MICHAEL FU TIESHAN (not recognized by the Vatican).

Chinese Patriotic Catholic Association: Chair. Mgr ZONG HUAIDE; Sec.-Gen. ZHU SHICHANG; c. 3m. mems (1988).

CONFUCIANISM

Confucianism is a philosophy and a system of ethics, without ritual or priesthood. The respects that adherents accord to Confucius are not bestowed on a prophet or god, but on a great sage whose teachings promote peace and good order in society and whose philosophy encourages moral living.

DAOISM

Daoism was founded by Zhang Daoling during the Eastern Han dynasty (AD 125–144). Lao Zi, a philosopher of the Zhou dynasty (born 604 BC), is its principal inspiration, and is honoured as Lord the Most High by Daoists. According to official sources, there were 1,500 Daoist temples in China in 1997.

China Daoist Association: Temple of the White Cloud, Xi Bian Men, 100045 Beijing; tel. (10) 6367179; f. 1957; Chair. FU YUANTIAN.

ISLAM

According to Muslim history, Islam was introduced into China in AD 651. There were some 18m. adherents in China in 1997, chiefly among the Wei Wuer (Uygur) and Hui people.

Beijing Islamic Association: Dongsi Mosque, Beijing; f. 1979; Chair. Imam Al-Hadji SALAH AN SHIWEI.

China Islamic Association: Beijing 100053; tel. (10) 63546384; telex 222571; fax (10) 63529483; f. 1953; Pres. SALAH AN SHIWEI.

The Press

In 1996 China had 2,235 newspaper titles (including those below provincial level) and in 1995 there were 7,543 magazine titles. Each province publishes its own daily. Only the major newspapers and periodicals are listed below.

PRINCIPAL NEWSPAPERS

Anhui Ribao (Anhui Daily): 206 Jinzhai Lu, Hefei, Anhui 230061; tel. (551) 2827842; fax (551) 2825843; Editor-in-Chief WANG HONG.

Beijing Ribao (Beijing Daily): 34 Xi Biaobei Hutong, Dongdan, Beijing 100743; tel. (10) 65132233; fax (10) 65126581; f. 1952; organ of the Beijing municipal cttee of the CCP; Dir MAN YUNLAI; Editor-in-Chief LIU HUSHAN; circ. 700,000.

Beijing Wanbao (Beijing Evening News): 34 Xi Biaobei Hutong, Dongdan, Beijing 100743; tel. (10) 65132233; telex 283642; fax (10) 65126581; f. 1958; Editor LI BINGREN; circ. 800,000.

Beijing Youth Daily: Beijing; national and local news; promotes ethics and social service; circ. 3m.–4m.

Changsha Wanbao (Changsha Evening News): 161 Caie Zhong Lu, Changsha, Hunan 410005; tel. (731) 4424457; fax (731) 4445167.

Chengdu Wanbao (Evening News): Qingyun Nan Jie, Chengdu 610017; tel. (28) 664501; fax (28) 666597; circ. 700,000.

China Business Times: Beijing; f. 1989; Editor HUANG WENFU; circ. 500,000.

Chungcheng Wanbao (Chungcheng Evening News): 51 Xinwen Lu, Kunming, Yunnan 650032; tel. and fax (871) 4141896.

Dazhong Ribao (Masses Daily): 46 Jinshi Lu, Jinan, Shandong 250014; tel. (531) 2968911; telex 9993; fax (531) 2962450; f. 1939; Dir LIU XUEDE; Editor-in-Chief LIU GUANGDONG; circ. 550,000.

Economic News: Editor-in-Chief DU ZULIANG.

Fujian Ribao (Fujian Daily): Hualin Lu, Fuzhou, Fujian Province; tel. (591) 57756; daily; Deputy Editor-in-Chief HUANG ZHONGSHENG.

Gongren Ribao (Workers' Daily): Liupukang, Andingmen Wai, Beijing; tel. (10) 64211561; telex 210423; fax (10) 64214890; f. 1949; trade union activities and workers' lives; also major home and overseas news; Dir and Editor-in-Chief QU ZUGENG; circ. 2.5m.

Guangming Ribao (Guangming Daily): 106 Yongan Lu, Beijing 100050; tel. (10) 63010636; telex 20021; fax (10) 63016716; f. 1949; literature, art, science, education, history, economics, philosophy; Editor-in-Chief WANG CHEN; circ. 920,000.

Guangxi Ribao (Guangxi Daily): Guangxi Region; Dir and Editor-in-Chief LI MINGDE.

Guangzhou Ribao (Canton Daily): 10 Dongle Lu, Renmin Zhonglu, Guangzhou, Guangdong Province; tel. (20) 81887294; fax (20) 81862022; f. 1952; daily; social, economic and current affairs; Editor-in-Chief LI YUANJIANG; circ. 600,000.

Guizhou Ribao (Guizhou Daily): Guiyang, Guizhou Province; tel. (851) 627779; f. 1949; circ. 300,000; Editor-in-Chief LIU XUEZHU.

Hainan Ribao (Hainan Daily): Xinhua Nan Lu, Haikou, Hainan 570001; tel. (898) 6222021.

Hebei Ribao (Hebei Daily): Yuhuazhong Lu, Shijiazhuang, Hebei 050013; tel. (311) 6048901; fax (311) 6046969; f. 1949; Dir LIU HAIQUAN; Editor-in-Chief YE ZHEN; circ. 500,000.

Heilongjiang Ribao (Heilongjiang Daily): Heilongjiang Province; Editor-in-Chief JIA SHIXIANG.

Henan Ribao (Henan Daily): 1 Weiyi Lu, Zhengzhou, Henan Province; tel. (371) 5958319; telex 1032; fax (371) 5955636; f. 1949; Editor-in-Chief YANG FENGGE; circ. 390,000.

Huadong Xinwen (Eastern China News): f. 1995; published by Renmin Ribao.

Huanan Xinwen (South China News): Guangzhou; f. 1997; published by Renmin Ribao.

Hubei Ribao (Hubei Daily): 65 Huangli Lu, Wuhan, Hubei 430077; tel. (27) 6833522; telex 5590; fax (27) 6813989; f. 1949; Dir LU JIAN; Editor-in-Chief YANG RENBEN; circ. 800,000.

Hunan Ribao (Hunan Daily): 435 Jiangxiang Zhong Lu, Changsha, Hunan 410005; tel. (731) 4444999; fax (731) 4441029; Dir and Editor-in-Chief JIANG XIANLI.

Jiangxi Ribao (Jiangxi Daily): 175 Yangming Jie, Nanchang, Jiangxi Province; tel. (791) 6849888; fax (791) 6772590; f. 1949; Editor-in-Chief DUAN FURUI; circ. 300,000.

Jiefang Ribao (Liberation Daily): 300 Han Kou Lu, Shanghai 200001; tel. (21) 63521111; fax (21) 63515461; f. 1949; Chief Editor QIN SHAODE; circ. 1m.

Jiefangjun Bao (Liberation Army Daily): Beijing; f. 1956; official organ of the Central Military Comm.; Dir Lt-Gen. XU CAIHOU; Editor-in-Chief SUN ZHONGTONG; circ. 800,000.

Jilin Ribao (Jilin Daily): Jilin Province; Editor-in-Chief YI HONGBIN.

Jingji Ribao (Economic Daily): 277 Wang Fujing Dajie, Beijing 100746; tel. (10) 65232854; fax (10) 65125015; f. 1983; financial affairs, domestic and foreign trade; administered by the State Council; Editor-in-Chief YANG SHANGDE; circ. 1.2m.

Jinrong Shibao (Financial News): 44 Taipingqiao Fengtaiqu, Beijing 100073; tel. (10) 63269233; fax (10) 68424931.

Liaoning Ribao (Liaoning Daily): Liaoning Province; Dir ZHU SHILIANG; Editor-in-Chief XIE ZHENGQIAN.

Nanfang Ribao (Nanfang Daily): 289 Guangzhou Da Lu, Guangzhou, Guangdong 510601; tel. (20) 8763998; fax (20) 87375203; f. 1949; Dir LIU TAO; Editor-in-Chief FAN YIJIN; circ. 1m.

Nanjing Ribao (Nanjing Daily): 53 Jiefang Lu, Nanjing, Jiangsu 210016; tel. (25) 4496564; fax (25) 4496544.

Nongmin Ribao (Farmers' Daily): Shilipu Beili, Chao Yang Qu, Beijing 100025; tel. (10) 65005522; telex 6592; fax (10) 65071154; f. 1980; 6 a week; circulates in rural areas nation-wide; Dir SUN YONGREN; circ. 1m.

Renmin Ribao (People's Daily): 2 Jin Tai Xi Lu, Beijing; tel. (10) 5092121; telex 22320; fax (10) 65091982; f. 1948; organ of the CCP; also publishes overseas edn; Editor-in-Chief SHAO HUAZE; circ. 2.15m.

Shaanxi Ribao (Shaanxi Daily): Shaanxi Province; Pres. and Editor-in-Chief QIAN GUOZHENG.

Shanxi Ribao (Shanxi Daily): 24 Shuangtasi Jie, Taiyuan, Shanxi Province; tel. (351) 446561; fax (351) 441771; Dir WANG XIYI; Editor-in-Chief LI DONGXI; circ. 300,000.

Shenzhen Commercial Press: Shenzhen; Editor-in-Chief GAO XINGLIE.

Shenzhen Tequ Bao (Shenzhen Special Economic Zone Daily): 4 Shennan Zhonglu, Shenzhen 518009; tel. (755) 2244566; telex 1032; fax (755) 2243919; f. 1982; reports on special economic zones, as well as mainland, Hong Kong and Macau; Pres. and Editor-in-Chief WU SONGYING.

Sichuan Ribao (Sichuan Daily): 70 Hongxing Zhong Lu, Erduan, Chengdu, Sichuan 610012; tel. (28) 6678900; fax (28) 6665035; f. 1952; Editor YAO ZHINENG; circ. 8m.

Tianjin Ribao (Tianjin Daily): 54 Anshan Dao, Heping Qu, Tianjin 300020; tel. (22) 7301024; fax (22) 7305803; f. 1949; Dir QIU YUNSHENG; Editor-in-Chief WU BINGJING; circ. 600,000.

Wenhui Bao (Wenhui Daily): 50 Huqiu Lu, Shanghai 200002; tel. (21) 63211410; telex 33080; fax (21) 63233533; f. 1938; Editor-in-Chief SHI JUNSHENG; circ. 800,000m.

Xin Min Wan Bao (Xin Min Evening News): 839 Yan An Lu, Shanghai 200040; tel. (21) 62791234; fax (21) 62473220; f. 1929; specializes in public policy, education and social affairs; Editor-in-Chief DING FAZHANG; circ. 1.75m.

Xinhua Ribao (New China Daily): 55 Zhongshan Lu, Nanjing, Jiangsu 210005; tel. (21) 741757; fax (21) 741023; Editor-in-Chief LIU XIANGDONG; circ. 900,000.

Xinjiang Ribao (Xinjiang Daily): Xinjiang Region; Dir TIAN YUMIAN; Editor-in-Chief HUANG YANCAI.

Xizang Ribao (Tibet Daily): Tibet; Editor-in-Chief LI CHANGWEN.

Yangcheng Wanbao (Yangcheng Evening News): 733 Dongfeng Dong Lu, Guangzhou, Guangdong 510085; tel. (20) 87776211; fax (20) 87765103; f. 1957; Editor-in-Chief CAO CHUNLIANG; circ. 1.2m.

Yunnan Ribao (Yunnan Daily): Yunnan Province; Editor-in-Chief WANG ZIMING.

Zhejiang Ribao (Zhejiang Daily): Zhejiang Province; Editor-in-Chief JIANG PING.

Zhongguo Qingnian Bao (China Youth News): 2 Haiyuncang, Dong Zhi Men Nei, Beijing 100702; tel. (10) 64032233; fax (10) 64033961; f. 1951; daily; aimed at 14–40 age-group; Dir and Editor-in-Chief XU ZHUQING; circ. 1.0m.

Zhongguo Ribao (China Daily): 15 Huixin Dongjie, Chao Yang Qu, Beijing 100029; tel. (10) 64918366; telex 22022; fax (10) 64918377; f. 1981; English; China's political, economic and cultural developments; world, financial and sports news; also publishes *Business Weekly* (f. 1985), *Beijing Weekend* (f. 1991), *Shanghai Star* (f. 1992), *Reports from China* (f. 1992), *21st Century* (f. 1993); Editor-in-Chief ZHU YINGHUANG; circ. 300,000.

Zhongguo Xinwen (China News): 12 Baiwanzhuang Nanjie, Beijing; tel. (10) 68315012; f. 1952; daily; Editor-in-Chief WANG XIJIN; current affairs.

SELECTED PERIODICALS

Ban Yue Tan (Fortnightly Review): Beijing; tel. (10) 6668521; f. 1980; in Chinese and Wei Wuer (Uygur); Editor-in-Chief MIN FANLU; circ. 6m.

Beijing Review: 24 Baiwanzhuang Lu, Beijing 100037; tel. (10) 68328115; telex 222374; fax (10) 68326628; weekly; edns in English, French, Spanish, Japanese and German; also **Chinafrica** (monthly in English and French); Editor-in-Chief LIN LIANGQI.

BJ TV Weekly: 2 Fu Xing Men Wai Zhenwumiao Jie, Beijing 100045; tel. (10) 6366036; fax (10) 63262388; circ. 1m.

China TV Weekly: 15 Huixin Dong Jie, Chaoyang Qu, Beijing 100013; tel. (10) 64214197; telex 22022; circ. 1.7m.

Chinese Literature Press: 24 Baiwanzhuang Lu, Beijing 100037; tel. (10) 68326010; fax (10) 68326678; f. 1951; quarterly; in English and French; contemporary and classical writing, poetry, literary criticism and arts; Exec. Editor TANG JIALONG.

Chinese Science Abstracts: Science Press, 16 Donghuangchenggen Beijie, Beijing 100717; tel. (10) 64018833, ext. 391; telex 210247; fax (10) 64019810; f. 1982; monthly in English; science and technology; Chief Editor LI RUIXU.

Dianying Xinzuo (New Films): 796 Huaihai Zhonglu, Shanghai; tel. (21) 64379710; f. 1979; bi-monthly; introduces new films.

Dianzi yu Diannao (Electronics and Computers): Beijing; f. 1985; popularized information on computers and microcomputers.

Elle (China): 14 Lane 955, Yanan Zhong Lu, Shanghai; tel. (21) 62472890; fax (21) 62475100; f. 1988; monthly; fashion; Pres. YANG XINCI; Chief Editor WU YING; circ. 250,000.

Family Magazine: 14 Siheng Lu, Xinhepu, Dongshan Qu, Guangzhou 510080; tel. (20) 7777718; fax (20) 7185670; monthly; circ. 2.5m.

Feitian (Fly Skywards): 50 Donggan Xilu, Lanzhou, Gansu; tel. (931) 25803; f. 1961; monthly.

Guoji Xin Jishu (New International Technology): Zhanwang Publishing House, Beijing; f. 1984; also publ. in Hong Kong; international technology, scientific and technical information.

Guowai Keji Dongtai (Recent Developments in Science and Technology Abroad): Institute of Scientific and Technical Information of China, 15 Fuxing Lu, Beijing 100038; tel. (10) 68515544, ext. 2557; telex 20079; fax (10) 68514025; f. 1962; monthly; scientific journal; Editor-in-Chief BAI YIRAN; circ. 100,000.

Hai Xia (The Strait): 27 De Gui Xiang, Fuzhou, Fujian Province; tel. (10) 33656; f. 1981; quarterly; literary journal; CEOs YANG YU, JWO JONG LIN.

Huasheng Monthly (Voice for Overseas Chinese): 12 Bai Wan Zhuang Nan Jie, Beijing 100037; tel. (10) 68311578; fax (10) 68315039; f. 1995; monthly; intended mainly for overseas Chinese and Chinese nationals resident abroad; Editor-in-Chief FAN DONG-SHENG.

Jianzhu (Construction): Baiwanzhuang, Beijing; tel. (10) 68992849; f. 1956; monthly; Editor FANG YUEGUANG; circ. 500,000.

Jinri Zhongguo (China Today): 24 Baiwanzhuang Lu, Beijing 100037; tel. (10) 68326037; fax (10) 68328338; f. 1952; fmrly *China Reconstructs*; monthly; edns in English, Spanish, French, Arabic, German, Chinese and English braille; economic, social and cultural affairs; illustrated; Vice-Pres. and Deputy Editor-in-Chief SHEN XINGDA.

Liaowang (Outlook): 57 Xuanwumen Xijie, Beijing; tel. (10) 63073049; f. 1981; weekly; current affairs; Gen. Man. ZHOU YICHANG; Editor CHEN DABIN; circ. 500,000.

Luxingjia (Traveller): Beijing; tel. (10) 6552631; f. 1955; monthly; Chinese scenery, customs, culture.

Meishu Zhi You (Friends of Art): 32 Beizongbu Hutong, East City Region, Beijing; tel. (10) 65122583; telex 5019; f. 1982; every 2 months; art review journal, also providing information on fine arts publs in China and abroad; Editors PENG SHEN, BAOLUN WU.

Nianqingren (Young People): 169 Mayuanlin, Changsha, Hunan Province; tel. (731) 23610; f. 1981; monthly; general interest for young people.

Nongye Zhishi (Agricultural Knowledge): 21 Ming Zi Qian Lu, Jinan, Shandong 250100; tel. (531) 8932238; f. 1950; monthly; popular agricultural science; Dir YANG LIJIAN; circ. 650,000.

Qiushi (Seeking Truth): 2 Shatan Beijie, Beijing 100727; tel. (10) 64011155; telex 1219; fax (10) 64018174; f. 1988 to succeed *Hong Qi* (Red Flag); 2 a month; theoretical journal of the CCP; Editor-in-Chief XING BENSI; circ. 1.83m.

Renmin Huabao (China Pictorial): Huayuancun, West Suburbs, Beijing 100044; tel. (10) 68411144; fax (10) 68413023; f. 1950; monthly; edns: 2 in Chinese, 1 in Tibetan and 12 in foreign languages; Dir and Editor-in-Chief ZHANG JIAHUA.

Shichang Zhoubao (Market Weekly): 2 Duan, Sanhao Jie, Heping Qu, Shenyang, Liaoning Province; tel. (24) 482983; f. 1979; weekly in Chinese; trade, commodities and financial and economic affairs; circ. 1m.

Shufa (Calligraphy): 81 Qingzhou Nan Lu, Shanghai 200233; tel. (21) 64519008; fax (21) 64519015; f. 1977; every 2 months; journal on ancient and modern calligraphy; Chief Editor LU FUSHENG.

Tiyu Kexue (Sports Science): 8 Tiyuguan Lu, Beijing 100763; tel. (10) 67112233; telex 22323; f. 1981; sponsored by the China Sports Science Soc.; every 2 months; summary in English; Chief Officer YUAN WEIMIN; in Chinese; circ. 20,000.

Wenxue Qingnian (Youth Literature Journal): Mu Tse Fang 27, Wenzhou, Zhejiang Province; tel. (577) 3578; f. 1981; monthly; Editor-in-Chief CHEN YUSHEN; circ. 80,000.

Xian Dai Faxue (Modern Law Science): Chongqing, Sichuan 630031; tel. (811) 961671; f. 1979; bi-monthly; with summaries in English; Dirs XU JINGCUN, XIE XOUPING.

Yinyue Aihaozhe (Music Lovers): 74 Shaoxing Lu, Shanghai 200020; tel. (21) 64372608; telex 33384; fax (21) 64332019; f. 1979; every 2 months; music knowledge; illustrated; Editor-in-Chief CHEN XUEYA; circ. 50,000.

Zhongguo Duiwai Maoyi (China's Foreign Trade): CCPIT Bldg, 1 Fu Xing Men Wai Jie, Beijing 100860; tel. (10) 68513344; fax (10) 68510201; e-mail cft@public.gb.co.cn; f. 1956; monthly; edns in Chinese and English; information on Chinese imports and exports, foreign trade and economic policies; Editor-in-Chief YANG HAIQING.

Zhongguo Ertong (Chinese Children): 21 Xiang 12, Dongsi, Beijing; tel. (10) 6444761; telex 4357; f. 1980; monthly; illustrated journal for elementary school pupils.

Zhongguo Funu (Women of China): 15 Jiang Guo Men Dajie, Beijing 100730; tel. (10) 65134616; fax (10) 65225380; f. 1956; monthly; administered by All-China Women's Federation; women's rights and status, marriage and family, education, family planning, arts, cookery, etc.; Editor-in-Chief Ms WANG XIULIN.

Zhongguo Guangbo Dianshi (China Radio and Television): 12 Fucheng Lu, Beijing; tel. (10) 6896217; f. 1982; monthly; sponsored by Ministry of Radio, Film and Television; reports and comments.

Zhongguo Jin Rong Xin Xi: Beijing; f. 1991; monthly; economic news.

Zhongguo Sheying (Chinese Photography): 61 Hongxing Hutong, Dongdan, Beijing 100005; tel. (10) 65252277; f. 1957; monthly; photographs and comments; Editor LIU BANG.

Zhongguo Zhenjiu (Chinese Acupuncture and Moxibustion): China Academy of Traditional Chinese Medicine, Dongzhimen Nei, Beijing 100700; tel. (10) 64014411; telex 210340; f. 1981; 2 a month; publ. by Chinese Soc. of Acupuncture and Moxibustion; abstract in English; Editor-in-Chief Prof. WEI MINGFENG.

Zijing (Bauhinia): Pres. CHEN HONG.

Other popular magazines include **Gongchandang Yuan** (Communists, circ. 1.63m.) and **Nongmin Wenzhai** (Peasants Digest, circ. 3.54m.).

NEWS AGENCIES

Xinhua (New China) News Agency: 57 Xuanwumen Xidajie, Beijing 100803; tel. (10) 63073767; telex 22316; fax (10) 63073735; f. 1931; offices in all Chinese provincial capitals, and about 100 overseas bureaux; news service in Chinese, English, French, Spanish, Portuguese, Arabic and Russian, feature and photographic services; Pres. GUO CHAOREN; Editor-in-Chief NAN ZHENZHONG.

Zhongguo Xinwen She (China News Agency): POB 1114, Beijing; f. 1952; office in Hong Kong; supplies news features, special articles and photographs for newspapers and magazines in Chinese printed overseas; services in Chinese; Dir WANG SHIGU.

Foreign Bureaux

Agence France-Presse (AFP) (France): 11-11 Jian Guo Men Wai, Diplomatic Apts, Beijing 100600; tel. (10) 65321409; fax (10) 65322371; Bureau Chief GILLES CAMPION.

Agencia EFE (Spain): 2-2-132 Jian Guo Men Wai, Beijing 100600; tel. (10) 65323449; telex 22167; fax (10) 65323688; Rep. CARLOS REDONDO.

Agenzia Nazionale Stampa Associata (ANSA) (Italy): 1-11 Ban Gong Lu, San Li Tun, Beijing; tel. (10) 65323651; telex 22290; fax (10) 65321954; Bureau Chief BARBARA ALIGHIERO.

Allgemeiner Deutscher Nachrichtendienst (ADN) (Germany): Jian Guo Men Wai, Qi Jia Yuan Gong Yu 7-2-61, Beijing 100600; tel. and fax (10) 65321115; telex 22109; Correspondent Dr LUTZ POHLE.

Associated Press (AP) (USA): 6-2-22 Jiang Guo Men Wai, Diplomatic Quarters, Beijing; tel. (10) 65326650; telex 22196; fax (10) 65323419; Bureau Chief ELAINE KURTENBACH.

Deutsche Presse-Agentur (dpa) (Germany): Ban Gong Lou, Apt 1-31, San Li Tun, Beijing 100600; tel. (10) 65321473; fax (10) 65321615; Bureau Chief ANDREAS LANDWEHR.

Informatsionnoye Telegrafnoye Agentstvo Rossii—Telegrafnoye Agentstvo Suverennykh Stran (ITAR—TASS) (Russia): 6-1-41 Tayuan Diplomatic Office Bldg, Beijing; tel. (10) 65324821; telex 22115; fax (10) 65324820; Bureau Chief GRIGORII KURBANOVICH ARSLANOV.

Inter Press Service (IPS) (Italy): 15 Fu Xing Lu, POB 3811, Beijing 100038; tel. (10) 68514046; fax (10) 68518210; e-mail tips@sunlo.sti.ac.cn; Dir WANG XIAOYING.

Jiji Tsushin (Japan): 9-1-13 Jian Guo Men Wai, Waijiao, Beijing; tel. (10) 65322924; telex 22381; fax (10) 65323413; Correspondents YOSHIHISA MURAYAMA, TETSUYA NISHIMURA.

Korean Central News Agency (Democratic People's Republic of Korea): Beijing; Bureau Chief SONG YONG SONG.

Kyodo News Service (Japan): 3-901 Jian Guo Men Wai, Beijing; tel. (10) 6532680; telex 22324; fax (10) 65322273; Bureau Chief KAZUYOSHI NISHIKURA.

Magyar Távirati Iroda (MTI) (Hungary): 1-42 Ban Gong Lu, San Li Tun, Beijing 100600; tel. (10) 65321744; telex 22106; Correspondent GYÖRGY BARTA.

Prensa Latina (Cuba): 6-2-12 Qi Ji Yuan, Beijing; tel. (10) 65321831, ext. 539; telex 22284; Correspondent MARÍA ELENA LLANA CASTRO.

Press Trust of India: 5-131 Diplomatic Apts, Jiang Guo Men Wai, Beijing 100600; tel. and fax (10) 65322221.

Reuters (UK): Beijing Hilton, 4 Bei Dong Sanhuan Lu, Beijing 100027; tel. (10) 65321921; fax (10) 65324978; Bureau Man. RICHARD PASCOE.

United Press International (UPI) (USA): 7-1-11 Qi Jia Yuan, Beijing; tel. (10) 65323271; telex 22197; Bureau Chief CHRISTIAAN VIRANT.

The following are also represented: Rompres (Romania), Tanjug (Yugoslavia) and VNA (Viet Nam).

PRESS ORGANIZATIONS

All China Journalists' Association: Xijiaominxiang, Beijing 100031; tel. (10) 66023981; telex 222719; fax (10) 66014658; Exec. Chair. WU LENGXI.

China Newspapers Association: Beijing; Chair. XU ZHONGTIAN.

The Press and Publication Administration of the People's Republic of China: 85 Dongsi Nan Dajie, Beijing 100703; tel. (10) 65124433; telex 22024; fax (10) 65127875; Dir YU YOUXIAN.

Publishers

In 1996 there were 528 publishing houses in China. A total of 112,813 titles were published in 1996.

Beijing Chubanshe (Beijing Publishing House): 6 Bei Sanhuan Zhong Lu, Beijing 100011; tel. (10) 62016699; telex 8909; fax (10) 62012339; f. 1956; politics, history, law, economics, geography, science, literature, art, etc.; Dir ZHU SHUXIN; Editor-in-Chief TAO XINCHENG.

Beijing Daxue Chubanshe (Beijing University Publishing House): Beijing University, Haidian Qu, Beijing 100871; tel. (10) 62502024; telex 22239; fax (10) 62556201; f. 1979; academic and general.

China International Book Trading Corpn: POB 399, Chegongzhuang Xilu 35, Beijing; tel. (10) 68414284; telex 22496; fax (10) 68412023; f. 1949; foreign trade org. specializing in publs, including books, periodicals, art and crafts, microfilms, etc.; import and export distributors; Pres. LIU ZHIBIN.

CITIC Publishing House: Beijing; Pres. WANG MINGHUI.

Dianzi Gongye Chubanshe (Publishing House of the Electronics Industry—PHEI): POB 173, Wan Shou Lu, Beijing 100036; tel. (10) 68159028; fax (10) 68159025; f. 1982; electronic sciences and technology; Pres. LIANG XIANGFENG; Vice-Pres. WANG MINGJUN.

Dolphin Books: 24 Baiwanzhuang Lu, Beijing 100037; tel. (10) 68326332; telex 22475; fax (10) 68326642; f. 1986; children's books in Chinese and foreign languages; Dir WANG YANRONG.

Falü Chubanshe (Law Publishing House): POB 111, Beijing 100036; tel. (10) 6815325; f. 1980; current laws and decrees, legal textbooks, translations of important foreign legal works; Dir LAN MINGLIANG.

Foreign Languages Press: 24 Baiwanzhuang Lu, Beijing 100037; tel. (10) 68326641; telex 22475; fax (10) 68326642; f. 1952; books in 20 foreign languages reflecting political and economic developments in People's Republic of China and features of Chinese culture; Dir GUO JIEXIN; Editor-in-Chief XU MINGQIANG.

Gaodeng Jiaoyu Chubanshe (Higher Education Press): 55 Shatan Houjie, Beijing 100009; tel. (10) 64014043; fax (10) 64054602; e-mail linm@public.bta.net.cn; f. 1954; academic, textbooks; Pres. and Editor-in-Chief YU GUOHUA.

Gongren Chubanshe (Workers' Publishing House): Liupukeng, Andingmen Wai, Beijing; tel. (10) 64215278; f. 1949; labour movement, trade unions, science and technology related to industrial production.

Guangdong Keji Chubanshe (Guangdong Science and Technology Press): 11 Shuiyin Lu, Huanshidong Lu, Guangzhou, Guangdong 510075; tel. (20) 87768688; telex 3934; fax (20) 87764169; f. 1978; natural sciences, technology, agriculture, medicine, computing, English language teaching; Dir OUYANG LIAN.

Heilongjiang Kexue Jishu Chubanshe: (Heilongjiang Science and Technology Press): 41 Jianshe Jie, Nangang Qu, Harbin 150001, Heilongjiang; tel. and fax (451) 3642127; f. 1979; industrial and agricultural technology, natural sciences, economics and management, popular science, children's and general.

Huashan Wenyi Chubanshe (Huashan Literature and Art Publishing House): 45 Bei Malu, Shijiazhuang, Hebei; tel. 22501; f. 1982; novels, poetry, drama, etc.

Kexue Chubanshe (Science Press): 16 Donghuangchenggen Beijie, Beijing 100717; tel. (10) 64010642; fax (10) 64020094; f. 1954; books and journals on science and technology.

Lingnan Meishu Chubanshe (Lingnan Art Publishing House): 11 Shuiyin Lu, Guangzhou, Guangdong 510075; tel. 87771044; fax 87771049; f. 1981; works on classical and modern painting, picture albums, photographic, painting techniques; Pres. CAO LIXIANG.

Minzu Chubanshe (Nationalities Publishing House): 14 Hepingli Beijie, Beijing 100013; tel. (10) 64211261; f. 1953; books and periodicals in minority languages, e.g. Mongolian, Tibetan, Uygur, Korean, Kazakh, etc.; Editor-in-Chief ZHU YINGWU.

Qunzhong Chubanshe (Masses Publishing House): Bldg 15, Part 3, Fangxingyuan, Fangzhuan Lu, Beijing 100078; tel. (10) 67633344; f. 1956; politics, law, judicial affairs, criminology, public security, etc.

Renmin Chubanshe (People's Publishing House): Dir and Editor-in-Chief XUE DEZHEN.

Renmin Jiaoyu Chubanshe (People's Education Press): 55 Sha Tan Hou Jie, Beijing 100009; tel. (10) 64035745; fax (10) 64010370; f. 1950; school textbooks, guidebooks, teaching materials, etc.

Renmin Meishu Chubanshe (People's Fine Arts Publishing House): 32 Beizongbu Hutong, Beijing 100735; tel. (10) 65122371; fax (10) 65122370; f. 1951; works by Chinese and foreign painters, sculptors and other artists, picture albums, photographic, painting techniques; Dir CHEN YUNHE; Editor-in-Chief LIU YUSHAN.

Renmin Weisheng Chubanshe (People's Medical Publishing House): 10 Tian Tan Xi Li, Beijing 100050; tel. (10) 67015802; fax (10) 67025429; f. 1953; medicine (Western and traditional Chinese), pharmacology, dentistry, public health; Pres. LIU YIQING.

Renmin Wenxue Chubanshe (People's Literature Publishing House): 166 Chaoyangmen Nei Dajie, Beijing 100705; tel. (10) 65138394; telex 2192; f. 1951; largest publr of literary works and translations into Chinese; Dir and Editor-in-Chief CHEN ZAOCHUN.

Shanghai Guji Chubanshe (Shanghai Classics Publishing House): 272 Ruijin Erlu, Shanghai 200020; tel. (21) 64370011; fax (21) 64339287; f. 1956; classical Chinese literature, history, philosophy, geography, linguistics, science and technology.

Shanghai Jiaoyu Chubanshe (Shanghai Educational Publishing House): 123 Yongfu Lu, Shanghai 200031; tel. (21) 64377165; telex 3413; fax (21) 64339995; f. 1958; academic; Dir and Editor-in-Chief CHEN HE.

Shanghai Yiwen Chubanshe (Shanghai Translation Publishing House): 14 Xiang 955, Yanan Zhonglu, Shanghai 200040; tel. (21) 62472890; fax (21) 62475100; f. 1978; translations of foreign classic and modern literature; philosophy, social sciences, dictionaries, etc.

Shangwu Yinshuguan (Commercial Publishing House): 36 Wangfujing Dajie, Beijing; tel. (10) 65252026; f. 1897; dictionaries and reference books in Chinese and foreign languages, translations of foreign works on social sciences; Pres. YANG DEYAN.

Shaonian Ertong Chubanshe (Juvenile and Children's Publishing House): 1538 Yan An Xi Lu, Shanghai 200052; tel. (21) 62823025; telex 5801; fax (21) 62821726; f. 1952; children's educational and literary works, teaching aids and periodicals; Gen. Man. ZHOU SHUIPEI.

Shijie Wenhua Chubanshe (World Culture Publishing House): Dir ZHU LIE.

Wenwu Chubanshe (Cultural Relics Publishing House): 29 Wusi Dajie, Beijing 100009; tel. (10) 64048057; fax (10) 64010698; f. 1956; books and catalogues of Chinese relics in museums and those recently discovered; Dir YANG JIN.

Wuhan Daxue Chubanshe (Wuhan University Press): Suojia Hill, Wuhan, Hubei; tel. (27) 7820651; fax (27) 7812661; f. 1981; reference books, academic works, etc.; Pres. and Editor-in-Chief Prof. NIU TAICHEN.

Xiandai Chubanshe (Modern Press): 504 Anhua Li, Andingmenwai, Beijing 100011; tel. (10) 64263515; telex 210215; fax (10) 64214540; f. 1981; directories, reference books, etc.; Dir ZHOU HONGLI.

Xinhua Chubanshe (Xinhua Publishing House): 57 Xuanwumen Xidajie, Beijing 100803; tel. (10) 63073885; telex 22316; fax (10) 63073880; f. 1979; social sciences, economy, politics, history, geography, directories, dictionaries, etc.; Dir and Editor-in-Chief QIU YUNSHENG.

Xuelin Chubanshe (Scholar Books Publishing House): 120 Wenmiao Lu, Shanghai 200010; tel. and fax (21) 63768540; f. 1981; academic, including personal academic works at authors' own expense; Dir LEI QUNMING.

Zhongguo Caizheng Jingji Chubanshe (China Financial and Economic Publishing House): 8 Dafosi Dongjie, Dongcheng Qu, Beijing; tel. (10) 64011805; f. 1961; finance, economics, commerce and accounting.

Zhongguo Dabaike Quanshu Chubanshe (Encyclopaedia of China Publishing House): 17 Fu Cheng Men Bei Dajie, Beijing 100037; tel. (10) 68315610; fax (10) 68316510; f. 1978; specializes in encyclopaedias; Dir SHAN JIFU.

Zhongguo Ditu Chubanshe (China Cartographic Publishing House): 3 Baizhifang Xijie, Beijing 100054; tel. and fax (10) 63014136; f. 1954; cartographic publr; Dir ZHANG XUELIANG.

Zhongguo Funü Chubanshe (China Women Publishing House): 24A Shijia Hutong, 100010 Beijing; tel. (10) 65126986; f. 1981; women's movement, marriage and family, child-care, etc.; Dir LI ZHONGXIU.

Zhongguo Qingnian Chubanshe (China Youth Press): 21 Dongsi Shiertiao, Beijing 100708; tel. (10) 64032266; telex 4357; fax (10) 64031803; e-mail cyph@eastnet.co.cn; f. 1950; literature, social and natural sciences, youth work, autobiography; also periodicals; Editor-in-Chief CHEN HAOZENG.

Zhongguo Shehui Kexue Chubanshe (China Social Sciences Publishing House): 158A Gulou Xidajie, Beijing 100720; tel. (10) 64073837; telex 1531; fax (10) 64074509; f. 1978; Dir ZHENG WENLIN.

Zhongguo Xiju Chubanshe (China Theatrical Publishing House): 52 Dongsi Batiao Hutong, Beijing; tel. (10) 64015815; telex 0489; f. 1957; traditional and modern Chinese drama.

Zhongguo Youyi Chubanshe (China Friendship Publishing House): Pres. DONG WEIKANG.

Zhonghua Shuju (Chung Hwa Book Co): 36 Wangfujing Dajie, Beijing; tel. (10) 6554504; f. 1912; general; Pres. DENG JINGYUAN.

PUBLISHERS' ASSOCIATION

Publishers' Association of China: Beijing; f. 1979; arranges academic exchanges with foreign publrs; Chair. SONG MUWEN; Sec.-Gen. FANG ZHENJIANG.

Broadcasting and Communications

TELECOMMUNICATIONS

Ministry of Posts and Telecommunications: 13 Xichangan Jie, Beijing 100716; tel. (10) 66014249; telex 222187; fax (10) 62016362; regulates all issues concerning the telecommunications sector.

China Telecom: f. 1997 as a vehicle for foreign investment in telecommunications sector; operating division of the Ministry of Posts and Telecommunications.

China United Telecommunications Corpn (UNICOM): Huibin Bldg, Yayun Village, Beijing; tel. (10) 64934151; fax (10) 64934153; f. 1994; Chair. ZHAO WEICHEN; Pres. LI HUIFEN.

BROADCASTING

At the end of 1996 there were 1,244 radio broadcasting stations, 746 medium- and short-wave radio transmitting and relay stations (covering 84.2% of the population), 880 television stations and 1,245 television transmitting and relay stations with a capacity of over 1,000 watts (covering 86.2% of the population).

Ministry of Radio, Film and Television: 2 Fu Xing Men Wai Dajie, POB 4501, Beijing 100866; tel. (10) 66093114; telex 22236; fax (10) 68512174; controls the Central People's Broadcasting Station, the Central TV Station, Radio Beijing, China Record Co., Beijing Broadcasting Institute, Broadcasting Research Institute, the China Broadcasting Art Troupe, etc.

Radio

China National Radio (CNR): 2 Fu Xing Men Wai Dajie, Beijing 100866; f. 1945; domestic service in Chinese, Zang Wen (Tibetan), Min Nan Hua (Amoy), Ke Jia (Hakka), Hasaka (Kazakh), Wei Wuer (Uygur), Menggu Hua (Mongolian) and Chaoxian (Korean); Dir TONG XIANGRONG.

China Radio International (CRI): 16A Shijingshan Jie, Beijing 100039; tel. (10) 68891297; telex 222271; fax (10) 68891582; e-mail crieng@public.bta.net.cn; f. 1941; fmrly Radio Beijing; foreign service in 38 languages incl. Arabic, Burmese, Czech, English, Esperanto, French, German, Indonesian, Italian, Japanese, Lao, Polish, Portuguese, Russian, Spanish, Turkish and Vietnamese; Dir ZHANG ZHENHUA.

Television

China Central Television (CCTV): Bureau of Broadcasting Affairs of the State Council, Beijing; f. 1958; operates eight networks; 24-hour global satellite service commenced in 1996; Dir AN JINGLIN.

In April 1994 foreign companies were prohibited from establishing or operating cable TV stations in China. By mid-1996 there were more than 3,000 cable television stations in operation, with networks covering 45m. households. The largest subscriber service is Beijing Cable TV (Dir GUO JUNJIN). Satellite services are available in some areas, and by 1993 millions of satellite receivers were in use. In October of that year the Government approved new regulations, attempting to restrict access to foreign satellite broadcasts.

Finance

(cap. = capital; auth. = authorized; p.u. = paid up; res = reserves; dep. = deposits; m. = million; amounts in yuan unless otherwise stated)

BANKING

Radical economic reforms, introduced in 1994, included the strengthening of the role of the central bank and the establishment of new commercial banks. The Commercial Bank Law took effect in July 1995. The establishment of private banks was to be permitted.

Central Bank

People's Bank of China: Sanlihe Lu, Xicheng Qu, Beijing 100800; tel. (10) 66015522; telex 22612; fax (10) 66016704; f. 1948; bank of issue; decides and implements China's monetary policies; Gov. DAI XIANGLONG; 2,204 brs.

Other Banks

Agricultural Bank of China: 23 Fuxing Lu, Beijing 100036; tel. (10) 68475321; telex 22017; fax (10) 68297160; f. 1951; serves mainly China's rural financial operations, providing services for agriculture, industry, commerce, transport, etc. in rural areas; cap. 35,926m., res 2,915m., dep. 901,905m. (Dec. 1995); Pres. SHI JILIANG; 2,500 brs.

Agricultural Development Bank of China: 23A Dong Jiao Min Xiang, Dongcheng Qu, Beijing 100006; tel. (10) 65243311; fax (10) 65235059; cap. 20,000m.; Pres. ZHU YUANLIANG.

Bank of China: Bank of China Bldg, 410 Fu Cheng Men Nei Dajie, Beijing 100818; tel. (10) 66016688; telex 22254; fax (10) 66016869; f. 1912; handles foreign exchange and international settlements; cap. p.u. 52,000m., res 46,953m., dep. 1,887,432m. (Dec. 1996); Chair. WANG XUEBING; 3,136 brs.

Bank of Communications Ltd: 18 Xian Xia Lu, Shanghai 200335; tel. (21) 62751234; telex 337340; fax (21) 62752191; f. 1908; commercial bank; cap. 11,391m., res 6,616m., dep. 368,584m. (Dec. 1996); Chair. PAN QICHANG; Pres. WANG MINGQUAN; 90 brs.

Beijing City United Bank: 65 You An Men Nei Lu, Xuanwu Qu, Beijing 100054; tel. and fax (10) 63518301; f. 1996; cap. 1,000m., res 3,466m., dep. 26,660m. (Dec. 1996); 90 brs.

China and South Sea Bank Ltd: 17 Xi Jiao Min Xiang, Beijing 100031; tel. (10) 68317711; f. 1921; cap. 1,200m., res 2,616m., dep. 32,463m. (Dec. 1995); Chair. CUI PING.

China Construction Bank (CCB): 12C Fuxing Lu, Beijing 100810; tel. (10) 68527351; telex 222977; fax (10) 68527344; f. 1954; fmrly People's Construction Bank of China; makes payments for capital construction projects in accordance with state plans and budgets; issues medium- and long-term loans to enterprises and short-term loans to construction enterprises and others; also handles foreign exchange business; cap. 35,438m., res 9,113m., dep. 1,347,858m. (Dec. 1996); Pres. WANG QISHAN; 49 brs.

China International Capital Corporation (CICC): C12 Fuxing Lu, Beijing 100810; tel. (10) 66068401; f. 1995; international investment bank; 42.5% owned by People's Construction Bank of China; registered cap. US $100m.; CEO EDWIN LIM.

China International Trust and Investment Corporation (CITIC): Capital Mansion, 6 Xianyuannan Lu, Chao Yang Qu, Beijing 100004; tel. (10) 64660088; telex 210026; fax (10) 64661186; f. 1979; economic and technological co-operation; finance, banking, investment and trade; registered cap. 3,000m.; Chair. WANG JUN; Pres. QIN XIAO.

China Investment Bank: 88 Xuanwumenwai Jie, Xuanwu Qu, Beijing 100052; tel. (10) 63031599; telex 22537; fax (10) 63031944; f. 1981; cap. 1,500m.; specializes in raising foreign funds for domestic investment and credit; Chair. WANG QISHAN; Pres. LIU DAWEI.

China Merchants Bank: 2 Shennan Lu, Shenzhen 518001; tel. (755) 2243888; telex 420034; fax (755) 2243666; f. 1987; cap. 1,123m., res 2,075m., dep. 56,626m. (Dec. 1995); Chair. LIU SONGJIN; Pres. WANG SHIZHEN; 8 brs.

China Minsheng Banking Corporation: 2nd Floor, Tower B, Vantone New World Plaza, 2 Fu Cheng Men, Xicheng Qu, Beijing; tel. (10) 68588440; telex 22418; fax (10) 68588570; first privately-funded bank, opened Jan. 1996; registered cap. 1,380m.; dep. 12,600m. (Sept. 1997); Chair. JING SHUPING; Pres. CAI LULUN.

China State Bank Ltd: 17 Xi Jiao Min Xiang, Beijing 100031; f. 1927; cap. 1,100m., res 2,642m., dep. 31,699m. (Dec. 1995); Gen. Man. LI PINZHOU.

Chinese Mercantile Bank: Ground and 23rd Floors, Dongfeng Bldg, 2 Yannan Lu, Futian Qu, Shenzhen 518031; tel. (755) 3257880; fax (755) 3257801; f. 1993; cap. US $34.5m., res US $1.2m., dep. US $384.7m. (Dec. 1996); Pres. HUANG MINGXIANG.

CITIC Industrial Bank: 1-3F, Capital Mansion, 6 Xianyuannan Lu, Chao Yang Qu, Beijing 100027; f. 1987; tel. (10) 64661058; telex 210716; fax (10) 64661061; cap. 3,938m., res 30.5m., dep. 67,881m. (Dec. 1995); Chair. HONG YUNCHENG; Pres. DOU JIANZHONG; 17 brs.

Everbright Bank of China: Everbright Tower, 6 Fu Xing Men Wai Lu, Beijing 100045; tel. (10) 68565577; telex 221115; fax (10) 68561260; e-mail EBBC@public.bta.net.cn; f. 1992; cap. 5,000m., res 826m., dep. 32,700m. (Dec. 1996); Chair. and Pres. ZHU XIAOHUA; 13 brs.

Export and Import Bank of China: Beijing; tel. (10) 67626688; fax (10) 67638940; f. 1994; provides trade credits for export of large machinery, electronics, ships, etc.; Chair. DONG ZHIGUANG; Pres. LEI ZUHUA.

Fujian Asia Bank Ltd: 2nd Floor, Yuan Hong Bldg, 32 Wuyi Lu, Fuzhou, Fujian 350005; tel. (591) 3330788; telex 924888; fax (591) 7820301; f. 1993; cap. US $25.0m., res US $257,000, dep. US $15.6m. (Dec. 1995); Chair. SONG QIN; Gen. Man. DENNIS H. LAM.

Fujian Industrial Bank: Zhong Shan Bldg, 154 Hudong Lu, Fuzhou, Fujian 350003; tel. (591) 7844196; telex 92235; fax (591) 7841932; f. 1982; cap. 816.3m., res 771.4m., dep. 18,519.7m. (Dec. 1996); Pres. and Gen. Man. YUN CHEN; 10 brs.

Guangdong Development Bank: Guangdong Development Bank Centre, 83 Nonglinxia Lu, Guangzhou, Guangdong 510080; tel. (20) 87310888; telex 441086; fax (20) 87310779; f. 1988; cap. 1,698.8m., res 1,595.6m., dep. 45,170.9m. (Dec. 1995); Pres. LI RUOHONG; Chair. and Gen. Man. WU CHIXIN; 12 brs.

Guangdong (Kwangtung) Provincial Bank: 410 Fuchengmen Nei Dajie, Beijing 100818; f. 1924; cap. 1,500m., res 5,437m., dep. 75,216m. (Dec. 1996).

Hainan Development Bank: 7th Floor, Funan Bldg, 12 Binhai Dajie, Haikou, Hainan 570011; tel. (898) 6239063; f. 1995; commercial bank; registered cap. 1,677m.; Pres. REN JUNYIN.

Huaxia Bank: Changdongmen, Shijingshan Qu, Beijing 100041; tel. (10) 68294148; fax (10) 68293645; f. 1992 as part of Shougang Corpn; registered cap. 2,500m.; Chair. ZHANG YANLIN; Pres. LI XIKUI.

Industrial and Commercial Bank of China: 15 Cuiwei Lu, Haidian Qu, Beijing 100036; tel. (10) 68217601; telex 22770; fax (10) 68217920; f. 1984; handles industrial and commercial credits and international business; cap. 86,024m., res 4,288m., dep. 1,900,885m. (Dec. 1996); Chair. and Pres. LIU TINGHUAN; 138 brs.

International Bank of Paris and Shanghai: 93 Guangdong Lu, Shanghai 200002; tel. (21) 63217518; telex 33318; fax (21) 63216968; f. 1992; cap. US $30m., res US $522,009, dep. US $61m. (Dec. 1995); Chair. and Dir SHEN RUOLEI.

Kincheng Banking Corporation: 17 Xi Jiao Min Xiang, Beijing 100031; tel. (10) 68317711; fax (10) 66014030; f. 1917; cap. 2,200m., res 5,146m., dep. 66,133m. (Dec. 1996); Chair. ZHANG GUOWEN.

National Commercial Bank Ltd: 410 Fu Cheng Men Nei Da Jie, Beijing; f. 1907; cap. 1,200m., res 3,750m., dep. 40,592m. (Dec. 1996).

Qingdao International Bank: 117 Yan'an San Lu, Qingdao, Shandong 266071; tel. (532) 3870921; telex 321351; fax (532) 3870306; f. 1996; joint venture between Industrial and Commercial Bank of China and Korea First Bank; cap. 900m.; Pres. DUCK SUNG YUN.

Shanghai Pudong Development Bank: 50 Ningbo Lu, Shanghai 200002; tel. (21) 63296188; telex 337139; fax (21) 63232036; f. 1993; cap. 200m., total assets 75,000m. (Dec. 1996); Pres. JIN YUN.

Shenzhen Development Bank Co Ltd: Shenzhen Development Bank Bldg, 178 Shennan Zhong Lu, Shenzhen 518010; tel. (755) 2081069; fax (755) 2081031; f. 1987; cap. 1,000m., res 550m., dep. 22,800m. (Dec. 1996); Pres. ZHOU LIN.

Sin Hua Bank Ltd: 17 Xi Jiao Min Xiang, Beijing 100031; subsidiary of Bank of China; cap. 2,200m., res 6,482m., dep. 76,103m. (Dec. 1996); Chair. JIANG ZU QI.

State Development Bank (SDB): 40 Fucheng Lu, Haidian Qu, Beijing 100046; tel. (10) 68473229; fax (10) 68472977; f. 1994; handles low-interest loans for infrastructural projects and basic industries; Pres. YAO ZHENYAN.

Xiamen International Bank: 10 Hu Bin Bei Lu, Xiamen, Fujian 361012; tel. (592) 5310686; telex 93062; fax (592) 5310685; e-mail xib@public.xm.fj.cn; f. 1985; cap. HK $620m., res HK $346m., dep. HK $7,094m. (Dec. 1996); Chair. WANG ZIYING.

Yien Yieh Commercial Bank Ltd: 17 Xi Jiao Min Xiang, Beijing 100031; f. 1915; cap. 800m., res 3,228m., dep. 34,976m. (Dec. 1996); Gen. Man. WU GUO RUI; 27 brs.

Zhejiang Commercial Bank Ltd: 88 Xi Zhongshan Lu, Ningbo 315010; tel. (574) 7245060; telex 37005; fax (574) 7245409; f. 1993; cap. US $40m., dep. US $79m. (Dec. 1996); Pres. HUANG KAIJIAN; Chair. SHEN SONGJUN.

Zhongxin Shiye Bank is a nation-wide commercial bank. Other commercial banks include the Fujian Commercial Bank, Zhaoshang Bank, Bengbu Housing Deposit Bank and Yantai Housing Deposit Bank.

Foreign Banks

By the end of 1995 a total of 120 branches of foreign banks had been established in various Chinese cities. In Beijing representative offices only were permitted until mid-1995 (when the Bank of Tokyo became the first foreign bank to establish a full branch in the capital). In March 1997 foreign banks were allowed for the first time to conduct business in yuan. Representative offices totalled 519 in December 1996.

STOCK EXCHANGES

Several stock exchanges were in the process of development in the mid-1990s, and by early 1995 the number of shareholders had reached 38m. By 1995 a total of 15 futures exchanges were in operation, dealing in various commodities, building materials and currencies. By the end of 1996 the number of companies listed on the Shanghai and Shenzhen Stock Exchanges had reached 540. In August 1997, in response to unruly conditions, the Government ordered the China Securities Regulatory Commission (see below) to assume direct control of the Shanghai and Shenzhen exchanges.

Stock Exchange Executive Council (SEEC): Tongguang Jindu Office Bldg, Beijing 100026; tel. (10) 64935210; f. 1989 to oversee the development of financial markets in China; mems comprise leading non-bank financial institutions authorized to handle securities; Vice-Pres. WANG BOMING.

Securities Association of China (SAC): Olympic Hotel, 52 Baishiqiao Lu, Beijing 100081; tel. (10) 68316688; fax (10) 68318390; f. 1991; non-governmental organization comprising 122 mems (stock exchanges and securities cos) and 35 individual mems; Pres. GUO ZHENQIAN.

Beijing Securities Exchange: 5 Anding Lu, Chao Yang Qu, Beijing 100029; tel. (10) 64939366; fax (10) 64936233.

Shanghai Stock Exchange: 15 Huangpu Lu, Shanghai 200080; f. 1990; tel. (21) 63063195; fax (21) 63063076; Chair. GONG HAOCHENG; Pres. TU GUANGSHAO.

Shenzhen Stock Exchange: 15/F, International Trust and Investments Bldg, Hongling Zhong Lu, Shenzhen, Guangdong 518005; tel. and fax (755) 5594074; telex 420592; f. 1991; Chair. LUO XIANRONG.

Regulatory Authorities

Operations are regulated by the State Council Securities Policy Committee and by the following:

China Securities Regulatory Commission (CSRC): Bldg 3, Area 3, Fangqunyuan, Fangzhuang, Beijing 100078; tel. (10) 67617343; fax (10) 67653117; f. 1993; Chair. ZHOU ZHENGQING; Sec.-Gen. ZHU LIN.

INSURANCE

A new Insurance Law, formulated to standardize activities and to strengthen the supervision and administration of the industry, took effect in October 1995. Changes included the separation of life insurance and property insurance businesses. By late 1996 the number of insurance companies totalled 25. Total premiums rose from 44,000m. yuan in 1994 to 55,600m. yuan in 1995. In 1996 life insurance premiums alone reached 33,000m. yuan, an increase of 70% compared with the previous year.

China Insurance Co Ltd: 22 Xi Jiao Min Xiang, POB 20, Beijing 100032; tel. (10) 6654231; telex 22102; fax (10) 66011869; f. 1931; cargo, hull, freight, fire, life, personal accident, industrial injury, motor insurance, reinsurance, etc.; Man. SONG GUO HUA.

China Insurance Group: 410 Fu Cheng Men Nei Dajie, Beijing; tel. (10) 66016688; telex 22102; fax (10) 66011869; f. 1996 (fmrly People's Insurance Co of China (PICC), f. 1949); hull, marine cargo, aviation, motor, life, fire, accident, liability and reinsurance, etc.; in process of division into three subsidiaries (life insurance (China Life Insurance Co—CLIC), property-casualty insurance and reinsurance) by mid-1996, in preparation for transformation into joint-stock cos; registered cap. 20,000m., res 1,029,000m.; Chair. and Pres. MA YONGWEI.

China Pacific Insurance Co Ltd (CPIC): Hengshan Hotel, 534 Hengshan Lu, Shanghai 200001; tel. (21) 84377050; telex 33207; fax (21) 84339259; f. 1991; joint-stock co; registered cap. 1,000m.; Chair. WANG MINGQUAN; Pres. LIN ZHONGJIE.

China Ping An Insurance Co: 2/F, Citic Bldg, 7 Hong Ling Zhong Lu, Shenzhen; tel. (755) 5564232; fax (755) 5564225; f. 1988.

Hua Tai Property Insurance Co Ltd: Everbright Bldg, 6 Fuwai Dajie, Beijing 100045; tel. (10) 68565588; fax (10) 68561750; f. 1996 by 63 industrial cos.

Tai Ping Insurance Co Ltd: 410 Fu Cheng Men Nei Dajie, Beijing 100034; tel. (10) 66016688; telex 42001; fax (10) 66011869; marine freight, hull, cargo, fire, personal accident, industrial injury, motor insurance, reinsurance, etc.; Pres. SUN XIYUE.

Taikang Life Insurance Co Ltd: Beijing; f. 1996; Chair. CHEN DONGSHENG.

Joint-stock companies include the Xinhua (New China) Life Insurance Co Ltd (Gen. Man. SUN BING). By October 1995 a total of 77 foreign insurance companies had established 119 offices in China, being permitted to operate in Shanghai and Guangzhou only.

Trade and Industry

GOVERNMENT AGENCIES

China Council for the Promotion of International Trade (CCPIT): 1 Fu Xing Men Wai Jie, Beijing 100860; tel. (10) 68513344; telex 22315; fax (10) 68511370; e-mail ccpiteid@netchina.co.cn; f. 1952; encourages foreign trade and economic co-operation; sponsors and arranges Chinese exhbns abroad and foreign exhbns in China; helps foreigners to apply for patent rights and trade-mark registration in China; promotes foreign investment and organizes tech. exchanges with other countries; provides legal services; publishes trade periodicals; Chair. YU XIAOSONG: Sec.-Gen. ZHONG MIN.

Chinese General Association of Light Industry: B22 Fuwai Dajie, Beijing 100833; tel. (10) 68396114; under supervision of State Council; Chair. YU CHEN.

Chinese General Association of Textile Industry: 12 Dong Chang An Jie, Beijing 100742; tel. (10) 65129545; under supervision of State Council; Chair. WU WENYING.

Ministry of Foreign Trade and Economic Co-operation: (see under Ministries).

State Administration for Industry and Commerce: 8 Sanlihe Dong Lu, Xichengqu, Beijing 100820; tel. (10) 68010463; telex 222431; fax (10) 68020843; responsible for market supervision and administrative execution of industrial and commercial laws; functions under the direct supervision of the State Council; Dir WANG ZHONGFU.

CHAMBERS OF COMMERCE

All-China Federation of Industry and Commerce: 93 Beiheyan Dajie, Beijing 100006; tel. (10) 65136677; fax (10) 65122631; f. 1953; promotes overseas trade relations; Chair. JING SHUPING; Sec.-Gen. HUAN YUSHAN.

China Chamber of International Commerce—Shanghai: 14/F New Town Mansion, 55 Loushanguan Lu, Shanghai 200335; tel. (21) 62757178; fax (21) 62756364.

China Chamber of International Commerce—Zhuhai: 127 Xinguangli, Zhuhai, Guangdong 519000; tel. (756) 2218954; fax (756) 2228640.

TRADE AND INDUSTRIAL ORGANIZATIONS

Anshan Iron and Steel Co: Angang Daibailou, Anshan, Liaoning Province; tel. (412) 6724947; Pres. LIU JIE.

Aviation Industries of China: 67 Nan Dajie, Jiaodaokou, Beijing; tel. (10) 64013322; telex 211244; fax (10) 64013648; Pres. ZHU YULI.

Baoshan Iron and Steel Complex Corpn (Group): 2 Mundangjiang Lu, Shanghai 201900; tel. (21) 5646944; telex 33901; fax (21) 56600260; registered cap. 100m. yuan; Chair. LI MING; Pres. XIE QIHUA.

Baotou Iron and Steel Co: Baogangchang Qu, Baotou, Inner Mongolia; tel. (472) 2183450; fax (472) 2183708; Pres. ZENG GOAN.

China Aviation Supplies Corpn: 155 Xi Dongsi Jie, Beijing 100013; tel. (10) 64012233; telex 22101; fax (10) 64016392; f.1980; Pres. LIU YUANFAN.

China Civil Engineering Construction Corpn (CCECC): 4 Beifeng Wo, Haidian Qu, Beijing 100038; tel. (10) 63263392; telex 22471; fax (10) 63263864; f. 1953; Pres. WANG GUOQING.

China Construction International Inc: 9 Sanlihe Lu, Haidian Qu, Beijing; tel. (10) 68394086; fax (10) 68394097; Pres. FU RENZHANG.

China Electronics Corpn: 27 Wanshou Lu, Beijing 100005; tel. (10) 68212233; fax (10) 68213745; Pres. YU ZHONGYU.

China Gold Co: Anwaiqingnianhu, Beijing; tel. (10) 64214831; Pres. CUI LAN.

China Great Wall Computer Group: 48 Baishiqiao Lu, Haidian Qu, Beijing 100081; tel. (10) 68342714; fax (10) 68316065; Pres. LU MING.

China Great Wall Industry Corpn: 30 Haidian Nanlu, Beijing 100080; tel. (10) 68748810; telex 22651; fax (10) 68748865; e-mail cgwic@cgwic.com; registered cap. 200m. yuan; Pres. ZHANG TONG.

China International Book Trading Corpn: (see under Publishers).

China International Futures Trading Corpn: 24/F Capital Mansion, 6 Xinyuan Nan Lu, Chao Yang Qu, Beijing 100004; tel. (10) 64665388; telex 210747; fax (10) 64665140; Chair. TIAN YUAN; Pres. LU JIAN.

China International Telecommunications Construction Corpn (CITCC): 22 Yuyou Lane, Xicheng Qu, Beijing; tel. (10) 66012244; telex 22080; fax (10) 6024103; Pres. QI FUSHENG.

China National Aerotechnology Import and Export Corpn: 5 Liangguochang Dongcheng Qu, Beijing 100010; tel. (10) 64017722; telex 22318; fax (10) 64015381; f.1952; exports signal flares, electric detonators, tachometers, parachutes, general purpose aircraft, etc.; Pres. YANG CHUNSHU; Gen. Man. LIU GUOMIN.

China National Animal Breeding Stock Import and Export Corpn (CABS): 10 Yangyi Hutong Jia, Dongdan, Beijing 100005; tel. (10) 65131107; fax (10) 65128694; sole agency for import and export of stud animals including cattle, sheep, goats, swine, horses, donkeys, camels, rabbits, poultry, etc., as well as pasture and turf grass seeds, feed additives, medicines, etc.; Pres. YANG CHENGSHAN.

China National Arts and Crafts Import and Export Corpn: Jingxin Bldg 2A, Dong San Huan Bei Lu, Beijing 100027; tel. (10) 64663366; telex 210641; fax (10) 64661821; deals in jewellery, ceramics, handicrafts, embroidery, pottery, wicker, bamboo, etc.; Pres. LIU PEIJIN.

China National Automotive Industry Corpn: 46 Fucheng Lu, Haidian Qu, Beijing; tel. (10) 68127146; fax (10) 68125556; Pres. GU YAOTIAN.

China National Automotive Industry Import and Export Corpn (CAIEC): 5 Beisihuan Xilu, Beijing 100083; tel. (10) 62310650; fax (10) 62310688; e-mail caiechcn@public3.bta.net.cn; sales US $540m. (1995); Pres. CHEN XULIN; 1,100 employees.

China National Cereals, Oils and Foodstuffs Import and Export Corpn: 7th–13th Floors, Tower A, COFCO Plaza, No. 8, Jian Guo Men Wai Dajie, Beijing 100005; tel. (10) 65268888; telex 210238; fax (10) 65278612; imports and exports rice, cereals, pulses, sugar, vegetable oils and oil-seeds, meat, poultry, live animals, fresh fruit, vegetables and dairy produce, wines and spirits, canned foods and aquatic products, etc.; Pres. ZHOU MINGCHEN.

China National Chartering Corpn (SINOCHART): Rm 1306/1307, Jiu Ling Bldg, 21 Xisanhuan Bei Lu, Beijing 100081; tel. (10) 68405375; telex 222508; fax (10) 68405398; e-mail sinochrt@public.intercom.co.cn; f. 1950; functions under Ministry of Foreign Trade and Economic Co-operation; subsidiary of SINOTRANS (see below); arranges chartering of ships, reservation of space, managing and operating chartered vessels; Pres. LE TIANXIANG; Gen. Man. ZHANG JIANWEI.

China National Chemical Construction Corpn: 16-7 Hepingli, Beijing 100013; tel. (10) 64212961; telex 22492; fax (10) 64215982; registered cap. 50m.; Pres. CHEN LIHUA.

China National Chemicals Import and Export Corpn (SINOCHEM): Beijing; tel. (10) 65002010; telex 22243; fax (10) 65001534; deals in rubber products, crude petroleum, petroleum products, chemicals, etc.; Pres. ZHENG DUNXUN.

China National Coal Industry Import and Export Corpn (CNCIEC): 8 Xiaguangli, Chao Yang Qu, Beijing 100016; tel. (10) 64678866; telex 211273; fax (10) 64677038; f. 1982; sales US $800m. (1992); imports and exports coal and tech. equipment for coal industry, joint coal development and compensation trade; Chair. WEI GUOFU; Pres. JING TIANLIANG.

China National Coal Mine Corpn: 21 Bei Jie, Heipingli, Beijing 100013; tel. (10) 64217766; telex 2102877; Pres. WANG SENHAO.

China National Complete Plant Import and Export Corpn (Group): 28 Donghouxiang, Andingmenwai, Beijing; tel. (10) 64251029; fax (10) 64211382; Chair. BAI YUNLONG; Pres. ZHU JIMING.

China National Electronics Import and Export Corpn: A-23 Fuxing Lu, Beijing 100036; tel. (10) 68219550; telex 22475; fax (10) 68223916; e-mail ceiechq@ceiec.com.cn; imports and exports electronics equipment, light industrial products, ferrous and non-ferrous metals; advertising; consultancy; Pres. and CEO QIAN BENYUAN.

China National Export Bases Development Corpn: Bldg 16–17, District 3, Fang Xing Yuan, Fang Zhuang Xiaoqu, Fengtai Qu, Beijing 100078; tel. (10) 67628899; telex 22787; fax (10) 67019518; Pres. XUE ZHAO.

China National Foreign Trade Transportation Corpn (SINOTRANS): 21 Xisanhuan Bei Lu, Beijing 100081; tel. (10) 68415304; telex 22867; fax (10) 68405402; f. 1950; functions under Ministry of Foreign Trade and Economic Co-operation; agents for Ministry's import and export corpns; arranges customs clearance, deliveries, forwarding and insurance for sea, land and air transportation; registered cap. 150m. yuan; Pres. WU BINGZE.

China National Garments Corpn: A-9, Beisanhuandong Lu, Chaoyang Qu, Beijing 100028; tel. (10) 64215186; fax (10) 64239134; Pres. JIANG HENGJIE.

China National Import and Export Commodities Inspection Corpn: 12 Jian Guo Men Wai Jie, Beijing 100022; tel. (10) 65062221; telex 210076; fax (10) 65004625; inspects, tests and surveys import and export commodities for overseas trade, transport, insurance and manufacturing firms; Pres. HU BAISEN.

China National Instruments Import and Export Corpn (CNIIEC): POB 2811, Erligou, Xijiao, Beijing 100044; tel. (10) 68317393; telex 22304; fax (10) 68315925; f. 1955; imports and exports computers, communication and broadcasting equipment, audio and video systems, scientific instruments, etc.; Pres. ZHANG HANCHEN.

China National Light Industrial Products Import and Export Corpn: 82 Donganmen Jie, Beijing 100747; tel. (10) 65133239; telex 210037; fax (10) 65123763; imports and exports household electrical appliances, audio equipment, photographic equipment, films, paper goods, building materials, bicycles, sewing machines, enamelware, glassware, stainless steel goods, footwear, leather goods, watches and clocks, cosmetics, stationery, sporting goods, etc.; Pres. XIONG YAOHUA.

China National Machine Tool Corpn: 19 Fang Jia Xiaoxiang, An Nei, Beijing 100007; tel. (10) 64033767; telex 210088; fax (10) 64015657; f. 1979; imports and exports machine tools and tool products, components and equipment; supplies apparatus for machine building industry; Pres. QUAN YILU.

China National Machinery and Equipment Import and Export Corpn/Group: 16 Fu Xing Men Wai Jie, Beijing 100045; tel. (10) 63268694; telex 22186; fax (10) 63261865; f. 1978; imports and exports machine tools, all kinds of machinery, automobiles, hoisting and transport equipment, electric motors, photographic equipment, etc.; Pres. XI JIACHENG.

China National Machinery Import and Export Corpn: Sichuan Mansion, West Wing, 1 Fu Xing Men Wai Jie, Beijing 100037; tel. (10) 68991188; telex 22328; fax (10) 68991000; f. 1950; imports and exports machine tools, diesel engines and boilers and all kinds of machinery; imports aeroplanes, ships, etc.; Pres. LIU DESHU.

China National Medicine and Health Products Import and Export Corpn: 18 Guangming Zhong Jie, Chongwen Qu, Beijing 100061; tel. (10) 67116688; fax (10) 671215791; Pres. LIU GUOSHENG.

China National Metallurgical Import and Export Corpn (CMIEC): 46 Dongsi Xidajie, Beijing 100711; tel. (10) 65153322; telex 22461; fax (10) 65123792; f. 1980; imports ores, spare parts, automation and control systems, etc.; exports metallurgical products, technology and equipment; establishes joint ventures and trade with foreign companies; Pres. HE LIN.

China National Metals and Minerals Import and Export Corpn: Bldg 15, Block 4, Anhuili, Chao Yang Qu, Beijing 100101; tel. (10) 64916666; telex 22190; fax (10) 68315079; f. 1950; principal imports and exports include steel, antimony, tungsten concentrates and ferrotungsten, zinc ingots, tin, mercury, pig iron, cement, etc.; Pres. ZHOU KEREN.

China National Native Produce and Animal By-Products Import and Export Corpn (TUHSU): 208 An Ding Men Wai Jie, Beijing 100011; tel. (10) 64204697; fax (10) 64204099; f. 1949; imports and exports include tea, coffee, cocoa, fibres, etc.; 13 subsidiary enterprises; 18 tea brs; 19 overseas subsidiaries; Pres. JI XINGYA.

China National Non-ferrous Metals Import and Export Corpn (CNIEC): 12B Fuxing Lu, Beijing 100814; tel. (10) 68514423; telex 22086; fax (10) 68515368; Chair. WU JIANCHANG; Pres. XU HANJING.

China National Non-Ferrous Metals Industry Corpn (CNNC): 12B Fuxing Lu, Beijing 100814; tel. (10) 68514477; telex 22086; fax (10) 68515360; Pres. WU JIANCHANG.

China National Nuclear Corpn: 1 Nansanxiang, Sanlihe, Beijing; tel. (10) 68512211; telex 22240; fax (10) 68512393; Pres. JIANG XINXIONG.

China National Offshore Oil Corpn (CNOOC): Jia 2, North Dongsanhuan Lu, Chao Yang Qu, Beijing 100027; tel. (10) 64663696; telex 210561; fax (10) 64662994; sales 2,039m.; Pres. WANG YAN.

China National Oil Development Corpn: Liupukang, Beijing 100006; tel. (10) 6444313; telex 22312; Pres. CHENG SHOULI.

China National Packaging Import and Export Corpn: Block B, Xingfu Bldg, 3 Dong San Huan Bei Lu, Chao Yang Qu, Beijing 100027; tel. (10) 64616361; telex 22490; fax (10) 64616437; handles import and export of packaging materials, containers, machines and tools; contracts for the processing and converting of packaging machines and materials using raw materials supplied by foreign customers; produces packing materials in 249 factories; registered cap. US $30m.; Pres. ZHENG CHONGXIANG.

China National Petro-Chemical Corpn (SINOPEC): Jia 6, Dong Huixin Lu, Chao Yang Qu, Beijing 100029; tel. (10) 64225533; telex 210625; fax (10) 64216972; f. 1983; under direct control of the State Council; petroleum refining, petrochemicals, synthetic fibres, etc.; 61 subordinate enterprises; approx. 500,000 employees; Pres. SHENG HUAREN.

China National Petroleum Corpn: Liupukang, Beijing 100724; tel. (10) 62015544; telex 22312; fax (10) 64212347; responsible for onshore resources; Pres. ZHOU YONGKANG.

China National Publications Import and Export Corpn: 16 Gongrentiyuguandong Lu, Chao Yang Qu, Beijing; tel. (10) 65066688; telex 22131; fax (10) 65063101; imports principally foreign books, newspapers and periodicals, records, etc., exports principally Chinese scientific and technical journals published in foreign languages; Pres. CHEN WEIJIANG.

China National Publishing Industry Trading Corpn: POB 782, 504 An Hua Li, An Ding Men Wai, Beijing 100011; tel. (10) 64210403; fax (10) 64214540; f. 1981; imports and exports publications, printing equipment technology; holds book fairs abroad; undertakes joint publication; Pres. ZHOU HONGLI.

China National Seed Corpn: 31 Min Feng Hu Tong, Xidan, Beijing 100032; tel. (10) 64201729; telex 22598; fax (10) 66014770; imports and exports crop seeds, including cereals, cotton, oil-bearing crops, teas, flowers and vegetables; seed production for foreign seed companies etc.; Pres. WANG JIANMIN.

China National Silk Import and Export Corpn: 105 Bei He Yan Jie, Dongcheng Qu, Beijing 100006; tel. (10) 65123338; telex 210594; fax (10) 65136838; Pres. CHEN YOUZHE.

China National Star Petroleum Corpn: Beijing; f. 1997; Pres. ZHU JIAZHEN.

China National Technical Import and Export Corpn: Jiuling Bldg, 21 Xisanhuaibei Lu, Beijing 100081; tel. (10) 68404123; telex 22244; fax (10) 68414877; f. 1952; imports all kinds of complete plant and equipment, acquires modern technology and expertise from abroad, undertakes co-production and jt-ventures, and technical consultation and updating of existing enterprises; registered cap. 200m.; Pres. TONG CHANGYIN.

China National Textiles Import and Export Corpn: 82 Donganmen Jie, Beijing 100747; tel. (10) 65136229; telex 22280; fax (10) 65124711; imports synthetic fibres, raw cotton, wool, garment accessories, etc.; exports cotton yarn, cotton fabric, knitwear, woven garments, etc.; Pres. WANG RUIXIANG.

China National Tobacco Corpn: 11 Hufang Lu, Beijing 100052; tel. (10) 63013399; telex 22015; fax (10) 63015331; Pres. XUN XINGHUA.

China National United Oil Corpn: 57 Wangfujing Jie, Dongcheng Qu, Beijing 100005; tel. (10) 65223825; fax (10) 65223817; Chair. SHENG HUAREN; Pres. JIANG YUNLONG.

China No. 1 Automobile Group: 63 Dongfeng Jie, Chao Yang Qu, Changchun, Jilin; tel. (431) 5003030; fax (431) 5001309; f. 1953; mfr of passenger cars; Gen. Man. GENG ZHAOJIE.

China North Industries Group: B12 Guang An Men Nan Jie, Beijing 100053; tel. (10) 63529988; telex 22339; fax (10) 63540398; exports mechanical products, light industrial products, chemical products, opto-electronic products, military products, etc.; Pres. ZHANG JUNJIU.

China Nuclear Energy Industry Corpn (CNEIC): A-1 Dongkou, Yuetan Jie, Beijing 100045; tel. (10) 68350384; telex 22240; fax (10) 68512393; exports air filters, vacuum valves, dosimeters, radioactive detection elements and optical instruments; Pres. ZHOU YANQUAN.

China Petro-Chemical International Co: Huibin Bldg, 8 Beichendong Lu, Chao Yang Qu, Beijing 100101; tel. (10) 64211052; telex 22655; fax (10) 64216972; f. 1983; registered cap. 120m.; Pres. YANG SHUSHAN.

China Road and Bridge Corpn: C88, An Ding Men Wai Dajie, Beijing 100011; tel. (10) 64285646; telex 22336; fax (10) 64285686; overseas and domestic building of highways, urban roads, bridges, tunnels, industrial and residential buildings, airport runways and parking areas; contracts to do all surveying, designing, pipe-laying, water supply and sewerage, building, etc., and/or to provide technical or labour services; Gen. Man. ZHOU JICHANG.

China Shipbuilding Trading Corpn Ltd: 10 Yue Tan Bei Xiao Jie, Beijing 100861; tel. (10) 68582560; telex 22029; fax (10) 68583380; Pres. LI JIAN.

China State Construction Engineering Corpn: Baiwanzhuang, Xicheng Qu, Beijing; tel. (10) 68327766; telex 22477; fax (10) 68314326; Pres. MA TINGGUI.

China State Shipbuilding Corpn: 5 Yuetan Beijie, Beijing; tel. (10) 68318833; telex 22029; fax (10) 68313380; Gen. Man. XU PENGHANG.

China Tea Import and Export Corpn: 82 Donganmen Jie, Beijing 100747; tel. (10) 65124785; fax (10) 65124775; Pres. LI JIAZHI.

China Xinshidai (New Era) Corpn: 40 Xie Zuo Hu Tong, Dongcheng Qu, Beijing 100007; tel. (10) 64017383; telex 22338; fax (10) 64032935; Pres. QIN ZHONGXING.

China Xinxing Corpn (Group): Wanshouluxijie, Beijing 100005; tel. (10) 68516688; telex 222938; fax (10) 68514669; Pres. ZHU ZUOMAN.

Chinese General Co of Astronautics Industry (State Aerospace Bureau): 8 Funcheng Lu, Haidian Qu, Beijing 100712; tel. (10) 68370699; fax (10) 68370043; Pres. LIU JIYUAN.

Daqing Petroleum Administration Bureau: Sartu Qu, Daqing, Heilongjiang; tel. (459) 814649; fax (459) 322845; Gen. Man. WANG ZHIWU.

Dongfeng Automobile Corpn: 1 Checheng Lu, Zhangwan Qu, Shiyan, Hubei; tel. (719) 226987; fax (719) 226815; f. 1969; mfr of trucks; Gen. Man. MA YUE.

Maanshan Iron and Steel Co: 8 Hongqizhong Lu, Maanshan, Anhui; tel. (555) 2883492; fax (555) 2324350; Chair. HANG YONGYI; Pres. LI ZONGBI.

Shanghai Automobile Industrial Corpn: 390 Wukang Lu, Shanghai; tel. (21) 64336892; fax (21) 64330518; Gen. Man. LU JIAN.

Shanghai Automobile Industry Sales Corpn: 548 Caoyang Lu, Shanghai; tel. and fax (21) 62443223; Gen. Man. XU JIANYU.

Shanghai Foreign Trade Corpn: 27 Zhongshan Dong Yi Lu, Shanghai 200002; tel. (21) 63217350; telex 33034; fax (21) 63290044; f. 1988; handles import-export trade, foreign trade transportation, chartering, export commodity packaging, storage and advertising for Shanghai municipality; Gen. Man. WANG MEIJUN.

Shanghai International Trust Trading Corpn: 521 Henan Lu, POB 002-066, Shanghai 200001; tel. (21) 63226650; telex 33627; fax (21) 63207412; f. 1979, present name adopted 1988; handles import and export business, international mail orders, processing, assembling, compensation trade etc.

Shougang Corpn: Shijingshan, Beijing 100088; tel. (10) 68291114; telex 22619; fax (10) 68293307; Chair. BI QUN; Gen. Man. LUO BINGSHENG.

Wuhan Iron and Steel (Group) Co: Qingshan Qu, Wuhan, Hubei Province; tel. (27) 6863718; fax (27) 6862325; Pres. LIU BENREN.

Xinxing Oil Co (XOC): Beijing; f. 1997; exploration, development and production of domestic and overseas petroleum and gas resources; Gen. Man. ZHU JIAZHEN.

Yuxi Cigarette Factory: Yujiang Lu, Yuxi, Yunnan Province; tel. and fax (877) 2052343; Gen. Man. CHU SHIJIAN.

UTILITIES

Electricity

Beijing Datang Power Generation: one of China's largest independent power producers.

China International Water and Electric Corpn: No. 3, M-St, Block 1, Liupukang, Beijing 100011; tel. (10) 64015511; telex 22485; fax (10) 64014075; f. 1956 as China Water and Electric International Corpn, name changed 1983; imports and exports equipment for projects in the field of water and electrical engineering; undertakes such projects; provides technical and labour services; Pres. WANG SHUOHAO.

China Power Grid Development (CPG): f. to manage transmission and transformation lines for the Three Gorges hydroelectric scheme.

China Three Gorges Project Corpn: 80 Dongshandadao, Yichang, Hubei Province; tel. (717) 444572; fax (717) 444495; Pres. LU YOUMEI.

Huadong Electric Power Group Corpn: 201 Nanjing Dong Lu, Shanghai; tel. (21) 63290000; fax (21) 63290727; power supply.

Huazhong Electric Power Group Corpn: Liyuan, Donghu, Wuhan, Hubei Province; tel. (27) 6813398; fax (27) 6813143; electrical engineering; Gen. Man. LIN KONGXING.

National Grid Construction Co: established to oversee completion of the National Grid by 2009.

North China Power Group Corpn: service provider.

Water

The China Water Company: f. to develop investment opportunities for water projects.

Shanghai Municipal Waterworks Co: service provider for municipality of Shanghai.

TRADE UNIONS

All-China Federation of Trade Unions (ACFTU): 10 Fu Xing Men Wai Jie, Beijing 100865; tel. (10) 68512200; telex 222290; fax (10) 68512922; f. 1925; organized on an industrial basis; 15 affiliated national industrial unions, 30 affiliated local trade union councils; membership is voluntary; trade unionists enjoy extensive benefits; in 1995 there were 103,996,000m. members; Pres. WEI JIANXING; First Sec. ZHANG DINGHUA.

Principal affiliated unions:

All-China Federation of Railway Workers' Union: Chair. FENG ZUCHUN.

Architectural Workers' Trade Union: Sec. SONG ANRU.

China Self-Employed Workers' Association: Pres. REN ZHONGLIN.

Educational Workers' Trade Union: Chair. JIANG WENLIANG.

Light Industrial Workers' Trade Union: Chair. LI SHUYING.

Machinery Metallurgical Workers' Union: Chair. ZHANG CUNEN.

National Defence Workers' Union: Chair. GUAN HENGCAI.

Postal and Telecommunications Workers' Trade Union of China: Chair. LUO SHUZHEN.

Seamen's Trade Union of China: Chair. ZHANG SHIHUI.

Water Resources and Electric Power Workers' Trade Union: Chair. DONG YUNQI.

Workers' Autonomous Federation (WAF): f. 1989; aims to create new trade union movement in China, independent of the All-China Federation of Trade Unions.

Transport

RAILWAYS

Ministry of Railways: 10 Fuxing Lu, Haidian Qu, Beijing 100844; tel. (10) 63240114; telex 22483; controls all railways through regional divisions. The railway network has been extended to all provinces and regions except Tibet (Xizang), where construction is in progress. Total length in operation in December 1995 was 54,616 km, of which 16,909 km were double track and 9,703 km were electrified. The major routes include Beijing–Guangzhou, Tianjin–Shanghai, Manzhouli–Vladivostok, Jiaozuo–Zhicheng and Lanzhou–Badou. In addition, special railways serve factories and mines. There is an extensive development programme to improve the rail network. A new 2,536-km line from Beijing to Kowloon (Hong Kong) was completed in late 1995. Plans for a 1,300-km high-speed link between Beijing and Shanghai, to be completed by the year 2000, were announced in 1994. China's first high-speed service, linking Guangzhou and Shenzhen, commenced in December 1994. A direct service between Shanghai and Hong Kong commenced in 1997.

There is an underground system serving Beijing. Its total length was 42 km in 1995, and 78 km of further lines were to be built by the year 2010. In 1984 Tianjin city opened an underground line (10.3 km). In 1995 the Shanghai system opened (16.1 km, a further 13.5 km being planned). In addition, an underground line of 18.5 km was planned for Guangzhou (first section opened in 1997) and a line of 15.5 km for Qingdao. A 17.4-km light railway was to be built in Chongqing.

ROADS

At the end of 1996 China had 1,186,000 km of highways (of which at least 1,043,390 km were paved). Four major highways link Lhasa (Tibet) with Sichuan, Xinjiang, Qinghai Hu and Kathmandu (Nepal). A programme of expressway construction began in the mid-1980s. By 1997 there were 3,422 km of expressways, routes including the following: Shenyang–Dalian, Beijing–Tanggu, Shanghai–Jiading, Guangzhou–Foshan and Xian–Lintong. A new 123-km highway linking Shenzhen (near the border with Hong Kong) to Guangzhou opened in 1994. A 58-km road between Guangzhou and Zhongshan connects with Zhuhai, near the border with Macau. A bridge was to be constructed by 1999, linking Zhuhai with Macau. In 1997 some 20% of villages in China were not connected to the road infrastructure.

WATER TRANSPORT

At the end of 1995 there were 110,562 km of navigable inland waterways in China. The main navigable rivers are the Changjiang (Yangtze River), the Zhujiang (Pearl River), the Heilongjiang, the Grand Canal and the Xiangjiang. The Changjiang is navigable by vessels of 10,000 tons as far as Wuhan, more than 1,000 km from the coast. Vessels of 1,000 tons can continue to Chongqing upstream. There were 5,142 river ports at the end of 1996.

SHIPPING

China has a network of more than 2,000 ports, of which more than 80 are open to foreign vessels. The main ports include Dalian, Qinhuangdao, Tianjin, Yantai, Qingdao, Rizhao, Lianyungang, Shanghai, Ningbo, Guangzhou and Zhanjiang. More than 80% of the handling facilities are mechanical. In 1996 the main coastal ports handled 835m. tons of cargo. In December 1996 China's merchant fleet comprised 3,121 ships, totalling 17.0m. grt.

China National Chartering Corpn (SINOCHART): see p. 919.

China Ocean Shipping Group (COSG): 3 Dongsanhuan Lu, Beijing; tel. (10) 64661188; telex 210740; fax (10) 64669859; reorg. 1993, re-established 1997; head office transferred to Tianjin late 1997; br. offices: Shanghai, Guangzhou, Tianjin, Qingdao, Dalian; 200 subsidiaries (incl. China Ocean Shipping Agency—PENAVIC) and joint ventures in China and abroad, engaged in ship-repair, container-manufacturing, warehousing, insurance, etc.; merchant fleet of 600 vessels; 47 routes; serves China/Japan, China/SE Asia, China/Australia, China/Gulf, China/Europe and China/N America; Pres. CHEN ZHONGBIAO.

China Shipping Group: f. 1997; Pres. LI KELIN.

Minsheng Shipping Co: Minsheng Bldg, 83 Xinhua Lu, Chongqing 630011; tel. (811) 3845695; telex 62241; fax (811) 3832359; f. 1984; Gen. Man. LU GUOJI.

CIVIL AVIATION

Air travel is expanding very rapidly. In 1995 81 airports were equipped to handle Boeing-737 and larger aircraft. Chinese airlines carried a total of 51.2m. passengers in 1995. By 1996 more than 40 airlines, including numerous private operators, had been established in China.

General Administration of Civil Aviation of China (CAAC): POB 644, 155 Dongsixi Jie, Beijing 100710; tel. (10) 64014104; telex 22101; fax (10) 64016918; f. 1949 as Civil Aviation Administration of China; restructured in 1988 as a purely supervisory agency, its operational functions being transferred to new, semi-autonomous airlines (see below; also China United Airlines (division of Air Force) and China Capital Helicopter Service); domestic flights throughout China; external services are operated by **Air China** throughout Asia, to Australia, North America, Europe and the Middle East; Dir CHEN GUANGYI.

Air China: Capital Airport, Beijing 100621; tel. (10) 64563604; telex 222793; fax (10) 64563831; international and domestic scheduled passenger and cargo services; Pres. YIN WENLONG.

China Eastern Airlines: 2550 Hongqiao Rd, Hongqiao Airport, Shanghai 200335; tel. (21) 62558899; telex 331898; fax (21) 62558668; f. 1987; domestic services; overseas destinations include USA, Europe, Japan, Singapore, Seoul and Bangkok; Pres. WANG LIAN.

China Northern Airlines: Dongta Airport, Shenyang, Liaoning 110043; tel. (24) 4822563; telex 804062; fax (24) 728030; f. 1990; scheduled flights to the Democratic People's Republic of Korea, Russia, Hong Kong and Macau; charter flights to Japan; Pres. JIANG LIANYING.

China Northwest Airlines: Lao Dong Nan Lu, Xian, Shaanxi 710082; tel. (29) 4261763; telex 700224; fax (29) 4262022; f. 1992; domestic services and flights to Macau, Singapore and Nagoya; Pres. GAO JUNYUE.

China Southern Airlines: Baiyuan International Airport, Guangzhou, Guangdong 510406; tel. (20) 86678901; telex 44218; fax (20) 86667637; domestic services; overseas destinations include Bangkok, Hanoi, Ho Chi Minh City, Kuala Lumpur, Penang, Singapore, Manila, Vientiane, Jakarta and Surabaya; Chair. YU YANEN; Pres. YAN ZHIQING.

China Southwest Airlines: Shuangliu Airport, Chengdu, Sichuan 610202; tel. (28) 5703724; telex 600049; fax (28) 5582630; f. 1987; 148 domestic routes; international services to Singapore and Bangkok; also Lhasa (Tibet) to Kathmandu (Nepal); Pres. WANG RUOEN.

Changan Airlines: POB 2, Laodongnan Lu, Xian, Shaanxi 710082; tel. and fax (29) 792483; f. 1992; local passenger and cargo services; Pres. SHE YINING.

China General Aviation Corpn: Wusu Airport, Taiyuan, Shanxi 030031, tel. (351) 7040600; fax (351) 7040094; f. 1989; 58 domestic routes; Pres. ZHANG CHANGJING.

China Xinhua Airlines: Zhangguizhuang Airport, Tianjin; tel. (22) 5121585; telex 210404; fax (22) 5121581; f. 1993; Pres. JIANG BOYUE.

Fujian Airlines: Tielu Bldg, Wuyi Jie, Fuzhou 350005; tel. (591) 539073; fax (591) 7544696; f. 1993; domestic services; Pres. HOU ZHENSHAN.

Guizhou Airlines: 20 Shengfu Lu, Guiyang, Guizhou 550001; tel. (851) 525626; f. 1991; regional passenger and cargo services; Pres. MA YONGXING.

Hainan Airlines: Haihang Devt Bldg, 29 Haixiu Lu, Haikou, Hainan 570206; tel. (898) 6709602; fax (898) 6798976; f. 1989; domestic services; Pres. CHENG FENG.

Nanjing Airlines: Dajiaochang Airport, Nanjing; f. 1994; local services; Pres. JIANG HEPING.

Shandong Airlines: Yaoqiang Airport, Jinan, Shandong 250011; tel. (531) 554081; fax (531) 554082; f. 1994; domestic services; Pres. SUN DEHAN.

Shanghai Air Lines: North Gate of Hongqiao International Airport, Shanghai 200335; tel. (21) 62558558; telex 33536; fax (21) 62558107; f. 1985; domestic services; Chair. HE PENGNIAN; Pres. SUN ZHONGLI.

Shanxi Airlines: 36 Yingze Jie, Taiyun 030001; tel. and fax (351) 447178; f. 1991; domestic services; Pres. QIN JIANMING.

Shenzhen Airlines: Lingtian Tian, Lingxiao Garden, Shenzhen Airport, Shenzhen 518128; tel. (755) 7777243; fax (755) 7777242; f. 1993; domestic services; Pres. DUAN DAYANG.

Sichuan Airlines: 9 Nan Sanduan Yihuan Lu, Chengdu, Sichuan 610041; tel. (28) 5551161; fax (28) 5582641; f. 1986; fax (371) 56222542; f. 1986; domestic services; Pres. LAN XINGLIO.

Wuhan Air Lines: 230–1 Hangkong Lu, Wuhan 430030; tel. (27) 3854313; fax (27) 5853692; f. 1986; domestic services; CEO CHENG YAOKUN.

Xiamen Airlines: Gaoqi Airport, Xiamen, Fujian 361009; tel. (592) 6022961; fax (592) 6028263; f. 1992; domestic services; Pres. WU RONGNAN.

Xinjiang Airlines: Diwopu Airport, Urumqi, Xinjiang 830016; tel. (991) 335688; telex 79067; fax (991) 339771; f. 1985; domestic services and charter flights to the CIS; Pres. ZHANG RUIFU.

Yunnan Airlines: Wujiaba Airport, Kunming, Yunnan 650200; tel. (871) 7177528; fax (871) 3138675; f. 1992; Pres. XU XIAOMING.

Zhejiang Airlines: Jian Qiao Airport, 7 Yucheng Lu, Hangzhou, Zhejiang 310021; tel. (571) 8082490; fax (571) 5173015; f. 1990; regional services; Pres. LUO QIANG.

Zhong Yuan Airlines: 143 Minggong Lu, Zhengzhou, Henan 450000; tel. and fax (371) 6222542; f. 1986; domestic services; Pres. XIE YONGLIANG; Gen. Man. RONG LIANG.

Tourism

China has enormous potential for tourism, and the sector is developing rapidly. Attractions include dramatic scenery and places of historical interest such as the Temple of Heaven and the Forbidden City in Beijing, the Great Wall, the Ming Tombs, and also the terracotta warriors at Xian. Tibet (Xizang), with its monasteries and temples, has also been opened to tourists. Tours of China are organized for groups of visitors, and Western-style hotels have been built as joint ventures in many areas. By 1997 3,720 tourist hotels were in operation, comprising 486,000 guest rooms. A total of 51.1m. tourists visited China in 1996, when receipts totalled US $10,200m.

China International Travel Service (CITS): 103 Fu Xing Men Nei Dajie, Beijing 100800; tel. (10) 66011122; telex 22350; fax (10) 66012013; e-mail liluan@cits.co.cn; makes travel arrangements for foreign tourists; general agency in Hong Kong, business offices in London, Paris, New York, Los Angeles, Frankfurt, Sydney and Tokyo; Pres. LI LUAN.

China National Tourism Administration (CNTA): A9 Jian Guo Men Nei Dajie, Beijing 100740; tel. (10) 65138866; telex 210449; fax (10) 65122096; Dir HE GUANGWEI.

Chinese People's Association for Friendship with Foreign Countries: 1 Tai Ji Chang Dajie, Beijing 100740; tel. (10) 65122474; telex 210368; fax (10) 65128354; f. 1954; Pres. QI HUAIYUAN; Sec.-Gen. BIAN QINGZU.

CHINESE SPECIAL ADMINISTRATIVE REGION

HONG KONG

Introductory Survey

Location, Climate, Language, Religion, Flag, Capital

The Special Administrative Region (SAR) of Hong Kong, as the territory became on 1 July 1997, lies in east Asia, off the south coast of the People's Republic of China, and consists of the island of Hong Kong, Stonecutters Island, the Kowloon Peninsula and the New Territories, which are partly on the mainland. The climate is sunny and dry in winter, and hot and humid in summer. The average annual rainfall is 2,214 mm (87 in), of which about three-quarters falls between June and August. The official languages are English and Chinese: Cantonese is spoken by the majority of the Chinese community, while Putonghua (Mandarin) is widely understood and of increasing significance. The main religion is Buddhism. Confucianism, Islam, Hinduism and Daoism are also practised, and there are about 500,000 Christians. The flag of the Hong Kong SAR (proportions 3 by 2), introduced in July 1997 and flown subordinate to the flag of the People's Republic of China, displays a bauhinia flower consisting of five white petals, each bearing a red line and a red five-pointed star, at the centre of a red field. The capital is Victoria.

Recent History

Hong Kong Island was ceded to the United Kingdom under the terms of the Treaty of Nanking (Nanjing) in 1842. The Kowloon Peninsula was acquired by the Convention of Peking (Beijing) in 1860. The New Territories were leased from China in 1898 for a period of 99 years. From the establishment of the People's Republic in 1949, the Chinese Government asserted that the 'unequal' treaties giving Britain control over Hong Kong were no longer valid.

Japanese forces invaded Hong Kong in December 1941, forcing the British administration to surrender. In August 1945, at the end of the Second World War, the territory was recaptured by British forces. Colonial rule was restored, with a British military administration until May 1946. With the restoration of civilian rule, the territory was again administered in accordance with the 1917 Constitution, which vested full powers in the British-appointed Governor. In 1946 the returning Governor promised a greater measure of self-government but, after the communist revolution in China in 1949, plans for constitutional reform were abandoned. Thus, unlike most other British colonies, Hong Kong did not proceed, through stages, to democratic rule. The essential features of the colonial regime remained unaltered until 1985, when, following the Sino-British Joint Declaration (see below), the first changes were introduced into the administrative system. Prior to 1985 the Executive and Legislative Councils consisted entirely of nominated members, including many civil servants in the colonial administration. There were, however, direct elections for one-half of the seats on the Urban Council, responsible for public health and other amenities, but participation was low.

Between 1949 and 1964 an estimated 1m. refugees crossed from the People's Republic to Hong Kong, imposing serious strains on Hong Kong's housing and other social services. More than 460,000 Chinese immigrants arrived, many of them illegally, between 1975 and 1980. Strict measures, introduced in October 1980, reduced the continuous flow of refugees from China (at one time averaging 150 per day), but the number of legal immigrants remained at a high level—more than 50,000 per year in 1980 and 1981, although by 1984 the figure had declined to around 27,700.

In 1981–82 a new problem arose with the arrival of Vietnamese refugees: by January 1987 there were 8,254 in Hong Kong, of whom 62% had spent more than three years living in camps, and refugees continued to arrive in increasing numbers. The Hong Kong authorities, meanwhile, exerted pressure on the British Government to end its policy of granting first asylum to the refugees. In response, legislation was introduced in June 1988 to distinguish between political refugees and 'economic migrants'. The latter were to be denied refugee status, and in October the British and Vietnamese Governments agreed terms for their voluntary repatriation. In March 1989 the first group of co-operative 'economic migrants' flew back to Viet Nam.

More than 18,000 Vietnamese arrived in Hong Kong between June 1988 and May 1989, despite the extremely unpleasant conditions in the detention camps where they were confined on arrival, and the restricting of the definition of refugee status. The relative paucity of those who agreed to return to Viet Nam (totalling 1,225 by February 1990) caused the British Government to claim that the policy of voluntary repatriation was not effective. After the United Kingdom had failed on a number of occasions to gain general international endorsement for a policy of compulsory repatriation (which, it was claimed, would discourage further large-scale immigration), the Vietnamese Government announced in December 1989 that an agreement had been concluded between the United Kingdom and Viet Nam on a programme of 'involuntary' repatriation. Under the agreement, 'economic migrants' could be returned to Viet Nam against their will, on condition that no physical force were used. Reports that a group of 51 Vietnamese had been forcibly repatriated led to violent disturbances in many of the camps. The programme of involuntary repatriation was halted, in anticipation of a meeting in January 1990 of the UN steering committee for the Comprehensive Plan of Action on Indochinese refugees. The 29-nation committee failed to agree upon a policy, the USA and Viet Nam each adhering to the principle of a moratorium on involuntary repatriation, in order to allow more time to persuade 'economic migrants' to return voluntarily. By May 1990 no further cases of the repatriation of Vietnamese against their will had been reported. At an international conference held in that month, Hong Kong and the member countries of ASEAN threatened to refuse asylum to Vietnamese refugees altogether, unless the USA and Viet Nam gave approval to the policy of involuntary repatriation. In September Hong Kong, Viet Nam and the United Kingdom reached an agreement, supported by the UNHCR, to allow the repatriation of a new category of refugees—those who were not volunteering to return but who had indicated that they would not actively resist repatriation. By mid-1991, however, very few refugees had returned to Viet Nam, and the number of those arriving in Hong Kong had increased considerably. By June more than 60,000 Vietnamese were accommodated in permanent camps. In October, following protracted negotiations, it was announced that Viet Nam had agreed to the mandatory repatriation of refugees from Hong Kong. The first forcible deportation (mainly of recent arrivals) under the agreement was carried out in November. Tension in the camps continued, and in February 1992 23 refugees were burned to death and almost 130 were injured in rioting at one of the detention centres. In May the United Kingdom and Viet Nam signed an agreement providing for the forcible repatriation of all economic migrants. By the end of 1995 the detention camp population had been reduced to 21,704, of whom 1,479 were classified as refugees. Demonstrations and riots in the camps continued intermittently. Almost 200 people were injured during clashes in May 1995, when security officers attempted to transfer 1,500 inmates from a detention centre to a transit camp prior to repatriation. In May 1996 more than 100 asylum-seekers escaped from Whitehead Detention Centre following rioting during which 50 security officers were injured. In June there was an attempted mass escape from High Island Detention Centre in the New Territories. The People's Republic of China, meanwhile, continued to insist that all camps be cleared prior to the transfer of sovereignty in mid-1997. The Whitehead Detention Centre was closed in January 1997, and the refugees were transferred to other detention centres. Despite an acceleration in the repatriation programme, some 1,200 Vietnamese migrants remained in Hong Kong in December 1997.

Following a visit to Hong Kong by the British Prime Minister in September 1982, talks between the United Kingdom and China were held at diplomatic level about the territory's future status. In 1984 the United Kingdom conceded that in mid-1997, upon the expiry of the lease on the New Territories, China would regain sovereignty over the whole of Hong Kong. In September 1984 British and Chinese representatives met in Beijing and initialled a legally-binding agreement, the Sino-British Joint Declaration, containing detailed assurances on the future of Hong Kong. China guaranteed the continuation of the territory's capitalist economy and life-style for 50 years after 1997. The territory, as a special administrative region of the People's Republic, would be designated 'Hong Kong, China', and would continue to enjoy a high degree of autonomy, except in matters of defence and foreign affairs. It was agreed that

Hong Kong would retain its identity as a free port and separate customs territory, and its citizens would be guaranteed freedom of speech, of assembly, of association, of travel and of religious belief. In December 1984, after being approved by the National People's Congress (Chinese legislature) and the British Parliament, the agreement was signed in Beijing by the British and Chinese Prime Ministers, and in May 1985 the two Governments exchanged documents ratifying the agreement. A Joint Liaison Group (JLG), comprising British and Chinese representatives, was established to monitor the provisions of the agreement, and this group held its first meeting in July 1985. A 58-member Basic Law Drafting Committee (BLDC), including 23 representatives from Hong Kong, was formed in Beijing in June, with the aim of drawing up a new Basic Law (Constitution) for Hong Kong, in accordance with Article 31 of the Chinese Constitution, which provides for special administrative regions within the People's Republic.

A special office, which had been established in Hong Kong to assess the views of the people of the territory, reported that the majority of the population accepted the terms of the Joint Declaration, but the sensitive issue of the future nationality of Hong Kong residents proved controversial. The 1981 British Nationality Act had already caused alarm in the territory, where the reclassification of 2.3m. citizens was seen as a downgrading of their status. As holders of Hong Kong residents' permits, they have no citizenship status under British law. Following the approval of the Hong Kong agreement, the British Government announced a new form of nationality, to be effective from 1997, designated 'British National (Overseas)', which would not be transferable to descendants and would confer no right of abode in the United Kingdom.

In September 1985 indirect elections were held for 24 new members of an expanded Legislative Council, to replace the former appointees and government officials. The turn-out for the elections was low (less than 1% of the total population was eligible to vote, and only 35% of these participated). In March 1986 municipal elections were held for the urban and regional councils, which were thus, for the first time, wholly directly-elected. In December the Governor, Sir Edward Youde, died unexpectedly while on a visit to Beijing. The new Governor, Sir David Wilson (who had played a prominent part in the Sino-British negotiations on the territory's future), formally assumed office in April 1987. In May the Hong Kong Government published proposals regarding the development of representative government during the final decade of British rule. Among the options that it proposed was the introduction, in 1988, of direct elections to the Legislative Council, based upon universal adult franchise. In spite of the disapproval of the Chinese Government with regard to the introduction of direct elections before the new Constitution was promulgated in 1990, a survey, held in 1987, found the majority of people to be in favour of the introduction of direct elections before 1990. In February 1988 the Hong Kong Government published a policy document on the development of representative government; the principal proposal was the introduction, in 1991, of 10 (subsequently increased) directly-elected members of the Legislative Council.

In April 1988 the first draft of the Basic Law for Hong Kong was published, and a Basic Law Consultative Committee (BLCC) was established in Hong Kong, initially with 176 members, to collect public comments on its provisions, over a five-month period; the draft was to be debated by the Legislative Council and by the Parliament of the United Kingdom, but no referendum was to be held in Hong Kong, and final approval of the Basic Law rested with the National People's Congress of China. The draft offered five options for the election of a chief executive and four options were presented regarding the composition of the future Legislative Council, none of which, however, proposed that the Council should be elected entirely by universal suffrage. Although the legislature would be empowered to impeach the chief executive for wrongdoing, the Chinese Government would have final responsibility for his removal. Critics of the draft Basic Law complained that it failed to offer democratic representation or to guarantee basic human rights; they argued that Hong Kong's autonomy was not clearly defined, and would be threatened by the fact that power to interpret those parts of the Basic Law relating to defence, foreign affairs and China's 'executive acts' would be granted to the National People's Congress in Beijing and not to the Hong Kong judiciary.

In November 1988 the UN Commission on Human Rights criticized the British attitude to the transfer of Hong Kong, with particular reference to the lack of direct elections. A second draft of the Basic Law was approved by China's National People's Congress in February 1989, which ignored all five options previously proposed for the election of a chief executive. In May there were massive demonstrations in Hong Kong in support of the anti-Government protests taking place in China. In June, following the killing of thousands of protesters by the Chinese armed forces in Tiananmen Square in Beijing, further demonstrations and a general strike took place in Hong Kong, expressing the inhabitants' revulsion at the massacres and their doubts as to whether the Basic Law would, in practice, be honoured by the Chinese Government after 1997. The British Government refused to consider renegotiating the Sino-British Joint Declaration, but, in response to demands that the British nationality laws should be changed to allow Hong Kong residents the right to settle in the United Kingdom after 1997, it announced in December 1989 that the British Parliament would be asked to enact legislation enabling as many as 50,000 Hong Kong residents (chosen on a 'points system', which was expected to favour leading civil servants, business executives and professional workers), and an estimated 175,000 dependants, to be given the right of abode in the United Kingdom. The measure was intended to 'maintain confidence' in the colony during the transition to Chinese sovereignty, by stemming the emigration of skilled personnel (42,000 Hong Kong residents having left the colony in 1989). The announcement received a cautious welcome from the Hong Kong authorities. However, China warned prospective applicants that their British nationality would not be recognized by the Chinese Government after 1997. There were also widespread popular protests in Hong Kong itself over the unfairness of a scheme which was perceived as élitist. The bill containing the measures received approval at its second reading in the United Kingdom House of Commons in April 1990. (It was estimated that a record 66,000 Hong Kong residents left the colony in 1992, the number of emigrants fluctuating thereafter and declining to 43,100 in 1995.)

Among other recommendations made by the parliamentary select committee were the introduction of a Bill of Rights for Hong Kong and an increase in the number of seats subject to direct election in the Hong Kong Legislative Council, to one-half of the total in 1991, leading to full direct elections in 1995. A draft Bill of Rights, based on the UN International Covenant on Civil and Political Rights, was published by the Hong Kong Government in March 1990. The draft was criticized in principle because its provisions would have been subordinate, in the case of conflict, to the provisions of the Basic Law. Nevertheless, the Bill of Rights entered into law in June 1991, its enactment immediately being deemed unnecessary by the Government of China.

China's National People's Congress approved a final draft of the Basic Law for Hong Kong in April 1990. In the approved version, 24 of the 60 seats in the Legislative Council would be subject to direct election in 1999, and 30 seats in 2003; a referendum, to be held after 2007, would consult public opinion on the future composition of the Council, although the ultimate authority to make any changes would rest with China's National People's Congress. The British Government had agreed to co-operate with these measures by offering 18 seats for direct election in 1991 and 20 seats in 1995. Under the Basic Law, the Chief Executive of the Hong Kong Special Administrative Region (SAR), as the territory was to be designated in 1997, would initially be elected for a five-year term by a special 800-member election committee; a referendum was to be held during the third term of office in order to help to determine whether the post should be subject to a general election. However, no person with the right of residence in another country would be permitted to hold an important government post. Particular concern was expressed over a clause in the Law which would 'prohibit political organizations and groups in the Hong Kong SAR from establishing contacts with foreign political organizations or groups.' The British Government and the Hong Kong authorities expressed disappointment that the Basic Law did not allow the development of democratic government at a more rapid pace.

In October 1989 the Governor announced plans to construct a new international airport off the island of Lantau, together with extensive new port facilities in the west of the harbour and massive infrastructural development, at a projected cost (at 1989 prices) of HK $127,000m. The airport was expected to be completed by 1997/98. China, however, expressed serious concern about the high cost of the ambitious project, thus leading to fears that difficulties in raising the necessary finances might be encountered. By the beginning of 1991 relations between China and Hong Kong had deteriorated considerably, with several members of the Chinese Government claiming the right to be consulted about all major new projects undertaken in the colony before 1997. The Government of Hong Kong rejected China's demands, reasserting its responsibility for governing the territory until 1997, but agreed, however, that China should be kept informed about the project. China continued to express its fears that the scheme would drastically deplete the colony's public funds. In July 1991, following the holding of several rounds of senior-level negotiations, China and the United Kingdom reached agreement on a memorandum of understanding permitting the airport project to proceed, subject to certain conditions. China, however, subsequently raised objections to the revised costs and financing arrangements, and discussions were suspended in October 1992. Upon their resumption in June 1993, China approved plans for the construction of a third cross-harbour road tunnel, to link the airport with the central business district and to be funded by the private sector. In November 1994, the cost of the entire project now having reached HK $158,000m., the United Kingdom and China signed an accord relating to the overall financing arrangements for the airport and for its railway link. A detailed agreement was reached in June 1995. Plans for the construction of a second airport runway, to be completed by late 1998, received approval in May 1996.

In April 1990, meanwhile, liberal groups formed Hong Kong's first formal political party, the United Democrats of Hong Kong (UDHK), with Martin Lee as its Chairman. The party subsequently became the main opposition to the conservatives, and achieved considerable success in local elections in March and May 1991. In November 1990 it had been announced that less than one-half of Hong Kong's eligible voters had registered to vote in elections for 18 seats in the Legislative Council, which were due to be held in September 1991 and which were to be the territory's first direct legislative elections. Of the 18 seats open to election by universal suffrage, 17 were won by members of the UDHK and like-minded liberal and independent candidates. Only 39% of registered electors, however, were reported to have voted. Following their victory, the UDHK urged the Governor to consider liberal candidates when selecting his direct appointees to the Legislative Council. The Governor, however, resisted this pressure, appointing only one of the UDHK's 20 suggested candidates. Changes in the membership of the Executive Council were announced in October, liberal citizens again being excluded by the Governor.

In September 1991 the Sino-British JLG announced the future composition of the Hong Kong Court of Appeal, which in 1993 was to assume the function hitherto performed by the British Privy Council in London. Local lawyers, however, denounced the proposed membership, arguing that the new body would lack independence and flexibility. In December the Legislative Council voted overwhelmingly to reject the proposed composition of the Court.

Sir David Wilson was to retire in 1992. Months of speculation over the Governor's replacement were ended in April, with the appointment of Christopher Patten, hitherto Chairman of the Conservative Party in the United Kingdom, who took office in July. In the following month Patten held discussions with Zhou Nan, director of the Xinhua News Agency and China's most senior representative in Hong Kong. Ambitious plans for democratic reform in the territory, announced by the Governor in October, included the separation of the Executive Council from the Legislative Council. The former was reorganized to include prominent lawyers and academics. At the 1995 elections to the latter, the number of directly-elected members was to be increased to the maximum permissible of 20; the franchise for the existing 21 'functional constituencies', representing occupational and professional groups, was to be widened and nine additional constituencies were to be established, in order to encompass all categories of workers. Various social and economic reforms were also announced. In the same month Patten paid his first visit to China.

The proposed electoral changes were denounced by China as a contravention of the Basic Law and of the 1984 Joint Declaration. Although Patten's programme received the general support of the Legislative Council, many conservative business leaders were opposed to the proposals. In November 1992, following Hong Kong's announcement that it was to proceed with the next stage of preparations for the construction of the airport (without, as yet, the Chinese Government's agreement to the revised financing of the project), China threatened to cancel, in 1997, all commercial contracts, leases and agreements between the Hong Kong Government and the private sector that had been signed without its full approval. The dispute continued in early 1993, China's criticism of the territory's Governor becoming increasingly acrimonious. In February China announced plans to establish a 'second stove', or alternative administration for Hong Kong, if the Governor's proposed reforms were implemented. In April, however, the impasse was broken when the United Kingdom and China agreed to resume negotiations. In July the 57-member Preliminary Working Committee (PWC), established to study issues relating to the transfer of sovereignty in 1997 and chaired by the Chinese Minister of Foreign Affairs, held its inaugural meeting in Beijing. Negotiations between the United Kingdom and China continued intermittently throughout the year. In December, however, no progress having been made, proposed electoral reforms were submitted to the Legislative Council. The Governor's decision to proceed unilaterally was denounced by China, which declared that it would regard as null and void any laws enacted in Hong Kong.

In January 1994, during a visit to London for consultations, Patten urged China to resume negotiations. In the following month the Legislative Council approved the first stage of the reform programme, which included the lowering of the voting age from 21 to 18 years. China confirmed that all recently-elected bodies would be disbanded in 1997. The second stage was presented to the Legislative Council in March. Relations with China deteriorated further in April, upon the publication of a British parliamentary report endorsing Patten's democratic reforms. In the same month the UDHK and Meeting Point, a smaller party, announced their intention to merge and form the Democratic Party of Hong Kong. In April the trial in camera of a Beijing journalist (who worked for a respected Hong Kong newspaper) on imprecise charges of 'stealing state secrets' and his subsequent severe prison sentence aroused widespread concern in the territory over future press freedom. Hundreds of journalists took part in a protest march through the streets of Hong Kong.

In June 1994, in an unprecedented development that reflected growing unease with Patten's style of government, the Legislative Council passed a motion of censure formally rebuking the Governor for refusing to permit a debate on an amendment to the budget. Nevertheless, at the end of the month the Legislative Council approved further constitutional reforms, entailing an increase in the number of its directly-elected members and an extension of the franchise. Despite China's strong opposition to these reforms, shortly afterwards the People's Republic and the United Kingdom concluded an agreement on the transfer of defence sites, some of which were to be retained for military purposes and upgraded prior to 1997, while others were to be released for redevelopment. At the end of August, following the issuing of a report by the PWC in the previous month, the Standing Committee of the National People's Congress in Beijing approved a decision on the abolition, in 1997, of the current political structure of Hong Kong. . In September, during a visit to the territory, the British Foreign Secretary was accused by members of the Legislative Council of failing to give adequate support to Hong Kong, and was urged to permit the establishment of an independent commission to protect human rights in the territory after 1997.

In September 1994, at elections to the 18 District Boards (the first to be held on a fully democratic basis), 75 of the 346 seats were won by the Democratic Party of Hong Kong. The pro-Beijing Democratic Alliance for the Betterment of Hong Kong (DAB) won 37 seats, the progressive Association for Democracy and People's Livelihood (ADPL) 29 seats, and the pro-Beijing Liberal Party and Liberal Democratic Foundation 18 seats and 11 seats, respectively. Independent candidates secured 167 seats. The level of voter participation was a record 33.1%.

In early October 1994 the Governor of Hong Kong offered his full co-operation with China during the 1,000 remaining days of British sovereignty. In December the director of the State Council's Hong Kong and Macau Affairs Office and secretary-general of the PWC, Lu Ping, formally confirmed that the Legislative Council would be disbanded in 1997.

A new dispute with China, relating to the personal files of Hong Kong civil servants, arose in January 1995. China's demand for immediate access to these confidential files, ostensibly for the purposes of verifying integrity and of determining nationality (and thus eligibility for senior posts), was rejected by the Governor.

Elections for the 32 seats on the Urban Council and the 27 seats on the Regional Council took place in March 1995. The Democratic Party of Hong Kong took 23 seats, the DAB eight seats and the ADPL also eight seats. Fewer than 26% of those eligible voted in the polls. In the same month Donald Tsang was nominated as Financial Secretary, his predecessor, along with other expatriate senior officials, having been requested to take early retirement in order to make way for a local civil servant. Tsang took office in September.

Following a redrafting of the legislation, in June 1995 the United Kingdom and China reached agreement on the establishment of the Court of Final Appeal. Contrary to the Governor's original wishes, this new body would not now be constituted until after the transfer of sovereignty in mid-1997. The agreement was approved by the Legislative Council in July 1995. In the same month an unprecedented motion of 'no confidence' in the Governor was defeated at a session of the Legislative Council. Also in July the territory's Chief Secretary, Anson Chan, confirmed that she had had clandestine meetings with senior Chinese officials during a three-day visit to Beijing.

At elections to the Legislative Council in September 1995, for the first time all 60 seats were determined by election. The Democratic Party of Hong Kong won 12 of the 20 seats open to direct election on the basis of geographical constituencies and two of the 10 chosen by an electoral committee, bringing the party's total representation to 19. The Liberal Party took nine of the 60 seats, the pro-Beijing DAB six seats and the ADPL four seats. Independent candidates won 17 seats. The level of participation in the geographical constituencies was 35.8%.

The Governor aroused much controversy in September 1995, when he urged the United Kingdom to grant the right of abode to more than 3m. citizens of Hong Kong. The proposals were rebuffed by the British Home Secretary. In October, however, an improvement in Sino-British relations was confirmed by the visit of the Chinese Minister of Foreign Affairs to London. The two sides reached agreement on the establishment of a liaison office to improve bilateral contacts between civil servants. In November the Chinese Government rejected a request by the UN Commission on Human Rights that from mid-1997 it file reports on the situation in Hong Kong. China's disclosure of a plan to establish a parallel administration six months prior to the transfer of sovereignty provoked outrage in Hong Kong.

In January 1996 the 150-member Preparatory Committee of the Hong Kong SAR was formally established in Beijing to succeed the

PWC. The 94 Hong Kong delegates included representatives of the territory's business and academic communities. The Democratic Party of Hong Kong was excluded from the new body, which was to appoint a 400-member Selection Committee responsible for the choice of the territory's future Chief Executive.

In March 1996, during a visit to the territory, the British Prime Minister announced that more than 2m. holders of the forthcoming Hong Kong SAR passports would be granted visa-free access to (but not residency in) the United Kingdom. He also declared that China had a legal obligation to maintain the Legislative Council and to uphold basic rights in the territory. The Preparatory Committee in Beijing, however, approved a resolution to appoint a provisional body to replace the Legislative Council. Towards the end of March, as the final deadline approached, there were chaotic scenes in Hong Kong as thousands of residents rushed to submit applications for British Dependent Territories Citizenship (BDTC) which, although conferring no right of abode in the United Kingdom, would provide an alternative travel document to the new SAR passports. As tension continued to rise, in April the Chief Secretary of Hong Kong travelled to Beijing for discussions with Lu Ping. A visit to Hong Kong by Lu Ping earlier in the month had been disrupted by pro-democracy demonstrators. In early July eight pro-democracy politicians, including five members of the Legislative Council, were refused entry to China, having flown from Hong Kong in an attempt to deliver a petition of 60,000 signatures criticizing the proposed establishment of a provisional legislative body for Hong Kong. In mid-August nominations opened for candidacy for the 400-member Selection Committee. In the same month a new pro-democracy movement, The Frontier, comprising teachers, students and trade unionists, was established.

In September 1996 the United Kingdom and China finally reached agreement on the ceremonial arrangements to commemorate the transfer of sovereignty on 30 June 1997. In October 1996 the Chinese Minister of Foreign Affairs declared that from mid-1997 the annual protests against the Tiananmen Square massacre of 1989 (and similar demonstrations) would not be tolerated in Hong Kong; furthermore, criticism of the Chinese leadership by the territory's press would not be permitted.

In December 1996 the second ballot for the selection of Hong Kong's Chief Executive (the first having been held in November) resulted in the choice of Tung Chee-hwa, a shipping magnate and former member of the territory's Executive Council, who obtained 320 of the 400 votes, defeating the former Chief Justice, (Sir) Yang Ti-Liang, and a businessman, Peter Woo. Later in the month the Selection Committee reassembled to choose the 60 members of the SAR's controversial Provisional Legislative Council (PLC). More than 30 of the new appointees were members of the existing Legislative Council, belonging mainly to the DAB and to the Liberal Party. Despite much criticism of the PLC's establishment, the new body held its inaugural meeting in Shenzhen in January 1997, and elected Rita Fan as its President.

In early 1997 the Chief Executive-designate announced the composition of the Executive Council, which was to comprise three ex-officio members (as previously) and 11 non-official members. The latter included two members of the outgoing Executive Council. Anson Chan was to remain as Chief Secretary, while Donald Tsang was to continue as Financial Secretary; Elsie Leung was to become Justice Secretary, replacing the incumbent Attorney General. China's approval of Tung Chee-hwa's recommendations that senior civil servants be retained did much to enhance confidence in the territory's future. In February, however, relations with the outgoing administration deteriorated when the Preparatory Committee voted overwhelmingly in favour of proposals to repeal or amend 25 laws, thereby reducing the territory's civil liberties. The British Foreign Secretary reiterated concerns regarding the establishment of the PLC and the proposed curbs on civil liberties.

Meanwhile, Lawrence Leung had abruptly resigned as Director of Immigration in July 1996 for 'personal reasons'. In January 1997 he cast doubt on the integrity of the Hong Kong Government when he appeared before a hearing of the Legislative Council and claimed that he had in fact been dismissed, thus denying the official version of his departure from office. The scandal deepened with the revelation that Leung had been found to possess undisclosed business interests. Newspaper reports alleged that Leung had passed sensitive information to unauthorized parties, leading to speculation that the security of mainland dissidents in the territory, of civil servants who held foreign passports, and of others who had been granted British nationality, had been severely compromised. The Government finally admitted that Leung had indeed been dismissed, but denied that he had been involved in any espionage activities on behalf of China.

In May 1997 the PLC approved its first legislation (a bill on public holidays), despite protests from the British Government and pro-democracy groups in Hong Kong that the PLC was not entitled to pass laws during the transition period. However, the PLC declared that the legislation would come into effect only on 1 July. Following the circulation in April of a public consultation document on proposed legislation governing civil liberties and social order, a series of amendments, relating to the holding of public demonstrations and the funding of political organizations, was announced in May. Pro-democracy groups and the outgoing administration remained dissatisfied with the legislation.

Shortly after the handover of Hong Kong from British to Chinese sovereignty at midnight on 30 June 1997, the inauguration of the SAR Executive Council, the PLC and members of the judiciary was held. Some 4,000 dignitaries attended the ceremonies, although the British Prime Minister and Foreign Secretary, and the US Secretary of State, did not attend the inauguration of the PLC, to register their disapproval at the undemocratic nature of its formation. Pro-democracy groups and members of the former legislature staged peaceful demonstrations in protest at the abolition of the Legislative Council. More than 4,000 Chinese People's Liberation Army troops entered Hong Kong shortly after the handover ceremony, joining the small number of Chinese military personnel that had been deployed in the territory in April, following protracted negotiations with the British Government; a further 500 had entered the territory on 30 June, immediately prior to the handover.

Details of the procedure for elections to a new Legislative Council, which would replace the PLC, were announced by the SAR Government in early July 1997. The elections were scheduled to take place in May 1998, and were to be conducted under a new system of voting. Of the 60 seats in the legislature, 20 were to be directly elected by means of a revised system of proportional representation, 30 were to be elected by 'functional constituencies' and 10 by an 800-member electoral college. Legislative amendments governing the electoral arrangements were approved by the PLC in late September 1997. The significant reduction of the franchise, by comparison with the 1995 legislative elections, was condemned by the Democratic Party of Hong Kong. The appointment by indirect election of 36 Hong Kong delegates to the Chinese National People's Congress, in December 1997, also attracted criticism from pro-democracy activists. Nevertheless, the arrangements were defended by Anson Chan, who maintained that democracy and the rule of law were being upheld in Hong Kong. A campaign held in December 1997–January 1998 to register voters for the 1998 legislative elections received a low level of popular support.

Legislation approved by the PLC in July 1997 included the introduction of measures to restrict the immigration into the territory of mainland-born children of Hong Kong residents. The PLC also passed legislation suspending the operation of a number of labour laws, which had been approved by the former Legislative Council in June. An attempt to challenge the legitimacy of the PLC was rejected by the Court of Appeal in late July.

In his first policy address to the PLC, in early October 1997, Tung Chee-hwa confirmed that elections to the new Legislative Council would take place on 24 May 1998. In his speech, Tung concentrated on economic and social problems, in particular the severe housing shortage in the territory, one of the most pressing concerns facing the new administration, and investment of HK $88,000m. in education, infrastructure and information technology was promised. Pro-democracy groups criticized Tung for failing to address political and human rights issues. However, opinion polls conducted in the territory revealed a widespread confidence in Tung's performance as Chief Executive.

The regional currency crisis, which had affected much of South-East Asia in mid-1997, spread to Hong Kong in October. The Hong Kong dollar, which is pegged to the US dollar, became the target of currency speculators, resulting in a substantial decline in value of the stock-market index. The Hong Kong authorities acted swiftly to maintain the currency link, and the situation stabilized briefly in late 1997, before deteriorating in early January 1998, when the index again plummeted. China pledged to support the Hong Kong dollar.

The SAR Government was confronted by a new problem in December 1997, when a strain of influenza previously confined to poultry appeared to have been contracted by humans, resulting in several deaths. A mass slaughter of all chickens in Hong Kong was carried out, and restrictions were imposed on the import of chickens from the mainland. Fears of the extent of the disease were enhanced by concerns that the virus might be transferred from person to person.

Despite the tensions surrounding the transfer of sovereignty, many citizens of Hong Kong supported the Government of the People's Republic of China in its territorial dispute with Japan regarding the Diaoyu (or Senkaku) Islands (see p. 893). In September 1996 a Hong Kong activist, David Chan, was accidentally drowned during a protest against Japan's claim to the islands. As issues of patriotism assumed greater significance in Hong Kong, more than 10,000 people attended a demonstration to mourn the death of David Chan and to denounce Japan. In October protesters from Hong Kong joined a flotilla of small boats from Taiwan and Macau, which successfully evaded Japanese patrol vessels and raised the flags of China and Taiwan on the disputed islands.

Government

Since 1 July 1997 the Hong Kong SAR has been administered by a Chief Executive, chosen by a 400-member Selection Committee in December 1996. The Chief Executive is accountable to the State Council of China, and serves a five-year term, there being a limit of two consecutive terms. The 15-member Executive Council, appointed by the Chief Executive-designate in early 1997, comprises three ex-officio members and 11 non-official members, and includes the Chief Executive. The 60 members of the SAR's Provisional Legislative Council (PLC) were chosen by the Selection Committee in December 1996. The PLC was to remain in office until the establishment of the SAR's first Legislative Council, by 30 June 1998 at the latest.

Defence

The British army, navy and air force completed their final withdrawal on 30 June 1997. In December 1996 the Standing Committee of the National People's Congress in Beijing adopted the Hong Kong Garrison Law, which provided for the stationing in Hong Kong of troops of the People's Liberation Army (PLA). The Garrison Law defined the duties and obligations of the troops, jurisdiction over them and also the relationship between the troops and the Government of the Hong Kong SAR. The legislation took effect on 1 July 1997. Almost 200 unarmed members of the PLA were permitted to enter Hong Kong (in three stages) prior to the transfer of sovereignty. In July 1997 a garrison of 4,800 PLA troops was established in Hong Kong. The garrison can intervene in local matters only at the request of the Hong Kong Government, which remains responsible for internal security.

Economic Affairs

In 1995, according to estimates by the World Bank, Hong Kong's gross domestic product (GDP), measured at average 1993–95 prices, was US $142,332m., equivalent to US $22,990 per head. During 1985–95, it was estimated, GDP per head increased, in real terms, at an average annual rate of 4.8%. Over the same period, the population increased by an annual average of 1.3%. GDP was officially estimated to have risen by 5.4% in 1994, by 4.7% in 1995 and by 4.7% in 1996. Growth of between 5.25% and 5.5% was forecast for 1997.

Agriculture and fishing together employed only 0.4% of the working population in 1996, and contributed an estimated 0.1% of GDP in 1995. Crop production is largely restricted to flowers, vegetables and some fruit and nuts, while pigs and poultry are the principal livestock. Hong Kong relies heavily on imports for its food.

Industry (including mining, manufacturing, construction and power) provided an estimated 14.8% of GDP in 1995. In 1996 the sector employed 25.7% of the working population.

Manufacturing employed 16.0% of the working population in 1996, and contributed an estimated 8.2% of GDP in 1995. Measured by the value of output, the principal branches of manufacturing are textiles and clothing, plastic products, metal products and electrical machinery (particularly radio and television sets).

The services sector plays the most important role in the economy, accounting for 85.0% of GDP in 1995, and employing 73.9% of the working population in 1996. The value of Hong Kong's invisible exports (financial services, tourism, shipping, etc.) was HK $291,030m. in 1995. Revenue from tourism (excluding expenditure by visitors from the People's Republic of China) was HK $87,000m. in 1996, when 11.6m. people visited the territory. However, the number of people visiting Hong Kong declined sharply after the handover to Chinese sovereignty, with a decline of 21%, compared with the previous year, recorded in October. This was partly attributed to the regional economic crisis that affected South-East Asia in mid-1997. Hong Kong banking and mercantile houses have branches throughout the region, and the territory is regarded as a major financial centre, owing partly to the existence of an excellent international telecommunications network and to the absence of restrictions on capital inflows.

In 1996 Hong Kong recorded a visible trade deficit of HK $137,664m. Re-exports constituted 84.8% of total exports in 1996. The principal sources of Hong Kong's imports in 1996 were the People's Republic of China (37.1%) and Japan (13.6%); the principal markets for exports (including re-exports) were the People's Republic of China (34.3%) and the USA (21.2%). Other major trading partners included Taiwan, Germany and Singapore. In 1996 the principal domestic exports were clothing, textiles, electrical machinery, data-processing equipment, and photographic apparatus. The principal imports in that year were foodstuffs, chemicals, textiles, machinery, transport equipment, and other manufactured articles.

The 1996/97 budget recorded an estimated deficit of HK $14,918m. The annual rate of inflation averaged 7.7% in 1985–95. The composite consumer price index rose by 9.1% in 1995 and by 6.3% in 1996. In the year ending October 1997 the consumer price index increased by 5.7%. An estimated 2.3% of the labour force were unemployed, according to seasonally-adjusted figures for the quarter ending October 1997. The shortage of skilled labour continued.

Hong Kong is a member of the Asian Development Bank (ADB, see p. 110) and an associate member of the UN's Economic and Social Commission for Asia and the Pacific (ESCAP, see p. 27). The territory became a member of Asia-Pacific Economic Co-operation (APEC, see p. 108) in late 1991. Hong Kong joined the Bank for International Settlements (see p. 118) in 1996, and in early 1997 announced its participation in the IMF's New Arrangements to Borrow scheme (NAB, see p. 81). After mid-1997 Hong Kong remained a separate customs territory, within the World Trade Organization (WTO, see p. 244).

Under the terms of the Basic Law, Hong Kong's financial system remained unchanged following the transfer to Chinese sovereignty in mid-1997. The territory continued as a free port, and the Hong Kong dollar was retained, remaining freely convertible and linked to the US currency. Nevertheless, prior to the surrender of Hong Kong to the People's Republic of China, uncertainty over the territory's future had a destabilizing influence on Hong Kong's economy, and led to an exodus of skilled personnel. The territory's increasingly heavy dependence on the services sector, and the attendant decline in job opportunities in manufacturing, began to cause some concern in the mid-1990s. The rising rate of unemployment, which reached its highest level for more than 10 years in 1995, was also attributed to the return to Hong Kong of emigrants who had secured residency rights in other countries. Furthermore, the territory's competitiveness continued to decline, following sharp increases in labour costs and property prices in the early 1990s. Many companies, mainly in the manufacturing sector but also businesses such as data-processing, were obliged to relocate operations to southern China and elsewhere. In January 1997 the Government announced measures to curtail speculation in the territory's property market. In recognition of the worsening housing shortage, the new SAR administration pledged in late 1997 that 85,000 new housing units would be constructed annually over the next 10 years. In October the currency crisis experienced by much of South-East Asia in mid-1997 severely affected the Hong Kong stock-market index, which declined by some 30% over seven trading days, causing repercussions throughout the world's financial markets. The Hong Kong Monetary Authority maintained a strong defence of the Hong Kong dollar, by raising interest rates and by utilizing some of Hong Kong's extensive foreign exchange reserves. A positive assessment of the Hong Kong economy was given in November by the IMF, which described the territory's economy as 'sound', yet warned of a deceleration in economic growth as a result of the regional financial turmoil. However, in January 1998 the collapse of one of Asia's largest investment banks, Peregrine Investments (which was based in Hong Kong), caused a further sharp fall in the stock-market index. Rumours of a possible devaluation of the Hong Kong dollar were denied by the authorities.

Social Welfare

Social welfare is administered by the Social Welfare Department. Expansion of social welfare services in the 1990s was to continue in accordance with the objectives formulated in the 1991 White Paper on social welfare. The establishment of a government-administered pension scheme for the elderly was proposed in 1994. In December 1996 there were an estimated 9,196 registered physicians, 36,395 nurses (not all resident and working in Hong Kong) and 29,956 hospital beds in the territory. In 1996/97 budgetary expenditure on health services and social welfare was projected at HK $25,051m. and HK $18,227m., respectively.

Education

In September 1996 180,771 children attended kindergarten. Full-time education is compulsory between the ages of six and 15. Primary education has been free in all government schools and in nearly all aided schools since 1971 and junior secondary education since 1978. There are three main types of secondary school: grammar, technical and pre-vocational. The four government-run teacher-training colleges merged to form the Hong Kong Institute of Education in 1994. There are seven government-funded technical institutes. In 1994 total enrolment at primary and secondary schools was equivalent to 91% of the school-age population. Primary enrolment in that year was equivalent to 99% of children in the relevant age-group, while the comparable ratio for secondary enrolment was 85%. In December 1996 the six universities, Lingnan College and the Hong Kong Institute of Education had an estimated combined enrolment of 87,411 full-time and part-time students. The Open Learning Institute of Hong Kong, founded in 1989, had 20,451 students in September 1996. The adult illiteracy rate in 1995 was estimated by UNESCO at 7.8% (males 4.0%; females 11.8%). Budgetary expenditure (capital and recurrent) on education was estimated at HK $39,163m. in the financial year 1996/97.

Public Holidays

1998: 1 January (first weekday in January), 28–30 January (Chinese New Year), 6 April (day following Ching Ming), 10–13 April (Easter), 30 May (Tuen Ng, Dragon Boat Festival), 1 July (SAR Establishment Day), 17 August (Sino-Japanese War Victory Day), 1–2 October

(National Day and day following), 6 October (day following Chinese Mid-Autumn Festival), 28 October (Chung Yeung Festival), 25–26 December (Christmas).

1999 (provisional): 1 January (first weekday in January), mid-February (Chinese New Year), 2–5 April (Easter), 5 April (Ching Ming), May/June (Tuen Ng, Dragon Boat Festival), 1 July (SAR Establishment Day), 17 August (Sino-Japanese War Victory Day), September/October (Chinese Mid-Autumn Festival), 1–2 October (National Day and day following), October (Chung Yeung Festival), 25–26 December (Christmas).

Weights and Measures

The metric system is in force. Chinese units include: tsün (37.147 mm), chek or ch'ih (37.147 cm); kan or catty (604.8 grams), tam or picul (60.479 kg).

Statistical Survey

Source (unless otherwise stated): Census and Statistics Department, Wanchai Tower, 12 Harbour Rd, Hong Kong; tel. 25824736; fax 28021101.

Area and Population

AREA, POPULATION AND DENSITY

Land area (sq km)	1,095*
Population (census results)†	
11 March 1986	5,495,488
15 March 1991	
Males	2,900,344
Females	2,773,770
Total	5,674,114
Population (official estimates at mid-year)	
1994	6,035,400
1995	6,156,000
1996	6,311,000
Density (per sq km) at mid-1996	5,763

* 422.8 sq miles.

† All residents on the census date, including those who were temporarily absent from Hong Kong.

DISTRIBUTION OF RESIDENT POPULATION
(1991 census)

Hong Kong Island	Kowloon and New Kowloon	Marine	New Territories
1,250,993	2,030,683	17,620	2,374,818

BIRTHS, MARRIAGES AND DEATHS*

	Known live births		Registered marriages		Known deaths	
	Number	Rate (per '000)	Number	Rate (per '000)	Number	Rate (per '000)
1989†	69,621	12.3	43,947	7.8	28,745	5.1
1990†	67,731	12.0	47,168	8.3	29,136	5.2
1991	68,281	12.0	42,568	7.5	28,429	5.0
1992	70,949	12.3	45,702	7.9	30,550	5.3
1993	70,451	12.0	41,681	7.1	30,571	5.2
1994	71,646	11.9	38,264	6.3	29,905	5.0
1995	68,836	11.2	38,786	6.3	31,183	5.1
1996	64,559‡	10.0	37,045	n.a.	32,049‡	4.9

* Excluding Vietnamese migrants.

† Figures revised on the basis of the 1991 census results.

‡ Figure calculated by year of registration.

Expectation of life (years at birth, 1996, provisional): Males 75.9; Females 81.5.

ECONOMICALLY ACTIVE POPULATION
(1996, persons aged 15 years and over)*

	Employed	Unemployed
Agriculture and fishing	11,900	200
Mining and quarrying	500	—
Manufacturing	482,100	18,600
Electricity, gas and water	21,400	—
Construction	269,600	10,900
Trade, restaurants and hotels	887,400	26,500
Transport, storage and communications	331,800	8,000
Financing, insurance, real estate and business services	353,600	5,200
Community, social and personal services	649,500	7,100
Unemployed without previous job	—	9,600
Total labour force†	3,007,700	86,100

* Figures may not add up to the total of the component parts, owing to rounding.

† Including activities not adequately defined.

Source: General Household Survey.

Agriculture

PRINCIPAL CROPS

	1994	1995	1996
Field crops* (metric tons)	710	880	660
Vegetables† (metric tons)	89,000	88,000	76,000
Fresh fruit and nuts (metric tons)	5,340	4,820	5,230
Flowers (HK $'000)	163,352	205,956	186,802

* Includes yam, groundnut, sugar cane, sweet potato and water chestnut.

† Fresh, frozen or preserved.

Source: Agriculture and Fisheries Department, Hong Kong.

LIVESTOCK (estimates—head)

	1994	1995	1996
Cattle	1,790	1,950	1,550
Water buffaloes	150	220	170
Pigs	106,700	106,700	166,200
Goats	280	200	150
Chickens	3,512,100	3,290,000	3,184,500
Ducks	102,600	106,500	28,500
Quail	48,000	35,000	28,800
Pigeons (pairs)	358,100	365,813	412,210

Source: Agriculture and Fisheries Department, Hong Kong.

Fishing*

('000 metric tons, live weight)

	1994	1995	1996
Inland waters:			
Freshwater fish	5.5	5.3	5.1
Pacific Ocean:			
Marine fish	184.1	172.6	165.0
Crustaceans	9.5	8.8	8.0
Molluscs	17.4	13.6	11.0
Total catch	216.5	200.3	189.1

* Including estimated quantities landed directly from Hong Kong vessels in Chinese ports.

Source: Agriculture and Fisheries Department, Hong Kong.

Industry

SELECTED PRODUCTS

('000 metric tons, unless otherwise indicated)

	1993	1994	1995
Crude groundnut oil	29	22	16
Uncooked macaroni and noodle products	93	75	126
Soft drinks ('000 hectolitres)	3,248	3,435	3,273
Cigarettes (million)	25,759	24,747	22,767
Cotton yarn (pure and mixed)	166.0	169.6	147.9
Cotton woven fabrics (million sq m)	755	691.7	655.0
Knitted sweaters ('000)	185,702	166,935	166,467
Men's and boys' jackets ('000)	14,930	13,708	13,552
Men's and boys' trousers ('000)	94,388	61,788	49,499
Women's and girls' blouses ('000)	168,806	152,823	119,258
Women's and girls' dresses ('000)	10,846	8,103	10,433
Women's and girls' skirts, slacks and shorts ('000)	94,072	74,286	70,013
Men's and boys' shirts ('000)	132,108	119,456	96,323
Telephones ('000)	n.a.	n.a.	1,053
Watches ('000)	147,856	133,651	131,431
Electric energy (million kWh)	36,840	34,994	35,461

Finance

CURRENCY AND EXCHANGE RATES

Monetary Units

100 cents = 1 Hong Kong dollar (HK $).

Sterling and US Dollar Equivalents (30 September 1997)

£1 sterling = HK $12.5008;
US $1 = HK $7.7385;
HK $1,000 = £79.995 = US $129.224.

Average Exchange Rate (HK $ per US $)

1994 7.7284
1995 7.7358
1996 7.7343

BUDGET (HK $ million, year ending 31 March)

Revenue	1994/95	1995/96	1996/97*
Direct taxes:			
Earnings and profits tax	74,295	77,419	82,050
Estate duty	1,459	1,277	1,400
Indirect taxes:			
Duties on petroleum products, beverages, tobacco and cosmetics	7,583	7,899	8,334
General rates (property tax)	5,156	5,806	6,295
Motor vehicle taxes	4,662	2,880	3,162
Royalties and concessions	1,653	1,773	1,768
Others	23,202	23,491	30,649
Fines, forfeitures and penalties	1,520	1,607	1,617
Receipts from properties and investments	2,103	2,488	2,809
Reimbursements and contributions	4,048	4,597	5,311

Revenue — *continued*	1994/95	1995/96	1996/97*
Operating revenue from utilities:			
Airport and air services	3,046	3,482	3,875
Postal services	2,739	1,040	94
Water	2,308	2,378	2,475
Others	299	299	305
Fees and charges	9,562	9,879	10,756
Interest receipts (operating revenue)	4,942	5,910	5,643
Capital Works Reserve Fund (land sales and interest)	20,193	22,478	29,037
Capital Investment Fund	2,799	2,681	3,087
Loan funds	953	1,306	1,699
Other capital revenue	2,476	1,355	1,910
Total government revenue	174,998	180,045	202,276

Expenditure†	1994/95	1995/96	1996/97*
Economic affairs and services	7,374	8,707	10,542
Internal security	15,416	17,790	19,983
Immigration	1,517	1,719	1,881
Other security services	2,042	2,355	2,869
Social welfare	10,948	14,147	18,227
Health services	19,322	24,285	25,051
Education	28,878	33,610	39,163
Environmental services	4,401	5,626	6,550
Recreation, culture and amenities	7,924	9,120	11,132
Other community and external affairs	1,305	1,464	1,884
Transport	10,682	10,204	9,078
Land and buildings	10,573	10,787	9,053
Water supply	4,976	5,854	6,049
Support	20,891	26,601	29,887
Housing	19,701	19,069	25,845
Total	165,950	191,338	217,194
Recurrent	119,920	138,693	159,745
Capital	46,030	52,645	57,449

* Revised estimates.

† Figures refer to consolidated expenditure by the public sector. Of the total, government expenditure, after deducting grants, debt repayments and equity injections, was (in HK $ million): 143,170 in 1994/95; 161,633 in 1995/96; 177,722 (estimate) in 1996/97. Expenditure by other public-sector bodies (in HK $ million) was: 22,780 in 1994/95; 29,705 in 1995/96; 39,471 (estimate) in 1996/97.

INTERNATIONAL RESERVES (US $ '000 million at 31 December)

	1994	1995	1996
Gold*	0.03	0.03	0.03
Foreign exchange	49.25	55.40	63.81
Total	49.28	55.43	63.84

* National valuation.

Source: IMF, *International Financial Statistics.*

MONEY SUPPLY (HK $ '000 million at 31 December)

	1994	1995	1996
Currency outside banks	67.31	70.87	76.05
Demand deposits at banking institutions	83.38	80.32	98.33
Total money	150.70	151.19	174.38

Source: IMF, *International Financial Statistics.*

COST OF LIVING
(Consumer price index; base: October 1994–September 1995 = 100)

	1996
Foodstuffs	105.5
Housing	113.3
Fuel and light	106.8
Alcoholic drinks and tobacco	107.3
Clothing and footwear	110.2
Durable goods	102.8
Miscellaneous goods	103.5
Transport	108.0
Miscellaneous services	107.9
All items	108.3

NATIONAL ACCOUNTS
(HK $ million at current market prices)

Expenditure on the Gross Domestic Product

	1994	1995	1996
Government final consumption expenditure	83,658	95,283	106,083
Private final consumption expenditure	592,665	652,875	718,779
Change in stocks	21,263	48,461	16,871
Gross domestic fixed capital formation	301,112	326,184	365,493
Total domestic expenditure	998,698	1,122,803	1,207,226
Exports of goods and services	1,410,681	1,623,407	1,700,779
Less Imports of goods and services	1,398,494	1,661,640	1,712,690
GDP in purchasers' values	1,010,885	1,084,570	1,195,315
GDP at constant 1990 prices	727,506	762,007	798,031

Gross Domestic Product by Economic Activity

	1993	1994	1995*
Agriculture and fishing	1,612	1,596	1,453
Mining and quarrying	197	249	268
Manufacturing	92,582	87,354	89,719
Electricity, gas and water	17,591	22,175	23,562
Construction	43,089	46,325	49,753
Wholesale, retail and import/export trades, restaurants and hotels	224,462	249,167	278,581
Transport, storage and communications	78,993	92,109	100,129
Financing, insurance, real estate and business services	214,550	254,346	253,492
Community, social and personal services	130,408	151,293	174,448
Ownership of premises	89,862	115,659	128,864
Sub-total	893,346	1,020,273	1,100,269
Less Imputed bank service charges	63,177	70,101	81,866
GDP at factor cost	830,169	950,172	1,018,403
Indirect taxes, *less* subsidies	53,278	56,286	52,971
GDP in purchasers' values	883,447	1,006,458	1,071,374

* Preliminary estimates.

External Trade

PRINCIPAL COMMODITIES (HK $ million, excl. gold)

Imports	1994	1995	1996
Food and live animals	50,776	58,195	61,972
Crude materials (inedible) except fuels	23,816	32,398	31,429
Mineral fuels, lubricants and related materials	24,378	28,660	34,644
Petroleum, petroleum products and related materials	18,232	22,143	27,469
Chemicals and related products	84,122	111,777	105,461
Plastic in primary forms	28,438	44,078	37,811
Basic manufactures	259,536	305,588	308,694
Textile yarn, fabrics, made-up articles, etc.	118,205	130,422	127,730
Non-metallic mineral manufactures	39,790	43,960	43,391
Machinery and transport equipment	443,633	553,915	568,856
Office machines and automatic data-processing equipment	48,468	68,737	81,382
Telecommunications and sound recording and reproducing apparatus and equipment	120,621	145,976	141,033
Electrical machinery, apparatus and appliances n.e.s., and electrical parts thereof	138,881	185,943	195,942
Road vehicles	51,419	n. a.	n. a.
Miscellaneous manufactured articles	337,549	372,394	394,582
Clothing (excl. footwear)	96,277	97,886	105,419
Footwear	47,128	52,715	56,734
Photographic apparatus, equipment and supplies, optical goods, watches and clocks	54,314	62,759	62,745
Total (incl. others)	1,250,709	1,491,121	1,535,582

Domestic exports	1994	1995	1996
Chemicals and related products	8,418	9,178	8,691
Basic manufactures	26,455	25,711	24,538
Textile yarn, fabrics, made-up articles, etc.	15,038	14,030	13,693
Machinery and transport equipment	62,211	68,149	59,360
Office machines and automatic data-processing equipment	17,623	17,866	13,090
Telecommunications and sound recording and reproducing apparatus and equipment	11,622	10,587	8,586
Other electrical machinery, apparatus, etc.	24,815	31,889	30,357
Miscellaneous manufactured articles	112,472	115,304	107,193
Clothing (excl. footwear)	73,086	73,801	69,447
Photographic apparatus, equipment and supplies, optical goods, watches and clocks	16,207	17,091	15,084
Total (incl. others)	222,092	231,657	212,160

Re-exports	1994	1995	1996
Chemicals and related products	56,731	74,524	74,143
Plastic in primary forms	20,771	30,636	28,819
Basic manufactures	165,653	196,959	208,518
Textile yarn, fabrics, made-up articles, etc.	82,145	92,840	95,719
Machinery and transport equipment	304,789	367,077	391,077
General industrial machinery, equipment and parts	24,026	26,864	29,134
Office machines and automatic data-processing equipment	37,050	57,347	70,757
Telecommunications and sound recording and reproducing apparatus and equipment	99,552	119,009	115,959
Electric machinery, apparatus and appliances n.e.s., and electrical parts thereof	83,767	114,628	123,764
Miscellaneous manufactured articles	361,579	402,831	434,522
Clothing (excl. footwear)	92,335	90,951	100,524
Footwear	53,269	60,167	65,233
Photographic apparatus, equipment and supplies, optical goods, watches and clocks	41,865	50,767	55,519
Total (incl. others)	947,921	1,112,470	1,185,758

PRINCIPAL TRADING PARTNERS (HK $ million, excl. gold)

Imports	1994	1995	1996
China, People's Repub.	470,876	539,480	570,442
France	15,361	28,930	n. a.
Germany	28,660	32,038	33,884
Italy	22,778	27,637	31,799
Japan	195,036	221,254	208,239
Korea, Repub.	57,551	73,268	73,302
Malaysia	20,147	28,797	33,994
Singapore	61,968	78,027	81,495
Switzerland	14,836	n. a.	n. a.
Taiwan	107,310	129,266	123,202
Thailand	17,196	n. a.	n. a.
United Kingdom	25,405	30,448	33,264
USA	89,343	115,078	121,058
Total (incl. others)	1,250,709	1,491,121	1,535,582

Domestic exports	1994	1995	1996
Australia	2,565	n. a.	n. a.
Canada	4,173	4,324	3,885
China, People's Repub.	61,009	63,555	61,620
France	2,813	3,174	2,947
Germany	12,811	12,178	11,388
Japan	10,455	11,877	11,335
Malaysia	2,813	n. a.	n. a.
Netherlands	4,775	5,152	4,674
Philippines	2,912	n. a.	n. a.
Singapore	12,225	12,236	10,009
Taiwan	6,076	7,971	6,705
Thailand	2,524	n. a.	n. a.
United Kingdom	10,292	10,941	10,597
USA	61,419	61,250	53,860
Total (incl. others)	222,092	231,657	212,160

Re-exports	1994	1995	1996
Australia	13,877	n. a.	n. a.
Canada	14,199	n. a.	n. a.
China, People's Repub.	322,835	384,043	417,752
France	13,671	17,452	18,823
Germany	41,617	45,770	47,216
Italy	11,028	n. a.	n. a.
Japan	54,745	70,081	80,154
Korea, Repub.	16,483	19,292	20,091
Macau	10,748	n. a.	n. a.
Netherlands	13,542	16,702	18,261
Philippines	11,524	n. a.	n. a.
Singapore	20,346	26,011	28,388
Taiwan	22,416	27,758	26,638
United Kingdom	27,318	32,257	35,991
USA	210,077	230,997	242,342
Total (incl. others)	947,921	1,112,470	1,185,758

Transport

RAILWAYS (traffic)

	1994	1995	1996
Passengers:			
Arrivals	1,970	1,868	1,878
Departures	1,970	1,868	1,877
Freight (in metric tons)			
Loaded	345,206	315,742	255,054
Unloaded	1,146,078	996,633	683,907

ROAD TRAFFIC (registered motor vehicles at 31 December)

	1994	1995	1996
Private cars	311,929	318,233	325,131
Private buses	285	333	383
Public buses	9,007	9,599	10,265
Private light buses	2,589	2,585	2,481
Public light buses	4,350	4,350	4,348
Taxis	18,111	18,190	18,126
Goods vehicles	141,574	136,316	134,419
Motor cycles	28,372	29,073	30,164
Crown vehicles (excl. vehicles of HM Forces)	7,478	7,283	7,282
Total (incl. others)	524,021	526,296	532,946

Note: Figures do not include tramcars.

SHIPPING

Merchant Fleet (registered at 31 December)

	1994	1995	1996
Number of vessels	358	399	398
Total displacement ('000 grt)	7,703.4	8,794.8	7,863.0

Source: Lloyd's Register of Shipping, *World Fleet Statistics*.

Traffic (1996)

	Ocean-going Vessels	River Vessels
Vessels entered (number)*	40,688	177,600
Vessels cleared (number)*	40,767	177,100
Passengers landed ('000)	10,603†	—
Passengers embarked ('000)	10,772†	—
Cargo landed ('000 metric tons)	86,403*	14,723‡
Cargo loaded ('000 metric tons)	38,993*	14,009‡

* Provisional. † Includes helicopter passengers to/from Macau.
‡ 1995 figure.

CIVIL AVIATION

	1994	1995	1996
Passengers:			
Arrivals	9,889,567	10,631,000	11,692,000
Departures	10,027,849	10,739,000	11,786,000
Freight (in metric tons):			
Arrivals	605,782	685,450	733,934*
Departures	686,722	772,230	829,598*

* Provisional.

Tourism

VISITOR ARRIVALS BY COUNTRY OF RESIDENCE

	1994	1995	1996
Australia	267,158	280,080	310,597
Canada	185,290	174,656	165,887
China, People's Repub.	1,943,678	2,243,245	2,311,184
France	138,920	129,576	126,986
Germany	236,384	249,266	275,892
Indonesia	176,014	184,417	174,960
Japan	1,440,632	1,691,283	2,382,890
Korea, Repub.	282,392	352,981	396,549
Malaysia	202,181	222,319	263,670
Philippines	249,698	295,018	376,746
Singapore	270,585	279,514	349,768
Taiwan	1,665,330	1,761,111	1,821,279
Thailand	285,041	265,844	n. a.
United Kingdom	379,577	360,545	397,153
USA	776,039	748,911	751,275
Total (incl. others)*	9,331,156	10,199,994	11,702,735

* **Receipts from tourism:** HK$84,520m. in 1996 (excluding expenditure by visitors from the People's Republic of China).

Source: Hong Kong Tourist Association, Hong Kong.

Communications Media

	1994	1995	1996
Telephones*	4,050,000	4,230,000	4,440,000
Periodicals	663	675	625
Daily newspapers	76	59	58

* Estimates.

1994: Radio receivers in use: 3,950,000; Television receivers in use: 1,700,000; Telefax stations in use 256,960; Mobile cellular telephone subscribers 484,820 (Sources: UNESCO, *Statistical Yearbook*; UN, *Statistical Yearbook*).

Education

(1996)

	Institutions	Full-time Teachers*	Students
Kindergartens	734	8,438	180,771
Primary schools	856	19,710	466,507
Secondary schools	498	22,777	477,608
Special schools	68	1,424	8,697
Technical institutes	7	756	48,837
Technical colleges	2	354	13,872
Approved post-secondary college	1	133	2,434
Other post-secondary colleges	16	—	3,061
UGC-funded institutions‡	8	5,154	87,411†
Open Learning Institute	1	—	20,451
Adult education institutions	411	—	92,570

* 1995 figures. † Provisional figure.

‡ Funded by the University Grants Committee; includes Hong Kong Institute of Education.

Directory

The Constitution

Under the terms of the Basic Law of the Hong Kong SAR, from 1 July 1997 the Government comprised the Chief Executive, who was chosen by the 400-member Selection Committee in December 1996; the Executive Council announced by the Chief Executive-designate in early 1997; and the Provisional Legislative Council (PLC), chosen by the Selection Committee in December 1996. The Chief Executive must be a Chinese citizen of at least 40 years of age; he serves a five-year term, with a limit of two consecutive terms; he is accountable to the State Council of the People's Republic of China, and has no military authority; he appoints the Executive Council, judges and the principal government officials; he makes laws with the advice and consent of the legislature; he has a veto over legislation, but can be overruled by a two-thirds majority; he may dissolve the legislature once in a term, but must resign if the legislative impasse continues with the new body. The PLC is responsible for enacting, revising and abrogating laws, for approving the budget, taxation and public expenditure, for debating the policy address of the Chief Executive and for approving the appointment of the judges of the Court of Final Appeal and of the Chief Justice of the High Court. The PLC was to remain in office until the establishment (by 30 June 1998 at the latest) of the first Legislative Council of the Hong Kong SAR.

The Government

Chief Executive: TUNG CHEE-HWA (assumed office 1 July 1997).

EXECUTIVE COUNCIL
(January 1998)

Chairman: The Chief Executive.

Ex-Officio Members:

Chief Secretary for Administration: ANSON CHAN.

Financial Secretary: DONALD TSANG.

Secretary for Justice: ELSIE LEUNG.

Non-Official Members:

Dr CHUNG SZE-YUEN
Dr RAYMOND CHIEN KUO-FUNG
CHUNG SHUI-MING
FONG WONG KUT-MAN
LEE YEH-KWONG
LEUNG KAM-CHUNG
LEUNG CHUN-YING
TAM YIU-CHUNG
TANG YING-YEN
ROSANNA WONG YICK-MING
YANG TI-LIANG

PROVISIONAL LEGISLATIVE COUNCIL

The 60 members of the SAR's Provisional Legislative Council (PLC) were chosen from among 130 candidates at a meeting in Shenzhen of the 400-member Selection Committee on 21 December 1996. Thirty-three members of the PLC, which took office on 1 July 1997, had also served on the outgoing Legislative Council. (A new Legislative Council comprising 60 members—30 to be chosen by functional constituencies, 20 by direct election in five geographical constituencies and 10 by an Election Committee—was to be elected on 24 May 1998.)

President: RITA FAN.

GOVERNMENT OFFICES

Office of the Chief Executive: 705–708 Asia Pacific Finance Tower, Citibank Plaza, 3 Garden Rd; tel. 28783300; fax 25090580.

Government Secretariat: Central Government Offices, Lower Albert Rd, Hong Kong; tel. 28102717; fax 28457895.

Government Information Services: Murray Bldg, Garden Rd, Central; tel. 28428777; fax 28459078.

Political Organizations

After the signing of the Sino-British Joint Declaration in 1984, numerous associations advocating immediate democratic reforms for Hong Kong were formed.

Association for Democracy and People's Livelihood (ADPL): Room 1104, Sun Beam Commercial Bldg, 469–471 Nathan Rd, Kowloon; tel. 27822699; fax 27823137; advocates democracy; Sec. LEE YIU-KWAN.

Citizens' Party: Hong Kong; tel. 25372485; fax 25376937; f. 1997; urges mass participation in politics; Leader CHRISTINE LOH.

Democratic Alliance for the Betterment of Hong Kong (DAB): 12/F, SUP Tower, 83 King's Rd, North Point; tel. 25280136; fax 25284339; e-mail info@dab.org.hk; f. 1992; pro-Beijing; supports return of Hong Kong to the motherland and implementation of the Basic Law; Chair. TSANG YOK-SING; Hon. Sec. MA LIK.

Democratic Party of Hong Kong: Rooms 401/413, Central Government Offices, West Wing, 11 Ice House St, Central; tel. 25372471; fax 23978998; f. 1994 by merger of United Democrats of Hong Kong (UDHK—declared a formal political party in 1990) and Meeting Point; liberal grouping; advocates democracy; Chair. MARTIN LEE; Sec.-Gen. LAW CHI-KWONG.

The Frontier: Room 301, Hong Kong House, 11–19 Wellington St, Central; tel. 25372482; fax 28456203; f. 1996; pro-democracy movement, comprising teachers, students and trade unionists; Spokesperson EMILY LAU.

Hong Kong Democratic Foundation: Room 301, Hong Kong House, 17–19 Wellington St, Central; GPOB 12287; tel. 28696443; fax 28696318; advocates democracy; Chair. ALAN LUNG.

Hong Kong Progressive Alliance: Hong Kong; tel. 25262316; fax 28450127; f. 1994; advocates close relationship with the People's Republic of China; 52-mem. organizing cttee drawn from business and professional community; Spokesman AMBROSE LAU.

Liberal Democratic Foundation (LDF): Hong Kong; pro-Beijing.

Liberal Party: Shun Ho Tower, 2/F, 24–30 Ice House St, Central; tel. 28696833; fax 28453671; f. 1993 by mems of Co-operative Resources Centre (CRC); business-orientated; pro-Beijing; Leader ALLEN LEE PENG-FEI.

New Hong Kong Alliance: 4/F, 14–15 Wo On Lane, Central; fax 28691110; pro-China.

123 Democratic Alliance: Hong Kong.

The **Chinese Communist Party** (based in the People's Republic) and the **Kuomintang** (Nationalist Party of China, based in Taiwan) also maintain organizations.

Judicial System

The Court of Final Appeal was established on 1 July 1997 upon the commencement of the Hong Kong Court of Final Appeal Ordinance. It replaced the Privy Council in London as the highest appellate court in Hong Kong to safeguard the rule of law after 30 June 1997. The Court, when sitting, will comprise five judges—the Chief Justice, three permanent judges and one non-permanent Hong Kong judge or one judge from another common law jurisdiction.

The High Court consists of a Court of Appeal and a Court of First Instance. The Court of First Instance has unlimited jurisdiction in civil and criminal cases, while the District Court has limited jurisdiction. Appeals from these courts lie to the Court of Appeal, presided over by the Chief Judge or a Vice-President of the Court of Appeal with one or two Justices of Appeal. Appeals from Magistrates' Courts are heard by a Court of First Instance judge.

HIGH COURT

38 Queensway; tel. 28690869; fax 28690640.

Chief Justice of the Court of Final Appeal: ANDREW K. N. LI.

Permanent Judges of the Court of Final Appeal: H. LITTON, K. BOKHARY, A. C. CHING.

Justices of Appeal: N. P. POWER, G. P. NAZARETH, J. B. MORTIMER, G. M. GODFREY, B. T. M. LIU, S. H. MAYO.

Chief Judge of the High Court: PATRICK S. O. CHAN.

Judges of the Court of First Instance: M. K. C. WONG, R. A. W. SEARS, N. J. BARNETT, M. SAIED, T. M. GALL, B. R. KEITH, A. S. C. LEONG, K. H. WOO, F. STOCK, A. G. ROGERS, M. STUART-MOORE, D. Y. K. YAM, J. K. FINDLAY, P. C. Y. CHEUNG, W. S. Y. WAUNG, C. SEAGROATT, W. C. K. YEUNG, M. P. BURRELL, Mrs D. LE PICHON, Mrs V. S. BOKHARY, K. K. PANG, W. D. STONE.

OTHER COURTS

District Courts: There are 26 District Judges.

Magistrates' Courts: There are 60 Magistrates and 11 Special Magistrates, sitting in 10 magistracies.

Religion

The Chinese population is predominantly Buddhist. In 1994 the number of active Buddhists was estimated at between 650,000 and 700,000. Confucianism and Daoism are widely practised. The three religions are frequently found in the same temple. In 1990 there were more than 500,000 Christians, approximately 50,000 Muslims, 12,000 Hindus, 1,000 Jews and 3,000 Sikhs. The Bahá'í faith and Zoroastrianism are also represented.

BUDDHISM

Hong Kong Buddhist Association: 1/F, 338 Lockhart Rd; tel. 25749371; fax 28340789; Pres. Ven. KOK KWONG.

CHRISTIANITY

Hong Kong Christian Council: 9/F, 33 Granville Rd, Kowloon; tel. 23687123; fax 27242131; e-mail hkcc@hk.super.net; f. 1954; 21 mem. orgs; Chair. Rev. LI PING-KWONG; Gen. Sec. Rev. Dr TSO MAN-KING.

The Anglican Communion

Bishop of Hong Kong and Macau: Rt Rev. PETER K. K. KWONG, Bishop's House, 1 Lower Albert Rd; tel. 25265355; telex 62822; fax 25212199.

The Lutheran Church

Evangelical Lutheran Church of Hong Kong: 50A Waterloo Rd, Kowloon; tel. 23885847; fax 23887539; 12,400 mems; Pres. Rev. TSO SHUI-WAN.

The Roman Catholic Church

For ecclesiastical purposes, Hong Kong forms a single diocese, nominally suffragan to the archdiocese of Canton (Guangzhou), China. In 1995 there were an estimated 237,416 adherents in the territory, representing about 4% of the total population.

Bishop of Hong Kong: Cardinal JOHN BAPTIST WU CHENG-CHUNG, Catholic Diocese Centre, 16 Caine Rd; tel. 25241633; fax 25218737.

The Press

Hong Kong has a thriving press. In 1996, according to government figures, there were 58 daily newspapers, including 38 Chinese-language and 12 English-language dailies, and 625 periodicals.

PRINCIPAL DAILY NEWSPAPERS

English Language

Asian Wall Street Journal: GPOB 9825; tel. 25737121; fax 28345291; f. 1976; business; Editor URBAN C. LEHNER; circ. 51,009.

China Daily: Hong Kong edition of China's official English-language newspaper; launched 1997; Editor LIU DIZHONG.

Hong Kong Standard: Sing Tao Bldg, 4/F, 1 Wang Kwong Rd, Kowloon Bay, Kowloon; tel. 27982798; fax 27953009; f. 1949; Editor TERRY CHENG; circ. 55,000.

International Herald Tribune: 7/F, 50 Gloucester Rd; tel. 29221188; fax 29221190; Correspondent KEVIN MURPHY.

South China Morning Post: Morning Post Centre, Dai Fat St, Tai Po Industrial Centre, Tai Po, New Territories; tel. 26808888; fax 26616984; f. 1903; Editor JONATHAN FENBY; circ. 104,000.

Target Financial Service: Wah Tao Bldg, 4/F, 42 Wood Rd, Wanchai; tel. 25730379; fax 28381597; e-mail targnews@hkstar.com; f. 1972; financial news, commentary, politics, property, litigations, etc.

Chinese Language

Ching Pao: 3/F, 141 Queen's Rd East; tel. 25273836; f. 1956; Editor MOK KONG; circ. 120,000.

Hong Kong Commercial Daily: 1/F, 499 King's Rd, North Point; tel. 25905322; fax 25658947.

Hong Kong Daily News: All Flats, Hong Kong Industrial Bldg, 17/F, 444–452 Des Voeux Rd West; tel. 28555111; telex 83567; fax 28198717; f. 1958; morning; Man. Dir SIMON LUNG; Chief Editor K. P. FUNG; circ. 101,815.

Hong Kong Economic Journal: North Point Industrial Bldg, 22/F, 499 King's Rd; tel. 28567567; fax 28111070; Editor-in-Chief JOSEPH LIAN; circ. 70,000.

Hong Kong Economic Times: Kodak House, Block 2, Room 808, 321 Java Rd, North Point; tel. 28802888; fax 28111926; f. 1988; Publr PERRY MAK; Chief Editor ERIC CHAN; circ. 64,565.

Hong Kong Sheung Po (Hong Kong Commercial Daily): 499 King's Rd, North Point; tel. 25640788; f. 1952; morning; Editor-in-Chief H. CHEUNG; circ. 110,000.

Hsin Wan Pao (New Evening Post): 342 Hennessy Rd, Wanchai; tel. 28911604; fax 28382307; f. 1950; Editor-in-Chief CHAO TSE-LUNG; circ. 90,000.

Ming Pao Daily News: Block A, Ming Pao Industrial Centre, 15/F, 18 Ka Yip St, Chai Wan; tel. 25953111; fax 28982534; f. 1959; morning; Chief Editor PAUL CHEUNG; circ. 90,888.

Oriental Daily News: Oriental Press Centre, Wang Tai Rd, Kowloon Bay, Kowloon; tel. 27951111; fax 27955599; Chair. C. F. MA; Editor-in-Chief MA KAI LUN; circ. 650,000.

Ping Kuo Jih Pao (Apple Daily): Hong Kong; tel. 29908685; fax 23708908; f. 1995; Propr JIMMY LAI; Publr LOH CHAN; circ. 400,000.

Seng Weng Evening News: 5/F, 198 Tsat Tse Mui Rd; tel. 25637523; f. 1957; Editor WONG LONG-CHAU; circ. 60,000.

Sing Pao Daily News: Sing Pao Bldg, 101 King's Rd, North Point; tel. 25702201; telex 60587; fax 28870348; f. 1939; morning; Chief Editor HON CHUNG-SUEN; circ. 229,250.

Sing Tao Daily: Sing Tao Bldg, 3/F, 1 Wang Kwong Rd, Kowloon Bay, Kowloon; tel. 27982575; telex 40347; fax 27953022; f. 1938; morning; Editor-in-Chief LUK KAM WING; circ. 60,000.

Ta Kung Pao: 342 Hennessy Rd, Wanchai; tel. 25757181; telex 72859; fax 28345104; e-mail tkp@takungpao.com; f. 1902; morning; supports People's Republic of China; Editor T. S. TSANG; circ. 150,000.

Tin Tin Yat Pao: Culturecom Centre, 10/F, 47 Hung To Rd, Kwun Tong, Kowloon; tel. 29507300; fax 23452285; f. 1960; Chief Editor IP KAI-WING; circ. 199,258.

Wen Wei Po: Hing Wai Centre, 2–4/F, 7 Tin Wan Praya Rd, Aberdeen; tel. 28738288; fax 28730657; f. 1948; morning; communist; Dir CHANG YUN-FENG; Editor-in-Chief LIU ZAI-MING; circ. 180,000.

SELECTED PERIODICALS

English Language

Asia Magazine: Morning Post Centre, 4/F, Dai Fat St, Tai Po Industrial Estate, Tai Po, NT; tel. 26808572; fax 26808583; f. 1961; weekend magazine for English language newspapers; Editor JOYCE MOY; circ. 808,900.

Asian Business: c/o Far East Trade Press Ltd, Block C, 10/F, Seaview Estate, 2–8 Watson Rd, North Point; tel. 25668381; fax 25080255; monthly; Publr and Editor-in-Chief ANTHONY S. C. TEO; circ. 100,000.

Asian Medical News: Pacific Plaza, 8/F, 410 Des Voeux Rd West; tel. 25595888; fax 25596910; e-mail amn@medimedia.com.hk; f. 1979; monthly; Man. Editor LYNNE LARACY; circ. 28,050.

Asian Profile: Asian Research Service, GPOB 2232; tel. 25707227; telex 63899; fax 25128050; f. 1973; 6 a year; multi-disciplinary study of Asian affairs.

Asiaweek: Citicorp Centre, 34/F, 18 Whitfield Rd, Causeway Bay; tel. 25082688; fax 25710916; f. 1975; Asian news weekly; Editor ANN MORRISON; circ. 130,000.

Business Traveller Asia/Pacific: Tung Sun Commercial Bldg, 13/F, 200 Lockhart Rd, Wanchai; tel. 25119317; telex 62107; fax 25196846; e-mail biztrvlr@netvigator.com.; f. 1982; consumer business travel; 12 a year; Editor JONATHAN WALL; Assoc. Publr GEORGINA WONG; circ. 23,000.

Executive Magazine: Sunpress Company Ltd, Sing Tao Bldg, 4/F, 1 Wang Kwong Rd, Kowloon; tel. 28155221; fax 28542794; f. 1979; monthly; Publr JOAN HOWLEY; circ. 18,225.

Far East Business: POB 9765; tel. 25721116; telex 66381; fax 28650844; f. 1967; business, government and industry; 12 a year; Editor LEWIS H. YOUNG; circ. 70,000.

Far Eastern Economic Review: Citicorp Centre, 25/F, 18 Whitfield Rd, Causeway Bay, GPOB 160; tel. 25084338; fax 25031553; f. 1946; weekly; Editor NAYAN CHANDA; circ. 81,500.

Hong Kong Electronics: Office Tower, Convention Plaza, 38/F, 1 Harbour Rd; tel. 25844333; telex 73595; fax 28240249; f. 1985; quarterly; publ. by the Hong Kong Trade Development Council; circ. 40,000.

Hong Kong Enterprise: Office Tower, Convention Plaza, 38/F, 1 Harbour Rd; tel. 25844333; telex 73595; fax 28240249; f. 1967; monthly; also 2 a year in Chinese; publ. by the Hong Kong Trade Development Council; Editor SAUL LOCKHART; circ. 70,000.

Hong Kong Government Gazette: Govt Printing Dept, Cornwall House, Taikoo Trading Estate, 28 Tong Chong St, Quarry Bay; tel. 25649500; weekly.

Hong Kong Household: Office Tower, Convention Plaza, 38/F, 1 Harbour Rd; tel. 25844333; telex 73595; fax 28240249; f. 1983; publ. by the Hong Kong Trade Development Council; household and hardware products; 2 a year; Editor SAUL LOCKHART; circ. 30,000.

Hong Kong Industrialist: Federation of Hong Kong Industries, Hankow Centre, 4/F, 5–15 Hankow Rd, Tsimshatsui, Kowloon; tel. 27323188; telex 30101; fax 27213494; e-mail fhki@fhki.org.hk; monthly; publ. by the Federation of Hong Kong Industries; Editor SALLY HOPKINS; circ. 7,000.

Hong Kong Trader: Office Tower, Convention Plaza, 38/F, 1 Harbour Rd; tel. 25844333; fax 28240249; e-mail trader@tdc.org.hk; f. 1983; publ. by the Hong Kong Trade Development Council; trade, economics, financial and general business news; monthly; Man. Editor SOPHY FISHER; circ. 65,000.

Official Hong Kong Guide: Wilson House, 3/F, 19–27 Wyndham St, Central; tel. 25215392; telex 74523; fax 25218638; f. 1982; monthly; information on sightseeing, shopping, dining, etc. for overseas visitors; Editor-in-Chief DEREK DAVIES; circ. 9,300.

Orientations: 200 Lockhart Rd, 14/F; tel. 25111368; fax 25074620; e-mail info@orientations.com.hk; f. 1970; 11 a year; arts of East Asia, the Indian subcontinent and South-East Asia; Publr and Editorial Dir ELIZABETH KNIGHT.

Reader's Digest (Asia Edn): 3 Ah Kung Ngam Village Rd, Shaukiwan; tel. 28845678; telex 74700; fax 25689024; f. 1963; general topics; monthly; Editor-in-Chief JANIE COUCH; circ. 277,000.

Sunday Examiner: Catholic Diocese Centre, 11/F, 16 Caine Rd; tel. 25220487; fax 25213095; f. 1946; religious; weekly; Editor Fr JOHN J. CASEY; circ. 2,300.

Target Intelligence Report: Wah Tao Bldg, 4/F, 42 Wood Rd, Wanchai; tel. 25730379; fax 28381597; f. 1972; monthly; financial analysis, investigations, surveys, food, wine and car reviews, etc.; Editor RAYMONDE SACKLYN; circ. 120,000.

Textile Asia: c/o Business Press Ltd, California Tower, 11/F, 30–32 D'Aguilar St, GPOB 185, Central; tel. 25233744; fax 28106966; e-mail texasia@netvigator.com; f. 1970; monthly; textile and clothing industry; Publr and Editor-in-Chief KAYSER W. SUNG; circ. 17,000.

Tradefinance Asia: 16/F, 2 Wellington St; telex 84247; monthly; Editor RICHARD TOURRET.

Travel Business Analyst: GPOB 12761; tel. 25072310; fax 25074620; e-mail tba@asiaonline.net; f. 1982; travel trade; monthly; Editor MURRAY BAILEY.

Chinese Language

Affairs Weekly: Hong Kong; tel. 28950801; fax 25767842; f. 1980; general interest; Editor WONG WAI MAN; circ. 130,000.

Cheng Ming Monthly: Hennessy Rd, POB 20370; tel. 25740664; Chief Editor WAN FAI.

City Magazine: Hang Seng Bldg, 7/F, 200 Hennessy Rd, Wanchai; tel. 28931393; telex 84289; fax 28388761; f. 1976; monthly; fashion, wine, cars, society, etc.; Publr JOHN K. C. CHAN; Chief Editor PETER WONG; circ. 30,000.

Contemporary Monthly: Unit 705, Westlands Centre, 20 Westlands Rd, Quarry Bay; tel. 25638122; fax 25632984; f. 1989; monthly; current affairs; 'China-watch'; Editor-in-Chief CHING CHEONG; circ. 50,000.

Disc Jockey: Fuk Keung Ind. Bldg, B2, 14/F, 66–68 Tong Mei Rd, Taikoktsui, Kowloon; tel. 23905461; fax 27893869; f. 1990; monthly; music; Publr VINCENT LEUNG; circ. 32,000.

Eastweek: Oriental Press Centre, Wang Tai Rd, Kowloon Bay, Kowloon; tel. 27951111; fax 27955599; f. 1992; weekly; general interest; Chair. C. F. MA; circ. 238,000.

Elegance HK: Aik San Bldg, 14/F, 14 Westlands Rd, Quarry Bay; tel. 2963011; telex 84289; fax 25658217; f. 1977; monthly; for thinking women; Chief Editor WINNIE YUEN; circ. 75,000.

Kung Kao Po (Catholic Chinese Weekly): 11/F, 16 Caine Rd; tel. 25220487; fax 25213095; f. 1928; religious; weekly; Editor-in-Chief PETER CHEUNG KA HING.

Lisa's Kitchen Bi-Weekly: Fuk Keung Ind. Bldg, B2, 14/F, 66–68 Tong Mei Rd, Taikoktsui, Kowloon; tel. 23910668; fax 27893869; f. 1984; recipes; Publr VINCENT LEUNG; circ. 50,000.

Metropolitan Weekly: Toppan Bldg, Rm 1008, 10/F, 22A Westlands Rd, Quarry Bay; tel. 28113811; fax 28113822; f. 1983; weekly; entertainment, social news; Chief Editor CHARLES YOU; circ. 130,000.

Ming Pao Monthly: Ming Pao Industrial Centre, 15/F, Block A, 18 Ka Yip St, Chai Wan; tel. 25155107; fax 28982566; Chief Editor KOO SIU-SUN.

Motor Magazine: Flat D, 1/F, Prospect Mansion, 66–72 Paterson St, Causeway Bay; tel. 28822230; telex 49505; fax 28823949; f. 1990; Publr and Editor-in-Chief KENNETH LI; circ. 32,000.

Next Magazine: Hong Kong; tel. 28119686; fax 28113862; f. 1989; weekly; news, business, lifestyle, entertainment; Editor-in-Chief LEUNG TIN WAI; circ. 180,000.

The Nineties Monthly: Going Fine Ltd, Flats A & B, 1/F, Southward Mansion, 3 Lau Li St, Causeway Bay; tel. 28873997; fax 28873897; f. 1970; Editor LEE YEE; circ. 20,000.

Open Magazine: Causeway Bay, POB 31429; tel. 28939197; fax 28935591; f. 1990; monthly; Chief Editor JIN CHONG; circ. 15,000.

Oriental Sunday: Oriental Press Centre, Wang Tai Rd, Kowloon Bay, Kowloon; tel. 27951111; fax 27952299; f. 1991; weekly; leisure magazine; Chair. C. F. MA; circ. 120,000.

Reader's Digest (Chinese Edn): Reader's Digest Association Far East Ltd, 3 Ah Kung Ngam Village Rd, Shaukiwan; tel. 28845590; fax 25671479; f. 1965; monthly; Editor-in-Chief VICTOR FUNG KEUNG; circ. 315,000.

Today's Living: Flat D, 1/F, Prospect Mansion, 66–72 Paterson St, Causeway Bay; tel. 28822230; telex 49505; fax 28823949; f. 1987; monthly; interior design; Publr and Editor-in-Chief KENNETH LI; circ. 35,000.

TV Week: 1 Leighton Rd, Causeway Bay; tel. 28366147; fax 28346717; f. 1967; weekly; Publr PETER CHOW; circ. 59,082.

Yazhou Zhoukan: Block A, Ming Pao Industrial Centre, 15/F, 18 Ka Yip St, Chai Wan; tel. 25155358; telex 83540; fax 25059662; f. 1987; global Chinese news weekly; Man. Editor YAU LOP-POON; circ. 93,000.

Young Girl Magazine: Fuk Keung Ind. Bldg, B2, 14/F, 66–68 Tong Mei Rd, Taikoktsui, Kowloon; tel. 23910668; fax 27893869; f. 1987; biweekly; Publr VINCENT LEUNG; circ. 65,000.

Yuk Long TV Weekly: Hong Kong; tel. 25657883; fax 25659958; f. 1977; entertainment, fashion, etc.; Publr TONY WONG; circ. 82,508.

NEWS AGENCIES

International News Service: 2E Cheong Shing Mansion, 33–39 Wing Hing St, Causeway Bay; tel. 25665668; Rep. AU KIT MING.

Foreign Bureaux

Agence France-Presse (AFP): Telecom House, Room 1840, 18/F, 3 Gloucester Rd, Wanchai, GPOB 5613; tel. 28020224; telex 73415; fax 28027292; Regional Dir YVAN CHEMLA.

Agencia EFE (Spain): 10A Benny View House, 63–65 Wong Nai Chung Rd, Happy Valley; tel. 28080199; fax 28823101; Correspondent MIREN GUTIÉRREZ.

Associated Press (AP) (USA): 1282 New Mercury House, Waterfront Rd; tel. 25274324; telex 73265; Bureau Chief ROBERT LIU.

Central News Agency (CNA) Inc (Taiwan): 60 Tanner Rd, 8/F-A, North Point; tel. 25277885; fax 28656810; Bureau Chief CONRAD LU.

Jiji Tsushin-Sha (Japan): Room 1811, Hutchinson House, 10 Harcourt Rd; tel. 25237112; telex 73295; fax 28459013; Bureau Man. KATSUHIKO KABASAWA.

Kyodo News Service (Japan): Unit 1303, 13/F, 9 Queen's Rd, Central; tel. 25249750; telex 76499; fax 28105591; e-mail tyoko@po.iijnet.or.jp; Correspondent TSUKASA YOKOYAMA.

Reuters Asia Ltd (United Kingdom): Gloucester Tower, 5F, 11 Pedder St, Central; tel. 258436363; telex 73310; Bureau Man. GEOFF WEETMAN.

United Press International (UPI) (USA): 1287 Telecom House, 3 Gloucester Rd, POB 5692; tel. 28020221; telex 73418; fax 28024972; Vice-Pres. (Asia) ARNOLD ZEITLIN; Editor (Asia) PAUL H. ANDERSON.

Xinhua (New China) News Agency (People's Republic of China): 387 Queen's Rd East, Wanchai; tel. 28314126; telex 73383; Dir JIANG ENZHU.

PRESS ASSOCIATIONS

Chinese Language Press Institute: Hong Kong; tel. 25616211.

Hong Kong Chinese Press Association: 3/F, 48 Gage St; tel. 25439477.

Hong Kong Journalists Association: POB 11726; tel. 25910692; fax 25727329; f. 1968; 650 mems; Chair. TONG KAM-PIU.

Newspaper Society of Hong Kong: Culturecom Centre, 12/F, 47 Hung To Rd, Kwun Tong, Kowloon; tel. 29507129; fax 27639691; f. 1954; Chair. L. Y. TANG.

Publishers

Asian Research Service: GPOB 2232; tel. 25707227; fax 25128050; f. 1972; geography, maps, atlases, monographs on Asian studies and journals; authorized agent for China National Publishing Industry Trading Corporation; Dir NELSON LEUNG.

Business Press Ltd: California Tower, 11/F, 30–32 D'Aguilar St, GPOB 185, Central; tel. 25233744; fax 28106966; e-mail texasia@netvigator.com; f. 1970; textile magazine; Man. Dir KAYSER W. SUNG.

Chinese University Press: Chinese University of Hong Kong, Sha Tin, New Territories; tel. 26096508; fax 26036692; f. 1977; studies on China and Hong Kong and other academic works; Dir PAUL S. L. WONG.

Commercial Press (Hong Kong) Ltd: Kiu Ying Bldg, 2D Finnie St, Quarry Bay; tel. 25651371; telex 86564; fax 25645277; f. 1897; trade books, dictionaries, textbooks, Chinese classics, art, etc.; Man. Dir and Chief Editor CHAN MAN HUNG.

Excerpta Medica Asia Ltd: 8/F, 67 Wyndham St; tel. 25243118; telex 71866; fax 28100687; f. 1980; sponsored medical publications, abstracts, journals etc.

Far East Trade Press Ltd: Seaview Estate, Block C, 10/F, 2–8 Watson Rd, North Point; tel. 25668381; fax 25080255; trade magazines and directories; CEO ANTHONY TEO.

Hong Kong University Press: Hing Wai Centre, 14/F, 7 Tin Wan Praya Rd, Aberdeen; tel. 25502703; fax 28750734; e-mail hkupress@hkucc.hku.hk; internet http://www.hkupress.org; f. 1956; Publr BARBARA CLARKE; Man. Editor DENNIS CHEUNG.

Ling Kee Publishing Co Ltd: Zung Fu Industrial Bldg, 1067 King's Rd, Quarry Bay; tel. 25616151; fax 28111980; f. 1956; educational and reference; Chair. B. L. AU; Man. Dir K. W. AU.

Oxford University Press (China) Ltd: Warwick House, 18/F, 979 King's Rd, Taikoo Place, Quarry Bay; tel. 25163222; fax 25658491; e-mail oupchina@oupchina.com.hk; f. 1961; school textbooks, reference, academic and general works relating to Hong Kong and China; Regional Dir A. F. D. SCOTT.

Government Publishing House

Government Information Services: see p. 932.

PUBLISHERS' ASSOCIATIONS

Hong Kong Publishers' and Distributors' Association: National Bldg, 4/F, 240–246 Nathan Rd, Kowloon; tel. 23674412.

Society of Publishers in Asia: c/o Worldcom Hong Kong, 502–503 Admiralty Centre, Tower I, 18 Harcourt Rd, Admiralty; tel. 28654007; fax 28652559.

Broadcasting and Communications

TELECOMMUNICATIONS

Asia Satellite Telecommunications Co Ltd (AsiaSat): East Exchange Tower, 23–24/F, 38–40 Leighton Rd; tel. 28056666; fax 25043875.

Hong Kong Telecommunications Ltd: Hongkong Telecom Tower, 39/F, Taikoo Place, 979 King's Rd, Quarry Bay; tel. 28882888; fax 28778877; Non-Exec. Chair. RICHARD BROWN; CEO LINUS CHEUNG.

Telecommunications Authority: statutory regulator, responsible for implementation of the Govt's pro-competition and pro-consumer policies.

In late 1996 eight companies were licensed to provide mobile telecommunications services.

BROADCASTING

Broadcasting Authority: regulatory body; administers and issues broadcasting licences.

Radio Television Hong Kong: Broadcasting House, 30 Broadcast Drive, POB 70200, Kowloon Central PO; tel. 23396300; telex 45568; fax 23380279; f. 1928; govt-funded; 24-hour service in English and Chinese on seven radio channels; service in Mandarin inaugurated in 1997; television division produces drama, documentary and public affairs programmes; also operates an educational service for transmission by two local commercial stations; Dir M. Y. CHEUNG.

Radio

Hong Kong Commercial Broadcasting Co Ltd: GPO Box 3000; tel. 23365111; fax 23380021; f. 1959; broadcasts in English and Chinese on three radio frequencies; Chair. GEORGE HO; Man. Dir WINNIE YU.

Metro Radio: Site 11, Basement 1, Whampoa Gardens, Hunghom, Kowloon; tel. 23649333; fax 23646577; f. 1991; broadcasts on three channels in English, Cantonese and Mandarin; Gen. Man. CRAIG B. QUICK.

Star Radio: Hutchison House, 12/F, 10 Harcourt Rd, Central; f. 1995; satellite broadcasts in Mandarin and English; Gen. Man. MIKE MACKAY.

Television

Asia Television Ltd (ATV): Television House, 81 Broadcast Drive, Kowloon; tel. 29928888; telex 44680; fax 23384347; f. 1973; operates two commercial television services (English and Chinese) and produces television programmes; Dir and CEO LIM POR YEN.

Satellite Television Asian Region Ltd—STAR TV: One Harbourfront, 8/F, 18 Tak Fung St, Hunghom, Kowloon; tel. 26218888; fax 26218000; f. 1990; wholly-owned subsidiary of the News Corpn Ltd; broadcasts programming services via satellite to 260m. viewers in 53 countries across Asia, the Indian subcontinent and the Middle East; music, sport and entertainment broadcasts in English, Mandarin, Hindi, Japanese, Tagalog, Bahasa Indonesia, Thai and Malayalam; subscription and free-to-air services on several channels; CEO GARY DAVEY.

Television Broadcasts Ltd (TVB): TV City, Clearwater Bay Rd, Kowloon; tel. 27194828; telex 43596; fax 23581300; f. 1967; operates Chinese and English language services; two colour networks; Exec. Chair. Sir RUN RUN SHAW; Man. Dir LOUIS PAGE.

Wharf Cable Ltd: Wharf Cable Tower, 4/F, 9 Hoi Shing Rd, Tsuen Wan; tel. 26115533; fax 24171511; f. 1993; 24-hour subscription service of news, sport and entertainment initially on 16 channels; carries BBC World Service Television; Chair. PETER WOO; Man. Dir STEPHEN NG.

Finance

(cap. = capital; res = reserves; dep. = deposits; m. = million; brs = branches; amounts in Hong Kong dollars unless otherwise stated)

BANKING

In August 1997 there were 183 licensed banks, of which 31 were locally incorporated, operating in Hong Kong. There were also 64 restricted licence banks (formerly known as licensed deposit-taking companies), 120 deposit-taking companies, and 159 foreign banks' representative offices.

Hong Kong Monetary Authority (HKMA): 30/F, 3 Garden Rd, Central; tel. 28788196; fax 28788197; e-mail hkma@hkma.gov.hk;

f. 1993 by merger of Office of the Commissioner of Banking and Office of the Exchange Fund; carries out central banking functions; maintains Hong Kong dollar currency stability within the framework of the linked exchange rate system; supervises licensed banks, restricted licence banks and deposit-taking cos, their overseas brs and representative offices; manages foreign currency reserves; Chief Exec. JOSEPH YAM; Deputy Chief Execs DAVID CARSE, ANDREW SHENG, NORMAN CHAN.

Banks of Issue

Bank of China (People's Repub. of China): Bank of China Tower, 1 Garden Rd, Central; tel. 28266888; telex 73772; fax 28105963; f. 1917; became third bank of issue in May 1994; Gen. Man. YANG ZILIN; 27 brs.

The Hongkong and Shanghai Banking Corpn Ltd: 1 Queen's Rd, Central; tel. 28221111; telex 73201; fax 28101112; internet http://www.hongkongbank.com; f. 1865; personal and commercial banking; cap. 16,254m., res 67,176m., dep. 1,030,306m. (Dec. 1996); Chair. J. E. STRICKLAND; CEO D. G. ELDON; more than 600 offices world-wide.

Standard Chartered Bank: Standard Chartered Bank Bldg, 4–4A Des Voeux Rd, Central; tel. 28203333; fax 28569129; f. 1859; Group Exec. Dir MERVYN DAVIES; 100 brs.

Other Commercial Banks

Asia Commercial Bank Ltd: Asia Financial Centre, 120–122 Des Voeux Rd, Central; tel. 25419222; telex 73085; fax 25410009; f. 1934; fmrly Commercial Bank of Hong Kong; cap. 400.0m., res 752.3m., dep. 10,070.5m. (Dec. 1996); Chair. and CEO ROBIN Y. H. CHAN; Vice-Chair. and Exec. Dir JOHN C. C. CHEUNG; 16 brs.

Bank of East Asia Ltd: GPOB 31, 10 Des Voeux Rd, Central; tel. 28423200; telex 73017; fax 28459333; inc in Hong Kong in 1918; cap. 2,756.2m., res 8,931.6m., dep. etc. 95,106.9m. (Dec. 1996); Chair. and Chief Exec. DAVID K. P. LI; 77 brs in Hong Kong and 13 overseas brs.

Chekiang First Bank Ltd: Chekiang First Bank Centre, 1 Duddell St, Central; tel. 29221222; telex 73686; fax 28669133; f. 1950; cap. 525.0m., res 1,829.1m., dep. 22,061.1m. (Dec. 1996); Chair. JAMES Z. M. KUNG; 18 brs.

Dah Sing Bank Ltd: Dah Sing Financial Centre, 36/F, 108 Gloucester Rd, Central; tel. 25078866; telex 74063; fax 25987101; f. 1947; cap. 500.0m., res 2,211.5m., dep. 32,485.0m. (Dec. 1996); Chair. DAVID S. Y. WONG: Man. Dir RONALD CARSTAIRS; 43 brs.

Dao Heng Bank Ltd: Wu Chung House, 32–35/F, 213 Queen's Rd East, Central; tel. 28315000; telex 73345; fax 28916683; f. 1921; cap. 2,704.3m., res 6,530.1m., dep. 87,811.5m. (June 1996); Chair. QUEK LENG-CHAN; CEO KWEK LENG-HAI; 54 domestic brs, 5 overseas brs.

First Pacific Bank Ltd: First Pacific Bank Centre, 22/F, 56 Gloucester Rd; tel. 28239239; fax 28655151; f. 1922; fmrly The Hong Nin Savings Bank Ltd; merged with Far East Bank in 1989; cap. 1,073.0m., res 839.3m., dep. 24,403.5m. (Dec. 1996); Chair. M. PANGILINAN; Man. Dir J. C. NG; 27 brs.

Hang Seng Bank Ltd: 83 Des Voeux Rd, Central; tel. 28255111; telex 73311; fax 28459301; f. 1933; cap. and res 48,285m., dep. 320,845m. (Dec. 1996); Chair. Dr LEE QUO-WEI; Vice-Chair. and CEO A. S. K. AU; 146 brs.

Hongkong Chinese Bank Ltd: Lippo Centre, Floor Mezz. 1, 89 Queensway; tel. 28448833; telex 73749; fax 28459221; f. 1954; cap. 1,891m., res 950m., dep. 19,208m. (Dec. 1996); Chair. MOCHTAR RIADY; Man. Dir and Chief Exec. DAVID P. L. CHAN; 26 brs.

International Bank of Asia Ltd: 34–38 Des Voeux Rd, Central; tel. 28426222; telex 63394; fax 28101483; f. 1982 as Sun Hung Kai Bank Ltd, name changed 1986; subsidiary of Arab Banking Corpn; cap. 746m., res 1,128m., dep. 18,176m. (Dec. 1996); Chair. Sheikh ALI JARRAH AL-SABAH; Man. Dir and CEO M. M. MURAD; 25 brs.

Ka Wah Bank Ltd: 232 Des Voeux Rd, Central; tel. 25457131; telex 74636; fax 25417029; f. 1922; cap. 1,108.5m., res 987.1m., dep. 23,115.9m. (Dec. 1996); Chair. and Chief Exec. JIN DE-QIN; 31 brs.

Kwong On Bank Ltd: Asia Standard Tower, 59–65 Queen's Rd, Central; tel. 28153636; telex 73359; fax 28506129; f. 1938, inc 1954; cap. 750m., res 3,409m., dep. 20,562m. (Dec. 1996); Chair. RONALD LEUNG DING-BONG; Sr Man. Dir KENNETH T. M. LEUNG; 31 brs.

Liu Chong Hing Bank Ltd: POB 2535, 24 Des Voeux Rd, Central; tel. 28417417; telex 75700; fax 28459134; f. 1948; cap. 200m., res. 4,308.4m., dep. 22,095.5m. (Dec. 1996); Chair. LIU LIT-FOR; Man. Dir LIU LIT-MAN; 32 brs.

Nanyang Commercial Bank Ltd: 151 Des Voeux Rd, Central; tel. 28520888; telex 73412; fax 28153333; internet http://www.nanyangbankhk.com; f. 1949; cap. p.u. 600m., res 7,147m., dep. 60,254m. (Dec. 1996); Chair. ZHANG HONG-YI; 42 brs, 6 mainland brs, 1 overseas br.

Overseas Trust Bank Ltd: OTB Bldg, 160 Gloucester Rd, Central; tel. 28312161; telex 74545; fax 25727535; f. 1955; under govt control 1985–93; cap. 2,000m., res 2,322.3m., dep. 43,660.4m. (June 1996); acquired by Dao Heng Bank in 1993; Chair. QUEK LENG CHAN; 42 brs in Hong Kong, 6 overseas brs.

Po Sang Bank Ltd: 71 Des Voeux Rd, Central; tel. 28436111; telex 75164; fax 28101126; f. 1949; cap. 400m., res 5,535m., dep. 38,296.5m. (Dec. 1996); Chair. LAM KWONG-SUI; Gen. Man. GAO JI-LU; 19 brs.

Shanghai Commercial Bank Ltd: 12 Queen's Rd, Central; tel. 28415415; telex 73390; fax 28104623; e-mail contact@shacombank.com.hk; f. 1950; cap. US $205.1m., res US $594.9m., dep. US $5,060.6m. (1996); Chair. and Man. Dir PAO-CHU SHIH; Gen. Man. JOHN KAM-PAK YAN; 42 brs.

Union Bank of Hong Kong Ltd: Union Bank Tower, 122–126 Queen's Rd, Central; tel. 25343333; telex 73264; fax 28051166; f. 1964; cap. 487.8m., res 1,115m., dep. 13,241m. (Dec. 1996); Chair. LI YIN FEI; 22 brs.

Wing Hang Bank Ltd: POB 514, 161 Queen's Rd, Central; tel. 28525111; telex 73268; fax 25410036; f. 1937; cap. 245.0m., res 3,342.9m., dep. 33,088.6m. (Dec. 1996); Chair. and Chief Exec. PATRICK Y. FUNG; 24 brs.

Wing Lung Bank Ltd: 43–49 Des Voeux Rd, Central; tel. 28268333; telex 73360; fax 28100592; e-mail wlb@winglungbank.com.hk; f. 1933; cap. 1,160m. (April 1997), res 4,262m., dep. 37,256m. (Dec. 1996); Chair. MICHAEL PO-KO WU; Exec. Dir and Gen. Man. CHE-SHUM CHUNG; 35 brs.

Principal Foreign Banks

ABN AMRO Bank NV (Netherlands): Edinburgh Tower, 3–4/F, Landmark, 15 Queen's Rd, Central; tel. 28429211; telex 73453; fax 28459049; CEO (China) SERGIO RIAL; 10 brs.

American Express Bank Ltd (USA): One Pacific Place, 35/F, 88 Queensway, Central; tel. 28440688; telex 73675; fax 28453637; Exec. Dir and Regional Head JOHN FILMERIDIS; 4 brs.

Australia and New Zealand Banking Group Ltd: 27/F, One Exchange Square, 8 Connaught Place, Central; tel. 28437111; telex 86019; fax 28680089; Gen. Man. DAVID MORGAN.

Bangkok Bank Public Co Ltd (Thailand): 28 Des Voeux Rd, Central; tel. 28016688; telex 73679; fax 28105679; Gen. Man. DAVID KIANG; 4 brs.

Bank of America (Asia) Ltd (USA): Devon House, 17/F, 979 King's Rd, Quarry Bay; tel. 25972888; telex 73471; fax 25972500; Chair. JAMES E. HULIHAN; Pres. and CEO SAMUEL TSIEN; 17 brs.

Bank of Communications (People's Repub. of China): 20 Pedder St, Central; tel. 28419611; telex 73409; fax 28106993; Gen. Man. FANG LIANKUI; 1 br.

Bank of India: Ruttonjee House, 2/F, 11 Duddell St, Central; tel. 25240186; telex 75646; fax 28106149; Gen. Man. K. SUBRAMANI; 2 brs.

Bank Negara Indonesia (Persero) Tbk: Far East Finance Centre, 16 Harcourt Rd, Central; tel. 25299871; telex 73624; fax 28656500; Gen. Man. I. NYOMAN SENDER; 1 br.

Bank of Scotland: Jardine House, 11/F, Connaught Rd, Central; tel. 25212155; telex 73435; fax 28459007; Sr Man. I. A. MCKINNEY; 1 br.

Bank of Tokyo-Mitsubishi Ltd (Japan): Far East Finance Centre, 1/F, 16 Harcourt Rd, Central; tel. 28236666; fax 25293821; 3 brs.

Bank of Yokohama Ltd (Japan): Edinburgh Tower, 36/F, 15 Queen's Rd, Central; tel. 25236041; telex 63061; fax 28459022; Gen. Man. SUSUMU YAMADA; 1 br.

Banque Nationale de Paris SA (France): Central Tower, 4–13/F, 28 Queen's Rd, Central; tel. 25329288; telex 65384; fax 25302707; f. 1966; Chief Exec. Man. PHILIPPE COTTUS; 6 brs.

Banque Worms (France): Central Plaza, 39/F, 18 Harbour Rd, Wanchai; tel. 28028382; telex 60139; fax 28028065; Gen. Man. JEAN-FRANÇOIS FERRACHAT; 1 br.

Barclays Bank PLC (UK): Citibank Tower, 42/F, Citibank Plaza, 3 Garden Rd; tel. 29032000; telex 75144; fax 29032999; f. 1973; Regional CEO Asia ROGER DAVIS.

Belgian Bank (Belgium): Belgian Bank Tower, G/F, 77–79 Gloucester Rd, Wanchai; tel. 28230566; telex 73207; fax 25297966; Man. Dir GEORGES LEGROS; 33 brs.

Chase Manhattan Bank (USA): Chase Manhattan Tower, 15–22/F, Shatin, Central; tel. 26855111; telex 83830; fax 26855099; Sr Vice-Pres. RICHARD MOUNCE; 9 brs.

China and South Sea Bank Ltd (People's Repub. of China): 22–26 Bonham Strand East, Central; tel. 25429429; telex 73384; fax 25418242; Gen. Man. L. S. NG.

China State Bank Ltd (People's Repub. of China): China State Bank Bldg, 39–41 Des Voeux Rd, Central; tel. 28419333; telex 73410; fax 28450584; Gen. Man. CHAN SHUE BIU.

Chung Khiaw Bank Ltd (Singapore): Edinburgh Tower, Room 2508, 25/F, The Landmark, 15 Queen's Rd, Central; tel. 25250318; telex 75103; fax 28684598; Man. LIEW CHAN HARN; 2 brs.

Citibank, NA (USA): Citicorp Centre, 18 Whitfield Rd, Causeway Bay; tel. 28078211; telex 73243; fax 28078322; 27 brs.

Commerzbank AG (Germany): Hong Kong Club Bldg, 21/F, 3A Chater Rd, Central; tel. 28429666; telex 66400; fax 28681414; 1 br.

Crédit Agricole Indosuez (France): One Exchange Square, 44/F, 8 Connaught Rd, Central; tel. 28489000; telex 73766; fax 28681406; Sr Country Officer FRANÇOIS BEYLER; 1 br.

Dai-Ichi Kangyo Bank Ltd (Japan): Gloucester Tower, 31/F, 11 Pedder St, Central; tel. 25266591; telex 60489; fax 28681421; Gen. Man. TAKESHI TANIMURA.

Deutsche Bank AG (Germany): New World Tower, 37F, 16–18 Queen's Rd, Central, POB 3193; tel. 28430400; telex 73498; fax 28459056; Gen. Mans Dr MICHAEL THOMAS, REINER RUSCH; 1 br.

Equitable Banking Corpn (Philippines): 4 Duddell St, Central; tel. 28680323; telex 73382; fax 28100050; Vice-Pres. PAUL LANG; 1 br.

Indian Overseas Bank: Ruttonjee House, 3/F, 11 Duddell St, Central; tel. 25227249; telex 74795; fax 28451549; 2 brs.

Kincheng Banking Corpn (People's Repub. of China): Kincheng Bank Bldg, 55 Des Voeux Rd, Central; tel. 28430222; telex 73405; fax 28450116; f. 1917; Gen. Man. SUN HUNG-KAY; 34 brs.

Korea Exchange Bank (Repub. of Korea): Far East Finance Centre, 32/F, 16 Harcourt Rd, Central; tel. 25201221; telex 73459; fax 28612379; f. 1977; Gen. Man. KIM SUH-BONG; 1 br.

Kwangtung Provincial Bank (People's Repub. of China): Euro Trade Centre, G–3/F, 13–14 Connaught Rd, Central; tel. 28410410; telex 83654; fax 28459302; Gen. Man. ZHENG BAILIN; 30 brs.

Malayan Banking Berhad (Malaysia): Entertainment Bldg, 18–19/F, 30 Queen's Rd, Central; tel. 25225529; telex 60907; fax 58106013; trades in Hong Kong as Maybank; Man. HUAN WOON WAN; 2 brs.

National Bank of Pakistan: Central Bldg, Room 324, 21–27 Queen's Rd, Central; tel. 25217321; telex 75137; fax 28451703; Sr Vice-Pres. M. IQBAL SHEIKH; 2 brs.

National Commercial Bank Ltd (People's Repub. of China): 1–3 Wyndham St, Central; tel. 28432882; telex 83491; fax 28779432; Gen. Man. M. L. LAM; 26 brs.

National Westminster Bank PLC (UK): Natwest Tower, Time Square, 46/F, 1 Matheson St, Causeway Bay; tel. 29662800; telex 60111; fax 258104103; Chair. JOHN HOWLAND-JACKSON; 1 br.

Oversea-Chinese Banking Corpn Ltd (Singapore): 9/F, 9 Queen's Rd, Central; tel. 28682086; telex 73417; fax 28453439; Man. NA WU BENG; 3 brs.

Overseas Union Bank Ltd (Singapore): Edinburgh Tower, 5/F, 15 Queen's Rd, The Landmark, Central; tel. 25211521; telex 73258; fax 28105506; Vice-Pres. and Gen. Man. KWIK SAM AIK; 2 brs.

Philippine National Bank: Regent Centre Bldg, 7/F, 88 Queen's Rd, Central; tel. 25437171; telex 73019; fax 25253107; Sr Vice-Pres. and Gen. Man. A. O. QUEBAL; 1 br.

Royal Bank of Canada: Gloucester Tower, 18/F, 11 Pedder St, Central; tel. 28430888; telex 73171; fax 28681871; Vice-Pres. T. P. GIBBS; 1 br.

Sanwa Bank Ltd (Japan): Fairmont House, 8 Cotton Tree Drive, Central; tel. 28433888; telex 73423; fax 28400730; Gen. Man. Y. KIDA; 6 brs.

Sin Hua Bank Ltd (People's Repub. of China): 134–136 Des Voeux Rd, Central; tel. 28536388; telex 73416; fax 28542596; f. 1914; Gen. Man. WU JUN SHENG; 42 brs.

Sumitomo Bank Ltd (Japan): 2601 Edinburgh Tower, 15 Queen's Rd, Central; tel. 28421700; telex 73343; fax 28106452; Gen. Man. TOSIO MORIKAWA; 1 br.

Toyo Trust and Banking Co Ltd (Japan): Gloucester Tower, 15/F, The Landmark, 11 Pedder St, Central; tel. 25265657; telex 85198; fax 28459247; Gen. Man. MIKIO ITO; 1 br.

United Overseas Bank Ltd (Singapore): United Overseas Bank Bldg, 54–58 Des Voeux Rd, Central; tel. 28425666; telex 74581; fax 28105773; Sr Vice-Pres. and CEO ROBERT CHAN TZE LEUNG; 4 brs.

Yien Yieh Commercial Bank Ltd (People's Repub. of China): 242–252 Des Voeux Rd, Central; tel. 25411601; telex 83542; fax 25414037; Gen. Man. WU GUO RUI; 28 sub-brs.

Banking Associations

The Chinese Banks' Association: South China Bldg, 5/F, 1–3 Wyndham St, Central; tel. 25224789; fax 28775102; 1,601 mems; Chair. Bank of East Asia (represented by DAVID K. P. LI).

The Hong Kong Association of Banks: GPOB 11391; tel. 25211169; fax 28685035; f. 1981 to succeed The Exchange Banks' Assen of Hong Kong; all licensed banks in Hong Kong are required by law to be mems of this statutory body, whose function is to represent and further the interests of the banking sector; 181 mems; Chair. Standard Chartered Bank; Sec. PAUL LOWNDES.

STOCK EXCHANGE

The Stock Exchange of Hong Kong Ltd: Exchange Sq., Tower 1 & 2, 1/F; tel. 25221122; telex 86839; fax 28104475; e-mail info@sehk.com.hk; internet http://www.sehk.com.hk; f. 1986 by unification of four fmr exchanges; 557 mems; Chair. LEE HON CHIU; CEO ALEC TSUI.

FUTURES EXCHANGE

Hong Kong Futures Exchange Ltd: Asia Pacific Finance Tower, Suite 605–608, 6/F, Citibank Plaza, 3 Garden Rd; tel. 28429333; fax 25090555; Chair. FRANK WONG; CEO RANDY GILMORE.

SUPERVISORY BODY

Securities and Futures Commission (SFC): Edinburgh Tower, 12/F, The Landmark, 15 Queen's Rd, Central; tel. 28409222; telex 61919; fax 28459553; f. 1989 to supervise the stock and futures markets; Chair. ANTHONY NEOH; Exec. Dir LAURA CHA.

INSURANCE

In December 1995 there were 223 insurance companies, including 123 overseas companies, authorized to transact insurance business in Hong Kong. The following are among the principal companies:

Asia Insurance Co Ltd: World-Wide House, 16/F, 19 Des Voeux Rd, Central; tel. 28677988; telex 74542; fax 28100218; Chair. SEBASTIAN KI CHIT LAU.

General Accident Insurance Asia Ltd: World Trade Centre, 35–37/F, Causeway Bay; tel. 28940555; telex 75609; fax 28905741; Gen. Man. ANDREW LO.

Mercantile and General Reinsurance Co PLC: 13C On Hing Bldg, 1 On Hing Terrace, Central; tel. 28106160; telex 74062; fax 25217353; Man. T. W. HO.

Ming An Insurance Co (HK) Ltd: Ming An Plaza, 22/F, 8 Sunning Rd, Causeway Bay; tel. 28151551; telex 74172; fax 25416567; e-mail mai@mingan.com.hk; Vice-Chair. and Gen. Man. Y. W. SIU.

National Mutual Insurance Co (Bermuda) Ltd: 151 Gloucester Rd, Wanchai; tel. 25191111; fax 25987204; life and general insurance; Chair. Sir DAVID AKERS-JONES; CEO TERRY SMITH.

Prudential Assurance Co Ltd: Cityplaza 4, 10/F, 12 Taikoo Wan Rd, Taikoo Shing; tel. 29773888; fax 28776994; life and general; Gen. Man. EDDIE K. F. FONG.

South British Insurance Co Ltd: World Trade Centre, 36/F, Causeway Bay; tel. 28940666; telex 75609; fax 28950426; Regional Dir P. C. TSAO; Gen. Man. ANDREW LO.

Summit Insurance (Asia) Ltd: Devon House, 4–5F, 979 King's Rd, Quarry Bay; tel. 25798238; fax 25166992; CEO IU PO SING.

Sun Alliance and London Insurance plc: 2101-07 Office Tower, Convention Plaza, 1 Harbour Rd, Wanchai; tel. 28107383; fax 28450389.

Taikoo Royal Insurance Co Ltd: Dorset House, 32/F, Taikoo Place, 979 King's Rd, Quarry Bay; tel. 29683000; fax 29685111; Man. Dir ANDREW LEUNG.

Willis Faber (Far East) Ltd: 5108 Central Plaza, 18 Harbour Rd, Wanchai; tel. 28270111; telex 85240; fax 28270966; Man. Dir HOWARD H. K. TSANG.

Winterthur Swiss Insurance (Asia) Ltd: Dah Sing Financial Centre, 19/F, 108 Gloucester Rd, Wanchai; tel. 25986282; fax 25985838; Man. Dir RISTO LAHTI.

Insurance Associations

Hong Kong Federation of Insurers (HKFI): First Pacific Bank Centre, Room 902, 9/F, 56 Gloucester Rd, Wanchai; tel. 25201868; fax 25201967; e-mail hkfi@hkfi.org.hk; internet http://www.hkfi.org.hk; f. 1988; 121 general insurance and 45 life insurance mems; Chair. FRANK CHAN; Exec. Dir LOUISA FONG.

Insurance Institute of Hong Kong: First Pacific Bank Centre, 9/F, 56 Gloucester Rd, GPO Box 6747, Wanchai; tel. 28619301; fax 25201967; f. 1967; Pres. JACKIE CHUN.

Trade and Industry

Trade Department: Trade Department Tower, 700 Nathan Rd, Kowloon; tel. 27897555; telex 45126; fax 27892491; Dir-Gen. ALAN LAI.

Industry Department: Ocean Centre, 14/F, 5 Canton Rd, Kowloon; tel. 27372208; telex 50151; fax 27304633; Dir-Gen. FRANCIS HO.

DEVELOPMENT ORGANIZATIONS

Hong Kong Housing Authority: 33 Fat Kwong St, Homantin, Kowloon; tel. 27615002; fax 27621110; f. 1973; plans, builds and manages public housing; Chair. ROSANNA WONG YICK-MING; Dir of Housing J. A. MILLER.

Hong Kong Trade Development Council: Office Tower, Convention Plaza, 39/F, 1 Harbour Rd, Wanchai; tel. 25844333; telex 73595; fax 28240249; f. 1966; Chair. Dr VICTOR K. FUNG; Exec. Dir MICHAEL SZE.

Kadoorie Agricultural Aid Loan Fund: c/o Director of Agriculture and Fisheries, Canton Rd Govt Offices, 393 Canton Rd, Kowloon; tel. 27332211; fax 23113731; f. 1954; provides low-interest loans to farmers; HK $11,137,000 was loaned in 1996/97.

J. E. Joseph Trust Fund: c/o Director of Agriculture and Fisheries, Canton Rd Govt Offices, 393 Canton Rd, Kowloon; tel. 27332211; fax 23113731; f. 1954; grants low-interest credit facilities to farmers' co-operative socs; HK $3,252,000 was loaned in 1996/97.

CHAMBERS OF COMMERCE

Chinese Chamber of Commerce, Kowloon: 2/F, 8–10 Nga Tsin Long Rd, Kowloon; tel. 23822309; 250 mems; Chair. LEE CHEUK-FAN.

Chinese General Chamber of Commerce: 24 Connaught Rd, Central; tel. 25256385; fax 28452610; e-mail cgcc@cgcc.org.hk; f. 1900; 6,000 mems; Chair. Dr TSANG HIN-CHI.

Hong Kong General Chamber of Commerce: United Centre, 22/F, 95 Queensway, POB 852; tel. 25299229; telex 83535; fax 25279843; f. 1861; 4,000 mems; Chair. JAMES TIEN; Dir EDEN WOON.

Kowloon Chamber of Commerce: KCC Bldg, 3/F, 2 Liberty Ave, Homantin, Kowloon; tel. 27600393; fax 27610166; 1,700 mems; Chair. TONG KWOK-WAH; Exec. Dir CHENG PO-WO.

INDUSTRIAL AND TRADE ASSOCIATIONS

Hong Kong Productivity Council: HKPC Bldg, 78 Tat Chee Ave, Yau Yat Chuen, Kowloon Tong, Kowloon; tel. 27885678; telex 32842; fax 27885900; f. 1967 to promote increased productivity of industry and to encourage optimum utilization of resources; council of 23 mems appointed by the Government, representing management, labour, academic and professional interests, and govt depts associated with productivity matters; Chair. KENNETH FANG; Exec. Dir THOMAS S. K. CHAN.

Chinese Manufacturers' Association of Hong Kong: CMA Bldg, 64–66 Connaught Rd, Central; tel. 25456166; telex 63526; fax 25414541; e-mail cma@hkstar.com; internet http://www.cma.org.hk; f. 1934 to promote and protect industrial and trading interests; operates testing and certification laboratories; 3,700 mems; Pres. HERBERT H. Y. LIANG; Exec. Sec. FRANCIS T. M. LAU.

Federation of Hong Kong Garment Manufacturers: Room 401–3, Cheung Lee Commercial Bldg, 25 Kimberley Rd, Tsimshatsui, Kowloon; tel. 27211383; fax 23111062; 200 mems; Pres. WING-KEE CHAN; Sec.-Gen. ANTHONY K. K. TANG.

Federation of Hong Kong Industries (FKHI): Hankow Centre, 4/F, 5–15 Hankow Rd, Tsimshatsui, Kowloon; tel. 27323188; telex 30101; fax 27213494; f. 1960; 2,800 mems; Chair. HENRY Y. Y. TANG.

Federation of Hong Kong Watch Trades and Industries Ltd: Room 604, Peter Bldg, 58–62 Queen's Rd, Central; tel. 25233232; fax 28684485; f. 1947; 700 mems; Chair. ANTHONY WONG.

Hong Kong Chinese Enterprises Association: China Resources Bldg, Room 3203–4, 32/F, 26 Harbour Rd; tel. 28272831; fax 28272606; 1,100 mems; Chair. GU YONG-JIANG; Exec. Dir WANG MEIYUE.

Hong Kong Chinese Importers' and Exporters' Association: Champion Bldg, 7–8/F, 287–291 Des Voeux Rd, Central; tel. 25448474; fax 25444677; 2,842 mems; Pres. NG LIN-FUNG.

Hong Kong Chinese Textile Mills Association: 11/F, 38–40 Tai Po Rd, Kowloon; tel. 27778236; fax 27881836; 250 mems; Pres PANG WOON-TONG.

Hong Kong Construction Association Ltd: 3/F, 180–182 Hennessy Rd, Wanchai; tel. 25724414; fax 25727104; 350 mems; Pres. PETER LAM; Sec.-Gen. PATRICK CHAN.

Hong Kong Electronic Industries Association Ltd: Units 208–9, HK Industrial Technology Centre, 72 Tat Chee Ave, Kowloon; tel. 27788328; fax 27882200; e-mail hkeia@hkeia.com; internet http://www.hkeia.com; 445 mems; Chair. Dr M. W. LUI.

Hong Kong Exporters' Association: Room 825, Star House, 3 Salisbury Rd, Tsimshatsui, Kowloon; tel. 27309851; fax 27301869; f. 1955; 300 mems comprising leading merchants and manufacturing exporters; Chair. WILLY S. M. LIN; CEO MIMI YEUNG.

Hong Kong Garment Manufacturers Association: 3/F, 63 Tai Yip St, Kowloon Bay, Kowloon; tel. 23052893; fax 23052493; 36 mems; Chair. Dr HARRY N. S. LEE.

Hong Kong Information Technology Federation Ltd: 601 Glenealy Tower, 1 Glenealy, Central; tel. 25228118; fax 28682083; 69 mems; Pres. ANTHONY AU.

Hong Kong Jade and Stone Manufacturers' Association: Hang Lung House, 16/F, 184–192 Queen's Rd, Central; tel. 25430543; fax 28150164; f. 1965; 159 mems; Chair. CHARLES CHAN SING-CHUK; Sec. REBECCA LAW.

Hong Kong Jewelry Manufacturers' Association: Room 906, Block A, Focal Centre, 21 Man Lok St, Hunghom, Kowloon; tel. 27663002; fax 23623647; 178 mems; Chair. KARL SHIN.

Hong Kong Knitwear Exporters and Manufacturers Association: 3/F, Clothing Industry Training Authority, Kowloon Bay Training Centre, 63 Tai Yip St, Kowloon; tel. 27552621; fax 27565672; 100 mems; Chair. WILLY LIN; Exec. Sec. SHIRLEY LIU.

Hong Kong and Kowloon Footwear Manufacturers' Association: Kam Fung Bldg, 3/F, Flat D, 8 Cleverly St, Sheung Wan; tel. and fax 25414499; 90 mems; Pres. LOK WAI-TO; Sec. LEE SUM-HUNG.

Hong Kong Optical Manufacturers' Association: 2/F, 11 Fa Yuen St, Mongkok, Kowloon; tel. 23326505; fax 27705786; 106 mems; Pres. TONY CHOW CHING-LAM.

Hong Kong Plastics Manufacturers Association Ltd: 1/F, Flat B, Fu Yuen, 39–49 Wanchai Rd; tel. 25742230; fax 25742843; 200 mems; Chair. KENNETH W. S. TING; Pres. DENNIS H. S. TING.

Hong Kong Printers Association: 1/F, 48–50 Johnston Rd, Wanchai; tel. 25275050; fax 28610463; f. 1939; 430 mems; Chair. HO KA HUN; Exec. Dir LEE SHUN-HAY.

Hong Kong Rubber and Footwear Manufacturers' Association: Block A, 2/F, 185 Prince Edward Rd, Kowloon; tel. 23812297; fax 23976927; 230 mems; Chair. TANG KIM-KWAN; Sec. WENDY LAI.

Hong Kong Sze Yap Commercial and Industrial Association: Hang Lung House, 1/F, 184–192 Queen's Rd, Central; tel. 25438095; fax 25449495; 1,103 mems; Chair. AU KIT-MING; Exec. Dir and Sec. CHIU KING-WAN.

Hong Kong Toys Council: Hankow Centre, 4/F, 5–15 Hankow Rd, Tsimshatsui, Kowloon; tel. 27323188; telex 30101; fax 27213494; 190 mems; Chair. WONG TIT-SHING.

Hong Kong Watch Manufacturers' Association: Yu Wing Bldg, 3F/11F, Unit A, 64–66 Wellington St, Central; tel. 25225238; fax 28106614; 634 mems; Pres. KENNETH NG KAM-WING; Sec.-Gen. STANLEY LAU CHIN-HO.

New Territories Commercial and Industrial General Association Ltd: Cheong Hay Bldg, 2/F, 107 Hoi Pa St, Tsuen Wan; tel. 24145316; fax 24934130; 3,000 mems; Pres. LEUNG HIN-CHI; Sec.-Gen. SUNG WAI-CHEN.

Real Estate Developers Association of Hong Kong: Room 1403, Worldwide House, 19 Des Voeux Rd, Central; tel. 28260111; fax 28452521; 474 mems; Pres. Dr STANLEY HO; Exec. Vice-Pres. THOMAS KWOK PING-KONG.

Telecom Association of Hong Kong: GPOB 13461; tel. 25042732; fax 25042752; 120 mems; Chair. HUBERT NG; Vice-Chair. PRUDENCE CHAN.

Textile Council of Hong Kong Ltd: 3/F, 63 Tai Yip St, Kowloon Bay, Kowloon; tel. 23052893; fax 23052493; 10 mems; Chair. KENNETH FANG; Exec. Dir JOHN YUNG.

Toys Manufacturers' Association of Hong Kong Ltd: Level 12, Metroplaza, Tower 2, 223 Hing Fong Rd, Kwai Chung, New Territories; tel 24221209; fax 24221639; 150 mems; Pres. Dr C. L. LUK; Sec. BECKY TO.

EMPLOYERS' ORGANIZATIONS

Employers' Federation of Hong Kong: United Centre, Unit C3, 12/F, 95 Queensway; tel. 25280536; fax 28655285; f. 1947; 460 mems; Chair. F. K. HU; Exec. Dir MAY CHOW.

Hong Kong Factory Owners' Association: Wing Wong Bldg, 11/F, 557–559 Nathan Rd, Kowloon; tel. 23882372; fax 23857184; 1,168 mems; Pres. HWANG JEN; Sec. WONG KIN-WA.

UTILITIES

Electricity

China Light and Power Co Ltd: 147 Argyle St, Kowloon; tel. 23711511; telex 44488; fax 23691619; f. 1918; generation and supply of electricity to Kowloon and the New Territories; Chair. Sir SIDNEY GORDON; Man. Dir ROSS SAYERS.

Hongkong Electric Holdings Ltd: Electric Centre, 28 City Garden Rd, North Point; tel. 28433111; telex 73071; fax 28100506; generation and supply of electricity; Chair. GEORGE C. MAGNUS; Man. Dir E. L. Y. YEE.

Gas

Gas Authority: all gas supply cos, gas installers and contractors are required to be registered with the Gas Authority. In 1996 there were eight gas supply cos registered.

Hong Kong and China Gas Co Ltd: 23/F, 363 Java Rd, North Point; tel. 29633388; telex 86086; fax 25632233; production, distribution and marketing of town gas and gas appliances; operates three plants; Chair. LEE SHAU-KEE; Man. Dir ALFRED W. K. CHAN.

Water

Drainage Services Department: responsible for planning, designing, constructing, operating and maintaining the sewerage, sewage treatment and stormwater drainage infrastructures.

CO-OPERATIVES

(socs = societies; feds = federations; mems = membership; cap. = paid-up share capital in Hong Kong dollars)

Registrar of Co-operatives: c/o Director of Agriculture and Fisheries, Canton Rd Govt Offices, 393 Canton Rd, Kowloon; tel. 27332211; fax 23113731; 315 socs, 19,328 mems, cap. 2,092,954 (March 1997).

Co-operative Societies

Agricultural Credit: socs 2, mems 73, cap. 58,630.

Agricultural Thrift and Loan: soc. 1, mems 45, cap. 620.

Apartment Owners: soc. 1, mems 60, cap. 6,000.

Better Living: socs 28, mems 2,409, cap. 60,330.

Consumers: socs 12, mems 3,492, cap. 84,975.

Farmers' Irrigation: soc. 1, mems 30, cap. 155.

Federation of Co-operative Building Societies: fed. 1, mem.-socs 101, cap. 10,100.

Federation of Fisheries' Societies: feds 4, mem.-socs 40, cap. 4,375.

Federation of Pig Raising Societies: fed. 1, mem.-socs 15, cap. 46,575.

Federation of Vegetable Marketing Societies: fed. 1, mem.-socs 26, cap. 5,200.

Fishermen's Credit: socs 47, mems 751, cap. 10,835.

Fishermen's Credit and Housing: socs 2, mems 35, cap. 250.

Housing: socs 169, mems 3,519, cap. 1,239,400.

Pig Raising: socs 15, mems 947, cap. 466,100.

Salaried Workers' Thrift and Loan: soc. 1, mems 408, cap. 16,320.

Vegetable Marketing: socs 29, mems 7,376, cap. 83,089.

There were also 69 Credit Unions in March 1996.

TRADE UNIONS

In December 1996 there were 577 trade unions in Hong Kong, comprising 535 employees' unions, 25 employers' associations and 17 mixed organizations.

Hong Kong and Kowloon Trades Union Council (TUC): Labour Bldg, 11 Chang Sha St, Kowloon; tel. 23845150; telex 36866; f. 1949; 65 affiliated unions, mostly covering the catering and building trades; 27,600 mems; supports Taiwan; affiliated to ICFTU; Officer-in-Charge Wong Yiu Kam.

Hong Kong Confederation of Trade Unions: 19/F, Wing Wong Commercial Bldg, 557–559 Nathan Rd, Kowloon; tel. 27708668; fax 27707388; e-mail hkctu@hk.super.net; registered Feb. 1990; 42 affiliated independent unions; 130,000 mems.

Hong Kong Federation of Trade Unions (FTU): 7/F, 50 Ma Tau Chung Rd, Tokwawan, Kowloon; tel. 27120231; fax 27608477; f. 1948; 113 member unions, mostly concentrated in shipyards, public transport, textile mills, construction, department stores, printing and public utilities; supports the People's Republic of China; 229,400 mems; Chair. Cheng Yiu-tong; Pres. Lee Chark-tim; Gen. Sec. Chan Jik-kwei.

Also active are the **Federation of Hong Kong and Kowloon Labour Unions** (31 affiliated unions with 21,200 mems) and the **Federation of Civil Service Unions** (29 affiliated unions with 12,400 mems).

Transport

Transport Department: Immigration Tower, 41/F, 7 Gloucester Rd, Wanchai; tel. 28295258; fax 28240433.

RAILWAYS

Kowloon–Canton Railway: KCRC House, 9 Lok King St, Fo Tan, Sha Tin, New Territories; tel. 26881333; telex 51666; fax 26880983; operated by the Kowloon–Canton Railway Corpn, a public statutory body f. 1983 and wholly owned by the Hong Kong Govt; the 34-km East Rail runs from the terminus at Hung Hom to the frontier at Lo Wu; through passenger services to Guangzhou (Canton), suspended in 1949, were resumed in 1979; the electrification and double-tracking of the entire length and redevelopment of all stations has been completed, and full electric train service came into operation in 1983; in 1988 a light railway network serving Tuen Mun, Yuen Long and Tin Shui Wai in the north-western New Territories was opened; passenger service extended to Foshan and Zhaoqing in 1993; direct Kowloon–Beijing service commenced in May 1997; also freight services to several destinations in China; proposals for West Rail, incorporating a domestic passenger line and a cross-border passenger and freight service, were under consideration in 1997; Chair. and CEO Yueng Kai-yin.

Mass Transit Railway Corporation (MTRC): MTR Tower, Telford Plaza, 33 Wai Yip St, Kowloon Bay; tel. 29932111; telex 56257; fax 27988822; f. 1975; network of 43 km and 38 stations; the first section of the underground railway system opened in 1979; a 15.6-km line from Kwun Tong to Central opened in 1980; a 10.5-km Tsuen Wan extension opened in 1982; the 12.5-km Island Line opened in 1985–86; in 1989 a second harbour crossing between Cha Kwo Ling and Quarry Bay, known as the Eastern Harbour Crossing, commenced operation, adding 4.6 km to the railway system; 34-km link to new airport at Chek Lap Kok scheduled to open in mid-1998; two additional lines planned for completion by 2006; Chair. and Chief Exec. Jack C. K. So.

TRAMWAYS

Hong Kong Tramways Ltd: Whitty Street Tram Depot, Connaught Rd West, Western District; tel. 25598918; telex 73591; fax 28583697; f. 1904; operates six routes and 161 double-deck trams between Kennedy Town and Shaukeiwan; Operations Man. A. T. Leech.

ROADS

In December 1996 there were 1,743 km of roads, 420 km on Hong Kong Island, 400 km in Kowloon and 923 km in the New Territories. Almost all of them are concrete or asphalt surfaced. Owing to the hilly terrain, and the density of building development, the scope for substantial increase in the road network is limited.

The 123-km Hong Kong–Guangzhou (Canton) section of the Hong Kong–Macau highway was completed in 1994.

FERRIES

Conventional ferries, hydroferries and catamarans operate between Hong Kong, China and Macau. There is also an extensive network of ferry services to outlying districts.

Hongkong and Yaumati Ferry Co Ltd: West Kowloon Reclamation Area, Lot No. S.S.P. Misc. 58 (KX 1850), Po Lun St (extension), Lai Chi Kok, Kowloon; tel. 27869383; fax 27869001; 24 franchised and licensed routes on ferry services, incl. cross-harbour, to outlying islands, excursion, vehicular and dangerous goods; fleet of 82 vessels (passenger ferries, vehicular ferries, hoverferries and catamarans); also operates hoverferry services between Hong Kong and Shekou and catamaran service to Macau; Gen. Man. David C. S. Ho.

'Star' Ferry Co Ltd: Kowloon Point Pier, Tsimshatsui, Kowloon; tel. 21186228; fax 21186028; f. 1899; operates 12 passenger ferries between the Kowloon Peninsula and Central, the main business district of Hong Kong; between Central and Hung Hom; and between Tsimshatsui and Wanchai; Man. Johnny Leung.

SHIPPING

Hong Kong is one of the world's largest shipping centres. Hong Kong was a British port of registry until the inauguration of a new and independent shipping register in December 1990. At the end of 1996 the register comprised a fleet of 543 vessels, totalling 7.9m. grt. The eight container terminals at Kwai Chung, which are privately-owned and operated, comprised 19 berths in 1996. In September of that year plans to construct a ninth terminal (CT9) received approval from the People's Republic of China. CT9 was to be operational by 1999. The planning of a new container port on Lantau Island (to comprise twice the capacity of Kwai Chung) continued in 1997.

Hong Kong Government Marine Department: Harbour Bldg, 22/F, 38 Pier Rd, Central, GPOB 4155; tel. 28523001; telex 64553; fax 25449241; e-mail webmaster@mardep.gen.gov.hk; Dir of Marine I. B. Dale.

Shipping Companies

Anglo-Eastern Ship Management Ltd: Dominion Centre, 20/F, 43–59A Queen's Rd East, Hennessy Rd, POB 20587; tel. 28636111; telex 75478; fax 28612419; Chair. J. Savarys; Man. Dir K. P. McGuinness.

Chung Gai Ship Management Co Ltd: Admiralty Centre Tower 1, 31/F, 18 Harcourt Rd; tel. 25295541; telex 73556; fax 28656206; Chair. S. Koda; Man. Dir K. Ichihara.

Fairmont Shipping (HK) Ltd: Fairmont House, 21/F, 8 Cotton Tree Drive; tel. 25218338; telex 75228; fax 28104560; Man. Charles Leung.

Far East Enterprising Co (HK) Ltd: China Resources Bldg, 18–19/F, 26 Harbour Rd, Wanchai; tel. 28283668; telex 73333;

fax 28275584; f. 1949; shipping, chartering, brokering; Gen. Man. WEI KUAN.

Gulfeast Shipmanagement Ltd: Great Eagle Centre, 9/F, 23 Harbour Rd, Wanchai; tel. 28313344; telex 86204; Finance Dir A. T. MIRMOHAMMADI.

Hong Kong Borneo Shipping Co Ltd: 815 International Bldg, 141 Des Voeux Rd, Central; tel. 25413797; telex 74135; fax 28153473; Pres. Datuk LAI FOOK KIM.

Island Navigation Corpn International Ltd: Harbour Centre, 29/F, 25 Harbour Rd, Wanchai; tel. 28333222; telex 73108; fax 28270001; Man. Dir C. C. TUNG.

Jardine Ship Management Ltd: Jardine Engineering House, 11/F, 260 King's Rd, North Point; tel. 28074101; telex 74570; fax 28073351; Man. Dir Capt. PAUL UNDERHILL.

Oak Maritime (HK) Inc Ltd: 2301 China Resources Bldg, 26 Harbour Rd, Wanchai; tel. 25063866; telex 73005; fax 25063563; Chair. STEVE G. K. HSU; Man. Dir FRED C. P. TSAI.

Ocean Tramping Co Ltd: Hongkong Shipping Centre, 24–29/F, 167 Connaught Rd West; tel. 25892888; telex 73462; fax 25461041; Chair. Z. M. GAO.

Orient Overseas Container Line Ltd: Harbour Centre, 31/F, 25 Harbour Rd, Wanchai; tel. 28333888; fax 25318122; internet http://www.oocl.com; Chair. C. C. TUNG.

Teh-Hu Cargocean Management Co Ltd: Unit B, Belgian Bank Tower, 15/F, 77–79 Gloucester Rd, Wanchai; tel. 25988688; telex 73458; fax 28249339; f. 1974; Man. Dir KENNETH W. LO.

Wah Kwong Shipping Agency Co Ltd: Shanghai Industrial Investment Bldg, 26/F, 48–62 Hennessy Rd, POB 283; tel. 25279227; telex 73430; fax 28656544; Chair. TSONG-YEA CHAO.

Wah Tung Shipping Agency Co Ltd: China Resources Bldg, Rooms 2101–5, 21/F, 26 Harbour Rd, Wanchai; tel. 28272818; telex 89410; fax 28275361; f. 1981; Dir and Gen. Man. B. L. LIU.

Wallem Shipmanagement Ltd: Hopewell Centre, 48/F, 183 Queen's Rd East; tel. 28768200; telex 74147; fax 28761234; Man. Dir R. G. BUCHANAN.

Worldwide Shipping Agency Ltd: Wheelock House, 6–7/F, 20 Pedder St; tel. 28423888; telex 73247; fax 28100617; Man. J. WONG.

Associations

Hong Kong Cargo-Vessel Traders' Association: 2/F, 21–23 Man Wai Bldg, Ferry Point, Kowloon; tel. 23847102; fax 27820342; 978 mems; Chair. CHOW YAT-TAK; Sec. CHAN BAK.

Hong Kong Shipowners' Association: Queen's Centre, 12/F, 58–64 Queen's Rd East, Wanchai; tel. 25200206; telex 89157; fax 25298246; 220 mems; Chair. GEORGE CHAO; Dir MICHAEL FARLIE.

Hong Kong Shippers' Council: Wu Chung House, 31/F, 213 Queen's Rd East; tel. 28340010; fax 28919787; 66 mems; Chair. CHAN WING-KEE; Exec. Dir CLEMENT YEUNG.

CIVIL AVIATION

By the end of 1996 Hong Kong's international airport at Kai Tak was served by 66 foreign airlines. Its runway, which extends 3,390m. into Kowloon Bay, can accommodate all types of conventional wide-bodied and supersonic aircraft. The planned construction of a new international airport, on the island of Chek Lap Kok, near Lantau Island, was announced in 1989. Opening of the new airport, initially scheduled for April 1998, was postponed to July, following delays in the construction of a connecting high-speed rail-link. The airport will initially have one runway, with the capacity to handle 35m. passengers and 3m. metric tons of cargo per year. The second runway was to be commissioned in late 1998. A helicopter link with Macau was established in 1990.

Airport Authority of Hong Kong: Central Plaza, 25/F, 18 Harbour Rd, Wanchai; tel. 28247111; fax 28240717; f. 1995; Chair. WONG PO-YAN; CEO Dr HENRY TOWNSEND.

Civil Aviation Department: Queensway Government Offices, 46/F, 66 Queensway; tel. 28674332; telex 61361; fax 28690093; e-mail cadadmin@cad.gen.gov.hk; Dir RICHARD A. SIEGEL.

Air Hong Kong (AHK) Ltd: Block 2, Tien Chu Centre, 2/F, 1E Mok Cheong St, Kowloon; tel. 27618588; telex 37625; fax 27618586; f. 1986; international cargo carrier; Commercial Man. CHRISTINA H. L. SIAW; Chief Operating Office KENNETH TANG.

Cathay Pacific Airways Ltd: Swire House, 9 Connaught Rd, Central; tel. 27475000; telex 82345; fax 28680176; f. 1946; services to more than 40 major cities in the Far East, Middle East, North America, Europe, South Africa, Australia and New Zealand; Chair. PETER D. A. SUTCH; Man. Dir DAVID TURNBULL.

Hong Kong Dragon Airlines Ltd (Dragonair): Devon House, 22/F, Taikoo Place, 979 King's Rd, Quarry Bay; tel. 25901328; telex 45936; fax 25901333; f. 1985; scheduled and charter flights to numerous cities in China; scheduled regional services include Phuket (Thailand), Hiroshima and Sendai (Japan), Kaohsiung (Taiwan), Phnom-Penh (Cambodia), Dhaka (Bangladesh) and Kota Kinabalu (Malaysia); Chair. K. P. CHAO; Chief Operating Officer STANLEY HUI.

Tourism

Tourism is a major source of foreign exchange, contributing revenue of HK $104,800m. (including receipts from visitors from the People's Republic of China) in 1996. Some 11.7m. people visited Hong Kong in 1996. In December 1996 there were 87 hotels, and the number of rooms available totalled 33,500 in May 1997. The number of rooms was to be increased to 46,000 by December 2000.

Hong Kong Tourist Association: Citicorp Centre, 9–11/F, 18 Whitfield Rd, North Point; tel. 28076543; fax 28060303; f. 1957; co-ordinates and promotes the tourist industry; has govt support and financial assistance; 11 mems of the Board represent the Govt, the private sector and the tourism industry; Chair. Y. S. LO; Exec. Dir AMY CHAN.

CHINA (TAIWAN)

Introductory Survey

Location, Climate, Language, Religion, Flag, Capital

The Republic of China has, since 1949, been confined mainly to the province of Taiwan (comprising one large island and several much smaller ones), which lies off the south-east coast of the Chinese mainland. The territory under the Republic's effective jurisdiction consists of the island of Taiwan (also known as Formosa) and nearby islands, including the P'enghu (Pescadores) group, together with a few other islands which lie just off the mainland and form part of the province of Fujian (Fukien), west of Taiwan. The largest of these is Kinmen (Jinmen), also known as Quemoy, which (with three smaller islands) is about 10 km from the port of Xiamen (Amoy), while five other islands under Taiwan's control, mainly Matsu (Mazu), lie further north, near Fuzhou. Taiwan itself is separated from the mainland by the Taiwan (Formosa) Strait, which is about 130 km (80 miles) wide at its narrowest point. The island's climate is one of rainy summers and mild winters. Average temperatures are about 15°C (59°F) in the winter and 26°C (79°F) in the summer. The average annual rainfall is 2,580 mm (102 in). The official language is Northern Chinese (Mandarin), but Taiwanese, a dialect based on the language of Fujian Province, is widely spoken. The predominant religions are Buddhism and Daoism (Taoism), but there are also adherents of I-kuan Tao, Christianity (mainly Roman Catholics and Protestants) and Islam. The philosophy of Confucianism has a large following. The national flag (proportions 3 by 2) is red, with a dark blue rectangular canton, containing a white sun, in the upper hoist. The capital is Taipei.

Recent History

China ceded Taiwan to Japan in 1895. The island remained under Japanese rule until the end of the Second World War in 1945, when it was returned to Chinese control, becoming a province of the Republic of China, then ruled by the Kuomintang (KMT, Nationalist Party). The leader of the KMT was Gen. Chiang Kai-shek, President of the Republic since 1928. The KMT Government's forces were defeated in 1949 by the Communist revolution in China. President Chiang and many of his supporters withdrew from the Chinese mainland to Taiwan, where they established a KMT regime in succession to their previous all-China administration. This regime continued to assert that it was the rightful Chinese Government, in opposition to the People's Republic of China, proclaimed by the victorious Communists in 1949. The Nationalists successfully resisted attacks by their Communist rivals, and declared that they intended to recover control of mainland China.

Although its effective control was limited to Taiwan, the KMT regime continued to be dominated by politicians who had formerly been in power on the mainland. Unable to replenish their mainland representation, the National Assembly (last elected fully in 1947) and other legislative organs extended their terms of office indefinitely, although fewer than half of the original members were alive on Taiwan by the 1980s. The political domination of the island by immigrants from the mainland caused some resentment among native Taiwanese, and led to demands for increased democratization and for the recognition of Taiwan as a state independent of China. The KMT, however, consistently rejected demands for independence, restating the party's long-standing policy of seeking political reunification, although under KMT terms, with the mainland.

The KMT regime continued to represent China at the United Nations (and as a permanent member of the UN Security Council) until 1971, when it was replaced by the People's Republic. Nationalist China was subsequently expelled from several other international organizations. In November 1991, however, as 'Chinese Taipei', Taiwan joined the Asia-Pacific Economic Co-operation forum (APEC). In September 1992, under the name of the 'Separate Customs Territory of Taiwan, P'enghu, Kinmen and Matsu', Taiwan was granted observer status at the General Agreement on Tariffs and Trade (GATT), and by 1997 the island's application for full membership of the successor World Trade Organization (WTO) was well advanced. In June 1995 Taiwan offered to make a donation of US $1,000m., to be used for the establishment of an international development fund, if the island were permitted to rejoin the UN. In September 1997, for the fifth consecutive year, the General Committee of the UN General Assembly rejected a proposal urging Taiwan's participation in the UN. After 1971 a number of countries broke off diplomatic relations with Taiwan and recognized the People's Republic, and by early 1998, following South Africa's establishment of diplomatic links with the People's Republic, the Taiwan Government was recognized by some 30 countries.

In 1973 the Government of Taiwan rejected an offer from the People's Republic to hold secret discussions on the reunification of China. In October 1981 Taiwan rejected China's suggested terms for reunification, whereby Taiwan would become a 'special administrative region' and would have a substantial degree of autonomy, including the retention of its own armed forces. In 1983 China renewed its offer, including a guarantee to maintain the status quo in Taiwan for 100 years if the province agreed to reunification. In 1984, following the agreement between the People's Republic of China and the United Kingdom that China would regain sovereignty over the British colony of Hong Kong in 1997, mainland Chinese leaders urged Taiwan to accept similar proposals for reunification on the basis of 'one country—two systems'. The Taipei Government insisted that Taiwan would never negotiate with Beijing until the mainland regime renounced communism. In May 1986, however, the Government was forced to make direct contact with the Beijing Government for the first time, over the issue of a Taiwanese pilot who had defected to the mainland. In October 1987 the Government announced the repeal of the 38-year ban on visits to the mainland by Taiwanese citizens, with the exception of civil servants and military personnel.

In April 1989 the Government announced that it was considering a 'one China, two governments' formula, whereby China would be a single country under two administrations, one in Beijing and one in Taipei. In May a delegation led by the Minister of Finance attended a meeting of the Asian Development Bank (ADB) in Beijing, as representatives of 'Taipei, China', demonstrating a considerable relaxation in Taiwan's stance. Reconciliation initiatives were abruptly halted, however, by the violent suppression of the pro-democracy movement in Beijing in June. In May 1990 a proposal by the President of Taiwan to open direct dialogue on a government-to-government basis with the People's Republic was rejected by Beijing, which continued to maintain that it would negotiate only on a party-to-party basis with the KMT. In December Taiwan announced that the state of war with the People's Republic would be formally ended by May 1991 (see below).

In February 1991 the recently-formed National Unification Council, under the chairmanship of the President of Taiwan, put forward radical new proposals, whereby Taiwan and the People's Republic of China might recognize each other as separate political entities. In March a national unification programme, which incorporated the demand that Taiwan be acknowledged as an independent and equal entity, was approved by the Central Standing Committee of the KMT. The programme also included a proposal for direct postal, commercial and shipping links with the mainland.

In April 1991 a delegation from the Straits Exchange Foundation (SEF), established in late 1990 to deal with bilateral issues, travelled to Beijing for discussions, the first such delegation ever to visit the People's Republic. In August 1991 a Beijing magazine published an informal 10-point plan for the eventual reunification of China, whereby Taiwan would become a special administrative region and retain its own legislative, administrative and judicial authority. Two senior envoys of the mainland Chinese Red Cross were allowed to enter Taiwan in August on a humanitarian mission.

As the Beijing Government continued to warn against independence for Taiwan, in September 1991 the island's President asserted that conditions were not appropriate for reunification with the mainland and that Taiwan was a *de facto* sovereign and autonomous country. The President of the People's Republic indicated that force might be used to prevent the separation of

Taiwan. In December the non-governmental Association for Relations across the Taiwan Straits (ARATS) was established in Beijing. In January 1992 the SEF protested to the People's Republic over the detention of a former pilot of the mainland air force who had defected to Taiwan in 1965 and, upon returning to his homeland for a family reunion in December 1991, had been arrested. He subsequently received a 15-year prison sentence. In May 1992 the National Unification Council's proposal for a non-aggression pact between Taiwan and the People's Republic was rejected.

In July 1992 the Taiwanese Government reiterated that it would not consider party-to-party talks with Beijing. In the same month President Lee urged the establishment of 'one country, one good system'. In mid-July statutes to permit the further expansion of economic and political links with the People's Republic were adopted by the Legislative Yuan. In August the vice-president of the mainland Red Cross travelled to the island, thus becoming the most senior representative of the People's Republic to visit Taiwan since 1949. Delegates from the SEF and ARATS met in Hong Kong in October 1992 for discussions. The Chairman of the Mainland Affairs Council, however, insisted upon the People's Republic's renunciation of the use of military force prior to any dialogue on the reunification question. Upon taking office in February 1993, the new Premier of Taiwan confirmed the continuation of the 'One China' policy.

In 1993 divisions between Taiwan's business sector and political groupings (the former advocating much closer links with the People's Republic, the latter urging greater caution) became evident. In January, and again later in the year, the Secretary-General of the SEF resigned, following disagreement with the Mainland Affairs Council. Historic talks between the Chairmen of the SEF and of the ARATS were held in Singapore in April. Engaging in the highest level of contact since 1949, Taiwan and the People's Republic agreed on the establishment of a formal structure for future negotiations on economic and social issues.

In August 1993 the People's Republic issued a document entitled *The Taiwan Question and the Reunification of China,* reiterating its claim to sovereignty over the island. Relations were further strained by a series of aircraft hijackings to Taiwan from the mainland. A SEF-ARATS meeting, held in Taiwan in December, attempted to address the issue of the repatriation of hijackers. Incidents of air piracy continued in 1994, prison sentences of up to 13 years being imposed on the hijackers by the Taiwanese authorities.

Further meetings between delegates of the SEF and ARATS were held in early 1994. Relations between Taiwan and the mainland deteriorated sharply in April, however, when 24 Taiwanese tourists were among those killed on board a pleasure boat plying Qiandao Lake, in the People's Republic. The mainland authorities initially attributed the deaths to an accidental fire, but it was subsequently revealed that the tourists had been robbed and murdered. Taiwan suspended all commercial and cultural exchanges with the People's Republic. In June three men were convicted of the murders and promptly executed. In February 1995 compensation totalling 1.2m. yuan was awarded to the victims' families by the People's Republic.

In July 1994 the Taiwanese Government released a White Paper on mainland affairs, urging that the division be acknowledged and the island accepted as a separate political entity. In August the SEF-ARATS talks were resumed when Tang Shubei, Vice-Chairman and Secretary-General of the ARATS, flew to Taipei for discussions with his Taiwanese counterpart, Chiao Jen-ho. Tang thus became the most senior Communist Chinese official ever to visit the island. Although the visit was marred by opposition protesters, the two sides reached tentative agreement on several issues, including the repatriation of hijackers and illegal immigrants from Taiwan to the mainland. Procedures for the settlement of cross-Straits fishing disputes were also established. In mid-November relations were strained once again when, in an apparent accident during a training exercise, Taiwanese anti-aircraft shells landed on a mainland village, injuring several people. Nevertheless, in late November a further round of SEF-ARATS talks took place in Nanjing, at which agreement in principle on the procedure for the repatriation of hijackers and illegal immigrants was confirmed. Further progress was made at meetings in Beijing in January 1995, although no accord was signed. It was announced in March that the functions of the SEF were to be enhanced. To improve co-ordination, the SEF board of directors would henceforth include government officials, while meetings of the Mainland Affairs Council would be attended by officials of the SEF. In the same month the Mainland Affairs Council approved a resolution providing for the relaxation of restrictions on visits by mainland officials and civilians.

President Jiang Zemin's Lunar New Year address, incorporating the mainland's 'eight-point' policy on Taiwan, was regarded as more conciliatory than hitherto. In April 1995, in response, President Lee proposed a 'six-point' programme for cross-Straits relations: unification according to the reality of separate rules; increased exchanges on the basis of Chinese culture; increased economic and trade relations; admission to international organizations on an equal footing; the renunciation of the use of force against each other; and joint participation in Hong Kong and Macau affairs. In late April, however, the eighth round of working-level SEF-ARATS discussions was postponed, owing to disagreement over the agenda.

In May 1995 the SEF Chairman, Koo Chen-fu, and his mainland counterpart, Wang Daohan, formally agreed to meet in Beijing in July. In June, however, this proposed second session of senior-level negotiations was postponed by the ARATS, in protest at President Lee's recent visit to the USA. Tension between the two sides increased in July, when the People's Republic unexpectedly announced that it was about to conduct an eight-day programme of guided missile and artillery-firing tests off the northern coast of Taiwan. A second series of exercises took place in August, again arousing much anxiety on the island. In mid-August President Jiang Zemin confirmed that the People's Republic would not renounce the use of force against Taiwan. Nevertheless, at the end of that month President Lee reaffirmed the KMT's commitment to reunification. In October President Jiang Zemin's offer to visit Taiwan in person was cautiously received on the island. President Lee confirmed his Government's anti-independence stance in November.

In January 1996 the Taiwanese Premier again urged the early resumption of cross-Straits dialogue. In February unconfirmed reports indicated that as many as 400,000 mainland troops had been mobilized around Fujian Province. In the same month, upon his appointment as Chairman of the Mainland Affairs Council, Chang King-yuh pledged to attempt to improve relations with the mainland. In early March as Taiwan's first direct presidential election approached, the People's Republic began a new series of missile tests, including the firing of surface-to-surface missiles into coastal areas around Taiwan. Live artillery exercises continued in the Taiwan Strait until after the island's presidential election, arousing international concern. The USA deployed two naval task forces in the area (see below).

In early April 1996, as tension eased, the Mainland Affairs Council removed the ban on visits to Taiwan by officials of the People's Republic. The Ministry of Transportation and Communications announced that mainland container traffic was to be permitted direct entry to Taiwanese ports. At the end of April the SEF, which had lodged a strong protest with the ARATS during the missile tests of March, urged the resumption of bilateral discussions. Upon his inauguration in May, Taiwan's re-elected Head of State declared his readiness to visit the People's Republic for negotiations. In July President Lee reaffirmed his commitment to peaceful reunification, and urged the mainland to renounce the use of violence and to resume dialogue. In the same month visits to Taiwan by executives of the mainland's port authorities and of Air China (the flag carrier of the People's Republic) led to speculation that direct travel links between the two sides might be established. Other business delegations followed. The national oil corporations of Taiwan and of the People's Republic signed a joint exploration agreement.

In October 1996 the Taiwanese Vice-Minister of Education, the most senior official to date, visited the People's Republic for discussions with his mainland counterparts. In November the Mainland Affairs Council announced that the permanent stationing of mainland media representatives in Taiwan was to be permitted. President Lee's renewed offer to travel to the People's Republic was rejected and, despite repeated SEF requests, Tang Shubei of the ARATS continued to assert that cross-Straits discussions could not resume owing to Taiwan's pursuit of its 'two Chinas' policy (a reference to President Lee's attempts to raise the diplomatic profile of the island). In January 1997, however, as the reversion of the entrepôt of Hong Kong to Chinese sovereignty approached, shipping representatives of Taiwan and of the People's Republic reached a preliminary consensus on the establishment of direct sea links. The agreement permitted mainland cargoes to be transhipped at Kaohsiung for onward passage to a third country, but did not allow goods to enter the island's customs. Five Taiwanese and six mainland shipping companies were granted permission to conduct cross-Straits cargo services, which began in April, the first since 1949.

In March 1997 an unemployed journalist hijacked a Taiwanese airliner on an internal flight and, citing political repression on the island, forced the aircraft to fly to the mainland, where he requested asylum. He was subsequently extradited to Taiwan, where he faced criminal charges.

In July 1997, upon the reversion to Chinese sovereignty of the British colony of Hong Kong, President Lee firmly rejected the concept of 'one country, two systems' and any parallel with Taiwan, and strenuously refuted a suggestion by President Jiang Zemin that Taiwan would eventually follow the example of Hong Kong. In August Liu Gangchi, Deputy Secretary-General of the ARATS, arrived in Taipei, at the head of a 32-member delegation, to attend a seminar on the subject of China's modernization. In September the Taiwanese Minister of Finance and the Governor of the central bank were obliged to cancel a visit to Hong Kong, where they had planned to have informal discussions with delegates to the forthcoming IMF/World Bank meeting, owing to Hong Kong's failure to issue them with visas. The affair compounded fears that Taiwan's business dealings with Hong Kong might be jeopardized.

In October 1997 the alleged abduction to the mainland of a Taiwanese marine police officer, who was investigating a Chinese fishing vessel suspected of smuggling, caused tension in Taiwan's relations with the People's Republic. The police officer, who sustained head injuries in the incident and was hospitalized on the mainland, was permitted to return to Taiwan in December, following lengthy negotiations.

A call for the opening of political negotiations, made by the Minister of Foreign Affairs of the People's Republic in September 1997, was welcomed by the Mainland Affairs Council. However, the Taiwanese authorities continued to insist that Beijing remove all preconditions before the opening of dialogue. In November the Secretary-General of the SEF was invited by the ARATS to attend a seminar on the mainland in the following month. The SEF proposed instead that its Chairman head a delegation to the People's Republic. An interview given by President Lee to a Western newspaper, in which he referred to Taiwan's independence, caused anger on the part of the Beijing authorities. Nevertheless, relations with the mainland showed signs of improving in early December when senior SEF and ARATS officials resumed negotiations.

In December 1972 legislative elections were held, for the first time in 24 years, to fill 53 seats in the National Assembly. The new members, elected for a fixed term of six years, joined 1,376 surviving 'life-term' members of the Assembly. President Chiang Kai-shek remained in office until his death in April 1975. He was succeeded as leader of the ruling KMT by his son, Gen. Chiang Ching-kuo, who had been Premier since May 1972. Dr Yen Chia-kan, Vice-President since 1966, became the new President. In May 1978 President Yen retired and was succeeded by Gen. Chiang, who appointed Sun Yun-suan, hitherto Minister of Economic Affairs, to be Premier. At elections for 71 seats in the Legislative Yuan in December 1983, the KMT won an overwhelming victory, confirming its dominance over the independent 'Tangwai' (non-party) candidates. In March 1984 President Chiang was re-elected for a second six-year term, and Lee Teng-hui, a former Mayor of Taipei and a native Taiwanese, became Vice-President. In May a major government reshuffle took place, and Yu Kuo-hwa, formerly the Governor of the Central Bank, replaced Sun Yun-suan as Premier. President Chiang died in January 1988 and was succeeded by Lee Teng-hui.

In September 1986 135 leading opposition politicians formed the Democratic Progressive Party (DPP), in defiance of the KMT's ban on the formation of new political parties. Elections for 84 seats in the National Assembly and 73 seats in the Legislative Yuan were held in December. The KMT achieved a decisive victory, winning 68 seats in the National Assembly and 59 in the Legislative Yuan, but the DPP received about one-quarter of the total votes, and won 11 seats in the Assembly and 12 in the Legislative Yuan, thus more than doubling the non-KMT representation. In February 1987 the KMT began to implement a programme of political reform. Martial law (in force since 1949) was replaced by the National Security Law in July and, under the terms of the new legislation, political parties other than the KMT were permitted, and civilians were removed from the jurisdiction of military courts. In April seven major posts in a reorganization of the Executive Yuan were allocated to reformist members of the KMT.

In November 1987 the second annual Congress of the DPP approved a resolution declaring that Taiwanese citizens had the right to advocate independence. In January 1988, however, two opposition activists were imprisoned, on charges of sedition, for voicing such demands. In October Huang Hsin-chieh replaced Yao Chia-wen as Chairman of the DPP.

In February 1988 a plan to restructure the legislative bodies was approved by the Central Standing Committee of the KMT. Voluntary resignations were to be sought from 'life-term' members of the Legislative Yuan and National Assembly, and seats were no longer to be reserved for representatives of mainland constituencies. The 13th national Congress of the KMT was held in July. It was decided that, for the first time, free elections would be held for two-thirds of the members of the KMT's Central Committee. In the ensuing ballot, numerous new members were elected, and the proportion of native Taiwanese increased sharply. A reshuffle of the Executive Yuan, later in the month, resulted in a government comprising younger members. President Lee promoted three draft legislative measures: a revision of regulations concerning the registration of political parties; a retirement plan for those members of the three legislative assemblies who had been elected by mainland constituencies in 1947; and a new law aiming to give greater autonomy to the Taiwan Provincial Government and its assembly. In January 1989 the three measures were enacted, and in the following month the KMT became the first political party to register under the new legislation. However, the new laws were severely criticized by the DPP, which protested at the size of the retirement pensions being offered and at the terms of the Civic Organizations Law, which required that, in order to register, political parties undertook to reject communism and any notion of official political independence for Taiwan. Despite these objections, the DPP applied for official registration in April. In May Yu Kuo-hwa resigned as Premier of the Executive Yuan and was replaced by Lee Huan, the Secretary-General of the KMT.

Partial elections to the Legislative Yuan and the Taiwan Provincial Assembly were held on 2 December 1989. A total of 101 seats in the Legislative Yuan were contested, with the KMT obtaining 72 seats and the DPP winning 21, thus securing the prerogative to propose legislation in the Legislative Yuan. In February 1990 the opening of the National Assembly's 35-day plenary session, convened every six years to elect the country's President, was disrupted by DPP members' violent action in a protest against the continuing domination of the Assembly by elderly KMT politicians, who had been elected on the Chinese mainland prior to 1949 and who had never been obliged to seek re-election. More than 80 people were injured during street clashes between riot police and demonstrators. In March 1990 DPP members were barred from the National Assembly for refusing to swear allegiance to 'The Republic of China', attempting instead to substitute 'Taiwan' upon taking the oath. A number of amendments to the Temporary Provisions, which for more than 40 years had permitted the effective suspension of the Constitution, were approved by the National Assembly in mid-March. Revisions included measures to strengthen the position of the mainland-elected KMT members, who were granted new powers to initiate and veto legislation, and also an amendment to permit the National Assembly to meet annually. The revisions were opposed not only by the DPP but also by more moderate members of the KMT, and led to a large protest rally in Taipei, which attracted an estimated 10,000 demonstrators, who continued to demand the abolition of the National Assembly and the holding of direct presidential elections. Nevertheless, President Lee was duly re-elected, unopposed, by the National Assembly for a six-year term, two rival KMT candidates having withdrawn from the contest.

There was renewed unrest in May 1990, however, following President Lee's unexpected appointment as the new Premier of Gen. (retd) Hau Pei-tsun, the former Chief of the General Staff and, since December 1989, the Minister of National Defense. Outraged opposition members prevented Hau from addressing the National Assembly, which was unable to approve his nomination until the session was reconvened a few days later. Angry demonstrators, fearing a reversal of the process of democratic reform, again clashed with riot police on the streets of Taipei. A new Executive Yuan was appointed at the end of the month.

The National Affairs Conference (NAC) convened in late June 1990 to discuss proposals for reform. A Constitutional Reform Planning Group was subsequently established. The NAC reached consensus on the issue of direct presidential elections, which would permit the citizens of Taiwan, rather than the ageing members of the National Assembly, to select the Head of State. Meanwhile, the Council of Grand Justices had ruled that elderly members of the National Assembly and of the Legislative Yuan should step down by the end of 1991.

In October 1990 the National Unification Council, chaired by President Lee, was formed. In the same month the Mainland Affairs Council, comprising heads of government departments and led by the Vice-Premier of the Executive Yuan, was founded. The DPP urged the Government to renounce its claim to sovereignty over mainland China and also Mongolia. In December President Lee announced that Taiwan would formally end the state of war with the mainland; the declaration of emergency was to be rescinded by May 1991. Constitutional reform was to be implemented in several stages: in April 1991 the Temporary Provisions, adopted in 1948, were to be abolished; in late 1991 a new National Assembly was to be elected by popular vote, the number of members being reduced to 405 and all elderly mainland-elected delegates being obliged to relinquish their seats; elections to the new 161-member Legislative Yuan and the 52-member Control Yuan were to take place in 1992 and 1993 respectively. Meanwhile, in early December 1990 Huang Hwa, the leader of a faction of the DPP and independence activist, had received a 10-year prison sentence upon being found guilty of 'preparing to commit sedition'.

In April 1991 the resignation of Clement Chang, the Minister of Communications, was accepted, following investigations into an 'insider' share-trading scandal in which his wife and daughter were implicated. In the same month the National Assembly was convened, the session again being marred by violent clashes between KMT and DPP members. The DPP subsequently boycotted the session, arguing that a completely new constitution should be introduced and that elderly KMT delegates, who did not represent Taiwan constituencies, should not have the right to make amendments to the existing Constitution. As many as 20,000 demonstrators attended a protest march organized by the DPP. Nevertheless, the National Assembly duly approved the constitutional amendments, and at midnight on 30 April the 'period of mobilization for the suppression of the Communist rebellion' and the Temporary Provisions were formally terminated. The existence, but not the legitimacy, of the Government of the People's Republic was officially acknowledged by President Lee. Furthermore, Taiwan remained committed to its 'one China' policy. In May 1991, following the arrest of four advocates of independence for Taiwan (which led to student unrest and further opposition protests), the Statute of Punishment for Sedition was hastily abolished. The law had been adopted in 1949 and had been frequently employed by the KMT to suppress political dissent.

A senior UN official arrived on the island in August 1991, the first visit by such a representative since Taiwan's withdrawal from the organization in 1971. There were renewed clashes between demonstrators and the security forces in September, when as many as 15,000 citizens marched through Taipei to demand the holding of a referendum on the issue of Taiwan's readmission to the UN as an independent state. A similar rally, attended by more than 30,000 demonstrators, took place in Kaohsiung in October.

In August 1991 the opposition DPP officially announced its alternative draft constitution for 'Taiwan', rather than for 'the Republic of China', thus acknowledging the *de facto* position regarding sovereignty. In September, after being reinstated in the Legislative Yuan, Huang Hsin-chieh, the Chairman of the DPP, relinquished his seat in the legislature and urged other senior deputies to do likewise. Huang had been deprived of his seat and imprisoned in 1980, following his conviction on charges of sedition. At the party congress in October 1991, Huang was replaced as DPP Chairman by Hsu Hsin-liang. Risking prosecution by the authorities, the DPP congress adopted a resolution henceforth to advocate the establishment of 'the Republic of Taiwan', and urged the Government to declare the island's independence.

Elections to the new 405-member National Assembly, which was to be responsible for amending the Constitution, were held on 21 December 1991. The 225 seats open to direct election were contested by a total of 667 candidates, presented by 17 parties. The campaign was dominated by the issue of whether Taiwan should become independent or seek reunification with the mainland. The opposition's independence proposal was overwhelmingly rejected by the electorate, the DPP suffering a humiliating defeat. The KMT secured a total of 318 seats (179 of which were won by direct election), while the DPP won 75 seats (41 by direct election).

In late 1991, in a new campaign to curb illegal dissident activity, the authorities arrested 14 independence activists, including members of the banned, US-based World United Formosans for Independence (WUFI). Several detainees were indicted on charges of sedition. Furthermore, the four dissidents, whose arrest in May had provoked widespread unrest, were brought to trial and found guilty of sedition, receiving short prison sentences. In January 1992 four WUFI members were found guilty of plotting to overthrow the Government. In February 20,000 demonstrators protested against the sedition laws and demanded a referendum on the issue of independence.

In March 1992, at a plenary session of the KMT Central Committee, agreement was reached on a reduction in the President's term of office from six to four years. The principal question of arrangements for future presidential elections, however, remained unresolved. Liberal members continued to advocate direct election, while conservatives favoured a complex proxy system. In April street demonstrations were organized by the DPP to support demands for direct presidential elections. In May the National Assembly adopted eight amendments to the Constitution, one of which empowered the President to appoint members of the Control Yuan.

Meanwhile, the radical dissident, (Stella) Chen Wan-chen, who had established the pro-independence Organization for Taiwan Nation-Building upon her return from the USA in 1991, was sentenced to 46 months' imprisonment in March 1992, having been found guilty of 'preparing to commit sedition'. In May, however, Taiwan's severe sedition law was amended, non-violent acts ceasing to be a criminal offence. Several independence activists were released from prison and other dissidents were able to return from overseas exile. Nevertheless, in June (George) Chang Tsang-hung, the chairman of WUFI, who had returned from exile in the USA in December 1991, received a prison sentence of five (commuted from 10) years upon conviction on charges of sedition and attempted murder, involving the dispatch of letter-bombs to government officials in 1976. Chang was released for medical treatment in October 1992. In March 1993 Chang was acquitted of the sedition charges, on the grounds of insufficient evidence.

In October 1992 the Minister of Finance, Wang Chien-shien, resigned, owing to controversy arising from his proposed land-tax reforms. Taiwan's first full elections since the establishment of Nationalist rule in 1949 were held in December 1992. The KMT retained 102 of the 161 seats in the Legislative Yuan. The DPP, however, garnered 31% of the votes and more than doubled its representation in the legislature, winning 50 seats. Following this set-back, the Premier and the KMT Secretary-General resigned. In February 1993 President Lee nominated the Governor of Taiwan Province, Lien Chan, for the premiership. Lien Chan thus became the island's first Premier of Taiwanese descent.

There were violent scenes in the National Assembly in April 1993, when deputies of the DPP (which in recent months had modified its aggressive pro-independence stance, placing greater emphasis on the issues of corruption and social welfare) accused members of the KMT of malpractice in relation to the election of the Assembly's officers.

In May 1993 the growing rift between conservative and liberal members of the ruling party was illustrated by the resignation from the KMT of about 30 conservative rebels, and their formation of the New Alliance Nationalist Party. Furthermore, in June the Government was defeated in the Legislative Yuan, when a group of KMT deputies voted with the opposition to approve legislation on financial disclosure requirements for elected and appointed public officials. The unity of the KMT was further undermined in August, when six dissident legislators belonging to the New Kuomintang Alliance, which had registered as a political group in March, announced their decision to leave the ruling party in order to establish the New Party. The rebels included Wang Chien-shien, the former Minister of Finance. Nevertheless, in the same month, at the 14th KMT Congress, Lee Teng-hui was re-elected Chairman of the party. A new 31-member Central Standing Committee and 210-member Central Committee, comprising mainly Lee's supporters, were selected. In a conciliatory gesture by the KMT Chairman, four vice-chairmanships were created, the new positions being filled by representatives of different factions of the party.

In September 1993, following a series of bribery scandals, the Executive Yuan approved measures to combat corruption. The administrative reform plan included stricter supervision of public officials and harsher penalties for those found guilty of misconduct. In the same month a KMT member of the Legislative Yuan was sentenced to 14 years' imprisonment for bribery of voters during the 1992 election campaign; similar convictions followed. At local government elections held in November 1993, although its share of the votes declined to 47.5%, the KMT fared better than anticipated, securing 15 of the 23 posts at stake. The DPP, which accused the KMT of malpractice, received 41.5% of the votes cast, but won only six posts; it retained control of Taipei County. The DPP Chairman, Hsu Hsin-liang, resigned, and was replaced by Shih Ming-teh. Following allegations of extensive bribery at further local polls in early 1994 (at which the DPP and independent candidates made strong gains), the Ministry of Justice intensified its campaign against corruption. Proposals for constitutional amendments to permit the direct election in 1996 of the Taiwanese President by popular vote (rather than by electoral college) and to limit the powers of the Premier were approved by the National Assembly in July 1994.

At gubernatorial and mayoral elections in December 1994 the DPP took control of the Taipei mayoralty, in the first such direct polls for 30 years, while the KMT succeeded in retaining the provincial governorship of Taiwan, in the first ever popular election for the post, and the mayoralty of Kaohsiung. The New Party established itself as a major political force, its candidate for the mayoralty of Taipei receiving more votes than the KMT incumbent. Almost 77% of those eligible voted in the elections. A government reorganization followed.

In March 1995, in response to continuing allegations of corruption (the number of indictments now having exceeded 2,000), President Lee announced the appointment of a committee to investigate the financial activities of the KMT. In the same month, following the President's formal apology at a ceremony of commemoration in February, the Legislative Yuan approved a law granting compensation to the relatives of the victims of a massacre by Nationalist troops in 1947 (the 'February 28 Incident'), in which an estimated 18,000 native Taiwanese had been killed.

Fewer than 68% of those eligible voted at the elections to the Legislative Yuan held on 2 December 1995. A major campaign issue was that of corruption. The KMT received only 46% of the votes cast, and its strength declined to 84 of the 164 seats, faring particularly badly in Taipei. Although it performed less well than anticipated, the DPP increased its representation to 53 seats. The New Party, which favoured reconciliation with the mainland, secured 21 seats. At the Legislative Yuan's first session in February 1996, Liu Sung-pan of the KMT only narrowly defeated a strong challenge from Shih Ming-teh of the DPP to secure re-election as the chamber's President.

The first direct presidential election was scheduled for March 1996, to coincide with the National Assembly polls. President Lee had declared his intention to stand for re-election in August 1995. In January 1996 Lien Chan offered to resign as Premier in order to support President Lee and to concentrate on his own vice-presidential campaign. He remained in office in an interim capacity. Other contenders for the presidency included the independent candidate and former President of the Judicial Yuan, Lin Yang-kang, supported by former Premier Hau Pei-tsun (both conservative former KMT Vice-Chairmen having campaigned on behalf of New Party candidates at the December elections and therefore having had their KMT membership revoked); Peng Ming-min of the DPP; and Chen Li-an, former President of the Control Yuan and previously Minister of National Defense, an independent Buddhist candidate. Wang Chien-shien of the New Party withdrew his candidacy in favour of the Lin-Hau alliance. The campaign was dominated by the issue of reunification with the mainland. In mid-March a DPP demonstration on the streets of Taipei, in support of demands for Taiwan's independence, was attended by 50,000 protesters.

At the presidential election, held on 23 March 1996, the incumbent President Lee received 54.0% of the votes cast, thus securing his re-election for a four-year term. His nearest rival, Peng Ming-min of the DPP, took 21.1% of the votes. The independent candidates, Lin Yang-kang and Chen Li-an, received 14.9% and 10.0% of the votes, respectively. At the concurrent elections for the National Assembly, the KMT garnered 55% of the votes and took 183 of the 334 seats. The DPP won 99 seats and the New Party 46 seats. The Chairman of the DPP, Shih Ming-teh, resigned and Hsu Hsin-liang subsequently returned to the post.

In June 1996 the President's announcement of the composition of the new Executive Yuan aroused much controversy. Although several members retained their previous portfolios, the President (apparently under pressure from within the KMT and disregarding public concern at the rising levels of corruption and organized crime) demoted the popular Ministers of Justice, and of Transportation and Communications, who had exposed malpractice and initiated campaigns against corruption. Other changes included the replacement of the Minister of Foreign Affairs, Fredrick Chien (who became Speaker of the National Assembly), by John Chang, the grandson of Chiang Kai-shek. The most controversial nomination, however, was the reappointment as Premier of Lien Chan, despite his recent election as the island's Vice-President. As fears of a constitutional crisis grew, opposition members of the Legislative Yuan, along with a number of KMT delegates, demanded that the President submit the membership of the Executive Yuan to the legislature for approval, and threatened to boycott the chamber's business. In October the Constitutional Court opened its hearing regarding the question of the island's Vice-President serving concurrently as Premier.

In October 1996 the Taiwan Independence Party was established by dissident members of the DPP. In the same month, the Legislative Yuan approved the restoration of funding for a controversial fourth nuclear power plant, construction of which had been suspended in 1986. Thousands of anti-nuclear protesters clashed with police, following demonstrations at the legislature.

Public concern at the sharp increase in crimes of violence intensified in late 1996. The mass murder in Taoyuan in November of local politician and magistrate Liu Pang-you and seven colleagues, followed by the rape and murder of an eminent female professor, prompted the Government to announce an eight-point programme to combat crime and 'deteriorating social morals'.

In December 1996 the multi-party National Development Conference (NDC), established to review the island's political system, held its inaugural meeting. The convention approved KMT proposals to abolish the Legislative Yuan's right to confirm the President's choice of Premier, to permit the legislature to introduce motions of no confidence in the Premier and to empower the President to dismiss the legislature. The Provincial Governor, (James) Soong Chu-yu, subsequently tendered his resignation in protest at the NDC's recommendations that elections for the provincial governorship and assembly be abolished, as the first stage of the dissolution of the provincial apparatus. An historical legacy duplicating many of the functions of central and local government, the Provincial Government was responsible for the entire island, with the exception of the cities of Taipei and Kaohsiung. In January 1997 President Lee refused to accept the Governor's resignation, but the affair drew attention to the uneasy relationship between the island's President and its Governor, and brought to the fore the question of reunification with the mainland. In February, however, Vice-President and Premier Lien Chan declared that the Provincial Government would not be abolished and that the five-branch system of government (see Government, below) would be retained.

The abduction and brutal murder in April 1997 of the teenage daughter of a television celebrity provoked renewed outrage on the island. In early May more than 50,000 demonstrators, protesting against the Government's apparent inability to address the problem of increasing crime, demanded the resignation of President Lee. Three members of the Executive Yuan subsequently resigned, including the popular Minister without Portfolio and former Minister of Justice, Ma Yingjeou. The appointment of Yeh Chin-feng as Minister of the Interior (the first woman to oversee Taiwan's police force) did little to appease the public, which remained highly suspicious of the alleged connections between senior politicians and the perpetrators of organized crime. In mid-May thousands of protesters, despairing of the rapid deterioration in social order, again took to the streets of Taipei, renewing their challenge to President Lee's leadership and demanding the immediate resignation of Premier Lien Chan. In late June a 'Say No to China' rally attracted as many as 70,000 supporters.

In July 1997 the National Assembly approved a series of constitutional reforms, including the 'freezing' of the Provincial Government, which had been agreed by the NDC in December

1996. In August 1997 the Government resigned in order to permit a reallocation of portfolios. Vincent Siew, former Chairman of the Council for Economic Planning and Development and also of the Mainland Affairs Council, replaced Lien Chan as Premier (Lien Chan retained the post of Vice-President), and John Chang was appointed Vice-Premier. The new Premier pledged to improve social order, further develop the economy, raise the island's standard of living and improve links with the People's Republic of China. In the same month President Lee was re-elected unopposed as Chairman of the ruling KMT.

In mid-November 1997 the man suspected of the murder of the television celebrity's daughter, in April, took hostage a South African diplomat and several members of his family. All were subsequently released, having sustained minor injuries, and the kidnapper, who later confessed to other murders, including that of a prominent plastic surgeon earlier in 1997, was arrested.

The KMT experienced a serious set-back in elections at mayoral and magistrate levels, held on 29 November 1997. The opposition DPP, which had campaigned on a platform of more open government, secured 43% of the total votes, winning 12 of the 23 constituency posts contested, while the KMT achieved only 42% (eight posts). Voter turn-out was 65.9%. The outcome of the elections meant that more than 70% of Taiwan's population would come under DPP administration. Following the KMT's poor performance in the ballot, the Secretary-General of the party resigned, and was replaced by John Chang. A major reorganization of the party followed. Liu Chao-shiuan was appointed Vice-Premier in place of Chang.

At local elections, held in January 1998, the KMT won an overwhelming majority of the seats contested, while the DPP, in a reversal of fortune, performed badly. A minor cabinet reshuffle was carried out in early February.

In foreign relations, meanwhile, in January 1979 Taiwan suffered a serious set-back when the USA established full diplomatic relations with the People's Republic of China and severed relations with Taiwan. The USA also terminated the 1954 mutual security treaty with Taiwan. Commercial links are still maintained, however, and Taiwan's purchase of armaments from the USA has remained a controversial issue. In August 1982 a joint Sino-US communiqué was published, in which the USA pledged to reduce gradually its sale of armaments to Taiwan. In September 1992 President Bush announced the sale of up to 150 F-16 fighter aircraft to Taiwan. The announcement was condemned by the People's Republic. In December the US trade representative became the first senior US government official to visit the island since 1979. In September 1994 the USA announced a modification of its policy towards Taiwan, henceforth permitting senior-level bilateral meetings to be held in US government offices. In December the US Secretary of Transportation visited the Ministry of Foreign Affairs in Taipei, the first US official of cabinet rank to visit Taiwan for more than 15 years. In June 1995 President Lee was permitted to make a four-day unofficial visit to the USA, where he gave a speech at Cornell University, and met members of the US Congress. This visit provoked outrage in Beijing, and the Chinese ambassador to Washington was recalled. In early 1996 the Taiwanese Vice-President was twice granted transit visas permitting him to disembark in the USA en route to Central America. The new Vice-President was accorded similar privileges on two occasions.

In March 1996, as the mainland began a new series of missile tests off the Taiwanese coast (see above), the USA stationed two naval convoys in waters east of the island, representing the largest US deployment in Asia since 1975. US President Clinton agreed to the sale of Stinger anti-aircraft missiles and other defensive weapons to Taiwan. In September 1996 President Lee and the US Deputy Treasury Secretary met in Taipei for discussions, the most senior-level contact between the two sides since 1994. Some controversy arose in late 1996, however, when irregularities in the financing of President Clinton's re-election campaign, involving Taiwanese donors, were reported. Furthermore, it was alleged that a senior KMT official had offered an illicit contribution of US $15m. to the Democratic Party in Washington. In early 1997 the first of the Patriot anti-missile air defence systems, purchased from the USA under an arrangement made in 1993, were reported to have been deployed on the island. The first of the F-16s were delivered to Taiwan in April 1997. The Taiwanese Government expressed satisfaction at the USA's continued commitment to Taiwan's security, confirmed following the visit to the USA of the President of the People's Republic, Jiang Zemin, in October.

In January 1993 the official confirmation of Taiwan's purchase of 60 Mirage fighter aircraft from France again provoked strong protest from Beijing. In January 1994 Taiwan suffered a reverse when (following pressure from the People's Republic) France recognized Taiwan as an integral part of Chinese territory, and the French Prime Minister agreed not to sell weapons to the island. In March 1995, however, it was reported that Taiwan was to purchase shoulder-fired anti-aircraft missiles from a French company. The sale of these missiles, as well as the delivery of the Mirage aircraft and six frigates, was confirmed in 1996. Deliveries commenced in 1997.

Taiwan severed diplomatic relations with Japan in 1972, following Tokyo's *rapprochement* with Beijing. Mainland displeasure was compounded in February 1993, however, when, for the first time in two decades, the Taiwanese Minister of Foreign Affairs paid a visit to Japan. In September 1994 pressure from Beijing resulted in the withdrawal of President Lee's invitation to attend the forthcoming Asian Games in Hiroshima. Instead, however, the Taiwanese Vice-Premier was permitted to visit Japan. Similarly, in July 1995 Japan announced that the Taiwanese Vice-Premier would not be permitted to attend a meeting of APEC members to be held in Osaka in November. Instead, President Lee was represented by Koo Chen-fu, the SEF Chairman. The latter also attended the APEC meeting in the Philippines in November 1996. In 1996 Taiwan's relations with Japan continued to be strained by the issue of adequate compensation for the thousands of Asian (mostly Korean) women used by Japanese troops for sexual purposes during the Second World War. In October Taiwan rejected a Japanese offer of nominal compensation for Taiwanese women. Relations deteriorated further in 1996 on account of a dispute relating to a group of uninhabited islets in the East China Sea: known as the Tiaoyutai (Diaoyu Dao) in Chinese, or Senkaku in Japanese, the islands were claimed by Taiwan, China and Japan. In July, following the construction of a lighthouse on one of the islands by a Japanese right-wing group, the Taiwanese Ministry of Foreign Affairs lodged a strong protest over Japan's decision to incorporate the islands within its 200-mile (370-km) exclusive economic zone. In early October further discussions with Japan on the question of Taiwanese fishing rights within the disputed waters ended without agreement. In the same month a flotilla of small boats, operated by activists from Taiwan, Hong Kong and Macau, succeeded in evading Japanese patrol vessels. Having reached the disputed islands, protesters raised the flags of Taiwan and of China. In May 1997 the Taiwanese Minister of Foreign Affairs expressed grave concern, following the landing and planting of their national flag on one of the disputed islands by a Japanese politician. A flotilla of 20 ships, carrying about 200 protesters and journalists from Taiwan and Hong Kong, set sail from the port of Shenao, ostensibly to participate in an international fishing contest. The boats were intercepted by Japanese coastguard vessels and failed to gain access to the islands. In September an attempted parachute landing by Taiwanese activists also ended in failure. Reports in October that Japanese patrol boats were forcibly intercepting Taiwanese fishing vessels were a further cause for concern for the Taiwanese authorities.

In March 1989, meanwhile, President Lee paid a state visit to Singapore, the first official visit overseas by a President of Taiwan for 12 years. In February 1994 President Lee embarked upon an eight-day tour of South-East Asia. Although the tour was described as informal, President Lee had meetings with the Heads of State of the Philippines, Indonesia and Thailand, leading to protests from Beijing. In May the Taiwanese President visited Nicaragua, Costa Rica, South Africa (at that time the island's only remaining major diplomatic ally) and Swaziland. In April 1995 President Lee travelled to the United Arab Emirates and to Jordan, on what were described as private visits (Taiwan having no diplomatic relations with these countries). In June the Taiwanese Premier visited countries in Central Europe. Again, the visits provoked strong protest from China. In August 1996, as Beijing continued to urge Pretoria to sever its diplomatic links with Taipei, Vice-Premier Hsu Li-teh led a delegation of government and business representatives to South Africa. In September, however, the Taiwanese Minister of Foreign Affairs was obliged to curtail an ostensibly private visit to Jakarta, following protests from the People's Republic of China. In January 1997 the Vice-President was received by the Pope during a visit to the Holy See, the only European state that continued to recognize Taiwan. In the same month the Minister of Foreign Affairs embarked upon a tour of seven African nations, in order to consolidate relations. His itinerary included South Africa, despite that country's recent announcement of its intention to sever diplomatic relations with Taiwan (a major set-back to the island's campaign to gain wider international recognition). In March a six-day visit to Taiwan by the Dalai Lama was strongly condemned by the People's Republic of China, which denounced a meeting between President Lee and the exiled spiritual leader of Tibet as a 'collusion of splittists'.

In July 1997, following the Bahamas' withdrawal of recognition from Taiwan and establishment of diplomatic relations with the People's Republic of China, the Taiwanese Minister of Foreign Affairs undertook an extensive tour of the countries of Central America and the Caribbean, in an effort to maintain their support. In September, during a tour of Central America (the six nations of the region having become the core of Taiwan's remaining diplomatic allies), President Lee attended an international conference on the development of the Panama Canal. The USA granted a transit visa to the Taiwanese President. A visit to Europe in October by Vice-President Lien Chan was curtailed when pressure from Beijing forced the Spanish Government to withdraw an invitation. The Malaysian and Singaporean Prime Ministers met their Taiwanese counterpart in Taiwan in November, on their return from the APEC forum in Canada. The People's Republic expressed concern at the meetings.

The question of the sovereignty of the Spratly Islands, situated in the South China Sea and believed to possess petroleum resources, to which Taiwan and five other countries laid claim, remained unresolved in 1997. A contingent of Taiwanese marines is maintained on Taiping Island, the largest of the disputed islands, located some 1,574 km south-west of Taiwan. A satellite telecommunications link between Taiping and Kaohsiung was inaugurated in October 1995. In August 1993 Taiwan announced its intention to construct an airbase on Taiping Island, but in January 1996 the scheme was postponed.

Government

Under the provisions of the amended 1947 Constitution, the Head of State is the President, who is elected by popular vote for a four-year term. There are five Yuans (governing bodies), the highest legislative organ being the Legislative Yuan, to which the Executive Yuan (the Council of Ministers) is responsible. Following elections in December 1995, the Legislative Yuan comprised 164 members: 128 chosen by direct election, most of the remainder being appointed from separate lists of candidates on the basis of proportional representation. The Legislative Yuan serves a three-year term. There are also Control, Judicial and Examination Yuans. Their respective functions are: to investigate the work of the executive; to interpret the Constitution and national laws; and to supervise examinations for entry into public offices. The Legislative Yuan submits proposals to the National Assembly. Following elections in March 1996, the National Assembly comprised 334 members serving a four-year term. The Taiwan Provincial Government handles the general administrative affairs of the island (excluding the cities of Taipei and Kaohsiung). Its policy-making body is the Taiwan Provincial Government Council. The Governor of Taiwan is popularly elected for a four-year term. The Taiwan Provincial Assembly exercises the province's legislative power. The Fukien (Fujian) Provincial Government is responsible for the administration of Quemoy and Matsu.

Defence

In August 1997 the armed forces totalled an estimated 376,000: army 240,000 (with deployments of 35,000–40,000 and 8,000–10,000, respectively, on the islands of Quemoy and Matsu), air force 68,000 and navy 68,000 (including 30,000 marines). Paramilitary forces numbered 26,650. Reserves totalled 1,657,500. Military service lasts for two years. Defence expenditure for 1998 was projected at NT $308,000m.

Economic Affairs

In 1996 Taiwan's gross national product (GNP), at current prices, totalled US $274,568m., having increased, in real terms, by 5.4% compared with 1995. GNP per head reached US $12,838 in 1996. In 1986–96 the population increased at an average annual rate of 1.0%. Between 1986 and 1996 real gross domestic product (GDP) expanded at an average annual rate of 7.3%. In 1996 GDP increased by 5.7%, in real terms, to total NT $7,477,540m. GDP growth was estimated at 6.7% in 1997.

Agriculture (including hunting, forestry and fishing) contributed 3.2% of GDP, and employed 10.1% of the working population, in 1996. The principal crops are rice, sugar cane, maize and sweet potatoes. Agricultural GDP increased at an average annual rate of 1.0%, in real terms, during 1986–96, but decreased by 0.6% in 1996, compared with the previous year.

Industry (comprising mining, manufacturing, construction and utilities) employed 37.5% of the working population, and provided 34.2% of GDP, in 1996. Industrial GDP increased, in real terms, at an average rate of 5.3% per year between 1986 and 1996. In 1996 industrial GDP rose by 3.7%, compared with 1995.

Mining contributed 0.3% of GDP, and employed less than 0.2% of the working population, in 1996. Coal, marble and dolomite are the principal minerals extracted. Taiwan also has substantial reserves of natural gas. The GDP of the mining sector rose by an average annual rate of 0.9% in 1986–96. Mining GDP decreased by 4.6% in 1996, compared with 1995.

Manufacturing contributed 26.9% of GDP, and employed 26.7% of the working population, in 1996. The most important branches, measured by gross value of output, are electronics (particularly personal computers), plastic goods, synthetic yarns and the motor vehicle industry. The sector's GDP grew by an average annual rate of 4.9%, in real terms, in 1986–96. Growth in manufacturing GDP in 1996 was 4.5%.

In 1996 almost 53% of Taiwan's energy supply was derived from imported petroleum. Imports of petroleum accounted for 4.7% of total import expenditure in 1996. In that year nuclear power supplied 11.4% of Taiwan's energy requirements.

The services sector contributed 62.6% of GDP in 1996, while engaging 52.4% of the employed labour force. In 1986–96 the GDP of this sector increased by an average annual rate of 10.3%. In 1996 services GDP increased by 7.4%, compared with the previous year.

In 1996 Taiwan recorded a visible trade surplus of US $17,568m., and there was a surplus of US $11,027m. on the current account of the balance of payments. In 1996 the principal sources of imports were Japan (accounting for 26.8%) and the USA (19.5%). The principal markets for exports in that year were the USA (23.2%), Hong Kong (23.1%) and Japan (11.8%). Trade with the People's Republic of China (mainly via Hong Kong) is of increasing significance. Taiwan's principal imports in 1996 were valves and tubes, petroleum and data-processing machines. The principal exports in that year were electronic products, valves and tubes, office machinery and plastic material products.

In the financial year ending 30 June 1997 there was a projected budgetary deficit of NT $153,438m. The 1997/98 budget proposals envisaged expenditure of NT $1,240,000m. (excluding special procurements). At 31 December 1996 Taiwan's external public debt was US $165.0m. In that year the cost of debt-servicing was equivalent to only 0.1% of the value of exports of goods and services. The annual rate of inflation averaged 3.0% during the period 1985–95. Consumer prices rose by 3.1% in 1996, but increased by only 1.1% in the first 10 months of 1997. Only 2.8% of the labour force were unemployed in September 1997. There is a shortage of labour in the construction and manufacturing sectors.

Taiwan became a member of the Asian Development Bank (ADB, see p. 110) in 1966, and of the Asia-Pacific Economic Co-operation forum (APEC, see p. 108) in late 1991. In September 1992 Taiwan was granted observer status at the General Agreement on Tariffs and Trade (GATT), and in early 1998 continued to await approval of its application for full membership of the successor World Trade Organization (WTO, see p. 244).

Taiwan's economic growth since 1949 has been substantial, the economy proving to be very resilient to world recession. As a result of its repeated trade surpluses, particularly with the USA and Hong Kong (the latter inclusive of much indirect trade with the People's Republic of China), Taiwan possesses one of the world's largest reserves of foreign exchange (US $90,025m. at mid-1997). Plans to transfer numerous state enterprises to the private sector commenced in 1989, but were subject to various delays. In 1997, however, the programme was accelerated, the most significant transfer plans involving the state power, petroleum and telecommunications monopolies. Proposals for the privatization of three commercial banks were announced in mid-1997. The monopoly system having been cited as an obstacle to Taiwan's admission to the WTO, the Government also pledged to transfer the state alcohol and tobacco concerns to private ownership. In 1995, in the hope of attracting to the island the headquarters of multinational companies, the Government announced the proposed establishment in Taiwan of an Asia-Pacific Regional Operations Center (APROC), scheduled to begin functioning in the year 2000. The plan involved extensive liberalization of the services and manufacturing sectors, improvements in the infrastructure and the development of sub-centres for manufacturing, sea and air transport, financial services, telecommunications and media organizations. In April 1996 plans to transform Taiwan into a developed economy by the year 2006 were announced. In July 1997 new restrictions limiting Taiwanese investment in mainland projects to US $50m. entered into force. Support for increased economic integration with the People's Republic was growing within the Taiwanese business community, but the Government was keen to encourage investment elsewhere in Asia. (Direct investment by Taiwanese businesses into the mainland totalled US $3,482m. in 1996.) In late 1997 the regional economic crisis affected the Taiwan dollar, which suffered a sharp loss in value in relation to the US dollar, reaching its lowest level for 10 years in November. The central bank was forced to intervene to defend the currency.

Social Welfare

In August 1997 the Labour Insurance programme covered around 7,440,000 workers, providing benefits for injury, disability, birth, death and old age. At the same time, 640,000 government employees and their dependants were covered by a separate scheme. In 1978 a system of supplementary benefits for those with low incomes was introduced. An unemployment insurance scheme began in July 1994. A universal health insurance scheme took effect in March 1995. In 1996 Taiwan had a total of 16,645 medical institutions, hospitals and clinics, with a total of 114,923 beds. There were 24,790 physicians, 2,992 doctors of traditional Chinese medicine, 61,494 nurses, 774 midwives and 7,332 dentists working in the country. Of total government expenditure in 1996/97, 13.2% (NT $157,903m.) was allocated to social welfare.

Education

Education at primary schools and junior high schools is free and compulsory between the ages of six and 15 years. Secondary schools consist of junior and senior middle schools, normal schools for teacher-training and vocational schools. There are also a number of private schools. Higher education is provided in universities, colleges, junior colleges and graduate schools. Government expenditure on education, science and culture in 1996/97 totalled NT $179,842m. In that year there were almost 2.0m. pupils enrolled in state primary schools. There were more than 1.9m. children in secondary schools. There were 137 universities and other institutes of higher education. The adult literacy rate in 1996 was 93.3%.

Public Holidays

1998: 1–2 January (Founding of the Republic/New Year), 27–30 January (Chinese New Year), 5 April (Ching Ming/Tomb-Sweeping Day and Death of President Chiang Kai-shek), 30 May (Dragon Boat Festival), 28 September (Teachers' Day/Birthday of Confucius), 5 October (Mid-Autumn Moon Festival), 10 October (Double Tenth Day, anniversary of 1911 revolution), 25 October (Retrocession Day, anniversary of end of Japanese occupation), 12 November (Birthday of Sun Yat-sen), 25 December (Constitution Day).

1999: 1–2 January (Founding of the Republic/New Year), 16–19 February (Chinese New Year), 5 April (Ching Ming/Tomb-Sweeping Day and Death of President Chiang Kai-shek), 18 June (Dragon Boat Festival), 24 September (Mid-Autumn Moon Festival), 28 September (Teachers' Day/Birthday of Confucius), 10 October (Double Tenth Day, anniversary of 1911 revolution), 25 October (Retrocession Day, anniversary of end of Japanese occupation), 12 November (Birthday of Sun Yat-sen), 25 December (Constitution Day).

Weights and Measures

The metric system is officially in force, but some traditional Chinese units are still used.

Statistical Survey

Source (unless otherwise stated): Bureau of Statistics, Directorate-General of Budget, Accounting and Statistics (DGBAS), Executive Yuan, 2 Kwang Chow St, Taipei 10729; tel. (2) 23710208; fax (2) 23319925; e-mail edp@emc.dgbasey.gov.tw.

Area and Population

AREA, POPULATION AND DENSITY

Area (sq km)	36,000*
Population (census results)	
28 December 1980	17,968,797
16 December 1990	
Males	10,533,921
Females	9,751,705
Total	20,285,626
Population (official figures at 31 December)	
1994	21,125,792
1995	21,304,181
1996	21,471,448
Density (per sq km) at 31 December 1996	596.4

* 13,900 sq miles.

Population (official figure at 30 September 1997): 21,615,000.

PRINCIPAL TOWNS

(population at 31 December 1996)

Taipei (capital)	2,605,374	Hsinchuang	345,954
Kaohsiung	1,433,621	Fengshan	309,062
Taichung	876,384	Chungli	306,473
Tainan	710,954	Taoyuan	283,861
Panchiao	524,323	Chiayi	262,860
Chungho	383,715	Hsintien	254,078
Shanchung	377,498	Yungho	230,734
Keelung	374,199	Changhwa	224,066
Hsinchu	345,954	Pingtung	214,627

BIRTHS, MARRIAGES AND DEATHS (registered)

	Live births		Marriages		Deaths	
	Number	Rate (per 1,000)	Number	Rate (per 1,000)	Number	Rate (per 1,000)
1990	334,872	16.55	142,753	7.06	105,322	5.21
1991	321,276	15.71	162,766	7.96	105,933	5.18
1992	320,963	15.54	169,234	8.19	110,140	5.33
1993	324,944	15.59	157,539	7.56	110,563	5.30
1994	322,263	15.32	170,580	8.11	113,486	5.40
1995	328,904	15.50	159,943	7.54	118,737	5.60
1996	324,874	15.19	169,106	7.91	122,152	5.71

Expectation of life (years at birth, 1995): Males 72.17; Females 78.00.

ECONOMICALLY ACTIVE POPULATION
(annual averages, '000 persons aged 15 years and over*)

	1994	1995	1996
Agriculture, forestry and fishing	976	954	918
Mining and quarrying	18	15	14
Manufacturing	2,485	2,449	2,422
Construction	967	1,003	928
Electricity, gas and water	36	36	35
Commerce	1,875	1,919	1,976
Transport, storage and communications	473	469	472
Finance, insurance and real estate	290	311	334
Business services	214	223	233
Social, personal and related community services	1,288	1,347	1,412
Public administration	317	317	324
Total employed	8,939	9,045	9,068
Unemployed	142	165	242
Total labour force	9,081	9,210	9,310
Males	5,595	5,659	5,662
Females	3,485	3,551	3,648

* Excluding members of the armed forces and persons in institutional households.

Agriculture

PRINCIPAL CROPS ('000 metric tons)

	1994	1995	1996
Potatoes	36.4	33.5	38.7
Rice*	1,678.8	1,686.5	1,577.3
Sweet potatoes	181.5	195.9	203.9
Asparagus	7.4	7.6	7.6
Soybeans	12.0	8.9	9.7
Sorghum	105.3	97.6	66.8
Maize	397.1	375.6	395.4
Tea	24.5	20.9	23.1
Tobacco	18.5	12.7	11.2
Groundnuts	80.6	92.2	79.9
Cassava (Manioc)	1.4	1.1	0.7
Sugar cane	5,503.6	4,861.8	4,384.2
Bananas	184.3	172.6	141.0
Pineapples	252.2	256.4	274.1
Citrus fruit	468.0	472.4	463.0
Vegetables	2,593.8	2,853.5	3,059.4
Mushrooms	9.9	8.6	12.1

* Figures are in terms of brown rice. The equivalent in paddy rice is approximately 31% greater (1 metric ton of paddy rice = 763.66 kg of brown rice).

LIVESTOCK ('000 head at 31 December)

	1994	1995	1996
Cattle	149.4	151.9	151.9
Buffaloes	14.9	12.9	11.2
Pigs	10,065.6	10,508.5	10,698.4
Sheep and goats	310.8	318.8	309.1
Chickens	97,827	101,838	110,535
Ducks	12,843	13,084	12,977
Geese	3,427	2,979	3,021
Turkeys	215	204	180

LIVESTOCK PRODUCTS

	1994	1995	1996
Beef (metric tons)	5,189	6,113	5,968
Pig meat (metric tons)	1,458,904	1,494,572	1,538,611
Goat meat (metric tons)	5,442	8,148	10,139
Chickens ('000 head)*	301,914	319,820	345,509
Ducks ('000 head)*	40,886	42,580	41,759
Geese ('000 head)*	8,521	7,744	7,078
Turkeys ('000 head)*	458	415	398
Milk (metric tons)	289,574	317,806	315,927
Duck eggs ('000)	472,555	517,945	538,845
Hen eggs ('000)	5,200,777	5,718,589	6,288,783

* Figures refer to numbers slaughtered.

Forestry

ROUNDWOOD REMOVALS ('000 cubic metres)

	1994	1995	1996
Industrial wood	37.8	35.6	36.1
Fuel wood	6.5	17.2	9.8
Total	44.3	52.8	45.9

Fishing*

('000 metric tons, live weight)

	1993	1994	1995
Tilapias	57.6	48.0	46.8
Other freshwater fishes	27.7	33.9	31.2
Japanese eel	40.0	33.4	25.5
Milkfish	45.5	66.8	63.3
Pacific saury	36.4	12.6	13.8
Skipjack tuna†	116.9	138.2	158.8
Albacore†	70.3	67.8	56.5
Yellowfin tuna†	166.2	98.2	83.1
Bigeye tuna†	41.3	47.5	59.3
Chub mackerel	41.9	54.9	54.2
Sharks, rays, skates, etc.†	56.1	39.5	44.1
Other fishes (incl. unspecified)†	375.7	309.5	332.5
Total fish	1,075.7	950.2	969.0
Marine shrimps and prawns	37.6	31.2	48.6
Other crustaceans	11.2	13.2	20.2
Pacific cupped oyster	27.7	24.9	25.4
Common squids†	74.5	56.6	20.5
Argentine shortfin squid	123.7†	104.5†	100.4
Flying squids	17.7†	18.3†	54.0
Other molluscs	44.5	47.2	47.6
Other aquatic animals	3.2	2.9	2.7
Total catch	1,415.8	1,248.9	1,288.4
Inland waters	192.1	190.3	175.6
Atlantic Ocean†	170.7	163.5	171.2
Indian Ocean†	134.5	79.5	86.8
Pacific Ocean†	918.5	815.6	854.8

* Figures exclude aquatic plants, totalling (in '000 metric tons): 8.1 in 1993; 6.2 in 1994; 8.3 in 1995. Also excluded are aquatic mammals, crocodiles and alligators, pearls, corals and sponges.

† FAO estimate(s).

Source: FAO, *Yearbook of Fishery Statistics*.

1996 ('000 metric tons): Total catch 1,240.

Mining

(metric tons, unless otherwise indicated)

	1994	1995	1996
Coal	285,099	234,965	147,497
Crude petroleum ('000 litres)	68,578	62,310	59,731
Natural gas ('000 cu m)	866,627	889,321	873,872
Salt	185,987	220,531	233,321
Gypsum	2,876	3,135	n.a.
Sulphur	154,778	167,468	181,600
Marble	17,740,499	16,974,726	17,527,940
Talc	4,290	3,500	n.a.
Dolomite	264,099	195,905	116,096

Industry

SELECTED PRODUCTS
('000 metric tons, unless otherwise indicated)

	1994	1995	1996
Wheat flour	682.3	711.3	707.9
Granulated sugar	474.9	402.1	366.0
Carbonated beverages ('000 litres)	433,541	420,764	449,935
Alcoholic beverages—excl. beer ('000 hectolitres)	2,391.4	2,374.9	2,301.4
Cigarettes (million)	28,825	27,562	26,731
Cotton yarn	341.2	323.5	339.0
Man-made fibres	2,505	2,601	2,737
Paper	1,114.5	1,138.6	1,049.8
Paperboard	3,046	3,030	3,213
Sulphuric acid	727.3	769.5	751.4
Spun yarn	504.9	507.0	490.8
Motor spirit—petrol (million litres)	4,376.3	n.a.	n.a.
Diesel oil (million litres)	5,002.5	6,329.2	n.a.
Cement	22,721.7	22,478.0	21,537.3
Pig-iron	27.0	25.3	n.a.
Steel ingots	12,102.3	12,320.9	12,471.7
Sewing machines ('000 units)	3,671	3,213	3,305
Electric fans ('000 units)	17,548	15,337	15,855
Personal computers ('000 units)	4,793	6,868	8,540
Monitors ('000 units)	14,070	17,751	19,048
Radio cassette recorders ('000 units)	6,433	6,975	6,562
Radio receivers ('000 units)	3,823.1	3,777.4	2,954.7
Television receivers ('000 units)	1,903	1,423	1,045
Picture tubes ('000 units)	13,184	14,614	13,004
Integrated circuits (million units)	7,294	8,566	9,147
Electronic condensers (million units)	36,974	39,578	41,324
Telephone sets ('000 units)	6,715	6,162	4,797
Passenger motor cars (units)	406,029	385,222	362,544 (incl. trucks and buses)
Trucks and buses (units)	4,954	5,238	
Bicycles ('000 units)	7,537	7,656	7,381
Ships ('000 dwt)*	1,036.2	780.3	1,245.9
Electric energy (million kWh)	118,917	126,973	134,977
Liquefied petroleum gas	552.0	623.9	689.1

* Excluding motor yachts.

Finance

CURRENCY AND EXCHANGE RATES

Monetary Units
100 cents = 1 New Taiwan dollar (NT $).

Sterling and US Dollar Equivalents (30 September 1997)
£1 sterling = NT $46.20;
US $1 = NT $28.60;
NT $1,000 = £21.65 = US $34.97.

Average Exchange Rate (NT $ per US $)
1994 26.457
1995 26.486
1996 27.458

BUDGET
(central government accounts, NT $ million, year ending 30 June)

Revenue	1994/95	1995/96	1996/97
Taxes	705,725	706,108	773,322
Monopoly profits	39,915	36,373	37,369
Non-tax revenue from other sources	191,777	254,276	230,132
Total	937,417	996,757	1,040,823

Expenditure	1994/95	1995/96	1996/97
General administration	93,135	104,752	109,427
National defence	234,073	244,149	252,371
Education, science and culture	156,582	166,812	179,842
Economic development	137,059	125,243	117,663
Social welfare	134,182	148,205	157,903
Community development and environmental protection	24,820	19,950	16,176
Pensions and survivors' benefits	95,947	109,032	143,945
Obligations	87,715	141,365	168,960
Subsidies to provincial and municipal governments	29,443	28,824	37,494
Other expenditure	3,741	3,047	10,479
Total	996,697	1,091,379	1,194,261

INTERNATIONAL RESERVES (US $ million at 31 December)

	1994	1995	1996
Gold*	5,819	5,601	5,559
Foreign exchange	92,454	90,310	88,038
Total	98,273	95,911	93,597

* National valuation.

MONEY SUPPLY (NT $ million at 31 December)

	1994	1995	1996
Currency outside banks	497,747	506,694	498,513
Demand deposits at deposit money banks	2,641,523	2,656,407	2,927,545
Total	3,139,270	3,163,101	3,426,058

COST OF LIVING
(Consumer Price Index; base: 1991 = 100)

	1994	1995	1996
Food	119.43	124.51	129.16
Clothing	97.61	101.00	103.52
Housing	111.95	116.00	118.39
Transport and communications	99.98	102.55	103.91
Medicines and medical care	109.02	111.86	113.71
Education and entertainment	117.52	122.89	131.13
All items (incl. others)	111.94	116.06	119.62

NATIONAL ACCOUNTS (NT $ million in current prices)

National Income and Product

	1994	1995	1996
Compensation of employees	3,408,726	3,696,125	3,975,063
Operating surplus	1,705,614	1,841,934	2,100,723
Domestic factor incomes	5,114,340	5,538,059	6,075,786
Consumption of fixed capital	573,671	629,315	706,171
Gross domestic product (GDP) at factor cost	5,688,011	6,167,374	6,781,957
Indirect taxes	696,997	734,355	712,172
Less Subsidies	8,510	9,683	16,589
GDP in purchasers' values	6,376,498	6,892,046	7,477,540
Factor income from abroad	194,084	221,456	220,021
Less Factor income paid abroad	116,080	147,204	157,911
Gross national product (GNP)	6,454,502	6,966,298	7,539,650
Less Consumption of fixed capital	573,671	629,315	706,171
National income in market prices	5,880,831	6,336,983	6,833,479
Other current transfers from abroad	57,683	61,801	69,469
Less Other current transfers paid abroad	93,589	137,350	132,814
National disposable income	5,844,925	6,261,434	6,770,134

Expenditure on the Gross Domestic Product

	1994	1995	1996
Government final consumption expenditure	960,822	1,002,398	1,082,323
Private final consumption expenditure	3,772,529	4,123,356	4,519,289
Increase in stocks	61,378	49,109	23,079
Gross fixed capital formation	1,460,716	1,581,211	1,565,392
Total domestic expenditure	6,255,445	6,756,074	7,190,083
Exports of goods and services	2,812,830	3,362,138	3,630,443
Less Imports of goods and services	2,691,777	3,226,166	3,342,986
GDP in purchasers' values	6,376,498	6,892,046	7,477,540
GDP at constant 1991 prices	5,817,402	6,168,052	6,517,625

Gross Domestic Product by Economic Activity

	1994	1995	1996
Agriculture, hunting, forestry and fishing	227,568	244,887	245,735
Mining and quarrying	21,021	21,583	20,212
Manufacturing	1,849,216	1,939,051	2,087,727
Construction	338,845	360,023	355,959
Electricity, gas and water	168,200	177,474	188,429
Transport, storage and communications	417,526	458,122	507,006
Trade, restaurants and hotels	979,030	1,100,328	1,222,084
Finance, insurance and real estate*	1,206,097	1,317,664	1,460,106
Business services	123,554	139,028	155,438
Community, social and personal services	473,134	549,339	627,324
Government services	677,720	724,687	789,230
Other services	77,083	80,732	97,117
Sub-total	6,558,994	7,112,918	7,756,367
Value-added tax	150,349	152,802	155,683
Import duties	160,639	172,095	150,456
Less Imputed bank service charge	493,484	545,769	584,966
GDP in purchasers' values	6,376,498	6,892,046	7,477,540

* Including imputed rents of owner-occupied dwellings.

BALANCE OF PAYMENTS (US $ million)

	1994	1995	1996
Exports of goods f.o.b.	92,719	111,214	115,462
Imports of goods f.o.b.	−80,872	−97,979	−97,894
Trade balance	11,847	13,235	17,568
Exports of services	13,205	15,016	16,260
Imports of services	−21,068	−24,053	−24,381
Balance on goods and services	3,984	4,198	9,447
Other income received	7,125	8,119	7,757
Other income paid	−3,586	−4,620	−4,517
Balance on goods, services and income	7,523	7,697	12,687
Current transfers received	2,168	2,312	2,498
Current transfers paid	−3,193	−4,535	−4,158
Current balance	6,498	5,474	11,027
Capital account (net)	−344	−650	−653
Direct investment abroad	−2,640	−2,983	−3,843
Direct investment from abroad	1,375	1,559	1,864
Portfolio investment assets	−1,997	−2,236	−4,368
Portfolio investment liabilities	2,902	2,729	3,256
Other investment assets	−7,511	−8,063	−11,594
Other investment liabilities	6,474	804	5,883
Net errors and omissions	−135	−565	−470
Overall balance	4,622	−3,931	1,102

External Trade

SELECTED COMMODITIES (NT $ million)

Imports c.i.f.	1994	1995	1996
Maize	20,580	25,469	32,130
Oil seeds and oleaginous fruits	17,684	18,382	24,154
Coal	30,409	36,146	39,705
Petroleum	72,737	100,408	133,438
Hydrocarbons	33,782	57,171	48,431
Polymers and copolymers	29,548	33,459	34,250
Rough wood	10,932	9,719	8,657
Cotton	9,860	13,473	15,458
Gold	40,094	35,249	31,441
Semi-finished products of iron or non-alloy steel	23,676	34,595	22,870
Steel or non-alloy steel and articles thereof, hot-rolled or cold-rolled	28,823	43,921	32,395
Alloy steel and high-carbon steel	24,610	35,173	26,220
Copper	31,634	46,354	38,999
Automatic data-processing machines and units thereof	33,036	41,119	57,858
Electric motors and generators, etc., electronic goods	28,296	38,064	34,210
Transmission apparatus for radio-telephony, radio-telegraphy, radio-broadcasting or television	24,511	29,383	25,481
Electrical resistors, printed circuits, switches, electrical circuits	37,712	45,469	44,306
Cold cathode and photo-cathode valves and tubes, diodes, crystals	285,020	402,937	423,659
Motor vehicles for the transport of persons, goods or materials	70,488	66,131	49,534
Electrical measuring, checking, analysing or automatically controlling instruments and apparatus	15,534	19,967	34,580
Total (incl. others)	2,261,651	2,742,842	2,815,103

Exports f.o.b.	1994	1995	1996
Meat and edible offals, fresh, chilled or frozen	33,831	41,543	42,599
Polymerization and copolymerization products	52,894	70,613	69,721
Artificial resins and plastic material products	72,369	79,183	84,307
Travel goods, handbags and similar containers	12,200	11,560	10,611
Yarn of man-made fibres, regenerated fibres	34,839	45,483	39,690
Woven fabrics of synthetic filaments yarn, woven fabrics of artificial filaments yarn	47,426	55,625	57,172
Woven fabrics of synthetic staple fibres	23,084	25,013	25,551
Knitted or crocheted chenille fabric	50,494	53,946	62,400
Women's and girls' outer garments	11,681	10,267	10,278
Footwear with outer soles of rubber, plastic, leather or composition leather and uppers of textile materials	13,943	11,908	9,081
Screws, bolts, nuts and similar articles	26,307	35,468	34,888
Sewing machines	16,335	16,988	16,905
Automatic data-processing machines and units thereof	154,078	241,200	337,676
Office machinery	151,181	187,997	185,970
Electric motors and generators	46,413	54,569	59,669
Transmission apparatus for radio-telephony, radio-telegraphy, radio-broadcasting or television	90,817	89,997	89,330
Thermionic, cold cathode or photo-cathode valves and tubes, diodes, transistors, semiconductors, electronic integrated circuits and microassemblies	149,725	240,689	262,462
Photographic cameras	12,784	13,897	14,143
Festival, carnival or other entertainment articles	9,172	7,563	5,831
Articles and equipment for gymnastics, athletics, other sports and outdoor games	43,076	44,768	48,864
Total (incl. others)	2,456,011	2,949,580	3,176,621

PRINCIPAL TRADING PARTNERS (US $ '000)

Imports c.i.f.	1994	1995	1996
Australia	2,224,988	2,575,298	2,845,058
Canada	1,250,712	1,593,815	1,356,732
Germany	4,784,285	5,683,348	5,023,379
Hong Kong	1,532,958	1,842,873	1,704,663
Indonesia	2,114,386	2,150,425	1,884,483
Italy	1,464,413	1,565,257	1,557,930
Japan	24,785,822	30,265,880	27,492,964
Korea, Republic	3,015,198	4,327,379	4,161,720
Kuwait	286,493	455,979	550,143
Malaysia	2,326,856	2,953,718	3,565,236
Philippines	460,680	623,225	840,302
Saudi Arabia	1,332,875	1,763,397	1,763,340
Singapore	2,412,279	2,957,975	2,789,115
Thailand	1,108,777	1,485,292	1,671,718
United Kingdom	1,529,102	1,643,210	1,805,433
USA	18,042,642	20,771,393	19,971,851
Total (incl. others)	85,349,194	103,550,044	102,370,021

Exports f.o.b.	1994	1995	1996
Australia	1,632,446	1,755,641	1,836,932
Canada	1,458,206	1,429,521	1,397,373
Germany	3,251,303	3,839,174	3,644,109
Hong Kong	21,262,326	26,105,855	26,787,641
Indonesia	1,433,032	1,868,877	1,955,334
Italy	813,141	1,004,060	1,080,322
Japan	10,221,109	13,156,727	13,658,783
Korea, Republic	1,740,090	2,571,771	2,661,602
Kuwait	83,007	90,197	95,618
Malaysia	2,224,156	2,898,592	2,953,726
Philippines	1,222,485	1,653,555	1,931,207
Saudi Arabia	456,420	449,864	467,522
Singapore	3,365,837	4,404,987	4,573,182
Thailand	2,440,238	3,071,726	2,789,603
United Kingdom	2,172,524	2,408,718	2,807,366
USA	24,336,757	26,407,389	26,866,357
Total (incl. others)	93,048,783	111,658,800	115,942,064

Transport

RAILWAYS (traffic)

	1994	1995	1996
Passengers ('000)	160,991	160,926	160,058
Passenger-km ('000)	9,515,175	9,499,387	8,975,193
Freight ('000 metric tons)	31,233	30,122	27,410
Freight ton-km ('000)	2,006,710	1,899,537	1,584,857

ROAD TRAFFIC (motor vehicles in use at 31 December)

	1994	1995	1996
Passenger cars	3,570,501	3,874,203	4,146,475
Buses and coaches	21,252	21,598	21,772
Goods vehicles	711,810	748,150	777,884
Motorcycles and scooters	8,034,509	8,517,024	9,283,914

SHIPPING

Merchant Fleet (at 31 December)

	1994	1995	1996
Number of vessels	642	683	681
Total displacement ('000 grt)	5,996.1	6,104.3	6,174.5

Source: Lloyd's Register of Shipping, *World Fleet Statistics*.

Sea-borne freight traffic ('000 metric tons)

	1994	1995	1996
Goods loaded	148,371	156,230	162,198
Goods unloaded	254,248	263,938	270,427

CIVIL AVIATION (traffic on scheduled services)

	1994	1995	1996
Passengers carried ('000)	36,972.0	43,727.5	52,031.6
Passenger-km (million)	36,770.2	38,247.2	39,803.8
Freight carried ('000 metric tons)	880.3	1,105.7	1,172.4
Freight ton-km (million)	2,772.8	3,410.3	3,567.9

Tourism

TOURIST ARRIVALS BY COUNTRY OF ORIGIN

	1994	1995	1996
Japan	816,665	907,338	911,777
Korea, Republic	124,116	140,469	121,399
Malaysia	47,577	53,620	55,430
Philippines	69,468	89,490	n.a.
Singapore	65,259	69,665	77,642
Thailand	114,613	146,632	n.a.
USA	266,115	273,606	277,236
Overseas Chinese*	270,564	265,601	269,682
Total (incl. others)	2,127,249	2,331,934	2,358,221

* i.e. those bearing Taiwan passports.

Tourist receipts (US $ million): 3,210 in 1994; 3,286 in 1995; 3,636 in 1996.

Communications Media

	1994	1995	1996
Newspapers	300	357	361
Magazines	4,984	5,247	5,480
Telephone subscribers ('000)	8,503	9,175	10,011
Mobile telephones ('000 in use)	584	770	n.a.

Radio receivers (1994): more than 16 million in use.
Television receivers (1994): 5,050,000 in use.
Book production (1993): 14,743 titles.

Education

(1996/97)

	Schools	Full-time teachers	Pupils/ Students
Pre-school	2,660	16,076	235,830
Primary	2,519	90,127	1,934,756
Secondary (incl. vocational)	1,138	98,437	1,908,935
Higher	137	37,779	795,547
Special	17	1,386	5,203
Supplementary	885	3,348	281,638
Total (incl. others)	7,357	247,246	5,191,219

Directory

The Constitution

On 1 January 1947 a new Constitution was promulgated for the Republic of China (confined to Taiwan since 1949). The form of government that was incorporated in the Constitution is based on a five-power system and has the major features of both cabinet and presidential government. A process of constitutional reform, initiated in 1991, continued in 1998. The following is a summary of the Constitution, as subsequently amended:

PRESIDENT

The President shall be directly elected by popular vote for a term of four years. Both the President and Vice-President are eligible for re-election to a second term. The President represents the country at all state functions, including foreign relations; commands land, sea and air forces, promulgates laws, issues mandates, concludes treaties, declares war, makes peace, declares martial law, grants amnesties, appoints and removes civil and military officers, and confers honours and decorations. The President convenes the National Assembly and, subject to certain limitations, may issue emergency orders to deal with national calamities and ensure national security; may dissolve the Legislative Yuan; also nominates the Premier (who may be appointed without the Legislative Yuan's confirmation), and the officials of the Judicial Yuan, the Examination Yuan and the Control Yuan.

NATIONAL ASSEMBLY

The National Assembly is elected by popular vote for a four-year term, and shall comprise 334 members: 228 regional representatives; six aboriginal delegates; 20 overseas Chinese delegates; and 80 delegates from one national constituency. The functions of the National Assembly are: to amend the Constitution; to vote on proposed constitutional amendments submitted by the Legislative Yuan; to confirm the appointment of personnel nominated by the President; to hear a report on the state of the nation by the President, to discuss national affairs and to offer counsel; to elect a new Vice-President should the office become vacant; to recall the President and the Vice-President; and to pass a resolution on the impeachment of the President or Vice-President instituted by the Control Yuan.

EXECUTIVE YUAN

The Executive Yuan is the highest administrative organ of the nation and is responsible to the Legislative Yuan; has three categories of subordinate organization:

- Executive Yuan Council (policy-making organization)
- Ministries and Commissions (executive organization)
- Subordinate organization (19 bodies, including the Secretariat, Government Information Office, Directorate-General of Budget, Accounting and Statistics, Council for Economic Planning and Development, and Environmental Protection Administration).

LEGISLATIVE YUAN

The Legislative Yuan is the highest legislative organ of the state, empowered to hear administrative reports of the Executive Yuan, and to change government policy. It may hold a binding vote of no confidence in the Executive Yuan. It comprises 164 members, 128 chosen by direct election, the remaining delegates being appointed on the basis of proportional representation. Members serve for three years and are eligible for re-election.

JUDICIAL YUAN

The Judicial Yuan is the highest judicial organ of state and has charge of civil, criminal and administrative cases, and of cases concerning disciplinary measures against public functionaries (see Judicial System).

EXAMINATION YUAN

The Examination Yuan supervises examinations for entry into public offices, and deals with personnel questions of the civil service.

CONTROL YUAN

The Control Yuan is the highest control organ of the State, exercising powers of impeachment, censure and audit. Comprising 29 members serving a six-year term, nominated and (with the consent of the National Assembly) appointed by the President, the Control Yuan may impeach or censure a public functionary at central or local level, who is deemed guilty of violation of law or dereliction of duty, and shall refer the matter to the law courts for action in cases involving a criminal offence; may propose corrective measures to the Executive Yuan or to its subordinate organs.

The Government

HEAD OF STATE

President: LEE TENG-HUI (took office 13 January 1988, re-elected by the National Assembly 20 March 1990, directly elected by popular vote 23 March 1996).

Vice-President: LIEN CHAN.

Secretary-General: HUANG KUN-HUEI.

THE EXECUTIVE YUAN
(February 1998)

Premier: VINCENT C. SIEW (HSIAO WAN-CHANG).

Vice-Premier and Chairman of the Consumer Protection Commission: LIU CHAO-SHIUAN.

Minister without Portfolio and Director-General of the Council for Economic Planning and Development: CHIANG PIN-KUNG.

Ministers without Portfolio: LIN FENG-CHENG, HUANG TA-CHOU, CHEN CHIENG-MING, CHAO SHU-PO, SHIRLEY W. Y. KUO, YANG SHIH-CHIEN.

Secretary-General: CHANG YU-HUI.

Minister of the Interior: HUANG CHU-WEN.

Minister of Foreign Affairs: JASON HU.

Minister of National Defense: Gen. CHIANG CHUNG-LING.

Minister of Finance: PAUL CHENG-HSIUNG CHIU.

Minister of Education: LIN CHING-JIANG.

Minister of Economic Affairs: WANG CHIH-KANG.

Minister of Justice: LIAO CHENG-HAO.

Minister of Transportation and Communications: TSAY JAW-YANG.

Chairman of the Mainland Affairs Council: CHANG KING-YUN.

Chairman of the Overseas Chinese Affairs Commission: CHIAO JEN-HO.

Chairman of the Mongolian and Tibetan Affairs Commission: KAO KOONG-TIAN.

Director-General of the Government Information Office: CHEN CHIEN-JEN.

Director-General of Directorate-General of Budget, Accounting and Statistics: WEI TUAN.

Director-General of Central Personnel Administration: WEA CHI-LIN.

Director-General of the Department of Health: CHAN CHI-HSIEN.

Director-General of the Environmental Protection Administration: TSAI HSUN-HSIUNG.

Chairman of the National Science Council: HWANG CHEN-TAI.

Chairman of the Council of Agriculture: PENG TSO-KUAI.

Chairwoman of the Council for Cultural Affairs: LIN CHENG-CHI.

Chairman of the Research, Development and Evaluation Commission: YANG CHAUI-CHIN.

Chairman of Vocational Assistance Commission for Retired Servicemen: Gen. YANG TING-YU.

Chairwoman of the National Youth Commission: LEE CHI-CHU.

Chairman of the Atomic Energy Council: HU CHIN-PIAO.

Chairman of the Council of Labor Affairs: CHAN HUO-SHENG.

Chairman of the Fair Trade Commission: CHAO YANG-CHING.

Chairman of the Public Construction Commission: OU CHIN-TEH.

Chairman of the Aboriginal Affairs Commission: HUA CHIA-CHIH.

Chairwoman of the Physical Education Commission: CHAO LI-YUN.

MINISTRIES, COMMISSIONS, ETC.

Office of the President: Chiehshou Hall, 122 Chungking South Rd, Sec. 1, Taipei 100; tel. (2) 23113731; fax (2) 23825580; e-mail webmaster@www.oop.gov.tw.

Ministry of Economic Affairs: 15 Foo Chou St, Taipei; tel. (2) 23212200; telex 19884; fax (2) 23919398; e-mail service@moea.-gov.tw.

Ministry of Education: 5 Chung Shan South Rd, Taipei 10040; tel. (2) 23566051; telex 10894; fax (2) 23976978.

Ministry of Finance: 2 Ai Kuo West Rd, Taipei; tel. (2) 23228000; telex 11840; fax (2) 23965829; e-mail root@www.mof.gov.tw.

Ministry of Foreign Affairs: 2 Chiehshou Rd, Taipei 10016; tel. (2) 23119292; telex 11299; fax (2) 23144972.

Ministry of the Interior: 5th–9th Floors, 5 Hsu Chou Rd, Taipei; tel. (2) 23565005; fax (2) 23566201; e-mail gethics@mail.moi.gov.tw.

Ministry of Justice: 130 Chungking South Rd, Sec. 1, Taipei 10036; tel. (2) 23146871; fax (2) 23896759.

Ministry of National Defense: POB 9001, Taipei; tel. (2) 23181320; fax (2) 23616199.

Ministry of Transportation and Communications: 2 Chang Sha St, Sec. 1, Taipei; tel. (2) 23492900; fax (2) 23118587; e-mail motceyes@motc.gov.tw.

Mongolian and Tibetan Affairs Commission: 4th Floor, 5 Hsu Chou Rd, Sec. 1, Taipei; tel. (2) 23566166; fax (2) 23566432.

Overseas Chinese Affairs Commission: 4th Floor, 5 Hsu Chou Rd, Taipei; tel. (2) 23566166; fax (2) 23566323; e-mail ocacinfo@mail .ocac.gov.tw.

Directorate-General of Budget, Accounting and Statistics: 2 Kwang Chow St, Taipei 10729; tel. (2) 23814910; fax (2) 23319925; e-mail d44x@emc.dgbasey.gov.tw.

Government Information Office: 2 Tientsin St, Taipei; tel. (2) 23228888; fax (2) 23568733; e-mail service@mail.gio.gov.tw.

Aboriginal Affairs Commission: 3rd Floor, 6 Chung Hsiao West Rd, Sec. 1, Taipei; tel. (2) 23882122; fax (2) 23891967.

Council of Agriculture: see p. 960.

Atomic Energy Council: 67 Lane 144, Kee Lung Rd, Sec. 4, Taipei; tel. (2) 23634180; fax (2) 23635377.

Central Personnel Administration: 109 Huai Ning St, Taipei; tel. (2) 23111720; fax (2) 23715252.

Consumer Protection Commission: 1 Chung Hsiao East Rd, Sec. 1, Taipei; tel. (2) 23566600; fax (2) 23214538.

Council for Cultural Affairs: 102 Ai Kuo East Rd, Taipei; tel. (2) 25225300; fax (2) 25519011; e-mail wwwadm@ccpdunx.ccpd.gov.tw.

Council for Economic Planning and Development: 9th Floor, 87 Nanking East Rd, Sec. 2, Taipei; tel. (2) 25225300; fax (2) 25519011.

Environmental Protection Administration: 41 Chung Hua Rd, Sec. 1, Taipei; tel. (2) 23228751; fax (2) 23516227; e-mail www@sun .epa.gov.tw.

Fair Trade Commission: Taipei; tel. (2) 25455501; fax (2) 25450107; e-mail ftcpd@ftc.gov.tw.

Department of Health: 100 Ai Kuo East Rd, Taipei; tel. (2) 23210151; fax (2) 23122907.

Council of Labor Affairs: 5th–15th Floors, 132 Min Sheng East Rd, Sec. 3, Taipei; tel. (2) 27182512; fax (2) 25149240.

Mainland Affairs Council: 5th–13th Floors, 2–2 Chi-nan Rd, Sec. 1, Taipei; tel. (2) 23975589; fax (2) 23975700; e-mail macst@mac .gov.tw.

National Science Council: 17th–22nd Floors, 106 Ho Ping East Rd, Sec. 2, Taipei; tel. (2) 27377501; fax (2) 27377668; e-mail nsc@nsc.gov.tw.

National Youth Commission: 14th Floor, 5 Hsu Chou Rd, Taipei; tel. (2) 23566271; fax (2) 23566290.

Research, Development and Evaluation Commission: 7th Floor, 2–2 Chi-nan Rd, Sec. 1, Taipei; tel. (2) 23419066; fax (2) 23928133; e-mail service@rdec.gov.tw.

Vocational Assistance Commission for Retired Servicemen: 222 Chung Hsiao East Rd, Sec. 5, Taipei; tel. (2) 27255700; fax (2) 27230170; e-mail hsc@www.vacrs.gov.tw.

President and Legislature

PRESIDENT

Election, 23 March 1996

Candidate	Votes	% of votes
LEE TENG-HUI (Kuomintang—KMT)	5,813,699	54.0
PENG MING-MIN (Democratic Progressive Party—DPP)	2,274,586	21.1
LIN YANG-KANG (Independent)	1,603,790	14.9
CHEN LI-AN (Independent)	1,074,044	10.0

KUO-MIN TA-HUI
(National Assembly)

The National Assembly comprises 334 members: 228 regional representatives, three mountain aborigines, three plains aborigines, 20 overseas Chinese and 80 representatives of a national constituency. Members serve a four-year term.

Speaker: FREDRICK CHIEN.

Election, 23 March 1996

Party	% of votes	Seats
Kuomintang (KMT)	54.8	183
Democratic Progressive Party (DPP)	29.6	99
New Party (NP)	13.8	46
Independents	1.8	5
Green Party		1
Total	100.0	334

LI-FA YUAN
(Legislative Yuan)

The Legislative Yuan is the highest legislative organ of state. It comprises 164 seats. The 128 directly-elected members include six representatives of aboriginal communities and six overseas Chinese. The remaining delegates are appointed on a proportional basis according to the parties' share of the popular vote, six seats being reserved for overseas Chinese. Members serve a three-year term.

President: LIU SUNG-PAN.

General Election, 2 December 1995

Party	Seats
Kuomintang (KMT)	85
Democratic Progressive Party (DPP)	54
New Party (NP)	21
Independents	4
Total	164

Note: The Taiwan Independence Party, founded by dissident members of the DPP in October 1996, held two seats in early 1998.

Political Organizations

Legislation adopted in 1987 permitted political parties other than the KMT to function. By early 1997 a total of 83 parties had registered.

China Democratic Socialist Party (CDSP): 6 Lane 357, Ho Ping East Rd, Sec. 2, Taipei; tel. (2) 27072883; f. 1932 by merger of National Socialists and Democratic Constitutionalists; aims to promote democracy, to protect fundamental freedoms, and to improve public welfare and social security; 30,000 mems; Chair. WANG PEIR-JI; Sec.-Gen. KAO SHAO-CHUNG.

China Young Party: 12th Floor, 2 Shin Sheng South Rd, Sec. 3, Taipei; tel. (2) 23626715; f. 1923; aims to recover sovereignty over mainland China, to safeguard the Constitution and democracy, and to foster understanding between Taiwan and the non-communist world; Chair. JAW CHWEN-SHIAW.

Chinese Republican Party (CRP): 3rd Floor, 26 Lane 90, Jong Shuenn St, Sec. 2, Taipei; tel. (2) 29366572; f. 1988; advocates peaceful struggle for the salvation of China and the promotion of world peace; 10,200 mems; Chair. WANG YING-CHYUN.

Democratic Liberal Party (DLP): Taipei; f. 1989; aims to promote political democracy and economic liberty for the people of Taiwan.

Democratic Progressive Party (DPP): 8th Floor, 39 Pei Ping East Rd, Taipei; tel. and fax (2) 23929989; f. 1986; advocates 'self-determination' for the people of Taiwan and UN membership; supports establishment of independent Taiwan following plebiscite; 50,000 mems; Chair. HSU HSIN-LIANG; Sec.-Gen. CHIOU I-JEN.

Green Party: 10th Floor, 281 Roosevelt Rd, Sec. 3, Taipei; tel. (2) 23621362; f. 1996 by breakaway faction of the DPP; Chair. GAU CHERNG-YAN.

Kungtang (KT) (Labour Party): 2nd Floor, 22 Kai Feng St, Sec. 2, Taipei; tel. (2) 23121472; f. 1987; aims to become the main political movement of Taiwan's industrial work-force; 4,500 mems; Chair. JENG JAU-MING; Sec.-Gen. SHIEH JENG-I.

Kuomintang (KMT) (Nationalist Party of China): 53 Jen Ai Rd, Sec. 3, Taipei; tel. (2) 23434567; fax (2) 23434524; f. 1894; ruling party; aims to supplant communist rule in mainland China; supports democratic, constitutional government, and advocates the unification of China under the 'Three Principles of the People'; aims to promote market economy and equitable distribution of wealth; c. 2.4m. mems; Chair. LEE TENG-HUI; Sec.-Gen. JOHN CHANG (CHANG HSIAO-YEN).

New Party (NP): 4th Floor, 65 Guang Fuh South Rd, Taipei; tel. (2) 27562222; e-mail npncs@ms2.hinet.net; f. 1993 by dissident KMT legislators (hitherto mems of New Kuomintang Alliance faction); merged with China Social Democratic Party in late 1993; advocates co-operation with the KMT and DPP in negotiations with the People's Republic, the maintenance of security in the Taiwan Straits, the modernization of the island's defence systems, measures to combat government corruption, the support of small and medium businesses and the establishment of a universal social security system; 70,000 mems; Sec.-Gen. (vacant).

Taiwan Independence Party: c/o Legislative Yuan, Taipei; f. 1996 by dissident mems of DPP; Chair. LI CHEN-YUAN; Sec.-Gen. LI SHENG-HSIUNG.

Workers' Party: 2nd Floor, 181 Fu-hsing South Rd, Taipei; tel. (2) 27555868; f. 1989 by breakaway faction of the Kungtang; radical; Leader LOU MEIWEN.

Various pro-independence groups (some based overseas and, until 1992, banned in Taiwan) are in operation. These include the **World United Formosans for Independence** (WUFI—4,000 mems world-wide; Chair. GEORGE CHANG) and the **Organization for Taiwan Nation-Building**.

Diplomatic Representation

EMBASSIES IN THE REPUBLIC OF CHINA

Burkina Faso: 3rd Floor, 5 Chung Cheng Rd, Sec. 2, Taipei; tel. (2) 28383776; fax (2) 26342701; Ambassador: JACQUES SAWADOGO.

Central African Republic: 7th Floor, 59 Yung Ho Rd, Sec. 2, Yung Ho, Taipei; tel. (2) 29246600; fax (2) 29202266; diplomatic relations suspended Jan. 1998; Chargé d'affaires a.i.: GUILLAUME MOKEMAT-KENGUEMBA.

Costa Rica: 6th Floor, 1-1, 16 Lane 189, Sec. 1, Cheng Tai Rd, Wu Ku Rural, Taipei; tel. (2) 22933446; fax (2) 22933548; Ambassador: ELENA WACHONG STORER.

Dominican Republic: 6th Floor, 76 Tun Hua South Rd, Sec. 2, Taipei; tel. (2) 27079006; fax (2) 27091429; Ambassador: VÍCTOR MANUEL SÁNCHEZ PEÑA.

El Salvador: 15 Lane 34, Ku Kung Rd, Shih Lin, Taipei 11102; tel. (2) 28817995; fax (2) 28819887; Ambassador: DAVID ERNESTO PANAMÁ S.

The Gambia: 3rd Floor, 92 Hwang Chi St, Shih Lin, Taipei; tel. (2) 28332434; fax (2) 28324336; Ambassador: ANTOUMAN SAHO.

Guatemala: 12 Lane 88, Chien Kuo North Rd, Sec. 1, Taipei; tel. (2) 25077043; fax (2) 25060577; Ambassador: LUIS ALBERTO NORIEGA MORALES.

Guinea-Bissau: 6-1, Lane 77, Sung Chiang Rd, Taipei; tel. (2) 25099052; telex 29380; fax (2) 25073111; Ambassador: INACIO SEMEDO JÚNIOR.

Haiti: 3rd Floor, 246 Chungshan North Rd, Sec. 6, Taipei; tel. (2) 28384945; fax (2) 28317086; Ambassador: SONNY SERAPHIN.

Holy See: 87 Ai Kuo East Rd, Taipei 10605 (Apostolic Nunciature); tel. (2) 3216847; fax (2) 3911926; Chargé d'affaires a.i.: Mgr JOSEPH CHENNOTH.

Honduras: Room B, 10th Floor, 167 Tun Hua North Rd, Taipei; tel. and fax (2) 27120743; Ambassador: DANIEL EDGARDO MILLA VILLEDA.

Liberia: 13th Floor, 2 Lane 10, Hsing Yi Rd, Peitou, Taipei; tel. (2) 28745768; Ambassador: JOHN CUMMINGS.

Nicaragua: 3rd Floor, 222-6 Jyi Shyan Rd, Lu Chow, Taipei; tel. (2) 282814512; fax (2) 282814515; Ambassador: SALVADOR STADTHAGEN.

Panama: 6th Floor, 111 Sung Chiang Rd, Taipei; tel. (2) 25099189; fax (2) 25099801; Ambassador: CARLOS ALBERTO MENDOZA.

Paraguay: 1st Floor, 110 Chung Cheng Rd, Sec. 2, Taipei; tel. (2) 28736310; telex 13744; fax (2) 28736312; Ambassador: CEFERINO ADRIÁN VÁLDEZ PERALTA.

Judicial System

The power of judicial review is exercised by the Judicial Yuan's Grand Justices nominated and appointed for nine years by the President of Taiwan with the consent of the National Assembly. The President of the Judicial Yuan is also the *ex officio* chairman for the Plenary Session of the Grand Justices. The Ministry of Justice is under the jurisdiction of the Executive Yuan.

Judicial Yuan: 124 Chungking South Rd, Sec. 1, Taipei; tel. (2) 23618577; fax (2) 23821739; Pres. SHIH CHI-YANG; Sec.-Gen. LIN KUO-HSIEN; the highest judicial organ, and the interpreter of the constitution and national laws and ordinances; supervises the following:

Supreme Court: 6 Chang Sha St, Sec. 1, Taipei; tel. (2) 23141160; fax (2) 23114246; Court of third and final instance for civil and criminal cases; Pres. KO YIH-TSAIR.

High Courts: Courts of second instance for appeals of civil and criminal cases.

District Courts: Courts of first instance in civil, criminal and non-contentious cases.

Administrative Court: Court of final resort in cases brought against govt agencies; Pres. LIN MING-TEH.

Committee on the Discipline of Public Functionaries: decides on disciplinary measures against public functionaries impeached by the Control Yuan; Chair. CHU SHIH-YEN.

Religion

According to the Ministry of the Interior, in 1996 43% of the population were adherents of Buddhism, 34% of Daoism (Taoism), 8% of I-Kuan Tao and 6% of Christianity.

BUDDHISM

Buddhist Association of Taiwan: Mahavana and Theravada schools; 1,613 group mems and more than 9.61m. adherents; Leader Ven. CHIN-HSIN.

CHRISTIANITY

The Roman Catholic Church

Taiwan comprises one archdiocese, six dioceses and one apostolic administrative area. In December 1996 there were 304,000 adherents.

Bishops' Conference: Regional Episcopal Conference of China, 34 Lane 32, Kuangfu South Rd, Taipei 10552; tel. (2) 25782355; fax (2) 25773874; f. 1967; Pres. Cardinal PAUL SHAN KUO-HSI.

Archbishop of Taipei: Most Rev. JOSEPH TI-KANG, Archbishop's House, 94 Loli Rd, Taipei 10668; tel. (2) 27371311; fax (2) 27373710.

The Anglican Communion

Anglicans in Taiwan are adherents of the Protestant Episcopal Church. In 1995 the Church had 6,201 members.

Bishop of Taiwan: Rt Rev. JOHN CHIH-TSUNG CHIEN, 7 Lane 105, Hangchow South Rd, Sec. 1, Taipei 100; tel. (2) 23411265; fax (2) 23962014.

Presbyterian Church

Tai-oan Ki-tok Tiu-Lo Kau-Hoe (Presbyterian Church in Taiwan): No. 3, Lane 269, Roosevelt Rd, Sec. 3, Taipei 106; tel. (2) 23625282; fax (2) 23628096; f. 1865; Gen. Sec. Rev. C. S. YANG; 220,000 mems (1996).

DAOISM (TAOISM)

In 1996 there were about 4.32m. adherents. Temples numbered 8,248, and clergy totalled 32,500.

I-KUAN TAO

Introduced to Taiwan in the 1950s, this 'Religion of One Unity' is a modern, syncretic religion, drawn mainly from Confucian, Buddhist and Daoist principles and incorporating ancestor worship. In 1995 there were 87 temples and 18,000 family shrines. Adherents totalled 942,000.

ISLAM

Leader MOHAMMED WU HUAN-HUNG; 52,000 adherents in 1996.

The Press

By mid-1996 the number of registered newspapers had increased to 344. The majority of newspapers are privately owned. The total circulation of all daily newspapers was approximately 5.7m. in mid-1990.

PRINCIPAL DAILIES

Taipei

Central Daily News: 260 Pa Teh Rd, Sec. 2, Taipei; tel. (2) 27765368; telex 24884; fax (2) 27775835; f. 1928; morning; Chinese; official Kuomintang organ; Publr and Editor-in-Chief HUANG HUI-TSEN; circ. 600,000.

China News: 10th Floor, 109-2 Tung Hsing St, Taipei; tel. (2) 27686002; fax (2) 27686773; f. 1949; morning; English; Chair. and Publr SIMONE WEI; Man. Editor (vacant); circ. 100,000.

The China Post: 8 Fu Shun St, Taipei 104; tel. (2) 25969971; fax (2) 25957962; e-mail cpost@pc2.hinet.net; f. 1952; morning; English; Publr and Editor JACK HUANG; circ. 150,000.

China Times: 132 Da Li St, Taipei; tel. (2) 23087111; telex 26464; fax (2) 23082745; f. 1950; morning; Chinese; Chair. YU CHI-CHUNG; Publr YU ALBERT CHIEN-HSIN; Editor HUANG CHAO-SONG; circ. 1.2m.

China Times Express: 132 Da Li St, Taipei; tel. (2) 23087111; telex 26464; fax (2) 23048138; f. 1988; evening; Chinese; Publr ALICE YU; Editor LIN KUO-CHING; circ. 400,000.

Commercial Times: 132 Da Li St, Taipei; tel. (2) 23087111; telex 26464; fax (2) 23084708; f. 1978; morning; Chinese; Publr YU CHI-CHENG; Editor-in-Chief JIMMY CHANG; circ. 250,000.

Economic Daily News: 555 Chung Hsiao East Rd, Sec. 4, Taipei; tel. (2) 27681234; telex 27710; f. 1967; morning; Chinese; Publr WANG PI-LY; Editor LU SHIH HSIANG.

Independence Evening Post: 15 Chi Nan Rd, Sec. 2, Taipei; tel. (2) 23519621; fax (2) 23419054; f. 1947; afternoon; Chinese; Publr CHEN TSEN-HUEI; Editor LEE SEN-HONG; circ. 307,071.

Independence Morning Post: 15 Chi Nan Rd, Taipei; tel. (2) 23519621; fax (2) 23514219; f. 1988; Chinese; Publr KUO CHENG-CHAU; Editor SU JENG-PING; circ. 310,087.

Liberty Times: 137 Nanking East Rd, 11th Floor, Sec. 2, Taipei; tel. (2) 25042828; fax (2) 25042212; f. 1988; Publr YEN WEN-SHUN; Editor-in-Chief LIN JIAN-LIAN; circ. 500,000.

Mandarin Daily News: 4 Foo Chou St, Taipei; tel. (2) 23213479; f. 1948; morning; Publr LIN LIANG.

Min Sheng Daily: 555 Chung Hsiao East Rd, Sec. 4, Taipei; tel. (2) 27681234; telex 27710; fax (2) 27626542; f. 1978; sport and leisure; Publr WANG SHAW-LAN; Editor-in-Chief GLORIA HSU RONG-HUN; circ. 556,639.

Taiwan Hsin Sheng Pao: 12th Floor, 110 Yengping South Rd, Taipei; tel. (2) 23117000; fax (2) 23115319; f. 1945; morning; Chinese; also southern edn publ. in Kaohsiung; Publr SU YU-CHEN; Editor WANN TSU; circ. 460,000.

The Great News: 216 Chen Teh Rd, Sec. 3, Taipei; tel. (2) 25973111; f. 1988; morning; also *The Great News Daily-Entertainment* (circ. 460,000) and *The Great News Daily-Sport* (circ. 410,000); Publr CHEN CHE-CHIA; circ. 310,000.

United Daily News: 555 Chung Hsiao East Rd, Sec. 4, Taipei; tel. (2) 27681234; fax (2) 27632303; f. 1951; morning; Publr WANG SHAW-LAN; Editor SHUANG KUO-NING; circ. 1.2m.

Youth Daily News: 3 Hsinyi Rd, Sec. 1, Taipei; tel. (2) 23222722; f. 1984; morning; Chinese; armed forces; Publr TIEN TUAN-YUAN; Editor CHIAO CHENG-CHONG.

Provincial

Chien Kuo Daily News: 36 Min Sheng Rd, Makung, Chen, Penghu; tel. (6) 9272675; f. 1949; morning; Editor LU KUO-HSIUNG; circ. 15,000.

China Daily News (Southern Edn): 57 Hsi Hwa St, Tainan; tel. (6) 2296381; telex 054; fax (6) 2201804; f. 1946; morning; Publr LIN SHE-CHI; Man. Dir and Editor TIEN SHING CHAN; circ. 670,000.

China Evening News: 71 Linhai St, Fengshan, Kaohsiung; tel. (7) 8122525; fax (7) 8416565; f. 1955; afternoon; Publr LAI JUNG TSEN; circ. 200,000.

Keng Sheng Daily News: 36 Wuchuan St, Hualien; tel. (38) 340131; fax (38) 329664; f. 1947; morning; Publr HSIEH YING-YIN; Editor CHEN HSING; circ. 50,000.

Kinmen Daily News: Chin Hu Village, Kinmen; tel. (823) 2874; f. 1965; morning; Publr CHEN SHOEI-TZOY; Editor YANG CHERNG-YEH; circ. 5,000.

Matsu Daily News: 1 Jenai Village, Nankan Hsiang, Matsu; tel. (836) 2276; f. 1957; morning; Publr HWANG NAN-TUNG; Editor YU CHANG-CHAO.

Min Chung Daily News: 180 Min Chuan 2 Rd, Kaohsiung; tel. (7) 3363131; fax (7) 3363604; f. 1950; morning; Publr LEE JER-LANG; Editor LEE WANG-TAI; circ. 148,000.

Shin Wen Evening News: 249 Chung Cheng 4 Rd, Kaohsiung; tel. (7) 2212858; f. 1985; afternoon; Publr and Dir YEH CHIEN-LI; Editor LIU TII-CHANG; circ. 12,000.

Taiwan Daily News: 361 Wen Shin Rd, Sec. 3, Taichung; tel. (4) 2958511; fax (4) 2958950; f. 1964; morning; Publr ANTHONY CHIANG; Editor CHAO LI-NAIN; circ. 250,000.

Taiwan Hsin Wen Daily News: 249 Chung Cheng 4 Rd, Kaohsiung; tel. (7) 2958951; f. 1949; morning; southern edn of *Hsin Sheng Pao*; Publr CHAO LI-NIEN; Editor HSIEH TSUNG-MIN.

Taiwan Times: 110 Chung Shan 1 Rd, Kaohsiung; tel. (7) 2155666; fax (7) 2150264; f. 1971; Publr WANG YUH-CHEN; Editor HWANG DONG-LIEH; circ. 148,000.

SELECTED PERIODICALS

Artist Magazine: 6th Floor, 147 Chung Ching South Rd, Sec. 1, Taipei; tel. (2) 23719692; fax (2) 23317096; f. 1975; monthly; Publr HO CHENG KUANG; circ. 28,000.

Car Magazine: 1st Floor, 3 Lane 3, Tun-Shan St, Taipei; tel. (2) 23218128; fax (2) 23935614; e-mail carguide@ms13.hinet.net; f. 1982; monthly; Publr H. K. LIN; Editor-in-Chief WILLIAM CHOU; circ. 85,000.

China Times Weekly: 5th Floor, 25 Min Chuan East Rd, Sec. 6, Taipei; tel. (2) 27929688; fax (2) 27929568; f. 1978; weekly; Chinese; Editor CHANG KUO-LI; Publr CHIEN CHIH-SHIN; circ. 180,000.

Continent Magazine: 3rd Floor, 11-6 Foo Chou St, Taipei; tel. (2) 23518310; f. 1950; monthly; archaeology, history and literature; Publr HSU CHO-YU.

Country Road: 14 Wenchow St, Taipei; tel. (2) 23628148; fax (2) 23636724; f. 1975; monthly; Editor CHRISTINE S. L. YU; Publr HONG PI-FENG.

Crown Magazine: 50 Lane 120, Tun Hua North Rd, Taipei; tel. (2) 27168888; fax (2) 27133422; f. 1954; monthly; literature and arts; Publr PING HSIN TAO; Editor CHEN LIH-HWA; circ. 76,000.

Elle-Taipei: 5th Floor, 67-4 Chung Hsiao East Rd, Sec. 4, Taipei; tel. (2) 27212421; fax (2) 27514583; f. 1991; monthly; women's magazine; Publr OLIVIER BURLOT; Editor-in-Chief LENA YANG; circ. 25,000.

Evergreen Monthly: 11th Floor, 2 Pa Teh Rd, Sec. 3, Taipei; tel. (2) 25785078; fax (2) 25786838; f. 1983; health care knowledge; Publr LEE SHENG-WEN; circ. 50,000.

Excellence Magazine: 1st Floor, 17 Lane 3, Sec. 2, Chien Kuo North Rd, Taipei; tel. (2) 25093548; telex 10196; fax (2) 25173607; f. 1984; monthly; business; Man. Dir CHRIS J. F. LIN; Editor-in-Chief LIN JE-HUEN; circ. 66,000.

Families Monthly: 11th Floor, 2 Pa Teh Rd, Sec. 3, Taipei; tel. (2) 25785078; fax (2) 25786838; f. 1976; family life; Publr LEE SHENG-WEN; Editor-in-Chief THELMA KU; circ. 155,000.

Foresight Investment Weekly: 7th Floor, 52 Nanking East Rd, Sec. 1, Taipei; tel. (2) 25512561; fax (2) 25681999; f. 1980; weekly; Dir and Publr SUN WUN HSIUNG; Editor-in-Chief WU WEN SHIN; circ. 55,000.

Free China Review: 2 Tientsin St, Taipei 10041; tel. (2) 23516419; fax (2) 23516227; f. 1951; monthly; English; illustrated; Publr DAVID TAWEI LEE; Editor-in-Chief JIANG PING-LUN.

Free China Journal: 2 Tientsin St, Taipei 10041; tel. (2) 23970180; fax (2) 23568233; f. 1964 (fmrly Free China Weekly); weekly; English; news review; Publr DAVID TAWEI LEE; Exec. Editor HENRY HU; circ. 37,000.

The Gleaner: 7th Floor, 7 Chung Ching South Rd, Sec. 1, Taipei; tel. (2) 23813781; fax (2) 23899801; Publr CHIN KAI-YIN.

Global Views Monthly: 4th Floor, 87 Sung Chiang Rd, Taipei; tel. (2) 25078627; fax (2) 25079011; f. 1986; Pres. CHARLES H. C. KAO; Publr and Editor-in-Chief WANG LI-HSING.

Harvest Farm Magazine: 14 Wenchow St, Taipei; tel. (2) 23628148; fax (2) 23636724; f. 1951; every 2 weeks; Publr HONG PI-FENG; Editor KAO MING-TANG.

Information and Computer: 6th Floor, 153 Hsinyi Rd, Sec. 3, Taipei; tel. (2) 23255750; fax (2) 23255749; f. 1980; monthly; Chinese; Publr FANG HSIEN-CHI; Editor JENNIFER CHIU; circ. 28,000.

Issues and Studies: Institute of International Relations, 64 Wan Shou Rd, Wenshan, Taipei 116; tel. (2) 9394921; fax (2) 2344919; e-mail scchang@cc.nccu.edu.tw; f. 1965; monthly; English; Chinese studies and international affairs; Publr SHAW YU-MING; Editor HO SZU-YIN.

Jade Biweekly Magazine: 7th Floor, 222 Sung Chiang Rd, Taipei; tel. (2) 25811665; fax (2) 25210586; f. 1982; economics, social affairs, leisure; Publr HSU CHIA-CHUNG; circ. 98,000.

Ladies Magazine: 11F-3, 187 Shin Yi Rd, Sec. 4, Taipei; tel. (2) 27026908; fax (2) 27014090; f. 1978; monthly; Publr CHENG CHIN-SHAN; Editor-in-Chief THERESA LEE; circ. 60,000.

Management Magazine: 3rd Floor, 143 Sim-Yi Rd, Sec. 4, Hsichih, Taipei; tel. (2) 26485828; fax (2) 26484666; e-mail flhung@email.gcn.net.tw; internet http://www.harment.com; monthly; Chinese; Publr and Editor FRANK L. HUNG; circ. 65,000.

Money Monthly: 12th Floor, 102 Tun Hua North Rd, Taipei; tel. (2) 25149822; fax (2) 27154657; f. 1986; monthly; personal financial management; Publr PATRICK SUN; Man. Editor JENNIE SHUE; circ. 55,000.

Music and Audiophile: 88 Ming Sheng East Rd, Sec. 2, Taipei; tel. (2) 25684607; fax (2) 25232376; f. 1973; Publr CHANG KUO-CHING; Editor-in-Chief CHARLES HUANG.

National Palace Museum Bulletin: Wai Shuang Hsi, Shih Lin, Taipei 11102; tel. (2) 28812021; fax (2) 28821440; e-mail bulletin@ss20.npm.gov.tw; f. 1966; every 2 months; Chinese art history research in English; Publr and Dir CHIN HSIAO-YI; Editor-in-Chief LIN PO-TING; circ. 1,000.

National Palace Museum Monthly of Chinese Art: Wai Shuang Hsi, Shih Lin, Taipei 11102; tel. (2) 28821230; fax (2) 28821440; f. 1983; monthly in Chinese; Publr CHIN HSIAO-YI; Editor-in-Chief CHANG YUEH-YUN; circ. 10,000.

The Nineties: 2nd–10th Floors, 2 Lane 199, Sin-yi Rd, Sec. 4, Taipei; tel. (2) 27091388; fax (2) 27553959; Publr CHIOU JEAN-SSU; Editor-in-Chief LEE YEE.

Nong Nong Magazine: 7th Floor, 531-1 Chung Cheng Rd, Hsin Tien, Taipei; tel. (2) 22181828; fax (2) 22181081; e-mail group@nongnong.com.tw; f. 1984; monthly; women's interest; Publr LISA WU; Editor DIANA LIU; circ. 70,000.

Reader's Digest (Chinese Edn): 2nd Floor, 2 Ming Sheng East Rd, Taipei; tel. (2) 27607262; fax (2) 27461588; monthly; Editor-in-Chief ANNIE CHENG.

Sinorama: 8th Floor, 15-1 Hangchow South Rd, Sec. 1, Taipei 100; tel. (2) 23922256; fax (2) 23970655; f. 1976; monthly; cultural; bilingual magazine with edns in Chinese with Japanese, Spanish and English; Publr DAVID TAWEI LEE; Editor-in-Chief ANNA Y. WANG; circ. 110,000.

Sinwen Tienti (Newsdom): 10th Floor, 207 Fuh Hsing North Rd, Taipei; tel. (2) 27139668; fax (2) 27131763; f. 1945; weekly; Chinese; Dir PU SHAO-FU.

Tien Hsia (CommonWealth Monthly): 4th Floor, 87 Sung Chiang Rd, Taipei; tel. (2) 25078627; fax (2) 25079011; f. 1981; monthly; business; Pres. CHARLES H. C. KAO; Publr and Editor DIANE YING; circ. 83,000.

TV Weekly: 11th Floor, 2 Pa Teh Rd, Taipei; tel. (2) 25785078; fax (2) 25786838; f. 1962; Publr LEE SHENG-WEN; circ. 160,000.

Unitas: 7th Floor, 180 Keelung Rd, Sec. 1, Taipei; tel. (2) 27666759; fax (2) 27567914; monthly; Chinese; literary journal; Publr CHANG PAO-CHING; Editor-in-Chief CHU AN-MIN.

Vi Vi Magazine: 7th Floor, 550 Chung Hsiao East Rd, Sec. 5, Taipei; tel. (2) 27275336; fax (2) 27592031; f. 1984; monthly; women's interest; Pres. TSENG CHING-TANG; circ. 60,000.

Wealth Magazine: 7th Floor, 52 Nanking East Rd, Sec. 1, Taipei; tel. (2) 25512561; fax (2) 25316438; f. 1974; monthly; finance; Pres. TSHAI YEN-KUEN; Editor ANDY LIAN; circ. 75,000.

NEWS AGENCIES

Central News Agency Inc. (CNA): 209 Sung Chiang Rd, Taipei; tel. (2) 25051180; telex 11548; fax (2) 25014806; f. 1924; news service in Chinese, English and Spanish; feature and photographic services; 7 domestic and 28 overseas bureaux; Pres. KERMIN SHIH; Editor-in-Chief W. L. LEE.

Chiao Kwang News Agency: 4th Floor, 28 Tsinan Rd, Sec. 2, Taipei; tel. (2) 23214803; fax (2) 23516416; Dir HUANG HER.

Foreign Bureaux

Agence France-Presse (AFP): Room 617, 6th Floor, 209 Sung Chiang Rd, Taipei; tel. (2) 25016395; fax (2) 25011881; Correspondents YANG HSIN-HSIN, LAWRENCE CHUNG, JOYCE CHIANG.

Associated Press (AP) (USA): Room 630, 6th Floor, 209 Sung Chiang Rd, Taipei; tel. (2) 25015109; fax (2) 25007133; Correspondents PAN YUEH-KAN, ANNIE HUANG, YANG CHI-HSIEN, PATRICIA KUO.

Reuters (UK): 8th Floor, 196 Chien Kuo North Rd, Taipei; tel. (2) 25004881; fax (2) 25080204; Bureau Chief JEFFREY PARKER.

United Press International (UPI) (USA): Room 624, 6th Floor, 209 Sung Chiang Rd, Taipei; tel. and fax (2) 25052549; Correspondent MARK A. LEWIS.

PRESS ASSOCIATION

Taipei Journalists Association: 209 Sung Chiang Rd, Taipei; tel. (2) 25056530; fax (2) 25021069; 3,147 mems representing editorial and business executives of newspapers and broadcasting stations; Chair. KERMIN SHIH; Sec.-Gen. HUANG CHING-CHIH.

Publishers

There are more than 5,524 publishing houses. In 1996 a total of 20,000 titles were published.

Art Book Co: 4th Floor, 18 Lane 283, Roosevelt Rd, Sec. 3, Taipei; tel. (2) 23620578; Publr HO KUNG SHANG.

Cheng Wen Publishing Co: 3rd Floor, 277 Roosevelt Rd, Sec. 3, Taipei; tel. (2) 23628032; fax (2) 23660806; Publr LARRY HUANG.

China Economic News Service (CENS): 555 Chung Hsiao East Rd, Sec. 4, Taipei 110; tel. (2) 26422629; fax (2) 26427422; e-mail webmaster@www.cens.com; f. 1974; trade magazines.

China Times Publishing Co: 5th Floor, 240 Hoping West Rd, Sec. 3, Taipei; tel. (2) 23027845; fax (2) 23027844; f. 1975; Pres. MO CHAO-PING.

Chinese Culture University Press: 55 Hua Kang Rd, Yangmingshan, Taipei; tel. (2) 28611861; fax (2) 28617164; Publr LEE FU-CHEN.

Chung Hwa Book Co Ltd: 14th Floor, 51 Keelung Rd, Sec. 2, Taipei; tel. (2) 23780215; fax (2) 27355887; humanities, social sciences, medicine, fine arts, school books, reference books; Publr LIN WIN-RONG.

The Commercial Press Ltd: 37 Chungking South Rd, Sec. 1, Taipei; tel. (2) 23116118; fax (2) 23710274; Publr REX HOW.

Crown Publishing Co: 50 Lane 120, Tun Hua North Rd, Taipei; tel. (2) 27168888; fax (2) 27133422; Publr PHILIP PING.

The Eastern Publishing Co Ltd: 121 Chungking South Rd, Sec. 1, Taipei; tel. (2) 23114514; Publr CHENG LI-TSU.

Elite Publishing Co: 1st Floor, 33-1 Lane 113, Hsiamen St, Taipei 100; tel. (2) 23671021; fax (2) 23657047; f. 1975; Publr KO CHING-HWA.

Far East Book Co: 10th Floor, 66-1 Chungking South Rd, Sec. 1, Taipei; tel. (2) 23118740; fax (2) 23114184; art, education, history, physics, mathematics, law, literature, dictionaries, textbooks, language tapes; Publr GEORGE C. L. PU.

Hilit Publishing Co Ltd: 11th Floor, 79 Hsin Tai Wu Rd, Sec. 1, Hsichih Town, Taipei County; tel. (2) 26984565; fax (2) 26984980; Publr DIXON D. S. SUNG.

Hua Hsin Culture and Publications Center: 2nd Floor, 133 Kuang Fu North Rd, Taipei; tel. (2) 27658190; f. 1960; Dir CHENG CHI.

International Cultural Enterprises: 5th Floor, 25 Po Ai Rd, Taipei 100; tel. (2) 23318080; fax (2) 23318090; e-mail itstpeh@MS8.hinet.net; internet http://www.spring.net.tw; Publr LAKE HU.

Kwang Fu Book Enterprises Co Ltd: 6th Floor, 38 Fu Hsing North Rd, Taipei; tel. (2) 27716622; fax (2) 27315982; Publr LIN CHUN-HUI.

Kwang Hwa Publishing Co: 8th Floor, 15-1 Hangchow South Rd, Sec. 1, Taipei; tel. (2) 23922256; fax (2) 23970655; Publr DAVID TAWEI LEE.

Li-Ming Cultural Enterprise Co: 2nd Floor, 49 Chungking South Rd, Sec. 1, Taipei 100; tel. (2) 23821233; telex 27877; fax (2) 23821244; Pres. HSU MING-SHIUNG.

Linking Publishing Co Ltd: 555 Chung Hsiao East Rd, Sec. 4, Taipei; tel. (2) 27683708; Publr LIU KUO-JUEI.

San Min Book Co Ltd: 5th Floor, 386 Fushing North Rd, Sec. 1, Taipei; tel. (2) 5006600; fax (2) 5064000; e-mail sanmin@msz.hinet.net; internet http://www.sanmin.com.tw; f. 1953; literature, history, philosophy, social sciences, dictionaries, art, politics, law; Publr LIU CHEN-CHIANG.

Sitak Publishing & Book Corpn: 10th Floor, 15 Lane 174, Hsin Ming Rd, Neihu Dist, Taipei; tel. (2) 27911197; fax (2) 27955824; e-mail kellychu@tptsl.seed.net.tw; Publr CHU PAU-LUNG; Dir KELLY CHU.

Taiwan Kaiming Book Co: 77 Chung Shan North Rd, Sec. 1, Taipei; tel. (2) 25415369; Publr LUCY CHOH LIU.

Tung Hua Book Co Ltd: 105 Ermei St, Taipei; tel. (2) 23114027; Publr CHARLES CHOH.

The World Book Co: 99 Chungking South Rd, Sec. 1, Taipei; tel. (2) 23311616; fax (2) 23317963; f. 1921; literature, textbooks; Chair. YEN FENG-CHANG; Publr YEN ANGELA CHU.

Youth Cultural Enterprise Co Ltd: 3rd Floor, 66-1 Chungking South Rd, Sec. 1, Taipei; tel. (2) 23112832; Publr LEE CHUNG-KUEI.

Yuan Liou Publishing Co Ltd: 7F/5, 184 Ding Chou Rd, Sec. 3, Taipei 100; tel. (2) 23651212; fax (2) 23657979; e-mail ylib@yuanliou.ylib.com.tw; internet http://www.ylib.com.tw; f. 1975; fiction, non-fiction, children's; Publr WANG JUNG-WEN.

Broadcasting and Communications

TELECOMMUNICATIONS

Directorate-General of Telecommunications: regulatory authority.

Chunghwa Telecommunications Co Ltd: 31 Ai Kuo East Rd, Taipei; f. 1996; state-controlled company, scheduled for privatization; sole provider of telephone services.

BROADCASTING

Broadcasting stations are mostly commercial. The Ministry of Communications determines power and frequencies, and the Government Information Office supervises the operation of all stations, whether private or governmental.

Radio

In mid-1997 there were 55 radio broadcasting corporations in operation, and permission for the establishment of a further 92 radio stations had been given. The ban on FM broadcasting was removed in 1993.

Broadcasting Corpn of China (BCC): 53 Jen Ai Rd, Sec. 3, Taipei; tel. (2) 27710151; fax (2) 27813845; f. 1928; domestic (6 networks) and external services in 13 languages and dialects; 9 local stations, 126 transmitters; Pres. LEE TSU-YUAN; Chair. WANG SUH-CHING.

Cheng Sheng Broadcasting Corpn Ltd: 6th–8th Floors, 66-1 Chungking South Rd, Sec. 1, Taipei; tel. (2) 23617231; f. 1950; 6 stations, 9 relay stations; Chair. YANG SHYUE-YENN; Pres. CHEN SHENG-CHUAN.

Fu Hsing Broadcasting Corpn: 5, Lane 280, Sec. 5, Chung Shan North Rd, Taipei; tel. (2) 28823450; fax (2) 28818218; 27 stations; Dir LO SHENG-HSIUNG.

Television

Legislation to place cable broadcasting on a legal basis was adopted in mid-1993, and by July 1997 154 cable television companies were in operation. A non-commercial station, Public Television (PTV), was to go on air in early 1998.

China Television Co (CTV): 120 Chung Yang Rd, Nan Kang District, Taipei; tel. (2) 27838308; telex 25080; f. 1969; Pres. JIANG FENG-CHYI; Chair. SUMING CHENG.

Chinese Television System (CTS): 100 Kuang Fu South Rd, Taipei 10658; tel. (2) 27510321; telex 24195; fax (2) 27775414; f. 1971; cultural and educational; Chair. CHOU SHIH-PIN; Pres. CHANG CHIA-HSIANG.

Formosa Television Co (FTV): 14th Floor, 30 Pa Teh Rd, Sec. 3, Taipei; tel. (2) 25702570; fax (2) 25773522; f. 1997; Chair. TSAI TUNG-RONG: Pres. LEE GUANG-HUEI.

Taiwan Television Enterprise (TTV): 10 Pa Teh Rd, Sec. 3, Taipei; tel. (2) 25781515; telex 25714; fax (2) 25799626; f. 1962; Chair. CHIEN MING-CHING; Pres. LEE SHENG-WEN.

Finance

(cap. = capital; p.u. = paid up; dep. = deposits; m. = million; brs = branches; amounts in New Taiwan dollars unless otherwise stated)

BANKING

In June 1991 the Ministry of Finance granted 15 new banking licences to private banks. A 16th bank was authorized in May 1992; further authorizations followed. Restrictions on the establishment of offshore banking units were relaxed in 1994.

Central Bank

Central Bank of China: 2 Roosevelt Rd, Sec. 1, Taipei 10757; tel. (2) 23936161; telex 21532; fax (2) 235719733; e-mail admirol@cbciso.cbc.gov.tw; f. 1928; bank of issue; cap. 55,000m., dep. 2,313,365m. (June 1997); Gov. (vacant).

Domestic Banks

Bank of Taiwan: 120 Chungking South Rd, Sec. 1, Taipei 10036; tel. (2) 23493456; telex 11201; fax (2) 23613203; internet http://www.bot.com.tw; f. 1899; cap. 22,000m., dep. 1,277,191m. (June 1997); Chair. JAMES C. T. LO; Pres. HO KUO-HWA; 96 brs, incl. 9 overseas.

Chiao Tung Bank: 91 Heng Yang Rd, Taipei 100; tel. (2) 23613000; telex 11341; fax (2) 23612046; f. 1907; fmrly Bank of Communications; cap. 15,300m., dep. 160,360m. (June 1997); Chair. CHEN S. YU; Pres. Dr CHAO CHIEH-CHIEN; 34 brs, incl. 3 overseas.

Export-Import Bank: 8th Floor, 3 Nan Hai Rd, Taipei 100; tel. (2) 23210511; telex 26044; fax (2) 23940630; f. 1979; cap. 10,000m. (June 1997); Chair. T. Y. CHU; Pres. PAULINE FU; 2 brs.

Farmers Bank of China: 85 Nanking East Rd, Sec. 2, Taipei 10408; tel. (2) 25517141; telex 21610; fax (2) 25622162; f. 1933; cap. 9,000m., dep. 321,497m. (June 1997); Chair. Y. S. LEE; Pres. W. L. CHEN; 72 brs.

International Commercial Bank of China: 100 Chi Lin Rd, Taipei 10424; tel. (2) 25633156; telex 11300; fax (2) 25632614; f. 1912; cap. 18,514m., dep. 310,881m. (June 1997); Chair. P. Y. PAI; Pres. JAMES T. T. YUAN; 75 brs, incl. 21 overseas.

Land Bank of Taiwan: 46 Kuan Chien Rd, Taipei 10038; tel. (2) 23483456; telex 14564; fax (2) 23819548; f. 1945; cap. 15,000m., dep. 1,015,139m. (June 1997); Chair. DONALD T. CHEN; Pres. LIN PONG-LONG; 95 brs.

Taiwan Co-operative Bank: 77 Kuan Chien Rd, Taipei 10038; tel. (2) 23118811; telex 23749; fax (2) 23316567; e-mail sphsu@www.tcb-bankcon.tw; f. 1946; acts as central bank for co-operatives, and as major agricultural credit institution; cap. 15,120m., dep. 1,405,377m. (June 1997); Chair. W. H. LEE; Pres. T. N. HSU; 136 brs.

Commercial Banks

Asia Pacific Bank: 66 Minchuan Rd, Taichung; tel. (4) 2271799; telex 51388; fax (4) 2204297; f. 1992; cap. 10,358m., dep. 777,623m. (June 1997); Chair. CHIOU JIA-SHYONG; Pres. CHIANG PO-HSUN; 27 brs.

Bank of Kaohsiung: 168 Po Ai 2nd Rd, Kaohsiung; tel. (7) 3480535; telex 73266; fax (7) 3480529; f. 1982; cap. 2,368m., dep. 110,099m. (June 1997); Chair. PAUL S. C. HSU; Pres. WAYNE CHEN; 32 brs.

Bank SinoPac: 1st–3rd Floors, 4 Chung Hsiao West Rd, Sec. 1, Taipei 100; tel. (2) 23881111; fax (2) 23810225; cap. 10,743m., dep. 95,316m. (June 1997); f. 1992; Chair. L. S. LIN; Pres. PAUL C. Y. LO; 24 brs.

Bao-Dao Commercial Bank: 68 Sung Chiang Rd, Taipei; tel. (2) 25615888; fax (2) 25219889; f. 1992; cap. 10,000m., dep. 95,152m. (1997); Chair. CHEN CHUN-KUAN; Pres. T. H. CHUNG; 18 brs.

Central Trust of China: 49 Wu Chang St, Sec. 1, Taipei 100; tel. (2) 23111511; telex 11379; fax (2) 23118107; f. 1935; cap. 8,000m., dep. 98,837m. (June 1997); Chair. PERNG FAI-NAN; Pres. LEE YE-TSAN; 20 brs.

Chang Hwa Commercial Bank Ltd: 38 Tsuyu Rd, Sec. 2, Taichung 40010; tel. (4) 2222001; telex 51248; fax (4) 2231170; f. 1905; 53% govt-owned; cap. 24,652m., dep. 669,211m. (June 1997); Chair. MOU HSING-TSAI; Pres. HONG TO TSOU; 140 brs, 7 overseas.

Chinatrust Commercial Bank: 3 Sung Shou Rd, Taipei; tel. (2) 27222002; telex 24654; fax (2) 27233872; f. 1966; cap. 18,222m., dep. 301,086m. (June 1997); Chair. JEFFREY L. S. KOO; Pres. KENNETH C. M. LO; 34 brs, 5 overseas.

The Chinese Bank: 68 Nanking East Rd, Sec. 3, Taipei; tel. (2) 25168686; fax (2) 25170797; f. 1992; dep. 72,411m. (June 1997); Chair. WANG YOU-THENG; Pres. TEN CHEN; 22 brs.

Chinfon Commercial Bank: 1 Nanyang St, Taipei 10039; tel. (2) 23114881; fax (2) 23712395; f. 1994; cap 10,000m., dep. 117,331m. (June 1997); Chair. HUANG SHI-HUI; Pres HU TZU-HUEI; 22 brs, 2 overseas.

Chung Shing Bank: 228–230 Sung Chiang Rd, Taipei; tel. (2) 25616601; fax (2) 25114389; f. 1992; cap. 13,500m., dep. 75,574m. (Dec. 1996); Chair. Y. Y. WANG; Pres. ABEL S. WANG; 25 brs.

Cosmos Bank: 39 Tun Hua South Rd, Sec. 2, Taipei; tel. (2) 27011777; telex 26505; fax (2) 27541742; f. 1992; cap. 12,000m., dep. 101,247m. (June 1997); Chair. HSUI SHENG-FA; Pres. WANG SHAO-KING; 23 brs.

Da Chong Bank: 58 Chungcheng 2nd Rd, Kaohsiung; tel. (7) 2242220; fax (7) 2241620; f. 1992; cap. 10,500m., dep. 102,569m. (June 1997); Chair. CHEN TIEN-MAO; Pres. P. W. CHANG; 26 brs.

Dah An Commercial Bank: 117 Ming Sheng East Rd, Sec. 3, Taipei; tel. (2) 27126666; fax (2) 27197415; f. 1992; cap. 10,886m., dep. 89,841m. (June. 1997); Chair. J. K. LOH; Pres. KENG PING; 23 brs.

E. Sun Commercial Bank: 77 Wuchang St, Sec. 1, Taipei; tel. (2) 23891313; fax (2) 23125125; f. 1992; cap. 10,690m., dep. 117,200m. (June 1997); Chair. LIN JONG-SHONG; Pres. HUANG YUNG-JEN; 26 brs.

En Tie Commercial Bank: 3rd Floor, 158 Ming Sheng East Rd, Sec. 3, Taipei; tel. (2) 27189999; fax (2) 27175940; f. 1993; cap. 10,700m., dep. 68,274m. (June 1997); Chair. YEE TEH-MING; Pres. LEE JYE-CHENG; 21 brs.

Far Eastern International Bank: 27th Floor, 207 Tun Hua South Rd, Sec. 2, Taipei; tel. (2) 23786868; fax (2) 23779000; f. 1992; cap. 10,548m. (Dec. 1996); dep. 73,200m. (June 1997); Chair. DOUGLAS T. HSU; Pres. ELI HONG; 27 brs.

First Commercial Bank: POB 395, 30 Chungking South Rd, Sec. 1, Taipei; tel. (2) 23111111; telex 11310; fax (2) 23610036; f. 1899; 71.35% govt-owned; cap. 27,367m., dep. 900,565m. (June 1997); Chair. T. L. HUANG; Pres. A. C. CHEN; 138 brs, 12 overseas.

Fubon Commercial Bank: 2nd Floor, 169 Jen Ai Rd, Sec. 4, Taipei; tel. (2) 27716699; telex 26277; fax (2) 27730763; f. 1992; cap. 10,731m., dep. 96,168m. (June 1997); Chair. TSAI WAN-TSAI; Pres. WANG CHUAN-HSI; 22 brs.

Grand Commercial Bank: 17 Chengteh Rd, Sec. 1, Taipei; tel. (2) 25562088; telex 26462; fax (2) 25561579; f. 1991; cap. 13,230m., dep. 99,972m. (June 1997); Chair. WU TSUN-HSIENG; Pres. and Man. Dir ALEXANDER T. Y. DEAN; 27 brs.

Hua Nan Commercial Bank Ltd: 38 Chungking South Rd, Sec. 1, Taipei; tel. (2) 23713111; telex 11307; fax (2) 23711972; f. 1919; cap. 25,605m., dep. 683,051m. (June 1997); Chair. KENNETH B. K. TSAN; Pres. H. T. CHEN; 151 brs, 8 overseas.

Overseas Chinese Bank: 8 Hsiang Yang Rd, Taipei 10014; tel. (2) 23715181; telex 21571; fax (2) 23814056; f. 1961; general banking and foreign exchange; cap. p.u. 12,500m., dep. 128,155m. (June 1997); Chair. LININ DAY; Pres. RICHARD L. C. CHERN; 49 brs.

Pan Asia Bank: 3rd–4th Floors, 60-8 Chungkang Rd, Taichung; tel. (4) 3232468; fax (4) 3292216; f. 1992; cap. 10,586m., dep. 80,290m. (June 1997); Chair. CHANG CHUN-SHYONG; Pres. WANG TSAI-WONG; 18 brs.

Shanghai Commercial and Savings Bank Ltd: 2 Min Chuan East Rd, Sec. 1, Taipei 104; tel. (2) 25817111; telex 22507; fax (2) 25671921; f. 1915; cap. p.u. 6,060m., dep. 174,459m. (June 1997); Chair. H. C. YUNG; Pres. C. S. CHOU; 44 brs.

Taipeibank: 50 Chung Shan North Rd, Sec. 2, Taipei 10419; tel. (2) 25425656; telex 11722; fax (2) 25428870; f. 1969; fmrly City Bank of Taipei; cap. 14,000m., dep. 407,214m. (June 1997); Chair. K. H. YEH; Pres. J. H. HUANG ; 66 brs, 5 overseas.

Taishin International Bank: 44 Chung Shan North Rd, Sec. 2, Taipei; tel. (2) 25683988; fax (2) 25234564; f. 1992; cap. 10,300m., dep. 98,208m. (June 1997); Chair. THOMAS T. L. WU; Pres. JULIUS H. C. CHEN; 27 brs.

Union Bank of Taiwan: 109 Ming Sheng East Rd, Sec. 3, Taipei; tel. (2) 27180001; telex 26354; fax (2) 27137515; f. 1992; cap. 12,300m., dep. 95,310m. (June 1997); Chair. C. C. HUANG; Pres. S. C. LEE; CEO SHERMAN CHUANG; 23 brs.

United World Chinese Commercial Bank: 65 Kuan Chien Rd, POB 1670, Taipei 10038; tel. (2) 23125555; telex 21378; fax (2) 23311093; e-mail ho8p@uwccb.com.tw; f. 1975; dep. 406,639m. (June 1997); Chair. SNIT VIRAVAN; Pres. GREGORY K. H. WANG; 61 brs.

There are also a number of Medium Business Banks throughout the country.

Community Financial System

The community financial institutions include both credit co-operatives and credit departments of farmers' and fishermen's associations. These local financial institutions focus upon providing savings and loan services for the community. At the end of 1996 there were 73 credit co-operatives, 285 credit departments of farmers' associations and 27 credit departments of fishermen's associations, with a combined total deposit balance of NT $2,892,800m., or 20.68% of the market share, while outstanding loans amounted to NT $1,864,400m., or 16.25% of the market share.

Foreign Banks

In 1997 44 foreign banks maintained 70 branches in Taiwan.

STOCK EXCHANGE

In January 1991 the stock exchange was opened to direct investment by foreign institutions, and in March 1996 it was also opened to direct investment by foreign individuals. Various liberalization measures have been introduced since 1994. In November 1996 the limit on aggregate foreign investment in domestic shares was raised to 25% of total market capitalization. From July 1997 Taiwanese companies were permitted to list shares on domestic and foreign stock exchanges simultaneously.

Taiwan Stock Exchange Corpn: 10th Floor, City Bldg, 85 Yen-Ping South Rd, Taipei 10034; tel. (2) 23114020; fax (2) 23114004; f. 1962; Chair. C. Y. LEE.

Supervisory Body

Securities and Futures Commission: 12th Floor, 3 Nan Hoi Rd, Taipei; tel. (2) 23413101; fax (2) 23963617; Chair. LU DAUNG-YEN; Sec.-Gen. NING KOU-HUEI.

INSURANCE

In 1993 the Ministry of Finance issued eight new insurance licences, the first for more than 30 years. Two more were issued in 1994.

Cathay Life Insurance Co Ltd: 296 Jen Ai Rd, Sec. 4, Taipei; tel. (2) 27551399; telex 24994; fax (2) 27551322; f. 1962; premium income NT $222,587m. (1995); Chair. TSAI HONG-TU; Gen. Man. DAVID K. H. FAN.

Central Insurance Co Ltd: 6 Chung Hsiao West Rd, Sec. 1, Taipei; tel. (2) 23819910; telex 22871; fax (2) 23116901; f. 1962; Chair. H. K. SHE; Gen. Man. C. C. HUANG.

Central Reinsurance Corpn: 53 Nanking East Rd, Sec. 2, Taipei; tel. (2) 25115211; telex 11471; fax (2) 25235350; f. 1968; Chair. C. K. LIU; Pres. C. T. YANG.

Central Trust of China, Life Insurance Dept: 3rd–8th Floors, 69 Tun Hua South Rd, Sec. 2, Taipei; tel. (2) 27849151; fax (2) 27052214; f. 1941; life insurance; Pres. EDWARD LO; Man. S. TSAU.

China Life Insurance Co Ltd: 122 Tun Hua North Rd, Taipei; tel. (2) 27134511; fax (2) 27125966; f. 1963; Chair. C. F. KOO; Gen. Man. CHESTER C. Y. KOO.

China Mariners' Assurance Corpn Ltd: 11th Floor, 2 Kuan Chien Rd, Taipei; tel. (2) 23757676; fax (2) 23756363; f. 1948; Chair. K. S. FAN; Gen. Man. VINCENT M. S. FAN.

Chinfon Life Insurance Co Ltd: 12th Floor, 550 Chung Hsiao East Rd, Sec. 4, Taipei; tel. (2) 27582727; fax (2) 27586758; f. 1962; fmrly First Life Insurance Co; Chair. C. Y. CHENG; Gen. Man. C. S. TU.

Chung Kuo Insurance Co Ltd: 10th–12th Floors, ICBC Bldg, 100 Chilin Rd, Taipei 10424; tel. (2) 25513345; telex 21573; fax (2) 25414046; f. 1931; fmrly China Insurance Co Ltd; Chair. J. T. LEE; Pres. S. N. TAUNG.

Chung Shing Life Insurance Co Ltd: 18th Floor, 200 Keelung Rd, Sec. 1, Taipei 110; tel. (2) 27583099; fax (2) 23451635; f. 1993; Chair. T. H. CHAO; Gen. Man. TERRY W. Y. CHEN.

Eagle Star President Life Insurance Co Ltd: 11th Floor, 69 Ming-Sheng East Road, Sec. 3, Taipei; tel. (2) 25151888; fax 5151777; f. 1995; Chair. C. S. LIN; Gen. Man. EDWARD TASI.

Eurich Insurance Taiwan Ltd: 56 Tun Hua North Rd, Taipei; tel. (2) 27752888; telex 11122; fax (2) 27416004; f. 1961; Chair. and Gen. Man. CHARLES C. T. WANG.

The First Insurance Co Ltd: 54 Chung Hsiao East Rd, Sec. 1, Taipei; tel. (2) 23913271; telex 28971; fax (2) 23930685; f. 1962; Chair. C. H. LEE; Gen. Man. M. C. CHEN.

Fubon Insurance Co Ltd: 237 Chien Kuo South Rd, Sec. 1, Taipei; tel. (2) 27067890; telex 11143; fax (2) 27042915; f. 1961; Chair. TSAI MING-CHUNG; Gen. Man. T. M. SHIH.

Fubon Life Insurance Co Ltd: 237 Chien Kuo South Rd, Sec. 1, Ta-an District, Taipei; tel. (2) 27067890; fax (2) 27042915; f. 1993; premium income NT $29,328m. (1995); Chair. RICHARD M. TSAI; Gen. Man. Y. Y. HO.

Global Life Insurance Co Ltd: 502 San Ho St, Sec. 2, Peitou, Taipei 11235; tel. (2) 8967899; fax (2) 8958312; f. 1993; Chair. JOHN TSENG; Gen. Man. ROBERT KUO.

Hung Fu Life Insurance Co Ltd: 7th Floor, 70 Cheng Teh Rd, Sec. 1, Taipei; tel. (2) 25595151; fax (2) 25562840; f. 1994; Chair. ROBERT CHEN; Gen. Man. HIRO TSEN.

Kuo Hua Insurance Co Ltd: 166 Chang An East Rd, Sec. 2, Taipei; tel. (2) 27514225; telex 22554; fax (2) 27817802; f. 1962; premium income NT $7,073m. (1995); Chair. J. B. WANG; Gen. Man. CHI HSIUNG-HUNG.

Kuo Hua Life Insurance Co Ltd: 42 Chung Shan North Rd, Sec. 2, Taipei; tel. (2) 25621101; telex 22486; fax (2) 25374083; f. 1963; Chair. JASON CHANG; Gen. Man. CHEN TUNG-CHENG.

Mercuries Life Insurance Co Ltd: 6th Floor, 2 Lane 150, Sin-Yi Rd, Sec. 5, Taipei; tel. (2) 23455511; fax (2) 23456616; f. 1993; Chair. GEORGE C. S. WONG; Gen. Man. STEVE WANG.

Mingtai Fire and Marine Insurance Co Ltd: 1 Jen Ai Rd, Sec. 4, Taipei; tel. (2) 27725678; telex 22792; fax (2) 27729932; f. 1961; Chair. LARRY P. C. LIN; Pres. H. T. CHEN.

Nan Shan Life Insurance Co Ltd: 144 Min Chuan East Rd, Sec. 2, Taipei 104; tel. (2) 25013333; fax (2) 25012555; internet http://www.nanshanlife.com.tw; f. 1963; premium income NT $52,687m. (1995); Chair. EDMUND TSE; Pres. SUNNY LIN.

Shin Fu Life Insurance Co Ltd: 6th Floor, 123 Chung Hsiao East Rd, Sec. 2, Taipei; tel. (2) 23563921; fax (2) 23563927; f. 1993; Chair. M. H. KAO; Gen. Man. NING HAI JIN.

Shin Kong Fire and Marine Insurance Co Ltd: 7th–12th Floors, 13 Chien Kuo North Rd, Sec. 2, Taipei; tel. (2) 25075335; telex 11393; fax (2) 25074580; f. 1963; Chair. ANTHONY T. S. WU; Pres. Y. H. CHANG.

Shin Kong Life Insurance Co Ltd: 243 Tun Hua South Rd, Sec. 1, Taipei; tel. (2) 23895858; telex 21471; fax (2) 23758688; f. 1963; premium income NT $104,207m. (1995); Chair. EUGENE T. C. WU; Gen. Man. C. M. SU.

Shinung Life Insurance Co Ltd: 11-2F, 155 Tsu Chih St, Taichung; tel. (4) 3721653; fax (4) 3722008; f. 1993; Chair. YANG WEN-BEN; Gen. Man. P. T. LAI.

South China Insurance Co Ltd: 5th Floor, 560 Chung Hsiao East Rd, Sec. 4, Taipei; tel. and fax (2) 27298022; telex 21977; f. 1963; Chair. C. F. LIAO; Pres. ALLAN I. R. HUANG.

Tai Ping Insurance Co Ltd: 3rd–5th Floors, 550 Chung Hsiao East Rd, Sec. 4, Taipei; tel. (2) 27582700; telex 21641; fax (2) 27295681; f. 1929; Chair. T. C. CHEN; Gen. Man. T. Y. TUNG.

Taian Insurance Co Ltd: 59 Kuan Chien Rd, Taipei; tel. (2) 23819678; telex 21735; fax (2) 23816057; f. 1961; Chair. C. H. CHEN; Gen. Man. Y. H. LEE.

Taiwan Fire and Marine Insurance Co Ltd: 49 Kuan Chien Rd, Taipei; tel. (2) 23317261; telex 21694; fax (2) 23145287; f. 1946; Chair. HSU HUNG-CHIH; Gen. Man. JOHN F. KAO.

Taiwan Life Insurance Co Ltd: 14th–19th Floors, 17 Hsu Chang St, Taipei; tel. (2) 23116411; fax (2) 23710854; f. 1947; Chair. KUAN-YI LU; Pres. FRANK C. H. CHENG.

Tong Tai Insurance Co Ltd: 5th Floor, 296 Jen Ai Rd, Sec. 4, Taipei; tel. (2) 27551299; fax (2) 27093699; f. 1993; Chair. S. T. LIAO; Gen. Man. C. Y. LEE.

Union Insurance Co Ltd: 12th Floor, 219 Chung Hsiao East Rd, Sec. 4, Taipei; tel. (2) 27765567; telex 27616; fax (2) 27737199; f. 1963; Chair. S. H. CHIN; Gen. Man. FRANK S. WANG.

In 1995 there were 26 foreign insurance companies operating in Taiwan.

Trade and Industry

GOVERNMENT AGENCIES

Board of Foreign Trade (Ministry of Economic Affairs): 1 Houkow St, Taipei; tel. (2) 23510271; fax (2) 23513603; Dir-Gen. Y. F. LIN.

Council of Agriculture (COA): 37 Nan Hai Rd, Taipei 100; tel. (2) 23812991; fax (2) 23310341; e-mail webmaster@www.coa.gov.tw; f. 1984; govt agency directly under the Executive Yuan, with ministerial status; a policy-making body in charge of national agriculture, forestry, fisheries, the animal industry and food administration; promotes technology and provides external assistance; Chair. Dr PENG TSO-KWEI; Sec.-Gen. Dr KU TE-YEH.

Industrial Development Bureau (Ministry of Economic Affairs): 41-3 Hsin Yi Rd, Sec. 3, Taipei; tel. (2) 27541255; fax (2) 27043784; Dir-Gen. C. M. YIN.

Industrial Development and Investment Center (Ministry of Economic Affairs): 19th Floor, 4 Chung Hsiao West Rd, Sec. 1, Taipei; tel. (2) 23892111; fax (2) 23820497; f. 1959 to assist investment and planning; Dir CHOU YAN.

CHAMBER OF COMMERCE

General Chamber of Commerce of the Republic of China: 6th Floor, 390 Fu Hsing South Rd, Sec. 1, Taipei; tel. (2) 27012671; telex 11396; fax (2) 27542107; f. 1946; 39 mems, incl. 14 nat. feds of trade asscns, 22 district export asscns and 3 district chambers of commerce; Chair. Dr Y. T. WANG; Sec.-Gen. CHIU JAW-SHIN.

INDUSTRIAL AND TRADE ASSOCIATIONS

China External Trade Development Council: 4th–8th Floors, CETRA Tower, 333 Keelung Rd, Sec. 1, Taipei 110; tel. (2) 27255200; telex 21676; fax (2) 27576653; trade promotion body; Sec.-Gen. RICKY Y. S. KAO.

China Productivity Center: 2nd Floor, 79 Hsin Tai 5 Rd, Sec. 1, Hsichih, Taipei County; tel. (2) 26982989; fax (2) 26982976; f. 1956; management, technology, training, etc.; Pres. BEN WAN.

Chinese National Association of Industry and Commerce: 13th Floor, 390 Fu Hsing South Rd, Sec. 1, Taipei; tel. (2) 27070111; telex 10774; fax (2) 27017601; Chair. JEFFREY L. S. KOO.

Chinese National Federation of Industries (CNFI): 12th Floor, 390 Fu Hsing South Rd, Sec. 1, Taipei; tel. (2) 27033500; telex 14565; fax (2) 27033982; f. 1948; 136 mem. asscns; Chair. KAO CHIN-YUAN; Sec.-Gen. HO CHUN-YIH.

Taiwan Handicraft Promotion Centre: 1 Hsu Chou Rd, Taipei; tel. (2) 23933655; fax (2) 23937330; f. 1956; Pres. Y. C. WANG.

Trading Department of Central Trust of China: 49 Wuchang St, Sec. 1, Taipei 10006; tel. (2) 23111511; telex 26254; fax (2) 23821047; f. 1935; export and import agent for private and govt-owned enterprises.

UTILITY

Electricity

Taiwan Power Co: 242 Roosevelt Rd, Sec. 3, Taipei 100; tel. (2) 23651234; telex 11520; fax (2) 23678593; f. 1946; electricity generation; Chair. CHANG CHUNG-CHIEN; Pres. S. C. HSI.

CO-OPERATIVES

In December 1996 there were 5,324 co-operatives, with a total membership of 7,098,000m. and total capital of NT $59,322m. Of the specialized co-operatives the most important was the consumers' co-operative (4,558 co-ops).

The Co-operative League (f. 1940) is a national organization responsible for co-ordination, education and training and the movement's national and international interests (Chair. K. L. CHEN).

TRADE UNIONS

Chinese Federation of Labour: 11th Floor, Back Bldg, 201–18 Tun Hua North Rd, Taipei; tel. (2) 27135111; fax (2) 27135116; f. 1958; mems: c. 3,110 unions representing 2,938,446 workers; Pres. LEE CHENG-CHONG; Gen. Sec. CHIU CHING-HWEI.

National Federations

Chinese Federation of Postal Workers: 9th Floor, 45 Chungking South Rd, Sec. 2, Taipei 100; tel. (2) 23921380; fax (2) 23414510; f. 1930; 27,957 mems; Pres. CHEN SHIAN-JUH.

Chinese Federation of Railway Workers Union: Room 6048, 6th Floor, 3 Peiping West Rd, Taipei; tel. (2) 23815226; fax (2) 23831523; f. 1947; 17,595 mems; Pres. LIN HUI-KUAN.

National Chinese Seamen's Union: 8th Floor, 25 Nanking East Rd, Sec. 3, Taipei; tel. (2) 25150259; telex 13665; fax (2) 25078211; f. 1913; 26,391 mems; Pres. CHANG KAI-FENG.

Regional Federations

Taiwan Federation of Textile and Dyeing Industry Workers' Unions (TFTDWU): 2 Lane 64, Chung Hsiao East Rd, Sec. 2, Taipei; tel. (2) 23415627; f. 1958; 11,906 mems; Chair. LEE CHIN-CHIH.

Taiwan Provincial Federation of Labour: 11th Floor, 44 Roosevelt Rd, Sec. 2, Taipei; tel. and fax (2) 23938181; f. 1948; 77 mem.

unions and 1.8m. mems; Pres. WU HAI-RAY; Sec.-Gen. HUANG YAO-TUNG.

Transport

RAILWAYS

Taiwan Railway Administration (TRA): 3 Peiping West Rd, Taipei 10026; tel. (2) 23815226; fax (2) 23831367; f. 1891; a public utility under the provincial govt of Taiwan; operates both the west line and east line systems, with a route length of 1,107.7 km, of which 497.5 km are electrified; the west line is the main trunk line from Keelung, in the north, to Fangliao, in the south, with several branches; electrification of the main trunk line was completed in 1979; the east line runs along the east coast, linking Hualien with Taitung; the north link line, with a length of 79.2 km from New Suao to Hualien, connecting Suao and Hualien, was opened in 1980; the south link line, with a length of 98.2 km from New Taitung to Fangliao, opened in late 1991, completing the round-the-island system; construction of a high-speed link between Taipei and Kaohsiung (345 km) was to begin in 1998, completion of the project being scheduled for the year 2003; Man. Dir T. P. CHEN.

There are also 1,212.1 km of private narrow-gauge track, operated by the Taiwan Sugar Corpn in conjunction with the Taiwan Forestry Bureau and other organizations. These railroads are mostly used for freight, but they also offer a limited public passenger service.

Construction of a five-line, 86.8km, mass rapid-transit system (MRTS) in Taipei, incorporating links to the airport, began in 1987. The first 10.9km section of the Mucha line opened in March 1996. The remainder of the network was scheduled for completion by 2006. A 42.7-km system is planned for Kaohsiung, scheduled for completion in the year 2005. MRT systems are also projected for Taoyuan, Hsinchu, Taichung and Tainan.

ROADS

There were 20,118.4 km of highways in 1996, most of them asphalt-paved. The Sun Yat-sen (North–South) Freeway was completed in 1978. Construction of a 505-km Second Freeway, which is to extend to Pingtung, in southern Taiwan, began in July 1987 and was scheduled to be completed by the end of 2003. Work on the Taipei–Ilan freeway began in 1991.

Taiwan Area National Freeway Bureau: POB 75, Sinchwang, Taipei 242; tel. (2) 29096141; fax (2) 29093218; f. 1970; Dir-Gen. OU HUEI-JENG.

Taiwan Highway Bureau: 70 Chung Hsiao West Rd, Sec. 1, Taipei; tel. (2) 23113456; fax (2) 23810394; f. 1946; responsible for planning, design, construction and maintenance of provincial and county highways and administration of motor vehicles and drivers; Dir-Gen. LIANG YUEH.

Taiwan Motor Transport Co Ltd: 5th Floor, 17 Hsu Chang St, Taipei; tel. (2) 23715364; fax (2) 23810268; f. 1980; operates national bus service; Chair. KIANG CHING-CHIEN; Gen. Man. CHEN WU-SHIUNG.

SHIPPING

Taiwan has five international ports: Kaohsiung, Keelung, Taichung, Hualien and Suao. In 1996 the merchant fleet comprised 681 vessels, with a total displacement of 6,174,500 grt.

Evergreen Marine Corpn: 166 Ming Sheng East Rd, Sec. 2, Taipei; tel. (2) 25057766; telex 11476; fax (2) 25055256; f. 1968; world-wide container liner services; Indian subcontinent feeder service; two-way round-the-world services; Chair. CHANG JUNG-FA; Pres. GEORGE HSU.

Taiwan Navigation Co Ltd: 7th Floor, 17 Hsuchang St, Taipei; tel. (2) 23113882; telex 11233; Chair. L. S. CHEN; Pres. I. Y. CHANG.

U-Ming Marine Transport Corpn: 29th Floor, Taipei Metro Tower, 207 Tun Hua South Rd, Sec. 2, Taipei; tel. (2) 27338000; telex 15459; fax (2) 27359900; world-wide tramp services; Chair. D. T. HSU; Pres. C. S. CHEN.

Uniglory Marine Corpn: 6th Floor, 172 Ming Sheng East Rd, Sec. 2, Taipei; tel. (2) 25016711; telex 24720; fax (2) 25017592; Chair. LOH YAO-FON; Pres. LEE MUN-CHI.

Wan Hai Lines Ltd: 10th Floor, 136 Sung Chiang Rd, Taipei; tel. (2) 25677961; telex 21742; fax (2) 25216000; f. 1965; regional container liner services; Chair. CHAO CHUAN CHEN; Pres. T. S. CHEN.

Yang Ming Marine Transport Corpn (Yang Ming Line): 4th–6th Floors, Hwai Ning Bldg, 53 Hwai Ning St, Taipei 10037; tel. (2) 23812911; telex 11572; fax (2) 23148058; f. 1972; world-wide container liner services, bulk carrier and supertanker services; Chair. T. H. CHEN; Pres. FRANK LU.

CIVIL AVIATION

There are two international airports, Chiang Kai-shek at Taoyuan, near Taipei, which opened in 1979 (a second passenger terminal and expansion of freight facilities being scheduled for completion by 1999), and Hsiaokang, in Kaohsiung (where similar improvements were in progress in 1997). There are also 14 domestic airports.

China Air Lines Ltd (CAL): 131 Nanking East Rd, Sec. 3, Taipei; tel. (2) 7152626; fax (2) 27152233; internet http://www.china-airlines.com; f 1959; domestic services and international services to destinations in the Far East, Europe, the Middle East and the USA; Chair. CHIANG HUNG-I; Pres. FU CHUN-FANG.

EVA Airways: Eva Air Bldg, 376 Hsin-nan Rd, Sec. 1, Luchu, Taoyuan Hsien; tel. (3) 3515151; fax (3) 3352093; f. 1989; subsidiary of Evergreen Group; commenced flights in 1991; services to destinations in Asia (incl. Hong Kong and Macau), Europe, North America, Australia and New Zealand; Pres. RICHARD HUANG.

Far Eastern Air Transport Corpn (FAT): 5, Alley 123, Lane 405, Tun Hua North Rd, Taipei 10592; tel. (2) 27121555; fax (2) 27122428; f. 1957; domestic scheduled and chartered flights; Pres. LEE YUN-LING.

Formosa Airlines: 12th Floor, 1 Nanking East Rd, Sec. 4, Taipei; tel. (2) 25149811; fax (2) 25149817; f. 1966; domestic services; Pres. H. H. SUN.

Great China Airlines: 9th Floor, 260 Pa Teh Rd, Sec. 2, Taipei; tel. (2) 27755317; fax (2) 27755385; f. 1989; scheduled domestic and chartered international services; Chair. PETER SZU; Gen. Man. JAMES JENG.

Mandarin Airlines (AE): 13th Floor, 134 Ming Sheng East Rd, Sec. 3, Taipei; tel. (2) 27171188; fax (2) 27170716; f. 1991; subsidiary of CAL; services to Auckland, Brisbane, Sydney and Vancouver; Chair. CHIANG HUNG-I; Pres. MICHAEL LO.

Taiwan Airlines: 8th Floor, 59 Sung Chiang Rd, Taipei; tel. (2) 25168801; fax (2) 25168807; domestic services; Chair. CHU LIN LI-CHEN; Pres. HAN JYA-YANG.

Transasia Airways: 9th Floor, 139 Chengchou Rd, Taipei; tel. (2) 25575767; fax (2) 25570840; f. 1989; fmrly Foshing Airlines; scheduled domestic flights and international services to Macau and Indonesia; Chair. CHARLES C. LIN; Pres. ITOY WANG.

U-Land Airlines: 2nd Floor, 25 Hein Tai Wu Rd, Sec. 1, His-chih, Taipei Hsien; tel. (2) 26981280; fax (2) 26982890; fmrly China Asia Airlines; domestic services; Chair. WANG KER-GER; Pres. TING ZEAN.

UNI Airways Corpn: 2-6 Chung Shan 4th Rd, Kaohsiung; tel. (7) 7917611; fax (7) 7917511; f. 1989; fmrly Makung Airlines; domestic and international charter services; Chair. HSU JUI-YUAN; Pres. JOSEPH LIN.

Tourism

The principal tourist attractions are the festivals, the ancient art treasures and the island scenery. In 1996 there were 2,358,221 visitor arrivals (including 269,682 overseas Chinese) in Taiwan. Receipts from tourism in that year totalled US $3,636m.

Tourism Bureau, Ministry of Transportation and Communications: 9th Floor, 290 Chung Hsiao East Rd, Sec. 4, Taipei; tel. (2) 23491635; fax (2) 27735487; f. 1966; Dir-Gen. CHANG TZU-CHYANG.

Taiwan Visitors' Association: 5th Floor, 9 Min Chuan East Rd, Sec. 2, Taipei; tel. (2) 25943261; fax (2) 25943265; f. 1956; promotes domestic and international tourism; Chair. STANLEY C. YEN.

COLOMBIA

Introductory Survey

Location, Climate, Language, Religion, Flag, Capital

The Republic of Colombia lies in the north-west of South America, with the Caribbean Sea to the north and the Pacific Ocean to the west. Its continental neighbours are Venezuela and Brazil to the east, and Peru and Ecuador to the south, while Panama connects it with Central America. The coastal areas have a tropical rain forest climate, the plateaux are temperate, and in the Andes mountains there are areas of permanent snow. The language is Spanish. Almost all of the inhabitants profess Christianity, and about 95% are Roman Catholics. There are small Protestant and Jewish minorities. The national flag (proportions 3 by 2) has three horizontal stripes, of yellow (one-half of the depth) over dark blue over red. The capital is Santafé de Bogotá (formerly Bogotá).

Recent History

Colombia was under Spanish rule from the 16th century until 1819, when it achieved independence as part of Gran Colombia, which included Ecuador, Panama and Venezuela. Ecuador and Venezuela seceded in 1830, when Colombia (then including Panama) became a separate republic. In 1903 the province of Panama successfully rebelled and became an independent country. For more than a century, ruling power in Colombia has been shared between two political parties, the Conservatives (Partido Conservador, PC) and the Liberals (Partido Liberal, PL), whose rivalry has often led to violence. President Laureano Gómez of the PC, who was elected 'unopposed' in November 1949, ruled as a dictator until his overthrow by a coup in June 1953, when power was seized by Gen. Gustavo Rojas Pinilla. President Rojas established a right-wing dictatorship but, following widespread rioting, he was deposed in May 1957, when a five-man military junta took power. According to official estimates, lawlessness during 1949–58, known as 'La Violencia', caused the deaths of about 280,000 people.

In an attempt to restore peace and stability, the PC and the PL agreed to co-operate in a National Front. Under this arrangement, the presidency was to be held by the PC and the PL in rotation, while cabinet portfolios would be divided equally between the two parties and both would have an equal number of seats in each house of the bicameral Congress. In December 1957, in Colombia's first vote on the basis of universal adult suffrage, this agreement was overwhelmingly approved by a referendum and was subsequently incorporated in Colombia's Constitution, dating from 1886.

In May 1958 the first presidential election under the amended Constitution was won by the National Front candidate, Dr Alberto Lleras Camargo, a PL member who had been President in 1945–46. He took office in August 1958, when the ruling junta relinquished power. As provided by the 1957 agreement, he was succeeded by a member of the PC, Dr Guillermo León Valencia, who was, in turn, succeeded by a PL candidate, Dr Carlos Lleras Restrepo, in 1966.

At the presidential election of 19 April 1970, the National Front candidate, Dr Misael Pastrana Borrero (PC) narrowly defeated Gen. Rojas, the former dictator, who campaigned as leader of the Alianza Nacional Popular (ANAPO), with policies that had considerable appeal for the poorer sections of the population. At elections to Congress, held simultaneously, the National Front lost its majority in each of the two houses, while ANAPO became the main opposition group in each. The result of the presidential election was challenged by supporters of ANAPO, who demonstrated against alleged electoral fraud, and an armed wing of the party, the Movimiento 19 de Abril (M-19), began to organize guerrilla activity against the Government. It was joined by dissident members of a pro-Soviet guerrilla group, the Fuerzas Armadas Revolucionarias de Colombia (FARC), which had been established in 1966.

The bipartisan form of government ended formally with the presidential and legislative elections of April 1974, although the 1974–78 Cabinet remained subject to the parity agreement. The PC and the PL together won an overwhelming majority of seats in Congress, and support for ANAPO was greatly reduced. The presidential election was won by the PL candidate, Dr Alfonso López Michelsen, who received 56% of the total votes.

At elections to Congress in February 1978, the PL won a clear majority in both houses, and in June the PL candidate, Dr Julio César Turbay Ayala, won the presidential election. President Turbay continued to observe the National Front agreement, and attempted to address the problems of urban terrorism and drugs-trafficking. In early 1982 the guerrillas suffered heavy losses after successful counter-insurgency operations, combined with the activities of a new anti-guerrilla group which was associated with drugs-smuggling enterprises, the Muerte a Secuestradores (MAS, Death to Kidnappers), whose targets later became trade union leaders, academics and human rights activists.

At congressional elections in March 1982, the PL maintained its majority in both houses. In the presidential election in May, the PC candidate, Dr Belisario Betancur Cuartas, received the most votes, benefiting from a division within the PL. President Betancur, who took office in August, declared a broad amnesty for guerrillas in November, reconvened the Peace Commission (first established in 1981) and ordered an investigation into the MAS. An internal pacification campaign, which was begun in November, met with only moderate success. Despite the Peace Commission's successful negotiation of cease-fire agreements with the FARC, the M-19 group (now operating as a left-wing guerrilla movement) and the Ejército Popular de Liberación (EPL) during 1984, factions of all three groups which were opposed to the truce continued to conduct guerrilla warfare against the Government. In May 1984 the Government's campaign for internal peace was severely hampered by the assassination of the Minister of Justice, Rodrigo Lara Bonilla. His murder was regarded as a consequence of his energetic attempts to eradicate the flourishing drugs industry, and Colombia's leading drugs dealers were implicated in the killing. The Government immediately declared a nation-wide state of siege and announced its intention to enforce its hitherto unobserved extradition treaty with the USA.

Relations between the M-19 and the armed forces deteriorated during 1985, and in June the M-19 formally withdrew from the cease-fire agreement, accusing the armed forces of attempting to sabotage the truce. In November a dramatic siege by the M-19 at the Palace of Justice in the capital, during which more than 100 people (including 41 guerrillas and 11 judges) were killed, resulted in severe public criticism of the Government and the armed forces for their handling of events. Negotiations with the M-19 were suspended indefinitely.

At congressional elections in March 1986, the traditional wing of the PL secured a clear victory over the PC and obtained 49% of the votes cast. The Unión Patriótica (UP), formed by the FARC in 1985, won seats in both houses of Congress. At the presidential election in May, Dr Virgilio Barco Vargas, candidate of the PL, was elected President with 58% of the votes cast. The large majority that the PL secured at both elections obliged the PC to form the first formal opposition to a government for 30 years.

Attempts by the new administration to address the problems of political violence and the cultivation and trafficking of illicit drugs enjoyed little success during 1986–87. Hopes that an indefinite cease-fire agreement, concluded between the FARC and the Government in March 1986, would facilitate the full participation of the UP in the political process were largely frustrated by the Government's failure to respond effectively to a campaign of assassinations of UP members, conducted by paramilitary 'death squads' during 1985–87, which resulted in an estimated 450 deaths. The crisis was compounded in October 1987 by the decision of six guerrilla groups, including the FARC, the Ejército de Liberación Nacional (ELN) and the M-19, to form a joint front, the Coordinadora Guerrillera Simón Bolívar (CGSB). Although in 1987 the Government authorized an extension of police powers against drugs dealers, its efforts were severely hampered by the Colombian Supreme Court's rulings, in December 1986 and June 1987, that Colombia's extradition treaty with the USA was unconstitutional.

In mid-1988 the Comisión de Convivencia Democrática (Commission of Democratic Cohabitation) was established, with the aim of holding further meetings between all sides in the internal conflict in Colombia. Moreover, in September President Barco announced a peace initiative, composed of three phases: pacification; transition; and definitive reintegration into the democratic system. Under the plan, the Government was committed to entering into a dialogue with those guerrilla groups that renounced violence and intended to resume civilian life. However, violence continued to escalate, and in December it was estimated that some 18,000 murders had occurred in Colombia in 1988, of which at least 3,600 were attributed to political motives or related to drugs-trafficking.

In January 1989 the Government and the M-19 concluded an agreement to initiate direct dialogue between the Government, all political parties in Congress and the CGSB. In March the M-19 and the Government signed a seven-point document providing for the reintegration of the guerrillas within Colombian society. In the same month, the ELN, the EPL and the FARC publicly confirmed their willingness to participate in peace talks with the Government; in July the leading guerrilla groups (including the M-19) held a summit meeting, at which they agreed to the formation of a commission, which was to draft proposals for a peace dialogue with the Government. In September the M-19 announced that it had reached agreement with the Government on a peace treaty, under which its members were to demobilize and disarm in exchange for a full pardon. In addition, the movement was to enter the political mainstream; in October the M-19 was formally constituted as a political party, and its leader, Carlos Pizarro León Gómez, was named presidential candidate for the movement. By March 1990 all M-19 guerrilla forces had surrendered their weapons. In exchange for firm commitments from the Barco administration that a referendum would be held to decide the question of constitutional reform and that proposals for comprehensive changes to the electoral law would be introduced in Congress, members of the M-19 were guaranteed a general amnesty, reintegration into civilian life and full political participation in forthcoming elections.

The increasingly destabilizing influence of the drugs cartels, meanwhile, continued to undermine government initiatives. The murder, in August 1989, of the popular PL politician Luis Galán Sarmiento, an outspoken critic of the drugs-traffickers, was the latest in a series of assassinations of prominent Colombians, ascribed to the drugs cartels of Cali and Medellín, and was widely deplored, prompting President Barco to introduce emergency measures, including the reactivation of Colombia's extradition treaty with the USA. The US administration requested the arrest by the Colombian authorities of 12 leading drugs-traffickers, popularly known as the 'Extraditables', who responded to the USA's request by issuing a declaration of 'total war' against the Government and all journalists, judges and trade unionists opposed to their activities.

At the congressional and municipal elections in March 1990 the PL won 72 of the 114 seats in the Senate and an estimated 60% of the 199 contested seats in the House of Representatives, as well as regaining the important mayorships of Bogotá and Medellín. Ballot papers had also presented the opportunity to vote for the convening of a National Constituent Assembly (a measure which was heavily endorsed) and the selection procedure for the PL's presidential candidate, from which César Gaviria Trujillo emerged as a clear winner, with 60% of the votes cast.

Bernardo Jaramillo, the presidential candidate of the UP (who had secured the only left-wing seat in the Senate), was assassinated by a hired gunman at Bogotá airport later in March 1990, and in April Carlos Pizarro became the third presidential candidate to be killed by hired assassins since August 1989; he was shot dead aboard an aircraft on a domestic flight. Pizarro was replaced by Antonio Navarro Wolff as presidential candidate for the M-19, in conjunction with the recently established Convergencia Democrática (later Alianza Democrática), an alliance of 13 (mainly left-wing) groups and factions. Although responsibility for the murder of Pizarro was officially ascribed to the Medellín drugs cartels (as in the case of Jaramillo), spokesmen representing the cartels strenuously denied the allegations, leading to further speculation that both men had been the victims of political extremists.

A presidential election was held on 27 May 1990. César Gaviria Trujillo of the PL, who had been the most vociferous opponent of the drugs cartels among the surviving candidates, was proclaimed the winner, with 47% of the votes cast, ahead of Alvaro Gómez Hurtado of the conservative Movimiento de Salvación Nacional (MSN), with 24%. Antonio Navarro Wolff of the Alianza Democrática—M-19 (ADM-19) received 13% of the votes. Voters were also required to indicate support for, or opposition to, more detailed proposals for the creation of a National Constituent Assembly in a *de facto* referendum held simultaneously with the presidential ballot. Some 90% of voters indicated their approval of the proposal.

Gaviria's Cabinet, which was announced shortly before his inauguration on 7 August 1990, was described as a cabinet of 'national unity' and comprised seven members of the PL, four of the Partido Social Conservador Colombiano (PSC) and, most surprisingly, Navarro Wolff, who was appointed Minister of Public Health. President Gaviria emphasized, however, that the diversity in composition of the Cabinet did not represent the installation of a coalition government.

In his inaugural address in August 1990, President Gaviria confirmed his administration's commitment to continuing the strenuous efforts to combat drugs-trafficking, having previously made comprehensive changes to police and military personnel in an apparent attempt to strengthen the Government's resistance to infiltration by the cartels. In October the Government proposed an initiative by which some articles of law would be relaxed and others not invoked (including the extradition treaty) for suspected drugs-traffickers who were prepared to surrender to the authorities. By early 1991 Jorge Luis Ochoa (who had narrowly avoided extradition in 1987) and two brothers, members of one of Medellín's most notorious cartels and all sought by US courts for drugs-related offences in the USA, had surrendered. In January 1991 the deaths of two hostages, who had been held by the 'Extraditables', threatened to undermine the recent success of the Government's latest initiative.

In October 1990 the creation of the National Constituent Assembly was declared constitutionally acceptable by the Supreme Court, and later in the month Navarro Wolff resigned the health portfolio in order to head the list of candidates representing the ADM-19 in elections to the Assembly which took place in December. Candidates for the ADM-19 secured around 27% of the votes cast and 19 of the 70 contested Assembly seats, forcing the ruling PL (with a total of 24 seats) and the Conservatives (with a combined total of 20 seats) to seek support from the ADM-19 members and seven elected independents (including two members of the Evangelical Church and two representatives of indigenous Indian groups) for the successful enactment of reform proposals.

In February 1991 the five-month session of the National Constituent Assembly was inaugurated. The composition of the Assembly had been expanded from 70 to 73 members in order to incorporate three invited members of former guerrilla groupings (two from the EPL and one from the Partido Revolucionario de Trabajadores—PRT) and was later expanded further to accommodate a representative of the Comando Quintín Lame. By June a political pact had been negotiated between President Gaviria and representatives of the three largest parties within the Assembly (the PL, the ADM-19 and the MSN), and an agreement was reached that, in order to facilitate the process of political and constitutional renovation, Congress should be dissolved prematurely. The Assembly subsequently voted to dismiss Congress in early July, pending new congressional and gubernatorial elections, to be conducted in October 1991 (although congressional elections had not been scheduled to take place until 1994). Incumbent government ministers and members of the National Constituent Assembly, which was itself to be dissolved on 5 July, were declared to be ineligible for congressional office.

At midnight on 5–6 July 1991 the new Constitution became effective. At the same time, the state of siege, which had been imposed in 1984 in response to the escalation in political and drugs-related violence, was ended. Although the new Constitution preserved the existing institutional framework of a president and a bicameral legislature (reduced in size to a 102-seat Senate and a 161-seat House of Representatives), considerable emphasis was placed upon provisions to encourage greater political participation and to restrict electoral corruption and misrepresentation. The Constitution also identified and sought to protect a comprehensive list of civil liberties. The duration of the state of siege was to be restricted to 90 days (only to be extended with the approval of the Senate). The judiciary was to be restructured with the creation of the posts of Public Prosecutor and Defender of the People (Defensor del Pueblo).

All marriages were to be placed under civil jurisdiction, with the guaranteed right to divorce. Most controversially, extradition of Colombian nationals was to be prohibited (see below). While the Constitution was welcomed enthusiastically by the majority of Colombians, reservations were expressed that clauses relating to the armed forces remained largely unchanged and that provisions which recognized the democratic rights of indigenous groups did not extend to their territorial claims.

Relations with the Medellín cartel improved considerably following the release, in May 1991, of two remaining hostages, and in June, following the decision to prohibit constitutionally the practice of extradition, the Government's efforts were rewarded with the surrender of Pablo Escobar, the supposed head of the Medellín cartel. Fourteen charges were later brought against Escobar, including several of murder, kidnapping and terrorism. In July spokesmen for the Medellín drugs cartel announced that its military operations were to be suspended and that the 'Extraditables' were to be disbanded. Hopes that Escobar's surrender might precipitate a decline in drugs-related violence were frustrated by reports that Escobar was continuing to direct the operations of the Medellín cocaine cartels from his purpose-built prison at Envigado, and by the emergence of the powerful Cali drugs cartel, which was expected to compensate for any shortfall in the supply of illicit drugs resulting from the demise of the Medellín cartel.

Congressional and gubernatorial elections, conducted in October 1991, were distinguished by a high level of voter apathy, attributed to the busy electoral schedule of the previous 18 months. The Liberals, who presented a confusing number of electoral lists, were most successful, with a clear majority of seats in each chamber of Congress, and victory in the gubernatorial elections in 18 of the 27 contested departments. The traditional Conservative opposition suffered from a division in their support between the PSC, the MSN and the Nueva Fuerza Democrática, securing around one-quarter of the seats in both houses between them. The ADM-19 received only 10% of the votes cast (compared with 27% in December 1990), equivalent to nine seats in the Senate and 15 seats in the House of Representatives.

Meanwhile, in February 1990 the Government had established the National Council for Normalization, in an attempt to repeat the success of recent peace initiatives with the M-19 in negotiations with other revolutionary groups. The EPL announced the end of its armed struggle in August 1990 and joined the political mainstream (retaining the Spanish acronym EPL as the Partido de Esperanza, Paz y Libertad), along with the Comando Quintín Lame and the PRT, in early to mid-1991. Attempts to negotiate with the FARC and the ELN, however, proved fruitless, and violent clashes between the remaining guerrilla groups (now co-ordinating actions as the Coordinadora Nacional Guerrillera Simón Bolívar—CNGSB) and security forces persisted in the early 1990s.

The results of municipal elections, conducted in March 1992, represented a significant reversal for the PL and for the M-19. In the capital, support for candidates for council seats, from both parties, was undermined by the popularity of two former PL ministers who had campaigned as vociferous opponents of recent government policy regarding drugs-trafficking and urban terrorism. Coalition candidates proved most successful in mayoral contests to several major cities including Medellín, Cali and Barranquilla. In June President Gaviria effected a comprehensive reorganization of the Cabinet, while maintaining a multi-party composition, in preparation for the new congressional term, scheduled to begin in July. In January 1993 the Minister of Government, Humberto de la Calle, resigned in order to prepare for the forthcoming presidential election.

An escalation in guerrilla activity during May and September 1992 prompted the Government to intensify anti-insurgency measures and to exclude the possibility of future peace negotiations with rebel groups. In October Congress approved government proposals for an increased counterinsurgency budget and for the creation of new armed units to combat terrorism. The Government's rejection of any agenda for renewed negotiations provoked an intensification of the conflict, and this, together with a resurgence of drugs-related violent incidents following the death of the supposed military commander of the Medellín cartel, prompted President Gaviria, in November, to declare a 90-day state of emergency or 'internal disturbance', thereby extending wide-ranging powers to the security forces and imposing restrictions on media coverage. In late November the M-19 announced that, in view of the Government's uncompromising armed response to recent internal disturbances, the party was to withdraw from the Government and resume an active opposition role. Later in the month a new Minister of Public Health was duly appointed to replace the outgoing M-19 minister.

The security situation continued to deteriorate during 1993, following increased activity from guerrilla groups in response to the capture of several prominent rebel leaders in January and February, and the internecine activities of the drugs cartels (see below). In February the Government announced a significant increase in its budget allocation for security, and in April it was revealed that the duration of terms of imprisonment awarded for acts of terrorism resulting in death or injury was to be doubled. The state of internal disturbance was extended for 90 days in February, and again in November. Attempts by the Government and the ELN to negotiate a truce were frustrated by a perceived lack of commitment to compromise on both sides, and the prospects for future successful discussions were severely undermined by the insistence of security forces that ELN members were responsible for the murder of the Vice-President of the Senate, Darío Londoño Carmona, in November. In December negotiations with the Corriente de Renovación Socialista (CRS), a dissident faction of the ELN more disposed to political assimilation, produced an agreement for the guerrillas' reincorporation into civilian life and transformation into a legitimate political force. However, agreement had been reached somewhat tentatively, owing to the experience of other former guerrilla groups which had effected a similar move to the political mainstream only to be persecuted by less compromising guerrilla factions. (In January 1994 more than 30 EPL members were murdered, allegedly by FARC activists, during a demonstration in the Urabá region.) However, in April 1994, under the supervision of international observers, the CRS duly surrendered its weapons, and was subsequently awarded two seats in the newly-elected House of Representatives (see below). In January the ELN claimed responsibility for an unsuccessful bomb attack on the Minister of Finance and Public Credit.

An intensification of drugs-related violence in the capital during early 1993 was attributed to an attempt by Pablo Escobar (who had escaped from prison in July 1992) to force the Government to negotiate more favourable conditions for his surrender, and prompted the formation of a vigilante group, Pepe (Perseguidos por Pablo Escobar—those Persecuted by Pablo Escobar), which launched a campaign of retaliatory violence against Escobr's family, associates and and property. Pepe was thought to number among its members several of Escobar's disgruntled rivals from the Medellín cartel. A simultaneous and sustained assault by Pepe and by the security forces against the remnants of the Medellín cartel resulted in the death and surrender of many notable cartel members, culminating in the death of Escobar himself in Medellín, in December, during an exchange of fire with security forces attempting to effect his arrest. In late December it was reported that the Government was again considering the negotiation of a rehabilitation programme for prominent members of the Cali cartel, following their offer to dismantle all illicit operations in return for lenient prison sentences and negligible financial penalties.

The dispatch of a contingent of US troops to the Valle del Cauca region in December 1993, described as a humanitarian mission to improve communications and health and education facilities, aroused widespread political outrage from the Government's opponents, who interpreted the accommodation of the troops as capitulation to US demands for military participation in the region, in order to ensure the destruction of the Cali cartel. By late February 1994, however, the troops had been withdrawn, the Council of State having ruled earlier in the month that President Gaviria had abused his authority by endorsing their deployment prior to consultation with the Senate. Relations with the USA deteriorated further during March following US criticism of the lenient terms of surrender being offered to leaders of the Cali cartel by the Colombian authorities. A suspension of co-operation with regard to the exchange of evidence relating to drugs offences ensued. The situation was exacerbated in May following a Constitutional Court ruling which recognized the legal right of the individual to possess small quantities of drugs (including cocaine) for personal use. An unsuccessful attempt by Gaviria to amend the ruling by emergency decree, together with his statement of intent to revoke the decision by means of a referendum, did little to allay US fears that the Colombian judiciary was attempting to destroy the wealth of the cartels by legalizing the trade in illicit drugs.

Changes to the Cabinet were effected in February 1993, after the dismissal of the Minister of Agriculture and Livestock following allegations of ministerial misconduct during land purchase proceedings, and in March 1993, January 1994 and March 1994, when ministers resigned in order to participate in electoral campaigns for the forthcoming polls. Colombia's first Minister of the Environment was appointed in January 1994.

The results of congressional and local elections conducted in March 1994 represented a serious reversal for the political left in Colombia and re-established the traditional two-party dominance of the PL and the PSC. The elections were particularly disappointing for the ADM-19, whose congressional representation was reduced from 13 seats to two in the House of Representatives and from nine seats to just one in the Senate. The PL retained a comfortable congressional majority. No candidate secured the margin of victory necessary to be declared outright winner in the presidential election conducted on 29 May, and a second poll was contested on 19 June between Ernesto Samper Pizano (PL) and Andrés Pastrana Arango (PSC), who had been placed first and second respectively in the first round. The similarity in the two contestants' campaign manifestos (advocating economic liberalization, job creation and improved social welfare) resulted in a second close contest. Samper was eventually declared President-elect, with 50.9% of the valid votes cast. Samper was inaugurated on 7 August and a new Cabinet was installed simultaneously. PL candidates were also successful in departmental and municipal elections conducted in October, securing 22 of the 32 contested governorships. However, the PL lost control of a number of crucial cities including Cali, Medellín and the capital.

Shortly after President Samper's inauguration, allegations emerged that his election campaign had been partly funded by contributions from the Cali cartel. Tape-recordings of conversations which appeared to provide evidence that contact had at least been made with the cartels were subsequently dismissed by the Public Prosecutor as insufficient proof of such contributions actually having been made. In July 1994 a similar recording, which appeared to implicate the Colombian Chief of National Police in the payment of a bribe by the Cali cartel, prompted the US Senate to vote to make the disbursement of future aid to Colombia dependent on an assessment of the level of its co-operation in anti-drugs programmes. The existence of the tape-recordings was widely attributed to the US Drugs Enforcement Agency (DEA) which the Colombian media accused of fomenting mistrust in an attempt to ensure that the new administration would pursue an uncompromising anti-drugs policy. Restrictions were subsequently imposed on DEA operations and access to information in Colombia. However, it was hoped that bilateral relations would improve following the appointment of a new Public Prosecutor and a new Chief of the National Police in late 1994, and the House of Representatives' rejection, in December, of the 'narco bill' which sought to limit the powers of the authorities to confiscate funds and assets proceeding from illicit activities and which had received support from a congressional committee in November.

CNGSB offensives during 1994 were launched to coincide with campaigning for the March legislative elections, and to disrupt the weeks preceding the transfer of power from Gaviria to Samper in early August. Fighting between guerrillas and the security forces resulted in numerous deaths on both sides and considerable damage was inflicted on power installations and the transport infrastructure. Prospects for the swift negotiation of a peace agreement between the new administration and the CNGSB were immediately undermined by the murder of the UP's Manuel Cepeda Vargas (the only left-wing member of the Senate) and deteriorated as guerrilla activities intensified in late 1994. However, in November Samper complied with a guerrilla request that rebel leaders currently in detention should be moved from military installations to civilian prisons, and also declared the Government's willingness to enter into unconditional dialogue with the guerrillas, preferably outside of Colombia.

Meanwhile, during 1994 the Government was subject to intense international pressure to formalize a greater commitment to respect for human rights, following a series of revelations in which members of the security forces were implicated in abuses of human rights, and the publication of a report by Amnesty International in which it was claimed that the vast majority of infringements of human rights in Colombia were perpetrated by the armed forces and associated paramilitary groups. In September the Minister of the Interior, Horacio Serpa Uribe, announced an initiative to address the human rights crisis, including plans to reform the National Police and to disband all paramilitary units. In September 1995 Brig.-Gen. Alvaro Velandia Hurtado was removed from active duty by the Government, after a report by the office of the Prosecutor for Human Rights had pronounced him responsible for the detention and murder of a prominent M-19 member in 1987. Velandia's dismissal marked the first such action undertaken by the Government against senior army personnel in response to abuses of human rights.

In February 1995, in the context of the US Government's persistence in attaching preconditions to the disbursement of financial aid to Colombia, President Samper reiterated his commitment to the eradication of all illegal drugs-related activities in the country. A number of initiatives to address the problem were launched in Cali, resulting in the capture of the head of the Cali cartel, Gilberto Rodríguez Orejuela, and four other cartel leaders in mid-1995. Meanwhile, in April nine prominent PL politicians were suspended from the party pending their investigation by the office of the Public Prosecutor, following allegations of their maintaining links with the Cali drugs cartel. In the following months it was confirmed that the Comptroller-General and the Attorney-General were also to be the subject of investigation as a result of similar allegations, while Samper's former election campaign treasurer, Santiago Medina, was arrested on charges related to the processing of drugs cartel contributions through Samper's election fund. In August the Minister of National Defence, Fernando Botero Zea, resigned, having been implicated in the affair by evidence submitted to the authorities by Medina. Medina also insisted that Samper had been fully aware of the origin of the funds, prompting opposition demands for the President's resignation. Samper's former campaign manager, Juan Manuel Avella, was arrested in September, in which month Samper protested his own innocence before a congressional accusations committee. In October the Constitutional Court confirmed the jurisdiction of the congressional committee to conduct further investigations into the allegations.

In May 1995 the Government extended an offer of participation in legislative and consultative processes to the FARC, in the hope of securing their commitment to surrender arms. While the FARC general secretariat responded positively to the initial proposal, further progress was to be dependent on the Government's successful execution of its stated intention to demilitarize the sensitive north-eastern region of La Uribe. A Government proposal for the exchange of armed struggle for a political agenda, issued to the ELN and dissident groups of the EPL and the M-19 at the same time, received a more cautious response from the guerrillas. However, all negotiations were severely hampered by renewed FARC and ELN offensives in late May. An escalation in the number of acts of violence perpetrated by guerrilla forces and by paramilitary defence groups in the north-western Urabá region had resulted in the deaths during 1995 of some 600 civilians (mainly banana plantation workers) by August, prompting Samper to declare a state of internal disturbance for a 90-day period. In October, however, the Constitutional Court rejected the terms of the state of emergency, forcing the President to seek immediate congressional approval for alternative powers to extend the period of detention of some 3,500 suspected insurgents. Following the assassination, in November, of a prominent Conservative politician, Alvaro Gómez Hurtado, the President immediately declared a new 90-day state of internal disturbance. Responsibility for the assassination was claimed by the little known Movimiento por la Dignidad de Colombia, an organization which, in September, had claimed responsibility for a failed attempt on the life of Samper's lawyer. (In April 1996 the group kidnapped the brother of former President Gaviria and demanded that the latter resign as Secretary-General of the Organization of American States—OAS; the hostage was released in June, even though the demand was not met.) However, negotiations between the President and the PSC leader, Andrés Pastrana Arango, for a 'national agreement against violence' were frustrated by the latter's insistence that the establishment of an independent commission of inquiry into the allegations of Samper's campaign funding by the Cali drugs cartel should be a precondition to any political negotiation. Increased emergency powers for regional evacuations were assumed by the President in November as part of an initiative to re-establish the military supremacy of the armed forces in all regions.

In December 1995 the congressional accusations committee voted against the initiation of a full-scale inquiry into allegations of Samper's impropriety in the use of funds proceeding from drugs cartels, on the grounds of insufficient evidence at that time. The repercussions of the scandal, however, were considered to have severely undermined the political integrity of the Government, both at home and abroad. Relations between the US Government and the Samper administration deteriorated dramatically during 1995, culminating in allegations—made by official sources in Colombia—that the US Government was attempting to destabilize the administration through the covert actions of the DEA. (In September the Minister of the Interior, Horacio Serpa Uribe, had accused the DEA of involvement in a failed attempt to assassinate President Samper's lawyer, earlier in the month.)

In January 1996 Botero reiterated Medina's claim that Samper had been in full possession of the facts regarding the cartel's funding of his election campaign, prompting the PSC to announce an immediate suspension of co-operation with the Government and the resignation of the Ministers of Transport and of Foreign Trade, two of the four incumbent PSC members of the Cabinet. (The PL Minister of Public Health also resigned, in protest at the Government's failure to refute the mounting evidence of widespread corruption which had been presented.) Samper subsequently urged Congress to reopen investigations into his involvement in the affair, seeking to demonstrate his innocence. Evidence collected by the Public Prosecutor, Alfonso Valdivieso, was submitted to the accusations committee in February, together with four formal charges to be brought against the President, including that of illegal enrichment. Later in the month congressional commissions of both parliamentary chambers decided to launch a new and public investigation into the funding of Samper's election campaign. In March Samper testified before the accusations committee and denied further allegations made by Medina and Botero that he had contrived the plan to solicit funding from the Cali cartel; however, he did concede that the cartel had part-financed the campaign, albeit without his knowledge.

In March 1996, in the context of the Supreme Court's investigation into the financing of Samper's election campaign, the Ministers of the Interior, Foreign Affairs and Communications were summoned to face charges of illegal enrichment. In the following month Rodrigo Pardo García-Peña (who had since announced his temporary retirement as Minister of Foreign Affairs) admitted that he had been aware of the Cali cartel's role in the financing of the campaign. In May the charges of illegal enrichment against the three ministers were abandoned, although they were formally accused of the lesser charge of deliberately concealing the use of illicit funds in the campaign. Meanwhile, in April the Supreme Court took the unprecedented step of requesting that the Senate suspend the Attorney-General, Orlando Vásquez Velásquez, in order that he face charges of obstructing the course of justice (he had allegedly fabricated evidence to discredit the Public Prosecutor). In October Vásquez Velásquez was found guilty of the charges; he was dismissed as Attorney-General and banned from holding public office for a five-year period. Moreover, in December 1997 he was sentenced to eight years' imprisonment on drugs charges. Also in October 1996 it was confirmed that Botero would serve a 63-month prison sentence after pleading guilty to charges of illegal enrichment and forging a private document. (In July Medina and a former PL Senator, María Izquierdo, were found guilty of illegal enrichment and imprisoned for their involvement in the Samper affair.)

In May 1996 the PL-dominated accusations committee voted in favour of recommending that the House of Representatives abandon its investigation into Samper's conduct during the presidential campaign, arguing that there was insufficient evidence to implicate him. In the following month the House of Representatives (also dominated by the PL) voted in favour of exonerating Samper of all penal and political responsibility regarding the election campaign funding. The US administration immediately condemned the result and threatened to impose trade sanctions against Colombia. (In March the US Congress had refused to 'certify' Colombia as a co-operating nation with regard to US anti-drugs activities after a leading Cali cartel member escaped from prison.) In July, following the release of a prominent Medellín cartel member after only five-and-a-half years in prison, the US Government accused Samper of failing to take appropriate measures to deter drugs-trafficking and revoked his visa to travel to the USA.

Meanwhile, civil unrest and guerrilla activity continued during 1996. The state of internal disturbance was extended for a further 90 days in January, and then again in April following a CNGSB-organized nation-wide 'armed industrial strike', which had resulted in as many as 40 deaths. In March a FARC attack on a drugs-control police unit had renewed speculation of links between guerrilla groups and the drugs cartels. Moreover, it was suggested that a major offensive launched in August by FARC and ELN rebels (resulting in as many as 100 fatalities) had been deliberately timed to coincide with large-scale protests by coca growers demanding a review of the coca eradication programme, particularly the use of aerial spraying. Serious clashes between guerrillas and the security forces continued in September, prompting the Government to announce the imminent mobilization of thousands of reserves. Although 26 members of the FARC and some 250 dissident EPL rebels surrendered to the authorities during September and October, violent skirmishes continued unabated, and disaffected members of the ELN were reported to have regrouped as the Ejército Revolucionario del Pueblo. Some 780 guerrillas and 500 members of the armed forces were estimated to have been killed during 1996.

In September 1996 Samper's credibility was undermined by the resignation of the Vice-President, Humberto de la Calle, who appealed to the President to renounce his office in order to prevent the country from descending into 'total chaos'. (Congress subsequently elected Carlos Lemos-Simmonds as the new Vice-President.) Later in September Samper was again humiliated by the discovery of 3.7 kg of heroin aboard the aircraft in which he had been scheduled to fly to the USA (using a diplomat visa) to attend a meeting of the UN General Assembly. (A subsequent investigation into the drugs seizure did not implicate the President in any way.) In an apparent attempt to appease the US administration, Samper announced that Colombia's Congress would debate whether to amend the Constitution in order to permit the extradition of Colombian nationals. Moreover, in December Congress approved controversial legislation to allow for the confiscation of drugs-traffickers' assets. (Many members of the congressional constitutional committees had been reluctant to adopt or even debate the law for fear of reprisals from the drugs cartels.) In addition, the authorities continued their campaign to destroy the drugs cartels in Colombia, arresting six prominent Cali cartel members during 1996.

In early 1997 the Samper administration encountered increasing pressure from the USA to address the issues of drugs-trafficking and corruption. The appointment of Guillermo Alberto González as Colombia's Minister of National Defence was condemned by the USA, which alleged that he had maintained links with drugs-traffickers, notably with Justo Pastor Perafán, who currently was sought by the authorities. In March González resigned as a result of the allegations; in the same month Perafán was arrested in Venezuela. In late February, meanwhile, the USA again refused to 'certify' Colombia, claiming that there had been a substantial increase in the production of illicit drugs in that country during 1996. The US administration had also been critical of the lenient prison sentences imposed on two notorious drugs-traffickers in January. In response, Samper announced the temporary suspension of Colombia's drugs-crop eradication programme. The programme was resumed shortly afterwards, but relations with the USA remained strained until August, when it agreed to grant Colombia US $70m. in military aid to counter drugs-trafficking in return for Colombia's commitment to investigate reports of human rights violations. Although legislation permitting the extradition of Colombian nationals sought for criminal offences abroad was finally approved in November, it was strongly criticized by he US administration as it would not have retroactive effect.

Meanwhile, in January 1997 President Samper risked civil unrest by decreeing a state of economic emergency. In the following month, after an eight-day nation-wide strike, the Government agreed to substantial pay awards for public-sector employees and to the establishment of a joint commission with labour unions to analyze the effects of its privatization plans. In March the Constitutional Court legally annulled the economic emergency, obliging Samper to seek congressional approval for the measures announced in January, and prompting him to threaten legislation that would limit the Court's jurisdiction.

The activities of guerrilla and paramilitary groups in Colombia intensified during 1997. In May the Government agreed to the demilitarization of part of the Caquetá department for a 32-day period in order to secure the release of 70 members of the armed forces captured by the FARC in August 1996 and January 1997. The release of the captives in mid-June received widespread media coverage and led to speculation that a peace agreement might be imminent. Notably, President Samper acknowledged that paramilitary groups had increasingly instigated violent attacks (sometimes with the tacit support of the security forces) and agreed that they should be included in peace negotiations. In the following month, after a series of assaults on the security forces by FARC and ELN rebels, Samper reorganized the military and police command, replacing the Commander-in-Chief of the Armed Forces, Gen. Harold Bedoya Pizzaro (who had vehemently opposed negotiating with the guerrillas), with Gen. Manuel José Bonett Locarno, hitherto Chief of Staff of the Army. In addition, Samper presented legislation to Congress that would lead to the establishment of a national peace commission.

In mid-1997 there was a marked increase in violent attacks by guerrilla and paramilitary groups, apparently intent on sabotaging departmental and municipal elections which were scheduled to be held in late October. In the months preceding the elections more than 40 candidates were killed, some 200 were kidnapped and as many as 1,900 were persuaded to withdraw after receiving death threats. Voting was cancelled in numerous municipalities, while in August the vulnerability of the Government to rebel attacks was emphasized by the assassination (most probably by the ELN) of a PL senator who was a close ally of President Samper. Meanwhile, reports of secret preliminary peace negotiations between representatives of the Government and the FARC were undermined by a major military offensive in the Llanos del Yarí region in September, in which 652 FARC guerrillas were killed and a further 1,600 were captured. The Government's subsequent conciliatory gestures to the guerrillas, including a promise by the President to submit legislation to Congress granting an amnesty in return for the signing of a peace accord, were met with little enthusiasm by the FARC and the ELN. In October Samper categorically rejected a peace proposal presented by Juan Manuel Santos (a possible PL presidential candidate), requiring his resignation followed by the establishment of a constituent assembly charged with commencing peace negotiations with the guerrillas.

Departmental and municipal elections took place on 26 October 1997, despite the campaign of intimidation by guerrilla and paramilitary groups. According to preliminary results, the PL won 19 of the 32 departmental governorships (the PSC obtained four) and took control of 412 local councils (compared with 301 by the PSC). An independent Liberal won the mayorship of the capital, while a PSC candidate became mayor of Medellín. There were reports of widespread electoral fraud and of false voter registration, and opposition parties claimed that the official rate of voter participation (some 49% of the electorate) was unrealistically high. Meanwhile, in early November the ELN secured significant concessions from the Government in return for the release of two OAS election observers abducted in mid-October. During November there was a sharp increase in attacks by paramilitary groups; some 47 people were killed in an eight-day period.

Changes to the Cabinet took place on numerous occasions during 1997, affecting most of the principal ministries. In May Horacio Serpa Uribe, a prominent member of the PL and a close ally of President Samper, resigned as Minister of the Interior; shortly afterwards he announced his intention to contest the presidential election, scheduled to be held in May 1998. Serpa was considered a strong contender for the presidency, although his candidature was opposed by the US administration as he remained under investigation for alleged links with drugs-traffickers and for his involvement in Samper's 1994 presidential campaign. (Meanwhile, in July Juan Manuel Avella, Samper's former campaign manager, was sentenced to more than six years' imprisonment for personal illicit enrichment and forgery in connection with the affair.) Earlier in May the resignation of Alfonso Valdivieso, the Public Prosecutor, led to speculation that he also would contest the presidential election; Valdivieso's vigorous investigations into corruption and drugs-trafficking had bolstered his popularity both at home and abroad. Other potential presidential candidates included Gen. Harold Bedoya (the erstwhile Commander-in-Chief of the Armed Forces), Antanas Mockus (a former mayor of Santafé de Bogotá), and Andrés Pastrana Arango, who came second in the 1994 election.

Colombia has a long-standing border dispute with Venezuela. However, relations between the countries improved following the signing, in October 1989, of a border integration agreement, which included a provision on joint co-operation in the campaign to eradicate drugs-trafficking. (A permanent reconciliation commission to investigate the border dispute had been established in March 1989.) In March 1990 the San Pedro Alejandrino agreement, signed by the two countries, sought to initiate the implementation of recommendations made by existing bilateral border commissions and to establish a number of new commissions, including one to examine the territorial claims of both sides. Colombia's efforts to improve relations with Venezuela were hampered by the activities of FARC guerrillas in the border region, although in early 1997 it was reported that negotiations were in progress on settling the maritime boundary between the two countries. In February Colombia and Venezuela signed an agreement to improve border co-operation; however, in April Venezuela deployed 5,000 troops along its frontier with Colombia in an attempt to halt repeated incursions by Colombian guerrillas. In June Panama also announced its intention to station 1,200 soldiers along its border with Colombia to counter an increase in the activities of Colombian guerrilla and paramilitary groups in the country. In 1980 Nicaragua laid claim to the Colombian-controlled islands of Providencia and San Andrés. Colombia has a territorial dispute with Honduras over cays in the San Andrés and Providencia archipelago. In October 1986 the Colombian Senate approved a delimitation treaty of marine and submarine waters in the Caribbean Sea, which had been signed by the Governments of Colombia and Honduras in August.

In April 1991 the ministers with responsibility for foreign affairs of Colombia, Mexico and Venezuela (known as the Group of Three) announced their intention to create a free-trade zone by mid-1994. In October 1993 the Group of Three announced the implementation, as of 1 January 1994, of a 10-year trade liberalization programme.

In December 1991 the leaders of the countries of the Andean Pact agreed to remove trade barriers between their countries in early 1992 and to adopt unified external tariffs by 1993. In March 1993 it was announced that full customs union would take effect from 1 January 1994 (see p. 107). However, subsequent negotiations failed to produce agreement on a common external tariff. In February 1995 a three-level tariff system was implemented to cover 90% of imports (the remainder to be incorporated by 1999). In March 1996 the Presidents of the member nations of the Pact signed the Reform Protocol of the Cartagena Agreement, whereby the Pact was superseded by the Andean Community.

A free trade agreement, the Acuerdo de Complementación Económica (ACE), concluded with Chile in December 1993, took effect from 1 January 1994, and was expected to have eliminated tariffs on most goods by the time of its full implementation on 1 January 1999.

Government

Executive power is exercised by the President (assisted by a Cabinet), who is elected for a four-year term by universal adult suffrage. Legislative power is vested in the bicameral Congress, consisting of the Senate (102 members elected for four years) and the House of Representatives (165 members elected for four years). The country is divided into 32 Departments and one Capital District.

Defence

At 18 years of age, every male (with the exception of students) must present himself as a candidate for military service of between one and two years. In August 1997 the strength of the army was 121,000 (including 63,800 conscripts), the navy 18,000 (including 9,000 marines) and the air force 7,300. The paramilitary police force numbers about 87,000 men. Some 2,200,000m. pesos were allocated to defence expenditure as part of the state budget for 1997.

Economic Affairs

In 1995, according to estimates by the World Bank, Colombia's gross national product (GNP), measured at average 1993–95 prices, was US $70,263m., equivalent to $1,910 per head. During 1985–95, it was estimated, GNP per head increased, in real terms, by 2.8% per year. Over the same period, the population increased by an annual average of 1.8%. Colombia's gross domestic product (GDP) increased, in real terms, by an average of 4.2% per year in 1985–95.

Agriculture (including hunting, forestry and fishing) contributed an estimated 11.1% of GDP in 1996, and employed some 23.5% of the labour force. The principal cash crops are coffee (which accounted for 14.9% of official export earnings in 1996), cocoa, sugar cane, bananas, tobacco, cotton and cut flowers. Rice, cassava, plantains and potatoes are the principal food crops. Timber and beef production are also important. During 1985–95 agricultural GDP increased by an annual average of 3.9%. Growth in agricultural GDP was estimated by the World Bank at 11.1% in 1995.

Industry (including mining, manufacturing, construction and power) employed 23.1% of the labour force in 1995, and contributed an estimated 33.1% of GDP in 1996. During 1985–95 industrial GDP increased by an annual average of 3.9%. The World Bank estimated growth in industrial GDP at 5.9% in 1995.

Mining contributed an estimated 5.4% of GDP in 1996, and employed 0.8% of the labour force in 1995. Petroleum, natural gas, coal, nickel, emeralds and gold are the principal minerals exploited. Silver, platinum, iron, lead, zinc, copper, mercury, limestone and phosphates are also mined.

Manufacturing contributed an estimated 17.1% of GDP in 1996 and employed 15.7% of the labour force in 1995. During 1985–95 manufacturing GDP increased by an annual average of 3.8%. Growth in manufacturing GDP was estimated by the World Bank at 1.0% in 1995. Based on the value of output, the most important branches of manufacturing in 1992 were food products (accounting for 25.4% of the total), chemical products (13.8%), textiles, beverages and transport equipment.

In 1987 hydroelectricity provided about 75% of Colombia's electricity requirements. The country is self-sufficient in petroleum and coal, and minerals accounted for 35.3% of export revenues in 1996.

The services sector contributed an estimated 55.8% of GDP in 1996, and engaged 54.6% of the labour force in 1995. During 1985–95 the combined GDP of the service sectors increased, in real terms, at an estimated average rate of 4.1% per year.

In 1996 Colombia recorded a visible trade deficit of US $2,133m. and there was a deficit of $4,754m. on the current account of the balance of payments. The country's principal trading partner in 1996 was the USA, which (together with Puerto Rico) provided 40.9% of imports and took 39.8% of exports. Other Latin American countries (especially Venezuela, Ecuador, Peru and Mexico), Japan and the European Union are important trading partners. The principal exports in 1996 were minerals (particularly petroleum and its derivatives and coal), coffee, other agricultural products (chiefly cut flowers and bananas), chemicals, textiles and foodstuffs, beverages and tobacco. The principal imports were machinery and transport equipment, chemicals, vegetables and vegetable products, metals, foodstuffs, beverages and tobacco, and minerals. A significant amount of foreign exchange is believed to be obtained from illegal trade in gold, emeralds and, particularly, the drug cocaine: in 1995 it was estimated that some $3,500m. (equivalent to around 4% of GDP) was entering Colombia each year as the proceeds of drugs-trafficking activities.

In 1993 there was a budgetary deficit of 238,200m. pesos in central government spending, equivalent to 0.5% of GDP. Colombia's external debt amounted to US $20,760m. at the end of 1995, of which $12,983m. was long-term public debt. In that year the cost of debt-servicing was equivalent to 25.2% of the value of exports of goods and services. In 1986–96 the average annual rate of inflation was 25.1%. Some 13.6% of the labour force were unemployed in mid-1997.

Colombia is a member of ALADI (see p. 261) and of the Andean Community (see p. 106). Both organizations attempt to increase trade and economic co-operation within the region.

Colombia's principal export commodities are petroleum and coffee, although the export of other agricultural products and manufactured goods has become increasingly important. Unlike most Latin American countries, Colombia avoided the need to reschedule its foreign debt during the 1980s, and in recent years the country has recorded strong economic growth, not least because of the discovery in the early 1990s of significant petroleum reserves. During 1990–94 the Gaviria administration adopted a programme of structural reform, resulting in the liberalization of trade and the reorganization of the public sector. Since 1994 the Samper administration has given priority to increasing public expenditure on social sectors and infrastructure, while it has also pledged to reduce inflation and address the problem of high unemployment. In January 1997, following an unexpected inflow of foreign currency in the previous year and the consequent appreciation of the peso (adversely affecting the country's exports), the Government decreed a state of economic emergency in an attempt to stem the widening budget deficit. However, in February, following a nation-wide strike, the Government was forced to award substantial pay increases to public-sector workers. In addition, the state of economic emergency was ruled unconstitutional in March, prompting the Government to announce a series of new measures in April, including a reduction in value-added tax. An increase in the coffee harvest, combined with a substantial rise in the international price for that commodity, contributed to strong economic growth in the latter half of the year. Meanwhile, the Government altered regulations concerning petroleum and gas exploration and production in an attempt to attract foreign investment to Colombia. Investment in the country had declined, primarily as a result of the continued sabotage of petroleum installations by guerrilla groups.

Social Welfare

There is compulsory social security, paid for by the Government, employers and employees, and administered by the Institute of Social Security. It provides benefits for disability, old age, death, sickness, maternity, industrial accidents and unemployment. Large enterprises are required to provide life insurance schemes for their employees, and there is a comprehensive system of pensions. Implementation of a system of private pension funds (modelled on the AFP system in Chile) was under consideration in 1995. In 1984 there were 23,520 physicians working in Colombia, and in 1980 the country had 849 hospital establishments, with a total of 44,495 beds. Of total expenditure by the central Government in 1996, an estimated 1,309,354m. pesos (8.0%) was for health.

Education

Primary education is free and compulsory for five years, to be undertaken by children between six and 12 years of age. No child may be admitted to secondary school unless these five years have been successfully completed. Secondary education, beginning at the age of 11, lasts for up to six years. Following completion of a first cycle of four years, pupils may pursue a further two years of vocational study, leading to the Bachiller examination. In 1994 the total enrolment at primary schools included 87% of pupils in the relevant age-group, while the comparable ratio for secondary education was 46%. In the late 1990s there were 25 public universities in Colombia. Government expenditure on education in the 1996 budget was 2,950,304m. pesos, representing 18.0% of total spending. The rate of adult illiteracy averaged 19.2% in 1973, but, according to estimates by UNESCO, had declined to 8.7% (males 8.8%; females 8.6%) by 1995.

Public Holidays

1998: 1 January (New Year's Day), 12 January (for Epiphany), 23 March (for St Joseph's Day), 9 April (Maundy Thursday), 10 April (Good Friday), 1 May (Labour Day), 25 May (for Ascension Day), 15 June (for Corpus Christi), 29 June (SS Peter and Paul), 20 July (Independence), 7 August (Battle of Boyacá), 17 August (for Assumption), 12 October (Discovery of America), 2 November (for All Saints' Day), 16 November (for Independence of Cartagena), 8 December (Immaculate Conception), 25 December (Christmas Day).

1999: 1 January (New Year's Day), 11 January (for Epiphany), 22 March (for St Joseph's Day), 1 April (Maundy Thursday), 2 April (Good Friday), 1 May (Labour Day), 17 May (for Ascension Day), 7 June (for Corpus Christi), 5 July (for SS Peter and Paul), 20 July (Independence), 7 August (Battle of Boyacá), 16 August (for Assumption), 18 October (for Discovery of America), 1 November (All Saints' Day), 15 November (for Independence of Cartagena), 8 December (Immaculate Conception), 25 December (Christmas Day).

Weights and Measures

The metric system is in force.

Statistical Survey

Sources (unless otherwise stated): Departamento Administrativo Nacional de Estadística (DANE), Centro Administrativo Nacional (CAN), Avda El Dorado, Apdo Aéreo 80043, Santafé de Bogotá, DC; tel. (1) 222-1100; telex 44573; fax (1) 222-2107; Banco de la República, Carrera 7, No 14-78, Apdo Aéreo 3531, Santafé de Bogotá, DC; tel. (1) 342-1111; telex 044560.

Area and Population

AREA, POPULATION AND DENSITY

Area (sq km)	
Total	1,141,748*
Population (census results)†	
15 October 1985	
Males	14,642,835
Females	14,838,160
Total	29,480,995
24 October 1993	37,664,711
Population (official estimates at mid-year)	
1995	38,814,162
1996	39,510,657
1997	40,214,723
Density (per sq km) at mid-1997	35.2

* 440,831 sq miles.

† Revised figures, including adjustment for underenumeration. The enumerated total was 27,853,436 (males 13,785,523; females 14,067,913) in 1985 and 33,109,840 (males 16,296,539; females 16,813,301) in 1993.

DEPARTMENTS (census of 24 October 1993)

Department	Area (sq km)	Population	Capital (with population)
Amazonas	109,665	56,399	Leticia (30,045)
Antioquia	63,612	4,919,619	Medellín (1,834,881)
Arauca	23,818	185,882	Arauca (59,805)
Atlántico	3,388	1,837,468	Barranquilla (1,090,618)
Bolívar	25,978	1,702,188	Cartagena (747,390)
Boyacá	23,189	1,315,579	Tunja (112,807)
Caldas	7,888	1,055,577	Manizales (345,539)
Caquetá	88,965	367,898	Florencia (107,620)
Casanare	44,640	211,329	Yopal (57,279)
Cauca	29,308	1,127,678	Popayán (207,700)
César	22,905	827,219	Valledupar (278,216)
Chocó	46,530	406,199	Quibdó (122,371)
Córdoba	25,020	1,275,623	Montería (308,506)
Cundinamarca	22,623	1,875,337	Santafé de Bogotá*
Guainía	72,238	28,478	Puerto Inírida (18,270)
La Guajira	20,848	433,361	Riohacha (109,474)
Guaviare	42,327	97,602	San José del Guaviare (48,237)
Huila	19,890	843,798	Neiva (278,350)
Magdalena	23,188	1,127,691	Santa Marta (313,072)
Meta	85,635	618,427	Villavicencio (272,118)
Nariño	33,268	1,443,671	Pasto (331,866)
Norte de Santander	21,658	1,162,474	Cúcuta (538,126)
Putumayo	24,885	264,291	Mocoa (25,910)
Quindío	1,845	495,212	Armenia (258,990)
Risaralda	4,140	844,184	Pereira (401,909)
San Andrés y Providencia Islands	44	61,040	San Andrés (56,361)
Santander del Sur	30,537	1,811,740	Bucaramanga (472,461)
Sucre	10,917	701,105	Sincelejo (194,962)
Tolima	23,562	1,286,078	Ibagué (399,838)
Valle del Cauca	22,140	3,736,090	Cali (1,847,176)
Vaupés	65,268	24,671	Mitú (13,177)
Vichada	100,242	62,073	Puerto Carreño (11,452)
Capital District			
Santafé de Bogotá, DC	1,587	5,484,244	Bogotá*
Total	1,141,748	37,664,711	

* The capital city, Santafé de Bogotá, exists as the capital of a department as well as the Capital District. The city's population is included only in Santafé de Bogotá, DC.

PRINCIPAL TOWNS
(estimated population at mid-1997)

Santafé de Bogotá, DC (capital)	6,004,782	Montería	327,249
Cali	1,985,906	Neiva	305,625
Medellín	1,970,691	Bello	304,819*
Barranquilla	1,157,826	Villavicencio	299,296
Cartagena	812,595	Valledupar	296,624
Cúcuta	589,196	Armenia	283,842
Bucaramanga	508,240	Buenaventura	266,988*
Pereira	434,267	Soacha	266,817*
Ibagué	419,883	Soledad	264,583*
Pasto	362,227	Palmira	256,823*
Manizales	358,194	Floridablanca	246,834*
Santa Marta	343,038	Popayán	218,057
		Sincelejo	213,916

* Mid-1995.

BIRTHS, MARRIAGES AND DEATHS*

	Registered live births	Registered deaths
1983	829,348	140,292
1984	825,842	137,189
1985	835,922	153,947
1986	931,956	146,346
1987	937,426	151,957

Registered deaths: 167,743 in 1992; 168,647 in 1993; 168,568 in 1994.
Registered marriages: 102,448 in 1980; 95,845 in 1981; 70,350 in 1986.

* Data are tabulated by year of registration rather than by year of occurrence, although registration is incomplete. According to UN estimates, the average annual rates in 1985–90 were: births 25.9 per 1,000; deaths 6.1 per 1,000; and in 1990–95: births 24.0 per 1,000; deaths 6.0 per 1,000 (Source: UN, *World Population Prospects: The 1994 Revision*).

Expectation of life (UN estimates, years at birth, 1990–95): 69.3 (males 66.4; females 72.3) (Source: UN, *World Population Prospects: The 1994 Revision*).

ECONOMICALLY ACTIVE POPULATION
(household survey, 1995)

Agriculture, hunting, forestry and fishing	3,370,557
Mining and quarrying	121,763
Manufacturing	2,381,687
Electricity, gas and water	77,262
Construction	922,255
Trade, restaurants and hotels	3,296,685
Transport, storage and communications	841,026
Financing, insurance, real estate and business services	701,166
Community, social and personal services	3,450,590
Activities not adequately described	6,699
Total labour force	15,169,690*

* Males 9,715,167; females 5,454,523.

Mid-1996 (estimates, '000 persons): Agriculture, etc. 3,682; Total labour force 15,651 (Source: FAO, *Production Yearbook*).

Agriculture

PRINCIPAL CROPS ('000 metric tons)

	1994	1995	1996
Wheat	105.2	74.1*	64.9*
Rice (paddy)	1,657.2	1,784.6*	1,664.7*
Barley	57.7	44.9*	45.3*
Maize	1,161.1	1,019.7*	999.9*
Sorghum	649.3	553.8*	452.0*
Potatoes	2,938.6	2,891.9*	2,788.2*
Cassava (Manioc)	1,794.6	1,751.9	1,804.9
Soybeans	109.4	95.0*	60.2*
Seed cotton	145.6	146.2*	193.9*
Cane sugar (raw)	2,943.1	3,199.2	3,336.4
Bananas†	1,845.0	1,513.2	1,430.0
Plantains	2,395.6	2,783.5	3,212.4
Coffee (green)	721.9	821.8	833.4
Cocoa beans	50.6	53.0	65.0
Tobacco (blond and black)	26.9	26.2*	31.1*

Fruit ('000 metric tons): 2,051.6 in 1994; 2,135.8 in 1995; 2,306.6 in 1996.

Vegetables ('000 metric tons): 1,249.1 in 1994; 1,277.6 in 1995; 1,303.1 in 1996.

* Preliminary figure.

† For export only.

Source: Ministerio de Agricultura.

LIVESTOCK ('000 head, year ending September)

	1994	1995	1996
Horses	2,000*	2,450	2,450*
Mules	622*	586	586*
Asses*	710	710	710
Cattle	25,634†	25,551	26,088†
Pigs	2,600*	2,500	2,431
Sheep	2,540*	2,540†	2,540†
Goats	960*	965†	963†
Poultry*	90,000	100,000	110,000

* FAO estimate(s).

† Unofficial figure.

Source: FAO, *Production Yearbook*.

LIVESTOCK PRODUCTS ('000 metric tons)

	1994	1995	1996
Beef and veal	669	665	698
Mutton and lamb*	10	10	12
Goat meat*	4	4	4
Pig meat	133	133*	135*
Horse meat*	5	5	5
Poultry meat	443	553	579
Cows' milk	4,768	5,078	5,000*
Cheese*	51	51	51
Butter and ghee*	15	15	15
Poultry eggs	293	315*	315*
Cattle hides*	77	81	78

* FAO estimate(s).

Source: FAO, *Production Yearbook*.

Forestry

ROUNDWOOD REMOVALS
(FAO estimates, '000 cu metres, excl. bark)

	1992	1993	1994
Sawlogs, veneer logs and logs for sleepers*	2,686	2,686	2,686
Pulpwood*	589	589	589
Other industrial wood†	408	408	408
Fuel wood	16,936	17,220	17,504
Total	20,619	20,903	21,187

* Assumed to be unchanged from 1986 official estimate.

† Assumed to be unchanged from 1982 official estimate.

Source: FAO, *Yearbook of Forest Products*.

SAWNWOOD PRODUCTION
('000 cu metres, incl. railway sleepers)

	1984*	1985*	1986
Coniferous (softwood)	181	196	244
Broadleaved (hardwood)	422	459	569
Total	603	655	813

* FAO estimates.

1987–94: Annual production as in 1986 (FAO estimates).

Source: FAO, *Yearbook of Forest Products*.

Fishing

('000 metric tons, live weight)

	1993	1994	1995
Inland waters	47.2	51.7	52.1
Atlantic Ocean	16.5	17.2	22.8
Pacific Ocean	84.1	54.8	92.2
Total catch	147.8	123.7	167.1

Source: FAO, *Yearbook of Fishery Statistics*.

Mining

('000 metric tons, unless otherwise indicated)

	1994	1995	1996
Gold ('000 troy oz)*	675.0	194.7	48.9
Silver ('000 troy oz)	187.0	21.5	5.9
Salt (refined)	135.9	281.4	560.3
Coal†	23,532	26,800	n.a.
Iron ore‡	552.1	571.6	605.7
Crude petroleum ('000 barrels)	165,675	213,627	228,778

* Figures refer to purchases by the Banco de la República.

† Estimate.

‡ Figures refer to the gross weight of ore. The estimated iron content is 46%.

Industry

SELECTED PRODUCTS ('000 metric tons, unless otherwise indicated)

	1994	1995	1996
Sugar	1,964.3	2,057.7	2,149.2
Cement	9,209.2	9,229.3	8,590.1
Steel ingots	256.3	294.7	298.4
Diesel oil ('000 barrels)	20,650	21,989	24,552
Fuel oil ('000 barrels)	19,453	20,039	19,453
Motor fuel ('000 barrels)	30,126	33,822	41,160

Finance

CURRENCY AND EXCHANGE RATES

Monetary Units

100 centavos = 1 Colombian peso.

Sterling and Dollar Equivalents (30 September 1997)

£1 sterling = 2,013.2 pesos;
US $1 = 1,246.3 pesos;
10,000 Colombian pesos = £4.967 = $8.024.

Average Exchange Rate (pesos per US $)

1994 844.84
1995 912.83
1996 1,036.69

BUDGET (million pesos)

Revenue	1994	1995	1996
Direct taxation	3,227,689	4,007,700	4,804,878
Indirect taxation	4,429,303	5,502,797	7,720,075
Rates and fines	296,962	493,466	102,746
Revenue under contracts	5,406	545,997	290,786
Credit resources	2,206,006	3,248,411	5,380,155
Other	2,322,507	1,688,610	2,387,473
Total	12,487,873	15,486,981	20,686,113

Expenditure*	1994	1995	1996
Congress and comptrollership	118,066	144,627	186,359
General administration	501,870	620,870	880,041
Home office and foreign affairs	105,247	135,903	123,196
Finance and public credit	2,154,616	1,845,578	3,184,648
Public works and transportation	766,500	1,138,585	1,370,592
Defence	982,375	1,318,142	2,039,513
Police	538,803	731,319	972,974
Agriculture	396,707	464,618	811,808
Health	616,267	938,401	1,309,354
Education	1,638,210	1,970,654	2,950,304
Development, labour, mines and communications	515,689	1,013,441	1,411,375
Justice and legal affairs	584,859	776,247	947,694
Trade	8,760	15,603	31,068
Environment	3,691	113,885	138,982
Total	8,931,660	11,227,873	16,357,908

* Excluding public debt.

Source: *Informe Anual de la Contraloría General de la República.*

INTERNATIONAL RESERVES
(US $ million at 31 December)

	1994	1995	1996
Gold*	111.9	103.2	93.2
IMF special drawing rights	169.9	176.6	176.3
Reserve position in IMF	126.6	201.1	236.9
Foreign exchange	7,455.9	7,725.0	9,184.4
Total	7,864.3	8,205.9	9,690.8

* Valued at market-related prices.

MONEY SUPPLY ('000 million pesos at 31 December)

	1994	1995	1996
Currency outside banks	2,376.1	3,003.2	3,550.3
Demand deposits at commercial banks	3,624.3	4,241.5	5,229.8
Total money (incl. others)	6,542.6	8,057.0	9,937.3

Source: IMF, *International Financial Statistics.*

COST OF LIVING (Consumer price index for low-income families in Santafé de Bogotá; base: 1988 = 100)

	1994	1995	1996
Food	381.1	444.0	545.3
Clothing	356.5	410.0	462.7
Rent	436.7	525.4	647.2
All items (incl. others)	419.2	498.6	614.5

NATIONAL ACCOUNTS ('000 million pesos at current prices)

Composition of the Gross National Product

	1993	1994	1995*
Compensation of employees	17,510.1	23,528.3	29,960.3
Operating surplus / Consumption of fixed capital	21,627.1	27,611.0	34,761.1
Gross domestic product (GDP) at factor cost	39,137.2	51,139.3	64,721.4
Indirect taxes	5,044.3	7,222.2	9,351.4
Less Subsidies	283.3	379.2	681.0
GDP in purchasers' values	43,898.2	57,982.3	73,391.9
Net factor income from abroad	245.2	–314.6	n.a.
Gross national product (GNP)	44,143.4	57,667.7	n.a.

* Provisional.

Expenditure on the Gross Domestic Product

	1994	1995*	1996†
Government final consumption expenditure	7,652.7	10,937.0	14,247.9
Private final consumption expenditure	39,269.6	49,063.9	60,256.4
Increase in stocks	1,615.9	2,222.2	1,602.5
Gross fixed capital formation	11,872.7	14,529.0	15,499.7
Total domestic expenditure	60,411.0	76,752.1	91,606.5
Exports of goods and services	8,934.6	11,085.5	13,239.8
Less Imports of goods and services	11,363.2	14,445.7	16,018.6
GDP in purchasers' values	57,982.3	73,391.9	88,827.8

* Provisional. † Preliminary.

Gross Domestic Product by Economic Activity

	1994	1995*	1996†
Agriculture, hunting, forestry and fishing	7,465.1	9,305.4	10,110
Mining and quarrying	2,581.7	3,584.6	4,909
Manufacturing	11,353.4	13,762.6	15,587
Electricity, gas and water	1,836.3	2,295.5	3,158
Construction	4,387.0	5,435.7	6,413
Wholesale and retail trade	9,664.8	12,440.1	14,655
Transport, storage and communications	5,731.3	7,195.1	9,042
Finance, insurance, real estate and business services	7,037.4	9,367.0	11,828
Government services	5,508.9	7,108.7	9,492
Other services	3,161.4	4,218.2	5,721
Sub-total	58,727.4	74,713.1	90,914
Import duties	1,481.0	1,813.8	2,008
Less Imputed bank service charge	2,226.1	3,135.0	4,094
Total	57,982.3	73,391.9	88,828

* Provisional. † Preliminary.

BALANCE OF PAYMENTS (US $ million)

	1994	1995	1996
Exports of goods f.o.b.	8,749	10,222	10,651
Imports of goods f.o.b.	–11,040	–12,921	–12,784
Trade balance	–2,292	–2,699	–2,133
Exports of services	3,342	3,522	3,867
Imports of services	–2,719	–3,338	–4,094
Balance on goods and services	–1,668	–2,514	–2,360
Other income received	791	1,299	958
Other income paid	–3,098	–3,563	–3,883
Balance on goods, services and income	–3,975	–4,779	–5,285
Current transfers received	1,055	861	701
Current transfers paid	–193	–182	–170
Current balance	–3,113	–4,101	–4,754
Direct investment abroad	–152	–284	–68
Direct investment from abroad	1,667	2,317	3,322
Portfolio investment liabilities	584	–170	1,656
Other investment assets	–1,773	158	–1,193
Other investment liabilities	2,457	2,641	3,069
Net errors and omissions	482	–210	–434
Overall balance	153	351	1,598

Source: IMF, *International Financial Statistics.*

External Trade

PRINCIPAL COMMODITIES (US $ million)

Imports c.i.f.	1994	1995	1996
Vegetables and vegetable products	748.3	898.2	1,176.7
Prepared foodstuffs, beverages and tobacco	393.8	529.9	645.0
Mineral products	547.2	684.7	641.2
Petroleum and its derivatives	313.5	382.6	355.4
Chemical products	2,266.7	2,928.7	2,936.8
Paper and paper products	401.4	513.2	476.7
Textiles and leather products	452.5	550.8	532.4
Metals	655.5	884.1	789.7
Mechanical, electrical and transport equipment	5,545.1	5,833.0	5,439.2
Total (incl. others)	11,882.9	13,853.1	13,683.6

Source: Dirección de Impuestos y Aduanas Nacionales.

Exports f.o.b.	1994	1995	1996
Agricultural, livestock, forestry and fisheries products	3,229.1	3,058.4	n.a.
Coffee	1,990.1	1,831.7	1,576.8
Bananas	489.7	431.0	459.5
Flowers	426.3	475.8	509.5
Coal	552.9	595.7	849.1
Petroleum and its derivatives	1,312.7	2,185.0	2,892.0
Prepared foodstuffs, beverages and tobacco	425.3	521.0	560.5
Textiles and leather products	802.1	824.6	666.3
Paper and publishing	214.1	254.6	223.0
Chemicals	544.8	828.0	895.2
Electrical and transport equipment	164.0	190.8	120.0
Total (incl. others)	8,478.9	10,125.9	10,586.9

Source: Departamento Administrativo Nacional de Estadísticas.

PRINCIPAL TRADING PARTNERS (US $ million)

Imports c.i.f.	1994	1995	1996
Argentina	155.4	147.3	159.8
Brazil	339.9	385.6	356.9
Canada	263.1	364.5	364.1
Chile	128.7	197.5	204.1
Ecuador	264.4	276.9	332.0
France	275.6	334.6	317.4
Germany	678.1	810.6	831.4
Italy	295.9	300.1	385.7
Japan	984.1	1,046.1	707.3
Mexico	292.6	452.3	477.0
Netherlands	148.3	109.7	138.6
Spain	267.4	287.1	287.4
United Kingdom	185.8	223.4	247.5
USA*	4,575.6	5,415.7	5,599.7
Venezuela	1,143.2	1,355.8	1,261.9
Total (incl. others)	11,882.9	13,853.2	13,683.5

* Including Puerto Rico.

Source: Dirección de Impuestos y Aduanas Nacionales.

Exports f.o.b.	1994	1995	1996
Belgium-Luxembourg	320.4	294.3	293.8
Brazil	57.7	103.8	119.1
Canada	91.0	157.5	109.3
Chile	119.4	148.6	182.7
Denmark	69.6	70.1	108.1
Ecuador	318.3	419.8	421.1
France	171.4	261.9	273.5
Germany	873.1	738.2	602.0
Italy	167.4	185.4	167.1
Japan	352.3	363.5	348.7
Mexico	109.4	90.3	89.3
Netherlands	293.8	340.9	364.5
Peru	245.5	617.4	610.1
Spain	166.7	186.6	157.7
United Kingdom	193.6	189.5	195.7
USA*	3,117.4	3,531.0	4,217.0
Venezuela	532.4	553.0	781.7
Total (incl. others)	8,478.9	10,125.9	10,586.9

* Including Puerto Rico.

Source: Departamento Administrativo Nacional de Estadísticas.

Transport

RAILWAYS (traffic)

	1994	1995	1996
Freight ('000 metric tons)	357	288	321
Freight ton-km ('000)	666,138	753,219	746,544

Source: Sociedad Colombiana de Transporte Ferroviario, SA.

ROAD TRAFFIC (motor vehicles in use)

	1986	1987	1988
Passenger cars	611,978	655,201	706,922
Buses	52,136	53,354	55,111
Goods vehicles	282,386	291,070	300,254
Heavy-duty vehicles	230,034	233,555	239,524
Total (incl. others)	1,242,650	1,301,802	1,375,405

1993 (vehicles in use at 31 December, estimates): Passenger cars 762,000; Goods vehicles (incl. vans) 672,000; Total 1,434,000 (Source: IRF, *World Road Statistics*).

SHIPPING

Merchant Fleet (registered at 31 December)

	1994	1995	1996
Number of vessels	106	116	118
Total displacement ('000 grt)	142.1	144.2	121.7

Source: Lloyd's Register of Shipping, *World Fleet Statistics.*

Domestic Sea-borne Freight Traffic ('000 metric tons)

	1987	1988	1989
Goods loaded and unloaded	772.1	944.8	464.6

International Sea-borne Freight Traffic ('000 metric tons)

	1994	1995	1996
Goods loaded	23,291	26,284	38,053
Goods unloaded	13,610	13,806	13,257

CIVIL AVIATION (traffic)

	1994	1995	1996
Domestic			
Passengers carried ('000)	7,332	8,058	8,293
Freight carried ('000 metric tons)	138,113	130,255	n.a.
International			
Passengers ('000):			
arrivals	1,018	1,146	1,173
departures	1,086	1,221	1,257
Freight ('000 metric tons):			
loaded	190,897	191,164	n.a.
unloaded	211,684	215,993	n.a.

Source: Departamento Administrativo de Aeronáutica Civil.

Tourism

('000 visitors)

Country of origin	1992	1993	1996*
Argentina	9.4	6.6	9.9
Canada	25.6	35.6	28.4
Chile	6.2	4.6	5.6
Costa Rica	17.3	11.5	16.8
Ecuador	108.8	157.7	193.8
France	9.5	7.7	8.6
Germany	14.3	20.7	14.9
Italy	10.8	12.6	11.2
Panama	18.2	11.1	16.9
Peru	22.6	16.3	39.4
Spain	17.1	14.9	19.7
United Kingdom	9.3	8.2	10.9
USA	145.9	114.7	155.1
Venezuela	606.1	574.0	664.3
Total (incl. others)	1,075.9	1,047.3	1,253.9

* Detailed figures for 1994 and 1995 are not available; total tourist arrivals in those years were 1,207,000 and 1,400,000 (estimate) respectively.

Source: Corporación Nacional de Turismo.

Communications Media

	1992	1993	1994
Telephones ('000 main lines in use)	2,822	3,221	3,518
Telefax stations ('000 in use)	53	65	80
Mobile cellular telephones ('000 subscribers)	n.a.	n.a.	101
Radio receivers ('000 in use)	5,900	6,020	6,150
Television receivers ('000 in use)	3,900	4,000	4,070
Daily newspapers: number	46	n.a.	46

Book production: 1,481 titles in 1991.

Sources: UN, *Statistical Yearbook*, and UNESCO, *Statistical Yearbook*.

Education

(1996, estimates)

	Institutions	Teachers	Pupils
Nursery	16,591	45,888	919,680
Primary	48,933	193,911	4,916,934
Secondary			
General	7,895	165,976	2,323,653
teacher-training			65,654
Vocational			862,820
Higher (incl. universities)	266	75,568	673,353

Source: Ministerio de Educación Nacional.

Directory

The Constitution

A new, 380-article Constitution, drafted by a 74-member National Constituent Assembly, took effect from 6 July 1991. The new Constitution retained the institutional framework of a directly-elected President with a non-renewable four-year term of office, together with a bicameral legislature composed of an upper house or Senate (with 102 directly-elected members) and a lower house or House of Representatives (with 161 members, to include at least two representatives of each national department).

The new Constitution also contained comprehensive provisions for the recognition and protection of civil rights, and for the reform of the structures and procedures of political participation and of the judiciary.

The fundamental principles upon which the new Constitution is based are embodied in articles 1–10.

Article 1: Colombia is a lawful state, organized as a single Republic, decentralized, with autonomous territorial entities, democratic, participatory and pluralist, founded on respect for human dignity, on the labour and solidarity of its people and on the prevalence of the general interest.

Article 2: The essential aims of the State are: to serve the community, to promote general prosperity and to guarantee the effectiveness of the principles, rights and obligations embodied in the Constitution, to facilitate the participation of all in the decisions which affect them and in the economic, political, administrative and cultural life of the nation; to defend national independence, to maintain territorial integrity and to ensure peaceful coexistence and the validity of the law.

The authorities of the Republic are instituted to protect the residents of Colombia, in regard to their life, honour, goods, beliefs and other rights and liberties, and to ensure the fulfilment of the obligations of the State and of the individual.

Article 3: Sovereignty rests exclusively with the people, from whom public power emanates. The people exercise power directly or through their representatives in the manner established by the Constitution.

Article 4: The Constitution is the highest authority. In all cases of incompatability between the Constitution and the law or other juridical rules, constitutional dispositions will apply.

It is the duty of nationals and foreigners in Colombia to observe the Constitution and the law, and to respect and obey the authorities.

Article 5: The State recognizes, without discrimination, the primacy of the inalienable rights of the individual and protects the family as the basic institution of society.

Article 6: Individuals are solely responsible to the authorities for infringements of the Constitution and of the law. Public servants are equally accountable and are responsible to the authorities for failure to fulfil their function or abuse of their position.

Article 7: The State recognizes and protects the ethnic diversity of the Colombian nation.

Article 8: It is an obligation of the State and of the people to protect the cultural and natural riches of the nation.

Article 9: The foreign relations of the State are based on national sovereignty, with respect for self-determination of people and with recognition of the principles of international law accepted by Colombia.

Similarly, Colombia's external politics will be directed towards Caribbean and Latin American integration.

Article 10: Spanish (Castellano) is the official language of Colombia. The languages and dialects of ethnic groups are officially recognized within their territories. Education in communities with their own linguistic traditions will be bilingual.

The Government

HEAD OF STATE

President: Ernesto Samper Pizano (took office 7 August 1994).

CABINET
(January 1998)

Minister of Government (Interior): Alfonso López Caballero (PL).

Minister of Foreign Affairs: María Emma Mejía (PL).

Minister of Justice: Alma Beatriz Renjifo (PL).

Minister of Finance and Public Credit: Antonio José Urdinola (PL).

Minister of National Defence: Gilberto Echeverry Mejía (PL).

Minister of Agriculture: Antonio Gómez Merlano (PL).

Minister of Labour and Social Security: Carlos Bula Camacho (MOIR).

Minister of Foreign Trade: Carlos Ronderos Torres (PL).

Minister of Public Health: María Teresa Forero de Saade (PL).

Minister of Economic Development: Carlos Julio Gaitan (PL).

Minister of Mines and Energy: Orlando Cabrales (PSC).

Minister of Education: Jaime Niño Diez (PSC).

Minister of Communications: José Fernando Bautista (PL).

Minister of Transport: Rodrigo Marin Bernal (PL).

Minister of the Environment: Eduardo Verano de la Rosa (PL).

Minister of Culture: Ramiro Osorio (PL).

MINISTRIES

Office of the President: Palacio de Nariño, Carrera 8A, No 7-26, Santafé de Bogotá, DC; tel. (1) 284-3300; telex 44281; fax (1) 289-3377.

Ministry of Agriculture: Avda Jiménez, No 7-65, Santafé de Bogotá, DC; tel. (1) 334-1199; fax (1) 284-1285.

Ministry of Communications: Edif. Murillo Toro, Carreras 7A y 8A, Calle 12A y 13, Apdo Aéreo 14515, Santafé de Bogotá, DC; tel. (1) 286-6911; fax (1) 286-1185; internet http://www.colomsat.net.co/mincom.

Ministry of Culture: Calle 8, No 6-97, Santafé de Bogotá, DC; tel. (1) 282-0666; fax (1) 282-0854.

Ministry of Economic Development: Carrera 13, No 28-01, 5°–9°, Santafé de Bogotá, DC; tel. (1) 287-4765; fax (1) 287-6025.

Ministry of Education: Centro Administrativo Nacional (CAN), Of. 501, Avda El Dorado, Santafé de Bogotá, DC; tel. (1) 222-2800; fax (1) 222-4578; internet http://www.icfes.gov.co/menhome.

Ministry of the Environment: Carrera 16, No 6-66, 3° y 4°, Santafé de Bogotá, DC; tel. (1) 336-1166; fax (1) 336-3984.

Ministry of Finance and Public Credit: Carrera 7A, No 6-45, Of. 308, Santafé de Bogotá, DC; tel. (1) 284-5400; fax (1) 284-5396.

Ministry of Foreign Affairs: Palacio de San Carlos, Calle 10A, No 5-51, Santafé de Bogotá, DC; tel. (1) 282-7811; fax (1) 341-6777; internet http://www.minrelext.gov.co.

Ministry of Foreign Trade: Calle 28, No 13A-15, 35°–40°, Santafé de Bogotá, DC; tel. (1) 286-9111; fax (1) 283-6323.

Ministry of Government (Interior): Palacio Echeverry, Carrera 8A, No 8-09, Santafé de Bogotá, DC; tel. (1) 283-0676; fax (1) 281-5884; internet http://www.presidencia.gov.co/mininterior.

Ministry of Justice: Avda Jiménez, No 8-89, Santafé de Bogotá, DC; tel. (1) 286-0211; fax (1) 281-6443; internet http://www.minjusticia.gov.co.

Ministry of Labour and Social Security: Carrera 7, No 34-50, Santafé de Bogotá, DC; tel. (1) 287-7189; fax (1) 285-7091.

Ministry of Mines and Energy: Centro Administrativo Nacional (CAN), Avda El Dorado, Santafé de Bogotá, DC; tel. (1) 222-4555; fax (1) 222-4680.

Ministry of National Defence: Centro Administrativo Nacional (CAN), 2°, Avda El Dorado, Santafé de Bogotá, DC; tel. (1) 266-9300; fax (1) 222-1874; internet http://www.mindefensa.gov.co.

Ministry of Public Health: Carrera 16, No 7-39, Santafé de Bogotá, DC; tel. (1) 282-2851; fax (1) 282-0003.

Ministry of Transport: Centro Administrativo Nacional (CAN), Of. 409, Avda El Dorado, Santafé de Bogotá, DC; tel. (1) 222-4411; telex 45656; fax (1) 222-1647.

President and Legislature

PRESIDENT

Presidential elections, 29 May and 19 June 1994

	Votes		
	First ballot*	Second ballot	Second ballot %
Ernesto Samper Pizano (PL)	2,581,193	3,679,632	50.9
Andrés Pastrana Arango (PSC)	2,562,481	3,553,146	49.1
Antonio Navarro Wolff (ADM-19)	217,067	—	—
Regina Betancourt de Liska (MUM)	64,871	—	—
Gen. (retd) Miguel Alfredo Maza	54,919	—	—

* Figures with 97.3% of vote counted.

CONGRESO

Senado
(Senate)

President: Carlos Espinosa Faccio-Lince.

General Election, 13 March 1994

	Seats
Partido Liberal (PL)	56
Partido Social Conservador (PSC)	20
Independent groups*	24
Indigenous groups†	2
Total	102

* Including the Alianza Democrática (ADM-19) which won one seat.
† Under the reforms of the Constitution in 1991, two Senate seats are reserved for indigenous groups.

Cámara de Representantes
(House of Representatives)

President: César Pérez García.

General Election, 13 March 1994

	Seats
Partido Liberal (PL)	88
Partido Social Conservador (PSC)	40
Independent groups*	33
Corriente de Renovación Socialista (CRS)†	2
Ethnic and minority groups‡	2
Total	165

* Including the Alianza Democrática (ADM-19) and the Movimiento de Salvación Nacional (MSN) which won two seats each.

† In compliance with the terms of the peace agreements between the Government of César Gaviria Trujillo and the former guerrilla groups, two seats in the House of Representatives were reserved for members of the CRS.

‡ Under the reforms of the Constitution in 1991, two seats in the House of Representatives are reserved for ethnic and minority groups.

Political Organizations

Alianza Democrática (ADM-19): Santafé de Bogotá, DC; f. 1990; alliance of centre-left groups (including factions of Unión Patriótica, Colombia Unida, Frente Popular and Socialismo Democrático) which supported the M-19 campaign for elections to the National Constituent Assembly in December 1990; Leader DIEGO MONTAÑA CUÉLLAR.

Alianza Nacional Popular (ANAPO): Santafé de Bogotá, DC; f. 1971 by supporters of Gen. Gustavo Rojas Pinilla; populist party; Leader MARÍA EUGENIA ROJAS DE MORENO DÍAZ.

Democracia Cristiana: Avda 42, No 18-08, Apdo 25867, Santafé de Bogotá, DC; tel. (1) 285-6639; telex 45572; f. 1964; Christian Democrat party; 10,000 mems; Pres. JUAN A. POLO FIGUEROA; Sec.-Gen. DIEGO ARANGO OSORIO.

Frente por la Unidad del Pueblo (FUP): Santafé de Bogotá, DC; extreme left-wing front comprising socialists and Maoists.

Movimiento 19 de Abril (M-19): f. 1970 by followers of Gen. Gustavo Rojas Pinilla and dissident factions from the FARC (see below); left-wing urban guerrilla group, until formally constituted as a political party in Oct. 1989; Leaders ANTONIO NAVARRO WOLFF, OTTY PATIÑO.

Movimiento Colombia Unida (CU): Santafé de Bogotá, DC; left-wing group allied to the UP; Leader ADALBERTO CARVAJAL.

Movimiento Nacional Conservador (MNC): Santafé de Bogotá, DC.

Movimiento Nacional Progresista (MNP): Santafé de Bogotá, DC.

Movimiento Obrero Independiente Revolucionario (MOIR): Santafé de Bogotá, DC; left-wing workers' movement; Maoist; Leader MARCELO TORRES.

Movimiento de Salvación Nacional (MSN): Santafé de Bogotá, DC; f. 1990; split from the Partido Social Conservador Colombiano.

Movimiento Unitario Metapolítico (MUM): Calle 13, No 68D–40, Santafé de Bogotá, DC; tel. (1) 292-1330; fax (1) 292-5502; f. 1985; populist-occultist party; Leader REGINA BETANCOURT DE LISKA.

Mujeres para la Democracia: Santafé de Bogotá, DC; f. 1991; women's party; Leader ANGELA CUEVAS DE DOLMETSCH.

Nueva Fuerza Democrática (NFD): Santafé de Bogotá, DC; conservative; Leader ANDRÉS PASTRANA.

Partido Liberal (PL): Avda Caracas, No 36-01, Santafé de Bogotá, DC; tel. (1) 287-9311; fax (1) 287-9540; f. 1815; divided into two factions, the official group (HERNANDO DURÁN LUSSÁN, MIGUEL PINEDO) and the independent group, Nuevo Liberalismo (New Liberalism, led by Dr ALBERTO SANTOFIMIO BOTERO, ERNESTO SAMPER, EDUARDO MESTRE); Pres. LUIS FERNANDO JARAMILLO.

Partido Nacional Cristiano (PNC): Santafé de Bogotá, DC.

Partido Social Conservador Colombiano (PSC): Avda 22, No 37-09, Santafé de Bogotá, DC; tel. (1) 369-0011; fax (1) 369-0053; f. 1849; fmrly Partido Conservador; 2.9m. mems; Leader MISAEL PASTRANA BORRERO; Sec.-Gen. Dr EUGENIO MERLANO DE LA OSSA.

Unidad Democrática de la Izquierda (Democratic Unity of the Left): Santafé de Bogotá, DC; f. 1982; left-wing coalition incorporating the following parties:

Firmes: Santafé de Bogotá, DC; democratic party.

Partido Comunista Colombiano (PCC): Calle 18A, No 14-56, Apdo Aéreo 2523, Santafé de Bogotá, DC; tel. (1) 334-1947; telex 45152; fax (1) 281-8259; f. 1930; Marxist-Leninist party; Sec.-Gen. ALVARO VÁSQUEZ DEL REAL.

Partido Socialista de los Trabajadores (PST): Santafé de Bogotá, DC; workers' socialist party; Leader MARÍA SOCORRO RAMÍREZ.

Unión Patriótica (UP): f. 1985; Marxist party formed by the FARC (see below); obtained legal status in 1986; Pres. ERNÁN PASTRANA; Exec. Sec. OVIDIO SALINAS.

The following guerrilla groups and illegal organizations were active in the late 1980s and in the 1990s:

Comando Ricardo Franco-Frente Sur: f. 1984; common front formed by dissident factions from the FARC and M-19 (see below); Leader JAVIER DELGADO.

Ejército de Liberación Nacional (ELN—Unión Camilista): Castroite guerrilla movement; f. 1965; 930 mems; Leaders FABIO VÁSQUEZ CASTAÑO, MANUEL PÉREZ; factions include:

Corriente de Renovación Socialista (CRS): (ceased hostilities in December 1993).

Frente Simón Bolívar: (ceased hostilities in December 1985).

Frente Antonio Nariño: (ceased hostilities in December 1985).

Frente Domingo Laín: formed splinter group in October 1993; armed wing.

Ejército Popular de Liberación (EPL): Maoist guerrilla movement; splinter group from Communist Party; abandoned armed struggle in March 1991; joined the political mainstream as the **Partido de Esperanza, Paz y Libertad (EPL)**; Leader FRANCISCO CARABALLO.

Frente Popular de Liberación Nacional (FPLN): f. 1994 by dissident members of the ELN and the EPL.

Fuerzas Armadas Revolucionarias de Colombia (FARC): fmrly military wing of the Communist Party; composed of 39 armed fronts; 4,400 armed supporters in 1987; Leader MANUEL MARULANDA VÉLEZ (alias TIROFIJO).

Movimiento de Autodefensa Obrera (MAO): workers' self-defence movement; Trotskyite; Leader ADELAIDA ABADIA REY.

Movimiento de Restauración Nacional (MORENA): right-wing; Leader ARMANDO VALENZUELA RUIZ.

Muerte a Secuestradores (MAS) (Death to Kidnappers): right-wing paramilitary organization; funded by drugs-dealers.

Nuevo Frente Revolucionario del Pueblo: f. 1986; faction of M-19; active in Cundinamarca region.

Partido Revolucionario de Trabajadores (PRT): left-wing; abandoned its armed struggle, in January 1991, and announced its intention to join the political mainstream as part of the Alianza Democrática.

Patria Libre: f. 1985; left-wing guerrilla movement.

In late 1985 the M-19, the Comando Ricardo Franco-Frente Sur and the **Comando Quintín Lame** (an indigenous organization active in the department of Cauca) announced the formation of a united front, the **Coordinadora Guerrillera Nacional (CGN)**. In 1986 the CGN participated in joint campaigns with the Movimiento Revolucionario Tupac Amarú (Peru) and the Alfaro Vive ¡Carajo! (Ecuador). The alliance operated under the name of **Batallón América.** In October 1987 six guerrilla groups, including the ELN, the FARC and the M-19, formed a joint front, to be known as the **Coordinadora Guerrillera Simón Bolívar (CGSB)** and subsequently as the **Coordinadora Nacional Guerrillera Simón Bolívar (CNGSB).** In early 1989 the ELN, the FARC, the EPL and the M-19 all confirmed their willingness to hold peace talks with the Government. At a summit meeting held with the Government, in July, these groups agreed to the formation of a Comisión de Notables, which was to draft proposals for a peace dialogue. In September the M-19 announced that it had reached agreement with the Government on a peace treaty, allowing the M-19 a full pardon and recognition as a political party in exchange for total demobilization and disarmament. Having received recognition as a political party, the M-19 joined the legitimate political system in early 1990. Similar transfers to political legitimacy were effected by the PRT, in January 1991, the EPL, in March 1991, and the Comando Quintín Lame, in May 1991. However, the political status of all three groups was annulled by the National Electoral Board in August 1992, following their failure to attract the 50,000 votes required to secure a congressional seat at elections conducted in October 1991.

Diplomatic Representation

EMBASSIES IN COLOMBIA

Argentina: Avda 40A, No 13-09, 16°, Santafé de Bogotá, DC; tel. (1) 288-0900; telex 44576; Ambassador: HÉCTOR SAINZ BALLESTEROS.

Austria: Carrera 11, No 75-29, Santafé de Bogotá, DC; tel. (1) 235-6628; telex 41489; Ambassador: OMAR KOLER.

Belgium: Calle 26, No 4A-45, 7°, Santafé de Bogotá, DC; tel. (1) 282-8881; telex 41203; fax (1) 282-8862; Ambassador: JEAN-PAUL WARNIMONT.

Bolivia: Transversal 12, No 119-95, Santafé de Bogotá, DC; tel. (1) 215-3274; telex 45583; Ambassador: OSCAR EDUARDO LAZCANO HENRY.

Bosnia and Herzegovina: Carrera 13A, No 89-38, Of. 607, Santafé de Bogotá, DC; tel. (1) 618-4869; fax (1) 618-4847; Chargé d'affaires: NARCISA ABDULAGIĆ.

Brazil: Calle 93, No 14-20, 8°, Santafé de Bogotá, DC; tel. (1) 218-0800; Ambassador: SYNÉSIO SAMPAIO GOES FILHO.

Bulgaria: Calle 81, No 7-71, Santafé de Bogotá, DC; tel. (1) 212-8028; fax (1) 345-3791; Ambassador: (vacant).

Canada: Calle 76, No 11-52, Apdo Aéreo 53531, Santafé de Bogotá, DC; tel. (1) 313-1355; fax (1) 313-3046; Ambassador: C. WILLIAM ROSS.

Chile: Calle 100, No 11B-44, Santafé de Bogotá, DC; tel. (1) 214-7926; telex 44404; Ambassador: ARMANDO JARAMILLO LYON.

China, People's Republic: Calle 71, No 2A-41, Santafé de Bogotá, DC; tel. (1) 211-8251; telex 45387; fax (1) 217-8985; Ambassador: HUANG SHIKANG.

Costa Rica: Carrera 15, No 102-25, Santafé de Bogotá, DC; tel. (1) 622-8830; fax (1) 623-0205; Ambassador: Dr FERNANDO DEL CASTILLO RIGGIONI.

Czech Republic: Carrera 7, No 113-16, 4°, Santafé de Bogotá, DC; tel. (1) 215-0633; fax (1) 612-8205.

Dominican Republic: Carrera 16A, No 86A-33, Santafé de Bogotá, DC; tel. (1) 621-1925; fax (1) 236-2588; Ambassador: MIGUEL A. FERSOBE PICHARDO.

Ecuador: Calle 89, No 13-07, Santafé de Bogotá, DC; tel. (1) 257-0066; telex 45776; fax (1) 257-9799; Ambassador: Dr FERNANDO CÓRDOVA.

Egypt: Carrera 19A, No 98-17, Santafé de Bogotá, DC; tel. (1) 236-4832; Ambassador: AHMED FATHI ABULKHEIR.

El Salvador: Carrera 9A, No 80-15, Apdo 89394, Santafé de Bogotá, DC; tel. (1) 211-0012; fax (1) 255-9482; Ambassador: ALEXANDER A. KRAVETZ.

Finland: Carrera 7, No 35–33, Santafé de Bogotá, DC; tel. (1) 232-1202; fax (1) 285-7752.

France: Avda 39, No 7-84, Santafé de Bogotá, DC; tel. (1) 285-4311; telex 44558; Ambassador: CHARLES CRETTIEN.

Germany: Edif. Sisky, 6°, Carrera 4, No 72-35, Apdo Aéreo 91808, Santafé de Bogotá, DC; tel. (1) 212-0511; telex 44765; fax (1) 210-4256; Ambassador: Dr GEERT-HINRICH AHRENS.

Guatemala: Transversal 29A, No 139A-41, Santafé de Bogotá, DC; tel. (1) 259-1496; fax (1) 274-5365; e-mail emguacol@colomsat.net.co; Ambassador: DANTE MARINELLI GOLOM.

Haiti: Carrera 11A, No 96-63, Santafé de Bogotá, DC; tel. (1) 256-6236; fax (1) 218-0326; Chargé d'affaires: CARLO TOUSSAINT.

Holy See: Carrera 15, No 36-33, Apdo Aéreo 3740, Santafé de Bogotá, DC (Apostolic Nunciature); tel. (1) 320-0289; fax (1) 285-1817; e-mail nunciapo@colomsat.net.co; Apostolic Nuncio: Most Rev. PAOLO ROMEO, Titular Archbishop of Vulturia.

Honduras: Carrera 16, No 85-15, Of. 302, Santafé de Bogotá, DC; tel. (1) 236-0357; telex 45540; fax (1) 616-0774; Ambassador: HERNÁN ANTONIO BERMÚDEZ.

Hungary: Carrera 6A, No 77-46, Santafé de Bogotá, DC; tel. (1) 217-8578; telex 43244; Chargé d'affaires: DÁNOS KORNÉL.

India: Calle 71A, No 6-30, Of. 501, Santafé de Bogotá, DC; tel. (1) 217-5143; telex 44323; fax (1) 212-7648; e-mail indembog@colomsat.net.co; Ambassador: PRAMATHESH RATH.

Iran: Calle 96, No 11A-16/20, Santafé de Bogotá, DC; tel. (1) 218-6205; fax (1) 610-2556; Ambassador: HOSSEIN SHEIKH ZEINEDDIN.

Israel: Calle 35, No 7-25, 14°, Santafé de Bogotá, DC; tel. (1) 232-0932; telex 44755; Ambassador: PINCHAS AVIVI.

Italy: Calle 93B, No 9-92, Apdo Aéreo 50901, Santafé de Bogotá, DC; tel. (1) 218-6680; telex 45588; fax (1) 610-5886; Ambassador: FRANCESCO CAPECE GALEOTA.

Japan: Carrera 9A, No 99-02, 6°, Edif. Latinoamericano de Seguros, Santafé de Bogotá, DC; tel. (1) 618-2800; telex 43327; fax (1) 618-2828; Ambassador: MAKOTO ASAMI.

Korea, Republic: Transversal 29, No 118-25, Santafé de Bogotá, DC; tel. (1) 213-6285; fax (1) 612-9565; Ambassador: JOUNG SOO LEE.

Lebanon: Calle 74, No 12-44, Santafé de Bogotá, DC; tel. (1) 212-8360; telex 44333; fax (1) 212-4446; Ambassador: JOSEPH AKL.

Mexico: Calle 99, No 12-08, Santafé de Bogotá, DC; tel. (1) 256-6121; telex 41264; Ambassador: RAÚL VALDÉS A.

Morocco: Carrera 13A, No 98-33, Santafé de Bogotá, DC; tel. (1) 218-7147; telex 43468; fax (1) 218-8068; Ambassador: MOHAMED AYACHI.

Netherlands: Carrera 13, No 93-40, 5°, Apdo Aéreo 4385, Santafé de Bogotá, DC; tel. (1) 611-5080; telex 44629; fax (1) 623-3020; Ambassador: G. J. A. M. BOS.

Nicaragua: Transversal 19A, No 108-77, Santafé de Bogotá, DC; tel. (1) 214-1445; telex 45388; fax (1) 215-9582; Ambassador: DONALD CASTILLO RIVAS.

Panama: Calle 92, No 7-70, Santafé de Bogotá, DC; tel. (1) 257-5068; Ambassador: JAIME RICARDO FERNÁNDEZ URRIOLA.

Paraguay: Calle 57, No 7-11, Of. 702, Apdo Aéreo 20085, Santafé de Bogotá, DC; tel. (1) 255-4160; Ambassador: GERARDO FOGEL.

Peru: Carrera 10, No 93-48, Santafé de Bogotá, DC; tel. (1) 257-6292; fax (1) 623-5102; Ambassador: ALEJANDRO GORDILLO FERNÁNDEZ.

Poland: Calle 104A, No 23-48, Santafé de Bogotá, DC; tel. (1) 214-0143; telex 44591; Ambassador: MIECZYSŁAW BIERNACKI.

Portugal: Calle 71, No 11-10, Of. 703, Santafé de Bogotá, DC; tel. (1) 212-4223; Ambassador: PINTO MACHADO.

Romania: Carrera 7, No 92-58, Santafé de Bogotá, DC; tel. (1) 256-6438; telex 41238; Ambassador CRISTIAN LAZARESCU.

Russia: Carrera 4, No 75-00, Apdo Aéreo 90600, Santafé de Bogotá, DC; tel. (1) 235-7960; telex 44503; Ambassador: EDNAN AGAYEV.

Slovakia: Avda 13, No 104A-30, Santafé de Bogotá, DC; tel. (1) 214-2240; telex 44590.

Spain: Calle 92, No 12-68, Santafé de Bogotá, DC; tel. (1) 618-1888; telex 44779; fax (1) 616-6104; Ambassador: YAGO PICO DE COAÑA.

Sweden: Calle 72, No 5-83, 9°, Santafé de Bogotá, DC; tel. (1) 255-3777; telex 44626; fax (1) 210-3401; Ambassador: SVEN JULIN.

Switzerland: Carrera 9, No 74-08/1101, Santafé de Bogotá, DC; tel. (1) 255-3945; telex 41230; fax (1) 235-9630; Ambassador: JEAN-MARC BOULGARIS.

United Kingdom: Torre Propaganda Sancho, Calle 98, No 9-03, 4°, Apdo Aéreo 4508, Santafé de Bogotá, DC; tel. (1) 218-5111; fax (1) 218-2460; Ambassador: Sir LEYCESTER COLTMAN.

USA: Calle 22D-bis, No 47-51, Apdo Aéreo 3831, Santafé de Bogotá, DC; tel. (1) 315-0811; telex 44843; fax (1) 315-2197; Ambassador: CURTIS WARREN KAMMAN.

Uruguay: Carrera 9A, No 80-15, 11°, Apdo Aéreo 101466, Santafé de Bogotá, DC; tel. (1) 235-2748; fax (1) 217-2320; Ambassador: DOMINGO SCHIPANI.

Venezuela: Calle 33, No 6-94, 10°, Santafé de Bogotá, DC; tel. (1) 285-2286; telex 44504; fax (1) 285-7372; Ambassador: GERMÁN CARRERA DAMAS.

Yugoslavia: Calle 93A, No 9A-22, Apdo Aéreo 91074, Santafé de Bogotá, DC; tel. (1) 257-0290; telex 45155; Ambassador: RADOMIR ZECEVIĆ.

Judicial System

The constitutional integrity of the State is ensured by the Constitutional Court. The Constitutional Court is composed of seven judges who are elected by the Senate for eight years. Judges of the Constitutional Court are not eligible for re-election.

Judges of the Constitutional Court: JAIME SANIN GREIFFENSTEIN, FABIO MORÓN DÍAZ, SIMÓN RODRÍGUEZ RODRÍGUEZ, JOSÉ GREGORIO HERNÁNDEZ, EDUARDO CIFUENTES, ALEJANDRO RAMÍREZ, CIRO ANGARITA.

The ordinary judicial integrity of the State is ensured by the Supreme Court of Justice. The Supreme Court of Justice is composed of the Courts of Civil, Penal and Laboral Cassation. Judges of the Supreme Court of Justice are selected from the nominees of the Higher Council of Justice and serve an eight-year term of office which is not renewable.

Public Prosecutor: ALFONSO GÓMEZ MÉNDEZ.

SUPREME COURT OF JUSTICE

President: PEDRO LAFONT PIANETTA.

Vice-President: DÍDIMO PÁEZ VELANDIA.

Court of Civil Cassation (six judges): President: CARLOS ESTEBAN JARAMILLO.

Court of Penal Cassation (eight judges): President: RICARDO CALVETE RANGEL.

Court of Laboral Cassation (six judges): President: ERNESTO JIMÉNEZ DÍAZ.

Religion

Roman Catholicism is the religion of 95% of the population.

CHRISTIANITY

The Roman Catholic Church

Colombia comprises 12 archdioceses, 41 dioceses, two territorial prelatures, eight Apostolic Vicariates and five Apostolic Prefectures.

Bishops' Conference: Conferencia Episcopal de Colombia, Carrera 47, No 84-85, Apdo Aéreo 7448, Santafé de Bogotá, DC; tel. (1) 311-4277; telex 44740; fax (1) 311-5575; f. 1978; Pres. ALBERTO GIRALDO JARAMILLO, Archbishop of Popayán.

Archbishop of Barranquilla: FÉLIX MARÍA TORRES PARRA, Carrera 42F, No 75B-220, Apdo Aéreo 1160, Barranquilla 4; tel. (58) 358-4929; fax (58) 345-2118.

Archbishop of Bucaramanga: DARÍO CASTRILLÓN HOYOS, Calle 33, No 21-18, Bucaramanga, Santander; tel. (7) 42-4387; fax (7) 42-1361.

Archbishop of Cali: ISAÍAS DUARTE CANCINO, Carrera 4, No 7-17, Apdo Aéreo 8924, Cali; tel. (2) 889-0562; fax (2) 83-7980.

Archbishop of Cartagena: CARLOS JOSÉ RUISECO VIEIRA, Apdo Aéreo 400, Cartagena; tel. (5) 664-5308; fax (5) 664-4974.

Archbishop of Ibagué: JUAN FRANCISCO SARASTI JARAMILLO, Calle 10, No 2-58, Ibagué, Tolima; tel. (82) 61-1680; fax (82) 63-2681.

Archbishop of Manizales: FABIO BETANCUR TIRADO, Carrera 23, No 19-22, Manizales, Caldas; tel. (68) 84-3344; fax (68) 84-3890.

Archbishop of Medellín: HÉCTOR RUEDA HERNÁNDEZ, Calle 57, No 49-44, 3°, Medellín; tel. (4) 251-7700; fax (4) 251-8306.

Archbishop of Nueva Pamplona: VÍCTOR MANUEL LÓPEZ FORERO, Carrera 5, No 4-109, Nueva Pamplona; tel. (4) 68-2886; fax (4) 68-4540.

Archbishop of Popayán: ALBERTO GIRALDO JARAMILLO, Calle 5, No 6-71, Apdo Aéreo 593, Popayán; tel. (928) 24-1710; telex 240098; fax (928) 24-0101.

Archbishop of Santa Fe de Antioquia: IGNACIO GÓMEZ ARISTIZÁBAL, Plazuela Martínez Pardo, No 12-11, Santa Fe de Antioquia; tel. (94) 826-1155; fax (94) 826-1308.

Archbishop of Santafé de Bogotá: PEDRO RUBIANO SÁENZ, Carrera 7A, No 10-20, Santafé de Bogotá, DC; tel. (1) 334-5500; fax (1) 334-7867.

Archbishop of Tunja: AUGUSTO TRUJILLO ARANGO, Calle 17, No 9-85, Apdo Aéreo 1019, Tunja, Boyacá; tel. (987) 42-2094.

The Anglican Communion

Anglicans in Colombia are members of the Episcopal Church in the USA.

Bishop of Colombia: Rt Rev. BERNARDO MERINO BOTERO, Carrera 6, No 49-85, Apdo Aéreo 52964, Santafé de Bogotá, DC; tel. (1) 288-3167; fax (1) 288-3228; there are 3,500 baptized mems, 2,000 communicant mems, 29 parishes, missions and preaching stations; 5 schools and 1 orphanage; 8 clergy.

Protestant Churches

The Baptist Convention: Apdo Aéreo 51988, Medellín; tel. (4) 38-9623; Pres. RAMÓN MEDINA IBÁÑEZ; Exec. Sec. Rev. RAMIRO PÉREZ HOYOS.

Iglesia Evangélica Luterana de Colombia: Calle 75, No 20-54, Apdo Aéreo 51538, Santafé de Bogotá, DC; tel. (1) 212-5735; 2,000 mems; Pres. VIESTURS PAVASARS.

BAHÁ'Í FAITH

National Spiritual Assembly: Apdo Aéreo 51387, Santafé de Bogotá, DC; tel. (1) 268-1658; adherents in 1,013 localities.

JUDAISM

There is a community of about 25,000 with 66 synagogues.

The Press

DAILIES

Santafé de Bogotá, DC

El Espacio: Carrera 61, No 45-35, El Dorado, Santafé de Bogotá, DC; tel. (1) 410-5066; fax (1) 410-4595; f. 1965; evening; Dir JAIME ARDILA CASAMITJANA; circ. 165,000.

El Espectador: Carrera 68, No 23-71, Apdo Aéreo 3441, Santafé de Bogotá, DC; tel. (1) 260-6044; telex 44718; f. 1887; morning; Dir JUAN GUILLERMO CANO; Editor FERNANDO CANO; circ. 215,000.

El Nuevo Siglo: Calle 45A, No 102-02, Apdo Aéreo 5452, Santafé de Bogotá, DC; tel. (1) 413-9200; fax (1) 413-8547; f. 1925; Conservative; Dirs JUAN PABLO URIBE, JUAN GABRIEL URIBE; circ. 68,000.

La Prensa: Calle 123, No 20-80, Santafé de Bogotá, DC; tel. (1) 612-6366; fax (1) 215-9467; Dir JUAN CARLOS PASTRANA.

La República: Calle 16, No 103-59, Santafé de Bogotá, DC; tel. (1) 413-5077; fax (1) 413-3725; f. 1953; morning; economics; Dir RODRIGO OSPINA HERNÁNDEZ; Editor JORGE EMILIO SIERRA M.; circ. 55,000.

El Tiempo: Avda El Dorado, No 59-70, Apdo Aéreo 3633, Santafé de Bogotá, DC; tel. (1) 294-0100; telex 44812; f. 1911; morning; Liberal; Dir HERNANDO SANTOS CASTILLO; Editor ENRIQUE SANTOS CALDERÓN; circ. 263,086 (weekdays), 510,034 (Sundays).

Barranquilla, Atlántico

Diario del Caribe: Calle 42, No 50B-32, Barranquilla, Atlántico; tel. (5) 41-5200; telex 33473; f. 1956; daily; Liberal; Dir EDUARDO POSADA CARBÓ; circ. 30,000.

El Heraldo: Calle 53B, No 46-25, Barranquilla, Atlántico; tel. (5) 41-6066; telex 33348; f. 1933; morning; Liberal; Dir JUAN B. FERNÁNDEZ; circ. 65,000.

La Libertad: Carrera 53, No 55-166, Barranquilla, Atlántico; tel. (5) 31-1517; Liberal; Dir ROBERTO ESPER REBAJE; circ. 25,000.

Bucaramanga, Santander del Sur

El Frente: Calle 35, No 12-40, Apdo Aéreo 665, Bucaramanga, Santander del Sur; tel. (7) 24949; telex 77777; f. 1942; morning; Conservative; Dir Dr RAFAEL ORTIZ GONZÁLEZ; circ. 13,000.

Vanguardia Liberal: Calle 34, No 13-42, Bucaramanga, Santander del Sur; tel. (7) 33-4000; fax (7) 30-2443; f. 1919; morning; Liberal; Sunday illustrated literary supplement and women's supplement; Dir and Man. ALEJANDRO GALVIS RAMÍREZ; circ. 60,000.

Cali, Valle del Cauca

Occidente: Calle 12, No 5-22, Cali, Valle del Cauca; tel. (2) 85-1110; telex 55509; fax (2) 83-6097; f. 1961; morning; Conservative; Dir ALVARO H. CAICEDO GONZÁLEZ; circ. 50,000.

El País: Carrera 2A, No 24-46, Apdo Aéreo 1608, Cali, Valle del Cauca; tel. (2) 89-3011; telex 55527; fax (2) 83-5014; f. 1950; Conservative; Dir RODRIGO LLOREDA C.; circ. 65,071 (weekdays), 72,938 (Saturdays), 108,304 (Sundays).

El Pueblo: Avda 3A, Norte 35-N-10, Cali, Valle del Cauca; tel. (2) 68-8110; telex 55669; morning; Liberal; Dir LUIS FERNANDO LONDOÑO CAPURRO; circ. 50,000.

Cartagena, Bolívar

El Universal: Calle 31, No 3-81, Cartagena, Bolívar; tel. (5) 40484; telex 37788; daily; Liberal; Dir GONZALO ZÚÑIGA; Man. GERARDO ARAÚJO; circ. 28,000.

Cúcuta, Norte de Santander

La Opinión: Avda 4, No 16-12, Cúcuta, Norte de Santander; tel. (75) 71-9999; fax (75) 71-7869; f. 1960; morning; Liberal; Dir Dr JOSÉ EUSTORGIO COLMENARES OSSA; circ. 26,000.

Manizales, Caldas

La Patria: Carrera 20, No 21-51, Apdo Aéreo 70, Manizales, Caldas; tel. (68) 84-2460; fax (68) 84-7158; f. 1921; morning; Independent; Dir Dr LUIS FELIPE GÓMEZ RESTREPO; circ. 22,000.

Medellín, Antioquia

El Colombiano: Carrera 48, No 30 sur-119, Apdo Aéreo 80636, Medellín, Antioquia; tel. (4) 331-5252; fax (4) 331-3950; f. 1912; morning; Conservative; Dir ANA MERCEDES GÓMEZ MARTÍNEZ; circ. 120,000.

El Mundo: Calle 53, No 74-50, Apdo Aéreo 53874, Medellín, Antioquia; tel. (4) 264-2800; fax (4) 264-3729; f. 1979; Dir GUILLERMO GAVIRIA; Man. ANÍBAL GAVIRIA CORREA; circ. 40,000.

Neiva

Diario del Huila: Calle 8A, No 6-30, Neiva; tel. (88) 22619; Dir MARÍA M. RENGIFO DE D.; circ. 10,000.

Pasto, Nariño

El Derecho: Calle 20, No 26-20, Pasto, Nariño; tel. (277) 2170; telex 53740; f. 1928; Conservative; Pres. Dr JOSÉ ELÍAS DEL HIERRO; Dir EDUARDO F. MAZUERA; circ. 12,000.

Pereira, Risaralda

Diario del Otún: Carrera 8A, No 22-75, Apdo Aéreo 2533, Pereira, Risaralda; tel. (63) 51313; telex 8754; fax (1) 34-2897; f. 1982; Financial Dir JAVIER IGNACIO RAMÍREZ MÚNERA; circ. 30,000.

La Tarde: Carrera 9A, No 20-54, Pereira, Risaralda; tel. (63) 35-7976; telex 08832; fax (63) 35-5187; f. 1975; Dir LUIS FERNANDO BAENA MEJÍA; circ. 15,000.

Popayán, Cauca

El Liberal: Carrera 3, No 2-60, Apdo Aéreo 538, Popayán; tel. (928) 23-2418; fax (928) 23-3888; f. 1938; Dir CARLOS ALBERTO CABAL JIMÉNEZ; circ. 10,000.

Santa Marta, Magdalena

El Informador: Santa Marta, Magdalena; f. 1921; Liberal; Dir JOSÉ B. VIVES; circ. 9,000.

Tunja, Boyacá

Diario de Boyacá: Tunja, Boyacá; Dir-Gen. Dr CARLOS H. MOJICA; circ. 3,000.

Villavicencio, Meta

Clarín del Llano: Villavicencio, Meta; tel. (866) 23207; Conservative; Dir ELÍAS MATUS TORRES; circ. 5,000.

PERIODICALS

Santafé de Bogotá, DC

Antena: Santafé de Bogotá, DC; television, cinema and show business; circ. 10,000.

Arco: Carrera 6, No 35-39, Apdo Aéreo 8624, Santafé de Bogotá, DC; tel. (1) 285-1500; telex 45153; f. 1959; monthly; history, philosophy, literature and humanities; Dir ALVARO VALENCIA TOVAR; circ. 10,000.

ART NEXUS/Arte en Colombia: Avda 68, No 23-52, 2°, Apdo Aéreo 90193, Santafé de Bogotá, DC; tel. (1) 262-5178; fax (1) 413-6335; e-mail artnex@colomsat.net.co; f. 1976; quarterly; Latin-American art, architecture, films and photography; editions in English and Spanish; Dir CELIA SREDNI DE BIRBRAGHER; Exec. Editor IVONNE PINI; circ. 15,000.

El Campesino: Carrera 39A, No 15-11, Santafé de Bogotá, DC; f. 1958; weekly; cultural; Dir JOAQUÍN GUTIÉRREZ MACÍAS; circ. 70,000.

Consigna: Diagonal 34, No 5-11, Santafé de Bogotá, DC; tel. (1) 287-1157; fortnightly; Turbayista; Dir (vacant); circ. 10,000.

Coyuntura Económica: Calle 78, No 9-91, Apdo Aéreo 75074, Santafé de Bogotá, DC; tel. (1) 312-5300; fax (1) 212-6073; e-mail fedesarr@openway.com.co; f. 1970; quarterly; economics; published by Fundación para Educación Superior y el Desarrollo (FEDESARROLLO); Editor MARÍA ANGÉLICA ARBELAEZ; circ. 1,500.

Cromos Magazine: Calle 70A, No 7-81, Apdo Aéreo 59317, Santafé de Bogotá, DC; f. 1916; weekly; illustrated; general news; Dir ALBERTO ZALAMEA; circ. 102,000.

As Deportes: Calle 20, No 4-55, Santafé de Bogotá, DC; f. 1978; sports; circ. 25,000.

Economía Colombiana: Edif. de los Ministerios, Of. 126A, No 6-40, Santafé de Bogotá, DC; f. 1984; published by Contraloría General de la República; monthly; economics.

Escala: Calle 30, No 17-70, Santafé de Bogotá, DC; tel. (1) 287-8200; fax (1) 232-5148; f. 1962; monthly; architecture; Dir DAVID SERNA CÁRDENAS; circ. 16,000.

Estrategia: Carrera 4A, 25A-12B, Santafé de Bogotá, DC; monthly; economics; Dir RODRIGO OTERO.

Guión: Carrera 16, No 36-89, Apdo Aéreo 19857; Santafé de Bogotá, DC; tel. (1) 232-2660; f. 1977; weekly; general; Conservative; Dir JUAN CARLOS PASTRANA; circ. 35,000.

Hit: Calle 20, No 4-55, Santafé de Bogotá, DC; cinema and show business; circ. 20,000.

Hoy Por Hoy: Santafé de Bogotá, DC; weekly; Dir DIANA TURBAY DE URIBE.

Menorah: Apdo Aéreo 9081, Santafé de Bogotá, DC; tel. (1) 611-2014; f. 1950; independent monthly review for the Jewish community; Dir ELIÉCER CELNIK; circ. 10,000.

Nueva Frontera: Carrera 7A, No 17-01, 5°, Santafé de Bogotá, DC; tel. (1) 334-3763; f. 1974; weekly; politics, society, arts and culture; Liberal; Dir CARLOS LLERAS RESTREPO; circ. 23,000.

Pluma: Apdo Aéreo 12190, Santafé de Bogotá, DC; monthly; art and literature; Dir (vacant); circ. 70,000.

Que Hubo: Santafé de Bogotá, DC; weekly; general; Editor CONSUELO MONTEJO; circ. 15,000.

Revista Diners: Carrera 10, No 64-65, 3°, Santafé de Bogotá, DC; tel. (1) 346-0800; telex 45304; fax (1) 212-8931; f. 1963; monthly; Editor JOSÉ FERNANDO LÓPEZ; circ. 130,000.

Semana: Calle 93B, No 13-47, Santafé de Bogotá, DC; tel. (1) 622-2277; fax (1) 621-0475; general; Pres. FELIPE LÓPEZ CABALLERO.

Síntesis Económica: Calle 70A, No 10-52, Santafé de Bogotá, DC; tel. (1) 212-5121; fax (1) 212-8365; f. 1975; weekly; economics; Dir FÉLIX LAFAURIE RIVERA; circ. 16,000.

Teorema: Calle 70A, No 8-17, Santafé de Bogotá, DC; tel. (1) 217-2266; fax (1) 212-0639; f. 1983; computer technology; Dir DIONISIO IBÁÑEZ; circ. 5,000.

Tribuna Médica: Calle 8B, No 68A-41 y Calle 123, No 8-20, Santafé de Bogotá, DC; tel. (1) 262-6085; telex 43195; fax (1) 262-4459; f. 1961; monthly; medical and scientific; Editor JACK ALBERTO GRIMBERG; circ. 50,000.

Tribuna Roja: Apdo Aéreo 19042, Santafé de Bogotá, DC; tel. (1) 243-0371; f. 1971; quarterly; organ of the MOIR (pro-Maoist Communist party); Dir CARLOS NARANJO; circ. 300,000.

Vea: Calle 20, No 4-55, Santafé de Bogotá, DC; weekly; popular; circ. 90,000.

Voz La Verdad del Pueblo: Carrera 8, No 19-34, Of. 310–311, Santafé de Bogotá, DC; tel. (1) 284-5209; fax (1) 342-5041; weekly; left-wing; Dir CARLOS A. LOZANO G.; circ. 45,000.

NEWS AGENCIES

Ciep—El País: Carrera 16, No 36-35, Santafé de Bogotá, DC; tel. (1) 232-6816; telex 44707; fax (1) 288-0236; Dir JORGE TÉLLEZ.

Colprensa: Diagonal 34, No 5-63, Apdo Aéreo 20333, Santafé de Bogotá, DC; tel. (1) 287-2200; fax (1) 287-6267; f. 1980; Dir OSCAR DOMÍNGUEZ GIRALDO.

Foreign Bureaux

Agence France-Presse (AFP): Carrera 5, No 16-14, Of. 807, Apdo Aéreo 4654, Santafé de Bogotá, DC1; tel. (1) 281-8613; telex 44726; Dir MARIE SANZ.

Agencia EFE (Spain): Carrera 16, No 39A-69, Apdo Aéreo 16038, Santafé de Bogotá, DC; tel. (1) 285-1576; telex 44577; fax (1) 285-1598; Bureau Chief ANTONIO MARTÍNEZ MARTÍN.

Agenzia Nazionale Stampa Associata (ANSA) (Italy): Carrera 4, No 67-30, Apdo Aéreo 16077, Santafé de Bogotá, DC; tel. (1) 211-9617; telex 42266; fax (1) 212-5409; Bureau Chief ALBERTO ROJAS MORALES.

Associated Press (AP) (USA): Transversal 14, No 122-36, Apdo Aéreo 093643, Santafé de Bogotá, DC; tel. (1) 619-3487; fax (1) 213-8467; e-mail apbogota@bigfoot.com; Bureau Chief FRANK BAJAK.

Central News Agency Inc. (Taiwan): Carrera 13A, No 98-34, Santafé de Bogotá, DC; tel. (1) 25-6342; Correspondent CHRISTINA CHOW.

Deutsche Presse-Agentur (dpa) (Germany): Carrera 7A, No 17-01, Of. 909, Santafé de Bogotá, DC; tel. (1) 284-7481; telex 45555; fax (1) 281-8065; Correspondent RODRIGO RUIZ TOVAR.

Informatsionnoye Telegrafnoye Agentstvo Rossii—Telegrafnoye Agentstvo Suverennykh Stran (ITAR—TASS) (Russia): Calle 20, No 7-17, Of. 901, Santafé de Bogotá, DC; tel. (1) 243-6720; telex 43329; Correspondent GENNADII KOCHUK.

Inter Press Service (IPS) (Italy): Calle 19, No 3-50, Of. 602, Apdo Aéreo 7739, Santafé de Bogotá, DC; tel. (1) 341-8841; fax (1) 334-2249; Correspondent MARÍA ISABEL GARCÍA NAVARRETE.

Prensa Latina: Carrera 3, No 21-46, Apdo Aéreo 30372, Santafé de Bogotá, DC; tel. (1) 282-4527; fax (1) 281-7286; Bureau Chief FAUSTO TRIANA.

Reuters (United Kingdom): Calle 94A, No 13-34, 4°, Apdo Aéreo 29848, Santafé de Bogotá, DC; tel. (1) 610-7633; fax (1) 610-7733; Correspondent MICHAEL STOTT.

United Press International (UPI) (USA): Carrera 4A, No 67-30, 4°, Apdo Aéreo 57570, Santafé de Bogotá, DC; tel. (1) 211-9106; telex 44892; Correspondent FEDERICO FULLEDA.

Xinhua (New China) News Agency (People's Republic of China): Calle 74, No 4-26, Apdo Aéreo 501, Santafé de Bogotá, DC; tel (1) 211-5347; telex 45620; Dir HOU YAOQI.

PRESS ASSOCIATIONS

Asociación Colombiana de Periodistas: Avda Jiménez, No 8-74, Of. 510, Santafé de Bogotá, DC; tel. (1) 243-6056.

Asociación Nacional de Diarios Colombianos (ANDIARIOS): Calle 61, No 5-20, Apdo Aéreo 13663, Santafé de Bogotá, DC; tel. (1) 212-8694; telex 41261; fax (1) 212-7894; f. 1962; 30 affiliated newspapers; Pres. LUIS MIGUEL DE BEDOUT; Vice-Pres. LUIS FERNANDO BAENA.

Asociación de la Prensa Extranjera: Pedro Meléndez, No 87-93, Santafé de Bogotá, DC; tel. (1) 288-3011.

Círculo de Periodistas de Santafé de Bogotá, DC (CPB): Calle 26, No 13A-23, 23°, Santafé de Bogotá, DC; tel. (1) 282-4217; Pres. MARÍA TERESA HERRÁN.

Publishers

Santafé de Bogotá, DC

Comunicadores Técnicos Ltda: Carrera 18, No 46-58, Apdo Aéreo 28797, Santafé de Bogotá, DC; technical; Dir PEDRO P. MORCILLO.

Cultural Colombiana Ltd: Calle 72, No 16-15 y 16-21, Apdo Aéreo 6307, Santafé de Bogotá, DC; tel. (1) 347-2180; fax (1) 217-6570; f. 1951; textbooks; Dir JOSÉ PORTO VÁSQUEZ.

Ediciones Lerner Ltda: Calle 8A, No 68A-41, Apdo Aéreo 8304, Santafé de Bogotá, DC; tel. (1) 262-4284; telex 43195; fax (1) 262-4459; f. 1959; general; Man. Dir JACK A. GRIMBERG.

Editora Cinco, SA: Calle 61, No 13-23, 7°, Apdo Aéreo 15188, Santafé de Bogotá, DC; tel. (1) 285-6200; telex 15188; recreation, culture, textbooks, general; Man. PEDRO VARGAS G.

Editorial El Globo, SA: Calle 16, No 4-96, Apdo Aéreo 6806, Santafé de Bogotá, DC.

Editorial Interamericana, SA: Carrera 17, No 33-71, Apdo Aéreo 6131, Santafé de Bogotá, DC; tel. (1) 288-1255; fax (1) 245-4786; university textbooks; Gen. Man. VÍCTOR CORTES.

Editorial Pluma Ltda: Carrera 20, No 39B-50, Santafé de Bogotá, DC; tel. (1) 245-7606; telex 45422; politics, psychology, philosophy; Man. Dir ERNESTO GAMBOA.

Editorial Presencia, Ltda: Calle 23, No 24-20, Apdo Aéreo 41500, Santafé de Bogotá, DC; tel. (1) 269-2188; fax (1) 269-6830; textbooks, tradebooks; Gen. Man. MARÍA UMAÑA DE TANCO.

Editorial Temis SA: Calle 13, No 6-45, Apdo Aéreo 5941, Santafé de Bogotá, DC; tel. (1) 269-0713; fax (1) 292-5801; f. 1951; law, sociology, politics; Man. Dir JORGE GUERRERO.

Editorial Voluntad, SA: Carrera 7A, No 24-89, 24°, Apdo Aéreo 4692, Santafé de Bogotá, DC; tel. (1) 286-0666; telex 42481; fax (1) 286-5540; e-mail voluntad@colomsat.net.co; f. 1930; school books; Pres. GASTÓN DE BEDOUT.

Fundación Centro de Investigación y Educación Popular (CINEP): Carrera 5A, No 33A-08, Apdo Aéreo 25916, Santafé de Bogotá, DC; tel. (1) 285-8977; fax (1) 287-9089; f. 1977; education and social sciences; Dir P. GABRIEL IZQUIERDO S. J.

Instituto Caro y Cuervo: Carrera 11, No 64-37, Apdo Aéreo 51502, Santafé de Bogotá, DC; tel. (1) 255-8289; fax (1) 217-0243; e-mail carocuerv@openway.com.co; f. 1942; philology, general linguistics and reference; Man. Dir IGNACIO CHAVES CUEVAS; Gen. Sec. GUILLERMO RUIZ LARA.

Inversiones Cromos SA: Calle 70A, No 7-81, Apdo Aéreo 59317, Santafé de Bogotá, DC; tel. (1) 217-1754; fax (1) 211-2642; f. 1916; Dir ALBERTO ZALAMEA; Gen. Man. JORGE EDUARDO CORREA ROBLEDO.

Legis, SA: Avda El Dorado, No 81-10, Apdo Aéreo 98888, Santafé de Bogotá, DC; tel. (1) 263-4100; fax (1) 295-2650; f. 1952; economics, law, general; Man. MAURICIO SERNA.

Publicar, SA: Avda 68, No 75A-50, 4°, Centro Comercial Metrópolis, Apdo Aéreo 8010, Santafé de Bogotá, DC; tel. (1) 225-5555; telex 44588; fax (1) 225-4015; f. 1954; directories; Man. Dr FABIO CABAL P.

Siglo XXI Editores de Colombia Ltda: Santafé de Bogotá, DC; tel. (1) 281-3905; f. 1976; arts, politics, anthropology, history, fiction, etc.; Man. SANTIAGO POMBO.

Suprimir Ediciones Paulinas (SSP): San Pablo, Carrera 46, No 22A–90, Quintaparedes, Apdo 100383, Santafé de Bogotá, DC; tel. (1) 244-4502; fax (1) 268-4288; f. 1951; religion, culture, humanism; Dir Editor ARCÁNGEL CÁRDENAS.

Tercer Mundo Editores SA: Transversal 2A, No 67-27, Apdo 4817, Santafé de Bogotá, DC; tel. (1) 255-1539; fax (1) 201-0209; f. 1961; social sciences, fiction; Gen. Man. SANTIAGO POMBO VEJARANO.

ASSOCIATIONS

Cámara Colombiana del Libro: Carrera 17A, No 37-27, Apdo Aéreo 8998, Santafé de Bogotá, DC; tel. (1) 288-6188; fax (1) 287-3320; f. 1951; Pres. GONZALO ARBOLEDA; Exec. Dir JUAN ORLANDO BUITRAGO D'LLEMAN;120 mems.

Colcultura: Calle 8, No 6-97, 2°, Santafé de Bogotá, DC; tel. (1) 282-8656; fax (1) 282-5104; Dir ISADORA DE NORDEN.

Fundalectura: Avda 40, No 16-46, Santafé de Bogotá, DC; tel. (1) 320-1511; fax (1) 287-7071; e-mail fundalec@impsat.net.co; Exec. Dir SILVIA CASTRILLÓN.

Broadcasting and Communications

Ministerio de Comunicaciones, Dirección de Telecomunicaciones: Edif. Murillo Toro, Carreras 7A y 8A, Calle 12A y 13, Apdo Aéreo 14515, Santafé de Bogotá, DC; tel. (1) 286-6911; telex 41249; fax (1) 286-1185; broadcasting authority; Dir Minister of Communications.

Instituto Nacional de Radio y Televisión—INRAVISION: Centro Administrativo Nacional (CAN), Avda El Dorado, Santafé de Bogotá, DC; tel. (1) 222-0700; telex 43311; fax (1) 222-1426; f. 1954; govt-run TV and radio broadcasting network; educational and commercial broadcasting; Dir DARÍO RESTREPO VÉLEZ.

TELECOMMUNICATIONS

Celumóvil SA: Calle 71A, No 6-30, 18°, Santafé de Bogotá, DC; tel. (1) 346-1666; fax (1) 211-2031; Sec.-Gen. CARLOS BERNARDO CARREÑO R.

Empresa Nacional de Telecomunicaciones (TELECOM): Calle 23, No 13-49, Santafé de Bogotá, DC; tel. (1) 269-4077; telex 44280; fax (1) 284-2171; f. 1947; national telecommunications enterprise; Pres. Dr JULIO MOLANO GONZÁLEZ.

RADIO

In 1988 there were 516 radio stations officially registered with the Ministry of Communications. Most radio stations belong to ASOMEDIOS. The principal radio networks are as follows:

Cadena Radial La Libertad Ltda: Carrera 53, No 55-166, Apdo Aéreo 3143, Barranquilla; tel. (5) 31-1517; fax (5) 32-1279; news and music programmes for Barranquilla, Cartagena and Santa Marta; stations include Emisora Ondas del Caribe (youth programmes), Radio Libertad (classical music programmes) and Emisora Fuentes.

Cadena Super: Calle 39A, No 18-12, Apdo Aéreo 23316, Santafé de Bogotá, DC; tel. (1) 287-7777; telex 45345; fax (1) 287-4293; stations include Radio Super and Super Stereo FM.

Cadena Melodía de Colombia: Calle 45, No 13-70, Santafé de Bogotá, DC; tel. (1) 245-4064; fax (1) 232-1425; Vice-Pres. GERARDO PAEZ MEJÍA.

CARACOL, SA (Primera Cadena Radial Colombiana, SA): Carretera 39A, No 15-81, Apdo Aéreo 9291, Santafé de Bogotá, DC; tel. (1) 337-8866; fax (1) 337-7126; f. 1948; 126 stations; Pres. RICARDO ALARCÓN GAVIRIA.

Circuito Todelar de Colombia: Avda 13, No 84-42, Apdo Aéreo 27344, Santafé de Bogotá, DC; tel. (1) 616-1011; fax (1) 616-0056; f. 1953; 74 stations; Pres. BERNARDO TOBÓN DE LA ROCHE.

Colmundo Radio, SA ('La Cadena de la Paz'): Diagonal 58, 26A-29, Apdo Aéreo 36750, Santafé de Bogotá, DC; tel. (1) 217-8911; fax (1) 217-9358; f. 1989; Pres. Dr NÉSTOR CHAMORRO P.

Organización Radial Olímpica, SA: Calle 72, No 48-37, 2°, Apdo Aéreo 51266, Barranquilla; tel. (5) 45-4102; fax (5) 45-9080; programmes for the Antioquia and Atlantic coast regions.

RCN (Radio Cadena Nacional, SA): Calle 37, No 13A-19, Santafé de Bogotá, DC; tel. (1) 314-7070; fax (1) 288-6130; 116 stations; official network; Gen. Man. RICARDO LONDOÑO LONDOÑO.

Radiodifusora Nacional de Colombia: Centro Administrativo Nacional (CAN), Avda El Dorado, Santafé de Bogotá, DC; tel. (1) 222-0415; Dir ATHALA MORRIS.

Radiodifusores Unidos, SA (RAU): Carrera 13, No 85-51, Of. 705, Santafé de Bogotá, DC; tel. (1) 617-0584; commercial network of independent local and regional stations throughout the country.

TELEVISION

Television services began in 1954, and are operated by the state monopoly, INRAVISION, which controls two national commercial stations and one national educational station. There are also three regional stations. Broadcasting time is distributed among competing programmers through a public tender and most of the commercial broadcast time is dominated by 35 programmers. Both channels broadcast around 77 hours per week. The educational station broadcasts some 39 hours per week. The NTSC colour television system was adopted in 1979.

Major Production Companies

Jorge Barón Televisión Ltda: Avda 15, No 123-31, 5°, Apdo Aéreo 003040, Santafé de Bogotá, DC; tel. (1) 215-0211; telex 42147; fax (1) 215-5581; light entertainment, news, children's programmes.

Caracol Televisión, SA: Calle 19, No 3-16, Santafé de Bogotá, DC; tel. (1) 282-2088; telex 41480; fax (1) 286-3160; general; Programme Head RUT ECHEVERDI.

CENPRO Televisión: Corporación Social para las Comunicaciones, Carrera 6, No 69A-20, Apdo Aéreo 057931, Santafé de Bogotá, DC; tel. (1) 232-3076; fax (1) 245-7526; imported US programmes, documentaries and magazine format programmes.

Colombiana de Televisión, SA: Calle 92, No 9-17, Santafé de Bogotá, DC; tel. (1) 218-1914; fax (1) 218-1775; general.

Intervisión, SA: Empresa Interamericana de Medios de Comunicación Social, Carrera 13A, No 38-22, Santafé de Bogotá, DC; tel. (1) 288-0599; telex 42537; fax (1) 285-3704; news, sport and imported US serials.

Noticiero Veinticuatro Horas Ltda: Calle 42, No 56-21, 20°, Apdo Aéreo 9268, Santafé de Bogotá, DC; tel. (1) 221-5040; telex 42289; fax (1) 222-0798; 24-hour news service for Channel 1.

Procívica TV: Carrera 41, No 5B-71, Cali; tel. (2) 553-6449; fax (2) 553-6422; news magazine programmes serving the Pacific coast region.

Producciones Punch, SA: Calle 43, No 27-47, Apdo Aéreo 14427, Santafé de Bogotá, DC; tel. (1) 269-4711; fax (1) 269-3539; f. 1956; light entertainment; Pres. ALEJANDRO PÉREZ V. BRANTEGHEM; Sec.-Gen. PATRICIA RODRÍGUEZ GÓMEZ.

RCN-Televisión de Colombia: Avda de las Américas, No 65-82, Santafé de Bogotá, DC; tel. (1) 290-6088; fax (1) 290-9241; general.

RTI: Calle 19, No 4-56, 2°, Santafé de Bogotá, DC; tel. (1) 282-7700; fax (1) 284-9012; Programme Head PATRICIO WILLS.

RTM-Radio Televisión Medios: Calle 8, No 37A-59, Medellín; tel. (4) 68-3030; fax (4) 246-0734; programmes serving the Antioquia region.

Televista Ltda: Calle 82, No 51B-64, Apdo Aéreo 51027, Barranquilla; tel. (5) 45-8475; fax (5) 45-2745; general.

ASSOCIATIONS

Asociación Nacional de Medios de Comunicación (ASOMEDIOS): Carrera 22, No 85-72, Santafé de Bogotá, DC; tel. (1) 611-1300; fax (1) 621-6292; f. 1978 and merged with ANRADIO

(Asociación Nacional de Radio, Televisión y Cine de Colombia) in 1980; Pres. Dr SERGIO ARBOLEDA CASAS.

Federación Nacional de Radio (FEDERADIO): Santafé de Bogotá, DC; Dir LIBARDO TABORDA BOLÍVAR.

Finance

(cap. = capital; res = reserves; dep. = deposits; m. = million; amounts in pesos, unless otherwise indicated)

Contraloría General de la República: Carrera 10, No 17-18, Torre Colseguros, 27°, Santafé de Bogotá, DC; tel. (1) 282-7905; fax (1) 282-3549; Controller-General Dr MANUEL FRANCISCO BECERRA.

BANKING

In August 1989 the Government authorized plans to return to private ownership 65% of the assets of all financial institutions nationalized after the financial crisis of 1982.

Supervisory Authority

Superintendencia Bancaria: Carrera 7A, No 4-49, 11°, Apdo Aéreo 3460, Santafé de Bogotá, DC; tel. (1) 280-1187; telex 41443; fax (1) 280-0864; e-mail superban@impsat.net.co; Banking Superintendent JOSÉ ELÍAS MELO ACOSTA.

Central Bank

Banco de la República: Carrera 7A, No 14-78, Apdo Aéreo 3531, Santafé de Bogotá, DC; tel. (1) 343-0190; telex 45407; fax (1) 286-1731; f. 1923; sole bank of issue; Gov. MIGUEL URRUTIA MONTOYA; 28 brs.

Commercial Banks

Santafé de Bogotá, DC

Banco America Colombia (fmrly Banco Colombo-Americano): Carrera 7, No 71-52, Torre B, 4°, Apdo Aéreo 12327, Santafé de Bogotá, DC; tel. (1) 312-1583; telex 44511; fax (1) 312-1816; cap. 3,268m., res 6,205m., dep. 14,475m. (Dec. 1993); wholly-owned subsidiary of Bank of America; Pres. JESÚS DUVÁN GÓMEZ; 1 br.

Banco Andino Colombia, SA (fmrly Banco de Crédito y Comercio): Carrera 7A, No 71-52, Torre B, 1°, 18° y 19°, Apdo Aéreo 6826, Santafé de Bogotá, DC; tel. (1) 312-3666; telex 45646; fax (1) 312-3273; f. 1954; cap. 7,206.5m., res 10,705.9m., dep. 121,367.4m. (Dec. 1993); Pres. JOSÉ VALLEJO GÓMEZ; 21 brs.

Banco Anglo-Colombiano (Lloyds Bank): Carrera 8A, No 15-46/60, 3°, Apdo Aéreo 3532, Santafé de Bogotá, DC; tel. (1) 334-5088; telex 44884; fax (1) 286-1383; f. 1976; cap. 10,173.0m., res 11,511.0m., dep. 209,087.0m. (Dec. 1995); Pres. DAVID J. HUTCHINSON; 45 brs.

Banco de Bogotá: Calle 36, No 7-47, 15°, Apdo Aéreo 3436, Santafé de Bogotá, DC; tel. (1) 288-1188; telex 44628; fax (1) 338-3375; f. 1870; acquired Banco del Comercio in 1992; cap. and res 238,786.2m., dep. 1,180,304.6m. (June 1996); Pres. Dr ALEJANDRO FIGUEROA JARAMILLO; 265 brs.

Banco Cafetero (Bancafe): Calle 28, No 13A-15, Apdo Aéreo 240332, Santafé de Bogotá, DC; tel. (1) 341-1511; telex 43422; f. 1953; cap. US $57.9m., res $134.8m., dep. $909.3m. (Dec. 1992); Pres. GILBERTO GÓMEZ ARANGO; 301 brs.

Banco Caja Social: Calle 72, No 10-71, 8°, Santafé de Bogotá, DC; tel. (1) 310-0099; telex 45685; fax (1) 310-1095; f. 1911; savings bank; cap. 93,077m., res 13,543m., dep. 559,729m. (Dec. 1996); Pres. EULALIA ARBOLEDA DE MONTES; 135 brs.

Banco de Colombia, SA: Calle 30A, No 6-38, Apdo Aéreo 6836, Santafé de Bogotá, DC; tel. (1) 285-0300; telex 44744; fax (1) 287-0595; f. 1874; cap. 57,964m., dep. 978,415m. (Dec. 1992); Pres. FEDERICO ALONSO RENJIFO VÉLEZ; 245 brs.

Banco Colpatria, SA: Carrera 7A, No 24-89, 10°, Apdo Aéreo 30241, Santafé de Bogotá, DC; tel. (1) 234-0600; telex 43404; fax (1) 286-1186; f. 1955; cap. 1,002m., res 15,575m., dep. 197,390m. (Dec. 1994); Pres. SANTIAGO PERDOMO MALDONADO; 26 brs.

Banco de Comercio Exterior de Colombia, SA—BANCOLDEX: Calle 28, No 13A-15, 40°, Apdo Aéreo 240092, Santafé de Bogotá, DC; tel. (1) 341-0677; telex 44452; fax (1) 282-5071; f. 1992; provides financing alternatives for Colombian exporters; affiliate trust company FIDUCOLDEX, SA manages PROEXPORT (Export Promotion Trust); Pres. Dr GABRIEL TURBAY.

Banco de Crédito: Calle 27, No 6-48, 4°, Apdo Aéreo 6800, Santafé de Bogotá, DC; tel. (1) 286-8400; telex 44789; fax (1) 286-7236; f. 1963; cap. 33,060.1m., res 36,405.6m., dep. 457,276.8m. (Dec. 1995); Pres. LUIS F. MESA; 23 brs.

Banco Exterior de Los Andes y de España de Colombia, SA—EXTEBANDES de Colombia, SA: Calle 74, No 6-65, Apdo Aéreo 241247, Santafé de Bogotá, DC; tel. (1) 217-7200; telex 43184; fax (1) 212-5786; f. 1982; cap. 10,312m., res 5,574m., dep. 84,200m. (Dec. 1996); Pres. MARÍA DEL ROSARIO SINTES ULLOA; 11 brs.

Banco Ganadero: Carrera 9A, No 72-21, 11°, Apdo Aéreo 53859, Santafé de Bogotá, DC; tel. (1) 217-0100; telex 45121; fax (1) 235-1248; f. 1956; cap. 27,911.0m., res 412,249.0m., dep. 1,488,672.0m. (Dec. 1995); Exec.-Pres. JOSÉ MARÍA AYALA VARGAS; 123 brs.

Banco Mercantil de Colombia, SA (fmrly Banco de los Trabajadores): Avda 82, No 12-18, 8°, Santafé de Bogotá, DC; tel. (1) 635-0035; telex 41430; fax (1) 623-7512; f. 1974; wholly-owned subsidiary of Banco Mercantil (Venezuela); cap. 19,409.9m., res 9,591.3m., dep. 99,483.2m. (Dec. 1995); Pres. GUSTAVO SINTES ULLOA; 10 brs.

Banco Nacional del Comercio (fmrly Banco de Caldas): Calle 72, No 7-64, 10°, Santafé de Bogotá, DC; tel. (1) 210-1600; Pres. RENÉ CAVANZO ALZUGARATTE.

Banco del Pacífico, SA: Calle 100, 19-05, Santafé de Bogotá, DC; tel. (1) 416-5945; fax (1) 611-2339; f. 1994; wholly-owned by Banco del Pacífico, SA, Guayaquil (Ecuador); cap. 12,000.0m., res 3,811.7m., dep. 141,657.3m. (Dec. 1995); Pres. JUAN CARLOS BERNAL.

Banco Popular, SA: Calle 17, 7-43, 4°, Apdo Aéreo 6796, Santafé de Bogotá, DC; tel. (1) 283-3964; telex 45840; fax (1) 281-9448; f. 1951; govt-owned; cap. 1,353m., res 55,159m., dep. 348,548m. (Dec. 1992); Pres. HERNÁN RINCÓN-GÓMEZ; 158 brs.

Banco Real de Colombia (fmrly Banco Real SA): Carrera 7A, No 33-80, Apdo Aéreo 34262, Santafé de Bogotá, DC; tel. (1) 879-9300; telex 44688; fax (1) 287-0507; f. 1975; cap. 8,110.5m., res 6,217.7m., dep. 56,787.7m. (Dec. 1993); Pres. PAULO CÉZAR DA ROCHA DIAS; 17 brs.

Banco Sudameris Colombia (fmrly Banco Francés e Italiano): Carrera 8, 15-42, 3°, Apdo Aéreo 3440, Santafé de Bogotá, DC; tel. (1) 337-4700; telex 44555; fax (1) 281-6191; cap. 10,989.7m., res 27,335.6m., dep. 269,243.0m. (Dec. 1995); Pres. GIANFRANCO ORONZO; 6 brs.

Banco Tequendama, SA: Diagonal 27, No 6-70, 4°, Santafé de Bogotá, DC; tel. (1) 205-9900; telex 45496; fax (1) 287-7020; f. 1976; wholly-owned subsidiary of Banco Construcción (Venezuela); cap. 12,049m., dep. 53,522m. (Dec. 1992); Pres. PEDRO RUBIO FEIJOO; 11 brs.

Banco Unión Colombiano (fmrly Banco Royal Colombiano): Torre Banco Unión Colombiano, Carrera 7A, No 71-52, 2°, Apdo Aéreo 3438, Santafé de Bogotá, DC; tel. (1) 312-0411; fax (1) 312-0843; f. 1925; cap. 12,350.3m. res 27,667.2m., dep. 131,063.0m. (Dec. 1995); Pres. FERNANDO E. SUESCUN; 29 brs.

Caja Agraria: Carrera 8A, No 15-43, 13°, Apdo Aéreo 3534, Santafé de Bogotá, DC; tel. (1) 241-1160; telex 44738; f. 1931; cap. 71,527m., res 196m., dep. 463,200m. (Nov. 1992); development bank; Vice-Pres. PABLO JOSÉ RAMÍREZ HERNÁNDEZ; 878 brs.

CITIBANK-Colombia, SA: Carrera 9A, No 99-02, 3°, Santafé de Bogotá, DC; tel. (1) 610-4455; telex 44721; fax (1) 618-2402; wholly-owned subsidiary of Citibank (USA); cap. 483m., res 9,399m., dep. 152,139m. (Dec. 1992); Pres. ERIC R. MAYER; 23 brs.

Cali

Banco de Occidente: Carrera 4, No 7-61, 12°, Apdo Aéreo 4400, Cali; tel. (2) 886-1117; fax (2) 886-1297; cap. and res 107,861m., dep. 809,097m. (June 1997); Pres. EFRAIN OTERO ÁLVAREZ; 110 brs.

Medellín

Banco Comercial Antioqueño, SA: Edif. Vicente Uribe Rendón, Carrera 46, No 52-36, 14°, Apdo Aéreo 54769, Medellín; tel. (4) 511-5200; telex 66643; fax (4) 251-2154; f. 1912; cap. 1,107.5m., res 195,214.6m., dep. 1,007,360.4m., (Dec. 1995); Pres. JORGE JULIÁN TRUJILLO AGUDELO; 131 brs.

Banco Industrial Colombiano, SA: Calle 50, No 51-66, Apdo Aéreo 768, Medellín; tel. (4) 511-5516; telex 66887; fax (4) 251-4716; f. 1945; cap. 1,349m., res 55,815m., dep. 342,983m. (June 1992); Pres. JORGE LONDONO SALDARRIAGA; 99 brs.

Banking Association

Asociación Bancaria de Colombia: Carrera 7A, No 17-01, 3°, Apdo Aéreo 13994, Santafé de Bogotá, DC; tel. (1) 282-1066; f. 1936; 56 mem. banks; Pres. FLORÁNGELA GÓMEZ ORDÓÑEZ; Vice-Pres. SANTIAGO GUTIÉRREZ.

Asociación Nacional de Instituciones Financieras (ANIF): Santafé de Bogotá, DC; Pres. JAVIER FERNÁNDEZ RIVA.

STOCK EXCHANGES

Superintendencia de Valores: Calle 16, No 5-13, Apdo Aéreo 39600, Santafé de Bogotá, DC; tel. (1) 342-0366; fax (1) 334-0072; f. 1979 to regulate the securities market; Supt. Dr LUIS FERNANDO LÓPEZ ROCA.

Bolsa de Bogotá: Carrera 8A, No 13-82, 8°, Apdo Aéreo 3584, Santafé de Bogotá, DC; tel. (1) 243-6501; telex 44807; fax (1) 281-3170; f. 1928; Pres. CARLOS CABALLERO; Sec.-Gen. MARÍA FERNANDA TORRES.

Bolsa de Medellín, SA: Carrera 50, No 50-48, 2°, Apdo Aéreo 3535, Medellín; tel. (4) 260-3000; telex 66788; fax (4) 251-1981; e-mail info@medellin.impsat.net.co; f. 1961; Pres. LUIS FERNANDO URIBE; Vice-Pres. SANTIAGO CÁRDENAS.

Bolsa de Occidente, SA: Calle 10, No 4-40, 13°, Apdo Aéreo 11718, Cali; tel. (2) 889-8400; fax (2) 889-8731; e-mail bolsaocc@cali.cetcol.net.co; internet http://www.bolsadeoccidente.com.co; f. 1983; Pres. JULIÁN DOMÍNGUEZ RIVERA; Vice-Pres. JORGE ALBERTO DURÁN CABAL.

INSURANCE

Principal National Companies

Aseguradora Colseguros, SA: Calle 28, No 13-22, 5°, Santafé de Bogotá, DC; tel. (1) 281-1502; telex 44710; fax (1) 285-7956; f. 1874; Pres. JAIRO MEJÍA HERRERA.

Aseguradora Grancolombiana, SA: Calle 93, No 11-26, 2°, 3°, 4° y 5°, Apdo Aéreo 10454, Santafé de Bogotá, DC; tel. (1) 635-6649; telex 41328; fax (1) 635-6797; Pres. Dr RICARDO MEJÍA OCHOA.

Aseguradora El Libertador, SA: Carrera 13, No 26-45, 9°, Santafé de Bogotá, DC; tel. (1) 281-2427; fax (1) 286-0662; e-mail aselib@impsat.net.co; Pres. FERNANDO ROJAS CÁRDENAS.

Chubb de Colombia Cía de Seguros, SA: Carrera 7A, No 71-52, Torre B, 10°, Santafé de Bogotá, DC; tel. (1) 312-3700; fax (1) 312-2434; e-mail na@chubb.com; Pres. Dr ALVARO SALAMANCA VILLEGAS.

Cigna Seguros de Colombia, SA: Calle 72, No 10-51, 6°, 7° y 8°, Santafé de Bogotá, DC; tel. (1) 212-0352; telex 43120; fax (1) 212-7902; Pres. ALVARO A. ROZO PALOU.

Cía Agrícola de Seguros, SA: Carrera 11, No 93-46, Santafé de Bogotá, DC; tel. (1) 635-5827; fax (1) 635-5876; e-mail secragr@impsat.net.co; f. 1952; Pres. Dr JOSÉ F. JARAMILLO HOYOS.

Cía Aseguradora de Fianzas, SA (Confianza): Calle 82, No 11-37, 7°, Santafé de Bogotá, DC; tel. (1) 610-8566; fax (1) 610-8866; Pres. JOAQUÍN VEGA GARZÓN.

Cía Central de Seguros: Carrera 13, No 27-47, 7° y 8°, Edif. Banco de Occidente, Apdo Aéreo 5764, Santafé de Bogotá, DC; tel. (1) 288-6226; telex 45664; fax (1) 288-6152; e-mail recursos@centralseguros.com.co; f. 1956; Pres. SYLVIA LUZ RINCÓN LEMA.

Cía de Seguros Antorcha de Colombia, SA: Calle 70, No 7-40, Santafé de Bogotá, DC; tel. (1) 217-9088; telex 43196; fax (1) 235-6578; f. 1972; Gen. Man. Dr JADIR GUILHERME FERNANDES.

Cía de Seguros Bolívar, SA: Carrera 10, No 16-39, Apdo Aéreo 4421, Santafé de Bogotá, DC; tel. (1) 281-8481; telex 44873; fax (1) 281-8262; e-mail bolivar@aldato.com.co; f. 1939; Pres. JORGE E. URIBE MONTAÑO.

Cía de Seguros Colmena, SA: Calle 72, No 10-07, 7° y 8°, Apdo Aéreo 6774, Santafé de Bogotá, DC; tel. (1) 211-4975; telex 45217; fax (1) 211-4952; e-mail esegv@col1.telecom.com.co; Pres. JUAN MANUEL DÍAZ-GRANADOS.

Cía de Seguros Generales Aurora, SA: Edif. Seguros Aurora, 1°, 2° y 3°, Carrera 7, No 74-21, Santafé de Bogotá, DC; tel. (1) 212-2252; telex 43186; fax (1) 212-2138; Pres. Dr ANTONIO PABÓN CASTRO.

Cía Mundial de Seguros, SA: Calle 33, No 6-94, 2° y 3°, Santafé de Bogotá, DC; tel. (1) 285-2580; telex 43183; fax (1) 285-1220; e-mail mundial@impsat.com.co; Dir-Gen. CAMILO FERNÁNDEZ ESCOVER.

Cía Suramericana de Seguros, SA: Centro Suramericana, Carrera 64B, No 49A-30, Apdo Aéreo 780, Medellín; tel. (4) 435-5201; telex 66639; fax (4) 260-3194; e-mail nrestrepo@suramericana.com.co; f. 1944; Pres. Dr NICANOR RESTREPO SANTAMARÍA.

Generali Colombia—Seguros Generales, SA: Carrera 7, No 72-13, 8°, Apdo Aéreo 076478, Santafé de Bogotá, DC; tel. (1) 217-8411; fax (1) 255-1164; Pres. JOHN S. PHILLIPS.

La Interamericana Cía de Seguros Generales, SA: Calle 78, No 9-57, 4° y 5°, Santafé de Bogotá, DC; tel. (1) 310-1030; telex 44631; fax (1) 210-2021; Pres. MIGUEL E. SILVA.

La Nacional Cía de Seguros de Vida, SA: Calle 28, No 13-22, 5°, Santafé de Bogotá, DC; tel. (1) 281-1502; telex 44567; fax (1) 285-7956; f. 1952; Pres. Dr BERNARDO BOTERO MORALES.

Latinoamericana de Seguros, SA: Calle 71A, No 6-30, 2° y 3°, Apdo Aéreo 57227, Santafé de Bogotá, DC; tel. (1) 212-0510; telex 44582; fax (1) 212-4034; e-mail lhernandez@impsat.net.co; f. 1954; Pres. MARIO HERNÁNDEZ NEIRA.

Pan American de Colombia Cía de Seguros de Vida, SA: Carrera 7A, No 75-09, Apdo Aéreo 76000, Santafé de Bogotá, DC; tel. (1) 211-8890; fax (1) 217-8799; e-mail 110130.321@compuserve.com; Gen. Man. and Vice-Pres. OSVALDO J. CASTRO PÉREZ.

Seguros Alfa, SA: Carrera 13, No 27-47, 22° y 23°, Apdo Aéreo 27718, Santafé de Bogotá, DC; tel. (1) 287-8225; telex 42191; fax (1) 287-8929; e-mail sistemas@andinet.lat.net; Pres. SONIA GALVIS SEGURA.

Seguros Caribe, SA: Carrera 7A, No 74-36, 5° y 6°, Apdo Aéreo 28525, Santafé de Bogotá, DC; tel. (1) 212-8299; telex 42122; fax (1) 212-0390; Pres. Dr FERNANDO ESCALLÓN MORALES; Dir-Gen. ANTONIO BOFARULL CAÑELLAS.

Seguros Colpatria, SA: Carrera 7, No 24-89, 9°, Apdo Aéreo 7762, Santafé de Bogotá, DC; tel. (1) 616-6655; telex 42066; fax (1) 281-5053; e-mail capricolc@openway.com.co; Pres. Dr MARIO PACHECO CORTÉS.

Seguros La Equidad, OC: Calle 19, No 6-68, 10°, 11° y 12°, Apdo Aéreo 30261, Santafé de Bogotá, DC; tel. (1) 281-8612; fax (1) 286-5124; e-mail equidad@colomsat.net.co; Gen. Man. Dr JULIO ENRIQUE MEDRANO LEÓN.

Seguros del Estado, SA: Carrera 11, No 90-20, Apdo Aéreo 6810, Santafé de Bogotá, DC; tel. (1) 218-6977; telex 45116; fax (1) 218-0971; e-mail seguros2@latino.net.co; Pres. Dr JORGE MORA SÁNCHEZ.

Seguros Fénix, SA: Carrera 7A, No 32-33, 5°, 6° y 7°, Santafé de Bogotá, DC; tel. (1) 243-2102; telex 41335; fax (1) 281-1962; e-mail cinternet@colomsat.net.co; Pres. Dr GONZALO SANÍN POSADA.

Seguros Tequendama, SA: Carrera 7A, No 26-20, 6° y 7°, Apdo Aéreo 7988, Santafé de Bogotá, DC; tel. (1) 334-1774; telex 41426; fax (1) 285-4221; Pres. FRANK DARÍO GÓMEZ.

Seguros Uconal: Calle 19, No 13A-12, 1°, Apdo Aéreo 16721, Santafé de Bogotá, DC; fax (1) 283-5936; Gen. Man. Dr CARLOS DUQUE GUTIÉRREZ.

Skandia Seguros Generales, SA: Avda 19, No 113-30, Apdo Aéreo 100327, Santafé de Bogotá, DC; tel. (1) 214-1200; telex 43398; fax (1) 214-0038; Pres. MAURICIO GARCÍA ORTÍZ.

Numerous foreign companies are also represented.

Insurance Association

Federación de Aseguradores Colombianos—FASECOLDA: Carrera 7A, No 26-20, 11° y 12°, Apdo Aéreo 5233, Santafé de Bogotá, DC; tel. (1) 287-6611; fax (1) 287-5764; e-mail fasecold@anditel.andinet.lat.net; f. 1976; 33 mems; Pres. Dr WILLIAM R. FADUL VERGARA.

Trade and Industry

GOVERNMENT AGENCIES

Departamento Nacional de Planeación: Calle 26, No 13-19, 14°, Santafé de Bogotá, DC; tel. (1) 336-1600; telex 45634; fax (1) 281-3348; f. 1958; supervises and administers development projects; approves foreign investments; Dir JOSÉ ANTONIO OCAMPO GAVIRIA.

Instituto Colombiano de Comercio Exterior—INCOMEX: Calle 28, No 13A-15, 5°, Apdo Aéreo 240193, Santafé de Bogotá, DC; tel. (1) 283-3284; telex 44860; fax (1) 281-2560; sets and executes foreign trade policy; Dir. MARTA RAMIREZ DE RINCÓN.

Instituto Colombiano de la Reforma Agraria—INCORA: Centro Administrativo Nacional (CAN), Avda El Dorado, Apdo Aéreo 151046, Santafé de Bogotá, DC; tel. (1) 222-0963; f. 1962; a public institution which, on behalf of the govt, administers public lands and those it acquires; reclaims land by irrigation and drainage facilities, roads, etc. to increase productivity in agriculture and stock-breeding; provides technical assistance and loans; supervises the distribution of land throughout the country; Dir GERMÁN BULA E.

Superintendencia de Industria y Comercio—SUPERINDUSTRIA: Carrera 13, No 27-00, 5°, Santafé de Bogotá, DC; tel. (1) 234-2035; fax (1) 281-3125; supervises chambers of commerce; controls standards and prices; Supt MARCO AURELIO ZULUAGA GIRALDO.

Superintendencia de Sociedades—SUPERSOCIEDADES: Avda El Dorado, No 46-80, Apdo Aéreo 4188, Santafé de Bogotá, DC; tel. (1) 222-0566; fax (1) 221-1027; e-mail supersoc1@sinpro.gov.co; f. 1931; oversees activities of local and foreign corpns; Supt DARÍO LAGUADO MONSALVE.

DEVELOPMENT ORGANIZATIONS

Fondo Nacional de Proyectos de Desarrollo—FONADE: Calle 26, No 13-19, 18°-21°, Apdo Aéreo 24110, Santafé de Bogotá, DC; tel. (1) 282-9400; telex 45634; fax (1) 282-6018; f. 1968; responsible for channelling loans towards economic development projects; administered by a committee under the head of the Departamento Nacional de Planeación; FONADE works in close association with other official planning orgs; Dir Dr ALBERTO VILLATE PARÍS.

Fundación para el Desarrollo Integral del Valle del Cauca—FDI: Calle 8, No 3-14, 17°, Apdo Aéreo 7482, Cali; tel. (2) 80-6660; telex 7482; fax (2) 82-4627; f. 1969; industrial development org.; Pres. GUNNAR LINDAHL HELLBERG; Exec. Pres. FABIO RODRÍGUEZ GONZÁLEZ.

CHAMBERS OF COMMERCE

Confederación Colombiana de Cámaras de Comercio—CONFECAMARAS: Carrera 13, No 27-47, Of. 502, Apdo Aéreo 29750, Santafé de Bogotá, DC; tel. (1) 288-1200; telex 44416; fax (1) 288-

4228; f. 1969; 53 mem. orgs; Exec.-Pres. NICOLÁS DEL CASTILLO MATHIEU.

Cámara de Comercio de Bogotá: Carrera 9A, No 16-21, Santafé de Bogotá, DC; tel. (1) 334-7900; fax (1) 284-8506; internet http://www.ccb.org.co; f. 1878; 3,650 mem. orgs; Dir ARIEL JARAMILLO JARAMILLO; Exec.-Pres. GUILLERMO FERNÁNDEZ DE SOTO.

There are also local Chambers of Commerce in the capital towns of all the Departments and in many of the other trading centres.

INDUSTRIAL AND TRADE ASSOCIATIONS

Carbones de Colombia, SA—CARBOCOL: Carrera 7, No 31-10, 5°, Apdo Aéreo 29740, Santafé de Bogotá, DC; tel. (1) 287-3100; telex 45779; fax (1) 287-3278; f. 1976; initial cap. 350m. pesos; state enterprise for the exploration, mining, processing and marketing of coal; Pres. Dr ANTONIO PRETELT EMILIANI; Vice-Pres. ARMANDO VERGARA BUSTILLO.

Colombiana de Minería—COLMINAS: Santafé de Bogotá, DC; state mining concern; Man. ALFONSO RODRÍGUEZ KILBER.

Corporación de la Industria Aeronáutica Colombiana, SA (CIAC SA): Aeropuerto Internacional El Dorado, Entrada 1 y 2, Apdo Aéreo 14446, Santafé de Bogotá, DC; tel. (1) 413-9735; fax (1) 413-8673; Gen. Man. ALBERTO MELENDEZ.

Empresa Colombia de Niquel—ECONIQUEL: Santafé de Bogotá, DC; tel. (1) 232-3839; telex 43262; administers state nickel resources; Dir JAVIER RESTREPO TORO.

Empresa Colombiana de Petróleos—ECOPETROL: Carrera 13, No 36-24, Apdo Aéreo 5938, Santafé de Bogotá, DC; tel. (1) 285-6400; fax (1) 287-0041; f. 1948; responsible for exploration, production, refining and transportation of petroleum; Pres. ANDRÉS RESTREPO LONDOÑO; 11,000 employees.

ECOPETROL Internacional: Santafé de Bogotá, DC; f. 1988; conducts exploration activities in Peru and other countries in the region.

Instituto Colombiano de Petróleo: f. 1985; research into all aspects of the hydrocarbon industry; Dir Dr MEDARDO GAMBOA MALDONADO.

Empresa Colombiana de Uranio—COLURANIO: Centro Administrativo Nacional (CAN), 4°, Ministerio de Minas y Energía, Santafé de Bogotá, DC; tel. (1) 244-5440; telex 45898; f. 1977 to further the exploration, processing and marketing of radio-active minerals; initial cap. US $750,000; Dir JAIME GARCÍA.

Empresa de Comercialización de Productos Perecederos—EMCOPER: Santafé de Bogotá, DC; tel. (1) 235-5507; attached to Ministry of Agriculture; Dir LUIS FERNANDO LONDOÑO RUIZ.

Industria Militar—INDUMIL: Diagonal 40, No 47-75, Apdo Aéreo 7272, Santafé de Bogotá, DC; tel. (1) 222-3001; telex 45816; fax (1) 222-4889; attached to Ministry of National Defence; Man. Adm. (retd) MANUEL F. AVENDAÑO.

Instituto Colombiano Agropecuario (ICA): Calle 37, No 8-43, 4° y 5°, Apdo Aéreo 7984, Santafé de Bogotá, DC; tel. (1) 285-5520; telex 44309; fax (1) 285-4351; f. 1962; institute for promotion, co-ordination and implementation of research into and teaching and development of agriculture and animal husbandry; Dir Dr HERNÁN MARIN GUTIÉRREZ.

Instituto de Crédito Territorial (ICT): Carrera 13, No 18-51, Apdo Aéreo 4037, Santafé de Bogotá, DC; tel. (1) 234-3560; telex 44826; Gen. Man. GABRIEL GIRALDO.

Instituto de Fomento Industrial (IFI): Calle 16, No 6-66, 7°-15°, Apdo Aéreo 4222, Santafé de Bogotá, DC; tel. (1) 282-2055; telex 44642; fax (1) 286-4166; f. 1940; state finance corpn for the promotion of manufacturing activities; cap. 115,190.2m. pesos, res 4,714.3m. pesos (Dec. 1994); Gen. Man. CARLOS WOLFF ISAZA.

Instituto de Hidrología, Meteorología y Estudios Ambientales—IDEAM: Diagonal 97, No 17-60, 1°, 2°, 3° y 7°, Santafé de Bogotá, DC; tel. (1) 283-6927; telex 44345; fax (1) 635-6218; f. 1995; responsible for irrigation, flood control, drainage, hydrology and meteorology; Dir PABLO LEYVA.

Instituto de Investigaciones en Geociencias, Minería y Química—INGEOMINAS: Diagonal 53, No 34-53, Apdo Aéreo 4865, Santafé de Bogotá, DC; tel. (1) 222-1811; telex 44909; fax (1) 222-3597; f. 1968; responsible for mineral research, geological mapping and research including hydrogeology, remote sensing, geochemistry and geophysics; Dir Dr ADOLFO ALARCÓN GUZMÁN.

Instituto de Mercadeo Agropecuario—IDEMA: Carrera 10A, No 16-82, Of. 1003, Santafé de Bogotá, DC; tel. (1) 342-2596; telex 43315; fax (1) 283-1838; state enterprise for the marketing of agricultural products; Gen. Man. GLORIA C. BARNEY DURÁN.

Instituto Nacional de Fomento Municipal—INSFOPAL: Centro Administrativo Nacional (CAN), Santafé de Bogotá, DC; tel. (1) 222-3177; telex 45328; Gen. Man. JAIME MARIO SALAZAR VELÁSQUEZ.

Instituto Nacional de los Recursos Naturales Renovables y del Ambiente—INDERENA: Diagonal 34, No 5-18, 3°, Apdo Aéreo 13458, Santafé de Bogotá, DC; tel. (1) 285-4417; telex 44428; f. 1968; govt agency regulating the development of natural resources; Dir (vacant).

Minerales de Colombia, SA (MINERALCO): Calle 32, No 13-07, Apdo Aéreo 17878, Santafé de Bogotá, DC; tel. (1) 287-7136; fax (1) 87-4606; administers state resources of emerald, copper, gold, sulphur, gypsum, phosphate rock and other minerals except coal, petroleum and uranium; Gen. Man. ORLANDO ALVAREZ PÉREZ.

Sociedad Minera del Guainía (SMG): Santafé de Bogotá, DC; f. 1987; state enterprise for exploration, mining and marketing of gold; Pres. Dr JORGE BENDECK OLIVELLA.

There are several other agricultural and regional development organizations.

EMPLOYERS' AND PRODUCERS' ORGANIZATIONS

Asociación Colombiana Popular de Industriales (ACOPI): Carrera 23, No 41-94, Apdo Aéreo 16451, Santafé de Bogotá, DC; tel. (1) 244-2741; fax (1) 268-8965; f. 1951; asscn of small industrialists; Pres. JUAN A. PINTO SAAVEDRA; Man. MIGUEL CARRILLO M.

Asociación de Cultivadores de Caña de Azúcar de Colombia (ASOCAÑA): Calle 58N, No 3N-15, Apdo Aéreo 4448, Cali; tel. (2) 64-7902; telex 51136; fax (2) 64-5888; f. 1959; sugar planters' asscn; Pres. Dr RICARDO VILLAVECES PARDO.

Asociación Nacional de Exportadores (ANALDEX): Carrera 10, No 27-27, Int. 137, Of. 902, Apdo Aéreo 29812, Santafé de Bogotá, DC; tel. (1) 342-0788; telex 43326; fax (1) 284-6911; exporters' asscn; Pres. JORGE RAMÍREZ OCAMPO.

Asociación Nacional de Exportadores de Café de Colombia: Calle 72, No 10-07, Of. 1101, Santafé de Bogotá, DC; tel. (1) 210-2181; telex 44802; fax (1) 210-2072; f. 1938; private asscn of coffee exporters; Pres. GABRIEL ROSAS VEGA.

Asociación Nacional de Industriales (ANDI) (National Asscn of Manufacturers): Calle 52, No 47-48, Apdo Aéreo 997, Medellín; tel. (4) 511-1177; telex 6631; fax (4) 251-8830; f. 1944; Pres. ALEJANDRO CEBALLOS ZULUAGA; 9 brs; 756 mems.

Expocafé Ltda: Edif. Seguros Caribe, Carrera 7A, No 74-36, 3°, Apdo Aéreo 41244, Santafé de Bogotá, DC; tel. (1) 217-8900; telex 42379; fax (1) 217-3554; f. 1985; coffee exporting org.; Gen. Man. LUIS JOSÉ ALVAREZ L.

Federación Colombiana de Ganaderos (FEDEGAN): Carrera 14, No 36-65, Apdo Aéreo 9709, Santafé de Bogotá, DC; tel. (1) 245-3041; fax (1) 232-7153; f. 1963; cattle raisers' asscn; about 350,000 affiliates; Pres. JOSÉ RAIMUNDO SOJO ZAMBRANO.

Federación Nacional de Cacaoteros: Carrera 17, No 30-39, Apdo Aéreo 17736, Santafé de Bogotá, DC; tel. (1) 288-7188; fax (1) 288-4424; fed. of cocoa growers; Gen. Man. Dr MIGUEL URIBE.

Federación Nacional de Cafeteros de Colombia (National Federation of Coffee Growers): Calle 73, No 8-13, Apdo Aéreo 57534, Santafé de Bogotá, DC; tel. (1) 345-6600; telex 44723; fax (1) 217-1021; f. 1927; totally responsible for fostering and regulating the coffee economy; Gen. Man. JORGE CÁRDENAS GUTIÉRREZ; 203,000 mems.

Federación Nacional de Cultivadores de Cereales (FENALCE): Carrera 14, No 97-62, Apdo Aéreo 8694, Santafé de Bogotá, DC; tel. (1) 218-9366; fax (1) 218-9463; f. 1960; fed. of grain growers; Gen. Man. ADRIANO QUINTANA SILVA; 12,000 mems.

Federación Nacional de Comerciantes (FENALCO): Carrera 4, No 19-85, 7°, Santafé de Bogotá, DC; tel. (1) 286-0600; telex 44706; fax (1) 282-7573; fed. of businessmen; Pres. SABAS PRETELT DE LA VEGA.

Sociedad de Agricultores de Colombia (SAC) (Colombian Farmers' Society): Carrera 7A, No 24-89, 44°, Apdo Aéreo 3638, Santafé de Bogotá, DC; tel. (1) 281-0263; fax (1) 284-4572; e-mail socdeagr @impsat.net.co; f. 1871; Pres. JUAN MANUEL OSPINA RESTREPO; Sec.-Gen. Dr GABRIEL MARTÍNEZ TELÁEZ.

There are several other organizations, including those for rice growers, engineers and financiers.

UTILITIES

Electricity

Corporación Eléctrica de la Costa Atlántica: Calle 55, No 72-109, 9°, Barranquilla; tel. (5) 56-0247; fax (5) 56-2370; responsible for supplying electricity to the Atlantic departments; generates more than 2,000m. kWh annually from thermal power-stations; Man. Dir. ENRIQUE JAVIER PACHECO.

Empresa de Energía Eléctrica de Bogotá, SA: Avda El Dorado, No 55-51, Santafé de Bogotá, DC; tel. (1) 221-1665; telex 41242; fax (1) 221-6858; owned by the city authorities; provides electricity for Bogotá area by generating capacity of 680 MW, mainly hydroelectric; Man. Dir. FABIO CHAPARRO.

Instituto Colombiano de Energía Eléctrica—ICEL: Carrera 13, No 27-00, 3°, Apdo Aéreo 16243, Santafé de Bogotá, DC; tel. (1) 342-0181; telex 43319; fax (1) 286-2934; formulates policy for the development of electrical energy; constructs systems for the generation, transmission and distribution of electrical energy; Man. DOUGLAS VELÁSQUEZ JACOME; Sec.-Gen. PATRICIA OLIVEROS LAVERDE.

Interconexión Eléctrica, SA (ISA): Calle 12 Sur, No 18-168, Apdo Aéreo 8915, Medellín; tel. (4) 317-1331; telex 65259; fax (4) 317-0848; f. 1967; created by Colombia's principal electricity production and distribution cos to form a national network; installed capacity of 2,641m. kWh; operates major power-stations at Chivor and San Carlos; Man. Dir. JAVIER GUTIÉRREZ.

Gas

Gas Natural ESP: Avda 40A, No 13-09, 9°, Santafé de Bogotá, DC; tel. (1) 338-1199; fax (1) 288-0807; f. 1987; private gas corpn; Pres. ANTONI PERIS MINGOT.

TRADE UNIONS

According to official figures, an estimated 900 of Colombia's 2,000 trade unions are independent.

Central Unitaria de Trabajadores (CUT): Calle 35, No 7-25, 9°, Apdo Aéreo 221, Santafé de Bogotá, DC; tel. (1) 288-8577; fax (1) 287-5769; f. 1986; comprises 50 feds and 80% of all trade union members; Pres. JORGE CARILLO ROJAS; Sec.-Gen. MIGUEL ANTONIO CARO.

Frente Sindical Democrática (FSD): f. 1984; centre-right trade union alliance; comprises:

Confederación de Trabajadores de Colombia (CTC) (Colombian Confederation of Workers): Calle 39, No 26A-23, 5°, Apdo Aéreo 4780, Santafé de Bogotá, DC; tel. (1) 269-7119; f. 1934; mainly Liberal; 600 affiliates, including 6 national orgs and 20 regional feds; admitted to ICFTU; Pres. ALVIS FERNÁNDEZ; 400,000 mems.

Confederación de Trabajadores Democráticos de Colombia (CTDC): Carrera 13, No 59-52, Of. 303, Santafé de Bogotá, DC; tel. (1) 255-3146; fax (1) 484-581; f. 1988; comprises 23 industrial feds and 22 national unions; Pres. MARIO DE J. VALDERRAMA.

Confederación General de Trabajadores Democráticos (CGTD): Calle 39A, No 14-48, Apdo Aéreo 5415, Santafé de Bogotá, DC; tel. (1) 288-1560; fax (1) 288-1504; Christian Democrat; Sec.-Gen. JULIO ROBERTO GÓMEZ ESGUERRA.

Transport

Land transport in Colombia is rendered difficult by high mountains, so the principal means of long-distance transport is by air. As a result of the development of the El Cerrejón coal field, Colombia's first deep-water port has been constructed at Bahía de Portete and a 150 km rail link between El Cerrejón and the port became operational in 1989.

Instituto Nacional del Transporte (INTRA): Edif. Minobras (CAN), 6°, Apdo Aéreo 24990, Santafé de Bogotá, DC; tel. (1) 222-4100; govt body; Dir Dr GUILLERMO ANZOLA LIZARAZO.

RAILWAYS

In 1989, following the entry into liquidation of the Ferrocarriles Nacionales de Colombia (FNC), the Government created three new companies, which assumed responsibility for the rail network in 1992. However, the new companies were beset by financial difficulties, and many rail services were subsequently suspended.

Empresa Colombiana de Vías Férreas: Calle 31, No 6-41, 20°, Santafé de Bogotá, DC; tel. (1) 287-9888; fax (1) 287-2515; responsible for the maintenance and development of the national rail network; Pres. L. B. VILLEGAS GIRALDO.

Fondo de Pasivo Social de Ferrocarriles Nacionales de Colombia: Santafé de Bogotá, DC; administers welfare services for existing and former employees of the FNC.

Sociedad Colombiana de Transporte Ferroviario, SA (STF): Calle 72, No 13-23, 2°, Santafé de Bogotá, DC; tel. (1) 255-8684; fax (1) 255-8704; operates public rail services; 1,830 km (1993); Pres. Dr L. F. ZEA LLANO.

El Cerrejón Mine Railway: International Colombia Resources Corpn, Carrera 54, No 72-80, Apdo Aéreo 52499, Barranquilla; tel. and fax (5) 77-7898; f. 1989 to link the mine and the port at Bahía de Portete; 150 km (1993); Supt M. MENDOZA.

Metro de Medellín Ltda: Calle 44, No 46-001, Apdo Aéreo 9128, Medellín; tel. (4) 452-6000; fax (4) 452-4450; e-mail emetro@col3.telecom.com.co; construction began in 1985 on this 29 km urban transport project for Medellín; the first stage was scheduled to open in late 1995; Gen. Man. ALBERTO VALENCIA RAMÍREZ.

A similar transit project has been proposed for Santafé de Bogotá and, in 1988, it was announced that Italy had been selected by the Colombian Government to construct the 44 km underground system, which is at the preliminary study stage.

ROADS

In 1996 there were an estimated 107,000 km of roads, of which 25,600 km were highways and main roads and 43,900 km were secondary roads. About 12% of the total road network was paved in the same year. The country's main highways are the Caribbean Trunk Highway, the Eastern and Western Trunk Highways, the Central Trunk Highway and there are also roads into the interior. There are plans to construct a Jungle Edge highway to give access to the interior, a link road between Turbo, Bahía Solano and Medellín, a highway between Bogotá and Villavicencio and to complete the short section of the Pan-American highway between Panama and Colombia. In 1992 the World Bank granted a loan of US $266m. to Colombia for the construction of 400 km of new roads and the completion of 2,000 km of roads begun under an earlier programme.

There are a number of national bus companies and road haulage companies.

Fondo Vial Nacional: Santafé de Bogotá, DC; f. 1966; administered by the Ministry of Transport; to execute development programmes in road transport.

INLAND WATERWAYS

The Magdalena–Cauca river system is the centre of river traffic and is navigable for 1,500 km, while the Atrato is navigable for 687 km. The Orinoco system has more than five navigable rivers, which total more than 4,000 km of potential navigation (mainly through Venezuela); the Amazonas system has four main rivers, which total 3,000 navigable km (mainly through Brazil). There are plans to connect the Arauca with the Meta, and the Putamayo with the Amazon, and also to construct an Atrato–Truandó inter-oceanic canal.

Dirección de Navegación y Puertos: Edif. Minobras (CAN), Of. 562, Santafé de Bogotá, DC; tel. (1) 222-1248; telex 45656; responsible for river works and transport; the waterways system is divided into four sectors: Magdalena, Atrato, Orinoquia, and Amazonia; Dir ALBERTO RODRÍGUEZ ROJAS.

SHIPPING

The four most important ocean terminals are Buenaventura on the Pacific coast and Santa Marta, Barranquilla and Cartagena on the Atlantic coast. The port of Tumaco on the Pacific coast is gaining in importance and there are plans for construction of a deep-water port at Bahía Solano.

In 1996 Colombia's merchant fleet totalled 121,696 grt.

Port Authorities

Port of Barranquilla: Sociedad Portuaria Regional de Barranquilla, Barranquilla; tel. (5) 379-9555; fax (5) 379-9557; e-mail sportuaria@rednet.net.co; internet http://www.colombiaexport.com/baqport.htm; privatized in 1993; Gen. Man. CIRO AVILA V.

Port of Buenaventura: Empresa Puertos de Colombia, Edif. El Café, Of. 1, Buenaventura; tel. (222) 22543; fax (222) 22503; Port Man. VÍCTOR GONZÁLEZ.

Port of Cartagena: Empresa Puertos de Colombia, Calle 26, Cartagena; tel. (5) 666-3751; telex 37718; fax (5) 666-3944; f. 1959; Port Man. Capt. ALFONSO SALAS; Harbour Master Capt. GONZALO PARRA.

Port of Santa Marta: Empresa Puertos de Colombia, Calle 15, No 3-25, 11°, Santa Marta; tel. (54) 210739; telex 38869; fax (54) 210711; Port Man. JULIÁN PALACIOS.

Principal Shipping Companies

Flota Mercante Grancolombiana, SA: Edif. Grancolombiana, Carrera 13, No 27-75, Apdo Aéreo 4482, Santafé de Bogotá, DC; tel. (1) 286-0200; telex 44853; fax (1) 286-9028; f. 1946; owned by the Colombian Coffee Growers' Federation (80%) and Ecuador Development Bank (20%); f. 1946; one of Latin America's leading cargo carriers serving 45 countries worldwide; Pres. ENRIQUE VARGAS.

Colombiana Internacional de Vapores, Ltda (Colvapores): Avda Caracas, No 35-02, Apdo Aéreo 17227, Santafé de Bogotá, DC; cargo services mainly to the USA.

Líneas Agromar, Ltda: Calle 73, Vía 40-350, Apdo Aéreo 3256, Barranquilla; tel. (5) 353-1049; telex 31405; fax (5) 353-1042; Pres. MANUEL DEL DAGO FERNÁNDEZ.

Petromar Ltda: Bosque, Diagonal 23, No 56-152, Apdo Aéreo 505, Cartagena; tel. (5) 662-7208; telex 37672; fax (5) 662-7592; Chair. SAVERIO MINERVINI S.

Transportadora Colombiana de Graneles, SA (GRANELCO, SA): K. 21, No 88-51, Apdo Aéreo 240187, Santafé de Bogotá, DC;

tel. (1) 617-0162; telex 45400; fax (1) 256-2463; Gen. Man. JAIME SÁNCHEZ CORTES.

Several foreign shipping lines call at Colombian ports.

CIVIL AVIATION

Colombia has more than 100 airports, including 11 international airports: Santafé de Bogotá, DC (El Dorado International Airport), Medellín, Cali, Barranquilla, Bucaramanga, Cartagena, Cúcuta, Leticia, Pereira, San Andrés and Santa Marta.

Airports Authority

Unidad Administrativa Especial de Aeronáutica Civil: Aeropuerto Internacional El Dorado, 4°, Santafé de Bogotá, DC; tel. (1) 413-9500; telex 44620; fax (1) 413-9878; f. 1967 as Departamento Administrativo de Aeronáutica Civil, reorganized 1993; Dir CARLOS FERNANDO ZARAMA VÁSQUEZ.

National Airlines

Aerolíneas Centrales de Colombia, SA (ACES): Edif. del Café, Calle 49, No 50-21, 34°, Apdo Aéreo 6503, Medellín; tel. (4) 511-2237; fax (4) 251-1677; f. 1971; operates scheduled domestic passenger services throughout Colombia, and charter flights to the USA and the Caribbean; Pres. JUAN E. POSADA.

Aerotaca, SA (Aerotransportes Casanare): Avda El Dorado, Entrada 2, Interior 7, Santafé de Bogotá, DC; tel. (1) 413-9884; fax (1) 413-5256; f. 1965; scheduled regional and domestic passenger services; Gen. Man. RAFAEL URDANETA.

AVIANCA (Aerovías Nacionales de Colombia, SA): Avda El Dorado, No 93-30, 5°, Santafé de Bogotá, DC; tel. (1) 413-9511; telex 44427; fax (1) 413-8325; f. 1919; operates domestic services to all cities in Colombia and international services to the USA, France, Spain and throughout Central and Southern America; Chair. AUGUSTO LÓPEZ; Pres. GUSTAVO A. LENIS.

Intercontinental de Aviación: Avda El Dorado, Entrada 2, Interior 6, Santafé de Bogotá, DC; tel. (1) 413-8888; telex 42241; fax (1) 413-9893; f. 1965 as Aeropesca Colombia (Aerovías de Pesca y Colonización del Suroeste Colombiano): operates scheduled domestic, regional and international passenger and cargo services: Pres. Capt. LUIS HERNÁNDEZ ZIA.

Servicio de Aeronavegación a Territorios Nacionales (Satena): Avda El Dorado, Entrada 1, Interior 11, Apdo Aéreo 11163, Santafé de Bogotá, DC; tel. (1) 413-8438; telex 42332; fax (1) 413-8178; f. 1962; commercial enterprise attached to the Ministry of National Defence; internal services; CEO and Gen. Man. Brig.-Gen. ALFREDO GARCÍA ROJAS.

Sociedad Aeronáutica de Medellín Consolidada, SA (SAM): Edif. SAM, Calle 53, No 45-211, 21°, Apdo Aéreo 1085, Medellín; tel. (4) 251-5544; telex 6774; fax (4) 251-0711; f. 1945; subsidiary of AVIANCA; internal services; and international cargo services to Central America and the Caribbean; Pres JULIO M. SANTO D., GUSTAVO LENIS.

Transportes Aéreos Mercantiles Panamericanos (Tampa): Carrera 76, No 34A-61, Apdo Aéreo 494, Medellín; tel. (4) 250-2939; telex 66601; fax (4) 250-5639; f. 1973; operates international cargo services to destinations throughout South America, also to Puerto Rico and the USA; Chair. FABIO ECHEVERREY; Pres. JORGE COULSON RODRÍGUEZ.

In addition, the following airlines operate international and domestic charter cargo services: Aerosucre Colombia, Aerotransportes Colombianos (ATC), Aerovías Colombianas (ARCA), Líneas Aéreas del Caribe (LAC Airlines Colombia), and Líneas Aéreas Suraméricanas (LAS).

Tourism

The principal tourist attractions are the Caribbean coast (including the island of San Andrés), the 16th-century walled city of Cartagena, the Amazonian town of Leticia, the Andes mountains rising to 5,700 m above sea-level, the extensive forests and jungles, pre-Columbian relics and monuments of colonial art. In 1996 there were 1,253,916 visitors (compared with an estimated 1,400,000 in 1995), most of whom came from Venezuela, Ecuador and the USA.

Corporación Nacional de Turismo: Calle 28, No 13A-15, 18°, Apdo Aéreo 8400, Santafé de Bogotá, DC; tel. (1) 283-9566; telex 411350; fax (1) 284-3818; f. 1968; Gen. Man. GUSTAVO TORO VELÁSQUEZ; 4 brs throughout Colombia and brs in Europe, the USA and Venezuela.

Asociación Colombiana de Agencias de Viajes y Turismo—ANATO: Carrera 21, No 83-63/71, Apdo Aéreo 7088, Santafé de Bogotá, DC; tel. (1) 256-2290; telex 45675; fax (1) 218-7103; f. 1949; Pres. Dr OSCAR RUEDA GARCÍA.

THE COMOROS*

Introductory Survey

Location, Climate, Language, Religion, Flag, Capital

The Federal Islamic Republic of the Comoros is an archipelago in the Mozambique Channel, between the island of Madagascar and the east coast of the African mainland. The group comprises four main islands (Njazidja, Nzwani and Mwali, formerly Grande-Comore, Anjouan and Mohéli respectively, and Mayotte) and numerous islets and coral reefs. The climate is tropical, with average temperatures ranging from 23°C (73.4°F) to 28°C (82.4°F). Average annual rainfall is between 1,500 mm (59 ins) and 5,000 mm (197 ins). The official languages are Comorian (a blend of Swahili and Arabic), French and Arabic. Islam is the state religion. The flag is green, with a white crescent moon and four five-pointed white stars in the centre; the white Arabic inscriptions 'Allah' and 'Muhammad' appear respectively in the upper fly and lower hoist corners of the flag. The capital, which is situated on Njazidja, is Moroni.

Recent History

Formerly attached to Madagascar, the Comoros became a separate French Overseas Territory in 1947. The islands achieved internal self-government in December 1961, with a Chamber of Deputies and a Government Council responsible for local administration.

Elections in December 1972 resulted in a large majority for parties advocating independence, and Ahmed Abdallah became President of the Government Council. In June 1973 he was restyled President of the Government. At a referendum in December 1974 96% of the voters expressed support for independence, despite the opposition of the Mayotte Party, which sought the status of a French Department for the island of Mayotte.

On 6 July 1975, despite French insistence that any constitutional settlement should be ratified by all the islands voting separately, the Chamber of Deputies voted for immediate independence. The Chamber elected Abdallah to be first President of the Comoros and was reconstituted as the National Assembly. Although France made no attempt to intervene, it maintained control of Mayotte. Abdallah was deposed in August, and the National Assembly was abolished. A National Executive Council was established, with Prince Saïd Mohammed Jaffar, leader of the opposition party, the Front national uni, as its head, and Ali Soilih, leader of the coup, among its members. In November the Comoros was admitted to the UN, as a unified state comprising the whole archipelago. In December France officially recognized the independence of Njazidja, Nzwani and Mwali, but all relations between France and the Comoros were effectively suspended. In February 1976 Mayotte voted overwhelmingly to retain its links with France.

In January 1976 Ali Soilih was elected Head of State, and adopted extended powers under the terms of a new Constitution. In May 1978 Soilih was killed, following a coup by a group of about 50 European mercenaries, led by a Frenchman, Bob Denard, on behalf of the exiled former President, Ahmed Abdallah, and the Comoros was proclaimed a Federal Islamic Republic. Shortly afterwards, diplomatic relations with France were restored. In July the Comoran delegation was expelled from the Organization of African Unity (OAU, see p. 215) as a result of the continued presence of the mercenaries (but was readmitted in February 1979).

In October 1978 a new Constitution was approved in a referendum, on the three islands excluding Mayotte, by 99.31% of the votes cast. Abdallah was elected President in the same month, and in December elections for a new legislature, the Federal Assembly, took place. In January 1979 the Federal Assembly approved the formation of a one-party state. Unofficial opposition groups, however, continued to exist, and 150 people were arrested in February 1981, following reports (which were officially denied) of an attempted coup. Ali Mroudjae, hitherto Minister of Foreign Affairs and Co-operation, was appointed Prime Minister in February 1982, and legislative elections took place in March. Constitutional amendments, which were adopted in October, vested additional powers in the President. Abdallah was the sole candidate at a presidential election in September 1984. Despite appeals by the opposition for voters to boycott the election, 98% of the electorate participated. Abdallah was re-elected President for a further six-year term by 99.44% of the votes cast. In January 1985, following further amendments to the Constitution, the position of Prime Minister was abolished, and Abdallah assumed the office of Head of Government.

In March 1985 an attempt by members of the presidential guard to overthrow Abdallah, while he was in France, failed. In November 17 people, including Mustapha Saïd Cheikh, the Secretary-General of the banned opposition movement, Front démocratique (FD), were sentenced to forced labour for life for their involvement in the coup attempt. In February 1987 Abdallah indicated that independent opposition candidates would be permitted to contest legislative elections scheduled for 22 March. In the event, however, opposition candidates were only allowed to contest 20 seats on Njazidja, where they received 35% of the total votes, and pro-Government candidates retained full control of the 42-seat Federal Assembly. There were allegations of widespread fraud and intimidation of opposition candidates, and, according to Comoran dissidents in Réunion, about 400 people were arrested, 200–300 of whom were later imprisoned. In November a further coup attempt by a left-wing group, which was composed of former members of the presidential guard and members of the Comoran armed forces, was suppressed by the authorities, with, it was believed, assistance from French mercenaries and South African military advisers.

In early November 1989 a constitutional amendment, which permitted Abdallah to remain in office for a third six-year term, was approved by 92.5% of votes cast in a popular referendum. The result of the referendum, however, was disputed by the President's opponents. Violent demonstrations followed, and opposition leaders were detained.

On the night of 26–27 November 1989, Abdallah was assassinated at the presidential palace by members of the presidential guard (which included a number of European advisers), under the command of Bob Denard. Under the terms of the Constitution, the President of the Supreme Court, Saïd Mohamed Djohar, was appointed interim Head of State, pending a presidential election. Denard, however, staged a coup, in which 27 members of the security forces were reportedly killed, and the regular army was defeated by Denard and his supporters. The mercenaries' action provoked international condemnation, despite denials by Denard of complicity in Abdallah's death. (In June 1997 it was announced that Denard was to stand trial in France in connection with the assassination.) A French naval force was sent to the area, ostensibly to prepare for the evacuation of French citizens from the Comoros. In mid-December Denard finally agreed to relinquish power, and, following the arrival of French paratroops in Moroni, was transported to South Africa, together with the remaining mercenaries. Djohar subsequently announced that the French Government's troops were to remain in the Comoros for up to two years in order to train local security forces.

At the end of December 1989 the main political groups agreed to form a provisional Government of National Unity. An amnesty for all political prisoners was proclaimed, and an inquiry into the death of Abdallah was instigated. It was announced that a multi-candidate presidential election, which was to end the system of single-party rule, was to take place in January 1990. The first round of the presidential election (which had been postponed until 18 February) was, however, abandoned, following allegations of widespread irregularities, and rescheduled for 4 March, with a second round of voting to take place on 11 March if necessary. After an inconclusive first round, Djohar,

* Some of the information contained in this chapter refers to the whole Comoros archipelago, which the independent Comoran state claims as its national territory. However, the island of Mayotte (Mahoré) is, in fact, administered by France. Separate information on Mayotte may be found in the chapter on French Overseas Possessions.

the official candidate for the Union comorienne pour le progrès (Udzima), was elected President, with 55.3% of the votes cast, while Mohamed Taki Abdulkarim, the leader of the Union nationale pour la démocratie aux Comores (UNDC), secured 44.7% of the votes. In late March Djohar appointed a new Government, in which the eight political parties that had supported his presidential candidacy were represented. In the following month Djohar announced plans for the formal constitutional restoration of a multi-party political system and indicated that extensive economic reforms were to be undertaken.

In August 1990 an attempted coup was staged by armed rebels, who attacked various French installations on Njazidja. The revolt was allegedly organized by a small group of European mercenaries, who intended to provoke Djohar's resignation through the enforced removal of French forces from the islands; however, supporters of Mohamed Taki were also implicated in the conspiracy. In September the Minister of the Interior and Administrative Reforms, Ibrahim Halidi, was dismissed for his alleged involvement in the attempted coup, and more than 20 arrests were made. In October it was reported that the leader of the conspirators, Max Veillard, had been killed by Comoran security forces. In the same month Djohar implemented an extensive ministerial reorganization.

In March 1991 the Government announced that a conference, comprising three representatives of each political association, was to be convened to discuss constitutional reform. The conference took place in May, but several principal opposition parties, which objected to arrangements whereby Djohar reserved the right to modify the conference's recommendations, refused to attend. However, the conference presented draft constitutional amendments, which were to be submitted for endorsement by a national referendum.

On 3 August 1991 the President of the Supreme Court, Ibrahim Ahmed Halidi, announced the dismissal of Djohar, on the grounds of negligence, and proclaimed himself interim President with the support of the Supreme Court. Opposition leaders declared the seizure of power to be legitimate under the terms of the Constitution. However, the Government condemned the coup attempt, and Halidi and several other members of the Supreme Court were arrested. A state of emergency was imposed, and remained in force until early September. A number of demonstrations in favour of Djohar took place in early August, although members of Udzima did not express support for the Government. Later that month, however, the Government banned all public demonstrations, following clashes between members of the opposition and pro-Government demonstrators.

In late August 1991 Djohar established a new coalition Government, which included two members of the FD. In an attempt to appease increasing discontent on the island of Mwali, which had repeatedly demanded greater autonomy, and had threatened to secede from the Comoros, Djohar also appointed two members of the Mwalian opposition to the Government. However, the two leading political associations represented in the coalition Government, Udzima and the Parti comorien pour la démocratie et le progrès (PCDP), objected to the ministerial reshuffle, and accused Djohar of attempting to reduce their power; shortly afterwards the ministers belonging to the two parties resigned.

In November 1991 Udzima (which had been officially renamed Parti Udzima—Udzima) announced that it was to withdraw its support for Djohar and join the parties opposing the government coalition. It also condemned the proposed constitutional amendments that had been drafted in May. Opposition leaders demanded the dissolution of the Federal Assembly (which was declared to be invalid on the grounds that it had been elected under the former one-party system) and the formation of a government of national unity. In the same month, despite efforts at appeasement by Djohar, Mwali announced plans to conduct a referendum on self-determination for the island. Later in November, agreement was reached between Djohar and the principal opposition leaders to initiate a process of national reconciliation, which would include the formation of a government of national unity and the convening of a constitutional conference. The accord also guaranteed the legitimacy of Djohar's election as President. In January 1992 a new transitional Government of National Unity was formed, under the leadership of Mohamed Taki, who was named as its Co-ordinator, pending legislative elections, which were scheduled for April. Later in January a national conference, comprising representatives of political parties and other organizations, was convened to draft a new constitution. (Mwalian representatives, however, refused to attend the conference.)

In early May 1992 opposition parties demanded the resignation of Djohar's son-in-law, Mohamed Saïd Abdallah M'Changama, as Minister of Finance, Commerce and Planning, following allegations of irregularities in the negotiation of government contracts. Djohar subsequently formed a new interim Council of Ministers, in which, however, M'Changama retained his portfolio. At a constitutional referendum, held on 7 June, the reform proposals, which had been submitted in April, were approved by 74.25% of the votes cast, despite opposition from eight parties, notably Udzima and the FD. The new Constitution limited the presidential tenure to a maximum of two five-year terms of office, and provided for a bicameral legislature, comprising a Federal Assembly, elected for a term of four years, and a 15-member Senate, selected for a six-year term by the regional Councils. In early July Djohar dismissed Mohamed Taki, following the latter's appointment of a former mercenary to a financial advisory post in the Government. Later that month Djohar formed a new Government, although the post of Co-ordinator remained vacant.

In mid-1992 social and economic conditions on the Comoros deteriorated, following renewed strikes in a number of sectors. In early September Djohar announced that legislative elections were to commence in late October, contrary to the recommendation of an electoral commission that they take place in December. Opposition parties claimed that the schedule allowed insufficient time for preparation, and indicated that they would boycott the elections. Later that month a demonstration, organized by Udzima, the UNDC and the FD, in support of demands for Djohar's resignation, was suppressed by security forces. In an apparent attempt to restore order, Djohar subsequently anounced a new electoral schedule, whereby legislative elections would take place in early November, and local government elections in December.

In late September 1992 an abortive coup attempt was staged by disaffected members of the armed forces, who seized the radio station at Moroni and announced that the Government had been overthrown. Six opposition leaders and six members of the armed forces, including two sons of the former President, Ahmed Abdallah, were subsequently arrested, and, in October, were charged with involvement in the attempted coup. In mid-October some 100 rebel troops, led by a former member of Abdallah's presidential guard, Lt Saïd Mohamed, attacked the military garrison of Kandani, in an attempt to release the members of the armed forces accused of instigating the coup attempt. Shortly afterwards government forces attacked the rebels at Mbeni, to the north-east of Moroni; fighting was also reported on the island of Nzwani. Later in October a demonstration was staged in protest at the French Government's support of Djohar, following French consignments of food rations to government forces, which prompted speculation that armaments had also been dispatched. By the end of October some 25 people had been killed in clashes between rebels and government forces in Moroni.

In October 1992 Djohar agreed to reschedule the legislative elections until late November, although opposition parties demanded a further postponement, and Udzima and the UNDC continued to support a boycott of the elections. Later that month, in accordance with a presidential decree, nine government ministers who intended to contest the legislative elections officially resigned for the period of the electoral campaign. The first round of the legislative elections, which took place on 22 November, was contested by some 320 candidates representing 21 political parties. Numerous electoral irregularities and violent incidents were reported, however, and several opposition parties demanded that the results be declared invalid, and joined the boycott implemented by Udzima and the UNDC. Election results in six constituencies were subsequently annulled, while the second round of voting on 29 November took place in only 34 of the 42 constituencies. Following partial elections on 13 and 30 December, reports indicated that candidates supporting Djohar—including seven members of the Union des démocrates pour la démocratie (UDD), a pro-Government organization based on Nzwani—had secured a narrow majority in the Federal Assembly. In accordance with the terms of the Constitution, the leader of the UDD, Ibrahim Abdérémane Halidi, was appointed Prime Minister on 1 January 1993, and formed a new Council of Ministers. Later in January a Mwalian, Amir Attoumane, was elected as Speaker of the Federal Assembly in response to demands by Mwalian deputies in the Assembly.

Shortly after the new Government took office, however, disagreement between Djohar and Halidi was reported, while the presidential majority in the Federal Assembly fragmented into three dissenting factions. In mid-February 1993 representatives of several pro-Djohar parties (which had criticized the appointment of a number of ministers by Halidi) proposed a vote of censure against the Government in the Federal Assembly; the motion was, however, rejected by 23 of the 42 deputies. Later that month Halidi effected an extensive reorganization of the Council of Ministers, although the political parties that supported Djohar remained dissatisfied with the composition of the Government.

In April 1993 nine people, including Abdallah's sons and two prominent members of Udzima, were convicted on charges of involvement in the coup attempt in September 1992, and sentenced to death. Following considerable domestic and international pressure, however, Djohar subsequently commuted the sentences to terms of imprisonment. In May 1993 eight supporters of M'Changama, allied with a number of opposition deputies, proposed a motion of 'no confidence' in the Government (apparently with the tacit support of Djohar), which was approved by 23 of the 42 deputies in the Federal Assembly. Shortly afterwards, Djohar appointed an associate of M'Changama, Saïd Ali Mohamed, as Prime Minister, replacing Halidi. Mohamed subsequently formed a new Council of Ministers. In mid-June an alliance of parliamentary deputies, who were supporters of Halidi, proposed a motion of censure against the new Government, on the grounds that the Prime Minister had not been appointed from a party that commanded a majority in the Federal Assembly. Djohar, however, declared the motion to be unconstitutional, and, in view of the continued absence of a viable parliamentary majority, dissolved the Federal Assembly, and announced that legislative elections were to take place within 40 days, as stipulated in the Constitution. He subsequently dismissed Mohamed, and appointed a former presidential adviser, Ahmed Ben Cheikh Attoumane, as Prime Minister. Shortly afterwards, an interim Council of Ministers was formed (although two of the newly-appointed ministers immediately announced their resignation).

Following the dissolution of the Federal Assembly, opposition parties declared Djohar to be unfit to hold office, in view of the increasing political confusion, and demanded that legislative elections take place within the stipulated period of 40 days. In early July 1993, however, Djohar announced that the legislative elections (which were to take place concurrently with local government elections), were to be postponed until October. Also in July Djohar attracted additional criticism, following his refusal (despite pressure from the French Government) to release the prisoners who had received custodial sentences in connection with the coup attempt in September 1992. Later in July 1993 opposition parties organized a one-day strike, in support of demands that Djohar bring forward the date of the legislative elections or resign. Shortly afterwards, several members of the opposition, including two parliamentary deputies, who had allegedly participated in the campaign of civil disobedience, were temporarily detained.

In early September 1993 a number of opposition movements, notably Udzima and the UNDC, established an informal electoral alliance, known as the Union pour la République et le progrès, while the FD, the PCDP, CHUMA (Islands' Fraternity and Unity Party), and the Mouvement pour la démocratie et le progrès (MDP) agreed to present joint candidates. Later in September Djohar postponed the legislative elections until November, officially on the grounds that the Government had inadequate resources to conduct the elections. There was, however, widespread speculation that Djohar intended to gain further time in order to establish an alliance of his supporters to contest the elections.

In October 1993 Djohar (who had failed to induce the political parties that supported him to form an electoral alliance, owing to their hostility towards M'Changama) established a political organization, known as Rassemblement pour la démocratie et le renouveau (RDR), principally comprising supporters of M'Changama and several prominent members of the Government. Later that month 16 political parties, including several pro-Djohar organizations, threatened to boycott the elections unless the Government repealed legislation that provided for the establishment of alternative electoral boundaries and the appointment of a new electoral commission. In subsequent weeks opposition supporters effectively prevented government candidates from convening political meetings, in an effort to disrupt the electoral campaign. In November the legislative elections were rescheduled for 12 and 19 December, while the local government elections were postponed indefinitely. Later that month Djohar reorganized the Council of Ministers, and established a new National Electoral Commission, in compliance with the demands of the opposition (which had objected to the composition of the former commission).

In the first round of the legislative elections, which took place peacefully on 12 December 1993, four opposition candidates secured seats in the Federal Assembly, apparently prompting concern in the Government. Following the second round of the polls, which was postponed until 20 December, it was reported that three people had been killed in violent incidents in Nzwani, where the authorities had assumed control of the electoral process. The National Electoral Commission subsequently declared the results in several constituencies to be invalid. Opposition candidates refused to participate in further elections in these constituencies, on the grounds that voting was again to be conducted under the supervision of the authorities, rather than that of the National Electoral Commission; RDR candidates consequently secured all 10 contested seats, and 22 seats overall, thereby securing a narrow majority in the Federal Assembly. In early January 1994 Djohar appointed the Secretary-General of the RDR, Mohamed Abdou Madi, as Prime Minister. Abdou Madi subsequently formed a new Council of Ministers, which included several supporters of M'Changama. Shortly afterwards, M'Changama was elected Speaker of the Federal Assembly. Later in January 12 principal opposition parties, which claimed that the RDR had assumed power illegally, formed a new alliance, known as the Forum pour le redressement national (FRN).

In February 1994 security forces seized the transmitters of a private radio station, owned by Udzima, which had broadcast independent news coverage. In the same month a demonstration took place in protest at the continued detention of an opposition candidate, Mohamed Ahmed Fuad, who had been arrested in connection with one of the deaths that had occurred during the legislative elections. In March the Comoros protested to the French Government after a French periodical published an article claiming that M'Changama was implicated in a number of fraudulent business transactions. At a religious ceremony later that month, which was attended by Djohar, a former bodyguard of an RDR candidate was arrested by security forces and discovered to be in possession of a firearm. A former Governor of Njazidja and member of the FRN, Mohamed Abdérémane, was subsequently arrested on suspicion of involvement in an assassination attempt against Djohar, while two other prominent opposition leaders were also questioned in connection with the incident. Abdérémane was later released, however, and there was speculation that the Government had arranged the episode in an attempt to discredit the opposition.

In April 1994 pressure increased from both the Comoran opposition and the French Government in support of an amnesty for political prisoners. In the same month division emerged between M'Changama and Abdou Madi regarding the appointment of a number of prominent government officials. In early May a court ruling in favour of Fuad's release prompted criticism from the Government, which dismissed the magistrate concerned. At the end of that month teachers initiated strike action (which was later joined by health workers) in support of demands for an increase in salaries and the reorganization of the public sector. In early June a motion of censure against Abdou Madi, which was proposed by supporters of the FRN in the Federal Assembly, was rejected by 26 of the 42 deputies. In mid-June it was reported that five people had been killed on Mwali, following an opposition demonstration in support of the strike, which was violently suppressed by the security forces. Later that month legislation (which had been approved by Djohar) providing for the sale of the state-owned airline, Air Comores, to an alleged international financier, known as Rowland Ashley, was rescinded, following protests from both opposition and government supporters in the Federal Assembly. Under a compromise arrangement, Ashley's privately-owned company was granted management of the airline's operations. In August, however, Ashley's background was proved to be fraudulent, and the existence of his company fabricated. Ashley subsequently claimed that prominent members of the Government had accepted financial inducements in connection with the proposed sale of the airline. Later that month the political management committee of the RDR, which was headed by M'Changama, criticized Abdou Madi's involvement in the affair.

In early September 1994 public-sector workers initiated further strike action; union officials refused to enter into negotiations with the authorities while Abdou Madi's Government remained in power. In mid-September the Government suspended the salaries of workers joining the general strike. In the same month the French national airline, Air France, threatened to suspend flights to the Comoros, in protest at debts incurred by Air Comores under Ashley's management. Despite previous expressions of support for Abdou Madi, in October Djohar dismissed him from the office of Prime Minister (apparently owing to his involvement in the Air Comores affair), and appointed Halifa Houmadi to the post. The resultant new Council of Ministers included only two members of the former administration.

In December 1994 Djohar failed to accede to a request by the Federal Assembly that political prisoners who had been implicated in the abortive coup attempt in September 1992 be granted amnesty. In January 1995 public-sector workers suspended strike action, after the Government agreed to a number of union demands. In the same month Djohar condemned a decision by the French Government to reimpose visa requirements for Comoran nationals entering Mayotte (which further undermined the Comoros' claim of sovereignty over the territory). A demonstration at the French embassy in Moroni, which was staged in protest at the measure, was suppressed by security forces, after degenerating into violence. It was subsequently reported that threats had been issued against French nationals resident in the Comoros. Later in January division emerged within the RDR, after the party Chairman and Secretary-General (Abdou Madi) both criticized the Government's failure to contain the hostility towards French citizens. At a congress of the RDR in early February the two officials were removed from the party, and Houmadi became Chairman. In the same month the Government announced that elections to the regional councils were to take place in April, and were to be followed by the establishment of a Senate and a Constitutional Council (in accordance with the terms of the Constitution). The opposition, however, accused Djohar of perpetrating a number of unconstitutional measures in the preparation for elections, and claimed that he planned to assume control of the electoral process. In March Djohar announced that the forthcoming elections to the regional councils were to be rescheduled for July, ostensibly owing to lack of finance; it was widely speculated, however, that the postponement had been decided in response to an opposition campaign in support of an electoral boycott.

In April 1995 reports emerged of a widening rift between Djohar and Houmadi, after the Prime Minister apparently claimed that Djohar and M'Changama had engaged in financial malpractice. At the end of that month Djohar dismissed Houmadi from the premiership and appointed a former Minister of Finance, Mohamed Caabi El Yachroutu, as his successor. A 13-member Council of Ministers, which included only five members of the previous administration, was subsequently established. In May three former Prime Ministers (Mohamed, Abdou Madi and Houmadi) conducted a series of political meetings urging public support for the removal of M'Changama, who, they claimed, exerted undue influence over Djohar, and demanded that the Federal Assembly be dissolved. In July further tension developed within the Government over an agreement whereby Air Comores was to be transferred to the joint management of an airline based in the United Arab Emirates, Menon Airways; M'Changama and the Minister of Transport and Tourism, Ahmed Saïd Issilame, claimed that the agreement was technically invalid on the grounds that it had been signed by Djohar before legislation providing for the privatization of Air Comores had been approved in the Federal Assembly. Meanwhile, it was feared that the further postponement of elections to the regional councils would delay the presidential election. In an effort to facilitate the organization of the presidential election, the Government introduced minor constitutional amendments, which included the relaxation of regulations governing the registration of political candidates and a provision empowering the Prime Minister to act as interim Head of State. At the end of July Djohar removed Issilame and a further three associates of M'Changama from the Council of Ministers.

In late September 1995 about 30 European mercenaries, led by Denard (who had hitherto been under investigation in France for involvement in the assassination of President Ahmed Abdallah in 1989), staged a military coup, seizing control of the garrison at Kandani and capturing Djohar. The mercenaries, who were joined by some 300 members of the Comoran armed forces, released a number of prisoners (including those detained for involvement in the failed coup attempt in September 1992), and installed a former associate of Denard, Capt. Ayouba Combo, as leader of a Transitional Military Committee. The French Government denounced the coup and suspended economic aid to the Comoros, but initially refused to take military action, despite requests for assistance from El Yachroutu, who had taken refuge in the French embassy. In early October Combo announced that he had transferred authority to Mohamed Taki and the leader of CHUMA, Saïd Ali Kemal (who had both welcomed the coup), as joint civilian Presidents, apparently in an attempt to avert military repercussions by the French Government, which had dispatched additional troops to the region of the Indian Ocean. The FRN, however, rejected the new leadership and entered into negotiations with El Yachroutu. Following a further appeal for intervention from El Yachroutu, who apparently invoked a defence co-operation agreement that had been established between the two countries in 1978, some 900 French military personnel landed on the Comoros and surrounded the mercenaries at Kandani. Shortly afterwards, Denard and his associates, together with the disaffected members of the Comoran armed forces, surrendered to the French troops. The mercenaries were subsequently placed under arrest and transported to France. (In October 1996, following his release from imprisonment in France in July, Denard claimed that the coup attempt had been planned at the request of several Comoran officials, including Mohamed Taki.)

Following the French military intervention, El Yachroutu declared himself interim President in accordance with the Constitution and announced the formation of a Government of National Unity, which included members of the constituent parties of the FRN. Djohar (who had been transported to Réunion by the French in order to receive medical treatment) rejected El Yachroutu's assumption of power and announced the reappointment of Saïd Ali Mohamed as Prime Minister. Later in October a National Reconciliation Conference decided that El Yachroutu would remain interim President, pending the forthcoming election, which was provisionally scheduled for early 1996; two electoral commissions were established. The incumbent administration opposed Djohar's stated intention to return to the Comoros, on the grounds that it would impede the restoration of civil order, and announced that measures would be taken to prevent him from entering the country. At the end of October El Yachroutu granted an amnesty to all Comorans involved in the coup attempt and appointed representatives of the UNDC and Udzima (which had supported the coup) to the new Council of Ministers. In early November Djohar announced the formation of a rival Government, headed by Mohamed. El Yachroutu, who was supported by the Comoran armed forces, refused to recognize the legitimacy of Djohar's appointments, while opposition parties equally opposed his return to power; only elements of the RDR continued to support Djohar's authority. It was reported that representatives of the OAU, who visited the Comoros and Réunion in mid-November in an effort to resolve the situation, had unofficially concluded that only El Yachroutu's administration was capable of governing. There was also widespread speculation that the French Government had believed Djohar's authority to be untenable, in view of his increasing domestic unpopularity, and had, in consequence, tacitly supported his removal from power. Later that month, however, supporters of Djohar, including M'Changama, organized a political gathering to demand the resignation of El Yachroutu's administration. Meanwhile, political leaders on Mwali rejected the authority of both rival Governments, urged a campaign of civil disobedience and established a 'citizens' committee' to govern the island; discontent with the central administration also emerged on Nzwani.

In December 1995 a decision by El Yachroutu's Government to schedule the presidential election for the end of January 1996 was opposed by a number of political leaders (including Mohamed Taki, Kemal and M'Changama), who demanded a postponement until March, ostensibly on the grounds that the stipulated date would coincide with the Islamic festival of Ramadan. In January 1996 the Government agreed to reschedule the presidential election for March. (Some 15 presidential candidates subsequently emerged.) Later that month Djohar returned to the Comoros, after apparently signing an agreement stipulating that he would retain only symbolic presidential powers. In February it was reported that the island of Mwali had unilaterally proclaimed itself a democratic republic. In the first round of the presidential election, which took place on 6 March,

Mohamed Taki obtained the highest number of votes, with 21%, while the leader of the FRN, Abbas Djoussouf, secured about 15% of votes; it was subsequently reported that 12 of the 13 unsuccessful candidates had urged support for Mohamed Taki in the second round of the election. Taki was duly elected to the presidency on 16 March, obtaining 64% of the vote. International observers, including delegates from the UN and OAU, were satisfied with the electoral process; officials reported that 62% of the electorate had participated in the second round. The new Head of State was sworn in on 25 March. On 28 March Taki appointed a new Council of Ministers, which included five of the presidential candidates who had supported him in the second round of the election.

In early April 1996 Taki dissolved the Federal Assembly and announced that legislative elections would take place on 6 October, despite the constitutional requirement that elections be held within a period of 40 days following the dissolution of the legislature. Taki further announced proposals for an early referendum on constitutional changes. New Governors, all belonging to the UNDC, were appointed to each of the three islands. In mid-June, during a visit to France, discussions took place between Taki and the French President, Jacques Chirac. Taki requested financial aid to enable him to pay the wage arrears owed to civil servants, and confirmed his wish for French troops to remain on the Comoros.

In mid-August 1996 Taki passed a decree awarding himself absolute powers. This measure was widely criticized in the media, and by opposition groups, notably CHUMA, the Forces pour l'action républicaine (FAR) and the FRN, as being in violation of the Constitution. In a government reorganization later in August, Saïd Ali Kemal and a representative of FAR were dismissed, following their parties' refusal to disband in order to join the single pro-presidential party that Taki intended to establish. At the end of that month Taki established an Islamic judicial commission. In September the first public execution to take place in the Comoros for 18 years prompted international concern.

In September 1996 Taki established a constitutional consultative committee, comprising 42 representatives of political parties and other organizations, which was to provide advice concerning a new constitution; the FRN refused to participate in the committee. Also in that month the forthcoming legislative elections were postponed until November. At the beginning of October the committee submitted a draft Constitution to Taki; a national referendum to endorse the new Constitution was scheduled for 20 October. In order to comply with a constitutional proposal, which effectively restricted the number of political parties to a maximum of three, 24 political organizations, including most of those which had supported Taki in the second round of the presidential elections, merged to form one presidential party, the Rassemblement national pour le développement (RND). The opposition condemned the extensive powers that the draft Constitution vested in the President, and the rapidity with which it was to be installed, and urged a boycott of the constitutional referendum. On 20 October, however, the new Constitution was approved by 85% of votes cast; according to official estimates, about 64% of the electorate voted. The new Constitution vested legislative power in a unicameral parliament, the Federal Assembly (thereby abolishing the Senate), and extended the presidential term to six years, with an unrestricted number of consecutive mandates. Political parties were required to have two parliamentary deputies from each island (following legislative elections) to be considered legal; organizations that did not fulfil these stipulations were to be dissolved. Extensive executive powers were vested in the President, who was to appoint the Governors of the islands, and gained the right to initiate constitutional amendments. The opposition parties disputed the official result of the referendum, insisting that only about 20% of the electorate had voted, and subsequently announced their decision to boycott the legislative elections, which were delayed further, until December.

Prior to the legislative elections, constituency boundaries were revised; Mwali was allocated a sixth constituency. Following unsuccessful negotiations with the Government, which rejected demands for the creation of an independent electoral commission and the revision of electoral lists, the opposition parties (having formed a new alliance, the Forum pour le rétablissement de la démocratie) again refused to participate in the electoral process. Consequently, the elections, which took place, in two rounds, on 1 and 8 December 1996, were only contested by the RND and the Front national pour la justice (FNJ), a fundamentalist Islamic organization, together with 23 independent candidates (in apparent contravention of a stipulation in the new Constitution that only legally-created political parties were entitled to participate in national elections). The RND secured 36 of the 43 seats in the Federal Assembly, while the FNJ won three, and four seats were taken by independent candidates. The opposition parties claimed that the elections were undemocratic, and had resulted in the establishment of a legislative body under Taki's control. On 26 December Salim Djabir was elected as Chairman of the Federal Assembly, securing the votes of all of the RND deputies. On the following day Taki nominated Ahmed Abdou, who had served in the administration of the former President Ahmed Abdallah, as Prime Minister. A new Council of Ministers was appointed later that month.

In late December 1996 industrial action in the public sector in support of demands by civil servants for the payment of some 10 months of salary arrears resulted in severe disruption in government services. A grouping of teachers' and hospital workers' unions joined the strike action in January 1997, and up to 30 people were injured when the security forces violently suppressed a demonstration organized by trade unions in Moroni. Civil unrest, exacerbated by severe shortages of water and electricity, continued, and in mid-February a one-day general strike, organized by the opposition, was widely supported. Meanwhile, discontent with the Government intensified on Nzwani; in mid-March a general strike escalated into riots, during which four people were killed, when some 3,000 demonstrators (now reported to be secessionists) clashed with the security forces in Mutsamudu, the main town. Taki replaced the Governor of Nzwani and other senior island officials and carried out a government reshuffle. In late May it was reported that, in an attempt to alleviate the crisis, Taki and Djoussouf had agreed to establish a joint commission to define terms for the participation of the FRN in the governing of internal affairs. However, sympathy for the separatist movements on both Nzwani and Mwali continued to increase, amid claims that the Government had consistently ignored their political and economic interests, and on 14 July (France's national day) two people were killed in skirmishes between the security forces and demonstrators who had blocked roads around Mutsamudu and raised the French flag, as they had done previously, in late June and on 6 July (Comoran independence day). Separatist leaders declared their intention to seek the restoration of French rule and established a 'political directorate' on Nzwani, chaired by Abdallah Ibrahim, a septuagenarian Koranic teacher and leader of the Mouvement populaire anjouanais, a grouping of separatist movements on Nzwani. (The relative prosperity of neighbouring Mayotte appeared to have prompted the demand for a return to French rule; it was reported that up to 200 illegal migrants a day attempted to enter Mayotte from Nzwani.) Military reinforcements were sent to Nzwani and the Governor of the island was replaced once again. Separatist leaders, including Ibrahim, were subsequently arrested, although the Government was forced to release them a week later, at the end of July, following a series of violent demonstrations in the main towns of the island. The French Government denounced the separatist actions and insisted on its respect for the 'territorial integrity' of the Comoros.

On 3 August 1997 the 'political directorate' unilaterally declared Nzwani's secession from the Comoros, despite an earlier proposal made by Taki to decentralize power and give increased autonomy to the islands. The separatists subsequently elected Ibrahim as president of a 13-member 'politico-administrative co-ordination' which included Abdou Madi, a former Prime Minister during Djohar's presidency, as spokesperson. The declaration of independence was condemned by Djoussouf who appealed for French mediation in the crisis. France, however, while denoucing the secession, declared itself in favour of the intervention of the OAU. The OAU responded by sending a special envoy, Pierre Yéré (Côte d'Ivoire's ambassador to Ethiopia and the OAU), to the Comoros. Meanwhile, separatist movements on Mwali held demonstrations, erecting barricades and raising the French flag. Separatist activity intensified, and on 11 August secessionists declared Mwali's independence from the Comoros, appointed a president and a prime minister to head a 12-member government, and called for reattachment to France.

As OAU mediation efforts continued, it was announced in mid-August 1997 that secessionist leaders on Mwali and Nzwani had agreed to negotiate with the authorities in Moroni, although those on Nzwani had insisted on the immediate withdrawal of the military reinforcements that had been sent to the island in July. By late August the Government had complied with this demand and the OAU announced its intention to hold a reconciliation conference in mid-September in Addis Ababa, Ethiopia, although the organization maintained its position that secession was unacceptable. Nzwani's Governor, who had been appointed in July, resigned and was not replaced. Meanwhile, in Moroni, some 500 opposition members demonstrated in support of demands for their participation in the OAU-sponsored talks and for the resignation of Taki.

At the end of August 1997 Yéré returned to the Comoros in order to prepare for the forthcoming conference. However, in early September, despite OAU and French opposition to military intervention, Taki despatched some 300 troops to Nzwani in an attempt to suppress the separatist insurrection. After two days of heavy fighting between secessionist and government forces, the OAU declared that the government troops had failed to quash the rebellion, despite earlier claims from Moroni that order had been restored. It was reported that many government soldiers had deserted,while others had apparently joined the separatist fighters. The Government claimed that the separatists had been aided by foreign elements and expressed regret at France's refusal to support the military operation. As it emerged that some 40 Comoran soldiers and 16 Nzwani residents had been killed in the fighting, with many more injured, demonstrators demanding Taki's resignation clashed violently with the security forces in Moroni during a protest against the unsuccessful military intervention. The separatists on Nzwani reaffirmed their independence and empowered Ibrahim to rule by decree. Taki subsequently declared a state of emergency, assumed absolute power and dismissed the Government of Ahmed Abdou and his military and civilian advisers. (Abdou, from Mutsamudu, had reportedly resigned his position in late August, although this had not been announced publicly.) Shortly afterwards, Taki established a State Transition Commission, which included three representatives from Nzwani and two from Mwali, although it was reported that one of the Mwalians had defected soon after. The reconciliation conference was postponed indefinitely by the OAU. Later in September the separatists released a number of government soldiers who had been taken captive during the military operation, apparently to demonstrate their desire for peace, having earlier threatened to kill the prisoners if Taki attempted another military offensive. The League of Arab States (Arab League) agreed to a request from Taki for assistance, and following talks with the OAU regarding the co-ordination of the mediation effort, all three islands hosted discussions in late September, which were convened by envoys from both organizations. A delegation of the Comoran State Transition Commission also addressed the UN General Assembly and held talks with US officials. The opposition continued to call for Taki's resignation, the decentralization of power through constitutional reform and the organization of new elections.

In late September 1997, despite the misgivings of some members of the 'politico-administrative co-ordination', notably Abdou Madi, Ibrahim announced his decision to hold a referendum on self-determination for Nzwani on 26 October, prior to a reconciliation conference sponsored by both the OAU and the Arab League, which all parties had agreed to attend. Despite international opposition, the referendum was conducted as scheduled; according to separatist officials, 99.88% of the electorate voted in favour of independence for Nzwani, with a turnout of 94%. The following day Ibrahim dissolved the 'politico-administrative co-ordination' and appointed a temporary government which was charged with preparing a constitution and organizing a presidential election, although it did not receive international recognition.

Taki reacted by cutting Nzwani's telephone lines, suspending air and maritime links and establishing a commission to liaise with opposition leaders prior to the appointment of a government of national unity. However, the opposition refused to participate in such a government before the reconciliation conference had taken place. The conference had been postponed several times, largely owing to disagreements regarding the composition and strength of the delegations. On completion of a five-day mission to the Comoros in mid-November 1997, Yéré revealed that only the list of delegates from Mwali had been submitted, while the secessionist government in Nzwani and the opposition parties remained dissatisfied with the OAU's proposals. The OAU also announced plans to deploy a force of military observers from Tunisia, Senegal and Niger in the Comoros, despite the separatists' insistence that the force would not be allowed to land on Nzwani; an initial eight-member contingent, which arrived later that month, was subsequently to be increased to 25 and was to receive logistical support from France. Meanwhile, amid reports of dissension within the separatist government on Nzwani, it was reported that Abdou Madi (believed to hold more moderate views than Ibrahim) was in Moroni, having fled Nzwani.

In early December 1997 Taki formed a new Council of Ministers, appointing Nourdine Bourhane as Prime Minister. The inter-Comoran reconciliation conference was held later that month; some agreement was reached on proposals for the establishment of an international commission of inquiry to investigate September's military intervention and on the holding of a Comoran inter-island conference to discuss institutional reform. In late January 1998, following the first meeting in Fomboni, Mwali, of a committee charged with pursuing negotiations on the crisis, the OAU announced that both the Comoran Government and the Nzwani separatists had agreed to a number of conciliatory measures, including the release of 18 federal soldiers still detained on Nzwani. In early February, however, tension increased on Nzwani, where several rival separatist factions had emerged and, following Abdou Madi's return to the island, fighting broke out between his supporters and those of Ibrahim.

Diplomatic relations between the Comoros and France, suspended in December 1975, were restored in July 1978; in November of that year the two countries signed agreements on military and economic co-operation, apparently deferring any decision on the future of Mayotte. In subsequent years, however, member countries of the UN General Assembly repeatedly voted in favour of a resolution affirming the Comoros' sovereignty over Mayotte, with only France dissenting. Following Djohar's accession to power, diplomatic relations were established with the USA in June 1990. In September 1993 the Arab League (see p. 195) accepted an application for membership from the Comoros.

Government

Under the Constitution of 20 October 1996, each of the islands in the Comoros has a Council and Governor. The Head of State is the President, who is elected by direct universal suffrage for an unlimited number of six-year terms. The President appoints the Prime Minister, who heads the Council of Ministers. The Constitution provides for a unicameral legislature, a 43-member Federal Assembly, which is directly-elected for a term of five years.

Defence

In mid-1997 the national army, the Force Comorienne de Défense (FCD), numbered about 1,500 men. Government expenditure on defence in 1987 was 910.8m. Comoros francs. In December 1996 an agreement was ratified with France, which provided for the permanent presence of a French military contingent in the Comoros, which was to be renewed by rotation. In July 1997, however, it was reported that the rotations had ceased several months previously.

Economic Affairs

In 1995, according to estimates from the World Bank, the gross national product (GNP) of the Comoros (excluding Mayotte), measured at average 1993–95 prices, was US $237m., equivalent to $470 per head. During 1985–95, it was estimated, GNP per head declined, in real terms, at an average rate of 1.4% per year. Over the same period, the population increased by an annual average of 2.8%. The Comoros' gross domestic product (GDP) increased, in real terms, by an annual average of 0.6% in 1985–95; GDP declined by 2.3% in 1994, and again in 1995, according to the World Bank.

Agriculture (including hunting, forestry and fishing) contributed an estimated 38.7% of GDP in 1995. Approximately 74.8% of the labour force were employed in the agricultural sector in 1996. In 1989 the sector accounted for more than 98% of total export earnings. The principal cash crops are vanilla, ylang-ylang, cloves and basil. Cassava, sweet potatoes, rice, maize, pulses, coconuts and bananas are also cultivated. Agricultural GDP increased by an annual average of 2.0% in 1985–95, according to the World Bank; growth was estimated at 1.5% in 1995.

Industry (including manufacturing, construction and power) contributed an estimated 12.8% of GDP in 1995. About 6% of the labour force were employed in the industrial sector at mid-

1980. Industrial GDP increased by an annual average of 1.3% in 1985–95, according to the World Bank; industrial GDP increased by 0.1% in 1994, and by an estimated 1.0% in 1995.

The manufacturing sector contributed an estimated 5.3% of GDP in 1995. The sector consists primarily of the processing of agricultural produce, particularly of vanilla and essential oils. According to the World Bank, manufacturing GDP increased by an annual average of 4.2% in 1985–95; the rate of growth was 1.0% in 1994.

Electrical energy is derived from wood (78%), and from thermal installations. Imports of fuel and energy comprised an estimated 11.8% of the total cost of imports in 1995.

The services sector contributed an estimated 48.4% of GDP in 1995. Strong growth in tourism since 1991 has led to a significant expansion in trade, restaurant and hotel activities. According to the World Bank, the GDP of the services sector increased by an average of 0.6% per year in 1985–95; services GDP declined by 5.6% in 1994 and by an estimated 6.3% in 1995.

In 1994 the Comoros recorded a visible trade deficit of US $34.1m., and there was a deficit of $10.7m. on the current account of the balance of payments. In 1995 the principal source of imports (32.2%) was France, which was also the principal market for exports (36.5%). The USA, Germany and South Africa were also major trading partners. The leading exports in 1995 were vanilla (54.8%) and ylang-ylang. The principal imports in that year were rice (20.7%), petroleum products, iron and steel, and meat.

The overall budget deficit for 1994 was estimated at 5,887m. Comoros francs (equivalent to 7.0% of GDP). The Comoros' external public debt at the end of 1995 totalled US $203.3m., of which $186.7m. was long-term public debt. In that year the cost of debt-servicing was equivalent to 0.9% of the value of exports of goods and services. The annual rate of inflation, which averaged 1.9% in 1993, increased to 21.7% in 1994, following the 33.3% devaluation of the Comoros franc in January 1994, but slowed to 7.1% in 1995. About 20% of the labour force were unemployed at the 1991 census.

In 1985 the Comoros joined the Indian Ocean Commission (IOC, see p. 261).

The Comoros has a relatively undeveloped economy, with high unemployment, a limited transport system, a severe shortage of natural resources and heavy dependence on foreign aid, particularly from France. A three-year structural adjustment programme, introduced in 1991, in agreement with the World Bank and IMF, which emphasized the reduction of public expenditure, the encouragement of private investment and the transfer of state-owned enterprises to the private sector, had limited success. In January 1994 the devaluation of the Comoros franc by 33.3% in relation to the French franc resulted in a dramatic increase in the price of imported goods. In March the IMF approved further credit in support of the Government's structural adjustment efforts. In mid-1995, in response to a further deterioration in the fiscal situation, the Government introduced measures to limit budgetary expenditure under a public finance recovery programme. However, political instability continued to impede economic progress. Falling prices and increased competition on the international market for the Comoros' principal export products contributed to economic decline in 1996–97. In February 1997 the Government agreed a six-month surveillance programme with the IMF and the World Bank, which laid emphasis on fiscal reform, greater control of public-sector wage costs and the effective privatization of state-owned enterprises. It had been hoped that this would lead to the approval of an enhanced structural adjustment facility by the end of that year, but the ongoing political uncertainty resulting from the unilateral secession of Nzwani and Mwali in August (see Recent History) seemed certain to hinder severely the implementation of economic reforms.

Social Welfare

In 1978 the Government administered six hospital establishments, with a total of 698 beds, and in 1984 there were 31 physicians working in the country. In 1989 it was estimated that there was one hospital bed per 342 inhabitants, and one physician per 7,500 inhabitants in the country. Expenditure on health services by the central Government in 1987 was 1,527.2m. Comoros francs (7.3% of total spending).

Education

Education is officially compulsory for nine years between seven and 16 years of age. Primary education begins at the age of six and lasts for six years. Secondary education, beginning at 12 years of age, lasts for seven years, comprising a first cycle of four years and a second of three years. Enrolment at primary schools in 1993 included an estimated 51% of children in the relevant age-group (boys 55%; girls 46%). Children may also receive a basic education through traditional Koranic schools, which are staffed by Comoran teachers. Enrolment at secondary schools in 1993 was equivalent to 19% of children in the relevant age-group (boys 21%; girls 17%). Expenditure by the central Government on education in 1992 was 2,829m. Comoros francs, representing 25.1% of total spending. In 1980, according to census results, the average rate of adult illiteracy was 52.1% (males 44.0%; females 60.0%). In 1995, according to estimates by UNESCO, the average rate of adult illiteracy was 42.7% (males 35.8%; females 49.6%).

Public Holidays

1998: 30 January* (Id al-Fitr, end of Ramadan), 8 April* (Id al-Adha, Feast of the Sacrifice), 28 April* (Muharram, Islamic New Year), 7 May* (Ashoura), 6 July (Independence Day), 7 July* (Mouloud, Birth of the Prophet), 17 November* (Leilat al-Meiraj, Ascension of the Prophet), 27 November (Anniversary of President Abdallah's assassination), 20 December* (Ramadan begins).

1999: 19 January* (Id al-Fitr, end of Ramadan), 28 March* (Id al-Adha, Feast of the Sacrifice), 17 April* (Muharram, Islamic New Year), 26 April* (Ashoura), 26 June* (Mouloud, Birth of the Prophet), 6 July (Independence Day), 6 November* (Leilat al-Meiraj, Ascension of the Prophet, 27 November (Anniversary of President Abdallah's assassination), 9 December* (Ramadan begins).

* Religious holidays, which are dependent on the Islamic lunar calendar, may differ by one or two days from the dates given.

Weights and Measures

The metric system is in force.

Statistical Survey

Source (unless otherwise stated): Ministry of Finance, the Budget and the Economy, BP 324, Moroni; tel. 2767; telex 219.

Note: Unless otherwise indicated, figures in this Statistical Survey exclude data for Mayotte.

AREA AND POPULATION

Area: 1,862 sq km (719 sq miles) *By island:* Njazidja (Grande-Comore) 1,146 sq km, Nzwani (Anjouan) 424 sq km, Mwali (Mohéli) 290 sq km.

Population: 335,150 (males 167,089; females 168,061), excluding Mayotte (estimated population 50,740), at census of 15 September 1980; 484,000 (official estimate), including Mayotte, at 31 December 1986; 446,817 (males 221,152; females 225,665), excluding Mayotte, at census of 15 September 1991. *By island* (1991 census): Njazidja (Grande-Comore) 233,533, Nzwani (Anjouan) 188,953, Mwali (Mohéli) 24,331.

Density (per sq km, 1991 census): 240.0 (Njazidja 203.8; Nzwani 445.6; Mwali 83.9).

Principal Towns (population at 1980 census): Moroni (capital) 17,267; Mutsamudu 13,000; Fomboni 5,400.

Births and Deaths (including figures for Mayotte, UN estimates): Average annual birth rate 48.5 per 1,000 in 1980–85, 48.5 per 1,000 in 1985–90, 48.5 per 1,000 in 1990–95; average annual death rate 14.4 per 1,000 in 1980–85, 13.0 per 1,000 in 1985–90, 11.7 per 1,000 in 1990–95. Source: UN, *World Population Prospects: The 1994 Revision*.

Expectation of life (UN estimates, years at birth, 1990–95): 56.0 (males 55.5; females 56.5). Source: UN, *World Population Prospects: The 1994 Revision*.

Economically Active Population (ILO estimates, '000 persons at mid-1980, including figures for Mayotte): Agriculture, forestry and fishing 150; Industry 10; Services 20; Total 181 (males 104, females 77). Source: ILO, *Economically Active Population Estimates and Projections, 1950–2025*. **1991 census** (persons aged 12 years and over, excluding Mayotte): Total labour force 126,510 (males 88,034; females 38,476). Source: UN, *Demographic Yearbook*.

AGRICULTURE, ETC.

Principal Crops (FAO estimates, '000 metric tons, 1996): Rice (paddy) 17, Maize 4, Cassava (Manioc) 50, Sweet potatoes 13, Pulses 8, Coconuts 60, Bananas 57. Source: FAO, *Production Yearbook*.

Livestock (FAO estimates, '000 head, year ending September 1996): Asses 5, Cattle 50, Sheep 15, Goats 128. Source: FAO, *Production Yearbook*.

Livestock Products (FAO estimates, '000 metric tons, 1996): Meat 2 (beef and veal 1); Cows' milk 4. Source: FAO, *Production Yearbook*.

Fishing ('000 metric tons, live weight): Total catch 11.6 in 1993; 13.0 in 1994; 13.2 (FAO estimate) in 1995. Source: FAO, *Yearbook of Fishery Statistics*.

INDUSTRY

Electric energy (production by public utilities): 17 million kWh in 1994. Source: UN, *Industrial Commodity Statistics Yearbook*.

FINANCE

Currency and Exchange Rates: 100 centimes = 1 Comoros franc. *Sterling and Dollar Equivalents* (30 September 1997): £1 sterling = 718.7 Comoros francs; US $1 = 444.9 Comoros francs; 1,000 Comoros francs = £1.391 = $2.248. *Average Exchange Rate* (Comoros francs per US $): 416.40 in 1994; 374.36 in 1995; 383.66 in 1996. Note: The Comoros franc was introduced in 1981, replacing (at par) the CFA franc. The fixed link to French currency was retained, with the exchange rate set at 1 French franc = 50 Comoros francs. This remained in effect until January 1994, when the Comoros franc was devalued by 33.3%, with the exchange rate adjusted to 1 French franc = 75 Comoros francs.

Budget (million Comoros francs, 1994): *Revenue:* Tax revenue 9,799 (Taxes on income and profits 1,399; Taxes on goods and services 929; Taxes on international trade 4,045; Unified tax on petroleum products and rice 3,132); Other revenue 1,268 (Proceeds from services 525); Total 11,067, excluding grants received (12,833). *Expenditure:* Budgetary current expenditure 14,783 (Wages and salaries 6,871; Goods and services 6,008; Transfers 1,048; Interest payments 857); Current expenditure under technical assistance programmes 5,300; Budgetary capital expenditure 638; Capital expenditure financed with external resources 7,582; Total 28,303, excluding net lending (393) and civil service action plan (1,091). Source: IMF, *Comoros—Recent Economic Developments* (October 1996).

International Reserves (US $ million at 31 December 1996): Gold 0.21; IMF special drawing rights 0.05; Reserve position in IMF 0.78; Foreign exchange 49.72; Total 50.76. Source: IMF, *International Financial Statistics*.

Money Supply (million Comoros francs at 31 December 1996): Currency outside deposit money banks 5,639; Demand deposits at deposit money banks 4,487; Total money (incl. others) 12,845. Source: IMF, *International Financial Statistics*.

Expenditure on the Gross Domestic Product (million Comoros francs at current prices, 1993): Government final consumption expenditure 15,033; Private final consumption expenditure 57,347; Gross fixed capital formation 10,497; Change in stocks 2,721; *Total domestic expenditure* 85,598; Exports of goods and services 11,247; *Less* Imports of goods and services 22,583; *GDP in purchasers' values* 74,261. Source: IMF, *Comoros—Recent Economic Developments* (October 1996).

Gross Domestic Product by Economic Activity (million Comoros francs at current prices, 1993): Agriculture, hunting, forestry and fishing 29,044; Manufacturing 3,340; Electricity, gas and water 889; Construction 4,652; Trade, restaurants and hotels 21,547; Transport and communications 3,190; Finance, insurance, real estate and business services 3,452; Government services 9,669; Other services 400; *Sub-total* 76,183; *Less* Imputed bank service charge 1,922; *GDP in purchasers' values* 74,261. Source: IMF, *Comoros—Recent Economic Developments* (October 1996).

Balance of Payments (US $ million, 1994): Exports of goods f.o.b. 10.8; Imports of goods f.o.b. −44.9; *Trade balance* −34.1; Services and other income (net) −15.7. *Balance on goods, services and income* −49.7; Current transfers (net) 39.0; *Current balance* −10.7; Capital account (net) −0.6; *Overall balance* −11.3. Source: IMF, *Comoros—Recent Economic Developments* (October 1996).

EXTERNAL TRADE

Principal Commodities (million Comoros francs, 1995): *Imports c.i.f.:* Rice 5,252; Meat 1,617; Petroleum products 2,897; Cement 1,652; Iron and steel 887; Total (incl. others) 25,411. *Exports f.o.b.:* Vanilla 2,320; Clove buds 133; Ylang-ylang 855; Total (incl. others) 4,236. Source: IMF, *Comoros—Recent Economic Developments* (October 1996).

Principal Trading Partners (US $'000, 1994): *Imports:* France 21,114; Kenya 5,463; Southern African Customs Union 3,341; Total (incl. others) 52,784. *Exports:* France 5,340; Germany 638; USA 3,273; Total (incl. others) 11,388. Source: UN, *International Trade Statistics Yearbook*. **1995** (percentage of trade): *Imports:* France 32.2%; Japan 1.3%; Kenya 4.3%; Madagascar 1.1%; Mauritius 1.3%; Réunion 3.3%; South Africa 6.7%. *Exports:* France 36.5%; Germany 8.0%; USA 28.4%. Source: IMF, *Comoros—Recent Economic Developments* (October 1996).

TRANSPORT

Road Traffic (estimates, motor vehicles in use, 1996): Passenger cars 9,100; Lorries and vans 4,950. Source: International Road Federation, *World Road Statistics*.

International Shipping (estimated sea-borne freight traffic, '000 metric tons, 1991): Goods loaded 12; Goods unloaded 107. Source: UN Economic Commission for Africa, *African Statistical Yearbook*.

Civil Aviation (traffic on scheduled services, 1994): Passengers carried ('000) 26; Passenger-km (million) 3. Source: UN, *Statistical Yearbook*.

TOURISM

Tourist Arrivals (by air): 18,921 in 1992; 23,671 in 1993; 27,061 in 1994.

Receipts from Tourism (US $ million): 8 in 1992; 8 in 1993; 9 in 1994.

Source: UN, *Statistical Yearbook*.

COMMUNICATIONS MEDIA

Radio Receivers (1994): 81,000 in use. Source: UNESCO, *Statistical Yearbook*.

Television Receivers (1994): 200 in use. Source: UNESCO, *Statistical Yearbook*.

Telephones (1994): 4,000 main lines in use. Source: UN, *Statistical Yearbook*.

Telefax Stations (1993): 100 in use. Source: UN, *Statistical Yearbook*.

EDUCATION

Pre-Primary (1980/81): 600 teachers; 17,778 pupils.

Primary (1993/94): 275 schools; 1,737 teachers; 77,837 pupils.

Secondary: Teachers: general education 613 (1991/92); teacher training 11 (1991/92); vocational 31 (1986/87). Pupils (1993/94): 17,637 (general education 17,474; teacher training 37; vocational 126).

Higher (1992/93): 32 teachers (1989/90); 229 pupils.

Source: UNESCO, *Statistical Yearbook*.

Directory

The Constitution

The Constitution of the Federal Republic of the Comoros was approved by popular referendum on 20 October 1996. The following is a summary of the main provisions:

PREAMBLE

The preamble affirms the will of the Comoran people to derive from the state religion, Islam, inspiration for the principles and laws that the State and its institutions govern, to adhere to the principles laid down by the Charters of the UN, the Organization of African Unity and the Organization of the Islamic Conference and by the Treaty of the League of Arab States, and to guarantee the rights of all citizens, without discrimination, in accordance with the UN Declaration of Human Rights and the African Charter of Human Rights.

GENERAL PROVISIONS

The Comoros archipelago constitutes a federal Islamic republic. Sovereignty belongs to the people, and is exercised through their elected representatives or by the process of referendum. There is universal secret suffrage, which can be direct or indirect, for all citizens who are over the age of 18 and in full possession of their civil and political rights. Political parties and groups operate freely, respecting national sovereignty, democracy and territorial integrity. However, political parties which are not represented by at least two deputies from each island, as a result of the first legislative election to follow the adoption of the Constitution, will be dissolved, unless those parties merge with others which are legitimately represented in the Federal Assembly. If only one political party has representation in the Federal Assembly, the party which has obtained the second highest number of votes will continue to operate freely. Only political parties and groups active throughout the Republic may participate in national elections. Political parties must be democratic both in their internal structure and their activities.

PRESIDENT OF THE REPUBLIC

The President is the Head of State and is elected by direct universal suffrage for a six-year term, which is renewable for an unrestricted number of mandates. He is also Head of the Armed Forces and ensures the legitimate functioning of public powers and the continuation of the State. He is the guarantor of national independence, the unity of the Republic, the autonomy of the islands, territorial integrity and adherence to international agreements. Candidates for the presidency must be aged between 40 and 75 years, of Comoran nationality by birth, and resident in the archipelago for at least 12 consecutive months prior to elections. The President presides over the Council of Ministers. He is empowered to ask the Federal Assembly to reconsider a Bill. The President can, having consulted with the Prime Minister and the Presidents of the Federal Assembly and the High Council of the Republic in writing, dissolve the Federal Assembly. The President determines and implements the Republic's foreign policy.

THE GOVERNMENT

The President appoints the Prime Minister, and on his recommendations, the other members of the Government. Under the authority of the President of the Republic, the Council of Ministers determines and implements domestic policy.

LEGISLATIVE POWER

Legislative power is vested in the Federal Assembly, which represents the Comoran nation. Deputies in the Federal Assembly are elected for five years by direct suffrage. Legislative elections take place between 30 and 90 days after the expiry of the mandate of the incumbent Federal Assembly. The electoral law dictates the number of members of the Federal Assembly, but there is a minimum of five deputies from each island. The deputies elect the President of the Federal Assembly at the beginning of their mandate. The Federal Assembly sits for two sessions each year and, if necessary, for extraordinary sessions. Matters covered by federal legislation include constitutional institutions, defence, posts and telecommunications, transport, civil and penal law, public finance, external trade, federal taxation, long-term economic planning, education and health.

JUDICIAL POWER

Judicial power is independent of executive and legislative power. The President is the guarantor of the independence of the judicial system and chairs the Higher Council of the Magistracy (Conseil Supérieur de la Magistrature), of which the Minister of Justice is Vice-President.

HIGH COUNCIL OF THE REPUBLIC

The High Council of the Republic considers constitutional matters and the control of public finance, and acts as a High Court of Justice. It has a renewable mandate of seven years and is composed of four members appointed by the President, three members elected by the Federal Assembly and one member elected by the Council of each island. The High Council oversees and proclaims the results of presidential and legislative elections and referendums.

COUNCIL OF THE ULÉMAS

The Council of the Ulémas offers opinions on projects for laws, ordinances and decrees. The President of the Republic, the Prime Minister, the President of the Federal Assembly, the Presidents of the Councils and the Governors of the islands may consult the Council of the Ulémas on any religious issue. The Council of the Ulémas may submit recommendations to the Federal Assembly, the Government or the Governors of the islands if it considers legislation to be in contravention of the principles of Islam.

ISLAND INSTITUTIONS

While respecting the unity of the Republic, each island is an autonomous territorial entity which freely controls its own administration through a Governor and a Council. The Governor of each island is appointed by the President of the Republic, from three candidates proposed by the Council of the island. The Council of each island is composed of the mayors of the communes and sits for not more than 15 days at a time, in March and December, and, if necessary, for extraordinary sessions. The Council is responsible for such matters as the budget of the island, taxes, culture, health, primary education and the environment.

REVISION OF THE CONSTITUTION

The power to initiate constitutional revision is vested in the President of the Republic. However, one-third of the members of the Federal Assembly may propose amendments to the President. Constitutional revision must be approved by a majority of two-thirds of the deputies in the Federal Assembly, and is subject to approval by national referendum. However, the President of the Republic may decide to promulgate a constitutional project, without submitting it to a referendum, if it has been adopted at a congress of deputies and the councillors of the islands, by a majority of two-thirds. The Republican and Islamic nature of the State cannot be revised.

The Government

HEAD OF STATE

President: MOHAMED TAKI ABDOULKARIM (elected President by popular vote 16 March 1996; took office 25 March 1996).

COUNCIL OF MINISTERS

(January 1998)

Prime Minister, also responsible for the Interior, Security and Information: NOURDINE BOURHANE.

Minister of National Education and Scientific Research, Spokesperson: MOUZAOIR ABDALLAH.

Minister of Development, Urban Affairs and Housing: OMAR TAMOU.

Minister of the Civil Service, Decentralization and Labour: SAÏD ALI MOHAMED.

Minister of the Economy, Domestic and External Trade and Energy: ABDÉRÉMANE MOHAMED.

Minister of Transport, Tourism, Posts and Telecommunications: MTARA MAECHA.

Minister of Public Health and Population: BEN CHEIKH MZE CHEIKH.

Minister of Finance and the Budget: MOHAMED ALI SOILIHI.

Minister of Justice and Prison Administration: SAÏD ALI YOUSSOUF.

Minister of Foreign Affairs and Diplomacy: IBRAHIM ALI MZIMBA.

Minister of Relations with Arab Countries: ABOUBACAR ABDALLAH.

Minister of Culture, Francophone Affairs, Youth and Sports: NOURDINE AHMED ABDOU.

MINISTRIES

Ministry of the Civil Service, Decentralization and Labour: Moroni.

Ministry of Culture, Francophone Affairs, Youth and Sports: Moroni.

Ministry of Development, Urban Affairs and Housing: Moroni.

Ministry of the Economy, Domestic and External Trade and Energy: Moroni; tel. (73) 2767; telex 219.

Ministry of Finance and the Budget: BP 324, Moroni; telex 245.

Ministry of Foreign Affairs and Diplomacy: Moroni.

Ministry of Justice and Prison Administration: Moroni.

Ministry of National Education and Scientific Research: BP 421, Moroni; telex 219.

Ministry of Public Health and Population: BP 42, Moroni; tel. (73) 2277; telex 219.

Ministry of Relations with Arab Countries: Moroni.

Ministry of Transport, Tourism, Posts and Telecommunications: Moroni; tel. (73) 2098; telex 244.

President and Legislature

PRESIDENT

In the first round of voting, which took place on 6 March 1996, none of the 15 candidates received 50% of the total votes cast. A second round of voting took place on 16 March, when voters chose between the two leading candidates. MOHAMED TAKI ABDOULKARIM received 64.3% of the votes, while ABBAS DJOUSSOUF obtained 35.7%.

ASSEMBLÉE FÉDÉRALE

Chairman: SALIM DJABIR.

General Election, 1 and 8 December 1996

	Seats
Rassemblement national pour le développement	36
Front national pour la justice	3
Independent	4
Total	43

Political Organizations

The Union comorienne pour le progrès (Udzima) was the sole legal party between 1982 and December 1989, when formal restrictions on multi-party activity were ended. Under the terms of a new Constitution, which was adopted in October 1996, however, existing political parties that failed to fulfil certain conditions, were to be dissolved; following legislative elections, held in December, the only legal political organizations were:

Front national pour la justice (FNJ): Islamic fundamentalist orientation; Leader AHMED ABDALLAH MOHAMED.

Rassemblement national pour le développement (RND): f. 1996 by 24 parties supporting President Taki; Chair. ALI BAZI SELIM; Sec. Gen. ABDOULHAMID AFFRAITANE.

The following opposition groups were active in late 1997:

CHUMA (Islands' Fraternity and Unity Party): Moroni; Leader Prince SAÏD ALI KEMAL.

Comité de suivi et d'orientation pour l'autonomie de Mohéli.

Forces pour l'action républicaine (FAR): Leader Maj. ABDURAZAK.

Forum pour le rétablissement de la démocratie (FRD): f. 1996; alliance of opposition parties; Leader ABBAS DJOUSSOUF.

Front démocratique (FD): BP 758, Moroni; tel. (73) 2939; f. 1982; Leader MOUSTAPHA SAÏD CHEIKH.

Front populaire comorien (FPC): Mwali; Leader MOHAMED HASSANALY.

Mkoutrouo: principal separatist group on Mwali (Mohéli); Leader SAÏD MOHAMED SOUEF.

Mouvement mohélien pour l'égalité des îles: f.1995.

Mouvement populaire anjouanais (MPA): f. 1997 by merger of Organisation pour l'indépendance d'Anjouan and Mouvement séparatiste anjouanais; principal separatist movement on Nzwani (Anjouan).

Mouvement pour la démocratie et le progrès (MDP): Moroni; founder-mem. of the FRD (see above); Leader ABBAS DJOUSSOUF.

Mouvement pour la rénovation et l'action démocratique (MOURAD): Moroni; f. 1990; aims to promote economic and financial rehabilitation; Leader ABDOY ISSA.

Nguzo: Moroni; Leader TAKI MBOREHA.

Parti comorien pour la démocratie et le progrès (PCDP): Route Djivani, BP 179, Moroni; tel. (73) 1733; fax (73) 0650; Leader ALI MROUDJAE.

Parti socialiste des Comores (PASOCO): POB 720, Moroni; tel. (73) 1328; Leader ALI IDAROUSSE.

Parti du salut national (PSN): f. 1993; breakaway faction of PCDP; Islamic orientation; Leader SAÏD ALI MOHAMED.

Diplomatic Representation

EMBASSIES IN THE COMOROS

China, People's Republic: Moroni; tel. (73) 2721; Ambassador: XU DAIJIE.

France: blvd de Strasbourg, BP 465, Moroni; tel. (73) 0753; telex 220; Ambassador: GASTON LE PAUDERT.

Korea, Democratic People's Republic: Moroni; Ambassador: KIM RYONG YONG.

Libya: Moroni.

Mauritius: Moroni.

Seychelles: Moroni.

Judicial System

Under the terms of the Constitution of October 1996, the President is the guarantor of the independence of the judicial system, and chairs the Higher Council of the Magistracy (Conseil Supérieur de la Magistrature), of which the Minister of Justice is Vice-President. The High Council of the Republic, which comprises four members appointed by the President, three members elected by the Federal Assembly and one member elected by the Council of each island, acts as a High Court of Justice.

Religion

The majority of the population are Muslims. At 31 December 1995 there were an estimated 5,000 adherents of the Roman Catholic Church, equivalent to 1.0% of the total population.

CHRISTIANITY

The Roman Catholic Church

Office of Apostolic Administrator of the Comoros: Mission Catholique, BP 46, Moroni; tel. and fax (73) 0570; Apostolic Pro-Admin. Fr JEAN PÉAULT.

The Press

Al Watwan: Nagoudjou, BP 984, Moroni; tel. (73) 2861; f. 1985; weekly; state-owned; Dir-Gen. MOHAMED IBRAHIM; Editor-in-Chief (vacant); circ. 1,500.

L'Archipel: Moroni; f. 1988; weekly; independent; Publrs ABOUBACAR MCHANGAMA, SAINDOU KAMAL.

NEWS AGENCIES

Agence Comores Presse (ACP): Moroni.

Foreign Bureau

Agence France-Presse (AFP): BP 1327, Moroni; telex 242; Rep. ABOUBACAR MICHANGAMA.

Broadcasting and Communications

TELECOMMUNICATIONS

Société Nationale des Postes et des Télécommunications: Moroni; operates post and telecommunications services.

RADIO

Transmissions to the Comoros from Radio France Internationale commenced in early 1994.

Radio-Comoros: BP 250, Moroni; tel. (73) 0531; telex 241; govt-controlled; domestic service in Comoran and French; international services in Swahili, Arabic and French; Tech. Dir KOMBO SOULAIMANA.

Finance

BANKING

(cap. = capital; res = reserves; dep. = deposits; m. = million; brs = branches; amounts in Comoros francs)

Central Bank

Banque Centrale des Comores: BP 405, Moroni; tel. (73) 1002; telex 213; f. 1981; bank of issue; cap. and res 2,202.8m. (Dec. 1989); Dir-Gen. SAÏD AHMED SAÏD ALI.

Commercial Bank

Banque pour l'Industrie et le Commerce—Comores (BIC): place de France, BP 175, Moroni; tel. (73) 0243; telex 242; fax (73) 1229; f. 1990; 51% owned by Banque Nationale de Paris Intercontinentale; 34% state-owned; cap. 300.0m., res 838.1m., dep. 10,494.3m. (Dec. 1993); Pres. MOHAMED MOUMINI; Dir-Gen. JEAN-PIERRE BAJON-ARNAL; 6 brs.

Development Bank

Banque de Développement des Comores: place de France, BP 298, Moroni; tel. (73) 0818; telex 213; fax (73) 0397; f. 1982; provides loans, guarantees and equity participation for small and medium-scale projects; 50% state-owned; cap. 300m. (Dec. 1992); Pres. AHMED EL-HARIF HAMIDI; Dir-Gen. AZALI AMBARI DAROUECHE.

Trade and Industry

GOVERNMENT AGENCIES

Office National du Commerce: Moroni, Njazidja; state-operated agency for the promotion and development of domestic and external trade.

Société de Développement de la Pêche Artisanale des Comores (SODEPAC): state-operated agency overseeing fisheries development programme.

DEVELOPMENT ORGANIZATIONS

CEFADER: a rural design, co-ordination and support centre, with brs on each island.

Mission de Coopération et d'Action Culturelle: BP 85, Moroni; tel. (73) 0391; fax (73) 1274; f. 1978; centre for administering bilateral aid from France; Dir JEAN-FRANCIS GOSPODAROWICZ.

CHAMBER OF COMMERCE

Chambre de Commerce, d'Industrie et d'Agriculture: BP 763, Moroni; privatized in 1995.

UTILITIES

Electricité et Eau des Comores (EEDC): Moroni; telex 251; state-controlled enterprise responsible for the production and distribution of electricity and water; transfer to private management pending in 1997.

TRADE UNION

Union des Syndicats Autonomes des Travailleurs des Comores: Moroni.

Transport

ROADS

In 1996 there were an estimated 900 km of classified roads, of which 440 km were principal roads and 230 km secondary roads. About 76.5% of the network was paved in 1995. In January 1996 the European Union granted over US $7m. to finance urgent repairs on a major road on Nzwani.

SHIPPING

The port of Mutsamudu, on Njazidja, can accommodate vessels of up to 11 m draught. Goods from Europe are routed via Madagascar, and coastal vessels connect the Comoros with the east coast of Africa. The development of the port of Moroni, with support from the European Community (EC, now European Union), was completed in mid-1991. In 1993 the EC pledged US $4m. to finance the construction of a port at Fomboni, on Mwali, to improve shipping access to the island.

Société Comorienne de Navigation: Moroni; services to Madagascar.

CIVIL AVIATION

The international airport is at Moroni-Hahaya on Njazidja. Each of the three other islands has a small airfield. At the end of 1995 it was announced that Air Comores, the national airline, was to be liquidated. In 1996 the Government was considering the establishment of a new airline, with the majority of shares to be held by the private sector.

Tourism

The principal tourist attractions are the beaches, underwater fishing and mountain scenery. In 1991 hotel capacity increased from 112 to 294 rooms, following the implementation of a number of hotel development projects, which resulted in a considerable increase in tourism receipts that year. In 1994 there were 27,061 tourist arrivals by air in the Comoros, and receipts from tourism totalled US $9m.

Société Comorienne de Tourisme et d'Hôtellerie (COMOTEL): Itsandra Hotel, Njazidja; tel. (73) 2365; national tourist agency.

THE DEMOCRATIC REPUBLIC OF THE CONGO

Introductory Survey

Location, Climate, Language, Religion, Flag, Capital

The Democratic Republic of the Congo (formerly Zaire) lies in central Africa, bordered by the Republic of the Congo to the north-west, by the Central African Republic and Sudan to the north, by Uganda, Rwanda, Burundi and Tanzania to the east and by Zambia and Angola to the south. There is a short coastline at the outlet of the River Congo. The climate is tropical, with an average temperature of 27°C (80°F) and an annual rainfall of 150cm–200cm (59ins–97ins). French is the official language. More than 400 Sudanese and Bantu dialects are spoken; Kiswahili, Kiluba, Kikongo and Lingala being the most widespread. An estimated 50% of the population is Roman Catholic, and there is a smaller Protestant community. Many inhabitants follow traditional (mostly animist) beliefs. The national flag (proportions 3 by 2) is blue with a large central yellow star and six smaller yellow stars arranged vertically at the hoist. The capital is Kinshasa.

Recent History

The Democratic Republic of the Congo, formerly called the Belgian Congo, became independent from Belgium as the Republic of the Congo on 30 June 1960. Five days later the armed forces mutinied. Belgium's actions during the ensuing unrest and its support for the secession of Katanga region were condemned by the UN, which dispatched troops to the region to maintain order. In September the Head of State, Joseph Kasavubu, dismissed the Prime Minister, Patrice Lumumba. Later in that month government was assumed temporarily by Col (later Gen. and, from December 1982, Marshal) Joseph-Désiré Mobutu. Mobutu returned power to President Kasavubu in February 1961. Shortly afterwards Lumumba, who had been imprisoned in December 1960, was murdered. In August 1961 a new Government was formed, with Cyrille Adoula as Prime Minister. In July 1964 Kasavubu appointed Moïse Tshombe, the former leader of the Katangan secessionists, as interim Prime Minister, pending elections, and in August the country was renamed the Democratic Republic of the Congo. Following elections in March and April 1965, a power struggle developed between Tshombe and Kasavubu; in November 1965 Mobutu intervened, seizing power and proclaiming himself head of the 'Second Republic'. In June 1967 a new Constitution was adopted. In October–November 1970 Gen. Mobutu was elected President, unopposed, and took office for a seven-year term. (From January 1972 he became known as Mobutu Sese Seko.) In November 1970 elections took place to a new National Assembly (subsequently renamed the National Legislative Council). In October 1971 the Democratic Republic of the Congo was redesignated the Republic of Zaire, and a year later the Government of Zaire and the Executive Committee of the Mouvement populaire de la révolution (MPR), Zaire's sole legal political party, merged into the National Executive Council.

In March 1977 and May 1978 the Front national pour la libération congolaise (FNLC), established in 1963 by Katangan separatists, invaded Zaire from Angola, taking much of Shaba (formerly Katanga) region; however, the FNLC was repulsed on both occasions by the Zairean army, with armed support from a number of Western Governments.

The invasion of 1977 prompted Mobutu to introduce a number of political reforms, including the introduction of a new electoral code. Legislative elections took place in October and, at a presidential election held in December, Mobutu (the sole candidate) was re-elected for a further seven-year term. In March 1979 the President appointed a new Government, with Bo-Boliko Lokonga, former head of the National Legislative Council, as First State Commissioner (equivalent to Prime Minister). In January 1980, as part of a large-scale campaign against corruption, Mobutu reorganized the National Executive Council, dismissing 13 of the 22 Commissioners.

Among a number of political reforms introduced in August 1980, was the creation of the new post of Chairman of the MPR, to be held by the President in his capacity as leader of the MPR. Thus the President became the central organ of decision-making and assumed more effective control of the party's activities. In the same month Nguza Karl-I-Bond was appointed First State Commissioner; in April 1981, however, he went into self-imposed exile in Belgium and was replaced by N'Singa Udjuu Ongwakebi Untube, who also became Executive Secretary of the MPR when the posts were merged in October 1981. In early 1982 opponents of Zaire's one-party system of government formed the Union pour la démocratie et le progrès social (UDPS). This was followed by the formation, later in that year, of the Front congolais pour le rétablissement de la démocratie (FCD), a coalition of opposition parties, for which Karl-I-Bond was the spokesman. Léon Kengo Wa Dondo was appointed First State Commissioner in a ministerial reshuffle in November.

In May 1983, following the publication of a highly critical report on Zaire by the human rights organization Amnesty International, Mobutu offered an amnesty to all political exiles who returned to Zaire by the end of June. A number of exiles accepted the offer, but a substantial opposition movement remained in Belgium, and violent opposition to Mobutu's regime was demonstrated in Zaire during 1984. However, Mobutu was re-elected President in July of that year, and was inaugurated in December. In July 1985 restrictions were lifted on seven members of the outlawed UDPS under the terms of another amnesty for political opponents, and Karl-I-Bond returned from exile.

In March 1986 Amnesty International published another unfavourable report on Zaire, citing the alleged illegal arrest, torture or killing of UDPS supporters in November and December 1985. In October 1986 Mobutu admitted that some of the allegations in the report were justified, and announced the appointment of a State Commissioner for Citizens' Rights. Elections to the 210-member National Legislative Council (reduced from 310 members) were held in September 1987. In November 1988, in the fourth ministerial reshuffle of the year, Mobutu replaced about one-third of the members of the National Executive Council and reappointed Kengo Wa Dondo to the post of First State Commissioner, from which he had been removed in October 1986. Further government reshuffles took place in May 1989 and January 1990.

The organization of opposition demonstrations (violently suppressed by the security forces) during 1989 and early 1990, prompted Mobutu's announcement, in late April 1990, that a multi-party political system, initially comprising three parties (including the MPR), would be introduced after a transitional period of one year; the UDPS was immediately legalized. At the same time Mobutu declared the inauguration of the 'Third Republic' and announced his resignation from both the post of Chairman of the MPR and from the post of State Commissioner for National Defence in the National Executive Council. However, he remained as the country's Head of State. N'Singa Udjuu Ongwakebi Untube, formerly First State Commissioner and Executive Secretary of the MPR, was subsequently appointed the new Chairman of the MPR. The National Executive Council was dissolved and Kengo Wa Dondo was replaced as First State Commissioner by Prof. Lunda Bululu, hitherto the Secretary-General of the Communauté économique des états de l'Afrique centrale. In early May a new, and smaller, transitional National Executive Council was formed. Furthermore, Mobutu announced the imminent 'depoliticization' of the security forces and of the administration in general. In late June Mobutu relinquished presidential control over the National Executive Council and over foreign policy, and authorized the establishment of independent trade unions. In early October Mobutu announced that a full multi-party political system would be established, thereby reversing his former decision to permit the existence initially of only three parties. In November legislation to this effect was introduced. In the same month the USA announced its decision to end all military and economic aid to

Zaire. This development followed renewed allegations of abuses of human rights by the Mobutu regime, and also reflected speculation that for many years Mobutu had misappropriated large amounts of foreign economic aid for his personal enrichment.

By February 1991 a large number of new parties had been established. Prominent among these was the Union des fédéralistes et républicains indépendants (UFERI), led by Karl-I-Bond. An enlarged transitional Government, appointed in late March and reshuffled in April, was reported to include members of minor opposition groups. None of the larger opposition parties, including the UDPS and the UFERI, agreed to join the new Government. Lunda Bululu was replaced as First State Commissioner by Prof. Mulumba Lukoji, a prominent economist who had served in previous administrations.

In early April 1991 Mobutu announced that a national conference would be convened at the end of that month, at which members of the Government and of opposition organizations would draft a new constitution. However, the Conference was postponed, owing to widespread disturbances and anti-Government demonstrations in several parts of the country. In late April Mobutu resumed the chairmanship of the MPR. In July some 130 opposition movements formed a united front, the Union sacrée. Later in July Mulumba Lukoji resigned as First State Commissioner. Etienne Tshisekedi Wa Mulumba, leader of the UDPS, was appointed in his place, but refused the post following threats to his life, and Mulumba Lukoji was subsequently reappointed. The National Conference was convened at the beginning of August, but was repeatedly suspended, initially owing to the dissatisfaction of the Union sacrée with the composition of its participants, and eventually by the Government, prompting renewed civil unrest, and the dispatch of French and Belgian troops to Zaire to evacuate nationals of those countries. In late September Tshisekedi finally accepted the post of First State Commissioner. In mid-October, however, he refused to swear allegiance to the President and the Constitution; shortly afterwards he was replaced as First State Commissioner by Bernardin Mungul Diaka, also a member of the opposition. In late November Mobutu dismissed Mungul from the premiership, and appointed Karl-I-Bond as the new First State Commissioner. The Union sacrée denounced the appointment, and expelled UFERI members from its ranks. Despite the expiry of his mandate as President in early December, Mobutu remained in office. In mid-December the Roman Catholic Archbishop of Kisangani, Most Rev. Laurent Monsengwo Pasinya, was elected President of the National Conference.

In mid-January 1992 further demonstrations took place in Kinshasa in protest against the continued suspensions of the National Conference. Shortly afterwards an alleged attempted military coup was suppressed (17 soldiers were subsequently sentenced to death in connection with this), and rioting by members of the armed forces was reported in the capital. In early April the National Conference reopened, and in mid-April it declared its status to be sovereign and its decisions to be binding. Mobutu reacted with cautious opposition to the erosion of his powers, anxious to secure confirmation of his position as Head of State.

In mid-August 1992 the National Conference employed its new sovereign powers by electing Tshisekedi as First State Commissioner, following the resignation of Karl-I-Bond, who had not stood for re-election. A 'transition act', adopted by the Conference in early August, afforded Tshisekedi a mandate to govern for 24 months, pending the promulgation of a new constitution which would curtail the powers of the President. On 30 August Tshisekedi, whose election was widely applauded as a victory for pro-democratic forces within Zaire, appointed a transitional Government of 'national union', which included opponents of Mobutu. The election of the State Commissioner was also welcomed by the international community, and it was hoped that renewed financial commitments from foreign donors would be promptly negotiated.

The political interests of Tshisekedi and Mobutu clashed almost immediately when the President declared his intention to promote the adoption of a 'semi-presidential constitution', in opposition to the parliamentary system favoured by the Conference. In October 1992 attacks on opposition leaders and the offices of newspapers critical of the President became increasingly frequent in Kinshasa, while Shaba was beset by ethnic violence. On 14 November the National Conference (without the participation of Mobutu's supporters) adopted a draft Constitution providing for the establishment of a 'Federal Republic of the Congo', the introduction of a bicameral parliament and the election of the President, by universal suffrage, to fulfil a largely ceremonial function. (Executive and military power was to be exercised by the Prime Minister.) The draft document was vigorously opposed by Mobutu who, having failed to persuade Tshisekedi to broaden his Government in order to accommodate the President's own supporters, unsuccessfully attempted in early December to declare the Tshisekedi Government dissolved. On 6 December the National Conference dissolved itself and was succeeded by a 453-member High Council of the Republic, headed by Monsengwo, which, as the supreme interim executive and legislative authority, was empowered to amend and adopt the new Constitution and to organize legislative and presidential elections. At the same time, Monsengwo declared that the report of a special commission, established by the Conference in order to examine allegations of corruption brought against the President and his associates, would be considered by the High Council. In response to this effective expropriation of his powers, Mobutu ordered the suspension of the High Council and the Government, and decreed that civil servants should usurp ministers in the supervision of government ministries (a demand which they refused). Attempts by the presidential guard to obstruct the convening of the High Council ended following the organization of a parade through the streets of Kinshasa, undertaken by Monsengwo and other members of the High Council, in protest at the actions of the armed forces. Bolstered by support from the USA, Belgium and France, Monsengwo reiterated the High Council's recognition of Tshisekedi as head of Zaire's Government.

In mid-January 1993 the High Council declared Mobutu to be guilty of treason, on account of his mismanagement of state affairs, and threatened impeachment proceedings unless he recognize the legitimacy of the transitional Government headed by Tshisekedi. A short-lived general strike and campaign of civil disobedience, organized by the Union sacrée, failed in their stated aims of forcing the resignation of the President and liberating the national radio and television stations from Mobutu's control. At the end of the month several units of the army rioted in protest at an attempt by the President to pay them with discredited banknotes. Order was eventually restored, but not before the deaths of some 65 individuals (including the French ambassador to Zaire) and the intervention of French troops.

In early March 1993, in an attempt to reassert his political authority, Mobutu convened a special 'conclave' of political forces to debate the country's future. The High Council and the Union sacrée declined an invitation to attend. In mid-March the 'conclave' appointed Faustin Birindwa, a former UDPS member and adviser to Tshisekedi, as Prime Minister, charged with the formation of a 'government of national salvation'. The somewhat perfunctory National Legislative Council was also revived to rival the High Council, and was reconvened to operate within the terms of reference of the old Mobutu-inspired Constitution. In early April Birindwa appointed a Cabinet which included Karl-I-Bond (as First Deputy Prime Minister in charge of Defence) and three members of the Union sacrée, who were immediately expelled from that organization. While the Birindwa administration was denied widespread official international recognition, Tshisekedi became increasingly frustrated at the impotence of his own Government (the armed forces recommenced blocking access to the High Council), and the deteriorating stability of the country. During April the army embarked upon a campaign of intimidation of opposition members, while tribal warfare re-emerged in Shaba and also erupted in the north-eastern region of Kivu. Tshisekedi urged the intervention of the UN to address these problems. In July the Secretary-General of the UN appointed Lakhdar Brahimi, a former Minister of Foreign Affairs in Algeria, as his Special Envoy to Zaire, entrusted with a humanitarian mission of mediation. Meanwhile, in late June, six of Birindwa's ministers, all former activists in the Union sacrée, had announced the formation of the Union sacrée rénovée (USR), claiming that the Union sacrée had abandoned its political objectives in the pursuit of extremist policies.

At the end of September 1993 an agreement was concluded between representatives of President Mobutu and of the principal opposition groups, providing for the adoption of a single constitutional text for the transitional period, which would be subject to approval by a national referendum. Under the provisions of the agreement, national transitional institutions would include the President of the Republic, a reorganized transitional parliament (a unicameral legislature to include all existing members of the High Council and most members of the National Legislative Council, as well as independent legislators, to be co-opted in order to ensure full national representation), the transitional Government and the national judiciary. As previously agreed, the organization of presidential and legislative elections would provide for the establishment of a new republic in January 1995. During October 1993, however, attempts to finalize the terms of the agreement were complicated by the insistence of Tshisekedi's supporters that he should continue in the office of Prime Minister, despite the objections of Mobutu's representatives that Tshisekedi's mandate, proceeding from the National Conference, had been superseded by the September agreement. The opposing positions of the principal political parties (largely polarized as the pro-Tshisekedi Union sacrée de l'opposition radicale—USOR and the pro-Mobutu Forces politiques du conclave—FPC) became more firmly entrenched during November and December.

Reports published by Amnesty International in September 1993 and February 1994 accused security forces of the Mobutu administration of having perpetrated numerous violations of human rights against civilians and political opponents during the previous four years.

An ultimatum, issued to all political parties by President Mobutu in early January 1994, in an attempt to end the political impasse, resulted in the conclusion of an agreement to form a government of national reconciliation, signed by all major constituent parties of the FPC and the USOR (with the notable exception of Tshisekedi's own UDPS). Encouraged by the unexpected level of political support for the initiative, on 14 January Mobutu announced the dissolution of the High Council and the National Legislative Council, the dismissal of the Government of National Salvation, headed by Birindwa, and the candidacy for the premiership of two contestants, Tshisekedi and Mulumba Lukoji, to be decided by the transitional legislature (to be known as the Haut Conseil de la République-Parlement de Transition—HCR-PT). Despite condemnation of Mobutu's procedural circumvention of the High Council's authority, and a well-supported 24-hour general strike, organized in Kinshasa on 19 January in protest at Mobutu's unilateral declarations, the HCR-PT convened for the first time on 23 January. The HCR-PT promptly rejected Mobutu's procedure for the selection of a new Prime Minister. Subsequent attempts by the legislature to formulate a new procedure were frustrated by the increasingly divergent interests of the member parties of the USOR, and by Tshisekedi's insistence of his legitimate claim to the office.

On 8 April 1994 the HCR-PT endorsed a new Transitional Constitution Act, reiterating the provisions of previous accords for the organization of a constitutional referendum and presidential and legislative elections, and defining the functions of and relationship between the President of the Republic, the transitional Government and the HCR-PT, during a 15-month transitional period. The Government, to be accountable to the HCR-PT, was to assume some former powers of the President, including the control of the Central Bank and the security forces and the nomination of candidates for important civil service posts. A new Prime Minister was to be appointed from opposition candidates, to be nominated within 10 days of the President's promulgation of the Act (on 9 April). Widening divisions within the USOR frustrated attempts to unite the opposition behind Tshisekedi as sole candidate, prompting the expulsion, in May, of 10 dissident parties from the USOR (including the Union pour la République et la démocratie—URD, whose members occupied several ministerial posts in the transitional Government).

In June 1994 the HCR-PT ratified the candidature of seven opposition representatives for the premiership, rejecting that of Tshisekedi for having failed to attend a parliamentary commission in order to explain the promotion of his position as 'Prime Minister awaiting rehabilitation', rather than candidate for the office. On 14 June it was reported that Léon Kengo Wa Dondo had been elected Prime Minister by 322 votes to 133 in the HCR-PT. However, Kengo Wa Dondo's election was immediately denounced as illegitimate, under the terms of the April Constitution Act, by opposition spokesmen and by the Speaker of the HCR-PT, Monsengwo Pasinya (who refused to endorse the actions of the legislature). A new transitional Government, announced on 6 July, was similarly rejected by the radical opposition, despite the offer of two cabinet posts to the UDPS. On 11 July, during a motion of confidence, the Government received overwhelming support from the HCR-PT. The new Prime Minister swiftly sought to restore the confidence of the international donor community in the commitment of the new administration to the implementation of political change and economic adjustment. In early October an expanded radical opposition grouping (the Union sacrée de l'opposition radicale et ses alliés–USORAL) resumed its participation in the HCR-PT, having boycotted proceedings since the election of Kengo Wa Dondo in June. By early November a reformist wing of the UDPS, led by Joseph Ruhana Mirindi, had agreed to participate in the Government, and a reallocation of portfolios, effected in mid-November, included the appointment of two ministers and two deputy ministers who were (or had previously been) members of the UDPS.

Despite the successful adoption, in May 1995, of the electoral law establishing the National Electoral Commission, a lack of government funds and the logistical problems presented by the presence in Zaire of as many as 2.5m. refugees seemed likely to force the extension of the 15-month period of transitional government beyond the 9 July deadline. In late June political consensus between the FPC and the USORAL resulted in the HCR-PT's adoption of a constitutional amendment (approved by Mobutu) whereby the period of national transition was to be extended by two years. On 1 July deputies from both groups voted to remove Monsengwo Pasinya from the post of President of the transitional legislature. Meanwhile, opposition frustration at the Government's failure to publish an electoral timetable continued to escalate. In late July, at an anti-Government demonstration organized in the capital, some 2,000 supporters of the Parti lumumbiste unifié (PALU—an organization which supported the aims of the murdered former Prime Minister, Patrice Lumumba) clashed with the security forces and violence erupted, resulting in the deaths of nine civilians and one police-officer. A subsequent anti-Government protest in Kinshasa, organized by the USORAL in early August, denounced international endorsement of Prime Minister Kengo Wa Dondo and urged his removal. The demonstration, which was conducted peacefully, was attended by an estimated 5,000 of Tshisekedi's supporters. In early December opposition groups voiced a unanimous rejection of a Government offer to participate in a national coalition government, and reiterated their demands for the prompt announcement of a timetable for multi-party elections. At the end of December the HCR-PT formalized the establishment of the National Electoral Commission, to be composed of 44 members (22 from both of the major political groupings), and headed by Bayona Bameya, a close political associate of President Mobutu. The Commission was formally installed in early April 1996.

In mid-April 1996 it was announced that multi-party presidential and legislative elections would be conducted in May 1997. Regional and municipal elections would be organized for June and July of the same year. All elections would be preceded by a referendum on a new constitution, to be conducted in December 1996. President Mobutu immediately announced his intention to contest the presidential poll. (However, neither the elections nor the referendum took place, as the security situation in the country deteriorated—see below.) A draft of the new Constitution, which provided for a federal state with a semi-presidential parliamentary system of government, was adopted by the Government in late May. Meanwhile, by late 1995 tensions within the UDPS appeared to be intensifying, with support divided between Tshisekedi and the USORAL President, Frédéric Kibassa-Maliba.

In the mid-1990s existing ethnic tensions in eastern Zaire were severely exacerbated by the presence of an estimated 1m. Hutu refugees from Rwanda (see below). The plight of the region's Zairean Tutsis (Banyamulenge) aroused international concern in late 1996, following reports of the organized persecution of Banyamulenge communities by elements of the Zairean security forces and by extremist Hutu refugees. Although Banyamulenge communities have existed within the country's modern borders for hundreds of years, legislation enacted by the Government in 1981 sought to undermine their claim to citizenship, and aroused concerns regarding the increasingly vulnerable existence of the tribe in the region. In October 1996 the Deputy Governor of Sud-Kivu, Lwasi Ngabo Lwabanji, ordered all Banyamulenge to leave the region within one week or risk internment or forced expulsion. Although Ngabo Lwabanji was subsequently suspended, this threat provoked the mobilization of armed Banyamulenge rebels, who launched a violent counter-offensive, allegedly supported by the Tutsi-dominated authorities in Rwanda and Burundi. Support for the rebels from dissidents of diverse ethnic origin (including Shaba and Kasaï secessionists, and local Mai-Mai warriors) increased during the month, and later in October the rebels announced the formation of the Alliance des forces démocratiques pour la libération du Congo-Zaïre (AFDL), under the leadership of Laurent-Désiré Kabila (hitherto leader of the Parti de la révolution populaire, and a known opponent of the Mobutu regime since the 1960s). AFDL forces made rapid territorial gains, in what initially appeared to be a regional movement which sought to defend the Tutsi population and to disempower extremist Hutus, but which soon gathered momentum and emerged as a national rebellion aiming to overthrow the Mobutu Government. In late January 1997 a counter-offensive by Zairean troops, reportedly assisted by foreign mercenaries, failed to recapture any significant area of territory. In March, after a brief battle, the AFDL entered the strategically-important northern town of Kisangani (which had served as the centre of military operations for the Government), and in early April Mbuji-Mayi fell to the rebels. Nguza Karl-I-Bond called on his followers (for the most part Shaba secessionists) to support the AFDL. According to international media reports, AFDL troops entering Zaire's 'second city', Lubumbashi, on 9 April, were cheered by crowds and greeted as liberators, as Government troops withdrew from the city. The Zairean Government continued to make allegations that the AFDL offensive was being supported by government troops from Rwanda, Uganda, Burundi and Angola, while the AFDL, in turn, claimed that the Zairean army was being supplemented by white mercenary soldiers and by forces of the União Nacional para a Independência Total de Angola (UNITA). Several attempts at mediation between the two sides, undertaken by various foreign governments (most notably South Africa) and international organizations, during February–April, failed to halt the escalation of the conflict.

Meanwhile, in August 1996 Mobutu had travelled to Switzerland to receive treatment for cancer. His absence, and uncertainties as to the state of his health, contributed to the poor coordination of the Zairean Government's response to the AFDL, which by the end of November was in control of most of Kivu. In that month the HCR-PT urged the expulsion of all Tutsis from Zairean territory; following attacks on Tutsis and their property, many Tutsi residents of Kinshasa fled to Brazzaville (Republic of the Congo). In the same month repeated public demonstrations demanded the resignation of Kengo Wa Dondo (himself, part-Tutsi in origin) for having failed to respond effectively to the insurrection. In December Mobutu finally returned to Zaire. He immediately appointed Gen. Mahele Bokungu as Chief of General Staff, and re-organized the Government, retaining Kengo Wa Dondo as Prime Minister. The continued exclusion of Tshisekedi from the Government prompted his supporters to mount a campaign of civil disobedience, and in January 1997 his faction of the UDPS announced its support for the AFDL. In February, following a highly effective general strike in Kinshasa, Mobutu banned all demonstrations and industrial action. In March, following the capture of Kisangani, the HCR-PT voted to dismiss Kengo Wa Dondo, who tendered his resignation as Prime Minister towards the end of the month. He was replaced at the beginning of April by Tshisekedi, who, having offered government posts to members of the AFDL (which they refused), announced that he was dissolving the HCR-PT. Parliament, in turn, voted to dismiss Tshisekedi, whose supporters organized a demonstration of support in Kinshasa, only to come under attack from the security forces. On 8 April Mobutu declared a national state of emergency, dismissing the Government and ordering the deployment of security forces throughout Kinshasa. Gen. Likulia Bolongo was appointed Prime Minister at the head of a new 28-member National Salvation Government, in which the USORAL refused to participate. An arrest warrant was subsequently issued for Kengo Wa Dondo, who was alleged to have fled to Switzerland with funds from the national treasury.

Following inconclusive peace talks between Mobutu and Kabila, mediated by the South African President, Nelson Mandela, in early May 1997, Mobutu refused to resign (despite intense international pressure to do so and thereby avoid a violent battle for Kinshasa) and Kabila reiterated his intention to take the capital by force. A hastily-assembled regional initiative to transfer interim executive power to Monsengwo Pasinya (recently re-elected Speaker of the HCR-PT) was rejected by the rebels, and was widely dismissed as a procedural device designed to afford Mobutu a dignified withdrawal from office.

On 16 May 1997 Mobutu left Kinshasa (travelling to Togo, and then to Morocco, where he died in September), whilst many of his supporters and family fled across the border to Brazzaville. On the night of 16 May Chief of General Staff Mahele Bokungu was murdered by elements of the presidential guard (reportedly led by Mobutu's son, Kongolo) who suspected him of attempting to negotiate a peaceful transfer of power to the rebels. On 17 May AFDL troops entered Kinshasa (encountering no resistance) and Kabila, speaking from Lubumbashi, declared himself President of the Democratic Republic of the Congo (DRC—the name used between 1964 and 1971), which swiftly gained international recognition. He immediately announced plans to form a provisional government within 72 hours and a commission to draft a new constitution within 60 days; presidential and parliamentary elections were to be held in April 1999. On 20 May Kabila arrived in Kinshasa, and on 22 May AFDL forces captured Matadi, giving the AFDL control of most of the country. On 23 May Kabila announced the formation of a transitional Government, which, whilst dominated by members of the AFDL, also included members of the UDPS and of the Front patriotique, and avoided a potentially unpopular preponderance of ethnic Tutsis. No Prime Minister was appointed, and Tshisekedi was not offered a cabinet post; he refused to recognize the new Government, and advocated public protest against the administration, but failed to raise the mass support that he had previously enjoyed. Following several demonstrations, including one in Uvira in which a number of people were reportedly killed by the security forces, Kabila issued a decree on 26 May banning all political parties and public demonstrations 'until further notice'. On 28 May Kabila issued a constitutional decree, which was to remain in force pending the adoption of a new constitution. The international community expressed concern that the decree allowed the President to wield near-absolute power, since it accorded him legislative and executive power as well as control over the armed forces and the treasury. Of the previously existing institutions, only the judiciary was not disbanded. On 29 May Kabila was sworn in as President of the DRC, assuming full executive legislative and military powers. Despite the concerns of a number of humanitarian organizations regarding the new administration's treatment of refugees (see below), Kabila's assumption of power was widely welcomed by the international community. In early June it was announced that a number of high-ranking officials from the Mobutu period, including the Secretary-General of the MPR and the Governor of the Central Bank, had been arrested, whilst the directors of all parastatal companies had been suspended, pending further investigations. Later in the month, the detention overnight of Tshisekedi, following a political address to students, prompted renewed scepticism regarding the Kabila Government's commitment to future political pluralism. In late July it was reported that the Minister of Finance, Ferdinand Mawapanga Mwana Nanga, had been arrested following accusations of fraud. Although any wrongdoing on the part of the minister (who was obliged to resign from his post) was swiftly denied by the Government, it aroused fears of high-level corruption. Instability continued throughout 1997; several businessmen and politicians were arrested, and in July a protest march against the ban on political activity was reported to have resulted in three civilian deaths following clashes between troops and demonstrators. Also in July, reports emerged that four of Mobutu's generals who had fled to South Africa were planning to lead a rebel movement to fight for the secession of the southern regions of the DRC.

In mid-1997 the Government blocked attempts by a UN investigation team to enquire into the alleged massacre of thousands of Rwandan Hutu refugees by Kabila's troops and his Rwandan Tutsi allies during the rebellion against Mobutu. The Government's refusal to collaborate with the UN was expected to jeopardize the DRC's prospects of receiving crucial foreign aid. In October, however, following intensive negotiations, President Kabila, while professing his army's innocence, agreed to permit the UN team to carry out its investigations between November 1997 and the end of February 1998.

Meanwhile, in late August 1997, a military Court of Justice was established by decree, and at the end of October two statutory orders were signed by Kabila; one updated and defined the new designation of administrative areas and local authorities of the DRC (regions were, henceforth, to be known as provinces) and the other created a paramilitary force—the Service National—which, under the control of the President, was to monitor and facilitate activities to rebuild the country. In late October Kabila appointed a 42-member Constitutional

Commission (originally due to be appointed in June), which was to draft a new constitution by March 1998. In the following month Kabila reaffirmed that the activities of political parties were suspended until the holding of presidential and legislative elections, scheduled for 1999. At the end of November President Kabila's Special Adviser for Security and the acting Army Chief of Staff, Gen. Masasu Nindanga, was arrested by troops in Kinshasa and accused of maintaining a private militia and of fraternizing with state enemies. It was subsequently reported that up to 20 people had been killed in clashes between rival army factions. By late 1997 Kabila had yet to gain full military control over the eastern province, where ethnic violence continued between the Tutsi and Bantu groups.

From the late 1980s relations between Zaire and Belgium deteriorated. In November 1988 a serious dispute arose between the two countries, following reports in the Belgian press criticizing the degree of corruption in Zaire, and alleging that funds granted annually by Belgium for development purposes in Zaire had been misappropriated by President Mobutu. Mobutu responded by ordering all Zairean nationals living in Belgium to return to Zaire, and to sell their assets or move them from Belgium; it was announced in January 1989 that the Belgian-based operations of Zairean state companies had relocated elsewhere. In that month Mobutu announced the abrogation of the two treaties of friendship and co-operation upon which post-colonial relations between the two countries had been based. In late July, however, following mediation by King Hassan II, an agreement was signed in Rabat, Morocco, restoring 'full and amicable relations' between Zaire and Belgium, and in March 1990 a new treaty of co-operation was signed. In early May, however, Belgian sources reported that members of the security forces, acting on Mobutu's orders, had killed between 50 and 150 Lubumbashi University students who were attending an anti-Government demonstration. Strong condemnation was voiced by many humanitarian organizations, and the Belgian Government announced the immediate suspension of all official bilateral assistance to Zaire. Subsequent relations between the two countries remained tense, although in January 1992 Mobutu finally agreed to permit an international investigation into the alleged massacre. Following the fall of Mobutu in 1997, relations with Belgium improved and the Belgian Government stated that it intended gradually to resume co-operation with the DRC (although this remained dependent upon Kabila's Government adhering to the conditions of strict respect for human rights and democratization).

Zaire's relations with its neighbours were complicated by the presence of large numbers of refugees in the border areas, and by the activities of rebels opposed to various regional governments. In May 1986 Zaire's relations with a number of southern African countries deteriorated, owing to allegations that the USA was covertly supplying weapons, through Zaire, to the South African-backed UNITA, which was in conflict with the Angolan Government. Although the Zairean Government denied these allegations and, in July, President Mobutu visited Angola and declared his support for the Angolan Government, reports that military equipment was reaching UNITA through Zaire nevertheless continued.

From mid-1994 the credibility of Mobutu's Transitional Government was somewhat enhanced by its support for French and US initiatives to address the humanitarian crisis presented by the flight to Zaire of more than 2m. Rwandan refugees hoping to escape the violent aftermath of the death of President Habyarimana. In late July 1994 President Mobutu met President Bizimungu of Rwanda and concluded an agreement for the disarmament and gradual repatriation of Rwandan refugees. By mid-August 1995, however, the security situation in refugee camps along the Zairean border had deteriorated to such an extent that the Zairean Government initiated a programme of forcible repatriation. Some 15,000 Rwandans were deported in a number of days, prompting widespread international concern for their welfare. Later in the month in Geneva, at a meeting with the office of the UN High Commissioner for Refugees (UNHCR), the Zairean Prime Minister, Kengo Wa Dondo, agreed to entrust the repatriation process to UNHCR officials until the end of the year, after which time the Zairean Government would resume the forcible return of all remaining refugees. In early September a formal agreement was concluded between UNHCR and the Zairean Government for a more regulated and bilateral approach to the refugee crisis, and later in the month further commitments were made by the Zairean and Rwandan Governments to improve security conditions on both sides of the border. At a conference of the Great Lakes Countries, convened in Cairo (Egypt) in late November, and attended by the Presidents of Burundi, Rwanda, Uganda and Zaire and by a Tanzanian presidential envoy, the member nations recognized the need to disarm and demilitarize displaced groups within their borders which threatened the security of neighbouring nations. President Mobutu also indicated (and in December confirmed) that the forcible return of remaining refugees in early 1996 was no longer a realistic objective.

By October 1996, despite reports that large numbers of refugees were beginning to return to Rwanda from Burundi and Tanzania, little progress had been made in repatriating displaced Rwandans in Zaire. In that month UNHCR warned that the distribution of food to the refugees was being prevented by the prevailing instability in eastern Zaire. Hundreds of thousands of Rwandan Hutus fled in advance of the arrival of AFDL troops (see above), who, in early November, declared a cease-fire for returning refugees, and later in the month announced the creation of a humanitarian corridor to the Rwandan border, in the hope that the estimated 700,000 Rwandan refugees now seeking shelter at the Mugunga camp, west of Goma, would return to Rwanda. (An additional 300,000 refugees were believed to have scattered into the surrounding hills.) However, the large-scale return of refugees was finally prompted by an AFDL attack on extremist Hutu units operating from the camp. In mid-November UNHCR reported the return of some 400,000 refugees in recent weeks, which did much to reassure the international aid community that the immediate humanitarian crisis had abated (a number of initiatives for multinational intervention were cancelled), but failed to allay continuing concern as to the whereabouts and welfare of a vast number of refugees who could not be accounted for. As the AFDL advance continued as far west as Kisangani, reports began to emerge that relief supplies for the estimated 200,000 remaining refugees were being intercepted by the rebels, who were also accused of forcing refugees to flee nearby camps, and of refusing to allow aid workers and journalists to enter the camps. In late April 1997 the AFDL leader, Laurent Kabila, demanded that the UN complete full repatriation of the refugees within 60 days, after which time their return would be undertaken unilaterally by the rebels. By early May the AFDL had initiated an organized repatriation programme which encountered almost immediate condemnation from the UN, owing to the overcrowded conditions in which the refugees were being transported. Allegations continued to emerge during 1997 that elements of the AFDL had committed massacres of Hutu refugees, and in May the EU Commissioner for Humanitarian Affairs accused the AFDL of complicity in the death of refugees from disease and starvation. In the same month the UN Security Council urged the immediate cessation of violence against refugees in the Democratic Republic of the Congo.

In the months following June 1997, relations with the Republic of the Congo deteriorated, owing to the outbreak of civil war in that country. Several shells exploded in Kinshasa that had been fired from Brazzaville, and in late September 17 people were killed in the DRC's capital by such shellfire. Consequently, in early October it was announced that a monitoring team from the DRC was to be dispatched to Brazzaville. Relations between the DRC and Uganda were also strained in 1997, owing to the reported presence in the DRC of Ugandan rebel groups, which resulted in the deployment, in August, of Ugandan government troops along the border to prevent rebel attacks.

Government

Under the terms of a constitutional decree promulgated in May 1997, legislative and executive power is exercised by the President, in consultation with the Government. A 42-member Constitutional Commission was appointed in October 1997, which was to draft a new constitution by March 1998. Presidential and legislative elections were scheduled to be held in 1999.

Defence

Following the overthrow of Mobutu's regime in May 1997, the former Zairean armed forces (which totalled 28,100 men in August 1996) were disbanded. The AFDL troops of the new President, Laurent Kabila, were estimated to number 20,000-40,000 men.

Economic Affairs

In 1995, according to estimates by the World Bank, Zaire's gross national product (GNP), measured at average 1993–95 prices, was US $5,313m., equivalent to $120 per head. During 1985–95, it was estimated, GNP per head decreased, in real terms, at an average annual rate of 8.5%. Over the same period the population increased by an annual average of 3.2%. Zaire's gross domestic product (GDP) increased, in real terms, by an annual average of 1.2% in 1980–90, but decreased by 6.2% per year in 1987–95. Real GDP was expected to decline by 0.7% in 1995, compared with a 14.5% decline in 1993 and a contraction of 7.2% in 1994.

Agriculture (including forestry and fishing) contributed an estimated 59% of GDP in 1995. About 65.8% of the working population were employed in agriculture at mid-1996. The principal cash crops are coffee (which accounted for 12.5% of export earnings in 1994), palm oil and palm kernels, sugar, tea, cocoa, rubber and cotton. In recent years the Mobutu Government sought to revitalize the forestry industry (an estimated 6% of the world's woodlands are located in the republic). During 1987–95 agricultural GDP increased by an annual average of 2.3%.

Industry (including mining, processing of minerals, manufacturing, power and construction) contributed an estimated 14.9% of GDP in 1995. Some 15.9% of the working population were employed in industry in 1991. During 1987–95 industrial GDP decreased by an annual average of 13.3%, although an estimated increase of 6.4%, in real terms, was predicted for the sector's GDP in 1995.

Mining and metallurgy contributed about 10% of GDP in 1990, but this percentage declined to an estimated 4.4% of GDP in 1995. Mineral products accounted for about 92% of export earnings in 1993. The most important minerals are copper and cobalt (of which the country has 65% of the world's reserves). Manganese, zinc, tin and gold are also mined. There are rich diamond deposits, and in the late 1980s Zaire was the world's second largest producer of industrial diamonds. (Diamonds became Zaire's principal source of foreign exchange—US $532m.—in 1993.) There are also extensive offshore reserves of petroleum (revenue from petroleum accounts for about 20% of total government income). In 1993 and 1994, however, production of copper decreased dramatically. During 1987–95 the sector's GDP (including the processing of minerals) decreased, in real terms, by an estimated annual average of 17.6%; an 8.2% decline, in real terms, was estimated for 1995.

Manufacturing contributed an estimated 6.5% of GDP in 1995. The most important sectors are textiles, cement, engineering and agro-industries producing consumer goods. During 1980–90 manufacturing production increased by an annual average of 2.3%. The sector was thought to have suffered a considerable reversal in 1993, with production of cement alone declining by some 28% compared with 1992. During 1987–95 manufacturing GDP declined, in real terms, by an estimated annual average of 10.5%; the sector's GDP increased, in real terms, by 19.4% in 1995.

Energy is derived principally from hydroelectric power. In 1994 an estimated 99.9% of electric energy was generated by hydroelectric plants. In 1995 imports of fuel and energy comprised 6.0% of the value of total merchandise imports.

The services sector contributed an estimated 26.6% of GDP in 1995, and employed some 19.0% of the working population in 1991. During 1987–95 the GDP of the services sector decreased by an annual average of 11.2%. Services GDP decreased by an estimated 5.3% in 1995.

In 1990 Zaire recorded a visible trade surplus of US $599m., but there was a deficit of $643m. on the current account of the balance of payments. In 1995 the trade surplus was estimated at $581m., while the deficit on the current account of the balance of payments was estimated at $631m. As the former colonial power, Belgium (which received 40% of the country's exports and provided 20% of imports in 1993) is the principal trading partner. Other important trading partners include the USA, France and the United Kingdom. The principal exports are mineral products (mainly copper, cobalt, industrial diamonds and petroleum) and agricultural products (primarily coffee). The principal imports are manufactured goods, food and raw materials.

In 1995 there was an estimated budgetary deficit of 1,169,000m. new zaires. At the end of 1995 national external debt totalled US $13,137m., of which $9,621m. was long-term public debt. In 1990, when the external debt totalled $10,270m., the cost of debt-servicing was equivalent to 15.1% of the value of exports of goods and services. Annual inflation averaged 1,091% in 1985–95. Consumer prices increased by an average of 23,773.1% in 1994, by 541.9% in 1995 and by 658.8% in 1996. The inflation rate was 479% in the year to April 1997, but prices declined in May and June.

The DRC maintains economic co-operation agreements with its neighbours, Burundi and Rwanda, through the Economic Community of the Great Lakes Countries (see p. 260). The DRC is also a member of the International Coffee Organization (see p. 257) and of the Common Market for Eastern and Southern Africa—COMESA (see p. 124). In September 1997 the DRC became a member of the Southern African Development Community (SADC, see p.236).

Potentially one of Africa's richest states, the DRC has extensive agricultural, mineral and energy resources. However, the country has experienced severe economic decline in recent years, with the result that, since the late 1980s, GNP per head has been among the lowest in the world. Economic difficulties have been exacerbated by hyperinflation, which precipitated widespread public unrest and industrial action, and by the suspension of financial assistance by the IMF, Belgium, France and the USA (see Recent History). During the early 1990s most foreign investment in the country was withdrawn. By February 1994 government revenues had declined to such an extent (by 84% between 1989 and 1994) that the World Bank closed its office in the capital, Kinshasa, having declared the country 'insolvent'; in June 1994 Zaire was suspended from the IMF. The Kabila administration, which came to power in May 1997, announced its plans to rebuild the country's economy and rapidly secured foreign investment to revive the highly lucrative mining sector. The new Government began proceedings in Switzerland and Belgium to reclaim state assets allegedly misappropriated by former President Mobutu, and international aid was received to improve the transport infrastructure. Although plans to introduce a new currency have been postponed, the new zaire improved its trading position in the latter half of 1997 and the DRC acquired negative inflation. The Government also announced plans to organize and monitor the labour force through a central computer system. The railway network and its assets were nationalized in May 1997, but no large-scale programme of nationalization was envisaged.

Social Welfare

There is an Institut National de la Sécurité Sociale, guaranteeing insurance coverage for sickness, pensions and family allowances under an obligatory scheme of national insurance. In 1995, of total expenditure by the central Government, 25,000m. new zaires (less than 1%) were allocated to public health. In 1979 Zaire had 942 hospitals, with a total of 79,244 beds, and there were 1,900 physicians working in the country. In 1988–91, it was estimated, there were, on average, 14,286 inhabitants for every doctor and 1,351 inhabitants for every nurse in the country.

Education

Primary education, beginning at six years of age and lasting for six years, is officially compulsory. Secondary education, which is not compulsory, begins at 12 years of age and lasts for up to six years, comprising a first cycle of two years and a second of four years. In 1993 the total enrolment at primary and secondary schools was equivalent to 49% of the school-age population (males 58%; females 39%). In 1993 primary enrolment included 54% of students in the relevant age-group (boys 60%; girls 47%). The comparable ratio for secondary enrolment in 1993 was 17% (boys 23%; girls 11%). The country has four universities, situated at Kinshasa, Kinshasa/Limete, Kisangani and Lubumbashi. According to estimates by UNESCO, the average rate of adult illiteracy in 1995 was 22.7% (males 13.4%; females 32.3%). In the budget for 1995 a total of 27,000m. new zaires (less than 1% of total expenditure by the central Government) was allocated to education.

Public Holidays

1998: 1 January (New Year's Day), 4 January (Commemoration of the Martyrs of Independence), 1 May (Labour Day), 24 June (Promulgation of the 1967 Constitution and Day of the Fishermen), 30 June (Independence Day), 1 August (Parents' Day), 14 October (Youth Day), 17 November (Army Day), 24 November (Anniversary of the Second Republic), 25 December (Christmas Day).

1999: 1 January (New Year's Day), 4 January (Commemoration of the Martyrs of Independence), 1 May (Labour Day), 24 June (Promulgation of the 1967 Constitution and Day of the Fishermen), 30 June (Independence Day), 1 August (Parents' Day), 14 October (Youth Day), 17 November (Army Day), 24 November (Anniversary of the Second Republic), 25 December (Christmas Day).

Weights and Measures

The metric system is in force.

Statistical Survey

Sources (unless otherwise stated): Département de l'Economie Nationale, Kinshasa; Institut National de la Statistique, Office Nationale de la Recherche et du Développement, BP 20, Kinshasa; tel. (12) 31401.

Area and Population

AREA, POPULATION AND DENSITY

Area (sq km)	2,344,885*
Population (census result)	
1 July 1984	
Males	14,543,800
Females	15,373,000
Total	29,916,800
Population (official estimates at mid-year)	
1989	34,491,000
1990	35,562,000
1991	36,672,000
Density (per sq km) at mid-1991	15.6

* 905,365 sq miles.

REGIONS*

	Area (sq km)	Population (31 Dec. 1985)†
Bandundu	295,658	4,644,758
Bas-Zaïre	53,920	2,158,595
Equateur	403,293	3,960,187
Haut-Zaïre	503,239	5,119,750
Kasaï Occidental	156,967	3,465,756
Kasaï Oriental	168,216	2,859,220
Kivu	256,662	5,232,442
Shaba (formerly Katanga)	496,965	4,452,618
Kinshasa (city)‡	9,965	2,778,281
Total	2,344,885	34,671,607

* In October 1997 a statutory order redesignated the regions as provinces. Kivu was divided into three separate provinces, and some of the other provinces were renamed. The 11 provinces are: Bandundu, Bas-Congo, Equateur, Haut-Congo, Kasaï Occidental, Kasaï Oriental, Katanga (formerly Shaba), Kivu-Manyema, Nord-Kivu, Sud-Kivu, Kinshasa (city).

† Provisional. ‡ Including the commune of Maluku.

Source: Département de l'Administration du Territoire.

PRINCIPAL TOWNS (population at census of July 1984)

Kinshasa	2,653,558
Lubumbashi	543,268
Mbuji-Mayi	423,363
Kananga	290,898
Kisangani	282,650
Kolwezi	201,382
Likasi	194,465
Bukavu	171,064
Matadi	144,742
Mbandaka	125,263

Source: UN, *Demographic Yearbook*.

BIRTHS AND DEATHS (UN estimates, annual averages)

	1980–85	1985–90	1990–95
Birth rate (per 1,000)	48.3	47.8	47.5
Death rate (per 1,000)	16.2	15.0	14.5

Expectation of life (UN estimates, years at birth, 1990–95): 52.0 (males 50.4; females 53.7).

Source: UN, *World Population Prospects: The 1994 Revision*.

1990–95 (revised UN estimates, annual averages): Birth rate 48.1 per 1,000; Death rate 14.6 per 1,000 (Source: UN, *Population and Vital Statistics Report*).

ECONOMICALLY ACTIVE POPULATION

Mid-1996 (estimates in '000): Agriculture, etc. 12,885; Total labour force 19,595 (Source: FAO, *Production Yearbook*).

Agriculture

PRINCIPAL CROPS ('000 metric tons)

	1994	1995	1996
Rice (paddy)	414	425	430†
Maize	1,198	1,170	1,100†
Millet	35†	39	39†
Sorghum†	55	55	55
Potatoes†	35	35	35
Sweet potatoes	385†	407	410†
Cassava (Manioc)	18,051	17,500†	18,000†
Yams†	315	315	315
Taro (Coco yam)†	41	41	41
Dry beans†	124	125	125
Dry peas†	65	66	66
Groundnuts (in shell)	547	581	580†
Cottonseed†	50	50	50
Palm kernels†	72	72	72
Cabbages†	30	30	30
Tomatoes†	41	41	41
Onions (dry)†	32	32	32
Pumpkins†	44	44	44
Sugar cane†	1,350	1,300	1,300
Oranges†	156	156	156
Grapefruit†	14	14	14
Avocados†	47	47	47
Mangoes†	212	212	212
Pineapples†	145	145	145
Bananas†	410	412	412
Plantains	2,424	2,262	2,270†
Papayas†	210	210	210
Coffee (green)*	76	62	60
Cocoa beans†	7	7	7
Tea (made)†	3	3	3
Tobacco (leaves)†	3	3	3
Cotton (lint)†	26	26	26
Natural rubber (dry weight)	12*	11*	11†

* Unofficial figure(s). † FAO estimate(s).

Source: FAO, *Production Yearbook*.

LIVESTOCK ('000 head, year ending September)

	1994	1995	1996
Cattle	1,475	1,480†	1,480†
Sheep	1,047	1,080*	1,043*
Goats	4,212	4,315*	4,172*
Pigs	1,192	1,170	1,157

Poultry (FAO estimates, million): 35 in 1994; 36 in 1995; 34 in 1996.

* Unofficial figure. † FAO estimate.

Source: FAO, *Production Yearbook*.

LIVESTOCK PRODUCTS (FAO estimates, '000 metric tons)

	1993	1994	1995
Beef and veal	28	28	28
Mutton and lamb	3	3	3
Goat meat	10	10	10
Pig meat	43	42	41
Poultry meat	30	30	29
Other meat	127	130	130
Cows' milk	8	8	8
Hen eggs	9	9	9

Source: FAO, *Production Yearbook*.

Forestry

ROUNDWOOD REMOVALS
(FAO estimates, '000 cubic metres, excl. bark)

	1992	1993	1994
Sawlogs, veneer logs and logs for sleepers	391	391	391
Other industrial wood	2,763	2,853	2,944
Fuel wood	40,152	41,352	42,592
Total	43,306	44,596	45,927

Source: FAO, *Yearbook of Forest Products*.

SAWNWOOD PRODUCTION
('000 cubic metres, incl. railway sleepers)

	1989	1990	1991
Total (all broadleaved)	131	117	105

1992–94: Annual production as in 1991 (FAO estimates).

Source: FAO, *Yearbook of Forest Products*.

Fishing

('000 metric tons, live weight)

	1993	1994	1995
Inland waters	193.3	152.1	154.8
Atlantic Ocean	4.2	3.8	3.9
Total catch	197.5	155.9	158.6

Source: FAO, *Yearbook of Fishery Statistics*.

Mining

('000 metric tons, unless otherwise indicated)

	1994	1995	1996*
Copper ore†	40.6	38.0	39.6
Cobalt ore†	3.4	4.0	4.0
Zinc ore†	0.6	4.5	3.2
Gold ore (kg)†	780	1,180	1,252
Tin ore†	0.9	n.a.	n.a.
Crude petroleum ('000 barrels)	8,971.5	n.a.	n.a.
Diamonds ('000 carats)	16,259	22,024	22,240

* Provisional figures.

† Figures refer to the metal content of ores.

Sources: Mining Journal Ltd, *Mining Annual Review — 1997*, and IMF, *Zaire—Background Information and Statistical Data* (April 1996).

Industry

SELECTED PRODUCTS
('000 metric tons, unless otherwise indicated)

	1992	1993	1994
Maize flour	13.0	12.8	10.3
Sugar	81.7	82.3	79.0
Cigarettes ('000 cartons)	2,682.1	2,472.5	2,535.0
Beer (million litres)	165.4	148.8	160.7
Soft drinks (million litres)	85.3	71.1	75.9
Soaps	38.7	38.6	37.4
Acetylene	39.2	54.3	62.0
Tyres	41.0	26.0	35.6
Cement	208.0	161.7	165.7
Glassware	10.9	12.5	12.9
Diesel and gas oil	52.6	30.7	20.7
Fuel oil	34.3	32.8	9.1
Jet fuel and kerosene	31.4	31.2	1.1
Butane	0.1	10.2	0.2
Premium gasoline	28.3	30.8	8.3
Cotton fabrics ('000 sq metres)	20,510	15,099	17,804
Printed fabrics ('000 sq metres)	30,994	28,400	25,900
Footwear ('000 pairs)	934	1,661	1,061
Blankets ('000 units)	54	177	94
Metallic furniture ('000 pieces)	9.0	6.0	7.5
Sheet metal ('000 pieces)	144.6	163.4	151.0
Motor cars (units)	131	150	140
Electric energy (million kWh)	5,883	5,351	5,006

Source: IMF, *Zaire—Background Information and Statistical Data* (April 1996).

Finance

CURRENCY AND EXCHANGE RATES

Monetary Units

100 new makuta (singular: likuta) = 1 new zaire (NZ).

Sterling and Dollar Equivalents (30 September 1996)

£1 sterling = 104,138 new zaires;
US $1 = 66,610 new zaires;
1,000,000 new zaires = £9.603 = $15.013.

Average Exchange Rate (new zaires per US $)

1993	2.5
1994	1,194.1
1995	7,024

Note: The new zaire (NZ), equivalent to 3m. old zaires, was introduced in October 1993. Some of the figures in this Survey are still in terms of old zaires.

BUDGET ('000 million new zaires, unless otherwise indicated)

Revenue*	1993†	1994	1995
Taxation	934	184	1,955
Taxes on income, profits, etc.	282	34	700
Social security contributions	17	n.a.	n.a.
Taxes on payroll and workforce	7	3	27
Turnover tax	16	19	109
Excises	245	29	286
Other domestic taxes on goods and services	4	0	1
Import duties	218	71	642
Export duties	114	20	50
Other tax revenue	31	7	140
Administrative fees and charges, etc.	25	13	48
Other current revenue	256	11	117
Total	1,216	208‡	2,120‡

Expenditure§	1993†	1994	1995
General public services‖	2,616	205	1,646
Defence	1,258	11	122
Education	8	2	27
Health	2	2	25
Social security and welfare	55	n.a.	n.a.
Housing and community amenities	2	9	1
Recreational, cultural and religious affairs and services	1	0	19
Economic affairs and services	307	59	1,194
Fuel and energy	11	0	8
Agriculture, forestry and fishing	33	18	1,183
Mining, manufacturing and construction	4	2	1
Transport and communications	259	39	2
Other purposes	582	43	255
Interest payments	304	43	21
Total	4,831	331‡	3,289‡

* Excluding grants received (million new zaires): 30 in 1993; 17,000 in 1994; 1,177,000 in 1995.

† Figures in million new zaires.

‡ Excluding the operations of the social security system. In 1993 the system had revenue of 111m. new zaires and expenditure of 99m. new zaires.

§ Excluding lending minus repayments (million) new zaires: 109 in 1993; 17,000 in 1994; none in 1995.

‖ Including public order and safety.

Source: IMF, *Government Finance Statistics Yearbook.*

INTERNATIONAL RESERVES (US $ million at 31 December)

	1993	1994	1995
Gold	8.59	10.71	10.83
Foreign exchange	46.20	120.69	146.60
Total	54.79	131.40	157.43

1996: (US $ million at 31 December): Foreign exchange 82.50.

Source: IMF, *International Financial Statistics.*

MONEY SUPPLY (million new zaires at 31 December)

	1993	1994	1995
Currency outside banks	4,693	277,000	1,684,000
Demand deposits at deposit money banks	1,618	92,000	187,000
Total money (incl. others)	6,495	373,000	1,889,000

Source: IMF, *International Financial Statistics.*

COST OF LIVING

(Consumer Price Index for Kinshasa; base: 1988 = 100)

	1990	1991	1992
Food	785.2	33,900	1,002,187
Rent	771.6	29,658	973,432
Health	1,046.7	50,004	1,881,696
Clothing	488.1	21,019	689,652
Transport and other	930.7	44,134	797,283
All items	782.4	33,867	958,367

All items (base: 1990 = 0.01): 47,501 in 1994; 304,915 in 1995; 2,313,781 in 1996. (Source: IMF, *International Financial Statistics.*)

NATIONAL ACCOUNTS

Expenditure on the Gross Domestic Product

('000 million old zaires at current prices, unless otherwise indicated)

	1993	1994*	1995*†
Government final consumption expenditure	12,462,186	522.2	3,356.1
Private final consumption expenditure	64,305,274	5,417.7	31,924.1
Gross capital formation	1,817,933	162.1	982.4
Total domestic expenditure	78,585,393	6,102.0	36,262.6
Exports of goods and services	10,648,434	825.6	5,527.2
Less Imports of goods and services	8,462,269	627.7	5,167.5
GDP in purchasers' values	80,771,558	6,300.0	36,622.3

* Figures in '000 million new zaires (1 new zaire = 3m. old zaires).

† Estimates.

Source: IMF, *Zaire—Background Information and Statistical Data* (April 1996).

Gross Domestic Product by Economic Activity

('000 million old zaires at current prices, unless otherwise indicated)

	1993	1994*	1995*†
Agriculture, forestry, livestock, hunting, and fishing	41,443,328	3,631.2	21,247.6
Mining‡	5,111,950	296.1	1,590.7
Manufacturing	5,523,985	338.6	2,364.8
Construction and public works	797,646	126.2	845.1
Electricity and water	1,793,098	100.8	603.6
Transportation and telecommunications	2,833,538	176.0	1,022.6
Trade and commerce	17,074,694	1,021.9	6,114.4
Public administration	2,743,993	195.4	482.9
Other services	2,796,040	349.5	2,038.1
GDP at factor cost	80,118,272	6,241.7	36,309.8
Import duties	653,286	58.3	312.5
GDP at market prices	80,771,558	6,300.0	36,622.3

* Figures in '000 million new zaires (1 new zaire = 3m. old zaires).

† Estimates.

‡ Including processing.

Source: IMF, *Zaire—Background Information and Statistical Data* (April 1996).

BALANCE OF PAYMENTS (US $ million)

	1988	1989	1990
Exports of goods f.o.b.	2,178	2,201	2,138
Imports of goods f.o.b.	–1,645	–1,683	–1,539
Trade balance	533	518	599
Exports of services	150	137	157
Imports of services	–895	–921	–907
Balance on goods and services	–212	–266	–151
Other income received	36	28	14
Other income paid	–563	–539	–642
Balance on goods, services and income	–739	–777	–779
Current transfers received	226	276	217
Current transfers paid	–67	–109	–81
Current balance	–580	–610	–643
Investment assets	–54	86	111
Investment liabilities	43	–146	–331
Net errors and omissions	–133	111	102
Overall balance	–724	–559	–761

Source: IMF, *International Financial Statistics.*

External Trade

PRINCIPAL COMMODITIES (UN estimates, million old zaires)

Imports c.i.f.	1989	1990	1991
Food and live animals	63,380	121,824	2,172,956
Beverages and tobacco	3,436	6,605	117,812
Crude materials (inedible) except fuels	9,545	18,347	327,252
Mineral fuels, lubricants, etc.	24,436	46,968	837,761
Chemicals	33,217	63,848	1,138,847
Basic manufactures	68,343	131,365	2,343,137
Machinery and transport equipment	102,706	197,414	3,521,243
Miscellaneous manufactured articles	16,418	31,557	562,877
Other commodities and transactions	2,673	5,137	91,628
Total	324,154	623,066	11,113,531

Exports f.o.b.	1989	1990	1991
Food and live animals	93,541	148,201	2,535,635
Beverages and tobacco	5,071	8,035	137,474
Crude materials (inedible) except fuels	14,087	22,319	381,865
Mineral fuels, lubricants, etc.	36,064	57,138	977,599
Chemicals	49,024	77,672	1,328,924
Basic manufactures	100,866	159,807	2,734,207
Machinery and transport equipment	151,581	240,157	4,108,950
Miscellaneous manufactured articles	24,230	38,389	656,814
Other commodities and transactions	3,944	6,249	106,917
Total	478,409	757,967	12,968,384

Source: UN Economic Commission for Africa, *African Statistical Yearbook.*

1994 (US $ million): *Imports c.i.f.:* Mineral fuels 45.4; Total 628.8. *Exports f.o.b.:* Copper 42.8; Cobalt 140.3; Zinc 0.5; Diamonds 293.6; Crude petroleum 123.5; Coffee 158.6; Total 1,271.6. (Source: IMF, *Zaire—Background Information and Statistical Data*, April 1996).

1996 (US $ million): Total imports 921; Total exports 1,629 (Source: *African Economic Digest).*

SELECTED TRADING PARTNERS (US $'000)

Imports c.i.f.	1982	1984*	1985
Belgium-Luxembourg	156,600	116,994	240,918
Brazil	n.a.	87,031	157,716
France	53,400	52,293	118,834
Japan	7,400	20,704	50,147
Netherlands	7,700	31,152	46,107
United Kingdom	29,500	24,339	59,164
USA	60,800	73,600	134,457
Total (incl. others)	475,600	658,741	1,299,282

* Figures for 1983 are not available.

1986 (US $'000): Belgium-Luxembourg 243,929; Brazil 75,238; France 125,981; Japan 47,165; Netherlands 76,275; United Kingdom 49,809; USA 108,143; *Total* (incl. others) 1,331,531.

Exports f.o.b.	1981	1982	1985*
Belgium-Luxembourg	521,300	385,100	165,784
France	25,500	68,100	42,018
Italy	400	200	57,676
Netherlands	2,100	1,500	44,579
Switzerland	71,500	60,500	32,971
United Kingdom	13,700	10,700	21,444
USA	10,900	20,100	228,391
Total (incl. others)	685,200	585,700	796,905

* Figures for 1983 and 1984 are not available.

Source: UN, *International Trade Statistics Yearbook.*

Transport

RAILWAYS (Total traffic, million)*

	1986	1988†	1990†
Passenger-km	330	200	260
Freight (net ton-km)	1,785	1,901	1,732

* Figures are for services operated by the Société Nationale des Chemins de Fer Zaïrois (SNCZ), which controls 4,772 km of railway line out of the country's total facility of 5,252 km.

† Figures for 1987 and 1989 are not available.

Source: *Railway Directory: A Railway Gazette Yearbook.*

ROAD TRAFFIC (motor vehicles in use at 31 December)

	1992	1993	1994
Passenger cars	665,853	693,974	698,672
Buses and coaches	44,357	46,265	51,578
Lorries and vans	399,222	416,385	464,205
Total vehicles	1,109,432	1,156,624	1,214,455

Source: IRF, *World Road Statistics.*

SHIPPING

Merchant Fleet (registered at 31 December)

	1994	1995	1996
Number of vessels	27	27	27
Total displacement ('000 grt)	15	15	15

Source: Lloyd's Register of Shipping, *World Fleet Statistics.*

International Sea-borne Freight Traffic
(estimates, '000 metric tons)

	1988	1989	1990
Goods loaded	2,500	2,440	2,395
Goods unloaded	1,400	1,483	1,453

Source: UN, *Monthly Bulletin of Statistics.*

CIVIL AVIATION (traffic on scheduled services)

	1992	1993	1994
Kilometres flown (million)	4	4	6
Passengers carried ('000)	116	84	178
Passenger-km (million)	295	218	480
Total ton-km (million)	56	42	87

Source: UN, *Statistical Yearbook.*

Tourism

	1992	1993	1994
Tourist arrivals ('000)	22	22	18
Tourist receipts (US $ million)	7	6	5

Source: UN, *Statistical Yearbook.*

Communications Media

	1992	1993	1994
Radio receivers ('000 in use)	3,870	4,000	4,150
Television receivers ('000 in use)	55	62	63
Telephones ('000 main lines in use)	36	36	36
Daily newspapers	9	n.a.	9

Book production (titles published): 64 in 1992.

Sources: UNESCO, *Statistical Yearbook;* UN Economic Commission for Africa, *African Statistical Yearbook.*

Education

	Institutions	Teachers	Students
Pre-primary (1992/93)	429	768	33,235
Primary (1993/94)	12,987	112,041	4,939,297
Secondary (1993/94)	n.a.	59,325	1,341,446
Higher (1988/89)	n.a.	3,873	61,422

Source: UNESCO, *Statistical Yearbook.*

Directory

Note: Following the proclamation of the Democratic Republic of the Congo in May 1997 it was assumed that the names of public- and private-sector businesses and organizations would be revised to reflect this change in the country's designation. Some entries in this section have been revised in anticipation of this development.

The Constitution

Following the proclamation of the Democratic Republic of the Congo, a 15-point constitutional decree was promulgated on 28 May 1997, which abrogated all previous constitutional dispositions. The decree declared the institutions of the Republic to be the President, the Government and the courts and tribunals; all institutions of the previous regime were suspended, except for the judiciary. All power was to be vested in the Head of State, pending the adoption of a new constitution. In October 1997 President Kabila appointed a 42-member Constitutional Commission, which was to draft a new constitution by March 1998.

EXECUTIVE POWER

The President of the Republic exercises legislative power by decree, following consultation with the Cabinet; he is chief of the executive and of the armed forces and has the authority to issue currency; he has the power to appoint and dismiss members of the Government, ambassadors, provincial governors, senior army officers, senior civil servants and magistrates.

POLITICAL PARTIES

A decree of 26 May 1997 banned all political parties.

PROVINCIAL GOVERNMENTS

Local government in each province is administered by a provincial governor and deputy governor, who are appointed and dismissed by the President.

The Government

HEAD OF STATE

President: LAURENT-DÉSIRÉ KABILA (assumed power 17 May 1997; inaugurated 29 May 1997).

CABINET
(January 1998)

President and Minister of Defence: LAURENT-DÉSIRÉ KABILA.

Minister of Foreign Affairs: BIZIMA KARAHA.

Minister of Finance and the Budget: TALA NGAI.

Minister of Industry: BABI MBAYI.

Minister of Commerce: PAUL BANDOMA.

Minister of Justice: MWENZE KONGOLO.

Minister of Information and Culture: RAPHAEL GHENDA.

Minister of the Civil Service: PAUL-GABRIEL KAPITA SHABANGI.

Minister of Environment and Tourism: EDDY ANGULU MABANGI.

Minister of Agriculture and Animal Husbandry: FERDINAND MAWAPANGA MWANA NANGA.

Minister of Health: Dr JEAN-BAPTISTE NSONJI.

Minister of International Co-operation: CÉLÉSTIN LUANGI.

Minister of Transport: HENRI MOVA SAKANI.

Minister of Youth and Sports: TSHIBAL MUTOMBO.

Minister of National Education: KAMARA WA KAHIKARA.

Minister of Public Works, Territorial Administration and Urban and Habitat Development: ANATOLE TSHUBAKA BISIKUABO.

Minister of Mines: FRÉDÉRIC KIBASA MALIBA.

Minister of Post and Telecommunications: KINKELA VINKASI.

Minister of Labour and Social Security: THOMAS KANZA.

Minister of Energy: PIERRE LOKOMBE KITETE.

Minister of Planning: ETIENNE RICHARD MBAYA.

Minister of State for Internal Affairs: GAETAN KAKUDJI.

Minister of State for Economy and Petroleum: PIERRE-VICTOR MPOYO.

Deputy Minister of Social Affairs: MILULU MAMBOLEO.

MINISTRIES

All ministries are in Kinshasa.

Office of the President: Hotel du Conseil Exécutif, ave des 3Z, Kinshasa-Gombe; tel. (12) 30892.

Ministry of Agriculture and Animal Husbandry: Building SOZACOM, 3rd floor, blvd du 30 juin, BP 8722 KIN I, Kinshasa-Gombe; tel. (12) 31821.

Ministry of the Civil Service: ave des Ambassadeurs, BP 3, Kinshasa-Gombe.

Ministry of Defence: Kinshasa-Gombe.

Ministry of Economy, Industry and Trade: Building ONATRA, blvd du 30 juin, BP 8500 KIN I, Kinshasa-Gombe.

Ministry of Energy: Building SNEL, 239 ave de la Justice, BP 5137 KIN I, Kinshasa-Gombe.

Ministry of Environment and Tourism: 15 ave des Cliniques, BP 12348 KIN I, Kinshasa-Gombe.

Ministry of Finance and the Budget: blvd du 30 juin, BP 12998 KIN I, Kinshasa-Gombe; tel. (12) 31197; telex 21161.

Ministry of Foreign Affairs: place de l'Indépendance, BP 7100, Kinshasa-Gombe; tel. (12) 32450; telex 21364.

Ministry of Health: blvd du 30 juin, BP 3088 KIN I, Kinshasa-Gombe; tel. (12) 31750.

Ministry of Information and Culture: ave du 24 novembre, BP 3171 KIN I, Kinshasa-Kabinda; tel. (12) 23171.

Ministry of Internal Affairs: Kinshasa-Gombe.

Ministry of International Co-operation: Enceinte SNEL, ave de la Justice, Kinshasa-Gombe.

Ministry of Justice: 228 ave des 3Z, BP 3137, Kinshasa-Gombe; tel. (12) 32432.

Ministry of Mines: Building SNEL, 239 ave de la Justice, BP 5137 KIN I, Kinshasa-Gombe.

Ministry of National Education: Enceinte de l'Institut de la Gombe, BP 3163, Kinshasa-Gombe; tel. (12) 30098; telex 21460.

Ministry of Planning: 4155 ave des Côteaux, BP 9378 KIN I, Kinshasa-Gombe 1; tel. (12) 31346; telex 21781.

Ministry of Post and Telecommunications: Building KILOU, 4484 ave des Huiles, BP 800 KIN I, Kinshasa-Gombe; tel. (12) 24854; telex 21403.

Ministry of Public Works, Territorial Administration and Urban and Habitat Development: Building TRAVAUX PUBLICS, Kinshasa-Gombe.

Ministry of Reconstruction and Emergency Works: Building TRAVAUX PUBLICS, blvd Colonel Tshatshi, BP 26, Kinshasa-Gombe.

Ministry of Transport: Building ONATRA, blvd du 30 juin, BP 3304, Kinshasa-Gombe; tel. (12) 23660; telex 21404.

Ministry of Youth and Sports: 77 ave de la Justice, BP 8541 KIN I, Kinshasa-Gombe.

President

Laurent-Désiré Kabila declared himself President on 17 May 1997, and was inaugurated on 29 May 1997. Presidential elections were scheduled to be held in 1999.

Legislature

The Head of State legislates by decree. Legislative elections were scheduled to be held in 1999.

Political Organizations

Alliance des forces démocratiques pour la libération du Congo-Zaïre (AFDL): Kinshasa; f. 1996; asscn of parties formed originally to overthrow Mobutu Govt; eight-mem. Exec. Committee; Leader LAURENT-DÉSIRÉ KABILA; Sec.-Gen. DEOGRATIAS BUGERA.

Front patriotique: Kinshasa; joined AFDL in July 1997; Leaders JEAN-BAPTISTE SONDJI, KINKELA VINKASI.

All political parties except the AFDL were banned on 26 May 1997. These organizations include:

Alliance des nationalistes africains (ANA): Kinshasa; f. 1994; agricultural manifesto; Chair. THÉOPHANE KINGOMBO MULULA.

Alliance des républicains pour le développement et le progrès (ARDP): Kinshasa; f. 1994; Chair. JOHN MILALA MBONO-MBUE; Sec.-Gen. MATAMO KUAKA.

Fédération des libéraux du Zaïre (FLZ): Kinshasa; f. 1994; asscn of 10 liberal political groups.

Forces novatrices pour l'union et la solidarité (FONUS): Kinshasa; advocates political pluralism; Pres. JOSEPH OLENGHAKOY; Sec.-Gen. JOHN KWET.

Forces politiques du conclave (FPC): Kinshasa; f. 1993; alliance of pro-Mobutu groups, incl the UFERI, led by MPR; Chair. NGUZA KARL-I-BOND.

Front Lumumba pour l'unité et la paix en Afrique (FLUPA): Kinshasa; f. 1963, obtained legal recognition 1994; supports aims of fmr Prime Minister, Patrice Lumumba.

Front national pour la libération du Katanga: Johannesburg, South Africa; f. 1997; seeks autonomy for province of Katanga; Leader Gen. KPAMA BARAMOTO KATA.

Front populaire de résistance armée: Paris, France; f. 1997; advocates armed resistance to Kabila regime; Leader JACQUES MATANDA MA MBOYO.

Katanga Gendarmes: based in Angola; guerrilla group which aims to win independence for the province of Katanga.

Mouvement national du Congo–Lumumba (MNC–Lumumba): Kinshasa; f. 1994; coalition of seven parties, incl. the Parti lumumbiste unifié (PALU), led by ANTOINE GIZENGA; supports the aims of the fmr Prime Minister, Patrice Lumumba; Co-ordinating Cttee PASCAL TABU, MBALO MEKA, OTOKO OKITASOMBO.

Mouvement populaire de la révolution (MPR): Palais du Peuple, angle ave des Huileries et ave Kasa-Vubu, Kinshasa; tel. (12) 22541; f. 1966; sole legal political party until Nov. 1990; advocates national unity and opposes tribalism; Leader (vacant); Sec.-Gen. KITHIMA BIN RAMAZANI.

Parti démocrate et social chrétien (PDSC): 32B ave Tombalbaye, Kinshasa-Gombe; tel. (12) 21211; f. 1990; centrist; Pres. ANDRÉ BO-BOLIKO; Sec. Gen. TUYABA LEWULA.

Parti démocrate et social chrétien national (PDSCN): Kinshasa; f. 1994; centrist; Chair. ANDRÉ BO-BOLIKO LOKONGA.

Parti des nationalistes pour le développement integral (PANADI): Kinshasa; f. 1994; Leader BALTAZAR HOUNGANGERA.

Parti ouvrier et paysan du Congo (POP): f. 1986; Marxist-Leninist.

Rassemblement des démocrates libéraux: Kinshasa; Leader MWAMBA MULANDA.

Rassemblement des patriotes congolais (RPC): Brussels, Belgium; f. 1997; opposed to Kabila's regime; advocates free elections; Founders GÉRARD KAMANDA WA KAMANDA, MULUMBA KIN-KIEY.

Sacré alliance pour le dialogue (SAD): Kinshasa; f. 1993; alliance of 10 political groups; Leader Gen. NATHANIEL MBUMBA.

Union des fédéralistes et républicains indépendants (UFERI): Kinshasa; f. 1990; seeks autonomy for province of Katanga; dominant party in the USOR; Pres. NGUZA KARL-I-BOND; Leader KOUYOUMBA MUCHULI MULEMBE.

Union pour la démocratie et le progrès social (UDPS): Twelfth St, Limete Zone, Kinshasa; f. 1982; Leader ETIENNE TSHISEKEDI WA MULUMBA; Sec.-Gen. Dr ADRIEN PHONGO KUNDA.

Union pour la démocratie et le progrès social national: Kinshasa; f. 1994; Chair. CHARLES DEOUNKIN ANDEL.

Union pour la République (UPR): Kinshasa; f. 1997 by former members of the MPR; Leader CHARLES NDAYWEL.

Union pour la République et la démocratie (URD): Kinshasa; centrist; expelled from USOR in May 1994; Chair. GÉRARD KAMANDA WA KAMANDA.

Union sacrée de l'opposition radicale (USOR): Kinshasa; f. July 1991; comprised c. 130 movements and factions opposed to Pres. Mobutu; led by the UDPS. The existence, within the transitional legislature, of an umbrella radical opposition grouping, known as the **Union sacrée de l'opposition radicale et ses alliés (USORAL)**, was announced in late 1994. In May 1996 FRÉDÉRIC KIBASSA MALIBA was re-elected President of the USORAL.

Union sacrée rénovée (USR): Kinshasa; f. 1993 by several ministers in Govt of Nat. Salvation; Leader KIRO KIMATE.

Diplomatic Representation

EMBASSIES IN THE DEMOCRATIC REPUBLIC OF THE CONGO

Algeria: 50/52 ave Colonel Ebeya, BP 12798, Kinshasa; tel. (12) 22470; Chargé d'affaires a.i.: HOCINE MEGHLAOUI.

Angola: 4413–4429 blvd du 30 juin, BP 8625, Kinshasa; tel. (12) 32415; Ambassador: MIGUEL GASPARD NETO.

Argentina: 181 blvd du 30 juin, BP 16798, Kinshasa; tel. (12) 25485; Ambassador: WERNER ROBERTO JUSTO BURGHARDT.

Austria: 39 ave Lubefu, BP 16399, Kinshasa-Gombe; tel. (12) 22150; telex 21310; Ambassador: Dr HANS KOGLER.

Belgium: Immeuble Le Cinquantenaire, place du 27 octobre, BP 899, Kinshasa; tel. (12) 20110; telex 21114; fax 22120; Ambassador: JOHAN VAN DESSEL.

Benin: 3990 ave des Cliniques, BP 3265, Kinshasa-Gombe; tel. (12) 33156; Ambassador: PIERRE DÉSIRÉ SADELER.

Brazil: 190 ave Basoko, BP 13296, Kinshasa; tel. (12) 21781; telex 21515; Ambassador: AYRTON G. DIEGUEZ.

Burundi: 17 ave de la Gombe, BP 1483, Kinshasa; tel. (12) 31588; telex 21655; Ambassador: LONGIN KANUMA.

Cameroon: 171 blvd du 30 juin, BP 10998, Kinshasa; tel. (12) 34787; Chargé d'affaires a.i.: DOMINIQUE AWONO ESSAMA.

Canada: BP 8341, Kinshasa 1; tel. (12) 21801; telex 21303; Ambassador: VERONA EDELSTEIN.

Central African Republic: 11 ave Pumbu, BP 7769, Kinshasa; tel. (12) 30417; Ambassador: SISSA LE BERNARD.

Chad: 67–69 ave du Cercle, BP 9097, Kinshasa; tel. (12) 22358; Ambassador: MAITINE DJOUMBE.

China, People's Republic: 49 ave du Commerce, BP 9098, Kinshasa; tel. 23972; Ambassador: AN GUOZHENG.

Congo, Republic: 179 blvd du 30 juin, BP 9516, Kinshasa; tel. (12) 30220; Ambassador: MAURICE OGNAMY.

Côte d'Ivoire: 68 ave de la Justice, BP 9197, Kinshasa; tel. (12) 30440; telex 21214; Ambassador: GASTON ALLOUKO FIANKAN.

Cuba: 4660 ave Cateam, BP 10699, Kinshasa; telex 21158; Ambassador: ENRIQUE MONTERO.

Czech Republic: 78 ave des 3Z, Gombé, BP 8242, Kinshasa 1; tel. (12) 45843; fax (12) 45847; Chargé d'affaires: PAVEL PROCHÁZKA.

Egypt: 519 ave de l'Ouganda, BP 8838, Kinshasa; tel. (12) 30296; Ambassador: AZIZ ABDEL HAMID HAMZA.

Ethiopia: BP 8435, Kinshasa; tel. (12) 23327; Ambassador: Col LEGESSE WOLDE-MARIAM.

France: 97 ave de la République du Tchad, BP 3093, Kinshasa; tel. (12) 30513; telex 21074; Ambassador: MICHEL ROUGAGNOU.

Gabon: ave du 24 novembre, BP 9592, Kinshasa; tel. (12) 68325; telex 21455; Ambassador: JOSEPH KOUMBA MOUNGUENGUI.

Germany: 82 ave des 3Z, BP 8400, Kinshasa-Gombe; tel. (12) 21529; telex 21110; fax (12) 21527; Ambassador: KLAUS BÖNNEMANN.

Ghana: 206 ave du 24 novembre, BP 8446, Kinshasa; tel. (12) 31766; Ambassador: KWAKU ADU BEDIAKO.

Greece: 72 ave des 3Z, BP 478, Kinshasa; tel. (12) 33169; Ambassador: PANAYOTIS TH. BAIZOS.

Guinea: 7–9 ave Lubefu, BP 9899, Kinshasa; tel. (12) 30864; Ambassador: FÉLIX FABER.

Holy See: 81 ave Goma, BP 3091, Kinshasa; tel. (12) 33128; telex 21527; fax (12) 33346; Apostolic Nuncio: Mgr FAUSTINO SAINZ MUÑOZ, Titular Archbishop of Novaliciana.

India: 188 ave des Batétéla, BP 1026, Kinshasa; tel. (12) 33368; telex 21179; Ambassador: ARUN KUMAR.

Iran: 76 blvd du 30 juin, BP 16599, Kinshasa; tel. (12) 31052; telex 21429.

Israel: 12 ave des Aviateurs, BP 8343, Kinshasa; tel. (12) 21955; Ambassador: SHLOMO AVITAL.

Italy: 8 ave de la Mongala, BP 1000, Kinshasa; tel. (12) 23416; telex 21560; Ambassador: VITTORIO AMEDEO FARINELLI.

Japan: Immeuble Marsavco, 2e étage, ave Colonel Lusaka, BP 1810, Kinshasa; tel. (871) 684400510; fax (871) 1205613; Ambassador: KYOICHI OMURA.

Kenya: 5002 ave de l'Ouganda, BP 9667, Kinshasa; tel. (12) 30117; telex 21359; Ambassador: MWABILI KISAKA.

Korea, Democratic People's Republic: 168 ave de l'Ouganda, BP 16597, Kinshasa; tel. (12) 31566; Ambassador: KIM PONG HUI.

Korea, Republic: 2A ave des Orangers, BP 628, Kinshasa; tel. (12) 31022; Ambassador: CHUN SOON-KYU.

Kuwait: Suite 232, Intercontinental Hotel, Kinshasa.

Lebanon: 3 ave de l'Ouganda, Kinshasa; tel. (12) 32682; telex 21423; Ambassador: MUSTAFA HOREIBE.

Liberia: 3 ave de l'Okapi, BP 8940, Kinshasa; tel. (12) 82289; telex 21205; Ambassador: JALLA D. LANSANAH.

Libya: BP 9198, Kinshasa.

Mauritania: BP 16397, Kinshasa; tel. (12) 59575; telex 21380; Ambassador: Lt-Col M'BARECK OULD BOUNA MOKHTAR.

Morocco: 4497 ave Lubefu, BP 912, Kinshasa; tel. (12) 30255; Ambassador: ABOUBKEUR CHERKAOUI.

Netherlands: 11 ave Zongo Ntolo, BP 10299, Kinshasa; tel (12) 30733; Chargé d'affaires a.i.: J. G. WILBRENNINCK.

Nigeria: 141 blvd du 30 juin, BP 1700, Kinshasa; tel. (12) 43272; Ambassador: DAG S. CLAUDE-WILCOX.

Pakistan: Kinshasa; Chargé d'affaires a.i.: SHAFQAT ALI SHAIKH.

Poland: 63 ave de la Justice, BP 8553, Kinshasa; tel. (12) 33349; telex 21057; Ambassador: ANDRZEJ M. LUPINA.

Portugal: 270 ave des Aviateurs, BP 7775, Kinshasa; tel. (12) 24010; telex 221328; Ambassador: LUÍS DE VASCONCELOS PIMENTEL QUARTIN BASTOS.

Romania: 5 ave de l'Ouganda, BP 2242, Kinshasa; tel. (12) 33127; telex 21316; Ambassador: EMINESCU DRAGOMIR.

Russia: 80 ave de la Justice, BP 1143, Kinshasa 1; tel. (12) 33157; telex 21690; fax (12) 45575; Ambassador: YURII SPIRINE.

Rwanda: 50 ave de la Justice, BP 967, Kinshasa; tel. (12) 30327; telex 21612; Ambassador: ANTOINE NYILINKINDI.

South Africa: 17 ave Pumbu, BP 7829, Kinshasa-Gombe; tel. (12) 34676; fax (satellite) 1-212-3723510; Ambassador: J. W. J. VAN DEVENTER.

Spain: Immeuble de la Communauté Hellénique, 4e étage, blvd du 30 juin, BP 8036, Kinshasa; tel. (12) 21881; fax (12) 24388; Ambassador: ANTONIO LÓPEZ MARTÍNEZ.

Sudan: 83 ave des Treis, BP 7347, Kinshasa; Ambassador: MUBARAK ADAM HADI.

Sweden: 89 ave des 3Z, BP 11096, Kinshasa; tel. (12) 33201; Chargé d'affaires a.i.: L. EKSTRÖM.

Switzerland: 654 ave Colonel Tshatshi, BP 8724, Kinshasa 1; tel. (12) 34243; fax (12) 34246; Ambassador: WILHELM SCHMID.

Togo: 3 ave de la Vallée, BP 10197, Kinshasa; tel. (12) 30666; telex 21388; Ambassador: MAMA GNOFAM.

Tunisia: ave du Cercle, BP 1498, Kinshasa; tel. (12) 31632; telex 21171; Ambassador: ABDEL KRIM MOUSSA.

Turkey: 18 ave Pumbu, BP 7817, Kinshasa; tel. (88) 01207; Ambassador: DENIZ UZMEN.

Uganda: 177 ave Tombalbaye, BP 1086, Kinshasa; tel. (12) 22740; telex 21618; Ambassador: Dr AJEAN.

United Kingdom: ave des 3Z, BP 8049, Kinshasa; tel. (12) 34775; fax (satellite) 871-144-5470; Ambassador: MARCUS HOPE.

USA: 310 ave des Aviateurs, BP 697, Kinshasa; tel. (12) 21532; telex 21405; fax 21232; Ambassador: DANIEL SIMPSON.

Yugoslavia: 112 quai de l'Etoile, BP 619, Kinshasa; tel. (12) 32325; Ambassador: (vacant).

Zambia: 54–58 ave de l'Ecole, BP 1144, Kinshasa; tel. (12) 23038; telex 21209; Ambassador: C. K. C. KAMWANA.

Judicial System

A Justice Department, under the control of the Minister of Justice, is responsible for the organization and definition of competence of the judiciary; civil, penal and commercial law and civil and penal procedures; the status of persons and property; the system of obligations and questions pertaining to nationality; international private law; status of magistrates; organization of the legal profession, counsels for the defence, notaries and of judicial auxiliaries; supervision of cemeteries, non-profit-making organizations, cults and institutions working in the public interest; the operation of prisons; confiscated property.

There is a Supreme Court in Kinshasa, and there are also nine Courts of Appeal and 36 County Courts.

The Head of State is empowered to appoint and dismiss magistrates.

President of the Supreme Court: GÉRARD KAMANDA WA KAMANDA.

Procurator-General of the Republic: MONGULU T'APANGANE.

Courts of Appeal

Bandundu: Pres. MUNONA NTAMBAMBILANJI.

Bukavu: Pres. TINKAMANYIRE BIN NDIGEBA.

Kananga: Pres. MATONDO BWENTA.

Kinshasa: Pres. KALONDA KELE OMA.

Kisangani: Pres. MBANGAMA KABUNDI.

Lubumbashi: Pres. BOKONGA W'ANZANDE.

Matadi: Pres. TSHIOVO LUMAMBI.

Mbandaka: Pres. MAKUNZA WA MAKUNZA.

Mbuji-Mayi: Pres. LUAMBA BINDU.

Religion

Many of the country's inhabitants follow traditional beliefs, which are mostly animistic. A large proportion of the population is Christian, predominantly Roman Catholic.

In 1971 new national laws officially recognized the Roman Catholic Church, the Protestant (ECC) Church and the Kimbanguist Church. The Muslim and Jewish faiths and the Greek Orthodox Church were granted official recognition in 1972.

CHRISTIANITY

The Roman Catholic Church

The Democratic Republic of the Congo comprises six archdioceses and 41 dioceses. An estimated 50% of the population are Roman Catholics.

Bishops' Conference: Conférence Episcopale du Congo, BP 3258, Kinshasa-Gombe; tel. (12) 30082; telex 21571; f. 1981; Pres. Rt Rev. FAUSTIN NGABU, Bishop of Goma.

Archbishop of Bukavu: (vacant), Archevêché, BP 3324, Bukavu; tel. 2707; fax (16) 82060067.

Archbishop of Kananga: Most Rev. MARTIN-LÉONARD BAKOLE WA ILUNGA, Archevêché, BP 70, Kananga; tel. 2477.

Archbishop of Kinshasa: Cardinal FRÉDÉRIC ETSOU-NZABI-BAMUNGWABI, Archevêché, ave de l'Université, BP 8431, Kinshasa 1; tel. (12) 3723-546.

Archbishop of Kisangani: Most Rev. LAURENT MONSENGWO PASINYA, Archevêché, ave Mpolo 10B, BP 505, Kisangani; tel. (761) 608334; fax (761) 608336.

Archbishop of Lubumbashi: Most Rev. EUGÈNE KABANGA SONGASONGA, Archevêché, BP 72, Lubumbashi; tel. (2) 34-1442.

Archbishop of Mbandaka-Bikoro: Joseph Kumuondala Mbimba, Archevêché, BP 1064, Mbandaka; tel. 2234.

The Anglican Communion

The Church of the Province of Zaire comprises six dioceses.

Archbishop of the Province of Zaire and Bishop of Boga-Zaïre: Most Rev. Patrice Byankya Njojo, c/o POB 21285, Nairobi, Kenya.

Bishop of Bukavu: Rt Rev. Fidèle Balufuga Dirokpa, BP 2876, Bukavu.

Bishop of Kindu-Maniema: Rt Rev. Zacharia Masimange Katanda, c/o BP 53435, Nairobi, Kenya.

Bishop of Kisangani: Rt Rev. Sylvestre Tibafa Mugera, BP 861, Kisangani.

Bishop of Nord Kivu: Rt Rev. Methusela Munzenda Musubaho, BP 322, Butembo.

Bishop of Shaba: Rt Rev. Emmanuel Kolini Mbona, c/o United Methodist Church, POB 22037, Kitwe, Zambia.

Kimbanguist

Eglise de Jésus Christ sur la Terre par le Prophète Simon Kimbangu: BP 7069, Kinshasa; tel. (12) 68944; telex 21315; f. 1921 (officially est. 1959); c. 5m. mems (1985); Spiritual Head HE Diangienda Kuntima; Sec.-Gen. Rev. Luntadilla.

Protestant Churches

Eglise du Christ au Congo (ECC): ave de la Justice (face no. 75), BP 4938, Kinshasa-Gombe; f. 1902; a co-ordinating agency for all the Protestant churches, with the exception of the Kimbanguist Church; 62 mem. communities and a provincial org. in each province; c. 10m. mems (1982); Pres. Bishop Bokeleale Itofo; includes:

Communauté Baptiste du Congo-Ouest: BP 4728, Kinshasa 2; f. 1970; 450 parishes; 170,000 mems (1985); Gen. Sec. Rev. Lusakweno-Vangu.

Communauté des Disciples du Christ: BP 178, Mbandaka; tel. 31062; telex 21742; f. 1964; 250 parishes; 650,000 mems (1985); Gen. Sec. Rev. Dr Elonda Efefe.

Communauté Episcopale Baptiste en Afrique: 2 ave Jason Sendwe, BP 3866, Lubumbashi 1; tel. (2) 24724; f. 1956; 1,300 episcopal communions and parishes; 150,000 mems (1993); Pres. Bishop Kitobo Kabweka-Leza.

Communauté Evangélique: BP 36, Luozi; f. 1961; 50 parishes; 33,750 mems (1985); Pres. Rev. K. Lukombo Ntontolo.

Communauté Lumière: BP 10498, Kinshasa 1; f. 1931; 150 parishes; 220,000 mems (1985); Patriarch Kayuwa Tshibumbu Wa Kahinga.

Communauté Mennonite: BP 18, Tshikapa; f. 1960; 40,000 mems (1985); Gen. Sec. Rev. Kabangy Djeke Shapasa.

Communauté Presbytérienne: BP 117, Kananga; f. 1959; 150,000 mems (1985); Gen. Sec. Dr M. L. Tshihamba.

Eglise Missionaire Apostolique: BP 15859, Kinshasa 1; f. 1986; 3 parishes; 1,000 mems.; Apostle for Africa L. A. Nanandana.

The Press

DAILIES

L'Analyste: 129 ave du Bas-Zaïre, BP 91, Kinshasa-Gombe; tel. (12) 80987; Dir and Editor-in-Chief Bongoma Koni Botahe.

Boyoma: 31 blvd Mobutu, BP 982, Kisangani, Dir and Editor Badriyo Rova Rovatu.

Elima: 1 ave de la Révolution, BP 11498, Kinshasa; tel. (12) 77332; f. 1928; evening; Dir and Editor-in-Chief Essolomwa Nkoy ea Linganga.

Mjumbe: BP 2474, Lubumbashi; tel. (2) 25348; f. 1963; Dir and Editor Tshimanga Koya Kakona.

Le Palmarès: Kinshasa; supports Union pour la démocratie et le progrès social; Editor Michel Ladeluya.

La Référence Plus: Kinshasa; Dir André Ipakala.

Salongo: 143 10e rue Limete, BP 601, Kinshasa/Limete; tel. (12) 77367; morning; operations suspended by Govt in Nov. 1993; Dir and Editor Bondo-Nsama; circ. 10,000.

PERIODICALS

Allo Kinshasa: 3 rue Kayange, BP 20271, Kinshasa-Lemba; monthly; Editor Mbuyu Wa Kabila.

Annales Aequatoria: Centre Aequatoria, BP 276, Mbandaka; f. 1980; central African culture, history and language; annually; Editor Honoré Vinck; circ. 400.

BEA Magazine de la Femme: 2 ave Masimanimba, BP 113380, Kinshasa 1; every 2 weeks; Editor Mutinga Mutwishayi.

Beto na Beto: 75 ave Tatamena, BP 757, Matadi; weekly; Dir-Gen. and Editor Bia Zanda ne Nanga.

Bibi: 33 ave Victoria, Kinshasa; f. 1972; French; general interest; monthly.

Bingwa: ave du 30 juin, zone Lubumbashi no 4334; weekly; sport; Dir and Editor Mateke Wa Mulamba.

Cahiers Economiques et Sociaux: BP 257, Kinshasa XI, (National University of the Congo); sociological, political and economic review; quarterly; Dir Prof. Ndongala Tadi Lewa; circ. 2,000.

Cahiers des Religions Africaines: Faculté de Théologie Catholique de Kinshasa, BP 712, Kinshasa/Limete; tel. (12) 78476; f. 1967; English and French; religion; 2 a year; circ. 1,000.

Le Canard Libre: Kinshasa; f. 1991; Editor Joseph Castro Mulebe.

Circulaire d'Information: Association Nationale des Entreprises du Congo, 10 ave des Aviateurs, BP 7247, Kinshasa 1; tel. (12) 22565; f. 1959; French; legal and statutory texts for the business community; monthly; circ. (variable).

La Colombe: 32b ave Tombalbaye, Kinshasa-Gombe; tel. (12) 21211; organ of Parti démocrate et social chrétien; circ. 5,000.

Congo-Afrique: Centre d'Etudes pour l'Action Sociale, 9 ave Père Boka, BP 3375, Kinshasa-Gombe; tel. (12) 34682; f. 1961; economic, social and cultural; monthly; Editors Kikassa Mwanalessa, René Beeckmans; circ. 4,500.

Conseiller Comptable: Immeuble SNCC, 17 ave du Port, BP 308, Kinshasa; f. 1974; French; public finance and taxation; quarterly; circ. 1,000.

Le Courrier du Zaïre: aut. no 04/DIMOPAP 0018/84, 101 Lukolela, Kinshasa; weekly; Editor Nzonzila Ndonzuau.

Cultures au Zaïre et en Afrique: BP 16706, Kinshasa; f. 1973; French and English; quarterly.

Dionga: Immeuble Amassio, 2 rue Dirna, BP 8031, Kinshasa; monthly.

Documentation et Informations Africaines (DIA): BP 2598, Kinshasa 1; tel. (12) 33197; fax (12) 33196; Roman Catholic news agency reports; 3 a week; Dir Rev. Père Vata Diambanza.

Documentation et Informations Protestantes (DIP): Eglise du Christ au Zaïre, BP 4938, Kinshasa-Gombe; French and English; religion.

L'Entrepreneur Flash: Association Nationale des Entreprises du Congo, 10 ave des Aviateurs, BP 7247, Kinshasa 1; tel. (12) 22565; f. 1978; French; business news; monthly; circ. 1,000.

Etudes d'Histoire Africaine: National University of the Congo, BP 1825, Lubumbashi; f. 1970; French and English; history; annually; circ. 1,000.

Etudes Zaïrois: c/o Institut National d'Etudes Politiques, BP 2307, Kinshasa 1; f. 1961; quarterly.

Horizons 80: Société Congolaise d'Edition et d'Information, BP 9839, Kinshasa; economy; weekly.

JUA: BP 1613, Bukavu; weekly; Dir and Editor Mutiri Wa Bashara.

Les Kasaï: 161 9e rue, BP 575, Kinshasa/Limete; weekly; Editor Nsenga Ndomba.

Kin-Média: BP 15808, Kinshasa 1; monthly; Editor Ilunga Kasambay.

KYA: 24 ave de l'Equateur, BP 7853, Kinshasa-Gombe; tel. (12) 27502; f. 1984; weekly for Bas-Zaïre; Editor Sassa Kassa Yi Kiboba.

Libération: Kinshasa; f. 1997; French; politics; pro-AFDL; weekly; Man. Ngoyi Kabuya Dikateta M'miana.

Maadini: Générale des Carrières et des Mines, BP 450, Lubumbashi; quarterly.

Mambenga 2000: BP 477, Mbandaka; Editor Bosange Yema Bof.

Ngabu: Société Nationale d'Assurances, Immeuble Sonas Sankuru, blvd du 30 juin, BP 3443, Kinshasa-Gombe; tel. (12) 23051; f. 1973; insurance news; quarterly.

Njanja: Société Nationale des Chemins de Fer Congolais, 115 place de la Gare, BP 297, Lubumbashi; tel. (2) 23430; telex 41056; fax (2) 61321; railways and transportation; annually; circ. 10,000.

NUKTA: 14 chaussée de Kasenga, BP 3805, Lubumbashi; weekly; agriculture; Editor Ngoy Bunduki.

L'Opinion: BP 15394, Kinshasa; weekly; Editor Sable Fwamba Kiependa.

Presse et Information Kimbanguiste (PIK): ave Bongolo, Kinshasa-Kalamu.

Problèmes Sociaux Zaïrois: Centre d'Exécution de Programmes Sociaux et Economiques, Université de Lubumbashi, 208 ave Kasavubu, BP 1873, Lubumbashi; f. 1946; quarterly; Editor N'Kashama Kadima.

Promoteur Congolais: Centre du Commerce International du Congo, 119 ave Colonel Tshatshi, BP 13, Kinshasa; f. 1979; French; international trade news; six a year.

La Revue Juridique du Congo: Société d'Etudes Juridiques du Congo, Université de Lubumbashi, BP 510, Lubumbashi; f. 1924; 3 a year.

Sciences, Techniques, Informations: Centre de Recherches Industrielles en Afrique Centrale (CRIAC), BP 54, Lubumbashi.

Le Sport Africain: 13è niveau Tour adm., Cité de la Voix du Congo, BP 3356, Kinshasa-Gombe; monthly; Pres. TSHIMPUMPU WA TSHIMPUMPU.

Taifa: 536 ave Lubumba, BP 884, Lubumbashi; weekly; Editor LWAMBWA MILAMBU.

Telema: 7–9 ave Père Boka, BP 3277, Kinshasa-Gombe; f. 1974; religious; quarterly; Editor BOKA DI MPASI LONDI; circ. 3,000.

Umoja: Kinshasa; weekly.

Zaïre-Afrique: Centre d'Etudes pour l'Action Sociale, 9 ave Père Boka, BP 3375, Kinshasa; tel. (12) 34682; f. 1961; economic, social and cultural; monthly; Editors KIKASSA MWANALESSA, RENÉ BEECKMANS; circ. 1,500.

Zaïre Agricole: 5 rue Bonga-Equateur, Matonge, Zone de Kalamu; monthly; Editor DIAYIKWA KIMPAKALA.

Zaïre Business: Immeuble Amasco, 3968 rue ex-Belgika, BP 9839, Kinshasa; f. 1973; French; weekly.

Zaïre Informatique: Conseil Permanent de l'Informatique au Zaïre, BP 9699, Kinshasa 1; f. 1978; French; quarterly.

Zaïre Ya Sita: Direction Générale et Administration, 1 rue Luozi Kasavubu, BP 8246, Kinshasa; f. 1968; Lingala; political science; 6 a year.

NEWS AGENCIES

Congolese News Agency (CNA): 44–48 ave Tombalbaye, BP 1595, Kinshasa 1; tel. (12) 22035; telex 21096; f. 1957; state-controlled; Dir-Gen. ALI KALONGA.

Documentation et Informations Africaines (DIA): BP 2598, Kinshasa 1; tel. (12) 34528; telex 2108; f. 1957; Roman Catholic news agency; Dir Rev. Père VATA DIAMBANZA.

Foreign Bureaux

Agence France-Presse (AFP): Immeuble Wenge 3227, ave Wenge, Zone de la Gombe, BP 726, Kinshasa 1; tel. (12) 27009; telex 21648; Bureau Chief JEAN-PIERRE REJETTE.

Agencia EFE (Spain): BP 2653, Lubumbashi; Correspondent KANKU SANGA.

Agência Lusa de Informação (Portugal): BP 4941, Kinshasa; tel. (12) 24437; telex 21605.

Agenzia Nazionale Stampa Associata (ANSA) (Italy): BP 2790, Kinshasa 15; tel. (12) 30315; Bureau Chief (vacant).

Pan-African News Agency (PANA) (Senegal): BP 1400, Kinshasa; tel. (12) 23290; telex 21475; f. 1983; Bureau Chief ADRIEN HONORÉ MBEYET.

Xinhua (New China) News Agency (People's Republic of China): 293 ave Mfumu Lutunu, BP 8939, Kinshasa; tel. (12) 25647; telex 21259; Correspondent CHEN WEIBIN.

PRESS ASSOCIATIONS

Médias Libres—Médias pour Tous: Kinshasa; org. representing Kinshasa newspapers.

Union de la Presse du Congo: BP 4941, Kinshasa 1; tel. (12) 24437; telex 21605.

Publishers

Centre Protestant d'Editions et de Diffusion (CEDI): 209 ave Kalémie, BP 11398, Kinshasa 1; tel. (12) 22202; fax (12) 26730; f. 1935; fiction, poetry, biography, religious, juvenile; Christian tracts, works in French, Lingala, Kikongo, etc.; Dir-Gen. HENRY DIRKS.

Maison d'Editions 'Jeunes pour Jeunes': BP 9624, Kinshasa 1; youth interest.

MEDIASPAUL: BP 127 Limete, Kinshasa; tel. (12) 40531; religion, education, literature; Dir LUIGI BOFFELLI.

Le Potentiel: Kinshasa; Chair. LUNGA MUTUSHA.

Les Presses Africaines: place du 27 Octobre, BP 12924, Kinshasa 1; general non-fiction, poetry; Man. Dir MWAMBA DI MBUYI.

Presses Universitaires du Congo (PUC): 290 rue d'Aketi, BP 1682, Kinshasa 1; tel. (12) 30652; telex 21394; f. 1972; scientific pubs; Dir Prof. MUMBANZA MWA BAWELE.

Broadcasting and Communications

TELECOMMUNICATIONS

Comcell: Kinshasa; provides satellite communications network.

Office Congolais des Postes et des Télécommunications (OCPT): Kinshasa; state-owned; 13,000 lines.

Telecel: Kinshasa; provides satellite communications network; largest private operator.

BROADCASTING

Radio-Télévision Nationale Congolaise (RTNC): BP 3171, Kinshasa-Gombe; tel. (12) 23171; telex 21583; state radio terrestrial and satellite television broadcasts; Dir-Gen. JOSE KAJANGUA.

Radio

Several private radio broadcasters operate in Kinshasa.

Voice of the People: Centre d'Animation et de Diffusion Pedagogique, BP 373, Bunia; state-controlled.

La Voix du Congo: Station Nationale, BP 3164, Kinshasa-Gombe; tel. (12) 23175; telex 21583; state-controlled; operated by RTNC; home service broadcasts in French, Swahili, Lingala, Tshiluba, Kikongo; regional stations at Kisangani, Lubumbashi, Bukavu, Bandundu, Kananga, Mbuji-Mayi, Matadi, Mbandaka and Bunia.

Television

Several private television broadcasters operate in Kinshasa.

Tele Kin Malebo (TKM): Kinshasa; private television station; nationalization announced 1997; Dir-Gen. NGONGO LUWOWO.

Télévision Congolais: BP 3171, Kinshasa-Gombe: tel. (12) 23171; telex 21583; govt commercial station; operated by RTNC; broadcasts for 5 hours daily on weekdays and 10 hours daily at weekends.

Finance

(cap. = capital; res = reserves; dep. = deposits; m. = million; brs = branches; amounts in old zaires unless otherwise indicated)

BANKING

Central Bank

Banque du Congo: blvd Colonel Tshatshi au nord, BP 2697, Kinshasa; tel. (12) 20701; telex 21365; f. 1964; cap. and res 50,088.4m. (Dec. 1988); Gov. MASANGU MULONGO; 8 brs, 34 agencies.

Commercial Banks

Banque Commerciale du Congo SARL: blvd du 30 juin, BP 2798, Kinshasa; tel. (12) 23772; telex 21127; f. 1909 as Banque du Congo Belge, name changed as above 1997; cap. NZ 36.6m., res NZ 166,358.7m., dep. NZ 221,416.7m., total assets NZ 393,602.2m. (Dec. 1994); Chair. KANDOLO WA KASHALA; Gen. Man. KASONGO TAIBU; 27 brs.

Banque Continentale Africaine (Congo) SCARL: 4 ave de la Justice, BP 7613, Kinshasa-Gombe; tel. (12) 28006; telex 21508; fax (12) 25243; f. 1983; total assets 28,786.5m. (Dec. 1994); Chair. PAUL LENOIR.

Banque de Crédit Agricole: angle ave Kasa-Vubu et ave M'Polo, BP 8837, Kinshasa-Gombe; tel. (12) 21800; telex 21383; fax (12) 27221; f. 1982 to expand and modernize enterprises in agriculture, livestock and fishing, and generally to improve the quality of rural life; state-owned; cap. 5m. (Dec. 1991); Pres. MOLOTO MWA LOPANZA.

Banque Internationale de Crédit SCARL (BIC): 191 ave de l'Equateur, BP 1299, Kinshasa 1; tel. (12) 20342; telex 21113; fax (12) 123769600; f. 1994; cap. NZ 5,473.7m., res NZ 2,881.7m., dep. NZ 21,973.4m., total assets 35,077.9m. (Dec. 1995); Pres. PASCAL KINDUELO LUMBU; Man. Dir THARCISSE K. M. MILEMBWE.

Banque Paribas Congo: Immeuble Unibra, ave Colonel Ebeya, BP 1600, Kinshasa 1; tel. (12) 24747; telex 21020; f. 1954; cap. and res 1.4m. (Dec. 1980).

Banque Congolaise du Commerce Extérieur SARL: blvd du 30 juin, BP 400, Kinshasa 1; tel. (12) 20393; telex 21108; fax (12) 27947; f. 1947, reorg. 1987; state-owned; cap. NZ 133.0m., res NZ 19,170.1m., dep. NZ 27,419.9m. (Dec. 1994); Chair. and Gen. Man. GBENDO NDEWA TETE; Dirs MAKUMA NDESEKE, ZIKONDOLO BIWABEKI; 31 brs.

Caisse Générale d'Epargne du Congo: 38 ave de la Caisse d'Epargne, BP 8147, Kinshasa-Gombe; tel. (12) 33701; telex 21384; f. 1950; state-owned; Chair. and Man. Dir NSIMBA M'VUEDI; 45 brs.

Caisse Nationale d'Epargne et de Crédit Immobilier: BP 11196, Kinshasa; f. 1971; state-owned; cap. 2m. (Dec. 1983); Dir-Gen. BIANGALA ELONGA MBAÜ.

Citibank (Congo) SARL: Immeuble Citibank Congo, angle aves Col Lukusa et Ngongo Lutete, BP 9999, Kinshasa 1; tel. (12) 20554; telex 21622; fax (12) 21064; f. 1971; cap. and res 152,120.0m., dep. 1,613,301.9m. (Dec. 1991); Chair. SHAUKAT AZIZ; Man. Dir MICHEL ACCAD; 1 br.

Compagnie Immobilière du Congo: BP 332, Kinshasa; f. 1962; cap. 150m. (Dec. 1983); Chair. A. S. GERARD; Man. Dir M. HERALY.

Crédit Foncier de l'Afrique Centrale: BP 1198, Kinshasa; f. 1961; cap. 40,000 (Dec. 1983).

Fransabank (Congo) SARL: Immeuble Congo-Shell 14/16, ave du Port, BP 9497, Kinshasa 1; tel. (12) 20119; telex 21430; fax (12) 27864; f. 1989; cap. 300m. (1993); Pres. ADNAN WAFIC KASSAR.

Nouvelle Banque de Kinshasa: 1 place du Marché, BP 8033, Kinshasa 1; tel. (12) 26361; telex 21304; fax (12) 20587; f. 1969 as Banque de Kinshasa; nationalized 1975; control assumed by National Union of Congolese Workers in 1989; cap. NZ 2,000 (1990), res NZ 92,179.4m., dep. NZ 25,396.8m. (Dec. 1994); Pres. DOKOLO SANU; 15 brs.

Société de Crédit aux Classes Moyennes et à l'Industrie: BP 3165, Kinshasa-Kauna; f. 1947; cap. 500,000 (Dec. 1983).

Société Financière de Développement SCARL (SOFIDE): Immeuble SOFIDE, 9–11 angle aves Ngabu et Kisangani, BP 1148, Kinshasa 1; tel. (12) 20676; telex 21476; fax (12) 20788; f. 1970; partly state-owned; provides tech. and financial aid, primarily for agricultural development; cap. and res NZ 16,303.3m. (Dec. 1995); Pres. and Dir-Gen. KIYANGA KI-N'LOMBI; 4 brs.

Stanbic Bank (Congo) SCARL: 12 ave de Mongala, BP 16297, Kinshasa 1; tel. (12) 20074; telex 21507; fax (12) 46216; f. 1973 as Grindlays Bank; acquired by Standard Bank Investment Corpn (South Africa) in 1992; adopted current name in 1997; cap. NZ 358.0m. (April 1996), res NZ 2,698.2m., dep. NZ 32,587.7m., total assets 35,672.6m. (Dec. 1994); Chair. A. D. B. WRIGHT; Man. Dir JOHN CALLAGHAN; 1 br.

Union Congolaise de Banques SARL: angle ave de la Nation et ave des Aviateurs 19, BP 197, Kinshasa 1; tel. (12) 25180; telex 21026; fax (12) 25527; f. 1929, renamed as above in 1997; cap. NZ 34,497.0m. (Dec. 1995), res 3,077,897m., dep. 2,975,182,180m. (Dec. 1993); Pres. RAOUL ISUNGU KY-MAKA; 11 brs.

INSURANCE

Société Nationale d'Assurances (SONAS): 3473 blvd du 30 juin, Kinshasa-Gombe; tel. (12) 23051; telex 21653; f. 1966; state-owned; cap. 23m.; 9 brs.

Trade and Industry

At November 1994 the Government's portfolio of state enterprises numbered 116, of which 56 were wholly owned by the Government. The heads of all state-owned enterprises were suspended by decree in June 1997.

DEVELOPMENT ORGANIZATIONS

Caisse de Stabilisation Cotonnière (CSCo): BP 3058, Kinshasa-Gombe; tel. (12) 31206; telex 21174; f. 1978 to replace Office National des Fibres Textiles; acts as an intermediary between the Govt, cotton ginners and textile factories, and co-ordinates international financing of cotton sector.

La Générale des Carrières et des Mines (GÉCAMINES): BP 450, Lubumbashi; tel. (2) 13039; telex 41034; f. 1967 as state holding co to acquire assets of Union Minière du Haut-Katanga; privatization announced in 1994; subsequently delayed; Man. Dir MBAKA KAWAYA SWANA; operates the following three enterprises which were merged in 1995:

GÉCAMINES—Commercial: marketing of mineral products.

GÉCAMINES—Développement: operates agricultural and stockfarming ventures in Katanga province.

GÉCAMINES—Exploitation: mining operations.

Institut National pour l'Etude et la Recherche Agronomiques: BP 1513, Kisangani, Haut-Congo; f. 1933; agricultural research.

Office Congolais du Café: ave Général Bobozo, BP 8931, Kinshasa 1; tel. (12) 77144; telex 20062; f. 1979; state agency for coffee and also cocoa, tea, quinquina and pyrethrum.

Pêcherie Maritime Congolaise: Kinshasa; DRC's only sea-fishing enterprise.

PetroCongo: 1513 blvd du 30 juin, BP 7617, Kinshasa 1; tel. (12) 25356; telex 21066; f. 1974; state-owned; petroleum refining, processing, stocking and transporting.

CHAMBERS OF COMMERCE

Chambre de Commerce, d'Industrie et d'Agriculture du Congo: 10 ave des Aviateurs, BP 7247, Kinshasa 1; tel. (12) 22286; telex 21071.

INDUSTRIAL AND TRADE ASSOCIATIONS

Association Nationale des Entreprises du Congo: 10 ave des Aviateurs, BP 7247, Kinshasa; tel. (12) 24623; telex 21071; f. 1972; represents business interests for both domestic and foreign institutions; Man. Dir EDOUARD LUBOYA DIYOKA; Gen. Sec. ATHANASE MATENDA KYELU.

Fédération des Entreprises du Congo (FEC): Kinshasa; Head JOSE ENDUNDO.

UTILITIES

Electricity

Société National d'Electricité (SNEL): Kinshasa; state-owned.

TRADE UNIONS

The Union Nationale des Travailleurs was founded in 1967 as the sole trade union organization. In 1990 the establishment of independent trade unions was legalized, and by early 1991 there were 12 officially recognized trade union organizations.

Union Nationale des Travailleurs du Congo: BP 8814, Kinshasa; f. 1967; embraces 16 unions; Pres. KATALAY MOLELI SANGOL.

Transport

Office National des Transports (ONATRA): BP 98, Kinshasa 1; tel. (12) 24761; fax (12) 24892; operates 12,174 km of waterways, 366 km of railways and road and air transport; administers ports of Kinshasa, Matadi, Boma and Banana; Dir-Gen. I. BANGONDA LOOLA.

RAILWAYS

The main line runs from Lubumbashi to Ilebo. International connections run to Dar es Salaam (Tanzania) and Lobito (Angola), and also connect with the Zambian, Zimbabwean, Mozambican and South African systems. In 1994 an agreement was concluded with the South African Government for the provision of locomotives, rolling stock and fuel, to help rehabilitate the rail system. In May 1997 the railway network and its assets were nationalized.

Kinshasa–Matadi Railway: BP 98, Kinshasa 1; 366 km operated by ONATRA; Pres. K. WA NDAYI MULEDI.

Société Nationale des Chemins de Fer du Congo (SNCC): 115 place de la Gare, BP 297, Lubumbashi; tel. (2) 23430; telex 41056; f. 1974; 4,772 km (including 858 km electrified); administers all internal railway sections as well as river transport and transport on Lakes Tanganyika and Kivu; man. contract concluded with a Belgian-South African corpn, Sizarail, in 1995 for the man. of the Office des Chemins de Fer du Sud (OCS) and the Société des Chemins de Fer de l'Est (SFE) subsidiaries, with rail networks of 2,835 km and 1,286 km respectively; assets of Sizarail nationalized and returned to SNCC control in May 1997; Dir-Gen. TSHISOLA KANGOA.

ROADS

In 1996 there were approximately 157,000 km of roads, of which some 33,100 km were main roads. In general road conditions are poor, owing to inadequate maintenance. In August 1997 a rehabilitation plan was announced by the Government under which 28,664 km of roads were to be built or repaired. The project was to be partly financed by external sources.

INLAND WATERWAYS

The River Congo is navigable for more than 1,600 km. Above the Stanley Falls the Congo becomes the Lualaba, and is navigable along a 965-km stretch from Bubundu to Kindu and Kongolo to Bukama. The River Kasai, a tributary of the River Congo, is navigable by shipping as far as Ilebo, at which the line from Lubumbashi terminates. The total length of inland waterways is 13,700 km.

Régie des voies fluviales: 109 ave Lumpungu, Kinshasa-Gombe, BP 11697, Kinshasa 1; administers river navigation; Gen. Man. MONDOMBO SISA EBAMBE.

Société Congolaise des Chemins de Fer des Grands Lacs: River Lualaba services: Bubundu–Kindu and Kongolo–Malemba N'kula; Lake Tanganyika services: Kamina–Kigoma–Kalundu–Moba–Mpulungu.

SHIPPING

The principal seaports are Matadi, Boma and Banana on the lower Congo. The port of Matadi has more than 1.6 km of quays and can accommodate up to 10 deep-water vessels. Matadi is linked by rail with Kinshasa. The country's merchant fleet numbered 27 vessels and amounted to 14,917 gross registered tons at 31 December 1996.

Compagnie Maritime Congolaise SARL: Immeuble CMC (AMIZA), place de la Poste, BP 9496, Kinshasa; tel. (12) 25816; telex 21626; fax (12) 26234; f. 1946; services: North Africa, Europe, North America and Asia to West Africa, East Africa to North Africa; Chair. MAYILUKILA LUSIASIA.

CIVIL AVIATION

International airports are located at Ndjili (for Kinshasa), Luano (for Lubumbashi), Bukavu, Goma and Kisangani. There are smaller airports and airstrips dispersed throughout the country.

Air Charter Service: Place Salongo, BP 5371, Kinshasa 10; tel. (12) 27891; telex 21573; passenger and cargo charter services; Dir TSHIMBOMBO MAKUNA; Gen. Man. N. MCKANDOLO.

Alliance Airlines: 210 bis 6e rue, Limete-Kinshasa, BP 12847, Kinshasa; tel. (12) 43862; fax (12) 372-3156; f.1996 as Zaire Airlines in merger of Zaire Express and Shabair, name changed as above in 1997; regional and domestic scheduled services for passengers and cargo; Pres. JOSE ENDUNO; CEO STAVROS PAPAIOANNOU.

Blue Airlines: BP 1115, Kinshasa 1; tel. (12) 20455; f. 1991; regional and domestic charter services for passengers and cargo; Man. T. MAYANI.

Congolese Airlines: 3555-3560 blvd du 30 Juin, BP 2111, Kinshasa; tel. (12) 24624; telex 21525; international, regional and domestic services for passengers and cargo; f. 1981; Delegate-Gen. Maj. PAUL MUKANDILA MBAYABO.

Eastern Congo Airlines: Bukavu; f. 1997; 60% state-owned, 40% by Belgian nationals; Chair. Chief NAKAZIBA CIMANYE.

Express City: BP 12847, Kinshasa; tel. (12) 275748; regional and domestic passenger and cargo services.

Filair: BP 14671, Kinshasa; tel. (88) 45702; fax (USA) 1-212-3769367; f. 1987; regional and domestic charter services; Pres. DANY PHILEMOTTE.

Scibe Airlift: BP 614, Kinshasa; tel. (12) 26237; fax (12) 24386; f. 1979; domestic and international passenger and cargo charter services between Kinshasa, Lubumbashi, Bujumbura (Burundi) and Brussels; Pres. BEMBA SAOLONA; Dir-Gen. BEMBA GOMBO.

Local charter services are also provided by Trans Service Airlift, Transair Cargo and Wetrafa Airlift.

Tourism

The DRC has extensive lake and mountain scenery. Tourist arrivals totalled about 18,000 in 1994, generating some US $5m. in revenue.

Office National du Tourisme: 2A/2B ave des Orangers, BP 9502, Kinshasa-Gombe; tel. (12) 30070; f. 1959; Man. Dir BOTOLO MAGOZA.

Société Congolaise de l'Hôtellerie: Immeuble Memling, BP 1076, Kinshasa; tel. (12) 23260; Man. N'JOLI BALANGA.

THE REPUBLIC OF THE CONGO

Introductory Survey

Location, Climate, Language, Religion, Flag, Capital

The Republic of the Congo is an equatorial country on the west coast of Africa. It has a coastline of about 170 km on the Atlantic Ocean, from which the country extends northward to Cameroon and the Central African Republic. The Republic of the Congo is bordered by Gabon to the west and the Democratic Republic of the Congo (formerly Zaire) to the east, while in the south there is a short frontier with the Cabinda exclave of Angola. The climate is tropical, with temperatures averaging 21°C–27°C (70°F–80°F) throughout the year. The average annual rainfall is about 1,200 mm (47 ins). The official language is French; Kikongo, Lingala and other African languages are also used. At least one-half of the population follow traditional animist beliefs and about 45% are Roman Catholics. There are small Protestant and Muslim minorities. The national flag (proportions 3 by 2) comprises a yellow stripe running diagonally from lower hoist to upper fly, separating a green triangle at the hoist from a red triangle in the fly. The capital is Brazzaville.

Recent History

Formerly part of French Equatorial Africa, Middle Congo became the autonomous Republic of the Congo, within the French Community, in November 1958, with Abbé Fulbert Youlou as the first Prime Minister. In November 1959 Youlou was elected President of the Republic by the National Assembly. The Congo became fully independent on 15 August 1960. Under the provisions of a new Constitution, approved by the National Assembly in March 1961, Youlou was re-elected President (unopposed) by popular vote in that month. Proposals to establish a one-party state were overwhelmingly approved by the National Assembly in April 1963. However, on 15 August (the third anniversary of independence and the date scheduled for the introduction of one-party rule) Youlou was forced to resign, following anti-Government demonstrations and strikes by trade unionists. On the following day a provisional Government was formed, with the support of military and trade union leaders. Alphonse Massamba-Débat, a former Minister of Planning, became Prime Minister. In December a new Constitution was approved in a referendum, a general election was held for a new National Assembly, and Massamba-Débat was elected President for a five-year term. He was replaced as Prime Minister by Pascal Lissouba, hitherto Minister of Agriculture. The Mouvement national de la révolution (MNR) was established as the sole political party in July 1964. In June 1965 Youlou was sentenced to death *in absentia*. Lissouba resigned as Prime Minister in April 1966 and was succeeded by Ambroise Noumazalay, the First Secretary of the MNR's Political Bureau. However, Noumazalay was dismissed in January 1968 by Massamba-Débat, who assumed the Prime Minister's functions himself.

Tension between the armed forces and the MNR culminated in a military coup in August 1968. The leader of the coup was Capt. (later Maj.) Marien Ngouabi, a paratroop officer, who became head of the armed forces. The National Assembly was replaced by the National Council of the Revolution, led by Ngouabi. The President was briefly restored to office, with reduced powers, but was dismissed again in September, when Capt. (later Maj.) Alfred Raoul, the new Prime Minister, also became Head of State, a position that he relinquished in January 1969 to Ngouabi, while remaining Prime Minister until the end of that year.

Ngouabi's regime proclaimed itself Marxist but maintained close economic ties with France. The People's Republic of the Congo, as it became in January 1970, was governed by a single political party, the Parti congolais du travail (PCT). In 1973 Ngouabi introduced a new Constitution and a National Assembly with delegates elected from a single party list. Ngouabi was assassinated in March 1977, reportedly by supporters of ex-President Massamba-Débat, who was subsequently charged with attempting to overthrow the Government and executed. Power was assumed by an 11-member Military Committee of the PCT, and in April Col (later Brig.-Gen.) Jacques-Joachim Yhombi-Opango, the head of the armed forces (and, like Ngouabi, a member of the Kouyou ethnic group), became the new Head of State.

In February 1979, faced with mounting unpopularity, Yhombi-Opango and the Military Committee transferred their powers to a Provisional Committee appointed by the PCT. Following an election in March the head of the Provisional Committee, Col (later Gen.) Denis Sassou-Nguesso (a member of the northern M'Bochi ethnic group), became Chairman of the PCT Central Committee and President of the Republic. In July a National People's Assembly and regional councils were also elected, and a new socialist Constitution was overwhelmingly approved in a national referendum. At the PCT Congress in July 1984 Sassou-Nguesso was unanimously re-elected Chairman of the party Central Committee and President of the Republic for a second five-year term. Under the provisions of a constitutional amendment, he also became Head of Government. As a result of an extensive government reshuffle in August, Ange-Edouard Poungui, a former Vice-President, became Prime Minister in succession to Col (later Gen.) Louis Sylvain Goma, who had held the post since December 1975. Sassou-Nguesso assumed personal control of the Ministry of Defence and Security. Legislative elections were held in September 1984, and in November Yhombi-Opango, who had been imprisoned since March 1979, was placed under house arrest.

Persistent ethnic rivalries, together with disillusionment with the Government's response to the country's worsening economic situation, resulted in an increase in opposition to the Sassou-Nguesso regime during the late 1980s. In July 1987 some 20 army officers, most of whom were members of the Kouyou tribe, were arrested for alleged complicity in a coup plot. Shortly afterwards fighting broke out in the northern Cuvette region between government forces and troops led by Pierre Anga, a supporter of Yhombi-Opango. In September government troops suppressed the rebellion with French military assistance. Yhombi-Opango was returned to prison. Anga evaded arrest; however, in July 1988 it was reported that he had been killed by Congolese security forces.

In August 1988 an amnesty was announced for all political prisoners sentenced before July 1987, to commemorate the 25th anniversary of the overthrow of the Youlou regime. During August 1988 a faction of the PCT published a document accusing the Government of having lost its revolutionary momentum, and criticizing its recourse to the IMF and its alleged links with the South African Government.

At the PCT Congress in July 1989 Sassou-Nguesso, the sole candidate, was re-elected Chairman of the party and President of the Republic for a third five-year term. In August Alphonse Mouissou Poaty-Souchalaty, formerly the Minister of Trade and Small and Medium-sized Enterprises, was appointed Prime Minister. At legislative elections in September the PCT-approved single list of 133 candidates was endorsed by 99.2% of voters. The list included, for the first time, candidates who were not members of the party. In November Sassou-Nguesso announced plans for economic reforms, signifying a departure from socialist policies. In the following month 40 prisoners who had been detained without trial since July 1987 were released.

Progress towards political reform dominated the latter half of 1990. In July the Government announced that an extraordinary Congress of the PCT would be convened to formulate legislation enabling the introduction of a multi-party system. The regime also approved measures that would limit the role of the ruling party in the country's mass and social organizations. In August, on the occasion of the 30th anniversary of the country's independence, several political prisoners were released, among them Yhombi-Opango. In September the Confederation of Congolese Trade Unions (CSC) was refused permission by the Government to disaffiliate itself from the ruling PCT. The CSC had also demanded the immediate transition to a plural political system and increased salaries for workers in the public sector. However, in response to a two-day general strike, Sassou-Nguesso agreed to permit free elections to the leadership of the trade union organization, and in late September the Central Committee of the PCT decided to allow the immediate registration of new political parties. In early December Poaty-Souchalaty resigned. On the following day the extraordinary Congress of the PCT commenced. The party abandoned Marxism-Leninism as its official ideology, and formulated constitutional amendments legalizing a multi-party system. The amendments were subsequently approved by the National People's Assembly, and took effect in January 1991. Gen. Louis Sylvain Goma was appointed Prime Minister (a position he had previously held between December 1975 and August 1984), and shortly afterwards an interim Government was installed.

A National Conference on the country's future was convened in February 1991. Opposition movements were allocated seven of the 11 seats on the Conference's governing body, and were represented by 700 of the 1,100 delegates attending the Conference. The Roman Catholic Bishop of Owando, Ernest N'Kombo, was elected as Chairman. The Conference voted to establish itself as a sovereign body, the decisions of which were to be binding and not subject to approval by the transitional Government. In April the Conference announced proposals to draft legislation providing for the abrogation of the Constitution and the abolition of the National People's Assembly, several national institutions and regional councils. In June, prior to the dissolution of the Conference, a 153-member legislative Higher Council of the Republic was established, under the chairmanship of N'Kombo; this was empowered to supervise the implementation of the resolutions made by the National Conference, pending the adoption of a new constitution and the holding of legislative and presidential elections in 1992. From June 1991 the President was replaced as Chairman of the Council of Ministers by the Prime Minister, and the country reverted to its previous official name, the Republic of the Congo. A new Prime Minister, André Milongo (a former World Bank official), was appointed in June, and during that month the Government agreed to permit workers to form independent trade unions. In December the Higher Council of the Republic adopted a draft Constitution, which provided for legislative power to be vested in an elected National Assembly and Senate and for executive power to be held by an elected President.

In January 1992, following a reorganization of senior army posts by the Prime Minister, members of the army occupied strategic positions in Brazzaville and demanded the reinstatement of military personnel who had allegedly been dismissed because of their ethnic allegiances, the removal of the newly-appointed Secretary of State for Defence and the immediate payment of overdue salaries. Shortly afterwards the Higher Council of the Republic requested that the interim Government cancel the appointments. Milongo refused to comply with these demands, whereupon the mutinous soldiers demanded his resignation as Prime Minister, and he was temporarily forced to go into hiding. Five supporters of Milongo were reportedly shot dead by security forces at a pro-Government demonstration in Brazzaville. The crisis was eventually resolved by the resignation of the Secretary of State for Defence and the installation of a candidate preferred by the army as Minister of Defence in a reorganization of the Council of Ministers in late January. Milongo appointed himself Chief of the Armed Forces.

The draft Constitution was approved by 96.3% of voters at a national referendum in March 1992. In May Milongo appointed a new Council of Ministers, membership of which was drawn from each of the country's regions, in order to avoid accusations of domination by any one ethnic group. Following two rounds of elections to the new National Assembly, in late June and mid-July, the Union panafricaine pour la démocratie social (UPADS) became the major party, winning 39 of the 125 contested seats; the Mouvement congolais pour la démocratie et le développement intégral (MCDDI) took 29 seats and the PCT secured 18 seats. At elections to the Senate, held in late July, the UPADS again won the largest share (23) of the 60 contested seats, followed by the MCDDI, with 13 seats. At the first round of presidential voting, in early August, former Prime Minister Pascal Lissouba, the leader of the UPADS, won the largest share of the votes cast (35.9%); of the 15 other candidates, his closest rival was Bernard Kolelas of the MCDDI (22.9%). Sassou-Nguesso took 16.9% of the votes cast. Lissouba and Kolelas thus proceeded to a second round of voting, held two weeks later, at which Lissouba won 61.3% of the votes cast. He was inaugurated as President at the end of August. Shortly afterwards Lissouba appointed Maurice-Stéphane Bongho-Nouarra (a member of the UPADS) as Prime Minister, and a new Council of Ministers was formed. Meanwhile, however, the Union pour le renouveau démocratique (URD), a new alliance of seven parties, including the MCDDI, formed a coalition with the PCT, thereby establishing a parliamentary majority. In October the URD-PCT coalition won a vote of no confidence in the Government, on the grounds that the Prime Minister now belonged to a minority parliamentary grouping. In November Bongho-Nouarra announced the resignation of his Government, and shortly afterwards Lissouba dissolved the National Assembly and announced that fresh legislative elections would be held in 1993. The URD-PCT coalition, which demanded the right to form the Government, commenced a protest campaign of civil disobedience. In December Claude Antoine Dacosta, a former FAO and World Bank official, was appointed Prime Minister. Later in that month Dacosta formed a transitional Government, comprising members of all the main political parties.

At the first round of legislative elections, which took place in early May 1993, the so-called Mouvance présidentielle, comprising the UPADS and its allies, won 62 of the 125 seats in the National Assembly, while the URD-PCT coalition secured 49. Protesting that serious electoral irregularities had occurred, the URD-PCT refused to contest the second round of elections in early June (for seats where a clear majority had not been achieved in the first round) and demanded that some of the first-round polls should be repeated. At the second round the Mouvance présidentielle secured an absolute majority (69) of seats in the National Assembly. In late June President Lissouba appointed a new Council of Ministers, with former President Yhombi-Opango as Prime Minister. During June Bernard Kolelas, the leader of the MCDDI and of the URD-PCT coalition, urged his supporters to force the Government to organize new elections by means of a campaign of civil disobedience. However, the political crisis soon precipitated violent conflict between armed militia, representing party political and ethnic interests, and the security forces. At the end of June the Supreme Court ruled that electoral irregularities had occurred at the first round of elections. In mid-July Lissouba declared a state of emergency, but by the end of the month the Government and the opposition had negotiated a truce, and in early August, following mediation by the Organization of African Unity (OAU—see p. 215), France and President Omar Bongo of Gabon, the two sides agreed that the disputed first-round election results should be examined by a committee of impartial international arbitrators and that the second round of elections should be rerun (the second round that had been held in June was consequently annulled by the Supreme Court). The state of emergency was revoked in mid-August.

Following the repeated second round of legislative elections, which took place at the beginning of October 1993, the Mouvance présidentielle, which had secured 65 seats, retained its overall majority in the National Assembly. (Therefore the Council of Ministers appointed in June, with Yhombi-Opango as Prime Minister, remained unchanged.) The URD-PCT coalition, which had taken 57 seats, agreed to participate in the new Assembly. In November, however, confrontations erupted once again between armed militia affiliated to political parties and the security forces. During the second half of 1993 activities by militia resulted in serious social and economic disruption and, reportedly, at least 2,000 deaths. A cease-fire was agreed by the Mouvance présidentielle and the opposition at the end of January 1994; nevertheless, fighting subsequently continued to erupt sporadically.

In February 1994 the committee of international arbitrators, which had been investigating the conduct of the first round of legislative elections held in May 1993, ruled that the results in eight constituencies were unlawful. In September 1994 six opposition parties formed an alliance, the Forces démocratiques unies (FDU), which was headed by the leader of the PCT, Sassou-Nguesso, and affiliated with the URD. In early December the Government announced its intention to re-form as a coalition administration, including members of the opposition, in the near future. At the end of the month, following the holding of reconciliation talks between the Government and the opposition, a co-ordinating body was established to oversee the disarmament of the party militia and the restoration of judicial authority. Meanwhile, Lissouba and the two main opposition leaders—Sassou-Nguesso and Kolelas—signed an agreement seeking a permanent end to hostilities between their respective supporters. In January 1995 it was announced that 2,000 places would be set aside in the national army for former militiamen when their units were finally disbanded. By the end of 1995, however, the party militia had been neither disarmed nor disbanded (see below).

In mid-January 1995 the Government resigned, and a new coalition Council of Ministers was appointed later in the month, including members of the MCDDI and headed by Yhombi-Opango. The FDU, however, refused to participate in the new administration. Some 12 parliamentary deputies defected from the majority UPADS in protest at the lack of representation for south-western Congolese in the newly-appointed Council of Ministers; they subsequently established a new party, the Union pour la République, which remained affiliated to the Mouvance présidentielle.

During early 1995 by-elections were contested for seven seats in the National Assembly (outstanding since the partially annulled elections of May 1993): five were won by opposition parties and two by the UPADS. In March 1995 the Government announced the introduction of measures to restrain state expenditure, including significant reductions in the number of civil service personnel, in order to secure continued assistance from the IMF. The Lissouba administration banned all public demonstrations in August, in order to restrict anti-Government protest activities by trade unions. In the following month the National Assembly approved legislation to restrict the freedom of the press, providing for a five-year term of imprisonment for journalists, printing houses and newspaper distributors convicted of libel, and prohibiting media coverage of libel cases, except where permission had previously been granted by the Ministry of Justice.

In October 1995 the Government announced the impending restructuring of the armed forces, with the aim of achieving a more balanced representation of ethnic and regional interests. In late December political parties from the Mouvance présidentielle and opposition groupings signed a peace pact that required the imminent disarmament of all party militia and the integration into the national security forces of 1,200 former militia members. In February 1996 about 100 soldiers who had previously belonged to militias staged a short-lived mutiny, in order to demand improved pay and conditions; five people were reportedly killed during the unrest. Later in that month the FDU suspended the integration of its militia associates into the national armed forces, claiming that the peace pact favoured pro-Government militias while under-representing those affiliated to opposition organizations. In March the Government agreed to increase the quota of opposition recruits into the security forces and, consequently, the integration of FDU-affiliated militia members resumed. During 1994–96 some 4,000 militiamen were integrated into the defence and security forces. Nevertheless, activities by armed militia groups continued to be reported. In August 1996, following a local dispute, some 200 armed militiamen professing allegiance to the FDU (which was subsequently renamed the Forces démocratiques et patriotiques—FDP) occupied a small town in central Congo for several days.

In late August 1996 Yhombi-Opango resigned as Prime Minister; he was replaced shortly afterwards by David Charles Ganao, the leader of the Union des forces démocratiques and a former Minister of Foreign Affairs. In early September Ganao appointed an expanded Council of Ministers, including representatives of the URD. The Ganao administration undertook to continue with the implementation of an economic reform programme agreed with the IMF in June. In early October elections were held for 23 of the 60 seats in the Senate. The Mouvance présidentielle retained its majority, winning 12 of the seats, while opposition organizations took 10 seats and one seat was secured by an independent candidate.

Factional divisions remained apparent in early 1997. Opposition politicians accused Lissouba of political and ethnic partiality when, on several occasions, he was perceived to grant preferential treatment to army members from his native southern Congo, while, during April and May, dismissing several high-ranking northern officers installed under the Sassou-Nguesso administration. In February 19 opposition parties (including the PCT and the MCDDI) published a memorandum demanding the expedited establishment of republican institutions, the free movement of people and goods, and more equitable access to the media and to public funds; in the short term they also requested, as matters of urgency, the creation of an independent electoral commission, the disarmament of civilians and the deployment of a multinational peace-keeping force, on the basis that the continued existence of armed militias was otherwise likely to lead to a resumption of large-scale factional violence. During May inter-militia unrest did erupt once again, and in early June an attempt by the Government forceably to disarm the militia group associated with Sassou-Nguesso's FDP (in preparation for legislative and presidential elections scheduled for July and August) precipitated a fierce national conflict along ethnic and political lines, involving the militias and also opposing factions within the regular armed forces. Barricades were erected in Brazzaville, and the capital was divided into three zones, controlled by supporters of Lissouba, Sassou-Nguesso and Kolelas. The conflict soon became polarized between troops loyal to the Lissouba administration and the rebel forces of Sassou-Neguesso; both sides were allegedly reinforced by mercenaries and by fighters from foreign rebel groups. Despite efforts to mediate—led by Kolelas at a national level and, on behalf of the international community, President Bongo of Gabon and Muhammad Sahnoun, the joint UN-OAU special representative to the Great Lakes region—none of the numerous cease-fires signed during mid-1997 led to more than a brief lull in hostilities. An attempt by Lissouba to postpone the impending elections and prolong his presidential mandate beyond the end of August was strongly opposed by Sassou-Nguesso, and both sides were unable to agree on the nature or composition of a proposed government of national unity. In early June French troops assisted in the evacuation of foreign residents from Brazzaville; in mid-June they themselves departed, despite mediators' requests that they remain to protect the civilian population and to attempt to forestall further hostilities. Fighting between forces loyal to the Government and to Sassou-Nguesso intensified in August, spreading to the north. In early September Lissouba appointed a Government of National Unity, under the premiership of Kolelas, thereby compromising the latter's role as a national mediator and impeding the ongoing negotiations in the Gabonese capital, Libreville. Sassou-Nguesso refused to accept the offer of five seats for his allies in the Council of Ministers. In September political organizations loyal to Lissouba formed the Espace républicain pour la défense de la démocratie et l'unité nationale.

In mid-October 1997 Sassou-Nguesso's forces, assisted by Angolan government troops, won control of Brazzaville and the strategic port of Pointe-Noire. Lissouba was ousted from the presidential palace, and, with Kolelas, found refuge in Burkina Faso. In late October Sassou-Nguesso was inaugurated as President, having retaken by force the office which he lost at the 1992 presidential election. He appointed a new transitional Government in early November. A Forum for Unity and National Reconciliation was established in January 1998. Subsequently, a National Transitional Council was to hold legislative power, pending the organization of legislative elections. Upon his accession to power, President Sassou-Nguesso decreed that party militias would be disarmed and outlawed as a matter of priority.

It was reported that some 10,000 people were killed during the civil war and that about 800,000 people were displaced. Brazzaville was ransacked and largely destroyed, while the national infrastructure and institutions were severely disrupted.

After the mid-1970s the Republic of the Congo moved away from the sphere of influence of the former USSR, fostering links with France (the former colonial power and source of more than one-half of total assistance to the Congo), with neighbouring francophone countries, and also with the USA and the People's Republic of China. Nevertheless, Cuban troops were stationed in the Congo from 1977 until 1991. In 1988 the Congo mediated in negotiations between Angola, Cuba, South Africa and the USA, which resulted in the signing, in December, of the Brazzaville accord, regarding the withdrawal of Cuban troops from Angola and progress towards Namibian independence. Diplomatic relations with the Republic of Korea (severed in 1964) were restored in June 1990, and relations with Israel (severed in 1973) were resumed in August 1991. The Congo established diplomatic relations with South Africa in March 1993.

During the 1997 civil war President Lissouba accused France of favouring the rebel forces of Sassou-Nguesso (who was reported to have allied himself with French petroleum interests) over the elected administration. Angolan government troops facilitated Sassou-Nguesso's victory by providing tactical support, including the occupation of Pointe-Noire, the Congo's main seaport and focus of the petroleum industry. Angola had accused the Lissouba Government of providing assistance both to rebels of the União Nacional para a Independência Total de Angola and to Cabindan separatist guerrillas.

Government

The 1992 Constitution, providing for an elected President, National Assembly and Senate, was suspended following the assumption of power by Gen. Denis Sassou-Nguesso on 15 October 1997. A Forum for Unity and National Reconciliation was established in January 1998. Subsequently a National Transitional Council was to be appointed, to act as a legislative body pending the organization of national elections.

Defence

In August 1997 the army numbered 8,000, the navy about 800 and the air force 1,200. There were 5,000 men in paramilitary forces. National service is voluntary for men and women, and lasts for two years. The estimated defence budget for 1997 was 32,000m. francs CFA.

Economic Affairs

In 1995, according to estimates by the World Bank, the Congo's gross national product (GNP), measured at average 1993–95 prices, was US $1,784m., equivalent to $680 per head. During 1985–95, it was estimated, GNP per head declined, in real terms, at an average rate of 3.2% annually. Over the same period, the population increased by an annual average of 3.1%. The Congo's gross domestic product (GDP) increased, in real terms, by an annual average of 0.3% in 1985–95. Negative growth of 1.5% and 5.5% was recorded in 1993 and 1994 respectively. GDP increased by 0.9% in 1995. An estimated 6.8% increase in GDP in 1996 was attributed to a substantial rise in petroleum production.

Agriculture (including forestry and fishing) contributed an estimated 11.2% of GDP in 1995 and employed about 43.8% of the total labour force in 1996. The staple crops are cassava and plantains, while the major cash crops are sugar cane, oil palm, cocoa and coffee. Forests cover about 55% of the country's total land area, and forestry is a major economic activity. Sales of timber provided an estimated 8.4% of export earnings in 1995. During 1985–95 agricultural GDP increased by an annual average of 1.0%.

Industry (including mining, manufacturing, construction and power) contributed 41.2% of GDP in 1995, and employed an estimated 12.7% of the labour force in 1984. During 1985–95 industrial GDP increased by an annual average of 3.5%.

Mining contributed 28.6% of GDP in 1989. The hydrocarbons sector is the only significant mining activity. In 1995 sales of petroleum and petroleum products provided an estimated 84.6% of export earnings. Annual petroleum production (8.4m. metric tons in 1995, according to UN figures) was expected to reach about 13m. tons by 2000, as a result of major exploration and development planned at various offshore deposits. Deposits of natural gas are also exploited. Lead, zinc, gold and copper are produced in small quantities, and magnesium production was expected to commence by 2000. There are also exploitable reserves of diamonds, gold, phosphate, iron ore and potash. In addition, the Congo has bauxite reserves.

Manufacturing contributed an estimated 6.9% of GDP in 1995. The most important industries are the processing of agricultural and forest products. The textile, chemical and construction materials industries are also important. During 1985–95 manufacturing GDP increased by an annual average of 0.4%.

Energy is derived principally from hydroelectric power. Imports of fuel and energy comprised an estimated 26.1% of the value of total imports in 1995.

The services sector contributed an estimated 47.7% of GDP in 1995. During 1985–95, it was estimated, the GDP of the services sector declined at an average annual rate of 1.5% (compared with growth averaging 11.3% per year in 1975–84). The sector's GDP declined by 16.3% in 1994, and by an estimated 8.6% in 1995.

In 1996 the Congo recorded a visible trade surplus of US $62.9m., but there was a deficit of $1,033.9m. on the current account of the balance of payments. In 1990 the principal source of imports (36.8%) was France, while the USA was the principal market for exports (36.3%). Italy is also an important trading partner. The principal exports in 1990 were petroleum and petroleum products. The principal imports were machinery, chemical products, iron and steel and transport equipment.

The budget deficit for 1994 was estimated at 79,000m. francs CFA. The country's external debt totalled US $6,032. at the end of 1995, of which $4,955m. was long-term public debt. In that year the cost of debt-servicing was equivalent to 14.4% of the value of exports of goods and services. The annual rate of inflation averaged 5.1% in 1986–95; it increased from 2.0% in 1993 to 49.8% in 1994, falling to 21.4% in 1995.

The Republic of the Congo is a member of the Central African organs of the Franc Zone (see p. 181) and of the Communauté économique des Etats de l'Afrique centrale (CEEAC, see p. 260).

From 1985 the decline in international petroleum prices significantly reduced government revenue, leading to a decline in the construction industry and a lack of industrial investment and growth. The agricultural sector, however, remained strong. The greatest impediment to development is the country's large external debt. In January 1994 the devaluation by 50% of the CFA franc, as in the other CFA franc zone countries, resulted in an immediate sharp increase in the prices of consumer goods. In May the Government agreed a programme of economic measures with the IMF, which aimed to stimulate growth in non-petroleum GDP and to contain the effect on the inflation rate of the January currency devaluation. The privatization of the major state-owned companies was envisaged, as well as a substantial reduction in the number of civil service personnel. In July the Government signed a debt-rescheduling agreement with members of the Paris Club of creditor countries. In June 1996 the IMF agreed to support an economic reform programme for 1996–99. This aimed to consolidate the reforms introduced in 1994, envisaging the stabilization of public finances, a reduction in external indebtedness and an acceleration in GDP growth and job creation. The programme was, however, jeopardized by the debilitating 1997 civil war. In November 1997 the World Bank suspended relations with the Congo in protest at the non-payment of debt arrears. Petroleum revenues (which were expected to be largely unaffected by the 1997 conflict), were forecast to rise substantially during the late 1990s, although the strengthening of the non-petroleum sectors of the economy remained an essential long-term goal.

Social Welfare

There is a state pension scheme and a system of family allowances and other welfare services. Both social welfare and health provision have, however, been seriously impeded by a lack of government funds and by the devastating effects of the 1997 civil war. In 1987 there were 43 hospitals, providing a total of 7,917 hospital beds. There were about 460 physicians working in the Congo in that year. Since the late 1980s rising numbers of AIDS cases have placed considerable strain on resources.

Education

Education is officially compulsory for 10 years between six and 16 years of age. Primary education begins at the age of six and lasts for six years. Secondary education, from 12 years of age, lasts for seven years, comprising a first cycle of four years and a second of three years. In 1996 there were 489,546 pupils enrolled at primary schools, while 190,409 pupils were receiving general secondary education. In addition, 23,606 students were attending vocational institutions. The Marien Ngouabi University, at Brazzaville, was founded in 1971. In 1995 there were 16,602 students at university level. Some Congolese students attend further education establishments in France and Russia. The provision of education was severely disrupted by the 1997 civil war. In 1995, according to estimates by UNESCO, the average rate of adult illiteracy was 25.1% (males 16.9%, females 32.8%), one of the lowest in Africa. Expenditure on education by all levels of government was 57,092m. francs CFA in 1991.

Public Holidays

1998: 1 January (New Year's Day), 10 April (Good Friday), 13 April (Easter Monday), 1 May (Labour Day), 15 August (Independence Day), 25 December (Christmas).

1999: 1 January (New Year's Day), 2 April (Good Friday), 5 April (Easter Monday), 1 May (Labour Day), 15 August (Independence Day), 25 December (Christmas).

Weights and Measures

The metric system is in force.

Statistical Survey

Source (unless otherwise stated): Centre National de la Statistique et des Etudes Economiques, BP 2093, Brazzaville; tel. 81-06-20; telex 5210.

Area and Population

AREA, POPULATION AND DENSITY

Area (sq km)	342,000*
Population (census results)	
7 February 1974	1,319,790
22 December 1984	1,843,421
Population (UN estimates at mid-year)	
1994†	2,516,000
1995†	2,590,000
1996‡	2,668,000
Density (per sq km) at mid-1996	7.8

* 132,047 sq miles.

† Source: UN, *World Population Prospects: The 1994 Revision.*

‡ Source: UN, *World Population Prospects: The 1996 Revision.*

REGIONS (estimated population at 1 January 1983)*

Brazzaville	456,383	Kouilou	78,738
Pool	219,329	Lékoumou	67,568
Pointe-Noire	214,466	Sangha	42,106
Bouenza	135,999	Nkayi	40,419
Cuvette	127,558	Likouala	34,302
Niari	114,229	Loubomo	33,591
Plateaux	110,379	**Total**	1,675,067

* Figures have not been revised to take account of the 1984 census results.

PRINCIPAL TOWNS (population at 1984 census)

Brazzaville (capital)	596,200
Pointe-Noire	298,014

BIRTHS AND DEATHS (UN estimates, annual averages)

	1980–85	1985–90	1990–95
Birth rate (per 1,000)	43.9	44.3	44.7
Death rate (per 1,000)	15.6	14.7	14.9

Expectation of life (UN estimates, years at birth, 1990-95): 51.3 (males 48.9; females 53.8).

Source: UN, *World Population Prospects: The 1994 Revision.*

EMPLOYMENT ('000 persons at 1984 census)

	Males	Females	Total
Agriculture, etc.	105	186	291
Industry	61	8	69
Services	123	60	183
Total	289	254	543

Mid-1996 (FAO estimates, '000 persons): Agriculture, etc. 485; Total labour force 1,107 (Source: FAO, *Production Yearbook*).

Agriculture

PRINCIPAL CROPS (FAO estimates, '000 metric tons)

	1994	1995	1996
Maize	26	26	26
Sugar cane	340	440	460
Sweet potatoes	23	24	25
Cassava (Manioc)	650	700	720
Yams	15	16	17
Other roots and tubers	39	40	42
Dry beans	6	6	6
Tomatoes	10	10	10
Other vegetables (incl. melons)	35	36	37
Avocados	25	25	26
Pineapples	12	12	13
Bananas	45	45	46
Plantains	95	97	99
Palm kernels	3	3	3
Palm oil	16	16	17
Groundnuts (in shell)	26	27	28
Coffee (green)	1	1	1
Cocoa beans	1	2	2
Natural rubber	2	2	2

Source: FAO, *Production Yearbook.*

LIVESTOCK (FAO estimates, '000 head, year ending September)

	1994	1995	1996
Cattle	68	69	70
Pigs	57	58	59
Sheep	112	113	114
Goats	308	310	312

Poultry (FAO estimates, million): 2 in 1994; 2 in 1995; 2 in 1996.

Source: FAO, *Production Yearbook.*

LIVESTOCK PRODUCTS (FAO estimates, '000 metric tons)

	1994	1995	1996
Beef and veal	2	2	2
Pig meat	3	3	3
Poultry meat	6	6	6
Other meat	12	12	13
Cows' milk	1	1	1
Hen eggs	1	1	1

Source: FAO, *Production Yearbook.*

Forestry

ROUNDWOOD REMOVALS ('000 cubic metres, excluding bark)

	1992	1993*	1994*
Sawlogs, veneer logs and logs for sleepers	635	635	635
Pulpwood	391	391	391
Other industrial wood*	306	315	325
Fuel wood	2,156	2,222	2,288
Total	3,488	3,563	3,639

* FAO estimates.

Source: FAO, *Yearbook of Forest Products.*

SAWNWOOD PRODUCTION
('000 cubic metres, including railway sleepers)

	1992	1993	1994
Total	52	52*	52*

* FAO estimate.

Source: FAO, *Yearbook of Forest Products*.

Fishing

('000 metric tons, live weight)

	1993	1994	1995
Freshwater fishes	19.3	19.0	19.8
Boe drum*	0.9	0.7	0.6
West African croakers*	2.1	1.7	0.6
Sardinellas	8.8	10.9	10.4
Other marine fishes (incl. unspecified)*	4.1	3.3	5.1
Crustaceans*	0.3	0.3	0.3
Total catch	36.9	37.0	36.8

* FAO estimate(s).

Source: FAO, *Yearbook of Fishery Statistics*.

Mining

('000 metric tons, unless otherwise indicated)

	1992	1993*	1994*
Crude petroleum	8,654	8,710	9,158
Gold (kg)†	5	5	5

* Provisional or estimated figures.

† Data from the US Bureau of Mines, referring to the metal content of ores.

Source: UN, *Industrial Commodity Statistics Yearbook*.

Crude petroleum ('000 metric tons): 8,448 in 1995; 8,040 in 1996. (Source: UN, *Monthly Bulletin of Statistics*.)

Industry

SELECTED PRODUCTS ('000 metric tons, unless otherwise indicated)

	1992	1993	1994
Raw sugar	27	28	29*
Beer ('000 hectolitres)	708	759	n.a.
Soft drinks ('000 hectolitres)	294	300	n.a.
Cigarettes (metric tons)	431	n.a.	n.a.
Veneer sheets ('000 cu metres)	35	35†	35†
Soap	3.2	1.5	n.a.
Jet fuels‡	14	15	15
Motor spirit (petrol)	53	55	58‡
Kerosene	49	50‡	52‡
Distillate fuel oils	90	92†	95‡
Residual fuel oils	267	285‡	288‡
Cement	124	95	n.a.
Electric energy (million kWh)	428	431‡	435‡

* Data from the International Sugar Organization.

† Data from the FAO.

‡ Provisional figure(s).

Source: UN, *Industrial Commodity Statistics Yearbook*.

Finance

CURRENCY AND EXCHANGE RATES

Monetary Units

100 centimes = 1 franc de la Coopération financière en Afrique centrale (CFA).

French Franc, Sterling and Dollar Equivalents (30 September 1997)

1 French franc = 100 francs CFA;
£1 sterling = 958.3 francs CFA;
US $1 = 593.2 francs CFA;
1,000 francs CFA = £1.044 = $1.686.

Average Exchange Rate (francs CFA per US $)

1994 555.20
1995 499.15
1996 511.55

Note: The exchange rate of 1 French franc = 50 francs CFA, established in 1948, remained in force until January 1994, when the CFA franc was devalued by 50%, with the exchange rate adjusted to 1 French franc = 100 francs CFA.

BUDGET ('000 million francs CFA)

Revenue*	1993	1994	1995†
Petroleum revenue	93.9	138.9	131.0
Royalties	44.1	74.4	78.5
Profits tax	0.8	0.2	13.1
Dividends	49.0	64.3	39.4
Tax revenue	83.8	77.8	116.9
Taxes on income and profits	31.8	34.1	31.4
Excise duty	36.6	30.6	47.8
Domestic petroleum tax	0.1	10.3	13.0
Other indirect taxes	15.3	2.8	24.7
Other revenue	5.4	3.4	1.5
Total	183.1	220.1	249.4

Expenditure	1993	1994	1995†
Current expenditure	266.4	333.3	315.0
Wages and salaries	136.2	130.8	111.1
Local authority subsidies	7.3	11.1	4.4
Interest payments	56.1	119.0	148.9
Other current expenditure	66.8	72.3	50.6
Capital expenditure	12.7	27.3	31.6
Sub-total	279.1	360.6	346.6
Less Adjustment for payment arrears	37.9	95.1	71.9
Total (cash basis)	241.2	265.5	274.7

* Excluding grants received ('000 million francs CFA): 0.1 in 1993; 10.4 in 1994; 10.7 in 1995.

† Provisional figures.

Source: IMF, *Republic of Congo—Statistical Annex* (August 1996).

CENTRAL BANK RESERVES (US $ million at 31 December)

	1994	1995	1996
Gold*	4.21	4.29	4.10
IMF special drawing rights	0.05	0.03	0.02
Reserve position in IMF	0.68	0.75	0.77
Foreign exchange	49.63	58.52	90.20
Total	54.57	63.59	95.09

* National valuation.

Source: IMF, *International Financial Statistics*.

MONEY SUPPLY ('000 million francs CFA at 31 December)

	1994	1995	1996
Currency outside banks	69.49	81.58	87.35
Demand deposits at commercial and development banks	60.57	49.16	61.08

Source: IMF, *International Financial Statistics*.

COST OF LIVING
(Consumer Price Index for Africans in Brazzaville; base: 1964 = 100)

	1993	1994	1995
Food	179.6	265.1	282.9
Fuel and light	181.6	207.4	229.6
Clothing	276.6	357.6	430.6
Rent (incl. construction)	247.7	321.5	355.9
Health care	210.7	330.4	377.2
Transportation and leisure	267.7	375.1	422.6
All items	206.2	293.7	320.1

Source: IMF, *Republic of Congo—Statistical Annex* (August 1996).

NATIONAL ACCOUNTS (million francs CFA at current prices)

National Income and Product

	1986	1987	1988
Compensation of employees	264,296	253,198	245,033
Operating surplus	133,347	183,843	188,612
Domestic factor incomes	397,643	437,041	433,645
Consumption of fixed capital	156,074	164,360	144,647
Gross domestic product (GDP) at factor cost	553,717	601,401	578,292
Indirect taxes	91,444	90,790	82,358
Less Subsidies	4,754	1,668	1,686
GDP in purchasers' values	640,407	690,523	658,964
Factor income from abroad	2,781	9,333	3,112
Less Factor income paid abroad	44,717	86,030	93,328
Gross national product	598,471	613,826	568,748
Less Consumption of fixed capital	156,074	164,360	144,647
National income in market prices	442,397	449,466	424,101
Other current transfers from abroad	17,470	25,403	24,100
Less Other current transfers paid abroad	25,512	36,255	36,264
National disposable income	434,355	438,614	411,937

Source: UN, *National Accounts Statistics*.

Expenditure on the Gross Domestic Product

	1993	1994	1995*
Government final consumption expenditure	210,000	213,600	165,200
Private final consumption expenditure	391,300	531,700	586,300
Increase in stocks	400	13,800	—
Gross fixed capital formation	220,000	480,000	293,600
Total domestic expenditure	821,700	1,239,100	1,045,100
Exports of goods and services	336,900	619,400	669,000
Less Imports of goods and services	398,500	894,100	710,100
GDP in purchasers' values	760,100	964,400	1,003,900
GDP at constant 1990 prices	792,800	749,200	755,800

* Provisional figures.

Source: IMF, *Republic of Congo—Statistical Annex* (August 1996).

Gross Domestic Product by Economic Activity

	1993	1994	1995*
Agriculture, hunting, forestry and fishing	85,500	101,300	107,800
Mining and quarrying† } Manufacturing† }	245,400	397,900	410,900
Electricity, gas and water	14,900	14,200	14,800
Construction	8,000	16,800	16,100
Trade, restaurants and hotels	104,300	113,000	119,000
Transport, storage and communication	71,300	76,900	87,300
Government services	133,800	135,000	130,300
Other services	68,200	80,300	78,700
Sub-total	731,400	935,400	964,900
Import duties	28,700	29,000	39,100
GDP in purchasers' values	760,100	964,400	1,003,900

* Provisional figures.

† Includes petroleum sector (million francs CFA): 184,700 in 1993; 322,400 in 1994; 329,400 (provisional figure) in 1995.

Source: IMF, *Republic of Congo—Statistical Annex* (August 1996).

BALANCE OF PAYMENTS (US $ million)

	1994	1995	1996
Exports of goods f.o.b.	968.9	1,174.6	1,487.2
Imports of goods f.o.b.	−612.7	−650.1	−1,424.3
Trade balance	346.2	524.5	62.9
Exports of services	67.0	76.3	96.4
Imports of services	−995.8	−778.3	−708.4
Balance on goods and services	−582.7	−177.5	−549.1
Other income received	2.0	3.0	3.9
Other income paid	−291.1	−401.5	−459.2
Balance on goods, services and income	−871.8	−576.0	−1,004.4
Current transfers received	111.3	40.9	22.9
Current transfers paid	−33.0	−38.3	−52.4
Current balance	−793.4	−573.4	−1,033.9
Investment assets	35.5	−10.4	5.1
Investment liabilities	569.9	−69.9	573.4
Net errors and omissions	33.1	88.7	84.7
Overall balance	−154.9	−565.0	−370.8

Source: IMF, *International Financial Statistics*.

External Trade

Note: Figures exclude trade with other states of the Customs and Economic Union of Central Africa (UDEAC).

PRINCIPAL COMMODITIES (US $ '000)

Imports c.i.f.	1988	1989	1990
Fresh meat etc	14,237	9,643	16,098
Fish and fish preparations	19,927	17,806	18,523
Wheat flour	11,410	12,790	12,819
Chemicals and related products	68,114	57,313	76,867
Medicines	35,050	30,089	42,849
Paper and paperboard products	19,249	13,031	14,068
Iron and steel	41,550	34,335	69,304
General industrial machinery	80,088	66,233	107,873
Electrical machinery	41,610	48,355	39,694
Road vehicles	58,855	85,742	53,984
Precision instruments, watches, etc.	16,520	14,916	22,175
Total (incl. others)	543,693	503,340	594,491

Exports f.o.b.	1988	1989	1990
Petroleum and petroleum products	598,123	747,880	830,173
Sawlogs and veneer logs	83,240	96,598	43,901
Veneer sheets etc	21,424	19,475	23,669
Total (incl. others)*	751,109	908,851	977,670

* Including special transactions and commodities not classified according to kind (US $ 000): 24,409 in 1988; 29,422 in 1989; 51,979 in 1990.

Source: UN, *International Trade Statistics Yearbook.*

Exports of petroleum and petroleum products ('000 million francs CFA): 272.9 in 1993; 454.0 in 1994; 527.9* in 1995.
Exports of wood and wood products ('000 million francs CFA): 26.6 in 1993; 48.6 in 1994; 52.3* in 1995.
Total exports ('000 million francs CFA): 316.8 in 1993; 532.4 in 1994; 624.1* in 1995.

* Provisional figure.

Source: IMF, *Republic of Congo—Statistical Annex* (August 1996).

PRINCIPAL TRADING PARTNERS (US $ '000)

Imports c.i.f.	1988	1989	1990
France (incl. Monaco)	233,510	246,413	218,645
Germany, Fed. Repub.	24,983	35,471	29,066
Italy	39,831	29,247	62,559
Japan	23,157	19,988	23,877
Netherlands	20,169	19,130	27,175
Spain	14,106	6,484	9,419
USA	35,873	27,262	66,152
Total (incl. others)	543,693	503,340	594,491

Exports f.o.b.	1988	1989	1990
France (incl. Monaco)	165,262	175,305	240,506
Italy	33,154	70,128	112,803
Netherlands	79,027	66,474	54,196
Spain	13,525	55,059	23,727
USA	307,186	419,185	354,503
Total (incl. others)	752,000	911,000	976,000

Source: UN, *International Trade Statistics Yearbook.*

Transport

RAILWAYS (traffic)

	1993	1994	1995
Passenger-km (million)	312	227	302
Freight ton-km (million)	259	222	266

Source: mainly IMF, *Republic of Congo—Statistical Annex* (August 1996).

ROAD TRAFFIC (estimates, '000 motor vehicles in use at 31 December)

	1993	1994	1995
Passenger cars	33.4	33.5	36.1
Goods vehicles	15.2	14.5	15.6

Source: IRF, *World Road Statistics.*

SHIPPING
Merchant Fleet (registered at 31 December)

	1994	1995	1996
Number of vessels	23	24	20
Total displacement ('000 grt)	9.2	12.1	6.3

Source: Lloyd's Register of Shipping, *World Fleet Statistics.*

International Sea-borne Freight Traffic ('000 metric tons)

	1988	1989	1990
Goods loaded	9,400	9,295	8,987
Goods unloaded	686	707	736

Source: UN, *Monthly Bulletin of Statistics.*

Inland Waterways (freight traffic, '000 metric tons)

Port of Brazzaville	1985	1986	1987
Goods loaded	77	77	62
Goods unloaded	407	309	331

CIVIL AVIATION (traffic on scheduled services)*

	1992	1993	1994
Kilometres flown (million)	3	3	3
Passengers carried ('000)	229	231	232
Passenger-km (million)	250	256	264
Total ton-km (million)	39	38	40

* Including an apportionment of the traffic of Air Afrique.

Source: UN, *Statistical Yearbook.*

Tourism

	1992	1993	1994
Foreign tourist arrivals	36,072	34,027	30,338
Tourist receipts (US $ million)	7	6	3

Source: UN, *Statistical Yearbook.*

Communications Media

	1992	1993	1994
Radio receivers ('000 in use)	270	280	290
Television receivers ('000 in use)	14	17	18
Telephones ('000 main lines in use)	18	19	21
Telefax stations (number in use)	110	n.a.	n.a.
Daily newspapers	6	n.a.	6

Sources: UNESCO, *Statistical Yearbook*; UN, *Statistical Yearbook.*

Education

(1996)

	Teachers	Pupils
Primary	6,926	489,546
Secondary		
General	5,466	190,409
Vocational	1,746	23,606
Higher*	1,341	16,602

* 1995 figures.

Directory

The Constitution

The 1992 Constitution, which provided for legislative power to be exercised by a directly-elected National Assembly and Senate and for executive power to be held by a directly-elected President, was suspended following the assumption of power by Gen. Denis Sassou-Nguesso on 15 October 1997. A Forum for Unity and National Reconciliation was established in January 1998. Subsequently a National Transitional Council was to be appointed, to act as a legislative body pending the organization of national elections.

The Government

HEAD OF STATE

President: Gen. DENIS SASSOU-NGUESSO (assumed power 15 October 1997; inaugurated 25 October 1997).

COUNCIL OF MINISTERS
(January 1998)

Minister of State for Programming, Privatization and Promotion of National Private Enterprises: PAUL KAYA.

Minister of State for Reconstruction and Urban Development: ITIHI LEKOUNZOU OSSETOUMBA.

Minister of State for Justice and Keeper of the Seals: PIERRE NZE.

Minister of State for Agriculture and Livestock: NKOUA CÉLESTIN GONGARA.

Minister for Labour and Social Security: JEAN-MARTIN M'BEMBA.

Minister for Transport and Civil Aviation in charge of the Merchant Navy: MARTIN M'BERI.

Minister of Territorial and Regional Development: PIERRE MOUSSA.

Minister of Foreign Affairs and Co-operation: RODOLPHE ADADA.

Minister of Youth Redeployment and Sports in charge of Civic Education: CLAUDE-ERNEST NDALLA-GRAILLE.

Minister of Social Amenities and Public Works: Col. FLORENT TSIBA.

Minister of Finance and the Budget: MATHIAS DZON.

Minister of the Interior, Security and Territorial Administration: Col. PIERRE OBA.

Minister of Petroleum Affairs: JEAN-BAPTISTE TATY-LOUTARD.

Minister of Energy and Water Resources: JEAN-MARIE TASSOUA.

Minister of Higher Education and Scientific Research: FRANÇOIS LOUMOUAMOU.

Minister of Culture and the Arts in charge of Francophone Affairs: MAMBOU ELIE NIAMY.

Minister of State Control: GÉRARD BITSINDOU.

Minister of Health and Population: MAMADOU DEKAMO.

Minister of National Solidarity, Disasters and War Victims in charge of Relief Actions: LÉON ALFRED OPIMBA.

Minister of Industry and Mines: MICHEL MAMPOYA.

Minister of Forestry: HENRI DJOMBO.

Minister of Small and Medium-sized Enterprises in charge of Handicrafts: PIERRE DAMIEN BOUSSOUKOU BOUMBA.

Minister of the Civil Service and Administrative Reforms: CHARLES DAMBENZET.

Minister of Tourism and the Environment: NOBERT NGOUA.

Minister of Communications and Spokesman for the Government: FRANÇOIS IBOVI.

Minister of Primary and Secondary Education: PIERRE TSIBA.

Minister for the Organization of the National Forum in charge of Relations with the National Council: FULMIN AYESSA.

Minister of Fishing and Fish Resources: PIERRE GASSAY.

Minister of Trade, Consumer Affairs and Supplies: FÉLIX NGOULOU.

Minister of Family Affairs and Women's Integration in Development: CÉCILE MATINGOU.

Minister of Posts and Telecommunications: JEAN-FÉLIX DEMBA DELO.

Minister of Technical Education and Vocational Training: ANDRÉ OKOMBI SALISSAN.

MINISTRIES

All Ministries are in Brazzaville.

Office of the President: Palais du Peuple, Brazzaville; telex 5210.

Ministry of Education: BP 169, Brazzaville; tel. 83-24-60; telex 5210.

Ministry of Foreign Affairs and Co-operation: BP 2070, Brazzaville; tel. 83-20-28; telex 5210.

Ministry of Health and Population: Palais du Peuple, Brazzaville; tel. 83-29-35; telex 5210.

Ministry of Industry and Mines: Brazzaville; tel. 83-18-27; telex 5210.

Ministry of Programming, Privatization and Promotion of National Private Enterprises: Centre Administratif, Quartier Plateau, BP 2093, Brazzaville; tel. 81-06-20; telex 5210.

President and Legislature

Gen. Denis Sassou-Nguesso assumed power on 15 October 1997, ousting the elected administration of President Pascal Lissouba. Sassou-Ngesso was sworn in as President on 25 October 1997. A Forum for Unity and National Reconciliation was established in January 1998. Subsequently a National Transitional Council was to be appointed to act as a legislative body pending the organization of national elections.

Political Organizations

Espace républicain pour la défense de la démocratie et l'unité nationale (ERDDUN); f. 1997; coalition of political organizations opposed to Pres. SASSOU-NGUESSO.

Forces démocratiques et patriotiques (FDP): Brazzaville; f. 1994 as an alliance of six political parties; Leader Gen. DENIS SASSOU-NGUESSO; Deputy Leader PIERRE NZE.

- **Convention pour l'alternative démocratique:** Leader ALFRED OPIMBA.
- **Parti congolais du travail (PCT):** Brazzaville; telex 5335; f. 1969; sole legal political party 1969–90; Pres. Gen. DENIS SASSOU-NGUESSO; Sec.-Gen. LEON ZOKONI.
- **Parti libéral républicain:** Leader NICÉPHORE FYLA.
- **Union nationale pour la démocratie et le progrès (UNDP):** f. 1990; Leader PIERRE NZE.
- **Union patriotique pour la réconstruction nationale:** Leader MATHIAS DZON.
- **Union pour le renouveau nationale:** Leader GABRIEL BOKILO.

Front uni des républicains congolais (FURC): f. 1994, regd 1995; promotes national development on a non-ethnic and non-regional basis; Chair. RAYMOND TIMOTHÉE MAKITA.

Horizon 2000: Brazzaville; f. 1997; coalition of independent republican parties.

Mouvement africain pour la réconstruction sociale: Leader JEAN ITADI.

Mouvement patriotique du Congo (MPC): Paris, France.

Mouvement pour la réconciliation congolaise: Paris, France; f. 1996; Leader Gen. JEAN-MARIE MICHEL MOKOKO.

Mouvement pour l'unité et la réconstruction: f. 1997 as an alliance of three political parties; mems:

- **Mouvement pour la démocratie et la solidarité (MDS):** Pres. PAUL KAYA.
- **Rassemblement pour la démocratie et le progrès social (RDPS):** Pointe-Noire; f. 1990; Pres. JEAN-PIERRE THYSTÈRE-TCHICAYA; Sec.-Gen. JEAN-FÉLIX DEMBA DELO.
- **Union pour la République (UR):** Brazzaville; f. 1995 by breakaway faction of UPADS; Leader BENJAMIN BOUNKOULOU.

Parti africain des pauvres: f. 1996; Leader ANGÈLE BANDOU.

Parti congolais pour la réconstruction (PCR): Brazzaville.

Parti libéral congolais: f. 1990; Gen. Sec. MARCEL MAKON.

Parti du renouvellement et du progrès: Leader HENRI MARCEL DOUMANGUELE.

Parti social-démocrate congolais (PSDC): f. 1990; Pres. CLÉMENT MIERASSA.

Parti du travail: f. 1991; Leader Dr AUGUSTE MAYANZA.

Parti pour l'unité, le travail et le progrès (PUTP): f. 1995 by defectors from the MCDDI; Leader DIDIER SENGHA.

Programe national de la jeunesse unie: f. 1996; Chair. LUDOVIC MIYOUNA.

Rassemblement pour la démocratie et le développement (RDD): f. 1990; advocates a mixed economy; Chair. SATURNIN OKABE.

Rassemblement démocratique et populaire du Congo: Leader JEAN-MARIE TASSOUA.

Rassemblement pour la République et la démocratie (RRD): f. 1996; Leader Maj.-Gen. RAYMOND DAMASSE NGOLLO.

Union du centre: Leader OKANA MPAN.

Union pour la démocratie congolaise (UDC): f. 1989; advocates economic liberalization; Chair. FÉLIX MAKOSSO.

Union pour la démocratie et la République–Mouinda (UDR—Mouinda): f. 1992; Leader ANDRÉ MILONGO.

Union pour la démocratie et le progrès social (UDPS): f. 1994 by merger of the Union pour le développement et le progrès social and the Parti populaire pour la démocratie sociale et la défense de la République; Leader JEAN-MICHEL BOUKAMBA-YANGOUMA.

Union des forces démocratiques (UFD): Chair. SÉBASTIEN EBAO.

Union panafricaine pour la démocratie sociale (UPADS): Pres. PASCAL LISSOUBA; Sec.-Gen. CHRISTOPHE MOUKOUEKE.

Union patriotique pour la démocratie et le progrès: Sec.-Gen. CÉLESTIN NKOUA.

Union pour le progrès: Pres. JEAN-MARTIN M'BEMBA.

Union pour le progrès du peuple congolais: f. 1991; advocates democracy and national unity; Leader ALPHONSE NBIHOULA.

Union pour le progrès social et la démocratie (UPSD): Brazzaville; f. 1991; Pres. ANGE-EDOUARD POUNGUI.

Union pour le renouveau démocratique (URD): f. 1992 as an alliance of seven political parties; Chair. BERNARD KOLELAS; prin. mems:

Mouvement congolais pour la démocratie et le développement intégral (MCDDI): Brazzaville; f. 1990; mainly Kongo support; Leader BERNARD KOLELAS.

Rassemblement pour la démocratie et le progrès social (RDPS): see under Mouvement pour l'unité et la réconstruction.

Diplomatic Representation

EMBASSIES IN THE CONGO

Algeria: BP 2100, Brazzaville; tel. 83-39-15; telex 5303; Ambassador: MOHAMED NACER ADJALI.

Angola: BP 388, Brazzaville; tel. 81-14-71; telex 5321; Ambassador: JOSÉ AGOSTINHO NETO.

Belgium: BP 225, Brazzaville; tel. 83-29-63; telex 5216; fax 83-71-18; Ambassador: ERNEST STAES.

Cameroon: BP 2136, Brazzaville; tel. 83-34-04; telex 5242; Ambassador: JEAN-HILAIRE MBEA MBEA.

Central African Republic: BP 10, Brazzaville; tel. 83-40-14; Ambassador: CHARLES GUEREBANGBI.

Chad: BP 386, Brazzaville; tel. 81-22-22; Chargé d'affaires a.i.: NEATOBEI BIDI.

China, People's Republic: BP 213, Brazzaville; tel. 83-11-20; Ambassador: YE HONGLIANG.

Congo, Democratic Republic: 130 ave de l'Indépendance, BP 2450, Brazzaville; tel. 83-29-38; Ambassador: (vacant).

Cuba: BP 80, Brazzaville; tel. 81-29-80; telex 5308; Ambassador: JUAN CÉSAR DÍAZ.

Egypt: BP 917, Brazzaville; tel. 83-44-28; telex 5248; Ambassador: MOHAMED ABDEL RAHMAN DIAB.

France: rue Alfassa, BP 2089, Brazzaville; tel. 83-14-23; telex 5239; Ambassador: HERVÉ BELOT.

Gabon: ave Fourneau, BP 2033, Brazzaville; tel. 81-05-90; telex 5225; Ambassador: CONSTANT TSOUMOU.

Germany: place de la Mairie, BP 2022, Brazzaville; tel. 83-29-90; telex 5235; Ambassador: ADOLF EDERER.

Guinea: BP 2477, Brazzaville; tel. 81-24-66; Ambassador: BONATA DIENG.

Holy See: rue Colonel Brisset, BP 1168, Brazzaville; tel. 83-15-46; fax 83-65-39; Apostolic Nuncio: Most Rev. DIEGO CAUSERO, Titular Archbishop of Meta.

Italy: 2-3 blvd Lyauté, BP 2484, Brazzaville; tel. 83-40-47; telex 5251; Ambassador: TIBOR HOOR TEMPIS LIVI.

Korea, Democratic People's Republic: BP 2032, Brazzaville; tel. 83-41-98; Ambassador: HAN BONG CHUN.

Libya: BP 920, Brazzaville; Secretary of People's Bureau: (vacant).

Nigeria: BP 790, Brazzaville; tel. 83-13-16; telex 5263; Ambassador: LAWRENCE OLUFOLAHAN OLADEJO OYELAKIN.

Romania: BP 2413, Brazzaville; tel. 81-32-79; telex 5259; Chargé d'affaires a.i.: DIACONESCO MILCEA.

Russia: BP 2132, Brazzaville; tel. 83-44-39; telex 5455; fax 83-69-17; Ambassador: ANATOLII SAFRONOVICH ZAITSEV.

USA: ave Amílcar Cabral, BP 1015, Brazzaville; tel. 83-20-70; telex 5367; fax 83-63-38; Ambassador: AUBREY HOOKS.

Viet Nam: BP 988, Brazzaville; tel. 83-26-21; Ambassador: BUI VAN THANH.

Judicial System

Supreme Court: Brazzaville; telex 5298; acts as a cour de cassation; Pres. GASTON MAMBOUANA.

Religion

At least one-half of the population follow traditional animist beliefs. Most of the remainder are Christians (mainly Roman Catholics).

CHRISTIANITY

The Roman Catholic Church

The Congo comprises one archdiocese and five dioceses. At 31 December 1995 there were an estimated 1.3m. adherents (about 45% of the total population).

Bishops' Conference: Conférence Episcopale du Congo, BP 200, Brazzaville; tel. 83-06-29; fax 83-79-08; f. 1967; Pres. Rt Rev. BERNARD NSAYI, Bishop of Nkayi.

Archbishop of Brazzaville: Most Rev. BARTHÉLÉMY BATANTU, Archevêché, BP 2301, Brazzaville; tel. and fax 83-17-93.

Protestant Church

Eglise Evangélique du Congo: BP 3205, Bacongo-Brazzaville; tel. 83-43-64; fax 83-77-33; f. 1909; autonomous since 1961; 135,811 mems (1993); Pres. Rev. ALPHONSE MBAMA.

ISLAM

In 1997 an estimated 2% of the population were Muslims. There were 49 mosques in the Congo in 1991.

Comité Islamique du Congo: 77 Makotipoko Moungali, BP 55, Brazzaville; tel. 82-87-45; f. 1988; Leaders HABIBOU SOUMARE, BACHIR GATSONGO, BOUILLA GUIBIDANESI.

The Press

In 1995 legislation was introduced which provided for a five-year term of imprisonment for journalists, printing houses and newspaper distributors convicted of libel, and prohibited media coverage of libel cases, except where permission had previously been granted by the Ministry of Justice. In July 1996 further legislation was approved, requiring all independent newspaper and periodical publishers to obtain a commercial licence. In August the Government issued a decree banning several unlicensed publications.

DAILIES

ACI: BP 2144, Brazzaville; tel. 83-05-91; telex 5285; daily news bulletin publ. by Agence Congolaise d'Information; circ. 1,000.

Aujourd'hui: BP 1171, Brazzaville; tel. and fax 83-77-44; f. 1991; Man. Dir and Chief Editor FYLLA DI FUA DI SASSA.

L'Eveil de Pointe-Noire: BP 66, Pointe-Noire.

Mweti: BP 991, Brazzaville; tel. 81-10-87; national news; Dir MATONGO AVELEY; Chief Editor HUBERT MADOUABA; circ. 7,000.

PERIODICALS

Bakento Ya Congo: BP 309, Brazzaville; tel. 83-27-44; quarterly; Dir MARIE LOUISE MAGANGA; Chief Editor CHARLOTTE BOUSSE; circ. 3,000.

Bulletin Mensuel de la Chambre de Commerce de Brazzaville: BP 92, Brazzaville; monthly.

Bulletin de Statistique: Centre Nationale de la Statistique et des Etudes Economiques, BP 2031, Brazzaville; tel. 83-36-94; f. 1977; quarterly; Dir-Gen. JEAN-PAUL TOTO.

Le Choc: Brazzaville; fortnightly; satirical; Chief Editor: JEAN-BAPTISTE BAKOUVOUKA.

Combattant Rouge: Brazzaville; tel. 83-02-53; monthly; Dir SYLVIO GEORGES ONKA; Chief Editor GILLES OMER BOUSSI.

Congo-Magazine: BP 114, Brazzaville; tel. 83-43-81; monthly; Dir GASPARD MPAN; Chief Editor THÉODORE KIAMOSSI; circ. 3,000.

Effort: BP 64, Brazzaville; monthly.

Etumba: Brazzaville; weekly; circ. 8,000.

Le Forum: Brazzaville.

Le Guardien: Brazzaville.

Jeunesse et Révolution: BP 885, Brazzaville; tel. 83-44-13; weekly; Dir JEAN-ENOCH GOMA-KENGUE; Chief Editor PIERRE MAKITA.

Le Madukutsekele: Brazzaville; f. 1991; weekly; satirical; Editor MATHIEU BAKIMA-BALIELE; circ. 5,000.

Le Pays: f. 1991; weekly; Dir ANTOINE MALONGA.

La Rue Meurt: Brazzaville.

La Semaine: Brazzaville; weekly; circ. 7,000.

La Semaine Africaine: BP 2080, Brazzaville; tel. 81-03-28; f. 1952; weekly; general information and social action; circulates widely in francophone equatorial Africa; Dir JEAN-PIERRE GALLET; Chief Editor JOACHIM MBANZA; circ. 6,500.

Le Soleil: f. 1991; weekly; organ of the Rassemblement pour la démocratie et le développement.

Le Stade: BP 114, Brazzaville; tel. 81-47-18; telex 5285; f. 1985; weekly; sports; Dir HUBERT-TRÉSOR MADOUABA-NTOUALANI; Chief Editor LELAS PAUL NZOLANI; circ. 6,500.

Voix de la Classe Ouvrière (Voco): BP 2311, Brazzaville; tel. 83-36-66; six a year; Dir MICHEL JOSEPH MAYOUNGOU; Chief Editor MARIE-JOSEPH TSENGOU; circ. 4,500.

NEWS AGENCIES

Agence Congolaise d'Information (ACI): BP 2144, Brazzaville; tel. 83-46-76; telex 5285; f. 1961; Dir RIGOBERT DOUNIAMA-ETOUA.

Foreign Bureaux

Agence France-Presse (AFP): c/o Agence Congolaise d'Information, BP 2144, Brazzaville; tel. 83-46-76; telex 5285; Correspondent JOSEPH GOUALA.

Associated Press (AP) (USA): BP 2144, Brazzaville; telex 5477; Correspondent ARMAND BERNARD MASSAMBA.

Informatsionnoye Telegrafnoye Agentstvo Rossii—Telegrafnoye Agentstvo Suverennykh Stran (ITAR—TASS) (Russia): BP 379, Brazzaville; tel. 83-44-33; telex 5203; Correspondent MAKSIM Y. KORSHUNOV.

Inter Press Service (IPS) (Italy): POB 964, Brazzaville; tel. 810565; telex 5285.

Pan-African News Agency (PANA) (Senegal): BP 2144, Brazzaville; tel. 83-11-40; telex 5285; fax 83-70-15.

Reuters (United Kingdom): BP 2144, Brazzaville; telex 5477; Correspondent ANTOINE MOUYAMBALA.

Rossiyskoye Informatsionnoye Agentstvo—Novosti (RIA—Novosti) (Russia): BP 170, Brazzaville; tel. 83-43-44; telex 5227; Bureau Chief DMITRII AMVROSIEV.

Xinhua (New China) News Agency (People's Republic of China): 40 ave Maréchal Lyauté, BP 373, Brazzaville; tel. 83-44-01; telex 5230; Chief Correspondent XU ZHENQIANG.

Publishers

Imprimerie Centrale d'Afrique (ICA): BP 162, Pointe-Noire; f. 1949; Man. Dir M. SCHNEIDER.

Société Congolaise Hachette: Brazzaville; telex 5291; general fiction, literature, education, juvenile, textbooks.

Government Publishing House

Imprimerie Nationale: BP 58, Brazzaville; Man. KIALA MATOUBA.

Broadcasting and Communications

TELECOMMUNICATIONS

Office National des Postes et Telecommunications (ONPT): Brazzaville; operates national telecommunications network; mobile cellular telephone system introduced in 1996.

RADIO AND TELEVISION

Canal Liberté: Brazzaville; f. 1997 by supporters of Sassou-Nguesso.

Radio Congo Liberté: Brazzaville; f. 1997; operated by supporters of Sassou-Nguesso.

Radiodiffusion-Télévision Congolaise: BP 2241, Brazzaville; tel. 81-24-73; telex 5299; Dir JEAN-FRANÇOIS SYLVESTRE SOUKA.

Radio Nationale Congolaise: BP 2241, Brazzaville; tel. 83-03-83; radio programmes in French, Lingala, Kikongo, Subia, English and Portuguese; transmitters at Brazzaville and Pointe-Noire; Dir of Broadcasting THÉOPHILE MIETE LIKIBI.

Télévision Nationale Congolaise: BP 2241, Brazzaville; tel. 81-51-52; began transmission in 1963; operates for 46 hours per week, with most programmes in French but some in Lingala and Kikongo; Dir JEAN-GILBERT FOUTOU.

Finance

(cap. = capital; res = reserves; m. = million; dep. = deposits; br. = branch;amounts in francs CFA)

BANKING

Central Bank

Banque des Etats de l'Afrique Centrale (BEAC): BP 126, Brazzaville; tel. 83-28-14; telex 5200; fax 83-63-42; headquarters in Yaoundé, Cameroon; f. 1973 as the central bank of issue for mem. states of the Customs and Economic Union of Central Africa (UDEAC), comprising Cameroon, the Central African Republic, Chad, the Republic of the Congo, Equatorial Guinea and Gabon; cap. and res 209,766m. (April 1997); Gov. JEAN-FÉLIX MAMALEPOT; Dir in Repub. of Congo ANGE-EDOUARD POUNGUI; br. at Pointe-Noire.

Commercial Banks

Banque Internationale du Congo (BIDC): ave Amílcar Cabral, BP 33, Brazzaville; tel. 83-03-08; telex 5339; fax 83-53-82; f. 1983; 62% state-owned; privatization pending in 1997; cap. and res 2,454.8m., dep. 37,301.8m. (Dec. 1992); Pres. and Chair. EDOUARD EBOUKA BABACKAS; Gen. Man. FRANÇOIS BITA; 1 br.

Crédit Rural du Congo: BP 2889, Brazzaville; tel. 83-53-50; telex 5532; fax 83-53-52; 50% state-owned; Chair. EDOUARD EBOUKA BABACKAS; Man. Dir DELPHINE MBOUNGOU.

Financial Bank Congo: BP 602, Pointe-Noire; tel. and fax 94-16-30; f. 1994; cap. 1,110m. (1994); Dir-Gen. JEAN-LOUIS CHAPUIS.

Union Congolaise de Banques SA (UCB): ave Amílcar Cabral, BP 147, Brazzaville; tel. 83-30-00; telex 5206; fax 83-68-45; f. 1974; state-owned, privatization pending; cap. and res 3,212.1m. (Dec. 1995); Pres. JOSEPH KOMBO KINTOMBO; Man. Dir GUY VALERO; 8 brs.

Co-operative Banking Institution

Mutuelles Congolaises de l'Epargne et du Crédit: Brazzaville; f. 1994; Dir. SERGE BAGETA.

Development Bank

Banque de Développement des États de l'Afrique Centrale: (see Franc Zone, p. 182).

Financial Institution

Caisse Congolaise d'Amortissement: 410 allée du Chaillu, BP 2090, Brazzaville; tel. 83-32-41; telex 5294; fax 83-63-42; f. 1971; management of state funds; Dir-Gen. EMMANUEL NGONO.

INSURANCE

Assurances et Réassurances du Congo (ARC): ave Amílcar Cabral, BP 977, Brazzaville; tel. 83-01-71; telex 5236; f. 1973 to acquire the businesses of all insurance cos operating in the Congo; 50% state-owned; Dir-Gen. RAYMOND IBATA; brs at Pointe-Noire, Loubomo and Ouesso.

Trade and Industry

DEVELOPMENT ORGANIZATIONS

Caisse Française de Développement: BP 96, Brazzaville; tel. 83-15-95; telex 5202; French fund for economic co-operation; Dir JACQUES BENIER.

Mission Française de Coopération: BP 2175, Brazzaville; tel. 83-15-03; f. 1959; administers bilateral aid from France; Dir JEAN-BERNARD THIANT.

Office des Cultures Vivrières (OCV): BP 894, Brazzaville; tel. 82-11-03; f. 1979; state-owned; food-crop development; Dir-Gen. GILBERT PANA.

Société Nationale d'Elevage (SONEL): BP 81, Loutété, Massangui; f. 1964; development of semi-intensive stock-rearing; exploitation of by-products; Man. Dir THÉOPHILE BIKAWA.

CHAMBERS OF COMMERCE

Chambre de Commerce, d'Agriculture et d'Industrie de Brazzaville: BP 92, Brazzaville; tel. 83-21-15; Pres. MAURICE OGNAOY; Sec.-Gen. FRANÇOIS DILOU-YOULOU.

Chambre de Commerce, d'Agriculture et d'Industrie de Loubomo: BP 78, Loubomo.

Chambre de Commerce, d'Industrie et d'Agriculture et des Métiers de Pointe-Noire: 8 ave Charles de Gaulle, BP 665, Pointe-Noire; tel. 94-12-80; fax 94-07-13; f. 1948; Chair. NARCISSE POATY PACKA; Sec.-Gen. JEAN-BAPTISTE SOUMBOU.

INDUSTRIAL AND TRADE ASSOCIATIONS

Office du Café et du Cacao (OCC): BP 2488, Brazzaville; tel. 83-19-03; telex 5273; f. 1978; marketing and export of coffee and cocoa; Man. Dir PAUL YORA.

Office Congolais des Bois (OCB): 2 ave Moe Vangoula, BP 1229, Pointe-Noire; tel. 94-22-38; telex 8248; f. 1974; purchase and marketing of timber products; Man. Dir ALEXANDRE DENGUET-ATTIKI.

Office National de Commercialisation des Produits Agricoles (ONCPA): Brazzaville; tel. 83-24-01; telex 5273; f. 1964; marketing of all agricultural products except sugar; promotion of rural co-operatives; Dir JEAN-PAUL BOCKONDAS.

Office National du Commerce (OFNACOM): BP 2305, Brazzaville; tel. 83-43-99; telex 5309; f. 1964; importer and distributor of general merchandise; monopoly importer of salted and dried fish, cooking salt, rice, tomato purée, buckets, enamelled goods and blankets; Dir-Gen. VALENTIN ENOUSSA NCONGO.

EMPLOYERS' ORGANIZATION

Union Patronale et Interprofessionnelle du Congo (UNICONGO): BP 42, Brazzaville; tel. 83-33-73; fax 83-68-16; f. 1960; employers' asscn; Pres. E. HANNA; Sec.-Gen. J. FUMEY.

UTILITIES

Electricity

Société Nationale d'Electricité: Brazzaville; f. 1967; state-owned, transfer to private ownership pending; operates hydroelectric plants at Bouenza and Djoué; total generating capacity of 149 MW (1990).

Water

Société Nationale de Distribution d'Eau (SNDE): rue du Sergent Malamine, BP 229 and 365, Brazzaville; tel. 83-73-26; telex 5272; fax 83-38-91; f. 1967; proposals for transfer to private-sector ownership pending; water supply and sewerage; holds monopoly over wells and import of mineral water; Chair. and Man. Dir S. MPINOU.

TRADE UNIONS

Independent trade unions were legalized in 1991.

Confédération Générale des Travailleurs du Congo (CGTC): Brazzaville; f. 1995; Chair. PAUL DOUNA.

Confédération Nationale des Syndicats Libres (CNASYL): Brazzaville; f. 1994; Sec.-Gen. MICHEL KABOUL MAOUTA.

Confédération Syndicale Congolaise (CSC): BP 2311, Brazzaville; tel. 83-19-23; telex 5304; f. 1964; 80,000 mems.

Confédération Syndicale des Travailleurs Congolais (CSTC): Brazzaville; f. 1993; fed. of 13 trade unions; Chair. DAMAS KIKONI; Sec.-Gen. LOUIS GOUNDOU; 40,000 mems.

Confédération des Syndicats Libres et Autonomes du Congo (COSYLAC): Brazzaville; Pres. RENÉ BLANCHARD SERGE OBA.

Transport

Agence Transcongolaise des Communications (ATC): BP 711, Pointe-Noire; tel. 94-15-32; telex 8345; f. 1969; transfer to private-sector ownership pending; three divisions: Congo-Océan Railways, inland waterways and Brazzaville inland port, and the Atlantic port of Pointe-Noire; Man. Dir Col JEAN-FÉLIX ONGOUYA.

RAILWAYS

There are 515 km of track from Brazzaville to Pointe-Noire. A 286-km section of privately-owned line links the manganese mines at Moanda (in Gabon), via a cableway to the border with the Republic of the Congo at M'Binda, with the main line to Pointe-Noire. Rail traffic was severely disrupted by the 1997 civil war.

ATC—Chemin de Fer Congo-Océan (CFCO): BP 651, Pointe-Noire; tel. 94-11-84; telex 8231; fax 94-12-30; transfer to private ownership pending; Dir DÉSIRÉ GOMA.

INLAND WATERWAYS

The Congo and Oubangui rivers form two axes of a highly developed inland waterway system. The Congo river and seven tributaries in the Congo basin provide 2,300 km of navigable river, and the Oubangui river, developed in co-operation with the Central African Republic, an additional 2,085 km.

ATC—Direction des Voies Navigables, Ports et Transports Fluviaux: BP 2048, Brazzaville; tel. 83-06-27; waterways authority; Dir MÉDARD OKOUMOU.

Compagnie Congolaise de Transports: BP 37, Loubomo; f. 1960; Pres. and Dir-Gen. ROBERT BARBIER.

Société Congolaise de Transports (SOCOTRANS): BP 617, Pointe-Noire; tel. 94-23-31; f. 1977; Man YVES CRIQUET.

Transcap-Congo: BP 1154, Pointe-Noire; tel. 94-01-46; telex 8218; f. 1962; Chair. J. DROUAULT.

SHIPPING

The deep-water Atlantic seaport at Pointe-Noire is the main port, and Brazzaville is the principal port on the Congo river. A major expansion programme, undertaken during the 1980s, aimed to establish Brazzaville port as a container traffic centre for several central African countries. In 1989 Congolese seaports handled 10m. metric tons of goods for international transport.

ATC—Direction du Port de Brazzaville: BP 2048, Brazzaville; tel. 83-00-42; port authority; Dir JEAN-PAUL BOCKONDAS.

ATC—Direction du Port de Pointe-Noire: BP 711, Pointe-Noire; tel. 94-00-52; telex 8318; fax 94-20-42; port authority; Dir DOMINIQUE BEMBA.

La Congolaise de Transport Maritime (COTRAM): f. 1984; national shipping co; state-owned.

ROADS

In 1995 there were an estimated 12,760 km of roads and tracks, including 3,430 km of main roads and 4,140 km of secondary roads. Only about 9.7% of the total network was paved. The principal routes link Brazzaville with Pointe-Noire, in the south, and with Ouesso, in the north.

Régie Nationale des Transports et des Travaux Publics: BP 2073, Brazzaville; tel. 83-35-58; f. 1965; civil engineering, maintenance of roads and public works; Man. Dir HECTOR BIENVENU OUAMBA.

CIVIL AVIATION

There are international airports at Brazzaville (Maya-Maya) and Pointe-Noire (Agostinho Neto). There are airports at six regional capitals, as well as 37 smaller airfields. In 1994 the state monopoly on internal flights was terminated.

Air Afrique: BP 1126, Pointe-Noire; tel. 94-17-00; telex 8342; see under Côte d'Ivoire; Dir at Pointe-Noire GUY C. CODIJA; Dir at Brazzaville AHMED LAMINE-ALI.

Congo-Aviation: Brazzaville; f. 1994.

Lina Congo (Lignes Nationales Aériennes Congolaises): ave Amílcar Cabral, BP 2203, Brazzaville; tel. 81-30-65; telex 5243; fax 82-80-34; f. 1965; 33% state-owned; operates an extensive internal network; Man. Dir JEAN-JACQUES ONTSA-ONTSA.

Trans Air Congo: Brazzaville; f. 1994; private airline operating internal flights.

Tourism

The tourism sector has been severely disrupted by political instability and violent unrest during the 1990s. Tourist visitors numbered 30,338 in 1994, when earnings from the sector were estimated at US $3m. (compared with tourist arrivals of 36,072 and estimated earnings of $7m. in 1992).

Direction Générale du Tourisme et des Loisirs: BP 456, Brazzaville; tel. 83-09-53; telex 5210; f. 1980; Dir-Gen. ANTOINE KOUNKOU-KIBOUILOU.

COSTA RICA

Introductory Survey

Location, Climate, Language, Religion, Flag, Capital

The Republic of Costa Rica lies in the Central American isthmus, with Nicaragua to the north, Panama to the south, the Caribbean Sea to the east and the Pacific Ocean to the west. The climate is warm and damp in the lowlands (average temperature 27°C (81°F)) and cooler on the Central Plateau (average temperature 22°C (72°F)), where two-thirds of the population live. The language spoken is Spanish. Almost all of the inhabitants profess Christianity, and the majority adhere to the Roman Catholic Church, the state religion. The national flag (proportions 5 by 3) has five horizontal stripes, of blue, white, red, white and blue, the red stripe being twice the width of the others. The state flag, in addition, has on the red stripe (to the left of centre) a white oval enclosing the national coat of arms, showing three volcanic peaks between the Caribbean and the Pacific. The capital is San José.

Recent History

Costa Rica was ruled by Spain from the 16th century until 1821, when independence was declared. The only significant interruption in the country's constitutional government since 1920 occurred in February 1948, when the result of the presidential election was disputed. The legislature annulled the election in March but a civil war ensued. The anti-Government forces, led by José Figueres Ferrer, were successful, and a revolutionary junta took power in April. Costa Rica's army was abolished in December. After the preparation of a new Constitution, the victorious candidate of the 1948 presidential election took office in January 1949.

Figueres, who founded the socialist Partido de Liberación Nacional (PLN), dominated national politics for decades, holding presidential office in 1953–58 and 1970–74. Under his leadership, Costa Rica became one of the most democratic countries in Latin America. Since the 1948 revolution, there have been frequent changes of power, all achieved by constitutional means. Figueres's first Government nationalized the banks and instituted a comprehensive social security system. The presidential election of 1958, however, was won by a conservative, Mario Echandi Jiménez, who reversed many PLN policies. His successor, Francisco Orlich Bolmarich (President from 1962 to 1966), was supported by the PLN but continued the encouragement of private enterprise. Another conservative, José Joaquín Trejos Fernández, held power in 1966–70. In 1974 the PLN candidate, Daniel Oduber Quirós, was elected President. He continued the policies of extending the welfare state and of establishing friendly relations with communist states. Communist and other left-wing parties were legalized in 1975. In 1978 Rodrigo Carazo Odio of the conservative Partido Unidad Opositora (PUO) coalition (subsequently the Coalición Unidad) was elected President. During Carazo's term of office increasing instability in Central America led to diplomatic tension, and in 1981 the President was criticized for his alleged involvement in illegal arms-trafficking between Cuba and El Salvador.

At presidential and legislative elections in February 1982, Luis Alberto Monge Alvarez of the PLN gained a comfortable majority when his party won 33 of the 57 seats in the Legislative Assembly. Following his inauguration in May, President Monge announced a series of emergency economic measures, in an attempt to rescue the country from near-bankruptcy. A policy of neutrality towards the left-wing Sandinista Government of Nicaragua was continued. However, following a number of cross-border raids, a national alert was declared in May. The rebel Nicaraguan leader, Edén Pastora Gómez, was expelled so as to reduce Costa Rican involvement in the Nicaraguan conflict. Relations with Nicaragua deteriorated as guerrilla activity spread to San José.

Throughout 1983 President Monge came under increasing pressure from liberal members of the Cabinet and PLN supporters to adopt a more neutral stance in foreign policy. Three leading members of the anti-Sandinista (Contra) movement were expelled from Costa Rica in May, and 80 of Pastora's supporters were arrested in September. In addition, some 82 guerrilla camps were dismantled by the Civil Guard. In November 1983 President Monge declared Costa Rica's neutrality in an attempt to elicit foreign support for his country. This declaration was opposed by the USA and led to the resignation of the Costa Rican Minister of Foreign Affairs.

In early 1984 there were increasing reports of incursions into Costa Rica by the Sandinista forces. Public opposition to any renunciation of neutrality was emphasized by a demonstration in support of peace and neutrality, held in San José and attended by over 20,000 people. An attempt was made to defuse the tense situation with the establishment of a commission, supported by the Contadora group (Colombia, Mexico, Panama and Venezuela), to monitor events in the border area. In late May, however, the attempt to assassinate Edén Pastora Gómez near the Costa Rican border exacerbated the rift within the Cabinet concerning government policy towards Nicaragua.

Relations with Nicaragua deteriorated further in December 1984, following an incident involving a Nicaraguan refugee at the Costa Rican embassy in Managua. Subsequently, diplomatic relations were reduced to a minimal level. Reports of clashes between Costa Rican Civil Guardsmen and Sandinista forces along the joint border became increasingly frequent. In 1985 the Government's commitment to neutrality was disputed when it decided to establish an anti-guerrilla battalion, trained by US military advisers.

During 1983 there were signs of increasing urban unrest in response to the Government's austerity measures and to the agrarian crisis, which had produced high levels of unemployment, principally among workers on banana plantations. By August 1984 the Government's position was regarded as unstable. The division within the Cabinet over policy towards Nicaragua, coupled with the effects of the unpopular austerity programme and a protracted strike by banana plantation workers, which had resulted in two deaths, led to fears of a coup. At President Monge's request, the Cabinet resigned, and in the subsequent reshuffle four ministers were replaced.

At presidential and legislative elections in February 1986, Oscar Arias Sánchez, the candidate of the PLN, was elected President, with 52% of the votes cast. The PLN also obtained a clear majority in the Legislative Assembly. The new Government was committed to the development of a welfare state, whereby 25,000 new jobs and 20,000 new dwellings were to be created each year. In addition, the Government planned to renegotiate the country's external debt and to reach agreement on a social pact with the trade unions. Furthermore, President Arias was resolved to maintain and reinforce Costa Rica's policy of neutrality, a decision which was expected to antagonize the US administration.

In February 1986 diplomatic relations with Nicaragua were fully restored, and it was decided to establish a permanent inspection and vigilance commission at the common border. In accordance with the Government's pledge to protect neutrality, Costa Rica objected to the allocation of US $100m. in US aid to the Contra forces in mid-1986. In addition, the Government embarked on a series of arrests and expulsions of Contras resident in Costa Rica. A degree of Costa Rican complicity in anti-Sandinista activity became apparent, however, in 1986, when the existence of a secret airstrip in Costa Rica, which was used as a supply base for the Contras, was made public. The airstrip had been constructed by the USA during President Monge's administration but had been closed on President Arias's accession to power.

Throughout 1986 and 1987 President Arias became increasingly involved in the quest for peace in Central America. In August 1987 the Presidents of El Salvador, Nicaragua, Guatemala, Honduras and Costa Rica signed a peace agreement based on proposals presented by President Arias, who was subsequently awarded the Nobel Peace Prize.

In January 1988 President Arias brought Nicaraguan government officials and Contra leaders together in San José for their first discussions concerning the implementation of a cease-fire. Prior to this meeting, President Arias ordered three Contra leaders to leave Costa Rica or cease their military activities. President Arias maintained his independent position by supporting discussions between the Contras and Sandinistas, held in Nicaragua in March, and by condemning any continuation of aid to the Contras. In November a border agreement was signed with Nicaragua.

In 1988 there were renewed indications of internal unrest as a result of the Government's economic policies. In March there were two one-day stoppages by public employees, to protest against concessions made to the IMF and the World Bank. In June UNSA, the co-ordinating organization for agricultural unions, proposed a week-long protest against the Government's agricultural policies. In August there were strikes by farmers who were aggrieved at the Government's 'Agriculture for Change' policy of promoting the cultivation of cash crops, and thereby sacrificing the interests of many smallholders, to appease the IMF. The Government established a commission to consider the farmers' complaints.

During 1989 there was increased labour unrest throughout the country. In September the Minister of Finance resigned, as his efforts to impose stringent austerity measures were being undermined by the increase in the budgetary deficit. He also opposed the Government's plan to reduce a tax on coffee production, claiming that the resultant increase in the government deficit might jeopardize agreements with the IMF.

In September 1989 the Legislative Assembly's commission of enquiry into the extent of drug-trafficking and related activities published its findings. As a result, a number of public figures were asked to resign. Among these were the former President (then a senior PLN official), Daniel Oduber Quirós, a PLN deputy, Leonel Villalobos, the general manager of a leading bank and the head of the Civil Aviation Authority.

At presidential and legislative elections in February 1990, Rafael Angel Calderón Fournier, the candidate of the Partido Unidad Social Cristiana (PUSC), was elected President, with 51.3% of the votes cast. The PUSC obtained a clear majority in the Legislative Assembly, with 29 seats. It was widely believed that the decline in public support for the PLN was partly a result of the party's involvement in the drug scandal in the previous year. On assuming office in May, President Calderón inherited a fiscal deficit of US $150m. and was therefore forced to renege on his pre-election promise of improvements in welfare and income distribution. In an attempt to reduce the deficit, the Government introduced an adjustment programme of austerity measures, which included a rise in the price of fuel by 30% and of many goods and services by as much as 20%, and proposed tax increases. In early October 70,000–100,000 public- and private-sector employees participated in a one-day national strike to protest against the Government's economic policies. On 30 October the Minister of Labour, Erick Thompson Piñeres, resigned, stating that his decision to do so reflected the rift between 'economic and social groups' within the Cabinet. Thompson was associated with a group of ministers (reportedly led by the First Vice-President, Germán Serrano) who were critical of the Government's structural adjustment policies.

In August 1991 the Minister of Public Security, Víctor Emilio Herrera Alfaro, and the Minister of National Planning and Economic Policy, Dr Helio Fallas, resigned, following disagreements with President Calderón. The Minister of the Interior and Police, Luis Fishman, was subsequently appointed acting Minister of Public Security. The Civil Guard and the Rural Guard (which had previously been responsible to the Ministry of Public Security and the Ministry of the Interior and Police, respectively) therefore came under the sole charge of Fishman. Opposition groups expressed concern at this concentration of power, in view of the continuing decline in popular support for President Calderón and the level of public unrest. In November, in response to pressure from student and public-sector unions, President Calderón abandoned austerity measures involving a reduction in the education budget and the dismissal of thousands of public employees. This decision prompted the resignation of the Minister of Finance, Thelmo Vargas, who claimed that the President's action would make it impossible to curb the rapidly increasing fiscal deficit and thus attain IMF-agreed targets.

In January 1992 President Calderón was summoned before the Legislative Assembly's commission on drug-trafficking to answer allegations that the PUSC had been the recipient of the proceeds of illegal drug-trafficking during its election campaign in 1990. Calderón denied any knowledge of such payments. Following the decision made by the Government in March 1992 to remove foreign exchange controls, there was mounting concern that Costa Rican banking institutions were being increasingly used for the purposes of 'laundering' money obtained from illegal drug-trafficking.

In March 1993 some 25 people, including the Nicaraguan Ambassador to Costa Rica, were taken hostage at the Nicaraguan embassy in San José by three armed men whose demands included the dismissals of the head of the Nicaraguan armed forces, Gen. Humberto Ortega Saavedra, and the Nicaraguan President's chief adviser, Antonio Lacayo Oyanguren. The hostages were later released unharmed in return for a ransom and safe passage out of the country. A similar incident, which took place in April and involved members of the Supreme Court being taken hostage, served to heighten concern about the security situation in Costa Rica.

In July 1993 the Minister of Finance, Rodolfo Méndez Mata, resigned from his post and was replaced by his deputy, Carlos Muñoz. In the same month trade unions organized consecutive strikes in support of demands for wage increases and in protest at government austerity policies.

Presidential and legislative elections were held in February 1994. José María Figueres Olsen, the candidate presented by the PLN, secured 49.6% of the votes cast in the presidential poll, thus obtaining a narrow victory over the candidate of the PUSC, Miguel Angel Rodríguez Echeverría, who received 47.6% of the votes. The PLN failed to obtain an outright majority in the Legislative Assembly securing only 28 of the 57 seats, while the PUSC won 25 seats and the Fuerza Democrática gained two seats. The remaining two seats were won by independent candidates. Figueres assumed office in early May.

In May 1994 industrial action by employees of the Geest banana company resulted in violent clashes with the security forces. The strike was organized in protest at the dismissal of some 400 workers for attempting to join a union. The dispute, which was resolved following government intervention, came in the wake of allegations by a US trade union body, the American Federation of Labor and Congress of Industrial Organizations, of violations of labour rights in Costa Rica. In late 1993 the Costa Rican authorities avoided an investigation into the country's labour practices by the US trade representative office and the possible loss of trading benefits enjoyed under the Generalized System of Preferences by introducing legislation reforming the labour code.

In mid-1994 a multi-party commission of the Legislative Assembly was appointed to consider proposals for the reform of the electoral system. Draft legislation for the reform, including provision for the extension of the presidential and legislative terms from four to five years, was approved by the legislature in March 1995. (However, following a second reading of the legislation in 1997, only minor changes to the electoral system were adopted, and the presidential and legislative terms remained unchanged.) Consecutive ministerial reshuffles in March 1995, aimed in part at rationalizing the administration in order to reduce public expenditure, included the disbanding of the ministries of Rural Development and Sustainable Development.

In July 1995 some 50,000 teachers began strike action in protest at proposed reforms to the state pension system. Growing dissatisfaction among other public-sector employees at Government economic policy, in particular proposals for the deregulation and privatization of state enterprises, resulted in an escalation of the unrest, which culminated, in August, in a 100,000-strong demonstration in the capital. Following the protest, the Government reached an accord with the teachers, under which it agreed to establish a commission, to include representatives of the teachers' unions, to debate the proposed reform of the pension system and to review certain other of the Government's economic policies.

In early 1995 relations with Nicaragua became strained, following a series of incidents concerning immigration and the policing of the countries' joint border. In February the Nicaraguan Government issued a formal protest at the allegedly violent manner in which a group of illegal Nicaraguan immigrants had been expelled from Costa Rica. A recent tightening of immigration policy in Costa Rica had led to the automatic expulsion of illegal immigrants who had previously been tolerated (providing, as they did, a source of cheap labour for agriculture and the construction industry). The change in government policy had been prompted by the excessive burden placed on Costa Rica's social services by a recent rapid increase in immigrant arrivals, and by a downturn in the country's economy. In 1997 the Costa Rican Government estimated the number of Nicaraguan immigrants living in the country at about 420,000, most of whom were residing illegally. According to official Nicaraguan figures, as many as 30,180 Nicaraguans were expelled from Costa Rica in the first half of 1997.

In January 1996, in an incident that had serious repercussions for the country's important tourism sector, two European women, one a resident and the other a tourist, were abducted from a hotel in San Carlos in northern Costa Rica, close to the border with Nicaragua. An insurgent group, the Viviana Gallardo Commando, claimed responsibility for the abduction and reportedly demanded a ransom of US $1m. The women were released unharmed in March. In July, in what was widely interpreted as an attempt to bolster his Government's flagging popularity, Figueres conducted a reorganization of the Cabinet. In November Bernardo Arce resigned from his position as Minister of Security, following an investigation by the Comptroller General's Office into allegations that he had been involved in corrupt practices. He was replaced by Laura Chinchilla.

Presidential and legislative elections were held in February 1998. Miguel Angel Rodríguez Echeverría, the candidate of the PUSC, received 46.9% of the votes cast in the presidential contest, thus securing a narrow victory over the candidate of the PLN, José Miguel Corrales Bolaños, who obtained 44.4% of the votes. The PUSC failed to obtain an outright majority in the legislature, securing only 27 of the 57 seats, while the PLN won 23, the Fuerza Democrática (FD) obtained three, the Partido Movimiento Libertario (PML) won two, and the Partido Integración Nacional (PIN) and the Partido Acción Laborista Agrícola (PALA) each secured one seat. Rodríguez, who was to take office on 1 May, announced that he would seek to form a 'government of national unity'.

In February 1989 the Presidents of Costa Rica, El Salvador, Guatemala, Honduras and Nicaragua met and agreed to draft a plan to remove the Contra forces from base camps in Honduras, in exchange for the introduction of political reforms and the holding of free elections in Nicaragua. The plan was ratified at a second summit meeting, held in August in Honduras, with the signing of the Tela Agreement. Peace proposals for El Salvador and Guatemala were also elaborated, as was an agreement on co-operation in the campaign against the trafficking and use of illicit drugs. In November, however, the conflicts in Nicaragua and El Salvador intensified. In December the deadline for the disbanding of Contra forces, agreed at Tela, passed unfulfilled, and the Presidents of the five Central American countries, meeting in Costa Rica, agreed on measures to revive the regional peace process. In February 1990, after being defeated in elections, Nicaragua's Sandinista Government decreed an immediate cease-fire. The Contras accepted this, and a cease-fire agreement was concluded in April.

The first inter-American summit meeting for 22 years, which was attended by 17 heads of state, was held in San José in October 1989, to celebrate a centenary of democracy in Costa Rica. In April 1990 an extradition treaty between Costa Rica and the USA was approved by the Legislative Assembly. The treaty, which does not apply to Costa Rican citizens, was aimed at combating crime, particularly international drug-trafficking.

Government

Under the Constitution of 1949, executive power is vested in the President, assisted by two Vice-Presidents (or, in exceptional circumstances, one Vice-President) and an appointed Cabinet. The President is elected for a four-year term by compulsory adult suffrage, and a successful candidate must receive at least 40% of the votes. The legislative organ is the unicameral Asamblea Legislativa (Legislative Assembly), with 57 members who are similarly elected for four years.

Defence

There have been no Costa Rican armed forces since 1948. In August 1997 Rural and Civil Guards totalled 2,000 and 3,000 men, respectively. In addition, there were 2,000 Border Security Police. In 1985 an anti-terrorist battalion was formed, composed of 750 Civil Guards; in 1994 it was superseded by the Immediate Action Unit. Expenditure on the security forces was budgeted at 5,800m. colones in 1997.

Economic Affairs

In 1995, according to estimates by the World Bank, Costa Rica's gross national product (GNP), measured at average 1993–95 prices, was US $8,884m., equivalent to $2,610 per head. During 1985–95, it was estimated, GNP per head increased, in real terms, at an average annual rate of 2.9%. Over the same period, the population increased by an annual average of 2.5%. Costa Rica's gross domestic product (GDP), at purchasers' values, increased, in real terms, by an annual average of 4.6% in 1985–95. Real GDP declined by 0.7% in 1996.

Agriculture (including forestry and fishing) contributed 17.3% of GDP in 1995 and employed an estimated 21.6% of the economically active population in 1996. The principal cash crops are bananas (which accounted for an estimated 22.4% of export earnings in 1996), coffee (13.4% of export earnings), flowers and tropical fruit. Seafood and meat exports were also significant. Sugar cane, rice, maize and beans are also cultivated. Agricultural GDP increased by an annual average of 4.3% during 1985–95, but declined by an estimated 0.6% in 1996.

Industry (including mining, manufacturing, construction and power) employed 24.1% of the economically active population and provided 24.4% of GDP in 1995. Industrial GDP increased by an annual average rate of 4.5% during 1985–95, but declined by an estimated 4.1% in 1996. Mining and manufacturing employed 16.7% of the economically active population and contributed 18.8% of GDP in 1995. The mining sector employed only 0.2% of the economically active population in 1995. In terms of the value of output, the principal branches of manufacturing in 1994, according to provisional figures, were food products (37.5%), chemical products (13.0%), beverages (8.3%) and electrical machinery (7.0%).

Energy is derived principally from petroleum and hydroelectric power. By the late 1980s hydroelectric power provided 20% of commercial energy consumption. The Arenal hydroelectricity project was inaugurated in 1979, and, at its full generating capacity of 1,974 MW, was expected to fulfil Costa Rica's entire electricity requirements. Imports of fuels and lubricants accounted for an estimated 6.5% of the value of total imports in 1996.

The services sector employed 53.5% of the economically active population and provided 58.2% of GDP in 1995. The GDP of this sector increased at an average annual rate of 4.9% during 1985–95, and by an estimated 0.9% in 1996. Tourism is the country's most important source of foreign-exchange earnings, accounting for some 17.5% of the total in 1993. The tourism sector grew by an annual average of some 17% in 1990–95, but experienced a significant downturn in growth as a result of concerns about security following the abduction of two Europeans in early 1996.

In 1995 Costa Rica recorded a visible trade deficit of US $473.5m. and there was a deficit of $143.0m. on the current account of the balance of payments. According to official estimates, in 1996 the principal source of imports (45.5%) was the USA; other major suppliers were Mexico, Venezuela and Japan. The USA was also the principal market for exports (36.8%) in that year; in 1995 other significant purchasers were Germany, Italy and Guatemala. The principal exports in 1996 were bananas and coffee. The principal imports in that year were raw materials for industry, consumer durables, consumer non-durables, and capital goods for industry.

In 1996 there was an estimated budgetary deficit of 98,131m. colones (equivalent to some 5.2% of GDP). Costa Rica's total external debt at the end of 1995 was US $3,800m., of which $3,132m. was long-term public debt. The cost of debt-servicing in that year was equivalent to 16.4% of the total value of exports of goods and services. The annual rate of inflation averaged 18.1% in 1985–95. Consumer prices increased by an annual average of 17.5% in 1996. An estimated 5.2% of the labour force (including those seeking work for the first time) were unemployed in 1995.

Costa Rica is a member of the Central American Common Market (CACM, see p. 122) and the Inter-American Development Bank (IDB, see p. 183).

Following strong growth in the early 1990s, Costa Rica's economy experienced a downturn in 1994. An escalating public-sector deficit forced the Figueres administration, inaugurated in mid-1994, to adopt the austerity policies of the previous Government, despite election pledges to the contrary. Under the third phase of Costa Rica's structural adjustment programme, agreed with multilateral creditors in late 1994, the Government committed itself to a reduction, by 25,000, of the public-sector work-force. Further austerity measures were introduced in February in an effort to reduce the budgetary deficit and to address the problems of rising inflation and depleted international reserves. In November 1995, following the adoption by the Government of further corrective measures, the IMF approved a 15-month stand-by credit, totalling US $78m., in support of the Government's economic programme for 1996, and thereby facilitated the release of further substantial loans from the World Bank and the IDB. Structural reforms, initiated in 1995, included the reform of the pensions system and of tax administration. Measures promoting increased foreign investment and enabling private-sector participation in activities formerly confined to the state sector, including the deregulation of the banking system, were implemented in 1996. In 1997 the Government introduced a privatization programme the proceeds of which were intended to contribute to redressing the country's internal debt, which was estimated at more than $3,500m. It was hoped that the programme, which envisaged the sale of assets including two banks and the state telecommunications company, would facilitate a new agreement with the IMF following the Government's failure to meet economic targets stipulated for 1996.

Social Welfare

Costa Rica possesses an advanced social welfare system, which provides a complete programme of care and assistance for all wage-earners and their dependants.

All social services are co-ordinated by the National Development Plan, administered by the Ministry of Planning, and are organized by state institutions. The Social Security Fund provides health services and general social insurance, the National Insurance Institute provides professional insurance, and the Ministry of Public Health operates a preventive health programme through a network of health units throughout the country. Benefits include disability and retirement pensions, workers' compensation and family assistance. In 1984 there were 2,539 physicians (10.1 per 10,000 inhabitants) and 5,400 nursing personnel working in the country. In 1982 there were 28 hospitals and 76 health centres, with a total of 7,706 beds. Of total expenditure by the central Government in 1995, about 97,550m. colones (20.7%) was for health services, and a further 94,200m. colones (19.9%) for social security and welfare.

Education

Education at all levels is available free of charge, and is officially compulsory for children between six and 15 years of age. Primary education begins at six years of age and lasts for six years. Secondary education consists of a three-year basic course, followed by a more highly specialized course of two years. In 1994 total enrolment at primary and secondary schools was equivalent to 81% of the school-age population (males 81%; females 82%). In that year primary enrolment included an estimated 90% of children in the relevant age-group, while the comparable ratio for secondary enrolment was 43%. There are six universities, one of which is an 'open' university. Costa Rica has the highest adult literacy rate in Central America. In 1995, according to estimates by UNESCO, the average rate of adult illiteracy was only 5.2% (males 5.3%; females 5.0%). Government expenditure on education in 1994 was 58,699m. colones (19.2% of total spending).

Public Holidays

1998: 1 January (New Year's Day), 19 March (Feast of St Joseph), 9 April (Maundy Thursday), 10 April (Good Friday), 11 April (Anniversary of the Battle of Rivas), 1 May (Labour Day), 11 June (Corpus Christi), 29 June (St Peter and St Paul), 25 July (Anniversary of the Annexation of Guanacaste Province), 2 August (Our Lady of the Angels), 15 August (Assumption), 15 September (Independence Day), 12 October (Columbus Day), 1 December (Abolition of the Armed Forces Day), 8 December (Immaculate Conception), 25 December (Christmas Day), 28–31 December (San José only).

1999: 1 January (New Year's Day), 19 March (Feast of St Joseph), 1 April (Maundy Thursday), 2 April (Good Friday), 11 April (Anniversary of the Battle of Rivas), 1 May (Labour Day), 3 June (Corpus Christi), 29 June (St Peter and St Paul), 25 July (Anniversary of the Annexation of Guanacaste Province), 2 August (Our Lady of the Angels), 15 August (Assumption), 15 September (Independence Day), 12 October (Columbus Day), 1 December (Abolition of the Armed Forces Day), 8 December (Immaculate Conception), 25 December (Christmas Day), 28–31 December (San José only).

Weights and Measures

The metric system is in force.

Statistical Survey

Sources (unless otherwise stated): Dirección General de Estadística y Censos, Ministry of the Economy, Industry and Commerce, Apdo 10.163, 1000 San José; tel. 221-0983; fax 223-0813; Banco Central de Costa Rica, Avdas Central y Primera, Calles 2 y 4, Apdo 10.058, 1000 San José; tel. 233-4233; telex 2163; fax 223-4658.

Area and Population

AREA, POPULATION AND DENSITY

Area (sq km)	
Land	51,060
Inland water	40
Total	51,100*
Population (census results)†	
14 May 1973	1,871,780
11 June 1984	
Males	1,208,216
Females	1,208,593
Total	2,416,809
Population (official estimates at mid-year)	
1994	3,265,920
1995	3,333,223
1996	3,398,000
Density (per sq km) at mid-1996	66.5

* 19,730 sq miles.

† Excluding adjustment for underenumeration.

PROVINCES (1 January 1996)

	Area (sq km)	Population (estimates)	Capital (with population)
Alajuela	9,757	601,674	Alajuela (175,129)
Cartago	3,125	378,188	Cartago (120,420)
Guanacaste	10,141	266,198	Liberia (41,009)
Heredia	2,657	270,096	Heredia (74,857)
Limón	9,189	255,248	Limón (77,234)
Puntarenas	11,266	375,639	Puntarenas (102,291)
San José	4,966	1,220,412	San José (324,011)
Total	51,100	3,367,455	—

BIRTHS, MARRIAGES AND DEATHS

	Registered live births		Registered marriages		Registered deaths	
	Number	Rate (per 1,000)	Number	Rate (per 1,000)	Number	Rate (per 1,000)
1991	81,110	26.5	22,348	7.3	11,792	3.8
1992	80,164	25.6	20,888	6.7	12,253	3.9
1993	79,714	24.6	21,715	6.7	12,543	3.8
1994	80,391	24.6	21,520	6.5	13,313	4.0
1995	80,306	24.1	24,274	7.3	14,061	4.2

Expectation of life (UN estimates, years at birth, 1990–95): males 72.89; females 77.60 (Source: UN, *Demographic Yearbook*).

ECONOMICALLY ACTIVE POPULATION*
(persons aged 12 years and over, household survey, July 1995)

	Males	Females	Total
Agriculture, hunting, forestry and fishing	230,431	21,933	252,364
Mining and quarrying	2,520	193	2,713
Manufacturing	122,684	70,111	192,795
Electricity, gas and water	10,316	1,980	12,296
Construction	72,116	1,170	73,286
Trade, restaurants and hotels	137,126	88,685	225,811
Transport, storage and communications	55,278	7,005	62,283
Financing, insurance, real estate and business services	38,142	11,632	49,774
Community, social and personal services	140,877	146,237	287,114
Activities not adequately defined	7,685	1,934	9,619
Total	817,175	350,880	1,168,055

* Figures exclude persons seeking work for the first time, totalling 9,119, and other unemployed persons, totalling 54,398.

Agriculture

PRINCIPAL CROPS ('000 metric tons)

	1994	1995	1996
Rice (paddy)	174	178	186
Maize	34	28	25
Beans (dry)	35	28	23
Palm kernels*	18	19	19
Palm oil	89	93	97
Sugar cane*	3,200	3,450	3,620
Bananas	2,000†	2,400†	2,100*
Coffee (green)†	150	156	143
Cocoa beans†	3	3	3

* FAO estimate(s). † Unofficial figure(s).

Source: FAO, *Production Yearbook.*

LIVESTOCK ('000 head, year ending September)

	1994	1995	1996
Horses*	114	115	115
Cattle	1,894†	1,700	1,585†
Pigs	350	300	300
Chickens*	15,000	17,000	17,000

* FAO estimates. † Unofficial figure.

Source: FAO, *Production Yearbook.*

LIVESTOCK PRODUCTS ('000 metric tons)

	1994	1995	1996
Beef and veal	91	92	96
Pig meat	23	24	20
Poultry meat	54	64	66
Cows' milk	519	539	536
Cheese*	3	3	6
Butter and ghee*	4	4	4
Hen eggs	23*	26*	27
Cattle hides (fresh)*	15	15	15

* FAO estimate(s).

Source: FAO, *Production Yearbook.*

Forestry

ROUNDWOOD REMOVALS
('000 cubic metres, excluding bark)

	1992	1993	1994
Sawlogs, veneer logs and logs for sleepers	840	870	870*
Pulpwood*	8	8	8
Other industrial wood*	221	227	232
Fuel wood*	3,136	3,210	3,289
Total	4,205	4,315	4,399*

* FAO estimate(s).

Source: FAO, *Yearbook of Forest Products.*

SAWNWOOD PRODUCTION ('000 cubic metres)

	1992	1993	1994*
Coniferous (softwood)*	12	12	12
Broadleaved (hardwood)	760	786	786
Total	772	798	798

* FAO estimates.

Source: FAO, *Yearbook of Forest Products.*

Fishing

('000 metric tons, live weight)

	1993	1994	1995
Inland waters	3.5	4.1	5.3
Atlantic Ocean	0.2	0.3	0.4
Pacific Ocean	15.2	16.4	22.2
Total catch	18.9	20.8	27.9

Source: FAO, *Yearbook of Fishery Statistics.*

Industry

SELECTED PRODUCTS
('000 metric tons, unless otherwise indicated)

	1992	1993	1994
Fish (tinned)*	5.0	4.6	n.a.
Raw sugar	284*	283*	325†
Nitrogenous fertilizers‡	42	38	n.a.
Motor spirit (petrol)§	61	63	102
Kerosene	4	5	6
Distillate fuel oils	150	151	162
Residual fuel oils	237	253	221
Bitumen	1	10	16
Electric energy (million kWh)	4,144	4,386	4,772

* Source: FAO.
† Source: International Sugar Organization.
‡ Production in terms of nitrogen.
§ Including alcohol.

Source: UN, *Industrial Commodity Statistics Yearbook.*

Finance

CURRENCY AND EXCHANGE RATES

Monetary Units

100 céntimos =1 Costa Rican colón.

Sterling and Dollar Equivalents (30 September 1997)

£1 sterling = 385.45 colones;
US $1 = 238.61 colones;
1,000 Costa Rican colones = £2.594 = $4.191.

Average Exchange Rate (colones per US $)

1994 157.07
1995 179.73
1996 207.69

GENERAL BUDGET (million colones)

Revenue	1994	1995	1996*
Taxation	192,253	259,777	308,750
Income tax	34,789	47,164	53,379
Other direct taxes	9,022	11,936	14,991
Taxes on external transactions	42,978	61,783	40,300
Taxes on internal transactions	105,464	138,894	200,080
Other revenues	1,443	1,807	2,294
Transfers	3,304	2,941	3,456
Total	197,000	264,525	314,500

Expenditure	1994	1995	1996*
Current expenditure	256,876	306,585	377,476
Consumption expenditure	91,697	115,607	137,528
Current transfers	111,688	100,031	126,109
Internal debt-servicing	43,841	78,425	100,698
External debt-servicing	9,650	12,522	13,140
Capital expenditure	30,082	31,079	35,155
Investment	10,727	14,564	13,734
Capital transfers	19,356	16,515	21,421
Total	286,959	337,663	412,631

* Preliminary figures.

INTERNATIONAL RESERVES (US $ million at 31 December)*

	1994	1995	1996
IMF special drawing rights	0.18	0.06	0.01
Reserve position in IMF	12.74	12.97	12.55
Foreign exchange	880.28	1,033.61	987.67
Total	893.20	1,046.64	1,000.23

* Figures exclude gold reserves ($95.97 million at 31 December 1992).

Source: IMF, *International Financial Statistics.*

MONEY SUPPLY ('000 million colones at 31 December)

	1994	1995	1996
Currency outside banks	74.9	84.8	91.7
Demand deposits at commercial banks	86.6	67.0	84.9
Total money (incl. others)	161.6	151.9	177.5

Source: IMF, *International Financial Statistics.*

COST OF LIVING

(Consumer Price Index for San José metropolitan area; base: January 1995 = 100)

	1995	1996
Food, beverages and tobacco	105.8	125.7
Clothing	105.4	117.5
Housing	110.9	124.2
All items (incl. others)	107.4	126.3

NATIONAL ACCOUNTS (million colones at current prices)

Expenditure on the Gross Domestic Product

	1994	1995	1996
Government final consumption expenditure	223,549	284,971	323,842
Private final consumption expenditure	779,307	958,024	1,127,726
Increase in stocks	86,365	67,648	100,607
Gross fixed capital formation	258,940	312,635	340,008
Total domestic expenditure	1,348,161	1,623,278	1,892,183
Exports of goods and services	518,370	693,390	830,092
Less Imports of goods and services	560,734	695,024	849,846
GDP in purchasers' values	1,305,796	1,621,644	1,872,429
GDP at constant 1990 prices	639,981	655,354	650,870

Source: IMF, *International Financial Statistics.*

Gross Domestic Product by Economic Activity

	1993	1994	1995
Agriculture, hunting, forestry and fishing	171,589	216,216	285,838
Mining and quarrying } Manufacturing }	206,877	243,044	310,005
Electricity, gas and water	39,610	47,104	55,159
Construction	29,283	35,446	38,494
Trade, restaurants and hotels	222,302	263,561	331,560
Transport, storage and communications	58,023	69,340	88,755
Finance, insurance and business services	90,052	114,608	145,208
Real estate	31,559	37,774	47,464
Government services	144,723	186,814	232,583
Other services	75,242	92,396	116,973
GDP in purchasers' values	1,069,259	1,306,302	1,652,038

BALANCE OF PAYMENTS (US $ million)

	1993	1994	1995
Exports of goods f.o.b.	1,866.8	2,122.0	2,480.2
Imports of goods f.o.b.	–2,627.6	–2,727.8	–2,953.7
Trade balance	–760.8	–605.8	–473.5
Exports of services	1,039.3	1,195.0	1,309.9
Imports of services	–816.4	–860.1	–947.1
Balance on goods and services	–537.9	–270.9	–110.7
Other income received	111.2	154.6	154.5
Other income paid	–333.6	–283.0	–340.3
Balance on goods, services and income	–763.3	–399.3	–296.5
Current transfers received	149.3	164.5	161.8
Current transfers paid	–6.2	–9.2	–8.3
Current balance	–620.2	–244.0	–143.0
Direct investment abroad	–2.3	–4.7	–5.5
Direct investment from abroad	246.7	297.6	395.5
Portfolio investment liabilities	–5.1	–1.2	–24.4
Other investment assets	–54.5	–76.2	–10.0
Other investment liabilities	–231.0	–323.9	–76.3
Net errors and omissions	299.0	249.1	94.4
Overall balance	–258.4	–103.3	230.7

Source: IMF, *International Financial Statistics.*

External Trade

PRINCIPAL COMMODITIES (US $ million)

Imports c.i.f.	1994	1995*	1996†
Raw materials for industry	1,125.9	1,360.6	1,389.7
Raw materials for agriculture	51.5	71.3	73.3
Consumer non-durables	567.0	597.5	495.2
Consumer durables	330.2	252.3	508.2
Capital goods for industry	435.3	479.8	465.0
Capital goods for transport	157.6	150.4	121.4
Building materials	118.2	109.9	113.4
Fuels and lubricants	203.3	208.0	222.4
Total (incl. others)	3,025.1	3,260.0	3,427.0

Exports f.o.b.	1993‡	1994	1995
Industrial goods	632.3	815.4	950.9
Consumables§	167.4	191.7	249.3
Textiles‖	111.7	117.3	121.4
Wood and paper products	34.8	36.4	39.5
Chemical and petroleum products	143.0	154.5	163.2
Machinery and metal products	101.1	122.4	127.9
Medicine	44.9	49.1	51.6
Agricultural and marine goods	1,241.6	1,194.5	1,455.6
Coffee	201.5	307.6	417.3
Bananas	560.1	561.0	683.8
Meat	62.5	51.0	43.6
Seafood	90.9	76.3	87.2
Plants and flowers	90.0	96.2	112.6
Tropical fruit	87.0	102.5	111.2
Total	1,873.9	2,242.5	2,657.3

1996 (estimates, US $million): *Exports f.o.b.*: Coffee 367.8; Bananas 616.0; Meat 40.2; Sugar 44.9; Seafood 172.6; Total (incl. others) 2,752.9.

* Preliminary figures. † Estimates.

‡ Source: IMF, *Costa Rica—Statistical Appendix*.

§ Including food products and tobacco.

‖ Including leather products and shoes.

PRINCIPAL TRADING PARTNERS (US $ million)

Imports c.i.f.*	1993	1994	1995
Canada	35.3	42.0	41.8
Colombia	75.1	86.8	100.9
El Salvador	69.2	76.4	83.7
Germany	104.3	100.2	101.8
Guatemala	104.7	109.2	110.7
Italy	50.3	50.4	63.2
Japan	222.0	166.4	124.6
Mexico	115.6	136.7	180.7
Netherlands	27.0	28.3	39.8
Panama	60.7	65.2	90.8
United Kingdom	29.6	30.9	25.8
USA	1,253.2	1,336.6	1,478.0
Venezuela	144.1	164.9	215.4
Total (incl. others)	2,885.6	3,024.8	3,252.8

* Figures are provisional. Revised totals: 2,884.7 in 1993; 3,025.1 in 1994; 3,260.0 in 1995 (estimate).

Exports f.o.b.	1993	1994	1995
Belgium-Luxembourg	125.5	151.7	146.0
Canada	36.6	28.5	33.4
El Salvador	63.0	72.8	90.9
Finland	7.6	17.2	34.7
Germany	175.1	203.7	168.8
Guatemala	85.6	102.7	117.0
Honduras	51.8	44.9	54.6
Italy	86.2	107.0	127.6
Japan	12.3	18.2	27.7
Mexico	28.2	21.8	16.5
Netherlands	42.0	60.5	87.5
Nicaragua	67.5	67.7	87.3
Panama	67.1	65.0	78.2
United Kingdom	36.9	65.8	100.6
USA	947.6	933.0	1,020.3
Total (incl. others)	1,995.3	2,242.5	2,657.3

1996 (estimates, US $ million): *Imports c.i.f.*: Colombia 119.3; El Salvador 85.8; Guatemala 134.0; Japan 135.0; Mexico 266.6; USA 1,560.0; Venezuela 223.4; Total (incl. others) 3,427.0. *Exports f.o.b.*: Colombia 20.5; Japan 31.9; Mexico 54.5; USA 1,013.2; Venezuela 11.2; Total (incl. others) 2,752.9.

Transport

RAILWAYS

	1992	1993	1994
Passenger journeys	11,580	367,803	335,276

Source: Ministry of Public Works and Transport.

ROAD TRAFFIC (motor vehicles in use at 31 December)

	1993*	1994	1995
Private cars	220,142	238,522	254,811
Buses and coaches	6,885	7,957	8,849
Goods vehicles	108,026	119,183	132,538
Motorcycles and mopeds	46,000	57,162	63,669

* Source: IRF, *World Road Statistics*.

Source: Ministry of Public Works and Transport.

SHIPPING

Merchant Fleet (registered at 31 December)

	1994	1995	1996
Number of vessels	19	16	14
Total displacement ('000 grt)	8	7	6

Source: Lloyd's Register of Shipping, *World Fleet Statistics*.

International Sea-borne Freight Traffic ('000 metric tons)

	1993	1994	1995
Goods loaded	2,713	2,885	2,643
Goods unloaded	3,557	3,835	4,054

Source: Ministry of Public Works and Transport.

CIVIL AVIATION (traffic on scheduled services)

	1992	1993	1994
Kilometres flown (million)	14	17	19
Passengers carried ('000)	623	690	773
Passenger-km (million)	1,202	1,429	1,611
Total ton-km (million)	165	188	213

Source: UN, *Statistical Yearbook*.

Tourism

	1993	1994	1995*
Visitors ('000)	684.0	761.4	792.3
Revenue (US $ million)	573.7	624.1	664.4

* Preliminary figures.

Source: IMF, *Costa Rica—Statistical Appendix*.

Communications Media

	1992	1993	1994
Radio receivers ('000 in use)	823	844	870
Television receivers ('000 in use)	450	465	475
Telephones ('000 main lines in use)	327	364	430
Telefax stations (number in use)	2,177	2,190	2,190
Mobile cellular telephones (subscribers)	3,008	4,533	6,990
Daily newspapers:			
Number	4	n.a.	5
Circulation	322	n.a.	333

Non-daily newspapers: 12 in 1991 (average circulation 106,000 copies).

Book production: 963 titles (excluding pamphlets) in 1994.

Sources: UNESCO, *Statistical Yearbook*, and UN, *Statistical Yearbook*.

Education

(1996)

	Institutions	Teachers	Students		
			Males	Females	Total
Pre-primary	1,128	2,435*	35,083	33,115	68,198
Primary	3,623	15,806*	267,215	253,180	520,395
Secondary	358	8,845*	103,427	104,806	208,233
Tertiary					
University level	36	n.a.	n.a.	n.a.	65,268†
Distance learning	n.a.	235‡	n.a.	n.a.	10,666†
Other higher	n.a.	n.a.	n.a.	n.a.	12,390†

* 1994 figure. † 1992 figure. ‡ 1991 figure.

Source: partly UNESCO, *Statistical Yearbook*

Directory

The Constitution

The present Constitution of Costa Rica was promulgated in November 1949. Its main provisions are summarized below:

GOVERNMENT

The government is unitary: provincial and local bodies derive their authority from the national Government. The country is divided into seven Provinces, each administered by a Governor who is appointed by the President. The Provinces are divided into Cantons, and each Canton into Districts. There is an elected Municipal Council in the chief city of each Canton, the number of its members being related to the population of the Canton. The Municipal Council supervises the affairs of the Canton. Municipal government is closely regulated by national law, particularly in matters of finance.

LEGISLATURE

The government consists of three branches: legislative, executive and judicial. Legislative power is vested in a single chamber, the Legislative Assembly, which meets in regular session twice a year—from 1 May to 31 July, and from 1 September to 30 November. Special sessions may be convoked by the President to consider specified business. The Assembly is composed of 57 deputies elected for four years. The chief powers of the Assembly are to enact laws, levy taxes, authorize declarations of war and, by a two-thirds' majority, suspend, in cases of civil disorder, certain civil liberties guaranteed in the Constitution.

Bills may be initiated by the Assembly or by the Executive and must have three readings, in at least two different legislative periods, before they become law. The Assembly may override the presidential vote by a two-thirds' majority.

EXECUTIVE

The executive branch is headed by the President, who is assisted by the Cabinet. If the President should resign or be incapacitated, the executive power is entrusted to the First Vice-President; next in line to succeed to executive power are the Second Vice-President and the President of the Legislative Assembly.

The President sees that the laws and the provisions of the Constitution are carried out, and maintains order; has power to appoint and remove Cabinet ministers and diplomatic representatives, and to negotiate treaties with foreign nations (which are, however, subject to ratification by the Legislative Assembly). The President is assisted in these duties by a Cabinet, each member of which is head of an executive department.

ELECTORATE

Suffrage is universal, compulsory and secret for persons over the age of 18 years.

DEFENCE

A novel feature of the Costa Rican Constitution is the clause outlawing a national army. Only by a continental convention or for the purpose of national defence may a military force be organized.

The Government

HEAD OF STATE

President: JOSÉ MARÍA FIGUERES OLSEN (took office 8 May 1994)*.

First Vice-President: RODRIGO OREAMUNO BLANCO.

Second Vice-President and Minister of Housing: REBECA GRYNSPAN MAYUFIS.

* To be succeeded on 1 May 1998 by MIGUEL ANGEL RODRÍGUEZ ECHEVERRÍA of the PUSC, who was the victorious candidate at the presidential election of 1 February 1998.

THE CABINET
(January 1998)

Minister of Foreign Affairs: FERNANDO NARANJO VILLALOBOS.

Minister of Security: LAURA CHINCHILLA.

Minister of the Interior and of Justice: JUAN DIEGO CASTRO FERNÁNDEZ.

Minister of Culture, Youth and Sports: ARNOLDO MORA RODRÍGUEZ.

Minister of Planning: LEONARDO GARNIER RIMOLO.

Minister of Public Health: HERMAN WEINSTOCK WOLFOWICZ.

Minister of Education: EDUARDO DORYAN GARRÓN.

Minister of Finance: FRANCISCO DE PAULA GUTIÉRREZ.

Minister of the Economy, Industry and Commerce: JOSÉ LEÓN DESANTI.

Minister of Agriculture and Livestock: RICARDO GARRÓN FILGUS.

Minister of Foreign Trade: JOSÉ MANUEL SALAZAR XIRINACHS.

Minister of Natural Resources, Energy and Mines: RENÉ CASTRO SALAZAR.

Minister of Public Works and Transport: RODOLFO SILVA.

Minister of the Presidency: MARCOS ANTONIO VARGAS.

Minister of Information and Communication: ALEJANDRO SOTO ZÚÑIGA.

Minister of Labour and Social Security: FARID AYALES ESNA.

Minister of Tourism: CARLOS ROESCH CARRANZA.

MINISTRIES

Ministry of Agriculture and Livestock: Apdo 10.094, 1000 San José; tel. 232-4496; telex 3558; fax 232-2103.

Ministry of Culture, Youth and Sports: Apdo 10.227, 1000 San José; tel. 223-1658; fax 233-7066.

Ministry of the Economy, Industry and Commerce: Avdas 2 y Central, Calle 10, Apdo 10.216, 1000 San José; tel. 222-1016; telex 2414; fax 222-2305.

Ministry of Education: Apdo 10.087, 1000 San José; tel. 222-0229; fax 233-0390.

Ministry of Finance: Apdo 5.016, San José; tel. 222-2481; telex 2277; fax 255-4874.

Ministry of Foreign Affairs: Apdo 10.027, 1000 San José; tel. 223-7555; telex 2107; fax 223-9328.

Ministry of Foreign Trade: Montes de Oca, Apdo 96, 2050 San José; tel. 222-5910; telex 2936; fax 233-5090.

Ministry of Housing: Paseo de los Estudiantes, Apdo 222, 1002 San José; tel. 257-9166; fax 255-1976.

Ministry of Information and Communication: Apdo 520, 1000 San José; tel. 234-2310; fax 253-7569; e-mail alesoto@casapres.go.cr.

Ministry of the Interior: Apdo 10.006, 1000 San José; tel. 223-8354; telex 3434; fax 222-7726.

Ministry of Justice: Apdo 5.685, 1000 San José; tel. 223-9739; fax 223-3879.

Ministry of Labour and Social Security: Apdo 10.133, 1000 San José; tel. 221-0238.

Ministry of Natural Resources, Energy and Mines: Avdas 8 y 10, Calle 25, Apdo 10.104, 1000 San José; tel. 257-1417; telex 2363; fax 257-0697.

Ministry of Planning: Avdas 3 y 5, Calle 4, Apdo 10.127, 1000 San José; tel. 221-9524; telex 2962; fax 253-6243.

Ministry of the Presidency: 2010 Zapote, Apdo 520, San José; tel. 224-4092; telex 2106; fax 253-6984.

Ministry of Public Health: Apdo 10.123, 1000 San José; tel. 233-0683; fax 255-4997.

Ministry of Public Works and Transport: Apdo 10.176, 1000 San José; tel. 226-7311; telex 2478; fax 227-1434.

Ministry of Security: Apdo 55, 4874 San José; tel. 226-0093; telex 3308; fax 226-6581.

Ministry of State Reorganization: Apdo 10.127, 1000 San José; tel. 223-7858; fax 223-8232.

Ministry of Tourism: Edif. Genaro Valverde, Calles 5 y 7, Avda 4, Apdo 777, 1000 San José; tel. 233-9605; telex 2281; fax 255-4997.

President and Legislature

PRESIDENT

Presidential Election, 1 February 1998

Candidate	Votes	% of votes cast
MIGUEL ANGEL RODRÍGUEZ ECHEVERRÍA (PUSC)*	650,399	46.9
JOSÉ MIGUEL CORRALES BOLAÑOS (PLN)	616,600	44.4
VLADIMIR DE LA CRUZ DE LEMOS (FD)	41,922	3.0
WÁLTER MUÑOZ CÉSPEDES (PIN)	20,226	1.5
SHERMAN THOMAS JACKSON (PRC)	19,103	1.4
ALVARO GONZÁLEZ ESPINOZA (PD)	13,559	1.0
Total (incl. others)†	1,387,287	100.0

* MIGUEL ANGEL RODRÍGUEZ ECHEVERRÍA was to assume office as President on 1 May 1998.

† Excluding 6,080 blank ballots.

ASAMBLEA LEGISLATIVA

General Election, 1 February 1998

Party	Seats
Partido Unidad Social Cristiana (PUSC)	27
Partido de Liberación Nacional (PLN)	23
Fuerza Democrática (FD)	3
Partido Movimiento Libertario (PML)	2
Partido Integración Nacional (PIN)	1
Partido Acción Laborista Agrícola (PALA)	1
Total	57

Political Organizations

Acción del Pueblo (AP): San José; Pres. ANGEL RUIZ ZÚÑIGA; Sec. HENRY MORA JIMÉNEZ.

Acción Agrícola Cartaginesa: Cartago; provincial party; Pres. JUAN BRENES CASTILLO; Sec. RODRIGO FALLAS BONILLA.

Acción Democrática Alajuelense: Alajuela; provincial party; Pres. FRANCISCO ALFARO FERNÁNDEZ; Sec. JUAN BAUTISTA CHACÓN SOTO.

Alianza Nacional Cristiana (ANC): Pres. VÍCTOR HUGO GONZÁLEZ MONTERO; Sec. JUAN RODRÍGUEZ VENEGAS.

Fuerza Democrática (FD): Pres. ISAAC FELIPE AZOFEIFA; coalition comprising:

- **Movimiento Humanista Ecologista.**
- **Partido del Progreso.**
- **Partido Unión Patriótica.**
- **Pueblo Unido (PU):** Calle 4, Avdas 7 y 9, San José; tel. 223-0032; Sec. ALBERTO SALOM ECHEVERRÍA; left-wing coalition comprising:
  - **Partido del Pueblo Costarricense:** Apdo 6.613, 1000 San José; tel. 222-5517; f. 1931; communist; Sec.-Gen. LENIN CHACÓN VARGAS.
  - **Partido Socialista Costarricense:** San José; socialist; Pres. ALVARO MONTERO MEJÍA; Sec. ALBERTO SALOM ECHEVERRÍA.
  - **Partido de los Trabajadores:** San José; Maoist; Pres. JOHNNY FRANCISCO ARAYA MONGE; Sec. ILSE ACOSTA POLONIO.

Movimiento Nacional (MN): San José; Pres. MARIO ECHANDI JIMÉNEZ; Sec. RODRIGO SANCHO ROBLES.

Partido Acción Laborista Agrícola (PALA): San José.

Partido Alajuelita Nueva: Alajuelita Centro, 100W Escuela Abraham Lincoln, San José; tel. 254-3879; telex 3076; fax 254-6072; f. 1981; Pres. ANNIE BADILLA CALDERÓN; Sec. CARLOS RETANA RETANA.

Partido Auténtico Limonense: Limón; provincial party; Pres. MARVIN WRIGHT LINDO; Sec. GUILLERMO JOSEPH WIGNALL.

Partido Concordia Costarricense: Calles 2 y 4, Avda 10, San José; tel. 223-2497; Pres. EMILIO PIEDRA JIMÉNEZ; Sec. ROBERTO FRANCISCO SALAZAR MADRIZ.

Partido Demócrata (PD): San José.

Partido Independiente (PI): San José; Pres. EUGENIO JIMÉNEZ SANCHO; Sec. GONZALO JIMÉNEZ CHAVES.

Partido Integración Nacional (PIN): San José.

Partido de Liberación Nacional (PLN): Sabana Oeste, San José; tel. 231-4022; f. 1948; social democratic party; affiliated to the Socialist International; 400,000 mems; Pres. ROLANDO ARAYA MONGE; Sec.-Gen. WALTER COTO MOLINA.

Partido Movimiento Libertario (PML): San José.

Partido Nacional Democrático: San José; Pres. RODOLFO CERDAS CRUZ; Sec. ELADIO JARA JIMÉNEZ.

Partido Renovación Costarricense (PRC): San José.

Partido Revolucionario de los Trabajadores (PRT): San José; worker's revolutionary party.

Partido Radical Demócrata: San José; Pres. JUAN JOSÉ ECHEVERRÍA BREALEY; Sec. RODRIGO ESQUIVEL RODRÍGUEZ.

Partido Republicano Nacional: San José; Pres. ROLANDO RODRÍGUEZ VARELA; Sec. FERNANDO PEÑA HERRERA.

Partido Unidad Social Cristiana (PUSC): San José; Pres. ABEL PACHECO; Sec. LORENA VÁSQUEZ.

Partido Unión Generaleña: Pérez Zeledón, Apdo 440-8.000, San José; tel. 771-0524; fax 771-0737; f. 1981; Pres. Dr CARLOS A. FERNÁNDEZ VEGA; Sec. VÍCTOR HUGO SOTO BARQUERO.

Partido Unión Nacional: San José; Pres. OLGA MARTA ULATE ROJAS; Sec. RODRIGO GONZÁLEZ SABORÍO.

Diplomatic Representation

EMBASSIES IN COSTA RICA

Argentina: Calle 27, Avda Central, Apdo 1.963, San José; tel. 221-3438; telex 2117; Chargé d'affaires a.i.: BERNARDO JUAN OCHOA.

Belgium: Los Yoses, 4a entrada, 25 metros sur, Apdo 3.725, 1000 San José; tel. 225-6255; telex 2909; fax 225-0351; Ambassador: WILLY J. STEVENS.

Brazil: Paseo Colón frente a Nissan Lachner y Sáenz, San José; tel. 233-1544; telex 2270; fax 223-4325; Ambassador: LUIZ JORGE RANGEL DE CASTRO.

Bulgaria: Edif. Delcoré, 3°, 100 metros sur Hotel Balmoral, Apdo 4.752, San José; Ambassador: KIRIL ZLATKOV NIKOLOV.

Canada: Oficentro Ejecutivo La Sabana, Edif. 5, 3°, detrás de la Contracoría, Centro Colón, Apdo 351, 1007 San José; tel. 296-4149; fax 296-4270; Ambassador: DAN GOODLEAF.

Chile: De la Pulpería La Luz 125 metros norte, Casa 116, Apdo 10.102, San José; tel. 224-4243; telex 2207; Ambassador: PEDRO PALACIOS CAMERÓN.

China (Taiwan): 500 metros al sur del ICE en San Pedro, Apdo 907, San José; tel. 224-8180; telex 2174; Ambassador: EDWARD Y. KUAN.

Colombia: Apdo 3.154, 1000 San José; tel. 221-0725; telex 2918; fax 255-1705; Ambassador: MARÍA CRISTINA ZULETA DE PATIÑ.

Czech Republic: 75 metros oeste de la entrada principal del Colegio Humboldt, Apdo 12041, 1000 San José; tel. 296-5671; fax 296-5595; Ambassador: Ing. VÍT KORSELT.

Dominican Republic: Lomas de Ayarco, Curridabat, de la Embajada de Rusia 100 metros oeste, 300 metros sur, 300 metros oeste y 150 metros norte, Apdo 4.746, San José; tel. and fax 272-2398; Ambassador: ALFONSO ARIA JIMÉNEZ.

Ecuador: Edif. de la esquina sureste del Museo Nacional, 125 metros al este, Avda 2, Calles 19 y 21, Apdo 1.374, 1000 San José; tel. 223-6281; telex 2601; Ambassador: Lic. ANDRÉS CÓRDOVA GALARZA.

El Salvador: Edif. Trianón, 3°, Avda Central y Calle 5, Apdo 1.378, San José; tel. 222-5536; telex 2641; Ambassador: CARLOS MATAMOROS GUIROLA.

France: Carretera a Curridabat, del Indoor Club 200 metros sur y 25 metros oeste, Apdo 10.177, San José; tel. 225-0733; telex 2191; fax 253-7027; Ambassador: PIERRE BOILLOT.

Germany: Barrio Rohrmoser, de la Embajada de España 200 metros norte, 50 metros oeste, Apdo 4.017, San José; tel. 232-5533; telex 2183; fax 231-6403; Ambassador Dr WILFRIED RUPPRECHT.

Guatemala: De Pops Curridabat 500 metros sur y 30 metros este, 2ª Casa Izquierda, Apdo 328, 1000 San José; tel. 231-6654; fax 231-6645; Ambassador: JULIO GANDARA VALENZUELA.

Holy See: Urbanización Rohrmoser, Sabana Oeste, Centro Colón, Apdo 992, 1007 San José (Apostolic Nunciature); tel. 232-2128; fax 231-2557; Apostolic Nuncio: Most Rev. GIACINTO BERLOCO, Titular Archbishop of Fidene.

Honduras: Los Yoses sur, del ITAN hacia la Presidencia la primera entrada a la izquierda, 200 metros norte y 100 metros este, Apdo 2.239, San José; tel. 234-9502; fax 253-2209; Ambassador: EDGARDO SEVILLA IDIÁQUEZ.

Hungary: Los Yoses, 5a entrada, 50 metros sur, No 1099, Apdo 765, 2010 San José; tel. 225-0908; telex 3589; fax 225-9741; Ambassador: Dr ZSOLT HORVÁTH.

Israel: Calle 2, Avdas 2 y 4, Apdo 5.147, San José; tel. 221-6444; telex 2258; fax 257-0867; Ambassador: SHLOMO TAL.

Italy: Los Yoses, 5a entrada, Apdo 1.729, San José; tel. 224-6574; telex 2769; fax 225-8200; Ambassador: Dr ARRIGO LÓPEZ CELLY.

Japan: De la primera entrada del Barrio Rohrmoser (Sabana Oeste) 500 metros oeste y 100 metros norte, Apdos 501 y 10.145, San José; tel. 232-1255; telex 2205; fax 231-3140; Ambassador: AKIMOTO KENSHIRO.

Korea, Republic: Calle 28, Avda 2, Barrio San Bosco, Apdo 3.150, San José; tel. 221-2398; telex 2512; Ambassador: JAE HOON KIM.

Mexico: Avda 7, No 1371, Apdo 10.107, San José; tel. 257-0633; telex 2218; fax 222-6080; Ambassador: ENRIQUE BERRUGA FILLOY.

Netherlands: Los Yoses, Avda 8, Calles 35 y 37, Apdo 10.285, 1000 San José; tel. 296-1490; telex 2187; fax 296-2933; Ambassador: F. B. A. M. VAN HAREN.

Nicaragua: Edif. Trianón, Calles 25 y 27, Avda Central, San José; tel. 222-4749; telex 2316; Ambassador: CLAUDIA CHAMORRO BARRIOS.

Panama: 200 metros sur, 25 metros este de Higuerón, La Granja, San Pedro, Montes de Oca, San José; tel. 225-3401; Ambassador: WALTER MYERS.

Peru: Barrio Pops de Curridabat, del Indoor Club 100 metros sur y 75 metros oeste, Apdo 4.248, 1000 San José; tel. 225-9145; telex 3515; fax 253-0457; Ambassador: ALBERTO VARILLAS MONTENEGRO.

Romania: Urbanización Rohrmoser, al costado norte de la Nunciatura Apostólica, Sabana Oeste, Centro Colón, Apdo 10.321, San José; tel. 231-0741; telex 2337; fax 232-6461; Ambassador: NICOLAE TURTUREA.

Russia: Apdo 6.340, San José; tel. 225-5780; telex 2299; Ambassador: YURII PAVLOV.

Slovakia: 200 metros sur de McDonald's en Plaza del Sol, Residencial El Prado, Curridabat, Apdo 3.910, San José; tel. 224-6467; fax 224-9184; Chargé d'affaires a.i.: VLADIMIR GRÁCZ.

Spain: Calle 32, Paseo Colón, Avda 2, Apdo 10.150, San José; tel. 221-1933; telex 2438; Ambassador: J. A. ORTIZ RAMOS.

Switzerland: Paseo Colón, Centro Colón, Apdo 895, San José; tel. 221-4829; telex 2512; Ambassador: Dr JOHANN BUCHER.

United Kingdom: Edif. Centro Colón, 11°, Apdo 815, 1007 San José; tel. 221-5566; telex 2169; fax 233-9938; Ambassador: RICHARD MICHAEL JACKSON.

USA: Pavas San José; tel. 220-3939; fax 220-2305; Ambassador: PETER JON DE VOS.

Uruguay: Calle 2, Avda 1, San José; tel. 223-2512; Ambassador: JORGE JUSTO BOERO-BRIAN.

Venezuela: Avda Central, Los Yoses, 5a entrada, Apdo 10.230, San José; tel. 225-5813; telex 2413; Ambassador: Dr FRANCISCO SALAZAR MARTÍNEZ.

Judicial System

Ultimate judicial power is vested in the Supreme Court, the 22 justices of which are elected by the Assembly for a term of eight years, and are automatically re-elected for an equal period, unless the Assembly decides to the contrary by a two-thirds vote. Judges of the lower courts are appointed by the Supreme Court's five-member Supreme Council.

The Supreme Court may also meet as the Corte Plena, with power to declare laws and decrees unconstitutional. There are also four appellate courts, criminal courts, civil courts and special courts. The jury system is not used.

La Corte Suprema: San José; tel. 295-3000; telex 1548; fax 257-0801.

President of the Supreme Court: EDGAR CERVANTES VILLALTA.

Religion

Under the Constitution, all forms of worship are tolerated. Roman Catholicism is the official religion of the country. Various Protestant Churches are represented. There are an estimated 7,000 members of the Methodist Church.

CHRISTIANITY

The Roman Catholic Church

Costa Rica comprises one archdiocese and five dioceses. At 31 December 1995 Roman Catholics represented some 90% of the total population.

Bishops' Conference: Conferencia Episcopal de Costa Rica, Arzobispado, Apdo 497, 1000 San José; tel. 221-3053; fax 221-6662; f. 1977; Pres. ROMÁN ARRIETA VILLALOBOS, Archbishop of San José de Costa Rica.

Archbishop of San José de Costa Rica: ROMÁN ARRIETA VILLALOBOS, Arzobispado, Apdo 497, 1000 San José; tel. 233-6029; fax 221-2427.

The Anglican Communion

Costa Rica comprises a single diocese (extra-provincial) in Province IX of the Episcopal Church in the USA.

Bishop of Costa Rica: Rt Rev. CORNELIUS JOSHUA WILSON, Apdo 2.773, 1000 San José; tel. 225-0209; fax 253-8331.

Other Churches

Baptist Convention of Costa Rica: Apdo 1.631, 2100 Guadalupe; tel. 253-5820; fax 253-4723; f. 1946; Pres. Ing. ARTHUR SAMUELS DOUGLAS.

Iglesia Evangélica Metodista de Costa Rica (Evangelical Methodist Church of Costa Rica): Apdo 5.481, 1000 San José; tel. 236-2171; fax 236-5921; autonomous since 1973; 6,000 mems; Pres. Bishop LUIS F. PALOMO.

BAHÁ'Í FAITH

Bahá'í Information Centre: Apdo 553, 1150 San José; tel. 231-0647; fax 296-1033; adherents resident in 242 localities.

National Spiritual Assembly of the Bahá'ís of Costa Rica: Apdo 553, 1150 La Uruca; tel. 231-0647; fax 296-1033; e-mail bahaiscr@sol.racsa.co.cr.

The Press

DAILIES

Boletín Judicial: La Uruca, Apdo 5.024, San José; tel. 231-5222; f. 1878; journal of the judiciary; Dir ISAÍAS CASTRO VARGAS; circ. 2,500.

Diario Extra: Calle 4, Avda 4, Apdo 177, 1009 San José; tel. 223-9505; fax 223-6101; f. 1978; morning; independent; Dir WILLIAM GÓMEZ; circ. 100,000.

La Gaceta: La Uruca, Apdo 5.024, San José; tel. 231-5222; f. 1878; official gazette; Dir ISAÍAS CASTRO VARGAS; circ. 5,300.

La Nación: Llorente de Tibás, Apdo 10.138, San José; tel. 247-4747; telex 2358; fax 240-6480; f. 1946; morning; independent; Dir EDUARDO ULIBARRI; circ. 113,000.

La Prensa Libre: Calle 4, Avda 4, Apdo 10.121, San José; tel. 223-6666; fax 223-4671; f. 1889; evening; independent; Dir ANDRÉS BORRASÉ SANOU; circ. 50,000.

La República: Barrio Tournón, Guadalupe, Apdo 2.130, San José; tel. 223-0266; fax 255-3950; f. 1950, reorganized 1967; morning; independent; Dir Lic. JOAQUÍN VARGAS GENE; circ. 60,000.

PERIODICALS

Abanico: Calle 4, esq. Avda 4, Apdo 10.121, San José; tel. 223-6666; fax 223-4671; weekly supplement of *La Prensa Libre*; women's interests; Editor MARÍA DEL CARMEN POZO C.; circ. 50,000.

Acta Médica: Sabana Sur, Apdo 548, San José; tel. 232-3433; f. 1954; organ of the Colegio de Médicos; 3 issues per year; Editor Dr BAUDILIO MORA MORA; circ. 2,000.

Contrapunto: La Uruca, Apdo 7-1.980, San José; tel. 231-3333; f. 1978; fortnightly; publication of Sistema Nacional de Radio y Televisión; Dir FABIO MUÑOZ CAMPOS; circ. 10,000.

Eco Católico: Calle 22, Avdas 3 y 5, Apdo 1.064, San José; tel. 222-7451; fax 222-6156; f. 1931; Catholic weekly; Dir ARMANDO ALFARO; circ. 20,000.

Mujer y Hogar: Avda 15, Casa 1916, Apdo 89, Barrio Aránjuez, San José; tel. 236-3128; f. 1943; weekly; women's journal; Editor and Gen. Man. CARMEN CORNEJO MÉNDEZ; circ. 15,000.

Noticiero del Café: Calle 1, Avdas 18 y 20, Apdo 37, San José; tel. 222-6411; telex 2279; f. 1964; bi-monthly; coffee journal; owned by the Instituto del Café de Costa Rica; Dir MELVYN ALVARADO SOTO; circ. 5,000.

Perfil: Llorente de Tibás, Apdo 10.138, San José, 1000; tel. 247-4355; telex 2358; fax 247-4477; fortnightly; women's interest; Dir GRETTEL ALFARO CAMACHO; circ. 20,000.

Polémica: Icadis, Paseo de los Estudiantes, Apdo 1.006, San José; tel. 233-3964; f. 1981; every 4 months; left-wing; Dir GABRIEL AGUILERA PERALTA.

Primera Plana: Sabana Este, San José; tel. 255-1590.

Rumbo: Llorente de Tibás, Apdo 10.138, 1000 San José; tel. 240-4848; telex 2358; fax 240-6480; f. 1984; weekly; general; Dir ROXANA ZÚÑIGA; circ. 15,000.

San José News: Apdo 7-2.730, San José; 2 a week; Dir CHRISTIAN RODRÍGUEZ.

Semanario Libertad: Calle 4, Avdas 8 y 10, Apdo 6.613, 1000 San José; tel. 225-5857; f. 1962; weekly; organ of the Partido del Pueblo Costarricense; Dir RODOLFO ULLOA B.; Editor JOSÉ A. ZÚÑIGA; circ. 10,000.

Semanario Universidad: Ciudad Universitaria Rodrigo Facio, San Pedro, Montes de Oca, San José; tel. 207-5355; telex 2544; fax 207-4774; f. 1970; weekly; general; Dir Lic. RENATO CAJAS CORSI; circ. 15,000.

The Tico Times: Calle 15, Avda 8, Apdo 4.632, San José; tel. 222-8952; fax 223-6378; weekly; in English; Dir DERY DYER; circ. 15,210.

PRESS ASSOCIATIONS

Colegio de Periodistas de Costa Rica: Sabana Este, Calle 42, Avda 4, Apdo 5.416, San José; tel. 233-5850; fax 223-8669; f. 1969; 550 mems; Exec. Dir Licda ADRIANA NÚÑEZ.

Sindicato Nacional de Periodistas: Sabana Este, Calle 42, Avda 4, Apdo 5.416, San José; tel. 222-7589; f. 1970; 200 mems; Sec.-Gen. ADRIÁN ROJAS JAÉN.

FOREIGN NEWS BUREAUX

ACAN-EFE (Central America): Costado Sur, Casa Matute Gómez, Casa 1912, Apdo 84.930, San José; tel. 222-6785; telex 3197; Correspondent WILFREDO CHACÓN SERRANO.

Agence France-Presse (France): Calle 13, Avdas 9 y 11 bis, Apdo 5.276, San José; tel. 233-0757; telex 2403; Correspondent DOMINIQUE PETTIT.

Agencia EFE (Spain): Avda 10, Calles 19 y 21, No 1912, Apdo 84.930, San José; tel. 222-6785; telex 3197.

Agenzia Nazionale Stampa Associata (ANSA) (Italy): c/o Diario La República, Barrio Tournón, Guadalupe, Apdo 545-1200, San José; tel. 231-1140; fax 231-1140; Correspondent LUIS CARTÍN S.

Associated Press (AP) (USA): San José; tel. 221-6146; Correspondent REID MILLER.

Deutsche Presse-Agentur (dpa) (Germany): Edif. 152, 3°, Calle 11, Avdas 1 y 3, Apdo 7.156, San José; tel. 233-0604; telex 2608; fax 233-0604; Correspondent ERNESTO RAMÍREZ.

Informatsionnoye Telegrafnoye Agentstvo Rossii—Telegrafnoye Agentstvo Suverennykh Stran (ITAR—TASS) (Russia): De la Casa Italia 1000 metros este, 50 metros norte, Casa 675, Apdo 1.011, San José; tel. 224-1560; telex 2711; Correspondent ENRIQUE MORA.

Inter Press Service (IPS) (Italy): Latin American Regional Center, Calle 11, Avdas 1 y 3, No 152, Paseo de los Estudiantes, Apdo 70, 1002 San José; tel. 255-3861; telex 3239; fax 233-8583; Regional Dir GONZALO ORTIZ-CRESPO.

Prensa Latina (Cuba): Avda 11, No 3185, Calles 31 y 33, Barrio Escalante (de la parrillada 25 metros al oeste), San José; tel. 253-1457; Correspondent FRANCISCO A. URIZARRI TAMAYO.

Rossiyskoye Informatsionnoye Agentstvo—Novosti (RIA—Novosti) (Russia): De la Casa Italiana 100 metros este, 50 metros norte, San José; tel. 224-1560; telex 2711.

United Press International (UPI) (USA): Calle 15, Avda 2, Radioperiódicos Reloj, Apdo 4.334, San José; tel. 222-2644; Correspondent WILLIAM CESPEDES CHAVARRÍA.

Xinhua (New China) News Agency (People's Republic of China): Apdo 4.774, San José; tel. 231-3497; telex 3066; Correspondent XU BIHUA.

Publishers

Alfalit Internacional: Apdo 292, 4050 Alajuela; f. 1961; educational; Dirs GILBERTO BERNAL, OSMUNDO PONCE.

Antonio Lehmann Librería, Imprenta y Litografía, Ltda: Calles 1 y 3, Avda Central, Apdo 10.011, San José; tel. 223-1212; telex 2540; f. 1896; general fiction, educational, textbooks; Man. Dir ANTONIO LEHMANN STRUVE.

Editorial Caribe: Apdo 1.307, San José; tel. 222-7244; f. 1949; religious textbooks; Dir JOHN STROWEL.

Editorial Costa Rica: 100 metros sur y 50 metros este del Supermercado Periféricos en San Francisco de Dos Ríos, Apdo 10.010, San José; tel. 286-1817; f. 1959; government-owned; cultural; Gen. Man. SHEILA DI PALMA GAMBOA.

Editorial Fernández Arce: Apdo 6.523, 1000 San José; tel. 224-5201; fax 234-1300; f. 1967; textbooks for primary, secondary and university education; Dir Dr MARIO FERNÁNDEZ LOBO.

Editorial Texto Ltda: Calle 26, Avda 3, Apdo 2.988, 1000 San José; tel. 255-3106; f. 1963; Dir FRANK THOMAS GALLARDO; Asst Man. FRANK THOMAS ECHEVERRÍA.

Editorial de la Universidad Autónoma de Centroamérica (UACA): Apdo 7.637, 1000 San José; tel. 234-0701; fax 224-0391; e-mail lauaca@sol.racsa.co.cr; f. 1981; Editor ALBERTO DI MARE.

Editorial de la Universidad Estatal a Distancia (EUNED): Paseo de los Estudiantes, Apdo 597, 1002 San José; tel. 223-5430; telex 3003; fax 257-5042; f. 1979; Dir AUXILIADORA PROTTI QUESADA.

Editorial Universitaria Centroamericana (EDUCA): Ciudad Universitaria Rodrigo Facio, San Pedro, Montes de Oca, Apdo 64, 2060 San José; tel. 224-3727; telex 3011; fax 253-9141; f. 1969; organ of the CSUCA; science, art, philosophy; Dir SEBASTIÁN VAQUERANO.

Mesén Editores: Urbanización El Cedral, 52, Cedros de Montes de Oca, Apdo 6.306, 1000 San José; tel. 253-5203; fax 283-0681; f. 1978; general; Dir DENNIS MESÉN SEGURA.

Trejos Hermanos Sucs, SA: Curridabat, Apdo 10.096, San José; tel. 224-2411; telex 2875; f. 1912; general and reference; Man. ALVARO TREJOS.

PUBLISHING ASSOCIATION

Cámara Costarricense del Libro: San José; Pres. LUIS FERNANDO CALVO FALLAS.

Broadcasting and Communications

TELECOMMUNICATIONS

Cámara Costarricense de Telecomunicaciones: Edif. Centro Colón, Of. 1–6, Apdo 591-1007, 1000 San José; tel. and fax 255-3422; Pres. EVITA ARGUEDAS MAKLOUF.

Cámara Nacional de Medios de Comunicación Colectiva (CANAMECC): Apdo 6.574, 1000 San José; tel. 222-4820; f. 1954; Pres. ANDRÉS QUINTANA CAVALLINI.

RADIO

Asociación Costarricense de Información y Cultura (ACIC): Apdo 365, 1009 San José; f. 1983; independent body; controls private radio stations; Pres. JUAN FCO. MONTEALEGRE MARTÍN.

Cámara Nacional de Radio (CANARA): Paseo de los Estudiantes, Apdo 1.583, 1002 San José; tel. 233-1845; fax 255-4483; e-mail canara@sol.racsa.co.cr; internet www.elparaiso.com/canara; f. 1947; Exec. Dir LUZMILDA VARGAS GONZÁLEZ.

Control Nacional de Radio (CNR): Dirección Nacional de Comunicaciones, Ministerio de Gobernación y Policia, Apdo 10.006, 1000 San José; tel. 221-0992; telex 3420; fax 221-9910; f. 1954; governmental supervisory department; Dir WARREN MURILLO MARTÍNEZ.

Non-commercial

Faro del Caribe: Apdo 2.710, 1000 San José; tel. 226-2573; fax 227-1725; f. 1948; religious and cultural programmes in Spanish and English; Man. CARLOS ROZOTTO PIEDRASANTA.

Radio Costa Rica: Apdo 6.462, 1000 San José; tel. 227-4693; f. 1985; broadcasts Voice of America news bulletins (in Spanish) and locally-produced educational and entertainment programmes; Dir MARIO ALBERTO SALGADO.

Radio Fides: Avda 4, Curia Metropolitana, Apdo 5.079, 1000 San José; tel. 222-1252; fax 233-2387; f. 1952; Roman Catholic station; Dir Rev. WILLIAM LIZANO A.

Radio Santa Clara: Santa Clara, San Carlos, Ciudad Quesada, Alajuela; tel. 479-1264; f. 1986; Roman Catholic station; Dir Rev. MARCO A. SOLÍS V.

Radio U: Ciudad Universitaria Rodrigo Facio, San Pedro, Montes de Oca, Apdo 2060, 1000 San José; tel. 207-5315; fax 207-4652; f. 1996; popular music; Dir CARLOS MORALES.

Commercial

There are about 40 commercial radio stations, including:

Cadena de Emisoras Columbia: Apdo 708, 1002 San José; tel. 234-0355; fax 225-9275; operates Radio Columbia, Radio Uno, Radio Sabrosa, Radio Puntarenas; Dir C. ARNOLDO ALFARO CHAVARRA.

Cadena Musical: Apdo 854, 1000, San José; tel. 257-2789; fax 233-9975; f. 1954; operates Radio Musical, Radio Emperador; Gen. Man. JORGE JAVIER CASTRO.

Grupo Centro: Apdo 6.133, San José; tel. 240-7591; fax 236-3672; operates Radio Centro 96.3 F.M., Radio 820 A.M., Televisora Guanacasteca Channels 16 and 28;Dir ROBERTO HERNÁNDEZ RAMÍREZ.

Radio Chorotega: Apdo 92, 5175 Santa Cruz de Guanacaste; tel. 663-2757; fax 663-0183; f. 1983; Roman Catholic station; Dir Rev. EMILIO MONTES DE OCA CORDERO.

Radio Emaus: San Vito de Coto Brus; tel. and fax 773-3101; f. 1962; Roman Catholic station; Dir Rev. LUIS PAULINO CABRERA SOTO.

Radio Monumental: Apdo 800, 1000 San José; tel. 222-0000; fax 222-8237; f. 1929; all news station; Dir-Gen. ADRIANA NÚÑEZ ARTILES.

Radio Sinaí: Apdo 262, 8000 San Isidro de El General; tel. 771-0367; f. 1957; Roman Catholic station; Dir Mgr ALVARO COTO OROZCO.

Sistema Radiofónico: Edif. Galería La Paz, 3°, Avda 2, Calles 2 y 4, Apdo 341, 1000 San José; tel. 222-4344; fax 255-0587; operates Radio Reloj; Dir Dr HERNÁN BARQUERO MONTES DE OCA.

TELEVISION

Government-owned

Sistema Nacional de Radio y Televisión Cultural (SINART): Apdo 7-1.980, San José; tel. 231-0839; telex 2374; cultural; Dir-Gen. GUIDO SÁENZ G.

Commercial

Canal 2: Apdo 2.860, San José; tel. 231-2222; Pres. RAMÓN COLL MONTERO.

Corporación Costarricense de Televisión, SA (Canal 6): Apdo 2.860, 1000 San José; tel. 232-9255; telex 2443; fax 232-6087; Gen. Man. MARIO SOTELA BLEN.

Multivisión de Costa Rica, Ltda (Canales 4 y 9): Apdo 4.666, 1000 San José; tel. 233-4444; fax 221-1734; operates Radio Sistema Universal A.M. (f. 1956), Channel 9 (f. 1962) and Channel 4 (f. 1964) and FM (f. 1980); Gen. Man. ARNOLD VARGAS V.

Televisora de Costa Rica (Canal 7), SA (Teletica): Apdo 3.876, San José; tel. 232-2222; telex 2220; fax 231-7545; f. 1960; operates Channel 7; Pres. OLGA DE PICADO; Gen. Man. RENÉ PICADO COZZA.

Televisora Sur y Norte (Canal 11): Apdo 99, 1000 San José; tel. 233-4988; Gen. Man. FEDERICO ZAMORA.

Finance

(cap. = capital; p.u. = paid up; res = reserves; dep. = deposits; m. = million; brs = branches; amounts in colones, unless otherwise indicated)

BANKING

Banco Central de Costa Rica: Avdas Central y Primera, Calles 2 y 4, Apdo 10.058, 1000 San José; tel. 233-4233; telex 2163; fax 223-4658; f. 1950; cap. 5.0m., res 10.0m., total resources 664,808.6m. (Dec. 1994); Pres. RODRIGO BOLAÑOS ZAMORA; Man. LUIS CARLOS MORA O.

State-owned Banks

Banco de Costa Rica: Avdas Central y 2, Calles 4 y 6, Apdo 10.035, 1000 San José; tel. 255-1100; telex 2103; fax 255-3316; f. 1877; responsible for industry; cap. 2,385.4m., surplus and res 5,995.9m., dep. 86,080.3m. (Dec. 1993); Pres. HERNÁN ACUÑA; Gen. Man. RODOLFO MONTERO B.; 44 brs and agencies.

Banco Crédito Agrícola de Cartago: Avda 2, Calles 3 y 5, Apdo 297, Cartago; tel. 551-3011; telex 8006; fax 552-0364; f. 1918; responsible for housing; cap. and res 1,056m., dep. 8,966m. (Aug. 1991); Pres. Lic. DANIEL GAMBOA P.; Gen. Man. Lic. ALBERTO CAMPOS C.; 10 brs.

Banco Nacional de Costa Rica: Calles 2 y 4, Avda Primera, Apdo 10.015, 1000 San José; tel. 223-2166; telex 2120; fax 255-2436; f. 1914; responsible for the agricultural sector; cap. 3,546.6m., surplus, profit and reserves 6,935.0m., dep. 143,295.2m. (Dec. 1992); Gen. Man. Lic. OMAR GARRO V.; 125 brs and agencies.

Banco Popular y de Desarrollo Comunal: Calle 1, Avdas 2 y 4, Apdo 10.190, San José; tel. 222-8122; telex 2844; fax 233-2350; f. 1969; cap. 260m., res 6m., dep. 940m. (June 1981); Pres. Ing. RODOLFO NAVAS ALVARADO; Gen. Man. ALVARO UREÑA ALVAREZ.

Private Banks

Banco BANEX, SA: Avda Primera y Calle Central, Apdo 7.893, 1000 San José; tel. 257-0522; telex 3065; fax 223-7192; f. 1981 as Banco Agro Industrial y de Exportaciones, SA; adopted present name 1987; cap. 1,300.1m., res 434.6m., dep. 11,971.6m. (June 1995); Pres. RICHARD BECK; Gen. Man. Ing. OSCAR RODRÍGUEZ ULLOA; 3 brs.

Banco BCT, SA: Calle Central No. 160, Apdo 7.698, San José; tel. 233-6611; telex 3153; fax 233-6833; f. 1984; cap. and res 279m. (Aug. 1991); Pres. ANTONIO BURGUÉS; Gen. Man. Lic. LEONEL BARUCH.

Banco BFA, SA: Centro Comercial CAFESA, La Uruca, Apdo 6.531, 1000 San José; tel. 231-4444; telex 3508; fax 232-7476; f. 1984 as Banco de Fomento Agrícola; present name adopted 1994; cap. 850m.; res 74.8m.; dep. 6,471m. (Dec. 1994); Pres. ERNESTO ROHRMOSER; Gen. Man. and CEO ALBERTO DENT.

Banco de COFISA, SA: Barrio Tournón, San Francisco de Goicoechea, Apdo 10.067, San José; tel. 257-6363; telex 2305; fax 233-4594; f. 1986; cap. and res 378m. (Aug. 1991); Pres. Lic. OMAR DENGO; Gen. Man. WILLIAM J. PHELPS.

Banco del Comercio, SA: Avda Primera y Calle Central, Apdo 1.106, 1000 San José; tel. 233-6011; telex 3301; fax 222-3706; f. 1978; cap. and res 348m. (Aug. 1991), dep. 1,653.7m. (Dec. 1989); Pres. JAVIER QUIRÓS RAMOS DE ANAYA; Gen. Man. JAVIER FILLOY ESNA.

Banco Continental, SA: Edif. LAICA, Barrio Tournón, Apdo 7.969, San José; tel. 257-1155; telex 3114; fax 255-3983; f. 1984; cap. and res 782m. (Oct. 1993); Pres. RODOLFO SALAS; Gen. Man. Ing. JUAN J. FLÓREZ.

Banco Cooperativo Costarricense, RL: Avda 7, Calles 3 y 5, Apdo 8.593, 1000 San José; tel. 233-5044; telex 3230; fax 233-0334; f. 1982; cap. and res 656m. (Dec. 1995); Pres. RODOLFO NAVAS ALVARADO; Gen. Man. JUAN RAFAEL ARAYA MARÍN.

Banco de Crédito Centroamericano, SA (Bancentro): Calles 26 y 38, Paseo Colón, de la Mercedes Benz 200 metros norte y 150 metros oeste, Apdo 5.099, 1000 San José; tel. 257-5811; telex 2473; fax 256-6147; f. 1974; cap. 492m. (1996); Pres. ROBERTO J. ZAMORA LLANES; Gen. Man GILBERTO SERRANO GUTIÉRREZ.

Banco FINCOMER, SA: Calles 7 y 9, Avda 2, Apdo 1.002, Paseo de los Estudiantes, San José; tel. 233-7822; telex 3306; fax 222-0405; f. 1977; cap. 600m., dep. 2,300m. (Sept. 1993); Pres. Lic. DANIEL CASAFONT FLORES; Gen. Man. Lic. RAFAEL A. MORA BADILLA.

Banco Federado, RL: 150 metros norte Fuente de la Hispanidad, San Pedro Montes de Oca, Apdo 806, 1000 San José; tel. 253-5108; telex 2902; fax 253-4803; f. 1985; cap. and res 505m. (Aug. 1991); Pres. Dr OLMAN MONTERO; Gen. Man. WALTER MORA.

Banco Germano Centroamericano, SA: 50 metros norte Iglesia El Carmen, Apdo 22.559, San José; tel. 233-8022; telex 3441; fax 222-2648; f. 1987; cap. and res 264m. (Aug. 1991); Pres. Lic. MANUEL QUESADA; Gen. Man. Ing. JOACHIM VON KOELLER.

Banco de la Industria, SA: Calle 9, Avdas Central y Primera, Apdo 4.254, 1000 San José; tel. 221-3355; telex 3177; fax 233-8383; f. 1985; cap. and res 200m. (Aug. 1993); Pres. Lic. ALBÁN BRENES IBARRA; Gen. Man. Dr ABELARDO BRENES IBARRA.

Banco Interfin, SA: Calle 3, Avdas 2 y 4, Apdo 6.899, San José; tel. 287-4000; telex 2868; fax 233-4823; f. 1982; cap. and res 2,198.6m. (Dec. 1996); Pres. Ing. LUIS LUKOWIECKI; Gen. Man. Dr LUIS LIBERMAN.

Banco Internacional de Costa Rica, SA: Edif. Inmobiliaria BICSA, Barrio Tournón, Apdo 6.116, San José; tel. 257-0855; telex

2771; fax 233-8413; f. 1987; cap. and res 1,625m. (Nov. 1994); Pres. Lic. FERNANDO SUÑOL PREGO; Gen. Man. MARCO ALFARO CHAVARRÍA.

Banco Internacional de Exportación, SA: Calle Central, Avda 3, Apdo 5.384, San José; tel. 222-3033; telex 2948; f. 1981; Pres. HOJABAR YAZDANI; Gen. Man. HERNÁN VOLIO.

Banco Latinoamericano (Costa Rica), SA: San José; f. 1974; cap. 5m.; Pres. FERNANDO BERROCAL S.; Man. FRED O'NEILL G.

Banco Lyon, SA: Calle 2, Avdas Primera y Central, Apdo 10.184, 1000 San José; tel. 221-2611; telex 2577; fax 221-6795; f. 1871; cap. 592.5m., res 78.4m., dep. 636.5m. (Dec. 1993); Pres. ALBERTO VALLARINO CLEMENT; Gen. Man. MARCIAL DÍAZ DEL VALLE.

Banco Mercantil de Costa Rica, SA: Avda Primera, Calles Central y 2, Apdo 5.395, San José; tel. 257-6868; fax 255-3076; f. 1987; cap. and res 750m. (Sept. 1994); Pres. IGNACIO AIZENMAN; Gen. Man. JACOBO AIZENMAN.

Banco Metropolitano, SA: Calle Central, Avda 2, Apdo 6.714, 1000 San José; tel. 257-3030; telex 2955; fax 255-3826; f. 1985; cap. and res US $5.0m., dep. $15.2m. (Dec. 1995); Pres. ABRAHAM MELTZER SPIGEL.; Gen. Man. FRANCISCO LAY SOLANO; 3 brs.

Banco de San José, SA: Calle Central, Avdas 3 y 5, Apdo 5.445, 1000 San José; tel. 221-9911; telex 2242; fax 222-8208; f. 1968; fmrly Bank of America, SA; cap. 405.0m., surplus, profits and reserves 1,606m., dep. 15,234.3m. (Dec. 1994); Pres. ERNESTO CASTEGNARO ODIO; Gen. Man. MARIO MONTEALEGRE-SABORÍO.

Banco de Santander (Costa Rica), SA: Avda 2, Calle Central, Apdo 6.714, San José; tel. 222-8066; telex 2666; fax 222-8840; f. 1977; cap. 60m. (1986); Pres. ABRAHAM WAIESLEDER; Gen. Man. LUIS MIER ABANS.

Credit Co-operatives

Federación Nacional de Cooperativas de Ahorro y Crédito (Fedecrédito, RL): Calle 20, Avdas 8 y 10, Apdo 4.748, 1000 San José; tel. 233-5666; fax 257-1724; f. 1963; 55 co-operatives, with 150,000 mems; combined cap. US $82m.; Pres. Lic. CARLOS BONILLA AYUB; Gen. Man. Lic. MARIO VARGAS ALVARADO.

STOCK EXCHANGE

Bolsa Nacional de Valores, SA: Edif. Cartagena, 4°, Calle Central, Avda Primera, Apdo 1.736, 1000 San José; tel. 256-1180; telex 2863; fax 255-0131; f. 1976; Exec. Pres. Lic. LEONEL BARUCH GOLDBERG; Gen. Man. ROBERTO VENEGAS RENAULD (acting).

INSURANCE

Instituto Nacional de Seguros: Calles 9 y 9 bis, Avda 7, Apdo 10.061, 1000 San José; tel. 223-5800; telex 2290; fax 222-2310; f. 1924; administers the state monopoly of insurance; services of foreign insurance companies may be used only by authorization of the Ministry of the Economy, and only after the Instituto has certified that it will not accept the risk; cap. and res 3,389m. (Dec. 1983); Pres. LUIS-JAVIER GUIER; Gen. Man. EDGAR SEQUEIRA.

Trade and Industry

GOVERNMENT AGENCIES

Instituto Nacional de Vivienda y Urbanismo (INVU): Apdo 2.534, San José; tel. 221-5266; telex 2908; fax 223-4006; housing and town planning institute; Exec. Pres. Ing. Lic. VICTOR EVELIO CASTRO; Gen. Man. Lic. PEDRO HERNÁNDEZ RUIZ.

Ministry of Planning: Avdas 3 y 5, Calle 4, Apdo 10.127, 1000 San José; tel. 221-9524; telex 2962; fax 253-6243; f. 1963; formulates and supervises execution of the National Development Plan; main aims: to increase national productivity; to improve distribution of income and social services; to increase citizen participation in solution of socio-economic problems; Pres. Dr LEONARDO GARNIER.

Promotora de Comercio Exterior de Costa Rica (PROCOMER): Calle 40, Avdas Central y 3, Centro Colón, Apdo 1.278, 1007 San José; tel. 256-7111; telex 2385; fax 223-0120; f. 1968 to encourage increased investment in export-orientated activities and greater exports of non-traditional products; Dir-Gen. EDUARDO ALONSO.

DEVELOPMENT ORGANIZATIONS

Cámara de Azucareros: Calle 3, Avda Fernández Güell, Apdo 1.577, 1000 San José; tel. 221-2103; fax 222-1358; f. 1949; sugar growers; Pres. RODRIGO ARIAS SÁNCHEZ.

Cámara Nacional de Bananeros: Edif. Urcha, 3°, Calle 11, Avda 6, Apdo 10.273, 1000 San José; tel. 222-7891; fax 233-1268; f. 1967; banana growers; Pres. Lic. HERNÁN ROBLES OREAMUNO; Exec. Dir Lic. ALEJANDRO BEJARANO CASTILLO.

Cámara Nacional de Cafetaleros: Calle 3, Avdas 6 y 8, No. 652, Apdo 1.310, San José; tel. 221-8207; fax 257-5381; f. 1948; 70 mems; coffee millers and growers; Pres. RONALD PETERS SEEVERS; Exec. Dir JOAQUÍN VALVERDE B.

Cámara Nacional de Ganaderos: Edif. Ilifilán, 4°, Calles 4 y 6, Avda Central, Apdo 5.539, 1000 San José; tel. 222-1652; cattle farmers; Pres. Ing. ALBERTO JOSÉ AMADOR ZAMORA.

Cámara Nacional de Artesanía y Pequeña Industria de Costa Rica (CANAPI): Calle 17, Avda 10, detrás estatua de San Martín, Apdo 1.783-2.100 Goicoechea, San José; tel. 223-2763; fax 255-4873; f. 1963; development, marketing and export of small-scale industries and handicrafts; Pres. and Exec. Dir RODRIGO GONZÁLEZ.

CINDE (Costa Rican Investment and Development Board): Apdo 7.170, 1000 San José; tel. 220-0366; telex 3514; fax 220-4750; f. 1983; coalition for development of initiatives to attract foreign investment for production and export of new products; Chair. EMILIO BRUCE; CEO ENRIQUE EGLOFF.

Instituto del Café de Costa Rica: Calle 1, Avdas 18 y 20, Apdo 37, San José; tel. 222-6411; telex 2279; fax 222-2838; f. 1948 to develop the coffee industry, to control production and to regulate marketing; Pres. Lic. LUIS DIEGO ESCALANTE.

CHAMBERS OF COMMERCE

Cámara de Comercio de Costa Rica: Urbanización Tournón, 150 metros noroeste del parqueo del Centro Comercial El Pueblo, Apdo 1.114, 1000 San José; tel. 221-0005; fax 233-7091; e-mail biofair@sol.racsa.co.cr; f. 1915; 1,200 mems; Pres. CARLOS A. FEDERSPIEL PINTO; Exec. Dir Lic. JULIO UGARTE TATÚM.

Cámara de Industrias de Costa Rica: Calles 13–15, Avda 6, Apdo 10.003, 1000 San José; tel. 223-2411; telex 2474; fax 222-1007; f. 1943; Pres. Ing. MIGUEL SCHYFTER LEPAR; Exec. Dir HELIO FALLAS V.

Unión Costarricense de Cámaras y Asociaciones de la Empresa Privada (UCCAEP): 1002 Paseo de los Estudiantes, Apdo 539, San José; tel. 290-5595; telex 3644; fax 290-5596; f. 1974; business federation; Pres. Ing. SAMUEL YANKELEWITZ BERGER; Exec. Dir ALVARO RAMÍREZ BOGANTES.

INDUSTRIAL AND TRADE ASSOCIATIONS

Cámara Nacional de Agricultura: Avda 10-10 bis, Cv. 23, Apdo 1.671, 1000 San José; tel. 221-6864; telex 3489; fax 233-8658; f. 1947; Pres. Ing. LEONEL PERALTA; Exec. Dir Lic. JOSÉ CARLOS BARQUERO ARCE.

CODESA: Apdo 10.254, 1000 San José; tel. 222-2344; telex 2405; fax 233-1355; f. 1972; development corporation; Pres. MÁSTER RENÁN MURILLO PIZARRO.

Consejo Nacional de Producción: Calle 36 a 12, Apdo 2.205, San José; tel. 223-6033; telex 2273; fax 233-9660; f. 1948 to encourage agricultural and fish production and to regulate production and distribution of basic commodities; Pres. Ing. JAVIER FLORES GALAGARZA; Man. Lic. VIRGINIA VALVERDE DE MOLINA.

Instituto de Desarrollo Agrícola (IDA): Apdo 5.054, 1000 San José; tel. 224-6066; Exec. Pres. Ing. ROBERTO SOLÓRZANO SANABRIA; Gen. Man. Ing. JORGE ANGEL JIMÉNEZ CALDERÓN.

Instituto de Fomento y Asesoría Municipal: Apdo 10.187, 1000 San José; tel. 223-3714; fax 233-1817; f. 1970; municipal development institute; Exec. Pres. ETELBERTO JIMÉNEZ PIEDRA; Exec. Dir Prof. GUILLERMO SABORÍO MORA.

Instituto Mixto de Ayuda Social (IMAS): Calle 29, Avdas 2 y 4, Apdo 6.213, San José; tel. 225-5555; telex 1559; fax 224-8783; Pres. CLOTILDE FONSECA QUESADA.

Instituto Nacional de Fomento Cooperativo: Apdo 10.103, 1000 San José; tel. 223-4355; telex 3040; fax 255-3835; f. 1973; to encourage the establishment of co-operatives and to provide technical assistance and credit facilities; cap. 11m. (May 1986); Pres. Lic. RAFAEL ANGEL ROJAS JIMÉNEZ; Exec. Dir Lic. LUIS ANTONIO MONGE ROMÁN.

UTILITIES

Electricity

Instituto Costarricense de Electricidad—ICE (Costa Rican Electricity Institute): Apdo 10.032, 1000 San José; tel. 220-7720; telex 2140; fax 220-4078; state power and telecommunications agency; Exec. Pres. Ing. TEÓFILO DE LA TORRE ARGÜELLO; Gen. Man. Ing. MARIO HIDALGO PACHECO.

Water

Instituto Costarricense de Acueductos y Alcantarillados: Avda Central, Calle 5, Apdo 5.120, 1000 San José; tel. 233-2155; telex 2724; fax 222-2259; water and sewerage; Exec. Pres. Ing. ANA GABRIELA ROSS.

TRADE UNIONS

By the end of 1987 there were only 19 unions, with a total of 4,313 members nation-wide; membership of 'solidarista' associations had risen to 16,229. A new labour code, adopted in 1988, has encouraged the further growth of these associations (in which employers' interests tend to predominate) at the expense of the trade unions.

Central de Trabajadores Costarricenses (CTC) (Costa Rican Workers' Union): Calle 20, Avdas 3 y 5, Apdo 4.137, 1000 San José; tel. 221-7701; telex 3091; fax 229-3893; Sec.-Gen. ALSIMIRO HERRERA TORRES.

Confederación Auténtica de Trabajadores Democráticos (Democratic Workers' Union): Calle 13, Avdas 10 y 12, Solera; tel. 253-2971; Pres. LUIS ARMANDO GUTIÉRREZ; Sec.-Gen. Prof. CARLOS VARGAS.

Confederación Costarricense de Trabajadores Democráticos (Costa Rican Confederation of Democratic Workers): Calles 3 y 5, Avda 12, Apdo 2.167, San José; tel. 222-1981; telex 2167; f. 1966; mem. ICFTU and ORIT; Sec.-Gen. LUIS ARMANDO GUTIÉRREZ R.; 50,000 mems.

Confederación Unitaria de Trabajadores (CUT): Calles 1 y 3, Avda 12, Casa 142, Apdo 186, 1009 San José; tel. 233-4188; f. 1980 from a merger of the Federación Nacional de Trabajadores Públicos and the Confederación General de Trabajadores; 53 affiliated unions; Sec.-Gen. GILBER BERMÚDEZ UMAÑA; c. 75,000 mems.

Federación Sindical Agraria Nacional (FESIAN) (National Agrarian Confederation): Apdo 2.167, 1000 San José; tel. 233-5897; 20,000 member families; Sec.-Gen. JUAN MEJÍA VILLALOBOS.

The **Consejo Permanente de los Trabajadores,** formed in 1986, comprises six union organizations and two teachers' unions.

Transport

Ministry of Public Works and Transport: Apdo 10.176, 1000 San José; tel. 226-7311; telex 2478; fax 227-1434; the ministry is responsible for setting tariffs, allocating funds, maintaining existing systems and constructing new ones.

Cámara Nacional de Transportes: Calle 20, Avda 7, San José; tel. 222-5394; national chamber of transport.

RAILWAYS

Instituto Costarricense de Ferrocarriles (INCOFER): Calle 2, Avda 20, Apdo 1-1009, San José; tel. 221-0777; fax 257-7220; f. 1985; government-owned; 471 km, of which 388 km are electrified; Exec. Pres. Lic. JOSÉ FRANCISCO BOLAÑOS ARQUÍN.

INCOFER comprises:

División I: Atlantic sector running between Limón, Río Frío, Valle la Estrella and Siquirres. Main line of 109 km, with additional 120 km of branch lines, almost exclusively for transport of bananas.

División II: Pacific sector running from San José to Puntarenas and Caldera; 116 km of track, principally for transport of cargo.

Plans for the introduction of a third division of the rail network, comprising 43 km linking Alajuela, Heredia, San José and Cartago, were being pursued in 1997.

Note: In 1995 INCOFER suspended operations, pending privatization.

ROADS

In 1996 there were 35,597 km of roads, of which 7,405 km were main roads and 28,192 km were secondary roads. An estimated 17% of the total road network was paved.

SHIPPING

Local services operate between the Costa Rican ports of Puntarenas and Limón and those of Colón and Cristóbal in Panama and other Central American ports. The multi-million dollar project at Caldera on the Gulf of Nicoya is now in operation as the main Pacific port; Puntarenas is being used as the second port. The Caribbean coast is served by the port complex of Limón/Moín. In April 1991 the complex was severely damaged by the effects of an earthquake. International services are operated by various foreign shipping lines.

Junta de Administración Portuaria y de Desarrollo Económico de la Vertiente Atlántica (JAPDEVA): Calle 17, Avda 7, Apdo 8-5.330, 1000 San José; tel. 233-5301; telex 2435; state agency for the development of Atlantic ports; Exec. Pres. Ing. JORGE ARTURO CASTRO HERRERA.

Instituto Costarricense de Puertos del Pacífico (INCOP): Calle 36, Avda 3, Apdo 543, 1000 San José; tel. 223-7111; telex 2793; fax 223-9685; state agency for the development of Pacific ports; Exec. Pres. GERARDO MEDINA MADRIZ.

CIVIL AVIATION

Costa Rica's main international airport is the Juan Santamaría Airport, 16 km from San José at El Coco. There is a second international airport, the Daniel Oduber Quirós Airport, at Liberia and there are regional airports at Limón and Pavas (Tobías Bolaños Airport).

Aero Costa Rica: San Pedro, Montes de Oca, Apdo 1.328, San José; tel. 296-1111; fax 232-1815; regional carrier; Chair. CALIXTO CHAVEL; Gen. Man. JUAN FERNÁNDEZ.

Líneas Aéreas Costarricenses, SA—LACSA (Costa Rican Airlines): Edif. Lacsa, La Uruca, Apdo 1.531, San José; tel. 290-2727; telex 2188; fax 232-4178; f. 1945; operates international services within Latin America and to North America; Chair. ALONSO LARA; Gen. Man. JOSÉ G. ROJAS.

Servicios Aéreos Nacionales, SA (SANSA): Paseo Colón, Centro Colón, Apdo 999, 1.007 San José; tel. 233-2714; telex 2914; fax 255-2176; subsidiary of LACSA; international, regional and domestic scheduled passenger and cargo services; Man. Dir CARLOS MANUEL DELGADO AGUILAR.

Servicios de Carga Aérea (SERCA): Aeropuerto Internacional Juan Santamaría, Apdo 6.855, San José; f. 1982; operates cargo service from San José.

Tourism

Costa Rica boasts a system of nature reserves and national parks unique in the world, which cover one-third of the country. The main tourist features are the Irazú and Poás volcanoes, the Orosí valley, the ruins of the colonial church at Ujarras and the jungle train to Limón. Tourists also visit San José, the capital, the Pacific beaches of Guanacaste and Puntarenas, and the Caribbean beaches of Limón. In 1995 plans were being pursued for the construction of a US $2,300m. tourism development at Papagayo Gulf in Guanacaste province. The project, for which the majority concession was held by the Mexican development company, Situr, envisaged the construction of a marina and as many as 25,000 hotel rooms. According to preliminary figures, a total of 792,300 tourists visited Costa Rica in 1995, when tourism receipts totalled an estimated $664.4m. There were 11,650 hotel rooms in Costa Rica in 1993.

Instituto Costarricense de Turismo: Edif. Genaro Valverde, Calles 5 y 7, Avda 4, Apdo 777, 1000 San José; tel. 223-1733; telex 2281; fax 223-5107; f. 1955; Exec. Pres. Ing. CARLOS ROESCH CARRANZA.

CÔTE D'IVOIRE

(THE IVORY COAST)

Introductory Survey

Location, Climate, Language, Religion, Flag, Capital

The Republic of Côte d'Ivoire lies on the west coast of Africa, between Ghana to the east and Liberia to the west, with Guinea, Mali and Burkina Faso to the north. Average temperatures vary between 21°C and 30°C (70°F and 86°F). The main rainy season, from May to July, is followed by a shorter wet season, in October–November. The official language is French, and a large number of African languages are also spoken. At the time of the 1988 census some 39% of the population were Muslims, 26% Christians (mainly Roman Catholics), and about 17% followed traditional beliefs. The national flag (proportions 3 by 2) has three equal vertical stripes, of orange, white and green. The political and administrative capital is Yamoussoukro, although most government ministries and offices remain in the former capital, Abidjan, which is the major centre for economic activity.

Recent History

Formerly a province of French West Africa, Côte d'Ivoire achieved self-government, within the French Community, in December 1958. Dr Félix Houphouët-Boigny, leader of the Parti démocratique de la Côte d'Ivoire—Rassemblement démocratique africain (PDCI—RDA), became Prime Minister in 1959. The country became fully independent on 7 August 1960; a new Constitution was adopted in October 1960, and Houphouët-Boigny became President in November.

Until 1990 the PDCI—RDA, founded in 1946, was Côte d'Ivoire's only legal political party. Despite constitutional provision for the existence of other political organizations, no opposition party was granted official recognition (although from November 1980 more than one candidate was permitted to contest each seat in the legislature, the Assemblée nationale). A high rate of economic growth (particularly during the 1970s), together with strong support from France, contributed, until the late 1980s, to the stability of the regime, and sporadic political unrest was without strong leadership.

In October 1985 the PDCI—RDA voted to amend Article 11 of the Constitution, thereby abolishing the post of Vice-President of the Republic and allowing for the President of the Assemblée nationale to succeed the Head of State, on an interim basis, in the event of a vacancy. Later that month Houphouët-Boigny was re-elected President for a sixth five-year term. Municipal and legislative elections took place in November, and in January 1986 Henri Konan Bédié was re-elected to the presidency of the legislature. In September Houphouët-Boigny hosted a series of 'days of national dialogue', at which Côte d'Ivoire's political, economic and social problems were discussed by state and party officials, senior officers of the armed forces and representatives of the country's trade unions and professional organizations. Houphouët-Boigny rejected appeals that Article 7 of the Constitution, which provides for the principle of a multi-party political system, be brought into effect, asserting that such a reform would impede progress towards national unity.

The announcement in early 1990 of austerity measures, in compliance with a new, IMF-sponsored economic revival programme, precipitated an unprecedented level of student and labour unrest, particularly following the announcement of reductions in salaries for all state employees and of a 'solidarity tax' on private-sector incomes. In April, as it became clear that the measures would, in any case, fail to generate the revenue necessary to reduce Côte d'Ivoire's increasingly burdensome foreign debt, Houphouët-Boigny appointed Alassane Ouattara, the Governor of the Banque centrale des états de l'Afrique de l'ouest, to chair a special commission whose task would be to formulate new measures that would be both more economically effective and politically acceptable. Economic reform was accompanied by political change, and in May it was announced that Article 7 of the Constitution be implemented. Hitherto unofficial political organizations were formally recognized, and many new parties were formed. In June the post of Chief of the General Staff of the Armed Forces was assigned to Col (later Gen.) Robert Gueï: his predecessor, Gen. Félix Ory, was transferred to a diplomatic post, apparently as a consequence of a mutiny by conscripts in the previous month. A new Minister of the Economy and Finance, Daniel Kablan Duncan, was appointed in July. Pope John Paul II visited Côte d'Ivoire in September, in order to consecrate a basilica in Yamoussoukro (Houphouët-Boigny's birthplace), which had been constructed, officially at the President's own expense, at a cost of some 40,000m. francs CFA.

Côte d'Ivoire's first contested presidential election was held on 28 October 1990. During the campaign period security forces had intervened at several opposition rallies and demonstrations, and Houphouët-Boigny's opponents had frequently accused the Government of impeding the political reform process. Houphouët-Boigny—challenged by Laurent Gbagbo, the candidate of the Front populaire ivoirien (FPI)—was re-elected for a seventh term with the support of 81.67% of those who voted. The FPI and its allies alleged malpractice, and appealed unsuccessfully to the Supreme Court to declare the election invalid. In November the legislature approved two constitutional amendments. The first concerned the procedure to be adopted if the presidency should become vacant: Article 11 was again amended to the effect that the President of the Assemblée nationale would assume the functions of the President of the Republic until the expiry of the previous incumbent's mandate. Secondly, provision was made for the appointment of a Prime Minister, who would be accountable to the President; Ouattara was subsequently designated premier.

Almost 500 candidates, representing some 17 political parties, contested legislative elections on 25 November 1990. Malpractice and the harassment of opposition supporters by the authorities was again alleged. The PDCI—RDA returned 163 deputies to the 175-member Assemblée nationale; Gbagbo and eight other members of the FPI were elected, as were Francis Wodié (the leader of the Parti ivoirien des travailleurs—PIT), and two independent candidates. Bédié was subsequently re-elected President of the Assemblée nationale. Ouattara's first Council of Ministers was named following the elections, in which the Prime Minister—assisted by Duncan—assumed personal responsibility for the economy and finance.

Tensions between the authorities and the education sector were revived in May 1991, after security forces used violent methods to disperse a students' meeting at the University of Abidjan. About 180 students were said to have been arrested, and the regional director of the Agence France-Presse news agency, which had published reports that four students had been killed by the security forces, was expelled from the country. Subsequent protests by students and academic staff were dispersed by the security forces. In June Houphouët-Boigny announced that a commission would be established to investigate the campus violence, but the crisis deepened when the death of a student who had defied an order to boycott classes, following an attack by members of the Fédération estudiantine et scolaire de Côte d'Ivoire (FESCI), prompted the Government to order that FESCI be disbanded, and that security forces be deployed at the university. Academic staff began an indefinite strike, and further protests followed the arrest, in July, of 11 FESCI activists, on suspicion of involvement in the student's death. The situation was temporarily resolved in August, when the Government withdrew the troops, suspended legal proceedings against FESCI members and restored the right of 'non-academic assembly' at the university (although the ban on FESCI remained in force). The commission of inquiry's report, published in January 1992, held the armed forces Chief of the General Staff ultimately responsible for the violent acts of the security forces. However, Houphouët-Boigny made it clear that neither Gueï nor anyone under his command would be subject to disciplinary proceedings. Demonstrations erupted at the university, prompting the arrest of FESCI activists, and in February Gbagbo and the President of the Ligue ivoirienne des droits de l'homme (LIDHO), René Degny-Segui, were among more than 100 people arrested during a violent anti-Government demonstration in Abidjan. It was subsequently announced that Gbagbo and other opposition leaders were to be prosecuted under the terms of a presidential ordinance, said by the Government to have been issued by Houphouët-Boigny (while on a private visit to Europe) on the eve of the demonstration, that rendered political leaders responsible for violent acts committed by their supporters during demonstrations. Later in the month the Secretary-General of FESCI was fined and sentenced to three years' imprisonment, convicted of reconstituting a banned organization and of responsibility for offences committed by students. The trials of other opposition activists followed, with, in all, some 75 custodial sentences being imposed: among those convicted were Gbagbo and Degny-Segui, who each received two-year prison sentences. In April FPI deputies began a boycott of the Assemblée nationale, in protest against the imprisonment of Gbagbo and another FPI member of parliament; the PIT leader joined the boycott in May.

Houphouët-Boigny returned to Côte d'Ivoire in June 1992, after an absence of almost five months (much of which had been spent in France). In July he proclaimed an amnesty for all persons convicted of political offences since the time of the 1990 disturbances. PDCI—RDA deputies approved the amnesty later in the month (and also endorsed legislation formalizing the presidential ordinance of February 1992); opposition deputies maintained their boycott of the legislature, protesting that the amnesty not only prevented detainees from pursuing the right of appeal, but also exempted members of the security forces from charges relating to alleged offences committed during the period covered by the measure.

In March 1993 there was a brief rebellion by members of the élite presidential guard in Abidjan. The mutineers, who were demanding pay increases commensurate with those recently granted to civilian employees at the presidency, ended their protest following discussions with Houphouët-Boigny. In the following month, however, presidential guards mutinied in Yamoussoukro, returning to barracks only after negotiations with Houphouët-Boigny, Gueï and the Minister of Defence regarding their salary demands. These incidents were cited by Ouattara's opponents (including, within the PDCI—RDA, supporters of Bédié) as evidence of the Prime Minister's inability to reconcile the demands of economic austerity with the need to maintain domestic harmony.

Houphouët-Boigny left Côte d'Ivoire in May 1993, and spent the following six months receiving medical treatment in France and Switzerland. As his health failed, controversy was revived concerning the presidential succession. Many senior politicians, including Ouattara and Gbagbo (both of whom were known to have presidential aspirations), asserted that the process defined in the Constitution effectively endorsed an 'hereditary presidency' (Bédié, like Houphouët-Boigny, was a member of the Baoulé ethnic group) and demanded that Article 11 again be revised to permit the President of the Assemblée nationale to assume the post of President of the Republic on an interim basis only, pending new elections.

Houphouët-Boigny died, officially aged 88, in Yamoussoukro on 7 December 1993. Later the same day Henri Konan Bédié made a television broadcast announcing that, in accordance with the Constitution, he was assuming the duties of President of the Republic with immediate effect. Ouattara initially refused to recognize Bédié's right of succession, but tendered his resignation two days later, thereby effectively strengthening the new President's position. Duncan was subsequently designated Prime Minister and Minister of the Economy, Finance and Planning. The Government retained senior members of the previous administration in charge of defence, foreign affairs, the interior and raw materials, and included two close associates of Bédié as Ministers of State. In January 1994 Charles Donwahi (the Vice-President of the legislature since 1991) was elected President of the Assemblée nationale.

Several months of sporadic labour unrest were brought to an end by Houphouët-Boigny's death, and, largely owing to a two-month period of national mourning, reactions to the 50% devaluation, in January 1994, of the CFA franc were generally more muted in Côte d'Ivoire than in other countries of the Franc Zone in Africa. In the months that followed his accession to the presidency Bédié appointed close associates to positions of influence in government, the judiciary and in the state-owned media. Bédié's position was further consolidated by his election to the chairmanship of the PDCI—RDA, in April, and by Ouattara's departure for the USA following his appointment, in May, to the post of Deputy Managing Director of the IMF. Disaffected members of the PDCI—RDA, who were reported to be supporters of Ouattara, left the party in June to form what they termed a moderate, centrist organization, the Rassemblement des républicains (RDR). Ouattara did not formally announce his membership of the RDR until early 1995.

The new regime used far-reaching legislation (introduced under Houphouët-Boigny) governing the press to bring charges against several journalists deemed to have been disrespectful to Bédié or to other state officials. Among those prosecuted was the director of an influential daily, *La Voie*, Abou Drahamane Sangaré (also the deputy leader of the FPI). Sangaré was, together with other journalists of his newspaper, imprisoned in April 1994, but was released in December, in accordance with a presidential amnesty for some 2,000 detainees. In June 1995 Sangaré was severely beaten by security forces at the office of the Minister of Security, Gaston Ouassénan Koné, following the publication in a satirical review owned by Sangaré's publishing group of remarks that were interpreted by Koné as insulting to him and his family.

An increase in recent years in the rate of violent crime in Côte d'Ivoire was of particular concern to the Bédié Government, and in June 1995 the Assemblée nationale approved proposals for legislation permitting the extension of the death penalty (already in existence for murder convictions, although there was no record of its implementation since independence) to cases of robbery with violence. Security operations accompanying the Government's anti-crime measures, which frequently targeted non-Ivorian groups, were denounced by Bédié's opponents as indicative of xenophobic tendencies within the new regime.

A new electoral code was adopted by parliament in December 1994. Among its stated aims was to increase the rate of electoral registration and participation. The new code also imposed new restrictions on eligibility for public office, notably stipulating that candidates for the Presidency or for the Assemblée nationale must be of direct Ivorian descent. The RDR in particular expressed concern that these restrictions might prevent Ouattara from contesting the presidency, since the former Prime Minister was of Burkinabè descent and would also be affected by the code's requirement that candidates have been continuously resident in Côte d'Ivoire for five years prior to seeking election. An opposition Front républicain (FR), comprising the RDR, the FPI and the Union des forces démocratiques (a coalition of several parties, among them the PIT), formed in April 1995, organized a series of mass demonstrations in Abidjan to demand the withdrawal of the electoral code and the establishment of an independent electoral commission. In August Ouattara, who had been invited by the RDR to be the party's presidential candidate, announced that, while he wished to contest the presidency, he would not attempt to do so in violation of the law. In the same month the PDCI—RDA formally adopted Bédié as its presidential candidate (Gbagbo was again to represent the FPI). The FR persisted in its demands for a revision of the electoral code, as well as guarantees regarding the autonomy of the electoral commission and the revision of voters' lists. In September, citing the need to ensure the continuation of economic activity, the Government imposed a three-month ban on political demonstrations. The FR countered that the ban was in violation of constitutional recognition of the right to demonstrate, emphasizing that it would continue to hold protest marches.

In early October 1995 the FPI and the RDR (whose Secretary-General, Djény Kobina, was to have replaced Ouattara as the party's candidate) stated that they would not be contesting the presidential election as long as the conditions were not 'clear and open'. An eruption of violence in Abidjan and in other major towns coincided with the opening of an international investment forum in Abidjan. Shortly afterwards the Constitutional Council announced that, of the six prospective candidates for the presidency, two—Bédié and (for the PIT) Wodié—had fulfilled the necessary criteria to contest the election. Negotiations involving Bédié, the FPI and other opposition groups subsequently took place; however, the RDR (which was later involved in separate talks with the authorities) claimed that it was being isolated from those discussions. No effective progress was made, despite mediation efforts by a group comprising religious and trade union leaders, as well as representatives of LIDHO and of other non-governmental organizations. The FR refused to accept a government offer to include opposition representatives on the commission responsible for scrutinizing voters' lists and the results of the elections as sufficient guarantee of the commission's autonomy, while the Government rejected the opposition's demand that the elections be postponed. Furthermore, the authorities emphasized that one of the principal grounds for the FR's proposed boycott of the presidential election—that the stipulation regarding continuous residency was directly aimed at preventing Ouattara's candidature—was invalid, since this did not apply to individuals selected by the Government to serve abroad.

The presidential election took place on 22 October 1995, following a week of violent incidents in several towns. The FR claimed that its campaign for an 'active boycott' of the poll had been largely successful (despite appeals by Wodié for the support of opposition sympathizers), while the Government claimed that voters had participated peacefully and in large numbers. Troops were deployed, ostensibly to prevent the disruption of voting by the opposition, although it was reported that polling had proceeded in only one of 60 designated centres in the FPI stronghold of Gagnoa, in the Centre-Ouest region. Bédié's overwhelming victory, with 95.25% of the valid votes cast, was confirmed by the Constitutional Council five days after the poll. While most areas remained generally calm following the election, reports of the persecution of Baoulé around Gagnoa by members of the local majority Bété ethnic group became a cause of concern, as large numbers of Baoulé converged on the town from surrounding areas. In November the Government announced the establishment of a commission of inquiry to investigate the situation. At this time official reports stated that there had been some 25 deaths in the region (although it later transpired that only one death had resulted from the unrest); more than 3,500 people, mainly Baoulé, had been displaced, and numerous settlements had been destroyed.

In early November 1995 it was announced that the FR had agreed to abandon its threatened boycott of the legislative elections, which were scheduled for 26 November, in return for government concessions regarding the revision of voters' lists; representatives of both the FPI and the RDR were subsequently appointed to the electoral commission. The opposition suffered a considerable reverse when the authorities announced that voting in three of Gagnoa's four constituencies (including the constituency that was to have been contested by Gbagbo) was to be postponed, owing to the disruption arising from the recent disturbances; moreover, Kobina's candidacy (in Abidjan's Adjamé constituency) was disallowed, on the grounds that he had been unable to prove direct Ivorian descent. Voting for the legislature was reported to have proceeded generally without incident, and the earliest indications were that the PDCI—RDA had retained a decisive majority—despite a notable loss of support for the party in the Nord region, in favour of the RDR. The FPI secured strong representation in the Centre-Ouest region, while the PDCI—RDA secured overwhelming victories in the Centre, Ouest and Sud-Ouest regions, and registered strong support in Abidjan and other major towns. Wodié failed to secure re-election to the Assemblée nationale. In late December the Constitutional Council annulled the results of the elections in three constituencies, including the one seat in Gagnoa for which voting had been permitted. The PDCI—RDA thus held 146 seats, the RDR 14, and the FPI nine. Also in December Donwahi was re-elected President of the Assemblée nationale.

In October 1995, shortly before the presidential election, Gueï was appointed to the Government as Minister of Employment and the Civil Service. He was replaced in his armed forces command by his former deputy, Cdre Lassana Timité. Duncan reorganized the Government in January 1996: Léon Konan Koffi was transferred from the post of Minister of Defence to that of Minister of State responsible for Religious Affairs and Dialogue with the Opposition, while Gueï became Minister of Sports.

Reports emerged in the independent press in May 1996 of a coup attempt by disaffected members of the armed forces at the time of the civil unrest that preceded the 1995 presidential election. Gueï's appointment, prior to the election, to a relatively minor government post was thus interpreted as a reaction to unrest in the forces under his command. In a televised statement, the Minister of Defence, Bandama N'Gatta, confirmed that members of the military high command had recently sought an audience with Bédié, at which they had affirmed their loyalty to the Head of State and had demanded that 'exemplary sanctions' be taken against armed forces personnel involved in 'disloyal' actions in September and October 1995. Also in May 1996 a prominent human rights organization, Amnesty International, alleged that opposition members in Côte d'Ivoire were, notably since the 1995 election campaign, the target of systematic repression: particular concern was expressed regarding the detention of opposition activists (many of whom had yet to be tried) under anti-riot legislation. Bédié and his ministers gave assurances of Côte d'Ivoire's respect for human rights and for correct judicial procedure, emphasizing that all those in detention had been convicted of, or were awaiting trial for, specific violations of the country's laws. In the following month *La Voie* reported the release, on appeal, of several opposition members who had been detained during pre-election unrest and subsequently convicted in unpublicized trials. The release on bail of a further 39 detainees was reported by the same newspaper in October. *La Voie* also drew attention to the death in custody of several opposition activists who had been arrested in connection with the so-called 'active boycott'. (In an interview published by a French journal in mid-1997, Gbagbo stated that, of some 450 opposition activists questioned in connection with election violence, 70 remained in detention without trial.)

A reorganization of government portfolios in August 1996 reflected Bédié's concern both to remove from positions of influence figures connected with the insecurity prior to the 1995 elections and to strengthen national security. Among those to leave the Government were Koffi, Koné and Gueï; a new Minister of Justice and Public Freedom was appointed, and the Secretary-General of the country's new National Security Council (which had been established in late July 1996 to co-ordinate all issues of national security) took the rank of Minister-delegate to the Presidency. In September LIDHO wrote to N'Gatta, expressing concern at the continued detention, in an unknown location, of several members of the armed forces on charges of plotting an armed insurrection. In November the Government announced the dismissal of seven members of the armed forces (six of them commissioned officers) and the suspension of several other members of the military, in accordance with investigations into what was now apparently confirmed as a destabilization plot. In late January 1997, moreover, Gueï was dismissed from the army, having been found to have committed 'serious disciplinary offences' in the discharge of his duties. At the end of March it was announced that Bédié had instructed N'Gatta to effect the release from custody of military personnel detained in connection with the events of late 1995.

The issue of press censorship had, meanwhile, been revived in late 1995 and early 1996 by the imprisonment of several journalists linked to the opposition. Notably, Sangaré and two other *La Voie* journalists had been sentenced to two years' imprisonment for publishing an article that was judged insulting to the Head of State. All three were pardoned by Bédié in December 1996. In August they had refused to submit to preconditions for their release under a presidential amnesty, whereby they would be required to write directly to the Head of State seeking a pardon and renouncing any appeal against sentence.

A congress of the PDCI—RDA held in October 1996 re-elected Bédié as party Chairman and Laurent Dona-Fologo (also Minister of State with responsibility for National Solidarity) as Secretary-General. Bédié, opening the congress, had urged a campaign against corruption. The President additionally advocated the opening of government to the parliamentary and non-parliamentary opposition: to this end, he stated, the process of bringing to trial detained members of the military and opposition activists must be expedited. The RDR and the FPI did not exclude the possibility of participating in government; however, the former stipulated that advance agreement be reached on the allocation of ministerial portfolios and on the government's programme, while the latter indicated that it would require, in particular, amendment of Article 11 of the Constitution (concerning the presidential succession) and revision of the electoral code. A commission of inquiry into the 1995 pre-election unrest was inaugurated in December 1996. The RDR and the FPI refused to take up their allotted seats, however, protesting that the opposition had been judged responsible in advance of the inquiry.

By-elections for eight parliamentary seats (including those for which voting did not take place or was cancelled in 1995) took place in December 1996: the FPI won five seats, and the PDCI—RDA three.

There was renewed unrest in the higher education sector from the end of 1996. In December university students in

Abidjan began a protest against the late payment of grants and to demand changes to the examinations system. Four members of FESCI (which remained outlawed) were arrested in connection with a disturbance outside the Ministry of Security. Three of the students were fined and sentenced to two years' imprisonment in early January 1997, provoking further disturbances at the university. Later in the month a student died while fleeing police who had stormed a FESCI meeting, and shortly afterwards two students were seriously injured in clashes with security forces at the Yopougon campus in Abidjan, on the eve of a planned boycott of classes. Further protests followed the arrest, in early February, of the Secretary-General and other leading members of FESCI. At the end of the month, however, Bédié issued a decree pardoning the three students who had been sentenced in January, and ordered the release of all detained student activists. This, together with the proposed establishment of a permanent committee, chaired by the president of the University of Cocody, to mediate or arbitrate in future disputes, served briefly to restore calm. In early April, however, disturbances at the University of Bouaké resulted in considerable material damage, prompting the Government to announce the closure of the university and its halls of residence. FESCI, adding the reopening of the university to its demands regarding improvements in conditions of study and accommodation and in the allocation and disbursement of grants, gave notice of a five-day strike. In early May the authorities ordered the closure of university residences in Abidjan, in an effort to curb persistent disturbances. (Lectures were to continue, and the resumption of classes at Bouaké was announced by the Government at the end of the month.) The university year was extended until December, in view of the disruption of recent months, but many students failed to resume classes at the beginning of a new term in September. National consultations on higher education began at the end of that month, apparently at Bédié's instigation. Addressing the closing session after 10 days of discussions, the Head of State revoked the ban on FESCI; the students' union responded the following day by announcing an end to the boycott of classes.

Inaugurating the National Security Council in early August 1997, Bédié emphasized that Côte d'Ivoire's political stability and economic development depended on guaranteed national security and effective measures to combat crime. The President announced that a general audit of the military, paramilitary and national police was to be undertaken, with a view to their restructuring, and that the armed forces were to be given additional responsibilities in countering illegal immigration, smuggling and organized crime, as well as in areas such as humanitarian assistance. Opponents of the Government denounced the Council, which was to be directly responsible to the Head of State, as a means of supporting the Bédié regime through espionage, intelligence and propaganda.

Also in August 1997 Bédié submitted draft legislation on institutional reforms for consideration by the Assemblée nationale. Foremost among the proposed changes was the establishment of a Senate as a second legislative chamber. Article 11 of the Constitution would then be revised once again, to the effect that, in the event of the death or incapacity of the Head of State, the President of the Senate would assume the Presidency of the Republic, on an interim basis, and would be responsible for organizing a presidential election (in which the Senate President would not be eligible to stand) within a period of between three and six months. The interim President would be empowered only to expedite outstanding matters of state, and would have no authority to appoint government ministers. For the first time, conditions of eligibility to seek office as President of the Republic were to be enshrined in the Constitution: presidential candidates would be required to be of direct Ivorian descent through the paternal line (the electoral code adopted in late 1994 had stipulated that both parents be of Ivorian birth), and would be required to have been resident in Côte d'Ivoire continuously for 15 years, either from birth or immediately preceding the date of their nomination. The electoral code would be revised to allow for a partial system of proportional representation for local elections, and a new election control and arbitration commission was to be established, with the participation of those parties presenting candidates as well as international observers. The leaders of political parties and parliamentary groups represented in the Assemblée nationale would, under the changes, have formal status, entailing special allowances and access to official vehicles. The proposed reforms were broadly welcomed by the main opposition parties.

Charles Donwahi died in early August 1997, he was succeeded as President of the Assemblée nationale by Emile Brou, hitherto Deputy President of the legislature.

In October 1997 the Government announced a 'freeze' in most areas of public expenditure until the end of the year, in an effort to redress the imbalance between revenue receipts and spending commitments. This followed reports of difficulties in negotiations with the IMF regarding a new funding arrangement. The Ministry of Handicrafts Development was abolished in early December, and its functions transferred to the Ministry of Technical Education and Professional Training.

President Houphouët-Boigny was widely respected as an active participant in regional and international affairs, although his commitment to a policy of dialogue between black Africa and the apartheid regime in South Africa prompted frequent criticism. In April 1992 (once the process of dismantling apartheid had begun) Côte d'Ivoire became the first black African country to establish diplomatic relations with South Africa. In the final years of his life, moreover, Houphouët-Boigny's role in the civil conflict in Liberia (see below) was a focus of considerable external scrutiny. It was expected that Côte d'Ivoire's foreign policy orientation would remain largely unaltered under the Bédié administration. Relations with France, the country's principal trading partner and provider of bilateral assistance, which had remained close since independence, were apparently enhanced following the election of the Gaullist Jacques Chirac to the presidency in May 1995—Chirac's predecessor, François Mitterrand, having latterly shown considerable support for Gbagbo and the FPI. Chirac began his first presidential visit to sub-Saharan Africa in Côte d'Ivoire in July of that year, and the Presidents of Benin, Burkina Faso, Niger and Togo travelled to Yamoussoukro for informal discussions with the new French leader. The Bédié administration has sought assurances from France that its programme of armed forces restructuring will not entail any significant reduction of French military commitments in Côte d'Ivoire. Details of the intended reduction of French forces in Africa, announced by the Government of Lionel Jospin in August 1997, apparently confirmed that a military base would be maintained at Port-Bouët. The new French Secretary of State responsible for co-operation, Charles Josselin, visited Côte d'Ivoire in July, and the Minister of Foreign Affairs, Hubert Védrine, and Minister of Defence, Alain Richard, visited in October; Richard announced that France would assist Côte d'Ivoire both in restructuring its armed forces and in establishing a centre for the training of African military personnel for peace-keeping operations. Relations with the USA remain close, while Bédié has also forged stronger links with other countries of the European Union and in the Far East.

Despite evidence to the contrary, Houphouët-Boigny consistently denied suggestions that his Government was supporting Charles Taylor's rebel National Patriotic Front of Liberia (NPFL), which was instrumental in the overthrow of President Samuel Doe of that country in mid-1990. (The Doe administration had maintained that rebel forces had entered Liberia via Côte d'Ivoire.) During 1991 the Ivorian authorities assumed an active role in attempts to achieve a peaceful dialogue between opposing forces in Liberia, and negotiations involving rival factions began in Yamoussoukro in the second half of the year. In December, none the less, the Liberian interim President, Dr Amos Sawyer, accused Côte d'Ivoire of providing the NPFL with arms and training facilities. Although Côte d'Ivoire did not contribute troops to the ECOMOG force that was dispatched to Liberia by the Economic Community of West African States (ECOWAS) in August 1990 (see p. 146), Houphouët-Boigny attended an ECOWAS summit meeting, convened in November 1992 in the Nigerian capital, Abuja, to discuss the Liberian problem, and supported in principle a communiqué proposing that ECOMOG be extended to all ECOWAS member states and appealing for UN intervention in the peace process.

Relations with other ECOWAS members deteriorated in February 1993, when (following recent allegations that NPFL units were operating from Ivorian territory) aircraft under ECOMOG command bombed the Ivorian border region of Danané. Côte d'Ivoire protested to ECOWAS, which expressed its regret at the incident, claiming that the area attacked had been mistaken for Liberian territory. Rumours persisted that Ivorian authorities were violating the international economic and military blockade of Liberia by (either actively or passively) allowing the NPFL access to the sea via the port of San Pedro in south-western Côte d'Ivoire, and there were reports that several of

Taylor's close and influential associates had taken up residence in Abidjan.

The presence in Côte d'Ivoire of a large number of refugees from Liberia (variously estimated at 300,000–400,000 in mid-1996) has been increasingly cited by the Ivorian authorities as a cause of the perceived escalation in insecurity in the country, and periodic incursions on to Ivorian territory by members of armed factions in the Liberian conflict have provoked considerable disquiet. In September 1994—shortly after a coup attempt in Liberia had prompted a renewed influx of refugees—four people, including two Ivorian civilians, were killed following an attack (which was suppressed by the Ivorian armed forces), apparently by members of the NPFL, on a village in the Danané region. Clashes around Taï between partisans of the Liberia Peace Council (LPC) faction and the NPFL in June 1995, as a result of which some 32 people, including 10 Ivorians, were killed, prompted a major security operation by Côte d'Ivoire's armed forces to regain control of border areas where infiltration by Liberian fighters was frequent.

In July 1995 Côte d'Ivoire, which had hitherto promoted the full integration of refugees into Ivorian society, announced the establishment of the first reception centre for Liberian refugees at Guiglo, and stated that further camps would also be established. Côte d'Ivoire expressed support for the Liberian peace agreement that was signed in Abuja in August, and Taylor was a member of a high-level Liberian delegation that visited Côte d'Ivoire in October, where discussions took place with the Ivorian authorities on joint concerns including border security and the repatriation of refugees. An agreement was signed in Abidjan in January 1996 regarding a major programme of assistance (valued at about US $100m.), to be co-ordinated by the office of the UN High Commissioner for Refugees and the World Food Programme, for refugees from the conflicts in Liberia and Sierra Leone displaced in those countries and in Côte d'Ivoire and Guinea. It was, however, increasingly suspected that Liberian militias operating near the border with Côte d'Ivoire were, either by looting or by registering as refugees, exploiting humanitarian assistance schemes in operation in Côte d'Ivoire. In February of that year a suspected looting raid, attributed to LPC fighters, on an oil-palm plantation near the border resulted in the deaths of five civilians, and in June some 14 deaths were reported following a cross-border attack in the Toulépleu area by suspected NPFL rebels. The Ivorian Government announced that security measures were to be increased in the west (in an effort to prevent further rebel incursions and the infiltration of refugee groups by Liberian fighters, and in July the Government proclaimed western Côte d'Ivoire to be a military 'operational zone', extending the powers of the armed forces to act in response to rebel activity.

The reinforcement of security and military operations in western Côte d'Ivoire additionally followed a period of concern regarding the integrity of the border with Guinea (the demarcation of part of which had long been disputed by the latter). Bilateral relations had been strained in August 1995, after Guinea established a border post in an area assumed to be part of Ivorian territory, claiming the need to prevent incursions into Guinea by Liberian rebels. Despite an announcement in September that the two countries were to co-operate in resolving this and other joint border issues, it was reported in March 1996 that Guinean soldiers had occupied a village in the Sipilou sub-prefecture. Ivorian troops in the region were mobilized in preparation for a military response, although Côte d'Ivoire's Minister of Defence reaffirmed his Government's desire to resolve such border disputes through dialogue.

In June 1997 Côte d'Ivoire's Minister of Foreign Affairs, Amara Essy, became (together with his counterparts from Ghana, Guinea and Nigeria) a member of the 'Committee of Four' charged with implementing ECOWAS decisions and recommendations pertaining to Sierra Leone in response to the overthrow, in May, of the elected Government of Ahmed Tejan Kabbah.

In April 1986 it was announced that the country wished to be known internationally by its French name of Côte d'Ivoire, rather than by translations of it. The request was subsequently endorsed by the UN.

Government

Executive power is vested in the President, who is directly elected for a five-year term. The President of the Republic appoints the Prime Minister, who is responsible to the former, and who in turn appoints the Council of Ministers. Legislative power is vested in the unicameral, 175-member Assemblée nationale, which is directly elected for five years. Elections are by universal suffrage, in the context of a multi-party political system. The minimum age for voters is 21 years. Constitutional reforms proposed in August 1997 include the establishment of a Senate as a second legislature chamber. The country is divided into 16 Regions, and further sub-divided into 49 Departments, each with its own elected Council.

Defence

In August 1997 Côte d'Ivoire's active armed forces comprised an army of 6,800 men, a navy of about 900, an air force of 700, a presidential guard of 1,100 and a gendarmerie of 4,400. There was also a 1,500-strong militia. Reserve forces numbered 12,000 men. Military service is by selective conscription and lasts for six months. France supplies equipment and training, and maintains a military presence in Côte d'Ivoire (520 men in 1997). The estimated defence budget for 1996 was 48,000m. francs CFA.

Economic Affairs

In 1995, according to estimates by the World Bank, Côte d'Ivoire's gross national product (GNP), measured at average 1993–95 prices, was US $9,248m., equivalent to $660 per head. During 1985–95, it was estimated, GNP per head declined at an average annual rate of 4.3% in real terms, while the population increased by an annual average of 3.4%. During 1985–95 Côte d'Ivoire's gross domestic product (GDP) declined by an average of 0.5% per year, in real terms. GDP increased by 7.0% in 1995 and by an estimated 6.8% in 1996, with growth in excess of 6% forecast for 1997.

Agriculture (including forestry and fishing) contributed an estimated 32.9% of GDP in 1995, and employed about 56.6% of the labour force in 1996. Côte d'Ivoire is the world's foremost producer of cocoa, and exports of cocoa and related products contributed 33.4% of total export earnings in 1995. Côte d'Ivoire is also among the world's largest producers and exporters of coffee. Other major cash crops are cotton, rubber, palm kernels, bananas and pineapples. The principal subsistence crops are maize, yams, cassava, plantains and, increasingly, rice (although large quantities of the last are still imported). Excessive exploitation of the country's forest resources has led to a decline in the importance of this sector, although measures have now been instigated to preserve remaining forests. Abidjan is among sub-Saharan Africa's principal fishing ports; however, the participation of Ivorian fishing fleets is minimal. During 1985–95 agricultural GDP increased by an annual average of 1.9%; the World Bank estimated growth of 5.5% in 1995.

Industry (including mining, manufacturing, construction and power) contributed an estimated 20.4% of GDP in 1995. According to UN estimates, 11.5% of the labour force were employed in the sector in 1994. Industrial GDP declined by an annual average of 0.3% in 1985–95, according to World Bank estimates, compared with average growth of 5.3% annually in 1975–84. However, growth in industrial GDP was 6.7% in 1994, and an estimated 8.5% in 1995.

Mining contributed only 0.2% of GDP in 1994. The sector's contribution was, however, expected to increase considerably following the commencement, in 1995, of commercial exploitation of important new offshore reserves of petroleum and natural gas. Gold and diamonds are also mined, although illicit production of the latter has greatly exceeded commercial output. There is believed to be significant potential for the development of nickel deposits, and there are also notable reserves of manganese, iron ore and bauxite.

The manufacturing sector, which, according to World Bank estimates, contributed 16.0% of GDP in 1995, is dominated by agro-industrial activities (such as the processing of cocoa, coffee, cotton, palm kernels, pineapples and fish). Crude petroleum (much of which has hitherto been imported) is refined at Abidjan, while the tobacco industry uses mostly imported tobacco. Manufacturing GDP increased by an estimated 7.0% in 1995.

Côte d'Ivoire has both thermal and hydroelectric power-generating installations. Through the exploitation, from 1995, of indigenous reserves of natural gas, the country expected to generate sufficient energy for its own requirements by 2000, and for regional export thereafter. Imports of fuel and energy accounted for an estimated 17.5% of the value of total imports in 1995.

An important aim of economic policy in the second half of the 1990s was to be the expansion of the services sector, which contributed an estimated 46.6% of GDP in 1995, and (according to UN estimates) employed 37.4% of the labour force in 1994.

Emphasis was to be placed on the promotion of tourism—already an important source of foreign exchange—as well as on furthering Côte d'Ivoire's role as a centre for financial services—Abidjan's stock exchange was to become a regional exchange for the member states of the Union économique et monétaire ouest-africaine (see p. 182) in early 1998—for communications and for regional trade. The GDP of the sector, which had, according to the World Bank, declined by an average of 2.1% per year in 1985–95, increased by an estimated 6.0% in 1995.

In 1996 Côte d'Ivoire recorded a visible trade surplus of US $1,859.8m., although there was a deficit of $203.5m. on the current account of the balance of payments. In 1995 the principal sources of imports were France (which supplied 32.0% of the total), Nigeria (19.6%) and the USA (5.9%). France was also the principal market for exports in 1995 (taking 18.1% of total exports); other significant purchasers were the Netherlands, Germany, Italy, Mali and Burkina Faso. The principal exports in 1994 were cocoa, wood, coffee and cotton. The principal imports were petroleum products, machinery and apparatus, cereals and fish and shellfish.

Côte d'Ivoire's overall budget deficit in 1995 was estimated at 184.3m. francs CFA (equivalent to 3.7% of GDP); the primary budget surplus in that year was equivalent to 3.2% of GDP). The country's total external debt was US $18,952m. at the end of 1995, of which $11,899m. was long-term public debt. In that year the cost of debt-servicing was equivalent to 23.1% of the value of exports of goods and services. The annual rate of inflation averaged 3.9% in 1985–93; consumer prices increased by an average of 26.1% in 1994 (following the devaluation of the currency at the beginning of the year); the rate slowed to an annual average of 14.3% in 1995, and only 2.5% in 1996. Some 114,880 persons were registered as unemployed at the end of 1992.

Côte d'Ivoire is a member of numerous regional and international organizations, including the Economic Community of West African States (ECOWAS, see p. 145), the West African organs of the Franc Zone (see p. 181), the African Petroleum Producers' Association (APPA, see p. 256), the Association of Coffee Producing Countries (ACPC, see p. 256), the International Cocoa Organization (ICCO, see p. 257), the International Coffee Organization (see p. 257) and the Conseil de l'Entente (see p. 260). The African Development Bank (see p. 104) has its headquarters in Abidjan.

Côte d'Ivoire's return to GDP growth in 1994, after seven years of recession, was in large part attributable to the beneficial effects of the 50% devaluation of the CFA franc. Higher demand for traditional exports coincided with an increase in world prices for cocoa and coffee, together with growth in the non-traditional agricultural sector and in manufacturing. Meanwhile, the self-sufficiency in hydrocarbons that was forecast to result from the exploitation of new petroleum and natural gas reserves was a further cause for optimism, especially with the introduction, in 1996, of a new mining code, which was expected to attract increased foreign participation in the sector. GDP growth in 1995–97, moreover, was in excess of the rate of population increase. In co-operation with the international financial community, the Bédié administration has pursued policies of economic liberalization embraced in the final years of Houphouët-Boigny's presidency, with the reduction of the country's vulnerability to, in particular, fluctuations in international prices for cocoa and coffee, the dismantling of marketing monopolies and an acceleration of the privatization programme being particular priorities. State controls on retail prices for petroleum products were removed in 1996, and important divestment measures included the sale of blocks of the oil-palm monopoly during 1996–97 and the transfer to majority private ownership of the telecommunications company in early 1997. The sizeable external debt was partially alleviated in late 1996, when creditor banks agreed major debt-relief measures (Côte d'Ivoire had been unable to service its commercial debt since 1987). Further debt reduction measures were, none the less, much needed (Côte d'Ivoire was, notably, expected to be eligible for the Bretton Woods institutions' Heavily Indebted Poor Countries Initiative). However, it was reported in the second half of 1997 that negotiations with the IMF regarding a new three-year (1997–2000) funding arrangement were experiencing difficulties, owing to IMF concerns at what was termed 'slippage' in the Government's management of public finances, and at delays in the dismantling of the cocoa and coffee export monopoly. A moratorium on public expenditure was announced in October 1997 (although this was to exclude spending on salaries, education and health), in an effort to redress the imbalance between revenue received and spending commitments. The World Bank has, meanwhile, expressed concern at the lack of progress hitherto in addressing serious disparities in levels of income per head.

Social Welfare

Medical services are organized by the State. In 1994 the country had 7,928 hospital beds, 4,971 nurses and 1,592 midwives. There were some 700 physicians in the mid-1990s. There is a minimum wage for workers in industry and commerce. Total government expenditure on health in 1995 was estimated at 62,700m. francs CFA, equivalent to 6.4% of total spending (excluding expenditure on the external debt). Expenditure by the Caisse nationale de prévoyance sociale and the Caisse générale de retraite des agents de l'Etat was estimated at 74,300m. francs CFA in 1995.

Education

At the time of the 1988 census adult illiteracy averaged 65.9% (males 55.6%; females 76.6%); UNESCO estimated the average in 1995 to be 59.9% (males 50.1%; females 70.0%). Education at all levels is available free of charge. Primary education, which is officially compulsory for six years between the ages of seven and 13 years, usually begins at seven years of age. Total enrolment at primary schools in 1994/95 was equivalent to 68% of the relevant age-group (males 78%; females 59%). The Ivorian Government anticipated that the rate of attendance at primary schools would have reached 90% by 2000. Secondary education, usually beginning at the age of 12, lasts for up to seven years, comprising a first cycle of four years and a second cycle of three years. In 1993/94 total enrolment at secondary schools was equivalent to 25% of children in the relevant age-group (males 33%; females 17%). The National University at Abidjan has six faculties, and in 1993/94 had 40,000–50,000 enrolled students. University-level facilities have been constructed in Yamoussoukro. Expenditure on education in 1995 was estimated at 241,100m. francs CFA, equivalent to 24.6% of total government expenditure (excluding spending on the public debt).

Public Holidays

1998: 1 January (New Year's Day), 30 January* (Id al-Fitr, end of Ramadan), 8 April* (Id al-Adha, Feast of the Sacrifice), 10 April (Good Friday), 13 April (Easter Monday), 1 May (Labour Day), 21 May (Ascension Day), 1 June (Whit Monday), 7 August (National Day), 15 August (Assumption), 1 November (All Saints' Day), 7 December (Félix Houphouët-Boigny Remembrance Day), 25 December (Christmas).

1999: 1 January (New Year's Day), 19 January* (Id al-Fitr, end of Ramadan), 28 March* (Id al-Adha, Feast of the Sacrifice), 2 April (Good Friday), 5 April (Easter Monday), 1 May (Labour Day), 13 May (Ascension Day), 24 May (Whit Monday), 7 August (National Day), 15 August (Assumption), 1 November (All Saints' Day), 7 December (Félix Houphouët-Boigny Remembrance Day), 25 December (Christmas).

* These holidays are dependent on the Islamic lunar calendar and may vary by one or two days from the dates given.

Weights and Measures

The metric system is in force.

Statistical Survey

Source (unless otherwise stated): Institut National de la Statistique, BP V55, Abidjan; tel. 21-05-38.

Area and Population

AREA, POPULATION AND DENSITY

Area (sq km)	322,462*
Population (census results)	
30 April 1975	6,702,866
1 March 1988	
Males	5,527,343
Females	5,288,351
Total	10,815,694
Population (official estimates at mid-year)	
1994	13,695,000
1995	14,230,000
1996	14,781,000
Density (per sq km) at mid-1995	45.8

* 124,503 sq miles.

POPULATION BY ETHNIC GROUP (1988 census)

Ethnic group	Number	%
Akan	3,251,227	30.1
Voltaïque	1,266,235	11.7
Mane Nord	1,236,129	11.4
Krou	1,136,291	10.5
Mane Sud	831,840	7.7
Naturalized Ivorians	51,146	0.5
Others	3,039,035	28.1
Unknown	3,791	0.0
Total	10,815,694	100.0

Source: UN, *Demographic Yearbook*.

POPULATION BY REGION (1988 census)

Region	Population
Centre	815,664
Centre-Est	300,407
Centre-Nord	915,269
Centre-Ouest	1,542,945
Nord	745,816
Nord-Est	514,134
Nord-Ouest	522,247
Ouest	968,267
Sud	3,843,249
Sud-Ouest	647,696
Total	10,815,694

Source: UN, *Demographic Yearbook*.

Note: In January 1997 the Government adopted legislation whereby Côte d'Ivoire's regions were to be renamed. The new regions (with their regional capitals) were to be: Lagoon (Abidjan), Upper Sassandra (Daloa), Savannah (Korhogo), Bandama Valley (Bouaké), Lakes (Yamoussoukro), Middle Comoé (Abengourou), Mountains (Man), Zanzan (Bondoukou), Lower Cavally (San Pedro), Denguélé (Odienné), Marahoué (Bouaflé), Nzi Comoé (Dimbroko), South Comoé (Aboisso), Worodougou (Seguéla), South Bandama (Divo), Agneby (Agboville).

PRINCIPAL TOWNS (population at 1988 census)

Abidjan*	1,929,079	Korhogo	109,445
Bouaké	329,850	Yamoussoukro*	106,786
Daloa	121,842		

* The process of transferring the official capital from Abidjan to Yamoussoukro began in 1983.

Source: UN, *Demographic Yearbook*.

BIRTHS AND DEATHS (UN estimates, annual averages)

	1980–85	1985–90	1990–95
Birth rate (per 1,000)	50.2	49.9	49.9
Death rate (per 1,000)	15.8	14.8	15.1

Expectation of life (UN estimates, years at birth, 1990–95): 51.0 (males 49.7; females 52.4).

Source: UN, *World Population Prospects: The 1994 Revision*.

ECONOMICALLY ACTIVE POPULATION

Mid-1996 (estimates in '000): Agriculture, etc. 2,883; Total 5,098 (Source: FAO, *Production Yearbook*).

Agriculture

PRINCIPAL CROPS ('000 metric tons)

	1994	1995	1996
Maize	517	552	597
Millet	81	85*	85*
Sorghum	31	32*	32*
Rice (paddy)	988	1,045	1,223
Sweet potatoes	36	36*	36*
Cassava (Manioc)	1,564	1,564*	1,564*
Yams	2,824	2,824*	2,824*
Taro (Coco yam)	337	337*	337*
Pulses*	8	8	8
Tree nuts*	15	15	15
Sugar cane	1,318	1,171	1,236
Palm kernels	32	31	30
Groundnuts (in shell)	138	147*	150*
Cottonseed	133	109	112
Coconuts	213	213*	213*
Copra*	34	34	34
Tomatoes	129	129*	129*
Aubergines (Eggplants)*	40	40	40
Green peppers*	20	20	20
Other vegetables*	343	343	343
Oranges*	28	28	28
Other citrus fruit*	28	28	28
Bananas	173	185	219
Plantains*	1,300	1,300	1,300
Mangoes*	14	14	14
Pineapples	205	206	236
Other fruit*	12	12	12
Coffee (green)	148	194	165
Cocoa beans	809	1,120	1,254
Tobacco (leaves)*	10	10	10
Cotton (lint)	116	93	96
Natural rubber (dry weight)	70	68	91

* FAO estimate(s).

Source: FAO, *Production Yearbook*.

LIVESTOCK ('000 head, year ending September)

	1994	1995	1996
Cattle	1,231	1,258	1,277
Pigs	403	414	290
Sheep	1,251	1,282	1,314
Goats	978	1,002	1,027

Poultry (million): 27 in 1994; 27 in 1995; 27 in 1996.

Source: FAO, *Production Yearbook*.

LIVESTOCK PRODUCTS
(FAO estimates unless otherwise indicated, '000 metric tons)

	1994	1995	1996
Beef and veal	40	38	41
Mutton and lamb	5	5	5
Goat meat	4	4	4
Pig meat	16	19	19
Poultry meat	48	48	49
Other meat	29	29	28
Cows' milk*	22	22	23
Poultry eggs*	16	16	16
Cattle hides	5	5	5
Sheepskins	1	1	1
Goatskins	1	1	1

* Official figures.

Source: FAO, *Production Yearbook*.

Forestry

ROUNDWOOD REMOVALS ('000 cubic metres)

	1992	1993	1994
Sawlogs, veneer logs and logs for sleepers	1,994	1,961	2,416
Other industrial wood*	811	840	869
Fuel wood*	10,453	10,824	11,202
Total	13,258	13,625	14,487

* FAO estimates.

Source: FAO, *Yearbook of Forest Products*.

SAWNWOOD PRODUCTION
('000 cubic metres, including railway sleepers)

	1992	1993	1994
Total	623	587	708

Source: FAO, *Yearbook of Forest Products*.

Fishing

('000 metric tons, live weight)

	1993	1994	1995
Freshwater fishes	13.8	14.7	11.2
Bigeye grunt	4.3	5.0	5.0*
Sardinellas	17.3	16.3	16.4*
Bonga shad	9.5	10.0	10.1*
Other marine fishes (incl. unspecified)	24.1	26.9	27.2*
Total fish	69.0	72.9	69.8*
Crustaceans	1.2	1.2	0.7*
Total catch	70.2	74.1	70.5
Inland waters	14.8	15.7	11.7
Atlantic Ocean	55.3	58.4	58.9

* FAO estimates.

Source: FAO, *Yearbook of Fishery Statistics*.

Mining

	1992	1993	1994
Gold (kg)	1,665.1	1,714.9	1,859.5
Diamonds ('000 carats)	117.3	98.4	84.3

Crude petroleum (estimates, '000 metric tons): 325 in 1992; 324 in 1993; 335 in 1994 (Source: UN, *Industrial Commodity Statistics Yearbook*).

Industry

SELECTED PRODUCTS ('000 metric tons, unless otherwise indicated)

	1992	1993	1994
Salted, dried or smoked fish*	15.2	n.a.	n.a.
Tinned fish*	41.4	49.9	n.a.
Raw sugar	155*	130*	141‡
Cigarettes (million)§	4,500	n.a.	n.a.
Plywood ('000 cubic metres)	39	41	41
Jet fuel†	58	59	59
Motor gasolene (Petrol)	472	414	420†
Kerosene	670	484	672†
Gas-diesel (Distillate fuel) oils	847	665	695†
Residual fuel oils	468	410†	454†
Cement†	510	500	500

Palm and palm kernel oil ('000 metric tons): 218† in 1991.
Cocoa powder (exports, '000 metric tons): 22.1*† in 1988.
Cocoa butter (exports, '000 metric tons): 28.2*† in 1988.
Cotton yarn (pure and mixed, '000 metric tons): 24.7† in 1989.

* Data from the FAO.
† Provisional or estimated figures.
‡ Data from the International Sugar Organization.
§ Data from the US Department of Agriculture.

Source: UN, *Industrial Commodity Statistics Yearbook*.

Electric energy (million kWh): 1,811 in 1991; 1,847 in 1992; 2,252 in 1993; 2,368 in 1994; 2,915 in 1995 (Source: IMF, *Côte d'Ivoire—Statistical Annex*, December 1996).

Finance

CURRENCY AND EXCHANGE RATES

Monetary Units
100 centimes = 1 franc de la Communauté financière africaine (CFA).

French Franc, Sterling and Dollar Equivalents (30 September 1997)
1 French franc = 100 francs CFA;
£1 sterling = 958.3 francs CFA;
US $1 = 593.2 francs CFA;
1,000 francs CFA = £1.044 = $1.686.

Average Exchange Rate (francs CFA per US $)
1994 555.20
1995 499.15
1996 511.55

Note: An exchange rate of 1 French franc = 50 francs CFA, established in 1948, remained in force until January 1994, when the CFA franc was devalued by 50%, with the exchange rate adjusted to 1 French franc = 100 francs CFA.

BUDGET (estimates, '000 million francs CFA)

Revenue*	1993	1994	1995
Tax revenue	435.3	678.6	897.4
Direct taxes	100.6	126.4	202.1
Taxes on profits	19.4	33.9	91.2
Individual income taxes	49.7	58.0	68.8
Employers' contributions	13.6	16.3	17.0
Taxes on petroleum products	81.9	90.8	98.9
Excise taxes	57.1	63.2	59.2
Value-added tax (VAT)	23.3	23.5	23.5
Other indirect taxes	116.6	131.0	167.3
VAT	53.1	53.3	62.2
Prepayment levy for various taxes	21.3	29.6	45.5
Turnover tax on services	9.2	11.5	15.6
Excise taxes on alcohol and tobacco	10.5	9.7	12.0
Registration and stamp taxes	13.1	15.9	20.6
Other taxes on imports	130.4	189.8	251.7
Customs, fiscal and statistical duties	62.5	84.0	116.9
Other import charges	11.2	19.0	21.6
VAT	56.7	86.8	113.3
Taxes on exports	5.7	140.5	177.4
Coffee and cocoa	—	126.2	162.7
Other revenue	82.7	168.4	205.9
Price equalization fund surplus	11.2	2.3	0.0
Stabilization fund surplus	18.1	112.7	135.9
Social security contributions	37.6	42.6	52.2
Total	518.0	846.9	1,103.3

Expenditure	1993	1994	1995
Wages and salaries	314.6	328.0	346.3
Social security benefits	39.8	51.3	65.2
Subsidies and other current transfers	26.2	42.3	51.7
Other current expenditure	156.6	201.2	236.1
Investment expenditure	90.8	195.0	280.1
Interest due on public debt	255.9	334.2	343.2
Total	883.9	1,152.0	1,322.6

* Excluding grants received (estimates, '000 million francs CFA): 15.0 in 1993; 29.7 in 1994; 35.0 in 1995.

Source: IMF, *Côte d'Ivoire—Statistical Annex* (December 1996).

1996 (draft budget, '000 million francs CFA): Current expenditure 625.2; Investment expenditure 356.3.

1997 (draft budget, '000 million francs CFA): Current expenditure 1,356.1; Investment expenditure 430.0.

INTERNATIONAL RESERVES (US $ million at 31 December)

	1994	1995	1996
Gold*	16.6	17.1	16.7
IMF special drawing rights	0.2	1.8	1.2
Reserve position in IMF	0.1	0.1	0.2
Foreign exchange	204.0	527.0	604.4
Total	220.9	546.1	622.5

* Valued at market-related prices.

Source: IMF, *International Financial Statistics.*

MONEY SUPPLY ('000 million francs CFA at 31 December)

	1994	1995	1996
Currency outside banks	392.6	451.4	472.7
Demand deposits at deposit money banks*	403.3	490.7	497.7
Checking deposits at post office	2.1	1.5	2.4
Total money (incl. others)	798.8	944.5	974.6

* Excluding the deposits of public establishments of an administrative or social nature.

Source: IMF, *International Financial Statistics.*

COST OF LIVING (Consumer Price Index for African households in Abidjan; base: 1990 = 100)

	1994	1995	1996
All items	136.5	156.0	159.9

Source: IMF, *International Financial Statistics.*

NATIONAL ACCOUNTS ('000 million francs CFA at current prices)

Expenditure on the Gross Domestic Product

	1993	1994	1995
Government final consumption expenditure	484.1	543.7	598.3
Private final consumption expenditure	2,184.9	2,678.0	3,453.5
Increase in stocks	13.6	41.8	33.6
Gross fixed capital formation	231.4	454.9	630.5
Total domestic expenditure	2,914.0	3,718.4	4,716.0
Exports of goods and services	846.0	1,803.4	2,165.8
Less Imports of goods and services	814.0	1,385.6	1,850.4
GDP in purchasers' values	2,946.0	4,136.2	5,031.4

Gross Domestic Product by Economic Activity

	1993	1994	1995
Agriculture, livestock-rearing, forestry and fishing	1,028.0	1,274.9	1,572.9
Mining and quarrying } Manufacturing } Electricity, gas and water }	550.0	771.1	876.8
Construction and public works	59.0	78.2	99.1
Transport, storage and communications	266.0	324.9	362.9
Trade	275.0	742.3	1,024.6
Other marketable services	235.0	328.1	395.9
Public administration	381.0	426.7	442.2
Sub-total	2,794.0	3,946.2	4,774.4
Import duties and taxes	152.0	190.0	257.0
GDP in purchasers' values	2,946.0	4,136.2	5,031.4

Source: IMF, *Côte d'Ivoire—Statistical Annex* (December 1996).

BALANCE OF PAYMENTS (US $ million)

	1994	1995	1996
Exports of goods f.o.b.	2,811.4	3,819.7	4,375.3
Imports of goods f.o.b.	−1,507.4	−2,474.4	−2,515.5
Trade balance	1,304.0	1,345.3	1,859.8
Exports of services	560.7	730.6	734.4
Imports of services	−1,233.3	−1,396.0	−1,501.7
Balance on goods and services	631.4	680.0	1,092.6
Other income received	85.6	32.1	36.2
Other income paid	−706.4	−862.5	−950.8
Balance on goods, services and income	10.5	−150.4	177.9
Current transfers received	774.3	255.8	228.1
Current transfers paid	−416.6	−552.1	−609.5
Current balance	368.2	−446.7	−203.5
Direct investment from abroad	26.8	19.4	
Portfolio investment assets	28.8	—	
Portfolio investment liabilities	−0.7	—	−55.9
Other investment assets	−168.4	−44.9	
Other investment liabilities	−459.7	239.2	
Net errors and omissions	−107.8	−21.3	−103.4
Overall balance	−312.7	−254.2	−362.8

Source: IMF, *International Financial Statistics.*

External Trade

PRINCIPAL COMMODITIES (million francs CFA)

Imports c.i.f.	1992	1993	1994
Rice	23,011	28,497	44,002
Wheat	8,592	8,156	18,112
Dairy products and birds' eggs	14,959	16,484	14,854
Fish, crustaceans and molluscs	26,676	30,119	54,312
Pharmaceutical products	34,253	33,064	43,707
Petroleum products	135,082	130,085	203,661
Chemical products	15,815	13,748	28,175
Electrical plant	11,063	18,836	40,866
Non-electrical machinery and apparatus	41,380	34,753	67,930
Base metals	20,148	14,797	29,925
Paper and paperboard	26,282	15,382	29,135
Industrial parachemical products	18,555	16,604	23,709
Passenger cars, coaches, lorries and vans	26,851	18,288	35,985
Total	615,149	561,321	1,018,171

Exports f.o.b.	1992	1993	1994
Fresh pineapples	11,820	11,313	18,992
Fresh bananas	14,108	18,333	30,803
Green coffee	41,156	48,859	78,001
Instant coffee	17,335	12,156	32,715
Cocoa beans	186,426	222,656	424,905
Cocoa paste	14,930	13,384	27,200
Cocoa butter	26,782	21,434	38,612
Natural rubber	15,897	15,411	38,159
Sawlogs	8,711	11,683	28,052
Sawnwood	42,307	41,736	113,117
Veneer sheets and plywood	15,513	14,798	27,166
Palm oil	18,358	21,035	32,965
Cotton fabrics	10,508	9,335	16,791
Raw (unginned) cotton	29,523	30,666	64,254
Tinned fish	26,220	20,084	64,923
Total (incl. others)	791,322	747,282	1,530,361

PRINCIPAL TRADING PARTNERS (percentage of trade)

Imports	1993	1994	1995
Belgium-Luxembourg	2.6	3.2	2.5
Brazil	1.3	1.7	1.0
China, People's Repub.	2.6	1.0	1.7
France	30.4	27.7	32.0
Germany	2.4	3.3	3.9
Ghana	3.9	4.9	4.0
Italy	3.8	3.1	3.8
Japan	2.7	2.6	3.2
Mauritania	1.3	1.5	1.3
Netherlands	3.4	2.8	2.7
Nigeria	24.3	26.5	19.6
Spain	2.7	1.4	2.5
United Kingdom	2.5	1.6	2.7
USA	4.3	5.7	5.9

Exports	1993	1994	1995
Belgium-Luxembourg	4.8	4.8	4.7
Burkina Faso	4.9	5.0	5.0
France	16.4	15.8	18.1
Germany	8.6	9.7	7.8
Italy	7.0	7.0	7.6
Mali	5.8	5.9	5.9
Netherlands	7.3	8.8	8.3
Niger	1.3	1.3	1.3
Nigeria	1.3	1.1	1.0
Spain	3.7	4.0	4.5
Togo	1.7	1.7	1.7
United Kingdom	2.9	1.9	3.2
USA	5.7	5.0	4.6

Source: IMF, *Direction of Trade Statistics.*

Transport

RAILWAYS (traffic)

	1991	1992	1993
Passengers ('000)	926	820	744
Passenger-km (million)	199	189	173
Freight ('000 metric tons)	488	484	292
Freight (million net ton-km)	272	266	168

Source: Société Ivoirienne des Chemins de Fer, Abidjan.

ROAD TRAFFIC (estimates, '000 motor vehicles in use)

	1994	1995	1996
Passenger cars	255	271	293
Lorries and vans	140	150	163

Source: IRF, *World Road Statistics.*

SHIPPING

Merchant Fleet (registered at 31 December)

	1994	1995	1996
Number of vessels	50	46	45
Total displacement ('000 grt)	61.5	40.0	12.7

Source: Lloyd's Register of Shipping, *World Fleet Statistics.*

International Sea-borne Freight Traffic
(freight traffic at Abidjan, '000 metric tons)

	1993	1994	1995
Goods loaded	3,882.4	3,702.3	4,172.9
Goods unloaded	5,936.4	6,183.9	7,227.8

Freight Traffic at San Pedro ('000 metric tons, 1994): Goods loaded 883.8; Goods unloaded 184.9.

Source: Banque centrale des états de l'Afrique de l'ouest.

CIVIL AVIATION (traffic on scheduled services)*

	1992	1993	1994
Kilometres flown (million)	4	4	3
Passengers carried ('000)	195	186	157
Passenger-km (million)	297	295	282
Total ton-km (million)	43	41	40

* Including an apportionment of the traffic of Air Afrique.

Source: UN, *Statistical Yearbook.*

Tourism

	1994
Tourist arrivals ('000)	200
Tourist receipts (US $ million)	66

Source: Haut Commissariat au Tourisme, Abidjan.

Communications Media

	1992	1993	1994
Radio receivers ('000 in use)	1,835	1,905	1,975
Television receivers ('000 in use)	765	805	822
Telephones ('000 main lines in use)	86	94	108
Daily newspapers			
Number	1	n.a.	1
Average circulation ('000 copies)	90	n.a.	90

Sources: UNESCO, *Statistical Yearbook*; UN, *Statistical Yearbook*.

Education

(1993/94)

	Institutions	Teachers	Students: Males	Students: Females	Students: Total
Pre-primary	128	39,691*	11,507*	10,951*	22,458*
Primary	7,249		902,932	650,608	1,553,540
Secondary					
General	395	10,378	294,951	150,554	445,505
Teacher training	13	538	n.a.	n.a.	2,821
Vocational	48	1,388	6,301	2,581	8,882

* Data refer only to schools attached to the Ministry of National Education.

Source: the former Ministère de l'Education nationale, Abidjan.

1994/95: *Students:* Pre-primary 25,638 (males 13,315; females 12,323). Primary 1,612,417 (males 919,233; females 693,184).

University level (1988/89): 15,501 students (males 12,600; females 2,901) (Source: UNESCO, *Statistical Yearbook*).

Directory

The Constitution

The Constitution was promulgated on 31 October 1960. It was amended in June 1971, October 1975, August 1980, November 1980, October 1985, January 1986 and November 1990.

PREAMBLE

The Republic of Côte d'Ivoire is one and indivisible. It is secular, democratic and social. Sovereignty belongs to the people who exercise it through their representatives or through referendums. There is universal, equal and secret suffrage. French is the official language.

HEAD OF STATE

The President is elected for a five-year term by direct universal suffrage and is eligible for re-election. He is Head of the Administration and the Armed Forces and has power to ask the Assemblée nationale to reconsider a Bill, which must then be passed by two-thirds of the members of the legislature; he may also have a Bill submitted to a referendum. In case of the death or incapacitation of the President of the Republic, the functions of the Head of State are assumed by the President of the Assemblée nationale, until the expiry of the previous incumbent's mandate.

EXECUTIVE POWER

Executive power is vested in the President. He appoints the Prime Minister, who, in turn, appoints the Council of Ministers. Any member of the Assemblée nationale appointed minister must renounce his seat in the legislature, but may regain it on leaving the Government.

LEGISLATIVE POWER

Legislative power is vested in the 175-member Assemblée nationale, elected for a five-year term of office. Legislation may be introduced either by the President or by a member of the National Assembly.

JUDICIAL POWER

The independence of the judiciary is guaranteed by the President, assisted by the High Council of Judiciary.

ECONOMIC AND SOCIAL COUNCIL

This is an advisory commission of 120 members, appointed by the President because of their specialist knowledge or experience.

POLITICAL ORGANIZATIONS

Article 7 of the Constitution stipulates that political organizations can be formed and can exercise their activities freely, provided that they respect the principles of national sovereignty and democracy and the laws of the Republic.

Note: In August 1997 the President of the Republic submitted proposals for constitutional change for consideration by the Assemblée nationale. Among the proposed amendments was the establishment of a Senate as a second chamber of the legislature. Provisions regarding the presidential succession would then be amended, to the effect that, in the event of the death or incapacity of the Head of State, the President of the Senate would assume the presidency of the Republic, on an interim basis, and would be responsible for organizing a presidential election within a period of between three and six months. The interim President would be ineligible to contest this election. It was also proposed to enshrine for the first time conditions of eligibility to contest the presidency (on grounds of nationality, residency, etc.) in the Constitution.

The Government

HEAD OF STATE

President: Aimé Henri Konan Bédié (took office 7 December 1993; elected President 22 October 1995).

COUNCIL OF MINISTERS

(January 1998)

Prime Minister and Minister of Planning and Industrial Development: Daniel Kablan Duncan.

Minister of State with responsibility for Relations with the Organs of State: Timothée N'Guetta Ahoua.

Minister of State with responsibility for National Solidarity: Laurent Dona-Fologo.

Minister of Foreign Affairs: Amara Essy.

Minister of the Interior and National Integration: Emile Constant Bombet.

Minister of Defence: Bandama N'Gatta.

Minister of Justice and Public Freedom, Keeper of the Seals: Brou Kacou.

Minister in charge of Presidential Affairs: Me Faustin Kouamé.

Minister of Agriculture and Animal Resources: Lambert Kouassi Konan.

Minister with responsibility for Raw Materials: Guy-Alain Emmanuel Gauze.

Minister of the Economy and Finance: N'Goran Niamien.

Minister of Economic Infrastructure: Ezan Akele.

Minister of Higher Education, Scientific Research and Technological Innovation: Saliou Touré.

Minister of National Education and Basic Training: Pierre Kipre.

Minister of Technical Education, Professional Training and Handicrafts: KOMENAN ZAKPA.

Minister of Security: MARCEL DIBONAN KONÉ.

Minister of Public Health: MAURICE KAKOU GUIKAHUE.

Minister of Mines and Petroleum Resources: LAMINE FADIKA.

Minister of Employment, the Civil Service and Social Welfare: PIERRE ACHI ATSAIN.

Minister of Trade: NICOLAS KOUASSI AKON.

Minister of Housing, Living Conditions and the Environment: ALBERT KAKOU TIAPANI.

Minister of Communications and Spokesperson for the Government: DANIÈLE BONI-CLAVERIE.

Minister of Culture: BERNARD ZADI ZAHOUROU.

Minister of the Family and Women's Promotion: ALBERTINE GNANAZAN HEPIE.

Minister of Youth Promotion and Civil Education: VLAMI BI DOU.

Minister of Sports: SITUIDÉ SOUMAHORO.

Resident Minister for the Autonomous District of Yamoussoukro: JEAN KONAN BANNY.

High Commissioner for the Development of the Savannah Regions of the North and Centre: TIMITÉ AMADOU.

High Commissioner for the Integrated Development of the Semi-mountainous Region of the West: TCHÉRÉ SEKA.

High Commissioner for Water Resources: TOURÉ SEKOU.

High Commissioner for Tourism: EUGÈNE KINDO BOUADI.

There are Ministers-delegate responsible for Planning and Industrial Development, the Promotion of Young Farmers and for Energy and Transport; the Secretary-General of the National Security Council also holds the rank of Minister-delegate.

MINISTRIES AND HIGH COMMISSIONS

Office of the President: Abidjan.

Office of the Prime Minister and Minister of Planning and Industrial Development: 01 BP 1533, Abidjan 01; tel. 21-11-00; fax 21-70-41.

Office of the Minister of State with responsibility for Relations with the Organs of State: Abidjan; tel. 22-00-20.

Office of the Minister of State with responsibility for National Solidarity: Abidjan; tel. 22-04-69.

Office of the High Commissioner for the Development of the Savannah Regions of the North and Centre: Abidjan.

Office of the High Commissioner for the Integrated Development of the Semi-mountainous Region of the West: Abidjan.

Office of the High Commissioner for Tourism: Immeuble EECI, place de la République, 01 BP 8538, Abidjan 01; tel. 20-65-00; fax 22-59-24.

Office of the High Commissioner for Water Resources: Abidjan.

Ministry of Agriculture and Animal Resources: BP V82, Abidjan; tel. 21-38-02; telex 23612; fax 21-46-18.

Ministry of Communications: BP V138, Abidjan; tel. 21-11-16; fax 22-22-97.

Ministry of Culture: Abidjan; tel. 21-40-34; fax 21-33-59.

Ministry of Defence: BP V11, Abidjan; tel. 21-26-74; fax 22-28-18.

Ministry of Economic Infrastructure: BP V6, Abidjan; tel. 34-73-15.

Ministry of the Economy and Finance: Immeuble SCIAM, ave Marchand, BP V163, Abidjan; tel. 21-65-61; telex 23747.

Ministry of Employment, the Civil Service and Social Welfare: BP V193, Abidjan; tel. 21-42-90; fax 22-84-15.

Ministry of the Family and Women's Promotion: BP V200, Abidjan; tel. 21-77-02; fax 21-44-61.

Ministry of Foreign Affairs: BP V109, Abidjan; tel. 22-71-50; fax 33-23-08.

Ministry of Higher Education, Scientific Research and Technological Innovation: BP V151, Abidjan; tel. 21-33-16.

Ministry of Housing, Living Conditions and the Environment: BP V153, Abidjan; tel. 21-94-06; fax 21-45-61.

Ministry of the Interior and National Integration: BP V241, Abidjan; tel. 21-68-23; fax 32-47-35.

Ministry of Justice and Public Freedom: BP V107, Abidjan; tel. 21-17-27; fax 33-12-59.

Ministry of Mines and Petroleum Resources: BP V50, Abidjan; tel. 21-66-17; fax 21-53-20.

Ministry of National Education and Basic Training: BP V259, Abidjan; tel. 22-44-17.

Ministry of Public Health: Cité Administrative, Tour C, 16e étage, BP V4, Abidjan; tel. 21-08-71; telex 22597; fax 21-10-85.

Ministry of Raw Materials: Abidjan; tel. 21-76-35.

Ministry of Security: BP V241, Abidjan; tel. 21-26-82.

Ministry of Sports: BP V136, Abidjan; tel. 21-17-02; fax 22-48-21.

Ministry of Technical Education, Professional Training and Handicrafts: Abidjan.

Ministry of Trade: Abidjan; tel. 22-20-04.

Ministry of Youth Promotion and Civil Education: BP V136, Abidjan; telex 22719; fax 22-48-21.

Office of the Resident Minister for the Autonomous District of Yamoussoukro: Yamoussoukro.

President and Legislature

PRESIDENT

Presidential Election, 22 October 1995

Candidate	Votes	% of votes
AIMÉ HENRI KONAN BÉDIÉ	1,640,635	95.25
ROMAIN FRANCIS WODIÉ	65,486	3.80
Abstentions	16,385	0.95
Total	1,722,506	100.00

ASSEMBLÉE NATIONALE

President: EMILE ATTA AMOAKAN BROU.

General Election, 26 November 1995

Party	Seats
PDCI—RDA	146
RDR	14
FPI	9
Total	169*

* Voting for three further seats was postponed prior to the election, and the results of voting in three constituencies was annulled by the Constitutional Court in December 1995. By-elections for these and for two other seats took place in December 1996: the FPI won five seats and the PDCI—RDA three.

Advisory Councils

Conseil Constitutionnel: Abidjan; f. 1994; Pres. NOËL NÉMIN.

Conseil Economique et Social: 04 BP 301, Abidjan 04; tel. 21-14-54; Pres. PHILIPPE GRÉGOIRE YACÉ; Vice-Pres BEDA YAO, GLADYS ANOMA, AUGUSTE DAUBREY, MARTIN KOUAKOU KOUADIO, BERNARD ANO BOA; 120 mems.

Political Organizations

Despite constitutional provision for the existence of more than one political organization, President Houphouët-Boigny's Parti démocratique de la Côte d'Ivoire—Rassemblement démocratique africain (PDCI—RDA) was the sole legal party until May 1990. By late 1997 there were some 90 registered political organizations. The following parties are represented in the Assemblée nationale:

Front populaire ivoirien (FPI): 22 BP 302, Abidjan 22; f. 1982 in France; Chair. LAURENT KOUDOU GBAGBO; Sec.-Gen. ABOU DRAHAMANE SANGARÉ.

Parti démocratique de la Côte d'Ivoire—Rassemblement démocratique africain (PDCI—RDA): Maison du Parti, Abidjan; f. 1946 as the local section of the Rassemblement démocratique africain; Chair. AIMÉ HENRI KONAN BÉDIÉ; Sec.-Gen. LAURENT DONA-FOLOGO.

Rassemblement des républicains (RDR): Abidjan; f. 1994, following split from PDCI—RDA; Pres. HYACINTHE LEROUX; Sec.-Gen. DJÉNY KOBINA.

Other registered parties include:

The **Congrès démocrate national (CDN):** Nat. Exec. Sec. MOCTAR HAIDARA; the **Front ivoirien du salut (FIS):** Sec.-Gen. N'TAKPE AUCHORET MONNON'GBA; the **Front de redressement national (FRN):** Sec.-Gen. VICTOR ATSEPI; the **Groupement pour la solidarité (GPS):** Pres. ACHI KOMAN; the **Mouvement démocratique et social (MDS):** First Nat. Sec.-Gen. SIAKA TOURÉ; the **Mouvement**

indépendantistes ivoirien (MII): Pres. ADOU YAPI; the **Mouvement progressiste de Côte d'Ivoire (MPCI):** Sec.-Gen. AUGUSTIN NANGONE BI DOUA; the **Organisation populaire de la jeunesse (OPJ):** Sec.-Gen. DENIS LATTA; the **Parti africain pour la renaissance ivoirienne (PARI):** Sec.-Gen. DANIEL ANIKPO; the **Parti communiste ivoirien (PCI):** Sec.-Gen. DENIS GUEU DRO; the **Parti fraternel des planteurs, des parents d'élèves et industriels ivoiriens (PFPPEI):** Pres. ERNEST AMESSAN; the **Parti ivoirien pour la démocratie (PID):** Sec.-Gen. FAUSTIN BOTOKO LÉKA; the **Parti ivoirien des travailleurs (PIT):** First Nat. Sec. ROMAIN FRANCIS WODIÉ; the **Parti ivoirien de justice et de solidarité (PIJS):** Pres. KEKONGO N'DIEN; the **Parti libéral de Côte d'Ivoire (PLCI):** Sec.-Gen. YADY SOUMAH; the **Parti pour la libération totale de la Côte d'Ivoire (PLTCI):** Sec.-Gen. ELISE ALLOUFOU NIAMIEN; the **Parti pour les libertés et la démocratie (PLD):** Pres. JEAN-PIERRE OUYA; the **Parti national socialiste (PNS):** Pres. RAPHAËL YAPI BEDA; the **Parti ouvrier et paysan de Côte d'Ivoire (POPCI):** Exec. Pres. KOUASSI ADOLPHE BLOKON; the **Parti pour le progrès et la solidarité (PPS):** Sec.-Gen. BAMBA MORIFÉRÉ; the **Parti progressiste ivoirien (PPI):** Pres. SOUMAHORO KASSINDOU; the **Parti pour la protection de l'environnement (PPE):** Sec.-Gen. DIOBA COULIBALY; the **Parti du rassemblement du peuple pour la jeunesse de Côte d'Ivoire (PRJCI):** Sec.-Gen. PHILIPPE ESSIS KHOL; the **Parti pour la reconstruction nationale et la démocratie (PRND):** Pres. MARC JOSEPH BEHED; the **Parti réformiste démocratique ivoirien (PRDI):** Sec.-Gen. RAPHAËL BEUGRÉ KOAMÉ; the **Parti pour la réhabilitation ivoirienne du social et de l'économie (PRISE):** Exec. Pres. GEORGES GRAHOU; the **Parti républicain de Côte d'Ivoire (PRCI):** Sec.-Gen. ROBERT GBAI TAGRO; the **Parti socialiste ivoirien (PSI):** First Nat. Sec. MANDOU-ADJOA KOUAKOU; the **Rassemblement des forces démocratiques (RFD):** Pres. FAKOUROU TOURÉ; the **Rassemblement pour le progrès social (RPS):** Pres. MAMADOU KONÉ; the **Rassemblement pour la République (RPR):** Sec.-Gen. BLAISE BONOUA KODJO; the **Rassemblement des sociaux-démocrates (RSD):** Sec.-Gen. MAHI GUINA; the **Union des libéraux pour la République (ULR):** Pres. CÉLESTIN AMON; the **Union nationale des démocrates (UND):** Sec.-Gen. AMADOU KONÉ; the **Union des paysans, des ouvriers et des salariés de Côte d'Ivoire (UPOSCI):** Sec.-Gen. COA KIÉMOKO; the **Union pour le progrès social (UPS):** Sec.-Gen. ALBERT SÉHÉ; and the **Union des sociaux-démocrates (USD):** Sec.-Gen. BERNARD ZADI ZAOUROU.

Note: In April 1995 the **FPI**, the **RDR** and the **Union des forces démocratiques** (a coalition of parties including the PPS, the PIT, the PLCI and the UND) formed an opposition **Front républicain**.

Diplomatic Representation

EMBASSIES IN CÔTE D'IVOIRE

Algeria: 53 blvd Clozel, 01 BP 1015, Abidjan 01; tel. 21-23-40; telex 23243; Ambassador: MOHAMED SENOUSSI.

Angola: Lot 190, Cocody-les-Deux-Plateaux, derrière l'Ecole Nationale d'Administration, 16 BP 1734, Abidjan 16; tel. 41-38-79; telex 27187; fax 41-28-89; Ambassador: SIMEÃO ADÃO MANUEL 'KAFUXI'.

Austria: Immeuble N'Zarama, blvd Lagunaire-Charles de Gaulle, Plateau, 01 BP 1837, Abidjan 01; tel. 21-25-00; telex 22664; fax 22-19-23; Ambassador: Dr EWALD JÄGER.

Belgium: Immeuble Alliance, ave Terrasson de Fougères, 01 BP 1800, Abidjan 01; tel. 21-00-88; telex 23633; Ambassador: PIERRE COLOT.

Benin: rue des Jardins, 09 BP 238, Abidjan 09; tel. 41-44-14; telex 27103; Ambassador: (vacant).

Brazil: Immeuble Alpha 2000, rue Gourgas, 01 BP 3820, Abidjan 01; tel. 22-23-41; telex 23443; Chargé d'affaires a.i.: FERNANDO JABLONSKI.

Burkina Faso: 2 ave Terrasson de Fougères, 01 BP 908, Abidjan 01; tel. 32-13-55; telex 23453; fax 32-66-41; Ambassador: LÉANDRE BASSOLE.

Cameroon: 01 BP 2886, Abidjan 01; tel. 32-33-31; Ambassador: PAUL KAMGA NJIKE.

Canada: Immeuble Trade Centre, 01 BP 4104, Abidjan 01; tel. 21-20-09; telex 23593; fax 21-77-28; Ambassador: SUZANNE LAPORTE.

Central African Republic: 7 rue des Jasmins, Cocody Danga, Abidjan; tel. 44-86-29; Ambassador: EMMANUEL BONGOPASSI.

China, People's Republic: 01 BP 3691, Abidjan 01; tel. 44-59-00; telex 22104; fax 44-67-81; Ambassador: LIU LIDE.

Colombia: 01 BP 3874, Abidjan 01; tel. 33-12-44; fax 32-47-31; Ambassador: MARÍA EUGENIA CORREA OLARTE.

Congo, Democratic Republic: 29 blvd Clozel, 01 BP 3961, Abidjan 01; tel. 22-20-80; telex 23795; Ambassador: BAMBI MAVUNGU.

Czech Republic: Immeuble Tropique III, 01 BP 1349, Abidjan 01; tel. 21-20-30; fax 22-19-06; Chargé d'affaires a.i.: ZDENEK MRKLOVSKY.

Egypt: Immeuble El Nasr, ave du Général de Gaulle, 01 BP 2104, Abidjan 01; tel. 32-79-25; telex 23537; Ambassador: ABEDLMONEIM ABDELAZIZ SEOUDY.

Ethiopia: Immeuble Nour Al-Hayat, ave Chardy, Plateau, 01 BP 3712, Abidjan 01; tel. 21-33-65; fax 21-37-09; Ambassador: WESSEN BESHAH.

France: rue Lecoeur, quartier du Plateau, 17 BP 175, Abidjan 17; tel. 20-04-04; telex 23699; fax 22-42-54; Ambassador: CHRISTIAN DUTHEIL DE LA ROCHÈRE.

Gabon: Cocody Danga Nord, derrière la Direction de la Géologie, 01 BP 3765, Abidjan 01; tel. 41-51-54; telex 27188; fax 44-75-05; Ambassador: VICTOR MAGNAGNA.

Germany: Immeuble Le Mans, angle blvd Botreau Roussel et ave Nogues, 01 BP 1900, Abidjan 01; tel. 21-47-27; telex 23642; fax 32-47-29; Ambassador: HANS-ALBRECHT SCHRAEPLER.

Ghana: Résidence de la Corniche, blvd du Général de Gaulle, 01 BP 1871, Abidjan 01; tel. 33-11-24; Ambassador: AKUMFI AMEYAW MUNIFIE.

Guinea: Immeuble Crosson Duplessis, 08 BP 2280, Abidjan 08; tel. 32-86-00; telex 22865; Ambassador: DOMINIQUE KOLY.

Holy See: 08 BP 1347, Abidjan 08 (Apostolic Nunciature); tel. 44-38-35; fax 44-72-40; Apostolic Nuncio: Most Rev. LUIGI VENTURA, Titular Archbishop of Equilio.

India: Lot 36, impasse Ablaha Pokou, Cocody, Danga Nord, 06 BP 318, Abidjan 06; tel. 44-52-31; telex 28103; fax 44-01-11; Ambassador: PRADEEP K. GUPTA.

Israel: Immeuble Nour Al-Hayat, ave Chardy, Plateau, 01 BP 1877, Abidjan 01; tel. 21-49-53; fax 21-87-04; Ambassador: JAACOV REVAH.

Italy: 16 rue de la Canebière, Cocody, 01 BP 1905, Abidjan 01; tel. 44-61-70; telex 26123; fax 44-35-87; Ambassador: RAFFAELE CAMPANELLA.

Japan: Immeuble Alpha 2000, Tour A, 18e étage, ave Chardy, 01 BP 1329, Abidjan 01; tel. 21-28-63; fax 21-30-51; Ambassador: HIROMI SATO.

Korea, Republic: Immeuble Le Général, 01 BP 3950, Abidjan 01; tel. 32-22-90; telex 23638; Ambassador: BAE SANG-KIL.

Lebanon: 01 BP 2227, Abidjan 01; tel. 33-28-24; telex 22245; Ambassador: MOHAMED DAHER.

Liberia: Immeuble Taleb, 20 ave Delafosse, Abidjan; tel. 32-39-73; telex 23535; Chargé d'affaires a.i.: TIAHKWEE JOHNSON.

Libya: Immeuble Shell, 48 ave Lamblin, 01 BP 5725, Abidjan 01; tel. 22-01-27; Chargé d'affaires a.i.: BADREDDIN M. RABIE.

Mali: Maison du Mali, rue du Commerce, 01 BP 2746, Abidjan 01; tel. 32-31-47; telex 23429; Ambassador: LASSANA KEITA.

Mauritania: blvd Latrille, rue de la Paroisse St Jacques, Cocody-les-Deux-Plateaux, 01 BP 2275, Abidjan 01; tel. 44-16-43; telex 27181; fax 41-05-77; Ambassador: Dr DIAGANA YOUSSOUF.

Morocco: 24 rue de la Canebière, Cocody, 01 BP 146, Abidjan 01; tel. 44-58-78; telex 26147; Ambassador: AHMED ASSOULI.

Netherlands: Immeuble Les Harmonies, 2e étage angle blvd Carde et ave Dr Jamot, Plateau, 01 BP 1086, Abidjan 01; tel. 22-77-12; telex 22694; fax 21-17-61; Ambassador: W. O. SERVATIUS.

Niger: 01 BP 2743, Abidjan 01; tel. 26-28-14; telex 43185; Ambassador: MADI KONATÉ.

Nigeria: 35 blvd de la République, 01 BP 1906, Abidjan 01; tel. 21-38-17; telex 23532; Ambassador: JONATHAN OLUWOLE COKER.

Norway: Immeuble N'Zarama, blvd du Général de Gaulle, 01 BP 607, Abidjan 01; tel. 22-25-34; telex 23355; fax 21-91-99; Ambassador: JAN NAERBY.

Poland: 04 BP 308, Abidjan 04; tel. 44-10-67; fax 44-12-35; e-mail polska@globeaccess.net; Chargé d'affaires a.i.: PIOTR MYSLIWIEC.

Russia: Riviera SQ-1 Sud, 01 BP 7646, Abidjan 01; tel. 43-09-59; Ambassador: MIKHAIL V. MAIOROV.

Senegal: Résidence Nabil, blvd du Général de Gaulle, 08 BP 2165, Abidjan 08; tel. 32-28-76; telex 23897; Ambassador: OUSMANE CAMARA.

South Africa: Villa Marc André, rue Mgr René Kouassi, Cocody, 08 BP 1806, Abidjan 08; tel. 44-59-63; fax 44-74-50; Ambassador: S. NGOMBANE.

Spain: impasse Ablaha Pokou, Cocody, Danga Nord, 08 BP 876, Abidjan 08; tel. 44-48-50; fax 44-71-22; Ambassador: ALMUDENA MAZARRASA ALVEAR.

Sweden: Immeuble N'Zarama, 4e étage, blvd Lagunaire, 04 BP 992, Abidjan 04; tel. 21-24-10; telex 23293; fax 21-21-07; Ambassador: BO WILÉN.

Switzerland: Immeuble Alpha 2000, rue Gourgas, 01 BP 1914, Abidjan 01; tel. 21-17-21; telex 23492; fax 21-27-70; Ambassador: PIERRE DE GRAFFENRIED.

Tunisia: Immeuble Pelieu, 6e étage, ave Delafosse, Abidjan 01; tel. 22-61-22; Ambassador: MONCEF LARBI.

United Kingdom: Immeuble Les Harmonies, 3e étage, angle blvd Carde et ave Dr Jamot, Plateau, 01 BP 2581, Abidjan 01; tel. 22-68-50; fax 22-32-21; Ambassador: HAYDON WARREN-GASH.

USA: 5 rue Jesse Owens, 01 BP 1712, Abidjan 01; tel. 21-09-79; telex 23660; fax 22-32-59; Ambassador: LANNON WALKER.

Judicial System

Since 1964 all civil, criminal, commercial and administrative cases have come under the jurisdiction of the Tribunaux de première instance (magistrates' courts), the assize courts and the Court of Appeal, with the Supreme Court as highest court of appeal.

The Supreme Court: rue Gourgas, BP V30, Abidjan; has four chambers: constitutional, judicial, administrative and auditing; Pres. MICHEL KOUI MAMADOU.

Courts of Appeal: Abidjan and Bouaké; hear appeals from courts of first instance; Abidjan: First Pres. (vacant), Attorney-Gen. LOUIS FOLQUET; Bouaké: First Pres. AHIOUA MOULARE, Attorney-Gen. ANOMAN OGUIE.

The High Court of Justice: composed of Deputies elected from and by the National Assembly; has jurisdiction to impeach the President or other member of the Government.

Courts of First Instance: Abidjan, Pres. ANTOINETTE MARSOUIN; Bouaké: Pres. KABLAN AKA EDOUKOU; Daloa: Pres. WOUNE BLEKA; there are a further 25 courts in the principal centres.

A new **Court of Arbitration** (Pres. DESIRÉ AMON TANOE) was established in August 1997 with jurisdiction in commercial disputes.

Religion

At the time of the 1988 census some 39% of the population were Muslims and 26% Christians (mainly Roman Catholics); about 17% followed traditional animist beliefs.

ISLAM

Conseil National Islamique (CNI): f. 1993; Chair. El Hadj IDRISS KOUDOUSS KONÉ.

Conseil Supérieur Islamique (CSI): f. 1978; Chair. El Hadj MOUSTAPHA DIABY.

CHRISTIANITY

The Roman Catholic Church

Côte d'Ivoire comprises four archdioceses and 10 dioceses. At 31 December 1995 Roman Catholics comprised about 15% of the total population.

Bishops' Conference: Conférence Episcopale de la Côte d'Ivoire, 01 BP 1287, Abidjan 01; tel. 33-22-56; f. 1973; Pres. Most Rev. AUGUSTE NOBOU, Archbishop of Korhogo.

Archbishop of Abidjan: Most Rev. BERNARD AGRÉ, Archevêché, ave Jean Paul II, 01 BP 1287, Abidjan 01; tel. 21-12-46; fax 21-40-22.

Archbishop of Bouaké: Most Rev. VITAL KOMENAN YAO, Archevêché, 01 BP 649, Bouaké 01; tel. and fax 63-24-59.

Archbishop of Gagnoa: Most Rev. NOËL KOKORA-TEKRY, Archevêché, BP 527, Gagnoa; tel. 77-25-68; fax 77-20-96.

Archbishop of Korhogo: Most Rev. AUGUSTE NOBOU, Archevêché, BP 12, Korhogo; tel. 86-01-18; fax 86-05-26.

Protestant Churches

Assemblée de Dieu: 04 BP 266, Abidjan 04; tel. 37-05-79; fax 24-94-65; f. 1960; Pres. GBOAGNON SÉRY APPOLINAIRE.

CB International: BP 109, Korhogo; tel. 86-01-07; fax 86-11-50; f. 1947; fmrly Conservative Baptist Foreign Mission Society; active in evangelism, medical work, translation, literacy and theological education in the northern area and in Abidjan.

Christian and Missionary Alliance: BP 585, Bouaké 01; tel. 63-23-12; fax 63-54-12; f. 1929; 13 mission stations; Dir Rev. DAVID W. ARNOLD.

Eglise du Nazaréen (Church of the Nazarene): 22 BP 623, Abidjan 22; tel. 41-07-80; fax 41-07-81; e-mail awfcon@compuserve.com; f. 1988; active in evangelism, ministerial training and medical work; Dir JOHN SEAMAN.

Eglise Protestante Baptiste Oeuvres et Mission: 03 BP 1032, Abidjan 03; tel. 45-20-18; fax 45-56-41; f. 1975; active in evangelism, teaching and social work; medical centre, 677 places of worship, 285 missionaries and 100,000 mems; Pres. YAYE ROBERT DION.

Eglise Protestante Méthodiste de Côte d'Ivoire: 41 blvd de la République, 01 BP 1282, Abidjan 01; tel. 21-17-97; fax 22-52-03; c. 650,000 mems; Pres. LAMBERT AKOSSI N'CHO.

Mission Baptiste Méridionale: 01 BP 3722, Abidjan 01.

Mission Evangélique de l'Afrique Occidentale: BP 822, Bouaflé; tel. and fax 68-93-70; e-mail 105344.2207@compuserve.com; f. 1934; 11 mission centres, 59 missionaries; Field Dirs LINDA NAGEL, MARRY SCHOTTE; affiliated church: Alliance des Eglises Evangéliques de Côte d'Ivoire; 254 churches, 50 full-time pastors; Pres. BOAN BI ZRÈ EMMANUEL.

Mission Evangélique Luthérienne en Côte d'Ivoire (MELCI): BP 196, Touba; tel. and fax 70-71-78; f. 1984; active in evangelism and social work; Dir JOHANNES REDSE.

Union des Eglises Evangéliques du Sud-Ouest de la Côte d'Ivoire and **Mission Biblique:** 08 BP 20, Abidjan 08; f. 1927; c. 250 places of worship.

The Press

DAILIES

Le Démocrate: Maison du Parti à Treichville, 01 BP 1212, Abidjan 01; tel. 24-25-61; organ of the PDCI—RDA; Dir JEANE-PIERRE AYE.

Fraternité-Matin: blvd du Général de Gaulle, 01 BP 1807, Abidjan 01; tel. 37-06-66; telex 23718; f. 1964; organ of the PDCI—RDA; Man. Dir MICHEL KOUAMÉ; circ. 80,000.

Ivoir 'Soir: blvd du Général de Gaulle, 01 BP 1807, Abidjan 01; tel. 37-06-66; telex 23718; f. 1987; organ of the PDCI—RDA; social, cultural and sporting activities; Man. Dir MICHEL KOUAMÉ; circ. 50,000.

Le Jour: 26 ave Chardy, Plateau, 01 BP 2432, Abidjan 01; tel. 21-95-78; fax 21-95-80; e-mail lejour@africaonline.co.ci; f. 1994; Dirs DIEGOU BAILLY, ABDOULAYE SANGARÉ; circ. 16,000.

Nouvelle République: face Théâtre de la Cité, Cocody, 09 BP 960, Abidjan 09; tel. 44-90-96; fax 44-97-10.

L'Oeil du Peuple: 220 Logements, escalier P, porte 160, rez-de-chaussée, blvd du Général de Gaulle, Adjamé, 23 BP 1093, Abidjan 23; tel. 37-98-09.

Le Populaire: 19 blvd Angoulvand, résidence Neuilly, Plateau, 01 BP 5496, Abidjan 01; tel. 22-79-69.

Le Républicain: zone 3, rue des Carrossiers, 01 BP 1942, Abidjan 01; tel. 25-55-43; fax 25-49-80.

Le Réveil Hebdo: face Théâtre de la Cité, Cocody, 09 BP 960, Abidjan 09; tel. 44-90-96; fax 44-97-10.

Soir Info: derrière IBIS Marcory, 10 BP 2462, Abidjan 10; tel. 25-32-77; Propr NADY RAYESS; circ. 10,000–15,000.

La Voie: face Institut Marie-Thérèse Houphouët-Boigny, 17 BP 656, Abidjan 17; tel. 37-68-23; fax 37-74-76; organ of the FPI; Dir ABOU DRAHAMANE SANGARÉ; Man. MAURICE LURIGNAN.

PERIODICALS

Alif: Cité Fairmont, 20 BP 575, Abidjan 20; tel. 37-20-90; weekly.

Le Bélier: Immeuble Roum, 2e étage, blvd Roum, Plateau, 16 BP 465, Abidjan 16; tel. 22-68-12; weekly.

Bol Kotch: face Institut Marie-Thérèse Houphouët-Boigny, Adjamé, 17 BP 656, Abidjan 17; tel. 37-68-23; weekly.

Le Changement: Immeuble Ghadar, blvd Giscard d'Estaing, 16 BP 10, Abidjan 16; tel. 25-52-52; f. 1991; weekly; Dir GOGBÉ DELIWA DAVID; circ. 10,000.

Le Combat: Yopougon, 23 BP 2044, Abidjan 23; tel. 45-85-16; weekly.

L'Essentiel: Cocody St Jean, 08 BP 1163, Abidjan 08; tel. 44-96-11; weekly.

Journal Officiel de la Côte d'Ivoire: Service Autonome des Journaux Officiels, BP V70, Abidjan; tel. 22-67-76; weekly; circ. 1,000.

La Lettre de l'Afrique de l'Ouest: rue des Jardins, Cocody-les-Deux-Plateaux, 01 BP 8534, Abidjan 01; tel. 41-04-76; fax 41-04-15; e-mail jvieyra@africaonline.co.ci; f. 1995; publ. by Centre Africain de Presse et d'Edition; six a year; politics, economics, regional integration; Editors JUSTIN VIEYRA, JÉRÔME CARLOS.

Mousso: zone 4, prolongement blvd du 7 décembre, après Carrefour rue Paul Laugevin, à 100 m de La Pharmacie St Joseph, 16 BP 522, Abidjan 16; tel. 25-19-06; weekly.

Notre chance: Immeuble SICOGI, 1er étage, porte escalier E, blvd du Gabon (Marcory), 10 BP 654, Abidjan 10; tel. 26-44-28; weekly.

Nouvel Elan: rue des Banques, Plateau, 18 BP 577, Abidjan 18; weekly.

Le Nouvel Horizon: 220 Logements, blvd du Général de Gaulle, Adjamé, 17 BP 656, Abidjan 17; tel. 37-68-23; f. 1990; organ of the FPI; weekly; Dir ABOU DRAHAMANE SANGARÉ; circ. 15,000.

La Nouvelle Presse: rue des Jardins, Cocody-les-deux-Plateaux, 01 BP 8534, Abidjan 01; tel. 41-04-76; fax 41-04-15; e-mail jvieyra@africaonline.co.ci; f. 1992; publ. by Centre Africain de Presse et d'Edition; weekly; current affairs; Editors JUSTIN VIEYRA, JÉRÔME CARLOS; circ. 25,000.

Plume Libre: Petite Mosquée Riviera, 08 BP 2464, Abidjan 08; tel. 43-47-58; weekly; Dir DEMBÉLÉ FOUSSENI; Editor KÉMÉ BRAHMA.

Revue Ivoirienne de Droit: BP 3811, Abidjan; f. 1969; publ. by the Centre ivoirien de recherches et d'études juridiques; legal affairs; circ. 1,500.

Star Magazine: Immeuble SIAM, Plateau, 17 BP 464, Abidjan 17; tel. 22-73-76; fax 35-85-66; weekly.

Téré: 220 Logements, blvd du Général de Gaulle, Adjamé, 20 BP 43, Abidjan 20; tel. 37-79-42; organ of the PIT; weekly; Dir ANGÈLE GNONSOA.

L'Union: 04 BP 2295, Abidjan 04; tel. 22-49-59; weekly; Dir YACOUBA BALLO.

La Voix d'Afrique: rue des Jardins, Cocody-les-Deux-Plateaux, 01 BP 8534, Abidjan 01; tel. 41-04-76; fax 41-04-15; e-mail jvieyra@africaonline.co.ci; publ. by Centre Africain de Presse et d'Edition; monthly; Editor-in-Chief GAOUSSOU KAMISSOKO.

NEWS AGENCIES

Agence Ivoirienne de Presse (AIP): 04 BP 312, Abidjan 04; telex 23781; f. 1961; Dir KONÉ SEMGUÉ SAMBA.

Foreign Bureaux

Agence France-Presse (AFP): 18 ave du Docteur Crozet, 01 BP 726, Abidjan 01; tel. 21-90-17; telex 22481; fax 21-10-36; Dir FRANÇOIS-XAVIER HARISPE.

Associated Press (AP) (USA): 01 BP 5843, Abidjan 01; tel. 41-37-49; telex 28129; Correspondent ROBERT WELLER.

Reuters West Africa (United Kingdom): Résidence Les Acacias, 2e étage, appt 203–205, 20 blvd Clozel, 01 BP 2338, Abidjan 01; tel. 21-12-22; telex 23921; fax 21-30-77; e-mail rtr.wads@africaonline.co.ci; West Africa Man. MICHEL CLÉMENT; Bureau Chief NICHOLAS PHYTHIAN.

Xinhua (New China) News Agency (People's Republic of China): Cocody Danga Nord Lot 46, 08 BP 1212, Abidjan 08; tel. 44-01-24; Chief Correspondent XIONG SHANWU.

Central News Agency (Taiwan) is also represented in Abidjan.

PRESS ASSOCIATION

Association de la Presse Démocratique Ivoirienne (APDI): Abidjan; f. 1994; Chair. JEAN-BAPTISTE AKROU.

Publishers

Centre Africain de Presse et d'Edition (CAPE): rue des Jardins, Cocody-les-Deux-Plateaux, 01 BP 8534, Abidjan 01; tel. 41-04-76; fax 41-04-15; e-mail jvieyra@africaonline.co.ci; Man. JUSTIN VIEYRA.

Centre d'Edition et de Diffusion Africaines (CEDA): square Aristide Briand, 04 BP 541, Abidjan 04; tel. 22-22-42; telex 22451; fax 32-72-62; f. 1961; general non-fiction; Chair. and Man. Dir VENANCE KACOU.

Centre de Publications Evangéliques: 08 BP 900, Abidjan 08; tel. 44-48-05; fax 44-58-17; f. 1970; religious; Dir JULES OUOBA.

Nouvelles Editions Ivoiriennes: 01 BP 1818, Abidjan 01; tel. 32-12-51; telex 22564; f. 1972; literature, criticism, essays, drama, religion, art, history; Dir K. L. LIGUER-LAUBHOUET.

Université Nationale de Côte d'Ivoire: 01 BP V34, Abidjan 01; tel. 44-08-59; telex 26138; f. 1964; academic and general non-fiction and periodicals; Publications Dir GILLES VILASCO.

Government Publishing House

Imprimerie Nationale: BP V87, Abidjan; tel. 21-76-11; fax 21-68-68.

Broadcasting and Communications

TELECOMMUNICATIONS

Côte d'Ivoire-Telcom (CI-Telcom): Immeuble Postel 2000, rue Lecoeur, 17 BP 275, Abidjan; tel. 34-40-00; telex 22759; fax 34-48-65; f. 1991; transferred to majority private ownership in 1997; 51% owned by France Câble Radio; Pres. LÉON AKA BONNY; Man. Dir KOUAMÉ YAO.

RADIO AND TELEVISION

Legislation to end the state monopoly of the broadcast media was enacted in late 1991. A private television channel, operated by Canal Horizon, a subsidiary of Canal Plus (France), commenced broadcasts from Abidjan in 1994: the channel had some 15,000 subscribers in mid-1995. Broadcasts from Abidjan by BBC Afrique, the British Broadcasting Corporation's first FM station outside Europe, began in April 1994. By 1995 five new FM broadcasting licences had been issued.

Broadcasting facilities were expected to be enhanced following the inauguration, scheduled for mid-1995, of Côte d'Ivoire's Comsat satellite communications project. A television licence fee was introduced in February of that year.

Radiodiffusion-Télévision Ivoirienne (RTI): Dir OUATTARA GNONZIE:

Radiodiffusion Ivoirienne: BP V191, Abidjan 01; tel. 21-48-00; telex 22635; f. 1962; govt radio station broadcasting in French, English and local languages; MW station at Abidjan, relay at Bouaké; VHF transmitters at Abidjan, Bouaflé, Man and Koun-Abbrosso; Dir MAMADOU BERTÉ.

Télévision Ivoirienne: 08 BP 883, Abidjan 08; tel. 43-90-39; telex 22293; f. 1963; broadcasts in French; two channels; stations at Abidjan, Bouaflé, Bouaké, Binao, Digo, Dimbokro, Koun, Man, Niangbo, Niangué, Séguéla, Tiémé and Touba; Man. (vacant).

Radio Espoir: 12 BP 27, Abidjan 12; tel. 27-60-01; fax 27-69-70; f. 1990; broadcasts from Port-Bouët by Roman Catholic Church; Dir Fr GIANFRANCO BRIGNON.

Radio Nostalgie: Abidjan; f. 1993; subsidiary of Radio Nostalgie (France); FM station; Dirs HAMED BAKAYOKO, YVES ZOGBO, Jr.

Finance

(br. = branch; cap. = capital; res = reserves; dep. = deposits; m. = million; amounts in francs CFA)

BANKING

Central Bank

Banque Centrale des Etats de l'Afrique de l'Ouest (BCEAO): angle blvd Botreau Roussel et ave Delafosse, 01 BP 1769, Abidjan 01; tel. 21-04-66; telex 23474; fax 22-28-52; headquarters in Dakar, Senegal; bank of issue and central bank for the member states of the Union économique et monétaire ouest-africaine (UEMOA), f. 1962; cap. and res 657,592m. (Dec. 1995); Gov. CHARLES KONAN BANNY; Dir in Côte d'Ivoire TIÉMOKO MEYLIET KONÉ; 5 brs.

Other Banks

Bank of Africa—Côte d'Ivoire (BOA—CI): Immeuble ex-BNDA, rue Joseph Anoma, 01 BP 4132, Abidjan 01; tel. 33-15-36; telex 22321; fax 32-89-93; 52% owned by Groupe African Financial Holding; cap. and res 1,470m. (Dec. 1996); Chair. PAUL DERREUMAUX; Man. Dir FRANCIS SUEUR.

Banque Atlantique—Côte d'Ivoire: Immeuble El Nasr, ave du Général de Gaulle, Plateau, 04 BP 1036, Abidjan 04; tel. 21-82-18; telex 23834; fax 21-68-52; f. 1978; cap. and res 4,867m. (Dec. 1995); Chair. DOSSONGUI KONÉ; Man. Dir PAUL PEETERS.

Banque de l'Habitat de Côte d'Ivoire (BHCI): 22 ave Joseph Anoma, 01 BP 2325, Abidjan 01, tel. 22-60-00; telex 22544; fax 22-58-18; f. 1993 to finance housing projects, operations commenced 1994; cap. and res 736m. (Dec. 1995); Chair. and Man. Dir KONÉ KAFONGO.

Banque Internationale pour le Commerce et l'Industrie de la Côte d'Ivoire SA (BICICI): Tour BICICI, ave Franchet d'Espérey, 01 BP 1298, Abidjan 01; tel. 20-16-00; telex 23651; fax 20-17-00; f. 1962; 28% owned by Société Financière pour les Pays d'Outre-Mer, 21% by Banque Nationale de Paris, 20% state-owned; cap. and res 24,293m. (Dec. 1995); Chair. JOACHIM RICHMOND; Man. Dir PATRICK MATHIEU; 39 brs.

Banque Paribas Côte d'Ivoire (PARIBAS CI): Immeuble Alliance, 6e étage, 17 ave Terrasson de Fougères, 17 BP 09, Abidjan 17; tel. 21-86-86; telex 22870; fax 21-88-23; f. 1984; 84% owned by Banque Paribas (France); cap. and res 1,172m. (Dec. 1995); Chair. DANIEL BÉDIN; Man. Dir CHRISTIAN ARLOT.

BIAO—Côte d'Ivoire SA: 8–10 ave Joseph Anoma, 01 BP 1274, Abidjan 01; tel. 20-07-20; telex 23641; fax 20-07-00; f. 1980; transferred to majority private ownership in 1997; cap. and res 7,951m. (Dec. 1995); Chair. NICOLAS KOUASSI AKON YAO; Man. Dir MARC DEMEULENAERE; 37 brs.

BICI Bail de Côte d'Ivoire: Tour BICICI, 5e étage, ave Franchet d'Espérey, 01 BP 6495, Abidjan 01; tel. 22-24-31; telex 23870; fax 20-17-00; 75% owned by BICICI; cap. and res 1,510m. (Dec. 1995); Chair JOACHIM RICHMOND; Man. Dir PATRICK MATHIEU.

Compagnie Financière de la Côte d'Ivoire (COFINCI): Tour BICICI, 15e étage, ave Franchet d'Espérey, 01 BP 1566, Abidjan 01; tel. 21-27-32; telex 22228; fax 20-17-00; f. 1974; 72% owned by BICICI; cap. and res 1,937m. (Dec. 1995); Chair. and Man. Dir JOACHIM RICHMOND.

Ecobank—Côte d'Ivoire: Immeuble Alliance, 17 ave Terrasson de Fougères, 01 BP 4107, Abidjan 01; tel. 21-10-41; telex 23266; fax 21-88-16; f. 1989; 93% owned by Ecobank Transnational Inc (operating under the auspices of the Economic Community of West African States); cap. 3,226m. (Jan. 1997); Chair. ABDOULAYE KONÉ; Man. Dir LOUIS NALLET; 1 br.

Société Générale de Banques en Côte d'Ivoire SA (SGBCI): 5–7 ave Joseph Anoma, Plateau, 01 BP 1355, Abidjan 01; tel. 20-12-34; telex 23741; fax 20-14-82; f. 1962; 39% owned by Société Générale (France); cap. and res 23,186m. (Dec. 1995); Chair. TIÉMOKO YADÉ COULIBALY; Man. Dir LUC BARAS; 55 brs.

Société Générale de Financement et de Participations en Côte d'Ivoire (SOGEFINANCE): 5–7 ave Joseph Anoma, 01 BP 3904, Abidjan 01; tel. 22-55-30; telex 23502; fax 32-67-60; f. 1978; 58% owned by SGBCI; cap. and res 1,661m. (Dec. 1995); Chair. and Man. Dir TIÉMOKO YADÉ COULIBALY; Man. Dir ANTOINE CASSAIGNAN.

Société Ivoirienne de Banque (SIB): Immeuble Alpha 2000, 34 blvd de la République, 01 BP 1300, Abidjan 01; tel. 20-00-00; telex 22283; fax 21-97-41; f. 1962; 51% owned by Crédit Lyonnais (France); 49% state-owned; cap. and res 4,241m. (Dec. 1995); Man. Dir JEAN-PIERRE GREYFIE DE BELLECOMBE; 35 brs.

Financial Institution

Caisse Autonome d'Amortissement: Immeuble SCIAM, ave Marchand, 01 BP 670, Abidjan 01; tel. 21-06-11; telex 23798; fax 21-35-78; f. 1959; management of state funds; Chair. ABDOULAYE KONÉ; Man. Dir VICTOR KOUAMÉ.

Bankers' Association

Association Professionnelle des Banques et Etablissements Financiers de Côte d'Ivoire (APBEFCI): 01 BP 3810, Abidjan 01; tel. 21-20-08; Pres. JEAN-PIERRE MEYER.

STOCK EXCHANGE

Bourse des Valeurs d'Abidjan (BVA): Immeuble BVA, ave Joseph Anoma, 01 BP 1878, Abidjan 01; tel. 21-57-42; telex 22221; fax 22-16-57; f. 1976; Pres. LÉON NAKA.

The BVA was scheduled to become a regional stock exchange, serving the member states of the UEMOA, in early 1998.

INSURANCE

Assurances Générales de Côte d'Ivoire (AGCI): Immeuble AGCI, ave Noguès, 01 BP 4092, Abidjan 01; tel. 33-11-31; telex 22502; fax 33-25-79; f. 1979; cap. 3,750m.; Chair. JEAN KACOU DIAGOU; Man. Dir GILBERT HIS.

Assurances Générales de Côte d'Ivoire—Vie (AGCI—Vie): Immeuble AGCI, ave Nogues, 01 BP 4092, Abidjan 01; tel. 33-11-31; telex 22502; fax 33-25-79; f. 1988; cap. 300m.; life; Chair. JEAN KACOU DIAGOU; Man. Dir GILBERT HIS.

Colina SA: Immeuble Colina, blvd Roume, 01 BP 3832, Abidjan 01; tel. 21-65-05; telex 23570; fax 22-59-05; f. 1980; cap. 600m.; Chair. MICHEL PHARAON; Dir-Gen. RAYMOND FARHAT.

Mutuelle Universelle de Garantie (UNIWARRANT): 01 BP 301, Abidjan 01; tel. 32-76-32; telex 22120; fax 32-55-36; f. 1970; cap. 400m.; Chair. and Man. Dir FATIMA SYLLA.

La Nationale d'Assurances (CNA): 30 ave du Général de Gaulle, 01 BP 1333, Abidjan 01; tel. 22-08-00; telex 22176; fax 22-49-06; f. 1972; cap. 400m.; insurance and reinsurance; Chair. SOUNKALO DJIBO; Man. Dir RICHARD COULIBALY.

La Sécurité Ivoirienne: Immeuble La Sécurité Ivoirienne, blvd Roume, 01 BP 569, Abidjan 01; tel. 21-50-63; telex 23817; fax 21-05-67; f. 1971; cap. 300m.; general; Chair. DIA HOUPHOUËT-BOIGNY; Dir-Gen. JACQUES BARDOUX.

Société Africaine d'Assurances et de Réassurances en République de Côte d'Ivoire (SAFARRIV): Immeuble SAFARRIV, 2 blvd Roume, 01 BP 1741, Abidjan 01; tel. 21-91-57; telex 22159; fax 21-82-72; f. 1975; cap. 700m.; Pres. TIÉMOKO YADÉ COULIBALY; Man. Dir CHRISTIAN ARRAULT.

Société Ivoirienne d'Assurances Mutuelles—Mutuelle d'Assurances Transports (SIDAM—MAT): Immeuble SIDAM, ave Houdaille, 01 BP 1217, Abidjan 01; tel. 21-97-82; telex 22670; fax 32-94-39; f. 1970; cap. 150m.; Chair. ABOU DOUMBIA; Dir-Gen. SOULEYMANE MEITE.

L'Union Africaine-IARD (UA): ave de la Fosse Prolongée, 01 BP 378, Abidjan 01; tel. 21-73-81; telex 23568; fax 22-12-42; f. 1981; cap. 2,175m.; insurance and reinsurance; Chair. JOACHIM RICHMOND; Dir MAURICE GIBOUDOT.

Union Africaine Vie: ave Houdaille, 01 BP 2016, Abidjan 01; tel. 22-25-15; telex 22200; fax 22-37-60; f. 1985; cap. 825m.; life assurance; Chair. ERNEST AMOS DJORO; Dir JEAN-KACOU DIAGOU.

Trade and Industry

GOVERNMENT AGENCIES

Bureau Nationale d'Etudes Techniques et de Développement (BNETD): ancien hôtel le Relais, blvd de la Corniche, Cocody, 04 BP 945, Abidjan 04; tel. 44-28-05; telex 26193; fax 44-56-66; f. 1978 as Direction et Controle des Grands Travaux; cap. 2,000m. francs CFA; management and supervision of major public works projects; Man. Dir TIDJANE THIAM.

Caisse de Stabilisation et de Soutien des Prix des Productions Agricoles (Caistab): BP V132, Abidjan; tel. 20-27-00; telex 23712; fax 21-89-94; f. 1964; cap. 4,000m. francs CFA; fmrly controlled price, quality and export of agricultural products; role reduced in 1995 to comprise forward selling of cocoa and coffee on international markets; offices in Paris, London and New York; Man. Dir YVES-MARIE KOISSY.

Comité de Privatisation: 6 blvd de L'Indénié, 01 BP 1141, Abidjan 01; tel. 22-22-31; fax 22-22-35: state privatization authority; Dir NAZAIRE GOUNONGBE.

Compagnie Ivoirienne pour le Développement des Cultures Vivrières (CIDV): 01 BP 2049, Abidjan 01; tel. 21-00-79; telex 23612; f. 1988; production of food crops; Man. Dir BENOÎT N'DRI BROU.

Société pour le Développement Minier de la Côte d'Ivoire (SODEMI): 31 blvd André Latrille, 01 BP 2816, Abidjan 01; tel. 44-29-94; telex 26162; fax 44-08-21; f. 1962; cap. 600m. francs CFA; geological and mineral research; Pres. NICOLAS KOUANDI ANGBA; Man. Dir JOSEPH N'ZI.

Société pour le Développement des Plantations de Canne à Sucre, l'Industrialisation et la Commercialisation du Sucre (SODESUCRE): 16 ave du Docteur Crozet, 01 BP 2164, Abidjan 01; tel. 21-04-79; telex 23451; fax 21-07-75; f. 1971; cap. 30,500m. francs CFA; transfer to private ownership pending; management of sugar plantations, refining, marketing and export of sugar and by-products; Chair. and Man. Dir JOSEPH KOUAMÉ KRA.

Société de Développement des Plantations Forestières (SODEFOR): blvd François Mitterrand, 01 BP 3770, Abidjan 01; tel. 44-46-16; telex 26156; fax 44-02-40; f. 1966; cap. 50m. francs CFA; establishment and management of tree plantations, management of state forests, marketing of timber products; Pres. Minister of Agriculture and Animal Resources; Man. Dir JEAN-CLAUDE ANEH.

Société pour le Développement des Productions Animales (SODEPRA): Immeuble Les Harmonies, angle blvd Carde et ave Dr Jamot, 01 BP 1249, Abidjan 01; tel. 21-13-10; telex 22123; f. 1970; cap. 404m. francs CFA; rearing of livestock; Chair. CHARLES DONWAHI; Man. Dir PAUL LAMIZANA.

Société Nationale d'Opérations Pétrolières de la Côte d'Ivoire (PETROCI): Immeuble les Hévéas, BP V194, Abidjan 01; tel. 21-40-58; telex 22135; fax 21-68-24; f. 1975; transfer to private ownership pending; cap. 20,000m. francs CFA; all aspects of petroleum development; Pres. and Man. Dir (vacant).

DEVELOPMENT AGENCIES

Caisse Française de Développement: 01 BP 1814, Abidjan 01; tel. 44-53-05; telex 28113; fmrly Caisse Centrale de Coopération Economique, name changed 1992; Dir in Côte d'Ivoire PIERRE MARSET.

Centre pour la Promotion des Investissements en Côte d'Ivoire (CEPICI): BP V152; Abidjan 01; tel. 21-40-70; fax 21-40-71; investment promotion authority.

Mission Française de Coopération: 01 BP 1839, Abidjan 01; tel. 21-60-45; administers bilateral aid from France.

CHAMBERS OF COMMERCE

Chambre d'Agriculture de la Côte d'Ivoire: 11 ave Lamblin, 01 BP 1291, Abidjan 01; tel. 32-92-13; fax 32-92-20; Sec.-Gen. GAUTHIER N'ZI.

Chambre de Commerce et d'Industrie de Côte d'Ivoire: 6 ave Joseph Anoma, 01 BP 1399, Abidjan 01; tel. 33-16-00; telex 23224; fax 32-39-46; f.1992; Pres. SEYDOU DIARRA; Dir-Gen. KONAN KOFFI.

TRADE ASSOCIATION

Organisation de Commercialisation de l'Ananas et de la Banane (OCAB): Abidjan; pineapple and banana growers' assoc.

EMPLOYERS' ASSOCIATIONS

Fédération Maritime de la Côte d'Ivoire (FEDERMAR): 04 BP 723, Abidjan 04; tel. 21-25-83; Sec.-Gen. VACABA DE MOVALY TOURÉ.

Fédération Nationale des Industries de la Côte d'Ivoire: 01 BP 1340, Abidjan 01; tel. 21-71-42; fax 21-72-56; f. 1993; Pres. PIERRE MAGNE; Sec.-Gen. DANIEL TEURQUETIL; 150 mems.

Groupement Interprofessionnel de l'Automobile (GIPA): 01 BP 1340, Abidjan 01; tel. 21-71-42; fax 21-72-56; f. 1953; Pres. PIERRE TENEUR; Sec.-Gen. DANIEL TEURQUETIL; 30 mems.

Syndicat des Commerçants Importateurs, Exportateurs et Distributeurs de la Côte d'Ivoire (SCIMPEX): 01 BP 3792, Abidjan 01; tel. 21-54-27; Pres. JACQUES ROSSIGNOL; Sec.-Gen. M. KOFFI.

Syndicat des Entrepreneurs et des Industriels de la Côte d'Ivoire (SEICI): Immeuble Jean Lefèbvre, 14 blvd de Marseille, 01 BP 464, Abidjan 01; tel. 21-83-85; f. 1934; Pres. ABDEL AZIZ THIAM.

Syndicat des Exportateurs et Négociants en Bois de Côte d'Ivoire: Immeuble CCIA, 11e étage, 01 BP 1979, Abidjan 01; tel. 21-12-39; fax 21-26-42; Pres. JEAN-CLAUDE BERNARD.

Syndicat des Producteurs Industriels du Bois (SPIB): Immeuble CCIA, 11e étage, 01 BP 318, Abidjan 01; tel. 21-12-39; fax 21-26-42; f. 1973; Pres. BRUNO FINOCCHIARO.

Union des Entreprises Agricoles et Forestières: Immeuble CCIA, 11e étage, 01 BP 2300, Abidjan 01; tel. 21-12-39; fax 21-26-42; f. 1952; Pres. FULGENCE KOFFY.

UTILITIES

Compagnie Ivoirienne d'Electricité (CIE): ave Christiani, 01 BP 6932, Abidjan 01; f. 1990 to assume electricity distribution network fmrly operated by Energie Electrique de la Côte d'Ivoire; 20% state-owned, 51% controlled by Société Bouygues group (France) and Electricité de France; Pres. MARCEL ZADI KESSY; Dir GÉRARD THEURIAU.

Compagnie Ivoirienne de Production d'Electricité (CIPREL): Tour Cidam, 12e étage, ave Houdaille, 01 BP 4039, Abidjan 01; tel. 22-60-97; operates national electricity production network.

Gaz de Côte d'Ivoire (GDCI): 01 BP 1351, Abidjan; tel. 44-49-55; telex 28109; f. 1961; transfer to majority private ownership pending; cap. 1,000m. francs CFA; gas distributor; Man. Dir LAMBERT KONAN.

TRADE UNIONS

Union Générale des Travailleurs de Côte d'Ivoire (UGTCI): 05 BP 1203, Abidjan 05; tel. 21-26-65; f. 1962; Sec.-Gen. HYACINTHE ADIKO NIAMKEY; 100,000 individual mems; 190 affiliated unions.

There are also several independent trade unions, the most prominent independent federations being the **Fédération des Syndicats Autonomes de la Côte d'Ivoire**, which grouped 19 workers' organizations in early 1995, and **Dignité**.

Transport

RAILWAYS

Société Ivoirienne des Chemins de Fer (SICF): 01 BP 1551, Abidjan 01; tel. 21-02-45; telex 23564; fax 21-39-62; f. 1989, following dissolution of Régie du Chemin de Fer Abidjan–Niger (a jt venture with the Govt of Burkina Faso); 660 km of track; Pres. and Man. Dir ABDEL AZIZ THIAM.

SITARAIL: Immeuble SAGA-CI, rond-point du Nouveau Port, 16 BP 1216, Abidjan 16; tel. 23-23-23; fax 24-22-11; consortium of French, Belgian, Ivorian and Burkinabè interests managing rail line linking Abidjan with Kaya (Burkina Faso).

ROADS

There are about 68,000 km of roads, of which some 6,000 km are paved. A four year (1994–97) programme for the repair and extension of the road network, valued at its outset at 147,000m. francs CFA, was supported by the World Bank, the African Development Bank, the Banque ouest-africaine de développement and the Governments of Germany and Japan. In late 1995 France announced funding of 15,000m. francs CFA, in support of a project (costing 18,000m. francs CFA) to rehabilitate more than 2,000 km of roads in northern regions. Tolls were being introduced on some roads in the mid-1990s, to assist in funding the maintenance of the network.

Société des Transports Abidjanais (SOTRA): 01 BP 2009, Abidjan 01; tel. 24-90-80; telex 43101; fax 25-97-21; f. 1960; 60% state-owned; urban transport; Man. Dir PASCAL YÉBOUÉ-KOUAMÉ.

SHIPPING

Côte d'Ivoire has two major ports, Abidjan and San Pedro, both of which are industrial and commercial establishments with financial autonomy. Abidjan, which handled 11.4m. metric tons of goods in 1995, is the largest container and trading port in west Africa. Access to the port is via the 2.7-km Vridi Canal. The port at San Pedro, which handled 1.1m. tons of goods in 1994, remains the main gateway to the south-western region of Côte d'Ivoire. Construction of a new fishing port at San Pedro, financed by a grant of US $14m. from the Japanese Government, was scheduled for completion in mid-1996.

Port Autonome d'Abidjan (PAA): BP V85, Abidjan; tel. 24-26-40; telex 42318; fax 24-23-28; f. 1950; public undertaking supervised by the Govt; Man. Dir JEAN-MICHEL MOULOD.

Port Autonome de San Pedro (PASP): BP 339/340, San Pedro; tel. 71-20-80; telex 99102; fax 71-27-85; f. 1971; Man. Dir OGOU ATTEMENE.

Compagnie Maritime Africaine—Côte d'Ivoire (COMAF—CI): rond-point du Nouveau Port, 08 BP 867, Abidjan 08; tel. 32-40-77; telex 23357; f. 1973; navigation and management of ships; Dir FRANCO BERNARDINI.

Nouvelle SITRAM: rue des Pétroliers, 01 BP 1546, Abidjan 01; tel. 36-92-00; telex 42254; fax 35-73-93; f. 1967, nationalized in 1976; returned to private ownership in 1995; services between Europe and west Africa and the USA; Chair. BONIFACE PEGAWAGNABA; Dir Commdt FAKO KONÉ.

SAGA—CI: Immeuble SAGA—CI, rond-point du Nouveau Port, 01 BP 1727, Abidjan 01; tel. 23-23-23; telex 43312; fax 24-25-06; merchandise handling, transit and storage; Chair. CHARLES BENITAL; Dir DANIEL CHARRIER.

Société Agence Maritime de l'Ouest Africain—Côte d'Ivoire (SAMOA—CI): rue des Gallions, 01 BP 1611, Abidjan 01; tel. 21-29-65; telex 23765; f. 1955; shipping agents; Man. Dir CLAUDE PERDRIAUD.

Société Ivoirienne de Navigation Maritime (SIVOMAR): 5 rue Charpentier, zone 2b, Treichville, 01 BP 1395, Abidjan 01; tel. 21-73-23; telex 22226; fax 32-38-53; f. 1977; shipments to ports in Africa, the Mediterranean and the Far East; Dir SIMPLISSE DE MESSE ZINSOU.

Société Ouest-Africaine d'Entreprises Maritimes en Côte d'Ivoire (SOAEM—CI): 01 BP 1727, Abidjan 01; tel. 21-59-69; telex 23654; fax 32-24-67; f. 1978; merchandise handling, transit and storage; Chair. JACQUES PELTIER; Dir JACQUES COLOMBANI.

SOCOPAO—Côte d'Ivoire: km 1 blvd de Marseille, 01 BP 1297, Abidjan 01; tel. 24-13-14; telex 43261; fax 24-21-30; e-mail socopao@africaonline.co.ci; shipping agents; Shipping Dir OLIVIER RANJARD.

CIVIL AVIATION

There are three international airports: Abidjan—Félix Houphouët-Boigny, Bouaké and Yamoussoukro. In addition, there are smaller airports at Bouna, Korhogo, Man, Odienné and San Pedro.

Air Afrique (Société Aérienne Africaine Multinationale): 3 ave Joseph Anoma, 01 BP 3927, Abidjan 01; tel. 20-30-00; telex 23785; f. 1961; 70.4% owned jtly by the Govts of Benin, Burkina Faso, the Central African Republic, Chad, the Republic of the Congo, Côte d'Ivoire, Mali, Mauritania, Niger, Senegal and Togo; extensive regional flights and services to Europe, North America and the Middle East; Dir-Gen. Sir HARRY TIRVENGADUM.

Air Ivoire: 13 ave Barthe, 01 BP 1027, Abidjan 01; tel. 20-66-66; fax 33-26-26; f. 1960; state-owned since 1976, transfer to private ownership pending; internal flights and services within west Africa; Man. Dir NICOLAS ADOM.

Tourism

The game reserves, forests, lagoons, coastal resorts, rich tribal folklore and the lively city of Abidjan are tourist attractions; Côte d'Ivoire also has well-developed facilities for business visitors, including golfing centres. An estimated 200,000 tourists visited Côte d'Ivoire in 1994; receipts from tourism in that year totalled some US $66m. The Government aims to increase visitor arrivals to 500,000 annually by 2000.

Office Ivoirien du Tourisme et de l'Hôtellerie: Immeuble EECI, place de la République, 01 BP 8538, Abidjan 01; tel. 20-65-00; fax 22-59-24; f. 1992; Dir EUGÈNE KINDO BOUADI.

CROATIA

Introductory Survey

Location, Climate, Language, Religion, Flag, Capital

The Republic of Croatia (formerly the Socialist Republic of Croatia, a constituent republic of the former Socialist Federal Republic of Yugoslavia) is situated in south-eastern Europe and has a long western coastline on the Adriatic Sea. It is bordered to the north-west by Slovenia, to the north-east by Hungary and to the east by the Vojvodina area of Serbia, part of the Federal Republic of Yugoslavia (FRY). Bosnia and Herzegovina abuts into Croatia, forming a southern border along the Sava river. The Croatian territory of Dubrovnik (formerly known as Ragusa), which is situated at the southern tip of the narrowing stretch of Croatia (beyond a short coastal strip of Bosnia and Herzegovina), has a short border with Montenegro, also part of the FRY. The climate is continental in the hilly interior and Mediterranean on the coast. There is steady rainfall throughout the year, although summer is the wettest season. The average annual rainfall in Zagreb is 890 mm (35 ins). Both the ethnic Croats (who comprised 78.1% of the total population according to the 1991 census) and the Serb minority (12.2%) speak versions of Serbo-Croat, but the largely Roman Catholic Croats use the Latin script and the Eastern Orthodox Serbs use the Cyrillic script. Since 1991 the ethnic Croats have rejected the 1954 Novi Sad Agreement (which proclaimed Serbo-Croat to be one language with two scripts), and now claim the distinctness of a Croatian language (Croat). There are, in addition, a number of small minority communities in Croatia, notably the Muslim community (which comprised 0.9% of the total population in 1991). The national flag (proportions 2 by 1) consists of three horizontal stripes, of red, white and dark blue, with the arms of Croatia (a shield of 25 squares, alternately red and white, below a blue crown composed of five shields) fimbriated in red and white and set in the centre of the flag, overlapping all three stripes. The capital is Zagreb.

Recent History

For several hundred years, from the sixteenth century, the territory of what is today the Republic of Croatia was divided between the Ottoman (Turkish) and Habsburg (Austrian) empires (although Dalmatia and Istria were dominated at different times by Venice and by France). After the Hungarian revolution of 1848–49, Croatia and Slavonia were made Austrian crown-lands. The Habsburg Empire became the Dual Monarchy of Austria-Hungary in 1867, and the territories were restored to the Hungarian Crown in the following year. Croatia gained its autonomy and was formally joined with Slavonia in 1881. However, the central Hungarian authorities pursued a policy of 'Magyarization', and, together with the anti-Serbian commercial practices of the Habsburgs (from 1904), this transformed traditional Croat-Serb rivalries into Southern Slav ('Yugoslav') solidarity. Following the collapse of the Austro-Hungarian Empire at the end of the First World War in October 1918, a Kingdom of Serbs, Croats and Slovenes (under the Serbian monarchy) was proclaimed on 4 December. The new Kingdom united Serbia, including Macedonia and Kosovo, with Montenegro and the Habsburg lands (modern Croatia, Slovenia and Vojvodina).

The new Kingdom, however, was dominated by the Serbs, and the Croats, as the second largest ethnic group, sought a greater share of power. There was increasing unrest within the Kingdom, culminating in the meeting of a separatist assembly in Zagreb in 1928, which led King Aleksandar (Alexander) to impose a royal dictatorship in 1929, when he formally changed the country's name to Yugoslavia. In 1934 the King was assassinated in France by Croatian extremists.

Meanwhile, the fascist Ustaša movement was gaining support among the discontented Croat peasantry. When German and Italian forces invaded Yugoslavia in 1941, many Croats welcomed the Axis powers' support for the establishment of an Independent State of Croatia. The new Croatian state, which included most of Bosnia and Herzegovina and parts of Serbia as well as modern-day Croatia, was proclaimed on 9 April 1941 and was led by the leader of the Ustaša, the 'Poglavnik' Ante Pavelić. The Ustaša regime subjected Croatia's minorities to ruthless persecution: a vast number of Jews, Serbs, Roma (Gypsies) and political dissidents were murdered in extermination camps. At the same time a vicious civil war was being waged against the resistance forces, particularly the Partisans, led by Josip Broz, alias Tito, the leader of the Communist Party of Yugoslavia (CPY). By 1943 the fascist regime was beginning to lose control, and Tito's forces were able to proclaim a provisional government in areas under their control. The Ustaša state collapsed in 1944, and Croatia was restored to Yugoslavia as one unit of a federal communist republic.

During the 1960s there was an increase in nationalism in Croatia. This 'mass movement' (*Maspok*), which was led by organizations such as Matica Hrvatska (an ostensibly cultural association), was supported by Croatian members of the ruling League of Communists (as the CPY had been renamed), as well as by non-communists. The movement encouraged the local communist leadership, which was associated with the reform wing of the party, to defy central policy in certain areas. In December 1971 Tito committed himself to opposing the nationalist movement, and the Croatian communist leaders were obliged to resign. Together with others prominent in *Maspok*, they were arrested, and a purge of the League of Communists of Croatia (LCC) followed. The central authorities also took action against liberals in other republics, notably Serbia, thus avoiding the charge of being anti-Croat. In 1974, however, Tito introduced a new Constitution, which enshrined the federal (almost confederal) and collective nature of the Yugoslav state. Any manifestations of Croatian nationalism continued to be prosecuted, even after the death of Tito in 1980.

An added impetus to Croatian nationalism and the perception that the Yugoslav federation was Serb-dominated, was that the LCC contained a high proportion of Serbs. Any reaction against the communists was readily associated with Croatian nationalism. When communist power began to decline, from 1989 particularly, Croatian nationalism re-emerged as a significant force. Dissidents of the 1970s and 1980s were the main beneficiaries. Dr Franjo Tudjman, who had been imprisoned in 1972 and 1981, formed the Croatian Democratic Union (CDU) in 1990. This rapidly became a mass party and the main challenger to the ruling party, which had changed its name to the League of Communists of Croatia–Party of Democratic Reform (LCC–PDR). The communists introduced a plurality ('first-past-the-post') voting system for the multi-party elections to the republican legislature in April–May 1990. Tudjman campaigned as a nationalist, causing controversy by advocating a 'Greater Croatia' (that is, including Bosnia) and complaining of Serb domination, although he did promise the Croatian Serbs cultural autonomy. This rhetoric caused considerable anxiety among the Serbs, and there were demonstrations protesting against the CDU and accusations of Croat attempts to revive the Ustaša. In March an assassination attempt was made against Tudjman, which exacerbated ethnic tensions.

At the elections to the tricameral republican Assembly (Sabor), which took place on 24 April and 6–7 May 1990, the CDU benefited from the new voting system, taking a majority of the seats, despite winning only about 42% of the votes cast in the second round (in both the Socio-Political Chamber and the Chamber of Counties). The CDU obtained 54 of the 80 seats in the Socio-Political Chamber, 68 of the 115 seats filled in the Chamber of Counties, and 83 of the 156 seats filled in the Chamber of Associated Labour; thus, of the 351 seats of all three chambers of the Sabor (a maximum of 356 could have been filled), the CDU won 205. The next-largest party was the LCC–PDR, with a total of 73 seats. Both the leading parties won further seats in alliance with other parties. Tudjman was elected President of Croatia, but he attempted to allay Serb fears by offering the vice-presidency of the Sabor to Dr Jovan Rašković, the leader of the Serbian Democratic Party (SDP). Rašković eventually refused the post, but another Serb was appointed to it. However, Serb-dominated areas (notably the Krajina—borderlands—along the border with Bosnia and Herzegovina, where the Habsburgs had settled many Serbs), felt alienated by Tudjman's Croat nationalism and the republic's adoption of a new flag (not unlike the Ustaša emblem in design) and new police uniforms (which bore a resemblance to the old Ustaša uniform). A 'Serb National Council', based at Knin (in Krajina), was formed in July 1990 and organized a referendum on autonomy for the Croatian Serbs. Despite attempts by the Croatian authorities to prohibit its being held, the referendum took place, amid virtual insurrection in some areas, in late August and early September. The result of the referendum was an overwhelming endorsement of the proposal for Serbian autonomy. By December Serbian areas were issuing declarations of autonomy, the extent of which expanded as Croatia itself moved further from acceptance of the federal Yugoslav state. By October 1991 three 'Serbian Autonomous Regions' (SARs) had been established in Croatia: Krajina, with its headquarters at Knin (which had declared its unification with the self-proclaimed Serb 'Municipal Community of Bosanska Krajina' in neighbouring Bosnia and Herzegovina in June); Eastern Slavonia, Baranja and Western Srem (Sirmium), with its temporary headquarters in Dalj (transferred to Vukovar in November, following the surrender of the Croatian resistance); and Western Slavonia, most of which was held by the Croats. The three regions, none of which was officially recognized by the Croatian Government, stated their determination to remain in a federal Yugoslavia or in a 'Greater Serbian' state. In December the three SARs announced their union as a 'Republic of Serbian Krajina' (RSK).

Meanwhile, the new Croatian Government was intent on dismantling the structures of communist power. In August 1990 the Socialist Republic of Croatia became the Republic of Croatia. In the same month the Sabor voted to dismiss the republican member of the federal State Presidency, Dr Stipe Šuvar, and replace him with Stipe Mesić, then President of the Government (Premier) of Croatia. His appointment was confirmed in October. In December the Sabor enacted a new republican Constitution, which declared Croatia's sovereignty, its authority over its own armed forces and its right to secede from the federation. Tensions increased when, in January 1991, the federal State Presidency ordered the disarming of all paramilitary groups, and the Croatian authorities refused to comply. The Croatian Minister of Defence was then indicted on a charge of plotting armed rebellion, but the Croatian Government refused to arrest him and boycotted negotiations on the future of the federation. In March the Sabor resolved that republican legislation take precedence over federal legislation. In negotiations on the future of Yugoslavia, Croatia favoured a looser federation of sovereign states and, like Slovenia, warned that it intended to end its membership of the federation by mid-1991 if no agreement was forthcoming. In April the Croatian National Guard was formed, replacing the Territorial Defence Force, which had been under the jurisdiction of the Jugoslovenska Narodna Armija (JNA) (Yugoslav People's Army). On 19 May some 94% of the voters participating in a referendum in Croatia favoured the republic's becoming a sovereign entity, possibly within a confederal Yugoslavia, and 92% rejected a federal Yugoslavia. Some 84% of the registered electorate participated in the referendum, which was largely boycotted by the Serb population.

On 25 June 1991 Croatia and Slovenia declared their independence and began the process of dissociation from the Yugoslav federation. However, the federal and Serbian authorities were less prepared to accept the loss of Croatia than that of Slovenia, since Croatia contained a significant Serb minority. During July, despite EC peace efforts and the Serbian agreement to the election of Stipe Mesić as President of the Yugoslav State Presidency, civil war effectively began in Croatia.

In September 1991 the UN placed an embargo on the delivery of all weapons and other military equipment to the territories of the former Yugoslavia. The initial successes of the JNA were curbed during August and September, when the Croatians adopted the tactic of besieging army and naval bases. The JNA was also hindered by organizational problems and desertions, owing largely to its multi-ethnic (albeit Serb-dominated) character. By November, however, the JNA supported by Serbian irregulars, had secured about one-third of Croatian territory. The main area of conflict was Slavonia, in eastern Croatia, although Serbian and JNA attacks were also concentrated on the port of Zadar, in central Dalmatia. In October the JNA attacked and besieged the coastal city of Dubrovnik, despite the fact that it contained neither a JNA barracks nor a significant Serb minority. There were accusations that the JNA was attempting to secure the borders of a 'Greater Serbian' state by linking the RSK territories to Serbia; among the main obstacles to this alleged goal, however, were the eastern Slavonian cities of Osijek, Vinkovci and Vukovar, the last of which became a particular symbol of Croatian resistance, with about 3,000 people killed in its defence. Vukovar finally surrendered on 18 November, after the 13th cease-fire negotiated by the EC, which supervised the subsequent civilian evacuation. In the same week Western nations agreed that they would be prepared to send naval detachments to ensure the safe implementation of the work of the International Red Cross, and both Croatia and Serbia indicated readiness to accept a UN peace-keeping force. Military action continued, however, while negotiations on the terms for such a force were conducted. The 14th cease-fire, therefore, involved the UN, although the agreement did not bring an end to all the fighting. In mid-December the UN Security Council resolved to send observers to Yugoslavia as well as a small team of civilian and military personnel to prepare for a possible peace-keeping force.

In August 1991 Tudjman appointed a coalition Government, dominated by the CDU but containing members of almost all the parties in the legislature. The SDP was not included. The new Government continued to seek international recognition and to pursue negotiations at the EC-sponsored peace conference in The Hague (the Netherlands). However, in October, the Croatian Government refused to extend the three-month moratorium on the process of dissociation from the Yugoslav federation (which had been agreed during the first round of EC peace negotiations in July). In November, in accordance with the principles formulated at The Hague, the Sabor declared its readiness to enact legislation guaranteeing minority rights, to allay the anxieties of the Serbs. However, there were increasing allegations of atrocities on both sides. The CDU came under increasing pressure from its own right wing and more extreme groups not to make any concessions to the Serbs. One of the most prominent of the nationalist parties was the Croatian Party of Rights (CPR). Its armed wing, the Croatian Defence Association (HOS, from the Serbo-Croat), was actively involved in the fighting and was implicated in other anti-Serb incidents. Tudjman's ban on political activity in the armed forces was believed to be directed at the HOS, which denied accusations that it was plotting a coup.

Despite such domestic and military pressures, the Croatian Government continued the process of dissociation, and in November 1991 the Supreme Council (a special war cabinet, chaired by the President of the Republic, which had been established in Croatia following the outbreak of civil war) ordered all Croatians to vacate any federal posts that they held and to place their services at the disposal of the Croatian state. On 5 December Stipe Mesić, Yugoslavia's nominal Head of State, resigned, as did Ante Marković, the federal Prime Minister, on 19 December. On 23 December Germany recognized Croatia, and on 15 January 1992 the other members of the EC initiated general international recognition of Croatia, which culminated in its accession to the UN in May.

With more than 6,000 dead, 23,000 wounded and 400,000 homeless in Croatia, a UN-sponsored unconditional cease-fire was signed by the Croatian National Guard and the JNA on 2 January 1992. In late February a 14,000-strong United Nations Protection Force (UNPROFOR, see p. 52) was entrusted with ensuring the withdrawal of the JNA from Croatia and the complete demilitarization of three Serbian-held enclaves within Croatia, which were designated UN Protected Areas (UNPAs). In the same month UNPROFOR's mandate in Croatia was extended to cover the so-called 'pink zones' (areas occupied by JNA troops and with majority Serb populations, but outside the official UNPAs).

In mid-May 1992 the JNA began to withdraw from Croatia, in accordance with the UN demilitarization of Serb areas, and the 238-day siege of Dubrovnik ended on 28 May. Sporadic shelling continued, however, and UNPROFOR proved unable to prevent the expulsion of more than 1,000 non-Serbs by Serbian forces from Eastern Slavonia, and had only limited success in its enforcement of the demilitarization of the UNPAs. In June Croatian forces launched a series of offensives in Serbian areas, beginning with the shelling of Knin. This development provoked a UN Security Council resolution requiring the Croats to withdraw to the positions that they had held prior to 21 June and to refrain from entering Serbian areas. Relations between Croatia and the UN remained strained, and President Tudjman subsequently threatened to refuse the renewal of UNPROFOR's mandate in March 1993.

In late July 1992 a military court in Split convicted 19 leading figures from the RSK for 'threatening the territorial integrity' of the Republic of Croatia. Shortly afterwards, however, as a precondition of their participation in the EC/UN London peace conference on Yugoslavia in August, the leaders of the RSK renounced their claims to independence. In early September the Prime Minister of the Federal Republic of Yugoslavia (FRY, comprising Serbia and Montenegro), Milan Panić, announced Yugoslavia's willingness to recognize Croatia within the borders existing prior to the outbreak of civil war in mid-1991, on the condition that the Serbian enclaves be granted special status. During the London peace talks, agreement was reached on economic co-operation between representatives of the Croatian Government and of the RSK, and at the end of September Presidents Tudjman (of Croatia) and Dobrica Ćosić (of the FRY) agreed to work towards a normalization of relations between their respective countries.

Presidential and legislative elections were held in Croatia on 2 August 1992. These were the first elections to be held under the new Constitution (promulgated in December 1990), which provided for a bicameral legislature composed of a Chamber of Representatives and a Chamber of Municipalities; however, the legislative elections were to the former house only. The franchise was extensive because, although many ethnic Croats living in Serbian areas could not vote (having been unable to claim their Croatian nationality), voting rights were afforded to Croats in Bosnia and Herzegovina and to anyone who had a Croatian parent or who intended to apply for Croatian citizenship. The elections were contested by eight presidential candidates and 37 political parties. President Tudjman was re-elected, with 56% of the presidential votes, more than twice that of his nearest rival, Dražen Budiša of the Croatian Social-Liberal Party (CSLP), while the ruling CDU obtained an outright majority in the Chamber of Representatives, winning 85 of the 138 seats contested. The new Government, under the premiership of Hrvoje Šarinić (hitherto head of the President's office), was appointed shortly thereafter.

In late November 1992 the Chamber of Representatives approved legislation providing for the internal redivision of Croatia, for electoral purposes, into 21 counties, 420 municipalities and 61 towns, and in early January 1993 proportional representation was introduced to replace the former plurality electoral system. Elections to the Chamber of Counties were held on 7 February. The CDU won a clear victory, with 37 of the 63 seats, while the CSLP, together with allied parties, obtained 16 seats. The CPR boycotted the elections.

Meanwhile, in October 1992 one of the co-Chairmen of the EC/UN peace talks, Lord David Owen (a British politician), threatened to impose EC sanctions on Croatia if it did not withdraw its troops from Bosnia and Herzegovina, where Croatia was supporting the self-styled breakaway Croat state, the 'Croatian Union of Herzeg-Bosna', which proclaimed its independence, with Mostar as its capital and the Croatian National Guard as sole authority, on 24 October 1992. He also accused the Croats of 'ethnic cleansing' (involving the expulsion by one ethnic group of other ethnic groups in an attempt to create a homogenous population) in Bosnia and Herzegovina. The accusation was strenuously denied by the Croatian authorities. Croatia continued its military involvement in Bosnia and Herzegovina throughout 1993 and into 1994, in spite of EC threats of economic sanctions.

In late January 1993 Croatian troops launched an offensive across the UN peace-keeping lines into Serb-held Krajina, an action that was provoked, they claimed, by the failure of the UN to restore the Maslenica bridge, a vital communications link between northern Croatia and the Dalmatian coast, to Croatian control. The Serbian forces in Krajina reclaimed weapons that they had earlier surrendered to UNPROFOR in order to defend themselves. The UN responded by ordering Croatia to withdraw its troops and the Serbian forces to return their weapons. As Croatian forces advanced towards the coastal town of Zadar on 26 January, President Ćosić of Yugoslavia warned the UN that, if UNPROFOR did not intervene, Yugoslavia would dispatch troops to defend the Serbs in Croatia. Eight French UN troops were wounded, and two were killed, in fighting around Zadar on the following day; consequently the French Government dispatched an aircraft-carrier to the Adriatic Sea. The Croats regained control of the Maslenica bridge and Zemunik airport, and by the end of January the peace process in both Croatia and Bosnia and Herzegovina appeared to be in serious jeopardy, with President Tudjman openly promising to repulse the Serbs and to aid the Bosnian Croats.

There was extensive political unrest in Croatia throughout 1993. The issues of continuing civil strife in Krajina and of the quest for autonomy in the Istrian peninsula in the north-west of Croatia (see below) proved increasingly problematic for the Government and added to domestic dissatisfaction with the country's desperate economic situation and concern regarding Croatian involvement in the Bosnian conflict. In late March Šarinić's Government resigned, following a series of financial scandals and a rapid deterioration in the economic situation. A former executive of the Croatian petroleum company Industrija Nafte, Nikica Valentić, was appointed Prime Minister. The new Government, which consisted only of members of the CDU, won a vote of confidence in the Chamber of Representatives in late April. Despite growing opposition to his policies within the party, Tudjman was re-elected Chairman of the CDU in October.

Meanwhile, the problem of war refugees escalated rapidly, and in January 1993 the Croatian authorities appealed to the international community for humanitarian and financial aid to provide for the large number of those seeking asylum in Croatia. (The number of refugees from Bosnia and Herzegovina totalled more than 800,000 in early 1993.) A state committee for the normalization of Serb-Croat relations within Croatia was established in Zagreb in May, but tensions between the two ethnic communities were exacerbated by repeated allegations of abuses of Serbian human rights.

At local elections in Istria in early February 1993 the Istrian Democratic Assembly (IDA), a party advocating Istrian autonomy, obtained 72% of the total votes cast. The Croatian Government and the IDA were subsequently in conflict throughout 1993, with the latter accusing the former of hindering Istria's political and economic development. The IDA proposed that Istria become a trans-border region comprising Croatian, Slovenian and Italian areas. Tudjman and his Government, however, strongly opposed any suggestion of Istrian autonomy, fearing the destabilization of Croatia and renewed support for the reconstitution of a Yugoslav federation.

In early April 1993 a UN-sponsored agreement guaranteed the reconstruction and reopening of the Maslenica bridge, Zemunik airport and the Peruca hydroelectric plant (all of which are situated in Krajina) under UNPROFOR supervision. The Croats decided to reconstruct the bridge themselves, however, and it was duly reopened by President Tudjman in July. In the same month the Serbs, frustrated by the continued Croatian military presence in the area, launched an attack on Croatian forces. In mid-July the UN successfully negotiated the Erdut Agreement between the leaders of Croatia and Serbia, whereby Croat forces were to leave the Maslenica area (which would then be placed under the administration of UNPROFOR again) and return captured villages to the Serbs; in return, President Milošević of Serbia was to dissuade Serbian troops from attacking the bridge. The Croats did not withdraw from Maslenica by the deadline of 31 July, however, with the Croatian Government claiming that Serbian weapons had not been surrendered to UNPROFOR, and fighting resumed. In August the Croatian Minister of Foreign Affairs, Dr Mate Granić, declared the Erdut Agreement redundant. In the following month a full-scale mobilization was undertaken among the Serbs living in the SAR of Eastern Slavonia, Baranja and Western Srem, in response to the Croatian offensives in Krajina. Serb-Croat hostilities extended to Zagreb by mid-September. By this time most of the JNA had withdrawn from Croatia, and some Serb artillery had been placed under UN control, but UNPROFOR forces were not yet in effective control of Croatian borders. The Serbs still occupied approximately 30% of the territory of Croatia.

In late September 1993 the UN Secretary-General recommended the extension of the UNPROFOR mandate in the former Yugoslavia for a further six months; the Croatian Council of Defence and National Security, however, rejected the recommendation. A few days later a special commission for relations with UNPROFOR was established in Croatia, but anti-UNPROFOR demonstrations took place across the country. On 4 October the UN Security Council voted unanimously to extend UNPROFOR's mandate in Croatia by Resolution 871. This Resolution also required the return to Croatian sovereignty of all 'pink zones', the restoration of all communications links between these regions and the remainder of Croatia, and the disarmament of Serb paramilitary groups. UNPROFOR forces were empowered by the Resolution to act in self-defence while implementing the mandate. The Croat administration accepted the Resolution, but it was rejected by the assembly of the RSK, based in Beli Menastir, which proceeded to order the mobilization of all Serb conscripts in Krajina. Multi-party elections were held in the RSK in December, but these were declared illegal by the Constitutional Court of Croatia. In January 1994 Milan Martić, a candidate supported by President Milošević of Serbia, was elected to the post of 'President' of the RSK.

In mid-January 1994 Croatia and the FRY announced their intention to begin the normalization of relations, including the establishment of representative offices in Zagreb and Belgrade. A parallel agreement was also signed between representatives of the Bosnian Croats and the Bosnian Serbs. The question of Serb-occupied territories in Croatia was, however, not specifically addressed. The declarations prompted much criticism in Croatia, where opposition parties and also elements within the CDU protested that the Muslims, and not the Serbs, were the natural allies of the Croats. In the same month President Tudjman and senior government officials indicated the possibility of direct Croatian intervention in central Bosnia and Herzegovina in support of Bosnian Croat forces encircled by Bosnian government troops, prompting the USA's Permanent Representative to the UN, Madeleine Albright, to warn Croatia that international economic sanctions could be imposed in the event of Croatian military intervention in the Bosnian conflict. On 3 February the UN Security Council issued a warning to President Tudjman to withdraw Croatian troops and artillery from Bosnia and Herzegovina by 17 February or risk 'serious measures'.

In an apparent reversal of policy, in late February 1994, President Tudjman approved US proposals for a Muslim-Croat federation within Bosnia and Herzegovina, which would ultimately seek formal association with Croatia within a loose confederation (see chapter on Bosnia and Herzegovina). This development followed a cease-fire agreement, concluded on 23 February by Muslim and Croat forces in Bosnia and Herzegovina. In the RSK, meanwhile, a cease-fire, which had been agreed between Croatia and the rebel Serbs in December 1993, was extended for a third time, until 31 March. On 30 March a fresh cease-fire, negotiated by the Russian Special Envoy to the Former Yugoslavia, Vitaly Churkin, was agreed in Zagreb. According to the cease-fire, a 'buffer' zone, monitored by UNPROFOR, was to be created between the front lines.

Croatia's domestic affairs became turbulent in April 1994, when a long-standing public feud between President Tudjman and Josip Manolić, the President of the Chamber of Municipalities and a leading member of the CDU, led to a split in the party. Manolić and other prominent liberals in the CDU (and in other parties) were displeased with Tudjman's perceived anti-Muslim views and his collusion with Gojko Šušak, the Minister of Defence, who was widely considered responsible for Croatia's involvement against the Muslims in the Bosnian conflict. Manolić demanded Šušak's resignation on the grounds that Tudjman could not hope to adhere to the Muslim-Croat federation accords with Šušak as Minister of Defence. Tudjman responded by suspending Manolić from his position within the CDU (also attempting, unsuccessfully, to dismiss him from his legislative office). On 5 April it was announced that Manolić, together with Stipe Mesić (now the President of the Chamber of Representatives), had left the CDU to form a new party, the Croatian Independent Democrats (CID). The party was formally established in late April, with Mesić as Chairman. With some 18 deputies, the CID became the largest opposition party in the Sabor.

There was further internal controversy in May 1994, when a new currency, the kuna, was introduced (the kuna had been the official tender of the Ustaša regime). Throughout June the principal opposition parties staged a boycott of the Sabor in protest at the appointment of two CDU deputies as Presidents of the parliamentary Chambers (Manolić and Mesić having agreed to resign from their posts in mid-May). Opposition deputies only returned to the Sabor in September.

Meanwhile, the cease-fire in the RSK continued precariously, as Croatian officials threatened to terminate the UN peace-keeping mandate in the area and forcibly reclaim Serb-held territory, unless the Krajina Serbs co-operated more fully in international peace negotiations. In late September 1994 the Chamber of Representatives voted to end the existing mandate of UNPROFOR in Croatia, offering a renewed mandate on the condition that UNPROFOR disarm Serb troops in Krajina, facilitate the return of Croatian refugees to Krajina, and protect Croatia's official borders. On 30 September, however, the Government reversed its opposition to the continued presence of UN forces in Croatia, and on the same day the UN Security Council adopted a resolution renewing the UNPROFOR mandate in Croatia for a further six months.

In mid-October 1994 a new negotiating forum was established in Zagreb with the aim of resolving the Krajina question. The forum, known as the 'Zagreb Group' or 'Z4', comprised two representatives of the European Union (EU, as the EC had been restructured) and the US and Russian ambassadors to Croatia. The group initially proposed that the RSK be reintegrated into Croatia while receiving extensive autonomy. In late October, however, the RSK 'Prime Minister', Borislav Mikelić, rejected any notion of Krajina's reintegration. Nevertheless, in December the two sides concluded an economic accord, which provided for the re-establishment of basic infrastructural links between the RSK and Croatia. A motorway and a petroleum pipeline were subsequently reopened.

On 12 January 1995 President Tudjman, faced by pressure from nationalist factions of the CDU and public dissatisfaction at the Government's perceived failure to assert control over Croatian territory, announced that the Government would not renew the UNPROFOR mandate in Croatia upon its expiry at the end of March, claiming that the UN presence had merely reinforced the Serbs' position. In late January, amid growing fears of the outbreak of total war in the former Yugoslavia, the 'Zagreb Group' presented a fresh peace plan to President Tudjman and the Krajina Serbs. The plan, which emphasized Croatia's territorial integrity while affording rights to the Serb minority, envisaged the return of one-half of Serb-controlled territory to Croatia in exchange for extensive regional autonomy for the Krajina Serbs. (The areas to be reintegrated into Croatia would be demilitarized, and administered by the UN for a minimum of five years.) The Krajina Serbs initially refused to consider the plan, but on 3 February Martić announced that the RSK would be willing to consider peace proposals if the UNPROFOR mandate was renewed and the RSK received guarantees of protection against Croatian aggression. A few days later the RSK suspended the economic accord concluded with Croatia in December 1994, following Croatia's decision to terminate UNPROFOR's mandate. In early March international efforts to secure a mandate for UN peace-keepers in Croatia included an offer from the EU of privileged trading links for Croatia .

On 12 March, in response to international pressure, President Tudjman reversed his decision to expel UNPROFOR from Croatian territory, two weeks before the UN troops were due to begin their withdrawal from the area. Croatia had agreed to a revised peace-keeping plan, following intensive diplomatic negotiations conducted by the international community (by the USA in particular), as a result of which a compromise UN mandate was to provide for a reduced peace-keeping force (to be known as the UN Confidence Restoration Operation—UNCRO, see p. 55), including several hundred troops to be posted along Croatia's official frontiers with Bosnia and Herzegovina and the FRY (effectively isolating Serb-occupied territory in Croatia from sources of military aid). In April the UN Security Council authorized UNCRO's strength at 8,750.

In early March 1995, following talks in Zagreb, a formal military alliance was announced between the Croatian, Bosnian Croat and Bosnian government armies against the backdrop of general preparation for new offensive campaigns in Bosnia and Herzegovina. (A similar agreement establishing a military alliance between the Croatian Serbs and the Bosnian Serbs had been drawn up in Banja Luka in February.) UN relief supplies to Serb-held enclaves in Croatia were halted in March following the disruption of aid convoys by Croatian Serbs and their rebel Muslim allies in Bosnia and Herzegovina. It was subsequently announced that the relief operations would not be resumed until the Serb and rebel Muslim blockade of the Bihać enclave in north-western Bosnia and Herzegovina was lifted.

In early April 1995 President Tudjman warned of Croatia's determination to 'liberate' Serb-held territories within its borders. Three days later the Croatian Minister of Defence, Gojko Šušak, announced the demobilization of some 30,000 government troops (but denied that, in doing so, he was hoping to draw the Croatian Serbs into taking offensive military action against Croatia). On 13 April the town and airport of Dubrovnik were attacked by Bosnian Serb artillery, resulting in one death and prompting Mate Granić, to lodge a formal protest at the shelling with the UN. In late April the principal motorway in

Croatia, linking Zagreb and Belgrade, was closed by Croatian Serb forces; the RSK 'President', Milan Martić, announced that the closure was a protest against alleged UN plans to halt the supply of essential goods from Bosnia and Herzegovina and the FRY to the Serb enclaves within Croatia.

On 1-2 May 1995 Croatian government forces seized the SAR of Western Slavonia; large numbers of Serb troops fled the area during the offensive. Government sources claimed that the attack was necessary in order to restore the Zagreb-Belgrade motorway (which was subsequently re-opened to civilian traffic on 3 May). The Croatian Serbs retaliated almost immediately with artillery attacks on Zagreb (where six civilians were killed), Karlovak and Sisak. President Milošević of Serbia distanced himself from the attacks by condemning the bombing of civilian targets. The international community immediately intensified its efforts to achieve peace in Croatia, and on 3 May, under the mediation of the UN Special Envoy, Yasushi Akashi, the warring parties agreed a cease-fire according to which Serb artillery was to be surrendered to the UN in exchange for the safe passage of all Serb civilians and troops from Western Slavonia into Bosnia and Herzegovina (an evacuation was to be organized by the UN). Sporadic fighting continued in the enclave despite the cease-fire, however, and there were allegations of Croatian human rights abuses in the area.

On 21 May 1995 a vote in the 'Assembly' of the RSK in favour of the unification of Bosnian Serb and Croatian Serb territories exposed differences within the RSK leadership, as 'President' Martić voted in favour of unification, while 'Prime Minister' Borislav Mikelić remained strongly opposed to the idea.

In early June 1995 President Tudjman aroused international controversy when he threatened further offensive campaigns to seize Serb-held territories following the expiry date of UNCRO's mandate in Croatia on 31 October unless the Croatian Serbs accepted Croatian sovereignty and a peace agreement. A few days earlier Croatian government forces had taken the strategic heights overlooking the RSK 'capital' Knin from Croatian Serb troops. In late July a joint offensive campaign by Croatian government forces and Bosnian Croat troops resulted in the seizure of the strategic Serb-held town of Bosansko Grahovo in south-western Bosnia and Herzegovina, thus blocking the principal supply route from Serb-held areas of Bosnia to Serb-held Krajina. On 4 August Croatian government troops launched a massive military operation and rapidly recaptured the Krajina enclave from the Croatian Serbs. The Croatian Minister of Defence, Gojko Šušak, later conceded that Croatian government troops had killed three UN peace-keepers during the offensive and that UN personnel had been used as 'human shields'. The success of the Croatian operation led to what was widely reported to be the largest exodus of refugees since the Yugoslav crisis began in 1991; about 150,000 Croatian Serbs either fled or were forcibly expelled from Krajina and made for Serb-held areas in Bosnia or for Serbia itself. Following the capture of Krajina, it was reported that Serbian troops had been stationed along the Serbian border with Croatia (thus strengthening the position of the Serb-held enclave of Eastern Slavonia against possible Croatian attack). In early September the UN announced that some 10,500 peace-keeping troops were to be withdrawn from Croatia in the light of the reoccupation of Krajina. On 20 September the Croatian Chamber of Representatives voted to suspend sections of the law on minorities which had provided the Krajina Serbs with special rights in areas where they had been a majority; this move had been preceded two days earlier by a new electoral law reducing the representation of the Serb minority in the Croatian legislature from 13 seats to three. The law also provided for 12 seats in the Chamber of Representatives to represent some 470,000 Croatian emigrés, thus giving the right to vote to some 291,000 Bosnian Croats (many of whom supported the CDU's sister party in Bosnia and Herzegovina). At the end of September the Croatian Government, despite UN criticism, was reported to have rehoused some 100,000 Bosnian refugees (both Croat and Muslim) in Krajina. In late September it was announced that elections to the Chamber of Representatives would take place on 29 October. A few days later seven opposition parties formed an informal electoral alliance and agreed to field joint candidates in a number of constituencies.

During October 1995 fighting continued in parts of Croatia despite the UN-brokered cease-fire. Heavy clashes were reported between Croatian troops and Serb forces in Eastern Slavonia, and President Tudjman continued to threaten the recapture of the Eastern Slavonian enclave by force as part of the CDU's electoral manifesto. On 3 October, however, an 'agreement on basic principles' was signed between Croatian government officials and Serb leaders in Eastern Slavonia, following talks in the Serb-held town of Erdut, conducted under the mediation of the US ambassador to Croatia, Peter Galbraith, and UN negotiator Thorvald Stoltenberg. The 11-point agreement provided for a 'transitional period' during which authority over the enclave would be invested in an interim administration established by the UN. The area would be demilitarized and a joint Serb-Croat police force would be created. There was also a clause providing for the safe return of refugees.

The Croatian electoral campaign was marred by widespread allegations of media bias since the Government only allowed very limited access to television for opposition parties; in early October 1995 the state-owned television network actually banned opposition broadcasts. The elections duly took place on 29 October; the CDU secured about 45% of votes cast (although the party failed to gain sufficient votes to achieve the two-thirds parliamentary majority required to make constitutional amendments). A new Government was appointed in early November, under the premiership of the erstwhile Minister of the Economy, Zlatko Matesa.

On 12 November 1995 representatives of the Croatian Government and Eastern Slavonian Serbs signed an agreement in Erdut on the reintegration of the Eastern Slavonian enclave into Croatia. The signature of this accord followed peace negotiations between Tudjman, Milošević and the President of the Presidency of Bosnia and Herzegovina, Dr Alija Izetbegović, conducted in Dayton, USA (where the three leaders signed a comprehensive peace agreement, providing for the division of Bosnia and Herzegovina between a Muslim-Croat Federation and a Serb Republic—see chapter on Bosnia and Herzegovina). Under the terms of the accord, Eastern Slavonia was to be administered by a transitional administration appointed by the UN for a period of up to two years prior to its complete reintegration into Croatia. The interim administration and UN peace-keeping forces would supervise the demilitarization of the area and the return of refugees and displaced persons. Long-standing Serbian demands for the holding of a referendum at the end of the transitional period, in which citizens would vote for the region's integration into either Croatia or Serbia, were not included in the agreement. On 15 January 1996 the UN Security Council established the United Nations Transitional Administration for Eastern Slavonia, Baranja and Western Sirmium (UNTAES, see p. 55), with an initial mandate for one year. UNTAES, comprising some 5,000 UN troops, replaced UNCRO, whose mandate expired on that day. A US diplomat, Jacques Paul Klein, was subsequently appointed Transitional Administrator of the region.

In February 1996 Tudjman, Izetbegović and Milošević attended a meeting in Rome, Italy, where the Croat and Muslim delegations reached an agreement regarding the administration of Mostar, in Bosnia and Herzegovina. (In November 1995 Tudjman and Izetbegović, the Bosnian Muslim leader, signed an agreement providing for the unification of Mostar as the capital of the Muslim-Croat Federation—see chapter on Bosnia and Herzegovina.) In March a FRY delegation, headed by the Minister of Foreign Affairs, Milan Milutinović, visited Croatia; a number of co-operation agreements, in areas such as transport, communications, property restitution and the exchange of consular facilities, were signed. On 19 April the Regional Executive Council of Eastern Slavonia appointed a former RSK 'President' (1992–94), Goran Hadžić, as President of the region. A new Regional Assembly (comprising representatives of Krajina and the five Eastern Slavonian municipalities) and Regional Executive Council were subsequently established. In the same month the Chamber of Representatives approved legislation on co-operation between Croatia and the international tribunal on war crimes in the Hague, providing for the transfer of authority to conduct criminal proceedings to the tribunal and the extradition of the accused.

In early May 1996 Tudjman dissolved the Zagreb City Assembly and appointed a Government Commissioner in its place (on the grounds that the Assembly had approved unconstitutional legislation), following a protracted dispute with an alliance of opposition parties that had won the local elections and held a majority in the Assembly; Tudjman had repeatedly failed to endorse opposition nominees for the posts of mayor of Zagreb and Speaker of the Assembly, while the opposition had refused to accept candidates appointed by the President. In the same month the Government closed an independent newspaper, which had published an article critical of Tudjman, and ordered the arrest of the editor of another independent publication. Shortly afterwards the Ministers of Foreign Affairs of the member states of the Council of Europe (see p. 140) refused to endorse Croatia's admission to the organization (despite a favourable vote by the Council of Europe's parliamentary assembly in April), on the grounds that the Government had failed to meet EU democratic standards; particular concern was expressed regarding the Government's infringements of the rights of the press and elected local authorities. Further consideration of Croatia's application for membership was postponed, pending guarantees from the Government of its intention to comply with a number of preconditions on democracy and human rights.

In May 1996 the Croatian House of Representatives adopted legislation granting amnesty for crimes committed during the civil conflict in Eastern Slavonia from August 1990, excepting 'war crimes'; the legislation was designed to expedite the return of displaced persons to the region. Later that month the demilitarization of Eastern Slavonia commenced; the process was completed within a period of 30 days, as scheduled. In early July an international security force was installed in Eastern Slavonia for the transitional period. Later that month the Regional Assembly of Eastern Slavonia submitted an official request to the UN Security Council that the mandate of UNTAES, which was officially due to expire in January 1997, be extended for a further year. (The Croatian Government opposed the extension of the mandate for more than three months.)

In August 1996 Tudjman met President Clinton for discussions in Washington, USA. It was subsequently reported that Tudjman influenced the Bosnian Croats to abandon a boycott of Mostar city council, which they had staged in protest at the results of municipal elections. Later in August, following a meeting between Tudjman and Milošević in Athens, Greece, an agreement was signed, providing for the establishment of full diplomatic relations between Croatia and the FRY; remaining issues of contention, most notably the territorial dispute over the Prevlaka peninsula, south-east of Dubrovnik (which, under the terms of the Dayton agreement, was to be ceded to Bosnian Serb control), were to be resolved by further negotiations. In October the Council of Europe agreed to accept Croatia's application for membership, after the Government undertook to ratify the European Convention on Human Rights within a year of admission.

In November 1996 a demonstration was staged in Zagreb in protest at efforts by the Government to close an opposition radio station, Radio 101 (following the closure of other independent radio stations). (The Croatian authorities subsequently extended Radio 101's provisional licence until January 1997, when the station was granted a five-year licence.) Also in November 1996 the UN Security Council announced that the mandate of UNTAES had been extended for an additional six months, to mid-July 1997. In December 1996 the Minister of the Interior was replaced in a government reorganization, prompting reports in the independent media that he had been removed in response to his failure to prevent the protest in Zagreb (which was apparently unauthorized) against the closure of Radio 101. At the end of December, following a meeting between Tudjman and Klein, it was announced that local government elections in Eastern Slavonia were to take place in March 1997, at the same time as elections to the upper house (Chamber of Counties) in Croatia. Serbs in Eastern Slavonia subsequently objected to elections taking place concurrently in Croatia and Eastern Slavonia (on the grounds that this preempted the reintegration of the region). In January 1997 it was reported that the Croatian Government had submitted to the UN proposals for the reintegration of Eastern Slavonia whereby the Serb community would be allocated two seats in the Chamber of Counties and Serbs would be exempt from serving in the Croatian army for the first two years. In early February Tudjman announced that the elections to the Chamber of Counties, which had been scheduled to take place in mid-March, had been postponed until 13 April, apparently owing to difficulties in the organization of the concurrent local government elections in Eastern Slavonia. In March the Independent Democratic Serb Party (SDSS), headed by Vojislav Stanimirović (the President of the Regional Council of Eastern Slavonia), was established to contest the elections in the enclave.

In early April 1997 Serb officials in Eastern Slavonia conducted a referendum (which, however, the Croatian Government and UN officials declared to be illegitimate) regarding the future of the enclave; about 99.5% of the participating electorate voted in favour of Eastern Slavonia remaining a single administrative unit under Serb control after its return to Croatia. On 13 April elections to the Chamber of Counties and to a number of municipal and regional councils took place. Voting in the concurrent local government elections in Eastern Slavonia was extended for two days, owing to administrative irregularities (which, it was reported, resulted from the Government's failure to provide sufficient ballot papers for voters in the enclave). Nevertheless, OSCE representatives who monitored the elections declared that they had been largely 'free and fair'. The CDU secured 42 of the 63 elective seats in the Chamber of Counties, while the Croatian Peasants' Party (Hrvatska Seljačka Stranka—HSS) took nine, the CSLP six, the Social Democratic Party (which had been reconstituted from the former LCC–PDR) four, and the IDA two seats. (A further five deputies were to be nominated by Tudjman, of whom two were to be members of the Serb community in Eastern Slavonia). The SDSS gained control of 11 of the 28 municipalities contested in the enclave. In May the CDU secured a narrow majority in the Zagreb City Assembly, following protracted negotiations which resulted in the defection of two councillors from the HSS to the CDU. Marina Dropulić-Matulović (who had been appointed to act as mayor of Zagreb following the controversy between the Government and opposition parties in May 1996) was subsequently elected to the office by CDU councillors.

In May 1997 the Government announced that the forthcoming presidential election was to take place on 15 June. Tudjman had been formally nominated as the presidential candidate of the CDU earlier that year (despite persistent reports, which were denied by government officials, that he was seriously ill). During a visit to Eastern Slavonia in early June Tudjman publicly offered reconciliation to all Serbs who were willing to accept Croatian citizenship, following continued pressure from Madeleine Albright, who had met Tudjman in late May. The presidential election took place on 15 June as scheduled; Tudjman was re-elected by 61.4% of votes cast, with the Social Democratic Party candidate, Zdravko Tomac, securing 21.0% and the CSLP leader, Vlado Gotovac, 17.6% of the votes. However, OSCE monitors declared that the elections had not been conducted fairly, on the grounds that opposition parties had not been permitted coverage in the state-controlled media during the electoral campaign. Later in June the Constitutional Court endorsed the results of the elections.

At the end of June 1997 a former Serb mayor of Vukovar, who had been indicted by the UN International Criminal Tribunal for the Former Yugoslavia (based in the Hague, the Netherlands), was arrested for his alleged involvement in the killing of some 260 civilians in Vukovar in November 1991. In early July 1997 the Government announced that the programme for the return of some 80,000 Croatian refugees to Eastern Slavonia had commenced; it was planned that about 40,000 displaced civilians would resettle in the region by the end of that year. Despite previous objections from the Croatian Government, the UN Security Council adopted a resolution to extend the mandate of UNTAES (which had been due to expire in mid-July) until mid-January 1998, owing to UN concern over the continued stability of Eastern Slavonia in view of the planned return of refugees to the enclave. (However, a number of UN troops withdrew from the region, reducing the size of the contingent from about 5,000 to 2,800.) Later in July the Croatian Government refused to comply with instructions from the UN International Criminal Tribunal to release official documents (which would be used as evidence in the trial of a former Bosnian Croat army officer) on the grounds of national security. In the same month the Bretton Woods institutions postponed the disbursement of financial assistance to Croatia, as a result of pressure from the Governments of the USA, the United Kingdom and Germany, which continued to criticize, in particular, the slow progress in the resettlement of refugees, the Croatian administration's failure to comply with extradition orders on suspects issued by the International Criminal Tribunal, and continued state control of the media.

On 5 August 1997 Tudjman was officially inaugurated for a second presidential term. In the same month the President of the CPR, Dobroslav Paraga, submitted a proposal at the UN International Criminal Tribunal that Tudjman, Šušak and a number of Bosnian Croats be officially charged in connection with the former conflict in Bosnia and Herzegovina. Paraga and a human rights activist, Ivan Zvonimir Čičak, were subsequently charged by the Croatian authorities with disseminating false information, after publishing claims in a national newspaper that Tudjman had been actively involved in initiating the Bosnian conflict. In September a former member of a Croatian paramilitary unit was arrested, following his confession in a published inverview that he had committed atrocities against Serb civilians in central and south-western Croatia in 1991. In October the Government announced plans to adopt new legislation which would allow the prosecution of journalists for publishing information considered to be insulting to the authorities (rather than on charges of publishing 'false' reports). In the same month the IMF approved the resumption of credit payments to Croatia (see Economic Affairs); it was reported that the US Government had withdrawn objections to the disbursement of funds after 10 Bosnian Croats (who had been indicted in connection with the massacre of Muslim civilians in 1993) agreed to appear before the UN International Criminal Tribunal. In November the legislature approved constitutional amendments, proposed by Tudjman, which, notably, prohibited the re-establishment of a union of Yugoslav states. In December Gotovac left the CSLP and formed a breakaway faction of the party.

In mid-December 1997 control of the Transitional Police Force in Eastern Slavonia was transferred to the Ministry of Internal Affairs. At the end of that year only about 7,000 refugees (of the estimated total of 80,000) had returned to the region. In mid-January 1998 the mandate of UNTAES ended, and Eastern Slavonia was officially returned to Croatian authority.

Government

According to the 1990 Constitution, legislative power is vested in the bicameral Assembly (Sabor), comprising a Chamber of Representatives (Zastupnički dom), with 80 seats, and a 68-member Chamber of Counties (Županijski dom). Both chambers are elected for a four-year term by universal adult suffrage. (Five of the 68 deputies in the Chamber of Counties are appointed by the President.) Executive power is held by the President and the Ministers, who are appointed by the President. The President is elected by universal adult suffrage for a period of five years. The country is divided, for electoral purposes, into 21 counties, 420 municipalities and 61 towns.

Defence

Military service is compulsory for men and lasts for a period of 10 months. In August 1997 the estimated total strength of the armed forces was 58,000 (the number of reservists totalled 220,000), including an army of 50,000, a navy of 3,000 and an air force of 5,000. There were, in addition, 40,000 armed military police. Expenditure on defence by the central Government was 6,955.5m. kuna (14.4% of total spending) in 1996.

Economic Affairs

In 1995, according to estimates by the World Bank, Croatia's gross national product (GNP), measured at average 1993–95 prices, was US $15,508m., equivalent to $3,250 per head. During 1985–95, according to estimates by the World Bank, Croatia's population increased at an average rate of 0.2% per year. Croatia's gross domestic product (GDP) declined, in real terms, at an average annual rate of 10.4% during 1989–93. However, real GDP rose by 0.6% in 1994, by 1.7% in 1995, by 4.2% in 1996 and by an estimated 6.5% in 1997.

Agriculture (including forestry and fishing) contributed an estimated 12.4% of GDP in 1995. About 14.3% of the labour force were employed in the sector in 1996. The principal crops are maize, wheat and sugar beet. (However, the civil conflict, which began in 1991, destroyed much arable land.) The GDP of the agricultural sector declined, in real terms, by 9.9% in 1991 and by 15.0% in 1992, but increased by 3.3% in 1993. Agricultural GDP declined by 0.9% in 1994, but increased by 0.2% in 1995. According to the FAO, agricultural production increased by 8.4% in 1996.

Industry (including mining, manufacturing, construction and utilities) engaged 40.7% of the employed labour force in 1991. Excluding crafts, trades and utilities, industrial activity provided an estimated 24.1% of GDP in 1995. In real terms, industrial GDP declined at an average rate of 11.4% per year during 1990–94. However, in 1995, compared with the previous year, industrial GDP was almost unchanged. Industrial production (excluding construction) increased by 3.1% in 1996.

The mining sector engaged only 0.7% of the employed labour force in 1992. Croatia has many exploitable mineral resources, including petroleum, coal and natural gas.

The manufacturing sector, which contributed an estimated 19.3% of GDP in 1995, engaged about 33.6% of the employed labour force in 1992. In the latter year the principal branches of the manufacturing sector, measured by the value of output, were food products (accounting for 19.2% of the total), chemicals (12.8%), textiles and clothing (8.5%), transport equipment and electrical machinery. It was estimated that some 30% of Croatia's production facilities were destroyed during the civil conflict. Production of machinery and equipment declined at an average rate of 21.2% per year during 1990–94, but increased by 4.2% in 1995 and by 9.4% in 1996.

Approximately 30% of Croatia's electricity-generating capacity was destroyed in the civil conflict. Production of electricity increased by 4.9% in 1995 and by 25.3% in 1996. However, the country remains dependent on imported fuel, which accounted for some 11.0% of total imports in 1996.

The services sector engaged 40.8% of the employed labour force in 1991. Including crafts, trades and utilities, services provided an estimated 63.5% of GDP in 1995. In real terms, the GDP of services declined at an average annual rate of 8.6% in 1990–93, but increased by 2.1% in 1994 and by 3.8% in 1995. The virtual elimination of tourism in Croatia (which in the late 1980s accounted for some 82% of Yugoslavia's total tourist trade) represented the largest war-related economic loss for Croatia. The number of tourist nights spent by foreign visitors to Croatia declined from about 59m. per year in 1985–88 to less than 7m. in 1991. There was a significant recovery in 1993 and 1994, but tourism fell sharply again in 1995. Overnight stays increased considerably in 1996.

In 1996 Croatia recorded a visible trade deficit of US $2,497.3m., while there was a deficit of $1,452.2m. on the current account of the balance of payments. In 1996 the principal source of imports was Germany (20.6%); other major sources were Italy, Slovenia and Austria. The principal market for exports in that year was Italy (21.0%); other important purchasers were Germany, Slovenia, and Bosnia and Herzegovina. The principal exports in 1996 were miscellaneous manufactured articles (particularly clothing and accessories), machinery and transport equipment, chemical products and basic manufactures. The main imports in that year were machinery and transport equipment (most notably road vehicles), basic manufactures, miscellaneous manufactured articles, fuels (particularly petroleum and petroleum products), chemical products and foodstuffs.

Croatia's overall budget deficit for 1996 was 477.4m. kuna (equivalent to 0.5% of GDP). The country's total external debt was US $3,662m. at the end of 1995, of which $1,693m. was long-term public debt. In that year the cost of debt-servicing was equivalent to 5.7% of the value of exports of goods and services. Croatia's external debt increased to $4,847m. at the end of 1996 and to more than $5,900m. in October 1997. Consumer prices increased by an annual average of 254.8% in 1990–95. However, the average rate of inflation was only 4.0% in 1995 and 4.3% in 1996. In early 1997 an estimated 15% of the population were unemployed.

Croatia was admitted to the IMF in Janury 1993, and became a member of the European Bank for Reconstruction and Development (EBRD, see p. 148) in April of that year.

The outbreak of civil conflict in Croatia in the early 1990s resulted in a rapid deterioration of the economy. In 1993 the Government initiated a macro-economic programme, which achieved some success in slowing the rate of inflation and controlling public expenditure. The introduction of a new national currency, the kuna, in May 1994 rapidly restrained the rate of inflation. In October of that year the IMF extended its first stand-by loan to Croatia; conditions imposed by the organization included rapid progress in the Government's plans for the large-scale privatization of state utilities, which had been subject to continued delays (apparently for political reasons). The Government subsequently received reconstruction loans from other official creditors and concluded a rescheduling agreement with the 'Paris Club' of donor nations. In April 1996 an agreement was reached with the 'London Club' of commercial creditor banks, establishing Croatia's share of the foreign commercial bank debt incurred by the former Yugoslavia. In March 1997 the IMF approved a further three-year credit arrangement to support the Government's programme of economic reform. In July of that year the Bretton Woods institutions postponed the disbursement of funds, owing to pressure from foreign Governments (see Recent History). In October the IMF approved the resumption of payments; however, the Croatian Government announced that the funds were not required, owing to the country's existing high level of foreign exchange reserves and favourable balance-of-payments position. The Government initiated a further stage of its large-scale privatization programme with a vouchers scheme (which was available to civilians who had suffered during the civil conflict); the project was expected to generate the country's first investment funds. The continuing recovery in the tourism sector and the increase in construction activity contributed to improved financial stability.

Social Welfare

A state health service is available to all citizens. In 1992 there were 9,446 physicians, about 2,500 dentists and 1,747 pharmacists working in Croatia. Of total expenditure by the central Government in 1996, 7,441m. kuna (15.4%) was for health, and a further 15,689m. kuna (32.4%) for social security and welfare. Most government spending on social services is disbursed through extrabudgetary funds, principally the Health Insurance Fund and the Pension Fund.

Education

Pre-school education, for children aged from three to six years, is available free of charge. Education is officially compulsory for eight years, between seven and 15 years of age. Primary education, which is provided free, begins at the age of seven and (since the 1995/96 academic year) lasts for four years. Enrolment at primary schools in 1995 was equivalent to 86% of children in the appropriate age-group (boys 87%; girls 86%). Special education in foreign languages is provided for children of non-Croat ethnic origin, since all national minorities in Croatia have the right to learn their minority language. Secondary education is available free (although private schools also exist) and lasts for up to eight years, comprising two cycles of four years each. There are various types of secondary school: grammar, technical and specialized schools and mixed-curriculum schools. Enrolment at secondary schools in 1995 was equivalent to 82% of the relevant age-group (boys 81%; girls 83%). In 1995 there were four universities in Croatia—in Zagreb, Rijeka, Osijek and Split. In 1995/96 a total of 86,357 students were enrolled in higher education establishments. Expenditure on education by the central Government in 1996 was 3,166m. kuna (6.5% of total spending).

Public Holidays

1998: 1 January (New Year's Day), 6 January (Epiphany), 10 April (Good Friday), 13 April (Easter Monday), 1 May (Labour Day), 30 May (Independence Day), 5 August (National Day), 15 August (Assumption), 1 November (All Saints' Day), 25–26 December (Christmas).

1999: 1 January (New Year's Day), 6 January (Epiphany), 2 April (Good Friday), 5 April (Easter Monday), 1 May (Labour Day), 30 May (Independence Day), 5 August (National Day), 15 August (Assumption), 1 November (All Saints' Day), 25–26 December (Christmas).

Weights and Measures

The metric system is in force.

Statistical Survey

Source (unless otherwise stated): Central Bureau of Statistics of the Republic of Croatia, 10000 Zagreb, Ilica 3; tel. (1) 4554422; telex 21130; fax (1) 429413.

Area and Population

AREA, POPULATION AND DENSITY

Area (sq km)	56,610*
Population (census results)	
31 March 1981	4,601,469
31 March 1991	
Males	2,318,623
Females	2,465,642
Total	4,784,265
Population (official estimates at mid-year)	
1992	4,789,000
1993	4,779,000
1994	4,777,000
Density (per sq km) at mid-1994	84.4

* 21,857 sq miles.

POPULATION BY ETHNIC GROUP (census of 31 March 1991)

	Number ('000)	%
Croat	3,736.4	78.1
Serb	581.7	12.2
Muslim	43.5	0.9
Slovene	22.4	0.5
Hungarian	22.4	0.5
Italian	21.3	0.4
Czech	13.1	0.3
Albanian	12.0	0.3
Montenegrin	9.7	0.2
Gypsy	6.7	0.1
Macedonian	6.3	0.1
Slovak	5.6	0.1
Others*	303.3	6.3
Total	4,784.3	100.0

* Including (in '000) persons who declared themselves to be Yugoslav (106.0), persons with a regional affiliation (45.5), persons of unknown nationality (62.9) and persons who refused to reply (73.4).

PRINCIPAL TOWNS (population at 1991 census)

Zagreb (capital)	706,770	Vukovar	44,639
Split	189,388	Varaždin	41,846
Rijeka	167,964	Šibenik	41,012
Osijek	104,761	Vinkovci	35,347
Zadar	76,343	Servete	35,337
Pula	62,378	Velika Gorica	31,614
Karlovac	59,999	Bjelovar	26,926
Slavonski Brod	55,683	Koprivnica	24,238
Dubrovnik	49,728	Požega	21,046
Sisak	45,792	Djakovo	20,317

BIRTHS, MARRIAGES AND DEATHS

	Registered live births		Registered marriages		Registered deaths	
	Number	Rate (per 1,000)	Number	Rate (per 1,000)	Number	Rate (per 1,000)
1988	58,525	12.5	29,719	6.3	52,686	11.3
1989	55,651	11.9	28,938	6.2	52,569	11.2
1990	55,409	11.6	27,924	5.9	52,192	10.9
1991	51,829	10.8	21,583	4.5	54,832	11.4
1992	46,970	9.8	22,169	4.6	51,800	10.8
1993	48,535	10.2	23,021	4.8	50,846	10.6
1994	48,584	10.2	23,966	5.0	49,482	10.4
1995	50,182	10.5	n.a.	n.a.	50,536	10.6

Expectation of life (years at birth 1991): Males 68.6; Females 76.0.

ECONOMICALLY ACTIVE POPULATION
(*de jure,* persons aged 15 years and over, 1991 census)

	Males	Females	Total
Agriculture, hunting, forestry and fishing	161,729	108,781	270,510
Mining and quarrying Manufacturing	368,708	243,867	612,575
Electricity, gas and water. Construction.	105,925	19,499	125,424
Trade, restaurants and hotels.	106,549	137,171	243,720
Transport, storage and communications	97,982	21,961	119,943
Financing, insurance, real estate and business services	26,353	33,997	60,350
Community, social and personal services	127,618	187,090	314,708
Activities not adequately defined	40,434	23,420	63,854
Total employed	1,035,298	775,786	1,811,084

Total labour force (persons aged 15 years and over, 1991 census): 2,039,833 (males 1,165,728; females 874,105). Figures refer to usual residents in the country at the time of the census.

Source: UN, *Demographic Yearbook*.

31 December 1993: Total employed 1,641,180; Registered unemployed 243,096; Total labour force 1,884,276.
31 December 1994: Total employed 1,587,578; Registered unemployed 247,555; Total labour force 1,835,133.
31 December 1995: Total employed 1,538,469; Registered unemployed 249,070; Total labour force 1,787,539.
Note: The foregoing figures include employment in the private sector, based on the number of employees paying pension contributions.

Source: IMF, *Croatia—Selected Issues and Statistical Appendix* (May 1997).

EMPLOYMENT (annual averages, '000 persons)*

	1993	1994	1995
Mining, quarrying and manufacturing	384.7	368.3	349.2
Agriculture and fishing	42.3	39.6	35.2
Forestry.	10.8	10.9	10.9
Water management	4.3	4.0	4.0
Construction.	66.3	59.0	59.0
Transport and communications	90.0	84.9	84.1
Trade	125.2	116.5	109.8
Hotels, restaurants and tourism	50.5	48.8	44.6
Crafts and trades	23.9	21.8	20.1
Housing, utilities and public services	23.3	23.4	24.1
Financial and other services	51.4	50.1	51.3
Education, culture and the arts	88.9	89.4	88.8
Health care and social services	98.6	97.3	95.3
Government bodies and agencies, social and political organizations	48.2	47.5	50.4
Total	1,108.4	1,061.5	1,026.8
Males	601.6	569.9	549.1
Females	506.8	491.6	477.7

* Excluding members of the armed forces and police, and persons employed in the private sector of agriculture. Also excluded are self-employed workers and their employees ('000): 130 in 1993; 149 in 1994; 169 in 1995.

Agriculture

PRINCIPAL CROPS ('000 metric tons)

	1994	1995	1996
Wheat	750	877	741
Barley	108	103	88
Maize	1,687	1,735	1,883
Rye	7	5	6
Oats	42	38	40
Potatoes	563	691	665
Dry beans	21	22	20
Soybeans (Soya beans)	44	34	36
Sunflower seed	26	37	29
Rapeseed	28	24	12
Cabbages	96	109	115
Tomatoes	46	47	49
Cucumbers and gherkins	24	19*	19*
Onions (fresh)	41	43	39
Garlic	9	8*	8*
Carrots	20	22	20
Watermelons and melons	16	12*	12*
Grapes	363	339	373
Sugar beet	592	691	906
Apples	47	51	75
Pears	9	11	11*
Peaches and nectarines	7	5	5*
Plums	36	38	38*
Tobacco (leaves)	9	9	11

* FAO estimate.

Source: FAO, *Production Yearbook.*

LIVESTOCK ('000 head, year ending September)

	1994	1995	1996
Horses	22	21*	21*
Asses and mules	10	7*	7*
Cattle	519	493	462
Pigs	1,347	1,175	1,196
Sheep	444	453	427
Goats	108	107	105
Chickens	12,503	12,024	10,000*

* FAO estimate.

Source: mainly FAO, *Production Yearbook.*

LIVESTOCK PRODUCTS ('000 metric tons)

	1994	1995	1996
Beef and veal	31	28	26
Mutton and lamb*	2	2	2
Pigmeat	57	48	46
Poultry meat	40	34	37
Cows' milk	600	590	590†
Butter	2	2	3
Cheese (all kinds)	17	17	19
Hen eggs	53	52	52†
Honey	1	1	1†

* Unofficial figures. † FAO estimate.

Source: FAO, *Production Yearbook.*

Forestry

ROUNDWOOD REMOVALS ('000 cubic metres)*

	1993	1994	1995
Sawlogs and veneer logs	1,320	1,367	1,307
Pitprops (mine timber)	41	32	24
Pulpwood	224	266	248
Other industrial wood	133	165	140
Fuel wood	610	790	703
Total	2,328	2,620	2,422

* From state-owned forests only.

SAWNWOOD PRODUCTION ('000 cubic metres)

	1993	1994	1995
Coniferous (softwood)	146	119	101
Broadleaved (hardwood)	553	490	477
Total	699	609	578

Fishing

('000 metric tons, live weight)

	1993	1994	1995
Freshwater fishes	5.3	5.4	4.6
Marine fishes	23.2	14.5	13.5
Crustaceans and molluscs	2.5	2.1	1.9
Total catch	31.0	22.0	20.0

Mining

('000 metric tons, unless otherwise indicated)

	1993	1994	1995
Coal	105	96	75
Crude petroleum	1,729	1,577	1,500
Bauxite	2	1	—
Natural gas (million cu m)	2,068	1,792	1,966

Industry

SELECTED PRODUCTS ('000 metric tons, unless otherwise indicated)

	1993	1994	1995
Beer ('000 hectolitres)	2,481	3,122	3,166
Spirits ('000 hectolitres)	293	288	265
Cigarettes (million)	11,582	12,672	12,110
Cotton fabric blankets ('000 sq metres)	28,759	22,572	22,200
Household linen ('000 sq metres)	12,601	12,191	9,161
Ready-to-wear clothing ('000 sq metres)	36,393	34,327	32,353
Leather footwear ('000 pairs)	8,176	8,106	6,542
Paper and cardboard	180	197	160
Cardboard packaging	106	122	128
Motor spirit (petrol)	964	1,036	1,453
Gas oil (distillate fuels)	772	952	1,141
Compound fertilizers	483	554	548
Synthetic materials and resin	132	159	165
Cement	1,683	2,055	1,708
Tractors (number)	1,164	783	359
Tankers ('000 gross registered tons)	145	124	121
Cargo ships ('000 gross registered tons)	80	45	37
Chairs ('000)	1,017	982	821
Electric energy (million kWh)	9,437	8,717	9,146

Finance

CURRENCY AND EXCHANGE RATES

Monetary Unit

100 lipa = 1 kuna.

Sterling and Dollar Equivalents (30 September 1997)

£1 sterling = 10.078 kuna;
US $1 = 6.239 kuna;
1,000 kuna = £99.22 = $160.28.

Average Exchange Rate (kuna per US $)

1994 5.996
1995 5.230
1996 5.434

Note: The Croatian dinar was introduced on 23 December 1991, replacing (and initially at par with) the Yugoslav dinar. On 30 May 1994 the kuna, equivalent to 1,000 dinars, was introduced.

STATE BUDGET ('000 kuna)

Revenue*	1994	1995	1996†
Tax revenue	22,377,482	26,505,353	29,075,638
Taxes on income and profits	3,803,192	4,506,661	4,851,432
Domestic taxes on goods and services	14,920,740	17,746,173	19,634,594
Taxes on international trade	3,486,771	3,939,005	4,399,788
Other current revenue	411,400	781,766	1,071,680
Entrepreneurial and property income	186,238	329,488	325,874
Central Bank profits	141,473	165,889	147,520
Capital revenue	353,750	593,660	938,000
Total	23,142,632	27,880,779	31,085,318

Expenditure‡	1994	1995	1996†
General public services	1,674,965	1,911,166	2,071,704
Defence	7,650,165	9,910,927	7,760,190
Public order and safety	2,841,432	3,351,489	3,826,741
Education	2,864,662	3,277,776	3,695,723
Health	57,245	78,167	216,380
Social security and welfare	2,547,002	3,185,789	4,357,143
Housing and community amenities	462,741	1,343,216	2,458,580
Recreational, cultural and religious affairs	308,960	430,115	436,487
Agriculture, forestry and fisheries	652,968	511,479	555,613
Mining and mineral resources, manufacturing and construction	192,398	255,352	463,363
Transport and communications	1,498,506	2,232,489	3,407,823
Other economic affairs and services	273,661	226,887	316,031
Other purposes	1,258,087	1,760,731	2,055,913
Total	22,282,792	28,475,583	31,621,691

* Excluding grants received ('000 kuna): 100,000 in 1995.

† Figures for 1996 are projections. The outturn (in '000 kuna) was: *Revenue:* Tax revenue 28,530,426; Other current revenue 1,713,917; Capital revenue 1,123,138; Total 31,367,481. *Expenditure:* Total 30,972,816, excluding lending minus repayments (528,685).

‡ Excluding lending minus repayments ('000 kuna): 315,982 in 1994; 220,603 in 1995; 1,646,620 (provisional) in 1996.

1997 (projections, '000 kuna): *Revenue:* Tax revenue 29,609,310; Other current revenue 1,925,197; Capital revenue 1,420,963; Total 32,955,470. *Expenditure:* Total 33,859,738, excluding lending minus repayments (1,932,430).

Source: Ministry of Finance.

INTERNATIONAL RESERVES (US $ million at 31 December)

	1994	1995	1996
IMF special drawing rights	4.5	140.3	125.6
Foreign exchange	1,405.0	1,895.2	2,314.0
Total	1,409.5	2,035.5	2,439.6

Source: IMF, *International Financial Statistics*.

MONEY SUPPLY (million kuna at 31 December)

	1994	1995	1996
Currency outside banks	2,658.2	3,365.1	4,366.2
Demand deposits at deposit money banks	3,960.5	4,861.2	6,997.2
Total (incl. others)	6,639.6	8,274.8	11,409.3

Source: IMF, *International Financial Statistics*..

COST OF LIVING (Consumer price index; base: 1990 = 100)

	1993	1994	1995
Food (incl. beverages)	26,708.0	53,709.8	54,139.5
Fuel and light	26,279.1	52,085.2	51,199.8
Clothing (incl. footwear)	27,021.0	57,473.7	57,818.5
Rent	16,423.8	36,345.9	40,707.5
All items (incl. others)	26,104.2	54,087.8	56,251.3

1996: All items 58,670.2 (Source: UN, *Monthly Bulletin of Statistics*).

NATIONAL ACCOUNTS

Gross Domestic Product by Economic Activity
(million kuna at current prices)

	1993	1994	1995
Industry and mining	9,007	14,934	14,889
Agriculture and fisheries	4,172	8,097	8,380
Forestry	462	934	885
Water management	97	194	200
Construction	1,278	2,615	2,950
Transport and communication	2,382	5,077	5,499
Trade	2,734	5,019	6,123
Hotels, restaurants and tourism	1,158	2,739	2,512
Crafts and trades	892	2,227	2,873
Housing, utilities and public services	4,803	5,773	6,208
Financial and other services	2,905	6,562	6,844
Education, health care, central government, funds and associations	6,135	14,091	17,464
GDP at factor cost	36,023	68,263	74,828
Net indirect taxes	5,810	17,037	19,736
GDP at market prices	41,833	85,299	94,564

Source: IMF, *Croatia—Selected Issues and Statistical Appendix* (May 1997).

GDP at market prices (million kuna): 103,610 in 1996; 113,288 (estimate) in 1997 (Source: Ministry of Finance).

BALANCE OF PAYMENTS (US $ million)

	1994	1995	1996
Exports of goods f.o.b.	4,260.4	4,632.7	4,511.8
Imports of goods f.o.b.	–4,706.4	–6,758.9	–7,009.1
Trade balance	–446.0	–2,126.2	–2,497.3
Exports of services	2,292.5	2,569.2	3,496.3
Imports of services	–2,077.9	–2,707.5	–3,184.5
Balance on goods and services	–231.4	–2,264.5	–2,185.5
Other income received	101.0	173.4	226.5
Other income paid	–225.5	–266.7	–271.9
Balance on goods, services and income	–355.9	–2,357.8	–2,230.9
Current transfers received	602.1	814.6	929.5
Current transfers paid	–142.8	–168.8	–150.8
Current balance	103.4	–1,712.0	–1,452.2
Direct investment from abroad	97.6	80.5	348.9
Other investment assets	241.8	49.8	142.0
Other investment liabilities	–119.7	362.2	480.1
Net errors and omissions	102.6	1,307.1	823.9
Overall balance	425.8	87.6	342.6

Source: IMF, *International Financial Statistics*.

External Trade

PRINCIPAL COMMODITIES (distribution by SITC, US $ million)

Imports c.i.f.	1994	1995	1996
Food and live animals	498	780	767
Vegetables and fruit	131	222	194
Crude materials (inedible) except fuels	151	198	220
Mineral fuels, lubricants, etc.	589	871	857
Petroleum and petroleum products	436	736	707
Chemicals and related products	541	810	848
Medicinal and pharmaceutical products	99	177	188
Basic manufactures	801	1,304	1,384
Paper, paperboard, etc.	134	236	249
Textile yarn, fabrics, etc.	149	210	203
Iron and steel	142	243	257
Machinery and transport equipment	1,367	2,009	2,129
Machinery specialized for particular industries	176	281	318
General industrial machinery, equipment and parts	217	330	370
Electrical machinery, apparatus, etc.	241	376	399
Road vehicles and parts (excl. tyres, engines and electrical parts)	391	439	n.a.
Miscellaneous manufactured articles	776	1,013	1,117
Clothing and accessories (excl. footwear)	231	271	286
Footwear	202	214	240
Total (incl. others)	5,229	7,510	7,788

Exports f.o.b.	1994	1995	1996
Food and live animals	369	395	411
Beverages and tobacco	67	90	92
Crude materials (inedible) except fuels	214	251	247
Wood, lumber and cork	144	161	166
Mineral fuels, lubricants, etc.	386	391	416
Petroleum and petroleum products	344	366	371
Chemicals and related products	543	814	643
Medicinal and pharmaceutical products	133	137	139
Fertilizers (other than crude)	86	112	118
Plastics in primary forms	177	361	209
Basic manufactures	654	670	594
Paper, paperboard, etc.	98	107	62
Textile yarn, fabrics, etc.	129	124	110
Non-metallic mineral manufactures	126	126	135
Machinery and transport equipment	732	778	964
Electrical machinery, apparatus, etc.	172	211	219
Transport equipment (excl. road vehicles)	304	261	n.a.
Miscellaneous manufactured articles	1,257	1,233	1,133
Furniture and parts	138	151	120
Clothing and accessories (excl. footwear)	629	673	633
Footwear	279	234	235
Total (incl. others)	4,232	4,633	4,512

Source: IMF, *Croatia—Selected Issues and Statistical Appendix* (May 1997).

PRINCIPAL TRADING PARTNERS (US $ million)

Imports c.i.f.	1994	1995	1996
Austria	353	575	597
Belgium	55	85	100
Czech Republic	92	147	207
France	116	188	199
Germany	1,110	1,509	1,602
Hungary	100	158	193
Iran	292	90	n.a.
Italy	994	1,366	1,421
Japan	54	80	104
Libya	68	190	n.a.
Netherlands	115	174	176
Slovakia	53	78	84
Slovenia	541	805	769
Sweden	81	148	117
Switzerland	101	169	144
USSR (former)	254	224	253
United Kingdom	179	455	225
USA	172	201	213
Total (incl. others)	5,229	7,510	7,788

Exports f.o.b.	1994	1995	1996
Austria	149	200	198
Bosnia and Herzegovina	338	383	549
France	111	110	84
Germany	941	997	839
Hungary	68	71	55
Italy	910	1,098	949
Liberia	55	105	n.a.
Macedonia, former Yugoslav republic	73	70	59
Netherlands	94	80	69
Poland	45	49	56
Slovenia	556	608	611
Sweden	164	14	13
Switzerland	60	52	37
USSR (former)	176	185	172
United Kingdom	68	57	70
USA	88	83	89
Total (incl. others)	4,260	4,633	4,512

Source: IMF, *Croatia—Selected Issues and Statistical Appendix* (May 1997).

Transport

RAILWAYS (traffic)

	1993	1994	1995
Passenger journeys ('000)	18,760	19,243	17,455
Passenger-kilometres (million)	951	962	943
Freight carried ('000 metric tons)	11,685	11,279	13,318
Freight net ton-km (million)	1,592	1,563	1,974

ROAD TRAFFIC (registered motor vehicles at 31 December)

	1993	1994	1995
Passenger cars	646,210	698,391	710,910
Buses	3,895	4,026	3,897
Lorries	35,308	49,834 }	67,282
Special vehicles	11,499	9,378 }	
Motorcycles and mopeds	171,860	202,900	201,126

INLAND WATERWAYS (vessels and traffic)

	1993	1994	1995
Tugs	28	26	25
Motor barges	1	1	2
Barges	121	106	105
Goods unloaded (million metric tons)	0.4	0.5	0.8

SHIPPING

Merchant Fleet (registered at 31 December)

	1994	1995	1996
Number of vessels	205	210	232
Total displacement ('000 grt)	247.0	332.8	579.8

Source: Lloyd's Register of Shipping, *World Fleet Statistics*.

International Sea-borne Freight Traffic

	1993	1994	1995
Vessels entered (million net reg. tons)	7.2	7.8	8.7
Goods loaded ('000 metric tons)	3,178	3,253	2,789
Goods unloaded ('000 metric tons)	5,832	5,734	6,450
Goods in transit ('000 metric tons)	1,984	1,408	2,492

CIVIL AVIATION

	1993	1994	1995
Kilometres flown ('000)	6,837	8,287	8,699
Passengers carried ('000)	507	661	679
Passenger-kilometres (million)	316	444	444
Freight carried (metric tons)	3,894	4,431	4,605
Ton-kilometres ('000)	2,620	3,247	3,408

Tourism

FOREIGN TOURIST ARRIVALS BY COUNTRY OF ORIGIN ('000)

	1993	1994	1995
Austria	249	362	193
Czech Republic	238	435	119
France	20	27	19
Germany	194	356	211
Hungary	91	129	34
Italy	258	357	194
Netherlands	17	30	25
Slovakia	23	59	27
Slovenia	230	294	300
United Kingdom	18	22	23
Total (incl. others)	1,521	2,293	1,324

Communications Media

	1993	1994	1995
Radio receivers ('000 in use)	n.a.	1,174	1,200
Television receivers ('000 in use)	n.a.	1,138	1,150
Book production: titles*	2,094	2,671	n.a.
Daily newspapers:			
Number	n.a.	6	12
Average circulation ('000 copies)	n.a.	n.a.	225†

Non-daily newspapers (1990): 563 (average circulation 110,000 copies).
Other periodicals (1990): 352 (average circulation 6,357,000 copies).

* Including pamphlets (431 titles in 1993; 730 in 1994).
† Estimate.
Source: UNESCO, *Statistical Yearbook*.

Telephones ('000 main lines in use): 955 in 1992; 1,027 in 1993; 1,205 in 1994 (Source: UN, *Statistical Yearbook*).

Telefax stations (number in use): 9,079 in 1992; 14,322 in 1993; 28,350 in 1994 (Source: UN, *Statistical Yearbook*).

Mobile cellular telephones (subscribers): 6,320 in 1992; 11,239 in 1993; 21,660 in 1994 (Source: UN, *Statistical Yearbook*).

Education

(1995/96)

	Institu-tions	Teach-ers	Students		
			Males	Females	Total
Pre-primary	902	5,531	34,525	31,580	66,105
Primary	1,134	10,605	106,794	101,096	207,890
Secondary: general	n.a.	17,781	129,217	136,250	265,467
Secondary: vocational	n.a.	11,960	81,825	70,183	152,008
University level*	n.a.	6,325	44,240	42,117	86,357

* Excluding post-graduate students.
Source: UNESCO, *Statistical Yearbook*.

Directory

The Constitution

The Constitution of the Republic of Croatia was promulgated on 21 December 1990. Croatia issued a declaration of dissociation from the Socialist Federal Republic of Yugoslavia in June 1991, and formal independence was proclaimed on 8 October 1991. Constitutional amendments, which were adopted in November 1997, included a prohibition on the re-establishment of a union of Yugoslav states.

The following is a summary of the main provisions of the Constitution:

GENERAL PROVISIONS

The Republic of Croatia is a democratic, constitutional state where power belongs to the people and is exercised directly and through the elected representatives of popular sovereignty.

The Republic of Croatia is an integral state, while its sovereignty is inalienable, indivisible and non-transferable. State power in the Republic of Croatia is divided into legislative, executive and judicial power.

All citizens of the Republic of Croatia over the age of 18 years have the right to vote and to be candidates for election to public office. The right to vote is realized through direct elections, by secret ballot. Citizens of the Republic living outside its borders have the right to vote in elections for the Assembly and the President of the Republic.

In a state of war or when there is a direct threat to the independence and unity of the Republic, as well as in the case of serious natural disasters, some freedoms and rights that are guaranteed by the Constitution may be restricted. This is decided by the Assembly of the Republic of Croatia by a two-thirds majority of its deputies and, if the Assembly cannot be convened, by the President of the Republic.

BASIC RIGHTS

The following rights are guaranteed and protected in the Republic: the right to life (the death sentence has been abolished), fundamental freedoms and privacy, equality before the law, the right to be presumed innocent until proven guilty and the principle of legality, the right to receive legal aid, the right to freedom of movement and residence, the right to seek asylum, inviolability of the home, freedom and secrecy of correspondence, safety and secrecy of personal data, freedom of thought and expression of opinion, freedom of conscience and religion (all religious communities are equal before the law and are separated from the State), the right of assembly and peaceful association, the right of ownership, entrepreneurship and free trade (monopolies are forbidden), the right to work and freedom of labour, the right to a nationality, the right to strike, and the right to a healthy environment.

Members of all peoples and minorities in the Republic enjoy equal rights. They are guaranteed the freedom to express their nationality, to use their language and alphabet and to enjoy cultural autonomy.

GOVERNMENT

Legislature

Legislative power resides with the Assembly (Sabor), which consists of the 80-member Chamber of Representatives (Zastupnički dom), and the 68-member Chamber of Counties (Županijski dom).

The Chamber of Representatives decides on the adoption and amendment of the Constitution, approves laws, adopts the state budgets, decides on war and peace, decides on the alteration of the borders of the Republic, calls referendums, supervises the work of the Government and other public officials responsible to the Assembly, in accordance with the Constitution and the law, and deals with other matters determined by the Constitution.

The Chamber of Counties proposes laws and gives opinions on issues within the competence of the Chamber of Representatives; however, after the adoption of a law in the Chamber of Representatives, the Chamber of Counties may return the same law to the former for reconsideration. The citizens of each district elect, by direct and secret ballot, three deputies to the Chamber of Counties. A further five deputies are appointed by the President.

Members of the Chambers of the Assembly are elected by universal, direct and secret ballot for a term of four years, and their term is not mandatory. The Chambers of the Assembly may be dissolved, if the majority of all the deputies decides so, while the President of the Republic may, in accordance with the Constitution, dissolve the Chamber of Representatives.

President of the Republic

The President of the Republic is the Head of State of Croatia. The President represents the country at home and abroad and is responsible for ensuring respect for the Constitution, guaranteeing the existence and unity of the Republic and the regular functioning of state power. The President is elected directly for a term of five years.

The President determines elections for the Chambers of the Assembly, orders referendums, appoints and dismisses the Prime Minister, the Deputy Prime Ministers and members of the Government, appoints and recalls diplomatic representatives of the Republic and is the Supreme Commander of the Armed Forces of the Republic of Croatia. In the event of war or immediate danger, the President issues decrees having the force of law. The President may convene a meeting of the Government and place on its agenda items which, in his opinion, should be discussed. The President attends the Government's meetings and presides over them.

The President may dissolve the Chamber of Representatives, if it approves a vote of 'no confidence' in the Government or if it does not approve the state budget within a specified period.

Ministers

Executive power in the Republic resides with the President, the Prime Minister and the Ministers. The Government of the Republic consists of the Ministers and the Prime Minister. The Government issues decrees, proposes laws and the budget, and implements laws and regulations that have been adopted by the Assembly. In its work, the Government is responsible to the President of the Republic and the Chamber of Representatives.

JUDICATURE

Judicial power is vested in the courts and is autonomous and independent. The courts issue judgments on the basis of the Constitution and the law. The Supreme Court is the highest court and is responsible for the uniform implementation of laws and equal rights of citizens. Judges and state public prosecutors are appointed and relieved of duty by the Judicial Council of the Republic, which is elected, from among distinguished lawyers, by the Chamber of Representatives for a term of eight years.

The Government

(February 1998)

HEAD OF STATE

President of the Republic: Dr Franjo Tudjman (elected by the Sabor 30 May 1990; elected by direct vote 2 August 1992; re-elected 15 June 1997).

Office of the President: 10000 Zagreb, Banski Dvori.

GOVERNMENT

Prime Minister: Zlatko Mateša.

Deputy Prime Minister responsible for Finance and the Economy: Borislav Skegro.

Deputy Prime Minister and Minister of Foreign Affairs: Dr Mate Granić.

Deputy Prime Minister and Minister of Development and Reconstruction: Dr Jure Radić.

Deputy Prime Minister responsible for Humanitarian Issues and Minister of Science and Technology: Dr Ivica Kostović.

Deputy Prime Minister responsible for Internal Policy and Public Services: Dr Ljerka Mintas Hodak.

Minister of Defence: Gojko Šušak.

Minister of Internal Affairs: Ivan Jarnjak.

Minister of Trade and Industry: Davor Stern.

Minister of Privatization and Property Management: Ivan Penić.

Minister of Agriculture and Forestry: Matej Janković.

Minister of Maritime Affairs, Transport and Communications: Zeljko Lužaveč.

Minister of Health: Dr Andrija Hebrang.

Minister of Culture: Bozo Biskupić.

Minister of Education and Sports: Ljilja Vokić.

Minister of Tourism: Sergev Morsan.

Minister of Labour and Social Welfare: Joso Skara.

Minister for Urban Planning, Construction and Housing: Marina Dropulíc-Matulović.

Minister of Justice: Miroslav Separović.

Minister of Administration: Davorin Mlakar.

Minister for Co-ordination and Emigration: Marijan Petrović.

Minister without Portfolio: Branko Mocibob.

MINISTRIES

Office of the Prime Minister: Government of the Republic of Croatia, 10000 Zagreb, trg sv. Marka 2; tel. (1) 4569201; fax (1) 432041.

Ministry of Administration: 10000 Zagreb, Republike Austrije 16; tel. (1) 182111.

Ministry of Agriculture and Forestry: 10000 Zagreb, Ave Vukovar 78; tel. (1) 6133444; fax (1) 442070.

Ministry of Construction, Urban Planning and Housing: 10000 Zagreb, Republike Austrije 20; tel. (1) 182142; fax (1) 172822.

Ministry for Co-ordination and Emigration: 10000 Zagreb, trg sv. Marka 2; tel. (1) 4569222; fax (1) 432041.

Ministry of Culture: 10000 Zagreb, trg Burze 6; tel. (1) 4569000; fax (1) 410487.

Ministry of Defence: 10000 Zagreb, trg kralja Petra Krešimira IV 1; tel. (1) 4567111.

Ministry of Development and Reconstruction: 10000 Zagreb, Nazorova 1; tel. and fax 184550.

Ministry of the Economy: 10000 Zagreb, trg sv. Marka 2; tel. (1) 4569207; fax (1) 4550606.

Ministry of Education and Sport: 10000 Zagreb, trg Burze 6; tel. (1) 4569000; fax (1) 4569087.

Ministry of Finance: 10000 Zagreb, ul. Katančićeva 5; tel. (1) 4551555; fax (1) 432789.

Ministry of Foreign Affairs: 10000 Zagreb, trg Nikole Šubića Zrinskog 7-8; tel. (1) 4569964; fax (1) 4569977.

Ministry of Health: 10000 Zagreb, ul. Baruna Tranka 6; tel. (1) 431068; fax (1) 431067.

Ministry of Internal Affairs: 10000 Zagreb, Savska cesta 39; tel. (1) 6122129.

Ministry of Justice: 10000 Zagreb, Savska cesta 41; tel. (1) 535935; fax (1) 536321.

Ministry of Labour and Social Welfare: 10000 Zagreb, Prisavlje 14; tel. (1) 6113337; fax (1) 6113593.

Ministry of Maritime Affairs, Transport and Communications: 10000 Zagreb, Prisavlje 14; tel. (1) 6112017; fax (1) 6110691.

Ministry of Privatization and Property Management: 10000 Zagreb, Gajeva 30a; tel. (1) 4569103; fax (1) 4569133.

Ministry of Science and Technology: 10000 Zagreb, Strossmayera trg 4, tel. (1) 4594444; fax (1) 429543.

Ministry of Tourism: 10000 Zagreb, Ave Vukovar 78; tel. (1) 6113477; fax (1) 6113216.

Ministry of Trade and Industry: 10000 Zagreb, Ave Vukovar 78; tel. (1) 6133444; fax (1) 6114210.

Ministry of Urban Planning, Construction and Housing: 10000 Zagreb, Republike Austrije 20; tel. (1) 182142.

President and Legislature

PRESIDENT

Presidential Election, 15 June 1997

Candidate	% of votes
Dr Franjo Tudjman (CDU)	61.41
Dr Zdravko Tomac (Social Democratic Party)	21.03
Vladimir (Vlado) Gotovac (CSLP)	17.56
Total	100.00

SABOR

(Assembly)

President: Vlatko Pavletić; 10000 Zagreb, trg sv. Marka 617; tel. (1) 4569222; fax (1) 276483.

Vice-Presidents: Dr Žarko Domijan, Dražen Busiša, Jadranka Kosor, Stjepan Radić, Vladimir Šeks.

Secretary: Berislav Živković.

Zastupnički dom

(Chamber of Representatives)

President: Vlatko Pavletić.

Election, 29 October 1995

Party	% of votes	Seats
Croatian Democratic Union (CDU)	45.23	42
Opposition electoral alliance*	18.26	16
Croatian Social-Liberal Party (CSLP)	11.55	10
Social Democratic Party (SDP)	8.93	8
Croatian Party of Rights (CPR)	5.01	4
Others	11.02	—
Total	100.00	80

* An alliance of seven opposition parties, which agreed to present joint candidates in a number of constituencies. The alliance was composed of: the Croatian People's Party (CPP), the Croatian Peasants' Party, the Croatian Social-Liberal Party (CSLP), the Croatian Party of Rights (CPR), the Croatian Independent Democrats (CID), the Istrian Democratic Assembly (IDA) and the SDP.

Županijski dom
(Chamber of Counties)

President: KATICA IVANEŠEVIĆ.

Election, 13 April 1997

Party	Seats
Croatian Democratic Union (CDU)	42
Croatian Peasants' Party (HSS)	9
Croatian Social-Liberal Party (CSLP)	6
Social Democratic Party (SDP)	4
Istrian Democratic Assembly (IDA)	2
Total	63*

* An additional five deputies, of whom two were members of the Serb community, were appointed by the President.

Political Organizations

Action of Social Democrats of Croatia (ASDC): 10000 Zagreb; f. 1994; Pres. SILVIJE DEGEN.

Christian People's Party (CPP) (Kršćanska Narodna Stranka—KNS): 10000 Zagreb, Degenova 7; tel. (1) 427258; fax (1) 273595; Pres. ZDRAVKO MRŠIĆ.

Croatian Christian Democratic Union (CCDU) (Hrvatska Kršćanska Demokratska Unija—HKDU): 10000 Zagreb; tel. (1) 327233; fax (1) 325190; Pres. IVAN CESAR.

Croatian Democratic Party (CDP) (Hrvatska Demokratska Stranka—HDS): 10000 Zagreb; tel. (1) 431837; Pres. MARKO VESELICA.

Croatian Democratic Union (CDU) (Hrvatska Demokratska Zajednica—HDZ): 10000 Zagreb, trg hrvatskih velikana 4; tel. (1) 4553000; fax (1) 4552600; f. 1989; Christian Democrat; Chair. Dr FRANJO TUDJMAN; Sec.-Gen. Dr IVAN VALENT.

Croatian Independent Democrats (CID) (Hrvatski Nezavisni Demokrati—HND): 10000 Zagreb; f. 1994 by a faction from the CDU; Chair. STIPE MESIĆ.

Croatian Muslim Democratic Party (CMDP) (Hrvatska Muslimanska Demokratska Stranka—HMDS): 10000 Zagreb; tel. (1) 421562.

Croatian Party of Rights (CPR) (Hrvatska Stranka Prava—HSP): 10000 Zagreb, ul. Senoina 13; tel. and fax (1) 271064; f. 1861, re-established 1990; right-wing, nationalist; armed br. is the Croatian Defence Asscn or Hrvatske Odbrambene Snage (HOS); Pres. DOBROSLAV PARAGA.

Croatian Party of Slavonia and Baranja (CPSB) (Slavonsko-Baranjska Hrvatska Stranka—SBHS): Osijek.

Croatian Peasants' Party (Hrvatska Seljačka Stranka—HSS): 10000 Zagreb, Trsnkoga 8; tel. (1) 212325; fax (1) 217411; Pres. ZLATKO TOMČIĆ.

Croatian People's Party (CPP) (Hrvatska Narodna Stranka—HNS): 10000 Zagreb, Ilica 61; tel. (1) 427888; fax (1) 273552; Pres. RADIMIR ČAČIĆ.

Croatian Republican Party (CRP) (Hrvatska Republikanska Stranka—HRS): 10000 Zagreb, Nalješkovićeva 11; tel. (1) 533486; Pres. BORKO JURIN.

Croatian Social-Liberal Party (CSLP) (Hrvatska Socijalno-Liberalna Stranka—HSLS): 10000 Zagreb, Amruševa 19; tel. (1) 4810401; fax (1) 4810404; e-mail hsis@www.ring.net; f. 1989; Pres. DRAZEN BUDISA; Gen. Sec. KARL GORINSEK.

Dalmatian Action (DA) (Dalmatinska Akcija): 21000 Split, Ulica bana Jelačića 4/I; tel. (21) 344322; f. 1990; Pres. Dr MIRA LJUBIĆ-LORGER.

Independent Democratic Serb Party (Samostalne Demokratska Srpska Stranka—SDSS): Vukovar; f. March 1997 by Serbs in Eastern Slavonia; Pres. Dr VOJISLAV STANIMIROVIĆ.

Istrian Democratic Assembly (IDA) (Istarski Demokratski Sabor—IDS): Pula, Flanatička 29/I; tel. and fax (52) 43702; Pres. IVAN JAKOVČIĆ.

Istrian People's Party (IPP) (Istarska Pučka Stranka—IPS): Pula, trg revolucije 3; tel. (52) 23863; fax (52) 23832; Pres. JOSIP FABRIS.

Party of Serbs: 10000 Zagreb; f. 1993 by mems of Serb cultural asscn Prosveta (Enlightenment) and Serb Democratic Forum; promotes liberal, democratic values; Leader MILORAD PUPOVAĆ.

Rijeka Democratic Alliance (RDA) (Riječki Demokratski Savez—RDS): 51000 Rijeka, Žrtava fašizma 29; tel. (51) 423713; Pres. NIKOLA IVANIŠ; Sec. FRANJO BUTORAC.

Serb Democratic Party (SDP) (Srpska Demokratska Stranka—SDS): 10000 Zagreb, Preradovićeva 18/I; tel. (1) 423583; f. 1990; seeks equality with Croats for Serbs in Croatia; Pres. Dr JOVAN RAŠKOVIĆ.

Serb People's Party (SPP) (Srpska Narodna Stranka—SNS): 10000 Zagreb, Mažuranića trg 3; tel. and fax (1) 451090; promotes cultural and individual rights for ethnic Serbs in Croatia; 4,500–5,000 mems; Pres. MILAN DUKIĆ.

Social Democratic Party (SDP) (Socijaldemokratska Partija Hrvatske—SPH): 10000 Zagreb, Iblerov trg 9; tel. (1) 519490; fax (1) 518249; formerly the ruling League of Communists of Croatia (Party of Democratic Reform), renamed as above in 1993; 20,000 mems; Pres. IVICA RAČAN.

Social Democratic Union of Croatia (SDUC) (Socijalno Demokratska Unija Hrvatske—SDUH): 10000 Zagreb, Tratinska 27; tel. and fax (1) 394055; f. 1992; Pres. VLADIMIR BEBIĆ.

Socialist Party of Croatia (SPC) (Socijalistička Stranka Hrvatske—SSH): 10000 Zagreb, Prisavlje 14; tel. (1) 517835; fax (1) 510235; Pres. ŽELJKO MAŽAR.

Diplomatic Representation

EMBASSIES IN CROATIA

Australia: 10000 Zagreb, Kralja Zvonimira 43; tel. (1) 442885; fax (1) 410071.

Austria: 10000 Zagreb, Jabukovać 39; tel. (1) 273392; fax (1) 424065; Ambassador: ANDREAS BERLAKOVICH.

Bosnia and Herzegovina: 10000 Zagreb, Torbarova 9; tel. (1) 425899; fax (1) 4556177; Ambassador: KASIM TRNKA.

Bulgaria: 10000 Zagreb, Novi Gajeva 19; Chargé d'affaires: LYUBCHO TROHAROV.

Canada: 10000 Zagreb, Mihanovićeva 1; tel. (1) 4577905; fax (1) 4577913; Ambassador: GRAHAM N. GREEN.

China, People's Republic: 10000 Zagreb, Kvaternikova 111; tel. (1) 197277; Chargé d'affaires: GUAN YUSEN.

Czech Republic: 10000 Zagreb, Prilaz Djure Deželića 10; tel. (1) 430099; fax (1) 430121.

Denmark: 10000 Zagreb, Gornje Prekrižje 51; tel. (1) 270382; fax (1) 273933.

France: 10000 Zagreb, Schlosserove stube 5; tel. (1) 272985; fax (1) 274923; Ambassador: JEAN-JACQUES GAILLARDE.

Germany: 10000 Zagreb, Ave. Vukovar 64; tel. (1) 519200; fax (1) 518070; Ambassador: VOLKER HAAK.

Holy See: 10000 Zagreb, Ksaverska cesta bb; tel. (1) 4554995; fax (1) 4554997; Apostolic Delegate: Most Rev. GIULIO EINAUDI, Titular Archbishop of Villamagna in Tripolitania.

Hungary: 10000 Zagreb, Krležin gvozd 11a; tel. (1) 422654; fax (1) 420542; Ambassador: Dr ZSOLT G. SZALAY.

Iran: 10000 Zagreb, Pantovčak 125c; tel. (1) 4578983; fax (1) 4578987; Ambassador: MOHAMMAD JAVAD ASAYESH ZARCHI.

Italy: 10000 Zagreb, Medulićeva 22; tel. (1) 4846386; fax (1) 4846384; e-mail velezoslanstvo italije@zg.tel.hr; Ambassador: FRANCESCO OLIVIERI.

Korea, Republic: 10000 Zagreb, III. Cvjetno naselje 7; tel. (1) 516662.

Netherlands: 10000 Zagreb, Medvescak 5B; tel. (1) 423959; fax (1) 424205; Chargé d'affaires: JOZEF W. SCHEFFERS.

Norway: 10000 Zagreb, Petrinjska 9; Ambassador: KNUT MØRKVED.

Panama: 10000 Zagreb, Tribaljska 11/I; tel. (1) 325159.

Poland: 10000 Zagreb, Krležin Gvozd 3; tel. (1) 278818; fax (1) 420305; Chargé d'affaires a.i.: Dr WIESŁAW WALKIEWICZ.

Portugal: 10000 Zagreb, trg hrvatskih velikana 3; tel. (1) 413921.

Romania: 10000 Zagreb, Becićeve 2; tel. (1) 436754; Ambassador: Dr VASILE LECA.

Russia: 10000 Zagreb, Bosanska 44; tel. (1) 575444; fax (1) 572260; Ambassador: (vacant).

Slovakia: 10000 Zagreb, Prilaz Djure Deželića 10; tel. (1) 430099; fax (1) 430121; Ambassador MATÚŠ KUČERA.

Slovenia: 10000 Zagreb, Savska cesta 41/II; tel. (1) 517401; fax (1) 517837; Ambassador: MATIJA MALEŠIĆ.

Sri Lanka: 10000 Zagreb, trg Burze 1/I; tel. (1) 442687; fax (1) 442878.

Sudan: 10000 Zagreb, Tuškanac 68; tel. (1) 276694; fax (1) 276705; Ambassador: SALAH MOHAMED ALI.

Sweden: 10000 Zagreb, Frankopanska 22; tel. (1) 422116; fax (1) 428244; Ambassador: SUNE DANIELSSON.

Switzerland: 10000 Zagreb, Bogovićeva 3; tel. (1) 421573; fax (1) 425995; Ambassador: JACQUES RIAL.

Turkey: 10000 Zagreb, Masarykova 3/II; tel. (1) 424255; fax (1) 426419; Ambassador: DARYAL BATIBAY.

United Kingdom: 10000 Zagreb, Vlaska 121; tel. (1) 4555310; fax (1) 4551685; Ambassador: COLIN MUNRO.

USA: 10000 Zagreb, Andrije Hebranga 2; tel. (1) 4555500; fax (1) 440235; Ambassador: WILLIAM MONTGOMERY.

Venezuela: 10000 Zagreb, Strossmayera trg 11; tel. and fax (1) 423651.

Yugoslavia: 10000 Zagreb; Chargé d'affaires: VELJKO KNEZEVIĆ.

Judicial System

The judicial system of Croatia is administered by the Ministry of Justice. The Supreme Court is the highest judicial body in the country, comprising 15 judges who are elected for a period of eight years by the Chamber of Municipalities at the proposal of the Chamber of Representatives. The Constitutional Court consists of 11 judges, elected in the same way and for the same period.

Public Prosecutor: PETAR ŠALE.

Public Attorney: STJEPAN HERCEG.

Constitutional Court of Croatia: 10000 Zagreb, Radićev trg 4; tel. (1) 444822; Pres. Dr JADRANKO CRNIĆ.

Supreme Court: 10000 Zagreb, trg Nikole Zrinjskog 3; tel. (1) 257787; Pres. MILAN VUKOVIĆ.

Office of the Public Prosecutor: 10000 Zagreb, Proleterskih brig. 84; tel. (1) 515422.

Religion

Most of the population are Christian, the largest denomination being the Roman Catholic Church, of which most ethnic Croats are adherents. The Archbishop of Zagreb is the most senior Roman Catholic prelate in Croatia. The Croatian Old Catholic Church does not acknowledge the authority of Rome or the papal reforms of the 19th century. There is a significant Serbian Orthodox minority. According to the 1991 census, 76.5% of the population of Croatia were Roman Catholics, 11.1% were Serbian Orthodox, 1.2% Muslims and there were small communities of Protestants and Jews.

CHRISTIANITY

The Roman Catholic Church

For ecclesiastical purposes, Croatia comprises four archdioceses (including one, Zadar, directly responsible to the Holy See) and eight dioceses (including one for Catholics of the Byzantine rite). At 31 December 1995 adherents of the Roman Catholic Church comprised about 71.4% of the total population.

Latin Rite

Archbishop of Rijeka-Senj: Dr ANTON TAMARUT, Nadbiskupski Ordinarijat, 51000 Rijeka, Slaviše Vajnera Čiče 2; tel. (51) 337999; fax (51) 215287; 260,000 adherents (1994).

Archbishop of Split-Makarska: ANTE JURIĆ, 21001 Split, pp 142, ul. Zrinjsko-Frankopanska 14; tel. (21) 46798; fax (21) 361462; 417,578 adherents (1994).

Archbishop of Zadar: IVAN PRENDJA, Nadbiskupski Ordinarijat, 23000 Zadar, Zeleni trg 1; tel. (23) 315712; fax (23) 316299; 150,000 adherents (1996).

Archbishop of Zagreb: JOSIP BOZANIĆ, 10000 Zagreb, pp 553, Kaptol 31; tel. (1) 275911; fax (1) 271936; 1,958,465 adherents (1994).

Byzantine Rite

Bishop of Križevci: SLAVOMIR MIKLOVŠ, Ordinarijat Križevačke Eparhije, 10000 Zagreb, Kaptol 20; tel. (1) 270767; 48,975 adherents (1993).

Old Catholic Church

Croatian Catholic Church: Hrvatska Katolička Crkva Ordinariat, 10000 Zagreb, ul. Kneza Branimirova 11; tel. (1) 275224; f. 894, re-established 1923; Archbishop MIHOVIL DUBRAVČIĆ.

Serbian Orthodox Church

Metropolitan of Zagreb and Ljubljana: Bishop JOVAN, Srpska Biskupija, 10000 Zagreb.

The Press

PRINCIPAL DAILIES

Osijek

Glas Slavonije: 31000 Osijek, Hrvatske Republike 20; tel. and fax (31) 121100; telex 28276; morning; independent; Editor DARIO TOPIĆ; circ. 25,000.

Pula

Glas Istre: 52100 Pula, Riva 10; tel. (52) 212969; telex 25248; fax (52) 211434; morning; Dir ŽELJKO ŽMAK; circ. 20,000.

Rijeka

Novi List: 51000 Rijeka, POB 130, Zvonimirova 20A; tel. (51) 32122; fax (51) 213654; morning; Editor VELJKO VICEVIĆ; circ. 60,000.

La Voce del Popolo: 51000 Rijeka, Zvonimirova 20A; tel. (51) 211154; fax (51) 213528; f. 1944; morning; Italian; Editor RODOLFO SEGNAN; circ. 4,000.

Split

Nedjeljna Dalmacija: 21000 Split, Gundulićeva 23; tel. (21) 362821; fax (21) 362526; f. 1972; weekly; politics and culture; Editor DRAŽEN GUDIĆ; circ. 45,000.

Slobodna Dalmacija: 21000 Split, ul. Hrvatske mornarice 4; tel. (21) 513888; telex 26124; fax (21) 551220; morning; Editor JOSIP JOVIĆ; circ. 102,000.

Zagreb

Nedjeljna Dalmacija: 10000 Zagreb, Ilica 24/II; tel. (1) 433716; fax (1) 433916; f. 1972; weekly; politics and culture; Editor-in-chief DUBRAVKO GRAKALIĆ; circ. 45,000.

Novi Vjesnik: 10000 Zagreb, Slavonska Ave. 4; tel. (1) 333333; telex 21121; fax (1) 341650; f. 1940; morning; Editor RADOVAN STIPETIĆ; circ. 45,000.

Sportske novosti: 10000 Zagreb, Slavonska Ave. 4; tel. (1) 341920; fax (1) 341950; morning; Editor DARKO TIRONI; circ. 55,000.

Večernji list: 10000 Zagreb, Slavonska Ave. 4; tel. (1) 342780; fax (1) 341850; evening; Editor BRANKO TUDJEN; circ. 200,000.

Vjesnik: 10000 Zagreb, Slavonska Ave. 4, POB 104; tel. (1) 342760; telex 21121; fax (1) 341602; morning; Editor KRESIMIR FIJACKO; circ. 50,000.

PERIODICALS

Arena: 10000 Zagreb, Slavonska Ave 4; tel. (1) 6162795; fax (1) 6161572; e-mail arena@eph.hr; f. 1957; illustrated weekly; Editor MLADEN GEROVAĆ; circ. 135,000.

Glasnik: 10000 Zagreb, trg hrvatskih velikana 4; tel. (1) 453000; fax (1) 453752; fortnightly; Editor ZDRAVKO GAVRAN; circ. 9,000.

Globus: 10000 Zagreb, Slavonska Ave 4; tel. (1) 6162057; fax (1) 6162058; e-mail globus@eph.hr; f. 1990; political weekly; Editor DJURDJICA KLANCIR; circ. 110,000.

Gloria: 10000 Zagreb, Slavonska Ave 4; tel. (1) 6161288; fax (1) 6182042; e-mail gloria@eph.hr; weekly; Editor DUBRAVKA TOMEKOVIĆ-ARALICA: circ. 110,000.

Informator: 10000 Zagreb, Masarykova 1; tel. (1) 429222; fax (1) 424904; f. 1950; economic and legal matters; Dir Dr IVO BURIĆ.

Mila: 10000 Zagreb, Slavonska Ave 4; tel. (1) 6161982; fax (1) 6162021; e-mail mila@eph.hr; weekly; Editor ZOJA PADOVAN; circ. 110,000.

Nacionalni Oglasnik: 10000 Zagreb, Slavonska Ave 4; tel. (1) 6162061; fax (1) 6161541; weekly; Editor STANKO KUČAN; circ. 55,000.

OK: Croatia: 10000 Zagreb, Slavonska Ave 4; tel. 6162127; fax (1) 6162125; e-mail ok@eph.hr; f. 1989; illustrated monthly; Editor NEVEN KEPESKI; circ. 55,000.

Privredni vjesnik: 10000 Zagreb, Kačićeva 9A; tel. (1) 422182; telex 21524; fax (1) 422100; f. 1953; weekly; economic; Man. ANTE GAVRANOVIĆ; Editor-in-Chief FRANJO ŽILIĆ; circ. 10,000.

Republika: 10000 Zagreb, trg bana Josipa Jelačića; tel. (1) 274211; fax (1) 434790; f. 1945; monthly; published by Društvo hrvatskih književnika; literary review; Editor-in-Chief VELIMIR VISKOVIĆ.

Slobodni Tjednik: 10000 Zagreb, Gundulićeva 21A; tel. (1) 426766; fax (1) 423411; weekly; independent.

Studio: 10000 Zagreb, Slavonska Ave 4; tel. (1) 6162085; fax (1) 6162031; e-mail studio@eph.hr; f.1964; illustrated weekly; Editor ROBERT NAPRTA; circ. 45,000.

Vikend: 10000 Zagreb, Slavonska Ave 4; tel. and fax (1) 6162064; 2 a week; Editor JOSIP MUŠNJAK; circ. 50,000.

NEWS AGENCIES

HINA News Agency: 10000 Zagreb, Marulićev trg 16; tel. (1) 4550008; telex 22303; fax (1) 4550477; e-mail newsline@hina.hr; f. 1990; Man. BRANKO SALAJ.

ILA (Catholic Information Agency): 10000 Zagreb, Kaptol 4; tel. (1) 272607; fax (1) 273151; Man. Editor ANTE ŽIVKO KUSTIĆ.

Publishers

August Cesarec: 10000 Zagreb, Prilaz Gjure Deželića 57; tel. (1) 171071; fax (1) 573695; Croatian and foreign literature.

Europa Press: 10000 Zagreb, Slavonska Ave 4; tel. (1) 6190011; fax (1) 6190033; Dir MARJAN JURLEKA.

Hrvatska Akademija Znanosti i Umjetnosti: 10000 Zagreb, Zrinski trg 11; tel. (1) 4819983; fax (1) 4819979; e-mail kabpred@mahazu.hazu.hr; f. 1861; publishing dept of the Croatian Academy of Sciences and Arts; Pres. Dr IVO PADOVAN.

Informator IRO: 10000 Zagreb, Masarykova 1; tel. (1) 429333; fax (1) 424904; f. 1950; newspapers, periodicals, books, forms, etc.; Dir Dr IVO BURIĆ.

Leksikografski zavod 'Miroslav Krleža' (Miroslav Krleža Lexicographic Institute): 10000 Zagreb, Frankopanska 26; tel. (1) 4556244; fax (1) 434948; f. 1951; encyclopedias, bibliographies and dictionaries; Pres. DALIBOR BROZOVIĆ.

Mladost: 10000 Zagreb, Ilica 30; tel. (1) 453222; telex 21263; fax (1) 434878; f. 1947; fiction, science, art, children's books; Gen. Dir BRANKO VUKOVIĆ.

Motovun: 51424 Motovun, V. Nazora 1; tel. (53) 81722; fax (53) 81642; photomonographs and international co-productions.

Muzička naklada: 10000 Zagreb, Nicole Tesle 10/I; tel. (1) 424099; telex 22430; f. 1952; musical editions, scores; Dir RAJKO LATINOVIĆ.

Nakladni zavod Matice hrvatske: 10000 Zagreb, Ulica Matice hrvatske 2, POB 515; tel. (1) 272143; fax (1) 432430; f. 1960; fiction, popular science, politics, economics, sociology, history; Dir HRVOJE BOŽIČEVIĆ.

Nakladni zavod Znanje: 10000 Zagreb, Zvonimirova 17; tel. (1) 451500; fax (1) 414007; f. 1946; popular science, agriculture, fiction, poetry, essays; Pres. ŽARKO ŠEPETAVIĆ; Dir BRANKO JAZBEC.

Naprijed: 10000 Zagreb, POB 1029, Palmotićeva 30; tel. (1) 4557133; fax (1) 433424; f. 1946; philosophy, psychology, religion, sociology, medicine, dictionaries, children's books, art, politics, economics, etc.; Dir ZDENKO LJEVAK.

Naša Djeca: 10000 Zagreb, Gundulićeva 40; tel. (1) 4856046; fax (1) 4856613; picture books, postcards, etc.; Dir Prof. DRAGO KOZINA.

Školska Knjiga: 10001 Zagreb, POB 1039, Masarykova 28; tel. (1) 420784; telex 21894; fax (1) 274360; education, textbooks, art; Dir Dr DRAGOMIR MADERIĆ.

Tehnička Knjiga: 10000 Zagreb, Jurišičeva 10; tel. (1) 278172; fax (1) 423611; f. 1947; technical literature, popular science, reference books; Gen. Man. ZVONIMIR VISTRIČKA.

PUBLISHERS' ASSOCIATION

Croatian Publishers' and Authors' Business Union (Poslovna Zajednica Izdavača i Knjižara Hrvatske): 10000 Zagreb, Klaićeva 7; fax (1) 171624.

Broadcasting and Communications

TELECOMMUNICATIONS

Croatian Posts and Telecommunications (HPT): Zagreb.

BROADCASTING

Croatian Radio and Television (Hrvatska Radiotelevizija—HRT): 10000 Zagreb, Dezmanova 10; tel. (1) 276338; fax (1) 424654; govt-owned; Dir-Gen. Dr IVICA MUDRINIĆ.

Radio

Croatian Radio: 10000 Zagreb, HRT House, Prisavlje 3; tel. (1) 6163280; telex 21154; fax (1) 6163285; f. 1926; 3 radio stations; 7 regional stations (Sljeme, Osijek, Pula, Rijeka, Split, Zadar and Dubrovnik); broadcasts in Serbo-Croat; Dir TOMISLAV BAKARIĆ.

Radio 101: Zagreb; independent radio station; Editor-in-Chief ZRINKA VRABEC-MOJZES.

Radio Baranja: independent radio station; Dir KAROLJ JANESI.

Television

Croatian Television: 10000 Zagreb, Prisavlje bb; tel. (1) 537004; telex 21427; fax (1) 430663; f. 1956; 3 channels; broadcasts in Serbo-Croat; Head of TV KRUNO NOVAK; Editor-in-Chief MARIJA NEMCIĆ.

Finance

A new currency, the kuna (equivalent to 1,000 Croatian dinars), was introduced on 30 May 1994.

(d.d. = dioničko društvo (joint-stock company); cap. = capital; res = reserves; dep. = deposits; m. = million; amounts in kuna, unless otherwise indicated; HRD = Croatian dinars; brs = branches)

BANKING

Central Bank

National Bank of Croatia: 10000 Zagreb, trg Burze 3; tel. (1) 4564555; telex 22569; fax (1) 441684; e-mail marko.skreb@publicsrce.hr; in 1991 it assumed the responsibilities of a central bank empowered as the republic's bank of issue; Gov. MARKO ŠKREB.

Selected Banks

Bjelovarska Banka d.d., Bjelovar: 43000 Bjelovar, POB 68, Jurja Haulika 19a; tel. (43) 275115; telex 23330; fax 275144; f. 1961; cap. 71.2m., res 46.3m., dep. 310.3m. (Dec. 1996); Chair DRAGO SUŠEC.

Croatia Banka d.d.: 10000 Zagreb, Kvaternikov trg 9; tel. (1) 2391111; telex 21146; fax (1) 2332470; internet http://www.open.hr/com/crobanka/; f. 1989; cap. 171.7m., res 31.1m., dep. 1,814.8m. (Sept. 1997); Chair. IVAN TARLE; 29 brs.

Croatian Bank for Reconstruction and Development (Hrvatska Banka za Obnovu i Razvoj—HBOR): 10000 Zagreb, Gajeva 30A; tel. (1) 4569106; fax (1) 5569166; f. 1995; Dir ANTON KOVAČEV.

Dalmatinska Banka d.d., Zadar: 23000 Zadar, trg sv. Stošije 3; tel. (23) 311311; telex 27224; fax (23) 437867; f. 1957; 52% privately-owned; cap. 155.9m., res 41.0m., dep. 1,164.7m. (Dec. 1996); Chair. of Supervisory Bd DENKO PEROŠ; Gen. Man. NEVEN DOBROVIĆ; 2 brs.

Dubrovačka Banka d.d., Dubrovnik (Bank of Dubrovnik): 20000 Dubrovnik, put Republike 9; tel. (20) 431366; telex 27540; fax (20) 411035; f. 1956; cap. 179.5m., res 513.3m., dep. 1,457.0m. (Dec. 1996); Gen. Man. NEVEN BARAČ; Deputy Gen. Man. KREŠIMIR KRILE.

Glumina Banka d.d., Zagreb: 10000 Zagreb, POB 215, Trpinjska 9; tel. (1) 2394444; telex 21108; fax (1) 2395706; f. 1994; cap. 185.1m., res 3.0m., dep. 1,064.4m. (Dec. 1996); Chair. MARKO MARČINKO.

Gradska Banka d.d. Osijek: 31000 Osijek, Šetalište kardinala Franje Šepera 12; tel. (31) 145944; fax (31) 145595; f. 1993; cap. 92.7m., res 27.2m., dep. 696.9m.; Pres. IVAN PATARČIĆ.

Hrvatska Gospodarska Banka d.d., Zagreb: 10000 Zagreb, Metalceva 5; tel. (1) 351888; telex 21664; fax (1) 351819; f. 1992; cap. 65.0m., res 2.9m., dep. 328.0m. (Dec. 1995); Chair. ŽELJKO ŠUPE.

Istarska Kreditna Banka Umag d.d.: 52470 Umag, Ernesta Miloša 1; tel. (52) 741622; telex 24745; fax (52) 741275; f. 1956; commercial and joint-stock bank; cap. 59m., res 16.8m., dep. 404.7m. (Dec. 1996); Chair. VLATKO RESCHNER; 12 brs.

Kreditna Banka Zagreb d.d.: 10000 Zagreb, Ulica grada Vukovara 74; tel. (1) 6167333; telex 21197; fax (1) 6117666; f. 1994; cap. 89.6m., res 11.7m. (Dec. 1996); Pres. ANTE TODORIĆ.

Medimurska Banka d.d., Čakovec; 40000 Čakovec, Valenta Morandinija 37; tel. (40) 810676; telex 23251; fax (40) 314610; f. 1954; cap. 98.7m., res 10.7m., dep. 635.7m. (Dec. 1996); Gen. Man MAŠAN SREDANOVIĆ.

Privredna Banka Zagreb d.d.: 10000 Zagreb, POB 1032, Račkoga 6; tel. (1) 4550822; telex 21120; fax (1) 447234; f. 1966; commercial bank; cap. 1,666m., res 10m., dep. 7,286m. (Dec. 1996); CEO IVAN TEŠIJA; 22 brs.

Riječka Banka d.d.: 51000 Rijeka, POB 300, trg Jadranski 3A; tel. (51) 208211; telex 24143; fax (51) 330525; f. 1954 as Komunalna banka i štedionica, renamed 1967; cap. 306m., res 35.7m., dep. 3,578.9m. (Dec. 1996); Chair. IVAN ŠTOKIĆ; 18 brs.

Sisačka Banka d.d.: 44000 Sisak, trg Ljudevita Posavskog 1; tel. (44) 522566; telex 23645; fax (44) 522090; e-mail siba-uprava@sibank.hr; f. 1957; cap. 62.4m., res 41.3m., dep. 312m. (Dec. 1996); Pres. DINKO PINTARIĆ.

Slavonska Banka d.d., Osijek (Bank of Slavonia): 31000 Osijek, POB 108, Kapucinska 29; tel. (31) 131131; telex 28090; fax (31) 122588; f. 1989; cap. 149.2m., res 137.8m., dep. 1,411.6m. (Dec. 1996); Pres. IVO MARKOTIĆ; 6 brs.

Trgovačka Banka d.d.: 10000 Zagreb, Varšavska 3–5; tel. (1) 4561999; telex 22370; fax (1) 4561900; f. 1990; cap. 69.0m., res 2.5m., dep. 327.6m. (Dec. 1996); Pres. DAVOR MATAS; CEO BORIS NINIĆ.

Varaždinska Banka d.d.: 42001 Varaždin, POB 95, P. Preradovića 17; tel. (42) 55106; telex 23063; fax (42) 55114; f. 1869, adopted current name 1981; cap. 183.0m., res 175.8m., dep. 1,137.9m. (Dec. 1996); Pres. MATO LUKINIĆ; 17 brs.

Zagrebačka Banka Zagreb d.d. (Bank of Zagreb): 10000 Zagreb, Paromlinska 2; tel. (1) 6104000; telex 21211; fax (1) 536626; f. 1978; cap. 1,096.2m., res 431.5m., dep. 17,114.8m. (Dec. 1996); Chair. FRANJO LUKOVIĆ; 150 brs.

Zagrebačka Banka—Pomorska Banka d.d., Split: 21000 Split, Ivana Gundulića 26a; tel. (21) 352222; telex 26333; fax (21) 357079; f. 1992; cap. 65.0m., res 1.9m., dep. 1,076.8m. (Dec. 1996); Pres. Dr MLADEN RAKELIĆ.

Županjska Banka d.d., Županja: 32270 Županja, J.J. Strossmayera 9; tel. (32) 832644; telex 28216; fax (32) 832646; f. 1955; cap. 71.6m., res 29.0m., dep. 401.3m. (Dec. 1995); Chair. ZDRAVKO LEŠIČ.

STOCK EXCHANGE

Zagreb Stock Exchange: 10000 Zagreb, Ksaver 208; tel. (1) 428455; fax (1) 420293; f. 1990; Gen. Man. MARINKO PAPUGA.

Trade and Industry

GOVERNMENT AGENCY

Croatian Privatization Fund: 10000 Zagreb, Gajeva 30A; tel. (1) 469168; fax (1) 469138; f. 1994 by merger of the Croatian Fund for Development and the Restructuring and Development Agency.

CHAMBERS OF COMMERCE

Croatian Chamber of Economy (Hrvatska Gospodarska Komora): 10000 Zagreb, Rooseveltov trg 2; tel. (1) 4561555; fax (1) 4828380; e-mail hgk@alf.hr; Pres. NADAN VIDOŠEVIĆ.

There are county chambers in Bjelovar, Karlovac, Osijek, Pula, Rijeka, Sisak, Split, Varaždin, Zadar and Zagreb.

UTILITIES

Electricity

HEP—Hrvatska Elektroprivreda d.d.: 10000 Zagreb, Ave. Vukovar 37; tel. (1) 625111; telex 21191; fax (1) 511612; f. 1990; production and distribution of electricity; Dir DAMIR BEGOVIĆ; 14,492 employees.

Gas

Gradska Plinara: 10000 Zagreb, Radnička 1; tel. (1) 617811; telex 22442; fax (1) 614776; f. 1974; manufacture of gas, distribution of gaseous fuels through mains; Dir IVAN VULAS; 571 employees.

INA—Naftaplin: 10000 Zagreb, Subičeva 29; tel. (1) 418011; fax (1) 440604; subsidiary of Industrija Nafter; geological and geophysical exploration of petroleum, natural-gas and geothermal energy; petroleum and gas reservoir development; drilling and exploration of on- and offshore wells; testing and completion of wells; production and transportation systems; natural-gas refining; production of ethylene, ethane and LPG.

TRADE UNIONS

Association of Autonomous Trade Unions of Croatia: 10000 Zagreb; f. 1990; 26 branch unions with some 500,000 mems; Pres. DRAGUTIN LESAR.

Confederation of Independent Trade Unions of Croatia: 10000 Zagreb; f. 1990; 40,000 mems; Pres. MLADEN MESIĆ.

Croatian Association of Trade Unions: Zagreb, f. 1990; 200,000 mems. Pres. BERISLAV BELEC.

Transport

RAILWAYS

In 1995 there were 2,452 km of railway lines in Croatia, of which 36% were electrified. In mid-1996 railway links between Croatia and Serbia, via Eastern Slavonia, were reopened.

Croatian Railways Ltd (Hrvatske Željeznice p.o.): 10000 Zagreb, Mihanovićeva 12; tel. (1) 4577111; telex 21199; fax (1) 4577730; f. 1990 as Hrvatsko željezničko poduzeće, renamed 1992; state-owned; public railway transport, construction, modernization and maintenance of railway vehicles; Pres. J. BOŽIĆEVIĆ; Gen. Dir M. KLARIĆ.

ROADS

The Road Fund was responsible for the planning, construction, maintenance and rehabilitation of all interurban roads in Croatia. As of 1 January 1995 the Fund was under the control of the budgetary central Government. In 1996 there were 27,247 km of roads in Croatia, of which 318 km were motorways, 4,740 km were main roads and 7,588 km were secondary roads. In late 1995 a US $705m. project was announced to build a 75-km. motorway linking Dragonje, near the Slovenian border, with Pula in southern Istria. The construction of the road was to be undertaken by a French company, Bouygues, and would be financed by World Bank loans, tolls and a domestic debt. In 1996 there were plans to build a further 1,200 km of new roads over a period of 10 years. In May 1996 the motorway between Zagreb and Belgrade (Yugoslavia) was reopened.

Croatian Roads Authority (Hrvatske Ceste): 10000 Zagreb, Vončinina 3; tel. (1) 445422; fax (1) 445215; f. 1991; state-owned; maintenance, construction and reconstruction of public roads; Pres. J. ZAVOREO; Man. Dir ALEKSANDAR ČAKLOVIĆ.

SHIPPING

Atlantska Plovidba d.d.: 20000 Dubrovnik, od sv. Mihajla 1; tel. (20) 412666; telex 27516; fax (20) 20384; f. 1974; Dir ANTE JERKOVIĆ.

Croatia Line: 51000 Rijeka, POB 379, Riva 18; tel. (51) 205111; telex 24218; fax (51) 331915; f. 1986; cargo and passenger services; chartering and tramp service; Gen. Man. DARIO VUKIĆ; 377 employees.

Jadrolinija (Adriatic Shipping Line): 51000 Rijeka, Riva 16; tel. (51) 330899; telex 24225; fax (51) 213116; f. 1872; regular passenger and car-ferry services between Italian, Greek and Croatian ports; Pres. M. RUŽIĆ.

Jadroplov: 21000 Split, Obala kneza Branimira 16; tel. (21) 302666; telex 26138; fax (21) 342198; f. 1984; fleet of 17 vessels and 1,500 containers engaged in linear and tramp service; Gen. Man. NIKŠA GIOVANELLI.

Lošinjska Plovidba—Brodarstvo: 51550 Mali Lošinj, Privlaka bb; tel. (51) 231832; fax (51) 231811; f. 1980; Dir DUMANČIĆ MARINKO.

Slobodna Plovidba: 22000 Šibenik, Drage 2; tel. (22) 23755; telex 27325; fax (22) 27860; f. 1976; transport of goods by sea; tourism services; Dir VITOMIR JURAGA.

Tankerska Plovidba d.d.: 23000 Zadar, Božidara Petranovića 4; tel. (23) 311132; fax (23) 314375; f. 1976; Dir STANKO BANIĆ; 420 employees.

CIVIL AVIATION

There are 10 international airports in Croatia.

Croatia Airlines: 10000 Zagreb, Teslina 5; tel. (1) 427752; fax (1) 427935; f. 1989 as Zagreb Airlines; name changed 1990; operates domestic services and 24 international routes to European destinations; Pres. MATIJA KATIČIĆ.

Anić Airways: Zagreb; tel. (1) 200200; fax (1) 204253; f. 1992; first private airline company in Croatia; domestic and international flights; Pres. DAMIR ANIĆ.

Tourism

The attractive Adriatic coast and the country's 1,185 islands made Croatia a very popular tourist destination before the 1990s. However, the civil conflict, which began in mid-1991, greatly reduced tourist activity in the country. The industry showed signs of recovery after 1992, however, with foreign tourist arrivals reaching 1,521,000 in 1993 and 2,293,000 in 1994. In 1995 the number of foreign tourist arrivals declined to 1,324,000.

Atlas: 20000 Dubrovnik, Pile 1; tel. (20) 442222; fax (20) 411100; travel agency; f. 1923; 28 br. offices; 2 overseas offices.

Dalmacijaturist: 21000 Split, 0. hrv. nar. preporada; tel. (21) 45743; telex 26145; fax (21) 591104; f. 1923; 8 br. offices; 3 offices abroad.

Generalturist: 10000 Zagreb, Praška 5; tel. (1) 4550888; telex 21100; fax (1) 422633; f. 1923, renamed 1963; 19 br. offices.

Jadran-Turist d.d.: 55210 Rovinj, V. Nazora 6; tel. (52) 811400; telex 24229; fax (52) 811540; e-mail jadrantur-rovinj@pu.tel.hr; internet http://www.istra.com/rovinj/jadranturist; f. 1954; Dir IVAN ŠORIĆ; 1,259 employees.

Jadranka HIT: 51550 Mali Lošinj, Čikat 13; tel. (51) 231564; fax (51) 231904; f. 1947; Dir VLADIMIR ANTOLOVIĆ.

Kvarner Express International: 51410 Opatija, M. Tita 186; tel. (51) 271111; fax (51) 271549; f. 1952; arranges accommodation, tours, conventions, etc.; 16 brs.

Plava Laguna—Laguna Poreč d.d.: 52440 Poreč, Rade Končara 12; tel. (52) 410101; fax (52) 451044; f. 1990; Dir ŁENIO RADIĆ; 1,008 employees.

Tankerska Plovidba: 23000 Zadar, B. Petranovića 4; tel. (23) 311132; telex 27127; fax (23) 437372.

CUBA

Introductory Survey

Location, Climate, Language, Religion, Flag, Capital

The Republic of Cuba is an archipelago of two main islands, Cuba and the Isle of Youth (formerly the Isle of Pines), and about 1,600 keys and islets. It lies in the Caribbean Sea, 145 km (90 miles) south of Florida, USA. Other nearby countries are the Bahamas, Mexico, Jamaica and Haiti. The climate is tropical, with the annual rainy season from May to October. The average annual temperature is 25°C (77°F) and hurricanes are frequent. The language spoken is Spanish. Most of the inhabitants are Christians, of whom the great majority are Roman Catholics. The national flag (proportions 2 by 1) has five equal horizontal stripes, of blue, white, blue, white and blue, with a red triangle, enclosing a five-pointed white star, at the hoist. The capital is Havana (La Habana).

Recent History

Cuba was ruled by Spain from the 16th century until 1898, when the island was ceded to the USA following Spain's defeat in the Spanish–American War. Cuba became an independent republic on 20 May 1902, but the USA retained its naval bases on the island and, until 1934, reserved the right to intervene in Cuba's internal affairs. In 1933 an army sergeant, Fulgencio Batista Zaldivar, came to power at the head of a military revolt. Batista ruled the country, directly or indirectly, until 1944, when he retired after serving a four-year term as elected President.

In March 1952, however, Gen. Batista (as he had become) seized power again, deposing President Carlos Prío Socarrás in a bloodless coup. Batista's new regime soon proved to be unpopular and became harshly repressive. In July 1953 a radical opposition group, led by Dr Fidel Castro Ruz, attacked the Moncada army barracks in Santiago de Cuba. Castro was captured, with many of his supporters, but later released. He went into exile and formed a revolutionary movement which was committed to Batista's overthrow. In December 1956 Castro landed in Cuba with a small group of followers, most of whom were captured or killed. However, 12 survivors, including Castro and the Argentine-born Dr Ernesto ('Che') Guevara, escaped into the hills of the Sierra Maestra, where they formed the nucleus of the guerrilla forces which, after a prolonged struggle, forced Batista to flee from Cuba on 1 January 1959. The Batista regime collapsed, and Castro's forces occupied Havana.

The assumption of power by the victorious rebels was initially met with great popular acclaim. The 1940 Constitution was suspended in January 1959 and replaced by a new 'Fundamental Law'. Executive and legislative power was vested in the Council of Ministers, with Fidel Castro as Prime Minister and his brother Raúl as his deputy. Guevara reportedly ranked third in importance. The new regime ruled by decree but promised to hold elections within 18 months. When it was firmly established, the Castro Government adopted a radical economic programme, including agrarian reform and the nationalization of industrial and commercial enterprises. These drastic reforms, combined with the regime's authoritarian nature, provoked opposition from some sectors of the population, including former supporters of Castro, and many Cubans went into exile.

All US business interests in Cuba were expropriated, without compensation, in October 1960, and the USA severed diplomatic relations in January 1961. A US-sponsored force of anti-Castro Cuban émigrés landed in April 1961 at the Bahía de Cochinos (Bay of Pigs), in southern Cuba, but the invasion was thwarted by Castro's troops. Later in the year, all pro-Government groups were merged to form the Organizaciones Revolucionarias Integradas (ORI). In December 1961 Fidel Castro publicly announced that Cuba had become a communist state, and he proclaimed a 'Marxist-Leninist' programme for the country's future development. In January 1962 Cuba was excluded from active participation in the Organization of American States (OAS). The USA instituted a full economic and political blockade of Cuba. Hostility to the USA was accompanied by increasingly close relations between Cuba and the USSR. In October 1962 the USA revealed the presence of Soviet missiles in Cuba but, after the imposition of a US naval blockade, the weapons were withdrawn. The missile bases, capable of launching nuclear weapons against the USA, were dismantled, so resolving one of the most serious international crises since the Second World War. In 1964 the OAS imposed diplomatic and commercial sanctions against Cuba.

The ORI was replaced in 1962 by a new Partido Unido de la Revolución Socialista Cubana (PURSC), which was established, under Fidel Castro's leadership, as the country's sole legal party. Guevara resigned his military and government posts in April 1965, subsequently leaving Cuba to pursue revolutionary activities abroad. In October 1965 the PURSC was renamed the Partido Comunista de Cuba (PCC). Although ostracized by most other Latin American countries, the PCC Government maintained and consolidated its internal authority, with little effective opposition. Supported by considerable aid from the USSR, the regime made significant progress in social and economic development, including improvements in education and public health. At the same time, Cuba continued to give active support to left-wing revolutionary movements in Latin America and in many other parts of the world. Guevara was killed in Bolivia, following an unsuccessful guerrilla uprising under his leadership, in October 1967.

In July 1972 Cuba's links with the Eastern bloc were strengthened when the country became a full member of the Council for Mutual Economic Assistance (CMEA—dissolved in 1991), a Moscow-based organization linking the USSR and other communist states. As a result of its admission to the CMEA, Cuba received preferential trade terms and more technical advisers from the USSR and East European countries.

In June 1974 the country's first elections since the revolution were held for municipal offices in Matanzas province. Cuba's first 'socialist' Constitution was submitted to the First Congress of the PCC, held in December 1975, and came into force in February 1976, after being approved by popular referendum. In addition, the existing six provinces were reorganized to form 14. As envisaged by the new Constitution, elections for 169 municipal assemblies were held in October 1976. These assemblies later elected delegates to provincial assemblies and deputies to the National Assembly of People's Power, inaugurated in December 1976 as 'the supreme organ of state'. The National Assembly chose the members of a new Council of State, with Fidel Castro as President. The Second Congress of the PCC was held in December 1980, when Fidel and Raúl Castro were re-elected First and Second Secretaries respectively. In December 1981 Fidel Castro was re-elected by the Assembly as President of the Council of State, and Raúl Castro re-elected as First Vice-President.

Cuba continued to be excluded from the activities of the OAS, although the Organization voted in favour of allowing members to normalize their relations with Cuba in 1975. Relations with the USA deteriorated because of Cuban involvement in Angola in 1976 and in Ethiopia in 1977. The relaxation of restrictions on emigration in April 1980 resulted in the departure of more than 125,000 Cubans for Florida. Antagonism continued as Cuba's military and political presence abroad increased, threatening US spheres of influence.

In 1981 Cuba expressed interest in discussing foreign policy with the USA, and declared that the shipment of arms to guerrilla groups in Central America had ceased. High-level talks between the two countries took place in November 1981 but US hostility increased. Economic sanctions were tightened, the major air link was closed, and tourism and investment by US nationals was prohibited in April 1982. Cuba's support of Argentina during the 1982 crisis concerning the Falkland Islands improved relations with the rest of Latin America, and the country's legitimacy was finally acknowledged when it was elected to the chair of the UN General Assembly Committee on Decolonization in September 1982, while continuing to play a leading role in the Non-Aligned Movement (despite its firm alliance with the Soviet bloc).

An increase in US military activity in Honduras and the Caribbean region led President Castro to declare a 'state of national alert' in August 1983. The US invasion of Grenada in October, and the ensuing short-lived confrontation between US forces and Cuban personnel on the island, severely damaged hopes that the two countries might reach an agreement over the problems in Central America, and left Cuba isolated in the Caribbean, following the weakening of its diplomatic and military ties with Suriname in November.

In July 1984 official negotiations were begun with the USA on the issues of immigration and repatriation. In December agreement was reached on the resumption of Cuban immigration to the USA and the repatriation of 2,746 Cuban 'undesirables', who had accompanied other Cuban refugees to the USA in 1980. The repatriation of Cuban 'undesirables' began in February 1985, but, following the inauguration of Radio Martí (a radio station sponsored by the 'Voice of America' radio network, which began to broadcast Western-style news and other programmes to Cuba from Florida, USA), the Cuban Government suspended its immigration accord with the USA. Subsequently, all visits to Cuba by US residents of Cuban origin were banned. The US Government responded by restricting visits to the USA by PCC members and Cuban government officials. In September 1986, as a result of mediation by the Roman Catholic Church, more than 100 political prisoners and their families were permitted to leave Cuba for the USA.

In 1987 relations with the USA continued to deteriorate when, in February, the US Government launched a campaign to direct public attention to violations of human rights in Cuba. A resolution to condemn Cuba's record on human rights was narrowly defeated at a meeting of the UN Commission on Human Rights in March. The Cuban Government subsequently allowed 348 current and former political prisoners to return to the USA. The restoration of the 1984 immigration accord, in October 1987, provoked rioting by Cuban exiles detained in US prisons lasting several days until the US Government assured the exiles that their return to Cuba would be suspended indefinitely and that their cases would be studied individually. The accord allowed for the repatriation of 2,500 Cuban 'undesirables' in exchange for a US agreement to allow 23,000 Cubans to enter the USA annually. The USA continued its attempts to have Cuba condemned by the UN Commission on Human Rights in March 1988, but the proposal was again vetoed. A resolution was adopted, however, for a human rights' commission to visit Cuba in September. The commission published its findings in March 1989. Although it did not produce any firm conclusions or recommendations, it did document many cases in which fundamental rights had been infringed. Regarding prisoners of conscience, there had been some improvements. In 1988 the Government had released some 250 political prisoners, and in the following January President Castro pledged to release the remaining 225 political prisoners acknowledged by the regime. In 1989 human rights activists formed a co-ordinating body and increased their operations. The Government responded in August by imprisoning leading activists for up to two years for having published allegedly false information. In April 1990 the UN Commission on Human Rights, at a meeting in Geneva, voted in favour of a resolution to keep Cuba under continued UN scrutiny. In September 1991 eight Cuban dissident organizations united to form a single democratic opposition group, the Concertación Democrática Cubana—CDC (Cuban Democratic Convergence), to campaign for political pluralism and economic reform.

At the Third Congress of the PCC in February 1986 drastic changes were made within the Central Committee. Almost one-third of the 146 full members were replaced. Nine of the 24 members of the new Politburo were elected for the first time, with several senior members, veterans of the 1959 revolution, being replaced by younger persons. A new Council of State was elected in December. However, in 1987, despite the major reorganization of the Politburo, there was little sign that the reforms being advocated in the USSR would be pursued in Cuba.

In June 1989 President Castro was confronted by Cuba's most serious political crisis since the 1959 Revolution. It was discovered that a number of senior military personnel were not only involved in smuggling operations in Angola but were also aiding drug-traffickers from the infamous Medellín cartel by enabling them to use Cuban airstrips as refuelling points (en route from Colombia to the USA) in return for bribes. Following court-martial proceedings, Gen. Arnaldo Ochoa Sánchez, who had led the military campaign in Angola, was found guilty of high treason and executed. Three other officers were also executed. A further purge led to the imposition of harsh sentences on 14 senior officials, including the head of civil aviation and the Ministers of the Interior and of Transport, who had been found guilty of corruption. President Castro insisted that the bureaucracy in Cuba needed to undergo a process of 'purification' but not reform. However, the scandal had clearly undermined the regime's credibility at the international, as well as the domestic, level.

In Angola, where Cuban troops numbered an estimated 50,000, the peace process gathered momentum in 1988. In May a large Cuban offensive almost succeeded in expelling South African forces from Angola and gave new impetus to the peace negotiations. A cease-fire was implemented, and at discussions held in New York, in October, an agreement was reached for a phased withdrawal of Cuban troops over a period of 24–30 months. By December a timetable for the withdrawal of Cuban troops had been agreed. The withdrawal began in April 1989 and was completed in May 1991.

In April 1989 President Gorbachev of the USSR visited Cuba. It was the first visit by a Soviet leader since 1974. The two Heads of State discussed bilateral relations, in particular ways in which Cuba's dependence on Soviet aid might be reduced, and Central American issues. The discussions culminated in the signing of a treaty of friendship and economic co-operation. Ostensibly, relations remained good. However, tensions were present, owing to Castro's resistance to Soviet-style reforms. Gorbachev made it clear that, in future, general financial aid would be replaced by assistance for specific projects, thus giving the USSR greater power to influence policy decisions in Cuba. In July President Castro strongly attacked the ideas of *perestroika* and *glasnost*, which he blamed for the 'crisis in socialism'. He pledged to eradicate all market forms of economic activity, despite the fact that Cuba's failure to integrate into the new supply-and-demand system of many Eastern European factories had led to delays in imports and acute shortages.

In early October 1990 President Castro announced plans to reduce the PCC's bureaucracy by as much as 50%, including the reassignment of thousands of employees to more productive sectors. The number of advisory departments to the Central Committee was to be reduced from 19 to nine, the military department was to be completely disbanded and replaced by a military commission, and the Secretariat was to be reduced from seven to five members. The changes were intended to improve the efficiency of the PCC in preparation for its Congress in 1991 and to help the party to confront the prevailing economic crisis more effectively.

In November 1990 rationing was extended to all products. Cubans were told to prepare for the possibility of a 'special wartime period' by the Minister of the Revolutionary Armed Forces, Gen. Raúl Castro, who warned of a possible US military attack if the currently intensified US economic blockade should fail. In spite of the gravity of Cuba's political and economic situation, President Castro was defiant in his rejection of recommendations that, as a condition for the removal of the blockade, Cuba should adopt a market economy and political pluralism.

In March 1990 a new Spanish-speaking television station, TV Martí (based in Florida, USA), began broadcasting to Cuba. However, reception of the station, which intended to propagate anti-communist feeling in Cuba, was successfully interrupted by electronic equipment in Cuban aircraft and naval vessels within an hour of beginning transmission. In mid-April Cuban officials commenced the systematic interruption of Radio Martí, which had been operating since 1985.

In early July 1990 a serious political and diplomatic crisis arose when five members of the dissident Asociación por Arte Libre (Association for Free Art) took refuge in the Czechoslovak embassy in Havana. This action prompted a succession of events involving the entry of Cuban dissidents into European embassies and diplomatic residences in Havana. At the height of the crisis, more than 50 Cubans were taking refuge, 18 of them in the Spanish embassy. One refuge-seeker had been pursued by the Cuban police and captured within the grounds of the Spanish embassy. The Spanish Government issued a strong protest against this violation of diplomatic immunity and called into question Cuba's record on human rights. As the diplomatic row escalated, the Spanish Government recalled its ambassador and suspended official aid of US $2.5m. to Cuba. Of those seeking asylum, it was widely believed in the diplomatic community that as many as one-half were *agents provocateurs* sent in with the full knowledge of the Cuban Ministry of the Interior to intimidate diplomats and to frustrate the efforts of genuine asylum-seekers. In early September the 58-day crisis finally came to an end when the last of the refugees voluntarily surrendered.

In September 1991 the USSR announced that it intended to withdraw the majority of its military personnel (some 3,000 troops and advisers) from Cuba. The decision, which was condemned by Cuba as presenting a major threat to its national security, came as the result of US demands that the USSR reduce its aid to Cuba as a precondition to the provision of US aid to the USSR. Cuba's subsequent demands that the US withdraw its troops from the naval base at Guantánamo were rejected. In September 1992 it was announced that the 3,000-strong military body of the former Soviet Union stationed in Cuba was to be withdrawn by July 1993.

At the Fourth Congress of the PCC, held in October 1991, the structure of the party underwent a series of reforms. It was proposed that the National Assembly be elected by direct vote, the Secretariat of the Central Committee was abolished, and 12 new members were introduced into the Politburo. The appointment of alternate members to leading party bodies was also abolished. Of the 225 members of the Central Committee, more than one-half were replaced. In addition, adherents to the Christian faith were formally permitted to join the party. However, the party excluded the possibility of political pluralism and remained defiant in its rejection of capitalism, despite the developments in the USSR that had led to Cuba's virtual isolation.

In early 1992 President Castro's efforts to quiet internal dissent and bolster the country against the perceived US threat revealed an increasingly militant attitude, as several death sentences were imposed on Cuban dissidents. Eduardo Díaz Betancourt, the leader of a group of three Cuban-American exiles who had been captured while allegedly attempting to infiltrate the country armed with guns and explosives, was executed on 21 January, despite international pleas for clemency. Two men who had been convicted of killing four policemen at Tarara naval base during an unsuccessful attempt to escape Cuba for Miami, USA, were executed in February.

In 1992 the USA began to implement a series of measures tightening its economic blockade on Cuba. In April President Bush issued an executive order barring ships that were engaged in trade with Cuba from entering US ports. In October the Cuban Democracy Act, also known as the 'Torricelli Law', was adopted, making it illegal for foreign subsidiaries of US companies to trade with Cuba. These measures encountered widespread international criticism, including protests by the EC that they violated international law. In November the UN General Assembly adopted a non-binding resolution demanding the cessation of the trade embargo.

In July 1992 the National Assembly approved a number of amendments to the Constitution. Under the reforms, President Castro was granted the authority to declare a state of emergency and, in such an event, to assume full control of the armed forces at the head of a National Defence Council. An electoral reform, which had originally been proposed at the Fourth Congress of the PCC in October 1991, was formally adopted, providing for elections to the National Assembly to be conducted by direct vote. The constitutional revisions also included an updating of the business law, legitimizing foreign investment in approved state enterprises and recognizing foreign ownership of property in joint ventures. While these revisions merely lent legal validity to what had become common practice since the collapse of the preferential trade agreement with the former USSR in 1991, they reflected the Government's increasing eagerness to attract foreign investment.

In early September 1992 a major economic set-back occurred when the construction of Cuba's first nuclear power station, at Juraguá, was suspended, owing to lack of funds, with one reactor 90% complete and a second in the early stages of construction. The project, which had been funded by the USSR, was to have provided as much as 25% of Cuba's energy requirements. Against a background of severe energy shortages, the prospect of an assured source of energy had represented an essential condition for many potential foreign investors. The suspension of work on the plant threatened to jeopardize such foreign interest. However, in late 1995 Russia pledged US $349m. towards the completion of the first reactor. Cuba was to provide $208m., and foreign investors were being sought for an additional $191m. According to official sources, the reactor would be ready to begin operating within four years of construction resuming.

In what was widely viewed as a move to consolidate power in the hands of President Castro, it was announced in late September 1992 that Carlos Aldana Escalante, the country's third most important leader, had been dismissed as the PCC's head of ideology, foreign policy and culture. The official reason given for Aldana's dismissal was his alleged involvement in a financial scandal. In late October Aldana was expelled from the PCC.

On 24 February 1993 elections to the National Assembly and the 14 provincial assemblies were, for the first time, conducted by direct secret ballot. Only candidates nominated by the PCC were permitted to contest the elections. According to official results, there was an abstention rate of only 1.2%, and 87.3% of the electorate cast a 'united' ballot (a vote for the entire list of candidates). Only 7.2% of votes cast were blank or spoilt. All 589 deputies of the National Assembly were elected with more than the requisite 50% of the votes. In the following month Fidel Castro and Gen. Raúl Castro were unanimously re-elected by the National Assembly to their respective posts as President and First Vice-President of the Council of State.

In June 1993, in accordance with a unilateral decision by the Soviet Union announced in September 1991 (see above), the 3,000-strong military unit of the former Soviet Union was withdrawn from Cuba. A number of Russian military personnel remained to operate military intelligence facilities. In the same month the Cuban Government announced that, owing to the adverse economic situation, the Cuban armed forces would be reduced.

In July 1993, with the economic crisis deepening and international reserves exhausted, Castro announced that a 30-year ban on Cuban citizens' possessing foreign currency was to be lifted. The measure, which represented a significant departure from the country's centrally-planned socialist economy, was intended to attract the large sums of foreign currency (principally US dollars) in circulation on the black market into the economy, and to encourage remittances from Cuban exiles. Restrictions on Cuban exiles travelling to Cuba were also to be relaxed. Concerns that the measures were socially divisive, affording privileges to those receiving currency from relatives abroad, were acknowledged by the Government.

In September 1993, in a further move away from traditional economic policy, the Government authorized limited individual private enterprise in a range of 117 occupations. In the same month plans were announced for the introduction of agricultural reforms allowing for the decentralization and reorganization of state farms into 'Units of Basic Co-operative Production', to be managed and financed by the workers themselves.

In April 1994, in a reorganization of the Government, four new ministries were created and a number of state committees and institutes dissolved. The creation of the new ministries (of economy and planning, finance and prices, foreign investment and economic co-operation, and tourism) reflected a significant change in the economic management of the country. In the following month an extraordinary session of the legislature empowered the Government to introduce a series of fiscal measures in order to address the problems of a rapidly contracting economy and increasing budget deficit. The measures included the introduction of a graduated income tax, price increases on goods and services, and the reduction of subsidies on unprofitable state enterprises.

On 5 August 1994 increasing discontent at deteriorating economic conditions resulted in rioting in the capital, precipitated by a confrontation between police and a large number of Cubans attempting to commandeer a ferry in order to take the vessel to the USA. In a public speech broadcast on the following day Castro indicated that, if the USA failed to halt the promotion of such illegal departures, Cuba would suspend its travel restrictions. The resultant surge of Cubans attempting to reach the USA by sea reached crisis proportions, and on 19 August President Clinton was forced to adopt measures to deter them. The automatic refugee status conferred on Cubans under the 1966 Cuban Adjustment Act was revoked, and Cubans were warned that those intercepted by the US Coast Guard would be transported to Guantánamo naval base and would not be allowed entry into the USA. On 20 August further measures were imposed, including the halting of cash remittances from Cuban exiles in the USA. However, these measures failed to stem the flow of Cubans seeking refuge in the USA, and on 27 August the US Government agreed to hold bilateral talks with Cuba to seek a resolution to the crisis. The talks concluded on 9 September with an agreement providing a commitment by the USA to grant visas allowing for the migration of a minimum of 20,000 Cubans annually (despite the 1984 immigration accord, a total of only 11,222 US entry visas had been granted to Cubans between December 1984 and July 1994). An additional

4,000–6,000 Cubans already on waiting lists for US visas would be granted them. In return, Cuba reintroduced border restrictions on 13 September. In excess of 30,000 Cubans were estimated to have left the country during the period when travel restrictions were suspended. The majority of these were detained by the US authorities and transported to camps in Guantánamo and the Panama Canal Zone.

Talks continued with the USA throughout 1995 to assess the progress of the September 1994 immigration accord. In February the transfer began of refugees to Guantánamo from the Panama Canal Zone. In May a further immigration accord was signed, bringing to an official end the automatic refugee status which had been revoked in August 1994. The accord also stated that all Cuban refugees intercepted at sea by the USA would thenceforth be repatriated. In addition, the USA agreed to grant visas to the majority of the approximately 20,000 Cuban refugees detained at Guantánamo, although the figure was to be deducted, over a period of four years, from the annual quota of visas granted under the September 1994 accord.

The Council of Ministers underwent reorganizations in January and May 1995. In January six portfolios were reassigned, most of which were concerned with the economic management of the country. In November the UN General Assembly voted in favour of a resolution demanding that the USA repeal its economic embargo against Cuba, with a majority higher than in similar votes conducted in the previous three years.

In early 1995 legislative proposals seeking to tighten the US embargo against Cuba were introduced to the US Congress by the Chairman of the Senate Foreign Relations Committee, Jesse Helms, and the Chairman of the House of Representatives Sub-Committee on the Western Hemisphere, Dan Burton. The proposals, referred to as the Helms-Burton bill, sought to impose sanctions on countries trading with or investing in Cuba, and threatened to reduce US aid to countries providing Cuba with financial assistance, notably Russia. The bill provoked international criticism, and a formal complaint was registered by the EU, which claimed that the legislation would be in violation of international law and the rules of the World Trade Organization (WTO). The bill was approved by the House of Representatives in September but was considerably modified by the Senate.

In May 1995, following the first visit to Cuba by an international human rights mission since the 1959 revolution, the Government authorized the release of six political prisoners. The mission had been co-ordinated by the human rights organization France-Libertés. According to Cuban human rights groups, however, more than 1,000 political prisoners remained in detention in the country.

In February 1996 Cuban MiG fighters shot down two US light aircraft piloted by members of the Cuban-American exile group Brothers to the Rescue, killing all four crew members. The action was vigorously condemned by the USA, which rejected Cuban claims that the aircraft had violated Cuban airspace. Further US sanctions were immediately implemented, including the indefinite suspension of charter flights to Cuba. In June, following an investigation, the International Civil Aviation Organization issued a report confirming US claims that the aircraft had been shot down over international waters. As a result of the incident, President Clinton reversed his previous opposition to certain controversial elements of the Helms-Burton bill, and on 12 March he signed the legislation, officially entitled the Cuban Liberty and Solidarity Act, thus making it law. However, Clinton was empowered to issue executive orders, at six-monthly intervals, postponing the implementation of a section of the law, Title III, which allowed US citizens, including naturalized Cuban exiles, to prosecute through US courts any foreign corporation or investor with business dealings involving property that had been expropriated during the Castro regime. Approval of the Helms-Burton bill prompted strenuous criticism from Cuba's major trading partners. The EU announced its intention to challenge the extra-territorial provisions of the Act through the WTO, while Mexico and Canada sought to dispute the law under the provisions of the North American Free Trade Agreement. International opposition to the Helms-Burton Act increased following the issue, in May, by the US State Department of letters to companies in Canada, Mexico and Italy, warning of possible prosecution. In June Canada initiated a series of legal measures to protect Canadian companies against the Helms-Burton Act. Similar legislation was subsequently adopted by Mexico and the EU. In July Clinton imposed a six-month moratorium on Title III of the Helms-Burton Act, which had been due to come into force in August. In November, in its annual vote on the US embargo, the UN General Assembly voted for its repeal with the largest majority to date. Notably, the United Kingdom, Germany and the Netherlands, which had all previously abstained on this question, voted in favour of a repeal. In the same month the WTO adopted a resolution to establish a disputes panel to rule on the legality of the Helms-Burton Act.

In December 1996 agreement was reached by the members of the EU to make the extent of economic co-operation with Cuba contingent upon progress towards democracy in the country. In that month the Cuban Government adopted legislation to counteract the application of the Helms-Burton Act in an attempt to protect foreign investment in the country. The Government also expressed its readiness to negotiate with the USA regarding the compensation of US citizens with property claims in Cuba. In January 1997 Clinton suspended Title III for a further six-month period. In early February the EU requested that the WTO postpone the appointment of a disputes panel in order that further discussions be conducted with the USA in an effort to reach a negotiated settlement. However, these efforts were not successful, and on 20 February a disputes panel was appointed and given six months to reach a decision on whether the extra-territorial provisions of the Helms-Burton Act contravened WTO rules on multilateral trade, or whether, as the USA maintained, the Act was a matter of national security and therefore not within the jurisdiction of the WTO. In March, in a futher attempt to avoid confrontation, the EU and the USA resumed discussions concerning the Helms-Burton Act, and in the following month agreement was reached in principle on a resolution of the dispute. Under the terms of the agreement, the USA was to continue deferring the implementation of Title III indefinitely, while the EU was to withdraw its petition to the WTO until October. In the interim, negotiations were to continue towards a multilateral accord defining investment principles, with particular emphasis on expropriated foreign assets. Although a resolution of the dispute was not reached by the specified deadline of 15 October, both sides agreed that sufficient progress had been made to justify the continuation of negotiations beyond that date.

In November 1996, following a meeting in the Vatican between Castro and the Pope, it was announced that Cuba was to receive its first ever papal visit. The date of the Pope's visit was subsequently set for 21–25 January 1998.

In April 1997 the Government sent a report to the UN Secretary-General, in which it accused the USA of perpetrating a deliberate act of biological aggression against Cuba. The Government claimed that a US crop-spraying aeroplane had flown over Cuban territory in October 1996, releasing an infestation of *Thrips palmi,* an insect which destroys agricultural crops. The insect had previously been unknown on the island. In August 1997 Cuba filed its complaint with the UN International Convention on Biological Weapons. The USA rejected the accusation, although it did admit that a US aircraft used for spraying drug crops had overflown Cuba *en route* to Colombia on the date specified. Later that month the Convention indicated that there was insufficient evidence to prove a direct link between the appearance of the insect and the flight of the US aircraft. A final report was due to be released in December.

In May 1997 the Council of State issued a decree-law authorizing the creation of a new bank, the Banco Central de Cuba (BCC), to assume the central banking functions of the Banco Nacional de Cuba (BNC). The BCC was to be responsible for issuing currency, proposing and implementing monetary policy and the regulation of financial institutions. The BNC was to continue functioning as a commercial bank and servicing the country's foreign debt.

In mid-1997 a spate of bombings directed against hotels and tourist locations began in the capital. In September an Italian businessman was killed by an explosion in a Havana hotel. The Government claimed that the bombings were an attempt to undermine the country's vital tourism industry, and that the campaign had been organized from within the USA. In that month a Salvadorean national was arrested and reportedly confessed to the bombings. The Government maintained that he was a mercenary and that the campaign had been organized by the anti-Castro Cuban-American National Foundation from its base in Miami, USA.

At the Fifth Congress of the PCC in October 1997 efforts were made to lessen the bureaucracy of the party, with the Central Committee being reduced in number from 225 members to 150, and the Politburo from 26 to 24 members.

On 11 January 1998 elections to the National Assembly (enlarged from 589 to 601 seats) and to the 14 provincial assemblies were conducted. All 601 candidates who contested the legislative ballot were elected. Of the 7.8m. registered voters, 98.35% participated in the elections. Only 5% of votes cast were blank or spoilt.

Since 1985 Cuba has succeeded in establishing stronger ties with other Latin American countries, notably Argentina, Brazil, Peru and Uruguay. In September 1988 diplomatic relations were established with the EC (restyled the European Union—EU—in late 1993). In February 1989 President Castro visited Venezuela, for the first time since 1959, to attend the inauguration of President Carlos Andrés Pérez. In October 1989 Cuba was elected to the UN Security Council (for a two-year term from January 1990) for the first time in the 30 years of President Castro's rule.

Relations with Spain reached a low point between July and September 1990, during the embassy crisis (see above); however, by October they were reported to be improving, with representatives from both countries holding talks to decide on a date for a meeting of the Spanish-Cuban commission. Since 1993 Spain has played a significant role in advising Cuba on economic affairs and mediating in negotiations with the IMF, with a view to future co-operation. In 1994 Cuba and Spain concluded an agreement providing for the compensation of Spanish citizens whose property was expropriated during the Cuban revolution of 1959. In 1996, following the succession in Spain of the socialist Government by the centre-right administration of José María Aznar, relations between Spain and Cuba began to deteriorate. In October Spain suspended its programme of aid to Cuba, and in the following month Cuba revoked its approval of a newly-appointed Spanish ambassador who had expressed his intention to maintain contacts with and assist Cuban dissidents.

A conference of Ibero-American leaders that took place in Guadalajara, Mexico, in July 1991 led to a partial resumption of diplomatic relations with Chile; full relations were resumed in 1995. In 1992 Cuba signed a number of accords and protocols establishing diplomatic relations with republics of the former Soviet Union, including Belarus, Georgia, Kyrgyzstan and Ukraine. Full diplomatic relations with Colombia, which were suspended in 1981, were resumed in October 1993.

Government

Under the 1976 Constitution (the first since the 1959 revolution, amended in July 1992), the supreme organ of state, and the sole legislative authority, is the National Assembly of People's Power (Asamblea Nacional del Poder Popular), with 601 deputies elected for five years by direct vote. The National Assembly elects 31 of its members to form the Council of State, the Assembly's permanent organ. The Council of State is the highest representative of the State, and its President is both Head of State and Head of Government. Executive and administrative authority is vested in the Council of Ministers, appointed by the National Assembly on the proposal of the Head of State. Municipal, regional and provincial assemblies have also been established. The Partido Comunista de Cuba (PCC), the only authorized political party, is 'the leading force of society and the State'. The PCC's highest authority is the Party Congress, which elects a Central Committee (150 members in December 1997) to supervise the Party's work. To direct its policy, the Central Committee elects a Politburo (24 members in 1997).

Defence

Conscription for military service is for a two-year period, and conscripts also work on the land. In August 1997, according to Western estimates, the armed forces totalled 53,000 (including ready reserves serving 45 days per year to complete active and reserve units): the army numbered 38,000, the navy 5,000 and the air force 10,000. Army reserves were estimated to total 39,000. Paramilitary forces include 15,000 State Security troops, 4,000 border guards, a civil defence force of 50,000 and a Youth Labour Army of 65,000. A local militia organization (Milicias de Tropas Territoriales—MTT), comprising an estimated 1m. men and women, was formed in 1980. Expenditure on defence and internal security for 1997 was budgeted at US $700m. Despite Cuban hostility, the USA maintains a base at Guantánamo Bay, with 1,000 naval and 640 marine personnel in 1997. In June 1993, in accordance with the unilateral decision of the Soviet Union in September 1991, the 3,000-strong military unit of the former Soviet Union, which had been stationed in Cuba since 1962, was withdrawn. A number of Russian military personnel remained to operate military intelligence facilities. Following the political changes in eastern Europe, previously high levels of military aid to Cuba were dramatically reduced in the early 1990s, and the size of the army has been reduced by some 60,000 personnel.

Economic Affairs

In 1994, according to official estimates, Cuba's gross domestic product (GDP), measured at constant 1981 prices, was 12,868.3m. pesos. During 1990–93, it was estimated, GDP declined, in real terms, by 34.8%. However, GDP increased by 0.7% in 1994, by 2.5% in 1995, and by an estimated 7.8% in 1996. During 1985–95 the population increased by an annual average of 0.9%.

Agriculture (including forestry and fishing) contributed 6.9% of GDP in 1995. About 15.2% of the labour force were employed in this sector in 1996. The principal cash crop is sugar cane, with sugar and its derivatives accounting for 73.2% of export earnings in 1989. Other important crops are tobacco, rice, citrus fruits, plantains and bananas. In real terms, the net material product (NMP) of the agricultural sector declined at an average rate of 3.5% per year during 1981–86, but increased by an annual average of 2.5% in 1986–89. According to the FAO, Cuba's agricultural production declined by 19.5% in 1993, by 6.9% in 1994 and by 2.6% in 1995, before increasing by 6.0% in 1996.

Mining, manufacturing and construction contributed 31.3% of GDP in 1995. Mining, manufacturing and power employed 18.9% of the labour force in 1981. Construction contributed 3.1% of GDP in 1995, and employed 8.9% of the labour force in 1981. The NMP of the industrial sector (including the production of water and power, but excluding construction) increased, in real terms, at an average rate of 9.3% per year in 1981–85, but declined by an annual average of 1.9% during 1985–89.

Mining contributed 1.2% of GDP in 1995. Nickel is the principal mineral export. In 1996 nickel output reached a record level of 55,800 metric tons, an increase of some 30% compared with the previous year. Cuba also produces considerable amounts of chromium, cobalt and copper, and there are workable deposits of gold and silver.

Manufacturing contributed 27.0% of GDP in 1995. Measured by the value of output, the principal branches of manufacturing in 1989 were food products (34.3% of the total), beverages and tobacco, machinery and industrial chemicals.

Energy is derived principally from petroleum and natural gas. Imports of mineral fuels accounted for 32.4% of the total cost of imports in 1989.

Services employed 46.3% of the total labour force in 1981 and accounted for 42.3% of total NMP in 1989. Tourism is one of the country's principal sources of foreign exchange, earning US $1,380m. in 1996, and development of the sector remains a priority of the Government. In real terms, the NMP of the service sectors increased at an average rate of 3.9% per year during 1981–86, but declined by an annual average of 2.7% in 1986–89.

In 1995 Cuba recorded a trade deficit of US $1,330m. and there was a deficit of $41m. on the current account of the balance of payments. In 1989 the principal source of imports (68.0%) was the USSR, which was also the principal market for exports (59.9%). Other major trading partners were the German Democratic Republic, the People's Republic of China, Czechoslovakia and Bulgaria. The principal imports in 1989 were mineral fuels, machinery and transport equipment. The principal exports in the same year were sugar, minerals and concentrates, and agricultural produce. The re-export of mineral fuels was a major source of convertible currency, earning Cuba an estimated US $500m. in 1989. In 1990, however, imports of subsidized petroleum from the USSR, which had, hitherto, provided 95% of Cuba's total petroleum requirements, were dramatically reduced.

In 1996 Cuba recorded an estimated budget deficit of 570m. pesos (equivalent to 2.4% of GDP). Cuba's external debt to Western creditor nations was estimated to be between US $9,000m. and $11,000m. in 1997. Cuba's debt to the USSR was estimated to be $24,780m. at mid-1990. According to official figures, some 6.5% of the labour force were unemployed in mid-1996. No index of consumer prices is published.

Cuba is a member of the Latin American Economic System (see p. 261) and of the Group of Latin American and Caribbean Sugar Exporting Countries (see p. 257).

In the early 1990s Cuba suffered severe economic decline, prompted by the collapse of the Soviet Union and by the consequent termination of the favourable aid and trade arrangements that had supported the Cuban economy. Resultant shortages, particularly of petroleum and basic raw materials, seriously affected production in all sectors and necessitated wide-ranging austerity measures. In 1994, in a significant departure from the country's traditional command economy, a series of adjustment measures was introduced in an attempt to reduce the budget deficit and to address the problem of excess liquidity. The measures included the introduction of new taxes and a drastic reduction (by some 40%) of subsidies to loss-making state enterprises. In December 1994 a new 'convertible peso' was introduced to regulate the circulation of foreign currency. A new investment law, approved in September 1995, opened all sectors of the economy, with the exception of defence, health and education, to foreign participation and introduced the possibility of 100% foreign ownership (foreign participation had previously been limited to 49%). Further legislation, approved in mid-1996, provided for the creation of free-trade zones and export manufacturing centres. A restructuring of the banking system, to accommodate Cuba's transformation to a more market-orientated economy, was proceeding in 1997, with the creation of a specialized central bank.

In 1996 the USA intensified its sanctions against Cuba with the introduction of the Helms-Burton Act. Denied access to medium- and long-term loans, Cuba's indebtedness increased substantially as high-interest short-term loans were contracted in order to finance production, most notably in the sugar industry. A shortfall in revenue, owing to a 6% decrease in sugar production in 1996/97, contributed to considerably reduced economic growth in 1997, when the rise in real GDP was expected to slow to 2.1% (from 7.8% in 1996).

Social Welfare

Through the State Social Security System, employees receive benefits for sickness, accidents, maternity, disability, retirement and unemployment. Health services are available free of charge. In 1993 there were 65,640 hospital beds, and there were 51,045 physicians working in the country. In 1997 the number of physicians was estimated at more than 63,000. In 1996 the infant mortality rate was an estimated 8.0 per 1,000 live births. The 1989 budget allocation for health and education was 2,906.2m. pesos.

Education

Education is universal and free at all levels. Education is based on Marxist-Leninist principles and combines study with manual work. Day nurseries are available for all children after their 45th day, and national schools at the pre-primary level are operated by the State for children of five years of age. Primary education, from six to 11 years of age, is compulsory, and secondary education lasts from 12 to 17 years of age, comprising two cycles of three years each. In 1994 total enrolment at primary and secondary schools was equivalent to 90% of the school-age population (males 88%; females 92%). In that year primary enrolment included almost 100% of children in the relevant age-group, while secondary enrolment was equivalent to 75% of the population in the appropriate age-group (males 70%; females 79%). In 1994/95 there were 140,800 students in higher education. Workers attending university courses receive a state subsidy to provide for their dependants. Courses at intermediate and higher levels lay an emphasis on technology, agriculture and teacher training. In 1995, according to estimates by UNESCO, the illiteracy rate among persons aged 15 years and over was 4.3% (males 3.8%; females 4.7%). In 1990 budgetary expenditure on education was estimated at 1,748m. pesos (12.3% of total spending).

Public Holidays

1998: 1 January (Liberation Day), 1 May (Labour Day), 25–27 July (Anniversary of the 1953 Revolution), 10 October (Wars of Independence Day).

1999: 1 January (Liberation Day), 1 May (Labour Day), 25–27 July (Anniversary of the 1953 Revolution), 10 October (Wars of Independence Day).

Weights and Measures

The metric system is in force.

Statistical Survey

Source (unless otherwise stated): Cámara de Comercio de la República de Cuba, Calle 21, No 661/701, esq. Calle A, Apdo 4237, Vedado, Havana; tel. (7) 30-3356; telex 511752; fax (7) 33-3042; Comité Estatal de Estadísticas, Calle Sta y Paseo, Vedado Havana, Cuba; tel. (7) 31-5171; telex 511257.

Area and Population

AREA, POPULATION AND DENSITY

Area (sq km)	110,860*
Population (census results)	
6 September 1970	8,569,121
11 September 1981	
Males	4,914,873
Females	4,808,732
Total	9,723,605
Population (official estimates at mid-year)	
1994	10,950,000
1995	10,980,000
1996	11,019,000
Density (per sq km) at mid-1996	99.4

* 42,803 sq miles.

PRINCIPAL TOWNS

(estimated population at 31 December 1993)

La Habana (Havana, the capital)	2,175,995	Bayamo	137,663
Santiago de Cuba	440,084	Cienfuegos	132,038
Camagüey	293,961	Pinar del Río	128,570
Holguín	242,085	Las Tunas	126,930
Guantánamo	207,796	Matanzas	123,843
Santa Clara	205,400	Ciego de Avila	95,641
		Sancti Spíritus	93,832

BIRTHS, MARRIAGES AND DEATHS*

	Registered live births†		Registered marriages‡		Registered deaths	
	Number	Rate (per 1,000)	Number	Rate (per 1,000)	Number	Rate (per 1,000)
1989	184,891	17.6	85,535	8.1	67,356	6.4
1990	186,658	17.6	101,515	9.5	72,144	6.8
1991	173,896	16.2	162,020	15.1	71,709	6.7
1992	157,349	14.5	191,837	17.7	75,457	7.0
1993	152,226	14.0	n.a.	n.a.	78,504	7.2

1996: Registered live births† 148,276 (birth rate 13.5 per 1,000); Registered deaths 79,654 (death rate 7.2 per 1,000).

* Data are tabulated by year of registration rather than by year of occurrence.

† Births registered in the National Consumers Register, established on 31 December 1964.

‡ Including consensual unions formalized in response to special legislation.

Expectation of life (UN estimates, years at birth, 1990–95): 75.3 (males 73.5; females 77.3). Source: UN, *World Population Prospects: The 1994 Revision.*

ECONOMICALLY ACTIVE POPULATION (1981 census)

	Males	Females	Total
Agriculture, hunting, forestry and fishing	677,565	113,304	790,869
Mining and quarrying Manufacturing Electricity, gas and water	472,399	195,941	668,340
Construction	279,327	33,913	313,240
Trade, restaurants and hotels	170,192	135,438	305,630
Transport, storage and communications	205,421	43,223	248,644
Financing, insurance, real estate and business services Community, social and personal services	541,387	544,665	1,086,052
Activities not adequately defined	87,778	40,139	127,917
Total labour force	2,434,069	1,106,623	3,540,692

1988 (sample survey, persons aged 15 years and over): Total employed labour force 4,570,236 (males 2,920,698; females 1,649,538).

Source: ILO, *Yearbook of Labour Statistics*.

CIVILIAN EMPLOYMENT IN THE STATE SECTOR
(annual averages, '000 persons)

	1987	1988	1989
Industry*	726.9	742.8	767.5
Construction	314.1	339.4	344.3
Agriculture	602.7	653.2	690.3
Forestry	30.1	26.8	30.8
Transport	196.9	199.9	204.4
Communications	28.4	30.1	31.5
Trade	376.2	387.3	395.3
Social services	116.5	121.5	124.5
Science and technology	28.7	27.5	27.4
Education	383.0	388.2	396.4
Arts and culture	42.2	42.1	43.9
Public health	222.4	232.5	243.5
Finance and insurance	20.6	20.9	21.7
Administration	161.4	155.1	151.7
Total (incl. others)	3,299.2	3,408.4	3,526.6

* Fishing, mining, manufacturing, electricity, gas and water.

Agriculture

PRINCIPAL CROPS ('000 metric tons)

	1994	1995	1996
Rice (paddy)	226	223	223*
Maize*	90	85	85
Potatoes	188	282	364†
Sweet potatoes*	190	220	220
Cassava (Manioc)*	290	250	250
Dry beans*	17	18	19
Groundnuts (in shell)*	15	15	15
Coconuts*	26	26	26
Cabbages*	26	28	28
Tomatoes	96	139	139*
Pumpkins, squash and gourds*	45	47	47
Cucumbers and gherkins*	35	36	36
Other vegetables	81	85	85*
Melons*	32	30	30
Sugar cane*	39,000	36,000	40,000
Oranges	256	275	275*
Tangerines, mandarins, clementines and satsumas*	15	16	16
Lemons and limes	15	19	19*
Grapefruit and pomelos	224	261	261*
Mangoes	44	72	72*
Pineapples*	21	19	19
Bananas*	180	160	160
Plantains*	115	100	100
Other fruits and berries	77	72	73*
Coffee (green)	19†	18†	18*
Tobacco (leaves)	35*	30†	30*

* FAO estimate(s). † Unofficial figure.

Source: FAO, *Production Yearbook*.

LIVESTOCK ('000 head, year ending September)

	1994	1995	1996
Cattle	4,617	4,632	4,650*
Horses*	580	580	580
Mules*	32	32	32
Pigs*	1,750	1,750	1,500
Sheep*	310	310	310
Goats*	95	95	95

* FAO estimate(s).

Poultry (FAO estimates, million): 18 in 1994; 19 in 1995; 19 in 1996.

Source: FAO, *Production Yearbook*.

LIVESTOCK PRODUCTS ('000 metric tons)

	1994	1995	1996
Beef and veal	60	65	65*
Pig meat	69	72	72*
Poultry meat	63	69	69*
Cows' milk*	950	920	920
Butter*	8	8	8
Cheese*	15	15	15
Hen eggs	70	64	64*

FAO estimate(s).

Source: FAO, *Production Yearbook*.

Forestry

ROUNDWOOD REMOVALS
(FAO estimates, '000 cubic metres, excl. bark)

	1992	1993	1994
Sawlogs, veneer logs and logs for sleepers	193	193	193
Other industrial wood	418	418	418
Fuel wood	2,529	2,535	2,535
Total	3,140	3,146	3,146

Source: FAO, *Yearbook of Forest Products*.

SAWNWOOD PRODUCTION
('000 cubic metres, incl. railway sleepers)

	1987	1988	1989
Coniferous (softwood)	40	46	59
Broadleaved (hardwood)	75	73	72
Total	114	118	130

1990–94: Annual production as in 1989 (FAO estimates).

Source: FAO, *Yearbook of Forest Products*.

Fishing

('000 metric tons, live weight)

	1993	1994	1995
Inland waters	18.7	20.4	22.5
Atlantic Ocean	75.0	67.4	71.7
Total catch	93.7	87.7	94.2

Source: FAO, *Yearbook of Fishery Statistics*.

Mining

('000 metric tons, unless otherwise indicated)

	1987	1988	1989
Crude petroleum	894.5	716.8	718.4
Natural gas (million cu metres)	23.9	21.9	33.6
Copper concentrates*	3.5	3.0	2.8
Nickel and cobalt*	36.8	43.9	46.6
Refractory chromium	52.4	52.2	50.6
Salt (unrefined)	230.5	200.3	206.1
Silica and sand ('000 cu metres)	5,826.3	6,467.7	6,396.7
Crushed stone ('000 cu metres)	11,102.3	12,676.6	12,510.1

1990: Crude petroleum 726,000 metric tons; Nickel and cobalt 40,000* metric tons; Salt (unrefined) 200,000 metric tons.

1991: Crude petroleum 748,000 metric tons; Nickel and cobalt 36,500* metric tons; Salt (unrefined) 200,000 metric tons.

1992: Crude petroleum 936,000 metric tons; Nickel and cobalt 33,400* metric tons.

1993: Crude petroleum 975,000 metric tons; Nickel and cobalt 29,800* metric tons.

1994: Crude petroleum 1,016,000 metric tons; Nickel and cobalt 32,000 metric tons.

* Figures refer to the metal content of ores and concentrates.

Source (for 1990–94): UN, *Industrial Commodity Statistics Yearbook.*

Industry

SELECTED PRODUCTS

('000 metric tons, unless otherwise indicated)

	1987	1988	1989
Crude steel	401.5	320.5	314.2
Corrugated steel bars	312.9	359.7	367.1
Grey cement	3,535.3	3,565.8	3,758.8
Mosaics ('000 sq metres)	3,443.8	3,987.9	4,478.1
Motor spirit (Gasoline)	960.3	1,011.8	1,025.7
Kerosene	546.5	558.5	640.1
Sulphuric acid (98%)	372.0	392.7	381.4
Fertilizers	996.3	840.4	898.6
Tyres ('000)	324.7	428.1	315.0
Woven textile fabrics ('000 sq metres)	258,400	260,400	220,300
Cigarettes (million)	15,397.6	16,885.2	16,500
Cigars (million)	278.6	270.2	308.5
Raw sugar*	6,961.5	7,815.6	7,328.8
Leather footwear ('000 pairs)	14,200	13,300	11,000
Electric energy (million kWh)	13,593.5	14,542.3	15,239.8

* Corresponding to calendar year.

1990: Crude steel 270,000 metric tons; Grey cement 3,696,000 metric tons; Motor spirit (gasoline) 945,000 metric tons; Kerosene 575,000 metric tons; Raw sugar 8,050,000 metric tons; Leather footwear 13,400,000 pairs; Electric energy 14,678m. kWh.

1991: Crude steel 270,000 metric tons; Grey cement 2,599,000 metric tons; Motor spirit (gasoline) 700,000 metric tons; Kerosene 510,000 metric tons; Raw sugar 7,233,000 metric tons; Leather footwear 13,000,000 pairs; Electric energy 12,741m. kWh.

1992: Crude steel 200,000 metric tons; Motor spirit (gasoline) 700,000 metric tons (estimate); Kerosene 500,000 metric tons (estimate); Raw sugar 7,104,000 metric tons (FAO figure); Leather footwear 13,400,000 pairs; Electric energy 11,127m. kWh.

1993: Crude steel 100,000 metric tons; Motor spirit (gasoline) 690,000 metric tons (estimate); Kerosene 490,000 metric tons (estimate); Raw sugar 4,200,000 metric tons (FAO figure); Electric energy 11,054m. kWh.

1994: Crude steel 80,000 metric tons; Motor spirit (gasoline) 700,000 metric tons (estimate); Kerosene 500,000 metric tons (estimate); Raw sugar 4,016,000 metric tons; Electric energy 10,982m. kWh.

Source: UN, *Industrial Commodity Statistics Yearbook*.

Finance

CURRENCY AND EXCHANGE RATES

Monetary Units:
100 centavos = 1 Cuban peso.

Sterling and Dollar Equivalents (30 September 1997)
£1 sterling = 1.6154 pesos;
US $1 = 1.0000 pesos;
100 Cuban pesos = £61.90 = $100.00.

Note: The foregoing information relates to non-commercial exchange rates, applicable to tourism. For the purposes of foreign trade, the peso was at par with the US dollar during each of the nine years 1987–95. A 'convertible peso' was introduced in December 1994. The free market rate of exchange in September 1997 was US $1 = 23 Cuban pesos.

STATE BUDGET (million pesos)

	1987	1988*	1989*
Total revenue	11,272	11,386	11,903.5
Total expenditure	11,881	12,532	13,527.5
Productive sector	4,575	4,713	4,975.1
Housing and community services	680	787	859.8
Education and public health	2,725	2,857	2,906.2
Other social, cultural and scientific activities	1,850	2,060	2,300.8
Government administration and judicial bodies	565	561	524.5
Defence and public order	1,242	1,274	1,377.4
Other	244	280	583.7

* Preliminary.

Source: State Committee for Finance, Havana.

INTERNATIONAL RESERVES (million pesos at 31 December)

	1987	1988
Gold and other precious metals	17.5	19.5
Cash and deposits in foreign banks (convertible currency)	36.5	78.0
Sub-total	54.0	97.5
Deposits in foreign banks (in transferable roubles)	142.5	137.0
Total	196.5	234.5

NATIONAL ACCOUNTS

Net Material Product (NMP) by Economic Activity*
(million pesos at current prices)

	1987	1988	1989
Agriculture, forestry and fishing	1,440.8	1,532.9	1,554.6
Industry†	4,498.5	4,782.2	4,656.2
Construction	997.6	1,082.5	1,171.8
Trade, restaurants, etc.	4,205.1	4,209.5	4,294.5
Transport and communications	986.3	1,073.4	1,037.8
Other activities of the material sphere	88.4	83.4	76.0
Total	12,284.3	12,763.9	12,790.9
NMP at constant 1981 prices	13,273.2	13,565.0	13,495.5

* NMP is defined as the total net value of goods and 'productive' services, including turnover taxes, produced by the economy. This excludes economic activities not contributing directly to material production, such as public administration, defence and personal and professional services.

† Principally manufacturing, mining, electricity, gas and water.

External Trade

PRINCIPAL COMMODITIES (million pesos)

Imports	1987	1988	1989
Food and live animals	716.2	730.4	925.3
Crude materials (inedible) except fuels	301.5	281.1	307.2
Mineral fuels, lubricants, etc.	2,621.0	2,589.0	2,629.9
Chemicals and related products	447.2	433.8	530.2
Basic manufactures	821.1	816.3	838.0
Machinery and transport equipment	2,353.7	2,409.5	2,530.7
Miscellaneous manufactured articles	244.7	233.8	276.5
Total (incl. others)	7,583.6	7,579.8	8,124.2

Exports	1987	1988	1989
Sugar and sugar products	4,012.6	4,116.5	3,948.5
Minerals and concentrates	332.2	455.0	497.7
Tobacco and tobacco products	90.5	98.4	83.6
Fish and fish preparations	144.3	149.0	128.8
Other agricultural products	250.9	248.2	211.3
Total (incl. others)	5,402.1	5,518.3	5,392.0

1990 (million pesos): Total imports c.i.f. 6,745; Total exports f.o.b. 4,910.
1991 (million pesos): Total imports c.i.f. 3,690; Total exports f.o.b. 3,550.
1992 (million pesos): Total imports c.i.f. 2,185; Total exports f.o.b. 2,050.
1993 (million pesos): Total imports c.i.f. 1,990; Total exports f.o.b. 1,275.
1994 (million pesos): Total imports c.i.f. 2,055; Total exports f.o.b. 1,385.
1995 (million pesos): Total imports c.i.f. 2,825; Total exports f.o.b. 1,600.

Source (for 1990–95): UN, *Monthly Bulletin of Statistics*.

PRINCIPAL TRADING PARTNERS ('000 pesos)

Imports c.i.f.	1987	1988	1989
Argentina	124,339	127,506	179,198
Bulgaria	183,980	171,797	177,501
China, People's Republic	100,750	175,886	255,483
Czechoslovakia	200,134	219,453	216,283
German Democratic Republic	338,836	340,950	358,688
Italy	45,825	75,850	62,577
Japan	106,503	88,563	49,456
Mexico	72,064	108,022	79,954
Poland	81,481	64,027	57,795
Romania	182,112	179,918	155,970
Spain	165,405	146,139	184,865
USSR	5,445,979	5,364,418	5,522,391
United Kingdom	70,195	59,746	81,769
Total (incl. others)	7,583,600	7,579,800	8,124,200

Exports f.o.b.	1987	1988	1989
Bulgaria	169,073	164,339	176,940
Canada	36,848	38,490	54,835
China, People's Republic	85,468	226,253	216,071
Czechoslovakia	143,998	183,542	136,026
France	57,585	66,854	54,429
German Democratic Republic	281,597	311,430	285,913
Germany, Federal Republic	28,360	73,015	71,395
Hungary	66,710	35,533	55,437
Japan	77,171	109,206	104,074
Poland	43,849	37,569	54,122
Romania	108,953	96,663	121,986
Spain	84,903	81,521	86,031
Switzerland	48,746	12,163	72,615
USSR	3,868,736	3,683,073	3,231,222
United Kingdom	13,365	42,491	113,782
Total (incl. others)	5,402,060	5,518,316	5,392,004

Transport

RAILWAYS

	1987	1988	1989
Passengers ('000)	23,600	25,200	26,400
Passenger-kilometres (million)	2,189.0	2,626.7	2,891.0
Freight carried ('000 metric tons)	15,738.5	15,531.0	15,732.4
Freight ton-kilometres (million)	2,407.6	2,429.1	2,416.2

1996: 2,346.7m. passenger-kilometres; 644.5m. freight ton-kilometres (Source: *Railway Directory*).

ROAD TRAFFIC ('000 motor vehicles in use)

	1986	1987	1988
Passenger cars	217.2	229.5	241.3
Commercial vehicles	184.2	194.9	208.4

Source: UN, *Statistical Yearbook*.

1993 (estimates, motor vehicles in use): 20,000 passenger cars; 33,000 commercial vehicles (Source: IRF, *World Road Statistics*).

SHIPPING

Merchant Fleet (registered at 31 December)

	1994	1995	1996
Number of vessels	361	355	324
Total displacement ('000 grt)	444	410	291

Source: Lloyd's Register of Shipping, *World Fleet Statistics*.

International Sea-borne Freight Traffic ('000 metric tons)

	1988	1989	1990
Goods loaded	8,600	8,517	8,092
Goods unloaded	15,500	15,595	15,440

Source: UN, *Monthly Bulletin of Statistics*.

CIVIL AVIATION (traffic on scheduled services)

	1992	1993	1994
Kilometres flown (million)	12	11	13
Passengers carried ('000)	733	624	731
Passenger-kilometres (million)	1,370	1,321	1,556
Total ton-kilometres (million)	149	138	174

Source: UN, *Statistical Yearbook*.

Tourism

	1992	1993	1994
Tourist arrivals ('000)	455	544	617
Receipts (US $ million)	567	729	850

Source: UN, *Statistical Yearbook*.

1995: Tourist arrivals 741,700; Receipts US $1,100m.

Communications Media

	1992	1993	1994
Radio receivers ('000 in use)	3,732	3,768	3,800
Television receivers ('000 in use)	1,750	1,850	1,870
Telephones ('000 main lines in use)	337	349	350
Telefax stations (number in use)	392	n.a.	n.a.
Mobile cellular telephones (subscribers)	234	500	1,150
Book production (titles)	957	568	932

Sources: UNESCO, *Statistical Yearbook*, and UN, *Statistical Yearbook*.

Education

(1994/95)

	Institu-tions	Teachers	Students		
			Males	Females	Total
Pre-primary	n.a.	6,512	n.a.	n.a.	160,283
Primary	9,425	74,225	517,148	490,621	1,007,769
Secondary:					
General	n.a.	43,633	206,141	239,037	445,178
Teacher training	n.a.	627	785	2,994	3,779
Vocational	n.a.	24,700	117,562	107,633	225,195
Universities and equivalent institutions	n.a.	23,300	n.a.	n.a.	140,800

Source: UNESCO, *Statistical Yearbook*.

Directory

The Constitution

Following the assumption of power by the Castro regime, on 1 January 1959, the Constitution was suspended and a Fundamental Law of the Republic was instituted, with effect from 7 February 1959. In February 1976 Cuba's first socialist Constitution came into force after being submitted to the first Congress of the Communist Party of Cuba, in December 1975, and to popular referendum, in February 1976; it was amended in July 1992. The main provisions of the Constitution, as amended, are summarized below:

POLITICAL, SOCIAL AND ECONOMIC PRINCIPLES

The Republic of Cuba is a socialist, independent, and sovereign state, organized with all and for the sake of all as a unitary and democratic republic for the enjoyment of political freedom, social justice, collective and individual well-being and human solidarity. Sovereignty rests with the people, from whom originates the power of the State. The Communist Party of Cuba is the leading force of society and the State. The State recognizes, respects and guarantees freedom of religion. Religious institutions are separate from the State. The socialist State carries out the will of the working people and guarantees work, medical care, education, food, clothing and housing. The Republic of Cuba bases its relations with other socialist countries on socialist internationalism, friendship, co-operation and mutual assistance. It reaffirms its willingness to integrate with and co-operate with the countries of Latin America and the Caribbean.

The State organizes and directs the economic life of the nation in accordance with a central social and economic development plan. The State directs and controls foreign trade. The State recognizes the right of small farmers to own their lands and other means of production and to sell that land. The State guarantees the right of citizens to ownership of personal property in the form of earnings, savings, place of residence and other possessions and objects which serve to satisfy their material and cultural needs. The State also guarantees the right of inheritance.

Cuban citizenship is acquired by birth or through naturalization.

The State protects the family, motherhood and matrimony.

The State directs and encourages all aspects of education, culture and science.

All citizens have equal rights and are subject to equal duties.

The State guarantees the right to medical care, education, freedom of speech and press, assembly, demonstration, association and privacy. In the socialist society work is the right and duty, and a source of pride for every citizen.

GOVERNMENT

National Assembly of People's Power

The National Assembly of People's Power (Asamblea Nacional del Poder Popular) is the supreme organ of the State and is the only organ with constituent and legislative authority. It is composed of deputies, over the age of 18, elected by free, direct and secret ballot, for a period of five years. All Cuban citizens aged 16 years or more, except those who are mentally incapacitated or who have committed a crime, are eligible to vote. The National Assembly of People's Power holds two ordinary sessions a year and a special session when requested by one-third of the deputies or by the Council of State. More than half the total number of deputies must be present for a session to be held.

All decisions made by the Assembly, except those relating to constitutional reforms, are adopted by a simple majority of votes. The deputies may be recalled by their electors at any time.

The National Assembly of People's Power has the following functions:

to reform the Constitution;

to approve, modify and annul laws;

to supervise all organs of the State and government;

to decide on the constitutionality of laws and decrees;

to revoke decree-laws issued by the Council of State and the Council of Ministers;

to discuss and approve economic and social development plans, the state budget, monetary and credit systems;

to approve the general outlines of foreign and domestic policy, to ratify and annul international treaties, to declare war and approve peace treaties;

to approve the administrative division of the country;

to elect the President, First Vice-President, the Vice-Presidents and other members of the Council of State;

to elect the President, Vice-President and Secretary of the National Assembly;

to appoint the members of the Council of Ministers on the proposal of the President of the Council of State;

to elect the President, Vice-President and other judges of the People's Supreme Court;

to elect the Attorney-General and the Deputy Attorney-Generals;

to grant amnesty;

to call referendums.

The President of the National Assembly presides over sessions of the Assembly, calls ordinary sessions, proposes the draft agenda, signs the Official Gazette, organizes the work of the commissions appointed by the Assembly and attends the meetings of the Council of State.

Council of State

The Council of State is elected from the members of the National Assembly and represents that Assembly in the period between sessions. It comprises a President, one First Vice-President, five Vice-Presidents, one Secretary and 23 other members. Its mandate ends when a new Assembly meets. All decisions are adopted by a simple majority of votes. It is accountable for its actions to the National Assembly.

The Council of State has the following functions:

to call special sessions of the National Assembly;

to set the date for the election of a new Assembly;

to issue decree-laws in the period between the sessions of the National Assembly;

to decree mobilization in the event of war and to approve peace treaties when the Assembly is in recess;

to issue instructions to the courts and the Office of the Attorney General of the Republic;

to appoint and remove ambassadors of Cuba abroad on the proposal of its President, to grant or refuse recognition to diplomatic representatives of other countries to Cuba;

to suspend those provisions of the Council of Ministers that are not in accordance with the Constitution;

to revoke the resolutions of the Executive Committee of the local organs of People's Power which are contrary to the Constitution or laws and decrees formulated by other higher organs.

The President of the Council of State is Head of State and Head of Government and for all purposes the Council of State is the highest representative of the Cuban state.

Head of State

The President of the Council of State is the Head of State and the Head of Government and has the following powers:

to represent the State and Government and conduct general policy;

to convene and preside over the sessions of the Council of State and the Council of Ministers;

to supervise the ministries and other administrative bodies;

to propose the members of the Council of Ministers to the National Assembly of People's Power;

to receive the credentials of the heads of foreign diplomatic missions;

to sign the decree-laws and other resolutions of the Council of State;

to exercise the Supreme Command of all armed institutions and determine their general organization;

to preside over the National Defence Council;

to declare a state of emergency in the cases outlined in the Constitution.

In the case of absence, illness or death of the President of the Council of State, the First Vice-President assumes the President's duties.

The Council of Ministers

The Council of Ministers is the highest-ranking executive and administrative organ. It is composed of the Head of State and Government, as its President, the First Vice-President, the Vice-Presidents, the Ministers, the Secretary and other members determined by law. Its Executive Committee is composed of the President, the First Vice-President, the Vice-Presidents and other members of the Council of Ministers determined by the President.

The Council of Ministers has the following powers:

to conduct political, economic, cultural, scientific, social and defence policy as outlined by the National Assembly;

to approve international treaties;

to propose projects for the general development plan and, if they are approved by the National Assembly, to supervise their implementation;

to conduct foreign policy and trade;

to draw up bills and submit them to the National Assembly;

to draw up the draft state budget;

to conduct general administration, implement laws, issue decrees and supervise defence and national security.

The Council of Ministers is accountable to the National Assembly of People's Power.

LOCAL GOVERNMENT

The country is divided into 14 provinces and 169 municipalities. The provinces are: Pinar del Río, Habana, Ciudad de la Habana, Matanzas, Villa Clara, Cienfuegos, Sancti Spíritus, Ciego de Avila, Camagüey, Las Tunas, Holguín, Granma, Santiago de Cuba and Guantánamo.

Voting for delegates to the municipal assemblies is direct, secret and voluntary. All citizens over 16 years of age are eligible to vote. The number of delegates to each assembly is proportionate to the number of people living in that area. A delegate must obtain more than half the number of votes cast in the constituency in order to be elected. The Municipal and Provincial Assemblies of People's Power are elected by free, direct and secret ballot. Nominations for Municipal and Provincial Executive Committees of People's Power are submitted to the relevant assembly by a commission presided over by a representative of the Communist Party's leading organ and consisting of representatives of youth, workers', farmers', revolutionary and women's organizations. The President and Secretary of each of the regional and the provincial assemblies are the only full-time members, the other delegates carrying out their functions in addition to their normal employment.

The regular and extraordinary sessions of the local Assemblies of People's Power are public. More than half the total number of members must be present in order for agreements made to be valid. Agreements are adopted by simple majority.

JUDICIARY

Judicial power is exercised by the People's Supreme Court and all other competent tribunals and courts. The People's Supreme Court is the supreme judicial authority and is accountable only to the National Assembly of People's Power. It can propose laws and issue regulations through its Council of Government. Judges are independent but the courts must inform the electorate of their activities at least once a year. Every accused person has the right to a defence and can be tried only by a tribunal.

The Office of the Attorney-General is subordinate only to the National Assembly and the Council of State and is responsible for ensuring that the law is properly obeyed.

The Constitution may be totally or partially modified only by a two-thirds majority vote in the National Assembly of People's Power. If the modification is total, or if it concerns the composition and powers of the National Assembly of People's Power or the Council of State, or the rights and duties contained in the Constitution, it also requires a positive vote by referendum.

The Government

(December 1997)

Head of State: Dr FIDEL CASTRO RUZ (took office 2 December 1976; re-elected December 1981, December 1986 and March 1993).

COUNCIL OF STATE

President: Dr FIDEL CASTRO RUZ.

First Vice-President: Gen. RAÚL CASTRO RUZ.

Vice-Presidents:
JUAN ALMEIDA BOSQUE.
Gen. ABELARDO COLOMÉ IBARRA.
CARLOS LAGE DÁVILA.
JUAN ESTEBAN LAZO HERNÁNDEZ.
JOSÉ RAMÓN MACHADO VENTURA.

Secretary: Dr JOSÉ M. MIYAR BARRUECO.

Members*:
JOSÉ RAMÓN BALAGUER CABRERA.
VILMA ESPÍN GUILLOIS DE CASTRO.
Dr ARMANDO HART DÁVALOS.
ORLANDO LUGO FONTE.
ROBERTO ROBAINA GONZÁLEZ.
LUIS ABREU MEJÍAS.
HIPÓLITO ABRIL.
ENITH ALERM PRIETO.
SIXTO BATISTA SANTANA.
CONCEPCIÓN CAMPA.
OSMANY CIENFUEGOS GORRIARÁN.
PEDRO MIRET PRIETO.
CARLOS DOTRES.
JUAN ESCALONA REGUERA.
ESLINDA OROZCO.
FELIPE PÉREZ ROQUE.
MARCOS PORTAL.
ABEL PRIETO JIMÉNEZ.
Gen. ULISES ROSALES DEL TORO.
PEDRO ROSS.
Dra ROSA ELENA SIMEÓN NEGRÍN.
NELSON TORRES.

* One post remained vacant, owing to the death, in 1996, of Gen. SENÉN CASAS REGUEIRO.

COUNCIL OF MINISTERS

President: Dr FIDEL CASTRO RUZ.

First Vice-President: Gen. RAÚL CASTRO RUZ.

Vice-Presidents:
CARLOS RAFAEL RODRÍGUEZ RODRÍGUEZ.
JOSÉ RAMÓN FERNÁNDEZ ALVAREZ.
ADOLFO DÍAZ SUÁREZ.
OSMANY CIENFUEGOS GORRIARÁN.
PEDRO MIRET PRIETO.
JOSÉ LUIS RODRÍGUEZ GARCÍA.

Secretary: CARLOS LAGE DÁVILA.

Minister of Agriculture: ALFREDO JORDÁN MORALES.

Minister of Foreign Trade: RICARDO CABRISAS RUIZ.

Minister of Internal Trade: BÁRBARA CASTILLO CUESTA.

Minister of Communications: Gen. SILVANO COLÁS SÁNCHEZ.

Minister of Construction: JUAN MARIO JUNCO DEL PINO.

Minister of Culture: ABEL ENRIQUE PRIETO JIMÉNEZ.

Minister of Economy and Planning: JOSÉ LUIS RODRÍGUEZ GARCÍA.

Minister of Education: LUIS IGNACIO GÓMEZ GUTIÉRREZ.

Minister of Higher Education: FERNANDO VECINO ALEGRET.

Minister of the Revolutionary Armed Forces: Gen. RAÚL CASTRO RUZ.

Minister of Finance and Prices: MANUEL MILLARES RODRÍGUEZ.

Minister of the Food Industry: ALEJANDRO ROCA IGLESIAS.

Minister of Foreign Investment and Economic Co-operation: IBRAHÍM FERRADAZ GARCÍA.

Minister of Sugar: Gen. ULISES ROSALES DEL TORO.

Minister of the Construction Materials Industry: JOSÉ M. CAÑETE ALVAREZ.

Minister of Light Industry: JESÚS PÉREZ OTHÓN.

Minister of the Fishing Industry: ORLANDO FELIPE RODRÍGUEZ ROMAY.

Minister of the Iron and Steel, Metallurgical and Electronic Industries: ROBERTO IGNACIO GONZÁLEZ PLANAS.

Minister of Basic Industries: MARCOS J. PORTAL LEÓN.

Minister of the Interior: Gen. ABELARDO COLOMÉ IBARRA.

Minister of Justice: ROBERTO DÍAZ SOTOLONGO.

Minister of Foreign Affairs: ROBERTO ROBAINA GONZÁLEZ.

Minister of Labour and Social Security: SALVADOR VALDÉS MESA.

Minister of Public Health: CARLOS DOTRES MARTÍNEZ.

Minister of Science, Technology and the Environment: Dra ROSA ELENA SIMEÓN NEGRÍN.

Minister of Transport: ALVARO PÉREZ MORALES.

Minister of Tourism: OSMANY CIENFUEGOS GORRIARÁN.

Minister, President of the State Committee for Technical and Material Supplies: SONIA RODRÍGUEZ CARDONA.

Minister, President of the State Committee for Statistics: FIDEL EMILIO VASCOS GONZÁLEZ.

Minister, President of the State Committee for Standardization: RAMÓN DARIAS RODÉS.

Minister, President of the Banco Central de Cuba: FRANCISCO SOBERÓN VALDEZ.

Minister without Portfolio: WILFREDO LÓPEZ RODRÍGUEZ.

MINISTRIES

Ministry of Agriculture: Avda Independencia, entre Conill y Sta Ana, Havana; tel. (7) 84-5770; telex 511154; fax (7) 33-5086.

Ministry of Basic Industries: Avda Salvador Allende 666, Havana; tel. (7) 70-7711; telex 511183.

Ministry of Communications: Plaza de la Revolución 'José Martí', CP 10600, Havana; tel. (7) 81-7654; telex 511490.

Ministry of Construction: Avda Carlos M. de Céspedes y Calle 35, Havana; tel. (7) 81-8385; telex 511275; fax (7) 33-5585; e-mail dirinter@ceniai.inf.cu.

Ministry of the Construction Materials Industry: Calle 17, esq. 0, Vedado, Havana; tel. (7) 32-2541; telex 511517; fax (7) 33-3176.

Ministry of Culture: Calle 2, No 258, entre 11 y 13, Vedado, Havana; tel. (7) 3-9945; telex 511400; fax (7) 33-3013.

Ministry of Economy and Planning: 20 de Mayo y Ayestarán, Plaza de la Revolución, Havana; tel. (7) 81-6444; telex 511158.

Ministry of Education: Obispo 160, Havana; tel. (7) 61-4888; telex 511188.

Ministry of Finance and Prices: Obispo 211, esq. Cuba, Havana; tel. (7) 60-4111; telex 511101; fax (7) 62-0252.

Ministry of the Fishing Industry: Avda 5 y 248 Jaimenitas, Santa Fe, Havana; tel. (7) 29-7034; telex 51-1309; fax (7) 24-9168; e-mail cubafish@ceniai.inf.cu.

Ministry of the Food Industry: Calle 41, No 4455, Playa, Havana; tel. (7) 2-6801; telex 511163.

Ministry of Foreign Affairs: Calzada 360, Vedado, Havana; tel. (7) 32-4074; telex 511122.

Ministry of Foreign Investment and Economic Co-operation: Calle 1, No 201, Vedado, Havana; tel. (7) 3-6661; telex 511297.

Ministry of Foreign Trade: Infanta 16, Vedado, Havana; tel. (7) 78-6230; telex 511174; fax (7) 78-6234.

Ministry of Higher Education: Calle 23, No 565, esq. a F, Vedado, Havana; tel. (7) 3-6655; telex 511253; fax (7) 33-3090; e-mail dri@reduniv.edu.cu.

Ministry of the Interior: Plaza de la Revolución, Havana.

Ministry of Internal Trade: Calle Habana 258, Havana; tel. (7) 62-5790; telex 511171.

Ministry of the Iron and Steel, Metallurgical and Electronic Industries: Avda Rancho Boyeros y Calle 100, Havana; tel. (7) 20-4861; telex 511179.

Ministry of Justice: Calle 0, No 216, entre 23 y Humboldt, Vedado, CP 10400, Havana 4; tel. (7) 32-6319; telex 511331.

Ministry of Labour and Social Security: Calle 23, esq. Calle P, Vedado, Havana; tel. (7) 70-4571; telex 511225; fax (7) 33-5816.

Ministry of Light Industry: Empedrado 302, Havana; tel. (7) 62-4041; telex 511141.

Ministry of Public Health: Calle 23, No 301, Vedado, Havana; tel. (7) 32-2561; telex 511149.

Ministry of the Revolutionary Armed Forces: Plaza de la Revolución, Havana.

Ministry of Science, Technology and the Environment: Havana.

Ministry of Sugar: Calle 23, No 171, Vedado, Havana; tel. (7) 30-5061; telex 511664.

Ministry of Tourism: Havana.

Ministry of Transport: Avda Independencia y Tulipán, Havana; tel. (7) 81-2076; telex 511181.

Legislature

ASAMBLEA NACIONAL DEL PODER POPULAR

The National Assembly of People's Power was constituted on 2 December 1976. In July 1992 the National Assembly adopted a constitutional amendment providing for legislative elections by direct vote. Only candidates nominated by the PCC were permitted to contest the elections. At elections to the National Assembly conducted on 11 January 1998 all 601 candidates were elected. Of the 7.8m. registered voters, 98.35% participated in the elections. Only 5% of votes cast were blank or spoilt.

President: RICARDO ALARCÓN DE QUESADA.

Vice-President: JAIME CROMBET HERNÁNDEZ MAURELL.

Secretary: Dr ERNESTO SUÁREZ MÉNDEZ.

Political Organizations

Partido Comunista de Cuba (PCC) (Communist Party of Cuba): Havana; f. 1961 as the Organizaciones Revolucionarias Integradas (ORI) from a fusion of the Partido Socialista Popular (Communist), Fidel Castro's Movimiento 26 de Julio and the Directorio Revolucionario 13 de Marzo; became the Partido Unido de la Revolución Socialista Cubana (PURSC) in 1962; renamed as the Partido Comunista de Cuba in 1965; 150-member Central Committee, Political Bureau (24 mems in 1997), and five Commissions; 706,132 mems (1994).

Political Bureau: Dr FIDEL CASTRO RUZ, Gen. RAÚL CASTRO RUZ, JUAN ALMEIDA BOSQUE, JOSÉ RAMÓN MACHADO VENTURA, ESTEBAN LAZO HERNÁNDEZ, Gen. ABELARDO COLOMÉ IBARRA, PEDRO ROSS LEAL, CARLOS LAGE DÁVILA, ROBERTO ROBAÍNA GONZÁLEZ, ALFREDO JORDÁN MORALES, Gen. ULISES ROSALES DEL TORO, CONCEPCIÓN CAMPA HUERGO, YADIRA GARCÍA VERA, ABEL ENRIQUE PRIETO JIMÉNEZ, Gen. JULIO CASAS REGUEIRO, Gen. LEOPOLDO CINTRA FRÍAS, RICARDO ALARCÓN DE QUESADA, JOSÉ RAMÓN BALAGUER CABRERA, MISAEL ENAMORADO DAGER, Gen. RAMÓN ESPINOSA MARTÍN, MARCOS J. PORTAL LEÓN, JUAN CARLOS ROBINSON AGRAMONTE, PEDRO SÁEZ MONTEJO, JORGE LUIS SIERRA CRUZ.

There are a number of dissident groups operating in Cuba. These include:

Concertación Democrática Cubana—CDC: f. 1991; alliance of eight dissident organizations campaigning for political pluralism and economic reform.

Partido pro-Derechos Humanos: f. 1988 to defend human rights in Cuba; Pres. HIRAM ABI COBAS; Sec.-Gen. TANIA DÍAZ.

Diplomatic Representation

EMBASSIES IN CUBA

Afghanistan: Calle 24, No 106, entre 1 y 3, Miramar, Havana; tel. (7) 22-1145; Ambassador: NUR AHMAD NUR.

Albania: Calle 13, No 851, Vedado, Havana; tel. (7) 30-2788; Ambassador: CLIRIM CEPANI.

Algeria: Avda 5, No 2802, esq. 28, Miramar, Havana; tel. (7) 2-6538; Ambassador: ABDELHAMID LATRECHE.

Angola: Avda 5, No 1012, entre 10 y 12, Miramar, Havana; tel. (7) 33-2474; telex 511105; fax (7) 33-2117; Ambassador: ANTÓNIO BURITY DA SILVA NETO.

Argentina: Calle 36, No 511, entre 5 y 7, Miramar, Havana; tel. (7) 22-5540; telex 511138; Ambassador: JUAN CARLOS OLIMA.

Austria: Calle 4, No 101, entre 1 y 3, Miramar, Havana; tel. (7) 33-2825; telex 511618; fax (7) 33-1235; Ambassador: Dr YURI STANDENAT.

Belgium: Avda 5, No 7408, Miramar, Havana; tel. (7) 29-6440; telex 511482; Ambassador: Count LOUIS CORNET D'ELZIUS DU CHENOY.

Benin: Calle 20, No 119, entre 1 y 3, Miramar, Havana; tel. (7) 29-6142; Ambassador: JOSEPH VICTOR MENARD.

Bolivia: Calle 24, No 108, entre 1 y 3, Miramar, Havana; tel. (7) 2-4426; Ambassador: OSCAR PEÑA FRANCO.

Brazil: Calle 16, No 503, entre 5 y 7, Miramar, Havana; tel. (7) 33-2917; fax (7) 33-2328; Ambassador: JOSÉ NOGUEIRA FILHO.

Bulgaria: Calle B, No 252, entre 11 y 13, Vedado, Havana; tel. (7) 33-3125; fax (7) 33-3297; Chargé d'affaires a.i.: KIRIL KOTZALIEV.

Burkina Faso: Calle 7, No 8401, entre 84 y 84A, Miramar; tel. (7) 24-2895; telex 2423; fax (7) 24-1942; Ambassador: SALIF NEBIE.

Cambodia: Avda 6, No 7001, esq. 70, Miramar, Havana; tel. (7) 33-6151; fax (7) 33-6400; Ambassador: ROS KONG.

Canada: Calle 30, No 518, esq. a 7, Miramar, Havana; tel. (7) 33-2516; telex 511586; fax (7) 33-2044; Ambassador: MARK A. ENTWISTLE.

Cape Verde: Calle 98, No 508, entre 5 y 5B, Miramar, Havana; tel. (7) 33-2979; fax (7) 33-1072; Chargé d'affaires a.i.: ARNALDO DELGADO.

Chile: Avda 33, No 1423, entre 16 y 18, Mitamar, Havana.

China, People's Republic: Calle 13, No 551, Vedado, Havana; tel. (7) 32-5205; Ambassador: LIU PEIGEN.

Colombia: Calle 6, No 106, entre 1 y 3, Miramar, Havana; tel. (7) 33-1246; Ambassador: ALBERTO VILLAMIZAR CARDENAS.

Congo, Democratic Republic: Calle 36, No 716, entre 7 y 9, Miramar, Havana; tel. (7) 29-1580; Ambassador: SIMBA NDOMBE.

Congo, Republic: Avda 5, No 1003, Miramar, Havana; tel. (7) 2-6513; Ambassador: MARCEL TOUANGA.

Czech Republic: Avda Kohly 259, entre 41 y 43, Nuevo Vedado, Havana; tel. (7) 33-3201; telex 512325; fax (7) 33-3596; Chargé d'affaires a.i.: PETR MIKYSKA.

Denmark: Paseo de Martí 20, Apto 4-C, Havana; tel. (7) 33-8128; telex 511100; fax (7) 33-8127; Consul: INGER ARREDONDO.

Ecuador: Avda 5-A, No 4407, Miramar, Havana; tel. (7) 29-6839; telex 511770; Ambassador: GUSTAVO JARRÍN AMPUDIA.

Egypt: Avda 5, No 1801, Miramar, Havana; tel. (7) 22-2541; telex 511551; Ambassador: ESMAT ABDEL HALIM MOHAMMAD.

Ethiopia: Calle 6, No 318, Miramar, Havana; tel. (7) 22-1260; Ambassador: ABEBE BELAYNEH.

Finland: Avda 5, No 9202, Miramar, Playa, Apdo. 3304, Havana; tel. (7) 33-2698; telex 511485; Ambassador: HEIKKI PUURUNEN.

France: Calle 14, No 312, entre 3 y 5, Miramar, Havana; tel. (7) 33-2132; telex 511195; fax (7) 33-1439; Ambassador: YVON ROE D'ALBERT.

Germany: Calle 28, No 313, entre 3 y 5, Miramar, Havana; tel. (7) 33-2539; telex 511433; fax (7) 33-1586; Ambassador: Dr GEORG TREFFTZ.

Ghana: Avda 5, No 1808, esq. Calle 20, Miramar, Havana; tel. (7) 24-2153; Ambassador: Dr KWAKU DANSO-BOAFO.

Greece: Avda 5, No 7802, esq. 78, Miramar, Havana; tel. (7) 33-2995; telex 51-2377; Ambassador: MARINOS RAFTOPOULOS.

Guinea: Calle 20, No 504, Miramar, Havana; tel. (7) 2-6428; Ambassador: LAMINE SOUGOULÉ.

Guinea-Bissau: Calle 14, No 313, entre 3 y 5, Miramar, Havana; tel. (7) 33-2689; fax (7) 33-2794; Ambassador: CONSTANTINO LOPES DA COSTA.

Guyana: Calle 18, No 506, Miramar, Havana; tel. (7) 24-2094; telex 511498; fax (7) 24-2867; Chargé d'affaires: RITA R. RAMLALL.

Holy See: Calle 12, No 514, Miramar, Havana (Apostolic Nunciature); tel. (7) 33-2700; fax (7) 33-2257; Apostolic Nuncio: Most Rev. BENIAMINO STELLA, Titular Archbishop of Midila.

Hungary: Avda de los Presidentes 458, entre 19 y 21, Vedado, Havana; tel. (7) 33-3365; fax (7) 33-3286; e-mail embhuncu@ceniai.-inf.cu; Ambassador: Dr JÓZSEF NÉMETH.

India: Calle 21, No 202, esq. a K, Vedado, Havana; tel. (7) 33-3777; telex 511414; fax (7) 33-3287; Ambassador: RAJENDRA SINGH RATHORE.

Indonesia: Avda 5, No 1607, esq. a 18, Miramar, Havana; tel. (7) 33-9618; fax (7) 80-5517.

Iran: Avda 5, No 3002, esq. a 30, Miramar, Havana; tel. (7) 29-4575; telex 512186; Ambassador: SEYED MAHMOUD SADRI TABALE ZAVAREH.

Iraq: Avda 5, No 8201, Miramar, Havana; tel. (7) 2-6461; telex 511413; Ambassador: WALEED A. ABBASS.

Italy: Paseo No 606, entre 25 y 27, Vedado, Havana; tel. (7) 33-3334; telex 511352; fax (7) 33-3416; Ambassador: GIOVANNI FERRERO.

Jamaica: Havana; Ambassador: CORDELL WILSON.

Japan: Calle 62, esq. 15, Vedado, Havana; tel. (7) 32-5554; telex 511260; Ambassador: RYO KAWADE.

Korea, Democratic People's Republic: Calle 17, No 752, Vedado, Havana; tel. (7) 30-5132; telex 511553; Ambassador: KIM GIL HWAN.

Laos: Avda 5, No 2808, esq. 30, Miramar, Havana; tel. (7) 2-6198; Ambassador: PONMEK DELALOY.

Lebanon: Calle 174, No 1707, entre 17 y 17A, Sihoney, Havana; tel. (7) 21-8974; Chargé d'affaires a.i.: ZOUHAIR KAZZAZ.

Libya: Calle 8, No 309, Miramar, Havana; tel. (7) 2-4892; telex 511570; Ambassador: ALI MUHAMMAD AL-EJILI.

Mexico: Calle 12, No 518, Miramar, Playa, Havana; tel. (7) 33-2383; telex 511298; fax (7) 33-2717; Ambassador: CLAUDE HELLER.

Mongolia: Calle 66, No 505, Miramar, Havana; tel. (7) 33-2763; fax (7) 33-0639; Ambassador: PUNTSAG DARIIN.

Mozambique: Avda 7, No 2203, entre 22 y 24, Miramar, Havana; tel. (7) 26445; Ambassador: JULIO BRAGA.

Netherlands: Calle 8, No 307, Miramar, Havana; tel. (7) 33-2511; telex 511279; Ambassador: GERHARD JOHAN VAN HATTUM.

Nicaragua: Calle 20, No 709, entre 7 y 9, Miramar, Havana; tel. (7) 33-1025; fax (7) 33-6323; Chargé d'affaires a.i.: AURA ESTELA CANO ARAGÓN.

Nigeria: Avda 5, No 1401, Apdo 6232, Miramar, Havana; tel. (7) 29-1091; telex 1589; Ambassador: SOLOMON KIKIOWO OMOJOKUN.

Panama: Calle 26, No 109, entre 1 y 3, Miramar, Havana; tel. (7) 33-1673; fax (7) 33-1674; Ambassador: RAFAEL MORENO SAAVEDRA.

Peru: Calle 36, No 109, entre 3 y 5, Miramar, Havana; tel. (7) 29-4477; telex 511289; Ambassador: JOSÉ TORRES MURGA.

Philippines: Avda 5, No 2207, esq. 24, Miramar, Havana; tel. (7) 24-1372; fax (7) 33-2915; Ambassador: RONALD B. ALLAREY.

Poland: Avda 5, No 4407, esq. a 46, Miramar, Havana; tel. and fax (7) 33-1323; telex 511037; Chargé d'affaires a.i.: SLAWOMIR KLIMKIEWICZ.

Portugal: Avda 5, No 6604, entre 66 y 68, Miramar, Havana; tel. (7) 24-2871; telex 511411; fax (7) 24-2593; Ambassador: Dr ANTÓNIO CARVALHO DE FARIA.

Romania: Calle 21, No 307, Vedado, Havana; tel. (7) 32-4303; Ambassador: ION SIMINICEANU.

Russia: Avda 5, No 6402, entre 62 y 66, Miramar, Havana; tel. (7) 22-6444; Ambassador: YURII VLADIMIROVICH PETROV.

Slovakia: Calle 66, No 521, entre 5 y 7, Miramar, Havana; tel. (7) 33-1884; fax (7) 33-1883; Chargé d'affaires a.i.: BETER SULOVSKY.

Spain: Cárcel No 51, esq. Zulueta, Havana; tel. (7) 62-6061; telex 511367; Chargé d'affaires a.i.: FRANCISCO JAVIER SANDOMINGO NÚÑEZ.

Sri Lanka: Calle 32, No 307, entre 3 y 5, Miramar, Havana; tel. (7) 24-2562; telex 512310; fax (7) 24-2183; Chargé d'affaires: DON BERNARD KALIDASA WITHANAGE.

Sweden: Avda 31, No 1411, entre 14 y 18, Miramar, Havana; tel. (7) 33-2831; telex 511208; Ambassador: KARIN OLDFELT HJERTONSSON.

Switzerland: Calzada, Calle L y M, Vedado, Havana; tel. (7) 2-4611; telex 511194; Ambassador: MARCUS KAISER.

Syria: Avda 5, No 7402, Miramar, Havana; tel. (7) 22-5266; telex 511394; Chargé d'affaires: R. F. JAJHAI.

Turkey: Avda 1-A, No 4215, entre 42 y 44, Miramar, Havana; tel. (7) 22-3933; telex 511724; Ambassador: MEHMET GÜNEY.

United Kingdom: Calle 34, No 708, entre 7 y 17, Miramar, Havana; tel. (7) 24-1771; fax (7) 24-8104; Ambassador: PHILIP A. MCLEAN.

USA: (Relations broken off in 1961); Interests Section: Calzada, entre L y M, Vedado, Havana; tel. (7) 32-0551; Counsellor and Principal Officer: ALAN H. FLANIGAN.

Uruguay: Calle 14, No 506, entre 5 y 7, Miramar, Havana; tel. (7) 33-2311; fax (7) 33-2246; Ambassador: CARLOS ALEJANDRO BARROS.

Venezuela: Calle 36-A, No 704, entre 7 y 42, Miramar, Havana; tel. (7) 29-4631; telex 511384; Ambassador: M. C. LÓPEZ.

Viet Nam: Avda 5, No 1802, Miramar, Havana; tel. (7) 2-5214; Ambassador: DO VAN TAI.

Yemen: Avda 7, No 2207, esq. 24, Miramar, Havana; tel. (7) 22-2594; telex 511488; Ambassador: MUHAMMAD ABDULRAHMAN HUSSEIN.

Yugoslavia: Calle 42, No 115, Miramar, Havana; tel. (7) 2-4982; Ambassador: MIHAJLO POPOVIĆ.

Zimbabwe: Avda 3, No 1001, esq. a 10, Miramar, Havana; tel. (7) 24-2857; Ambassador: AGRIPPAH MUJERE MUTAMBARA.

Judicial System

The judicial system comprises the People's Supreme Court, the People's Provincial Courts and the People's Municipal Courts. The People's Supreme Court exercises the highest judicial authority.

PEOPLE'S SUPREME COURT

The People's Supreme Court comprises the Plenum, the five Courts of Justice in joint session and the Council of Government. When the Courts of Justice are in joint session they comprise all the professional and lay judges, the Attorney-General and the Minister of Justice. The Council of Government comprises the President and Vice-President of the People's Supreme Court, the Presidents of each Court of Justice and the Attorney-General of the Republic. The Minister of Justice may participate in its meetings.

President: Dr José Raúl Amaro Salup.

Vice-President: Dr Zenaida Osorio Vizcaino.

Criminal Court:

President: Dr Graciela Prieto Martín.

Eight professional judges and 64 lay judges.

Civil and Administrative Court:

President: Andrés Bolaños Gasso.

Two professional judges and 32 lay judges.

Labour Court:

President: Dr Antonio R. Martín Sánchez.

Three professional judges and 32 lay judges.

Court for State Security:

President: Dr Everildo Domínguez Domínguez.

Three professional judges and 32 lay judges.

Military Court:

President: Col Juan Marino Fuentes Calzado.

Three professional judges and 32 lay judges.

Attorney-General: Juan Escalona Reguera.

Religion

There is no established Church, and all religions are permitted, though Roman Catholicism predominates.

CHRISTIANITY

Consejo Ecuménico de Cuba (Ecumenical Council of Cuba): Calle 14, No 304, entre 3 y 5, Miramar, Playa, Havana; tel. (7) 33-1792; fax (7) 33-178820; f. 1941; 11 mem. churches; Pres. Rev. Orestes González; Exec. Sec. Rev. José López.

The Roman Catholic Church

Cuba comprises two archdioceses and eight dioceses. At 31 December 1995 there were an estimated 4,701,000 adherents in the country, representing about 40% of the total population.

Bishops' Conference: Calle 26, No 314, entre 3 y 5, Miramar, Apdo 594, Havana; tel. (7) 33-2001; telex 512381; fax (7) 33-2168; f. 1983; Pres. Cardinal Jaime Lucas Ortega y Alamino, Archbishop of San Cristóbal de la Habana.

Archbishop of San Cristóbal de la Habana: Cardinal Jaime Lucas Ortega y Alamino, Calle Habana 152, esq. a Chacón, Apdo 594, Havana; tel. (7) 62-4000; fax (7) 33-8109.

Archbishop of Santiago de Cuba: Pedro Claro Meurice Estíu, Sánchez Hechevarría 607, Apdo 26, Santiago de Cuba; tel. (7) 226-5480; telex 61374.

The Anglican Communion

Anglicans are adherents of the Iglesia Episcopal de Cuba (Episcopal Church of Cuba).

Bishop of Cuba: Rt Rev. Jorge Perera Hurtado, Calle 6, No 273, Vedado, Havana 4.

Protestant Churches

Convención Bautista de Cuba Oriental (Baptist Convention of Eastern Cuba): San Jerónimo, No 467, entre Calvario y Carnicería, Santiago; tel. 2-0173; f. 1905; Pres. Rev. Dr Roy Acosta; Sec. Rafael Mustelier.

Iglesia Metodista en Cuba (Methodist Church in Cuba): Calle K, No 502, 25 y 27, Vedado, Apdo 10400, Havana; tel. (7) 32-2991; fax (7) 33-3135; autonomous since 1968; 6,000 mems; Bishop Francisco Gustavo Cruz Díaz.

Iglesia Presbiteriana-Reformada en Cuba (Presbyterian-Reformed Church in Cuba): Apdo 154, Matanzas; autonomous since 1967; 8,000 mems; Gen. Sec. Rev. Dr Sergio Arce.

Other denominations active in Cuba include the Apostolic Church of Jesus Christ, the Bethel Evangelical Church, the Christian Pentecostal Church, the Church of God, the Church of the Nazarene, the Free Baptist Convention, the Holy Pentecost Church, the Pentecostal Congregational Church and the Salvation Army.

The Press

DAILY

In October 1990 President Castro announced that, in accordance with other wide-ranging economic austerity measures, only one newspaper, *Granma*, would henceforth be published as a nationwide daily. The other national dailies were to become weeklies or were to cease publication.

Granma: Avda Gen. Suárez y Territorial, Plaza de la Revolución, Apdo 6187, Havana; tel. (7) 70-3521; telex 511221; fax (7) 33-5176; f. 1965 to replace *Hoy* and *Revolución*; official Communist Party organ; Dir Frank Aguero Gómez; circ. 400,000.

PERIODICALS

Adelante: Avda A, Rpto Jayamá, Camagüey; f. 1959; morning; Dir Evaristo Sardiñas Vera; circ. 42,000.

Ahora: Salida a San Germán y Circunvalación, Holguín; f. 1962; Dir Radobaldo Martínez Pérez; circ. 50,000.

ANAP: Línea 206, entre H e I, Vedado, Havana; f. 1961; monthly; information for small farmers; Dir Leonel Váldez Alonso; circ. 30,000.

Bastión: Territorial esq. a Gen. Suárez, Plaza de la Revolución, Havana; tel. (7) 79-3361; telex 512373; organ of the Revolutionary Armed Forces; Dir Frank Agüero Gómez; circ. 65,000.

Bohemia: Avda Independencia y San Pedro, Apdo 6000, Havana; tel. (7) 81-9213; telex 511256; fax (7) 33-5511; f. 1908; weekly; politics; Dir Caridad Miranda Martínez; circ. 100,000.

Boletín Alimentaria de Cuba: Amargura 103, 10100 Havana; tel. (7) 62-9245; telex 511123; f. 1996; quarterly; food industry; Dir Antonio Campos; circ. 10,000.

El Caimán Barbudo: Paseo 613, Vedado, Havana; f. 1966; monthly; cultural; Dir Alex Pausides; circ. 47,000.

Cinco de Septiembre: Calle 35, No 5609, entre 56 y 58, Cienfuegos; f. 1980; Dir Francisco Valdés Petitón; circ. 18,000.

Cómicos: Calle 28, No 112, entre 1 y 3, Miramar, Havana; tel. (7) 22-5892; monthly; humorous; circ. 70,000.

Con la Guardia en Alto: Avda Salvador Allende 601, Havana; tel. (7) 79-4443; f. 1961; monthly; for mems of the Committees for the Defence of the Revolution; Dir Omelia Guerra Pérez; circ. 60,000.

Cuba Internacional: Calle 21, No 406, Vedado, Havana 4, Apdo 3603 Havana 3; tel. (7) 32-3578; fax (7) 32-3268; f. 1959; monthly; political; Dir Félix Albisú; circ. 30,000.

Dedeté: Territorial esq. a Gen. Suárez, Plaza de la Revolución, Havana; tel. (7) 82-0134; f. 1969; 2 a month; Dir Alen Lauzán; circ. 150,000.

La Demajagua: Amado Estévez, esq. Calle 10, Rpto R. Reyes, Bayamo; f. 1977; Dir Pedro Mora Estrada; circ. 21,000.

El Deporte, Derecho del Pueblo: Vía Blanca y Boyeros, Havana; tel. (7) 40-6838; telex 511583; f. 1968; monthly; sport; Dir Manuel Vaillant Carpente; circ. 15,000.

Escambray: Adolfo del Castillo 10, Sancti Spíritus; f. 1979; Dir Aramis Arteaga Pérez; circ. 14,000.

Girón: Avda Camilo Cienfuegos No 10505, P. Nuero, Matanzas; f. 1960; Dir Othoniel González Quevedo; circ. 25,000.

Guerrillero: Colón esq. Delicias y Adela Azcuy, Pinar del Río; f. 1969; Dir Ronald Suárez; circ. 33,000.

El Habanero: Gen. Suárez y Territorial, Plaza de la Revolución, Apdo 6269, Havana; tel. (7) 6160; telex 1839; f. 1987; Dir Tubal Páez Hernández; circ. 21,000.

Invasor: Marcial Gómez 401, esq. Estrada Palma, Ciego de Avila; f. 1979; Dir Migdalia Utrera Peña; circ. 10,500.

Juventud Rebelde: Territorial esq. Gen. Suárez, Plaza de la Revolución, Apdo 6344, Havana; tel. (7) 81-9087; telex 511168; fax (7) 81-8621; f. 1965; organ of the Young Communist League; Dir Rogelio Polanco Fuentes; circ. 250,000.

Juventud Técnica: Prado 553, esq. Teniente Rey, Habana Vieja, Havana; tel. (7) 31-1825; f. 1965; monthly; scientific-technical; Dir Germán Fernández Burguet; circ. 100,000.

Mar y Pesca: San Ignacio 303, Havana; tel. (7) 61-5518; fax 33-8438; f. 1965; quarterly; fishing; Dir Gustavo López; circ. 20,000.

El Militante Comunista: Calle 11, No 160, Vedado, Havana; tel. (7) 32-7581; f. 1967; monthly; Communist Party publication; Dir Manuel Menéndez; circ. 200,000.

Moncada: Belascoaín esq. Zanja, Havana; tel. (7) 79-7109; f. 1966; monthly; Dir Ricardo Martínez; circ. 70,000.

Muchacha: Galiano 264, esq. Neptuno, Havana; tel. (7) 61-5919; f. 1980; monthly; young women's magazine; Dir Silvia Martínez; circ. 120,000.

Mujeres: Galiano 264, esq. Neptuno, Havana; tel. (7) 61-5919; f. 1961; monthly; women's magazine; Dir REGLA ZULUETA; circ. 270,000.

El Muñe: Calle 28, No 112, entre 1 y 3, Mirimar, Havana; tel. (7) 22-5892; weekly; circ. 50,000.

Opciones: Territorial esq. Gen. Suárez, Plaza de la Revolucíon, Havana; weekly; finance, commerce and tourism.

Opina: Edif. Focsa, M entre 17 y 19, Havana; f. 1979; 2 a month; consumer-orientated; published by Institute of Internal Demand; Dir EUGENIO RODRÍGUEZ BALARI; circ. 250,000.

Pablo: Calle 28, No 112, entre 1 y 3, Mirimar, Havana; tel. (7) 22-5892; 16 a year; circ. 53,000.

Palante: Calle 21, No 954, entre 8 y 10, Vedado, Havana; tel. (7) 3-5098; f. 1961; weekly; humorous; Dir ROSENDO GUTIÉRREZ ROMÁN; circ. 235,000.

Pionero: Calle 17, No 354, Havana 4; tel. (7) 32-4571; f. 1961; weekly; children's magazine; Dir PEDRO GONZÁLEZ (PÉGLEZ); circ. 210,000.

Prisma de Cuba y las Américas: Calle 21 y Avda G, No 406, Vedado, Havana; tel. (7) 8-7995; f. 1979; fortnightly; international news; Man. Dir LUIS MANUEL ARCE; circ. 15,000 (Spanish), 10,000 (English).

RIL: O'Reilly 358, Havana; tel. (7) 62-0777; telex 511592; f. 1972; 2 a month; technical; Dir Exec. Council of Publicity Dept, Ministry of Light Industry; Chief Officer MIREYA CRESPO; circ. 8,000.

Sierra Maestra: Avda de Los Desfiles, Santiago de Cuba; tel. (7) 2-2813; telex 061250; f. 1957; weekly; Dir ARNALDO CLAVEL CARMENATY; circ. 45,000.

Sol de Cuba: Calle 19, No 60, entre M y N, Vedado, Havana 4; tel. (7) 32-9881; telex 511955; f. 1983; every 3 months; Spanish, English and French editions; Gen. Dir ALCIDES GIRO MITJANS; Editorial Dir DORIS VÉLEZ; circ. 200,000.

Somos Jóvenes: Calle 17, No 354, esq. H, Vedado, Havana; tel. (7) 32-4571; f. 1977; monthly; Dir GUILLERMO CABRERA; circ. 200,000.

Trabajadores: Territorial esq. Gen. Suárez, Plaza de la Revolución, Havana; tel. (7) 79-0819; telex 511402; f. 1970; organ of the trade-union movement; Dir JORGE LUIS CANELA CIURANA; circ. 150,000.

Tribuna de la Habana: Territorial esq. Gen. Suárez, Plaza de la Revolución, Havana; tel. (7) 81-5932; f. 1980; weekly; Dir ANGEL ZÚÑIGA SUÁREZ; circ. 90,000.

Vanguardia: Céspedes 5 (altos), Santa Clara, Matanzas; f. 1962; Dir PEDRO HERNÁNDEZ SOTO; circ. 24,000.

Venceremos: Carretera Jamaica, Km 1½, Guantánamo; f. 1962; tel. (7) 35980; telex 62151; Dir HAYDÉE LEÓN MOYA; circ. 28,000.

Ventiseis: Avda Carlos J. Finley, Las Tunas; f. 1977; Dir JOSÉ INFANTES REYES; circ. 21,000.

Verde Olivo: Avda de Rancho Boyeros y San Pedro, Havana; tel. (7) 79-8373; f. 1959; monthly; organ of the Revolutionary Armed Forces; Dir EUGENIO SUÁREZ PÉREZ; circ. 100,000.

Victoria: Carretera de la Fe, Km 1½, Plaza de la Revolución, Nueva Gerona, Isla de la Juventud; f. 1967; Dir NIEVE VARONA PUENTE; circ. 9,200.

PRESS ASSOCIATIONS

Unión de Periodistas de Cuba: Calle 23, No 452, esq. I, Vedado, 10400 Havana; tel. (7) 32-7098; telex 512297; fax (7) 33-3079; f. 1963; Pres. TUBAL PÁEZ HERNÁNDEZ.

Unión de Escritores y Artistas de Cuba: Calle 17, No 351, Vedado, Havana; tel. (7) 32-4571; telex 511563; fax (7) 33-3158; Pres. ABEL E. PRIETO JIMÉNEZ; Exec. Vice-Pres. LISANDRO OTERO.

NEWS AGENCIES

Agencia de Información Nacional (AIN): Calle 23, No 358, esq. a J, Vedado, Havana; tel. (7) 32-5541; fax (7) 66-2049; e-mail RPT@ain.sld.cu; national news agency; Dir ROBERTO PAVÓN TAMAYO.

Prensa Latina (Agencia Informativa Latinoamericana, SA): Calle 23, No 201, esq. a N, Vedado, Havana; tel. (7) 32-5561; telex 511132; fax (7) 33-3069; f. 1959; Dir PEDRO MARGOLLES VILLANUEVA.

Foreign Bureaux

Agence France-Presse (AFP): Calle 17, No 4, 13°, entre N y 0, Vedado, Havana; tel. (7) 33-3503; fax (7) 33-3034; Bureau Chief DENIS ROUSSEAU.

Agencia EFE (Spain): Calle 36, No 110, entre 1 y 3, Miramar, Apdo 5, Havana; tel. (7) 22-4958; telex 511395; Bureau Chief JUAN J. AZNARES MOZAS.

Agenzia Nazionale Stampa Associata (ANSA) (Italy): Edif. Fomeillán, Línea 5, Dpt 12, Vedado, Havana; tel. (7) 33-3542; telex 511903; Correspondent KATTY SALERNO.

Bulgarska Telegrafna Agentsia (BTA) (Bulgaria): Edif. Focsa, Calle 17, esq. M, Vedado, Apdo 22-E, Havana; tel. (7) 32-4779; Bureau Chief VASIL MIKOULACH.

Česká tisková kancelář (ČTK) (Czech Republic): Edif. Fajardo, Calle 17 y M, Vedado, Apdo 3-A, Vedado, Havana; tel. (7) 32-6101; telex 511397; Bureau Chief PAVEL ZOVADIL.

Deutsche Presse-Agentur (dpa) (Germany): Edif. Focsa, Calle 17 y M, Vedado, Apdo 2-K, Havana; tel. (7) 33-3501.

Informatsionnoye Telegrafnoye Agentstvo Rossii-Telegrafnoye Agentstvo Suverennykh Stran (ITAR-TASS) (Russia): Calle 96, No 317, entre 3 y 5, Miramar, Havana 4; tel. (7) 29-2528; telex 511382; Bureau Chief ALEKSANDR KANICHEV.

Inter Press Service (IPS) (Italy): Calle 36-A, No 121 Bajos, esq. a 3, Miramar, Apdo 1, Havana; tel. (7) 22-1981; telex 512649; Bureau Chief CLAUDE JOSEPH HACKIN; Correspondent CARLOS BASTISTA MORENO.

Korean Central News Agency (Democratic People's Republic of Korea): Calle 10, No 613, esq. 25, Vedado, Apdo 6, Havana; tel. (7) 31-4201; Bureau Chief CHANG YON CHOL.

Magyar Távirati Iroda (MTI) (Hungary): Edif. Fajardo, Calle 17 y M, Apdo 2-C, Havana; tel. (7) 32-8353; telex 51-1324; Bureau Chief: ZOLTÁN TAKACS; Correspondent TIBOR CSÁSZÁR.

Novinska Agencija Tanjug (Yugoslavia): Calle 5-F, No 9801, esq. 98, Miramar, Havana; tel. (7) 22-7671; Bureau Chief DUŠAN DAKOVIĆ.

Polska Agencja Prasowa (PAP) (Poland): Calle 6, No 702, Apdo 5, entre 7 y 9, Miramar; Havana; tel. (7) 20-7067; telex 51-1254; Bureau Chief PIOTR SOMMERFED.

Reuters (United Kingdom): Edif. Someillón, Linea 5, 9°, Vedado, Havana 4; tel. (7) 33-3145; telex 511584; Bureau Chief FRANCES KERRY.

Rossiyskoye Informatsionnoye Agentstvo—Novosti (RIA—Novosti) (Russia): Calle 28, No 510, entre 5 y 7, Miramar, Havana; tel. (7) 22-4129; Bureau Chief YURII GOLOVIATENKO.

Viet Nam Agency (VNA): Calle 16, No 514, 1°, entre 5 y 7, Miramar, Havana; tel. (7) 2-4455; telex 511794; Bureau Chief PHAM DINH LOI.

Xinhua (New China) News Agency (People's Republic of China): Calle G, No 259, esq. 13, Vedado, Havana; tel. (7) 32-4616; telex 511692; Bureau Chief GAO YONGHUA.

Publishers

Casa de las Américas: Calle 3 y Avda G, Vedado, Havana; tel. (7) 32-3587; telex 511019; fax (7) 32-7272; e-mail casa@arsoft.cult.cu; f. 1960; Latin American literature and social sciences; Dir ROBERTO FERNÁNDEZ RETAMAR.

Ediciones Unión: Calle 17, No 354 esq. a H, Vedado, Havana; tel. (7) 32-5252; telex 511563; fax (7) 33-3158; f.1962; publishing arm of the Unión de Escritores y Artistas de Cuba; Cuban literature, art; Dir DANIEL GARCÍA SANTOS.

Editora Política: Belascoaín No 864, esq. a Desagüe y Peñalver, Havana; tel. (7) 79-8553; fax (7) 81-1024; f. 1963; publishing institution of the Cuban Communist Party; Dir HUGO CHINEA CABRERA.

Editorial Abril: Prado 553, esq. Teniente Rey, Habana Vieja, Havana; tel. (7) 62-7871; fax (7) 62-7871; e-mail eabril@tinored.cu; f. 1980; attached to the Union of Young Communists; children's literature; Dir IROEL SÁNCHEZ ESPINOSA.

Editorial Academia: Industria No 452, esq. a San José, Habana Vieja, Havana; tel. (7) 62-9501; telex 511290; f. 1963; attached to the Ministry of Science, Technology and the Environment; scientific and technical; Dir MIRIAM RAYA HERNÁNDEZ.

Editorial de Ciencias Médicas y Centro Nacional de Información de Ciencias Médicas: Calle E, No 452, entre 19 y 21, Vedado, Apdo 6520, Havana 10400; tel. (7) 32-4519; telex 511202; fax (7) 32-5008; attached to the Ministry of Public Health; books and magazines specializing in the medical sciences; Dir AUGUSTO HERNÁNDEZ BATISTA.

Editorial Ciencias Sociales: Calle 14, No 4104, entre 41 y 43, Miramar, Playa, Havana; tel. (7) 23-3959; f. 1967; attached to the Instituto Cubano del Libro; social and political literature, history, philosophy, juridical sciences and economics; Dir RICARDO GARCÍA PAMPÍN.

Editorial Científico-Técnica: Calle 2, No 58, entre 3 y 5, Vedado, Havana; tel. (7) 3-9417; f. 1967; attached to the Ministry of Culture; technical and scientific literature; Dir ISIDRO FERNÁNDEZ RODRÍGUEZ.

Editorial Gente Nueva: Palacio del Segundo Cabo, Calle O'Reilly, No 4, esq. a Tacón, Havana; tel. (7) 62-4753; telex 511881; f. 1967; books for children; Dir ELENIA RODRÍGUEZ OLIVA.

Editorial José Martí/Arte y Literatura: Calzada 259, entre I y J, Apdo 4208, Havana; tel. (7) 33-3541; fax (7) 33-8187; f. 1983; attached to the Ministry of Culture; foreign-language publishing; Dir CECILIA INFANTE GUERRERO.

Editorial Letras Cubanas: Calle O'Reilly, No 4, esq. a Tacón, Habana Vieja, Havana; tel. (7) 62-4378; telex 511881; fax (7) 33-8187; e-mail probiz@artsof.cult.cu; f. 1977; attached to the Ministry of Culture; general, particularly classic and contemporary Cuban literature and arts; Dir DANIEL GARCÍA SANTOS.

Editorial Oriente: Santa Lucía 356, Santiago de Cuba; tel. 2-2496; telex 061170; f. 1971; publishes works from the Eastern provinces; general; Dir Lic. EUCLIDES RODRÍGUEZ.

Editorial Pueblo y Educación: Avda 3-A 4601, entre 46 y 60, Playa, Havana; tel. (7) 22-1490; telex 511763; fax (7) 24-0844; f. 1967; textbooks; Dir CATALINA LAJUD HERRERO.

Government Publishing Houses

Instituto Cubano del Libro: Palacio del Segundo Cabo, Calle O'Reilly, No 4, esq. a Tacón, Havana; tel. (7) 62-4789; fax (7) 33-8187; printing and publishing organization attached to the Ministry of Culture which combines several publishing houses and has direct links with others; presides over the National Editorial Council (CEN); Pres. OMAR GONZÁLEZ JIMÉNEZ.

Oficina de Publicaciones: Calle 17, No 552, esq. a D, Vedado, Havana; tel. (7) 32-1883; fax (7) 33-5106; attached to the Council of State; books, pamphlets and other printed media on historical and political matters; Dir PEDRO ALVAREZ TABÍO.

Broadcasting and Communications

Ministerio de Comunicaciones (Dirección de Frecuencias Radioeléctricas): Plaza de la Revolución, CP 10600, Havana; tel. (7) 70-6932; telex 511490; Dir CARLOS MARTÍNEZ ALBUERNE.

Empresa Cubana de Radio y Televisión (INTERTV): Calle 23, No 156, entre N y O, Vedado, Havana; tel. (7) 32-7571; telex 511600; fax (7) 33-3939; Dir ANDRÉS SALCEDO GANCEDO.

Instituto Cubano de Radio y Televisión (ICRT): Edif. ICRT, Calle 23, No 258, entre L y M, Vedado, Havana 4; tel. (7) 32-1568; telex 511613; fax (7) 31-1723; f. 1962; Pres. ENRIQUE ROMÁN HERNÁNDEZ.

Instituto de Investigación y Desarrollo de las Telecomunicaciones (LACETEL): Rancho Boyeros, Km 14½, Santiago de las Vegas, Rancho Boyeros, Havana; tel. (7) 20-2929; telex 512262; fax (7) 33-5812; Dir EDUARDO TRUFFÍN TRIANA.

TELECOMMUNICATIONS

Empresa de Telecomunicaciones de Cuba, SA (ETECSA): Calle Egido, No 610, entre Gloria y Apodaca, Habana Vieja, Havana; tel. (7) 33-4848; telex 51914; fax (7) 33-5144; Exec. Pres. RAFAEL MARRERO GÓMEZ.

Empresa de Telecomunicaciones (EMTELCUBA): Zanja, No 855, 6°, Havana; tel. (7) 70-8794; telex 512243; fax (7) 78-3722; Dir REGINO GONZÁLEZ TOLEDO.

Teléfonos Celulares de Cuba, SA (CUBACEL): Calle 28, No 510, entre 5 y 7, Playa, Havana; tel. (7) 33-2222; fax (7) 33-1737.

RADIO

In 1997 there were 5 national networks and 1 international network, 14 provincial radio stations and 31 municipal radio stations, with a total of some 170 transmitters.

Radio Enciclopedia: Calle N, No 266, entre 21 y 23, Vedado, Havana; tel. (7) 81-2809; national network; instrumental music programmes; 24 hours daily; Dir EDELSA PALACIOS GORDO.

Radio Habana Cuba: Infanta 105 esq. a 25, 6°, Apdo 6240, Havana; tel. (7) 78-4954; telex 1334; fax (7) 79-5810; f. 1961; shortwave station; broadcasts in Spanish, English, French, Portuguese, Arabic, Esperanto, Quechua, Guaraní and Creole; Dir MILAGROS HERNÁNDEZ CUBA.

CMBF—Radio Musical Nacional: Avda 23, No 258, Vedado, Havana; tel. (7) 70-4561; telex 1766; f. 1948; national network; classical music programmes; 17 hours daily; Dir PEDRO PABLO RODRÍGUEZ.

Radio Progreso: Infanta 105, Havana; tel. (7) 70-4561; national network; mainly entertainment and music; 24 hours daily; Dir JULIO PÉREZ MUÑOZ.

Radio Rebelde: Edif. ICRT, Calle 23, No 258, entre L y M, Vedado, Apdo 6277, Havana; tel. (7) 32-3531; fax (7) 33-4270; f. 1984 (after merger of former Radio Rebelde and Radio Liberación); national network; 24-hour news programmes, music and sports; Dir MARIO ROBAINA DÍAZ.

Radio Reloj: Edif. Radiocentro, Calle 23, No 258, entre L y M, Vedado, Havana; tel. (7) 32-9689; telex 511226; f. 1947; national network; 24-hour news service; Dir OSVALDO RODRÍGUEZ MARTÍNEZ.

TELEVISION

Televisión Cubana (Cubavisión and Tele-Rebelde): Calle M, No 313, entre 21 y 23, Vedado, Havana; tel. (7) 32-5000; broadcasts in colour on channel 2 and channel 6; Dirs GARY GONZÁLEZ BENÍTEZ, RODOBALDO DÍAZ OLIVER.

CHTV: Habana Libre Hotel, Havana; f. 1990; subsidiary station of Tele-Rebelde.

Finance

Comité Estatal de Finanzas: Obispo 211, esq. Cuba, Havana; tel. (7) 60-4111; fax (7) 62-0252; f. 1976; charged with the direction and control of the State's financial policy, including preparation of the budget.

BANKING

All banks were nationalized in 1960. Legislation establishing the national banking system was approved by the Council of State in 1984. A restructuring of the banking system, initiated in 1995, to accommodate Cuba's transformation to a more market-orientated economy was proceeding in 1997, when a new central bank, the Banco Central de Cuba (BCC), was created to supersede the Banco Nacional de Cuba (BNC). The BCC was to be responsible for issuing currency, proposing and implementing monetary policy and the regulation of financial institutions. The BNC was to continue functioning as a commercial bank and servicing the country's foreign debt. Also envisaged in the restructuring of the banking system was the creation of an investment bank, the Banco de Inversiones, to provide medium- and long-term financing for investment, and the Banco Financiero Internacional, SA, to offer short-term financing. A new agro-industrial and commercial bank was also to be created to provide services for farmers and co-operatives. The new banking system is under the control of Grupo Nueva Banca, which holds a majority share in each institution.

Central Bank

Banco Central de Cuba (BCC): Havana; f. 1997; sole bank of issue; Pres. FRANCISCO SOBERÓN VALDEZ.

Commercial Banks

Banco Financiero Internacional, SA: Edif. Someillán, Calle Línea, No 1, Vedado, Havana; tel. (7) 33-3514; telex 512405; fax (7) 33-3006; f. 1984; autonomous; capital US $10m. (1985); mainly short-term financing; Chair. EDUARDO BENCOMO ZURDOS; Gen. Man. ARNALDO ALAYÓN.

Banco Internacional de Comercio, SA: 20 de Mayo y Ayestarán, Havana; tel. (7) 33-5115; telex 514055; fax (7) 33-5112; f. 1993; cap. and res US $13.7m., dep. $139.7m. (Dec. 1995); Chair. JOSÉ VAZ; Gen. Man. JOSÉ LEBREDO.

Banco Metropolitano: Línea, No 63, esq. Calle M, Vedado, Havana; tel. (7) 32-9894; telex 512920; fax (7) 33-4241; f. 1996; offers foreign currency and deposit account facilities; Dir PEDRO DE LA ROSA GONZÁLEZ.

Banco Nacional de Cuba (BNC): Cuba 402, esq. a Lamparilla, Apdo 736, Havana; tel. (7) 62-8001; telex 511124; fax (7) 63-4061; f. 1950, reorganized 1997.

Savings Bank

Banco Popular del Ahorro: Calle 16, No 306, entre 3 y 5, Playa, Havana; tel. and fax (7) 33-1180; telex 511608; f. 1983; savings bank; cap. 30m. pesos; dep. 5,363.7m. pesos; Pres. MARISELA FERREYRA DE LA GÁNDARA; 520 brs.

INSURANCE

State Organizations

Empresa del Seguro Estatal Nacional (ESEN): Obispo No 211, 3°, Apdo 109, 10100 Havana; tel. (7) 60-4111; f. 1978; motor and agricultural insurance; Man. Dir PEDRO MANUEL ROCHE ALVAREZ.

Seguros Internacionales de Cuba, SA—Esicuba: Cuba No 314, Apdo 79, Havana; tel. (7) 33-8057; telex 511616; fax (7) 33-8038; f. 1963, reorganized 1986; all classes of insurance except life; Chair. RAQUEL HERNÁNDEZ HERRERA; Deputy Chair. and Man. Dir RAMÓN MARTÍNEZ CARRERA.

Trade and Industry

CHAMBER OF COMMERCE

Cámara de Comercio de la República de Cuba: Calle 21, No 661/701, esq. Calle A, Apdo 4237, Vedado, Havana; tel. (7) 30-3356; telex 511752; fax (7) 33-3042; f. 1963; mems include all Cuban foreign trade enterprises and the most important agricultural and industrial enterprises; Pres. CARLOS MARTÍNEZ SALSAMENDI; Sec.-Gen. MARTA CAMACHO FUNDORA.

AGRICULTURAL ORGANIZATION

Asociación Nacional de Agricultores Pequeños—ANAP (National Association of Small Farmers): Calle I, No 206, entre Linea y 13, Vedado, Havana; tel. (7) 32-4541; fax (7) 33-4244; f. 1961; 220,000 mems; Pres. ORLANDO LUGO FONTE; Vice-Pres. EVELIO PAUSA BELLO.

STATE IMPORT-EXPORT BOARDS

Alimport (Empresa Cubana Importadora de Alimentos): Infanta 16, 3°, Apdo 7006, Havana; tel. (7) 70-2437; telex 511454; fax (7) 79-1274; controls import of foodstuffs and liquors; Man. Dir ARMANDO PERDOMO.

Autoimport (Empresa Central de Abastecimiento y Venta de Equipos de Transporte Ligero): Galiano 213, entre Concordia y Virtudes, Havana; tel. (7) 62-8180; telex 511417; imports cars, light vehicles, motor cycles and spare parts; Man. Dir EDELIO VERA RODRÍGUEZ.

Aviaimport (Empresa Cubana Importadora y Exportadora de Aviación): Calle 182, No 126, entre 1 y 5, Reparto Flores, Playa, Havana; tel. (7) 21-7609; telex 512328; import and export of aircraft and components; Man. Dir MARCOS LAGO MARTÍNEZ.

Caribex (Empresa Exportadora del Caribe): Edif. 7, Avda 5 y Calle 248, Barlovento, Santa Fe, Playa, Havana; tel. (7) 21-8277; telex 511471; fax (7) 33-1534; import and export of seafood and marine products; Dir ENRIQUE FRAXEDAS MAYOR.

Construimport (Empresa Central de Abastecimiento y Venta de Equipos de Construcción y sus Piezas): Carretera de Varona, Km. 1½, Capdevila, Havana; tel. (7) 45-2567; telex 511213; fax (7) 66-6180; controls the import and export of construction machinery and equipment; Man. Dir JESÚS SERRANO.

Consumimport (Empresa Cubana Importadora de Artículos de Consumo General): Calle 23, No 55, 9°, Apdo 6427, Vedado, Havana; tel. (7) 70-0302; telex 512355; fax (7) 33-3847; f. 1962; imports and exports general consumer goods; Dir HILARIO VEGA GONZÁLEZ.

Copextel (Combinado Productor y Exportador de Tecnología Electrónica): Calle 194 y 7, Miramar, Playa, Havana; tel. (7) 20-1715; telex 512242; fax (7) 20-1735; f. 1986; exports LTEL personal computers and micro-computer software; Man. Dir LUIS J. CARRASCO.

Coprefil (Empresa Comercial y de Producciones Filatélicas): Zanja No 855, 2°, esq. San Francisco e Infanta, Havana 1; tel. (7) 7-8812; telex 512479; fax (7) 33-5077; imports and exports postage stamps, postcards, calendars, handicrafts, communications equipment, electronics, watches, etc.; Dir NELSON IGLESIAS FERNÁNDEZ.

Cubaelectrónica (Empresa Importadora y Exportadora de Productos de la Electrónica): Calle 22, No 510, entre 5 y 7, Miramar, Havana; tel. (7) 22-7316; telex 512484; fax (7) 33-1233; f. 1986; imports and exports electronic equipment and devices; Pres. GUSTAVO LORET DE MOLA.

Cubaequipos (Empresa Cubana Importadora de Productos Mecánicos y Equipos Varios): Calle 23, No 55, Vedado, Apdo 6052, Havana; tel. (7) 70-6985; telex 512443; fax (7) 7-1350; f. 1982; imports of mechanical goods and equipment; Dir VÍCTOR MENÉNDEZ MORALES.

Cubaexport (Empresa Cubana Exportadora de Alimentos y Productos Varios): Calle 23, No 55, entre Infanta y P, 8°, Vedado, Apdo 6719, Havana; tel. (7) 74-3130; telex 511178; fax (7) 33-3587; export of foodstuffs and industrial products; Man. Dir MILDA PICOS RIVERS.

Cubafrutas (Empresa Cubana Exportadora de Frutas Tropicales): Calle 23, No 55, Apdo 6647, Vedado, Havana; tel. and fax (7) 79-5653; telex 511849; f. 1979; controls export of fruits, vegetables and canned foodstuffs; Dir JORGE AMARO MOREJÓN.

Cubalse (Empresa para Prestación de Servicios al Cuerpo Diplomático): Calle 3 y Final, Miramar, Havana (also at Apdo 634, Marianao 13); tel. (7) 33-2284; telex 511235; fax (7) 33-2282; f. 1974; imports consumer goods for the diplomatic corps and foreign technicians residing in Cuba; exports beverages and tobacco, leather goods and foodstuffs; Dir Dr JOSÉ M. MANRESA NARANJO.

Cubametales (Empresa Cubana Importadora de Metales, Combustibles y Lubricantes): Infanta 16, 4°, Apdo 6917, Vedado, Havana; tel. (7) 70-2561; telex 511452; controls import of metals (ferrous and non-ferrous), crude petroleum and petroleum products; also engaged in the export of petroleum products and ferrous and non-ferrous scrap; Dir RAFAEL PRIEDE GONZÁLEZ.

Cubaniquel (Empresa Cubana Exportadora de Minerales y Metales): Calle 23, No 55, Apdo 6128, Havana; tel. (7) 7-8460; telex 511178; fax (7) 33-3332; f. 1961; sole exporter of minerals and metals; Man. Dir ARIEL MASÓ MARZAL.

Cubatabaco (Empresa Cubana del Tabaco): Calle O'Reilly, No 104, Apdo 6557, Havana; tel. (7) 61-2778; telex 511760; fax (7) 33-8214; f. 1962; controls export of leaf tobacco, cigars and cigarettes to France; Dir JUAN MANUEL DÍAZ TENORIO.

Cubatécnica (Empresa de Contratación de Asistencia Técnica): Calle 12, No 513, entre 5 y 7, Miramar, Havana; tel. and fax (7) 22-7455; e-mail cubatec@ceniai.inf.cu; controls export and import of technical assistance; Dir RAFAEL JIMENO LÓPEZ.

Cubatex (Empresa Cubana Importadora de Fibras, Tejidos, Cueros y sus Productos): Calle 23, No 55, Apdo 7115, Vedado, Havana; tel. (7) 70-2531; telex 512361; fax (7) 79-4861; controls import of fibres, textiles, hides and by-products and export of fabric and clothing; Dir LUISA AMPARO SESÍN VIDAL.

Cubazúcar (Empresa Cubana Exportadora de Azúcar y sus Derivados): Calle 23, No 55, 7°, Vedado, Apdo 6647, Havana; tel. (7) 74-2175; telex 511147; fax (7) 33-3482; f. 1962; controls export of sugar, molasses and alcohol; Dir (vacant).

Ecimact (Empresa Comercial de Industrias de Materiales, Construcción y Turismo): Calle 1, C No 15220, entre 152 y 154, Rpto Náutico, Playa, Havana; tel. (7) 21-9783; telex 511926; controls import and export of engineering services and plant for industrial construction and tourist complexes; Dir OCTAVIO CASTILLA CANGAS.

Ecimetal (Empresa Comercial para la Industria Metalúrgica y Metalmecánica): Calle 23, No 55, esq. P, Vedado, Havana; tel. (7) 33-4737; fax (7) 70-3269; f. 1977; controls import of plant and equipment for all major industrial sectors; Dir ADALBERTO DUMENIGO CABRERA.

Ediciones Cubanas (Empresa de Comercio Exterior de Publicaciones): Obispo 527, Apdo 43, Havana; tel. (7) 63-1989; telex 512337; fax (7) 33-8943; controls import and export of books and periodicals; Dir NANCY MATOS LACOSTA.

Egrem (Estudios de Grabaciones y Ediciones Musicales): Avda 3, No 1008, entre 10 y 12, Miramar, Havana; tel. (7) 33-1925; telex 512171; fax (7) 33-8043; f. 1964; controls the import and export of records, tapes, printed music and musical instruments; Dir Gen. JULIO BALLESTER GUZMÁN.

Emexcon (Empresa Importadora y Exportadora de la Construcción): Calle 25, No 2602, Miramar, Havana; tel. (7) 22-3694; telex 511693; f. 1978; consulting engineer services, contracting, import and export of building materials and equipment; Dir ELEODORO PÉREZ.

Emiat (Empresa Importadora y Exportadora de Abastecimientos Técnicos): Calle 20, No 519, entre 5 y 7, Miramar, Havana; tel. (7) 22-1163; telex 511802; fax (7) 22-5176; f. 1983; imports technical materials, equipment and special products; exports furniture, kitchen utensils and accessories; Dir MARTA ALFONSO SÁNCHEZ.

Emidict (Empresa Especializada Importadora, Exportadora y Distribuidora para la Ciencia y la Técnica): Calle 16, No 102, esq. 1, Miramar, Playa, Havana 13; tel. (7) 23-5316; telex 512233; fax (7) 62-5604; controls import and export of scientific and technical products and equipment, live animals and ornamental fishes; Dir MIGUEL JULIO PÉREZ FLEITAS.

Energoimport (Empresa Importadora de Objetivos Electro-energéticos): Calle 7, No 2602, esq. a 26, Miramar, Havana; tel. (7) 23-8156; telex 511812; fax (7) 33-0147; f. 1977; controls import of equipment for electricity generation; Dir JORGE LUIS COTERÓN QUIÑONES.

Eprob (Empresa de Proyectos para las Industrias de la Básica): Avda 31-A, entre 18 y 20, Miramar, Playa, Apdo 12100, Havana; tel. (7) 33-2146; telex 512413; fax (7) 33-2146; f. 1967; exports consulting services and processing of engineering construction projects, consulting services and supplies of complete industrial plants and turn-key projects; Man. Dir RAÚL RIVERO MARTÍNEZ.

Eproyiv (Empresa de Proyectos para Industrias Varias): Calle 33, No 1815, entre 18 y 20, Playa, Havana; tel. (7) 33-2149; fax (7) 33-0773; f. 1967; consulting services, feasibility studies, development of basic and detailed engineering models, project management and turn-key projects; Dir GONZALO RÍOS ANDRÉS.

Esi (Empresa de Suministros Industriales): Calle Aguiar, No 556, entre Teniente Rey y Muralla, Havana; tel. (7) 62-0696; telex 511495; fax (7) 33-8951; f. 1985; imports machinery, equipment and components for industrial plants; Dir-Gen. FRANCISCO DÍAZ CABRERA.

Fecuimport (Empresa Cubana Importadora y Exportadora de Ferrocarriles): Avda 7, No 6209, entre 62 y 66, Miramar, Havana; tel. (7) 23-3764; telex 512419; imports and exports railway equipment; Dir ANTONIO CONEJO MESA.

Ferrimport (Empresa Cubana Importadora de Artículos de Ferretería): Calle 23, No 55, 2°, Vedado, Apdo 6258, Havana; tel. (7) 70-2531; telex 511144; importers of industrial hardware; Dir ENRIQUE DÍAZ DE VILLEGAS.

Fondo Cubano de Bienes Culturales: Calle 36, esq. 47, Reparto Kohly, Playa, Havana; tel. (7) 23-6523; telex 512278; fax (7) 24-0391; f. 1978; controls export of fine handicraft and works of art; Dir ANGEL ARCOS.

Habanos, S.A.: Calle O'Reilly, No 104, Apdo 6557, Havana; tel. 33-8998; fax 33-8946; f. 1994; controls export of leaf tobacco, cigars and cigarettes (except to France—see Cubatabaco).

ICAIC (Instituto Cubano del Arte e Industria Cinematográficos): Calle 23, No 1155, Vedado, Havana 4; tel. (7) 3-4400; telex 511419;

fax (7) 32-1444; f. 1959; production, import and export of films and newsreel; Dir Antonio Rodríguez Rodríguez.

Imexin (Empresa Importadora y Exportadora de Infraestructura): Avda 5, No 1007, esq. a 12, Miramar, Havana; tel. (7) 23-9293; telex 511404; f. 1977; controls import and export of infrastructure; Man. Dir Raúl Bence Vijande.

Imexpal (Empresa Importadora y Exportadora de Plantas Alimentarias, sus Complementos y Derivados): Calle 22, No 313, entre 3 y 5, Miramar, Havana; tel. (7) 29-1671; telex 511216; controls import and export of food-processing plants and related items; Man. Dir Ing. Concepción Bueno Campos.

Maprinter (Empresa Cubana Importadora y Exportadora de Materias Primas y Productos Intermedios): Infanta 16, Apdo 2110, Havana; tel. (7) 74-2971; telex 511453; fax (7) 33-3535; controls import and export of raw materials and intermediate products; Dir Enrique Díaz de Villegas Otero.

Maquimport (Empresa Cubana Importadora de Maquinarias y Equipos): Calle 23, No 55, Vedado, Apdo 6052, Havana; tel. (7) 70-2305; telex 511371; fax (7) 33-5443; controls import of machinery and equipment; Dir Francisco Benjamín Santos González.

Marpesca (Empresa Cubana Importadora y Exportadora de Buques Mercantes y de Pesca): Conill No 580, esq. Avda 26, Nuevo Vedado, Havana; tel. (7) 81-6704; telex 511687; imports and exports ships and port and fishing equipment; Dir José Cereijo Casas.

Medicuba (Empresa Cubana Importadora y Exportadora de Productos Médicos): Máximo Gómez 1, esq. a Egido, Havana; tel. (7) 62-3983; telex 511658; fax (7) 61-7995; enterprise for the export and import of medical and pharmaceutical products; Dir Orlando Romero Mérida.

Produimport (Empresa Central de Abastecimiento y Venta de Productos Químicos y de la Goma): Calle Consulado 262, entre Animas y Virtudes, Havana; tel. (7) 62-0581; telex 512390; fax (7) 62-9588; f. 1977; imports and exports spare parts for motor vehicles; Dir José Guerra Matos.

Quimimport (Empresa Cubana Importadora y Exportadora de Productos Químicos): Calle 23, No 55, Apdo 6088, Vedado, Havana; tel. (7) 33-3394; telex 511283; fax (7) 33-3190; controls import and export of chemical products; Dir Armando Barrera Martínez.

Suchel (Empresa de Jabonería y Perfumería): Calzada de Buenos Aires 353, esq. a Durege, Apdo 6359, Havana; tel. (7) 33-8008; telex 512159; fax (7) 33-5311; f. 1985; exports and imports materials for the detergent, perfumery and cosmetics industry, exports cosmetics, perfumes, hotel amenities and household products; Dir José García Díaz.

Tecnoazúcar (Empresa de Servicios Técnicos e Ingeniería para la Agro-industria Azucarera): Calle 12, No 310, entre 3 y 5, Miramar, Playa, Havana; tel. (7) 29-5441; telex 511022; fax (7) 33-1218; imports machinery and equipment for the sugar industry, provides technical and engineering assistance for the sugar industry; exports sugar-machinery equipment and spare parts; provides engineering and technical assistance services for sugar-cane by-product industry; Gen. Man. Victor R. Hernández Martínez.

Tecnoimport (Empresa Cubana Importadora y Exportadora de Productos Técnicos): Edif. de la Marina, Avda del Puerto, entre Justi y Obrapía, Habana Vieja, Havana; tel. (7) 23-0925; telex 511572; fax (7) 24-1682; imports technical products; Dir Lt-Col Adel Izquierdo Rodríguez.

Tecnotex (Empresa Cubana Exportadora e Importadora de Servicios, Artículos y Productos Técnicos Especializados): Avda 47, No 3419, Playa, Havana; tel. (7) 81-3989; telex 515172; fax (7) 33-1682; f. 1983; imports specialized technical and radiocommunications equipment, exports outdoor equipment and geodetic networks; Dir Adel Izquierdo Rodríguez.

Tractoimport (Empresa Central de Abastecimiento y Venta de Maquinaria Agrícola y sus Piezas de Repuesto): Avda Rancho Boyeros y Calle 100, Apdo 7007, Havana; tel. (7) 20-3474; telex 511162; fax (7) 33-8786; f. 1960 for the import of tractors and agricultural equipment; also exports pumps and agricultural implements; Dir Manuel Castro del Aguila.

Transimport (Empresa Central de Abastecimiento y Venta de Equipos de Transporte Pesados y sus Piezas): Calle 102 y Avda 63, Marianao, Apdo 6665, 11500 Havana; tel. (7) 20-0325; telex 511150; f. 1962; controls import and export of vehicles and transportation equipment; Dir Jesús Dennes Rivero.

UTILITIES

Electricity

Empresa Consolidada de Electricidad: Avda Salvador Allende 666, Havana; public utility.

TRADE UNIONS

All workers have the right to become members of a national trade union according to their industry and economic branch.

The following industries and labour branches have their own unions: Agriculture, Chemistry and Energetics, Civil Workers of the Revolutionary Armed Forces, Commerce and Gastronomy, Communications, Construction, Culture, Education and Science, Food, Forestry, Health, Light Industry, Merchant Marine, Mining and Metallurgy, Ports and Fishing, Public Administration, Sugar, Tobacco and Transport.

Central de Tradajadores de Cuba—CTC (Confederation of Cuban Workers): Palacio de los Trabajadores, San Carlos y Peñalver, Havana; tel. (7) 78-4901; telex 511403; f. 1939; affiliated to WFTU and CPUSTAL; 19 national trade unions affiliated; Gen. Sec. Pedro Ross Leal; 2,767,806 mems (1996).

Transport

The Ministry of Transport controls all public transport.

RAILWAYS

The total length of railways in 1990 was 14,519 km, of which 9,638 km were used by the sugar industry. The remaining 4,881 km were public service railways operated by Ferrocarriles de Cuba (reduced to 4,677 km in 1994). All railways were nationalized in 1960.

Ferrocarriles de Cuba: Edif. Estación Central, Egido y Arsenal, Havana; tel. (7) 62-1530; fax (7) 33-8628; f. 1960; operates public services; Dir Gen. P. Pérez Fleites; divided as follows:

División Occidente: serves Pinar del Río, Ciudad de la Habana, Havana Province and Matanzas.

División Centro: serves Villa Clara, Cienfuegos and Sancti Spíritus.

División Centro-Este: serves Camagüey, Ciego de Avila and Tunas.

División Oriente: serves Santiago de Cuba, Granma, Guantánamo and Holguín.

División Camilo Cienfuegos: serves part of Havana Province and Matanzas.

ROADS

In 1996 there were an estimated 27,700 km of roads, of which 15,484 km were paved. The Central Highway runs from Pinar del Río in the west to Santiago, for a length of 1,144 km. In addition to this paved highway, there are a number of secondary and 'farm-to-market' roads. A small proportion of these secondary roads is paved but many can be used by motor vehicles only during the dry season.

SHIPPING

Cuba's principal ports are Havana (which handles 60% of all cargo), Santiago de Cuba, Cienfuegos, Nuevitas, Matanzas, Antilla, Guayabal and Mariel. Maritime transport has developed rapidly since 1959, and at 31 December 1996 Cuba had a merchant fleet of 324 ships (with a total displacement of 291,394 grt). In 1988 there was a coastal trading and deep-sea fleet of 82 ships. In the early 1990s a port to accommodate supertankers was under construction at Matanzas, with co-operation from French enterprises. A major development of the port of Nuevitas has been planned.

Coral Container Lines, SA: Oficios 170, 1°, Habana Vieja, Havana; tel. (7) 62-5622; telex 512181; fax (7) 33-8275; f. 1994; liner services to Europe, Canada, Brazil and Mexico; 11 containers; Chair. and Man. Dir Q. Gutiérrez.

Empresa Consignataria Mambisa: San José No 65, entre Prado y Zulueta, Habana Vieja, Havana; tel. (7) 62-2061; telex 511890; fax (7) 33-8111; shipping agent, bunker suppliers; Man. Dir Eduardo Denis Valcárcel.

Empresa Cubana de Fletes (Cuflet): Calle Oficios No 170, entre Teniente Rey y Amargura, Apdo 6755, Havana; tel. (7) 61-2604; telex 512181; freight agents for Cuban cargo; Man. Dir Carlos Sánchez Perdomo.

Empresa de Navegación Caribe (Navecaribe): San Martín, 4°, Agramonte y Pasco de Martí, Habana Vieja, Havana; tel. (7) 61-9830; telex 511268; fax (7) 33-8564; f. 1966; operates Cuban coastal fleet; Dir Ramón Durán Suárez.

Empresa de Navegación Mambisa: San Ignacio No 104, Apdo 543, Havana; tel. (7) 62-7031; telex 511810; fax (7) 61-0044; operates dry cargo, reefer and bulk carrier vessels; Gen. Man. Gumersindo González Feliú.

Naviera Frigorífica Marítima: Avda 26, No 560, entre 31 y 33, Nuevo Vedado, Havana; tel. (7) 35743; telex 511284; fax (7) 33-5185.

Naviera Mar América: Calle de San Ignacio 104, Havana; tel. (7) 62-3560; telex 511875; fax (7) 61044.

Naviera Poseidon: Altos de la Aduana, San Pedro 1, Habana Vieja, Havana; tel. (7) 62-5618; telex 212085; fax (7) 33-8627.

Nexus Reefer: Avda de la Pesquera y Atarés, Habana Vieja, Havana 1; tel. (7) 33-8478; telex 511159; fax (7) 33-8046; merchant reefer ships; Gen. Dir QUIRINO L. GUTIÉRREZ LÓPEZ.

There are regular passenger and cargo services by Cuban vessels between Cuba and northern Europe, the Baltic, the Mediterranean, the Black Sea and Japan and by eastern European vessels between Cuba and the Baltic and the Black Sea. A regular Caribbean service is maintained by Empresa Multinacional del Caribe (Namucar). The Cuban fleet also runs regular container services to northern Europe, the Mediterranean and the Black Sea.

CIVIL AVIATION

There are international airports at Havana, Santiago de Cuba, Camagüey, Varadero and Holguín. In 1996 Canada granted financing of US $26m. for the construction of a third terminal at Havana International Airport.

Empresa Consolidada Cubana de Aviación (Cubana): Calle 23, Pt 64, La Rampa, Vedado, Apdo 4299, Havana; tel. (7) 78-4961; telex 511366; fax (7) 79-3333; f. 1929; international services to North America, Central America, the Caribbean, South America and Europe; internal services from Havana to 13 other cities; Gen. Dir. HERIBERTO PRIEGO.

Aero Caribbean de Cuba: Calle 23, No 113, esq. 0, Vedado, Havana; tel. (7) 33-7096; telex 512191; fax (7) 33-5016; f. 1982; international and domestic charter services; Pres. ALBERTO SÁNCHEZ.

Instituto de Aeronáutica Civil de Cuba (IACC): Calle 23, No 64, La Rampa, Vedado, Havana; tel. (7) 33-4471; telex 511737; fax (7) 33-3082; f. 1985; Pres. ROGELIO ACEVEDO GONZÁLEZ.

Tourism

Tourism began to develop after 1977, with the repeal of travel restrictions by the USA, and Cuba subsequently attracted European tourists. At the Fourth Congress of the PCC, held in 1991, emphasis was placed on the importance of expanding the tourist industry, and, in particular, on its promotion within Latin America. Receipts totalled an estimated US $1,380m. in 1996, when there were some 1,001,740 visitors. In that year there were more than 26,800 hotel rooms. The Government planned to increase the number of hotel rooms to some 50,000 and annual visitor arrivals to 2.5m. by 2000.

Cubanacán: Calle 148, entre 11 y 13, Playa, Apdo 16046, Havana; tel. (7) 133-1658; telex 511609; fax (7) 33-2251; f. 1987; Senior Vice-Pres. CARLOS GARCÍA.

Empresa de Turismo Internacional (Cubatur): Calle 23, No 156, entre N y O, Apdo 6560, Vedado, Havana; tel. (7) 32-4521; telex 511212; fax (7) 33-3104; Dir GUILLERMO BENÍTEZ BARBOSA.

Empresa de Turismo Nacional (Viajes Cuba): Calle 20, No 352, entre 21 y 23, Vedado, Havana; tel. (7) 30-0587; telex 511768; f. 1981; Dir ANA ELIS DE LA CRUZ GARCÍA.

CYPRUS

Introductory Survey

Location, Climate, Language, Religion, Flag, Capital

The Republic of Cyprus is an island in the eastern Mediterranean Sea, about 100 km south of Turkey. The climate is mild, although snow falls in the mountainous south-west between December and March. Temperatures in Nicosia are generally between 5°C (41°F) and 36°C (97°F). About 75% of the population speak Greek and almost all of the remainder speak Turkish. The Greek-speaking community is overwhelmingly Christian, and almost all Greek Cypriots adhere to the Orthodox Church of Cyprus, while most of the Turks are Muslims. The national flag (proportions 5 by 3) is white, with a gold map of Cyprus, above two crossed green olive branches, in the centre. The capital is Nicosia.

Recent History

A guerrilla war against British rule in Cyprus was begun in 1955 by Greek Cypriots seeking unification (*Enosis)* with Greece. Their movement, the National Organization of Cypriot Combatants (EOKA), was led politically by Archbishop Makarios III, head of the Greek Orthodox Church in Cyprus, and militarily by Gen. George Grivas. Archbishop Makarios was suspected by the British authorities of being involved in EOKA's campaign of violence, and in March 1956 he and three other leaders of the *Enosis* movement were deported. After a compromise agreement between the Greek and Turkish communities, a constitution for an independent Cyprus was finalized in 1959. Following his return from exile, Makarios was elected the country's first President in December 1959. Cyprus became independent on 16 August 1960, although the United Kingdom retained sovereignty over two military base areas.

Following a constitutional dispute, the Turks withdrew from the central Government in December 1963 and serious intercommunal fighting occurred. In March 1964 the UN Peacekeeping Force in Cyprus (UNFICYP, see p. 54) was established to prevent a recurrence of fighting between the Greek and Turkish Cypriot communities. The effective exclusion of the Turks from political power led to the creation of separate administrative, judicial and legislative organs for the Turkish community. Discussions concerning the establishment of a more equitable constitutional arrangement began in 1968, and continued sporadically for six years, without achieving any agreement, as the Turks favoured some form of federation, while the Greeks advocated a unitary state. Each community received military aid from its mother country, and the Greek Cypriot National Guard was controlled by officers of the Greek Army.

In 1971 Gen. Grivas returned to Cyprus, revived EOKA, and began a terrorist campaign for *Enosis,* directed against the Makarios Government and apparently supported by the military regime in Greece. Gen. Grivas died in January 1974, and in June Makarios ordered a purge of EOKA sympathizers from the police, National Guard and civil service, accusing the Greek regime of subversion. On 15 July President Makarios was deposed by a military coup, led by Greek officers of the National Guard, who appointed Nikos Sampson, an extremist Greek Cypriot politician and former EOKA terrorist, to be President. Makarios escaped from the island on the following day and travelled to the United Kingdom. At the invitation of Rauf Denktaş, the Turkish Cypriot leader, the Turkish army intervened to protect the Turkish community and to prevent Greece from using its control of the National Guard to take over Cyprus. Turkish troops landed on 20 July and rapidly occupied the northern third of Cyprus, dividing the island along what became the Attila Line, which runs from Morphou through Nicosia to Famagusta. President Sampson resigned on 23 July, and Glavkos Klerides, the President of the House of Representatives, became acting Head of State. The military regime in Greece collapsed on the same day. In December Makarios returned to Cyprus and resumed the presidency. However, the Turkish Cypriots' effective control of northern Cyprus enabled them to establish a *de facto* government, and in February 1975 to declare the establishment of the 'Turkish Federated State of Cyprus' ('TFSC'), with Denktaş as President.

President Makarios died in August 1977. He was succeeded by Spyros Kyprianou, a former Minister of Foreign Affairs, who had been President of the House of Representatives since 1976. In September 1980 a ministerial reshuffle by President Kyprianou caused the powerful communist party, the Anorthotiko Komma Ergazomenou Laou (AKEL—Progressive Party of the Working People), to withdraw its support from the ruling Dimokratiko Komma (DIKO—Democratic Party). Kyprianou therefore lost his overall majority in the House of Representatives. At the next general election, held in May 1981, the AKEL and the Dimokratikos Synagermos (DISY—Democratic Rally) each won 12 seats in the House. The DIKO, however, won only eight seats, so the President remained dependent on the support of the AKEL.

In the 'TFSC' a new Council of Ministers was formed in December 1978 under a former minister belonging to the Ulusal Bırlık Partisi (UBP—National Unity Party), Mustafa Çağatay. At the elections held in June 1981, President Denktaş was returned to office, but his party, the UBP, lost its majority, and the Government that was subsequently formed by Çağatay was defeated in December. In March 1982 a coalition Government, comprising the UBP, the Demokratik Halk Partisi (Democratic People's Party) and the Türkiye Bırlık Partisi (Turkish Unity Party), was formed by Çağatay.

In September 1980 the intermittent UN-sponsored intercommunal peace talks were resumed. The constitutional issue remained the main problem: the Turkish Cypriots demanded equal status for the two communities, with equal representation in government and strong links with the mother country, while the Greeks, although accepting the principle of an alternating presidency, favoured a strong central government, and objected to any disproportionate representation for the Turkish community, who formed less than 20% of the population. In November 1981 a UN plan (involving a federal council, an alternating presidency and the allocation of 70% of the island to the Greek community) was presented, but discussions faltered in February 1982, when the Greek Prime Minister, Andreas Papandreou, proposed the withdrawal of all Greek and Turkish troops and the convening of an international conference, rather than the continuation of intercommunal talks.

In February 1983 Kyprianou was re-elected President, with the support of the AKEL, gaining 56.5% of the votes. In May the UN General Assembly voted in favour of the withdrawal of Turkish troops from Cyprus, whereupon Denktaş threatened to boycott any further intercommunal talks and to seek recognition for the 'TFSC' as a sovereign state; simultaneously it was announced that the Turkish lira was to replace the Cyprus pound as legal tender in the 'TFSC'.

On 15 November 1983 the 'TFSC' made a unilateral declaration of independence as the 'Turkish Republic of Northern Cyprus' ('TRNC'), with Denktaş continuing as President. An interim Government was formed in December, led by Nejat Konuk (Prime Minister of the 'TFSC' from 1976 to 1978 and President of the Legislative Assembly from 1981), pending elections in 1984. Like the 'TFSC', the 'TRNC' was recognized only by Turkey, and the declaration of independence was condemned by the UN Security Council. The establishment of diplomatic links between the 'TRNC' and Turkey in April 1984 was followed by a formal rejection by the 'TRNC' of UN proposals for a suspension of its declaration of independence prior to further talks.

During 1984 a 'TRNC' Constituent Assembly, comprising the members of the Legislative Assembly and 30 nominated members, drafted a new Constitution, which was approved by a referendum in May 1985. At the 'TRNC' presidential election on 9 June, Denktaş was returned to office with over 70% of the vote. A general election followed on 23 June, with the UBP, led by Dr Derviş Eroğlu, winning 24 of the 50 seats in the Legislative Assembly. In July Dr Eroğlu became Prime Minister of the 'TRNC', leading a coalition Government formed by the UBP and the Toplumcu Kurtuluş Partisi (Communal Liberation Party).

In November 1985, following a debate on President Kyprianou's leadership, the House of Representatives was dissolved.

A general election for an enlarged House was held in December. The DISY won 19 seats, President Kyprianou's DIKO won 16 seats and the AKEL won 15 seats. The AKEL and the DISY therefore failed to secure the two-thirds majority required to amend the Constitution and thus challenge the President's tenure of power. The election result was regarded as a vindication of President Kyprianou's policies.

In July 1985 the UN Secretary-General proposed a settlement plan, which was based on the idea of establishing a two-zone federal republic, with participation in the federal government according to a specified ratio for the Greek and Turkish Cypriots. The plan was, however, rejected by the Turkish Cypriots who were demanding that Turkey be one of the international guarantors of the new republic and that Turkish troops remain on the island. A similar peace proposal, which the UN Secretary-General presented in April 1986, was this time rejected by the Greek Cypriots. Their principal objections were that the plan failed to envisage: the withdrawal of the Turkish troops in Cyprus prior to implementation of the plan; the removal from Cyprus of settlers from the Turkish mainland; the provision of suitable international guarantors for the settlement, with the exclusion of Turkey; and the assurance of the 'three basic freedoms', namely the right to reside, move and own property anywhere in Cyprus. In July 1987 it was reported that the Cyprus Government had proposed to the UN Secretary-General that the Cypriot National Guard be dissolved, and orders for military equipment cancelled, in return for the withdrawal of Turkish forces from the island. In an address to the UN General Assembly in October, President Kyprianou proposed the creation of an international peace-keeping force to replace the armed forces of both the Greek and Turkish Cypriots. Denktaş, however, maintained that negotiations on the establishment of a two-zone, federal republic should precede any demilitarization.

A presidential election, held in the Greek Cypriot zone in February 1988, was won by Georghios Vassiliou, an economist, who presented himself as an independent, but who was unofficially supported by the communist party, the AKEL. He took office later in February and promised to re-establish the National Council (originally convened by President Makarios), which was to include representatives of all the main Greek Cypriot political parties, to discuss the resolution of the Cyprus problem.

In April 1988 the Prime Minister of the 'TRNC', Dr Eroğlu, and the other members of the Council of Ministers resigned from their posts, following a disagreement between the UBP and its coalition partner (since September 1986), the Yeni Doğuş Partisi (New Dawn Party), which was demanding greater representation in the Government. At the request of President Denktaş, however, Dr Eroğlu resumed his post and formed a new Council of Ministers in May, comprising mainly UBP members but also including independents.

In March 1988 President Vassiliou rejected various proposals that had been submitted, via the UN, by President Denktaş of the 'TRNC', and which included a plan to form committees to study the possibilities of intercommunal co-operation. Following a meeting with the newly-revived National Council in June, however, President Vassiliou agreed to a proposal by the UN Secretary-General to resume intercommunal talks, without preconditions, with President Denktaş, in their capacity as the leaders of two communities. After consulting the Turkish Government in July, Denktaş also approved the proposal. Accordingly, a summit meeting, under UN auspices, took place in Geneva in August, the first such meeting between Greek and Turkish Cypriot leaders since January 1985. As a result of this meeting, Vassiliou and Denktaş began direct negotiations, under UN auspices, in September 1988. A target date of 1 June 1989 was agreed for the conclusion of a comprehensive political settlement. By the end of 1989, however, it was apparent that no real progress had been achieved. In February 1990 Vassiliou and Denktaş resumed negotiations at the UN, but these were abandoned in March, chiefly because Denktaş demanded recognition of the right to self-determination for Turkish Cypriots.

In April 1990 Denktaş was the successful candidate in an early presidential election in the 'TRNC', securing nearly 67% of the votes cast. In May, at the elections to the 'TRNC' Legislative Assembly, the UBP won 34 of the 50 seats, and its leader, Dr Eroğlu, retained the office of Prime Minister.

In July 1990 the Government of Cyprus formally applied to join the European Community (EC, now European Union—EU). Denktaş condemned the application, on the grounds that the Turkish Cypriots had not been consulted, and stated that the action would prevent the resumption of intercommunal talks. None the less, the Government of Cyprus continued to make overtures regarding admission to the EC, and in September 1992 Vassiliou visited Brussels, Belgium, to present the Cypriot case. In June 1993 the European Commission approved the eligibility of Cyprus for EC membership, but insisted that the application be linked to progress in the latest UN-sponsored talks concerning the island. The Commission's recommendation was endorsed by the EC Council of Ministers in October.

At the Greek Cypriot general election held on 19 May 1991, the conservative DISY, in alliance with the Komma Phileleftheron (Liberal Party), received 35.8% of the votes cast, thereby securing 20 seats in the House of Representatives. The AKEL, contrary to pre-election predictions, made the most significant gains, obtaining 30.6% of the votes and 18 seats.

At by-elections to 12 seats in the Turkish Cypriot Legislative Assembly, conducted in October 1991, the UBP increased its representation in the 50-seat Assembly to 45 members.

Following unsuccessful attempts to promote the resumption of discussions between Vassiliou and Denktaş by the UN, the EC and the USA during 1990 and 1991, the new UN Secretary-General, Dr Boutros Boutros-Ghali, made the resolution of the Cyprus problem one of his priorities in 1992. In February UN envoys visited Cyprus, Turkey and Greece, and in January and March Dr Boutros-Ghali himself held separate meetings in New York, USA, with Vassiliou and Denktaş. However, in his report to the UN Security Council in April, Dr Boutros-Ghali was unable to announce any progress on the basic differences between the two sides concerning territory and displaced persons.

In mid-1992 Dr Boutros-Ghali held a second round of talks with Vassiliou and Denktaş in New York, initially separately, but subsequently involving direct discussions between the two leaders. The talks aimed to arrive at a draft settlement based on a 'set of ideas', compiled by Dr Boutros-Ghali and endorsed by a UN Security Council resolution, which advocated 'uninterrupted negotiations' until a settlement was reached. Discussions centred on UN proposals for the demarcation of Greek Cypriot and Turkish Cypriot areas of administration under a federal structure. However, following the publication of what was described as a 'non-map' in the Turkish Cypriot press, which showed the proposed area of Turkish administration about 25% smaller than the 'TRNC', Denktaş asserted that the UN's territorial proposals were totally unacceptable to the 'TRNC' Government, while political opinion in the Greek Cypriot area was divided. The five weeks of talks in New York came to an end in August, again without having achieved significant progress. A third round of UN-sponsored talks opened in New York in late October 1992. The talks were suspended in the following month with no discernible progress having been made in the main areas of discussion, i.e. refugees, constitutional and territorial issues. The UN Security Council held Denktaş responsible for the lack of progress, and adjourned the talks until March 1993.

In February 1993 a presidential election was held in two rounds in the Greek Cypriot zone. In the second round of voting, which was held on 14 February, Glavkos Klerides, the leader of the DISY, defeated the incumbent President, Georghios Vassiliou, by a margin of less than 1%, to become the new President. Following his defeat, Vassiliou founded a new party called the Kinema ton Eleftheron Dimokraton (KED—Movement of Free Democrats).

The negotiations, which were reconvened in May 1993 under UN auspices in New York, were concerned with the Secretary-General's plan to introduce a series of 'confidence-building measures' (CBMs). These included the proposed reopening, under UN administration, of the international airport at Nicosia, and the resettlement, also under UN directives, of a fenced suburb of Famagusta. Denktaş presented separate demands at the talks, which included the removal of the embargo against 'TRNC' airports, ports and sporting activities. The talks were abandoned in June, when the Turkish Cypriot negotiators declined to respond to the UN proposals. In September the UN Security Council urged both parties to co-operate in the implementation of the CBMs. In December two teams of UN experts, having studied the likely effects of the proposals, reported that the measures would bring significant benefits to both communities. In the same month the Council of Ministers of the EU decided to appoint an observer to monitor and report on the UN talks. Negotiations between the Greek Cypriots and Turkish Cypriots were to be resumed following the holding of the general election in the 'TRNC'.

In November 1993 Klerides and the newly-appointed Prime Minister of Greece, Andreas Papandreou, agreed at a meeting in Athens that their countries would take joint decisions in negotiations for the settlement of the Cyprus problem. The two leaders also agreed on a common defence doctrine, whereby Greece was to provide Cyprus with a guarantee of air, land and naval protection. In October 1994 the Greek airforce participated for the first time in an exercise of the Cypriot National Guard.

In December 1993 an early general election was held in the 'TRNC', partly in response to increasing conflict between President Denktaş and Prime Minister Eroğlu over the handling of the UN-sponsored peace talks. The UBP lost its majority in the Legislative Assembly, winning only 17 of the 50 seats, and at the end of the month a coalition Government was formed by the Demokrat Parti (DP—Democrat Party), which had been supported by Denktaş, and the left-wing Cumhuriyetçi Türk Partisi (CTP—Republican Turkish Party). Together, the DP and the CTP won 53.4% of the votes cast and 28 seats. The leader of the DP, Hakkı Atun (hitherto the Speaker of the Assembly), was appointed as Prime Minister of the new administration.

In February 1994, following the confirmation by both authorities of their acceptance, in principle, of the CBMs, UN officials began conducting so-called 'proximity talks' separately with the two leaders. The negotiations focused on practical arrangements for the implementation of the CBMs. Denktaş insisted, however, that the proposals under discussion differed from the intention of the original measures that had been agreed upon, and therefore refused to accept the document that was presented to both sides in March. At the end of May a report issued by the UN Secretary-General for consideration by the Security Council placed responsibility for the breakdown of the peace efforts on the 'TRNC' authorities. The following month the resident representative of the Secretary-General, Gustave Feissel, conducted negotiations to reclarify the CBM package. Denktaş accepted certain UN requests on the implementation of the measures, including the withdrawal of Turkish Cypriot troops from the access road to Nicosia international airport, but no substantive progress was made.

In July 1994 the UN Security Council adopted resolution 939, which advocated a new initiative on the part of the Secretary-General to formulate a solution for peace, but one that should be based on a single nationality, international identity and sovereignty. The 'TRNC' Legislative Assembly responded to the resolution by approving a policy, in August, establishing principles of future foreign policy. It stated that no peace solution based on the concept of a federation would be acceptable, and urged greater integration with Turkey. During October five informal meetings between Klerides and Denktaş, held on the initiative of the UN Secretary-General and hosted by Feissel, failed to achieve any progress towards an agreement on issues of the peace settlement.

The issue of Cyprus's bid to accede to the EU had greatly unsettled the progress of peace negotiations. In June 1994 EU heads of government, meeting in Corfu, Greece, confirmed that Cyprus (together with Malta) would be included in the next round of expansion of the Union. Denktaş remained adamant that any approach by the Greek Cypriots to the EU would prompt the 'TRNC' to seek further integration with Turkey. In early 1995 US officials commenced discussions with the two sides in an attempt to break the existing deadlock: while Denktaş insisted that the 'TRNC' would oppose Cyprus's EU membership application until a settlement for the island had been reached, the Greek Cypriot Government demanded 'TRNC' acceptance of the application as a pre-condition to pursuing the talks. In March the Council of Ministers of the EU agreed to consider Cyprus's membership application without discrimination based on the progress (or otherwise) of settlement talks. Negotiations were to commence six months after the conclusion of the EU's 1996 Intergovernmental Conference.

In February 1995 the 'TRNC' Prime Minister and his coalition Government resigned as a result of serious disagreements with Denktaş, concerning the redistribution of Greek Cypriot-owned housing and land. However, in the following month, after the UBP failed to negotiate the formation of a new government, Atun was reappointed as Prime Minister. At a presidential election, held in April, Denktaş achieved conclusive victory only in the second round of voting (having obtained 40.4% of votes cast in the first poll), when he obtained 62.5% of the votes, compared with 37.5% for his opponent, Dr Eroğlu. Protracted inter-party negotiations were subsequently undertaken in order to form a new government. In early June a new coalition of the DP and CTP, under Atun's premiership, took office, having concluded a joint protocol agreement on economic and foreign policy.

In May 1995 so-called 'secret' negotiations between representatives of the two Cypriot communities, held in London on the initiative of the USA and the United Kingdom, achieved little apparent progress in furthering agreement on the island's future or in securing agreement for direct talks between Denktaş and Klerides. Meanwhile, public statements by the two leaders were not conducive to reaching agreement, although both declared their support for the talks, with Klerides having violated the agreement on secrecy and Denktaş continuing to express his strong opposition to the Greek Cypriot application for EU membership. In June a meeting of the EU-Cyprus Association Council ratified the conclusions of the EU Council of Ministers in March regarding the Greek Cypriot membership application and agreed to commence pre-accession 'structured dialogue' talks. In late June Klerides, for the first time, attended a summit meeting of EU heads of government, which was held in Cannes, France. In July a new political obstacle to inter-communal negotiations emerged over allegations that Turkish Cypriot construction work in the capital was, in fact, part of efforts to fortify the buffer zone. Despite the unpromising political climate, US-led efforts to reactivate settlement negotiations were pursued.

In August 1995 the 'TRNC' Legislative Assembly adopted new legislation concerning compensation for Greek-owned property in the north (the issue which had provoked Atun's resignation earlier in the year). At the end of October Özker Özgür resigned as Deputy Prime Minister, reportedly owing to his disapproval of Denktaş's uncompromising attitude to the Cyprus issue. In early November Denktaş rejected a new list of CTP ministers, which Atun subsequently refused to amend since it had been approved by both parties in the coalition administration. Temporary appointments were made to replace three ministers who resigned. On 11 November, however, Atun submitted the resignation of his entire Government. A new DP-CTP coalition, again under Atun's leadership with Mehmet Ali Talat replacing Özgür as Deputy Prime Minister, took office in early December.

In November 1995 the detention of a Greek Cypriot guardsman by the 'TRNC' authorities provoked hostile demonstrations on both sides of the zone of separation in Nicosia. In December the US administration declared its intention to strengthen efforts in Cyprus, led by the Assistant Secretary of State with responsibility for Europe, Richard Holbrooke, with the aim of achieving significant progress towards a final settlement during 1996. Early in the new year, however, Holbrooke postponed a visit to the region, owing to renewed tension between Greece and Turkey in the Aegean and the absence of a Turkish Government following elections in that country in December 1995. Representatives of the British Government and of the EU did hold discussions with both sides in late February 1996 to assess the potential success of a new political initiative to achieve a peaceful settlement. In March a representative of the Italian Government (in its capacity as President of the Council of the EU) pursued meetings with the two authorities.

In May 1996 the results of elections for the Greek Cypriot House of Representatives produced little change in the composition of the legislature. DISY retained its 20 seats, obtaining 34.5% of the votes cast, while AKEL took 19 seats, an increase of one, with 33.0% of the votes. DIKO secured 10 seats (16.4%), EDEK five (8.1%) and KED two (3.7%). In December KED and Ananeotiko Dimokratiko Sosialistiko Kinema (ADISOK—Democratic Socialist Reform Movement) merged to form the Enomeni Demokrates (EDE—United Democrats).

In May 1996 the 'TRNC' governing party, the DP, elected Serdar Denktaş, the President's son, as its new leader, although Atun, now honorary party leader, was to continue to serve as Prime Minister. However, the stability of the Government was increasingly undermined by persisting policy differences between the two coalition parties. In early July the Government resigned. Negotiations to establish a new administration were undertaken by the DP and the UBP. A protocol coalition agreement, whereby UBP leader Dr Eroğlu would become Prime Minister, was finally signed by the leaders of the two parties in mid-August and the Government secured a confidence motion in the Legislative Assembly later in that month.

In April 1996 the permanent members of the UN Security Council, convened by Dr Boutros-Ghali, endorsed an initiative of the US Government to promote a settlement in Cyprus, based on a federal arrangement. The Cyprus issue subsequently assumed a higher profile. In May the United Kingdom appointed Sir David Hannay, a former Permanent Representative to the UN, as its first special representative to Cyprus. In June Dr Boutros-Ghali held discussions, separately, with Presidents Denktaş and Klerides, with the intention of generating support for future direct bilateral negotiations. The meetings preceded a visit to the island by the UN Secretary-General's newly-appointed Special Representative in Cyprus, Han Sung-Joo. A high-level delegation of the US Government visited the island in July, and at the end of that month the new EU envoy (representing the Irish Government) held meetings with both leaders. However, all efforts towards international mediation were diminished by a sharp escalation in intercommunal hostilities. In June an unarmed Greek Cypriot solider was killed by Turkish Cypriot forces. The situation deteriorated in August when a Greek Cypriot died and an estimated 50 others were injured during violence that erupted at a mass demonstration which violated the 'buffer' zone. UN forces judged both sides responsible for the violence. Shortly afterwards a protester, attending the victim's funeral, was shot dead by Turkish Cypriot officials following a further breach of the border area. In early September a Turkish Cypriot guard was killed, and another seriously wounded, at the demarcation line near Famagusta. The Greek Cypriot Government denied any involvement of its soldiers in the incident. President Klerides appealed to both communities to work towards an end to the civil unrest, a sentiment endorsed by Denktaş. In October there was renewed animosity following the fatal shooting of a Greek Cypriot civilian by Turkish Cypriot police.

Amid the tension Sir David Hannay made a scheduled visit to revive the possibility of a meeting of the two Cypriot leaders in 1997. At the end of October 1996 a military dialogue, involving senior commanders of both armies on the island, commenced under UN mediation. The talks were to consider the following UN proposals for reducing intercommunal tension: the prohibition of loaded weapons along the buffer zone; the removal of military personnel from the most volatile parts of the demarcation line; and the formulation of a code of conduct to specify permissible activities in the border area. In November further efforts at mediation, including a visit by an official of the US Department of State, Carey Cavanaugh, were undermined by allegations of violations of Greek Cypriot airspace by Turkish military aircraft, efforts by the Greek Cypriot community to prevent tourists from visiting the 'TRNC' and the continued opposition of the 'TRNC' to the Cypriot application to join the EU. In mid-December the British government minister, Malcolm Rifkind, became the first Secretary of State for Foreign and Commonwealth Affairs officially to visit the island since 1960. During meetings with both leaders Rifkind presented a 10-point document aimed at promoting a peaceful settlement, and expressed concern at the escalating militarization of the island.

In December 1996 the European Court of Human Rights ruled that Turkey was in breach of the European Convention on Human Rights by, as a result of its occupation in the north, denying a woman (involved in the 1989 demonstration—see above) access to her property. The ruling implicated Turkey as fully responsible for activities in the 'TRNC' and for the consequences of the military action in 1974.

In January 1997 the purchase of an advanced anti-aircraft missile system by the Greek Cypriot authorities became the focus of political hostilities between the two sides and the cause of considerable international concern. The purchase agreement, which had been an issue of contention in the previous year, was reportedly concluded between the Cypriot authorities and the Russian Government at the beginning of the month, in order to secure Greek Cypriot defences. Deployment of the missiles would have the effect of challenging the air superiority that Turkish forces had enjoyed snce 1974. The purchase agreement was criticized by the USA and by other European countries, and condemned by the 'TRNC' as an 'act of aggression'. The potential for conflict over the issue increased when the Turkish Government declared its willingness to use military force to prevent the deployment of the system. The Greek Government, in turn, insisted that it would defend Cyprus against any Turkish attack. Cavanaugh sought urgent meetings with the Cypriot leaders, and was assured by the Greek Cypriot Government that the system would not be deployed until, at the earliest, May 1998, and that its deployment would be dependent upon the progress made in talks. In addition, both sides approved measures, supported by the UN, to reduce tension along the border area, although a US proposal for a ban on all military flights over the island was rejected by the Greek Cypriots. Later in January Turkey threatened to establish air and naval bases in the 'TRNC' if Greece continued to promote plans for the establishment of military facilities in the south, and at the end of the month Turkish warships arrived in the 'TRNC' port of Famagusta. Turkey and the 'TRNC' also declared their commitment to a joint military concept, whereby any attack on the 'TRNC' would be deemed a violation against Turkey.

In April 1997 Klerides announced a reorganization of the Council of Ministers, in which Yiannakis Kasoulides, a government spokesman, was appointed Minister of Foreign Affairs. In June, following proximity talks between Klerides and Denktaş that had begun in March, the Cypriot leaders agreed to take part in direct UN-sponsored negotiations in the USA in July, under the chairmanship of the UN Special Envoy for Cyprus, Dr Diego Córdovez. The talks took place under the auspices of the UN Secretary-General, Kofi Annan, and with the participation of Richard Holbrooke, whose appointment as the US Special Envoy to Cyprus in June had been welcomed by both Klerides and Denktaş. Further private direct talks took place in Nicosia at the end of July, when agreement was reached to co-operate in efforts to trace persons missing since the hostilities in 1974.

A second formal round of UN-sponsored peace negotiations in Switzerland in August 1997 collapsed without agreement, as Denktaş demanded the suspension of Cyprus's application for EU membership. The EU had formally agreed that Cyprus would be included in the next phase of the organization's enlargement at an EU summit in July. Denktaş opposed the application on the grounds that the negotiations, scheduled to begin in 1998, were to be conducted with the Greek Cypriot Government, ignoring the issue of Turkish Cypriot sovereignty. Prior the UN-sponsored meeting in August, the 'TRNC' and Turkey agreed to create a joint committee to co-ordinate the partial integration of the 'TRNC' into Turkey. This was widely regarded as a response to the EU's decision to negotiate with the Greek Cypriot Government concerning future membership of the EU while excluding Turkey. Despite Denktaş's threat to suspend discussions pending the resolution of the EU dispute, further UN-sponsored peace negotiations concerning security issues were held in September.

During October and November 1997 US and UN efforts to promote progress in the talks, including visits to Cyprus by both Holbrooke and Córdovez, achieved little success, partly due to the imminence of the Greek Cypriot presidential election. Denktaş rejected Holbrooke's attempts to persuade the 'TRNC' to join the Greek Cypriot Government at EU accession talks in 1998, insisting on EU recognition of the 'TRNC' and the simultaneous admission of Turkey to EU membership. Tensions between the two sides remained high, as Turkish fighter aircraft violated Cyprus's airspace in October 1997, in retaliation for Greek participation in Greek Cypriot military manoeuvres.

In November 1997 DIKO voted to leave the Greek Cypriot ruling coalition in advance of the presidential election. On the following day the five DIKO ministers resigned from their government positions; they were subsequently replaced by members of the business community and civil servants. On 15 February 1998, in the second round of voting in the presidential election, Glavkos Klerides defeated Georghios Iacovou, an independent candidate (supported by AKEL and DIKO), by a margin of 1.6%, thus retaining the presidency.

Government

The 1960 Constitution provided for a system of government in which power would be shared by the Greek and Turkish communities in proportion to their numbers. This Constitution officially remains in force, but since the ending of Turkish participation in the Government in 1963, and particularly since the creation of a separate Turkish area in northern Cyprus in 1974, each community has administered its own affairs, refusing to recognize the authority of the other's Government. The Greek Cypriot administration claims to be the Government of all Cyprus, and is generally recognized as such, although it has no Turkish participation. The northern area is under the *de facto* control of the 'Turkish Republic of Northern Cyprus' (for which a new Constitution was approved by a referendum in May 1985).

Each community has its own President, Council of Ministers, legislature and judicial system.

Defence

The formation of the National Guard was authorized by the House of Representatives in 1964, after the withdrawal of the Turkish members. Men between 18 and 50 years of age are liable to 26 months' conscription. At 1 August 1997 the National Guard comprised an army of 10,000 regulars, mainly composed of Cypriot conscripts but with an additional 1,300 seconded Greek Army officers and NCOs, and 88,000 reserves. A further 950 Greek army personnel were stationed in Cyprus at that time. There is also a Greek Cypriot paramilitary police force of 3,700. In 1997 the defence budget for the Greek Cypriot area was C£259m.

At 1 August 1997 the 'TRNC' had an army of about 4,000 regulars and 26,000 reserves. Men between 18 and 50 years of age are liable to 24 months' conscription. In 1996 it was estimated that the 'TRNC' forces were being supported by 25,000–30,000 Turkish troops. In 1995 defence expenditure in the 'TRNC' was an estimated US $510m.–$540m.

The UN Peace-keeping Force in Cyprus (UNFICYP) consisted of 1,266 military and police personnel at 30 September 1997 (see p. 54). There are British military bases (with personnel numbering 3,800 in August 1997) at Akrotiri, Episkopi and Dhekelia.

Economic Affairs

In 1993, according to estimates by the World Bank, Cyprus's gross national product (GNP), measured at average 1991–93 prices, was US $7,539m., equivalent to $10,380 per head. During 1985–94, it was estimated, GNP per head increased, in real terms, by an annual average of 5.2%. In 1985–95 the population increased by an annual average of 1.2%. Cyprus's gross domestic product (GDP), according to official figures, increased by 9.7% in 1992, by 1.6% in 1993 and by 5.1% in 1994. The rate of GDP growth was estimated at 4.7% in 1995. In the 'TRNC' GNP per head was valued at $3,093 in 1994. There was an increase in GDP of 8.1% in 1989 and an estimated 5.7% in 1990. However, in 1992 GDP per head in the 'TRNC' remained less than one-half that of the remainder of the island.

Agriculture (including forestry and fishing) contributed approximately 5.5% of GDP in 1995. In the government-controlled area of the country 10.7% of the employed labour force were engaged in this sector in 1995. The principal crops of the government-controlled area are barley, potatoes (which accounted for 18.0% of domestic export earnings in 1995), grapes and citrus fruit. During 1985–94 the area's agricultural output increased by an annual average of 3.2%. In the 'TRNC' 22.7% of the working population were employed in agriculture (mainly in the production of citrus fruit), forestry and fishing, and the sector contributed an estimated 10.9% of GDP, in 1995. The principal crops of the 'TRNC' are wheat, barley, potatoes and citrus fruit.

Industry (comprising mining, manufacturing, construction and utilities) engaged 25.3% of the employed labour force in the government-controlled area in 1995, and accounted for 24.7% of GDP. In the 'TRNC' the industrial sector contributed 18.0% of GDP in 1995 and engaged 23.5% of the working labour force.

Mining provided only 0.3% of GDP and engaged a mere 0.3% of the employed labour force in the government-controlled area in 1995. Minerals accounted for less than 2% of domestic exports (by value) from the government-controlled sector in 1989. In the 'TRNC' mining and quarrying contributed 0.7% of GDP in 1995.

Manufacturing accounted for 12.8% of GDP in the government-controlled area in 1995, and engaged 15.4% of the employed labour force. Clothing represents the southern sector's main export commodity, yielding C£44.3m., or 18.6% of total export earnings (excluding re-exports), in 1995. In the 'TRNC' the manufacturing sector provided about 9.0% of GDP in 1995.

Energy is derived principally from imported petroleum, which comprised 2.7% of total imports in the government-controlled area in 1995. Mineral fuels, lubricants, etc. comprised 9.1% of total imports in the 'TRNC' in that year.

The services sector in the government-controlled area contributed an estimated 69.8% of GDP and engaged 64.0% of the employed labour force in 1995. Within the sector, financial and business services provided an estimated 17.7% of GDP and generated 7.9% of employment in that year. By 1997 the government-controlled area supported 32 'offshore' banking units; an estimated 26,000 'offshore' enterprises had been registered in the sector since incentives were introduced in 1975. In the 'TRNC' the services sector contributed 71.1% of GDP in 1995 and engaged 53.8% of the employed labour force. Both Cypriot communities have undertaken measures to expand their tourist industries, which are important sources of revenue and employment. Tourist arrivals to the government-controlled area declined from 1,991,000 in 1992 to 1,841,000 in 1993, as a result of relatively high tourist prices, but recovered in 1994 to 2,069,000 and reached 2,100,000 in 1995. Receipts from tourism in 1995 amounted to C£813m. In 1995 a total of 385,759 tourists (298,026 of whom were from the Turkish mainland) visited the 'TRNC', and net tourism receipts in that year totalled US $172.9m.

In 1995 the government-controlled area recorded a visible trade deficit of US $2,085.5m. and a current account deficit of $212.6m. The trade deficit in the 'TRNC' in 1995 was $298.8m., while the current account deficit was $12.3m. In 1995 the principal sources of imports to the government-controlled area were the United Kingdom (11.8%) and the USA (13.0%); the former was also the principal market for domestic exports (28.2%). Other major trading partners are Arab countries, France, Greece, Germany, Japan, Italy and Russia. The principal domestic exports in 1995 were clothing, potatoes and pharmaceutical products. The principal imports were textiles, vehicles, minerals, metals and foodstuffs (including beverages, spirits and vinegar and tobacco and manufactured tobacco substitutes). In 1994 the principal imports of the 'TRNC' were basic manufactures, machinery and transport equipment, and food and live animals; the principal exports were citrus fruit and industrial products. In 1995 the Turkish Cypriot area's main source of imports was Turkey (53.2%). The principal destination for exports was the United Kingdom (35.4%).

The 1995 budget estimates for the government-controlled area provided for total expenditure of C£1,306.1m. and total revenue of C£1,266.9m., thus envisaging a deficit of C£39.2m. External debt totalled C£1,199.7m. at the end of 1994, of which C£694.7m. was medium- and long-term public debt. In that year the cost of debt-servicing was equivalent to 12.9% of the value of exports of goods and services. The annual rate of inflation averaged 3.9% in 1985–95. Consumer prices increased by an average of 6.5% in 1992, following the introduction of value-added tax (VAT), and by 4.9% in 1993. They rose by 4.7% in 1994, but by only 2.6% in 1995. The average level of unemployment in the government-controlled area was 2.5% of the labour force in 1994.

The 1995 budget of the 'TRNC' recorded expenditure of TL 13,655,393.2m. and revenue of TL 9,758,343.6m. (with aid from Turkey contributing TL 1,253,647.9m. to revenue), resulting in a deficit of TL 3,897,049.6m. (equivalent to 11.2% of GDP). The average annual rate of inflation in the 'TRNC' was 87.5% in 1996. According to census figures, 6.5% of the labour force were unemployed in December 1996.

In 1972 Cyprus concluded an association agreement with the European Community (EC, now European Union—EU), improving access for Cypriot exports and ensuring financial assistance for Cyprus. In 1987 an agreement was signed on the progressive establishment of a customs union with the Community, with effect from 1 January 1988. An application to become a full member of the EC was submitted by the Greek Cypriot Government in July 1990; accession negotiations were scheduled to commence in April 1998. The 'TRNC' is a member of the Economic Co-operation Organization (ECO, see p. 260).

In the mid-1990s the failure of efforts to conclude a political settlement continued to dominate the economy and future prospects of the island. The Greek Cypriot Government's principal concern was to develop further relations with the EU and to achieve the necessary economic criteria to secure accession to the grouping (which itself was a factor in achieving a political settlement). In June 1992 the Cypriot pound was linked to the narrow band of the EC's exchange rate mechanism. In May 1993 the Government announced a programme of austerity measures (including an increase in the VAT rate to 8%), in an attempt to reduce the budget deficit and public debt to comply with the 'Maastricht' targets (which determine the conditions for economic and monetary union) of 3% and 60% of GDP respectively. In June 1995 a fourth EU-Cyprus financial protocol was signed, which awarded ECU 74m. in grants and loans to assist the process of economic convergence and the modernization of transport, communications and financial services' infrastructure in preparation for the eventual accession of Cyprus to the EU. Economic growth in the Greek Cypriot part of the island has been dominated by the service sectors, in particular tourism, banking and the 'offshore' sector. Following rapid growth, Cyprus's shipping registry, by mid-1995, was ranked as the fourth largest in the world. In February 1997 the legislation governing foreign investment was relaxed in accordance with EU legislation, and, following a slight economic downturn in 1996, the 1997 budget announced measures to promote tourism, manufacturng, exports and agriculture.

The economy of the 'TRNC', although substantially less prosperous and affected by diplomatic isolation, has also achieved significant growth since the 1980s, with considerable assistance from Turkey. The principal growth area in the economy is tourism. The close linkage with the Turkish economy, including the use of the Turkish lira as currency in the 'TRNC', has, however, resulted in persistently high levels of inflation. In July 1994 the 'TRNC' economy suffered a potential set-back with a ruling by the Court of Justice of the European Communities that effectively prohibited EU member states from importing agricultural goods (unless certified by the recognized Cypriot authorities) and ended preferential treatment of textiles. While there was little prospect of an imminent resolution of the political issue in Cyprus, the economic divergence of the two communities remained evident, with GNP per head estimated at US $13,300 in the government-controlled area in 1995, more than three times the estimated 'TRNC' figure of $4,000. In mid-1997 a five-year plan to reduce the economic disparity with the government-controlled area was announced by the 'TRNC'.

Social Welfare

A comprehensive social insurance scheme, covering every working male and female and their dependants, is in operation in the government-controlled area. It includes provisions for protection against arbitrary and unjustified dismissal, for industrial welfare and for tripartite co-operation in the formulation and implementation of labour policies and objectives. Benefits and pensions from the social insurance scheme cover unemployment, sickness, maternity, widows, orphans, injury at work, old age and death. An improved scheme, involving income-related contributions and benefits, was introduced in October 1980. The provision of health services to Greek Cypriots in 1981 included 134 hospital establishments, with a total of 3,535 beds. In 1994, in the government-controlled area, there was one doctor for every 415 inhabitants, a nurse for every 233 inhabitants and a hospital bed for every 195 inhabitants. Of total estimated expenditure by the central Government in the Greek Cypriot area in 1995, C£81.1m. (6.6%) was for health services, and a further C£312.9m. (25.3%) for social security and welfare. In 1995 the state health service in the Turkish Cypriot zone included nine hospital establishments, with a total of 902 beds, while there were 229 private establishments, with 201 beds. In that year there were 400 physicians and dentists, of whom 170 worked in the state health service.

Education

In the Greek Cypriot sector elementary education, which is compulsory and available free of charge, is provided in six grades for children between five-and-a-half and 12 years of age. Enrolment at primary level included 96% of children in the relevant age-group in 1994 (males 96%; females 96%). Secondary education is free for all years of study and lasts six years, with three compulsory years at the Gymnasium being followed by three non-compulsory years at a technical school or a Lyceum. There are five options of specialization at the Lyceums: classical, science, economics, commercial/secretarial and foreign languages. In 1994 enrolment in secondary education included 92% of school-age children (males 90%; females 93%). There are 11 three-year technical schools. Higher education for teachers, technicians, engineers, hoteliers and caterers, foresters, nurses and health inspectors is provided by technical and vocational colleges. The University of Cyprus was inaugurated in September 1992, and there were a further 31 post-secondary institutions in 1994/95. In 1994/95 a total of 9,188 students from the Greek Cypriot area were studying in universities abroad. In 1994 enrolment at tertiary level was equivalent to 17.0% of the relevant age-group (males 15.0%; females 19.0%). Estimated budgetary expenditure on education by the central Government in the Greek Cypriot area was C£150.7m. (12.2% of total spending) in 1995. In 1992, according to census results, 5.6%. of the adult population (males 2.2%; females 8.9%) were illiterate.

Education in the Turkish Cypriot zone is controlled by the 'TRNC'. Pre-primary education is provided by kindergartens for children of 5 and 6 years of age. Primary education is free and compulsory: it comprises elementary schools for the 7–11 age group, and secondary-junior schools for the 12–14 age group. Secondary education, for the 15–17 age group, is provided by high schools (Lycées) and vocational schools, including colleges of agriculture, nursing and hotel management. It is free, but not compulsory. In 1994/95 14,262 students proceeded to higher education in the 'TRNC', which is provided by seven institutions: the Eastern Mediterranean University in Gazi Mağusa (Famagusta); the Near East University College in Lefkoşa (Nicosia); the Girne (Kyrenia) American University; Lefke (Levka) University; the International American University; the Open University; and a Teachers' Training College in Lefkoşa (Nicosia). In 1996, according to census figures, the rate of adult illiteracy in the 'TRNC' was 6.5%.

Public Holidays

1998: 1 January (New Year's Day), 6 January (Epiphany)*, 29–31 January (Ramazam Bayram—end of Ramadan)†, 2 March (Green Monday)*, 25 March (Greek Independence Day)*, 1 April (Anniversary of Cyprus Liberation Struggle), 7–9 April (Kurban Bayram—Feast of the Sacrifice)†, 17–20 April (Easter)*, 23 April (National Sovereignty and Children's Day)†, 1 May (May Day), 19 May (Youth and Sports Day)†, 8 June (Pentecost)*, 20 July (Peace and Freedom Day, anniversary of the Turkish invasion in 1974)†, 29 July (Birth of the Prophet)†, 1 August (Communal Resistance Day)†, 15 August (Assumption)*, 30 August (Victory Day)†, 1 October (Independence Day)*, 28 October (Greek National Day)*, 29 October (Turkish Republic Day)†, 15 November (TRNC Day)†, 25–26 December (Christmas)*.

1999: 1 January (New Year's Day), 6 January (Epiphany)*, 18–20 January (Ramazam Bayram—end of Ramadan)†, 22 February (Green Monday)*, 25 March (Greek Independence Day)*, 27–29 March (Kurban Bayram—Feast of the Sacrifice)†, 1 April (Anniversary of Cyprus Liberation Struggle), 9–12 April (Easter)*, 23 April (National Sovereignty and Children's Day)†, 1 May (May Day), 19 May (Youth and Sports Day)†, 31 May (Pentecost)*, 20 July (Peace and Freedom Day, anniversary of the Turkish invasion in 1974)†, 1 August (Communal Resistance Day)†, 9 August (Birth of the Prophet)†, 15 August (Assumption)*. 30 August (Victory Day)†, 1 October (Independence Day)*, 28 October (Greek National Day)*, 29 October (Turkish Republic Day)†, 15 November (TRNC Day)†, 25–26 December (Christmas)*.

* Greek and Greek Orthodox.

† Turkish and Turkish Muslim.

Weights and Measures

Although the imperial and the metric systems are understood, Cyprus has a special internal system:

Weights: 400 drams = 1 oke = 2.8 lb (1.27 kg.).
44 okes = 1 Cyprus kantar.
180 okes = 1 Aleppo kantar.

Capacity: 1 liquid oke = 2.25 pints (1.28 litres).
1 Cyprus litre = 5.6 pints (3.18 litres).

Length and Area: 1 pic = 2 feet (61 cm).

Area: 1 donum = 14,400 sq ft (1,338 sq m).

Statistical Survey

Source (unless otherwise indicated): Department of Statistics and Research, Ministry of Finance, Nicosia; tel. (2) 309301; telex 3399; fax (2) 374830.

Note: Since July 1974 the northern part of Cyprus has been under Turkish occupation. As a result, some of the statistics relating to subsequent periods do not cover the whole island. Some separate figures for the 'TRNC' are given on pp. 1100–1101.

AREA AND POPULATION

Area: 9,251 sq km (3,572 sq miles), incl. Turkish-occupied region.

Population: 735,900 (males 367,000; females 368,900), incl. 90,600 in Turkish-occupied region, at 31 December 1995 (official estimate). Note: Figures for the Turkish-occupied region exclude settlers from Turkey, estimated at more than 90,000 in 1995.

Ethnic Groups (estimates, 31 December 1995): Greeks 623,200 (84.7%), Turks 90,600 (12.3%), others 22,100 (3.0%); Total 735,900.

Principal Towns (population at 1 October 1992): Nicosia (capital) 181,234 (excl. Turkish-occupied portion); Limassol 139,424; Larnaca 62,178; Famagusta (Gazi Mağusa) 39,500 (mid-1974); Paphos 33,246; (estimated population at 31 December 1995): Nicosia 191,000 (excl. Turkish-occupied portion); Limassol 148,700; Larnaca 66,400; Paphos 36,300.

Births and Deaths (government-controlled area, 1995): Registered live births 9,869 (birth rate 15.4 per 1,000); Registered deaths 4,935 (death rate 7.7 per 1,000).

Expectation of Life (government-controlled area, years at birth, 1992–93): males 74.6; females 79.1. Source: UN, *Demographic Yearbook*.

Employment (government-controlled area, provisional figures, '000 persons aged 15 years and over, excl. armed forces, 1995): Agriculture, hunting, forestry and fishing 30.5; Mining and quarrying 0.8; Manufacturing 44.0; Electricity, gas and water 1.5; Construction 25.7; Trade, restaurants and hotels 74.6; Transport, storage and communications 18.5; Financing, insurance, real estate and business services 22.6; Community, social and personal services 63.8; employment on British sovereign bases 3.1; Total 285.1 (males 173.0, females 112.1).

AGRICULTURE, ETC.

Principal Crops (government-controlled area, '000 metric tons, 1996): Wheat 13; Barley 131; Potatoes 220; Olives 10; Tomatoes 40; Watermelons 29*; Melons 9*; Grapes 122; Apples 9; Oranges 50; Tangerines, mandarins, etc. 20; Grapefruit 58; Lemons and limes 25. *FAO estimate. Source: FAO, *Production Yearbook*.

Livestock (government-controlled area, '000 head, 1995): Cattle 69; Sheep 250; Goats 220; Pigs 374; Chickens 3,400.

Livestock Products (government-controlled area, '000 metric tons, 1996): Beef and veal 5; Mutton and lamb 4; Goat meat 4; Pig meat 46; Poultry meat 31; Cows' milk 138; Sheep's milk 19; Goats' milk 24; Cheese 5; Hen eggs 10. Source: FAO, *Production Yearbook*.

Forestry (government-controlled area, '000 cubic metres, 1995): Roundwood removals (excl. bark) 39; Sawnwood production (incl. railway sleepers) 20.

Fishing (metric tons, live weight, government-controlled area): Total catch 3,022 in 1995.

MINING AND QUARRYING

Selected Products (metric tons, government-controlled area, 1995): Sand and gravel 6,200,000; Marble 30,000; Gypsum 148,275; Bentonite 51,234.

INDUSTRY

Selected Products (government-controlled area, 1995): Cement 1,021,703 metric tons; Bricks 54.6 million; Mosaic tiles 1.6 million sq metres; Cigarettes 2,528 million; Footwear (excluding plastic and semi-finished shoes) 3.4 million pairs; Beer 34.9 million litres; Wines 59.1 million litres; Carbonated soft drinks 58.9 million litres.

FINANCE

Currency and Exchange Rates: 100 cents = 1 Cyprus pound (Cyprus £). *Sterling and Dollar Equivalents* (30 September 1997): £1 sterling = 84.52 Cyprus cents; US $1 = 52.32 Cyprus cents; Cyprus £100 = £118.31 sterling = $191.12. *Average exchange rate* (US $ per Cyprus £): 2.0347 in 1994; 2.2113 in 1995; 2.1446 in 1996.

Budget (estimates, Cyprus £ million, government-controlled area, 1995): *Revenue:* Taxation 1,022.36 (Taxes on income 241.41, Social security contributions 180.97, Taxes on payroll 20.03, Taxes on property 25.98, Excises 118.53, Value-added tax 191.86, Other domestic taxes on goods and services 46.41, Import duties 101.40, Other taxes 95.77); Entrepreneurial and property income 154.20; Administrative fees and charges, non-industrial and incidental sales 63.75; Other current revenue 25.84; Capital revenue 0.79; Total 1,266.94, excl. grants from abroad (3.90). *Expenditure:* General public services 85.89; Defence 46.24; Public order and safety 77.59; Education 150.74; Health 81.14; Social security and welfare 312.91; Housing and community amenities 59.97; Recreational, cultural and religious affairs and services 17.93; Economic affairs and services 195.43 (Agriculture, forestry, fishing and hunting 86.12, Mining 0.11, Road transport 40.10, Other transport and communication 34.40, Other economic affairs 34.70); Other purposes 209.10; Sub-total 1,236.93 (Current 1,083.70, Capital 153.23); Adjustment 69.21; Total 1,306.14, excl. lending minus repayments (4.57).

International Reserves (US $ million at 31 December 1996): Gold (national valuation) 17.0; Reserve position in IMF 36.6; Foreign exchange 1,505.3; Total 1,558.9. Source: IMF, *International Financial Statistics*.

Money Supply (Cyprus £ million at 31 December 1996, government-controlled area): Currency outside banks 265.8, Demand deposits at deposit money banks 387.4; Total money 653.2.

Cost of Living (Retail Price Index, government-controlled area; base: 1992 = 100): 109.78 in 1994; 112.65 in 1995; 116.01 in 1996.

Gross Domestic Product in Purchasers' Values (Cyprus £ million at current prices, government-controlled area): 3,250.5 in 1993; 3,599.6 in 1994; 3,905.1 in 1995.

Gross Domestic Product by Economic Activity (provisional, Cyprus £ million at current prices, government-controlled area, 1995): Agriculture, hunting, forestry and fishing 199.5; Mining and quarrying 11.4; Manufacturing 465.6; Electricity, gas and water 84.0; Construction 338.8; Wholesale and retail trade, restaurants and hotels 759.6; Transport, storage and communications 299.7; Finance, insurance, real estate and business services 644.9; Government services 507.1; Other community, social and personal services 296.9; Other services 31.9; *Sub-total* 3,639.4; Import duties 185.6; Value-added Tax 191.6; *Less* Imputed bank service charges 111.5; *Total* 3,905.1.

Balance of Payments (US $ million, government-controlled area, 1995): Exports of goods f.o.b. 1,228.7, Imports of goods f.o.b. –3,314.2, *Trade balance* –2,085.5; Exports of services 2,960.1, Imports of services –1,102.7, *Balance on goods and services* –228.1; Other income received 142.3, Other income paid –244.0, *Balance on goods, services and income* –329.8; Current transfers received 134.8; Current transfers paid –17.7, *Current balance* –212.6; Direct investment abroad –6.6, Direct investment from abroad 119.1; Portfolio investment assets –23.7, Portfolio investment liabilities –29.4, Other investment assets –1,060.7, Other investment liabilities 945.8, Net errors and omissions –94.9, *Overall balance* –363.1. Source: IMF, *International Financial Statistics*.

EXTERNAL TRADE

Principal Commodities (Cyprus £ '000, government-controlled area, 1995): *Imports c.i.f.:* Textiles and textile articles 122,798 (Clothing and clothing accessories 29,594); Road vehicles, parts and accessories 166,864; Mineral products 132,882 (Crude oil 45,286); Base metals and articles of base metal 109,303; Products of chemical or allied industries 116,527; Prepared foodstuffs, beverages, spirits and vinegar, tobacco and manufactured tobacco substitutes 241,878 (Tobacco and manufactured tobacco substitutes 165,573); Plastics and articles thereof 52,280; Paper, paperboard and articles thereof 47,374; Live animals and animal products 29,788; Total (incl. others) 1,670,408. *Exports f.o.b.:* Clothing 44,303; Footwear 4,937; Potatoes 43,072; Citrus fruit 16,797; Cement 7,801; Pharmaceutical products 17,841; Alcoholic beverages 9,647 (Wines 9,105); Fruit and vegetable juices 7,690; Total (incl. others) 238,675. Figures for exports exclude re-exports (Cyprus £'000): 316,932.

Total Trade (Cyprus £ '000, government-controlled area): *Imports c.i.f.* (incl. military equipment): 1,316,078 in 1993; 1,482,222 in 1994; 1,670,408 in 1995. *Exports f.o.b.* (incl. re-exports): 431,462 in 1993; 475,978 in 1994; 555,607 in 1995.

Principal Trading Partners (Cyprus £ '000, government-controlled area, 1995): *Imports c.i.f.:* France 68,674; Germany 136,264; Greece 120,058; Italy 163,589; Japan 111,658; Russia 66,417; United Kingdom 196,718; USA 217,433; Total (incl. others) 1,670,408. *Exports f.o.b.* (excl. re-exports): Belgium-Luxembourg 7,024; France

6,878; Germany 23,820; Greece 11,469; Israel 6,093; Lebanon 12,568; Russia 12,183; United Kingdom 67,337; Total (incl. others) 238,675.

TRANSPORT

Road Traffic (licensed motor vehicles, government-controlled area, 31 December 1995): Private passenger cars 212,152; Taxis and self-drive cars 7,597; Buses and coaches 2,670; Lorries and vans 101,182; Motorcycles 50,393; Total (incl. others) 387,559.

Shipping (freight traffic, '000 metric tons, government-controlled area, 1995): Goods loaded 2,255, Goods unloaded 5,023. At 31 December 1996 a total of 1,652 merchant vessels (combined displacement 23.8 m. grt) were registered in Cyprus. (Source: Lloyd's Register of Shipping, *World Fleet Statistics*).

Civil Aviation (government-controlled area, 1995): Overall passenger traffic 4,665,276; Total freight transported 39,701 metric tons.

TOURISM

Foreign Visitors by Country of Origin (excluding one-day visitors and visitors to the Turkish-occupied zone, 1995): Germany 235,000, Greece 65,000, Middle East and Gulf countries 105,000, Russia 95,000, Scandinavian countries 230,000, Switzerland 110,000, United Kingdom 850,000; Total (incl. others) 2,100,000.

Tourist Arrivals (government-controlled area): 1,841,000 in 1993; 2,069,000 in 1994; 2,100,000 in 1995.

Tourist Receipts (Cyprus £ million, government-controlled area): 698 in 1993; 812 in 1994; 813 in 1995.

COMMUNICATIONS MEDIA

Radio Receivers (government-controlled area): 210,000 in 1992; 215,000 in 1993*; 220,000 in 1994*. (* Source: UNESCO, *Statistical Yearbook.*)

Television Receivers (government-controlled area): 235,000 in 1994 (Source: UNESCO, *Statistical Yearbook.*)

Telephones (main lines in use): 311,000 in 1993; 330,000 in 1994; 347,000 in 1995.

Telefax Stations (number in use): 6,000 in 1992; 7,000 in 1993. Source: UN, *Statistical Yearbook*.

Mobile Telephones (subscribers): 9,739 in 1992; 15,288 in 1993; 22,940 in 1994. Source: UN, *Statistical Yearbook*.

Book Production (government-controlled area): 1,040 titles and 1,551,700 copies in 1994; 1,128 titles and 1,723,400 copies in 1995.

Newspapers (1995): 10 daily (circulation 84,000 copies); 27 non-daily (circulation 165,000 copies).

EDUCATION

1995/96 (government-controlled area): Kindergarten: 647 institutions, 1,323 teachers, 26,254 pupils; Primary schools: 381 institutions, 3,411 teachers, 64,660 pupils; Secondary schools (Gymnasia and Lyceums): 112 institutions, 4,258 teachers, 55,435 pupils; Technical colleges: 11 institutions, 574 teachers, 4,410 pupils; University of Cyprus: 201 teachers, 1,962 students; Other post-secondary: 32 institutions, 527 teachers, 6,912 students.

'Turkish Republic of Northern Cyprus'*

Source: Office of the London Representative of the 'Turkish Republic of Northern Cyprus', 29 Bedford Sq., London WC1B 3EG (tel. (171) 631-1920; telex 8955363; fax (171) 631-1948).

AREA AND POPULATION

Area: 3,355 sq km (1,295 sq miles).

Population (census, 15 December 1996): 200,587 (males 105,978; females 94,609).

Ethnic Groups (estimates, 1996): Turks 180,207, Greeks 476, Maronites 187, Others 2,420; Total 183,290.

Principal Towns (estimated population within the municipal boundary, 1996): Lefkoşa (Nicosia) 42,767 (Turkish-occupied area only); Gazi Mağusa (Famagusta) 22,216; Girne (Kyrenia) 7,893.

Births, Marriages and Deaths (registered, 1996): Birth rate 18.0 per 1,000; Marriage rate 6.1 per 1,000; Death rate 8.0 per 1,000.

Employment (1995): Agriculture, forestry and fishing 17,383; Industry 8,348; Construction 9,584; Trade and tourism 8,367; Transport and communications 6,510; Financial institutions 2,397; Business and personal services 7,276; Public Services 16,589; *Total employed* 76,454. Total unemployed 567; *Total labour force* 77,021.

AGRICULTURE, ETC.

Principal Crops ('000 metric tons, 1995): Wheat 16.1; Barley 84.6; Potatoes 15.1; Legumes 3.1; Tomatoes 1.1; Onions 2.4; Artichokes 0.8; Water-melons 4.3; Melons 1.0; Cucumbers 0.9; Carobs 1.5; Olives 2.7; Lemons 12.2; Grapefruit 53.2; Oranges 138.0; Tangerines 1.3.

Livestock ('000 head, 1995): Cattle 20.0; Sheep 207.6; Goats 57.3; Chickens 3,519.7.

Livestock Products ('000 metric tons, unless otherwise indicated, 1995): Sheep's and goats' milk 10.4; Cows' milk 28.5; Mutton and lamb 3.1; Goat meat 0.8; Beef 1.3; Poultry meat 5.2; Wool 0.3; Eggs (million) 34.0.

Fishing (metric tons, 1994); Total catch 400.

FINANCE

Currency and Exchange Rates: Turkish currency: 100 kuruş = 1 Turkish lira (TL) or pound. *Sterling and Dollar Equivalents* (30 September 1997): £1 sterling = 280,482 liras; US $1 = 173,630 liras; 1,000,000 Turkish liras = £3.565 = $5.759. *Average Exchange Rate* (liras per US dollar): 29,609 in 1994; 45,845 in 1995; 81,405 in 1996.

Budget (million Turkish liras, 1995): *Revenue:* Internal revenue 8,463,386.0 (Direct taxes 3,661,102.4, Indirect taxes 2,541,579.4, Non-tax revenue 1,609,116.6); Aid from Turkey 1,253,647.9; Aid from other countries 41,309.7; Loans 3,897,049.6; Total 13,655,393.2. *Expenditure:* Personnel 5,509,473.8; Other goods and services 753,885.6; Transfers 5,794,161.5; Investments 850,372.3; Defence 747,500.0; Total 13,655,393.2

Cost of Living (Retail Price Index at December; base: December of previous year = 100): 315.0 in 1994; 172.1 in 1995; 187.5 in 1996.

Expenditure on the Gross Domestic Product (million Turkish liras at current prices, 1995): Government final consumption expenditure 8,078,733.9; Private final consumption expenditure 22,846,169.6; Increase in stocks 579,670.0; Gross fixed capital formation 4,247,018.7; *Total domestic expenditure* 35,751,592.2; Exports of goods and services, *less* Imports of goods and services –1,033,975.7; *GDP in purchasers' values* 34,717,616.5; *GDP at constant 1977 prices* 7,360.0.

Gross Domestic Product (GDP) by Economic Activity (million Turkish liras, 1995): Agriculture, forestry and fishing 3,530,103.8; Mining and quarrying 239,268.5; Manufacturing 2,928,154.4; Electricity and water 1,352,971.7; Construction 1,291,235.6; Wholesale and retail trade 4,657,853.1; Restaurants and hotels 1,797,093.8; Transport and communications 3,006,231.4; Finance 3,879,119.3; Ownership of dwellings 634,713.2; Business and personal services 1,884,287.4; Government services 7,155,640.7; *Sub-total* 32,356,672.9; Import duties 2,360,943.6; *GDP in purchasers' values* 34,717,616.5.

Balance of Payments (US $ million, 1995): Merchandise exports f.o.b. 67.3; Merchandise imports c.i.f. –366.1; *Trade balance* –298.8; Services and unrequited transfers (net) 286.5; *Current balance* –12.3; Capital movements (net) 76.5; Net errors and omissions 1.9; *Total* (net monetary movements) 66.1.

EXTERNAL TRADE

Principal Commodities (US $ million, 1995): *Imports c.i.f.:* Food and live animals 54.3; Beverages and tobacco 20.0; Mineral fuels, lubricants, etc. 33.8; Chemicals 27.2; Basic manufactures 94.5; Machinery and transport equipment 98.7; Miscellaneous manufactured articles 28.5; Total (incl. others) 366.1. *Exports f.o.b.:* Food and live animals 34.9 (Citrus fruit 22.0, Potatoes 1.4, Concentrated citrus 4.8, Carobs 1.8); Beverages and tobacco 2.8; Crude materials (inedible) except fuels 1.9; Chemicals 1.5; Basic manufactures 1.9; Clothing 23.8; Total (incl. others) 67.3.

Principal Trading Partners (US $ million, 1995): *Imports c.i.f:* Belgium 4.4; France 8.8; Germany 16.6; Hong Kong 22.5; Italy 13.2; Japan 6.7; Lebanon 6.5; Netherlands 4.6; Romania 4.7; Sri Lanka 5.5; Turkey 194.8; United Kingdom 49.4; Total (incl. others) 366.1. *Exports f.o.b.:* Belgium 1.8; Germany 8.0; Kuwait 0.8; Netherlands 2.6; Romania 1.3; Russia 5.1; Turkey 20.2; United Kingdom 23.8; Total (incl. others) 67.3.

TRANSPORT

Road Traffic (registered motor vehicles, 1995): Saloon cars 49,422; Estate cars 6,564; Pick-ups 2,649; Vans 5,651; Buses 1,453; Trucks 751; Lorries 4,475; Motor cycles 13,526; Agricultural tractors 5,730; Total (incl. others) 91,724.

Shipping (1995): Freight traffic ('000 metric tons): Goods loaded 238.6, Goods unloaded 712.4; Vessels entered 3,468.

Civil Aviation: Kilometres flown (Turkish Cypriot Airlines) 1,126,848 (1985); Passenger arrivals and departures 624,189 (1994); Freight landed and cleared (metric tons) 3,303 (1994).

TOURISM

Visitors (1995): 385,759 (including 298,026 Turkish); **Accommodation** (1995): Hotels 40, Tourist beds (in all tourist accommodation, including pensions and hotel-apartments) 7,774; **Net Receipts** (US $ million, 1995): 218.9.

COMMUNICATIONS MEDIA

Radio Receivers (1994, provisional): 56,450 in use.

Television Receivers (1994, provisional): 52,300 in use.

Telephones (31 December 1995): 70,448 subscribers.

EDUCATION

1995/96: *Primary and pre-primary education:* 262 institutions, 1,314 teachers, 18,893 pupils; *High schools:* 14 institutions, 439 teachers, 5,649 students; *Vocational schools:* 11 institutions, 348 teachers, 2,477 students; *Higher education:* 8 institutions, 6,149 students.

* Note: Following a unilateral declaration of independence in November 1983, the 'Turkish Federated State of Cyprus' became known as the 'Turkish Republic of Northern Cyprus'.

Directory

The Constitution

The Constitution, summarized below, entered into force on 16 August 1960, when Cyprus became an independent republic.

THE STATE OF CYPRUS

The State of Cyprus is an independent and sovereign Republic with a presidential regime.

The Greek Community comprises all citizens of the Republic who are of Greek origin and whose mother tongue is Greek or who share the Greek cultural traditions or who are members of the Greek Orthodox Church.

The Turkish Community comprises all citizens of the Republic who are of Turkish origin and whose mother tongue is Turkish or who share the Turkish cultural traditions or who are Muslims.

The official languages of the Republic are Greek and Turkish.

The Republic shall have its own flag of neutral design and colour, chosen jointly by the President and the Vice-President of the Republic.

The Greek and the Turkish Communities shall have the right to celebrate respectively the Greek and the Turkish national holidays.

THE PRESIDENT AND VICE-PRESIDENT

Executive power is vested in the President and the Vice-President, who are members of the Greek and Turkish Communities respectively, and are elected by their respective communities to hold office for five years.

The President of the Republic as Head of the State represents the Republic in all its official functions; signs the credentials of diplomatic envoys and receives the credentials of foreign diplomatic envoys; signs the credentials of delegates for the negotiation of international treaties, conventions or other agreements; signs the letter relating to the transmission of the instruments of ratification of any international treaties, conventions or agreements; confers the honours of the Republic.

The Vice-President of the Republic, as Vice-Head of the State, has the right to be present at all official functions; at the presentation of the credentials of foreign diplomatic envoys; to recommend to the President the conferment of honours on members of the Turkish Community, which recommendation the President shall accept unless there are grave reasons to the contrary.

The election of the President and the Vice-President of the Republic shall be direct, by universal suffrage and secret ballot, and shall, except in the case of a by-election, take place on the same day but separately.

The office of the President and of the Vice-President shall be incompatible with that of a Minister or of a Representative or of a member of a Communal Chamber or of a member of any municipal council including a Mayor or of a member of the armed or security forces of the Republic or with a public or municipal office.

The President and Vice-President of the Republic are invested by the House of Representatives.

The President and the Vice-President of the Republic in order to ensure the executive power shall have a Council of Ministers composed of seven Greek Ministers and three Turkish Ministers. The Ministers shall be designated respectively by the President and the Vice-President of the Republic who shall appoint them by an instrument signed by them both. The President convenes and presides over the meetings of the Council of Ministers, while the Vice-President may ask the President to convene the Council and may take part in the discussions.

The decisions of the Council of Ministers shall be taken by an absolute majority and shall, unless the right of final veto or return is exercised by the President or the Vice-President of the Republic or both, be promulgated immediately by them.

The executive power exercised by the President and the Vice-President of the Republic conjointly consists of:

Determining the design and colour of the flag.

Creation or establishment of honours.

Appointment of the members of the Council of Ministers.

Promulgation by publication of the decisions of the Council of Ministers.

Promulgation by publication of any law or decision passed by the House of Representatives.

Appointments and termination of appointments as in Articles provided.

Institution of compulsory military service.

Reduction or increase of the security forces.

Exercise of the prerogative of mercy in capital cases.

Remission, suspension and commutation of sentences.

Right of references to the Supreme Constitutional Court and publication of Court decisions.

Address of messages to the House of Representatives.

The executive powers which may be exercised separately by the President and Vice-President include: designation and termination of appointment of Greek and Turkish Ministers respectively; the right of final veto on Council decisions and on laws concerning foreign affairs, defence or security; the publication of the communal laws and decisions of the Greek and Turkish Communal Chambers respectively; the right of recourse to the Supreme Constitutional Court; the prerogative of mercy in capital cases; and addressing messages to the House of Representatives.

THE COUNCIL OF MINISTERS

The Council of Ministers shall exercise executive power in all matters, other than those which are within the competence of a Communal Chamber, including the following:

General direction and control of the government of the Republic and the direction of general policy.

Foreign affairs, defence and security.

Co-ordination and supervision of all public services.

Supervision and disposition of property belonging to the Republic.

Consideration of Bills to be introduced to the House of Representatives by a Minister.

Making of any order or regulation for the carrying into effect of any law as provided by such law.

Consideration of the Budget of the Republic to be introduced to the House of Representatives.

THE HOUSE OF REPRESENTATIVES

The legislative power of the Republic shall be exercised by the House of Representatives in all matters except those expressly reserved to the Communal Chambers.

The number of Representatives shall be 50, subject to alteration by a resolution of the House of Representatives carried by a majority comprising two-thirds of the Representatives elected by the Greek

Community and two-thirds of the Representatives elected by the Turkish Community.

Out of the number of Representatives 70% shall be elected by the Greek Community and 30% by the Turkish Community separately from amongst their members respectively, and, in the case of a contested election, by universal suffrage and by direct and secret ballot held on the same day.

The term of office of the House of Representatives shall be for a period of five years.

The President of the House of Representatives shall be a Greek, and shall be elected by the Representatives elected by the Greek Community, and the Vice-President shall be a Turk and shall be elected by the Representatives elected by the Turkish Community.

THE COMMUNAL CHAMBERS

The Greek and the Turkish Communities respectively shall elect from amongst their own members a Communal Chamber.

The Communal Chambers shall, in relation to their respective Community, have competence to exercise legislative power solely with regard to the following:

All religious, educational, cultural and teaching matters.

Personal status; composition and instances of courts dealing with civil disputes relating to personal status and to religious matters.

Imposition of personal taxes and fees on members of their respective Community in order to provide for their respective needs.

THE PUBLIC SERVICE AND THE ARMED FORCES

The public service shall be composed as to 70% of Greeks and as to 30% of Turks.

The Republic shall have an army of 2,000 men, of whom 60% shall be Greeks and 40% shall be Turks.

The security forces of the Republic shall consist of the police and gendarmerie and shall have a contingent of 2,000 men. The forces shall be composed as to 70% of Greeks and as to 30% of Turks.

OTHER PROVISIONS

The following measures have been passed by the House of Representatives since January 1964, when the Turkish members withdrew:

The amalgamation of the High Court and the Supreme Constitutional Court (see Judicial System section).

The abolition of the Greek Communal Chamber and the creation of a Ministry of Education.

The unification of the Municipalities.

The unification of the Police and the Gendarmerie.

The creation of a military force by providing that persons between the ages of 18 and 50 years can be called upon to serve in the National Guard.

The extension of the term of office of the President and the House of Representatives by one year intervals from July 1965 until elections in February 1968 and July 1970 respectively.

New electoral provisions; abolition of separate Greek and Turkish rolls; abolition of post of Vice-President, which was re-established in 1973.

The Government*

HEAD OF STATE

President: GLAVKOS KLERIDES (took office 28 February 1993; re-elected 15 February 1998).

COUNCIL OF MINISTERS

(January 1998)

Minister of Foreign Affairs: YIANNAKIS KASOULIDES.

Minister of Defence: GEORGHIOS CHARALAMBIDES.

Minister of the Interior: GEORGHIOS STAVRINAKIS.

Minister of Finance: CHRISTODOULOS CHRISTODOULOU.

Minister of Justice and Public Order: NIKOS KOSHIS.

Minister of Commerce, Industry and Tourism: MICHALAKIS MICHAELIDES.

Minister of Education and Culture: GEORGHIOS HADJINIKOLAOU.

Minister of Health: CHRISTOS SOLOMIS.

Minister of Labour and Social Insurance: EFSTATHIOS PAPADAKIS.

Minister of Communications and Works: LEONTIOS IERODIAKONOU.

Minister of Agriculture, Natural Resources and the Environment: ANDREAS MANTOVANIS.

* Under the Constitution of 1960, the vice-presidency and three posts in the Council of Ministers are reserved for Turkish Cypriots. However, there has been no Turkish participation in the Government since December 1963. In 1968 President Makarios announced that he considered the office of Vice-President in abeyance until Turkish participation in the Government is resumed, but the Turkish community elected Rauf Denktaş Vice-President in February 1973.

MINISTRIES

Ministry of Agriculture, Natural Resources and the Environment: Loukis Akritas Ave, Nicosia; tel. (2) 302171; fax (2) 781156.

Ministry of Commerce, Industry and Tourism: 2 Andreas Araouzos St, Nicosia; tel. (2) 308041; fax (2) 375120.

Ministry of Communications and Works: Dem. Severis Ave, 1424 Nicosia; tel. (2) 302830; fax (2) 465462.

Ministry of Defence: 4 Emmanuel Roides St, Nicosia; tel. (2) 303187; fax (2) 366225.

Ministry of Education and Culture: Greg. Afxentiou St, 1434 Nicosia; tel. (2) 303331; fax (2) 445021.

Ministry of Finance: Ex Secretariat Compound, 1439 Nicosia; tel. (2) 302164; fax (2) 366080.

Ministry of Foreign Affairs: 18–19 Dem. Severis Ave, Nicosia; tel. (2) 300600; fax (2) 451881.

Ministry of Health: Ex Secretariat Compound, Nicosia; tel. (2) 303243; fax (2) 303498.

Ministry of the Interior: Dem. Severis Ave, Ex Secretariat Compound, Nicosia; tel. (2) 302238; fax (2) 453465.

Ministry of Justice and Public Order: 12 Helioupoleos, Nicosia; tel. (2) 302355; fax (2) 461427.

Ministry of Labour and Social Insurance: Byron Ave, Nicosia; tel. (2) 303481; telex 6011; fax (2) 450993.

President and Legislature

PRESIDENT

Election, 8 and 15 February 1998*

Candidates	Votes	%
GLAVKOS KLERIDES (Democratic Rally)	206,879 (158,763)	50.8 (40.1)
GEORGHIOS IACOVOU (Independent, with AKEL/DIKO support)	200,222 (160,918)	49.2 (40.6)
VASSOS LYSSARIDES (EDEK—Socialist Party)	— (41,978)	— (10.6)
ALEXIS GALANOS (Independent)	— (16,003)	— (4.0)
GEORGHIOS VASSILIOU (United Democrats)	— (11,908)	— (3.0)
NIKOS KOUTSOU (New Horizons)	— (3,625)	— (0.9)
NIKOS ROLANDIS (Liberal Party)	— (3,104)	— (0.8)
Total	407,101 (396,299)	100.0 (100.0)

* Figures from the first round of voting appear in brackets.

HOUSE OF REPRESENTATIVES

The House of Representatives originally consisted of 50 members, 35 from the Greek community and 15 from the Turkish community, elected for a term of five years. In January 1964 the Turkish members withdrew and set up the 'Turkish Legislative Assembly of the Turkish Cypriot Administration' (see p. 1104). At the 1985 elections the membership of the House was expanded to 80 members, of whom 56 were to be from the Greek community and 24 from the Turkish community (according to the ratio of representation specified in the Constitution).

President: SPYROS KYPRIANOU.

Elections for the Greek Representatives, 26 May 1996

Party	Votes	% of Votes	Seats
DISY (Democratic Rally)/Liberal Party	127,380	34.5	20
AKEL (Communist Party)	121,958	33.0	19
DIKO (Democratic Party)	60,726	16.4	10
EDEK (Socialist Party)	30,033	8.1	5
KED (Free Democrats)*	13,623	3.7	2
New Horizons	6,317	1.7	—
ADISOK*	5,311	1.4	—
Ecologists	3,710	1.0	—
Independents	463	0.1	—
Total	369,521	100.0	56

* Merged in December 1996 to form Enomeni Dimokrates (United Democrats—EDE).

Political Organizations

Anorthotiko Komma Ergazomenou Laou (AKEL) (Progressive Party of the Working People): POB 1827, 4 Akamantos St, Nicosia; tel. (2) 441121; fax (2) 461574; f. 1941; successor to the Communist Party of Cyprus (f. 1926); Marxist-Leninist; supports demilitarized, non-aligned and independent Cyprus; over 14,000 mems; Sec.-Gen. DEMETRIS CHRISTOFIAS.

Dimokratiko Komma (DIKO) (Democratic Party): POB 3979, 50 Grivas Dhigenis Ave, Nicosia; tel. (2) 472002; fax (2) 366488; f. 1976; absorbed Enosi Kentrou (Centre Union, f. 1981) in 1989; supports settlement of the Cyprus problem based on UN resolutions; Pres. SPYROS KYPRIANOU; Vice-Pres. DINOS MICHAELIDES; Sec.-Gen. STATHIS KITTIS.

Dimokratikos Synagermos (DISY) (Democratic Rally): POB 5305, 23 Pindarou St, Nicosia; tel. (2) 449791; fax (2) 442751; f. 1976; absorbed Democratic National Party (DEK) in 1977 and New Democratic Front (NEDIPA) in 1988; advocates entry of Cyprus into the European Union and greater active involvement by the EU in the settlement of the Cyprus problem; 25,000 mems; Pres. NIKOS ANASTASIADES; Gen. Sec. ELENI VRAHIMI.

Enomeni Dimokrates (EDE) (United Democrats): POB 3494, 8 Iassonos St, Nicosia; tel. (2) 474460; fax (2) 474757; f. Dec. 1996 by merger of Ananeotiko Dimokratiko Socialistiko Kinema (ADISOK—Democratic Socialist Reform Movement) and Kinema ton Eleftheron Dimokraton (KED—Movement of Free Democrats); Pres. GEORGHIOS VASSILIOU; Gen. Sec. KOSTAS THEMISTOKLEOUS.

Komma ton Phileleftheron (Liberal Party): POB 7282, 19 Gregoriou Xenopoulou St, 1st Floor, Nicosia; tel. (2) 452117; telex 2483; fax (2) 368900; f. 1986; supports settlement of the Cyprus problem based on UN resolutions; Pres. NIKOS A. ROLANDIS; Gen. Sec. PHIVOS MAVROVOUNIOTIS.

Neyi Orizontes (NEO) (New Horizons): POB 2064, 9 Byzantiou St, Strovolos, Nicosia; tel. (2) 475333; fax (2) 476044; e-mail neo@logos.cy.net; f. 1996; supports settlement of the Cyprus problem through political means and the establishment of a non-federal unitary state with single sovereignty throughout the whole territory of the island; Pres. NIKOS KOUTSOU; Gen. Sec. STELIOS AMERIKANOS.

Pankyprio Komma Prosfygon ke Pligenton (PAKOP) (Pancyprian Party of Refugees and Stricken Persons): POB 1216, 7 Androkleous St, Nicosia; tel. (2) 458764; fax (2) 367053; f. 1991; Pres. YIANNAKIS EROTOKRITOU; Gen. Sec. CHRISTOS IOANNOU.

Socialistiko Komma Kyprou EDEK (EDEK Socialist Party of Cyprus): POB 1064, 40 Byron Ave, Nicosia; tel. (2) 458617; telex 3182; fax (2) 458894; f. 1969 as Ethniki Dimokratiki Enosi Kyprou (EDEK) (Cyprus National Democratic Union); supports independent, non-aligned, unitary, demilitarized Cyprus; advocates the establishment of a socialist structure; Pres. Dr VASSOS LYSSARIDES; First Vice-Pres. YIANNAKIS OMIROU.

Diplomatic Representation

EMBASSIES AND HIGH COMMISSIONS IN CYPRUS

Australia: 4 Annis Komninis St, 2nd Floor, Nicosia; tel. (2) 473001; fax (2) 366486; High Commissioner: J. W. SULLIVAN.

Bulgaria: POB 4029, 13 Konst. Paleologos St, 2406 Engomi, Nicosia; tel. (2) 472486; fax (2) 456598; Ambassador: ALEXEI IVANOV.

China, People's Republic: POB 4531, 28 Archimedes St, 2411 Engomi, Nicosia; tel. (2) 352182; telex 6376; fax (2) 353530; Ambassador: YIN ZUOJIN.

Cuba: 7 Yiannis Taliotis St, Strovolos 147, Nicosia; tel. (2) 512332; fax (2) 512331; Ambassador: MANUEL PARDIÑAS AJENO.

Czech Republic: POB 5202, 48 Arsinois St, 1307 Nicosia; tel. (2) 421118; fax (2) 421059; Chargé d'affaires: JIŘÍ MICHOVSKY.

Egypt: POB 1752, 3 Egypt Ave, 1097 Nicosia; tel. (2) 465144; telex 2102; fax (2) 462287; Ambassador: FADEL EL-KADI.

France: POB 1671, 6 Ploutarchou St, Engomi, Nicosia; tel. (2) 465258; telex 2389; fax (2) 452289; Ambassador: HENRI JACOLIN.

Germany: POB 1795, 10 Nikitaras St, Ay. Omoloyitae, 1513 Nicosia; tel. (2) 444362; telex 2460; fax (2) 365694; Ambassador: Dr GABRIELE VON MALSEN-TILBORCH.

Greece: POB 1799, 8/10 Byron Ave, Nicosia; tel. (2) 441880; telex 2397; fax (2) 511290; Ambassador: KYRIAKOS RODOUSSAKIS.

Holy See: POB 1964, Holy Cross Catholic Church, Paphos Gate, Nicosia (Apostolic Nunciature); tel. (2) 462132; fax (2) 466767; Apostolic Pro-Nuncio: Most Rev. ANDREA CORDERO LANZA DI MONTEZEMOLO, Titular Archbishop of Tuscania (with residence in Jerusalem).

Hungary: POB 4067, 13/A Princess Anne St, 1700 Nicosia; tel. (2) 779074; fax (2) 779243; e-mail hungcomm@spidernet.com.cy; Ambassador: JÁNOS HERMAN.

India: POB 5544, 3 Indira Gandhi St, Engomi, Nicosia; tel. (2) 351741; telex 4146; fax (2) 350402; High Commissioner: YOGESH TIWARI.

Iran: POB 8145, 42 Armenias St, Akropolis, Nicosia; tel. (2) 314459; telex 6416; fax (2) 315446; Chargé d'affaires: ALI AKBAR FARAZI.

Israel: POB 1049, 4 I. Gryparis St, Nicosia; tel. (2) 445195; fax (2) 453486; Ambassador: SHEMI TZUR.

Italy: 11 25th March St, Engomi 2408, Nicosia; tel. (2) 357635; telex 3847; fax (2) 357616; Ambassador: FRANCESCO BASCONE.

Lebanon: POB 1924, 1 Vasilissis Olgas St, Nicosia; tel. (2) 442216; telex 3056; fax (2) 267662; Ambassador: ZEIDAN ZEIDAN.

Libya: POB 3669, 14 Estias St, 1041 Nicosia; tel. (2) 317366; telex 3277; fax (2) 316152; Chargé d'affaires: MUFTAH FITOURI.

Poland: 11 Acharnon St, Strovolos, Nicosia; tel. (2) 427077; fax (2) 510611.

Romania: 83 Kennedy Ave, Nicosia; tel. (2) 379303; fax (2) 379121; Chargé d'affaires: FLORIAN UNCHIASU.

Russia: Ay. Prokopias St and Archbishop Makarios III Ave, Engomi, Nicosia; tel. (2) 772141; telex 5808; fax (2) 774854; Ambassador: GEORGII MURATOV.

Slovakia: POB 1165, 4 Kalamatas St, Akropolis, Nicosia; tel. (2) 311683; fax (2) 311715; Chargé d'affaires a.i.: DUŠAN ROZBORA.

Switzerland: POB 729, MEDCON Bldg, 6th Floor, 46 Themistoklis Dervis St, Nicosia; tel. (2) 446261; fax (2) 446008; Chargé d'affaires a.i.: WALTER BOPP.

Syria: POB 1891, Cnr Androkleous and Thoukidides Sts, Nicosia; tel. (2) 474481; telex 2030; fax (2) 446963; Chargé d'affaires a.i.: Dr AHMED HAJ-IBRAHIM.

United Kingdom: POB 1978, Alexander Pallis St, Nicosia; tel. (2) 771131; telex 2208; fax (2) 777198; High Commissioner: DAVID MADDEN.

USA: 7 Ploutarchou, 2406 Engomi, Nicosia; tel. (2) 476100; fax (2) 465944; Ambassador: KENNETH BRILL.

Yugoslavia: 2 Vasilissis Olgas St, Nicosia; tel. (2) 445511; fax (2) 445910; Chargé d'affaires a.i.: IVAN MRKIĆ.

Judicial System

Supreme Council of Judicature: Nicosia. The Supreme Council of Judicature is composed of the President and Judges of the Supreme Court. It is responsible for the appointment, promotion, transfer, etc., of the judges exercising civil and criminal jurisdiction in the District Courts and the Assize Courts.

SUPREME COURT

Supreme Court: Char. Mouskos St, Nicosia; tel. (2) 302398. The Constitution of 1960 provided for a separate Supreme Constitutional Court and High Court but in 1964, in view of the resignation of their neutral presidents, these were amalgamated to form a single Supreme Court.

The Supreme Court is the final appellate court in the Republic and the final adjudicator in matters of constitutional and administrative law, including recourses on conflict of competence between state organs on questions of the constitutionality of laws, etc. It deals with appeals from Assize Courts and District Courts as well as from the decisions of its own judges when exercising original jurisdiction in certain matters such as prerogative orders of *habeas corpus, mandamus, certiorari*, etc., and in admiralty cases.

President: GEORGHIOS M. PIKIS.

Judges: I. C. CONSTANTINIDES, T. ELIADES, CHR. C. ARTEMIDES, G. NIKOLAOU, P. KALLIS, FR. G. NIKOLAIDES, Y. CHR. CHRYSOSTOMIS, S. NIKITAS, P. CH. ARTEMIS, M. KRONIDES, A. KRAMVIS, R. GAVRIELIDES.

Attorney-General: ALEKOS MARKIDES.

OTHER COURTS

As required by the Constitution a law was passed in 1960 providing for the establishment, jurisdiction and powers of courts of civil and criminal jurisdiction, i.e. of six District Courts and six Assize Courts. In accordance with the provisions of new legislation, approved in 1991, a permanent Assize Court, with powers of jurisdiction in all districts, was established.

In addition to a single Military Court, there are specialized Courts concerned with cases relating to industrial disputes, rent control and family law.

'Turkish Republic of Northern Cyprus'

The Turkish intervention in Cyprus in July 1974 resulted in the establishment of a separate area in northern Cyprus under the control of the Autonomous Turkish Cypriot Administration, with a Council of Ministers and separate judicial, financial, police, military and educational machinery serving the Turkish community.

On 13 February 1975 the Turkish-occupied zone of Cyprus was declared the 'Turkish Federated State of Cyprus', and Rauf Denktaş declared President. At the second joint meeting held by the Executive Council and Legislative Assembly of the Autonomous Turkish Cypriot Administration, it was decided to set up a Constituent Assembly which would prepare a constitution for the 'Turkish Federated State of Cyprus' within 45 days. This Constitution, which was approved by the Turkish Cypriot population in a referendum held on 8 June 1975, was regarded by the Turkish Cypriots as a first step towards a federal republic of Cyprus. The main provisions of the Constitution are summarized below:

The 'Turkish Federated State of Cyprus' is a democratic, secular republic based on the principles of social justice and the rule of law. It shall exercise only those functions which fall outside the powers and functions expressly given to the (proposed) Federal Republic of Cyprus. Necessary amendments shall be made to the Constitution of the 'Turkish Federated State of Cyprus' when the Constitution of the Federal Republic comes into force. The official language is Turkish.

Legislative power is vested in a Legislative Assembly, composed of 40 deputies, elected by universal suffrage for a period of five years. The President is Head of State and is elected by universal suffrage for a period of five years. No person may be elected President for more than two consecutive terms. The Council of Ministers shall be composed of a prime minister and 10 ministers. Judicial power is exercised through independent courts.

Other provisions cover such matters as the rehabilitation of refugees, property rights outside the 'Turkish Federated State', protection of coasts, social insurance, the rights and duties of citizens, etc.

On 15 November 1983 a unilateral declaration of independence brought into being the 'Turkish Republic of Northern Cyprus', which, like the 'Turkish Federated State of Cyprus', was not granted international recognition.

The Constituent Assembly, established after the declaration of independence, prepared a new constitution, which was approved by the Turkish Cypriot electorate on 5 May 1985. The new Constitution is very similar to the old one, but the number of deputies in the Legislative Assembly was increased to 50.

HEAD OF STATE

President of the 'Turkish Republic of Northern Cyprus': Rauf R. Denktaş (assumed office as President of the 'Turkish Federated State of Cyprus' 13 February 1975; became President of the 'TRNC' 15 November 1983; re-elected for five-year terms on 9 June 1985, on 22 April 1990 and on 22 April 1995).

COUNCIL OF MINISTERS

(January 1998)

A coalition of the Demokrat Parti (DP) and the Ulusal Bırlık Partisi (UBP).

Prime Minister: Dr Derviş Eroğlu (UBP).

Minister of State and Deputy Prime Minister: Serdar Denktaş (DP).

Minister of Foreign Affairs and Defence: Taner Etkin (DP).

Minister of the Interior and Rural Affairs: İlkay Kamil (UBP).

Minister of Finance: Salih Coşar (DP).

Minister of the Economy: Erdal Onurhan (UBP).

Minister of Education, Culture, Youth and Sports: Günay Caymaz (UBP).

Minister of Agriculture and Forestry: Kenan Akin (DP).

Minister of Communications, Works and Tourism: Mehmet Bayram (UBP).

Minister of Social Welfare and Rehabilitation: Ali Özkan Altinişik (DP).

Minister of Health and the Environment: Dr Ertuğrul Hasipoğlu (UBP).

MINISTRIES

All ministries are in Lefkoşa (Nicosia). Address: Lefkoşa (Nicosia), Mersin 10, Turkey.

Prime Minister's Office: tel. (22) 83141; fax (22) 87280; e-mail talsin@cc.emu.edu.tr.

Ministry of State and Deputy Prime Minister's Office: tel. (22) 77283; telex 5744; fax (22) 73976.

Ministry of Agriculture and Forestry: tel. (22) 83735; telex 57419; fax (22) 86945.

Ministry of Communications, Works and Tourism: tel. (22) 83666; telex 57169; fax (22) 81891.

Ministry of the Economy and Finance: tel. (22) 83116; telex 57268; fax (22) 73049.

Ministry of Education, Culture, Youth and Sports: tel. (22) 83136; fax (22) 82334.

Ministry of Foreign Affairs and Defence: tel. (22) 83241; telex 57612; fax (22) 84290.

Ministry of Health and the Environment: tel. (22) 83173; fax (22) 83893.

Ministry of the Interior and Rural Affairs: tel. (22) 85453; fax (22) 83043.

Ministry of Social Welfare and Rehabilitation: tel. (22) 78765; fax (22) 76349.

PRESIDENT

Election, 15 April 1995* and 22 April 1995

Candidates	Votes	%
Rauf R. Denktaş (Independent)	53,235 (37,541)	62.48 (40.40)
Dr Derviş Eroğlu (UBP)	31,972 (22,476)	37.52 (24.19)
Özker Özgür (CTP)	— (17,639)	— (18.98)
Mustafa Akinci (TKP)	— (13,179)	— (14.18)
Alpay Durduran (YKP)	— (1,619)	— (1.74)
Ayhan Kaymak (Independent)	— (345)	— (0.37)
Sami Güdenoğlu (Independent)	— (133)	— (0.14)
Total	85,207†(92,932)‡	100.00 (100.00)

* Figures from the first round of voting appear in brackets.

† Excluding 5,684 invalid votes.

‡ Excluding 3,560 invalid votes.

LEGISLATIVE ASSEMBLY

Speaker: Hakki Atun (DP).

Deputy Speaker: Olgun Paşalar (UBP).

General Election, 12 December 1993

Party	% of votes	Seats
Ulusal Bırlık Partisi	29.9	16
Demokrat Parti	29.2	16
Cumhuriyetçi Türk Partisi	24.2	13
Toplumcu Kurtuluş Partisi	13.3	5
Others*	3.5	—
Total	100.0	50

* The other parties that contested the election were the National Struggle Party, which won 2% of the votes; the Yeni Kıbrıs Partisi, which obtained 1.2%; and the Unity and Sovereignty Party, which won 0.3%.

POLITICAL ORGANIZATIONS

Cumhuriyetçi Türk Partisi (CTP) (Republican Turkish Party): 99A Şehit Salahi, Şevket Sok., Lefkoşa (Nicosia), Mersin 10, Turkey; tel. (22) 73300; fax (22) 81914; f. 1970 by members of the Turkish community in Cyprus; socialist principles with anti-imperialist stand; district organizations at Gazi Mağusa (Famagusta), Girne (Kyrenia), Güzelyurt (Morphou) and Lefkoşa (Nicosia); Leader Mehmet Ali Talat; Gen. Sec. Mustafa Ferdi Soyer.

Demokrat Parti (DP) (Democrat Party): Lefkoşa (Nicosia), Mersin 10, Turkey; tel. (22) 83795; fax (22) 87130; f. 1992 by disaffected UBP representatives; merged with the Yeni Doğuş Partisi (New Dawn Party; f. 1984) and Sosyal Demokrat Partisi (Social Democrat Party) in May 1993; Leader Serdar Denktaş; Sec.-Gen. (vacant).

Hür Demokrat Parti (Free Democrat Party): Lefkoşa (Nicosia), Mersin 10, Turkey; f. 1991. Leader Özel Tahsin.

Toplumcu Kurtuluş Partisi (TKP) (Communal Liberation Party): 44 İkinci Selim Sok., Lefkoşa (Nicosia), Mersin 10, Turkey; tel. (22) 72555; f. 1976; merged with the Atılımcı Halk Partisi (Progressive People's Party, f. 1979) in 1989; democratic left party; wants a solution of Cyprus problem as an independent, non-aligned, bi-zonal and bi-communal federal state; Leader Mustafa Akinci; Gen. Sec. Hüseyin Angolemli.

Ulusal Bırlık Partisi (UBP) (National Unity Party): 9 Atatürk Meydanı, Lefkoşa (Nicosia), Mersin 10, Turkey; tel. (22) 73972; f. 1975; right of centre; based on Atatürk's reforms, social justice, political equality and peaceful co-existence in an independent, bi-zonal, bi-communal, federal state of Cyprus; Leader Dr Derviş Eroğlu; Sec.-Gen. Dr Vehbi Zeki Serter.

Unity and Sovereignty Party (BEP): Lefkoşa (Nicosia), Mersin 10, Turkey; Leader Arif Salih Kirdağ.

Yeni Doğus Partisi (New Dawn Party): Lefkoşa (Nicosia); f. 1984; merged with DP in May 1993, revived 1997; Leader ENVER EMIN.

Yeni Kıbrıs Partisi (YKP) (New Cyprus Party): Lefkoşa (Nicosia), Mersin 10, Turkey; tel. (22) 74917; fax (22) 71476; e-mail YKP@cc.emu.edu.tr; f. 1989; Leader ALPAY DURDURAN.

DIPLOMATIC REPRESENTATION

Embassy in the 'TRNC'

Turkey: Bedrettin Demirel Cad., Lefkoşa Büyükelçisi, Lefkoşa (Nicosia), Mersin 10, Turkey; tel. (22) 72314; fax (22) 82289; Ambassador: ERTUĞRUL APAKAN.

Turkey is the only country officially to have recognized the 'Turkish Republic of Northern Cyprus'.

JUDICIAL SYSTEM

Supreme Court: The highest court in the 'TRNC' is the Supreme Court. The Supreme Court functions as the Constitutional Court, the Court of Appeal and the High Administrative Court. The Supreme Court, sitting as the Constitutional Court, has exclusive jurisdiction to adjudicate finally on all matters prescribed by the Constitution. The Supreme Court, sitting as the Court of Appeal, is the highest appellate court in the 'TRNC'. It also has original jurisdiction in certain matters of judicial review. The Supreme Court, sitting as the High Administrative Court, has exclusive jurisdiction on matters relating to administrative law.

The Supreme Court is composed of a president and seven judges.

President: SALİH S. DAYIOĞLU.

Judges: GÖNÜL ERÖNEN, NEVVAR NOLAN, CELÂL KARABACAK, TANER ERGİNEL, METİN A. HAKKI, MUSTAFA ÖZKÖK, SEYİT A. BENSEN.

Subordinate Courts: Judicial power other than that exercised by the Supreme Court is exercised by the Assize Courts, District Courts and Family Courts.

Supreme Council of Judicature: The Supreme Council of Judicature, composed of the president and judges of the Supreme Court, a member appointed by the President of the 'TRNC', a member appointed by the Legislative Assembly, the Attorney-General and a member elected by the Bar Association, is responsible for the appointment, promotion, transfer and matters relating to the discipline of all judges. The appointments of the president and judges of the Supreme Court are subject to the approval of the President of the 'TRNC'.

Attorney-General: SAİT AKIN.

Religion

Greeks form 77% of the population and most of them belong to the Orthodox Church, although there are also adherents of the Armenian Apostolic Church, the Anglican Communion and the Roman Catholic Church (including Maronites). Most Turks (about 18% of the population) are Muslims.

CHRISTIANITY

The Orthodox Church of Cyprus

The Autocephalous Orthodox Church of Cyprus, founded in AD 45, is part of the Eastern Orthodox Church; the Church is independent, and the Archbishop, who is also the Ethnarch (national leader of the Greek community), is elected by representatives of the towns and villages of Cyprus. The Church comprises six dioceses, and in 1995 had an estimated 600,000 members.

Archbishop of Nova Justiniana and all Cyprus: Archbishop CHRYSOSTOMOS, POB 1130, Arch. Kyprianos St, Nicosia; tel. (2) 430696; fax (2) 432470.

Metropolitan of Paphos: Bishop CHRYSOSTOMOS.

Metropolitan of Kitium: Bishop CHRYSOSTOMOS, Dem. Lipertis St, Larnaca; fax (41) 55588.

Metropolitan of Kyrenia: Bishop PAULUS.

Metropolitan of Limassol: Bishop CHRYSANTHOS.

Metropolitan of Morphou: (vacant).

The Roman Catholic Church

Latin Rite

The Patriarchate of Jerusalem covers Israel, Jordan and Cyprus. The Patriarch is resident in Jerusalem (see the chapter on Israel).

Vicar Patriarchal for Cyprus: Father UMBERTO BARATO.

Maronite Rite

Most of the Roman Catholics in Cyprus are adherents of the Maronite rite. Prior to June 1988 the Archdiocese of Cyprus included part of Lebanon. At December 1995 the archdiocese contained an estimated 10,000 Maronite Catholics.

Archbishop of Cyprus: Most Rev. BOUTROS GEMAYEL, POB 2249, Maronite Archbishop's House, 8 Ayios Maronas St, Nicosia; tel. (2) 458877; fax (2) 368260.

The Anglican Communion

Anglicans in Cyprus are adherents of the Episcopal Church in Jerusalem and the Middle East, officially inaugurated in January 1976. The Church has four dioceses. The diocese of Cyprus and the Gulf includes Cyprus, Iraq and the countries of the Arabian peninsula.

Bishop in Cyprus and the Gulf: Rt Rev. CLIVE HANDFORD, c/o POB 2075, Diocesan Office, 2 Grigoris Afxentiou St, 1517 Nicosia; tel. (2) 451220; fax (2) 466553.

Other Christian Churches

Among other denominations active in Cyprus are the Armenian Apostolic Church and the Greek Evangelical Church.

ISLAM

Most adherents of Islam in Cyprus are Sunni Muslims of the Hanafi sect. The religious head of the Muslim community is the Mufti.

Mufti of Cyprus: AHMET CEMAL İLKTAÇ (acting), PK 142, Lefkoşa (Nicosia), Mersin 10, Turkey.

The Press

GREEK CYPRIOT DAILIES

Agon (Struggle): POB 1417, Makarios Ave and Agapinoros St, Nicosia; tel. (2) 477181; fax (2) 457887; f. 1964; morning; Greek; right of centre; Founder NIKOS KOSHIS; Dir LEONIDAS KOSHIS; Chief Editor PANAYIOTIS PAPADEMETRIS; circ. 5,000.

Alithia (Truth): POB 1695, 26A Pindaros and Androklis St, 1060 Nicosia; tel. (2) 463040; fax (2) 463945; f. 1952 as a weekly, 1982 as a daily; morning; Greek; right-wing; Dir SOCRATIS HASIKOS; Chief Editor ALEKOS KONSTANTINIDES; circ. 11,000.

Apogevmatini (Afternoon): POB 5603, 5 Aegaleo St, Strovolos, Nicosia; tel. (2) 353603; fax (2) 353223; f. 1972; afternoon; Greek; independent, Dirs EFTHYMIOS HADJIEFTHIMIOU, ANTONIS STAVRIDES; Chief Editor ALKIS ANDREOU; circ. 8,000.

Cyprus Mail: POB 1144, 24 Vassilios Voulgaroktonos St, Nicosia; tel. (2) 462074; fax (2) 366385; f. 1945; morning; English; independent; Dir. KYRIACOS IAKOVIDES; Editor STEVEN MYLES; circ. 4,000.

Phileleftheros (Liberal): POB 1094, Commercial Centre, 1 Diogenous St, 3rd, 6th–7th Floor, Engomi, 1501 Nicosia; tel. (2) 590000; fax (2) 590122; f. 1955; morning; Greek; independent, moderate; Dir N. PATTICHIS; Editorial Dir A. LYKAVGIS; Chief Editor T. KOUNNAFIS; circ. 31,000.

Haravghi (Dawn): POB 1556, ETAK Bldg, 6 Akamantos St, Nicosia; tel. (2) 476356; fax (2) 365154; f. 1956; morning; Greek; organ of AKEL (Communist Party); Dir NIKOS KATSOURIDES; circ. 9,000.

Machi (Battle): POB 7628, 4A Danaes, Engomi, Nicosia; tel. (2) 356676; fax (2) 356701; f. 1961; morning; Greek; right-wing; Dir SOTIRIS SAMSON; Chief Editor DEMETRIS SAVVIDES; circ. 4,200.

Simerini (Today): POB 1836, 31 Archangelos Ave, Strovolos, Nicosia; tel. (2) 353532; fax (2) 352237; f. 1976; morning; Greek; right-wing; supports DISY party; Dir COSTAS HADJICOSTIS; Chief Editor SAVVAS IAKOVIDES; circ. 9,000.

TURKISH CYPRIOT DAILIES

Bırlık (Unity): 43 Yediler Sok., PK 841, Lefkoşa (Nicosia), Mersin 10, Turkey; tel. (22) 72959; fax (22) 83959; f. 1980; Turkish; organ of UBP; Editor LÜTFI ÖZTER.

Halkın Sesi (Voice of the People): 172 Kyrenia Sok., Lefkoşa (Nicosia), Mersin 10, Turkey; tel. (22) 73141; telex 57173; f. 1942; morning; Turkish; independent Turkish nationalist; Editor AKAY CEMAL; circ. 6,000.

Kıbrıs: Dr Fazil Küçük Bul., Lefkoşa (Nicosia), Mersin 10, Turkey; tel. (22) 81922; telex 57177; fax 81934; Editor MEHMET ALI AKPINAR; circ. 13,000.

Ortam (Political Conditions): 158A Girne Cad., Lefkoşa (Nicosia), Mersin 10, Turkey; tel. (22) 74872; Turkish; organ of the TKP; Editor ÖZAL ZIYA; circ. 1,250.

Vatan (Homeland): Lefkoşa (Nicosia), Mersin 10, Turkey; Editor ERTEN KASIMOĞLU.

Yeni Demokrat (New Democrat): 1 Cengiz Han Cad., Köskluçiftlik, Lefkoşa (Nicosia), Mersin 10, Turkey; tel. (22) 81485; fax (22) 72558; Turkish; organ of the DP; Editor MUSTAFA OKAN; circ. 450.

Yeni Düzen (New System): Yeni Sanayi Sok., Lefkoşa (Nicosia), Mersin 10, Turkey; tel. (22) 74906; fax (22) 75240; Turkish; organ of the CTP; Editor ÖZKAN YORGANCIOĞLU; circ. 1,000.

GREEK CYPRIOT WEEKLIES

Athltiki tis Kyriakis: 5 Epias, Engomi, Nicosia; tel. (2) 352966; fax (2) 348835; f. 1996; Greek; athletic; Dir PANAYIOTIS FELLOUKAS; Chief Editor SAWAS KOSHARIS; circ. 4,000.

Cyprus Financial Mirror: POB 4280, 80B Thermopylon St, 2007 Nicosia; tel. (2) 495790; fax (2) 495907; e-mail finmir@logos.cy.net; internet http://www.cfm.com.cy; f. 1993; English (with Greek-language supplement, Russian edition); independent; Dirs MASIS DER PARTHOGH, SHAVASB BOHDJALIAN; circ. 3,500.

Cyprus Weekly: POB 4977, Suite 102, Trust House, Gryparis St Nicosia; tel. (2) 456047; fax (2) 458665; f. 1979; English; independent; Dirs GEORGES DER PARTHOGH, ALEX EFTHYVOULOS, A. HADJIPAPAS; Chief Editor MARTYN HENRY; circ. 22,000.

Epilogi: 19 Nikitara St, Ay. Omologiles, Nicosia; tel. (2) 367345; fax (2) 367511; f. 1997; Greek; Chief Editor COSTAS ZACHARIADES.

Ergatiki Phoni (Workers' Voice): POB 5018, SEK Bldg, 23 Alkeou St, Engomi, Nicosia; tel. (2) 441142; fax (2) 476360; f. 1947; Greek; organ of SEK trade union; Dir MICHALAKIS IOANNOU; Chief Editor XENIS XENOFONTOS; circ. 10,000.

Ergatiko Vima (Workers' Tribune): POB 1185, 31-35 Archemos St, Nicosia; tel. (2) 349400; fax (2) 349382; f. 1956; Greek; organ of the PEO trade union; Editor-in-Chief KOSTAS GREKOS; circ. 14,000.

Official Gazette: Printing Office of the Republic of Cyprus, Nicosia; tel. (2) 302202; fax (2) 303175; f. 1960; Greek; published by the Government of the Republic of Cyprus.

Paraskinio (Behind the Scenes): 39 Kennedy Ave, Nicosia; tel. (2) 313334; fax (2) 314193; f. 1987; Greek; Dir and Chief Editor D. MICHAEL; cir. 3,000.

Selides (Pages): POB 1094, 1501 Nicosia; tel. (2) 590000; fax (2) 590516; f. 1991; Greek; Dir N. PATTICHIS; Chief Editor A. MICHAELIDES; circ. 17,000.

Ta Nea (News): POB 4349, 40 Vyronos Ave, Nicosia; tel. (2) 476575; fax (2) 476512; f. 1968; Greek; organ of EDEK (Socialist Party); Chief Editor PHYTOS SOCRATOUS; circ. 3,000.

Tharros (Courage): POB 7628, 4A Danaes, Engomi, Nicosia; tel. (2) 356676; fax (2) 356701; f. 1961; Greek; right-wing; Dir SOTIRIS SAMSON; Chief Editor DIMITRIS SAVVIDES; circ. 3,500.

To Periodiko: POB 1836, Dias Bldg, 31 Archangelos Ave, Strovolos, Nicosia; tel. (2) 353646; fax (2) 352268; f. 1986; Greek; Dir COSTAS HADJICOSTIS; Chief Editor PHILIPPOS STYLIANOU; circ. 14,000.

TURKISH CYPRIOT WEEKLIES

Cyprus Today: A. N. Graphics Ltd, Dr Fazil Küçük Bul., PK 831, Lefkoşa (Nicosia), Mersin 10, Turkey; tel. (22) 81922; fax (22) 81934; f. 1991; English; political, social, cultural and economic; Editor GILL FRASER; circ. 5,000.

Ekonomi (The Economy): Bedrettin Demirel Cad. No.90, Lefkoşa (Nicosia), Mersin 10, Turkey; tel. (22) 83760; telex 57511; fax (22) 83089; f. 1958; Turkish; published by the Turkish Cypriot Chamber of Commerce; Editor-in-Chief SAMİ TAŞARKAN; circ. 3,000.

Safak: PK 228, Lefkoşa (Nicosia), Mersin 10, Turkey; tel. (22) 71472; fax (22) 87910; f. 1992; Turkish; circ. 1,000.

Yeni Çağ: 28 Ramadan Cad., Lefkoşa (Nicosia), Mersin 10, Turkey; tel. (22) 74917; fax (22) 71476; f. 1990; Turkish; publ. of the YKP; circ. 500.

OTHER WEEKLIES

Lion: 55 AEC Episkopi, British Forces Post Office 53; tel. (5) 263263; fax (5) 263181; e-mail carl@dial.cylink.com.cy; distributed to British Sovereign Base Areas, United Nations Forces and principal Cypriot towns; weekly; includes British Forces Broadcasting Services programme guide; Editor CARL BEAUMONT; circ. 5,000.

Middle East Economic Survey: Middle East Petroleum and Economic Publications (Cyprus), POB 4940, 1355 Nicosia; tel. (2) 445431; telex 2198; fax (2) 474988; e-mail mees@spidernet.com.cy; f. 1957 (in Beirut); weekly review and analysis of petroleum, economic and political news; Publr BASIM W. ITAYIM; Editor IAN SEYMOUR.

GREEK CYPRIOT PERIODICALS

Cool: POB 8205, 86 Iphigenias St, 2091 Nicosia; tel. (2) 378900; fax (2) 378916; f. 1994; Greek; youth magazine; Chief Editor: PROMETHEAS CHRISTOPHIDES; circ. 4,000.

Cypria (Cypriot Woman): POB 8506, 56 Kennedy Ave, 11th Floor, 1076 Nicosia; tel. (2) 494907; fax (2) 427051; f. 1983; every 2 months; Greek; Owner MARO KARAYIANNI; circ. 7,000.

Cyprus Bulletin: 1465 Nicosia; tel. (2) 801102; fax (2) 366123; e-mail pioxx@cytanet.com.cy; internet http//:www.pio.gov.cy; f. 1964; fortnightly; Arabic, English, Greek; published by the Cyprus Press and Information Office; Principal Officers M. CHARALAMPIDES, A. LYRITSAS, A. STYLIANOU; circ. 17,500.

Cyprus P.C.: POB 4989, 15 Dhigenis Akritas Ave, Nicosia; tel. (2) 343044; fax (2) 349867; f. 1990; monthly; Greek; computing magazine; Dir LAKIS VARNAVA; circ. 5,000.

Cyprus Time Out: POB 3697, 4 Pygmalionos St, 1010 Nicosia; tel. (2) 472949; fax (2) 360668; f. 1978; monthly; English; Dir ELLADA SOPHOCLEOUS; Chief Editor LYN HAVILAND; circ. 8,000.

Cyprus Today: c/o Ministry of Education and Culture, Nicosia; tel. (2) 303337; fax (2) 443565; f. 1963; quarterly; English; cultural and information review; published and distributed by Press and Information Office; Principal Officer NIKOS PANAYIOTOU; circ. 15,000.

Dimosios Ypallilos (Civil Servant): 3 Dem. Severis Ave, 1066 Nicosia; tel. (2) 442278; fax (2) 465189; fortnightly; published by the Cyprus Civil Servants' Association (PASYDY); circ. 14,000.

Eso-Etimos (Ever Ready): POB 4544, Nicosia; tel. (2) 443587; f. 1913; quarterly; Greek; publ. by Cyprus Scouts' Asscn; Editor TAKIS NEOPHYTOU; circ. 2,500.

Eva: 39 Kennedy, Nicosia; tel. (2) 493510; fax (2) 314193; f. 1996; Greek; Dir DINOS MICHAEL; Chief Editors CHARIS PONTIKIS, KATIA SAVVIDOU; circ. 4,000.

Hermes International: POB 4706, Nicosia; tel. (2) 581880; fax (2) 581884; f. 1992; quarterly; English; lifestyle, business, finance, management; Chief Editor ALAN GATHERGOOD; circ. 8,500.

Nicosia This Month: POB 1015, Nikoklis Publishing House, Ledras and Pygmalionos St, Nicosia; tel. (2) 472949; telex 5374; fax (2) 360668; f. 1984; monthly; English; Chief Editor ELLADA SOPHOCLEOUS; circ. 3,000.

Omicron: POB 5211, 1 Commercial Centre Diogenous, 2nd Floor, 1307 Nicosia; tel. (2) 590110; fax (2) 590410; f. 1996; Greek; Dir NIKOS CHR. PATTICHIS; Chief Editor STAVROS CHRISTODOULOU; circ. 8,000.

Paediki Chara (Children's Joy): 18 Archbishop Makarios III Ave, 1065 Nicosia; tel. (2) 442638; fax (2) 360410; e-mail poed@logos.cy.net; f. 1962; monthly; for pupils; publ. by the Pancyprian Union of Greek Teachers; Editor SOFOCLES CHARALAMBIDES; circ. 14,000.

Super Flash: POB 9246, 11 Kolokotronis St, Kaimakli, Nicosia; tel. (2) 437887; fax (2) 434197; f. 1979; fortnightly; Greek; Dir ANTHI VATI; circ. 6,000.

Synergatiko Vima (The Co-operative Tribune): Paloma Court, 6th Floor, No. 601, 16 Stasikratou St, Nicosia; tel. (2) 458757; fax (2) 446833; f. 1983; monthly; Greek; official organ of the Pancyprian Co-operative Confederation Ltd; circ. 5,000.

Synthesis (Composition): 39 Kennedy Ave, Nicosia; tel. (2) 429589; fax (2) 314193; f. 1988; every 2 months; Greek; interior decorating; Dir DINOS MICHAEL; circ. 6,000.

Tele Ores: POB 8205, 2nd Floor, 86 Iphighenias St, 2091 Nicosia; tel. (2) 378900; fax (2) 378916; f. 1993; Greek; fortnightly; television guide; Chief Editor PROMETHEAS CHRISTOPHIDES; circ. 17,000.

TV Kanali (TV Channel): POB 5603, 5 Aegaleo St, Strovolos, Nicosia; tel. (2) 353603; fax (2) 353223; f. 1993; Greek; Dirs A. STAVRIDES, E. HADJIEFTHYMIOU; Chief Editor CHARIS TOMAZOS; circ. 13,000.

TV Radio Programme: POB 4824, Cyprus Broadcasting Corpn, 1397 Nicosia; tel. (2) 422231; telex 2333; fax (2) 314050; e-mail rik@cybc.com.cy; fortnightly; Greek and English; published by the CyBC; radio and TV programme news; circ. 7,000.

TURKISH CYPRIOT PERIODICALS

Güvenlik Kuvvetleri Magazine: Lefkoşa (Nicosia), Mersin 10, Turkey; tel. (22) 75880; publ. by the Security Forces of the 'TRNC'.

Halkbilimi: Has-Der, PK 199, Lefkoşa (Nicosia), Mersin 10, Turkey; tel. (22) 83146; fax (22) 84125; f. 1986; 2 a year; publ. of Folk Arts Assoc.; academic; Turkish; Editors ENGIN ANIL, ÖCAL ERTEN; circ. 750.

Kıbrıs—Northern Cyprus Monthly: Ministry of Foreign Affairs and Defence, Lefkoşa (Nicosia), Mersin 10, Turkey; tel. (22) 83241; telex 57612; fax (22) 84290; f. 1963; Editors AHMET ERDENGİZ, HAKKI MÜFTÜZADE.

Kültür Sanat Dergisi: Girne Cad. 92, Lefkoşa (Nicosia), Mersin 10, Turkey; tel. (22) 83313; telex 82432; publ. of Türk Bankası; circ. 1,000.

Kuzey Kıbrıs Kültür Dergisi (North Cyprus Cultural Journal): PK 157, Lefkoşa (Nicosia), Mersin 10, Turkey; tel. (22) 31298; f. 1987; monthly; Turkish; Chief Editor GÜNSEL DOĞASAL.

New Cyprus: PK 327, Lefkoşa (Nicosia), Mersin 10, Turkey; tel. (22) 78914; telex 2585; fax (22) 72592; English; publ. by the North Cyprus Research and Publishing Centre; also Turkish edition *Yeni Kıbrıs*; Editor AHMET C. GAZİOĞLU.

Pan Magazine: Atü Apt 4, Sht. İbrahim Yusuf Sok., Lefkoşa (Nicosia), Mersin 10, Turkey; tel. (22) 77813; f. 1980; Dir ARMAN RATİP.

OTHER PERIODICALS

The Blue Beret: POB 1642, HQ UNFICYP, Nicosia; tel. (2) 359550; fax (2) 359752; monthly; English; circ. 1,000.

International Crude Oil and Product Prices: Middle East Petroleum and Economic Publications (Cyprus), POB 4940, 1355 Nicosia; tel. (2) 445431; telex 2198; fax (2) 474988; e-mail mees@spidernet.com.cy; f. 1971 (in Beirut); 2 a year; review and analysis of petroleum price trends in world markets; Publisher BASIM W. ITAYIM.

NEWS AGENCIES

Cyprus News Agency: POB 3947, 7 Kastorias St, 2002 Strovolos, 1685 Nicosia; tel. (2) 319009; telex 4787; fax (2) 319006; e-mail cna@cytanet.com.cy; f. 1976; English and Greek; Dir ANDREAS CHRISTOFIDES.

Kuzey Kıbrıs Haber Ajansı (Northern Cyprus News Agency): Alirizin Efendi Cad., Vakiflar Işhani, Kat 2, No. 3, Ortaköy, Lefkoşa (Nicosia), Mersin 10, Turkey; tel. (22) 81922; telex 57536; fax (22) 81934; f. 1977; Dir-Gen. M. ALI AKPINAR.

Papyrus General Press Distribution Agency: POB 12669, 5 Arch. Kyprianou, Latsia, Nicosia; tel. (2) 488855; fax (2) 488883.

TürkAjansı-Kıbrıs (TAK) (Turkish News Agency of Cyprus): POB 355, 30 Mehmet Akif Cad., Lefkoşa (Nicosia), Mersin 10, Turkey; tel. (22) 71818; telex 57448; fax (22) 71213; f. 1973; Dir EMİR HÜSEYİN ERSOY.

Foreign Bureaux

Agence France-Presse (AFP) (France): POB 7242, Loizides Centre, 7th Floor, 36 Kypranoros St, Nicosia; tel. (2) 365050; telex 2824; fax (2) 365125; e-mail nicosie.redaction@afp.com; Bureau Chief MICHEL GARIN.

Agencia EFE (Spain): 64 Metochiou St, Office 401, Nicosia; tel. (2) 775725; fax (2) 781662; Correspondent MARIA SAAVEDRA.

Agenzia Nazionale Stampa Associata (ANSA) (Italy): Middle East Office, 10 Katsonis St, Ayii Omoloyites, Nicosia; tel. (2) 491699; telex 4139; fax (2) 492732; Rep. VITTORIO FRENQUELLUCCI.

Associated Press (AP) (USA): POB 4853, Neoelen Marina, 10 Katsonis St, Nicosia; tel. (2) 492599; telex 2459; fax (2) 491617; Correspondent ALEX EFTY.

Athinaikon Praktorion Eidiseon (Greece): Flat 64, Tryfonos Bldg, Eleftherias Sq., 1011 Nicosia; tel. (2) 441110; fax (2) 457418; Rep. GEORGE LEONIDAS.

Bulgarian News Agency: 1 Konstantinou Kavafi St, Limassol; tel. (5) 332187.

Informatsionnoye Telegrafnoye Agentstvo Rossii-Telegrafnoye Agentstvo Suverennykh Stran (ITAR-TASS) (Russia): POB 2235, 5–6 Evangelias St, Archangelos, Nicosia; tel. (2) 382486; telex 2368; Rep. ALEXEI YEROVTCHENKOV.

Iraqi News Agency: POB 1098, Flat 201, 11 Ippocratous St, Nicosia; tel. (2) 472095; telex 2197; fax (2) 472096; Correspondent AHMED SULEIMAN.

Jamahiriya News Agency (JANA) (Libya): Flat 203, 12 Kypranoros, Nicosia; tel. (2) 361129; Rep. MOHAMED ALI ESHOWEIHIDI.

Polska Agencja Prasowa (PAP) (Poland): POB 2373, Prodromos St 24, Nicosia; Rep. MICHALAKIS PANTELIDES.

Prensa Latina (Cuba): 12 Demophon St, 5th Floor, Apt 501, Nicosia; tel. (2) 464131; telex 4505; Rep. LEONEL NODAL.

Reuters: POB 5725, 5th Floor, George and Thelma Paraskevaides Foundation Bldg, 36 Grivas Dhigenis Ave, Nicosia; tel. (2) 365087; telex 4922; fax (2) 475487; Correspondent MICHELE KAMBAS.

Sofia-Press Agency (Bulgaria): 9 Roumeli St, Droshia, Larnaca; tel. (4) 494484; Rep. IONKA VERESIE.

United Press International (UPI) (USA): 24A Heroes Ave, Nicosia 171; tel. (2) 456643; telex 2260; fax (2) 455998; Rep. GEORGES DER PARTHOGH.

Xinhua (New China) News Agency (People's Republic of China): 12 Byzantiou St, Flat 201, Ayios Dhometios, Nicosia; tel. (2) 590133; telex 5265; fax (2) 590146; Rep. HUANG JIANMING.

Publishers

GREEK CYPRIOT PUBLISHERS

Action Publications: POB 4676, 35 Ayiou Nicolaou St, Egkomi, Nicosia; tel. (2) 590555; fax (2) 590048; e-mail actionpr@spidernet.com.cy; f. 1971; travel; Pres. TONY CHRISTODOULOU.

Alithia (Truth): POB 1695, 5 Pindaros and Adroklis St, Nicosia; tel. (2) 463040; fax (2) 463945.

Andreou Chr. Publications: POB 2298, 67a Regenis St, Nicosia; tel. (2) 466813; fax (2) 466649; f. 1979.

Chrysopolitissa: 27 Al. Papadiamantis St, 2400 Nicosia; tel. (2) 353929; e-mail rina@spidernet.com.cy.

MAM (The House of Cyprus Publications): POB 1722, Phaneromeni Library Building, 46 Phaneromeni St, Nicosia; tel. (2) 472744; fax (2) 465411; f. 1965.

Nikoklis Publishing House: POB 3697, Nicosia; tel. (2) 456544; fax (2) 360668; Man. ELLADA SOPHOCLEOUS.

Romantic Cyprus: POB 2375, Nicosia; fax (2) 445155.

TURKISH CYPRIOT PUBLISHERS

Birlik Gazetesi: Yediler Sok., Lefkoşa (Nicosia), Mersin 10, Turkey; tel. (22) 72959; f. 1980; Dir MEHMET AKAR.

Bolan Matbaası: 35 Pençizade Sok., Lefkoşa (Nicosia), Mersin 10, Turkey; tel. (22) 74802.

Devlet Basımevi (Turkish Cypriot Government Printing House): Şerif Arzik Sok., Lefkoşa (Nicosia), Mersin 10, Turkey; tel. (22) 72010; Dir S. KÜRŞAD.

Halkın Sesi Ltd: 172 Girne Cad., Lefkoşa (Nicosia), Mersin 10, Turkey; tel. (22) 73141.

Kema Matbaası: 1 Tabak Hilmi Sok., Lefkoşa (Nicosia), Mersin 10, Turkey; tel. (22) 72785.

K. Rüstem & Bro.: 22–24 Girne Cad., Lefkoşa (Nicosia), Mersin 10, Turkey; tel. (22) 71418.

Sebil International Press: 59 Atatürk Ave, Gönyeli, PK 7, Lefkoşa (Nicosia), Mersin 10, Turkey; tel. (22) 46805; fax (22) 31080; f. 1985; technical and scientific; Principal Officer E. BAŞARAN.

Tezel Matbaası: 35 Şinasi Sok., Lefkoşa (Nicosia), Mersin 10, Turkey; tel. (22) 71022.

Broadcasting and Communications

TELECOMMUNICATIONS

Cyprus Telecommunications Authority (CYTA): POB 4929, Nicosia; tel. (2) 313111; internet http://www.cytanet.com.cy; responsible for the the telephone network in Cyprus.

RADIO

Cyprus Broadcasting Corporation (CyBC): POB 4824, Broadcasting House, 1397 Nicosia; tel. (2) 422231; telex 2333; fax (2) 314050; e-mail rik@cybc.com.cy; radio f. 1952; Programme I in Greek, Programme II in Greek, Turkish, English and Armenian, Programme III in Greek; two medium wave transmitters of 100 kW in Nicosia with relay stations at Paphos and Limassol; three 30 kW ERP VHF FM stereo transmitters on Mount Olympus; and three relay stations; Chair. ANTONIS DRAKOS; Dir-Gen. PAVLOS SOTERIADES; Head of Radio KYRIACOS CHARALAMBIDES.

Logos: Church of Cyprus, POB 7400, 1644 Nicosia; tel. (2) 355444; fax (2) 355737; Chair. ANDREAS PHILIPPOU; Gen. Man. CHRISTODOULOS PROTOPAPAS.

Radio Astra: 145 Athalassas Ave, Strovolos, 2045 Nicosia; tel. (2) 313200; fax (2) 319261; Chair. ANDREAS ALONEFTIS; Dir TAKIS HADJIGEORGIOU.

Radio Proto: POB 3477, 31 Archangelos St, Parissinos, 2054 Nicosia; tel. (2) 353545; fax (2) 352266; Chair. CHR. MELARIS; Gen. Man. PAVLOS PAPACHRISTODOULOU.

Services Sound and Vision Corpn, Cyprus: Akrotiri, British Forces Post Office 57; tel. (5) 252009; fax (5) 252006; f. 1948; incorporates the British Forces Broadcasting Service, Cyprus; broadcasts a two-channel 24-hour radio service in English on VHF; Station Man. PATRICK EADE; Engineering Man. DAVE RAMSAY.

Bayrak Radio and TV Corpn (BRTK): Atatürk Sq., Lefkoşa (Nicosia), Mersin 10, Turkey; tel. (22) 85555; telex 57264; fax (22) 81991; e-mail brt@cc.emu.edu.tr; internet http://www.cc.emu.edu.tr/press/brt/brt.htm; in July 1983 it became an independent Turkish Cypriot corpn, partly financed by the Govt; Radio Bayrak f. 1963; home service in Turkish, overseas service in Turkish, Greek, English, Arabic and German; broadcasts 52.5 hours per day; Chair. GÜNAY YORGANCIOĞLU; Dir. ISMET KOTAK; Head of Radio ŞIFA NESIM.

Türkiye Radyo Televizyon (TRT): 3 channels of radio programmes in Turkish, transmitted to the Turkish sector of Cyprus.

First fm: f. 1996.

Tempo: f. 1996.

Emu fm: f. 1995.

TELEVISION

In 1991, under an agreement between Cyprus and Greece, Cypriot viewers were to be given access to Greek television channels for several hours daily via satellite.

Antenna T.V.: POB 923, 1655 Nicosia: tel. (2) 311111; fax (2) 314959; Chair. LOUCIS PAPAPHILIPPOU; Gen. Man. IOANNIS PAPOUTSANIS (acting).

Cyprus Broadcasting Corporation (CyBC): POB 4824, Broadcasting House, 1397 Nicosia; tel. (2) 422231; telex 2333; fax (2) 314050; e-mail rik@cybc.com.cy; television f. 1957; **Channel 1:** one

Band III 40/4 kW transmitter on Mount Olympus. **Channel 2:** one Band IV 100/10 kW ERP transmitter on Mount Olympus. **ET 1:** one Band IV 100/10 kW ERP transmitter on Mount Olympus for transmission of the ETI Programme received, via satellite, from Greece. The above three TV channels are also transmitted from 77 transposer stations; Chair. ANTONIS DRAKOS; Dir-Gen. PAVLOS SOTERIADES.

Lumier T.V. Ltd.: 1 Diogenous, Block A, 1st and 2nd Floors, 2122 Nicosia; tel. (2) 357272; fax (2) 354638; encoded signal; Chair. CHRIS ECONOMIDES; Gen. Man. AKIS AVRAAMIDES.

O Logos: POB 7400, 1644 Nicosia; tel. (2) 355444; fax (2) 355737; Chair. and Gen. Man. CHRISTODOULOS PROTOPAPAS.

Services Sound and Vision Corpn, Cyprus: Akrotiri, British Forces Post Office 57; tel. (5) 252009; fax (5) 252006; f. 1948; incorporates the British Forces Broadcasting Service, Cyprus; broadcasts a daily TV service; Station Man. PATRICK EADE; Engineering Man. DAVE RAMSAY.

Sigma: POB 1836, 1513 Nicosia; tel. (2) 357070; fax (2) 352237; island-wide coverage; Chair. and Dir COSTIS HADJICOSTIS; Head of News DINOS MENELAOU.

Bayrak Radio and TV Corpn (BRTK): Atatürk Sq., Lefkoşa (Nicosia), Mersin 10, Turkey; tel. (22) 85555; telex 57264; fax (22) 81991; e-mail brt@cc.emu.edu.tr; internet http://www.cc.emu.edu.tr/press/brt/brt.htm; in July 1983 it became an independent Turkish Cypriot corpn, partly financed by the Govt; Bayrak TV f. 1976; transmits programmes in Turkish, Greek, English and Arabic on nine channels; Chair. GÜNAY YORGANCIOĞLU; Dir. ISMET KOTAK; Head of Television TÜLIN URAL.

Türkiye Radyo Televizyon (TRT): 2 channels of television programmes in Turkish, transmitted to the Turkish sector of Cyprus.

Finance

(brs = branches; cap. = capital; p.u. = paid up; auth. = authorized; dep. = deposits; res = reserves; m. = million; amounts in Cyprus pounds)

BANKING

Central Bank

Central Bank of Cyprus: POB 5529, 80 Kennedy Ave, 1395 Nicosia; tel. (2) 379800; telex 2424; fax (2) 378153; e-mail cbcinfo@centralbank.gov.cy; f. 1963; cap. p.u. 15m., res 15m., dep. 838m. (Dec. 1996); Gov. A. C. AFXENTIOU.

Greek Cypriot Banks

Bank of Cyprus Group: POB 1472, 51 Stassinos St, Ayia Paraskevi, Strovolos 140, 1599 Nicosia; tel. (2) 378000; telex 2451; fax (2) 378111; e-mail tsolakis@logos.cy.net; f. 1899, reconstituted 1943 by the amalgamation of Bank of Cyprus, Larnaca Bank Ltd and Famagusta Bank Ltd; cap. 74.0m., res 46.8m. (Dec. 1996); Chair. SOLON A. TRIANTAFYLLIDES; Group Chief Exec. CHR. PANTZARIS; 199 brs.

Co-operative Central Bank Ltd: POB 4537, 8 Gregoris Afxentiou St, 1389 Nicosia; tel. (2) 442921; telex 2313; fax (2) 360261; f. 1937 under the Co-operative Societies Law; banking and credit facilities to member societies, importer and distributor of agricultural requisites, insurance agent; cap. 0.1m., res 4.9m. (Dec. 1995), dep. 402m. (Dec 1996); Chair. A. SOTERIADES; Sec.-Gen. D. PITSILLIDES; 4 brs.

The Cyprus Popular Bank Ltd: POB 2032, Popular Bank Bldg, 154 Limassol Ave, 1598 Nicosia; tel. (2) 450000; telex 2494; fax (2) 811491; f. 1901; full commercial banking; cap. 63.2m., res 88.3m. dep. 1,724.7m. (Dec. 1995); Chair. and Group Chief Exec. KIKIS N. LAZARIDES; 143 local brs.

Hellenic Bank Ltd: POB 4747, 1394 Nicosia; tel. (2) 360000; telex 3311; fax (2) 454074; e-mail hellenic@hellenicbank.com; f. 1974; financial services group; cap. p.u. 21.3m., res 25.7m., dep. 850.5m. (1996); Chair. and Chief Exec. PANOS CHR. GHALANOS; 115 brs.

Housing Finance Corpn: POB 3898, 41 Themistoklis Dervis St, Hawaii Tower, Nicosia; tel. (2) 452777; telex 4134; fax (2) 452870; f. 1980; provides long-term loans for home-buying; cap. 5.0m., dep. 85.0m. (Dec. 1994); Chair. I. TYPOGRAPHOS; Gen. Man. CH. SHAMBARTAS; 6 brs.

Lombard NatWest Bank Ltd: POB 1661, Cnr of Chilon and Gladstone St, Stylianos Lenas Square, Nicosia; tel. (2) 474333; telex 2262; fax (2) 457870; f. 1960; locally incorporated although foreign-controlled; cap. p.u. 4m., dep. 309.0m. (Sept. 1996); Chair. M. G. COLOCASSIDES; Man. Dir E. IOANNOU; 25 brs.

National Bank of Greece (Cyprus) Ltd: POB 1191, Galaxias Centre, 2nd Floor, 36 Ayias Elenis St, 1597 Nicosia; tel. (2) 362262; telex 2445; fax (2) 362090; f. 1994 by incorporating all local business of the National Bank of Greece SA; full commercial banking; cap. p.u. 15m. (Jan. 1997); Chair. TH. KARATZAS; Man. Dir M. TAGAROULIAS; 26 brs.

Turkish Cypriot Banks

(amounts in Turkish liras)

Akdeniz Garanti Bankası Ltd: PK 149, 2–4 Celaliye Sok. Inönu Meydan, Lefkoşa (Nicosia), Mersin 10, Turkey; tel. (22) 86742; telex 57572; fax (22) 86741; f. 1989 as Mediterranean Guarantee Bank; cap. 5.4m., res 1.1m., dep. 73.6m. (Dec. 1991); Chair. and Gen. Man. YUSUF DEGIRMENCIOĞLU.

Asbank Ltd: 8 Mecidiye Sok., PK 448, Lefkoşa (Nicosia), Mersin 10, Turkey; tel. (22) 83023; telex 57305; fax (22) 81244; f. 1986; cap. and res 322,730m., dep. 2,941,766m. (Dec. 1996); Chair. MUSTAFA ALTUNER; Exec. Dir M. ERGUN OLGUN; 6 brs.

Cyprus Altinbaş Bank Ltd: PK 843, 2 Müftü Ziyai Efendi Sok., Lefkoşa (Nicosia), Mersin 10, Turkey; tel. (22) 82222; telex 57347; fax (22) 83603; f. 1993; cap. 50,000m., res 3,941m., dep. 292,342m. (Dec. 1995); Chair. VAKKAS ALTINBAŞ; Gen. Man. OLGUN BEYOĞLU.

Everest Bank Ltd: Sarayönü 23A, Lefkoşa (Nicosia), Mersin 10, Turkey; tel. (22) 88281; telex 57624; fax (22) 89787; f. 1993; cap. 50,000m., res 28,366m., dep. 680,344m. (Dec. 1995); Chair. MEHMET CIVA; Gen. Man. NURHAN CANDEMIR; 6 brs.

Kıbrıs Endüstri Bankası Ltd: (Industrial Bank of Cyprus Ltd): Bedrettin Demirel Cad., Başbakanlık Kavşağı, Lefkoşa (Nicosia), Mersin 10, Turkey; tel. (22) 83770; telex 57397; fax (22) 71830.

Kıbrıs Eurobank Ltd: PK 35, 18 Mecidiye Sok., Lefkoşa (Nicosia), Mersin 10, Turkey; tel. (22) 87382; telex 57629; fax (22) 87670; f. 1993; cap. 25,000m., dep. 36,835m. (Dec. 1994); Pres. and Chair. KEMAL AKKAYA; Gen. Man. YALÇIN POYRAZ.

Kıbrıs Hürbank Ltd (Cyprus Liberal Bank Ltd): Sht. Tekin Yurdabak Cad., POB 887, Göçmenköy, Lefkoşa (Nicosia), Mersin 10, Turkey; tel. (22) 36612; telex 57631; fax (22) 36707; f. 1993; Chair. Dr ERDOĞAN MIRATA; Gen. Man. MAHMUT SEZINLER; 6 brs.

Kıbrıs İktisat Bankası Ltd: 151 Bedrettin Demirel Cad., Lefkoşa (Nicosia), Mersin 10, Turkey; tel. (22) 85300; fax (22) 86860; f. 1990; cap. 50,000m., res 41,219m., dep. 775,869m. (Dec. 1995); Chair. METİN MENTESH; Gen. Man. METE OZMERTER; 5 brs.

Kıbrıs Kredi Bankası Ltd (Cyprus Credit Bank Ltd): 5–7 İplik Pazarı Sok., Lefkoşa (Nicosia), Mersin 10, Turkey; tel. (22) 75026; telex 57336; fax (22) 76999; f. 1978; cap. p.u. 30,930m., res 164,131m., dep. 2,628,193m. (Dec. 1994); Chair. SALİH BOYACI; Gen. Man. (acting) HALIL OKUR; 12 local brs.

Kıbrıs Ticaret Bankası Ltd (Cyprus Commercial Bank Ltd): 111 Bedrettin Demirel Ave, Lefkoşa (Nicosia), Mersin 10, Turkey; tel. (22) 83180; telex 57395; fax (22) 82278; f. 1982; cap. p.u. 89,860m., res 169,317m., dep. 3,229,137m. (Dec. 1996); Chair. YÜKSEL AHMET RAŞİT; Gen. Man. PEKER M. TURGUD; 9 brs.

Kıbrıs Türk Kooperatif Merkez Bankası Ltd (Cyprus Turkish Co-operative Central Bank): 49–55 Mahmut Paşa Sok., PK 823, Lefkoşa (Nicosia), Mersin 10, Turkey; tel. (22) 73398; telex 57558; fax (22) 76787; e-mail ataman@coopcb.com; f. 1959; cap. and res 914,817m., dep. 12,236,327m. (Dec. 1996); banking and credit facilities to member societies aindividuals; Chair. EREN RIFAT ERTANIN; Gen. Man. TAŞKENT ATASAYAN; 9 brs.

Kıbrıs Vakiflar Bankası Ltd: 58 Yediler Sok., PK 212, Lefkoşa (Nicosia), Mersin 10, Turkey; tel. (22) 75109; telex 57122; fax (22) 75169; f. 1982; cap. and res 32,220m., dep. 922,750m. (Dec. 1994); Chair. Dr RAUF UNSAL; 6 brs.

Limassol Turkish Co-operative Bank Ltd: Orhaneli Sok., Kyrenia, PK 27, Mersin 10, Turkey; tel. (2) 8156786; telex 57607; fax (2) 8156959; f. 1939; cap. 4,516m., res 102,076m, dep. 2,092,820m. (Dec. 1995); Chair. GÜZEL HALIM; Gen. Man. ATTILA BERBEROĞLU.

Türk Bankası Ltd (Turkish Bank Ltd): 92 Girne Cad., PK 242, Lefkoşa (Nicosia), Mersin 10, Turkey; tel. (22) 83313; telex 2585; fax (22) 82432; f. 1901; cap. p.u. 500,009m., res 1,314,196m., dep. 16,184,923m. (Dec. 1995); Chair. M. TANJU ÖZYOL; Gen. Man. C. YENAL MUSANNIF; 12 brs.

Turkish Cypriot Bankers' Association

Northern Cyprus Bankers' Association: Lefkoşa (Nicosia), Mersin 10, Turkey; f. 1987; tel. (22) 83180; fax (22) 82278; 25 mems (1996).

Investment Organization

Cyprus Investment and Securities Corpn: POB 597, Ghinis Bldg, 4th Floor, 58–60 Dhigenis Akritas Ave, Nicosia; tel. (2) 451535; fax (2) 445481; f. 1982 to promote development of capital market; member of Bank of Cyprus Group; issued cap. 1m. (1990); Chair. J. CL. CHRISTOPHIDES; Gen. Man. SOCRATES R. SOLOMIDES.

Development Bank

The Cyprus Development Bank Ltd: POB 1415, Alpha House, 50 Archbishop Makarios III Ave, 1508 Nicosia; tel. (2) 457575; telex 2797; fax (2) 464322; f. 1963; share cap. p.u. 12.0m. (Jan. 1997); res 4.5m. (Dec. 1995); aims to accelerate the economic development of Cyprus by providing medium- and long-term loans for productive projects, developing the capital market, encouraging joint ventures and providing technical and managerial advice to productive private enterprises; Chair. J. CHR. STRONGYLOS; Gen. Man. JOHN G. JOANNIDES; 1 br.

Savings Bank

Universal Savings Bank Ltd (Designated Financial Institution): POB 8510, 26 Santaroza St, Nicosia; tel. (2) 472972; fax (2) 450280; f. 1908 (closed 1974, reopened 1990); provides loan facilities and other banking services; cap. p.u. 4.0m., res 0.3m. (Dec. 1995); Chair. GEORGE SYRIMIS; Gen. Man. D. MESSIOS; 3 brs.

Foreign Banks

Arab Bank PLC: POB 5700, 28 Santaroza St, 1393 Nicosia; tel. (2) 457111; telex 5717; fax (2) 457890; f. 1984; commercial; Area Exec. T. DAJANI; 18 brs.

Commercial Bank of Greece SA: POB 5151, 4 Ionos St, 2015 Nicosia; tel. (2) 363646; telex 4055; fax (2) 473923; f. 1992; Country Man. G. KANTIANIS; 2 brs.

Türkiye Cumhuriyeti Ziraat Bankası: Girnekapi Cad., Ibrahimpaşa Sok. 105, Lefkoşa (Nicosia), Mersin 10, Turkey; tel. (22) 83050; telex 57499; fax (22) 82041.

Türkiye Halk Bankası AŞ: Osman Paşa Cad., Ümit Office, Lefkoşa (Nicosia), Mersin 10, Turkey; tel. (22) 72145; telex 57241; fax (22) 72146.

Türkiye İş Bankası AŞ: Girne Cad. 9, Lefkoşa (Nicosia), Mersin 10, Turkey; tel. (22) 83133; telex 57569; fax (22) 78315; f. 1924; Man. KEMAL AĞANOĞLU.

Offshore Banking Units

Cyprus-based Offshore Banking Units (OBUs) are fully-staffed units which conduct all forms of banking business from within Cyprus with other offshore or foreign entities and non-resident persons. (OBUs are not permitted to accept deposits from persons of Cypriot origin who have emigrated to the United Kingdom and taken up permanent residence there.) Although exempt from most of the restrictions and regulatory measures applicable to onshore banks, OBUs are subject to supervision and inspection by the Central Bank of Cyprus. OBUs may conduct business with onshore and domestic banks in all banking matters which the latter are allowed to undertake with banks abroad. OBUs are permitted to grant loans or guarantees in foreign currencies to residents of Cyprus (conditional on obtaining an exchange control permit from the Central Bank of Cyprus). Interest and other income earned from transactions with residents is subject to the full rate of income tax (20%), but the Minister of Finance is empowered by law to exempt an OBU from the above tax liability if satisfied that a specific transaction substantially contributes towards the economic development of the Republic. In 1997 there were 32 OBUs operating in Cyprus.

Agropromstroybank (Cyprus Offshore Banking Unit): POB 5297, Maximos Court B, 17 Leontiou St, Limassol; tel. (5) 384747; telex 5065; fax (5) 384858; Man. ALEXANDRE MOKHONKO.

Allied Business Bank SAL: POB 4232, 3rd Floor, Flat 31, Lara Court, 276 Archbishop Makarios III Ave, Limassol; tel. (5) 363759; telex 6040; fax (5) 372711; Sr Man. SAMIR BADR.

Arab Jordan Investment Bank SA (Cyprus Offshore Banking Unit): POB 4384, Libra Tower, 23 Olympion St, Limassol; tel. (5) 351351; telex 3809; fax (5) 360151; f. 1978; cap. and dep. US $216m., total assets $315m. (Dec. 1996); Man. ABED ABU-DAYEH.

AvtoVAZbank: 5 Promitheos St, Flat No. 2, POB 2025, 1516 Nicosia; tel. (2) 361561; fax. (2) 361525; Local Man. A. TSELOUNOV.

Banca de Credit Cooperatist BankCoop SA (BankCoop): 24 Stassikratous St, Office 101-102, 1065 Nicosia; tel. (2) 360788; fax (2) 360795; Local Man. BOGDAN BELCIU.

Banca Română de Comerţ Exterior (Bancorex) SA: Margarita House, 5th Floor, 15 Them. Dervis St, POB 2538, 1309 Nicosia; tel. (2) 367992; telex 4815; fax (2) 367945; Local Man. GRIGORE IOAN BUDISAN.

Bank Menatep: 1 Lambousas St, 4th Floor, 1095 Nicosia; tel. (2) 442444; fax (2) 442464; CEO VICTOR S. PHILARETOV.

Bank of Beirut and the Arab Countries SAL: POB 6201, Emelle Bldg, 1st Floor, 135 Archbishop Makarios III Ave, Limassol; tel. (5) 381290; telex 5444; fax (5) 381584; Man. O. S. SAAB.

Banque de l'Europe Méridionale SA: POB 6232, Doma Court, 1st-2nd Floors, 227 Archbishop Makarios III Ave, Limassol; tel. (5) 368668; telex 5575; fax (5) 368611; Local Man. N. A. HCHAIME.

Banque du Liban et d'Outre-Mer SAL: POB 3243, P. Lordos Centre Roundabout, Byron St, Limassol; tel. (5) 376433; telex 4424; fax (5) 376292; Local Man. S. FARAH.

Banque Nationale de Paris Intercontinentale SA: POB 58, Hanseatic House, 111 Spyrou Araouzou Ave, Limassol; tel. (5) 360166; telex 5519; fax (5) 376519; Local Man. M. PIANO.

Banque SBA (Cyprus Offshore Banking Unit): POB 4405, Iris House, Kanika Enaerios Complex, 8C Kennedy St, Limassol; tel. (5) 368650; telex 3569; fax (5) 351643; branch of Banque SBA (fmrly Société Bancaire Arabe), Paris; Local Man. N. DAGISTANI.

Barclays Bank PLC, Cyprus Offshore Banking Unit: POB 7320, 88 Dhigenis Akritas Ave, Nicosia; tel. (2) 464777; telex 5200; fax (2) 464233; Senior Man. CLIVE BRITTON.

Beogradska Banka: POB 530, 34 Kennedy Ave, Nicosia; tel. (2) 453493; telex 6413; fax (2) 453207; Man. Dir B. VUČIĆ.

Byblos Bank SAL: POB 218, Loucaides Bldg, 1 Archbishop Kyprianou St/St Andrew St, Limassol; tel. (5) 341433; telex 5203; fax (5) 367139; Local Man. R. T. CHEMALY.

Commercial Bank of Greece SA: 1 Iona Nicolaou, POB 7587, Engomi, 2431 Nicosia, tel. (2) 363686; fax (2) 363688; Man. G. KANTIANIS.

Crédit Libanais SAL (Cyprus Offshore Banking Unit): POB 3492, Chrysalia Court, 1st Floor, 206 Archbishop Makarios III Ave, 3030 Limassol; tel. (5) 376444; telex 4702; fax (5) 376807; e-mail credub@inco.com.lb; Local Man. HAYAT HARFOUCHE.

Federal Bank of the Middle East Ltd: POB 5566, Megaron Lavinia, Santa Rosa Ave and Mykinon St, Nicosia; tel. (2) 461716; telex 4700; fax (2) 461751; f. 1983; cap. and res US $31.4m., dep. $142.1m. (Dec. 1996); Chair. A. F. M. SAAB; Chief Exec. JAMES V. HOEY.

First Merchant Bank OSH Ltd.: 1 Kubilay Altayli Sok., Nicosia; tel. (22) 75373; telex 57376; fax (22) 75377; f. 1993; cap. 10m., res 0.7m., dep. 178.8m. (Dec. 1995); Chair. and Gen. Man. Dr H. YAMAN.

First Private Bank Ltd, Cyprus Offshore Banking Unit: POB 6656, 36 Kypranorou St, 2nd Floor, 1646 Nicosia; tel. (2) 362850; telex 4264; fax (2) 362983; Gen. Man. ENU NEDELEV.

HSBC Investment Bank Cyprus Ltd: POB 5718, 7 Dositheou, Block C, Nicosia; tel. (2) 376116; telex 4980; fax (2) 376121; f. 1984, as Wardley Cyprus Ltd; Man. Dir T. TAOUSHANIS.

Inkombank: 67 Spyros Araouzos St, Karmozi House, POB 3349, 3302 Limassol; tel. (5) 745949; telex 5817; fax (5) 747067; Gen. Man. ANDREI A. TIOURIAKOV.

Jordan National Bank PLC, Cyprus Offshore Banking Unit: POB 3587, 1 Anexartissias St, Pecora Tower, 2nd Floor, 3303 Limassol; tel. (5) 356669; telex 5471; fax (5) 356673; e-mail jnb@cytanet.com.cy; f. 1984; Reg. Man. KHALIL NASR.

Karić Banka, COBU: Flat 22, Cronos Court, 66 Archbishop Makarios III Ave, Nicosia; tel. (2) 374977; telex 6510; fax (2) 374151; Man. Dir BILJANA CAMILOVIĆ.

Lebanon and Gulf Bank SAL: POB 337, Akamia Court, 3rd Floor, corner of G. Afxentiou and Archbishop Makarios III Ave, Larnaca; tel. (4) 620500; telex 5779; fax (4) 620708; Local Man. M. HAMMOUD.

Permcombank (Permanent Joint-Stock Commercial Bank): POB 6037, 66 Archbishop Makarios III Ave, Of. 43, Nicosia; tel. (2) 361566; telex 4572; fax (2) 361466; Man. V. NOVIKOV.

Russian Commercial Bank (Cyprus) Ltd: POB 6868, 2 Amathuntos St, 3310 Limassol; tel. (5) 342190; telex 4561; fax (5) 342192; Gen. Man. O. I. LAPUSHKIN.

Société Générale Cyprus Ltd: POB 8560, 7–9 Grivas Dhigenis Ave, Nicosia; tel. (2) 464885; telex 5342; fax (2) 464471; Gen. Man. GÉRARD MALHAME.

STOCK EXCHANGE

Cyprus Stock Exchange: POB 5427, 54 Grivas Dhigenis Ave, 1309 Nicosia; tel. (2) 368782; telex 2077; fax (2) 368790; official trading commenced in March 1996; 41 companies listed in 1997; Chair. DINOS PAPADOPOULOS; Gen. Man. N. METAXAS.

INSURANCE

Office of the Superintendent of Insurance: Treasury Department, Ministry of Finance, Nicosia; tel. (2) 303256; telex 3399; fax (2) 302938; f. 1969 to control insurance companies, insurance agents, brokers and agents for brokers in Cyprus.

Greek Cypriot Insurance Companies

Aegis Insurance Co Ltd: POB 3450, 7 Klimentos St, Ayios Antonios, 1061 Nicosia; tel. (2) 343644; fax (2) 369359; Chair. ARISTOS KAISIDES; Principal Officer PANTELAKIS SOUGLIDES.

Allied Assurance & Reinsurance Co Ltd: POB 5509, 66 Grivas Dhigenis Ave, Nicosia; tel. (2) 457131; fax (2) 441975; f. 1982; offshore company operating outside Cyprus; Chair. HENRI J. G. CHALHOUB; Principal Officer DEMETRIOS DEMETRIOU.

Alpha Insurance Ltd: 59–61 Strovolos Ave, Nicosia; tel. (2) 318883; fax (2) 318925; Chair. ROGER AKELIOUS; Principal Officer IOANNIS LOIZOW.

Antarctic Insurance Co Ltd: POB 613, 199 Archbishop Makarios III Ave, Neokleou Bldg, 3030 Limassol; offshore captive company operating outside Cyprus; Principal Officer ANDREAS NEOKLEOUS.

Apac Ltd: POB 5403, 5 Mourouzi St, Apt 1, Nicosia; tel. (2) 455186; telex 2766; f. 1983; captive offshore company operating outside Cyprus; Chair. KYPROS CHRYSOSTOMIDES; Principal Officer GEORGHIOS POYATZIS.

APOL Insurance Ltd: 24 Perea St, Mocassino Centre, 3rd Floor, Strovolos, Nicosia; tel. (2) 425550; fax (2) 425147; offshore company operating outside Cyprus; Chair. M. ARBOUZOV; Principal Officer STELIOS MICHAEL.

Asfalistiki Eteria I 'Kentriki' Ltd: POB 5131, Greg Tower, 3rd Floor, 7 Florinis St, Nicosia 136; tel. (2) 473931; telex 4987; fax (2) 366276; f. 1985; Chair. ARISTOS CHRYSOSTOMOU; Principal Officer GEORGHIOS GEORGALLIDES.

Atlantic Insurance Co Ltd: POB 4579, 37 Prodromou St, 2nd Floor, Nicosia; tel. (2) 444052; telex 6446; fax (2) 474800; f. 1983; Chair. and Man. Dir ZENIOS PYRISHIS.

Axioma Insurance (Cyprus) Ltd: 2 Ionni Klerides St, Demokritos No. 2 Bldg, Flat 83, Nicosia; offshore company operating outside Cyprus; Principal Officer KONSTANTINOS KYAMIDES.

Commercial Union Assurance (Cyprus) Ltd: POB 1312, Commercial Union House, 101 Archbishop Makarios III Ave, Nicosia; tel. (2) 377373; telex 2547; fax (2) 376155; e-mail mailbox@commercial-union.com.cy; f. 1974; Chair. J. CHRISTOPHIDES; Gen. Man. KONSTANTINOS P. DEKATRIS.

Cosmos (Cyprus) Insurance Co Ltd: POB 1770, 1st Floor, Flat 12, 6 Ayia Eleni St, 1060 Nicosia; tel. (2) 441235; fax (2) 457925; f. 1982; Chair. and Gen. Man. KYRIACOS M. TYLLIS.

Crown Insurance Co Ltd: POB 4690, Royal Crown House, 20 Mnasiadou St, Nicosia 136; tel. (2) 455333; fax (2) 455757; Principal Officer ANTHIE ZACHARIADOU.

Cyprialife Ltd: POB 2535, 2 Amphipoleos St, Strovolos, 1522 Nicosia; tel. (2) 360030; fax (2) 428569; Chair. KIKIS LAZARIDES; Principal Officer ANDREAS ALONEFTIS.

E.F.U. General Insurance Ltd: POB 1612, 3 Themistoklis Dervis St, Julia House, Nicosia; tel. (2) 453053; fax (2) 475194; offshore company; Chair. ROSHEN ALI BHIMJEE.

Eurolife Ltd: POB 1655, 40 Them. Dervis St, Eurolife House, Nicosia; tel. (2) 442044; telex 3313; fax (2) 451040; Chair. ANDREAS PATSALIDES; Principal Officer ANDREAS KRITOTIS.

Eurosure Insurance Co Ltd: POB 1961, 8 Michalaki Karaoli St, Anemomylos Office Bldg, 3rd Floor, Nicosia; tel. (2) 463439; telex 2302; fax (2) 459084; Chair. STELIOS IOANNOU.

Excelsior General Insurance Co Ltd: POB 6106, 339 Ayiou Andreou St, Andrea Chambers, Of. 303, Limassol; tel. (5) 427021; fax (5) 312446; f. 1995; Chair. CLIVE E. K. LEWIS; Principal Officer MARIA HADJIANTONIOU.

Financial and Mercantile Insurance Co Ltd: POB 132, 284 Archbishop Makarios III Ave, Fortuna Bldg, Block 'B', 2nd Floor, Limassol; tel. (5) 362424; telex 2566; fax (5) 370055; offshore captive company operating outside Cyprus; Principal Officer CHR. GEORGHIADES.

General Insurance Co of Cyprus Ltd: POB 1668, 2–4 Themistoklis Dervis St, Nicosia; tel. (2) 450444; telex 2311; fax (2) 446682; f. 1951; Chair. A. PATSALIDES; Gen. Man. A. STYLIANOU.

Geopolis Insurance Ltd: POB 8530, 6 Neoptolemou St, Nicosia; tel. (2) 490094; fax (2) 490494; Principal Officer NIKOS DRYMIOTIS.

Granite Insurance Co Ltd: POB 613, 199 Archbishop Makarios III Ave, Neokleou Bldg, 3030 Limassol; tel. (5) 362818; telex 2948; fax (5) 359262; captive offshore company operating outside Cyprus; Chair. and Gen. Man. KOSTAS KOUTSOKOUMNIS; Principal Officer ANDREAS NEOKLEOUS.

Greene Insurances Ltd: POB 132, 4th Floor, Vereggaria Bldg, 25 Spyrou Araouzou St, Limassol; tel. (5) 362424; telex 2566; f. 1987; Chair. GEORGHIOS CHRISTODOULOU; Principal Officer JOSIF CHRISTOU.

Hellenic Hull Mutual Association (HMA) Ltd: POB 6777, 232 Archbishop Makarios III Ave, Apollon Bldg, Of. 101, 1st Floor, Limassol; tel. (5) 353554; telex 4743; fax (5) 354414; f. 1994; Principal Officer ANDREAS GEORGHADJIS.

Hermes Insurance Co Ltd: POB 4828, 1st Floor, Office 101–103, Anemomylos Bldg, 8 Michalakis Karaolis St, Nicosia; tel. (2) 448130; telex 3466; fax (2) 461888; f. 1980; Chair. and Man. Dir P. VOGAZIANOS.

Holloway Reinsurance Co Ltd: Artemis Ave, 4 Landways Mantion II, Larnaca; tel. (5) 365773; telex 3439; fax (5) 359770; f. 1994; Principal Officer PANIKOS ONOUFRIOU.

Interamerican Insurance Co Ltd: POB 819, 64 Archbishop Makarios III Ave and I Karpenisiou, 1077 Nicosia; tel. (2) 374100; fax (2) 374030; Principal Officer PETROS ADAMIDES.

Iris Insurance Co Ltd: POB 4841, Flat A5–A6, 1st Floor, 'Aspelia' Bldg, 34 Costis Palamas St, Nicosia; tel. (2) 448302; telex 3675; fax (2) 449579; Chair. and Gen. Man. PAVLOS CL. GEORGHIOU.

Laiki Insurance Co Ltd: POB 2069, 6 Evgenias & Antoniou Theodotou St, 1517 Nicosia; tel. (2) 449900; telex 5916; fax (2) 466890; f. 1981; Chair. K. N. LAZARIDES; Man. Y. E. SOLOMONIDES.

LCF Reinsurance Co Ltd: POB 3589, 3 Themistoklis Dervis St, Julia House, Nicosia; tel. (2) 453053; telex 2046; f. 1984; Chair. LELLOS DEMETRIADES; Principal Officer SOPHIA XINARI.

Ledra Insurance Ltd: POB 3942, 93 Kennedy Ave, 1077 Nicosia; tel. (2) 378200; fax (2) 378330; f. 1994; Principal Officer ALEKOS PULCHERIOS.

Liberty Life Insurance Ltd: POB 6070, 75 Limassol Ave, 5th Floor, Nicosia; tel. (2) 319300; fax (2) 429134; f. 1994; Principal Officer EVRIPIDES NEOKLEOUS.

Medlife Insurance Ltd: POB 1675, Themistoklis Dervis St and Florinis St, Nicosia; tel. and fax (2) 453390; e-mail office@medlife.net; f. 1995; Chair. Dr WOLFGANG GOSHNIK.

Metropolitan Insurance Ltd: POB 6516, 2 Kretes St, Pelekanos Court, Of. 1, Nicosia; tel. (2) 360655; fax (2) 360483; e-mail metropolitan@cytanet.com.cy; Chair. MICHALAKIS ZIVANARIS; Principal Officer PAVLOS DEKATRIS.

Minerva Insurance Co Ltd: POB 3554, 8 Epaminondas St, Nicosia 137; tel. (2) 445134; telex 2608; fax (2) 455528; f. 1970; Chair. and Gen. Man. K. KOUTSOKOUMNIS.

Pancypian Insurance Ltd: POB 1352, Mepa Tower, 66 Grivas Dhigenis Ave, Nicosia; tel. (2) 442235; telex 3015; fax (2) 477656; Chair. HENRI CHALHOUB; Principal Officer VASSOS STYLIANIDES.

Paneuropean Insurance Co Ltd: POB 553, 45 Bysantium St, 2064 Strovolos, 1660 Nicosia; tel. (2) 472000; fax (2) 472706; f. 1980; Chair. N. K. SHACOLAS; Gen. Man. POLIS MICHAELIDES.

Philiki Insurance Co Ltd: POB 2274, 45 Byzantium St, Strovolos, Nicosia; tel. (2) 444433; telex 2353; fax (2) 442026; f. 1982; Principal Officer DOROS ORPHANIDES.

Progressive Insurance Co Ltd: POB 2111, 6 Themistoklis Dervis St, 3rd Floor, Of. C1 and C2, Nicosia; tel. (2) 448787; fax (2) 453588; Principal Officer TAKIS HADJIANDREOU.

Saviour Insurance Co Ltd: POB 3957, 8 Michalakis Karaolis St, Anemomylos Bldg, Flat 104, 1687 Nicosia; tel. (2) 365085; fax (2) 446097; f. 1987; Chair. ROBERT SINCLAIR; Principal Officer KONSTANTINOS KITTIS.

Sunlink Insurance Co Ltd: POB 3585, 3 Themistoklis Dervis St, Julia House, Nicosia, tel. (2) 453328; telex 4857; fax (2) 461447; f. 1995; offshore captive company operating outside Cyprus; Chair. CHARALAMBOS ZAVALLIS; Principal Officer MARIA LAMBROU.

Tercet Insurance Ltd: 3 Themistoklis Dervis St, Julia House, Nicosia; tel. (2) 453053; telex 2046; fax (2) 475194; f. 1994; Chair. ANDREAS STYLIANOU; Principal Officer CH. ZAVALLIS.

Tortoise Insurance Services Ltd: POB 7233, Konstantinos Paleologos and Halkousis, Nicosia; tel. (2) 377370; telex 6149; fax (2) 377115; f. 1994; Chair. VALERIE PIROGOV; Principal Officer DOROS ORPHANIDES.

Trust International Insurance Co (Cyprus) Ltd: POB 132, 284 Archbishop Makarios III Ave, Fortuna Bldg, 2nd Floor, Limassol; tel. (5) 335856; telex 5054; fax (5) 335268; f. 1992; Principal Officer CHR. GEORGHIADES.

Universal Life Insurance Company Ltd: POB 1270, Universal Tower, 85 Dhigenis Akritas Ave, 1505 Nicosia; tel. (2) 461222; fax (2) 461343; f. 1970; Chair. J. CHRISTOPHIDES; Principal Officer ANDREAS GEORGHIOU.

UPIC Ltd: POB 7237, Nicolaou Pentadromos Centre, 10th Floor, Ayias Zonis St, 3314 Limassol; tel. (5) 347664; fax (5) 347081; f. 1992; Principal Officer POLAKIS SARRIS.

VTI Insurance Co Ltd: POB 613, 199 Archbishop Makarios III Ave, Neokleou Bldg, Limassol; tel. (5) 362818; telex 2948; fax (5) 359262; f. 1994; Chair. SOTTERIS PITTAS; Principal Officer ANDREAS NEOKLEOUS.

Warwick Insurance Co Ltd: POB 1612, 3 Themistoklis Dervis St, Julia House, Nicosia; tel. (2) 453053; telex 2046; fax (2) 475446; f. 1987; Chair. CHARALAMBOS ZAVALLIS.

WOB Insurances Ltd: 199 Archbishop Makarios III Ave, Neokleou Bldg, 3030 Limassol; tel. (5) 362818; telex 2948; fax (5) 359262; captive offshore company operating outside Cyprus; Principal Officer ANDREAS NEOKLEOUS.

Zako Insurance Ltd: POB 7106, 170 Ledra St, Nicosia; tel. (2) 454316; telex 2250; fax (2) 486596; Chair. GEORGE PETRO.

Turkish Cypriot Insurance Companies

Akfinans Sigorta Insurance AŞ: 16 Osman Paşa Cad., Lefkoşa (Nicosia), Mersin 10, Turkey; tel. (22) 84506; fax (22) 85713.

Ankara Sigorta: 50–58 Muzaffer Paşa Cad., Lefkoşa (Nicosia), Mersin 10, Turkey; tel. (22) 85815; fax (22) 83099.

Gold Insurance Ltd: Mehmet Akif Cad., Okay 7 Apt 1, Kumsal, Lefkoşa (Nicosia), Mersin 10, Turkey; tel. (22) 86479.

Güven Sigorta (Kıbrıs) Sirketi AŞ: Mecidiye Sok. 8, Lefkoşa (Nicosia), Mersin 10, Turkey; tel. (22) 81431; fax (22) 81244.

Işlek Sigorta: Bahçelievler Bul., Güzelyurt (Morphou), Mersin 10, Turkey; tel. (71) 42473; fax (71) 45507.

Kıbrıs Sigorta Şirketi: 27 Cengiz Topel Sok., Köşklüçiftlik, Lefkoşa (Nicosia), Mersin 10, Turkey; tel. (22) 83022; fax (22) 83838.

Liberty Sigorta: 25 Şehit Azrık Sok. Köşklüçiftlik, Lefkoşa (Nicosia), Mersin 10, Turkey; tel. (22) 81848; fax (22) 81844.

Saray Sigorta: 182 Girne Cad., Lefkoşa (Nicosia), Mersin 10, Turkey; tel. (22) 72976; fax (22) 79001.

Şeker Sigorta (Kibris) Ltd: 27–29 Mecidiye Sok., PK 664, Lefkoşa (Nicosia), Mersin 10, Turkey; tel. (22) 85883; fax (22) 74074.

Sigma Reasürans AŞ: 25 Şehit Arzık Sok., Köşklüçiftlik, Lefkoşa (Nicosia), Mersin 10, Turkey; tel. (22) 88511; fax (22) 88122.

Trade and Industry

GREEK CYPRIOT CHAMBERS OF COMMERCE AND INDUSTRY

Cyprus Chamber of Commerce and Industry: POB 1455, 38 Grivas Dhigenis Ave, 1509 Nicosia; tel. (2) 449500; telex 2077; fax (2) 449048; e-mail wtccy@wtca.geis.com; f. 1963; Pres. Vassilis Rologis; Sec.-Gen. Panayiotis Loizides; 6,000 mems, 84 affiliated trade asscns.

Famagusta Chamber of Commerce and Industry: POB 3124, 339 Ayiou Andreou St, Andrea Chambers Bldg, 2nd Floor, Office No 201–202, 3300 Limassol; tel. (5) 370165; telex 4519; fax (5) 370291; f. 1952; Pres. Photis Papathomas; Sec. Iacovos Hadjivarnavas; 450 mems.

Larnaca Chamber of Commerce and Industry: POB 287, 12 Gregoriou Afxentiou St, Skouros Bldg, Apt 43, 4th Floor, 6302 Larnaca; tel. (4) 655051; telex 3187; fax (4) 628281; Pres. Iacovos Demetriou; Sec. Othon Theodoulou; 450 mems.

Limassol Chamber of Commerce and Industry: POB 347, 25 Spyrou Araouzou St, Veregaria Bldg, 3rd Floor, 3603 Limassol; tel. (5) 362556; fax (5) 371655; e-mail chamberl@dial.cylink.com.cy; f. 1962; Pres. Michalis Polydorides; Sec. Christos Nicolaou; 750 mems.

Nicosia Chamber of Commerce and Industry: POB 1455, 38 Grivas Dhigenis Ave, Chamber Bldg, 1509 Nicosia; tel. (2) 449500; telex 2077; fax (2) 367433; f. 1962; Pres. George Argyropoulos; Sec. Panikos Michaelides; 1,200 mems.

Paphos Chamber of Commerce and Industry: POB 82, Athinon Ave & corner Alexandrou Papayou Ave, 8100 Paphos; tel. (6) 235115; telex 2888; fax (6) 244602; Pres. Theodoros Aristodemou; Sec. Kendeas Zampirinis; 450 mems.

TURKISH CYPRIOT CHAMBERS OF COMMERCE AND INDUSTRY

Turkish Cypriot Chamber of Industry: 14 Osman Paşa Cad., PK 563, Köşklüçiftlik, Lefkoşa (Nicosia), Mersin 10, Turkey; tel. (22) 84596; fax (22) 84595; Pres. Eren Ertanin.

Turkish Cypriot Chamber of Commerce: Bedrettin Demirel Cad., PK 718, Lefkoşa (Nicosia), Mersin 10, Turkey; tel. (22) 83645; telex 57511; fax (22) 83089; f. 1958; more than 6,000 regd mems; Chair. Salih Boyaci; Sec.-Gen. Janel Burcan.

GREEK CYPRIOT EMPLOYERS' ORGANIZATION

Cyprus Employers' & Industrialists' Federation: POB 1657, 30 Grivas Dhigenis Ave, 1511 Nicosia; tel. (2) 445102; fax (2) 459459; e-mail OEB@dial.cylink.com.cy; f. 1960; 40 member trade associations, 400 direct and 2,500 indirect members; Dir-Gen. Antonis Pierides; Chair. Andreas Pittas. The largest of the trade association members are: Cyprus Building Contractors' Association; Cyprus Hotel Keepers' Association; Clothing Manufacturers' Association; Cyprus Shipping Association; Shoe Makers' Association; Cyprus Metal Industries Association; Cyprus Bankers Employers' Association; Motor Vehicles Importers' Association.

TURKISH CYPRIOT EMPLOYERS' ORGANIZATION

Kıbrıs Türk İşverenler Sendikası (Turkish Cypriot Employers' Association): PK 674, Lefkoşa (Nicosia), Mersin 10, Turkey; tel. (22) 76173; Chair. Alpay Ali Riza Görgüner.

UTILITIES

Electricity

Electricity Authority of Cyprus (EAC): Nicosia; generation, transmission and distribution of electric energy in government-controlled area; total capacity 690 MW at power stations.

Water

Water Development Department: Ministry of Agriculture, Natural Resources and the Environment, Loukis Akritis Ave, Nicosia; tel. (2) 302171; fax (2) 445156; dam storage capacity 300m. cu m.

TRADE UNIONS

Greek Cypriot Trade Unions

Cyprus Civil Servants' Trade Union: 3 Dem. Severis Ave, Nicosia; tel. (2) 442278; fax (2) 465199; f. 1949, registered 1966; restricted to persons in the civil employment of the Government and public authorities; 6 brs with a total membership of 15,383; Pres. N. Panayiotou; Gen. Sec. A. Polyviou.

Demokratiki Ergatiki Omospondia Kyprou (Democratic Labour Federation of Cyprus): POB 1625, 40 Byron Ave, Nicosia; tel. (2) 456506; fax (2) 449494; f. 1962; 4 unions with a total membership of 6,329; Gen. Sec. Renos Prentzas.

Pankypria Ergatiki Omospondia—PEO (Pancyprian Federation of Labour): POB 1885, 31–35 Archermos St, Nicosia; tel. (2) 349400; fax (2) 349382; e-mail PEO@cytanet.com.cy; f. 1946, registered 1947; previously the Pancyprian Trade Union Committee f. 1941, dissolved 1946; 10 unions and 176 brs with a total membership of 75,000; affiliated to the WFTU; Gen. Sec. Avraam Antoniou.

Pankyprios Omospondia Anexartition Syntechnion (Pancyprian Federation of Independent Trade Unions): 4B Dayaes St, 2369 Ay. Dhometios; POB 7521, 2430 Nicosia; tel. (2) 356414; fax (2) 354216; f. 1956, registered 1957; has no political orientations; 8 unions with a total membership of 798; Gen. Sec. Kyriacos Nathanael.

Synomospondia Ergaton Kyprou (Cyprus Workers' Confederation): POB 5018, 23 Alkaiou St, Engomi, Nicosia; tel. (2) 441142; telex 6180; fax (2) 476360; f. 1944, registered 1950; 7 federations, 5 labour centres, 47 unions, 12 brs with a total membership of 56,935; affiliated to the ICFTU and the ETUC; Gen. Sec. Michael Ioannou; Deputy Gen. Sec. Demetris Kittenis.

Union of Cyprus Journalists: POB 3495, 2 Kratinos St, Strovolos, Nicosia; tel. (2) 454680; fax (2) 464598; f. 1959; Chair. Andreas Kannaouros.

Turkish Cypriot Trade Unions

In 1992 trade union membership totalled 20,711.

Devrimci İşçi Sendikaları Federasyonu (Dev-İş) (Revolutionary Trade Unions' Federation): 8 Serabioğlu Sok., Lefkoşa (Nicosia), Mersin 10, Turkey; tel. (22) 72640; f. 1976; two unions with a total membership of 570 (1992); affiliated to WFTU; Pres. (acting) and Gen.-Sec. Bayram Çelik.

Kıbrıs Türk İşçi Sendikaları Federasyonu (TÜRK-SEN) (Turkish Cypriot Trade Union Federation): POB 829, 7-7A Şehit Mehmet R. Hüseyin Sok., Lefkoşa (Nicosia), Mersin 10, Turkey; tel. (22) 72444; fax (22) 87831; f. 1954, regd 1955; 12 unions with a total membership of 7,093 (1992); affiliated to ICFTU, ETUC, CTUC and the Confederation of Trade Unions of Turkey (Türk-Iş); Pres. Önder Konuloğlu; Gen. Sec. Aslan Biçakli.

Transport

There are no railways in Cyprus.

ROADS

In December 1995 there were 25,378 km of roads in the government-controlled areas, of which 5,942 km were paved and the remainder were earth or gravel roads. The Nicosia–Limassol four-lane dual carriageway, which was completed in 1985, was subsequently extended with the completion of the Limassol and Larnaca bypasses. New highways between Nicosia and Larnaca, and Larnaca and Kophinou have been completed, as well as the Aradippo–Dhekelia and Larnaca Airport bypasses. The Nicosia–Anthoupolis–Kokkinotrimithia highway was completed in 1994. At December 1995 the total extent of the highway network was 178.4 km., which was expected to be increased further with the construction of a Limassol–Paphos highway (the first section of which opened in January 1997). The north and south are now served by separate transport systems, and there are no services linking the two sectors. In 1984 the road network in the Turkish Cypriot area consisted of about 5,278 km of paved and 838 km of unpaved roads. Between 1988 and 1990 some 250 km of new highways were constructed in the area.

SHIPPING

Until 1974 Famagusta, a natural port, was the island's most important harbour, handling about 83% of the country's cargo. Since its capture by the Turkish army in August 1974 the port has been officially declared closed to international traffic. However, it continues to serve the Turkish-occupied region.

The main ports which serve the island's maritime trade at present are Larnaca and Limassol, which were constructed in 1973 and 1974 respectively. Both ports have since been expanded and improved. There is also an industrial port at Vassiliko and there are three specialized petroleum terminals, at Larnaca, Dhekelia and Moni. A second container terminal became operational at Limassol in 1995.

In 1994, 4,946 vessels, with a total net registered tonnage of 15,338,000, visited Cyprus, carrying 8,134,000 metric tons of cargo to and from Cyprus. In addition to serving local traffic, Limassol and Larnaca ports act as transhipment load centres for the Eastern Mediterranean, North Adriatic and Black Sea markets and as regional warehouse and assembly bases for the Middle East, North Africa and the Persian (Arabian) Gulf. Containerized cargo handled at Cypriot ports amounted to 3,560,300 metric tons in 1994.

Both Kyrenia and Karavostassi are under Turkish occupation and have been declared closed to international traffic. Karavostassi used to be the country's major mineral port, dealing with 76% of the total mineral exports. However, since the war minerals have been passed through Vassiliko which is a specified industrial port. A hydrofoil service operates between Kyrenia and Mersin on the Turkish mainland. Car ferries sail from Kyrenia to Taşucu and Mersin, in Turkey.

The total number of merchant vessels registered in Cyprus on 31 December 1996 was 1,652, amounting to a total displacement of 23.8m. grt.

Department of Merchant Shipping: POB 6193, 15 Nafpliou St, 3005 Limassol; tel. (5) 330320; fax (5) 330264; e-mail dms@cytanet.com.cy; Dir. SERGHIOS SERGHIOU.

Cyprus Ports Authority: POB 2007, 23 Crete St, 1516 Nicosia; tel. (2) 450100; telex 2833; fax (2) 365420; e-mail cpa@cytanet.com.cy; f. 1973; Chair. COSTAS EROTOKRITOU; Gen. Man. MICHAEL VASSILIADES.

Cyprus Shipping Council: POB 6607, 3309 Limassol; tel. (5) 360717; fax (5) 358642; e-mail csc@dial.cylink.com.cy; internet http://www.swaypage.com/csc; Gen. Sec. THOMAS A. KAZAKOS.

Greek Cypriot Shipping Companies

Amer Shipping Ltd: 6th Floor, Ghinis Bldg, 58–60 Dhigenis Akritas Ave, Nicosia; tel. (2) 751707; telex 6513; fax (2) 751460; Reps SHASHI K. MEHROTRA, DEMETRI ANGELOU.

C. F. Ahrenkiel Shipmanagement (Cyprus) Ltd: 4th Floor, O & A Tower, 25 Olympion St, 3035 Limassol; tel. (5) 359731; telex 6309; fax (5) 359714; Reps PETER DE JONGH, JOHN CONSTANTINOU.

Columbia Shipmanagement Ltd: POB 1624, Columbia House, Dodekanissou and Kolonakiou Corner, Limassol; tel. (5) 320900; telex 3206; fax (5) 320325; f. 1978; Chair H. SCHOELLER, Man. Dir D. FRY.

Hanseatic Shipping Co Ltd: POB 127, 111 Spyrou Araouzou St, Limassol; tel. (5) 345111; telex 3282; fax (5) 342879; f. 1972; Man. Dirs A. J. DROUSSIOTIS, B. BEHRENS.

Interorient Navigation Co Ltd: POB 1309, 3 Thalia St, 3504 Limassol; tel. (5) 341616; telex 2629; fax (5) 345895; e-mail Management@Interorient.com.cy; Man. Dir JAN LISSOW.

Louis Cruise Lines: POB 1301, 54-58 Evagoras I Ave, Nicosia; tel. (2) 442114; telex 2341; fax (2) 459800; Reps COSTAKIS LOIZOU, STELIOS KILIARIS.

Marlow Navigation Co Ltd: POB 4077, Marlow Bldg, cnr 28th October St and Sotiris Michaelides St, Limassol; tel. (5) 348888; telex 2019; fax (5) 748222; Gen. Man. ANDREAS NEOPHYTOU.

Oldendorff Ltd, Reederei Nord Klaus E: POB 6345, Libra Tower, 23 Olympion St, 3306 Limassol; tel. (5) 370262; telex 5938; fax (5) 345077; e-mail a14cy288@gncomtext.com; Chair. and Man. Dir KLAUS E. OLDENDORFF.

Seatankers Management Co Ltd: POB 3562, Flat 411, Deana Beach Apartments, Promachon Eleftherias St, 4103 Limassol; tel. (5) 326111; telex 5606; fax (5) 323770; Man. Dir DANIEL IONNIDES; Gen. Man. DEMETRIS HANNAS.

Turkish Cypriot Shipping Companies

Armen Denizcilik Ltd: Altun Tabya Yolu No. 10–11, Gazi Mağusa (Famagusta), Mersin 10, Turkey; tel. (36) 63565; fax (36) 65860; e-mail armden@escortnet.com; Dir AYHEN VARER.

Compass Shipping Ltd: Seagate Court, Gazi Mağusa (Famagusta), Mersin 10, Turkey; tel. (36) 66393; fax (36) 66394.

Denko Koop Marine Cargo Department: PK 4, Gazi Mağusa (Famagusta), Mersin 10, Turkey; tel. (36) 65419; telex 57608; fax (36) 62773; Dir MEHMET EFE.

Ertürk Ltd: Kyrenia (Girne), Mersin 10, Turkey; tel. (81) 55834; fax (81) 51808; Dir KEMAL ERTÜRK.

Fergun Maritime Co: Kyrenia (Girne), Mersin 10, Turkey; tel. (81) 54993; ferries to Turkish ports; Owner FEHIM KUÇUK.

Kıbrıs Türk Denizcilik Ltd, Şti (Turkish Cypriot Maritime Co Ltd): 3 Bülent Ecevit Bul., Gazi Mağusa (Famagusta), Mersin 10, Turkey; tel. (36) 65995; telex 57547; fax (36) 67840.

Medusa Marine Shipping Ltd: Aycan Apt, Gazi Mağusa (Famagusta), Mersin 10, Turkey; tel. (36) 63945; fax (36) 67800; Dir ERGÜN TOLAY.

Orion Navigation Ltd: Seagate Court, Gazi Mağusa (Famagusta), Mersin 10, Turkey; tel. (36) 62643; telex 57583; fax (36) 64773; f. 1976; shipping agents; Dir O. LAMA; Shipping Man. L. LAMA.

Özari Shipping Ltd: Seagate Court, Gazi Mağusa (Famagusta), Mersin 10, Turkey; tel. (36) 66555; fax (36) 67098; Dir YALÇIN RUHI.

Tahsin Transtürk ve Oğlu Ltd: 11 Kizilkule Yolu, Gazi Mağusa (Famagusta), Mersin 10, Turkey; tel. (36) 65409.

CIVIL AVIATION

There is an international airport at Nicosia, which can accommodate all types of aircraft, including jets. It has been closed since July 1974 following the Turkish invasion. A new international airport was constructed at Larnaca, from which flights operate to Europe, the USA, the Middle East and the Gulf. Another international airport at Paphos began operations in November 1983.

Cyprus Airways: 21 Alkeou St, Engomi 2404, POB 1903, 1514, Nicosia; tel. (2) 443054; telex 2225; fax (2) 443167; f. 1947; jointly owned by Cyprus Government and local interests; wholly-owned charter subsidiaries Cyprair Tours Ltd, Eurocypria Airlines Ltd and Duty Free Shops Ltd; Chair. TAKIS KYRIAKIDES; CEO DEMETRIS PANTAZIS; Gen. Man. CHRISTOS KYRIAKIDES; services throughout Europe and the Middle East.

In 1975 the Turkish authorities opened Ercan (formerly Tymbou) airport, and a second airport was opened at Geçitkale (Lefkoniko) in 1986.

Kıbrıs Türk Hava Yolları (Turkish Cypriot Airlines): Bedrettin Demirel Cad., PK 793, Lefkoşa (Nicosia), Mersin 10, Turkey; tel. (22) 83901; telex 57350; fax (22) 81468; f. 1974; jointly owned by the Turkish Cypriot Community Assembly Consolidated Improvement Fund and Turkish Airlines Inc; Gen. Man. Dr FERDA ÖNEŞ; services to Turkey and five European countries.

Tourism

In 1996 a total of 1,950,000 foreign tourists visited the Greek Cypriot area, and receipts from tourism amounted to C£780m. In 1995 an estimated 385,759 tourists visited the Turkish Cypriot area, and in 1994 revenue from tourism reached US $172.9m.

Cyprus Tourism Organization (CTO): POB 4535, 19 Limassol Ave, 2112 Nicosia; tel. (2) 337715; fax (2) 331644; e-mail cto@cyta.com.cy; Chair. A. EROTOCRITOU; Dir-Gen. FRYNI MICHAEL.

Turkish Cypriot Tourism Enterprises Ltd: Kyrenia (Girne), Mersin 10, Turkey; tel. (81) 52165; telex 57128; fax (81) 52073; f. 1974; Chair. YALÇIN VEHIT.

THE CZECH REPUBLIC

Introductory Survey

Location, Climate, Language, Religion, Flag, Capital

The Czech Republic lies in central Europe. It comprises the Czech Lands of Bohemia and Moravia and part of Silesia. Its neighbours are Poland to the north, Germany to the north-west and west, Austria to the south and Slovakia to the east. The climate is continental, with warm summers and cold winters. The average mean temperature is 9°C (49°F). The official language is Czech, a member of the west Slavonic group. There is a sizeable Slovak minority and also small Polish, German, Silesian, Romany, Hungarian and other minorities. The major religion is Christianity (about 43% of the population are Roman Catholics). The national flag (proportions 3 by 2) has two equal horizontal stripes, of white and red, on which is superimposed a blue triangle (half the length) at the hoist. The capital is Prague (Praha).

Recent History

In October 1918, following the collapse of the Austro-Hungarian Empire at the end of the First World War, the Republic of Czechoslovakia was established. The new state united the Czech Lands of Bohemia and Moravia, which had been incorporated into the Austrian Empire in the 16th and 17th centuries, and Slovakia, which had been under Hungarian rule for almost 1,000 years. In the inter-war period (1918–39) a stable democratic system of government flourished in Czechoslovakia, and the country's economy was considered to be the most industrialized and prosperous in eastern Europe. After the Nazis, led by Adolf Hitler, came to power in Germany in 1933, there was increased agitation in the Sudetenland (an area in northern Bohemia that was inhabited by about 3m. German-speaking people) for autonomy within, and later secession from, Czechoslovakia. In 1938, to appease German demands, the British, French and Italian Prime Ministers concluded an agreement with Hitler, whereby the Sudetenland was ceded to Germany, while other parts of Czechoslovakia were transferred to Hungary and Poland. The remainder of Czechoslovakia was invaded and occupied by Nazi armed forces in March 1939, and a German protectorate was established in Bohemia and Moravia. In Slovakia, which had been granted self-government in late 1938, a separate Slovak state was formed, under the pro-Nazi 'puppet' regime of Jozef Tiso.

After Germany's defeat in the Second World War (1939–45), the pre-1938 frontiers of Czechoslovakia were restored, although a small area in the east was ceded to the USSR in June 1945. Almost all of the German-speaking inhabitants of Czechoslovakia were expelled, and the Sudetenland was settled by Czechs from other parts of Bohemia. In response to Slovak demands for greater autonomy, a legislature (the Slovak National Council) and an executive Board of Commissioners were established in Bratislava, the Slovak capital. At elections in 1946 the Communist Party of Czechoslovakia (CPCz) emerged as the leading party, winning 38% of the votes. The CPCz's leader, Klement Gottwald, became Prime Minister in a coalition Government. After ministers of other parties resigned, communist control became complete on 25 February 1948. A People's Republic was established on 9 June 1948. Gottwald replaced Edvard Beneš as President, a position that he held until his death in 1953. The country aligned itself with the Soviet-led eastern European bloc, joining the Council for Mutual Economic Assistance (CMEA) and the Warsaw Pact.

Under Gottwald, government followed a rigid Stalinist pattern, and in the early 1950s there were many political trials. Although these ended under Gottwald's successors, Antonín Zápotocký and, from 1956, Antonín Novotný, 'de-Stalinization' was late in coming to Czechoslovakia, and there was no relaxation until 1963, when a new Government, with Jozef Lenárt as Prime Minister, was formed. Meanwhile, the country was renamed the Czechoslovak Socialist Republic, under a new Constitution, proclaimed in July 1960.

In January 1968 Alexander Dubček succeeded Novotný as CPCz Secretary, and in March Gen. Ludvík Svoboda succeeded Novotný as President. Oldřich Černík became Prime Minister in April. The policies of the new Government were more independent and liberal, and envisaged widespread reforms, including the introduction of more genuine elections, a greater freedom of expression and a greater degree of separation between party and state. A federal system of government was also to be introduced. The Government's reformist policies were regarded by other members of the eastern European bloc as endangering their unity, and in August Warsaw Pact forces (numbering an estimated 600,000 men) invaded Czechoslovakia, occupying Prague and other major cities. Mass demonstrations in protest at the invasion were held throughout the country, and many people were killed in clashes with occupation troops. The Soviet Government exerted heavy pressure on the Czechoslovak leaders to suppress their reformist policies, and in April 1969 Dubček was replaced by a fellow Slovak, Dr Gustáv Husák, as First (subsequently General) Secretary of the Central Committee of the CPCz. Under Husák's leadership, there was a severe purge of CPCz membership, and most of Dubček's supporters were removed from the Government. All the reforms of the so-called 'Prague Spring' of 1968 were duly abandoned, with the exception of the federalization programme. This was implemented in January 1969, when the unitary Czechoslovak state was transformed into a federation, with separate Czech and Slovak Republics, each having its own National Council (legislature) and Government. A Federal Government was established as the supreme executive organ of state power, while the country's existing legislature, the National Assembly, was transformed into a bicameral Federal Assembly. The first legislative elections since 1964 were held in November 1971 and produced a 99.81% vote in favour of candidates of the National Front (the communist-dominated organization embracing all the legal political parties in Czechoslovakia).

In May 1975 Husák was appointed to the largely ceremonial post of President of Czechoslovakia, while still holding the positions of Chairman of the National Front and General Secretary of the CPCz. He held the latter post until December 1987, when he was replaced by Miloš Jakeš, an economist and member of the Presidium of the party's Central Committee. However, Husák remained as President of the Republic.

Although Jakeš affirmed his commitment to the moderate programme of reform, initiated by his predecessor, there was little indication of a policy more liberal than that of Husák, as repressive measures against the Roman Catholic Church and dissident groups continued. Of the latter, the most influential was Charter 77, which had been established in January 1977 by intellectuals, former politicians and others to campaign for the observance of civil and political rights. Despite the regime's continued attempts to suppress it, the movement's sphere of influence broadened, and it played a leading role in anti-Government demonstrations, which began in 1988. In February 1989, following one such demonstration, the Czech playwright, Václav Havel (a leader of Charter 77), was sentenced to nine months' imprisonment. (He was released in May, following international condemnation.) Anti-Government demonstrations followed in May, August and October 1989.

In November 1989 the protest actions of preceding months evolved into a process of dramatic, yet largely peaceful, political change, which subsequently became known as the 'velvet revolution'. On 17 November some 50,000 people, mainly students, participated in an anti-Government demonstration in Prague, the largest public protest for 20 years. The demonstration was violently dispersed by the police, and more than 500 people were injured. Following rumours (which later proved to be unfounded) that a student had been killed, a series of demonstrations of escalating size took place, culminating in gatherings of as many as 500,000 people in Prague, while large-scale demonstrations took place in other towns throughout the country.

A new opposition group, Civic Forum, was established in November 1989 as an informal alliance embracing several existing opposition and human rights organizations, including Charter 77, and rapidly gained widespread popular support. Meanwhile, Alexander Dubček addressed mass rallies in Bratislava and Prague, expressing his support for the opposition's demands for reform. On 24 November it was announced that Jakeš and the entire membership of the Presidium of the Central Committee had resigned. Karel Urbánek, a member of the Presidium, replaced Jakeš as General Secretary of the party, and a new Presidium was elected.

The increasing strength of Civic Forum and its Slovak counterpart, Public Against Violence (PAV), was demonstrated during discussions on reform with the Federal Prime Minister, Ladislav Adamec. The opposition's demands for the ending of censorship and the release of all political prisoners were fulfilled, and, in late November 1989, the articles guaranteeing the CPCz's predominance were deleted from the Constitution. In the following month the CPCz condemned the invasion of Czechoslovakia by Warsaw Pact forces in 1968 as 'unjustified and mistaken'. Shortly afterwards, the Governments of the five countries that had invaded Czechoslovakia issued a joint statement condemning their action.

In early December 1989 a reshuffle of the Federal Government took place. Civic Forum and PAV denounced the new Government, as the majority of its ministers had been members of the previous administration, and it included only five non-communists. Adamec subsequently resigned as Prime Minister, and was replaced by Marián Čalfa, the newly-appointed First Deputy Prime Minister. In the following week a new, interim Federal Government was formed, with a majority of non-communist members, including seven non-party supporters of Civic Forum. Husák resigned as President of the Republic and, at the end of December, was replaced by Václav Havel. Alexander Dubček was elected Chairman of the Federal Assembly. At an emergency congress of the CPCz, held in December, Urbánek was dismissed from the post of General Secretary of the Central Committee and this position was abolished. Adamec was appointed to the new post of Chairman of the party.

In April 1990 the Federal Assembly voted to rename the country the Czech and Slovak Federative Republic (CzSFR). The decision, which followed intense controversy between Czech and Slovak deputies, satisfied Slovak demands that the new title should reflect the equal status of Slovakia within the federation.

On 8–9 June 1990 the first free legislative elections since 1946 were held in Czechoslovakia. About 97% of the electorate voted for a total of 27 parties and movements for representation in the Federal Assembly (now numbering 300 seats) and in the National Councils of each republic. In the elections at federal level, the largest share of the total votes cast (about 46%) was won by Civic Forum, in the Czech Lands, and by PAV, in Slovakia. The CPCz won a larger proportion of the total votes (about 14%) than had been expected, obtaining the second largest representation in the Federal Assembly. The Christian Democratic Union—a coalition of the Czechoslovak People's Party, the Christian Democratic Party (Chr.DP) and the Slovak-based Christian Democratic Movement (CDM)—obtained approximately 12% of the total votes. Contrary to expectations, two parties which had campaigned for regional autonomy or secession secured more than the 5% of the vote required for representation in the legislature: the Movement for Autonomous Democracy–Society for Moravia and Silesia (MAD–SMS), and the separatist Slovak National Party (SNP). The newly-elected Federal Assembly was to serve a transitional two-year term until the holding of fresh legislative elections in 1992, before which time it was to have drafted new federal and republican constitutions and elected a new President of the Republic. In late June 1990 Alexander Dubček was re-elected Chairman of the Federal Assembly. A new Federal Government, announced in that month, comprised 16 members: four from Civic Forum, three from PAV, one from the CDM and eight independents. In early July Václav Havel was re-elected to the post of President.

In the latter half of 1990 there was increasing unrest in Slovakia, as several newly-established parties and groups, most prominently the SNP, organized demonstrations and rallies as part of a campaign for Slovak autonomy. In an attempt to alleviate the increasing ethnic tension in the country, the Federal Assembly voted overwhelmingly, in December, to transfer broader powers to the Czech and Slovak Governments, while the Federal Government was to retain jurisdiction over defence, foreign affairs and monetary policy. None the less, the Slovak question remained the dominant topic of political debate during 1991 and 1992. A widening division appeared between the more moderate Slovak movements, such as PAV and the CDM (which advocated the preservation of the federation, albeit in a looser form), and a minority of more radical parties, which campaigned for full independence. In early March 1991 Vladimír Mečiar, the Slovak Prime Minister and a founding member of PAV, announced the formation of a minority faction within PAV—the Movement for a Democratic Slovakia (MDS)—in support of greater Slovak autonomy. However, leading officials in PAV and some of its representatives in the Slovak Government viewed Mečiar's policies and aggressive style of leadership as detrimental to the future of Czech–Slovak relations, and in April the Slovak National Council voted to remove Mečiar from the Slovak premiership. He was replaced by Ján Čarnogurský, the Chairman of the CDM. In response, Mečiar and his supporters left PAV, and the MDS was established as a separate political group.

Meanwhile, disagreement over the direction of post-communist politics and economic management had led to a split within Civic Forum. Two main groups emerged in February 1991—the conservative Civic Democratic Party (CDP), led by Václav Klaus, and the liberal Civic Movement (CM), led by Jiří Dienstbier. However, it was announced that, in the interests of national unity, the two new groups were to remain as coalition partners in the Federal Government until the holding of the next legislative elections, due in June 1992.

In March 1991 representatives of all political forces in Czechoslovakia reached agreement on the framework of a new federal Constitution. This stipulated, *inter alia,* that the country would remain a federative state comprising two 'sovereign and equal republics, linked voluntarily and by the free will of their citizens'. However, by late 1991, the Federal Assembly's discussions on the new Constitution had reached an impasse, as deputies failed to agree on the status of the two republics within any future federation. President Havel repeatedly proposed the holding of a referendum on the possible division of Czechoslovakia into two separate states, as the only democratic means of resolving the issue. His proposals, however, were rejected by the Federal Assembly. The constitutional debate continued in the first half of 1992, with increasing Slovak support for the loosest possible confederation, comprising two nominally independent states. The majority of Czech politicians, however, were in favour of preserving the existing state structure, and rejected Slovak proposals as impracticable. In March it was agreed to postpone the constitutional talks until after the legislative elections at federal and republican level, in June. Meanwhile, the results of public opinion polls indicated that the majority of Czechoslovaks favoured a continued federation.

The legislative elections of 5–6 June 1992 proved to be decisive in the eventual dismantling of Czechoslovakia, particularly as the MDS, led by Mečiar, emerged clearly as the dominant political force in Slovakia. With about 34% of the total Slovak votes, the party obtained 57 seats (the second largest representation) in the 300-member Federal Assembly. The leading party in the Slovak Government, the CDM (which advocated a continued federation), won only 9% of the Slovak votes, securing 14 seats in the Federal Assembly, one seat less than the separatist SNP. As had been expected, Václav Klaus's party, the CDP (in coalition with the Chr.DP), won the largest share (about 34%) of the total votes in the Czech Lands. The CDP was one of only two parties to contest the elections in both republics, and in Slovakia it received 4% of the votes cast. In total, the CDP won 85 seats in the Federal Assembly, thus becoming the largest party in the legislature. Two other splinter groups of the former Civic Forum—Dienstbier's CM and the Civic Democratic Alliance (CDA)—failed to win representation in the Federal Assembly, as did the Civic Democratic Union (formerly PAV), in Slovakia. The successor organizations to the communist parties of the two republics achieved considerable success: the Left Bloc (which included the Communist Party of Bohemia and Moravia, CPBM) won a total of 34 seats in the Federal Assembly, while the Slovak-based Party of the Democratic Left secured 23 seats. The representation of parties in the new republican legislatures did not differ greatly from that of the Federal Assembly, although the CDA and the MAD–SMS succeeded in winning seats in the Czech National Council.

Negotiations on the formation of a new federal government were initiated forthwith by the CDP and the MDS, but only served to emphasize the two leading parties' fundamental divergence of opinion on the future of the CzSFR. Nevertheless, a transitional Federal Government, dominated by members of the CDP and the MDS, was appointed in early July 1992. The new Prime Minister was Jan Stráský of the CDP, who had served as a Deputy Prime Minister in the outgoing Czech Government. There was now increasing recognition by Czech politicians that the constitutional talks on the future of Czechoslovakia were no longer viable and that a complete separation was preferable to the compromise measures that most Slovak parties favoured. The principal task of the new Federal Government, it was acknowledged, was to supervise the eventual dissolution of the CzSFR. Meanwhile, in late June, the new Slovak Government was announced, with Mečiar as Prime Minister. All but one of the ministers were members of the MDS. A new coalition Czech Government, dominated by the CDP and with Klaus as Prime Minister, was appointed in early July. In three rounds of presidential elections, held in the same month, the Federal Assembly failed to elect any of the candidates. Havel's re-election as President had effectively been blocked by the MDS and the SNP, and in mid-July he resigned from the post. Further rounds of voting, in August and October, were aborted, as no candidates presented themselves.

The events of June and July 1992 had ensured that the emergence of two independent states was now inevitable. On 17 July the Slovak National Council overwhelmingly approved a (symbolic) declaration of Slovak sovereignty, and in the following week the Czech and Slovak Prime Ministers agreed, in principle, to the dissolution of the CzSFR, the terms of which were to be settled shortly. In the following months extensive negotiations were conducted to determine the modalities of the division, which was to take effect from 1 January 1993. International observers expressed surprise not only that the dissolution of Czechoslovakia should be effected in so short a time, but also that the majority of Czechs and Slovaks (more than 60%, according to the results of public opinion polls) were still opposed to the country's division. Moreover, it now appeared that Slovak leaders were less intent to leave the federation. Indeed, the Federal Assembly's failure, in early October 1992 and again in mid-November, to adopt legislation permitting the dissolution of the CzSFR was due to opposition by (mainly) MDS deputies. However, the two republican Prime Ministers, supported by their respective governments, stressed that the process of partition was now irreversible. In late October the Czech and Slovak Governments ratified a number of accords, including a customs union treaty to abolish trade restrictions between the two republics following their independence. Finally, on 25 November, the Federal Assembly adopted legislation providing for the constitutional disbanding of the federation, having secured the necessary three-fifths majority by a margin of only three votes. Accordingly, the Federal Government accelerated the process of dividing the country's assets and liabilities as well as its armed forces, applying, in as far as was practically possible, a ratio of 2 to 1, to reflect the relative size of the Czech and Slovak populations. In most cases federal property was divided territorially (according to its location in either of the republics). It was agreed, however, that the two states would continue to share some federal infrastructure and would retain a single currency for the immediate future, although respective central banks were established. (Two separate currencies, the Czech and the Slovak koruna, were introduced in February 1993.)

On 17 December 1992 a treaty of good-neighbourliness, friendly relations and co-operation was signed, followed by the exchange of diplomatic relations between the two republics. At midnight on 31 December all federal structures were dissolved and the Czech Republic and the Slovak Republic came into being. The dissolution of the CzSFR, like the 'velvet revolution' of 1989, had thus been effected in an entirely peaceful fashion. As legal successors to Czechoslovakia, the two republics were quickly recognized by the states that had maintained diplomatic relations with the CzSFR, as well as by those international bodies of which the CzSFR had been a member. Existing treaties and agreements, to which the CzSFR had been a party, were to be honoured by both republics.

In anticipation of the establishment of the Czech Republic as an independent state, the existing legislature was replaced by a bicameral body, in accordance with the Czech Constitution (adopted in mid-December 1992); the Czech National Council was transformed into a Chamber of Deputies (lower house), which retained the Council's 200 members, while an upper house, or Senate, was due to be elected at a later date. In late January 1993 the Chamber of Deputies elected Václav Havel to be the Czech Republic's first President. The composition of the Government remained largely unchanged. It included among its principal objectives the pursuance of the former Federal Government's economic reforms, including its programme of large-scale privatization. Another of its priorities was to curb the recent rise in organized crime.

Relations between the Czech Republic and Slovakia were troubled in early 1993 by a number of disagreements over former Czechoslovak assets and property that still remained to be divided. In March the Czech Government announced that, until the resolution of all such issues, it would suspend Slovak investment in privatized Czech companies. Relations improved in May, however, when the two states concluded an agreement on former federal property, following which the Czech Government recommenced the issue of shares to Slovak investors.

In late 1993 the Government was divided over the issue of the restitution of property that had been expropriated from Czech Jews during the period of Nazi occupation (1938–45). There were fears that any such restitution would lead to claims for compensation by those surviving Sudeten Germans who were expelled from Czechoslovakia in 1945 (see below). (The country's existing legislation on restitution of property covered only the communist period, 1948–89.) Nevertheless, in April 1994 the Chamber of Deputies adopted legislation permitting the restitution of Jewish property.

In November 1994 local elections were held, at which the CDP was confirmed as the party with the broadest support (receiving some 31% of the total votes), followed by the CPBM (with 13%). The electoral turn-out was about 60%.

There was renewed controversy in 1995 over the so-called 'lustration' or screening law, which had been adopted by the Czechoslovak Federal Assembly in October 1991. The law effectively banned former communist functionaries as well as members of the former state security service and the People's Militia (the CPCz's paramilitary force) from holding senior political, economic and judicial posts. In September 1995 the Chamber of Deputies voted to extend until the year 2000 the legislation on screening (which had been due to expire in late 1996). In the following month President Havel rejected the decision, but the Chamber approved it for a second time, and the extension of the screening law entered into force.

The first general election to be held since the dissolution of the CzSFR took place on 31 May and 1 June 1996. Eighteen parties and two political movements contested the election to the Chamber of Deputies, and it was expected that the CDP (which had merged with the Chr.DP in April) would retain its position as the largest party in the legislature by a clear margin. In the event, the CDP won 68 of the 200 seats (with 29.6% of the total votes), while the Czech Social Democratic Party (CSDP), which had become a major force of the centre-left under the leadership of Miloš Zeman, almost quadrupled its parliamentary representation, winning 61 seats (26.4%). As a result, the coalition of the CDP, the Christian Democratic Union–Czechoslovak People's Party (CDU–CPP, which obtained 18 seats) and the CDA (13 seats) lost its overall majority, achieving a total of 99 seats. The CPBM and the Association for the Republic–Republican Party of Czechoslovakia were the only other parties to exceed the 5% threshold required for representation in the legislature, securing 22 seats and 18 seats, respectively. Despite losing its parliamentary majority, the governing coalition remained intact. The CSDP ruled out the possibility of joining the coalition, but agreed to give tacit support on most issues to a minority government. In early July Václav Klaus formed a new Government, comprising eight CDP members, four CDU–CPP members and four from the CDA, and, in a major concession to the CSDP, Miloš Zeman was appointed Chairman of the Chamber of Deputies. The Government survived a vote of confidence in late July, despite CSDP opposition to government proposals to return some 175,000 ha of land, confiscated by the communists, to the Catholic Church, without seeking the approval of the legislature. Although the CSDP achieved considerable success in the elections, overall support for the ruling coalition had not actually declined; in fact, its share of the vote had increased from 41% in 1992 to 44% in 1996, and, in retaining his position as Prime Minister, Klaus became the only conservative leader in Central Europe to win a second term of office following the collapse of communism in 1989.

In November 1996 preparations for elections to the 81-seat Senate were overshadowed by the resignation of the acting head of the counterintelligence service, Stanislav Devaty, amid allegations that he had placed Josef Lux, a Deputy Prime Minister and Minister of Agriculture, under surveillance, and by Zeman's ensuing accusation that the secret service was being used to promote party interests. The turn-out for the elections, held in mid-November, was low (35%), but the ruling coalition gained a majority of the votes, winning 52 seats. The CSDP won 25 seats, and the CPBM won two, while the remaining two seats went to the Democratic Union and an independent candidate. At the first meeting of the Senate (whose main role would be to scrutinize legislation), held in December, Petr Pithart was elected Chairman. In late January 1997 a parliamentary commission investigating Zeman's claims found them to be unsubstantiated, and in the following month Devaty was awarded substantial compensation after winning a libel case against the CSDP.

Economic problems and growing divisions within the ruling coalition created considerable pressure for government change in May 1997. Vladimír Dlouhý, the Minister for Industry and Trade (who had earlier proposed that the entire Council of Ministers should step down), Ivan Kočárník, the Minister of Finance, and Jan Ruml, the Minister of the Interior, all resigned, although Ruml's resignation was later rejected by Havel. Despite severe criticism from the President, Klaus dismissed suggestions that he or his administration should resign and presented a programme for economic stabilization and recovery. In June the Government narrowly won a vote of confidence in the Chamber of Deputies, relying on the vote of one independent deputy.

In July 1997 severe flooding in Moravia and eastern Bohemia resulted in some 50 deaths and the destruction of property and infrastructure; overall damage was estimated at 60,000m. koruny. Meanwhile, disagreements within the ruling coalition continued, particularly over defence and economic policy. Furthermore, in mid-September the Government was forced to withdraw plans to levy a surcharge on income tax to raise funds for reconstruction work, following the flooding, when several CDA and CDP deputies joined the opposition in rejecting the measure.

In August 1997 the Government was forced to address the problems of the Romany population (unofficially estimated at some 300,000) as hundreds of Romanies, claiming to have suffered persecution in the Czech Republic, attempted to gain political asylum in Canada (which subsequently reimposed visa requirements for Czech visitors) and the United Kingdom. The Government established an interministerial commission for Romany community affairs in October and outlined further measures aimed at improving the situation of Romanies in the Czech Republic.

Czech–Slovak relations, which had been strained in recent years (mainly because of disagreements over the division of former federal property), improved to some extent in October 1997, when the Prime Ministers of the two countries held their first official meeting since the dissolution of the CzSFR. Negotiations on the restitution of gold reserves to Slovakia, the repayment of debts to the Czech Republic and the exchange of bank shares between the two countries continued in December.

Tension within the CDP and between the coalition parties intensified in October 1997. Josef Zieleniec resigned from his position as Minister of Foreign Relations and as Deputy Chairman of the CDP, citing a lack of consultation on important party decisions (notably in the selection of a replacement for Ruml, who had announced his intention to resign from the Government by the end of the year) and the fact that he had not been informed of changes to the financial management of the CDP as the reasons for his departure. Zieleniec was replaced by Jaroslav Šedivý, hitherto ambassador to Belgium and NATO (and unaffiliated to any political party). Josef Lux, Chairman of the CDU–CPP, subsequently demanded that a new government policy statement be presented, and submitted to a vote of confidence in early 1998 (a demand which Klaus rejected).

In early November 1997, while coalition leaders failed to reach agreement on a solution to the political and economic situation, at least 60,000 trade-union members demonstrated in Prague against the Government's social welfare and economic policies. At the end of that month, allegations of impropriety in the funding of the CDP led to the resignation of the Klaus administration, following the withdrawal of the CDU–CPP and the CDA from the coalition, and appeals from both the President and senior members of the CDP for the Government to stand down. It had emerged that a substantial donation, received by the CDP in 1995, had been donated by a businessman who had successfully bid for the privatization tender for a steelworks. It was also reported that the CDP had access to funds held in a secret account in a Swiss bank. Klaus insisted that he had not known the identity of the sponsor, although Zieleniec subsequently claimed to have informed Klaus of his identity before the 1996 general election; Klaus continued to deny all allegations of corruption. In December 1997 Josef Lux was asked to lead talks on the formation of a new government. Klaus was re-elected Chairman of the CDP at the party's national conference later that month, defeating Jan Ruml, who subsequently formed a new faction within the party. Josef Tošovský, hitherto Governor of the Czech National Bank, was designated Prime Minister in mid-December, and a new temporary Government, comprising seven non-political ministers, four CDP members, three CDU–CPP members and three CDA members, was appointed in early January 1998. The CDP was divided over its participation in the new administration. The party's leadership in the Chamber of Deputies recommended that the four CDP ministers should retain their positions, while Klaus, as leader of the party's executive council, claimed that the ministers had infringed CDP statutes, by not receiving the council's approval, and should leave either the Government or the party. The ministers subsequently resigned from the party and joined the Freedom Union, a newly-established breakaway party, which had 31 seats in the Chamber of Deputies by mid-February, leaving the CSDP as the largest party in the chamber.

In the presidential election, which took place on 20 January 1998, Havel was narrowly re-elected in a second round of voting, having failed to win an absolute majority in the first round, in which he defeated the only other candidates, who represented the Communist Party of Bohemia and Moravia, and the Association for the Republic–Republican Party of Czechoslovakia. At the end of that month the Government won a vote of confidence when its policy statement was adopted in the Chamber of Deputies; main objectives included the establishment of political stability, further preparations for membership of NATO and the EU, and the organization of early elections (expected to be held in June). In late February Jiří Skalický resigned as Deputy Prime Minister and Minister of the Environment, and as Chairman of the CDA, after admitting that, prior to the 1996 elections (when the CDA controlled the ministries responsible for privatization and industry), the party had received donations from a number of companies.

An important focus of the Czech Republic's foreign policy is to maintain close relations with Slovakia and other neighbouring eastern European states. It is a member, with Slovakia, Hungary and Poland, of the Visegrad Group (established, following the collapse of communist rule, to promote economic, defence and other co-operation in the region). However, the Czech Republic also actively pursues a policy of European integration and co-operation, and envisages early full membership of the EU (for which it officially applied in January 1996). The Czech Republic was one of a number of central and eastern European states invited to begin negotiations in March 1998 on possible entry to the EU. In this connection, the Czech Government has emphasized the importance of close ties with western European states, particularly neighbouring Germany (the Czech Republic's most important trading partner).

Nevertheless, since the end of the Second World War Czech-German relations have been dominated by two issues: the question of compensation for Czech victims of Nazism, and demands for the restitution of property to the Sudeten Germans who were driven from Czechoslovakia in 1945. From 1993 negotiations were held to formulate a declaration on bilateral relations, but progress was hampered by these two outstanding issues. However, a joint declaration was finally signed by both Ministers of Foreign Affairs on 20 December 1996, and by Václav Klaus of the Czech Republic and Chancellor Kohl of Germany on 21 January 1997. In the declaration, Germany admitted that it was to blame for the Nazi occupation and the partition of Czechoslovakia in 1939, while the Czech Republic apologized for the abuses of human rights that were committed during the deportation of ethnic Germans in 1945–46. The declaration did not, however, condemn the expulsion of the Sudeten Germans as a crime, which would have meant that those people expelled could have made claims for compensation. A joint Czech-German fund was established in January 1998 to finance joint projects, in particular benefiting victims of the Nazis.

In August 1993 the Czech Republic and the Russian Federation signed a treaty of friendship and co-operation (replacing the Russian-Czechoslovak treaty of 1992). In March 1994, despite Russia's apparent opposition, the Czech Republic joined NATO's 'Partnership for Peace' programme of military co-operation. In 1996 the Chamber of Deputies approved legislation prohibiting the storage of nuclear weapons on Czech territory, except where international treaties are concerned, thereby allowing for full membership of NATO. In July 1997 the Czech Republic, together with Hungary and Poland, was invited to join NATO. A protocol providing for the accession of the three states to NATO was signed in December and was subsequently to be presented for ratification to the legislatures of member states. The Czech Republic is a member of the Council of Europe (see p. 140) and the Organization for Security and Co-operation in Europe (OSCE, see p. 212).

Government

Legislative power is held by two chambers, the 200-member Chamber of Deputies (lower house) and the 81-member Senate. Members of the Chamber of Deputies and the Senate are elected for four and six years, respectively, by universal adult suffrage. The President of the Republic (Head of State) is elected for a term of five years by a joint session of the legislature. The President, who is also Commander of the Armed Forces, may be re-elected for a second consecutive term. He/she appoints the Prime Minister and, on the latter's recommendation, the other members of the Council of Ministers (the highest organ of executive power). For administrative purposes, the Czech Republic is divided into 72 districts. Legislation providing for the creation of 14 regions was to take effect from 1 January 2000.

Defence

In August 1997 total armed forces numbered 61,700 (including an estimated 37,000 conscripts): an army of 27,000 and an air force of 17,000; there were also some 17,700 troops attached to the Ministry of Defence and centrally-controlled formations. In addition, there were an estimated 4,000 border guards and 1,600 internal security forces. Military service is compulsory and lasts for 12 months. The defence budget for 1997 was projected at 27,800m. koruny. In March 1994 the Czech Republic joined NATO's 'Partnership for Peace' programme of military co-operation, and in July 1997 it was invited to become a full member of NATO.

Economic Affairs

In 1995, according to estimates by the World Bank, the Czech Republic's gross national product (GNP), measured at average 1993–95 prices, was US $39,990m., equivalent to $3,870 per head. During 1985–94, it was estimated, GNP per head decreased, in real terms, at an average annual rate of 1.8%. During 1985–95 the population remained virtually unchanged. Gross domestic product (GDP) declined, in real terms, by an average of 2.6% annually during 1990–95; GDP increased by 4.1%, however, in 1996.

Agriculture (including forestry and fishing) contributed 4.4% of GDP in 1994. In 1996 the sector provided 6.0% of employment. The principal crops are wheat, sugar beet, barley, potatoes and hops (the Czech Republic is a major beer producer and exporter). In 1994 agricultural production declined by 19.1%. Annual growth of 1.2% in agricultural production was recorded in 1995, but a decline of 0.7% was registered in 1996.

Industry (including manufacturing, mining, construction and power) contributed 39.7% of GDP in 1994. In 1996 the sector provided 40.9% of employment. Industrial production (excluding construction) increased by 8.8% in 1995, and by 6.5% in 1996.

The principal minerals extracted are coal and lignite. In 1996 the mining sector provided 1.7% of employment. In 1993 mining production declined by 7.1%, compared with the previous year.

In 1993, according to preliminary figures, thermal power provided 76% of total electricity production, nuclear power 21% and hydroelectric power 3%. Imports of mineral fuels comprised 8.7% of the value of total imports in 1996.

The services sector contributed 55.9% of GDP in 1994, and engaged 53.1% of the employed labour force in 1996. Tourism is an important source of revenue, providing receipts of US $1,966m. in 1994, when the sector accounted for some 5.5% of GDP.

In 1996 the Czech Republic recorded a visible trade deficit of US $5,877m. and there was also a deficit, of US $4,299m., on the current account of the balance of payments. In 1996 the principal source of imports (29.8%) was Germany; other major sources were Slovakia, Russia, Italy and Austria. Germany was also the principal market for exports (35.9%) in that year; other important purchasers were Slovakia and Austria. The principal exports were machinery and transport equipment, basic manufactures and miscellaneous manufactured articles. The principal imports were machinery and transport equipment, basic manufactures, chemicals and related products, and miscellaneous manufactured articles.

In 1996 there was a budgetary deficit of 1,800m. koruny (equivalent to 0.1% of GDP). The Czech Republic's total external debt was US $16,576m. at the end of 1995, of which $11,504m. was long-term public debt. In that year the cost of debt-servicing was equivalent to 10.5% of the value of exports of goods and services. The annual rate of inflation averaged 12.1% in 1992–96; the average annual rate in 1996 was 8.9%. About 4.9% of the labour force were unemployed in October 1997.

The Czech Republic is a member of the IMF and the World Bank and an associate member of the EU. It is also a member of the European Bank for Reconstruction and Development (EBRD, see p. 148) and, in late 1995, became the first post-communist state in eastern Europe to be admitted to the Organisation for Economic Co-operation and Development (OECD, see p. 208).

Of all the post-communist states of eastern Europe, the Czech Republic is considered to have undertaken the transition to a market economic system with greatest success. The country's programme of rapid privatization, price and currency stabilization and the establishment of a new banking system, while preserving a low level of unemployment, won strong popular support during 1992–95; at the same time these economic reforms, together with the country's political stability, attracted widespread foreign investment in the republic. In 1996, however, economic growth decelerated and the first budgetary deficit since the transition to a market economy was recorded, largely owing to a mounting trade deficit. Difficulties were experienced in the banking sector in that year, with several banks forced to cease operations. By mid-1996 some 11 banks had failed since the implementation of economic reforms. In 1997 a number of senior bankers were charged with fraud and embezzlement, and the privatization of the republic's largest banks was delayed. Economic performance deteriorated, and investor confidence was dented by cases of embezzlement of investment funds. In April the Government outlined measures to cut public spending, reduce imports and regulate the capital market. In May, following a series of speculative attacks on the koruna (which had prompted the introduction of a floating exchange rate), further measures, including additional cuts in public expenditure, were announced as part of a programme for economic recovery. In July severe damage caused by flooding badly affected the industrial sector, placing further demands on government spending. By the end of 1997 signs of a narrowing of the trade deficit and increased industrial output was largely attributed to the depreciation of the koruna in May. Following the resignation of Klaus's administration in late 1997, it was hoped that the new Government, headed by the former Governor of the Czech National Bank, would achieve its objectives of successfully tackling financial crime and stabilizing the economy prior to a return to growth.

Social Welfare

A single and universal system of social security was established in Czechoslovakia after the Second World War. Protection of health was stipulated by law, and medical care, treatment, medicines, etc., were, in most cases, available free of charge to the entire Czechoslovak population. Following the dissolution of Czechoslovakia in January 1993, the two successor states announced plans to introduce changes to the existing social welfare system. In the Czech Republic the privatization programme was to extend to the health-care system, although at a slower rate than in many other parts of the economy. By September 1994 the Government had approved the privatization of 11 hospitals. In 1992 there were 31 physicians (in the state sector) per 10,000 inhabitants, and 82.4 hospital beds per 10,000 inhabitants. Expenditure on social welfare and health care in 1995 was 227,627m. koruny (some 45.2% of total budgetary spending). A new pensions insurance law was to come into effect in the late 1990s, which would gradually increase the retirement age for men to 65 years (from 60) and for women to 57–61 (from 53–57, according to the number of children born) by 2007.

Education

Almost 90% of children between the ages of three and six years attend kindergarten. After kindergarten children attend basic school, which covers both primary (grades 1–5) and lower secondary (grades 6–9) level, and is attended by almost 97% of pupils aged between six and 14 years. Education is compulsory for nine years. Most children (almost 97%) continue their education at an upper secondary school, of which there were four types in 1997: gymnasia (grammar schools), secondary vocational schools, secondary technical schools and integrated schools. Students follow three- to four-year courses. Tertiary education consists of non-university schools and universities, at which most courses last from five to six years. Since 1990 many private schools, particularly at upper secondary level, have been established.

In the 1996/97 academic year 1,100,096 children attended basic schools, while 465,945 attended the different types of upper secondary school. In the same year there were 195,820 students in higher education. In 1996 budgetary expenditure on education was 81,700m. koruny (some 12% of total budgetary spending).

Public Holidays

1998: 1 January (New Year's Day), 13 April (Easter Monday), 1 May (Labour Day), 8 May (Liberation Day), 5 July (Day of the Apostles St Cyril and St Methodius), 6 July (Anniversary of the Martyrdom of Jan Hus), 28 October (Independence Day), 24–25 December (Christmas), 26 December (St Stephen's Day).

1999: 1 January (New Year's Day), 5 April (Easter Monday), 1 May (Labour Day), 8 May (Liberation Day), 5 July (Day of the Apostles St Cyril and St Methodius), 6 July (Anniversary of the Martyrdom of Jan Hus), 28 October (Independence Day), 24–25 December (Christmas), 26 December (St Stephen's Day).

Weights and Measures

The metric system is in force.

Statistical Survey

Source: mainly Czech Statistical Office, Sokolovská 142, 186 04 Prague 8; tel. (2) 66042451; fax (2) 66310429.

Area and Population

AREA, POPULATION AND DENSITY

Area (sq km)	78,866*
Population (census results)	
1 November 1980	10,291,927
3 March 1991	
Males	4,999,935
Females	5,302,280
Total	10,302,215
Population (official estimates at 31 December)	
1994	10,333,161
1995	10,321,344
1996	10,309,137
Density (per sq km) at 31 December 1996	130.7

* 30,450 sq miles.

POPULATION BY NATIONALITY (census of 3 March 1991)

	Number	%
Czech (Bohemian)	8,363,768	81.2
Moravian	1,362,313	13.2
Slovak	314,877	3.1
Polish	59,383	0.6
German	48,556	0.5
Silesian	44,446	0.4
Roma (Gypsy)	32,903	0.3
Hungarian	19,932	0.2
Others	34,020	0.3
Unknown	22,017	0.2
Total	10,302,215	100.0

REGIONS (estimates, 1 January 1997)

	Area (sq km)*	Population	Density (per sq km)
Central Bohemia	11,013	1,105,234	100
Southern Bohemia	11,345	700,595	62
Western Bohemia	10,875	859,306	79
Northern Bohemia	7,799	1,178,977	151
Eastern Bohemia	11,240	1,234,781	110
Southern Moravia	15,028	2,054,989	137
Northern Moravia	11,068	1,970,302	178
Prague (city)	496	1,204,953	2,429
Total	78,864	10,309,137	131

* Figures are provisional. The revised total is 78,866 sq km.

PRINCIPAL TOWNS (estimated population, 1 January 1997)

Praha (Prague, capital)	1,204,953	Hradec Králové	100,280
Brno	387,570	České Budějovice (Budweis)	99,593
Ostrava	323,870	Ústí nad Labem	97,041
Plzeň (Pilsen)	170,449	Pardubice	93,134
Olomouc	104,380	Havířov	87,756
Liberec	100,356	Zlín*	82,590

* During the period of communist rule this town was renamed Gottwaldov, but it has since reverted to its former name.

BIRTHS, MARRIAGES AND DEATHS

	Registered live births		Registered marriages		Registered deaths	
	Number	Rate (per 1,000)	Number	Rate (per 1,000)	Number	Rate (per 1,000)
1989	128,356	12.4	81,262	7.8	127,747	12.3
1990	130,564	12.6	90,953	8.8	129,166	12.5
1991	129,354	12.5	71,973	7.0	124,290	12.1
1992	121,705	11.8	74,060	7.2	120,337	11.7
1993	121,025	11.7	66,033	6.4	118,185	11.4
1994	106,579	10.3	58,440	5.7	117,373	11.4
1995	96,097	9.3	54,956	5.3	117,913	11.4
1996	90,446	8.8	53,896	5.2	112,782	10.9

EMPLOYMENT (annual averages)*

	1994	1995	1996
Agriculture, forestry and fishing	340,348	313,900	303,200
Mining and quarrying	100,558	91,500	86,500
Manufacturing	1,428,206	1,445,200	1,441,800
Electricity, gas and water	90,432	91,400	87,700
Construction	444,360	450,200	452,500
Trade, restaurants and hotels	838,791	890,500	937,200
Transport, storage and communications	352,875	355,200	363,200
Finance, insurance, real estate and business services	416,591	473,800	471,800
Public administration, defence and compulsory social security	146,266	161,600	168,700
Education	321,458	321,600	321,100
Health and social welfare	258,257	262,400	268,300
Other community, social and personal services	146,611	154,300	152,100
Total	4,884,753	5,011,600	5,054,100

* Excluding women on maternity leave.

Agriculture

PRINCIPAL CROPS ('000 metric tons)

	1994	1995	1996
Wheat and spelt	3,713	3,823	3,727
Barley	2,419	2,140	2,262
Maize	91	113	169
Rye*	276	262	204
Oats	208	187	214
Potatoes	1,231	1,330	1,800
Peas (dry)	149	130	136
Rapeseed	452	662	227
Cabbages	133	116	153
Tomatoes	36	38	28
Cauliflowers	40	38	36
Cucumbers and gherkins	51	46	53
Onions (dry)	78	94	100
Carrots	68	73	91
Other vegetables	116	44	50
Grapes	65	43	70
Sugar beet	3,240	3,712	4,316
Apples	244	226	251
Pears	23	27	19
Peaches and nectarines	9	12	8
Plums	20	14	26
Hops	9	10	9

* Including mixed crops of wheat and rye.

LIVESTOCK ('000 head at 1 March)

	1995	1996	1997
Horses	18	19	19
Cattle	2,030	1,989	1,866
Pigs	3,867	4,016	4,080
Sheep	165	134	121
Goats	45	42	151
Poultry	26,688	27,875	27,573

LIVESTOCK PRODUCTS
('000 metric tons, unless otherwise indicated)

	1994	1995	1996
Beef and veal*	313.3	322.9	310.4
Pig meat*	682.0	725.8	727.0
Poultry meat*	127.8	180.0	172.0
Milk (million litres)	3,134	3,031	3,039
Eggs (million)	2,999	3,047	2,948

* Slaughter weight.

Forestry

LOGGING ('000 cubic metres)

	1994	1995	1996
Coniferous (softwood)	11,157	11,308.1	9,287.1
Broadleaved (hardwood)	793	1,057.3	1,098.4
Total	11,950	12,365.4	10,385.5

Fishing*

(metric tons)

	1994	1995	1996
Common carp	19,220	19,219	18,462
Others	3,393	3,389	3,262
Total catch	22,613	22,608	21,724

* Figures refer only to fish caught by the Fishing Association (formerly State Fisheries) and members of the Czech and Moravian Fishing Union.

Mining

('000 metric tons)

	1994	1995	1996
Brown coal and lignite	59,568	57,163	58,846
Kaolin	648	759	741

Hard coal ('000 metric tons): 12,300 in 1992; 11,139 in 1993; 10,886 in 1994.

Crude petroleum ('000 metric tons): 82 in 1992; 111 in 1993; 128 in 1994.

(Source: UN, *Industrial Commodity Statistics Yearbook.*)

Industry

SELECTED PRODUCTS
('000 metric tons, unless otherwise indicated)

	1994	1995	1996
Wheat flour and meal	800	916	868
Refined sugar	428	494	588
Wine ('000 hectolitres)	483.5	459.2	515.6
Beer ('000 hectolitres)	17,671	17,715	18,420
Cotton yarn (metric tons)	61,401	63,644	57,864
Woven cotton fabrics ('000 metres)	364,640†	355,209	329,097
Woollen fabrics ('000 metres)	39,299†	31,535	29,728
Linen fabrics ('000 metres)	54,773†	43,906	27,329
Paper and paperboard (metric tons)	615,584	n.a.	n.a.
Footwear ('000 pairs)	20,255‡	18,898	22,003
Nitrogenous fertilizers	246.6	264.0	253.0
Soap	30.3	35.9	44.3
Plastics	538	n.a.	n.a.
Motor spirit (petrol)	970	n.a.	n.a.
Diesel and fuel oil	3,440	n.a.	n.a.
Coke	5,125	4,945	n.a.
Cement	5,303	4,825	5,016
Bricks and breeze blocks (million)	1,359	n.a.	n.a.
Pig iron	5,287	5,289	n.a.
Crude steel	7,075	7,184	n.a.
Trucks (number)	3,495	3,686	n.a.
Motorcycles and mopeds (number)	11,305	6,558	n.a.
Bicycles (number)	420,461	519,580	500,525
Tractors (number)	12,907	n.a.	n.a.
Electric energy (million kWh)	58,705	60,847	64,257
Manufactured gas (million cu metres)	1,126	n.a.	n.a.

* Production in terms of nitrogen.
† '000 sq metres.
‡ Production from plastics, hide and rubber only.

Finance

CURRENCY AND EXCHANGE RATES

Monetary Units

100 haléřů (singular: haléř—heller) = 1 Czech koruna (Czech crown or Kč.; plural: koruny).

Sterling and Dollar Equivalents (30 September 1997)

£1 sterling = 52.97 koruny;
US $1 = 32.79 koruny;
1,000 koruny = £18.88 = $30.50.

Average Exchange Rate (koruny per US $)

1994 28.785
1995 26.541
1996 27.145

Note: Figures for average exchange rates prior to February 1993 refer to the Czechoslovak koruna. In February 1993 the Czech Republic introduced its own currency, the Czech koruna, to replace (at par) the Czechoslovak koruna.

BUDGET (million koruny)*

Revenue	1993	1994	1995
Taxation	357,856	394,273	446,381
Taxes on income, profits and capital gains	72,389	69,428	71,828
Corporate	70,880	63,624	63,337
Social security contributions	134,492	164,912	195,800
From employees	39,218	46,295	54,834
From employers	95,274	118,617	140,966
Domestic taxes on goods and services	121,443	136,387	155,434
Value-added tax	77,104	85,849	94,801
Excises	39,983	46,360	56,650
Motor vehicle taxes	4,335	4,147	n.a.
Taxes on international trade and transactions	15,170	17,359	17,410
Import duties	15,170	17,359	17,410
Other current revenue	27,015	31,259	39,965
Entrepreneurial and property income	11,342	8,853	11,035
From non-financial public enterprises and public financial institutions	10,849	51	n.a.
Administrative fees and charges, non-industrial and incidental sales	8,442	8,170	14,659
Capital revenue	161	100	150
Total	385,032	425,632	486,496

Expenditure†	1993	1994	1995
General public services	23,061	27,700	31,333
Defence	24,151	27,515	28,390
Public order and safety	21,533	25,715	29,733
Education	41,998	49,453	57,836
Health	69,373	73,592	83,568
Social security and welfare	100,799	124,207	144,059
Housing and community amenities	7,658	5,139	2,707
Recreational, cultural and religious affairs and services	3,390	4,508	5,019
Economic affairs and services	47,937	61,197	68,809
Fuel and energy	4,362	3,746	3,583
Agriculture, forestry, fishing and hunting	10,036	8,926	9,000
Mining and mineral resources, manufacturing and construction	6,371	15,169	2,560
Transport and communications	17,516	21,621	26,033
Road transport	9,003	12,484	n.a.
Other purposes	46,252	46,155	51,841
Sub-total	386,152	445,181	503,295
Adjustment‡	−2,831	−3,967	−3,937
Total	383,321	441,214	499,358
Current§	351,850	390,786	438,601
Capital	31,471	50,428	60,757

* Figures represent a consolidation of transactions by the central Government, including the operations of the Central Budget, social security funds (controlled by the General Health Insurance Organization) and extrabudgetary accounts.

† Excluding lending minus repayments (million koruny): −22,619 in 1993; −24,715 in 1994; −18,584 in 1995.

‡ Relating to employer's contributions to social security schemes at the same level of government.

§ Including interest payments (million koruny): 17,739 in 1993; 15,030 in 1994; 15,366 in 1995.

Source: IMF, *Government Finance Statistics Yearbook*.

INTERNATIONAL RESERVES (US $ million at 31 December)

	1994	1995	1996
Gold*	140	141	137
Foreign exchange	6,145	13,843	12,352
Total	6,285	13,984	12,489

* Valued at 60.685 koruny per gram.

Source: IMF, *International Financial Statistics*.

MONEY SUPPLY ('000 million koruny at 31 December)

	1994	1995	1996
Currency outside banks	83.58	104.27	118.90
Demand deposits at deposit money banks	307.64	310.89	317.46
Total money (incl. others)	403.97	431.08	451.55

Source: IMF, *International Financial Statistics*.

COST OF LIVING

(Consumer Price Index; base: 1994 = 100)

	1995	1996
Food, beverages and tobacco	110.3	119.4
Clothing and footwear	110.3	121.7
Housing, water, fuel and light	110.1	123.5
Furnishings, household equipment and maintenance	105.5	110.1
All items (incl. others)	109.1	118.8

NATIONAL ACCOUNTS (million koruny at current prices)

Expenditure on the Gross Domestic Product

	1994	1995	1996
Government final consumption expenditure	255,540	288,200	327,600
Private final consumption expenditure	571,547	663,800	760,900
Increase in stocks	5,294	10,800	39,700
Gross fixed capital formation	335,068	435,700	503,800
Total domestic expenditure	1,167,449	1,398,500	1,632,000
Exports of goods and services	607,964	755,900	818,800
Less Imports of goods and services	632,454	815,500	926,100
GDP in purchasers' values	1,142,959	1,338,900	1,524,700
GDP at constant 1994 prices	1,142,959	1,211,000	1,260,300

Gross Domestic Product by Economic Activity

	1992	1993	1994
Agriculture, hunting, forestry and fishing	38,259	49,398	47,078
Mining and quarrying Manufacturing Electricity, gas and water	335,861	308,654	346,321
Construction	44,870	67,890	81,882
Trade, restaurants and hotels	98,530	137,207	173,595
Transport, storage and communications	57,362	72,731	77,011
Finance, insurance, real estate and business services	119,590	191,685	202,724
Government services	46,809	40,038	48,231
Other community, social and personal services	38,113	63,722	75,632
Other services	18,860	18,423	25,243
Sub-total	798,254	949,748	1,077,717
Import duties	22,443	19,557	27,304
Turnover tax	90,030	116,067	127,003
Other adjustments	−14,914	−21,160	−20,396
Less Imputed bank service charge	48,970	61,952	68,669
GDP in purchasers' values	846,845	1,002,260	1,142,959

BALANCE OF PAYMENTS (US $ million)

	1994	1995	1996
Exports of goods f.o.b.	16,003	21,477	21,693
Imports of goods f.o.b.	−17,369	−25,162	−27,571
Trade balance	−1,366	−3,685	−5,877
Exports of services	5,167	6,725	8,181
Imports of services	−4,685	−4,882	−6,264
Balance on goods and services	−884	−1,842	−3,961
Other income received	791	1,197	1,170
Other income paid	−812	−1,301	−1,892
Balance on goods, services and income	−905	−1,946	−4,683
Current transfers received	298	664	617
Current transfers paid	−171	−92	−233
Current balance	−778	−1,374	−4,299
Capital account (net)	—	7	1
Direct investment abroad	−116	−37	−41
Direct investment from abroad	878	2,568	1,435
Portfolio investment assets	−47	−325	−50
Portfolio investment liabilities	893	1,695	771
Other investment assets	−2,536	−2,492	−2,370
Other investment liabilities	5,431	6,816	4,571
Net errors and omissions	−243	596	−843
Overall balance	3,483	7,453	−825

Source: IMF, *International Financial Statistics*.

External Trade

COMMODITY GROUPS (distribution by SITC, million koruny)*

Imports f.o.b.	1994	1995*	1996
Food and live animals	29,897	37,149	43,217
Crude materials (inedible) except fuels	21,157	29,942	27,773
Mineral fuels, lubricants, etc.	42,967	52,483	65,592
Chemicals and related products	56,656	79,236	88,882
Basic manufactures	70,989	135,959	145,632
Machinery and transport equipment	150,947	248,465	288,492
Miscellaneous manufactured articles	50,884	79,325	86,646
Total (incl. others)	430,853	670,445	755,278

Exports f.o.b.	1994	1995*	1996
Food and live animals	21,580	27,688	23,985
Crude materials (inedible) except fuels	28,107	29,673	27,905
Mineral fuels, lubricants, etc.	23,246	24,519	26,924
Chemicals and related products	41,132	53,428	54,146
Basic manufactures	125,065	185,213	171,596
Machinery and transport equipment	106,263	174,727	194,572
Miscellaneous manufactured articles	58,424	73,413	87,921
Total (incl. others)	410,250	574,722	594,952

* Beginning in 1995, the value of goods for processing is included in total trade on a gross basis. According to the methodology in use up to 1994, the value of total 1995 trade (in million koruny) was: Imports 554,282; Exports 453,634.

SELECTED TRADING PARTNERS (million koruny)

Imports f.o.b.	1994	1995*	1996*
Austria	34,714	46,327	43,411
China, People's Republic	2,931	5,552	8,119
France	15,781	26,971	31,629
Germany	109,744	212,379	225,039
Hungary	4,919	5,788	7,522
Italy	22,133	35,617	44,424
Japan	8,735	11,715	12,962
Russia	36,024	49,789	55,861
Slovakia	61,326	79,177	72,181
United Kingdom	13,050	25,259	28,404
USA	14,589	22,602	25,516
Total (incl. others)	430,853	670,445	755,278

Exports f.o.b.	1994	1995*	1996*
Austria	29,242	37,810	38,430
France	10,507	15,100	16,996
Germany	120,539	215,860	213,685
Hungary	10,887	10,025	10,607
Italy	18,195	21,338	19,656
Russia	16,025	16,749	18,826
Slovakia	67,369	79,756	84,948
United Kingdom	11,570	18,230	14,952
USA	8,905	11,010	12,636
Total (incl. others)	410,250	574,722	594,952

* Figures based on revised methodology (see above).

Transport

RAILWAYS (traffic)

	1994	1995	1996
Passenger-km (million)	8,481	8,023	8,111
Freight net ton-km (million)	24,401	25,468	24,294

ROAD TRAFFIC (motor vehicles in use at 31 December)

	1994	1995	1996
Passenger cars*	2,967,253	3,113,476	3,349,008
Buses and coaches	22,761	21,912	21,460
Goods vehicles†	160,793	182,326	235,114
Motorcycles	476,453	457,560	439,247

* Including vans.
† Excluding special-purpose lorries.

INLAND WATERWAYS (freight carried, '000 metric tons)

	1994	1995	1996
Imports	354	359	436
Exports	667	1,028	909
Internal	3,608	2,782	1,448
Total (incl. others)	4,811	4,332	2,879

AIR TRANSPORT

	1994	1995	1996
Kilometres flown ('000)	36,170	37,944	37,767
Passengers carried ('000)	1,718	1,857	1,982
Freight carried (metric tons)	10,936	17,562	13,959
Passenger-km ('000)	2,605,299	3,052,744	3,170,030
Freight ton-km ('000)	26,063	33,473	25,920

Tourism

FOREIGN TOURIST ARRIVALS*

Country of origin	1994	1995	1996
Austria	188,863	183,462	199,355
Belgium	62,904	69,564	81,269
Denmark	66,466	75,825	95,112
France	121,207	123,175	149,295
Germany	1,146,611	1,243,385	1,668,846
Italy	178,633	207,007	250,237
Netherlands	191,421	228,669	312,043
Poland	116,706	129,694	213,543
Spain	81,093	129,386	134,730
United Kingdom	124,587	128,739	188,312
USA	129,002	120,336	185,691
Total (incl. others)	3,036,473	3,381,186	4,558,322

* Figures refer to visitors staying for at least one night at registered accommodation facilities.

Communications Media

	1993	1994	1995
Radio licences	2,931,000	n.a.	n.a.
Television licences	3,389,901	n.a.	n.a.
Telephones in use	3,536,407	3,703,558	3,017,530
Book production: titles	9,309	8,994	10,244
Daily newspapers (number)	51	75	90
Other periodicals (number)	1,926	4,305	4,938

Telefax stations (number in use, 1994): 58,460.
Mobile cellular telephones (subscribers, 1994): 20,000.

(Source: UN, *Statistical Yearbook.*)

Education

(1996/97)

	Institutions	Teachers	Students
Pre-primary	6,344	27,636	317,159
Basic:			
Primary	4,166	32,057	636,986
Lower secondary		37,521	463,110
Upper secondary:			
Gymnasia	367	12,487	126,124
Technical schools	827	25,571	158,074
Vocational schools	733	33,724	181,750
Higher:			
Universities	23	13,332	166,123
Professional schools	158	4,189	29,697

Source: Institute for Information on Education, Prague.

Directory

The Constitution

The following is a summary of the main provisions of the Constitution of the Czech Republic, which was adopted on 16 December 1992 and entered into force on 1 January 1993:

GENERAL PROVISIONS

The Czech Republic is a sovereign, unified and democratic law-abiding state, founded on the respect for the rights and freedoms of the individual and citizen. All state power belongs to the people, who exercise this power through the intermediary of legislative, executive and judicial bodies. The fundamental rights and freedoms of the people are under the protection of the judiciary.

The political system is founded on the free and voluntary operation of political parties respecting fundamental democratic principles and rejecting force as a means to assert their interests. Political decisions derive from the will of the majority, expressed through the free ballot. Minorities are protected in decision-making by the majority.

The territory of the Czech Republic encompasses an indivisible whole, whose state border may be changed only by constitutional law. Procedures covering the acquisition and loss of Czech citizenship are determined by law. No one may be deprived of his or her citizenship against his or her will.

GOVERNMENT

Legislative Power

Legislative power in the Czech Republic is vested in two chambers, the Chamber of Deputies and the Senate. The Chamber of Deputies has 200 members, elected for a term of four years. The Senate has 81 members, elected for a term of six years. Every two years one-third of the senators are elected. Both chambers elect their respective Chairman and Deputy Chairmen from among their members. Members of both chambers of the legislature are elected on the basis of universal, equal and direct suffrage by secret ballot. All citizens of 18 years and over are eligible to vote.

The legislature enacts the Constitution and laws; approves the state budget and the state final account; and approves the electoral law and international agreements. It elects the President of the Republic (at a joint session of both chambers), supervises the activities of the Government, and decides upon the declaration of war.

President of the Republic

The President of the Republic is Head of State. He/she is elected for a term of five years by a joint session of both chambers of the legislature. The President may not be elected for more than two consecutive terms.

The President appoints, dismisses and accepts the resignation of the Prime Minister and other members of the Government, dismisses the Government and accepts its resignation; convenes sessions of the Chamber of Deputies; may dissolve the Chamber of Deputies; names the judges of the Constitutional Court, its Chairman and Deputy Chairmen; appoints the Chairman and Deputy Chairmen of the Supreme Court; has the right to return adopted constitutional laws to the legislature; initials laws; and appoints members of the Council of the Czech National Bank. The President also represents the State in external affairs; is the Supreme Commander of the Armed Forces; receives heads of diplomatic missions; calls elections to the Chamber of Deputies and to the Senate; and has the right to grant amnesty.

Council of Ministers

The Council of Ministers is the highest organ of executive power. It is composed of the Prime Minister, the Deputy Prime Ministers and Ministers. It is answerable to the Chamber of Deputies. The President of the Republic appoints the Prime Minister, on whose recommendation he/she appoints the remaining members of the Council of Ministers and entrusts them with directing the ministries or other offices.

JUDICIAL SYSTEM

Judicial power is exercised on behalf of the Republic by independent courts. Judges are independent in the exercise of their function. The judiciary consists of the Supreme Court, the Supreme Administrative Court, high, regional and district courts.

The Constitutional Court is a judicial body protecting constitutionality. It consists of 15 judges appointed for a 10-year term by the President of the Republic with the consent of the Senate.

The Government

HEAD OF STATE

President: VÁCLAV HAVEL (elected 26 January 1993; re-elected 20 January 1998).

COUNCIL OF MINISTERS
(February 1998)

An interim coalition comprising independents, the Christian Democratic Union–Czechoslovak People's Party (CDU–CPP), the Civic Democratic Alliance (CDA) and the Freedom Union (FU).

Prime Minister: JOSEF TOŠOVSKÝ (Ind.).

Minister of Foreign Relations: JAROSLAV ŠEDIVÝ (Ind.).

Minister of Defence: MICHAL LOBKOWICZ (FU).

Minister of the Interior: CYRIL SVOBODA (CPU–CPP).

Minister of Finance: IVAN PILIP (FU).

Minister of Agriculture: JOSEF LUX (CDU–CPP).

Minister of the Environment: (vacant).

Minister of Health: ZUZANA ROITHOVÁ (Ind.).

Minister of Labour and Social Affairs: STANISLAV VOLÁK (FU).

Minister of Education, Youth and Sport: JAN SOKOL (Ind.).

Minister of Transport and Communications: PETR MOOS (Ind.).

Minister of Justice: VLASTA PARKANOVÁ (CDA).

Minister of Culture: MARTIN STROPNICKÝ (Ind.).

Minister for Regional Development: JAN ČERNÝ (FU).

Minister of Industry and Trade: KAREL KÜHNL (CDA).

Minister, Chairman of the Legislative Council: MILOSLAV VÝBORNÝ (CDU–CPP).

Minister, Government Spokesman: VLADIMÍR MLYNÁŘ (Ind.).

MINISTRIES

Office of the Government of the Czech Republic: nábř. E. Beneše 4, 125 11 Prague 1; tel. (2) 24002111; fax (2) 24810231.

Ministry of Agriculture: Těšnov 17, 117 05 Prague 1; tel. (2) 2862111; telex 121041; fax (2) 2315725; e-mail vicenova@mze.cz.

Ministry of Culture: Milady Horákové 139, Prague 6; tel. (2) 24318051; fax (2) 24323304.

Ministry of Defence: Tychonova 1, 160 00 Prague 6; tel. (2) 20201111; fax (2) 3116238.

Ministry of Education, Youth and Sport: Karmelitská 8, 118 12 Prague 1; tel. (2) 5193111; fax (2) 5193790.

Ministry of the Environment: Vršovická 65, 100 10 Prague 10; tel. (2) 67121111; fax (2) 67310308.

Ministry of Finance: Letenská 15, 118 00 Prague 1; tel. (2) 24541111; fax (2) 24542788.

Ministry of Foreign Relations: Loretánské nám. 5, 118 00 Prague 1; tel. (2) 24181111; fax (2) 24310017.

Ministry of Health: Palackého nám. 4, POB 81, 128 01 Prague 2; tel. (2) 24971111; fax (2) 24972111; e-mail mzcr@mzcr.cz.

Ministry of Industry and Trade: Na Františku 32, 110 15 Prague 1; tel. (2) 2317718; fax (2) 24811089.

Ministry of the Interior: Nad štolou 3, 170 34 Prague 7; tel. (2) 3351111; fax (2) 378216.

Ministry of Justice: Vyšehradská 16, 128 10 Prague 2; tel. (2) 24915228; fax (2) 24915140.

Ministry of Labour and Social Affairs: Na poříčním právu 1, 128 00 Prague 2; tel. (2) 293108; fax (2) 299832.

Ministry of Regional Development: Prague.

Ministry of Transport and Communications: nábř. L. Svobody 12, 110 15 Prague 1; tel. (2) 23031111; fax (2) 24810596.

Legislature

The Czech Constitution, which was adopted in December 1992, provided for the creation of a bicameral legislature as the highest organ of state authority in the Czech Republic (which was established as an independent state on 1 January 1993, following the dissolution of the Czech and Slovak Federative Republic). The lower house, the Chamber of Deputies, retained the structure of the Czech National Council (the former republican legislature). The upper chamber, or Senate, was first elected in November 1996.

CHAMBER OF DEPUTIES
(Poslanecká sněmovna)

Chairman: MILOŠ ZEMAN.

General election, 31 May–1 June 1996

Parties and Groups	% of votes	Seats
Civic Democratic Party*	29.62	68
Czech Social Democratic Party	26.44	61
Communist Party of Bohemia and Moravia	10.33	22
Christian Democratic Union–Czechoslovak People's Party	8.08	18
Association for the Republic–Republican Party of Czechoslovakia	8.01	18
Civic Democratic Alliance	6.36	13
Others	11.16	—
Total	100.00	200

* By mid-February 1998 31 deputies from the Civic Democratic Party had joined the breakaway Freedom Union.

SENATE
(Senát)

Chairman: PETR PITHART.

Election, 15, 16, 22 and 23 November 1996

Parties and Groups	% of votes	Seats
Civic Democratic Party*	49.19	32
Czech Social Democratic Party	31.80	25
Christian Democratic Union–Czechoslovak People's Party	10.74	13
Civic Democratic Alliance	5.19	7
Communist Party of Bohemia and Moravia	1.96	2
Others	1.16	2
Total	100.00	81

* By mid-February 1998 three senators from the Civic Democratic Party had joined the Freedom Union.

Political Organizations

Association for the Republic–Republican Party of Czechoslovakia (Sdružení pro republiku–Republikánská strana Československa): Bělohorská 74, 169 00 Prague 6; tel. (2) 375089; fax (2) 350608; f. 1989; extreme right-wing; Chair. MIROSLAV SLÁDEK; Sec. JAN VÍK.

Christian Democratic Union–Czechoslovak People's Party (Křesťanská a demokratická unie–Československá strana lidová): Revoluční 5, 110 15 Prague 1; tel. (2) 2328086; fax (2) 24812114; f. 1992; Chair. JOSEF LUX.

Civic Democratic Alliance (CDA) (Občanská demokratická aliance): Rytířská 10, 110 00 Prague 1; tel. (2) 24214134; fax (2) 24214390; f. 1991 as a formal political party, following a split in Civic Forum (f. 1989); fmrly an informal group within Civic Forum; conservative; Chair. (vacant).

Civic Democratic Party (CDP) (Občanská demokratická strana): Sněmovní 3, 110 00 Prague 1; tel. (2) 3114809; fax (2) 24510731; e-mail foreign@ods.cz; f. 1991 following a split in Civic Forum (f. 1989); merged with Christian Democratic Party in 1996; liberal-conservative; 35,000 mems; Chair. VÁCLAV KLAUS.

Communist Party of Bohemia and Moravia (Komunistická strana Čech a Moravy): Politických vězňů 9, 111 21 Prague 1; tel. (2) 24210172; fax 24264572; e-mail leftnews@kscm.cz; internet http://www.ksm.cz; f. 1991 as a result of the reorganization of the Communist Party of Czechoslovakia; c. 200,000 mems; Leader MIROSLAV GREBENÍČEK.

Countryside Party: f. 1996 to promote interests of rural areas; c. 3,000 mems; Chair. JAN VELEBA.

Czech Social Democratic Party (CSDP) (Česká strana sociálně demokratická): Lidový dům, Hybernská 7, 110 00 Prague 1; tel. and fax (2) 24226222; f. 1878; prohibited 1948; re-established 1989; formerly the Czechoslovak Social Democratic Party; Chair. Ing. MILOŠ ZEMAN.

Democratic Left (Demokratická levice): Moravské nám. 2, 602 00 Brno; tel. and fax (5) 42211677; Chair. LOTAR INDRUCH.

Free Democrats–Liberal National Social Party (Svobodní demokraté–Liberální strana národně sociální): Jungmannovo nám. 9, 110 00 Prague 1; tel. (2) 24226626; fax (2) 24226568; f. 1995 by merger of Free Democrats (fmrly Civic Movement) and Liberal National Social Party (fmrly Czechoslovak Socialist Party); Chair. JIŘÍ DIENSTBIER, JOSEF LESAK.

Freedom Union (FU): Prague; f. 1998, following a split in the Civic Democratic Party; Leader JAN RUML.

Green Party: Jandova 2, 190 00 Prague 9; tel. and fax (2) 824267; f. 1989; Chair. JAROSLAV VLČEK.

Left Bloc–Party of the Democratic Left: f. 1997 by merger of Left Bloc and Party of the Democratic Left; c. 9,000 mems; Chair. MARIE STIBOROVA.

Moravian Democratic Party: Brno; f. 1997 by merger of Bohemian–Moravian Union of the Centre and Moravian National Party; Chair. IVAN DRIMAL.

Party of Czechoslovak Communists: f. 1995; 19,980 mems; Leader MIROSLAV STEPAN.

Diplomatic Representation

EMBASSIES IN THE CZECH REPUBLIC

Afghanistan: V tišině 6, 160 00 Prague 6; tel. (2) 372417; telex 121752; Chargé d'affaires a.i.: WAZIR AHMAD FAIZI.

Albania: Pod kaštany 22, 160 00 Prague 6; tel. (2) 379329; fax (2) 371742; Ambassador: SHERIF BINAK ÇAUSHI.

Algeria: Na Marně 16, 225 21 Prague 6; tel. and fax (2) 24311150; Ambassador: CHERIF MEZIANE.

Argentina: Washingtonova 25, 225 22 Prague 1; tel. (2) 24212448; fax (2) 266384; Ambassador: HORACIO ADOLFO BASABE.

Austria: Viktora Huga 10, 225 43 Prague 5; tel. (2) 57321282; telex 121849; fax (2) 549626; Ambassador: PETER NIESNER.

Belarus: Sádky 626, 171 00 Prague 7; tel. (2) 6888216; fax (2) 6888217; Ambassador: ULADZIMIR PETROVIČ BELSKY.

Belgium: Valdštejnská 6, 118 00 Prague 1; tel. (2) 57314430; fax (2) 24510966; Ambassador: BERNARD PIERRE.

Brazil: Sušická 12, 160 41 Prague 6; tel. (2) 3116694; fax (2) 3118274; Ambassador: SERGIO PAULO ROUANET.

Bulgaria: Krakovská 6, 125 25 Prague 1; tel. (2) 22211258; fax (2) 22211728; Ambassador: OGNIAN GARKOV.

Cambodia: Na Hubálce 1, 169 00 Prague 6; tel. (2) 352603; fax (2) 351078; Chargé d'affaires a.i.: MAKANA YOUS.

Canada: Mickiewiczova 6, 125 33 Prague 6; tel. (2) 24311108; fax (2) 24310294; internet http://www.dfait-maeci.gc.ca/~prague/; Ambassador: RONALD HALPIN.

Chile: U Vorlíků 4/623, 160 00 Prague 6; tel. (2) 24315064; fax (2) 24316069; Ambassador: RICARDO CONCHA GAZMURI.

China, People's Republic: Pelléova 22, 160 00 Prague 6; tel. (2) 24311323; Ambassador: YAN PENG.

Colombia: Washingtonova 25, 110 00 Prague 1; tel. (2) 21674200; fax (2) 24225538; Ambassador: ENRIQUE GAVIRIA LIEVANO.

Costa Rica: Eliášova 21, 160 00 Prague 6; tel. (2) 3123750; Chargé d'affaires a.i.: JOHNNY JOSÉ SUÁREZ SANDÍ.

Croatia: V Průhledu 9, 162 00 Prague 6; tel. (2) 3120479; fax (2) 3123464; Ambassador: ZLATKO STAHULJAK.

Cuba: Na Kazance 7/634, apts. 18 až 19, 170 00 Prague 7; tel. (2) 24311253; fax (2) 3121029; Chargé d'affaires a.i.: ALCIDES DE LA ROSA DEL TORO.

Cyprus: Eliasova 21, 160 00 Prague 6; tel. (2) 3124111; fax (2) 4314225; Ambassador: ATHENA MAVRONICOLA.

Denmark: U páté baterie 7, POB 70, 162 00 Prague 6; tel. (2) 24311919; telex 122209; fax (2) 24311946; Ambassador: MICHAEL WAGTMANN.

Egypt: Pelléova 14, 160 00 Prague 6; tel. (2) 24311506; fax (2) 24311157; Ambassador: ASSEM A. MEGAHED.

Estonia: Hotel InterContinental, Curieových nám. 43/5, 110 00 Prague 1; tel. (2) 24881111; Ambassador: RIHO LAANEMÄE.

Finland: Hellichova 1, 110 00 Prague 1; tel. (2) 57007130; Ambassador: ROINE ESKO RAJAKOSKI.

France: Velkopřevorské nám. 2, 125 27 Prague 1; tel. (2) 57320352; fax (2) 57321024; e-mail ambafrcz@mbox.vol.cz; Ambassador: PHILIPPE COSTE.

Germany: Vlašská 19, 118 01 Prague 1; tel. (2) 57113111; telex 122701; fax (2) 57320043; Ambassador: MICHAEL STEINER.

Ghana: V tišině 4, 160 00 Prague 6; tel. (2) 373058; fax (2) 371603; e-mail ghanaemb@mbox.vol.cz; Ambassador: S. VALIS-AKYIANU.

Greece: Na Ořechovce 19, 162 00 Prague 6; tel. (2) 3121702; fax (2) 3121849; Ambassador: GEORGES LINARDOS.

Holy See: Voršilská 12, 110 00 Prague 1; tel. (2) 24912192; fax (2) 24914160; Apostolic Nuncio: Most Rev. GIOVANNI COPPA, Titular Archbishop of Serta.

Hungary: Badeniho 1, 125 37 Prague 6; tel. (2) 365041; fax (2) 329425; Ambassador: ZOLTÁN VEZÉR.

India: Valdštejnská 6, 125 28 Prague 1; tel. (2) 57320255; telex 121901; fax (2) 539495; Ambassador: GIRISH DHUME.

Indonesia: Nad Budánkami II/7, 150 00 Prague 5; tel. (2) 526041; telex 121443; fax (2) 522825; Ambassador: LEONARD TOBING.

Iran: Na Zátorce 18, 160 00 Prague 6; tel. (2) 20570454; fax (2) 371468; Ambassador: SEYED-JAFAR HASHEMI.

Iraq: Trojská 90, 171 00 Prague 7; tel. (2) 8540668; Ambassador: SADIQ KH. R. AHMED.

Ireland: Tržiště 13, 118 00 Prague 1; tel. (2) 530902; Ambassador: MARIE THERESE CROSS.

Israel: Badeniho 2, 170 00 Prague 7; tel. (2) 322453; fax (2) 322732; e-mail israemba@bohem-net.cz; Ambassador: RAPHAEL GVIR.

Italy: Nerudova 20, 125 31 Prague 1; tel. (2) 57320011; fax (2) 24510363; Ambassador: MAURIZIO MORENO.

Japan: Maltézské nám. 6, 118 01 Prague 1; tel. (2) 57320561; telex 121199; fax (2) 539997; Ambassador: SHUNJI MARUYAMA.

Kazakhstan: Fetrovská 15, 160 00 Prague 6; tel. (2) 3114596; Chargé d'affaires a.i.: SOVETKALI KAMAUBOJEVIČ KARTBAJEV.

Korea, Democratic People's Republic: Na Zátorce 6, 160 00 Prague 6; tel. (2) 24324307; fax (2) 329432; Chargé d'affaires a.i.: KIM JONG NAM.

Korea, Republic: U Mrázovky 1985/17, 150 00 Prague 5; tel. (2) 542671; fax (2) 530204; Ambassador: JAE SUP KIM.

Kuwait: Pod kaštany 2, 160 00 Prague 6; tel. (2) 24311966; fax (2) 378688; Ambassador: KAZIM Haji Y. MARAFIE.

Latvia: Hradešínská 3, POB 54, 101 00 Prague 10; tel. (2) 24252454; fax (2) 24255099; Ambassador: VALDIS KRASTIŅŠ.

Lebanon: Masarykovo nábřeží 14, 110 00 Prague 1; tel. (2) 293633; fax (2) 293406; Ambassador: SLEIMAN YOUNES.

Libya: Na baště sv. Jiří 5–7, 160 00 Prague 6; tel. (2) 323410; Chargé d'affaires a.i.: MILUD MOHAMED JADID.

Lithuania: Pod Klikovkou 1916/2, 150 00 Prague 5; tel. (2) 57210122; fax (2) 57210124; e-mail ltembcz@mbox.vol.cz; Ambassador: JURGIS BRĖDIKIS.

Malta: Lázeňská 4, 118 00 Prague 1; tel. (2) 537222; fax (2) 536874; Chargé d'affaires a.i.: MAX TURNAUER.

Mexico: Nad Kazankou 8, 171 00 Prague 7; tel. (2) 8555554; fax (2) 8550477; Ambassador: GONZALO AGUIRRE ENRILE.

Mongolia: Na Marně 5, 160 00 Prague 6; tel. (2) 24311198; Chargé d'affaires: NAIDANSUREN JARGALSAIKHAN.

Morocco: Ke starému Bubenči 4, 160 00 Prague 6; tel. (2) 329404; fax (2) 321758; Ambassador: ABDESSELEM OUAZZANI.

Netherlands: Gotthardská 6/27, 225 40 Prague 6; tel. (2) 24312190; telex 122643; fax (2) 24312160; Ambassador: P. F. C. KOCH.

Nigeria: Před bateriemi 18, 162 00 Prague 6; tel. (2) 24312065; fax (2) 24312072; Chargé d'affaires a.i.: YAKUBU D. BALA.

Norway: Na Ořechovce 69, 162 00 Prague 6; tel. (2) 3111411; telex 122200; fax (2) 3123797; Ambassador: METTE KONGSHEM.

Pakistan: Šmolíkova 1009, 161 00 Prague 6; tel. (2) 3025869; telex 122715; fax (2) 3025852; Ambassador: FREDA SHAH.

Peru: Muchova 9, 160 00 Prague 6; tel. (2) 24316210; fax (2) 24314749; e-mail emba.peru.praga.ms.anet.cz; Ambassador: JULIO MUÑOZ DEACON.

Philippines: Karolíny Světlé 34, 110 00 Prague 1; tel. (2) 21635300; Ambassador: CARMELITA RODRÍGUEZ SALAS.

Poland: Valdštejnská 8, 118 01 Prague 1; tel. (2) 5732068; telex 121841; fax (2) 57320764; e-mail ambpolcz@mbox.vol.cz; Ambassador: MAREK PERNAL.

Portugal: Kinských nám. 7, 150 00 Prague 5; tel. (2) 57311230; telex 121354; fax (2) 57311234; Ambassador: ANTÓNIO CASCAIS.

Romania: Nerudova 5, 118 10 Prague 1; tel. (2) 57320494; telex 121506; fax (2) 534393; Ambassador: NICOLAE VULPAŞIN.

Russia: Pod kaštany 1, 160 00 Prague 6; tel. (2) 381943; fax (2) 373800; Ambassador: NIKOLAI T. RYABOV.

Slovakia: Pod hradbami 1, 160 00 Prague 6; tel. (2) 320521; fax (2) 320401; Ambassador: IVAN MJARTAN.

Slovenia: Pod hradbami 15, 160 00 Prague 6; tel. (2) 24315106; fax (2) 320864; Chargé d'affaires a.i.: SMILJANA KNEZ.

South Africa: Ruská 65, 100 00 Prague 10; tel. (2) 67311114; fax (2) 67311395; e-mail saprague@terminal.cz; Ambassador: THOMAS LANGLEY.

Spain: Pevnostní 9, 162 00 Prague 6; tel. (2) 24311222; fax (2) 3121770; Ambassador: JUAN M. DE BARANDICA Y LUXÁN.

Sweden: Úvoz 13-Piradčany, POB 35, 160 12 Prague 612; tel. (2) 20313200; telex 121840; fax (2) 20313240; e-mail sweemb@termin al.cz; Ambassador: INGMAR KARLSSON.

Switzerland: Pevnostní 7, 162 01 Prague 6; tel. (2) 24311228; fax (2) 3123058; Ambassador: WALTER FETSCHERIN.

Syria: Pod kaštany 16, 160 00 Prague 6; tel. (2) 24310952; telex 121532; fax (2) 325360; Chargé d'affaires a.i.: HAYSSAM MASHFEJ.

Thailand: Romaina Rollanda 3, 160 00 Prague 6; tel. (2) 20571435; fax (2) 20570049; e-mail thai@thaiemb.cz; internet http://www .bohemia.net/thai; Ambassador: NARIM PONTHAM.

Tunisia: Sadky 462/12, 170 00 Prague 7; tel. (2) 8543524; fax (2) 8543523; Ambassador: MONDHER MAMI.

Turkey: Pevnostní 3, 160 00 Prague 6; tel. (2) 24311402; fax (2) 3122546; Ambassador: ÜSTÜN DINÇMEN.

Ukraine: Ch. de Gaulla 29, 160 00 Prague 6; tel. (2) 3122000; fax (2) 3124366; Ambassador: ANDRIY OZADOVSKY.

United Kingdom: Thunovská 14, 118 00 Prague 1; tel. (2) 57320355; fax (2) 57321023; e-mail britemb@bohem-net.cz; Ambassador: DAVID BROUCHER.

USA: Tržiště 15, 118 01 Prague 1; tel. (2) 57320663; fax (2) 24511001; Ambassador: JENONNE WALKER.

Uruguay: Malátova 12, 150 00 Prague 5; tel. (2) 545455; fax (2) 548852; Ambassador: Dr JOSÉ LUIS REMEDI.

Venezuela: Jánský vršek 2/350, 118 00 Prague 1; tel. (2) 57313740; telex 122146; fax (2) 57313742; e-mail embaven@mbox.vol.cz; Ambassador: GERMÁN CARRERA DAMAS.

Viet Nam: Plzeňská 214, 150 00 Prague 5; tel. (2) 57211540; fax (2) 536127; Ambassador: NGUYEN VAN KHIEU.

Yemen: Sibeliova 39, 162 00 Prague 6; tel. (2) 20514486; fax (2) 325808; Chargé d'affaires a.i.: MOHAMED HUSSEIN A. AL-SHARAFI.

Yugoslavia: Mostecká 15, 118 00 Prague 1; tel. (2) 57320031; telex 123284; fax (2) 57320491; Ambassador: DJOKO STOJIČIĆ.

Judicial System

The judicial system comprises the Supreme Court (which sits in Brno), the Supreme Administrative Court, chief, regional and district courts. There is also a 15-member Constitutional Court.

Chairman of the Supreme Court: Dr OTAKAR MOTEJL.

Attorney-General: BOHUMÍRA KOPEČNÁ.

Chairman of the Constitutional Court: ZDENĚK KESSLER.

Religion

The principal religion in the Czech Republic is Christianity. The largest denomination in 1995 was the Roman Catholic Church. About 30% of the population professed no religious belief.

CHRISTIANITY

Ecumenical Council of Churches in the Czech Republic (Ekumenická rada církví v České republice): Donská 370/5, 101 00 Prague 10; tel. and fax (2) 746247; f. 1955; 11 mem. churches; Pres. Rev. PAVEL SMETANA; Gen. Sec. NADĚJE MANDYSOVÁ.

The Roman Catholic Church

Latin Rite

The Czech Republic comprises two archdioceses and six dioceses. At 31 December 1995 there were 4.1m. adherents in the country, representing about 39% of the population.

Czech Bishops' Conference (Česká biskupská konference): Thákurova 3, 160 00 Prague 6; tel. (2) 20181421; fax (2) 24310144; e-mail cbk@ktf.cuni.cz; f. 1990; Pres. Cardinal Dr MILOSLAV VLK, Archbishop of Prague.

Archbishop of Olomouc: Most Rev. JAN GRAUBNER, Wurmova 9, 771 01 Olomouc; tel. (68) 5500211; fax (68) 5224840.

Archbishop of Prague: Cardinal Dr MILOSLAV VLK, Hradčanské nám. 16, 119 02 Prague 1; tel. (2) 20181424; fax (2) 350353.

Byzantine Rite

Apostolic Exarch of the Czech Republic: Rt Rev. IVAN LJAVINEC (Titular Bishop of Acalissus), Haštalské nám. 4, 110 00 Prague 1; tel. (2) 2312817.

The Eastern Orthodox Church

Orthodox Church (Pravoslavná církev): V jámě 6, 111 21 Prague 1; divided into two eparchies: Prague and Olomouc; Head of the Orthodox Church, Metropolitan of Prague and of all Czechoslovakia His Holiness Patriarch DOROTEJ.

Protestant Churches

Baptist Union in the Czech Republic: Na Topolce 14, 140 00 Prague 4; tel. and fax (2) 61222179; f. 1994; 2,395 mems; Pres. Rev. DOBROSLAV STEHLÍK; Sec. Rev. PETR ČERVINSKÝ.

Brethren Church: Soukenická 15, 110 00 Prague 1; tel. and fax (2) 2318131; e-mail etspraha@login.cz; internet http://www .cbchurch.cz; f. 1880; 8,331 mems, 46 churches; Pres. PAVEL ČERNÝ; Sec. KAREL TASCHNER.

Christian Corps: nám. Konečného 5, 602 00 Brno; tel. (5) 756365; 3,200 mems; 123 brs; Rep. Ing. PETR ZEMAN.

Evangelical Church of Czech Brethren (Presbyterian): Jungmannova 9, 111 21 Prague 1; tel. (2) 24222219; fax (2) 24222218; f. 1781; united since 1918; activities extend over Bohemia, Moravia and Silesia; 150,371 adherents and 264 parishes (1995); Pres. Rev. PAVEL SMETANA; Synodal Curator Dr ZDENĚK SUSA.

Silesian Evangelical Church of the Augsburg Confession in the Czech Republic (Silesian Lutheran Church): Na nivách 7, 737 01 Český Těšín; tel. (659) 56656; fax (659) 56737; founded in the 16th century during the Lutheran Reformation, reorganized in 1948; 49,588 mems (1994); Bishop VLADISLAV VOLNÝ.

United Methodist Church: Ječná 19, 120 00 Prague 2; tel. (2) 290623; fax (2) 290167; 2,298 mems; 15 parishes; Supt JOSEF ČERVEŇÁK.

Unity of Brethren (Moravian Church): Kollárova 456, 509 01 Nová Paka; tel. and fax (434) 621258; f. 1457; 2,447 mems; 21 parishes; Pres. Rev. ONDŘEJ HALAMA.

Other Christian Churches

Apostolic Church in the Czech Republic: V Zídkách 402, 280 02 Kolín; tel. (321) 20457; fax (321) 27668; e-mail hqbishopac@clever.cz; f. 1989; 3,232 mems; Bishop RUDOLF BUBÍK.

Church of the Seventh-day Adventists: Zálesí 50, 142 00 Prague 4; tel. (2) 4723745; fax (2) 4728222; e-mail casd.csunieapha .pvtnet.cz; f. 1919; 9,866 mems; 184 churches; Pres. KAREL NOWAK.

Czechoslovak Hussite Church: Wuchterlova 5, 166 26 Prague 6; tel. (2) 24311395; fax (2) 320045; f. 1920; 131,000 mems; five dioceses, divided into 310 parishes; Bishop-Patriarch JOSEF ŠPAK.

Old Catholic Church: Hládkov 3, 169 00 Prague 6; tel. and fax (2) 352395; f. 1871; 3,300 mems, eight parishes; Bishop Mgr DUŠAN HEJBAL.

JUDAISM

Federation of Jewish Communities in the Czech Republic (Federace židovských obcí v České republice): Maiselova 18, 110 01 Prague 1; tel. (2) 24811090; fax (2) 24810912; 3,000 mems; Pres. Dr JAN MUNK; Chief Rabbi KAROL SIDON.

The Press

PRINCIPAL DAILIES

Brno

Brněnský večerník (Brno Evening Paper): Jakubské nám. 7, 658 44 Brno; tel. (5) 42321227; fax (5) 45215150; f. 1968; Editor-in-Chief PETR HOSKOVEC; circ. 16,000.

Rovnost (Equality): M. Horákové 9, 658 22 Brno; tel. (5) 45321121; fax (5) 45212873; f. 1885; morning; Editor-in-Chief LUBOMÍR SELINGER; circ. 62,000.

České Budějovice

Jihočeské listy (South Bohemia Paper): Vrbenská 23, 370 45 České Budějovice; tel. (38) 22081; f. 1991; morning; Editor-in-Chief VLADIMÍR MAJER; circ. 53,000.

Hradec Králové

Hradecké noviny (Hradec News): Škroupova 695, 501 72 Hradec Králové; tel. (49) 613511; fax (49) 615681; Editor-in-Chief JAROMÍR FRIDRICH; circ. 30,000.

Karlovy Vary

Karlovarské noviny (Karlovy Vary News): třída TGM 32, 360 21 Karlovy Vary; tel. (17) 3224496; fax (17) 3225115; f. 1991; Editor-in-Chief JIŘÍ LINHART ; circ. 15,000.

Ostrava

Moravskoslezský den (Moravia-Silesia Daily): Novinářská 7, 700 00 Ostrava 1; tel. (69) 55134; fax (69) 57021; f. 1991; Editor-in-Chief VLADIMÍR VAVRDA; circ. 130,000.

Svoboda (Freedom): Mlýnská 10, 701 11 Ostrava; tel. (69) 2472311; fax (69) 2472312; f. 1991; morning; Editor-in-Chief JOSEF LYS; circ. 100,000.

Pardubice

Pardubické noviny (Pardubice News): Tříd Míru 60, 530 02 Pardubice; tel. (40) 517366; fax (40) 517156; f. 1991; Editor-in-Chief ROMAN MARČÁK; circ. 15,000.

Plzeň

Plzeňský deník (Plzeň Daily): Husova 15, 304 83 Plzeň; tel. (19) 551111; fax (19) 551234; f. 1991 (fmrly *Pravda*, f. 1919); Editor-in-Chief JAN PERTL; circ. 50,000.

Prague

Hospodářské noviny (Economic News): Na Florenci 19, 115 43 Prague 1; tel. (2) 24213535; fax (2) 2327236; f. 1957; morning; Editor-in-Chief PETR ŠTĚPÁNEK; circ. 130,000.

Lidové noviny (People's News): Žerotínova 32, 130 00 Prague 3; tel. (2) 67098444; fax (2) 67098608; f. 1893, re-established 1988; morning; Editor-in-Chief PAVEL ŠAFR; circ. 68,230.

Mladá fronta Dnes (Youth Front Today): Senovážná 4, 110 00 Prague 1; tel. (2) 21007111; fax (2) 21007229; f. 1990; morning; independent; Editor-in-Chief PETR ŠABATA; circ. 350,000.

Právo (Right): Slezská 13, 120 00 Prague 2; tel. (2) 21001111; fax (2) 21001361; f. 1920, as *Rudé právo*: name changed as above 1995; morning; Editor-in-Chief ZDENĚK PORYBNÝ; circ. 250,000.

Slovo (Word): Václavské nám. 36, 112 12 Prague 1; tel. (2) 24227258; fax (2) 24229477; f. 1945; Editor-in-Chief LIBOR ŠEVČÍK; circ. 95,000.

Večerník Praha (Evening Prague): Na Florenci 19, 111 21 Prague 1; tel. (2) 24227625; fax (2) 2327361; f. 1991 (fmrly *Večerní Praha*, f. 1955); evening; Editor-in-Chief IVAN ČERVENKA; circ. 130,000.

Ústí nad Labem

Severočeský deník (North Bohemia Daily): Velká Hradební 50, 400 90 Ústí nad Labem; tel. (47) 5220525; fax (47) 5220587; f. 1920; Editor-in-Chief MARIE SRPOVÁ; circ. 95,000.

PRINCIPAL PERIODICALS

100+1 ZZ: Karlovo nám. 5, 120 00 Prague 2; tel. (2) 293291; fax (2) 299824; f. 1964; fortnightly foreign press digest; Editor-in-Chief VÁCLAV DUŠEK; circ. 85,000.

Ateliér (Studio): Masarykovo nábř. 250, 110 01 Prague 1; tel. and fax (2) 291884; f. 1988; visual arts; fortnightly; Editor-in-Chief BLANKA JIRÁČKOVÁ.

Auto Tip: Střelnična 1680/8, 182 00 Prague 8; tel. (2) 66193173; fax (2) 66193172; f. 1990; fortnightly for motorists; Editor-in-Chief VLADIMÍR ŠULC; circ. 45,000.

Českomoravský profit (Czech–Moravia Profit): Domažlická 3, 130 00 Prague 3; tel. (2) 277084; fax (2) 278514; weekly; Editor-in-Chief JAN BALTUS.

Divadelní noviny (Theatre News): c/o Divadelní ústav, Celetná 17, 110 00 Prague 1; tel. and fax (2) 2315912; fortnightly; Editor-in-Chief JAN KOLÁŘ.

Ekonom (Economist): Na Poříčí 30, 112 86 Prague 1; tel. (2) 2822207; fax (2) 2321168; weekly; Editor-in-Chief MIROSLAV KAŇA.

Filip pro-náctileté (Filip for Teenagers): U Prašné brány 3, 116 29 Prague 1; tel. (2) 2328215; fax (2) 2328415; f. 1991; monthly cultural magazine for young people; Editors-in-Chief MARCELA TITZLOVÁ, MILAN POLÁK; circ. 125,000.

Hudební rozhledy (Musical Review): Maltézské nám. 1, 110 00 Prague 1; tel. and fax (2) 531343; f. 1947; monthly; Editor JAN ŠMOLÍK; circ. 3,000.

Katolický týdeník (Catholic Weekly): Londýnská 44, 120 00 Prague 2; tel. (2) 24250385; fax (2) 24257041; e-mail tydenik@mbox.vol.cz; f. 1989; weekly; Editor-in-Chief NORBERT BADAL; circ. 70,000.

Kino revue (Cinema Review): Ve Smečkách 22, 110 00 Prague 1; tel. and fax (2) 24231583; f. 1991; fortnightly; Editor-in-Chief MICHAELA VAŇKOVÁ; circ. 40,000.

Květy (Flowers): Na Florenci 3, 117 14 Prague 1; tel. and fax (2) 24219549; f. 1834; illustrated family weekly; Editor-in-Chief JINDŘICH MAŘAN; circ. 320,000.

Mladý svět (Young World): Na Poříčí 30, 112 86 Prague 1; tel. (2) 24229087; fax (2) 24210211; f. 1956; illustrated weekly; Editor-in-Chief OLGA DOUBRAVOVÁ; circ. 110,000.

Obchod-Kontakt-Marketing(Trade-Contact-Marketing):Korunní 87, 130 00 Prague 3; tel. and fax (2) 255440; monthly; Editor-in-Chief MARCELA NOVÁKOVÁ.

Reflex: Jeseniova 51, 130 00 Prague 3; tel. (2) 67097542; fax (2) 61216239; f. 1990; social weekly; Editor-in-Chief PETR BÍLEK; circ. 220,000.

Respekt: Sokolská 66, 120 00 Prague 2; tel. (2) 24941962; fax (2) 24941965; e-mail redakce@respekt.cz; f. 1990; political weekly; Editor-in-Chief MARTIN FENDRYCH; circ. 30,000.

Romano Kurko (Romany Week): Černovické nábř. 7, 618 00 Brno; tel. and fax (5) 330785; f. 1991; weekly; in Czech with Romany vocabulary; Dir M. SMOLEŇ; circ. 8,000.

Sondy (Soundings): W. Churchilla 2, 130 00 Prague 3; tel. (2) 24462328; fax (2) 24462313; f. 1990; weekly; Editor-in-Chief JANA KAŠPAROVÁ; circ. 40,000.

Týdeník Rozhlas (Radio Weekly): Na Florenci 3, 112 86 Prague 1; tel. and fax (2) 2323261; f. 1923; Editor-in-Chief AGÁTA PILÁTOVÁ; circ. 170,000.

Vesmír (Universe): Národní 3, 111 42 Prague 1; tel. (2) 24229181; fax (2) 24240513; e-mail vesmir@mbox.cesnet.cz; f. 1871; monthly; popular science magazine; Editor IVAN M. HAVEL; circ. 8,000–10,000.

Vlasta: Žitná 18, 120 00 Prague 2; tel. (2) 298641; fax (2) 294535; f. 1947; weekly; illustrated magazine for women; Editor-in-Chief MARIE FORMÁČKOVÁ; circ. 380,000.

Zahrádkář (Gardener): Kloknerova 720, 149 00 Prague 4; tel. (2) 766346; fax (2) 768042; monthly; Editor-in-Chief ANTONÍN DOLEJŠÍ; circ. 200,000.

Zora: Krakovská 21, 115 17 Prague 1; tel. (2) 24228126; fax (2) 24228120; f. 1917; bimonthly; for the visually handicapped; Editor-in-Chief JIŘÍ REICHEL.

FOREIGN LANGUAGES

Amaro Lav (Our Word): Černovické nábř. 7, 618 00 Brno; tel. and fax (5) 330785; f. 1990; monthly; in Romany and Czech; Dir M. SMOLEŇ; circ. 3,000.

Czech Business and Trade: V jirchářích 8, 110 00 Prague 1; tel. (2) 290329; fax (2) 24912355; f. 1960; monthly; publ. in English, German, Spanish and French; Editor-in-Chief Dr PAVLA PODSKALSKÁ; circ. 15,000.

Prager Wochenblatt (Prague Weekly): Vítkovická 373, 199 00 Prague 9; tel. (2) 6282029; weekly; politics, culture, economy; in German; Editor-in-Chief FELIX SEEBAUER; circ. 30,000.

Prague Post: Na Poříčí 12, 115 30 Prague 1; tel. (2) 24875000; fax (2) 24875050; e-mail marketing@praguepost.cz; f. 1991; political, economic and cultural weekly; in English; Editor-in-Chief ALAN LEVY; circ. 15,000.

Prognosis: Africká 17, 160 00 Prague 6; tel. (2) 3167007; fax (2) 368139; f. 1991; political, economic and cultural fortnightly; in English; Editor-in-Chief BEN SULLIVAN; circ. 10,000.

NEWS AGENCIES

Česká tisková kancelář (ČTK) (Czech News Agency): Opletalova 5–7, 111 44 Prague 1; tel. (2) 22098111; fax (2) 24220553; f. Nov. 1992, assuming control of all property and activities (in the Czech Lands) of the former Czechoslovak News Agency; news and photo exchange service with all international and many national news agencies; maintains network of foreign correspondents; Czech and English general and economic news service; publishes daily bulletins in Czech and English; Gen. Dir Dr MILAN STIBRAL.

Foreign Bureaux

Agence France-Presse (AFP): Žitná 10, 120 00 Prague 2; tel. (2) 24915554; telex 121124; fax (2) 294818; Bureau Chief DANIEL PRIOLLET.

Agencia EFE (Spain): Ubrinivenka 65, 100 00 Prague 1; tel. (2) 67313620; fax (2) 67313975; Bureau Chief MIGUEL FERNÁNDEZ.

Agenzia Nazionale Stampa Associata (ANSA) (Italy): Ve Smečkách 2, 110 00 Prague 1; tel. and fax (2) 24222793; telex 122734; Bureau Chief LUCIO ATTILIO LEANTE.

Allgemeiner Deutscher Nachrichtendienst (ADN) (Germany): Milevská 835, 140 00 Prague 4; tel. (2) 6921911; fax (2) 6921627; Bureau Chief STEFFI GENSICKE.

Associated Press (AP) (USA): Růžová 7, 110 00 Prague 1; tel. (2) 24224346; telex 121987; fax (2) 24227445; Correspondent ONDŘEJ HEJMA.

Deutsche Presse-Agentur (dpa) (Germany): Petrské nám. 1, 110 00 Prague 1; tel. (2) 24810290; fax (2) 2315196; Bureau Chief SYLVIE JANOVSKÁ.

Informatsionnoye Telegrafnoye Agentstvo Rossii—Telegrafnoye Agentstvo Suverennykh Stran (ITAR—TASS) (Russia): Pevnostní 5, 162 00 Prague 6; tel. (2) 328307; fax (2) 327527; Bureau Chief ALEKSANDR YAKOVLEV.

Magyar Távirati Iroda (MTI) (Hungary): U Smaltovny 17, 6th Floor, 170 00 Prague 7; tel. and fax (2) 66710131; Bureau Chief GYÖRGY HARSÁNYI.

Novinska Agencija Tanjug (Yugoslavia): U Smaltovny 19, 170 00 Prague 7; tel. (2) 2674401; Correspondent BRANKO STOŠIĆ.

Polska Agencja Prasowa (PAP) (Poland): Petrské nám. 1, 110 00 Prague 1; tel. and fax (2) 24812205; Correspondent ZBYGNIEW KRZYSTYNJAK.

Rossiiskoye Informatsionnoye Agentstvo—Novosti (RIA—Novosti) (Russia): Italská 36, 130 00 Prague 3; tel. (2) 24218069; telex 122235; fax (2) 24223734; Bureau Chief VALERII YENIN.

Tlačová agentúra Slovenskej republiky (TASR) (Slovakia): Šmeralova 7, 170 00 Prague 7; tel. and fax (2) 370525; Correspondent BOHDAN KOPČÁK.

Xinhua (New China) News Agency (People's Republic of China): Pelléova 22, 169 00 Prague 6; tel. and fax (2) 24311325; telex 121561; Correspondent SAN XI-YOU.

PRESS ASSOCIATION

Syndicate of Journalists of the Czech Republic: Pařížská 9, 116 30 Prague 1; tel. (2) 2325109; fax (2) 2327782; e-mail sncr@mbox.vol.cz; f. 1877; reorganized in 1990; 5,000 mems; Chair. RUDOLF ZEMAN.

Publishers

Academia: Legerova 61, 120 00 Prague 2; tel. (2) 24942584; fax (2) 24941982; f. 1953; scientific books, periodicals; Dir ALEXANDER TOMSKÝ.

Akcent-Blok: Rooseveltova 4, 657 00 Brno; tel. and fax (5) 42214516; f. 1957; regional literature, fiction, general; Dir JAROSLAV NOVÁK.

Albatros: Truhlářská 9, 110 01 Prague 1; tel. (2) 24810704; fax (2) 24810850; f. 1949; literature for children and young people; Dir MILADA MATĚJOVICOVÁ.

Horizont: Francouzská 6, 120 00 Prague 2; tel. (2) 257942; f. 1968; Dir Dr VLADIMÍR TROJÁNEK.

Kalich, evangelické nakladatelství (Evangelical Publishing House): Jungmannova 9, 111 21 Prague 1; tel. (2) 2350342; fax (2) 2357594; f. 1920; Dir Ing. JAN RYBÁŘ.

Kartografie Praha, a.s.: Fr. Křížka 1, 170 30 Prague 7; tel. (2) 375541; fax (2) 375555; f. 1954; cartographic publishing and printing house; Dir Ing. JIŘÍ KUČERA.

Kruh (Circle): Dlouhá 108, 500 21 Hradec Králové; tel. (49) 22076; f. 1966; regional literature, fiction and general; Dir Dr JAN DVOŘÁK.

Lidové nakladatelství (People's Publishing House): Václavské nám. 36, 110 00 Prague 1; tel. (2) 226383; f. 1968; classical and contemporary fiction, general, magazines; Dir Dr KORNEL VAVRINČÍK.

Melantrich: Václavské nám. 36, 112 12 Prague 1; tel. (2) 260341; telex 121432; fax (2) 225012; f. 1919; general, fiction, humanities, newspapers and magazines; Dir MILAN HORSKÝ.

Mladá fronta (Young Front): Radlická 61, 150 02 Prague 5; tel. (2) 24511587; fax (2) 533492; f. 1945; literature for young people, fiction and non-fiction, magazines; Dir MARIE KOŠKOVÁ.

Nakladatelství dopravy a spojů (Transport and Communications): Hybernská 5, 115 78 Prague 1; tel. (2) 2365774; fax (2) 2356772; Dir Ing. ALOIS HOUDEK.

Nakladatelství Svoboda (Freedom): Na Florenci 3, POB 704, 113 03 Prague 1; tel. (2) 24224705; fax (2) 24226026; f. 1945 as the publishing house of the Communist Party; restructured in 1992–94 as a limited company; in voluntary liquidation since Sept. 1997; politics, history, philosophy, fiction, general; Dir STEFAN SZERYŃSKI.

Odeon: Národní tř. 36, 115 87 Prague 1; tel. (2) 24225248; fax (2) 24225262; f. 1953; literature, poetry, fiction (classical and modern), literary theory, art books, reproductions; Dir MILUŠE SLAPNIČKOVÁ.

Olympia: Klimentská 1, 110 15 Prague 1; tel. (2) 2314861; fax (2) 2312137; e-mail olympia@mbox.vol.cz; f. 1954; sports, tourism, illustrated books; Dir Ing. KAREL ZELNÍČEK.

Panton: Radlická 99, 150 00 Prague 5; tel. and fax (2) 548627; f. 1958; publishing house of the Czech Musical Fund; books on music, sheet music, records; Dir KAREL ČERNÝ.

Práce (Labour): Václavské nám. 17, 112 58 Prague 1; tel. (2) 24009100; fax (2) 2320989; f. 1945; trade union movement, fiction, general, periodicals; Dir JANA SCHMIDTOVÁ.

Profil: Ciklářská 51, 702 00 Ostrava 1; regional literature, fiction and general; Dir IVAN ŠEINER.

Rapid, a.s.: 28. října 13, 112 79 Prague 1; tel. (2) 24195111; telex 121142; fax (2) 2327520; advertising; Dir-Gen. ČESTMÍR ČEJKA.

Růže (Rose): 370 96 České Budějovice; f. 1960; regional literature, fiction and general; Dir MIROSLAV HULE.

Severočeské nakladatelství (North Bohemian Publishing House): Ústí nad Labem; tel. (47) 28581; regional literature, fiction and general; Dir JIŘÍ ŠVEJDA.

SNTL—Nakladatelství technické literatury (Technical Literature): Spálená 51, 113 02 Prague 1; tel. (2) 297670; fax (2) 203774; f. 1953; technology, applied sciences, dictionaries, periodicals; Dir Dr KAREL ČERNÝ (acting).

Státní pedagogické nakladatelství: Ostrovní 30, 113 01 Prague 1; tel. and fax (2) 24912206; f. 1775; state publishing house; school and university textbooks, dictionaries, literature; Dir MILAN KOVÁŘ.

Vyšehrad: Karlovo nám. 5, 120 00 Prague 2; tel. (2) 297726; fax (2) 268390; f. 1934; religion, philosophy, history, fiction; Dir PRAVOMIL NOVÁK; Chief Editor VLASTA HESOUNOVÁ.

Západočeské nakladatelství (West Bohemian Publishing House): Plzeň; tel. (19) 34783; f. 1955; regional literature, fiction, general; Dir KATEŘINA RUBÍŠOVÁ.

WRITERS' UNION

Community of Writers (Obec spisovatelů): POB 669, 111 21 Prague 1; tel. (2) 2358968; fax (2) 269072; f. 1989; 720 mems; Dir EVA KANTŮRKOVÁ.

Broadcasting and Communications

TELECOMMUNICATIONS

SPT Telecom: Olsanska 5, 130 00 Prague 3; partially privatized 1995; 27%-owned by Dutch/Swiss consortium; monopoly operator of long-distance and international services; CEO SVATOSLAV NOVAK.

RADIO

The national networks include Radio Prague (medium wave and VHF), Radio Vltava (VHF from Prague—programmes on Czech and world culture), Radio Regina (medium and VHF—programme of regional studios), and Interprogramme (medium and VHF—for foreign visitors to the Czech Republic, in English, German and French). Radio Free Europe and Radio Liberty also broadcast from Prague (programmes in 19 languages).

Local stations broadcast from Prague (Central Bohemian Studio), Brno, České Budějovice, Hradec Králové, Ostrava, Plzeň, Ústí nad Labem and other towns. By August 1993 44 private stations had been licensed, 37 of which were in operation (14 in Prague).

Český rozhlas (Czech Radio): Vinohradská 12, 120 99 Prague 2; tel. (2) 24094111; fax (2) 24222223; 4 nation-wide stations; Dir-Gen. VLASTIMIL JEŽEK.

TELEVISION

In 1995 there were four main television stations: the two state-run channels, ČT1 and ČT2, reached 98% and 71% of the population, respectively, while the two private commercial stations, Nova TV and Premiera TV, were received by 99% and approximately 50%, respectively.

Česká televize (Czech Television): Kavčí hory, 140 70 Prague 4; tel. (2) 61212914; fax (2) 421562; f. 1992; state-owned; two channels; studios in Prague, Brno and Ostrava; Dir-Gen. JAKUB PUCHALSKY.

Nova TV: Celakovského sady 4, 110 00 Prague 1; tel. (2) 2363044; fax (2) 2431041; f. 1994; 93.5%-owned by Central European Media Enterprises; the first independent commercial station; Dir-Gen. VLADIMÍR ŽELEZNÝ.

Premiera TV: Prague; f. 1993; 55%-owned by FTV Premiera, 45%-owned by Investiční a Poštovní banka.

Finance

(cap. = capital; res = reserves; dep. = deposits; m. = million; brs = branches; amounts in Czech koruny)

BANKING

With the establishment of independent Czech and Slovak Republics on 1 January 1993, the State Bank of Czechoslovakia was divided and its functions were transferred to the newly-created Czech National Bank and National Bank of Slovakia. The Czech National Bank is independent of the Government.

In December 1996 there were 58 banks licensed to operate in the Czech Republic (53 actively operating and five under forced administration), with combined total assets of some 2,004,000m. Czech koruny.

Central Bank

Czech National Bank (Česká národní banka): Na Příkopě 28, 115 03 Prague 1; tel. (2) 24411111; telex 121555; fax (2) 24413708; f. 1993; bank of issue, the central authority of the Czech Republic in the monetary sphere, legislation and foreign exchange permission; central bank for directing and securing monetary policy, supervision of activities of other banks and savings banks; cap. 1,400m., res 25,380m., dep. 137,854m. (Dec. 1996); Gov. PAVEL KYSILKA (acting); 7 brs.

Commercial Banks

Agrobanka Praha, a.s.: Hybernská 18, 111 21 Prague 1; tel. (2) 24441111; fax (2) 24441500; f. 1990; universal bank with foreign exchange licence; provides a wide range of financial services, participates in privatization programmes; placed under forced administration Sept. 1996; cap. 3,993m., dep. 54,039m. (Dec. 1995); Chair. STANISLAV LABOUNEK; 28 brs.

Československá obchodní banka, a.s. (Czechoslovak Commercial Bank): Na Příkopě 14, 115 20 Prague 1; tel. (2) 24111111; telex 122201; fax (2) 2327562; f. 1965; commercial and foreign trade transactions; cap. 5,105m., res 6,540m., dep. 152,628m. (Dec. 1995); Chair. and Gen. Man. PAVEL KAVÁNEK; 40 brs.

COOP banka, a.s.: Benešova 14/16, 601 78 Brno; tel. (5) 42130111; fax (5) 42214337; f. 1992; placed under forced administration April 1996; cap. 625m., res 302m., dep. 5,473m. (Dec. 1995); Chair. ANTON VAVRO; 19 brs.

Foresbank, a.s.: Přílucká 360, 760 01 Zlín; tel. (67) 7626111; fax (67) 7626833; f. 1992; cap. 1,010m., res. 83m., dep. 5,506m. (Dec. 1995); Chair. MIROSLAV ŠKRABAL.

Giro Credit-Sparkassen Banka Praha, a.s.: Václavské nám. 56, POB 749, 111 21 Prague 1; tel. (2) 24033333; telex 121235; fax (2) 265886; f. 1993; cap. 500m., res 82m., dep. 12,265m. (Dec. 1995); Chair. and Gen. Man. Dr WILHELM REICHMANN.

HYPO-BANK CZ, a.s.: Štěpánská 33, 110 00 Prague 1; tel. (2) 21106204; telex 122821; fax (2) 21106112; f. 1991; cap. 740m., res 149m., dep. 5,971m. (Dec. 1995); Chair. Dr JAN KOLLERT; 12 brs.

Investiční a Poštovní banka, a.s.: Senovážné nám. 32, 114 03 Prague 1; tel. (2) 24071111; telex 122459; fax (2) 24244035; e-mail info@ipb.cz; internet http://www.ipb.cz; f. 1990; cap. 5,681m., res 12,422m., dep. 180,755m. (Dec. 1996); Chair. and Gen. Man. JIŘÍ TESAŘ; 157 brs.

Komerční banka, a.s.: Na Příkopě 33, POB 839, 114 07 Prague 1; tel. (2) 24021111; telex 121831; fax (2) 24243065; f. 1990; cap. 9,502m., res 22,122m., dep. 343,427m. (Dec. 1995); Chair. and CEO RICHARD SALZMANN; 379 brs.

Konsolidační banka Praha, s.p.ú.: Janovského 2, 170 00 Prague 7; tel. (2) 20141111; telex 122931; fax (2) 378244; f. 1991; cap. 5,950m., res 32,403m., dep. 73,833m. (Dec. 1995); Chair. VLADIMÍR ŠULC.

Pragobanka, a.s.: Vinohradská 230, 100 00 Prague 10; tel. (2) 67007111; telex 121776; fax (2) 67007255; f. 1990; cap. 1,860m. (Dec. 1996), res 1,598m., dep. 10,076m. (Dec. 1995); Gen. Man. Ing. RUDOLF KRÁL; 41 brs.

Union banka, a.s.: ul. 30. dubnač. 35, 702 00 Ostrava; tel. (69) 6108111; telex 52189; fax (69) 211586; f. 1991; cap. 1,390m., res 232m., dep. 8,116m. (Dec. 1995); Gen. Man. and Chair. of Bd MARIE PARMOVÁ.

Živnostenská banka, a.s.: Na Příkopě 20, 113 80 Prague 1; tel. (2) 24121111; telex 122313; fax (2) 24125555; e-mail info@ziba.cz; f. 1868; cap. 1,360m., res 876m., dep. 23,541m. (Dec. 1996); Chair. of Bd JIŘÍ KUNERT; 5 brs.

Foreign and Joint-Venture Banks

Bank Austria (ČR), a.s.: Revoluční 15, 110 15 Prague 1; tel. (2) 24892111; fax (2) 24892680; f. 1991; shareholders: Bank Austria AG, Vienna (80%), CARIPLO SpA, Milan (20%); cap. 750m., res 200m., dep. 6,837m. (Dec. 1995); Chair. of Bd MANFRED MEIER.

Banka Haná, a.s.: Rooseveltova 10, 602 00 Brno; tel. (5) 42219548; fax (5) 42215681; f. 1990; cap. 1,000m., res 321m., dep. 17,300m. (Dec. 1995); Chair. and Gen. Man. PAVEL RUCKI; 7 brs.

BNP—Dresdner Bank (ČR), a.s.: Vítězná 1, POB 229, 150 00 Prague 5; tel. (2) 57006111; fax (2) 57006202; f. 1991; ownership: Banque Nationale de Paris (50%), Dresdner Bank (50%); cap. and res 1,204m., dep. 2,900m. (Dec. 1996); Chair. and Gen. Man. ROLF D. BECK.

Citibank, a.s.: Evropská 178, 166 40 Prague 6; tel. (2) 4304111; telex 122196; fax (2) 3164706; f. 1991; wholly-owned subsidiary of Citibank Overseas Investment Corpn (Delaware, USA); cap. 350m., res 110m., dep. 11,836m. (Dec. 1994); Chair. DAVID ANSELL.

Crédit Lyonnais Bank Prague, a.s.: Ovocny Trh 8, 110 00 Prague 1; tel. (2) 24233543; telex 121346; fax (2) 24238356; wholly-owned subsidiary of Crédit Lyonnais, SA (France); cap. 500m., res 214m., dep. 11,246m. (Dec. 1995).

Creditanstalt, a.s.: Široká 5, 110 01 Prague 1; tel. (2) 21102111; telex 122015; fax (2) 24812185; f. 1991; wholly-owned subsidiary of Creditanstalt-Bankverein (Austria); cap. 1,700m., res 94,429m., dep. 20,395m. (Dec. 1995); Chair. GUIDO SCHMIDT-CHIARI; 9 brs.

Moravia banka, a.s.: Palackého 133, 738 02 Frýdek-Místek; tel. (658) 606111; telex 52171; fax (658) 606225; f. 1992; cap. 650m. Kč., dep. 8,563m. (Dec. 1995); Chair. PTER GERLICH; Gen. Man. JIŘÍ BARTON; 17 brs.

Société Générale banka, a.s.: Pobřežní 3, POB 74, 186 00 Prague 8; tel. (2) 24832300; telex 122735; fax (2) 24832487; f. 1990; cap. 774m. (Oct. 1994); Gen. Man. CLAUDE ARMAND BLANOT.

Savings Bank

Czech Savings Bank (Česká spořitelna, a.s.): Na Příkopě 29, POB 838, 113 98 Prague 1; tel. (2) 61071111; telex 121010; fax (2) 61073006; f. 1825; 45% state-owned; accepts deposits and issues loans; 15,239,363 depositors (June 1990); cap. 7,600m., res 13,097m., dep. 326,423m. (Dec. 1996); Chair. and Gen. Man. Ing. JAROSLAV KLAPAL; 2,090 brs.

Bankers' Organization

Association of Banks, Prague: Vodičkova 30, 110 00 Prague 1; tel. (2) 24225926; fax (2) 24225957.

STOCK EXCHANGE

Prague Stock Exchange (Burza cenných papírů Praha, a.s.): Rybná 14, 110 00 Prague 1; tel. (2) 21832116; fax (2) 21833040; f. 1992; Chair. TOMÁŠ JEŽEK.

INSURANCE

Czech Association of Insurers: f. 1994; 27 members.

Czech Co-operative Insurance Company (Česká Kooperativa, družstevní pojišťovna, a.s.): Templová, 110 01 Prague 1; tel. (2) 21000111; fax (2) 2322633; f. 1993.

Czech Insurance and Reinsurance Corporation (Česká pojišťovna, a.s.): Spálená 16, 113 04 Prague 1; tel. (2) 24051111; fax (2) 24052200; internet http://www.cpoj.cz; f. 1827; many home brs and some agencies abroad; issues life, accident, fire, aviation, industrial and marine policies, all classes of reinsurance; Lloyd's agency; Chair. of the Bd. IVAN KOČÁRNÍK; Gen. Man. LADISLAV BARTONÍČEK.

Pojišťovna IB, a.s.: V jámě 1, 114 09 Prague 1; tel. (2) 21422492.

Trade and Industry

GOVERNMENT AGENCIES

Česká agentura pro zahraniční investice (CzechInvest): Politických vězňů 20, 112 49 Prague 1; tel. (2) 24221540; fax (2) 24221804; e-mail czinvest@ms.anet.cz; internet http://www. czechinvest.com; f. 1992; foreign investment agency; Dir Ing. JAN HAVELKA.

National Property Fund: Rašínovo nábřeží 42, 12800 Prague 2; tel. (2) 24991285; fax (2) 24991379; responsible for state property and state-owned companies in the period up to their privatization; Chair. ROMAN CEŠKA.

CHAMBER OF COMMERCE

Economic Chamber of the Czech Republic (Hospodářská komora České republiky): Argentinská 38, 170 05 Prague 7; tel. (2) 66794880; fax (2) 875438; f. 1850; has almost 20,000 members (trading corporations, industrial enterprises, banks and private enterprises); Chair. Dr ZDENĚK SOMR.

EMPLOYERS' ORGANIZATIONS

Association of Entrepreneurs of the Czech Republic (Sdružení podnikatelů České republiky): Škrétova 6/44, 120 59 Prague 2; tel. and fax (2) 24230572; Chair. RUDOLF BARÁNEK.

Association of Industry of the Czech Republic (Svaz průmyslu a dopravy České Republiky): Mikulamdská 7, 113 61 Prague 1; tel. (2) 24915679; fax (2) 297896; e-mail spet@spct. amet.cz.

UTILITIES

Electricity

Central Bohemian Electricity Distribution Company (Středočeská Energetická—STE a.s.): Na Přikopě 15, 113 20 Prague 1; tel. (2) 24224469; fax (2) 24216424.

ČEZ (České Energeticke Zavody): Hlavni Sprava, Jungmannova 29, 111 48 Prague 1; tel. (2) 24081111; fax (2) 24082440; production company; Gen. Dir PETR KARAS; 16,062 employees.

Dukovany Nuclear Plant: Dukovany.

East Bohemian Electricity Company (Východočeská Energetika—VCE): Hradec Králové; Dir PETR ZEMAN.

North Bohemian Electricity (Severočeská Energetika—SČE a.s.): Teplická 8, 405 49 Děčín IV; Chair. JIRI STASTNY.

North Moravian Electricity (Severomoravská Energetika—SME a.s.): Ostrava; tel. (69) 6612821; fax (69) 6611187; distribution company; Dir Gen. THOMAS HUNER.

South Bohemian Electricity (Jihočeská Energetika—JČE a.s.): Lannova 16, 370 49 České Budějovice; tel. (38) 7312682; fax (38) 59803; Gen. Dir JAN ŠPIKA.

South Moravian Electricity (Jihomoravska Energetika—JME): Brno; Man. Dir MILOSLAV VACEK.

State Office for Nuclear Safety (Statni urad pro jadernou bezpečnost): Slejzska 9; 120 29 Prague 2; tel. (2) 24171111; fax (2) 255262; state supervision of nuclear safety, co-ordination of international relations in the sphere of nuclear safety; Chair. JAN STULLER.

Gas

North Moravian Gas (Severomoravsjká Plynarenska—SMP): distribution company; Man. Dir LIBOR JURICEK.

South Moravian Gas (Jihomoravska Plynarenska—JMP a.s.): Plynárenská 1, 657 00 Brno; tel. (5) 5148 111; fax (5) 578571; distribution company; Chair. LIBOR MARTINEK.

Transgas: Vinohradská 8, 120 00 Prague 2; tel. (2) 70771111; import and distribution company; Man. Dir MIROSLAV GREC.

TRADE UNIONS

Czech-Moravian Chamber of Trade Unions (Českomoravská komora odborových svazů): nám. W. Churchilla 2, 113 59 Prague 3; tel. (2) 24461111; fax (2) 24226163; f. 1990; 35 affiliated unions (1995); Pres. RICHARD FALBR.

Affiliated unions include the following:

Czech-Moravian Trade Union of Workers in Education (Českomoravský odborový svaz školství): nám. W. Churchilla 2, 113 59 Prague 3; tel. (2) 24226491; fax (2) 24218010; Pres. JAROSLAV RÖSSLER; 164,000 mems.

Czech-Moravian Trade Union of Workers in Services (Českomoravský odborový svaz pracovníků služeb): nám. W. Churchilla 2, 113 59 Prague 3; tel. (2) 24463172; fax (2) 24463185; f. 1990; Pres. RICHARD FALBR; 44,000 mems.

Trade Union Association of Railwaymen (Odborové sdružení železničářů): nám. W. Churchilla 2, 113 59 Prague 3; tel. (2) 2356813; fax (2) 2361928; f. 1990; Chair. JAROMÍR DUSEK; 324,360 mems.

Trade Union of Workers in Health Service and Social Care in the Czech Republic (Odborový svaz pracovníků zdravotnictví a sociální péče v ČR): Koněvova 54, 130 00 Prague 3; tel. (2) 61216114; fax (2) 61216118; e-mail bonase@mbox .vol.cz; Pres. JIŘÍ SCHLANGER; 100,000 mems.

Trade Union of Workers in Textile, Clothing and Leather Industry of Bohemia and Moravia (Odborový svaz pracovníků textilního, oděvního a kožedělného průmyslu Čech a Moravy): nám. W. Churchilla 2, 113 59 Prague 3; tel. (2) 24222123; fax (2) 273589; Pres. KAREL NOCOTNY; 79,600 mems.

Trade Union of Workers in Woodworking Industry, Forestry and Management of Water Supplies in the Czech Republic (Odborový svaz pracovníků dřevozpracujícího odvětví, lesního a vodního hospodářství v České republice): nám. W. Churchilla 2, 113 59 Prague 3; tel. (2) 24463091; telex 121484; fax (2) 24224520; Pres. RUDOLF KYNCL; 82,000 mems.

Transport

RAILWAYS

In 1994 the total length of the Czech railway network was 9,413 km.

České dráhy (Czech Railways): nábř. L. Svobody 12, 110 15 Prague 1; tel. (2) 23031111; fax (2) 24812569; f. 1993, as successor to Czechoslovak State Railways; Gen. Dir Ing. VLADIMÍR SOSNA.

Prague Metropolitan Railway: Dopravní podnik hlavního města Prahy, Sliačská 1, 141 41 Prague 4; tel. (2) 763657; fax (2) 764762; the Prague underground railway opened in 1974 and, by Oct. 1997, 43.4 km were operational; 46 stations; Gen. Dir Ing. LADISLAV HOUDEK.

ROADS

In 1996 there were an estimated 55,489 km of roads in the Czech Republic, including 423 km of motorways.

INLAND WATERWAYS

The total length of navigable waterways in the Czech Republic is 303 km. The Elbe (Labe) and its tributary, the Vltava, connect the Czech Republic with the North Sea via the port of Hamburg (Germany). The Oder provides a connection with the Baltic Sea and the port of Szczecin (Poland). The Czech Republic's river ports are Prague Holešovice, Prague Radotín, Kolín, Mělník, Ústí nad Labem and Děčín, on the Vltava and Elbe.

Czechoslovak Elbe Navigation Ltd (Československá plavba labská, a.s.): K. Čapka 1, 405 91 Děčín; tel. (412) 561111; telex 184241; fax (412) 510140; f. 1922; river transport of goods to Germany, Poland, the Netherlands, Belgium, Luxembourg, France and Switzerland; Man. Dir KAREL HORYNA.

SHIPPING

Since August 1997 no ships have operated under the Czech flag. All Czech-owned ships operate under the Maltese flag.

Czech Ocean Shipping, Joint-Stock Company (Česká námořní plavba, akciová společnost): Počernická 168, 100 99 Prague 10; tel. (2) 778941; telex 122137; fax (2) 773962; f. 1959; 15 ships totalling 361,339 dwt; Man. Dir Capt. PAVEL TRNKA.

CIVIL AVIATION

There are main civil airports at Prague (Ruzyně), Brno, Karlovy Vary and Ostrava, operated by the Czech Airport Administration. The opening of a new terminal at Ruzyně in June 1997 was expected to increase the airport's capacity from 2.3m. passengers to 4.8m.

Air Ostrava: Ostrava International Airport, 742 51 Mosnov; tel. (69) 6659433; fax (69) 58206; f. 1977; services to international, regional and domestic destinations; Man. Dir PAVEL HRADEC.

ČSA (České aerolinie, a.s.) (Czech Airlines): Ruzyně Airport, 160 08 Prague 6; tel. (2) 20104111; telex 120338; fax (2) 24314273; f. 1995; external services to most European capitals, the Near, Middle and Far East, North Africa and North America; Pres. ANTONÍN JAKUBSE.

Topair: Ruzyně Airport, U Silnice 42, 161 00 Prague 6; tel. (2) 3165554; fax (2) 3166561; f. 1991; charter flights throughout Europe; Gen.-Dir. MILOSLAV TUTTER.

Tourism

The Czech Republic has magnificent scenery, with winter sports facilities. Prague, Karlovy Vary (Carlsbad), Olomouc, Český Krumlov and Telč are among the best known of the historic towns, and there are famous castles and cathedrals, numerous resorts as well as spas with natural mineral springs. Registered accommodation establishments recorded some 4.6m. stays of at least one night by foreigners in 1996. In 1994 tourist receipts totalled US $1,970m.

Czech Tourist Authority: Staromestské nám. 6, 110 15 Prague 1; tel. (2) 248128529; fax (2) 2314227; f. 1993; Dir KAREL NEJDL.

Čedok Travel Corpn: Na Příkopě 18, 111 35 Prague 1; tel. (2) 24197111; telex 121064; fax (2) 2321656; internet http://www .cedok.cz; f. 1920; 90 domestic travel offices; eight branches throughout Europe; Pres. ČESTMÍR SAJDA.

DENMARK

Introductory Survey

Location, Climate, Language, Religion, Flag, Capital

The Kingdom of Denmark is situated in northern Europe. It consists of the peninsula of Jutland, the islands of Zealand, Funen, Lolland, Falster and Bornholm, and 401 smaller islands. The country lies between the North Sea, to the west, and the Baltic Sea, to the east. Denmark's only land frontier is with Germany, to the south. Norway lies to the north of Denmark, across the Skagerrak, while Sweden, whose most southerly region is separated from Zealand by a narrow strait, lies to the north-east. Outlying territories of Denmark are Greenland and the Faroe Islands in the North Atlantic Ocean. Denmark is low-lying and the climate is temperate, with mild summers and cold, rainy winters. The language is Danish. Almost all of the inhabitants profess Christianity: the Evangelical Lutheran Church, to which some 87% of the population belong, is the established Church, and there are also small communities of other Protestant groups and of Roman Catholics. The national flag (proportions 37 by 28) displays a white cross on a red background, the upright of the cross being to the left of centre. The capital is Copenhagen (København).

Recent History

In 1945, following the end of German wartime occupation, Denmark recognized the independence of Iceland, which had been declared in the previous year. Home rule was granted to the Faroe Islands in 1948 and to Greenland in 1979. Denmark was a founder member of NATO in 1949 and of the Nordic Council in 1952. In January 1973, following a referendum, Denmark entered the European Communities (including the EEC), later more commonly referred to as simply the European Community (EC), and from 1993 restyled as the European Union (EU).

In 1947 King Frederik IX succeeded to the throne on the death of his father, Christian X. Denmark's Constitution was radically revised in 1953: new provisions allowed for female succession to the throne, abolished the upper house of Parliament and amended the franchise. King Frederik died in January 1972, and his eldest daughter, Margrethe, became the first queen to rule Denmark for nearly 600 years.

The system of proportional representation which is embodied in the 1953 Constitution makes it difficult for a single party to gain a majority in the Folketing (Parliament). The Liberal Party's minority Government, led by Poul Hartling and formed in 1973, was followed in 1975 by a minority Social Democratic Government under the leadership of Anker Jørgensen. Jørgensen led various coalitions and minority governments until 1982. There were general elections in 1977, 1979 and 1981, held against a background of growing unemployment and attempts to tighten control of the economy. By September 1982 Jørgensen's economic policy, including attempts to reduce the budget deficit by introducing new taxes, had once more led to disagreements within the Cabinet, and the Government resigned.

The Conservatives, who had been absent from Danish coalitions since 1971, formed a centre-right four-party Government (with the Liberals, the Centre Democrats and the Christian People's Party), led by Poul Schlüter, who became Denmark's first Conservative Prime Minister since 1894. Holding only 66 of the Folketing's 179 seats, the coalition narrowly avoided defeat in October 1982, when it introduced stringent economic measures (including a six-month 'freeze' on wages), and again in September 1983, when larger reductions in public spending were proposed. In December the right-wing Progress Party withdrew its support for further cuts in expenditure, and the Government was defeated. A general election to the Folketing was held in January 1984, and Schlüter's Government remained in office, with its component parties holding a total of 77 seats, and relying on the support of the Social Liberal members.

In January 1986 the left-wing parties in the Folketing combined to reject the ratification by Denmark of the Single European Act (which amended the Treaty of Rome—the agreement that founded the EC—so as to establish the EC's single market and allow the EC Council of Ministers to take decisions by a qualified majority vote if a unanimous one was not achieved). Opponents of ratification, led by the Social Democrats, argued that it would lead to a diminution of Denmark's power to maintain strict environmental controls. In a national referendum in February, however, 56.2% of the votes cast were in favour of ratification, and the Folketing formally approved it in May.

A general election took place in September 1987 and was contested by 16 political parties, nine of which won seats in the Folketing. Schlüter's coalition retained only 70 seats, while the opposition Social Democratic Party lost two of its 56 seats. Jørgensen later resigned as leader of the latter party. Several of the smaller and extremist parties made considerable gains, with the result that the outgoing coalition was weakened, while the main opposition parties were unable to command a working majority. Schlüter eventually formed a new Cabinet comprising representatives of the former four-party governing coalition. However, the Social Liberals had earlier declared that they would not support any administration that depended on the support of the Progress Party. This therefore left a precarious balance of power within the Folketing.

In April 1988 the Folketing adopted an opposition-sponsored resolution requiring the Government to inform visiting warships of the country's ban on nuclear weapons. The British and US Governments were highly critical of the resolution. Schlüter therefore announced an early general election for May 1988, on the issue of Denmark's membership of NATO and defence policy. For the main parties the election result was inconclusive, and negotiations lasting three weeks were necessary before Schlüter was appointed to seek a basis for viable government. At the beginning of June a new minority coalition, comprising Conservatives, Liberals and Social Liberals, formed a Cabinet under Schlüter. The new Government restored good relations with its NATO allies by adopting a formula that requested all visiting warships to respect Danish law in its territorial waters, while making no specific reference to nuclear weapons. The Schlüter Government did receive some criticism from NATO, however, for its refusal to increase defence expenditure.

The Government proposed large reductions in social welfare provision for 1989, and attacked Progress Party demands for less taxation as unrealistic. The Progress Party, however, continued to increase in popularity, and in November 1989 its share of the vote rose significantly in municipal elections, while the Conservatives lost support. The Government therefore proposed to reduce the rates of taxation in 1990, despite Social Democratic opposition to the accompanying decreases in welfare expenditure. The budget proposals for 1990 were enacted in December 1989, relying on the support of the six right-wing parties in the Folketing. An early general election was organized for 12 December 1990. Although the Social Democratic Party retained the largest share of the vote (winning an additional 14 seats to bring its total to 69), Schlüter formed a minority coalition Government, comprising the Conservative party, which had lost five seats in the election, and the Liberal Party, which had gained an additional seven seats. As expected, the Social Liberals, while no longer part of the Government, continued to support the majority of the new coalition Government's policies.

In May 1992 the Folketing voted, by 130 votes to 25, to approve the Treaty on European Union (the 'Maastricht Treaty'—see p. 158), which further expands the scope of the Treaty of Rome. In a referendum held in Denmark in June, however, 50.7% of those who participated voted against ratification of the Treaty, compared with 49.3% in favour. This unexpected result caused consternation among Denmark's European partners, and during the rest of the year discussions took place among representatives of EC countries, who sought to establish a formula that, without necessitating the renegotiation of the Treaty, would allow the Danish Government to conduct a second referendum with some hope of success. In December EC heads of government agreed that Denmark should be allowed exemption from certain provisions of the Treaty, namely the final stage of European monetary union (including the adoption of a single currency); participation in a common defence policy; common European citizenship; and co-operation in legal and home affairs: all provisions that had been regarded as a threat to national sovereignty by Danish opponents of ratification. Despite uncertainty as to how far these exemptions were legally binding, the agreement was endorsed by seven of the eight parties represented in the Folketing (the exception being the Progress Party), and in a second referendum, held in May 1993, 56.7% of the votes were cast in favour of ratification, and 43.3% against. In June 1994 the Government announced that it would seek an amendment to the Maastricht Treaty to ensure that environmental safety took precedence over European free trade initiatives. In October 1997 Prime Minister Rasmussen announced that a further referendum was to be organized in order to ascertain levels of popular support for and against Denmark's future ratification of the Amsterdam Treaty on European integration (see p. 159), drafted at a meeting of EU member nations in the Netherlands in June. Urging support for the Treaty's ratification, Rasmussen asserted that acceptance of the new Treaty would not compromise the exemptions secured from the Maastricht Treaty, and that the Amsterdam accord provided for greater levels of environmental protection than its predecessor.

On 14 January 1993 Schlüter resigned from the premiership after a judicial enquiry disclosed that he had misled the Folketing in April 1989 over a scandal that had its origin in 1987, when the then Minister of Justice, Erik Ninn-Hansen, had illegally ordered civil servants to delay issuing entry visas to the families of Tamil refugees from Sri Lanka. (In June 1995 Ninn-Hansen was given a suspended four-month prison sentence for contravening immigration laws.) In subsequent negotiations between political parties, Poul Nyrup Rasmussen, the leader of the Social Democratic Party, obtained enough support to form a new government, and on 25 January a majority coalition Government (the first majority Government in Denmark for 11 years, controlling 90 of the 179 seats in the legislature) took office: it comprised members of the Social Democratic Party and three small centre parties (the Social Liberal Party, the Centre Democrats and the Christian People's Party). The new Government gave priority to securing an affirmative vote for the Maastricht Treaty (see above).

In February 1994 the Government lost its parliamentary majority, when the Minister of Social Affairs resigned from both the Cabinet and the Centre Democrats. At elections to the European Parliament, held in June, the Social Democratic Party's share of the vote was reduced, whereas parties that opposed the EU increased their support. Of more concern to the Government, however, with a general election imminent, was the growth in support for the Conservatives and the Liberal Party. In the subsequent general election, which took place on 21 September, three months earlier than scheduled, the Social Democratic Party won a reduced number of seats, although it retained the larger share of the vote. The Liberal Party, led by Uffe Ellemann-Jensen, gained an additional 13 seats, but the Christian People's Party, a member of the coalition, failed to secure representation in the new legislature. Rasmussen, however, was able to form a minority Government with his two remaining coalition partners, the Social Liberal Party and the Centre Democrats, and denied that the Government would be dependent for support on the left-wing Socialist People's Party. In December 1996, however, the Centre Democrats withdrew from the coalition, following the Government's decision to seek support from left-wing parties in order to achieve parliamentary approval for legislation relating to the 1997 budget.

In late October 1997 Thorkild Simonsen was appointed as the new Minister of the Interior and of Health, following mounting public concern at reports of increasingly high levels of immigration. The new appointment was expected to signal a new government initiative to enforce stricter immigration policy.

The results of local elections conducted on 18 November 1997 indicated that the Social Democratic Party, which received some 33% of the votes, was continuing to attract the largest share of popular support. In February 1998 Prime Minister Rasmussen announced that an early general election would be conducted on 11 March (see Late Information). A referendum on ratification of the Amsterdam Treaty (see above) was to be held on 28 May.

In August 1988 the Danish Government decided to submit a dispute with Norway, concerning maritime economic zones between Greenland and Jan Mayen island, to the International Court of Justice (ICJ) at The Hague. A delimitation line was fixed by the ICJ in June 1993. In 1991 the construction of a bridge across the Great Belt, between the Danish islands of Zealand and Funen, was the subject of an objection submitted by Finland to the ICJ that the proposed bridge's clearance would not allow Finland to move oil-drilling rigs through the strait and would, therefore, be in contravention of Denmark's international treaty obligations to permit the free passage of shipping through the Great Belt. In September 1992, however, the ICJ was informed by the parties that the dispute had been settled.

In August 1991 Denmark and Sweden signed an agreement on the proposed construction of a 15.9-km road and rail system across the Oresund strait between Copenhagen and Malmö. The total cost of the project was projected at an estimated 14,400m. kroner. Although construction was initially delayed, owing to objections raised by environmentalists in Sweden and Germany, the agreement was finally ratified by the Swedish Government in 1994, construction contracts were awarded in 1995 and the project was expected to be completed by 2000.

Following the dissolution of the USSR at the end of 1991, Denmark rapidly established diplomatic relations with (and began investing in) the former Soviet Baltic states of Estonia, Latvia and Lithuania, and was a founder member of the Council of Baltic Sea States, established in 1992.

Government

Denmark is a constitutional monarchy. Under the 1953 constitutional charter, legislative power is held jointly by the hereditary monarch (who has no personal political power) and the unicameral Folketing (Parliament), with 179 members, including 175 from metropolitan Denmark and two each from the Faroe Islands and Greenland. Members are elected for four years (subject to dissolution) on the basis of proportional representation. A referendum in September 1978 reduced the age of suffrage from 20 to 18. Executive power is exercised by the monarch through a Cabinet, which is led by the Prime Minister and is responsible to the Folketing. Denmark comprises 14 counties (amtskommuner), one city and one borough, all with elected councils.

Defence

In August 1997 Denmark maintained an army of some 19,000 (including 6,900 conscripts), a navy of 6,000 (480 conscripts) and an air force of 7,900 (430 conscripts). There were, in total, 70,450 reservists, and a volunteer Home Guard numbering 64,300. Military service is for nine–12 months, although some ranks are required to serve for 27 months. Denmark abandoned its neutrality after the Second World War and has been a member of NATO since 1949. In 1992 Denmark assumed observer status in the Western European Union (WEU, see p. 240). The defence budget for 1996 was initially estimated at 18,000m. kroner, representing some 4.7% of total budget spending, and annual expenditure on defence was forecast to remain at 17,500m.–18,000m. kroner for 1997 and 1998.

Economic Affairs

In 1995, according to estimates by the World Bank, Denmark's gross national product (GNP), measured at average 1993–95 prices, was US $156,027m., equivalent to $29,890 per head. Denmark's level of GNP per head is one of the highest among industrialized countries. It was estimated that GNP per head increased, in real terms, at an average rate of 1.5% per year between 1985 and 1995. Over the same period, Denmark's population grew at an average annual rate of 0.2%. Denmark's gross domestic product (GDP) increased, in real terms, by an average annual rate of 2.0% in 1990–95. In 1995 and 1996 growth in GDP was estimated at 2.7% and 2.4%, respectively; official sources forecast a rise of 2%–3% in 1997.

Agriculture (including forestry and fishing) employed about 4.8% of the working population and contributed 4.1% of GDP in 1995. In 1995 about 55% of Denmark's land area was used for agriculture. The principal activities are pig-farming (Denmark is a major exporter of pork products and pig meat accounts for some 8% of total exports) and dairy farming. Most of Denmark's agricultural production is exported, and the sector accounted for 23.2% of total exports in 1995. Agricultural GDP increased, in real terms, by an annual average of 3.6% in 1980–90; rises of 9.7% and 15.2% were recorded in 1994 and 1995, respectively. The fishing industry accounted for about 5% of total export earnings in 1995.

Industry (including mining, manufacturing, construction, power and water) employed 27.0% of the working population and provided 27.8% of GDP in 1995. Industrial GDP increased by an annual average of 1.9% (in real terms) in 1980–90; growth of 7.3% was recorded in both 1994 and 1995.

In 1995 mining accounted for only 0.1% of employment and 0.8% of GDP. Denmark has few natural resources, but exploration for petroleum reserves in the Danish sector of the North Sea in the 1970s proved successful. Natural gas has also been extensively exploited. In 1989, in north-western Jutland, it was established that there was a significant reserve of sand which could be exploited for rich yields of titanium, zirconium and yttrium.

Manufacturing employed about 19.6% of the working population and contributed 19.6% of GDP in 1995. The most important manufacturing industries, measured by the value of output, are food-processing, steel and metals, chemicals and pharmaceuticals, printing and publishing, machinery, electronic goods and transport equipment. Manufacturing GDP increased, in real terms, by an annual average of 1.0% in 1980–90; rises of 8.4% and 7.9% were recorded in 1994 and 1995, respectively.

Energy is derived principally from petroleum and natural gas. In 1994 output of crude petroleum reached 9.2m. metric tons and in 1993 oil equivalents of gas amounted to 4m. metric tons, enough to satisfy Denmark's own energy requirements. In 1995 mineral fuels comprised about 5% of the total cost of imports. The use of renewable sources of energy (including wind power) has been encouraged.

In 1996 Denmark recorded a visible trade surplus of US $7,313m., and there was a surplus of US $1,920m. on the current account of the balance of payments. Most Danish trade is with the EU (69.7% of imports and 64.6% of exports in 1995). The principal sources of imports in 1995 were Germany (22.5%) and Sweden (12.2%), which were also the principal markets for exports (23.2% and 9.9%, respectively). Other major trading partners include the United Kingdom, the Netherlands and Norway. The principal exports are food and food products, chemicals and manufactures such as industrial machinery. The principal imports are chemicals, food and live animals, machinery and basic manufactures such as iron, steel and paper.

In 1997 there was an actual budget surplus of some 3,700m. kroner. Denmark has one of the highest levels of debt per head of population among industrialized nations. By the end of 1995 Denmark's net external debt stood at an estimated 266,000m. kroner (equivalent to about 27% of annual GDP). The average annual rate of inflation was 2.9% in 1985–96. Consumer prices increased by 2.0% in 1994, by 2.1% in 1995, and by 2.1% in 1996. The average annual rate of unemployment decreased from 10.2% of the labour force in 1995 to some 8.6% in 1996.

Denmark is a member of the EU (see p. 152), the Nordic Council (p. 200) and the Nordic Council of Ministers (p. 201).

During the 1980s progress towards the formation of a European single market (with effect from 1992) caused pressure for the creation of larger economic units that were able to compete more effectively. In 1989 legislation permitted the formation of larger farms, signifying a change in the policy that had protected the traditional family farms, many of which had become seriously indebted. The Danish Government came under considerable pressure to reform the rates of taxation in preparation for 1992 and the single European market. Serious obstacles to such reform were the comprehensive nature of welfare provision and the size of the national debt. In 1990–95 there was a surplus on the current account of the balance of payments, and inflation was low, at around 2% annually; however, economic growth was initially slow, and the high level of unemployment was a cause for concern. In 1993 the Government adopted a programme of measures designed to accelerate economic growth and lower the rate of unemployment by reducing income tax and increasing investment in infrastructure. It also embarked on a programme of privatization. In May 1997, in an attempt to consolidate public finances, the Government announced new legislation on taxes, and restrictions on central government spending. In August the economy ministry forecast GDP growth of 3.1% for 1997 and 3.0% for 1998. The rate of unemployment was expected to continue to decrease to 7.8% in 1997, and to 7.4% in 1998. The draft budget for 1998, announced later in August on the strength of Denmark's first fiscal surplus for 10 years, envisaged an increased surplus for 1998.

Social Welfare

Denmark was one of the first countries to introduce state social welfare schemes. The principal benefits cover unemployment, sickness, old age and disability, and are financed largely by state subventions. The Government introduced a new system in 1984, whereby social benefits are regulated according to the individual's means. In 1985 Denmark had 120 hospital establishments. In 1994 there were 21,900 hospital beds, and in 1992 there were 14,657 physicians working in the country. In 1996 some 24% of proposed budget expenditure was allocated to social services.

Education

Education is compulsory for nine years between seven and 16 years of age. The State is obliged to offer a pre-school class and a tenth voluntary year. State-subsidized private schools are available, but about 90% of pupils attend municipal schools. The 1975 Education Act increased parental influence, introduced a comprehensive curriculum for the first 10 years and offered options on final tests or a leaving certificate thereafter. A new Education Act, with effect from August 1994, emphasized the comprehensive aspect of education.

Primary and lower secondary education begins at six or seven years of age and lasts for nine (optionally 10) years. This includes at least six years at primary school. The first three-year cycle of secondary education begins at 13 years of age. At the age of 16 or 17, pupils may transfer to a three-year course at an upper secondary school (Gymnasium), leading to the Upper Secondary School Leaving Examination (Studentereksamen), or they may take a two-year course, leading to the Higher Preparatory Examination (Højere Forberedelseseksamen); they may also take a three-year course leading to the Higher Commercial Examination or the Higher Technical Examination; all four courses give admission to university studies. Students may transfer to vocational courses at this stage. Total enrolment at the approximately 1,800 primary and lower secondary schools (Folkeskole) is equivalent to about 90% of the school-age population, including attendance by pupils outside the normal age range.

There are five universities and many other institutions of further and higher education. The traditional folk high schools offer a wide range of further education opportunities, which do not confer any professional qualification. In 1996 proposed government expenditure on education represented 6.7% of total budget spending.

Public Holidays

1998: 1 January (New Year's Day), 9–13 April (Easter), 8 May (General Prayer Day), 21 May (Ascension Day), 1 June (Whit Monday), 5 June (Constitution Day), 25–26 December (Christmas).

1999: 1 January (New Year's Day), 1–5 April (Easter), 30 April (General Prayer Day), 13 May (Ascension Day), 24 May (Whit Monday), 5 June (Constitution Day), 25–26 December (Christmas).

Weights and Measures

The metric system is in force.

Statistical Survey

Note: The figures in this survey relate only to metropolitan Denmark, excluding the Faroe Islands and Greenland, which are dealt with in separate chapters (see pp. 1152 and 1155 respectively).

Source (unless otherwise stated): Danmarks Statistik, Sejrøgade 11, POB 2550, 2100 Copenhagen Ø; tel. 39-17-39-17; telex 16236; fax 31-18-48-01.

Area and Population

AREA, POPULATION AND DENSITY

Area (sq km)	43,094*
Population (census results)	
1 January 1981	5,123,989
1 January 1991	
Males	2,536,391
Females	2,610,078
Total	5,146,469
Population (official estimates at 1 January)	
1995	5,215,718
1996	5,251,027
1997	5,275,000†
Density (per sq km) at 1 January 1997	122.4†

* 16,639 sq miles.

† Provisional.

PRINCIPAL TOWNS (population at 1 January 1996)

København (Copenhagen, the capital)	1,362,264*	Kolding	60,040
Århus (Aarhus)	279,759	Herning	57,965
Odense	183,564	Helsingør (Elsinore)	57,421
Ålborg (Aalborg)	159,980	Horsens	55,747
Esbjerg	82,905	Vejle	53,261
Randers	62,013	Roskilde	51,423
		Sikeborg	51,166

* Copenhagen metropolitan area, including Frederiksberg and 26 suburb municipalities. The estimated population of the Copenhagen municipality was 476,751 at 1 January 1996.

BIRTHS, MARRIAGES AND DEATHS

	Registered live births		Registered marriages		Registered deaths	
	Number	Rate (per 1,000)	Number	Rate (per 1,000)	Number	Rate (per 1,000)
1989	61,351	12.0	30,894	6.0	59,397	11.6
1990	63,433	12.3	31,513	6.1	60,926	11.9
1991	64,358	12.5	31,099	6.0	59,581	11.6
1992	67,726	13.1	32,188	6.2	60,821	11.8
1993	67,371	13.0	31,638	6.1	62,809	12.1
1994	69,684	13.4	35,321	6.8	61,099	11.7
1995	69,796	13.2	34,736	6.6	63,216	12.0
1996*	67,675	12.9	n.a.	n.a.	61,085	11.6

* Provisional.

Expectation of life (years at birth, 1994/95): Males 72.6; Females 77.8.

CIVILIAN LABOUR FORCE EMPLOYED
(ISIC Major Divisions, '000 persons)

	1993	1994	1995
Agriculture, forestry and fishing	126.6	120.9	120.4
Mining and quarrying	2.3	2.3	2.3
Manufacturing	475.0	477.2	492.0
Electricity, gas and water	16.5	15.9	16.1
Construction	157.2	162.3	168.8
Trade, restaurants and hotels	327.3	326.7	337.8
Transport, storage and communications	173.9	172.7	174.6
Financing, insurance, real estate and business services	251.6	251.4	256.0
Community, social and personal services	955.3	941.9	943.8
Total	2,485.7	2,471.3	2,511.8

Agriculture

PRINCIPAL CROPS ('000 metric tons)

	1994	1995	1996
Wheat	3,725	4,599	4,758
Barley	3,446	3,898	3,953
Rye	423	495	343
Oats	206	158	164
Potatoes	1,359	1,441	1,617
Pulses	377	282	n.a.
Rapeseed	371	315	251
Sugar beet	3,138	3,130	3,064

LIVESTOCK ('000 head at June-July)

	1993	1994	1995
Horses	20.4	18.5	17.6
Cattle	2,195.5	2,104.9	2,090.4
Pigs	11,567.8	10,922.6	11,083.9
Sheep	157.4	144.9	145.2
Chickens	18,916.0	18,954.4	18,673.3
Turkeys	504.1	367.9	449.4
Ducks	448.8	509.1	472.0
Geese	29.0	20.2	24.7

1996 (mid-year estimates, '000 head): Horses 20; Cattle 2,093; Sheep 170; Pigs 10,842; Poultry 19,224.

LIVESTOCK PRODUCTS ('000 metric tons)

	1993	1994	1995
Beef and veal	223.7	210.2	200.3
Pig meat	1,588.4	1,604.3	1,581.8
Poultry meat	172.2	185.4	184.0
Cows' milk	4,660.4	4,642.2	4,676.2
Butter	59.4	59.3	54.4
Cheese	323.3	288.1	311.2
Eggs	87.1	90.1	94.9

1996 ('000 metric tons): Cows' milk 4,695; Eggs 88.

Forestry

ROUNDWOOD REMOVALS ('000 cu m, excl. bark)

	1992	1993	1994
Sawlogs, veneer logs and logs for sleepers	880	886	875
Pulpwood	513	633	644
Other industrial wood	350*	352	351
Fuel wood	491	469	491
Total	2,234	2,340	2,361

* FAO estimate.

Source: FAO, *Yearbook of Forest Products.*

SAWNWOOD PRODUCTION ('000 cu m, incl. railway sleepers)

	1992	1993	1994*
Coniferous (softwood)	368	338	338
Broadleaved (hardwood)	252	245	245
Total	620	583	583

* FAO estimates.

Source: FAO, *Yearbook of Forest Products.*

Fishing*

('000 metric tons, live weight)

	1993	1994	1995
Trouts	41.1	42.3	41.3
European plaice	27.2	28.0	24.1
Atlantic cod	47.9	55.2	78.3
Norway pout	190.1	166.9	262.5
Blue whiting (Poutassou)	69.4	22.8	46.2
Sandeels (Sandlances)	631.5	839.8	844.5
Atlantic horse mackerel	49.4	53.6	56.2
Atlantic herring	169.5	177.5	191.4
European pilchard (sardine)	53.4	39.3	36.2
European sprat (brisling)	136.9	240.2	258.2
Atlantic mackerel	42.1	46.8	36.8
Other fishes (incl. unspecified)	48.3	55.5	39.8
Total fish	1,506.6	1,768.1	1,915.5
Crustaceans	10.3	16.2	15.1
Blue mussel	136.7	129.3	107.4
Other aquatic animals	2.2	2.8	3.1
Total catch	1,655.8	1,916.4	2,041.1
Inland waters	35.7	36.4	35.7
Atlantic Ocean	1,620.1	1,880.0	2,005.5

* Data include quantities landed by Danish fishing craft in foreign ports and exclude quantities landed by foreign fishing craft in Danish ports.

Source: FAO, *Yearbook of Fishery Statistics.*

Mining

('000 metric tons)

	1992	1993	1994
Crude petroleum	7,611	8,298	9,161
Salt (unrefined)	528	591	634
Sulphur*	7	10	7
Limestone flux and calcareous stone	1,024	803	955

* Sulphur of all kinds, other than sublimed sulphur, precipitated sulphur and colloidal sulphur.

Natural gas ('000 terajoules): 157 in 1992; 175 in 1993; 191 in 1994 (Source: UN, *Industrial Commodity Statistics Yearbook*).

Industry

SELECTED PRODUCTS ('000 metric tons, unless otherwise indicated)

	1992	1993	1994
Pig meat:			
Fresh, chilled or frozen	845	918	1,009
Salted, dried or smoked	112	106	119
Poultry meat and offals	138	151	149
Fish fillets: fresh, chilled, frozen	87	43	76
Salami, sausages, etc.	89	100	107
Meat in airtight containers:			
Hams	57	62	70
Other meat	34	36	40
Beet and cane sugar (solid)	501	484	496
Beer ('000 hectolitres)	9,775	9,435	9,410
Flours, meals and pastes of fish	359	342	402
Oil cake and meal	215	207	197
Cigarettes (million)	11,439	10,980	11,448
Cement	2,072	2,270	2,427
Motor spirit (Petrol)	1,499	1,930	1,868
Motor and fuel oils	5,844	6,541	5,863
Powder asphalt	1,203	1,451	1,421
Washing powders, etc	n.a.	193	n.a.
Refrigerators for household use ('000)	164	143	161
New dwellings completed (number)	16,355	14,131	12,845
Electric energy (million kWh)	32,097	32,739	33,051
Manufactured gas ('000 gigajoules)	1,515	1,496	1,337

Finance

CURRENCY AND EXCHANGE RATES

Monetary Units

100 øre = 1 Danish krone (plural: kroner).

Sterling and Dollar Equivalents (30 September 1997)

£1 sterling = 10.863 kroner;
US $1 = 6.725 kroner;
1,000 Danish kroner = £92.05 = $148.70.

Average Exchange Rate (kroner per US $)

1994 6.361
1995 5.602
1996 5.799

BUDGET (million kroner)

Revenue	1994*	1995*	1996†
Income and property taxes	138,678	139,838	126,533
Customs and excise duties	141,658	149,355	157,060
Other revenue Interest (net)	62,175	66,029	71,963
Total	342,511	355,222	355,556

Expenditure	1994*	1995*	1996†
Ministry of Social Affairs	98,500	98,145	92,864
Ministry of Education	23,798	24,757	25,654
Ministry of Defence	16,409	15,944	14,860
Public corporations	2,682	4,240	4,754
Ministry of Agriculture and Fisheries‡	1,843	2,345	2,637
Ministry of Justice	7,956	7,965	7,787
Ministry of Finance	4,883	4,896	7,837
Other expenditure	226,166	224,499	223,901
Total	382,237	382,791	380,294

* Approved.
† Estimates.
‡ Until 1995 figure excluded expenditure on the fishing industry.

1997 (budget proposals, million kroner): Revenue 379,800; Expenditure 385,600.

1998 (budget proposals, million kroner): Revenue 397,100; Expenditure 390,900.

NATIONAL BANK RESERVES (million kroner)

	1993	1994	1995
Gold	4,339	3,789	3,531
IMF special drawing rights	580	1,107	880
European currency units	4,947	3,460	4,521
Gross foreign assets	62,818	44,658	53,578
Reserve position in IMF	2,876	2,616	8,818
Total official reserves	75,560	55,630	71,328

MONEY SUPPLY ('000 million kroner at 31 December)*

	1993	1994	1995
Notes and coins	25.8	28.9	30.6
Deposits at commercial and savings banks:			
Demand deposits	246.4	243.4	251.7
Savings deposits	29.7	27.0	31.8
Time savings deposits	114.7	94.6	96.0
Total	416.6	393.9	410.1

* Figures refer to the national definition of 'broad money'.

COST OF LIVING (Consumer Price Index; base: 1980 = 100)

	1993	1994	1995
Food	168	173	178
Fuel and power	186	185	185
Clothing and footwear	178	180	180
Rent	214	220	225
All items (incl. others)	187.8	191.6	195.6

NATIONAL ACCOUNTS

National Income and Product (million kroner at current prices)

	1993	1994	1995
Compensation of employees	469,864	485,088	512,222
Operating surplus	148,235	169,117	175,780
Domestic factor incomes	618,099	654,205	688,002
Consumption of fixed capital	139,200	141,800	143,731
Gross domestic product at factor cost	757,299	796,005	831,733
Indirect taxes	153,180	168,259	175,032
Less Subsidies	35,569	35,667	35,987
GDP in purchasers' values	874,910	928,597	970,778
Factor income from abroad	153,733	147,944	163,312
Less Factor income paid abroad	182,891	178,490	188,935
Gross national product	845,752	898,050	945,155
Less Consumption of fixed capital	139,200	141,800	143,731
National income in market prices	706,552	756,250	801,424
Other current transfers from abroad	12,006	10,850	12,135
Less Other current transfers paid abroad	18,892	20,908	21,155
National disposable income	699,666	746,193	792,404

Expenditure on the Gross Domestic Product
('000 million kroner at current prices)

	1994	1995	1996
Government final consumption expenditure	238.5	243.9	254.2
Private final consumption expenditure	498.3	519.7	544.1
Increase in stocks	−1.5	12.4	1.3
Gross fixed capital formation	134.7	152.0	167.6
Total domestic expenditure	870.0	928.0	967.2
Exports of goods and services	327.8	330.4	341.6
Less Imports of goods and services	272.3	290.8	298.4
GDP in purchasers' values	925.6	967.7	1,010.4
GDP at constant 1990 prices	859.1	881.8	903.3

Source: IMF, *International Financial Statistics.*

Gross Domestic Product by Economic Activity
(million kroner at factor cost)

	1993	1994	1995
Agriculture and hunting	25,463	27,943	32,198
Forestry and logging	910	982	906
Fishing	1,411	1,386	1,895
Mining and quarrying	7,106	7,667	7,225
Manufacturing	143,583	155,654	167,943
Electricity, gas and water	15,425	16,049	16,172
Construction	40,965	42,744	47,015
Wholesale and retail trade	94,380	98,721	96,683
Restaurants and hotels	10,909	12,169	11,921
Transport, storage and communication	72,088	77,214	79,261
Finance and insurance	14,263	20,511	20,593
Owner-occupied dwellings	77,657	79,097	80,057
Business services	52,243	53,082	57,649
Market services of education and health	10,397	10,653	10,779
Recreational and cultural services	8,789	10,118	10,414
Household services (incl. vehicle repairs)	22,057	23,661	24,515
Government services	171,911	176,675	183,466
Other producers	6,421	7,005	7,227
Sub-total	775,978	821,331	855,918
Less Imputed bank service charges	18,679	25,326	24,185
Total	757,299	796,005	831,733

BALANCE OF PAYMENTS (US $ million)

	1994	1995	1996
Exports of goods f.o.b.	41,741	48,901	48,660
Imports of goods f.o.b.	−34,300	−42,080	−41,347
Trade balance	7,441	6,820	7,313
Exports of services	13,661	14,800	15,699
Imports of services	−12,067	−14,074	−14,819
Balance on goods and services	9,035	7,546	8,193
Other income received	22,743	28,433	38,097
Other income paid	−27,385	−32,982	−42,544
Balance on goods, services and income	4,394	2,998	3,746
Current transfers received	2,261	2,580	2,137
Current transfers paid	−3,466	−3,970	−3,963
Current balance	3,189	1,607	1,920
Direct investment abroad	−4,162	−2,969	−2,510
Direct investment from abroad	5,006	4,139	773
Portfolio investment assets	−1,175	−1,171	−2,349
Portfolio investment liabilities	−10,596	7,487	7,865
Other investment assets	12,136	−1,330	−9,279
Other investment liabilities	−6,856	−6,341	8,532
Net errors and omissions	606	1,075	−1,390
Overall balance	−1,851	2,498	3,563

Source: IMF, *International Financial Statistics.*

External Trade

PRINCIPAL COMMODITIES (distribution by SITC, million kroner)

Imports c.i.f.	1993	1994*	1995*
Food and live animals	22,517	24,001.3	24,067.0
Fish (not marine mammals), crustaceans, molluscs and aquatic invertebrates	6,208	6,834.1	6,840.2
Animal feeding-stuff (excl. cereals)	4,462	4,253.0	3,732.7
Crude materials (inedible) except fuels	6,953	8,766.4	9,116.3
Mineral fuels, lubricants, etc.	12,115	11,726.5	10,885.0
Petroleum, petroleum products, etc	9,339	9,103.4	7,596.0
Chemicals and related products	22,417	25,142.1	27,349.0
Medicinal and pharmaceutical products	3,926	4,612.4	5,008.7
Plastics in primary forms	4,108	4,631.8	5,539.0
Basic manufactures	33,663	40,276.2	44,611.9
Paper, paperboard and manufactures	7,075	7,881.3	8,779.2
Textile yarn, fabrics, etc.	5,073	5,714.1	5,937.7
Iron and steel	6,745	8,878.0	10,214.0
Machinery and transport equipment	57,947	71,081.4	77,125.5
Machinery specialized for particular industries	4,996	6,042.8	7,033.4
General industrial machinery, equipment and parts	7,898	8,838.8	10,248.2
Office machines and automatic data-processing equipment	10,455	12,299.7	12,943.7
Telecommunications and sound equipment	6,098	7,446.8	8,189.0
Other electrical machinery, apparatus, etc.	8,857	10,239.6	11,358.0
Road vehicles (incl. air-cushion vehicles) and parts†	11,619	16,877.8	18,325.5
Other transport equipment†	4,143	4,875.1	3,637.0
Miscellaneous manufactured articles	27,114	30,021.6	30,667.1
Clothing and accessories (excl. footwear)	8,498	9,533.6	10,089.2
Total (incl. others)	191,325	219,213.9	232,279.5

* Provisional figures.
† Data on parts exclude tyres, engines and electrical parts.

Exports f.o.b.	1993	1994*	1995*
Food and live animals	58,430	61,408.8	61,188.2
Meat and meat preparations	21,901	24,524.0	22,983.2
Dairy products and birds' eggs	9,230	9,433.9	9,657.5
Fish (not marine mammals), crustaceans, molluscs and aquatic invertebrates	13,363	12,374.6	12,238.5
Cereals and cereal preparations	4,678	4,529.9	5,424.2
Crude materials (inedible) except fuels	10,051	11,583.8	11,707.6
Mineral fuels, lubricants, etc.	8,384	9,743.9	8,318.8
Petroleum, petroleum products, etc.	6,650	7,832.3	6,700.0
Chemicals and related products	24,163	26,402.9	28,714.7
Medicinal and pharmaceutical products	9,501	10,848.4	12,601.5
Basic manufactures	25,029	28,021.7	31,140.0

Exports f.o.b. — *continued*	1993	1994*	1995*
Machinery and transport equipment	59,502	67,157.9	70,156.1
Power-generating machinery and equipment	3,934	4,715.7	5,714.2
Machinery specialized for particular industries	9,088	9,826.9	10,995.7
General industrial machinery, equipment and parts	17,310	18,575.4	20,444.6
Office machines and automatic data-processing equipment	3,875	5,730.5	4,782.8
Telecommunications and sound equipment	4,932	6,262.3	7,386.0
Other electrical machinery, apparatus, etc.	7,707	8,719.5	8,924.6
Road vehicles (incl. air-cushion vehicles) and parts†	4,639	4,609.0	5,038.7
Other transport equipment†	7,296	7,944.3	5,978.6
Miscellaneous manufactured articles	39,940	42,269.5	43,602.4
Furniture and parts	10,170	11,116.5	11,712.4
Clothing and accessories (excl. footwear)	6,726	6,744.4	7,110.6
Professional, scientific and controlling instruments, etc.	5,291	5,893.9	5,827.0
Total (incl. others)	232,884	254,929.7	263,502.8

* Provisional figures.
† Data on parts exclude tyres, engines and electrical parts.

PRINCIPAL TRADING PARTNERS (million kroner)

Imports c.i.f.	1993	1994*	1995*
Austria	2,273.4	2,249.1	2,310.5
Belgium/Luxembourg.	6,881.2	7,882.2	8,515.0
China, People's Republic	3,690.8	4,162.1	4,236.4
Finland	5,483.7	6,650.3	6,842.7
France (incl. Monaco)	10,071.0	11,893.2	12,538.9
Germany	43,350.4	47,839.8	52,221.3
Ireland	1,157.8	1,659.4	2,370.4
Italy	7,393.5	9,140.7	10,032.5
Japan	6,630.0	7,550.6	6,387.6
Korea, Republic	1,525.0	2,235.1	1,317.7
Netherlands	12,264.6	14,738.8	17,025.4
Norway	9,888.8	10,923.1	11,893.2
Poland	2,972.7	3,834.8	4,063.8
Portugal.	2,107.7	2,807.7	2,624.5
Russia	2,304.7	2,329.2	2,669.0
Spain	2,174.6	2,515.1	2,815.1
Sweden	20,819.6	24,920.4	28,316.0
Switzerland	4,282.6	4,072.2	4,071.1
United Kingdom	14,291.3	14,671.2	15,859.7
USA	9,188.7	11,100.3	11,511.3
Total (incl. others)	191,325.2	219,213.9	232,279.5

Exports f.o.b.	1993	1994*	1995*
Austria	2,486.3	2,689.9	2,785.4
Belgium/Luxembourg.	4,445.8	4,607.8	5,293.4
Finland	4,448.0	6,061.0	6,854.6
France (incl. Monaco)	12,491.4	13,354.7	14,604.9
Germany	55,354.3	57,701.6	61,135.5
Italy	9,402.3	9,466.4	9,871.0
Japan	9,467.5	10,484.4	10,531.6
Netherlands	9,973.9	10,699.4	11,943.8
Norway	16,156.5	16,308.7	16,113.0
Poland	3,100.2	3,630.8	3,752.7
Russia	1,797.4	2,707.2	3,645.6
Spain (excl. Canary Is.)	4,012.5	4,282.4	4,977.5
Sweden	23,392.2	26,349.4	26,188.3
Switzerland	4,245.4	4,831.2	4,920.9
United Kingdom	20,377.4	21,990.9	21,341.3
USA	12,300.6	13,909.6	11,004.6
Total (incl. others)	232,884.2	254,929.7	263,502.8

* Provisional figures.

Revised figures (million kroner): *Exports:* 262,365 in 1994; 278,515 in 1995; 290,609 in 1996. *Imports c.i.f.:* 220,769 in 1994; 252,343 in 1995; 258,010 in 1996. (Source: IMF, *International Financial Statistics.*)

Transport

RAILWAYS (traffic)

	1993	1994	1995
Number of journeys ('000)	139,982	141,127	140,382
Passenger-kilometres (million)	4,700	4,784	4,834
Ton-kilometres (million)	1,751	2,008	1,985

ROAD TRAFFIC (motor vehicles in use at 31 December)

	1993	1994	1995
Private cars	1,618,330	1,610,955	1,674,263
Taxis, hire cars, etc.	14,565	18,551	22,620
Buses, coaches	12,978	13,564	13,649
Vans, lorries	312,336	321,330	332,844
Tractors	130,271	127,610	125,875
Trailers	362,627	384,097	408,848
Motor cycles	47,405	49,194	51,946

SHIPPING

Danish Merchant Marine

(vessels exceeding 100 gross registered tons, at 1 January)

	1994		1995	
	Number	Gross tonnage	Number	Gross tonnage
Dry cargo	441	3,108,000	429	3,361,000
Tankers	109	1,612,000	105	1,573,000
Total	550	4,720,000	534	4,934,000

Sea-borne Freight Traffic at Danish Ports*

('000 metric tons loaded and unloaded)

	1993	1994	1995
Ålborg	2,790	2,765	2,976
Århus	5,268	6,321	6,283
Copenhagen	5,776	6,157	6,434
Fredericia	10,262	11,465	11,117
Kalundborg	6,137	5,933	7,208
Skaelskør	4,889	4,419	5,135
Others	35,350	37,636	40,729
Total	70,472	74,696	79,882

* Including domestic traffic, excluding international ferry traffic.

International Sea-borne Shipping* (freight traffic, '000 metric tons)

	1993	1994	1995
Goods loaded	19,297	20,682	20,284
Goods unloaded	33,056	35,885	37,314

* Excluding international ferry traffic.

CIVIL AVIATION (Scandinavian Airlines System)

	1993	1994	1995
Kilometres flown ('000)	225,583	217,185	218,483
Passengers carried ('000)	18,584	18,775	18,704
Passenger-kilometres (million)	18,137	18,466	18,506
Cargo and mail ton-kilometres (million)	470	496	502

Tourism

(income from visitors, million kroner)

	1993	1994	1995
Scandinavian visitors	5,070	4,399	4,400
German visitors	7,484	8,197	8,159
All other visitors	7,700	8,254	8,267
Total	20,254	20,850	20,827

OVERNIGHT STAYS (foreign visitors)

	1993	1994	1995
In hotels	5,913,000	5,932,247	5,885,205
At camping sites	4,104,300	4,233,520	4,448,611
Total	10,017,300	10,165,767	10,333,816

Source: The Danish Tourist Board.

Communications Media

	1993	1994	1995
Radio licences	2,131,000	2,148,000	2,155,000
Television licences (black and white)	101,000	82,000	64,000
Television licences (colour)	1,938,000	1,972,000	1,997,000
Number of newspapers	42	37	37
Total circulation (weekdays)	1,668,000	1,616,000	1,610,000
Books published (titles)*	11,492	11,973	12,478

* Including pamphlets (3,701 titles in 1993; 3,950 titles in 1994; 4,131 titles in 1995).

Telephones ('000 subscribers): 3,060 in 1993; 3,123 in 1994 (Source: UN, *Statistical Yearbook*).

Telefax stations: 185,000 in use in 1993 (Source: UN, *Statistical Yearbook*).

Mobile cellular telephones (subscribers): 357,590 in 1993; 503,500 in 1994 (Source: UN, *Statistical Yearbook*).

Education

(1993/94)

	Institutions	Teachers	Students
Pre-primary	2,341*	58,500†	605,704*
Primary			
Secondary: first stage			
Secondary: second stage			
General	153	11,000	102,277
Vocational	231	12,000	120,638
Teacher-training	18	8,000	166,614
Technical education	n.a.		
Universities	5		
Other university-level	146		

* Including 206 special schools.

† Full-time equivalents.

Directory

The Constitution

The constitutional charter (*Grundlov*), summarized below, was adopted on 5 June 1953.

GOVERNMENT

The form of government is a limited (constitutional) monarchy. The legislative authority rests jointly with the Crown and Parliament. Executive power is vested in the Crown, and the administration of justice is exercised by the courts. The Monarch can constitutionally 'do no wrong'. She exercises her authority through the Ministers appointed by her. The Ministers are responsible for the government of the country. The Constitution establishes the principle of Parliamentarism under which individual Ministers or the whole Cabinet must retire when defeated in Parliament by a vote of no confidence.

MONARCH

The Monarch acts on behalf of the State in international affairs. Except with the consent of the Parliament, she cannot, however, take any action which increases or reduces the area of the Realm or undertake any obligation, the fulfilment of which requires the co-operation of the Parliament or which is of major importance. Nor can the Monarch, without the consent of the Parliament, terminate any international agreement which has been concluded with the consent of the Parliament.

Apart from defence against armed attack on the Realm or on Danish forces, the Monarch cannot, without the consent of the Parliament, employ military force against any foreign power.

PARLIAMENT

The Parliament is an assembly consisting of not more than 179 members, two of whom are elected in the Faroe Islands and two in Greenland. It is called the Folketing. Danish nationals, having attained 18 years of age, with permanent residence in Denmark, have the franchise and are eligible for election. The members of the Folketing are elected for four years. Election is by a system of proportional representation, with direct and secret ballot on lists in large constituencies. A bill adopted by the Folketing may be submitted to referendum, when such referendum is claimed by not less than one-third of the members of the Folketing and not later than three days after the adoption. The bill is void if rejected by a majority of the votes cast, representing not less than 30% of all electors.

The Government

HEAD OF STATE

Queen of Denmark: HM Queen MARGRETHE II (succeeded to the throne 14 January 1972).

THE CABINET

(January 1998)

A coalition of the Social Democratic Party (SD) and the Social Liberals (SL).

Prime Minister: POUL NYRUP RASMUSSEN (SD).

Minister of Foreign Affairs: NIELS HELVEG PETERSEN (SL).

Minister of Economic Affairs and of Nordic Co-operation: MARIANNE JELVED (SL).

Minister of Finance: MOGENS LYKKETOFT (SD).

Minister of Business and of Industry: JAN TRØJBORG (SD).

Minister of Taxation: CARSTEN KOCH (SD).

Minister of Justice: FRANK JENSEN (SD).

Minister of Food, Agriculture and Fisheries: HENRIK DAM KRISTENSEN (SD).

Minister of Defence: HANS HÆKKERUP (SD).

Minister of the Interior and of Health: THORKILD SIMONSEN (SD).

Minister of Labour: JYTTE ANDERSEN (SD).

Minister of Transport: BJØRN WESTH (SD).

Minister of Development Co-operation: POUL NIELSON (SD).

Minister of Education and of Ecclesiastical Affairs: OLE VIG JENSEN (SL).

Minister of the Environment and of Energy: SVEND AUKEN (SD).

Minister of Social Affairs: KAREN JESPERSEN (SD).

Minister of Culture: EBBE LUNDGAARD (SL).

Minister of Housing and Building: OLE LØVIG SIMONSEN (SD).

Minister of Research: JYTTE HILDEN (SD).

MINISTRIES

Office of the Prime Minister: Christiansborg, Prins Jørgens Gård 11, 1218 Copenhagen K; tel. 33-92-33-00; telex 27027; fax 33-11-16-65.

Ministry of Business and Industry: Slotsholmsgade 10–12, 1216 Copenhagen K; tel. 33-92-33-50; telex 22373; fax 33-12-37-78; e-mail em@em.dk.

Ministry of Culture: Nybrogade 2, 1203 Copenhagen K; tel. 33-92-33-70; telex 27385; fax 33-91-33-88.

Ministry of Defence: Holmens Kanal 42, 1060 Copenhagen K; tel. 33-92-33-20; telex 27190; fax 33-32-06-55; e-mail fmn@fmn.dk.

Ministry of Economic Affairs: Ved Stranden 8, 1061 Copenhagen K; tel. 33-92-33-22; telex 16833; fax 33-93-60-20.

Ministry of Education: Frederiksholms Kanal 21, 1220 Copenhagen K; tel. 33-92-50-00; telex 16243; fax 33-92-55-47; e-mail uvm@uvm.dk.

Ministry of the Environment and of Energy: Højbro Plads 4, 1200 Copenhagen K; tel. 33-92-76-00; fax 33-32-22-27.

Ministry of Finance: Christiansborg Slotsplads 1, 1218 Copenhagen K; tel. 33-92-33-33; telex 43333; fax 33-32-80-30.

Ministry of Food, Agriculture and Fisheries: Holbergsgade 2, 1057 Copenhagen K; tel. 33-92-33-01; telex 27157; fax 33-14-50-42.

Ministry of Foreign Affairs: Asiatisk Plads 2, 1448 Copenhagen K; tel. 33-92-00-00; telex 31292; fax 31-54-05-33; e-mail um@um.dk.

Ministry of Health: Holbergsgade 6, 1057 Copenhagen K; tel. 33-92-33-60; fax 33-93-15-63; e-mail sum@sum.dk.

Ministry of Housing and Building: Slotsholmsgade 1, 1216 Copenhagen K; tel. 33-92-61-00; fax 33-92-61-04.

Ministry of the Interior: Christiansborg Slotsplads 1, 1218 Copenhagen K; tel. 33-92-33-80; fax 33-11-12-39.

Ministry of Justice: Slotsholmsgade 10, 1216 Copenhagen K; tel. 33-92-33-40; telex 15530; fax 33-93-35-10.

Ministry of Labour: Holmens Kanal 20, 1060 Copenhagen K; tel. 33-92-59-00; telex 19320; fax 33-12-13-78.

Ministry of Research and Information Policy: Bredgade 43, 1260 Copenhagen K; tel. 33-92-97-00; fax 33-32-35-01.

Ministry of Social Affairs: Holmens Kanal 22, 1060 Copenhagen K; tel. 33-92-93-00; telex 27343; fax 33-93-25-18.

Ministry of Transport: Frederiksholms Kanal 25–27, 1220 Copenhagen K; tel. 33-92-33-55; telex 22275; fax 33-12-38-93; e-mail trm@trm.dk; internet http://www.trm.dk.

Legislature

FOLKETING

President of the Folketing: ERLING OLSEN.

Secretary-General: OLE ANDERSEN.

General Election, 21 September 1994
(metropolitan Denmark only)

	% of votes	Seats
Social Democratic Party	34.6	62
Liberals	23.3	42
Conservative People's Party	15.0	27
Socialist People's Party	7.3	13
Progress Party	6.4	11
Social Liberals	4.6	8
Red-Green Alliance	3.1	6
Centre Democrats	2.8	5
Others	2.8	1
Total	100.0	175

The Folketing also includes two members from Greenland and two from the Faroe Islands.

Political Organizations

Centrum-Demokraterne (Centre Democrats): Folketinget, Christiansborg, 1240 Copenhagen K; tel. 33-37-48-77; fax 33-14-54-20; f. 1973; opposes extreme ideologies, supports EU and NATO; Leader MIMI JAKOBSEN; Nat. Chair. INGER BORIIS.

Danmarks Kommunistiske Parti (Danish Communist Party): Studiestræde 24, 1455 Copenhagen K; tel. 33-91-66-44; fax 33-32-03-72; f. 1919; Chair. MOGENS HØVER.

Danmarks kommunistiske Parti/Marxister Leninister: (Marxist-Leninist Party): Griffenfeldsgade 26, 2200 Copenhagen N; tel. 31-35-60-69; fax 35-37-20-39; Sec.-Gen. JØRGEN PETERSEN.

Danmarks Retsforbund (Justice Party): Landssekretariatet, Lyngbyvej 42, 2100 Copenhagen Ø; tel. 31-20-44-88; fax 31-20-44-50; f. 1919; programme is closely allied to Henry George's teachings (single tax, free trade); Chair. POUL GERHARD C. KRISTIANSEN.

Dansk Folkeparti (Danish People's Party): Copenhagen; f. 1995 by defectors from the Progress Party; Leader PIA KJAERSGAARD.

Enhedslisten–de rød-grønne (Red–Green Alliance): Studiestraede 24, 1455 Copenhagen K; tel. 33-93-33-24; fax 33-32-03-72; f. 1989 by three left-wing parties; membership of individual socialists; 21-mem. collective leadership.

Europæiske Centrum-Demokrater (European Centre Democrats): Christiansborg, 1240 Copenhagen K; tel. 33-11-66-00; f. 1974; supports co-operation within EU and provides information about the workings of the EU; Chair. MIMI JAKOBSEN.

Fælles Kurs (Common Course): Herluf Trolles Gade 5, 1052 Copenhagen K; tel. 33-14-44-18; fax 33-32-40-16; f. 1986; socialist; Chair. PREBEN MØLLER HANSEN.

Folkebevægelsen mod EF-Unionen (Danish People's Movement Against the European Union): Sigurdsgade 39A, 2200 Copenhagen N; tel. 35-82-18-00; fax 35-82-18-06; e-mail katte.ud@post/.tele.dk; opposes membership of the EU, in favour of self-determination for Denmark and all European countries; 21-mem. collective leadership.

Fremskridtspartiet (Progress Party): Folketinget, Christiansborg, 1240 Copenhagen K; tel. 33-37-46-49; fax 33-15-13-99; f. 1972; movement whose policies include gradual abolition of income tax, disbandment of most of the civil service, and abolition of diplomatic service and about 90% of legislation; Chair. JOHANNES SØRENSEN; Leader KIRSTEN JACOBSEN; Sec. Gen. MARTIN IPSEN.

De Grønne/Økologisk-realistik Alternativ (Green Party/The Realistic Ecological Alternative): Willemoesgade 16, 2100 Copenhagen Ø; tel. 31-38-00-97 f. 1983, reformed 1991.

Det Humanistiske Parti (The Humanist Party): Skt Jorgens Alle 7, 1615 Copenhagen V; tel. 31-24-70-60; pro-democratic, non-violent; Chair. CHRISTIAN ADAMSEN.

JuniBevægelsen (June Movement): Copenhagen; tel. 33-93-00-46; fax 33-93-30-67; e-mail juninet@inform-bbs.dk; f. 1992; opposes the EU; Leader JENS-PETER BONDE.

Kommunistisk Arbejderparti (Communist Workers' Party): Studiestraede 24, 1455 Copenhagen K; tel. 33-15-21-33; fax 33-33-86-56; f. 1968.

Det Konservative Folkeparti (Conservative People's Party): Nyhavn 4, POB 1515, 1020 Copenhagen K; tel. 33-13-41-40; fax 33-93-37-73; e-mail konservative@konservative.dk; f. 1916; advocates free initiative and the maintenance of private property, but recognizes the right of the State to take action to keep the economic and social balance; Leader PER STIG MOLLER ; Sec.-Gen. PETER STERUP.

Kristeligt Folkeparti (Christian People's Party): Bernhard Bangs Allé 23, 2000 Frederiksberg; tel. 38-88-51-52; fax 38-88-31-15; e-mail krf@krf.dk; internet http://www.krf.dk; f. 1970; emphasizes the need for political decisions based on Christian ethics; Chair. JANN SJURSEN; Sec.-Gen. PER BREINDAHL.

Det Radikale Venstre (Social Liberal Party): Christiansborg, 1240 Copenhagen K; tel. 33-37-47-47; fax 33-13-72-51; f. 1905; supports international *détente* and co-operation within regional and world organizations, social reforms without socialism, incomes policy, workers' participation in industry, state intervention in industrial disputes, state control of trusts and monopolies, strengthening private enterprise; Chair. JOHANNES LEBECH; Leader MARIANNE JELVED; Gen. Sec. ANDERS KLOPPENBORG.

Schleswigsche Partei (Schleswig Party): Vestergade 30, 6200 Åbenrå; tel. 74-62-38-33; fax 74-62-79-39; f. 1920; represents the German minority in North Schleswig; Chair. PETER BIELING.

Socialdemokratiet (Social Democratic Party): Thorvaldsensvej 2, 1780 Copenhagen V; tel. 31-39-15-22; fax 31-39-40-30; e-mail socialdemokratiet@net.dialog.dk; internet http://www.socialdemokratiet.dk; f. 1871; finds its chief adherents among workers, employees and public servants; 70,000 mems; Leader POUL NYRUP RASMUSSEN; Gen. Sec. WILLY STIG ANDERSEN.

Socialistisk Arbejderparti (Socialist Workers' Party): Norre Allé 11A, POB 547, 2200 Copenhagen N; tel. 31-39-79-48; fax 35-37-32-17.

Socialistisk Folkeparti (Socialist People's Party): Folketinget, Christiansborg, 1240 Copenhagen K; tel. 33-12-70-11; fax 33-14-70-10; internet http://www.sf.dk; f. 1959 by Aksel Larsen; socialist; Chair. HOLGER K. NIELSEN; Parliamentary Leader JES LUNDE; Sec. OLE HVAS KRISTIANSEN.

Venstre (Liberal Party): Søllerødvej 30, 2840 Holte; tel. 42-80-22-33; fax 42-80-38-30; f. 1870; supports free trade, a minimum of state interference, and the adoption, in matters of social expenditure, of a modern general social security system; 82,300 mems; Pres. UFFE ELLEMANN-JENSEN; Sec.-Gen. CLAUS HJORT FREDERIKSEN.

Diplomatic Representation

EMBASSIES IN DENMARK

Argentina: Store Kongensgade 45, 1264 Copenhagen K; tel. 33-15-80-82; fax 33-15-55-74; Ambassador: VICENTE ERNESTO BERASATEGUI.

Austria: Sølundsvej 1, 2100 Copenhagen Ø; tel. 39-29-41-41; telex 27023; fax 39-29-20-86; Ambassador: Dr ROBERT MARSCHIK.

Belgium: Øster Allé 7, 2100 Copenhagen Ø; tel. 35-25-02-00; telex 22624; fax 35-25-02-11; Ambassador: BAUDOUIN DE LA KETHULLE DE RYHOVE.

Bolivia: Amaliegade 16C, 2nd Floor, 1256 Copenhagen K; tel. 33-12-49-00; fax 33-12-49-03; e-mail embodk-1@inet.uni-c.dk; Chargé d'affaires: ESTHER MARIA ASHTON.

Bosnia and Herzegovina: Nytorv 3, 1450 Copenhagen K; tel. 33-33-80-40; fax 33-33-80-17; e-mail iobih@inet.uni-c.dk; Chargé d'affaires a.i.: Dr NENAD TANOVIĆ.

Brazil: Ryvangs Allé 24, 2100 Copenhagen Ø; tel. 31-20-64-78; fax 39-27-36-07; Ambassador: JOSÉ VIEGAS FILHO.

Bulgaria: Gamlehave Allé 7, 2920 Charlottenlund; tel. 39-64-24-84; telex 27020; fax 39-63-49-23; Ambassador: KROUM DIMITROV SLAVOV.

Burkina Faso: Svanemøllevej 20, 2100 Copenhagen Ø; tel. 31-18-40-22; telex 19375; fax 39-27-18-86; Ambassador: ANNE KONATÉ.

Canada: Kr. Bernikowsgade 1, 1105 Copenhagen K; tel. 33-12-22-99; fax 33-14-05-85; Ambassador: BRIAN ELLISON BAKER.

Chile: Kastelsvej 15, 3rd Floor, 2100 Copenhagen Ø; tel. 31-38-58-34; telex 15099; fax 31-38-42-01; Ambassador: RAÚL SCHMIDT.

China, People's Republic: Øregårds Allé 25, 2900 Hellerup; tel. 39-46-08-89; telex 27019; fax 39-62-54-84; Ambassador: YANG HEXIONG.

Colombia: Kastelsvej 15, 2100 Copenhagen Ø; tel. 35-26-30-26; telex 27072; fax 35-26-22-97; Chargé d'affaires a.i.: CARLOS ARTURO MORALES.

Côte d'Ivoire: Gersonsvej 8, 2900 Hellerup; tel. 39-62-88-22; telex 22351; fax 39-62-01-62; Ambassador: LILIANE MARIE-LAURE BOA.

Croatia: Dronningens Tværgade 5, 1st Floor, 1302 Copenhagen K; tel. 33-91-33-94; fax 33-91-71-31; Ambassador: MARIO MIKOLIĆ.

Cuba: Esplanaden 14, 2nd Floor, 1263 Copenhagen K; tel. 33-16-10-18; fax 33-16-10-18; Chargé d'affaires a.i.: TERESITA VICENTE SOTOLONGO.

Czech Republic: Ryvangs Allé 14-16, 2100 Copenhagen Ø; tel. 39-29-18-88; fax 39-29-09-30; Ambassador: ALOIS BUCHTA.

Egypt: Kristianiagade 19, 2100 Copenhagen Ø; tel. 35-43-70-70; telex 19892; fax 35-43-36-49; Ambassador: TAHER A. KHALIFA.

Estonia: Aurehøjvej 19, 2900 Hellerup; tel. 39-40-26-66; fax 39-40-26-30; e-mail jkhan@estemb.dk; Ambassador: JÜRI KAHN.

Finland: Skt Annae Plads 24, 1250 Copenhagen K; tel. 33-13-42-14; fax 33-32-47-10; e-mail webmaster@finamb.dk; Ambassador: RALF FRIBERG.

France: Kongens Nytorv 4, 1050 Copenhagen K; tel. 33-15-51-22; fax 33-93-97-52; Ambassador: JACQUES-ALAIN DE SÉDOUY.

Germany: Stockholmsgade 57, POB 2712, 2100 Copenhagen Ø; tel. 35-26-16-22; telex 27166; fax 35-26-71-05; Ambassador: JOHANN DREHER.

Ghana: Egebjerg Allé 13, 2900 Hellerup; tel. 39-62-82-22; telex 19471; fax 39-62-16-52; Ambassador: Prof. MARTHA DODOO-TAMAKLOE.

Greece: Borgergade 16, 1300 Copenhagen K; tel. 33-11-45-33; telex 22911; fax 33-93-16-46; Ambassador: ANASTASE SCOPELITIS.

Holy See: Immortellevej 11, 2950 Vedbaek (Apostolic Nunciature); tel. 42-89-35-36; fax 45-66-17-71; Apostolic Nuncio: Most Rev. GIOVANNI CEIRANO, Titular Archbishop of Tagase.

Hungary: Strandvejen 170, 2920 Charlottenlund; tel. 39-63-16-88; fax 39-63-00-52; e-mail ambassador.cph@humfa.kum.hu; Ambassador: Dr ANDRÁS HAJDU.

Iceland: Dantes Plads 3, 1556 Copenhagen V; tel. 33-15-96-04; fax 33-93-05-06; Ambassador: RÓBERT TRAUSTI ÁRNASON.

India: Vangehusvej 15, 2100 Copenhagen Ø; tel. 31-18-28-88; telex 15964; fax 39-27-02-18; e-mail inemb@euroconnect.dk; Ambassador: NEELAM DEO.

Indonesia: Ørehøj Allé 1, 2900 Hellerup; tel. 39-62-44-22; telex 16274; fax 39-62-44-83; e-mail indon-dkocybernet.dk; internet http://www.cybernet.dk/users/indon.dk; Ambassador: ANDJAR SOEDJITO MANGKOEWIJOTO.

Iran: Grønningen 5, 1270 Copenhagen K; tel. 33-14-91-34; telex 16979; fax 33-14-98-94; Ambassador: MOHAMMAD MEHDI POURMOHAMMADI.

Ireland: Østbanegade 21, 2100 Copenhagen Ø; tel. 31-42-32-33; fax 35-43-18-58; Ambassador: JAMES ANTHONY SHARKEY.

Israel: Lundevangsvej 4, 2900 Hellerup; tel. 39-62-62-88; fax 39-62-19-38; e-mail israel@pip.dknet.dk; Ambassador: ABRAHAM SETTON.

Italy: Gammel Vartov Vej 7, 2900 Hellerup; tel. 39-62-68-77; telex 27078; fax 39-62-25-99; Ambassador: GIACOMO IVANCICH-BIAGGINI.

Japan: Pilestræde 61, 1112 Copenhagen K; tel. 33-11-33-44; telex 27082; fax 33-11-33-77; Ambassador: MASAKI ORITA.

Korea, Democratic People's Republic: Skelvej 2, 2900 Hellerup; tel. and fax 39-62-50-70; Ambassador: RI THAE GYUN.

Korea, Republic: Svanemøllevej 104, 2900 Hellerup; tel. 39-46-04-00; fax 39-46-04-22; Ambassador: JONG-KI PARK.

Latvia: Rosbæksvej 17, 2100 Copenhagen Ø; tel. 39-27-60-00; fax 39-27-61-73; Ambassador: GVIDO ZEMRIBO.

Lesotho: Tuborg Nord, Strandvejen 64H, 2900 Hellerup; tel. 39-62-43-43; telex 16687; fax 39-62-15-38; Ambassador: SEYMOUR REHAUHELE KIKINE.

Libya: Rosenvaengets Hovedvej 4, 2100 Copenhagen Ø; tel. 35-26-36-11; telex 22652; fax 35-26-56-06; Chargé d'affaires a.i.: FAUZI MILAD ABU-ARGUB.

Lithuania: Bernstorffsvej 214, 2920 Charlottenlund; tel. 39-63-62-07; fax 39-63-65-32; Ambassador: Dr RAIMUNDAS JASINEVIČIUS.

Luxembourg: Fridtjof Nansens Plads 5, 1st Floor, 2100 Copenhagen Ø; tel. 35-26-82-00; telex 40883; fax 35-26-82-08; Ambassador: FRANÇOIS BREMER.

Macedonia, former Yugoslav republic: Vestagervej 7, 2100 Copenhagen Ø; tel. 39-27-43-14; fax 39-27-43-15; Ambassador: MUHAMED HALILI.

Mexico: Strandvejen 64E, 2900 Hellerup; tel. 39-61-05-00; fax 39-61-05-12; e-mail embmxdin@inet.uni-c.dk; Ambassador: WALTER ASTIÉ-BURGOS.

Morocco: Øregårds Allé 19, 2900 Hellerup; tel. 39-62-45-11; telex 22913; fax 39-62-24-49; Ambassador: (vacant).

Netherlands: Toldbodgade 33, 1253 Copenhagen K; tel. 33-15-62-93; fax 33-14-03-50; Ambassador: JOHANNES HUBERTUS WILHELMUS FIETELAARS.

Norway: Amaliegade 39, 1256 Copenhagen K; tel. 33-14-01-24; fax 33-14-06-24; Ambassador: THORVALD STOLTENBERG.

Pakistan: Valeursvej 17, 2900 Hellerup; tel. 39-62-11-88; telex 19348; fax 39-40-10-70; e-mail parep-dk@post4.tele.dk; Ambassador: ASIF EZDI.

Peru: Rosenvaengets Allé 20, 2100 Copenhagen Ø; tel. 35-26-58-48; fax 35-26-84-06; e-mail perudk@post6.tele.dk; Chargé d'affaires: JOSÉ BERAÚN ARANIBAR.

Poland: Richelieus Allé 12, 2900 Hellerup; tel. 39-62-72-44; telex 19264; fax 39-62-71-20; e-mail ambaspol@post4.tele.dk; Ambassador: JAN GÓRECKI.

Portugal: Hovedvagtsgade 6, 1103 Copenhagen K; tel. 33-13-13-01; telex 16586; fax 33-14-92-14; Ambassador: RUI FERNANDO DE MEIRA FERREIRA.

Romania: Strandagervej 27, 2900 Hellerup; tel. 39-40-71-77; fax 39-62-78-99; Ambassador: Dr GRETE TARTLER TĂBĂRAŞI.

Russia: Kristianiagade 5, 2100 Copenhagen Ø; tel. 31-42-55-85; telex 16943; fax 31-42-37-41; Ambassador: ALEKSANDR CHEPURIN.

Saudi Arabia: Lille Strandvej 27, 2900 Hellerup; tel. 31-62-12-00; telex 15931; fax 39-62-60-09; Ambassador: (vacant).

Slovakia: Vesterled 26–28, 2100 Copenhagen Ø; tel. 31-20-99-11; fax 31-20-99-13; e-mail dko12084@vip.cybercity.dk; Chargé d'affaires a.i.: IVAN SURKOŠ.

South Africa: Gammel Vartov Vej 8, POB 128, 2900 Hellerup; tel. 31-18-01-55; fax 31-18-40-06; Ambassador: THEMBA MUZIWAKHE NICHOLAS KUBHEKA.

Spain: Upsalagade 26, 1st Floor, 2100 Copenhagen Ø; tel. 31-42-47-00; fax 35-26-30-99; Ambassador: JOSÉ LUIS PARDOS PÉREZ.

Swaziland: Kastelsvej 19, 2100 Copenhagen Ø; tel. 31-42-61-11; telex 15810; fax 31-42-63-00; Ambassador: Prince DAVID DLAMINI.

Sweden: Skt Annæ Plads 15A, 1250 Copenhagen K; tel. 33-36-03-70; telex 22933; fax 33-36-03-95; Ambassador: HÅKAN BERGGREN.

Switzerland: Amaliegade 14, 1256 Copenhagen K; tel. 33-14-17-96; fax 33-33-75-51; Ambassador: ANDRÉ VON GRAFFENRIED.

Thailand: Norgesmindevej 18, 2900 Hellerup; tel. 39-62-50-10; telex 16216; fax 39-62-50-59; Ambassador: APIPHONG JAYANAMA.

Turkey: Rosbæksvej 15, 2100 Copenhagen Ø; tel. 31-20-27-88; telex 27476; fax 31-20-51-66; Ambassador: TURAN MORALI.

Uganda: Sofievej 15, 2900 Hellerup; tel. 39-62-09-66; telex 15689; fax 39-61-01-48; Ambassador: OMAR MIGADDE LUBULWA.

Ukraine: Toldbodgade 37A, 1st Floor, 1253 Copenhagen K; tel. 33-16-16-35; fax 33-16-00-74; Chargé d'affaires a.i.: VASSYL YAKOVENKO.

United Kingdom: Kastelsvej 36–40, 2100 Copenhagen Ø; tel. 35-44-52-00; fax 35-44-52-93; e-mail brit-emb@post6.tele.dk; Ambassador: ANDREW PHILIP FOLEY BACHE.

USA: Dag Hammarskjølds Allé 24, 2100 Copenhagen Ø; tel. 35-55-31-44; telex 22216; fax 35-43-02-23; Ambassador: EDWARD E. ELSON.

Venezuela: Holbergsgade 14, 3rd Floor, 1057 Copenhagen K; tel. 33-93-63-11; fax 33-15-69-11; e-mail emvendk@post7.tele.dk; Ambassador: HUGO ALVAREZ PIFANO.

Yugoslavia: Svanevænget 36, 2100 Copenhagen Ø; tel. 39-29-71-61; fax 39-29-79-19; Ambassador: (vacant).

Judicial System

In Denmark the judiciary is independent of the Government. Judges are appointed by the Crown on the recommendation of the Minister of Justice and cannot be dismissed except by judicial sentence.

The ordinary courts are divided into three instances, the Lower Courts, the High Courts and the Supreme Court. There is one Lower Court for each of the 82 judicial districts in the country. These courts must have at least one judge trained in law and they hear the majority of minor cases. The two High Courts serve Jutland and the islands respectively. They serve as appeal courts for cases from the lower courts, but are also used to give first hearing to the more important cases. Each case must be heard by at least three judges. The Supreme Court, at which at least five judges must sit, is the court of appeal for cases from the Higher Courts. Usually only one appeal is allowed from either court, but in special instances the Board of Appeal may give leave for a second appeal, to the Supreme Court, from a case which started in a lower court. Furthermore, in certain minor cases, appeal from the Lower Courts to the High Courts is allowed only by leave of appeal from the Board of Appeal.

There is a special Maritime and Commercial Court in Copenhagen, consisting of a President and two Vice-Presidents with legal training and a number of commercial and nautical assessors; and also a Labour Court, which deals with labour disputes.

An Ombudsman is appointed by Parliament, after each general election, and is concerned with defects in the laws or administrative provisions. He must present an annual report to Parliament.

President of the Supreme Court: N. E. PONTOPPIDAN.

President of the East High Court: SVEN ZIEGLER.

President of the West High Court: BJARNE CHRISTENSEN.

President of the Maritime and Commercial Court: EMIL FRANK POULSEN.

President of the Labour Court: PALLE KIIL.

Ombudsman: HANS GAMMELTOFT-HANSEN.

Religion

CHRISTIANITY

Det Økumeniske Faellesraad i Danmark (Ecumenical Council of Denmark): Dag Hammarskjölds Allé 17/3, 2100 Copenhagen Ø; tel. 35-43-29-43; fax 35-43-29-44; e-mail kill@inform-66s.dk; f. 1939; associate council of the World Council of Churches; six mem. churches, one observer; Chair. Dr ANNA-MARIE AAGAARD; Gen. Sec. HOLGER LAM.

The National Church

Den evangelisk-lutherske Folkekirke i Danmark (Evangelical Lutheran Church in Denmark): Nørregade 11, 1165 Copenhagen K; tel. 33-13-35-08; fax 33-14-39-69; the established Church of Denmark, supported by the State; no bishop exercises a presiding role, but the Bishop of Copenhagen is responsible for certain co-ordinating questions. The Church of Denmark Council on Inter-Church Relations (Vestergade 8, 1456 Copenhagen K; tel. 33-11-44-88) is responsible for ecumenical relations. Membership in 1995 was 4,539,773 (87% of the population).

Bishop of Copenhagen: ERIK NORMAN SVENDSEN.

Bishop of Helsingør: LISE LOTTE REBEL.

Bishop of Roskilde: B. WIBERG.

Bishop of Lolland-Falster: HOLGER JEPSEN.

Bishop of Odense: KRESTEN DREJERGAARD.

Bishop of Ålborg: SØREN LODBERG HVAS.

Bishop of Viborg: KARSTEN NISSEN.

Bishop of Århus: KJELD HOLM.

Bishop of Ribe: NIELS HOLM.

Bishop of Haderslev: O. LINDEGÅRD.

The Roman Catholic Church

Denmark comprises a single diocese, directly responsible to the Holy See. At 31 December 1996 there were an estimated 32,756 adherents in the country. The Bishop participates in the Scandinavian Episcopal Conference (based in Sweden).

Bishop of Copenhagen: Czeslaw Kozon, Katolsk Bispekontor, Bredgade 69a, 1260 Copenhagen K; tel. 33-11-60-80; fax 33-14-60-86.

Other Churches

Apostolic Church in Denmark: Lykkegaards vej 100, 6000 Kolding; tel. 75-54-12-01; fax 75-52-11-64; e-mail akm@apostolic.dk; Nat. Leader Jens Erik Jacobsen.

Church of England: St Alban's House, Stigårdsvej 6, 2900 Hellerup; tel. and fax 39-62-77-36; f. 1728; Chaplain Rev. T. O. Mendel.

Church of Jesus Christ of Latter-day Saints (Mormons): Rødovre; tel. 31-70-90-43; f. in Denmark 1850; 4,500 mems.

Danish Mission Covenant Church: Rosenlunden 17, 5000 Odense C; tel. 66-14-83-99; fax 66-14-83-00; Rev. Leo Hansen.

Det Danske Baptistsamfund (Baptist Union of Denmark): Købnerhus, Laerdalsgade 7, 2300 Copenhagen S; tel. 31-59-07-08; fax 31-59-01-33; f. 1839; 6,000 mems; Pres. Knud Rønne-Hansen; Gen. Sec. Rev. Ole Jörgensen.

First Church of Christ, Scientist: Nyvej 7, 1851 Frederiksberg C; tel. 33-13-08-91; also in Århus; tel. 86-16-22-78.

German Lutheran Church: Skt Petri Church Office, Larslejsstraede 11, 1451 Copenhagen K; tel. 33-13-38-34; fax 33-13-38-35.

Methodist Church: Metodistkirkens Social Arbejde, Rigensgade 21a, 1316 Copenhagen K; f. 1910; tel. 33-93-25-96; Chair. Thomas Hjorth; Pastor Ejler Busch Andersen.

Moravian Brethren: The Moravian Church, 6070 Christiansfeld; f. in Denmark 1773; Pastor Helge Rønnow, Lindegade 26, 6070 Christiansfeld; tel. 74-56-14-20.

Norwegian Lutheran Church: Kong Håkons Kirke, Ved Mønten 9, 2300 Copenhagen S; tel. 31-57-11-03; fax 31-57-40-05; f.1958.

Reformed Church: Reformed Synod of Denmark, Nørrebrogade 32a, 7000 Fredericia; tel. 75-92-05-51; Rev. Sabine Hofmeister.

Russian Orthodox Church: Alexander Nevski Church, Bredgade 53, 1260 Copenhagen K; tel. 33-13-60-46.

Seventh-day Adventists: Adventistsamfundet, Concordiavej 16, 2850 Naerum; tel. 45-80-56-00; fax 45-80-70-75; f. 1863; Pres. Carl-David Andreassen; Sec. Richard Müller.

Society of Friends: Danish Quaker Centre, Vendersgade 29, 1363 Copenhagen K; tel. 33-11-82-48.

Swedish Lutheran Church: Svenska Gustafskyrkan, Folke Bernadottes Allé, 2100 Copenhagen Ø; tel. 33-15-54-58; fax 33-15-02-94.

Unitarians: Unitarernes Hus, Dag Hammarskjølds Allé 30, 2100 Copenhagen Ø; Chair. P. Bovin; mems: 100 families.

The Salvation Army is also active in the country (Frederiksberg Allé 9, 1621 Copenhagen V; tel. 31-31-41-92).

BAHÁ'Í FAITH

Bahá'í: Det Nationale Åndelige Råd, Sofievej 28, 2900 Hellerup; tel. 39-62-35-18; fax 39-62-17-80; e-mail bahaidenmarknsa@vip.cybercily.dk; National Centre for the Bahá'í faith in Denmark.

ISLAM

The Muslim Community: Nusrat Djahan Mosque (and Ahmadiyya Mission), Eriksminde Allé 2, 2650 Hvidovre, Copenhagen; tel. 36-75-35-02; telex 16600; fax 36-75-00-07.

JUDAISM

Jewish Community: The Synagogue, Krystalgade 12, Copenhagen; Mosaisk Trossamfund, Ny Kongensgade 6, 1472 Copenhagen K; tel. 33-12-88-68; fax 33-12-33-57; 5,000 mems; Chief Rabbi Bent Lexner.

The Press

There are more than 220 separate newspapers, including some 37 principal dailies. The average total circulation of newspapers in 1995 was 1,610,000 on weekdays.

Most newspapers and magazines are privately owned and published by joint concerns, co-operatives or limited liability companies. The main concentration of papers is held by the Berlingske Tidende Group which owns *Berlingske Tidende, Weekendavisen, B.T.,* the provincial *Jydske Vestkysten* and *Amtsavisen,* and three weekly magazines. Another company, Politiken A/S, owns several dailies, including *Politiken* and *Ekstra Bladet*, one weekly and a large publishing house. De Bergske Blade owns a group of four Liberal papers.

There is no truly national press. Copenhagen accounts for 20% of the national dailies and about half the total circulation. No paper is directly owned by a political party, although all papers show a fairly pronounced political leaning.

PRINCIPAL DAILIES

Ålborg

Aalborg Stiftstidende: Langagervej 1, 9220 Ålborg Ø; tel. 99-35-35-35; telex 69747; fax 99-35-33-75; f. 1767; weekday evenings; Saturday and Sunday mornings; Liberal independent; Publr and Editor-in-Chief Erling Bröndum; approx. circ. weekdays 131,738, Sundays 192,068.

Århus

Århuus Stiftstidende: Olof Palmes Allé 39, 8200 Århus N; tel. 86-78-40-00; fax 86-78-44-00; f. 1794; evening and weekend mornings; Liberal independent; Editors Åge Lundgård, Hans Petersen; circ. weekdays 64,384, Sundays 82,755.

Copenhagen

Berlingske Tidende: Pilestraede 34, 1147 Copenhagen K; tel. 33-75-75-75; telex 27143; fax 33-75-20-20; f. 1749; morning; Conservative independent; Editor-in-Chief Anne E. Jensen; circ. weekdays 160,000, Sundays 195,000.

Børsen: Møntergade 19, 1140 Copenhagen K; tel. 33-32-01-02; fax 33-12-24-45; f. 1896; morning; independent; business news; Editor-in-Chief Leif Beck Fallesen; circ. 41,800.

B.T.: Kr. Bernikowsgade 6, 1147 Copenhagen K; tel. 33-75-75-33; fax 33-75-20-33; f. 1916; morning; Conservative independent; Editor-in-Chief Poul-Erik Thomsen; circ. weekdays 175,648, Sundays 201,033.

Ekstra Bladet: Rådhuspladsen 37, 1785 Copenhagen V; tel. 33-11-13-13; telex 22300; fax 33-14-10-00; f. 1904; evening; Liberal independent; Editor-in-Chief S. O. Gade; Man. Dir N. Meyer; circ. weekdays 170,983, Sundays 193,052.

Det Fri Aktuelt: Rådhuspladsen 45–47, 1595 Copenhagen V; tel. 33-32-40-01; telex 19785; fax 33-13-00-48; f. 1871; morning; Social Democratic; Editor-in-Chief and Man. Dir Lisbeth Knudsen; circ. weekdays 40,000.

Information: Store Kongensgade 40, POB 188, 1006 Copenhagen K; tel. 33-69-60-00; fax 33-69-61-32; f. 1943 (underground during occupation), legally 1945; morning; independent; Editors Jacob Mollerup, Jørgan Steen Nielsen; circ. 25,000.

Kristeligt Dagblad: Rosengården 14, 1174 Copenhagen K; tel. 33-48-05-00; fax 33-48-05-01; f. 1896; morning; independent; Editor Erik Bjerager; circ. 15,844.

Politiken: Politikens Hus, Rådhuspladsen 37, 1585 Copenhagen V; tel. 33-11-85-11; telex 16885; fax 33-15-41-17; f. 1884; morning; Liberal independent; Editor-in-Chief Toeger Seidenfaden; circ. weekdays 158,876, Sundays 207,136.

Esbjerg

Jydske Vestkysten: Banegårdspladsen, 6700 Esbjerg; tel. 75-12-45-00; telex 54123; fax 75-13-62-62; f. 1917 as *Vestkysten,* merged with *Jydske Tidende* in 1991 to form present daily; evening; Liberal; Editors Jörgen Ejböl, Egon Hansen; circ. weekdays 79,386, Sundays 92,058.

Herning

Herning Folkeblad: Østergade 25, 7400 Herning; tel. 97-12-37-00; fax 97-22-36-00; f. 1869; evening; Liberal; Editor-in-Chief Gorm Albrechtsen; circ. 16,714 (Wednesday 48,000).

Hillerød

Frederiksborg Amts Avis: Milnersvej 44–46, 3400 Hillerød; tel. 48-24-41-00; fax 42-25-48-40; f. 1874; morning; Liberal; Editor Torben Dalley Larsen; circ. weekdays 38,000, Sundays 35,800.

Hjørring

Vendsyssel Tidende: Frederikshavnsvej 79–81, 9800 Hjørring; tel. 98-92-17-00; fax 98-92-16-70; f. 1872; evening; Liberal; Editor Claus Dindler; Man. Dir L. Juhl Andersen; circ. weekdays 23,978, Sundays 90,215.

Holbaek

Holbaek Amts Venstreblad: Ahlgade 1, 4300 Holbaek; tel. 53-43-20-48; telex 44148; fax 53-44-28-10; f. 1905; evening; Social Liberal; Editor Alfred Hansen; circ. 21,492.

Holstebro

Dagbladet Holstebro-Struer: Laegårdvej 86, 7500 Holstebro; tel. 99-12-83-00; fax 97-41-03-20; evening; Liberal independent; Editor Erik Møller; circ. 13,276.

Horsens

Horsens Folkeblad: Søndergade 47, 8700 Horsens; tel. 75-62-45-00; telex 61626; fax 75-61-07-97; f. 1866; evening; Liberal; Editor MOGENS AHRENKIEL; circ. 23,277.

Kolding

Kolding Folkeblad: Jernbanegade 33–35, 6000 Kolding; tel. 75-52-20-00; fax 75-53-21-44; f. 1871; restructured 1996 as an edition of the Esbjerg daily, *Jydske Vestkysten*; evening; Liberal; Editor TAGE RASMUSSEN; circ. 17,497.

Naestved

Naestved Tidende: Ringstedgade 13, 4700 Naestved; tel. 55-72-45-11; fax 55-77-01-57; f. 1866; Liberal; 6 days a week; Editor SØREN BAUMANN; circ. 19,240.

Nykøbing

Folketidende: Tvaergade 14, 4800 Nykøbing F; tel. 54-88-02-00; fax 54-85-38-52; f. 1873; evening; Liberal; Editor BO BISCHOFF; circ. 27,245.

Odense

Fyens Stiftstidende: POB 418, 5220 Odense SØ; tel. 66-11-11-11; fax 65-93-25-74; internet http://www.fyensstiftstidende.dk; f. 1772; morning; independent; Editor-in-Chief HANS DAM; circ. weekdays 66,147, Sundays 94,276.

Randers

Amtsavisen: Lille Voldgade 5, 8900 Randers; tel. 86-42-75-11; telex 65173; fax 86-41-81-50; f. 1810; evening; independent; Editor-in-Chief OLE C. JØRGENSEN; circ. 29,859.

Ringkøbing

Ringkøbing Amts Dagblad: Skt Blichersvej 5, 6950 Ringkøbing; tel. 99-75-73-00; fax 97-32-05-46; evening; Editor KRISTIAN SAND; circ. 16,700.

Rønne

Bornholms Tidende: Nørregade 11–13, 3700 Rønne; tel. 56-95-14-00; fax 56-95-31-19; f. 1866; evening; Liberal; Editor-in-Chief JØRGEN BAUNGAARD; circ. 14,300.

Silkeborg

Midtjyllands Avis: Vestergade 30, 8600 Silkeborg; tel. 86-82-13-00; fax 86-81-35-77; f. 1857; daily except Sundays; Editor-in-Chief VIGGO SØRENSEN; circ. 21,673.

Skive

Skive Folkeblad: Gemsevej 7, 7800 Skive; tel. 97-51-34-11; fax 97-51-28-35; f. 1880; Social Liberal; Editor OLE DALL; circ. 13,909.

Slagelse

Sjaellands Tidende: Korsgade 4, 4200 Slagelse; tel. 53-52-37-00; fax 53-52-34-97; f. 1815; evening; Liberal; for western part of Zealand; Editor SØREN BAUMANN; circ. 15,247.

Svendborg

Fyns Amts Avis: Skt Nicolaigade 3, 5700 Svendborg; tel. 62-21-46-21; fax 62-22-06-10; e-mail post@fynsamtsavis.dk; f. 1863; Liberal; Editor KARSTEN MADSEN; circ. 21,500.

Thisted

Thisted Dagblad: Jernbanegade 15–17, 7700 Thisted; tel. 97-92-33-22; fax 97-91-07-20; Liberal independent; Editor HANS PETER KRAGH; circ. 11,165.

Vejle

Vejle Amts Folkeblad: Bugattivej 8, 7100 Vejle; tel. 75-85-77-88; fax 75-85-74-76; f. 1865; evening; Liberal; Editor ARNE MARIAGER; circ. 32,626.

Viborg

Viborg Stifts Folkeblad: Skt Mathiasgade 7, 8800 Viborg; tel. 89-27-63-00; fax 89-27-63-70; f. 1877; evening; Liberal Democrat; also published: *Viborg Nyt* (weekly); Editor PER SUNESEN; circ. 13,131.

Viby

Jyllands-Posten Morgenavisen: Grøndalsvej 3, 8260 Viby J; tel. 87-38-38-38; telex 68747; fax 86-11-26-29; independent; Editor-in-Chief JØRGEN EJBØL; circ. weekdays 172,758, Sundays 269,259.

OTHER NEWSPAPERS

Den Blå Avis (East edition): Generatorvej 8D, 2730 Herlev; tel. 44-85-44-44; 2 a week; circ. 73,000.

Den Blå Avis (West edition): Frederiksgade 45, POB 180, 8000 Århus C; tel. 86-19-14-11; fax 86-20-20-02; Thursday; circ. 46,160.

Det halve Sjaelland: POB 129, 4760 Vordingborg; tel. 53-77-16-66; fax 55-34-05-04; weekly; circ. 180,300.

Ugeavisen Lørdag: Vestergade 70–74, 5100 Odense C; tel. 66-14-14-10; fax 65-91-37-06; weekly; circ. 150,000.

Weekendavisen Berlingske: Pilestræde 34, 1147 Copenhagen K; tel. 33-75-75-75; fax 33-75-20-50; e-mail weekendavisen@berlingske.dk; f. 1749; independent Conservative; Friday; Editor-in-Chief PETER WIVEL; circ. 49,823.

POPULAR PERIODICALS

Ældre Sagen: Allégade 8F, 2000 Frederiksberg; tel. 31-22-20-20; fax 31-22-99-59; 6 a year; for senior citizens; circ. 240,000.

ALT for damerne: Hellerupvej 51, 2900 Hellerup; tel. 39-45-74-00; fax 39-45-74-80; f. 1946; weekly; women's magazine; Editor-in-Chief HANNE HØIBERG; circ. 90,721.

Alt om Mad: Strandboulevarden 130, 2100 Copenhagen Ø; tel. 39-29-55-00; fax 31-18-43-66; f. 1991; quarterly; food; Editor JETTE JULIUSSON: circ. 34,870.

Anders And & Co: Vognmagergade 11, 1148 Copenhagen K; tel. 33-14-31-00; fax 33-11-70-10; weekly; children's magazine; Editor TOMMY MELLE; circ. 99,826.

Arte-Nyt: Hvidkildevej 64, 2400 Copenhagen NV; tel. 38-88-49-00; fax 38-33-20-83; 3 a year; arts; Editor MOGENS HJORTH; circ. 50,000.

Basserne: Copenhagen; tel. 33-33-75-35; fax 33-33-75-05; fortnightly; children and youth; circ. 49,000.

Det Bedste fra Reader's Digest A/S: Jagtvej 169B, 2100 Copenhagen Ø; tel. 39-18-12-13; fax 39-18-12-36; e-mail Det-Bedste@internet.dk; monthly; Danish *Reader's Digest*; Editor YNGVE SKOVMAND; circ. 69,556.

Billed-Bladet: Vesterbrogade 16, 1506 Copenhagen; tel. 31-23-16-11; fax 31-24-10-08; f. 1938; weekly; family picture magazine; Editor ANDERS THISTED; circ. 222,951.

Bo Bedre: Strandboulevarden 130, 2100 Copenhagen Ø; tel. 39-29-55-00; fax 39-29-01-99; monthly; homes and gardens; Editor-in-Chief BIRGITTE ENGEN; circ. 85,408.

Camping: Lillehøjvej 10, 8600 Silkeborg; tel. 86-82-55-00; telex 22611; fax 86-81-63-02; monthly; circ. 44,107.

Facts & Fænomener: Strandboulevarden 130, 2100 Copenhagen Ø; tel. 39-29-55-00; fax 39-29-01-99; f. 1991; monthly; popular science; Editor ANKER TIEDEMANN; circ. 32,471.

Familie Journalen: Vigerslev Allé 18, 2500 Valby, Copenhagen; tel. 36-30-33-33; telex 22390; fax 36-30-30-25; f. 1877; weekly; Editor-in-Chief ANKER SVENDSEN-TUNE; circ. 275,000.

Femina: Vigerslev Allé 18, 2500 Valby, Copenhagen; tel. 36-30-33-33; fax 36-44-19-79; f. 1873; weekly; Editor JUTTA LARSEN; circ. 93,866.

Gør Det Selv: Strandboulevarden 130, 2100 Copenhagen Ø; tel. 39-29-55-00; telex 15712; fax 39-29-01-99; f. 1975; 14 a year; do-it-yourself; Editor KARL OLOFSEN; circ. 72,000.

Helse—Familiens Laegemagasin: Classensgade 36, 2100 Copenhagen Ø; tel. 35-25-05-25; fax 35-26-87-60; monthly; family health; circ. 300,000.

Hendes Verden: Hellerupvej 51, 2900 Hellerup; tel. 39-45-75-50; fax 39-45-75-99; f. 1937; weekly; for women; Editor IBEN NIELSEN; circ. 58,302.

Hjemmet (The Home): Vognmagergade 10, 1145 Copenhagen K; tel. 33-15-15-95; fax 33-91-05-85; weekly; Editor-in-Chief BJARNE RAUNSTED; circ. 257,799.

I form: Strandboulevarden 130, 2100 Copenhagen Ø; tel. 39-29-55-00; fax 39-29-01-99; monthly; sport, health, nutrition, sex, psychology; Editor HANNE-LUISE DANIELSEN; circ. 70,766.

Idé-nyt: Gl. Klausdalsbrovej 480, 2730 Herlev; tel. 44-53-40-00; fax 44-92-11-21; e-mail idenyt@idenyt.dk; f. 1973; 5 a year; free magazine (regional editions); homes and gardens; circ. 2,490,000.

Illustreret Videnskab: Strandboulevarden 130, 2100 Copenhagen Ø; tel. 39-29-55-00; fax 39-29-01-99; monthly; popular science; Editor JENS E. MATTHIESEN; circ. 88,132.

Mad og Bolig: Vesterbrogade 16, POB 484, 1506 Copenhagen V; tel. 31-23-16-11; fax 31-23-16-08; f. 1991; 6 a year; gastronomy and interiors; Editor JETTE ØSTERLUND; circ. 60,596.

Månedsmagasinet Bilen: Strandboulevarden 130, 2100 Copenhagen Ø; tel. 39-29-55-00; fax 39-27-11-24; e-mail bilen@ppp.dknet.dk; monthly; cars, motor sport; Editor ALLAN STRAUSS; circ. 38,405.

Månedsmagasinet IN: Vesterbrogade 16, POB 484, 1506 Copenhagen V; fashion magazine; tel. 31-23-16-11; fax 31-23-16-08; Editor CAMILLA LINDEMANN; circ. 49,582.

Motor: Firskovvej 32, POB 500, 2800 Lyngby; tel. 45-27-07-07; fax 45-27-09-89; e-mail motor@fdm.dk; monthly; cars and motoring; circ. 200,000.

Penny: Vognmagergade 11, 1148 Copenhagen K; tel. 33-15-19-25; fax 33-91-05-85; monthly; children's magazine; circ. 43,000.

Rapport: Vigerslev Allé 18, 2500 Valby; tel. 36-30-33-33; f. 1971; men's weekly; Editor-in-Chief JAN SCHIWE NIELSEN; circ. 36,964.

Samvirke: Roskildevej 65, 2620 Albertslund; tel. 43-86-43-86; fax 43-86-44-89; f. 1928; consumer monthly; Publr and Editor-in-Chief POUL DINES; circ. 500,000.

Se og Hør: Vigerslev Allé 18, 2500 Valby; tel. 36-30-33-33; telex 22390; fax 36-30-01-60; f. 1940; news and TV; Editor NIELS SMIOT-JENSEN; circ. 315,083.

Sofus' Lillebror: Copenhagen; tel. 33-33-75-35; fax 33-33-75-05; monthly; children and youth; circ. 44,000.

TIPS-bladet: Alsgarde Centret 2, 3140 Alsgarde; tel. 49-70-89-00; fax 49-70-88-30; weekly; sport; circ. 39,467.

Ud og Se: Allégade 8F, 2000 Frederiksberg; tel. 31-22-20-20; fax 31-22-99-59; travel monthly; circ. 290,000.

Ude og Hjemme: Vigerslev Allé 18, 2500 Valby, Copenhagen; tel. 36-30-33-33; fax 36-30-74-44; f. 1926; family weekly; Editor JØRN BAUENMAND; circ. 208,400.

Ugebladet Søndag: Vesterbrogade 16, 1505 Copenhagen V; tel. 33-85-34-00; f. 1921; weekly; family magazine; Editor JOHNNY JOHANSEN; circ. 129,700.

Wendy: Vognmagergade 9, 1148 Copenhagen K; tel. 33-30-50-00; fax 33-30-55-10; fortnightly; children's comics; circ. 30,000.

SPECIALIST PERIODICALS

ABF-Nyt: Carsten Ekström, Bagsværdhovedgade 296–298, 2880 Bagsværd; tel. 44-44-77-47; fax 44-44-67-47; 6 a year; Editor JAN HANSEN; circ. 26,837.

Aktive Kvinder: Niels Hemmingsensgade 10, 1153 Copenhagen K; tel. 33-13-12-12; fax 33-33-03-28; e-mail ddhfak@inet.uni-c.dk; 6 a year; home management; Editor KIRSTEN WULFF; circ. 25,000.

Aktuel Elektronik: Skelbaekgade 4, 1780 Copenhagen V; tel. 31-21-68-01; fax 31-21-23-96; 22 a year; computing and information technology; circ. 21,642.

Alt om Data: St. Kongensgade 72, 1264 Copenhagen K; tel. 33-91-28-33; fax 33-91-01-21; e-mail redaktion@aod.dk; f. 1983; monthly; Editor-in-Chief TORBEN OKHOLM; circ. 35,000.

Automatik: Algade 10, POB 80, 4500 Nykøbing; tel. 53-41-23-10; engineering; monthly; circ. 39,250.

Bådnyt (Boats): Strandboulevarden 130, 2100 Copenhagen Ø; tel. 39-29-55-00; fax 39-27-24-02; monthly; Editor KNUT IVERSEN; circ. 18,351.

Beboerbladet: Allégade 8F, 2000 Frederiksberg; tel. 31-22-20-20; fax 31-22-99-59; quarterly; for tenants in public housing; circ. 475,000.

Beredskab: Nørrebrogade 66D, 2200 Copenhagen N; tel. 35-37-75-00; fax 35-37-73-95; f. 1934; 6 a year; civil protection and preparedness; publ. by the Danish Civil Protection League; circ. 20,500.

Bilsnak: Park Allé 355, 2605 Brøndby; tel. 43-28-82-00; fax 43-63-27-22; quarterly; cars; circ. 150,000.

Boligen: Studiestræde 50, 1554 Copenhagen V; tel. 33-11-11-22; fax 33-93-37-47; monthly; housing associations, architects; Editor HELGE MØLLER; circ. 30,000.

BygTek: Stationsparken 29, 2600 Glostrup; tel. 43-43-29-00; fax 43-43-13-28; e-mail odsgard@odsgard.dk; monthly; building and construction; circ. 30,000.

Computerworld: Carl Jacobsensvej 25, 2500 Valby; tel. 36-19-91-00; fax 36-44-25-69; f. 1981; weekly; computing; Chief Officers PETER HVIDTFELDT, JENS JØRGEN KRAG HANSEN, KIM MARQUART; circ. 26,000.

Cyklister: Dansk Cyklist Forbund, Rømersgade 7, 1362 Copenhagen K; tel. 33-32-31-21; fax 33-32-76-83; f. 1905; 6 a year; organ of Danish Cyclists' Asscn; Editor POUL JENSEN; circ. 22,000.

Effektivt Landbrug: Skelbaekgade 4, 1780 Copenhagen V; tel. 31-21-68-01; fax 31-21-53-50; 21 a year; farming; circ. 31,407.

FINANS: Langebrogade 5, 1411 Copenhagen K; tel. 32-96-46-00; 16 a year; for employees in the financial sector; circ. 53,000.

Folkeskolen: Vandkunsten 12, POB 2139, 1015 Copenhagen K; tel. 33-69-63-00; fax 33-69-64-26; e-mail folkeskolen@dk-online.dk; 43 a year; teaching; Editor THORKILD THEJSEN; circ. 78,400.

Forbrugsforeningsbladet: Knabrostraede 12, 1210 Copenhagen K; tel. 33-15-88-26; monthly; for civil servants and doctors; circ. 60,000.

Havebladet: Hvidehusv 24, POB 173, 3450 Allerød; tel. 42-27-14-09; fax 42-27-72-88; 6 a year; gardening; circ. 47,000.

Hi-Fi & Elektronik: Rønnegade 1, 2100 Copenhagen Ø; tel. 39-16-02-30; fax 39-27-24-02; f. 1980; monthly; audio, video, car stereo, computer tests; Editor CHRISTIAN HOLM; circ. 21,441.

High Fidelity: Blegdamsvej 112A, 2100 Copenhagen Ø; tel. 70-23-70-01; fax 70-23-70-02; e-mail hifired@hifi.dk; f. 1968; 11 a year; Editor-in-Chief MICHAEL MADSEN; circ. 24,833.

Hunden: Parkvej 1, 2680 Solrød Strand; tel. 53-14-74-00; fax 53-14-30-03; 10 a year; organ of the kennel club; circ. 25,000.

Ingeniøren: POB 373, Skelbaekgade 4, 1503 Copenhagen V; tel. 31-21-68-10; fax 31-21-67-01; weekly engineers' magazine; circ. 72,000.

Jaeger: Hojnæsvej 56, 2610 Rødovre; tel. 36-72-42-00; fax 36-72-09-11; monthly except July; circ. 89,000.

Jern- og Maskinindustrien: Falkoner Allé 90, 2000 Frederiksberg; tel. 35-36-37-00; telex 21317; fax 35-36-37-90; 22 a year; iron and metallic industries; circ. 25,295.

Jyllands Ringens program: Vilvordevej 102, 2920 Charlottenlund; tel. 31-64-46-92; 5 a year; cars and motor cycles; circ. 280,000.

Kommunalbladet: Park Allé 9, 8000 Aarhus C; tel. 86-76-13-22; 22 a year; municipal administration, civil servants; Editor ULLA KRAG JESPERSEN; circ. 75,500.

KontorBladet: Sydvestvej 49, 2600 Glostrup; tel. 43-63-02-22; fax 43-63-01-13; e-mail kontorbladet@visholm.dk; internet http://www.kontorbladet.dk; monthly; management in trade and industry; Editor JANN KALF LARSEN; circ. 32,539.

Landsbladet Kvæg: Vester Farimagsgade 6, 1606 Copenhagen V; tel. 33-11-22-22; fax 33-11-31-48; monthly; for cattle-breeders and dairy-farmers; (related titles *Landsbladet Mark* for arable farmers, *Landbladet Svin* for pig-farmers); circ. 15,000.

Lederne: Vermlandsgade 65, 2300 Copenhagen S; tel. 32-83-32-83; fax 32-83-32-84; e-mail lh@lederne.dk; 12 a year; for managers; circ. 80,136.

Metal: Nyropsgade 38, 1602 Copenhagen V; tel. 33-63-20-00; fax 33-63-21-00; 16 a year; metal industries; circ. 150,571.

Praktisk Foto & Video: POB 239, 9900 Frederikshavn; tel. 38-88-32-22; fax 38-88-30-38; f. 1960; 2 a year; photography; Editors E. STEEN SØRENSEN; circ. 24,000.

Produktion: Copenhagen; tel. 35-82-28-88; fax 35-82-22-66; 8 a year; farming; circ. 120,000.

Spejd: Lundsgade 6, 2100 Copenhagen Ø; tel. 35-25-00-50; fax 35-25-00-75; 8 a year; organ of the Scout Movement; circ. 40,000.

Stat, Amt og KommuneInformation: 2600 Glostrup; tel. 43-43-31-21; fax 43-43-15-13; e-mail saki@post4.tele.dk; monthly; public works and administration; circ. 21,000.

Sundhedsbladet: Odense; tel. 66-15-88-43; fax 66-15-57-43; 6 a year; health; circ. 27,000.

Sygeplejersken: Vimmelskaftet 38, POB 1084, 1008 Copenhagen K; tel. 33-15-15-55; 50 a year; nursing; circ. 70,000.

Tidsskrift for Sukkersyge—Diabetes: Filosofgangen 24, 5000 Odense C; tel. 66-12-90-06; fax 65-91-49-08; f. 1940; 6 a year; diabetes; Dir FLEMMING KJERSGAARD JOHANSEN; circ. 40,000.

Ugeskrift for Laeger: Trondhjemsgade 9, 2100 Copenhagen Ø; tel. 31-38-55-00; weekly; medical; circ. 21,000.

NEWS AGENCY

Ritzaus Bureau I/S: St. Kongensgade 14, 1264 Copenhagen K; tel. 33-30-00-00; telex 22362; fax 33-30-00-01; e-mail rb@ritzau.dk; f. 1866; general, financial and commercial news; owned by all Danish newspapers; Chair. of Board of Dirs HANS DAM; Gen. Man. and Editor-in-Chief UFFE RIIS SØRENSEN.

Foreign Bureaux

Agence France-Presse (AFP): Mikkel Bryggersgade 5, 1460 Copenhagen K; tel. 33-13-23-31; telex 19584; Bureau Chief SLIM ALLAGUI.

Agencia EFE (Spain): Copenhagen; Correspondent MARÍA CAMINO SÁNCHEZ.

Agenzia Nazionale Stampa Associata (ANSA) (Italy): Vestergade 2, 1456 Copenhagen K; tel. 33-32-03-59; fax 33-32-03-69; Correspondent DANIELA ROMITI.

Allgemeiner Deutscher Nachrichtendienst (ADN) (Germany): 2660 Brøndbystrand, Kisumparken 65 st. th., Copenhagen; Bureau Chief HERBERT HANSCH.

Associated Press (AP) (USA): Bremerholm 1, 1069 Copenhagen K; tel. 33-11-15-04; fax 33-32-36-60; Bureau Chief ED MCCULLOUGH.

Deutsche Presse-Agentur (dpa) (Germany): Mikkel Bryggersgade 5, 1460 Copenhagen K; tel. 33-14-22-19; fax 33-14-66-72; Chief Correspondent THOMAS BORCHERT.

Informatsionnoye Telegrafnoye Agentstvo Rossii-Telegrafnoye Agentstvo Suverennykh Stran (ITAR-TASS) (Russia): Uraniavej 9B, 1878 Frederiksberg C; tel. 31-31-88-48; Correspondent TARAS B. LARIOKHIN.

Reuters (UK): Badstuestraede 18, 1209 Copenhagen K; tel. 33-96-96-96; telex 16846; fax 33-12-32-72; e-mail copenhagen.newsroom@reuters.com; Bureau Chief PER BECH THOMSEN.

Rossiyskoye Informatsionnoye Agentstvo—Novosti (RIA—Novosti) (Russia): Copenhagen; tel. 31-20-04-44; telex 15618; fax 31-20-19-42; Editor-in-Chief IGOR PAVLOV.

PRESS ASSOCIATIONS

Dansk Fagpresse (Danish Periodical Press Association): Sommerstedgade 7, 1718 Copenhagen V; tel. 31-22-12-10; fax 31-23-43-10.

Dansk Magasinpresses Udgiverforening (Danish Magazine Publishers' Association): Hammerensgade 6, 1267 Copenhagen K; tel. 33-11-88-44; fax 33-15-01-86; e-mail dmu-mags@internet.dk; Chair. NILS PRIENCE; Dir TORBEN HOLMBÄCK.

Danske Dagblades Forening (Danish Newspaper Publishers' Association): Pressens Hus, Skindergade 7, 1159 Copenhagen K; tel. 33-12-21-15; telex 27183; fax 33-14-23-25; e-mail ddf@danskedagblade.dk; comprises managers and editors-in-chief of all newspapers; general spokesperson for the Danish press; Man. Dir EBBE DAL.

Publishers

Aarhus Universitetsforlag: Ole Worms Allé, Bygning 170, 8000 Aarhus C; tel. 86-19-70-33; fax 86-19-84-33; e-mail unipress@aau.dk; non-fiction and educational; Man. Dir TØNNES BEKKER-NIELSEN.

Forlaget åløkke A/S: Porskaervej 15, Nim, 8700 Horsens; tel. 75-67-11-19; fax 75-67-10-74; f. 1977; educational, children's books, audio-visual and other study aids; Pres. BERTIL TOFT HANSEN; Man. Dir EVA B. HANSEN.

Akademisk Forlag A/S (Danish University Press): Nørre Voldgade 90, POB 54, 1002 Copenhagen K; tel. 33-11-98-26; fax 33-32-05-70; e-mail info@akademisk.dk; f. 1962; history, health, linguistics, university textbooks, educational materials; Man. Dir HENRIK BORBERG.

Forlaget Amanda: Nørre Søgade 49C, 1370 Copenhagen K; tel. 33-11-20-11; fax 33-15-07-20; art, culture, school books, non-fiction; Editorial Dir GERT EMBORG.

Forlaget Apostrof ApS: Berggreensgade 24, 2100 Copenhagen Ø; tel. 39-20-84-20; fax 39-20-84-53; f. 1980; fiction and non-fiction for children, humour; Publrs MIA THESTRUP, OLE THESTRUP.

Arkitektens Forlag: Strandgade 27A, 1408 Copenhagen K; tel. 32-83-69-00; fax 32-83-69-41; architecture, planning; Dir KIM DIRCKINCK-HOLMFELD.

Forlaget Artia (Ars Audiendi ApS); Vognmagergade 9, 1120 Copenhagen K; tel. 33-12-28-98; fax 33-14-12-63; fiction, non-fiction, science fiction, music, horror; Publr ERIK LÆSSØE STILLING; Dir PETER SCHANTZ.

Aschehoug Dansk Forlag A/S: Vognmagergade 7, POB 2179, 1017 Copenhagen K; tel. 33-91-55-22; fax 33-91-07-76; imprints: Aschehoug (fiction), Aschehoug Fakta (non-fiction, reference, children's books), Sesam (educational, children's books, history); Man. Dir (Aschehoug) STIG ANDERSEN.

Peter Asschenfeldt's Stjernebøger A/S: Gerdasgade 37, 2500 Valby; tel. 36-44-11-20; telex 19387; fax 36-44-11-62; book clubs and fiction; Man. Dir SØREN FOGTDAL.

Thomas Bloms Forlag ApS: Skovenggaardsvej 8, 9490 Pandrup; tel. 98-24-85-25; fax 98-24-80-60; fiction, non-fiction, children's books, talking books; Publrs CONNIE BLOM, THOMAS BLOM.

Bogans Forlag: Kastaniebakken 8, POB 39, 3540 Lynge; tel. 48-18-80-55; fax 48-18-87-69; f. 1974; general paperbacks, popular science, non-fiction, humour, health; Publr EVAN BOGAN.

Borgens Forlag A/S: Valbygårdsvej 33, 2500 Valby; tel. 36-46-21-00; fax 36-44-14-88; f. 1948; fiction, poetry, children's books, humour, general non-fiction; Man. Dir NIELS BORGEN.

Børnegudstjeneste-Forlaget: Korskærvej 25, 7000 Fredericia; tel. 75-93-44-55; fax 75-92-42-75; religion, children's books; Dir FINN ANDERSEN; Editorial Dir JØRGEN HEDAGER.

Carit Andersens Forlag A/S: Upsalagade 18, 2100 Copenhagen Ø; tel. 35-43-62-22; fax 35-43-51-51; illustrated books, non-fiction, fiction, science fiction; Publr ERIK ALBRECHTSEN.

Forlaget Carlsen A/S: Krogshøjvej 32, 2880 Bagsværd; tel. 44-44-32-33; fax 44-44-36-33; children's books; Man. Dir JESPER HOLM.

Forlaget Centrum: St. Kongensgade 10, 3TV, 1264 Copenhagen K; tel. 33-32-12-06; fax 33-32-12-07; fiction, non-fiction, travel guides, management; Man. Dir CLAES HVIDBAK.

Forlaget Cicero (Chr. Erichsens Forlag A/S): Nørrebrogade 53B, 2200 Copenhagen N; tel. 31-35-03-08; fax 31-39-40-54; f. 1902; fiction, non-fiction, art, culture; Publrs NIELS GUDBERGSEN, ALIS CASPERSEN.

DA-Forlag/Dansk Arbejdsgiverforening: Vester Voldgade 113, 1790 Copenhagen V; tel. 33-93-40-00; fax 33-91-09-32; e-mail smh@da.di; non-fiction and reference; Publishing Dir SØREN MELDORF HANSEN.

Dansk BiblioteksCenter A/S: Tempovej 7-11, 2750 Ballerup; tel. 44-86-77-77; fax 44-86-78-91; e-mail dbc@dbc.dk; bibliographies, library literature, talking books; Man. Dir MOGENS BRABRAND JENSEN.

Dansk Historisk Håndbogsforlag A/S: Buddingevej 87A, 2800 Lyngby; tel. 45-93-48-00; fax 45-93-47-47; e-mail mrjensen@image.dk; f. 1976; genealogy, heraldry, law, culture and local history, facsimile editions, microfiches produced by subsidiary co; Owners and Man. Dirs RITA JENSEN, HENNING JENSEN.

Dansklærerforeningens Forlag: Nørre Søgade 49, 1370 Copenhagen K; tel. 33-15-04-99; fax 33-15-07-20; Dir CAMILLA GELLERT NIELSEN.

Dansk psykologisk Forlag: Stockholmsgade 29, 2100 Copenhagen Ø; tel. 35-38-16-55; fax 35-38-16-65; e-mail dk-psych@dpf.dk; educational books, health, psychology; Man. Dir HANS GERHARDT.

Det Danske Bibelselskabs Forlag/Det Kongelige Vajsenshus' Forlag: Frederiksborggade 50, 1360 Copenhagen K; tel. 33-12-78-35; fax 33-93-21-50; religious and liturgical books, children's books; Sec.-Gen. MORTEN M. AAGAARD.

Christian Ejlers' Forlag ApS: Brolaeggerstraede 4, POB 2228, 1018 Copenhagen K; tel. 33-12-21-14; fax 33-12-28-84; e-mail liber@ce-publishers.dk; f. 1967; art, cultural, educational and academic; Publr CHRISTIAN EJLERS.

Forlaget for Faglitteratur A/S: Vandkunsten 6, 1467 Copenhagen K; tel. 33-13-79-00; fax 33-14-51-56; medicine, technology.

FinansSupport: Hovedvejen 9, POB 70, 2600 Glostrup; tel. 43-44-04-44; fax 43-44-07-44; educational books; Pres. ERLING JENSEN.

Flachs: Øverødvej 98, 2840 Holte; tel. 45-42-48-30; fax 45-42-48-29; fiction, non-fiction, reference, educational and children's books; Publrs ALLAN FLACHS, ANETTE FLACHS.

Palle Fogtdal A/S: Østergade 22, 1100 Copenhagen K; tel. 33-15-39-15; fax 33-93-35-05; Danish history; Man. Dir PALLE FOGTDAL.

Forum: Snaregade 4, 1205 Copenhagen K; tel. 33-14-77-14; fax 33-14-77-91; f. 1940; history, fiction, biographies, quality paperbacks and children's books; Man. Dir WERNER SVENDSEN.

Fremad: Kronprinsensgade 1, POB 2252, 1019 Copenhagen K; tel. 33-93-43-40; fax 33-93-52-74; f. 1912; general trade, fiction, non-fiction, juveniles, reference, children's books; Man. Dir NIELS KØLLE.

Forlaget FSR: Nytorv 5, 1450 Copenhagen K; tel. 33-74-07-74; fax 33-93-30-77; textbooks, legal, economic, financial, management, business, accounting; Editorial Dir VIBEKE CHRISTIANSEN.

Gad & Grafisk I/S: Møntergade 5, POB 2152, 1016 Copenhagen K; tel. 33-91-46-66; fax 33-91-17-46; school books; Dir JAN B. THOMSEN.

G.E.C. Gad Publishers Ltd: Vimmelskaftet 32, 1161 Copenhagen K; tel. 33-15-05-58; fax 33-11-08-00; biographies, natural science, history, reference, fiction, educational materials, food and drink, travel guides; Man. Dir AXEL KIELLAND.

Gyldendalske Boghandel, Nordisk Forlag A/S: Klareboderne 3, 1001 Copenhagen K; tel. 33-11-07-75; fax 33-11-03-23; e-mail gyldendal@gyldendal.dk; f. 1770; fiction, non-fiction, reference books, paperbacks, children's books, textbooks; Man. Dir KURT FROMBERG.

P. Haase & Søns Forlag A/S: Løvstraede 8, 1152 Copenhagen K; tel. 33-14-41-75; fax 33-11-59-59; f. 1877; educational books, audio-visual aids, children's books, humour, fiction, non-fiction; Man. Dir MICHAEL HAASE.

Edition Wilhelm Hansen A/S: Bornholmsgade 1, 1266 Copenhagen K; tel. 33-11-78-88; fax 33-14-81-78; e-mail ewh@post1.tele.dk; internet http://www.wilhelm-hansen.dk; f. 1855; music books, school and educational books; Man. Dir TINE BIRGER CHRISTENSEN.

Hernovs' Forlag: Siljangade 6, 2300 Copenhagen S; tel. 32-96-33-14; fax 32-96-04-46; f. 1941; fiction, non-fiction, children's; Publr JOHS. G. HERNOV.

Holkenfeldt 3: Fuglevadsvej 71, 2800 Lyngby; tel. 45-93-12-21; fax 45-93-82-41; fiction, non-fiction, reference, sport, humour; Publr KAY HOLKENFELDT.

Høst & Søns Forlag: Købmagergade 62, POB 2212, 1018 Copenhagen K; tel. 33-15-30-31; fax 33-15-51-55; e-mail host@euroconnect.dk; f. 1836; crafts and hobbies, languages, books on Denmark, children's books; Skarv imprint (travel, ecology, etc.); Man. Dir ERIK C. LINDGREN.

Forlaget Hovedland: Stenvej 21, 8270 Højbjerg; tel. 86-27-65-00; fax 86-27-65-37; e-mail hovedland@isa.dknet.dk; internet http://www.hovedland.dk; fiction, non-fiction, environment, sport, health, crafts; Publr STEEN PIPER.

Forlaget Klematis A/S: Østre Skovvej 1, 8240 Risskov; tel. 86-17-54-55; fax 86-17-59-59; fiction, non-fiction, crafts, children's books; Dir CLAUS DALBY.

Forlaget Per Kofod ApS: Nikolaj Plads 32, 1067 Copenhagen K; tel. 33-15-03-47; fax 33-93-14-93; fiction, non-fiction, art and culture; Publr PER KOFOD.

Krak: Virumgaardsvej 21, 2830 Virum; tel. 45-95-65-00; fax 45-95-65-65; e-mail krak@krak.dk; f. 1770; reference works, maps and yearbooks; Dir IB LE ROY TOPHOLM.

Egmont Lademann A/S: Gerdasgade 37, 2500 Valby; tel. 36-15-66-00; telex 19387; fax 36-44-11-62; f. 1954; non-fiction, reference; Man. Dir SØREN FOGTDAL; Editor-in-Chief LISELOTTE NELSON.

Lindhardt og Ringhof A/S: Frederiksborggade 1, 1360 Copenhagen K.

Lindhardt og Ringhof (incl. Jespersen and Pios Forlag): tel. 33-69-50-00; fax 33-69-50-01; e-mail bonnier@inet.uni-c.dk; f. 1971; general fiction and paperbacks; Man. Dir HENRIK HJORTH; Publr LIV BENTSEN.

L & R FAKTA: tel. 33-69-50-70; fax 33-69-50-01; e-mail bonnier@inet.uni-c.dk; f. 1997; non-fiction; Man. Dir HENRIK HJORTH; Publr ANNEMARIE ELKJÆR.

Lohses Forlag (incl. Forlaget Korskaer): Korskaervej 25, 7000 Fredericia; tel. 75-93-44-55; fax 75-92-42-75; f. 1868; religion, children's, biographies, devotional novels; Man. Dir FINN ANDERSEN.

Forlaget Lotus: Knudslundvej 19, 2605 Brøndby; tel. 43-45-78-74; fax 43-45-97-71; management, health, religion, the occult, educational; Publr FINN ANDERSEN.

Forlaget Magnus A/S Skattekartoteket: Informationskontor, Palægade 4, POB 9026, 1022 Copenhagen K; tel. 33-11-78-74; fax 33-93-80-09; e-mail magnus@cddk.dk; f. 1962; guidebooks, journals, law; Man. Dirs PETER TAARNHØJ, HANNE TOMMERUP.

Medicinsk Forlag ApS: Tranevej 2, 3650 Ølstykke; tel. and fax 42-17-65-92; astrology, medical and scientific books; Man. Dir ANNI LINDELØV.

Modtryk AmbA: Anholtsgade 4, 8000 Århus C; tel. 86-12-79-12; fax 86-13-27-78; f. 1972; children's and school books, fiction, thrillers and non-fiction; Man. Dir ILSE NØRR.

Munksgaard International Publishers Ltd: Nørre Søgade 35, POB 2148, 1016 Copenhagen K; tel. 33-12-70-30; fax 33-12-93-87; e-mail headoffice@mail.munksgaard.dk; f. 1917; medicine, nursing, dentistry, social science, psychology, fiction, non-fiction, art and culture, reference books, dictionaries, multimedia, scientific journals; Man. Dir JOACHIM MALLING.

Rasmus Navers Forlag A/S: Løvstraede 8, 1152 Copenhagen K; tel. 33-14-41-75; fax 33-11-59-59; humour; Man. Dir MICHAEL HAASE.

Nyt Nordisk Forlag-Arnold Busck A/S: Købmagergade 49, 1150 Copenhagen K; tel. 33-11-11-03; fax 33-93-44-90; f. 1896; textbooks, school books, guidebooks, fiction and non-fiction; Man. Dir OLE ARNOLD BUSCK.

OP-Forlag Dafolo A/S: Suderbovej 22-24, 9900 Frederikshavn; tel. 98-42-28-22; fax 98-43-13-88; educational books; Publr MICHAEL SCHELDE.

Jørgen Paludans Forlag ApS: Fiolstraede 10, 1171 Copenhagen K; tel. 33-15-06-75; fax 33-15-06-76; language teaching, non-fiction, psychology, history, politics, economics, reference, children's books; Man. Dir JØRGEN PALUDAN.

Politikens Forlag A/S: Vestergade 26, 1456 Copenhagen K; tel. 33-47-07-07; fax 33-47-07-08; f. 1946; non-fiction, reference, history, family, health, biography, travel; Ekstra Bladets imprint; Man. Dir JOHANNES RAVN.

C.A. Reitzels Boghandel og Forlag A/S: Nørregade 20, 1165 Copenhagen K; tel. 33-12-24-00; fax 33-14-02-70; f. 1819; reference books, philosophy, educational and academic books, Hans Christian Andersen, Kierkegaard; Dir SVEND OLUFSEN.

Hans Reitzels Forlag A/S: Købmagergade 62, POB 1073, 1008 Copenhagen K; tel. 33-14-04-51; fax 33-15-51-55; f. 1949; education, philosophy, psychology, sociology, Hans Christian Andersen; Man. Dir ERIK C. LINDGREN.

Rhodos, International Science and Art Publishers: Niels Brocks Gård, Strandgade 36, 1401 Copenhagen K; tel. 31-54-30-20; fax 32-95-47-42; e-mail rhodos@rhodos.com; f. 1959; university books, art, science, fiction, poetry; Man. Dir NIELS BLAEDEL; Dir RUBEN BLAEDEL.

Roths Forlag A/S: Milnersvej 7, 3400 Hillerød; tel. 42-25-49-94; fax 48-24-24-13; fiction, non-fiction, art and culture, guides, travel, humour; Dir JOHN ROTH.

Samlerens Forlag A/S: Snaregade 4, 1205 Copenhagen K; tel. 33-13-10-23; fax 33-14-43-14; Danish and foreign fiction, contemporary history and politics, biographies; Man. Dir PETER HOLST.

Scandinavia Publishing House Copenhagen: Nørregade 32, 1165 Copenhagen K; tel. 33-14-00-91; fax 33-32-00-91; f. 1973; children's books, religion, Hans Christian Andersen; Dir JØRGEN VIUM OLESEN.

Det Schønbergske Forlag A/S: Landemaerket 5, 1119 Copenhagen K; tel. 33-11-30-66; fax 33-33-00-45; f. 1857; fiction, humour, psychology, biography, children's books, paperbacks, textbooks; Man. JOAKIM WERNER; Editor ARVID HONORÉ.

Spektrum: Snaregade 4, 1205 Copenhagen K; tel. 33-14-77-14; fax 33-14-77-91; non-fiction, history, biographies, science, psychology, religion, philosophy, arts; Man. Dir WERNER SVENDSEN.

Strandbergs Forlag ApS: Vedbaek Strandvej 475, 2950 Vedbaek; tel. 42-89-47-60; fax 42-89-47-01; cultural history, travel; Publr HANS JØRGEN STRANDBERG.

Strubes Forlag og Boghandel ApS: Dag Hammerskjølds Allé 36, 2100 Copenhagen Ø; tel. 31-42-53-00; fax 31-42-23-98; health, astrology, philosophy, the occult; Man. Dir JONNA STRUBE.

Teknisk Forlag A/S: Skelbaekgade 4, 1780 Copenhagen V; tel. 31-21-68-01; fax 31-21-09-83; f. 1948; computing, technical books, reference, business, educational, science; Man. Dir PETER MÜLLER.

Tiderne Skifter: Pilestraede 51, 1001 Copenhagen K; tel. 33-32-57-72; fax 33-14-42-05; fiction, sexual and cultural politics, psychology, science, religion, arts; Man. Dir CLAUS CLAUSEN.

Unitas Forlag: Valby Langgade 19, 2500 Valby; tel. 36-16-64-81; fax 36-16-08-18; religion, fiction, education, children's books; Man. PEDER GUNDERSEN.

Forlaget Vindrose A/S: Valbygaardsvej 33, 2500 Valby; tel. 36-46-21-00; fax 36-44-14-88; f. 1980; general trade, fiction and non-fiction; Man. Dir NIELS BORGEN.

Vitafakta ApS: Kohavevej 28, 2950 Vedbaek; tel. and fax 42-89-21-03; health books, nutrition, school books; Dir INGER MARIE HAUT.

Wisby & Wilkens: Vestergade 6, 8464 Galten; tel. 86-94-46-22; fax 86-94-47-22; e-mail wisby@image.dk; f. 1986; children's book, crafts, fiction, health, humour, science, religion; Publr JACOB WISBY.

Mikro: f. 1960; drama, poetry and humour.

Falkenlöwe: f. 1995; debate, gay literature and contemporary history.

Government Publishing House

Statens Information (State Information Service): Nørre Farimagsgade 65, POB 1103, 1009 Copenhagen K; tel. 33-37-92-00; fax 33-37-92-99; e-mail si@si.dk; f. 1975; acts under the purview of the Ministry of Research, as public relations and information body for the public sector; publishes Statstidende (Official Gazette), etc.; Dir LEON ØSTERGAARD.

PUBLISHERS' ASSOCIATION

Den danske Forlaeggerforening: Købmagergade 11, 1150 Copenhagen K; tel. 33-15-66-88; fax 33-15-65-88; f. 1837; 75 mems; Chair. ERIK C. LINDGREN; Man. Dir ERIK V. KRUSTRUP.

Broadcasting and Communications

TELECOMMUNICATIONS

Telecommunications services are administered by the Post- og Telegrafvæsenet (the general directorate of posts and telecommunications) and the National Telecom Agency.

Denmark participates in the Nordic Mobile Telephone (NMT) system, an integrated cellular-radio network which is compatible throughout Scandinavia.

Telecommunications links with the Faroe Islands are provided by satellite ground stations at Tórshavn and Herstedvester. The latter also provides international data communication links via the EUTELSAT system and the French Telecom 1 satellite system, while a station at Blåvand receives signals from INTELSAT.

Regulatory Organization

National Telecom Agency: Holsteinsgade 63, 2100 Copenhagen Ø; tel. 35-43-03-33; telex 31100; fax 35-43-14-34; f. 1991; under the general directorate for posts and telecommunications, in charge of administration and regulation of the telecommunications sector as laid down in telecommunications legislation; works on legislation; government's centre of expertise in telecommunications; Dir JØRGAN ABILD ANDERSEN; Deputy Dir TAGE M. IVERSEN.

Major Service Providers

GN Store Nordiske Telegraf-Selskab as (GN Great Northern Telegraph Co Ltd): Kongens Nytorv 26, POB 2167, 1016 Copenhagen; tel. 33-95-09-09; telex 5522371; fax 33-95-09-09; e-mail info@gn.dk; Pres. and CEO JORGEN LINDEGAARD.

Lasat Communications A/S: Skalhuse 13, 9240 Nibe; tel. 96-71-10-00; fax 96-71-10-99; e-mail hedehus@lasat.dk; Dir KIM HEDEUS.

Telecom A/S: Telegade 2, 2630 Tåstrup; tel. 42-52-91-11; fax 42-52-93-31; Man. Dir GREGERS MOGENSEN.

Tele Danmark A/S: Norregade 21, 4th Floor, 0900 Copenhagen; tel. 33-43-77-77; fax 33-43-73-89; state-owned telecommunications company; scheduled for partial privatization in 1998; Man. Dir HANS MUNK JENSEN.

RADIO

DR RADIO: Mørkhøjvej 500, 2860 Söborg; tel. 35-20-30-40; telex 22695; fax 35-20-21-09; fmrly Danmarks Radio; independent statutory corpn; Dir-Gen. CHR. S. NISSEN; Dir of Radio Programmes HANS JØRGEN SKOV; operates a foreign service (Radio Denmark), nine regional stations and three national channels:

Channel 1 broadcasts for 110 hours per week on FM, in Danish (Greenlandic programmes weekly); Head FINN SLUMSTRUP.

Channel 2, a music channel, broadcasts on FM, for 45 hours per week nationally, in Danish, as well as regional and special (for foreign workers) programmes; Head STEEN FREDERIKSEN.

Channel 3 broadcasts on FM for 24 hours per day, in Danish; primarily a popular music channel, there is news in Greenlandic, Faroese and in English; Head JESPER GRUNWALD.

There are also some 300 operators licensed for low-power FM transmissions of local and community radio, etc.

TELEVISION

DK4: CIAC A/S, Falkoner Allé 3,2000 Frederiksberg; tel. 38-34-34-90; fax 38-34-34-85; f. 1994; broadcasts 24 hours a day; political, environmental, cultural and educational programming; reaches 23% of the country via cable.

DR TV: TV-Byen, 2860 Søborg; tel. 35-20-30-40; telex 22695; fax 35-20-26-44; e-mail dr-kontakten@dr.dk; Dir-Gen. CHR. S. NISSEN; Dir of Television Programmes BJØRN ERICHSEN.

TV 2/DANMARK: Rugaardsvej 25, 5100 Odense C; tel. 65-91-12-44; telex 59660; fax 65-91-33-22; began broadcasts in October 1988; Denmark's first national commercial TV station; 20% of its finances come from licence fees, the rest from advertising and sponsorship; Dir-Gen. JØRGEN FLINDT PEDERSEN.

TV 3: Indiakaj 6, 2100 Copenhagen Ø; tel. 35-25-90-00; fax 35-25-90-10; reaches 60% of the country via cable and satellite; Man. Dir JENS TORPE; Dir of Programmes JØRGEN STEEN NIELSEN.

There are some 35 operators licensed for local television transmission.

Finance

The first Danish commercial bank was founded in 1846. In January 1975 restrictions on savings banks were lifted, giving commercial and savings banks equal rights and status, and restrictions on the establishment of full branches of foreign banks were removed. In October 1988 all remaining restrictions on capital movements were ended. In 1995 there were some 186 banks and savings banks in operation. All banks are under government supervision, and public representation is obligatory on all bank supervisory boards.

BANKING

(cap. = capital; p.u. = paid up; res = reserves; dep. = deposits; m. = million; brs = branches; amounts in kroner)

Supervisory Authority

Finanstilsynet (Danish Financial Supervisory Authority): Gammel Kongevej 74A, 1850 Frederiksberg C; tel. 33-55-82-82; fax 33-55-82-99; agency of the Ministry of Economic Affairs; Man. Dir HENRIK BJERRE-NIELSEN.

Central Bank

Danmarks Nationalbank: Havnegade 5, 1093 Copenhagen K; tel. 33-63-63-63; telex 27051; fax 33-63-71-06; f. 1818; self-governing; sole right of issue; conducts monetary policy; administers reserves of foreign exchange; general capital fund 50m.; total net cap. 38,752m., dep. 28,070m.; gold in coin and bullion 3,652m.; notes in circ. 33,187m. (Dec. 1996); Govs BODIL NYBOE ANDERSEN (Chair.), TORBEN NIELSEN, JENS THOMSEN.

Commercial Banks

Alm. Brand Bank: Jarmers Plads 7, 1551 Copenhagen V; tel. 33-30-70-30; fax 33-14-11-88; f. 1988; cap. 300m.; res 0.1m.; dep. 5,750m. (Dec. 1996); Chair. CHRISTIAN N. B. ULRICH; Man. Dir HENRIK NORDAM; 24 brs.

Amagerbanken A/S: Amagerbrogade 25, 2300 Copenhagen S; tel. 32-95-60-90; telex 31262; fax 31-54-45-34; f. 1903; dep. 6,080.0m. (Dec. 1996); Chair. N. E. NIELSEN; Man. Dirs KNUD CHRISTENSEN, BENT SCHØN HANSEN; 26 brs.

Arbejdernes Landsbank A/S: Vesterbrogade 5, 1502 Copenhagen V; tel. 33-38-80-00; telex 15633; fax 33-38-89-06; f. 1919; cap. 300m., res 135m., dep. 11,388m. (Dec. 1996); Chair. ANTON JOHANNSEN; Gen. Mans E. MIDTGAARD, P. E. LETH, E. CASTELLA; 59 brs.

Bikuben Girobank: Silkegade 8, 1113 Copenhagen K; tel. 43-30-30-30; fax 33-15-90-33; f. 1996 by merger of Sparekassen Bikuben A/S (f. 1857) and Girobank A/S (f. 1990); cap. 2,927m.; res 1,690m.; dep. 142,319m. (Dec. 1996); Chair. HENRIK THUFASON; Vice-Chair. BJARNE WIND; 271 brs.

Codan Bank A/S: Borgergade 24, 1790 Copenhagen V; tel. 33-55-55-55; telex 22396; fax 33-15-96-48; f. 1993 by merger of Alliance Bank of Copenhagen, Hafnia Bank A/S and Hafnia Börs-Börsmaeglerselskab; cap. 825m., res 52m., dep. 5,090m. (Dec. 1996); CEO JENS OLE PEDERSEN; Gen. Man. THORKILD KOKHOLM.

Den Danske Bank A/S: Holmens Kanal 2–12, 1092 Copenhagen K; tel. 33-44-00-00; telex 27000; fax 31-18-58-73; f. 1871 as Danske Landmandsbank; merged with Copenhagen Handelsbank and Provinsbanken in 1990 to form Den Danske Bank A/S; in 1995 the bank acquired the insurance group, Danica; cap. 5,293m., res 20,586m., dep. 380,523m. (Dec. 1996); Chair. KNUD SØRENSEN; Dep. Chair. PETER STRAARUP; 430 brs.

Egnsbank Nord A/S: Jernbanegade 4–6, POB 701, 9900 Frederikshavn; tel. 99-21-22-23; telex 67102; fax 99-21-22-67; f. 1979; cap. 50m., res 296m., dep. 2,397m. (Dec. 1996); Chair. KNUD UGGERHØJ; Gen. Mans JENS OLE JENSEN, OLE KRISTENSEN; 17 brs.

Forstaedernes Bank A/S: Malervangen 1, 2600 Glostrup; tel. 43-96-17-20; telex 33261; fax 43-63-32-36; f. 1902; cap. 250m., res 3m., dep. 2,984m. (Dec. 1996); subsidiary, Den Fri Bank, f. 1994, provides telephone banking service to individual customers; Chair. HELMER OLSEN; Man. Dir KJELD MOSEBO CHRISTENSEN; 19 brs.

A/S Jyske Bank: Vestergade 8–16, 8600 Silkeborg; tel. 89-22-22-22; fax 89-22-24-96; f. 1855, established in 1967; cap. 900m., res 3,482m., dep. 39,293m. (Dec. 1996); Chair. LEON RASMUSSEN; Chief Exec. ANDERS DAM; 123 brs.

Midtbank A/S: Østergade 2, 7400 Herning; tel. 96-26-26-26; telex 62142; fax 96-26-28-98; e-mail midtbank@midtbank.dk; f. 1965; cap. 282m., res 232m., dep. 5,076m. (Dec. 1996); Chair. GUNNAR PEDERSEN; Gen. Man. STEEN HOVE; 23 brs.

Nørresundby Bank A/S: Torvet 4, 9400 Nørresundby; tel. 98-17-33-33; telex 69776; fax 98-19-18-78; f. 1898; cap. 44m., res 0.6m., dep. 3,035m. (Dec. 1996); Chair. KJELD KOLIND JENSEN; Gen. Mans TORBEN HOLM, ANDREAS RASMUSSEN; 16 brs.

Nykredit Bank: Bredgade 40, POB 3033, 1021 Copenhagen K; tel. 33-42-18-00; fax 33-42-18-01; f. 1986; cap. 1,000m., res 278m., dep. 13,786m. (Dec. 1996); Chair. HENNING KRUSE PETERSEN; Man. Dir HANS MØLLER CHRISTENSEN.

Ringkjøbing Landbobank A/S: Torvet 1, 6950 Ringkøbing; tel. 97-32-11-66; telex 60385; fax 97-32-18-18; f. 1886; cap. 27m., res 462m., dep. 2,765m. (Dec. 1995); Chair. KR. OLE KRISTENSEN; Gen. Man. BENT NAUR KRISTENSEN; 13 brs.

Roskilde Bank A/S: Algade 14, POB 39, 4000 Roskilde; tel. 46-35-17-00; telex 43122; fax 46-34-83-52; f. 1884; cap. 77m., res 94m., dep. 2,949m. (Dec. 1996); Chair. JØRØGEN WESTERGAARD; Man. NIELS VALENTIN HANSEN; 13 brs.

Sparbank Vest: Adelgade 8, POB 505, 7800 Skive; tel. 96-14-14-14; telex 66724; fax 96-14-14-15; f. 1857; cap. 121m., res 485m., dep. 3,730m.; Chair. OLE BROENDUM JENSEN; Gen. Man. PREBEN RASMUSSEN; 31 brs.

Sydbank A/S: Peberlyk 4, POB 1038, 6200 Åbenrå; tel. 74-36-36-36; telex 52114; fax 74-36-35-36; e-mail intl@sydbank.dk; f. 1970, established in 1990; cap. 871m., res 1,535m., dep. 25,817m. (Dec. 1996); Chair. VAGN JACOBSEN; CEO CARSTEN ANDERSEN; 125 brs.

Unibank A/S: Torvegade 2, 1786 Copenhagen V; tel. 33-33-33-33; telex 27543; fax 33-33-63-63; f. 1990 by merger of Andelsbanken, Privatbanken and SDS; part of the Unidanmark A/S group; cap. 5,323m., res 11,116m., dep. 296,337m. (Dec. 1996); Man. Dir THORLEIF KRARUP; 400 brs.

Savings Banks

Amtssparekassen Fyn: Vestre Stationsvej 7, POB 189, 5100 Odense C; tel. 66-14-04-74; telex 59778; fax 65-91-01-10; f. 1974; cap. 194m., res 633.3m., dep. 10,062.7m. (Dec. 1996); Chair. CLAUS HANSEN; Man. Dirs POUL BALLE, NIELS CHR. KNUDSEN; 40 brs.

Lån & Spar Bank: Højbro Plads 9-11, POB 2117, 1014 Copenhagen K; tel. 33-14-87-48; telex 15908; fax 33-14-18-48; f. 1880 (present name 1990); cap. 281m., res 42m., dep. 4,674m. (Dec. 1996); Chair. TOMMY AGERSKOV THOMSEN; Man. Dir, CEO PETER SCHOU; 11 brs.

Sparekassen Nordjylland A/S: Karlskogavej 4, POB 162, 9100 Ålborg; tel. 96-34-40-00; telex 69662; fax 96-34-45-75; f. 1967; cap. 430m., res 150m., dep. 19,391m. (Dec. 1996); Chair. POUL LAURITSEN; Man. Dirs OLE JØRGENSEN, LASSE NYBY; 74 brs.

Bankers' Organization

Finansrådet—Danske Pengeinstitutters Forening (Danish Bankers Association): Finansrådets Hus, Amaliegade 7, 1256 Copenhagen K; tel. 33-12-02-00; telex 16102; fax 33-93-02-60; f. 1990; 173 mems; Chair. THORLEIF KRARUP; Man. Dir LARS BARFOED.

STOCK EXCHANGE

Københavns Fondsbørs (Copenhagen Stock Exchange): Nikolaj Plads 6, POB 1040, 1007 Copenhagen K; tel. 33-93-33-66; fax 33-12-86-13; f. 1861; Pres. BENT MEBUS; Chair. LARS JOHANSEN.

INSURANCE

Principal Companies

Alm. Brand af 1792: Lyngby Hovedgade 4, POB 1792, 2800 Lyngby; tel. 45-96-70-00; telex 37512; fax 45-87-17-92; f. 1792; subsidiaries: finance, life, non-life and reinsurance; Chief Gen. Man. BENT KNIE-ANDERSEN.

Forsikringsselskabet Codan A/S: Codanhus, Gl. Kongevej 60, 1790 Copenhagen V; tel. 31-21-21-21; telex 15469; fax 31-21-21-22; f. 1915; controlled by Royal and Sun Alliance Group Ltd (UK); acquired insurance operations of Hafnia Holdings in 1993; accident, life; CEO PETER ZOBEL.

Danica Liv I, Livsforsikringsaktieselskab: Parallelvej 17, 2800 Lyngby; tel. 45-23-23-23; fax 45-23-20-20; e-mail information@danica.dk; f. 1842 as state insurance co; privatized in 1990; pensions, life and non-life.

ERC Frankona Reinsurance A/S: Grønningen 25, 1270 Copenhagen K; tel. 33-97-95-93; telex 15367; fax 33-97-94-41; f. 1894; reinsurance, life and non-life, international; Gen. Mans WALTHER HAMMERSTROEM, ANNETTE SADOLIN, AAGE LYTT JENSEN.

A/S Det Kjøbenhavnske Reassurance-Compagni: Lyngby Hovedgade 4, POB 325, 2800 Lyngby; tel. 45-96-75-75; fax 45-96-72-72; f. 1915; reinsurance; Gen. Man. LEIF CORINTH-HANSEN.

Købstaedernes almindelige Brandforsikring: Grønningen 1, 1270 Copenhagen K; tel. 33-14-37-48; fax 33-32-27-27; f. 1761; fire; Chair. JENS J. VILDBRAD; Gen. Man. LARS ØSTENFIELD.

Kompas Rejseforsikring A/S: Lautruphøj 1, 2750 Ballerup; tel. 44-68-81-00; telex 16375; fax 44-68-84-00; travel, health; Chief Gen. Man. PETER BOESEN.

Kgl. Brand A/S (The Royal Chartered General Fire Insurance Co. Ltd): Stamholmen 159, 2650 Hvidovre; tel. 36-87-47-47; fax 36-87-47-87; f. 1798; all branches; subsidiaries: workers' liability, life; Gen. Man. JØRN OLE JØRGENSEN.

Max Levig & Cos Eft. A/S: Vesterbrogade 2B, 1620 Copenhagen V; tel. 33-14-67-00; telex 27519; fax 33-93-67-01; f. 1890; Gen. Man. ERNST KAAS WILHJELM.

PFA Pension: Marina Park, Sundkrogsgade 4, 2100 Copenhagen Ø; tel. 39-17-50-00; telex 16183; fax 39-17-59-50; f. 1917; life; non-life, property; Gen. Mans ANDRÉ LUBLIN, A. KÜHLE.

Topdanmark A/S: Borupvang 4, 2750 Ballerup; tel. 44-68-33-11; telex 35107; fax 44-68-12-64; f. 1985; all classes, with subsidiaries; Man. Dir MICHAEL PRAM RASMUSSEN.

Tryg-Baltica Forsikring A/S: Klausdalsbrovej 601, 2750 Ballerup; tel. 44-20-20-20; telex 37449; fax 44-20-66-00; f. 1995 by merger of Tryg Forsikring A/S and Baltica Forsikring A/S; 92% owned by Tryg General Ltd; all classes, with subsidiaries; Group Chief Exec. HUGO ANDERSEN.

Insurance Association

Assurandør-Societetet (Association of Danish Insurance Companies): Amaliegade 10, 1256 Copenhagen K; tel. 33-13-75-55; fax 33-11-23-53; f. 1918; Chair. BENT KNIE-ANDERSEN; Dir STEEN LETH JEPPESEN; 169 mems.

Trade and Industry

GOVERNMENT AGENCIES

Dansk Industri (Confederation of Danish Industries): 1787 Copenhagen V; tel. 33-77-33-77; telex 112217; fax 33-77-33-00; e-mail di@di.dk; f. 1992; Dir HANS SKOV CHRISTENSEN.

Elektricitetsrådet (Electricity Council): Gothersgade 160, 1123 Copenhagen K; tel. 33-11-65-82; f. 1907; responsible for the general planning, operation and safety of the electricity-supply industry in Denmark; Pres. JØRGEN ERIKSEN; Man. Dir H. KASTOFT JANSEN.

Landsforeningen Dansk Arbejde (The National Association for Danish Enterprise): Gravene 2, 8800 Viborg; tel. 86-62-42-22; fax 86-62-45-88.

DEVELOPMENT ORGANIZATIONS

Dansk Gasteknisk Forening (Danish Technical Gas Association): Rønnehaven 12, 5320 Agedrup; f. 1911; promotes the use of gas; 680 mems.

Det Økonomiske Råd (Danish Economic Council): Copenhagen; tel. 33-13-51-28; fax 33-32-90-29; f. 1962 to supervise national economic development and help to co-ordinate the actions of economic interest groups; 26 members representing both sides of industry, the Government and independent economic experts; Co-Chairs Prof. NINA SMITH; Prof. NIELS KIERGAARD, Prof. PETER BIRCH SØRENSEN; Sec.-Gen. PEDER ANDERSEN.

CHAMBER OF COMMERCE

Det Danske Handelskammer (Danish Chamber of Commerce): Børsen, 1217 Copenhagen K; tel. 33-95-05-00; fax 33-32-52-16; f. 1742; approx. 12,000 mems; Man. Dir LARS KROBAEK; Pres. OVE ANDERSEN.

INDUSTRIAL AND TRADE ASSOCIATIONS

Dansk Elvaerkers Forening (Association of Danish Electric Utilities): Rosenørns Allé 9, 1970 Frederiksberg C; tel. 31-39-01-11; telex 16147; f. 1923; promotes the interests of Danish producers and suppliers of electricity; 105 mem. companies.

Det Kgl. Danske Landhusholdningsselskab (The Royal Danish Agricultural Society): Mariendalsvej 27, 2, 2000 Frederiksberg; tel. 38-88-66-88; fax 38-88-66-11; e-mail njf-gs@inet.uni-c.dk; f. 1769 to promote agricultural progress; Pres JON KRABBE, BRITTA SCHALL HOLBERG, NIELS KÆRGÅRD, KIRSTEN JAKOBSEN, IVER TESDORPF; Dir JENS WULFF; 1,700 mems.

Landbrugsrådet (Agricultural Council): Axelborg, Axeltorv 3, 1609 Copenhagen V; tel. 33-14-56-72; telex 16772; fax 33-14-95-74; f. 1919; Pres. (vacant); Dir KLAUS BUSTRUP; 38 mems.

Mejeriforeningen(Danish Dairy Board): Frederiks Allé 22, 8000 Århus; tel. 87-31-20-00; telex 64307; fax 87-31-20-01; e-mail ddb@mejeri.dk; f. 1912; Chair. KNUD HARCK MADSEN; Man. Dir K. THAYSEN; 30 mems.

Oliebranchens Fællesrepræsentation—OFR (Danish Petroleum Industry Association): Vognmagergade 7, POB 120, 1004 Copenhagen K; tel. (01) 33-11-30-77; fax (01) 33-32-16-18; representative organization for petroleum industry; Chair. S. GULLEV; Sec.-Gen. JØRGEN POSBORG.

EMPLOYERS' ORGANIZATIONS

Bryggeriforeningen (Danish Brewers' Association): Frederiksberggade 11, 1459 Copenhagen K; tel. 33-12-62-41; fax 33-14-25-13; e-mail info@bryggeriforeningen.dk; f. 1899; Chair. FLEMMING LINDELØV; Dir NIELS HALD; 11 mems.

Dansk Arbejdsgiverforening (Danish Employers' Confederation): Vester Voldgade 113, 1790 Copenhagen V; tel. 33-93-40-00; fax 33-12-29-76; f. 1896; Chair. NIELS FOG; Dir-Gen. JØRN NEERGAARD LARSEN; 22 mem. orgs.

Dansk Pelsdyravlerforening (DPF) (Danish Fur Breeders' Association): Langagervej 60, POB 79, 2600 Glostrup; tel. 43-26-10-00; telex 33171; fax 43-26-11-26; co-operative of 3,000 mems.

Danske Husmandsforeninger (Danish Family Farmers' Association): Landbrugsmagasinet, Vester Farimagsgade 6, 1606 Copenhagen V; tel. 33-12-99-50; fax 33-93-63-62; f. 1906; Chair. CHR. SØRENSEN; Sec.-Gen. OLAV POVLSGÅRD; 30,000 mems.

Danske Landboforeninger (Danish Farmers' Union): Axelborg, Vesterbrogade 4A, 1620 Copenhagen V; tel. 33-12-75-61; telex 327662; fax 33-32-76-62; e-mail ddl@ddl.dk; f. 1893; Pres. PETER GÆMELKE; Dir CARL AAGE DAHL; 59,000 mems.

Håndvaerksrådet (Danish Federation of Small- and Medium-Sized Enterprises): Amaliegade 31, 1256 Copenhagen K; tel. 33-93-20-00; telex 16600; fax 33-32-01-74; f. 1879; Chair. SVEND ERIK LAURSEN; Man. LARS JØRGEN NIELSEN; 135 asscns with 35,000 mems.

Industriens Arbejdsgivere i København (The Copenhagen Employers' Federation): 1787 Copenhagen V; tel. 33-77-33-77; telex 112217; fax 33-77-34-10; e-mail di@di.dk; internet http://www.di.dk; Chair. GERHARD ALBRECHTSEN; Sec. H. ENGELHARDT; 475 mems.

Provinsindustriens Arbejdsgiverforening (Federation of Employers in the Provincial Industry): 1787 Copenhagen V; tel. 33-77-33-77; telex 112217; fax 33-77-33-00; e-mail di@di.dk; internet http://www.di.dk; f. 1895; Chair. SVEND-AAGE NIELSEN; Sec. GLENN SØGÅRD.

Sammenslutningen af Landbrugets Arbejdsgiverforeninger (SALA) (Danish Confederation of Employers' Associations in Agriculture): Vester Farimagsgade 1, 1606 Copenhagen V; tel. 33-13-46-55; fax 33-11-89-53.

Skibsvaerftsforeningen (Association of Danish Shipbuilders): St. Kongensgade 128, 1264 Copenhagen K; tel. 33-13-24-16; fax 33-11-10-96.

UTILITIES

Danish Energy Agency: Landenmærket 11, 1119 Copenhagen K; tel. 33-92-67-00; telex 22450; fax 33-11-47-43; f. 1976; department of the Danish Ministry of the Environment and of Energy; Dir IB LARSEN.

Electricity

Elkraft Power Company Ltd: Lautruphøj 5, 2750 Ballerup; tel. 44-66-00-22; telex 35158; fax 42-65-61-04; f. 1978; co-ordinates supply of electricity and co-generated heat to eastern Denmark; Man. Dir JOHN HEBO NIELSEN.

Foreningen af Kommunale Elvaeker: Gyldenløvesgade 11, 1600 Copenhagen V; tel. 33-12-27-88; fax 33-14-40-51; 43 municipal power-station mems.

Københavns Belyningsvaesen (The Copenhagen Lighting Department): Vognmagergade 8, 1149 Copenhagen K; tel. 33-12-72-90; fax 33-12-72-91; one of the largest distributors of electricity in Denmark; also supplier of gas, district-heating and public-lighting systems; 2,055 employees.

NESA A/S: Strandvejen 102, 2900 Hellerup; tel. 31-62-41-41; telex 37500; fax 31-62-63-36; f. 1902; largest distributor of electricity in Denmark; Man. Dir PREBEN SCHOU.

SK Power Company, Denmark: Strandvejen 102, 2900 Hellerup; tel. 31-62-41-41; telex 37500; fax 31-61-28-88; f. 1992; power production; owns and operates Asnæs, Avedøre, Kyndby, Masnedø and Stigsnæs power stations and a number of local stations; Man. Dir PREBEN SCHOU.

Gas

Dansk Olie og Naturgas A/S (DONGAS): Agern Allé 24-26, 2970 Hørsholm; tel. 45-57-10-22; telex 37322; fax 45-17-10-44; f. 1972; oil and natural gas exploration, production and distribution; acts as consultant in other countries; Chair. HOLGER LAVESEN; cap. 1,200m. kroner; 418 employees.

CO-OPERATIVE

Faellesforeningen for Danmarks Brugsforeninger (Co-operative of Denmark): Roskildevej 65, 2620 Albertslund; f. 1896; Chair. BJARNE MØGELHØJ; 1,113,506 mems.

TRADE UNIONS

Landsorganisationen i Danmark (LO) (Danish Confederation of Trade Unions): Rosenørns Allé 12, 1634 Copenhagen V; tel. 32-24-60-00; fax 35-24-63-00; Pres. HANS JENSEN; Vice-Pres. TINE A. BRØNDUM; 1,495,850 mems (1 Jan. 1997); 1,087 brs.

Principal Affiliated Unions

Blik- og Rørarbejderforbundet i Danmark (Metal and Steel Workers): Ålholmvej 55, 2500 Valby; tel. 38-71-30-22; fax 38-71-29-97; Pres. PER FREDERIKSEN; 9,237 mems.

Dansk Artist Forbund: Vendersgade 24, 1363 Copenhagen K; tel. 33-32-66-77; fax 33-33-73-30; e-mail artisten@image.dk; f. 1918; Pres. NICK OLANDER; Gen. Sec. ANDY FILIPSEN; 1,550 mems.

Dansk Beklaednings- og Textilarbejderforbund (Textile and Garment Workers): Nyropsgade 14, 1602 Copenhagen V; tel. 33-11-67-65; fax 33-32-99-94; Pres. ANNE M. PEDERSEN; 18,450 mems.

Dansk El-Forbund (Electricians' Union): Vodroffsvej 26, 1900 Frederiksberg C; tel. 33-29-70-00; fax 33-29-70-70; Pres. ERIK ANDERSSON; 29,989 mems.

Dansk Funktionaerforbund—Serviceforbundet (Danish Federation of Salaried Employees): Upsalagade 20, 2100 Copenhagen Ø; tel. 31-38-65-95; fax 31-38-71-59; Pres. KARSTEN HANSEN; 21,435 mems.

Dansk Jernbaneforbund (Railway Workers): Svanemøllevej 65, 2900 Hellerup; tel. 39-40-11-66; fax 39-40-17-71; f. 1899; Pres. KURT CHRISTIANSEN; 8,567 mems.

Dansk Metalarbejderforbund (Metalworkers): Nyropsgade 38, POB 308, 1780 Copenhagen V; tel. 33-63-20-00; fax 33-63-21-00; f. 1888; Pres. JENS BOE ANDERSEN; 143,808 mems.

Dansk Postforbund (Post Office Civil Servants): Vodroffsvej 13A, 1900 Frederiksberg C; tel. 31-21-41-24; fax 31-21-06-42; f. 1908; Pres. JAN SVENDSEN; 11,770 mems.

Forbundet af Offentligt Ansatte (Public Employees): POB 11, Staunings Plads 1–3, 1790 Copenhagen V; tel. 33-13-40-00; fax 33-13-40-42; Pres. POUL WINCKLER; 202,479 mems.

Forbundet Trae-Industri-Byg i Danmark (Timber Industry and Construction Workers): Mimersgade 41, 2200 Copenhagen N; tel. 31-81-99-00; fax 35-82-07-44; Pres. ARNE JOHANSEN; 72,000 mems.

Frisør- og Kosmetiker Forbund (Hairdressers and Beauticians): Lersø Park Allé 21, 2100 Copenhagen Ø; tel. 31-83-18-80; fax 35-82-14-62; Pres. POUL MONGGAARD; 5,288 mems.

Grafisk Forbund (Printing Workers): Lygten 16, 2400 Copenhagen NV; tel. 31-81-44-89; fax 31-81-24-25; f. 1993 by merger of 4 unions; Pres. TOM DURBING; 24,025 mems.

Haerens Konstabel- og Korporal-Forening: Kronprinsensgade 8, 1114 Copenhagen K; tel. 33-93-65-22; fax 33-93-65-23; e-mail hkkf@hkkf.dk; Pres. SVEND-ERIK LARSEN; 4,586 mems.

Handels- og Kontorfunktionaerernes Forbund i Danmark (Commercial and Clerical Employees): H. C. Andersens Blvd 50, POB 268, 1780 Copenhagen V; tel. 33-30-43-43; fax 33-30-40-99; f. 1900; Pres. JOHN DAHL; 360,980 mems.

Kvindeligt Arbejderforbund i Danmark (Women Workers): Applebys Plads 5, 1411 Copenhagen K; tel. 32-83-83-83; fax 32-83-86-67; f. 1901; Pres. LILLIAN KNUDSEN; 92,516 mems.

Malerforbundet i Danmark (Housepainters): Tomsgårdsvej 23C, 2400 Copenhagen NV; tel. 38-34-75-22; fax 38-33-75-22; f. 1890; Pres. JØRN ERIK NIELSEN; 14,042 mems.

Naerings- og Nydelsesmiddelarbejder Forbundet (Food, Sugar Confectionery, Chocolate, Dairy Produce and Tobacco Workers): C.F. Richsvej 103, POB 1479, 2000 Frederiksberg; tel. 38-18-72-72; fax 38-18-72-00; Pres. ANTON JOHANNSEN; 43,307 mems.

Paedagogisk Medhjaelper Forbund (Nursery and Child-care Assistants): St. Kongensgade 79, 1017 Copenhagen K; tel. 33-11-03-43; fax 33-11-31-36; f. 1974; Pres. JAKOB BANG; 32,162 mems.

Restaurations-og Bryggeriarbejder Forbundet (Restaurant and Brewery Workers): Thoravej 29-33, 2400 Copenhagen NV; tel. 38-33-89-00; fax 38-33-67-91; Chair. PREBEN RASMUSSEN; 30,770 mems.

Socialpaedagogernes Landsforbund (National Federation of Social Educators in Denmark): Brolaeggerstraede 9, 1211 Copenhagen K; tel. 33-14-00-58; fax 33-14-04-15; Pres. KIRSTEN NISSEN; 21,864 mems.

Specialarbejderforbundet i Danmark (General Workers' Union in Denmark): Kampmannsgade 4, POB 392, 1790 Copenhagen V; tel. 33-14-21-40; fax 33-97-24-60; Pres.POUL ERIK SKOV CHRISTENSEN; Int. Sec. CLAUS LARSEN-JENSEN; 306,763 mems.

Teknisk Landsforbund: Nørre Voldgade 12, 1358 Copenhagen K; tel. 33-12-22-00; fax 33-11-42-72; f. 1919; Pres. ESKE PEDERSEN; 33,915 mems.

Telekommunikations Forbundet (Telecommunications): Rolfsvej 37, 2000 Frederiksberg; tel. 38-88-00-55; fax 38-88-15-11; Pres. BO STENØR LARSEN; 11,500 mems.

Other Unions

Akademikernes Centralorganisation (Danish Confederation of Professional Associations): Nørre Voldgade 29, 1358 Copenhagen K; tel. 33-69-40-40; fax 33-93-85-40; e-mail ac@ac.dk.

Den Almindelige Danske Laegeforening (Danish Medical Association): Trondhjemsgade 9, 2100 Copenhagen Ø; tel. 31-38-55-00; fax 31-38-55-07; e-mail dadl@dadl.dk.

Dansk Journalistforbund (Journalists): Gammel Strand 46, 1202 Copenhagen K; tel. 33-14-23-88; fax 33-14-23-01; f. 1961; Pres. LARS POULSEN; 8,000 mems.

Funktionaerernes og Tjenestemaendenes Faellesråd (Civil Servants' and Salaried Employees' Confederation): Niels Hemmingsens Gade 12, POB 1169, 1010 Copenhagen K; tel. 33-36-88-00; fax 33-36-88-80; f. 1952; Chair. ANKER CHRISTOFFERSEN; 400,000 mems.

Transport

In 1997 a 20-km combined tunnel-and-bridge link across the Great Belt, linking the islands of Zealand and Funen was completed, at a cost of 20,000m. kroner. In August 1991 Denmark and Sweden signed an agreement on the construction of a 15.9-km road and rail link across the Oresund strait, between Copenhagen and Malmö. Although reservations expressed in the parliaments of both countries, on financial and environmental grounds, initially delayed the project, it was announced in 1994 that construction was expected to be completed by 2000. In October 1992 the Danish, German and Swedish State Railways announced a plan to develop a high-speed rail system linking Stockholm and Oslo with Copenhagen, and Copenhagen with Berlin, Hamburg and Köln. The plan, which was estimated to cost 40,000m.–50,000m. kroner, would include the bridge over the Oresund and would require new track between Copenhagen and Hamburg and the construction of a tunnel under the Fehmern Belt. In 1996 contracts were signed for the construction of a 22-km underground light railway system in Copenhagen.

RAILWAYS

Banestyrelsen (Danish National Railway Agency): Solvgade 40, 1349 Copenhagen; tel. 33-14-04-00; fax 33-11-20-38; f. 1997 to assume, from the DSB (see below), responsibility for the maintenance and development of the national rail network; CEO E. ELSBORG.

DSB (Danish State Railways): Sølvgade 40, 1349 Copenhagen K; tel. 33-14-04-00; telex 22225; fax 33-14-04-40; controls 2,344 km of line, of which 170 km are electrified; also operates passenger train and motor car ferries between the mainland and principal islands. Train and motor car ferries are also operated between Denmark, Sweden and Germany in co-operation with German and Swedish state railways. In 1997 it was announced that DSB was to become an independent public enterprise from January 1999.

A total of 526 km, mostly branch lines, is run by 15 private companies.

ROADS

At 31 December 1996 Denmark had an estimated 71,600 km of paved roads, including 880 km of motorways, 3,690 km of national roads and 7,090 km of secondary roads.

SHIPPING

The Port of Copenhagen is the largest port in Denmark and the only one including a Free Port Zone. The other major ports are Århus, Fredericia, Ålborg and Esbjerg, all situated in Jutland. There are oil terminals, with adjacent refineries, at Kalundborg, Stigsnaes and Fredericia. Ferry services are provided by DSB (see above) and by private companies.

Farvandsvaesenet (Royal Danish Administration of Navigation and Hydrography): Overgaden oven Vandet 62B, POB 1919, 1023 Copenhagen K; tel. 32-68-95-00; fax 31-57-43-41.

Port Authorities

Århus: Port Authority of Århus, Mindet 2, POB 130, 8100 Århus; tel. 86-13-32-66; fax 86-12-76-62; Gen. Man. KAJ SCHMIDT.

Copenhagen: Port of Copenhagen Authority, Nordre Tolbod 7, 1259 Copenhagen K; tel. 33-47-99-99; telex 15439; fax 33-47-99-33; Gen. Man. E. SCHAFER; Harbour Master S. ANDERSEN.

Esbjerg: Port of Esbjerg Authority, POB 2, 6701 Esbjerg; tel. 75-12-92-00; fax 75-13-31-67; Gen. Man. V. V. LEISNER; Harbour Master IB MOLLER NIELSEN.

Fredericia: Port Authority of Fredericia, Vesthavnsvej 33, 7000 Fredericia; tel. 75-92-02-55; fax 75-92-51-04; Harbour Dir P. E. SKOTT.

Frederikshavn: Frederikshavn Havnekontor, Oliepieren 7, POB 129, 9900 Frederikshavn; tel. 98-42-19-88; fax 96-20-09-88; Harbour Master JESPER THOMSEN.

Kalundborg: Kalundborg Port Authority, POB 50, 4400 Kalundborg; tel. 53-51-33-11; fax 53-51-00-89.

Sønderborg: Sønderborg Havn, Norrebro 1, 6400 Sønderborg; tel. 74-42-27-65; fax 74-43-30-19; Harbour Master LASS ANDERSEN.

Principal Shipping Companies

Rederiet Otto Danielsen: Kongevejen 272A, 2830 Virum; tel. 45-83-25-55; telex 15837; fax 45-83-50-55; f. 1944; 6 general cargo vessels, totalling 16,400 grt, under foreign flags; general tramp trade, chartering, ship sales; Fleet Man. JØRN STAUREBY.

Dannebrog Rederi A/S: Rungsted Strandvej 113, 2960 Rungsted Kyst; tel. 45-17-77-77; telex 37204; fax 45-17-77-70; f. 1883; 4 ro-ro vessels, ferry and product chemical tanker services; liner service US–Europe, US Gulf–Caribbean, Mediterranean–Caribbean; CEO DITLEV WEDELL-WEDELLSBORG.

DFDS A/S: Skt Annae Plads 30, 1295 Copenhagen K; tel. 33-42-33-42; telex 19435; fax 33-42-33-41; f. 1866; 8 car/passenger ships of 174,221 grt and 8 ro-ro vessels of 121,690 grt (incl. Swedish and German subsidiaries); passenger and car ferry services between Denmark, Sweden, the UK, the Netherlands, Germany and Norway, liner trade between Denmark, Sweden, the UK, the Netherlands, eastern Europe and Belgium; Lauritzen owns majority share; Man. Dir NIELS BACH.

The East Asiatic Co Ltd A/S: Holbergsgade 2, 1099 Copenhagen K; tel. 35-27-27-27; telex 12100; fax 33-12-37-00; f. 1897; trading, industry, food processing, plantations, shipping; totally owned and managed tonnage: 4 bulk/log carriers of 94,400 grt and 2 tankers of 33,700 grt under foreign flags; worldwide services; Chair. JAN ERLUND; Man. Dir MICHAEL FIORINI.

Elite Shipping A/S: H.C. Andersens Blvd 12, 3rd floor, 1553 Copenhagen V; tel. 33-15-32-33; telex 15301; fax 33-15-32-06; 29 dry cargo vessels of 80,200 grt; tramp, world-wide; Man. Dirs RINO LANGE, TORBEN PALLE HANSEN.

H. Folmer & Co: Fredericiagade 57, 1310 Copenhagen K; tel. 33-13-25-10; telex 15910; fax 33-13-54-64; f. 1955; 14 general cargo vessels of 14,100 grt; world-wide tramping; Man. Owners J. J. FOLMER, UFFE MARTIN JENSEN.

Rederiet Knud I. Larsen A/S: Enrum, Vedbaek Strandvej 341, POB 40, 2950 Vedbaek; tel. 45-66-00-90; telex 27150; fax 45-66-09-90; f. 1942; 11 container vessels totalling 126,125 dwt under the Danish Flag and 1 general cargo vessel of 4,500 dwt under a foreign flag, 17 chemical carriers totalling 124,473 dwt, 3 under the Danish flag and 14 under foreign flags, and 6 gas carriers totalling 16,005 dwt under foreign flags; Man. Dir BJARNE TUILDE.

J. Lauritzen A/S: Skt Annae Plads 28, POB 2147, 1291 Copenhagen K; tel. 33-11-12-22; telex 15522; fax 33-11-85-13; f. 1884; operates pool of 39 reefer ships, 27 Kosan tankers and 24 bulk ships; Pres. CLAUS V. IPSEN.

Lauritzen Kosan Tankers: Skt Annae Plads 28, 1291 Copenhagen K; tel. 33-14-34-00; telex 22214; fax 33-91-00-39; f. 1951; 25 gas carriers of 83,532 grt; Man. Dir LEIF SVANBERG.

Mercandia Rederierne: Amaliegade 27, 1256 Copenhagen K; tel. 33-12-01-55; telex 19762; fax 33-32-55-47; f. 1964; 24 ro-ro vessels and car ferries totalling 238,200 grt; tramp and liner services; Man. Owner PER HENRIKSEN.

A. P. Møller: Esplanaden 50, 1098 Copenhagen K; tel. 33-63-33-63; telex 19632; fax 33-14-15-15; f. 1904; fleet of 38 container vessels, 13 products tankers, 5 crude oil tankers, 13 gas carriers, 26 offshore vessels and 7 drilling rigs, totalling 3,081,900 grt under the Danish flag; further tonnage owned by subsidiary cos in Singapore and the UK; world-wide liner and feeder services under the name of **Maersk Line**, and world-wide tanker, bulk, offshore and rig services; Man. Owner JESS SØDERBERG.

A/S Em. Z. Svitzer: Park Allé 350B, 2605 Brøndby; tel. 43-43-43-71; telex 15983; fax 43-43-60-22; f. 1833; wholly-owned subsidiary of A. P. Møller; 22 tugs and salvage vessels and a barge fleet; salvage, towage and barge services; Gen. Man. KELD BALLE-MORTENSEN.

Mortensen & Lange A/S: Kongevejen 2, 2480 Fredensborg; tel. 48-40-85-85; telex 15100; fax 42-28-00-57; f. 1961; general cargo vessels of 13,800 grt and 6 reefer vessels of 8,000 grt; worldwide tramping; Man. Dir TORBEN JANHOLT.

Dampskibsselskabet Norden A/S: Amaliegade 49, 1256 Copenhagen K; tel. 33-15-04-51; telex 22374; fax 33-15-61-99; f. 1871; 5 bulk carriers of 224,600 grt, 1 product tanker of 43,700 grt and 1 oil tanker of 55,000 grt; worldwide tramping; Man. Dir STEEN KRABBE.

Sønderborg Rederiaktieselskab: Havnevej 18, POB 20, 6320 Egernsund; tel. 74-44-14-35; telex 52815; fax 74-44-14-75; 6 livestock carriers of 5,700 grt; shipowners, managers, chartering agents; worldwide; Chair. B. CLAUSEN.

Terkol-Rederierne: Jaegergårdsvej 107, 8000 Århus C; tel. 86-13-36-88; telex 64578; fax 86-18-15-10; 2 container vessels of 21,100 grt and 17 chemical tankers of 42,400 grt; world-wide tanker services; Gen. Man. N. B. TERKILDSEN.

A/S D/S Torm: Marina Park, Sundkrogsgade 10, 2100 Copenhagen Ø; tel. 39-17-92-00; telex 22315; fax 39-17-93-93; f. 1889; 3 bulk carriers of 110,524 grt, 12 product tankers totalling 445,810 grt and 3 multipurpose vessels of 43,798 grt (1996); operator of a time-chartered fleet; liner services USA–West Africa; Man. Dir ERIK BEHN.

Association

Danmarks Rederiforening (Danish Shipowners' Asscn): Amaliegade 33, 1256 Copenhagen K; tel. 33-11-40-88; telex 16492; fax 33-11-62-10; f. 1884; 21 members, representing 4,500,000 grt (July 1995); Chair. of the Board NIELS BACH; Man. Dir PETER BJERREGAARD.

CIVIL AVIATION

The main international airport is Copenhagen Airport, situated about 10 km from the centre of the capital. The following domestic airports have scheduled flights to European and Scandinavian destinations: Ålborg, Århus and Billund in Jutland. Other domestic airports include Roskilde (30 km south-west of Copenhagen); Esbjerg, Karup, Skrydstrup, Stauning, Sønderborg and Thisted in Jutland; Odense in Funen; and Bornholm Airport on the island of Bornholm.

Statens Luftfartsvæsen (Civil Aviation Administration): Luftfartshuset, POB 744, 2450 Copenhagen SV; tel. 36-44-48-48; telex 27096; fax 36-44-03-03; e-mail dcaa@slv.dk; Dir-Gen. OLE ASMUSSEN.

Det Danske Luftfartselskab A/S—DDL (Danish Airlines): Industriens Hus, H. C. Andersens Blvd 18, 1553 Copenhagen V; tel. 33-14-13-33; fax 33-14-28-28; f. 1918; 50% govt-owned; Danish parent company of the designated national carrier, Scandinavian Airlines System—SAS (see under Sweden), SAS Commuter; Chair. HUGO SCHRØDER; Man. Dir GUNNAR TIETZ.

National Airlines

Cimber Air Denmark: Sønderborg Airport, 6400 Sønderborg; tel. 74-42-22-77; telex 52367; fax 74-42-65-11; f. 1950; operates domestic service in co-operation with Lufthansa and SAS; operates charter flights and total route systems for other cos throughout Europe; markets electronic data systems for airlines and industry; Pres., CEO JORGEN NIELSEN; Vice-Pres. (Airline Division) HANS I. NIELSEN.

Maersk Air: Copenhagen Airport South, 2791 Dragør; tel. 32-31-44-44; telex 31125; fax 32-31-44-90; e-mail mail@maersk-air.dk; f. 1969; provides charter flights for Scandinavian tour operators, operates domestic services and international flights to Belgium, Germany, Sweden, the Netherlands, Norway, and the UK; owned by Møller Group (see under Shipping); subsidiaries: Maersk Helicopters, Maersk Air Cargo; Maersk DFDS Travel; Chair. BJARNE HANSEN; Pres. FLEMMING KNUDSEN.

Muk Air: Copenhagen Airport South, 2791 Dragør; tel. 32-82-00-00; telex 37697; fax 32-82-00-79; f. 1979; operates scheduled services to destinations in Scandinavia and Germany; Pres. Capt. KNUT LINDAU; Vice-Pres. FRANK HOLTON.

Premiair: Copenhagen Airport South, 2791 Dragør; tel. 32-47-72-00; telex 31923; fax 32-45-12-20; f. 1994 by merger of Conair A/S (Denmark) and Scanair (Sweden); controlling stake acquired by Airtours in 1996; flights to major destinations in Europe; Pres. TOM CLAUSEN.

Star Air: Copenhagen Airport South, 2791 Dragør; tel. 32-31-43-43; telex 31459; fax 32-31-43-90; f. 1987; operates cargo services in Europe and the Middle East; Pres. BJARNE HANSEN.

Tourism

There were 27,007,143 overnight stays in all types of accommodation (10,350,832 in hotels and camping sites) by foreign visitors in 1996.

Danmarks Turistråd (The Danish Tourist Board): Vesterbrogade 6D, 1620 Copenhagen V; tel. 33-11-14-15; fax 33-93-14-16; e-mail dt@dt; internet http://www.dt.dk; f. 1967; Dir BJARNE EKLUND.

DANISH EXTERNAL TERRITORIES

THE FAROE ISLANDS

Introductory Survey

Location, Climate, Language, Religion, Flag, Capital

The Faroe Islands are a group of 18 islands (of which 17 are inhabited) in the Atlantic Ocean, between Scotland and Iceland. The main island is Streymoy, where more than one-third of the population resides. The climate is mild in winter and cool in summer, with a mean temperature of 7°C (45°F). Most of the inhabitants profess Christianity: the majority of Faroese belong to the Evangelical Lutheran Church of Denmark. The principal language is Faroese, but Danish is a compulsory subject in all schools. The flag (proportions 22 by 16) displays a red cross, bordered with blue, on a white background, the upright of the cross being to the left of centre. The capital is Tórshavn, which is situated on Streymoy.

History and Government

The Faroe Islands have been under Danish administration since Queen Margrethe I of Denmark inherited Norway in 1380. The islands were occupied by the United Kingdom while Denmark was under German occupation during the Second World War, but they were restored to Danish control immediately after the war. The Home Rule Act of 1948 gave the Faroese control over all their internal affairs. The Faroe Islands did not join the EC with Denmark in 1973. There is a local parliament (the Løgting), but the Danish Folketing, to which the Faroese send two members, is responsible for defence and foreign policy, constitutional matters and the judicial and monetary systems. The Faroes control fishing resources within their fisheries zone, and in September 1992 a long-standing dispute between Denmark and the Faroes was settled when the Danish Government agreed to give the Faroese authorities legislative and administrative power over mineral resources, including those beneath the bed of the sea in the area adjacent to the islands. This agreement removed one of the major obstacles to exploration for hydrocarbons off the Faroe Islands, where geologists consider that prospects for discovering reserves of petroleum and natural gas are favourable. In 1994 the Faroe Islands accordingly awarded a US company a licence to begin exploratory surveys, despite the existence of a dispute between Denmark and the United Kingdom over the demarcation of the continental shelf west of the Shetland Islands and south-east of the Faroe Islands, which had threatened to delay prospecting.

The centre-left coalition Government of the Social Democratic Party (SDP), Republicans and the People's Party, formed in 1975, collapsed in 1980 over a plan, opposed by the conservative People's Party, to extend through the winter months a government-owned ferry service linking the islands with Denmark, Norway and Scotland. At a general election, held in November, conservative political groups slightly increased their share of the popular vote. Although there was no material change in the balance of party representation in the Løgting, the Union Party formed a centre-right coalition with the People's Party and the Home Rule Party in January 1981. A general election was held in November 1984, and in December a four-party, centre-left coalition government was formed under the premiership of Atli Dam, comprising his SDP, the Home Rule Party, the Republican Party and the Christian People's Party combined with the Progressive and Fishing Industry Party (CPP-PFIP).

Elections in 1988 demonstrated a shift to the right in the Faroes, to the benefit of the People's Party. Its one member in the Danish Folketing increased his support in the national elections of September 1987 and May 1988. At a Faroese general election in November 1988 the incumbent Government lost its majority, and the People's Party became the largest party in the Løgting. In January 1989, after 10 weeks of negotiations, a centre-right coalition comprising the People's Party, the Republican Party, the Home Rule Party and the CPP-PFIP, and led by Jógvan Sundstein (Chairman of the People's Party), was formed. The coalition was committed to economic austerity and support for the fishing industry. In June 1989, however, the CPP-PFIP and the Home Rule Party withdrew their support for the Government. After three weeks a new coalition was formed. Sundstein remained Løgmadur (Prime Minister), and his People's Party was supported by the Republican and Union Parties. In October 1990, however, the Republican Party and the Union Party withdrew their support for the coalition Government. As a result, an early general election was held on 17 November. The SDP obtained the largest share of the vote, winning 10 seats (an increase of three), while the People's Party, which led the outgoing coalition, won seven seats (a loss of one seat). In January 1991 a coalition between the SDP and the People's Party was formed, under the leadership of Atli Dam. He was replaced in January 1993 by Marita Petersen (also of the SDP). In April the People's Party withdrew from the coalition, and was replaced by the Republican Party and the Home Rule Party. At a general election, held on 7 July 1994, the Union Party became the largest party in the Løgting, winning eight seats (an increase of two), while the SDP's allocation of seats was reduced from 10 to five. In September a coalition of the Union Party, the SDP, the Home Rule Party and the newly-formed Labour Front took office. Edmund Joensen replaced Petersen as Prime Minister. In 1996 the People's Party replaced the SDP in the governing coalition. Joensen remained Prime Minister, while Anfinn Kallsberg succeeded Jóannes Eidesgaard as Minister of Finance and Economics.

In international affairs, the Faroe Islanders earned opprobrium for their traditional slaughter of pilot whales, an important source of food. After foreign journalists publicized the whaling in 1986, stricter regulations were imposed on whaling operations. In July 1992 the Faroes Government threatened to leave the International Whaling Commission (IWC, see p. 253), following the latter's criticism of whaling methods practised in the Faroe Islands. It was, however, claimed that the Faroese did not have the legal right to withdraw from the Commission independently of Denmark. In September the Faroe Islands, Greenland, Norway and Iceland agreed to establish the North Atlantic Marine Mammal Commission, in protest at what they viewed as the IWC's preoccupation with conservation.

Responsibility for foreign policy lies in Copenhagen, but in 1983 the Løgting unanimously declared the Faroe Islands a 'nuclear-free zone', and in 1987, as a consequence of this policy, requested the Danish Government to curtail a US naval visit. There have also been several declarations of 'non-aligned' status, notwithstanding NATO membership as part of the Kingdom of Denmark. When the People's Party changed its policy, however, to advocate closer co-operation with the NATO alliance, the party ended political unanimity on the issue and made gains in the elections of 1987 and 1988.

Economic Affairs

In 1995 gross national product (GNP), estimated at 1990 prices, was US $829m., equivalent to $19,000 per head. Between 1973 and 1988, it was estimated, GNP increased, in real terms, at an average rate of 4.5% per year, with real GNP per head rising by 3.3% annually. Between 1989 and 1993, however, real GNP decreased dramatically, at an average rate of 9.4% per year. During 1994–95 real GNP increased by 4.2%. The average annual rate of population growth between 1977 and 1988 was 1.2%. Since then, however, the population has decreased at an average annual rate of 1.3%, although it was expected to increase by some 2% in 1996.

Agriculture (principally sheep-farming) and fishing contributed 13% of gross domestic product (GDP) in 1994. Potatoes and other vegetables are the main crops. Only about 6% of the land surface is cultivated.

Fishing is the dominant industry. In 1994 fishing and fish-processing accounted for 18% of GDP, employed 23% of the labour force and provided 96% of exports. Most fishing takes place within the 200-nautical-mile (370-km) fisheries zone imposed around the Faroes in 1977, and in the 1980s there was massive investment in developing the fishing fleet and the processing plants on the islands. The fishing industry has considerably declined, however, since 1991. In the 1980s fish farming began to be encouraged, and in 1994 farmed fish amounted to about 12,400 metric tons and earned some 363m. kroner. The traditional hunting of whales (see Recent History) is an important source of meat.

Industry (including mining, manufacturing, construction and power) contributed 18% of GDP in 1994. The dominant sector is fish-processing. Coal is mined on Suðuroy, and a small textile industry exports traditional Faroese woollens. Manufacturing alone accounted for 12% of GDP in 1994. The export of machinery and transport equipment accounted for some 3% of total exports in 1994, and consists mainly of sea-going vessels. About 48% of the islands' energy requirements are provided by a hydroelectric power plant. The potential for petroleum production around the islands is believed to be significant.

In 1995 the Faroe Islands recorded a trade surplus of 523m. kroner, and there was an estimated surplus of 700m. kroner on the current account of the balance of payments. Denmark remains the Faroes' principal trading partner, supplying 34% of imports and receiving 22% of exports in 1995. The EU as a whole took 79% of exports in that year, the UK receiving 26% and Germany 10%. Norway is also a major source of imports, supplying about 16% of the total in 1995. The principal imports from Norway are animal food and live animals, and machinery and transport equipment.

Danish subsidies are an important source of income to the islands, and accounted for about 31% of total government revenue in 1995. In that year, including the central government grant of 852m. kroner as revenue, the Faroese Government recorded a budget deficit of 79m. kroner. At the end of 1995 the net foreign debt was estimated at 4,700m. kroner, or some 83% of GNP. The annual rate of inflation averaged 4.0% between 1987 and 1991, falling to 0.4% in 1992. However, in 1993 it rose sharply to 6.8%, largely owing to the introduction of a value-added tax. In 1994 and 1995 the average annual rate of inflation stood at 2.3% and 3.2%, respectively. In the 1980s there was an acute labour shortage in the Faroes, but by mid-1995 unemployment had increased to 3,200, equivalent to some 16% of the labour force. By the end of 1996 unemployment had declined to some 10% of the labour force.

The Faroe Islands did not join the EC with Denmark in 1973, but did secure favourable terms of trade with Community members and special concessions in Denmark and the United Kingdom. Agreements on free trade were concluded between the Faroe Islands and Iceland, Norway, Sweden, Finland and Austria in 1992 and 1993. In international fisheries organizations, where Denmark is represented by the EU, the Kingdom maintains separate membership in respect of the Faroe Islands (and Greenland). The Faroe Islands is also a member of the Nordic Council (see p. 200).

During the 1980s the Faroes' principal source of income, the fishing industry, was expanded with the help of substantial investment and official subsidies, financed by external borrowing. However, depletion of stocks and the resulting decline in catches, together with a fall in export prices, led to a reduction in export earnings and a financial crisis in the early 1990s (GDP was estimated to have declined by some 20% in 1993). The Danish Government attempted to stabilize the economy by restructuring the banking sector and by extending significant loans (by the end of 1997 it was estimated that the Faroes owed some 5,500m. kroner to the Danish Government, equivalent to 140,000 kroner per head). The report of an independent commission of inquiry into Denmark's response to the crisis in the Faroes, which had been established by the islanders in 1995, was published in early 1998 and levelled accusations of serious mismanagement at Danish government officials, and at the Danish Den Danske Bank. It was widely anticipated that some form of compensation would be offered to the islanders during 1998.

Education and Social Welfare

The education system is similar to that of Denmark, except that Faroese is the language of instruction. Danish is, however, a compulsory subject in all schools. The Faroese Academy was upgraded to the University of the Faroe Islands in May 1990.

In 1995 government medical services included three hospitals, with a total of 297 beds.

In 1995 government expenditure on social welfare represented 28% of total budget spending, while education received a further 13% of the total.

Statistical Survey

Sources (unless otherwise stated): Statistical Bureau of the Faroe Islands, POB 355, 110 Tórshavn; tel. 14636; fax 18696; Faroese Government Office, Højbro Plads 7, 1200 Copenhagen K; tel. 33-14-08-66; fax 33-93-85-75; *Yearbook of Nordic Statistics*.

AREA AND POPULATION

Area: 1,398.9 sq km (540.1 sq miles).

Population: 43,382 (males 22,412, females 20,970) at 31 December 1995.

Density (1995): 31.0 per sq km.

Principal Town: Tórshavn (capital), population 15,272 at 31 December 1995.

Births and Deaths (1995): Registered live births 638 (birth rate 14.6 per 1,000); Deaths 361 (death rate 8.3 per 1,000).

Labour Force (estimate, Dec. 1995): Total 20,345.

AGRICULTURE AND FISHING

Principal Crop (FAO estimate, 1996): Potatoes 2,000 metric tons. Source: FAO, *Production Yearbook*.

Livestock (FAO estimates, '000 head, year ending September 1996): Cattle 2; Sheep 68. Source: FAO, *Production Yearbook*.

Fishing ('000 metric tons, live weight, 1995): Cod 43.4, Haddock 8.3, Saithe (Pollock) 30.1, Redfish 14.2, Blue whiting (Poutassou) 26.7, Norway pout 9.7, Herring 62.0, Horse mackerel 1.0, Mackerel 29.5, Capelin 3.7, Scallop 2.8, Prawn 9.4; Total catch by Faroese vessels (incl. other species) 285.0. Number of cetaceans caught (1995): 228 pilot whales.

INDUSTRY

Selected Products ('000 metric tons, unless otherwise indicated, 1995): Frozen or chilled fish 129.4; Salted and processed fish products 14.1; Aquamarine products 6.0; Oils, fats and meal of aquatic animals 29.7; Electric energy (million kWh) 174.9.

FINANCE

Danish currency is in use.

Government Accounts ('000 kroner, 1995): Revenue 1,874,000; Danish state subsidy 852,000; Expenditure 2,805,000.

Cost of Living (Consumer Price Index; base: 1983 = 100): *1995:* Food 206.1; Fuel and power 77.1; Clothing 157.1; Dwellings 140.3; Other 147.7; All items 157.3.

Gross Domestic Product by Economic Activity (million kroner at current factor cost, 1994): Agriculture, fishing, etc. 639; Mining and quarrying 6; Manufacturing 574; Electricity, gas and water 93; Construction 171; Trade, restaurants and hotels 538; Transport, storage and communications 372; Financing 370; Dwellings 685; Business services, etc. 126; Domestic services 11; Government services 1,215; Sub-total (incl. adjustment) 4,791; *Less* imputed bank service charges 457; Gross domestic product at factor cost 4,334.

Balance of Payments (US $ million, 1995): Merchandise exports f.o.b. 362; Merchandise imports c.i.f. –315; *Trade balance* 46; Services, other income and private unrequited transfers (net) –114; Official unrequited transfers (net) 193; *Current balance* 125.

EXTERNAL TRADE

Principal Commodities (million kroner, 1995): *Imports c.i.f.:* Food and live animals 111; Mineral fuels, lubricants, etc. 202 (Petroleum products 190); Chemicals and related products 69; Commodities for final consumption 625; Machinery and transport equipment 248 (Machinery specialized for particular industries 45, General industrial machinery, equipment and parts 64, Electric machinery, apparatus, etc. 37, Road vehicles and parts 91); Total (incl. others) 1,766. *Exports f.o.b.:* Food and live animals 1,874; Machinery and transport equipment 35; Total (incl. others) 2,026.

Principal Trading Partners (million kroner, 1995): *Imports c.i.f.:* Denmark 608; Germany 138; Iceland 48; Japan 53; Norway 279; Sweden 102; United Kingdom 149; USA 27; Total (incl. others) 1,767. *Exports f.o.b.:* Denmark 449; France (incl. Monaco) 168; Germany 196; Greece 6; Italy 102; Japan 77; Spain 98; Sweden 53; United Kingdom 523; USA 41; Total (incl. others) 2,026.

TRANSPORT

Road Traffic (registered motor vehicles, 31 December 1995): Private motor cars 11,528; Goods vehicles 2,673; Buses 106; Coaches 116; Trailers 949; Motor cycles 132.

Shipping (30 June 1995): Merchant fleet (displacement) 86,002 gross registered tons (fishing vessels 53,953 grt); International seaborne freight traffic (1994, '000 metric tons): Goods loaded 130, Goods unloaded 367.

COMMUNICATIONS MEDIA

Radio Receivers (1994): 24,000 registered.

Television Receivers (1994): 14,000 registered.

Book Production (1995): 155 titles.

Newspapers (1995): 5 titles (average circulation 7,000 copies per issue).

Telephones ('000 main lines in use, 1994): 23 (Source: UN, *Statistical Yearbook*).

Telefax Stations (1993): 1,400 in use (Source: UN, *Statistical Yearbook*).

Mobile Cellular Telephones (subscribers, 1994): 1,960 (Source: UN, *Statistical Yearbook*).

Directory

The Government

The legislative body is the Løgting (Lagting in Danish) which consists of 27 members, elected on a basis of proportional representation in seven constituencies, with up to five supplementary seats dependent upon the discrepancy between the distribution of seats among the parties and the numbers of people voting. All Faroese over the age of 18 years have the right to vote. Based on the strength of the parties in the Løgting, a Government, the Landsstýri, is formed. This is the administrative body in certain spheres, chiefly relating to Faroese economic affairs. The Løgmaður (Prime Minister) has to ratify all Løgting laws. Power is decentralized and there are about 50 local authorities. The Ríkisumboðsmaður, or High Commissioner, represents the Danish Government, and has the right to address the Løgting and to advise on joint affairs. All Danish legislation must be submitted to the Landsstýri before becoming law in the Faroe Islands.

LANDSSTÝRI

(February 1998)

A coalition of the Union Party (UP), the People's Party (PP), the Labour Front (LF) and the Home Rule Party (HRP).

Prime Minister (with responsibility for Constitutional Affairs, Foreign Affairs, Administration and Judicial Affairs): EDMUND JOENSEN (UP).

Minister of Finance and Economics: ANFINN KALLSBERG (PP).

Minister of the Fishing Industry: JOHN PETERSEN (PP).

Minister of Social Affairs, Labour Matters and the Health Service: KRISTIAN MAGNUSSEN (LF).

Minister of Education, Energy, Environment, Nordic Affairs and Municipal Affairs: EILIF SAMUELSEN (UP).

Minister of Industry, Trade, Agriculture and Insurance: IVAN JOHANNESEN (UP).

Minister of Communications, Shipping, Culture and Tourism: SÁMAL PETUR Í GRUND (HRP).

Government Offices

Ríkisumboðsmaðurin (Danish High Commission): POB 12, Amtmansbrekkan 4, 110 Tórshavn; tel. 11040; fax 10864; High Commissioner VIBEKE LARSEN.

Løgtingsskrivstovan (Parliament Office): POB 208, 110 Tórshavn; tel. 10850; fax 10686; Leader SÚSANNA DANIELSEN.

Faroese Government Office: Højbro Plads 7, 1200 Copenhagen K; tel. 33-14-08-66; fax 33-93-85-75.

LØGTING

The Løgting has between 27 and 32 members, elected by universal adult suffrage.

Speaker: JÓGVAN I. OLSEN (Union Party).

Election, 7 July 1994

	Votes	Seats
Sambandsflokkurin (Union Party)	5,974	8
Fólkaflokkurin (People's Party)	4,080	6
Javnaðarflokkurin (Social Democratic Party)	3,917	5
Tjóðveldisflokkurin (Republican Party)	3,489	4
Verkmannafylkingin (Labour Front)	2,417	3
Kristiligi Fólkaflokkurin, Føroya Framburðs- og Fiskivinnuflokkurin (Christian People's Party, Progressive and Fishing Industry Party)	1,606	2
Miðflokkurin (Centre Party)	1,485	2
Sjálvstýrisflokkurin (Home Rule Party)	1,434	2
Total (incl. others)	25,501	32

Political Organizations

Unless otherwise indicated, the address of each of the following organizations is: Aarvegur, POB 208, 110 Tórshavn; tel. 10850; fax 10686.

Fólkaflokkurin (People's Party): f. 1940; conservative-liberal party, favours free enterprise and wider political and economic autonomy for the Faroes; Chair. ÓLI BRECKMANN.

Hin Føroyski Flokkurin (The Faroese Party): f. 1994; seeks to abolish Home Rule and fully to re-integrate the Faroes into the Kingdom of Denmark; Chair. ÓLAVUR CHRISTIANSEN.

Javnaðarflokkurin (Social Democratic Party—SDP): Argjavegur 26, 160 Argir; tel. 11820; fax 14720; f. 1928; Chair. JÓANNES EIDESGAARD.

Kristiligi Fólkaflokkurin, Føroya Framburðs- og Fiskivinnuflokkurin (Christian People's Party, Progressive and Fishing Industry Party—CPP-PFIP): à Brekku 5, 700 Klaksvík; tel. 57580; fax 57581; f. 1954; centre party; Chair. NIELS PAULI DANIELSEN; Parliamentary Chair. LASSE KLEIN.

Miðflokkurin (Centre Party): POB 3237, 110 Tórshavn; f. 1991; Chair. TORDUR NICLASEN.

Sambandsflokkurin (Union Party): f. 1906; favours the maintenance of close relations between the Faroes and the Kingdom of Denmark; conservative in internal affairs; Chair. EDMUND JOENSEN.

Sjálvstýrisflokkurin (Home Rule Party): f. 1906; social-liberal party advocating eventual political independence for the Faroes within the Kingdom of Denmark; Chair. HELENA DAM Á NEYSTABØ.

Tjóðveldisflokkurin (Republican Party): Villingadalsvegi, 100 Tórshavn; tel. 14412; f. 1948; left-wing party, advocates the secession of the Faroes from Denmark; Chair. FINNBOGI ÍSAKSON.

Verkmannafylkingin (Labour Front): f. 1994 by Union leaders and former members of the SDP.

Religion

CHRISTIANITY

The Faroes Church (Evangelical Lutheran Church of Denmark) regained its diocese in November 1990, and the suffragan bishop became Bishop of the Faroe Islands. The largest independent group is the 'Plymouth Brethren'. There is also a small Roman Catholic community.

Evangelical Lutheran Church

Føroya Biskupur (Bishop of the Faroe Islands): HANS J. JOENSEN, J. Paturssonargøta 20, POB 8, 110 Tórshavn; tel. 11995; fax 15889.

The Press

There are no daily papers in the Faroe Islands. In 1996 there were six general interest newspapers.

Dagblaðið: Reynagøta 9, 100 Tórshavn; tel. 19833; fax 19823; weekly; People's Party.

Dimmalætting: Smyrilsvegur, POB 19, 110 Tórshavn; tel. 11212; telex 81222; fax 10941; 4 a week; Union Party; circ. 11,000.

FF/FA-Blaðið: Vágsbotnur, POB 58, 110 Tórshavn; tel. 12169; fax 18769; weekly; Editor VILMUND JACOBSEN; circ. 2,500.

Norðlýsið: á Hædd, POB 58, 700 Klaksvík; tel. 56285; fax 56498; weekly; circ. 1,200.

Oyggjatíðindi: R. C. Effersøesgøta 7, POB 3312, 110 Tórshavn; tel. 14411; fax 16410; 2 a week; circ. 4,500.

Tíðindablaðið Sosialurin: POB 76, 110 Tórshavn; tel. 11820; fax 14720; f. 1927; 5 a week; Editor JAN MÜLLER; Social Democratic Party; circ. 7,000.

NEWS AGENCY

Ritzaus Bureau: Gamli Vegur 3; tel. 16366; f. 1980; Man. RANDI MOHR.

Broadcasting and Communications

RADIO

Útvarp Føroya (Faroese Broadcasting Corporation): Norðari Ringvegur, POB 328, 110 Tórshavn; tel. 16566; telex 81226; fax 10471; e-mail uf@utvarp.olivant.fo; internet http://utvarp.olivant.fo: f. 1957; Man. JÓGVAN JESPERSEN.

TELEVISION

Sjónvarp Føroya (Faroese Television): M. A. Winthersgøta, POB 21, 110 Tórshavn; tel. 17780; telex 81391; fax 11345; f. 1984; Gen. Man. J. A. SKAALE.

Finance

BANKS

(cap. = capital; res = reserves; dep. = deposits; m. = million; amounts in kroner; brs = branches)

Føroya Banki P/f: Husagøta 3, POB 3048, 110 Tórshavn; tel. 11350; telex 81227; fax 15850; f. 1906; amalgamated with Sjóvinnubankin P/F in 1994; cap. 175m., res 478m., dep. 2,968m., total assets 3,838m. (Dec. 1996); Chair. JÓHAN PÁLL JOENSEN; Mans JORN ASTRUP HANSEN, JANUS PETERSEN; 25 brs.

Føroya Sparikassi (Faroese Savings Bank): Tinghúsvegur 14, POB 34, 110 Tórshavn; tel. 14800; telex 81318; fax 19948; f. 1832; res 588m., dep. 2,494m., total assets 3,175m. (Dec. 1995); Man. EYÐUN Á RÓGVU OLSEN.

Landsbanki Føroya: Müllers Hús, Gongin, POB 229, 110 Tórshavn; tel. 18305; fax 18537; e-mail landsbankin@lbk.olivant.fo; Man. SIGURÐ POULSEN.

Norðoya Sparikassi: Ósávegur 1, POB 149, 700 Klaksvík; tel. 56366; fax 56761.

Suðuroya Sparikassi: 900 Vágur.

INSURANCE

Tryggingarsambandið Føroyar: Kongabrúgvin, POB 329, 110 Tórshavn; tel. 14590; telex 81253; fax 15590; marine, fire, accident and life; only insurance co. in islands; Man. JENS PETUR ARGE.

Trade and Industry

GOVERNMENT AGENCY

Fiskivinnuumsitingin (Fisheries Administration): POB 87, 110 Tórshavn; tel. 13068; telex 81310; fax 14942.

INDUSTRIAL AND TRADE ASSOCIATIONS

L/F Føroya Fiskasøla—Faroe Seafood Prime P/F: Yviri við Strond 2, POB 68, 110 Tórshavn; tel. 14960; fax 12520; f. 1948, restructured 1995; joint stock company of fish producers; exports all marine produce; Man. Dir POUL MICHELSEN.

Føroya Reiðarafelag (Faroe Fishing Vessel-Owners' Association): R.C. Effersøesgøta, POB 179, 110 Tórshavn; tel. 11864; telex 81388; fax 17278.

TRADE UNION

Føroya Arbeiðarafelag (Faroese Labour Organization): Tjarnð eild 5, POB 56, 110 Tórshavn; tel. 12101; telex 82416; fax 15374.

Transport

There are about 458 km of roads in the Faroe Islands. The main harbour is at Tórshavn; the other ports are at Fuglafjørður, Klaksvík, Skálafjørður, Tvøroyri, Vágur and Vestmanna. Between mid-May and mid-September, a summer roll-on, roll-off ferry service links the Faroe Islands with Iceland, Shetland (United Kingdom), Denmark and Norway.

There is an airport on Vágar.

Atlantic Airways Faroe Islands: Vágar Airport, 380 Sørvágur; tel. 33344; telex 82440; fax 33380; f. 1987; owned by Faroes Govt; scheduled passenger and cargo services to Copenhagen; Pres. MAGNI ARGE.

Tourism

Ferðaráð Føroya (Faroe Islands Tourist Board): Gongin, POB 118, 110 Tórshavn; tel. 16055; fax 10858; f. 1984; Man. JAN MORTENSEN.

GREENLAND

Introductory Survey

Location, Climate, Language, Religion, Flag, Capital

Greenland (Kalaallit Nunaat) is the world's largest island, with a total area of 2,166,086 sq km, and lies in the North Atlantic Ocean, east of Canada. Most of it is permanently covered by ice, but 410,449 sq km of coastland are habitable. Greenlandic, an Inuit (Eskimo) language, and Danish are the official languages. The majority of the population profess Christianity and belong mainly to the Evangelical Lutheran Church of Denmark. There are also small communities of other Protestant groups and of Roman Catholics. The flag (proportions 3 by 2) consists of two equal horizontal stripes (white above red) on which is superimposed a representation of the rising sun (a disc divided horizontally, red above white) to the left of centre. Nuuk (Godthåb) is the capital.

Recent History

Greenland first came under Danish rule in 1380. In the revision of the Danish Constitution in 1953, Greenland became part of the Kingdom and acquired the representation of two members in the Danish Folketing. In October 1972 the Greenlanders voted, by 9,658 to 3,990, against joining the EC but, as part of Denmark, were bound by the Danish decision to join. Resentment of Danish domination of the economy, education and the professions continued, taking expression when, in 1977, the nationalist Siumut movement formed a left-wing party. In 1975 the Minister for Greenland appointed a commission to devise terms for Greenland home rule, and its proposals were approved, by 73.1% to 26.9%, in a referendum among the Greenland electorate in January 1979. The Siumut, led by a Lutheran pastor, Jonathan Motzfeldt, secured 13 seats in the 21-member Landsting (the local legislature) at a general election in April, and a five-member Landsstyre, with Motzfeldt as Prime Minister, took office in May. Since 1979 the island has been gradually assuming full administration of its internal affairs.

In February 1982 a referendum was held to decide Greenland's continued membership of the EC. This resulted in a 53% majority in favour of withdrawal. Negotiations were begun in May 1982, with the Danish Government acting on Greenland's behalf, and were concluded in March 1984 (with effect from 1 February 1985): Greenland was accorded the status of an overseas territory in association with the Community, with preferential access to EC markets.

At the April 1983 general election to the Landsting (enlarged, by measures adopted in 1982, to between 23 and 26 seats, depending on the proportion of votes cast), the Siumut and the conservative Atassut parties won 12 seats each, while the Inuit Ataqatigiit (IA) won two seats. The Siumut party once again formed a Government, led by Motzfeldt, dependent on the support of the IA members in the Landsting: this support was withdrawn in March 1984, when the IA members voted against the terms of withdrawal from the EC, and Motzfeldt resigned. In the ensuing general election, held in June, the Siumut and Atassut parties won 11 seats each, while the IA won three. Motzfeldt again formed a coalition Government, comprising the Siumut party and the IA.

In March 1987 the coalition Government collapsed, following a dispute between the Siumut party and the IA over policy towards the modernization of the US radar facility at Thule, which was claimed by the IA to be in breach of the 1972 US-Soviet Anti-Ballistic Missile Treaty. A general election was held in May. Each party retained 11 seats in the Landsting (which had been enlarged in 1986, to 27 seats—23 of which were to be obtained by election in multi-member constituencies, while four were to be supplementary seats); the IA won four seats, and the remaining seat was won by the newly-formed Issittup Partiia, which was demanding the privatization of the trawler fleet. Motzfeldt eventually formed a new coalition Government with the IA. In May 1988, at elections to the Danish Folketing, Siumut was the most successful party. In June the coalition between Siumut and the IA collapsed, and Motzfeldt formed a new Siumut Government, with support from the Atassut party. In the municipal elections of April 1989, Siumut's share of the votes increased to 41.8%, while support for Atassut fell to only 31.3%. In December 1990, when the Atassut party withdrew its support for the Siumut administration (following allegations that government ministers had misused public funds), Motzfeldt organized an early general election for 5 March 1991, at which both Siumut and Atassut obtained a reduced share of the vote. Siumut received 37.3%, and Atassut 30.1%, of the votes cast, while the IA's share rose to 19.4%. Accordingly, Siumut retained 11 seats in the Landsting, while Atassut's representation decreased to eight seats and the IA's increased to five. A new party, the liberal Akulliit Partiiaat, won two seats, and the remaining place was taken by the Issittup Partiia. Siumut and the IA formed a coalition Government and elected the Chairman of Siumut, Lars Emil Johansen, as Prime Minister. In muncipal elections in April 1993 Siumut received 38.2% of the votes cast, Atassut 24.6% and the IA 17.1%.

At the general election held in March 1995 Siumut secured 38.4% of the votes cast and increased to 12 seats its representation in the Landsting (enlarged to 31 seats). Atassut received 30.1% of the votes (10 seats) and the IA obtained 20.3% (6 seats). A coalition Government was formed between Siumut and Atassut, following the withdrawal from negotiations of the IA, which failed to reach agreement with Siumut on the question of independence. Johansen retained the premiership, while Daniel Skifte, the leader of Atassut, was appointed Minister of Finance and Housing. In early 1997 Johansen asserted that Greenland could achieve economic independence from Denmark on the basis of its unexploited mineral resources. In September Motzfeldt replaced Johansen as Prime Minister at the head of the coalition. Johansen was reported to have taken a senior position with the Royal Greenland fishing group.

Denmark remains responsible for Greenland's foreign relations. Greenland does have separate representation on the Nordic Council (see p. 200), and is a member of the Inuit Circumpolar Conference (see p. 204). Denmark, a member of NATO, retains its responsibility for defence, and Danish-US military co-operation in Greenland began in 1951. Under a 1981 agreement on the defence of Greenland, two US radar bases were established on Greenland, at Thule and at Kangerlussuaq (Søndre Strømfjord). An agreement between the USA and Denmark for the reduction of the bases from 325,000 ha to 160,000 ha took effect from 1 October 1986, and the land thus becoming available was returned to the Inuit. In March 1991 the USA agreed to transfer ownership and control of the base at Kangerlussuaq to the Greenland Government in September 1992, in exchange for the right to use it again in the future. In July 1996 it was announced that the base at Thule would be opened to aircraft.

In June 1980 the Danish Government declared an economic zone extending 200 nautical miles (370 km) off the east coast of Greenland. This, however, caused a dispute with Norway over territorial waters, owing to the existence of the small Norwegian island of Jan Mayen, 460 km off the east coast of Greenland. In 1988 Denmark requested the International Court of Justice to arbitrate on the issue of conflicting economic zones. A delimitation line was established by the Court in June 1993. A subsequent accord on maritime delimitation, agreed between the Governments of Norway, Greenland and Iceland in November 1997, established the boundaries of a 1,934-sq km area of Arctic sea which had been excluded from the terms of the 1993 settlement.

Government

Greenland is part of the Kingdom of Denmark, and the Danish Government, which remains responsible for foreign affairs, defence and justice, is represented by the Rigsombudsmand, or High Commissioner, in Nuuk (Godthåb). Most functions of government are administered by the 'Home Rule Government', the Landsstyre. The formation of this executive is dependent upon support in the local legislature, the Landsting. The Landsting has 31 members elected for a maximum term of four years, on a basis of proportional representation. Greenland also elects two members to the Danish Folketing. For administration purposes, Greenland is divided into 18 municipalities, of which the largest is Nuuk.

Defence

The Danish Government, which is responsible for Greenland's defence, co-ordinates military activities through its Greenland Command. The Greenland Command, which also undertakes fisheries control and sea rescues, is based at the Grønnedal naval base, in south-west Greenland. Greenlanders are not liable for military service. As part of the Kingdom of Denmark, Greenland belongs to NATO. The USA operates an air base, at Pituffik in Thule (see Recent History). In 1993 the Danish Government spent 315m. kroner (10.6% of total central government expenditure on Greenland) on the territory's defence, of which 253m. kroner was spent on the Fisheries Inspectorate.

Economic Affairs

In 1994, according to preliminary official estimates, Greenland's gross national product (GNP) was 6,381m. kroner, equivalent to some 114,800 kroner per head. The economy enjoyed overall growth during the 1970s and 1980s, but gross domestic product (GDP) declined by 9%, in real terms, in 1990, and continued to decline significantly (owing to depleted fish stocks and the discontinuation of lead and zinc mining) until 1994 and 1995, when real growth rates of 5% and 3%, respectively, were recorded.. The population increased at an average annual rate of 0.5% between 1985 and 1996.

Fishing dominates the commercial economy, as well as being important to the traditional way of life. In 1995 the fishing industry accounted for almost all of Greenland's total export revenue. It was estimated that the industry, including the processing of the catch, employed about one-sixth of the paid labour force in the late 1980s. The cod catch has declined substantially, however, since 1989. The traditional occupation of the Greenlanders is seal-hunting, which remains important in the north. The only feasible agricultural activity in the harsh climate is livestock-rearing, and only sheep-farming has proved to be of any commercial significance. There are also herds of domesticated reindeer.

Industry (including mining, manufacturing, construction and public works) employed some 25% of those in paid employment in March 1987. Mining earned 13.0% of total export revenue in 1990. A Swedish company extracted lead, zinc and some silver at the important mine at Marmorilik in the north-west. The mine was closed, however, in 1990. In recent years there have been several discoveries of petroleum, natural gas and other mineral deposits, which, it is hoped, can be exploited.

Manufacturing is mainly dependent upon the fishing industry. Water power (meltwater from the ice-cap and glaciers) is an important potential source of electricity. All mineral fuels are imported. Mineral fuels accounted for 8% of total imports in 1995.

In 1995 Greenland recorded a visible trade deficit of 350m. kroner. The principal trading partner remains Denmark, although its monopoly on trade ceased in 1950. Denmark supplied 75% of imports and received 89% of exports in 1995. Trade is still dominated by companies owned by the Home Rule Government. The principal exports are fish and fish products, and the principal imports are machinery and transport equipment.

Greenland is dependent upon large grants from the central Danish Government. In 1995 central government expenditure on Greenland included some 2,393m. kroner in the form of a direct grant to the Home Rule Government. Greenland has few debts, and also receives valuable revenue from the EU (see below) for fishing licences. The annual rate of inflation averaged 3.3% in 1985–96, and stood at 1.6% in 1996. In August 1997 8.4% of the urban labour force were unemployed.

Greenland, although a part of the Kingdom of Denmark, withdrew from the (then) EC in 1985 (see Recent History). It remains a territory in association with the EU, however, and has preferential access to European markets. The loss of EU development aid has been offset by the annual payment (ECU 37.7m. during 1995–2000) for member countries to retain fishing rights in Greenlandic waters.

Greenland's economy is dominated by the fishing industry, but remains a subsistence, barter economy for a large part of the population. Migration to the towns and the rejection of a traditional life-style by many young people have, however, created new social and economic problems. Dependence on a single commodity leaves the economy vulnerable to the effects of depletion of fish stocks and fluctuating international prices. Any development or progress is possible only with Danish aid, which is already fundamental to Greenlandic finances. In an effort to generate revenue from the tourist industry, the Home Rule Government undertook, in 1990, to achieve a target of 35,000 tourist arrivals (equivalent to 500m. kroner) annually by 2025; by 1994 the campaign was showing positive results and tourist arrivals had doubled compared with levels in previous years.

Education and Social Welfare

The educational system is based on that of Denmark, except that the main language of instruction is Greenlandic. Danish is, however, widely used. There is a school in every settlement. In 1992/93 there were 86 primary and lower secondary schools, with 9,785 pupils and 725 full-time and 219 part-time teachers. In the same year there were also three upper secondary schools, with 168 students. There is a teacher-training college in Nuuk, and a university centre opened in 1987. In 1995 current expenditure on education by the Home Rule Government (including allocations to the municipalities) represented 11% of total current budget spending.

There is a free health service for all residents, comprising examination, treatment and nursing, and dental services. In 1995 there were 114 physicians and dentists, and the territory had 17 regional health centres and one central hospital. The Home Rule Government assumed control of health services on 1 January 1992 (and Denmark's annual subsidy to Greenland was increased accordingly thereafter). In the budget for 1995 some 577m. kroner (17% of total current spending) was allocated to health services. The social welfare system is based on the Scandinavian welfare model. In 1995 it was allocated 18.5% of total current budget expenditure. Public aid for the unemployed is administered locally, and trade union members also have a system of unemployment insurance. Old age pensions (beginning at the age of 60), disability pensions, housing benefits and maternity and child benefits are also provided.

Statistical Survey

Sources: Greenland Bureau of Statistics, *Statistical Yearbook*; Greenland Home Rule Government—Denmark Bureau, Pilestræde 52, POB 2151, 1122 Copenhagen K; tel. 33-13-42-24; fax 33-13-49-71; Greenland Bureau of Statistics, Box 1025, 3900 Nuuk; tel. 23000; fax 22954.

AREA, POPULATION AND DENSITY

Area: Total 2,166,086 sq km (836,330 sq miles); Ice-free portion 410,449 sq km (158,475 sq miles).

Population: 55,863 (males 29,817; females 26,046) at 1 January 1996 (incl. 48,679 born in Greenland).

Density (1996): 0.026 per sq km.

Capital: Nuuk (Godthåb), population 13,286 (1996).

Births, Marriages and Deaths (1994): Registered live births 1,156 (birth rate 20.6 per 1,000); Registered marriages (1993) 436 (marriage rate 7.8 per 1,000); Registered deaths 440 (death rate 7.9 per 1,000).

Labour Force (census of 26 October 1976): Males 14,234; Females 7,144; Total 21,378. **1994:** Total 28,300 (incl. 23,000 employed).

AGRICULTURE AND FISHING

Livestock (1995): Sheep 19,464, Reindeer 4,600.

Hunting (1995): Fox skins 74, Polar bears 72, Seals 47,675 (Ringed seal 32,493), Minke whales 155.

Fishing ('000 metric tons, live weight, 1995): Greenland halibut 18.6, Atlantic cod 9.2, Other fishes 11.1, Crabs 1.0, Northern prawn 82.7, Scallops 5.3; Total catch 127.9. The total excludes seals and whales, which are recorded by number rather than by weight (see Hunting, above).

MINING

Production (concentrates, '000 metric tons, 1989): Lead 36; Zinc 131. The estimated metal content ('000 metric tons) was: Lead 20.0; Zinc 71.5 (source: US Bureau of Mines). Note: The mine producing lead and zinc closed in 1990.

INDUSTRY

Selected Products: Frozen fish (1994) 11,000 metric tons; Salted, dried or smoked fish (1993) 300 metric tons; Electric energy (1995 estimate) 257 million kWh. Source: partly UN, *Industrial Commodity Statistics Yearbook.*

FINANCE

Danish currency is in use.

Central Government Expenditure (by Ministry, million kroner, 1994): *Current:* Prime Minister's Office 8, Transport 41, Justice 116, Defence 321 (Fisheries Inspectorate 253), Finance 2,375 (Grant to Home Rule Govt 2,375), Energy 123, Other 10, Total 2,994. *Capital:* 12. *Total:* 3,006.

Home Rule Government Accounts (million kroner, 1995): *Revenue:* Current 3,786 (Income tax 524, Import and production duties 540, Fishing licences 281, Danish central govt grant 2,393, Other 48), Capital 169, Total 3,955. *Expenditure:* Current 3,318 (Grants to municipalities 621, Education, church and culture 513, Social security and welfare 613, Health and environment 609), Capital 595 (Housing 243), Total 3,913, excl. net lending (–6).

Cost of Living (consumer price index; annual averages; base: 1990 = 100): 106.0 in 1992; 107.2 in 1993; 107.7 in 1994 (Source: ILO, *Yearbook of Labour Statistics*).

Gross Domestic Product (provisional, million kroner at current market prices): 6,386 in 1992; 6,365 in 1993; 6,731 in 1994.

Gross National Product by Economic Activity (million kroner at factor cost, 1988): Agriculture and fisheries 971; Mineral resources 328; Manufacturing 171; Electricity, gas and heating 195; Construction 1,063, Other private services 1,989; Public sector 1,648; Total 6,365.

EXTERNAL TRADE

Principal Commodities (provisional, million kroner, 1995): *Imports c.i.f.:* Food and live animals 248.8 (Meat and meat preparations 81.9); Beverages and tobacco 85.4 (Beverages 64.3); Mineral fuels, lubricants etc. 195.4 (Petroleum products 193.1); Chemicals 100.8; Basic manufactures 419.3; Machinery and transport equipment 582.0 (Machinery 384.0, Transport equipment 198.0); Miscellaneous manufactured articles 305.0; Total (incl. others) 2,430.8. *Exports f.o.b.:* Shrimps 1,516; Cod 58; Other fish products 318; Total (incl. others) 2,081.

Principal Trading Partners (US $ million, 1995): *Imports c.i.f.:* Denmark 314.9, Japan 14.1, Norway 13.1; Total (incl. others) 421.1. *Exports f.o.b.:* Denmark 322.5, Japan 16.9, United Kingdom 16.9; Total (incl. others) 363.6. Source: UN, *International Trade Statistics Yearbook.*

TRANSPORT

Road Traffic (registered vehicles, excl. those on radio, weather or military stations, 1994): Passenger cars 1,944, Lorries and trucks 1,039, Total (incl. others) 3,551 (of which 2,666 privately owned).

Shipping (number of fishing vessels, 1994): 280.

International Sea-borne Freight Traffic ('000 metric tons, 1990): Goods loaded 298; Goods unloaded 288. Source: UN, *Monthly Bulletin of Statistics.*

International Transport (passengers conveyed between Greenland and Denmark): Ship (1983) 94; Aircraft (1994) 66,135.

TOURISM

Registered Hotel Accommodations (nights, 1995): 70,273 (incl. 52,761 by Danish visitors).

COMMUNICATIONS MEDIA

Radio Receivers (1995): 25,000 in use.

Television Receivers (1995): 20,000 in use.

Telephones ('000 main lines, 1994): 18.

Telefax Stations (1992): 1,150 in use.

Mobile Cellular Telephones (subscribers, 1994): 1,110.

Sources: UNESCO, *Statistical Yearbook*, and UN, *Statistical Yearbook.*

EDUCATION

(1995/96)

Pre-primary and Primary: 88 schools; 1,019 teachers; 10,616 pupils.

Secondary: 3 schools; 459 pupils.

Directory

The Government

The legislative body is the Landsting, with 31 members elected for four years, on a basis of proportional representation. Greenlanders and Danes resident in Greenland for at least six months prior to an election and over the age of 18 years have the right to vote. Based on the strength of the parties in the Landsting, an executive, the Landsstyre, is formed. During a transitional period the Landsstyre will gradually assume control of the administration of Greenland's internal affairs. Jurisdiction in constitutional matters, foreign affairs and defence remains with the Danish Government, the highest representative of which, in Greenland, is the Rigsombudsmand or High Commissioner.

LANDSSTYRE

(February 1998)

A coalition of Siumut (S) and Atassut (A).

Prime Minister: Jonathan Motzfeldt.

Minister of Finance and Housing: Daniel Skifte (A).

Minister of Trade, Industry, Transportation and Public Works: Peter Grønvold Samuelsen (S).

Minister of Fisheries, Hunting and Agriculture: Påviâraq Heilmann (S).

Minister of Health, Environment and Research: Marianne Jensen (S).

Minister of Culture, Education and Church: Konrad Steenholdt (A).

Minister of Social Affairs and Labour: Benedikte Thorsteinsson (S).

Government Offices

Rigsombudsmanden i Grønland (High Commission for Greenland): POB 1030, 3900 Nuuk; tel. 32-10-01; telex 90604; fax 32-41-71; e-mail riomgr@stm.dk; High Commissioner Gunnar Martens.

Grønlands Hjemmestyre (Greenland Home Rule Government): POB 1015, 3900 Nuuk; tel. 23000; telex 90613; fax 25002; Denmark Bureau, Pilestraede 52, POB 2151, 1112 Copenhagen K; tel. 33-13-42-24; fax 33-32-20-24.

LANDSTING

Election, 4 March 1995

	Votes	%	Seats
Siumut (Forward)	9,794	38.4	12
Atassut (Solidarity)	7,674	30.1	10
Inuit Ataqatigiit (Inuit Brotherhood)	5,180	20.3	6
Akulliit Partiiat (Centre Party)	1,560	6.1	2
Issittup Partiia (Polar Party)	90	0.4	—
Others	1,193	4.7	1
Total	25,491	100.0	31

Political Organizations

Akulliit Partiiat (Centre Party): POB 456, 3900 Nuuk; f. 1991; liberal, supports open-sea fishing industry; Chair. Bjarne Kreutzmann.

Atassut (Solidarity): POB 399, 3900 Nuuk; tel. 32-33-66; fax 32-58-40; e-mail atassut.landsorganisation@partiit.centadm.gh.gl; f. 1978 and became political party in 1981; supports close links with Denmark and favours EU membership for Greenland; part of Venstre (Liberal) party in the Danish legislature, and of Liberal group in the Nordic Council; Leader Daniel Skifte.

Inuit Ataqatigiit (Inuit Brotherhood): POB 321, 3900 Nuuk; f. 1978; socialist organization, demanding that Greenland citizenship be restricted to those of Inuit parentage; advocates Greenland's eventual independence from Denmark; Chair. JOSEF MOTZFELDT.

Siumut (Forward): POB 357, 3900 Nuuk; tel. 32-20-77; fax 32-23-19; e-mail siumut@greennet.gl; f. 1971 and became political party in 1977; aims to promote collective ownership and co-operation, and to develop greater reliance on Greenland's own resources; favours greatest possible autonomy within the Kingdom of Denmark; social democratic party; Chair. MICHAEL PETERSEN.

Judicial System

The island is divided into 18 court districts and these courts all use lay assessors. For most cases these lower courts are for the first instance and appeal is to the Landsret, the higher court in Nuuk, which is the only one with a professional judge. This court hears the more serious cases in the first instance and appeal in these cases is to the High Court (Østre Landsret) in Copenhagen.

Religion

CHRISTIANITY

The Greenlandic Church, of which most of the population are adherents, forms an independent diocese of the Evangelical Lutheran Church in Denmark and comes under the jurisdiction of the Landsstyre and of the Bishop of Greenland. There are 17 parishes and in 1995 there were 23 ministers serving in Greenland.

Biskoppen over Grønlands Stift (Bishop of Greenland): SOFIE PETERSEN, Evangelical Lutheran Church, POB 90, 3900 Nuuk.

There are also small groups of other Protestant churches and of Roman Catholics.

The Press

There are no daily newspapers in Greenland.

Atuagagdliutit/Grønlandsposten: POB 39, 3900 Nuuk; tel. 21083; fax 23147; e-mail actuag@greennet.gl; 2 a week; Editor JENS BRØNDEN.

Niviarsiaq: POB 357, 3900 Nuuk; tel. 32-20-77; fax 32-23-19; e-mail siumut@greennet.gl; organ of Siumut; monthly; Editor J. WAEVER JOHANSEN.

Sermitsiaq: Spindlers Bakke 10B, POB 150, 3900 Nuuk; tel. 21903; fax 22499; weekly; Editor POUL KRARUP.

Publisher

Atuakkiorfik/Greenland Publishers: Hans Egedesvej 3, POB 840, 3900 Nuuk; tel. 22122; fax 22500; f. 1956; general fiction and non-fiction, children's and textbooks, public relations; Man. NUKAARAQ EUGENIUS.

Broadcasting and Communications

TELECOMMUNICATIONS

TELE Greenland A/S: Nuuk; f. 1994; owned by Home Rule Govt.

RADIO

Kalaallit Nunaata Radioa (KNR)—Grønlands Radio: POB 1007, 3900 Nuuk; tel. 21172; telex 90606; fax 24703; 5 AM stations, 45 FM stations; bilingual programmes in Greenlandic and Danish, 17 hours a day; Man. Dir JENS LYBERTH.

Kujataata Radioa: POB 158, 3920 Qaqortoq; regional station in south Greenland.

Avannaata Radioa: POB 223, 3952 Ilulissat; tel. 43633; fax 43618; regional station in north Greenland.

Thule Air Base Radio—50Z20: DAC POB 1117, 3970 Dundas; FM, non-commercial station; broadcasts 24 hours a day; news, music, etc.; Station Man. KURT CHRISTENSEN.

TELEVISION

Kalaallit Nunaata Radioa TV: POB 1007, 3900 Nuuk; tel. 25333; fax 25042; broadcasts by VHF transmitter to all Greenland; commercial; most programmes in Danish; Man. Dir JENS LYBERTH.

Finance

BANKS

(cap. = capital; dep. = deposits; m. = million; amounts in kroner; br. = branch)

Grønlandsbanken A/S—The Bank of Greenland: POB 1033, 3900 Nuuk; tel. 32-13-80; fax 32-39-18; e-mail grbank@greennet.gl; f. 1967; cap. 191.8m., res 267.1m., dep. 2,217.9m. (June 1997); Pres. SVEND-ERIK DANIELSEN; Man. FRANK KRISTENSEN.

Nuna Bank A/S: Skibshavnsvej 33, POB 1031, 3900 Nuuk; tel. 21360; telex 90610; fax 21346; f. 1985; cap. 150m., res 20.2m., dep. 854.6m. (Dec. 1994); commercial bank; Chair. STEEN AAGE BACHE; Gen. Man. POUL ERIK OLSEN; 5 brs.

Trade and Industry

GOVERNMENT AGENCY

Government of Greenland, Minerals Office: POB 1015, 3900 Nuuk; tel. 23000; fax 24302; f. 1995; Pres. LARS VESTERBIRK.

STATE-OWNED COMPANIES

KNI Udvikling A/S: POB 1008, 3900 Nuuk; tel. 25211; fax 24431; f. 1774; Home Rule Govt assumed control 1986, reorganized 1993; Chair. JONATHAN MOTZFELDT; Man. Dir STIG BENDTSEN.

Kalaallit Niuerfiat Detail A/S (KNI Detail A/S)—Greenland Trade Retail Ltd: POB 1009, 3911 Sisimiut; tel. 14711; fax 14758; f. 1993; statutory wholesale and retail trading co.; Chair. PETER OSTERMANN; Man. BENT ASKJAR.

Kalaallit Pilersuisoq A/S (KNI Service A/S)—Greenland Trade Service Ltd: POB 193, 3912 Maniitsoq; tel. 13844; fax 13814; f. 1993; statutory wholesale and retail trading co., mail service, oil and fuel supply; Chair. JONATHAN MOTZFELDT; Pres. KELD ASKÆR; Mans HANS THOMSEN, GERHARDT PETERSEN.

Royal Greenland A/S: POB 1073, 3900 Nuuk; tel. 24422; fax 23349; internet http://www.royalgreenland.com; f. 1774; trade monopoly ended 1950; Home Rule Govt assumed control 1986; established as share company 1990 (all shares owned by Home Rule Govt); fishing group based in Greenland with subsidiaries in Japan, the United Kingdom, Scandinavia, the USA, Italy, France, Germany and Spain; main products are coldwater prawns and halibut; six trawlers; factories in Greenland, Denmark and Germany; Chair. OVE ROSING OLSEN; Pres. and CEO OLE RAMLAU-HANSEN.

Transport

Domestic traffic is mainly by aircraft (fixed-wing and helicopter), boat and dog-sled. There are airports or heliports in all towns for domestic flights.

The main port is at Nuuk; there are also all-year ports at Paamiut (Frederikshåb), Maniitsoq (Sukkertoppen) and Sisimiut (Holsteinsborg). In addition, there are shipyards at Nuuk, Qaqortoq, Paamiut, Maniitsoq, Sisimiut and Aasiaat. Coastal motor vessels operate passenger services along the west coast from Upernavik to Nanortalik.

Shipping Company

Royal Arctic Line A/S: POB 1580, 3900 Nuuk; tel. 32-24-20; telex 90401; fax 32-24-50; e-mail royal.arctic.line@greennet.gl; f. 1993; owned by Home Rule Govt; 5 general cargo vessels of 31,519 grt; Pres. KARSTEN STOCK ANDRESEN.

Airline

Grønlandsfly A/S (Greenlandair Inc.): POB 1012, 3900 Nuuk; tel. 28888; telex 90602; fax 27288; f. 1960; air services to the 19 principal centres in Greenland, and to Copenhagen (Denmark), Reykjavík and Keflavík (Iceland) and Ottawa (Canada); supply, survey, ice-reconnaissance services and helicopter/fixed-wing charters; owned by Danish and Home Rule Govts and SAS; Chair. JONATHAN MOTZFELDT; Pres. OLE BJERREGAARD.

Tourism

Tourist arrivals traditionally did not exceed 5,000–7,000 per year. In order to stimulate increased revenue, it was decided in 1990 to set a target of 30,000–35,000 tourist arrivals per year (generating income of some 500m. kroner) to be achieved by 2005. Some 13,000 tourist arrivals were registered in 1994.

Greenland Tourism: POB 1552, 3900 Nuuk; tel. 20588; fax 27288; Chair. JENS VEINO; Pres. KIM FOLMANN JØRGENSEN.

DJIBOUTI

Introductory Survey

Location, Climate, Language, Religion, Flag, Capital

The Republic of Djibouti is in the Horn of Africa, at the southern entrance to the Red Sea. It is bounded on the north by Eritrea, on the north, west and south-west by Ethiopia, and on the south-east by Somalia. The land is mainly volcanic desert, and the climate hot and arid. There are two main ethnic groups, the Issa, who are of Somali origin and comprise 50% of the population, and the Afar, who comprise 40% of the population and are of Ethiopian origin. Both groups are Muslims, and they speak related Cushitic languages. The official languages are Arabic and French. The flag has two equal horizontal stripes, of light blue and light green, with a white triangle, enclosing a five-pointed red star, at the hoist. The capital is Djibouti.

Recent History

In 1945 the area now comprising the Republic of Djibouti (then known as French Somaliland) was proclaimed an overseas territory of France, and in 1967 was renamed the French Territory of the Afars and the Issas. The Afar and the Issa have strong connections with Ethiopia and Somalia respectively. Until the 1960s ethnic divisions were not marked; subsequently, however, conflicting international tensions in the Horn of Africa, together with France's policy of favouring the minority Afar community, combined to create internal tensions. Demands for independence were led by the Issa community, and, under pressure from the Organization of African Unity to grant full independence to the territory, France acted to improve relations between the two communities. A unified political movement, the Ligue populaire africaine pour l'indépendance (LPAI) was formed, and, following an overwhelming vote favouring independence at a referendum held in May 1977, the territory became independent on 27 June. Hassan Gouled Aptidon, a senior Issa politician and leader of the LPAI, became the first President of the Republic of Djibouti.

Initial intentions to maintain an ethnic balance in government were not sustained. In March 1979 Gouled replaced the LPAI with a new political party, the Rassemblement populaire pour le progrès (RPP), which was placed under his personal direction. Afar opposition groups, led by the Mouvement populaire pour la libération de Djibouti (MPLD), responded by forming a clandestine movement, the Front démocratique pour la libération de Djibouti, based in Ethiopia. In June 1981 Gouled, as sole candidate, was elected to a further six-year term as President, and in October the RPP was declared the sole legal party. Legislative elections were held in May 1982, when candidates were chosen from a single list approved by the RPP. At the next presidential and legislative elections, held in April 1987, President Gouled, the sole candidate, was re-elected, while RPP-sponsored candidates for all 65 seats in the Chamber of Deputies were elected unopposed. Successive government reorganizations failed, however, to achieve national unity.

Until the mid-1980s there was little overt opposition to the RPP under Gouled's leadership. In May 1986 Aden Robleh Awalleh, a former political associate of President Gouled, fled to Ethiopia and announced the formation of an opposition group, the Mouvement national djiboutien pour l'instauration de la démocratie (MNDID), with the stated aim of restoring a multi-party parliamentary democracy. Within Djibouti, political tensions began to escalate during 1987, prompting Gouled to reorganize the Government and to undertake a personal tour of remote areas of the country in early 1988. In April 1989 inter-tribal hostilities erupted in the capital and the Afar town of Tadjourah. Inter-ethnic tensions persisted, and in May 1990 fighting broke out between the Issa and the Gadabursi communities in the capital. In June units of the Djibouti armed forces raided the town of Tadjourah and arrested Afars who were suspected of involvement in the MPLD.

In April 1991 a new and powerful armed opposition group, the Front pour la restauration de l'unité et de la démocratie (FRUD), was formed by a merger of three insurgent Afar movements. In mid-November the FRUD, with a force of about 3,000 men, launched a full-scale insurrection against the Government. By late November the FRUD controlled many towns and villages in the north of the country, and was besieging the northern towns of Tadjourah and Obock, which were held by the national army. The Government instituted mass conscription, and requested military assistance from France (see below) to repel what it described as 'external aggression' by soldiers loyal to the deposed President Mengistu of Ethiopia. The FRUD denied that it constituted a foreign aggressor (although many of its officers had received training in Ethiopian military camps), claiming that its aim was to secure fair political representation for all ethnic groups in Djibouti.

In December 1991 President Gouled announced that a national referendum regarding proposed changes in the system of government would be held, but only when the 'external aggressors' had been expelled from the country. At the end of the month, 14 Afar deputies resigned from the RPP (and, therefore, from the Chamber of Deputies), claiming that its leaders were seeking to protect their privileges rather than the national interest. In January 1992 two ministers resigned, in protest at the Government's policy of continuing the civil war.

In January 1992, under pressure from the French Government to accommodate opposition demands for democratic reform, President Gouled appointed a commission to draft a new constitution, which was to restore the multi-party system and provide for free elections. The FRUD, following meetings with French officials, stated its willingness to negotiate with Gouled, and undertook to observe a cease-fire, subject to satisfactory progress on democratic reforms. Gouled, however, reasserted that the FRUD was controlled by 'foreign interests', and accused France of failing to honour its defence agreement. By late January, most of northern Djibouti was under FRUD control. In the following month, after further mediation by France, a cease-fire was implemented under the supervision of a French peace-keeping force. These arrangements collapsed in March, however, and armed conflict between the FRUD and the Government was resumed. In June Ahmed Dini, who had been Djibouti's first Prime Minister after independence, assumed the leadership of the FRUD.

President Gouled's constitutional plan, which was announced in April 1992, conceded the principle of political pluralism, but proposed few other changes and retained a strong executive presidency. The plan was rejected by the opposition parties and by the FRUD, although cautiously welcomed by France. However, Gouled's intention that a constitutional referendum should take place in June, with legislative elections to follow in July, was recognized as unrealistic, especially with large areas of the country no longer under government control. The referendum, which was held in September, was boycotted by all the opposition groups; the Government, however, stated that, with 75% of the electorate participating, 97% of voters had endorsed the new Constitution. At the end-September deadline for party registration, only the RPP and the Parti du renouveau démocratique (PRD), an opposition group formed earlier in 1992 under the leadership of Mohamed Djama Elabe (a former minister), were granted legal status. The application for registration by the opposition Parti national démocratique (PND) was initially rejected, although it was allowed in October. Parliamentary elections were held on 18 December, and all 65 seats were won by the RPP. Elabe accused the Government of electoral irregularities. More than 51% of the electorate abstained from voting in the elections, leading to charges from the PND that the chamber was unrepresentative.

Renewed fighting was reported in January 1993, when dozens of people were said to have been killed in what appeared to be a new government offensive against the FRUD in the Tadjourah area. The army claimed a series of successes during February and March, recapturing FRUD strongholds in the south of the country and severing the rebels' supply routes to the sea. In mid-March the FRUD carried out its first guerrilla attack on the capital.

Gouled reshuffled the Council of Ministers in February 1993, preserving the traditional ethnic balance, with Issa ministers receiving eight portfolios, and Afar representatives seven, and one portfolio each being given to members of the Arab, Issaq and Gadabursi minorities. However, these appointments did not alter the Government's policy of refusing to negotiate with the FRUD. Five candidates stood in Djibouti's first contested presidential election, which was held on 7 May: Gouled himself, Elabe (for the PRD), Aden Robleh Awalleh (PND) and two independents, Mohamed Moussa Ali 'Tourtour' and Ahmed Ibrahim Abdi. The election was again notable for a low level of participation (49.9% of the electorate), indicating an Afar boycott, but resulted in a clear victory for Gouled, who, according to official results, obtained 60.8% of the valid votes cast, compared with 22.0% for Elabe and 12.3% for Awalleh. 'Tourtour' and Abdi won 3.0% and 2.0% of the votes cast respectively. The opposition alleged that there had been widespread electoral fraud.

Following his re-election as President, Gouled appealed to the FRUD to negotiate with the Government. His appeal was rejected, as he proposed that discussions should take place in Djibouti, while the FRUD insisted that it would only meet the Government abroad, in the presence of foreign mediators. In July 1993 the army launched a successful offensive on FRUD positions in the centre and north of the country, capturing the FRUD's headquarters on the plateau of Asa Gayla, as well as other towns and areas held by the rebel group. As a result of the hostilities, thousands of the inhabitants of these largely Afar-populated areas fled towards the Ethiopian border. Many of the rebels retreated into the mountains in the far north of the country. The FRUD continued its struggle, however, and began launching armed attacks on government forces, including an assault on the army's camp at Tadjourah. By July an estimated 80,000 civilians had been displaced by the fighting. In September the Gouled administration was strongly criticized by Amnesty International for abuses of human rights, inflicted by the army.

The extent of the military reverses inflicted on the FRUD was reflected in the intensification of political activity during late 1993. In October the PRD and the FRUD issued joint proposals for a cease-fire, to be followed by negotiations aimed at forming a transitional 'government of national unity' to supervise the implementation of democratic reforms. These objectives were also defined by two new parties formed in the same month: the Organisation des masses Afars and the Parti centriste et des reformes démocratiques (PCRD). The PCRD, whose leadership comprised former members of the FRUD, announced that it was to seek legal recognition. In December the PRD and the PND launched a co-ordinated campaign to persuade the Government to agree to new parliamentary elections under the supervision of an independent electoral commission. In early 1994, again under economic pressure from France, the Government agreed to reduce its military expenditure, although operations against the FRUD continued in February.

During March 1994 serious divisions emerged within the FRUD leadership. It was reported that the political bureau, led by Ahmed Dini, had been dissolved and that dissident members had formed an 'executive council' under the leadership of Ougoureh Kifleh Ahmed. This dissident leadership (Ali Mohamed Daoud was subsequently declared President) sought support within the movement for a negotiated political settlement of the conflict. In June Kifleh Ahmed and the Government agreed preliminary terms for a cease-fire, and formal negotiations for a peace settlement began in July. Executive bodies of both FRUD factions continued to operate during the latter half of 1994, and parallel national congresses rejected the legitimacy of the opposing faction's leadership. In December an agreement signed by Kifleh Ahmed and the Minister of the Interior, Idris Harbi Farah, contained provisions for a permanent cessation of hostilities, the incorporation of FRUD armed forces into the national force, the recognition of the FRUD as a legal political party, the multi-ethnic composition of a new council of ministers and the reform of electoral procedures prior to the next general election. In accordance with the peace agreement, 300 members of the FRUD armed forces were integrated into the national army in March 1995. However, there was little further implementation of the accord, and there was considerable criticism of the agreement by the radical faction of the FRUD (which, under the leadership of Ahmed Dini, favoured a continuation of military operations and launched a number of small-scale attacks against government targets in late 1995) and other opposition groups. Nevertheless, Ali Mohamed Daoud and Kiflen Ahmed were appointed to posts in the Government in June. In March 1996 the Government granted legal recognition to the FRUD, which became the country's fourth and largest political party. However, at approximately the same time, Ibrahim Chehem Daoud, a former high-ranking official in the FRUD, rejected the reconciliation between the Government and the group, and formed a new group, called FRUD-Renaissance.

Meanwhile in September 1995 trade unions organized a widely-observed one-day general strike. Several trade union leaders were arrested. In some sectors, work stoppages continued until mid-September, when the unions recommended a return to work. In October a demonstration organized by the PND, to protest at the Government's economic austerity policy, resulted in the arrest of several protesters, including the PND leader, Awalleh. In November Awalleh was released, but subsequently he was reported to have begun a hunger strike in support of other demonstrators who remained in prison. In January 1996, after demonstrations organized by school teachers against the economic reforms, some 500 protesters were reported to have been arrested. They were released later in the month and further strikes were staged in April and May. Also in May 34 people were arrested and one person was reported to have been killed during clashes between the security forces and supporters of the former Paymaster-General, Nouh Omar Miguil, who had been detained by the police. Miguil was dismissed from his post in October 1995 on suspicion of embezzlement, although his followers alleged that he had been the victim of a political power struggle.

In December 1995 President Gouled received medical treatment in France, where he remained in convalescence until March 1996. His prolonged absence from Djibouti prompted a succession crisis within the RPP, between the President's nephew and chief minister, Ismael Omar Gelleh, and his private secretary, Ismael Gedi Hared. In February a prison riot in the capital (which resulted in two deaths and 29 injuries) provoked a confrontation between the Minister of Justice and Islamic Affairs, Moumin Bahdon Farah (who suggested that the incident had occurred because the cost of maintaining a sizeable army had resulted in poor staffing levels at the prison), and the Minister of the Interior, Idris Harbi Farah, who attributed the uprising to inadequate prison food supplies. Bahdon Farah's remarks reflected his opposition to Gelleh (whom Harbi Farah supported), who was known to favour a large standing army. In March Bahdon Farah was dismissed from the Council of Ministers, together with Ahmed Bulaleh Barreh, the Minister of Defence. Both ministers had openly opposed the December 1994 peace agreement with the FRUD, on the grounds that it strengthened the position of Gelleh and his followers. In April 1996 Bahdon Farah established a splinter group of the RPP, the Groupe pour la démocratie de la république (RPP–GDR), which included 13 of the 65 members of the Chamber of Deputies. The President of the Chamber subsequently claimed that the RPP–GDR would remain illegal while Bahdon Farah continued to hold his position as Secretary-General of the RPP. In May Gouled expelled Gedi Hared from the RPP's executive committee, together with Bahdon Farah and former ministers Barreh and Ali Mahamade Houmed, all of whom opposed Gelleh. In June Gedi Hared formed an opposition alliance, the Coordination de l'opposition djiboutienne, embracing the PND, the Front uni de l'opposition djiboutienne (a coalition of internal opposition groups) and the RPP–GDR. In August Gedi Hared, Bahdon Farah and Barreh were among five people sentenced to six months' imprisonment, and the suspension of their civil rights for five years, for 'insulting the Head of State'. The accused reportedly signed a document in May alleging that President Gouled ruled by force and terror. The detainees were released from prison in January 1997, following a presidential pardon, although their civil rights were not restored.

In September 1996 an internal dispute arose in the RPP when Gelleh began a discreet campaign against the holding of several positions concurrently, which was aimed at the Prime Minister and Deputy Chairman of the RPP, Barkad Gourad Hamadou. In an apparent attempt to end these internecine disputes, President Gouled announced his intention to remain as Head of State until the expiry of his term of office in 1999. Gouled was re-elected President of the RPP in March 1997.

In April 1997 the FRUD faction led by Ali Mohamed Daoud announced its intention to participate in the forthcoming legislative elections (scheduled to be held in December) and to present joint electoral lists with the RPP. Meanwhile, in September an attack on an army division in northern Djibouti (during which 11 soldiers were killed and 16 were wounded) was attributed to the armed wing of the FRUD, under the leadership of Ahmed Dini.

At the legislative elections, held on 19 December 1997, the RPP-FRUD alliance won all 65 seats in the Chamber of Deputies. According to official results, 63.8% of the electorate participated nation-wide, but only 47.8% voted in the capital and 32.9% in Ali-Sabieh. The PRD and the PND presented candidates in some districts, but neither succeeded in gaining representation in the Chamber. The PRD had suffered a split in May when Abdillahi Hamareiteh was elected as the party's new President (to succeed Elabe, who died in late 1996). A rival faction, led by Kaireh Allaleh Hared, was refused legal recognition. In late December President Gouled announced the formation of a new Council of Ministers; minor reshuffles had been effected in April and November.

Meanwhile, problems concerning the Government's programme of demobilization emerged in May 1997 when some 200 troops demonstrated in the capital, claiming that they had not been paid for more than three months. The Gouled administration also encountered criticism from the US Government for alleged violations of human rights by the security forces, including the arbitrary arrest of political dissidents.

Separate treaties of friendship and co-operation were signed in 1981 with Ethiopia, Somalia, Kenya and Sudan, with the aim of resolving regional conflicts. In August 1984 the Minister of Foreign Affairs reaffirmed Djibouti's policy of maintaining a neutral stance in the conflict between its neighbours in the Horn of Africa, and expressed his Government's willingness to act as a mediator. A joint ministerial committee, which held its first session in July 1985, was formed between Djibouti and Ethiopia, to strengthen existing relations and co-operation between the two countries. These relations, however, were overshadowed in 1986 by Ethiopia's support for the MNDID.

Djibouti's interest in promoting regional co-operation was exemplified by the creation, in February 1985, of the Intergovernmental Authority on Drought and Development (IGADD, now the Intergovernmental Authority on Development, IGAD, see p. 261), with six (now seven) member states; Djibouti was chosen as the site of its permanent secretariat, and President Gouled became the first Chairman. Under the auspices of IGADD, the Heads of State of Ethiopia and Somalia met in January 1986 for the first time in 10 years, and in March 1988 they held a further meeting. In the following month the two countries agreed to re-establish diplomatic relations, to withdraw troops from their common border and to exchange prisoners of war.

Following the overthrow of the Ethiopian President, Mengistu Haile Mariam, in May 1991, Djibouti established good relations with the successor transitional Government in that country. In June Djibouti hosted a preliminary conference of groups from southern Somalia, aimed at forming a transitional Somali government. In October the borders between Djibouti and Somalia were reopened for the first time since May 1989, when they had been closed as a result of civil unrest in Somalia. Relations with the self-proclaimed 'Republic of Somaliland', which declared independence in 1991, were increasingly strained during 1995. In August there were reports of clashes along the border, apparently between local militia groups from Djibouti and Somaliland troops. In June 1996, however, Djibouti and Somaliland concluded an agreement, which included provisions for co-operation on border security and the establishment of trade relations. Moreover, in November 1997 Djibouti granted official recognition to Somaliland. In December 1995 the Djibouti Government protested to the Eritrean authorities about alleged incursions by Eritrean troops into north-eastern Djibouti. These allegations were vehemently denied by Eritrea. Relations between the two countries were strained in April 1996, when President Gouled rejected a map of Eritrea submitted by the Eritrean Minister of Foreign Affairs, which reportedly included a 20-km strip of territory belonging to Djibouti. Concurrently, reports emerged of exchanges of artillery fire at a frontier post in northern Djibouti; Eritrea denied the incident. Relations with Israel improved during 1995. After a meeting between officials in September, plans were announced to open liaison offices in the countries' capitals, prior to the possible establishment of diplomatic relations between the two states.

In August 1986 a new scheme for repatriating Ethiopian refugees, under the auspices of the UN High Commissioner for Refugees (UNHCR), was begun. The burden that 'official' refugees imposed on the economy was exacerbated by an influx of illegal immigrants from Somalia and Ethiopia, and in June 1987 the Djibouti Government announced tighter controls on border crossings and identity papers. Following discussions in February 1988, Djibouti and Ethiopia agreed to control movements across their common border and to curb the influx of refugees into Djibouti. In January 1989 illegal immigrants were alleged to have taken part in a violent confrontation between the security forces and inhabitants of Balbala, a densely-populated shanty-town close to the capital, in which four people died and 100 were injured. In response, President Gouled announced that measures were to be taken against illegal refugees, who, he claimed, were not only an economic burden on the country, but also a source of instability. In early June 1991 there were an estimated 35,000 Somali and 5,000 Ethiopian official refugees in Djibouti. Although the Government maintained that by early 1993 the number of Somali refugees in Djibouti had risen to 120,000, UNHCR argued that many of these were economic migrants. In September 1994 UNHCR initiated a programme of voluntary repatriation for Ethiopian refugees in Djibouti. According to UNHCR, some 35,000 Ethiopians returned voluntarily to their homes between early 1995 and April 1996. According to the US Committee for Refugees, in early 1996 there were some 20,000 Somali and 5,000 Ethiopian refugees in Djibouti. Fighting between government forces and the FRUD led some 10,000 Djiboutians to seek refuge in Ethiopia, and caused another 50,000 to become internally displaced.

President Gouled has consistently fostered cordial relations with France, and has encouraged the maintenance of French troops in Djibouti. However, the French military presence became more controversial following Iraq's invasion of Kuwait in August 1990 and the onset of the 'Gulf crisis', during which Djibouti became the base of operations connected with France's participation in the multinational force deployed in Saudi Arabia. By supporting the UN resolutions that were formulated against Iraq, Djibouti jeopardized its future relations with that country, which was emerging as an important supplier of economic and military aid. However, Djibouti's stance during the Gulf War of January–February 1991 strengthened its ties with France, and in February the Djibouti and French Governments signed defence treaties, extending military co-operation, although France refused to intervene militarily in the conflict between the Government and the FRUD. The failure of the Government to conclude a peace agreement with the FRUD strained relations with France in 1993–94. Relations improved as a result of the peace accord of December 1994, but tensions remained between the two countries, largely owing to Djibouti's reluctance to adopt a strict economic reform programme. Although in January 1996 the French Minister of Defence pledged to maintain a military presence in Djibouti, it was subsequently announced that the French military contingent would be reduced by some 14%. In December 1997 it was announced that the number of French troops stationed in Djibouti was to be reduced still further, from 3,200 to 2,600, although no timetable was given for the planned reduction. Meanwhile, in November the Djibouti Government adopted legislation imposing visa requirements on French nationals, including members of the armed forces stationed in Djibouti.

Meanwhile, in April 1996 a French judge issued warrants for the arrest of the Chairman of the PND, Aden Robleh Awalleh, and his wife, both of whom were suspected of involvement in a grenade attack on a cafeteria in Djibouti in 1990, during which a French child was killed and 15 others were injured.

Government

Executive power is vested in the President, who is directly elected by universal adult suffrage for a six-year term. Legislative power is held by the Chamber of Deputies, consisting of 65 members elected for five years. The Council of Ministers, presided over by a Prime Minister, is responsible to the President. The Republic forms a single electoral district.

Defence

Since independence, a large portion of the annual budget has been allocated to military expenditure, and defence (excluding demobilization) absorbed 13.2% of total government budgetary expenditure in 1994. In August 1997 there were about 3,900 French troops stationed in Djibouti. The total armed forces of Djibouti itself, in which all services form part of the army, was estimated at 9,600 (including 200 naval and 200 air force personnel), and there was a paramilitary force of 1,200 gendarmes as well as a 3,000-strong national security force. The defence budget for 1997 was expected to amount to 4,000m. Djibouti francs.

Economic Affairs

In 1993, according to estimates by the World Bank, Djibouti's gross national product (GNP), measured at average 1991–93 prices, was US $448m., equivalent to $780 per head. Djibouti's overall gross domestic product (GDP) expanded, in real terms, at an average annual rate of 1.2% in 1980–85 and 2.0% in 1985–89, reversing an average annual decline of 2.7% in 1977–79. However, as a result of rapid population increase, GDP per head declined, in real terms, during 1980–86. According to estimates by the IMF, GDP declined, in real terms, in each of the five years 1992–96. Real GDP fell by 2.9% in 1994, by 4.0% in 1995 and by an estimated 5.1% in 1996. During 1985–95 the population increased by an annual average of 4.8% (according to World Bank estimates), owing partly to the influx of refugees from neighbouring Ethiopia and Somalia.

Agriculture (including hunting, forestry and fishing) provided only 3.3% of GDP in 1995, although an estimated 75.2% of the labour force were employed in the sector in 1991. There is little arable farming, owing to Djibouti's unproductive terrain, and the country is able to produce only about 3% of its total food requirements. More than one-half of the population are pastoral nomads, herding goats, sheep and camels.

Industry (comprising manufacturing, construction and utilities) provided 19.5% of GDP in 1995 and engaged 11.0% of the employed labour force in 1991. Industrial activity is mainly limited to a few small-scale enterprises.

The manufacturing sector contributed 5.4% of GDP in 1995. Almost all consumer goods have to be imported.

In 1986 work commenced on a major geothermal exploration project, funded by the World Bank and foreign aid. In that year Saudi Arabia granted Djibouti US $21.4m. for the purchase and installation of three electricity generators, with a combined capacity of 15 MW. Total electricity generating capacity rose from 40 MW to 80 MW in 1988, when the second part of the Boulaos power station became operative. Imported fuels satisfy 90% of Djibouti's energy requirements.

Djibouti's economic viability is based on trade through the international port of Djibouti, and on the developing service sector, which accounted for 77.2% of GDP in 1995, and engaged 13.8% of the employed labour force in 1991.

In 1995 Djibouti recorded a visible trade deficit of US $171.5m., and there was a deficit of $23.0m. on the current account of the balance of payments. In 1995 the principal sources of imports were Thailand (15.8%), France (13.4%), Ethiopia (8.2%) and Saudi Arabia (6.1%). The principal markets for exports in that year were Ethiopia (41.4%), Somalia (35.3%) and the Republic of Yemen (7.6%). The principal imports were food and beverages, qat (a narcotic leaf), machinery and electrical appliances, clothing and footwear, petroleum and chemical products, and vehicles and transport equipment. Most exports are unclassified.

Djibouti's overall budget deficit for 1995 was 4,300m. Djibouti francs (equivalent to 4.9% of GDP). The country's total external debt was US $260.2m. at the end of 1995, of which $218.0m. was long-term public debt. In that year the cost of debt-servicing was equivalent to 4.8% of revenue from exports of goods and services. The annual rate of inflation averaged 5.4% during 1989–95. In 1996 unemployment was estimated to affect some 58% of the labour force.

Djibouti is heavily dependent on foreign assistance. Since 1986, however, there has been a reduction in foreign aid, resulting in financial problems. In 1992 Djibouti's primary bilateral donors included France (US $43.4m.) and Italy ($38m.). Co-operation agreements have been signed with Pakistan, the People's Republic of China, the Republic of Korea and Uganda. The Intergovernmental Authority on Development (see p. 261) has its headquarters in Djibouti. The country is a member of numerous other international organizations, including the African Development Bank (see p. 104), the Arab Fund for Economic and Social Development (see p. 259) and the Islamic Development Bank (see p. 194). In May 1995 Djibouti became a member of the World Trade Organization (see p. 244).

Djibouti suffers from periodic drought, and serious flooding in November 1994 led to a disruption in supplies on the Djibouti–Addis Ababa railway, and considerable damage to buildings and roads. The high level of military expenditure in 1991–94, in response to internal insurgency, caused a substantial deficit in the government budget. Attempts by aid donors, notably France, to insist on structural reforms to the economy were initially resisted by the Government, but in May 1995 considerable reductions in government spending were announced. In April 1996 the IMF approved Djibouti's first stand-by credit, equivalent to US $6.7m. Djibouti agreed to implement a 14-month programme of austerity measures, concentrating on budgetary adjustment and structural reform. France subsequently released funds for a variety of projects in Djibouti, primarily in the sectors of health and education. French aid to Djibouti for 1996 amounted to 162.5m. French francs. The IMF later extended the stand-by agreement until March 1998 and disbursed additional credits in mid-1997. Meanwhile, Djibouti also received grants from the European Union (EU) and the International Development Association. In recent years Djibouti port has experienced increasing competition from nearby developing Arab ports. However, with French assistance, Djibouti port and the Djibouti–Addis Ababa railway have been undergoing modernization, with a view to establishing Djibouti as a major entrepôt for trade between East Africa and the Arab countries.

Social Welfare

The social insurance scheme in Djibouti is divided into three categories, according to whether the worker is employed in the private sector, the civil service or the army. Employees receive benefits in case of accidents at work, and are allocated retirement pensions after the age of 55 years. In 1990 there were 20 hospital establishments, with a total of 1,369 beds, and more than 660 medical personnel, including 73 physicians and four dentists. Budgetary current expenditure on health for 1995 was 1,653m. Djibouti francs (equivalent to 5.3% of total spending).

Education

The Government has overall responsibility for education. Primary education generally begins at six years of age and lasts for six years. Secondary education, usually starting at the age of 12, lasts for seven years, comprising a first cycle of four years and a second of three years. In 1994 the total enrolment at primary and secondary schools was equivalent to 26% of the school-age population (30% of boys; 22% of girls), while primary enrolment included 32% of pupils in the relevant age-group (36% of boys; 28% of girls). Budgetary current expenditure on education in 1995 was 3,202m. Djibouti francs, equivalent to 10.2% of total government expenditure. In 1994 there were 35,024 primary school pupils and 11,562 pupils receiving general secondary and vocational education (including teacher training). As Djibouti has no university, students seeking further education travel abroad to study, mainly to France. In 1995, according to UNESCO estimates, the rate of illiteracy among the population aged 15 years and over was 53.8% (males 39.7%; females 67.3%).

Public Holidays

1998: 1 January (New Year's Day), 30 January* (Id al-Fitr, end of Ramadan), 8 April* (Id al-Adha, Feast of the Sacrifice), 28 April* (Muharram, Islamic New Year), 1 May (Workers' Day), 27 June (Independence Day), 7 July* (Mouloud, Birth of the Prophet), 25 December (Christmas Day).

1999: 1 January (New Year's Day), 19 January* (Id al-Fitr, end of Ramadan), 28 March* (Id al-Adha, Feast of the Sacrifice), 17 April* (Muharram, Islamic New Year), 1 May (Workers' Day), 26 June* (Mouloud, Birth of the Prophet), 27 June (Independence Day), 25 December (Christmas Day).

* These holidays are dependent on the Islamic lunar calendar and may vary by one or two days from the dates given.

Weights and Measures

The metric system is in force.

Statistical Survey

Source (unless otherwise stated): the former Ministère de l'Economie et du Commerce, BP 1846, Djibouti; tel. 351682; telex 5871.

AREA AND POPULATION

Area: 23,200 sq km (8,958 sq miles).

Population: 220,000 (1976 estimate), including Afars 70,000, Issas and other Somalis 80,000, Arabs 12,000, Europeans 15,000, other foreigners 40,000; 519,900 (including refugees and resident foreigners) at 31 December 1990 (official estimate).

Density (1990): 22.4 per sq km.

Principal Towns: Djibouti (capital), population 200,000 (1981); Dikhil; Ali-Sabieh; Tadjourah; Obock.

Births and Deaths (UN estimates, 1990–95): Average annual birth rate 38.1 per 1,000; Average annual death rate 16.1 per 1,000. Source: UN, *World Population Prospects: The 1994 Revision*.

Expectation of life (years at birth, 1990–95): 48.3 (males 46.7; females 50.0). Source: UN, *World Population Prospects: The 1994 Revision*.

Economically Active Population (estimates, '000 persons, 1991): Agriculture, etc. 212; Industries 31; Services 39; *Total* 282 (males 167, females 115). Source: UN Economic Commission for Africa, *African Statistical Yearbook*.

AGRICULTURE, ETC.

Principal Crops (FAO estimate, '000 metric tons, 1996): Vegetables 22. Source: FAO, *Production Yearbook*.

Livestock (FAO estimates, '000 head, year ending September 1996): Cattle 190; Sheep 470; Goats 507; Asses 8; Camels 62. Source: FAO, *Production Yearbook*.

Livestock Products: (FAO estimates, '000 metric tons, 1996): Beef and veal 3; Mutton and lamb 2; Goat meat 2; Cows' milk 7; Cattle hides 1. Source: FAO, *Production Yearbook*.

Fishing (FAO estimates, metric tons, live weight): Total catch 300 in 1993; 320 in 1994; 350 in 1995. Source: FAO, *Yearbook of Fishery Statistics*.

INDUSTRY

Electric energy (million kWh): 180 in 1992; 182 in 1993; 185 in 1994. Source: UN, *Industrial Commodity Statistics Yearbook*.

FINANCE

Currency and Exchange Rates: 100 centimes = 1 Djibouti franc. *Sterling and Dollar Equivalents* (30 September 1997): £1 sterling = 287.09 Djibouti francs; US $1 = 177.72 Djibouti francs; 1,000 Djibouti francs = £3.483 = $5.627. *Exchange Rate:* Fixed at US $1 = 177.721 Djibouti francs since February 1973.

Budget (million Djibouti francs, 1995): *Revenue:* Tax revenue 23,569 (Taxes on incomes and profits 4,839, Other direct taxes 4,595, Indirect taxes 12,725; Registration fees, etc. 1,411); Other revenue (incl. property sales) 1,821; Total 25,390, excl. grants received from abroad (1,779). *Expenditure:* Current expenditure 31,036 (General administration 12,304, Defence 4,481, Mobilization and demobilization 4,875, Education 3,202, Health 1,653, Economic services 1,033, Transfers 1,735); Capital expenditure 3,206; Sub-total 34,242; *Less* Payment arrears 2,773; Total 31,469. Source: IMF, *Djibouti—Statistical Annex* (July 1997).

International Reserves (US $ million at 31 December 1996): IMF special drawing rights 0.15; Foreign exchange 76.82; Total 76.97. Source: IMF, *International Financial Statistics*.

Money Supply (million Djibouti francs at 31 December 1996): Currency outside banks 9,686; Demand deposits at commercial banks 18,738; Total money (incl. others) 35,925. Source: IMF, *International Financial Statistics*.

Cost of Living: (Consumer Price Index for expatriates; base: 1989 = 100): All items 122.8 in 1993; 130.8 in 1994; 137.2 in 1995. Source: IMF, *Djibouti—Statistical Annex* (July 1997).

Expenditure on the Gross Domestic Product (million Djibouti francs at current purchasers' values, 1995): Government final consumption expenditure 33,395; Private final consumption expenditure 61,400; Gross capital formation 7,463; *Total domestic expenditure* 102,258; Exports of goods and services 35,510; *Less* Imports of goods and services 50,527; *GDP in purchasers' values* 87,241. Source: IMF, *Djibouti—Statistical Annex* (July 1997).

Gross Domestic Product by Economic Activity (million Djibouti francs at current factor cost, 1995): Agriculture, hunting, forestry and fishing 2,517; Manufacturing 4,105; Electricity, gas and water 6,297; Construction 4,440; Trade, restaurants and hotels 13,378; Transport, storage and communications 12,618; Finance, insurance, real estate and business services 7,928; Public administration 21,107; Other services 3,861; *GDP at factor cost* 76,251; Indirect taxes *less* subsidies 10,990; *GDP in purchasers' values* 87,241. Source: IMF, *Djibouti—Statistical Annex* (July 1997).

Balance of Payments (US $ million, 1995): Exports of goods f.o.b. 33.5; Imports of goods f.o.b. −205.0; *Trade balance* −171.5; Exports of services 151.4; Imports of services −87.2; *Balance on goods and services* −107.3; Other income received 25.9; Other income paid −8.7; *Balance on goods, services and income* −90.0; Current transfers received 85.4; Current transfers paid −18.4; *Current balance* −23.0; Direct investment from abroad 3.2; Other investment liabilities −5.4; Net errors and omissions 0.7; *Overall balance* −24.5. Source: IMF, *International Financial Statistics*.

EXTERNAL TRADE

Principal Commodities: *Imports c.i.f.* (million Djibouti francs, 1995): Food and beverages 9,918; Qat 4,547; Petroleum products 2,803; Chemical products 1,832; Clothing and footwear 3,115; Metals and metal products 1,386; Machinery and electrical appliances 3,614; Vehicles and transport equipment 2,076; Total (incl. others) 34,284. Note: figures refer only to imports for domestic use. Source: IMF, *Djibouti—Statistical Annex* (July 1997). *Exports f.o.b.* (distribution by SITC, US $'000, 1992): Food and live animals 3,393 (Rice 726, Coffee and coffee substitutes 1,773); Crude materials (inedible) except fuels 715; Basic manufactures 833; Machinery and transport equipment 1,260 (Road vehicles and parts 585, Other transport equipment 501); Commodities not classified according to kind 9,487; Total (incl. others) 15,919. Source: UN, *International Trade Statistics Yearbook*.

Principal Trading Partners (US $'000, 1992): *Imports c.i.f.*: People's Republic of China 6,724; Ethiopia 17,157; France (incl. Monaco) 58,003; Italy 12,064; Japan 14,810; Netherlands 7,771; Saudi Arabia 8,750; Thailand 6,207; United Kingdom 6,955; USA 6,764; Total (incl. others) 219,926. *Exports f.o.b.:* Ethiopia 523; France (incl. Monaco) 9,144; Saudi Arabia 1,587; Somalia 664; Yemen 686; Total (incl. others) 15,919. Source: UN, *International Trade Statistics Yearbook*.

TRANSPORT

Railways (1995): Passenger-km (million) 279; Freight ton-km (million) 273. Source: IMF, *Djibouti—Statistical Annex* (July 1997).

Road Traffic ('000 motor vehicles, 1992): Passenger cars 13; Commercial vehicles 3. Source: UN, *Statistical Yearbook*.

Shipping: *Merchant Fleet* (registered at 31 December 1996): 11 vessels (displacement 3,784 grt). Source: Lloyd's Register of Shipping. *Freight Traffic* ('000 metric tons, 1995): Goods loaded and unloaded 736. Source: IMF, *Djibouti—Statistical Annex* (July 1997).

Civil Aviation (1995): Passengers arriving and departing 120,145; Freight loaded and unloaded 12,291 metric tons. Source: IMF, *Djibouti—Statistical Annex* (July 1997).

TOURISM

Tourist arrivals: 24,715 in 1993; 46,595 in 1994; 20,000 in 1995. Source: IMF, *Djibouti—Statistical Annex* (July 1997).

COMMUNICATIONS MEDIA

Newspapers (1988): 2 non-dailies (estimated combined circulation 7,000).

Periodicals (1989): 7 (estimated combined circulation 6,000).

Radio Receivers (1994): 46,000 in use.

Television Receivers (1994): 25,000 in use.

Telephones (1996): 8,169 main lines in use.

Telefax Stations (1996): 142 in use.

Source: mainly UNESCO, *Statistical Yearbook*.

EDUCATION

Pre-primary (1994/95): 2 schools; 259 pupils.

Primary (1994/95): 81 schools; 35,024 pupils; 932 teachers.

Secondary (1994/95): 11,562 pupils (general 9,755, teacher-training 110, vocational 1,697); 385 teachers.

Higher (1992/93): 61 students.

Source: UNESCO, *Statistical Yearbook*.

Directory

The Constitution

In February 1981 the National Assembly approved the first constitutional laws controlling the election and terms of office of the President, who is elected by universal adult suffrage for six years and may serve for no more than two terms. Candidates for the presidency must be presented by a regularly constituted political party and represented by at least 25 members of the Chamber of Deputies. The Chamber, comprising 65 members, is elected for a five-year term.

In October 1984 a new constitutional law was proposed, specifying that, when the office of President falls vacant, the President of the Supreme Court will assume the power of Head of State for a minimum of 20 days and a maximum of 35 days, during which period a new President shall be elected.

Laws approving the establishment of a single-party system were adopted in October 1981. A new Constitution, providing for the establishment of a maximum of four political parties, was approved by national referendum on 4 September 1992 and entered into force on 15 September.

The Government

HEAD OF STATE

President and Commander-in-Chief of the Armed Forces: Hassan Gouled Aptidon (took office 27 June 1977; re-elected June 1981, April 1987 and May 1993).

COUNCIL OF MINISTERS

(January 1998)

Prime Minister and Minister of National and Regional Development: Barkad Gourad Hamadou.

Minister of Justice and Human Rights: Mohamed Dini Farah.

Minister of the Interior and Decentralization: Elmi Obsieh Wa'ays.

Minister of Defence: Abdallah Cherwa Djibrill.

Minister of Foreign Affairs and Co-operation: Muhammad Musa Chehem.

Minister of the Economy, Finance and Planning, and Privatization: Yacin Elmi Bouh.

Minister of Trade and Industry: Mohamed Barkat Abdillahi.

Minister of Transport and Communications: Abdallah Abdillahi Miguil.

Minister of Education: Ahmed Gireh Waberi.

Minister of Labour and Vocational Training: Mohamed Ali Mohamed.

Minister of the Civil Service and Administrative Reform: Ougoureh Kifleh Ahmed.

Minister of Health and Social Affairs: Ali Mohamed Daoud.

Minister of Public Works, Town Planning and Housing: Hassan Farah Miguil.

Minister of Agriculture and Water Resources: Ibrahim Idriss Djibril.

Minister of Energy and Natural Resources: Ali Abdi Farah.

Minister of Youth, Sports and Culture: Rifki Abdulkader Bamakhrama.

Minister of the Environment, Tourism and Handicrafts: Ougoureh Robleh Dahach.

MINISTRIES

Office of the Prime Minister: BP 2086, Djibouti; tel. 351494; telex 5871; fax 355049.

Ministry of Agriculture and Water Resources: BP 453, Djibouti; tel. 351297; telex 5871.

Ministry of the Civil Service and Administrative Reform: BP 155, Djibouti; tel. 351464; telex 5871.

Ministry of Defence: BP 42, Djibouti; tel. 352034; telex 5871.

Ministry of the Economy, Finance and Planning, and Privatization: BP 13, Djibouti; tel. 350297; telex 5871; fax 35601.

Ministry of Education: BP 2102, Djibouti; tel. 350850; telex 5871.

Ministry of Energy and Natural Resources: BP 175, Djibouti; tel. 350340; telex 5871.

Ministry of the Environment, Tourism and Handicrafts: Djibouti.

Ministry of Foreign Affairs and Co-operation: BP 1863, Djibouti; tel. 352471; telex 5871.

Ministry of Health and Social Affairs: BP 296, Djibouti; tel. 353331; telex 5871.

Ministry of the Interior and Decentralization: BP 33, Djibouti; tel. 350791; telex 5990.

Ministry of Justice and Human Rights: BP 12, Djibouti; tel. 351506; telex 5871; fax 354012.

Ministry of Labour and Vocational Training: BP 170, Djibouti; tel. 350497; telex 5871.

Ministry of National and Regional Development: Djibouti.

Ministry of Public Works, Town Planning and Housing: BP 11, Djibouti; tel. 350006; telex 5871.

Ministry of Trade and Industry: BP 1846, Djibouti; tel. 351682; telex 5871.

Ministry of Transport and Communications: Djibouti; tel. 350971; telex 5871.

Ministry of Youth, Sports and Culture: Djibouti.

President and Legislature

PRESIDENT

Presidential Election, 7 May 1993

Candidates	Votes	%
Hassan Gouled Aptidon (RPP)	45,470	60.76
Mohamed Djama Elabe (PRD)	16,485	22.03
Aden Robleh Awalleh (PND)	9,170	12.25
Mohamed Moussa Ali 'Tourtour' (Independent)	2,239	2.99
Ahmed Ibrahim Abdi (Independent)	1,474	1.97
Total	74,838	100.00

CHAMBRE DES DÉPUTÉS

Elections for the 65-seat Chamber of Deputies were held on 19 December 1997. The election was contested by the governing Rassemblement populaire pour le progrès (RPP), in alliance with the Front pour la restauration de l'unité et de la démocratie (FRUD), and by the Parti national démocratique (PND) and the Parti du renouveau démocratique (PRD). All 65 seats were won by the RPP-FRUD alliance.

President of the Chamber: Said Ibrahim Badoul.

Political Organizations

Constitutional reforms permitting a maximum of four political parties took effect in September 1992. By late 1997 the following parties were legally recognized:

Front pour la restauration de l'unité et de la démocratie (FRUD): f. 1991 by merger of three militant Afar groups; advocates fair representation in government of Djibouti's different ethnic groups; commenced armed insurgency in Nov. 1991; split into two factions in March 1994; the dissident group, which negotiated a settlement with the Govt, obtained legal recognition in March 1996 and recognizes the following leaders: Pres. Ali Mohamed Daoud; Sec.-Gen. Ougoureh Kifleh Ahmed; the faction favouring a continuation of mil. operations is led by Ahmed Dini Ahmed; another dissident group, FRUD–Renaissance (led by Ibrahim Chehem Daoud), was formed in 1996.

Parti national démocratique (PND): f. 1992; seeks formation of a 'govt of national unity' to supervise implementation of democratic reforms; Chair. Aden Robleh Awalleh.

Parti du renouveau démocratique (PRD): BP 2198, Djibouti; tel. 356235; fax 351474; f. 1992; seeks to establish democratic parliamentary govt; Pres. Abdillahi Hamareiteh; Sec.-Gen. Maki Houmed Gaba.

Rassemblement populaire pour le progrès (RPP): Djibouti; f. 1979; sole legal party 1981–92; Pres. Hassan Gouled Aptidon; Sec.-Gen. Mohamed Ali Mohamed.

The following organizations are banned:

Coordination de l'opposition djiboutienne: f. 1996; alliance of PND, FUOD and RPP–GDR; Leader Ismael Gedi Hared.

Front des forces démocratiques (FFD): Leader Omar Elmi Khaireh.

Front de libération de la côte des Somalis (FLCS): f. 1963; Issa-supported; has operated from Somalia; Chair. ABDALLAH WABERI KHALIF; Vice-Chair. OMAR OSMAN RABEH.

Front uni de l'opposition djiboutienne (FUOD): f. 1992; based in Ethiopia; united front of internal opposition groups, incl. some fmr mems of the RPP; Leader MOHAMED AHMED ISSA ('CHEIKO').

Groupe pour la démocratie de la république (RPP–GDR): f. 1996 by a dissident faction of the RPP; Leader MOUMIN BAHDON FARAH.

Mouvement de la jeunesse djiboutienne (MJD): Leader ABDOULKARIM ALI AMARKAK.

Mouvement pour l'unité et la démocratie (MUD): advocates political pluralism; Leader MOHAMED MOUSSA ALI ('TOURTOUR').

Organisation des masses Afar (OMA): f. 1993 by mems of the fmr Mouvement populaire de libération; Chair. AHMED MALCO.

Parti centriste et des reformes démocratiques (PCRD): f. 1993 in Addis Ababa, Ethiopia, by a breakaway faction of the FRUD; seeks official registration as an opposition party; Chair. HASSAN ABDALLAH WATTA.

Parti populaire djiboutien (PPD): f. 1981; mainly Afar-supported; Leader MOUSSA AHMED IDRIS.

Union des démocrates djiboutiens (UDD): affiliated to the FUOD; Chair. MAHDI IBRAHIM AHMED.

Union démocratique pour le progrès (UDP): f. 1992; advocates democratic reforms; Leader FARAH WABERI.

Union des mouvements démocratiques (UMD): f. 1990 by merger of two militant external opposition groups; Pres. MOHAMED ADOYTA.

Diplomatic Representation

EMBASSIES IN DJIBOUTI

China, People's Republic: Djibouti; tel. 352246; telex 5926; Ambassador: SUN ZHIRONG.

Egypt: BP 1989, Djibouti; tel. 351231; telex 5880; Ambassador: IBRAHIM ELCHOUMI.

Eritrea: Djibouti; Ambassador: DANIEL YOHANNES HAGDU.

Ethiopia: BP 230, Djibouti; tel. 350718; fax 354803; Ambassador: BERHANU DINKA.

France: 45 blvd du Maréchal Foch, BP 2039, Djibouti; tel. 350963; telex 5861; fax 350272; e-mail ambfrdj@intnet.dj; Ambassador: BERNARD LE TOURNEAU.

Iraq: BP 1983, Djibouti; tel. 353469; telex 5877; Ambassador: ABDEL AZIZ AL-GAILANI.

Libya: BP 2073, Djibouti; tel. 350202; telex 5874; Ambassador: KAMEL AL-HADI ALMARASH.

Oman: BP 1996, Djibouti; tel. 350852; telex 5876; Ambassador: SAOUD SALEM HASSAN AL-ANSI.

Russia: BP 1913, Djibouti; tel. 352051; telex 5906; fax 355990; Ambassador: MIKHAIL TSVIGOUN.

Saudi Arabia: BP 1921, Djibouti; tel. 351645; telex 5865; fax 352284; Chargé d'affaires a.i.: MOWAFFAK AL-DOLIGANE.

Somalia: BP 549, Djibouti; tel. 353521; telex 5815; Ambassador: MOHAMED SHEK MOHAMED MALINGUR.

Sudan: BP 4259, Djibouti; tel. 351404; fax 356662; Ambassador: SAYED SHARIF AHMED SHARIF.

USA: Villa Plateau du Serpent, blvd du Maréchal Joffre, BP 185, Djibouti; tel. 353995; fax 353940; Ambassador: LANGE SCHERMERHORN.

Yemen: BP 194, Djibouti; tel. 352975; Ambassador: MUHAMMAD ABDOUL WASSI HAMID.

Judicial System

The Supreme Court was established in 1979. There is a high court of appeal and a court of first instance in Djibouti; each of the five administrative districts has a 'tribunal coutumier'.

President of the Court of Appeal: KADIDJA ABEBA.

Religion

ISLAM

Almost the entire population are Muslims.

Qadi of Djibouti: MOGUE HASSAN DIRIR, BP 168, Djibouti; tel. 352669.

CHRISTIANITY

The Roman Catholic Church

Djibouti comprises a single diocese, directly responsible to the Holy See. There were an estimated 8,000 adherents in the country at 31 December 1995.

Bishop of Djibouti: Rt Rev. GEORGES PERRON, Evêché, blvd de la République, BP 94, Djibouti; tel. 350140; fax 354831.

The Anglican Communion

Within the Episcopal Church in Jerusalem and the Middle East, Djibouti lies within the jurisdiction of the Bishop in Egypt.

Other Christian Churches

Eglise Protestante: blvd de la République, BP 416, Djibouti; tel. 351820; fax 350706; f. 1957; Pastor PHILIPPE GIRARDET.

Greek Orthodox Church: blvd de la République, Djibouti; tel. 351325; c. 350 adherents; Archimandrite STAVROS GEORGANAS.

The Ethiopian Orthodox Church is also represented in Djibouti.

The Press

L'Atout: Palais du peuple, Djibouti; twice a year; publ. by the Centre National de la Promotion Culturelle et Artistique.

Carrefour Africain: BP 393, Djibouti; fax 354916; fortnightly; publ. by the Roman Catholic mission; circ. 500.

La Nation de Djibouti: place du 27 juin, BP 32, Djibouti; tel. 352201; fax 353937; weekly; Dir ISMAEL H. TANI; circ. 4,300.

Le Progrès: Djibouti; weekly; publ. by the RPP; Publr ALI MOHAMED HUMAD.

Revue de l'ISERT: BP 486, Djibouti; tel. 352795; telex 5811; twice a year; publ. by the Institut Supérieur d'Etudes et de Recherches Scientifiques et Techniques (ISERT).

NEWS AGENCIES

Agence Djiboutienne d'Information (ADJI): place du 27 juin, BP 32, Djibouti; tel. 355672; fax 353957.

Foreign Bureau

Agence France-Presse (AFP): BP 97, Djibouti; tel. 352294; telex 5863; Correspondent KHALID HAIDAR ABDALLAH.

Broadcasting and Communications

TELECOMMUNICATIONS

Société des Télécommunications Internationales (STID): c/o Ministry of the Interior and Decentralization, BP 33, Djibouti; tel. 350791; telex 5990.

RADIO AND TELEVISION

Radiodiffusion-Télévision de Djibouti (RTD): BP 97, Djibouti; tel. 352294; telex 5863; fax 356502; f. 1957; state-controlled; programmes in French, Afar, Somali and Arabic; 17 hours radio and 5 hours television daily; Dir-Gen. MOHAMED DJAMA ADEN.

Finance

(cap. = capital; res = reserves; dep. = deposits; m. = million; br. = branch; amounts in Djibouti francs)

BANKING

Central Bank

Banque Nationale de Djibouti: BP 2118, Djibouti; tel. 352751; telex 5838; fax 356288; e-mail bndj@intnet.dj; f. 1977; bank of issue; Gov. DJAMA M. HAID.

Commercial Banks

Banque al-Baraka Djibouti: ave Pierre Pascal, BP 2607, Djibouti; tel. 355046; telex 5739; fax 355038; f. 1991; cap. 600.0m., res 27.8m., dep. 4,692.1m. (Dec. 1995); Chair. OSMAN AHMED SOULEIMAN; Dir-Gen. ABDOUL-WAHED ALAWI.

Banque Indosuez Mer Rouge: 10 place Lagarde, BP 88, Djibouti; tel. 353016; telex 5829; fax 351638; f. 1908; owned by Banque Indosuez (France); cap. 1,500.0m., res 150.0m., dep. 20,679.5m. (Dec. 1995); Chair. and CEO BERNARD PARDIGON.

Banque pour le Commerce et l'Industrie-Mer Rouge (BCIMR): place Lagarde, BP 2122, Djibouti; tel. 240857; telex 5821; fax 354260; f. 1977; 51% owned by Banque Nationale de Paris Intercontinentale; cap. and res 3,623m., dep. 27,971.7m. (Dec. 1997); Pres. MOHAMED ADEN; Vice-Pres. VINCENT DE ROUX; Gen. Man. JOSEPH DETRAUX; 8 brs.

Development Bank

Banque de Développement de Djibouti: angle ave Georges Clemenceau et rue Pierre Curie, BP 520, Djibouti; tel. 353391; telex 5717; fax 355022; f. 1983; 39.2% govt-owned; cap. 1,557m. (Dec. 1993); Dir-Gen. ABDOURAHMAN ISMAEL GUELLEH.

Banking Association

Association Professionnelle des Banques: c/o Banque pour le Commerce et l'Industrie (Mer Rouge), place Lagarde, BP 2122, Djibouti; tel. 350857; telex 5821; fax 354260; Pres. MOHAMED ADEN.

INSURANCE

Ets Marill 'La Prudence': 8 rue Marchand, BP 57, Djibouti; tel. 351150; fax 355623; f.1896.

Trade and Industry

CHAMBER OF COMMERCE

Chambre Internationale de Commerce et d'Industrie: place Lagarde, BP 84, Djibouti; tel. 351070; telex 5957; fax 350096; f. 1906; 24 mems; 12 assoc. mems; Pres. SAID ALI COUBECHE; First Vice-Pres. ABDOURAHMAN MAHAMOUD BOREH.

TRADE ASSOCIATION

Office National d'Approvisionnement et de Commercialisation (ONAC): BP 119, Djibouti; tel. 350327; telex 5933.

UTILITIES

Electricity

Electricité de Djibouti (EdD): c/o Ministry of Trade and Industry, BP 1846, Djibouti; tel. 351682; telex 5871; Dir-Gen. DJAMA ALI GELLEH.

Water

Office National des Eaux de Djibouti (ONED): c/o Ministry of Trade and Industry, BP 1846, Djibouti; tel. 351682; telex 5871.

Société des Eaux de Tadjourah: c/o Ministry of Trade and Industry, BP 1846, Djibouti; tel. 351682; telex 5871.

TRADE UNION

Union Générale du Travail: Djibouti; f. 1992 to succeed Union Générale des Travailleurs de Djibouti; confed. of 22 unions; Chair. AHMED DJAMA EGUEH (OBOLEY); Sec.-Gen. ADEN MOHAMED ARDOU.

Transport

RAILWAYS

Chemin de Fer Djibouti-Ethiopien (CDE): BP 2116, Djibouti; tel. 350280; telex 5953; fax 351256; POB 1051, Addis Ababa; tel. 517250; telex 21414; fax 513533; f. 1908, adopted present name in 1981; jtly-owned by Govts of Djibouti and Ethiopia; 781 km of track (100 km in Djibouti) linking Djibouti with Addis Ababa; Pres. SALEH OMAR HILDID; Gen. Man. BOUH HOUSSEIN OMAR.

ROADS

In 1996 there were an estimated 2,890 km of roads, comprising 1,090 km of main roads and 1,800 km of regional roads; some 12.6% of the roads were paved. Of the remainder, 1,000 km are serviceable throughout the year, the rest only during the dry season. About one-half of the roads are usable only by heavy vehicles. In 1981 the 40-km Grand Bara road was opened, linking the capital with the south. In 1986 the Djibouti–Tadjourah road, the construction of which was financed by Saudi Arabia, was opened, linking the capital with the north. In mid-1996 the Islamic Development Bank granted Djibouti a loan of US $3.6m. to finance road construction projects.

SHIPPING

Djibouti, which was established as a free port in 1981, handled 736,000 metric tons of freight in 1995.

Port Autonome International de Djibouti: BP 2107, Djibouti; tel. 352331; telex 5836; fax 356187; Dir ADEN AHMED DOUALE.

Maritime and Transit Service: rue de Marseille, BP 680, Djibouti; tel. 353204; telex 5845; fax 354149.

Principal Shipping Agents

Almis Shipping Line & Transport Co: BP 85, Djibouti; tel. 356996; telex 5958; fax 356998; Man. Dir MOHAMED NOOR.

Compagnie Générale Maritime: 3 rue Marchand, BP 182, Djibouti; tel. 353825; telex 5817; fax 354778; agents for Mitsui OSK, CGM, CGM-SUD, SNC, Capricorne, WAKL, Hapaglloyd, Sea Consortium, Total Transport and others; Gen. Man. HENRI FERRAND.

Compagnie Maritime et de Manutention de Djibouti: ave des Messageries Maritimes, BP 89, Djibouti; tel. 351028; telex 5825; fax 350466; agents for Wec Lines, Zim Line, Mitsui Osk Line, Western Bulk Carriers, Metalink, Portserv; also stevedores and freight forwarders; Man. Dir ALI A. HETTAM.

Inchcape Shipping Services & Co (Djibouti) SA: 9–11 rue de Genève, BP 81, Djibouti; tel. 353844; telex 3856; fax 353294; f. 1942; agents for Lloyds and DHL; shipping agents for Nippon Yusen Kaisha, Waterman Steamship Co, Harrison Lines, Ellerman Lines, Shell, Mobil, and others; Dir-Gen. JOHN MCCAULEY.

J. J. Kothari & Co Ltd: rue d'Athens, BP 171, Djibouti; tel. 350219; telex 5860; fax 351778; agents for Shipping Corpn of India, Pacific International Lines, Shipping Corpn of Saudi Arabia, Egyptian Navigation, Sealift NV, India Shipping Co, Mediterranean Shipping Co, and others; also ship managers, stevedores, freight forwarders; Dirs S. J. KOTHARI, NALIN KOTHARI.

Mitchell Cotts Djibouti SARL: blvd de la République, BP 85, Djibouti; tel. 351204; telex 5812; fax 355851; agents for Central Gulf, Cunard Ellerman, Dry Tank/Piraeus, Harrison, Khan Shipping, Mobil/Fairfax/London, Scan-Shipping/Denmark and others; Dir FAHMY SAID CASSIM.

Société Maritime L. Savon et Ries: blvd Cheikh Osman, BP 2125, Djibouti; tel. 352351; telex 5823; fax 351103; agents for DRML, Conti Lines, SUDGARCO, Lloyd Triestino, Messina, Polish Ocean Lines and others; Gen. Man. J. P. DELARUE.

CIVIL AVIATION

The international airport is at Ambouli, 6 km from Djibouti, and there are six other airports providing domestic services.

Air Djibouti (Red Sea Airlines): BP 505, rue Marchand, Djibouti; tel. 352651; telex 5820; fax 354363; f. 1971; former govt-owned co; ceded to privately-owned co in 1997; internal flights and international services to points in the Middle East and Europe; Chair. SAAD BEN MOUSSA AL-JANAIBI.

Daallo Airlines: BP 1954, Djibouti; tel. 353401; fax 351765; f. 1992; regional carrier operating services to Somalia, Saudi Arabia and the United Arab Emirates; Man. Dir MOHAMED I. YASSIN.

Tourism

Djibouti offers desert scenery in its interior and watersport facilities on its coast. In addition, a casino opened in the capital in January 1997. In 1995 there were some 20,000 tourist arrivals.

Office National du Tourisme et de l'Artisanat (ONTA): place du 27 juin, BP 1938, Djibouti; tel. 353790; telex 5938; fax 356322; Dir ALI MOHAMED ABDALLAH.

DOMINICA

Introductory Survey

Location, Climate, Language, Religion, Flag, Capital

The Commonwealth of Dominica is situated in the Windward Islands group of the West Indies, lying between Guadeloupe, to the north, and Martinique, to the south. The climate is tropical, though tempered by sea winds which sometimes reach hurricane force, especially from July to September. The average temperature is about 27°C (80°F), with little seasonal variation. Rainfall is heavy, especially in the mountainous areas, where the annual average is 6,350 mm (250 ins), compared with 1,800 mm (70 ins) along the coast. English is the official language, but a local French patois, or Creole, is widely spoken. In parts of the north-east an English dialect, known as Cocoy, is spoken by the descendents of Antiguan settlers. There is a small community of Carib Indians on the east coast. Almost all of the inhabitants profess Christianity, and about 80% are Roman Catholics. The national flag (proportions 2 by 1) has a green field, with equal stripes of yellow, white and black forming an upright cross, on the centre of which is superimposed a red disc containing a parrot surrounded by ten five-pointed green stars (one for each of the island's parishes). The capital is Roseau.

Recent History

Dominica was first settled by Arawaks and then Caribs. Control of the island was fiercely contested by the Caribs, British and French during the 17th and 18th centuries. The British eventually prevailed and Dominica formed part of the Leeward Islands federation until 1939. In 1940 it was transferred to the Windward Islands and remained attached to that group until the federal arrangement was ended in December 1959. Under a new Constitution, effective from January 1960, Dominica (like each other member of the group) achieved a separate status, with its own Administrator and an enlarged Legislative Council.

At the January 1961 elections to the Legislative Council, the ruling Dominica United People's Party was defeated by the Dominica Labour Party (DLP), formed from the People's National Movement and other groups. Edward LeBlanc, leader of the DLP, became Chief Minister. In March 1967 Dominica became one of the West Indies Associated States, gaining full autonomy in internal affairs, with the United Kingdom retaining responsibility for defence and foreign relations. The Legislative Council was replaced by the House of Assembly, the Administrator became Governor and the Chief Minister was restyled Premier. At elections to the House in October 1970, LeBlanc was returned to power as Premier.

In July 1974 LeBlanc retired, and was replaced as DLP leader and Premier by Patrick John, formerly Deputy Premier and Minister of Finance. At elections to the enlarged House of Assembly in March 1975 the DLP was returned to power. Following a decision in 1975 by the Associated States to seek independence separately, Dominica became an independent republic within the Commonwealth on 3 November 1978. John became Prime Minister, and Frederick Degazon, formerly Speaker of the House of Assembly, was eventually elected President.

In May 1979 two people were killed by the Defence Force at a demonstration against the Government's attempts to introduce legislation which would restrict the freedom of the trade unions and the press. The killings fuelled increasing popular opposition to the Government, and a pressure group, the Committee for National Salvation (CNS), was formed to campaign for John's resignation. On his refusal to do so, opponents of the Government organized a general strike which lasted 25 days, with John relinquishing power only after all his cabinet ministers had resigned and President Degazon had gone into hiding abroad (there was a succession of Acting Presidents; Degazon finally resigned in February 1980). Oliver Seraphin, the candidate proposed by the CNS, was elected Prime Minister, and an interim Government was then formed to prepare for elections after six months.

Elections were eventually held in July 1980, when the Dominica Freedom Party (DFP) gained a convincing victory, winning 17 of the 21 elective seats in the House of Assembly. Eugenia Charles, the party's leader, became the Caribbean's first female Prime Minister. Both John, who contested the elections as leader of the DLP, and Seraphin, who stood as leader of the newly-formed Democratic Labour Party (DEMLAB), lost their seats. The DFP's victory was attributed to its continued integrity, while the DLP and DEMLAB had suffered from major political scandals.

Fears for the island's security dominated 1981. In January the Government disarmed the Defence Force, following reports that weapons were being traded for marijuana. Against a background of increasing violence and the declaration of a state of emergency, however, there were two coup attempts involving former Defence Force members. John, the former Prime Minister, was also implicated and imprisoned. In June 1982 John and his fellow prisoners were tried and acquitted but the Government secured a retrial in October 1985. John and the former Deputy Commander of the Defence Force each received a prison sentence of 12 years (they were released in May 1990). In 1986 the former Commander of the Defence Force was hanged for the murder of a police officer during the second coup attempt. The death sentences on five other soldiers were commuted to life imprisonment.

After his release in June 1982, John attempted to form a new left-wing coalition party. By 1985 the DLP, DEMLAB, the United Dominica Labour Party and the Dominica Liberation Movement had united to form a left-wing grouping, known as the Labour Party of Dominica (LPD). The new leader, however, was Michael Douglas, a former Minister of Finance. At elections in July 1985 the DFP was returned to power, winning 15 of the 21 elective seats in the House of Assembly. The opposition LPD won five seats, with the remaining seat being won by Rosie Douglas, the brother of the LPD leader, whose candidature was not officially endorsed by the LPD. Following the election, the LPD began an 18-month boycott of the House, in protest at the Government's decision to curtail live broadcasts of parliamentary proceedings. By July 1987, the DFP's strength in the House had increased to 17 seats, with four seats still being held by the LPD.

Dissatisfaction at continued government austerity measures was offset by the success of the land reform programme. Since independence, the Government had acquired nearly all the large estates, often in an attempt to forestall violence. In 1986 the first of the estates was divided, and tenure granted to the former workers. Despite the success of this programme, the opposition DLP and the Dominica United Workers' Party (UWP—formed in 1988) bitterly denounced many other government policies and criticized Charles's style of leadership. The two opposition parties failed to agree on the formation of an electoral alliance, however, and the DFP was returned for a third term in government at the general election in May 1990. There was a relatively low level of participation in the election, in which the DFP won a total of 11 seats, the UWP became the official opposition (with six seats) and the LPD won four seats. The results were reported to indicate the electorate's disenchantment with the traditional parties; participation and voting preferences were determined by personality rather than policy.

A programme, introduced in August 1991, granting Dominican citizenship to foreigners in return for a minimum investment of US $35,000 in the country caused considerable controversy during 1992. The UWP expressed opposition to the policy, and a pressure group, 'Concerned Citizens', organized several demonstrations demanding that the programme be modified. In response to such pressure (including vociferous opposition from the Dominica Association of Industry and Commerce), the Government announced in July that the minimum investment was to be increased substantially, the number of applications was to be limited to 800 and restrictions were to be placed on the investors' right to vote in Dominica. By early 1995 some 615 people (mainly Taiwanese) had been granted citizenship under the scheme, and an estimated US $7.1m. had been invested in the country.

In August 1993 the DFP elected Brian Alleyne, the Minister of External Affairs, to succeed to the leadership of the party upon Charles's retirement, which was expected to occur prior to the next general election. Following the retirement of President Seignoret, Crispin Sorhaindo, formerly the Speaker of the House of Assembly, was appointed to the presidency and assumed office in October.

At the general election of 12 June 1995 the DFP's 15-year tenure was finally ended, with the party losing four of its 11 seats to the UWP and two to the LPD. The LPD won five seats, while the UWP secured a narrow victory, with 11 seats and 34.5% of total votes cast (compared with 35.8% for the DFP). Some observers attributed the DFP's poor performance in the election to Charles's failure to give full support to her successor, Brian Alleyne, upon her retirement. Edison James was subsequently appointed as Prime Minister, and the LPD and DFP leaders agreed to occupy the position of Leader of the Opposition in alternate years, commencing with Brian Alleyne. In the following month a legal dispute arose concerning the eligibility to serve in the House of Assembly of one of the DFP's members, Charles Savarin, who, as General Manager of the National Development Corporation, was deemed to occupy a public role in the country. As a result of the dispute, which continued during 1995, the position of Leader of the Opposition was transferred to the LPD leader, Rosie Douglas. In April 1996, however, Savarin was elected leader of the DFP following Alleyne's resignation, which had been prompted by his appointment as a judge in Grenada. A by-election for Alleyne's seat, which took place in August, was won by the UWP candidate, thus increasing the Government's representation in the House of Assembly to 12 seats. The Government's support for a long-term programme to divest several state-owned enterprises to the private sector and to implement structural adjustment measures (recommended by the IMF) attracted criticism from the opposition in 1996 and 1997, as well as from the Civil Service Association, which pledged its resistance to any retrenchment in the sector.

In April 1997 an investigation of the police force was conducted, following allegations of corruption. In November the Prime Minister announced that the Police Commissioner, Desmond Blanchard, his deputy, Hansel Valerie, and five other officers had been sent on leave, owing to the findings of the report. Meanwhile, the Government established a Constitutional Commission to examine several issues, including civil rights, standards in public service, the responsibility of politicians and public involvement in government. The Commission was expected to publish its conclusions in late 1998. In late 1997 the Ministries of Trade and Marketing and of Foreign Affairs were merged for reasons of finance and efficiency; responsibility for the respective portfolios was, however, retained by Norris Charles and the Prime Minister.

An attempt by the British Government in January 1996 to deport an exiled Saudi Arabian opposition leader to Dominica aroused controversy in both countries. The proposal was criticized by the leaders of the DFP and DLP and by former Prime Minister Dame Eugenia Charles. James, who had agreed to the plan following a request from the United Kingdom in December 1995, vehemently denied suggestions that the scheme may have had a financial motive, despite speculation to that effect, prompted by an increase in aid from the United Kingdom from £0.5m. in 1995 to £2m. for 1996. Following a legal challenge to the proposed deportation (concluded in April), the dissident was granted permission to remain in Britain for a total of four years.

In foreign policy, Dominica has close links with France and the USA. France helped in suppressing the coup attempts against the DFP Government, and Dominica was the first Commonwealth country to benefit from the French aid agency, FAC. In October 1983 Dominica, as a member of the Organization of Eastern Caribbean States (OECS—see p. 122), contributed forces to the US-backed invasion of Grenada. In 1988 four countries of the Windward group (Dominica, Grenada, Saint Lucia and Saint Vincent and the Grenadines) decided to proceed with plans for the formation of a political union. In 1990 the four countries decided to convene a constituent assembly, and in early 1992 this assembly agreed a draft constitution, which included provision for the election of an executive president by universal suffrage. Following its election in mid-1995, the Government of Edison James stated its commitment to the increased economic integration of the Windward Islands, leading to political union. Dominica is also a member of the Caribbean Community and Common Market (CARICOM—see p. 119) and the Association of Caribbean States (see p. 259).

Government

Legislative power is vested in the unicameral House of Assembly, comprising 30 members (nine nominated and 21 elected for five years by universal adult suffrage). Executive authority is vested in the President, elected by the House, but in most matters the President is guided by the advice of the Cabinet and acts as the constitutional Head of State. He appoints the Prime Minister, who must be able to command a majority in the House, and (on the Prime Minister's recommendation) other ministers. The Cabinet is responsible to the House. The island is divided into 10 administrative divisions, known as parishes, and there is limited local government in Roseau and in the Carib Territory.

Defence

The Dominican Defence Force was officially disbanded in April 1981. There is a police force of about 300, which includes a coastguard service. A patrol boat was received from the USA in 1983. The country participates in the US-sponsored Regional Security System.

Economic Affairs

In 1995, according to estimates by the World Bank, Dominica's gross national product (GNP), measured at average 1993–95 prices, was US $218m., equivalent to US $2,990 per head. Between 1985 and 1995, it was estimated, GNP per head increased, in real terms, at an average rate of 4.0% per year. Over the same period, the population decreased by an annual average of 0.1%. Gross domestic product (GDP), in real terms, increased by an annual average of 5.0% in 1986–90, but the average annual growth rate declined to 2.1% in 1991–95. Real GDP growth was estimated at 3.2% in 1996.

Agriculture (including forestry and fishing) is the principal economic activity, accounting for an estimated 18.4% of GDP in 1995. In 1991 the sector engaged 30.8% of the employed labour force. The principal cash crop is bananas, of which an estimated 40,327 metric tons were produced in 1996, with exports earning EC $44.6m. (compared with EC $104m. in 1988). The industry, which was already experiencing difficulties (owing to a decline in banana prices), was likely to be adversely affected by a ruling of the World Trade Organization (WTO—see p. 244) against Dominica's preferential access to the European (particularly the British) market. Other important crops include coconuts (which provide copra for export as well as edible oil and soap), mangoes, avocados, papayas, ginger, citrus fruits and, mainly for domestic consumption, vegetables. Livestock-rearing and fishing are also practised for local purposes. In July 1997 construction of a fishing port and market in Roseau, which commenced in 1994 with financial assistance from Japan, was completed. Dominica has extensive timber reserves (more than 40% of the island's total land area is forest and woodland), and international aid agencies are encouraging the development of a balanced timber industry. In real terms, agricultural GDP, which contracted by 8.1% in 1995 (largely as a result of hurricane damage), increased by an estimated 5.7% in 1996.

Industry (comprising mining, manufacturing, construction and utilities) provided 19.3% of GDP in 1995, and employed 21.6% of the labour force in 1991. Industrial activity is mainly small-scale and dependent upon agriculture. The mining sector contributed only 0.8% of GDP in 1995 and employed 0.3% of the labour force in 1991. There is some quarrying of pumice, and there are extensive reserves of limestone and clay. In 1996 an Australian mining company began investigations into the possible exploitation of extensive copper deposits in north-eastern Dominica. Pumice is useful to the construction industry, which accounted for 8.1% of GDP in 1995 and employed 11.8% of the labour force in 1991. Extensive infrastructure development by the Government maintained high levels of activity in the construction sector. The GDP of the construction sector increased at an annual average rate of 4.9% in 1991–95, but decreased by an estimated 7.5% in 1996. The Government has also encouraged the manufacturing sector in an attempt to diversify the economy. In 1995 manufacturing contributed 6.5% of GDP. Manufacturing GDP increased by only 0.1% in 1995 but by an estimated 6.5% in 1996, largely owing to a 32.2% increase in the output of soap products. The sector employed 8.2% of the labour force in 1991. There is a banana-packaging plant and factories for the manufacturing and refining of crude and edible vegetable oils and for the production of soap, canned juices and cigarettes. A brewery was established in 1995 to supply domestic requirements. Furniture, paint, cardboard boxes and candles are also significant manufactures. Soap accounted for an estimated 35.7% of total domestic exports in 1996.

In 1996 60% of Dominica's energy requirements were supplied by hydroelectric power. Investment in a hydroelectric development scheme and in the water supply system has been partially financed by the export of water, from Dominica's extensive reserves, to drier Caribbean islands such as Aruba. A hydroelectric power station, with a generating capacity of 1.24 MW, began operation at Laudat in 1990. By 1991 Dominica had reduced imports of mineral fuels to 7.9% of the value of total imports. In 1995 a US company announced that it would invest EC $25m. in a geothermal energy project in Soufrière, which aimed to begin producing electricity by 1998. In December 1996 the state-owned Dominica Electricity Services (DOMLEC) was privatized, with the British Government's overseas private finance institution, the Commonwealth Development Corporation (CDC), buying 73% of the company. The CDC outlined plans to improve transmission lines and to increase electricity generation by 80% by the year 2000.

The tourist industry is an increasingly important sector of the economy and exploits Dominica's natural history and scenery. The majority of tourists are cruise-ship passengers. Arrivals from cruise ships increased from 6,777 in 1990 to 64,762 in the following year, and by 1996 totalled an estimated 193,484. In 1990 the Government decided to proceed with the construction of an international airport. However, in early 1997 the administration was still experiencing problems in securing the necessary finance for the project, although the CDC was reported to be assisting with the cost of the scheme (which was estimated to total EC $700m., rather than the original budgetary estimate of EC $76m.).

In 1994 Dominica recorded a visible trade deficit of US $51.85m., and a deficit of US $35.73m. on the current account of the balance of payments. The principal source of imports in 1996 was the USA (including Puerto Rico), which accounted for 40.6% of total imports, followed by the United Kingdom (13.0%). Members of the Caribbean Community and Common Market (CARICOM—see p. 119) provided a total of 24.7% of imports. The principal market for exports is the United Kingdom, which receives virtually all Dominica's banana production. In 1996 the United Kingdom received 36.0% of total domestic exports, while CARICOM countries received 47.4%. The principal imports are food and live animals, basic manufactures such as paper, and machinery and transport equipment. The principal exports are bananas and soap.

For the financial year ending 30 June 1996 there was a budget deficit of EC $3.5m. Recurrent expenditure for 1997/98 was expected to increase by 3.7%, to EC $205.5m., and a 4.5% increase in revenue, to total EC $194.8m., was also anticipated. At the end of 1995 Dominica's total external debt was US $93.0m., of which US $84.6m. was long-term public debt. In that year the cost of debt-servicing was equivalent to 6.1% of the value of exports of goods and services. The annual rate of inflation averaged 3.2% in 1986–96; consumer prices increased by 1.7% in 1996. An estimated 23% of the labour force were unemployed in 1994. Labour shortages have occurred in the agricultural and construction sectors.

Dominica is a member of the Organization of American States (OAS—see p. 219), CARICOM, the OECS and is a signatory of the Lomé Conventions with the EU (see p. 178). Under the Charles administration, the island received considerable aid from the United Kingdom, France, the USA and various international aid agencies.

The Dominican economy is heavily dependent on the production of coconut-based products and bananas, and their export to a limited market, and is thus vulnerable to adverse weather conditions, price fluctuations and economic conditions in its principal markets. In the 1990s growth in the economy slowed, owing to the uncertainty surrounding Dominica's preferential access to the European market and the devastation of the 1995 banana crop by a hurricane. Efforts to expand the country's economic base have been impeded by poor infrastructure and, in terms of tourism, a paucity of desirable beaches. Foreign investment was deterred by discrimination against foreign capital, while tariffs and trade restrictions hindered exports. This was likely to be addressed, however, as the secretariat of the OECS was urging members to create a single market and economy by September 1998, prior to the creation of a CARICOM single market, planned for 1999. In September 1997 the WTO finally ruled against the EU's banana import regime, putting intense pressure on Dominica to diversify. Financial experts urged monetary restraint and economic restructuring to avoid further deterioration in Dominica's fiscal performance. However, the 1997/98 budget was expansionary in character, envisaging borrowing to finance capital expenditure on roads, sewerage and education, and relying on a reorganization within government departments to achieve savings, rather than introducing new methods of taxation.

Social Welfare

There are main hospitals at Roseau and Portsmouth, with 136 and 50 beds respectively, and two cottage hospitals, at Marigot and Grand Bay. There is a polyclinic at the Princess Margaret Hospital, Roseau. There are 51 health centres, located throughout the island. In 1996 Dominica had one hospital bed for every 88 citizens, and one physician for every 225 inhabitants.

Education

Education is free and is provided by both government and denominational schools. There are also a number of schools for the mentally and physically handicapped. Education is compulsory for 10 years between five and 15 years of age. Primary education begins at the age of five and lasts for seven years. Enrolment of children in the primary age-group was 70.7% in 1992. Secondary education, beginning at 12 years of age, lasts for five years. A teacher-training college provides further education, and there is also a branch of the University of the West Indies on the island. In 1997 the Government announced plans to invest EC $17.9m. in a Basic Education Reform project. The rate of adult illiteracy was only 5.6% in 1986.

Public Holidays

1998: 1 January (New Year's Day), 23–24 February (Masquerade, Carnival), 10 April (Good Friday), 13 April (Easter Monday), 1 May (May or Labour Day), 1 June (Whit Monday), 3 August (Emancipation, August Monday), 3 November (Independence Day), 4 November (Community Service Day), 25–26 December (Christmas).

1999: 1 January (New Year's Day), 15–16 February (Masquerade, Carnival), 2 April (Good Friday), 5 April (Easter Monday), 1 May (May or Labour Day), 24 May (Whit Monday), 2 August (Emancipation, August Monday), 3 November (Independence Day), 4 November (Community Service Day), 25–26 December (Christmas).

Weights and Measures

The imperial system is in use, although the metric system is to be introduced.

Statistical Survey

Sources (unless otherwise stated): Ministry of Finance, Roseau; OECS Economic Affairs Secretariat, *Annual Digest of Statistics*.

AREA AND POPULATION

Area: 751 sq km (290 sq miles).

Population: 69,548 at census of 7 April 1970; 73,795 at census of 7 April 1981; 71,183 (males 35,471, females 35,712) at census of 12 May 1991; 74,000 (official estimate) at mid-1996.

Density (mid-1996): 98.5 per sq km.

Population by Ethnic Group (*de jure* population, excl. those resident in institutions, 1981): Negro 67,272; Mixed race 4,433; Amerindian (Carib) 1,111; White 341; Total (incl. others) 73,795 (males 36,754, females 37,041). Source: UN, *Demographic Yearbook*.

Principal Town (population at 1991 census): Roseau (capital) 15,853.

Births, Marriages and Deaths (1996): Live births 1,419 (birth rate 19.1 per 1,000); Marriages (1995) 229 (marriage rate 3.1 per 1,000); Deaths 575 (death rate 7.7 per 1,000).

Expectation of Life (UN estimates, years at birth, 1990–95): 67.8 (males 64.1; females 71.4). Source: ECLAC Demography Unit.

Economically Active Population (persons aged 15 years and over, excl. institutional population, at census of May 1991): Agriculture, hunting, forestry and fishing 7,344; Mining and quarrying 65; Manufacturing 1,947; Electricity, gas and water 304; Construction 2,819; Trade, restaurants and hotels 3,658; Transport, storage and communications 1,202; Financing, insurance and real estate 810; Public administration, defence and social security 1,520; Community services 2,400; Other services 1,046; Activities not adequately defined 699; Total employed 23,814; Unemployed 2,541; Total labour force 26,355 (males 17,275; females 9,080).

AGRICULTURE, ETC.

Principal Crops (FAO estimates, '000 metric tons, 1996): Sweet potatoes 2; Cassava 1; Yams 7; Taro (Dasheen) 11; Other roots and tubers 4; Coconuts 18; Cabbages 1; Pumpkins 1; Cucumbers 2; Carrots 1; Other vegetables 1; Sugar cane 5; Oranges 3; Lemons and limes 1; Grapefruit 13; Avocados 1; Mangoes 3; Bananas 40; Plantains 6. Source: FAO, *Production Yearbook*.

Livestock (FAO estimates, '000 head, year ending September 1996): Cattle 13; Pigs 5; Sheep 8; Goats 10. Source: FAO, *Production Yearbook*.

Livestock Products (FAO estimates, '000 metric tons, 1996): Beef and veal 1; Cows' milk 6. Source: FAO, *Production Yearbook*.

Fishing (metric tons, live weight): Total catch 797 in 1993; 885 in 1994; 842 in 1995. Source: FAO, *Yearbook of Fishery Statistics*.

MINING

Pumice ('000 metric tons): Estimated production 100 per year in 1987–94 (Source: US Bureau of Mines).

INDUSTRY

Production (1996, metric tons, unless otherwise indicated): Soap 14,815; Crude coconut oil 753 (estimate); Edible coconut oil 82 (estimate); Coconut meal 350 (estimate); Electricity 52.4 million kWh (1994).

FINANCE

Currency and Exchange Rates: 100 cents = 1 East Caribbean dollar (EC $). *Sterling and US Dollar Equivalents* (30 September 1997): £1 sterling = EC $4.362; US $1 = EC $2.700; EC $100 = £22.93 = US $37.04. *Exchange Rate:* Fixed at US $1 = EC $2.70 since July 1976.

Budget (EC $ million, year ending 30 June 1996): *Revenue:* Tax revenue 148.8; Other current revenue 17.2; Capital revenue 1.6; Total 167.5, excl. grants received (40.6). *Expenditure:* Current expenditure 155.7 (Wages and salaries 88.5); Fixed investment 59.3; Other capital expenditure and net lending –3.3; Total 211.7. Source: IMF, *Dominica—Recent Economic Developments* (July 1997).

International Reserves (US $ million at 31 December 1996): Reserve position in IMF 0.01; Foreign exchange 22.88; Total 22.89. Source: IMF, *International Financial Statistics*.

Money Supply (EC $ million at 31 December 1996): Currency outside banks 28.53; Demand deposits at commercial banks 67.43; Total money (incl. others) 97.04. Source: IMF, *International Financial Statistics*.

Cost of Living (Retail Price Index, base: 1990 = 100): All items 113.1 in 1994; 114.6 in 1995; 116.5 in 1996. Source: IMF, *International Financial Statistics*.

National Accounts (EC $ million at current prices): Gross domestic product in purchasers' values 537.8 in 1993; 584.3 in 1994; 597.7 in 1995. Source: IMF, *International Financial Statistics*.

Expenditure on the Gross Domestic Product (EC $'000 at current prices, 1991): Government final consumption expenditure 95,670; Private final consumption expenditure 341,860; Increase in stocks 5,150; Gross fixed capital formation 192,500; *Total domestic expenditure* 635,180; Exports of goods and services 222,280; *Less* Imports of goods and services 378,630; GDP in purchasers' values 478,830. Source: UN, *National Accounts Statistics*.

Gross Domestic Product by Economic Activity (EC $ million at current prices, 1995): Agriculture, hunting, forestry and fishing 100.9; Mining and quarrying 4.4; Manufacturing 35.8; Electricity, gas and water 21.0; Construction 44.3; Wholesale and retail trade 61.6; Restaurants and hotels 15.1; Transport 52.0; Communications 36.3; Finance and insurance 57.8; Real estate 17.8; Government services 92.9; Other services 7.1; Sub-total 547.0; *Less* imputed bank service charge 36.8; GDP at factor cost 510.3. Source: IMF, *Dominica—Recent Economic Developments* (July 1997).

Balance of Payments (US $ million, 1994): Exports of goods f.o.b. 43.98; Imports of goods f.o.b. –95.83; *Trade balance* –51.85; Exports of services 51.58; Imports of services –32.97; *Balance on goods and services* –33.24; Other income received 3.07; Other income paid –13.98; *Balance on goods, services and income* –44.14; Current transfers received 14.82; Current transfers paid –6.41; *Current balance* –35.73; Capital account (net) 8.20; Direct investment from abroad 22.13; Other investment assets 5.96; Other investment liabilities –2.26; Net errors and omissions –1.36; *Overall balance* –3.24. Source: IMF, *International Financial Statistics*.

EXTERNAL TRADE

Principal Commodities (EC $ '000, 1993): *Imports c.i.f.:* Food and live animals 48,546; Beverages and tobacco 10,648; Crude materials (inedible) except fuels 5,250; Mineral fuels, lubricants, etc. 16,100; Animal and vegetable oils and fats 9,777; Chemicals and related products 35,363; Basic manufactures 56,473; Machinery and transport equipment 48,059; Miscellaneous manufactured articles 23,010; Total 253,225. *Exports f.o.b.:* Food and live animals 84,924; Beverages and tobacco 38; Crude materials (inedible) except fuels 508; Animal and vegetable oils and fats 2; Chemicals and related products 35,260; Basic manufactures 3,453; Machinery and transport equipment 107; Miscellaneous manufactured articles 2,278; Total 126,570 (excl. re-exports 3,062).

Principal Trading Partners (EC $ '000, 1993): *Imports c.i.f.:* Barbados 8,618; Canada 5,600; Germany 3,283; Jamaica 4,945; Netherlands 4,518; Saint Lucia 8,153; Saint Vincent and the Grenadines 8,081; Trinidad and Tobago 28,090; United Kingdom 31,905; USA 82,120; Total (incl. others) 253,225. *Exports f.o.b.:* Antigua and Barbuda 3,938; Barbados 3,173; Grenada 3,266; Guyana 3,954; Italy 4,273; Jamaica 11,815; Saint Kitts and Nevis/Anguilla 1,732; Saint Lucia 4,420; Saint Vincent and the Grenadines 1,874; Trinidad and Tobago 4,013; United Kingdom 65,880; USA 4,024; Total (incl. others) 129,631.

TRANSPORT

Road Traffic (motor vehicles licensed in 1994): Private cars 6,491; Taxis 90; Buses 559; Motorcycles 94; Trucks 2,266; Jeeps 461; Tractors 24; Total 9,985.

Shipping (international sea-borne freight traffic, '000 metric tons, estimates, 1993): Goods loaded 103.2; Goods unloaded 181.2.

Civil Aviation (1994): Aircraft arrivals and departures 18,066; Freight loaded 592 metric tons; Freight unloaded 385 metric tons.

TOURISM

Tourist Arrivals: *Stop-overs:* 56,522 in 1994; 60,471 in 1995; 63,259 in 1996. *Cruise-ship passengers:* 125,541 in 1994; 134,921 in 1995; 193,484 in 1996.

Tourist Receipts (US $ million): 31.7 in 1994; 35.0 in 1995; 38.0 (estimate) in 1996.

COMMUNICATIONS MEDIA

Radio Receivers (1994, estimate): 43,000 in use.

Television Receivers (1994, estimate): 5,000 in use.

Telephones (1993): 15,283 in use.

Telefax Stations (1992): 290 in use.

Non-daily Newspapers (1993): 3.

Source: mainly UNESCO, *Statistical Yearbook*.

EDUCATION

Institutions (1994/95): Pre-primary 73 (1992/93); Primary 64; Secondary 14; Tertiary 2.

Teachers (1994/95): Pre-primary 108 (1992/93); Primary 643; Secondary 269; Tertiary 39 (1992/93).

Pupils (1994/95): Pre-primary 2,369 (1992/93); Primary 14,632; Secondary 4,511; Tertiary 482.

Directory

The Constitution

The Constitution came into effect at the independence of Dominica on 3 November 1978. Its main provisions are summarized below:

FUNDAMENTAL RIGHTS AND FREEDOMS

The Constitution guarantees the rights of life, liberty, security of the person, the protection of the law and respect for private property. The individual is entitled to freedom of conscience, of expression and assembly and has the right to an existence free from slavery, forced labour and torture. Protection against discrimination on the grounds of sex, race, place of origin, political opinion, colour or creed is assured.

THE PRESIDENT

The President is elected by the House of Assembly for a term of five years. A presidential candidate is nominated jointly by the Prime Minister and the Leader of the Opposition and on their concurrence is declared elected without any vote being taken; in the case of disagreement the choice will be made by secret ballot in the House of Assembly. Candidates must be citizens of Dominica aged at least 40 who have been resident in Dominica for five years prior to their nomination. A President may not hold office for more than two terms.

PARLIAMENT

Parliament consists of the President and the House of Assembly, composed of 21 elected Representatives and nine Senators. According to the wishes of Parliament, the latter may be appointed by the President—five on the advice of the Prime Minister and four on the advice of the Leader of the Opposition—or elected. The life of Parliament is five years.

Parliament has the power to amend the Constitution. Each constituency returns one Representative to the House who is directly elected in accordance with the Constitution. Every citizen over the age of 18 is eligible to vote.

THE EXECUTIVE

Executive authority is vested in the President. The President appoints as Prime Minister the elected member of the House who commands the support of a majority of its elected members, and other ministers on the advice of the Prime Minister. Not more than three ministers may be from among the appointed Senators. The President has the power to remove the Prime Minister from office if a resolution expressing 'no confidence' in the Government is adopted by the House and the Prime Minister does not resign within three days or advise the President to dissolve Parliament.

The Cabinet consists of the Prime Minister, other ministers and the Attorney-General in an ex officio capacity.

The Leader of the Opposition is appointed by the President as that elected member of the House who, in the President's judgement, is best able to command the support of a majority of the elected members who do not support the Government.

The Government

HEAD OF STATE

President: Crispin Sorhaindo (assumed office 25 October 1993).

CABINET

(February 1998)

Prime Minister and Minister of Legal and Foreign Affairs and Labour: Edison James.

Minister of Finance, Industry and Planning: Julius Timothy.

Minister of Tourism, Ports and Employment: Senator Norris Prevost.

Minister of Health and Social Security: Doreen Paul.

Minister of Trade and Marketing: Norris Charles.

Minister of Community Development and Women's Affairs: Gertrude Roberts.

Minister of Housing, Communications, Public Works and Road Construction: Earl Williams.

Minister of Agriculture and the Environment: Peter Carbon.

Minister of Education, Sports and Youth Affairs: Ron Green.

Attorney-General: Anthony Laronde.

MINISTRIES

Office of the President: Morne Bruce, Roseau; tel. 4482054; fax 4498633.

Office of the Prime Minister: Government Headquarters, Kennedy Ave, Roseau; tel. 4482401.

All other ministries are at Government Headquarters, Kennedy Ave, Roseau; tel. 4482401.

CARIB TERRITORY

This reserve of the remaining Amerindian population is located on the central east coast of the island. The Caribs enjoy a measure of local government and elect their chief.

Chief: Hilary Frederick.

Waitukubuli Karifuna Development Committee: Salybia, Carib Territory.

Legislature

HOUSE OF ASSEMBLY

Speaker: Osborne Symes.

Clerk: Albertha Jno Baptiste.

Senators: 9.

Elected Members: 21.

Election, 12 June 1995

Party	Votes cast	%	Seats
Dominica United Workers' Party	12,792	34.5	11
Dominica Freedom Party	13,296	35.8	5*
Labour Party of Dominica	11,007	29.6	5
Independents	29	0.1	—
Total	37,124	100.0	21

* A legal dispute regarding the eligibility of a DFP assembly member resulted in that party controlling only four seats for much of 1995.

Political Organizations

Dominica Freedom Party (DFP): Cross St, Roseau; tel. 4482104; Leader Charles Savarin.

Dominica Progressive Party: Roseau; f. 1990; Leader Leonard (Pappy) Baptiste.

Dominica United Workers' Party (UWP): Roseau; tel. 4485051; f. 1988; Leader Edison James; Chair. Garnet L. Didier.

Labour Party of Dominica (LPD): Roseau; f. 1985; merger and reunification of left-wing groups, incl. the Dominica Labour Party (f. 1961); Leader Rosie Douglas; Deputy Leader Pierre Charles.

Diplomatic Representation

EMBASSIES IN DOMINICA

China (Taiwan): Checkhall Estate, POB 56, Roseau; tel. 4491385; fax 4492085; Chargé d'affaires: Philip T. Y. Wang.

Venezuela: 37 Cork St, 3rd Floor, POB 770, Roseau; tel. 4483348; telex 8643; fax 4486198; Ambassador: HERNANI ESCOBAR.

Judicial System

Justice is administered by the Eastern Caribbean Supreme Court (based in Saint Lucia), consisting of the Court of Appeal and the High Court. One of the six puisne judges of the High Court is resident in Dominica and presides over the Court of Summary Jurisdiction. The District Magistrate Courts deal with summary offences and civil offences involving limited sums of money (specified by law).

Religion

Most of the population profess Christianity, but there are some Muslims and Bahá'ís. The largest denomination is the Roman Catholic Church (with some 80% of the inhabitants in 1991).

CHRISTIANITY

The Roman Catholic Church

Dominica comprises the single diocese of Roseau, suffragan to the archdiocese of Castries (Saint Lucia). At 31 December 1995 there were an estimated 57,000 adherents in the country, representing a large majority of the inhabitants. The Bishop participates in the Antilles Episcopal Conference (currently based in Port of Spain, Trinidad).

Bishop of Roseau: Rt Rev. EDWARD J. GILBERT; Bishop's House, 20 Virgin Lane, POB 790, Roseau; tel. 4482837; fax 4483404.

The Anglican Communion

Anglicans in Dominica are adherents of the Church in the Province of the West Indies. The country forms part of the diocese of the North Eastern Caribbean and Aruba. The Bishop, who is also Archbishop of the Province, is resident in Antigua.

Other Christian Churches

There are churches of various denominations, including Methodist, Pentecostal, Baptist, Church of God, Presbyterian, the Assemblies of Brethren, Moravian and Seventh-day Adventist groups, and the Jehovah's Witnesses.

BAHÁ'Í FAITH

National Spiritual Assembly: 9 James Lane, POB 136, Roseau; tel. 4484269; fax 4483881; e-mail coolesp@cwdom.dm.

The Press

The Independent Newspaper: POB 462, 9 Great Marlborough St, Roseau; tel. 4480221; fax 4484368.

The New Chronicle: Wallhouse, POB 1724, Roseau; tel. 4482121; telex 8625; fax 4488031; f. 1909; Friday; progressive independent; Gen. Man. J. A. WHITE; Editor RASCHID OSMAN; circ. 2,500.

Official Gazette: Government Printery, Roseau; tel. 4482401, ext. 330; telex 8613; weekly; circ. 550.

The Tropical Star: Roseau; circ. 3,000.

Broadcasting and Communications

RADIO

Dominica Broadcasting Corporation: Victoria St, POB 1, Roseau; tel. 4483283; fax 4482918; government station; daily broadcasts in English; 2 hrs daily in French patois; 10 kW transmitter on the medium wave band; programmes received throughout Caribbean excluding Jamaica and Guyana; Gen. Man. CHARLES JAMES; Programme Dir SHERMAINE GREEN-BROWN.

Kairi FM: Great George St, POB 931, Roseau; tel. 4487330; fax 4487332.

Voice of Life Radio—ZGBC: Gospel Broadcasting Corpn, Loubiere, POB 205, Roseau; tel. 4487017; fax 4487094; e-mail volradio @tod.dm; linked to the US Christian Reformed Church; 112 hrs weekly AM, 24 hrs daily FM; Man. Dir GRANT HOEPPNER.

Voice of the Islands Radio—VOI: Pte Michel, POB 2402, Roseau; tel. 4484042; fax 4480938; religious; f. 1986; 105 hrs weekly; broadcasts were suspended in early 1997; Gen. Man. J.F.R. CASIMIR.

TELEVISION

There is no national television service, although there is a cable television network serving one-third of the island.

Marpin-TV: POB 2381, Roseau; tel. 4484107; fax 4482965; e-mail manager@marpin.dm; internet http://www.marpin.dm; commercial; cable service; Programme Man. RON ABRAHAM.

Finance

(cap. = capital; res = reserves; dep. = deposits; m. = million; amounts in East Caribbean dollars)

The Eastern Caribbean Central Bank (see p. 122), based in Saint Christopher, is the central issuing and monetary authority for Dominica.

BANKS

Agricultural, Industrial and Development (AID) Bank: 64 Hillsborough St, POB 215, Roseau; tel. 4482853; fax 4484903; f. 1971; state-owned; planned privatization suspended in 1997; cap. 9.5m. (1991).

Bank of Nova Scotia (Canada): 28 Hillsborough St, POB 520, Roseau; tel. 4485800; telex 8672; fax 4485805; Man. C. M. SMITH.

Banque Française Commerciale (France): Cnr Queen Mary St and Gt Marlborough St, POB 166, Roseau; tel. 4484040; telex 8629; fax 4485335; Man. P. INGLISS.

Barclays Bank (United Kingdom): Old St, POB 4, Roseau; tel. 4482571; telex 8618; fax 4483471; Man. VICTOR EUDORIE; sub-br. in Portsmouth.

Dominica Co-operative Bank: 9 Great Marlborough St, Roseau; tel. 4482580.

International Bank of Roseau: 14 Cork St, Roseau; tel. 4488106.

National Commercial Bank of Dominica: 64 Hillsborough St, POB 271, Roseau; tel. 4484401; telex 8620; fax 4483982; f. 1976; cap. 10.0m., res 10.0m., dep. 167.2m. (June 1995); 51% govt-owned; Chair. NICHOLAS WALDRON; Gen. Man. LAMBERT V. LEWIS; 2 brs.

Royal Bank of Canada: Bay Front, POB 19, Roseau; tel. 4482771; telex 8637; fax 4485398; Man. H. PINARD.

INSURANCE

Several British, regional and US companies have agents in Roseau. Local companies include the following:

First Domestic Insurance Co Ltd. 19-21 King George V St, POB 1931, Roseau; tel. 4483337; fax 4485778; e-mail: insurance@tod.dm.

Insurance Specialists and Consultants: 19-21 King George V St, POB 20, Roseau; tel. 4482022; fax 4485778.

J. B. Charles and Co Ltd: Old St, POB 121, Roseau; tel. 4482876.

Tonge Inc Ltd: 19–21 King George V St, POB 20, Roseau; tel. 4484027; fax 4485778.

Windward Islands Crop Insurance Co (Wincrop): Vanoulst House, Goodwill, POB 469, Roseau; tel. 4483955; fax 4484197; f. 1987; regional; coverage for weather destruction of, mainly, banana crops; total assets 10m. (1994); Man. KERWIN FERREIRA; brs in Grenada, Saint Lucia and Saint Vincent.

Trade and Industry

DEVELOPMENT ORGANIZATIONS

National Development Corporation (NDC): Valley Rd, POB 293, Roseau; tel. 4482045; telex 8462; fax 85840; f. 1988 by merger of Industrial Development Corpn (f. 1974) and Tourist Board; promotes local and foreign investment to increase employment, production and exports; promotes and co-ordinates tourism development; Chair. HUGH PINARD; Gen. Man. CHARLES SAVARIN.

Eastern Caribbean States Export Development Agency (ECSEDA): POB 371, Old St, Roseau; f. 1990; OECS regional development org.; Officer-in-Charge ELROY TURNER.

INDUSTRIAL AND TRADE ASSOCIATIONS

Dominica Association of Industry and Commerce (DAIC): 111 Bath Rd, POB 85, Roseau; tel. 4482874; fax 4486868; f. 1972 by a merger of the Manufacturers' Association and the Chamber of Commerce; represents the business sector, liaises with the Government, and stimulates commerce and industry; 100 mems; Pres. LENNOX LINTON; CEO JEANILIA R. V. DE SMET.

Dominica Banana Marketing Corporation (DBMC): Vanoulst House, POB 1620, Roseau; tel. 4482671; fax 4486445; f. 1934 as Dominica Banana Growers' Association; restructured 1984; state-supported; Chair. VANOULST JNO CHARLES; Gen. Man. (vacant).

Dominica Export-Import Agency (Dexia): Bay Front, POB 173, Roseau; tel. 4483494; fax 4486308; e-mail dexia@tod.dm; f. 1986; replaced the Dominica Agricultural Marketing Board and the External Trade Bureau; exporter of Dominican agricultural products, trade facilitator and importer of bulk rice and sugar.

EMPLOYERS' ORGANIZATION

Dominica Employers' Federation: 14 Church St, POB 1783, Roseau; tel. 4482314; fax 4484474; Pres. GERARD COOLS-LARTIGUE; Dir SHIRLEY A. GUYE.

UTILITIES

Electricity

Dominica Electricity Services Ltd (DOMLEC): 18 Castle St, POB 1593, Roseau; tel. 4482681; fax 4485397; e-mail mandomlec@tod.dm; national electricity service; 73%-owned by the Commonwealth Development Corporation (UK).

TRADE UNIONS

Civil Service Association: Cnr Valley Rd and Windsor Lane, Roseau; tel. 4482102; fax 4488060; f. 1940 and registered as a trade union in 1960; representing all grades of civil servants, including firemen, prison officers, nurses, teachers and postal workers; Pres. SONIA D. WILLIAMS; Gen. Sec. THOMAS LETANG; 1,400 mems.

Co-operative Citrus Growers' Association: 21 Hanover St, Roseau; tel. 4482062; telex 8615.

Dominica Amalgamated Workers' Union (DAWU): 40 Kennedy Ave, POB 137, Roseau; tel. 4483048; f. 1960; Gen. Sec. DARRYL D. GAGE; 500 mems.

Dominica Farmers' Union: 17 Church St, Roseau; tel. 4484244.

Dominica Trade Union: 70–71 Queen Mary St, Roseau; tel. 4498139; f. 1945; Pres. KENNEDY PASCAL; Gen. Sec. LEO J. BERNARD NICHOLAS; 800 mems.

Media Workers' Association: Roseau; Pres. MATTHIAS PELTIER.

National Workers' Union: 69 Queen Mary St, Roseau; tel. 4484465; f. 1977; Pres. RAWLINS JERMOTT; Gen. Sec. PATRICK JOHN; 800 mems.

Waterfront and Allied Workers' Union: 43 Hillsborough St, Roseau; tel. 4482343; f. 1965; Pres. LOUIS BENOIT; Gen. Sec. NEVILLE LEE; 1,500 mems.

Transport

ROADS

At the end of 1984 there were 370 km (231 miles) of first-class, 262 km (163 miles) of second-class and 117 km (73 miles) of third-class motorable roads, as well as 454 km (282 miles) of tracks. In 1997 the Government announced plans to spend EC $ 33m. on a road and bridge reconstruction project.

SHIPPING

A deep-water harbour at Woodbridge Bay serves Roseau, which is the principal port. Several foreign shipping lines call at Roseau, and there is a high-speed ferry service between Martinique and Guadeloupe which calls at Roseau eight times a week. Ships of the Geest Line call at Prince Rupert's Bay, Portsmouth, to collect bananas, and cruise-ship facilities were constructed there during 1990. There are other specialized berthing facilities on the west coast.

Dominica Ports Authority: POB 243, Roseau; tel. 4484431; fax 4486131.

CIVIL AVIATION

Melville Hall Airport, 64 km (40 miles) from Roseau, and Canefield Airport, 5 km (3 miles) from Roseau, are the two airports on the island. In 1990 it was decided to proceed with the construction of an international airport, although the project still lacked sufficient funding in early 1998. A feasibility study on the expansion and upgrading of Melville Hall Airport was expected to be completed in 1998. Canefield Airport was also to be improved. The regional airline, LIAT (based in Antigua and Barbuda, and in which Dominica is a shareholder), provides daily services and, with Air Caraibe, Air Guadeloupe and Air BVI, connects Dominica with all the islands of the Eastern Caribbean, including the international airports of Puerto Rico, Antigua, Guadeloupe and Martinique.

Tourism

The Government has designated areas of the island as nature reserves, to preserve the beautiful, lush scenery and the rich natural heritage that is Dominica's main tourist attraction. Birdlife is particularly prolific, and includes several rare and endangered species, such as the Imperial parrot. There are also two marine reserves. Tourism is not as developed as it is among Dominica's neighbours. There were an estimated 262,132 visitors in 1996 (of whom 193,484 were cruise-ship passengers) and 764 hotel rooms.

National Development Corporation (NDC)—Division of Tourism: Valley Rd, POB 73, Roseau; tel. 4482351; telex 8642; fax 4485840; f. 1988, when Tourist Board merged with Industrial Development Corpn; Dir of Tourism MARIE-JOSE EDWARDS.

Dominica Hotel Association: POB 384, Roseau; tel. 4486565; fax 4480299.

THE DOMINICAN REPUBLIC

Introductory Survey

Location, Climate, Language, Religion, Flag, Capital

The Dominican Republic occupies the eastern part of the island of Hispaniola, which lies between Cuba and Puerto Rico in the Caribbean Sea. The country's only international frontier is with Haiti, to the west. The climate is sub-tropical, with an average annual temperature of 27°C (80°F). In Santo Domingo, temperatures are generally between 19°C (66°F) and 31°C (88°F). The west and south-west of the country are arid. Hispaniola lies in the path of tropical cyclones. The official language is Spanish. Almost all of the inhabitants profess Christianity, and some 89% are Roman Catholics. There are small Protestant and Jewish communities. The national flag (proportions 8 by 5) is blue (upper hoist and lower fly) and red (lower hoist and upper fly), quartered by a white cross. The state flag has, in addition, the national coat of arms, showing a quartered shield in the colours of the flag (on which are superimposed national banners, a cross and an open Bible) between scrolls above and below, at the centre of the cross. The capital is Santo Domingo.

Recent History

The Dominican Republic became independent in 1844, although it was occupied by US military forces between 1916 and 1924. General Rafael Leónidas Trujillo Molina overthrew the elected President, Horacio Vázquez, in 1930 and dominated the country until his assassination in May 1961. The dictator ruled personally from 1930 to 1947 and indirectly thereafter. His brother, Héctor Trujillo, was President from 1947 until August 1960, when he was replaced by Dr Joaquín Balaguer Ricardo, hitherto Vice-President. After Rafael Trujillo's death, President Balaguer remained in office, but in December 1961 he permitted moderate opposition groups to participate in a Council of State, which exercised legislative and executive powers. Balaguer resigned in January 1962, when the Council of State became the Provisional Government. A presidential election in December 1962, the country's first free election for 38 years, was won by Dr Juan Bosch Gaviño, the founder and leader of the Partido Revolucionario Dominicano (PRD), who had been in exile since 1930. President Bosch, a left-of-centre democrat, took office in February 1963 but was overthrown in the following September by a military coup. The leaders of the armed forces transferred power to a civilian triumvirate, led by Emilio de los Santos. In April 1965 a revolt by supporters of ex-President Bosch overthrew the triumvirate. Civil war broke out between pro-Bosch forces and military units headed by Gen. Elías Wessin y Wessin, who had played a leading role in the 1963 coup. The violence was eventually suppressed by the intervention of some 23,000 US troops, who were formally incorporated into an Inter-American peace force by the Organization of American States (OAS) after they had landed. The peace force withdrew in September 1965.

Following a period of provisional government under Héctor García Godoy, a presidential election in June 1966 was won by ex-President Balaguer, the candidate of the Partido Reformista Social Cristiano (PRSC), who won 57% of the votes cast, while ex-President Bosch won 39%. The PRSC, founded in 1964, also won a majority of seats in both houses of the new National Congress. President Balaguer took office in July. A new Constitution was promulgated in November. Despite his association with the Trujillo dictatorship, Balaguer initially proved to be a popular leader, and in May 1970 he was re-elected for a further four years. In February 1973 a state of emergency was declared when guerrilla forces landed on the coast. Captain Francisco Caamaño Deño, the leader of the 1965 revolt, and his followers were killed. Bosch and other opposition figures went into hiding. Bosch later resigned as leader of the PRD (founding the Partido de la Liberación Dominicana—PLD), undermining hopes of a united opposition in the May 1974 elections, when President Balaguer was re-elected with a large majority.

In the May 1978 presidential election, Dr Balaguer was defeated by the PRD candidate, Silvestre Antonio Guzmán Fernández. This was the first occasion in the country's history when an elected President yielded power to an elected successor. An attempted military coup in favour of Dr Balaguer was prevented by pressure from the US Government. On assuming office in August, President Guzmán undertook to professionalize the armed forces by removing politically ambitious high-ranking officers. In June 1981 he declared his support for Jacobo Majluta Azar, his Vice-President, as his successor, but in November the PRD rejected Majluta's candidacy in favour of Dr Salvador Jorge Blanco, a left-wing senator, who was elected President in May 1982. In the congressional elections, held at the same time, the PRD gained a majority in both the Senate and the Chamber of Deputies. President Guzmán committed suicide in July after allegations of fraud were made against his Government and members of his family. Vice-President Majluta was immediately sworn in as interim President until Dr Blanco assumed office in August. Although a member of the Socialist International, Blanco maintained good relations with the USA (on which the country is economically dependent) and declared that he would not resume relations with Cuba.

In 1983 popular discontent with the Government's austerity programme led to the occupation of the Ministry of Agriculture by peasants, and calls for agrarian reform. In August a two-week purge of subversives took place on the orders of President Blanco. Two visiting Cuban academics were deported, and Socialist and Communist Party sympathizers were arrested. The Government's move came in response to a report which implicated Cubans and Nicaraguans in the increased left-wing activity in the country.

In April 1984 a series of public protests against substantial increases in the cost of essential items erupted into violent confrontations between government forces and demonstrators in Santo Domingo and four other cities, which lasted for three days. In the course of the protests, more than 50 people were killed. The Government held opposition groups of the extreme right and left responsible for the unrest. In May the Government responded to the prospect of further demonstrations by ordering the arrest of more than 100 trade union and left-wing leaders. In August, in anticipation of civil unrest at the announcement of new price increases, more arrests were made among trade union and opposition leaders. Further demonstrations, including one attended by 40,000 people in Santo Domingo, were held in protest at the continuing economic decline.

In February 1985 a further series of substantial price increases led to violent clashes between demonstrators and police, during which four people died and more than 50 were injured. Public unrest was exacerbated by the Government's decision, in April, to accept the IMF's terms for further financial aid. In June a 24-hour general strike was organized by trade unions, in protest at the Government's economic policy and its refusal to increase the minimum wage. In July, however, the threat of a 48-hour general strike prompted the Government to order an immediate increase in the minimum wage.

Further violence preceded the presidential and legislative elections of May 1986. Several people were killed, and many more injured, in clashes between rival political supporters. The three principal candidates in the presidential election were all former Presidents: Dr Joaquín Balaguer of the PRSC; Jacobo Majluta, who, having registered La Estructura, his right-wing faction of the PRD, as a separate political party in July 1985, nevertheless secured the candidacy of the ruling PRD; and Dr Juan Bosch of the PLD. The counting of votes was suspended twice, following allegations by Majluta of fraud by the PRSC and by the Central Electoral Board, two of the three members of which then resigned. Dr Balaguer was finally declared the winner by a narrow margin of votes over Majluta, his closest rival. In the simultaneous legislative elections, the PRSC won 21 of the 30 seats in the Senate and 56 of the 120 seats in the Chamber of Deputies.

Upon taking office as President (for the fifth time) in August 1986, Dr Balaguer initiated an investigation into alleged corrupt practices by members of the outgoing administration. Dr Blanco, the former President, was charged with embezzlement and the illegal purchase of military vehicles. (In August 1991 he was finally convicted of 'abuse of power' and misappropriation of public funds, and sentenced to 20 years' imprisonment. However, in September 1994 legislation granting him amnesty was approved by the Chamber of Deputies.) The financial accounts of the armed forces were examined, and the former Secretary of State for the Armed Forces was subsequently imprisoned. In July 1987 a general strike was organized by the trade unions, in support of a demand for an increase of 62% in the minimum wage. In September the Cabinet resigned, at the request of the President, to enable him to restructure the Government. Some 35,000 government posts were abolished, in an attempt to reduce public spending, and the money thus becoming available was to be used to finance a programme of public works projects which were expected to create almost 100,000 new jobs. Nevertheless, strike action continued. The situation deteriorated in February 1988, when demonstrations took place throughout the country, to protest against the high cost of living, following an increase in the price of staple foods. Six people were killed as the police intervened to quell the protests. Subsequently, the Roman Catholic Church mediated between the opposing sides, and President Balaguer agreed to stabilize prices of staple foods and to increase the minimum wage by 33%. However, prices continued to rise, provoking a new wave of strikes in June.

In 1989 opposition to the Government's economic policies intensified. The elimination of preferential exchange rates, which took effect in January, resulted in further price increases for basic commodities. In an unpopular measure to stabilize the peso, the Government had earlier curbed the activities of unlicensed money-traders, so restricting the flow of dollars from remittances from *émigrés* in the USA. Thus, a major source of foreign exchange was eliminated. Popular discontent was aggravated by the deterioration of public utilities, particularly water and electricity. In June a national strike committee called a 48-hour general strike. More than 300 organizations supported the action, which reportedly paralysed the country for two days. The major demands were the doubling of the minimum wage, the implementation of the 1988 tripartite agreement on workers' conditions and benefits, a reduction in the prices of staple commodities, and the ending of interruptions in the supplies of water and electricity. Four people were killed and an estimated 3,000 were arrested during the protests. Despite mediation efforts by the Roman Catholic Church, the Government made no concessions to union demands. In October, following a 66% rise in fuel prices, there were further violent demonstrations.

With presidential and legislative elections due to take place in May 1990, President Balaguer's prospects for re-election were hampered considerably by the continuing deterioration of the economy (particularly rapid inflation), the worsening energy crisis, and criticism of government spending on expansive public works programmes which had resulted in a severe depletion of the country's reserves of foreign exchange. The principal contender for the presidency was the PLD candidate, Dr Juan Bosch, who concentrated his election campaign on seeking support from the private sector, promising privatization of state-owned companies. In opinion polls conducted in the period preceding the presidential election, Bosch appeared to have a clear advantage. When the initial results indicated a narrow victory for Balaguer, Bosch accused the ruling PRSC and the Central Electoral Board of a 'colossal fraud', necessitating a re-count, supervised by monitors from the OAS. Almost two months after the election, Balaguer was declared the official winner. The PRSC secured a narrow majority in the Senate, with 16 of the 30 seats; the PLD won 12 and the PRD two. At elections to the Chamber of Deputies the PLD obtained 44 of the 120 seats, while the PRSC won 42, the PRD 32 and the Partido Revolucionario Independiente (PRI) two. However, the lack of an outright majority in the Chamber of Deputies did not threaten seriously to impede government policies, in view of President Balaguer's extensive powers to govern by decree.

In August 1990, in an attempt to reduce inflation by cutting government subsidies, the Government announced a programme of austerity measures, including substantial increases in the cost of fuel and food. Petrol and essential foodstuffs were almost doubled in price. The trade unions reacted angrily to the austerity measures, calling a 48-hour general strike. This action was violently suppressed by the army, and the ensuing conflict resulted in as many as 14 deaths. The price increases were partially offset by an increase of 30% in the salaries of army personnel and civilian employees in the public sector. The trade unions, however, rejected an identical offer by the private sector and threatened further strike action if their demands for basic food subsidies and considerable wage increases were not satisfied. In September a three-day general strike, organized by the Organizaciones Colectivas Populares (OCP), led to further arrests, injuries and at least one death. In the following month another general strike was called by the OCP and the Central General de Trabajadores (CGT), with the stated aim of ousting Balaguer from power. Violent clashes with the army in Santo Domingo resulted in a further four deaths.

In July 1991 a government announcement that a stand-by agreement had been concluded with the IMF prompted a series of general strikes in opposition to the accord and its concomitant economic guidelines. The strikes, called by the Confederación de Trabajadores Unitaria (CTU), also supported demands for a 100% rise in the minimum wage for state employees. Despite the adverse public response, the IMF agreement was formally signed in late August.

In April 1992 evidence emerged of a serious rift within the PLD. Following the expulsion from the party, by the PLD's predominantly right-wing political committee, of Nélsida Marmolejos, a deputy and trade unionist who had criticized the party's position on a new labour code under discussion in Congress, 47 high-ranking, and mainly left-wing, members announced their resignation from the PLD. Those resigning included 10 deputies and one Senate representative, Max Puig. In mid-June more than 400 former PLD members held a 'national assembly' to form a new political movement, the Alianza por la Democracia (APD), which was officially established in early August. The APD was represented by all 11 former PLD deputies in the Chamber of Deputies, and by Max Puig in the Senate.

Cabinet changes in February and August 1992 prompted speculation that President Balaguer would be seeking a further term in office, despite previous statements that he would not be contesting the 1994 presidential election. Luis Taveras A., who had played a key role in Balaguer's election success in 1990, was appointed Minister of Tourism, while the appointment of Dr Elías Wessin Chávez, the Secretary-General of the Partido Quisqueyano Demócrata (PQD), to a cabinet position signalled Balaguer's desire to secure right-wing support.

In late September 1992 a Dominican human rights leader, Rafael Efraín Ortiz, was shot dead by police during a demonstration in Santo Domingo, protesting at government plans to celebrate the 500th anniversary of the arrival in the Caribbean of Christopher Columbus. The demonstrations were the result of increasing public anger at the inordinate expense of the construction of the commemorative Columbus Lighthouse (estimated to have cost in excess of US $25m.). Protesters also denounced the celebration of the Spanish conquest, which had led to the enslavement and destruction of the indigenous Taino Indian population. In response to the death of Efraín, general strikes were called in several cities, and violent protests broke out, resulting in a further death as rioters clashed with police. In view of this popular discontent, the Pope, who was in the Dominican Republic to attend a Latin American Bishops' Conference, declined to preside over the inauguration of the Columbus Lighthouse on 6 October.

In April 1993 the APD split into two factions, led, respectively, by Max Puig and Nélsida Marmolejos. The split reportedly resulted from a dispute over efforts made by the group led by Marmolejos to establish an electoral alliance between the APD and the PRD. In September a reorganization of ministerial portfolios prompted further speculation that Balaguer was seeking to improve his standing in readiness to contest the presidential election in May 1994. In January 1994 the PLD announced that it had formed an alliance with the right-wing Fuerza Nacional Progresista (FNP) in order to contest the forthcoming general election. At a special convention of the PRSC held that month, Balaguer officially announced his intention to contest the forthcoming presidential election, and his nomination received the support of the majority of the party delegates. However, his decision prompted 20 members of the PRSC executive to withdraw from the party in order to support the presidential candidate of the Unidad Democrática (UD), Fernando Alvarez Bogaert, himself a defecting member of the PRSC. The UD subsequently signed an electoral pact with the PRD, with Alvarez to contest the vice-presidency and José Francisco Peña Gómez, of the PRD, the presidency.

The official results of the presidential and legislative elections of 16 May 1994 were delayed, amid accusations of widespread voting irregularities. Interim results, announced on 24 May, indicated a narrow victory for Balaguer in the presidential election. However, the PRD claimed that polling stations had been issued with abbreviated electoral rolls and that the PRSC, which had effective control of the Central Electoral Board, had removed the names of some 200,000 PRD supporters from the lists. A full recount began on 25 May. In June the Central Electoral Board rejected a request, made by the US Department of State, that fresh elections be conducted wherever voting irregularities had been detected. In the same month Dr Juan Bosch Gaviño resigned as leader of the PLD.

In July 1994 an investigative commission, comprising three members of the Central Electoral Board (two from the PRSC and one from the PRD) and two independent academics, confirmed that, as a result of serious irregularities, some 73,000 of the registered electorate had been denied a vote. Despite an atmosphere of growing political instability, Balaguer rejected opposition demands for the formation of a provisional government. Strike action in protest at the electoral irregularities was reported to have seriously affected several regions, including the capital, during that month.

On 2 August 1994 the Central Electoral Board announced the final election results, having apparently overlooked the findings of the electoral investigative commission. Balaguer was proclaimed the winner of the presidential election by a margin of less than 1% of the votes cast, with 43.6%. Peña Gómez received 42.9% of the votes and Bosch obtained the remaining 13.5%. In the Senate the alliance of the PRD and the UD secured 15 seats, while the PRSC won 14 and the PLD one seat. In the Chamber of Deputies the PRD/UD alliance obtained 57 seats, while the PRSC gained 50 and the PLD 13 seats.

Talks aimed at ending the political crisis caused by the election were held in early August 1994, with the mediation of the OAS and the Roman Catholic Church, and resulted in the signing of the Pact for Democracy. Under the terms of the accord (agreed by all the major parties), a fresh presidential election was to be held in November 1995 and a series of constitutional reforms would be adopted, providing for the prohibition of the re-election of a president to a consecutive term, the replacement of the Central Electoral Board, and the reorganization of the judiciary. As a result of the accord, Peña Gómez cancelled a series of planned strikes and demonstrations organized by the PRD. However, at a session of the National Congress, held on 14 August, the deputies of the PRSC, with the support of those of the PLD, voted to extend Balaguer's mandate from 18 months to two years. The PRD withdrew from the legislature in protest, and Peña Gómez announced that his party would boycott Congress and resume strike action. The OAS also criticized Congress for violating the terms of the Pact for Democracy. The constitutional amendments that the Pact envisaged were, however, approved by Congress. On 16 August Balaguer was inaugurated as President for a seventh term. The Cabinet was appointed in the following days, with a further minor reorganization in early September.

The year 1995 was marked by a series of protests and disturbances, largely provoked by the deteriorating standards of public services. In March four people were killed when protest at increases in public transport fares erupted into violence and the security forces were dispatched to restore order. The fare increases, which had been imposed unilaterally by certain transport companies, were declared illegal by the Government. In April, following the most severe electricity shortages since the energy crisis of 1990, the administrator of the state electricity company, the Corporación Dominicana de Electricidad (CDE), was dismissed. In May a 24-hour general strike was conducted in protest at increases in food prices and at the deterioration of electricity and transport services, although it received only partial support. During the following month there were renewed disturbances in Santo Domingo and in towns to the north of the capital, as protesters demanding the provision of basic services clashed with the security forces. Protests continued in August, following the implementation by the Government of a 25% increase in public transport fares. In September as many as three people were killed during violent confrontations between the security forces and workers at a sugar plantation in San Luis, east of the capital. The workers had been protesting at the decision of the state sugar council, the Consejo Estatal de Azúcar, to dismiss some 12,700 of its work-force.

In April 1996 the energy shortfall again reached crisis proportions, with power cuts averaging between 14 and 20 hours per day, following the decision by a major private power station, owned by the US consortium Smith-Enron, to withdraw from the national grid pending the settlement of a debt of US $4.5m. owed to it by the CDE. Although the dispute was resolved later that month, the crisis prompted renewed demands for Congress to approve delayed legislation enabling the privatization of CDE, which, owing largely to inefficiency and corruption, operated at a considerable loss.

The presidential election of 16 May 1996, the first for some 30 years in which Balaguer was not a candidate, was conducted according to a new system, introduced since 1994, whereby a second round of voting would be conducted between the two leading candidates should no candidate secure an absolute majority in the initial ballot. In the first round Peña Gómez won 45.9% of the votes, while the candidate of the PLD, Leonel Fernández Reyna, obtained 38.9%. The candidate of the PRSC, Jacinto Peynado (who had received only nominal support from Balaguer), obtained just 15.0% of the votes. The appointment, immediately prior to the election, to the post of chief of police, of Gen. Enrique Pérez y Pérez, a figure associated with the political repression of the late 1960s and 1970s, was widely interpreted as an attempt to intimidate supporters of the PRD. Gen. Pérez was, however, dismissed in June 1996, following a protest by international observers of the election process that he had ordered the arrest of some 10,000 PRD supporters for failing to produce identity cards.

At the second round of the presidential election, conducted on 30 June 1996, Fernández secured a narrow victory, winning 51.25% of the votes, while Peña Gómez obtained 48.75%. The establishment, earlier in the month, of an electoral alliance between the PLD and PRSC, entitled the Frente Nacional Patriótico, had ensured Fernández the support of the PRSC voters. Peña Gómez accepted the result of the ballot but attributed his defeat to a defamation campaign conducted by Balaguer, for which he claimed the President had drawn extensively from state resources. While the PRSC failed to retain the presidency, Balaguer appeared to have succeeded in retaining considerable influence in the new administration, since the PLD had only minority representation in Congress and would be dependent on the support of the PRSC to implement planned institutional reforms. However, in early August relations between Fernández and Balaguer appeared to have deteriorated when the PRSC signed an unexpected agreement with the PRD, which guaranteed the PRSC the presidency of the Senate while the PRD obtained that of the Chamber of Deputies. On 16 August Fernández was inaugurated, and the Cabinet, consisting almost exclusively of PLD members, was sworn in.

In October 1996, in what Fernández presented as a key component of his campaign to combat official corruption (which was estimated to cost the State some 30,000m. pesos per year), sizeable salary increases for leading government officials were announced, provoking strong criticism from opposition politicians and trade union leaders. In the same month Fernández ordered the retirement of 24 generals from active service in the armed forces.

In 1997, as part of a campaign to eliminate deep-seated corruption in the country's institutions, Fernández restructured both the police and the judiciary. In May several senior police-officers, including the head of the Dirección Nacional de Control de Drogas (National Drug Control Directorate), Julio César Ventura Bayonet, were dismissed. Ventura's dismissal reflected concern that assets seized from imprisoned drugs-traffickers were being misappropriated. In the same month a new body, under the direct control of the Consejo Nacional de Drogas (National Drug Council), was created to deal with such confiscated assets. In August Fernández, in his role as Chairman of the Consejo Nacional de la Magistratura (National Judiciary Council), oversaw a restructuring of the Supreme Court, including the appointment of 15 new judges. Responsibility for appointing judges at all other levels of the judicial system was transferred from the Senate to the Supreme Court, principally to avoid appointments being influenced by political considerations.

Growing dissatisfaction with the continuing deterioration of public services and Fernández's failure to honour promises made during his election campaign provoked widespread disturbances and strike action throughout the country in 1997. Between July and September numerous violent confrontations between demonstrators and security forces resulted in several deaths. In October, in an effort to defuse the volatile social and political climate, Fernández introduced a recovery plan aimed at overcoming electricity and food shortages. However, in the following month a two-day general strike was organized by an 'umbrella' protest group, the Coordinadora de Organizaciones Populares, in support of demands for pay increases, reductions in the price of fuel and basic foodstuffs and improved public services.

Further industrial action was threatened for early 1998 if the Government failed to meet the organization's demands.

Relations with Haiti remained tense in 1988. Dominican soldiers were accused of arresting immigrant Haitians in order to use them as cutters during the sugar harvest. The situation improved somewhat when the deposed Haitian leader, Gen. Henri Namphy, was refused permission to remain in the Dominican Republic. Subsequently, however, Gen. Namphy was unable to find a country willing to accept him as a political exile, and the Dominican Government was obliged to allow him to stay. In January 1989 a traffic accident, in which 47 Haitian sugar workers were killed, focused attention on the continuing illegal import of plantation labour into the Dominican Republic from Haiti. In June 1991, in reaction to increasing criticism of the Dominican Republic's human rights record (and, in particular, the Government's apparent acquiescence in the exploitation of Haitian child labourers), President Balaguer ordered the repatriation of all Haitian residents aged under 16 or over 60 years. Protests made by the Haitian Government that such a unilateral measure contravened normal diplomatic procedure were rejected by Balaguer. Following the army coup of September 1991 in Haiti, tens of thousands of Haitians were estimated to have fled to the Dominican Republic. However, only some 700 had been granted refugee status by mid-1993, according to the United Nations High Commissioner for Refugees. In mid-1994 reports of smuggling on a large scale from the Dominican Republic to Haiti, in defiance of UN sanctions against the Haitian military dictatorship, prompted the UN to seek assurances of co-operation from President Balaguer. In June an agreement was reached, providing for the UN to send a monitoring mission to observe the enforcement of the embargo on the Dominican border with Haiti. The first contingent of UN observers arrived in August. The border remained closed after the US occupation of Haiti in mid-September and was reopened in mid-October, following the lifting of UN sanctions. In early 1997 relations with Haiti became strained following the expulsion from the Dominican Republic over a three-month period of some 20,000 Haitians who had been residing illegally in the country. In late February Fernández and his Haitian counterpart met in Antigua to discuss the situation, and agreement was reached to put an immediate end to large-scale repatriations. Accord was also achieved providing for the repatriation process to be monitored by an international body to ensure the observance of human rights.

Government

The Dominican Republic comprises 26 provinces, each administered by an appointed governor, and a Distrito Nacional (DN) containing the capital. Under the 1966 Constitution, legislative power is exercised by the bicameral National Congress, with a Senate of 30 members and a Chamber of Deputies (120 members). Members of both houses are elected for four years by universal adult suffrage. Executive power lies with the President, who is also elected by direct popular vote for four years. He is assisted by a Vice-President and a Cabinet comprising Secretaries of State.

Defence

Military service is voluntary and lasts for four years. In August 1997 the armed forces totalled 24,500 men: army 15,000, air force 5,500 and navy 4,000. Paramilitary forces number 15,000. The defence budget for 1997 was an estimated RD $1,300m.

Economic Affairs

In 1995, according to estimates by the World Bank, the Dominican Republic's gross national product (GNP), measured at average 1993–95 prices, was US $11,390m., equivalent to $1,460 per head. During 1985–95, it was estimated, GNP per head increased, in real terms, at an average rate of 2.1% annually. Over the same period, the population increased by an annual average of 2.0%. The Dominican Republic's gross domestic product (GDP) increased, in real terms, by an annual average of 3.5% in 1985–95. Real GDP increased by 7.3% in 1996.

Agriculture, including forestry and fishing, contributed an estimated 12.9% of GDP and employed an estimated 14.5% of the labour force in 1996. The principal cash crops are sugar cane (raw sugar accounted for 12.7% of total export earnings in 1995), coffee and cocoa beans. Agricultural GDP increased, in real terms, by an annual average of 0.6% during 1985–95, and by an estimated 10.3% in 1996.

Industry (including mining, manufacturing, construction and power) employed an estimated 23.2% of the labour force and contributed an estimated 31.6% of GDP in 1996. Industrial GDP increased, in real terms, by an annual average of 1.6% during 1985–95, and by an estimated 8.5% in 1996.

Mining contributed an estimated 2.6% of GDP but employed only an estimated 0.4% of the labour force in 1996. The major mineral export is ferronickel (providing 30.0% of total export earnings in 1995). Gold and silver are also exploited, and there are workable deposits of gypsum, limestone and mercury. The GDP of the mining sector increased, in real terms, by an annual average of 2.1% during 1991–95, and by an estimated 2.4% in 1996.

Manufacturing contributed an estimated 17.0% of GDP and employed an estimated 17.5% of the labour force in 1996. Based on the value of sales, the most important branches of manufacturing in 1984 were food products (accounting for 38.9% of the total), petroleum refineries (11.3%), beverages (11.3%) and chemicals (8.4%). The GDP of the manufacturing sector increased, in real terms, at an average rate of 1.9% per year during 1985–95, and by an estimated 5.2% in 1996.

Energy is derived principally from petroleum. Imports of mineral fuels accounted for an estimated 13.2% of the total cost of imports in 1996.

The services sector contributed an estimated 55.4% of GDP and employed an estimated 61.7% of the labour force in 1996. The GDP of the services sector expanded at an average annual rate of 5.4% during 1985–95, and by an estimated 6.3% in 1996. Tourism accounted for approximately 13.3% of GDP in 1995.

In 1996 the Dominican Republic recorded a visible trade deficit of US $1,764.5m., and there was a deficit of $110.1m. on the current account of the balance of payments. In 1986 the principal source of imports (37.9%) was the USA; other major suppliers were Venezuela, Mexico and Japan. In 1995 the USA was the principal market for exports (51.1% of the total, excluding exports from free trade zones); other significant purchasers were the Netherlands and Belgium. The principal exports in 1995 were ferro-nickel and sugar. The principal imports in 1986 were petroleum and petroleum products, and machinery.

In 1996 there was an estimated budgetary surplus of RD $903m. (equivalent to 0.5% of GDP). The Dominican Republic's total external debt at the end of 1995 was US $4,259m., of which $3,550m. was long-term public debt. In that year the cost of debt-servicing was equivalent to 12.9% of total revenue from exports of goods and services. In 1985–95 the average annual rate of inflation was 24.3%. Consumer prices increased by an average of 5.4% in 1996. An estimated 16.7% of the economically active population were unemployed in 1996.

In July 1984 the Dominican Republic was granted observer status in CARICOM (see p. 119). In December 1989 the country was accepted as a member of the ACP nations covered by the Lomé Convention (see p. 178). In 1990 the Dominican Republic's application for full membership of CARICOM was threatened when ACP nations accused the Dominican Republic of breaking an agreement made under the Lomé Convention concerning the export of bananas to countries of the European Community (now the European Union).

In the 1990s the economy of the Dominican Republic was severely affected by the unstable nature of the country's electricity supply. The situation reached crisis proportions in 1990 and again in 1995–97, when interruptions in the supply of electricity lasted up to 20 hours per day. A plan for the restructuring of the state electricity company (Corporación Dominicana de Electricidad—CDE), with substantial financial support from the World Bank and the Inter-American Development Bank, was agreed in principle in 1993. However, implementation of the plan was repeatedly delayed, while the CDE continued to operate at a significant loss (although in late 1997 plans for the divestment of the CDE appeared to be gathering momentum). In June legislation was instituted allowing private capital to be invested in almost all sectors, including the electricity and sugar industries. In 1996 an emergency plan had been introduced to revive the ailing sugar company, the Consejo Estatal de Azúcar (CEA), including a renegotiation of its debt of 3,000m. pesos. The CEA's sugar production levels had declined significantly in recent years, and in 1996 it was, for the first time, unable to fulfil its export quota to the USA. In 1997 the Government granted the CEA an emergency subsidy of US $25m. for the forthcoming harvest. Despite the structural difficulties in the state power and sugar sectors, GDP increased by 7.3% in 1996 and was forecast to grow by more than 6% in 1997, based on continued expansion in tourism and the free trade zones. In

1997 production in the free trade zones appeared to be thriving despite competition from Mexico, which, under the provisions of NAFTA, enjoys trade preferences on exports to the USA. In 1997 the IMF urged further restructuring, including that of the social security system and the civil service, as well as the implementation of tax and trade reforms. However, in the light of escalating social unrest owing to the deterioration in living standards, such structural adjustment would prove difficult to implement.

Social Welfare

A voluntary national contributory scheme, introduced in 1947, provides insurance cover for sickness, unemployment, accidental injury, maternity, old age and death. Only 42% of the population are thought to benefit from the system. In 1980 there were 571 hospitals and clinics, 2,142 physicians and 8,953 hospital beds under the auspices of the public health and welfare department and the Institute of Social Security. In 1984 the number of physicians stood at 3,555. The central Government's 1994 budget allocated 4,093m. pesos (17.4% of total expenditure) to the health sector.

Education

Education is, where possible, compulsory for children between the ages of six and 14 years. Primary education begins at the age of six and lasts for eight years. Secondary education, starting at 14 years of age, lasts for four years. In 1994 the total enrolment at primary and secondary schools was equivalent to 84% of the school-age population (males 81%; females 86%). In that year primary enrolment included an estimated 81% of children in the relevant age-group (males 79%; females 83%), while secondary enrolment included an estimated 22% of children in the relevant age-group (males 18%; females 26%). In 1994/95 there were 4,001 primary schools, and in 1983/84 there were an estimated 1,664 secondary schools. There are eight universities. Budgetary expenditure on education by the Secretariat of State for Education and Culture in 1994 was 2,606m. pesos, representing 11.1% of total government spending. In 1995, according to UNESCO estimates, the average rate of adult illiteracy was 17.9% (males 18.0%; females 17.8%).

Public Holidays

1998: 1 January (New Year's Day), 6 January (Epiphany), 21 January (Our Lady of Altagracia), 26 January (Duarte), 27 February (Independence), 10 April (Good Friday), 14 April (Pan-American Day), 1 May (Labour Day), 16 July (Foundation of Sociedad la Trinitaria), 16 August (Restoration Day), 24 September (Our Lady of Mercedes), 12 October (Columbus Day), 24 October (United Nations Day), 1 November (All Saints' Day), 25 December (Christmas Day).

1999: 1 January (New Year's Day), 6 January (Epiphany), 21 January (Our Lady of Altagracia), 26 January (Duarte), 27 February (Independence), 2 April (Good Friday), 14 April (Pan-American Day), 1 May (Labour Day), 16 July (Foundation of Sociedad la Trinitaria), 16 August (Restoration Day), 24 September (Our Lady of Mercedes), 12 October (Columbus Day), 24 October (United Nations Day), 1 November (All Saints' Day), 25 December (Christmas Day).

Weights and Measures

The metric system is officially in force but the imperial system is often used.

Statistical Survey

Source (unless otherwise stated): Oficina Nacional de Estadísticas, Edif. de Oficinas Públicas, Avda México esq. Leopoldo Navarro, Santo Domingo; Banco Central de la República Dominicana, Calle Pedro Henríquez Ureña, esq. Leopoldo Navarro, Apdo 1347, Santo Domingo; tel. 221-9111; telex 3460052; fax 678-7488.

Area and Population

AREA, POPULATION AND DENSITY

Area (sq km)	
Land	48,072
Inland water	350
Total	48,422*
Population (census results)†	
24 September 1993	
Males	3,550,797
Females	3,742,593
Total	7,293,390
Population (official estimates at mid-year)‡	
1994	7,769,000
1995	7,915,000
1996	8,052,000
Density (per sq km) at mid-1996	166.3

* 18,696 sq miles.

† Excluding adjustment for underenumeration.

‡ Not adjusted to take account of the results of the 1993 census.

Births and Deaths: Registered live births 135,056 (birth rate 17.4 per 1,000) in 1994; Registered deaths 10,103 (death rate 1.3 per 1,000) in 1994.

Expectation of life (UN estimates, years at birth, 1990–95): 69.6 (males 67.6; females 71.7 (Source: UN, *World Population Prospects: The 1994 Revision*).

PRINCIPAL TOWNS (population at 1993 census)

Santo Domingo, DN (capital)	2,138,262
Santiago de los Caballeros	364,447
La Romana	132,693
San Pedro de Macorís	123,855

ECONOMICALLY ACTIVE POPULATION (1981 census)*

	Males	Females	Total
Agriculture, hunting, forestry and fishing	378,274	42,189	420,463
Mining and quarrying	4,304	439	4,743
Manufacturing	166,748	57,689	224,437
Electricity, gas and water	12,090	1,801	13,891
Construction	77,880	2,970	80,850
Trade, restaurants and hotels	131,634	60,547	192,181
Transport, storage and communications	36,577	3,893	40,470
Financing, insurance, real estate and business services	14,944	7,425	22,369
Community, social and personal services	157,398	205,727	363,125
Activities not adequately defined	284,822	136,806	421,628
Total	1,264,671	519,486	1,784,157

* Figures exclude persons seeking work for the first time, totalling 131,231 (males 96,438; females 34,793), but include other unemployed persons, totalling 220,163 (males 144,823; females 75,340).

Source: ILO, *Yearbook of Labour Statistics*.

Mid-1996 (estimates in '000): Agriculture, etc. 666. Total labour force 3,369 (Source: FAO, *Production Yearbook*).

Agriculture

PRINCIPAL CROPS ('000 metric tons)

	1994	1995	1996
Rice (paddy)	376	523	555
Maize	46	47	69
Sorghum	13	19	18
Potatoes	31	36	32
Sweet potatoes	50	48	51
Cassava (Manioc)	99	137	137
Yams	7	10	10
Other roots and tubers	33	46	45
Dry beans	37	37	44
Groundnuts (in shell)	1	4	3
Coconuts*	185	175	175
Copra*	30	30	30
Tomatoes	85*	94	58
Sugar cane	6,285	5,442	5,252
Oranges	27	49	33
Lemons and limes*	9	9	9
Avocados*	165	155	155
Mangoes*	200	185	185
Pineapples	145	116	116*
Bananas	283	361	361*
Plantains	581	442†	442*
Coffee (green)	37	42	47
Cocoa beans	58	59	63
Tobacco (leaves)	17	29	23

* FAO estimate(s). † Unofficial figure.

Source: FAO, *Production Yearbook*.

LIVESTOCK ('000 head, year ending September)

	1994	1995	1996
Horses*	329	329	329
Mules*	135	135	135
Asses*	145	145	145
Cattle	2,366†	2,302	2,435
Pigs*	900	950	950
Sheep*	130	135	135
Goats*	570	570	570

* FAO estimates. † Unofficial figure.

Chickens (million): 34 in 1994 (FAO estimate); 34 in 1995; 43 in 1996.

Source: FAO, *Production Yearbook*.

LIVESTOCK PRODUCTS ('000 metric tons)

	1994	1995	1996
Beef and veal	81	80	80*
Poultry meat	131	167	150
Cows' milk	371	493	437
Butter*	2	2	2
Cheese*	3	3	3
Hen eggs	43	45	43
Cattle hides (fresh)*	7	8	8

* FAO estimate(s).

Source: FAO, *Production Yearbook*.

Forestry

ROUNDWOOD REMOVALS ('000 cubic metres, excl. bark)

	1983	1984	1985
Industrial wood	6	6	6
Fuel wood	951	963	976
Total	957	969	982

1986–94: Annual output as in 1985 (FAO estimates).

Source: FAO, *Yearbook of Forest Products*.

Fishing

('000 metric tons, live weight)

	1993	1994	1995
Inland waters	3.4	7.4	4.0
Atlantic Ocean	11.0	19.4	16.2
Total catch	14.4	26.9	20.2

Source: FAO, *Yearbook of Fishery Statistics*.

Mining

	1992	1993	1994
Ferro-nickel ('000 metric tons)	69	63	81
Gold (kg)	2,380	1,500*	1,300
Silver (metric tons)	15	13	10

* Estimate.

Source: US Bureau of Mines (Washington, DC).

Industry

SELECTED PRODUCTS

	1992	1993	1994
Refined sugar ('000 metric tons)	89	117*	101*
Cement ('000 metric tons)	1,365	1,271†	1,276†
Beer ('000 hectolitres)	1,956	1,992*	2,200*
Cigarettes (million)	4,432	4,356*	4,446*
Electricity (million kWh)*	5,581	5,874	6,182

* Estimate(s).

† Source: United Nations Economic Commission for Latin America and the Caribbean (ECLAC).

Source: UN, *Industrial Commodity Statistics Yearbook*.

Finance

CURRENCY AND EXCHANGE RATES

Monetary Units

100 centavos = 1 Dominican Republic peso (RD $ or peso oro)

Sterling and Dollar Equivalents (30 September 1997)

£1 sterling = 23.028 pesos;
US $1 = 14.255 pesos;
1,000 Dominican Republic pesos = £43.43 = US $70.15.

Average Exchange Rate (RD $ per US $)

1994 13.160
1995 13.597
1996 13.775

BUDGET (RD $ million)

Revenue	1994	1995	1996*
Tax revenue	18,729	21,681	24,031
Taxes on income and profits	3,212	4,121	4,629
Taxes on goods and services	9,210	10,770	12,143
Taxes on international trade and transactions	6,064	6,509	6,947
Other current revenue	1,402	2,337	2,409
Property income	392	338	331
Fees and charges	461	1,109	1,481
Capital revenue	123	159	482
Total	20,254	24,177	26,922

* Preliminary figures.

Expenditure	1993	1994	1995
Health	3,610	4,093	3,560
Education	2,007	2,606	3,019
Welfare	1,592	1,617	1,678
Defence	1,007	1,106	940
Administration	2,252	2,154	2,319
Financial services	1,224	1,461	1,746
Others*	8,391	10,488	10,552
Total	20,084	23,526	23,816
Current	9,498	10,776	12,708
Capital	10,606	12,750	11,108

* Including public works.

1996 (preliminary figure, RD $ million): Total expenditure 27,825 (current 14,129; capital 13,697).

Source: IMF, *Dominican Republic—Statistical Annex* (October 1997).

INTERNATIONAL RESERVES (US $ million at 31 December)

	1994	1995	1996
Gold*	6.8	6.8	6.7
IMF special drawing rights	3.7	0.5	0.4
Foreign exchange	248.4	365.0	349.8
Total	258.9	372.4	356.9

* Valued at market-related prices.

Source: IMF, *International Financial Statistics.*

MONEY SUPPLY (RD $ million at 31 December)

	1994	1995	1996
Currency outside banks	7,679	8,875	9,632
Demand deposits at commercial banks	6,014	7,178	11,201
Total money (incl. others)	13,742	16,092	20,884

Source: IMF, *International Financial Statistics.*

COST OF LIVING
(Consumer Price Index; base: year ending April 1977 = 100)

	1990	1991	1992*
Food, beverages and tobacco	1,376.6	2,048.0	2,048.8
Housing	948.2	1,388.7	1,581.7
Clothing, shoes and accessories	1,871.8	2,982.0	3,196.9
Others	975.8	1,778.2	1,929.3
All items	1,231.7	1,895.2	1,892.3

* Provisional figures.

All items (base: 1990 = 100): 169.4 in 1993; 183.4 in 1994; 206.4 in 1995; 217.5 in 1996 (Source: IMF, *International Financial Statistics*).

NATIONAL ACCOUNTS (RD $ million at current prices)

National Income and Product

	1994	1995	1996
GDP in purchasers' values	136,206	160,587	181,466
Net factor income from abroad	−4,498	−5,851	−8,965
Gross national product (GNP)	131,708	154,605	172,505
Less Consumption of fixed capital	8,172	9,627	10,891
National income in market prices	123,536	144,978	161,614

Source: IMF, *International Financial Statistics.*

Expenditure on the Gross Domestic Product

	1994	1995	1996
Government final consumption expenditure	6,559	7,961	9,155
Private final consumption expenditure	102,653	117,443	135,642
Increase in stocks	175	210	227
Gross fixed capital formation	30,670	37,524	42,830
Total domestic expenditure	140,057	163,138	187,854
Exports of goods and services	33,153	43,139	46,062
Less Imports of goods and services	37,005	45,689	52,450
GDP in purchasers' values	136,206	160,587	181,466
GDP at constant 1990 prices	70,681	74,054	79,476

Source: IMF, *International Financial Statistics.*

Gross Domestic Product by Economic Activity

	1994	1995	1996*
Agriculture	8,971	10,976	13,106
Livestock	7,320	8,469	9,407
Forestry and fishing	765	885	951
Mining	3,570	4,392	4,738
Manufacturing	25,213	28,163	30,906
Construction	12,862	15,288	18,202
Utilities	2,830	3,053	3,548
Wholesale and retail trade	15,946	19,473	22,365
Hotels and restaurants	7,805	10,235	11,997
Transport	9,121	10,861	12,362
Communications	4,158	5,584	6,842
Finance	6,928	7,854	8,430
Housing	7,298	8,347	8,935
Government services	12,010	13,557	15,099
Other	11,409	13,319	14,580
Total	136,206	160,456	181,466

* Preliminary figures.

Source: IMF, *Dominican Republic—Statistical Annex* (October 1997).

BALANCE OF PAYMENTS (US $ million)

	1994	1995	1996
Exports of goods f.o.b.	3,361.5	3,652.8	3,962.7
Imports of goods f.o.b.	−4,903.4	−5,145.0	−5,727.2
Trade balance	−1,541.9	−1,492.2	−1,764.5
Exports of services	1,746.3	1,912.7	2,132.4
Imports of services	−772.2	−854.2	−961.9
Balance on goods and services	−567.8	−433.7	−594.0
Other income received	99.7	114.2	119.1
Other income paid	−723.0	−773.6	−715.1
Balance on goods, services and income	−1,191.1	−1,093.1	−1,190.0
Current transfers received	964.3	992.2	1,083.1
Current transfers paid	—	−0.2	−3.2
Current balance	−226.8	−101.1	−110.1
Capital account (net)	659.5	68.0	72.0
Direct investment abroad	−12.4	−14.6	−13.8
Direct investment from abroad	360.2	404.4	394.1
Other investment assets	−72.0	−39.0	4.4
Other investment liabilities	51.5	66.9	36.6
Net errors and omissions	−659.8	−256.6	−384.1
Overall balance	100.2	128.0	−0.9

Source: IMF, *International Financial Statistics.*

External Trade

PRINCIPAL COMMODITIES (US $ '000)

Imports f.o.b.	1984*	1985*	1986*
Cars and other vehicles (incl. spares)	65,300	84,633	161,619
Chemical and pharmaceutical products	59,649	64,436	106,229
Cotton and manufactures	9,660	15,212	7,045
Foodstuffs	112,295	171,793	115,248
Petroleum and petroleum products	504,842	426,782	253,849
Iron and steel manufactures (excl. building materials)	56,874	43,500	56,357
Machinery (incl. spares)	83,360	119,311	218,185
Total (incl. others)	1,257,134	1,285,910	1,351,732

* Figures are provisional.

Total imports f.o.b. (US $ million): 1,591.5 in 1987; 1,608.0 in 1988; 1,963.8 in 1989; 1,792.8 in 1990; 1,728.8 in 1991; 2,174.6 in 1992; 2,118.4 in 1993; 2,283.8 in 1994; 2,588.0 in 1995; 3,205.1 in 1996 (Source: IMF, *International Financial Statistics*). Note: Figures exclude imports into free-trade zones.

Exports f.o.b.	1992	1993	1994
Food and live animals	284,746	285,755	334,951
Vegetables and fruit	53,867	54,096	55,347
Sugar, sugar preparations and honey	138,676	127,196	129,085
Sugar and honey	138,282	126,826	128,672
Refined sugars	123,776	109,600	113,345
Coffee, tea, cocoa, spices, and manufactures thereof	63,467	63,186	118,685
Coffee (not roasted), husks and skins	27,091	25,667	62,919
Cocoa	35,256	36,908	55,014
Cocoa beans (raw or roasted)	33,236	33,885	51,380
Beverages and tobacco	76,852	69,476	64,111
Tobacco and tobacco manufactures	72,746	66,288	60,247
Unmanufactured tobacco (not stripped)	42,224	39,080	29,679
Chemicals and related products	46,559	50,029	51,732
Basic manufactures	314,078	316,833	400,157
Leather, leather manufactures, and dressed furskins	94,806	95,874	110,292
Prepared parts of footwear	94,612	94,615	108,488
Textile yarn, fabrics and related products	41,800	52,334	64,780
Iron and steel	144,423	133,635	190,191
Ferro-alloys	143,930	126,903	182,438
Machinery and transport equipment	171,404	190,325	232,422
Electrical machinery, apparatus and appliances (excl. telecommunications and sound equipment)	152,784	163,438	192,268
Switchgear and parts thereof	117,036	103,719	115,995
Miscellaneous manufactured articles	783,485	822,362	847,584
Articles of apparel and clothing accessories	486,593	526,939	509,263
Outer garments, men's and boys', of textile fabrics (not knitted)	148,507	160,738	173,671
Outer garments, women's, girls' and infants', of textile fabrics (not knitted)	76,821	104,420	91,497
Under garments of textile fabrics (not knitted)	153,896	158,299	151,505
Apparel and clothing accessories of other than textile fabrics; headgear of all materials	65,255	59,415	29,661
Professional, scientific and controlling instruments and apparatus	111,767	145,013	159,110
Medical instruments and appliances	111,660	144,976	158,999
Jewellery, goldsmiths' and silversmiths' wares	113,279	85,786	87,475
Total (incl. others)	1,715,375	1,758,898	2,007,775

Source: UN, *International Trade Statistics Yearbook*.

1995 (Exports f.o.b., US $ million): Raw sugar 102.3; Unprocessed coffee 81.4; Raw cocoa 54.3; Ferro-nickel 242.2; Total 806.0 (excl. exports from free-trade zones 2,592.1, and goods sold in parts 99.0) (Source: IMF, *Dominican Republic—Statistical Annex* October 1997).

PRINCIPAL TRADING PARTNERS (US $ '000)

Imports f.o.b.	1984	1985*	1986*
Brazil	21,537	22,514	23,491
Canada	19,222	17,507	24,351
France	9,351	8,598	15,096
Germany, Federal Republic	33,396	48,611	45,164
Italy	9,745	13,073	28,499
Japan	58,621	78,357	105,630
Mexico	147,660	101,795	112,981
Netherlands	14,752	11,789	12,693
Netherlands Antilles (incl. Aruba)	23,159	6,715	2,932
Puerto Rico	21,869	19,378	23,901
Spain	27,942	21,712	26,028
United Kingdom	11,661	13,462	14,266
USA	407,646	452,786	511,700
Venezuela	332,726	332,250	134,307
Total (incl. others)	1,257,134	1,285,910	1,351,732

* Figures are provisional.

Exports f.o.b.	1992	1993	1994
Belgium and Luxembourg	39,930	44,898	21,623
Canada	92,934	22,120	18,998
Japan	5,322	19,485	15,532
Korea, Republic	23,251	22,940	37,643
Netherlands	9,279	42,432	103,683
United Kingdom	16,491	17,769	12,910
USA (incl. Puerto Rico)	1,412,629	1,482,993	1,678,812
Total (incl. others)	1,690,441	1,753,063	1,988,365

Source: UN, *International Trade Statistics Yearbook*.

Transport

ROAD TRAFFIC (motor vehicles in use at 31 December, estimates)

	1994	1995	1996
Passenger cars	183,000	209,000	224,000
Buses and coaches	13,440	15,520	14,550
Lorries and vans	112,000	126,000	137,000

Source: IRF, *World Road Statistics*.

SHIPPING

Merchant Fleet (registered at 31 December)

	1994	1995	1996
Number of vessels	28	27	27
Total displacement ('000 grt)	12	12	12

Source: Lloyd's Register of Shipping, *World Fleet Statistics*.

International Sea-borne Freight Traffic ('000 metric tons)

	1988	1989	1990
Goods loaded	2,515	2,520	2,550
Goods unloaded	4,210	4,342	4,182

Source: UN, *Monthly Bulletin of Statistics*.

CIVIL AVIATION (traffic on scheduled services)

	1992	1993	1994
Kilometres flown (million)	4	3	2
Passengers carried ('000)	323	328	300
Passengers-km (million)	283	280	234
Total ton-km (million)	26	28	24

Source: UN, *Statistical Yearbook*.

Tourism

	1992	1993	1994
Tourist arrivals ('000)	1,415	1,609	1,717
Tourist receipts (US $ million)	1,054	1,234	1,148

Source: UN, *Statistical Yearbook*.

Communications Media

	1992	1993	1994
Radio receivers ('000 in use)	1,280	1,300	1,330
Television receivers ('000 in use)	650	680	695
Telephones ('000 main lines in use)	479	552	605
Telefax stations (number in use)	2,061	2,500	n.a.
Mobile cellular telephones (subscribers)	7,190	11,020	20,040

Daily newspapers: 11 in 1994 (estimated average circulation 264,000 copies).

Non-daily newspapers: 39 in 1986.

Other periodicals: 277 in 1986.

Sources: UNESCO, *Statistical Yearbook*; UN, *Statistical Yearbook*.

Education

(1994/95)

	Institu-tions	Teachers	Students		
			Males	Females	Total
Pre-primary*	n.a.	n.a.	73,055	75,380	148,435
Primary	4,001	42,135	735,224	727,498	1,462,722
Secondary:					
general	n.a.	10,757	102,279	138,162	240,441
teacher training	n.a.	86	549	743	1,292
vocational	n.a.	1,211	9,147	12,356	21,503
Higher†	n.a.	6,539	n.a.	n.a.	123,748

* 1993/94 figures. † 1985/86 figures.

Source: UNESCO, *Statistical Yearbook*.

Directory

The Constitution

The Constitution of the Dominican Republic was promulgated on 28 November 1966. Its main provisions are summarized below:

The Dominican Republic is a sovereign, free, independent state; no organizations set up by the State can bring about any act which might cause direct or indirect intervention in the internal or foreign affairs of the State or which might threaten the integrity of the State. The Dominican Republic recognizes and applies the norms of general and American international law and is in favour of and will support any initiative towards economic integration for the countries of America. The civil, republican, democratic, representative Government is divided into three independent powers: legislative, executive and judicial.

The territory of the Dominican Republic is as laid down in the Frontier Treaty of 1929 and its Protocol of Revision of 1936.

The life and property of the individual citizen are inviolable; there can be no sentence of death, torture nor any sentence which might cause physical harm to the individual. There is freedom of thought, of conscience, of religion, freedom to publish, freedom of unarmed association, provided that there is no subversion against public order, national security or decency. There is freedom of labour and trade unions; freedom to strike, except in the case of public services, according to the dispositions of the law.

The State will undertake agrarian reform, dedicating the land to useful interests and gradually eliminating the latifundios (large estates). The State will do all in its power to support all aspects of family life. Primary education is compulsory and all education is free. Social security services will be developed. Every Dominican has the duty to give what civil and military service the State may require. Every legally entitled citizen must exercise the right to vote, i.e. all persons over 18 years of age and all who are or have been married even if they are not yet 18.

GOVERNMENT

Legislative power is exercised by Congress which is made up of the Senate and Chamber of Deputies, elected by direct vote. Senators, one for each of the 26 Provinces and one for the Distrito Nacional, are elected for four years; they must be Dominicans in full exercise of their citizen's rights, and at least 25 years of age. Their duties are to elect judges, the President and other members of the Electoral and Accounts Councils, and to approve the nomination of diplomats. Deputies, one for every 50,000 inhabitants or fraction over 25,000 in each Province and the Distrito Nacional, are elected for four years and must fulfil the same conditions for election as Senators.

Decisions of Congress are taken by absolute majority of at least half the members of each house; urgent matters require a two-thirds' majority. Both houses normally meet on 27 February and 16 August each year for sessions of 90 days, which can be extended for a further 60 days.

Executive power is exercised by the President of the Republic, who is elected by direct vote for a four-year term. The President must be a Dominican citizen by birth or origin, over 30 years of age and in full exercise of citizen's rights. The President must not have engaged in any active military or police service for at least a year prior to election. The President takes office on 16 August following the election. The President of the Republic is Head of the Public Administration and Supreme Chief of the armed forces and police forces. The President's duties include nominating Secretaries and Assistant Secretaries of State and other public officials, promulgating and publishing laws and resolutions of Congress and seeing to their faithful execution, watching over the collection and just investment of national income, nominating, with the approval of the Senate, members of the Diplomatic Corps, receiving foreign Heads of State, presiding at national functions, decreeing a State of Siege or Emergency or any other measures necessary during a public crisis. The President may not leave the country for more than 15 days without authorization from Congress. In the absence of the President, the Vice-President will assume power, or failing him, the President of the Supreme Court of Justice.

LOCAL GOVERNMENT

Government in the Distrito Nacional and the Municipalities is in the hands of local councils, with members elected proportionally to the number of inhabitants, but numbering at least five. Each Province has a civil Governor, designated by the Executive.

JUDICIARY

Judicial power is exercised by the Supreme Court of Justice and the other Tribunals; no judicial official may hold another public office or employment, other than honorary or teaching. The Supreme Court is made up of at least nine judges, who must be Dominican citizens by birth or origin, at least 35 years old, in full exercise of their citizen's rights, graduates in law and have practised professionally for at least 12 years. There are also five Courts of Appeal, a Lands Tribunal and a Court of the First Instance in each judicial district; in each Municipality and in the Distrito Nacional there are also Justices of the Peace.

Elections are directed by the Central Electoral Board. The armed forces are essentially obedient and apolitical, created for the defence of national independence and the maintenance of public order and the Constitution and Laws.

The artistic and historical riches of the country, whoever owns them, are part of the cultural heritage of the country and are under the safe-keeping of the State. Mineral deposits belong to the State. There is freedom to form political parties, provided they conform to the principles laid down in the Constitution. Justice is administered without charge throughout the Republic.

This Constitution can be reformed if the proposal for reform is supported in Congress by one-third of the members of either house or by the Executive. A special session of Congress must be called and any resolutions must have a two-thirds' majority. There can be no reform of the method of government, which must always be civil, republican, democratic and representative.

Note: In August 1994 Congress resolved that the current President's term of office should be restricted to two years. Presidential elections were, therefore, scheduled for 1996. Other constitutional amendments included provisions for the prohibition of the re-election of the President to a consecutive term in office, the adoption of a two-round voting system for presidential elections, the reorganization of the judicial system and the replacement of the Central Electoral Board.

The Government

HEAD OF STATE

President: Leonel Fernández Reyna (took office 16 August 1996).

Vice-President: Jaime David Fernández Mirabal.

CABINET
(February 1998)

Secretary of State to the Presidency: Danilo Medina.

Secretary of State for External Relations: Eduardo Latorre.

Secretary of State for the Interior and Police: Norge Botello.

Secretary of State for the Armed Forces: Rear-Adm. Rubén Paulino Alvarez.

Secretary of State for Finance: Daniel Toribio.

Secretary of State for Energy: Celestino Armas.

Secretary of State for Education and Culture: Ligia Amada Melo de Cardona.

Secretary of State for Agriculture: Frank Rodríguez.

Secretary of State for Public Works and Communications: Jaime Durán Hernando.

Secretary of State for Public Health and Social Welfare: Erasmo Vásquez.

Secretary of State for Industry and Commerce: Luis Manuel Bonetti.

Secretary of State for Labour: Rafael Albuquerque.

Secretary of State for Tourism: Félix Jiménez.

Secretary of State for Sport, Physical Education and Recreation: Juan Marichal.

Secretary of State without Portfolio: Lidio Cadet.

Administrative Secretary to the Presidency: Diandino Peña.

Technical Secretary to the Presidency: Eduardo Selman.

Attorney-General: Abel Rodríguez del Orbe.

Governor of the Central Bank: Héctor Váldez Albizú.

SECRETARIATS OF STATE

Secretariat of State for Agriculture: Centro de los Héroes de Constanza, Santo Domingo, DN; tel. 533-7171; telex 3460393.

Secretariat of State for Defence: Plaza de la Independencia, Avda 27 de Febrero, Santo Domingo, DN; tel. 530-5193; telex 3460652; fax 530-5017.

Secretariat of State for Education and Culture: Avda Máximo Gómez, Santo Domingo, DN; tel. 689-9161.

Secretariat of State for Energy: Santo Domingo, DN.

Secretariat of State for External Relations: Avda Independencia, Santo Domingo, DN; tel. 533-4121; telex 3264192.

Secretariat of State for Finance: Avda México 45, Santo Domingo, DN; tel. 687-5131; telex 3460437; fax 688-6561.

Secretariat of State for Industry and Commerce: Edif. de Oficinas Gubernamentales, 7°, Avda México, Santo Domingo, DN; tel. 685-5171; fax 686-1973; e-mail ind.comercio@codetel.net.do.

Secretariat of State for the Interior and Police: Edif. de Oficinas Gubernamentales, 3°, Avda Leopoldo Navarro a esq. México, Santo Domingo, DN; tel. 689-1979.

Secretariat of State for Labour: Santo Domingo, DN.

Secretariat of State for the Presidency: Santo Domingo, DN.

Secretariat of State for Public Health and Social Welfare: Santo Domingo, DN.

Secretariat of State for Public Works and Communications: Ensanche La Fe, Santo Domingo, DN; tel. 567-4929.

Secretariat of State for Sport, Physical Education and Recreation: Calle Pedro Henríquez Ureña, Apdo 1484, Santo Domingo, DN; tel. 688-0126; telex 3460471.

Secretariat of State for Tourism: Edif. D, Oficinas Gubernamentales, Avda México, esq. 30 de Marzo, Apdo 497, Santo Domingo, DN; tel. 221-4660; telex 3460303; fax 682-3806.

President and Legislature

PRESIDENT

Elections of 16 May and 30 June 1996

Candidate	Votes cast in first ballot	Votes cast in second ballot
José Francisco Peña Gómez (PRD)	1,333,925	1,394,641
Leonel Fernández Reyna (PLD)	1,130,523	1,466,382
Jacinto Peynado (PRSC)	435,504	—
Dr José Rafael Abinader (ASD)	3,907	—
Total	2,903,859	2,861,023

CONGRESO NACIONAL

The National Congress comprises a Senate and a Chamber of Deputies.

President of the Senate: Amable Aristy Castro (PRSC).

President of the Chamber of Deputies: Rafael Peguero Méndez (PRD).

General Election, 16 May 1994

	Seats	
	Senate	Chamber of Deputies
Partido Reformista Social Cristiano (PRSC)	14	50
Partido Revolucionario Dominicano (PRD)*/Unidad Democrática (UD)	15	57
Partido de la Liberación Dominicana (PLD)	1	13
Total	30	120

* Including seats held by the Partido Revolucionario Independiente (PRI).

Political Organizations

Alianza por la Democracia (APD): Santo Domingo, DN; f. 1992 by breakaway group of the PLD; split into two factions (led, respectively, by MAX PUIG and NÉLSIDA MARMOLEJOS) in 1993; Sec.-Gen. VICENTE BENGOA.

Fuerza Nacional Progresista (FNP): Santo Domingo, DN; right-wing; Leader MARIO VINICIO CASTILLO.

Movimiento de Conciliación Nacional (MCN): Calle Pina 207, Santo Domingo, DN; f. 1969; centre party; 659,277 mems; Pres. Dr JAIME M. FERNÁNDEZ; Sec. VÍCTOR MENA.

Movimiento de Integración Democrática (MIDA): Las Mercedes 607, Santo Domingo, DN; tel. 687-8895; centre-right; Leader Dr FRANCISCO AUGUSTO LORA.

Movimiento Popular Dominicano: Santo Domingo, DN; left-wing; Leader JULIO DE PEÑA VALDÉS.

Participación Ciudadana: Santo Domingo, DN; Leaders ANTONIO ISA CONDE, JUAN BOLÍVAR DÍAZ.

Partido Comunista Dominicano: Avda Independencia 89, Santo Domingo, DN; tel. 685-3540; f. 1944; outlawed 1962–77; Leader JOSÉ ISRAEL CUELLO; Sec.-Gen. NARCISO ISA CONDE.

Partido Demócrata Popular: Arz. Meriño 259, Santo Domingo, DN; tel. 685-2920; Leader LUIS HOMERO LÁJARA BURGOS.

Partido de la Liberación Dominicana (PLD): Avda Independencia 401, Santo Domingo, DN; tel. 685-3540; f. 1973 by breakaway group of PRD; left-wing; Leader LEONEL FERNÁNDEZ REYNA; Sec.-Gen. LIDIO CADET.

Partido Quisqueyano Demócrata (PQD): 27 de Febrero 206 (Altos), Santo Domingo, DN; tel. 565-0244; f. 1968; right-wing; 600,000 mems; Pres. Lic. PEDRO BERGÉS; Sec.-Gen. Dr ELÍAS WESSIN CHÁVEZ.

Partido Reformista Social Cristiano (PRSC): Avda San Cristóbal, Ensanche La Fe, Apdo 1332, Santo Domingo, DN; tel. 566-7089; f. 1964; centre-right party; Leader Dr JOAQUÍN BALAGUER RICARDO.

Partido Revolucionario Dominicano (PRD): Espaillat 118, Santo Domingo, DN; tel. 687-2193; f. 1939; democratic socialist; mem. of Socialist International; 400,000 mems; Pres. JOSÉ FRANCISCO PEÑA GÓMEZ; Sec.-Gen. HATUEY DECAMPS.

Partido Revolucionario Independiente (PRI): Santo Domingo; f. 1985 after split by the PRD's right-wing faction; Pres. JOSÉ RAFAEL MOLINA UREÑA; Sec.-Gen. STORMI REYNOSO.

Partido Revolucionario Social Cristiano: Las Mercedes 141, Santo Domingo, DN; tel. 688-3511; f. 1961; left-wing; Pres. Dr CLAUDIO ISIDORO ACOSTA; Sec.-Gen. Dr ALFONSO LOCKWARD.

Partido de los Trabajadores Dominicanos: Avda Duarte 69 (Altos), Santo Domingo, DN; tel. 685-7705; f. 1979; workers' party; Sec.-Gen. JOSÉ GONZÁLEZ ESPINOZA.

Unidad Democrática (UD): Santo Domingo; Leader FERNANDO ALVAREZ BOGAERT.

Other parties include Unión Cívica Nacional (UCN), Partido Alianza Social Demócrata (ASD—Leader Dr JOSÉ RAFAEL ABINADER), Movimiento Nacional de Salvación (MNS—Leader LUIS JULIÁN PÉREZ), Partido Comunista del Trabajo de la República Dominicana (Sec.-Gen. RAFAEL CHALJUB MEJÍA), Partido de Veteranos Civiles (PVC), Partido Acción Constitucional (PAC), Partido Unión Patriótica (PUP—Leader ROBERTO SANTANA), Partido de Acción Nacional (right-wing) and Movimiento de Acción Social Cristiana (ASC).

An opposition front, the Frente Izquierda Dominicana, has been formed by 53 political organizations and trade unions.

Diplomatic Representation

EMBASSIES IN THE DOMINICAN REPUBLIC

Argentina: Avda Máximo Gómez 10, Santo Domingo, DN; tel. 682-2977; fax 221-2206; Ambassador: ADRIÁN GUILLERMO MIRSON.

Brazil: Avda Winston Churchill 32, Edif. Franco-Acra y Asociados, 2°, Apdo 1655, Santo Domingo, DN; tel. 532-0868; telex 3460155; Ambassador: P. G. VILAS-BÔAS CASTRO.

Chile: Avda Anacaona 11, Mirador del Sur, Santo Domingo, DN; tel. 532-7800; telex 3460395; fax 530-8310; Ambassador: PATRICIO POZO RUIZ.

China (Taiwan): Edif. Palic, 1°, Avda Abraham Lincoln, esq. José Amado Soler, Apdo 4797, Santo Domingo, DN; tel. 562-5555; fax 563-4139; Ambassador: KUO KANG.

Colombia: Avda Abraham Lincoln 502, 2°, Santo Domingo, DN; tel. 567-6836; telex 3460448; Ambassador: (vacant).

Costa Rica: Andrés Julio Aybar 15, Santo Domingo, DN; tel. 565-7294; Chargé d'affaires: ODALISCA AUED RODRÍGUEZ.

Ecuador: Calle Rafael Augusto Sánchez 17, Ensanche Naco, Apdo 808, Santo Domingo, DN; tel. 563-8363; fax 563-8153; e-mail mecuador@codetel.net.do; Ambassador: LUIS NARVÁEZ RIVADENEIRA.

El Salvador: Calle José A. Brea Peña 12, Ensanche Evaristo Morales, Santo Domingo, DN; tel. 565-4311; fax 541-7503; Ambassador: Dr BYRON F. LARIOS L.

France: Avda Jorge Washington 353, Santo Domingo, DN; tel. 681-2161; telex 3460392; fax 221-8408; Ambassador: FRANÇOIS-XAVIER DENIAU.

Germany: Calle Rafael Augusto Sánchez 33, esq. Avda Lope de Vega, Ensanche Naco, Santo Domingo, DN; tel. 565-8811; telex 3264125; fax 567-5014; Ambassador: IMMO VON KESSEL.

Guatemala: Z No 8, Ensanche Naco, Santo Domingo, DN; tel. 567-0110; fax 567-0115; Ambassador: Gen. ROBERTO MATA.

Haiti: 33 Juan Sánchez Ramírez, Santo Domingo, DN; tel. 686-5778; fax 686-6096; Chargé d'affaires: GUY G. LAMOTHE.

Holy See: Avda Máximo Gómez 27, Apdo 312, Santo Domingo, DN (Apostolic Nunciature); tel. 682-3773; fax 687-0287; Apostolic Nuncio: Most Rev. FRANÇOIS BACQUÉ, Titular Archbishop of Gradisca.

Honduras: Calle Porfirio Herrera 9, esq. Respaldo Federico Geraldino, Ensanche Piantini, Santo Domingo, DN; tel. 566-5707; telex 3464104; Ambassador: IVÁN ROMERO MARTÍNEZ.

Israel: Pedro Henríquez Ureña 80, Santo Domingo, DN; tel. 541-8974; fax 562-3555; Ambassador: PINCHAS LAVIE.

Italy: Rodríguez Objío 4, Santo Domingo, DN; tel. 689-3684; telex 3460543; Ambassador: RUGGERO VOZZI.

Japan: Torre BHD, 8°, Avda Winston Churchill, esq. Luis F. Thomén, Santo Domingo, DN; tel. 567-3365; telex 4154; fax 566-8013; Ambassador: TSUNODA KATSUHIKO.

Korea, Republic: Avda Sarasota 98, Santo Domingo, DN; tel. 532-4314; telex 3264368; fax 532-3807; Ambassador: YUN PARK.

Mexico: Rafael Hernández 11, Ensanche Naco, Santo Domingo, DN; tel. 565-2744; telex 3264187; Ambassador: HUMBERTO LIRA MORA.

Nicaragua: El Recodo, Santo Domingo, DN; tel. 532-8846; telex 3264542; Ambassador: Dr DANILO VALLE MARTÍNEZ.

Panama: Hotel Embajador, Apdo 25338, Santo Domingo, DN; tel. 685-6950; Chargé d'affaires a.i.: Lic. ANTONIO PUELLO.

Peru: Cancillería, Avda Winston Churchill, Santo Domingo, DN; tel. 565-5851; Ambassador: RAÚL GUTIÉRREZ.

Russia: Santo Domingo, DN; Ambassador: VLADIMIR GONCHARENKO.

Spain: Independencia 1205, Santo Domingo, DN; tel. 535-1615; telex 3460158; fax 535-1595; Ambassador: RICARDO DÍEZ HOCHLEITNER.

United Kingdom: Suite 1108, Hotel Santo Domingo, Avda Independencia esq. Abraham Lincoln, Santo Domingo; tel. 534-7534; fax 534-7609; Ambassador: RICHARD THOMSON.

USA: César Nicolás Pensón, esq. Leopoldo Navarro, Santo Domingo, DN; tel. 541-2171; telex 3460013; Ambassador: MARI CARMEN APONTE.

Uruguay: Avda México 169, Santo Domingo, DN; tel. 565-2669; telex 3460442; Ambassador: JAIME WOLFSON KOT.

Venezuela: Cancillería, Avda Anaconda 7, Mirador Sur, Santo Domingo, DN; tel. 537-8578; telex 3264279; fax 537-8780; Ambassador: Lic. MARÍA CLEMENCIA LÓPEZ-JIMÉNEZ.

Judicial System

The Judicial Power resides in the Supreme Court of Justice, the Courts of Appeal, the Tribunals of the First Instance, the municipal courts and the other judicial authorities provided by law. The Supreme Court is composed of at least nine judges (15 in December 1997) and the Attorney-General, and exercises disciplinary authority over all the members of the judiciary. The Attorney-General of the Republic is the Chief of Judicial Police and of the Public Ministry which he represents before the Supreme Court of Justice. The Consejo Nacional de la Magistratura (National Judiciary Council) appoints the members of the Supreme Court, which in turn appoints judges at all other levels of the judicial system.

Corte Suprema: Centro de los Héroes de Constanza, Santo Domingo, DN; tel. 533-3522.

President: JORGE SUBERO ISA.

Attorney-General: ABEL RODRÍGUEZ DEL ORBE.

Religion

The majority of the inhabitants belong to the Roman Catholic Church, but freedom of worship exists for all denominations. The Baptist, Evangelist and Seventh-day Adventist churches and the Jewish faith are also represented.

CHRISTIANITY

The Roman Catholic Church

The Dominican Republic comprises two archdioceses and eight dioceses. At 31 December 1995 adherents represented about 89% of the population.

Bishops' Conference: Conferencia del Episcopado Dominicano, Apdo 186, Santo Domingo, DN; tel. 685-3141; fax 698-9454; f. 1985; Pres. Cardinal NICOLÁS DE JESÚS LÓPEZ RODRÍGUEZ, Archbishop of Santo Domingo.

Archbishop of Santiago de los Caballeros: Most Rev. JUAN ANTONIO FLORES SANTANA, Arzobispado, Calle 30 de Marzo 1, Apdo 679, Santiago de los Caballeros; tel. 582-2094; fax 581-3580.

Archbishop of Santo Domingo: Cardinal NICOLÁS DE JESÚS LÓPEZ RODRÍGUEZ, Arzobispado, Isabel la Católica 55, Apdo 186, Santo Domingo, DN; tel. 685-3141; fax 688-7270.

The Anglican Communion

Anglicans in the Dominican Republic are under the jurisdiction of the Episcopal Church in the USA. The country is classified as a missionary diocese, in Province IX.

Bishop of the Dominican Republic: Rt Rev. JULIO CÉSAR HOLGUÍN, Calle Santiago 114, Apdo 764, Santo Domingo, DN; tel. 688-6016; fax 686-6364; e-mail h.khoury@codetel.net.do.

BAHÁ'Í FAITH

National Spiritual Assembly of the Bahá'ís of the Dominican Republic: Cambronal 152, esq. Beller, Santo Domingo, DN; f. 1961; tel. 687-1726; fax 687-7606; e-mail bahai.rd.aen@codetel.net.do; 392 localities.

The Press

DAILIES

Santo Domingo, DN

El Caribe: Autopista Duarte, Km 7½, Apdo 416, Santo Domingo, DN; tel. 566-8161; f. 1948; morning; Dir GERMÁN E. ORNES; circ. 28,000.

Diario Las Américas: Avda Tiradentes, Santo Domingo, DN; tel. 566-4577.

Hoy: Santo Domingo, DN.

Listín Diario: Paseo de los Periodistas 52, Ensanche Miraflores, Santo Domingo, DN; tel. 686-6688; fax 686-6595; f. 1889; morning; Dir RAFAEL HERRERA; circ. 55,000.

El Nacional: San Martín 236, Santo Domingo, DN; tel. 565-5581; f. 1966; evening and Sunday; Dir MARIO ALVAREZ DUGAN; circ. 45,000.

La Noticia: Julio Verne 14, Santo Domingo, DN; tel. 687-3131; f. 1973; evening; Pres. JOSÉ A. BREA PEÑA; Dir SILVIO HERASME PEÑA.

El Sol: Santo Domingo, DN; tel. 532-9511; morning; Pres. QUITERIO CEDEÑO; Dir-Gen. MIGUEL ANGEL CEDEÑO.

Ultima Hora: Paseo de los Periodistas 52, Ensanche Miraflores, Santo Domingo, DN; tel. 688-3361; telex 3460206; fax 688-3019; f. 1970; evening; Dir ANÍBAL DE CASTRO; circ. 50,000.

Puerto Plata

El Porvenir: Calle Imbert 5, Apdo 614, Puerto Plata; f. 1872; Dir CARLOS ACEVEDO.

Santiago de los Caballeros, SD

La Información: Carretera Licey, Km 3, Santiago de los Caballeros, SD; tel. 581-1915; fax 581-7770; f. 1915; morning; Editor ADRIANO MIGUEL TEYADA; circ. 15,000.

PERIODICALS AND REVIEWS

Agricultura: Santo Domingo, DN; organ of the State Secretariat of Agriculture; f. 1905; monthly; Dir MIGUEL RODRÍGUEZ, Jr.

Agroconocimiento: Apdo 345-2, Santo Domingo, DN; monthly; agricultural news and technical information; Dir DOMINGO MARTE; circ. 10,000.

¡Ahora!: San Martín 236, Apdo 1402, Santo Domingo, DN; tel. 565-5581; telex 3460423; f. 1962; weekly; Dir MARIO ALVAREZ DUGAN.

La Campiña: San Martín 236, Apdo 1402, Santo Domingo, DN; f. 1967; Dir Ing. JUAN ULISES GARCÍA B.

Carta Dominicana: Avda Tiradentes 56, Santo Domingo, DN; tel. 566-0119; f. 1974; monthly; economics; Dir JUAN RAMÓN QUIÑONES M.

Deportes: San Martín 236, Apdo 1402, Santo Domingo, DN; f. 1967; sports; fortnightly; Dir L. R. CORDERO; circ. 5,000.

Eva: San Martín 236, Apdo 1402, Santo Domingo, DN; f. 1967; fortnightly; Dir MAGDA FLORENCIO.

Horizontes de América: Santo Domingo, DN; tel. 565-9717; f. 1967; monthly; Dir ARMANDO LEMUS CASTILLO.

Letra Grande, Arte y Literatura: Leonardo da Vinci 13, Mirador del Sur, Avda 27 de Febrero, Santo Domingo, DN; tel. 531-2225; f. 1980; monthly; art and literature; Dir JUAN RAMÓN QUIÑONES M.

Renovación: Calle José Reyes, esq. El Conde, Santo Domingo, DN; fortnightly; Dir OLGA QUISQUEYA VIUDA MARTÍNEZ.

FOREIGN PRESS BUREAUX

Agencia EFE (Spain): Galerías Comerciales, 5°, Of. 507, Avda 27 de Febrero, Santo Domingo, DN; tel. 567-7617; telex 2024176; Bureau Chief ANTONIO CASTILLO URBERUAGA.

Agenzia Nazionale Stampa Associata (ANSA) (Italy): Calle Leopoldo Navarro 79, 3°, Sala 17, Apdo 20324, Huanca, Santo Domingo, DN; tel. 685-8765; telex 2014537; fax 685-8765; Bureau Chief HUMBER ANDRÉS SUAZO.

Inter Press Service (IPS) (Italy): Calle Cambronal, No. 4-1, Ciudad Nueva, Santo Domingo, DN; tel. 593-5153; Correspondent VIANCO MARTÍNEZ.

United Press International (UPI) (USA): Carrera A. Manoguaybo 16, Manoguaybo, DN; tel. 689-7171; telex 3460206; Chief Correspondent SANTIAGO ESTRELLA VELOZ.

Publishers

Santo Domingo, DN

Arte y Cine, C por A: Isabel la Católica 42, Santo Domingo, DN.

Editora Alfa y Omega: José Contreras 69, Santo Domingo, DN; tel. 532-5577.

Editora de las Antillas: Calle Pedro Henríquez Ureña, Santo Domingo, DN; tel. 685-2197.

Editora Colonial, C por A: Calle Moca 27-B, Apdo 2569, Santo Domingo, DN; tel. 688-2394; Pres. DANILO ASENCIO.

Editora Dominicana, SA: 23 Oeste, No 3 Lup., Santo Domingo, DN; tel. 688-0846.

Editora El Caribe, C por A: Autopista Duarte, Km 7½, Apdo 416, Santo Domingo, DN; tel. 566-8161; f. 1948; Dir Dr GERMÁN E. ORNES.

Editora Hoy, C por A: San Martín, 236, Santo Domingo, DN; tel. 566-1147; telex 3460423.

Editora Listín Diario, C por A: Paseo de los Periodistas 52, Ensanche Miraflores, Apdo 1455, Santo Domingo, DN; tel. 686-6688; telex 3460206; fax 686-6595; f. 1889; Pres. Dr ROGELIO A. PELLERANO.

Editorama, SA: Calle Justiniano Bobea, esq. Eugenio Contreras, Apdo 2074, Santo Domingo, DN; tel. 596-6669; fax 594-1421.

Editorial Padilla: San F. de Macorís 14, Santo Domingo, DN; tel. 682-3101.

Editorial Santo Domingo: Santo Domingo, DN; tel. 532-9431.

Editorial Stella: 19 de Marzo, Santo Domingo, DN; tel. 682-2281.

Julio D. Postigo e Hijos: Santo Domingo, DN; f. 1949; fiction; Man. J. D. POSTIGO.

Publicaciones América: Santo Domingo, DN; Dir PEDRO BISONÓ.

Santiago de los Caballeros, SD

Editora el País, SA: Carrera Sánchez, Km 6½, Santiago de los Caballeros, SD; tel. 532-9511.

Broadcasting and Communications

Dirección General de Telecomunicaciones: Isabel la Católica 73, Santo Domingo, DN; tel. 682-2244; fax 682-3493; government supervisory body; Dir-Gen. RUBÉN MONTAS.

TELECOMMUNICATIONS

Compañía Dominicana de Teléfonos (Codetel): Avda Lincoln 1101, Santo Domingo, DN; tel. 220-2000.

Tricom Telecomunicaciones de Voz, Data y Video: Avda Lope de Vega 95, Santo Domingo, DN; tel. 542-7556; fax 567-4412; Chief of Int. Relations CÉSAR A. FRANCO.

RADIO

There were some 100 commercial stations in 1997. The government-owned broadcasting network, Radio Televisión Dominicana, operates nine radio stations.

Asociación Dominicana de Radiodifusoras (ADORA): Calle Paul Harris 3, Centro de los Héroes, Santo Domingo; tel. 535-4057; Pres. IVELISE DE TORRES.

TELEVISION

Radio Televisión Dominicana: Dr Tejada Florentino 8, Apdo 869, Santo Domingo, DN; tel. 689-2120; government station; three channels, two relay stations; Dir-Gen. ADRIANO RODRÍGUEZ; Gen. Man. AGUSTÍN MERCADO.

Rahintel Televisión: Centro de los Héroes de Constanza, Avda Independencia, Apdo 1220, Santo Domingo, DN; tel. 532-2531; telex 3460213; fax 535-4575; commercial station; two channels; Pres. LEONEL ALMONTE V.

Color-Visión (Corporación Dominicana de Radio y Televisión): Calle Emilio A. Morel, esq. Luis E. Pérez, Ensanche La Fe, Apdo 30043, Santo Domingo, DN; tel. 556-5876; fax 544-3607; commercial station; Channel 9; Dir-Gen. MANUEL QUIROZ.

Teleantillas: Autopista Duarte, Km 7½, Apdo 30404, Santo Domingo, DN; tel. 567-7751; telex 3460863; Gen. Man. MARITZA DE LOS SANTOS.

Telecentro, SA: Avda Pasteur 204, Santo Domingo, DN; tel. 687-9161; telex 3460091; fax 542-7582; Channel 13 for Santo Domingo and east region; Pres. JASINTO PEYNADO.

Tele-Inde Canal 13: 30 de Marzo 80, Santo Domingo, DN; commercial station; Proprietor JOSÉ A. SEMORILE.

Telesistema Dominicana: Avda 27 de Febrero, Santo Domingo, DN; tel. 567-1251; Pres. JOSÉ L. CORREPIO.

Finance

(cap. = capital; dep. = deposits; m = million; p.u. = paid up; res = reserves; amounts in pesos)

BANKING

Supervisory Body

Superintendencia de Bancos: Avda México, esq. Leopoldo Navarro, Apdo 1326, Santo Domingo, DN; tel. 685-8141; telex 3460653; fax 685-0859; f. 1947; Superintendent Lic. PERSIA ALVAREZ DE HERNÁNDEZ.

Central Bank

Banco Central de la República Dominicana: Calle Pedro Henríquez Ureña, esq. Leopoldo Navarro, Apdo 1347, Santo Domingo, DN; tel. 221-9111; telex 3460052; fax 687-7488; f. 1947; cap. 0.7m., res 92.3m., dep. 6,321.7m. (Dec. 1996); Gov. HÉCTOR VÁLDEZ ALBIZÚ; Man. NIEVES MÁRMOL DE PERICHE.

Commercial Banks

Banco BHD, SA: Avda 27 de Febrero, esq. Winston Churchill, Apdo 266-2, Santo Domingo, DN; tel. 243-3232; fax 562-4396; e-mail bhd@codetel.net.do; internet http://www.codetel.net.do.BHD; f. 1972; cap. and res 364.3m., dep. 3,431.8m.; Pres. JOSÉ ANTONIO CARO; Gen. Man. LUIS MOLINA A.; 35 brs.

Banco del Comercio Dominicano, SA: Avda 27 de Febrero, esq. Winston Churchill, Apdo 1440, Santo Domingo, DN; tel. 545-5100; telex 3464533; fax 566-3694; f. 1980; cap. and res. 407.3m., dep. 3,606.0m. (Dec. 1993); Pres. JOSÉ UREÑA ALMONTE; 42 brs.

Banco Dominicano del Progreso, SA: Avda John F. Kennedy 3, Apdo 1329, Santo Domingo, DN; tel. 563-3233; telex 3264321; fax 563-2455; f. 1974; cap. 118.9m., dep. 1,213.9m. (Dec. 1995); Chair. TOMÁS A. PASTORIZA; Exec. Vice-Pres. MICHAEL A. KELLY; 17 brs.

Banco Gerencial y Fiduciario Dominicano, SA: San Martín 122, Apdo 1101, Santo Domingo, DN; tel. 565-9971; f. 1983; cap. and res 5.1m., dep. 17.8m. (June 1985); Exec. Vice-Pres. GEORGE MANUEL HAZOURY PEÑA.

Banco Metropolitano: Avda Lope de Vega, esq. Gustavo Mejía Ricart, Apdo 1872, Santo Domingo, DN; tel. 562-2442; telex 346 0419; f. 1974; cap. and res 17.1m., dep. 196.4m. (Dec. 1986); Gen. Dir ADALBERTO PÉREZ PERDOMO; 7 brs.

Banco Nacional de Crédito, SA: Avda John F. Kennedy, esq. Tiradentes, Santo Domingo, DN; tel. 540-4441; f. 1981; cap. 212.3m., dep. 1,700.0m. (Sept. 1993); Vice-Pres. ANGEL BALIÑO.

Banco Popular Dominicano: Avda John F. Kennedy 20, Torre Popular, Apdo 1441, Santo Domingo, DN; tel. 544-8000; telex 3264157; fax 544-5899; f. 1963; cap. 456.5m., res 151.0m., dep. 7,463.9m. (Dec. 1995); Pres. MANUEL A. GRULLÓN; 45 brs.

Banco de Reservas de la República Dominicana: Isabel la Católica 201, Apdo 1353, Santo Domingo, DN; tel. 687-5366; telex 3460012; fax 542-0017; f. 1941; cap. 250.0m., res 443.0m., dep. 8,880.4m. (Dec. 1995); Gen. Man. ROBERTO SALADÍN S.; 20 brs.

Banco de los Trabajadores Dominicanos: Avda México, esq. Calle Altagracia, Apdo 1446, Santo Domingo, DN; tel. 682-0171; telex 3264500; fax 685-6536; f. 1972; state-controlled; cap. and res 21.8m., dep. 39.6m. (June 1992); Pres. Lic. JOSÉ A. RODRÍGUEZ ESPAILLAT; 4 brs.

Development Banks

Banco Agrícola de la República Dominicana: Avda G. Washington 601, Apdo 1057, Santo Domingo, DN; tel. 533-1171; telex 3460026; f. 1945; government agricultural development bank; cap. and res 230.9m., dep. 115.5m. (Dec 1985); Pres. Lic. RAFAEL ANGELES SUÁREZ; Gen. Administrator PEDRO BRETÓN.

Banco Hipotecario Bancomercio, SA: Avda Máximo Gómez, Santo Domingo, DN; tel. 541-6231.

Banco Hipotecario de la Construcción, SA (BANHICO): Avda Tiradentes (Altos Plaza Naco), Santo Domingo, DN; tel. 562-1281; f. 1977; cap. and res 8.4m., dep. 0.4m. (June 1985); Man. Dr JAIME ALVAREZ DUGAN.

Banco Hipotecario Popular, SA: Avda 27 de Febrero 261, Santo Domingo, DN; tel. 544-6700; f. 1978; cap. 43.5m., dep. 232.2m. (Aug. 1989); Pres. MANUEL E. JIMÉNEZ F.

Banco Inmobiliario Dominicano, SA: Calle Del Sol 10, Santiago; tel. 581-0121; telex 3461111; fax 688-3419; f. 1979; cap. and res 13.6m., dep. 0.5m. (June 1985); Dir Dr J. MANUEL PITTALUGA NIVAR; 3 brs.

Banco Nacional de la Construcción: Avda Alma Mater, esq. Pedro Henríquez Ureña, Santo Domingo, DN; tel. 685-9776; f. 1977; cap. and res 3.7m., dep. 0.9m. (June 1985); Gen. Man. LUIS MANUEL PELLERANO.

Foreign Banks

Bank of Nova Scotia (Canada): Avda John F. Kennedy, esq. Lope de Vega, Apdo 1494, Santo Domingo, DN; tel. 544-1700; telex 3460145; fax 542-6302; f. 1920; Vice-Pres. A. D. PÉREZ; 13 brs.

Citibank NA (USA): Avda John F. Kennedy 1, Apdo 1492, Santo Domingo, DN; tel. 566-5611; telex 3460083; fax 567-2255; f. 1962; Vice-Pres. ROBERT MATTHEWS; 7 brs.

STOCK EXCHANGE

Santo Domingo Securities Exchange Inc: Edif. Disesa, Suite 302, Avda Abraham Lincoln, Santo Domingo; tel. 567-6694; fax 567-6697; Pres. FELIPE AUFFANT.

INSURANCE

Supervisory Body

Superintendencia de Seguros: Secretaría de Estado de Finanzas, Avda México, esq. Leopoldo Navarro, Santo Domingo, DN; tel. 688-1245; f. 1969; Superintendent Dr JUAN ESTEBAN OLIVERO FELIZ.

National Companies

American Life and General Insurance Co, C por A: Edif. ALICO, 5°, Avda Abraham Lincoln, Santo Domingo, DN; tel. 533-7131; telex 3460366; fax 533-5969; general; Gen. Man. FRANK CABREJA.

La Americana, SA: Edif. La Cumbre, Avda Tiradentes, Apdo 25241, Santo Domingo, DN; tel. 567-1211; telex 3460034; f. 1975; life; Pres. MARINO GINEBRA H.

Aseguradora Dominicana Agropecuaria C por A (ADACA): Isabel la Católica 212, Santo Domingo, DN; tel. 685-6191; agriculture; Pres. Ing. PEDRO BRETÓN.

Centro de Seguros La Popular, C por A: Gustavo Mejía Ricart 61, Apdo 1123, Santo Domingo, DN; tel. 566-1988; fax 567-9389; f. 1965; general except life; Pres. Lic. FABIO A. FIALLO.

Centroamericana de Seguros, SA: Edif. BHD, Avda 27 de Febrero, esq. Tiradentes, Santo Domingo, DN; tel. 566-5151; general; Pres. Lic. JOSÉ E. DE POOL.

Citizens Dominicana, SA: Avda Winston Churchill esq. Paseo de los Locutores, 4°, Santo Domingo, DN; tel. 562-2705; f. 1978; Pres. MIGUEL E. SAVIÑÓN TORRES.

Cía Dominicana de Seguros, C por A: Edif. Buenaventura, Avda Independencia 201, esq. Dr Delgado, Apdo 176, Santo Domingo, DN; tel. 689-6127; general except life; Pres. Lic. HUGO VILLANUEVA.

Cía Nacional de Seguros, C por A: Avda Máximo Gómez 31, Apdo 916, Santo Domingo, DN; tel. 685-2121; telex 3460117; fax 682-3269; f. 1964; general; Pres. Dr MÁXIMO A. PELLERANO.

La Colonial, SA: Edif. Haché, 2°, Avda John F. Kennedy, Santo Domingo, DN; tel. 565-9926; f. 1971; general; Pres. Dr MIGUEL FERIS IGLESIAS.

El Condor Seguros, SA: Avda 27 de Febrero 12, Apdo 20077, Santo Domingo, DN; tel. 689-4146; telex 3460210; f. 1977; general; Pres. JUAN PABLO REYES.

General de Seguros, SA: Avda Sarasota 55, Bella Vista, Santo Domingo, DN; tel. 535-8888; fax 532-4451; f. 1981; general; Pres. Dr FERNANDO A. BALLISTA DÍAZ.

Inter-Oceania de Seguros, SA: Calle el Conde 105, Santo Domingo, DN; tel. 689-2688; general; Pres. LEONEL ALMONTE.

La Intercontinental de Seguros, SA: Plaza Naco, 2°, Avda Tiradentes, Apdo 825, Santo Domingo, DN; tel. 562-1211; telex 3460034; general; Pres. Lic. RAMÓN BÁEZ ROMANO.

Latinoamericana de Seguros, SA: Santo Domingo, DN; tel. 541-5400; life; Pres. Rafael Castro Martínez.

Magna Compañía de Seguros, SA: Edif. Magna Motors, Avda Abraham Lincoln, esq. John F. Kennedy, Santo Domingo, DN; tel. 544-1400; telex 3460812; fax 562-5723; f. 1974; general and life; Pres. E. Antonio Lama S.; Man. Milagros de los Santos.

La Metropolitana de Seguros, C por A: Edif. ALICO, 4a, Avda Abraham Lincoln, Apdo 131, Santo Domingo, DN; tel. 532-0541; telex 3460366; managed by American International Underwriters (AIU); Gen. Man. Rafael Armando Pichardo.

La Mundial de Seguros, SA: Avda Máximo Gómez, No 31, Santo Domingo, DN; tel. 685-2121; telex 3460466; fax 682-3269; general except life and financial; Pres. Dr Máximo A. Pellerano.

Patria, SA: Avda 27 de Febrero 10, Santo Domingo, DN; tel. 687-3151; general except life; Pres. Rafael Bolívar Nolasco.

La Peninsular de Seguros, SA: Edif. Corp. Corominas Pepín, 3°, Avda 27 de Febrero 233, Santo Domingo, DN; tel. 472-1166; fax 563-2349; general; Pres. Lic. Ernesto Romero Landrón.

La Principal de Seguros, SA: Max Henríquez Ureña, esq. Virgilio Díaz Ordóñez, Santo Domingo, DN; tel. 566-8141; telex 4112; fax 541-4868; f. 1986; general; Pres. Virtudes González de Céspedes.

Reaseguradora Internacional, SA: Avda Pasteur 17, Santo Domingo, DN; tel. 685-3909; general; Pres. Lic. Fabio A. Fiallo.

Reaseguradora Nacional, SA: Avda Máximo Gómez 31, Apdo 916, Santo Domingo, DN; tel. 685-2121; f. 1971; general; Pres. Máximo A. Pellerano.

Reaseguradora Profesional, SA: Edif. La Universal de Seguros, 4°, Avda Winston Churchill 1100, Santo Domingo, DN; tel. 544-7400; telex 3264545; fax 544-7099; f. 1981; Gen. Man. Lic. Manuel de Js Colón.

Reaseguradora Santo Domingo, SA: Centro Comercial Jardines del Embajador, 2°, Avda Sarasota, Apdo 25005, Santo Domingo, DN; tel. 532-2586; telex 3460566; general; Man. Douglas Harmand.

Seguros San Rafael, C por A: Leopoldo Navarro 61, esq. San Francisco de Macorís, Santo Domingo, DN; tel. 688-2231; telex 3460169; general; Admin. Francisco Reyes Peguero.

Seguros La Alianza: Edif. La Cumbre, 8°, Centro Comercial Naco, Avda Tiradentes, Santo Domingo, DN; tel. 567-0181; general; Pres. Milton Rubén Gómez.

Seguros América, C por A: Edif. La Cumbre, 4°, Centro Comercial Naco, Avda Tiradentes, Santo Domingo, DN; tel. 567-0181; telex 3460185; fax 567-8909; f. 1966; general except life; Pres. Dr Luis Ginebra Hernández.

Seguros La Antillana, SA: Avda Abraham Lincoln 708, Apdo 146 y 27, Santo Domingo, DN; tel. 567-4481; telex 3460411; fax 541-2927; f. 1947; general and life; Pres. Andrés A. Freites V.

Seguros Bancomercio, SA: Avda Lope de Vega 29, Apdo 1440, Santo Domingo, DN; tel. 541-3366; fax 567-9350; f. 1985; general; Pres. José A. Ureña.

Seguros del Caribe, SA: Avda. México 105, Santo Domingo, DN; tel. 567-0242; general; Pres. Carlos P. Portes.

Seguros Pepín, SA: Edif. Corp. Corominas Pepín, Avda 27 de Febrero 233, Santo Domingo, DN; tel. 472-1006; general; Pres. Dr Bienvenido Corominas.

El Sol de Seguros, SA: Torre Hipotecaria, 2°, Avda Tiradentes 25, Santo Domingo, DN; tel. 542-6063; general; Pres. Guillermo Armenteros.

Unión de Seguros, C por A: Calle Beller 98, Santiago de los Caballeros, SD; tel. 582-5195; f. 1964; general and life; Pres. Belarminio Cortina.

La Universal de Seguros, C por A: Torre La Universal de Seguros, Avda Winston Churchill 1100, Apdo 1052, Santo Domingo, DN; tel. 544-7200; fax 544-7999; general; Pres. Ing. Ernesto Izquierdo.

There are also 11 foreign-owned insurance companies in the Dominican Republic.

Insurance Association

Cámara Dominicana de Aseguradores y Reaseguradores, Inc: Torre BHD, 5a, Calle Luis F. Thomen, esq. Winston Churchill, Santo Domingo, DN; tel. 566-0019; fax 566-2600; e-mail cadoar@codetel.net.do; f. 1972; Pres. Milagros de los Santos.

Trade and Industry

GOVERNMENT AGENCIES

Consejo Estatal del Azúcar (CEA) (State Sugar Council): Centro de los Héroes, Apdo 1256/1258, Santo Domingo, DN; tel. 533-1161; telex 3460043; f. 1966; autonomous administration for each of the 12 state sugar mills; Dir Ignacio Rodríguez Chiappini.

Corporación Dominicana de Empresas Estatales (CORDE) (Dominican State Corporation): Avda General Antonio Duvergé, Apdo 1378, Santo Domingo, DN; tel. 533-5171; telex 3460311; f. 1966 to administer, direct and develop 26 state enterprises; auth. cap. RD $25m.; Dir Euclides Gutiérrez Feliz.

Instituto de Estabilización de Precios (INESPRE): Avda Luperón, Santo Domingo, DN; tel. 530-0020; fax 530-0343; f. 1969; price commission; Dir Manuel Amezquita.

Instituto Nacional de la Vivienda: Antiguo Edif. del Banco Central, Avda Pedro Henríquez Ureña, esq. Leopoldo Navarro, Apdo 1506, Santo Domingo, DN; tel. 685-4181; f. 1962; low-cost housing institute; Dir Ing. Serapio Terrero.

DEVELOPMENT ORGANIZATIONS

Departamento de Desarrollo y Financiamento de Proyectos—DEFINPRO: c/o Banco Central de la República Dominicana, Calle Pedro Henríquez Ureña, esq. Leopoldo Navarro, Apdo 1347, Santo Domingo, DN; tel. 221-9111; telex 3460052; fax 687-7488; f. 1993; associated with AID, IDB, WB, KFW; resources US $250m.; encourages economic development in productive sectors of economy, excluding sugar; authorizes complementary financing to private sector for establishing and developing industrial and agricultural enterprises and free-zone industrial parks; Dir Lic. Virgilio Malagón Alvarez.

Fundación Dominicana de Desarrollo (Dominican Development Foundation): Calle Mercedes No 4, Apdo 857, Santo Domingo, DN; f. 1962 to mobilize private resources for collaboration in financing small-scale development programmes; 384 mems; assets US $10.7m.; Dir Eduardo La Torre.

Instituto de Desarrollo y Crédito Cooperativo (IDECOOP): Centro de los Héroes, Apdo 1371, Santo Domingo, DN; tel. 533-8131; fax 535-5148; f. 1963 to encourage the development of co-operatives; cap. 100,000 pesos; Dir Rafael Méndez.

CHAMBERS OF COMMERCE

Cámara de Comercio y Producción de Santo Domingo: Arz. Nouel 206, Zona Colonial, Apdo 815, Santo Domingo, DN; tel. 682-7206; fax 685-2228; e-mail cámara.sto.dgo.@codetel.net.do; f. 1910; 1,500 active mems; Pres. José Manuel Armenteros; Exec. Dir Milagros J. Puello.

Cámara Americana de Comercio de la República Dominicana: Torre BHD, 4°, Avda Winston Churchill, Santo Domingo, DN; tel. 544-2222; fax 544-0502; e-mail amcham@codetel.net.do; internet http://www.amcham.org.do; Pres. José Vitienes.

There are official Chambers of Commerce in the larger towns.

INDUSTRIAL AND TRADE ASSOCIATIONS

Asociación Dominicana de Hacendados y Agricultores Inc: Avda Sarasota 20, Santo Domingo, DN; tel. 565-0542; farming and agricultural org.; Pres. Lic. Silvestre Alba de Moya.

Asociación de Industrias de la República Dominicana Inc: Avda Sarasota 20, Apdo 850, Santo Domingo, DN; tel. 535-9111; fax 533-7520; f. 1962; industrial org.; Pres. Nassim Alemany.

Centro Dominicano de Promoción de Exportaciones (CEDOPEX): Plaza de la Independencia, Apdo 199-2, Santo Domingo, DN; tel. 530-5505; telex 3460351; fax 530-8208; organization for the promotion of exports; Dir Francisco Amézquita Candelier.

Consejo Promotor de Inversiones (Investment Promotion Council): Avda Abraham Lincoln, 2°, Santo Domingo; tel. 532-3281; fax 533-7029; Exec. Dir and CEO Frederic Emam Zadé.

Corporación de Fomento Industrial (CFI): Avda 27 de Febrero, Plaza Independencia, Apdo 1452, Santo Domingo, DN; tel. 530-0010; telex 3460049; fax 530-1303; f. 1962 to promote agro-industrial development; auth. cap. RD $25m.; Dir José Tomás Pérez.

Dirección General de Minería e Hidrocarburos: Edif. de Oficinas Gubernamentales, 10°, Avda México, esq. Leopoldo Navarro, Santo Domingo, DN; tel. 687-7557; fax 686-8327; f. 1947; government mining and hydrocarbon org.; Dir-Gen. Ing. Gerard Marten Ellis.

Instituto Agrario Dominicano (IAD): Avda 27 de Febrero, Santo Domingo, DN; tel. 530-8272; Dir Wilton Guerrero.

Instituto Azucarero Dominicano (INAZUCAR): Avda Jiménez Moya, Apdo 667, Santo Domingo, DN; tel. 532-5571; sugar institute; f. 1965; Exec. Dir M. Federico Echenique N.

EMPLOYERS' ORGANIZATIONS

Confederación Patronal de la República Dominicana: Edif. Mella, Cambronal/G. Washington, Santo Domingo, DN; tel. 688-3017; Pres. Ing. Heriberto de Castro.

Consejo Nacional de Hombres de Empresa Inc: Edif. Motorámbar, 7°, Avda Abraham Lincoln 1056, Santo Domingo, DN; tel. 562-1666; Pres. José Manuel Paliza.

Federación Dominicana de Comerciantes: Carretera Sánchez Km 10, Santo Domingo, DN; tel. 533-2666; Pres. IVAN GARCÍA.

UTILITIES

Electricity

Corporación Dominicana de Electricidad (CDE): Centro de los Héroes, Apdo 1428, Santo Domingo, DN; tel. 535-1100; fax 535-7472; f. 1955; state electricity company; privatization pending; Admin. TEMISTOCLES MONTAS.

TRADE UNIONS

It is estimated that about 13% of the total work-force are trade union members.

Central General de Trabajadores (CGT): Calle 26, esq. Duarte, Santo Domingo, DN; tel. 688-3932; f. 1972; 13 sections; Sec.-Gen. FRANCISCO ANTONIO SANTOS; 65,000 mems.

Central de Trabajadores Independientes (CTI): Calle Juan Erazo 133, Santo Domingo, DN; tel. 688-3932; f. 1978; left-wing; Sec.-Gen. RAFAEL SANTOS.

Central de Trabajadores Mayoritarias (CTM): Tunti Cáceres 222, Santo Domingo, DN; tel. 562-3392; Sec.-Gen. NÉLSIDA MARMOLEJOS.

Confederación Autónoma de Sindicatos Clasistas (CASC) (Autonomous Confederation of Trade Unions): J. Erazo 39, Santo Domingo, DN; tel. 687-8533; f. 1962; supports PRSC; Sec.-Gen. GABRIEL DEL RÍO.

Confederación Nacional de Trabajadores Dominicanos (CNTD) (National Confederation of Dominican Workers): Santo Domingo, DN; f. 1988 by merger; 11 provincial federations totalling 150 unions are affiliated; Sec.-Gen. JULIO DE PEÑA VÁLDEZ; 188,000 mems (est.).

Confederación de Trabajadores Unitaria (CTU) (United Workers Confederation): Santo Domingo, DN; f. 1991.

Transport

RAILWAYS

Dirección General de Tránsito Terrestre: Avda San Cristóbal, Santo Domingo, DN; tel. 567-4610; f. 1966; run by Secretary of State for Public Works and Communications; Dir-Gen. Ing. ARIF ABUD ABREU.

Ferrocarriles Unidos Dominicanos: Santo Domingo; government-owned; 142 km of track from La Vega to Sánchez and from Guayubín to Pepillo principally used for the transport of exports.

There are also a number of semi-autonomous and private railway companies for the transport of sugar cane, including:

Ferrocarril de Central Romana: La Romana; 375 km open; Pres. C. MORALES.

Ferrocarril Central Río Haina: Apdo 1258, Haina; 113 km open.

ROADS

In 1996 there were an estimated 12,600 km of roads, of which about 6,225 were paved. There is a direct route from Santo Domingo to Port-au-Prince in Haiti. In 1991 the World Bank approved a loan of US $79m. to support the first three years of a five-year road reconstruction project covering 830 km of roads.

SHIPPING

The Dominican Republic has 14 ports, of which Santo Domingo is by far the largest, handling about 80% of imports.

A number of foreign shipping companies operate services to the island.

Armadora Naval Dominicana, SA: Isabel la Católica 165, Apdo 2677, Santo Domingo, DN; tel. 689-6191; telex 3460465; Man. Dir Capt. EINAR WETTRE.

Líneas Marítimas de Santo Domingo, SA: José Gabriel García 8, Apdo 1148, Santo Domingo, DN; tel. 689-9146; telex 3264274; fax 685-4654; Pres.C. LLUBERES; Vice-Pres. JUAN T. TAVARES.

CIVIL AVIATION

There are international airports at Santo Domingo (Aeropuerto Internacional de las Américas), Puerto Plata and Barahona (Aeropuerto Internacional María Móntez). The airport at La Romana is authorized for international flights, providing that three days' notice is given. Most main cities have domestic airports.

Aerochago: Aeropuerto Internacional de las Américas, Santo Domingo; tel. 549-0709; fax 549-0708; f. 1973; operates cargo and charter service in Central America and the Caribbean; Gen. Man. PEDRO RODRÍGUEZ.

Aerolíneas Argo: Avda 27 de Febrero 409, Santo Domingo, DN; tel. 566-1844; telex 3460531; f. 1971; cargo and mail services to the USA, Puerto Rico and the US Virgin Islands.

Aerolíneas Dominicanas (Dominair): Calle el Sol, Apdo 202, Santiago; tel. 247-4010; telex 3461023; fax 582-5074; scheduled and charter passenger services; Pres. J. ARMANDO BERMÚDEZ; Gen. Man. MARÍA TERESA VELÁSQUEZ.

Aerolíneas de Santo Domingo: Santo Domingo; f. 1995; operates charter flights to North and South America and Europe.

Alas del Caribe, C por A: Avda Luperón, Aeropuerto de Herrera, Santo Domingo, DN; tel. 566-2141; f. 1968; internal routes; Pres. JACINTO B. PEYNADO; Dir MANUEL PÉREZ NEGRÓN.

Compañía Dominicana de Aviación C por A: Avda Jiménez de Moya, esq. José Contreras, Apdo 1415, Santo Domingo, DN; tel. 532-6269; telex 3460390; fax 535-1656; f. 1944; operates on international routes connecting Santo Domingo with the Netherlands Antilles, Aruba, the USA, Haiti and Venezuela; operations suspended 1995, privatization pending; Chair. Dr RODOLFO RINCÓN; CEO MARINA GINEBRA DE BONNELLY.

Tourism

The total number of visitors to the Dominican Republic in 1996 was 1,623,824. In 1995 receipts totalled US $1,490m. In 1996 there were 35,750 hotel rooms in the Dominican Republic. Strenuous efforts were made in the 1980s and early 1990s to improve the tourist infrastructure, with 200m. pesos spent on increasing the number of hotel rooms by 50%, road improvements and a new development, costing 160m. pesos, planned at Bahía de Manzanillo.

Secretaría de Estado de Turismo: Edif. D, Oficinas Gubernamentales, Avda México, esq. 30 de Marzo, Apdo 497, Santo Domingo, DN; tel. 221-4660; telex 3460303; fax 682-3806; Sec. of State for Tourism FÉLIX JIMÉNEZ.

Asociación Dominicana de Agencias de Viajes: Carrera Sánchez 201, Santo Domingo, DN; tel. 687-8984; Pres. RAMÓN PRIETO.

ECUADOR

Introductory Survey

Location, Climate, Language, Religion, Flag, Capital

The Republic of Ecuador lies on the west coast of South America. It is bordered by Colombia to the north, by Peru to the east and south, and by the Pacific Ocean to the west. The Galápagos Islands, about 960 km (600 miles) off shore, form part of Ecuador. The climate is affected by the Andes mountains, and the topography ranges from the tropical rain forest on the coast and in the eastern region to the tropical grasslands of the central valley and the permanent snowfields of the highlands. The official language is Spanish, but Quechua and other indigenous languages are very common. Almost all of the inhabitants profess Christianity, and more than 90% are Roman Catholics. The national flag (proportions 2 by 1) has three horizontal stripes, of yellow (one-half of the depth), blue and red. The state flag has, in addition, the national emblem (an oval cartouche, showing Mt Chimborazo and a steamer on a lake, surmounted by a condor) in the centre. The capital is Quito.

Recent History

Ecuador was ruled by Spain from the 16th century until 1822, when it achieved independence as part of Gran Colombia. In 1830 Ecuador seceded and became a separate republic. A long-standing division between Conservatives (Partido Conservador), whose support is generally strongest in the highlands, and Liberals (Partido Liberal, subsequently Partido Liberal Radical), based in the coastal region, began in the 19th century. Until 1948 Ecuador's political life was characterized by a rapid succession of presidents, dictators and juntas. Between 1830 and 1925 the country was governed by 40 different regimes. From 1925 to 1948 there was even greater instability, with a total of 22 heads of state.

Dr Galo Plaza Lasso, who was elected in 1948 and remained in power until 1952, was the first President since 1924 to complete his term of office. He created a climate of stability and economic progress. Dr José María Velasco Ibarra, who had previously been President in 1934–35 and 1944–47, was elected again in 1952 and held office until 1956. A 61-year-old tradition of Liberal Presidents was broken in 1956, when a Conservative candidate, Dr Camilo Ponce Enríquez, took office. He was succeeded in September 1960 by Dr Velasco, who campaigned as a non-party Liberal. In November 1961, however, President Velasco was deposed by a coup, and was succeeded by his Vice-President, Dr Carlos Julio Arosemena Monroy. The latter was himself deposed in July 1963 by a military junta, led by Capt. (later Rear-Adm.) Ramón Castro Jijón, the Commander-in-Chief of the Navy, who assumed the office of President. In March 1966 the High Command of the Armed Forces dismissed the junta and installed Clemente Yerovi Indaburu, a wealthy business executive and a former Minister of Economics, as acting President. Yerovi was forced to resign when the Constituent Assembly, elected in October 1966, proposed a new Constitution which prohibited the intervention of the armed forces in politics. In November he was replaced as provisional President by Dr Otto Arosemena Gómez, who held office until the elections of June 1968, when Dr Velasco returned from exile to win the presidency for the fifth time.

In June 1970 Velasco, with the support of the army, suspended the Constitution, dissolved the National Congress and assumed dictatorial powers to confront a financial emergency. In February 1972 he was overthrown for the fourth time by a military coup, led by Brig.-Gen. Guillermo Rodríguez Lara, the Commander-in-Chief of the Army, who proclaimed himself Head of State. In January 1976 President Rodríguez resigned, and power was assumed by a three-man military junta, led by Vice-Adm. Alfredo Poveda Burbano, the Chief of Staff of the Navy. The new junta announced its intention to lead the country to a truly representative democracy. A national referendum approved a newly-drafted Constitution in January 1978 and presidential elections took place in July. No candidate achieved an overall majority, and a second round of voting was held in April 1979, when a new Congress was also elected. Jaime Roldós Aguilera of the Concentración de Fuerzas Populares (CFP) was elected President and he took office in August, when the Congress was inaugurated and the new Constitution came into force. Roldós promised social justice and economic development, and guaranteed freedom for the press, but he encountered antagonism from both the conservative sections of the Congress and the trade unions. In May 1981 the President died in an air crash and was replaced by the Vice-President, Dr Osvaldo Hurtado Larrea. He encountered opposition from left-wing politicians and unions for his efforts to reduce government spending and from right-wing and commercial interests, which feared encroaching state intervention in the private economic sector.

A dispute between Hurtado and Vice-President León Roldós Aguilera in January 1982 led to the resignation of two ministers belonging to Roldós' party, Pueblo, Cambio y Democracia (PCD), which subsequently joined the opposition. Hurtado replaced the ministers with members of the CFP, creating a new pro-Government majority with a coalition of members of Democracia Popular-Unión Demócrata Cristiana (DP-UDC), CFP, Izquierda Democrática (ID) and seven independents. The heads of the armed forces resigned and the Minister of Defence was dismissed in January, when they opposed Hurtado's attempts to settle amicably the border dispute with Peru (see below).

In March 1983 the Government introduced a series of austerity measures, which encountered immediate opposition from the trade unions and workers in the private sector. Discontent with the Government's performance was reflected in the results of the presidential and congressional elections of January 1984, when the ruling party, DP-UDC, lost support. At a second round of voting in May León Febres Cordero, leader of the Partido Social Cristiano (PSC) and presidential candidate of the conservative Frente de Reconstrucción Nacional (FRN), unexpectedly defeated Dr Rodrigo Borja Cevallos, representing the left-wing ID, with 52.2% of the votes cast. He took office in August.

Opposition to the new Government's austerity programme led to a number of protests and strikes in late 1984 and early 1985, organized by the Frente Unitario de Trabajadores (FUT) and opposition groups.

The dismissal of the Chief of Staff of the Armed Forces, Lt-Gen. Frank Vargas Pazzos, brought about a military crisis in March 1986. Lt-Gen. Vargas and his supporters barricaded themselves inside the Mantas military base until they had forced the resignation of both the Minister of Defence, Gen. Luis Piñeiros, and the army commander, Gen. Manuel Albuja, who had been accused by Vargas of embezzlement. Vargas then staged a second rebellion at the military base where he had been detained. Troops loyal to the President made an assault on the base, captured Vargas and arrested his supporters. In January 1987 President Febres Cordero was abducted and, after being held for 11 hours, was released in exchange for Vargas, who was granted an amnesty. In July 58 members of the air force were sentenced to up to 16 years' imprisonment for involvement in the abduction of the President.

In June 1986 President Febres Cordero lost the majority that his coalition of parties had held in the Congress. A total of 10 candidates (including Lt-Gen. Vargas) contested the presidential election of January 1988. At a second round of voting in May Dr Rodrigo Borja Cevallos (of the ID) secured 46% of the votes cast, defeating Abdalá Bucaram Ortiz of the Partido Roldosista Ecuatoriano (PRE), who won 41%. Borja took office as President in August, promising to act promptly to address Ecuador's increasing economic problems and to change the country's isolationist foreign policy. In September there were large demonstrations in protest against the rise in the price of fuel and against other economic measures that had been implemented to combat inflation. In October the guerrilla organization, Montoneros Patria Libre (MPL), proposed the establishment of dialogue between the Government and the rebels. In the same month the President of the Supreme Court of Justice, Ivan Martínez Vela, was murdered in Quito by unknown assassins.

In February 1989 the Government conducted a campaign to confiscate weapons belonging to paramilitary organizations. This measure followed an incident in which armed men prevented security police from arresting Miguel Orellana, the former private secretary to ex-President Febres Cordero, who was accused of misusing public funds. In March Alfaro Vive ¡Carajo! (AVC), a leading opposition (hitherto guerrilla) group, urged paramilitary groups across the political spectrum to surrender their weapons. The Government agreed to guarantee the civil rights of AVC members and promised to initiate a national dialogue in return for the group's demobilization. In the same month the MPL dissociated itself from the agreement between the Government and the AVC and pledged to continue violent opposition.

In October 1989 a plot to organize a coup to overthrow the President and replace him with Vice-President Luis Parodí Valverde was revealed in a Federal German newspaper. The alleged conspirators were based in the Guayaquil municipality, where the local business community resented the perceived growing centralization of power in Quito. Radical right-wing groups, headed by former President Febres Cordero, led the movement. In January 1990 Febres Cordero was detained and charged with embezzlement of public funds.

In October 1989 a leading figure of the Medellín drugs-trafficking cartel was arrested in Ecuador and extradited to Colombia. In January 1990 the Government expressed opposition to the operation of US warships in Ecuador's territorial waters, but affirmed its support for President Bush's intention to confront the drugs-trafficking problem in the region. The US Government provided Ecuador with US $1.7m. in aid towards a programme to combat drugs-trafficking later that year.

At the mid-term legislative elections, which were held in June 1990, the ID lost 16 seats and conceded control of Congress to an informal alliance of the PSC and the PRE.

In October 1990 a serious conflict arose between the Government and Congress when the newly-elected President of Congress, Dr Averroes Bucaram, attempted to stage a legislative coup against President Borja. Bucaram initially impeached several ministers, who were subsequently dismissed by Congress. Congress then dismissed the 16 Supreme Court justices and other high-ranking members of the judiciary, and appointed new courts with shortened mandates. Both the Government and the judiciary refused to recognize these actions, on the grounds that Congress had exceeded its constitutional powers. Bucaram then announced that Congress would initiate impeachment proceedings against President Borja himself. However, this move was averted when three opposition deputies transferred their allegiance, so restoring Borja's congressional majority. Bucaram was subsequently dismissed as President of Congress. Impeachment proceedings against government ministers continued into 1991, and, consequently, by August of that year a total of six ministers had been dismissed. The Government accused the opposition of using the impeachment proceedings as part of a deliberate campaign to undermine the prospects of the ID in the forthcoming elections.

In May 1990 about 1,000 indigenous Indians, representing 70 socio-political Indian organizations, marched into Quito to present President Borja with a 16-point petition demanding official recognition of land rights for the indigenous population. In the following month the Confederación Nacional de Indígenas del Ecuador (CONAIE) (National Confederation of the Indigenous Population of Ecuador) organized an uprising covering seven Andean provinces. Roads were blockaded, *haciendas* occupied, and supplies to the cities interrupted. Following the arrest of 30 Indians by the army, the rebels took military hostages. The Government offered to hold conciliatory negotiations with CONAIE, in return for the release of the hostages. Among the demands made by the Indians were the return of traditional community-held lands, recognition of Quechua as an official language and compensation from petroleum companies for environmental damage. Discussions between CONAIE and President Borja collapsed in August. In January 1991 the FUT announced a joint anti-Government campaign with CONAIE. The FUT was protesting against the Government's decision to increase the minimum monthly wage by only 38%, to 44,000 sucres, and insisted that the minimum should be raised to 150,000 sucres. In February discussions between CONAIE and the Government were resumed, following the seizure by Indian groups in the Oriente of eight oil wells. The protest was halted two weeks later, when the Government promised to consider the Indians' demands for stricter controls on the operations of the petroleum industry, and for financial compensation.

In September 1991 the British Embassy in Quito was occupied by eight members of a dissident faction of the AVC. The siege, which ended peacefully after two days, formed part of a campaign to win the release of Patricio Baquerizo, the dissidents' leader, from prison. In February 1991 the AVC had concluded the process of demobilization that it had begun in February 1989. In October 1991 the party was absorbed by the ID.

In April 1992 several thousand Amazon Indians, representing four indigenous communities, marched from the Oriente to Quito to demand that their historical rights to their homelands be recognized. In mid-May President Borja agreed to grant legal title to more than 1m. ha of land in the province of Pastaza to the Indians.

General elections, including the selection of 926 representatives to municipal and provincial councils, were held in May 1992. In the legislative elections the PSC gained the highest number of seats in the enlarged National Congress, winning 21 of the 77 seats, while the PRE secured 13. The Partido Unidad Republicano (PUR) was formed prior to the elections by the former PSC presidential candidate, Sixto Durán Ballén, in order to contest the presidential election (since the PSC had nominated the President of the party, Jaime Nebot Saadi, as its candidate). The PUR won 12 seats in the congressional elections, the ID only seven and the Partido Conservador (PC) six seats. In the presidential election no candidate secured an absolute majority of the votes. The two leading contenders, Durán and Nebot, who secured 32.9% and 25.2% of the votes respectively, proceeded to a second round of voting July, at which Durán secured 58% of the votes cast, defeating Nebot, who won 38%. The PUR was to govern with its ally, the PC. However, as the two parties' seats did not constitute a majority in Congress, support from other centre-right parties, particularly the PSC, was sought. The appointment of prominent business executives to most of the principal portfolios in the new Cabinet reflected Durán's commitment to free-market policies.

In September 1992 the Government's announcement of a programme of austerity measures, aimed at controlling inflation, reducing the budget deficit and restructuring the public sector, prompted widespread protest. Following violent demonstrations and several bomb attacks in Quito and Guayaquil, the Government dispatched units of the armed forces to restore order. Widespread opposition to the Government's economic policies continued to manifest itself, however, in demonstrations and protests, and a general strike in May 1993. The 'Modernization Law', a crucial part of the controversial austerity programme (which was to provide for the privatization of some 160 state-owned companies and the reduction in the number of employees in the public sector by 100,000), was approved by Congress in August. In November striking teachers organized demonstrations throughout the country, demanding wage increases and reforms in the education system. During the protests two demonstrators were killed and many injured.

In January 1994 Congress approved a reform of the Constitution that would increase the number of deputies from 77 to 113. It remained unclear, however, when this reform would be implemented.

Environmental concerns regarding the exploitation of the Oriente by the petroleum industry continued to be expressed by national and international groups during 1993. In November five Amazon Indian tribes initiated legal proceedings against the international company Texaco to claim compensation totalling US $1,500m. for its part in polluting the rain forest. (It was estimated that some 17m. barrels of oil had been spilt during the company's 25 years of operations in the region.) Protests intensified in January 1994, when the Government initiated a round of bidding for petroleum-exploration licences for 10 hydrocarbon regions, including sites in the eastern Oriente, previously withheld because of opposition from environmentalists and indigenous communities. During the demonstrations, Indian groups occupied the Ministry of Energy and Mines and CONAIE renewed its demand for a 15-year moratorium on further bidding. In mid-1997 a US court provoked outrage among indigenous organizations by rejecting their claim for compensation from Texaco. The organizations announced their intention to pursue the matter.

Meanwhile, the Government's economic programme of austerity measures and privatizations continued to arouse widespread hostility, and its decision in January 1994 to increase the price of fuel by more than 70% provoked violent demonstrations throughout the country and a general strike. In the following month the Tribunal of Constitutional Guarantees declared the rise to be unconstitutional, although Durán refused to recognize the ruling.

At mid-term congressional elections in May 1994 President Durán's PUR-PC governing alliance suffered a serious defeat, winning only nine of the 77 seats in Congress. The PSC secured 26 seats, while the PRE remained the second-largest party in Congress, winning 11 seats. Despite the fact that voting is compulsory in Ecuador, only some 70% of eligible voters participated in the poll, and of these 18% returned void ballot papers, reflecting a widespread disillusionment among the electorate with the democratic process.

In June 1994 the increasingly vociferous indigenous movement organized large-scale demonstrations across the country, in protest at a recently-approved Land Development Law. The law, which allowed for the commercialization of Amerindian lands for farming and resource extraction, provoked serious unrest and a general strike, during which a state of emergency was declared and the army mobilized. Seven protesters were killed, and many injured, in clashes with the security forces. The law was subsequently judged to be unconstitutional by the Tribunal of Constitutional Guarantees, although Durán refused to accept the ruling. In early July, however, the law was modified to extend the rights of landowners and those employed to work on the land.

On 28 August 1994 President Durán's referendum on constitutional reform finally took place, following much disagreement between the Government and the judiciary and opposition parties, who argued that the proposals had not been properly debated and that the plebiscite was merely an attempt by Durán to undermine the new Congress. All but one of the eight proposed reforms (which included measures to alter the electoral system and the role of Congress and the establishment of a bicameral legislature) were approved; however, only some 50% of eligible voters participated, of whom some 20% returned void ballot papers.

Protests against the Government's economic programme of austerity measures and privatizations in January 1995 resulted in the deaths of two students in Quito during clashes with riot police. In March Modesto Correa became the administration's third Minister of Finance to resign, apparently because of differences within the Cabinet concerning economic policy. Industrial unrest continued during May and June, when the FUT launched a national strike against a new series of 'corrective' economic measures, introduced by the Government in an attempt to reduce the impact of the financial crisis caused by the border conflict with Peru (see below). These measures included the elimination of fuel subsidies to major industries, the introduction of a more efficient system for the collection of taxes and increases of 140% in the price of electricity for domestic use. Continued industrial unrest was compounded in July, when oil workers initiated a strike in protest at the impact of government policy on the petroleum industry. Later in the month, however, the country was plunged into a serious political crisis when Vice-President Alberto Dahik admitted giving funds from the state budget to opposition deputies (allegedly for use in local public works projects) in return for their support for the Government's economic reform programme. Dahik announced that he would not resign, despite the initiation of impeachment proceedings, and rejected the criminal charges against him. Two secretaries from Dahik's office, who were also seriously implicated in the affair, were reported to have fled the country. In a further development (believed by some observers to be an attempt to obstruct the case against Dahik) the President of the Supreme Court and two other justices were dismissed. Critics of the Government's action claimed that the dismissals themselves were unconstitutional, as they did not respect the separation of powers of the judiciary from the legislature and executive. In September impeachment proceedings began against the Minister of Finance, Mauricio Pinto, for his role in various alleged financial irregularities. Meanwhile, the Superintendent of Banks resigned his post, following accusations that he had attempted to hinder the case against Dahik in the Supreme Court. Impeachment proceedings against Dahik began on 2 October, and on 11 October, following an appeal by Durán, the Vice-President resigned. A former Minister of Education, Dr Eduardo Peña Triviño, was subsequently elected as Vice-President by Congress. A further two cabinet ministers offered their resignations in support of Dahik, and on 13 October the entire Cabinet resigned in order that a reorganization of portfolios could take place.

In addition to the political crisis provoked by the scandal surrounding the Vice-President during mid-1995, the administration continued to be troubled by various industrial disputes and strikes. In September troops were dispatched to the Galápagos Islands, following disturbances among the islanders, who had blocked principal points of entry to the islands and had occupied public buildings (including one of the airports), as well as threatening to take tourists hostage. The protesters were demanding the Government's acceptance of a special law granting increased political and financial autonomy to the islands, in addition to some US $16m. in priority economic aid. Concerned about the potentially disastrous effect of the protests on the country's important tourist industry, the Government quickly withdrew its opposition to the proposed legislation and agreed to establish a specialist commission to draft a new law acceptable to all parties. Moreover, in October petroleum workers resumed strike action in protest at the Government's privatization plans, and in one incident occupied the PETROECUADOR building, taking two cabinet ministers hostage for several hours, in order to prevent the signing of a contract to sell the Trans-Ecuadorean oil pipeline. The dispute ended following the resignation of the Minister of Energy and Mines, Galo Abril Ojeda, at the end of the month. The strike, however, together with a severe drought, which halted production at the Paute hydroelectric plant (which provides 60%–70% of the country's electricity), resulted in serious energy shortages in October and November, which further exacerbated the country's troubled political and economic situation.

A referendum on the Government's proposals for constitutional reform was held on 26 November 1995. All of the 11 proposed changes were rejected in the plebiscite, which was widely regarded as a reflection of the Government's continued unpopularity. Despite its decisive defeat, the Government announced its intention to pursue its programme of reforms.

Widespread strikes and demonstrations by teachers and students in November 1995, in which one student was killed in clashes with police, led to the resignation of the Minister of Education. The initiation of impeachment proceedings against one cabinet minister, and the resignation of another, further weakened the President's position, and pressure for him to resign intensified. Ex-President Borja was particularly vociferous in demanding Durán's resignation. Industrial action among employees in the energy sector continued, and in January 1996 army units were deployed at prominent sites throughout the country in order to prevent further unrest and a worsening of the energy crisis. Furthermore, an industrial dispute by transport workers in March resulted in serious disruption in the capital and prompted a series of strikes in other sectors. The Government's decision to concede to some of the transport workers' demands led the Secretary-General of Public Administration to resign his post in protest at what he described as the Government's weak approach to resolving disputes.

A presidential election, held on 19 May 1996, failed to produce an outright winner, thus necessitating a second round of voting for the two leading contenders. The PSC candidate, Jaime Nebot Saadi, secured 27.1% of the votes during the first round, while Abdalá Bucaram Ortiz of the PRE won 25.6%. An increasingly vocal and politically-organized indigenous movement resulted in the strong performance of Freddy Ehlers, a former journalist, who was the candidate for the newly-formed Movimiento Nuevo País-Pachakutik (MNPP), a coalition organization composed of Amerindian and labour groups. Ehlers secured 21% of the votes. At legislative elections held concurrently the PSC won 27 of the 82 seats in the enlarged National Congress, while the PRE secured 19 and Democracia Popular (DP—formerly DP-UDC) won 12. The MNPP emerged as a significant new force in Congress, with a total of eight seats. At the second round of voting in the presidential election, on 7 July, Bucaram was the unexpected victor, receiving 54.5% of total votes. The success of Bucaram, a populist figure and former Olympic athlete (who had held political office as mayor of Guayaquil in the 1980s and had contested three previous presidential elections), was widely interpreted as a rejection of the policies of the outgoing Government (which Nebot had promised to continue) and an expression of disenchantment with established party politics. Bucaram's electoral campaign had focused on promises to establish 'a government for the poor', and included proposals to extend social security benefits to indigenous families, to provide low-cost housing for 200,000 families, to increase the salaries of teachers and health workers and to introduce subsidies for rice, meat, milk and fuel. Following his inauguration on 10 August, however, Bucaram sought to allay the fears of the business community (prompted by his proposals for costly social reform), stating that existing economic arrangements would be maintained. Moreover, a team of prominent businessmen was assigned the role of advising the President on economic policy. Appointments to a new Cabinet included Bucaram's brother and brother-in-law and several close personal friends.

A scandal at the Ministry of Finance in September 1996, which resulted in the arrest of seven senior officials on charges of embezzlement (estimated at more than US $300m.) was claimed by Bucaram as a victory for his anti-corruption policies. However, concern at the President's idiosyncratic style of leadership and increasingly eccentric behaviour began to intensify in late 1996. It was reported that Bucaram had failed to attend a number of important meetings, while his television appearances (which often involved the President dancing and performing rock music) became more frequent. Moreover, a perceived inconsistency in many of Bucaram's policies and the apparently arbitrary nature of his decisions, together with his use of undiplomatic language, contributed to a rapid decline in his popularity.

A 48-hour general strike took place in early January 1997, prompted by increases of up to 600% in the price of certain commodities and a climate of considerable dissatisfaction with the President's leadership. Demonstrations in the capital continued throughout January and trade union leaders announced an indefinite extension of the general strike. Protests intensified in early February when several hundred thousand demonstrators marched through the streets of Quito demanding Bucaram's resignation. The President responded by declaring a national holiday and a one-week closure of schools across the country, and stated his support for the strike. Meanwhile, troops were deployed throughout the capital as violent clashes erupted between protesters and security personnel and Bucaram was barricaded inside the presidential palace. On 6 February, at an emergency session, Congress voted by 44 votes to 34 to dismiss the President on the grounds of mental incapacity; by questioning the President's sanity Congress was able to evade the normal impeachment requirements of a two-thirds' majority. A state of emergency was declared and acting President, the former Speaker, Fabián Alarcón Rivera urged demonstrators to storm the presidential palace. Bucaram, however, refused to leave office and claimed that he would retain power by force if necessary. The situation was further complicated by the claim of the Vice-President, Rosalia Arteaga, to be the legitimate constitutional successor to Bucaram. Political confusion over the correct procedure prompted fears of a military coup, despite a declaration of neutrality by the armed forces. Bucaram reportedly fled from the presidential palace on 9 February, and on the following day Arteaga was declared interim President after narrowly winning a congressional vote. However, by 11 February Arteaga had resigned, amid continued constitutional uncertainty, and Alarcón was reinstated as President following a congressional vote on the same day, at which 57 members indicated their support for him. Alaracón, who stated that his priorities as President were political reform and the restoration of economic confidence, announced a reorganization of cabinet portfolios (which included no members of the two largest parties in Congress, the PSC and the PRE) and the creation of a commission to investigate allegations of corruption against Bucaram and his administration. In March Bucaram's extradition from Panama (where he had fled and successfully sought political asylum) was requested in order that he face charges of misappropriating some US $90m. of government funds. Bucaram responded by stating that if he were fit to face criminal charges he could not be insane and should, therefore, be reinstated as President. He also reiterated his view that his removal from office constituted a *coup d'état*. In the following month the President of the Supreme Court announced that extradition would only be possible once a prison sentence had been issued. Furthermore, in May Bucaram declared his intention to present himself as a presidential candidate at Ecuador's next elections. The announcement prompted Congress to vote almost unanimously in favour of a motion to impose an indefinite ban on Bucaram's candidacy in any future presidential election in the country. The legislature similarly voted to curtail the term of office of the Vice-President, Rosalia Arteaga, such that it would terminate, along with that of the interim President, in August 1998 when elections would take place. Arteaga, however, who had urged that fresh elections be held immediately, criticized the decision as unconstitutional, claiming that, as she had been elected legitimately and not appointed by Congress following the dismissal of Bucaram, she was entitled to remain in office for the full term. However, the Minister of Government, César Verduga, insisted that all senior positions should be renewed simultaneously in order to maintain institutional stability.

On 25 May 1997 a referendum comprising 14 questions sought public opinion on a variety of matters, including electoral reform, the modernization of the judiciary and the authenticity of Alarcón's position. Although some 40.7% of the electorate did not participate, the vote revealed considerable support for the decision to remove Bucaram from office (75.7%) and for the appointment of Alarcón as interim President (68.3%). Some 64.5% of voters also favoured the creation of a national assembly to consider constitutional reform. Alarcón's apparent success in the referendum, however, was undermined in early June by a scandal which threatened the stability of the administration. Allegations that leading drugs-traffickers in the country had contributed to political party funds, and, particularly, to Alarcón's Frente Radical Alfarista (FRA), were to be investigated in an official inquiry established by Congress.

In July 1997 Congress dismissed all 31 judges of the Supreme Court, claiming that its action was in accordance with the views on the depoliticization of the judiciary (which is nominated by the legislature) expressed in the recent referendum. The President of the Supreme Court, Carlos Solorzano, condemned the action as unconstitutional.

The announcement in August 1997 that a national assembly to review the Constitution (as proposed in the referendum of May 1997) would be elected and installed in August 1998 was widely opposed, and provoked a 48-hour strike to demand that the assembly be established sooner. The strike led by CONAIE, which virtually paralyzed the country by means of numerous roadblocks, was supported most strongly by Indian and peasant organizations, who insisted that an assembly should be convened as soon as possible in order to discuss indigenous rights and the proposed privatization of key areas of the economy. In response to the apparent strength of public opinion it was announced in September that elections for the 70 representatives to the assembly would take place in late November. However, 11 indigenous organizations demonstrated their lack of confidence in the Government to address their concerns by convening a mass rally in Quito to establish guidelines for their own Constitution.

Criticism of the Government increased during the second half of 1997, with both the Roman Catholic Church and ex-President Rodrigo Borja urging Alarcón to resign. The uneasy relationship between Alarcón and Arteaga also became more apparent in August when the Vice-President publicly expressed support for the striking indigenous groups, and when Alarcón refused to transfer power to Arteaga while he left the country on a brief foreign tour. Alarcón's problems in office were further exacerbated by charges of embezzlement filed against him in the Supreme Court by a former FRA colleague, Cecilia Calderón.

The long-standing border dispute with Peru over the Cordillera del Cóndor erupted into war in January 1981. A cease-fire was declared a few days later under the auspices of the guarantors of the Rio Protocol of 1942 (Argentina, Brazil, Chile and the USA). The Protocol was not recognized by Ecuador as it awarded the area, which affords access to the Amazon river system, to Peru. Further clashes occurred along the border with Peru in December 1982 and January 1983. In January 1992 discussions on the border dispute were resumed. A number of minor incidents along the border were reported during 1994. However, in January 1995 serious fighting broke out between the two sides, following reports of Peruvian incursions into Ecuadorean territory, and border towns were evacuated as air and mortar attacks, as well as hand-to-hand fighting, took place in the region. Both Governments denied responsibility for initiating hostilities and issued contradictory reports concerning subsequent clashes. Following offers from the Organization of American States (OAS) and the four guarantor nations of the Rio Protocol, representatives of the two Governments met for negotiations in Rio de Janeiro, Brazil. A cease-fire was announced on 31 January but did not appear to have the full support of the Peruvian delegation. An agreement was signed in mid-February but was not observed by troops on either side. On 28 February a further cease-fire agreement was concluded, and an observer mission, representing the four guarantor nations, was dispatched to the border, to oversee the separation of forces and demilitarization of the border area. However, in late March Ecuador accused Peru of breaking the cease-fire, when an Ecuadorean observation post was attacked by a Peruvian patrol, during which one soldier was killed and several others injured. Similarly, in May a Peruvian post was reported to have been attacked, and one soldier killed, by Ecuadorean forces. However, the separation of forces continued and both Governments ordered the release of a number of prisoners taken during the conflict. Intensive negotiations continued to take place in Brazil, and, as a result, agreement on the delimitation of the demilitarized zone in the disputed area was reached in July. In October Ecuador finally repealed the state of emergency. Official discussions between the Ministers of Foreign Affairs of Peru and Ecuador began in January 1996, amid renewed controversy that the two countries were engaged in a campaign to strengthen their military capability by negotiating contracts for the supply of weapons from a number of foreign countries, reported to include the People's Republic of China, Argentina, Israel and the Democratic People's Republic of Korea. A resumption of negotiations in September resulted in the signing of the Santiago Agreement by both sides in the following month, which was to provide a framework for a definitive solution on the border issue. In March 1997 Ecuador lodged an official complaint against the Peruvian army's use of land-mines along the border, claiming that many of its security personnel had been killed or maimed while deactivating some 5,000 devices. A new round of talks (which had been postponed twice as a result of the Japanese embassy hostage crisis in Lima and the political crisis in Ecuador) began in Brasilia in April. It was reported in the following month that Ecuadorean troops had been captured during an incursion into Peruvian territory. The soldiers denied Peruvian accusations that they had been planting land-mines, and claimed rather that they had been deactivating devices. The troops were subsequently released and both sides agreed that the incident should not affect ongoing negotiations. In August the two countries signed an agreement aimed at ensuring transparent mechanisms in arms procurement. The agreement, however, failed to prevent a series of rumours that Ecuador had secretly purchased considerable quantities of armaments from Israel. Negotiations continued to take place in Brasilia during 1997. However, in October it was suggested that Peru might withdraw from the talks if the Ecuadorean delegation continued to insist on including the issue of a sovereign outlet to the Amazon river. The Peruvian Government reiterated that it considered this to be an unacceptable demand.

Government

Executive power is vested in the President, who is directly elected by universal adult suffrage for a four-year term. The President is not eligible for re-election. Legislative power is held by the 82-member unicameral Congress, which is also directly elected: 12 members are elected on a national basis and serve a four-year term, while 65 members are elected on a provincial basis and are replaced every two years, being ineligible for re-election. Ecuador comprises 21 provinces, composed of 193 cantons, 322 urban parishes and 757 rural parishes. Each province has a Governor, who is appointed by the President.

Defence

Military service, which lasts one year, is selective for men at the age of 20. In August 1997 there were 57,100 men in the armed forces: army 50,000, navy 4,100 (including 1,500 marines) and air force 3,000. Defence expenditure in 1996 was estimated to be 1,600,000m. sucres.

Economic Affairs

In 1995, according to estimates by the World Bank, Ecuador's gross national product (GNP), measured at average 1993–95 prices, was US $15,997m., equivalent to $1,390 per head. During 1985–95, it was estimated, GNP per head increased, in real terms, at an average annual rate of 0.8%. Over the same period, the population increased by an annual average of 2.3%. Ecuador's gross domestic product (GDP) increased, in real terms, by an annual average of 2.0% in 1980–90, by 3.4% per year in 1990–95 and by 2.0% in 1996.

Agriculture (including forestry and fishing) contributed an estimated 12.5% of GDP at current prices in 1996. An estimated 28.0% of the economically active population were employed in the agricultural sector in that year. The principal cash crops are bananas, coffee and cocoa. The seafood sector, particularly the shrimp industry, expanded rapidly in the 1980s, and in 1995 Ecuador was the second largest producer of shrimps in the world. Ecuador's extensive forests yield valuable hardwoods, and the country is a leading producer of balsawood. Exports of cut flowers increased from US $0.5m. in 1985 to $99m. in 1996. During 1990–95 agricultural GDP increased by an annual average of 2.5%.

Industry (including mining, manufacturing, construction and power) employed 18.1% of the labour force in 1990, and provided an estimated 39.0% of GDP in 1996. During 1990–95 industrial GDP increased by an annual average of 4.9%.

Mining and petroleum-refining contributed an estimated 11.1% of GDP in 1996, although the mining sector employed only 0.6% of the labour force in 1990. Petroleum and its derivatives remained the major exports in 1996. In that year some 84.4m. barrels of crude petroleum were exported, earning some US $1,521m. in export revenue. Natural gas is extracted, but only a small proportion is retained. Gold, silver, copper, antimony and zinc are also mined.

Manufacturing contributed an estimated 22.7% of GDP (excluding petroleum-refining) in 1996, and employed 11.2% of the labour force in 1990. Measured by the value of output, the most important branches of manufacturing in 1994 were food products (accounting for 26.8% of the total), petroleum refineries (19.3%), chemicals (17.3%) and transport equipment (5.2%). During 1990–95 manufacturing GDP increased by an annual average of 3.2%.

Energy is derived principally from thermoelectric and hydroelectric plants. Imports of mineral fuels and lubricants comprised only 3.0% of the value of total imports in 1994.

The services sector contributed an estimated 48.5% of GDP in 1996. Around 46% of the active population were employed in this sector in 1990. The sector's GDP increased at an average annual rate of 2.7% during 1990–95.

In 1996 Ecuador recorded a visible trade surplus of US $1,402m., and a surplus of $293m. on the current account of the balance of payments. In 1995 the principal source of imports (31.2%) was the USA, which was also the principal market for exports (42.7%). Other major trading partners were Japan, Colombia, Germany, Italy and the Republic of Korea. The principal exports in 1996 were petroleum and petroleum derivatives (36.3%), bananas (19.9%) and seafood and seafood products (18.8%). The principal imports in 1994 were machinery and transport equipment (48.0%), chemicals (16.6%) and basic manufactures (15.9%).

In 1996 there was an estimated budgetary deficit of some 1,611,600m. sucres. In that year some 40% of government expenditure was financed by revenue from petroleum. Ecuador's total external debt was US $13,957m. at the end of 1995, of which $12,032m. was long-term public debt. In that year the cost of debt-servicing was equivalent to 26.7% of the total value of exports of goods and services. Official development assistance was equivalent to 1.4% of GNP in 1994. The average annual rate of inflation in 1985–93 was 47.1%. The rate averaged 27.4% in 1994, declining further to 22.9% in 1995, before increasing to some 24.4% in 1996. An estimated 14.3% of the labour force were unemployed in 1990. In 1994 some 7.1% of the labour force in urban areas were unemployed.

Ecuador is a member of the Andean Community (see p. 106), the Organization of American States (OAS—see p. 219) and of the Asociación Latinoamericana de Integración (ALADI—p. 261). In November 1992 Ecuador withdrew from the Organization of the Petroleum Exporting Countries (OPEC—p. 227) and announced its intention of seeking associate status. In August 1995 Ecuador joined the World Trade Organization (WTO—p. 244).

In early 1993 Ecuador's proven petroleum reserves almost tripled, following discoveries in the Amazon region, and in 1994 and 1995 the Government signed contracts with numerous companies for further exploration and drilling (including rights to explore areas in the eastern Amazon, which had previously been withheld owing to indigenous and environmental protests). Production continued to increase in 1996, and in August 1997 work to expand the capacity of the trans-Ecuadorean pipeline from 330,000 b/d to 410,000 b/d began. Ecuador's economy was adversely affected in 1995 by the border conflict with Peru (which, according to some analysts, cost the country a total of US $680m. directly and indirectly), and in 1997 by the political crisis (see above), which resulted in economic instability and a decrease in foreign investment. The implementation of a privatization programme, first proposed in 1992, was repeatedly impeded by political turmoil and trade union opposition (including several general strikes). Flooding of the coastal lowlands in mid-1997, caused by El Niño (a periodic warming of the tropical Pacific Ocean), adversely affected various cash crops and fishing catches.

Social Welfare

Social insurance is compulsory for all employees. Benefits are available for sickness, industrial accidents, disability, maternity, old age, widowhood and orphanhood. Hospitals and welfare institutions are administered by Central Public Assistance Boards. Budgetary expenditure on social welfare and labour was 134,697m. sucres (2.4% of total spending) in 1994. In 1993 there were 433 hospitals and 12,149 physicians in the country. Budgetary expenditure on health and community development by the central Government was 319,470m. sucres (5.8% of total spending) in 1994.

Education

Education is compulsory for six years, to be undertaken between six and 14 years of age, and all state schools are free. Private schools continue to play a vital role in the educational system. Primary education begins at six years of age and lasts for six years. Secondary education, in general and specialized technical or humanities schools, begins at the age of 12 and lasts for up to six years, comprising two equal cycles of three years each. In 1992 the total enrolment at primary and secondary schools was equivalent to 90% of the school-age population (123% in primary schools and 55% in secondary schools). In 1993/94 there were 16,825 primary schools and 2,868 secondary schools. University courses extend for up to six years, and include programmes for teacher training. A number of adult schools and literacy centres have been built, aimed at reducing the rate of adult illiteracy, which averaged an estimated 9.9% (males 8.0%; females 11.8%) in 1995. Budgetary expenditure on education and culture by the central Government was estimated at 1,066,535m. sucres (19.3% of total spending) in 1994. In many rural areas, Quechua and other indigenous Indian languages are used in education.

Public Holidays

1998: 1 January (New Year's Day), 6 January (Epiphany), 23–24 February (Carnival), 9 April (Holy Thursday), 10 April (Good Friday), 11 April (Easter Saturday), 1 May (Labour Day), 24 May (Battle of Pichincha), 11 June (Corpus Christi), 24 July (Birth of Simón Bolívar), 10 August (Independence of Quito), 9 October (Independence of Guayaquil), 12 October (Discovery of America), 1 November (All Saints' Day), 2 November (All Souls' Day), 3 November (Independence of Cuenca), 6 December (Foundation of Quito), 25 December (Christmas Day).

1999: 1 January (New Year's Day), 6 January (Epiphany), 15–16 February (Carnival), 1 April (Holy Thursday), 2 April (Good Friday), 3 April (Easter Saturday), 1 May (Labour Day), 24 May (Battle of Pichincha), 3 June (Corpus Christi), 24 July (Birth of Simón Bolívar), 10 August (Independence of Quito), 9 October (Independence of Guayaquil), 12 October (Discovery of America), 1 November (All Saints' Day), 2 November (All Souls' Day), 3 November (Independence of Cuenca), 6 December (Foundation of Quito), 25 December (Christmas Day).

Weights and Measures

The metric system is in force.

Statistical Survey

Sources (unless otherwise stated): Banco Central del Ecuador, Quito; Ministerio de Industrias, Comercio, Integración y Pesquería, Quito; Instituto Nacional de Estadística y Censos, 10 de Agosto 229, Quito; tel. (2) 519-320.

Area and Population

AREA, POPULATION AND DENSITY

Area (sq km)	272,045*
Population (census results)†	
28 November 1982	8,060,712
25 November 1990	
Males	4,796,412
Females	4,851,777
Total	9,648,189
Population (official estimates at mid-year)†	
1994	11,221,070
1995	11,460,117
1996	11,698,496
Density (per sq km) at mid-1996	43.0

* 105,037 sq miles.

† Figures exclude nomadic tribes of indigenous Indians. Census results also exclude any adjustment for underenumeration, estimated to have been 5.6% in 1982 and 6.3% in 1990.

PROVINCES (official estimates, mid-1995)*

	Population	Capital
Azuay	578,229	Cuenca
Bolívar	175,342	Guaranda
Cañar	205,818	Azogues
Carchi	156,803	Tulcán
Cotopaxi	296,647	Latacunga
Chimborazo	402,914	Riobamba
El Oro	500,707	Machala
Esmeraldas	372,303	Esmeraldas
Guayas	3,055,907	Guayaquil
Imbabura	308,047	Ibarra
Loja	411,010	Loja
Los Ríos	608,402	Babahoyo
Manabí	1,172,814	Portoviejo
Morona Santiago	124,133	Macas
Napo	137,234	Tena
Pastaza	54,139	Puyo
Pichincha	2,181,315	Quito
Sucumbíos	117,629	Nueva Loja
Tungurahua	415,372	Ambato
Zamora Chinchipe	83,379	Zamora
Archipiélago de Colón (Galápagos)	13,239	Puerto Baquerizo (Isla San Cristóbal)
Total	11,371,383	

* Figures exclude persons in unspecified areas, totalling 88,734.

PRINCIPAL TOWNS (estimated population at mid-1995)

Guayaquil	1,877,031	Ambato	151,134
Quito (capital)	1,401,389	Manta	149,353
Cuenca	239,896	Milagro	114,229
Machala	184,588	Esmeraldas	113,488
Santo Domingo	165,090	Riobamba	111,416
Portoviejo	159,566	Loja	111,086

BIRTHS, MARRIAGES AND DEATHS
(excluding nomadic Indian tribes)

	Registered live births		Registered marriages		Registered deaths	
	Number	Rate (per 1,000)	Number	Rate (per 1,000)	Number	Rate (per 1,000)
1992	309,683	28.8	68,337	6.4	53,430	5.0
1993	314,522	28.6	68,193	6.2	52,453	4.8
1994	350,838	31.3	71,289	6.4	51,165	4.6

Expectation of life (UN estimates, years at birth, 1990-95): 68.8 (males 66.4, females 71.4) (Source: UN, *World Population Prospects: The 1994 Revision*).

ECONOMICALLY ACTIVE POPULATION*
(ISIC Major Divisions, 1990 census)

	Males	Females	Total
Agriculture, hunting, forestry and fishing	904,701	131,011	1,035,712
Mining and quarrying	18,849	2,021	20,870
Manufacturing	248,157	122,181	370,338
Electricity, gas and water	10,741	1,919	12,660
Construction	192,034	4,682	196,716
Trade, restaurants and hotels	295,855	180,875	476,730
Transport, storage and communications	123,807	7,277	131,084
Financing, insurance, real estate and business services	54,043	27,314	81,357
Community, social and personal services	483,821	354,308	838,129
Activities not adequately defined	111,919	45,811	157,730
Total labour force	2,443,927	877,399	3,321,326

* Figures refer to persons aged 8 years and over, excluding those seeking work for the first time, totalling 38,441 (males 27,506; females 10,935).

Agriculture

PRINCIPAL CROPS ('000 metric tons)

	1994	1995	1996
Wheat	20	20	23
Rice (paddy)	1,420	1,291	1,346
Barley	32	32	40
Maize	581	613	855
Potatoes	531	473	460
Cassava (Manioc)	77	76	76*
Dry beans	39	41	51
Soybeans (Soya beans)	194	91	88
Seed cotton	15	17	18
Palm kernels	32	30	39*
Coconuts	57	73	73*
Pumpkins, squash and gourds*	45	40	40
Sugar cane*	7,000	6,750	6,750
Oranges	88	86	87
Other citrus fruits	73	65	75*
Pineapples	62	53	54
Bananas	5,086	5,403	5,309
Plantains	922	681	681*
Coffee (green)	187	148	155
Cocoa beans	81	86	88

* FAO estimate(s).

Source: FAO, *Production Yearbook*.

LIVESTOCK ('000 head)

	1994	1995	1996
Cattle	4,937	4,995	5,105
Sheep	1,690	1,692	1,709
Pigs	2,546	2,618	2,621
Horses*	515	520	520
Goats	369	295	307
Asses*	264	265	265
Mules*	153	154	154
Poultry	60,000	62,000	63,000

* FAO estimates.

Source: FAO, *Production Yearbook*.

LIVESTOCK PRODUCTS ('000 metric tons)

	1994	1995	1996
Beef and veal	127	149	150
Mutton and lamb*	5	6	6
Pig meat*	82	89	103
Goat meat*	2	2	2
Poultry meat*	95	103	112
Cows' milk	1,823	1,870	1,848
Butter*	5	5	5
Cheese*	6	6	6
Hen eggs	54	55	55*
Wool:			
greasy*	2	2	2
clean*	1	1	1
Cattle hides (fresh)*	28	33	33

* FAO estimate(s).

Source: FAO, *Production Yearbook*.

Forestry

ROUNDWOOD REMOVALS ('000 cubic metres, excluding bark)

	1992	1993	1994
Sawlogs, veneer logs and logs for sleepers	2,793	680	884
Pulpwood	184	692	900
Other industrial wood	291	82	107
Fuel wood	4,231	5,000	5,800
Total	7,499	6,454	7,691

Source: FAO, *Yearbook of Forest Products*.

SAWNWOOD PRODUCTION ('000 cubic metres, including railway sleepers)

	1992	1993	1994
Coniferous (softwood)	8*	39	51
Broadleaved (hardwood)	900	157	204
Total	908	196	255

* FAO estimate.

Source: FAO, *Yearbook of Forest Products*.

Fishing

('000 metric tons, live weight)

	1993	1994	1995
Freshwater fishes	3.5	0.6	0.6
South American pilchard	n.a.	n.a.	75.9
Red-eye round herring	23.5	23.3	4.9
Pacific thread herring	20.3	35.9	40.9
Chub mackerel	45.3	28.2	63.6
Pacific anchoveta	57.7	17.5	9.7
Skipjack tuna	23.8	16.0	31.6
Yellowfin tuna	17.5	23.6	15.9
Chilean jack mackerel	9.9	23.7	174.4
Other fishes	25.0	68.2	67.0
Whiteleg shrimp	92.1	89.9	91.0
Other aquatic creatures	12.8	13.1	16.1
Total catch	331.4	339.9	591.6

Source: FAO, *Yearbook of Fishery Statistics*.

Mining

	1992	1993	1994
Crude petroleum ('000 metric tons)	17,949	19,797	17,391
Natural gas (petajoules)	11	11	10
Natural gasoline ('000 metric tons)	40	48	43
Gold-bearing ores (kilograms)*	1,310	940	1,500

* Estimated gold content (data from the US Bureau of Mines).

Source: UN, *Industrial Commodity Statistics Yearbook*.

1995: Crude petroleum 20.1 million metric tons; Natural gas 10.3 petajoules (Source: UN, *Monthly Bulletin of Statistics*).

Industry

SELECTED PRODUCTS ('000 metric tons, unless otherwise indicated)

	1992	1993	1994
Jet fuels	198	198	181
Kerosene	194	135	80
Motor spirit (gasoline)	1,257	1,288	1,302
Distillate fuel oils	1,497	1,616	1,533
Residual fuel oils	2,627	2,612	2,999
Liquefied petroleum gas	219	255	253
Crude steel	20	27	22
Cement	2,072	2,155	2,085
Electric energy (million kWh)	7,165	7,447	8,163

Source: UN, *Industrial Commodity Statistics Yearbook*.

1995 ('000 metric tons): Motor spirit (gasoline) 1,156; Distillate fuel oils 1,554; Residual fuel oils 3,208 (Source: UN, *Monthly Bulletin of Statistics*).

Finance

CURRENCY AND EXCHANGE RATES

Monetary Units

100 centavos = 1 sucre.

Sterling and Dollar Equivalents (30 September 1997)

£1 sterling = 6,691.0 sucres;
US $1 = 4,142.0 sucres;
10,000 sucres = £1.495 = $2.414.

Average Exchange Rate (sucres per US dollar)

1994 2,196.7
1995 2,564.5
1996 3,189.5

BUDGET (million sucres)

Revenue	1992	1993	1994
Petroleum revenue	1,537,698	2,069,852	2,345,187
Tax revenue	68,627	31,197	42,965
Non-tax revenue	1,469,071	2,038,655	2,302,222
Price increases on petroleum by-products for internal consumption	470,993	851,920	1,172,573
For export	998,078	1,186,735	1,129,649
Non-petroleum revenue	1,570,059	2,162,669	3,138,030
Tax revenue	1,368,994	2,034,925	2,808,630
External trade	274,413	392,470	606,631
Exports	—	—	—
Imports	274,413	392,470	606,631
Domestic taxes	1,094,581	1,642,455	2,201,999
Income tax	253,415	331,231	503,864
Taxes on financial transactions	66,246	43,013	110,576
Taxes on production and consumption	744,757	1,152,491	1,495,902
Other taxes	30,163	115,720	91,657
Non-tax revenue	201,065	127,744	329,400
Transfers	22,034	82,051	164,426
Total	3,129,791	4,314,572	5,647,643

Expenditure	1992	1993	1994
General services	736,416	1,144,175	1,679,092
Education and culture	605,075	746,993	1,066,535
Social welfare and labour	43,092	99,421	134,697
Health and community development	200,421	202,593	319,470
Farming and livestock development	88,631	146,023	230,227
Natural and energy resources	14,121	31,323	47,144
Industry and trade	43,041	25,507	33,674
Transport and communications	126,629	327,585	446,366
Public debt interest	473,826	500,841	898,153
Other purposes	216,730	539,389	677,075
Total	2,547,982	3,763,850	5,532,433

Source: Banco Central del Ecuador.

INTERNATIONAL RESERVES (US $ million at 31 December)

	1994	1995	1996
Gold*	165.6	166.6	166.6
IMF special drawing rights	4.3	3.1	2.7
Reserve position in IMF	25.0	25.5	24.7
Foreign exchange	1,814.9	1,599.0	1,831.1
Total	2,009.8	1,794.2	2,025.1

* National valuation ($400 per troy ounce at 31 December 1994; $402 per ounce at 31 December 1995 and 1996).

Source: IMF, *International Financial Statistics*.

MONEY SUPPLY ('000 million sucres at 31 December)

	1994	1995	1996
Currency outside banks	1,122.4	1,375.8	1,882.4
Demand deposits at deposit money banks	2,217.8	2,339.2	2,977.2
Total money*	4,041.5	4,151.2	5,349.5

* Includes private-sector deposits at the Central Bank.

Source: IMF, *International Financial Statistics*.

COST OF LIVING

(Consumer Price Index; annual averages for middle- and low-income families in urban area; base: 1990 = 100)

	1992	1993	1994
Food (incl. beverages)	228.9	324.7	405.2
Rent	229.5	347.7	514.5
Clothing (incl. footwear)	222.5	308.8	367.5
Fuel and light	179.1	276.9	307.5
All items (incl. others)	230.0	333.9	424.4

Source: ILO, *Yearbook of Labour Statistics*.

1995: Food 489.3; All items 521.5

1996: Food 605.8; All items 648.8.

Source (for 1995 and 1996): UN, *Monthly Bulletin of Statistics*.

NATIONAL ACCOUNTS

Expenditure on the Gross Domestic Product

('000 million sucres at current prices)

	1994	1995	1996
Government final consumption expenditure	3,427	5,789	7,171
Private final consumption expenditure	25,025	30,701	38,207
Increase in stocks	82	60	40
Gross fixed capital formation	6,852	8,537	10,385
Statistical discrepancy	—	-2	—
Total domestic expenditure	35,386	45,085	55,803
Exports of goods and services	9,743	13,230	17,143
Less Imports of goods and services	8,651	12,310	15,312
GDP in purchasers' values	36,478	46,005	57,634
GDP at constant 1990 prices	9,502	9,723	10,008

Source: IMF, *International Financial Statistics*.

Gross Domestic Product by Economic Activity

(million sucres at constant 1975 prices)

	1991	1992	1993
Agriculture, hunting, forestry and fishing	33,988	35,154	34,555
Petroleum and other mining*	23,251	24,599	27,298
Manufacturing*	28,951	29,989	30,731
Electricity, gas and water	2,841	2,919	2,980
Construction	5,274	5,256	5,032
Trade, restaurants and hotels	28,557	29,420	29,919
Transport, storage and communications	16,289	17,223	17,992
Finance, insurance, real estate and business services	20,806	21,479	23,455
Community, social and personal services	10,757	11,112	11,264
Sub-total	170,714	177,151	183,226
Less Imputed bank service charge	5,661	5,984	7,811
Domestic product of industries	165,053	171,167	175,415
Government services	16,169	16,114	15,754
Domestic services of households	844	864	881
Sub-total	182,066	188,145	192,050
Customs duties (net of import subsidies)	8,572	9,291	9,397
GDP in purchasers' values	190,638	197,436	201,447

*Petroleum-refining is included in mining and excluded from manufacturing.

Source: UN, *National Accounts Statistics*.

BALANCE OF PAYMENTS (US $ million)

	1994	1995	1996
Exports of goods f.o.b.	3,843	4,411	4,890
Imports of goods f.o.b.	-3,280	-4,057	-3,488
Trade balance	563	354	1,402
Exports of services	745	854	858
Imports of services	-922	-983	-975
Balance on goods and services	386	225	1,285
Other income received	52	82	73
Other income paid	-1,262	-1,273	-1,355
Balance on goods, services and income	-824	-966	3
Current transfers received	164	250	358
Current transfers paid	-19	-19	-68
Current balance	-679	-735	293
Capital account (net)	43	—	7
Direct investment from abroad	531	470	447
Other investment assets	-9	-16	-5
Other investment liabilities	-630	1,098	668
Net errors and omissions	-22	-1,336	-1,494
Overall balance	-766	-519	-84

Source: IMF, *International Financial Statistics*.

External Trade

PRINCIPAL COMMODITIES (distribution by SITC, US $ million)

Imports c.i.f.	1992	1993	1994
Food and live animals	82.9	100.0	178.9
Cereals and cereal preparations	34.7	59.2	70.7
Crude materials (inedible) except fuels	59.4	70.6	84.3
Mineral fuels, lubricants, etc.	101.0	42.9	108.5
Chemicals and related products	437.3	390.4	602.6
Organic chemicals	69.9	62.7	90.3
Medicinal and pharmaceutical products	82.0	95.1	115.2
Medicaments	36.0	71.9	84.2
Artificial resins, plastic materials, etc.	79.1	62.8	140.7
Products of polymerization, etc.	60.9	44.2	79.0
Basic manufactures	404.0	445.8	576.6
Paper, paperboard and manufactures	48.8	49.6	103.6
Paper and paperboard (not cut to size or shape)	41.2	44.5	91.1
Iron and steel	134.6	178.9	186.9
Ingots and other primary forms	24.9	63.8	58.6
Machinery and transport equipment	1,113.3	1,250.7	1,737.3
Power-generating machinery and equipment	85.3	105.0	99.2
Machinery specialized for particular industries	164.0	221.4	184.0
General industrial machinery, equipment and parts	188.2	219.5	235.0
Telecommunications and sound equipment	59.4	77.8	93.1
Other electrical machinery, apparatus, etc.	130.3	87.5	117.1
Road vehicles and parts*	415.7	468.9	915.9
Passenger motor cars (excl. buses)	209.9	266.1	418.4
Motor vehicles for goods transport, etc.	131.7	130.3	297.6
Lorries and trucks	125.1	126.7	287.5
Other road motor vehicles	2.4	18.6	98.4
Parts and accessories for cars, buses, lorries, etc.*	62.6	42.8	77.3
Miscellaneous manufactured articles	260.5	209.0	281.8
Printed matter	117.4	68.9	72.9
Total (incl. others)	2,501.3	2,552.7	3,622.0

*Excluding tyres, engines and electrical parts.

Exports f.o.b.	1992	1993	1994
Food and live animals	1,506.6	1,407.5	2,056.4
Fish, crustaceans and molluscs	631.3	593.8	734.9
Fresh, chilled, frozen, salted or dried crustaceans and molluscs	529.2	468.2	557.4
Prepared or preserved fish, crustaceans and molluscs.	44.2	71.7	102.8
Prepared or preserved fish	43.6	70.8	102.2
Vegetables and fruit	707.3	588.2	742.6
Fruit and nuts (excl. oil nuts), fresh or dried	679.0	560.7	712.4
Bananas and plantains	675.9	557.5	708.4
Coffee, tea, cocoa and spices	147.3	190.5	517.4
Coffee and coffee substitutes	71.8	107.4	413.8
Coffee (incl. husks and skins) and substitutes containing coffee	53.9	80.2	368.8
Unroasted coffee, husks and skins	51.0	79.2	365.7
Cocoa	68.7	78.4	101.0
Crude materials (inedible) except fuels	58.6	67.2	101.3
Mineral fuels, lubricants, etc.	1,336.7	1,249.9	1,304.9
Petroleum, petroleum products, etc.	1,336.7	1,249.9	1,304.9
Crude petroleum oils, etc.	1,251.0	1,149.0	1,185.0
Refined petroleum products	85.7	100.8	119.9
Basic manufactures	61.0	83.9	118.8
Machinery and transport equipment	21.3	70.0	91.4
Total (incl. others)	3,042.3	3,020.0	3,843.4

Source: UN, *International Trade Statistics Yearbook.*

PRINCIPAL TRADING PARTNERS (US $ million)

Imports c.i.f.	1993	1994	1995
Argentina	41.2	50.0	74.6
Belgium and Luxembourg	20.2	34.5	59.4
Brazil	99.3	227.0	186.8
Canada	29.4*	53.3*	84.7*
Chile	48.9	66.6	111.1
Colombia	99.5	297.9	396.2
France	49.3	37.5	59.2
Germany	131.1	217.0	192.5
Italy	193.3	138.1	104.2
Japan	344.7	515.5	328.2
Korea, Republic	43.4*	102.8*	102.1*
Mexico	59.2	150.8	153.4
Panama	80.7*	74.0*	68.7*
Peru	34.8	52.4	39.7
Spain	119.3	82.9	92.6
Switzerland	35.5	40.0	42.5
Taiwan	34.4	59.9	61.2
United Kingdom	37.5	35.0	51.5
USA	823.6	950.3	1,290.4
Venezuela	48.6	160.0	253.6
Total (incl. others)	2,562.2	3,622.0	4,137.8

Exports f.o.b.	1993	1994	1995
Argentina	53.4*	71.5*	n.a.
Belgium and Luxembourg	60.1	105.8	93.2
Chile	117.5	166.5	193.2
Colombia	147.3	226.0	246.3
France	45.7*	64.0*	n.a.
Germany	81.7	188.8	166.3
Italy	122.5	155.3	172.0
Japan	52.6	76.0	116.7
Korea, Republic	281.6*	289.6*	n.a.
Mexico	42.7	76.4	54.0
Netherlands	43.3*	49.3*	n.a.
Panama	88.1*	101.4*	n.a.
Peru	130.9	156.8	68.3
Poland	14.3*	41.6*	n.a.
Russia	24.2*	53.3*	n.a.
Spain	82.6	114.6	148.7
USA	1,410.2	1,630.1	1,847.4
Total (incl. others)	3,061.6	3,843.4	4,321.9

* Provisional (Source: UN, *International Trade Statistics Yearbook*).

Source: mainly Banco Central del Ecuador.

Transport

RAILWAYS (traffic)

	1992	1993	1994
Passenger-kilometres (million)	53	39	27
Net ton-kilometres (million)	3	3	9

Source: UN, *Statistical Yearbook.*

ROAD TRAFFIC (motor vehicles in use at 31 December)

	1994	1995	1996*
Passenger cars	380,684	446,192	485,000
Buses and coaches	9,388	8,753	6,580
Lorries and vans	49,070	43,340	44,550
Road tractors	2,441	2,813	3,200

* Estimates.

Source: IRF, *World Road Statistics.*

SHIPPING

Merchant Fleet (registered at 31 December)

	1994	1995	1996
Number of vessels	147	136	145
Total displacement ('000 grt)	270	168	178

Source: Lloyd's Register of Shipping, *World Fleet Statistics.*

International Sea-borne Freight Traffic ('000 metric tons)

	1988*	1989*	1990
Goods loaded	8,402	10,020	11,783
Goods unloaded	2,518	2,573	1,958

* Source: UN, *Monthly Bulletin of Statistics.*

CIVIL AVIATION (traffic on scheduled services)

	1992	1993	1994
Passengers carried ('000)	1,120	1,243	1,126
Passenger-km (million)	1,604	1,800	1,410
Total ton-km (million)	214	245	162

Source: UN, *Statistical Yearbook.*

Tourism

	1992	1993	1994
Tourist arrivals ('000)	403	471	482
Tourism receipts (US $ million)	192	230	252

Source: UN, *Statistical Yearbook*.

Communications Media

	1992	1993	1994
Radio receivers ('000 in use)	3,510	3,580	3,670
Television receivers ('000 in use)	940	970	990
Daily newspapers	36	n.a.	24
Telephones ('000 main lines in use)	531	598	658

Source: mainly UNESCO, *Statistical Yearbook*.

Mobile Cellular Telephones: 17,860 subscribers in 1994; **Telefax Stations:** 30,000 in use in 1993 (Source: UN, *Statistical Yearbook*).

Education

(1993/94)

	Teachers	Pupils/ Students
Pre-primary	7,020	127,355
Primary	63,708	1,742,984
Secondary:		
General	59,449	785,522
Teacher-training	n.a.	7,888
Vocational	16,838*	260,850*
Higher:		
Universities, etc	12,520*	186,456*
Distance-learning	150*	11,158*
Other institutions	n.a.	2,795†

* 1989 figure. † 1984 figure.

Source: mainly Ministerio de Educación y Cultura.

Directory

The Constitution

The 1945 Constitution was suspended in June 1970. In January 1978 a referendum was held to choose between two draft Constitutions, prepared by various special constitutional committees. In a 90% poll, 43% voted for a proposed new Constitution and 32.1% voted for a revised version of the 1945 Constitution. The new Constitution came into force on 10 August 1979. In November 1997 a national assembly was elected for the purpose of reviewing the Constitution. The main provisions of the Constitution are summarized below:

CHAMBER OF REPRESENTATIVES

The Constitution of 1979 states that legislative power is exercised by the Chamber of Representatives which sits for a period of 60 days from 10 August. The Chamber is required to set up four full-time Legislative Commissions to consider draft laws when the House is in recess. Special sessions of the Chamber of Representatives may be called.

Representatives are elected for four years from lists of candidates drawn up by legally recognized parties. Twelve are elected nationally; two from each Province with over 100,000 inhabitants, one from each Province with fewer than 100,000; and one for every 300,000 citizens or fractions of over 200,000. Representatives are eligible for re-election.

In addition to its law-making duties, the Chamber ratifies treaties, elects members of the Supreme and Superior Courts, and (from panels presented by the President) the Comptroller-General, the Attorney-General and the Superintendent of Banks. It is also able to overrule the President's amendment of a bill which it has submitted for Presidential approval. It may reconsider a rejected bill after a year or request a referendum, and may revoke the President's declaration of a state of emergency. The budget is considered in the first instance by the appropriate Legislative Commission and disagreements are resolved in the Chamber.

PRESIDENT

The presidential term is four years, and there is no re-election. The President appoints the Cabinet, the Governors of Provinces, diplomatic representatives and certain administrative employees, and is responsible for the direction of international relations. In the event of foreign invasion or internal disturbance, the President may declare a state of emergency and must notify the Chamber, or the Tribunal for Constitutional Guarantees if the Chamber is not in session.

As in other post-war Latin-American Constitutions, particular emphasis is laid on the functions and duties of the State, which is given wide responsibilities with regard to the protection of labour; assisting in the expansion of production; protecting the Indian and peasant communities; and organizing the distribution and development of uncultivated lands, by expropriation where necessary.

Voting is compulsory for every Ecuadorean citizen who is literate and over 18 years of age. An optional vote has been extended to illiterates (under 15% of the population by 1981). The Constitution guarantees liberty of conscience in all its manifestations, and states that the law shall not make any discrimination for religious reasons.

The Government

HEAD OF STATE

President: Dr FABIÁN ALARCÓN RIVERA (assumed office as acting President in February 1997).

Vice-President: Dra ROSALIA ARTEAGA.

CABINET
(January 1998)

Minister of Government and Justice (Interior): CÉSAR VERDUGA.

Minister of Foreign Affairs: JOSÉ AYALA LASSO.

Minister of Finance and Public Credit: MARCOS FLORES.

Minister of Industry, Trade, Integration and Fisheries: BENIGNO SOTOMAYOR.

Minister of Agriculture and Livestock: ALFREDO SALTOS GUALE.

Minister of Energy and Mines: RAÚL BACA CARBO.

Minister of the Environment: JAIME GALARZA ZAVALA.

Minister of Labour and Human Resources: EDGAR RIVADENEIRA.

Minister of Education and Culture: MARIO JARAMILLO.

Minister of National Defence: Gen. RAMIRO RICAURTE.

Minister of Public Health: ASDRUBAL DE LA TORRE.

Minister of Social Welfare: GUSTAVO BAQUERO.

Minister of Public Works and Communications: HOMERO TORRES.

Minister of Tourism: JUANA VALLEJO.

Minister of Housing and Urban Development: DIEGO PONCE.

Secretary-General for Public Administration: WILSON MERINO.

National Secretary of Administrative Development: JOSÉ ZURITA MARCIAL.

Secretary of State for Communication: MARIANA ORDOÑEZ DE LARREA.

Co-ordinator of the Social Expenditure Fund (FISE): JORGE BUSTAMENTE.

State Comptroller-General: BENJAMÍN TERÁN.

State Procurator-General: Dr Leonidas Plaza.

The following are, *ex officio*, members of the Cabinet: the Chairman of the National Monetary Board, the General Manager of the State Bank, the General Manager of the Central Bank, the Secretary-General of the National Planning Council (CONADE), the President of the National Financial Corporation, the President of the National Modernization Council (CONAM), the Presidential Private Secretary, the Subsecretary-General of Public Administration and the Presidential Press Secretary.

MINISTRIES

Office of the President: Palacio Nacional, García Moreno 1043, Quito; tel. (2) 216-300; telex 23751.

Office of the Vice-President: Manuel Larrea y Arenas, Edif. Consejo Provincial de Pichincha, 21°, Quito; tel. (2) 504-953; telex 22058; fax (2) 503-379.

Ministry of Agriculture and Livestock: Avda Eloy Alfaro y Amazonas, Quito; tel. (2) 504-433; fax (2) 564-531.

Ministry of Education and Culture: Mejía 322, Quito; tel. (2) 216-224; telex 1267.

Ministry of Energy and Mines: Santa Prisca 223 y Manuel Larrea, Quito; tel. (2) 570-141; telex 2271; fax (2) 2271.

Ministry of the Environment: Quito.

Ministry of Finance and Public Credit: Avda 10 de Agosto 1661 y Jorge Washington, Quito; tel. (2) 544-500; telex 2358; fax (2) 530-703.

Ministry of Foreign Affairs: Avda 10 de Agosto y Carrión, Quito; tel. (2) 230-100; telex 22705; fax (2) 564-873.

Ministry of Housing and Urban Development: Quito.

Ministry of Industry, Trade, Integration and Fisheries: Avda Eloy Alfaro y Amazonas, Quito; tel. (2) 527-988; telex 2166; fax (2) 503-549.

Ministry of the Interior (Government and Justice): Espejo y Benalcázar, Quito; tel. (2) 580-970; telex 2354; fax (2) 442-771.

Ministry of Labour and Human Resources: Ponce y Luis Felipe Borja, Quito; tel. (2) 524-666; telex 2898.

Ministry of National Defence: Exposición 208, Quito; tel. (2) 216-150; telex 3986.

Ministry of Public Health: Juan Larrea 444, Quito; tel. (2) 529-163; telex 2677; fax 569-786.

Ministry of Public Works and Communications: Avda Juan León Mera y Orellana, Quito; tel. (2) 222-749; fax (2) 223-077.

Ministry of Social Welfare: Robles 850 y Amazonas, Quito; tel. (2) 540-750; telex 2497.

Ministry of Tourism: Avda 6 de Diciembre 1184, Quito; tel. (2) 561-180; telex 2663.

Office for Public Administration: Palacio Nacional, García Morena 1043, Quito; tel. (2) 515-990.

Office of the Secretary of Administrative Development: Quito.

Office of State Communication: Quito.

Office of the State Comptroller-General: Quito.

Office of the State Procurator-General: Quito.

President and Legislature

PRESIDENT*

Elections of 19 May and 7 July 1996

Candidate	% of votes cast in first ballot	% of votes cast in second ballot
Jaime Nebot Saadi (PSC)	27.4	45.5
Abdalá Bucaram Ortiz (PRE)	25.5	54.5
Freddy Ehlers (Movimiento Nuevo País-Pachakutik)	20.9	—
Rodrigo Paz (DP)	13.5	—
Total (incl. others)	100.0	100.0

* In accordance with the election results, Abdalá Bucaram Ortiz took office as President on 10 August 1996. However, on 6 February 1997 the National Congress voted to dismiss him, on grounds of mental incapacity.

CONGRESO NACIONAL

Cámara Nacional de Representantes

President: Dr Heinz Moeller Freile.

Election, 19 May 1996

Political parties	Seats
Partido Social Cristiano (PSC)	27
Partido Roldosista Ecuatoriano (PRE)	19
Democracia Popular (DP)	12
Movimiento Nuevo País-Pachakutik (MNPP)	8
Izquierda Democrática (ID)	4
Movimiento Popular Democrático (MPD)	3
Partido Conservador (PC)	2
Frente Radical Alfarista (FRA)*	2
Acción Popular Revolucionaria Ecuatoriana (APRE)	2
Concentración de Fuerzas Populares (CFP)	1
Independents	2
Total	82

* In alliance with the Partido Liberal Radical (PLR).

Political Organizations

Acción Popular Revolucionaria Ecuatoriana (APRE): centrist; Leader Lt-Gen. Frank Vargas Pazzos.

Coalición Nacional Republicana (CNR): Quito; f. 1986; fmrly Coalición Institucionalista Demócrata (CID).

Concentración de Fuerzas Populares (CFP): Quito; f. 1946; Leader Galo Vayas; Dir Dr Averroes Bucaram Saxida.

Democracia Popular (DP): Calle Luis Saá 153 y Hnos Pazmiño, Casilla 17-01-2300, Quito; tel. (2) 547-654; fax (2) 502-995; f. 1978 as Democracia Popular-Unión Demócrata Cristiana; Christian democrat; Pres. Lic. Absalón Rocha.

Frente Amplio de la Izquierda (FADI): Quito; f. 1977; left-wing alliance comprising the following parties: Partido Comunista Ecuatoriano, Partido Socialista Revolucionario, Movimiento para la Unidad de la Izquierda, Movimiento Revolucionario de la Izquierda Cristiana; Dir Dr René Maugé M.

Frente Radical Alfarista (FRA): Quito; f. 1972; Leader Fabián Alarcón Rivera.

Izquierda Democrática (ID): Polonia 161, entre Vancouver y Eloy Alfaro, Quito; tel. (2) 564-436; telex 21396; fax (2) 569-295; f. 1977; absorbed Fuerzas Armadas Populares Eloy Alfaro—Alfaro Vive ¡Carajo! (AVC) (Eloy Alfaro Popular Armed Forces—Alfaro Lives, Damn It!) in October 1991; Leader Rodrigo Borja Cevallos; National Dir Andrés Vallejo.

Movimiento Independiente para una República Auténtica (MIRA): Quito; f. 1996; Leader Dra Rosalia Arteaga.

Movimiento Nuevo País-Pachakutik (MNPP): Quito; represents indigenous, environmental and social groups; Leader Rafael Pandam.

Movimiento Popular Democrático (MPD): Maoist; Leader Dr Jaime Hurtado González.

Partido Comunista Marxista-Leninista de Ecuador: Sec.-Gen. Camilo Almeyda.

Partido Conservador (PC): Wilsón 578, Quito; tel.(2) 505-061; f. 1855; incorporated Partido Unidad Republicano in 1995; centre-right; Leader Sixto Durán Ballén.

Partido Demócrata (PD): Quito; Leader Dr Francisco Huerta Montalvo.

Partido de Liberación Nacional (PLN): Quito.

Partido Liberal Radical (PLR): Quito; f. 1895; held office from 1895 to 1944 as the Liberal Party, which subsequently divided into various factions; perpetuates the traditions of the Liberal Party; Dir Carlos Julio Plaza A.

Partido Nacionalista Revolucionario (PNR): Calle Pazmiño 245, Of. 500, Quito; f. 1969; supporters of fmr President Dr Carlos Julio Arosemena Monroy; Dir Dr Mauricio Gándara.

Partido Republicano (PR): Quito; Leader Guillermo Sotomayor.

Partido Roldosista Ecuatoriano (PRE): Quito; f. 1982; Dir Abdalá Bucaram Ortiz.

Partido Social Cristiano (PSC): Carrión 548 y Reina Victoria, Casilla 9454, Quito; tel. (2) 568-560; telex 21270; fax (2) 568-562; f. 1951; centre-right party; Pres. Jaime Nebot Saadi; Leaders León Febres Cordero Rivadeneira, Lic. Camilo Ponce Gangotena, Dr Heinz Moeller Freile; Lic. Pascual del Cioppo Aragundi.

Partido Socialista-Frente Amplia (PS-FA): Avda Gran Colombia y Yaguachi, Quito; tel. (2) 221-764; fax (2) 222-184; f. 1926; Pres. Dr MANUEL SALGADO TAMAYO.

Pueblo, Cambio y Democracia (PCD) Popular Roldosista: Quito; f. 1980; centre-left; committed to policies of fmr Pres. Jaime Roldós; Dir LEÓN ROLDÓS AGUILERA; Sec.-Gen. ERNESTO BUENANO CABRERA.

Unión Democrática Popular (UDP): Leader JORGE CHIRIBOGA.

Unión del Pueblo Patriótico (UPP): Quito; Leader Lt-Gen. FRANK VARGAS PAZZOS.

The following guerrilla groups are active:

Combatientes Populares: claims to defend human rights and to fight poverty.

Montoneros Patria Libre (MPL): f. 1986; advocates an end to authoritarianism.

Partido Maoísta-Comunista 'Puka Inti': Sec.-Gen. RAMIRO CELI.

Diplomatic Representation

EMBASSIES IN ECUADOR

Argentina: Avda Amazonas 477, Apdo 2937, Quito; tel. (2) 562-292; telex 2136; Ambassador: RICARDO H. ILLIA.

Austria: Edif. Cofiec, 11°, Avda Patria y Amazonas, Quito; tel. (2) 545-336; fax (2) 564-560; Ambassador: ARTUR SCHUSCHNIGG.

Belgium: Austria 219 e Irlanda, Quito; telex 2767; Ambassador: F. FRANZ.

Bolivia: Calle Ramirez Davalos 258, Quito; Ambassador: EUSEBIO MOREIRA.

Brazil: Avda Amazonas 1429 y Colón, Apdo 231, Quito; tel. (2) 563-846; fax (2) 509-468; Ambassador: OSMAR CHOHFI.

Bulgaria: Calle Colina 331 y Orellana, Quito; tel. (2) 552-553; telex 22047; Chargé d'affaires: LUBOMIR IVANOV.

Canada: Edif. Belmonte, 6°, Avda Corea 126 y Amazonas, Quito; tel. (2) 458-102.

Chile: Edif. Xerox, 4°, Juan Pablo Sanz y Amazonas, Quito; telex 2167; Ambassador: ROBERTO PIZARRO HOFER.

China, People's Republic: Quito; Ambassador: YANG BINWEI.

Colombia: Calle San Javier 169, Casilla 2923, Quito; telex 2156; Ambassador: LAUREANO ALBERTO ARELLANO.

Costa Rica: Roca 536, Reina Victoria, Apdo 9A, Quito; Ambassador: FÉLIX CÓRTEZ.

Cuba: Mercurio 365, entre La Razón y El Vengador, Quito; tel. (2) 458-282; telex 21493; fax (2) 430-594; Ambassador: RENÉ CASTRO.

Dominican Republic: Avda 6 de Diciembre 4629, Quito; Ambassador: MARIO PEÑA.

Egypt: Edif. Araucaria, 9°, Baquedano 222 y Reina Victoria, Apdo 9355, Sucursal 7, Quito; tel. (2) 235-046; telex 2154; Ambassador: KHAIRAT ISSA.

El Salvador: Edif. Albatros, Avda de los Shyris 1240 y Portugal, Apdo 17-17-1402, Quito; tel. (2) 433-823; telex 22931; Ambassador: MAURICIO CASTRO ARAGÓN.

France: Plaza 107 y Avda Patria, Apdo 536, Quito; tel. (2) 560-789; telex 2146; fax (2) 566-424; Ambassador: JOSEPH LAURENT RAPIN.

Germany: Edif. Banco de Colombia, 6°, Avda Patria y 9 de Octubre, Apdo 17-01-537, Quito; tel. (2) 232-660; telex 22222; fax (2) 563-697; Ambassador: Dr WERNER PIECK.

Guatemala: Avda 6 de Diciembre 2636, Quito; Ambassador: JUAN RENDÓN M.

Holy See: (Apostolic Nunciature), Avda Orellana 692, Apdo 17-07-8980, Quito; tel. (2) 505-200; fax (2) 564-810; Apostolic Nuncio: Most Rev. FRANCESCO CANALINI, Titular Archbishop of Valeria.

Honduras: Cordero 279 y Plaza, Quito; telex 2805; Ambassador: ANTONIO MOLINA O.

Hungary: Avda República de El Salvador 733 y Portugal, Casilla 17-03-4549, Quito; tel. (2) 459-700; telex 2255; Chargé d'affaires: GÁBOR KALMÁR.

Israel: Avda Eloy Alfaro 969 y Amazonas, Quito; tel. (2) 565-509; telex 2174; e-mail isremuio@vio.telconet.net; Ambassador: YAAKOV PARAN.

Italy: Calle La Isla 111, Casilla 17-03-72, Quito; tel. (2) 561-077; telex 22715; fax (2) 502-818; Ambassador: PATRIZIO IVAN ARDEMAGNI.

Japan: Juan León Mera 130 y Avda Patria, 7°, Quito; telex 2185; fax (2) 503-670; Ambassador: TETSUO HANAWA.

Korea, Republic: Edif. Banco de Guayaquil, 11°, Calle Reina Victoria 1539 y Colón, Quito; tel. (2) 560-573; telex 2868; Ambassador: CHAI KI OH.

Mexico: Avda 6 de Diciembre 4843 y Naciones Unidas, Casilla 17-11-6371, Quito; tel. (2) 457-820; telex 22395; fax (2) 448-245; Ambassador: ANTONIO RIVA PALACIO LÓPEZ.

Netherlands: Edif. Club de Leones Central, 3°, Avda de las Naciones Unidas entre Avdas 10 de Agosto y Amazonas, Apdo 2840, Quito; telex 2576; Ambassador: Dr J. WEIDEMA.

Panama: Edif. Posada de las Artes, 3°, Diego de Almagro 1550 y Pradera, Apdo 17-07-9017, Quito; tel. (2) 565-234; fax (2) 566-449; Ambassador: JOSÉ MARÍA CABRERA JOVANÉ.

Paraguay: Avda Gaspar de Villarroel 2013 y Amazonas, Casilla 139-A, Quito; tel. (2) 245-871; telex 2260; Ambassador: Dr GILBERTO CANIZA SÁNCHEZ.

Peru: Avda República de El Salvador 495 e Irlanda, Quito; tel. (2) 468-410; fax (2) 252-560; e-mail embpeecuuio.satnet.net; Ambassador: HUGO PALMO.

Poland: Avda Eloy Alfaro 2897 y Portugal, Apdo 6637, Quito; tel. (2) 453-466; telex 21349; fax (2) 446-288; Chargé d'affaires: BOGUSŁAW GAJDAMOWICZ.

Romania: Avda República del Salvador 482 e Irlanda, Quito; telex 2230; Ambassador: GHEORGHE DOBRA.

Russia: Reina Victoria 462 y Roca, Quito; Ambassador: MIKHAIL P. YEMELYANOV.

Slovakia: Gen. Francisco Salazar 459 y Coruña, Quito; telex 2478.

Spain: La Pinta 455 y Amazonas, Casilla 9322, Quito; tel. (2) 564-373; telex 22816; Ambassador: JUAN MANUEL EGEA IBÁÑEZ.

Switzerland: Edif. Xerox, 2°, Juan Pablo Sanz 120 y Amazonas, Casilla 17-11-4815, Quito; tel. (2) 434-948; telex 2592; fax (2) 449-314; Ambassador: PETER VON GRAFFENRIED.

United Kingdom: Avda González Suárez 111, Casilla 17-01-314, Quito; tel. (2) 560-670; fax (2) 560-730; Ambassador: JOHN FORBES-MEYLER.

USA: Avda 12 de Octubre y Patria 120, Quito; tel. (2) 562-890; telex 2329; fax (2) 502-052; Ambassador: LESLIE ALEXANDER.

Uruguay: Edif. Josueth González, 9°, Avda 6 de diciembre 2816 y James Orton, Casilla 17-12-282, Quito; tel. (2) 563-762; fax (2) 563-763; Ambassador: JOSÉ MARÍA ALZAMORA.

Venezuela: Coruña 1733 y Belo Horizonte, Apdo 17-01-688, Quito; tel. (2) 564-626; telex 22160; fax (2) 502-630; Ambassador: FREDDY CHRISTIAN.

Yugoslavia: Gen. Francisco Salazar 958 y 12 de Octubre, Quito; tel. (2) 526-218; telex 2633; Ambassador: SAMUILO PROTIĆ.

Judicial System

Attorney-General: ROBERTO GÓMEZ MERA.

Supreme Court of Justice: Palacio de Justicia, Avda 6 de Diciembre y Piedrahita, Quito; tel. (2) 236-550; telex 22976; fax (2) 551-516; f. 1830; Pres. HÉCTOR ROMERO.

Higher or Divisional Courts: Ambato, Azogues, Babahoyo, Cuenca, Esmeraldas, Guaranda, Guayaquil, Ibarra, Latacunga, Loja, Machala, Portoviejo, Quito, Riobamba and Tulcán; 90 judges.

Provincial Courts: there are 40 Provincial Courts in 15 districts; other courts include 94 Criminal; 219 Civil; 29 dealing with labour disputes; 17 Rent Tribunals.

Special Courts: National Court for Juveniles.

Religion

There is no state religion but more than 90% of the population are Roman Catholics. There are representatives of various Protestant Churches and of the Jewish faith in Quito and Guayaquil.

CHRISTIANITY

The Roman Catholic Church

Ecuador comprises four archdioceses, 11 dioceses, seven Apostolic Vicariates and one Apostolic Prefecture. At 31 December 1995 there were an estimated 11,018,538 adherents in the country, equivalent to some 93.8% of the population.

Bishops' Conference: Conferencia Episcopal Ecuatoriana, Avda América 1805 y La Gasca, Apdo 17-01-1081, Quito; tel. (2) 223-144; fax (2) 501-429; f. 1939; Pres. JOSÉ MARIO RUIZ NAVAS, Archbishop of Portoviejo.

Archbishop of Cuenca: LUIS ALBERTO LUNA TOBAR, Arzobispado, Calle Bolívar 7-64, Apdo 01-01-0046, Cuenca; tel. (7) 831-651; fax (7) 827-792.

Archbishop of Guayaquil: JUAN IGNACIO LARREA HOLGUÍN, Arzobispado, Calle Clemente Ballén 501 y Chimborazo, Apdo 09-01-0254, Guayaquil; tel. (4) 322-778; fax (4) 329-695.

Archbishop of Portoviejo: JOSÉ MARIO RUIZ NAVAS, Arzobispado, Calle Alajuela, Apdo 24, Portoviejo; tel. (5) 637-127; fax (5) 634-428.

Archbishop of Quito: ANTONIO JOSÉ GONZÁLEZ ZUMÁRRAGA, Arzobispado, Calle Chile 1140 y Venezuela, Apdo 17-01-00106, Quito; tel. (2) 214-429; fax (2) 572-898.

The Anglican Communion

Anglicans in Ecuador are under the jurisdiction of Province IX of the Episcopal Church in the USA. The country is divided into two dioceses, one of which, Central Ecuador, is a missionary diocese.

Bishop of Littoral Ecuador: Rt Rev. ALFREDO MORANTE, Calle Bogotá 1010, Barrio Centenario, Apdo 5250, Guayaquil.

Bishop of Central Ecuador: Rt Rev. JOSÉ NEPTALI LARREA MORENO, Apdo 353-A, Quito.

The Baptist Church

The Baptist Convention of Ecuador: Casilla 3236, Guayaquil; tel. (4) 384-865; Pres. Rev. HAROLT SANTE MATA; Sec. JORGE MORENO CHAVARRÍA.

The Methodist Church

The Methodist Church: Evangelical United Church, Rumipamba 915, Casilla 17-03-236, Quito; tel. (2) 456-714; fax (2) 529-933; 800 mems, 2,000 adherents.

BAHÁ'Í FAITH

The National Spiritual Assembly of the Bahá'ís: Apdo 869-A, Quito; tel. (2) 563-484; e-mail sec@nsa.ecuanex.net; mems resident in 1,121 localities.

The Press

PRINCIPAL DAILIES

Quito

El Comercio: Km 6 Sur, Apdo 57, Quito; tel. (2) 260-020; telex 2246; fax (2) 614-466; f. 1906; morning; independent; Proprs Compañía Anónima El Comercio; Dir SANTIAGO JERVIS; circ. 130,000.

Hoy: Avda Occidental, Apdo 17-07-09069, Quito; tel. (2) 490-888; fax (2) 491-881; e-mail hoy@edimpres.com.ec; f. 1982; independent; Dir BENJAMÍN ORTIZ BRENNAN; Man. JAIME MANTILLA ANDERSON; circ. 60,000.

El Tiempo: Avda América y Villalengua, Apdo 3117, Quito; f. 1965; morning; independent; Proprs Editorial La Unión, CA; Pres. ANTONIO GRANDA CENTENO; Editor EDUARDO GRANDA GARCÉS; circ. 35,000.

Ultimas Noticias: Calle Chile 1345, Apdo 57, Quito; tel. (2) 260-020; fax (2) 614-923; f. 1938; evening; independent; commercial; Proprs Compañía Anónima El Comercio; Dir DAVID MANTILLA CASHMORE; circ. 90,000.

Guayaquil

Expreso: Avda 9 de Octubre 427 y Chimborazo, Guayaquil; morning; independent; Dir GALO MARTÍNEZ; circ. 30,000.

El Extra: Venezuela 1018 y Mejía, Guayaquil; tel. (4) 201-111; fax (4) 200-291; f. 1975; evening.

La Razón: Frente al Terminal Aéreo, Junto a Canal 10, Casilla 5832, Guayaquil; tel. (4) 280-100; f. 1965; evening; independent; Dir JIMMY JAIRALA VALLAZZA; circ. 28,000.

El Telégrafo: Avda 10 de Agosto 601 y Boyacá, Apdo 415, Guayaquil; tel. (4) 326-500; telex 3473; fax (2) 323-265; f. 1884; morning; independent; commercial; Proprs El Telégrafo CA; Dir Dr ROBERTO HANZE SALEM; Man. MICHAEL SHANK K.; circ. 45,000 (weekdays), 55,000 (Sundays).

El Universo: Escobedo 1204 y 9 de Octubre, Apdo 09-01-531, Guayaquil; tel. (4) 490-000; fax (4) 492-925; f. 1921; morning; independent; Dir CARLOS PÉREZ PERASSO; Man. CÉSAR PÉREZ; circ. 174,000 (weekdays), 290,000 (Sundays).

There are local daily newspapers of very low circulation in other towns.

PERIODICALS

Quito

La Calle: Casilla 2010, Quito; f. 1956; weekly; politics; Dir CARLOS ENRIQUE CARRIÓN; circ. 20,000.

Cámara de Comercio de Quito: Avda Amazona y República, Casilla 202, Quito; tel. (2) 443-787; telex 2638; fax (2) 435-862; f. 1906; monthly; commerce; Pres. ANDRÉS PÉREZ ESPINOSA; Exec. Dir ARMANDO TOMASELLI; circ. 10,000.

Carta Económica del Ecuador: Toledo 1448 y Coruña, Apdo 3358, Quito; f. 1969; weekly; economic, financial and business information; Pres. Dr LINCOLN LARREA B.; circ. 8,000.

El Colegial: Calle Carlos Ibarra 206, Quito; tel. (2) 216-541; f. 1974; weekly; publ. of Student Press Association; Dir WILSON ALMEIDA MUÑOZ; circ. 20,000.

Ecuador Guía Turística: Mejía 438, Of. 43, Quito; f. 1969; fortnightly; tourist information in Spanish and English; Propr Prensa Informativa Turística; Dir JORGE VACA O.; circ. 30,000.

Integración: Solano 836, Quito; quarterly; economics of the Andean countries.

Letras del Ecuador: Casa de la Cultura Ecuatoriana, Avda 6 de Diciembre, Casilla 67, Quito; f. 1944; monthly; literature and art; non-political; Dir Dr TEODORO VANEGAS ANDRADE.

El Libertador: Olmedo 931 y García Moreno, Quito; f. 1926; monthly; Pres. Dr BENJAMÍN TERÁN VAREA.

Mensajero: Benalcázar 478, Apdo 17-01-4100, Quito; tel. (2) 219-555; f. 1884; monthly; religion, culture, economics and politics; Man. OSWALDO CARRERA LANDÁZURI; circ. 5,000.

Nueva: Apdo 3224, Quito; tel. (2) 542-244; f. 1971; monthly; left-wing; Dir MAGDALENA JARAMILLO DE ADOUM.

Quince Dias: Sociedad Periodistica Ecuatoriana, Los Pinos 315, Panamericana Norte km 5½, Quito; tel. (2) 474-122; fax (2) 566-741; fortnightly; news and regional political analysis.

Solidaridad: Calle Oriente 725, Quito; tel. (2) 216-541; f. 1982; monthly; publ. of Confederation of Catholic Office Staff and Students of Ecuador; Dir WILSON ALMEIDA MUÑOZ; Man. JOHNY MERIZALDE; circ. 15,000.

This is Ecuador: La Niña 555 y Amazonas, Quito; f. 1968; monthly; English; tourism; Dir GUSTAVO VALLEJO.

Guayaquil

Análisis Semanal: Elizalde 119, 10°, Apdo 4925, Guayaquil; tel. (4) 326-590; fax (4) 326-842; weekly; economic and political affairs; Editor WALTER SPURRIER BAQUERIZO.

Ecuador Ilustrado: Guayaquil; f. 1924; monthly; literary; illustrated.

El Financiero: Casilla 6666, Guayaquil; tel. (4) 304-050; weekly; business and economic news.

Revista Estadio: Aguirre 730 y Boyacá, Apdo 1239, Guayaquil; tel. (4) 327-200; telex 3423; fax (4) 320-499; f. 1962; fortnightly; sport; Editor JOSÉ CALDERÓN; circ. 70,000.

Hogar: Aguirre 724 y Boyacá, Apdo 1239, Guayaquil; tel. (4) 327-200; telex 3423; f. 1964; monthly; Man. Editor ROSA AMELIA ALVARADO; circ. 35,000.

Vistazo: Aguirre 724 y Boyacá, Apdo 1239, Guayaquil; tel. (4) 327-200; fax (4) 320-499; e-mail vistazo@vistazo.coh; f. 1957; fortnightly; general; Pres. XAVIER ALVARADO ROCA; circ. 85,000.

NEWS AGENCIES

Foreign Bureaux

Agencia EFE (Spain): Palacio Arzobispal, Chile 1178, Apdo 4043, Quito; tel. (2) 512-427; telex 2602; Bureau Chief EMILIO CRESPO.

Agenzia Nazionale Stampa Associata (ANSA) (Italy): Calle Venezuela 1013 y esq. Mejía, Of. 26, Quito; tel. (2) 580-794; telex 1362; fax (2) 580-782; Correspondent FERNANDO LARENAS.

Associated Press (AP) (USA): Edif. Sudamérica, 4°, Of. 44, Calle Venezuela 1018 y Mejía, Apdo 3056, Quito; tel. (2) 570-235; telex 2296; Correspondent CARLOS CISTERNAS.

Deutsche Presse-Agentur (dpa) (Germany): Edif. Atrium, Of. 5-7, González Suárez 894 y Gonnessiat, Quito; tel. (2) 568-986; Correspondent JORGE ORTIZ.

Informatsionnoye Telegrafnoye Agentstvo Rossii—Telegrafnoye Agentstvo Suverennykh Stran (ITAR—TASS) (Russia): Calle Roca 328 y 6 de Diciembre, 2°, Dep. 6, Quito; tel. (2) 511-631; telex 3566; Correspondent VLADIMIR GOSTEV.

Inter Press Service (IPS) (Italy): Guayanas 137 e Inglaterra, Casilla 17-01-1284, Quito; tel. (2) 529-911; fax (2) 623-156; Correspondent MARIO GONZÁLEZ.

Prensa Latina (Cuba): Edif. Sudamérica, 2°, Of. 24, Calle Venezuela 1018 y Mejía, Quito; tel. (2) 519-333; telex 2625; Bureau Chief ENRIQUE GARCÍA MEDINA.

Reuters (United Kingdom): Avda Amazonas 3655, 2°, Casilla 17-01-4112, Quito; tel. (2) 431-753; telex 22620; fax (2) 432-949; Correspondent JORGE AGUIRRE CHARVET.

United Press International (UPI) (USA): Quito; Correspondent RICARDO POLIT.

Xinhua (New China) News Agency (People's Republic of China): Edif. Portugal, Avda Portugal y Avda de la República del Salvador 730, 10°, Quito; telex 2268; Bureau Chief LIN MINZHONG.

Publishers

Artes Gráficas Ltda: Avda 12 de Octubre 1637, Apdo 533, Casilla 456-A, Quito; Man. MANUEL DEL CASTILLO.

Cromograf, SA: Coronel 2207, Casilla 4285, Guayaquil; tel. (4) 346-400; telex 3387; children's books, paperbacks, art productions.

Editorial de la Casa de la Cultura Ecuatoriana 'Benjamín Carrión': Avda 6 de Diciembre 794, Apdo 67, Quito; tel. (2) 566-070; f. 1944; general fiction and non-fiction, general science; Pres. MÍLTON BARRAGÁN DUMET.

Editorial Claridad: Quito; tel. (2) 517-442; economics, history, sociology and politics.

Editorial y Librería Selecciones: Avda 9 de Octubre 724 y Boyacá, Guayaquil; tel. (4) 305-807; history, geography and sociology.

Libros Técnicos Litesa Cía Ltda: Avda América 542, Apdo 456A, Quito; tel. (2) 528-537; Man. MANUEL DEL CASTILLO.

Pontificia Universidad Católica del Ecuador: Avda 12 de Octubre 1076 y Carrión, Apdo 2184, Quito; tel. (2) 529-240; fax (2) 567-117; e-mail puce.edu.ec; internet http://www.puce.edu.ec; f. 1946; literature, natural science, law, anthropology, sociology, politics, economics, theology, philosophy, history, archaeology, linguistics, languages and business; Rector Dr HERNÁN ANDRADE TOBAR.

Universidad Central del Ecuador: Departamento de Publicaciones, Servicio de Almacén Universitario, Ciudad Universitaria, Quito.

Universidad de Guayaquil: Departamento de Publicaciones, Biblioteca General 'Luis de Tola y Avilés', Apdo 09-01-3834, Guayaquil; tel. (4) 282-440; f. 1930; general literature, history, philosophy, fiction; Man. Dir LEONOR VILLAO DE SANTANDER.

Broadcasting and Communications

TELECOMMUNICATIONS

Asociación Ecuatoriana de Radiodifusión: Casilla 6014, Quito; independent association; Pres. EDGAR YÁNEZ V.

Empresa Estatal de Telecomunicaciones—EMETEL: Quito; scheduled for privatization as two separate bodies (Andinatel and Pacifictel) in 1998.

Instituto Ecuatoriano de Telecomunicaciones—IETEL: Casilla 3066, Quito; telex 2202; Gen. Man. Ing. MARIO CUESTA BASTIDAS.

RADIO

There are nearly 300 commercial stations, 10 cultural stations and 10 religious stations. The following are some of the most important commercial stations:

CRE (Cadena Radial Ecuatoriana): Edif. El Torreón, 9°, Avda Boyacá 642, Apdo 4144, Guayaquil; tel. (4) 564-290; fax (4) 328-806; e-mail cortel@gye.satnet.net; Dir RAFAEL GUERRERO VALENZUELA.

Emisoras Gran Colombia: Vasco de Contreras 689 y Pasaje A, Quito; tel. (2) 211-670; fax (2) 580-170; f. 1943; Dir EDUARDO CEVALLOS CASTEÑEDA.

Nueva Emisora Central Cía Ltda: Roca 331, Quito; tel (2) 566-017; national coverage of sports events.

Radio Centro Cía Ltda: Eloy Alfaro 355; Quito; tel. (2) 555-311; fax (2) 554-870.

Radio Colón: Avda América y Diguja 327, Casilla 81-67, Quito; tel. (2) 453-288; Dir ATAHUALPA RUIZ RIVA.

Radio Nacional del Ecuador: Chile 1267, Quito.

Radio Quito-La Voz de la Capital: Avda 10 de Agosto 2441, Apdo 17-21-1971, Quito; tel. (2) 508-300; fax (2) 503-311; f. 1940; Dir G. DE ACQUAVIVA.

Radio Tropicana: Edif. El Torreón, 9°, Avda Boyacá 642, Apdo 4144, Guayaquil; tel. (4) 564-290; fax (4) 328-806; Dir ANTONIO GUERRERO GÓMEZ.

La Voz de los Andes (HCJB): Villalengua 884, Casilla 17-17-691, Quito; tel. (2) 466-808; fax (2) 447-263; e-mail helpdesk@hcjb.org.ec; f. 1931; operated by World Radio Missionary Fellowship; programmes in 44 languages and dialects, including Spanish, English and Quechua; private, non-commercial, cultural, religious; Programme Dir JOHN BECK; Man. Dir GLEN VOLKHARDT.

TELEVISION

Corporación Ecuatoriana de Televisión: Calle del Carmen, Casilla 10992, Guayaquil; tel. (4) 300-150; telex 3409; fax (4) 303-677; f. 1967; Pres. XAVIER ALVARADO ROCA; Gen. Man. FRANCISCO AROSEMENA ROBLES.

Cadena Ecuatoriana de Televisión: Avda de las Américas, frente al Aeropuerto, Casilla 673, Guayaquil; tel. (4) 393-248; telex 3530; fax (4) 287-544; f. 1969; commercial; Gen. Man. JORGE E. PÉREZ P.

Canal Universitario Católica: Avda Humbolt 3170, Cuenca; tel. (7) 827-862; telex 48775; fax (7) 831-040; Dir Dr CÉSAR CORDERO MOSCOSO.

El Diario: Apdo 50, 13-01 Portoviejo; tel. (5) 633-777; fax (5) 636-151; Dir PEDRO EDUARDO ZAMBRANO.

Ecuavisa–Canal 8: Bosmediano 447 y José Carbo, Bellavista, Quito; tel. (2) 448-100; fax (2) 445-488; commercial.

Organización Ecuatoriana de Televisión (ORTEC): Eloy Alfaro 2236 y 6 de Diciembre, Casilla 2779, Quito; tel. (2) 459-934; fax (2) 446-660; commercial.

Teleamazonas Cratel, CA: Casilla 17-11-04844, Quito; tel. (2) 430-313; fax (2) 442-151; commercial; Pres. EDUARDO GRANDA GARCÉS; Vice-Pres. ALFREDO ESCÓBAR C.

Tele Cuatro Guayaquil, SA: Edif. Casa de Cultura, 5°, Avda 9 de Octubre 1200, Guayaquil; tel. (4) 560-431; fax (4) 566-436; Pres. Dr CARLOS MUÑOZ INSUA.

Televisión Esmeraldeña Compañía de Economía Mixta—TECEM: Edif. Mutual L.V. Torres, Casilla 17-21-108, Esmeraldas; tel. (2) 710-090; Dir Gen. HÉCTOR ENDARA E.

Televisión del Pacífico, SA (Telenacional): Murgeón 732, Casilla 3977, Guayaquil; tel. (4) 300-359; fax (4) 314-998; commercial; Man. MODESTO LUQUE BENÍTEZ.

Finance

(cap. = capital; p.u. = paid up; res = reserves; dep. = deposits; m. = million; amounts in sucres)

Junta Monetaria Nacional (National Monetary Board): Quito; tel. (2) 514-833; telex 2182; fax (2) 570-258; f. 1927; Pres. DANILO CARRERA.

Supervisory Authority

Superintendencia de Bancos y Seguros: Avda 12 de Octubre 1561, Apdo 424, Quito; tel. (2) 569-526; telex 22148; fax (2) 563-652; f. 1927; supervises national banking system, including state and private banks and other financial institutions; Superintendent (vacant).

BANKING

Central Bank

Banco Central del Ecuador: Avda 10 de Agosto y Briceño, Plaza Bolívar, Casilla 339, Quito; tel. (2) 519-384; telex 2359; fax (2) 570-701; f. 1927; cap. 1,482m., res 2,533m., dep. 666,608m. (Dec. 1987); Chair. Econ. ANA LUCÍA ARMIJOS HIDALGO; Gen. Man. Dr AUGUSTO DE LA TORRE; 19 brs.

Other State Banks

Banco Ecuatoriano de la Vivienda: Avda l0 de Agosto 2270 y Cordero, Casilla 3244, Quito; tel. (2) 521-311; telex 2399; f. 1962; cap. 5,006m., res 952m., dep. 7,389m. (Dec. 1986); Pres. Abog. JUAN PABLO MONCAGATTA; Gen. Man. Dr PATRICIO CEVALLOS MORÁN.

Banco del Estado (BDE): Avda Atahualpa 628 y 10 de Agosto, Casilla 17-01-00373, Quito; tel. (2) 250-800; fax (2) 250-320; f. 1979; cap. 115,587.5m., res 8,481.5m. (Aug. 1991); Pres. Econ. CÉSAR ROBALINO; Gen. Man. Econ. MARTÍN COSTA MARCH.

Banco Nacional de Fomento: Ante 107 y 10 de Agosto, Casilla 685, Quito; tel. (2) 230-010; telex 22256; f. 1928; cap. 3,000m., res 14,914m., dep. 117,067m. (Dec. 1987); Pres. Dr IGNACIO HIDALGO VILLAVICENCIO; Gen. Man. MARCELO PEÑA DURINI; 70 brs.

Corporación Financiera Nacional (CFN): Avda Juan León Mera 130 y Patria, Casilla 17-21-01924, Quito; tel. (2) 564-900; fax (2) 562-519; f. 1964; cap. 2,000m., res 8,417m. (July 1987); Pres. TOMMY SCHWARZKOPF; Gen. Man. Ing. RAFAEL CUESTA.

Commercial Banks

Quito

Banco Amazonas, SA: Avda Amazonas y Santa María, Casilla 121, Quito; tel. (2) 545-315; telex 2393; fax (2) 560-310; f. 1976; affiliated to Banque Paribas; cap. 21,400m., res 8,970m., dep. 145,740m. (Dec. 1994); Pres. Dr FRANCISCO PARRA GIL; Vice-Pres. MICHAEL MANCY MARCHLAND.

Banco de los Andes: Avda Amazonas 477 y Robles, Casilla 3761, Quito; tel. (2) 554-215; telex 22214; fax (2) 564-786; f. 1973; affiliated to Banco de Bogotá; cap. 247m., res 57m., dep. 1,298m. (June 1984); Pres. and Gen. Man. GUILLERMO DUEÑAS ITURRALDE; 11 brs.

Banco Caja de Crédito Agrícola Ganadero, SA: Avda 6 de Diciembre 225 y Piedrahita, Quito; tel. (2) 528-521; telex 2559; f. 1949; cap 132m., res 41m., dep. 592m. (Aug. 1984); Man. HUGO GRIJALVA GARZÓN; Pres. NICOLÁS GUILLÉN.

Banco Consolidado del Ecuador: Avda Patria 740 y 9 de Octubre, Apdo 9150, Suc. 7, Quito; tel. (2) 560-369; telex 2634; fax (2) 560-719; f. 1981; cap. 4,937.0m., res 290.9m., dep. 15,890.3m. (Sept. 1993); Pres. Ing. GONZALO VORBECK; Gen. Man. Ing. GIOVANNI DI MELLA VESPA; 11 brs.

Banco General Rumiñahui: Avda Orellana y Amazonas, Casilla 2952, Quito; tel. (2) 505-446; telex 21498; fax (2) 505-366; Gen. Man. Gen. GUSTAVO HERRERA.

Banco Internacional, SA: Avda Patria 640 y 9 de Octubre, Casilla 17-01-2114, Quito; tel. (2) 565-547; fax (2) 565-758; f. 1973; cap. 11,000m. (Dec. 1995); Pres. FRANCISCO URIBE LASSO; Gen. Man. Econ. RAÚL GUERRERO ANDRADE; 7 brs.

Banco del Pichincha, CA: Avda 10 de Agosto y Bogotá, Casilla 261, Quito; tel. (2) 561-531; telex 2618; fax (2) 560-463; f. 1906; cap. 92,000m., dep. 1,544,000m. (Sept. 1995); Exec. Pres. Lic. JAIME ACOSTA VELASCO; Chair. Dr FIDEL EGAS GRIJALVA; 82 brs.

Banco Popular del Ecuador: Avda Amazonas 3535 y Juan Pablo Sanz, Casilla 696, Quito; tel. (2) 444-700; telex 2234; fax (2) 444-794; f. 1953; cap. 92,645m., res 384,318m., dep. 526,299m. (Dec. 1996); Pres. and Gen. Man. NICOLÁS LANDES; 6 brs.

Banco de Préstamos, SA: Avda Patria y 10 de Agosto, Casilla 17-01-529, Quito; tel. (2) 561-680; telex 22195; fax (2) 565-357; f. 1909; cap. 9,600m., res 8,225m., dep. 112,745m. (Dec. 1992); Pres. Econ. ALEJANDRO PEÑAFIEL; Gen. Man. Dr MARIO LARREA; 29 brs.

PRODUBANCO: Avda Amazonas 3775 y Japón, Apdo 17-03-38-A, Quito; tel. (2) 250-150; telex 22376; fax (2) 447-319; f. 1978; name changed from Banco de la Producción in April 1996; cap. 55,0000m., res 21,960m., dep. 442,695m. (Dec. 1995); Pres. RODRIGO PAZ DELGADO; Exec. Pres. Econ. ABELARDO PACHANO BERTERO.

UniBanco: Avda 10 de Agosto 937 y Buenos Aires, Casilla 2244, Quito; tel. (2) 544-188; fax (2) 227-898; f. 1964 as Banco de Cooperativas del Ecuador, name changed in 1995; Pres. Dr JACINTO MONTERO ZAMORA; 4 brs.

Ambato

Banco de Tungurahua: Montalvo 630, Casilla 173, Ambato; tel. (2) 821-122; telex 7186; fax (2) 840-426; f. 1979; cap. 50m., res 2m., dep. 329m. (June 1984); Pres. GEORG SONNENHOLZNER; Gen. Man. Econ. CAMILO AMPUERO SÁNCHEZ.

Cuenca

Banco del Austro: Sucre y Borrero (esq.), Casilla 01-01-0167, Cuenca; tel. (7) 831-646; telex 8560; fax (7) 832-633; f. 1977; cap. 34,000m., dep. 141,000m. (July 1994); Pres. JUAN ELJURI ANTÓN; Gen. Man. PATRICIO ROBAYO IDROVO; 19 brs.

Banco del Azuay, SA: Bolívar 7-67 y Borrero, Casilla 33, Cuenca; tel. (7) 831-811; telex 48579; fax (7) 833-655; f. 1913; cap. 267m., res 33m., dep. 1,860m. (June 1984); Exec. Pres. CARLOS JULIO MIRANDA; Gen. Man. ANTONIO CHAMOUN; 4 brs.

Guayaquil

Banco Bolivariano: Pichincha 412 y Aguirre, Casilla 09-01-10184, Guayaquil; tel. and fax (4) 325-654; telex 3659; f. 1980; cap. 24,000m., res 6,226m., dep. 78,839m. (Dec. 1994); Exec. Pres. JOSÉ SALAZAR BARRAGÁN; 9 brs.

Banco Continental, SA: General Córdova 811 y V. M. Rendón, Casilla 9348, Guayaquil; tel. (4) 303-300; telex 3418; fax (4) 312-669; f. 1974; cap. 3,000m., res 1,847m., dep. 34,965m. (Dec. 1988); Pres. and Gen. Man. LEONIDAS ORTEGA; 23 brs.

Banco de Crédito e Hipotecario: Plaza Ycaza 302 y Córdova, Casilla 09-01-4173, Guayaquil; tel. (4) 563-055; telex 3336; fax (4) 372-397; f. 1871; cap. 10,000m., dep. 31,898m. (June 1993); Pres. LUIS NOBOA NARANAJO; Exec. Vice-Pres. FERNANDO LEÓN BARBA.

Banco Industrial y Comercial—Baninco: Pichincha 335 e Illingworth, Casilla 5817, Guayaquil; tel. (4) 323-488; telex 3199; f. 1965; cap. and res 2m., dep. 10m. (June 1988); Pres. Ing. CARLOS MANZUR PERES; Gen. Man. GABRIEL MARTÍNEZ INTRIAGO; 2 brs.

Banco del Pacífico, SA: Plaza Ycaza 200 y Pichincha, Casilla 988, Guayaquil; tel. (4) 566-010; telex 43240; fax (4) 564-636; f. 1972; cap. 10,051m., res 3,544m., dep. 200,456m. (1990); total assets US $1,897m. (Dec. 1996); Chair. VÍCTOR MASPONS Y BIGAS; Exec. Pres. MARCEL J. LANIADO DE WIND; 117 brs.

Banco del Progreso, SA: Primero de Mayo y Pedro Moncayo, Casilla 09-01-11100, Guayaquil; tel. (4) 563-800; fax (4) 560-312; f. 1981; cap. 192,304m., res 117,720m., dep. 1,965,390m. (Dec. 1996); Pres. FERNANDO ASPIAZU S.; Gen. Man. ERNESTO BALDA.

Banco La Previsora: Avda 9 de Octubre 100 y Malecón, Casilla 1324, Guayaquil; tel. (4) 566-100; fax (4) 563-390; e-mail mcampo@b-previsora.fin.ec; f. 1920; cap. 9,400m., res 39,119m., dep. 175,522m. (June 1993); Exec. Pres. Ing. ALVARO GUERRERO FERBER; 14 brs.

Banco Sociedad General de Crédito, CA: Avda 9 de Octubre 1404 y Machala, Casilla 5501, Guayaquil; tel. (4) 286-490; telex 43138; fax (4) 283-952; f. 1972; cap. 8,437m., res 6,344m., dep. 39,558m. (Dec. 1993); Pres. SANTIAGO MASPONS GUZMÁN; Gen. Man. Dr GONZALO NOBOA ELIZALDE; 3 brs.

Banco Territorial, SA: Panamá 814 y V. M. Rendón, Casilla 09-01-227, Guayaquil; tel. (4) 566-695; telex 42359; fax (4) 566-695; f. 1886; cap. 3,800m., res 3,769m. (June 1993), dep. 516m. (Sept. 1991); Pres. ROBERTO GOLDBAUM; Gen. Man. Ing. GUSTAVO HEINERT.

FILANBANCO, SA: Avda 9 de Octubre 203 y Pichincha, Apdo 149, Guayaquil; tel. (4) 322-780; telex 43173; fax (4) 326-916; f. 1908; cap. 330,000m., res 169,629m., dep. 2,266,241m. (Dec. 1996); Exec. Pres. ROBERTO ISAIAS DASSUM; Gen. Man. PEDRO GÓMEZ-CENTURIÓN; 73 brs.

Loja

Banco de Loja: esq. Bolívar y Rocafuerte, Casilla 11-01-300, Loja; tel. (4) 571-682; telex 4132; fax (4) 573-019; f. 1968; cap. 10,000m., res 4,207m., dep. 70,900m. (Dec. 1996); Pres. Lic. AUGUSTO EGUIGUREN EGUIGUREN; Man. Lic. FERNANDO BURBANO TORAL.

Machala

Banco de Machala, SA: Avda 9 de Mayo y Rocafuerte, Casilla 711, Machala; tel. (4) 930-100; telex 4479; fax (4) 922-744; f. 1972; Pres. Dr RODOLFO VINTIMILLA FLORES; Exec. Pres. and Gen. Man. ESTEBAN QUIROLA FIGUEROA; 2 brs.

Portoviejo

Banco Comercial de Manabí, SA: Avda 10 de Agosto 600 y 18 Octubre, Portoviejo; tel. (4) 653-888; telex 6180; fax (4) 635-527; f. 1980; cap. 117m., res 21m., dep. 720m. (June 1985); Pres. Dr RUBÉN DARÍO MORALES; Gen. Man. ARISTO ANDRADE DÍAZ.

Foreign Banks

Banco Holandés Unido, SA (Netherlands): Avda Amazonas 4272, Casilla 17-01-42, Quito; tel. (2) 460-333; telex 2153; fax (2) 443-151; f. 1959; cap. 3,880m., res 2,343m., dep. 22,769m. (June 1992); Gen. Man. GERRIT THISSEN; 10 brs.

Bank of America (USA): Calle Guayaquil 1938, Casilla 344, Quito; tel. (2) 550-510; telex 3143; f. 1966; cap. 250m., res 180m., dep. 1,500m. (Dec. 1986); Gen. Man. EDUARDO GAETE; Vice-Pres. JOHN TURNER; br. at Guayaquil.

Citibank, NA (USA): Juan León Mera 130 y Patria, Casilla 17-01-1393, Quito; tel. (2) 563-300; fax (2) 566-895; f. 1959; cap. 7,000m., res 1,000m., dep. 62,000m. (Dec. 1996); Gen. Man. BENJAMÍN FRANCO; 3 brs.

Lloyds Bank (BLSA) Ltd (United Kingdom): Avda Amazonas 580, esq. Jerónimo Carrión, Casilla 17-03-556, Quito; tel. (2) 564-177; fax (2) 568-997; f. 1988 (in succession to the Bank of London and South America, f. 1936); cap. 6,500m., res 6,200m., dep. 60,692m. (Nov. 1997); Man. G. BELTRÁN M.

'Multibanco'

Banco de Guayaquil, SA: Plaza Ycaza 105 y Pichincha, Casilla 09-01-1300, Guayaquil; tel. (4) 517-100; telex 3153; fax (4) 514-976; e-mail servicios@bankguay.com; f. 1923; absorbed the finance corpn, FINANSUR, in 1990 to become Ecuador's first 'multibanco', carrying out commercial and financial activities; cap. 35m., dep. 246.4m. (Sept. 1997); Exec. Pres. GUILLERMO LASSO MENDOZ; Pres. Econ. DANILO CARRERA DROUET; 48 brs.

Finance Corporations

Banco COFIEC SA: Edif. COFIEC, 14°, Avda Patria y Amazonas, Casilla 17-01-411, Quito; tel. (2) 546-177; telex 2131; fax (2) 564-224; f. 1966; fmrly Compañía Financiera Ecuatoriana de Desarrollo; cap. 21,300m., res 4,593m. (Jan. 1997); Pres. JUAN JOSÉ AVELLÁN; Exec. Pres. RAÚL ANDRADE GÁNDARA; Gen. Man. ARTURO QUIROZ MARTÍN.

Financiera Guayaquil, SA: Carchi 702 y 9 de Octubre, 6°, Casilla 2167, Guayaquil; telex 43431; f. 1976; cap. 900m., res 142m. (June 1987); Gen. Man. Dr MIGUEL BABRA LYON.

FINANSA—Financiera Nacional, SA: Avda 6 de Diciembre 2417, entre Orellana y la Niña, Casilla 6420-CCI, Quito; tel. (2) 546-200; telex 2884; f. 1976; cap. 694m., res 103.6m. (June 1986); Gen. Man. RICHARD A. PEARSE; Dir LEONARDO STAGG.

Associations

Asociación de Bancos Privados del Ecuador: Edif. Delta, 7°, Avda República de El Salvador 890 y Suecia, Casilla 17-11-6708, Quito; tel. (2) 466-670; fax (2) 466-701; f. 1965; 34 mems; Pres. ANTONIO ACOSTA ESPINOSA; Exec. Pres. Econ. ANA LUCÍA ARMIJOS HIDALGO.

Asociación de Compañías Financieras del Ecuador—AFIN: Robles 653 y Amazonas, 13°, Of. 1310-1311, Casilla 17-07-9156, Quito; tel. (2) 550-623; telex 21444; fax (2) 567-912; Pres. Ing. FRANCISCO ORTEGA.

STOCK EXCHANGES

Bolsa de Valores de Guayaquil: Baquerizo Moreno 1112, Guayaquil; tel. (4) 307-310; fax (4) 561-871; Dir Gen. ENRIQUE AROSEMENA; Dir of Operations ERNESTO MURILLO.

Bolsa de Valores de Quito: Avda Amazonas 540 y J. Carrión, Quito; tel. (2) 225-434; fax (2) 500-942; e-mail pazosc@ccbuq.com; internet http://www.ccbuq.com; f. 1969; volume of operations US $1,700m. (1995); Pres Dr. ERNESTO ANDRADE VELOZ; Exec. Pres. ARTURO QUIROZ RIUMALLÓ.

INSURANCE

Instituto Ecuatoriano de Seguridad Social: Avda 10 de Agosto y Bogotá, Apdo 2640, Quito; tel. (2) 547-400; telex 221459; fax (2) 504-572; f. 1928; various forms of state insurance provided; directs the Ecuadorean social insurance system; provides social benefits and medical service; Dir-Gen. Dr RAÚL ZAPATER HIDALGO.

National Companies

In 1992 there were some 35 insurance companies operating in Ecuador. The following is a list of the eight principal companies, selected by virtue of capital.

Amazonas Cía Anónima de Seguros: V. M. Rendón 401 y Córdova, Apdo 3285, Guayaquil; tel. (4) 566-300; telex 3176; fax (4) 563-192; f. 1966; cap. 600m. sucres (1991); Exec. Pres. ANTONIO AROSEMENA G.-L.

Cía Reaseguradora del Ecuador, SA: Junín 105 y Malecón Simón Bolívar, Casilla 09-01-6776, Guayaquil; tel. (4) 566-326; telex 42960; fax (4) 564-454; e-mail oespinoz@ecuare.fin.ec; f. 1977; cap. 200m. sucres (1993); Man. Dir Ing. OMAR ESPINOSA ROMERO.

Cía de Seguros Condor, SA: Plaza Ycaza 302, Apdo 09-01-5007, Guayaquil; tel. (4) 565-888; telex 43755; fax (4) 560-144; f. 1966; cap. 151m. sucres; Gen. Man. OCTAVIO SARMIENTO MARTÍNEZ.

Cía de Seguros Ecuatoriano-Suiza, SA: Avda 9 de Octubre 2101 y Tulcán, Apdo 09-01-0937, Guayaquil; tel. (4) 372-222; telex 3386; f. 1954; cap. 440m. sucres (1991); Gen. Man. Econ. ENRIQUE SALAS CASTILLO.

La Nacional Cía de Seguros Generales, SA: Panamá 809 y V. M. Rendón, Apdo 19-01-1085, Guayaquil; tel. (4) 560-700; fax (4) 566-327; f. 1940; cap. 1,200m. sucres (1994); Gen. Man. Ab. LUIS AVELLÁN W.

Panamericana del Ecuador, SA: Edif. Banco de los Andes, 4°, Avda Amazonas 477 entre Roca y Robles, Apdo 3902, Quito; tel. (2) 235-358; telex 22352; fax (2) 563-875; f. 1973; cap. 320m. sucres (1991); Gen. Man. HANS G. GRIESBACH S.

Seguros Rocafuerte, SA: Plaza Carbo 505 y 9 de Octubre, Apdo 6491, Guayaquil; f. 1967; cap. 40m. sucres; Gen. Man. Ing. DANIEL CAÑIZARES AGUILAR.

La Unión Cía Nacional de Seguros: Km. 5½, Vía a la Costa, Apdo 09-01-1294, Guayaquil; tel. (4) 851-500; fax (4) 851-700; f. 1943; cap. 4,761m. sucres; Man. DAVID ALBERTO GOLDBAUM MORALES.

Trade and Industry

GOVERNMENT AGENCIES

Consejo Nacional de Modernización del Estado—CONAM: Edif. CFN, 9°, Avda Juan León Mera 130 y Patria, Quito; tel. (2) 509-432; fax (2) 509-437; f. 1992; Pres. OMAR QUINTANA; Exec. Dir LEONARDO ESCOBAR.

Empresa de Comercio Exterior (ECE): Quito; f. 1980 to promote non-traditional exports; State owns 33% share in company; share capital 25m. sucres.

Fondo de Promoción de Exportaciones—FOPEX: Juan León Mera 130 y Patria, Casilla 163, Quito; tel. (2) 564-900; telex 2193; fax (2) 562-519; f. 1972; export promotion; Dir Econ. DANIEL OCAMPO C.

Instituto Ecuatoriano de Reforma Agraria y Colonización (IERAC): f. 1973 to supervise the Agrarian Reform Law under the auspices and co-ordination of the Ministry of Agriculture and Livestock; Dir LUIS LUNA GAYBOR.

Superintendencia de Compañías del Ecuador: Roca 660 y Amazonas, Casilla 17-01-687, Quito; tel. (2) 525-022; telex 22595; fax (2) 566-685; e-mail estudi@q.supercias.gov.ecj; f. 1964; responsible for the legal and accounting control of commercial enterprises; Supt Dr IGNACIO VIDAL MASPONS.

DEVELOPMENT ORGANIZATIONS

Centro Nacional de Promoción de la Pequeña Industria y Artesanía—CENAPIA: Quito; agency to develop small-scale industry and handicrafts; Dir Econ. EDGAR GUEVARA (acting).

Centro de Reconversión Económica del Azuay, Cañar y Morona Santiago (CREA): Avda México entre Unidad Nacional y las Américas, Casilla 01-01-1953, Cuenca; tel. (7) 817-500; fax (7) 817-134; f. 1959; development organization; Dir Dr JUAN TAMA.

Consejo Nacional de Desarrollo—CONADE: Juan Larrea y Arenas, Quito; formerly Junta Nacional de Planificación y Coordinación Económica; aims to formulate a general plan of economic and social development and supervise its execution; also to integrate local plans into the national; Chair. GALO ABRIL OJEDA; Sec. PABLO LUCIO PAREDES.

Fondo de Desarrollo del Sector Rural Marginal—FODERUMA: f. 1978 to allot funds to rural development programmes in poor areas.

Fondo Nacional de Desarrollo—FONADE: f. 1973; national development fund to finance projects as laid down in the five-year plan.

Instituto de Colonización de la Región Amazónica—INCREA: f. 1978 to encourage settlement in and economic development of the Amazon region; Dir Dr DIMAS GUZMÁN.

Instituto Ecuatoriano de Recursos Hidráulicos—INERHI: undertakes irrigation and hydroelectric projects; Man. Ing. EDUARDO GARCÍA GARCÍA.

Organización Comercial Ecuatoriana de Productos Artesanales (OCEPA): Carrión 1236 y Versalles, Casilla 17-01-2948, Quito; tel. (2) 541-992; fax (2) 565-961; f. 1964; to develop and promote handicrafts; Gen. Man. MARCELO RODRÍGUEZ.

Programa Nacional del Banano y Frutas Tropicales: Guayaquil; to promote the development of banana and tropical-fruit cultivation; Dir Ing. JORGE GIL CHANG.

Programa Regional de Desarrollo del Sur del Ecuador—PREDESUR: Pasaje María Eufrasia 100 y Mosquera Narváez, Quito; tel. (2) 544-415; f. 1972 to promote the development of the southern area of the country; Dir Ing. LUIS HERNÁN EGUIGUREN CARRIÓN.

CHAMBERS OF COMMERCE AND INDUSTRY

Federación Nacional de Cámaras de Comercio del Ecuador: Avda Olmedo 414 y Boyacá, Guayaquil; tel. (4) 323-130; telex 3466; fax (4) 323-478; Pres. Ing. LUIS TRUJILLO BUSTAMANTE; Exec. Vice-Pres. Dr ROBERTO ILLINGWORTH.

Cámara de Comercio de Cuenca: Avda Federico Malo 1-90, Casilla 4929, Cuenca; tel. (7) 827-531; fax (7) 833-891; f. 1919; 5,329 mems; Pres. ENRIQUE MORA VÁZQUEZ.

Cámara de Comercio de Quito: Edif. Las Cámaras, 6°, Avda República y Amazonas, Casilla 17-01-202, Quito; tel. (2) 443-787; telex 2638; fax (2) 435-862; f. 1906; 8,000 mems; Pres. DOMINGO CÓRDOVEZ PÉREZ.

Cámara de Comercio de Guayaquil: Avda Olmedo 414 y Boyacá, Guayaquil; tel. (4) 323-130; telex 43466; fax (4) 323-478; f. 1889; 16,500 mems; Pres. Ing. LUIS TRUJILLO BUSTAMENTE; Exec. Sec. Dr ROBERTO ILLINGWORTH CABANILLA.

Federación Nacional de Cámaras de Industrias: Avda República y Amazonas, Casilla 2438, Quito; tel. (2) 452-994; telex 2770; fax (2) 448-118; f. 1974; Pres. Ing. PEDRO KOHN.

Cámara de Industrias de Cuenca: Edif. Las Cámaras, Avda Federico Malo 1-90, Casilla 01-01-326, Cuenca; tel. (7) 830-845; telex 8631; fax (7) 830-945; f. 1936; Pres. Ing. FRANK TOSI IÑIGUEZ.

Cámara de Industrias de Guayaquil: Avda 9 de Octubre 910, Casilla 09-01-4007, Guayaquil; tel. (4) 562-705; telex 3686; fax (4) 320-924; f. 1936; Pres. Ing. ERNESTO NOBOA BEJARANO.

INDUSTRIAL AND TRADE ASSOCIATIONS

Centro de Desarrollo Industrial del Ecuador—CENDES: Avda Orellana 1715 y 9 de Octubre, Casilla 2321, Quito; tel. (2) 527-100; f. 1962; carries out industrial feasibility studies, supplies technical and administrative assistance to industry, promotes new industries, supervises investment programmes; Gen. Man. CLAUDIO CREAMER GUILLÉN.

Corporación de Desarrollo e Investigación Geológico-Minero-Metalúrgica—CODIGEM: Quito; f. 1991 to direct mining exploration and exploitation.

Empresa Pesquera Nacional: Guayaquil; tel. (4) 524-913; state fishing enterprise.

Fondo Nacional de Preinversión—FONAPRE: Jorge Washington 624 y Amazonas, Casilla 17-01-3302, Quito; tel. (2) 563-261; telex 2772; f. 1973 to undertake feasibility projects before investment; Pres. LUIS PARODÍ VALVERDE; Gen. Man. Ing. EDUARDO MOLINA GRAZZIANI.

Petróleos del Ecuador—PETROECUADOR: Avda 6 de Diciembre, Casilla 5007-8, Quito; tel. (2) 229-043; state petroleum company; expected to be divested to the private sector in 1998; Exec. Pres. LUIS ROMÁN LAZO.

EMPLOYERS' ORGANIZATIONS

Asociación de Cafecultores del Cantón Piñas: García Moreno y Abdón Calderón, Quito; coffee growers' association.

Asociación de Comerciantes e Industriales: Avda Boyacá 1416, Guayaquil; traders' and industrialists' association.

Asociación de Industriales Textiles del Ecuador (AITE): Edif. Las Cámaras, 8°, Avda República y Amazonas, Casilla 2893, Quito; telex 2770; f. 1938; textile manufacturers' association; 33 mems; Pres. RICHARD C. HANDAL; Sec.-Gen. JOSÉ LUIS ALARCÓN.

Asociación de Productores Bananeros del Ecuador—APROBANA: Malecón 2002, Guayaquil; banana growers' association; Pres. NICOLÁS CASTRO.

Asociación Nacional de Empresarios—ANDE: Edif. España, 6°, Of. 67, Avda Amazonas 1429 y Colón, Casilla 17-01-3489, Quito; tel. (2) 238-507; fax (2) 509-806; e-mail ande@vio.satnet.net; internet http://www.ande.net; national employers' association.

Asociación Nacional de Exportadores de Cacao y Café: Casilla 4774, Manta; cocoa and coffee exporters' association.

Asociación Nacional de Exportadores de Camarones: Pres. LUIS VILLACÍS.

Cámara de Agricultura: Casilla 17-21-322, Quito; tel. (2) 230-195; Pres. ALBERTO ENRÍQUEZ PORTILLA.

Consorcio Ecuatoriano de Exportadores de Cacao y Café: cocoa and coffee exporters' consortium.

Corporación Nacional de Exportadores de Cacao y Café: Guayaquil; cocoa and coffee exporters' corporation.

Federación Nacional de Cooperativas Cafetaleras: Quito; coffee co-operatives federation.

Unión Nacional de Periodistas: Joaquín Auxe Iñaquito, Quito; national press association.

There are several other coffee and cocoa organizations.

UTILITIES

Regulatory Authorities

Ministry of Energy and Mines: see section on The Government (Ministries).

Comisión Ecuatoriana de Energía Atómica: Avda González Suarez 2351 y Bosmediano, Quito; tel. (2) 458-013; telex 21461; fax (2) 253-097; atomic energy commission; Exec. Dir CELIANO ALMEIDA.

Dirección General de Hidrocarburos: Avda 10 de Agosto 321, Quito; supervision of the enforcement of laws regarding the exploration and development of petroleum.

Instituto Nacional de Energía: 007-C, Quito; tel. (2) 434-153; telex 22991; energy planning and research and development of new and renewable energy sources; Dir HORACIO M. YEPEZ.

Electricity

Empresa Eléctrica del Ecuador: V. M. Rendón 511 y Escobedo 301700, Casilla 1320, Guayaquil; telex 43159; major producer and distributor of electricity, mostly using oil-fired or diesel generating capacity.

Empresa Eléctrica Quito, SA: Avda 10 de Agosto y Las Casas, Quito; telex 22528; produces electricity for the region around Quito, mostly from hydroelectric plants.

Instituto Ecuatoriano de Electrificación—INECEL: Avda 6 de Diciembre 2427 y Orellana, Casilla 17-03-565 y 9076, Suc. 7, Quito; tel. (2) 237-422; telex 2243; fax (2) 503-762; f. 1961; state enterprise for the generation, transmission and distribution of electric energy, through 19 regional companies; under the control of the Ministry of Energy and Mines; scheduled for privatization in the 1990s; installed capacity of 1,692.6 MW in 1993; Gen. Man. Ing. IVAN RODRÍGUEZ RAMOS.

TRADE UNIONS

Frente Unitario de Trabajadores (FUT): f. 1971; left-wing; 300,000 mems; Pres. EDGAR PONCE; comprises:

Confederación Ecuatoriana de Organizaciones Clasistas—CEDOC: Calle Río de Janeiro 407 y Juan Larrea, Casilla 3207, Quito; tel. (2) 548-086; f. 1938; affiliated to CMT and CLAT; humanist; Pres. RAMIRO ROSALES NARVÁEZ; Sec.-Gen. JORGE MUÑOZ;150,000 mems (est.) organized in 20 provinces.

Confederación Ecuatoriana de Organizaciones Sindicales Libres (CEOSL): Casilla 17-01-1373, Quito; tel. (2) 522-511; fax (2) 500-836; f. 1962; affiliated to ICFTU and ORIT; Pres. JOSÉ CHÁVEZ CHÁVEZ; Sec.-Gen. WILSON BECERRA ROSERO.

Confederación de Trabajadores del Ecuador (CTE) (Confederation of Ecuadorean Workers): Olmedo y Benalcázar, 3°, Casilla 4166, Quito; telex 22582; fax (2) 580-747; f. 1944; admitted to WFTU and CPUSTAL; Leaders EDGAR PONCE; 1,200 affiliated unions, 70 national federations.

Central Católica de Obreros: Avda 24 de Mayo 344, Quito; tel. (2) 213-704; f. 1906; craft and manual workers and intellectuals; Pres. CARLOS E. DÁVILA ZURITA.

A number of trade unions are not affiliated to the above groups. These include the Federación Nacional de Trabajadores Marítimos y Portuarios del Ecuador (FNTMPE) (National Federation of Maritime and Port Workers of Ecuador) and both railway trade unions.

Transport

Ministerio de Obras Públicas y Comunicaciones: Avda Juan León Mera y Orellana, Quito; tel. (2) 222-749; fax (2) 223-077.

RAILWAYS

All railways are government-controlled. In 1993 the total length of track was 966 km; extensive construction work was being undertaken.

Empresa Nacional de Ferrocarriles del Estado: Calle Bolívar 443, Casilla 159, Quito; tel. (2) 216-180; Gen. Man. M. ARIAS SALAZAR.

There are divisional state railway managements for the following lines: Guayaquil–Quito, Sibambe–Cuenca and Quito–San Lorenzo.

ROADS

There were 43,249 km of roads in 1996, of which 13.3% were paved. The Pan-American Highway runs north from Ambato to Quito and to the Colombian border at Tulcán and south to Cuenca and Loja. In 1994 the Government announced plans to transfer responsibility for several major roads to private concerns.

SHIPPING

The following are Ecuador's principal ports: Guayaquil, Esmeraldas, Manta and Puerto Bolívar.

Ecuanave, CA: Junin 415 y Córdova, 4°, Casilla 09-01-30H, Guayaquil; tel. (4) 293-808; fax (4) 289-257; e-mail ecuanav@ecua.net.ec.; Chair. Ing. P. ERNESTO ESCOBAR; Gen. Man. ALFREDO ESCOBAR.

Flota Bananera Ecuatoriana, SA: Edif. Gran Pasaje, 9°, Plaza Ycaza 437, Casilla 6883, Guayaquil; tel. (4) 309-333; telex 43218; f. 1967; owned by Govt of Ecuador and private stockholders; Pres. DIEGO SÁNCHEZ; Gen. Man. JORGE BARRIGA.

Flota Mercante Grancolombiana, SA: Calle 2 Aguirre 104 y Malecón Simón Bolívar, Casilla 3714, Guayaquil; tel. (4) 512-791; telex 3210; f. 1946 with Colombia and Venezuela; on Venezuela's withdrawal, in 1953, Ecuador's 10% interest was increased to 20%; operates services from Colombia and Ecuador to European ports, US Gulf ports and New York, Mexican Atlantic ports and East Canada; offices in Quito, Cuenca, Bahía, Manta and Esmeraldas; Man. Naval Capt. J. ALBERTO SÁNCHEZ.

Flota Petrolera Ecuatoriana—FLOPEC: Edif. FLOPEC, Avda Amazonas 1188 y Cordero, Casilla 535-A, Quito; tel. (2) 552-167; telex 22211; fax (2) 501-428; f. 1973; Pres. S. CORAL.

Logística Marítima, CA (LOGMAR): Avda Córdova 812 y V. M. Rendón, 1°, Casilla 9622, Guayaquil; tel. (4) 307-041; telex 43591; Pres. J. COELLOG; Man. IGNACIO RODRÍGUEZ BAQUERIZO.

Naviera del Pacífico, CA: El Oro 101 y La Ría, Apdo 09-01-529, Guayaquil; tel. (4) 442-055; telex 3144.

Servicios Oceánicos Internacionales, SA: Avda Domingo Comin y Calle 11, Casilla 79, Guayaquil; Pres. CARLOS VALDANO RAFFA; Man. FERNANDO VALDANO TRUJILLO.

Transportes Navieros Ecuatorianos—Transnave: Edif. Citibank, 4°–7°, Avda 9 de Octubre 416 y Chile, Apdo 4706, Guayaquil; tel. (4) 308-400; telex 43249; fax (4) 329-273; transports general cargo within the European South Pacific Magellan Conference, Japan West Coast South America Conference and Atlantic and Gulf West Coast South America Conference; Pres. Vice-Adm. YÉZID JARAMILLO SANTOS; Gen. Man. Vice-Adm. ANDRÉS L. ARRATA MENESES.

CIVIL AVIATION

There are two international airports: Mariscal Sucre, near Quito, and Simón Bolívar, near Guayaquil.

Aerolíneas Nacionales del Ecuador, SA—ANDES: Aeropuerto Simón Bolívar, Apdo 3317, Guayaquil; tel. (4) 284-490; telex 3228; fax (4) 283-352; f. 1961; regular scheduled and charter cargo services linking Quito and Guayaquil with Miami, USA and Panama; Dir HÉCTOR PONCE; Gen. Man. VINICIO DONOSO.

Empresa Ecuatoriana de Aviación (EEA): Condominios Almagro, Avda Reina Victoria y Colón, Torres de Almagro, Apdo 505, Quito; tel. (2) 563-003; telex 21143; fax (2) 563-920; nationalized 1974; ceased operations in 1993, aircraft subsequently sold or repossessed, and routes to the USA assigned to SAETA.

SAETA (Sociedad Ecuatoriana de Transportes Aereos): Santa María y Amazonas, Apdo 2943, Quito; tel. (4) 200-277; telex 22570; fax (2) 200-791; f. 1967; domestic and regional scheduled flights; charter cargo services; Exec. Pres. ROBERTO DUNN BARREIRO; Exec. Vice-Pres. Capt. LUIS YÉPEZ G.

Servicios Aereos Nacionales (SAN): 2½ Km Avda Carlos Julio Arrosemena, Apdo 7138, Guayaquil; tel. (4) 202-559; fax (4) 201-152; f. 1964; scheduled passenger and cargo services linking Guayaquil with Quito and the Galápagos Islands and Quito with Cuenca; Pres. PATRICIO SUÁREZ.

Transportes Aéreos Militares Ecuatorianos (TAME): Avda Amazonas 13–54 y Colón, 6°, Casilla 8736, Sucursal Almagro, Quito; tel. (2) 509-375; telex 2567; fax (2) 509-594; f. 1962; domestic scheduled and charter services for passengers and freight; Pres. Gen. JULIO ESPINOSA.

The following airlines also offer national and regional services: Aerotaxis Ecuatorianos, SA (ATESA); Cía Ecuatoriana de Transportes Aéreos (CEDTA); Ecuastol Servicios Aéreos, SA; Ecuavia Cía Ltda; Aeroturismo Cía Ltda (SAVAC).

Tourism

Tourism has become an increasingly important industry in Ecuador, with around 482,000 tourists visiting the country in 1994. Of total visitors in 1993, some 38% came from Colombia, 11% were from Peru, 13% from other Latin American countries, 20% from the USA and 17% from Europe. Receipts from the industry amounted to US $252m. in 1994, but declined to US $188m. in the following year, owing to the border conflict with Peru, a series of strikes, an energy crisis and unrest in the Galápagos Islands.

Asociación Ecuatoriana de Agencias de Viajes y Turismo—ASECUT: Edif. Banco del Pacífico, 5°, Avda Amazonas 720 y Veintimilla, Casilla 9421, Quito; tel. (2) 503-669; telex 2749; fax (2) 285-872; f. 1953; Pres. KATBE I. TOUMA ABUHAYAR.

Corporación Ecuatoriana de Turismo—CETUR: Avda Eloy Alfaro y Carlos Tobar, Quito; tel. (2) 507-555; fax (2) 507-564; f. 1964; govt-owned; Exec. Dir KATBE TOUMA ABUHAYAR.

EGYPT

Introductory Survey

Location, Climate, Language, Religion, Flag, Capital

The Arab Republic of Egypt occupies the north-eastern corner of Africa, with an extension across the Gulf of Suez into the Sinai Peninsula, sometimes regarded as lying within Asia. Egypt is bounded to the north by the Mediterranean Sea, to the north-east by Israel, to the east by the Red Sea, to the south by Sudan, and to the west by Libya. The climate is arid, with a maximum annual rainfall of only 200 mm (8 ins) around Alexandria. More than 90% of the country is desert, and some 99% of the population live in the valley and delta of the River Nile. Summer temperatures reach a maximum of 43°C (110°F) and winters are mild, with an average day temperature of about 18°C (65°F). Arabic is the official language. Many educated Egyptians also speak English or French. More than 80% of the population are Muslims, mainly of the Sunni sect. The remainder are mostly Christians, principally Copts, who number some 6m. The national flag (proportions 3 by 2) has three equal horizontal stripes, of red, white, and black; the white stripe has, in the centre, the national emblem (a striped shield superimposed on an eagle, with a cartouche beneath bearing the inscription, in Kufic script, 'Arab Republic of Egypt') in gold. The capital is Cairo.

Recent History

Egypt, a province of Turkey's Ottoman Empire from the 16th century, was occupied by British forces in 1882. The administration was controlled by British officials, although Egypt remained nominally an Ottoman province until 1914, when a British protectorate was declared. Egypt was granted titular independence on 28 February 1922. Fuad I, the reigning Sultan, became King of Egypt. He was succeeded in 1936 by his son, King Faruq (Farouk). The Anglo-Egyptian Treaty of 1936 recognized full Egyptian sovereignty and provided for the gradual withdrawal of British troops, while giving the United Kingdom the right to maintain a garrison on the Suez Canal, and to use Alexandria and Port Said as naval bases. The Italian invasion of Egypt in 1940 and the subsequent Libyan campaign postponed the departure of British forces. After the Second World War, British forces withdrew from Egypt, except for a military presence in the Suez Canal Zone. When the British mandate in Palestine was ended in 1948, Arab armies intervened to oppose the newly-proclaimed State of Israel. A cease-fire was agreed in 1949, leaving Egyptian forces occupying the Gaza Strip.

On 23 July 1952 King Farouk's unpopular regime was overthrown in a bloodless military coup. Power was seized by a group of young army officers, led by Lt-Col Gamal Abd an-Nasir (Nasser). Farouk abdicated in favour of his infant son, Ahmad Fuad II, and went into exile. Gen. Muhammad Nagib (Neguib) was appointed Commander-in-Chief of the army and Chairman of the Revolution Command Council (RCC). In September Gen. Neguib was appointed Prime Minister and Military Governor, with Col Nasser as Deputy Prime Minister. In December the 1923 Constitution was abolished, and in January 1953 all political parties were dissolved. On 18 June 1953 the monarchy was abolished, and Egypt was proclaimed a republic, with Gen. Neguib as President and Prime Minister. In April 1954 President Neguib was succeeded as Prime Minister by Col Nasser. In October Egypt and the United Kingdom signed an agreement providing for the withdrawal of all British forces from the Suez Canal by June 1956. In November 1954 President Neguib was relieved of all his remaining posts, and Col Nasser became acting Head of State.

The establishment of military rule was accompanied by wide-ranging reforms, including the redistribution of land, the promotion of industrial development and the expansion of social welfare services. In foreign affairs, the new regime was strongly committed to Arab unity, and Egypt played a prominent part in the Non-Aligned Movement. In 1955, having failed to secure Western armaments on satisfactory terms, Egypt accepted military assistance from the USSR.

On 23 June 1956 a new Constitution was approved by a national referendum, and Nasser was elected President (unopposed). The RCC was dissolved. In July, following the departure of British forces, the US and British Governments withdrew their offers of financial assistance for Egypt's construction of the Aswan High Dam. In response, President Nasser announced the nationalization of the Suez Canal Company, so that revenue from Canal tolls could be used to finance the dam's construction. The take-over of the Canal was a cause of great concern to Israel, Britain and France, and Israel invaded the Sinai Peninsula on 29 October. Britain and France launched military operations against Egypt two days later. Strong pressure from the UN and the US Government resulted in a cease-fire on 6 November, and supervision by the UN of the invaders' withdrawal.

Egypt and Syria merged in February 1958 to form the United Arab Republic (UAR), with Nasser as President. The new nation strengthened earlier ties with the USSR and other countries of the East European bloc. In September 1961 Syria seceded from the UAR, but Egypt retained this title until September 1971. In 1958 the UAR and Yemen formed a federation called the United Arab States, but this was dissolved in 1961.

President Nasser enjoyed immense prestige throughout the Arab world and beyond. Internally, he was regarded as the founder of modern Egypt. In December 1962 he established the Arab Socialist Union (ASU) as the country's only recognized political organization. In May 1967 he secured the withdrawal of the UN Emergency Force from Egyptian territory. Egypt subsequently reoccupied Sharm esh-Sheikh, on the Sinai Peninsula, and closed the Straits of Tiran to Israeli shipping. This provoked the 'Six-Day War' of June 1967, when Israel quickly defeated neighbouring Arab states, including Egypt. The war left Israel in control of the Gaza Strip and a large area of Egyptian territory, including the whole of the Sinai Peninsula. The Suez Canal was blocked, and remained closed until June 1975.

President Nasser died suddenly in September 1970, and was succeeded by Col Anwar Sadat, hitherto the Vice-President. In September 1971 the UAR was renamed the Arab Republic of Egypt, and a new Constitution took effect. The Federation of Arab Republics (Egypt, Libya and Syria) was founded in 1972, but proved to be ineffective. In 1976 Egypt terminated its Treaty of Friendship with the USSR. Relations with the USA, however, became closer, as President Sadat came to rely increasingly on US aid.

An uneasy cease-fire with Israel lasted until October 1973, when Egyptian troops crossed the Suez Canal to recover territory lost in 1967. After 18 days of fighting, a cease-fire was achieved. In 1974–75 Dr Henry Kissinger, the US Secretary of State, negotiated disengagement agreements whereby Israel evacuated territory in Sinai, and Israeli and Egyptian forces were separated by a buffer zone under the control of UN forces. In a dramatic peace-making initiative, President Sadat visited Israel in 1977 and addressed the Knesset. Many Arab countries opposed the visit. The leaders of Syria, Libya, Algeria, Iraq, the People's Democratic Republic of Yemen (PDRY) and the Palestine Liberation Organization (PLO) condemned Egypt, which responded by severing diplomatic relations with the five dissenting countries. In September 1978, following talks held at Camp David in the USA, President Sadat and the Prime Minister of Israel, Menachem Begin, signed two agreements. The first provided for a five-year transitional period during which the inhabitants of the Israeli-occupied West Bank of Jordan and the Gaza Strip would obtain full autonomy and self-government. The second agreement provided for a peace treaty between Egypt and Israel. This was signed in March 1979, and Israel subsequently made phased withdrawals from the Sinai Peninsula, the last of which took place in April 1982. Syria, Algeria, Libya and the PLO had condemned the Camp David agreements, and in March 1979 the Arab League expelled Egypt and introduced political and economic sanctions. Egypt, however, continued to strengthen relations with Israel, and in February 1980 the two countries exchanged ambassadors for the first time.

In 1974 Sadat began to introduce a more liberal political and economic regime. Political parties (banned since 1953) were allowed to participate in the 1976 elections for the People's

Assembly, and in July 1978 Sadat formed the National Democratic Party (NDP), with himself as leader. In 1979 the special constitutional status of the ASU was ended. In October 1981 Sadat was assassinated by members of Islamic Jihad, a group of Muslim fundamentalists. Sadat was succeeded by Lt-Gen. Hosni Mubarak, his Vice-President and a former Commander-in-Chief of the air force. A new electoral law required parties to receive a minimum of 8% of the total vote in order to be represented in the People's Assembly. This prompted opposition parties to boycott elections to local councils and to the Shura (Advisory) Council. At legislative elections in May 1984 the ruling NDP received 72.9% of the total vote. Of the four other participating parties, only the New Wafd Party, with 15.1%, crossed the 8% threshold. Dr Ahmad Fuad Mohi ed-Din, Prime Minister since 1982, died in June 1984, and was succeeded by Gen. Kamal Hassan Ali. The campaign by Muslim fundamentalists for the Egyptian legal system fully to adopt the principles of the *Shari'a* (Islamic holy law) intensified in 1985. The People's Assembly rejected proposals for immediate changes and advocated a thorough study of the small proportion of Egyptian law that did not conform to Islamic precepts. Dr Ali Lutfi was appointed Prime Minister in September, following the resignation of Gen. Kamal Hassan Ali and his Council of Ministers.

In foreign affairs, a division in the Arab world between a 'moderate' grouping (including Jordan, Iraq and the Gulf States), which viewed the participation of Egypt as indispensable to any diplomatic activities for solving the problems of the region, and a 'radical' grouping, led by Syria, became increasingly evident. The PLO leader, Yasser Arafat, visited President Mubarak for discussions in December 1983, signifying the end of an estrangement between Egypt and the PLO. In 1984 Jordan resumed diplomatic relations with Egypt. Egypt proposed two formulas for a peaceful settlement of the Iran–Iraq War, but neither was adopted by Iran or Iraq. President Mubarak, accompanied by King Hussein of Jordan, made an unexpected visit to Baghdad in March 1985, to demonstrate his support for the Iraqi President, Saddam Hussain, although there had been no formal diplomatic relations between Egypt and Iraq since 1979. Relations with Libya continued to deteriorate.

President Mubarak, King Hussein of Jordan and Yasser Arafat of the PLO continued their discussions in pursuit of a negotiated settlement of the Palestinian question during 1984–85. Mubarak endorsed the agreement concluded by Arafat and King Hussein, establishing the principle of a joint Jordanian-Palestinian delegation to participate in a proposed Middle East peace conference. The credibility of the PLO as a participant in peace negotiations, and of the Jordanian-Palestinian agreement, was compromised in 1985, when an Italian cruise liner, the *Achille Lauro*, was hijacked by Palestinians belonging to a faction of the Palestine Liberation Front (PLF). In November an EgyptAir airliner was hijacked to Malta by Palestinians, whom Egypt linked with the renegade PLO leader, Abu Nidal, and his Libyan supporters. Egypt's handling of the crisis, resulting in 58 deaths, was strongly criticized.

Relations between Egypt and Israel were strained by the latter's invasion of Lebanon in 1982, and Israel repeatedly accused Egypt of contraventions of the 1979 peace treaty. In 1985 Israel and Egypt began a series of negotiations to determine the sovereignty of a small coastal strip at Taba, on the Red Sea, which Israel did not vacate when it withdrew from the Sinai Peninsula in 1982. The dispute was referred to international arbitration. In 1988 sovereignty was awarded to Egypt, but an important border was left undefined. Egypt assumed control over the Taba enclave in March 1989.

In November 1986 President Mubarak accepted the resignation of the Prime Minister, Dr Ali Lutfi. A new Council of Ministers was appointed, under the premiership of Dr Atif Sidqi, hitherto the head of the Central Auditing Agency. A general election was held in April 1987, following a campaign marred by clashes between Christians and Muslims, and by accusations of government corruption. The election resulted in a large majority for the ruling NDP. Of the 448 elective seats, the NDP won 346, the opposition parties together won 95, and independents seven. The Socialist Labour Party (SLP), the Liberal Socialist Party (LSP) and the Muslim Brotherhood had formed an electoral alliance, and won a combined total of 60 seats, of which the Brotherhood took 37, thus becoming the largest single opposition group in the new Assembly. In October Hosni Mubarak was confirmed as President for a second six-year term of office. In March 1988 the national state of emergency first declared after the assassination of President Sadat was renewed for a further three years. Anti-Government demonstrations, not only by Muslim fundamentalists but also by striking workers, occurred later in the year. In May 1989, faced with increasing popular discontent over price increases and food shortages, the Government acted to pre-empt disturbances during Ramadan by detaining more than 2,000 Muslim fundamentalists. In June elections to the Shura Council were contested by opposition parties for the first time since the Council's establishment in 1980. It was subsequently alleged that the NDP had achieved its victory by fraudulent means. In July and August 1989 large numbers of alleged 'leftists' and Shi'ite Muslims were arrested, but most were released within a month, following international protests. In December there was speculation that Muslim fundamentalists had been responsible for the attempted assassination of the Minister of the Interior, Maj.-Gen. Zaki Badr. In January 1990 Badr was replaced by Muhammad Abd al-Halim Moussa. In April three new political parties, the Green Party, the Democratic Unionist Party (DUP) and the Young Egypt Party (YEP), were legalized, bringing the total number of officially recognized political parties to nine.

The legislative elections held in November and December 1990 were boycotted by the principal opposition parties, despite the fact that polling was conducted under new electoral laws. The former requirement for a party to win a minimum of 8% of the total vote in order to gain representation in the Assembly was abolished, and restrictions on independent candidates were removed; the Government refused, however, to concede the opposition parties' demands that the elections be removed from the supervision of the Ministry of the Interior, and that the state of emergency be repealed. The credibility of any mandate that the Government might receive in the elections was thus undermined in advance. Moreover, the electoral turn-out was estimated to have been no greater than 20%–30%. Of the 444 elective seats in the new Assembly, the NDP won 348, the National Progressive Unionist Party won six, and independent candidates 83. Voting in the remaining seven seats was suspended.

In November 1987, at a summit conference in Jordan which was attended by the majority of Arab leaders, the Syrian President, Hafiz Assad, obstructed proposals to readmit Egypt to the League of Arab States. However, recognizing Egypt's support for Iraq in the Iran–Iraq War and acknowledging the influence that Egypt could exercise on the problems of the region, the conference approved a resolution placing the establishment of diplomatic links with Egypt at the discretion of member governments. Such links had previously been prohibited.

Following Jordan's decision, in 1988, to sever its legal and administrative links with the West Bank region (under Israeli occupation since 1967), President Mubarak urged the PLO to exercise caution in its plans to declare an independent Palestinian state and to form a government-in-exile. In September 1988, during a tour of western Europe, the Egyptian President expressed reservations regarding the PLO's commitment to renouncing terrorism and recognizing Israel. In November, however, Egypt granted full recognition to the newly-declared independent Palestinian State.

The visit of King Fahd of Saudi Arabia to Cairo in March 1989 was a further indication of Egypt's improved status in the Arab world. In May Egypt was readmitted to the Arab League, despite Libya's opposition. President Mubarak represented Egypt at an emergency summit conference of the League, convened to rally support for the diplomatic initiatives of Yasser Arafat, following the Palestinian declaration of independence. Col Qaddafi of Libya attended the meeting and had separate discussions with President Mubarak. In June it was announced that Egypt was preparing to reopen its border with Libya, and in October Col Qaddafi visited Egypt for further discussions.

In April 1989, in response to increasing international diplomatic pressure, Israel announced details of a four-point peace initiative for a resolution of the Middle East conflict. The most important component of the plan was a proposal to hold elections in the West Bank and Gaza Strip. However, the initiative was ambiguous with regard to several crucial aspects of the Middle East conflict. In August the Egyptian Minister of State for Foreign Affairs, Dr Boutros Boutros-Ghali, visited Israel to confer with the Israeli Prime Minister, Itzhak Shamir. However, his offer to mediate between Israel and the PLO was rejected. In September President Mubarak sought to persuade the Israeli Government to accept 10 points clarifying its peace initiative, so that direct Palestinian-Israeli negotiations concerning the election plans could begin. In December following two months of US diplomatic support for the 'Cairo initiative', Egypt accepted, with conditions, a five-point US framework for the holding of Palestinian elections in the Occupied Territories.

By early 1990 there had been no appreciable progress in the Middle East peace process, which had been further complicated by Israel's apparent intention to settle in the Occupied Territories some of the Soviet Jewish immigrants who were arriving in the country in large numbers. Egypt's increasing frustration at the lack of progress, and its concern about the escalation of the Palestinian *intifada* ('uprising'—launched in 1987), led it to assume a more critical stance towards the Israeli Government. Following the suspension by the US Government of its dialogue with the PLO in June 1990, Egypt attributed the disintegration of the peace process to 'Israeli intransigence'.

Following Iraq's invasion and annexation of Kuwait in August 1990, Egypt convened an emergency summit meeting of Arab leaders. Egypt demanded the withdrawal of Iraqi forces from Kuwait, and 12 of the 20 Arab League states voted to send an Arab force to the Persian (Arabian) Gulf region, in response to Saudi Arabia's request for multinational assistance to deter aggression by Iraq. Following the outbreak of hostilities between Iraq and a UN-sponsored multinational force in January 1991, the Egyptian Government continued to support the anti-Iraq coalition. Egypt's contingent within the multinational force, eventually augmented to 35,000 troops, sustained only light casualties in the fighting. Egypt emerged from the conflict in the Gulf region with its international reputation enhanced, largely as a result of President Mubarak's firm leadership of 'moderate' Arab opinion.

In early March 1991 the Ministers of Foreign Affairs of Egypt, Syria and the member states of the Gulf Co-operation Council (GCC, see p. 136) met in Damascus. A statement that was issued after the meeting appeared to foresee the formation of an Arab regional security force, of which it was proposed that the Egyptian and Syrian troops already deployed in Saudi Arabia and other Gulf states should constitute the nucleus. In May, however, Egypt unexpectedly announced the withdrawal of most of its 35,000 troops in Saudi Arabia and Kuwait. It had reportedly been angered by the decision of the Gulf states to reduce the amount of aid that they had pledged to Egypt and Syria in March, and considered that the Egyptian role in the liberation of Kuwait had not been duly recognized.

The first regular meeting of the Arab League since the outbreak of hostilities in the Gulf region in January 1991 commenced in Cairo in late March. A further meeting took place in May, at which Egypt's Minister of Foreign Affairs, Dr Ahmad Esmat Abd al-Meguid, was endorsed as the League's new Secretary-General. The holding of the League's meetings at its original headquarters in Cairo, under its new Secretary-General, was a further indication of the rehabilitation of Egypt's reputation within the Arab world.

Following a reshuffle of the Council of Ministers in May 1991, President Mubarak stated that domestic political reform, in particular the extension of the democratic franchise, was to be one of the new Government's principal aims. However, in June the national state of emergency was renewed for a further three years, the Government citing the continued threat of internal and external subversion.

President Mubarak was formally nominated for a third term of office in July 1993, and in early October his nomination was approved by some 94.9% of the valid votes cast in a national referendum. The Government's claim that 84% of the electorate had participated in the referendum was regarded with scepticism by many observers. None of Egypt's opposition parties had endorsed Mubarak's candidature for a third term of office. Rather, they criticized the Government for its attempts to monopolize political life and urged reforms on the President. These included changing the Constitution to allow direct presidential elections; the unrestricted formation of political parties; and the introduction of a two-term limit to the presidency. In mid-October the Prime Minister, Dr Atif Sidqi, was invited to form a new Council of Ministers. The new Government included 10 new ministers, but most key portfolios remained in the charge of their previous holders. No members of the principal opposition blocks were included, and the President gave no indication that he was prepared to concede any other reforms. In May 1994 representatives of all the country's legal political parties and of its professional associations were chosen to form preparatory committees for a National Dialogue Congress, the terms of reference of which were political, economic and social reform. The Muslim Brotherhood, which was legally barred from forming its own political party, was excluded from the Congress, although it was believed that some of its supporters might attend as trade union representatives. Before it commenced, the credibility of the national dialogue was undermined by the withdrawal of the New Wafd Party and the Nasserist Party from the preparatory committees. The New Wafd Party accused the Government of seeking to predetermine the outcome of the national dialogue by manipulating the agenda of the Congress. The National Dialogue Congress held its first procedural session on 25 June and ended, sooner than expected, on 7 July. Three committees (charged, respectively, to consider political, economic and social affairs)—into which the Congress had divided—were reported to have forwarded to the President only general, non-binding recommendations. With regard to political reform, the Congress was reported to have suggested that the electoral register should be updated; that elections should be supervised by the judiciary; and that the electoral system should be changed into one based on party lists. In January 1995, however, the NDP announced that the legislative election scheduled to take place later in the year would not be contested on the party list system, as recommended by the National Dialogue Congress, but that the individual list system would be retained. Most opposition parties, including the Muslim Brotherhood, indicated that they would not boycott the elections as they had in 1990.

In the elections to the People's Assembly, which were held in November–December 1995, candidates of the ruling NDP won the majority—316—of seats. Independent candidates gained 115 legislative seats, but it was reported that 99 of them had immediately either joined or rejoined the NDP. The New Wafd Party obtained six seats, the National Progressive Unionist Party five and the LSP and the Nasserist Party one seat each. It was widely alleged that the supporters of opposition candidates had been intimidated at the polls, and that agents acting for the NDP had resorted to various electoral malpractices. In early January 1996 a new Council of Ministers was appointed, with Kamal Ahmad al-Ganzouri (hitherto the Minister of Planning) replacing Dr Atif Sidqi as Prime Minister. In June the People's Assembly adopted more liberal legislation governing the activities of the press. New laws replaced those enacted in May 1995, which had attracted severe criticism from all sections of the press, including those that supported the Government.

In July 1997 President Mubarak announced a reorganization of the Council of Ministers, including the appointment of Youssef Boutros-Ghali, who had played a leading role in Egypt's economic liberalization programme, to the post of Minister of Economy. The following day the President appointed new governors to 10 of the country's governorates; these included Menia, where the former head of the state security services, Gen. Mustafa Abdel Qader, was selected as governor in an attempt to restore order in an area that had been the scene of persistent Islamist attacks and recent violent demonstrations against an unpopular new land law.

Since early 1992 the Government's attempts to suppress an Islamic fundamentalist movement that frequently resorts to violence in order to further its aims have dominated the domestic political agenda. During 1992 some 70 people were reportedly killed as a result of militant violence, which increasingly targeted foreign tourists visiting Egypt. Attacks on foreign tourists and violent confrontations between Islamic militants and the security forces, occurred regularly during 1993. In late May the UK-based human rights organization Amnesty International published a report in which it alleged that the Government was systematically maltreating political detainees, and in November the organization accused the Government of breaching the UN Convention Against Torture. The number of Islamists executed in Egypt in 1993 totalled 29.

In January 1994 the Egyptian security forces were reported to have detained some 1,000 suspected fundamentalist activists in response to attacks on their members during that month. In the following month militant Islamist groups intensified their attacks on tourists and also targeted foreign investors. In March nine members of the Vanguard of Conquest (a faction of Islamic Jihad) were sentenced to death after having been convicted of conspiring to assassinate the Prime Minister in November 1993. On 9 April 1994 the chief of the anti-terrorist branch of the State Security Investigation Section, Maj.-Gen. Raouf Khairat, was assassinated by members of Jama'ah al-Islamiyah (one of Egypt's main militant Islamic groups), prompting an extensive retaliatory security operation. On 11 April emergency laws giving the security forces wide powers to arrest and detain suspects were renewed for a further three years. In mid-July a further five members of the Vanguard of Conquest were sentenced to death, having been found guilty of attempting to assassinate the Minister of the Interior in August 1993. Islamic militants carried out further attacks on tourists during August–October 1994. In September Amnesty International again criticized Egypt's human rights record, in particular methods employed by the police and the security forces in their campaign against the Islamic fundamentalist movement.

In early 1995 the Government began to take steps to isolate the more moderate Muslim Brotherhood and to weaken its political influence in the approach to the parliamentary elections planned for later that year. Several leading members of the Brotherhood were arrested in late January and both President Mubarak and the Minister of the Interior claimed that there was evidence of links between the movement and Islamist extremists. The Government also acted to curb Islamist influence within professional organizations; in February the People's Assembly passed an amendment to legislation governing such organizations, giving the judiciary wide powers to intervene in union elections and to prevent Muslim Brotherhood members from standing. Clashes between extremists and the security forces in Upper Egypt claimed 87 lives in January 1995, the highest number for any month in three years. Security officials announced that 123 people had been killed in Menia governorate alone in the first three months of 1995, compared with 77 in the whole of the previous year. In early 1995 some 20 members of the SLP were arrested in Menia and charged with distributing anti-Government leaflets and with supporting the Jama'ah al-Islamiyah. In February the US Department of State published a highly critical report on the methods employed by the Egyptian security forces. In June President Mubarak escaped an assassination attempt in Ethiopia while he was travelling to the opening session of the OAU summit meeting in Addis Ababa. It was widely believed that the attackers belonged to either Islamic Jihad or the Jama'ah al-Islamiyah. The Government claimed that the gunmen were helped by Sudan, an accusation denied by the Sudanese Government. (In September 1996 three Egyptians, who were reported to be members of unspecified Islamist groups, were sentenced to death by the Ethiopian Supreme Court for their involvement in the assassination attempt.) The Government's decision, in September, to refer the cases of 45 detained members of the Muslim Brotherhood for trial by military court was condemned by the Brotherhood as an attempt to undermine its effective participation in the forthcoming legislative elections. A further 14 Muslim Brotherhood leaders were arrested in October, the Government claiming that they had assisted members of proscribed Islamist organizations.

In February 1996 more than 30 people were reported to have been killed in clashes between security forces and Islamic extremists in the Upper Egypt governorates of Menia and Asyut. In April 12 prominent members of the Muslim Brotherhood were arrested and charged with attempting to resume the movement's clandestine activities and restore its links with extremist groups. For the first time, the Egyptian authorities detained a member of the Brotherhood's Supreme Guidance Council. Three of those arrested had founded a new political organization, the Al-Wasat (Centre) Party. While the authorities claimed that the new party was serving as a front for Brotherhood activities, its founders—who included Islamists, Christians, leftists and Nasserist activists—insisted that they were seeking to create a political group that occupied the middle ground between the State and its Islamist opponents. In mid-April 18 Greek tourists were killed in an attack on a hotel in Cairo. The Jama'ah al-Islamiyah admitted responsibility for the attack, but claimed that it had intended to kill Israeli tourists in order to avenge the victims of Israeli military operations in Lebanon. In early May the Government was reported to have rejected a peace initiative by Islamist groups, offering a halt to their campaign of violence against security forces and terrorists; the Government insisted that it would not negotiate with 'militant groups'. In July Amnesty International published further allegations of the systematic use of torture by the Government against its opponents. In October it was reported that the security forces had arrested members of a Shi'ite Muslim group accused of planning to stage an Iranian-style revolution in Egypt. Further arrests of supporters of the Muslim Brotherhood and the SLP were made in December. The detention of these activists was widely regarded as an attempt by the Government to weaken political opposition prior to the local elections scheduled for April 1997. The Government continued in its attempt to curb political dissidence and Islamist violence throughout 1997; in February the national state of emergency, first declared in 1981, was renewed for a further three years. Nevertheless, despite the extension of emergency provisions (including trial of civilians by military court, lengthy detention without trial and press censorship), a number of people were killed by Islamic extremists in Upper Egypt in the following month and, again, in August. In mid-September a military court in Haekstep, north of the capital, held Egypt's largest-single military trial to date of suspected Islamic militants; 98 people, in total, were convicted, four of whom were sentenced to death and eight to life imprisonment. In apparent retaliation, a few days later suspected Islamist extremists opened fire on and launched petrol bombs at a tourist bus in Cairo, killing nine German tourists and injuring 11 others. Although the perpetrators of the attack were widely believed to be members of the Jama'ah al-Islamiyah, in an apparent attempt to protect the country's vital tourism industry, the Government claimed that the attack was an isolated incident carried out by 'mentally deranged' individuals with no terrorist connections. Government claims to have suppressed Islamist extremist activity appeared invalidated in October when 10 policemen and one civilian were killed by suspected members of the Jama'ah al-Islamiyah in the southern governorate of Menia. In the following month both the Government and the Egyptian tourism industry suffered a serious set-back following the massacre of 70 people, including 58 foreign tourists, by members of the Jama'ah al-Islamiyah near the ancient city of Luxor. President Mubarak criticized the security services for failing to protect tourists and publicly accused the Minister of the Interior, Hussein Muhammad al-Alfi, who had drawn up the Government's hardline policies aimed at eradicating Islamist militancy, of having failed. The disgraced Minister was forced to resign immediately and was replaced by Habib Ibrahim el-Adli, hitherto the head of the state security services. President Mubarak ordered a heightened security presence at all tourist sites and placed the Prime Minister at the head of a special committee, which was to devise a plan to safeguard the lucrative tourism industry. Later that month, in an apparent attempt to deflect some of the responsibility for the attack, the Government published a wanted list of exiled Islamic militants and accused the countries that permitted them residency rights (particularly the United Kingdom) of condoning terrorist acts of violence. In December internal dissension within the Jama'ah al-Islamiyah became evident when a number of the group's exiled leaders claimed that the massacre at Luxor had been perpetrated by a rogue element acting without the authorization of the group's central leadership; at the same time, these leaders in exile announced that the Jama'ah al-Islamiyah (at least, those members under their specific authority) would no longer target tourists in their conflict with the Government.

Egypt played an important role in the diplomatic efforts which led to the convening of a Middle East peace conference in Madrid, Spain, on 30 October 1991, and an Egyptian delegation attended the first, symbolic session of the conference. At later stages of the conference Egypt also attended bilateral sessions as an observer and multilateral sessions as a participant. Despite the procedural delays and the slow progress of the negotiations, the Egyptian Government felt that the conference represented the best hope for a durable peace in the region and that it had an important 'behind-the-scenes' role to play in co-ordinating Arab strategy and providing diplomatic expertise. In late July 1992 the Israeli Prime Minister, Itzhak Rabin, visited Cairo for talks with President Mubarak, who reportedly emphasized to him his opinion that progress in the peace process was dependent on a halt to Israeli settlements in the Occupied Territories. Egyptian mediators were influential in the secret negotiations between Israel and the PLO that led to the signing of the Declaration of Principles on Palestinian Self-Rule on 13 September 1993. In October PLO and Israeli delegations began to meet regularly in Cairo or at Taba, on the Red Sea, to discuss the detailed implementation of the Declaration of Principles. In November King Hussein of Jordan visited Cairo for talks on the Middle East peace process, his first visit since the Gulf crisis of 1990–91, which had damaged relations between the two countries. In December 1993 President Mubarak convened an emergency summit meeting in Cairo between Itzhak Rabin and the PLO leader, Yasser Arafat, in an unsuccessful attempt to achieve an agreement on the withdrawal of Israeli armed forces from the Gaza Strip and the Jericho area, which had been due to begin on 13 December.

The massacre of some 30 Palestinians in Hebron on the West Bank by an Israeli settler in February 1994 provoked angry demonstrations in Cairo, where supporters of the Nasserist Party and the Muslim Brotherhood remained opposed to the terms of the Declaration of Principles on Palestinian Self-Rule. Egypt recalled its ambassador from Israel for consultations, but at the same time sought to persuade the PLO to resume the suspended peace negotiations. Talks between Israel and the PLO recommenced in Cairo in late March. On 4 May an agreement on Palestinian self-rule in the Gaza Strip and the Jericho area was signed in Cairo by the Israeli Prime Minister and the PLO Chairman at a ceremony presided over by President Mubarak. Under the terms of the agreement, Israeli forces withdrew from the Jericho area on 13 May and from the Gaza Strip on 18 May.

In July 1994 President Mubarak travelled to Damascus in an effort to break the deadlock in the peace negotiations between Syria and Israel. Despite the first official Israeli presidential visit to Egypt by Ezer Weizman, in December relations between Egypt and Israel began to deteriorate. Egypt was concerned that the Middle East peace process might collapse unless Israel showed more flexibility and the Palestinians secured some real benefits from the peace agreement as quickly as possible.

In December 1994 and February 1995 Egypt hosted two meetings which some observers viewed as an attempt by the Government to demonstrate its continuing role as the key intermediary in the region and to refute the view, expressed by some members of the new Republican majority in the US Congress, that Egypt no longer deserved substantial US aid. The meeting between Syrian President Assad, King Fahd of Saudi Arabia and President Mubarak took place on 28–29 December 1994 in Alexandria and, according to some reports, was convened in response to Syrian anxiety about the number of Arab states seeking to normalize their relations with Israel before significant progress had been made in peace negotiations between Syria and Israel. The Israeli Government interpreted the summit as being hostile to Israel and as a negative response to President Weizman's invitation to Mubarak to make a reciprocal visit to Israel. Further tension arose when President Mubarak reiterated his threat that Egypt would not sign the Nuclear Non-Proliferation Treaty (NPT), which was due for renewal in April 1995, unless Israel also agreed to sign it; and urged other states to do likewise.

President Mubarak met King Hussein of Jordan at Aqaba in January 1995, his first visit to Jordan since the Gulf crisis of 1990. The visit was regarded as a sign of an improvement in relations between the two countries now that Jordan had signed a peace treaty with Israel. King Hussein, together with Yasser Arafat and Itzhak Rabin, attended a hastily convened meeting in Cairo in early February 1995 after a suicide bomb attack on an Israeli civilian target threatened to halt the peace process. Tension between Egypt and Israel over the NPT continued. In March Israel offered to sign the NPT once it had concluded peace treaties with all of the Arab states and Iran, and to allow Egypt to inspect its research nuclear reactor at Nahal Shorek (but not the nuclear facility at Dimona). Egypt rejected both offers, but adopted a more conciliatory line on the issue.

Egypt's position regarding the NPT antagonized the USA, which insisted that the continuation of US aid depended on Egypt's signing the Treaty. When President Mubarak visited Washington, DC, in April 1995 Egypt's relations with the USA were at their lowest level for many years. Despite President Mubarak's pledge that Egypt would not withdraw from the NPT, nor seek to persuade other states to suspend their membership, the possibility of a reduction in US aid to Egypt continued to be openly discussed. The dispute over the NPT culminated at the headquarters of the UN in New York, USA, in May. The Arab states agreed to a resolution which did not mention Israel by name, but instead urged all states in the Middle East, without exception, to sign the NPT. Relations between Egypt and Israel deteriorated again in August, after it was revealed that Israeli soldiers had killed a large number of Egyptian prisoners of war during the Suez crisis in 1956 and the Six-Day War in 1967. Nevertheless, Egypt continued its mediatory role in the complex negotiations that eventually led to the signing of the Israeli-Palestinian Interim Agreement on the West Bank and the Gaza Strip in Washington, DC, USA, in September 1995. In November Mubarak made his first visit to Israel as President of Egypt, in order to attend the funeral of Itzhak Rabin. Egypt also participated in meetings which led to the resumption of peace negotiations between Israel and Syria at the end of 1995.

After a number of suicide bomb attacks in Israel in February and March 1996, Egypt and the USA co-hosted a one-day 'Summit of Peacemakers' at the Red Sea resort of Sharm esh-Sheikh in March. At the meeting, while Israel and the USA sought to devise new ways of combating terrorism through increased regional and international co-operation, President Mubarak, together with other Arab leaders, concentrated on preventing the collapse of the Middle East peace process. Egypt's relations with Israel deteriorated again in April, as a consequence of Israeli military operations in Lebanon. Diplomatic efforts by the Egyptian Minister of Foreign Affairs to achieve a cease-fire in Lebanon were unsuccessful, and the Minister complained that Israel's actions were threatening the entire peace process.

In June 1996 Mubarak stated that the new Israeli administration led by Prime Minister Binyamin Netanyahu, which came to power in the previous month, had to be given time 'to clarify its viewpoints and intentions towards the peace process'. However, at the end of June, after Netanyahu had repeated his rejection of the principle of exchanging land for peace, President Mubarak convened an emergency summit meeting of the Arab League in Cairo—the first such summit meeting for six years. Only Iraq was not invited to attend, owing to what President Mubarak described as 'continuing sensitivities'. In response to what had become known as the three noes of Israeli policy—no to a Palestinian state, no to Palestinian sovereignty over East Jerusalem and no to Israeli withdrawal from the Golan Heights—the summit's final communiqué reaffirmed the Arab states' commitment to peace, but warned that peace and any further *rapprochement* between them and Israel depended on Israel's returning of all the Arab land that it occupied in 1967. Israel rejected all of the resolutions adopted at the summit meeting. In July Netanyahu visited Egypt for talks with Mubarak; this was the Israeli Prime Minister's first official visit to an Arab country since his election to the premiership. In response to a serious escalation in Palestinian–Israeli fighting, the Arab League met in emergency session in Cairo in September and demanded that the UN Security Council halt Israel's 'aggression' against the Palestinians. In March 1997 Egypt condemned the Israeli Government for ordering the start of construction work on the new Israeli settlement of Har Homa in East Jerusalem; this controversial decision by Israel effectively brought about the collapse of the peace process. For the remainder of that year the Egyptian Government, in its role as principal mediator, attempted unsuccessfully to revive the peace process. In October Egypt announced a prohibition of imports of Israeli goods produced in the occupied territories. In the following month Egypt was one of a large number of Arab countries that boycotted the fourth Middle East and North Africa economic conference in Doha, Qatar, in protest at Israel's failure to honour its commitments to the Palestinians under the terms of the 1993 Oslo peace agreements.

Relations with the USA remained strained. The US Secretary of Defense, William Perry, visited Cairo in April 1996 and denied rumours that the USA had signed a secret defence agreement with Israel. Perry announced that the USA would supply advanced military equipment to Egypt, including 21 F-16 fighter aircraft, in acknowledgement of its key role in the peace process.

Egypt's relations with Libya have been dominated by the repercussions of the Lockerbie affair (see chapter on Libya) and allegations, by the USA and its western allies, of Libya's involvement. As there are more than 1m. Egyptian expatriate workers in Libya, Egypt has used its diplomacy to try to avert a confrontation between Libya and the West, which could threaten not only the jobs of its workers but also a steadily growing market for its exports. During his visit to Egypt in April 1996 the US Secretary of Defense was reported to have shown President Mubarak conclusive evidence that Libya was constructing a huge chemical weapons factory at Tarhuna. While offering to mediate with the Libyan leader, Col Qaddafi, on this issue, President Mubarak warned against any new US military action against Libya. In May Mubarak sought to persuade Col Qaddafi to reconsider his decision to expel Palestinians from Libya.

Egypt's relations with Sudan deteriorated following the visit, in December 1991, of an Iranian delegation, led by President Rafsanjani, to Sudan. Aware of the dangers posed by the activities of its own Islamic militants, Egypt was alarmed by Iran's support of Sudan's military regime, which is dominated by the fundamentalist National Islamic Front. In October 1992 an Egyptian-Sudanese committee that had been established in order to study the issue of the disputed Halaib border area met for the first time. In June 1993 President Mubarak held talks with the Sudanese President, Lt-Gen. al-Bashir, who was visiting Cairo for the annual meeting of the OAU, in an attempt to reduce tensions between Egypt and Sudan. However, relations worsened again in August 1994, when each side accused the other of mistreating its nationals. In the following month Sudan alleged that Egyptian troops had entered the disputed border area of Halaib. Relations deteriorated sharply in June 1995, after the unsuccessful attempt to assassinate President Mubarak in Addis Ababa (see above). The Egyptian Government accused Sudan of complicity in the attack, and Egypt immediately strengthened its control of the Halaib triangle. In July, in contravention of an agreement concluded with Sudan in 1978, Egypt imposed visa and permit requirements on Sudanese nationals visiting or resident in Egypt. Relations between Egypt and Sudan deteriorated further in September 1995, when the OAU accused Sudan of direct involvement in the attempted assassination, and in December, when it demanded that Sudan should immediately extradite three individuals who were sought in connection with the attack. In February 1996 Sudan introduced permit requirements for Egyptian nationals resident in Sudan. Presidents Mubarak and al-Bashir met at the Arab League summit meeting in Cairo in May. In July, however, Egypt accused Sudan of harbouring Egyptian terrorists, contrary to an agreement concluded at the summit meeting. None the less, Egypt opposed the imposition of more stringent economic sanctions against Sudan by the UN (in addition to diplomatic sanctions and an embargo on international flights operated by Sudan Airways), on the grounds that they would harm the Sudanese people more than the Sudanese regime. In January 1997 Egypt refused to provide the Sudanese Government with military support in its struggle against rebel advances in southern Sudan. In June Sudan accused Egypt of providing the opposition with military training, and in October the Sudanese press reported that Egypt was obstructing the import of medical supplies to Halaib. Despite such accusations, there was evidence of attempts to improve bilateral relations: in August security talks between the two countries resumed after a year-long suspension, and in October the Sudanese First Vice-President, Maj.-Gen. Zubair Muhammad Salih, visited Egypt to discuss specifically the normalization of relations.

Government

Legislative power is held by the unicameral Majlis ash-Sha'ab (People's Assembly), which has 454 members: 10 nominated by the President and 444 directly elected for five years from 222 constituencies. The Assembly nominates the President, who is elected by popular referendum for six years (renewable). The President has executive powers and appoints one or more Vice-Presidents, a Prime Minister and a Council of Ministers. There is also a 210-member advisory body, the Shura Council. The country is divided into 27 governorates.

Defence

In August 1997 Egypt had total armed forces of 450,000 (army 320,000, air defence command 80,000, navy 20,000, air force 30,000), with 254,000 reserves. There is a selective three-year period of national service. Defence expenditure for 1997 was budgeted at £E8,700m. ($2,600m.).

Economic Affairs

In 1995, according to estimates by the World Bank, Egypt's gross national product (GNP), measured at average 1993–95 prices, was US $45,507m., equivalent to $790 per head. During 1985–95, it was estimated, GNP per head increased, in real terms, by an annual average of 1.1%. Over the same period, the population increased by an annual average of 2.2%. The average annual growth of overall gross domestic product (GDP), measured in constant prices, was 2.1% in 1985–95. GDP increased, in real terms, by 2% in 1994, by 2.4% in 1995 and by 3.3% in 1996.

Agriculture (including forestry and fishing) contributed 16.0% of GDP in 1995/96 and employed an estimated 31.9% of the economically active population in 1996. The principal crops include cotton, rice, wheat, sugar cane, maize and tomatoes. Exports of food and live animals accounted for 10.2% of total exports in 1996. During 1990–95 agricultural GDP increased by an annual average of 2.1%. Agricultural GDP grew by 2.9% in 1994/95 and by 3.1% in 1995/96.

Industry (including mining, manufacturing, construction and power) employed 21.9% of the working population in 1995, and provided 33.8% of GDP in 1995/96. During 1990–95 industrial GDP rose by an annual average of 0.4%. Industrial GDP grew by 5.0% in 1994/95 and by 4.9% in 1995/96.

Mineral resources include petroleum, natural gas, phosphates, manganese, uranium, coal, iron ore and gold. The petroleum industry contributed 16.1% of GDP in 1985/86, and petroleum and petroleum products accounted for 47.6% of total export earnings in 1996. However, the mining sector employed only 0.3% of the working population in 1995.

Manufacturing contributed 17.2% of GDP in 1995 and employed 14.2% of the working population in that year. Based on the value of output, the main branches of manufacturing in 1992 were food products (accounting for 18.9% of the total), petroleum refineries (16.0%) and textiles (12.2%).

Energy is derived principally from hydroelectric power and coal. Petroleum production averaged 830,000 barrels per day in 1996, and at the beginning of that year Egypt's proven published petroleum reserves totalled 3,900m. barrels. Egypt has proven natural gas reserves of about 594,000m. cu m. In 1996 all the natural gas produced (about 1,300m. cu ft per day) was consumed locally. In 1996 imports of fuel and energy accounted for about 4% of the value of all imports.

Services contributed 50.2% of GDP in 1995/96 and employed 44.1% of the working population in 1995. In the late 1980s tourism became one of the most dynamic sectors of the Egyptian economy. However, the sector's prospects have been damaged by a campaign of Islamic fundamentalist violence aimed at tourists. In 1990–95 the real GDP of the service sector grew by an annual average of 1.5%. The service sector grew by 4.4% in 1994, and a further 2.5% in 1995.

In 1996 Egypt recorded a visible trade deficit of US $8,390m., while there was a deficit of $192m. on the current account of the balance of payments. In 1996 the principal source of imports (20.0%) was the USA, which was also the principal market for exports (13.0%). Other major trading partners were Germany, France, the Netherlands and Italy. Egypt's principal exports in 1996 were petroleum and petroleum products, textiles, food, non-ferrous metals and clothing. The principal imports were cereals, chemicals, machinery and transport equipment, and basic manufactures.

For the financial year ending 30 June 1998 there was a projected budgetary deficit of £E6,838m. Egypt's external debt totalled US $34,116m. at the end of 1995, of which $31,325m. was long-term public debt. In that year the cost of servicing the foreign debt was equivalent to 14.6% of the value of exports of goods and services. The annual rate of inflation averaged 11.4% in 1990–96. Consumer prices increased by an average of 8.4% in 1995 and by 7.2% in 1996. In 1995 the number of unemployed persons was equivalent to 11.1% of the total labour force.

Egypt is a member of the Arab League (see p. 195), the Organization of Arab Petroleum Exporting Countries (see p. 223), the Arab Co-operation Council (see p. 259) and the Organization of the Islamic Conference (see p. 224).

Egypt's economic difficulties in 1990–96 were largely due to the economy's traditional reliance on an inflexible public sector; and its failure, in the 1980s, to respond adequately to the decline in the world price of petroleum and to rising interest rates. The most serious consequence of this was a huge, unsustainable level of debt which led, in turn, to a decline in investment and increased levels of inflation and unemployment. Between 1990 and 1996 the Egyptian economy was characterized by very weak growth in production, high unemployment and disappointing performances in the private and export sectors. From 1991 the Government implemented an economic reform programme, the short-term aims of which were to increase production and reduce unemployment. In the medium term the aim was to achieve the country's maximum sustainable rate of economic growth in order to alleviate the socio-economic crisis. A key feature of the economic reform programme was the aim to increase the role of the private sector at the expense of public enterprises. By mid-1996, however, it was clear that the reform programme had achieved only limited success and was in need of acceleration. For instance, the Government retained too many loss-making, inefficient companies, although this was partly due to a shortage of willing buyers. While GDP had risen consistently, it had not done so at a rate sufficient substantially to reduce unemployment. However, inflation had declined steadily and the Government had reduced its budget deficit (expressed as a percentage of GDP). In October the IMF approved a two-year stand-by credit agreement for Egypt, worth about US $391m. This agreement facilitated the completion of a debt-restructuring plan agreed in principle between Egypt and the 'Paris Club' of creditor governments in 1991. In 1997 the Government stated its intention of modernizing the stock market in an attempt to attract foreign investment. Other incentives included a reduction in bureaucracy and lower taxes for new businesses. Particular support would be given to companies established in outlying rural areas as part of a long-term strategy to encourage a shift in investment and population outside the congested Nile Valley. The Government hoped to extend the inhabited area of Egypt from 4% of the total land area to 25% within the next 20 years. Two large-scale attacks on foreign tourists, carried out by Islamist militants in late 1997, placed the economic reform programme in jeopardy; a deceleration in economic growth was consequently anticipated in 1998.

Social Welfare

Substantial progress has been made in social welfare services in recent years. There are comprehensive state schemes for sickness benefits, pensions, health insurance and training. In 1982 Egypt had 1,521 hospital establishments, with a total of 87,685 beds. (The number of hospital beds had increased to 119,463 by 1996.) There were 9,495 physicians working in the country in 1985. Of total expenditure by the central Government in the financial year 1992/93, £E1,370m. (2.4%) was for health services, and a further £E6,156m. (11.0%) for social security and welfare.

Education

Education is officially compulsory for five years between six and 13 years of age. Primary education, beginning at six years of age, lasts for five years, while secondary education, beginning at the age of 11 years, lasts for six years, comprising two cycles of three years each. In 1995 total enrolment at primary and secondary schools was equivalent to 87% of the school-age population (males 93%; females 80%). In that year primary enrolment was equivalent to 100% of children in the relevant age-group (males 107%; females 93%), while the comparable ratio for secondary enrolment was 74% (males 80%; females 68%). More than 13.8m. people were receiving state education in 1993. There are 13 universities. Education at all levels is available free of charge. Expenditure on education by the central Government in the financial year 1992/93 was £E6,921m. (12.3% of total spending). In 1995, according to UNESCO estimates, the rate of adult illiteracy stood at 48.6% (males 36.4%; females 61.2%).

Public Holidays

1998: 1 January (New Year), 30 January (Id al-Fitr, end of Ramadan), 8 April (Id al-Adha, Feast of the Sacrifice), 20 April (Sham an-Nessim, Coptic Easter Monday), 25 April (Sinai Day), 28 April (Islamic New Year), 18 June (Evacuation Day, proclamation of the republic), 7 July (Mouloud, Birth of Muhammad), 23 July (Revolution Day), 6 October (Armed Forces Day), 24 October (Popular Resistance Day), 17 November (Leilat al-Meiraj, Ascension of Muhammad), 23 December (Victory Day).

1999: 1 January (New Year), 19 January (Id al-Fitr, end of Ramadan), 28 March (Id al-Adha, Feast of the Sacrifice), 12 April (Sham an-Nessim, Coptic Easter Monday), 17 April (Islamic New Year), 25 April (Sinai Day), 18 June (Evacuation Day, proclamation of the republic), 26 June (Mouloud, Birth of Muhammad), 23 July (Revolution Day), 6 October (Armed Forces Day), 24 October (Popular Resistance Day), 6 November (Leilat al-Meiraj, Ascension of Muhammad), 23 December (Victory Day).

Coptic Christian holidays include: Christmas (7 January), Palm Sunday and Easter Sunday.

Weights and Measures

The metric system is in force, but some Egyptian measurements are still in use.

Statistical Survey

Sources (unless otherwise stated): Central Agency for Public Mobilization and Statistics, POB 2086, Cairo (Nasr City); tel. (2) 604632; telex 92395; Research Department, National Bank of Egypt, Cairo.

Area and Population

AREA, POPULATION AND DENSITY

Area (sq km)	1,002,000*
Population (census results)	
17–18 November 1986†	48,254,238
31 December 1996‡	
Males	30,330,804
Females	28,941,578
Total	59,272,382
Density (per sq km) at 31 December 1996	59.2

* 386,874 sq miles. Inhabited and cultivated territory accounts for 55,039 sq km (21,251 sq miles).

† Excluding Egyptian nationals abroad, totalling an estimated 2,250,000.

‡ Preliminary results, excluding Egyptian nationals abroad, totalling an estimated 2,180,000.

GOVERNORATES (population at 1996 census*)

Governorate	Area (sq km)†	Population ('000)	Capital
Cairo	457	6,789.5	Cairo
Alexandria	2,879	3,328.2	Alexandria
Port Said	1,351	496.5	Port Said
Ismailia	4,483	715.0	Ismailia
Suez	2,500	417.6	Suez
Damietta	1,029	914.6	Damietta
Dakahlia	3,459	4,223.7	Mansoura
Sharkia	4,190	4,287.8	Zagazig
Kalyubia	1,001	3,302.9	Benha
Kafr esh-Sheikh	3,748	2,222.9	Kafr esh-Sheikh
Gharbia	1,943	3,404.8	Tanta
Menufia	2,158	2,758.5	Shibin el-Kom
Behera	9,504	3,981.2	Damanhur
Giza	4,840	4,779.9	Giza
Beni Suef	9,576	1,860.2	Beni Suef
Fayum	4,949	1,989.9	Fayum
Menia	2,263	3,308.9	Menia
Asyut	1,558	2,802.2	Asyut
Suhag	1,574	3,123.0	Suhag
Qena	12,743	2,441.4	Qena
Aswan	34,608	973.7	Aswan
Luxor City	55	360.5	Luxor
Red Sea	130,000	155.7	Hurghada
Al-Wadi al-Jadid	376,505	141.7	Al-Kharijah
Matruh	212,000	211.9	Matruh
North Sinai	31,000	252.7	El-Arish
South Sinai	28,438	54.5	Et-Toor

* Preliminary results.

† The sum of these figures is 888,811 sq km, compared with the official national total of 1,002,000 sq km.

PRINCIPAL TOWNS (estimated population at 1 July 1992)

El-Qahira (Cairo, the capital)*	6,789,479	Asyut	321,000
El-Iskandariyah (Alexandria)*	3,328,196	Zagazig	287,000
El-Giza*	4,779,865	Ismailia	255,000
Shoubra el-Kheima	834,000	El-Fayoum (Fayum)	250,000
Bur Sa'id (Port Said)*	469,533	Kafr ed-Dawar	226,000
El-Mahalla el-Koubra	408,000	Damanhur	222,000
Es-Suweis (Suez)*	417,610	Aswan	220,000
Tanta	380,000	El-Minya (Menia)	208,000
El-Mansoura	371,000	Beni Suef	179,000
		Shebin el-Kom	158,000
		Suhag	156,000

* At census of December 1996.

Source: mainly UN, *Demographic Yearbook*.

BIRTHS, MARRIAGES AND DEATHS

	Registered live births		Registered marriages		Registered deaths	
	Number	Rate (per 1,000)	Number	Rate (per 1,000)	Number	Rate (per 1,000)
1989	1,743,000	32.1	392,000	7.5	417,000	7.7
1990	1,717,000	30.9	405,000	7.6	395,000	7.1
1991	1,662,000	29.9	400,000	7.3	393,000	6.9
1992	1,521,000	26.2	397,000	7.1	385,000	6.6
1993	1,623,000	27.4	432,000	7.6	382,000	6.5
1994*	1,748,000	28.9	452,000	7.8	408,000	6.7
1995*	1,714,000	27.7	519,000	8.7	432,000	7.0
1996*	1,746,000	27.6	489,000	8.0	396,000	6.2

* Provisional figures.

Expectation of life (years at birth, 1991): males 62.86; females 66.39.

ECONOMICALLY ACTIVE POPULATION*
(sample surveys, '000 persons aged 12 to 64 years)

	1993	1994	1995
Agriculture, hunting, forestry and fishing	5,188.4	5,360.5	5,215.6
Mining and quarrying	45.4	47.3	40.7
Manufacturing	2,045.2	2,055.1	2,183.5
Electricity, gas and water	147.6	154.1	166.8
Construction	949.5	1,019.4	967.6
Trade, restaurants and hotels	1,437.0	1,561.1	1,587.7
Transport, storage and communications	806.5	843.3	907.6
Finance, insurance, real estate and business services	276.4	295.3	282.7
Community, social and personal services	3,805.4	3,903.1	3,990.8
Activities not adequately defined	1.9	2.1	1.2
Total employed	14,703.4	15,241.4	15,344.2
Unemployed	1,800.6	1,877.4	1,917.0
Total labour force	16,504.0	17,118.8	17,261.2
Males	12,718.6	13,107.3	13,393.2
Females	3,785.4	4,011.5	3,868.0

* Figures for each year represent the average of two surveys, conducted in May and November.

Agriculture

PRINCIPAL CROPS ('000 metric tons)

	1994	1995	1996
Wheat	4,437	5,722	5,735
Rice (paddy)	4,583	4,888	4,895
Barley	129	368	120
Maize	5,112	5,115	5,165
Sorghum	731	769	604
Potatoes	1,325	2,599	1,133
Sweet potatoes	152	165	114
Taro (Coco yam)*	115	120	125
Dry broad beans	357	392	442
Other pulses	65	69	64
Soybeans (Soya beans)	67	64	40
Groundnuts (in shell)	117	131	125
Sunflower seed	51	68	69*
Cottonseed	411	380	540†
Cotton (lint)†	255	237	350
Olives	130	208	210*
Cabbages	496	477	354
Tomatoes	5,011	5,034	5,038
Cauliflowers*	76	78	80
Pumpkins, squash and gourds*	305	310	315
Cucumbers and gherkins*	248	250	253
Aubergines*	345	350	355
Green chillies and peppers*	192	198	200
Onions (dry)	481	574	448
Garlic	105†	119†	120*
Green beans*	107	108	109
Green peas*	105	106	107
Carrots	118	131	101
Other vegetables	681	691	697
Watermelons*	716	720	730
Melons*	450	460	470
Grapes	707	739	740*
Dates	646	678	680*
Sugar cane	13,822	13,827	14,105
Sugar beets	825	920	842
Apples	313	438	455*
Pears*	90	93	95
Peaches and nectarines*	58	58	60
Oranges	1,513	1,555	1,608†
Tangerines, mandarins, clementines and satsumas	250	471	475*
Lemons and limes	296	308	330*
Mangoes	180	232	240*
Bananas	459	499	500*
Other fruits and berries	559	564	570

* FAO estimate(s). † Unofficial figure(s).

Source: FAO, *Production Yearbook*.

LIVESTOCK ('000 head, year ending September)

	1994	1995	1996
Cattle	2,750*	2,700†	2,700†
Buffaloes	2,850*	2,800†	2,800†
Sheep*	4,000	3,648	3,491
Goats	3,100*	3,210†	3,250†
Pigs	27	27†	27†
Horses†	10	11	11
Asses†	1,650	1,680	1,690
Camels	133	133†	135†

Chickens (million): 38 in 1994; 40† in 1995; 42† in 1996.
Ducks (FAO estimates, million): 8 in 1994; 8 in 1995; 9 in 1996.

* Unofficial figure(s). † FAO estimate(s).

Source: FAO, *Production Yearbook*.

LIVESTOCK PRODUCTS ('000 metric tons)

	1994	1995	1996
Beef and veal*	170	168	163
Buffalo meat*	160	153	150
Mutton and lamb*	63	58	55
Goat meat*	42	43	44
Pig meat*	3	3	3
Poultry meat	383	409	429
Other meat*	89	90	92
Cows' milk	999	1,000	1,000*
Buffaloes' milk*	1,580	1,590	1,600
Sheep's milk*	16	16	16
Goats' milk*	43	43	44
Butter and ghee*	82	82	82
Cheese*	341	349	349
Hen eggs	154†	158†	160*
Honey*	10	10	11
Wool: greasy*	2	2	2
Cattle and buffalo hides*	38	37	37
Sheepskins*	8	7	7
Goatskins*	6	6	6

* FAO estimate(s). † Unofficial figure.

Source: FAO, mainly *Production Yearbook*.

Forestry

ROUNDWOOD REMOVALS
(FAO estimates, '000 cubic metres, excluding bark)

	1992	1993	1994
Industrial wood	117	120	123
Fuel wood	2,412	2,467	2,520
Total	2,529	2,587	2,643

Source: FAO, *Yearbook of Forest Products*.

Fishing

('000 metric tons, live weight)

	1993	1994	1995
Common carp	22.4	20.1	30.9
Nile tilapia	117.5	121.0	122.2
Mudfish	23.9	21.1	19.6
Other freshwater fishes	18.1	32.3	20.7
Flathead grey mullet	14.0	14.1	24.5
Jacks and crevalles	14.4	11.8	1.8
Sardinellas	14.4	11.1	11.9
Other marine fishes	68.8	63.0	66.4
Total fish	293.5	294.7	298.0
Crustaceans and molluscs	9.3	11.1	11.6
Total catch	302.8	305.7	309.6
Inland waters	207.5	220.3	226.2
Mediterranean and Black Sea	44.6	41.5	44.5
Indian Ocean	50.7	43.9	38.9

Source: FAO, *Yearbook of Fishery Statistics*.

Mining

('000 metric tons, year ending 30 June)

	1993/94	1994/95	1995/96
Crude petroleum	45,000	44,000	44,000
Iron ore*	2,703	2,433	2,098
Salt (unrefined)	1,116	1,193	1,632
Phosphate rock	864	1,044	1,238
Gypsum (crude)	1,481	2,361	2,092
Kaolin	195	233	293

* Figures refer to gross weight. The estimated iron content is 50%.

Natural gas (estimates, petajoules): 376 in 1993; 411 in 1994 (Source: UN, *Industrial Commodity Statistics Yearbook*).

Industry

SELECTED PRODUCTS ('000 metric tons, unless otherwise indicated)

	1992	1993	1994
Wheat flour	3,510	3,352	3,662
Raw sugar*	1,077	1,093	1,190
Cottonseed oil (refined)	312	329	318
Beer ('000 hectolitres)	420	350	360
Cigarettes (million)	42,516	38,844	39,145
Cotton yarn (pure)†	273.0	253.9	251.0
Jute yarn	25.0	21.6	20.8
Jute fabrics	20.1	18.2	n.a.
Wool yarn	20.0	19.2	15.2
Paper and paperboard*	201	220	270
Rubber tyres and tubes ('000)‡	3,371	3,368	3,858
Sulphuric acid (100%)	111	122	112
Caustic soda (Sodium hydroxide)	59	59	49
Nitrogenous fertilizers§	5,342	5,588	5,918
Phosphate fertilizers‖	825	689	765
Motor spirit (petrol)	3,638	4,073	4,356
Kerosene	1,983	1,930	1,405
Distillate fuel oils	4,332	4,747	5,246
Residual fuel oil (Mazout)	11,258	11,735	12,071
Petroleum bitumen (asphalt)	581	617	683
Cement	15,454	12,576	13,554
Pig-iron	60	92	109
Radio receivers ('000)	36	13	52
Television receivers ('000)	260	269	234
Passenger motor cars—assembly (number)	7,000	4,000	6,000
Electric energy (million kWh)	45,110	47,470	47,920

* Data from the FAO.

† Figures refer to the year ending 30 June.

‡ Tyres and inner tubes for road motor vehicles (including motorcycles) and bicycles.

§ Production in terms of nitrogen.

‖ Production in terms of phosphoric acid.

Source: mainly UN, *Industrial Commodity Statistics Yearbook*.

Finance

CURRENCY AND EXCHANGE RATES

Monetary Units

1,000 milliѐmes = 100 piastres = 5 tallaris = 1 Egyptian pound (£E).

Sterling and Dollar Equivalents (30 September 1997)

£1 sterling = £E5.475;
US $1 = £E3.389;
£E100 = £18.27 sterling = $29.51.

Note: From February 1991 foreign exchange transactions were conducted through only two markets, the primary market and the free market. With effect from 8 October 1991, the primary market was eliminated, and all foreign exchange transactions are effected through the free market. For external trade purposes, the average value of the Egyptian pound was 29.53 US cents in 1994, 29.48 US cents in 1995 and 29.49 US cents in 1996.

STATE PUBLIC BUDGET (£E million, year ending 30 June)

Revenue	1992/93	1993/94	1994/95
Current revenue	43,683	49,418	52,925
Central Government	41,020	46,384	49,889
Tax revenue	27,334	31,373	34,279
Taxes on income and profits	11,114	12,003	12,134
Domestic taxes on goods and services	7,191	8,080	9,333
Customs duties	5,009	6,120	7,017
Stamp duties	2,067	2,657	2,874
Other current revenue	13,686	15,011	15,610
Profit transfers	9,364	9,070	10,542
Petroleum Authority	4,626	4,610	4,443
Suez Canal Authority	3,013	2,610	3,132
Central Bank of Egypt	968	1,200	2,072
Local government	1,782	1,984	1,951
Service authorities	881	1,050	1,085
Capital revenue	3,020	3,149	2,794
Total	46,703	52,567	55,719

Expenditure	1992/93	1993/94	1994/95
Current expenditure	41,292	46,097	47,632
Wages	9,803	11,096	12,519
Pensions	3,526	3,914	4,146
Goods and services	2,423	2,857	2,986
Defence	5,572	5,873	6,410
Public debt interest	13,309	16,498	14,790
Local	9,315	11,816	11,177
Foreign	3,994	4,682	3,613
Subsidies	4,047	3,265	3,818
Capital expenditure (net)	10,931	10,167	10,624
Total	52,223	56,264	58,256

1995/96 (provisional, £E million, year ending 30 June): Revenue 60,600 (current 57,100, capital 3,500); Expenditure 63,500 (current 51,700, capital 11,800).
1996/97 (estimates, £E million, year ending 30 June): Revenue 65,300 (current 61,700, capital 3,600); Expenditure 68,100 (current 54,700, capital 13,400).
1997/98 (projections, £E million, year ending 30 June): Revenue 76,398 (current 70,107, capital 6,290); Expenditure 83,236 (current 64,993, capital 18,243).

INTERNATIONAL RESERVES (US $ million at 31 December)

	1994	1995	1996
Gold*	694	704	695
IMF special drawing rights	86	103	123
Reserve position in IMF	78	80	77
Foreign exchange	13,316	15,998	17,198
Total	14,175	16,885	18,093

* Valued at market-related prices.

Source: IMF, *International Financial Statistics.*

MONEY SUPPLY (£E million at 31 December)

	1994	1995	1996
Currency outside banks	20,612	22,750	24,954
Demand deposits at deposit money banks	15,919	17,282	18,026
Total money (incl. others)	38,275	41,540	44,521

Source: IMF, *International Financial Statistics.*

COST OF LIVING (Consumer Price Index; base: 1990 = 100)

	1993	1994	1995
Food	135.9	149.1	164.4
Clothing	157.7	170.1	184.1
Fuel and light	275.2	295.8	305.2
Rent	192.3	207.1	217.9
All items (incl. others)	152.5	164.9	178.7

Source: ILO, *Yearbook of Labour Statistics.*

1996: All items 191.6 (Source: UN, *Monthly Bulletin of Statistics*).

NATIONAL ACCOUNTS
(£E million, year ending 30 June)

Expenditure on the Gross Domestic Product (at current prices)

	1993/94	1994/95	1995/96
Government final consumption expenditure	18,000	21,500	23,600
Private final consumption expenditure	130,500	148,900	171,700
Increase in stocks	—	700	1,550
Gross fixed capital formation	35,600	38,600	42,100
Total domestic expenditure	184,100	209,700	238,950
Exports of goods and services	40,100	45,100	48,450
Less Imports of goods and services	49,200	49,800	59,100
GDP in purchasers' values	175,000	205,000	228,300

Source: IMF, *International Financial Statistics.*

Gross Domestic Product by Economic Activity
(at constant 1991/92 factor cost)

	1993/94	1994/95	1995/96
Agriculture, hunting, forestry and fishing	23,072	23,741	24,470
Mining and quarrying } Manufacturing }	37,640	39,452	41,335
Electricity	2,382	2,525	2,658
Construction	7,079	7,485	7,898
Trade, restaurants and hotels	25,315	26,929	28,545
Transport and communications	15,112	15,422	16,116
Finance, insurance and real estate	7,733	8,239	8,832
Government services	10,120	10,565	11,039
Other services	11,169	11,791	12,476
Total	139,622	146,149	153,369

BALANCE OF PAYMENTS (US $ million)

	1994	1995	1996
Exports of goods f.o.b.	4,044	4,670	4,779
Imports of goods f.o.b.	−9,997	−12,267	−13,169
Trade balance	−5,953	−7,597	−8,390
Exports of services	8,070	8,590	9,271
Imports of services	−5,645	−4,873	−5,084
Balance on goods and services	−3,528	−3,880	−4,023
Other income received	1,330	1,578	1,901
Other income paid	−2,114	−1,983	−1,556
Balance on goods, services and income	−4,312	−4,285	−3,858
Current transfers received	4,622	4,284	3,888
Current transfers paid	−279	−253	−222
Current balance	31	−254	−192
Direct investment abroad	−43	−93	−5
Direct investment from abroad	1,256	598	636
Portfolio investment liabilities	3	20	545
Other investment assets	−905	−396	−565
Other investment liabilities	−1,761	−1,974	−2,070
Net errors and omissions	255	272	−74
Overall balance	−1,164	−1,827	−1,725

Source: IMF, *International Financial Statistics.*

External Trade

Note: Figures exclude trade in military goods.

PRINCIPAL COMMODITIES (distribution by SITC, US $ million)

Imports c.i.f.	1994	1995	1996
Food and live animals	2,263.3	2,611.7	3,056.6
Cereals and cereal preparations	1,126.6	1,299.2	1,705.1
Wheat and meslin (unmilled)	766.6	875.7	1,231.3
Maize (unmilled)	263.8	349.3	435.2
Crude materials (inedible) except fuels	716.3	1,059.3	1,142.4
Cork and wood	377.4	551.0	501.9
Simply worked wood and railway sleepers	344.8	522.3	452.3
Simply worked coniferous wood	256.2	445.6	346.5
Sawn coniferous wood	256.1	445.6	346.5
Animal and vegetable oils, fats and waxes	193.4	510.3	512.8
Fixed vegetable oils and fats	172.4	466.7	481.7
Chemicals and related products	1,154.5	1,550.8	1,617.0
Organic chemicals	190.7	289.1	277.1
Artificial resins, plastic materials, etc.	358.3	448.4	496.2
Products of polymerization, etc.	288.3	72.4	33.0
Basic manufactures	1,821.4	2,360.3	2,580.6
Paper, paperboard and manufactures	282.6	530.1	406.6
Paper and paperboard (not cut to size or shape)	261.8	504.3	367.5
Textile yarn, fabrics, etc.	242.3	279.7	288.8
Iron and steel	546.1	777.5	1,007.5
Machinery and transport equipment	2,784.3	2,967.8	3,313.1
Machinery specialized for particular industries	439.1	481.4	613.4
General industrial machinery, equipment and parts	657.5	790.6	846.0
Telecommunications and sound equipment	201.4	212.0	237.8
Other electrical machinery, apparatus, etc.	444.7	96.3	97.4
Road vehicles and parts*	667.3	623.2	598.2
Passenger motor cars (excl. buses)	213.5	216.7	201.1
Parts and accessories for cars, buses, lorries, etc.*	228.1	228.4	201.5
Miscellaneous manufactured articles	370.6	392.1	427.7
Total (incl. others)	9,592.1	11,738.8	13,012.1

* Excluding tyres, engines and electrical parts.

Exports f.o.b.	1994	1995	1996
Food and live animals	266.3	324.2	359.2
Cereals and cereal preparations	86.0	60.3	122.7
Rice	79.2	56.7	117.7
Vegetables and fruit	121.0	206.8	169.9
Fresh or simply preserved vegetables	75.5	152.7	120.6
Crude materials (inedible) except fuels	305.2	241.3	180.0
Textile fibres (excl. wool tops) and waste	250.4	169.4	102.4
Cotton	237.6	157.8	92.3
Raw cotton (excl. linters)	233.8	152.2	91.8
Mineral fuels, lubricants, etc.	1,360.9	1,282.9	1,681.1
Petroleum, petroleum products, etc.	1,321.2	1,231.7	1,633.9
Crude petroleum oils, etc.	793.4	719.2	861.1
Refined petroleum products	503.8	496.3	809.6
Residual fuel oils	486.7	16.3	8.1
Chemicals and related products	159.3	201.4	176.5
Basic manufactures	1,047.4	1,033.2	785.4
Textile yarn, fabrics, etc.	619.2	570.1	425.3
Textile yarn	387.1	322.2	204.0
Cotton yarn	378.1	304.8	192.5
Woven cotton fabrics (excl. narrow or special fabrics)	121.3	109.2	88.7
Unbleached fabrics (not mercerized)	111.7	105.9	83.8
Iron and steel	134.8	159.8	68.8
Non-ferrous metals	168.3	199.8	157.4
Aluminium and aluminium alloys	167.3	149.7	164.7
Worked aluminium and alloys	139.4	47.8	20.3
Aluminium bars, wire, etc.	125.6	9.2	6.7
Other metal manufactures	70.7	47.5	44.0
Miscellaneous manufactured articles	305.4	331.4	325.9
Clothing and accessories (excl. footwear)	230.7	252.5	239.2
Men's and boys' outer garments of non-knitted textile fabrics	25.8	94.2	91.1
Knitted or crocheted undergarments (incl. foundation garments of non-knitted fabrics)	73.0	4.9	8.2
Cotton undergarments, non-elastic	72.9	n.a.	n.a.
Total (incl. others)	3,474.5	3,444.1	3,532.5

PRINCIPAL TRADING PARTNERS
(countries of consignment, US$ million)

Imports c.i.f.	1994	1995	1996
Argentina	93.5	115.1	237.5
Australia	403.3	82.4	386.0
Belgium-Luxembourg	214.6	236.8	211.8
Brazil	158.2	189.9	265.5
China, People's Repub.	194.5	295.9	283.4
Denmark	96.3	95.0	94.1
Finland	135.7	183.0	166.3
France (incl. Monaco)	592.6	685.2	576.6
Germany	913.9	1,044.6	1,088.6
India	123.9	170.6	184.3
Ireland	200.3	217.9	131.7
Italy	614.0	731.1	870.4
Japan	401.2	314.0	344.7
Korea, Republic	107.1	2.0	0.2
Malaysia	93.7	220.4	240.9
Netherlands	285.7	381.4	363.3
Romania	121.5	160.4	197.0
Russia	273.9	405.3	370.5
Saudi Arabia	194.2	249.0	290.4
Spain	143.1	184.4	210.7
Sweden	157.6	259.6	306.5
Switzerland-Liechtenstein	211.6	311.9	333.9
Turkey	143.4	179.6	352.7
United Kingdom	349.8	379.8	441.1
USA	1,616.9	2,211.0	2,607.2
Total (incl. others)	9,592.0	11,738.8	13,012.1

Exports f.o.b.	1994	1995	1996
Belgium-Luxembourg	71.3	110.4	50.5
France (incl. Monaco)	138.3	144.2	144.0
Germany	209.8	207.0	162.8
Greece	117.2	137.3	142.3
India	66.1	53.0	14.1
Israel	188.3	173.6	343.4
Italy	426.7	458.8	438.1
Japan	49.8	43.7	41.3
Jordan	21.0	30.9	44.6
Korea, Republic	106.3	0.0	0.2
Lebanon	35.1	43.4	33.0
Libya	44.1	52.9	51.7
Netherlands	207.2	166.7	364.6
Romania	43.4	41.3	36.9
Russia	41.0	31.9	37.7
Saudi Arabia	155.1	113.1	122.7
Singapore	146.7	92.8	90.0
Spain	149.1	157.1	98.2
Syria	57.5	56.1	55.0
Turkey	71.5	82.7	115.2
United Arab Emirates	40.8	41.0	44.4
United Kingdom	144.0	142.4	165.3
USA	364.6	521.8	459.7
Total (incl. others)	3,474.5	3,444.1	3,532.5

Source: UN, *International Trade Statistics Yearbook*.

Transport

RAILWAYS (traffic, year ending 30 June)

	1993/94	1994/95	1995/96
Passenger-km (million)	46,721	48,243	50,665

1991/92: Freight ton-km (million): 3,229 (Source: UN, *Statistical Yearbook*).

ROAD TRAFFIC (motor vehicles in use at 31 December)

	1994	1995*	1996*
Passenger cars	1,228,606	1,280,000	1,354,000
Buses and coaches	37,231	36,630	37,620
Lorries and vans	408,691	387,000	397,000
Motorcycles and mopeds	383,592	397,000	418,000

* Estimates.

Source: IRF, *World Road Statistics*.

SHIPPING

Merchant Fleet (registered at 31 December)

	1994	1995	1996
Number of vessels	393	385	375
Displacement ('000 grt)	1,262	1,269	1,230

Source: Lloyd's Register of Shipping, *World Fleet Statistics*.

Suez Canal Traffic

	1994	1995	1996
Transits (number)	16,370	15,051	14,731
Displacement ('000 net tons)	364,487	360,372	354,974
Northbound goods traffic ('000 metric tons)	142,872	144,024	136,092
Southbound goods traffic ('000 metric tons)	147,083	149,100	145,923
Net tonnage of tankers ('000)	107,201	96,930	85,895

Source: Suez Canal Authority.

CIVIL AVIATION (traffic on scheduled services)

	1992	1993	1994
Kilometres flown (million)	44	44	54
Passengers carried ('000)	3,609	2,881	3,538
Passenger-km (million)	6,323	5,277	6,342
Total ton-km (million)	687	606	763

Source: UN, *Statistical Yearbook*.

Tourism

	1992	1993	1994
Tourist arrivals ('000)	2,944	2,291	2,356
Tourist receipts (US $ million)	2,730	1,332	1,384

UN, *Statistical Yearbook*.

Communications Media

	1992	1993	1994
Radio receivers ('000 in use)	18,000	18,500	18,950
Television receivers ('000 in use)	6,500	6,800	6,700
Daily newspapers:			
Number	16	n.a.	17
Average circulation ('000 copies)	2,426	n.a.	3,949
Telephones ('000 main lines in use)*	2,028	2,235	2,456
Telefax stations (number in use)	13,640	17,610	21,590
Mobile cellular telephones (subscribers)	4,910	6,880	7,370

* Year ending 30 June.

Sources: UNESCO, *Statistical Yearbook*; UN, *Statistical Yearbook*.

Education

(1995/96, unless otherwise indicated)

	Schools	Teachers	Students
Pre-primary	2,060	10,913	266,502
Primary*	16,188	302,916	7,470,437
Secondary:			
General*	205,519†	235,313	4,242,245
Vocational	n.a.	133,794	1,900,406

* Excluding Al-Azhar education. † 1994/95.

Higher Education (excl. private institutions): *Universities and equivalent* (excl. Al-Azhar University): Teachers 38,828 in 1993/94; Students 620,145 in 1993/94, 696,988 in 1994/95. *Other institutions:* Students 107,737 in 1990/91.

Source: mainly UNESCO, *Statistical Yearbook*.

Directory

The Constitution

A new Constitution for the Arab Republic of Egypt was approved by referendum on 11 September 1971.

THE STATE

Egypt is an Arab Republic with a democratic, socialist system based on the alliance of the working people and derived from the country's historical heritage and the spirit of Islam.

The Egyptian people are part of the Arab nation, who work towards total Arab unity.

Islam is the religion of the State; Arabic is its official language and the Islamic code is a principal source of legislation. The State safeguards the freedom of worship and of performing rites for all religions.

Sovereignty is of the people alone which is the source of all powers.

The protection, consolidation and preservation of the socialist gains is a national duty: the sovereignty of law is the basis of the country's rule, and the independence of immunity of the judiciary are basic guarantees for the protection of rights and liberties.

THE FUNDAMENTAL ELEMENTS OF SOCIETY

Social solidarity is the basis of Egyptian society, and the family is its nucleus.

The State ensures the equality of men and women in both political and social rights in line with the provisions of Muslim legislation.

Work is a right, an honour and a duty which the State guarantees together with the services of social and health insurance, pensions for incapacity and unemployment.

The economic basis of the Republic is a socialist democratic system based on sufficiency and justice in a manner preventing exploitation.

Ownership is of three kinds, public, co-operative and private. The public sector assumes the main responsibility for the regulation and growth of the national economy under the development plan.

Property is subject to the people's control.

Private ownership is safeguarded and may not be sequestrated except in cases specified in law nor expropriated except for the general good against fair legal compensation. The right of inheritance is guaranteed in it.

Nationalization shall only be allowed for considerations of public interest in accordance with the law and against compensation.

Agricultural holding may be limited by law.

The State follows a comprehensive central planning and compulsory planning approach based on quinquennial socio-economic and cultural development plans whereby the society's resources are mobilized and put to the best use.

The public sector assumes the leading role in the development of the national economy. The State provides absolute protection of this sector as well as the property of co-operative societies and trade unions against all attempts to tamper with them.

PUBLIC LIBERTIES, RIGHTS AND DUTIES

All citizens are equal before the law. Personal liberty is a natural right and no one may be arrested, searched, imprisoned or restricted in any way without a court order.

Houses have sanctity, and shall not be placed under surveillance or searched without a court order with reasons given for such action.

The law safeguards the sanctities of the private lives of all citizens; so have all postal, telegraphic, telephonic and other means of communication which may not therefore be confiscated, or perused except by a court order giving the reasons, and only for a specified period.

Public rights and freedoms are also inviolate and all calls for atheism and anything that reflects adversely on divine religions are prohibited.

The freedom of opinion, the Press, printing and publications and all information media are safeguarded.

Press censorship is forbidden, so are warnings, suspensions or cancellations through administrative channels. Under exceptional circumstances, as in cases of emergency or in war time, censorship may be imposed on information media for a definite period.

Egyptians have the right to permanent or provisional emigration and no Egyptian may be deported or prevented from returning to the country.

Citizens have the right to private meetings in peace provided they bear no arms. Egyptians also have the right to form societies which have no secret activities. Public meetings are also allowed within the limits of the law.

SOVEREIGNTY OF THE LAW

All acts of crime should be specified together with the penalties for the acts.

Recourse to justice is a right of all citizens. Those who are financially unable will be assured of means to defend their rights.

Except in cases of *flagrante delicto,* no person may be arrested or their freedom restricted unless an order authorizing arrest has been given by the competent judge or the public prosecution in accordance with the provisions of law.

SYSTEM OF GOVERNMENT

The President, who must be of Egyptian parentage and at least 40 years old, is nominated by at least one-third of the members of the People's Assembly, approved by at least two-thirds, and elected by popular referendum. His term is for six years and he 'may be re-elected for another subsequent term'. He may take emergency measures in the interests of the State but these measures must be approved by referendum within 60 days.

The People's Assembly, elected for five years, is the legislative body and approves general policy, the budget and the development plan. It shall have 'not less than 350' elected members, at least half of whom shall be workers or farmers, and the President may appoint up to 10 additional members. In exceptional circumstances the Assembly, by a two-thirds vote, may authorize the President to rule by decree for a specified period but these decrees must be approved by the Assembly at its next meeting. The law governing the composition of the People's Assembly was amended in May 1979 (see People's Assembly, below).

The Assembly may pass a vote of no confidence in a Deputy Prime Minister, a Minister or a Deputy Minister, provided three days' notice of the vote is given, and the Minister must then resign. In the case of the Prime Minister, the Assembly may 'prescribe' his responsibility and submit a report to the President: if the President disagrees with the report but the Assembly persists, then the matter is put to a referendum: if the people support the President the Assembly is dissolved; if they support the Assembly the President must accept the resignation of the Government. The President may dissolve the Assembly prematurely, but his action must be approved by a referendum and elections must be held within 60 days.

Executive Authority is vested in the President, who may appoint one or more Vice-Presidents and appoints all Ministers. He may also dismiss the Vice-Presidents and Ministers. The President has 'the right to refer to the people in connection with important matters related to the country's higher interests.' The Government is described as 'the supreme executive and administrative organ of the state'. Its members, whether full Ministers or Deputy Ministers, must be at least 35 years old. Further sections define the roles of Local Government, Specialized National Councils, the Judiciary, the Higher Constitutional Court, the Socialist Prosecutor General, the Armed Forces and National Defence Council and the Police.

POLITICAL PARTIES

In June 1977 the People's Assembly adopted a new law on political parties, which, subject to certain conditions, permitted the formation of political parties for the first time since 1953. The law was passed in accordance with Article Five of the Constitution which describes the political system as 'a multi-party one' with four main parties: 'the ruling National Democratic Party, the Socialist Workers (the official opposition), the Liberal Socialists and the Unionist Progressive'. (The legality of the re-formed New Wafd Party was established by the courts in January 1984.)

1980 AMENDMENTS

On 30 April 1980 the People's Assembly passed a number of amendments, which were subsequently massively approved at a referendum the following month. A summary of the amendments follows:

(i) the regime in Egypt is socialist-democratic, based on the alliance of working people's forces.

(ii) the political system depends on multiple political parties; the Arab Socialist Union is therefore abolished.

(iii) the President is elected for a six-year term and can be elected for 'other terms'.

(iv) the President shall appoint a Consultative Council to preserve the principles of the revolutions of 23 July 1952 and 15 May 1971.

(v) a Supreme Press Council shall safeguard the freedom of the press, check government censorship and look after the interests of journalists.

(vi) Egypt's adherence to Islamic jurisprudence is affirmed. Christians and Jews are subject to their own jurisdiction in personal status affairs.

(vii) there will be no distinction of race or religion.

The Government

THE PRESIDENCY

President: MUHAMMAD HOSNI MUBARAK (confirmed as President by referendum, 13 October 1981, after assassination of President Sadat; re-elected and confirmed by referendum, 5 October 1987 and 4 October 1993).

COUNCIL OF MINISTERS
(February 1998)

Prime Minister and Minister for Planning and International Co-operation: Dr KAMAL AHMAD AL-GANZOURI.

Deputy Prime Minister and Minister of Agriculture and Land Reclamation: Dr YOUSUF AMIN WALI.

Minister of Transport and Communications: Eng. SULAYMAN MUTAWALLI SULAYMAN.

Minister of Defence and Military Production: Field Marshal MUHAMMAD HUSSAIN TANTAWI.

Minister of Electricity and Energy: Eng. MUHAMMAD MAHER ABAZAH.

Minister of Information: MUHAMMAD SAFWAT MUHAMMAD YOUSUF ASH-SHARIF.

Minister of Foreign Affairs: AMR MUHAMMAD MOUSSA.

Minister of Supply and Trade: AHMED GUEILY.

Minister of Finance: MOHIEDDIN EL-GHARIB.

Minister of Awqaf (Islamic Endowments): MAHMOUD HAMDI ZAKZOUK.

Minister of Justice: FAROUK MAHMOUD SAYF AN-NASR.

Minister of Culture: FAROUK ABD AL-AZIZ HOSNI.

Minister of Cabinet Affairs and Follow-Up: TALAAT SAID AHMED HAMMAD.

Minister of Rural Development: MAHMOUD SAYED AHMED SHARIF.

Minister of Training and Education: HUSSAIN KAMAL BAHAEDDIN.

Minister of Petroleum: Dr Eng. HAMDY AL-BANBI.

Minister of the Interior: HABIB IBRAHIM EL-ADLI.

Minister of Housing, Utilities and New Communities: Dr Eng. MUHAMMAD IBRAHIM SULAYMAN.

Minister of Tourism: Dr MAMDOUH EL-BELTAGI.

Minister of Economy: YOUSSEF BOUTROS-GHALI.

Minister of Public Works and Water Resources: Dr MAHMOUD ABD AL-HALIM ABU ZEID.

Minister of Health and Population: ISMAIL AWADALLAH SALAM.

Minister of Higher Education and Minister of State for Scientific Research: Dr MUFID MAHMOUD SHEHAB.

Minister of Industry and Mineral Wealth: SULAYMAN REDA.

Minister of Labour and Migration: AHMED AHMED EL-AMAWI.

Minister of Social Insurance and Social Affairs: MERVAT MIHANNA TALAWI.

Minister of the Public Enterprise Sector: Dr ATIF MUHAMMAD OBEID.

Minister of State for Parliamentary Affairs: KAMAL SHAZLI.

Minister of State for Administrative Development: MAHMOUD ABU AMER.

Minister of State for Military Production: Dr Eng. MUHAMMAD EL-GHAMRAWI DAWOUD.

Minister of State for Environment: NADIA MAKRAM OBEID.

Minister of State for Planning and International Co-operation: ZAFER SALIM EL-BESHRY.

MINISTRIES

Ministry of Agriculture and Land Reclamation: Sharia Wizaret az-Ziraa, Dokki, Giza; tel. (2) 702677; telex 93006.

Ministry of Awqaf (Islamic Endowments): Sharia Sabri Abu Alam, Ean el-Luk, Cairo; tel. (2) 746305.

Ministry of Civil Aviation: Sharia Matar, Cairo (Heliopolis); tel. (2) 969555.

Ministry of Communications: 26 Sharia Ramses, Cairo; tel. (2) 909090.

Ministry of Culture: 110 Sharia al-Galaa, Cairo; tel. (2) 971995.

Ministry of Defence and Military Production: 5 Sharia Ismail Abaza, Qasr el-Eini, Cairo; tel. (2) 3553063; telex 92167.

Ministry of Economic Co-operation: 9 Sharia Adly, Cairo; telex 348.

Ministry of Economy: 8 Sharia Adly, Cairo; tel. (2) 907344.

Ministry of Electricity and Energy: Sharia Ramses, Cairo (Nasr City); tel. (2) 2616317; fax (2) 2616302.

Ministry of Finance: Sharia Majlis ash-Sha'ab, Lazoughli Sq., Cairo; tel. (2) 24857; telex 22386.

Ministry of Foreign Affairs: Tahrir Sq., Cairo; tel. (2) 760518; telex 92220.

Ministry of Foreign Trade: Lazoughli Sq., Cairo; tel. (2) 25424.

Ministry of Health and Population: Sharia Majlis ash-Sha'ab, Cairo; tel. (2) 903939; telex 94107.

Ministry of Higher Education and Scientific Research: 4 Sharia Ibrahim Nagiv, Cairo (Garden City).

Ministry of Housing, New Communities and Public Utilities: 1 Ismail Abaza, Qasr el-Eini, Cairo; tel.: Development (2) 3540419; New Communities (2) 3540590; Public Utilities (2) 3540110; telex: Development and New Communities 20807; Public Utilities 92188.

Ministry of Industry and Mineral Resources: 2 Sharia Latin America, Cairo (Garden City); tel. (2) 3550641; telex 93112; fax (2) 3555025.

Ministry of Information: Radio and TV Bldg, Corniche en-Nil, Cairo (Maspiro); tel. (2) 974216.

Ministry of International Co-operation: 8 Sharia Adly, Cairo; tel. (2) 3909707; fax (2) 3915167.

Ministry of Justice: Justice Bldg, Cairo (Lazoughli); tel. (2) 31176.

Ministry of Labour and Migration: Sharia Yousuf Abbas, Abbassia, Cairo (Nasr City).

Ministry of Land Reclamation: Land Reclamation Bldg, Dokki, Giza; tel. (2) 703011.

Ministry of Maritime Transport: 4 Sharia Ptolemy, Alexandria; tel. (3) 4842119; telex 54142; fax (3) 4842096.

Ministry of Petroleum and Mineral Resources: Sharia el-Mokhayem el-Dayem, Cairo (Nasr City); tel. (2) 2622237; telex 92197; fax (2) 2636060.

Ministry of Planning: Sharia Salah Salem, Cairo (Nasr City); tel. (2) 604489.

Ministry of Public Works and Water Resources: Sharia Corniche en-Nil, Imbaba, Giza; tel. (2) 3123727; fax (2) 3123257.

Ministry of Social Affairs: Sharia Sheikh Rihan, Cairo; tel. (2) 70039; telex 705390; fax (2) 94105.

Ministry of Social Insurance: 3 Sharia el-Alfi, Cairo; tel. (2) 922717; fax (2) 5922717.

Ministry of Supply and Internal Trade: 99 Sharia Qasr el-Eini, Cairo; tel. (2) 3557598; telex 93497; fax (2) 3556835.

Ministry of Tourism: Misr Travel Tower, Abbassia Sq., Cairo; tel. (2) 2828439; telex 94040; fax (2) 2829771.

Ministry of Training and Education: Sharia el-Falaky, Cairo; tel. (2) 8544805.

Ministry of Transport: Sharia Qasr el-Eini, Cairo; tel. (2) 3555566; telex 92802; fax (2) 3555564.

Legislature

MAJLIS ASH-SHA'AB
(People's Assembly)

There are 222 constituencies, which each elect two deputies to the Assembly. Ten deputies are appointed by the President, giving a total of 454 seats.

Speaker: Dr AHMAD FATHI SURUR.

Deputy Speakers: Dr ABD AL-AHAD GAMAL AD-DIN, AHMAD ABU ZEID.

Elections, 29 November and 6 December 1995

	Seats
National Democratic Party*	316
New Wafd Party	6
National Progressive Unionist Party	5
Liberal Socialist Party	1
Nasserist Party	1
Independents	115
Total†	444

* Official candidates of the National Democratic Party (NDP) gained 316 seats in the two rounds of voting. However, after the elections it was reported that 99 of the 115 candidates who had successfully contested the elections as independents had either joined or rejoined the NDP.

† There are, in addition, 10 deputies appointed by the President.

MAJLIS ASH-SHURA
(Advisory Council)

In September 1980 elections were held for a 210-member **Shura (Advisory) Council**, which replaced the former Central Committee of the Arab Socialist Union. Of the total number of members, 140 are elected and the remaining 70 are appointed by the President. The opposition parties boycotted elections to the Council in October 1983, and again in October 1986, in protest against the 8% electoral threshold. In June 1989 elections to 153 of the Council's 210 seats were contested by opposition parties (the 'Islamic Alliance', consisting of the Muslim Brotherhood, the LSP and the SLP). However, all of the seats in which voting produced a result (143) were won by the NDP. NDP candidates won 88 of the 90 seats on the Council to which mid-term elections were held in June 1995. The remaining two elective seats were gained by independent candidates. The SLP and the LSP offered only 29 candidates for election and most of the remaining opposition parties did not participate. On 21 June new appointments were made to 47 vacant, non-elective seats.

Speaker: Dr MUSTAFA KAMAL HELMI.

Deputy Speakers: THARWAT ABAZAH, AHMAD AL-IMADI.

Political Organizations

Democratic People's Party: f. 1992; Chair. ANWAR AFIFI.

Democratic Unionist Party: f. 1990; Pres. MUHAMMAD ABD AL-MONEIM TURK.

El-Takaful: f. 1995; Chair. Dr USAMA MUHAMMAD SHALTOUT.

Green Party: f. 1990; Chair. ABD AL-MONEIM EL-AASAR.

Ikhwan (Brotherhood): f. 1928; officially illegal, the (Muslim) Brotherhood advocates the adoption of the *Shari'a*, or Islamic law, as the sole basis of the Egyptian legal system; Sec.-Gen. MAAMOUN AL-HODAIBY.

Liberal Socialist Party (LSP): Cairo; f. 1976; advocates expansion of 'open door' economic policy and greater freedom for private enterprise; Leader MUSTAFA KAMEL MURAD.

Nasserist Party: Cairo; f. 1991; Chair. DIAA ED-DIN DAOUD.

National Democratic Party (NDP): Cairo; f. 1978; government party established by Anwar Sadat; has absorbed Arab Socialist Party; Leader MUHAMMAD HOSNI MUBARAK; Sec.-Gen. Dr YOUSUF AMIN WALI; Political Bureau: Chair. MUHAMMAD HOSNI MUBARAK; mems: KAMAL HASSAN ALI, Dr MUSTAFA KHALIL, Dr RIFA'AT EL-MAHGOUB, Dr SUBHI ABD AL-HAKIM, Dr MUSTAFA KAMAL HILMI, FIKRI MAKRAM OBEID, Dr ISMAT ABD AL-MEGUID, Dr AMAL OSMAN, SAFWAT ASH-SHARIF, Dr YOUSUF AMIN WALI, HASSAN ABU BASHA, KAMAL HENRY BADIR, Dr AHMAD HEIKAL.

National Progressive Unionist Party (Tagammu): 1 Sharia Karim ed-Dawlah, Cairo; f. 1976; left-wing; Leader KHALED MOHI ED-DIN; Sec. Dr RIFA'AT ES-SAID; 160,000 mems.

New Wafd Party: Cairo; original Wafd Party f. 1919; banned 1952; re-formed as New Wafd Party Feb. 1978; disbanded June 1978; re-formed 1983; Leader FOUAD SERAG ED-DIN; Sec.-Gen. IBRAHIM FARAG.

Social Justice Party: f. 1993; Chair. MUHAMMAD ABD AL-AAL.

Socialist Labour Party (SLP): 12 Sharia Awali el-Ahd, Cairo; f. 1978; official opposition party; Leader IBRAHIM SHUKRI.

Umma (National) Party: Islamic religious party, based in Khartoum, Sudan; Leader SADIQ AL-MAHDI (fmr Prime Minister of Sudan).

Young Egypt Party: f. 1990; Chair. ALI ALDIN SALIH.

Diplomatic Representation

EMBASSIES IN EGYPT

Afghanistan: 59 Sharia El Orouba, Heliopolis, Cairo; tel. and fax (2) 417728; Ambassador: SAYED FAZLULLAH FAZIL.

Albania: 29 Sharia Ismail Muhammad, Cairo (Zamalek); tel. (2) 3415651; Ambassador: ARBEN PANDI CICI.

Algeria: 14 Sharia Bresil, Cairo (Zamalek); tel. (2) 3418527; Ambassador: MUHAMMAD ABRAHIMI EL-MILY.

Angola: 12 Foud Mohy Ed-Din Sq., Mohandessin, Cairo; tel. (2) 3498259; Ambassador: DANIEL JULIO CHIPENDA.

Argentina: 8 Sharia as-Saleh Ayoub, Cairo (Zamalek); tel. (2) 3401501; telex 92260; fax (2) 3414355; e-mail argemb@idsc.gov.eg; Ambassador: DOMINGO CULLEN.

Armenia: 20 Sharia Muhammad Mazhar, Cairo (Zamalek); tel. (2) 3416862; e-mail armenemb@idsc.gov.eg; Ambassador: EDWARD NALBANDIAN.

Australia: World Trade Centre, Corniche en-Nil, Cairo; tel. (2) 5750444; telex 92257; fax (2) 5780638; e-mail austremb@idsc.gov.eg; Ambassador: MICHAEL SMITH.

Austria: Sharia en-Nil, Cnr of Sharia Wissa Wassef, Cairo (Giza); tel. (2) 5702975; telex 92258; fax (2) 5702979; e-mail austemb @idsc.gov.eg; Ambassador: HEINRICH QUERNER.

Bahrain: 8 Sharia Gamiet an-Nisr, Dokki, Giza; tel. (2) 3407996; Ambassador: EBRAHIM AL-MAJED.

Bangladesh: 47 Sharia Ahmed Heshmat, Cairo (Zamalek); tel. (2) 3412642; Ambassador: M. NURUN NABI CHOWDHURY.

Belarus: 12-49 Misakha Sq., Cairo (Dokki); tel. and fax (2) 3493743; Chargé d'affaires: IGOR LESCHENYA.

Belgium: 20 Sharia Kamel esh-Shennawi, Cairo (Garden City); tel. (2) 3547494; telex 92264; Ambassador: ALAIN RENS.

Bolivia: Cairo; tel. and fax (2) 3546390; Ambassador: HERNANDO VELASCO.

Bosnia and Herzegovina: 26 July Square, (Sphinx) Agouza, Cairo; tel. (2) 3456091; fax (2) 3456029; Chargé d'affaires a.i.: AVDIJA HADROVIĆ.

Brazil: 1125 Corniche en-Nil, Cairo 11561 (Maspiro); tel. (2) 5756938; telex 92044; fax (2) 761040; e-mail brazemb@idsc.gov.eg; Ambassador: MARCIO DE OLIVEIRA DIAS.

Brunei: 11 Sharia Amer, Cairo (Dokki); tel. (2) 3485903; Dato Paduka Haji SUNI BIN Haji IDRALS.

Bulgaria: 6 Sharia El-Malek el-Ajdal, Cairo (Dokki); tel. (2) 3413025; fax (2) 3413826; Ambassador: PETKO DIMITROV.

Burkina Faso: POB 306, Ramses Centre, 9 Sharia el-Fawakeh, Mohandessin, Cairo; tel. (2) 3379098; telex 93871; fax (2) 3495310; Ambassador: AMADÉ OUÉDRAOGO.

Burundi: 22 Sharia el-Nakhil, Madinet ed-Dobbat, Cairo (Dokki); tel. (2) 3373078; telex 20091; Ambassador: GERVAIS NDIKUMAGNEGE.

Cambodia: 2 Sharia Tahawia, Cairo (Giza); tel. (2) 3489966; Ambassador: IN SOPHEAP.

Cameroon: POB 2061, 15 Sharia Israa, Madinet el-Mohandessin, Cairo; tel. (2) 3441101; telex 92088; fax (2) 3459208; Ambassador: MOUCHILI NJI MFOUAYO.

Canada: POB 1667, 5 Sharia Midan es-Saraya el-Kobra, Cairo (Garden City); tel. (2) 3543110; telex 92677; fax (2) 3563548; e-mail canademb@idsc.gov.eg; Ambassador: MICHAEL BELL.

Central African Republic: 41 Sharia Mahmoud Azmy, Mohandessin, Cairo (Dokki); tel. (2) 3446873; Ambassador: HENRY KOBA.

Chad: POB 1869, 12 Midan ar-Refaï, Cairo 11511 (Dokki); tel. (2) 3373379; telex 92285; fax (2) 3373232; Ambassador: ADOUM ATTIMEE.

Chile: 5 Sharia Chagaret ed-Dorr, Cairo (Zamalek); tel. (2) 3408711; telex 92519; fax (2) 3403716; e-mail chilemb@idsc.gov.eg; Ambassador: NELSON HADAD HERESI.

China, People's Republic: 14 Sharia Bahgat Aly, Cairo (Zamalek); tel. (2) 3417691; e-mail chinaemb@idsc.gov.eg; Ambassador: YANG FUCHANG.

Colombia: 6 Sharia Gueriza, Cairo (Zamalek); tel. (2) 3414203; fax (2) 3407429; e-mail colombemb@idsc.gov.eg; Ambassador: JAIME GIRÓN DUARTE.

Congo, Democratic Republic: 5 Sharia Mansour Muhammad, Cairo (Zamalek); tel. (2) 3403662; telex 92294; Ambassador: KAMIMBAYA WA DJONDO.

Côte d'Ivoire: 39 Sharia el-Kods esh-Sherif, Madinet el-Mohandessin, Cairo (Dokki); tel. (2) 699009; telex 2334; Ambassador: Gen. FÉLIX ORY.

Croatia: 13 Sharia Adel Hussain Nessim, Dokki, Giza; tel. (2) 3405812; Ambassador: DANIEL BUCAN.

Cuba: 6 Sharia el-Fawakeh, Madinet el-Mohandessin, Cairo (Dokki); tel. (2) 3350564; telex 93966; fax (2) 3612739; e-mail cubaemb@ idsc.gov.eg; Ambassador: ORLANDO MARINO LANCIS SUÁREZ.

Cyprus: 23A Sharia Ismail Muhammad, Cairo (Zamalek); tel. (2) 3411288; fax (2) 3415299; Ambassador: STAVROS ORPHANOU.

Czech Republic: 4 Sharia Dokki, Cairo 12511 (Giza); tel. (2) 3485531; fax (2) 3485892; Ambassador: BŘETISLAV VACHALA.

Denmark: 12 Sharia Hassan Sabri, Cairo (Zamalek); tel. (2) 3407411; telex 92254; fax (2) 3411780; e-mail rdemb@idsc.gov.eg; Ambassador: ERLING HARILD NIELSEN.

Djibouti: 11 Sharia el-Gazaer, Aswan Sq., Cairo (Agouza); tel. (2) 709787; telex 93143; Ambassador: ADEN Sheikh HASSEN.

Ecuador: Suez Canal Bldg, 4 Sharia Ibn Kasir, Cairo (Giza); tel. (2) 3496782; fax (2) 3609327; e-mail ecuademb@idsc.gov.eg; Ambassador: MANUEL ROMERO.

Ethiopia: 6 Sharia Abd ar-Rahman Hussein, Midan Gomhuria, Cairo (Dokki); tel. (2) 3353696; fax (2) 3353699; Ambassador: KONGIT SINEGIORGIS.

Finland: 3 Sharia Abu el-Feda, Cairo (Zamalek); tel. (2) 3411487; fax (2) 3405170; Ambassador: GARTH CASTRÉN.

France: POB 1777, 29 Sharia Giza, Cairo; tel. (2) 5703916; fax (2) 5710276; Ambassador: PATRICK LE CLERECQ.

Gabon: 15 Sharia Mossadek, Cairo (Dokki); tel. (2) 702963; telex 92323; Ambassador: MAMBO JACQUES.

Germany: 8B Sharia Hassan Sabri, Cairo (Zamalek); tel. (2) 3410015; telex 92023; fax (2) 3410530; e-mail germemb@idsc.gov.eg; Ambassador: Dr WOLF-DIETRICH SCHILLING.

Ghana: 1 Sharia 26 July, Cairo (Zamalek); tel. (2) 3444000; Ambassador: BON OHANE KWAPONG.

Greece: 18 Sharia Aicha at-Taimouria, Cairo (Garden City); tel. (2) 3551074; telex 92036; fax (2) 3563903; Ambassador: DIMITRIOUS VIDOURIS.

Guatemala: POB 8062, 8 Sharia Muhammad Fahmi el-Mohdar, Primer Zone, Madinet Nasr, Cairo; tel. (2) 2611813; fax (2) 2611814; Ambassador: JUAN ALFREDO RENDÓN.

Guinea: 46 Sharia Muhammad Mazhar, Cairo (Zamalek); tel. (2) 3408109; fax (2) 3411446; Ambassador: MOHAMED TSSIOGA KOUROUMA.

Guinea-Bissau: 37 Sharia Lebanon, Madinet el-Mohandessin, Cairo (Dokki).

Holy See: Apostolic Nunciature, Safarat al-Vatican, 5 Sharia Muhammad Mazhar, Cairo (Zamalek); tel. (2) 3402250; fax (2) 3406152; Apostolic Nuncio: Most Rev. PAOLO GIGLIO, Titular Archbishop of Tindari.

Hungary: 29 Sharia Muhammad Mazhar, Cairo (Zamalek); tel. (2) 3400659; fax (2) 3408648; Ambassador: ERNŐ JUHÁSZ.

India: 5 Sharia Aziz Abaza, Cairo (Zamalek); tel. (2) 3413051; telex 92081; fax (2) 3414038; e-mail indiaemb@idsc.gov.eg; Ambassador: KENWAL GIBAL; also looks after Iraqi interests at 5 Aziz Abaza St, Cairo (Zamalek) (tel. (2) 3409815).

Indonesia: POB 1661, 13 Sharia Aicha at-Taimouria, Cairo (Garden City); tel. (2) 3547200; telex 92555; fax (2) 3562495; Ambassador: Dr BOER MAUNA.

Iraq: *Interests served by India.*

Ireland: POB 2681, 3 Sharia Abu el-Feda, Cairo (Zamalek); tel. (2) 3408264; telex 92778; fax (2) 3412863; Ambassador: HUGH SWIFT.

Israel: 6 Sharia ibn el-Malek, Cairo (Giza); tel. (2) 3610545; fax (2) 3610414; Ambassador: ZVI MAZEL.

Italy: 1079 Corniche en-Nil, Cairo (Garden City); tel. (2) 3543194; telex 942229; Ambassador: FRANCESCO ALOISI DE LARDEREL.

Japan: Cairo Centre Bldg, 2nd and 3rd Floors, 2 Sharia Abd al-Kader Hamza or 106 Sharia Qasr el-Eini, Cairo (Garden City); tel. (2) 3553962; fax (2) 3563540; e-mail japanemb@idsc.gov.eg; Ambassador: KUNIO KATAKURA.

Jordan: 6 Sharia Juhaini, Cairo; tel. (2) 3487543; Ambassador: NABIH AN-NIMR.

Kazakhstan: 4 Road 256 New Maadi, Cairo; tel. (2) 3508471; fax (2) 3521900; Ambassador: BOLATKHAN K. TAIZHANOV.

Kenya: POB 362, 7 Sharia el-Mohandess Galal, Cairo (Dokki); tel. (2) 3453628; telex 92021; fax (2) 3443400; Ambassador: ALI MOHAMED ABDI.

Korea, Democratic People's Republic: 6 Sharia as-Saleh Ayoub, Cairo (Zamalek); tel. (2) 650970; Ambassador: PAK YONG-HO.

Kuwait: 12 Sharia Nabil el-Wakkad, Cairo (Dokki); tel. (2) 701611; ABD AR-RAZAK ABD AL-KADER AL-KANDRI.

Lebanon: 5 Sharia Ahmad Nessim, Cairo (Giza); tel. (2) 3610474; telex 92227; fax (2) 3610463; Ambassador: HISHAM DIMASHKIEH.

Liberia: 3 Midan Amman, Cairo (Dokki); tel. (2) 3367046; telex 22474; fax (2) 3365701; Ambassador: Dr BRAHIMA D. KABA.

Libya: 7 Sharia as-Saleh Ayoub, Cairo (Zamalek); tel. (2) 3401864; Secretary of People's Bureau: AHMAD GADDAF'ADDAM.

Malaysia: 29 Sharia Taha Hussein, Cairo (Zamalek); tel. (2) 3410863; Ambassador: Dato RAJA MANSUR RAZMAN.

Mali: 3 Sharia al-Kawsar, Cairo (Dokki); tel. (2) 3371641; telex 94319; fax (2) 3371841; Ambassador: ALLAYE ALPHADY CISSÉ.

Malta: 25 Sharia 12, Ma'adi, Cairo; tel. (2) 3754451; fax (2) 3754452; e-mail maltaemb@idsc.gov.eg; Ambassador: IVES DE BARRO.

Mauritania: 114 Mohy ed-Din, Abu-el Ezz, Mohandessin, Cairo; tel. (2) 3490671; MUHAMMAD LEMINE OULD.

Mauritius: 5 Sharia 26 July, Lebanon Sq., Mohandessin, Cairo; tel. (2) 3470929; telex 93631; fax (2) 3452425; Ambassador: Dr SAHID MAUDARBOCUS.

Mexico: 6 Sharia Ahmed Shawki, 11111 Cairo (Giza); tel. (2) 5716155; fax (2) 623404; e-mail mexemb@idsc.gov.eg; Ambassador: HÉCTOR CÁRDENAS RODRÍGUEZ.

Mongolia: 3 Midan en-Nasr, Cairo (Dokki); tel. (2) 3460670; Ambassador: SONOMDORJIN DAMBADARJAA.

Morocco: 10 Sharia Salah Eddine, Cairo (Zamalek); tel. (2) 3409849; fax (2) 3411937; e-mail morocemb@idsc.gov.eg; Ambassador: ABD AL-LATIF MOULINE.

Myanmar: 24 Sharia Muhammad Mazhar, Cairo (Zamalek); tel. (2) 3404176; telex 20957; fax (2) 3416793; Ambassador: U AUNG GYI.

Nepal: 9 Sharia Tiba, Cairo (Dokki); tel. (2) 3603426; fax (2) 704447; Ambassador: JITENDRA RAJ SHARMA.

Netherlands: 18 Sharia Hassan Sabri, Cairo (Zamalek); tel. (2) 3406434; telex 92028; fax (2) 3415249; e-mail nlgovkai@rite.com.eg; Ambassador: RONALD H. LOUDON.

Niger: 101 Sharia Pyramids, Cairo (Giza); tel. (2) 3865607; telex 2880; Ambassador: MAMANE OUMAROU.

Nigeria: 13 Sharia Gabalaya, Cairo (Zamalek); tel. (2) 3406042; telex 92038; Chargé d'affaires a.i.: P. S. O. EROMOBOR.

Norway: 8 Sharia el-Gezireh, Cairo (Zamalek); tel. (2) 3403340; telex 92259; fax (2) 3420709; Ambassador: METTE RAVN.

Oman: 52 Sharia el-Higaz, Mohandessin, Cairo; tel. (2) 3035942; telex 92272; Ambassador: ABDULLA BIN HAMED AL-BUSAIDI.

Pakistan: 8 Sharia es-Salouli, Cairo (Dokki); tel. (2) 3487677; fax (2) 3480310; Ambassador: GUL HANEEF.

Panama: POB 62, 4A Sharia Ibn Zanki, 11211 Cairo (Zamalek); tel. (2) 3411093; telex 92776; fax (2) 3411092; Chargé d'affaires a.i.: ROY FRANCISCO LUNA GONZÁLEZ.

Peru: 8 Sharia Kamel esh-Shenawi, Cairo (Garden City); tel. (2) 3562973; telex 93663; fax (2) 3557985; Ambassador: MANUEL VERAMENDI I. SERRA.

Philippines: 5 Sharia Ibn el-Walid, Cairo (Dokki); tel. (2) 3480396; fax (2) 3480393; Ambassador: MENANDRO P. GALENZOGA.

Poland: 5 Sharia el-Aziz Osman, Cairo (Zamalek); tel. (2) 3417456; Ambassador: ROMAN CZYZYCKI.

Portugal: 15A Sharia Mansour Muhammad, Cairo (Zamalek); tel. (2) 3405583; telex 20325; Ambassador: FRANCISCO DO VALLE.

Qatar: 10 Sharia ath-Thamar, Midan an-Nasr, Madinet al-Mohandessin, Cairo; tel. (2) 704537; telex 92287; Ambassador: BADIR AL-DAFA.

Romania: 4 Sharia Aziz Abaza, Cairo (Zamalek); tel. (2) 3410107; telex 93807; fax (2) 3410851; Ambassador: RADU ONOFREI.

Russia: 95 Sharia Giza, Cairo (Giza); tel. (2) 3489353; fax (2) 3609074; Ambassador: VLADIMIR GOUDEV.

Rwanda: 23 Sharia Babel, Mohandessin, Dokki, Giza; tel. (2) 3461126; telex 92552; fax (2) 3461079; Ambassador: CÉLESTIN KABANDA.

Saudi Arabia: 2 Sharia Ahmad Nessim, Cairo (Giza); tel. (2) 3490775; Ambassador: ASSAD ABD AL-KAREM ABOU AN-NASR.

Senegal: 46 Sharia Abd al-Moneim Riad, Mohandessin, Cairo (Dokki); tel. (2) 3458479; telex 92047; Ambassador: SHAMS ED-DINE NDOYE.

Sierra Leone: *Interests served by Saudi Arabia.*

Singapore: POB 356, 40 Sharia Babel, Cairo (Dokki); tel. (2) 704744; telex 21353; fax (2) 3481682; Ambassador: V. K. RAJAN.

Slovakia: 3 Sharia Adel Hussein Rostom, 12511 Cairo (Giza); tel. (2) 718240; telex 22029; fax (2) 715810; Ambassador: JÁN BÓRY.

Slovenia: 5 Es-Saraya El-Kobra Sq., Cairo (Garden City); tel. (2) 3555798; Ambassador: ANDREJ ŽLEBNIK.

Somalia: 27 Sharia es-Somal, Dokki, Giza; tel. (2) 704038; Ambassador: ABDALLA HASSAN MAHMOUD.

South Africa: 18th Floor, Nile Tower Bldg, 21–23 Sharia Giza, Cairo; tel. (2) 5717238; fax (2) 5717241; Ambassador: JUSTUS DE GOEDE.

Spain: 41 Sharia Ismail Muhammad, Cairo (Zamalek); tel. (2) 3406397; telex 92255; fax (2) 3405829; e-mail spainemb@idsc.gov.eg; Ambassador: JUAN ALFONSO ORTIZ.

Sri Lanka: POB 1157, 8 Sharia Sri Lanka, Cairo (Zamalek); tel. (2) 3400047; fax (2) 3417138; e-mail srilanka@idsc.gov.eg; Ambassador: H. K. J. R. BANDARA.

Sudan: 4 Sharia el-Ibrahimi, Cairo (Garden City); tel. (2) 3549661; Ambassador: IZZ AD-DIN HAMID.

Sweden: POB 131, 13 Sharia Muhammad Mazhar, Cairo (Zamalek); tel. (2) 3414132; telex 92256; fax 3404357; e-mail sveamcai@link.com.eg; Ambassador: CHRISTER SYLVÉN.

Switzerland: POB 633, 10 Sharia Abd al-Khalek Saroit, Cairo; tel. (2) 5758133; fax (2) 5745236; Ambassador: BLAISE GODET.

Syria: 14 Sharia Ahmad Hechmar, Cairo (Zamalek); Ambassador: Dr ISSA DARWISH.

Tanzania: 9 Sharia Abd al-Hamid Lotfi, Cairo (Dokki); tel. (2) 704155; telex 23537; Ambassador: MUHAMMAD A. FOUM.

Thailand: 2 Sharia al-Malek el-Afdal, Cairo (Zamalek); tel. (2) 3410094; fax (2) 3400340; e-mail thaiemb@idsc.gov.eg; Ambassador: BUNTHAM BAIRAJ-VINICHAI.

Tunisia: 26 Sharia el-Jazirah, Cairo (Zamalek); tel. (2) 3404940; Ambassador: ABD AL-HAMID AMMAR.

Turkey: 25 Sharia Felaki, Cairo (Bab el-Louk); tel. and fax (2) 3548885; telex 21236; Ambassador: YAŞAR YAKIŞ.

Uganda: 9 Midan el-Messaha, Cairo (Dokki); tel. (2) 3485544; telex 92087; fax (2) 3485980; Ambassador: IBRAHIM MUKIIBI.

United Arab Emirates: 4 Sharia Ibn Sina, Cairo (Giza); tel. (2) 729955; Ambassador: HAMED HILAL SABIT EL-KUWAITI.

United Kingdom: 7 Sharia Ahmad Raghab, Cairo (Garden City); tel. (2) 3540852; fax (2) 3540859; Ambassador: Sir DAVID BLATHERWICK.

USA: 8 Sharia Kamal ed-Din, Cairo (Garden City); tel. (2) 3557371; telex 93773; fax (2) 3573200; Ambassador: CHARLES KURTZER.

Uruguay: 6 Sharia Lotfallah, Cairo (Zamalek); tel. (2) 3415137; telex 92435; fax (2) 3418123; Ambassador: JULIO CÉSAR FRANZINI.

Venezuela: 15A Sharia Mansour Muhammad, Cairo (Zamalek); tel. (2) 3413517; telex 93638; fax (2) 3417373; Ambassador: Dr JOSÉ RAFAEL ZANONI.

Viet Nam: 39 Sharia Kambiz, Cairo (Dokki); tel. (2) 3371494; fax (2) 3496597; Ambassador: NGUYEN LE BACH.

Yemen: 28 Sharia Amean ar-Rafai, Cairo (Dokki); tel. (2) 3604806; Ambassador: ABD AL-GHALIL GHILAN AHMAD.

Yugoslavia: 33 Sharia Mansour Muhammad, Cairo (Zamalek); tel. (2) 3404061; telex 21046; Ambassador: Dr IVAN IVEKOVIĆ.

Zambia: POB 253, Dokki; 6 Abd ar-Rahman Hossein, Mohandessin, Cairo 12311; tel. (2) 3610282; telex 92262; fax (2) 3610833; Ambassador: Dr ANGEL ALFRED MWENDA.

Zimbabwe: 36 Sharia Wadi en-Nil, Mohandessin, Cairo; tel. (2) 3471217; telex 21876; fax (2) 3474872; Ambassador: Dr HENRY MOYANA.

Judicial System

The Courts of Law in Egypt are principally divided into two juridical court systems: Courts of General Jurisdiction and Administrative Courts. Since 1969 the Supreme Constitutional Court has been at the top of the Egyptian judicial structure.

THE SUPREME CONSTITUTIONAL COURT

The Supreme Constitutional Court is the highest court in Egypt. It has specific jurisdiction over: (i) judicial review of the constitutionality of laws and regulations; (ii) resolution of positive and negative jurisdictional conflicts and determination of the competent court between the different juridical court systems, e.g. Courts of General Jurisdiction and Administrative Courts, as well as other bodies exercising judicial competence; (iii) determination of disputes over the enforcement of two final but contradictory judgments rendered by two courts each belonging to a different juridical court system; (iv) rendering binding interpretation of laws or decree laws in the event of a dispute in the application of said laws or decree laws, always provided that such a dispute is of a gravity requiring conformity of interpretation under the Constitution.

COURTS OF GENERAL JURISDICTION

The Courts of General Jurisdiction in Egypt are basically divided into four categories, as follows: (i) The Court of Cassation; (ii) The Courts of Appeal; (iii) The Tribunals of First Instance; (iv) The District Tribunals; each of the above courts is divided into Civil and Criminal Chambers.

(i) Court of Cassation: Is the highest court of general jurisdiction in Egypt. Its sessions are held in Cairo. Final judgments rendered by Courts of Appeal in criminal and civil litigation may be petitioned to the Court of Cassation by the Defendant or the Public Prosecutor in criminal litigation and by any of the parties in interest in civil litigation on grounds of defective application or interpretation of the law as stated in the challenged judgment, on grounds of irregularity of form or procedure, or violation of due process, and on grounds of defective reasoning of judgment rendered. The Court of Cassation is composed of the President, 41 Vice-Presidents and 92 Justices.

President: Hon. ABD AL-BORHAN NOOR.

(ii) The Courts of Appeal: Each has geographical jurisdiction over one or more of the governorates of Egypt. Each Court of Appeal is divided into Criminal and Civil Chambers. The Criminal Chambers try felonies, and the Civil Chambers hear appeals filed against such judgment rendered by the Tribunals of First Instance where the law so stipulates. Each Chamber is composed of three Superior Judges. Each Court of Appeal is composed of President, and sufficient numbers of Vice-Presidents and Superior Judges.

(iii) The Tribunals of First Instance: In each governorate there are one or more Tribunals of First Instance, each of which is divided into several Chambers for criminal and civil litigations. Each Chamber is composed of: (a) a presiding judge, and (b) two sitting judges. A Tribunal of First Instance hears, as an Appellate Court, certain litigations as provided under the law.

(iv) District Tribunals: Each is a one-judge ancillary Chamber of a Tribunal of First Instance, having jurisdiction over minor civil and criminal litigations in smaller districts within the jurisdiction of such Tribunal of First Instance.

PUBLIC PROSECUTION

Public prosecution is headed by the Attorney General, assisted by a number of Senior Deputy and Deputy Attorneys General, and a sufficient number of chief prosecutors, prosecutors and assistant prosecutors. Public prosecution is represented at all levels of the Courts of General Jurisdiction in all criminal litigations and also in certain civil litigations as required by the law. Public prosecution controls and supervises enforcement of criminal law judgments.

Attorney General: GAMAL SHOMAN.

Prosecutor-General: MUHAMMAD ABD AL-AZIZ EL-GINDI.

ADMINISTRATIVE COURTS SYSTEM (CONSEIL D'ETAT)

The Administrative Courts have jurisdiction over litigations involving the state or any of its governmental agencies. The Administrative Courts system is divided into two courts: the Administrative Courts and the Judicial Administrative Courts, at the top of which is the High Administrative Court. The Administrative Prosecutor investigates administrative crimes committed by government officials and civil servants.

President of Conseil d'Etat: Hon. MUHAMMAD HILAL QASIM.

Administrative Prosecutor: Hon. RIFA'AT KHAFAGI.

THE STATE COUNCIL

The State Council is an independent judicial body which has the authority to make decisions in administrative disputes and disciplinary cases within the judicial system.

THE SUPREME JUDICIAL COUNCIL

The Supreme Judicial Council was reinstituted in 1984, having been abolished in 1969. It exists to guarantee the independence of the judicial system from outside interference and is consulted with regard to draft laws organizing the affairs of the judicial bodies.

Religion

According to the 1986 census, some 94% of Egyptians are Muslims (and almost all of these follow Sunni tenets). According to government figures published in the same year, there are about 2m. Copts (a figure contested by Coptic sources, whose estimates range between 6m. and 7m.), forming the largest religious minority, and about 1m. members of other Christian groups. There is also a small Jewish minority.

ISLAM

There is a Higher Council for the Isamic Call, on which sit: the Grand Sheikh of al-Azhar (Chair); the Minister of Awqaf (Islamic Endowments); the President and Vice-President of Al-Azhar University; the Grand Mufti of Egypt; and the Secretary-General of the Higher Council for Islamic Affairs.

Grand Sheikh of al-Azhar: Sheikh MUHAMMAD SAYED ATTIYAH TANTAWI.

Grand Mufti of Egypt: NASR WASSEL.

CHRISTIANITY

Orthodox Churches

Coptic Orthodox Church: St Mark Cathedral, POB 9035, Anba Ruess, 222 Sharia Ramses, Abbassia, Cairo; telex 23281; fax (2) 2825983; f. AD 61; Leader Pope SHENOUDA III; c. 10m. followers in Egypt, Sudan, other African countries, the USA, Canada, Australia, Europe and the Middle East.

Greek Orthodox Patriarchate: POB 2006, Alexandria; tel. (3) 4835839; f. AD 64; Pope and Patriarch of Alexandria and All Africa His Beatitude PARTHENIOS III; 350,000 mems.

The Roman Catholic Church

Armenian Rite

The Armenian Catholic diocese of Alexandria, with an estimated 1,580 adherents at 31 December 1995, is suffragan to the Patriarchate of Cilicia. The Patriarch is resident in Beirut, Lebanon.

Bishop of Alexandria: BOUTROS TAZA, Patriarcat Arménien Catholique, 36 Sharia Muhammad Sabri Abou Alam, Cairo; tel. (2) 3938429; fax (2) 3932025.

Chaldean Rite

The Chaldean Catholic diocese of Cairo had an estimated 2,070 adherents at 31 December 1995.

Bishop of Cairo: YOUSSEF IBRAHIM SARRAF, Evêché Chaldéen, Basilique-Sanctuaire Notre Dame de Fatima, 141 Sharia Nouzha, 11361 Heliopolis, Cairo; tel. and fax (2) 2455718.

Coptic Rite

Egypt comprises the Coptic Catholic Patriarchate of Alexandria and five dioceses. At 31 December 1995 there were an estimated 192,955 adherents in the country.

Patriarch of Alexandria: His Beatitude STEPHANOS II (ANDREAS GHATTAS), Patriarcat Copte Catholique, POB 69, 34 Sharia Ibn Sandar, Koubbeh Bridge, Cairo; tel. (2) 2571740; fax (2) 4545766.

Latin Rite

Egypt comprises the Apostolic Vicariate of Alexandria (incorporating Heliopolis and Port Said), containing an estimated 5,200 adherents at 31 December 1995.

Vicar Apostolic: Fr EGIDIO SAMPIERI (Titular Bishop of Ida in Mauretania), 10 Sharia Sidi El-Metwalli, Alexandria; tel. (3) 4836065; also at 2 Sharia Banque Misr, Cairo; tel. (2) 41280.

Maronite Rite

The Maronite diocese of Cairo had an estimated 5,000 adherents at 31 December 1995.

Bishop of Cairo: JOSEPH DERGHAM, Evêché Maronite, 15 Sharia Hamdi, Daher, Cairo; tel. (2) 923327.

Melkite Rite

His Beatitude MAXIMOS V HAKIM (resident in Damascus, Syria) is the Greek-Melkite Patriarch of Antioch, of Alexandria and of Jerusalem.

Patriarchal Exarchate of Egypt and Sudan: Patriarcat Grec-Melkite Catholique, 16 Sharia Daher, Cairo; tel. (2) 5905790; 7,000 adherents (31 December 1995); Exarch Patriarchal Mgr PAUL ANTAKI, Titular Archbishop of Nubia.

Syrian Rite

The Syrian Catholic diocese of Cairo had an estimated 2,070 adherents at 31 December 1995.

Bishop of Cairo: JOSEPH HANNOUCHE, Evêché Syrien Catholique, 46 Sharia Daher, Cairo; tel. (2) 901234.

The Anglican Communion

The Anglican diocese of Egypt, suspended in 1958, was revived in 1974 and became part of the Episcopal Church in Jerusalem and the Middle East, formally inaugurated in January 1976. The Province has four dioceses: Jerusalem, Egypt, Cyprus and the Gulf, and Iran, and its President is the Bishop in Egypt. The Bishop in Egypt has jurisdiction also over the Anglican chaplaincies in Algeria, Djibouti, Eritrea, Ethiopia, Libya, Somalia and Tunisia.

Bishop in Egypt: Most Rev. GHAIS ABD AL-MALIK, Diocesan Office, POB 87, 5 Sharia Michel Lutfalla, Cairo (Zamalek); tel. (2) 3414019; fax (2) 3408941; e-mail diocese@intouch.com.

Other Christian Churches

Armenian Apostolic Church: 179 Sharia Ramses, Cairo, POB 48-Faggalah; tel. (2) 5901385; fax (2) 906671; Archbishop ZAVEN CHINCHINIAN; 7,000 mems.

Protestant Churches of Egypt: POB 1304, Cairo 11511; tel. (2) 5903925; f. 1902, independent since 1926; 200,000 mems (1985); Gen. Sec. (vacant).

Other denominations active in Egypt include the Coptic Evangelical Church (Synod of the Nile) and the Union of the Armenian Evangelical Churches in the Near East.

JUDAISM

The 1986 census recorded 794 Jews in Egypt.

Jewish Community: Office of the Chief Rabbi, Rabbi HAIM DOUEK, 13 Sharia Sebil el-Khazindar, Abbassia, Cairo.

The Press

Despite a fairly high illiteracy rate in Egypt, the country's press is well developed. Cairo is one of the largest publishing centres in the Middle East and Africa.

All newspapers and magazines are supervised, according to law, by of the Supreme Press Council. The four major publishing houses of al-Ahram, Dar al-Hilal, Dar Akhbar al-Yawm and Dar at-Tahrir, operate as separate entities and compete with each other commercially.

The most authoritative daily newspaper is the very long-established *Al-Ahram*.

DAILIES

Alexandria

Bareed ach-Charikat (Companies' Post): POB 813, Alexandria; f. 1952; Arabic; evening; commerce, finance, insurance and marine affairs, etc.; Editor S. BENEDUCCI; circ. 15,000.

Al-Ittihad al-Misri (Egyptian Unity): 13 Sharia Sidi Abd ar-Razzak, Alexandria; f. 1871; Arabic; evening; Propr ANWAR MAHER FARAG; Dir HASSAN MAHER FARAG.

Le Journal d'Alexandrie: 1 Sharia Rolo, Alexandria; French; evening; Editor CHARLES ARCACHE.

As-Safeer (The Ambassador): 4 Sharia as-Sahafa, Alexandria; f. 1924; Arabic; evening; Editor MUSTAFA SHARAF.

Tachydromos-Egyptos: 4 Sharia Zangarol, Alexandria; tel. (3) 35650; f. 1879; Greek; morning; liberal; Publr PENNY COUTSOUMIS; Editor DINOS COUTSOUMIS; circ. 2,000.

Cairo

Al-Ahram (The Pyramids): Sharia al-Galaa, Cairo 11511; tel. (2) 5747011; telex 92002; fax (2) 5747089; f. 1875; Arabic; morning, incl. Sundays (international edition published in London, England; North American edition published in New York, USA); Editor and Chair. IBRAHIM NAFEH; circ. 900,000 (weekdays), 1.1m. (Friday).

Al-Ahrar: 58 Manshyet Al-Sadr, Kobry-al Kobba, Cairo; tel. (2) 4823046; fax (2) 4823027; f. 1977; organ of Liberal Socialist Party; Editor-in-Chief SALAH QABADAYA.

Al-Akhbar (The News): Dar Akhbar al-Yawm, Sharia as-Sahafa, Cairo; tel. (2) 5782600; telex 20321; fax (2) 5782520; f. 1952; Arabic; Chair. IBRAHIM ABU SADAH; Man. Editor GALAL DEWIDAR; circ. 980,000.

Arev: 3 Sharia Soliman Halaby, Cairo; tel. (2) 754703; f. 1915; Armenian; evening; official organ of the Armenian Liberal Democratic Party; Editor AVEDIS YAPOUDJIAN.

Egyptian Gazette: 24–26 Sharia Zakaria Ahmad, Cairo; tel. (2) 5783333; telex 92475; fax (2) 5781717; f. 1880; English; morning; Editor-in-Chief MUHAMMAD ALI IBRAHIM; circ. 35,000.

Al-Gomhouriya (The Republic): 24 Sharia Zakaria Ahmad, Cairo; tel. (2) 5783333; telex 92475; fax (2) 5781717; f. 1953; Arabic; morning; Chair. SAMIR RAGAB; Editor MAHFOUZ AL-ANSARI; circ. 900,000.

Le Journal d'Egypte: 1 Sharia Borsa Guédida, Cairo; f. 1936; French; morning; Gen. Man. LITA GALLAD; Editor-in-Chief MUHAMMAD RACHAD; circ. 72,000.

Al-Misaa' (The Evening): 24 Sharia Zakaria Ahmad, Cairo; telex 92475; f. 1956; Arabic; evening; Editor-in-Chief SAMIR RAGAB; circ. 105,000.

Phos: 14 Sharia Zakaria Ahmad, Cairo; f. 1896; Greek; morning; Editor S. PATERAS; Man. BASILE A. PATERAS; circ. 20,000.

Le Progrès Egyptien: 24 Sharia Zakaria Ahmad, Cairo; tel. (2) (2) 5783333; telex 92475; fax (2) 5781717; f. 1890; French; morning including Sundays; Editor-in-Chief KHALED ANWAR BAKIR; circ. 21,000.

PERIODICALS

Alexandria

Al-Ahad al-Gedid (New Sunday): 88 Sharia Said M. Koraim, Alexandria; tel. (3) 807874; f. 1936; Editor-in-Chief and Publr GALAL M. KORAITEM; circ. 60,000.

Alexandria Medical Journal: 4 G. Carducci, Alexandria; f. 1922; English, French and Arabic; quarterly; publ. by Alexandria Medical Assn; Editor AMIN RIDA; circ. 1,500.

Amitié Internationale: 59 ave el-Hourriya, Alexandria; tel. (3) 23639; f. 1957; publ. by Assn Egyptienne d'Amitié Internationale; Arabic and French; quarterly; Editor Dr ZAKI BADAOUI.

L'Annuaire des Sociétés Egyptiennes par Actions: 23 Midan Tahrir, Alexandria; f. 1930; annually in Dec.; French; Propr ELIE I. POLITI; Editor OMAR ES-SAYED MOURSI.

L'Echo Sportif: 7 Sharia de l'Archevêché, Alexandria; French; weekly; Propr MICHEL BITTAR.

Egyptian Cotton Gazette: POB 433, Alexandria; tel. (3) 4806971; fax (3) 4833002; e-mail alcotexa@idsc.gov.eg; organ of the Alexandria Cotton Exporters' Association; English; 2 a year; Chief Editor GALAL REFAI.

Informateur des Assurances: 1 Sharia Sinan, Alexandria; f. 1936; French; monthly; Propr ELIE I. POLITI; Editor SIMON A. BARANIS.

Sina 'at en-Nassig (L'Industrie Textile): 5 rue de l'Archevêché, Alexandria; Arabic and French; monthly; Editor PHILIPPE COLAS.

Voce d'Italia: 90 Sharia Farahde, Alexandria; Italian; fortnightly; Editor R. AVELLINO.

Cairo

Al-Ahali (The People): 23 Sharia Abd al-Khalek, Tharwat, Cairo; tel. (2) 3923306; fax (2) 3900412; f. 1978; weekly; published by the National Progressive Unionist Party; Chair. Lotfi Wakid; Editor-in-Chief Abd el-Bakoury.

Al-Ahram al-Arabi: Sharia al-Galaa, Cairo 11511; f. 1997; Arabic; weekly; political, social and economic affairs; Editor-in-Chief Ibrahim Nafie.

Al-Ahram Hebdo: Sharia al-Galaa, Cairo 11511; tel. (2) 4180034; fax (2) 4182663; f. 1993; French; weekly; Editor-in-Chief Muhammad Salmawi.

Al-Ahram al-Iqtisadi (The Economic *Al-Ahram*): Sharia al-Galaa, Cairo 11511; telex 20185; fax (2) 5786833; Arabic; weekly; economic and political affairs; owned by Al-Ahram publrs; Chief Editor Issam Rifa'at; circ. 67,000.

Al-Ahram Weekly (The Pyramids): Al-Ahram Bldg, Sharia al-Galaa, Cairo; tel. (2) 5786064; telex 20185; fax (2) 5786833; f. 1989; English; weekly; published by Al-Ahram publications; Editor-in-Chief Hosny Guindy; circ. 150,000.

Akhbar al-Hawadith: 6 Sharia as-Sahafa, Cairo; tel. (2) 5782600; fax (2) 5782510; f. 1993; weekly; crime reports; Editor-in-Chief Samir Tawfik.

Akhbar al-Nogoome: 6 Sharia as-Sahafa, Cairo; tel. (2) 5782600; fax (2) 5782510; f. 1991; weekly; theatre and film news; Editor-in-Chief Muhammad Tabarak.

Akhbar ar-Riadah: 6 Sharia as-Sahafa, Cairo; tel. (2) 5782600; fax (2) 5782510; f. 1990; weekly; sport; Editor-in-Chief Fathi Sanad.

Akhbar al-Yaum (Daily News): 6 Sharia as-Sahafa, Cairo; tel. (2) 5782600; fax (2) 5782510; f. 1944; Arabic; weekly (Saturday); Chair. and Editor-in-Chief Ibrahim Abu Sedah; circ. 1,158,000.

Akher Sa'a (Last Hour): Dar Akhbar al-Yawm, Sharia as-Sahafa, Cairo; telex 92215; f. 1934; Arabic; weekly (Wed.); independent; Editor-in-Chief Muhammad Wajdi Kandil; circ. 150,000.

Al-Azhar: Idarat al-Azhar, Sharia al-Azhar, Cairo; f. 1931; Arabic; Islamic monthly; supervised by the Egyptian Council for Islamic Research of Al-Azhar University; Dir Muhammad Farid Wagdi.

Al-Bitrul (Petroleum): Cairo; monthly; published by the Egyptian General Petroleum Corporation.

Contemporary Thought: University of Cairo, Cairo; quarterly; Editor Dr Z. N. Mahmoud.

Ad-Da'wa (The Call): Cairo; Arabic; monthly; organ of the Muslim Brotherhood.

Ad-Doctor: 8 Sharia Hoda Shaarawy, Cairo; f. 1947; Arabic; monthly; Editor Dr Ahmad M. Kamal; circ. 30,000.

Echos: 1–5 Sharia Mahmoud Bassiouni, Cairo; f. 1947; French; weekly; Dir and Propr Georges Qrfali.

The Egyptian Mail: 24–26 Sharia Zakaria Ahmad; telex 92475; weekly; Sat. edn of *The Egyptian Gazette*; English; circ. 35,000.

Al-Fusoul (The Seasons): 17 Sharia Sherif Pasha, Cairo; Arabic; monthly; Propr and Chief Editor Samir Muhammad Zaki Abd al-Kader.

Al-Garidat at-Tigariyat al-Misriya (The Egyptian Business Paper): 25 Sharia Nubar Pasha, Cairo; f. 1921; Arabic; weekly; circ. 7,000.

Hawa'a (Eve): Dar al-Hilal, 16 Sharia Muhammad Ezz el-Arab, Cairo; tel. (2) 3625450; fax (2) 3625469; women's magazine; Arabic; weekly (Sat.); Chief Editor Ekbal Baraka; circ. 160,837.

Al-Hilal Magazine: Dar al-Hilal, 16 Sharia Muhammad Ezz el-Arab, Cairo; telex 92703; f. 1895; Arabic; literary monthly; Editor Moustafa Nabil.

Huwa wa Hiya (He and She): POB 525, Cairo 11511; tel. (2) 3506752; fax (2) 3508604; f. 1977; monthly; news, leisure, sport, health, religion, women's issues; Dir George Tawfik.

Industrial Egypt: POB 251, 26A Sharia Sherif Pasha, Cairo; tel. (2) 3928317; telex 92624; fax (2) 3928075; f. 1924; quarterly bulletin and year book of the Federation of Egyptian Industries in English and Arabic; Editor Ali Fahmy.

Informateur Financier et Commercial: 24 Sharia Soliman Pasha, Cairo; f. 1929; weekly; Dir Henri Politi; circ. 15,000.

Al-Iza'a wat-Television (Radio and Television): 13 Sharia Muhammad Ezz el-Arab, Cairo; f. 1935; Arabic; weekly; Editor and Chair. Sakeena Fouad; circ. 80,000.

Al-Kerazeh (The Sermon): Cairo; Arabic; weekly newspaper of the Coptic Orthodox Church.

Al-Kawakeb (The Stars): Dar al-Hilal, 16 Sharia Muhammad Ezz el-Arab, Cairo; tel. (2) 3625450; fax (2) 3625469; f. 1952; Arabic; weekly; film magazine; Editor-in-Chief Ragaa al-Nakkash; circ. 86,381.

Kitab al-Hilal: Dar al-Hilal, 16 Sharia Muhammad Ezz el-Arab, Cairo; monthly; Founders Emile and Shoukri Zeidan; Editor Moustafa Nabil.

Al-Liwa' al-Islami (Islamic Standard): 11 Sharia Sherif Pasha, Cairo; f. 1982; Arabic; weekly; govt paper to promote official view of Islamic revivalism; Propr Ahmad Hamza; Editor Muhammad Ali Sheta; circ. 30,000.

Lotus Magazine: 104 Sharia Qasr el-Eini, Cairo; f. 1992; English, French and Arabic; quarterly; computer software magazine; Editor Berend Harmens.

Magallat al-Mohandeseen (The Engineer's Magazine): 28 Sharia Ramses, Cairo; f. 1945; publ. by The Engineers' Syndicate; Arabic and English; 10 a year; Editor and Sec. Mahmoud Sami Abd al-Kawi.

Al-Magallat az-Zira'ia (The Agricultural Magazine): Cairo; monthly; agriculture; circ. 30,000.

Mayo (May): Sharia al-Galaa, Cairo; organ of National Democratic Party; Supervisor Muhammad Safwat ash-Sharif; Chair. Abdullah Abd al-Bary; Chief Editor Samir Ragab; circ. 500,000.

Medical Journal of Cairo University: Manyal University Hospital, Sharia Qasr el-Eini, Cairo; f. 1933; Kasr el-Eini Clinical Society; English; quarterly.

The Middle East Observer: 41 Sharia Sherif, Cairo; tel. (2) 3926919; fax (2) 3939732; f. 1954; English; weekly; specializing in economics of Middle East and African markets; also publishes supplements on law, foreign trade and tenders; agent for IMF, UN and IDRC publications, distributor of World Bank publications; Man. Owner Ahmad Foda; Chief Editor Muhammad Abdullah Hesham A. Raouf; circ. 30,000.

Al-Musawar: Dar al-Hilal, 16 Sharia Muhammad Ezz el-Arab, Cairo; tel. (2) 3625450; telex 92703; fax (2) 3625469; f. 1924; Arabic; weekly; Editor-in-Chief Makram Muhammad Ahmad; circ. 130,423.

Nesf ad-Donia: Sharia al-Galaa, Cairo 11511; tel. (2) 5786100; f. 1990; weekly; women's magazine; Editor-in-Chief Sanaa al-Besi.

October: 1119 Sharia Corniche en-Nil, Cairo; tel. (2) 777077; fax (2) 5744999; monthly; Chair. and Editor-in-Chief Ragab al-Bana; circ. 140,500.

Al-Omal (The Workers): 90 Sharia Galal, Cairo; telex 93255; publ. by the Egyptian Trade Union Federation: Arabic; weekly; Chief Editor Ahmad Harak.

Progrès Dimanche: 24 Sharia Galal, Cairo; tel. 741611; telex 92475; French; weekly; Sunday edition of *Le Progrès Egyptien*; Editor-in-Chief Khaled Anwar Bakir.

Radio and TV Magazine: At-Tahrir Printing and Publishing House, 24 Sharia Zakaria Ahmad, Cairo; tel. (2) 3643314; fax (2) 3543030; Arabic; weekly; Editor-in-Chief Mahmoud Ali.

Rose al-Yousuf: 89A Sharia Qasr el-Eini, Cairo; tel. (2) 3540888; fax (2) 3556413; f. 1925; Arabic; weekly; political; circulates throughout all Arab countries; Chair. of Board and Editor Mahmud Tuhami; circ. 35,000.

As-Sabah (The Morning): 4 Sharia Muhammad Said Pasha, Cairo; f. 1922; Arabic; weekly (Thurs.); Editor Raouf Tawfik.

Sabah al-Kheir (Good Morning): 18 Sharia Muhammad Said Pasha, Cairo; Arabic; weekly; light entertainment; Chief Editor Mofeed Fawzi; circ. 70,000.

Ash-Shaab (The People): 313 Sharia Port Said, Cairo; organ of Socialist Labour Party; weekly; Editor-in-Chief Adel Hussein; circ. 130,000.

At-Tahrir (Liberation): 5 Sharia Naguib, Rihani, Cairo; Arabic; weekly; Editor Abd al-Aziz Sadek.

At-Taqaddum (Progress): c/o 1 Sharia Jarim ed-Dawlah, Cairo; f. 1978; organ of National Progressive Unionist Party.

Tchehreh Nema: 14 Sharia Hassan el-Akbar (Abdine), Cairo; f. 1904; Iranian; monthly; political, literary and general; Editor Manuchehr Tchehreh Nema Moadeb Zadeh.

Up-to-Date International Industry: 10 Sharia Galal, Cairo; Arabic and English; monthly; foreign trade journal.

Al-Wafd: 1 Sharia Boulos Hanna, Cairo (Dokki); tel. (2) 3482079; fax (2) 3602007; f. 1984; weekly; organ of the New Wafd Party; Editor-in-Chief Gamal Badawi; circ. 360,000.

Watani (My Country): 27 Sharia Abdel Khalek Sarwat, Cairo; tel. (2) 3927201; fax (2) 3935946; f. 1958; Arabic; independent Sun. newspaper addressing Egyptians in general and the Christian Copts in particular; Chief Officers Y. Sidhom, S. Aziz, F. A. Sayed; circ. 50,000.

Yulio (July): July Press and Publishing House, Cairo; f. 1986; weekly; Nasserist; Editor Abdullah Imam; and a monthly cultural magazine, Editor Mahmoud al-Maraghi.

NEWS AGENCIES

Middle East News Agency: 17 Sharia Hoda Sharawi, Cairo; tel. (2) 3933000; telex 92252; fax (2) 3935055; f. 1955; regular service in Arabic, English and French; Chair. and Editor-in-Chief Moustafa Naguib.

Foreign Bureaux

Agence France-Presse (AFP): POB 1437-15511, 2nd Floor, 10 Misaha Sq, Cairo; tel. (2) 3481236; telex 92225; fax (2) 3603282; Chief SAMMY KETZ.

Agencia EFE (Spain): 35A Sharia Abu el-Feda, 4th Floor, Apt 14, Cairo (Zamalek); Correspondent DOMINGO DEL PINO.

Agenzia Nazionale Stampa Associata (ANSA) (Italy): 19 Sharia Abd al-Khalek Sarwat, Cairo; tel. (2) 3929821; telex 93365; fax (2) 3938642; Chief ANTONELLA TARQUINI.

Allgemeiner Deutscher Nachrichtendienst (ADN) (Germany): 17 Sharia el-Brazil, Apt 59, Cairo (Zamalek); tel. (2) 3404006; telex 92339; Correspondent RALF SCHULTZE.

Associated Press (AP) (USA): POB 1077, 1117 Sharia Corniche en-Nil, Maspiro, Cairo 11221; tel. (2) 5784091; telex 92211; fax (2) 5784094; Chief GERALD G. LABELLE.

Deutsche Presse-Agentur (dpa) (Germany): 14th Floor, 1125 Corniche en-Nil, Cairo; tel. (2) 5780351; telex 92054; fax (2) 5780354; Chief JÖRG FISCHER.

Informatsionnoye Telegrafnoye Agentstvo Rossii-Telegrafnoye Agentstvo Suverennykh Stran (ITAR-TASS) (Russia): 30 Sharia Muhammad Mazhar, Cairo (Zamalek); tel. 3419784; telex 93008; fax (2) 3417268; Dir MIKHAIL I. KROUTIKHIN.

Jiji Press (Japan): Room 2, 1st Floor, 3 Gezira el-Wosta, Cairo (Zamalek); tel. (2) 3411411; telex 20940; fax (2) 3405244; Chief FUMIHIKO SUGIYAMA.

Kyodo News Service (Japan): Flat 301, 15 Sharia Hassan Sabri, Cairo 11211 (Zamalek); tel. (2) 3411756; telex 20435; fax (2) 3406105; Chief JITSURO KIHARA.

Magyar Távirati Iroda (MTI) (Hungary): 6A Sharia el-Malek el-Afdal, Cairo (Zamalek); tel. (2) 3402892; fax (2) 3402898; Correspondent IMRE KERESZTES.

Reuters (United Kingdom): POB 2040, 21st Floor, Bank Misr Tower, 153 Sharia Muhammad Farid, Cairo; tel. (2) 777150; telex 92210; fax (2) 771133; Chief Correspondent JONATHAN WRIGHT.

United Press International (UPI) (USA): POB 872, 4 Sharia Eloui, Cairo; tel. (2) 3928106.

Xinhua (New China) News Agency (People's Republic of China): 2 Moussa Galal Sq., Mohandessin, Cairo; tel. (2) 3448950; telex 93812.

The Iraqi News Agency (INA) reopened its office in Cairo in 1985.

PRESS ASSOCIATION

Foreign Press Association: Room 2037, Mariot Hotel, Cairo; tel. (2) 3419957.

Publishers

General Egyptian Book Organization: 117 Sharia Corniche en-Nil, Boulac, Cairo; tel. (2) 775000; fax (2) 5754213; e-mail ssarhan@idsc.gov.eg; f. 1961; affiliated to the Ministry of Culture; Chair. Dr SAMIR SARHAN.

Alexandria

Alexandria University Press: Shatby, Alexandria.

Egyptian Printing and Publishing House: Ahmad es-Sayed Marouf, 59 Safia Zaghoul, Alexandria; f. 1947.

Maison Egyptienne d'Editions: Ahmad es-Sayed Marouf, Sharia Adib, Alexandria; f. 1950.

Maktab al-Misri al-Hadith li-t-Tiba wan-Nashr: 7 Sharia Noubar, Alexandria; also at 2 Sharia Sherif, Cairo; Man. AHMAD YEHIA.

Cairo

Al-Ahram Establishment: 6 Sharia al-Galaa, Cairo; tel. (2) 576069; telex 92001; fax 5786023; f. 1875; publ. newspapers, magazines and books, incl. *Al-Ahram*; Chief Ed. IBRAHIM NAFEI.

Akhbar al-Yawm Publishing Group: 6 Sharia as-Sahafa, Cairo; tel. (2) 5748100; telex 20321; fax (2) 5748895; f. 1944; publ. *Al-Akhbar* (daily), *Akhbar al-Yawm* (weekly), and colour magazine *Akher Sa'a* (weekly); Pres. IBRAHIM SAAD.

Argus Press: 10 Sharia Zakaria Ahmad, Cairo; Owners KARNIG HAGOPIAN and ABD AL-MEGUID MUHAMMAD.

Boustany Publishing House: 29 Sharia Faggalah, Cairo 11271; tel. (2) 5915315; fax 4177915; e-mail bph@ritsec3.com.eg; internet http://www.boustanys.com; f. 1900; fiction, poetry, history, biography, philosophy, Arabic language, literature, politics, religion, archaeology, Egyptology; Chief Exec. Dr FADWA BOUSTANY.

Dar al-Gomhouriya: 24 Sharia Zakaria Ahmad, Cairo; tel. (2) 5781010; fax (2) 5784747; affiliate of At-Tahrir Printing and Publishing House; publications include the dailies, *Al-Gomhouriya, Al-Misaa', Egyptian Gazette* and *Le Progrès Egyptien*; Pres. SAMIK RAGAB.

Dar al-Hilal Publishing Institution: 16 Sharia Muhammad Ezz el-Arab, Cairo; tel. (2) 20610; telex 92703; f. 1892; publ. *Al-Hilal, Riwayat al-Hilal, Kitab al-Hilal, Tabibak al-Khass* (monthlies); *Al-Mussawar, Al-Kawakeb, Hawaa, Samir, Mickey* (weeklies); Chair. MAKRAN MUHAMMAD AHMAD.

Dar al-Kitab al-Arabi: Misr Printing House, Sharia Noubar, Cairo (Bab el-Louk); f. 1968; Man. Dir Dr SAHAIR AL-KALAMAWI.

Dar al-Kitab al-Masri: POB 156, 33 Sharia Qasr en-Nil, Cairo; tel. (2) 3922168; telex 23081; fax (2) 3924614; f. 1929; religion, history, books for children, general interest, etc.; Man. Dir HASSAN EL-ZEIN.

Dar al-Maaref: 1119 Sharia Corniche en-Nil, Cairo; tel. (2) 759411; fax (2) 5744999; f. 1890; publishing, printing and distribution of all kinds of books in Arabic and other languages; publishers of *October* magazine; Chair. and Man. Dir RAGAB AL-BANA.

Dar an-Nashr (formerly Les Editions Universitaires d'Egypte): POB 1347, 41 Sharia Sherif, Cairo 11511; tel. (2) 3934606; fax (2) 3921997; f. 1947; university textbooks, academic works, encyclopaedia.

Dar ash-Shorouk: 16 Sharia Gawad Hosni, Cairo; tel. (2) 3929333; telex 93091; fax (2) 3934814; f. 1968; publishing, printing and distribution; publishers of books on modern Islamic politics, philosophy and art, and books for children; Chair. ABRAHIM EL-MOALLIM ADEL.

Editions Horus: 1 Midan Soliman Pasha, Cairo.

Editions le Progrès: 6 Sharia Sherif Pasha, Cairo; Propr WADI SHOUKRI.

Egyptian Co for Printing and Publishing: 40 Sharia Noubar, Cairo; tel. (2) 21310; Chair. MUHAMMAD MAHMOUD HAMED.

Higher University Council for Arts, Letters and Sciences: University of Cairo, Cairo.

Lagnat at-Taalif wat-Targama wan-Nashr (Committee for Writing, Translating and Publishing Books): 9 Sharia el-Kerdassi (Abdine), Cairo.

Librairie La Renaissance d'Egypte (Hassan Muhammad & Sons): POB 2172, 9 Sharia Adly, Cairo; f. 1930; religion, history, geography, medicine, architecture, economics, politics, law, philosophy, psychology, children's books, atlases, dictionaries; Man. HASSAN MUHAMMAD.

Maktabet Misr: POB 16, 3 Sharia Kamal Sidki, Cairo; tel. (2) 5898553; fax (2) 5907593; f. 1932; publs wide variety of fiction, biographies and textbooks for schools and universities; Man. AMIR SAID GOUDA ES-SAHHAR.

National Centre for Educational Research and Development: 12 Sharia Waked, el-Borg el-Faddy, POB 836, Cairo; tel. (2) 3930981; f. 1956; formerly Documentation and Research Centre for Education (Ministry of Education); bibliographies, directories, information and education bulletins; Dir Prof. ABD EL-FATTAH GALAL.

National Library Press (Dar al-Kutub): Midan Ahmad Maher, Cairo; bibliographic works.

Senouhy Publishers: 54 Sharia Abd al-Khalek Sarwat, Cairo; f. 1956; Dir LEILA A. FADEL.

Ash-Shaab: 313 Sharia Port Said, Sayeda Zeinab, Cairo; tel. (2) 3909716; fax (2) 3900283; e-mail elshaab@idsc.gov.eg; f. 1979; bi-weekly (Tuesday and Friday); Editor-in-Chief MAGDI AHMED HUSSEIN.

As-Syassa ad-Dawliah: Sharia al-Galaa, Cairo 11511; tel. (2) 5786022; fax (2) 5786023; f. 1965; political quarterly; Editor-in-Chief Dr OSAMA AL-GHAZALI HARB.

At-Tahrir Printing and Publishing House: 24 Sharia Zakaria Ahmad, Cairo; tel. (2) 5781010; telex 92475; fax (2) 5784747; f. 1953; affil. to Shura (Advisory) Council; Chair. and Man. Dir SAMIR RAGAB.

Watani: Sharia Talaat Harb, Cairo; tel. (2) 3927201; fax (2) 3935946; weekly; Editor-in-Chief Dr SAMI AZIZ.

Broadcasting and Communications

TELECOMMUNICATIONS

Egypt Telecommunications Co: Sharia Ramses, Cairo 11511; tel. (2) 7676244; telex 92100; fax (2) 771306; Chair. Eng. ABD AL-FATTAH ABU SEREE.

BROADCASTING

Egyptian Radio and Television Union (ERTU): POB 11511, Cairo 1186; tel. (2) 5787120; telex 22609; fax (2) 746989; f. 1928; 450 hours daily. Home Service radio programmes in Arabic, English and French; foreign services in Arabic, English, French, Swahili, Hausa, Bengali, Urdu, German, Spanish, Armenian, Greek, Hebrew, Indonesian, Malay, Thai, Hindi, Pushtu, Persian, Turkish, Somali,

Portuguese, Fulani, Italian, Zulu, Shona, Sindebele, Lingala, Afar, Amharic, Yoruba, Wolof, Bambara; Pres. AMIN BASSIOUNI.

Radio

Middle East Radio: Société Egyptienne de Publicité, 24-26 Sharia Zakaria Ahmad, Cairo; tel. (2) 744166; telex 924475.

Finance

(cap. = capital; p.u. = paid up;
dep. = deposits; res = reserves; m. = million; brs = branches;
amounts in Egyptian pounds unless otherwise stated)

BANKING

The whole banking system was nationalized in 1961. Since 1974 foreign and private-sector banks have been allowed to play a role in the economy, and in mid-1995 there were 84 banks operating in Egypt.

Central Bank

Central Bank of Egypt: 31 Sharia Qasr en-Nil, Cairo; tel. (2) 3931514; telex 92237; fax (2) 3926361; f. 1961; state-owned; cap. 100m., dep. 81,285m., res 3,447m., total assets 129,811m. (June 1996); Gov. and Chair. ESMAIEL HASSAN MUHAMMAD; 3 brs.

Commercial and Specialized Banks

Alexandria Commercial and Maritime Bank: POB 2376, 85 avenue el-Hourriya, Alexandria 21519; tel. (3) 4921556; telex 54553; fax (3) 4913706; f. 1981; the Almar Co has an 18.96% shareholding, the National Investment Bank has a 13.3% interest and the Egyptian Co for Maritime Transport has a 13.2% interest. Other interests 54.54%; cap. 60.1m., dep. 830.5m., total assets 1,090.1m. (Dec. 1996); Chair. MUHAMMAD ADEL EL-BARKOUKI; Gen. Man. KAMAL E. A. ZAYED; 5 brs.

Bank of Alexandria, SAE: 6 Sharia Salah Salem, Alexandria; and 49 Sharia Qasr en-Nil, Cairo; tel. (3) 4830159 (Alexandria), (2) 3913822 (Cairo); telex 54107 (Alexandria), 22218 (Cairo); fax (3) 4839968 (Alexandria), (2) 3919805 (Cairo); f. 1957; state-owned; cap. p.u. 700m., dep. 16,296.3m., res 1,888.6m., total assets 19,894.5m. (June 1996); Chair. ABDEL KARIM MUHAMMAD ABDEL HAMID; 184 brs.

Bank of Commerce and Development: POB 1373, 13 Sharia 26 July Sphinx Sq., Mohandessin, Cairo; tel. (2) 3472063; telex 21607; fax (2) 3450581; f. 1980; cap. 205.9m., dep. 500.0m., total assets 937.5m. (Dec. 1995); Chair. and Man. Dir SAMIR MUHAMMAD FOUAD EL-QASRI; 6 brs.

Banque du Caire, SAE: POB 1495, 30 Sharia Roushdy, Cairo; tel. (2) 3904554; telex 92022; f. 1952; state-owned; cap. 750.0m., res 167.3m., dep. 22,358.8m., total assets 26,897m. (June 1996); Chair. MUHAMMAD ABD EL-FATH; 238 brs.

Banque Misr: 151 Sharia Muhammad Farid, Cairo; tel. (2) 3912711; telex 92242; fax (2) 3919779; f. 1920; state-owned since 1960; cap. p.u. 1,000m., res 264.2m., dep. 41,792.6m., total assets 47,680m. (June 1996); Chair. ESSAM ED-DIN EL-AHMADY; 420 brs.

Commercial International Bank (Egypt), SAE: POB 2430, Nile Tower Bldg, 21-23 Sharia Giza, Giza; tel. (2) 5701949; telex 20202; fax (2) 5703172; f. 1975 as Chase National Bank (Egypt) SAE; adopted present name 1987; National Bank of Egypt has 42.15% interest, International Finance Corpn 5%; cap. 400m., dep. 4,121.6m., total assets 6,343.2m. (Dec. 1994); Exec. Chair. MAHMOUD ABD AL-AZIZ ; 16 brs.

Crédit Foncier Egyptien: 11 Sharia el-Mashadi, POB 141, Cairo; tel. (2) 3911977; telex 93863; fax (2) 3907363; f. 1880; state-owned; cap. p.u. 100m., total assets 1,173.5m. (June 1993); Chair. ADEL MAHMOUD ABD AL-BAKI; Gen Man. ABD AL-WAHAB EL-ILADYDY; 9 brs.

Egyptian British Bank SAE: POB 126 D, Abu el-Feda Bldg, 3 Sharia Abu el-Feda, Cairo (Zamalek); tel. (2) 3408938; telex 22505; fax (2) 3414010; f. 1982; the Hongkong and Shanghai Banking Corporation has a 40% shareholding, Egyptian interests 51%, other Arab interests 9%; cap. 100.8m., res 8.5m., dep. 1,384.7m., total assets 1,682.2m. (Dec. 1996); Chair. Dr IBRAHIM ABU EL-EYOUN A. KAMEL; 6 brs.

Export Development Bank of Egypt: Evergreen Bldg, 10 Sharia Talaat Harb, Cairo; f. 1983 to replace National Import-Export Bank; tel. (2) 777003; telex 20850; fax (2) 774553; cap. p.u. 69m., res 119.7m., dep. 1,395.6m., total assets 1,942m. (June 1996); Chair. MAHMOUD MOHAMED MAHMOUD; 3 brs.

Industrial Development Bank of Egypt: 110 Sharia al-Galaa, Faggalah, Cairo; tel. (2) 779087; telex 23377; fax (2) 777324; f. 1975; cap. p.u. 146.2m.; total assets 1,865m. (June 1993); Chair. Dr KAMAL ABOU EL-EID; 9 brs.

National Bank for Development: POB 647, 5 Sharia el-Borsa el-Gedida, Cairo; tel. (2) 3923245; f. 1980; cap. p.u. 150.7m., res 92.0m., dep. 4,460m., total assets 5,363m. (Dec. 1996); Pres. MUHAMMAD ZAKI EL-ORABI; 66 brs; there are affiliated National Banks for Development in 16 governorates.

National Bank of Egypt: POB 11611, 1187 Corniche en-Nil, Cairo; tel. (2) 5749101; telex 20069; fax (2) 762672; f. 1898; nationalized 1960; handles all commercial banking operations; cap. 1,000m., dep. 39,193m., total assets 53,224m. (June 1996); Chair. MAHMOUD ABD AL-AZIZ MUHAMMAD; 320 brs.

Principal Bank for Development and Agricultural Credit: POB 11669, 110 Sharia Qasr el-Eini, Cairo; tel. (2) 3551204; fax (2) 3548337; f. 1976 to succeed former credit organizations; state-owned; cap. p.u. 1,105m., res 245m., dep. 5,244m., total assets 10,257m. (June 1997); Chair. HASSAN KHIDR; 8 brs.

Société Arabe Internationale de Banque: POB 54, 56 Sharia Gamet ed-Dowal al-Arabia, Mohandessin, Cairo (Giza); tel. (2) 3499463; telex 22087; fax (2) 3603497; f. 1976; the Arab International Bank has a 39.3% share, other interests 60.7%; cap. p.u. US $28m., total assets 271m. (Dec. 1995); Chair. Dr HASSAN ABBAS ZAKI; 4 brs.

Social Bank

Nasser Social Bank: POB 2552, 35 Sharia Qasr en-Nil, Cairo; tel. (2) 744377; telex 92754; f. 1971; state-owned; interest-free savings and investment bank for social and economic activities, participating in social insurance, specializing in financing co-operatives, craftsmen and social institutions; cap. p.u. 20m.; Chair. NASSIF TAHOON.

Multinational Banks

Arab African International Bank: POB 60, 5 Midan es-Saray el-Koubra, Majlis ash-Sha'ab, Cairo 11516 (Garden City); tel. (2) 3545094; telex 93531; fax (2) 3558493; f. 1964; cap. p.u. US $100.0m., res US $21.6m., dep. US $921.8m., total assets US $1,151.0m. (Dec. 1996); commercial investment bank; shareholders are Govts of Kuwait, Egypt, Algeria, Jordan and Qatar, Bank Al-Jazira (Saudi Arabia), Rafidain Bank (Iraq), individuals and Arab institutions; Chair. Dr FAHED MOHAMED AR-RASHED; 5 brs in Egypt, 6 abroad.

Arab International Bank: POB 1563, 35 Sharia Abd al-Khalek Sarwat, Cairo; tel. (2) 3918794; telex 92098; fax (2) 3916233; f. 1971 as Egyptian International Bank, renamed 1974; cap. p.u. US $210m., res US $100.7m., dep. US $1,836.5m., total assets US $2,264.3m. (June 1996); offshore bank; aims to promote trade and investment in shareholders' countries and other Arab countries; owned by Egypt, Libya, UAE, Oman, Qatar and private Arab shareholders; Chair. Dr MUSTAFA KHALIL; 6 brs in Egypt, 1 in Bahrain.

Commercial Foreign Venture Banks

Alexandria-Kuwait International Bank: POB 92, 4th Floor, Evergreen Bldg, 10 Sharia Talaat Harb, Majlis ash-Sha'ab, Cairo; tel. (2) 779766; telex 21394; fax (2) 764844; f. 1978; Bank of Alexandria 71.68%, Kuwaiti Egyptian Real Estate Investment Co 1.8%, Principal Bank for Development and Agric. Credit 1.62%, Kato Aromatic 1.07%, other interests 23.83%; cap. 50m., res 11.5m., dep. 615m., total assets 855.4m. (Dec. 1993); Chair. MUHAMMAD ABD AL-WAHAD; 7brs.

Alwatany Bank of Egypt: POB 63, 13 Sharia Semar, Dr Fouad Mohy ed-Din Sq., Gameat ed-Dewal el-Arabia, Mohandessin, Cairo; tel. (2) 3379134; telex 93268; fax (2) 3379302; f. 1980; cap. p.u. 82.6m., res 62.2m., dep. 1,642m., total assets 2,002.3m. (Dec. 1996); Chair. ADEL HUSSEIN EZZI; 8 brs.

Banque du Caire Barclays International, SAE: POB 110, 12 Midan esh-Sheikh Yousuf, Cairo (Garden City); tel. (2) 3542195; telex 93734; fax (2) 3552746; f. 1975 as Cairo Barclays Int. Bank; name changed 1983; Banque du Caire has 51%, Barclays Bank 49%; cap. 50m., dep. 1,661m., total assets 2,033m. (Dec. 1996); Chair. MUHAMMAD ABO EL-FATH; 4 brs.

Banque du Caire et de Paris: POB 2441, 3 Sharia Latin America, Cairo (Garden City); tel. (2) 3548323; telex 93722; fax (2) 3540619; f. 1977; Banque du Caire has 51% interest and Banque Nationale de Paris 49%; cap. p.u. 50.5m., res 19.8m., dep. 716.1m., total assets 857.8m. (Dec. 1995); Chair. SAMIR MANSOUR; 4 brs.

Cairo Far East Bank SAE: POB 757, 104 Corniche en-Nil, Cairo (Dokki); tel. (2) 3362516; telex 93977; fax (2) 3483818; f. 1978; cap. p.u. 51.0m., dep. 180.9m., total assets 372.6m. (Dec. 1996); Chair. Dr HASSAN FAG EN-NOUR; 2 brs.

Crédit International d'Egypte: 46 Sharia el-Batal Ahmed Abd al-Aziz, Mohandessin, Cairo; tel. (2) 3361897; telex 21217; fax (2) 3608673; f. 1977; Crédit Commercial de France has 51% interest, National Bank of Egypt 20% and Berliner Handels und Frankfurter Bank 10%; cap. 44.4m., res 27.2m., dep. 289.1m., total assets 719.3m. (Dec. 1995); Gen. Man. MOUSTAFA KIWAN; 3 brs.

Delta International Bank: POB 1159, 1113 Corniche en-Nil, Cairo; tel. (2) 5753484; telex 93833; fax (2) 5743403; f. 1978; cap. p.u. 180m., dep. 1,075m. (Dec. 1996); Chair. and Man. Dir ALI MUHAMMAD NEGM; 16 brs.

Egyptian American Bank: POB 1825, 4 Sharia Hassan Sabri, Cairo (Zamalek); tel. (2) 3416150; telex 92683; fax (2) 3409430; f. 1976; Bank of Alexandria has 42.5% interest, Amex Holdings Inc. 40.8% and Public 16.7%; cap. p.u. 100m., res 202.0m., dep. 3,205.3m., total assets 3,650.4m. (Dec. 1995); Chair. ABD AL-KARIM MUHAMMAD ABD AL-HAMID; Man. Dir GARY L. JOHNS; 28 brs.

Egyptian Gulf Bank: POB 56, El-Orman Giza, 8–10 Sharia Ahmad Nessim, El-Orman, Cairo (Giza); tel. (2) 3606640; telex 20214; fax (2) 3606512; f. 1981; Misr Insurance Co has 24.4% interest; cap. 85.0m., res 14.8m., dep. 1,229.8m., total assets 1,486m. (Dec. 1996); Chair. SALAH ED-DIN MUHAMMAD MAHMOUD; 5 brs.

Egyptian-Saudi Finance Bank: Es-Sabbah Tower, 8 Sharia Ibrahim Naguib, Cairo (Garden City); tel. (2) 3546208; telex 21086; fax (2) 3542911; f. 1980 as Pyramids Bank; cap. 63.2m., res 5.7m., dep. 418.1m., total assets 695.4m. (Dec. 1995); Chair. Sheikh SALEH ABDULLAH KAMEL; Man. Dir ABD AL-LATIF YOUSEF ABD AL-LATIF; 6 brs.

Faisal Islamic Bank of Egypt: POB 2446, 1113 Corniche en-Nil, Cairo; tel. (2) 5753109; telex 93877; fax (2) 777301; f. 1979; all banking operations conducted according to Islamic principles; cap. p.u. US $155.0m., dep. US $5,842m., total assets US $6,424.8m. (May 1996); Chair. Prince MUHAMMAD AL-FAISAL AS-SAOUD; Gen. Man. YOUSUF AL-BAGKIR MUDAWI; 14 brs.

Misr Exterior Bank, SAE: POB 272, Cairo Plaza Bldg, Corniche en-Nil, Ataba, Cairo; tel. (2) 778701; telex 94061; fax (2) 762806; f. 1981; Misr International Bank has 30% interest, Banque Misr 19.5%, Domestic and International Funds 13%, Egyptian/Arab private investors 25%; cap. p.u. 51.1m., res 124.9m., dep. 3,345.2m., total assets 3,746.0m. (Dec. 1996); Chair. MUHAMMAD NABIL IBRAHIM; 9 brs.

Misr International Bank, SAE: POB 218, 54 Sharia al-Batal Ahmed Abd al-Aziz, Mohandessin, Cairo 12411; tel. (2) 3497091; telex 20840; fax (2) 3498072; f. 1975; the Banque Misr has 38.5% interest, Banco di Roma 10%, UBAF London 8.5%, Europartners 7.88%; cap. p.u. 52.4m., res 338.2m., dep. 6,218.2m., total assets 8,516m. (Dec. 1995); Chair. ESSAM ED-DIN MUHAMMAD EL-AHMADY; Vice-Chair. MUHAMMAD MONIEB; 14 brs.

Misr-America International Bank: POB 1003, 12 Sharia Nadi es-Seid, Dokki, Giza; tel. (2) 3616623; telex 23505; fax (2) 3616610; f. 1977; Banque du Caire has 33% interest, Misr Insurance Co 33%, Industrial Development Bank of Egypt 17%, S.A. for Investments, Luxembourg 17%; cap. p.u. 56m., res 10.8m., dep. 873.8m., total assets 984.9m. (Dec. 1995); Chair. and Man. Dir Dr YOUSRY ALI MOUSTAFA; 6 brs.

Misr-Romanian Bank, SAE: 54 Sharia Lebanon, Mohandessin, Cairo; tel. (2) 3039825; telex 92099; fax (2) 3039806; f. 1977; Banque Misr has 33% interest, Romanian Bank for Foreign Trade (Bucharest) 19%, Bank of Agriculture (Bucharest) 15%, and Romanian Bank for Development (Bucharest) 15%; cap. p.u. 58m., res 140.6m., dep. 1,011.5m. (Dec. 1996); Chair. Dr BAHAA ED-DIN HELMY ISMAIL; 5 brs in Egypt, 2 in Romania.

Mohandes Bank: POB 170, 3-5 Sharia Mossadek, Cairo (Dokki); tel. (2) 3362769; telex 20762; fax (2) 3362741; f. 1979; Engineers' Syndicate has 32.1% interest, National Investment Bank 12.5%, Becorb Holding Co 10%, Suez Canal Bank 9%, Suez Canal Authority 10%, other interests 36.4%; cap. p.u. 100,000m., res 0.1m., dep. 2,191m., total assets 2,910m. (Dec. 1996); Chair. Eng. HUSSEIN FAYEK SABBOUR; 9 brs.

Nile Bank, SAE: POB 2741, 35 Sharia Ramses, Cairo; tel. (2) 5741417; telex 20825; fax (2) 5756296; f. 1978; cap. p.u. 32.2m., res 86.7m., dep. 1,103.4m., total assets 1,330.7m. (Dec. 1993); Chair. and Man. Dir ISSA EL-AYOUTY; 18 brs.

Suez Canal Bank, SAE: POB 2620, 11 Sharia Muhammad Sabry Abu Alam, Cairo; tel. (2) 3931033; telex 93852; fax (2) 3913522; f. 1978; cap. p.u. 50m., res 170.8m., dep. 5,056.6m., total assets 5,589.1m. (Dec. 1996); Chair. and Man. Dir MOUSTAFA FAYEZ HABLAS; 14 brs.

Non-Commercial Banks

Arab Investment Bank: POB 826, Cairo Sky Center Bldg, 8 Sharia Abd el-Khalik Tharwa, Cairo; tel. (2) 5759267; telex 20191; fax (2) 770329; f. 1978 as Union Arab Bank for Development and Investment; Egyptian/Syrian/Libyan joint venture; cap. p.u. 18.5m., res 31.8m., dep. 625m., total assets 977m. (Dec. 1990); Chair. Prof. Dr MUHAMMAD AHMAD ER-RAZAZ; 13 brs.

Egypt Arab African Bank: POB 61, Majlis ash-Sha'ab, 5 Midan es-Saray, el-Koubra, Cairo (Garden City); tel. (2) 3550948; telex 21600; fax (2) 3556239; f. 1982; Arab African International Bank has 49% interest, Egyptian businessmen have 11.3%, Al Mansour and Al Maghraby Investment Co has 7.0%, Arab African International Bank's Pension Fund has 7%, other interests 25.7%; cap. p.u. 75m., res 50.0m., dep. 1,083.8m., total assets 1,290.7m. (Dec. 1996); merchant and investment bank services; Chair. Dr AHMED ABD EL-WAHAB EL-GHANDOUR; 6 brs.

Housing and Development Bank, SAE: POB 234, 12 Sharia Syria, Mohandessin, Cairo; tel. (2) 3492013; telex 94075; fax (2) 3600712; f. 1979; cap. p.u. 54m., res 121.9m., dep. 2,122.9m., (Dec. 1996); Chair. and Man. Dir Eng. MUHAMMAD HOSNI IBRAHIM ABUL ENEEN; 24 brs.

Islamic International Bank for Investment and Development: POB 180, 4 Sharia Ali Ismail, Mesaha Sq., Cairo (Dokki); tel. (2) 3489983; telex 20442; fax (2) 3600771; f. 1980; cap. p.u. 133.8m., res 1.7m., dep. 1,855.4m., total assets 2,037.4m. (Dec. 1995); Chair. MUHAMMAD ABD AL-WAKIL GABER; 7 brs.

Misr Iran Development Bank: POB 219, The Nile Tower, 21–23 Charles de Gaulle Ave, Sharia Giza, Giza; tel. (2) 5727311; telex 21407; fax (2) 5701185; f. 1975; the Bank of Alexandria has 39.73% interest, Misr Insurance Co 39.73%, Bank Melli, Iran, 10.27%, Bank of Industry and Mines 10.27%; cap. p.u. 196.3m., res 92.4m., dep. 756.1m. (Dec. 1995); Chair. Dr MAHMOUD SALAH ED-DIN HAMED; Man. Dir Dr AL-MOTAZ MANSOUR; 7 brs.

National Investment Bank: POB 3726, 37 Kwame Nkrumah Ave, Cairo; tel. (2) 669301; telex 2481; fax (2) 669307; f. 1980; state-owned; responsible for government projects; Chair. ZAFER EL-BESHRY.

National Société Générale Bank, SAE: POB 2664, 10 Sharia Talaat Harb, Cairo; tel. (2) 5749376; telex 22307; fax (2) 776249; f. 1978; the National Bank of Egypt has 18% interest, Société Générale de Paris 51%, other interests 31%; cap. p.u. 100m., res 98.3m., dep. 2,073.0m., total assets 3,197.9m. (Dec. 1996); Chair. MUHAMMAD MADBOULY; 8 brs.

STOCK EXCHANGES

Capital Market Authority: 20 Sharia Emad ed-Din, Cairo; tel. (2) 762626; fax (2) 5794176; f. 1979; Chair. ABD AL-HAMID IBRAHIM.

Cairo Stock Exchange: 4 Sharia esh-Sherifein, Cairo; tel. (2) 3921447; fax (2) 3928526; f. 1904; Chair. Dr MUHAMMAD HAMED.

Alexandria Stock Exchange: 11 Sharia Talaat Harb, Menshia, Alexandria; tel. (3) 4835432; fax (3) 4823039; f. 1861; Chair. EDWARD ANIS GEBRAYIL.

INSURANCE

Arab International Insurance Co: POB 2704, 28 Sharia Talaat Harb, Cairo; tel. (2) 5746322; telex 92599; fax (2) 760053; f. 1976; a joint-stock free zone company established by Egyptian and foreign insurance companies; Chair. and Man. Dir HASSAN MUHAMMAD HAFEZ.

Ach-Chark Insurance Co, SAE: 15 Sharia Qasr en-Nil, Cairo; tel. (2) 5753265; telex 92276; fax (2) 766963; f. 1931; Chair. Dr BORHAM ATALLAH; general and life.

Egyptian Reinsurance Co, SAE: POB 950, 7 Sharia Abdel Latif Boltia, Cairo (Garden City); tel. (2) 3543354; telex 92245; fax (2) 3557483; f. 1957; Chair. MUHAMMAD MUHAMMED AHMED ET-TEIR.

L'Epargne, SAE: POB 548, Immeuble Chemla, Sharia 26 July, Cairo; all types of insurance.

Al-Iktisad esh-Shabee, SAE: 11 Sharia Emad ed-Din, Cairo; f. 1948; Man. Dir and Gen. Man. W. KHAYAT.

Misr Insurance Co: POB 261, 44A Sharia Dokki, Giza; tel. (2) 3355350; telex 22080; fax (2) 3370428; f. 1934; all classes of insurance and reinsurance; Chair. MUHAMMAD ELTEIR.

Mohandes Insurance Co: POB 62, 3 El-Mesaha Sq., Dokki, Giza; tel. (2) 3352162; telex 93392; fax (2) 3352697.

Al-Mottahida: POB 804, 9 Sharia Soliman Pasha, Cairo; f. 1957.

National Insurance Co of Egypt, SAE: 41 Sharia Qasr en-Nil, Cairo; tel. (2) 3910731; telex 92372; fax (2) 3909133; f. 1900; cap. 100m.; Chair. MUHAMMAD ESH-SHAZLY.

Provident Association of Egypt, SAE: POB 390, 9 Sharia Sherif Pasha, Alexandria; f. 1936; Man. Dir G. C. VORLOOU.

Trade and Industry

GOVERNMENT AGENCIES

Egyptian Geological Survey and Mining Authority (EGSMA): 3 Sharia Salah Salem, Abbassia, Cairo; tel. (2) 4829935; telex 22695; fax (2) 4820128; f. 1896; state supervisory authority concerned with geological mapping, mineral exploration and other mining activities; Chair. GABER M. NAIM.

DEVELOPMENT ORGANIZATION

General Authority for Investment and Free Zones: POB 1007, 8 Sharia Adly, Cairo; tel. (2) 3906163; telex 92235; fax (2) 3907315; Exec. Pres. Dr IBRAKUM FAWZY.

CHAMBERS OF COMMERCE

Federation of Chambers of Commerce: 4 el-Falaki Sq., Cairo; tel. (2) 3551164; telex 92645; fax (2) 3557940; Pres. MAHMOUD EL-ARABY.

Alexandria

Alexandria Chamber of Commerce: 31 Sharia el-Ghorfa Altogariya, Alexandria; tel. (3) 809339; telex 4180; fax (2) 808993; Pres. MOSTAFA EL-NAGGAR.

Cairo

Cairo Chamber of Commerce: 4 el-Falaki Sq., Cairo; tel. (2) 3558261; telex 927753; fax (2) 3563603; f. 1913; Pres. MAHMOUD EL-ARABY; Sec.-Gen. MOSTAFA ZAKI TAHA.

In addition, there are 20 local chambers of commerce.

EMPLOYERS' ORGANIZATION

Federation of Egyptian Industries: POB 251, 26A Sharia Sherif Pasha, Cairo, and 65 Gamal Abdel Nasser Ave, Alexandria; tel. (2) 3928317 (Cairo), (3) 4928622 (Alexandria); fax (2) 3928075; f. 1922; Pres. MUHAMMAD FARID KHAMIS; represents the industrial community in Egypt.

PETROLEUM

Arab Petroleum Pipelines Co (SUMED): POB 158 es-Saray, 431 El-Geish Ave, Louran, Alexandria; tel. (3) 5864138; telex 55446; fax (3) 5871295; f. 1974; Suez-Mediterranean crude petroleum transportation pipeline (capacity: 117m. tons per year) and petroleum terminal operators; Chair. and Man. Dir Eng. HAZEM AMIN HAMMAD.

Egyptian General Petroleum Corporation (EGPC): POB 2130, 4th Sector, Sharia Palestine, New Maadi, Cairo; tel. (2) 3531340; telex 92049; state supervisory authority generally concerned with the planning of policies relating to petroleum activities in Egypt with the object of securing the development of the petroleum industry and ensuring its effective administration; Chair. MUSTAFA SHAARAWI.

General Petroleum Co (GPC): 8 Sharia Dr Moustafa Abou Zahra, Cairo (Nasr City); f. 1957; wholly-owned subsidiary of EGPC; operates mainly in Eastern Desert.

Belayim Petroleum Co (PETROBEL): POB 7074, Sharia El-Mokhayam Cairo (Nasr City); tel. (2) 2621738; fax (2) 2609792; f. 1978; capital equally shared between EGPC and International Egyptian Oil Co, which is a subsidiary of ENI of Italy; petroleum and gas exploration, drilling and production.

Gulf of Suez Petroleum Co (GUPCO): POB 2400, 4th Sector, Sharia Palestine, New Maadi, Cairo; tel. (2) 3520985; telex 92248; fax (2) 3521286; f. 1965; partnership between EGPC and Amoco-Egypt Oil Co, which is a subsidiary of Amoco Corpn, USA; developed the el-Morgan oilfield in the Gulf of Suez, also holds other exploration concessions in the Gulf of Suez and the Western Desert; Chair. AHMED SHAWKY ABDINE.

Western Desert Petroleum Co (WEPCO): POB 412, Alexandria; tel. (3) 4928710; telex 54075; f. 1967 as partnership between EGPC (50% interest) and Phillips Petroleum (35%) and later Hispanoil (15%); developed Alamein, Yidma and Umbarka fields in the Western Desert and later Abu Qir offshore gas field in 1978 followed by NAF gas field in 1987; Chair. Eng. MUHAMMAD MOHI ED-DIN BAHGAT.

Numerous foreign petroleum companies are prospecting for petroleum in Egypt under agreements with EGPC.

TRADE UNIONS

Egyptian Trade Union Federation (ETUF): 90 Sharia al-Galaa, Cairo; tel. (2) 5740362; fax (2) 5753427; f. 1957; 23 affiliated unions; 5m. mems; affiliated to the International Confederation of Arab Trade Unions and to the Organization of African Trade Union Unity; Pres. MUHAMMAD ES-SAYED RACHID; Gen. Sec. MUHAMMED ES-SAYED MORSI.

General Trade Union of Air Transport: 5 Sharia Ahmad Sannan, St Fatima, Heliopolis; 11,000 mems; Pres. ABD AL-MONEM FARAG EISA; Gen. Sec. SHEKATA ABD AL-HAMID.

General Trade Union of Banks and Insurance: 2 Sharia el-Kady el-Fadel, Cairo; 56,000 mems; Pres. MAHMOUD MUHAMMAD DABBOUR; Gen. Sec. ABDOU HASSAN MUHAMMAD ALI.

General Trade Union of Building Workers: 9 Sharia Emad ed-Din, Cairo; 150,000 mems; Pres. HAMID HASSAN BARAKAT; Gen. Sec. SALEM ABD AR-RAZEK.

General Trade Union of Chemical Workers: 90 Sharia al-Galaa, Cairo; fax (2) 5750490; 120,000 mems; Pres. IBRAHIM EL-AZHARY; Gen. Sec. GAAFER ABD EL-MONEM.

General Trade Union of Commerce: 70 Sharia el-Gomhouriya, Cairo; tel. (2) 914124; f. 1903; more than 100,000 mems; Pres. ABD AR-RAZEK ESH-SHERBEENI; Gen. Sec. KAMEL HUSSEIN A. AWAD.

General Trade Union of Food Industries: 3 Sharia Housni, Hadaek el-Koba, Cairo; 111,000 mems; Pres. SAAD M. AHMAD; Gen. Sec. ADLY TANOUS IBRAHIM.

General Trade Union of Health Services: 22 Sharia esh-Sheikh Qamar, es-Sakakiny, Cairo; 56,000 mems; Pres. IBRAHIM ABOU EL-MUTI IBRAHIM; Gen. Sec. AHMAD ABD AL-LATIF SALEM.

General Trade Union of Hotels and Tourism Workers: POB 606, 90 Sharia al-Galaa, Cairo; tel. and fax (2) 773901; 70,000 mems; Pres. MUHAMMAD HILAL ES-SHARKAWI.

General Trade Union of Maritime Transport: 36 Sharia Sharif, Cairo; 46,000 mems; Pres. THABET MUHAMMAD ES-SEFARI; Gen. Sec. MUHAMMAD RAMADAN ABOU TOR.

General Trade Union of Military Production: 90 Sharia al-Galaa, Cairo; telex 93255; 64,000 mems; Pres. MOUSTAFA MUHAMMAD MOUNGI; Gen. Sec. FEKRY IMAM.

General Trade Union of Mine Workers: 5 Sharia Ali Sharawi, Hadaek el-Koba, Cairo; 14,000 mems; Pres. ABBAS MAHMOUD IBRAHIM; Gen. Sec. AMIN HASSAN AMER.

General Trade Union of Petroleum Workers: 5 Sharia Ali Sharawi, Hadaek el-Koba, Cairo; tel. (2) 820091; telex 93255; fax (2) 834551; 60,000 mems; Pres. MUHAMMAD ZAD ED-DIN; Gen. Sec. ABD AL-KADER HASSAN ABD AL-KADER.

General Trade Union of Postal Workers: 90 Sharia al-Galaa, Cairo; telex 93255; 80,000 mems; Pres. HASSAN MUHAMMAD EID; Gen. Sec. SALEM MAHMOUD SALEM.

General Trade Union of Press, Printing and Information: 90 Sharia al-Galaa, Cairo; tel. (2) 740324; telex 93255; 55,000 mems; Pres. MUHAMMAD ALI EL-FIKKI; Gen. Sec. AHMED ED-DESSOUKI.

General Trade Union of Public and Administrative Workers: 2 Sharia Muhammad Haggag, Midan et-Tahrir, Cairo; tel. (2) 742134; telex 93255; 210,000 mems; Pres. ABD AR-RAHMAN KHEDR; Gen. Sec. MAHMOUD MUHAMMAD ABD EL-KHALEK.

General Trade Union of Public Utilities Workers: 30 Sharia Sharif, Cairo; tel. and fax (2) 3938293; telex 93255; 290,000 mems; Pres. MUHAMMAD ES-SAYED MORSI; Gen. Sec. MUHAMMAD TALAAT HASSAN.

General Trade Union of Railway Workers: POB 84 (el-Faggalah), 15 Sharia Emad ed-Din, Cairo; tel. (2) 5930305; fax (2) 5917776; 90,000 mems; Pres. SABER AHMED HUSSAIN; Gen. Sec. YASIN SOLUMAN.

General Trade Union of Road Transport: 90 Sharia al-Galaa, Cairo; tel. (2) 5740413; telex 93255; fax (2) 5752955; 245,000 mems; Pres. MOUNIR BADR CHETA; Gen. Sec. SALINI GUNIDI.

General Trade Union of Telecommunications Workers: POB 651, Cairo; telex 93255; 60,000 mems; Pres. KHAIRI HACHEM; Sec.-Gen. IBRAHIM SALEH.

General Trade Union of Textile Workers: 327 Sharia Shoubra, Cairo; 244,000 mems; Pres. ALI MUHAMMAD DOUFDAA; Gen. Sec. HASSAN TOULBA MARZOUK.

General Trade Union of Workers in Agriculture and Irrigation: 31 Sharia Mansour, Cairo (Bab el-Louk); tel. (2) 3541419; 150,000 mems; Pres. MUKHTAR ABD AL-HAMID; Gen. Sec. FATHI A. KURTAM.

General Trade Union of Workers in Engineering, Metal and Electrical Industries: 90 Sharia al-Galaa, Cairo; tel. (2) 742519; telex 93255; 160,000 mems; Pres. SAID GOMAA; Gen. Sec. MUHAMMAD FARES.

Transport

RAILWAYS

The area of the Nile Delta is well served by railways. Lines also run from Cairo southward along the Nile to Aswan, and westward along the coast to Salloum.

Egyptian Railways: Station Bldg, Midan Ramses, Cairo; tel. (2) 751000; telex 92616; fax (2) 540000; f. 1852; length 8,600 km; 42 km electrified; a 346-km line to carry phosphate and iron ore from the Bahariya mines, in the Western Desert, to the Helwan iron and steel works in south Cairo, was opened in 1973, and the Quena–Safaga line (length 223 km) came into operation in 1989; Chair. Eng. ABD AS-SALAM SHAATH.

Alexandria Passenger Transport Authority: POB 466, 3 Sharia Aflatone, esh-Shatby, Alexandria; tel. (3) 5975223; telex 54637; f. 1860; controls City Tramways (30 km), Ramleh Electric Railway (14.7 km), suburban buses (450 km); 129 tram cars, 42 light railway three-car sets; construction of the Alexandria Metro (55 km) began in 1997; Chair. Eng. ESSAM HASBY; Tech. Dir Eng. MEDHAT HAFEZ.

Cairo Metro: National Authority for Tunnels, Ministry of Transport, POB 466, Ramses Bldg, Ramses Sq., Cairo 11794; construction of the first underground transport system in Africa and the Middle East began in Cairo in 1982; connects electrified Helwan line of Egyptian railways with the diesel el-Marg line, via a 4.2-km tunnel with five stations beneath central Cairo, making a 42.5-km regional line with a total of 33 stations; gauge 1,435 mm, electrified; work on the first stage of the system was completed in July 1987, and it was opened in September; the second stage was completed in 1989; work on a second line linking Shubra el-Khaima with central Cairo and Giza commenced in 1992. This new line will have a total length of 19.5 km. (13 km in tunnel) and 18 stations, two of which will interconnect with the first line. The first stage started operating between Shubra el-Khaima and Ramses Square in 1996, the service extending to Tahrir Square in 1997. The rest of the line, extending to Cairo University, is under construction and is due to be completed in 1999; Chair. Eng. H. ABD ES-SALAM.

Cairo Transport Authority: POB 254, Madinet Nasr, Cairo; tel. (2) 830533; length 78 km (electrified); gauge 1,000 mm; operates 16 tram routes and 24 km of light railway; 720 cars.

Lower Egypt Railway: Mansura; f. 1898; length 160 km; gauge 1,000 mm; 20 diesel railcars.

ROADS

There are good metalled main roads as follows: Cairo–Alexandria (desert road); Cairo–Benna–Tanta–Damanhur–Alexandria; Cairo–Suez (desert road); Cairo–Ismailia–Port Said or Suez; Cairo–Fayum (desert road); in 1997 there were some 41,300 km of roads, including 22,000 km of highways. The Ahmad Hamdi road tunnel (1.64 km) beneath the Suez Canal was opened in 1980. A 320-km macadamized road linking Mersa Matruh, on the Mediterranean coast, with the oasis town of Siwa was completed in 1986.

General Authority for Roads and Bridges, Ministry of Transport: 105 Sharia Qasr el-Eini, Cairo; tel. (2) 3557429; fax (2) 3550591; e-mail garb@idsc.gov.eg; Chair. MUHAMMAD NABIL ELKOUSY.

SHIPPING

Egypt's principal ports are Alexandria, Port Said and Suez. A port constructed at a cost of £E315m. and designed to handle up to 16m. tons of grain, fruit and other merchandise per year (22% of the country's projected imports by the year 2000) in its first stage of development, was opened at Damietta in 1986. The second stage will increase handling capacity to 25m. tons per year. A ferry link between Nuweibeh and the Jordanian port of Aqaba was opened in 1985.

Alexandria Port Authority: 66 ave Gamal Abd an-Nasser, Alexandria; Head Office: 106 Sharia el-Hourriya, Alexandria; tel. (3) 445 8394; fax (3) 4458397; Gen. Man. Adm. HAMDY.

Major Shipping Companies

Alexandria Shipping and Navigation Co: POB 812, 557 ave el-Hourriya, Alexandria; tel. (3) 62923; telex 54029; services between Egypt, N. and W. Europe, USA, Red Sea and Mediterranean; 5 vessels; Chair. and Man. Dir Eng. MAHMOUD ISMAIL; Man. Dir ABD AL-AZIZ QADRI.

Egyptian Navigation Co: POB 82, 2 Sharia en-Nasr, Alexandria; tel. (3) 4800050; telex 54131; fax (3) 4831345; f. 1930; owners and operators of Egypt's mercantile marine; services Alexandria/Europe, USA, Black Sea, Adriatic Sea, Mediterranean Sea, Indian Ocean and Red Sea; 30 vessels; Chair. FATHI SOROUR.

Pan-Arab Shipping Co: POB 39, 404 ave el-Hourriya, Rouchdy, Alexandria; tel. (3) 5468835; telex 54123; fax (3) 5469533; f. 1974; Arab League Co; 5 vessels; Chair. Adm. SHERIF ES-SADEK; Gen. Man. Capt. MAMDOUH EL-GUINDY.

THE SUEZ CANAL

In 1996 a total of 14,731 vessels, with a net displacement of 355m. tons, used the Suez Canal, linking the Mediterranean and Red Seas.

Length of Canal 190 km; maximum permissible draught: 17.68 m (58 ft); breadth of canal at water level and breadth between buoys defining the navigable channel 365 m and 225 m respectively in the northern section and 365 m and 205 m in the southern section.

Suez Canal Authority (Hay'at Canal as-Suweis): Irshad Bldg, Ismailia; tel. (64) 330000; telex 63238; fax (64) 320784; Cairo Office: 6 Sharia Lazoughli, Cairo (Garden City); f. 1956; Chair. Adm. AHMED ALI FADEL.

CIVIL AVIATION

The main international airports are at Heliopolis (23 km from the centre of Cairo) and Alexandria (7 km from the city centre). An international airport was opened at Nuzhah in 1983.

EgyptAir: Cairo International Airport, Heliopolis, Cairo; tel. (2) 2454400; fax (2) 2449727; f. 1932 as Misr Airwork; known as United Arab Airlines 1960–1971; operates internal services in Egypt and external services throughout the Middle East, Far East, Africa, Europe and the USA; Chair. Eng. MUHAMMAD FAHIM RAYAN.

Egyptian Civil Aviation Authority: 31 Sharia 26 July, Cairo; tel. (2) 742853; telex 24430; fax (2) 2475473; Chair. ALI OSMAN ZIKO.

Tourism

Tourism is currently Egypt's second-largest source of revenue, generating around US $3,000m. annually. Traditionally the industry has attracted tourists to its pyramids and monuments. Recently the industry has diversified; the Red Sea coastline boasts 1,000 km of beaches along which developments, including two international airports at Taba and Suba Bay, are under construction.

Ministry of Tourism: Misr Travel Tower, Abbassia Sq., Cairo; tel. (2) 2828430; telex 94040; fax (2) 2829771; f. 1965; brs at Alexandria, Port Said, Suez, Luxor and Aswan; Minister of Tourism Dr MAMDOUH EL-BELTAGI.

Egyptian General Authority for the Promotion of Tourism: Misr Travel Tower, Abbassia Sq., Cairo; tel. (2) 2853576; fax (2) 2854363; Chair. ADEL ABD AL-AZIZ.

Egyptian General Co for Tourism and Hotels: 4 Sharia Latin America, Cairo (Garden City); tel. (2) 3026470; telex 92363; fax (2) 3024456; f. 1961; affiliated to the holding co for Housing, Tourism and Cinema.

EL SALVADOR

Introductory Survey

Location, Climate, Language, Religion, Flag, Capital

The Republic of El Salvador lies on the Pacific coast of Central America. It is bounded by Guatemala to the west and by Honduras to the north and east. The climate varies from tropical on the coastal plain to temperate in the uplands. The language is Spanish. About 86% of the population are Roman Catholics, and other Christian churches are represented. The civil flag (proportions 3 by 2) consists of three equal horizontal stripes, of blue, over white, over blue. The state flag differs by the addition, in the centre of the white stripe, of the national coat of arms. The capital is San Salvador.

Recent History

El Salvador was ruled by Spain until 1821, and became independent in 1839. Since then the country's history has been one of frequent coups and outbursts of political violence. General Maximiliano Hernández Martínez became President in 1931, and ruthlessly suppressed a peasant uprising, with an alleged 30,000 killings (including that of Farabundo Martí, the leader of the rebel peasants), in 1932. President Hernández was deposed in 1944, and the next elected President, Gen. Salvador Castañeda Castro, was overthrown in 1948. His successor as President, Lt-Col Oscar Osorio (1950–56), relinquished power to Lt-Col José María Lemus, who was deposed by a bloodless coup in 1960. He was replaced by a military junta, which was itself supplanted by another junta in January 1961. Under this Junta, the conservative Partido de Conciliación Nacional (PCN) was established and won all 54 seats in elections to the Asamblea Legislativa (Legislative Assembly) in December. A member of the Junta, Lt-Col Julio Adalberto Rivera, was elected unopposed to the presidency in 1962. He was succeeded by the PCN candidate, Gen. Fidel Sánchez Hernández, in 1967.

In the 1972 presidential election Col Arturo Armando Molina Barraza, candidate of the ruling PCN, was elected. His rival, José Napoleón Duarte, the leader of the left-wing coalition party, Unión Nacional de Oposición, launched an abortive coup in March, and Col Molina took office in July, despite allegations of massive electoral fraud. Similar allegations were made during the 1977 presidential election, after which the PCN candidate, Gen. Carlos Humberto Romero Mena, took office.

Reports of violations of human rights by the Government were widespread in 1979. The polarization of left and right after 1972 was characterized by an increase in guerrilla activity. In October 1979 President Romero was overthrown and replaced by a Junta of civilians and army officers. The Junta, which promised to install a democratic system and to organize elections, declared a political amnesty and invited participation from the guerrilla groups, but violence continued between government troops and guerrilla forces, and elections were postponed. In January 1980 an ultimatum from progressive members of the Government resulted in the formation of a new Government, a coalition of military officers and the Partido Demócrata Cristiano (PDC). In March the country moved closer to full-scale civil war following the assassination of the Roman Catholic Archbishop of San Salvador, Oscar Romero y Galdames, an outspoken supporter of human rights.

In December 1980 José Napoleón Duarte, the 1972 presidential candidate and a member of the Junta, was sworn in as President. In January 1981 the guerrillas launched their 'final offensive' and, after initial gains, the opposition front, Frente Democrático Revolucionario—FDR (allied with the guerrilla front, the Frente Farabundo Martí para la Liberación Nacional—FMLN), proposed negotiations with the USA. The US authorities referred them to the Salvadorean Government, which refused to recognize the FDR while it was linked with the guerrillas. The USA affirmed its support for the Duarte Government and provided civilian and military aid. During 1981 the guerrilla forces unified and strengthened their control over the north and east of the country. Attacks on economic targets continued, while the army retaliated by acting indiscriminately against the local population in guerrilla-controlled areas. By December there were an estimated 300,000 Salvadorean refugees, many of whom had fled to neighbouring countries.

At elections to a National Constituent Assembly, conducted in March 1982, the PDC failed to win an absolute majority against the five right-wing parties, which, together having obtained 60% of the total votes, formed a Government of National Unity. Major Roberto D'Aubuisson Arrieta, leader of the extreme right-wing Alianza Republicana Nacionalista (ARENA), emerged as the most powerful personality within the coalition and became President of the National Constituent Assembly. In April a politically independent banker, Dr Alvaro Magaña Borja, was elected interim President of El Salvador, after pressure from the armed forces. However, the Assembly voted to award itself considerable power over the President. Military leaders then demanded that five ministerial posts be given to members of the PDC, fearing that, otherwise, US military aid would be withdrawn. A presidential election was scheduled for 1983, and a new constitution was to be drafted.

During 1982 about 1,600 Salvadorean troops were trained in the USA, and US military advisers were reported to be actively participating in the conflict. In November a military coup was forestalled by Gen. José Guillermo García, the Minister of Defence, who removed several right-wingers from key military posts. President Magaña's position was strengthened in December, when a division within the PCN resulted in the moderates achieving a majority in the Assembly.

The presidential election, originally planned for 1983, was postponed until March 1984, as a result of disagreement in the National Constituent Assembly over the new Constitution, which finally became effective in December 1983. The issue of agrarian reform caused a serious dispute between Maj. D'Aubuisson's ARENA party and the PDC, and provoked a campaign by right-wing 'death squads' against trade unionists and peasant leaders. (In February–March 1980 the governing Junta had nationalized some 60% of the country's prime arable land as part of a three-phase agrarian reform initiative, which envisaged the eventual redesignation of 90% of El Salvador's farmland, thereby benefiting 80%–90% of the rural population. However, subsequent phases of the expropriation and reallocation programme had been suspended in March 1981 and May 1982, prompting US Government threats to withdraw financial and military assistance.) In December 1983 ARENA secured the support of the Assembly for the reactivation of a severely compromised reform programme which provided for a maximum permissible landholding of 245 ha (rather than 100 ha as originally envisaged). This represented an important victory for the ARENA party, which had been isolated in the Assembly following the collapse of its alliance with the PCN in February.

Following a period of intense activity by 'death squads' in September and October 1983, when the weekly total of murders exceeded 200, the US Government urged the removal of several high-level officials, military officers and political figures who were linked to the murders. The failure of the US-trained 'rapid reaction' battalions and frequent reports of army atrocities undermined both public confidence in the Government and US President Ronald Reagan's efforts to secure further US aid for El Salvador. In February 1984, following a number of strategic territorial advances, the FDR-FMLN proposed the formation of a broadly-based provisional government, as part of a peace plan without preconditions. The plan was rejected by the Government. The guerrillas refused to participate in the presidential election, conducted in March 1984, and attempted to prevent voting in various provinces. As no candidate emerged with a clear majority, a second round of voting was held in May, when the contest was between José Napoleón Duarte, the candidate of the PDC, and Maj. D'Aubuisson, the ARENA candidate. Duarte secured a clear majority over D'Aubuisson, obtaining 54% of the votes cast.

Following his inauguration in June 1984 President Duarte instituted a purge of the armed forces and the reorganization of the police force, including the disbanding of the notorious Treasury Police. Both the FDR-FMLN and the President expressed their willingness to commence peace negotiations. Following pressure from the Roman Catholic Church and trade unions, the Government opened discussions with guerrilla leaders in Chalatenango in October. A second round of negotiations, held in November, ended amid accusations of intransigence from both sides.

At legislative and municipal elections in March 1985 the PDC won a convincing victory over the ARENA-PCN electoral alliance, thereby securing a clear majority in the new Asamblea Nacional (National Assembly). The PDC's victory, coupled with internal divisions within the right-wing grouping, precipitated a decline in the popularity and influence of the alliance, which culminated in the resignation of ARENA's leader, Roberto D'Aubuisson, in September.

Despite a perceived decline in political violence and abuses of human rights in 1985–86, the failure of the Government and the rebels to agree an agenda for renewed negotiations during this period prompted speculation that a military solution would be sought to end the civil war. Such speculation was supported by reports of the armed forces' growing domination of the conflict and by the success of the army's 'Unidos para reconstruir' campaign, a social and economic programme, launched in July 1986, to recover areas that had been devastated by the protracted fighting. Although the guerrillas mounted a successful attack against the army garrison at San Miguel in June, they failed to make any significant gains in 1986.

In February 1987 the Government suffered a humiliating defeat when its attempt to introduce a 'war tax' was ruled unconstitutional by the Supreme Court. Furthermore, in March guerrillas carried out another successful attack on the army garrison at El Paraíso which enabled them to take the military initiative in the civil war. Later in 1987, however, the Salvadorean Government's participation in a peace plan for Central America, which was signed on 7 August in Guatemala City, encouraged hopes that a peaceful solution could be found to the conflict. Discussions between the Government and the FDR-FMLN were eventually held in October, when agreement was reached on the formation of two committees to study the possibility of a cease-fire and an amnesty.

Despite the inauguration, in September 1987, of a National Reconciliation Commission (CRN), appointed by the President in August, and the Government's proclamation, in November, of a unilateral cease-fire, no long-term cessation of hostilities was maintained by either side. In late 1987 the political situation deteriorated further, following President Duarte's public denunciation of Roberto D'Aubuisson's complicity in the murder of Archbishop Romero y Galdames in March 1980.

In early 1988 there were increasing reports of the resurgence of 'death squads', and it was suggested that abuses of human rights were rapidly returning to the level reached at the beginning of the internal conflict. In February the FMLN launched a campaign of bombings and transport disruptions, in order to undermine preparations for the forthcoming legislative and municipal elections. The elections took place, in March, in an atmosphere of public apathy. ARENA secured control of more than 200 municipalities, including San Salvador, hitherto held for more than 20 years by the PDC. However, a dispute developed over the distribution of seats in the legislature, with both ARENA and the PDC claiming the same seat in one region. Following protracted arguments, ARENA was able to resume an overall majority in the Asamblea, when a deputy of the PCN transferred allegiance to ARENA, thereby giving the party 31 seats, compared with the PDC's 23 seats. In May the PDC suffered another reverse when it was revealed that President Duarte was suffering from a terminal illness (he died in February 1990).

In mid-1988 the Convergencia Democrática (CD), a left-wing alliance comprising two of the leading groups within the FDR-FMLN and the Partido Social Demócrata, announced that Dr Guillermo Ungo would be its candidate at the forthcoming presidential election. In September, however, the guerrillas launched a major new offensive, and in November took advantage of a transitional period following the installation of a new military high command to attack the headquarters of the National Guard in San Salvador.

By the end of 1988, it was estimated that as many as 70,000 Salvadoreans had died in the course of the civil war, while the US administration had provided some US $3,000m. in aid to the Government. Moreover, by early 1989 many areas appeared to be without government, following the resignations of some 75 mayors and nine judges, purportedly because of death threats by the FMLN. In late January, however, radical new peace proposals were announced by the FMLN, which, for the first time, expressed its willingness to participate in the electoral process. The FMLN proposed that the presidential election be postponed from March to September, and offered a 60-day cease-fire (30 days on each side of a September election date). However, negotiations about this proposal failed to produce agreement. When Duarte announced that the election would proceed on the scheduled date of 19 March, the FMLN advocated a boycott of the election and intensified its campaign of violence, resulting in the deaths of more than 40 people on election day alone.

The election resulted in victory for the ARENA candidate, Alfredo Cristiani Burkard, who obtained 53.81% of the votes cast, thus obviating the need for a second round of voting. Dr Fidel Chávez Mena of the PDC received 36.59% of the votes. The level of abstention was estimated at almost 50%. Cristiani took office on 1 June 1989.

In August 1989 the Heads of State of five Central American countries signed an agreement in Tela, Honduras. The accord included an appeal to the FMLN to abandon its military campaign and to 'initiate dialogue' with the Salvadorean Government. In the spirit engendered by the Tela agreement, representatives of the Government and the FMLN began negotiations in Mexico City in September. A second round of discussions took place in San José, Costa Rica, in mid-October, but a third round, planned for Caracas, Venezuela, in November, was abandoned by the FMLN, following a bomb attack in late October, allegedly perpetrated by the Salvadorean army, on the headquarters of the Salvadorean Workers' National Union Federation (FENASTRAS), in which 10 people were killed. On 7 November, in accordance with the Tela agreement, the UN Security Council authorized the creation of the UN Observer Group for Central America (ONUCA), a multinational military force, to monitor developments in the region.

On 11 November 1989 the FMLN launched a military offensive, and throughout the month the fiercest fighting for nine years took place. The Government declared a state of siege, and stability was further undermined when, on 16 November, gunmen murdered the head of a San Salvador Jesuit university and five other Jesuit priests. Both the UN and the Organization of American States appealed for a cease-fire. Although the fighting moderated in December and in January 1990, no cease-fire was observed. On 12 January 1990, however, the FMLN announced that it would accept an offer made by the Salvadorean Government whereby the UN Secretary-General, Javier Pérez de Cuéllar, was to arrange the reopening of peace talks. In March President Cristiani announced that he was willing to offer a comprehensive amnesty, territorial concessions and the opportunity to participate fully in political processes to members of the FMLN, as part of a broad-based peace proposal. Later in 1990, however, hopes for the successful negotiation of a peaceful settlement (including the implementation of a cease-fire in mid-September) were frustrated by the failure of the two sides to reach a consensus, at a series of UN-sponsored discussions, on the crucial issue of the future role, structure and accountability of the armed forces.

In May 1990 guerrilla forces had launched their first major offensive since November 1989, coinciding with demonstrations in San Salvador by some 40,000 trade unionists and opposition supporters in protest at economic austerity measures and the breakdown of peace negotiations. By the end of September all hopes for a cease-fire had been abandoned, and the FMLN had publicly advocated a 'democratic revolution' to abolish the armed forces, to create a civilian-controlled public security force, to effect judicial, electoral and political reform, to expand existing proposals for agrarian reform and to introduce specific economic measures to benefit the poor. A renewed FMLN offensive, undertaken by the newly-proclaimed National Army for Democracy (the establishment of which marked the reorganization of the FMLN's previous divisions into a more conventional army structure) in several departments in November, was named 'Punishment for the Anti-Democratic Armed Forces'. The conflict was considered to have entered into a new phase when, in the same month, a government aircraft was shot down by guerrilla forces armed with surface-to-air missiles (supplied by Nicaraguan military personnel). In January 1991 a US military helicopter, en route to operations in Honduras, was shot down by rebel forces in El Salvador. Public and political outrage in the USA increased when it became known that two of the three US servicemen who died in the incident had been executed, following the crash, by members of the FMLN.

Negotiations between the Government and the FMLN continued throughout 1991 on a monthly basis, and were accompanied by fluctuations in the intensity of violent exchanges between the guerrillas and the security forces. In early March the FMLN announced that a three-day cease-fire to coincide with forthcoming elections would be observed by the rebel forces, although voting would not be permitted in those areas under rebel control.

On 10 March 1991 elections to the Asamblea (enlarged from 60 to 84 seats) and to 262 municipalities were conducted. While guerrilla forces refrained from disrupting the proceedings, it was reported that many voters were intimidated by an escalation in military operations, and more than 50% of the electorate failed to cast a vote. A long delay in announcing the final results prompted left-wing groups to level accusations of electoral fraud against the Central Electoral Commission, which was under right-wing control. The final results revealed that ARENA had lost its majority in the Asamblea, but continued to command considerable support, with 44.3% of the votes and 39 seats. The PDC obtained 28% of the votes and 26 seats in the Asamblea, while the PCN won 9% of the votes and nine seats, and the left-wing CD won 12.2% of the votes and secured eight seats. In the local elections ARENA also retained significant support, with victories in 175 of the 262 municipalities. However, it was hoped that ARENA's weakened position in the Asamblea might moderate the Government's uncompromising stance in recent negotiations with the FMLN.

In late March 1991 hopes for an early settlement to the conflict were renewed when a new initiative for negotiation was presented by the FMLN in Managua, Nicaragua, following a meeting between foreign affairs ministers from Central America and the European Community (EC, now European Union–EU). This new proposal dispensed with previous stipulations put forward by the guerrillas that military and constitutional reforms should be effected prior to any cease-fire, and suggested that concessions on both sides could be adopted simultaneously. The constitutional requirement that amendments to the Constitution be ratified by two successive legislative assemblies lent impetus to negotiations in April, the current Asamblea being scheduled to dissolve at the end of the month. Despite the attempts of uncompromising right-wing members of the Asamblea to sabotage the proceedings, a last-minute agreement on human rights (including the creation of a three-member 'truth commission', to be appointed by the UN Secretary-General) and on judicial and electoral reform was reached by the Government and the FMLN, and was swiftly approved by the Asamblea, prior to its dissolution. The working structure of a cease-fire and the detailed reform and purge of the armed forces were set aside for negotiation at a later date.

In May 1991 the UN Security Council voted to create an observer mission to El Salvador (ONUSAL), to be charged with the verification of accords reached between the Government and the FMLN. Initially the mission was to be resident in six regional centres for a 12-month period, at a cost of US $23m., and was expected to participate in any future cease-fire and peaceful reintegration programme. The creation of ONUSAL was denounced by right-wing groups within El Salvador as unwarranted interference and as an insult to national sovereignty.

In August 1991 the US Secretary of State and the USSR's Minister of Foreign Affairs urged the UN Secretary-General, Javier Pérez de Cuéllar, personally to intervene in negotiations between the Government and the guerrillas in El Salvador, in an attempt to reactivate a constructive dialogue. In response to a personal invitation from Pérez de Cuéllar, both sides attended a round of discussions in New York, where it was announced that a new framework for peace had been agreed. A National Commission for the Consolidation of Peace (COPAZ) was to be created (comprising representatives of both sides, as well as of all major political parties), which would supervise the enforcement of guarantees for the political integration of the guerrillas. The FMLN also secured guaranteed territorial rights for peasants settled in guerrilla-controlled areas, and the participation of former FMLN members in a National Civilian Police (PNC), which was to be under the control of a new Ministry of the Interior and Public Security. At the same time, the Asamblea approved constitutional reforms, whereby the Central Electoral Commission would be replaced by a Supreme Electoral Tribunal, composed of five magistrates (one from each of the five most successful parties at the previous presidential election), to be elected by the Asamblea.

In December 1991, following renewed discussions between the Government and the guerrilla leaders in New York, a new peace initiative was announced. Under the terms of the agreement, a formal cease-fire was to be implemented on 1 February 1992, under the supervision of some 1,000 UN personnel. The FMLN was to begin a process of disarmament, to be implemented in five stages (simultaneous with the dissolution of the notorious, military-controlled, 17,000-strong rapid deployment battalions), leading to full disarmament by 31 October. The success of the cease-fire agreement was expected to be dependent upon the adequate implementation, by the Government, of previously agreed reforms to the judiciary, the electoral system, guarantees of territorial rights, human rights, and guerrilla participation in civil defence, and of newly agreed reforms whereby the armed forces would be purged of those most responsible for abuses of human rights during the previous 12 years, and would be reduced in size by almost one-half, over a 22-month period.

In mid-January 1992 the UN Security Council approved the dispatch of some 1,000 police and military personnel to El Salvador to supervise the implementation of the first stage of the cease-fire. On 16 January, at Chapultepec Castle in Mexico City, the formal peace accord was ratified and was witnessed by the new UN Secretary-General, Boutros Boutros-Ghali, the US Secretary of State, James Baker, Heads of State from Central America, South America and Europe, representatives of El Salvador's military high command and all 84 members of the Asamblea. On 1 February some 30,000 Salvadoreans gathered in San Salvador to celebrate the first day of the cease-fire and to attend the formal installation of COPAZ.

Although mutual allegations of failure to comply with the terms of the peace accord persisted during 1992, prompting the temporary withdrawal, in May, of the FMLN from COPAZ, and resulting in further UN mediation and the negotiation of a revised timetable for disarmament, the cease-fire was carefully observed by both sides. In San Salvador on 15 December (declared National Reconciliation Day), at a ceremony attended by President Cristiani, FMLN leaders, the UN Secretary-General and Central American Heads of State and government representatives, the conflict was formally concluded, the terms of the December 1991 agreement having been fulfilled to the satisfaction of both sides. On the same day the FMLN was officially registered and recognized as a legitimate political party.

In November 1992, in accordance with the terms of the December 1991 peace accord, the Comisión de la Verdad (Truth Commission) announced the names of more than 200 military personnel alleged to have participated in abuses of human rights during the civil war. By early 1993, however, despite the urgences of the UN Secretary-General, the reluctance of the Government to comply with the conditions of the peace accord, relating to the removal from the armed forces of those personnel (particularly officers) identified by the Commission, threatened the further successful implementation of the process of pacification, and prompted the FMLN to delay the demobilization of its forces and the destruction of its remaining arsenals. The situation was exacerbated, in March 1993, by the publication of the report of the Commission, which attributed responsibility for the vast majority of the war's 75,000 fatalities to the counter-insurgency measures of the armed forces, including the systematic eradication, by the security forces, of civilians thought to harbour left-wing sympathies. Some 400 murders were attributed to the FMLN. Forty military personnel, identified by name as those responsible for various human rights atrocities, included the Minister of Defence and Public Security, Gen. René Emilio Ponce, his deputy, Gen. Orlando Zepeda, and the former air force chief, Gen. Juan Rafael Bustillo, who were believed to have ordered the murder of six prominent Jesuits in 1989 (see below), and ARENA founder Roberto D'Aubuisson Arrieta (who died in 1992), who was identified as the authority behind the organization of 'death squads' in the early 1980s, and the murder, in 1980, of the Archbishop of San Salvador, Oscar Romero y Galdames. The report recommended that the judiciary should be reorganized, having failed to protect human rights during the war, and that all individuals identified by the report should be permanently excluded from all institutions of national defence and public security, and should be barred from holding public office for a period of 10 years.

While the conclusions of the report were welcomed by the FMLN, representatives of the Government and the armed forces challenged the legal validity of the document, despite the insistence of UN officials that the recommendations of the report were mandatory under the terms of the peace accord. However, later in March 1993, the strength of ARENA's representation in the Asamblea overcame opposition from the PDC, the CD and the Movimiento Nacional Revolucionario (MNR), and secured the approval of an amnesty law to extend to all political crimes committed before 1992, prompting widespread public outrage, which was compounded, in April 1993, by the release of two prisoners sentenced in January 1992 for the murder of six prominent Jesuits (see below), as the first beneficiaries of the amnesty. In late June 1993 the Government compromised, to some extent, by announcing the compulsory retirement of several veteran military officers, including Gen. Ponce, although their immunity from prosecution was guaranteed.

The findings of the Truth Commission, together with the disclosure of information following the declassification by the US administration, in November 1993, of hitherto confidential documents relating to the administrations of former US Presidents Ronald Reagan and George Bush, suggested that detailed knowledge of abuses of human rights was suppressed by US officials in order to continue to secure congressional funding for the Government in El Salvador in the 1980s. Evidence also emerged that US military training had been provided, in at least one instance, for a civilian group in El Salvador operating as a 'death squad'.

Meanwhile, in June 1993 the FMLN had agreed to comply with an ultimatum issued by the UN, that the location and destruction of all remaining arms caches in El Salvador and neighbouring countries should be swiftly implemented. At the first national convention of the FMLN as a political organ, convened in September, the party confirmed its political alliance with the CD, selecting Francisco Lima as vice-presidential co-candidate with Rubén Zamora Rivas, the presidential candidate of the CD. In December this alliance was expanded to incorporate the MNR.

Voting to elect a new president, vice-president, legislature, 262 mayors and 20 members of the Central American parliament took place on 20 March 1994. Early indications were of a high level of support for ARENA's presidential candidate, Armando Calderón Sol, the mayor of San Salvador whose name had been linked to a 1981 plot to kidnap left-wing sympathisers by documents declassified by the US administration in November 1993. However, Calderón Sol failed to secure the clear majority needed for outright victory in the first poll, and was forced to contest a second round of voting against the second-placed candidate, Zamora Rivas, on 24 April 1994, which the ARENA candidate won with 68.2% of the votes. ARENA candidates also achieved considerable success in the legislative elections (retaining 39 seats in the Asamblea) and in the municipal poll (securing an estimated 200 municipalities). FMLN candidates were also considered to have performed well in the party's first electoral contest, winning 21 seats in the Asamblea and a number of rural municipalities. Calderón Sol was inaugurated on 1 June and a new Cabinet was installed simultaneously. In late June, in response to a recent intensification of political violence and organized crime, President Calderón Sol announced a new initiative for national security which attracted opposition for its virtual exclusion of the transitional National Civilian Police. In late November the Ministers of the Treasury and of Agriculture and Livestock resigned in order to facilitate judicial investigation of the alleged involvement of both ministries in an influence-peddling and tax evasion scandal.

Meanwhile, serious divisions emerged within the FMLN during 1994, and members of two constituent parties, the Resistencia Nacional (RN) and the Expresión Renovadora del Pueblo (ERP—formerly the Fuerzas Armadas de la Resistencia Nacional and the Ejército Revolucionario Popular guerrilla groups, respectively) became increasingly alienated following a decision, taken by the FMLN national council in May, to suspend several prominent members of the two parties from their positions within the FMLN executive for failing to comply with a party directive to boycott elections to the new directorate of the Asamblea. In December the RN and the ERP announced their withdrawal from the FMLN, owing to a divergence of political interests. In March 1995 the Secretary-General of the ERP, Joaquín Villalobos (who had been highly critical of the predominance of political extremism), announced the formation of a new centre-left political force, the Partido Demócrata (PD), comprising the ERP, the RN, the MNR and a dissident faction of the PDC. The new party demonstrated an immediate willingness to co-operate with the country's most prominent political forces. In May the PD and President Calderón Sol were the only signatories to a 'national' pact to promote a broad range of social, political and economic aims, and in June the support of five PD deputies, together with that of three independents, enabled the Government to secure the Asamblea's approval of a controversial increase in the rate of value-added tax (VAT). The Government had insisted that the increase was necessary to fund the costs of post-war economic reconstruction, despite vociferous opposition to the increase from both left- and right-wing parties and from the business community. An economic reform programme, announced in February, had also provoked widespread opposition to tax increases, and to a comprehensive divestment plan. However, in July the IMF announced a US $58m. stand-by credit in support of the Government's economic programme for 1995/96.

Political manoeuvring in preparation for congressional and municipal elections scheduled for March 1997, began in mid-1996 with the PD's announcement of its withdrawal from the legislative pact forged with ARENA in May 1995, owing to the Government's failure to honour pledges to increase spending on health and education and to safeguard the jobs of employees at state concerns scheduled for privatization. (The Government's divestment and rationalization programme had provoked industrial action in the public sector early in the year, and was causing considerable anxiety amongst employees at a number of state-owned companies, most prominently ANTEL—the large telecommunications organization—which was scheduled for privatization.) The PD subsequently announced that it would contest the March 1997 elections in an electoral alliance of the 'democratic centre', with the PDC. In early January 1997 ARENA's congressional strength was further undermined by the defection, to the PCN, of three prominent ARENA deputies, who complained of constrictive practices within the party.

The results of municipal and legislative elections, conducted on 16 March 1997, demonstrated a significant increase in support for the FMLN, particularly in the capital, where the party won seven of the 16 contested seats. Héctor Silva, the FMLN-led coalition candidate, was elected Mayor of San Salvador, defeating the incumbent ARENA candidate, Mario Valiente. The results of the legislative poll revealed a considerable erosion of ARENA's predominance in the Asamblea, with the party securing 29 seats, just one more than the FMLN. Widespread concern was expressed at the high level of voter abstention, estimated to be some 60%.

In May 1997 the FMLN secured sufficient support in the legislature to repeal a law providing for the privatization of ANTEL. However, a revised privatization bill prepared by an *ad hoc* joint commission, involving all parties with representation in the Asamblea Nacional, was approved by the legislature in July, despite the continued opposition of the FMLN. ANTEL was to be divided into two separate companies, Compañía de Telecomunicaciones de El Salvador (CTE), which would control the terrestrial network, and Internacional de Telecomunicaciones (Intel), which would manage the sale of telecommunications frequencies. In June Miguel Araújo was appointed Minister of the Environment, a new portfolio created to address the country's serious environmental problems.

In July 1997 ARENA suffered a serious embarrassment when a prominent party official, Mathies Hill, was arrested for his part in a financial scandal involving the illegal diversion of some US $113m. The Financial Superintendent, Rafael Rodríguez Loucel, was dismissed and charged with complicity in the fraud (although he was later acquitted). In October ARENA elected the former President, Alfredo Cristiani Burkard, as leader of the party.

A severe increase in violent criminal activity during late 1995 and early 1996 caused widespread concern and prompted the Government to introduce a number of uncompromising emergency laws, in March 1996, which sought to address the problem. However, a number of human rights organizations expressed concern that the new laws represented a serious infringement of civil liberties. These concerns were reiterated in October, following the Asamblea's approval of a constitutional amendment whereby the death penalty for civilians (abolished in 1971) was to be reinstated for a number of offences including rape, kidnapping and aggravated murder.

In early December 1993, bowing to pressure from the UN, President Cristiani inaugurated a four-member commission of investigation (the Joint Group for the Investigation of Illegal Armed Groups), comprising representatives of the Government, the Office of the Ombudsman for Human Rights, and of ONUSAL, to examine allegations of political motivation behind an escalation in violent attacks against members of the FMLN in late 1993. Publication of the group's report, scheduled for

May 1994, was initially suspended, after death threats were received by the members of the commission, apparently issued by the previously unknown Comando Domingo Monterrosa (CDM). The conclusions of the commission, which claimed that officials from numerous government departments, together with current and former members of the security forces, were continuing to participate in organized crime and in politically motivated acts of violence, were eventually published in late July, prompting President Calderón Sol to declare his full commitment to all efforts to bring to justice anyone engaged in criminal activity.

In September 1994 and January 1995, in protest at the Government's failure to honour the terms of the 1992 peace accord with regard to financial compensation and other benefits for demobilized military personnel, retired soldiers occupied the Asamblea and took a number of deputies hostage. On both occasions the occupation was ended swiftly and peacefully following the Government's agreement to enter into direct negotiations with the former soldiers. The Association of the Demobilized Armed Forces had earlier threatened to sabotage the economy by disrupting transport communications and foreign businesses throughout the country if the Government failed to meet its obligations, and had organized a series of co-ordinated protests throughout the country in early January 1995. Further demonstrations by army veterans during March and November were forcibly curtailed by the security forces, prompting concern that such incidents might provoke a renewed escalation of armed conflict.

In May 1994 the UN Security Council voted to extend the ONUSAL mandate for a further six months in order to supervise the full implementation of the outstanding provisions of the peace agreement. Of particular concern were delays in the reform of the judiciary, the initiation of the land reform programme and the full integration and activation of the National Civilian Police. It was estimated that some US $80m. would be needed to ensure the prompt fulfilment of the terms of the negotiated settlement and in September the UN Secretary-General appealed to the Government and to the international community for increased financial commitment to the peace process. In the same month, in the context of increasing levels of crime and social unrest, President Calderón Sol requested a further extension of the ONUSAL mandate pending the effective habilitation of the National Civilian Police. In November the UN Security Council approved the continued presence of the mission in El Salvador until the end of April 1995. A small contingent of UN observers, MINUSAL, was mandated to remain in El Salvador until April 1996 (the revised deadline for the fulfilment of the outstanding terms of the peace accord). By April 1996, however, full implementation of those terms of the accord relating to land allocation for refugees and former combatants, and to the reform of the judiciary and the electoral code, had yet to be achieved. A reduced MINUSAL contingent was further mandated to oversee Government efforts to fulfil the outstanding terms of the agreement, and the mission was formally terminated on 31 December 1996.

In January 1990 President Cristiani had admitted that members of the Salvadorean army were involved in the murder of the six Jesuits in the previous November. Nine soldiers, including a colonel, were charged in connection with the massacre. The successful prosecution of those implicated in the affair was, however, severely impeded by the disappearance of important evidence in May 1990. In January 1991 two leading state prosecutors resigned from the case, complaining of military obstruction and interference by the Attorney-General. In April the Supreme Court upheld a decision to bring to trial Col Guillermo Benavides and eight other military personnel who were accused of the murders. In September Col Benavides and an army lieutenant were found guilty of murder. Two other lieutenants and five soldiers were acquitted, on the grounds that they were simply following orders. In January 1992 the two guilty men were awarded prison sentences of a maximum of 30 years. However, doubts were expressed that justice had been administered, and allegations were made that evidence linking the murders to higher-ranking military personnel had been removed or destroyed.

In November 1989, meanwhile, Cristiani had suspended relations with Nicaragua, after an aircraft, en route from Nicaragua, made a crash landing in El Salvador and was found to contain 24 Soviet-made surface-to-air missiles. This confirmed the suspicions of the Salvadorean Government that Nicaragua had been supplying weapons to the FMLN. In January 1991 four officers of the Nicaraguan armed forces were placed under arrest by the Nicaraguan Government and charged with supplying anti-aircraft missiles to the FMLN guerrilla forces.

In an attempt to resolve a territorial dispute between El Salvador and Honduras over three islands in the Gulf of Fonseca and a small area of land on the joint border, President Duarte and President Azcona of Honduras submitted the dispute to the International Court of Justice (ICJ) for arbitration in December 1986. In September 1992 both countries accepted the ruling of the ICJ, which awarded one-third of the disputed mainland and two of the three disputed islands to El Salvador. Following the ruling, negotiations began towards a protocol defining the nationality and property rights of the inhabitants of the redesignated land. Although the ICJ recommended that all those involved should be granted dual nationality, a provision of the Honduran Constitution precluded this possibility. A resolution of the issue, which had led to numerous disputes between the two countries, was finally achieved in January 1998, when the parties signed a convention specifying the rights and obligations of those affected, including the right to choose between Honduran and Salvadorean citizenship.

Government

Executive power is held by the President, assisted by the Vice-President and the Council of Ministers. The President is elected for a five-year term by universal adult suffrage. Legislative power is vested in the Asamblea Nacional—National Assembly—which replaced the National Constituent Assembly in March 1985), with 84 members elected by universal adult suffrage for a three-year term.

Defence

Military service is by compulsory selective conscription of men between 18 and 30 years of age for one year. In early 1992 it was reported that, from February of that year, compulsory military service was to be abolished, as part of a peace accord negotiated between the Government and the FMLN. In August 1997 the armed forces totalled 28,400 men, comprising the army 25,700, the navy 1,100 and the air force 1,600. The creation of a National Civilian Police force (to include former members of the FMLN) was agreed in 1991 and the force numbered around 12,000 personnel by 1997. The defence budget for 1997 totalled 910m. colones.

Economic Affairs

In 1995, according to estimates by the World Bank, El Salvador's gross national product (GNP), measured at average 1993–95 prices, was US $9,057m., equivalent to $1,610 per head. During 1985–95, it was estimated, GNP per head increased, in real terms, by 2.9% per year. Over the same period, the population increased by an annual average of 1.8%. El Salvador's gross domestic product (GDP) increased, in real terms, by an annual average of 4.1% in 1985–95. GDP growth was 6.3% in 1995 and 3.0% in 1996.

Agriculture (including hunting, forestry and fishing) contributed an estimated 13.6% of GDP in 1996, and employed some 27.0% of the labour force in 1995. The principal cash crops are coffee (which accounted for an estimated 31.7% of export earnings in 1996) and sugar cane. Maize, beans, rice and millet are the major subsistence crops. Shrimps and honey are increasingly significant export commodities. During 1985–95 agricultural GDP was estimated to have increased by an annual average of 1.3%. The sector's GDP increased by an estimated 0.6% in 1996.

Industry (including mining, manufacturing, construction and power) contributed an estimated 27.2% of GDP in 1996, and employed 26.3% of the labour force in 1995. During 1985–95 industrial GDP increased by an annual average of 2.8%. The sector's GDP increased by an estimated 3.1% in 1996.

El Salvador has no significant mineral resources, and the mining sector employed less than 0.1% of the labour force in 1995, and contributed only an estimated 0.4% of GDP in 1996. Small quantities of gold, silver, sea-salt and limestone are mined or quarried.

Manufacturing contributed an estimated 21.3% of GDP in 1996, and employed 19.3% of the labour force in 1995. Measured by the gross value of output, the most important branches of manufacturing (excluding the in-bond industry) in 1995 were food products (about 29.1% of the total), chemical products (8.9%), beverages, textiles and petroleum products. During 1991–95 manufacturing GDP increased by an annual average of 5.6%. The sector's GDP increased by an estimated 3.5%, in real terms, in 1996. There is a thriving offshore (*maquila*) manufacturing sector.

Energy is derived principally from imported fuel, which accounted for an estimated 5.6% of the cost of merchandise imports in 1996. Some 46.9% of total electricity production in 1994 was contributed by hydroelectric installations.

The services sector contributed an estimated 59.1% of GDP in 1996 and employed 46.7% of the labour force in 1995. According to the World Bank, the GDP of the services sector increased by an average of 5.6% per year in 1985–95. Growth in the sector was estimated at 3.4% in 1996. The promising tourism sector was severely damaged by the civil war, but was expected to recover in the late 1990s.

In 1995 El Salvador recorded a visible trade deficit of US $1,523.2m., and there was a deficit of $322.2m. on the current account of the balance of payments. Workers' remittances from abroad were reported to be worth twice the value of coffee exports in the early 1990s. The country's principal trading partner is the USA, which took an estimated 18.1% of exports and provided some 38.3% of imports in 1996. Costa Rica, Guatemala, Honduras, Mexico, Venezuela, Germany and Japan are also important trading partners. In 1994 the main exports were coffee, sugar, textile yarn and fabrics, paper and paperboard manufactures, and chemicals and related products. In 1996 the principal imports were primary materials for industry, non-durable consumer goods, capital goods for transport, capital goods for industry and construction materials.

In 1996 there was an estimated budgetary deficit of 1,841.5m. colones, equivalent to some 2.0% of GDP. El Salvador's external debt totalled US $2,583m. at the end of 1995, of which $2,055m. was long-term public debt. In that year the cost of debt-servicing was equivalent to 8.9% of the value of exports of goods and services. In 1996 the average annual rate of inflation was 9.8% (compared with an annual average of 18.1% in 1985–95). An estimated 7.7% of the labour force in urban areas were unemployed in 1995.

El Salvador is a member of the Central American Common Market (CACM, see p. 122), which aims to increase trade within the region and to encourage monetary and industrial co-operation.

During the 1980s El Salvador's economy was devastated by the civil war and by guerrilla attacks on agricultural areas and sabotage of power installations and roads; natural disasters, including a major earthquake in October 1986, a hurricane in October 1988 and recurrent drought, also had a severe effect. The Government depended on US aid to counteract deficits on the balance of payments and on budgetary spending, and to finance military activity against its opponents. In July 1989 the newly-elected administration of President Cristiani introduced austerity measures to reduce public spending and to liberalize trade and price controls. The administration of Calderón Sol, which took office in 1994, achieved considerable progress in reducing financial imbalances and the rate of inflation and in stabilizing the balance of payments and addressing the problem of widespread poverty. Economic growth of some 6% in 1995 was fuelled by strong performances by the public utilities, construction and manufacturing sectors, and by higher world prices for coffee. Economic measures designed to encourage private investment and to increase spending on social programmes were introduced in mid-1996. In March 1997 the IMF approved a stand-by agreement for some US $58m. in support of the Government's economic programme for 1997/98. The programme aimed to strengthen public finances while continuing with structural reform. Real GDP growth of 3%–4% was envisaged in 1997, when inflation was expected to decline to 5%–6%.

Social Welfare

In 1952 the Instituto Salvadoreño del Seguro Social (ISSS) was established. This institute provides hospital facilities, medicines and benefits for industrial injury, sickness, accident, disability, maternity, old age and death. Health and welfare insurance is financed by contributions from workers, employers and the State. In 1981 El Salvador had 46 government-controlled hospital establishments, with a total of 7,375 beds, and in 1984 there were 1,664 physicians working in the country. The Ministry of Public Health and Social Welfare administers 250 medical units, including 14 hospitals. In 1994 budgetary expenditure by the central Government (excluding the ISSS) included 852.8m. colones (8.3% of total expenditure) on health and a further 748.7m. colones (7.3%) on social security and welfare.

Education

There are two national universities and more than 30 private universities. Education is provided free of charge in state schools, and there are also numerous private schools. Primary education, beginning at seven years of age and lasting for nine years, is officially compulsory. In 1993 enrolment at primary schools was equivalent to 79% of children in the relevant age-group (males 79%; females 80%). Secondary education begins at the age of 16 and lasts for three years. In 1993 enrolment at secondary schools was equivalent to just 29% of students in the relevant age-group (males 27%; females 30%). In 1995, according to estimates by UNESCO, the illiteracy rate among people aged 15 years and over was 28.5% (males 26.5%; females 30.2%). Budgetary expenditure on education by the central Government in 1994 was 1,351.7m. colones, equivalent to 13.2% of total expenditure.

Public Holidays

1998: 1 January (New Year's Day), 10–13 April (Easter), 1 May (Labour Day), 11 June (Corpus Christi), 4–6 August* (San Salvador Festival), 15 September (Independence Day), 12 October (Discovery of America), 2 November (All Souls' Day), 5 November (First Call of Independence), 24–25 December (Christmas).

1999: 1 January (New Year's Day), 2–5 April (Easter), 1 May (Labour Day), 3 June (Corpus Christi), 4–6 August* (San Salvador Festival), 15 September (Independence Day), 12 October (Discovery of America), 2 November (All Souls' Day), 5 November (First Call of Independence), 24–25 December (Christmas).

* 5–6 August in other cities.

Weights and Measures

The metric system is officially in force. Some old Spanish measures are also used, including:

25 libras = 1 arroba;
4 arrobas = 1 quintal (46 kg);
1 manzana = 0.699 ha.

Statistical Survey

Sources (unless otherwise stated): Banco Central de Reserva de El Salvador, Alameda Juan Pablo II y 17 Avda Norte, Apdo 01-106, San Salvador; tel. 271-0011; fax 271-4575; Dirección General de Estadística y Censos, 1a Calle Poniente y 43a Avda Norte, Apdo 2670, San Salvador; tel. 771-5011.

Area and Population

AREA, POPULATION AND DENSITY

Area (sq km)	
Land	20,721
Inland water	320
Total	21,041*
Population (census results)†	
28 June 1971	3,554,648
27 September 1992	
Males	2,485,613
Females	2,632,986
Total	5,118,599
Density (per sq km) at 27 September 1992	243.3

* 8,124 sq miles.
† Excluding adjustments for underenumeration.

PRINCIPAL TOWNS* (population at 1992 census)

San Salvador (capital)	422,570	Mejicanos	145,000
Soyapango	251,811	Nueva San Salvador	116,575
Santa Ana	202,337	Ciudad Delgado	104,790
San Miguel	182,817	Apopa	100,763

* Figures refer to *municipios*, which may each contain rural areas as well as an urban centre.

Source: UN, *Demographic Yearbook*.

BIRTHS, MARRIAGES AND DEATHS

	Registered live births		Registered marriages		Registered deaths	
	Number	Rate (per 1,000)	Number	Rate (per 1,000)	Number	Rate (per 1,000)
1985	139,514	28.7	18,097	3.7	27,225	5.6
1986	145,126	29.3	19,630	4.0	25,731	5.2
1987	148,355	29.1	22,327	4.4	27,581	5.5
1988	149,299	29.3	21,314	4.2	27,774	5.5
1989	151,859	29.2	20,787	4.0	27,768	5.3
1990*	148,360	28.7	22,360	4.3	28,195	5.5
1991	151,210	28.3	22,658	4.2	27,066	5.1
1992	154,014	28.1	23,050	4.2	27,869	5.1

* Rates based on UN population estimate.

1994: 152,943 registered live births; 28,694 registered deaths.

Note: Registration is incomplete. According to UN estimates, the average annual rates in 1985–90 were: births 34.6 per 1,000; deaths 8.6 per 1,000, and in 1990–95 were: births 33.5 per 1,000; deaths 7.1 per 1,000.

Expectation of life (UN estimates, years at birth, 1990–95): 66.4 (males 63.9; females 68.8) (Source: UN, *World Population Prospects: The 1994 Revision*).

EMPLOYMENT
('000 persons aged 10 years and over, 1995)

	Males	Females	Total
Agriculture, hunting, forestry and fishing	474.7	57.8	532.5
Mining and quarrying	1.0	—	1.0
Manufacturing	192.0	188.7	380.7
Electricity, gas and water	6.5	0.9	7.4
Construction	126.6	3.3	129.9
Trade, restaurants and hotels	172.8	226.5	399.3
Transport, storage and communication	76.5	5.2	81.7
Financing, insurance, real estate and business services	13.1	13.1	26.2
Community, social and personal services	163.6	250.6	414.2
Total	1,226.9	746.1	1,973.0

Source: ILO, *Yearbook of Labour Statistics*.

Agriculture

PRINCIPAL CROPS (production in '000 quintals*)

	1993	1994	1995†
Coffee (green)	3,349	3,106	3,100
Cotton (lint)	79	41	n.a.
Maize	13,716	10,405	12,000
Beans	1,367	1,344	1,425
Rice (milled)	1,619	1,405	1,489
Millet	4,410	3,957	4,140
Sugar cane‡	3,762	3,564	3,552

* Figures are in terms of the old Spanish quintal, equivalent to 46 kg (101.4 lb).
† Preliminary figures.
‡ Figures are in terms of '000 metric tons.

1996 (production in '000 metric tons, FAO estimates): Coffee (green) 126; Cotton (lint) 4; Maize 640; Beans (dry) 51; Rice (paddy) 51; Sugar cane 3,900 (Source: FAO, *Production Yearbook*).

LIVESTOCK ('000 head, year ending September)

	1994	1995	1996
Horses*	96	96	96
Mules*	24	24	24
Cattle	1,236	1,262	1,287
Pigs	336	372	400
Sheep*	5	5	5
Goats*	15	15	15

Chickens (million): 5 in 1994; 5 in 1995; 6* in 1996.

* FAO estimate(s).

Source: FAO, *Production Yearbook*.

LIVESTOCK PRODUCTS ('000 metric tons)

	1994	1995	1996
Beef and veal	27	27	34
Pig meat*	11	13	11
Poultry meat	49	54	53
Cows' milk	284	280*	290*
Cheese*	3	3	3
Hen eggs*	44	45	45

* FAO estimate(s).

Source: FAO, *Production Yearbook*.

Forestry

ROUNDWOOD REMOVALS
(FAO estimates, '000 cubic metres, excl. bark)

	1992	1993	1994
Sawlogs, veneer logs and logs for sleepers*	90	90	90
Other industrial wood*	56	56	56
Fuel wood	6,226	6,368	6,508
Total	6,372	6,514	6,654

* Annual output assumed to be unchanged since 1989.

Source: FAO, *Yearbook of Forest Products.*

SAWNWOOD PRODUCTION
(FAO estimates, '000 cubic metres, incl. railway sleepers)

	1987	1988	1989
Coniferous (softwood)	35	42	57
Broadleaved (hardwood)	12	13	14
Total	47	54	70

1990-94: Annual production as in 1989 (FAO estimates).

Source: FAO, *Yearbook of Forest Products.*

Fishing

(metric tons, live weight)

	1993	1994	1995
Nile tilapia	2,906	2,860	2,621
Other freshwater fishes	1,448	1,626	1,833
Marine fishes	3,080	2,909	4,075
Pacific seabobs	2,363	2,326	2,671
Other crustaceans	2,455	2,518	4,011
Molluscs	825	827	601
Total catch	13,077	13,066	15,812

Source: FAO, *Yearbook of Fishery Statistics.*

Industry

SELECTED PRODUCTS ('000 metric tons, unless otherwise indicated)

	1992	1993	1994
Raw sugar	346*	368*	275†
Cigarettes (million)	1,620	n.a.	n.a.
Motor spirit (petrol)	152	197	248
Distillate fuel oils	271	301	327
Residual fuel oils	268	290	315
Cement‡	421	365	598
Electric energy (million kWh)	2,457	2,858§	3,324§

* Source: Food and Agriculture Organization (Rome).

† Source: International Sugar Organization (London).

‡ Source: UN, Economic Commission for Latin America and the Caribbean.

§ Estimate.

Source: UN, *Industrial Commodity Statistics Yearbook.*

Finance

CURRENCY AND EXCHANGE RATES

Monetary Units

100 centavos = 1 Salvadorean colón.

Sterling and Dollar Equivalents (30 September 1997)

£1 sterling = 14.143 colones;
US $1 = 8.755 colones;
1,000 Salvadorean colones = £70.71 = $114.22.

Note: The foregoing information refers to the principal exchange rate, applicable to official receipts and payments, imports of petroleum and exports of coffee. In addition, there is a market exchange rate, applicable to other transactions. The principal rate (colones per US dollar) at 31 December was: 8.750 in 1994; 8.755 in 1995; 8.755 in 1996.

BUDGET (million colones)

Revenue*	1992	1993	1994
Current revenue	5,261.9	6,548.8	8,519.0
Taxation	4,915.7	6,071.5	7,609.1
Taxes on income, profits and capital gains	1,072.0	1,274.5	1,823.6
Taxes on property	331.3	266.1	317.1
Domestic taxes on goods and services	2,602.1	3,524.6	4,195.5
Sales or turnover taxes	1,939.3	2,880.5	3,464.5
Excises	591.2	578.5	612.0
Taxes on international trade and transactions	892.3	1,004.2	1,272.3
Customs duties	855.6	991.3	1,270.6
Entrepreneurial and property income	178.2	245.8	578.6
Non-financial public enterprises and public financial institutions	136.6	151.9	216.5
Capital revenue	0.4	1.6	135.4
Total	5,262.3	6,550.4	8,654.4

Expenditure†	1992	1993	1994
General public services	761.9	962.3	1,355.7
Defence	974.7	888.1	829.0
Public order and safety	445.0	761.0	1,007.5
Education	778.2	1,010.6	1,351.7
Health	446.2	662.7	852.8
Social security and welfare	205.1	338.0	748.7
Social security	147.5	238.8	626.6
Housing and community amenities	79.8	96.8	799.3
Recreational, cultural and religious affairs and services	90.6	126.1	113.5
Economic services	1,178.6	1,480.2	2,173.3
Fuel and energy	302.2	3.3	935.2
Agriculture, forestry and fishing	160.2	260.5	188.5
Mining and mineral resources, manufacturing and construction	4.7	5.2	125.8
Transport and communications	528.7	801.6	634.4
Other purposes	182.8	409.6	289.4
Other expenditure	1,102.8	1,026.9	1,311.0
Total expenditure	6,077.9	7,753.0	10,264.3
Current‡	5,150.7	6,156.5	7,937.5
Capital§	912.2	1,196.2	2,605.0

* Excluding grants received (million colones): 343.5 in 1992; 269.3 in 1993; 303.0 in 1994.

† Excluding lending minus repayments (million colones): –40.0 in 1992; –277.3 in 1993; –746.5 in 1994.

‡ Including interest payments (million colones): 1,072.3 in 1992; 1,024.1 in 1993; 1,131.1 in 1994.

§ Excluding adjustment to cash basis and expenditure under previous budgets (million colones): 15 in 1992; 400.3 in 1993; –278.2 in 1994.

Source: IMF, *Government Finance Statistics Yearbook.*

CENTRAL BANK RESERVES (US $ million at 31 December)

	1994	1995	1996
Gold*	19.8	19.8	19.8
IMF special drawing rights	0.1	37.1	35.9
Foreign exchange	649.3	721.2	901.0
Total	669.2	778.1	956.7

* Valued at US $42.22 per troy ounce.

Source: IMF, *International Financial Statistics.*

MONEY SUPPLY (million colones at 31 December)

	1994	1995	1996
Currency outside banks	2,999	3,161	3,130
Demand deposits at deposit money banks	3,539	3,934	4,996
Total money (incl. others)	7,569	8,766	9,898

Source: IMF, *International Financial Statistics.*

COST OF LIVING
(Consumer Price Index for urban areas; base: 1992 = 100)

	1994	1995	1996
Food	128.9	137.5	155.1
Clothing	111.6	117.5	121.0
Housing	110.8	131.7	142.9
All items (incl. others)	118.3	130.2	142.9

NATIONAL ACCOUNTS (million colones at current prices)

National Income and Product

	1990	1991	1992*
Domestic factor incomes†	37,168.5	43,049.5	49,247.0
Consumption of fixed capital	1,693.7	1,971.5	2,263.0
Gross domestic product at factor cost	38,862.2	45,021.0	51,510.0
Indirect taxes, *less* subsidies	2,194.8	2,771.0	3,252.0
GDP in purchasers' values	41,057.0	47,792.0	54,762.0
Net factor income from abroad	−775.2	−822.1	−498.0
Gross national product	40,281.8	46,969.9	54,264.0
Less Consumption of fixed capital	1,693.7	1,971.5	2,263.0
National income in market prices	38,588.1	44,998.4	52,001.0

* Provisional.

† Compensation of employees and the operating surplus of enterprises. The amount is obtained as a residual.

Expenditure on the Gross Domestic Product

	1994	1995	1996*
Government final consumption expenditure	5,762.3	6,540.2	7,083.5
Private final consumption expenditure	61,685.0	73,928.7	82,284.8
Increase in stocks	767.4	1,057.8	−1,127.0
Gross fixed capital formation	13,209.1	15,724.5	15,786.2
Total domestic expenditure	81,423.8	97,251.2	104,027.5
Exports of goods and services	14,104.3	18,069.6	19,425.0
Less Imports of goods and services	24,915.4	31,633.0	30,898.9
GDP in purchasers' values	70,612.7	83,687.8	92,553.6
GDP at constant 1990 prices	46,251.3	49,144.9	50,596.2

* Preliminary figures..

Gross Domestic Product by Economic Activity

	1994	1995	1996*
Agriculture, hunting, forestry and fishing	9,880.5	12,053.3	12,633.4
Mining and quarrying	299.2	354.6	384.9
Manufacturing	15,680.8	17,905.1	19,725.8
Construction	3,264.4	3,674.8	4,012.7
Electricity, gas and water	738.8	966.3	1,082.4
Transport, storage and communications	5,137.1	5,991.9	6,850.7
Wholesale and retail trade	13,570.5	16,391.4	18,619.6
Finance, insurance, etc.	1,930.4	2,488.7	3,169.8
Owner-occupied dwellings	5,887.6	6,643.5	7,512.3
Public administration	4,185.1	4,720.5	4,973.7
Other	10,038.3	12,497.7	13,588.4
Total	70,612.7	83,687.8	92,553.6

* Preliminary figures.

BALANCE OF PAYMENTS (US $ million)

	1993	1994	1995
Exports of goods f.o.b.	731.5	1,252.2	1,660.4
Imports of goods f.o.b.	−1,766.4	−2,407.4	−3,183.6
Trade balance	−1,034.9	−1,155.3	−1,523.2
Exports of services	406.3	387.2	388.5
Imports of services	−382.1	−443.9	−489.7
Balance on goods and services	−1,010.6	−1,212.0	−1,624.4
Other income received	30.8	35.5	54.0
Other income paid	−142.4	−130.1	−140.7
Balance on goods, services and income	−1,122.2	−1,306.6	−1,711.1
Current transfers received	1,004.7	1,290.9	1,388.9
Current transfers paid	−0.7	−2.4	—
Current balance	−118.2	−18.1	−322.2
Direct investment from abroad	16.4	—	38.0
Portfolio investment liabilities	—	—	68.5
Other investment assets	4.1	−7.9	−7.1
Other investment liabilities	66.1	91.8	333.0
Net errors and omissions	90.3	47.3	38.1
Overall balance	58.7	113.0	148.3

Source: IMF, *International Financial Statistics.*

External Trade

PRINCIPAL COMMODITIES (distribution by SITC, US $ '000)

Imports c.i.f.	1992	1993	1994
Food and live animals	174,821	178,467	257,479
Cereals and cereal preparations	48,892	53,256	100,130
Crude materials (inedible) except fuels	52,103	52,538	81,713
Mineral fuels, lubricants, etc.	215,753	210,854	215,378
Petroleum, petroleum products, etc.	204,153	199,841	201,482
Crude petroleum	145,071	137,941	112,014
Refined petroleum products	57,023	59,731	86,799
Gasoline, other light oils	18,606	8,282	13,929
Gas oils	—	38,355	56,592
Animal and vegetable oils, fats and waxes	40,788	41,337	59,562
Chemicals and related products	276,571	316,634	373,017
Medicinal and pharmaceutical products	80,352	88,747	97,022
Medicaments	63,374	70,288	79,530
Perfumes and cleaning preparations, etc.	33,775	43,412	53,457
Plastic materials, etc.	50,734	59,029	73,765
Products of polymerization, etc.	36,129	46,559	61,605

Imports c.i.f. — *continued*	1992	1993	1994
Basic manufactures	278,860	344,949	399,796
Paper, paperboard and manufactures	58,283	74,695	81,585
Paper and paperboard	48,679	62,139	67,452
Textile yarn, fabrics, etc.	36,550	44,880	54,355
Iron and steel	60,905	67,441	81,979
Other metal manufactures	62,463	76,424	88,589
Machinery and transport equipment	396,988	582,160	695,697
Power-generating machinery and equipment	37,578	48,393	55,610
Machinery specialized for particular industries	59,981	111,118	84,403
General industrial machinery, equipment and parts	56,190	57,960	71,168
Electrical machinery, apparatus, etc.	75,165	127,924	195,488
Road vehicles	162,690	228,676	279,463
Passenger motor cars (except buses)	136,917	97,439	96,376
Lorries and trucks	—	75,754	106,218
Miscellaneous manufactured articles	96,529	123,112	163,486
Total	1,537,506	1,858,343	2,261,800

Exports f.o.b.	1992	1993	1994
Food and live animals	247,115	344,901	399,022
Sugar, sugar preparations and honey	53,185	46,418	44,058
Sugar and honey	48,440	39,721	35,894
Sugars, beet and cane (raw, solid)	41,488	29,485	27,690
Coffee, tea, cocoa, etc.	137,082	224,075	268,710
Coffee and coffee substitutes	136,241	223,195	267,767
Coffee (incl. husks and skins) and substitutes containing coffee	136,125	223,074	263,920
Miscellaneous edible products and preparations	17,171	16,445	20,329
Crude materials (inedible) except fuels	18,485	12,317	13,477
Chemicals and related products	70,444	87,659	97,482
Medicinal and pharmaceutical products	28,139	34,326	34,412
Medicaments	26,494	32,103	32,568
Perfumes and cleaning preparations, etc.	15,269	20,580	27,919
Soap etc.	11,574	15,730	22,047

Exports f.o.b. — *continued*	1992	1993	1994
Basic manufactures	135,039	166,121	171,078
Paper, paperboard and manufactures	40,116	53,259	56,576
Shaped or cut articles of paper and paperboard	31,289	43,280	43,929
Boxes, bags, packing containers, etc.	22,471	29,469	29,393
Textile yarn, fabrics, etc.	60,556	61,057	61,638
Textile yarn	21,685	19,745	21,884
Cotton yard	17,165	14,194	13,918
Fabrics of woven, man-made fibres	15,825	16,670	15,048
Fabrics of woven, discontinuous synthetic fibres	14,233	15,573	13,474
Linens, etc.	10,690	12,473	14,788
Non-ferrous metals	13,257	18,540	19,306
Aluminium	13,061	17,502	18,435
Aluminium and alloys (unwrought)	13,061	17,502	18,408
Other metal manufactures	16,449	25,270	27,793
Machinery and transport equipment	16,088	23,500	24,781
Electrical machinery, apparatus, etc.	5,795	17,339	20,288
Miscellaneous manufactured articles	55,783	70,639	89,585
Clothing and accessories	25,398	29,456	37,509
Footwear	11,627	14,087	17,721
Total	555,111	716,286	812,718

Source: UN, *International Trade Statistics Yearbook.*

PRINCIPAL TRADING PARTNERS
(US $ '000)

Imports c.i.f.	1992	1993	1994
Brazil	22,455	24,542	40,290
Costa Rica	56,248	66,040	78,919
Germany	68,430	65,005	73,106
Guatemala	—	204,655	242,494
Honduras	28,635	34,754	46,065
Italy	12,456	17,388	22,837
Japan	79,407	97,604	143,277
Mexico	112,115	103,665	105,558
Netherlands	17,804	18,729	14,625
Panama	55,454	66,322	80,855
Spain	12,250	16,064	28,956
United Kingdom	18,171	17,863	25,117
USA	614,562	789,426	938,064
Venezuela	81,527	133,570	138,422
Total (incl. others)	1,537,424	1,858,178	2,261,595

Exports f.o.b.	1992	1993	1994
Belgium-Luxembourg	3,938	17,932	34,053
Canada	4,222	6,089	12,452
Costa Rica	54,954	65,994	72,259
Germany	42,986	75,232	120,824
Guatemala	—	157,137	178,147
Honduras	31,616	47,084	56,326
Japan	3,618	14,588	6,253
Mexico	12,350	17,176	21,277
Netherlands	3,868	15,566	22,320
Nicaragua	38,730	35,537	36,652
Panama*	11,275	12,847	12,105
USA	186,353	212,426	183,445
Total (incl. others)	555,111	716,286	812,718

Transport

RAILWAYS (traffic)

	1992	1993	1994
Passenger-km (million)	6	6	6
Net ton-km (million)	38	35	30

Source: UN, *Statistical Yearbook*.

ROAD TRAFFIC (motor vehicles in use at 31 December)

	1994	1995	1996
Passenger cars	136,080	151,081	168,234
Buses and coaches	27,655	29,293	32,238
Lorries and vans	110,361	125,101	142,016
Motorcycles and mopeds	25,586	28,888	38,330

Source: IRF, *World Road Statistics*.

SHIPPING

Merchant Fleet (registered at 31 December)

	1994	1995	1996
Number of vessels	12	12	12
Total displacement ('000 grt)	1.5	1.5	1.5

Source: Lloyd's Register of Shipping, *World Fleet Statistics*.

CIVIL AVIATION (traffic on scheduled services)

	1992	1993	1994
Kilometres flown (million)	29	17	17
Passengers carried ('000)	683	723	734
Passenger–km (million)	1,563	1,738	1,573
Total ton-km (million)	175	203	217

Source: UN, *Statistical Yearbook*.

Tourism

	1992	1993	1994
Tourist arrivals ('000)	314	267	181
Tourist receipts (US $ million)	128	121	86

Source: UN, *Statistical Yearbook*.

Communications Media

	1992	1993	1994
Radio receivers ('000 in use)	2,230	2,280	2,500
Television receivers ('000 in use)	501	520	n.a.
Telephones ('000 main lines in use)	165	174	236
Mobile cellular telephones (subscribers)	n.a.	1,632	6,480
Daily newspapers	8	n.a.	6

Source: mainly UNESCO, *Statistical Yearbook*.

Education

(1993)

	Institutions	Teachers	Students
Pre-primary	2,312	2,522	113,440
Primary	3,961	26,259*	1,042,256
Secondary	n.a.	n.a.	118,115
Higher†	n.a.	4,643	77,359

* Public schools only. † Universities and equivalent institutions only.

Source: UNESCO, *Statistical Yearbook*.

Directory

The Constitution

The Constitution of the Republic of El Salvador came into effect on 20 December 1983.

The Constitution provides for a republican, democratic and representative form of government, composed of three Powers—Legislative, Executive, and Judicial—which are to operate independently. Voting is a right and duty of all citizens over 18 years of age. Presidential and congressional elections may not be held simultaneously.

The Constitution binds the country, as part of the Central American Nation, to favour the total or partial reconstruction of the Republic of Central America. Integration in a unitary, federal or confederal form, provided that democratic and republican principles are respected and that basic rights of individuals are fully guaranteed, is subject to popular approval.

LEGISLATIVE ASSEMBLY

Legislative power is vested in a single chamber, the Asamblea Nacional, whose members are elected every three years and are eligible for re-election. The Asamblea's term of office begins on 1 May. The Asamblea's duties include the choosing of the President and Vice-President of the Republic from the two citizens who shall have gained the largest number of votes for each of these offices, if no candidate obtains an absolute majority in the election. It also selects the members of the Supreme and subsidiary courts; of the Elections Council; and the Accounts Court of the Republic. It determines taxes; ratifies treaties concluded by the Executive with other States and international organizations; sanctions the Budget; regulates the monetary system of the country; determines the conditions under which foreign currencies may circulate; and suspends and reimposes constitutional guarantees. The right to initiate legislation may be exercised by the Asamblea (as well as by the President, through the Council of Ministers, and by the Supreme Court). The Asamblea may override, with a two-thirds majority, the President's objections to a Bill which it has sent for presidential approval.

PRESIDENT

The President is elected for five years, the term beginning and expiring on 1 June. The principle of alternation in the presidential office is established in the Constitution, which states the action to be taken should this principle be violated. The Executive is responsible for the preparation of the Budget and its presentation to the Asamblea; the direction of foreign affairs; the organization of the armed and security forces; and the convening of extraordinary sessions of the Asamblea. In the event of the President's death, resignation, removal or other cause, the Vice-President takes office for the rest of the presidential term; and, in case of necessity, the Vice-President may be replaced by one of the two Designates elected by the Asamblea.

JUDICIARY

Judicial power is exercised by the Supreme Court and by other competent tribunals. The Magistrates of the Supreme Court are elected by the Legislature, their number to be determined by law. The Supreme Court alone is competent to decide whether laws, decrees and regulations are constitutional or not.

The Government

HEAD OF STATE

President: Dr ARMANDO CALDERÓN SOL (assumed office 1 June 1994).

Vice-President: Dr ENRIQUE BORGO BUSTAMENTE.

COUNCIL OF MINISTERS
(February 1998)

Minister of Foreign Affairs: RAMÓN ERNESTO GONZÁLEZ GINER.

Minister of the Interior: MARIO ACOSTA OERTEL.

Minister of Public Security: HUGO BARRERA.

Minister of Justice: RUBÉN ANTONIO MEJÍA PEÑA.

Minister of the Economy: EDUARDO ZABLAH TOUCHE.

Minister of Education: CECILIA GALLARDO DE CANO.

Minister of National Defence: Gen. JAIME GUZMÁN MORALES.

Minister of Labour and Social Security: Dr EDUARDO TOMASINO.

Minister of Public Health and Social Welfare: Dr EDUARDO INTERIANO.

Minister of the Treasury: MANUEL ENRIQUE HINDS.

Minister of Agriculture and Livestock: RICARDO QUINÓÑEZ AVILA.

Minister of Public Works: JORGE ALBERTO SANSIVIRINI MAGAÑA.

Minister of the Environment: MIGUEL ARAÚJO.

MINISTRIES

Ministry for the Presidency: Avda Cuba, Calle Darió González 806, Barrio San Jacinto, San Salvador; tel. 221-8483; telex 20552; fax 771-0950.

Ministry of Agriculture and Livestock: Alameda Roosevelt, San Salvador; tel. 779-1579; telex 20228; fax 779-1941.

Ministry of the Economy: 1A Calle Poniente 2310, Col. Escalón, San Salvador; tel. 224-2159; telex 20269; fax 998-1965.

Ministry of Education: Dirección de Publicaciones, 17 Avda Sur 430, San Salvador; tel. 222-0665; fax 271-1071.

Ministry of the Environment: San Salvador.

Ministry of Foreign Affairs: Alameda Dr Manuel Enrique Araújo, Km 6, Carretera a Santa Tecla, San Salvador; tel. 243-3805; telex 20179; fax 243-3710.

Ministry of the Interior: Centro de Gobierno, Alameda Juan Pablo II, San Salvador; tel. 298-5000.

Ministry of Justice: Avda Masferrer 612B, Col. Escalón, San Salvador; tel. 998-5413; fax 998-5232.

Ministry of Labour and Social Security: Avda La Capilla 223, Col. San Benito, San Salvador; tel. 779-0388; telex 20016; fax 779-0877.

Ministry of National Defence: Alameda Dr Manuel Enrique Araújo, Km 5, Carretera a Santa Tecla, San Salvador; tel. 223-0233; telex 30345; fax 998-2005.

Ministry of Public Health and Social Welfare: Calle Arce 827, San Salvador; tel. 771-0008; telex 20704.

Ministry of Public Security: 6A Col. Antiguo, Local Policia Nacional, San Salvador; tel. 245-2667; fax 245-2660.

Ministry of Public Works: 1A Avda Sur 603, San Salvador; tel. 222-1505; fax 771-2881.

Ministry of the Treasury: Edif. Las Tres Torres, San Salvador; tel. 771-0250; telex 20647; fax 771-0591.

President

In the first round of voting in the presidential election, held on 20 March 1994, Dr ARMANDO CALDERÓN SOL, candidate of the Alianza Republicana Nacionalista (ARENA), received 49% of the votes cast. RUBÉN ZAMORA RIVAS, candidate of the Convergencia Democrática (CD), received 25% of the votes cast. The Partido Demócrata Cristiano (PDC) candidate, FIDEL CHÁVEZ MENA, obtained 16% of the votes cast. In the second round of voting, held on 24 April 1994, CALDERÓN SOL received 68.2% of the votes cast, and ZAMORA RIVAS 31.6%. CALDERÓN SOL was duly elected President.

Legislature

ASAMBLEA NACIONAL

President: FRANCISCO FLORES (ARENA).

General Election, 16 March 1997

Party	Seats
Alianza Republicana Nacionalista (ARENA)	28
Frente Farabundo Martí de Liberación (FMLN)	27
Partido de Conciliación Nacional (PCN)	11
Partido Demócrata Cristiano (PDC)	7
PDC/Partido Demócrata (PD) coalition	3
Partido de Renovación Social Cristiano (PRSC)	3
Convergencia Democrática (CD)	2
Partido Liberal Democrático (PLD)	2
Movimiento de Unidad (MU)	1
Total	84

Political Organizations

Alianza Republicana Nacionalista (ARENA): San Salvador; f. 1981; right-wing; Leader ALFREDO CRISTIANI BURKARD.

Frente Farabundo Martí para la Liberación Nacional (FMLN): 27 Calle Poniente 1316 y 9a Avda Norte 229, San Salvador; tel. 225-2961; f. 1980 (see below), achieved legal recognition 1992; left-wing; Co-ordinator FACUNDO GUARDADO.

Movimiento Auténtico Cristiano (MAC): San Salvador; f. 1988; Leader JULIO ADOLFO REY PRENDES.

Movimiento Estable Republicano Centrista (MERECEN): San Salvador; f. 1982; centre party; Sec.-Gen. JUAN RAMÓN ROSALES Y ROSALES.

Partido Acción Democrática (AD): Apdo 124, San Salvador; f. 1981; centre-right; observer mem. of Liberal International; Leader RICARDO GONZÁLEZ CAMACHO.

Partido Acción Renovadora (PAR): San Salvador; f. 1944; advocates a more just society; Leader ERNESTO OYARBIDE.

Partido Auténtico Institucional Salvadoreño (PAISA): San Salvador; f. 1982; formerly right-wing majority of the PCN; Sec.-Gen. Dr ROBERTO ESCOBAR GARCÍA.

Partido de Conciliación Nacional (PCN): Calle Arce 1128, San Salvador; f. 1961; right-wing; Pres. CIRO ZEPEDA; Leader FRANCISCO JOSÉ GUERRERO; Sec.-Gen. RAFAEL MORÁN CASTANEDA.

Partido Demócrata (PD): San Salvador; f. 1995 by ERP, RN, MNR and a dissident faction of the PDC; centre-left.

Partido Demócrata Cristiano (PDC): 3a Calle Poniente 836, San Salvador; tel. 222-1815; fax 998-1526; f. 1960; 150,000 mems; anti-imperialist, advocates self-determination and Latin American integration; Sec.-Gen. RONALD UMAÑA.

Partido de Orientación Popular (POP): San Salvador; f. 1981; extreme right-wing.

Partido Liberal Democrático (PLD): San Salvador; f. 1994; right-wing.

Partido Popular Salvadoreño (PPS): Apdo 425, San Salvador; tel. 224-5546; fax 224-5523; f. 1966; right-wing; represents business interests; Sec.-Gen. FRANCISCO QUIÑÓNEZ AVILA.

Partido Unionista Centroamericana (PUCA): San Salvador; advocates reunification of Central America; Pres. Dr GABRIEL PILOÑA ARAÚJO.

Unión Social Cristiana (USC): f. 1997 by merger of Movimiento de Unidad, Partido de Renovación Social Cristiano and Movimiento de Solidaridad Nacional.

Other parties include Partido Centrista Salvadoreño (f. 1985; Leader TOMÁS CHAFOYA MARTÍNEZ); Partido de Empresarios, Campesinos y Obreros (ECO, Leader Dr LUIS ROLANDO LÓPEZ) and Partido Independiente Democrático (PID, f. 1985; Leader EDUARDO GARCÍA TOBAR); Partido de la Revolución Salvadoreña (Sec.-Gen. JOAQUÍN VILLALOBOS); Patria Libre (f. 1985; right-wing; Leader HUGO BARRERA); Partido Social Demócrata (PSD, f. 1987; left-wing; Sec.-Gen. MARIO RENI ROLDÁN); Partido Liberal Democrático (PLD, f. 1994; right-wing; Leader KIRIO WALDO SALGADO); Expresión Renovadora del Pueblo (ERP, f. 1994; left-wing; Leader JOAQUÍN VILLALOBOS); Resistencia Nacional (RN, f. 1994; left-wing; Leader EDUARDO SANCHO).

The following groups were active during the internal disturbances of the 1980s and early 1990s:

OPPOSITION GROUPING

Frente Democrático Revolucionario-Frente Farabundo Martí para la Liberación Nacional (FDR-FMLN): San Salvador;

f. 1980 as a left-wing opposition front to the PDC-military coalition Government; the FDR was the political wing and the FMLN was the guerrilla front; military operations were co-ordinated by the Dirección Revolucionaria Unida (DRU); Leader RUBÉN ZAMORA RIVAS; General Command (FMLN) FERMÁN CIENFUEGOS, ROBERTO ROCA, JOAQUÍN VILLALOBOS, LEONEL GONZÁLEZ, SHAFIK JORGE HANDAL; the front comprised *c.* 20 groups, of which the principal were:

Bloque Popular Revolucionario (BPR): guerrilla arm: Fuerzas Populares de Liberación (FPL; Leader 'Commander GERÓNIMO'); based in Chalatenango; First Sec. LEONEL GONZÁLEZ; Second Sec. DIMAS RODRÍGUEZ.

Frente de Acción Popular Unificado (FAPU): guerrilla arm: Fuerzas Armadas de la Resistencia Nacional (FARN); Leaders FERMÁN CIENFUEGOS, SAÚL VILLALTA.

Frente Pedro Pablo Castillo: f. 1985.

Ligas Populares del 28 de Febrero (LP-28): guerrilla arm: Ejército Revolucionario Popular (ERP); Leaders JOAQUÍN VILLALOBOS, ANA GUADALUPE MARTÍNEZ.

Movimiento Nacional Revolucionario (MNR): Blvd María Cristina 128, Urbanización La Esperanza, San Salvador; tel. 226-4194; fax 225-3166; f. 1967; Sec.-Gen. Dr VÍCTOR MANUEL VALLE.

Movimiento Obrero Revolucionario Salvado Cayetano Carpio (MOR).

Movimiento Popular Social Cristiano (MPSC): formed by dissident members of PDC; Leader RUBÉN ZAMORA RIVAS.

Partido Comunista Salvadoreño (PCS): guerrilla arm: Fuerzas Armadas de Liberación (FAL); Leader SHAFIK JORGE HANDAL; Deputy Leader AMÉRICO ARAÚJO RAMÍREZ.

Partido Revolucionario de los Trabajadores Centroamericanos (PRTC): Leaders ROBERTO ROCA, MARÍA CONCEPCIÓN DE VALLADARES (alias Commdr NIDIA DÍAZ).

Unión Democrática Nacionalista (UDN): f. 1969; Communist; Sec.-Gen. MARIO AGUINADA CARRANZA.

In November 1987 the PSD, MNR and MPSC united to form a left-wing alliance, the **Convergencia Democrática** (CD; Leader VINICIO PEÑATE). The MNR and MPSC, however, remained as members of the FDR-FMLN. In December 1994 the Expresión Renovadora del Pueblo (fmrly the Ejército Revolucionario Popular—the guerrilla arm of the LP-28) and the Resistencia Nacional (fmrly the Fuerzas Armadas de la Resistencia Nacional—the guerrilla arm of the FAPU) announced their withdrawal from the FMLN, and subsequently formed the Partido Demócrata (PD). In August 1995 the PRTC and the PCS announced their dissolution and absorption by the FMLN.

OTHER GROUPS

Partido de Liberación Nacional (PLN): political-military organization of the extreme right; the military wing was the Ejército Secreto Anti-comunista (ESA); Sec.-Gen. and C-in-C AQUILES BAIRES.

The following guerrilla groups were dissident factions of the Fuerzas Populares de Liberación (FPL):

Frente Clara Elizabeth Ramírez: f. 1983; Marxist-Leninist group.

Movimiento Laborista Cayetano Carpio: f. 1983.

There were also several right-wing guerrilla groups and 'death squads', including the Fuerza Nacionalista Roberto D'Aubuisson (FURODA), not officially linked to any of the right-wing parties.

Diplomatic Representation

EMBASSIES IN EL SALVADOR

Argentina: 79 Avda Norte 704, Col. Escalón, Apdo 384, San Salvador; tel. 224-4238; telex 20221; Ambassador: JUAN CARLOS IBÁÑEZ.

Brazil: Edif. la Centroamericana, 5°, Alameda Roosevelt 3107, San Salvador; tel. 998-2751; telex 20096; fax 779-3934; Ambassador: FRANCISCO DE LIMA E SILVA.

Chile: Pasaje Belle Vista 121, Entre 9a C.P. y 9a C.P. bis, Col. Escalón, San Salvador; tel. 223-7132; telex 20377; Ambassador: RENÉ PÉREZ NEGRETE.

China (Taiwan): 89a Avda Norte 335, Col. Escalón, Apdo 956, San Salvador; tel. 298-3464; telex 20152; Ambassador: Gen. LO YU-LUM.

Colombia: Edif. Inter-Capital, 2°, Paseo General Escalón y Calle La Ceiba, Col. Escalón, San Salvador; tel. 223-0126; telex 20247; Ambassador: Dr LUIS GUILLERMO VÉLEZ TRUJILLO.

Costa Rica: Edif. La Centroamericana, 3°, Alameda Roosevelt 3107, San Salvador; tel. 279-0303; telex 20171; fax 279-3079; Ambassador: FERNANDO JIMÉNEZ MAROTO.

Dominican Republic: San Salvador; tel. 223-6636; Ambassador: ALBERTO EMILIO DESPRADEL CABRAL.

Ecuador: 77 Avda Norte 208, Col. Escalón, San Salvador; tel. 223-1279; telex 20445; fax 779-3098; Ambassador: Dr LUIS GALLEGOS.

France: 1 Calle Poniente 3718, Col. Escalón, Apdo 474, San Salvador; tel. 223-0728; telex 20243; Ambassador: MICHÈLE DANTEC.

Germany: 7a Calle Poniente 3972 esq. 77a Avda Norte, Col. Escalón, Apdo 693, San Salvador; tel. 223-6140; telex 20149; fax 298-3368; Ambassador: RICHARD GIESEN.

Guatemala: 15 Avda Norte 135, San Salvador; tel. 221-6097; Ambassador: Brig.-Gen. LUIS FEDERICO FUENTES CORADO.

Holy See: 87a Avda Norte y 7a Calle Poniente, Col. Escalón, Apdo 01-95, San Salvador (Apostolic Nunciature); tel. 263-2931; fax 263-3010; Apostolic Nuncio: Most Rev. MANUEL MONTEIRO DE CASTRO, Titular Archbishop of Beneventum.

Honduras: 7a Calle Poniente 4326, Col. Escalón, San Salvador; tel. 223-3856; telex 20524; fax 779-0545; Ambassador: FRANCISCO ZEPEDA ANDINO.

Israel: 85 Avda Norte 619, Col. Escalón, Apdo 1776, San Salvador; tel. 298-5331; telex 20777; Ambassador: YOSEF LIVNE.

Italy: Calle la Reforma 158, Col. San Benito, Apdo 0199, San Salvador; tel. 223-7325; telex 20418; fax 778-3050; Ambassador: Dr MARIO FORESTI (also represents the interests of Somalia).

Japan: Avda La Capilla 615, Col. San Benito, San Salvador; tel. 24-4597; Chargé d'affaires: HIROYUKI KIMOTO.

Mexico: Calle Circunvalación y Pasaje 12, Col. San Benito, Apdo 432, San Salvador; tel. 243-3190; fax 243-0437; Ambassador: Lic. JOSÉ IGNACIO PIÑA.

Nicaragua: 71a Avda Norte y 1a Calle Poniente 164, Col. Escalón, San Salvador; tel. 223-7729; fax 223-7201; Ambassador: ROBERTO FERREY ECHAVERRY.

Panama: Edif. Balam Quitzé 68-1, Calle Circunvalación y 89a Avda Sur, Col. Escalón, San Salvador; tel. 223-7893; Ambassador: MIRIAM BERMÚDEZ.

Paraguay: Avda La Capilla 414, Col. San Benito, San Salvador; tel. 223-5951; Ambassador: JUAN ALBERTO LLÁNEZ.

Peru: Edif. La Centroamericana, 2°, Alameda Roosevelt 3107, Apdo 1579, San Salvador; tel. 223-0008; telex 20791; fax 223-5672; Ambassador: GUSTAVO TEIXEIRA.

Spain: 51a Avda Norte 138, entre 1a Calle Poniente y Alameda Roosevelt, San Salvador; tel. 223-7961; telex 20372; fax 998-0402; Ambassador: RICARDO PEIDRÓ CONDE.

United Kingdom: Edif. Inter Inversión, Paseo General Escalón 4828, Apdo 1591, San Salvador; tel. 298-1763; fax 298-3328; Ambassador: IAN GERKEN.

USA: Blvd Santa Elena Sur, Antiguo Cuscatlán, La Libertad; tel. 278-4444; fax 278-6011; Ambassador: ANNE W. PATTERSON.

Uruguay: Edif. Gran Plaza, 4°, Blvd del Hipódromo San Benito, San Salvador; tel. and fax 279-1626; Ambassador: Dr ENRIQUE DELGADO GENTA.

Venezuela: Calle La Mascota 319, Col. La Mascota, San Salvador; tel. 223-5809; telex 20388; Ambassador: Dra ELSA BOCCHECIAMPE.

Judicial System

Supreme Court of Justice: Centro de Gobierno José Simeón Cañas, San Salvador; tel. 771-3511; fax 771-3379; f. 1824; composed of 14 Magistrates, one of whom is its President. The Court is divided into four chambers: Constitutional Law, Civil Law, Penal Law and Litigation.

President: JOSÉ DOMINGO MÉNDEZ.

Chambers of 2nd Instance: 14 chambers composed of two Magistrates.

Courts of 1st Instance: 12 courts in all chief towns and districts.

Courts of Peace: 99 courts throughout the country.

Attorney-General: ROBERTO MENDOZA JEREZ.

Secretary-General: ERNESTO VIDAL RIVERA GUZMÁN.

Attorney-General of the Poor: Dr VICENTE MACHADO SALGADO.

Religion

Roman Catholicism is the dominant religion, but other denominations are also permitted. In 1982 there were about 200,000 Protestants. Seventh-day Adventists, Jehovah's Witnesses, the Baptist Church and the Church of Jesus Christ of Latter-day Saints (Mormons) are represented.

CHRISTIANITY

The Roman Catholic Church

El Salvador comprises one archdiocese and seven dioceses. About 86% of the country's inhabitants are adherents.

Bishops' Conference: Conferencia Episcopal de El Salvador, 15 Avda Norte 1420, Col. Layco, Apdo 1310, San Salvador; tel. 225-8997; telex 20420, fax 226-5330; f. 1974; Pres. Rev. MARCO RENÉ REVELO CONTRERAS, Bishop of Santa Ana.

Archbishop of San Salvador: Most Rev. FERNANDO SÁENZ LACALLE, Arzobispado, Urb. Isidro Menéndez, Calle San José y Avda Las Américas, Apdo 2253, San Salvador; tel. 226-0501; fax 226-4979.

The Anglican Communion

El Salvador is a missionary diocese of Province IX of the Episcopal Church in the USA.

Bishop of El Salvador: Rt Rev. MARTÍN BARHONA, 47 Avda Sur, 723 Col. Flor Blanca, Apdo 01-274, San Salvador.

The Baptist Church

Baptist Association of El Salvador: Avda Sierra Nevada 922, Col. Miramonte, Apdo 347, San Salvador; tel. 226-6287; f. 1933; Exec. Sec. Rev. CARLOS ISIDRO SÁNCHEZ.

The Press

DAILY NEWSPAPERS

San Miguel

Diario de Oriente: Avda Gerardo Barrios 406, San Miguel.

San Salvador

El Diario de Hoy: 11 Calle Oriente 271, Apdo 495, San Salvador; tel. 271-0100; fax 271-2040; f. 1936; independent; Dir ENRIQUE ALTAMIRANO MADRIZ; circ. 99,000 (weekdays), 95,000 (Sundays).

Diario Latino: 23a Avda Sur 225, Apdo 96, SanSalvador; tel. 221-3240; f. 1890; evening; Editor MIGUEL ÁNGEL PINTO; circ. 20,000.

Diario Oficial: 4a Calle Poniente 829, San Salvador; tel. 221-9101; f. 1875; Dir LUD DREIKORN LÓPEZ; circ. 2,100.

El Mundo: 2a Avda Norte 211, Apdo 368, San Salvador; tel. 771-4400; f. 1967; evening; Dir CRISTÓBAL IGLESIAS; circ. 58,032 (weekdays), 61,822 (Sundays).

La Noticia: Edif. España, Avda España 321, San Salvador; tel. 222-7906; fax 771-1650; f. 1986; evening; general information; independent; Dir CARLOS SAMAYOA MARTÍNEZ; circ. 30,000 (weekdays and Saturdays).

La Prensa Gráfica: 3a Calle Poniente 130, San Salvador; tel. 771-3333; f. 1915; general information; conservative, independent; Editor RODOLFO DUTRIZ; circ. 97,312 (weekdays), 115,564 (Sundays).

Santa Ana

Diario de Occidente: 1a Avda Sur 3, Santa Ana; tel. 441-2931; f. 1910; Editor ALEX E. MONTENEGRO; circ. 6,000.

PERIODICALS

Anaqueles: 8a Avda Norte y Calle Delgado, San Salvador; review of the National Library.

Cultura: Concultura, Ministerio de Educación, 17 Avda Sur 430, San Salvador; tel. 222-0665; fax 271-1071; quarterly; educational; Dir Dr RICARDO ROQUE BALDOVINOS.

El Salvador Filatélico: Avda España 207, Altos Vidrí Panades, San Salvador; f. 1940; publ. quarterly by the Philatelic Society of El Salvador.

Orientación: 1a Calle Poniente 3412, San Salvador; tel. 998-6838; fax 224-5099; f. 1952; Catholic weekly; Dir P. FABIAN AMAYA TORRES; circ. 8,000.

Proceso: Universidad Centroamericana, Apdo 01-575, San Salvador; tel. 224-0011; fax 273-3556; f. 1980; weekly newsletter, published by the Documentation and Information Centre of the Universidad Centroamericana José Simeón Cañas; Dir LUIS ARMANDO GONZÁLEZ.

Revista del Ateneo de El Salvador: 13a Calle Poniente, Centro de Gobierno, San Salvador; tel. 222-9686; f. 1912; 3 a year; official organ of Salvadorean Athenaeum; Pres. Lic JOSÉ OSCAR RAMÍREZ PÉREZ; Sec.-Gen. Lic. RUBÉN REGALADO SERMEÑO.

Revista Económica: Avda Bernal, Pasaje Recinos, Miramonte, San Salvador.

Revista Judicial: Centro de Gobierno, San Salvador; tel. 222-4522; organ of the Supreme Court; Dir Dr MANUEL ARRIETA GALLEGOS.

PRESS ASSOCIATIONS

Asociación de Corresponsales Extranjeros en El Salvador: Edif. Montecristo, 3°, Frente a Salvador del Mundo, comienzo del Paseo Gral Escalón, San Salvador; tel. 224-5507; Dir CRISTINA HASBÚN.

Asociación de Periodistas de El Salvador (Press Association of El Salvador): Edif. Casa del Periodista, Paseo General Escalón 4130, San Salvador; tel. 223-8943; Pres. JORGE ARMANDO CONTRERAS.

FOREIGN NEWS AGENCIES

Agencia EFE (Spain): Edif. OMSA, 2°, Of. 1, 21 Calle Poniente, San Salvador; tel. 226-0110; telex 20455; Bureau Chief CRISTINA HASBÚN DE MERINO.

Agenzia Nazionale Stampa Associata (ANSA) (Italy): Edif. 'Comercial 29', 29 Calle Poniente y 11 Avda Norte, San Salvador; tel. 226-8008; telex 20083; fax 774-5512; Bureau Chief RENÉ ALBERTO CONTRERAS.

Associated Press (AP) (USA): Hotel Camino Real, Suite 201, Blvd de Los Héroes, San Salvador; tel. 224-4885; telex 20463; Correspondent ANA LEONOR CABRERA.

Deutsche Presse-Agentur (dpa) (Germany): Avda España 225, 2°, Of. 1, Apdo 150, San Salvador; tel. 222-2640; Correspondent JORGE ARMANDO CONTRERAS.

Inter Press Service (IPS) (Italy): Apdo 05152, San Salvador; tel. 998-0760; telex 20523; Correspondent PABLO IACUB.

Reuters (United Kingdom): 7 Calle Poniente 3921, Col. Escalón, San Salvador; tel. 223-4736; telex 20634; Bureau Chief ALBERTO BARRERA.

United Press International (UPI) (USA): Calle y Pasaje Palneral, Col. Toluca, Apdo 05-185, San Salvador; tel. 225-4033; telex 30131; Correspondent (vacant).

Publishers

CENITEC (Centro de Investigaciones Tecnológicas y Científicas): 85 Avda Norte 905 y 15c Pte, Col. Escalón, San Salvador; tel. 223-7928; f. 1985; politics, economics, social sciences; Dir IVO PRÍAMO ALVARENGA.

Clásicos Roxsil, SA de CV: 4a Avda Sur 2–3, Nueva San Salvador; tel. 228-1832; fax 228-1212; f. 1976; textbooks, literature; Dir ROSA VICTORIA SERRANO DE LÓPEZ.

Editorial Delgado: Universidad 'Dr José Matías Delgado', Km 8.5, Carretera a Santa Tecla, Ciudad Merliot; tel. 278-1011; f. 1984; Dir LUCÍA SÁNCHEZ.

Editorial Universitaria: Ciudad Universitaria de El Salvador, Apdo 1703, San Salvador; tel. 226-0017; f. 1963; Dir TÍRSO CANALES.

D'TEXE (Distribuidora de Textos Escolares): Edif. C, Col., Paseo y Condominio Miralvalle, San Salvador; tel. 274-2031; f. 1985; educational; Dir JORGE A. LÓPEZ HIDALGO.

Dirección de Publicaciones e Impresos: Ministerio de Educación, 17a Avda Sur 430, San Salvador; tel. 222-0665; fax 271-1071; e-mail comunica@es.com.sv; f. 1953; educational and general; Dir MIGUEL HUEZO MIXCO.

UCA Editores: Apdo 01-575, San Salvador; tel. 273-4400; fax 273-3556; f. 1975; social science, religion, economy, literature and textbooks; Dir RODOLFO CARDENAL.

PUBLISHERS' ASSOCIATIONS

Asociación Salvadoreña de Agencias de Publicidad: Centro Profesional Presidente Loc. 33a, Col. San Benito, San Salvador; tel. 243-3535; f. 1962; Dir ANA ALICIA DE GONZÁLEZ.

Cámara Salvadoreña del Libro: 4a Avda Sur 2–3, Apdo 2296, Nueva San Salvador; tel. 228-1832; fax 228-1212; f. 1974; Pres. ROSA VICTORIA SERRANO DE LÓPEZ.

Broadcasting and Communications

TELECOMMUNICATIONS

Administración Nacional de Telecomunicaciones—ANTEL: Edif. Administrativo ANTEL, Centro de Gobierno, San Salvador; tel. 771-7171; telex 20252; fax 221-5456; f. 1963; state telecommunications company; scheduled for privatization in 1998; Pres. JUAN JOSÉ DABOUB; Man. CARLOS ANTONIO MEDINA NOVELLINO.

RADIO

Asociación Salvadoreña de Radiodifusores—ASDER: Avda Izalco, Bloco 6 No 33, Residencial San Luis, San Salvador; tel. 222-0872; fax 274-6870; f. 1965; Pres. JOSÉ ANDRÉS ROVIRA CANALES.

YSS Radio Nacional de El Salvador: Dirección General de Medios, Calle Monserrat, Plantel Ex-IVU, San Salvador; tel. 773-4170; telex 20145; non-commercial cultural station; Dir-Gen. ALFONSO PÉREZ GARCÍA.

There are 64 commercial radio stations. Radio Venceremos and Radio Farabundo Martí, operated by the former guerrilla group FMLN, were legalized in April 1992. A new station, Radio Mayavisión (operated by FMLN supporters), began broadcasting in November 1993.

TELEVISION

Canal 2, SA: Carretera Nueva San Salvador, Apdo 720, San Salvador; tel. 223-6744; telex 20443; fax 998-6565; commercial; Pres. B. ESERSKI; Gen. Man. SALVADOR I. GADALA MARÍA.

Canal 4, SA: Carretera a Nueva San Salvador, Apdo 444, San Salvador; tel. 224-4555; commercial; Pres. BORIS ESERSKI; Man. RONALD CALVO.

Canal 6, SA: Km 6, Alameda Dr Manuel Enrique Araújo, Apdo 06-1801, San Salvador; tel. 223-5122; commercial; Pres. BORIS ESERSKI; Man. Dr PEDRO LEONEL MORENO MONGE.

Canal 8 and 10 (Televisión Cultural Educativa): Avda Robert Baden Powell, Apdo 104, Nueva San Salvador; tel. 228-0499; fax 228-0973; f. 1964; government station; Dir TOMÁS PANAMEÑO.

Canal 12: Urb. Santa Elena 12, Antiguo Cuscatlán; Pres. JORGE EMILIO ZEDÁN.

Canal 19 Sistemas de Video y Audio INDESI: Final Calle Los Abetos 1, Col. San Francisco, San Salvador; Gen. Man. MARIO CAÑAS.

Canal 25 (Auvisa de El Salvador): Final Calle Libertad 100, Nueva San Salvador; commercial; Gen. Man. MANUEL BONILLA.

Finance

(cap. = capital; p.u. = paid up; res = reserves; dep. = deposits; m. = million; brs = branches; amounts in colones unless otherwise stated)

BANKING

The banking system was nationalized in March 1980. In October 1990 the Government announced plans to return the banking system to private ownership. In June 1991 the Government initiated the transfer to private ownership of six banks and seven savings and loans institutions, as part of a programme of economic reform.

Supervisory Body

Superintendencia del Sistema Financiero: 4a Calle Poniente 2223, Col. Flor Blanca, Apdo 2942, San Salvador; tel. 298-0133; fax 279-1819; Supt Lic. FRANCISCO RODOLFO BERTRÁND GALINDO.

Central Bank

Banco Central de Reserva de El Salvador: Alameda Juan Pablo II y 17 Avda Norte, Apdo 01-106, San Salvador; tel. 271-2006; telex 20088; fax 221-5128; f. 1934; nationalized Dec. 1961; sole right of note issue; cap. 800.0m., res 830.9m., dep. 9,639.5m. (Dec. 1995); Pres. JOSÉ ROBERTO ORELLANA MILLA; First Vice-Pres. MAURICIO ANTONIO GALLARDO.

Commercial and Mortgage Banks

Banco Agrícola Comercial de El Salvador: Paseo General Escalón y 69 Avda Sur 3635, Col. Escalón, San Salvador; tel. 771-2666; telex 20092; fax 223-6516; f. 1955; privately owned; cap. 30m., res 13.1m., dep. 1,113.8m. (June 1987); Pres. RODOLFO SANTOS MORALES; 8 brs.

Banco Capitalizador, SA: Alameda Roosevelt y 43 Avda Sur, Apdo 60, San Salvador; tel. 224-1039; fax 224-5516; f. 1955; cap. 24m., res 30.8m., dep. 575.6m. (Dec. 1988); Pres. OSCAR A. HINDS V.; 17 brs.

Banco de Comercio de El Salvador: Alameda Roosevelt y 43 Avda Norte, Apdo 237, San Salvador; tel. 224-3238; fax 224-0890; f. 1949; scheduled for transfer to private ownership in 1993; cap. 102m., dep. 497.6m. (June 1990); Pres. Lic. RAMÓN AVILA QUEHL; Gen. Man. Lic. MARCO TULIO MEJÍA; 23 brs.

Banco de Construcción y Ahorro SA—BANCASA: 75 Avda Sur 209, Col. Escalón, Apdo 2215, San Salvador; tel. 298-0122; fax 279-1692; f. 1964; saving and building finance; cap. 209m., dep. 4,318m. (Dec. 1996); Pres. JOSE LUIS ZABLAH; 29 brs.

Banco de Crédito Popular: 4a Calle Oriente y 2a Avda Sur, Apdo 994, San Salvador; tel. 771-1122; telex 20208; f. 1957; cap. 35m., res 1.8m., dep. 483.6m. (Dec. 1989); Pres. JUAN SAMUEL QUINTEROS; 11 brs.

Banco Cuscatlán: Edif. Pirámide Cuscatlán, La Libertad, Km 10, Carretera a Santa Tecla, San Salvador; tel. 228-7777; telex 20220; fax 229-2168; e-mail cuscatlan@sal.gbm.net; f. 1972; partially privatized in 1992; cap. 180m., res 254m., dep. 7,410m. (Dec. 1996); Pres. MAURICIO SAMAYOA; Gen. Man. ALVARO RENDEROS; 28 brs.

Banco de Desarrollo e Inversión, SA: 67a Avda Norte y Blvd San Antonio Abad, Plaza las Américas, San Salvador; tel. 223-7888; fax 224-4316; f. 1978; cap. 17m., res 7.5m., dep. 265.1m. (June 1988); Pres. Lic. GERARDO BALZARETTI KRIETE; 7 brs.

Banco Financiero: Edif. Torre Roble, Blvd Los Héroes, 1°, Apdo 1562, San Salvador; tel. 223-6066; telex 20319; f. 1977; cap. 5m., res 0.3m., dep. 86.9m. (June 1987); Pres. Lic. JOSÉ LUIS ZABLAH TOUCHÉ; 3 brs.

Banco Hipotecario: Pasaje Senda Florida Sur, Col. Escalón, Apdo 999, San Salvador; tel. 223-7713; telex 20309; fax 298-2071; f. 1934; state-owned commercial bank; cap. 104.0m., dep. 1,672.7m. (Dec. 1995); Pres. EDUARDO ENRIQUE BARRIENTOS; Gen. Man. Dr JOSÉ FELIPE LÓPEZ CUELLAR; 13 brs.

Banco Mercantil, SA: Avda Olímpica y 59 Avda Sur, Edif. La Tapachulteca, San Salvador; tel. 223-3022; fax 779-1159; f. 1978; cap. 10m., res 4.6m., dep. 187.8m. (June 1987); Pres. MAXIMINO BELLOSO; 4 brs.

Banco Salvadoreño, SA: Calle Rubén Darío 1236, Apdo 06-73, San Salvador; tel. 222-2144; telex 20382; fax 771-6135; f. 1885; privatization announced in 1992; cap. 145m., res 23.6m., dep. 2,957.9m. (Aug. 1993); Pres. Lic. FÉLIX SIMÁN J.; Vice-Pres. Ing. MOISÉS CASTRO MACEDA; 17 brs.

Public Institutions

Banco de Fomento Agropecuario: Km 10.5, Carretera al Puerto de la Libertad, Nueva San Salvador; tel. 228-3466; telex 20089; fax 228-2666; e-mail rgprieto@gbm.net; f. 1973; cap. 605.0m., dep. 872.0m. (Oct. 1997); Pres. RAÚL GARCÍA PRIETO; Gen. Man. JUAN A. MARTÍNEZ; 27 brs.

Banco Nacional de Fomento Industrial—BANAFI: 1a Calle Poniente 2310, San Salvador; tel. 224-6677; fax 224-4956; f. 1982; Pres. Lic. RENÉ ORLANDO SANTAMARÍA; Man. Lic. JUAN JOSÉ MANZANARES.

Financiera Nacional de la Vivienda (FNV): 49 Avda Sur 820, San Salvador; tel. 223-8822; fax 223-9985; national housing finance agency; f. 1963 to improve housing facilities through loan and savings associations; cap. 5.2m., res 20.8m. (June 1990); Pres. Lic. RICARDO F. J. MONTENEGRO PALOMO; Man. Lic. ADALBERTO ELÍAS CAMPOS.

Financiera Nacional de Tierras Agrícolas—FINATA: Blvd del Hipódromo 643, Col. San Benito, San Salvador; tel. 771-1230; fax 779-1231; Pres. Lic. OSCAR RENÉ DÍAZ; Gen. Man. Lic. JOSÉ MARÍA AVELAR.

Savings and Loan Associations

Asociación de Ahorro y Préstamo, SA (ATLACATL): 55 Avda Sur 221, San Salvador; tel. 779-0033; fax 224-4278; f. 1964; savings and loan association; cap. 19.2m., dep. 305.4m. (June 1987); Pres. Ing. GASTÓN DE CLAIRMONT DUEÑAS; 17 brs.

Ahorro, Préstamos e Inversiones, SA—APRISA: Edif. Metroplaza, Oficina Central, San Salvador; tel. 998-0411; fax 224-1288; f. 1977; cap. 3.1m., res 0.7m., dep. 105.8m. (June 1987); Pres. Lic. GINO ROLANDO BETTAGLIO; 9 brs.

Ahorros Metropolitanos, SA—AHORROMET: Paseo General Escalón, Contiguo a CURACAO, Salvador del Mundo, Edif. Ahorromet, San Salvador; tel. 771-0888; fax 224-2884; f. 1972; cap. 4.5m., res 0.5m., dep. 187.9m. (June 1987); Pres. Lic. JUAN FEDERICO SALAVERRIA; 12 brs.

La Central de Ahorros, SA: 43 Avda Sur, Alameda Roosevelt, San Salvador; tel. 224-4840; fax 223-3783; f. 1979; cap. 5m., dep. 60m. (June 1989); Pres. Lic. GUILLERMO ALFARO CASTILLO; 7 brs.

Crédito Inmobiliario, SA—CREDISA: Edif. CREDISA, Alameda Juan Pablo II, San Salvador; tel. 223-4111; fax 224-4378; f. 1964; cap. 9m., res 2.8m., dep. 240.2m. (June 1987); Pres. Ing. JOSÉ ALBERTO GÓMEZ; 14 brs.

Banking Associations

Federación de Asociaciones Cooperativas de Ahorro y Crédito de El Salvador, de Responsabilidad Limitada—FEDECACES DE R.L.: 23 Avda Norte y 25 Calle Poniente 1301, Col. San Jorge, Apdo 156, San Salvador; tel. 226-9014; fax 226-8925; e-mail fedecaces@itinet.net; f. 1966; Pres. MARCOS ANTONIO GONZÁLEZ ARÉVALO; Gen. Man. HÉCTOR DAVID CÓRDOVA ARTEAGA.

Federación de Cajas de Crédito—FEDECREDITO: 25a Avda Norte y 23 Calle Poniente, San Salvador; tel. 226-5191; telex 20392; fax 226-7059; f. 1943; Pres. Lic. GUILLERMO FUNES ARAUJO; Gen. Man. RODOLFO ELÍAS SEGOVIA BAIRES.

STOCK EXCHANGE

Mercado de Valores de El Salvador, SA de CV—Bolsa de Valores: Alameda Roosevelt 3107, 6°, Edif. La Centroamericana, San Salvador; tel. 298-4244; fax 223-2898; Pres. GUILLERMO HIDALGO-QUEHL.

INSURANCE

American Life Insurance Co.: Edif. Omnimotores, 2°, Km 4½, Carretera a Santa Tecla, Apdo 169, San Salvador; tel. 223-4925; telex 20627; f. 1963; Man. CARLOS F. PEREIRA.

Aseguradora Agrícola Comercial, SA: Alameda Roosevelt 3104, Apdo 1855, San Salvador; tel. 260-3344; telex 20288; fax 260-5526; f. 1973; Pres. Luis Alfredo Escalante; Gen. Man. Federico Peraza F.

Aseguradora Popular, SA: Paseo General Escalón 5338, Col. Escalón, San Salvador; tel. 998-0700; fax 224-6866; f. 1975; Exec. Pres. Dr Carlos Armando Lahúd.

Aseguradora Salvadoreña: Alameda Dr Manuel Enrique Araújo y Calle Nueva 2, Edif. Omnimotores, 2°, San Salvador; tel. 224-3816; fax 224-5990; f. 1974; Pres. José Mauricio Loucel.

Aseguradora Suiza Salvadoreña, SA: Calle la Reforma, Col. San Benito, Apdo 1490, San Salvador; tel. 298-5222; fax 298-5060; f. 1969; Pres. Mauricio M. Cohen; Gen. Man. Rodolfo Schildknecht.

Internacional de Seguros, SA: 79a Avda Norte 521, Col. Escalón, San Salvador; tel. 224-6935; fax 224-6935; f. 1958; Pres. Félix José Simán Jacir; Gen. Man. Alejandro Cabrera Rivas.

La Centro Americana, SA, Cía Salvadoreña de Seguros: Alameda Roosevelt 3107, Apdo 527, San Salvador; tel. 223-6666; fax 223-2687; f. 1915; Pres. Tomás Trigueros Alcaine; Gen. Man. Rufino Garay.

Compañía Anglo Salvadoreña de Seguros, SA: Paseo General Escalón 3848, San Salvador; tel. 224-2399; telex 20466; fax 224-4394; f. 1976; Pres. Lic. Ricardo Barrientos; Vice-Pres. Julio E. Payes.

Compañía General de Seguros, SA: Calle Loma Linda 223, Col. San Benito, Apdo 1004, San Salvador; tel. 779-2777; fax 998-2870; f. 1955; Pres. Lic. Antonio Perla Bustamente; Gen. Man. Lic. Heriberto Pérez Aguirre.

Seguros e Inversiones, SA (SISA): Alameda Dr Manuel Enrique Araújo 3530, Apdo 1350, San Salvador; tel. 998-1199; telex 20772; fax 998-2882; f. 1962; Pres. Jacobo Esteban Nasser.

Seguros Universales, SA: Paseo Escalón y 81 Avda Norte 205, Col. Escalón, San Salvador; tel. 779-3533; fax 779-1830; Pres. Dr Enrique García Prieto.

Unión y Desarrollo, SA: Calle Loma Linda 265, Col. San Benito, Apdo 92, San Salvador; tel. 298-5455; fax 298-5084; e-mail unidesa@sal.gbm.net; f. 1994 following merger of Unión de Seguros, SA and Seguros Desarrollo, SA; Exec. Pres. Francisco R. R. de Sola.

Trade and Industry

GOVERNMENT AGENCIES AND DEVELOPMENT ORGANIZATIONS

Consejo Nacional de Ciencia y Tecnología—CONACYT: Urb. Isidro Menéndez, Pasaje San Antonio 51, San Salvador; f. 1992; formulation and guidance of national policy on science and technology; Exec. Dir Carlos Federico Paredes Castillo.

Corporación de Exportadores de El Salvador—COEXPORT: Condomínios del Mediterráneo, Edif. A 23, Col. Jardines de Guadalupe, San Salvador; tel. 243-1328; telex 20235; fax 243-3159; f. 1973 to promote Salvadorean exports; Exec. Dir Lic. Silvia M. Cuéllar.

Corporación Salvadoreña de Inversiones—CORSAIN: 1a Calle Poniente, entre 43 y 45 Avda Norte, San Salvador; tel. 224-4242; telex 20257; fax 224-6877; Pres. Lic. Mario Emilio Redaelli.

Fondo de Financiamiento y Garantía para la Pequeña Empresa—FIGAPE: 9a Avda Norte 225, Apdo 1990, San Salvador; tel. 771-1994; f. 1994; government body to assist small-sized industries; Pres. Lic. Marco Tulio Guardado.

Fondo de Garantía para el Crédito Educativo—EDUCREDITO: Avda España 726, San Salvador; tel. 222-2181; f. 1973.

Fondo Social para la Vivienda (FSV): Calle Rubén Darío y 4a Calle Poniente, entre 15 y 17 Avda Sur 455, San Salvador; tel. 271-1662; fax 271-2910; f. 1973; Pres. Dr Francisco Rodolfo Bertrand Galindo.

Instituto Salvadoreño de Transformación Agraria (ISTA): Km 5½, Carretera a Santa Tecla, San Salvador; tel. 224-6000; fax 224-0259; f. 1976 to promote rural development; empowered to buy inefficiently cultivated land; Pres. José Roberto Molina Morales.

Instituto de Vivienda Urbana (IVU): Avda Don Bosco, Cento Urbano Libertad, San Salvador; tel. 225-3011; f. 1950; government housing agency, transferred to private ownership in 1991; Pres. Lic. Pedro Alberto Hernández P.

CHAMBER OF COMMERCE

Cámara de Comercio e Industria de El Salvador: 9a Avda Norte y 5a Calle Poniente, Apdo 1640, San Salvador; tel. 771-2055; telex 20753; fax 771-4461; f. 1915; 1,800 mems; Pres. Ricardo Simán; Exec. Dir Ing. Francisco Castro Funes; Gen. Man. Albero Padilla. Branch offices in San Miguel, Santa Ana and Sonsonate.

INDUSTRIAL AND TRADE ASSOCIATIONS

Asociación Cafetalera de El Salvador (ACES): 67 Avda Norte 116, Col. Escalón, San Salvador; tel. 223-3024; fax 223-7471; f. 1930; coffee growers' asscn; Pres. Ing. Eduardo E. Barrientos.

Asociación de Ganaderos de El Salvador: 1a Avda Norte 1332, San Salvador; tel. 225-7208; telex 20213; f. 1932; livestock breeders' asscn; Pres. Lic. Carlos Arturo Muyshondt.

Asociación Salvadoreña de Beneficiadores y Exportadores de Café—ABECAFE: 87a Avda Norte 720, Col. Escalón, Apdo A, San Salvador; tel. 223-3292; telex 20231; fax 223-3292; coffee producers' and exporters' asscn; Pres. Victoria Daltón de Díaz.

Asociación Salvadoreña de Industriales: Calles Roma y Liverpool, Col. Roma, Apdo 48, San Salvador; tel. 223-7788; telex 20235; fax 223-2994; f. 1958; 400 mems; manufacturers' asscn; Pres. Ing. Roberto Vilanova M.; Exec. Dir Lic. Roberto Ortiz Avalos.

Cooperativa Algodonera Salvadoreña, Ltda: 7a Avda Norte 418, Apdo 616, San Salvador; tel. 222-0399; telex 20112; fax 222-7359; f. 1940; 185 mems; cotton growers' asscn; Pres. Ulises Fernando González; Gen. Man. Lic. Manuel Rafael Arce.

Instituto Nacional del Azúcar: Paseo General Escalón y 87a Avda Norte, San Salvador; tel. 224-6044; telex 20430; fax 224-5132; national sugar institute, scheduled for privatization; Pres. Lic. Jaime Alvarez Gotán.

Instituto Nacional del Café—INCAFE: 6a Avda Sur 133, San Salvador; tel. 771-3311; telex 20138; f. 1942; national coffee institute, scheduled for privatization; Pres. Robert Suárez Suay; Gen. Man. Miguel Ángel Aguilar.

UCAFES: San Salvador; union of coffee-growing co-operatives; Pres. Francisco Alfaro Castillo.

EMPLOYERS' ORGANIZATIONS

There are several business associations, the most important of which is the Asociación Nacional de Empresa Privada (National Private Enterprise Association).

UTILITIES

Electricity

Comisión Ejecutiva Hidroeléctrica del Río Lempa (CEL): 9a Calle Poniente 950, San Salvador; tel. 271-0855; telex 20303; fax 228-1911; state energy agency dealing with electricity generation and transmission, and non-conventional energy sources; scheduled for privatization; Pres. Guillermo A. Sol.

TRADE UNIONS

Asociación de Sindicatos Independientes—ASIES (Association of Independent Trade Unions): San Salvador.

Central de Trabajadores Democráticos (CTD) (Democratic Workers' Confederation): 6 Avda Sur y 8 Calle Oriente 438, San Salvador; tel. 221-5405; Pres. Salvador Carazo.

Central de Trabajadores Salvadoreños (CTS) (Salvadorean Workers' Confederation): Calle Darío González 616, Barrio San Jacinto, San Salvador; f. 1966; Christian Democratic; 35,000 mems; Sec.-Gen. Miguel Angel Vásquez.

Confederación General de Sindicatos (CGS) (General Confederation of Unions): 3a Calle Oriente 226, San Salvador; f. 1958; admitted to ICFTU/ORIT; 27,000 mems.

Confederación General del Trabajo (CGT) (General Confederation of Workers): 2a Avda Norte 619, San Salvador; tel. 222-5980; f. 1983; 20 affiliated unions; Sec.-Gen. José Luis Grande Preza; 85,000 mems.

Coordinadora de Solidaridad de los Trabajadores (CST): San Salvador; f. 1985; conglomerate of independent left-wing trade unions.

Federación Campesina Cristiana de El Salvador-Unión de Trabajadores del Campo—FECCAS-UTC: Universidad Nacional, Apdo 4000, San Salvador; allied illegal Christian peasants' organizations.

Federación Nacional de Sindicatos de Trabajadores de El Salvador—FENASTRAS (Salvadorean Workers' National Union Federation): San Salvador; f. 1975; left-wing; 35,000 mems in 16 affiliates.

Federación Revolucionaria de Sindicatos (Revolutionary Federation of Unions): San Salvador; Sec.-Gen. Salvador Chávez Escalante.

Federación Unitaria Sindical Salvadoreña (FUSS) (United Salvadorean Union Federation): Centro de Gobierno, Apdo 2226, San Salvador; tel. and fax 225-3756; f. 1965; left-wing; Sec.-Gen. Juan Edito Genovez.

MUSYGES (United Union and Guild Movement): San Salvador; labour federation previously linked to FDR; 50,000 mems (est.).

Unión Comunal Salvadoreña (UCS) (Salvadorean Communal Union): 4a Calle Oriente 6-4, Santa Tecla, La Libertad; tel. 284-836; peasants' association; 100,000 mems; Gen. Sec. Guillermo Blanco.

Unidad Nacional de Trabajadores Salvadoreños (UNTS): San Salvador; f. 1986; largest trade union conglomerate; Leader MARCO TULIO LIMA; affiliated unions include:

Unidad Popular Democrática (UPD): San Salvador; f. 1980; led by a committee of 10; 500,000 mems.

Unión Nacional Obrera-Campesina (UNOC): San Salvador; f. 1986; centre-left labour organization; 500,000 mems.

Some unions, such as those of the taxi drivers and bus owners, are affiliated to the Federación Nacional de Empresas Pequeñas Salvadoreñas—Fenapes, the association of small businesses.

Transport

Comisión Ejecutiva Portuaria Autónoma (CEPA): Edif. Torre Roble, Blvd de Los Héroes, Apdo 2667, San Salvador; tel. 224-1133; telex 20194; fax 224-0907; f. 1952; operates and administers the ports of Acajutla (on Pacific coast) and Cutuco (on Gulf of Fonseca) and the El Salvador International Airport, as well as Ferrocarriles Nacionales de El Salvador; Pres. Ing. ARTURO ZABLAH; Gen. Man. Lic. ARTURO GERMÁN MARTÍNEZ.

RAILWAYS

There are about 674 km of railway track in the country. The main track links San Salvador with the ports of Acajutla and Cutuco and with San Jerónimo on the border with Guatemala. The International Railways of Central America run from Anguiatú on the El Salvador–Guatemala border to the Pacific ports of Acajutla and Cutuco and connect San Salvador with Guatemala City and the Guatemalan Atlantic ports of Puerto Barrios and Santo Tomás de Castilla.

A project to connect the Salvadorean and Guatemalan railway systems between Santa Ana and Santa Lucia (in Guatemala) is under consideration.

Ferrocarriles Nacionales de El Salvador—FENADESAL: Avda Peralta 903, Apdo 2292, San Salvador; tel. 271-5632; telex 20194; fax 271-5650; 562 km open; in 1975 Ferrocarril de El Salvador and the Salvadorean section of International Railways of Central America (429 km open) were merged and are administered by the Railroad Division of CEPA (see above); Gen. Man. T. O. VERGARA.

ROADS

The country's highway system is well integrated with its railway services. There are some 12,495 km of roads, including: the Pan-American Highway: 306 km; paved highways: 1,739 km; improved roads: 7,999 km; dry-weather roads: 2,692 km. A coastal highway, with interconnecting roads, was under construction in the early 1990s.

SHIPPING

The ports of Acajutla and Cutuco are administered by CEPA (see above). Services are also provided by foreign lines.

CIVIL AVIATION

AESA Aerolíneas de El Salvador, SA de CV: Avda Las Palmas 129, Col. San Benito, Apdo 1830, San Salvador; tel. 224-6166; fax 224-6588; cargo and mail service between San Salvador and Miami; Pres. E. CORNEJO LÓPEZ; Gen. Man. JOSÉ ROBERTO SANTANA.

TACA International Airlines: Edif. Caribe, 2°, Col. Escalón, San Salvador; tel. 339-9155; telex 20456; fax 223-3757; f. 1939; passenger and cargo services to Central America and the USA; Pres. FEDERICO BLOCH; Gen. Man. WILLIAM J. HANDAL.

Tourism

El Salvador was one of the centres of the ancient Mayan civilization, and the ruined temples and cities are of great interest. The volcanoes and lakes of the uplands provide magnificent scenery, while there are fine beaches along the Pacific coast. The civil war, from 1979 to 1992, severely affected the tourist industry. The number of tourist arrivals declined from 293,000 in 1978 to 82,000 in 1981, although the total rose to 314,000 in 1992 before declining to 181,000 in 1994.

Buró de Convenciones y Visitantes de la Ciudad de San Salvador: Edif. Olimpic Plaza, 73 Avda Sur 28, 2°, San Salvador; tel. 224-0819; telex 20037; fax 223-4912; f. 1973; assists in organization of national and international events; Pres. (vacant); Exec. Dir ROSY MEJÍA DE MARCHESINI.

Cámara Salvadoreña de Turismo: Hotel El Salvador, 89 Avda Norte y 11 Calle Poniente, Col. Escalón, San Salvador; tel. 223-9992; Pres. ARNOLDO JIMÉNEZ; co-ordinates:

Comité Nacional de Turismo—CONATUR: San Salvador; tel. 223-4566; comprises hotels, restaurants, tour operators, airlines and Instituto Salvadoreño de Turismo; Sec. MERCEDES MELÉNDEZ.

Feria Internacional de El Salvador—FIES: Km 6, Carretera a Santa Tecla, San Salvador; tel. 998-5644; fax 998-5388; Pres. MIGUEL ANGEL SALAVERRIA.

Instituto Salvadoreño de Turismo—ISTU (National Tourism Institute): Calle Rubén Darío 619, San Salvador; tel. 222-0960; telex 20775; fax 222-1208; f. 1950; Pres. CARLOS HIRLEMANN; Dir EDUARDO LÓPEZ RIVERA.

EQUATORIAL GUINEA

Introductory Survey

Location, Climate, Language, Religion, Flag, Capital

The Republic of Equatorial Guinea consists of the islands of Bioko (formerly Fernando Póo and subsequently renamed Macías Nguema Biyogo under the regime of President Macías), Corisco, Great Elobey, Little Elobey and Annobón (previously known also as Pagalu), and the mainland region of Río Muni (previously known also as Mbini) on the west coast of Africa. Cameroon lies to the north and Gabon to the east and south of Río Muni, while Bioko lies off shore from Cameroon and Nigeria. The small island of Annobón lies far to the south, beyond the islands of São Tomé and Príncipe. The climate is hot and humid, with average temperatures higher than 26°C (80°F). The official languages are Spanish and French. In Río Muni the Fang language is spoken, as well as those of coastal tribes such as the Combe, Balemke and Bujeba, while in Bioko the principal local language is Bubi, although pidgin English and Ibo are also widely understood. An estimated 90% of the population are adherents of the Roman Catholic Church, although traditional forms of worship are also followed. The national flag (proportions 3 by 2) has three equal horizontal stripes, of green, white and red, with a blue triangle at the hoist and the national coat of arms (a silver shield, containing a tree, with six yellow stars above and a scroll beneath) in the centre of the white stripe. The capital is Malabo (formerly Santa Isabel).

Recent History

Portugal ceded the territory to Spain in 1778. The mainland region and the islands were periodically united for administrative purposes. In July 1959 Spanish Guinea, as the combined territory was known, was divided into two provinces: Río Muni, on the African mainland, and Fernando Póo (now Bioko), with other nearby islands. From 1960 the two provinces were represented in the Spanish legislature. In December 1963 they were merged again, to form Equatorial Guinea, with a limited measure of self-government.

After 190 years of Spanish rule, independence was declared on 12 October 1968. Francisco Macías Nguema, Equatorial Guinea's first President, formed a coalition Government from all the parties represented in the new National Assembly. In March 1969 the Minister for Foreign Affairs, Atanasio Ndongo Miyone, was killed by security forces during a failed coup attempt.

In February 1970 the President outlawed all existing political parties and formed the Partido Unico Nacional (PUN), which later became the Partido Unico Nacional de los Trabajadores (PUNT). Macías appointed himself Life President in July 1972. A new Constitution, giving absolute powers to the President was adopted in July 1973. Macías controlled both radio and press and all citizens were forbidden to leave the country, although many fled during his rule. During 1975–77 there were many arrests and executions. Nigerian workers were repatriated in 1976, following reports of maltreatment and forced labour. The Macías regime maintained close relations with the Soviet bloc.

In August 1979 President Macías was overthrown in a coup led by his nephew, Lt-Col (later Brig.-Gen.) Teodoro Obiang Nguema Mbasogo, hitherto the Deputy Minister of Defence. (Obiang Nguema subsequently ceased to use his forename.) Macías was found guilty of treason, genocide, embezzlement and violation of human rights, and was executed in September. The Spanish Government, which admitted prior knowledge of the coup, was the first to recognize the new regime, and remained a major supplier of financial and technical aid. Obiang Nguema appointed civilians to the Government for the first time in December 1981. In August 1982 he was reappointed President for a further seven years, and later that month a new Constitution, which provided for an eventual return to civilian government, was approved by 95% of voters in a referendum. Equatorial Guinea held its first legislative elections for more than 19 years in August 1983, when 41 candidates were elected (unopposed) to a new House of Representatives.

The imposition, from 1979 to 1991, of a ban on organized political activity within Equatorial Guinea, and persistent allegations against Obiang Nguema's regime of human rights abuses and corruption, resulted in the development of a substantial opposition in exile. Opposition coalitions were formed in Spain and France during the 1980s. In 1991 the Coordinación Democrática de los Partidos de Oposición de Guinea Ecuatorial was established in Libreville, Gabon, and in 1997 the Consejo de Liberación Nacional, comprising political parties as well as civilian, military and religious interests opposed to the Equato-Guinean regime, was founded in Kinshasa, Democratic Republic of the Congo (see below).

During the 1980s Obiang Nguema's rule was threatened on a number of occasions. Attempted coups were reported in April 1981, May 1983 and November 1983. In January 1986 the President reinforced his control by assuming the post of Minister of Defence. An attempt in July by senior civilian and military officials to occupy the presidential palace in Malabo was quelled by loyalist forces. In the following month the alleged leader of the coup attempt, Eugenio Abeso Mondu (a former diplomat and a member of the House of Representatives), was sentenced to death and executed, while prison sentences were imposed on 12 others who had been convicted of complicity in the plot, including two government ministers and the national director of the Banque des Etats de l'Afrique Centrale. In August 1987 Obiang Nguema announced the establishment of a 'governmental party', the Partido Democrático de Guinea Ecuatorial (PDGE), while continuing to reject demands for the legalization of opposition parties. At legislative elections held in July 1988, 99.2% of voters endorsed a single list of candidates who had been nominated by the President. In September severe sentences of imprisonment were imposed on nine civilians and military officers who had been convicted of plotting to overthrow Obiang Nguema; these included the Secretary-General of the Partido del Progreso de Guinea Ecuatorial, José Luis Jones. Jones was, however, released in January 1989, prior to an official visit to Spain by Obiang Nguema.

The human rights organization Amnesty International has frequently reiterated accusations against the Equato-Guinean authorities of detaining and torturing political opponents.

In June 1989 Obiang Nguema was elected, unopposed, to the office of President, in the first presidential election to be held since independence. Voting was compulsory, and Obiang Nguema reportedly received the support of more than 99% of the electorate. Opposition groupings criticized the conduct of the election and declared the result invalid. Following his success, the President appealed to dissidents to return to Equatorial Guinea and declared an amnesty for political prisoners. However, Obiang Nguema reiterated his opposition to the establishment of a multi-party system, and in December 1990 it was reported that about 30 advocates of the introduction of a plural political system had been imprisoned.

In April 1991 opposition groups in exile in Gabon formed a coalition, the Coordinación Democrática de los Partidos de Oposición de Guinea Ecuatorial. In early August the ruling PDGE held its first national extraordinary congress, at which delegates demanded the introduction of a new democratic constitution, the legalization of other political parties and the removal of restrictions on the media. Nevertheless, in mid-August a prominent opposition leader in exile was refused a passport to travel to Equatorial Guinea in order to campaign for democracy, and shortly afterwards the Equato-Guinean Ambassador to Spain was reportedly arrested, during a return visit to Equatorial Guinea, for allegedly liaising with opposition movements. In the following month Amnesty International claimed that torture was 'accepted practice' in Equatorial Guinea, and reported the deaths in custody of at least six Equato-Guineans since 1988. Later in September the Government announced the formation of a human rights commission.

A new Constitution, containing provisions for a multi-party political system, was approved by an overwhelming majority of voters at a national referendum in November 1991. However, opposition movements rejected the Constitution, owing to the inclusion of clauses exempting the President from any judicial procedures arising from his tenure of office and prohibiting citizens who had not been continuously resident in Equatorial Guinea for 10 years from standing as election candidates, while requiring all political parties to submit an excessively large deposit (which could not be provided by funds from abroad) as a condition of registration. In addition, there was inadequate provision for the upholding of human rights. In mid-January 1992 a transitional Government was formed (comprising only members of the PDGE), and, during that month, a general amnesty was extended to all political exiles. The UN published a report in January which adversely criticized the human rights record of the Equato-Guinean authorities and some of the provisions incorporated in the new Constitution. Throughout 1992 the security forces continued to arrest members of opposition parties. In early November two Spanish businessmen were charged with plotting a coup against the Government; they were found guilty later in the month and sentenced to 12 years' imprisonment, but were pardoned on the same day. During November a new alliance of opposition organizations, the Plataforma de la Oposición Conjunta (POC), was created.

In January 1993 an electoral law was promulgated. In early February the UN released another report in which it alleged a serious disregard for human rights by the Obiang Nguema regime. During February and March the Government and several opposition organizations negotiated a national pact which established conditions for the conduct of legislative elections that were due to take place in 1993, including the freedom to organize political activity and the provision of equal access to the media for all political parties. However, the Government was soon accused of violating the pact, and further arrests and mistreatment of its political opponents were reported. During August violent clashes occurred on the island of Annobón between anti-Government demonstrators and the security forces. Accusations by the Equato-Guinean authorities that Spain had incited the unrest were strongly denied by the Spanish Government.

Multi-party legislative elections took place in November 1993. The elections were, however, boycotted by most of the parties in the POC, in protest at Obiang Nguema's refusal to review contentious clauses of the electoral law or to permit impartial international observers to inspect the electoral register. The UN declined a request by the Equato-Guinean authorities to monitor the elections, contending that correct electoral procedures were evidently being infringed. Representatives of the OAU were present and estimated that 50% of the electorate participated. The PDGE won 68 of the 80 seats in the House of Representatives, while, of the six opposition parties that presented candidates, the Convención Socialdemocrática Popular obtained six seats, the Unión Democrática y Social de Guinea Ecuatorial won five seats and the Convención Liberal Democrática secured one. Widespread electoral irregularities were alleged to have occurred and, prior to the elections, opposition politicians were reportedly subjected to intimidation by the security forces. In early December the Government announced that all party political gatherings would henceforth be subject to prior official authorization. In mid-December Silvestre Siale Bileka, hitherto Prime Minister of the interim Government,was appointed Prime Minister of the new administration. Shortly afterwards Bileka nominated a Council of Ministers, which included no opposition representatives.

In April 1994 Severo Moto Nsa, the founding leader of one of the most influential exiled opposition parties, the Partido del Progreso de Guinea Equatorial (PPGE), based in Spain, returned to Equatorial Guinea. In June, in response to pressure from international aid donors, the Government agreed to amend the controversial electoral law and to conduct a preliminary electoral census prior to the holding of local elections. In September, however, the authorities began to compile a full population census, instead of preparing for the local elections, which had been scheduled for November. The census was boycotted by opposition parties, and many people were arrested in ensuing clashes with the security forces. The local elections were postponed. In mid-October three members of the legalized opposition were arrested on their return from a political meeting in Gabon with representatives of illegal opposition parties. At the end of the month the Speaker and Deputy Speaker of the National Assembly resigned, accusing the Obiang Nguema administration of incompetence and disregard for human rights. In early November Moto Nsa alleged that the Government had sanctioned the assassination of Vicente Moto, who was his brother and a senior figure in the POC.

In early 1995 the Constitution and electoral law were amended to reduce from 10 to five the requisite number of years that election candidates must have been resident in Equatorial Guinea. In February several leading members of the PPGE, including Moto Nsa, were arrested for allegedly plotting to overthrow Obiang Nguema; in April they were found guilty by a military court and sentenced to terms of imprisonment. (Moto Nsa received a sentence of 28 years.) The convictions and sentences were widely condemned by foreign Governments and in August, following representations by President Chirac of France, Obiang Nguema unexpectedly pardoned all the convicted PPGE members.

Local elections (which had been postponed in 1994—see above) were staged, on a multi-party basis, in September 1995. According to the official results, the ruling PDGE won an overall victory, securing a majority of the votes cast in two-thirds of local administrations. Allegations by the opposition (which claimed to have obtained 62% of the votes) that serious electoral malpractice had occurred were supported by the Spanish Ambassador to Equatorial Guinea. A monitoring team of international observers agreed that some electoral irregularities had taken place.

At a presidential election held in February 1996 Obiang Nguema was returned to office, reportedly securing more than 90% of the votes cast. However, influential opposition leaders boycotted the election, in protest at alleged electoral irregularities and official intimidation. In late March Obiang Nguema appointed a new Prime Minister, Angel Serafin Seriche Dougan (hitherto a Deputy Minister) for a two-year term of office; an enlarged Council of Ministers was announced in early April. Representatives of opposition parties had declined a presidential invitation to participate in the new administration. During March the POC was dissolved.

In August 1996 Obiang Nguema awarded himself the military rank of General. In November a military court found 11 army officers guilty of conspiring to overthrow the Government; all were sentenced to terms of imprisonment.

In April 1997 representatives of the Government and of 14 opposition groupings signed a national pact, which preceded two months of negotiations. In May Moto Nsa was arrested by the Angolan authorities with a consignment of arms, which were reportedly intended for use in a planned *coup d'état* in Equatorial Guinea. Following his release in June, Moto Nsa was granted refuge in Spain; meanwhile, the PPGE was banned. During June Obiang Nguema dismissed two cabinet ministers. In August Moto Nsa and 11 others were convicted *in absentia* of treason; Moto Nsa was sentenced to 101 years' imprisonment. In September the Government protested strongly to Spain over its offer of political asylum to Moto Nsa. Shortly afterwards French was declared the second official national language. In October opposition parties (including the PPGE) and other anti-Government interests formed the Consejo de Liberación Nacional in Kinshasa, Democratic Republic of the Congo. Reports of arrests and intimidation of opposition members by the security forces continued thoughout 1997.

In January 1998 the Government resigned, having completed its two-year mandate (see above). Shortly afterwards Seriche Dougan was re-appointed as Prime Minister, and a new Council of Ministers was formed.

While Spain (the former colonial power) has traditionally been a major trading partner and aid donor, Equatorial Guinea's entry into the Customs and Economic Union of Central Africa (UDEAC, see p. 182) in 1983 represented a significant move towards a greater integration with neighbouring francophone countries. In 1985 Equatorial Guinea joined the Franc Zone (see p. 181), with financial assistance from France. In September 1988 Obiang Nguema made an official visit to France, and in November 1994 the President attended the Franco-African summit in Biarritz, France. In late 1988 Obiang Nguema postponed a visit to Spain, following allegations, in the Spanish legislature, of the misappropriation of Spanish development aid to the former colony; the visit was, however, eventually undertaken in January 1989, when the continuation of bilateral links between the two countries was confirmed and the Spanish Government agreed to cancel one-third of Equatorial Guinea's public debt to Spain. In 1991 Spain cancelled a further one-third of the bilateral debt, and in November of that year the Prime Minister of Spain made an official visit to Equatorial Guinea. From mid-1993, however, Equato-Guinean-Spanish relations deteriorated, and in January 1994 the Spanish Government withdrew one-half of its aid to Equatorial Guinea in retaliation for the expulsion in December 1993 of a Spanish diplomat whom the Equato-Guinean authorities had accused of interfering in the country's internal affairs. A tentative agreement for the gradual resumption of full Spanish assistance was made in mid-1994. In November 1994 the Equato-Guinean Government accused Spain of sponsoring the passage of a resolution adopted by the European Parliament condemning violations of human rights in Equatorial Guinea. In September 1997 the Obiang Nguema administration protested strongly to the Spanish Government over Spain's offer of political asylum to the opposition leader Severo Moto Nsa (see above). Later in that month it was announced that French would henceforth be the second national official language. During the 1990s the European Union has also withdrawn financial assistance to Equatorial Guinea, and the United Nations Development Programme has suspended some projects.

Despite Equatorial Guinea's close military links with Nigeria, relations between the two countries became strained in 1988, when evidence emerged that Equatorial Guinea, keen to attract foreign investment, had formed links with South Africa. However, reciprocal official visits in 1990 by the Equato-Guinean and Nigerian Heads of State indicated an improvement in relations between the two countries. In mid-1994, following a visit to Nigeria by Obiang Nguema, both countries agreed to cooperate in the establishment of an international committee to demarcate maritime borders in the Gulf of Guinea. Cameroon and São Tomé and Príncipe were also expected to become members. Relations with Gabon have come under strain, as the result of unresolved frontier disputes, revived by petroleum exploration activity in southern Mbini.

Government

In November 1991 a new Constitution was approved in a referendum, providing for the introduction of multi-party democracy. Executive power is vested in the President, whose seven-year term of office is renewable indefinitely. The President is immune from prosecution for offences committed before, during or after his tenure of the post. Legislative power is held by an 80-member House of Representatives, which serves for a term of five years. Both the President and the House of Representatives are directly elected by universal adult suffrage. The President appoints a Council of Ministers, headed by a Prime Minister, from among the members of the House of Representatives.

Defence

In August 1997 there were 1,100 men in the army, 120 in the navy and 100 in the air force. There was also a paramilitary force, trained by French military personnel. Military service is voluntary. The estimated defence budget for 1997 was 1,300m. francs CFA. Spain has provided military advisers and training since 1979, and military aid has also been received from the USA.

Economic Affairs

In 1995, according to estimates by the World Bank, Equatorial Guinea's gross national product (GNP), measured at average 1993–95 prices, was US $152m., equivalent to $380 per head. During 1985–93, it was estimated, GNP per head increased, in real terms, at an average annual rate of 1.5%. During 1985–95 the population increased by an annual average of 2.5%. Equatorial Guinea's gross domestic product (GDP) increased, in real terms, by an average of 4.0% annually during 1985–95. GDP grew by 7.3% in 1993, 6.8% in 1994 and 11.2% in 1995.

Agriculture (including hunting, forestry and fishing) contributed 48.3% of GDP in 1994, and employed an estimated 72.8% of the labour force in 1996. The principal cash crops are cocoa, which contributed 10.3% of export earnings in 1990, and coffee. The Government is encouraging the production of spices (vanilla, pepper and coriander) for export. The main subsistence crops are cassava and sweet potatoes. Exploitation of the country's vast forest resources (principally of okoumé and akoga timber) provided nearly 21% of export revenue in 1990. Almost all industrial fishing activity is practised by foreign fleets, notably by those of countries of the EU.

Industry (including manufacturing, construction and power) contributed 30.1% of GDP in 1994. Only 4.8% of the working population were employed in industrial activities in 1983.

Despite the existence of significant mineral resources, extractive activities were minimal during the 1980s, and the mining sector employed less than 0.2% of the working population in 1983. However, the development of onshore and offshore reserves of petroleum and of offshore deposits of natural gas has contributed significantly to Equatorial Guinea's economic growth during the 1990s. Exports of petroleum commenced in 1992, and were expected to become the primary source of foreign-exchange earnings by the late 1990s. In 1994 the petroleum sector contributed 20.6% of GDP. The existence of deposits of gold, uranium, iron ore, tantalum and manganese has also been confirmed.

The manufacturing sector contributed only 1.2% of GDP in 1994. Wood-processing constitutes the main commercial manufacturing activity.

A total of 20m. kWh of electric energy was generated in 1994. Bioko is supplied by a 3.6-MW hydroelectric installation, constructed on the Riaba river. There is a further 3.6-MW installation on the mainland. Imports of fuel products comprised 7.7% of the value of total imports in 1990.

In 1996 there was a visible trade deficit of US $116.73m., while the deficit on the current account of the balance of payments was $344.04m. In 1991 the USA (29.4%) was the principal source of imports, while Cameroon (54.8%) was the main market for exports. Other major trading partners were Liberia and Spain. In 1990 re-exported ships and boats, wood, textile fibres and waste and cocoa constituted the principal sources of export revenue, while the principal imports were ships and boats, petroleum and related products and food and live animals.

Budget estimates for 1995 envisaged a deficit of 142m. francs CFA. Equatorial Guinea's external debt was US $293.0m. at the end of 1995, of which $229.6m. was long-term public debt. In that year the cost of debt-servicing was equivalent to 2.5% of the value of exports of goods and services. The annual rate of inflation averaged –3.8% per year in 1985-93; consumer prices decreased by an annual average of 3.2% in 1991 and 7.2% in 1992. Prices increased by an annual average of 4.0% in 1993, but, following the devaluation of the currency (see below), they rose by 31.5% in the year to July 1996.

Equatorial Guinea is a member of the central African organs of the Franc Zone (see p. 181) and of the Communauté économique des états de l'Afrique centrale (CEEAC, see p. 260).

Equatorial Guinea suffered a severe economic decline under the Macías regime. The Obiang Nguema administration has achieved some success in rehabilitating and diversifying the primary sector and, during the 1990s, economic growth has been stimulated by the commencement in 1992 of petroleum exports. However, industrial activities remain minimal, the transport infrastructure and power-generating facilities are inadequate and the country is burdened by a large external debt. Meanwhile, revenue from the petroleum and timber sectors has been greatly undermined by the country's inefficient taxation system. The IMF supported an economic development programme for 1991–94, which aimed to encourage non-traditional agricultural exports, to promote the exploitation of the country's reserves of petroleum and natural gas, to reorganize the forestry sector, to attract private investment and to improve the efficiency of public-sector enterprises and the civil service. A further programme of economic reforms for 1994–96, also supported by the IMF, aimed to accelerate the diversification of the economy and envisaged the continued restructuring of the public and financial sectors. The devaluation of the CFA franc by 50% against the French franc in January 1994 was expected significantly to enhance export competitiveness and to provide the stimulus for domestic import-substitution. An immediate sharp rise in the prices of consumer goods, however, increased hardship for vulnerable sections of the population. Spain and France have traditionally been important bilateral donors.

Social Welfare

Health services are extremely limited, and diseases such as malaria, infectious hepatitis, whooping cough and dysentery are endemic.

Education

Education is officially compulsory and free for five years between the ages of six and 11 years. Primary education starts at six years of age and normally lasts for five years. Secondary education, beginning at the age of 12, spans a seven-year period, comprising a first cycle of four years and a second cycle of three years. In 1982 the total enrolment at primary and secondary schools was equivalent to 81% of the school-age population. In 1993/94 primary education was provided for 75,751 pupils in 781 schools with 1,381 teachers. More advanced education for 16,616 pupils was provided in that year, with 588 teachers. In 1990 there were 578 pupils in higher education.

Since 1979, assistance in the development of the educational system has been provided by Spain. Two higher education centres, at Bata and Malabo, are administered by the Spanish Universidad Nacional de Educación a Distancia. The French Government also provides considerable financial assistance. In 1995, according to UNESCO estimates, the average rate of adult illiteracy was 21.5% (males 16.9%; females 32.8%). In 1993 budgetary expenditure on education by the central Government amounted to 734m. francs CFA (1.8% of total expenditure).

Public Holidays

1998: 1 January (New Year's Day), 5 March (Independence Day), 10–13 April (Easter), 1 May (Labour Day), 25 May (OAU Day), 10 December (Human Rights Day), 25 December (Christmas).

1999: 1 January (New Year's Day), 5 March (Independence Day), 2–5 April (Easter), 1 May (Labour Day), 25 May (OAU Day), 10 December (Human Rights Day), 25 December (Christmas).

Weights and Measures

The metric system is in force.

Statistical Survey

Source (unless otherwise stated): Dirección Técnica de Estadística, Secretaría de Estado para el Plan de Desarrollo Económico, Malabo.

AREA AND POPULATION

Area: 28,051 sq km (10,831 sq miles): Río Muni 26,017 sq km, Bioko 2,017 sq km, Annobón 17 sq km.

Population: 246,941 (Río Muni 200,106, Bioko 44,820, Annobón 2,015) at December 1965 census; 300,000 (Río Muni 240,804, Bioko 57,190, Annobón 2,006), comprising 144,268 males and 155,732 females, at census of 4–17 July 1983. Source: Ministerio de Asuntos Exteriores, Madrid. 410,000 (UN estimate) at mid-1996.

Provinces (population, census of July 1983): Kié-Ntem 70,202, Litoral 66,370, Centro-Sur 52,393, Wele-Nzas 51,839, Bioko Norte 46,221, Bioko Sur 10,969, Annobón 2,006.

Principal towns (population at 1983 census): Malabo (capital) 15,253, Bata 24,100.

Births and Deaths (UN estimates, annual averages): Birth rate 43.8 per 1,000 in 1985–90, 43.5 in 1990–95; Death rate 19.6 per 1,000 in 1985–90, 18.0 in 1990–95. Source: UN, *World Population Prospects: The 1994 Revision*.

Expectation of life (UN estimates, years at birth, 1990–95): 48.0 (males 46.4; females 49.6) (Source: UN, *Demographic Yearbook*.)

Economically Active Population (persons aged 6 years and over, 1983 census): Agriculture, hunting, forestry and fishing 59,390; Mining and quarrying 126; Manufacturing 1,490; Electricity, gas and water 224; Construction 1,929; Trade, restaurants and hotels 3,059; Transport, storage and communications 1,752; Financing, insurance, real estate and business services 409; Community, social and personal services 8,377; Activities not adequately defined 984; Total employed 77,740 (males 47,893, females 29,847); Unemployed 24,825 (males 18,040, females 6,785); Total labour force 102,565 (males 65,933, females 36,632). Note: Figures are based on unadjusted census data, indicating a total population of 261,779. The adjusted total is 300,000. Source: International Labour Office, *Yearbook of Labour Statistics*.

AGRICULTURE, ETC.

Principal Crops (FAO estimates, '000 metric tons, 1996): Sweet potatoes 37; Cassava 49; Coconuts 8; Palm kernels 3; Bananas and plantains 17; Cocoa beans (unofficial estimate) 5; Green coffee 7. Source: FAO, *Production Yearbook*.

Livestock (FAO estimates, '000 head, year ending September 1996): Cattle 5; Pigs 5; Sheep 36; Goats 8. Source: FAO, *Production Yearbook*.

Forestry (1994): Roundwood removals (FAO estimates, '000 cu m): Fuel wood 447 (assumed to be unchanged since 1983); Sawlogs, veneer logs and logs for sleepers 267; Total 714. Source: FAO, *Yearbook of Forest Products*.

Fishing (FAO estimates, metric tons, live weight): Total catch 3,800 in 1993; 3,700 in 1994; 3,800 in 1995. Source: FAO, *Yearbook of Fishery Statistics*.

INDUSTRY

Palm oil (FAO estimates, '000 metric tons): 5.0 in 1994; 5.0 in 1995; 5.0 in 1996. Source: FAO, *Production Yearbook*.

Veneer sheets ('000 cubic metres): 7 in 1992; 8 in 1993; 8 in 1994. Source: FAO, *Yearbook of Forest Products*.

Electric energy (million kWh): 19 in 1992; 19 in 1993; 20 in 1994. Source: UN, *Industrial Commodity Statistics Yearbook*.

FINANCE

Currency and Exchange Rates: 100 centimes = 1 franc de la Coopération financière en Afrique centrale (CFA). *French Franc, Sterling and Dollar Equivalents* (30 September 1997): 1 French franc = 100 francs CFA; £1 sterling = 958.3 francs CFA; US $1 = 593.2 francs CFA; 1,000 francs CFA = £1.044 = $1.686. *Average Exchange Rate* (francs CFA per US dollar): 555.20 in 1994; 499.15 in 1995; 511.55 in 1996. *Note:* An exchange rate of 1 French franc = 50 francs CFA, established in 1948, remained in force until January 1994, when the CFA franc was devalued by 50%, with the exchange rate adjusted to 1 French franc = 100 francs CFA.

Budget (million francs CFA, 1995): *Revenue:* Petroleum sector 2,260; Taxation 8,395 (Taxes on income and profits 373; Taxes on domestic goods and services 3,223; Taxes on international trade 3,960; Other taxes 839); Other revenue 2,753; Total revenue 13,408, excl. grants from abroad (2,134). *Expenditure:* Current expenditure 14,396 (Wages and salaries 3,609; Other goods and services 5,068; Subsidies and transfers 893; Interest payments 4,826); Capital expenditure 3,628; Unclassified expenditure 2,114; Total expenditure 20,138. Source: IMF, *Equatorial Guinea—Recent Economic Developments* (December 1996).

International Reserves (US $ million at 31 December 1996): IMF special drawing rights 0.01; Foreign exchange 0.51; Total 0.52. Source: IMF, *International Financial Statistics*.

Money Supply ('000 million francs CFA at 31 December 1996): Currency outside deposit money banks 8.50; Demand deposits at deposit money banks 5.78; Total money 14.28. Source: IMF, *International Financial Statistics*.

Cost of Living (Consumer price index for Africans in Malabo; base: 1990 = 100): 96.84 in 1991; 89.90 in 1992; 93.49 in 1993. Source: IMF, *International Financial Statistics*.

Expenditure on the Gross Domestic Product (million francs CFA at current prices, 1994): Government final consumption expenditure 11,600; Private final consumption expenditure 42,700; Gross capital formation 17,300; *Total domestic expenditure* 71,600; Exports of goods and services 39,100; *Less* Imports of goods and services 39,200; *GDP in purchasers' values* 71,500; GDP at constant 1985 prices 49,237. Source: IMF, *Equatorial Guinea—Recent Economic Developments* (December 1996).

Gross Domestic Product by Economic Activity (million francs CFA at current prices, 1994): Agriculture, hunting, forestry and fishing 33,893; Petroleum sector 14,446; Manufacturing 835; Electricity, gas and water 2,452; Construction 3,391; Trade, restaurants and hotels 6,567; Transport and communications 1,452; Finance, insurance, real estate and business services 1,497; Government services 3,472; Other services 2,170; *Sub-total* 70,175; Import duties 1,330; *GDP in purchasers' values* 71,507. Source: IMF, *Equatorial Guinea—Recent Economic Developments* (December 1996).

Balance of Payments (US $ million, 1996): Exports of goods f.o.b. 175.31; Imports of goods f.o.b. –292.04; *Trade balance* –116.73; Exports of services 4.88; Imports of services –184.58; *Balance on goods and services* –296.43; Other income received 0.16; Other income paid –45.18; *Balance on goods, services and income* –341.45. Current transfers received 4.03. Current transfers paid –6.62; *Current balance* –344.04; Direct investment from abroad 376.18; Other investment liabilities –62.43; Net errors and omissions –24.82; *Overall balance* –5.46. Source: IMF, *International Financial Statistics*.

EXTERNAL TRADE

Principal Commodities (distribution by SITC, US $ '000, 1990): *Imports c.i.f.*: Food and live animals 4,340; Beverages and tobacco 3,198, (Alcoholic beverages 2,393); Crude materials (inedible) except fuels 2,589 (Crude fertilizers and crude minerals 2,102); Petroleum and petroleum products 4,738; Chemicals and related products 2,378; Basic manufactures 3,931; Machinery and transport equipment 35,880 (Road vehicles and parts 3,764, Ships, boats and floating structures 24,715); Miscellaneous manufactured articles 2,725; Total (incl. others) 61,601. *Exports f.o.b.*: Food and live animals 6,742 (Cocoa 6,372); Beverages and tobacco 3,217 (Tobacco and tobacco manufactures 2,321); Crude materials (inedible) except fuels 20,017 (Sawlogs and veneer logs 12,839, Textile fibres and waste 7,078); Machinery and transport equipment 24,574 (Ships, boats and floating structures 23,852); Total (incl. others) 61,705. Source: UN, *International Trade Statistics Yearbook*.

1995 (US $ '000): Imports c.i.f. 75,900; Exports f.o.b. 86,440. Source: IMF, *Equatorial Guinea—Recent Economic Developments* (December 1996).

Principal Trading Partners (US $'000, 1991): *Imports c.i.f.*: Cameroon 29,141; France 5,915; Italy 3,001; Liberia 22,032; Spain 11,640; USA 33,366; Total (incl. others) 113,545. *Exports f.o.b.*: Cameroon 47,212; Gabon 2,389; Netherlands 2,103; Nigeria 8,955; São Tomé and Príncipe 1,952; Spain 11,645; Total (incl. others) 86,151. Source: UN, *International Trade Statistics Yearbook*.

TRANSPORT

Shipping: *Merchant Fleet* (displacement, '000 grt at 31 December 1996): 20.6. Source: Lloyd's Register of Shipping, *World Fleet Statistics*. International Sea-borne Freight Traffic ('000 metric tons, 1990): Goods loaded 110; Goods unloaded 64. Source: UN, *Monthly Bulletin of Statistics*.

Civil Aviation (traffic on scheduled services, 1994): Passengers carried ('000) 14; Passenger-km (million) 7. Source: UN, *Statistical Yearbook*.

COMMUNICATIONS MEDIA

1994: 165,000 radio receivers in use; 4,000 television receivers in use; 3,000 main telephone lines in use; 100 telefax stations in use; 1 daily newspaper (estimated circulation 1,000); Book production 17 titles (1988). Sources: UNESCO, *Statistical Yearbook*; UN, *Statistical Yearbook*.

EDUCATION

Primary (1993/94): Schools 781; Teachers 1,381; Pupils 75,751.
Secondary and Further (1993/94): Teachers 588; Pupils 16,616.
Higher (1990/91): Teachers 58; Pupils 578.
Source: UNESCO, *Statistical Yearbook*.

Directory

The Constitution

The present Constitution was approved by a national referendum on 16 November 1991 and amended in January 1995. It provided for the introduction of multi-party democracy and for the establishment of an 80-member legislative House of Representatives. The term of office of the President is seven years, renewable on an indefinite number of occasions. The President is immune from prosecution for offences committed before, during or after his tenure of the post. The House of Representatives serves for a term of five years. Both the President and the House of Representatives are directly elected by universal adult suffrage. The President appoints a Council of Ministers, headed by a Prime Minister, from among the members of the House of Representatives.

The Government

HEAD OF STATE

President and Supreme Commander of the Armed Forces: Gen. (TEODORO) OBIANG NGUEMA MBASOGO (assumed office 25 August 1979; elected President 25 June 1989; re-elected 25 February 1996).

COUNCIL OF MINISTERS
(February 1998)

Prime Minister and Head of Government: ANGEL SERAFIN SERICHE DOUGAN.

Deputy Prime Minister and Minister for Foreign Affairs and Co-operation: MIGUEL OYONO NDONG MIFUMU.

Second Deputy Prime Minister and Minister for the Interior: DEMETRIO ELO NDONG MIFUMU.

Minister of State for Missions: ALEJANDRO EVUNA OWONO ASANGONO.

Secretary-General of the Presidency: RICARDO MANGUE OBAMA NFUBE.

Minister of State for Public Works and Urban Affairs: FRANCISCO PASCUAL EYEGUE OBAMA ASUE.

Minister of State for Planning and Economic Development, and Government Spokesman: ANTONIO FERNANDO NVE NGU.

Minister of State for Health and Social Welfare: SALOMÓN NGUEMA OWONO.

Minister of State for Labour and Social Security: CARMELO MODU AKUNE.

Minister of State for Transport and Communications: MARCELINO OYONO NTUTUMU.

Minister of Justice and Religious Affairs: RUBÉN MYE NSUE.

Minister of the Interior and Local Corporations: ANGEL ESONO ABAGA.

Minister of the Economy and Finance: BALTASAR ENGONGA EDJO.

Minister of Education, Science and Francophone Affairs: SANTIAGO NGUA NFUMU.

Minister of Industry, Commerce and Small and Medium-sized Enterprises: VIDAL DJONI BECOBA.

Minister of Mines and Energy: JUAN OLO MBA NSENG.

Minister of Agriculture, Fisheries and Animal Husbandry: CONSTANTINO EKONG NSUE.

Minister of Forestry and Environment: NGUEMA TEODORO OBIANG.

Minister of Information, Tourism and Culture: LUCAS NGUEMA ESONO.

Minister of Social Affairs and Women's Development: MARGARITA ALENE MBA.

Minister of Youth and Sports: IGNACIO MINLANE NTANG.

Minister of the Civil Service and Administrative Reforms: FERNANDO MABALE MBA.

MINISTRIES

All ministries are in Malabo.

Ministry of Agriculture: Apdo 504, Malabo.

Ministry of the Economy and Finance: Malabo; tel. (9) 31-05; fax (9) 32-05.

Ministry of Foreign Affairs and Co-operation: Malabo; tel. (9) 32-20.

Ministry of Mines and Energy: Calle 12 de Octobre s/n, Malabo; tel. (9) 35-67; fax (9) 33-53.

Legislature

CÁMARA DE REPRESENTANTES DEL PUEBLO
(House of Representatives)

Speaker: (vacant).

General Election, 21 November 1993

Party	Seats
Partido Democrático de Guinea Ecuatorial (PDGE)	68
Convención Socialdemocrática Popular (CSDP)	6
Unión Democrática y Social de Guinea Ecuatorial (UDS)	5
Convención Liberal Democrática (CLD)	1
Total	80

Political Organizations

Acción Popular (AP): Pres. MIGUEL ESONO.

Alianza Democrática Progresista (ADP): Pres. VICTORINO BOLEKIA.

Alianza Nacional para la Restauración Democrática de Guinea Ecuatorial (ANRDGE): 95 Ruperto Chapi, 28100 Madrid, Spain; tel. (1) 663-60-13; f. 1974; Sec.-Gen. LUIS ONDO AYANG.

Consejo de Liberación Nacional (COLINA): based in Kinshasa, Democratic Republic of the Congo; f. 1997; coalition of political parties and civilian, military and religious interests opposed to the Equato-Guinean Govt; includes:

Fuerza Demócrata Republicana: f. 1995; Leader FELIPE ONDO OBIANG.

Partido del Progreso de Guinea Ecuatorial (PPGE): f. 1983; Pres. SEVERO MOTO NSA.

Unión Democrática y Social de Guinea Ecuatorial (UDS): Pres. CARMELO MODÚ AKUNE.

Unión Popular (UP): f. 1992; Leader ANDRÉS MOISÉS MBA.

Convención Liberal Democrática (CLD): Pres. ALFONSO NSUE MIFUMU.

Convención Socialdemocrática Popular (CSDP): Leader SECUNDINO OYONO.

Convergencia para la Democracia Social (CPDS): Pres. SANTIAGO OBAMA; Sec.-Gen. PLÁCIDO MIKÓ ABOGO.

Coordinación Democrática de los Partidos de Oposición de Guinea Ecuatorial: based in Libreville, Gabon; f. 1991; coalition of the following groups:

Frente Democrático para la Reforma: Sec.-Gen. BIYONGO BITUNG.

Movimento Nacional para la Nueva Liberación de Guinea Ecuatorial.

Partido Republicano.

Partido de Reunificación (PR).

Unión para la Democracia y el Desarrollo Social (UDDS): f. 1990; Sec.-Gen. ANTONIO SIBACHA BUEICHEKU.

Movimento para la Autodeterminación de la Isla de Bioko (MAIB): f. 1993 by Bubi interests seeking independence of Bioko; Spokesman JOAQUÍN MAHO.

Partido de la Convergencia Social Demócrata (PCSD): Pres. BUENAVENTURA MOSUY.

Partido Democrático de Guinea Ecuatorial (PDGE): Malabo; f. 1987; sole legal party 1987–92; Chair. Gen. (TEODORO) OBIANG NGUEMA MBASOGO.

Partido Social Demócrata (PSD): Pres. BENJAMÍN BALINGA.

Partido Socialista (PS): Pres. TOMÁS MACHEBA.

Unión Democrática Nacional (UDEMA): Pres. JOSÉ MECHEBA.

Diplomatic Representation

EMBASSIES IN EQUATORIAL GUINEA

Cameroon: 37 Calle Rey Boncore, Apdo 292, Malabo; tel. and fax (9) 23-64; Ambassador: JOHN NCHOTU AKUM.

China, People's Republic: Malabo; Ambassador: XU SHAOHAI.

France: Carreterra del Aeropuerto, Apdo 326, Malabo; tel. (9) 20-05; Ambassador: GÉRARD BRUNET DE COURSSOU.

Gabon: Apdo 648, Douala, Malabo; tel. (9) 420; telex 1125; Ambassador: JEAN-BAPTISTE MBATCHI.

Korea, Democratic People's Republic: Malabo; Ambassador: RYOM THAE RYUL.

Nigeria: 4 Paseo de los Cocoteros, Apdo 78, Malabo; tel. (9) 23-86; Ambassador: JOHN SHINKAME.

Russia: Malabo; Ambassador: LEV ALEKSANDROVICH VAKHRAMEYEV.

Spain: Parque de las Avenidas de Africa, Malabo; tel. (9) 20-20; fax (9) 26-11; Ambassador: JACOBO GONZÁLEZ-ARNAO.

Judicial System

The structure of Judicial Administration was established in 1981. The Supreme Tribunal in Malabo, consisting of a President of the Supreme Tribunal, the Presidents of the three chambers (civil, criminal and administrative), and two magistrates from each chamber, is the highest court of appeal, There are Territorial High Courts in Malabo and Bata, which also sit as courts of appeal. Courts of first instance sit in Malabo and Bata, and may be convened in the other provincial capitals. Local courts may be convened when necessary.

President of the Supreme Tribunal: ALFREDO KING TOMÁS.

Religion

An estimated 90% of the population are adherents of the Roman Catholic Church. Traditional forms of worship are also followed.

CHRISTIANITY

The Roman Catholic Church

Equatorial Guinea comprises one archdiocese and two dioceses. There were an estimated 364,411 adherents in the country at 31 December 1995.

Bishops' Conference: Arzobispado, Apdo 106, Malabo; tel. (9) 24-16; f. 1984; Pres. Rt Rev. ANACLETO SIMA NGUA, Bishop of Bata.

Archbishop of Malabo: Most Rev. ILDEFONSO OBAMA OBONO, Arzobispado, Apdo 106, Malabo; tel. (9) 29-09; fax (9) 21-76.

Protestant Church

Iglesia Reformada Evangélica de Guinea Ecuatorial (Evangelical Reformed Church of Equatorial Guinea): Apdo 195, Malabo; f. 1960; c. 8,000 mems; Sec.-Gen. Rev. JAIME SIPOTO.

The Press

El Patio: Apdo 180, Malabo; tel. (9) 27-20; fax (9) 29-32; Spanish; cultural review; quarterly; publ. by Centro Cultural Hispano-Guineano; Editor DONATO NDONGO-BIDYOGO.

El Sol: 24 Calle Camerún, Apdo 944, Malabo; f. 1994; Spanish; weekly; Chief Editor NVO MBOMIO AVOMO; circ. 3,500.

Hoja Parroquial: Malabo; weekly.

La Gaceta: Malabo; f. 1996; bi-weekly.

La Verdad: Malabo; opposition monthly; publ. by the Convergencia para la Democracia Social; Editor PLÁCIDO MIKÓ ABOGO.

Voz del Pueblo: Malabo; publ. by the Partido Democrático de Guinea Ecuatorial.

FOREIGN NEWS BUREAU

Agencia EFE (Spain): 50 Calle del Presidente Nasser, Malabo; tel. (9) 31-65; Bureau Chief DONATO NDONGO-BIDYOGO.

Publisher

Centro Cultural Hispano-Guineano: Apdo 180, Malabo; tel. (9) 27-20; fax (9) 29-32.

Broadcasting and Communications

RADIO

Radio Africa and Radio East Africa: Apdo 851, Malabo; e-mail pabcomain@aol.com; commercial station; owned by Pan American Broadcasting; music and religious programmes in English.

Radio Malabo: Malabo; Spanish and French programmes.

Radio Nacional de Guinea Ecuatorial: Apdo 749, Barrio Comandachina, Bata; tel. (8) 83-82; fax (8) 20-93; and Apdo 195, 90 ave 30 de Agostó, Malabo; tel. (9) 22-60; fax (9) 20-97; govt-controlled; commercial station; programmes in Spanish, French and vernacular languages; Dir (Bata) SEBASTIÁN ELÓ ASEKO; Dir (Malabo) JUAN EYENE OPKUA NGUEMA.

TELEVISION

Televisión Nacional: Malabo; broadcasts in Spanish and French; Dir ANTONIO NKULU OYE.

Finance

(cap. = capital; p.u. = paid up; res = reserves; m. = million; br. = branch; amounts in francs CFA)

BANKING

Central Bank

Banque des Etats de l'Afrique Centrale (BEAC): Apdo 510 Malabo; tel. (9) 20–10; telex 5407; fax (9) 20–06; headquarters in Yaoundé, Cameroon; f. 1973 as the bank of issue for mem. states of the Customs and Economic Union of Central Africa (UDEAC), comprising Cameroon, the Central African Republic, Chad, the Congo, Equatorial Guinea and Gabon; cap. and res 209,766m. (April 1997); Gov. JEAN-FÉLIX MAMALEPOT; Dir in Equatorial Guinea MARTÍN-CRISANTO EBE MBA.

Commercial Banks

Banco Internacional para Africa Occidental y de la Guinea Ecuatorial: 6 Calle de Argelia, Apdo 686, Malabo; tel. (9) 28-87; telex 5403; fax (9) 27-42; f. 1986; cap. p.u. 300m. (Dec. 1993); Pres. CASTRO NVONO AKELE; Gen. Man. CHARLES SANLAVILLE; brs in Bata and Malabo.

Caisse Commune d'Epargne et d'Investissement Guinea Ecuatorial (CCEI): Malabo; f. 1995.

Development Bank

Banque de Développement des Etats de l'Afrique Centrale (see Franc Zone, p. 181).

Financial Institution

Caja Autónoma de Amortización de la Deuda Pública: Ministry of the Economy and Finance, Malabo; tel. (9) 31-05; fax (9) 32-05; management of state funds; Dir Patricio Eka Nguema.

Trade and Industry

GOVERNMENT AGENCIES

Cámaras Oficiales Agrícolas de Guinea: Bioko and Bata; purchase of cocoa and coffee from indigenous planters, who are partially grouped in co-operatives.

Empresa General de Industria y Comercio (EGISCA): Malabo; f. 1986; parastatal body jtly operated with the French Société pour l'Organisation, l'Aménagement et le Développement des Industries Alimentaires et Agricoles (SOMDIA); import-export agency.

Oficina para la Cooperación con Guinea Ecuatorial (OCGE): Malabo; f. 1981; administers bilateral aid from Spain.

DEVELOPMENT ORGANIZATION

Sociedad Anónima de Desarrollo del Comercio (SOADECO-Guinée): Malabo; f. 1986; parastatal body jtly operated with the French Société pour l'Organisation, l'Aménagement et le Développement des Industries Alimentaires et Agricoles (SOMDIA); development of commerce.

CHAMBER OF COMMERCE

Cámara de Comercio, Agrícola y Forestal de Malabo: Apdo 51, Malabo; tel. (9) 151.

INDUSTRIAL AND TRADE ASSOCIATIONS

INPROCAO: Malabo; production, marketing and distribution of cocoa.

Total Ecuatoguineana de Gestion (GE-Total): Malabo; f. 1984; 50% state-owned, 50% by CFP-Total (France); petroleum marketing and distribution; Chair. of Bd of Dirs Minister of Public Works, Housing and Town Planning.

TRADE UNIONS

A law permitting the establishment of trade unions was introduced in 1992.

Transport

RAILWAYS

There are no railways in Equatorial Guinea.

ROADS

In 1996 there were an estimated 2,880 km of roads and tracks.

Bioko: a semi-circular tarred road serves the northern part of the island from Malabo down to Batete in the west and from Malabo to Bacake Grande in the east, with a feeder road from Luba to Moka and Bahía de la Concepción.

Río Muni: a tarred road links Bata with the town of Mbini (Río Benito) in the west; another road, partly tarred, links Bata with the frontier post of Ebebiyín in the east and then continues into Gabon; other earth roads join Acurenam, Mongomo and Anisok.

SHIPPING

The main ports are Bata (general cargo and most of the country's export timber), Malabo (general), Luba (bananas, timber), Mbini and Cogo (timber).

CIVIL AVIATION

There is an international airport at Malabo. A larger international airport at Bata, constructed with Italian aid, was to be completed in the mid-1990s. The national carrier, EGA-Ecuato Guineana (which has been in liquidation since 1990), continues to provide limited regional and domestic services. During the mid-1990s scheduled services between Malabo and Madrid were being operated by IBERIA, Líneas Aéreas de España, while Cameroon Airlines (Cam-Air) carried passengers between Malabo and Douala (Cameroon) and provided air freight facilities linking Malabo with destinations in the EU and the USA. Air Gabon operates weekly services between Malabo, Bata, Douala and Libreville (Gabon). Air Afrique operates a cargo service linking Equatorial Guinea with 11 West African destinations.

EGA-Ecuato Guineana (Ecuato Guineana de Aviación): Apdo 665, Malabo; tel. (9) 23-25; fax (9) 33-13; regional and domestic passenger and cargo services.

Tourism

Few foreigners visit Equatorial Guinea, and tourism remains undeveloped.

ERITREA

Introductory Survey

Location, Climate, Language, Religion, Flag, Capital

The State of Eritrea, which has a coastline on the Red Sea extending for almost 1,000 km, is bounded to the north-west by Sudan, to the south and west by Ethiopia, and to the south-east by Djibouti. Its territory includes the Dahlak islands, a low-lying coralline archipelago off shore from Massawa. Rainfall is less than 500 mm per year in lowland areas, increasing to 1,000 mm in the highlands. The temperature gradient is similarly steep: average annual temperatures range from 17°C (63°F) in the highlands to 30°C (86°F) in Massawa. The Danakil depression in the south-east, which is more than 130 m below sea-level in places, experiences some of the highest temperatures recorded, frequently exceeding 50°C (122°F). The major language groups in Eritrea are Afar, Bilien, Hedareb, Kunama, Nara, Rashaida, Saho, Tigre and Tigrinya. English is rapidly becoming the language of business and is the medium of instruction at secondary schools and at university. Arabic is also widely spoken. The population is fairly evenly divided between Tigrinya-speaking Christians (mainly Orthodox), the traditional inhabitants of the highlands, and the Muslim communities of the western lowlands, northern highlands and east coast; there are also systems of traditional belief adhered to by a small number of the population. The national flag (proportions 2 by 1) consists of a red triangle with its base corresponding to the hoist and its apex at the centre of the fly, in which is situated, towards the hoist, an upright gold olive branch with six bunches of three leaves each, framed by a wreath of two gold olive branches; the remainder of the field is green at the top and light blue at the base. The capital is Asmara.

Recent History

Eritrea, as a political entity, first emerged following Italian occupation of the Red Sea port of Massawa and other coastal enclaves in the 1880s. Despite a strong interest in the region, the British were not opposed to Italian expansion inland as they regarded Italy as a useful counter to French influence in that area. In 1889 Italy signed the Treaty of Ucciali with the Ethiopian Emperor, Menelik, and in 1890 named its new possession 'Eritrea'. The treaty gave the Italian Government control over the colony, and the borders agreed upon therein are now the borders of modern-day Eritrea. Italian farmers were encouraged to settle on areas declared Italian Crown Land by the colonial government, covering, in particular, the fertile highland area. Italian exploitation of the colony continued until the defeat of the Axis powers by the Allied powers in East Africa during the Second World War. Between 1941 and 1952 Eritrea was under British administration. The Eritrean national identity, which was established during the Italian colonial period, was further subjugated under British rule, which was also instrumental in the neglect and decline of Eritrean industry and the continued exploitation of Eritrea's agricultural resources by Italian settler farmers. As the Allied powers and the newly-formed UN discussed the future of the former Italian colony, Ethiopian territorial claims helped to foment a more militant nationalism among the Eritrean population. In 1952 a compromise agreement was reached, largely as a result of US strategic interests and influence in the UN, whereby a federation was formed between Eritrea and Ethiopia. However, the absence of adequate provisions for the creation of federal structures allowed Ethiopia's Emperor, Haile Selassie, to succeed in reducing Eritrea's status to that of an Ethiopian province by 1962.

Resistance to the Ethiopian annexation was first organized in the late 1950s around emerging opposition groups, in particular the Eritrean Liberation Movement, founded in 1958, which was succeeded shortly afterwards by the Eritrean Liberation Front (ELF). The ELF launched an armed struggle in 1961. However, not until the mid-1970s, when a reformist group broke away from the ELF and formed the Popular Liberation Forces (which became the Eritrean People's Liberation Front—EPLF—in 1977), did the military confrontation with the Ethiopian Government begin in earnest. A major consequence of the split between the two groups was the civil war of 1972–74. After two phases of desertion from the ELF to the EPLF, firstly in 1977–78 and secondly in 1985 (following a second civil war), the ELF was left without a coherent military apparatus. However, a number of disaffected factions remained loyal to the ELF, particularly those associated with Ahmed Nasser, the leader of the ELF—Revolutionary Council (ELF—RC).

Following the 1974 revolution in Ethiopia and the assumption of power by Mengistu Haile Mariam in 1977, thousands of new recruits joined the EPLF. Even greater numbers joined after the regime launched its 'red terror' campaign in Asmara, and following its capture of smaller provincial cities such as Keren and Decamhare in 1977. The armed struggle intensified and was eventually transformed into full-scale warfare. The numerically and materially superior Ethiopian forces (armed mainly by the USSR) initially achieved significant victories over the EPLF. Following defeat in the highlands, the EPLF was forced to retreat to its stronghold in the north of Eritrea. During Ethiopia's 'red star' offensive in 1982, which aimed to destroy the Eritrean resistance, the EPLF captured sufficient quantities of heavy artillery and tanks to transform it from a guerrilla force into a regular army. From its secure base, the EPLF then launched counter-attacks throughout the late 1980s and slowly drove back the Ethiopian forces on all fronts. By 1989 the EPLF had gained control of the north and the west of the country. After the failure of US-sponsored peace talks in late 1989, the EPLF captured Massawa port and succeeded in severing a major supply-route to the Ethiopian forces, who were by now besieged in Asmara. In May 1991 units of the EPLF entered Asmara, after the Ethiopian troops had fled, and immediately established an interim EPLF administration.

Following the liberation of Asmara by the EPLF, and of Addis Ababa by the Ethiopian People's Revolutionary Democratic Front (EPRDF), a conference was convened in London, United Kingdom, in August 1991, under the chairmanship of the US Assistant Secretary of State for Africa. Representatives of the EPLF attended in a delegation separate from the EPRDF, now in control of Ethiopia and sympathetic to Eritrean national aspirations. Both the USA and the Ethiopian delegation accepted the EPLF administration as the legitimate provisional Government of Eritrea, and the EPLF agreed to hold a referendum on independence in 1993. The provisional Government, which was to administer Eritrea during the two years prior to the referendum, drew most of its members from the EPLF. The Government struggled to rehabilitate and develop Eritrea's war-torn economy and infrastructure, and to feed a population of whom 80% remained dependent on food aid. The agricultural sector had been severely disrupted by the war, and urban economic activity was almost non-existent. The Government was confronted by the additional problem of how to reintegrate some 750,000 refugees, of whom approximately 500,000 lived in Sudan, mostly at subsistence level.

The UN-supervised referendum on independence was held in April 1993; of the 1,102,410 Eritreans who voted, 99.8% endorsed national independence. The anniversary of the liberation of Asmara, 24 May, was proclaimed Independence Day, and on 28 May Eritrea formally attained international recognition. In the following month Eritrea was admitted to the Organization of African Unity (OAU). Following Eritrea's accession to independence, a four-year transitional period was declared, during which preparations were to proceed for establishing a constitutional and pluralist political system. At the apex of the transitional Government were three state institutions: the Consultative Council (the executive authority formed from the ministers, provincial administrators and heads of government authorities and commissions); the National Assembly (the legislative authority formed from the Central Committee of the EPLF with the addition of 30 members from the Provincial Assemblies and 30 individuals selected by the Central Committee); and the judiciary. One of the National Assembly's first acts was the election of a head of state. To little surprise, Issaias Afewerki, the Secretary-General of the EPLF, was elected, by a margin of 99 votes to five.

At its third congress, held in Asmara in February 1994, the EPLF debated its own dissolution and decided to transform itself into a political party, called the People's Front for Democracy and Justice (PFDJ). An 18-member Executive Committee and a 75-member Central Committee were elected; President Afewerki was elected Chairman of the latter. In March the National Assembly adopted a series of resolutions whereby the former executive body, the Consultative Council, was formally superseded by a State Council. Other measures adopted by resolutions of the Assembly included the creation of a 50-member Constitutional Commission, and the establishment of a committee charged with the reorganization of the country's administrative divisions. It was decided that the National Assembly would henceforth comprise the 75 members of the PFDJ Central Committee and 75 directly elected members. However, no mechanism was announced for their election. All but eight of the 50-member Constitutional Commission were government appointees, and there was no provision for any opposition participation in the interim system.

A draft constitution was discussed at international conventions, held by the Constitutional Commission, in July 1994 and January 1995, and more than 1,000 popular meetings took place in the first six months of 1995 to allow wider discussion of the proposed constitution. A third stage of consultation began in October, when former soldiers of the EPLF armed forces were invited to discuss the draft law. Meanwhile, in May the National Assembly approved proposals to create six administrative regions to replace the 10 regional divisions that had been in place since colonial rule. In November the Assembly approved new names for the regions, unrelated to the ethnic groups which inhabit them, and finalized details of their exact boundaries and sub-divisions.

Since the establishment of the EPLF Government, an effective ban on other political groups had been in effect. The opposition ELF claimed that many political activists remained in prison. In April 1994 26 members of the ELF—RC faction were detained in Ethiopia; other ELF—RC members were reported to have been forcibly repatriated to Eritrea. In 1994–95 there were allegations of discrimination against Jehovah's Witnesses resident in Eritrea. They did not take part in the independence referendum of 1993 and refused to recognize the state of Eritrea or to fulfil military service obligations. As a result, they were refused Eritrean citizenship and some were reportedly evicted from state-owned housing. During 1995 there were reports of anti-Government activity in several outlying areas of Eritrea. In July there were clashes in the west of the country between government troops and groups of young men who were refusing to report for national service.

In early 1997 the Government established a Constituent Assembly, comprising 527 members (150 from the National Assembly; the remainder selected from representatives of Eritreans residing abroad or elected by regional assemblies), to discuss and ratify the draft constitution. On 23 May the Constituent Assembly adopted the Constitution, authorizing 'conditional' political pluralism and instituting a presidential regime, with a President elected for a maximum of two five-year terms. The President, as Head of State, would appoint a Prime Minister and judges of the Supreme Court; his mandate could be revoked should two-thirds of the members of the National Assembly so demand. The Constituent Assembly was disbanded and a Transitional National Assembly (consisting of the 75 members of the PFDJ Central Committee, 60 members of the Constituent Assembly and 15 representatives of Eritreans residing abroad) was empowered to act as the legislature until the holding of elections to a new National Assembly. It was anticipated that legislative elections would be held in 1998. Meanwhile, in February 1997 President Afewerki carried out a wide-ranging reorganization of the State Council; notably, no public announcement was made of the changes.

External relations have proved problematic. The transitional Government has attempted to consolidate good relations with Eritrea's neighbours and to develop stronger links with the USA, China and other major powers. However, the complexity of regional relations, and of Eritrea's position therein, became evident in July 1993, when President Afewerki had to counter allegations, made during a visit to Saudi Arabia, that Israel was establishing a military presence in Eritrea. Prior to the referendum, harsh reactions had been provoked in the Arab press after Afewerki visited Israel for medical treatment. The Eritrean Government is keen to maintain good relations with its Arab neighbours (one of which, namely Saudi Arabia, had previously provided support to the ELF) but not to the detriment of what it regards as important ties with Israel.

Relations between the transitional Government and Sudan, which had supported the EPLF during the war, deteriorated in December 1993, following an incursion by members of an Islamist group, the Eritrean Islamic Jihad (EIJ), into Eritrea from Sudan. In a clash with Eritrean forces, all the members of the group, and an Eritrean commander, were killed. In response to the incident, President Afewerki stressed the links between the EIJ and the Sudanese National Islamic Front, led by Dr Hassan at-Turabi, implying that the latter had prior knowledge of the incursion. However, following a swift denial by the Sudanese Government that it would ever interfere in the affairs of neighbouring states, Afewerki reaffirmed his support for the Sudanese authorities and his commitment to improving bilateral relations. In August 1993 it was reported that the EIJ had split between its political faction, led by Sheikh Mohamed Arafa, and a military wing.

In August 1994 Eritrea and Sudan signed an agreement concerning borders, security and the repatriation of refugees, and in October Eritrea, Sudan and the UN High Commissioner for Refugees issued a joint statement giving details of a repatriation programme for Eritrean refugees currently in Sudan. The repatriation programme began in November. By June 1995 some 24,000 refugees had returned to Eritrea, but an estimated 100,000 remained in Sudan. A further phase in the repatriation process began in October.

Relations between Eritrea and Sudan deteriorated in November 1994, when the Eritrean authorities accused Sudan of training 400 terrorists since August. Sudan accused Eritrea of training some 3,000 Sudanese rebels in camps within Eritrea. In December Eritrea severed diplomatic relations with Sudan. Further destabilization was provoked in early 1995 by attacks and infiltration in Barka Province by commandos of the military wing of the EIJ. The Eritrean authorities subsequently claimed to have identified six training camps on the Sudanese side of the border, and also alleged that large numbers of Eritrean refugees in Sudan had been arrested by Sudanese security forces. Sudan responded by proposing Eritrea's suspension from the Intergovernmental Authority on Drought and Development (IGADD, now the Intergovernmental Authority on Development—IGAD, see p. 261), which had been attempting to mediate in Sudan's civil war. The Sudanese Government protested strongly against Eritrea's growing support for the Sudanese opposition grouping, the National Democratic Alliance, which held conferences in Asmara in December 1994, June 1995 and January 1996. In February 1996 Eritrea granted Sudanese opposition leaders permission to use Sudan's embassy in Asmara as their headquarters; limited radio transmissions to Sudan were also allowed. The EIJ claimed responsibility for several attacks on Eritrean government vehicles in April. In January 1997 Sudan accused Eritrean troops of launching an attack on Sudanese forces in the frontier region, resulting in numerous casualties. In May Sudan closed its border with Eritrea, apparently fearing an imminent Eritrean attack. Meanwhile, Eritrean security forces announced that they had foiled a plot by the Sudanese Government to assassinate President Afewerki in that month. Eritrea subsequently protested against alleged repeated violations of its airspace by Sudanese aircraft.

In November 1995 there were reports that Eritrean troops had attempted to land on the Red Sea island of Greater Hanish, one of three islands (the others being Lesser Hanish and Zuqar) claimed by both Eritrea and Yemen. The attempted invasion had apparently been prompted by Yemen's announced intention to develop Greater Hanish as a tourist resort, and its subsequent refusal to comply with an Eritrean demand that the island be evacuated. The disputed islands had been used by Eritrea (with apparent Yemeni approval) during its struggle for independence from Ethiopia. Yemen had subsequently resumed its claims to the islands, because of both their strategic importance (located close to a principal shipping lane) and the possibility of discovering lucrative petroleum reserves in their surrounding waters. Negotiations in Eritrea and Yemen failed to defuse the crisis, and in mid-December fighting broke out between the two sides, resulting in the deaths of six Eritrean and three Yemeni soldiers. Two days later Eritrea and Yemen agreed to a cease-fire, but fighting was renewed on the following day, and Eritrean forces succeeded in occupying Greater Hanish. The cease-fire was adhered to thenceforth, and some 180 Yemeni soldiers (captured during the fighting) were released at the end of the month. Attempts by the Ethiopian and Egyptian Governments to broker an agreement between the two sides proved unsuccessful. In late January 1996 France assumed the mediatory role and in

May representatives of Eritrea and Yemen signed an arbitration accord in Paris, France, whereby the two sides agreed to submit the dispute to an international tribunal. France subsequently undertook to observe and supervise military movements in the area around the disputed islands. In August, despite the accord, Eritrean troops occupied Lesser Hanish; however, later in the month Eritrea withdrew its soldiers after mediation by France and a UN Security Council edict to evacuate the island forthwith. In October Eritrea and Yemen confirmed that they would submit the dispute to an international tribunal, based in the United Kingdom. The two countries agreed to abide by the court's rulings on the territorial sovereignty of the disputed region, and on the demarcation of the maritime boundaries.

In November 1995 Eritrea and Djibouti pledged to enhance bilateral co-operation, following a meeting between Eritrea's Minister of Foreign Affairs, Petros Solomon, and Djibouti's President Gouled. However, relations between the two countries were strained in April 1996 when Gouled reportedly rejected a map (produced by Italy in 1935) submitted by Solomon, which apparently indicated that a 20-km strip of land currently claimed by Djibouti was, in fact, Eritrean territory. Meanwhile, Eritrea denied reports of an attempted occupation of a border post in Djibouti (within the disputed territory) by Eritrean troops.

In late September 1993 the first meeting of the Ethiopian-Eritrean joint ministerial commission was held in Asmara, during which agreement was reached on measures to allow the free movement of nationals between each country, and on co-operation regarding foreign affairs and economic policy. Meetings held between President Afewerki and the Ethiopian President, Meles Zenawi, in December underlined the good relations prevailing between the two Governments and their efforts to co-ordinate policy with regard to Somalia. In June the OAU had appointed Afewerki to work on behalf of Africa towards solving the Somalia problem, an appointment supported by the UN Security Council and other member states of the UN. Relations between Eritrea and Ethiopia were consolidated further by the signing of a bilateral extradition treaty in November 1996.

Government

In May 1991 the Eritrean People's Liberation Front (EPLF, restyled as the People's Front for Democracy and Justice—PFDJ—in February 1994) established a provisional Government to administer Eritrea, pending the holding of a national referendum on the issue of independence. The EPLF did not invite other organizations to participate, although it promised that free elections would be held following the referendum. The referendum was held in April 1993, and Eritrea was proclaimed an independent state in the following month. A transitional Government was established, at the apex of which were three state institutions: the Consultative Council (the executive authority formed from the ministers, provincial administrators and heads of government authorities and commissions); the National Assembly (the legislative authority comprising the Central Committee of the EPLF, 30 additional members from the Provincial Assemblies and 30 individuals selected by the Central Committee); and the judiciary. In March 1994 the Consultative Council was superseded by a State Council. At independence a four-year transitional period was declared, during which preparations were to proceed for the establishment of a constitutional and pluralist political system. Meanwhile, in March 1994 the National Assembly voted to alter its composition: it would thenceforth comprise the 75 members of the PFDJ Central Committee and 75 directly elected members. In May 1997, following the adoption of the Constitution, the Constituent Assembly empowered a Transitional National Assembly (comprising the 75 members of the PFDJ Central Committee, 60 members of the Constituent Assembly and 15 representatives of Eritreans residing abroad) to act as the legislature until elections were held for a new National Assembly. Elections to the National Assembly were scheduled to be held in 1998.

Defence

In August 1997 Eritrea's armed forces were estimated to number 46,000 (compared with a total of some 96,000 prior to the demobilization programme, which began in 1993). Following independence, the Eritrean authorities assumed control of the Ethiopian navy, based in the ports of Massawa and Assab. National service is compulsory for all Eritrean citizens between 18 and 40 years of age (with certain exceptions), for a two-year period, including six months of military training. The defence budget for 1997 was estimated at US $80m.

Economic Affairs

There is little statistical information available on the Eritrean economy. However, according to estimates by the IMF, Eritrea's gross domestic product (GDP) was 3,872.7m. birr in 1995, with a real growth rate of 3.0%. In 1996 GDP was estimated to be 4,253.7m. birr, with a real growth rate of 6.8%. It is estimated that Eritrea is one of the poorest countries in Africa, with an annual income of between US $75 and $150 per head. Although Eritrea has the distinction of being one of the very few non-debtor states in Africa, many of its people are without even a basic subsistence income; at the end of the war in 1991 it was estimated that more than 85% of the population were surviving on international relief. In 1993 it was estimated that it would cost some $3,000m. to begin the reconstruction of the economy and infrastructure.

By far the most important sector of the economy is agriculture, which, despite a reduction in food production of roughly 40% between 1980 and 1990, still sustains 90% of the population. In 1996 agricultural production (including forestry and fishing) accounted for an estimated 9.8% of GDP. In that year the sector employed an estimated 78.8% of the working population. Most sedentary agriculture is practised in the highlands, where rainfall is sufficient to cultivate the main crops: teff (an indigenous grain), maize, wheat, sorghum and millet. In 1992, which was described as a satisfactory year in agricultural terms, some 315,000 ha of land were cultivated, and the harvest was sufficient to satisfy an estimated 54% of Eritrea's food requirements. The 1994 harvest was considerably higher than in the previous few years, owing to high levels of rainfall and an extensive government programme of rehabilitation of communications and irrigation systems. Crop production declined in 1995 (despite good rainfall), owing to a severe locust infestation.

As a result of serious environmental degradation (caused directly and indirectly by the war), water scarcity and unreliable rainfall, projects have been undertaken to build water reservoirs and small dams, while badly eroded hillsides have been terraced and new trees planted in order to prevent soil erosion. Since 1994 several international organizations have granted loans for the development of the agricultural sector.

Fishing of sardines, anchovies, tuna, shark and mackerel is practised in the Red Sea. Although fishing activity is on a very small scale, the total catch has increased considerably in recent years, amounting to 3,826 metric tons in 1995. According to the UN, sustainable yields of as much as 70,000 tons per year may be possible. In 1994 the China State Construction and Engineering Co was awarded a contract to construct a new fishery centre in Massawa port, as part of a US $5m.-scheme, funded by the UN Development Programme, to develop fishery projects for Eritrea. Italian and Saudi Arabian companies also promised substantial investments in the fisheries sector.

Eritrea's industrial base traditionally centred on the production of glass, cement, footwear and canned goods, but most industrial enterprises were badly damaged during the war. In 1996 industrial production (comprising mining, manufacturing, construction and utilities) accounted for an estimated 27.4% of GDP. Although some of the 42 public-sector factories—producing textiles, footwear, beverages and other light industrial goods—were operating in 1991, they were doing so at only one-third of capacity. By 1995 production had increased considerably, mostly as a result of substantial government aid. The Government has calculated that the cost of industrial recovery would be US $20m. for the private sector and $66m. for the state sector.

The manufacturing sector provided an estimated 15.0% of GDP in 1996. Imported petroleum is usually processed at the Assab refinery, whose entire output of petroleum products is delivered to Ethiopia. However, the Assab refinery temporarily ceased operations in mid-1997. Eritrea purchases its own petroleum requirements from Ethiopia under a quota arrangement.

Eritrea's mineral resources are believed to be of significant potential value, although in 1996 mining and quarrying accounted for less than 0.1% of GDP. Of particular importance, in view of Eritrea's acute energy shortage, is the possibility of large reserves of petroleum and natural gas beneath the Red Sea. Production-sharing agreements for the exploration of petroleum and gas were signed with the Anadarko Petroleum Corpn of the USA in 1995 and 1997. The exploitation of gold was expected to resume in 1998. Other mineral resources include potash, zinc, magnesium, copper, iron ore and marble. Gold-bearing seams exist in many of the igneous rocks forming the highlands of Eritrea. New legislation on mining, adopted in

1995, declared all mineral resources to be state assets, but recognized an extensive role for private investors in their exploitation.

Most electric energy is provided by four thermal power stations, largely dependent on fuel imported from Ethiopia. However, electricity is provided to only some 10% of the population, the remainder relying on fuelwood and animal products. In 1994 the Kuwait Fund for Arab Economic Development allocated US $158m. for improvements in electricity production and distribution.

The services sector contributed an estimated 62.8% of GDP in 1996. The dominant services are trade, transport and public administration.

In 1996, according to estimates by the IMF, Eritrea recorded a trade deficit of US $418m., while there was a deficit of $49m. on the current account of the balance of payments. In 1996 the principal sources of non-petroleum imports were Saudi Arabia (accounting for 15.2% of the total) and Italy (14.0%). Exports in that year were mostly to Ethiopia (65.8%) and Sudan (9.9%). The principal exports to these countries were manufactured articles, crude materials, and food and live animals. The main non-petroleum imports were machinery and transport equipment (35.6% of the total), basic manufactures, and food and live animals.

In 1996 it was estimated that Eritrea's budget deficit reached 823.0m. birr, equivalent to some 19.3% of GDP. There are no overall price indices for Eritrea, but statistics for Asmara showed that prices rose by 3.4% in the year to December 1996, compared with 10.9% in the previous 12 months. Unemployment and underemployment are estimated to affect as many as 50% of the labour force.

In May 1993 Eritrea was admitted to the group of African, Caribbean and Pacific (ACP) countries party to the Lomé Convention (see p. 178). Eritrea became a member of the IMF in July 1994.

Since Eritrea achieved independence, the establishment of a strong market-based economy has been a government priority. In 1993 the authorities adopted a two-year Recovery and Rehabilitation Programme (funded by a series of loans on concessionary terms) to address the extensive economic problems generated by years of war and infrastructural neglect. Donor assistance and remittances from expatriate Eritreans accelerated the recovery process. Emphasis has been placed on improving agricultural productivity, promoting export-orientated industries, developing financial and tourism services, and restructuring the public administration. In addition, considerable government expenditure has been allocated to financing the demobilization and reintegration of ex-combatants, and the resettlement of refugees. (The cost of demobilizing ex-combatants during 1993–96 totalled some 310m. birr.) Significant progress has been made in attracting domestic and foreign investment, increasing receipts from exports, reforming taxation policy and improving revenue administration. However, during 1995 and 1996 the budget deficit rose sharply, primarily as a result of extraordinary capital expenditure (notably on rehabilitation, demobilization and reconstruction programmes). An increase in revenue and external grants, together with a decline in total expenditure, was expected to reduce the deficit significantly in 1997. Meanwhile, in November 1997 the Government introduced the nakfa as the national currency (Eritrea had retained the Ethiopian birr as its monetary unit since independence), initially at par with the birr. Priorities for the late 1990s included completing the privatization programme and civil service reforms, and addressing the problems of high unemployment, the country's dependence on food aid, and the severe housing shortage.

Social Welfare

One of the major problems facing the Government since the end of the war has been the need to occupy thousands of EPLF fighters. The costs of demobilizing and maintaining ex-combatants fall within the Government's defence budget, accounting for some 0.5% of total government expenditure in 1996. Government expenditure on health in that year was estimated at 143.7m. birr (5.3% of total spending).

In the early 1990s the infant mortality rate was estimated to be 135 per 1,000 live births, average life expectancy at birth was 46 years, and the population per physician was 48,000. By mid-1994, however, there were 17 hospitals, 32 health centres and 120 health stations under the administration of the Government (compared with eight, four and 45, respectively, in 1991). An estimated 60,000 children have been left crippled by the war, and another 45,000 orphaned. The overall rate of adult illiteracy in Eritrea is estimated to be 80% (among demobilized women fighters the rate is believed to be as high as 95%).

Education

Education is provided free of charge in government schools and at the University of Asmara. There are also some fee-paying private schools. Education is officially compulsory for children between seven and 13 years of age. Primary education begins at the age of seven and lasts for five years. Secondary education, beginning at 12 years of age, lasts for as much as six years, comprising a first cycle of two years and a second of four years. In 1994 the total enrolment at primary and secondary schools was equivalent to 32% of the school-age population (37% of boys; 28% of girls). In that year primary enrolment included 27% of children in the relevant age-group (males 28%; females 25%), while the comparable ratio for secondary enrolment was only 12% (males 13%; females 11%). Government expenditure on education and training in 1996 was estimated at 120m. birr (4.4% of total spending). By mid-1994 Eritrea had about 600 schools, almost three times as many as in 1991. In 1994 there were 3,081 students enrolled at the University of Asmara or at equivalent level institutions.

Public Holidays

1998: 1 January (New Year's Day), 6 January (Epiphany), 30 January* (Id al-Fitr, end of Ramadan), 8 April* (Id al-Adha/Arafat), 24 May (Independence Day), 20 June (Martyrs' Day), 1 September (anniversary of the start of the armed struggle), 25 December (Christmas).

1999: 1 January (New Year's Day), 6 January (Epiphany), 19 January* (Id al-Fitr, end of Ramadan), 28 March* (Id al-Adha/Arafat), 24 May (Independence Day), 20 June (Martyrs' Day), 1 September (anniversary of the start of the armed struggle), 25 December (Christmas).

* These holidays are dependent on the Islamic lunar calendar and may vary by one or two days from the dates given.

Weights and Measures

The metric system is in force.

Statistical Survey

Area and Population

AREA, POPULATION AND DENSITY*

Area (sq km)	121,144†
Population (census results)	
9 May 1984	
Males	1,374,452
Females	1,373,852
Total	2,748,304
Population (official estimates at mid-year)	
1989	3,239,400
1990	3,329,600
1991	3,435,500
Density (per sq km) at mid-1991	28.4

* Including the Assab district.
† 46,774 sq miles.

Note: In 1993 the domestic population was estimated to be about 2m., based on the total of 1.2m. people who registered to vote in the April 1993 referendum, 860,000 of whom lived in Eritrea.

PRINCIPAL TOWN (estimated population at mid-1990)

Asmara (capital) . . . 358,100

Source: UN, *Demographic Yearbook*.

BIRTHS AND DEATHS (UN estimates, annual averages)

	1980–85	1985–90	1990–95
Birth rate (per 1,000)	45.2	44.6	43.0
Death rate (per 1,000)	20.3	17.0	15.2

Expectation of life (UN estimates, years at birth, 1990–95): 50.4 (males 48.9; females 52.1).

Source: UN, *World Population Prospects: The 1994 Revision*.

Agriculture

PRINCIPAL CROPS ('000 metric tons)

	1994	1995	1996
Wheat	18	16*	17†
Barley	41	29*	35†
Maize	22	8*	10†
Millet	73	30†	35†
Sorghum	127	68*	80†
Potatoes†	39	39	40
Other roots and tubers†	70	70	70
Pulses	38	45†	45†
Groundnuts (in shell)†	—	1	1
Sesame seed	7	7†	7†
Linseed†	3	3	3
Vegetables†	34	35	35
Fruits and berries†	5	5	5

* Unofficial figure. † FAO estimate(s).

Source: FAO, *Production Yearbook*.

LIVESTOCK ('000 head, year ending September)

	1994	1995	1996
Cattle	1,290*	1,312*	1,320†
Sheep†	1,520	1,530	1,530
Goats†	1,400	1,400	1,400
Camels†	69	69	69

Poultry† (million): 4 in 1994; 4 in 1995; 4 in 1996.

* Unofficial figure.
† FAO estimate(s).

Source: FAO, *Production Yearbook*.

LIVESTOCK PRODUCTS (FAO estimates, '000 metric tons)

	1994	1995	1996
Beef and veal	10	10	10
Mutton and lamb	5	5	5
Goat meat	5	5	5
Poultry meat	6	6	6
Cows' milk	30	31	31
Goats' milk	7	7	7
Sheep's milk	4	4	4
Hen eggs	6	6	6
Wool: greasy	1	1	1
Cattle hides	2	2	2
Sheepskins	1	1	1
Goatskins	1	1	1

Source: FAO, *Production Yearbook*.

Fishing

(metric tons, live weight)

	1993	1994	1995
Inland waters	1	1	1
Indian Ocean	416	3,017	3,825
Total catch	417	3,018	3,826

Source: FAO, *Yearbook of Fishery Statistics*.

Total catch (metric tons, live weight): 3,272 in 1996 (Source: IMF, *Eritrea—Selected Issues* (October 1997)).

Finance

CURRENCY AND EXCHANGE RATES

Monetary Units

100 cents = 1 birr.

Sterling and Dollar Equivalents (30 September 1997)

£1 sterling = 10.998 birr;
US $1 = 6.808 birr;
1,000 birr = £90.93 = $146.89.

Note: Following its secession from Ethiopia in May 1993, Eritrea retained the Ethiopian currency. An exchange rate of US $1 = 5.000 birr was introduced in October 1992 and remained in force until April 1994, when it was adjusted to $1 = 5.130 birr. Further adjustments were made subsequently. In addition to the official exchange rate, the Bank of Eritrea applied a marginal auction rate (determined at fortnightly auctions of foreign exchange, conducted by the National Bank of Ethiopia) to aid-funded imports and to most transactions in services. A more depreciated preferential rate applied to remittances of foreign exchange by Eritreans abroad, to proceeds from exports and to most payments for imports. In November 1997 the Government introduced a separate national currency, the nakfa, replacing (and initially at par with) the Ethiopian birr.

BUDGET (million birr)

Revenue*	1994	1995	1996†
Tax revenue	657.5	715.6	830.4
Direct taxes	315.8	339.7	380.0
Taxes on personal income	79.1	74.2	113.6
Taxes on business profits	160.7	185.0	230.7
Rehabilitation tax	73.0	73.2	23.3
Domestic sales tax (incl. stamp duties)	142.8	151.0	180.7
Import duties and taxes	187.1	224.9	269.7
Export tax	11.8	—	—
Port fees and charges	152.9	233.5	281.9
Other current revenue	180.5	396.1	277.6
Capital revenue	35.6	—	—
Total	1,026.5	1,345.2	1,389.9

Expenditure	1994	1995	1996†
Current expenditure	1,551.8	2,131.3	1,883.3
General services	635.9	1,090.3	1,233.1
Internal affairs	38.0	110.7	74.7
Regional administration	32.7	48.6	40.6
Foreign affairs	54.0	71.5	77.1
Defence‡	438.7	770.5	968.1
Economic services	185.0	235.1	186.4
Agriculture and natural resources	18.0	30.1	15.4
Construction and urban development	57.7	88.5	61.8
Transport and communications	98.5	97.6	85.4
Social services	135.4	226.9	188.0
Education and training	64.9	97.6	70.7
Health	35.1	75.3	56.0
Demobilization of ex-combatants	153.6	41.8	14.0
Capital expenditure	453.9	548.7	838.2
General services	17.3	54.4	163.9
Economic development	339.4	410.4	471.4
Agriculture and natural resources	130.8	272.5	256.1
Trade, industry and tourism	69.7	25.1	35.0
Construction, transport and communications	55.4	93.8	73.6
Social development	73.4	83.9	202.9
Education	9.3	15.5	49.3
Health	13.5	35.5	87.7
Total	2,005.7	2,680.0	2,721.5

* Excluding grants received (million birr): 626.0 (current 456.3, capital 169.7) in 1994; 491.0 (current 170.6, capital 320.4) in 1995; 508.6 (provisional) in 1996 (current 194.6, capital 314.0).

† Provisional figures.

‡ Including some demobilization costs.

Source: IMF, *Eritrea—Selected Issues* (October 1997).

MONEY SUPPLY (million birr at 31 December)

	1994	1995	1996
Demand deposits at banks	1,258.4	1,295.8	1,670.9

Source: IMF, *Eritrea—Selected Issues* (October 1997).

COST OF LIVING*
(price index for Asmara at December; base: January 1992 = 100)

	1994	1995	1996
All items	127.4	141.3	146.1

* The index has been constructed using estimated weights for various categories of commodity prices, compiled by the Ministry of Trade and Industry.

Source: IMF, *Eritrea—Selected Issues* (October 1997).

NATIONAL ACCOUNTS (estimates, million birr at current prices)

Gross Domestic Product by Economic Activity

	1994	1995	1996
Agriculture, forestry and fishing	489.1	390.9	371.7
Mining and quarrying	1.5	2.1	3.6
Manufacturing*	372.7	501.9	571.4
Electricity and water	39.0	52.5	56.2
Construction	166.0	235.6	412.3
Wholesale and retail trade	857.5	921.9	1,050.2
Transport and communications	416.1	453.4	475.3
Financial services	39.8	57.8	68.1
Dwellings and domestic services	65.3	79.0	95.6
Public administration and services	550.5	758.8	648.3
Other services	41.7	43.0	50.5
GDP at factor cost	3,039.1	3,496.8	3,803.3
Indirect taxes, *less* subsidies	341.7	375.9	450.4
GDP in purchasers' values	3,380.9	3,872.7	4,253.7

* Including handicrafts and small-scale industry.

Source: IMF, *Eritrea—Selected Issues* (October 1997).

BALANCE OF PAYMENTS (US $ million)

	1994	1995	1996*
Exports of goods f.o.b.	64.5	80.6	95.3
Imports of goods c.i.f.	–395.9	–403.8	–513.7
Trade balance	–331.4	–323.2	–418.5
Exports of services	79.8	90.8	104.8
Imports of services	–6.9	–43.7	–53.7
Balance on goods and services	–258.5	–276.1	–367.3
Other income (net)	—	7.6	–7.3
Balance on goods, services and income	–258.5	–268.5	–374.6
Private unrequited transfers (net)	276.3	215.3	243.9
Official unrequited transfers (net)	79.7	71.0	81.7
Current balance	97.5	17.8	–49.0
Direct investment (net)	n.a.	n.a.	36.7
Official long-term capital (net)	29.2	7.5	3.6
Short-term capital (net) / Net errors and omissions	–48.5	–91.5	–66.5
Overall balance	78.2	–66.3	–75.2

* Estimates.

Source: IMF, *Eritrea—Selected Issues* (October 1997).

External Trade

PRINCIPAL COMMODITIES (million birr)

Imports c.i.f. (excl. petroleum)	1994	1995	1996*
Food and live animals	426.2	426.7	542.9
Beverages and tobacco	43.3	10.7	23.5
Crude materials (inedible) except fuels	49.1	65.9	116.5
Chemicals and related products	120.3	144.2	209.7
Basic manufactures	320.5	478.1	733.8
Machinery and transport equipment	752.6	1,166.0	1,091.1
Miscellaneous manufactured articles	234.9	166.9	250.8
Total (incl. others)	1,993.1	2,535.5	3,062.8

Exports f.o.b.	1994	1995	1996*
Food and live animals	117.7	141.3	92.4
Beverages and tobacco	9.2	19.7	26.2
Crude materials (inedible) except fuels	132.1	156.1	123.0
Chemicals and related products	7.5	12.0	13.4
Basic manufactures	67.8	100.3	88.3
Machinery and transport equipment	11.7	20.2	27.7
Miscellaneous manufactured articles	51.1	76.9	146.6
Total (incl. others)	397.1	528.8	520.4

* Estimates.

Source: IMF, *Eritrea—Selected Issues* (October 1997).

PRINCIPAL TRADING PARTNERS (million birr)

Imports c.i.f. (excl. petroleum)	1994	1995	1996*
Belgium	66.5	64.3	84.1
Djibouti	29.8	41.1	78.6
Ethiopia	90.9	146.9	261.8
Germany	147.4	142.5	217.0
Italy	431.0	459.0	429.1
Japan	34.4	58.9	111.2
Korea, Repub.	16.0	58.1	126.0
Netherlands	107.8	60.3	49.4
Saudi Arabia	328.0	490.4	465.6
Sudan	51.7	71.1	97.9
Sweden	16.1	31.7	19.3
United Arab Emirates	178.6	236.9	365.9
United Kingdom	79.1	78.5	68.5
USA	35.3	93.8	83.1
Yemen	20.5	19.6	3.6
Total (incl. others)	1,993.2	2,535.5	3,062.9

Exports f.o.b.	1994	1995	1996*
Ethiopia	207.5	354.2	342.4
Italy	10.2	15.2	22.3
Japan	16.3	6.3	n.a.
Saudi Arabia	50.3	15.9	20.0
Sudan	57.9	76.0	51.5
United Kingdom	10.2	1.8	4.0
USA	1.2	0.6	39.9
Yemen	7.4	27.4	n.a.
Total (incl. others)	397.1	528.8	520.4

* Estimates.

Source: IMF, *Eritrea—Selected Issues* (October 1997).

Transport

SHIPPING

Merchant Fleet (registered at 31 December)

	1994	1995	1996
Number of vessels	1	5	4
Displacement (grt)	104	12,403	830

Source: Lloyd's Register of Shipping, *World Fleet Statistics*.

Communications Media

	1993	1994
Radio receivers ('000 in use)	n.a.	300
Television receivers ('000 in use)	n.a.	1
Telephones ('000 main lines in use)	13	15
Telefax stations (number in use)	310	510

Book production (1993): 106 titles (including 23 pamphlets) and 420,000 copies (including 60,000 pamphlets). Figures for books, excluding pamphlets, refer only to school textbooks (64 titles; 323,000 copies) and government publications (19 titles; 37,000 copies).

Sources: UNESCO, *Statistical Yearbook*; UN, *Statistical Yearbook*.

Education

(1994/95)

	Institutions	Teachers	Pupils
Pre-primary	80	256	8,032
Primary	507	5,583	224,287
Secondary:			
General	n.a.	2,029	71,723
Teacher-training	n.a.	44	427
Vocational	n.a.	89	819
University level	n.a.	136	3,081
Other higher	n.a.	n.a.	56

Source: UNESCO, *Statistical Yearbook*.

Directory

The Constitution

On 23 May 1997 the Constituent Assembly unanimously adopted the Eritrean Constitution. A presidential regime was instituted, with the President to be elected for a maximum of two five-year terms. The President, as Head of State, has extensive powers and appoints the Prime Minister and the judges of the Supreme Court, although his mandate can be revoked if two-thirds of the members of the National Assembly (the Legislature) so demand. 'Conditional' political pluralism is authorized. Elections to the National Assembly were scheduled to be held in 1998; in the interim period the Transitional National Assembly was empowered to act as the legislature.

The Government

HEAD OF STATE

President: ISSAIAS AFEWERKI (assumed power May 1991; elected President by National Assembly 8 June 1993).

STATE COUNCIL
(January 1998)

President: ISSAIAS AFEWERKI.

Minister of Defence: Gen. SEBHAT EPHREM.

Minister of Justice: FAWZIYYAH HASHIM.

Minister of Foreign Affairs: HAILE WOLDE TENSAE.

Minister of Information and Culture: BARAKI GEBRE SELASSIE.

Minister of Finance and Development: GEBRE SELASSIE YOSEF.

Minister of Trade and Industry: ALI SAYYID ABDULLAH.

Minister of Agriculture: AREFAYNE BERHE.

Minister of Local Government: MAHMOUD AHMED MAHMOUD.

Minister of Labour and Social Security: OQBE ABRAHA.

Minister of Marine Resources: PETROS SOLOMON.

Minister of Construction: ABRAHA ASFAHA.

Minister of Energy and Mines: TESFAY GEBRE SELASSIE.

Minister of Education: OSMAN SALIH MUHAMMAD.

Minister of Health: DR SALIH MEKKI.

Minister of Transport and Communications: SALEH KEKIA.

Minister of Tourism: AHMED HAJI ALI.

Minister of Land, Water and the Environment: Dr TESFAY GHIRMAZION.

MINISTRIES AND COMMISSIONS

Ministry of Agriculture: POB 1024, Asmara; tel. (1) 181499; fax (1) 181415.

Ministry of Construction: POB 841, Asmara; tel. (1) 119077.

Ministry of Defence: POB 629, Asmara; tel. (1) 113349; fax (1) 114920.

Ministry of Education: POB 5610, Asmara; tel. (1) 113044; fax (1) 113866.

Ministry of Energy and Mines: POB 5285, Asmara; tel. (1) 116872; fax (1) 127652.

Ministry of Finance and Development: POB 896, Asmara; tel. (1) 113633; fax (1) 117947.

Ministry of Foreign Affairs: POB 190, Asmara; tel. (1) 113811; fax (1) 123788.

Ministry of Health: POB 212, Asmara; tel. (1) 112877; fax (1) 112899.

Ministry of Information and Culture: POB 242, Asmara; tel. (1) 115171; fax (1) 119847.

Ministry of Internal Affairs: POB 250, Asmara; tel. (1) 119299; fax (1) 114920.

Ministry of Justice: POB 241, Asmara; tel. (1) 127739; fax (1) 112193.

Ministry of Labour and Social Security: Asmara.

Ministry of Land, Water and the Environment: Asmara.

Ministry of Local Government: POB 225, Asmara; tel. (1) 113006.

Ministry of Marine Resources: POB 923, Asmara; tel. (1) 114271; fax (1) 112185.

Ministry of Tourism: POB 1010, Asmara; tel. (1) 126997; fax (1) 126949; e-mail ona@eol.com.er.

Ministry of Trade and Industry: POB 1515, Asmara; tel. (1) 117944; fax (1) 120586.

Ministry of Transport and Communications: POB 204, Asmara; tel. (1) 110444; fax (1) 127048.

Eritrean Relief and Refugee Commission: POB 1098, Asmara; tel. (1) 182222; fax (1) 182970; e-mail john@errec.er.punchdown.org.

Land and Housing Commission: POB 348, Asmara; tel. (1) 117400.

Provincial Administrators

There are six administrative regions in Eritrea, each with regional, sub-regional and village administrations.

Anseba Province: ALAMIN SHEIKH SALIH.

Debub Province: MESFIN HAGOS.

Debubawi Keyih Province: HAMID MUHAMMAD KARIKAREH.

Gash-Barka Province: MUSTAFA NUR HUSSEIN.

Maakel Province: WELDENKIEL ABRAHA.

Semenawi Keyih Bahri Province: IBRAHIM IDRIS TOTIL.

Legislature

NATIONAL ASSEMBLY

In accordance with transitional arrangements formulated in Decree No. 37 of May 1993, the National Assembly consists of the Central Committee of the People's Front for Democracy and Justice (PFDJ) and 60 other members: 30 from the Provincial Assemblies and an additional 30 members, including a minimum of 10 women, to be nominated by the PFDJ Central Committee. The legislative body 'outlines the internal and external policies of the government, regulates their implementation, approves the budget and elects a president for the country'. The National Assembly is to hold regular sessions every six months under the chairmanship of the President. In his role as Head of the Government and Commander-in-Chief of the Army, the President nominates individuals to head the various government departments. These nominations are ratified by the legislative body. In March 1994 the National Assembly voted to alter its composition: it would henceforth comprise the 75 members of the Central Committee of the PFDJ and 75 directly elected members. In May 1997, following the adoption of the Constitution, the Constituent Assembly empowered a Transitional National Assembly (comprising the 75 members of the PFDJ, 60 members of the Constituent Assembly and 15 representatives of Eritreans residing abroad) to act as the legislature until elections were held for a new National Assembly. Elections to the National Assembly were scheduled to be held in 1998.

Chairman of the Transitional National Assembly: ISSAIAS AFEWERKI.

Political Organizations

At independence in May 1993, many of the rival political organizations to the Eritrean People's Liberation Front (now the People's Front for Democracy and Justice) declared their support for the transitional Government.

Democratic Movement for the Liberation of Eritrea: opposition group; Leader HAMID TURKY.

Eritrean Islamic Jihad (EIJ): radical opposition group; in Aug. 1993 split into a mil. wing and a political wing, led by Sheikh MOHAMED ARAFA.

Eritrean Liberation Front (ELF): f. 1958; commenced armed struggle against Ethiopia in 1961; subsequently split into numerous factions (see below); mainly Muslim support; opposes the PFDJ; principal factions:

Eritrean Liberation Front–Central Command (ELF–CC): f. 1982; Chair. ABDALLAH IDRISS.

Eritrean Liberation Front–National Council (ELF–NC): Leader ABDULKADER JAILANY.

Eritrean Liberation Front–Revolutionary Council (ELF–RC): Leader AHMED NASSER.

People's Front for Democracy and Justice (PFDJ): POB 1081, Asmara; f. 1970 as the Eritrean Popular Liberation Forces, following a split in the Eritrean Liberation Front; renamed the Eritrean People's Liberation Front in 1977; adopted present name in Feb. 1994; Christian and Muslim support; in May 1991 took control of Eritrea and formed provisional Govt; formed transitional Govt in May 1993; Chair. ISSAIAS AFEWERKI; Sec.-Gen. AMIN MUHAMMAD SA'ID.

Diplomatic Representation

EMBASSIES IN ERITREA

China, People's Republic: POB 204, Asmara; tel. (1) 116988; Ambassador: SHI YONGJIU.

Denmark: Asmara; Ambassador: PETER TRUELSEN.

Djibouti: POB 5589, Asmara; tel. (1) 114189; Chargé d'affaires a.i.: DJAMA OMER IDLEH.

Egypt: POB 5577, Asmara; tel. (1) 119935; Ambassador: HUSSEIN ALI AL-ZEQBI.

Ethiopia: Franklin D. Roosevelt St, Asmara; tel. (1) 116365; fax (1) 116144; Ambassador: AWALOM WOLDU.

France: POB 209, Asmara; tel. (1) 126599; fax (1) 121036; Ambassador: LOUIS LE VERT.

Germany: Saba Development Bldg, Airport Rd, POB 4974, Asmara; tel. (1) 182670; fax (1) 182900; Ambassador: WOLFGANG RINGE.

Israel: POB 5600, Asmara; tel. (1) 120137; fax (1) 120187; Ambassador: RAPHAEL WALDEN.

Italy: Wedajo Ali St, POB 220, Asmara; tel. (1) 120914; fax (1) 121115; Ambassador: CLAUDIO BAY ROSSI.

Russia: POB 6557, Asmara; tel. (1) 182112; fax (1) 182033; Ambassador: RACHID IBRAGIMOV.

Saudi Arabia: POB 5599, Asmara; tel. (1) 120171; fax (1) 121027; Ambassador: ABDUL R. IBRAHIM AL-TOELMI.

USA: POB 211, Asmara; tel. (1) 120004; fax (1) 127584; Ambassador: (vacant).

Yemen: POB 5566, Asmara; tel. (1) 114434; fax (1) 127921; Chargé d'affaires a.i.: AHMED HASSEN BIN HASSEN.

Judicial System

The judicial system operates on the basis of transitional laws which incorporate pre-independence laws of the Eritrean People's Liberation Front, revised Ethiopian laws, customary laws and post-independence enacted laws. The independence of the judiciary in the discharge of its functions is unequivocally stated in Decree No. 37, which defines the powers and duties of the Government. It is subject only to the law and to no other authority. At present, the court structure is composed of first instance sub-zonal courts, appellate and first instance zonal courts, appellate and first instance high courts and a panel of high court judges, presided over by the president of the high court, as a court of last resort. With the implementation of the 1997 ratified Constitution, a supreme court will be established, whose judges will be appointed by the President of the State, subject to confirmation by the National Assembly.

Religion

Eritrea is almost equally divided between Muslims and Christians. Most Christians are adherents of the Orthodox Church, although there are Protestant and Roman Catholic communities. A small number of the population follow traditional beliefs.

CHRISTIANITY

The Eritrean Orthodox Church

In September 1993 the separation of the Eritrean Orthodox Church from the Ethiopian Orthodox Church was agreed by the respective church leaderships. The Eritrean Orthodox Church announced plans to appoint a bishop for each of the country's then 10 provinces. The first five bishops of the Eritrean Orthodox Church were consecrated in Cairo in September 1994. These consecrations signified the formal establishment of the Eritrean Orthodox Church as an independent body.

Leader: Bishop PHILIPPOS.

The Roman Catholic Church

At 31 December 1995 there were an estimated 125,564 adherents in the country.

Bishop of Asmara: Rt Rev. ZEKARIAS YOHANNES, 19 Gonder St, POB 244, Asmara; tel. (1) 120206; fax (1) 126519.

Bishop of Barentu: Rt Rev. LUCA MILESI, c/o 107 National Ave, POB 224, Asmara; tel. (1) 120631; fax (1) 122322.

Bishop of Keren: Rt Rev. TESFAMARIAN BEDHO, POB 460, Keren; tel. 401604.

The Anglican Communion

Within the Episcopal Church in Jerusalem and the Middle East, Eritrea lies within the jurisdiction of the Bishop in Egypt.

Leader: ASFAHA MAHARY.

ISLAM

There are substantial Muslim communities in the western lowlands, the northern highlands and the eastern coastal region.

Leader: Sheikh AL-AMIN OSMAN AL-AMIN.

The Press

Chamber News: POB 856, Asmara; tel. (1) 121388; fax (1) 120138; Tigrinya and English; publ. by Asmara Chamber of Commerce.

Eritrea Profile: POB 247, Asmara; f. 1994; weekly; English; publ. by the Ministry of Information and Culture.

Hadas Eritra (New Eritrea): Asmara; f. 1991; twice a week; in English, Tigrinya and Arabic; govt publ.; Editor YITBAREK ZEROM; circ. 25,000.

Trade and Development Bulletin: POB 856, Asmara; tel. (1) 121388; telex 42079; fax (1) 120138; monthly; Tigrinya and English; publ. by Asmara Chamber of Commerce; Editor TAAME FOTO.

Broadcasting and Communications

Communications and Postal Authority: POB 4918, Asmara; tel. (1) 115847; fax (1) 126966; Dir ESTIFANOS AFEWERKI.

TELECOMMUNICATIONS

Telecommunications Services of Eritrea: POB 234, Asmara; tel. (1) 117547; fax (1) 120938; Gen. Man. GOITOM OGBAZGHI.

RADIO

Voice of the Broad Masses of Eritrea (Dimseehafash): Ministry of Information, Radio Division, POB 872, Asmara; govt-controlled; programmes in Arabic, Tigrinya, Tigre, Amharic, Afar and Kunama.

TELEVISION

ERI-TV: Asmara; f. 1992; govt station providing educational, tech. and information service; broadcasting began in Jan. 1993 in Arabic and Tigrinya; transmissions limited to Asmara and surrounding areas.

Finance

(cap. = capital; brs = branches; amounts in Ethiopian birr)

In November 1997 Eritrea adopted the nakfa as its unit of currency, replacing the Ethiopian birr, which had been Eritrea's monetary unit since independence.

BANKING

Bank of Eritrea: POB 849, Asmara; tel. (1) 123036; telex 42065; fax (1) 123162; f. 1993; state central bank; Gov. TEKIE BEYENE.

Commercial Bank of Eritrea: POB 219, Asmara; tel. (1) 111065; fax (1) 124887; f. 1991; dep. 5,100m. (Dec. 1996); Gen. Man. YAMANE TESFAI; 15 brs.

Eritrean Investment and Development Bank: Asmara; f. 1996; cap. 45m.; provides medium- to long-term credit; 13 brs.

Housing and Commerce Bank of Eritrea: POB 235, Asmara; tel. (1) 120350; fax (1) 120401; f. 1994; cap. 5m.; finances residential and commercial construction projects; Gen. Man. and CEO Dr ARAIA TSEGGAI; 3 brs.

INSURANCE

National Insurance Corpn of Eritrea: POB 881, Asmara; tel. (1) 123000; fax (1) 123240; Gen. Man. ZERU WOLDEMICHAEL.

Trade and Industry

CHAMBER OF COMMERCE

Asmara Chamber of Commerce: POB 856, Asmara; tel. (1) 121388; fax (1) 120138.

TRADE ASSOCIATION

Red Sea Trading Corpn: 29/31 Ras Alula St, POB 332, Asmara; tel. (1) 127846; fax (1) 124353; f. 1983; import and export services; operated by the PFDJ; Gen. Man. KUBROM DAFLA.

Transport

Eritrea's transport infrastructure was severely damaged during the three decades of war. As part of the Government's Recovery and Rehabilitation Programme, US $27m. was allocated to road reconstruction and $10.2m. to improving port facilities.

Ministry of Transport: POB 204, Asmara; tel. (1) 110444; fax (1) 127048.

RAILWAYS

The 344-km railway connection between Agordat, Asmara and the port of Massawa was severely damaged during the war and ceased operation in 1978. In early 1997 the Asmara–Massawa line became operational (a short section of the railway had been reopened in 1994).

ROADS

In 1997 there were approximately 3,900 km of roads in Eritrea, of which some 900 km were paved. Roads that are paved require considerable repair, as do many of the bridges across seasonal water courses destroyed in the war. Road construction between Asmara and the port of Massawa was given particular priority in the Recovery and Rehabilitation Programme.

SHIPPING

Eritrea has two major seaports: Massawa, which sustained heavy war damage in 1990, and Assab, which has principally served Addis Ababa, in Ethiopia. Under an agreement signed between the Ethiopian and Eritrean Governments in 1993, the two countries will share the facilities of both ports. Since the end of the war, activity in Massawa has increased substantially. In mid-1996 Italy and the World Bank approved funding for a major programme of investment at both ports. In 1996 a total of 445 vessels docked at Massawa, handling 813,126 metric tons of goods; 676 vessels docked at Assab, which handled 2,982,654 tons of goods.

Department of Maritime Transport: POB 679, Asmara; tel. (1) 121317; fax (1) 121316; Dir-Gen. IBRAHIM SAÏD IDRIS.

Port and Maritime Transport Authority: POB 851, Asmara; tel. (1) 111399; fax (1) 113647; Dir WELDE MIKAEL ABRAHAM.

Eritrean Shipping Lines: 80 Semaetat Ave, POB 1110, Asmara; tel. (1) 120359; fax (1) 120331; f. 1992; provides shipping services in Red Sea and Persian (Arabian) Gulf areas and owns and operates four cargo ships; Gen. Man. TEWELDE KELATI.

CIVIL AVIATION

The international airport is at Asmara.

Civil Aviation Authority (Eritrean Airlines): POB 252, Asmara; tel. (1) 181822; fax (1) 181255; handles freight and passenger traffic for six scheduled carriers which use Asmara airport; Dir-Gen. ESTIFANOS AFEWERKI.

Tourism

With Eritrea's transport infrastructure still requiring massive repair, tourism remains undeveloped. However, the country possesses many areas of scenic and scientific interest, including the Dahlak Islands (a coralline archipelago rich in marine life), off the coast from Massawa, and the massive escarpment rising up from the coastal plain and supporting a unique ecosystem. In late 1993 the transitional Government inaugurated a programme of privatization of state-operated hotels in Asmara, Massawa, Keren and Assab. The Ministry of Tourism oversees the development of this sector. During 1996 some 417,000 tourists visited Eritrea.

Eritrean Tourism Service Corpn: Asmara; operates govt-owned hotels.

ESTONIA

Introductory Survey

Location, Climate, Language, Religion, Flag, Capital

The Republic of Estonia (formerly the Estonian Soviet Socialist Republic) is situated in north-eastern Europe. The country is bordered to the south by Latvia, and to the east by the Russian Federation. Estonia's northern coastline is on the Gulf of Finland and its territory includes more than 1,520 islands, mainly off its western coastline in the Gulf of Riga and the Baltic Sea. The largest of the islands are Saaremaa and Hiiumaa, in the Gulf of Riga. The climate is influenced by Estonia's position between the Eurasian land mass and the Baltic Sea and the North Atlantic Ocean. The mean January temperature in Tallinn is −0.6°C (30.9°F); in July the mean temperature is 17.1°C (62.8°F). Average annual precipitation is 568 mm. The official language is Estonian, which is a member of the Baltic-Finnic group of the Finno-Ugric languages, is written in the Latin script and is closely related to Finnish. Many of the Russian residents, who comprise nearly 30% of the total population, do not speak Estonian. Most of the population profess Christianity and, by tradition, Estonians belong to the Evangelical Lutheran Church. Smaller Protestant sects and the Eastern Orthodox Church are also represented. The national flag (proportions 11 by seven) consists of three equal horizontal stripes, of blue, black and white. The capital is Tallinn.

Recent History

The Russian annexation of Estonia, formerly under Swedish rule, was formalized in 1721. During the latter half of the 19th century, as the powers of the dominant Baltic German nobility declined, Estonians experienced a national cultural revival, which culminated in political demands for autonomy during the 1905 Russian Revolution, and for full independence after the beginning of the First World War. On 30 March 1917 the Provisional Government in Petrograd (St Petersburg), which had taken power after the abdication of Tsar Nicholas II in February, approved autonomy for Estonia. A Land Council was elected as the country's representative body. However, in October the Bolsheviks staged a coup in Tallinn, and declared the Estonian Soviet Executive Committee as the sole government of Estonia. As German forces advanced towards Estonia, in early 1918, the Bolshevik troops were forced to leave. The major Estonian political parties united to form the Estonian Salvation Committee, and on 24 February 1918 an independent Republic of Estonia was proclaimed. A Provisional Government, headed by Konstantin Päts, was formed, but Germany refused to recognize Estonia's independence and the country was occupied by German troops until the end of the First World War. Following the capitulation of Germany in November 1918, the Provisional Government assumed power. After a period of armed conflict between Soviet and Estonian troops, the Republic of Estonia and Soviet Russia signed the Treaty of Tartu on 2 February 1920. Under the terms of the Treaty, the Soviet Government recognized Estonia's independence and renounced any rights to its territory. Estonian independence was recognized by the major Western powers in January 1921, and Estonia was admitted to the League of Nations.

This period of independence lasted until 1940. During most of this time the country had a liberal-democratic political system, in which the Riigikogu (State Assembly) was the dominant political force. Significant social, cultural and economic advances were made in the 1920s, including radical land reform. However, the decline in trade with Russia and the economic depression of the 1930s, combined with the political problems of a divided parliament, caused public dissatisfaction with the regime. In March 1934 the Prime Minister, Konstantin Päts, seized power in a bloodless coup and introduced a period of authoritarian rule. The Riigikogu and political parties were disbanded, but in 1938 a new Constitution was adopted, which provided for a presidential system of government, with a bicameral legislature. In April 1938 Päts was elected President.

In August 1939 the USSR and Germany signed a non-aggression treaty (the Nazi-Soviet or Molotov-Ribbentrop Pact). The secret supplementary protocol to the treaty provided for the occupation of Estonia by the USSR. In September Estonia was forced to sign an agreement which permitted the USSR to base Soviet troops in Estonia. In June 1940 the Government, in accordance with a Soviet ultimatum, resigned, and a new administration was appointed by the Soviet authorities, with Johannes Vares-Barbarus as Prime Minister. In July elections were held, in which only candidates approved by the Soviet authorities were permitted to participate. On 21 July the Estonian Soviet Socialist Republic was proclaimed by the new legislature, and on 6 August the republic was formally incorporated into the USSR.

Soviet rule in Estonia lasted less than a year, before German forces occupied the country. In that short period, Soviet policy resulted in mass deportations of Estonians to Siberia (in one night, on 14 June 1941, more than 10,000 people were arrested and deported), the expropriation of property, severe restrictions on cultural life and the introduction of Soviet-style government in the republic.

German forces entered Estonia in July 1941 and remained in occupation until September 1944. After a short-lived attempt to reinstate Estonian independence, Soviet troops occupied the whole of the country, and the process of 'sovietization' was continued. By the end of 1949 most Estonian farmers had been forced to join collective farms. Heavy industry was expanded, with investment concentrated on electricity generation and the chemical sector. Structural change in the economy was accompanied by increased political repression, with deportations of Estonians continuing until the death of Stalin, in 1953. The most overt form of opposition to Soviet rule was provided by the 'forest brethren' (*metsavennad*), a guerrilla movement, which continued to conduct armed operations against Soviet personnel and institutions until the mid-1950s. In the late 1960s, as in other Soviet republics, more traditional forms of dissent appeared, concentrating on cultural issues, provoked by the increasing domination of the republic by immigrant Russians and other Slavs.

During the late 1970s and the 1980s the issues of 'russification' and environmental degradation became subjects of intense debate in Estonia. The policy of *glasnost,* introduced by the Soviet leader, Mikhail Gorbachev, in 1986, allowed such discussion to spread beyond dissident groups. The first major demonstrations of the 1980s were organized in protest against plans to escalate the scale of open-cast phosphorite mining in north-eastern Estonia. The public opposition to the plans caused the Soviet Government to reconsider its proposals, and this success prompted further protests. In August 1987 a demonstration, attended by some 2,000 people, commemorated the anniversary of the signing of the Nazi-Soviet Pact. Following the demonstration, an Estonian Group for the Publication of the Molotov-Ribbentrop Pact (MRP-AEG) was formed. During 1988 the Nazi-Soviet Pact was duly published, and the MRP-AEG re-formed as the Estonian National Independence Party (ENIP), proclaiming the restoration of Estonian independence as its political objective. Another opposition group, the Estonian Popular Front (EPF), which had been established in April, was formally constituted at its first congress, in October, and included many members of the ruling Communist Party of Estonia (CPE). The EPF was more cautious than the ENIP in its approach, advocating the transformation of the USSR into a confederal system. The CPE itself was forced to adapt its policies to retain a measure of public support. On 16 November the Estonian Supreme Soviet (legislature) adopted a declaration of sovereignty, which included the right to annul all-Union (USSR) legislation. The Presidium of the USSR Supreme Soviet declared the sovereignty legislation unconstitutional, but the Estonian Supreme Soviet affirmed its decision in December.

One of the main demands of the opposition—the adoption of Estonian as the state language—was accepted by the Supreme Soviet in January 1989, and the tricolour of independent Estonia was also reinstated as the official flag. Despite the successes of the opposition, differing political tactics were employed by the radical ENIP and the EPF. The ENIP refused to nominate candidates for elections to the all-Union Congress of People's Deputies in March. Instead, the ENIP leadership announced plans for the registration by citizens' committees of all citizens of the pre-1940 Republic of Estonia and their descendants. Voters on an electoral register, thus compiled, would elect a Congress of Estonia as the legal successor to the pre-1940 Estonian legislature. The EPF, however, participated in the elections to the Congress of People's Deputies and won 27 of the 36 contested seats. Five seats were won by the International Movement, a political group which was composed predominantly of Russian immigrants and was established in July 1988 to oppose the growing influence of the Estonian opposition movements in the republic.

In October 1989 delegates at the second congress of the EPF, influenced by the growing popularity of the ENIP and the citizens' committees, voted to adopt the restoration of Estonian independence as official policy. In November the Estonian Supreme Soviet voted to annul the decision of its predecessor in 1940 to enter the USSR, declaring that the decision had been reached under coercion from Soviet armed forces.

On 2 February 1990 a mass rally was held to commemorate the anniversary of the 1920 Treaty of Tartu. Deputies attending the rally later met to approve a declaration urging the USSR Supreme Soviet to begin negotiations on restoring Estonia's independence. On 22 February the Estonian Supreme Soviet approved the declaration, and on the following day it voted to abolish the constitutional guarantee of power enjoyed by the CPE. This formal decision permitted largely free elections to take place to the Estonian Supreme Soviet in March. The EPF won 43 of the 105 seats, while 35 were won by the Association for a Free Estonia and other pro-independence groups. The remainder were won by members of the International Movement. Candidates belonging to the CPE, which was represented in all these groups, won 55 seats.

At the first session of the new legislature, Arnold Rüütel, previously Chairman of the Presidium of the Supreme Soviet, was elected to the new post of Chairman of the Supreme Soviet, in which was vested those state powers that had previously been the preserve of the First Secretary of the CPE. On 30 March 1990 the Supreme Soviet adopted a declaration which proclaimed the beginning of a transitional period towards independence and denied the validity of Soviet power in the republic.

In late February and early March 1990 elections were held to the rival parliament to the Supreme Soviet, the Congress of Estonia. Some 580,000 people took part. The Congress convened on 11–12 March and declared itself the constitutional representative of the Estonian people. The participants adopted resolutions demanding the restoration of Estonian independence and the withdrawal of Soviet troops from Estonia.

In early April 1990 the Supreme Soviet elected Edgar Savisaar, a leader of the EPF, as Prime Minister. On 8 May the Soviet voted to restore the first five articles of the 1938 Constitution, which described Estonia's independent status. The formal name of pre-1940 Estonia, the Republic of Estonia, was also restored, as were the state emblems, flag and anthem. On 16 May a transitional system of government was approved.

Although formal economic sanctions were not imposed on Estonia (as was the case with Lithuania), the republic's declaration of independence severely strained relations with the Soviet authorities. In mid-May 1990 President Gorbachev annulled the declaration, declaring that it violated the USSR Constitution. The Estonian leadership's request for negotiations on the status of the republic was refused by Gorbachev, who insisted that the independence declaration be rescinded before negotiations could begin. There was also opposition within the republic, mostly from ethnic Russians affiliated to the International Movement.

When troops of the USSR's Ministry of Internal Affairs attempted military intervention in Latvia and Lithuania in January 1991, the Estonian leadership anticipated similar confrontation. Barricades and makeshift defences were erected, but no military action was taken. However, events in the other Baltic republics intensified popular distrust of Estonian involvement in a new union which was being negotiated by other Soviet republics. Consequently, Estonia refused to participate in a referendum on the future of the USSR, which took place in nine of the republics in March 1991. The Estonian authorities had conducted a poll on the issue of independence earlier in the same month. According to the official results, 82.9% of the registered electorate took part, of which 77.8% voted in favour of Estonian independence.

When the State Committee for the State of Emergency announced that it had seized power in the USSR on 19 August 1991, Estonia, together with the other Baltic republics, expected military intervention to overthrow the pro-independence governments. Gen. Fyodor Kuzmin, the Soviet commander of the Baltic military district, informed Arnold Rüütel, the Chairman of the Supreme Council (as the legislature was now known), that he was taking full control of Estonia. Military vehicles entered Tallinn on 20 August, and troops occupied the city's television station. However, the military command did not prevent a session of the Estonian Supreme Council from convening on the same day. Deputies adopted a resolution declaring the full and immediate independence of Estonia, thus ending the transitional period which had begun in March 1990. Plans were also announced for the formation of a government-in-exile, should the Government and the Supreme Council be disbanded by Soviet troops.

After it became evident, on 22 August 1991, that the Soviet coup had collapsed, the Government began to take measures against persons who had allegedly supported the coup. The anti-Government movements, the International Movement and the United Council of Work Collectives, were banned, as was the Communist Party of the Soviet Union. Several directors of Soviet enterprises were dismissed, and the Committee of State Security (KGB) was ordered to terminate its activities in Estonia.

As the Estonian Government moved to assert its authority over former Soviet institutions, other countries quickly began to recognize its independence. On 6 September the USSR State Council finally recognized the re-establishment of Estonian independence. Later in the month Estonia, together with the other Baltic states, was admitted to the UN as well as to the Conference on Security and Co-operation in Europe (CSCE, renamed Organization for Security and Co-operation in Europe, OSCE, in December 1994). During the remainder of 1991 Estonia re-established diplomatic relations with most major states and was offered membership of leading international organizations. In internal politics there was hope for a cessation of conflict between the radical Congress of Estonia and the Supreme Council, with the establishment of a Constitutional Assembly, composed of equal numbers of delegates from each body, which was to draft a new constitution.

In January 1992, following a series of disputes with the Supreme Council concerning economic management and the issue of citizenship, and the Government's failure to persuade the legislature to impose an economic state of emergency, Savisaar resigned as Prime Minister and was replaced by the erstwhile Minister of Transport, Tiit Vähi. A new Council of Ministers, which included seven ministers from the previous Government, was approved by the Supreme Council at the end of the month.

The draft Constitution that had been prepared by the Constitutional Assembly was approved by an overwhelming majority of the electorate (some 91%) in a referendum held in late June 1992. Under the recently adopted Citizenship Law, only persons who had been citizens of pre-1940 Estonia, and their descendants, or those who had successfully applied for citizenship, were entitled to vote. This ruling drew strong criticism from Russian leaders, concerned that the rights of the large Russian minority in Estonia, most of whom had not been granted citizenship and who were thus disenfranchised, were being violated. The new Constitution, which entered into force in early July 1992, provided for a parliamentary system of government, with a strong presidency. A new legislature, the Riigikogu, was to replace the Supreme Council (and the Congress of Estonia), and elections to the new body were to be held in September. A direct presidential election was to take place simultaneously (although subsequent presidents would be elected by the Riigikogu).

Legislative and presidential elections were duly held on 20 September 1992, with the participation of some 67% of the electorate. The country's Russian and other ethnic minorities, who now represented 42% of the total population, were again barred from voting (with the exception of those whose applications for citizenship had been granted). The elections to the 101-seat Riigikogu were contested by a total of 633 candidates, representing some 40 parties and movements, largely grouped into eight coalitions. The nationalist alliance Isamaa (Pro Patria, or Fatherland) emerged with the largest number of seats (29). Other right-wing parties and alliances performed well. The centrist Popular Front alliance (led by the EPF) won an unexpectedly low total of 15 seats. The ENIP, which was not part of a coalition, won 10 seats. The Secure Home alliance, which comprised some former communists, obtained 17 seats.

None of the four candidates in the presidential election, which was held simultaneously, won an overall majority of the votes. It thus fell to the Riigikogu to choose from the two most successful candidates, Arnold Rüütel, now a leading member of the Secure Home alliance, and Lennart Meri, a former Minister of Foreign Affairs, who was supported by Isamaa. In early October 1992 the Riigikogu, now dominated by members or supporters of Isamaa, elected Meri to be Estonia's President, by 59 votes to 31.

A new coalition Government, with a large representation of Isamaa members, as well as members of the Moderates electoral alliance and the ENIP, was announced in mid-October 1992. Earlier in the month Mart Laar, a 32-year-old historian and the leader of Isamaa, had been chosen as Prime Minister. Laar indicated that the principal objectives of his administration would be to negotiate the withdrawal of all Russian troops remaining in Estonia, as well as to accelerate the country's privatization programme. In late November four of the five constituent parties of the Isamaa alliance united to form the National Fatherland Party (NFP), with Laar as its Chairman. In the same month the CPE was renamed the Estonian Democratic Labour Party.

The NFP suffered a considerable loss of support at local elections held in October 1993. In Tallinn the party secured only five of the 64 seats on the city council. In the following month Laar survived a vote of 'no confidence', proposed to the Riigikogu by opposition deputies, who accused the Prime Minister of incompetence and 'strategic errors in foreign affairs'. In January 1994 Laar reshuffled four key portfolios in the Council of Ministers (finance, economy, defence and foreign affairs), overcoming initial opposition by President Meri to two of the nominees. Meanwhile, in November 1993, the EPF was disbanded; it was stated that the party had largely fulfilled its aims.

The NFP continued to lose popular support in early 1994. At the same time the governing coalition, led by the NFP, was increasingly afflicted by internal divisions, largely prompted by what was perceived as Laar's authoritarian style of leadership. In May–June four members of the Council of Ministers resigned their posts. Defections from the Isamaa faction within the Riigikogu resulted in supporters of Laar retaining control of only 19 seats in the legislature by early September. Following the revelation, in that month, that Laar had secretly contravened an agreement with the International Monetary Fund (IMF), a vote of 'no confidence in the Prime Minister' was endorsed by 60 members of the Riigikogu (with 27 votes against). In late October Andres Tarand, hitherto Minister of the Environment, was appointed to replace Laar. A new Council of Ministers—which included representatives of the Isamaa and Moderates groups, the ENIP, and liberal and right-wing parties—was announced in the following month.

In early January 1995 seven electoral alliances and eight parties were registered to participate in the general election scheduled for 5 March. The result of the election reflected widespread popular dissatisfaction with the parties of the governing coalition. The largest number of seats in the Riigikogu (41 of the total of 101) was won by an alliance of the centrist Estonian Coalition Party (ECP, led by the former Prime Minister, Tiit Vähi) and the Rural Union (comprising various agrarian parties, most prominently Arnold Rüütel's Estonian Rural People's Party, ERPP). A coalition of the newly-established Estonian Reform Party (ERP, led by Siim Kallas, the President of the Bank of Estonia) and liberal groups obtained 19 seats, followed by Edgar Savisaar's Estonian Centre Party (16). The NFP (in coalition with the ENIP) won only eight seats, while the Moderates alliance (which included Andres Tarand) gained six seats. The 'Estonia is Our Home' pact (which united three new parties representing the Russian-speaking minority) also won six seats; this development was broadly welcomed as a potentially stabilizing factor in both the domestic and foreign affairs of the country. The remaining five seats were taken by a coalition of right-wing parties. The electoral turnout was almost 70%.

In late March 1995 Tiit Vähi was nominated by President Meri to form a new Council of Ministers. Vähi was confirmed as Prime Minister by the legislature in early April, and the new Government—a coalition of the ECP/Rural Union and the Estonian Centre Party—was appointed later in the month. Vähi stated that his Government's main priorities were to further the reforms undertaken by the preceding administration, to seek full membership of the EU and to improve relations with the Russian Federation (see below).

The Government survived only until early October 1995, when it was revealed that Edgar Savisaar, the Minister of the Interior, had made secret tape and video recordings of conversations that he had held with other politicians, following the Riigikogu election in March, concerning the formation of a new coalition government. In the ensuing scandal, Savisaar was dismissed from his post by Vähi; however, the Estonian Centre Party (of which Savisaar was the leader) refused to accept his dismissal. As a result of the effective collapse of the coalition, Vähi and the remaining members of the Council of Ministers tendered their resignations. In mid-October President Meri reappointed Vähi as Prime Minister and charged him with the formation of a new Government. This emerged in late October, and represented a coalition of the ECP/Rural Union and Siim Kallas's ERP. Meanwhile, Savisaar resigned as Chairman of the Estonian Centre Party; he also announced his departure from political activity. In December the NFP and the ENIP, which had campaigned jointly in the legislative election in March, merged to form the Fatherland Union (FU), and appointed Toivo Jürgenson, a former Minister of the Economy, as Chairman. In March 1996 tension within the Estonian Centre Party, following the scandal surrounding Savisaar, resulted in the emergence of two factions: Andra Veidemann, the Chairman of the party, and six deputies from the Riigikogu established the New Democratic Association, subsequently to become the liberal-centrist Development Party, while Savisaar was re-elected as Chairman of the Estonian Centre Party. Criminal proceedings were initiated against Savisaar in May, for conducting illegal investigative activities, but these were later abandoned.

A presidential election was held in the Riigikogu on 26 August 1996, and was contested by the incumbent, Lennart Meri, and Arnold Rüütel of the ERPP. A further two rounds of voting took place on the following day, since neither candidate had secured the requisite 68 votes; however, these were also inconclusive. A larger electoral college, comprising the 101 deputies of the legislature and 273 representatives of local government, was therefore convened on 20 September. Five candidates contested the first round, but, as none of the contenders secured an overall majority of the votes, a second round of voting was held to choose between the leading candidates, Meri and Rüütel. The election was won by Meri, with some 52% of the votes, and in October he was duly sworn in as President for a second term in office.

In October 1996 local government elections were held, in which the ERP gained control of Tallinn city council. In the following month the ECP concluded a co-operation agreement with the Estonian Centre Party (which had been forced to leave the Government in October 1995), pledging to seek to involve the centrists in the governing coalition. Disagreements among the coalition partners led to the collapse of the Tallinn council leadership, and Savisaar was appointed as the new Chairman of the council, replacing the newly-elected ERP candidate. The ERP threatened to leave the Government unless the co-operation agreement with the Estonian Centre Party was cancelled, and on 22 November 1996 six ministers, including Siim Kallas, the Minister for Foreign Affairs, resigned, thus causing the collapse of the ruling coalition. Negotiations to form a new coalition were conducted by the ECP with the Estonian Centre Party and the Development Party, who between them commanded 16 seats in the Riigikogu, but no agreement was reached. A minority Government, comprising the ECP, the Rural Union and independent members, which had the support of 41 deputies, was therefore appointed in early December. In early 1997 a series of allegations, concerning the abuse of his office, were made against Vähi. A legislative motion of 'no confidence in the Prime Minister', presented by the leaders of four opposition parties (the Fatherland Union, the Reform Party, the Moderates' Party and the Republican Party) in early February, was defeated by a narrow margin, but Vähi nevertheless tendered his resignation at the end of that month, while denying the allegations made against him. Mart Siimann, the leader of the ECP parliamentary faction, was appointed Prime Minister, having received the support of the majority of parliamentary deputies, and was asked to form a new Government (the resignation of the Prime Minister automatically entailed that of the Government). In mid-March a new minority Government, which comprised a coalition of the ECP, the Rural Union and independent members, was appointed. Siimann immediately declared the new Government's commitment to continue to seek economic growth through reform initiatives pursued by the previous administration. In April Robert Lepikson, a former Mayor of Tallinn, was appointed Minister of Internal Affairs, replacing Riivo Sinijärv who was dismissed allegedly for his failure to address reports of abuses of official privileges at the ministry. In September Siimann refused offers to resign tendered by both the Minister of Defence, Andrus Öövel, and the Commander of the Armed Forces, Maj.-Gen. Johannes Kert, following an accident in which 14 Estonian soldiers of the Baltic Peace-keeping Battalion drowned, in adverse weather conditions, during a military training exercise in the Kurkse strait, off the north-western coast. A commission of inquiry into the incident, headed by the Minister of Justice, Paul Varul, concluded that 'management error' had contributed to the tragedy. Also in September, former Prime Minister Tiit Vähi announced his resignation from the ECP and his retirement from political life. His position as Chairman of the ECP was assumed by Prime Minister Siimann. In late January 1998 Robert Lepikson was dismissed as Minister of Internal Affairs, following harsh criticism, proceeding largely from Siimann, of his outspoken opinions of other members of the Government.

Since the restoration of Estonian independence in 1991, the republic's relations with its eastern neighbour, the Russian Federation, have been strained by a number of issues, most notably the presence of former Soviet troops (under Russian jurisdiction) and the rights of the large Russian minority in Estonia. Under the Citizenship Law of 1992 (a modified version of that adopted in 1938), non-ethnic Estonians who settled in the republic after its annexation by the USSR in 1940 were obliged to apply for naturalization (as were their descendants). Many of the requirements for naturalization—including two years' residency in Estonia as well as an examination in the Estonian language—were criticized by the Russian Government as being excessively stringent, and discriminatory against the Russian-speaking minority. A new citizenship law, adopted in January 1995, extended the residency requirement to five years. Non-citizens were given until 12 July 1995 to apply for residence and work permits, by which time almost 330,000 people (more than 80% of the total) had submitted applications. The deadline was extended until 30 November 1996, following which non-citizens were required to hold either an alien's passport (which served as an international travel document) or a residence permit. (Former Soviet passports were valid for identification purposes within Estonia until the relevant documents had been issued.) By October 1996 some 110,000 people had taken Russian citizenship, while continuing to live in Estonia. In May 1997 the Ministry of Internal Affairs announced that Soviet passports were no longer valid in Estonia. An amendment to the Language Law, adopted by the Riigikogu in November 1997, provoked outrage among the Russian-speaking minority. Under the terms of the amended law, parliamentary deputies and local government officials who had not received elementary education at an Estonian language school were to be required to demonstrate their knowledge of the language. The amendment was denounced by ethnic Russian members of the legislature (who had opposed the legislation) as unconstitutional, and the amendment was vetoed by President Meri in December 1997 and in January 1998.

With the dissolution of the USSR in 1991, several thousand former Soviet troops remained stationed (under Russian command) on Estonian territory. Their withdrawal was commenced in 1992, but the Russian leadership increasingly linked the progress of the troop withdrawals with the question of the citizenship, and other rights, of the Russian-speaking minority in Estonia. Withdrawals of the troops were suspended temporarily on several occasions in response to allegations of violations of the Russian minority's rights. In November 1993 a resolution by the UN General Assembly demanded a complete withdrawal of the ex-Soviet troops, and the Russian Government proposed 31 August 1994 as the final deadline for the withdrawals. Negotiations continued in 1994 on the terms for the withdrawal of the troops, but were complicated by Russian demands that the 12,000 retired Russian military servicemen (and their dependants) living in Estonia be granted unqualified citizenship rights and social guarantees. In July talks were held in Moscow between President Meri and President Yeltsin of the Russian Federation, at which Meri pledged that civil and social rights would be guaranteed to all Russian military pensioners in Estonia, while Yeltsin confirmed that Russia would remove its military presence by the end of August. The withdrawal of former Soviet troops from Estonia was finally completed on 29 August 1994. The agreements on the withdrawal of troops and on Russian military pensioners were ratified by the Russian and Estonian legislatures in 1995, despite opposition from many Estonian politicians who argued that, as Russia had been an occupying force, its servicemen should not be allowed to retire in Estonia. By December 1996 the Estonian Government had granted residence permits to over 20,000 retired servicemen and their dependants.

A further cause of tension in Estonian–Russian relations concerned Estonia's demand for the return of some 2,000 sq km (770 sq miles) of territory that had been ceded to Russia in 1944. This matter remained unresolved at inter-governmental talks held in 1992–93, with Estonia insisting that the Russian-Estonian state border be determined by the terms of the Treaty of Tartu of 1920, in which Russia recognized Estonia's independence. In June 1994 President Yeltsin ordered the unilateral demarcation of Russia's border with Estonia according to the Soviet boundary, although no agreement with Estonia had been concluded. During 1995 Estonia abandoned its demand for the return of the disputed territories. Instead, during Russian–Estonian border negotiations, the Estonian Government appealed only for minor amendments to be made to the existing line of demarcation in order to improve border security; more importantly, it insisted that Russia recognize the Treaty of Tartu as the basis of future relations between the two countries. However, the Russian Government maintained that the Treaty had lost its legal force, having been superseded by the declaration on bilateral relations signed by Russia and Estonia in 1991.

Relations between Russia and Estonia deteriorated in 1996. The re-establishment of the Estonian Apostolic Orthodox Church (see section on Religion) was perceived by Russia as a threat to the rights of the Russian-speaking minority in Estonia, and the assertion of jurisdiction in Estonia by the Ecumenical Patriarch of Constantinople in February led to a temporary break in relations with the Moscow Patriarchate. Relations were restored in May, when it was agreed that congregations should be permitted to decide which Patriarchate they wished to support. Tensions increased later in that month when Russia expelled an Estonian diplomat, allegedly for espionage; Estonia retaliated by expelling a Russian diplomat from Tallinn. Negotiations concerning the adoption of the border agreement were held at intervals throughout 1996, but Russia continued to reject the inclusion in the agreement of the Treaty of Tartu, fearing it would legitimize Estonia's claims on Russian territory (despite the fact that Estonia had abandoned such claims). In November it was announced that Estonia was prepared to omit the Treaty of Tartu from the border agreement. The Estonian Government approved the draft agreement in late November, and declared that it would be signed by Estonia and Russia at the Lisbon summit of the OSCE in December. However, the Russian Government refused to sign the agreement until other issues had been addressed, in particular the rights of the Russian-speaking minority in Estonia.

Estonia actively pursues close relations with its Baltic neighbours, Latvia and Lithuania. In late 1991 the three states established a consultative interparliamentary body, the Baltic Assembly, with the aim of developing political and economic co-operation. In early 1992 it was agreed to abolish almost all trade restrictions between the three countries and to introduce a common visa policy, and a tripartite agreement on free trade and regional security was signed in late 1993. A customs agreement came into force in June 1996, which constituted the first stage towards the establishment of a unified customs system. At two separate meetings during November 1997 the three countries agreed to reject Russian overtures to provide unilateral security guarantees, and to remove all non-tariff customs barriers between them, thus reiterating hopes for complete customs union by mid-1998. In January 1998 the Presidents of the three states met President Clinton of the USA in Washington, DC, and all parties signed a Charter of Partnership. The charter, which contained no specific military provision, was described as a framework for the development of closer political and economic ties. Estonia is a member of the Council of Baltic Sea States (established in March 1992). In July 1996 the member states signed a programme of co-operation aimed at encouraging economic development and integration between the countries of the Council. Further agreements on regional co-operation were concluded by the premiers of member nations of the Council at a summit meeting which took place in January 1998 in Riga, Latvia. The summit also marked the first meeting for more than two years of the Prime Ministers of Estonia and Russia.

An important focus of Estonia's foreign policy is the attainment of full membership of the European Union (EU). In July 1995 Estonia became an associate member of the EU, and in December it officially applied for full membership. At a meeting of the European Council of Ministers convened in Luxembourg in December 1997, the EU confirmed that Estonia was among six states with which it wished to begin bilateral negotiations on accession in April 1998. Among the EU states, Estonia enjoys particularly cordial relations with Finland (its largest trading partner), with which it shares close cultural and linguistic ties. Estonia is also a member of the Council of Europe (see p. 140), holding the Presidency for six months from May 1996. In addition, Estonia pursues the goal of membership of NATO (Estonia joined NATO's 'Partnership for Peace' programme of military co-operation in 1994). However, the likelihood of Estonia's early incorporation into NATO has diminished, owing, in part, to Russian opposition to the expansion of NATO into eastern Europe and, particularly, into the former USSR.

Government

Legislative authority resides with the Riigikogu (State Assembly), which has 101 members, elected by universal adult suffrage for a four-year term. The Riigikogu elects the President (Head of State) for a term of five years. The President is also Supreme Commander of Estonia's armed forces. Executive power is held by the Council of Ministers, which is headed by the Prime Minister, who is nominated by the President. For administrative purposes, Estonia is divided into 15 counties (*maakond*) and six towns. The counties are subdivided into communes (*vald*).

Defence

Before regaining independence in 1991, Estonia had no armed forces separate from those of the USSR. Following the establishment of its own Ministry of Defence in April 1992, Estonia began to form an independent army. By August 1997 total armed forces numbered 3,510 (army 3,350, navy 160). There was also a reserve militia of some 6,000. There is a paramilitary border guard numbering 2,800 troops, under the command of the Ministry of the Interior. Military service is for 12 months, but is to be reduced to nine months by mid-1998. In February 1994 Estonia joined NATO's 'Partnership for Peace' programme of military co-operation (see p. 206). Of total government expenditure for 1996, some 3.1% was for defence. Projected budgetary expenditure on defence for 1997 and 1998 was 736m. and 805m. kroons, respectively.

Economic Affairs

In 1995, according to preliminary estimates by the World Bank, Estonia's gross national product (GNP), measured at average 1993–95 prices, was US $4,252m., equivalent to $2,860 per head. During 1985–95, it was estimated, GNP per head declined, in real terms, at an average annual rate of 4.3%. Over the same period the population was estimated to have declined by an annual average of 0.3%. Estonia's gross domestic product (GDP) was estimated to have decreased, in real terms, by an average of 3.1% per year during 1991–96. Real GDP decreased by an estimated 12.4% in 1992. The IMF estimated real GDP growth of 4.2% in 1995 and 4.0% in 1996.

Agriculture (including forestry and fishing) contributed an estimated 7.3% of GDP in 1996. In that year the sector provided 10.0% of employment. Animal husbandry is the main activity in the agricultural sector. Some 30% of Estonia's land is cultivable. The principal crops are grains, potatoes and other vegetables. Forestry products are also important. During 1990–94, according to the World Bank, agricultural GDP declined by an average annual rate of 9.3%. According to the FAO, agricultural production increased by 5.4% in 1994 and by 57.6% in 1995, but declined by an estimated 4.0% in 1996.

Industry (including mining and quarrying, manufacturing, construction and power) contributed 27.6% of GDP in 1996. In the same year the sector provided 33.5% of employment. The sector is dominated by machine-building, electronics and electrical engineering. During 1990–94, according to the World Bank, industrial GDP declined by an average annual rate of 19.4%. However, according to government estimates, industrial production increased by 1.4% in 1995, and by 1.3% in 1996.

Mining and quarrying contributed 1.6% of GDP in 1996, and provided 1.4% of employment in the same year. Estonia's principal mineral resource is oil-shale, and there are also deposits of peat and phosphorite ore. There are total estimated reserves of oil-shale of some 4,000 metric tons. Annual extraction of oil-shale reached 31m. metric tons in 1980, but had decreased to 13.5m. tons in 1995. Phosphorite ore is processed to produce phosphates for use in agriculture, but development of the industry has been accompanied by increasing environmental problems.

In 1996 the manufacturing sector accounted for 15.9% of GDP and engaged an estimated 23.9% of the employed labour force. The sector is based on products of food- and beverage-processing (especially dairy products), textiles and clothing, fertilizers and other chemical products, and wood and timber products (particularly furniture). In 1994 production in the sector was estimated to have declined by 3.5%, but in 1995 it was reported that the sector's GDP increased by 3.7%.

The country relies on oil-shale for about 65% of its energy requirements. Some 50% of electricity produced in this way is exported. In 1995 imports of fuel and energy products accounted for an estimated 5.9% of total imports.

Estonia's services sector was the most developed in the former USSR. In 1996 the sector accounted for 65.1% of GDP and engaged 56.4% of the employed population. Although services GDP declined by an annual average of 27.1% in 1990–94, the sector subsequently expanded considerably, in response to increased tourism and Western investment. Services GDP increased by an estimated 3.5%, in real terms, in 1995.

In 1996 Estonia recorded a visible trade deficit of US $1,057.7m., while there was a deficit of $447.3m. on the current account of the balance of payments. Of all the former republics of the USSR, Estonia experienced the most rapid reorientation of its trade after 1991: trade with Western countries, particularly Scandinavia, increased considerably, while trade with former Soviet republics declined from about 90% of the pre-1991 total to some 30% in 1995. In 1996 Finland was Estonia's principal trading partner, accounting for 29.2% of imports and 18.3% of exports; other important trading partners were Russia, Sweden and Germany. In 1996 the principal exports were foodstuffs and animal products, textiles, timber products, base metals, mineral products, machinery and chemical products. The principal imports were machinery and transport equipment, mineral products, textiles, food products, base metals and chemical products.

In 1996, according to the IMF, there was a budget deficit of 96.6m. kroons (equivalent to 0.2% of GDP). Estonia's external debt totalled US $308.8m. at the end of 1995, of which $181.7m. was long-term public debt. In 1995 the cost of debt-servicing was equivalent to 0.8% of the value of exports of goods and services. The annual rate of inflation averaged 3.3% in 1980–89, rising to 17% in 1990, to 202% in 1991 and to as high as 1,069% in 1992. However, in 1993, following a programme of radical monetary reform, the average annual rate of inflation was reduced to 89%. During 1992–96 the annual rate of inflation averaged 45.2%. Consumer prices increased by an average of 23.1% in 1996 and by 11.9% in the year to August 1997. Some 37,350 people (approximately 4.3% of the labour force) were officially registered as unemployed in December 1996.

In 1992 Estonia became a member of the IMF and the World Bank. It also joined the European Bank for Reconstruction and Development (see p. 148). In 1994 Estonia signed a free-trade agreement with the EU; in June 1995 Estonia became an associate member of the EU, and in December it applied for full membership.

Even before it regained independence in mid-1991, Estonia had begun a transition to a market economic system, which included the nationalization of formerly Soviet-controlled enterprises and the establishment of a central bank as well as a private banking system. Further far-reaching economic reforms were continued in the early 1990s. Despite Estonia's relative prosperity during the Soviet period, the collapse of the USSR and its internal economic system resulted in serious economic difficulties. An annual decline in output was recorded in all sectors in 1991 and 1992. However, a rapid rise in the volume of exports and growing foreign investment in the country helped to reverse this trend from 1993 onwards. There was also a remarkable decrease in the rate of inflation during 1993–97. These successes were ascribed to the Government's effective budgetary and monetary reforms, which included the introduction, in June 1992, of a new currency, the kroon, replacing the rouble. During 1992–97 the kroon's value remained stable in relation to the Deutsche Mark, further enhancing international financial confidence in Estonia. Meanwhile, the country's privatization programme advanced considerably in some sectors. In late 1995 almost all small enterprises had been privatized, as well as some 75% of medium and large businesses. During 1997, despite a short-lived financial crisis on the Tallinn Stock Exchange in October–November, growth was recorded in most sectors (growth in industry was estimated at 13%), and greater foreign investment was encouraged by the continuing programme of divestment (one of the country's largest concerns, the Estonian Shipping Co, was successfully transferred to the private sector in June). In October 1997 it was estimated that total investment from abroad since independence amounted to some US $700m. However, some international financial institutions have continued to express concern regarding the slow pace of land reform and the growing current-account deficit.

Social Welfare

In pre-1940 Estonia health care was provided by both state and private facilities. A comprehensive state-funded health system was introduced under Soviet rule. This system was restructured in the early 1990s. Social security is administered by the state and provided through specialized agencies, while social assistance and social services are the responsibility of local municipalities. The system of social security comprises pensions insurance (introduced in 1993), health insurance (1991), family benefits (1994), unemployment benefits (1995) and funeral grants (1993). Under the social assistance programme, subsistence cash benefits are paid according to means-testing. There is a relatively high number of physicians, equivalent to 30 per 10,000 inhabitants in 1996, but a shortage of auxiliary staff. There were 76 hospital beds per 10,000 inhabitants in 1996. Of total expenditure by all levels of government in 1996, 16.2% was for health, and a further 28.0% for social security and welfare.

Education

The Estonian education system consists of pre-school, primary, secondary, vocational, university/higher, and adult education. Compulsory education begins at the age of seven and lasts for nine years: primary school (Grades 1-6) and lower secondary (Grades 7-9). Students may then attend either general secondary school (Grades 10-12) or vocational school. Higher education is provided at 71 institutes of higher education, including Tartu University (founded in 1632) and the Tallinn Technical University. In 1996/97 there were 43,468 students in higher education. The language of instruction at all levels is either Estonian or Russian. In 1992/93 the proportion of students instructed in Estonian was: primary and lower secondary 64%, upper secondary 76%, vocational and technical 65% and higher 81%. In 1995 the total enrolment at primary and secondary schools was equivalent to 97% of the school-age population (95% of boys, 98% of girls). In 1989, according to census results, only 0.3% of the adult population were illiterate. Expenditure on education by all levels of government represented 10.4% of total government spending in 1996.

Public Holidays

1998: 1 January (New Year's Day), 24 February (Independence Day), 10 April (Good Friday), 1 May (Labour Day), 23 June (Victory Day, anniversary of the Battle of Võnnu in 1919), 24 June (Midsummer Day), 25–26 December (Christmas).

1999: 1 January (New Year's Day), 24 February (Independence Day), 2 April (Good Friday), 1 May (Labour Day), 23 June (Victory Day, anniversary of the Battle of Võnnu in 1919), 24 June (Midsummer Day), 25–26 December (Christmas).

Weights and Measures

The metric system is in force.

Statistical Survey

Source (unless otherwise stated): State Statistical Office, Endla 15, Tallinn 0100; tel. 6259-202; fax (2) 453-923.

Area and Population

AREA, POPULATION AND DENSITY

Area (sq km)	45,227*
Population (census results)†	
17 January 1979	1,464,476
12 January 1989	
Males	731,392
Females	834,270
Total	1,565,662
Population (official estimates at 1 January)†	
1995	1,491,583
1996	1,476,301
1997	1,462,130
Density (per sq km) at 1 January 1997	32.3

* 7,462 sq miles.

† Figures refer to permanent inhabitants. The *de facto* total at the 1989 census was 1,572,916.

POPULATION BY NATIONALITY
(estimated permanent inhabitants at 1 January 1997)

	Number	%
Estonian	950,124	65.0
Russian	412,628	28.2
Ukrainian	37,306	2.6
Belarusian	21,883	1.5
Finnish	13,629	0.9
Tatar	3,315	0.2
Latvian	2,723	0.2
Jewish	2,553	0.2
Polish	2,374	0.2
Lithuanian	2,245	0.2
German	1,349	0.1
Others	12,001	0.8
Total	1,462,130	100.0

PRINCIPAL TOWNS
(estimated population, excluding suburbs, at 1 January 1997)

Tallinn (capital)	420,500	Kohtla-Järve	53,500
Tartu	101,900	Pärnu	51,800
Narva	75,200		

BIRTHS, MARRIAGES AND DEATHS

	Registered live births		Registered marriages		Registered deaths	
	Number	Rate (per 1,000)	Number	Rate (per 1,000)	Number	Rate (per 1,000)
1989	24,292	15.5	12,644	8.1	18,530	11.8
1990	22,308	14.2	11,774	7.5	19,530	12.4
1991	19,320	12.3	10,292	6.6	19,705	12.6
1992	18,006	11.7	8,878	5.7	20,115	13.0
1993	15,170	10.0	7,745	5.1	21,267	14.0
1994	14,178	9.5	7,378	4.9	22,150	14.8
1995	13,560	9.1	7,006	4.7	20,872	14.1
1996	13,291	9.0	5,517	3.8	19,019	12.9

Expectation of life (years at birth, 1995): 67.9 (males 61.7; females 74.3).

EMPLOYMENT
(labour force sample surveys, annual averages, '000 persons aged 15 years and over, excl. armed forces)

	1994	1995	1996
Agriculture, hunting and forestry	87.5	63.0	59.7
Fishing	13.5	6.0	5.0
Mining and quarrying	11.2	9.1	8.9
Manufacturing	143.2	162.9	154.4
Electricity, gas and water supply	19.5	15.8	16.4
Construction	49.9	35.6	36.8
Wholesale and retail trade	88.1	82.7	85.8
Hotels and restaurants	18.7	18.0	17.8
Transport, storage and communications	58.2	65.8	64.7
Financial intermediation	7.9	7.1	6.6
Real estate, renting and business activities	29.9	32.2	32.3
Public administration and defence	36.4	35.7	35.0
Education	48.2	55.8	56.3
Health and social work	47.0	36.5	35.9
Other community, social and personal service activities	27.0	29.3	28.8
Activities not adequately defined	6.5	0.5	1.2
Total employed	692.6	656.1	645.6

1989 census ('000 persons aged 15 years and over): Total labour force 856 (males 428; females 428).

Agriculture

PRINCIPAL CROPS ('000 metric tons)

	1994	1995	1996
Wheat	57	77	101
Barley	340	280	317
Rye	41	58	62
Oats	58	80	115
Other cereals	15	25	48
Potatoes	563	537	500
Cabbages	40	19	22
Tomatoes	3	3	3
Cucumbers and gherkins	6	6	5
Carrots	6	9	10
Other vegetables	23	20	15
Fruits and berries	21	37	15

LIVESTOCK ('000 head at 1 January)

	1995	1996	1997
Cattle	419.5	370.4	343.0
Pigs	459.8	448.8	298.4
Sheep and goats	61.5	49.8	39.2
Poultry	3,129.7	2,911.3	2,324.9

LIVESTOCK PRODUCTS
('000 metric tons, unless otherwise indicated)

	1994	1995	1996
Beef and veal	31	26	22
Mutton and lamb	1	1	1
Pig meat	30	35	32
Poultry meat	6	6	4
Cows' milk	772	707	675
Butter (metric tons)	18,900	15,600	17,224*
Cheese	10.7	8.6	8.9*
Poultry eggs (metric tons)	22,462	20,418	18,741
Honey (metric tons)	642	621	335

* Provisional.

Forestry

ROUNDWOOD REMOVALS ('000 cu m, excl. bark)

	1992	1993	1994*
Sawlogs, veneer logs and logs for sleepers	515	561	561
Pulpwood	600	634	634
Other industrial wood	224	196	196
Fuel wood	807	1,048	1,048
Total	2,146	2,439	2,439

* FAO estimates.

Source: FAO, *Yearbook of Forest Products*.

1995: Total roundwood removals 3,820,000 cu m.
1996: Total roundwood removals 4,029,000 cu m.

SAWNWOOD PRODUCTION ('000 cu m, incl. railway sleepers)

	1992	1993*	1994*
Coniferous (softwood)	270	270	270
Broadleaved (hardwood)	30	30	30
Total	300	300	300

* FAO estimates.

Source: FAO, *Yearbook of Forest Products*.

Fishing

('000 metric tons, live weight)

	1994	1995	1996
Blue whiting	4.3	13.7	11.0
Atlantic redfishes	18.0	17.7	7.1
Jack and horse mackerels	41.8	30.6	10.2
Other fishes*	56.3	69.6	80.1
Total catch	120.4	131.6	108.4

* Including crustaceans and molluscs.

Mining

('000 metric tons)

	1994	1995	1996*
Oil-shale	14,530	13,310	14,735
Peat	645	583	629

* Provisional.

Industry

SELECTED PRODUCTS ('000 metric tons, unless otherwise indicated)

	1994	1995	1996*
Wine and spirits ('000 hectolitres)	123	173	84
Beer ('000 hectolitres)	477	492	454
Soft drinks ('000 hectolitres)	368	435	571
Textile fabrics (million sq metres)	78	94	124
Footwear ('000 pairs)	800	682	897
Plywood ('000 cubic metres)	9.9	11.2	18
Paper	—	5.9	19.5
Paperboard	0.3	0.4	0.9
Building bricks (million)	48	31	24
Cement	403	418	388
Electric energy (million kWh)	9,152	8,693	9,102

* Provisional.

Finance

CURRENCY AND EXCHANGE RATES

Monetary Units
100 cents = 1 kroon.

Sterling and Dollar Equivalents (30 September 1997)
£1 sterling = 22.90 kroons;
US $1 = 14.17 kroons;
1,000 kroons = £43.67 = $70.55.

Average Exchange Rate (kroons per US $)
1994 12.991
1995 11.465
1996 12.034

Note: In June 1992 Estonia reintroduced its national currency, the kroon, replacing the rouble of the former USSR, initially at a rate of one kroon per 10 roubles (for details of the rouble, see the chapter on the Russian Federation).

BUDGET
(million kroons)*

Revenue	1994	1995	1996
Central government	6,910.1	8,909.7	10,747.3
Taxation	6,633.5	8,635.6	10,437.5
Taxes on income and profits	2,228.7	2,771.4	2,827.2
Taxes on property	29.7	44.4	—
Domestic taxes on goods and services	3,715.7	4,986.1	6,233.9
Taxes on international trade	505.4	571.5	1,086.1
Non-tax receipts	256.6	271.1	292.6
Local government	1,496.4	2,505.5	3,868.6
Taxation	1,313.7	1,986.0	2,669.6
Taxes on income and profits	1,197.8	1,871.3	2,404.4
Taxes on property	94.2	104.3	211.0
Taxes on goods and services	8.5	8.7	53.3
Non-tax receipts	148.8	206.9	318.8
Extrabudgetary funds	4,468.8	5,957.7	7,298.9
Taxation	3,919.0	5,201.1	6,508.3
Pollution tax	20.6	35.3	40.9
Social security and health tax	3,876.3	5,128.2	6,395.5
Gambling tax	22.1	37.6	71.9
Non-tax receipts	315.2	417.4	440.6
Total	12,875.3	17,372.9	21,914.8

Expenditure	1994	1995	1996
Central government	5,221.3	6,751.5	8,463.5
Current expenditure	4,334.8	5,813.7	7,303.3
Goods and services	3,602.8	5,096.1	6,471.6
Subsidies and current transfers	732.0	717.6	831.7
Capital expenditure	886.5	937.8	1,160.2
Local government	2,134.4	3,279.2	4,654.1
Current expenditure	1,711.9	2,608.9	3,287.0
Capital expenditure	422.5	670.3	1,367.1
Extrabudgetary funds	4,579.5	6,642.2	8,553.6
Social Fund	2,611.1	3,677.6	4,943.8
Health Security Fund	1,458.4	2,118.8	2,577.9
Other funds	510.0	845.8	1,031.9
Total	11,935.2	16,672.9	21,671.2

* Figures represent a consolidation of the operations of all Estonian government units, i.e. excluding transfers between different levels of government.

INTERNATIONAL RESERVES
(US $ million at 31 December)

	1994	1995	1996
Gold*	3.61	3.19	3.03
IMF special drawing rights	1.58	0.29	0.17
Reserve position in IMF	0.01	0.01	0.01
Foreign exchange	441.76	579.61	636.64
Total	446.96	583.10	639.85

* National valuation.

Source: IMF, *International Financial Statistics.*

MONEY SUPPLY (million kroons at 31 December)

	1994	1995	1996
Currency outside banks	3,131.3	3,837.5	4,270.5
Demand deposits at banks	3,248.6	4,399.6	6,513.9
Total money	6,379.9	8,237.1	10,784.4

Source: IMF, *International Financial Statistics.*

COST OF LIVING (Retail price index; base: 1990 = 100)

	1994	1995	1996
Food (incl. beverages)	8,011	9,275	10,966
Fuel and light	30,391	38,636	46,381
Clothing (incl. footwear)	6,067	7,285	8,391
Rent	14,354	24,021	28,671
All items (incl. others)	9,960	12,849	15,811

NATIONAL ACCOUNTS (million kroons at current prices)

Expenditure on the Gross Domestic Product

	1993	1994*	1995*
Government final consumption expenditure	4,473.8	6,790.1	9,701.6
Non-profit institutions	120.0	145.6	207.0
Private final consumption expenditure	12,416.9	17,532.1	23,490.6
Increase in stocks	541.0	786.0	774.5
Gross fixed capital formation	5,280.0	7,827.5	10,374.7
Total domestic expenditure	22,831.7	33,081.3	44,548.4
Exports of goods and services f.o.b.	15,197.0	23,799.0	31,326.9
Less Imports of goods and services f.o.b.	16,124.9	27,034.2	34,921.9
Statistical discrepancy	156.1	256.8	550.0
GDP in purchasers' values	22,059.9	30,102.9	41,503.4

* Figures are provisional.

Gross Domestic Product by Economic Activity

	1994	1995	1996*
Agriculture and forestry	2,560.5	2,767.7	3,101.6
Fishing	153.6	173.3	221.3
Mining and quarrying	478.2	601.3	719.3
Manufacturing	5,021.6	6,264.6	7,244.2
Electricity, gas and water supply	870.5	1,441.5	1,927.2
Construction	1,683.9	2,115.9	2,702.6
Trade	4,077.8	5,988.2	8,081.2
Hotels and restaurants	311.2	436.4	668.8
Transport, storage and communications	3,060.0	3,776.2	4,794.8
Financing, banking and insurance	847.8	1,321.3	2,226.5
Real estate, renting and business activities	2,211.0	3,698.8	4,567.2
Public administration	1,193.5	1,690.4	1,858.4
Education	1,510.0	2,173.0	2,482.5
Health and social care	947.2	1,459.9	2,114.8
Other personal and household services	1,551.8	2,376.6	2,897.9
GDP at factor cost	26,478.6	36,285.1	45,608.3
Indirect taxes	4,076.4	5,305.0	6,770.7
Less subsidies	287.1	311.0	
GDP in purchasers' values	30,276.9	41,279.1	52,379.0

* Figures are provisional.

BALANCE OF PAYMENTS (US $ million)

	1994	1995	1996
Exports of goods f.o.b.	1,327.4	1,856.3	2,063.8
Imports of goods f.o.b.	−1,682.5	−2,530.0	−3,121.5
Trade balance	−355.2	−673.6	−1,057.7
Exports of services	515.3	876.8	1,108.3
Imports of services	−410.2	−497.7	−608.4
Balance on goods and services	−250.0	−294.5	−557.7
Other income received	37.3	63.6	112.2
Other income paid	−66.9	−60.8	−110.3
Balance on goods, services and income	−279.6	−291.7	−555.8
Current transfers received	120.3	134.5	125.0
Current transfers paid	−5.7	−8.2	−16.4
Current balance	−165.0	−165.4	−447.3
Capital account (net)	−0.6	−0.8	−0.7
Direct investment abroad	−2.4	−2.5	−40.1
Direct investment from abroad	214.4	201.5	150.2
Portfolio investment assets	−22.5	−33.2	−52.7
Portfolio investment liabilities	8.4	11.1	198.1
Other investment assets	−146.7	−98.9	9.0
Other investment liabilities	115.9	155.4	325.2
Net errors and omissions	15.9	16.3	−35.6
Overall balance	17.5	83.5	106.3

Source: IMF, *International Financial Statistics*.

External Trade

PRINCIPAL COMMODITIES
(million kroons)

Imports	1994	1995	1996
Vegetable products	585.7	896.4	1,267.6
Prepared foodstuffs, beverages, spirits, vinegar and tobacco	2,135.0	2,190.2	3,252.1
Mineral products	3,034.7	3,341.3	3,791.7
Products of the chemical or allied industries	1,627.1	2,333.9	3,554.6
Plastics, rubber and articles thereof	843.1	1,319.8	1,711.1
Wood pulp, paper and paperboard	570.3	973.5	1,259.0
Textiles and textile articles	2,217.3	3,023.5	3,618.8
Footwear, headgear, etc.	339.8	383.0	464.1
Pearls, precious or semi-precious stones, precious metals and articles thereof	57.7	82.4	71.7
Base metals and articles of base metal	1,278.5	2,059.9	3,015.0
Machinery (incl. electrical) and parts	4,242.1	6,280.6	8,448.4
Transport equipment	1,849.5	2,307.2	2,877.5
Miscellaneous manufactured articles	596.5	850.6	1,057.4
Total (incl. others)	21,509.3	29,111.9	38,552.6

Exports	1994	1995	1996
Live animals and animal products	1,300.1	1,616.4	1,559.1
Animal or vegetable fats, oil and waxes	78.9	103.8	85.3
Prepared foodstuffs, beverages, spirits, vinegar and tobacco	2,077.5	1,472.5	1,952.0
Mineral products	1,382.9	1,707.4	1,799.7
Products of the chemical or allied industries	1,148.0	1,593.5	2,200.4
Plastics, rubber and articles thereof	302.5	559.8	545.1
Raw hides and skins, leather, furskins and articles thereof	208.6	239.3	310.7
Wood and cork products, etc.	1,730.1	2,622.6	2,857.6
Wood pulp, paper and paperboard	139.6	246.2	490.6
Textiles and textile articles	2,324.8	2,842.4	3,563.8
Footwear, headgear, etc.	249.2	304.9	393.9
Base metals and articles of base metal	1,350.1	1,437.1	1,596.5
Machinery (incl. electrical) and parts	1,572.2	2,741.1	3,355.2
Vehicles, aircraft, vessels and associated transport equipment	1,287.2	1,455.5	1,587.2
Miscellaneous manufactured articles	918.5	1,194.3	1,497.7
Total (incl. others)	16,924.4	21,048.8	24,988.3

PRINCIPAL TRADING PARTNERS (million kroons)

Imports	1994	1995	1996
Denmark	568.4	810.1	1,088.0
Finland	6,432.4	9,486.8	11,257.4
France	317.5	419.9	779.1
Germany	2,143.3	2,783.2	3,843.3
Italy	517.0	758.9	1,245.6
Japan	627.4	545.2	781.7
Latvia	313.1	577.2	747.5
Lithuania	553.5	470.2	603.3
Netherlands	661.5	902.8	1,098.7
Russia	3,620.0	4,687.4	5,201.6
Sweden	1,911.1	2,466.5	3,149.8
Ukraine	362.8	308.3	619.0
United Kingdom	458.7	643.2	1,275.6
USA	536.5	710.6	882.0
Total (incl. others)	21,509.3	29,111.9	38,552.6

Exports	1994	1995	1996
Denmark	577.0	691.7	885.3
Finland	3,022.6	4,526.1	4,583.6
Germany	1,153.7	1,517.5	1,764.0
Latvia	1,390.0	1,573.6	2,066.2
Lithuania	916.9	986.5	1,434.4
Netherlands	532.8	981.0	753.3
Poland	115.6	241.2	290.9
Russia	3,905.5	3,698.1	4,107.8
Sweden	1,836.7	2,292.6	2,890.2
Ukraine	518.2	789.3	1,254.7
United Kingdom	471.8	689.9	866.6
USA	308.9	503.2	552.4
Total (incl. others)	16,924.4	21,048.8	24,988.3

Transport

DOMESTIC PASSENGER TRAFFIC (million passenger-kilometres)

	1994	1995	1996
Railway traffic	537	421	309
Road traffic (bus traffic)	2,314	2,048	2,091
Sea traffic	286	244	272
Air traffic	159	138	158
Total public transport	3,296	2,851	2,830

DOMESTIC FREIGHT TRAFFIC (million ton-kilometres)

	1994	1995	1996
Railway traffic	3,652	3,846	4,198
Road traffic	1,415	1,549	1,897
Sea traffic	27,154	n.a.	28,918
River traffic	1	0	0
Total public transport	32,222	n.a.	35,013

ROAD TRAFFIC (motor vehicles in use at 31 December)

	1994	1995	1996
Passenger cars	337,812	383,444	406,598
Buses and coaches	6,340	7,009	6,829
Lorries and vans	70,663	89,685	100,580

SHIPPING

Merchant Fleet (registered at 31 December)

	1994	1995	1996
Number of vessels	262	235	220
Total displacement ('000 grt)	695	598	545

Source: Lloyd's Register of Shipping.

International Sea-borne Freight Traffic ('000 metric tons)

	1994	1995	1996
Goods loaded	7,064	10,964	11,465
Goods unloaded	4,310	3,424	3,993

Source: UN, *Monthly Bulletin of Statistics.*

CIVIL AVIATION (traffic on scheduled services)

	1992	1993	1994
Kilometres flown (million)	4	4	4
Passengers carried ('000)	146	128	157
Passenger-km (million)	102	86	92
Total ton-km (million)	10	8	9

Source: UN, *Statistical Yearbook.*

Tourism

	1994	1995	1996
Foreign tourist arrivals	586,818	1,284,891	1,354,101

Communications Media

(at 1 January)

	1994	1995	1996
Books published (titles)*	2,291	2,635	2,628
Books published ('000 copies)*	8,592	7,930	6,662
Daily newspapers (number)	15	19	15

* Including pamphlets (689 titles in 1996).

Radio receivers in use: 221,000 in 1996.

Television receivers in use: 455,000 in 1996.

Telephones (main lines) in use: 439,000 in 1997.

Telefax stations: 10,000 in use in 1994 (Source: UN, *Statistical Yearbook*).

Mobile cellular telephones (subscribers): 13,770 in 1994 (Source: UN, *Statistical Yearbook).*

Education

(1996/97)

	Institutions	Students
Pre-primary education	667	58,386
Primary education	735	126,800
General secondary education	565	95,877
Vocational secondary education	62	18,091
Higher education	71	43,468
Post-secondary technical	44	13,396
University	27	30,072

Directory

The Constitution

A new Constitution, based on that of 1938, was adopted by a referendum held on 28 June 1992. It took effect on 3 July. The following is a summary of its main provisions:

FUNDAMENTAL RIGHTS, LIBERTIES AND DUTIES

Every child with one parent who is an Estonian citizen has the right, by birth, to Estonian citizenship. Anyone who, as a minor, lost his or her Estonian citizenship has the right to have his or her citizenship restored. The rights, liberties and duties of all persons, as listed in the Constitution, are equal for Estonian citizens as well as for citizens of foreign states and stateless persons who are present in Estonia.

All persons are equal before the law. No one may be discriminated against on the basis of nationality, race, colour, sex, language, origin, creed, political or other persuasions. Everyone has the right to the protection of the state and the law. Guaranteeing rights and liberties is the responsibility of the legislative, executive and judicial powers, as well as of local government. Everyone has the right to appeal to a court of law if his or her rights or liberties have been violated.

The state organizes vocational education and assists in finding work for persons seeking employment. Working conditions are under state supervision. Employers and employees may freely join unions and associations. Estonian citizens have the right to engage in commercial activities and to form profit-making associations. The property rights of everyone are inviolable. All persons legally present in Estonia have the right to freedom of movement and choice of abode. Everyone has the right to leave Estonia.

Everyone has the right to health care [and to] education. Education is compulsory for school-age children. Everyone has the right to instruction in Estonian.

The official language of state and local government authorities is Estonian. In localities where the language of the majority of the population is other than Estonian, local government authorities may use the language of the majority of the permanent residents of that locality for internal communication.

THE PEOPLE

The people exercise their supreme power through citizens who have the right to vote by: i) electing the Riigikogu (legislature); ii) participating in referendums. The right to vote belongs to every Estonian citizen who has attained the age of 18 years.

THE RIIGIKOGU

Legislative power rests with the Riigikogu (State Assembly). It comprises 101 members, elected every four years in free elections on the principle of proportionality. Every citizen entitled to vote who has attained 21 years of age may be a candidate for the Riigikogu.

The Riigikogu adopts laws and resolutions; decides on the holding of referendums; elects the President of the Republic; ratifies or rejects foreign treaties; authorizes the candidate for Prime Minister to form the Council of Ministers; adopts the national budget and approves the report on its execution; may declare a state of emergency, or, on the proposal of the President, declare a state of war, order mobilization and demobilization.

The Riigikogu elects from among its members a Chairman (Speaker) and two Deputy Chairmen to direct the work of the Riigikogu.

THE PRESIDENT

The President of the Republic is the Head of State of Estonia. The President represents Estonia in international relations; appoints and recalls, on the proposal of the Government, diplomatic representatives of Estonia and accepts letters of credence of diplomatic representatives accredited to Estonia; declares regular (and early) elections to the Riigikogu; initiates amendments to the Constitution; nominates the candidate for the post of Prime Minister; and is the Supreme Commander of Estonia's armed forces.

The President is elected by secret ballot of the Riigikogu for a term of five years. No person may be elected to the office for more than two consecutive terms. Any Estonian citizen by birth, who is at least 40 years of age, may stand as a candidate for President.

Should the President not be elected after three rounds of voting, the Speaker of the Riigikogu convenes, within one month, an Electoral Body to elect the President.

THE GOVERNMENT

Executive power is held by the Government of the Republic (Council of Ministers). The Government implements national domestic and foreign policies; directs and co-ordinates the work of government institutions; organizes the implementation of legislation, the resolutions of the Riigikogu, and the edicts of the President; submits draft legislation to the Riigikogu, as well as foreign treaties; prepares a draft of the national budget and presents it to the Riigikogu; administers the implementation of the national budget; and organizes relations with foreign states.

The Government comprises the Prime Minister and Ministers. The President of the Republic nominates a candidate for Prime Minister, who is charged with forming a new government.

JUDICIAL SYSTEM

Justice is administered solely by the courts. They are independent in their work and administer justice in accordance with the Constitution and laws. The court system is comprised of rural and city, as well as administrative, courts (first level); district courts (second level); the National Court (the highest court in the land).

The Government

HEAD OF STATE

President: LENNART MERI (elected 5 October 1992, re-elected 20 September 1996).

COUNCIL OF MINISTERS
(February 1998)

A coalition of the Estonian Coalition Party/Rural Union (ECP/RU) electoral alliance and independents.

Prime Minister: MART SIIMANN (ECP/RU).

Minister of Internal Affairs: OLARI TAAL (Independent).

Minister of Foreign Affairs: TOOMAS HENDRIK ILVES (Farmers' Union*).

Minister of Justice: PAUL VARUL (Independent).

Minister of Economic Affairs: JAAK LEIMANN (Independent).

Minister of Finance: MART OPMANN (Independent).

Minister of Transport and Communications: RAIVO VARE (Independent).

Minister of the Environment: VILLU REILJAN (ECP/RU).

Minister of Culture: JAAK ALLIK (ECP/RU).

Minister of Education: MAIT KLAASSEN (Independent).

Minister of Agriculture: ANDRES VARIK (ECP/RU).

Minister of Social Affairs: TIIU ARO (ECP/RU).

Minister of Defence: ANDRUS ÖÖVEL (ECP/RU).

Minister without Portfolio: ANDRA VEIDEMANN (Development Party*).

Minister without Portfolio: PEEP ARU (ECP/RU).

* Not an official member of the coalition Government.

MINISTRIES

Office of the Prime Minister: Lossi plats 1A, Tallinn 0100; tel. 631-6701; fax 631-6704.

State Chancellery: Lossi plats 1A, Tallinn 0100; tel. 631-6860; fax 631-6914; e-mail riik@rk.ee.

Ministry of Agriculture: Lai 39/41, Tallinn 0100; tel. 625-6103; fax 625-6200.

Ministry of Culture: Suur-Karja 23, Tallinn 0001; tel. 628-2222; fax 6282-200; e-mail min@kul.ee.

Ministry of Defence: Sakala 1, Tallinn 0100; tel. 640-6010; fax 640-6001.

Ministry of Economic Affairs: Harju 11, Tallinn 0001; tel. 625-6304; fax 631-3660.

Ministry of Education: Tõnismägi 11, Tallinn 0100; tel. 6282-212; fax 631-1213; e-mail hm@hm.ee.

Ministry of the Environment: Toompuiestee 24, Tallinn 0100; tel. 626-2800; fax 626-2801; e-mail min@ekm.envir.ee; internet http://www.envir.ee.

Ministry of Finance: Suur-Ameerika 1, Tallinn 0100; tel. 631-7808; fax 631-7810; e-mail admin@fin.ee; internet http://www.netexpress.ee/rahmin.

Ministry of Foreign Affairs: Rävala 9, Tallinn 0100; tel. 631-7000; fax 631-7099; e-mail vminfo@vm.ee; internet http://www.vm.ee.

Ministry of Internal Affairs: Pikk 61, Tallinn 0100; tel. 612-5001; fax 612-5011; e-mail piret@sisemin.gov.ee.

Ministry of Justice: Tõnismägi 5A, Tallinn 0104; tel. 620-8100; fax 620-8109; e-mail sekretair@just.ee.

Ministry of Social Affairs: Gonsiori 29, Tallinn 0100; tel. 626-9701; fax 631-7909; e-mail lea@fsl.sm.ee; internet http://www.sm.ee.

Ministry of Transport and Communications: Viru 9, Tallinn 0100; tel. 639-7613; fax 639-7606; e-mail nei@mail.kbfi.ee.

President and Legislature

PRESIDENT

The presidential election was held on 26–27 August 1996 in the Riigikogu. LENNART MERI and ARNOLD RÜÜTEL were the contenders. A two-thirds' majority (68 votes) was needed, but, in three rounds of voting, neither contender achieved this. A larger electoral college, comprising the 101 parliamentary deputies and 273 representatives from local government, was convened on 20 September. Five candidates contested the first round of the election and, since no candidates achieved the necessary 188 votes, the leading two candidates, LENNART MERI and ARNOLD RÜÜTEL, went through to the second round of voting. The election was won by LENNART MERI, with 196 votes.

Election, 20 September 1996

Candidate	Votes: First Round	Votes: Second Round*
LENNART MERI	139	196
ARNOLD RÜÜTEL	85	126
TUNNE KELAM	76	—
ENN TOUGU	47	—
SIIRI OVIIR	25	—

* There were 44 abstentions and six invalid votes, with two electors absent.

RIIGIKOGU

(State Assembly)

Speaker: TOOMAS SAVI.

Deputy Speakers: ANTS KAARMA, TUNNE KELAM.

General Election, 5 March 1995

Coalitions and Parties	% of votes	Seats
Estonian Coalition Party/Rural Union*	32.23	41
Estonian Reform Party/Liberals	16.19	19
Estonian Centre Party†	14.17	16
National Fatherland Party/Estonian National Independence Party‡	7.86	8
Moderates	5.99	6
Our Home is Estonia§	5.87	6
Right-wingers	5.00	5
Others	12.69	—
Total	100.00	101

* The Rural Union comprised four agrarian parties, led by the Estonian Rural People's Party.

† Following a split in March 1996, seven deputies from the Estonian Centre Party formed a parliamentary faction known as the New Democratic Association. In May this faction formally established itself as a new political group and was named the Development Party.

‡ Merged in December 1995 as the Fatherland Union.

§ Comprising the Russian Party of Estonia, the Russian People's Party of Estonia and the United People's Party of Estonia.

Political Organizations

Estonian Centre Party (Eesti Keskerakond): POB 3737, Tallinn 0090; tel. (2) 499-304; fax (2) 493-881; e-mail keskerakand@teleport.ee; f. 1991; Chair. EDGAR SAVISAAR.

Estonian Coalition Party (ECP) (Eesti Koonderakond): Raekoja plats 16, Tallinn 0001; tel. 631-4161; fax 631-4041; f. 1991; Chair. MART SIIMANN.

Estonian Democratic Labour Party (Eesti Demokraatlik Tööpartei): Kentmanni 13, Tallinn 0001; tel. 646-6246; fax 646-6320; f. 1920 as the Communist Party of Estonia; renamed as above 1992; Chair. TIIT TOOMSALU; 1,024 mems (1996).

Estonian Greens (Eesti Rohelised): POB 1521, Tallinn 0004; tel. (2) 601-583; fax (2) 492-087; f. 1988; campaigns on environmental, social and economic issues; Chair. JÜRI MARTIN.

Estonian National Progressive Party: Tallinn; f. 1993; Chair. ANTS ERM.

Estonian Pensioners' and Families' Party: Tallinn; f. 1991; Chair. MAI TREIAL.

Estonian Reform Party (ERP) (Eesti Reformierakond): Tõnismagi 3A-15, Tallinn 0001; tel. 640-8740; fax 640-8741; f. 1994; Gen. Sec. HEIKI KRANICH; Chair. SIIM KALLAS.

Estonian Royalist Party (Eesti Rojalistlik Partei): POB 300, Tartu 2400; tel. (7) 432-986; fax (7) 431-466; f. 1989; advocates the establishment of a Kingdom of Estonia; Chair. KALLE KULBOK.

Estonian Rural People's Party (ERPP) (Eesti Maarahva Erakond): Lai 39/41, Tallinn 0001; tel. (2) 609-515; f. 1994; leading party of the Rural Union alliance; Chair. ARNOLD RÜÜTEL.

Estonian Rural Union (Eesti Maaliit): Lai 39, Tallinn 0001; tel. 641-1161; fax 631-6524; f. 1991; Chair. ARVO SIRENDI.

Farmers' Union (Põllumeeste Kogu): POB 543, Tallinn 0010; tel. (2) 437-733; f. 1992; Chair. ELDUR PARDER.

Fatherland Union (Isamaaliit): Endlatn 4A, Tallinn 0001; tel. (6) 263-325; fax (6) 263-324; f. 1995 by merger of the National Fatherland Party (Isamaa, f. 1992) and the Estonian National Independence Party (f. 1988); Chair. TOIVO JÜRGENSON; 2,000 mems.

Moderates' Party: (Erakond Mõõdukad): Rahukohtu 1-15, Tallinn 0001; POB 3437, Tallinn 0090; tel. (6) 316-651; fax (6) 316-653; f. 1996 by merger of the Estonian Rural Centre Party and and the Estonian Social Democratic Party; Chair. ANDRES TARAND; 800 mems.

Moderates' Women's Assembly (Moodukad Naiskogu): Tallinn; f. 1996 to encourage women to take part in politics; Pres. LIIA HANNI.

People's Party of Republicans and Conservatives (Vabariiklaste ja Konservatiivide Rahvaerakond, Parempoolsed): Rahukohtu 1-33, Tallinn 0100; tel. 631-6610; fax 631-6611; f. 1994; Chair. VOOTELE HANSEN.

Progressive Party (Arengupartei): c/o Riigikogu, Lossi plats 1A, Tallinn 0100; f. 1996 following a split in the Estonian Centre Party; Chair. ANDRA VEIDEMANN; Sec.-Gen. TOIVO KEVA; 1,300 mems.

Russian Christian Union: Tallinn; f. 1996; represents Russians in Estonia; Founder BORIS PILAR.

Russian Democratic Movement: Mere pst. 5, Tallinn 0001; tel. (2) 440-421; fax (2) 441-237; f. 1991 to promote domestic peace and mutual understanding between Estonians and Russians living in Estonia.

Russian Party of Estonia: c/o Riigikogu, Lossi plats 1A, Tallinn 0100; f. 1994; merged with the Russian People's Party of Estonia in early 1996; part of the Our Home is Estonia alliance; represents the Russian-speaking minority in Estonia; Chair. NIKOLAI MASPANOV; 500 mems.

Russian Unity Party (RUP): Tallinn; f. 1997 by former members of the Russian Party of Estonia; Leader IGOR SEDASHEV.

United People's Party of Estonia: c/o Riigikogu, Lossi plats 1A, Tallinn 0100; f. 1994; part of the Our Home is Estonia alliance; represents the Russian-speaking minority in Estonia; Chair. VIKTOR ANDREYEV.

Diplomatic Representation

EMBASSIES IN ESTONIA

China, People's Republic: Narva mnt. 98, Tallinn 0001; tel. 641-9041; fax 641-9044; Ambassador: SUN DADONG.

Denmark: Rävala 9, Tallinn 0001; tel. 631-3120; telex 173262; fax 631-3351; e-mail dan.emb@online.ee; Ambassador: SVEND ROED NIELSEN.

Finland: Kohtu 4, Tallinn 0100; tel. 6103-200; fax 6103-281; Ambassador: PEKKA OINONEN.

France: Toom-Kuninga 20, Tallinn 0100; tel. 631-1492; fax 631-1385; Ambassador: JACQUES FAURE.

Germany: Rävala 9, Floor 7, Tallinn 0100; tel. 631-3970; fax 631-6091; Ambassador: BERND MÜTZELBURG.

Italy: Müürivahe 3, Tallinn 0001; tel. 625-6444; fax 631-1370; Ambassador: ROBERTO G. MARTINI.

Japan: Harju 6, Tallinn 0100; tel. 631-0531; fax 631-0533; Chargé d'affaires a.i.: TOHRU KUMADA.

Latvia: Tõnismägi 10, Tallinn 0100; tel. 646-1313; fax 631-1366; Ambassador: ANDRIS PIEBALGS.

Lithuania: Uustn 15, Tallinn 0001; tel. 631-4030; fax 641-2013; Ambassador: RIMANTAS TOMKUNAS.

Norway: Pärnu mnt. 8, Tallinn 0100; tel. (2) 448-014; fax 631-3003; Ambassador: Dr KAI OLAF LIE.

Poland: Pärnu mnt. 8, Tallinn 0001; tel. (2) 440-609; telex 173061; fax (2) 445-221; Ambassador: JAKUB WOLASIEWICZ.

Russia: Pikk 19, Tallinn 0100; tel. 646-4175; fax 646-4178; Ambassador: ALEKSEI GLOUKHOV.

Sweden: Pikk 28, Tallinn 0100; tel. 640-5600; telex 173124; fax 640-5695; Ambassador: KATARINA BRODIN.

Ukraine: Endla 8, Tallinn; tel. 631-1555; Ambassador: YURI OLENENKO.

United Kingdom: Kentmanni 20, Tallinn 0100; tel. 631-3461; fax 631-3354; Ambassador: TIMOTHY JAMES CRADDOCK.

USA: Kentmanni 20, Tallinn 0001; tel. 631-2021; fax 631-2025; Chargé d'affaires: WALTER ANDRUSYSZYN.

Judicial System

National Court: Lossi 17, Tartu 2400; tel. (7) 441-411; fax (7) 441-433; e-mail nc@nc.ee.

Chief Justice: RAIT MARUSTE.

Chairman of the Constitutional Review Chamber: RAIT MARUSTE.

Chairman of the Civil Chamber: JAANO ODAR.

Chairman of the Criminal Chamber: JURI ILVEST.

Chairman of the Administrative Law Chamber: TONU ANTON.

State Prosecutor's Office: Wismari 7, Tallinn 0100; tel. (2) 445-226; fax (2) 451-475; e-mail riigipro@online.ee; State Prosecutor INDREK MEELAK.

Legal Chancellor's Office: Tõnismägi 16, Tallinn 0100; tel. 631-6582; fax 631-6583; e-mail lcer@online.ee; f. 1993; Legal Chancellor EERIK JUHAN TRUUVÄLI.

Religion

CHRISTIANITY

Protestant Churches

Consistory of the Estonian Evangelical Lutheran Church of Estonia: Kiriku plats 3, Tallinn 0001; tel. (2) 451-682; fax (2) 631-3738; Archbishop JAAN KIIVIT.

Estonian Conference of Seventh-day Adventists: Lille 18, Tartu 2400; tel. (7) 441-311; fax (7) 441-389; f. 1917; e-mail advent @uninet.ee; Chair. TÕNU JUGAR.

Union of Evangelical Christian and Baptist Churches of Estonia: Pargi 9, Tallinn 0016; tel. (2) 513-005; fax 650-6008; e-mail ecbu@safun.zzz.ee; Pres. JOOSEP TAMMO.

United Methodist Church in Estonia: Apteegi 3, Tallinn 0001; tel. (2) 445-447; fax 631-3482; f. 1907; Superintendent OLAV PÄRNAMETS.

The Eastern Orthodox Church

Between 1923 and 1940 the Estonian Apostolic Orthodox Church (EAOC) was subordinate to the Constantinople Ecumenical Patriarchate (based in Istanbul, Turkey). Following the Soviet occupation of Estonia in 1940, the EAOC was banned and its churches and communities were placed under the jurisdiction of the Moscow Patriarchate. The leaders of the EAOC went into exile in Stockholm (Sweden). After the restoration of Estonian independence in 1991, negotiations were held between the Constantinople and Moscow Patriarchates over the status of the more than 50 of Estonia's 84 Orthodox congregations that wished to return to Constantinople's jurisdiction. As no agreement was reached, in February 1996 the Constantinople Patriarchate decided unilaterally to restore the EAOC to its jurisdiction. In response, the Russian Orthodox Church suspended relations with Constantinople. The Estonian Government stated that freedom of worship would be guaranteed to the (predominantly Russian-speaking) congregations that wished to remain under the jurisdiction of the Moscow Patriarchate. Relations with Constantinople were restored in May 1996, when the holy synods of the two churches agreed that congregations should be permitted to decide under which jurisdiction they wished to remain.

Estonian Apostolic Orthodox Church: Tallinn; Chair. of Synod NIKOLAI SUURESOOT.

Council of the Russian Orthodox Diocese: Pikk 64/4, Tallinn 0001; tel. 641-1301; fax 641-1302; Archbishop KORNELIUS.

The Roman Catholic Church

At 31 December 1995 there were an estimated 3,500 Roman Catholic adherents in Estonia.

Office of the Apostolic Administrator: Poska Tanav 47, Tallinn; tel. (2) 691-400; fax (2) 426-440; Apostolic Administrator Most Rev. JUSTO MULLOR GARCÍA (Titular Archbishop of Bolsena), Apostolic Nuncio to Lithuania, Estonia and Latvia (resident in Vilnius, Lithuania).

Roman Catholic Parish of St Peter and St Paul in Tallinn: Vene 18, Tallinn 0001; tel. (2) 6446-367; fax (2) 6444-678; Parish Priest Fr ZBIGNIEW PIŁAT.

Tallinn Parish of the Ukrainian Catholic (Uniate) Church: Võrgu 13-6, Tallinn; tel. 632-4306; Chair. of Bd ANATOLIY LYUTYUK.

ISLAM

Estonian Islamic Congregation: Sütiste tee 52-76, Tallinn 0034; tel. (2) 522-403; f. 1928; Chair. of Bd TIMUR SEIFULLEN.

JUDAISM

Hineirry Jewish Progressive Community of Narva: Narva Partisani 2, Narva 2000; tel. (35) 409-97; Chair. of Bd YEVGENII BORINSKII.

Jewish Community of Estonia: POB 3576, Tallinn 0090; tel. and fax (2) 438-566; Chair. CILJA LAUD.

Jewish Progressive Community in Tallinn: POB 200, Tallinn; Chair. of Bd DAVID SLOMKA.

The Press

In 1993 there were 173 officially-registered newspapers published in Estonia, including 129 in Estonian, and 191 periodicals, including 149 in Estonian. There were 15 daily newspapers in 1994.

PRINCIPAL NEWSPAPERS

In Estonian except where otherwise stated.

Äripäev (Business Daily): Tulika 19, Tallinn 0006; tel. 650-5111; fax 654-1095; e-mail mbp@mbp.ee; f. 1989; five days a week; business and finance; Editor-in-Chief IGOR RÕTOV; circ. 16,000.

Den za Dnem-Estonia-M (Day After Day): Pärnu mnt. 67A, Tallinn 0001; tel. (2) 681-294; fax 646-1024; f. 1991; weekly; in Russian; Editor-in-Chief VALERII BELOBROVTSEV; circ. 15,800.

Eesti Ekspress (Estonian Express): Narva mnt. 11E, Tallinn 0001; tel. 611-8080; fax 611-8154; e-mail ekspress@ekspress.ee; f. 1989; weekly; Editor-in-Chief AAVO KONN; circ. 56,500.

Eesti Kirik (Estonian Church): Ülikooli, Tartu 2400; tel. (7) 431-437; fax (7) 441-231; f. 1923; weekly; Editor-in-Chief SIRJE SEMM; circ. 3,000.

Eesti Päevaleht (Estonian Daily): POB 433, Pärnu mnt. 67A, Tallinn 0090; tel. 646-1294; fax 631-1162; e-mail epl@epl.zzz.ee; f. 1905; daily; Editor-in-Chief KALLE MUULI; circ. 35,300.

Estonia: Mere pst. 5, Tallinn 0001; tel. (2) 445-865; fax 6418-402; f. 1940; five days a week in Russian (with Estonian edn Mon.); Editor-in-Chief VLADIMIR VELMAN; circ. 12,000.

Kultuurileht (Cultural Gazette): Pärnu mnt. 8, Tallinn 0001; tel. (2) 448-868; fax (2) 449-247; f. 1940; weekly; Editor-in-Chief TIINA TAMMER; circ. 3,400.

Maaleht (Country News): Toompuiestee 16, Tallinn 0100; tel. (2) 453-521; fax (2) 452-902; e-mail ml@maaleht.ee; f. 1987; weekly; problems and aspects of politics, culture, agriculture and country life; Editor-in-Chief RAUL KILGAS; circ. 40,000.

ME: Pärnu mnt. 67A, Tallinn 0001, tel. (2) 681-131; fax (2) 681-133; e-mail moles@teleport.ee; Editor-in-Chief SERGEI SERGEYEV; circ. 11,400.

Meie Meel (Our Mind): POB 104, Tallinn 0090; tel. (2) 681-253; fax 646-1625; e-mail meiemeel@zzz.ee; f. 1991; weekly; youth paper; Editor-in-Chief MARE VETEMAA; circ. 20,700.

Õhtuleht (Evening Gazette): Pärnu mnt. 67A, Tallinn 0090; tel. (2) 681-860; fax 631-1209; f. 1944; daily; in Estonian; Editor-in-Chief TÕNIS ERILAID; circ. 20,000.

Postimees (Postman): Gildi 1, Tartu 2400; tel. (7) 432-126; fax (7) 433-348; e-mail postimees@postimees.ee; f. 1857; daily; Editor-in-Chief VAHUR KALMRE; circ. 59,200.

Sõnumileht (Reports Newspaper): Vana-Lõuna 37, Tallinn 0001; tel. 640-8930; fax 640-8911; e-mail sleht@ruuter.sl.ee; f. 1995; daily; Editor-in-Chief MART LUIK; circ. 30,000.

PRINCIPAL PERIODICALS

Akadeemia: Ülikooli 21, Tartu 2400; tel. (7) 431-117; fax (7) 431-373; f. 1989; monthly; journal of the Union of Writers; Editor-in-Chief AIN KAALEP; circ. 2,800.

Eesti Arst (Estonian Physician): Piiskopi 3, Tallinn 0001; tel. (2) 444-370; f. 1922; 2 a month; Editor-in-Chief OKU TAMM.

Eesti Loodus (Estonian Nature): Veski 4, Tartu 2400; tel. (7) 421-186; fax (7) 433-472; f. 1933; monthly; popular science; illustrated; Editor-in-Chief UNO SIITAN; circ. 5,200.

Eesti Naine (Estonian Woman): Tartu mnt. 31, Tallinn 0001; tel. 641-9211; fax 641-9212; f. 1924; monthly; Editor-in-Chief KATRIN STREIMANN; circ. 20,000.

Horisont (Horizon): Narva mnt. 5, Tallinn 0001; tel. 641-8055; fax 641-8033; f. 1967; 8 a year; popular scientific; Editor-in-Chief INDREK ROHTMETS; circ. 4,800.

Keel ja Kirjandus (Language and Literature): Roosikrantsi 6, Tallinn 0001; tel. (2) 449-228; fax (2) 441-800; e-mail kk@eki.ee; f. 1958; monthly; joint edition of the Academy of Sciences and the Union of Writers; Editor-in-Chief MART MERI; circ. 1,500.

Kodukiri (Your Home): Regati 1–129A, Tallinn 0019; tel. 639-8083; fax 639-6715; e-mail kodukiri@spin.ee; f. 1992; monthly; Editor-in-Chief KATRIN KUUSEMÄE; circ. 50,000.

Linguistica Uralica: Roosikrantsi 6, Tallinn 0001; tel. (2) 440-745; f. 1965; Editor-in-Chief PAUL KOKLA; circ. 400.

Looming (Creation): Harju 1, Tallinn 0090; tel. (2) 441-365; f. 1923; journal of the Union of Writers; fiction, poetry, literary criticism; Editor-in-Chief ANDRES LANGEMETS; circ. 2,800.

Loomingu Raamatukogu (Library of Creativity): Harju 1, Tallinn 0001; tel. (2) 449-254; f. 1957; journal of the Union of Writers; poetry, fiction and non-fiction by Estonian and foreign authors; Editor-in-Chief TOOMAS HAUG; circ. 1,500.

Maakodu (Country Home): Lai 39, Tallinn 0001; tel. 641-1161; f. 1989; monthly; Editor-in-Chief ARVO SIRENDI; circ. 6,500.

Noorus (Youth): Narva mnt. 11A, Tallinn 0001; tel. 646-6284; fax 640-8399; f. 1946; monthly; youth issues, contemporary life in Estonia and worldwide, fashion, music, culture, business, cinema, essays, etc.; Editor-in-Chief SIIM NESTOR; circ. 8,000.

Oil Shale: Akadeemia tee 15, Tallinn 0026; tel. (2) 537-084; fax (2) 654-754; e-mail trilobite@argus.chemnet.ee; internet http://gaia .gi.ee/oilshale; f. 1984; 4 a year; geology, chemistry, mining, oil-shale industry; Editor-in-Chief JÜRI KANN; circ. 500.

Põllumajandus (Agriculture): Lai 39, Tallinn 0001; tel. 641-1161; f. 1932; monthly; Editor-in-Chief ARVO SIRENDI; circ. 1,000.

Täheke (Little Star): Pärnu mnt. 67A, Tallinn 0007; tel. (2) 681-495; f. 1960; illustrated; for 6–10-year-olds; Editor-in-Chief ELJU SILD; circ. 10,000.

Teater, Muusika, Kino (Theatre, Music, Cinema): POB 3200, Narva mnt. 5, Tallinn 0090; tel. (2) 440-472; fax (2) 434-172; f. 1982; monthly; Editor-in-Chief JÜRI AARMA; circ. 2,000.

Vikerkaar (Rainbow): Pikk 2, Tallinn 0001; tel. (2) 601-318; f. 1986; monthly; fiction, poetry, critical works; in Estonian and Russian; Editor-in-Chief MÄRT VÄLJATAGA; circ. 2,700.

NEWS AGENCIES

BNS (Baltic News Service): Rävala 10, Tallinn 0100 (until June 1998); tel. 610-8800; fax 610-8811; e-mail bns@bns.ee; internet http://www.bns.ee; f. 1990; Dir ALLAN MARTINSON.

ETA (Estonian Telegraph Agency): Pärnu mnt. 67A, Tallinn 0090; tel. 630-0800; telex 173193; fax 630-0817; f 1918; Dir MEELIS PIRN.

PRESS ORGANIZATIONS

Estonian Journalists' Union: Pärnu mnt. 67A, Tallinn 0001; tel. 646-1005; fax 631-1210; e-mail eall@netexpress.ee; f. 1919; Chair. TOIVO TOOTSEN.

Estonian Newspaper Association: Pärnu mnt. 67A, Tallinn 0001; tel. 646-1005; fax 631-1210; e-mail eall@netexpress.ee; f. 1990; 47 mem. newspapers; Man. Dir TARMU TAMMERK.

Publishers

Eesti Raamat (Estonian Book): Lakit 26, Tallinn 0006; tel. and fax (2) 6587-889; f. 1940; fiction; Dir HELLA LEMBER.

Estonian Encyclopaedia Publishers Ltd: Mustamäe tee 5, Tallinn 0006; tel. 6259-415; fax 6566-542; e-mail encyclo@online.ee; f. 1991; Man. Dir TÕNU KOGER.

Koolibri: Pärnu mnt. 10, Tallinn 0090; tel. (2) 445-223; fax (2) 446-813; f. 1991; textbooks, dictionaries, children's books; Dir ANTS LANG.

Kunst (Fine Art): Lai 34, Tallinn 0001; POB 105, Tallinn 0090; tel. 641-1764; fax 641-1762; f. 1957; fine arts, fiction, tourism, history, biographies; Dir SIRJE HELME.

Kupar: Pärnu mnt. 67A, Tallinn 0001; tel. (2) 681-257; fax 6462-076; e-mail kupar@netexpress.ee; f. 1987; contemporary fiction; Chair. of Bd MIHKEL MUTT.

Logos: Siili 21-72, Tallinn 0034; tel. (2) 525-522; fax 631-1501; f. 1991; religious publications; Chair. INGMAR KURG.

Monokkel: POB 311, Tallinn 0001; tel. 6501-6307; f. 1988; history, fiction; Dir ANTS ÖÖBIK.

Olion: Pikk 2, Tallinn 0090; tel. (2) 445-403; f. 1989; politics, economics, history, law; Dir HEINO KÄÄN.

Õllu: Harju 1, Tallinn 0001; tel. (2) 522-038; fiction; Chair. of Bd HEINO KIIK.

Olympia: Ümera 2-85, Tallinn 0001; tel. (2) 442-549; fax 634-4777; sports; Editor-in-Chief PAAVO KIVINE.

Perioodika (Periodicals): Pärnu mnt. 8, POB 107, Tallinn 0090; tel. (2) 441-262; fax (2) 442-484; f. 1964; newspapers, guidebooks, periodicals, fiction, children's books in foreign languages; Dir UNO SILLAJÕE.

Tartu University Press: Tiigi 78, Tartu 2400; tel. (7) 430-851; fax (7) 435-440; science, textbooks, etc; Chair. of Bd MART ORAV.

Tiritamm: Laki 15, Tallinn 0006; tel. and fax 656-3616; f. 1991; children's books; Dir SIRJE SAIMRE.

Valgus: Pärnu mnt. 10, Tallinn 0090; tel. (2) 443-702; fax (2) 445-197; f. 1965; popular science, dictionaries, medicine, engineering, etc.; Man. Dir ARVO HEINING.

PUBLISHERS' ASSOCIATION

Estonian Publishers' Association: Laki 17, Tallinn 0006; POB 3366, Tallinn 0090; tel. 650-5592; fax 650-5590; f. 1991; unites 31 publishing houses; Chair. of Bd TÕNU KOGER.

Broadcasting and Communications

TELECOMMUNICATIONS

Inspectorate of Telecommunications: Adala 4D, Tallinn 0006; tel. 639-9054; fax 639-9055; internet http://www.rei.ee; Dir JURI JOEMA.

RADIO

Eesti Raadio (Estonian Broadcasting Co): Gonsiori 21, Tallinn 0100; tel. (2) 434-115; telex 173271; fax (2) 434-457; internet http://www.er.ee; f. 1926; four channels (three in Estonian, one in Russian); external service (Radio Estonia) in Finnish, English and German; Dir-Gen. PEETER SOOKRUUS.

TELEVISION

Eesti Televisioon (Estonian Television): Faehlmanni 12, Tallinn 0100; tel. (2) 434-113; telex 173869; fax (2) 434-155; e-mail etv@etv.ee; internet http://www.etv.ee; f. 1955; one channel; programmes in Estonian and Russian; Dir-Gen. HAGI SHEIN.

EVTV: Peterburi 81, Tallinn 0014; tel. 632-8228; fax 632-3650; commercial station; Chair. VICTOR SIILATS.

Kanal Kaks (Channel 2): Harju 9, Tallinn 0001; tel. (2) 442-356; fax (2) 446-862; Commercial Station; Chair. ILMAR TASKA.

Reklaamitelevisioon Tallinn (Tallinn Commercial Television): Endla 3, Tallinn 0106; tel. (2) 666-743; fax 631-1077; f. 1992; one channel in Estonian and Russian; Dir-Gen. TOMAS LEPP.

TIPP TV: Regati pst. 1-6, Tallinn 0019; tel. (2) 238-535; fax (2) 238-555; Commercial Station; Pres. JURI MAKAROV.

Finance

(cap. = capital; res = reserves; dep. = deposits; m. = million; brs = branches; amounts in kroons, unless otherwise stated)

BANKING

Central Bank

Bank of Estonia (Eesti Pank): Estonia pst. 13, Tallinn 0100; tel. 631-0911; telex 173146; fax 631-0836; e-mail info@epbe.ee; internet http://www.ee/epbe; f. 1918, re-established 1990; central bank of Estonia; cap. and res. 1,727m. (Oct. 1997), dep. 1,020.8m. (Dec. 1994); Pres. VAHUR KRAFT.

Commercial Banks

In January 1997 there were 13 commercial banks operating in Estonia, as well as one foreign branch (Merita Bank Ltd, Finland).

AS ERA-Pank: Vallikraavi 2, Tartu 2400; tel. (7) 440-401; telex 173133; fax (7) 440-404; f. 1991; cap. 40.0m., res 1.3m. (Oct. 1996); Chair. of Bd YAAK KIIKER; 4 brs.

Bank of Tallinn (Tallinna Pank): Roosikrantsi 2, Tallinn 0100; tel. 6310-000; fax 6110-881; e-mail info@tp.ee; internet http://www.tp.ee; f. 1990; cap. US $22.7m., res US $5.3m., dep. US $98.0m. (Oct. 1997); Man. Dir GUIDO SAMMELSELG; 21 brs.

Eesti Maapank: Tallinna 12, Rakvere 2100; fax 324-3617; e-mail pank@emp.ee; f. 1989; cap. 72.2m., res 7.1m., dep. 625.2m. (Dec. 1996); Pres. MALLE EENMAA; 58 brs.

Estonian Credit Bank (Eesti Krediidipank): Narva mnt. 4, Tallinn 0100; tel. 640-5000; telex 64614901; fax 631-3533; cap. 84.0m., res 7.5m., dep. 345m. (Oct. 1997); Pres. REIN OTSASON; 7 brs.

Estonian Forexbank (Eesti Forekspank): Narva mnt. 11, Tallinn 0001; tel. 630-2100; fax 630-2200; f. 1992; cap. 57.9m., res 6.7m. (Oct. 1996), dep. 430.4m. (Dec 1995); Chair. of Bd IVAR LUKK; 6 brs.

Estonian Investment Bank (Eesti Investeerimispank): Narva mnt. 7, Tallinn 0001; tel. 6200-900; telex 173260; fax 6200-812; e-mail info@estib.ee; f. 1992; cap. 132.4m., res. 7.1m. (Oct. 1996), dep. ECU 12.4m. (Dec. 1994); Pres. HÄRMO VÄRK.

Estonian Savings Bank (Eesti Hoiupank): Rävala 5, Tallinn 0001; tel. 6136-600; telex 173076; fax 6136-700; e-mail kantselet@hoiupank.esb.ee; f. 1992; cap. 253.2m., res 27.7m. (Oct. 1996), total assets US $600m. (Oct. 1997); merger with Hansabank announced in Jan. 1998; Chair. AARE KILP; 170 brs.

EVEA Bank: Narva mnt. 40, Tallinn 0100; tel. (2) 422-122; telex 173184; fax 631-2063; f. 1989; cap. 55.0m., res 7.4m., dep. 290.3m. (Dec. 1996); Pres. BORIS ŠPUNGIN; 9 brs.

Hansabank: Liivalaia 8, Tallinn 0001; tel. 631-0311; telex 173005; fax 631-0410; e-mail webmaster@hansa.ee; cap. 292.4m., res 69.6m. (Oct. 1996), dep. 1,593.2m. (Dec. 1994); merger with Estonian Savings Bank announced in Jan. 1998; Chair. of Bd HANNES TAMJÄRV; 22 brs.

Tallinn Business Bank Ltd (Tallinna Äripanga Aktsiaselts): Estonia pst. 3–5, Tallinn 0100; tel. (2) 455-349; telex 173893; fax (2) 423-322; cap. 50.5m. (Oct. 1996); Chair. of Bd SERGEI SEMYONOV.

Union Bank of Estonia (Eesti Ühispank): Tartu mnt. 13, Tallinn 0001; tel. 610-4300; telex 173006; fax 610-4302; f. 1992; cap. 263.1m., res 29.9m. (Oct. 1996); merged with North Estonian Bank Jan. 1997; Chair. of Bd AIN HANSCHMIDT; 39 brs.

Foreign Bank

Merita Bank Ltd (Finland): Harju 6, Tallinn 0001; tel. 631-4040; fax 631-4153; e-mail merita@estpak.ee; f. 1995; Gen. Man. HEIKKI VIITANEN.

Banking Association

Estonian Banking Association (Eesti Pangaliit): Ahtri 12, Tallinn 0100; tel. 611-6567; fax 611-6568; e-mail post@pangaliit.ee; internet http://www.pangaliit.ee; f. 1992; Chair. of Bd PEETER VÄHI.

STOCK EXCHANGE

Tallinn Stock Exchange: Rävala 6, Tallinn 0001; tel. 640-8840; fax 640-8801; e-mail tse@tse.ee; f. 1995; Chair. HELO MEIGAS.

INSURANCE

Insurance Inspectorate of Estonia: Lauten 5, Tallinn 0001; tel. 610-6700; fax 610-6701; Dir-Gen. ELLEN RIDASTE.

Principal non-life companies include Asa Kindlustus Ltd, Balti Kindlustus (BICO) Ltd, Eesti Varakindlustus Ltd, ETAS Kindlustus Ltd, Hansa Kindlustus Ltd, Inges Kindlustus Ltd, Kalju Ltd, Leks Kindlustus Ltd, Nordika Kindlustus Ltd, Polaris-Vara Ltd, Salva Kindlustus Ltd, Sampo Kindlustus Ltd, Seesam Rahvusvaheline Kindlustus Ltd and Ühiskindlustus.

Principal life companies include AB Elukindlustus Ltd, Bico Elukindlustus Ltd, Eesti Elukindlustus Ltd, Hansapanga Kindlustus Ltd, Leks Elukindlustus Ltd, Nordika Elukindlustus Ltd, Polaris-Elu Ltd and Seesam Elukindlustus Ltd.

Trade and Industry

GOVERNMENT AGENCIES

Consumer Protection Board: Harju 11, Tallinn 0001; tel. 625-6480; fax 625-6481; Dir-Gen. HELLE ARUNIIT.

Estonian Grain Board: Hobujaama 1, Tallinn 0001; tel. (2) 432-815; fax (2) 438-832; Dir-Gen. AGO SOOTS.

Estonian Privatization Agency (Eesti Erastamisagentuur): Rävala 6, Tallinn 0100; tel. 630-5601; fax 630-5699; Dir-Gen. VÄINO SARNET.

Estonian Trade Council: Kiriku 2, Tallinn 0100; tel. (2) 444-703; fax 631-4117; f. 1991; Dir AARE PUUR.

CHAMBER OF COMMERCE

Trade and Investment Board: Rävala pst. 6-602B, Tallinn 0001; tel. 641-0166; fax 641-0312; e-mail info@eia.ee; internet http://www.eia.ee; Dir-Gen. JURI SAKKEUS.

Estonian Chamber of Commerce and Industry: Toom-Kooli 17, Tallinn 0001; tel. 646-0244; fax 646-0245; e-mail koda@koda.ee; internet http://www.koda.ee; f. 1925; Pres. TOOMAS LUMAN.

INDUSTRIAL AND TRADE ASSOCIATIONS

Association of Construction Material Producers of Estonia (Eesti Ehitusmaterjalide Tootjate Liit): Jaama 1A, Tallinn 0016; tel. (2) 512-230; fax 650-6178; Pres. VAMBOLA JUURMANN.

Association of Estonian Electrotechnical and Electronic Industry: Pirita tee 20, Tallinn 0001; tel. (2) 238-981; fax (2) 237-827; Pres. GUNNAR TOOMSOO.

Association of Estonian Food Industry: Gonsiori 29, Tallinn 0001; tel. (2) 422-246; fax 631-2718; Man. Dir HELVE REMMEL.

Association of Estonian International Road Carriers (Eesti Rahvusvaheliste Autovedajate Assotsiatsioon): Rävala pst 9, Tallinn 0001; tel. 6312-673; fax 6312-674; Pres. ENN SARAP.

Association of Estonian Leather Manufacturers (Eesti Nahaliit): Gonsiori 29, Tallinn 0100; tel. (2) 422-907; fax (2) 422-915; Man. Dir ENNU PEDOSK.

Association of Estonian Local Industry: Gonsiori 29, Tallinn 0100; tel (2) 422-367; fax (2) 424-962; Chair. HEINO VASAR.

Estonian Agricultural Producers Central Union (Eestimaa Pollumajandustootjate Keskliit): Lai 39/41, Tallinn 0100; tel. (2) 602-045; fax (2) 440-601; Chair. of Bd HEINO PRIIMÄGI.

Estonian Asphalt Pavement Association (Eesti Asfaldiliit): Ristiku põik 8, Tallinn 0006; tel. (2) 471-569; fax 654-1351; f. 1991; Chair. of Bd ALEKSANDER KALDAS.

Estonian Association of Construction Entrepreneurs (Eesti Ehitusettevõtjate Liit): Rävala pst. 8, Tallinn 0001; tel. and fax (2) 433-213; Chair. of Bd PRIIT VILBA.

Estonian Clothing Manufacturers' Association (Eesti Rõivatootjate Liit): Tartu mnt. 63, Tallinn 0001; tel. (2) 429-324; fax (2) 430-554; Chair. of Bd ANDRES SOOSAAR.

Estonian Dairy Association (Eesti Piimaliit): Vilmsi 53, Tallinn 0010; tel. (2) 427-468; fax (2) 430-418; Chair. of Bd JAAN KÄÄR.

Estonian Fisheries Association: Liivalaia 14, Tallinn 0100; tel. (2) 683-442; fax (2) 682-283; Chair. HEINO PALU.

Estonian Forest Federation (Eesti Metsaliit): Gonsiori 29, Tallinn 0001; tel. (2) 421-559; fax (2) 423-739; Pres. MART ERIK.

Estonian Gas Association (Eesti Gaasiliit): Liivalaia 9, Tallinn 0001; tel. 646-1571; fax 631-4340; Chair. of Bd ANDRES SAAR.

Estonian Hotel and Restaurant Association (Eesti Hotellide Ja Restoranide Liit): Pikk 71, Tallinn 0001; tel. (2) 602-433; fax (2) 601-907; Chair. of Bd TOOMAS SILDMÄE.

Estonian Meat Association (Eesti Lihaliit): Lai 39/41, Tallinn 0100; tel. and fax 641-1035; f. 1989; 22 mem. companies (1997); Chair. of Bd PEETER MASPANOV.

Estonian Small Business Association (EVEA): Pronksi str. 3, Tallinn 0001; tel. 640-3935; fax 631-2451; f. 1989; Man. Dir AIN NOORMÄGI.

Estonian Union of Automobile Enterprises (Eesti Autoettevõtete Liit): Magasini 31, Tallinn 0001; tel. (2) 439-476; fax (2) 443-345; Pres. MATI MÄGI.

ETK Industrial Managers' Club: Narva mnt. 7, Tallinn 0001; tel. (2) 438-242; fax 630-2333; f. 1991; Pres. GEORG ILVEST.

Federation of Estonian Chemical Industries: Tulika 19, Tallinn 0006; tel. and fax 659-1040; 24 mem. enterprises; Chair. REIN REILE.

Federation of Estonian Engineering Industry: Mustamäe tee 4, Tallinn 0006; tel. (2) 595-305; fax (2) 656-6640; e-mail eml@utnet.ee; f. 1991; 75 mem. enterprises; Chair. of Bd MICHAEL PIKNER.

Union of Estonian Breweries (Eesti Õlletootjate Liit): Tähtvere 58/62, Tartu 2400; tel. (7) 434-330; fax (7) 431-193; Chair. of Bd MADIS PADDAR.

Union of Estonian Paper Manufacturers (Eesti Paberitööstuse Liit): Tööstuse 19, Kohila 3420; tel. (48) 33-564; fax (48) 32-132; e-mail kohila pv@netexpress.ee; Chair. of Bd HENNO PAVELSON.

Union of Estonian Wine Producers (Eesti Veinitootjate Liit): Karksi, Polli vald 2944; tel. and fax (43) 31-533; Chair. of Bd JÜRI KERT.

EMPLOYERS' ORGANIZATION

Confederation of Estonian Industry and Employers: Gonsiori 29, Tallinn 0100; tel. (2) 422-235; fax (2) 424-962; f. 1991 as Confederation of Estonian Industry, name changed as above 1995; Man. Dir VILJAR VESKIVÄLI.

UTILITIES

Electricity

Eesti Energia (Estonian Energy): Estonia pst 1, Tallinn 0100; tel. 661-2222; fax 631-3031; producer of thermal and electric energy; electrical engineering.

Gas

Eesti Gaas (Estonian Gas): Liivalaia 9, Tallinn 0001; tel. 631-3883; fax 631-3884; produces and transports natural gas, constructs pipelines, calibrates gas meters.

TRADE UNIONS

Association of Estonian Trade Unions: Rävala 4, Tallinn 0100; tel. (2) 425-100; fax (2) 426-384; f. 1990; Chair. ILME OTSTAVEL.

Association of Estonian Chemical Industry Workers' Trade Unions: Järveküla tee 40, Kohtla-Järve 2020; tel. (33) 478-28; fax (33) 457-98; f. 1990; Chair. MIHKEL ISKÜL.

Association of Estonian Radio and Electronics Industry Workers' Trade Unions: Rävala 4, Tallinn 0100; tel. (2) 432-318; Chair. LYUBOV SEROVA.

Estonian Food and Agricultural Workers' Union: Rävala 4, Tallinn 0001; tel. (2) 430-404; fax (2) 430-865; Chair. AARE-LEMBIT NEEVE.

Estonian Light Industry Workers' Trade Union: Rävala 4, Tallinn 0100; tel. and fax (2) 431-640; Chair. EVI JAAGURA.

Trade Union of Estonian Engineering Workers: Rävala 4, Tallinn 0100; tel. (2) 430-879; Chair. MAIT-TOOMAS REIMANN.

Trade Union of Estonian Forest Industry Workers: Rävala 4, Tallinn 0001; tel. (2) 421-333; fax (2) 422-369; f. 1990; Chair. JÜRI MINJAJEV.

Trade Union of Oil-Shale Industry Workers: Jaama 10, Jõhvi 2045; tel. (33) 265-74; Chair. ENDEL PAAP.

Transport

RAILWAYS

In 1996 there were 1,020 km of railway track in use, of which 132 km were electrified. Main lines link Tallinn with Narva and St Petersburg (Russia), Tartu and Pskov (Russia), Tartu and Valga (Latvia), and Pärnu and Rīga (Latvia).

Estonian Railways (Eesti Raudtee): Pikk 36, Tallinn 0100; tel. 640-1610; fax 640-1710; Dir PARBO JUCHNEWITSCH.

ROADS

In 1997 Estonia had 15,304 km of state roads, of which 1,190 km were main roads, 2,666 km secondary roads and 11,448 km local roads. The motorway network totalled 64 km. About 53% of the total road network was asphalted.

Estonian Road Administration: Pärnu mnt. 24, Tallinn 0901; tel. 611-9300; fax 611-9360; e-mail mnt@online.ee; Gen. Dir RIHO SÕRMUS.

SHIPPING

Tallinn is the main port for freight transportation. There are regular passenger services between Tallinn and Helsinki (Finland). A service between Tallinn and Stockholm (Sweden) was inaugurated in 1991.

Estonian National Maritime Board: Sadama 29, Terminal B, Tallinn 0001; tel. 620-5500; telex 173027; fax 620-5506; internet http://www.enmb.ee; f. 1990; Gen. Dir Capt. KALLE PEDAK.

Shipowning Company

Estonian Shipping Company Ltd (Eesti Merelaevardus): Estonia pst. 3/5, Tallinn 0101; tel. 640-9500; telex 173272; fax 640-9595; f. 1992; transferred to private ownership in mid-1997; Chair. ENN PANT; Man. Dir TOIVO NINNAS.

Shipowners Association

Estonian Shipowners Association (Eesti Laevaomanike Liit): Endla 2-103, Tallinn 0001; tel. and fax 646-0109; Pres. ÜLO KOLLO.

Port Authority

Port of Tallinn: Sadama 25, Tallinn 0102; tel. 631-8002; fax 631-3060; Harbour Master E. HUNT.

CIVIL AVIATION

Estonia has air links with several major cities in the former USSR, including Moscow and St Petersburg (Russia), Kiev (Ukraine), Minsk (Belarus), Riga (Latvia) and Vilnius (Lithuania), and with several western European destinations.

Estonian Civil Aviation Administration: Pärnu mnt. 6, Tallinn 0001; tel. 631-3688; fax 631-2681; e-mail ecaa@trenet.ee; f. 1990; Dir Gen. EDUARD TÜÜR.

Elk Airways (Estonian Aviation Company Ltd): Eesti Vabariik, Majaka 26, Tallinn 0014; tel. (2) 211-929; fax 6211-978; scheduled flights to Finland; Chair. RITA LILLIPUN.

Estonian Air: Lennujaama tee 2, Tallinn 0011; tel. 640-1101; fax 631-2740; f. 1991; Gen. Dir BØRGE THORNBECH.

Tourism

Estonia has a wide range of attractions for tourists, including the historic towns of Tallinn and Tartu, extensive nature reserves and coastal resorts. In 1990 the National Tourism Board was established to develop facilities for tourism in Estonia. In 1997 there were an estimated 2.7m. visitors to Estonia.

Estonian Association of Travel Agents (Eesti Turismifirmade Liit): Pikk 71, Tallinn 0001; tel. 631-3013; fax 631-3622; e-mail info@etfl.travelnet.ee; f. 1990; Pres. ERKI URVA.

Estonian Hotel and Restaurant Association: Pikk 71, Tallinn 0001; tel. 641-1428; fax 641-1425; Man. Dir DONALD VISNAPUU.

Estonian Marine Tourism Association: Regan 1, 5th Floor, Tallinn 0019; tel. and fax 639-8933; f. 1990; Man. Dir HELLE HALLIKA.

Estonian Tourism Board: Mundi tn. 2, Tallinn 0001; tel. 641-1420; fax 641-1432; e-mail tallinn@tourism.uninet.ee; internet http://www.ee/etb/; f. 1990; Dir-Gen. SILVI BLJUMOVITŠ.

ETHIOPIA

Introductory Survey

Location, Climate, Language, Religion, Flag, Capital

The Federal Democratic Republic of Ethiopia is a land-locked country in eastern Africa; it has a long frontier with Somalia near the Horn of Africa. Sudan lies to the west, Eritrea to the north, Djibouti to the north-east and Kenya to the south. The climate is mainly temperate because of the high plateau terrain, with an average annual temperature of 13°C (55°F), abundant rainfall in some years and low humidity. The lower country and valley gorges are very hot and subject to recurrent drought. The official language is Amharic, but many other local languages are also spoken. English is widely used in official and commercial circles. The Ethiopian Orthodox (Tewahido) Church, an ancient Christian sect, has a wide following in the north and on the southern plateau. In much of the south and east the inhabitants include Muslims and followers of animist beliefs. The national flag (proportions 3 by 2) has three equal horizontal stripes, of green, yellow and red. The capital is Addis Ababa.

Recent History

Ethiopia was dominated for more than 50 years by Haile Selassie, who became Regent in 1916, King in 1928 and Emperor in 1930. He continued his autocratic style of rule (except during the Italian occupation of 1936–41) until September 1974, when he was deposed by the armed forces, in the wake of serious famine, economic problems and increasing demands for democratic reform. Haile Selassie died, a captive of the military regime, in August 1975.

The 1974 revolution was organized by an Armed Forces Co-ordinating Committee, known popularly as the Dergue (Shadow). It established a Provisional Military Government (PMG), headed by Lt-Gen. Aman Andom. In November, however, following a dispute within the military leadership, Andom was deposed and shot dead, and the PMG was replaced by a Provisional Military Administrative Council (PMAC), led by Brig.-Gen. Teferi Benti. In December Ethiopia was declared a socialist state, and in 1975 land, financial institutions and large industrial companies were nationalized. The regime introduced a programme of rural development, including land reform, education in health and literacy, and the establishment of peasant co-operatives. There was widespread unrest, however, throughout 1975 and 1976, despite promises by the Dergue to return to civilian rule at an unspecified date. In February 1977, following disagreements within the Dergue, Lt-Col Mengistu Haile Mariam executed Teferi and his closest associates, and replaced him as Chairman of the PMAC and as Head of State.

During 1977 and 1978, in an attempt to end armed and political opposition to the regime, the Government imprisoned or killed thousands of its opponents. In late 1979 all political groups were theoretically abolished, when a Commission for Organizing the Party of the Working People of Ethiopia (COPWE), largely dominated by military personnel, was formed. In September 1984, at the COPWE's third congress, the Workers' Party of Ethiopia (WPE) was formally inaugurated. Lt-Col Mengistu was unanimously elected Secretary-General of the party, which was modelled on the Communist Party of the Soviet Union. The congress also elected an 11-member Politburo and a 136-member Central Committee. In June 1986, in preparation for the eventual transfer of power from the PMAC to a civilian government, a draft Constitution was published. In February 1987 it was endorsed by a referendum, obtaining the support of some 81% of the votes cast. In June national elections were held to an 885-seat legislature, the National Shengo (Assembly). In September, at the inaugural meeting of the new legislature, the PMAC was abolished, and the People's Democratic Republic of Ethiopia (PDRE) was declared. The National Shengo unanimously elected Lt-Col Mengistu as President of the PDRE, and a 24-member Council of State was also elected, to act as the Shengo's permanent organ.

Numerous insurgent groups, encouraged by the confusion resulting from the 1974 revolution, engaged in armed struggle with the Ethiopian Government. The strongest movements were in the Ogaden, Eritrea and Tigre regions. Somalia laid claim to the Ogaden, which is populated mainly by ethnic Somalis. Regular Somali troops supported incursions by forces of the Western Somali Liberation Front, and in 1977 the Somalis made major advances in the Ogaden. In 1978, however, they were forced to retreat, and by the end of 1980 Ethiopian forces, assisted by Soviet military equipment and Cuban troops, had gained control of virtually the whole of the Ogaden region, although armed clashes continued.

The former Italian colony of Eritrea was merged with Ethiopia, in a federal arrangement, in September 1952, and annexed to Ethiopia as a province in November 1962. A secessionist movement, the Eritrean Liberation Front (ELF), was founded in Egypt in 1958. In the late 1960s and early 1970s the ELF enjoyed considerable success against government troops, but was weakened by internal dissension. It eventually split into several rival factions, the largest of which was the Eritrean People's Liberation Front (EPLF). In 1978 government troops re-established control in much of Eritrea, and the EPLF was forced to retreat to the remote northern town of Nakfa. In 1982 a military offensive by government troops failed to capture Nakfa, and in 1984 the EPLF made several successful counter-attacks. In mid-1985 the Government launched a large-scale offensive in Eritrea and made significant gains. The EPLF, however, continued to attack strategic targets, and in mid-1986 government forces abandoned the north-east coast to the rebels.

An insurgent movement also emerged in Tigre province in the late 1970s. The Tigre People's Liberation Front (TPLF) was armed and trained by the EPLF, but relations between the two groups deteriorated sharply in the mid-1980s. The TPLF was weakened by conflict with other anti-Government groups, and in 1985 and 1986 government forces had considerable success against the TPLF.

The conflict in the north of the country during 1984–85 compounded difficulties being experienced in areas of Ethiopia already severely affected by famine. In 1984 the rains failed for the third consecutive crop season, and in May it was estimated that 7m. people could suffer starvation. Emergency food aid was received from many Western nations, but distribution was hampered, both by the continuing conflict and by the inadequacy of Ethiopia's infrastructure. Some rainfall in 1985 eased the drought in the northern provinces, but there were further fears of famine in 1987, when the crops failed again.

In September 1987 the newly-elected National Shengo announced that five areas, including Eritrea and Tigre, were to become 'autonomous regions' under the new Constitution. Eritrea was granted a considerable degree of self-government, but both the EPLF and the TPLF rejected the proposals. In December EPLF forces launched a new offensive. In March 1988 they captured the town of Afabet, and claimed to have killed one-third of all Ethiopian troops in Eritrea. Following the capture of Afabet, the TPLF took advantage of the movement of government forces from Tigre to Eritrea and overran all the garrisons in north-western and north-eastern Tigre. In May the Government declared a state of emergency in Eritrea and Tigre, and in June government troops regained control of some of the captured garrison towns in Tigre, suffering heavy losses in the process. However, in early 1989, following major defeats in north-west Tigre, government forces abandoned virtually the whole region to the TPLF.

In May 1989 the Government acted to pre-empt an attempted *coup d'état*, which had been planned by numerous senior army officers, including the Chief of Staff, the Commander of the Air Force, and the Commander of the Army in Eritrea. The failed coup and the subsequent reorganization of the military command structure handicapped attempts by government forces (already weakend by heavy losses and low morale) to launch counter-offensives in Eritrea and Tigre. Nevertheless, while the EPLF and the TPLF continued their military campaigns during 1989, both groups agreed to enter negotiations with the Government, in an attempt to facilitate a diplomatic solution to the conflict.

US-sponsored negotiations held in late 1989 between representatives of the Ethiopian Government and the EPLF proved inconclusive. Meanwhile, negotiations between the TPLF and the Ethiopian Government, in late 1989 and early 1990, were also unsuccessful. The third round of negotiations, held in Rome, Italy, in March 1990, collapsed over the TPLF's insistence that substantive negotiations should involve a joint delegation of the TPLF and their allies, the Ethiopian People's Democratic Movement (EPDM).

Severe drought in 1989 threatened widespread famine, and the UN estimated that some 4m. people in northern areas would require food aid in 1990. Substantial aid was supplied by Western governments and non-governmental organizations, but its distribution to the most needy areas remained difficult, because of disruption of supply convoys by both rebel and government forces. The recurrent food crises prompted further criticism of the Mengistu Government's commitment to collectivist agricultural policies and its 'villagization' programme (combining several villages in single administrative units, mainly for security reasons), which adversely affected levels of agricultural production.

Following the capture of Massawa port by the EPLF in February 1990 (presenting a direct threat to the continued survival of the Ethiopian army in Eritrea), President Mengistu was obliged to make further concessions. (Meanwhile, the closure of the port and the continuation of hostilities further impeded the distribution of food aid.) In March Ethiopian socialism was virtually abandoned, when the ruling WPE was renamed the Ethiopian Democratic Unity Party, and membership was opened to non-Marxists. Mengistu also began introducing elements of a market economy and dismantling many of the economic structures that had been established after the 1974 revolution. However, heavy defeats of government forces continued during 1990 and early 1991. In February 1991 peace negotiations took place in the USA between representatives of the EPLF and the Ethiopian Government. They made no progress, however, and the military conflict continued.

By late April 1991, troops of the Ethiopian People's Revolutionary Democratic Front (EPRDF—an alliance of the TPLF and the EPDM, formed in September 1989) had captured Ambo, a town 130 km west of Addis Ababa, while EPLF forces were 50 km north of Assab, Ethiopia's principal port. On 21 May, faced with the prospect of the imminent defeat of his army, Mengistu fled the country. Lt-Gen. Tesfaye, the Vice-President, assumed control. On 28 May, following the failure of negotiations in the United Kingdom, and with the public support of the USA, units of the EPRDF entered Addis Ababa. They encountered little resistance, and the EPRDF established an interim Government, pending the convening, in July, of a multi-party conference, which was to elect a transitional government. Meanwhile, the EPLF had gained control of the Eritrean capital, Asmara, and announced the establishment of a provisional Government to administer Eritrea until the holding of a referendum, within two years, on the issue of independence.

A national conference in July 1991, organized by the EPRDF, was attended by some 20 political and ethnic organizations. The conference adopted amendments to a national charter, presented by the EPRDF, and elected an 87-member Council of Representatives, which was to govern for a transitional period of two years, after which free national elections were to be held. The national charter provided guarantees for freedom of association and expression, and for self-determination for Ethiopia's various ethnic groups. The EPLF was not officially represented at the conference, but came to an agreement with the EPRDF, whereby the EPRDF accepted the formation of the EPLF's provisional Government of Eritrea and the determination by referendum of the future of the region.

In late July 1991 the Council of Representatives established a commission to draft a new constitution and elected Meles Zenawi, the leader of the EPRDF (and of the TPLF), as Chairman of the Council, a position which made him President of the transitional Government and Head of State, and in August it appointed a Council of Ministers. However, violent conflict continued in many parts of the country in the latter half of the year, partly provoked by opposition to the domination of the transitional Government by the EPRDF and its allies. There were armed clashes between troops of the EPRDF and forces of the Ethiopian People's Revolutionary Party in the Gojam and Gondar regions, and in August and September supporters of the EPRDF clashed with those of the Oromo Liberation Front (OLF), despite co-operation between these two groups at government level. EPRDF troops (who are mainly Tigrean) also encountered violent opposition from the Afar, Issa and Gurgureh ethnic groups.

In November 1991, in accordance with the national charter's promise of self-determination for Ethiopia's peoples, the transitional Government announced the division of the country into 14 regional administrations, which would have autonomy in matters of regional law and internal affairs. The Government also approved a transitional economic policy, designed to accelerate economic reform in Ethiopia.

In early 1992 skirmishes continued between forces of the EPRDF and the OLF in the south and east of the country, severely hampering the distribution of food aid to some 6.5m. people affected by drought and to a further 1.4m. people displaced during the continuing conflict. In April a cease-fire between the two sides was agreed upon, under the auspices of the USA and the EPLF. Local elections were held in many parts of the country in April and May, and regional elections in June. These latter elections were boycotted by the OLF and other political groups, amid widespread allegations of intimidation of opposition candidates by the EPRDF. (There was also evidence, however, that the OLF itself had harassed civilians and election officials.) An international observer group, including representatives of the UN, the Organization of African Unity (OAU) and the European Community (EC, now European Union, EU), indicated that claims of electoral malpractice by the EPRDF in many areas were, at least in part, justified. Shortly after the elections, in which the EPRDF and associated parties obtained 90% of the votes cast, the OLF withdrew from the transitional Government, in which it had held four ministerial positions. In July 10 political organizations which were signatories to the national charter of July 1991 demanded the annulment of the results of the regional elections. The transitional Government established a board 'to correct election errors' at the end of the month, but by late August the regional councils were in place in all parts of the country except the Afar and Somali areas, where the elections had been postponed. Hopes that the transitional Government had truly democratic intentions were also undermined by reports from the Ethiopian Human Rights Council, which by mid-1992 had documented more than 2,000 cases of people who had been detained without being charged, of whom the majority were political opponents of the EPRDF. The Human Rights Council also reported 13 extra-judicial executions.

In June 1992 OLF troops reportedly captured the town of Asbe Teferi, about 150 km from Addis Ababa; the EPRDF's numerically greatly superior forces, however, ensured that the transitional Government's control of the capital was secure. In October talks between the EPRDF and the OLF, organized by the EPLF, ended in failure, with the OLF continuing to demand that the results of the June elections be annulled, while the EPRDF urged the OLF to rejoin the transitional Government. Hostilities between the two sides continued in various parts of the country, with the EPRDF taking prisoners in massive numbers: by mid-December there were an estimated 20,000 OLF prisoners of war being held.

Discontent with the transitional Government was also reported among ethnic Somalis, who made claims of harassment by the Oromo People's Democratic Organization (OPDO, which is in alliance with the EPRDF) and the EPRDF itself during the regional elections that were held in the south-east of the country in October 1992.

Throughout 1992 people in many parts of the country continued to suffer acute food shortages, caused by drought and ineffective distribution of aid: in August it was estimated that 13.5m. people were affected. In the following year inadequate rainfall resulted in further widespread crop failure in southern, northern and eastern Ethiopia.

Meanwhile the provisional Government of Eritrea announced in November 1992 that a UN-supervised referendum on the area's status would be held in April 1993. The Sudanese Government expressed its readiness to assist the Eritrean Referendum Commission in conducting a plebiscite among some 250,000 Eritrean refugees still residing in Sudan. The referendum revealed overwhelming support for Eritrean independence, which was duly proclaimed on 24 May 1993.

In January 1993 the Ethiopian security forces brutally suppressed a demonstration staged by students at Addis Ababa University, who were protesting at the UN's involvement in the Eritrean independence process (see below) on the occasion of UN-sponsored negotiations taking place in the Ethiopian capital between rival parties to the civil war in neighbouring Somalia. There was at least one death, and more than 30 demonstrators were injured.

In July 1993 the EPRDF experienced serious internal unrest when its executive committee issued a statement denouncing an undisclosed number of party members. It was believed that a purge was under way of middle-ranking TPLF members who had criticized the Government's policy of ethnic regionalization and the slow pace of economic liberalization. Delays in the dispatch of humanitarian aid in early 1994 resulted in the deaths (from hunger and disease) of some 5,000 people in southern Ethiopia. By August relief food was reaching those in need, and by October the threat of famine had been brought under control with help from international donors.

Elections to a new national assembly, the Constituent Assembly, were conducted in June 1994, in which the EPRDF won 484 of the 547 seats. The elections were boycotted by the All-Amhara People's Organization, the recently-formed Coalition of Alternative Forces for Peace and Democracy in Ethiopia (incorporating 30 opposition groups) and the OLF, whose leaders alleged that the Meles administration had intimidated their supporters and refused opposition parties permission to open offices. The Constituent Assembly was inaugurated in October to debate a draft Constitution, which it ratified in December. The new Constitution provided for the establishment of a federal government and the division of the country (renamed the Federal Democratic Republic of Ethiopia) into nine states. It provided for regional autonomy, including the right of secession. A new legislature, the Federal Parliamentary Assembly, was to be established, replacing the Constituent Assembly. It was to be composed of two chambers, the Council of People's Representatives (consisting of 548 directly elected members) and the Council of the Federation (comprising 117 deputies, elected by the new state assemblies).

The EPRDF and its allies won an overwhelming victory in elections to the Council of People's Representatives and state assemblies in May 1995. In Tigre region the TPLF won all the seats in both the federal and state assemblies; EPRDF parties were equally successful in Amhara and Oromia regions. The EPRDF itself won all 92 local assembly seats in Addis Ababa. The largest opposition party to participate in the elections, the Ethiopian National Democratic Movement, contested 80 seats, but none of its candidates was elected. Elections in Afar and Somali regions, where opposition to the EPRDF was strong, were postponed until June, when pro-EPRDF parties won narrow victories. Most opposition parties, however, boycotted the poll. International observers at the elections accepted that the polls were conducted in a largely free and fair manner. In July EU ambassadors to Ethiopia expressed concern that the overwhelming victory of the EPRDF would hinder the further development of political pluralism in the country.

On 21 August 1995 legislative power was transferred from the transitional Council of Representatives to the Federal Parliamentary Assembly. On 22 August the transitional administration was terminated, and the country's new Constitution and designation as the Federal Democratic Republic of Ethiopia were formally instituted. Later on the same day Dr Negasso Gidada (formerly the Minister of Information), a member of the OPDO and the nominee of the EPRDF, was elected President of the Federal Republic at a joint session of the assembly. A new Prime Minister, ex-President Meles Zenawi, was elected from among the members of the Council of People's Representatives; Meles nominated a 17-member Council of Ministers, which was duly approved by the Federal Parliamentary Assembly.

During late 1995 and early 1996 the Meles administration was criticized for its harsh treatment of the opposition, particularly journalists, editors, intellectuals and civil rights activists. In June 1996 Dr Taye Wolde Semayat, the Secretary-General of the Ethiopian Teachers' Association, was arrested with several associates and accused of leading a clandestine political organization (the Ethiopian National Patriotic Front), which, allegedly, had been responsible for terrorist acts, including the attempted assassination in 1994 of an employee of the US Agency for International Development (USAID) and a grenade attack in 1995 on USAID offices in Addis Ababa. The arrests were strongly criticized by human rights groups, which claimed that the detainees were guilty only of expressing discontent at certain government policies. Meanwhile, the Somali-based al-Ittihad al-Islam (Islamic Union Party—which has sought independence for Ethiopia's Ogaden province) claimed responsibility for bomb explosions at hotels in Addis Ababa and Dire Dawa in early 1996, and for the attempted assassination in July of Dr Abdul-Mejid Hussen, the Minister of Transport and Communications and current Chairman of the Ethiopian Somali Democratic League. Government forces launched reprisal attacks on al-Ittihad bases in Somalia on numerous occasions during 1996 and 1997, resulting in the deaths of several hundred al-Ittihad members.

In September 1996 the authorities announced a campaign to address the problem of corruption, which reportedly had become endemic in the country. In the following month Tamirat Layne was accused of 'indiscipline' (he was later implicated in corrupt activities) and removed from the post of Deputy Prime Minister and Minister of Defence; he was also dismissed as Secretary-General of the Amhara National Democratic Movement (as the EPDM had been renamed in 1994), and ejected from its central committee.

In late 1996 the transitional Government announced plans to establish a 25,000-strong Afar military force (under the command of the Afar People's Democratic Organization) to counter an increase in armed attacks on government troops by militant members of the Afar Revolutionary Democratic Unity Front (ARDUF). The authorities subsequently withdrew government forces from sensitive Afar regions and granted concessions regarding political prisoners in an attempt to persuade the ARDUF to cease its military activities. In August 1997 the ARDUF reportedly agreed to renounce the use of violence in its campaigning.

In February 1997 two people were killed and nine were injured in a grenade attack on a hotel in Harar. Similar attacks in Addis Ababa in April and September resulted in as many as 100 casualties, including three fatalities. The authorities attributed the incidents to the OLF, and in November the security forces claimed to have dismantled the OLF group responsible.

Meanwhile, in October 1997 the Somali Regional Council voted to dismiss the entire executive committee of the region's administration, following the apparent illegal arrest and replacement of several legislators by the committee. The Regional Council subsequently elected a provisional executive committee, while investigations began into the conduct of the former committee members.

The trial of 69 former government officials, including Mengistu himself, opened in Addis Ababa in December 1994, although proceedings were adjourned on numerous occasions. The defendants, 23 of whom were being tried *in absentia* (including Mengistu, who was in exile in Zimbabwe) and five of whom had died while awaiting trial, were accused of crimes against humanity and of genocide, perpetrated between 1974 and 1991. In February 1997 the office of the Special Prosecutor announced that an additional 5,198 people would be indicted for war crimes and genocide, of whom nearly 3,000 would be tried *in absentia*.

Ethiopia's foreign affairs after Mengistu's coup in 1977 were dominated by relations with the USSR, which replaced the USA as the principal supplier of armaments to Ethiopia and provided military advisers and economic aid. In the late 1980s, however, changes in Soviet foreign policy weakened the relationship, and the Soviet Government began to urge a political, rather than military, solution to Ethiopia's regional conflicts.

In April 1989 Ethiopia sought to upgrade its diplomatic relations with the USA, receiving a cautious initial response. The USA subsequently encouraged the EPRDF's seizure of power in May 1991 and expressed its approval of proposals for a transition to a multi-party democratic system. In late 1993 representatives of Ethiopia and the USA signed an agreement on economic and technical co-operation, the first such agreement for 17 years. In October 1996 the US Secretary of State, Warren Christopher, and the OAU Secretary-General, Salim Ahmed Salim, held talks with Prime Minister Meles in Ethiopia, who reportedly welcomed a US initiative to establish an African crisis reaction force.

Relations with Somalia were strained following the Ogaden War of 1977–78. In January 1986, however, following mediation by Kenya and Djibouti, President Mengistu met the Somali President, Mohamed Siad Barre, for the first time since 1977. Relations deteriorated in 1987, following a border clash between Ethiopian and Somali troops, but a further meeting between the two leaders took place in 1988. In April of that year Ethiopia and Somalia agreed to re-establish diplomatic relations, to withdraw troops from their common border and to exchange prisoners of war. During 1988–91 an estimated 600,000 Somali refugees entered Ethiopia from northern Somalia of whom more than 150,000 arrived in the first half of 1991. The transitional Government of Ethiopia declared a policy of non-interference in the affairs of neighbouring states and adopted a neutral stance in Somalia's civil conflict. In December 1992 Ethiopia permitted the USA to use its airspace and its principal airport in the US-led operation to facilitate the delivery of humanitarian relief in Somalia. During 1993–98 Ethiopia hosted reconciliation conferences between Somalia's warring factions.

Following the military coup in Sudan in April 1985 (which deposed President Nimeri), full diplomatic relations were restored between Ethiopia and Sudan. Relations between the two countries were strained, however, by the influx into Ethiopia, in the late 1980s, of thousands of Sudanese refugees, fleeing from famine and civil war in southern Sudan. The vast majority of an estimated 380,000 refugees were reported to have returned to Sudan by early 1991, as a result of the civil war in Ethiopia. The change of government in Ethiopia in May 1991 led to a considerable improvement in relations between Ethiopia and Sudan. In October President Meles and Sudan's leader, Lt-Gen. al-Bashir, signed an agreement on friendship and co-operation. Relations between the two countries deteriorated again in January 1994, when the Ethiopian Minister of Foreign Affairs accused the Sudanese National Islamic Front of supporting Islamic extremists in Ethiopia. In September 1995 the Ethiopian administration adopted a number of sanctions against Sudan, including the suspension of air flights between the two countries and a reduction in Sudanese diplomatic representation in Ethiopia. The measures were introduced in response to the refusal of the Sudanese authorities to extradite to Ethiopia three men allegedly involved in an assassination attempt on President Mubarak of Egypt in Addis Ababa in June. (The men were subsequently extradited to Ethiopia, and in September 1996 were sentenced to death by the High Court.) In December 1995 there were reports of military clashes between Ethiopian and Sudanese forces in the border region. Accusations of border incursions intensified during 1996–97. (Attacks against Sudanese positions were known to have been launched by the Sudan People's Liberation Army, operating from Ethiopia, although the Ethiopian authorities denied any knowledge of their activities.) In mid-1997 Ethiopia and Sudan reportedly agreed to 'normalize' relations.

In November 1991 the leaders of Ethiopia and Kenya signed a co-operation agreement, although in October 1992 it was reported that the Kenyan Government was secretly giving asylum to Ethiopian dissidents. In December the office of the UN High Commissioner for Refugees began a repatriation programme for Ethiopian refugees in Kenya, who had fled in May 1991. In April 1997 the two countries agreed to strengthen border controls following an attack by Ethiopian tribesmen in Kenya's frontier region; 41 civilians and 16 security personnel were killed during the incident. Relations with many Arab states improved substantially following the collapse of the Mengistu regime in 1991. In November 1993 Ethiopia removed all remaining sanctions against South Africa and announced that normal financial, trade and investment relations between the two countries would now be possible.

In 1984 some 13,000 Falashas, a Jewish group in Ethiopia, reached Sudan, from where they were flown to Israel in a secret airlift. Following the renewal of formal diplomatic relations (severed in 1973) between Ethiopia and Israel in 1989, the Ethiopian Government removed restrictions on Falashas' leaving the country, and Israel began to provide Ethiopia with more armaments and anti-guerrilla training. In May 1991 Israel evacuated a further 14,000 Falashas from Addis Ababa. During a visit to Israel in May 1993 by the Ethiopian Prime Minister, Tamirat Layne, a five-year protocol on bilateral co-operation between Ethiopia and Israel was signed.

After May 1991 the EPLF governed Eritrea as a *de facto* independent state and conducted its affairs with foreign countries accordingly. Ethiopia and the newly-independent Eritrea signed a treaty of co-operation during a visit by the Eritrean President, Issaias Afewerki, to Addis Ababa in July 1993. The agreement included provisions on the joint utilization of resources and co-operation in the energy, transport, defence and education sectors. A further agreement, signed in late 1994, provided for the free movement of goods between the two countries without payment of customs dues. In late 1996 Ethiopia and Eritrea signed a crime-prevention accord, including provisions for the extradition of criminals.

Government

In August 1995 the Council of Representatives, a body established in 1991 to govern the country during the transitional period after the overthrow of the Mengistu regime, formally transferred power to a newly elected legislature, the Federal Parliamentary Assembly. Under the provisions of a new Constitution, adopted in December 1994, the country became a federation, consisting of nine states and one metropolitan area, the capital, Addis Ababa. The states have their own parliamentary assemblies, which also elect representatives to the Council of the Federation, the upper chamber of the Federal Parliamentary Assembly. The lower chamber, the Council of People's Representatives, consists of 548 directly elected deputies. The Federal Parliamentary Assembly elects a President as Head of State. However, the President fulfils mainly ceremonial functions, executive power being the preserve of the Prime Minister. The Prime Minister, who is elected by the Council of People's Representatives, appoints the Council of Ministers (subject to approval by the legislature), and acts as Commander-in-Chief of the armed forces. Elections to the Council of People's Representatives and to the state assemblies took place in May and June 1995.

Defence

Following the fall of Mengistu's Government and the defeat of his army in May 1991, troops of the EPLF and the EPRDF were deployed in Eritrea and the remainder of Ethiopia respectively. In December Ethiopia's transitional Government announced that a 'national defence army' would constitute Ethiopia's armed forces during the transitional period. This army was to be based on already active EPRDF forces. In October 1993 the Minister of Defence announced that preparations were under way to create a 'multi-ethnic defence force', comprising members of all the different ethnic groups in Ethiopia. In 1993 Ethiopian armed forces were estimated to number some 120,000 (the majority of whom being former members of the TPLF and some 10,000–15,000 from the OLF). By December 1995 some 20,000 members of the EPRDF forces had been demobilized. In September 1996 the transitional Government sold its naval assets. The defence budget for 1997 was estimated at 823m. birr.

Economic Affairs

In 1995, according to estimates by the World Bank, the gross national product (GNP) of Ethiopia, measured at average 1993–95 prices, was US $5,722m., equivalent to $100 per head: one of the lowest recorded levels of GNP per caput for any country in the world. During 1985–95, it was estimated, GNP per head decreased, in real terms, at an average annual rate of 0.3%. Over the same period, the population increased by an annual average of 2.6%. Ethiopia's gross domestic product (GDP) increased, in real terms, by an annual average of 1.9% in the financial years 1989/90–1994/95. It rose by 7.7% in 1995/96 and by 7.0% in 1996/97.

Agriculture (including forestry and fishing) contributed 51.7% of GDP in 1993/94, and employed an estimated 85.3% of the economically active population in 1996. The principal cash crop is coffee (which accounted for 65.9% of export earnings in 1994/95). The principal subsistence crops are cereals (barley, maize, sorghum and teff) and sugar cane. During 1989/90–94/95 agricultural GDP increased by an annual average of 1.6%. It fell by 4.7% in 1993/94, but rose by 3.6% in 1994/95. In 1995 the Government initiated a five-year programme (supported by the World Bank), which aimed to make Ethiopia self-sufficient in food production. In 1996 agricultural production increased by 6.0%, compared with the previous year, while the cereal yield rose by 25.9%. However, drought and flooding severely disrupted agricultural output in 1997.

Industry (including mining, manufacturing, construction and power) employed 2.0% of the labour force in 1995, and provided 11.1% of GDP in 1993/94. During 1989/90–94/95 industrial GDP increased by an annual average of 1.6%. It rose by 7.1% in 1993/94 and by 8.0% in 1994/95.

Mining contributed only 0.3% of GDP in 1993/94, and employed less than 0.1% of the labour force in 1995. During 1989/90–94/95 mining GDP increased by an annual average of 16.8%. Ethiopia has reserves of petroleum, although these have not been exploited, and there are also deposits of copper and potash. The Government announced the discovery of a large salt deposit in late 1993, estimated to constitute 40,000 metric tons of sodium chloride and 53,000 tons of sodium bicarbonate. Gold reserves in excess of 500 tons have been identified; exploration for gold and base metals commenced in 1995.

Manufacturing employed only 1.6% of the labour force in 1995 and contributed 7.0% of GDP in 1993/94. During 1989/90–94/95 manufacturing GDP increased by an annual average of 0.9%. Measured by the value of output, the principal branches of manufacturing in the late 1980s were food products, petroleum refineries, beverages and textiles. During 1989/90–94/95 manufacturing GDP increased by an annual average of 0.9%. It rose by 9.0% in 1993/94 and in 1994/95.

Services, which consisted mainly of wholesale and retail trade, public administration and defence, and transport and communications, employed 9.5% of the labour force in 1995, and contributed 37.2% of GDP in 1993/94. The combined GDP of the service sectors increased, in real terms, at an average rate of 2.4% per year during 1989/90–94/95. It rose by 9.9% in 1993/94, and by 5.6% in 1994/95.

In years of normal rainfall, energy is derived principally from Ethiopia's massive hydroelectric power resources. Imports of mineral fuels accounted for 15.2% of the cost of total imports in 1994/95. In late 1993 agreement was reached with the World Bank on the financing of a project to construct a liquefied gas unit to exploit gas reserves in the Ogaden. In November 1995 the Government announced plans to develop geothermal energy sources at 15 sites in various regions of the country. In 1996 plans were announced to double the country's electricity generating capacity (to 756 MW) by 2002.

In 1996 Ethiopia recorded a visible trade deficit of US $817.3m., and there was a deficit of $102.3m. on the current account of the balance of payments. In 1994 the principal source of imports (15.0%) was Saudi Arabia, while the principal market for exports (31.7%) was Germany. Other major trading partners were the USA, Italy and Japan. The principal exports in 1994/95 were coffee, hides and skins and vegetables. The principal imports in that year were machinery and transport equipment, basic manufactures, mineral fuels and chemicals and related products.

In the fiscal year 1994/95 it was estimated that Ethiopia's budgetary deficit reached 1,277.5m. birr (equivalent to 3.8% of GDP). Ethiopia is the principal African recipient of concessionary funding, and the largest recipient of EU aid (US $387m. for the first five years of the period covered by the Lomé IV Convention). At the end of 1995 Ethiopia's total external debt was $5,221m., of which $4,958m. was long-term public debt. In that year the cost of debt-servicing was equivalent to an estimated 13.6% of total earnings from the export of goods and sevices. In late 1992 debts repayable to various countries and international organizations amounting to $595m., including interest, were cancelled. Commercial debts worth $250m. were cancelled in early 1996. The annual rate of inflation averaged 7.5% in 1986–96. Although the rate rose considerably in 1991 (to 35.7%), in the following years it remained constant at about 10%, and in 1996 consumer prices declined by 5.1%. There were 62,941 persons aged 18 to 55 years registered as applicants for work in the 12 months to June 1993.

Ethiopia is a member of the African Development Bank (see p. 104) and the Common Market for Eastern and Southern Africa (see p. 124), and adheres to the Lomé Convention of the EU (see p. 178).

Ethiopia's economy continues to suffer from the effects of recurrent, catastrophic drought, which severely disrupts agricultural production (the country's economic base). The economy remains dependent on foreign aid and is heavily indebted. Since May 1991 the transitional Government has adopted many elements of a market economy, resulting in a greater readiness on the part of developed countries to provide economic assistance to Ethiopia, and the resumption of relations with the World Bank in September 1991. As part of the economic reform programme that was agreed with the World Bank and the IMF, the transitional Government raised interest rates in October 1992, and devalued the birr by 57% in the same month. The IMF approved a three-year loan in 1992 to support the programme; a further three-year loan (totalling US $127m.) was approved in late 1996 under the IMF's enhanced structural adjustment facility. The transitional Government has made considerable progress in reforming public expenditure, liberalizing the economy, increasing private investment, allocating significant resources to social welfare and education, and transferring a measure of autonomy to the regional administrations. The diversification of agricultural products remains a priority, as Ethiopia's dependence on receipts from coffee exports has exposed the economy to fluctuations in the international price of that commodity. Advances in agricultural production remain subject to investment in the sector in order to address problems including land degradation, pest control and drought. Despite record cereal yields in 1995 and 1996 (which had prompted speculation that long-term food self-sufficiency might be possible), a period of drought, followed by severe flooding, in 1997 resulted in a poor harvest of cereals and left some 4.3m. people requiring food aid. Economic targets for the period 1996–99 included achieving real GDP growth of 6%, limiting the external current account deficit to some 9.2% of GDP, and maintaining inflation below 2%. Anticipated reforms included widening the tax base, improving tax collection, liberalizing the foreign exchange market further, and eliminating certain remaining subsidies (notably on fertilizers).

Social Welfare

The scope of modern health services has been greatly extended since 1960, but they still reach only a small section of the population. In 1977 free medical care for the needy was introduced. In 1980 Ethiopia had 86 hospital establishments. Between 1974 and 1987 26 new hospitals were built. By 1987 there were a total of 11,400 beds, while 1,204 physicians and 3,105 nurses were working in the health service. Relative to the size of the population, the provision of hospital beds and physicians was the lowest among African countries. By 1987 there were also 2,095 clinics and 159 health centres. With foreign assistance, health centres and clinics are steadily expanding into the rural areas. In times of famine, however, Ethiopian health services are totally inadequate. The 1994/95 budget allocated 6.0% (492m. birr) of total expenditure to public health.

Education

Education in Ethiopia is available free of charge, and, after a rapid growth in numbers of schools, it became compulsory between the ages of seven and 13 years. Since September 1976 most primary and secondary schools have been controlled by local peasant associations and urban dwellers' associations. Primary education begins at seven years of age and lasts for six years. Secondary education, beginning at 13 years of age, lasts for a further six years, comprising a first cycle of two years and a second of four years. In 1993 total enrolment at primary schools was equivalent to 27% of children in the relevant age-group (33% of boys; 21% of girls); the comparable ratio for secondary enrolment was only 11% (11% of boys; 10% of girls). The 1994/95 budget allocated 14.9% (1,212.2m. birr) of total expenditure to education and training. In 1995, according to UNESCO estimates, the rate of adult illiteracy stood at 64.5% (males 54.5%; females 74.7%). There is a university in Addis Ababa and another in Dire Dawa, and three institutions of higher education in the remainder of Ethiopia.

Public Holidays

1998: 7 January* (Christmas), 19 January* (Epiphany), 30 January† (Id al-Fitr, end of Ramadan), 2 March (Battle of Adowa), 6 April (Victory Day), 8 April† (Id al-Adha/Arafat), 13 April* (Palm Monday), 17 April* (Good Friday), 20 April* (Easter Monday), 6 May (May Day), 7 July† (Mouloud, Birth of the Prophet), 11 September (New Year's Day), 27 September* (Feast of the True Cross).

1999: 7 January* (Christmas), 19 January*† (Epiphany and Id al-Fitr, end of Ramadan), 2 March (Battle of Adowa), 28 March† (Id al-Adha/Arafat), 5 April* (Palm Monday), 6 April (Victory Day), 9 April* (Good Friday), 12 April* (Easter Monday), 6 May (May Day), 26 June† (Mouloud, Birth of the Prophet), 11 September (New Year's Day), 27 September* (Feast of the True Cross).

* Coptic holidays.

† These holidays are dependent on the Islamic lunar calendar and may vary by one or two days from the dates given.

Note: Ethiopia uses its own solar calendar; the Ethiopian year 1990 began on 11 September 1997.

Weights and Measures

The metric system is officially in use. There are also many local weights and measures.

Statistical Survey

Source (unless otherwise stated): Central Statistical Authority, POB 1143, Addis Ababa; tel. (1) 553010; fax (1) 550334.

Note: Unless otherwise indicated, figures in this Survey refer to the territory of Ethiopia after the secession of Eritrea in May 1993.

Area and Population

AREA, POPULATION AND DENSITY

Area (sq km)	1,133,380*
Population (census of 9 May 1984)†	
Males	20,062,453
Females	19,806,048
Total	39,868,501
Population (official estimates at mid-year)	
1994	54,938,000
1995	56,677,100
1996	58,506,000
Density (per sq km) at mid-1996	51.6

* 437,600 sq miles.

† Including an estimate for areas not covered by the census.

ADMINISTRATIVE REGIONS (census results of October 1994)

Region	Population
1 Tigre	3,136,267
2 Afar	1,106,383*
3 Amhara	13,834,297
4 Oromia	18,732,525
5 Somalia	2,514,399†
6 Metekel, Abosa, Metema	460,459
7–11 Southern Ethiopian Peoples‡	10,377,028
12 Gambela, Agriwak, Nuwar, Mezanger	181,862
13 Harar Town	131,139
14 Addis Ababa	2,112,737

* Population at July 1996.

† Estimated population at mid-1993.

‡ Comprising five separate regions.

Note: A new Constitution, ratified in December 1994, provided for the establishment of a federal government and the division of the country into nine states. The new states were formally instituted in August 1995.

PRINCIPAL TOWNS (census results of October 1994)

Addis Ababa (capital)	2,112,737	Dessie	97,314
Dire Dawa	164,851	Mekele	96,938
Harar	131,139	Bahir Dar	96,140
Nazret	127,842	Jimma	88,867
Gondar (incl. Azeso)	112,249		

BIRTHS AND DEATHS (UN estimates, annual averages)

	1980–85	1985–90	1990–95
Birth rate (per 1,000)	50.1	48.8	48.5
Death rate (per 1,000)	24.1	19.9	18.0

Expectation of life (UN estimates, years at birth, 1990–95): 47.5 (males 45.9; females 49.1).

Source: UN, *World Population Prospects: The 1994 Revision.*

ECONOMICALLY ACTIVE POPULATION (official estimates, ISIC Major Divisions, persons aged 10 years and over, mid-1995)*

	Males	Females	Total
Agriculture, hunting, forestry and fishing	12,681,037	8,924,280	21,605,317
Mining and quarrying	12,114	4,426	16,540
Manufacturing	224,106	160,889	384,995
Electricity, gas and water	14,799	2,267	17,066
Construction	55,906	5,326	61,232
Trade, restaurants and hotels	335,353	600,584	935,937
Transport, storage and communications	87,975	15,179	103,154
Financing, insurance, real estate and business services	14,513	4,938	19,451
Community, social and personal services	777,907	474,317	1,252,224
Total labour force	14,203,710	10,192,206	24,395,916

* The figures exclude persons seeking work for the first time, totalling 210,184 (males 100,790; females 109,394), but include other unemployed persons.

Source: ILO, *Yearbook of Labour Statistics.*

Mid-1996 (estimates in '000): Agriculture, etc. 21,763; Total labour force 25,509 (Source: FAO, *Production Yearbook*).

Agriculture

PRINCIPAL CROPS ('000 metric tons)

	1994	1995	1996
Wheat*	1,313	1,650	1,970
Barley*	1,284	1,417	1,570
Maize*	2,011	2,500	3,250
Oats*	46	52	63
Millet (Dagusa)*	172	248	360
Sorghum*	1,125	1,600	1,980
Other cereals*	1,325	1,700	1,935
Potatoes*	350	350	350
Sweet potatoes*	155	155	155
Yams*	263	263	263
Other roots and tubers*	1,250	1,250	1,250
Dry beans*	270	390	390
Dry peas*	120	150	150
Dry broad beans*	281	281	281
Chick-peas*	122	126	126
Lentils*	34	34	34
Other pulses*	127	127	127
Sugar cane*	1,200	1,200	1,600
Soybeans*	21	21	21
Groundnuts (in shell)*	54	54	54
Castor beans*	14	14	14
Rapeseed*	80	80	80
Sesame seed*	31	31	31
Linseed*	32	32	32
Safflower seed*	35	35	35
Cottonseed	28†	30†	30*
Cotton (lint)	14†	15†	15*
Vegetables and melons*	565	565	565
Bananas*	80	80	80
Other fruit (excl. melons)*	147	147	147
Tree nuts*	65	65	65
Coffee (green)†	207	228	230
Tobacco (leaves)*	4	4	4
Fibre crops (excl. cotton)*	17	17	17

* FAO estimate(s). † Unofficial figure(s).

Source: FAO, *Production Yearbook.*

LIVESTOCK (FAO estimates, '000 head, year ending September)

	1994	1995	1996
Cattle	29,450	29,825	29,900
Sheep	21,700	21,700	21,700
Goats	16,700	16,700	16,700
Asses	5,200	5,200	5,200
Horses	2,750	2,750	2,750
Mules	630	630	630
Camels	1,000	1,000	1,000
Pigs	20	20	20

Poultry (FAO estimates, million): 54 in 1994; 54 in 1995; 54 in 1996.

Source: FAO, *Production Yearbook*.

LIVESTOCK PRODUCTS (FAO estimates, '000 metric tons)

	1994	1995	1996
Beef and veal	230	231	236
Mutton and lamb	78	78	78
Goat meat	62	62	62
Pig meat	1	1	1
Poultry meat	72	72	72
Other meat	134	134	134
Cows' milk	738	738	740
Goats' milk	93	93	93
Sheep's milk	54	54	54
Butter	10	10	10
Cheese	5	5	5
Hen eggs	73	73	73
Honey	24	24	24
Wool:			
greasy	12	12	12
clean	6	6	6
Cattle hides	46	46	47
Sheepskins	14	14	14
Goatskins	13	13	13

Source: FAO, *Production Yearbook*.

Forestry

ROUNDWOOD REMOVALS ('000 cubic metres, excl. bark)

	1992*	1993	1994
Sawlogs, etc.	15	26	33
Other industrial wood†	1,693	1,693	1,693
Fuel wood	44,387	45,254	45,254
Total	46,095	46,973	46,980

* Including Eritrea.

† Assumed to be unchanged since 1983.

Source: FAO, *Yearbook of Forest Products*.

SAWNWOOD PRODUCTION
('000 cubic metres, incl. railway sleepers)

	1992*	1993	1994
Total	12	40	33

* Including Eritrea.

Source: FAO, *Yearbook of Forest Products*.

Fishing

('000 metric tons, live weight)

	1993	1994	1995
Total catch (freshwater fishes)	4.2	5.3	6.4

Source: FAO, *Yearbook of Fishery Statistics*.

Mining

('000 metric tons, including Eritrea, unless otherwise indicated)

	1989	1990	1991
Gold (kilograms)*	745	848	2,000†
Salt (unrefined)	188	110	94
Limestone ('000 cu metres)	150	100	85
Sand	775	1,250	1,000
Kaolin	0	1	0

* Figures for 1990 and 1991 exclude Eritrea.

† Provisional figure.

1992: Gold (kilograms) 2,652; Kaolin (provisional, metric tons) 1,000.
1993: Gold (kilograms) 3,404.

Source: US Bureau of Mines, quoted in UN, *Industrial Commodity Statistics Yearbook*.

Industry

SELECTED PRODUCTS
('000 metric tons, unless otherwise indicated; year ending 7 July)

	1992/93*	1993/94	1994/95
Edible oils	4.0	4.2	5.6
Wheat flour	62.3	74.7	116.0
Flour of other cereals	0.3	2.3	1.6
Macaroni and pasta	5.7	11.2	19.1
Raw sugar	136.7	123.3	129.3
Wine ('000 hectolitres)	68.9	57.3	70.9
Beer ('000 hectolitres)	522.3	634.4	723.5
Mineral waters ('000 hectolitres)	159.3	199.3	298.4
Soft drinks ('000 hectolitres)	553.8	546.2	710.5
Cigarettes (million)	1,932.0	1,468.4	1,582.8
Cotton yarn (metric tons)	3,448	5,669	4,934
Woven cotton fabrics ('000 sq metres)	36,423	60,591	50,016
Nylon fabrics ('000 sq metres)	3,840	3,752	4,910
Leather footwear ('000 pairs)	928.8	1,999.2	1,159.4
Canvas and rubber footwear ('000 pairs)	2,030.9	1,609.4	2,196.3
Plastic footwear ('000 pairs)	123.5	62.3	395.7
Paper	—	—	7.1
Soap	17.3	15.0	15.2
Tyres ('000)	99.8	171.3	167.5
Clay building bricks ('000)	19.8	19.5	19.3
Quicklime	3.7	2.7	4.9
Cement	377.1	464.4	609.3

* Including Eritrea.

Finance

CURRENCY AND EXCHANGE RATES

Monetary Units
100 cents = 1 birr.

Sterling and Dollar Equivalents (30 September 1997)
£1 sterling = 10.998 birr;
US $1 = 6.808 birr;
1,000 birr = £90.93 = $146.89.

Average Exchange Rate (birr per US $)
1994 5.4650
1995 6.1583
1996 6.3517

GENERAL BUDGET (provisional, million birr, year ending 7 July)

Note: The figures for 1992/93 include Eritrea.

Revenue*	1992/93	1993/94	1994/95
Taxation	2,135.3	3,535.1	3,890.3
Taxes on income and profits	670.5	880.9	1,210.1
Personal income	251.8	266.8	289.2
Business profits	376.8	557.3	848.2
Domestic production, sales and excise taxes†	711.2	816.5	925.6
Alcohol and tobacco	276.3	264.2	316.3
Import duties	697.0	1,774.0	1,472.7
Customs duties	348.8	1,182.0	771.4
Sales and other taxes‡	348.2	592.0	701.3
Export duties§	18.7	16.7	201.4
Customs duties§	11.0	15.1	190.1
Other revenue	956.3‖	833.2	1,948.9
Surplus, capital charges, interest payments and state dividends	437.9	476.8	1,399.3
Reimbursements and property sales	54.7	52.8	118.7
Total	3,091.6	4,368.3	5,839.2

* Excluding grants received from abroad (million birr): 1,067.0 in 1992/93; 1,218.1 in 1993/94; 1,034.9 in 1994/95.

† Sales tax until 1992/93; and excise taxes thereafter.

‡ Sales taxes until 1992/93; sales and excise taxes thereafter.

§ Figures refer to coffee only from December 1992.

‖ Including extraordinary transfer for evacuation of Felashas (Ethiopian Jews).

Expenditure	1992/93	1993/94	1994/95
Current expenditure	3,903.8	4,474.3	5,075.0
General services	1,173.4	1,452.5	1,560.5
Organs of state	80.0	195.3	189.8
Defence	697.0	709.3	672.5
Public order and security	165.1	226.0	289.5
Economic services	329.7	452.9	579.6
Agriculture and natural resources	164.4	261.3	366.0
Social services	876.9	1,224.9	1,520.3
Education and training	583.3	742.0	936.0
Public health	185.8	279.3	354.7
Pension payments	224.3	279.9	287.7
Interest and charges	530.3	951.5	855.2
External assistance (grants)*	600.0	0.0	0.0
Capital expenditure	2,150.4	3,018.0	3,076.6
Economic development	1,509.0	2,217.5	2,192.0
Agriculture, water and natural resources	530.2	732.3	656.5
Mining and industry	311.4	358.8	376.5
Electric power	75.1	115.8	212.4
Roads, transport and communications	532.7	967.0	811.4
Social development	267.9	718.2	593.0
Education	86.8	248.3	276.2
Public health	66.8	157.1	137.3
Community services†	114.3	312.8	179.5
General services and compensation	23.5	82.3	291.6
External assistance (grants)*	350.0	0.0	—
Total	6,054.2	7,492.3	8,151.6

* Imputed value of goods and services provided in kind.

† Including urban development and housing, social security, manpower and training, and sport.

Source: National Bank of Ethiopia.

NATIONAL BANK RESERVES (US $ million, at 31 December)

	1994	1995	1996
Gold*	11.4	11.4	0.4
IMF special drawing rights	0.4	0.3	—
Reserve position in IMF	10.2	10.5	10.1
Foreign exchange	533.6	760.8	722.0
Total	555.6	782.9	732.6

* National valuation.

Source: IMF, *International Financial Statistics.*

MONEY SUPPLY (million birr, at 31 December)

	1994	1995	1996
Currency outside banks	5,380	5,718	5,401
Demand deposits at commercial banks	3,646	3,562	3,872
Total money	9,027	9,280	9,273

Source: IMF, *International Financial Statistics.*

COST OF LIVING (General Index of Retail Prices for Addis Ababa, excluding rent; base: 1990 = 100)

	1993	1994	1995
Food	160.4	176.7	198.6
Fuel, light and soap*	133.1	134.1	n.a.
Clothing	189.9	170.3	n.a.
All items (incl. others)	155.3	167.1	183.9

* Including certain kitchen utensils.

Source: ILO, *Yearbook of Labour Statistics.*

1996: All items 174.6 (Source: IMF, *International Financial Statistics*).

NATIONAL ACCOUNTS

(million birr at current prices; year ending 7 July)

Expenditure on the Gross Domestic Product (excluding Eritrea)

	1992/93	1993/94	1994/95
Government final consumption expenditure	2,819	3,155	3,675
Private final consumption expenditure*	22,209	23,446	27,720
Gross capital formation	3,288	4,189	5,229
Total domestic expenditure	28,316	30,790	36,624
Exports of goods and services	2,223	3,223	4,899
Less Imports of goods and services	4,521	6,091	8,217
GDP in purchasers' values	26,018	27,922	33,306

* Including statistical discrepancies.

Source: National Bank of Ethiopia.

Gross Domestic Product by Economic Activity (at factor cost, including Eritrea)

	1991/92	1992/93	1993/94*
Agriculture, hunting, forestry and fishing	12,507.7	14,832.9	13,754.1
Mining and quarrying	45.5	132.8	85.3
Manufacturing	953.1	1,595.9	1,867.0
Electricity, gas and water	236.5	245.8	254.8
Construction	403.8	552.2	736.0
Trade, hotels and restaurants	1,468.4	2,187.5	2,551.3
Transport, storage and communications	779.3	1,041.0	1,163.5
Finance, insurance and real estate†	840.3	878.0	2,035.2
Public administration and defence	959.0	1,504.0	1,792.7
Education	505.1	617.6	752.5
Health	128.9	168.8	255.7
Domestic and other services	923.9	1,128.4	1,354.2
Subtotal	19,751.5	24,884.9	26,602.3
Less Imputed bank service charge	335.4	348.3	1,287.5
Total	19,416.1	24,536.6	25,314.8

* Figures are provisional.

† Including imputed rents of owner-occupied dwellings.

Source: National Bank of Ethiopia.

BALANCE OF PAYMENTS (US $ million)

	1994	1995	1996
Exports of goods f.o.b.	372.0	423.0	417.5
Imports of goods f.o.b.	-925.7	-1,136.7	-1,234.8
Trade balance	-553.7	-713.7	-817.3
Exports of services	294.6	344.4	391.2
Imports of services	-310.4	-357.9	-383.0
Balance on goods and services	-569.5	-727.1	-809.1
Other income received	42.9	68.3	51.3
Other income paid	-74.6	-87.2	-76.1
Balance on goods, services and income	-601.1	-745.9	-833.9
Current transfers received	728.5	737.3	739.2
Current transfers paid	-2.0	-1.1	-7.5
Current balance	125.4	-9.7	-102.3
Investment assets	-318.5	57.7	-306.8
Investment liabilities	144.6	118.7	64.2
Net errors and omissions	-13.1	-107.3	173.1
Overall balance	-61.5	59.5	-171.8

Source: IMF, *International Financial Statistics.*

External Trade

PRINCIPAL COMMODITIES (distribution by SITC, US $ '000)

Imports c.i.f.	1991*	1992*	1993
Food and live animals	20,151	83,418	93,928
Cereals and cereal preparations	14,172	76,285	78,942
Wheat and meslin (unmilled)	10,059	69,133	62,576
Mineral fuels, lubricants, etc.	50,196	149,749	166,612
Petroleum, petroleum products, etc.	50,134	149,546	165,633
Crude petroleum oils, etc.	29,148	99,993	71,393
Refined petroleum products	20,543	48,905	92,750
Animal and vegetable oils, fats and waxes	1,371	15,076	25,949
Fixed vegetable oils and fats	583	14,024	20,774
Chemicals and related products	72,735	58,256	106,125
Inorganic chemicals	6,629	8,015	20,813
Medicinal and pharmaceutical products	17,141	23,044	31,595
Medicaments	16,150	22,338	30,987
Manufactured fertilizers	23,613	159	18,736
Basic manufactures	76,327	99,432	124,232
Rubber manufactures	9,250	15,325	17,534
Textile yarn, fabrics, etc.	16,192	35,976	22,589
Iron and steel	15,559	13,913	38,552
Universals, plates and sheets	8,499	9,944	22,491
Machinery and transport equipment	210,482	192,831	208,897
Machinery specialized for particular industries	28,652	43,182	34,382
General industrial machinery, equipment and parts	13,268	7,349	14,344
Telecommunications and sound equipment	13,028	17,720	8,156
Other electrical machinery, apparatus, etc.	9,963	16,716	25,718
Road vehicles and parts†	77,506	96,703	113,440
Passenger motor cars (excl. buses)	26,561	21,283	29,589
Motor vehicles for goods transport, etc.	26,929	35,030	50,587
Goods vehicles (lorries and trucks)	25,906	34,482	48,989
Parts and accessories for cars, buses, lorries, etc.†	16,223	35,154	28,835
Other transport equipment†	54,633	1,127	2,336
Aircraft, etc., and parts†	53,056	630	1,949
Miscellaneous manufactured articles	30,092	43,160	30,421
Total (incl. others)	471,810	656,601	771,584

* Including Eritrea.

† Excluding tyres, engines and electrical parts.

Exports f.o.b.	1991*	1992*	1993
Food and live animals	126,325	113,228	138,541
Vegetables and fruit	6,292	3,609	3,053
Sugar, sugar preparations and honey	1,773	1,622	4,883
Coffee, tea, cocoa and spices	117,169	107,845	129,395
Coffee and coffee substitutes	116,233	107,310	129,177
Crude materials (inedible) except fuels	32,312	45,908	52,754
Raw hides, skins and furskins	25,068	32,288	32,697
Raw hides and skins (excl. furs)	25,068	32,288	32,697
Cattle hides	3,748	3,384	4,567
Goat skins	5,088	4,842	5,413
Sheep skins with the wool on	16,202	23,704	22,517
Mineral fuels, lubricants, etc.	1,836	13,162	8,020
Petroleum, petroleum products, etc.	1,836	13,162	8,020
Non-monetary gold (excl. ores and concentrates)	21,348	20,185	—
Total (incl. others)†	188,609	197,171	201,706

* Including Eritrea.

† Excluding platinum.

Source: UN, *International Trade Statistics Yearbook.*

1994 (US $ million): Imports c.i.f. 1,033; Exports f.o.b. 372.

PRINCIPAL TRADING PARTNERS (million birr)

Imports c.i.f.	1992*	1993	1994
Austria	20.2	10.6	15.1
Belgium-Luxembourg	37.6	103.4	111.5
Canada	38.2	73.1	136.8
China, People's Repub.	5.9	58.6	107.3
Denmark	31.5	70.5	46.9
Djibouti	129.9	172.3	239.5
France	24.6	59.9	134.6
Germany	196.1	407.8	450.7
Greece	5.4	39.9	24.5
India	25.5	53.7	101.0
Italy	143.8	397.8	627.5
Japan	103.9	156.5	296.5
Kenya	67.2	105.0	144.3
Korea, Repub.	8.8	27.4	74.0
Netherlands	98.6	141.7	228.1
Saudi Arabia	342.2	726.1	848.2
Sweden	45.5	93.9	103.6
Switzerland	66.2	61.8	54.6
United Kingdom	139.5	148.8	271.2
USA	106.0	366.3	694.5
Yemen	67.9	116.5	60.8
Total (incl. others)	1,987.8	3,852.3	5,650.8

Exports f.o.b.	1992*	1993	1994
Belgium-Luxembourg	6.6	30.1	37.8
Djibouti	35.8	121.7	153.3
France	25.1	37.0	102.0
Germany	48.9	198.4	654.3
Italy	32.5	76.4	166.8
Japan	108.4	191.7	300.0
Kuwait	—	—	76.4
Malaysia	2.3	8.9	20.8
Netherlands	7.2	21.1	44.1
Saudi Arabia	101.1	99.5	110.2
Sudan	—	13.2	18.3
United Kingdom	82.0	46.4	71.8
USA	19.6	92.1	133.2
Yemen	9.2	19.5	60.8
Total (incl. others)	504.0	1,007.5	2,062.4

* Including Eritrea.

Source: National Bank of Ethiopia.

Transport

RAILWAYS (traffic, year ending 7 July)*

	1994/95	1995/96	1996/97
Addis Ababa–Djibouti:			
Passenger-km (million)	151	167	157
Freight (million net ton-km)	93	104	106

* Including traffic on the section of the Djibouti–Addis Ababa line which runs through the Republic of Djibouti. Data pertaining to freight include service traffic.

Source: Ministry of Transport and Communications.

ROAD TRAFFIC (motor vehicles in use, year ending 7 July)

	1992/93	1993/94	1994/95
Cars	39,292	31,608	45,559
Buses and coaches	2,042	5,633	3,683
Lorries and vans	17,865	16,755	15,525
Motorcycles and mopeds	2,130	3,416	566
Road tractors	3,889	5,440	4,402
Total	65,218	62,852	69,735

Source: Ministry of Transport and Communications.

SHIPPING

Merchant Fleet (registered at 31 December)

	1995	1996	1997*
Number of vessels	15	15	11
Displacement (grt)	79,520	86,009	86,592

* Data from Ethiopian Shipping Lines Corpn.

Source: Lloyd's Register of Shipping, *World Fleet Statistics*.

International Sea-borne Shipping (freight traffic, '000 metric tons)

	1993	1994	1995
Goods loaded	137	177	234
Goods unloaded	1,129	824	1,242

Source: Ministry of Transport and Communications.

CIVIL AVIATION (traffic on scheduled services)

	1995	1996	1997
Kilometres flown (million)	25	26	28
Passengers carried ('000)	749	730	807
Passenger-km (million)	1,722	1,838	1,915
Total ton-km (million)	306	307	328

Source: Ministry of Transport and Communications.

Tourism

Note: The figures include Eritrea.

	1992	1993	1994
Tourist arrivals ('000)	83	93	98
Tourist receipts (US $ million)	23	20	23

Source: UN, *Statistical Yearbook*.

Communications Media

Note: Figures for 1990-93 include Eritrea.

	1992	1993	1994
Telephones ('000 main lines in use)	127*	132	138
Telefax stations (number in use)	521	760	1,060
Radio receivers ('000 in use)	9,900	10,200	10,550
Television receivers ('000 in use)	145	165	230
Daily newspapers:			
Number	4	n.a.	4
Average circulation ('000 copies)	70†	n.a.	81†

* Year ending 30 June.

† Estimate.

Book production: 240 titles (including 93 pamphlets) in 1991.

Non-daily newspapers: 4 in 1990.

Source: mainly UNESCO, *Statistical Yearbook*.

Education

(1993)

	Institutions	Teachers	Students
Pre-primary	652	1,638	66,086
Primary	8,674	75,736	2,283,638
Secondary: general	n.a.	21,598	714,622
Vocational*	n.a.	310	2,589
Universities†	n.a.	1,440	20,948
Other higher†	n.a.	257	5,270

* 1992 figures. † 1991 figures.

Source: UNESCO, *Statistical Yearbook*.

Directory

The Constitution

In July 1991 a national conference elected a transitional Government and approved a charter under the provisions of which the Government was to operate until the holding of democratic elections. The charter provided guarantees for freedom of association and expression, and for self-determination for Ethiopia's different ethnic constituencies. The transitional Government was to be responsible for drafting a new constitution to replace that introduced in 1987. A Constituent Assembly, dominated by representatives of the EPRDF, was elected in June 1994. It ratified the draft Constitution (already approved by the Council of Representatives) in December. The Constitution of the Federal Democratic Republic of Ethiopia provides for the establishment of a federal government and the division of the country into nine states. It also provides for regional autonomy, including the right of secession. Simultaneous elections of deputies to the federal and state parliaments were conducted on 7 May 1995. The new Constitution came into effect on 22 August 1995.

The Government

HEAD OF STATE

President: Dr NEGASSO GIDADA (took office 22 August 1995).

COUNCIL OF MINISTERS
(February 1998)

Prime Minister: MELES ZENAWI.

Deputy Prime Minister and Head of Economic Affairs at the Prime Minister's Office: Dr KASSA YLALA.

Deputy Prime Minister and Minister of Defence: TEFERA WALWA.

Minister of Foreign Affairs: SEYOUM MESFIN.

Minister of Health: ADEM IBRAHIM.

Minister of Energy and Mines: EZEDIN ALI.

Minister of Development and Economic Co-operation: GIRMA BIRU.

Minister of Information and Culture: WOLDE MIKAEL CHAMO.

Minister of Education: GENET ZEWDE.

Minister of Agriculture: SEIFU KEFEMA.

Minister of Commerce and Industry: KASAHUN AYELE.

Minister of Finance: SUFYAN AHMED.

Minister of Justice: WEREDE WOLDU WOLDE.

Minister of Works and Urban Development: HAILE SELASSIE ASEGIDE.

Minister of Transport and Communications: Dr ABDUL-MEJID HUSSEN.

Minister of Labour and Social Affairs: HASAN ABDELA.

Minister of Water Resources: SHIFERAW JARSO.

Minister and Head of the Revenue Collectors Board: DESTA AMARE.

MINISTRIES AND COMMISSIONS

Office of the Prime Minister: POB 1013, Addis Ababa; tel. (1) 123400.

Ministry of Agriculture: POB 62347, Addis Ababa; tel. (1) 518040; fax (1) 512984.

Ministry of Commerce and Industry: POB 704, Addis Ababa; tel. (1) 518025; telex 21514; fax (1) 515411.

Ministry of Defence: POB 125, Addis Ababa; tel. (1) 445555; telex 21261.

Ministry of Development and Economic Co-operation: POB 2559, Addis Ababa; tel. (1) 151066; telex 21320.

Ministry of Education: POB 1367, Addis Ababa; tel. (1) 553133.

Ministry of Energy and Mines: POB 486, Addis Ababa; tel. (1) 448250; telex 21448; fax (1) 517874.

Ministry of Finance: POB 1905, Addis Ababa; tel. (1) 552400; telex 21147; fax (1) 551355.

Ministry of Foreign Affairs: POB 393, Addis Ababa; tel. (1) 447345; telex 21050.

Ministry of Health: POB 1234, Addis Ababa; tel. (1) 516156.

Ministry of Information and Culture: POB 1020, Addis Ababa; tel. (1) 111124.

Ministry of Justice: POB 1370, Addis Ababa; tel. (1) 517390.

Ministry of Labour and Social Affairs: POB 2056, Addis Ababa; tel. (1) 517080.

Ministry of Transport and Communications: POB 1238, Addis Ababa; tel. (1) 516166; telex 21348; fax (1) 515665.

Ministry of Water Resources: POB 1043, Addis Ababa, tel. (1) 510455; fax (1) 513042.

Ministry of Works and Urban Development: POB 3386, Addis Ababa; tel. (1) 150000.

Legislature

FEDERAL PARLIAMENTARY ASSEMBLY

The legislature comprises an upper house, the Council of the Federation, with 117 seats (members are selected by state assemblies and are drawn one each from 22 minority nationalities and one from each professional sector of the remaining nationalities) and a lower house of 548 directly elected members, the Council of People's Representatives.

At elections conducted on 7 May 1995 the EPRDF secured 483 of the 537 confirmed seats, while 46 were won by regional political groupings and eight were won by independent candidates. The Federal Parliamentary Assembly assumed formal legislative power from the transitional Council of Representatives on 21 August 1995.

Speaker of the Council of the Federation: WEIZERO ALMAZ MEKO.

Speaker of the Council of People's Representatives: DAWIT YOHANES.

Political Organizations

Afar People's Democratic Organization (APDO): fmrly Afar Liberation Front (ALF); based in fmr Hararge and Wollo Admin. Regions; supported the Ethiopian transitional Govt; Leader ALI MIRAH.

Coalition of Alternative Forces for Peace and Democracy in Ethiopia (CAFPDE): f. 1993 as a broadly-based coalition of groups opposing the EPRDF; Chair. Dr BEYENE PETROS.

Coalition of Ethiopian Democratic Forces (COEDF): f. 1991 in USA by the Ethiopian People's Revolutionary Party–EPRP (the principal party involved), a faction of the Ethiopian Democratic Union (EDU) and the Ethiopian Socialist Movement (MEISON); opposes EPRDF; Chair. MERSHA YOSEPH.

Ethiopian Democratic Unity Party (EDUP): Addis Ababa; f. 1984 as Workers' Party of Ethiopia; adopted present name in March 1990, when its adherence to Marxist-Leninist ideology was relaxed and membership opened to non-Marxist and opposition groups; sole legal political party until May 1991; Sec.-Gen. Lt-Gen. TESFAYE GEBRE KIDAN.

Ethiopian National Democratic Party (ENDP): f. 1994 by merger of five pro-Govt orgs with mems in the Council of Representatives; comprises: the Ethiopian Democratic Organization, the Ethiopian Democratic Organization Coalition (EDC), the Gurage People's Democratic Front (GPDF), the Kembata People's Congress (KPC), and the Wolaita People's Democratic Front (WPDF); Chair. FEKADU GEDAMU.

Ethiopian People's Revolutionary Democratic Front (EPRDF): Addis Ababa; f. 1989 by the TPLF as an alliance of insurgent groups seeking regional autonomy and engaged in armed struggle against the EDUP Govt; Leader MELES ZENAWI; in May 1991, with other orgs, formed transitional Govt; alliance comprises:

Amhara National Democratic Movement (ANDM): based in Tigre; represents interests of the Amhara people; fmrly the Ethiopian People's Democratic Movement (EPDM); adopted present name in Jan. 1994; Sec.-Gen. TEFERA WALWA.

Oromo People's Democratic Organization (OPDO): f. 1990 by the TPLF to promote its cause in Oromo areas; based among the Oromo people in the Shoa region; Dep. Sec.-Gen. KUMA DEMEKSA.

Tigre People's Liberation Front (TPLF): f. 1975; the dominant org. within the EPRDF; Leader MELES ZENAWI.

Ethiopian Somali Democratic League (ESDL): f. 1994 by merger of 11 Ethiopian Somali orgs; comprises: Somali Democratic Union Party, the Issa and Gurgura Liberation Front, the Gurgura Independence Front, the Eastern Gabooye Democratic Organization, the Eastern Ethiopian Somali League, the Horyal Democratic Front, the Social Alliance Democratic Organization, the Somali Abo Democratic Union, the Shekhash People's Democratic Movement, the Ethiopian Somalis' Democratic Movement and the Per Barreh Party; Chair. Dr ABDUL-MEJID HUSSEN.

Oromo Liberation Front (OLF): seeks self-determination for the Oromo people; participated in the Ethiopian transitional Govt until June 1992; Sec.-Gen. GELASSA DILBO; Vice Sec.-Gen. LENCHO LETTA.

Somali Abo Liberation Front (SALF): operates in fmr Bale Admin. Region; has received Somali military assistance; Sec.-Gen. MASURAD SHU'ABI IBRAHIM.

Southern Ethiopian People's Democratic Union (SEPDU): f. 1992 as an alliance of 10 ethnically-based political groups from the south of the country; represented in the Council of Representatives, although five of the 10 groups were expelled from the Council in April 1993; Chair. Dr BEYENE PETROS.

Western Somali Liberation Front (WSLF): POB 978, Mogadishu, Somalia; f. 1975; aims to unite the Ogaden region with Somalia; maintains guerrilla forces of c. 3,000 men; has received support from regular Somali forces; Sec.-Gen. ISSA SHAYKH ABDI NASIR ADAN.

The following Oromo organizations are operating in a coalition (f. 1991):

Oromo Abo Liberation Front (OALF): Chair. MOHAMMED SIRAGE.

Oromo People's Democratic Organization (OPDO): see above.

United Oromo Liberation Front: f. 1995 by merger of United Oromo People's Liberation Front and Islamic Front for the Liberation of Oromia; Chair. AHMAD MUHAMMAD SARO.

Other organizations in opposition to the Ethiopian Government include: the **Democratic Unity Party (DUP):** Chair. AHMAD ABD AL-KARIM; the **Ethiopian Medhin Democratic Party:** Leader Col GOSHU WOLDE; the **Ethiopian National Democratic Organization**; the **Ethiopian People's Democratic Unity Organization (EPDUO):** Leader TADESE TILAHUN; the **Ethiopian People's Revolutionary Party (EPRP)**; the monarchist **Moa Ambessa Party** and the **National Democratic Union**.

Other ethnic organizations seeking self-determination for their respective groups include: the **Abugda Ethiopian Democratic Congress**; the **Afar Revolutionary Democratic Unity Front (ARDUF)**; the **All-Amhara People's Organization (AAPO)**: Chair. Prof. ASRAT WOLDYES; the **Burji People's Democratic Organization**; the **Daworo People's Democratic Movement**; the **Gedeo People's Democratic Organization (GPDO)**: Leader ALESA MENGESHA; the **Hadia People's Democratic Organization**; the **Harer National League**; the Somali-based **Islamic Union Party (al-Ittihad al-Islam),** seeking self-determination for the Ogaden; the **Jarso Democratic Movement**; the **Kaffa People's Democratic Union (KPDU)**; the **Kefa People's Democratic Movement**; the **Ogaden National Liberation Front (ONLF)**: Chair. BASHIR ABDI; the **Sidama Liberation Movement**; and the **Yem Nationality Movement**.

Other political organizations include the **Ethiopian Democratic Action Group:** Chair. EPHREM ZEMIKAEL; and **Forum 84**.

Diplomatic Representation

EMBASSIES IN ETHIOPIA

Algeria: POB 5740, Addis Ababa; tel. (1) 652300; telex 21799 fax (1) 650187; Ambassador: DELMI BOUDJEMAÂ.

Angola: Addis Ababa; tel. (1) 510085; fax (1) 514922; Ambassador: TOKO D. SERÃO.

Austria: POB 1219, Addis Ababa; tel. (1) 712144; telex 21060; Ambassador: THOMAS MICHAEL BAIER.

Belgium: POB 1239, Addis Ababa; tel. (1) 611813; fax (1) 613646; Ambassador: STEPHANE DE LOECKER.

Bulgaria: POB 987, Addis Ababa; tel. (1) 612971; telex 21450; Chargé d'affaires a.i.: LIBERT POPOV.

Burundi: POB 3641, Addis Ababa; tel. (1) 651300; telex 21069; Ambassador: ANTOINE NAMOBWA.

Cameroon: Bole Rd, POB 1026, Addis Ababa; telex 21121; fax (1) 518116; Ambassador: JEAN-HILAIRE MBÉA MBÉA.

Canada: Old Airport Area, Higher 23, Kebele 12, House No. 122, POB 1130, Addis Ababa; tel. (1) 713022; telex 21053; fax (1) 713033; Ambassador: GABRIEL M. LESSARD.

Chad: Addis Ababa; telex 21419; fax (1) 612050; Ambassador: MAHAMAT ABDELKERIM.

China, People's Republic: POB 5643, Addis Ababa; telex 21145; Ambassador: JIANG ZHENGYUN.

Congo, Democratic Republic: Makanisa Rd, POB 2723, Addis Ababa; tel. (1) 204385; telex 21043; Ambassador: (vacant).

Congo, Republic: POB 5571, Addis Ababa; tel. (1) 154331; telex 21406; Ambassador: VICTOR NIMI.

Côte d'Ivoire: POB 3668, Addis Ababa; tel. (1) 711213; telex 21061; Ambassador: PIERRE YÉRÉ.

Cuba: Jimma Road Ave, POB 5623, Addis Ababa; tel. (1) 202010; telex 21306; Ambassador: MARIANO M. L. BETANCOURT.

Czech Republic: POB 3108, Addis Ababa; tel. (1) 516132; fax (1) 513471; Ambassador: ZDENĚK POLAČEK.

Djibouti: POB 1022, Addis Ababa; tel. (1) 613200; telex 21317; fax (1) 612786; Ambassador: DILEITA MOHAMED DILEITA.

Egypt: POB 1611, Addis Ababa; tel. (1) 113077; telex 21254; Ambassador: MUHAMMAD ASIM IBRAHIM.

Equatorial Guinea: POB 246, Addis Ababa; Ambassador: SALVADOR ELA NSENG ABEGUE.

Eritrea: Addis Ababa; Ambassador: GRMAY ASMEROM.

Finland: Tedla Desta Bldg, Bole Rd, POB 1017, Addis Ababa; tel. (1) 513900; telex 21259; Chargé d'affaires a.i.: LAURI KANGAS.

France: Kabana, POB 1464, Addis Ababa; tel. (1) 550066; telex 21040; fax (1) 551441; Ambassador: ALAIN ROUQUIÉ.

Gabon: POB 1256, Addis Ababa; tel. (1) 611090; telex 21208; fax (1) 613700; Ambassador: EMMANUEL MENDOUME-NZE.

Germany: Kabana, POB 660, Addis Ababa; tel. (1) 550433; telex 21015; fax (1) 551311; Ambassador: WITRUD HOLIK.

Ghana: POB 3173, Addis Ababa; tel. (1) 711402; telex 21249; fax (1) 712511; Ambassador: BENJAMIN G. GODWYLL.

Greece: Africa Ave, POB 1168, Addis Ababa; tel. (1) 654912; telex 21092; fax (1) 654883; Ambassador: VASSILIOS N. VASSALOS.

Guinea: POB 1190, Addis Ababa; tel. (1) 651308; Ambassador: MAMADI DIAWARA.

Holy See: POB 588, Addis Ababa (Apostolic Nunciature); tel. (1) 712100; fax (1) 711499; Apostolic Nuncio: Most Rev. SILVANO M. TOMASI, Titular Archbishop of Cercina.

Hungary: Abattoirs Rd, POB 1213, Addis Ababa; tel. (1) 651850; telex 21176; Ambassador: Dr SÁNDOR ROBEL.

India: Kabena, POB 528, Addis Ababa; tel. (1) 552100; telex 21148; fax (1) 552521; Ambassador: GURCHARAN SINGH.

Indonesia: Mekanisa Rd, POB 1004, Addis Ababa; tel. (1) 712014; telex 21264; fax (1) 710877; Ambassador: ROCHSJAD DAHLAN.

Iran: 317/02 Jimma Rd, Old Airport Area, POB 1144, Addis Ababa; tel. (1) 200369; telex 21118; Ambassador: YOUSEF RAJAB.

Ireland: H-413, Higher 24, Kebele 13, Addis Ababa; tel. (1) 710835; Chargé d'affaires a.i.: DAVID BARRY.

Israel: POB 1266, Addis Ababa; tel (1) 610999; fax (1) 612456; Ambassador: AVI A. GRANOT.

Italy: Villa Italia, POB 1105, Addis Ababa; tel. (1) 551565; telex 21342; fax (1) 550218; Ambassador: MAURIZIO MELANI.

Jamaica: National House, Africa Ave, POB 5633, Addis Ababa; tel. (1) 613656; telex 21137; Ambassador: OWEN A. SINGH.

Japan: Sunshine Bldg, Bole Rd, POB 5650, Addis Ababa; tel. (1) 511088; telex 21108; fax (1) 511350; Ambassador: YASUHIRO HAMADA.

Kenya: Fikre Mariam Rd, POB 3301, Addis Ababa; tel. (1) 610303; telex 21103; Ambassador: G. K. MURITHI.

Korea, Democratic People's Republic: POB 2378, Addis Ababa; Ambassador: MUN SONG MO.

Korea, Republic: Jimma Rd, Old Airport Area, POB 2047, Addis Ababa; tel. (1) 444490; telex 21140; Ambassador: DEUK PO KIM.

Kuwait: Addis Ababa; Ambassador: MUHAMMAD AL-AWADHI.

Lesotho: POB 7483, Addis Ababa; tel. (1) 614368; fax (1) 612837; Ambassador: J. T. METSING.

Liberia: POB 3116, Addis Ababa; tel. (1) 513655; telex 21083; Ambassador: MARCUS M. KOFA.

Libya: POB 5728, Addis Ababa; telex 21214; Chargé d'affaires a.i.: OMAR ELHADI SHENSHEN.

Madagascar: Addis Ababa; Ambassador: JEAN DELCROCX BALKONIARIVO.

Malawi: POB 2316, Addis Ababa; tel. (1) 712440; telex 21087; fax (1) 710490; Ambassador: Mrs KALINDE.

Mali: Addis Ababa; Ambassador: S. Y. SIDIBE.

Mexico: Tsige Mariam Bldg 292/21, 4th Floor, Churchill Rd, POB 2962, Addis Ababa; tel. (1) 443456; telex 21141; Ambassador: CARLOS FERRER.

Morocco: POB 60033, Addis Ababa; Ambassador: ABD AL-LATIF NASIF.

Mozambique: POB 5671, Addis Ababa; telex 21008; Ambassador: ALEXANDRE ZANDAMELA.

Namibia: POB 1443, Addis Ababa; Ambassador: EDDIE S. AMKNOGO.

Netherlands: Old Airport Area, POB 1241, Addis Ababa; tel. (1) 711100; telex 21049; fax (1) 711577; Ambassador: PIETER J. T. MARRES.

Niger: Debrezenit Rd, Higher 18, Kebele 41, N-057, POB 5791, Addis Ababa; tel. (1) 651175; telex 21284; Ambassador: ASSANE IGODOE.

Nigeria: POB 1019, Addis Ababa; tel. (1) 550644; telex 21028; Ambassador: BROWNSON N. DEDE.

Norway: POB 8383, Addis Ababa; tel. (1) 710799; fax (1) 711255; Ambassador: SVEN A. HOLMSEN.

Poland: Bole Rd, POB 1123, Addis Ababa; tel. (1) 610197; telex 21185; Ambassador: TADEUSZ WUJEK.

Romania: Africa Ave, POB 2478, Addis Ababa; tel. (1) 610156; telex 21168; fax (1) 611191; Chargé d'affaires a.i.: BORIS RANGHET.

Russia: POB 1500, Addis Ababa; tel. (1) 552061; telex 21534; fax (1) 613795; Ambassador: VLADIMIR A. VOLKOV.

Rwanda: Africa House, Higher 17, Kebele 20, POB 5618, Addis Ababa; tel. (1) 610300; telex 21199; fax (1) 610411; Ambassador: CALLIXTE HABAMENSHI.

Saudi Arabia: Old Airport Area, POB 1104, Addis Ababa; tel. (1) 448010; telex 21194; Ambassador: SAOUD A. M. AL-YAHAYA.

Senegal: Africa Ave, POB 2581, Addis Ababa; tel. (1) 611376; telex 21027; Ambassador: PAPA LOUIS FALL.

Sierra Leone: POB 5619, Addis Ababa; tel. (1) 710033; telex 21144; Ambassador: IBRAHIM M. BABA KAMARA.

Somalia: Addis Ababa; Ambassador: ABRAHIM HAJI NUR.

South Africa: POB 1091, Addis Ababa; tel. (1) 713034; fax (1) 711330; Ambassador: W. NHLAPO.

Spain: Entoto St, POB 2312, Addis Ababa; tel. (1) 550222; telex 21107; fax (1) 551131; Ambassador: AURORA BERNÁLDEZ.

Sudan: Kirkos, Kebele, POB 1110, Addis Ababa; telex 21293; Ambassador: OSMAN AS-SAYED.

Sweden: Ras Ababa Aregaye Ave, POB 1029, Addis Ababa; tel. (1) 511255; telex 21039; fax (1) 515830; Ambassador: CARL OLOF CEDERBLAD.

Switzerland: Jimma Rd, Old Airport Area, POB 1106, Addis Ababa; tel. (1) 711107; telex 21123; fax (1) 712177; Ambassador: PAOLO BROGINI.

Tanzania: POB 1077, Addis Ababa; tel. (1) 441064; telex 21268; Ambassador: CHARLES BEHSTEVAN.

Tunisia: Kesetegna 20, Kebele 39, Addis Ababa; Ambassador: BECHIR BEN AISSA.

Turkey: POB 1506, Addis Ababa; tel. (1) 612321; fax (1) 611688; Ambassador: MURAT BILHAN.

Uganda: POB 5644, Addis Ababa; tel. (1) 513088; telex 21143; fax (1) 514355; Ambassador: B. W. K. MATOGO.

United Kingdom: Fikre Mariam Abatechan St, POB 858, Addis Ababa; tel. (1) 612354; telex 21299; fax (1) 610588; e-mail b.emb4@telecom.net.et; Ambassador: GORDON G. WETHERELL.

USA: Entoto St, POB 1014, Addis Ababa; tel. (1) 550666; telex 21282; fax (1) 551166; Ambassador: DAVID SHINN.

Venezuela: Debre Zeit Rd, POB 5584, Addis Ababa; tel. (1) 654790; telex 21102; Chargé d'affaires a.i.: ALFREDO HERNÁNDEZ-ROVATI.

Viet Nam: POB 1288, Addis Ababa; Ambassador: NGUYEN DUY KINH.

Yemen: POB 664, Addis Ababa; telex 21346; Ambassador: MANSUR ABD AL-JALIL ABD AL-RAB.

Yugoslavia: POB 1341; Addis Ababa; tel. (1) 517804; telex 21233; Ambassador: IGOR JOVOVIĆ.

Zambia: POB 1909; Addis Ababa; tel. (1) 711302; telex 21065; Ambassador: SIMATTA AKAPELWA.

Zimbabwe: POB 5624, Addis Ababa; tel. (1) 183872; telex 21351; Ambassador: T. A. G. MAKOMBE.

Judicial System

Special People's Courts were established in 1981 to replace the former military tribunals. Judicial tribunals are elected by members of the urban dwellers' and peasant associations. In 1987 the Supreme Court ceased to be administered by the Ministry of Law and Justice and became an independent body. In October 1993, however, the Council of Representatives approved draft amendments empowering the Ministry of Justice to assume, additionally, the functions of prosecutor; the office of prosecutor was to operate as a division under the Ministry.

The Supreme Court: Addis Ababa; comprises civil, criminal and military sections; in 1987 its jurisdiction (previously confined to hearing appeals from the High Court) was extended to include supervision of all judicial proceedings throughout the country; the Supreme Court is also empowered, when ordered to do so by the Procurator-General or at the request of the President of the Supreme Court, to review cases upon which final rulings have been made by the courts, including the Supreme Court, but where basic judicial errors have occurred; prior to May 1991, judges were elected by the National Shengo (the former national legislature); Pres. ASEFA LIBEN.

The High Court: Addis Ababa; hears appeals from the Provincial and sub-Provincial Courts; has original jurisdiction.

Awraja Courts: Regional courts composed of three judges, criminal and civil.

Warada Courts: Sub-regional; one judge sits alone with very limited jurisdiction, criminal only.

Religion

About 45% of the population are Muslims and about 40% belong to the Ethiopian Orthodox (Tewahido) Church. There are also significant Evangelical Protestant and Roman Catholic communities. The Pentecostal Church and the Society of International Missionaries carry out mission work in Ethiopia. There are also Hindu and Sikh religious institutions. Most of Ethiopia's small Jewish population was evacuated by the Israeli Government in May 1991. An estimated 5%–15% of the population adhere to animist rites and beliefs.

CHRISTIANITY

Ethiopian Orthodox (Tewahido) Church

The Ethiopian Orthodox (Tewahido) Church is one of the five oriental orthodox churches. It was founded in AD 328, and in 1989 had more than 22m. members, 20,000 parishes and 290,000 clergy. The Supreme Body is the Holy Synod and the National Council, under the chairmanship of the Patriarch. The Church comprises 25 archdioceses and dioceses (including those in Jerusalem, Sudan, Djibouti and the Western Hemisphere). There are 32 Archbishops and Bishops. The Church administers 1,139 schools and 12 relief and rehabilitation centres throughout Ethiopia.

Patriarchate Head Office: POB 1283, Addis Ababa; tel. (1) 116507; telex 21489; Patriarch Archbishop ABUNE PAULOS; Gen. Sec. L. M. DEMTSE GEBRE MEDHIN.

The Roman Catholic Church

At 31 December 1995 Ethiopia contained an estimated 66,546 adherents of the Alexandrian-Ethiopian Rite and 279,642 adherents of the Latin Rite.

Bishops' Conference: Ethiopian Episcopal Conference, POB 2454, Addis Ababa; tel. (1) 550300; telex 21381; fax (1) 553113; f. 1966; Pres. Cardinal PAULOS TZADUA, Archbishop of Addis Ababa.

Alexandrian-Ethiopian Rite

Adherents are served by one archdiocese (Addis Ababa) and three dioceses (Adigrat, Asmara, Keren).

Archbishop of Addis Ababa: Cardinal PAULOS TZADUA, Catholic Archbishop's House, POB 21903, Addis Ababa; tel. (1) 111667; fax (1) 553113.

Latin Rite

Aherents are served by the five Apostolic Vicariates of Awasa, Harar, Meki, Nekemte and Soddo-Hosanna, and by the Apostolic Prefecture of Jimma-Bonga.

Other Christian Churches

The Anglican Communion: Within the Episcopal Church in Jerusalem and the Middle East, the Bishop in Egypt has jurisdiction over seven African countries, including Ethiopia.

Armenian Orthodox Church: Deacon VARTKES NALBANDIAN, St George's Armenian Church, POB 116, Addis Ababa; f. 1923.

Ethiopian Evangelical Church (Mekane Yesus): Pres. Rev. YADESA DABA, POB 2087, Addis Ababa; tel. (1) 553280; telex 21528; fax (1) 552966; f. 1959; affiliated to Lutheran World Fed., All Africa Conf. of Churches and World Council of Churches; c. 2.1m. mems (1996).

Greek Orthodox Church: Metropolitan of Axum Most Rev. PETROS GIAKOUMELOS, POB 571, Addis Ababa.

Seventh-day Adventist Church: Pres. TINSAE TOLESSA, POB 145, Addis Ababa; tel. (1) 511319; telex 21549; f. 1907; 112,000 mems.

ISLAM

Leader: Haji MOHAMMED AHMAD.

JUDAISM

Following the phased emigration to Israel of about 21,000 Falashas (Ethiopian Jews), during 1984–91, there are now estimated to be fewer than 2,000 Falashas remaining in the country.

The Press

DAILIES

Addis Zemen: POB 30145, Addis Ababa; f. 1941; Amharic; publ. by the Ministry of Information and Culture; Editor-in-Chief MERID BEKELE; circ. 40,000.

Ethiopian Herald: POB 30701, Addis Ababa; tel. (1) 119050; f. 1943; English; publ. by the Ministry of Information and Culture; Editor-in-Chief KIFLOM HADGOI; circ. 37,000.

PERIODICALS

Abyotawit Ethiopia: POB 2549, Addis Ababa; fortnightly; Amharic.

Addis Tribune: Tambek International, POB 2395, Addis Ababa; tel. (1) 615228; fax (1) 615227; e-mail tambek@telecom.net.et; internet http://addistribune.ethiopiaonline.com; f. 1993; weekly; English; Editor-in-Chief T. BEKELE; circ. 6,000.

Addis Zimit: POB 2395, Addis Ababa; f. 1993; tel. (1) 118613; fax (1) 552110; weekly; Amharic; Editor-in-Chief T. BEKELE; circ. 8,000.

Al-Alem: POB 30232, Addis Ababa; weekly; Arabic; publ. by the Ministry of Information; Editor-in-Chief TELSOM AHMED; circ. 2,500.

Berisa: POB 30232, Addis Ababa; f. 1976; weekly; Oromogna; publ. by the Ministry of Information; Editor BULO SIBA; circ. 3,500.

Birhan Family Magazine: Addis Ababa; monthly; women's magazine.

Birritu: National Bank of Ethiopia, POB 5550, Addis Ababa; tel. (1) 517430; telex 21020; fax (1) 514588; f. 1968; six a year; Amharic and English; business, insurance and financial news; circ. 6,000; Editor-in-Chief SEMENEH ADGE.

Ethiopis Review: Editor-in-Chief TESFERA ASMARE.

Meskerem: Addis Ababa; quarterly; theoretical politics; circ. 100,000.

Negarit Gazzetta: POB 1031, Addis Ababa; irregularly; Amharic and English; official gazette.

Nigdina Limat: POB 2458, Addis Ababa; tel. (1) 513882; telex 21213; fax (1) 511479; monthly; Amharic; publ. by the Ethiopian Chamber of Commerce; circ. 6,000.

Tinsae (Resurrection): Addis Ababa; tel. (1) 116507; telex 21489; Amharic and English; publ. by the Ethiopian Orthodox Church.

Tobiya: Addis Ababa; weekly; Gen.-Man. HAILU WOLDETSADIK (acting).

Wetaderna Alamaw: POB 1901, Addis Ababa; fortnightly; Amharic.

Yezareitu Ethiopia (Ethiopia Today): POB 30232, Addis Ababa; weekly; Amharic and English; publ. by the Ministry of Information and Culture; Editor-in-Chief IMIRU WORKU; circ. 30,000.

NEWS AGENCIES

Ethiopian News Agency (ENA): Patriots' St, POB 530, Addis Ababa; tel. (1) 120014; telex 21068; Chief AMARE AREGAWI.

Foreign Bureaux

Agence France-Presse (AFP): POB 3537, Addis Ababa; tel. (1) 511006; telex 21031; Chief SABA SEYOUM.

Agenzia Nazionale Stampa Associata (ANSA) (Italy): POB 1001, Addis Ababa; tel. (1) 111007; Chief BRAHAME GHEBREZGHI-ABIHER.

Associated Press (AP): Addis Ababa; tel. (1) 161726; Correspondent ABEBE ANDUALAM.

Deutsche Presse-Agentur (dpa) (Germany): Addis Ababa; tel. (1) 510687; Correspondent GHION HAGOS.

Informatsionnoye Telegrafnoye Agentstvo Rossii—Telegrafnoye Agentstvo Suverennykh Stran (ITAR—TASS) (Russia): POB 998, Addis Ababa; tel. (1) 181255; telex 21091; Bureau Chief GENNADII G. GABRIELYAN.

Prensa Latina (Cuba): Gen. Makonnen Bldg, 5th Floor, nr Ghion Hotel, opp. National Stadium, POB 5690, Addis Ababa; tel. (1) 519899; telex 21151; Chief HUGO RIUS BLEIN.

Reuters (UK): Addis Ababa; tel. (1) 156505; telex 21407; Correspondent TSEGAYE TADESSE.

Rossiyskoye Informatsionnoye Agentstvo—Novosti (RIA—Novosti) (Russia): POB 239, Addis Ababa; telex 21237; Chief VITALII POLIKARPOV.

Xinhua (New China) News Agency (People's Republic of China): POB 2497, Addis Ababa; tel. (1) 515676; telex 21504; fax (1) 514742; Correspondent CHEN CAILIN.

PRESS ASSOCIATION

Ethiopian Journalists' Association: POB 5911, Addis Ababa; tel. (1) 128198; Chair. IMERU WORKU (acting).

Publishers

Addis Ababa University Press: POB 1176, Addis Ababa; tel. (1) 119148; telex 21205; f. 1968; educational and reference works in English; Editor MESSELECH HABTE.

Ethiopia Book Centre: POB 1024, Addis Ababa; tel. (1) 116844; f. 1977; privately-owned; publr, importer, wholesaler and retailer of educational books.

Kuraz Publishing Agency: POB 30933, Addis Ababa; tel. (1) 551688; telex 21512; state-owned.

Government Publishing House

Government Printing Press: Addis Ababa.

Broadcasting and Communications

TELECOMMUNICATIONS

Ethiopian Telecommunications Corpn: POB 1047, Addis Ababa; tel. (1) 510500; telex 21000; fax (1) 515777; Gen. Man. MESFIN HAILE.

RADIO

Radio Ethiopia: POB 1020, Addis Ababa; tel. (1) 121011; f. 1941; Amharic, English, French, Arabic, Afar, Oromifa, Tigre, Tigrinya and Somali; Gen. Man. KASA MILOKO.

Radio Voice of One Free Ethiopia: Amharic; broadcasts twice a week; opposes current govts of Ethiopia and Eritrea.

Torch: Addis Ababa; f. 1994; Amharic; Gen. Man. SEIFU TURE GETACHEW.

Voice of the Tigre Revolution: Mekele; supports Tigre People's Liberation Front.

TELEVISION

Ethiopian Television: POB 5544, Addis Ababa; tel. (1) 116701; telex 21429; f. 1964; state-controlled; commercial advertising accepted; programmes transmitted from Addis Ababa to 18 regional stations; Dir-Gen. WOLE GURMU.

Finance

(cap. = capital; p.u. = paid up; dep. = deposits; m. = million; res = reserves; brs = branches; amounts in birr)

BANKING

There are currently three state-owned and five privately-owned banks in Ethiopia.

Central Bank

National Bank of Ethiopia: POB 5550, Addis Ababa; tel. (1) 517430; telex 21020; fax (1) 514588; f. 1964; bank of issue; cap. and res 1,096.3m., dep. 3,305.3m. (Nov. 1997); Gov. DUBALE JALE; Vice-Gov. TEKLEWOLD ATNAFU; 1 br.

Other Banks

Awash Bank: POB 12638, Addis Ababa; tel. (1) 612919; telex 21688; fax (1) 614477; f. 1994; cap. and res 27.2m., dep. 212.5m. (Nov. 1996); Gen. Man. LEIKUN BERHANU; 11 brs.

Bank of Abyssinia: POB 12947, Addis Ababa; tel. (1) 159966; fax (1) 511575; e-mail abyssinia@telecom.net.et; f. 1905 (closed 1935 and reopened 1996); commercial banking service; cap. and res 17.7m., dep. 14.3m. (Nov. 1996); CEO TEKALIGN GEDAMU; 1 br.

Commercial Bank of Ethiopia: Unity Square, POB 255, Addis Ababa; tel. (1) 515004; telex 21037; fax (1) 517822; f. 1964, reorg. 1980; cap. and res 853.4m., dep. 11,868m. (Nov. 1996); Pres. TILAHUN ABBAY; 167 brs.

Construction and Business Bank: Higher 21, Kebele 04, POB 3480, Addis Ababa; tel. (1) 512300; telex 21869; fax (1) 515103; f. 1975 as Housing and Savings Bank; provides credit for construction projects and a range of commercial banking services; cap. and res 55.8m., dep. 447.7m. (Nov. 1996); Gen. Man. ADMASSU TECHANE; 20 brs.

Dashen Bank: POB 12752, Addis Ababa; tel. (1) 650286; telex 654073; cap. and res 14.9m., dep. 201.6m. (Nov. 1996); CEO TEKETEL HAPTE GIORGIS; 14 brs.

Development Bank of Ethiopia: Joseph Broz Tito St, POB 1700, Addis Ababa; tel. (1) 511188; telex 21173; fax (1) 511606; provides devt finance for industry and agriculture, technical advice and assistance in project evaluation; cap. and res 371.4m., dep. 8.9m. (June 1993); Gen. Man. MOGES CHEMERE; 19 brs.

Horn International Bank SC: Addis Ababa; f. 1997; commercial banking service; cap. p.u. 13.3m.

Wegagen Bank: Addis Ababa; commercial banking service; cap. p.u. 60m., res 30m. (Nov. 1996); CEO BRUTAYIT DAWIT ABDI; 4 brs.

INSURANCE

Africa Insurance Co: POB 12941, Addis Ababa; tel. (1) 517861; fax (1) 510376; Gen. Man. ALEM TESFATSION.

Awash Insurance Co: POB 34369, Addis Ababa; tel. (1) 614418; telex 21792; fax (1) 654788; Gen. Man. TSEGAYE KEMAI.

Ethiopian Insurance Corpn: POB 2545, Addis Ababa; tel. (1) 517974; telex 21120; fax (1) 517499; f. 1976; Gen. Man. MICHAEL KUMSA.

National Insurace Co of Ethiopia: POB 12645, Addis Ababa; tel. (1) 652448; fax (1) 650660; Gen. Man. HABTEMARIAM SHUMGIZAW.

Nile Insurance Co: POB 12836, Addis Ababa; tel. (1) 114041; fax (1) 550336; Gen. Man. MAHTSENTU FELEKE.

Nyala Insurance SC: POB 12753, Addis Ababa; tel. (1) 340532; fax (1) 654078; Man. Dir NAHU-SENAYE ARAYA.

United Insurance Co: POB 1156, Addis Ababa; tel. (1) 519847; fax (1) 513258; Gen. Man. EYESUSWORK ZAFU.

Trade and Industry

CHAMBER OF COMMERCE

Ethiopian Chamber of Commerce: Mexico Sq., POB 517, Addis Ababa; tel. (1) 518240; telex 21213; f. 1947; city chambers in Addis Ababa, Asella, Awasa, Bahir Dar, Dire Dawa, Nazret, Jimma, Gondar, Dessie, Mekele and Shashemene; Pres. KEBOUR GHENNA; Sec.-Gen. SOLOMON AZEZE.

INDUSTRIAL AND TRADE ASSOCIATIONS

Ethiopian Beverages Corpn: POB 1285, Addis Ababa; tel. (1) 186185; telex 21373; Gen. Man. MENNA TEWAHEDE.

Ethiopian Cement Corpn: POB 5782, Addis Ababa; tel. (1) 552222; telex 21308; fax (1) 551572; Gen. Man. REDI GEMAL.

Ethiopian Chemical Corpn: POB 5747, Addis Ababa; tel. (1) 184305; telex 21011; Gen. Man. ASNAKE SAHLU.

Ethiopian Coffee Marketing Corpn: POB 2591, Addis Ababa; tel. (1) 515330; telex 21174; fax (1) 510762; f. 1977; Gen. Man. GETACHW HAILE LEUL.

Ethiopian Food Corpn: Higher 21, Kebele 04, Mortgage Bldg, Addis Ababa; tel. (1) 158522; telex 21292; fax (1) 513173; f. 1975; produces and distributes food items including edible oil, ghee substitute, pasta, bread, maize, wheat flour etc.; Gen. Man. BEKELE HAILE.

Ethiopian Fruit and Vegetable Marketing Enterprise: POB 2374, Addis Ababa; tel. (1) 519192; telex 21106; fax (1) 516483; f. 1980; sole wholesale domestic distributor and exporter of fresh and processed fruit and vegetables, and floricultural products; Gen. Man. AGEGENHU SISSAY.

Ethiopian Handicrafts and Small-Scale Industries Development Organization: Addis Ababa; tel. (1) 157366.

Ethiopian Import and Export Corpn (ETIMEX): POB 2313, Addis Ababa; tel. (1) 511112; telex 21235; fax (1) 515411; f. 1975; state trading corpn under the supervision of the Ministry of Commerce and Industry; import of building materials, foodstuffs, stationery and office equipment, textiles, clothing, chemicals, general merchandise, capital goods; Gen. Man. ASCHENAKI G. HIWOT.

Ethiopian Livestock and Meat Corpn: POB 5579, Addis Ababa; tel. (1) 159341; telex 21095; f. 1984; state trading corpn responsible for the development and export of livestock and livestock products; Gen. Man. GELANA KEJELA.

Ethiopian National Metal Works Corpn: Addis Ababa; fax (1) 510714; Gen. Man. ALULA BERHANE.

Ethiopian Oil Seeds and Pulses Export Corpn: POB 5719, Addis Ababa; tel. (1) 550597; telex 21133; fax (1) 553299; f. 1975; Gen. Man. EPHRAIM AMBAYE.

Ethiopia Peasants' Association (EPA): f. 1978 to promote improved agricultural techniques, home industries, education, public health and self-reliance; comprises 30,000 peasant asscns with c. 7m. mems; Chair. (vacant).

Ethiopian Petroleum Corpn: POB 3375, Addis Ababa; telex 21054; fax (1) 512938; f. 1976; Gen. Man. ZEWDE TEWOLDE.

Ethiopian Pharmaceuticals and Medical Supplies Corpn: POB 21904, Addis Ababa; tel. (1) 134577; telex 21248; fax (1) 752555; f. 1976; manufacture, import, export and distribution of pharmaceuticals, chemicals, dressings, surgical and dental instruments, hospital and laboratory supplies; Gen. Man. BERHANU ZELEKE.

Ethiopian Sugar Corpn: POB 133, Addis Ababa; tel. (1) 519700; telex 21038; fax (1) 513488; Gen. Man. ABATE LEMENGH.

National Leather and Shoe Corpn: POB 2516, Addis Ababa; tel. (1) 514075; telex 21096; fax (1) 513525; f. 1975; produces and sells semi-processed hides and skins, finished leather, leather goods and footwear; Gen. Man. GIRMA W. AREGAI.

National Textiles Corpn: Addis Ababa; tel. (1) 157316; telex 21129; fax (1) 511955; f. 1975; production of yarn, fabrics, knitwear, blankets, bags, etc.; Gen. Man. FIKRE HUGIANE.

Natural Gums Processing and Marketing Enterprise: POB 62322, Addis Ababa; tel. (1) 159930; telex 21336; fax (1) 518110; Gen. Man. ESKINDER TAYE.

UTILITIES

Electricity

Ethiopian Electric Power Corpn: Addis Ababa; Chair. HAILE SELASSIE ASEGIDE.

TRADE UNIONS

Ethiopian Trade Union (ETU): POB 3653, Addis Ababa; tel. (1) 514366; telex 21618; f. 1975 to replace the Confed. of Ethiopian Labour Unions; comprises nine industrial unions and 22 regional unions with a total membership of 320,000 (1987); Chair. (vacant).

Transport

RAILWAYS

Djibouti-Ethiopian Railway (Chemin de Fer Djibouti-Ethiopien–CDE): POB 1051, Addis Ababa; tel. (1) 517250; telex 21414; fax (1) 513533; f. 1909, adopted present name in 1981; jtly-owned by Govts of Ethiopia and Djibouti; 781 km of track, of which 681 km in Ethiopia, linking Addis Ababa with Djibouti; Pres. SALAH OMAR HILDID; Vice-Pres. DR ABDUL-MEJID HUSSEN.

ROADS

In 1995 the total road network comprised an estimated 23,812 km of primary, secondary and feeder roads and trails, of which 15,709 km were main roads. A highway links Addis Ababa with Nairobi in Kenya, forming part of the Trans-East Africa Highway. In November 1995 a five-year programme of road construction was announced. Some US $200m. was allocated to the programme, mostly financed by loans from the World Bank and the European Union.

Ethiopian Roads Authority: POB 1770, Addis Ababa; tel. (1) 517170; telex 12180; fax (1) 514866; f. 1951; construction and maintenance of roads, bridges and airports; Gen. Man. TESFA MICHAEL NAHUSENAI.

Ethiopian Road Transport Authority: POB 2504, Addis Ababa; tel. (1) 510244; fax (1) 510715; enforcement of road transport regulations, registering of vehicles and issuing of driving licences; Gen. Man. ZEMEDKUN GIRMA.

National Freight Transport Corpn: POB 2538, Addis Ababa; tel. (1) 151841; telex 21238; f. 1974; truck and tanker operations throughout the country; restructured into five autonomous enterprises in 1994 and scheduled for privatization.

Public Transport Corpn: POB 5780, Addis Ababa; tel. (1) 153117; telex 21371; fax (1) 510720; f. 1977; urban bus services in Addis Ababa and Jimma, and services between towns; restructured into three autonomous enterprises in 1994 and scheduled for privatization; Gen. Man. TESFAYE SHENKUTE.

SHIPPING

The formerly Ethiopian-controlled ports of Massawa and Assab now lie within the boundaries of the State of Eritrea (q.v.). There is, however, an agreement between the two Governments allowing Ethiopian access to the two ports. There are regular services by foreign vessels to Massawa and Assab, which can handle more than 1m. metric tons of merchandise annually. Much trade passes through Djibouti (in the Republic of Djibouti) to Addis Ababa, and Ethiopia has access to the Kenyan port of Mombasa. At the end of 1997 Ethiopia's registered merchant fleet numbered 11 vessels, with a total displacement of 86,592 grt.

Ethiopian Shipping Lines Corpn: POB 2572, Addis Ababa; tel. (1) 518280; telex 21045; fax (1) 519525; e-mail esl@telecom.net.et; f. 1964; serves Red Sea, Europe, Mediterranean, Gulf and Far East with its own fleet and chartered vessels; Chair. G. TSADKAN GEBRE TENSAY; Gen. Man. AMBACHEW ABRAHA.

Marine Transport Authority: Maritime Dept, POB 1861, Addis Ababa; tel. (1) 158227; telex 21348; fax (1) 515665; f. 1993; regulates maritime transport services; Chair. TESHOME WOLDEGIORGIS.

Maritime and Transit Services Enterprise: POB 1186, Addis Ababa; tel. (1) 510666; telex 21290; fax (1) 514097; f. 1979; handles cargoes for import and export; operates shipping agency service; Chair. DESTA AMARE; Gen. Man. AHMED YASSIN.

CIVIL AVIATION

Ethiopia has two international airports (at Addis Ababa and Dire Dawa) and around 30 airfields. Bole International Airport in the capital handles 95% of international air traffic and 85% of domestic flights. A programme to modernize the airport, at an estimated cost of 819m. birr (US $130m.), was to be undertaken during 1997–2000. Construction of an international airport at Mekele began in November 1995. This airport was scheduled to become operational in 1997.

Civil Aviation Authority: POB 978, Addis Ababa; tel. (1) 610277; telex 21162; fax (1) 612533; constructs and maintains airports; provides air navigational facilities; Gen. Man. MESHESHA BELAYNEH.

Ethiopian Airlines: Bole International Airport, POB 1755, Addis Ababa; tel. (1) 612222; telex 21012; fax (1) 611474; f. 1945; operates regular domestic services and flights to 35 international destinations in Africa, Europe, Middle East and Asia; Chair. SEEYE ABRAHA; Dir-Gen. BISRAT NIGATU.

Tourism

Ethiopia's tourist attractions include the early Christian monuments and churches, the ancient capitals of Gondar and Axum, the Blue Nile Falls and the National Parks of the Semien and Bale Mountains. Tourist arrivals in 1994 totalled some 98,000 and provided an estimated US $23m. in foreign exchange.

Ethiopian Tourism Commission: POB 2183, Addis Ababa; tel. (1) 517470; telex 21067; fax (1) 513899; f. 1964; formulates national tourism policy, publicizes tourist attractions and regulates standards of tourist facilities; Commr YOUSUF ABDULLAHI SUKKAR.

FIJI

Introductory Survey

Location, Climate, Language, Religion, Flag, Capital

The Republic of Fiji comprises more than 300 islands, of which 100 are inhabited, situated about 1,930 km (1,200 miles) south of the equator in the Pacific Ocean. The four main islands are Viti Levu (on which almost 70% of the country's population lives), Vanua Levu, Taveuni and Kadavu. The climate is tropical, with temperatures ranging from 16° to 32°C (60°–90°F). Rainfall is heavy on the windward side. Fijian and Hindi are the principal languages but English is also widely spoken. In 1986 about 53% of the population were Christians (mainly Methodists), 38% Hindus and 8% Muslims. The national flag (proportions 2 by 1) is light blue, with the United Kingdom flag as a canton in the upper hoist. In the fly is the main part of Fiji's national coat of arms: a white field quartered by a red upright cross, the quarters containing sugar canes, a coconut palm, a stem of bananas and a dove bearing an olive branch; in chief is a red panel with a yellow crowned lion holding a white cocoa pod. The capital is Suva, on Viti Levu.

Recent History

The first Europeans to settle on the islands were sandalwood traders, missionaries and shipwrecked sailors, and in October 1874 Fiji was proclaimed a British possession. In September 1966 the British Government introduced a new Constitution for Fiji. It provided for a ministerial form of government, an almost wholly elected Legislative Council and the introduction of universal adult suffrage. Rather than using a common roll of voters, however, the Constitution introduced an electoral system that combined communal (Fijian and Indian) rolls with cross-voting. In September 1967 the Executive Council became the Council of Ministers, with Ratu Kamisese Mara, leader of the multiracial (but predominantly Fijian) Alliance Party (AP), as Fiji's first Chief Minister. Following a constitutional conference in April–May 1970, Fiji achieved independence, within the Commonwealth, on 10 October 1970. The Legislative Council was renamed the House of Representatives, and a second parliamentary chamber, the nominated Senate, was established. The British-appointed Governor became Fiji's first Governor-General, while Ratu Sir Kamisese Mara (as he had become in 1969) took office as Prime Minister.

Fiji was, however, troubled by racial tensions. Although the descendants of indentured Indian workers who were brought to Fiji in the late 19th century had grown to outnumber the native inhabitants, they were discriminated against in political representation and land ownership rights. A new electoral system was adopted in 1970 to ensure a racial balance in the legislature.

At the general election held in March and April 1977 the National Federation Party (NFP), traditionally supported by the Indian population, won 26 of the 52 seats in the House of Representatives but was unable to form a government and subsequently split into two factions. The AP governed in a caretaker capacity until the holding of a further general election in September, when it was returned with its largest-ever majority. While the two main parties professed multiracial ideas, the Fijian Nationalist Party campaigned in support of its 'Fiji for the Fijians' programme in order to foster nationalist sentiment.

In 1980 Ratu Sir Kamisese Mara's suggestion that a Government of National Unity be formed was overshadowed by renewed political disagreement between the AP and the NFP (whose two factions had drawn closer together again) over land ownership. Fijians owned 83% of the land and were strongly defending their traditional rights, while the Indian population was pressing for greater security of land tenure. The general election held in July 1982 was also dominated by racial issues. The AP retained power after winning 28 seats, but their majority had been reduced from 20 to four. The NFP won 22 seats and the Western United Front (WUF), which professed a multiracial outlook, took the remaining two seats.

A meeting of union leaders in May 1985 represented the beginning of discussions which culminated in the founding of the Fiji Labour Party (FLP), officially inaugurated in Suva in July. Sponsored by the Fiji Trades Union Congress (FTUC), and under the presidency of Dr Timoci Bavadra, the new party was formed with the aim of presenting a more effective parliamentary opposition, and declared the provision of free education and a national medical scheme to be among its priorities. The FLP hoped to work through farmers' organizations to win votes among rural electorates, which traditionally supported the NFP. During 1985 and 1986 disagreements between the Government and the FTUC over economic policies became increasingly acrimonious, leading to an outbreak of labour unrest and the withdrawal, in June 1986, of government recognition of the FTUC as the unions' representative organization.

At the general election held in April 1987 a coalition of the FLP and NFP won 28 seats (19 of which were secured by ethnic Indian candidates) in the House of Representatives, thus defeating the ruling AP, which won only 24 seats. The new Government, led by Dr Timoci Bavadra of the FLP, was therefore the first in Fijian history to contain a majority of ministers of Indian, rather than Melanesian, origin. Dr Bavadra, himself, was of Melanesian descent. On 14 May, however, the Government was overthrown by a military coup, led by Lt-Col (later Maj.-Gen.) Sitiveni Rabuka. The Governor-General, Ratu Sir Penaia Ganilau, responded by declaring a state of emergency and appointed a 19-member advisory council, including Bavadra and Rabuka. However, Bavadra refused to participate in the council, denouncing it as unconstitutional and biased in its composition.

Widespread racial violence followed the coup, and there were several public demands for Bavadra's reinstatement as Prime Minister. In July 1987 the Great Council of Fijian Chiefs, comprising the country's 80 hereditary Melanesian leaders, approved plans for constitutional reform. In September negotiations began, on the initiative of Ganilau, between delegations led by the two former Prime Ministers, Bavadra and Mara, to resolve the political crisis. On 22 September it was announced that the two factions had agreed to form an interim bipartisan Government.

On 25 September 1987, however, before the new plan could be implemented, Rabuka staged a second coup and announced his intention to declare Fiji a republic. Despite Ganilau's refusal to recognize the seizure of power, Rabuka revoked the Constitution on 1 October and proclaimed himself Head of State, thus deposing the Queen. Ganilau conceded defeat and resigned as Governor-General. At a meeting in Canada, Commonwealth Heads of Government formally declared that Fiji's membership of the Commonwealth had lapsed. An interim Cabinet, comprising mainly ethnic Fijians, was installed by Rabuka. In late October Rabuka announced that he would resign as Head of State as soon as he had appointed a new President of the Republic. Several cases of violations of human rights by the Fijian army were reported, as the regime assumed powers of detention without trial and suspended all political activity.

On 6 December 1987 Rabuka resigned as Head of State. Although he had previously refused to accept the post, Ganilau, the former Governor-General, became the first President of the Fijian Republic. Mara was reappointed Prime Minister, and Rabuka became Minister of Home Affairs. A new interim Cabinet was announced on 9 December, containing 11 members of Rabuka's administration, but no member of Bavadra's deposed Government.

In February 1988 Rotuma (the only Polynesian island in the country), which lies to the north-west of Vanua Levu, declared itself politically independent of Fiji, whose newly-acquired republican status it refused to recognize. Rotuma appealed to the Governments of Australia, New Zealand and the United Kingdom for assistance. Fijian troops were dispatched to the island, however, and soon quelled the dissent.

A new draft Constitution was approved by the interim Government in September 1988. The proposed Constitution was rejected, however, by a multiracial constitutional committee, which considered unnecessary the specific reservation of the principal offices of state for ethnic Fijians. In September 1989 the committee published a revised draft, which was still, however, condemned by Bavadra and the FLP-NFP coalition. In November Bavadra died and was replaced as leader of the FLP-NFP coalition by his widow, Adi Kuini Bavadra.

In January 1990 Rabuka resigned from the Cabinet and returned to his military duties. Mara agreed to remain as Prime Minister until the restoration of constitutional government. In June the Great Council of Chiefs approved the draft Constitution. At the same time, the Great Council of Chiefs stated its intention to form a new party, the Soqosoqo ni Vakavulewa ni Taukei (SVT) or Fijian Political Party, to advocate the cause of ethnic Fijians. The new Constitution was finally promulgated on 25 July by President Ganilau: a development which was reported to have been prompted by fears of another coup. The Constitution was immediately condemned by the FLP-NFP coalition, which announced that it would boycott any elections held in accordance with the Constitution's provisions. Angered by the fact that a legislative majority was guaranteed to ethnic Fijians (who were reserved 37 of the 70 elective seats, compared with 27 Indian seats), and that the Great Council of Chiefs was to nominate ethnic Fijians to 24 of the 34 seats in the Senate and to appoint the President of the Republic, the opposition organized anti-Constitution demonstrations. The new Constitution was similarly condemned for its racial bias by India, New Zealand and Australia at the UN General Assembly, meeting in New York in October. In May 1991 the Secretary-General of the Commonwealth stated that Fiji would not be readmitted to the organization until it changed its Constitution.

In April 1991, in a reorganization of cabinet portfolios, Rabuka was offered the post of Deputy Prime Minister and Minister of Home Affairs, and in July he officially resigned as Commander of the Armed Forces in order to join the Cabinet. The Rev. Manasa Lasaro, General Secretary of the Methodist Church and leader of the anti-Indian campaign during the coups of 1987, was also appointed to the Cabinet. Towards the end of 1991, Rabuka resigned from the Cabinet in order to assume the leadership of the SVT. Racial tensions were exacerbated after a number of arson attacks were perpetrated on Hindu temples in the latter part of 1991.

Disagreements between the Government and the FTUC re-emerged at the beginning of 1991. In February a strike by more than 900 members of the Fijian Miners' Union over union recognition, pay and poor working conditions led to the dismissal of some 400 of the workers. Despite support from several international mining organizations, employers claimed the strike action to be illegal, as the union did not have the 50% minimum membership required by Fijian law. Further reforms to the labour laws, announced by the Government in May, included the abolition of the minimum wage, restrictions on strike action and derecognition of unions that did not represent at least two-thirds of the work-force. A significant political development announced by the Government in late 1992 was the official recognition of the FTUC (withheld since 1986) as the sole representative of workers in Fiji.

In the legislative elections, which took place in May 1992, the SVT secured 30 of the 37 seats reserved for ethnic Fijians, while the NFP won 14 and the FLP 13 of the seats reserved for Indian representatives. Following the election, the FLP agreed to participate in Parliament and to support Rabuka in his campaign for the premiership, in return for a guarantee from the SVT of a full review of the Constitution and of trade union and land laws. Rabuka was, therefore, appointed Prime Minister and formed a coalition Government (consisting of 14 members of the SVT and five others).

In July 1992 a report was published, detailing the findings of a corruption inquiry, undertaken following the military coups of 1987. Rabuka aroused some controversy by ordering that the report remain 'classified'. Remarks made by the Prime Minister in an Australian television interview in October, expressing his implicit support for the repatriation of Fijian Indians, attracted similar controversy and prompted renewed fears that any reform of the Constitution would be merely superficial. Nevertheless, in December Rabuka formally invited the opposition leaders, Jai Ram Reddy of the NFP and Mahendra Chaudhry of the FLP (formerly the National Secetary of the FTUC), to form a Government of National Unity. The move was largely welcomed, but Indian politicians expressed reluctance to take part in a government whose political control remained fundamentally vested with ethnic Fijians. Rabuka was criticized equally by nationalist extremists of the Taukei Solidarity Movement, who, in a series of statements in early 1993, accused him of conceding too much political power to Fijian Indians. Following the appointment of a new Cabinet in June 1993, all 13 of the FLP members began an indefinite boycott of Parliament, in protest at Rabuka's failure to implement the reforms, which he had agreed to carry out in return for their support for his election to the premiership in June 1992.

The 1994 budget, which was presented to Parliament in November 1993, was widely criticized for failing to address the country's economic problems and did not achieve parliamentary approval, with seven SVT members voting against the Government. As a result of the Government's defeat, acting President Mara agreed to dissolve Parliament in preparation for legislative elections in February 1994. In January 1994 it was announced that several former members of the SVT had formed a new political party, the Fijian Association Party, under the leadership of Josefata Kamikamica.

In December 1993 President Ganilau died, following a long illness, and was replaced by Ratu Sir Kamisese Mara, who took office on 18 January 1994.

At legislative elections held on 18–24 February 1994 the SVT increased the number of its seats in the House of Representatives to 31, while, despite extremely favourable reports concerning the popularity of the Fijian Association Party, the newly-formed organization secured only five seats, of a total of 37 reserved for ethnic Fijians. Of the 27 seats reserved for ethnic Indian representatives, 20 were secured by the NFP. Following the election, Rabuka anounced the formation of a new Cabinet composed entirely of ethnic Fijians.

In response to international concern regarding the continued existence of Fiji's racially-biased Constitution, Rabuka announced in June 1994 that a commission had been established, which, it was hoped, would have completed a review of the Constitution by 1997. The opposition leader, Jai Ram Reddy, however, criticized the Prime Minister, whose appointment of an ethnic Fijian to head the commission contradicted his original assurance that the post would be held by an independent. In an attempt to reassure the opposition, Rabuka subsequently announced the creation of a joint select committee, comprising 45% Indian members and 55% Fijian and mixed-race members, to assist the commission. However, the committee was unable to agree on the composition of the commission, and in November the Cabinet announced that the commission should comprise only three members (one representing the Government, another representing the opposition and a third appointed with the approval of both sides).

In January 1995 the Government approved a scheme (similar to several others introduced in neighbouring Pacific islands in the early 1990s) which would involve providing residency in Fiji for as many as 28,000 ethnic Chinese from Hong Kong in return for a fee of US $30,000 and a minimum investment in economic development projects of US $100,000 per family. Opponents of the scheme expressed fears that the introduction of large numbers of immigrants would exacerbate existing racial tensions in Fiji. In the same month the Government announced that it was to recommend that Parliament vote to repeal the Sunday observance law (imposed after the coups of 1987), which prohibited work, organized entertainment and sport on that day. It was believed that the law had become increasingly unpopular, particularly among the Indian community. However, the announcement aroused intense opposition from nationalist politicians and Methodist church leaders, who organized demonstrations in three cities, attended by more than 12,000 people, in protest at the proposed repeal. Despite this vociferous opposition, in February the House of Representatives voted in favour of removing the regulations. The Senate, however, narrowly rejected the proposal (by 15 votes to 14), thus effectively delaying the implementation of any changes. Their campaign against the proposed legislation, together with their opposition to the immigration scheme for Hong Kong Chinese, led the Methodist leadership to announce the formation of a new political party, the Fiji Christian Party. The Sunday observance law was finally repealed in November 1995.

The issue of independence for the island of Rotuma was raised in September 1995 with the return of the King of Rotuma from exile in New Zealand. King Gagaj Sa Lagfatmaro, who had fled to New Zealand following death threats made against him during the military coups of 1987, appeared before the Constitutional Review Committee to petition for the island's independence within the Commonwealth, reiterating his view that Rotuma remains a British colony rather than a part of Fiji.

In September 1995 the Government decided to transfer all state land (comprising some 10% of Fiji's total land area), hitherto administered by the Government Lands Department, to the Native Lands Trust Board. The decision was to allow the allocation of land to indigenous Fijians on the basis of native custom. However, concern among the Fijian Indian population increased following reports in early 1996 that many would not be able to renew their land leases (most of which were due to expire between 1997 and 2024). The reports were strongly denied by the Government, despite statements by several Fijian land-owning clans that Indians' leases would not be renewed. Moreover, a recently-formed sugar cane growers' association solely for ethnic Fijians, the Taukei Cane Growers' Association, led by Koresi Matatolu, announced its intention to campaign for ethnic Fijian control of the sugar industry, largely by refusing to renew land leases to ethnic Indians (who held some 85% of sugar farm leases). The Government denied suggestions that Indian farmers would be evicted from their land, while expressing support for the Taukei Association and its aim of providing financial and technical assistance for ethnic Fijian farmers. In late 1997 the National Farmers' Union urged the Government to resolve the issue of land leases, following reports that many cane-growers whose leases were due to expire at the end of the year were being harassed by landowners.

Racial tension intensified in October 1995 following the publication of the SVT's submission to the Constitutional Review Commission. In its submission the party detailed plans to abandon the present multiracial form of government, recommending instead the adoption of an electoral system based on racial representation, in which each ethnic group selects its own representatives. The expression of numerous extreme anti-Indian sentiments in the document (including accusations that Indians were arrogant, disloyal and displayed unscrupulous political ambition) was widely condemned as offensive. Josefata Kamikamica of the Fijian Association Party was one of several political leaders to describe the submission as disgraceful and insulting to Fijian, as well as to Indian, sensibilities.

The issue of alleged state manipulation of the media re-emerged in late 1995 with the announcement that the Government was to review the Official Secrets Act. The statement came in response to the recent publication of a number of classified reports, including material concerning a serious financial scandal at the National Bank of Fiji (as a result of which several senior officials and former government members were charged with criminal offences). The FLP, the Law Society and various media associations were highly critical of the proposed review, which, they believed, would restrict the activities of the media and undermine its role in Fijian society.

A rift within the GVP in early 1996, which resulted in two of the four GVP members of the House of Representatives withdrawing their support for the Government, prompted Rabuka to seek alternative coalition partners from among the opposition, in an attempt to establish a more secure majority. However, the Prime Minister was unsuccessful in persuading parliamentary members of the Fijian Association Party to join the Government. The administration's troubles during 1996 contributed to the defeat of the SVT in virtually every municipality at local elections, which took place in September.

Existing divisions within the Government were further exacerbated by the presentation to the House of Representatives, in September 1996, of the Constitutional Review Commission's report. The report included recommendations to enlarge the House of Representatives to 75 seats, with 25 seats reserved on a racial basis (12 for ethnic Fijians, 10 for Fijian Indians, two for General Voters and one for Rotuma Islanders), and also proposed that the Prime Minister should be a Fijian of any race, while the President should continue to be an indigenous Fijian. Rabuka and Mara both endorsed the findings of the report, while several nationalist parties, including the Vanua Independent Party, the Fijian Nationalist United Front Party (FNUFP) and the Taukei Solidarity Movement, expressed extreme opposition to the proposals, and formed a coalition in an attempt to further their influence within Parliament. In addition, a number of SVT members of the House of Representatives aligned themselves with the nationalists, and in early 1997 were reported to be responsible for a series of political manoeuvres within the Cabinet, aimed at undermining Rabuka's position. The parliamentary committee reviewing the report agreed on a majority of the 700 recommendations, but proposed that the House of Representatives be enlarged to only 71 seats, with 46 seats reserved on a racial basis (23 for ethnic Fijians, 19 for Indians, three for general electors and one for Rotuma Islanders) and 25 seats open to all races. The committee's modified proposals were presented in May to the Great Council of Chiefs, which endorsed the recommendations on constitutional change, but demanded that the number of lower chamber seats reserved for ethnic Fijians be increased from 23 to 28. However, the Council approved the proposal to reduce the number of nominated senators to 15 (from 24). The reforms, as proposed by the committee, were officially endorsed by the Great Council of Chiefs in early June. The Constitution Amendment Bill was approved unanimously by the House of Representatives and the Senate on 3 and 10 July respectively. Although the new Constitution was not due to take effect until July 1998, Rabuka expressed his desire to establish a multi-party Cabinet as soon as possible. However, the idea was opposed by the Leader of the Opposition, Jai Ram Reddy, who favoured deferring such a development until after the general elections in 1999, in order that opposition parties could form a national coalition. Rabuka was also anxious to reassure extremist nationalist Fijians, who had vociferously opposed the reforms throughout the debate, that their interests would be protected under the amended Constitution and that indigenous Fijians would continue to play a pre-eminent role in the government of the country. Despite opposition from both the FLP and the nationalist parties, Fiji was readmitted to the Commonwealth at a meeting of member states in October 1997. In the same month Rabuka was granted an audience with Queen Elizabeth II in London, at which he formally apologized for the military coups of 1987. Opposition to his administration, however, continued during late 1997. A by-election held in October was won by the FNUFP, which declared its intention to win the next general election in order to overthrow the new Constitution. Furthermore, in the following month the Fijian Association Party, which had joined the Government in a cabinet reorganization in August, withdrew from the coalition, citing disagreement with the provisions of the 1998 budget, the poor state of the economy and increasing unemployment as the main reasons for its disaffection.

In November 1989 the Fijian Government expelled the Indian ambassador to Fiji for allegedly interfering in Fiji's internal affairs, and the status of the Indian embassy was downgraded to that of a consulate. Relations between Fiji and India deteriorated following the coup of May 1987, when many ethnic Indians (including many members of the professions) emigrated. In January 1989 statistical information, released by the interim Government, indicated that the islands' ethnic Fijians were in a majority for the first time since 1946. Following the adoption of significant constitutional reforms in 1997 diplomatic relations improved considerably, and in October the Indian Government invited Fiji to open a High Commission in New Delhi.

The decision by the French Government in June 1995 to resume nuclear testing in the region was widely condemned by the Pacific island nations and, in protest at the announcement, Fiji cancelled its annual military exercise with France. A demonstration by some 5,000 people in July against the tests typified the reaction of Pacific islanders throughout the region. Furthermore, in October the Minister for Foreign Affairs, Filipe Bole, suggested that France should consider the withdrawal of its ambassador from Fiji, as, given public anger over the tests, his safety could not be guaranteed.

Government

The 1990 Constitution provided for a parliamentary form of government with a bicameral legislature comprising the elected 70-seat House of Representatives and the appointed Senate with 34 members. The Constitution established a permanent majority of 37 seats in the House to be elected by indigenous Fijians, with 27 seats to be elected by those of Indian descent, four by other races (General Electors) and one by voters on the island of Rotuma. Only five Fijian seats were reserved for the urban centres, where approximately one-third of the ethnic Fijian population reside. The Senate was to be appointed by the President of the Republic, 24 members on the advice of the Great Council of Chiefs (an 80-member traditional body comprising every hereditary chief (Ratu) of a Fijian clan) from among their own number, one member on the advice of the Rotuma Island Council, and the remaining nine selected from 'prominent citizens' among the other racial communities, on the President's 'own deliberate judgement'. The Constitution Amendment Bill, which provided for major constitutional reforms, including the establishment of a multiracial Cabinet, was approved in July 1997 and was due to take effect in July 1998.

Defence

The Fiji Military Forces consist of men in the regular army, the Naval Squadron, the conservation corps and the territorials. The conservation corps was created in 1975 to make use of unemployed labour in construction work. In August 1996 the total armed forces numbered 3,600 men: 3,300 in the army and 290 in the navy. Budgetary expenditure on defence in 1995 was estimated at $F48.8m., equivalent to 6.1% of total government expenditure, and in 1996 was estimated at $F46m.

Economic Affairs

In 1995, according to estimates by the World Bank, Fiji's gross national product (GNP), measured at average 1993–95 prices, was US $1,895m., equivalent to $2,440 per head. During 1985–95, it was estimated, GNP per head increased, in real terms, at an average annual rate of 2.3%. Over the same period, the population increased by an annual average of 1.1%. Fiji's gross domestic product (GDP) increased by an annual average of 2.8% between 1987 and 1994, and GDP per head by 1.6% annually. GDP increased by some 1.4% in 1995, by 4.4% in 1996 and was projected to expand by 3.2% in 1997.

Agriculture (including forestry and fishing) contributed 17.9% of GDP (at constant 1989 prices) in 1996, and engaged 36.6% of the economically active population in 1994. The principal cash crop is sugar cane, which normally accounts for about 80% of total agricultural production. Sugar and its derivatives provided 31.7% of Fiji's total export earnings in 1995. Other important export crops are coconuts and ginger, while the most important subsistence crop is paddy rice (of which Fiji provided about 72% of its domestic requirements in 1989). Fishing was becoming an increasingly important activity in the mid-1990s, earning some $F56m. in 1995 in exports mainly to the Japanese market.

Industry (including mining, manufacturing, construction and power) engaged 35.1% of the employed labour force in 1995, and provided 24.5% of GDP in 1996. Industrial production increased by 5.8% in 1993. Mining contributed 3.2% of GDP in 1996, and employed 1.9% of the labour force in 1995. Gold and silver are the major mineral exports, with gold providing 9.0% of total export earnings in 1995. A copper mining project in Namosi, central Viti Levu, was expected to begin operations in the late 1990s, earning an estimated $F400m. annually in exports. Gold exploration activity increased dramatically in the mid-1990s and foreign mining companies expected to open at least two major new gold mines by the late 1990s in addition to the Mount Kasi and Vatukoula gold mines. It was forecast that exports of gold would total some 11,500 kg and earn an estimated $F200m. by 2003. The Vatukoula mine exported gold worth $F73m. in 1996. Production at the Mount Kasi gold mine began in 1996, and was expected to earn some $F20m.–35m. annually for 20 years. However, by October 1996 demands for the closure of the mine had already been expressed, prompted by the installation's adverse impact on the environment.

Manufacturing contributed 12.7% of GDP in 1996, and engaged 24.8% of the employed labour force in 1995. Manufacturing output (excluding the sugar industry) declined by 0.7% in 1992, but expanded by 5.4% in 1993. The most important branch of the sector is food-processing, in particular sugar, molasses and copra. The ready-made garment industry is also important and has particularly benefited from the tax-exemption scheme implemented by the Government in 1987. In 1995 there were 156 tax-exempt factories operating in the country, of which 103 were dedicated to garment manufacture. The ready-made garment industry accounted for 18.0% of total export earnings in 1994 and engaged 85.8% of the 13,400 people employed in the tax-free sector.

Energy is derived principally from hydroelectric power. Electricity, gas and water contributed 3.8% of GDP in 1996. Imports of mineral fuels represented 11.0% of the total cost of imports in 1995.

Tourism is Fiji's largest source of foreign exchange, earning some $F442.3m. in 1996, when visitor arrivals totalled 339,560.

In 1996 Fiji recorded a visible trade deficit of US $182.4m., but a surplus of US $10.2m. on the current account of the balance of payments. In 1995 the principal sources of imports were Australia (38.8%), New Zealand (15.8%), Japan (7.2%) and Singapopre (7.1%). The principal markets for exports were Australia (26.0%), the United Kingdom (22.9%) and the USA (13.0%). The principal imports in that year were machinery and transport equipment, basic manufactured goods, mineral fuels and food. The principal exports were sugar, gold, re-exported petroleum products and ready-made garments.

In 1995 there was a budgetary deficit of $F97.5m. and a projected budgetary deficit for 1997 of $F219.2m. The budgetary deficit for 1998 was forecast at 1.7% of GDP (compared with an estimated 9.2% for the previous year). Fiji's total external debt was US $252.8m. at the end of 1995, of which US $169.9m. was long-term public debt. In that year the cost of debt-servicing was equivalent to 5.9% of revenue from exports of goods and services. The annual rate of inflation averaged 5.6% in 1985–93, but declined to 1.2% in 1994, before rising to 2.0% in 1995. The rate was estimated at 3.5% in mid-1997. An estimated 5.8% of the labour force were unemployed in 1994, and in September 1995 there were 98,112 people in paid employment. Since 1987 Fiji's economy has suffered considerably from large-scale emigration. Between 1987 and 1995 some 72,688 citizens emigrated from Fiji, of which some 90% were Fijian Indians, with an estimated 30% described as professional or semi-professional workers.

Fiji is a member of the UN Economic and Social Commission for Asia and the Pacific (see p. 27), the South Pacific Forum (see p. 233), the Pacific Community (formerly the South Pacific Commission—see p. 232) and the International Sugar Organization (see p. 258). Fiji is also a signatory of the South Pacific Regional Trade and Economic Co-operation Agreement—SPARTECA (see p. 235) and the Lomé Convention with the European Union (EU—see p. 178). In 1995 Fiji sought membership of the Asia-Pacific Economic Co-operation (APEC) group (see p. 108), and in mid-1996 was admitted to the Melanesian Spearhead Group.

Fiji's economic performance in the 1980s was adversely affected by the world recession and by political instability resulting from the two coups of 1987. The subsequent recovery of the economy was aided by strong sugar prices on the international market, an increase in tourist arrivals, the introduction of tax-free zones, and growth in foreign investment (notably from Japan). It was hoped that the discovery of 20 potential petroleum-bearing sites in early 1993, as well as the identification of new gold reserves in the mid-1990s, would prove significant in the diversification of the economy. During the mid-1990s Fiji forged closer economic ties with several Asian countries, particularly the People's Republic of China, Taiwan and the Republic of Korea. The 1998 budget included a programme of reforms which aimed to increase revenue through privatization or corporatization of many government-owned enterprises, higher taxes on certain goods and increased tariff rates on imports.

Social Welfare

The Fiji National Provident Fund, established in 1966, contains provision for retirement pensions, widows' pensions, an insurance scheme and housing loans. Employers and employees contribute equally. In June 1987 there were 146,812 members. Medical and dental treatment is provided for all at a nominal charge. In 1992 Fiji had 25 hospitals (with a total of 1,747 beds) and 363 physicians. In late 1995 Parliament approved legislation providing for the establishment of a national non-contributory pension scheme. Of total budgetary expenditure by the central Government in 1995, $F68.56m. (8.6%) was estimated for health services, and a further $F35.2m. (4.4%) for social security and welfare.

Education

Education in Fiji is not compulsory, but in 1992 about 95% of school-age children were enrolled at the country's schools, and the Government provided free education for the first eight years of schooling. Primary education begins at six years of age and lasts for six years. Secondary education, beginning at the age of 12, lasts for a further six years. State subsidies are available for secondary and tertiary education in cases of hardship. In 1995 there were 709 primary schools (with a total enrolment of 146,900 pupils), 146 secondary schools (with an enrolment of 71,568 pupils) and in 1994 there were 31 vocational and technical institutions (with 6,653 students in 1992). In 1994 Fiji had four teacher-training colleges (with 630 students in 1992), and in 1989 there were two schools of medicine (with 493 students). In 1996 a total of about 4,000 students were enrolled on campus at the University of the South Pacific and there were a further 6,000 extension students. Budgetary expenditure on education by the central Government in 1995 was estimated at $F148.0m., representing 18.5% of total spending. The adult illiteracy rate in 1995 averaged an estimated 8.4% (males 6.2%; females 10.7%).

Public Holidays

1998: 1 January (New Year's Day), 13 March (National Youth Day), 10–13 April (Easter), 29 May (Ratu Sir Lala Sukuna Day), 15 June (Queen's Official Birthday), 6 July† (Birth of the Prophet Muhammad), 27 July (Constitution Day), 12 October (Fiji Day), 20 October (Diwali), 25–26 December (Christmas).

1999: 1 January (New Year's Day), 12 March (National Youth Day), 2–5 April (Easter), May/June* (Ratu Sir Lala Sukuna Day), June* (Queen's Official Birthday), 26 June† (Birth of the Prophet Muhammad), 19 July (Constitution Day), 4 October (Fiji Day), October/November (Diwali), 25–26 December (Christmas).

* Dates to be announced in 1998.

† This Islamic holiday is dependent on the lunar calendar and may vary by one or two days from the dates given.

Weights and Measures

The metric system is in force.

Statistical Survey

Sources (unless otherwise stated): Bureau of Statistics, POB 2221, Government Bldgs, Suva; tel. 315144; fax 303656; Reserve Bank of Fiji, POB 1220, Suva; tel. 313611; telex 2164; fax 301688.

AREA AND POPULATION

Area (incl. the Rotuma group): 18,376 sq km (7,095 sq miles). Land area of 18,333 sq km (7,078 sq miles) consists mainly of the islands of Viti Levu (10,429 sq km—4,027 sq miles) and Vanua Levu (5,556 sq km—2,145 sq miles).

Population: 588,068 (296,950 males, 291,118 females) at census of 13 September 1976; 715,375 (362,568 males, 352,807 females) at census of 31 August 1986; 772,655 at census of August 1996.

Density (August 1996): 42.0 per sq km.

Principal Towns (population at 1986 census): Suva (capital) 69,665; Lautoka 27,728; Nadi 7,709; Ba 6,515; Labasa 4,917.

Ethnic Groups (official estimate at 31 December 1995, provisional): Fijians 403,288; Indians 346,523; Others 46,267; Total 796,078.

Births, Marriages and Deaths (registrations, 1995): Live births 19,577 (birth rate 24.6 per 1,000); Marriages (1988) 6,892 (marriage rate 9.6 per 1,000); Deaths 4,959 (death rate 6.2 per 1,000).

Expectation of Life (UN estimates, years at birth, 1990–95): 71.5 (males 69.5; females 73.7). Source: UN, *World Population Prospects: The 1994 Revision*.

Economically Active Population (persons aged 15 years and over, census of 31 August 1986): Agriculture, hunting, forestry and fishing 106,305; Mining and quarrying 1,345; Manufacturing 18,106; Electricity, gas and water 2,154; Construction 11,786; Trade, restaurants and hotels 26,010; Transport, storage and communications 13,151; Financing, insurance, real estate and business services 6,016; Community, social and personal services 36,619; Activities not adequately defined 1,479; Total employed 222,971 (males 179,595, females 43,376); Unemployed 18,189 (males 10,334, females 7,855); Total labour force 241,160 (males 189,929, females 51,231). *1993* (total labour force at 31 December): 268,900.

AGRICULTURE, ETC.

Principal Crops (mostly FAO estimates, '000 metric tons, 1996): Sugar cane 4,100; Coconuts 210; Cassava 26; Rice (paddy) 18; Sweet potatoes 4; Bananas 6; Yams 3; Taro 22. Source: FAO, *Production Yearbook*.

Livestock (FAO estimates, '000 head, year ending September 1996): Cattle 354; Pigs 121; Goats 211; Horses 44; Chickens 4,000. Source: FAO, *Production Yearbook*.

Livestock Products (FAO estimates, metric tons, 1996): Poultry meat 7,000; Beef and veal 12,000; Goat meat 1,000; Pig meat 4,000; Hen eggs 3,000; Cows' milk 66,000; Honey 42 (1995). Source: FAO, *Production Yearbook*.

Forestry ('000 cubic metres, 1993): *Roundwood removals* (excl. bark): Sawlogs and veneer logs 244; Other industrial wood 1; Fuel wood 37 (FAO estimate); Total 282. *Sawnwood production* (incl. sleepers): 111. Source: FAO, *Yearbook of Forest Products*.

Fishing (metric tons, live weight): Total catch 31,399 in 1993; 32,000 (FAO estimate) in 1994; 34,577 in 1995. Figures exclude aquatic plants (metric tons, dry weight): 80 in 1993; 80 (FAO estimate) in 1994; 85 (FAO estimate) in 1995. Source: FAO, *Yearbook of Fishery Statistics*.

MINING

Production (1995): Gold 3,511 kg; Silver 2,095 kg; Crushed metal 133,891 cu m (1984).

INDUSTRY

Production (metric tons, 1994, unless otherwise stated): Beef 2,217 (1995); Sugar 516,589; Copra 10,724 (1995); Coconut oil 4,290; Soap 7,200; Cement 94,000; Paint 2,600 ('000 litres); Beer 16,000 ('000 litres); Soft drinks 9,000 ('000 litres); Cigarettes 483; Matches 142 ('000 gross boxes, 1992); Electric energy (million kWh) 520.

FINANCE

Currency and Exchange Rates: 100 cents = 1 Fiji dollar ($F). *Sterling and US Dollar Equivalents* (30 September 1997): £1 sterling = $F2.378; US $1 = $F1.472; $F100 = £42.06 = US $67.94. *Average Exchange Rate* ($F per US $): 1.4641 in 1994; 1.4063 in 1995; 1.4033 in 1996.

General Budget ($F million, 1995): *Revenue:* Taxation 615.31 (Taxes on income, profits and capital gains 225.47, Domestic taxes on goods and services 222.60, Taxes on international trade and transactions 161.40); Other current revenue 88.29 (Entrepreneurial and property income 67.47, Administrative fees and charges, non-industrial and incidental sales 9.56); Total 703.60, excl. grants received from abroad (6.27). *Expenditure:* General public services 234.30; Defence 48.80; Public order and safety 29.47; Education 148.02; Health 68.56; Social security and welfare 35.20; Housing and community amenities 29.07; Recreational, cultural and religious affairs and services 8.52; Economic affairs and services 111.47 (Agriculture, forestry, fishing and hunting 32.09, Transport and communications 15.83); Interest payments 87.73; Total 801.14 (current 723.10, Capital 78.04), excl. lending minus repayments (7.97). Figures exclude the accounts of central government units with individual budgets. Source: IMF, *Government Finance Statistics Yearbook*.

International Reserves (US $ million at 31 December 1996): Gold (valued at market-related prices) 0.31; IMF special drawing rights 11.49; Reserve position in IMF 14.45; Foreign exchange 401.30; Total 427.24. Source: IMF, *International Financial Statistics*.

Money Supply ($F million at 31 December 1996): Currency outside banks 125.4; Demand deposits at commercial banks 328.7; Total money 454.1. Source: IMF, *International Financial Statistics*.

Cost of Living (Consumer Price Index; base: 1990 = 100): 118.2 in 1994; 120.8 in 1995; 124.5 in 1996. Source: IMF, *International Financial Statistics*.

Expenditure on the Gross Domestic Product ($F million at current prices, 1996, provisional): Government final consumption expenditure 460.0; Private final consumption expenditure 2,079.0; Increase in stocks 40.0; Gross fixed capital formation 311.7; Statistical discrepancy 89.6; *Total domestic expenditure* 2,980.3; Exports of goods and services 1,629.4; *Less* Imports of goods and services 1,700.3; *GDP in purchasers' values* 2,909.4. Source: IMF, *Fiji—Selected Issues*.

Gross Domestic Product by Economic Activity ($F million at constant 1989 prices, 1996, provisional): Agriculture, forestry and fishing 358.1; Mining and quarrying 63.0; Manufacturing 253.5; Electricity, gas and water 75.6; Building and construction 96.1; Wholesale and retail trade 265.0; Hotels and restaurants 55.1; Transport and communications 224.2; Finance, real estate, etc. 264.5; Community, social and personal services 325.6; Other services 14.8; Sub-total 1,995.5; *Less* Imputed bank service charges 140.9; GDP at factor cost 1,854.6.

Balance of Payments (US $ million, 1996): Exports of goods f.o.b. 655.2; Imports of goods f.o.b. –837.7; *Trade balance* –182.4; Exports of services 623.6; Imports of services –412.6; *Balance on goods and services* 28.6; Other income received 63.6; Other income paid –91.6; *Balance on goods, services and income* 0.6; Current transfers received 44.1; Current transfers paid –34.6; *Current balance* 10.2; Capital account (net) 70.8; Direct investment abroad –9.8; Direct investment from abroad 9.8; Other investment assets -25.9; Other investment liabilities 36.8; Net errors and omissions -13.8; *Overall balance* 78.1. Source: IMF, *International Financial Statistics*.

EXTERNAL TRADE

Principal Commodities ($F million, 1995): *Imports c.i.f.* (distribution by SITC): Food and live animals 182.3; Beverages and tobacco 13.2; Crude materials excl. fuels 9.1; Mineral fuels 137.5; Oils and fats 16.5; Chemicals 92.8; Basic manufactures 337.0; Machinery and transport equipment 277.8; Miscellaneous manufactured items 139.3; Total (incl. others) 1,218.9. *Exports f.o.b.:* Food and live animals 397.7 (Sugar 276.1, Fish and preparations 56.3); Crude materials excl. fuels 51.5; Mineral fuels 65.1; Basic manufactures 43.7; Machinery and transport equipment 18.4; Miscellaneous manufactured articles 215.8; Goods not classified by kind 65.1; Total (incl. others) 869.9. Source: UN, *Statistical Yearbook for Asia and the Pacific*.

Principal Trading Partners (US $ '000, 1994): *Imports c.i.f.:* Australia 273,480; China, People's Republic 26,261; Hong Kong 17,520; Japan 66,292; New Zealand 139,584; Singapore 61,242; Thailand 12,743; United Kingdom 14,327; USA 122,635; Total (incl. others) 829,650. *Exports:* Australia 76,071; Canada 25,371; Japan 37,175; Malaysia 25,930; New Zealand 28,973; Tonga 15,071; United Kingdom 105,713; USA 97,587; Total (incl. others) 503,191. Note: Figures exclude trade in gold. The value of total trade (in US $ '000) was: Imports 830,477; Exports 544,472. Source: UN, *International Trade Statistics Yearbook*.

TRANSPORT

Road Traffic (motor vehicles registered at 31 December 1993): Passenger cars 24,586; Light goods vehicles 14,431; Heavy goods vehicles 2,455; Buses 1,145; Taxis 2,917; Rental vehicles 1,645; Motorcycles 638; Tractors 1,454; Total (incl. others) 50,560.

Shipping: *Merchant Fleet* (vessels registered, '000 grt at 31 December 1996): 36.3. Source: UN, *Statistical Yearbook. International Freight Traffic* ('000 metric tons, 1990): Goods loaded 568; Goods unloaded 625. Source: UN, *Monthly Bulletin of Statistics*.

Civil Aviation (traffic on scheduled services, 1994): Passengers carried 465,000; Passenger-kilometres 1,101 million; Total ton-kilometres 155 million. Source: UN, *Statistical Yearbook*.

TOURISM

Foreign Tourist Arrivals: 318,874 in 1994; 318,495 (139,508 visitors by air) in 1995; 339,560 in 1996.

COMMUNICATIONS MEDIA

Radio Receivers (1994): 468,000 in use*.

Television Receivers (1994): 13,000 in use*.

Telephones (1994): 59,000 main lines in use†.

Telefax Stations (1994): 2,500 in use†.

Mobile Cellular Telephones (1994): 1,100 subscribers†.

Book Production (1980): 110 titles (84 books, 26 pamphlets); 273,000 copies (229,000 books, 44,000 pamphlets).

Daily Newspaper (1994): 1 (estimated circulation 35,000)*.

Non-daily Newspapers (provisional, 1988): 7 (combined circulation 99,000)*.

* Source: UNESCO, *Statistical Yearbook*.

† Source: UN, *Statistical Yearbook*.

EDUCATION

Pre-primary (1992): 366 schools (1994); 422 teachers; 8,209 pupils.

Primary (1995): 709 schools; 4,923 teachers; 146,900 pupils.

General Secondary (1995): 146 schools; 3,045 teachers (1992); 71,568 pupils.

Vocational and Technical (1992): 31 institutions (1994); 586 teachers; 6,653 students.

Teacher Training (1992): 4 institutions (1994); 39 teachers; 630 students.

Medical (1989): 2 institutions; 493 students.

University (1991): 1 institution; 277 teachers; 7,908 students.

Source: mainly UNESCO, *Statistical Yearbook*.

Directory

The Constitution

On 25 July 1990 President Ganilau promulgated a new Constitution, after the Bose Levu Vakaturaga (Great Council of Chiefs—a traditional body, with some 70 members, consisting of every hereditary chief or Ratu of each Fijian clan) had approved the draft. The following is a summary of the main provisions:

The Constitution, which declares Fiji to be a sovereign, democratic republic, guarantees fundamental human rights, a universal, secret and equal suffrage and equality before the law for all Fijian citizens. Citizenship may be acquired by birth, descent, registration or naturalization and is assured for all those who were Fijian citizens before 6 October 1987. Parliament may make provision for the deprivation or renunciation of a person's citizenship. Ethnic Fijians, and the Polynesian inhabitants of Rotuma, receive special constitutional consideration, including positive discrimination for employment in the judiciary and by the Government (no less than 50% of those employed—although provision is made for exceptions). The Judicial and Legal Services Commission, the Public Service Commission and the Police Service Commission are established as supervisory bodies. The Constitution also declares that those involved in the two military coups of 1987 and the members of the military Government, which held office until 5 December 1987, will be immune from any consequent civil or criminal prosecution. The Constitution Amendment Bill which provided for major constitutional reforms, including the establishment of a multi-racial Cabinet, was approved in July 1997 and was due to take effect in July 1998.

THE GREAT COUNCIL OF CHIEFS

The Great Council of Chiefs (Bose Levu Vakaturaga) derives its authority from the status of its members and their chiefly lineage. The Great Council appoints the President of the Republic and selects the 24 Fijian nominees for appointment to the Senate, the upper chamber of the Parliament. Upon the introduction of constitutional reforms in July 1998, the Great Council of Chiefs will nominate only 15 senators to the upper chamber.

THE EXECUTIVE

Executive authority is vested in the President of the Republic, who is appointed by the Great Council of Chiefs, for a five-year term, to be constitutional Head of State and Commander-in-Chief of the armed forces. The Presidential Council advises the President on matters of national importance. The President, and Parliament, can be empowered to introduce any necessary measures in an emergency or in response to acts of subversion which threaten Fiji.

In most cases the President is guided by the Cabinet, which conducts the government of the Republic. The Cabinet is led by the Prime Minister, who must be an ethnic Fijian and is appointed by the President from among the members of Parliament, on the basis of support in the legislature. The Prime Minister selects the other members of the Cabinet (the Attorney-General, the minister responsible for defence and security and any other ministers) from either the House of Representatives or the Senate. The Cabinet is responsible to Parliament. Upon the introduction of constitutional reforms in July 1998, the Prime Minister will be a Fijian of any ethnic origin and the Cabinet will be selected on a multi-party and multiracial basis.

THE LEGISLATURE

Legislative power is vested in the Parliament, which comprises the President, the appointed upper house or Senate and an elected House of Representatives. The maximum duration of a parliament is five years.

The Senate has 34 members, appointed by the President of the Republic for the term of the Parliament. Twenty-four senators are ethnic Fijians, nominated by the Great Council of Chiefs; one Rotuman is appointed on the advice of the Rotuma Island Council; the remaining nine senators are appointed at the President's discretion from among other groups, with particular regard to minority communities. The Senate is a house of review, with some powers to initiate legislation, but with limited influence on financial measures. The Senate is important in the protection of ethnic Fijian interests, and its consent is essential to any attempt to amend, alter or repeal any provisions affecting ethnic Fijians, their customs, land or tradition.

The House of Representatives has 70 elected members, who themselves elect their presiding officials, the Speaker and Deputy Speaker, from outside the membership of the House. Voting is communal, with universal suffrage for all citizens of the Republic aged over 21 years. For general elections to the House, ethnic Fijians vote in five single-member urban constituencies and 14 rural constituencies, to elect 37 representatives in all. There are 27 seats for those on the Indian electoral roll, one seat for Rotumans and five seats for other races (General Electors). Elections must be held at least every five years and are to be administered by an independent Supervisor of Elections. An independent Boundaries Commission determines constituency boundaries.

Upon the introduction of constitutional reforms in July 1998, only 15 senators will be nominated by the Great Council of Chiefs, The House of Representatives will have 71 elected members with only 46 seats reserved on a racial basis (23 for ethnic Fijians, 19 for Indians, three for general electors and one for Rotuma Islanders) and 25 seats open to all races.

THE JUDICIARY

The judiciary is independent and comprises the High Court, the Fiji Court of Appeal and the Supreme Court. The High Court and the Supreme Court are the final arbiters of the Constitution. The establishment of Fijian courts is provided for, and decisions of the Native Lands Commission (relating to ethnic Fijian customs, traditions and usage, and on disputes over the headship of any part of the Fijian people, with the customary right to occupy and use any native lands) are declared to be final and without appeal.

The Government

HEAD OF STATE

President: Ratu Sir Kamisese Mara (took office 18 January 1994).

First Vice-President: Ratu Josefa Iloilo (acting).

Second Vice-President: Ratu Inoke Takiveikata.

THE CABINET
(January 1998)

Prime Minister and Minister for Multi-ethnic Affairs and Regional Development: Maj.-Gen. Sitiveni Rabuka.

Deputy Prime Minister and Minister for Education and Technology: Taufa Vakatale.

Minister for Agriculture, Fisheries, Forestry and the Agricultural, Landlords and Tenants Act: Militoni Leweniqila.

Minister for Finance: James Ah Koy.

Minister for Foreign Affairs and External Trade: Berenado Vunibobo.

Minister for Lands and Mineral Resources: Ratu Timoci Vesikula.

Minister for Justice and Home Affairs: Col Paul Manueli.

Minister for Commerce, Industry, Co-operatives and Public Enterprises: Isimeli Bose.

Minister for Communications, Works and Energy: Ratu Inoke Kubuabola.

Attorney-General: Ratu Etuati Tavai.

Minister for Labour and Industrial Relations: Vincent Lobendahn.

Minister for Local Government and the Environment: Vilisoni Cagimaivei.

Minister for National Planning: Filipe Bole.

Minister for Fijian Affairs: Ratu Finau Mara.

Minister for Information, Women and Culture: Seruwaia Hong Tiy.

Minister for Health: Leo Smith.

Minister for Tourism, Transport and Civil Aviation: David Pickering.

Minister for Youth, Employment and Sports: Jonetani Kaukimoce.

MINISTRIES

Office of the Prime Minister: Government Bldgs, POB 2353, Suva; tel. 211201; fax 306034.

Ministry of Agriculture, Fisheries and Forestry: Rodwell Rd, Suva; tel. 315986; fax 302478.

Ministry of Commerce, Trade and Industry: Naubati House, Suva; tel. 305411.

Ministry of Education, Women and Culture: Marela House, Suva; tel. 314477; fax 303511.

Ministry of Fijian Affairs: POB 2100, Suva.

Ministry of Finance and Economic Development: Government Bldgs, POB 2212, Suva; tel. 211425; fax 300834.

Ministry of Foreign Affairs: Government Bldgs, Suva; tel. 211458; fax 301741.

Ministry of Health: Government Bldgs, Flagstaff, POB 2223, Suva; tel. 306177; fax 306163.

Ministry of Home Affairs, Youth, Employment and Sports: Selbourne St, Suva; tel. 211210.

Ministry of Labour and Industrial Relations: 414 Victoria Parade, POB 2216, Government Bldgs, Suva.

Ministry of Public Works and Infrastructure, Information, Broadcasting and Telecommunications: Ganilau House, 7th Floor, Suva; tel. 315133; telex 2104; fax 301198.

Ministry of Regional Development and Multi-ethnic Affairs: POB 2219, Government Bldgs, Suva.

Ministry of Tourism, Transport and Civil Aviation: Vanua House, Suva; tel 312788.

All other ministries are based at the Government Buildings, Suva.

Legislature

PARLIAMENT

Senate

The upper chamber comprises 34 appointed members (see The Constitution).

House of Representatives

The lower chamber comprises 70 elected members: 37 representing ethnic Fijians, 27 representing ethnic Indians, five representing other races and one delegate from Rotuma Island.

Constitutional reforms approved in July 1997 and due to be implemented in July 1998 were to result in a lower chamber comprising 71 elected members: 23 representing ethnic Fijians, 19 representing ethnic Indians, three representing other races (general electors), one delegate from Rotuma Island and 25 seats open to all races.

Speaker: Dr Apenisa Kurisaqila.

General Election, 18–24 February 1994

	Seats
Seats reserved for ethnic Fijians	
Soqosoqo ni Vakavulewa ni Taukei	31
Fijian Association	5
Independent	1
Seats reserved for ethnic Indians	
National Federation Party	20
Fiji Labour Party	7
General Voters' Party	4
All Nationals Congress	1
Rotuma Island Representative	1
Total	70

Political Organizations

Fiji Christian Party: Suva; f. 1995 by the Methodist Church, in opposition to the repeal of the Sunday observance law.

Fiji Indian Congress: POB 3661, Samabula, Suva; tel. 391211; fax 340117; f. 1991; Gen. Sec. Vijay Raghwan.

Fiji Indian Liberal Party: Rakiraki; f. 1991; represents the interests of the Indian community, particularly sugar-cane farmers and students; Sec. Swani Kumar.

Fiji Labour Party (FLP): POB 2162, Suva; tel. 305811; fax 305808; f. 1985; Sec.-Gen. Mahendra Chaudhry; Pres. Jokapeci Koroi.

Fijian Association Party: Suva; f. 1995 by merger of Fijian Association (a breakaway faction of the SVT) and the multiracial All Nationals Congress; Leader Josefata Kamikamica; Pres. Epenisa Cakobau; Vice-Pres. Adi Kuini Speed.

Fijian Conservative Party: Suva; f. 1989 by former mems of the FNP and AP; Leader Isireli Vuibau.

Fijian Nationalist United Front Party (FNUFP): POB 1336, Suva; tel. 362317; f. 1992 to replace Fijian Nationalist Party; seeks additional parliamentary representation for persons of Fijian ethnic origin, the introduction of other pro-Fijian reforms and the repatriation of ethnic Indians; Leader Sakeasi Bakewa Butadroka.

General Voters' Party (GVP): Suva; f. 1990; fmrly the General Electors' Association, one of the three wings of the Alliance Party (AP, the ruling party 1970–87); represents the interests of the minority Chinese and European communities and people from other Pacific Islands resident in Fiji, all of whom are classed as General Electors under the 1990 Constitution; Leader DAVID PICKERING; Gen. Sec. GRAHAM RALPH.

Janata Party: Suva; f. 1995 by former mems of NFP and FLP.

National Democratic Party: Suva; Gen. Sec. ATUNAISA LACABUKA.

National Federation Party (NFP): POB 13534, Suva; tel. 665633; fax 664411; f. 1960 by merger of the Federation Party, which was multiracial but mainly Indian and the National Democratic Party; Leader JAI RAM REDDY; Pres. Dr BALWANT SINGH RAKKA; Gen. Sec. SHILI CHARAN.

New Labour Movement: Suva; Gen. Sec. MICHAEL COLUMBUS.

Soqosoqo ni Vakavulewa ni Taukei (SVT) (Fijian Political Party): Suva; f. 1990 by Great Council of Chiefs; supports constitutional dominance of ethnic Fijians but accepts multiracialism; Pres. Maj.-Gen. SITIVENI RABUKA; Sec. Dr FILIMONI WAINIQOLO.

Taukei Solidarity Movement: f. 1988, following merger of Taukei Liberation Front and Domo Ni Taukei; extreme right-wing indigenous Fijian nationalist group; Vice-Pres. MELI VESIKULA.

Vanua Independent Party: Leader ILIESA TUVALOVO; Sec. URAIA TUISOVISOVI.

Western United Front (WUF): POB 263, Sigatoka; f. 1981; mainly Fijian; advocates co-existence and co-operation among all communities; 10,000 mems; Pres. Ratu OSEA GAVIDI; Sec. ISIKELI NADALO.

Supporters of secession are concentrated in Rotuma.

Diplomatic Representation

EMBASSIES AND HIGH COMMISSIONS IN FIJI

Australia: 37 Princes Rd, POB 214, Suva; tel. 382211; fax 382065; High Commissioner: GREG URWIN.

China, People's Republic: 147 Queen Elizabeth Drive, PMB, Nasese, Suva; tel. 300215; telex 2136; fax 300950; Ambassador: HOU QINGRU.

France: Dominion House, 1st Floor, Thomson St, Suva; tel. 312925; telex 2152; fax 301894; Ambassador: MICHEL JOLIVET.

Japan: Dominion House, 2nd Floor, POB 13045, Suva; tel. 302122; telex 2253; fax 301452; Ambassador: JIRO KOBAYASHI.

Korea, Republic: Vanua House, 8th Floor, PMB, Suva; tel. 300977; fax 303410; Ambassador: KEUN-TAIK KANG.

Malaysia: Air Pacific House, 5th Floor, POB 356, Suva; tel. 312166; telex 2295; fax 303350; High Commissioner: NG BAK HAI.

Marshall Islands: 41 Borron Rd, Government Bldgs, POB 2038, Suva; tel. 387899; fax 387115; Ambassador: KINJA ANDRIKE.

Micronesia, Federated States: 37 Loftus St, POB 15493, Suva; tel. 304566; fax 304081; Ambassador: ALIK L. ALIK.

Nauru: Suva; High Commissioner: MILLICENT AROI.

New Zealand: Reserve Bank of Fiji Bldg, 10th Floor, Pratt St, POB 1378, Suva; tel. 311422; fax 300842; High Commissioner: TIA BARRETT.

Papua New Guinea: Credit House, Govt Bldgs, POB 2447, Suva; tel. 304244; telex 2113; fax 300178; High Commissioner: BABANI MARAGA.

Tuvalu: 16 Gorrie St, POB 14449, Suva; tel. 300697; fax 301023; High Commissioner: ENELE S. SOPOAGA.

United Kingdom: Victoria House, 47 Gladstone Rd, POB 1355, Suva; tel. 311033; fax 301406; e-mail ukrep@is.com.fj; High Commissioner: MICHAEL DIBBEN.

USA: 31 Loftus Rd, POB 218, Suva; tel. 314466; fax 300081; Ambassador: DON LEE GEVIRTZ.

Judicial System

Justice is administered by the Supreme Court, the Fiji Court of Appeal, the High Court and the Magistrates' Courts. The Supreme Court of Fiji is the superior court of record presided over by the Chief Justice. The Chief Justice and six senior judges were removed from office on 15 October 1987, following the military coup of 25 September. In January 1988 the former Chief Justice, Sir Timoci Tuivaga, resumed his post in a newly-constituted judicial system and a further three High Court judges were appointed. Many judicial appointees come from overseas. Since the 1987 coups about two-thirds of Fiji's lawyers have left the country. The judicial arrangements were regularized by the Constitution promulgated on 25 July 1990. This also provided for the establishment of Fijian customary courts and declared as final decisions of the Native Lands Commission in cases involving Fijian custom, etc.

Supreme Court: Suva; tel. 211481; fax 300674.

Chief Justice: Sir TIMOCI TUIVAGA.

President of the Fiji Court of Appeal: Sir MOTI TIKARAM.

Director of Public Prosecutions: NAZHAT SHAMEEM.

Solicitor-General: NAINENDRA NAND (acting).

Religion

CHRISTIANITY

Most ethnic Fijians are Christians. Methodists are the largest Christian group, followed by Roman Catholics. In the census of 1986 about 53% of the population were Christian (mainly Methodists).

Fiji Council of Churches: POB 2300, Government Bldgs, Suva; tel. (1) 313798; f. 1964; seven mem. churches; Pres. Rt Rev. JABEZ LESLIE BRYCE; Gen. Sec. EMI FRANCES.

The Anglican Communion

In April 1990 Polynesia, formerly a missionary diocese of the Church of the Province of New Zealand, became a full and integral diocese. The diocese of Polynesia is based in Fiji but also includes Wallis and Futuna, Tuvalu, Kiribati, French Polynesia, Cook Islands, Tonga, Samoa and Tokelau.

Bishop of Polynesia: Rt Rev. JABEZ LESLIE BRYCE, Bishop's House, 7 Disraeli Rd, POB 35, Suva; tel. 302553; fax 302687.

The Roman Catholic Church

Fiji comprises a single archdiocese. At 31 December 1995 there were an estimated 78,683 adherents in the country.

Bishops' Conference: Episcopal Conference of the Pacific Secretariat (CEPAC), 14 Williamson Rd, POB 289, Suva; tel. 300340; fax 303143; f. 1968; 17 mems; Gen. Sec. Rev. ARTHUR TIERNEY; Pres. Most Rev. MICHEL MARIE CALVET, Archbishop of Nouméa, New Caledonia.

Regional Appeal Tribunal for CEPAC: 14 Williamson Rd, POB 289, Suva; tel. 300340; fax 303143; e-mail cepac@is.com.fj; f. 1980; 17 mems; Judicial Vicar Rev. THEO KOSTER.

Archbishop of Suva: Most Rev. PETERO MATACA, Archdiocesan Office, Nicolas House, Pratt St, POB 109, Suva; tel. 301955; fax 301565.

Other Christian Churches

Methodist Church in Fiji (Lotu Wesele e Viti): Epworth Arcade, Nina St, POB 357, Suva; tel. 311477; fax 303771; f. 1835; autonomous since 1964; 214,697 mems (1995); Pres. Rev. Dr ILAITIA TUWERE; Gen. Sec. Rev. TOMASI KANAILAGI.

Other denominations active in the country include the Assembly of God (with c. 7,000 mems), the Baptist Mission, the Congregational Christian Church and the Presbyterian Church.

HINDUISM

Most of the Indian community are Hindus. According to the census of 1986, 38% of the population were Hindus.

ISLAM

In 1993 some 8% of the population were Muslim. There are several Islamic organizations:

Fiji Muslim League: POB 3990, Samabula, Suva; tel. 384566; fax 370204; f. 1926; Pres. Haji FAZAL KHAN; Gen. Sec. MASUM ALI BUKSH; 26 brs and 3 subsidiary orgs.

SIKHISM

Sikh Association of Fiji: Suva; Pres. TARA SINGH DHESI.

BAHÁ'Í FAITH

National Spiritual Assembly: National Office, POB 639, Suva; tel. 387574; fax 387772; e-mail nsafijiskm@suva.is.com.fj; mems resident in 490 localities; national headquarters for consultancy and co-ordination.

The Press

NEWSPAPERS AND PERIODICALS

Coconut Telegraph: POB 249, Savusavu, Vanua Levu; f. 1975; monthly; serves widely-scattered rural communities; Editor LEMA LOW.

Daily Post: 422 Fletcher Rd, POB 2071, Govt Bldgs, Suva; f. 1987 as *Fiji Post*, daily from 1989; English; Publr TANIELA BOLEA; Man. Editor LAISA TAGA.

Fiji Canegrower: POB 12095, Suva; tel. 305916; fax 305256.

Fiji Islands Business: 46 Gordon St, POB 12718; Suva; tel. 303108; fax 301423; e-mail editor@ibi.com.fj; monthly; English; Editor-in-Chief PETER LOMAS.

Fiji Magic: The Rubine Group, POB 12511, Suva; tel. 313944; fax 302852; monthly; English; Publr GEORGE RUBINE; Editor MABEL HOWARD; circ. 10,000.

Fiji Product Directory: POB 12095, Suva; tel. 305916; fax 301930; publ. by Associated Media Ltd; annually; English; Publr YASHWANT GAUNDER.

Fiji Republic Gazette: Printing Dept, POB 98, Suva; tel. 385999; fax 370203; f. 1874; weekly; English.

Fiji Times: 20 Gordon St, POB 1167, Suva; tel. 304111; telex 2124; fax 301521; f. 1869; publ. by Fiji Times Ltd; daily; English; Man. Dir ALAN ROBINSON; Editor SAMISONI KAKAIUALU; circ. 34,000.

Fiji Tourism Trade: POB 12095, Suva; tel. 305916; fax 301930; publ. by Associated Media Ltd; every 2 months; English; Publr YASHWANT GAUNDER.

Fiji Trade Review: The Rubine Group, POB 12511, Suva; tel. 313944; monthly; English; Publr GEORGE RUBINE; Editor MABEL HOWARD.

Islands Business: 46 Gordon St, POB 12718, Suva; tel. 303108; fax 301423; f. 1980; regional monthly news and business magazine; English; Publr ROBERT KEITH-REID; Editor-in-Chief PETER LOMAS; circ. 11,950.

Na Tui: 422 Fletcher Rd, POB 2071, Govt Bldgs, Suva; f. 1988; weekly; Fijian; Publr TANIELA BOLEA; Editor SAMISONI BOLATAGICI; circ. 7,000.

Nai Lalakai: 20 Gordon St, POB 1167, Suva; tel. 314111; telex 2124; f. 1962; publ. by Fiji Times Ltd; weekly; Fijian; Editor (vacant); circ. 18,000.

Pacific Islands Monthly: 177 Victoria Parade, POB 1167, Suva; tel. 304111; telex 2124; fax 303809; f. 1930; publ. by Fiji Times Ltd; monthly; English; political, economic and cultural affairs in the Pacific Islands; Publr ALAN ROBINSON; Editor MANIVANNAN NAIDU.

Pactrainer: PMB, Suva; tel. 303623; fax 303943; e-mail pina@is.com.fj; monthly; newsletter of Pacific Journalism Development Centre; Editor PETER LOMAS.

PINA Nius: Pacific Islands News Association, 46 Gordon St, PMB, Suva; tel. 303623; fax 303943; monthly newsletter of Pacific Islands News Association; Editor NINA RATULELE.

The Review: POB 12095, Suva; tel. 305916; fax 301930; publ. by Associated Media Ltd; monthly; English; Publr YASHWANT GAUNDER.

Sartaj: John Beater Enterprises Ltd, Raiwaqa, POB 5141, Suva; f. 1988; weekly; Hindi; Editor S. DASO; circ. 15,000.

Shanti Dut: 20 Gordon St, POB 1167, Suva; f. 1935; publ. by Fiji Times Ltd; weekly; Hindi; Editor M. C. VINOD; circ. 8,000.

Top Shot: Suva; f. 1995; golf magazine; monthly.

The Weekender: 2 Dension Rd, POB 15652, Suva; tel. 315477; fax 305346; publ. by Media Resources Ltd; weekly; English; Publr JOSEFATA NATA.

Welcome to Fiji and the South Pacific: Suva; f. 1994; tourist magazine.

What's On: POB 12095, Suva; tel. 305916; fax 301930; publ. by The Network; every 6 months; English; Publr YASHWANT GAUNDER.

PRESS ASSOCIATIONS

Fiji Islands Media Association: c/o Vasiti Ivaqa, POB 12718, Suva; tel. 303108; fax 301423; national press asscn; operates Fiji Press Club and Fiji Journalism Training Institute; Sec. NINA RATULELE.

Pacific Islands News Association: 46 Gordon St, PMB, Suva; tel. 303623; fax 303943; regional press asscn; defends freedom of information and expression, promotes professional co-operation, provides training and education; Administrator NINA RATULELE; Pres. WILLIAM PARKINSON.

Publishers

Fiji Times Ltd: POB 1167, Suva; tel. 304111; fax 302011; f. 1869; Propr News Corpn Ltd; largest newspaper publr; also publrs of books and magazines; Man. Dir ALAN ROBINSON.

Government Publishing House

Printing Department: POB 98, Suva; tel. 385999; fax 370203.

Broadcasting and Communications

TELECOMMUNICATIONS

Fiji International Telecommunicatons Ltd (FINTEL): Suva; 51% govt-owned.

Telcom Fiji Ltd: Suva; Chair. LIONEL YEE; CEO WINSTON THOMSON.

These two organizations were expected to be merged in 1998.

RADIO

Fiji Broadcasting Commission—FBC (Radio Fiji): Broadcasting House, POB 334, Suva; tel. 314333; telex 2142; fax 301643; f. 1954; statutory body; jointly funded by govt grant and advertising revenue; Chair. OLOTA ROKOVUNISEI; Gen. Man. BARRY FERBER.

Radio Fiji 1 broadcasts nationally on AM in English and Fijian.

Radio Fiji 2 broadcasts nationally on AM in English and Hindi.

Radio Fiji Gold broadcasts nationally on AM and FM in English.

104 FM and Radio Rajdhani 98 FM, mainly with musical programmes, broadcast in English and Hindi respectively, but are received only on Viti Levu.

Bula FM, musical programmes, broadcasts in Fijian, received only on Viti Levu.

Communications Fiji Ltd: 231 Waimanu Rd, PMB, Suva; tel. 314766; fax 303748; e-mail cfl@fm96.com.fj; f. 1985; operates three commercial stations; Man. Dir WILLIAM PARKINSON; Gen. Man. IAN JACKSON.

FM 96, f. 1985, broadcasts 24 hours per day, on FM, in English.

Navtarang, f. 1989, broadcasts 24 hours per day, on FM, in Hindi.

Viti FM, f. 1996, broadcasts 24 hours per day, on FM, in Fijian.

Radio Light: POB 319, Pacific Harbour; fax 450007; Station Man. ARNIE DYKES.

Radio Pasifik: POB 1168, University of the South Pacific, Suva; tel. 313900; fax 312591; e-mail schuster@usp.ac.fj; Gen. Man. ALFRED SCHUSTER.

TELEVISION

Film and Television Unit (FTU): c/o Ministry of Information, Govt Bldgs, POB 2225, Suva; tel. 314688; fax 300196; video library; production unit established by Govt and Hanns Seidel Foundation (Germany); a weekly news magazine and local documentary programmes.

Fiji Television Ltd: 20 Gorrie St, POB 2442, Suva; tel. 305100; fax 305077; e-mail fijitv@is.com.fj; f. 1994; subscription television; Chair. LAISENIA QARASE; CEO PETER WILSON; Head of Programmes CAROLYN JALAL.

Fiji Vision Ltd: Suva; f. 1997; subscription television; jointly-owned by Yasana Holdings Ltd and a Hawaiian consortium.

In 1990 two television stations were constructed at Suva and Monsavu, with aid from the People's Republic of China. A permanent television station became operational in July 1994.

Finance

In 1996 the Ministry of Finance announced that it had secured financial assistance for the undertaking of a study to investigate the possibility of developing an 'offshore' financial centre in Fiji.

BANKING

(cap. = capital; res = reserves; dep. = deposits; m. = million; brs = branches; amounts in Fiji dollars)

Central Bank

Reserve Bank of Fiji: PMB, Suva; tel. 313611; telex 2164; fax 301688; e-mail rbf@is.com.fj; f. 1984 to replace Central Monetary Authority of Fiji; bank of issue; administers Office of Commissioner of Insurance; cap. and res 28.1m., dep. 118.8m. (Oct. 1997); Chair. and Gov. Ratu JONE YAVALA KUBUABOLA.

Commercial Bank

National Bank of Fiji: 33 Ellery St, POB 1166, Suva; tel. 303499; telex 2135; fax 302190; f. 1974; cap. 9.2m. res 2.3m., dep. 115.2m. (June 1997); Chair. LIONEL YEE; Chief Man. KENNETH MCARTHUR; 13 brs; 66 agencies.

Development Bank

Fiji Development Bank: 360 Victoria Parade, POB 104, Suva; tel. 314866; telex 2578; fax 314886; f. 1967; finances the development of natural resources, agriculture, transportation and other industries and enterprises; statutory body; cap. 50.8m., res 14.0m., dep. 182.6m. (June 1993); Chair. CHARLES WALKER; 9 brs.

Merchant Banks

Merchant Bank of Fiji Ltd: Burns Philp Bldg, Usher St, POB 14213, Suva; tel. 314955; fax 300026; f. 1986; jointly owned by the Fijian Holdings Ltd (50%), Australian Guarantee Corpn Ltd (30%) and International Finance Ltd (20%); Gen. Man. LAISENIA QARASE; 3 brs.

National MBf Finance (Fiji) Ltd: Burns Philp Bldg, 2nd Floor, POB 13525, Suva; tel. 305113; fax 305097; e-mail mbf@is.com.fj;

f. 1991; 51% owned by the National Bank of Fiji, 49% by MBf Asia Capital Corpn Holding Ltd (Hong Kong); Chief Operating Officer K. C. WONG; 4 brs.

Foreign Banks

Australia and New Zealand (ANZ) Banking Group Ltd: ANZ House, 25 Victoria Parade, POB 10, Suva; tel. 302144; telex 2194; fax 300267; bought Bank of New Zealand in Fiji (8 brs) in 1990; Gen. Man. (Fiji) ROBIN TAYLOR; 10 brs; 9 agencies.

Bank of Baroda (India): Bank of Baroda Bldg, Marks St, POB 57, Suva; tel. 311400; telex 2300; fax 302510; f. 1908; CEO S. K. BAGCHI; 7 brs; 2 agencies.

Bank of Hawaii (USA): 67–69 Victoria Parade, POB 273, Suva; tel. 312144; fax 312464; f. 1993; Man. GREGORY AYAU; 3 brs.

Caisse Française de Développement (France): Suva; licensed to operate in Fiji in 1997.

Habib Bank (Pakistan): Narsey's Bldg, Renwick Rd, POB 108, Suva; tel. 304011; fax 304835; Chief Man. (Fiji) ABDUL MATIN; licensed to operate in Fiji 1990; 3 brs.

Westpac Banking Corporation (Australia): Civic House, 6th Floor, Town Hall Rd, POB 238, Suva; tel. 300666; telex 2133; fax 300718; Chief Man. (Pacific Islands region) TREVOR WISEMANTEL; 12 brs; 9 agencies.

STOCK EXCHANGE

Suva Stock Exchange: G. B. Hari Bldg, 2nd Floor, 12 Pier St, POB 1416, Suva; tel. 381460; fax 387511; Pres. NAVIN CHANDRA; Chair. LIONEL YEE; Man. MUSAKE NAWARI.

INSURANCE

Blue Shield (Pacific) Ltd: Parade Bldg, POB 15137, Suva; tel. 311733; fax 300318; Fijian co; subsidiary of Colonial Mutual Life Assurance Society Ltd; medical and life insurance; Chief Exec. SIALENI VUETAKI.

Colonial Mutual Life Assurance Society Ltd: CMLA Bldg, PMB, Suva; tel. 314400; telex 2254; fax 302277; f. 1876; inc in Australia; life; Man. TOMASI VUETILOVONI.

Dominion Insurance Ltd: Civic House, POB 14468, Suva; tel. 311055; fax 303475; partly owned by Flour Mills of Fiji Ltd; general insurance; Man. Dir GARY S. CALLAGHAN.

FAI Insurance (Fiji) Ltd: Suva.

Fiji Reinsurance Corpn Ltd: RBF Bldg, POB 12704, Suva; tel. 313471; fax 305679; 20% govt-owned; reinsurance; Chair. Ratu JONE Y. KUBUABOLA; Man. PETER MARIO.

Fijicare Mutual Assurance: 41 Loftus St, POB 15808, Suva; tel. 302717; fax 302119; f. 1992; CEO JEFF PRICE.

Insurance Trust of Fiji: Loftus St, POB 114; Suva; tel. 311242; fax 302541; Man. SAMUEL KRISHNA.

National Insurance Co of Fiji Ltd: McGowan Bldg, Suva; tel. 315955; fax 301376; owned by New Zealand interests; Gen. Man. GEOFF THOMPSON.

New India Assurance Co Ltd: Harifam Centre, POB 71, Suva; tel. 313488; fax 302679; Man. MILIND A. KHARAT.

Queensland Insurance (Fiji) Ltd: Queensland Insurance Center, Victoria Parade, POB 101, Suva; tel. 315455; fax 300285; owned by Australian interests; Gen. Man. PETER J. NICHOLLS.

There are also two Indian insurance companies operating in Fiji.

Trade and Industry

GOVERNMENT AGENCIES

Fiji National Training Council (FNTC): Beaumont Rd, POB 6890, Nasinu; tel. 392000; fax 340184; Dir-Gen. NELSON DELAILOMALOMA.

Fiji Trade and Investment Board: Civic House, 3rd Floor, Town Hall Rd, POB 2303, Govt Bldgs, Suva; tel. 315988; telex 2355; fax 301783; f. 1980, restyled 1988, to promote and stimulate foreign and local economic development investment; Chair. PETER LEE; Dir Ratu ISOA GAVIDI; CEO JESONI VITUSAGAVULU.

DEVELOPMENT ORGANIZATIONS

Fiji Development Company Ltd: POB 161, FNPF Place, 350 Victoria Parade, Suva; tel. 304611; fax 304171; f. 1960; subsidiary of the Commonwealth Development Corpn; Man. F. KHAN.

Fijian Development Fund Board: POB 122, Suva; tel. 312601; fax 302585; f. 1951; funds derived from payments of $F20 a metric ton from the sales of copra by indigenous Fijians; deposits receive interest at 2.5%; funds used only for Fijian development schemes; dep. $F1m. (1990); Chair. Minister for Fijian Affairs; CEO VINCENT TOVATA.

Land Development Authority: c/o Ministry for Agriculture, Fishery and Forestry, POB 358, Suva; tel. 311233; fax 302478; f. 1961 to co-ordinate development plans for land and marine resources; Chair. Ratu Sir JOSAIA TARAIQIA.

CHAMBERS OF COMMERCE

Ba Chamber of Commerce: POB 99, Ba; tel. 670134; fax 670132; Pres. DIJENDRA SINGH.

Labasa Chamber of Commerce: POB 121, Labasa; tel. 811262; fax 813009; Pres. SHIULAL NAGINDAS.

Lautoka Chamber of Commerce: POB 366, Lautoka; tel. 661834; fax 662379; Pres. NATWARLAL VAGH.

Levuka Chamber of Commerce: POB 85, Levuka; tel. 440164; fax 440252; Pres. ISHRAR ALI.

Nadi Chamber of Commerce: POB 2735, Nadi; tel. 723061; fax 702314; e-mail arunkumar@is.com.fj; Pres. RAMESH CHAUMAN.

Nausori Chamber of Commerce: POB 228, Nausori; tel. 478235; fax 400134; Pres. ROBERT RAJ KUMAR.

Sigatoka Chamber of Commerce: POB 882, Sigatoka; tel. 500064; fax 520006; Pres. NATWAR SINGH.

Suva Chamber of Commerce: 29 Ackland St, Vatuwara, POB 337, Suva; tel. 303854; fax 300475; f. 1902; Pres. NAVIN CHANDRA; 150 mems.

Tavua-Vatukoula Chamber of Commerce: POB 698, Tavua; tel. 680390; fax 680390; Pres. SOHAN SINGH.

Vanua Chamber of Chamber: 26 Carew St, Flagstaff, POB 13132, Suva; tel. 311022; f. 1988; Pres. PENI VEREKAUTA (acting); Sec. LITIA K. VAKAREWAKOBAU.

INDUSTRIAL AND TRADE ASSOCIATIONS

Fiji Forest Industries (FFI): Suva; Deputy Chair. Ratu SOSO KATONIVERE.

Fiji National Petroleum Co Ltd: Suva; f. 1991; govt-owned, distributor of petroleum products.

Fiji Sugar Cane Growers' Council: Dominion House, 4th Floor, Thomson St, Suva; tel. 314855; fax 301794; f. 1985; aims to develop the sugar industry and protect the interests of registered growers; CEO GRISH MAHARAJ; Chair. MARIKA V. SILIMAIBAU.

Fiji Sugar Corporation Ltd: Dominion House, 5th Floor, Thomson St, POB 283, Suva; tel. 313455; fax 302685; nationalized 1974; buyer of sugar-cane and raw sugar mfrs; Chair. LYLE N. CUPIT; Man. Dir JONETANI K. GALUINADI.

Fiji Sugar Marketing Co Ltd: Dominion House, 5th Floor, Thomson St, POB 1402, Suva; tel. 311588; telex 2271; fax 300607; Man. Dir JOHN MAY.

National Trading Corporation Ltd: POB 13673, Suva; tel. 315711; fax 302824; f. 1992; a govt-owned body set up to develop markets for agricultural and marine produce locally and overseas; processes and markets fresh fruit, vegetables and ginger products; Chair. MICHAEL DENNIS; CEO SOLOMONE MAKASIALE.

Native Lands Trust Board: Suva; manages holdings of ethnic Fijian landowners; Gen. Man. Ratu MOSESE VOLAVOLA.

Pacific Fishing Co: Suva; govt-owned.

Sugar Commission of Fiji: Dominion House, 4th Floor, Thomson St, Suva; tel. 315488; fax 301488; Chair. GERALD BARRACK.

EMPLOYERS' ORGANIZATIONS

Fiji Employers' Federation: 42 Gorrie St, POB 575, Suva; tel. 313188; fax 302183; e-mail employer@is.com.fj; represents 170 major employers; Pres. H. R. HATCH; CEO KENNETH A. J. ROBERTS.

Fiji Inter-Island Ship Owners' Association: POB 152, Suva; fax 303389; Pres. JUSTIN SMITH.

Fiji Manufacturers' Association: POB 1308, Suva; tel. 384455; fax 384766; f. 1902; Pres. DINESH SHANKAR; 75 mems.

Textile, Clothing and Footwear Council: POB 10015, Nabua; tel. 384777; fax 370446; Sec. R. DUNSTAN.

UTILITIES

Electricity

Fiji Electricity Authority: Suva.

Water

Water and Sewerage Section: Public Works Department, Ministry of Public Works and Infrastructure, Information, Broadcasting and Telecommunications, Ganilau House, 7th Floor, Suva; tel. 315133; telex 2104; fax 301198.

TRADE UNIONS

Fiji Trades Union Congress (FTUC): 32 Des Voeux Rd, POB 1418, Suva; tel. 315377; fax 300306; f. 1951; affiliated to ICFTU and

ICFTU—APRO; 35 affiliated unions; more than 42,000 mems; Pres. DANIEL URAI; Gen. Sec. PRATAP CHAND. Principal affiliated unions:

Association of USP Staff: POB 1168, Suva; tel. 313900; telex 2276; fax 301305; f. 1977; Pres. GANESH CHAND; Sec. D. R. RAO.

Building Workers' Union: POB 928, Lautoka; tel. 661989; Pres. EMORI TUISESE; Sec. JOHN PAUL.

Federated Airline Staff Association: Nadi Airport, POB 9259, Nadi; tel. 722877; fax 790068; Sec. RAM RAJEN.

Fiji Aviation Workers' Association: FTUC Complex, 32 Des Voeux Rd, POB 5351, Raiwaqa; tel. 303184; fax 300306; Pres. VALENTINE SIMPSON; Gen. Sec. ATTAR SINGH.

Fiji Bank Employees' Union: 101 Gordon St, POB 853, Suva; tel. 301827; fax 301956; Gen. Sec. DIWAN C. SHANKER.

Fiji Garment, Textile and Allied Workers' Union: c/o FTUC, Raiwaqa; f. 1992.

Fiji Nurses' Association: POB 1364, Suva; tel. 312841; Gen. Sec. KITI VATANIMOTO.

Fiji Public Service Association: 298 Waimanu Rd, POB 1405, Suva; tel. 311922; fax 301099; e-mail fpsa@is.com.fj; f. 1943; 3,434 mems; Pres. AISEA BATISARESARE; Gen. Sec. M. P. CHAUDHRY.

Fiji Sugar and General Workers' Union: 84 Naviti St, POB 330, Lautoka; tel. 660746; fax 664888; 25,000 mems; Pres. SHIU LINGAM; Gen. Sec. FELIX ANTHONY.

Fiji Teachers' Union: 1–3 Berry Rd, Govt Bldgs, POB 2203, Suva; tel. 314099; fax 305962; f. 1930; 3,200 mems; Pres. JAGDISH SINGH; Gen. Sec. PRATAP CHAND.

Fijian Teachers' Association: POB 14464, Suva; tel. 315099; Pres. JIUTA VOLATABU; Gen. Sec. ERONI BIUKOTO.

Insurance Officers' Association: POB 71, Suva; tel. 313488; Pres. JAGDISH KHATRI; Sec. DAVID LEE.

Mineworkers' Union of Fiji: POB 876, Tavua; f. 1986; Pres. HENNESY PETERS; Sec. KAVEKINI NAVUSO.

National Farmers' Union: POB 522, Labasa; tel. 811838; 10,000 mems (sugar-cane farmers); Pres. CHRISHNA CHAND SHARMA; Gen. Sec. M. P. CHAUDHRY; CEO MOHAMMED LATIF SUBEDAR.

National Union of Factory and Commercial Workers: POB 989, Suva; tel. 311155; 3,800 mems; Pres. CAMA TUILEVEUKA; Gen. Sec. JAMES R. RAMAN.

National Union of Hotel and Catering Employees: Nadi Airport, POB 9426, Nadi; tel. 70906; Pres. LEPANI VOSALEVU; Sec. ISMELI VOLAVOLA.

Public Employees' Union: POB 781, Suva; tel. 304501; 6,752 mems; Pres. SEMI TIKOICINA; Gen. Sec. FILIMONE BANUVE.

Transport and Oil Workers' Union: POB 903, Suva; tel. 302534; f. 1988; following merger of Oil and Allied Workers' Union and Transport Workers' Union; Pres. J. BOLA; Sec. MICHAEL COLUMBUS.

There are several independent trade unions, including Fiji Registered Ports Workers' Union (f. 1947; Pres. JIOJI TAHOLOSALE).

Transport

RAILWAYS

Fiji Sugar Corporation Railway: Rarawai Mill, POB 155, Ba; tel. 674044; fax 670505; for use in cane-harvesting season, May–Dec.; 595 km of permanent track and 225 km of temporary track (gauge of 600 mm), serving cane-growing areas at Ba, Lautoka and Penang on Viti Levu and Labasa on Vanua Levu; Gen. Man. ADURU KUVA.

ROADS

At the end of 1995 there were some 3,370 km of roads in Fiji, of which 49.1% were paved. A 500-km highway circles the main island of Viti Levu.

SHIPPING

There are ports of call at Suva, Lautoka, Levuka and Savusavu. The main port, Suva, handles more than 800 ships a year, including large passenger liners. Lautoka handles more than 300 vessels and liners and Levuka, the former capital of Fiji, mainly handles commercial fishing vessels. In 1996 a feasibility study into the possible establishment of a free port at Suva was commissioned. In May 1997 the Government approved 14 new ports of entry in the northern, western and central eastern districts of Fiji.

Ports Authority of Fiji (PAF): Administration Bldg, Princes Wharf, POB 780, Suva; tel. 312700; telex 2203; fax 300064; expected to be corporatized in 1998; CEO AKUILA T. P. SAVU (acting); Port Master Capt. GEORGE MACOMBER.

Burns Philp Shipping (Fiji) Ltd: Rodwell Rd, POB 15832, Suva; tel. 311777; telex 2168; fax 301127; shipping agents, customs agents and international forwarding agents; Gen. Man. HARI NARAIN.

Consort Shipping Line Ltd: Muaiwalu Complex, Rona St, Walubay, POB 152, Suva; tel. 313344; fax 303389; CEO HECTOR SMITH; Man. Dir JUSTIN SMIT.

Fiji Maritime Services Ltd: c/o Fiji Ports Workers and Seafarers Union, 36 Edinburgh Drive, Suva; f. 1989 by PAF and the Ports Workers' Union; services between Lautoka and Vanua Levu ports.

Inter-Ports Shipping Corpn Ltd: 25 Eliza St, Walu Bay; POB 152, Suva; tel. 313638; telex 2703; f. 1984; Man. Dir JUSTIN SMITH.

Transcargo Express Fiji Ltd: POB 936, Suva; f. 1974; Man. Dir LEO B. SMITH.

Wong's Shipping Co Ltd: Suite 647, Epworth House, Nina St, POB 1269, Suva; tel. 311867; telex 2343.

CIVIL AVIATION

There is an international airport at Nadi (about 210 km from Suva), a domestic airport at Nausori (Suva) and 15 other airfields. Nadi is an important transit airport in the Pacific and, in 1990, direct flights to Japan also began. In late 1993 projects to upgrade airfields at Labasa, Savusavu and Taveuni were initiated, and in 1996 the expansion of Nausori airport at a cost of $F1.5m. was announced.

Civil Aviation Authority of Fiji: Nadi International Airport, Nadi; expected to be corporatized in 1998.

Air Pacific Ltd: Air Pacific Centre, POB 9266, Nadi International Airport, Nadi; tel. 720777; fax 720512; f. 1951 as Fiji Airways, name changed in 1971; domestic services from Nausori Airport (serving Suva) to Nadi and international services to Tonga, Solomon Islands, Vanuatu, Samoa, Japan, the Republic of Korea, Australia and New Zealand; from November 1996 a weekly service to Vancouver (Canada) was to be introduced; 79.6% govt-owned, 17.5% owned by Qantas (Australia); Chair. GERALD BARRACK; Man. Dir and CEO ANDREW DRYSDALE.

Fiji Air Ltd: 219 Victoria Parade, POB 1259, Suva; tel. 314666; telex 2258; fax 300771; domestic airline operating 46 scheduled services a week to 13 destinations; charter operations, aerial photography and surveillance also conducted; partly owned by the Fijian Govt; Chair. DOUG HAZARD; CEO DAVID A. YOUNG.

Hibiscus Air Ltd: Nadi International Airport, Nadi; domestic airline operating charter and non-scheduled flights around Fiji.

Sunflower Airlines Ltd: POB 9452, Nadi International Airport, Nadi; tel. 723555; telex 5183; fax 720085; f. 1980; domestic airline; scheduled flights to 15 destinations, also charter services; Man. Dir DON IAN COLLINGWOOD.

Vanua Air Charters: Labasa; f. 1993; provides domestic charter and freight services; Proprs Ratu Sir KAMISESE MARA, CHARAN SINGH.

Tourism

Scenery, climate, fishing and diving attract visitors to Fiji, where tourism is an important industry. The number of foreign tourist arrivals remained almost constant in 1996 when 339,560 people visited the country and the industry earned $F442.3m. In 1995 some 24.6% of visitors came from Australia, 17.4% from Europe (with 7.7% from the United Kingdom alone), 18.5% from New Zealand, 12.5% from the USA and 14.2% from Japan. Expansion of the tourist industry is constrained by limited airline capacity and a shortage of skilled personnel. A total of 5,200 hotel rooms were available in 1995. The Tourism Council of the South Pacific is based in Suva.

Fiji Hotel Association (FHA): Suva; tel. 302980; fax 300331; represents 72 hotels; Pres. RADIKE QEREQERETABUA; Chief Exec. OLIVIA PARETI.

Fiji Visitors' Bureau: POB 92, Suva; tel. 302433; fax 300970; e-mail infodesk@fijifvb.gov.fj; f. 1923; Chair. WILLIAM G. J. CRUICKSHANK; Chief Exec. SITIVENI YARONA; Dir of Tourism RAJESHWAR SINGH.

FINLAND

Introductory Survey

Location, Climate, Language, Religion, Flag, Capital

The Republic of Finland lies in northern Europe, bordered to the far north by Norway and to the north-west by Sweden. Russia adjoins the whole of the eastern frontier. Finland's western and southern shores are washed by the Baltic Sea. The climate varies sharply, with warm summers and cold winters. The mean annual temperature is 5°C (41°F) in Helsinki and −0.4°C (31°F) in the far north. There are two official languages: 93.4% of the population speak Finnish and 5.9% speak Swedish. There is a small Lapp population in the north. Almost all of the inhabitants profess Christianity, and about 85.4% belong to the Evangelical Lutheran Church. The national flag (proportions 18 by 11) displays an azure blue cross (the upright to the left of centre) on a white background. The state flag has, at the centre of the cross, the national coat of arms (a yellow-edged red shield containing a golden lion and nine white roses). The capital is Helsinki.

Recent History

Finland formed part of the Kingdom of Sweden until 1809, when it became an autonomous Grand Duchy under the Russian Empire. During the Russian revolution of 1917 the territory proclaimed its independence. Following a brief civil war, a democratic Constitution was adopted in 1919. The Soviet regime which came to power in Russia attempted to regain control of Finland but acknowledged the country's independence in 1920.

Demands by the USSR for military bases in Finland and for the cession of part of the Karelian isthmus, in south-eastern Finland, were rejected by the Finnish Government in November 1939. As a result, the USSR attacked Finland, and the two countries fought the 'Winter War', a fiercely contested conflict lasting 15 weeks, before Finnish forces were defeated. Following its surrender, Finland ceded an area of 41,880 sq km (16,170 sq miles) to the USSR in March 1940. In the hope of recovering the lost territory, Finland joined Nazi Germany in attacking the USSR in 1941. However, a separate armistice between Finland and the USSR was concluded in 1944.

In accordance with a peace treaty signed in February 1947, Finland agreed to the transfer of about 12% of its pre-war territory (including the Karelian isthmus and the Petsamo area on the Arctic coast) to the USSR, and to the payment of reparations, which totalled about US $570m. when completed in 1952. Meanwhile, in April 1948, Finland and the USSR signed the Finno-Soviet Treaty of Friendship, Co-operation and Mutual Assistance (the YYA treaty), which was extended for periods of 20 years in 1955, 1970 and again in 1983. A major requirement of the treaty was that Finland repel any attack made on the USSR by Germany, or its allies, through Finnish territory. (The treaty was replaced by a non-military agreement in 1992, see below.)

Since independence in 1917, the politics of Finland have been characterized by coalition governments (including numerous minority coalitions) and the development of consensus between parties. The Social Democratic Party (SDP) and the Centre Party (Kesk) have usually been the dominant participants in government. The conservative opposition gained significant support at a general election in March 1979, following several years of economic crises. A new centre-left coalition Government was formed in May, however, by Dr Mauno Koivisto, a Social Democratic economist and former Prime Minister. This four-party Government, comprising Kesk, the SDP, the Swedish People's Party (SFP) and the Finnish People's Democratic League (SKDL—an electoral alliance, which included the communists), continued to pursue deflationary economic policies, although there were disagreements within the Council of State (Cabinet) in 1981, over social welfare policy and budgetary matters.

Dr Urho Kekkonen, President since 1956, resigned in October 1981. Dr Koivisto was elected President in January 1982. He was succeeded as head of the coalition by a former Prime Minister, Kalevi Sorsa, a Social Democrat. Towards the end of 1982 the SKDL refused to support austerity measures or an increase in defence spending. This led to the re-formation of the coalition in December, without the SKDL, until the general election of March 1983.

At this election the SDP won 57 of the 200 seats in the Eduskunta (Parliament), compared with 52 in the 1979 election; while the conservative opposition National Coalition Party (Kok) lost three seats. In May Sorsa formed another centre-left coalition, comprising the SDP, the SFP, Kesk and the Rural Party (SMP): the coalition parties held a total of 122 parliamentary seats.

At a general election held in March 1987, the combined non-socialist parties gained a majority in the Eduskunta for the first time since the election of 1945. Although the SDP remained the largest single party, losing one seat and retaining 56, the system of modified proportional representation enabled Kok to gain an additional nine seats, winning a total of 53, while increasing its share of the votes cast by only 1%. The communist parties (SKP and SKP—Y) suffered a decline in popularity: although the SKDL retained all of its 16 seats, the number of seats held by the Democratic Alternative was reduced from 10 to four. President Koivisto eventually invited Harri Holkeri, a former Chairman of Kok, to form a coalition Government comprising Kok, the SDP, the SFP and the SMP, thus avoiding a polarization of the political parties within the Eduskunta. The four parties controlled 131 of the 200 seats. Holkeri became the first conservative Prime Minister since 1946, and Kesk joined the opposition for the first appreciable length of time since independence.

In February 1988 Koivisto retained office after the first presidential election by direct popular vote (in accordance with constitutional changes adopted in the previous year). He campaigned for a reduction in presidential power. He did not win the required absolute majority, however, and an electoral college was convened. Koivisto was re-elected after an endorsement by the Prime Minister, Holkeri, who was third in terms of direct votes (behind Paavo Väyrynen, the leader of Kesk).

At a general election held in March 1991, Kesk obtained 55 of the 200 seats in the Eduskunta, the SDP gained 48 seats, and Kok 40 seats. In April a coalition Government, comprising Kesk, Kok, the SFP and the Finnish Christian Union (SKL), took office. The new coalition constituted the country's first wholly non-socialist Government for 25 years. The Chairman of Kesk, Esko Aho, became Prime Minister. In March 1993 President Koivisto announced that he would not present himself as a candidate for a third term in the forthcoming presidential election. In the first stage of the election, which took place in January 1994, the two most successful candidates were Martti Ahtisaari (the SDP candidate and a senior United Nations official), with 25.9% of the votes, and Elisabeth Rehn (the SFP candidate and Minister of Defence), with 22%. The Kesk candidate (Paavo Väyrynen) obtained 19.5% of the votes, and the Kok candidate 15.2%. Both of the leading candidates were firm supporters of Finland's application for membership of the European Union (EU), as the European Community (EC) had been restyled in late 1993. In accordance with constitutional changes adopted since the previous election (stipulating that, if no candidate gained more than 50% of the votes, the electorate should choose between the two candidates with the most votes), a second stage of the election took place on 6 February. It was won by Ahtisaari (with 53.9% of the votes), who took office on 1 March.

In June 1994 Pertti Salolainen, the Deputy Prime Minister, resigned from his duties as Chairman of Kok, following criticism of his role in negotiations for Finland's planned entry into the EU. In the same month the Government survived a parliamentary vote of 'no confidence' on the issue of accession to the EU, and the SKL withdrew from the coalition since it opposed EU membership.

At a general election, held on 19 March 1995, the SDP obtained 63 of the 200 seats in the Eduskunta, Kesk secured 44 seats, Kok 39 seats, and the Left-Wing Alliance (formed in 1990 by a merger of the SKP, the SKP—Y and the SKDL) 22 seats. A new coalition Government was formed in April, comprising the SDP, Kok, the SFP, the Left-Wing Alliance and the Green League. Paavo Lipponen, the leader of the SDP, replaced Aho as Prime Minister, and Sauli Niinistö, the Chairman of Kok, was appointed Deputy Prime Minister. The first election of Finnish representatives to the parliament of the EU was held in October 1996. The SDP performed relatively poorly, securing 21.5% of the votes cast, compared with 28.3% at the 1995 election to the Finnish Parliament, while Kesk achieved 24.6% (19.9% in 1995) and Kok 20.2% (17.9% in 1995). The disappointing result for the SDP was attributed, in part, to the Government's decision, a week earlier, to commit Finland to entering the exchange rate mechanism (ERM, see Economic Affairs, below) of the EU's European Monetary System.

In August 1997 the Government announced further reductions in expenditure and increased taxes on fuels, following the disclosure that an unforeseen statistical discrepancy had resulted in a budget deficit for 1996 which was incompatible with the agreed economic criteria for European economic and monetary union. The draft budget for 1998, presented in September, further reflected the Government's determination to reduce the fiscal deficit. A new junior finance minister with particular responsibility for taxation was appointed in October.

In foreign affairs, Finland has traditionally maintained a neutral stance, although the pursuance of friendly relations with the USSR has generally been regarded as a priority. In October 1989 Mikhail Gorbachev became the first Soviet Head of State to visit Finland since 1975, and recognized Finland's neutral status. The 1948 Finno-Soviet Treaty of Friendship, Co-operation and Mutual Assistance, which bound Finland to a military defence alliance with the USSR and prevented the country from joining any international organization (including the EU) whose members posed a military threat to the USSR, was replaced in January 1992 by a 10-year agreement, signed by Finland and Russia, which involved no military commitment. The agreement was to be automatically renewed for five-year periods unless annulled by either signatory. The new treaty also included undertakings by the two countries not to use force against each other and to respect the inviolability of their common border and each other's territorial integrity. During 1992 Finland established diplomatic relations with the former Soviet republics. A customs agreement was signed with Poland in November 1997.

Finland joined the United Nations and the Nordic Council (see p. 200) in 1955 but became a full member of EFTA (see p. 150) only in 1986. In 1989 Finland joined the Council of Europe (see p. 140). A free-trade agreement between Finland and the EC took effect in 1974. In March 1992 the Finnish Government formally applied to join the EC, despite opposition from farmers, who feared the impact of membership on Finland's strongly-protected agricultural sector. In a referendum on the question of Finland's accession to membership of the EU, which was held on 16 October 1994, 56.9% of the votes cast were in favour of membership, and in November the treaty of accession was ratified after protracted debate in Parliament. Opponents of EU membership highlighted the benefits of Finland's traditional policy of neutrality, particularly with regard to Russian national security considerations, and warned that the country would now be increasingly forced to identify with Western security policy. The Government declared, however, that Finland's neutral stance would not be compromised either by joining the EU or by its stated intention to participate in NATO's 'partnership for peace' programme, and announced that it would not seek full membership of NATO (see p. 204) or WEU (see p. 240). The decision not to apply for membership of NATO was reiterated in May 1995 by the new Prime Minister, Paavo Lipponen. Finland left EFTA and joined the EU, as scheduled, on 1 January 1995.

Government

Finland has a republican Constitution which combines a parliamentary system with a strong presidency. The unicameral Parliament (Eduskunta) has 200 members, elected by universal adult suffrage for four years (subject to dissolution by the President) on the basis of proportional representation. The President, entrusted with supreme executive power, is elected for six years by direct popular vote. Legislative power is exercised by Parliament in conjunction with the President. For general administration, the President appoints a Council of State (Cabinet), which is headed by a Prime Minister and is responsible to Parliament. Finland has 12 provinces, each administered by an appointed Governor, and is diyided into 452 municipalities. The province of Ahvenanmaa (the Åland Islands) has rights of legislation in internal affairs (see separate section at end of chapter).

Defence

In August 1997 the armed forces of Finland numbered 31,000 (of whom 23,700 were conscripts serving up to 11 months), comprising an army of 27,000 (21,000 conscripts), an air force of 1,900 (1,500 conscripts) and a navy of 2,100 (1,200 conscripts). There were also some 500,000 reserves and 3,400 frontier guards. The estimated defence budget for 1998 was 10,031m. markkaa.

Economic Affairs

In 1995, according to estimates by the World Bank, Finland's gross national product (GNP), measured at average 1993–95 prices, was US $105,174m., equivalent to US $20,580 per head. During 1985–95, it was estimated, GNP per head decreased, in real terms, at an average annual rate of 0.2%. Over the same period, the population increased by an annual average of 0.4%. The country's gross domestic product (GDP) increased, in real terms, by an annual average of 1.4% in 1986–96. Real GDP declined rapidly during 1991–93, but recovered in 1994 and 1995, when rises of 4.4% and 4.2%, respectively, were recorded; real growth of 3.7% was recorded for 1996.

Agriculture (including hunting, forestry and fishing) contributed an estimated 4.0% of GDP in 1996 and employed 7.6% of the working population in 1995. Forestry is the most important branch of the sector, providing about 31% of export earnings in 1996. Animal husbandry is the predominant form of farming. The major crops are oats, sugar beet and potatoes. During 1980–90 agricultural GDP decreased, in real terms, by an annual average of 0.2%, while no significant movement was recorded during 1990–95, on the same terms. Agricultural production declined by 3.7% in 1995, but increased by 0.3% in 1996.

Industry (including mining, manufacturing, construction and power), provided 33.8% of GDP in 1996 and employed 27.8% of the working population in 1995. Industrial GDP increased, in real terms, by an annual average of 3.5% during 1980-89, but declined at an average rate of 4.6% per year in 1989–92. Industrial production (excluding construction) grew by an annual average of 6.0% during 1991–94 and by 7.5% in 1995.

Mining and quarrying contributed 0.4% of GDP in 1996 and employed 0.2% of the working population in 1995. The GDP of the mining sector increased, in real terms, at an average rate of 5.7% per year during 1980–90, but declined by 7.8% in 1991 and by 2.3% in 1992. Mining output fell by an average of 4.9% annually in 1990–93, but rose by 11.7% in 1994. It decreased by 0.5% in 1995. Gold is the major mineral export, and zinc ore, silver, copper ore and lead ore are also mined in small quantities.

Manufacturing provided 26.2% of GDP in 1995 and in the same year employed 20.6% of the working population. In 1996 the most important branches of manufacturing, measured by value added in production, were metal products and electrical and transport equipment (accounting for 39.5% of the total), and food and beverages (9.3%). The GDP of the manufacturing sector increased, in real terms, at an average rate of 3.5% per year during 1980–89, but declined by 0.7% in 1990 and by 10.9% in 1991. Manufacturing GDP rose by 2.7% in 1992. The sector's output increased by 5.5% in 1993, by 12.1% in 1994 and by 8.7% in 1995.

Of total energy consumed in 1996, 28.6% was provided by petroleum, 16.6% by wood fuel, 16.4% by nuclear power, 14.6% by coal, 9.9% by natural gas and 7.0% by peat. At the end of 1996 there were four nuclear reactors in operation , and nuclear power provided 28.1% of total electricity generated. Imports of mineral fuels comprised 8.6% of the total cost of imports in 1995.

Services engaged 64.2% of the employed labour force in 1995 and provided 62.2% of GDP in 1996. In real terms, the combined GDP of the service sectors increased at an average rate of 3.7% per year during 1980–90, but declined by 4.0% in 1991 and by 4.8% in 1992. Growth in the sector's GDP was recorded at 3.1% in 1994 and 4.5% in 1995.

In 1996 Finland recorded a visible trade surplus of US $11,035m., and there was a surplus of US $4,790m. on the current account of the balance of payments. In 1996 the principal sources of imports were Germany (15.0%), Sweden (11.9%) and the United Kingdom (8.8%), which were also the principal customers for exports (12.1%, 10.7% and 10.2%, respectively). Other major trading partners were the USA and Russia. The EU accounted for some 54.5% of exports and 60.2% of imports in 1996. The principal exports in 1995 were paper and paper products, machinery and transport equipment, and crude materials (mainly wood and pulp). The principal imports were machinery and transport equipment, basic manufactures, mineral fuels, and chemicals and related products.

Finland's overall budget deficit for 1996 was 36,662m. markkaa (equivalent to 6.4% of GDP). A deficit of 28,990m. markkaa was forecast for 1997. At the end of September 1997 Finland's gross public debt amounted to some 426,000m. markkaa. The average annual rate of inflation was 3.3% during 1986–96. The rate declined from 2.1% in 1993 to 1.1% in 1994 and 1.0% in 1995, and was only 0.6% in 1996. Consumer prices increased by an estimated average of 1.6% in 1997. Unemployment increased from an average of 7.6% of the labour force in 1991 to 13.1% in 1992, to 17.9% in 1993 and to 18.4% in 1994; however, the rate of unemployment declined to an average of 17.2% in 1995, to 16.3% in 1996 and to 13.1% in October 1997.

Finland is a member of the Nordic Council (see p. 200) and the Organisation for Economic Co-operation and Development (p. 208). In January 1995 it left the European Free Trade Association and joined the European Union (EU, see p. 152).

Finland experienced a high rate of economic growth during the 1980s, but in 1991 the economy moved into recession. Political and economic upheaval in the USSR greatly reduced demand for Finnish exports there, while the market for forestry products and paper also diminished elsewhere. A rapid increase in business failures and unemployment occurred, and heavy loan losses led to a crisis in the financial sector, necessitating government assistance for banks in 1992 and 1993. Industrial production and exports improved from 1993. Unemployment, however, remained very high (averaging 17.2% of the labour force in 1995). GDP grew by 4.2% in 1995 and by an estimated 3.7% in 1996, and membership of the EU helped to stimulate investment and encourage competition. In September 1996 the Government announced that it had applied to join the exchange rate mechanism (ERM) of the EU, in order to prepare the Finnish economy to satisfy the terms of economic and monetary union (EMU) within the EU in 1998. Finland duly entered the ERM in October 1996. Economic initiatives undertaken during 1997 sought to meet the agreed criteria for EMU, and increased fiscal austerity ensured that the stipulations for budget deficit and public debt were successfully adhered to. The draft budget for 1998, presented in September 1997, envisaged economic growth of 4.5% for 1997 and 3.5% for 1998. A significant decrease in the rate of unemployment (to some 13%) was recorded during 1997.

Social Welfare

Benefits are paid to compensate for loss of income owing to sickness, unemployment, maternity, old age, disability and death of a family's principal source of income. Child allowances and living allowances are also paid. Pension coverage consists of a basic pension scheme, covering all persons who are permanently resident in Finland, and earnings-related pension schemes. Some 90% of employees are members of unemployment insurance funds. All children under seven years of age are entitled to day care provided by local authorities. (In 1995 about one-half of children of that age were exercising their entitlement.) All children under the age of three are entitled to public day care. The public health services (including both primary and specialized health care) cover the whole population, and are financed mainly by the state and local authorities. The National Health Act of 1972 provided for the establishment of health centres in every municipality. In 1994 Finland had 46,400 hospital beds and there were 14,500 physicians working in the country. Of total budgetary expenditure by the central Government in 1996, 48,317m. markkaa (24.2%) was for health and social security. The percentage of total expenditure devoted to health and social security was forecast to decrease to 23.9% in 1997.

Education

Compulsory education was introduced in 1921. By the 1977/78 school year, the whole country had transferred to a new comprehensive education system. Tuition is free and the core curriculum is the same for all students. Compulsory attendance lasts for nine years, and is divided into a six-year lower stage, beginning at the age of seven, and a three-year upper stage (or lower secondary stage), beginning at the age of 13. After comprehensive school, the pupil may continue his or her studies, either at a general upper secondary school, or a vocational upper secondary school. Courses leading to basic vocational qualifications take between two and three years to complete. The matriculation examination taken at the end of three years of general upper secondary school gives eligibility for a university education as do tertiary vocational diplomas. Higher education is provided by 20 universities, nine permanent and 19 experimental AMK institutions (polytechnics) and a number of vocational colleges. Total central government expenditure on education in 1996 was 26,561m. markkaa (13.3% of total expenditure).

Public Holidays

1998: 1 January (New Year's Day), 6 January (Epiphany), 10 April (Good Friday), 13 April (Easter Monday), 30 April–1 May (May Day), 21 May (Ascension Day), 31 May (Whitsun), 19–20 June (Midsummer Day), 31 October (for All Saints' Day), 6 December (Independence Day), 24–26 December (Christmas).

1999: 1 January (New Year's Day), 6 January (Epiphany), 2 April (Good Friday), 5 April (Easter Monday), 30 April–1 May (May Day), 13 May (Ascension Day), 23 May (Whitsun), 25–26 June (Midsummer Day), 1 November (All Saints' Day), 6 December (Independence Day), 24–26 December (Christmas).

Weights and Measures

The metric system is in force.

Statistical Survey

Source (unless otherwise specified): Statistics Finland, 00022 Helsinki; tel. (09) 17342220; fax (09) 17342279.

Note: Figures in this Survey include data for the autonomous Åland Islands, treated separately on p. 1326.

Area and Population

AREA, POPULATION AND DENSITY

Area (sq km)	
Land	304,592
Inland water	33,552
Total	338,144*
Population (census results)	
17 November 1985	4,910,619
31 December 1990	
Males	2,426,204
Females	2,572,274
Total	4,998,478
Population (official estimates at 31 December)	
1994	5,098,754
1995	5,116,826
1996	5,132,320
Density (per sq km) at 31 December 1996†	16.8

* 130,558 sq miles.

† Excluding inland waters.

PROVINCES (estimated population at 31 December 1996)

	Land Area (sq km)*	Population	Density (per sq km)
Uudenmaan (Nylands)	9,898	1,343,039	135.7
Turun-Porin (Åbo-Björneborgs)	19,954	703,146	35.2
Ahvenanmaa (Åland)	1,527	25,257	16.5
Hämeen (Tavastehus)	19,226	732,883	38.1
Kymen (Kymmene)	10,780	330,571	30.7
Mikkelin (St Michels)	16,326	204,194	12.5
Kuopion (Kuopio)	16,510	257,742	15.6
Pohjois-Karjalan (Norra Karelens)	17,782	176,220	9.9
Vaasan (Vasa)	26,418	446,708	16.9
Keski-Suomen (Mellersta Finlands)	16,249	259,096	15.9
Oulun (Uleåborgs)	56,858	452,885	8.0
Lapin (Lapplands)	93,066	200,579	2.2
Total	304,592	5,132,320	16.8

* Excluding inland waters, totalling 33,552 sq km.

PRINCIPAL TOWNS (estimated population at 31 December 1996)

Helsinki (Helsingfors) (capital)	532,053
Espoo (Esbo)	196,260
Tampere (Tammerfors)	186,026
Vantaa (Vanda)	168,778
Turku (Åbo)	166,929
Oulu (Uleåborg)	111,556
Lahti	95,501
Kuopio	85,255
Pori (Björneborg)	76,623
Jyväskylä	75,353
Lappeenranta (Villmanstrand)	56,902
Kotka	56,009
Vaasa (Vasa)	55,908
Joensuu	50,757
Hämeenlinna (Tavastehus)	45,141

BIRTHS, MARRIAGES AND DEATHS

	Registered live births*		Registered marriages†		Registered deaths*	
	Number	Rate (per 1,000)	Number	Rate (per 1,000)	Number	Rate (per 1,000)
1989	63,348	12.8	24,569	4.9	49,110	10.1
1990	65,549	13.1	24,997	5.0	50,058	10.0
1991	65,395	13.0	24,732	5.0	49,294	9.8
1992	66,877	13.2	23,093	4.6	49,523	9.8
1993	64,826	12.8	24,660	4.9	50,488	10.1
1994	65,231	12.8	24,898	4.9	48,000	9.4
1995	63,067	12.3	23,737	4.6	49,280	9.6
1996	60,723	11.8	24,464	4.8	49,167	9.6

* Including Finnish nationals temporarily outside the country.

† Data relate only to marriages in which the bride was domiciled in Finland.

Expectation of life (years at birth, 1996): males 73.0; females 80.5.

ECONOMICALLY ACTIVE POPULATION*
(annual averages, '000 persons aged 15 to 74 years)

	1993	1994	1995
Agriculture, forestry and fishing	173	167	158
Mining and quarrying	4	5	4
Manufacturing	396	398	426
Electricity, gas and water	23	23	24
Construction	125	114	120
Trade, restaurants and hotels	304	297	300
Transport, storage and communications	158	161	158
Finance, insurance, real estate and business services	209	202	208
Community, social and personal services	643	650	662
Activities not adequately defined	6	7	8
Total employed	2,040	2,024	2,068
Unemployed	444	456	430
Total labour force	2,484	2,480	2,498

* Excluding persons on compulsory military service (24,000 in 1993; 22,000 in 1994; 24,000 in 1995).

1996: Total employed 2,096,000 (males 1,100,000, females 996,000); Unemployed 408,000; Total labour force 2,503,000.

Agriculture

PRINCIPAL CROPS
('000 metric tons; farms with arable land of 1 hectare or more)

	1994	1995	1996
Wheat	337	379	459
Barley	1,858	1,764	1,860
Rye	22	58	87
Oats	1,150	1,097	1,261
Mixed grain	32	35	42
Potatoes	726	798	766
Rapeseed	108	128	89
Sugar beet	1,097	1,110	897

LIVESTOCK
('000 head at 1 June; farms with arable land of 1 hectare or more)

	1994	1995	1996*
Horses	16.9	25.7	52.0
Cattle	1,252.3	1,148.1	1,146.0
Sheep	121.1	158.6	150.0
Reindeer	346.1	333.0	213.0
Pigs†	1,308.8	1,400.3	1,395.0
Poultry	5,547.2	5,657.4	5,429.0
Beehives‡	45.0	45.0	n.a.

* Provisional figures.
† Including piggeries of dairies. ‡ '000 hives.

LIVESTOCK PRODUCTS ('000 metric tons)

	1993	1994	1995
Beef	105.7	107.4	95.5
Veal	0.1	0.1	0.1
Pig meat	167.9	170.7	164.6
Poultry meat	34.6	39.4	42.4
Cows' milk*	2,263.8	2,315.5	2,296.0
Butter	55.2	53.2	52.2
Cheese	89.1	92.2	95.7
Hen eggs	69.7	71.7	73.6

* Million litres.

1996 ('000 metric tons): Beef and veal 97; Pig meat 172; Poultry meat 49 (FAO estimate); Cows' milk 2,450; Butter 54; Cheese 95; Hen eggs 70. (Source: FAO, *Production Yearbook*).

Forestry

ROUNDWOOD REMOVALS ('000 cu m, excl. bark)

	1993	1994	1995
Sawlogs, veneer logs and logs for sleepers	17,098	24,946	24,748
Pulpwood	21,349	23,793	26,169
Other industrial wood	115	358	174
Fuel wood	79	98	85
Total	38,526	49,195	51,176

SAWNWOOD PRODUCTION ('000 cu m, incl. railway sleepers)

	1992	1993	1994
Coniferous (softwood)	6,917	8,305	9,700
Broadleaved (hardwood)	67	70	80
Total	6,983	8,375	9,780

Fishing

('000 metric tons, live weight)

	1993	1994	1995
Roaches	7.8	8.2	8.4
Northern pike	17.5	11.9	11.8
European perch	19.9	16.7	16.9
Other freshwater fishes	11.8	10.6	10.5
Rainbow trout	18.8	17.7	18.3
Other diadromous fishes	16.9	15.1	16.3
Atlantic herring	79.2	99.0	95.9
Other marine fishes	1.5	1.6	6.5
Crayfishes	0.4	0.2	0.2
Total catch	173.8	181.0	184.8
Inland waters	55.4	51.3	51.9
Atlantic Ocean	118.5	129.7	133.0

Source: FAO, *Yearbook of Fishery Statistics*.

Mining

('000 metric tons, unless otherwise indicated)

	1993	1994	1995†
Copper ore*	13.7	13.2	9.9
Zinc ore*	22.5	3.7	16.4
Silver (metric tons)	0.5	0.2	—
Gold (kilograms)	304	963	1,459

* Figures refer to metal content.
‡ Figures are provisional.

Industry

SELECTED PRODUCTS ('000 metric tons, unless otherwise indicated)

	1993	1994	1995*
Cellulose	6,424	6,845	5,782
Machine pulp (for sale)	99	187	25
Newsprint	1,414	1,468	1,413
Other paper, boards and cardboards	8,528	9,190	9,223
Plywoods and veneers ('000 cubic metres)	593	651	576
Cement	836	864	905
Pig iron and ferro-alloys	2,730	2,597	2,242
Electricity (million kWh)	57,887	62,069	60,628
Cotton yarn (metric tons)	2,051	2,714	3,264
Cotton fabrics (metric tons)	3,173	3,630	2,615
Sugar	312	285	154
Rolled steel products (metric tons)	3,636	3,840	4,406
Copper cathodes (metric tons)	73,373	69,187	72,626
Cigarettes (million)	7,237	7,232	6,369

* Figures are provisional.

Finance

CURRENCY AND EXCHANGE RATES

Monetary Units
100 penniä (singular: penni) = 1 markka (Finnmark).

Sterling and Dollar Equivalents (30 September 1997)
£1 sterling = 8.540 markkaa;
US $1 = 5.286 markkaa;
100 markkaa = £11.71 = $18.92.

Average Exchange Rate (markkaa per US $)
1994 5.2235
1995 4.3667
1996 4.5936

BUDGET (million markkaa)*

Revenue	1996	1997†	1998‡
Taxes and other levies	124,007	131,649	139,434
on income and property	48,359	49,495	54,730
on turnover	44,075	48,525	48,920
Excise duties	23,210	24,685	25,860
Miscellaneous revenues	33,097	26,639	28,366
Sub-total	162,764	161,324	170,871
Interest on investments and profits received	5,661	3,036	3,071
Borrowing (net)	35,628	28,997	16,014
Total	198,392	190,321	186,885

Expenditure	1996	1997†	1998‡
General administration	12,797	13,714	13,419
Public order and safety	6,286	6,327	6,669
National defence	9,121	9,579	10,031
Education, research and culture	26,561	25,280	25,892
Social security and health	48,317	45,498	43,753
Housing and environment	4,387	4,071	3,886
Labour force	14,058	13,578	12,920
Agriculture and forestry	12,320	12,200	11,958
Transport and communications	7,968	7,752	7,049
Industry and other economic activities	9,486	5,920	5,692
Other purposes	48,126	46,394	45,613
Total	199,426	190,314	186,883

* Figures refer to the General Budget only, excluding the operations of the Social Insurance Institution and of other social security funds with their own budgets.

† Projections.

‡ Proposals.

INTERNATIONAL RESERVES (US $ million at 31 December)

	1994	1995	1996
Gold*	459.6	399.7	375.1
IMF special drawing rights	325.1	359.2	289.9
Reserve position in IMF	286.3	385.8	421.1
Foreign exchange	10,050.6	9,293.4	6,205.3
Total	11,121.6	10,438.0	7,291.4

* Valued at market-related prices.

Source: IMF, *International Financial Statistics.*

MONEY SUPPLY (million markkaa at 31 December)

	1994	1995	1996
Currency outside banks	10,810	12,401	13,645
Demand deposits at deposit money banks	143,547	163,521	191,188
Total money	154,357	175,921	204,833

Source: IMF, *International Financial Statistics.*

COST OF LIVING (Consumer Price Index; base: 1990 = 100)

	1993	1994	1995
Food	102.1	102.3	94.8
Beverages and tobacco	118.0	118.6	120.5
Clothing and footwear	111.5	113.7	115.8
Rent, heating and lighting	100.1	98.8	100.6
Furniture, household equipment	109.7	111.6	113.9
All items	109.7	110.9	112.0

1996: All items 112.6.

NATIONAL ACCOUNTS (million markkaa at current prices)

National Income and Product

	1993	1994	1995*
Compensation of employees	258,075	263,775	281,549
Operating surplus	85,323	103,393	115,115
Domestic factor incomes	343,398	367,168	396,664
Consumption of fixed capital	83,819	85,480	87,384
Gross domestic product at factor cost	427,217	452,648	484,048
Indirect taxes	71,556	74,200	76,678
Less Subsidies	16,376	15,856	14,961
GDP in purchasers' values	482,397	510,992	545,765
Factor income received from abroad	6,814	10,201	14,176
Less Factor income paid abroad	36,577	33,627	34,389
Indirect taxes from the rest of the world (net)	—	—	1,029
Gross national product	452,634	487,566	524,523
Less Consumption of fixed capital	83,819	85,480	87,384
National income in market prices	368,815	402,086	437,139

* Provisional figures.

Expenditure on the Gross Domestic Product

	1993	1994	1995
Government final consumption expenditure	112,190	114,001	119,722
Private final consumption expenditure	275,252	284,425	295,779
Increase in stocks	–3,880	7,892	5,860
Gross fixed capital formation	71,194	74,186	83,289
Statistical discrepancy	1,653	–1,999	–4,979
Total domestic expenditure	456,409	478,505	499,671
Exports of goods and services	159,438	182,530	209,148
Less Imports of goods and services	133,450	150,043	163,054
GDP in purchasers' values	482,397	510,992	545,765

Gross Domestic Product by Economic Activity

	1993	1994	1995
Agriculture, hunting, forestry and fishing	22,081	25,264	20,107
Mining and quarrying	1,687	1,936	1,852
Manufacturing	101,816	112,737	128,561
Electricity, gas and water	11,334	12,281	13,261
Construction	20,998	23,303	27,832
Trade, restaurants and hotels	47,401	50,827	52,590
Transport, storage and communication	37,260	39,114	41,671
Finance, insurance and business services	17,388	16,665	16,153
Owner-occupied dwellings	41,109	42,443	43,649
Public administration and welfare	86,475	87,033	91,367
Other community, social and personal services	47,898	49,965	53,469
Sub-total	435,447	461,568	490,512
Less Imputed bank service charge	14,205	14,396	14,342
GDP in basic values	421,242	447,172	476,170
Commodity taxes	69,410	72,340	74,955
Less Commodity subsidies	8,255	8,520	5,360
GDP in purchasers' values	482,397	510,992	545,765

GDP in purchasers' values (million markkaa at current prices): 549,863 in 1995 (revised figure); 574,780 in 1996.

BALANCE OF PAYMENTS (US $ million)

	1994	1995	1996
Exports of goods f.o.b.	29,731	40,515	40,539
Imports of goods f.o.b.	–22,241	–28,169	–29,504
Trade balance	7,490	12,346	11,035
Exports of services	5,574	7,553	7,276
Imports of services	–7,187	–9,655	–8,773
Balance on goods and services	6,057	10,245	9,538
Other income received	1,748	2,837	2,810
Other income paid	–6,078	–7,283	–6,461
Balance on goods, services and income	1,727	5,799	5,887
Current transfers received	410	1,536	1,144
Current transfers paid	–863	–2,133	–2,242
Current balance	1,273	5,202	4,790
Capital account (net)	—	66	56
Direct investment abroad	–4,354	–1,494	–3,712
Direct investment from abroad	1,496	1,044	1,140
Portfolio investment assets	826	243	–4,122
Portfolio investment liabilities	6,186	–1,179	1,437
Other investment assets	–668	–2,863	–4,679
Other investment liabilities	607	–35	1,759
Net errors and omissions	–652	–1,354	297
Overall balance	4,714	–372	–3,036

Source: IMF, *International Financial Statistics.*

External Trade

PRINCIPAL COMMODITIES (distribution by SITC, million markkaa)

Imports c.i.f.	1993	1994	1995
Food and live animals	5,830.9	7,249.0	6,044.5
Crude materials (inedible) except fuels	7,264.3	7,995.1	9,291.6
Mineral fuels, lubricants, etc.	13,155.9	13,917.9	10,911.9
Petroleum, petroleum products, etc.	9,270.8	9,640.7	7,265.4
Crude petroleum oils, etc.	6,181.3	6,543.4	n.a.
Refined petroleum products	2,916.0	2,910.8	2,006.6
Chemicals and related products	13,739.6	15,414.2	15,489.8
Chemical elements and compounds	2,341.0	2,842.2	2,693.6
Plastic materials, etc.	2,410.0	2,678.1	2,803.9
Basic manufactures	14,617.7	17,756.4	19,384.5
Textile yarn, fabrics, etc.	2,630.1	2,955.6	2,626.3
Iron and steel	3,679.1	4,503.5	5,692.7
Machinery and transport equipment	35,009.9	43,318.4	49,001.2
Non-electric machinery	15,190.8	18,885.1	20,536.8
Electrical machinery, apparatus, etc.	11,442.8	15,504.0	18,186.8
Transport equipment	8,376.3	8,929.2	10,277.4
Road vehicles and parts*	5,147.9	7,357.5	8,243.5
Passenger motor cars (excl. buses)	2,313.1	1,927.5	3,705.4
Miscellaneous manufactured articles	12,683.3	13,956.6	12,994.1
Scientific instruments, watches, etc.	2,011.5	2,291.6	2,412.6
Total (incl. others)	103,167.0	120,546.6	126,329.8

* Excluding tyres, engines and electrical parts.

Exports f.o.b.	1993	1994	1995
Food and live animals	3,709.4	4,634.1	3,548.4
Crude materials (inedible) except fuels	11,718.2	15,255.8	15,562.3
Wood, lumber and cork	6,701.7	8,832.3	8,146.7
Shaped or simply worked wood	6,199.6	8,109.1	7,664.8
Sawn coniferous lumber	5,948.2	7,690.4	7,377.6
Pulp and waste paper	2,942.6	3,749.1	4,520.7
Chemical wood pulp	2,745.2	3,572.4	4,276.6
Mineral fuels, lubricants, etc.	3,659.0	3,478.4	3,372.7
Petroleum, petroleum products, etc.	3,565.9	3,331.8	3,295.5
Refined petroleum products	3,531.9	3,285.0	3,242.0

Exports f.o.b. — *continued*	1993	1994	1995
Chemicals and related products	8,698.0	10,194.2	10,446.4
Basic manufactures	54,409.3	59,937.3	67,550.6
Wood and cork manufactures (excl. furniture)	3,320.0	4,055.9	3,956.2
Paper, paperboard and manufactures	33,310.1	36,108.1	42,409.9
Paper and paperboard	30,953.8	33,165.2	38,491.5
Newsprint paper	2,973.6	2,899.5	3,170.6
Other printing and writing paper in bulk	17,641.2	19,190.4	23,699.6
Kraft paper and paperboard	2,552.9	2,842.6	3,012.6
Iron and steel	7,881.6	8,713.7	9,537.6
Non-ferrous metals	3,888.4	4,101.5	4,329.9
Machinery and transport equipment	42,174.7	49,147.9	61,355.1
Non-electric machinery	18,868.7	24,544.6	27,436.4
Electrical machinery, apparatus, etc.	12,400.5	16,949.5	22,600.7
Transport equipment	7,905.4	7,653.9	11,318.0
Ships and boats	4,159.6	2,691.2	5,585.0
Miscellaneous manufactured articles	9,133.5	10,765.4	10,475.9
Total (incl. others)	134,112.3	154,163.2	174,660.0

PRINCIPAL TRADING PARTNERS (million markkaa)*

Imports c.i.f.	1993	1994	1995
Austria	1,180.2	1,349.4	1,549.8
Belgium/Luxembourg	3,023.1	3,291.0	3,719.3
China, People's Republic	n.a.	1,829.5	1,702.1
Denmark	3,233.4	3,667.8	4,100.3
France	4,718.1	4,911.3	5,151.0
Germany	16,923.9	17,735.9	19,717.6
Italy	3,813.4	4,685.1	5,089.9
Japan	5,966.4	7,837.7	7,938.6
Netherlands	3,849.3	4,352.5	4,790.7
Norway	5,005.8	5,760.9	5,236.3
Poland	1,382.9	1,548.9	1,365.9
Russia	7,835.8	10,697.5	9,013.0
Spain	1,246.6	1,586.8	1,652.4
Sweden	10,544.7	12,576.1	14,754.7
Switzerland	2,044.0	2,108.7	2,141.9
United Kingdom	9,113.1	10,021.0	10,514.8
USA	7,502.6	9,137.3	8,976.1
Total (incl. others)	103,167.0	120,546.6	126,329.8

1996: Denmark 4,964; France 6,366; Germany 21,344; Japan 7,311; Netherlands 5,074; Norway 5,952; Russia 10,280; Sweden 16,911; United Kingdom 12,540; USA 10,387; **Total** (incl. others) 141,952.

Exports f.o.b.	1993	1994	1995
Belgium/Luxembourg	2,956.7	3,460.7	5,188.9
Denmark	4,480.5	5,287.4	5,563.7
Estonia	n.a.	3,381.5	4,117.5
France	7,115.1	7,783.5	7,970.3
Germany	17,633.2	20,678.2	23,490.7
Italy	4,350.8	4,605.2	4,934.0
Netherlands	6,733.9	7,874.2	7,376.4
Norway	4,280.2	4,881.4	5,229.2
Russia	6,059.1	8,029.0	8,440.8
Spain	3,263.1	3,549.9	4,394.6
Sweden	14,860.5	16,845.6	17,694.5
Switzerland	2,111.4	2,325.2	2,276.6
United Kingdom	14,033.5	15,917.1	18,196.1
USA	10,504.5	11,036.5	11,664.1
Total (incl. others)	134,112.3	154,163.2	174,660.0

1996: Denmark 5,652; France 7,863; Germany 22,515; Japan 4,844; Netherlands 7,377; Norway 5,322; Russia 11,373; Sweden 19,937; United Kingdom 19,010; USA 14,761; **Total** (incl. others) 186,334.

* Imports by country of production; exports by country of consumption.

Transport

RAILWAYS (traffic)

	1993	1994	1995
Passenger-km (million)	3,007	3,037	3,184
Freight ton-km (million)	9,259	9,949	9,293

ROAD TRAFFIC (registered motor vehicles at 31 December)

	1994	1995	1996
Passenger cars	1,872,588	1,900,855	1,942,752
Buses and coaches	8,054	8,083	8,233
Lorries and vans	249,400	252,032	258,697

SHIPPING

Merchant Fleet (registered at 31 December)

	1994	1995	1996
Number of vessels	272	274	274
Total displacement ('000 grt)	1,404	1,519	1,511

Source: Lloyd's Register of Shipping, *World Fleet Statistics*.

International Sea-borne Freight Traffic

	1994	1995	1996
Number of vessels entered	n.a.	23,699	22,891
Goods ('000 metric tons):			
Loaded	35,606	34,122	33,345
Unloaded	38,637	37,036	36,944

CANAL TRAFFIC

	1993	1994	1995
Vessels in transit	75,943	97,862	85,173
Timber rafts in transit	2,778	2,264	2,422
Goods carried ('000 metric tons)	3,920	4,630	5,100
Passengers carried ('000)	296	472	373

CIVIL AVIATION (traffic on scheduled services, '000)

	1993	1994	1995
Kilometres flown	64,013	67,238	76,828
Passenger-kilometres	5,589,469	6,719,806	8,562,000
Cargo ton-kilometres	169,605	205,418	226,675

Tourism

NUMBER OF NIGHTS AT ACCOMMODATION FACILITIES

Country of Domicile	1994	1995	1996
France	123,134	115,013	112,999
Germany	691,640	628,454	511,510
Italy	94,577	100,016	100,560
Japan	93,622	115,013	119,478
Netherlands	107,525	109,315	109,279
Norway	149,295	140,805	138,364
Russia	335,712	392,344	454,891
Sweden	666,802	485,454	540,869
United Kingdom	178,371	204,580	223,860
USA	176,909	190,751	187,032
Total (incl. others)	3,376,988	3,292,484	3,284,644

Source: Finnish Tourist Board.

Communications Media

	1994	1995	1996
Telephone lines ('000)	2,801	2,810	2,813
Mobile cellular telephones ('000 subscribers)	676	1,039	1,502
Television receivers ('000 in use)*	2,600	2,650	n.a.
Radio receivers ('000 in use)*	5,100	5,150	n.a.
Book production: titles	12,539	13,494	n.a.
Newspapers and periodicals	4,916	5,049	n.a.

* Source: UNESCO, *Statistical Yearbook*.

Education

(1995)

	Institutions	Teachers	Students
Comprehensive schools*	4,932 (combined with senior secondary)	41,524	588,162
Senior secondary schools		5,664	134,851
Vocational and professional institutions	458	17,053	203,134
Universities	20	7,552	135,121

* Comprising six-year primary stage (388,342 pupils in 1995) and three-year lower secondary stage.

Source: Ministry of Education.

Directory

The Constitution

The Constitution (summarized below) was adopted on 17 July 1919.

GOVERNMENT

For the general administration of the country, there is a Council of State, appointed by the President, and composed of the Prime Minister and the Ministers of the various Ministries. The members of the Council, who must enjoy the confidence of the Parliament, are collectively responsible to it for their conduct of affairs, and for the general policy of the administration, while each member is responsible for the administration of his or her own Ministry.

To this Council the President can appoint supernumerary Ministers, who serve either as assistant Ministers or as Ministers without portfolio. The President also appoints a Chancellor of Justice, who must see that the Council and its members act within the law. If, in the opinion of the Chancellor of Justice, the Council of State or an individual Minister has acted in a manner contrary to the law, the Chancellor must report the matter to the President of the Republic or, in certain cases, to the Parliament. In this way Ministers are rendered legally as well as politically responsible for their official acts.

Finland is divided into self-governing municipalities (452 in early 1997). Members of the municipal councils are elected by universal suffrage for a period of four years.

THE PRESIDENT

The President is elected for a term of six years by direct popular vote (in accordance with changes to the Constitution adopted in 1987 and subsequently). If no candidate obtains more than 50% of the votes, a second round of the election is contested by the two candidates who gained the largest share of the votes in the first round.

The President of the Republic is entrusted with supreme executive power. The President's decisions are made known in meetings of the Council of State on the basis of the recommendation of the minister responsible for the matter. The President has the right to depart even from a unanimous opinion reached by the Council of State. Legislative power is exercised by the Parliament in conjunction with the President. Both the President and the Parliament have the right of initiative in legislation. Laws passed by the Parliament are submitted to the President, who has the right of veto. If the President has not within three months assented to a law, this is tantamount to a refusal of assent. A law to which the President has not given assent will nevertheless come into force, if the Parliament elected at the next general election adopts it without alteration.

The President also has the right to issue decrees in certain circumstances, to order new elections to the Parliament, to grant pardons and dispensations, and to grant Finnish citizenship to foreigners.

The President's approval is necessary in all matters concerning the relations of Finland with foreign countries. The President is Supreme Commander of the Defence Forces of the Republic.

Such decisions as are arrived at by the President are made in the Council of State, except in matters pertaining to military functions and appointments.

THE PARLIAMENT

The Parliament is an assembly of one chamber with 200 members elected for four years by universal suffrage on a system of proportional representation, every man and woman aged 18 years or over being entitled to vote and everyone over 20 being eligible. It assembles annually at the beginning of February. The ordinary duration of a session is 120 days but the Parliament can, at its pleasure, extend or shorten its session. The opposition of one-third of the members can cause ordinary legislative proposals to be deferred until after the next elections. Discussion of questions relating to the constitutional laws belongs also to Parliament, but for the settlement of such questions certain delaying conditions (fixed majorities) are prescribed.

Furthermore, the Parliament has the right, in a large measure, to supervise the administration of the Government. For this purpose it receives special reports (the Government also submitting an account of its administration every year) and a special account of the administration of national finances. The Chancellor of Justice submits a yearly report on the administration of the Council of State. The Parliament elects five auditors, who submit to it annual reports of their work, to see that the estimates have been adhered to. The Parliament also appoints every four years a Parliamentary Ombudsman (Judicial Delegate of Parliament) who submits to it a report, to supervise the observance of the laws.

The Parliament has the right to interrogate the Government. It can impeach a member of the Council of State or the Chancellor of Justice for not having conformed to the law in the discharge of his duties. Trials are conducted at a special court, known as the Court of the Realm, of 13 members, six of whom are elected by Parliament for a term of four years.

The Government

(February 1998)

HEAD OF STATE

President: MARTTI AHTISAARI (elected 6 February 1994 and took office on 1 March 1994).

COUNCIL OF STATE

(Valtioneuvosto)

A coalition of the Social Democratic Party (SDP), National Coalition Party (Kok), Swedish People's Party (SFP), Left-Wing Alliance (V) and Green League (VL), with one independent.

Prime Minister: PAAVO LIPPONEN (SDP).

Deputy Prime Minister and Minister of Finance: SAULI NIINISTÖ (Kok).

Minister of Foreign Affairs: TARJA HALONEN (SDP).

Minister for European Affairs and Foreign Trade: OLE NORRBACK (SFP).

Minister of the Interior: JAN-ERIK ENESTAM (SFP).

Minister for Administrative Affairs: JOUNI BACKMAN (SDP).

Minister of Defence: ANNELI TAINA (Kok).

Minister at the Ministry of Finance: JOUKO SKINNARI (SDP).

Minister of Education: OLLI-PEKKA HEINONEN (Kok).

Minister at the Ministry of Education, responsible for culture, youth, universities and science: CLAES ANDERSSON (V).

Minister of Agriculture and Forestry: KALEVI HEMILÄ (Independent).

Minister of Transport and Communications: MATTI AURA (Kok).

Minister of Trade and Industry: ANTTI KALLIOMÄKI (SDP).

Minister of Social Affairs and Health: SINIKKA MÖNKÄRE (SDP)

Minister at the Ministries of Social Affairs and Health: TERTTU HUTTU-JUNTUNEN (V).

Minister of Justice: KARI HÄKÄMIES (Kok).

Minister of Labour: LIISA JAAKONSAARI (SDP).

Minister of the Environment: PEKKA HAAVISTO (VL).

MINISTRIES

Prime Minister's Office: Aleksanterinkatu 3D, 00170 Helsinki; tel. (09) 1601; fax (09) 1602099.

Ministry of Agriculture and Forestry: Hallituskatu 3A, 00170 Helsinki; tel. (09) 1601; telex 125621; fax (09) 1602190.

Ministry of Defence: Fabianinkatu 2, POB 31, 00130 Helsinki; tel. (09) 16161; fax (09) 653254.

Ministry of Education: Meritullinkatu 10, POB 293, 00171 Helsinki; tel. (09) 134171; telex 122079; fax (09) 1359335; e-mail pia.ekqvist@minedu.fi; internet http://www.minedu.fi.

Ministry of the Environment: POB 399, 00121 Helsinki; tel. (09) 19911; telex 123717; fax (09) 1991499.

Ministry of Finance: Snellmaninkatu 1A, 00170 Helsinki; tel. (09) 1601; telex 123241; fax (09) 1603090.

Ministry of Foreign Affairs: Merikasarmi, POB 176, 00161 Helsinki; tel. (09) 134151; telex 124636.

Ministry of the Interior: Kirkkokatu 12, 00170 Helsinki; tel. (09) 1601; telex 123644; fax (09) 1602927.

Ministry of Justice: Eteläesplanadi 10, POB 1, 00131 Helsinki; tel. (09) 18251; fax (09) 18257730.

Ministry of Labour: POB 524, 00101 Helsinki; tel. (09) 18561; fax (09) 1857950.

Ministry of Social Affairs and Health: Snellmaninkatu 4-6, 00170 Helsinki; tel. (09) 1601; telex 125073; fax (09) 1604716.

Ministry of Trade and Industry: Aleksanterinkatu 4, POB 230, 00171 Helsinki; tel. (09) 1601; fax (09) 1603666.

Ministry of Transport and Communications: Eteläesplanadi 16, POB 235, 00131 Helsinki; tel. (09) 1601; telex 125472; fax (09) 1602596; e-mail info@lm.vn.fi; internet http://www.vn.fi/lm.

President and Legislature

PRESIDENT

Elections of 16 January and 6 February 1994

	Popular vote (%)	
	First Round	Second Round
MARTTI AHTISAARI (SDP)	25.9	53.9
ELISABETH REHN (SFP)	22.0	46.1
PAAVO VÄYRYNEN (Kesk)	19.5	—
RAIMO ILASKIVI (Kok)	15.2	—
Other candidates	17.4	—
Total	100.0	100.0

EDUSKUNTA

(Parliament)

Speaker: RIITTA UOSUKAINEN (Kok).

Secretary-General: SEPPO TIITINEN.

General Election, 19 March 1995

	% of votes	Seats
Finnish Social Democratic Party	28.3	63
Finnish Centre Party	19.9	44
National Coalition Party	17.9	39
Left-Wing Alliance	11.2	22
Green League	6.5	9
Swedish People's Party	5.1	12
Finnish Christian Union	3.0	7
Young Finns	2.8	2
Finnish Rural Party	1.3	1
Ecological Party	0.3	1
Others	3.7	—
Total	100.0	200

Political Organizations

Kansallinen Kokoomus (Kok) (National Coalition Party): Kansakoulukuja 3, 00100 Helsinki; tel. (09) 69381; fax (09) 6943702; f. 1918; moderate conservative political ideology; 50,000 mems; Chair. SAULI NIINISTÖ; Sec.-Gen. MAIJA PERHO; Chair. Parliamentary Group BEN ZYSKOWICZ.

Liberaalinen Kansanpuolue (LKP) (Liberal People's Party): Fredrikinkatu 58A, 00100 Helsinki; tel. (09) 440227; fax (09) 440771; e-mail liberal@pp.iaf.fi; f. 1965 as a coalition of the Finnish People's Party and the Liberal Union; 4,000 mems; Chair. ALTTI MAJAVA; Sec.-Gen. KAARINA TALOLA.

Suomen Keskusta (Kesk) (Finnish Centre Party): Pursimiehenkatu 15, 00150 Helsinki; tel. (09) 172721; fax (09) 653589; f. 1906; a radical centre party founded to promote the interests of the rural population, now a reformist 'green' movement favouring individual enterprise, equality and decentralization; 270,000 mems; Chair. ESKO AHO; Sec.-Gen. PEKKA PERTTULA; Chair. Parliamentary Group AAPO SAARI.

Suomen Kristillinen Liitto (SKL) (Finnish Christian Union): Mannerheimintie 40D, 00100 Helsinki; tel. (09) 58400944; fax (09) 58400940; e-mail merja.erapolku@eduskunta.fi; f. 1958; 16,500 mems; Chair. BJARNE KALLIS; Sec. MILLA KALLIOMAA; Chair. Parliamentary Group JOUKO JÄÄSKELÄINEN.

Suomen Maaseudun Puolue (SMP) (Finnish Rural Party): Hämeentie 157, 00560 Helsinki; tel. (09) 790299; fax (09) 790299; f. 1959; non-socialist programme; represents lower-middle-class elements, small farmers, small enterprises etc.; Chair. RAIMO VISTBACKA; Sec. TIMO SOINI; Chair. Parliamentary Group LEA MÄKIPÄÄ.

Suomen Sosialidemokraattinen Puolue (SDP) (Finnish Social Democratic Party): Saariniemenkatu 6, 00530 Helsinki; tel. (09) 478988; fax (09) 712752; f. 1899; constitutional socialist programme; mainly supported by the urban working and middle classes; 72,000 mems; Chair. PAAVO LIPPONEN; Gen.-Sec. KARI LAITINEN; Chair. Parliamentary Group ERKKI TUOMIOJA.

Svenska folkpartiet (SFP) (Swedish People's Party): Gräsviksgatan 14, POB 282, 00181 Helsinki; tel. (09) 693070; fax (09) 6931968; f. 1906; a liberal party representing the interests of the Swedish-speaking minority; 42,000 mems; Chair. OLE NORRBACK; Sec. PETER HEINSTRÖM; Chair. Parliamentary Group EVA BIAUDET.

Vasemmistoliitto (Left-Wing Alliance): Siltasaarenkatu 6, 7th Floor, 00530 Helsinki; tel. (09) 774741; telex 123837; fax (09) 77474200; f. 1990 as a merger of the Finnish People's Democratic League (f. 1944), the Communist Party of Finland (f. 1918), the Democratic League of Finnish Women, and left-wing groups; Chair. CLAES ANDERSSON; Sec. RALF SUND; Chair. Parliamentary Group ESKO HELLE.

Vihreä Liitto (Green League): Eerikinkatu 27, 00180 Helsinki; tel. (09) 6933877; fax (09) 6933799; e-mail vihreat@vihrealitto.fi; f. 1988; Chair. TUIJA BRAX; Sec. SIRPA KURONEN.

Diplomatic Representation

EMBASSIES IN FINLAND

Argentina: Bulevardi 5A 11, 00120 Helsinki; tel. (09) 607630; telex 122794; fax (09) 646788; Ambassador: HUGO AUGUSTO URTUBEY.

Austria: Keskuskatu 1A, 00100 Helsinki; tel. (09) 171322; fax (09) 665084; austrian.embassy@pp.kolumbus.fi; Ambassador: Dr WENDELIN ETTMAYER.

Belgium: Kalliolinnantie 5, 00140 Helsinki; tel. (09) 170412; fax (09) 628842; Ambassador: E. DE WILDE.

Brazil: Itäinen puistotic 4B, 00140 Helsinki; tel. (09) 177922; fax (09) 650084; Ambassador: BERNARDO DE AZEVEDO BRITO.

Bulgaria: Kuusisaarentie 2B, 00340 Helsinki; tel. (09) 4584055; fax (09) 4584550; Ambassador: STOYAN DENTSHEV.

Canada: Pohjoisesplanadi 25B, 00100 Helsinki; tel. (09) 171141; telex 121363; fax (09) 601060; Ambassador: ISABELLE MASSIP.

Chile: Erottajankatu 11, 00130 Helsinki; tel. (09) 611699; telex 122119; fax (09) 611377; Ambassador: JAIME PARDO HUERTA.

China, People's Republic: Vanha Kelkkamäki 9–11, 00570 Helsinki; tel. (09) 6848371; fax (09) 6849551; Ambassador: ZHENG JINJIONG.

Colombia: Ratakatu 1B A1, 00120 Helsinki; tel. (09) 6802799; fax (09) 6802180; Chargé d'affaires a.i.: JOSÉ NEIRA-REY.

Czech Republic: Armfeltintie 14, 00150 Helsinki; tel. (09) 171169; fax (09) 630655; Ambassador: RADEK PECH.

Denmark: Keskuskatu 1A, POB 1042, 00101 Helsinki; tel. (09) 171511; telex 124782; fax (09) 171741; Ambassador: MARIE-LOUISE OVERVAD.

Egypt: Munkkiniemen puistotie 25, 00330 Helsinki; tel. (09) 4582299; Ambassador: ZEINAB SOHEIM.

Estonia: Itäinen puistotie 10, 00140 Helsinki; tel. (09) 6220260; fax (09) 62202610; e-mail sekretar@estemb.fi; Ambassador: MATI VAARMANN.

France: Itäinen puistotie 13, 00140 Helsinki; tel. (09) 171521; fax (09) 174440; Ambassador: GILLES D'HUMIÈRES.

Germany: Krogiuksentie 4B, 00340 Helsinki; tel. (09) 4582355; telex 124568; fax (09) 4582283; Ambassador: BERNHARD Freiherr VON PFETLEN-ARNBACH.

Greece: Maneesikatu 2A 4, 00170 Helsinki; tel. (09) 2781100; fax (09) 2781200; Ambassador: STELIO VALSAMAS-RHALLIS.

Holy See: Bulevardi 5 as. 12, 00120 Helsinki (Apostolic Nunciature); tel. (09) 644664; Apostolic Nuncio: Most Rev. GIOVANNI CEIRANO, Titular Archbishop of Tagase (resident in Denmark).

Hungary: Kuusisaarenkuja 6, 00340 Helsinki; tel. (09) 484144; fax (09) 480497; Ambassador: GYÖRGY KRAUSZ.

India: Satamakatu 2A 8, 00160 Helsinki; tel. (09) 608927; Ambassador: PRITHVI RAJ SOOD.

Indonesia: Kuusisaarentie 3, 00340 Helsinki; tel. (09) 4582100; telex 123240; fax (09) 4582882; Ambassador: I GUSTI NGURAH GEDHE.

Iran: Bertel Jungin tie 4, 00570 Helsinki; tel. (09) 6847133; Ambassador: SEYED ALI MAHMOUDI.

Iraq: Lars Sonckin tie 2, 00570 Helsinki; tel. (09) 6849177; fax (09) 6848977; Chargé d'affaires a.i.: NABIL ABDULLAH HUSSEIN AL-JANABI.

Ireland: Erottajankatu 7A, 00130 Helsinki; tel. (09) 646006; fax (09) 646022; Ambassador: DÁITHÍ O'CEALLAIGH.

Israel: Vironkatu 5A, 00170 Helsinki; tel. (09) 1356177; fax (09) 1356959; Ambassador: ALI ADEEB YIHYIA.

Italy: Itäinen puistotie 4, 00140 Helsinki; tel. (09) 175144; fax (09) 175976; Ambassador: MASSIMO MACCHIA.

Japan: Eteläranta 8, 00130 Helsinki; tel. (09) 633011; fax (09) 633012; Ambassador: ICHIRO OTAKA.

Korea, Democratic People's Republic: Kulosaaren puistotie 32, 00570 Helsinki; tel. (09) 6848195; fax (09) 6848995; Ambassador: KIM PHYONG IL.

Korea, Republic: Annankatu 32, 00100 Helsinki; tel. (09) 6866230; fax (09) 68662355; Ambassador: IN-HO LEE.

Latvia: Armfeltintie 10, 00150 Helsinki; tel. (09) 4764720; fax (09) 47647288; e-mail latemb.fin@latemb.inex.fi; Ambassador: ANNA ŽIGURE.

Lithuania: Rauhankatu 13A, 00170 Helsinki; tel. (09) 608210; fax (09) 608220; Ambassador: NERIS GERMANAS.

Mexico: Simonkatu 12A, 00100 Helsinki; tel. (09) 6949400; fax (09) 6949411; e-mail mexican.embassy@co.inex.fi; Ambassador: JORGE E. DOMÍNGUEZ.

Netherlands: Raatimiehenkatu 2A 7, 00140 Helsinki; tel. (09) 661737; fax (09) 654734; Ambassador: B. DE BRUYN OUBOTER.

Norway: Rehbinderintie 17, 00150 Helsinki; tel. (09) 171234; fax (09) 657807; Ambassador: DAGFINN STENSETH.

Peru: Annankatu 31-33C 44, 00100 Helsinki; tel. (09) 6933681; fax (09) 6933682; Chargé d'affaires a.i.: JOSE LUIS SALINAS.

Poland: Armas Lindgrenin tie 21, 00570 Helsinki; tel. (09) 6848077; fax (09) 6847477; Ambassador: JÓZEF WIEJACZ.

Portugal: Itäinen puistotie 11B, 00140 Helsinki; tel. (09) 171717; telex 121877; fax (09) 663550; Ambassador: MANUEL MOREIRA DE ANDRADE.

Romania: Stenbäckinkatu 24, 00250 Helsinki; tel. (09) 2413624; telex 121041; fax (09) 2413272; Ambassador: FLORICA IONEA.

Russia: Tehtaankatu 1B, 00140 Helsinki; tel. (09) 661876; fax (09) 661006; Ambassador: YURII S. DERYABIN.

Slovakia: Annankatu 25, 00100 Helsinki; tel. (09) 70018460; fax (09) 640105; e-mail skemb.hels@sci.fi; Chargé d'affaires a.i.: VLADIMÍR HALGAŠ.

South Africa: Rahapajankatu 1A 5, 00160 Helsinki; tel. (09) 658288; fax (09) 658365; Ambassador: Dr CHRIS STREETER.

Spain: Kalliolinnantie 6, 00140 Helsinki; tel. (09) 170505; telex 122193; fax (09) 660110; Ambassador: VICENTE BLASCO.

Sweden: Pohjoisesplanadi 7B, 00170 Helsinki; tel. (09) 651255; telex 124538; fax (09) 655285; Ambassador: MATS BERGQUIST.

Switzerland: Uudenmaankatu 16A, 00120 Helsinki; tel. (09) 649422; fax (09) 649040; Ambassador: SVEN MEILI.

Turkey: Puistokatu 1B A 3, 00140 Helsinki; tel. (09) 655755; telex 122632; fax (09) 655011; Ambassador: ONUR GÖKÇE.

Ukraine: Vähäniityntie 9, 00570 Helsinki; tel. (09) 2289000; fax (09) 2289001; Ambassador: KOSTIATYN MASYK.

United Kingdom: Itäinen puistotie 17, 00140 Helsinki; tel. (09) 22865100; fax (09) 22865262; Ambassador: GAVIN HEWITT.

USA: Itäinen puistotie 14A, 00140 Helsinki; tel. (09) 171931; telex 121644; fax (09) 174681; Ambassador: DEREK N. SHEARER.

Venezuela: Bulevardi 1A, POB 285, 00101 Helsinki; tel. (09) 641522; fax (09) 640971; e-mail embavene.finland@dlc.fi; Ambassador: LISÁN STRÉDEL BALLIACHE.

Yugoslavia: Kulosaarentie 36, 00570 Helsinki; tel. (09) 6848522; telex 122099; fax (09) 6848783; Chargé d'affaires a.i.: GRADIMIR GAJIĆ.

Judicial System

The administration of justice is independent of the Government and judges can be removed only by judicial sentence.

SUPREME COURT

Korkein oikeus/Högsta domstolen: Pohjoisesplanadi 3, POB 301, 00171 Helsinki; tel. (09) 12381; fax (09) 1238354; consists of a President and 20 Justices appointed by the President of the Republic. Final court appeal in civil and criminal cases, supervises judges and executive authorities.

President: OLAVI HEINONEN.

SUPREME ADMINISTRATIVE COURT

Korkeinhallinto-oikeus/Högstaförvaltningsdomstolen: Unioninkatu 16, POB 180, 00131 Helsinki; tel. (09) 18531; fax (09) 1853382; consists of a President and 20 Justices appointed by the President of the Republic. Highest tribunal for appeals in administrative cases.

President: PEKKA HALLBERG.

COURTS OF APPEAL

There are Courts of Appeal at Turku, Vaasa, Kuopio, Helsinki, Kouvola, and Rovaniemi, consisting of a President and an appropriate number of members.

DISTRICT COURTS

Courts of first instance for almost all suits. Appeals lie to the Court of Appeal, and then to the Supreme Court. The composition of the District Court is determined by the type of case to be heard. Civil cases and 'ordinary' criminal cases can be considered by one judge. Other criminal cases and family law cases are heard by a judge and a panel of three lay judges (jurors). Other civil cases are heard by three legally-qualified judges.

CHANCELLOR OF JUSTICE

The Oikeuskansleri is responsible for seeing that authorities and officials comply with the law. He is the chief public prosecutor, and acts as counsel for the Government.

Chancellor of Justice: JORMA S. AALTO.

PARLIAMENTARY SOLICITOR-GENERAL

The Eduskunnan Oikeusasiamies is the Finnish Ombudsman appointed by Parliament to supervise the observance of the law.

Parliamentary Solicitor-General: LAURI LEHTIMAJA.

Religion

CHRISTIANITY

Suomen ekumeeninen neuvosto/Ekumeniska Rådet i Finland (Finnish Ecumenical Council): Luotsikatu 1A, POB 185, 00161 Helsinki; tel. (09) 18021; fax (09) 174313; e-mail sen@pp.kolumbus.fi; f. 1917; 11 mem. churches; Pres. Archbishop JOHANNES (Archbishop of Karelia and All Finland, Orthodox Church of Finland); Gen. Sec. Rev. JAN EDSTRÖM.

National Churches

Suomen Evankelisluterilainen Kirkko (Evangelical Lutheran Church of Finland): Dept for International Relations, Satamakatu 11, POB 185, 00161 Helsinki; tel. (09) 18021; fax (09) 1802230; about 85.4% of the population are adherents; Archbishop Dr JOHN VIKSTRÖM.

Suomen Ortodoksinen Kirkko (Orthodox Church of Finland): Karjalankatu 1, 70110 Kuopio; tel. (017) 2872230; fax (017) 2872231; e-mail archbishop@ort.fi; 57,257 mems; Leader JOHANNES, Archbishop of Karelia and All Finland.

Other Churches

Anglican Church in Finland: Mannerheimintie 19A 7, 00250 Helsinki; tel. (09) 490424; fax (09) 447987; chaplaincy founded 1921; part of diocese of Gibraltar in Europe; 122 mems.

Finlands Svenska Baptistmission (Baptists, Swedish-speaking): Rådhusgatan 44A, 65100 Vaasa; tel. (06) 3178559; fax (06) 3178550; 1,461 mems.

Jehovan Todistajat (Jehovah's Witnesses): Puutarhatie 60, 01300 Vantaa; tel. (09) 825885; fax (09) 82588285; 19,631 mems.

Katolinen kirkko Suomessa (Roman Catholic Church in Finland): Rehbinderintie 21, 00150 Helsinki; tel. (09) 637907; fax (09) 639820; e-mail katpiispa@helsink.fi; Finland comprises the single diocese of Helsinki, directly responsible to the Holy See; 6,742 mems (Jan. 1997); Bishop of Helsinki PAUL M. VERSCHUREN; Vicar-Gen. Rev. JOHANNES AARTS.

Myöhempien Aikojen Pyhien Jeesuksen Kristuksen Kirkko (Church of Jesus Christ of Latter-day Saints—Mormon): Neitsytpolku 3A, 00140 Helsinki; tel. (09) 177311; 3,101 mems.

Suomen Adventtikirkko (Seventh-day Adventist Church in Finland): POB 94, 33101 Tampere; tel. (03) 3600866; fax (03) 3600454; e-mail advent@sdafin.org; f. 1894; 5,842 mems; Pres. PEKKA POHJOLA; Sec. JOEL NIININEN.

Suomen Baptistiyhdyskunta (Baptists, Finnish-speaking): Kissanmaankatu 19, 33530 Tampere; tel. (03) 2530901; fax (03) 2530913; e-mail kharis@sci.fi; 1,821 mems; Pres. Rev. JORMA LEMPINEN.

Suomen Vapaakirkko (Evangelical Free Church of Finland): POB 198, 13101 Hämeenlinna; tel. (03) 6445150; fax (03) 6122153; f. 1923; 13,849 mems; Pres. Rev. JORMA KUUSINEN.

Svenska Kyrkan i Finland (Church of Sweden in Finland): Minervagatan 6, 00100 Helsinki; tel. (09) 443831; fax (09) 4546059; f. 1919; 1,500 mems; Rector Dr JARL JERGMAR.

United Methodist Church in Northern Europe: Vänrikki Stoolinkatu 6, 00100 Helsinki; tel. (09) 444566; fax (09) 444074; Bishop HANS VÄXBY.

Finlands svenska metodistkyrka (United Methodist Church in Finland—Swedish-speaking): Apollonkatu 5, 00100 Helsinki; tel. (09) 449874; fax (09) 406098; 1,000 mems; District Superintendants Rev. BJÖRN ELFVING, Rev. GÖSTA SÖDERSTRÖM.

Suomen Metodistikirkko (United Methodist Church—Finnish-speaking): Punavuorenkatu 2, 00120 Helsinki; tel. (09) 628135; 776 mems; District Superintendant Rev. TAPANI RAJAMAA.

The Salvation Army is also active in the country.

BAHÁ'Í FAITH

Suomen Baha'i yhdyskunta (Bahá'í Community of Finland): POB 423, 00101 Helsinki; tel. (09) 790875; fax (09) 790058; 460 mems.

JUDAISM

Helsingin Juutalainen Seurakunta (Jewish Community of Helsinki): Synagogue and Community Centre, Malminkatu 26, 00100 Helsinki; tel. (09) 6941302; fax (09) 6948916; e-mail helsinki .jc@hjc.pp.fi; 1,100 mems; Pres. GIDEON BOLOTOWSKY; Exec. Dir DAN KANTOR.

ISLAM

Suomen Islamilainen Yhdyskunta (Islamic Community of Finland): POB 87, 00101 Helsinki; tel. (09) 3512190; fax (09) 6121156; 936 mems; Imam ENVER YILDIRIM.

The Press

In 1995 there were 223 daily newspapers in Finland (including 26 printed seven days a week), with a total circulation of some 3.6m. A number of dailies are printed in Swedish. The most popular daily papers are *Helsingin Sanomat, Aamulehti, Turun Sanomat* and *Ilta-Sanomat*. Most respected for its standard of news coverage and commentary is *Helsingin Sanomat,* an independent paper.

In 1996 there were about 2,500 periodicals. The principal 'consumer' periodicals, in terms of circulation, are the weekly family magazines *Apu* and *Seura*, the children's weekly *Aku Ankka*, and the monthlies *Kotivinkki* (for women) and *Valitut Palat* (Reader's Digest). A larger circulation is enjoyed by 'customer' magazines, such as *Pirkka* (distributed free to retail customers). Prominent business and management magazines include *Akava* and *Kunta ja me*.

PRINCIPAL DAILIES

Helsinki

Demari: Paasivuorenkatu 3, 00530 Helsinki; tel. (09) 701041; telex 124433; fax (09) 7010567; e-mail toimitus@demari.inet.fi; f. 1918; chief organ of the Social Democratic Party; Editor-in-Chief KARI AROLA; circ. 31,700.

Helsingin Sanomat: Ludviginkatu 2–10, POB 975, 00101 Helsinki; tel. (09) 1221; fax (09) 605709; f. 1889; independent; Publr SEPPO KIEVARI; Editor-in-Chief JANNE VIRKKUNEN; circ. 472,056 weekdays, 555,118 Sunday.

Hufvudstadsbladet: Mannerheimvägen 18, POB 217, 00101 Helsinki; tel. (09) 12531; fax (09) 642930; f. 1864; Swedish language; independent; Editor RAFAEL PARO; circ. 59,615 weekdays, 62,015 Sunday.

Iltalehti: POB 372, 00101 Helsinki; tel. (09) 507721; telex 124898; fax (09) 177313; f. 1981; independent; Editor-in-Chief PEKKA KARHUVAARA; circ. 101,980 weekdays, 129,443 Saturday.

Ilta-Sanomat: Korkeavuorenkatu 34, POB 375, 00101 Helsinki; tel. (09) 1221; telex 124897; fax (09) 1223419; f. 1932; afternoon; independent; Editor-in-Chief VESA-PEKKA KOLJONEN; circ. 218,185 weekdays, 258,815 weekend.

Kansan Uutiset: POB 43, 00501 Helsinki; tel. (09) 75881; telex 12663; f. 1957; organ of the Left-Wing Alliance; Editor YRJÖ RAUTIO; circ. 42,415.

Kauppalehti (The Commercial Daily): POB 189, 00101 Helsinki; tel. (09) 50781; telex 125827; f. 1898; morning; Editor-in-Chief LAURI HELVE; circ. 78,723.

Maaseudun Tulevaisuus: Simonkatu 6, 00100 Helsinki; tel. (09) 131151; fax (09) 6944766; circ. 105,523.

Hämeenlinna

Hämeen Sanomat: Vanajantie 7, POB 530, 13111 Hämeenlinna; tel. (03) 61511; f. 1879; independent; Man. ARTO KAJANTO; Editor-in-Chief TERTTU HÄKKINEN; circ. 30,638.

Joensuu

Karjalainen: Kosti Aaltosentie 9, POB 99, 80141 Joensuu; tel. (13) 1551; telex 46126; fax (13) 155363; e-mail toimitus@karjalainen.fi; f. 1874; independent; Editor PEKKA SITARI; circ. 49,000.

Jyväskylä

Keskisuomalainen: Aholaidantie 3, POB 159, 40101 Jyväskylä; tel. (014) 622000; fax (014) 622272; f. 1871; Editor ERKKI LAATIKAINEN; circ. 79,278.

Kajaani

Kainuun Sanomat: Viestitie 2, POB 150, 87101 Kajaani; tel. (08) 61661; fax (08) 623013; e-mail toimitus@kainuunsanomat.fi; f. 1918; independent; circ. 24,200.

Kemi

Pohjolan Sanomat: POB 17, 94101 Kemi; tel. 2911; telex 3643; f. 1915; organ of the Finnish Centre Party; Editors MATTI LAMMI, REIJO ALATÖRMÄNEN; circ. 35,538.

Kokkola

Keskipohjanmaa: Kosila, POB 45, 67101 Kokkola; tel. 8272000; fax 8225039; f. 1917; organ of the Finnish Centre Party; Editor LASSI JAAKKOLA; circ. 31,241.

Kotka

Kymen Sanomat: POB 27, 48101 Kotka; tel. (05) 2100111; fax (05) 216377; f. 1902; independent; Editor JUKKA VEHKASALO; circ. 29,283.

Lahti

Etelä-Suomen Sanomat: Ilmarisentie 7, POB 80, 15101 Lahti; tel. 75751; fax 575467; f. 1900; independent; Dir JAAKKO UKKONEN; Editors-in-Chief KAUKO MÄENPÄÄ, PENTTI VUORIO; circ. 62,279.

Lappeenranta

Etelä-Saimaa: POB 3, 53501 Lappeenranta; tel. 5591; fax 559209; f. 1885; independent; Man. Dir ESA LAVANDER; Editor KARI VÄISÄNEN; circ. 36,399.

Mikkeli

Länsi-Savo: POB 310, 50101 Mikkeli; tel.3501; fax 350337; Editor ILKKA JUVA; circ. 28,018.

Oulu

Kaleva: POB 70, 90101 Oulu; tel. (08) 5377111; telex 32112; fax (08) 5377195; f. 1899; Liberal independent; Editor TEUVO MÄLLINEN; circ. 85,222.

Pori

Satakunnan Kansa: POB 58, 28101 Pori; tel. 6328111; fax 6328392; f. 1873; independent; Editor ERKKI TEIKARI; circ. 58,086.

Rauma

Länsi-Suomi: Kaivopuistontie 1, 26100 Rauma; tel. 83361; fax 8240959; f. 1905; independent; circ. 18,067.

Rovaniemi

Lapin Kansa: Veitikantie 2, 96100 Rovaniemi; tel. (016) 320011; fax (016) 3200305; f. 1928; independent; Editor HEIKKI TUOMI-NIKULA; circ. 37,578.

Salo

Salon Seudun Sanomat: Örninkatu 14, POB 117, 24101 Salo; tel. (02) 77021; Editor JARMO VÄHÄSILTA; circ. 20,900.

Savonlinna

Itä-Savo: POB 35, 57231 Savonlinna; tel. 29171; telex 5611; organ of the Finnish Centre Party; Editor ESKO SUIKKANEN; circ. 23,502.

Seinäjoki

Ilkka: POB 60, Kouluk, 60101 Seinäjoki; tel. 4186555; fax 4186500; f. 1906; organ of the Finnish Centre Party; Editor KARI HOKKANEN; circ. 56,340.

Tampere

Aamulehti: POB 327, 33101 Tampere; tel. (03) 2666111; fax (03) 2666259; f. 1881; Editors SAKARI KUMPULAINEN, HANNU OLKINUORA; circ. 129,658 weekdays, 137,270 Sunday.

Turku

Turun Sanomat: Kauppiaskatu 5, 20100 Turku; tel. (02) 2693311; telex 62213; fax (02) 2693274; f. 1904; independent; Man. Dir KEIJO KETONEN; Editor ARI VALJAKKA; circ. 113,284, weekdays, 124,469 Sunday.

Tuusula

Keski-Uusimaa: Klaavolantie 5, 04300 Tuusula; tel. (09) 273000; independent; Editor-in-Chief REIJO HIRVONEN; circ. 24,090.

Vaasa

Pohjalainen: Pitkäkatu 37, POB 37, 65101 Vaasa; tel. (06) 3249111; fax (06) 3249352; e-mail kari.manty@pohjalainen.fi; f. 1903; independent; Editor KARI MANTY; circ. 35,500.

Vasabladet: Sandögatan 6, POB 52, 65101 Vaasa; tel. (06) 3260211; fax (06) 3129003; f. 1856; Swedish language; Liberal independent; Editor DENNIS RUNDT; circ. 26,700.

PRINCIPAL PERIODICALS

7 päivää: POB 124, 00151 Helsinki; tel. (09) 177777; fax (09) 177477; weekly; television and radio; circ. 127,810.

Ahjo: POB 107, 00531 Helsinki; tel. (09) 77071; fax (09) 7707400; e-mail ahjo@metalliliitto.fi; fortnightly; for metal industry employees; Editor-in-Chief HEIKKI PISKONEN; circ. 164,000.

Aku Ankka (Donald Duck): POB 40, 00040 Helsinki; tel. (09) 1201; fax (09) 1205569; f. 1951; weekly; children's; Editor-in-Chief MARKKU KIVEKÄS; circ. 283,334.

Apu: Hitsaajankatu 10, 00081 Helsinki; tel. (09) 75961; fax (09) 781911; f. 1933; weekly; family journal; Editor-in-Chief MARKKU VEIJALAINEN; circ. 250,380.

Avotakka: Hitsaajankatu 10, 00081 Helsinki; tel. (09) 75961; fax (09) 7591268; e-mail avotakka@a-lehdet.fi; monthly; interior decorating; Editor ANJA TUOMI; circ. 72,894.

Birka: Kanavakatu 3B, 00160 Helsinki; tel. (09) 1053010; fax (09) 105336235; quarterly; trade; in Swedish; circ. 76,322.

Diabetes: Kirjoniementie 15, 33680 Tampere; tel. (03) 2860111; fax (03) 3600462; e-mail lehdat@diabetes.fi; f. 1949; monthly; health; circ. 51,415.

Eeva: Hitsaajankatu 10, 00081 Helsinki; tel. (09) 75961; fax (09) 786858; f. 1933; monthly; women's; Editor-in-Chief MARJUT JOUSI; circ. 94,065.

Elbladet: POB 184, 00131 Helsinki; tel. (09) 6861676; fax (09) 68616786; e-mail ari.vesa@energia.fi; f. 1939; quarterly; Editor-in-Chief ARI J. VESA; circ. 101,575.

Erä: Maistraatinportti 1, 00240 Helsinki; tel. (09) 15661; fax (09) 15666206; era@kuvalehdet.fi; monthly; fishing and outdoor leisure; Editor SEPPO SUURONEN; circ. 51,290.

et-lehti: POB 100, 00040 Helsinki; tel. (09) 1201; fax (09) 1205428; monthly; over 50s magazine; Editor-in-Chief KAISA LARMELA; circ. 240,233.

Gloria: POB 107, 00381 Helsinki; tel. (09) 1201; fax (09) 1205427; monthly; women's; circ. 60,397.

Hippo: POB 480, 00101 Helsinki; tel. (09) 4041; fax (09) 4042213; 5 a year; Editor-in-Chief PETE-VEIKKO KAHARI; circ. 188,141.

Hymy: Maistraatinportti 1, 00240 Helsinki; tel. (09) 15661; fax (09) 15666206; monthly; family journal; Editor ESKO TULUSTO; circ. 94,527.

Hyvä Terveys: POB 100, 00040 Helsinki; tel. (09) 1201; fax (09) 1205456; e-mail hyva.terveys@helsinkimedia.fi; 10 a year; health; Editor-in-Chief JALI RUUSKANEN; circ. 61,248.

IT-Invaliditydö: Kumpulantie 1A, 00520 Helsinki; tel. (09) 613191; fax (09) 1461443; 11 a year; for handicapped people; Editor-in-Chief VOITTO KORHONEN; circ. 60,162.

Kaks' Plus: Maistraatinportti 1, 00240 Helsinki; tel. (09) 1566591; fax (09) 1566507; monthly; for families with young children; Editor MINNA JUTI; circ. 50,611.

Katso: Hitsaajankatu 7/5, 00081 Helsinki; tel. (09) 75961; telex 124732; fax (09) 7596342; f. 1960; weekly; TV, radio, film and video; Editor-in-Chief OONA TUOMI; circ. 60,450.

Kauneus ja terveys: Hitsaajankatu 10, 00081 Helsinki; tel. (09) 75961; fax (09) 786858; monthly; health and beauty; circ. 61,647.

Kirkko ja kaupunki: POB 137, 00201 Helsinki; tel. (09) 613021; fax (09) 61302342; weekly; church and community; Editor-in-Chief SEPPO SIMOLA; circ. 197,237.

Kodin Kuvalehti: POB 100, 00040 Helsinki; tel. (09) 1201; fax (09) 1205468; e-mail kodin.kuvalehti@helsinkimedia.fi; fortnightly; family magazine; Editor LEENA KARO; circ. 180,068.

Kotilääkäri: Maistraatinportti 1, 00240 Helsinki; tel. (09) 15661; telex 122772; fax (09) 15661; f. 1889; monthly; health and beauty; Editor-in-Chief TARJA HURME; circ. 58,074.

Kotiliesi: Maistraatinportti 1, 00240 Helsinki; tel. (09) 15661; fax (09) 147724; f. 1922; fortnightly; women's; Editor-in-Chief ELINA SIMONEN-HYVÄRINEN; circ. 200,474.

Kotivinkki: Kalevankatu 56, 00180 Helsinki; tel. (09) 773951; fax (09) 77395399; monthly; women's; Editor-in-Chief ANNELI MYLLER; circ. 207,550.

Me Naiset: POB 100, 00040 Helsinki; tel. (09) 1201; fax (09) 1205414; f. 1952; weekly; women's; Editor ULLA-MAIJA PAAVILAINEN; circ. 115,000.

Metsälehti: Soidink 4, 00700 Helsinki; tel. (09) 1562333; fax (09) 1562335; e-mail paavo.seppanen@metsalehti.mailnet.fi; internet http://www.metsalehti.fi; f. 1933; fortnightly; forestry; Editor PAAVO SEPPÄNEN; circ. 41,355.

MikroPC: POB 920, 00101 Helsinki; tel. (09) 148801; fax (09) 6856631; monthly; computers; circ. 50,574.

Muoti & Kauneus: Maistraatinportti 1, 00240 Helsinki; tel. (09) 15661; 6 a year; beauty, fashion; Editor ANJA SCHONE (acting); circ. 54,790.

Nykyposti: Maistraatinportti 1, 00240 Helsinki; tel. (09) 15661; fax (09) 144595; f. 1977; monthly; family journal; Editor JAANA LAUKKANEN; circ. 107,375.

Partio: Kylänvanhimmantie 29, 00640 Helsinki; tel. (09) 25331133; fax (09) 25331160; e-mail hanne.partanen@sp.partio.fi; 6 a year; the Scout movement; circ. 57,188.

Pellervo: POB 77, 00101 Helsinki; tel. (09) 4767501; fax (09) 6948945; e-mail toimisto@pellervo.inet.fi; f. 1899; monthly; agricultural and co-operative journal; organ of the Central Union of Agricultural Co-operative Societies; Editor-in-Chief KAISU RÄSÄNEN; circ. 45,712.

Pirkka: Kanavakatu 3B, 00160 Helsinki; tel. (09) 1053010; fax (09) 105336235; 10 a year; Swedish; trade; Editor-in-Chief KAISA PEUTERE; circ. 2,278,939.

Reserviläinen: Döbelninkatu 2, 00260 Helsinki; tel. (09) 40562018; fax (09) 499875; monthly; military; circ. 64,593.

Sähköviesti: POB 184, 00131 Helsinki; tel. (09) 68616716; fax (09) 68616786; e-mail ari.vesa@energia.fi; f. 1939; quarterly; publ. by Asscn of Finnish Electric Utilities; Editor-in-Chief ARI J. VESA; circ. 1,400,000.

Sampovisio: POB 2, 00040 Helsinki; tel. (09) 1205964; fax (09) 1205999; 6 a year; business, finance; circ. 65,000.

Seura: Maistraatinportti 1, 00240 Helsinki; tel. (09) 15661; telex 121364; fax (09) 1496472; f. 1934; weekly; family journal; Editor-in-Chief JOUNI FLINKKILÄ; circ. 268,553.

STTK—lehti: POB 248, 00171 Helsinki; tel. (09) 131521; fax (09) 652367; 11 a year; organ of Finnish Confederation of Salaried Employees; Editor-in-Chief MATTI HYNYNEN; circ. 40,000.

Suomen Kuvalehti: Maistraatinportti 1, 00015 Yhtyneet Kuvalehdet; tel. (09) 15661; telex 121364; fax (09) 144076; e-mail suomen.-kuvalehti@kuvalehdet.fi; f. 1916; weekly; illustrated news; Editor-in-Chief TAPANI RUOKANEN; circ. 98,465.

Suosikki: Maistraatinportti 1, 00240 Helsinki; tel. (09) 15661; telex 122722; fax (09) 145595; monthly; pop music; Editor-in-Chief JYRKI HÄMÄLÄINEN; circ. 77,445.

Suuri Käsityölehti: POB 100, 00040 Helsinki; tel. (09) 1201; telex 125848; fax (09) 1205428; f. 1974; monthly; needlework, knitting and dress-making magazine; Editor KRISTINA TÖTTERMAN; circ. 126,858.

Talouselämä: Malminkatu 30, POB 920, 00101 Helsinki; tel. (09) 148801; fax (09) 6856601; e-mail te@talentum.fi; 42 a year; economy, administration; Man. Dir HARRI ROSCHIER; Editor-in-Chief PERTTI MONTO; circ. 60,742.

Tekniikan Maailma: Maistraatinportti 1, 00240 Helsinki; tel. (09) 15661; telex 121364; fax (09) 15666313; e-mail tekniikan.maailma@kuvalehdet.fi; f. 1953; 20 a year; technical review; Editor-in-Chief MAURI J. SALO; circ. 124,847.

Trendi: Vilhovuorenkatu 12B, 00580 Helsinki; tel. (09) 773951; fax (09) 77395399; 6 a year; fashion; circ. 60,053.

Tuulilasi: Hitsaajankatu 7, 00081 Helsinki; tel. (09) 75961; fax (09) 787311; internet http://www.a-lehdet.fi/tuulilasi; monthly; motoring; Editor-in-Chief MATTI SAARI; circ. 78,815.

Työ Terveys Turvallisuus: Topeliuksenkatu 41A, 00250 Helsinki; tel. (09) 4747478; fax (09) 2414634; f. 1971; 14 a year; occupational safety and health; Editor-in-Chief MATTI TAPIAINEN; circ. 70,356.

Valitut Palat: POB 46, 00441 Helsinki; tel. (09) 503441; fax (09) 5034499; monthly; Finnish Reader's Digest; Editor-in-Chief TOM LUNDBERG; circ. 354,103.

Voi Hyvin: Hitsaajankatu 7, 000811 Helsinki; tel. (09) 75961; fax (09) 786858; 6 a year; health; circ. 64,675.

Yhteishyvä: POB 171, 00511 Helsinki; tel. (09) 1881; fax (09) 1882626; f. 1905; monthly; free to members of co-operative shops; Editor-in-Chief PENTTI TÖRMÄLÄ; circ. 492,074.

Ykköskl ubi: POB 140, 02631 Espoo; tel. (09) 133988; fax (09) 1339385; quarterly; banking; Editor-in-Chief RAUNO NIINIMÄKI; circ. 19,200.

NEWS AGENCIES

Oy Suomen Tietotoimisto-Finska Notisbyrån Ab (STTFNB): Albertinkatu 33, POB 550, 00101 Helsinki; tel. (09) 695811; telex 124534; fax (09) 69581203; f. 1887; eight provincial branches; independent national agency distributing domestic and international news in Finnish and Swedish; Chair. KEIJO KETONEN; Gen. Man. and Editor-in-Chief PER-ERIK LÖNNFORS.

Foreign Bureaux

Agence France-Presse (AFP) (France): c/o STT-FNB, POB 550, 00101 Helsinki; tel. (09) 695811; telex 124534; fax (09) 69581218.

Agenzia Nazionale Stampa Associata (ANSA) (Italy): JSO Roobertinkatu 46 B 31, 00120 Helsinki; tel. (09) 639799; Agent MATTI BROTHERUS.

Associated Press (AP) (USA): Etelaesplanadi 22A, 00130 Helsinki; tel. (09) 6802394; fax (09) 6802310; Correspondent MATTI HUUHTANEN.

Informatsionnoye Telegrafnoye Agentstvo Rossii—Telegrafnoye Agentstvo Suverennykh Stran (ITAR—TASS) (Russia): Ratakatu 1A B 10, 00120 Helsinki; tel. (09) 601877; fax (09) 601151; Correspondent VLADIMIR MOSTOVETS.

Inter Press Service (IPS) (Italy): Suomen IPS, Käenkuja 3-5N, 00500 Helsinki; tel. (09) 7536954; fax (09) 7536964; Editor MILLA SUNDSTRÖM.

Reuters (UK): Yrjönkatu 23 A 7, POB 550, 00101 Helsinki; tel. (09) 680501; fax (09) 601637; Correspondent FREDRIK DAHL.

Rossiyskoye Informatsionnoye Agentstvo—Novosti (RIA—Novosti) (Russia): Lönnrotinkatu 25A, 00180 Helsinki; tel. (09) 6820580; telex 124662; fax (09) 6927002; Dir YEVGENII ZHELEZNOV; Correspondents RUDOLF HILTUNEN, LEONID LAAKSO.

Xinhua (New China) News Agency (People's Republic of China): Hopeasalmentie 14, 00570 Helsinki; tel. (09) 6847587; fax (09) 6848629; Correspondent ZHENG HUANGING.

PRESS ASSOCIATIONS

Aikakauslehtien Liitto (Periodical Publishers' Association): Lönnrotinkatu 11, 00120 Helsinki; tel. (09) 22877280; fax (09) 603478; f. 1946; aims to further the interests of publishers of magazines and periodicals, to encourage co-operation between publishers, and to improve standards; Man. Dir MATTI AHTOMIES.

Suomen Journalistiliitto-Finlands Journalistförbund r.y. (Union of Journalists): Hietalahdenkatu 2B22, 00180 Helsinki; tel. (09) 6122330; telex 121394; fax (09) 644120; f. 1921; 10,839 mems; Pres. PEKKA LAINE; Sec.-Gen. EILA HYPPÖNEN.

Sanomalehtien Liitto—Tidningarnas Förbund (Finnish Newspapers Association): Lönnrotinkatu 11, 00120 Helsinki; tel. (09) 22877300; telex 123990; fax (09) 607989; e-mail info@sanomalehdet.fi; f. 1908; negotiates newsprint prices, postal rates; represents the press in relations with Government and advertisers; undertakes technical research; promotes newspaper advertising; 212 mems; Man. Dir VEIKKO LÖYTTYNIEMI.

Publishers

Art House Oy: Bulevardi 19C, 00120 Helsinki; tel. (09) 6932727; fax (09) 6949028; f. 1975; Finnish and foreign fiction, non-fiction, popular science, horror, fantasy, science fiction, detective fiction; Publr PAAVO HAAVIKKO.

Gummerus Kustannus Oy: Erottajankatu 5C, POB 2, 00131 Helsinki; tel. (09) 584301; fax (09) 58430200; f. 1872; fiction, non-fiction, encyclopaedias, dictionaries, textbooks and reference books; Man. Dir AHTI SIRKIÄ.

Helsinki Media Co Oy: POB 100, 00040 Helsinki; tel. (09) 1201; fax (09) 1205569; f. 1994; children's books, comics, non-fiction; Man. Dir TAPIO KALLIOJA.

Karisto Oy: Paroistentie 2, POB 102, 13101 Hämeenlinna; tel. (03) 6161551; telex 2348; fax (03) 6161555; f. 1900; non-fiction and fiction, the printing industry; Man. Dir SIMO MOISIO.

Kirjapaja: POB 137, 00101 Helsinki; tel. (09) 613021; fax (09) 61302341; f. 1942; Christian literature, general fiction, non-fiction, reference, juvenile; Man. Dir KALEVI VIRTANEN.

Kirjayhtymä Oy: Urho Kekkosen katu 4–6E, 00100 Helsinki; tel. (09) 6937641; fax (09) 69376366; f. 1958; fiction, non-fiction, textbooks; Man. Dir OLLI ARRAKOSKI.

Kustannus-Mäkelä Oy: POB 14, 03601 Karkkila; tel. (09) 2257995; fax (09) 2257660; f. 1971; juvenile, fiction; Man. Dir ORVO MÄKELÄ.

Oy Like Kustannus Ltd: Meritullinkatu 21, 00170 Helsinki; tel. (09) 1351385; fax (09) 1351372; e-mail likekustannus@dlc.fi; f. 1987; film literature, fiction, non-fiction, comics; Man. Dir HANNU PALOVIITA.

Otava Publishers: Uudenmaankatu 10, 00120 Helsinki; tel. (09) 19961; telex 124560; fax (09) 643136; f. 1890; non-fiction, fiction, the printing industry, science, juvenile, textbooks and encyclopaedias; Chair. HEIKKI A. REENPÄÄ; Man. Dir OLLI REENPÄÄ.

Schildts Förlags Ab: Rusthållargatan 1, 02270 Espoo; tel. (09) 8870400; fax (09) 8043257; e-mail schildts@schildts.fi; f. 1913; subjects mainly in Swedish; Man. Dir JOHAN JOHNSON.

Söderström & Co Förlags Ab: Wavulinsvägen 4, 00210 Helsinki; tel. (09) 6923681; fax (09) 6926346; e-mail soderstr@soderstrom.fi; f. 1891; all subjects in Swedish only; Man. Dir MARIANNE BARGUM.

Suomalaisen Kirjallisuuden Seura, SKS (Finnish Literature Society): POB 259, 00171 Helsinki; tel. (09) 131231; fax (09) 13123220; f. 1831; Finnish and other Finno-Ugric languages, Finnish literature, literary scholarship, folklore, comparative ethnology and cultural history; Publishing Dir MATTI SUURPÄÄ.

Tammi Publishers: Urho Kekkosen katu 4–6E, 00100 Helsinki; tel. (09) 6937621; fax (09) 69376266; f. 1943; fiction, non-fiction, juvenile; Man. Dir OLLI ARRAKOSKI.

Weilin & Göös: Ahertajantie 5, 02100 Espoo; tel. (09) 43771; fax (09) 4377390; f. 1872; non-fiction, encyclopaedias; Man. Dir JUHANI MIKOLA.

Werner Söderström Osakeyhtiö: Bulevardi 12, 00120 Helsinki; tel. (09) 61681; telex 122644; fax (09) 6168405; f. 1878; fiction and non-fiction, science, juvenile, textbooks, reference, comics, the printing industry; Pres., CEO ANTERO SILJOLA.

PUBLISHERS' ASSOCIATION

Suomen Kustannusyhdistys (Finnish Book Publishers' Association): POB 177, 00121 Helsinki; tel. (09) 22877258; fax (09) 6121226; e-mail finnpubl@skyry.pp.fi; f. 1858; Chair. ANTERO SILJOLA; Man. Dir VEIKKO SONNINEN; 85 mems.

Broadcasting and Communications

TELECOMMUNICATIONS

Telecommunications Administration Centre: POB 53, 00211 Helsinki; tel. (09) 69661; telex 124545; fax (09) 6966410; e-mail info@thk.fi; affiliated to Ministry of Transport and Communications; CEO REIJO SVENSSON.

Finnet International Ltd: POB 94, 00131 Helsinki; tel. (09) 69550212; fax (09) 69550301; Man. JAN C. M. VAN DER VEN.

Helsingin Puhelinyhdistys—HPY The Helsinki Telephone Company): Korkeavuorenkata 35–37, POB 148, 00130 Helsinki; tel. (09) 6061; telex 124939; fax (09) 664480; f. 1882; telecommunications in Helsinki and surrounding area; 3600 employees (1992).

Nokia Telecommunications: POB 45, 00211 Helsinki; tel. (09) 43761; telex 121440; fax (09) 43766227; Man. KARL LÄNG.

Telecom Finland Ltd: POB 106, 00051 Helsinki; tel. (09) 20401; fax (09) 20403526; scheduled for partial privatization; Pres. and CEO AULIS SALIN.

Telecon Ltd: POB 110, Teollisuuskatu 15, 00511 Helsinki; tel. (09) 20405390; fax (09) 20405389; e-mail yrjo.sirkeinen@telecon.telebox.fi; Man. Dir YRJÖ SIRKEINEN.

RADIO

Yleisradio Oy (YLE) (Finnish Broadcasting Company): POB 96, 00024 Yleisradio; tel. (09) 14801; fax (09) 14803588; internet http://www.yle.fi/fbc; f. 1926; 99.9% state-owned, with management appointed by the Administrative Council; YLE owns the networks that distribute radio and television programmes throughout Finland; Dir-Gen. ARNE WESSBERG; Dir of Radio and Deputy Dir-Gen. TAPIO SIIKALA; Dir of Television HEIKKI LEHMUSTO; Dir of Swedish-language programmes (Radio and Television) ANN SANDELIN.

YLE R1 (Ylen Ykkönen): 24-hour arts and culture in Finnish; Dir OLLI ALHO;

YLE R2 (Radiomafia): 24-hour popular culture for young people in Finnish; Dir LEENA PAKKANEN;

YLE R3 (Radio Suomi): 24-hour news, sport, regional programmes in Finnish; Dir RAIMO VANNINEN;

YLE R4 (Riksradion): Swedish-language programmes; Dir TOM MORING;

YLE R5 (Regionalradion): regional programmes in Swedish; Dir STEFAN FORSMAN;

Capital FM: 24-hour local service in the Helsinki area combining broadcasts by Radio Finland and several foreign radio stations;

Foreign Service (Radio Finland): broadcasts to Europe, Africa, Asia, Australia and America in Finnish, Swedish, German, Russian, French and English. There is also a Sámi-language radio service and a weekly news service in Latin.

Experimental Finnish local radio began operations in 1984, and in 1995 there were 61 local radio stations, of which two were broadcasting on a semi-national basis.

TELEVISION

Oy Yleisradio Ab (YLE) (see above) operates two national networks, TV 1 and TV 2, and leases the third network (TV 3) to the commercial company MTV Finland (see below).

YLE/TV 1: POB 97, 00024 Helsinki; tel. (09) 14801; telex 121270; fax (09) 14803424; f. 1957; programmes in Finnish; Dir ASTRID GARTZ.

YLE/TV 2: POB 196, 33101 Tampere; tel. (03) 3456111; fax (03) 3456892; f. 1964; programmes in Finnish and Swedish; Dir ARTO HOFFRÉN.

YLE/TV 4: relays programmes from Sweden for coastal areas in southern Finland.

MTV Finland: 00033 MTV3, 00240 Helsinki; tel. (09) 15001; fax (09) 1500707; f. 1957; independent nationwide commercial television company producing programmes on the third national network (MTV3), leased from YLE, the state broadcasting company (see above); about 120 hours per week; Pres. and CEO EERO PILKAMA.

Oy Kolmostelevisio Ab (MTV3 Finland): 00033 MTV3, 00240 Helsinki; tel. (09) 15001; telex 126068; fax (09) 1500673; subsidiary of MTV Finland; sport and other subcontracted programming on MTV 3; Man. Dir HEIKKI VAHALA.

Finance

The Bank of Finland is the country's central bank and the centre of Finland's monetary and banking system. It functions 'under guarantee and supervision of Parliament and the Bank supervisors delegated by Parliament'.

At the beginning of 1996 Finland's three groups of deposit banks (commercial banks, co-operative banks and savings banks) had a total of 1,953 branches. There were two large commercial banks and five smaller ones, and 301 co-operative banks, with their own extensive branch networks. In December 1995 (following a number of mergers in the early 1990s) there were 40 savings banks. There were also six mortgage banks and four specialized credit institutions. Insurance companies (numbering about 50) also grant credit. Foreign banks were permitted to open branches in Finland from the beginning of 1991.

In April 1992 the Government Guarantee Fund (GGF) was established to ensure the stability of deposit banking and to assist in rationalizing the Finnish banking system.

BANKING

(cap. = capital; dep. = deposits; m. = million; res = reserves; brs = branches; amounts in markkaa)

Supervisory Authorities

Financial Supervision Authority: Kluuvikatu 5, POB 159, 00101 Helsinki; tel. (09) 18351; fax (09) 1835328; f. 1995; maintains confidence in the financial markets by supervising the markets and the bodies working within them. It functions administratively in connection with the Bank of Finland, but operates as an independent decision-making body; Dir-Gen. KAARLO JÄNNÄRI.

Government Guarantee Fund: Fabianinkatu 8, 00130 Helsinki; tel. (09) 664344; fax (09) 662942; f. 1992 to safeguard the stability of the banking sector and the claims of depositors; operates in conjunction with the Ministry of Finance from May 1996; Chair. MATTI VUORIA; Deputy Dirs LIISA HALME, JARMO KILPELÄ.

Central Bank

Suomen Pankki/Finlands Bank (The Bank of Finland): Snellmaninaukio, POB 160, 00101 Helsinki; tel. (09) 1831; telex 121224;

fax (09) 174872; f. 1811; Bank of Issue under the guarantee and supervision of Parliament; cap. 5,000m., res 764m., dep. 25,367m. (Dec. 1996); Gov. SIRKKA HÄMÄLÄINEN; 4 brs.

Commercial and Mortgage Banks

Interbank Ltd: Bulevardi 10, POB 152, 00121 Helsinki; tel. (09) 166721; fax (09) 632700; internet http://www.interbank.fi; f. 1988; cap. 110.4m., res 35.6m., dep. 2,353.3m. (Dec. 1995); Chair. and Man. Dir PAAVO PREPULA.

Merita Pankki Oy (Merita Bank Ltd.): Aleksanterinkatu 30, 00010 Helsinki; tel. (09) 1651; telex 124407; fax (09) 16554213; f. 1995 by merger of Union Bank of Finland (SYP, f. 1862) and Kansallis-Osake-Pankki (KOP, f. 1889); cap. 6,024m., res. 6,172m., dep. 224,216m. (Dec. 1996); Chair. and CEO VESA VAINIO; Pres. PERTTI VOUTILAINEN; 479 brs.

OKO—Investointipankki Oy (OKO Mortgage Bank Ltd): Arkadiankatu 23B, POB 930, 00101 Helsinki; tel. (09) 4041; fax (09) 4044209; f. 1916; cap. and res 382m. (Dec. 1994); Chair. PAULI KOMI; Man. Dir HANNU JOENSIVU.

Okobank (Osuuspankkien Keskuspankki Oy) (Co-operative Banks of Finland Ltd): Teollisuuskatu 1B, 00510 Helsinki; tel. (09) 4041; telex 124714; fax (09) 4042624; f. 1902; cap. 1,098m., res 1,361m., dep. 44,864m. (Dec. 1996); Chair. and CEO ANTTI TANSKANEN; Man. Dir PENTTI HAKKARAINEN.

OP-Kotipankki Oy: Lummetie 2, 01300 Vantaa; tel. (09) 4041; fax (09) 4044042; cap. and res 96m., dep. 588m. (Dec. 1994); Man. Dir MATTI KORKEELA.

Postipankki Ltd: Unioninkatu 22, 00007 Helsinki; tel. (020) 42511; telex 121698; fax (09) 1642608; f. 1886, a limited company 1988; cap. 630m., res 2,549.8m., dep. 103,458.7m. (Dec. 1996); Chair. and CEO EINO KEINANEN; 63 brs.

PSP—Kuntapankki Oy (PSP Municipality Bank Ltd): Fabianinkatu 23, 00007 Helsinki; tel. (09) 2511; fax (09) 255272; cap. and res 153m. (Dec. 1994); Chair. ILKKA HALLAVO; Man. Dir PERTTI MATTILA.

Siltapankki Oy: Paasivuorenkatu 3, 05300 Helsinki; tel. (09) 73181; fax (09) 73182251; cap. 962m. (1994); Chair. INGA-MARIA GRÖHN; Man. Dir MARTTI ERMA.

Skopbank: Mikonkatu 4, POB 400,00101 Helsinki; tel. (09) 13341; telex 121154; fax (09) 1334896; f. 1908; taken over by the Bank of Finland in September 1991 and transferred to the control of the Government Guarantee Fund in June 1992; assets acquired by Svenska Handelsbanken in 1995, when plans announced to convert Skopbank into an asset management company; cap. 3,780m., dep. 2,714m. (Dec. 1996); Chief Gen. Man. JIPO NIITTI.

Suomen Hypoteekkiyhdistys (Mortgage Society of Finland): Yrjönkatu 9, POB 509, 00101 Helsinki; tel. (09) 228361; fax (09) 647443; f. 1860; cap. and res 220m. (Dec. 1996); Pres. RISTO PIEPPONEN.

Suomen Kiinteistöpankki Oy (Finnish Real Estate Bank Ltd): Erottajankatu 7A, POB 428, 00101 Helsinki; tel. (09) 13341; telex 122284; fax (09) 1335129; f. 1907; cap. and res 477m. (Dec. 1994); Man. Dir JYRKI JISALO.

Suomen Teollisuuspankki Oy (Industrial Bank of Finland Ltd): Aleksanterinkatu 36A, POB 165, 00101 Helsinki; tel. (09) 16542901; fax (09) 608951; f. 1924; cap. and res 374m. (Dec. 1995); Chair. KARI JORDAN; Man. Dir SEPPO LEINONEN.

Savings Bank

Aktia Sparbank Abp (Aktia Säästöpankki Oy): Mannerheimintie 14, 00100 Helsinki; tel. (09) 60921; telex 124269; fax (09) 6096356; current name adopted in September 1997; cap 412.7m., res 152.3m., dep. 8,937.3m. (Dec. 1996); Chair. PATRICK ENCKELL; Man. Dir JOHAN HORELLI.

Investment Bank

Nordiska Investeringsbanken (Nordic Investment Bank): Fabianinkatu 34, POB 249, 00171 Helsinki; tel. (09) 18001; telex 122121; fax (09) 1800210; f. 1976; owned by five Scandinavian Govts (incl. Finland, 20%); cap. ECU 304.3m., res ECU 640.5m., dep. ECU 7,092.4m. (Dec. 1996); Pres. and CEO JON SIGURDSSON.

Banking Associations

Säästöpankkiliitto (Finnish Savings Banks Association): Mannerheimintie 14A, 00100 Helsinki; tel. (09) 133986; fax (09) 1334077; f. 1906; 40 mems; 248 brs; Chair. EINO LINNAKANGAS; Man. Dir MARKKU RUUTU.

Suomen Pankkiyhdistys r.y. (Finnish Bankers' Association): Museokatu 8A, POB 1009, 00101 Helsinki; tel. (09) 4056120; fax (09) 40561291; f. 1914; Chair. PERTTI VOUTILAINEN; Man. Dir MATTI SIPILÄ.

STOCK EXCHANGE

Hex Ltd Helsinki Exchanges: Fabianinkatu 14, POB 361, 00131 Helsinki; tel. (09) 616671; fax (09) 61667366; f. 1912; current name adopted following merger between Helsinki Stock Exchange Ltd and SOM Ltd in December 1997; 126 listed companies at end of December 1997; Chair. of Bd of Dirs JUSSI LAITINEN; CEO JUHANI ERMA.

INSURANCE

A list is given below of some of the more important insurance companies:

A-Vakuutus keskinäinen yhtiö (A-Vakuutus Mutual Insurance Co): Hietalahdenranta 3, POB 165, 00151 Helsinki; tel. (10) 5040; fax (10) 5045200; non-life; Man. Dir ESKO RINKINEN.

Aurum Life Insurance Co. Ltd.: POB 308, 00101 Helsinki; tel. (09) 4043155; fax (09) 4043501; Man. Dir RAIMO VOUTILAINEN.

Eläkevakuutusosakeyhtiö Ilmarinen (Ilmarinen Pension Insurance Co Ltd): Eerikinkatu 41, 00180 Helsinki; tel. (09) 1841; fax (09) 1843445; f. 1961; statutory employment pensions; Man. Dir KARI PURO.

Eläke-Varma Keskinäinen Vakuutusyhtio (Pension-Varma Mutual Insurance Co): Annankatu 18, POB 175, 00121 Helsinki; tel. (09) 61651; fax (09) 61652714; Man. Dir PAAVO PITKÄNEN.

Eurooppalainen Insurance Co Ltd: Lapinmäentie 1, 00013 Pohjola; tel. (09) 55911; fax (09) 5592205; non-life; Pres. JIRO VIINANEN; Man. Dir JUKKA RANTALA.

Garantia Insurance Co Ltd: Salomonkatu 17A, POB 600, 00101 Helsinki; tel. (09) 685811; fax (09) 68581301; non-life; Man. Dir LAURI KOIVUSALO.

Henkivakuutusosakeyhtiö Nova (Nova Life Insurance Co Ltd): Bulevardi 7, POB 175, 00121 Helsinki; tel. (09) 616531; fax (09) 61653333; Man. Dir KARI STADIGH.

Henkivakuutusosakeyhtiö Salama (Salama Life Assurance Co): Lapinmäentie 1, 00300 Helsinki; tel. (09) 55911; fax (09) 5596799; Man. Dir JUKKA RANTALA.

Henkivakuutusosakeyhtiö Verdandi (Verdandi Pension Insurance Co Ltd): Olavintie 2, POB 133, 20101 Turku; tel. (02) 2690011; fax (02) 2690690; Man. Dir FOLKE LINDSTRÖM.

Insurance Co of Finland Ltd: Itälahdankatu 21A, POB 12, 00211 Helsinki; tel. (10) 51451512; fax (10) 5145833; non-life; Man. Dir ANTTI SAVOLAINEN.

Keskinäinen Eläkevakuutusosakeyhtiö Tapiola (Tapiola Mutual Pension Insurance Co): Revontulentie 7, POB 30, 02101 Espoo; tel. (09) 4531; fax (09) 4532146; CEO, ASMO KALPALA; Man. Dir TOM LILJESTRÖM.

Keskinäinen Henkivakuutusosakeyhtiö Suomi (Suomi Mutual Life Assurance Co): Lapinmäentie 1, 00300 Helsinki; tel. (09) 55911; fax (09) 5596799; Man. Dir JUKKA RANTALA.

Keskinäinen Henkivakuutusosakeyhtiö Tapiola (Tapiola Mutual Life Assurance Co): Revontulentie 7, POB 30, 02101 Espoo; tel. (09) 4531; fax (09) 4532146; CEO ASMO KALPALA; Man. Dir JARI SAINE.

Keskinäinen Vakuutusyhtiö Kaleva (Kaleva Mutual Insurance Co): Kluuvikatu 3, 00025 Sampo; tel. (10) 515311; fax (10) 5144229; Man. Dir MATTI RANTANEN.

Keskinäinen Vakuutusyhtiö Tapiola (Tapiola General Mutual Insurance Co): Revontulentie 7, POB 30, 02101 Espoo; tel. (09) 4531; fax (09) 4532146; non-life; CEO ASMO KALPALA; Man. Dir PERTTI HEIKKALA.

Keskinäinen Yhtiö Yrittäjäinvakuutus—Fennia (Enterprise Fennia Mutual Insurance Co): Asemamiehenkatu 3, 00520 Helsinki; tel. (09) 50351; fax (09) 5035300; non-life; Man. Dir KARI ELO.

Lähivakuutus Keskinäinen Yhtiö (Local Insurance Mutual Co): Lintuvaarantie 2, POB 50, 02601 Espoo; tel. (09) 511011; fax (09) 51101335; non-life; Man. Dir SIMO CASTRÉN.

Leijona Life Insurance Co Ltd: Kaivokatu 6/6, 00007 Helsinki; tel. (09) 1646296; fax (09) 1646299; Man. Dir MIKKO PALOMÄKI.

Merita Life Insurance Ltd: Asemakuja 2, POB 73, 02771 Espoo; tel. (09) 16527601; fax (09) 8594622; Man. Dir SEPPO ILVESSALO.

Palonvara Mutual Insurance Co: Saimaankatu 20, 15140 Lahti; tel. (03) 7522611; fax (03) 7522629; non-life; Man. Dir JUKKA HERTTI.

Pankavara Insurance Co Ltd: Kanavaranta 1, POB 309, 00101 Helsinki; tel. (09) 16291; fax (09) 1629447; non-life; Man. Dir JUKKA KÄHKÖNEN.

Pohjantähti Mutual Insurance Co: Raatihuoneenkatu 19, POB 164, 13101 Hämeenlinna; tel. (03) 62671; fax (03) 6169303; non-life; Man. Dir EERO YLÄ-SOININMÄKI.

Säästöpankkien Keskinäinen Vakuutusyhtiö (Mutual Insurance Co of the Savings Banks): Mannerheimintie 7, 00100 Helsinki; tel. (020) 4401; fax (020) 4407320; non-life; Man. Dir ESKO MÄKINEN.

Spruce Insurance Ltd: Porkkalankatu 3, 00101 Helsinki; tel. (10) 8611; fax (10) 8621568; e-mail jukka.liimatainen@kemira.com; non-life; Man. Dir JUKKA LIIMATAINEN.

Teollisuusvakuutus Oy (Industrial Insurance Co Ltd): Vattuniemenkuja 8A, POB 12, 00211 Helsinki; tel. (09) 51512; fax (09) 5145232; non-life; Man. Dir JUHA TOIVOLA.

Vakuutusosakeyhtiö Eläke-Sampo (Sampo Pension Insurance Co Ltd): Lapinlahdenkatu 1B, POB 1, 00026 Helsinki; tel. (09) 515311; fax (09) 5144434; Man. Dir MARKKU HYVÄRINEN.

Vakuutusosakeyhtiö Pohjola (Pohjola Insurance Co Ltd): Lapinmäentie 1, 00013 Pohjola; tel. (09) 55911; fax (09) 5592205; non-life; Pres. IIRO VIINANEN.

Vakuutusosakeyhtiö Sampo (Sampo Insurance Co Ltd): Yliopistonkatu 27, POB 216, 20101 Turku; tel. (02) 515300; fax (02) 5141811; non-life; Man. Dir JOUKO K. LESKINEN.

Insurance Associations

Federation of Accident Insurance Institutions: Bulevardi 28, 00120 Helsinki; tel. (09) 680401; fax (09) 68040389; f. 1920; Man. Dir TAPANI MIETTINEN.

Federation of Employment Pension Institutions: Lastenkodinkuja 1, 00180 Helsinki; tel. (09) 6940122; fax (09) 6944970; f. 1964; Man. Dir PENTTI KOSTAMO.

Federation of Finnish Insurance Companies: Bulevardi 28, 00120 Helsinki; tel. (09) 680401; fax (09) 68040216; f. 1942; Chair. ASMO KALPALA; Man. Dir ARTO OJALA; 50 mems.

Finnish Atomic Insurance Pool, Finnish Pool of Aviation Insurers, Finnish General Reinsurance Pool: Bulevardi 10, 00120 Helsinki; tel. (09) 61691; telex 121061; Man. Dir K.-M. STRÖMMER.

Finnish Motor Insurers' Centre: Bulevardi 28, 00120 Helsinki; tel. (09) 680401; fax (09) 68040391; f. 1938; Man. Dir PENTTI AJO.

Trade and Industry

GOVERNMENT AGENCIES

Finnish Foreign Trade Association: Arkadiankatu 2, POB 908, 00101 Helsinki; tel. (020) 6951; fax (020) 4695535; e-mail info@exports.finland.fi; f. 1919; Chair. JORMA OLLILA; Chair. of Board JOHANNES KOROMA; Pres. SEPPO HÄRKÖNEN.

Invest in Finland Bureau: Aleksanterinkatu 17, POB 800, 00101 Helsinki; tel. (09) 6969125; fax (09) 69692530: e-mail investinfinland@wtc.fi; internet http://www. investinfinland.fi.

DEVELOPMENT ORGANIZATION

Alko Group: Salmisaarenranta 7, POB 350, 00101 Helsinki; tel. (09) 13311; fax (09) 1333361; internet http://www.alko-yhtiot.fi; f. 1932; production, import, export and sale of alcoholic beverages and spirits; has monopoly of retail sale of all alcoholic beverages except fermented beverages under 4.7% volume; provision of hotel and restaurant services; 100% state-owned; Chair. of Board of Dirs ILKKA SUOMINEN; 4,350 employees.

CHAMBERS OF COMMERCE

Helsinki Chamber of Commerce: Kalevankatu 12, 00100 Helsinki; tel. (09) 228601; f. 1917; Pres. KURT NORDMAN; Man. Dir HEIKKI HELIÖ; 4,100 mems.

Keskuskauppakamari (Central Chamber of Commerce): Aleksanterinkatu 17, POB 1000, 00101 Helsinki; tel. (09) 69-69-69; fax (09) 650303; f. 1918; Pres. CURT LINDBOM; Gen. Man. MATTI AURA; represents 21 regional chambers of commerce.

INDUSTRIAL AND TRADE ASSOCIATIONS

Kalatalouden Keskusliitto (Federation of Finnish Fisheries Associations): Köydenpunojankatu 7B 23, 00180 Helsinki; tel. (09) 640126; fax (09) 608309; e-mail kalastus@kalataloudenkeskusliitto.fi; internet http://www.kalataloudenkeskusliitto.fi; f. 1891; Sec. M. MYLLYLÄ; 616,000 mems.

Kaukomarkkinat Oy: Kutojantie 4, 02630 Espoo; tel. (09) 5211; telex 124469; fax (09) 5216641; f. 1947; export, import and international trade; Pres. KARI ANSIO.

Kaupan Keskusliitto (Federation of Finnish Commerce and Trade): Mannerheimintie 76A, 00250 Helsinki; tel. (09) 441651; fax (09) 496142; f. 1992; Man. Dir GUY WIRES; 41 mem. asscns with over 13,000 firms.

Kesko Oy (Retailers' Wholesale Co): Satamakatu 3, 00160 Helsinki; tel. (09) 5311; telex 124748; fax (09) 655473; f. 1941; retailer-owned wholesale corporation, trading in foodstuffs, textiles, shoes, consumer goods, agricultural and builders' supplies, and machinery; Pres. EERO KINNUNEN.

Oy Labor Ab (Agricultural Machinery): Mikkolantie 1, 00640 Helsinki; tel. (09) 7291; telex 124660; f. 1898; Gen. Man. KIMMO VARJOVAARA.

Maa- ja metsataloustuottajain Keskusliitto MTK r.y. (Central Union of Agricultural Producers and Forest Owners): Simonkatu 6, 00100 Helsinki; tel. (09) 131151; telex 122474; fax (09) 13115425; f. 1917; Chair. of Board of Dirs ESA HÄRMÄLÄ; Sec.-Gen. PAAVO MÄKINEN; 223,511 mems.

Metsäteollisuus r.y. (Finnish Forest Industries Federation): Eteläesplanadi 2, 00130 Helsinki; tel. (09) 13261; telex 121823; fax (09) 174479; e-mail kari.vitie@forest.ttliitot.fi; f. 1918; Chair. JUHA NIEMELÄ; Man. Dir TIMO PORANEN; mems: 105 companies in the forestry industry and the following sales or trade associations:

Finncell (Finnish Pulp Exporters' Association): Eteläesplanadi 2, POB 60, 00101 Helsinki; tel. (09) 132480; telex 124459; fax (09) 1324892; f. 1918; Man. Dir T. NYKOPP; 4 mems.

Suomen Lastulevy-yhdistys (Finnish Particle Board Association): Rikhardinkatu 1B 19, 00130 Helsinki; tel. (09) 657122; fax (09) 657145; Man. Dir PENTTI SAARRO; 2 mems.

Suomen Vaneriyhdistys (Association of Finnish Plywood Industry): Rikhardinkatu 1B 19, 00130 Helsinki; tel. (09) 657122; fax (09) 657145; f. 1939; Man. Dir PENTTI SAARRO; 4 mems.

Suomalaisen Työn Liitto (Association for Finnish Work): Mannerheimintie 8, POB 429, 00101 Helsinki; tel. (09) 645733; fax (09) 645252; e-mail stl@avainlippu.fi; f. 1978; public relations for Finnish products and for Finnish work; Chair. of Council ANTTI KALLIOMÄKI; Chair. of Board of Dirs HANNU JAAKKOLA; Man. Dir LARS COLLIN; about 1,100 mems.

Suomen Betoniteollisuuden Keskusjärjestö r.y. (Association of the Concrete Industry of Finland): Helsinki; tel. (09) 648212; telex 121394; fax (09) 642597; f. 1929; Chair. ERKKI INKINEN; Man. Dir ERKKI TIKKANEN; 78 mems.

Suomen Osuuskauppojen Keskusliitto (SOKL) r.y. (Finnish Co-operative Union): POB 171, 00511 Helsinki; tel. (09) 1882222; fax (09) 1882580; f. 1908; Chair. MATTI VANTO; Man. Dir TAPIO PELTOLA; 44 mems.

Svenska Lantbruksproducenternas centralförbund (Central Union of Swedish-speaking Agricultural Producers): Fredriksgatan 61A, 00100 Helsinki; tel. (09) 6940533; fax (09) 6941358; f. 1945; Swedish-speaking producers; Chair. O. ROSENDAHL; 18,000 mems.

Teknisen Kaupan Liitto (Association of Finnish Technical Traders): Melkonkatu 24B, 00210 Helsinki; tel. (09) 5840311; fax (09) 58403200; f. 1918; organization of the main importers dealing in iron, steel, and non-ferrous metals, machines and equipment, heavy chemicals and raw materials; Chair. CHR. WESTERLUND; Man. Dir KLAUS KATARA; 190 mems.

EMPLOYERS' ORGANIZATIONS

Autoliikenteen Työnantajaliitto r.y. (Employers' Federation of Road Transport): Nuijamiestentie 7A, 00400 Helsinki; tel. (09) 47899480; fax (09) 5883995; Chair. PERTTI KORHONEN; Man. Dir HANNU PARVELA; 477 mems.

Autonrengasliitto r.y. (Tyre Federation): Helsinki; tel. (09) 492054; f. 1944; Chair. HANNA MAJA; Man. Dir AIMO WASENIUS; 52 mems, 15 assoc. mems.

Kultaseppien Työnantajaliitto r.y. (Employers' Association of Goldsmiths): Eteläranta 10, 00130 Helsinki; tel. (09) 172841; Chair., Man. Dir ILKKA KUNNAS; 25 mems.

Liiketyönantajain Keskusliitto (LTK) r.y. (Employers' Confederation of Service Industries): Eteläranta 10, 00130 Helsinki; tel. (09) 172831; fax (09) 655588; f. 1945; seven mem. asscns consisting of about 5,800 enterprises with 234,000 employees; Man. Dir JARMO PELLIKKA.

Suomen Lasitus- ja Hiomoliitto r.y. (Finnish Glaziers' Association): Eteläranta 10, 00130 Helsinki; tel. (09) 172841; fax (09) 179588; Chair. HARRI RAIKAA; Dir RAIMO KILPIÄINEN; 90 mems.

Suomen Tiiliteollisuusliitto r.y. (Finnish Brick Industry Association): Laturinkuja 2, 02600 Espoo; tel. (09) 519133; fax (09) 514017; Chair. LEO SEPPÄLÄ; Man. Dir JUKKA SUONIO; 6 mems.

Teollisuuden ja Työnantajain Keskusliitto (TT) (Confederation of Finnish Industry and Employers): Eteläranta 10, POB 30, 00131 Helsinki; tel. (09) 68681; fax (09) 68682812; f. 1907 (renamed 1992); aims to promote co-operation between companies and member organizations and to protect the interests of mems in employment issues; 29 asscns consisting of about 5,500 enterprises with 450,000 employees; Chair. JUKKA HÄRMÄLÄ; Dir-Gen. JOHANNES KOROMA.

Elintarviketeollisuus r.y. (Finnish Food and Drinks Industries): Pasilankatu 2, 00240 Helsinki; tel. (09) 148871; fax (09) 14887201; Chair. FELIX BJÖRKLUND; Man. Dir PEKKA HÄMÄLÄINEN.

Energia–alan Keskusliitto r.y. Finergy (Finnish Energy Industry Association): Eteläranta 10, 00130 Helsinki; tel. (09) 686161; fax (09) 6861630; Chair HEIKKI MARTTINEN.

Graafisen Teollisuuden Liitto r.y. (Federation of the Printing Industry): Lönnrotinkatu 11A, 00120 Helsinki; tel. (09) 22877200; fax (09) 603527; Chair. PEKKA SALOJÄRVI; Man. Dir MATTI SUTINEN.

Kemianteollisuus (KT) r.y. (Chemical Industry Federation): Eteläranta 10, POB 4, 00131 Helsinki; tel. (09) 172841; fax (09) 630225; Chair. JAAKKO IHAMUOTILA; Man. Dir HANNU VORNAMO.

Kenkä- ja Nahkateollisuus r.y. (Association of Finnish Shoe and Leather Industries): Eteläranta 10, 00130 Helsinki; tel. (09) 172841; fax (09) 179588; Chair. OLAVI VILJANMAA; Exec. Dir SARI VANNELA.

Kulutustavara- ja Erikoistuoteteollisuus Ket (Association of Consumer Goods and Special Products Industries): Eteläranta 10, 00130 Helsinki; tel. (09) 686121; fax (09) 653305; Chair. JUSSI KARINEN; Man. Dir MATTI JÄRVENTIE.

Kumiteollisuusyhdistys r.y. (Rubber Manufacturers' Association): Eteläranta 10, 00130 Helsinki; tel. (09) 172841; fax (09) 666561; Chair. LASSE KURKILAHTI; Man. Dir EEVA FRANCK.

Lääketeollisuusliitto r.y. (Finnish Pharmaceutical Industry Federation): Sörnäisten rantatie 23, POB 108, 00501 Helsinki; tel. (09) 5842400; fax (09) 58424728; Chair. MATTI LIEVONEN; Man. Dir JARMO LEHTONEN.

Metalliteollisuuden Keskusliitto r.y. (Federation of Finnish Metal, Engineering and Electrotechnical Industries): Eteläranta 10, POB 10, 00131 Helsinki; tel. (09) 19231; telex 124997; fax (09) 624462; f. 1903; Chair. MIKKO KIVIMÄKI; Man. Dir HARRI MALMBERG.

Metsäteollisuus r.y. (Finnish Forest Industries): Eteläesplanadi 2, 00130 Helsinki; tel. (09) 13261; fax (09) 174479; Chair. JUHA NIEMELÄ; Man. Dir TIMO PORANEN.

Palvelualojen Toimialaliitto r.y. (Association of Support Service Industries): Eteläranta 10, 00130 Helsinki; tel. (09) 172841; fax (09) 179588; Chair. ARNE WESSBERG; Man. Dir PETER FORSSTRÖM.

PT:n Työnantajaliitto r.y. (PT Employers' Federation): Mannerheiminaukio 1A, 00100 Helsinki; tel. (09) 613151; fax (09) 61315082; Chair. PEKKA VENNAMO; Man. Dir JUHA KIVINEN.

Puusepänteollisuuden Liitto r.y. (Employers' Association of the Finnish Furniture and Joinery Industries): Eteläesplanadi 2, POB 316, 00131 Helsinki; tel. (09) 13261; fax (09) 657923; f. 1917; Chair. HANNU ROINE; Man. Dir ARTO TÄHTINEN; 125 mems.

Rakennusteollisuuden Keskusliitto r.y. (Confederation of the Finnish Construction Industries): Unioninkatu 14 VI, 00130 Helsinki; tel. (09) 12991; fax (09) 1299252; f. 1920; Chair. HEIKKI PENTTI; Man. Dir TERHO SALO; 1,630 mems.

Rakennustuoteteollisuus r.y. (Finnish Association of Construction Product Industries): Eteläranta 10, 00130 Helsinki; tel. (09) 172841; fax (09) 17284444; Chair. CHRISTOFFER TAXELL; Man. Dir ERKKI INKINEN.

Rannikko- ja Sisävesiliikenteen Työnantajaliitto (RASILA) r.y. (Coastal and Inland Waterway Employers' Association): Satamakatu 4A, 00160 Helsinki; tel. (09) 62267312; fax (09) 669251; Chair. STEFAN HÅKANS; Man. Dir HENRIK LÖNNQVIST.

Sähkö- ja telealan työnantajaliitto r.y. (Finnish Association of Electrical and Telecommunications Employers): Yrjönkatu 13A, 00120 Helsinki; tel. (09) 642811; telex 124845; fax (09) 644383; Chair. ERKKI RIPATTI; Man. Dir MATTI HÖYSTI; 168 mems.

Suomen Kiinteistöliitto r.y. (Finnish Real-Estate Association): Annankatu 24, 00100 Helsinki; tel. (09) 166761; fax (09) 16676400; f. 1907; Chair. KARI RAHKAMO; Man. Dir UKKO LAURILA.

Suomen Lastauttajain Liitto (SLL) r.y. (Federation of Finnish Master Stevedores): Köydenpunojankatu 8, 00180 Helsinki; tel. (09) 6949800; fax (09) 6944585; f. 1906; Chair. HANS MARTIN; Man. Dir HARRI TUULENSU.

Suomen Muoviteollisuusliitto r.y. (Finnish Plastics Industries' Federation): Eteläranta 10, 00130 Helsinki; tel. (09) 172841; fax (09) 171164; Chair. JYRKI ANT-WUORINEN; Man. Dir KARI TEPPOLA.

Suomen Varustamoyhdistys r.y. (Finnish Shipowners' Association): see under Shipping.

Suunnittelu- ja konsulttitoimistojen liitto (SKOL) r.y. (Finnish Association of Consulting Firms—SKOL): Pohjantie 12A, 02100 Espoo; tel. (09) 460122; fax (09) 467642; e-mail skol.ry@kolumbus.fi; Chair. MATTI OLLILA; Man. Dir TIMO MYLLYS; 230 mems.

Teknokemian Yhdistys r.y. (Cosmetic, Toiletries and Detergent Association): Eteläranta 10, 00130 Helsinki; tel. (09) 172841; fax (09) 666561; Chair. JARL STORGÅRDS.

Tekstiili- ja vaatetusteollisuus r.y. (Federation of Finnish Textile and Clothing Industries): Aleksis Kiven katu 10, POB 50, 33211 Tampere; tel. (03) 3889111; fax (03) 3889120; f. 1905; Chair. HANNU JAAKKOLA; Man. Dir MATTI JÄRVENTIE.

Toimistoteknisen Kaupan Yhdistys (TTK) r.y. (Finnish Association of Office Technology Traders): Mannerheimintie 76A, 00250 Helsinki; tel. (09) 441651; fax (09) 496142; Chair. KARI SOLALA; Man. Dir EERO PERITALO.

Tupakkatehtaiden Yhdistys r.y. (Finnish Tobacco Manufacturers' Association): Lönnrotinkatu 4B, 00120 Helsinki; tel. (09) 644373; Chair. JUKKA ANT-WUORINEN; Man. Dir RAIMO LINTUNIEMI.

Työnantajain Yleinen Ryhmä r.y. (Finnish Employers' General Group): Eteläranta 10, 00130 Helsinki; tel. (09) 172841; fax (09) 179588; Chair. LASSE KURKILAHTI; Man. Dir SARI VANNELA.

Yleinen Teollisuusliitto r.y. (General Industry Association): Eteläranta 10, 00130 Helsinki; tel. (09) 6220410; fax (09) 176135; Chair. MARKKU TALONEN; Man. Dir MARKKU KÄPPI.

UTILITIES

Helsingin Kaupungin Energialaitos (Helsinki Energy Board): POB 469, 00101 Helsinki; tel. (09) 6171; telex 122290; fax (09) 6172360; f. 1909; municipal undertaking; generates and distributes electrical power and district heating; distributes natural gas.

Imatran Voima Oy: Malminkatu 16, 00100 Helsinki; tel. (09) 85611; telex 124608; fax (09) 5666235; f. 1932; electric power, including nuclear energy, district heating; provides consultancy services world-wide; 95.6% state-owned; merger with state oil and petrochemicals concern, Neste, announced in December 1997; CEO HEIKKI MARTTINEN; 5,000 employees.

Electricity

Kemijoki Oy: Valtakatu 9–11, POB 8131, 96101 Rovaniemi; tel. (016) 7401; fax (016) 7402325; f. 1954; electric power; 78.17% state-owned; Chair. of Supervisory Board LASSE NÄSI; Chair. of Board of Management MARKKU AUTTI; 417 employees.

Suomen Sähkölaitosyhdistys r.y. (Association of Finnish Electric Utilities): Mannerheimintie 76A, 00250 Helsinki; POB 100, 00101 Helsinki; tel. (09) 408188; fax (09) 442994; f. 1926; 122 mems; development of technical, economic and administrative functions of utilities; consultant services in electricity supply; educational activities; research and advice on electrical applications; collection and publication of electricity statistics; publishes consumer magazine *Sähköviesti/Elbladet*; domestic and international co-operation; safety at work and environmental conservation.

Suomen Voimalaitosyhdistys r.y.—SVY (Finnish Power Plant Association): Lönnrotinkatu 4B, 00120 Helsinki 12; tel. (09) 602944; fax (09) 644098; f. 1928; promotes progress in electricity supply and transmission; 235 individual mems, 51 companies, 5 other organizations.

CO-OPERATIVES

Finn Coop Pellervo (Confederation of Finnish Co-operatives): Simonkatu 6, POB 77, 00100 Helsinki; tel. (09) 4767501; fax (09) 6948845; f. 1899; central organization of co-operatives; Man. Dir SAMULI SKURNIK; 400 mem. societies (incl. 7 central co-operative societies).

Munakunta (Co-operative Egg Producers' Association): POB 6, 20761 Piispanristi; tel. 21214420; fax 212144222; f. 1921; Man. Dir HEIKKI PARVIAINEN; 3,472 mems.

Valio Ltd (Finnish Co-operative Dairies' Association): POB 390, 00101 Helsinki; tel. (10) 381121; fax (10) 3812039; f. 1905; marketing of dairy products; Pres., CEO MATTI KAVETVUO.

TRADE UNIONS

AKAVA (Confederation of Unions for Academic Professionals): Rautatieläisenkatu 6, 00520 Helsinki; tel. (09) 141822; fax (09) 142595; f. 1950; 32 affiliates, incl. asscns of doctors, engineers, social workers and teachers; total membership 330,000; Pres. MIKKO VIITASALO; Gen. Sec. RISTO PIEKKA.

Suomen Ammattiliittojen Keskusjärjestö (SAK) r.y. (Central Organization of Finnish Trade Unions): Siltasaarenkatu 3A, POB 157, 00531 Helsinki; tel. (09) 77211; fax (09) 7721447; internet http://www.sak.fi; f. 1907; 25 affiliated unions; 1,110,000 mems (1996); Pres. LAURI IHALAINEN; Dirs TUULIKKI KANNISTO, PEKKA AHMAVAARA.

Principal affiliated unions:

Auto- ja Kuljetusalan Työntekijäliitto (AKT) r.y. (Transport Workers): Haapaniemenkatu 7–9B, POB 313, 00531 Helsinki; tel. (09) 613110; fax (09) 739287; e-mail juhani.koivunen@akt.fi; f. 1948; Pres. KAUKO LEHIKOINEN; Secs MATTI VEHKAOJA, JUHANI KOIVUNEN; 48,204 mems.

Hotelli- ja Ravintolahenkilökunnan Liitto (HRHL) r.y. (Hotel and Restaurant Workers): Toinen linja 3, POB 327, 00531 Helsinki; tel. (09) 77561; fax (09) 7756223; e-mail hrhl@hrhl.fi; f. 1933; Pres. JORMA KALLIO; Sec. LEENA RAUTAVUORI; 52,504 mems.

Kemianliitto-Kemifacket r.y. (Chemical Workers): Haapaniemenkatu 7-9B, POB 324, 00531 Helsinki; tel. (09) 773971; fax (09) 7538040; f. 1993; Pres. TIMO VALLITTU; Sec. SULO KORHONEN; 35,000 mems.

Kiinteistötyöntekijäin Liitto r.y. (Caretakers): Vihermiemenkatu 5A, 00530 Helsinki; tel. (09) 750075; fax (09) 761427; f. 1948; Pres. RISTO SORSA; Sec. TAUNO ROSTEN; 12,645 mems.

Kunta-alan Ammattiliitto (KTV) r.y. (Municipal Sector): Kolmas linja 4, POB 101, 00531 Helsinki; tel. (09) 77031; fax (09) 7703397; f. 1931; Pres. JOUNI RISKILÄ; 229,622 mems.

Liikealan ammattiliitto r.y. (Commercial Employees): Paasivuorenkatu 4–6, POB 54, 00531 Helsinki; tel. (09) 77571; fax (09) 7011119; f. 1987; Pres. MAJ-LEN REMAHL; Secs NILS KOMI, JARMO KOSKI; 135,000 mems.

Metallityöväen Liitto r.y. (Metalworkers): Siltasaarenkatu 3–5A, POB 107, 00531 Helsinki; tel. (09) 77071; fax (09) 7707277; internet http://www.metalliliitto.fi; f. 1899; Pres. PER-ERIK LUNDH; Sec. ERIK LINDFORS; 164,000 mems.

Paperiliitto r.y. (Paperworkers): Paasivuorenkatu 4–6A, POB 326, 00531 Helsinki; tel. (09) 70891; fax (09) 7012279; f. 1906; Pres. JARMO LÄHTEENMÄKI; Gen. Sec. ARTTURI PENNANEN; 48,569 mems.

Puu- ja erityisalojen Liitto r.y. (Wood and Allied Workers): Haapaniemenkatu 7–9B, POB 318, 00531 Helsinki; tel. (09) 615161; fax (09) 761160; f. 1993 by merger of two unions; Pres. HEIKKI PELTONEN; Sec. KALEVI VÄISÄNEN; 55,000 mems.

Rakennusliitto r.y. (Construction Workers): Siltasaarenkatu 4, POB 307, 00531 Helsinki; tel. (09) 77021; fax (09) 7702241; f. 1930; Pres. PEKKA HYNÖNEN; 89,000 mems.

Sähköalojen ammattiliitto r.y. (Electrical Workers): Aleksanterinkatu 15, POB 747, 33101 Tampere; tel. (03) 2520111; fax (03) 2520210; f. 1955; Pres. SEPPO SALISMA; Sec. HEIMO RINNE; 30,000 mems.

Suomen Elintarviketyöläisten Liitto (SEL) r.y. (Food Workers): Siltasaarenkatu 6, POB 213, 00531 Helsinki; tel. (09) 393881; fax (09) 712059; f. 1905; Pres. RITVA SAVTSCHENKO; Sec. ARTO TALASMÄKI; 42,753 mems.

Suomen Merimies-Unioni r.y. (Seamen): Uudenmaankatu 16B, POB 249, 00121 Helsinki; tel. (09) 6152020; fax (09) 61520227; f. 1916; Pres. PER-ERIK NELIN; Sec. ERKKI UKKONEN; 9,650 mems.

Tekstiili- ja vaatetustyöväen liitto Teva r.y. (Textile and Garment Workers): Salhojankatu 27, POB 87, 33101 Tampere; tel. (03) 2593111; fax (03) 2593343; e-mail tevaliitto@tevaliitto.fi; f. 1970; Pres. PIRKKO OKSA; 20,000 mems.

Valtion yhteisjärjestö (VTY) r.y. (Joint Organization of State Employees): Haapaniemenkatu 7–9B, POB 317, 00531 Helsinki; tel. (09) 584211; fax (09) 739513; f. 1946; Pres. RAIMO RANNISTO; Sec.-Gen. PERTTI AHONEN; 40,000 mems.

Viestintäalan ammattiliitto r.y. (Media Union): Sutasarrntatu 4, 00530 Helsinki; tel. (09) 616581; fax (09) 61658333; f. 1894; Pres. PENTTI LEVO; Sec. PEKKA LAMTINEN; 32,000 mems.

STTK (Finnish Confederation of Salaried Employees): Pohjoisranta 4A, POB 248, 00171 Helsinki; tel. (09) 131521; fax (09) 652367.

The principal independent trade unions (formerly affiliated to the now-dissolved Confederation of Salaried Employees—TVK, f. 1922) include the following:

Erityisalojen Toimihenkilöliitto (ERTO) (Special Service and Clerical Employees): Asemamiehenkatu 2, 00520 Helsinki; tel. (09) 1551; f. 1968; Chair. MATTI HELLSTEN; 15,500 mems.

Hallintovirkailijoiden Keskusliitto (HVK) (Civil Servants): Ratamestarinkatu 11, 00520 Helsinki; tel. (09) 1551; f. 1992; Chair. HEIKKI KUJANPÄÄ; 12,500 mems.

Kunnallisvirkamiesliitto r.y. (KVL) (Municipal Officers): Asemamiehenkatu 4, 00520 Helsinki; tel. (09) 1551; fax (09) 1552333; f. 1918; Chair. KATRIINA PERKKA-JORTIKKA; 74,000 mems.

Maanpuolustuksen ja Turvallisuuden Ammattijärjestöt (MTAJ) r.y. (Defence and Security Employees): Ratamestarinkatu 11, 00520 Helsinki; tel. (09) 1551; f. 1992; Chair. PIRKKO MATTILA; 7,800 mems.

Opetus- ja tutkimusalan unioni (OTU) (Teaching and Research Employees): Ratamestarinkatu 11, 00520 Helsinki; tel. (09) 143515; f. 1992; Chair. SINIKKA OLANDER; 9,500 mems.

Pankkitoimihenkilöliitto (Bank Employees): Ratamestarinkatu 12, 00520 Helsinki; tel. (09) 22914300; fax (09) 229141; f. 1931; Pres. CHRISTINA HOLMLUND; Sec.-Gen. SIMO LEIVO; 42,000 mems.

Poliisijärjestöjen Liitto (Police): Asemamiehenkatu 2, 00520 Helsinki; tel. (09) 1551; f. 1990; Chair. TIMO MIKKOLA; 12,600 mems.

Suomen Perushoitajaliitto (Enrolled Nurses): Asemamiehenkatu 2, 00520 Helsinki; tel. (09) 141833; f. 1948; Chair. KAARINA MUHLI; 36,000 mems.

Suomen Teollisuustoimihenkilöiden Liitto (Salaried Employees in Industry): Asemamiehenkatu 4, 00520 Helsinki; tel. (09) 1551; fax (09) 1481930; internet http://www.stl.fi; f. 1917; Pres. HELENA RISSANEN; Admin. Dir MARJATTA VÄISÄNEN; 51,000 mems.

Tehy (The Union of Health and Social Care Services): POB 10,00060 Helsinki; tel. (09) 1551; telex 122505; fax (09) 1483038; f. 1982; Chair. JAANA LAITINEN-PESOLA; 110,000 mems.

Vakuutusväen Liitto r.y. (Insurance Employees): Asemamiehenkatu 2, 00520 Helsinki; tel. (09) 1552432; fax (09) 142413; e-mail pekka.portilla@jttpalvelut.fi; f. 1945; Chair. SIRPA KOMONEN; Exec. Dir PEKKA PORTTILA; 12,000 mems.

Valtion Laitosten ja Yhtiöiden Toimihenkilöliitto (Employees in State-owned Institutions and Companies): Topparikuja 7, 00520 Helsinki; tel. (09) 348050; fax (09) 145135; f. 1945; Gen. Sec. PEKKA ELORANTA; 10,000 mems.

Transport

RAILWAYS

Finland has 5,860 km of railways, providing internal services and connections with Sweden and Russia. An underground railway service has been provided by Helsinki City Transport since 1982.

Karhula Railway: Ratakatu 8, 48600 Karhula; tel. 298221; telex 53170; fax 298225; f. 1937; goods transport; operates 10 km of railway (1,524 mm gauge); Man. PERTTI HONKALA.

VR Group: Vilhonkatu 13, POB 488, 00101 Helsinki; tel. (09) 7071; telex 301151; fax (09) 7073700; began operating 1862; privatized in 1995; operates 5,864 km of railways; wide gauge (1,524 mm); 2,100 km of route are electrified; Pres. and CEO HENRI KUITUNEN; Exec. Vice-Pres. JUHANI KOPPERI.

ROADS

At 31 December 1996 there were 77,782 km of public roads, of which 431 km were motorways, 12,338 km other main roads, 29,073 km secondary or regional roads and 35,939 other roads.

Tielaitos (National Road Administration): POB 33, 00521 Helsinki; tel. (204) 44150; fax (204) 442202; f. 1799; supervises nine road districts; maintains the public road network, including bridges and ferries; Dir-Gen. LASSE WECKSTRÖM.

INLAND WATERWAYS

Lakes cover 31,500 sq km. The inland waterway system comprises 6,600 km of buoyed-out channels, 40 open canals and 26 lock canals. The total length of canals is 116 km. In 1995 the canals carried about 5.1m. metric tons of goods and 373,000 passengers.

In 1968 the southern part of the Saimaa Canal, which was leased to Finland by the USSR, was opened for vessels. In 1993 a total of 1.4m. tons of goods were transported along the canal.

SHIPPING

The chief port of export is Kotka; the main port of import is Helsinki, which has five specialized harbours. The West Harbour handles most of the transatlantic traffic, the East Harbour coastal and North Sea freight, and the South Harbour passenger traffic. North Harbour deals only in local launch traffic. Sörnäinen is the timber and coal harbour; Herttoniemi specializes in petroleum. Other important international ports are Turku (Åbo), Rauma and Hamina. The ports handled 71.2m. metric tons of cargo in 1995.

Port Authority Association

Suomen Satamaliitto (Finnish Port Association): Toinen Linja 14, 00530 Helsinki; tel. (09) 7711; fax (09) 7530474; Gen. Dir ALPO NASKI.

Port Authorities

Hamina: Haminan Kapungin Satamalaitos, POB 14, Hamina; tel. (05) 495400; fax (05) 495419; Port Dir HEIMC HEIKKILA; Harbour Master TAIPO MANSIKKA.

Helsinki: Helsinki Port Authority, Olympiaranta 3, 00140 Helsinki; tel. (09) 173331; fax (09) 17333232; Harbour Master K. WALLIN.

Kotka: Port Authority of Kotka, Laivurinkatu 7, 48100 Kotka; tel. (05) 2344280; fax (05) 2181375; Harbour Master Capt. JUHANI KAUTTONEN.

Rauma: Port of Rauma Authority, 26100 Rauma; tel. (02) 8344710; fax (02) 8226369.

Turku: Turku Port Authority, Linnankatu 80, 20100 Turku; tel. (02) 2674111; fax (02) 2674125; Harbour Master TOM JOUTSIA.

Shipowners' Association

Suomen Varustamoyhdistys r.y. (Finnish Shipowners' Association): Satamakatu 4, POB 155, 00161 Helsinki; tel. (09) 6226730; fax (09) 669251; f. 1932; Chair. ERKKI GRÖNQVIST; Man. Dir PER FORSSKÅHL; 10 mems.

Principal Companies

Bore: Veistämönaukio 1–3, POB 144, 20101 Turku; tel. (02) 2813600; telex 62287; fax (02) 2534036; f. 1897; Man. Dir KAJ ERIKSSON; 6 cargo ferries; 40,416 dwt.

ESL Shipping Oy: Suolakivenkatu 10, 00810 Helsinki; tel. (09) 7595777; telex 124453; fax (09) 787315; world-wide tramp services; Man. Dir H. HÖCKERT.

FG Shipping Oy Ab: Lönnrotinkatu 21, POB 406, 00121 Helsinki; tel. (10) 21640; telex 124462; fax (09) 2164243; e-mail fgs@fg-shipping.fi; f. 1947 (until 1989 Oy Finnlines Ltd); cargo traffic, chartering; ship management, marine consulting; Pres. ESKO MUSTAMÄKI.

Finncarriers Oy Ab: Porkkalankatu 7, POB 197, 00180 Helsinki; tel. (09) 1034350; telex 1001743; fax (09) 103435200; f. 1975; liner and contract services between Finland and other European countries; overland and inland services combined with direct sea links; contract services in the North Atlantic and bulk traffic in the Baltic; Man. Dir ASSER AHLESKOG; 3 cargo ferries; 28,335 dwt.

Finnish Maritime Agencies (Fimag) Oy: POB 124, 00241 Helsinki; tel. (09) 1483070; fax (09) 145737; Man. Dir REIJO NIIRANEN; 1 oil tanker; 11,474 dwt.

Finnlines Oy/Finnlines Ab: Lönnrotinkatu 21, POB 182, 00121 Helsinki; tel. (09) 1055440; fax (09) 105544425; Pres., CEO ANTTI LAGERROOS.

Alfons Håkans Oy Ab: Linnankatu 36C, 20100 Turku; tel. (02) 2516633; fax (02) 2515873; 2 tugs.

Neste Oy: POB 20, Keilaniemi 02151 Espoo; tel. (020) 4501; telex 124641; fax (020) 4504447; internet http://www.neste.com; f. 1948; CEO JAAKKO IHAMUOTILA; Exec. Vice-Pres. (Logistics Services) ERKKI GRÖNQVIST.

Oy Nielsen Shipping Co Ltd: Lönnrotinkatu 18, 00120 Helsinki; tel. (09) 68503435; telex 125417; fax (09) 68503439; f. 1923; managing owners for about 10,000 dwt tanker and dry cargo; shipbrokers, port agents; Man. Dir ASKO ARKKOLA.

Rederi Ab Engship: Slottsgatan 33B, 20100 Turku; tel. (02) 5125500; fax (02) 2502087; Man. Dir KAJ ENGBLOM; 12 dry cargo vessels; 78,000 dwt.

Silja Oy Ab: POB 659, 00101 Helsinki; tel. (09) 18041; fax (09) 176623; f. 1883; cruise and ferry traffic in the Baltic (Silja Line), the English Channel (Sally); Man. Dir JUKKA SUOMINEN; 9 passenger vessels.

CIVIL AVIATION

An international airport is situated at Helsinki-Vantaa, 19 km from Helsinki. International and domestic services also operate to and from airports at Ivalo, Joensuu, Jyväskylä, Kajaani, Kemi-Tornio, Kruunupyy, Kuopio, Lappeenranta, Mariehamn, Oulu, Pori, Rovaniemi, Savonlinna, Tampere-Pirkkala, Turku, Vaasa and Varkaus. Domestic services are available at airports at Enontekiö, Kittilä, Kuusamo and Mikkeli.

In 1996 10.6m. passengers passed through Finnish airports.

Ilmailulaitos (Civil Aviation Administration): POB 50, 01531 Vantaa; tel. (09) 82771; telex 121247; fax (09) 82772099; e-mail ilmailulaitos@fcaa.fi.

Principal Airlines

Air Botnia: POB 168, 01531 Vantaa; tel. (09) 8702530; fax (09) 822491; f. 1994; domestic services; acquired by Scandinavian Airlines System in early 1998; Man. Dir K. HOHTI.

Finnair Oy: Tietotie 11A, POB 15, 01053 Vantaa; tel. (09) 81881; telex 124946; fax (09) 8184401; f. 1923; 59.8% state-owned; 22 domestic services and 45 international services (to Europe, North America, the Middle East and the Far East); Pres. and CEO ANTTI POTILA.

Tourism

Europe's largest inland water system, vast forests, magnificent scenery and the possibility of holiday seclusion are Finland's main attractions. Most visitors come from other Nordic countries, Germany, Russia, the UK and the USA. Registered accommodation establishments recorded 3,292,484 overnight stays by foreigners in 1995. Travel account receipts amounted to 6,812m. markkaa in 1993.

Matkailun edistämiskeskus (Finnish Tourist Board): Töölönkatu 11, POB 625, 00101 Helsinki; tel. (09) 4176911; telex 122690; fax (09) 41769333; f. 1973; Chair. MATTI VUORIA; Dir PIRJO-RIITTA VATANEN.

FINNISH EXTERNAL TERRITORY

THE ÅLAND ISLANDS

Introductory Survey

Location, Language, Religion, Flag, Capital

The Åland Islands are a group of 6,554 islands (of which some 60 are inhabited) in the Gulf of Bothnia, between Finland and Sweden. About 95% of the inhabitants are Swedish-speaking, and Swedish is the official language. The majority profess Christianity and belong to the Evangelical Lutheran Church of Finland. The flag displays a red cross, bordered with yellow, on a blue background, the upright of the cross being to the left of centre. The capital is Mariehamn, which is situated on Åland, the largest island in the group.

History and Government

For geographical and economic reasons, the Åland Islands were traditionally associated closely with Sweden. In 1809, when Sweden was forced to cede Finland to Russia, the islands were incorporated into the Finnish Grand Duchy. However, following Finland's declaration of independence from the Russian Empire, in 1917, the Ålanders demanded the right to self-determination and sought to be reunited with Sweden. Their demands were supported by the Swedish Government and people. In 1920 Finland granted the islands autonomy but refused to acknowledge their secession, and in 1921 the Åland question was referred to the League of Nations. In June the League granted Finland sovereignty over the islands, while directing that certain conditions pertaining to national identity be included in the autonomy legislation offered by Finland and that the islands should be a neutral and non-fortified region. Elections were held in accordance with the new legislation, and the new provincial parliament (Landsting) held its first plenary session on 9 June 1922. The revised Autonomy Act of 1951 provided for independent rights of legislation in internal affairs and for autonomous control over the islands' economy. This Act could not be amended or repealed by the Finnish Eduskunta without the consent of the Åland Landsting.

In 1988 constitutional reform introduced the principle of a majority parliamentary government, to be formed by the Lantrådskandidat, the member of the Landsting nominated to conduct negotiations beween the parties. These negotiations may yield two alternative outcomes: either the nominee will submit a proposal to create a new government or the nominee will fail to reach agreement on a new government (in which case renewed negotiations will ensue). The first formal parliamentary government and opposition were duly established. The governing coalition consisted of the three largest parties that had been elected to the Landsting in October 1987 (the Centre Party, the Liberals and the Moderates), which together held 22 seats in the 30-member legislature.

At a general election held on 20 October 1991 the Centre Party increased its share of the seats in the Landsting to 10, while the Liberal Party secured seven seats and the Moderates and Social Democrats won six and four seats respectively. The parties forming the new coalition Government included the Centre and Moderate Parties, as before, while the Liberal Party was replaced by the Social Democratic Party.

A revised Autonomy Act, providing Åland with a greater degree of autonomous control, was adopted in 1991 and took effect on 1 January 1993. The rules regarding legislative authority were modernized, and the right of the Åland legislature (henceforth known as the Lagting) to enact laws was extended. Åland was given greater discretion with respect to its budget, and the revised Act also introduced changes in matters such as right of domicile, land ownership regulations and administrative authority. The Autonomy Act contains a provision that, in any treaty which Finland may conclude with a foreign state and to which Åland is a party, the Lagting must consent to the statute implementing the treaty in order for the provision to enter into force in Åland. This procedure gave Åland the opportunity not to consent to membership of the European Union (EU). A referendum on the issue of Åland's proposed accession to membership of the EU in 1995 was held in November 1994, immediately after similar referendums in Finland and Sweden had shown a majority in favour of membership. (A small majority of Åland citizens had supported Finland's membership.) Despite low participation in the referendum, 73.7% of the votes cast supported membership and Åland duly joined the EU, together with Finland and Sweden, on 1 January 1995. Under the terms of the treaty of accession, Åland was accorded special exemption from tax union with the EU in order to stimulate the ferry and tourist industries. (In November 1997 it was reported that two of Europe's largest ferry operators, Silja and Viking—both Finnish—were planning to re-route their major services via Åland in order to continue to conduct duty-free sales, which were expected to be abolished under EU proposals.)

A general election was held on 15 October 1995. The Centre Party secured nine seats and the Liberal Party won eight seats, while the Moderates and Social Democrats maintained the representation that they had achieved in the previous parliament. The new coalition Government was composed of members of the Centre and Moderate Parties and one independent.

Economic Affairs

In 1993 the gross domestic product (GDP) of the Åland Islands, measured at current prices, was 3,240m. marks. Forests cover most of the islands, and only 8% of the total land area is arable. The principal crops are cereals, sugar-beet, potatoes and fruit. Dairy-farming and sheep-rearing are also important.

Since 1960 the economy of the islands has expanded and diversified. Fishing has declined as a source of income, and shipping (particularly the operation of ferry services between Finland and Sweden), trade and tourism have become the dominant economic sectors. In 1993 services employed 29.9% of the labour force, while communications, including shipping, employed 18.2%. The political autonomy of the islands and their strategic location between Sweden and Finland have contributed to expanding banking and trade sectors, which employed 20.5% of the working population in 1993. Unemployment stood at 4% in 1996.

Education and Social Welfare

The education system is similar to that of Finland, except that Swedish is the language of instruction and Finnish an optional subject. In 1995 government medical services included two hospitals, with a total of 151 beds, and 44 physicians.

Statistical Survey

Source: Government of Åland, Department of Statistics and Economic Research, POB 60, 22101 Mariehamn; tel. (018) 25000; fax (018) 19495.

AREA, POPULATION AND DENSITY

Area: 1,552 sq km (599 sq miles), of which 25 sq km (9.7 sq miles) is inland waters.

Population (31 December 1996): 25,257.

Density (1996): 16.5 per sq km.

Births and Deaths (1995): Registered live births 338 (birth rate 13.4 per 1,000); Deaths 258 (death rate 10.2 per 1,000).

Economically Active Population (1993): Agriculture 1,219; Manufacturing 1,129; Construction 624; Trade 1,524; Transport 2,107; Financial services 851; Other services 3,466; Statistical discrepancy 660; Total employed 11,580.

Labour Force (1994): Males 6,349; Females 5,801; Total 12,150.

FINANCE

Currency: Finnish currency: 100 penni (penniä) = 1 mark (markka).

Government Accounts ('000 marks, 1995): Revenue 1,037,756; Expenditure 1,008,373.

Cost of Living (consumer price index; base: 1985 = 100): 139.0 in 1993; 140.1 in 1994; 141.1 in 1995.

Gross Domestic Product (million marks at current prices): 3,853 in 1991; 3,554 in 1992; 3,240 in 1993.

EXTERNAL TRADE

1993 (million marks): Imports 2,240; Exports 3,046.

TRANSPORT AND TOURISM

Shipping (1996): Merchant fleet 40 vessels; total displacement 315,896 grt.

Tourist Arrivals (1995): 1,120,697.

Directory

Government and Legislature

The Governor of Åland represents the Government of Finland and is appointed by the Finnish President (with the agreement of the Speaker of the Åland legislature). The legislative body is the Lagting, comprising 30 members, elected every four years on a basis of proportional representation. All Ålanders over the age of 18 years, possessing Åland regional citizenship, have the right to vote and to seek election. An executive council (Landskapsstyrelse), consisting of five to seven members, is elected by the Lagting, and its Chairman (Lantråd) is the highest-ranking politician in Åland after the Speaker (Talman) of the Lagting. The President has the right to veto Lagting decisions only when the Lagting exceeds its legislative competence, or when there is a threat to the security of the country.

Governor: HENRIK GUSTAFSSON.

LANDSKAPSSTYRELSE

(February 1998)

The governing coalition comprises members of the Centre Party, the Moderate Party and the Independents.

Chairman (Lantråd): ROGER JANSSON (Moderate Party).

Deputy Chairman: ROGER NORDLUND (Centre Party).

Members: ANDERS ERIKSSON (Centre Party), GUN CARLSSON (Centre Party), ANDERS ENGLUND (Centre Party), HARRIET LINDEMAN (Moderate Party), BENGT HÄGER (Independents).

LAGTING

Speaker (Talman): RAGNAR ERLANDSSON.

Election, 15 October 1995

	% of votes cast	Seats
Åländsk Center (Centre Party)	27.8	9
Liberalerna på Åland (Liberal Party)	26.6	8
Frisinnad samverkan (Moderate Party)	20.6	6
Ålands socialdemokrater (Social Democratic Party)	15.2	4
Independents	9.8	3
Total	100.0	30

Political Organizations

Unless otherwise indicated, the address of each of the following organizations is: Ålands Lagting, POB 69, 22101 Mariehamn; tel. (018) 25000; fax (018) 13302.

Åländsk Center (Centre Party): e-mail centern@lagtinget.aland.fi.; Chair. ROGER NORDLUND; Leader JAN-ERIK MATTSSON.

Ålands socialdemokrater (Social Democratic Party): Leader BARBRO SUNDBACK; Sec. PETER ANDERSSON.

Frisinnad samverkan (Moderate Party): Chair. HARRIET LINDEMAN; Leader MAX SIRÉN; Sec.-Gen. NINA HÄGERSTRAND.

Gröna på Åland (Green Party): 13 Mariegatan, 22100 Mariehamn; tel. (018) 11528; f. 1987; Chair. and Leader CHRISTINA HEDMAN-JAAKKOLA.

Liberalerna på Åland (Liberal Party): tel. (018) 25362; fax (018) 16075; e-mail liberalerna@lagtinget.aland.fi; Chair. OLOF ERLAND; Leader LISBETH ERIKSSON; Gen. Sec. BIRGITTA GUSTAVSSON.

Obunden samling (Independents): Chair. BERIT HAMPF; Leader ERIK TUDEER.

The Press

Åland: POB 50, 22101 Mariehamn; tel. (018) 26026; fax (018) 15505; 5 a week; circ. 11,502.

Nya Åland: POB 21, 22101 Mariehamn; tel. (018) 23450; fax (018) 23449; 4 a week; circ. 8,220.

Broadcasting and Communications

RADIO

Ålands Radio och TV: POB 140, 22101 Mariehamn; tel. (018) 26060; fax (928) 26520; broadcasts 70 hours a week; Man. Dir PIA ROTHBERG-OLOFSSON; Editor-in-Chief ASTRID OLHAGEN.

Finance

BANKS

(cap. = capital; res = reserves; dep. = deposits; m. = million; amounts in marks; brs = branches)

Ålandsbanken Ab (Bank of Åland Ltd): Nygatan 2, POB 3, 22101 Mariehamn; tel. (018) 29011; telex 63157; fax (018) 29228; f. 1919 as Ålands Aktiebank; name changed as above in 1980; merged with Ålands Hypoteksbank Ab in November 1995; cap. 72m., res 155.5m., dep. 3,208.0m. (Dec. 1995); Man. Dir FOLKE HUSELL; 25 brs.

Andelsbanken för Åland: POB 34, 22101 Mariehamn; tel. (018) 26000; Dirs HÅKAN CLEMES, ROLAND KARLSSON.

Lappo Andelsbank: 22840 Lappo; tel. (018) 56621; fax (018) 56699; Dir TORSTEN NORDBERG.

Merita Bank: Torggatan 10, 22100 Mariehamn; tel. (018) 5330; fax (018) 12499; Dirs ERLING GUSTAFSSON, JAN-ERIK RASK.

Postbanken: Torggatan 4, 22100 Mariehamn; tel. (018) 28055; fax (018) 28608.

INSURANCE

Alandia Group: Ålandsvägen 31, POB 121, 22101 Mariehamn; tel. (018) 29000; telex 63117; fax (018) 12290; e-mail info@alandiabolag-en.fi; f. 1938; life, non-life and marine; comprises three subsidiaries; Gen. Man. JOHAN DAHLMAN.

Ålands Ömsesidiga Försäkringsbolag (Åland Mutual Insurance Co): Köpmansgatan 6, POB 64, 22101 Mariehamn; tel. (018) 27600; telex 63191; fax (018) 27610; f. 1866; property; Man. Dir BJARNE OLOFSSON.

Cabanco Insurance Co Ltd: Köpmansgatan 6, POB 64, 22101 Mariehamn; tel. (018) 27690; fax (018) 27699; Man. Dir BO-STURE SJÖLUND.

Hamnia Reinsurance Co Ltd: Köpmansgatan 6, POB 64, 22101 Mariehamn; tel. (018) 27690; fax (018) 27699; Man. Dir BO-STURE SJÖLUND.

Trade and Industry

CHAMBER OF COMMERCE

Ålands Handelskammare: Nygatan 9, 22100 Mariehamn; tel. (018) 29029; fax (018) 21129; f. 1945; br. in Helsinki; Chair. PETER GRÖNLUND; Man. Dir AGNETA ERLANDSSON.

TRADE ASSOCIATION

Ålands Företagareförening (Åland Business Asscn): Nygatan 9, 22100 Mariehamn; tel. (018) 29033; fax (018) 21129; f. 1957; Chair. SIGVARD PERSSON; Sec. BO HELENIUS.

EMPLOYERS' ORGANIZATIONS

Ålands Arbetsgivareförening (Åland Employers' Asscn): Nygatan 9, 22100 Mariehamn; tel. (018) 291474; fax (018) 21129; f. 1969; Chair. ERIK SUNDBLOM; Man. Dir ANDERS KULVES.

Ålands Fiskodlarförening: (Åland Fish Farmers' Asscn): Storagatan 14, 22100 Mariehamn; tel. (018) 17834; fax (018) 17833; Chair. MARCUS ERIKSSON; Sec. OLOF KARLSSON.

Ålands köpmannaförening (Åland Businessmen's Asscn): Nygatan 9, 22100 Mariehamn; f. 1927; Chair. ROLF NORDLUND; Sec. VIKING GRANSKOG.

Ålands producentförbund (Åland Agricultural Producers' Asscn): Styrmansgatan 1B, 22100 Mariehamn; fax (018) 11410; f. 1946; Chair. JAN SUNDBERG; Man. Dir OLOF ÖSTRÖM.

Utrikesfartens Småtonnageförening (Shipowners Asscn for Smaller Ships in Foreign Trade): Norragatan 7A, 22100 Mariehamn; Chair. OLOF WIDÉN.

TRADE UNIONS

AKAVA-Åland (Professional Asscn): Storagatan 14, 22100 Mariehamn; tel. (018) 16348; fax (018) 12125; Chair. PEKKA ERÄMETSÄ Gen. Sec. Maj. BRITT LIND.

FFC/SAK; s Lokalorganisation på Åland (SAK Regional Trade Union in Åland): POB 108, 22101 Mariehamn; tel. (018) 16207; fax (018) 17207; e-mail kurt.gustafsson@sak.fi; Chair. FREJVID GRANQVIST; Gen. Sec. KURT GUSTAFSSON.

Fackorgan för offentliga arbetsomraden på Åland (FOA-Å) (Joint Organization of Civil Servants and Workers (VTY) in Åland): Ålandsvägen 55, 22100 Mariehamn; tel. (018) 16976; Chair. ULLA ANDERSSON; Gen. Sec. BRITT-MARIE LUND.

Tjänstemannaorganisationerna på Åland, TCÅ r.f. (Union of Salaried Employees in Åland): Strandgatan 23, 22100 Mariehamn; tel. (018) 16210; Chair. YVONNE ASPHOLM; Gen. Sec. TUULA MATTSSON.

Transport

The islands are linked to the Swedish and Finnish mainlands by ferry services and by air services from Mariehamn airport.

SHIPPING

Ålands Redarförening r.f. (Åland Shipowners' Association): Hamngatan 8, 22100 Mariehamn; tel. (018) 13430; fax (018) 22520; f. 1934; Chair. GUN ERIKSSON–HJERLING; Man. Dir HANS AHLSTRÖM.

Principal Companies

Birka Line Ab: POB 175, 22101 Mariehamn; tel. (018) 27027; telex 63163; fax (018) 15118; f. 1971; passenger service; Chair. K.–J. HAGMAN; Man. Dir WIKING JOHANSSON.

Lundqvist Rederierna: Norra Esplanadgatan 9B, 22100 Mariehamn; tel. (018) 26050; telex 63113; fax (018) 15411; f. 1927; tanker services; Pres. STIG LUNDQVIST; total tonnage 1.2m. dwt.

Rederi Ab Lillgaard: Nygatan 5, POB 136, 22101 Mariehamn; tel. (018) 13120; fax (018) 17220.

Rederiaktiebolaget Gustaf Erikson: POB 49, 22101 Mariehamn; tel. (018) 27070; telex 63112; fax (018) 12670; e-mail gustaf.erikson@co.inet.fi; f. 1913; Man. Dir GUN ERIKSON-HJERLING; manages 12 dry cargo and refrigerated vessels.

United Shipping Ltd Ab: Storagatan 11, POB 175, 22101 Mariehamn; tel. (018) 27320; fax (018) 23223.

Viking Line Ab: Norragatan 4, 22100 Mariehamn; tel. (018) 27000; telex 63151; fax (018) 16977; f. 1963; Chair. BEN LUNDQVIST; Man. Dir NILS-ERIK EKLUND; 6 car/passenger vessels; total tonnage 205,860 grt.

Viking Line Marketing: Storagatan 2, POB 35, 22101 Mariehamn; tel. (018) 26011; fax (018) 15811; Man. Dir BORIS EKMAN.

Tourism

Ålands TuristFörbund (Åland Tourist Asscn): Storagatan 8, 22100 Mariehamn; tel. (018) 24000; fax (018) 24265; internet http://www. turist.aland.fi; f. 1989; Chair. LASSE WIKLÖF; Man. Dir GUNILLA G. NORDLUND.

FRANCE

Introductory Survey

Location, Climate, Language, Religion, Flag, Capital

The French Republic is situated in western Europe. It is bounded to the north by the English Channel (la Manche), to the east by Belgium, Luxembourg, Germany, Switzerland and Italy, to the south by the Mediterranean Sea and Spain, and to the west by the Atlantic Ocean. The island of Corsica is part of metropolitan France, while four overseas departments, two overseas 'collectivités territoriales' and four overseas territories also form an integral part of the Republic. The climate is temperate throughout most of the country, but in the south it is of the Mediterranean type, with warm summers and mild winters. Temperatures in Paris are generally between 0°C (32°F) and 24°C (75°F). The principal language is French, which has numerous regional dialects, and small minorities speak Breton and Basque. Almost all French citizens profess Christianity, and about 81% are adherents of the Roman Catholic Church. Other Christian denominations are represented, and there are also Muslim and Jewish communities. The national flag (proportions three by two) has three equal vertical stripes, of blue, white and red. The capital is Paris.

Recent History

In September 1939, following Nazi Germany's invasion of Poland, France and the United Kingdom declared war on Germany, thus entering the Second World War. In June 1940, however, France was forced to sign an armistice, following a swift invasion and occupation of French territory by German forces. After the liberation of France from German occupation in 1944, a provisional Government took office under Gen. Charles de Gaulle, leader of the 'Free French' forces during the wartime resistance. The war in Europe ended in May 1945, when German forces surrendered at Reims. In 1946, following a referendum, the Fourth Republic was established and Gen. de Gaulle announced his intention to retire from public life.

France had 26 different Governments from 1946 until the Fourth Republic came to an end in 1958 with an insurrection in Algeria (then an overseas department) and the threat of civil war. In May 1958 Gen. de Gaulle was invited by the President, René Coty, to form a government. In June he was invested as Prime Minister by the National Assembly, with the power to rule by decree for six months. A new Constitution was approved by referendum in September and promulgated in October; thus the Fifth Republic came into being, with Gen. de Gaulle taking office as its first President in January 1959. The new system provided a strong, stable executive. Real power rested in the hands of the President, who strengthened his authority through direct appeals to the people in national referendums.

The early years of the Fifth Republic were overshadowed by the Algerian crisis. De Gaulle suppressed a revolt of French army officers and granted Algeria independence in 1962, withdrawing troops and repatriating French settlers. A period of relative tranquillity was ended in 1968, when dissatisfaction with the Government's authoritarian policies on education and information, coupled with discontent at low wage rates and lack of social reform, fused into a serious revolt of students and workers. For a month the republic was threatened, but the student movement collapsed and the general strike was settled by large wage rises. In April 1969 President de Gaulle resigned after defeat in a referendum on regional reform.

Georges Pompidou, who had been Prime Minister between April 1962 and July 1968, was elected President in June 1969. He attempted to continue Gaullism, while also responding to the desire for change. The Gaullist hold on power was threatened, however, by the Union of the Left, formed in 1972 by the Parti Socialiste (PS) and the Parti Communiste Français (PCF). Leaders of the PS and the PCF agreed a common programme for contesting legislative elections. At a general election for the National Assembly in March 1973, the government coalition was returned with a reduced majority.

President Pompidou died in April 1974. Valéry Giscard d'Estaing, formerly leader of the Républicains Indépendants (RI), supported by the Gaullist Union des Démocrates pour la République (UDR) and the centre parties, was elected President in May, narrowly defeating François Mitterrand, the First Secretary of the PS and the candidate of the Union of the Left (which was disbanded in 1977). A coalition Government was formed from members of the RI, the UDR and the centre parties. In August 1976 Jacques Chirac resigned as Prime Minister and was replaced by Raymond Barre, hitherto Minister of External Trade. Chirac undertook the transformation of the UDR into a new Gaullist party, the Rassemblement pour la République (RPR). In February 1978 the non-Gaullist parties in the Government formed the Union pour la Démocratie Française (UDF), to compete against RPR candidates in the National Assembly elections held in March, when the governing coalition retained a working majority.

In the April/May 1981 presidential elections, Mitterrand, the candidate of the PS, defeated Giscard d'Estaing, with the support of communist voters. Pierre Mauroy was appointed Prime Minister and formed France's first left-wing Council of Ministers for 23 years. At elections for a new Assembly, held in June, the PS and associated groups, mainly the Mouvement des Radicaux de Gauche (MRG), won an overall majority of the seats. The Government was reorganized to include four members of the PCF in the Council of Ministers. The new Government introduced a programme of reforms: social benefits and working conditions were substantially improved; several major industrial enterprises and financial institutions were brought under state control; and administrative and financial power was transferred from government-appointed Préfets to locally-elected departmental assemblies.

An election to the National Assembly (now enlarged from 491 to 577 seats) took place in March 1986. A system of proportional representation, with voters choosing from party lists in each department or territory (in accordance with legislation introduced in 1985), replaced the previous system of single-member constituencies. The PS remained the largest single party in the new Assembly, but the centre-right RPR-UDF alliance was able to command a majority of seats, with the support of minor right-wing parties. The PCF suffered a severe decline in support, while the extreme right-wing Front National (FN) won seats in the Assembly for the first time. At President Mitterrand's invitation, Jacques Chirac, the leader of the RPR, formed a new Council of Ministers, comprising mainly RPR-UDF members. The socialist President (whose term of office did not expire until 1988) was thus 'cohabiting' with a right-wing Government: a situation unprecedented in France.

In April 1986 Chirac introduced controversial legislation that allowed his Government to legislate by decree on economic and social issues and on the proposed reversion to a single-seat majority voting system for elections to the National Assembly. However, Mitterrand insisted on exercising the presidential right to withhold approval of decrees that reversed the previous Government's social reforms. Chirac was, therefore, forced to resort to the 'guillotine' procedure (setting a time-limit for parliamentary consideration of legislative proposals) to gain parliamentary consent for contentious legislation, which, if approved by the predominantly right-wing Senate and the Constitutional Council, the President would be legally bound to approve. In July this procedure was used to enact legislation for the transfer to the private sector of 65 state-owned companies.

In the second round of voting in the presidential election, held in May 1988, Mitterrand (with 54% of the votes) defeated Chirac (with 46%). Michel Rocard succeeded Chirac as Prime Minister. However, the Government formed by Rocard (comprising mostly PS members) failed to command a reliable majority in the National Assembly, which was dissolved: a general election took place in June, with voting based on the single-seat majority system that had been reintroduced by Chirac. The RPR and the UDF contested the election jointly (with some other right-wing candidates) as the Union du Rassemblement et du Centre (URC), winning 272 seats. The PS formed an alliance with the MRG, together securing a total of 276 seats. The PCF won 27 seats and the FN one. Rocard was reappointed Prime Minister, and formed an administration in which the principal portfolios were held by members of the previous Government, although six UDF members and a number of independents were also included.

The Government was criticized by members of the judiciary, following the introduction, in December 1989, of legislation which appeared to discriminate in favour of elected politicians by protecting them from prosecution for politically-related crimes; the amnesty was appended to a law which exonerated all persons guilty of offences relating to party finances that had been committed before June 1989, but instituted rigorous rules governing such finances in the future. Following revelations made in early 1990 that a consultancy firm, Urba, had made excessive and undisclosed contributions to Mitterrand's re-election campaign funds, the examining magistrate who was investigating the allegations was ordered by the Minister of Justice to stop seizing documents from the company. A motion of 'no confidence' (proposed by the RPR, UDF and UDC), which accused the Government of interfering with the judiciary, was defeated in the National Assembly. However, members of the judiciary claimed that there had been no legal infringement by the examining magistrate.

In April 1991 Rocard proved unable to negotiate majority support in the National Assembly for three government bills. This failure to guarantee success for the Government's legislative programme, and the apparent disunity within the PS, seriously undermined Rocard's position. In May he resigned and was replaced by Edith Cresson, who thus became France's first female Prime Minister. Cresson had resigned eight months previously from her post as Minister of European Affairs, in protest at Rocard's economic policies and the pace of their implementation. On assuming the premiership, she promised an increase in government control over economic and industrial planning.

The issues of urban deprivation, immigration and race relations featured in political debate throughout 1991. Certain politicians of the RPR, UDF and FN made public statements about immigration which were interpreted as inflammatory, and violent incidents in a number of cities exacerbated a widespread climate of hostility towards immigrants. In June Cresson announced emergency measures, designed to provide training opportunities for young people in poor areas. In addition, an increased police presence in the country's suburban areas was to be assured. In July the Government announced that more stringent measures would be taken against illegal immigrants and that stricter criteria would be applied in the consideration of requests for asylum. In October the National Assembly approved a law introducing heavy penalties for persons found guilty of employing illegal immigrants or conducting them into France.

The results of the regional elections that took place in late March 1992 revealed a notable decline in support for the main traditional parties, particularly for the PS. In metropolitan France the PS obtained only 18.3% of the total votes cast, while the Union pour la France (UPF, the electoral alliance of the RPR and the UDF, formed in 1990) received 33.0%, the FN 13.9%, and two environmental parties (Les Verts and Génération Ecologie) also 13.9%. The PS again performed very poorly in subsequent cantonal elections. In early April, in response to these electoral reversals, President Mitterrand replaced Edith Cresson as Prime Minister with Pierre Bérégovoy, hitherto the Minister of State for the Economy, Finance and the Budget. On assuming the premiership, Bérégovoy declared the Government's priority to be a reduction in the rate of unemployment, which had reached 9.9% of the labour force in February. In June Bérégovoy's Government survived a major challenge to its continuance in office, by narrowly defeating a motion of 'no confidence', introduced in the National Assembly by the RPR and the UDF in protest at the Government's support for a reform of the EC's Common Agricultural Policy (CAP, see p. 164). In the same month, the Assembly approved constitutional changes allowing French ratification of the EC's Treaty on European Union (the 'Maastricht Treaty', see p. 158) to be subject to approval in a referendum. In the referendum, which was held on 20 September, 69.7% of the electorate voted, of whom 51.05% were in favour of the ratification of the Treaty, and 48.95% against. The result was received with relief by the French and other European Governments.

Further allegations of corruption were made against a number of politicians in 1992. In May the Minister of Urban Development, Bernard Tapie, resigned, following allegations of business malpractice: he was reinstated in December, when charges against him were withdrawn. In September 1992 Henri Emmanuelli, the President of the National Assembly and a former treasurer of the PS, was charged with complicity in illegal party fund-raising during the electoral campaigns of at least 20 PS members of the National Assembly. (Emmanuelli was given an 18-month suspended prison sentence in May 1995 and excluded from public office for two years.) In December the National Assembly adopted new legislation aimed at preventing political corruption and ensuring freedom of information on the funds donated to political parties.

In October 1992 two senior health service officials received prison sentences, following the discovery that unscreened blood containing the human immunodeficiency virus (HIV) had been used in transfusions. It was estimated that more than 1,200 haemophiliacs had been infected with the virus (of whom more than 200 had since died) as a result of blood transfusions that were performed in 1985. Public pressure mounted in late 1992 to have three ex-ministers—including the former Prime Minister and current leader of the PS, Laurent Fabius—indicted for their alleged part in the scandal. In December the Senate voted by an overwhelming majority to endorse the decision of the National Assembly that the three should be brought to trial before the Conseil d'Etat.

In early 1993 the RPR and the UDF agreed to present joint candidates (as the UPF) in about 500 constituencies at the elections to the National Assembly, to be held in March. As widely predicted, the elections resulted in a resounding defeat for the PS, which was attributable, in part, to the high level of unemployment, and, in part, to the recent succession of scandals in which members of the ruling party had been implicated. Several government ministers failed to retain their seats, as did Michel Rocard. In the first round of voting the RPR and the UDF together received 39.5% of the total votes cast, while the PS obtained 17.6%. However, as a result of voting in the second round a week later, the RPR won 247 of the 577 seats in the Assembly, the UDF 213, and the PS only 54. Neither the FN nor the alliance of the two main environmental parties, Les Verts and Génération Ecologie, won any seats (although they had obtained, respectively, 12.4% and 7.6% of the votes cast in the first stage of the election).

The elections of March 1993 introduced a new period of 'cohabitation' between a socialist President and a centre-right Government. Chirac, the leader of the RPR, now the largest party in the legislature, had made it known that he was not available for the post of Prime Minister (since he intended to concentrate on his candidacy in the 1995 presidential election). Mitterrand therefore asked another RPR member, Edouard Balladur (Minister of Finance in the previous 'cohabitation' Government of 1986–88), to form a government. Balladur's new administration comprised members of the RPR and the UDF. Stricter laws on immigration and the conferral of French citizenship were adopted in the course of 1993 and 1994, together with controversial legislation giving the police wider powers to make random security checks.

In October 1993 Michel Rocard was elected First Secretary of the PS, having urged the widening of the party's membership to include environmentalists, social democrats and former communists. He resigned from the post, however, in June 1994, following the poor performance of the PS in elections to the European Parliament, and was replaced by Emmanuelli. The number of seats obtained by the RPR/UDF alliance in the new Parliament was also reduced, while lists led by Bernard Tapie, the former PS minister, and Philippe de Villiers, a right-wing politician opposing the EU, each secured 12% of the votes cast. In the same month the National Assembly voted to remove the immunity from judicial investigation accorded to Tapie as a parliamentary deputy, following a number of allegations of tax evasion, embezzlement and of unfairly influencing the outcome of a football match in favour of the Marseille team he owned. In December Tapie was declared to be personally bankrupt and thereby debarred from seeking elective office for a period of five years. (In May 1996 Tapie was sentenced to six months in prison, and received several suspended prison sentences. In July his appeal against being declared bankrupt was dismissed and in September the Constitutional Court found that he could no longer be considered a parliamentary deputy. In February 1997 Tapie also lost an appeal in the Supreme Court against his prison sentence. He resigned immediately as an MEP. He was sentenced to a further six months in prison in June 1997 for additional fraudulent practices.)

In November 1994 Chirac resigned as President of the RPR in order to concentrate on his candidacy in the forthcoming presidential election. In the first round of voting on 23 April 1995, Lionel Jospin, the candidate of the PS, won 23% of the votes, while Chirac and Balladur, both representing the RPR, gained 21% and 19% respectively. Jean-Marie Le Pen, the leader of the FN, won 15%. In the second round on 7 May Chirac (with 53% of the votes) defeated Jospin (with 47%). Balladur then resigned as Prime Minister, and Chirac appointed Alain Juppé (Minister of Foreign Affairs in the previous RPR Government) as his successor. Juppé formed an administration in which the principal portfolios were evenly shared between the RPR and the UDF. In October Juppé was elected President of the RPR, while Jospin was elected First Secretary of the PS, replacing Emmanuelli.

In June 1995 Chirac announced that France was to end a moratorium on nuclear testing imposed by Mitterrand in 1992. Eight tests were to be conducted on Mururoa and Fangataufa atolls in French Polynesia, in the Pacific Ocean, between September 1995 and May 1996. The announcement caused almost universal outrage in the international community, and was condemned for its apparent disregard for South Pacific regional opinion, as well as for undermining the considerable progress made by Western nations towards a world-wide ban on nuclear-weapons tests. Large-scale demonstrations throughout the South Pacific region, Europe and Japan were accompanied by boycotts of French products in many countries. The occasion of the first test in the series prompted riots in French Polynesia by protesters demanding an end to French rule, which left much of the capital, Papeete, in ruins. Following five further tests, conducted in defiance of world opinion, Chirac announced an end to testing in January 1996.

A series of strikes and demonstrations by public-sector workers in late 1995 caused widespread disruption to the public transport system. The strikes occurred in protest at government proposals to reform the welfare system, set public-sector wage restrictions in 1996 and change pension arrangements in the public sector. In November Juppé announced a major reorganization of the Council of Ministers, reportedly following internal disagreements over the proposed welfare reforms and budgetary policy. The following month Juppé agreed to abandon the pension reforms and the strikes largely came to an end, although trade unions expressed disappointment that no concessions had been made on the proposed reforms to the welfare system. In November 1995 Alain Carignon, a former Minister of Communications in the Balladur administration, was given a three-year prison sentence for financial irregularities in connection with the awarding of commercial contracts to supply water to the city of Grenoble. The sentence was increased, on appeal, to four years in July 1996.

The Juppé Government suffered frequent criticism throughout 1996 of its economic austerity measures, which were designed to prepare the French economy for monetary union within the EU (see Economic Affairs, below).

In May 1996 the French Government approved proposals submitted by President Chirac to restructure the armed forces. The restructuring was to take place in two stages and was scheduled to be completed by 2015. The first stage, covering the period 1997–2002, envisaged a 30% reduction in military personnel and the elimination of compulsory military service. The defence budget was to be restricted to 185,000m. francs a year during the six-year period and state-owned companies in the defence industry were to be reorganized and sold to the private sector. The restructuring appeared to be in response to the political changes in Europe in the 1990s: President Chirac emphasized the need for a modern army that could be deployed rapidly overseas and advocated a greater number of joint operations between European armed forces. Despite the announced reduction in French troops to be stationed in Germany, France reiterated its commitment to the 'Eurocorps' joint defence force (see below).

During 1997 representatives of the extreme right wing continued to enjoy significant levels of popular support in France. In February the FN candidate, Catherine Mégret (wife of Bruno Mégret, the prominent FN politician), won the mayoral election in Vitrolles, near Marseille. Mégret secured an absolute majority with 52.5% of total votes, despite Juppé's decision to withdraw the RPR candidate from the second round of the election and to urge voters to support the PS representative, in an attempt to block the FN. Meanwhile, the FN-controlled council in Toulon dismissed the director of a theatre and dance company based in the area, which it had frequently criticized for staging productions written or performed by members of ethnic minorities. After securing his dismissal, the council disbanded the company. At the FN congress in Strasbourg in March Le Pen was re-elected as leader of the party unopposed.

In late February 1997 immigration legislation approved in the National Assembly provoked a demonstration by some 100,000 people in Paris. The protests were widely believed to have resulted in the Government's decision to exclude a controversial clause in the bill, requiring French citizens to register the arrival and departure of any foreign guests with the local authorities. Renewed controversy surrounding the conduct of French institutions during the Second World War arose in early 1997, following reports that French banks had failed to transfer the deposits of Jews killed in the Holocaust to the State, as required by law. Similar revelations that museums in France, including the Louvre, continued to hold some 2,000 valuable works of art seized from Jews under the Vichy regime (1940–44) prompted the Government to announce the creation of a commission to trace and catalogue the misappropriated property.

In April 1997 Chirac announced that legislative elections would take place in May/June. His decision to organize the elections some 10 months earlier than required was widely viewed as an attempt to secure a mandate for a number of important policies relating to the Maastricht Treaty (see p. 158) for economic and monetary union (EMU). In the first round of voting, held on 25 May, the PS secured 23.5% of total votes, the RPR won 15.7% and the FN were the third most successful party, obtaining 14.9% of the votes, followed by the UDF with 14.2%. As a result of voting in the second round on 1 June, the PS secured 241 seats, the RPR won 134 and the UDF obtained 108. Despite its strong performance in the first round, the FN secured only one seat (with 5.6% of total votes), while the PCF won 38 seats (with 3.8%). The unexpected victory of the PS, led by Lionel Jospin, which signalled the beginning of a five-year period of 'cohabitation', was widely attributed to dissatisfaction with Juppé's administration and the imposition of economic austerity measures necessitated under the terms ('convergence criteria') of EMU. (Juppé resigned as leader of the RPR and was subsequently replaced by Philippe Séguin.) Jospin formed a coalition with several left-wing and ecologist parties and announced a 15-member Council of Ministers, which included five women. The new Government's stated objectives included the reduction of youth unemployment by the creation of some 700,000 new jobs and the shortening of the maximum working week from 39 to 35 hours. Another of the Government's priorities was the reform of immigration law. Shortly after its installation, the administration dismissed a Préfet in the Département of Var who had influenced the racist policies of the FN-controlled council in Toulon, particularly in its decision to close down a theatre company based in the area (see above). In August the Government announced that some 54,000 people had responded to its offer to grant residence permits to immigrants unsure of their legal status (the *'sans-papiers'*), 14,000 more than had been expected. The initiative fuelled criticism by right-wing groups, who claimed that it would encourage illegal immigration and increase unemployment. Legislation proposed by the new Government, which envisaged reinstating the right to French citizenship for anyone born in the country, granting residency to long-term settlers and reforming regulations surrounding political asylum, was similarly attacked by the opposition. The Government's subsequent decision not to repeal certain aspects of existing immigration law led to accusations by some left-wing and ecologist members of the coalition that Jospin had capitulated to pressure from right-wing groups.

In October 1997 the trial of Maurice Papon, a former civil servant and senior official in the pro-Nazi Vichy regime, opened in Bordeaux. Papon was accused of deporting some 1,500 Jews to Germany, where almost all were killed in Nazi concentration camps, in 1943–44. Defence lawyers for Papon, who denied the charges against him, argued that their client was unfit to stand trial, owing to ill health. The trial, which continued in early 1998, was suspended on several occasions when Papon was deemed too unwell to appear in court. As a result of evidence heard in the trial, the Government announced an inquiry into the killing of Algerian demonstrators during a protest march in Paris in 1961. According to official reports, two people were killed in clashes with riot police during the demonstration, which took place during Papon's tenure as chief of the Paris police. Historians and independent witnesses, however, estimated that as many as 300 people were killed. Police records, subsequently uncovered during the inquiry, revealed that the bodies of at least 90 demonstrators had been recovered from the river Seine.

The Government was beset by serious domestic problems in late 1997. In November industrial action by lorry drivers, involved in a dispute over pay, caused widespread disruption to the country's road transport network and impacted adversely on industry and agriculture. The dispute, which involved some 200 road-blocks at strategic junctions, border crossings and entrances to ports, ended after four days with the signing of an agreement between employers and trade union representatives. Many observers speculated that the dispute had been orchestrated by large haulage companies in an attempt to eliminate competition from smaller operators.

In December 1997 a series of demonstrations took place in Marseille in protest at the Government's alleged failure to address adequately the problem of unemployment. The demonstrations soon spread to other parts of the country, and in many towns erupted into violence when unemployed youths attacked public-service workers (leading to strikes by public transport operators), clashed with police and set fire to buildings and cars. Meanwhile, protesters began an occupation of welfare offices across the country (which lasted several weeks), demanding a review of the benefits system. A package of measures announced by the Government in January 1998, which aimed to placate the demonstrators, was rejected by groups representing the unemployed. Divisions within the governing coalition on the matter further compounded the Government's precarious position.

As a result of the decentralization legislation of 1982, Corsica was elevated from regional status to that of a 'collectivité territoriale', with its own directly-elected 61-seat Assembly, and an administration with greater executive powers in economic, social and other spheres. However, this measure failed to pacify the pro-independence Front de Libération Nationale de la Corse (FLNC) and the Consulte des Comités Nationalistes (CCN), which were banned in 1983, following a terrorist campaign. A new independence movement, the Mouvement Corse pour l'Autodétermination (MCA), was immediately formed by members of the banned CCN, and terrorist activities continued from 1984. In January 1987 the MCA, which had six members in the Corsican Assembly in alliance with the Union du Peuple Corse (UPC), was banned after police investigations suggested links with the FLNC, and the UPC later suspended the alliance. In November 1990 the French Government proposed legislation that would grant greater autonomy to Corsica. The proposals, known as the Joxe Plan (after the Minister of the Interior, Pierre Joxe), envisaged the formation of an executive council comprising seven members, chosen from a 51-member Corsican assembly, to be elected in 1992. The Joxe Plan was opposed both by militant Corsican separatists, and by right-wing members of the National Assembly. Despite a bombing campaign and a series of assassinations in December 1990 and January 1991, the legislation was adopted in April 1991. In the early 1990s, however, an unprecedented series of armed robberies, bombings and deliberately raised forest fires threatened to undermine the Corsican tourist industry. In January 1996 the FLNC announced a suspension of terrorist attacks: the truce was extended in April but ended in August. In October a faction of the FLNC (the FLNC–Historic Wing) admitted responsibility for the bombing, earlier in the month, of the town hall in Bordeaux. A number of Corsican separatists were subsequently arrested. The attack was deemed to be in reprisal for assertions made by Prime Minister Juppé that his Government would never negotiate with terrorists (Juppé was also Mayor of Bordeaux and had presided over a meeting in the town hall on the day of the explosion). In February 1997 an unprecedented series of explosions in Corsica followed the arrest, earlier in the month, of several high-profile Corsican separatists. In one of the most serious incidents of violence on Corsica in its recent history, the Préfet of the island, Claude Erignac, was assassinated in early February 1998. The killing was condemned by the FLNC, leading observers to speculate that the assassination had been carried out by one of the organized crime syndicates that were known to use the island's splintered nationalist terrorist movement to conceal their activities. (Proposals to declare Corsica a 'free zone' during 1997–2001, exempt from customs duty and tax, were approved by the EU in October 1996. The zone came into force on 1 January 1997.)

During the 1980s indigenous Melanesian (Kanak) separatists also campaigned for the independence of the Pacific overseas territory of New Caledonia, in conflict with the wishes of settlers of European origin (see French Overseas Territories, p. 1404). In 1988 it was agreed that, from July 1989, a high commissioner should administer the territory, assisted by three elected provincial assemblies, until the holding of a referendum on self-determination in 1998.

France granted independence to most of its former colonies after the Second World War. In Indo-China, after prolonged fighting, Laos, Cambodia and Viet Nam became fully independent in 1954. In Africa most of the French colonies in the West and Equatorial regions attained independence in 1960, but retained their close economic and political ties with France (particularly within the framework of the Franc Zone: see p. 181). In 1983, under the terms of a co-operation agreement, a large contingent of French troops was sent to Chad as a result of continuing hostilities between government forces and Libyan-backed rebels (see chapter on Chad for further details). The troops were withdrawn in September 1984, but, following a resumption of hostilities between government forces and rebels, France agreed in February 1986 to establish a defensive air-strike force in the capital, N'Djamena, in an intervention which was code-named *Opération Epervier*. In June 1994 France announced that the *Epervier* force (which then numbered some 800 troops) was to remain in Chad, despite demands from the Libyan Government that they be withdrawn.

In the early 1990s a contingent of French troops was dispatched to Rwanda to train forces of the Rwandan Government and to supply military equipment, following the outbreak of armed conflict between the Government and the opposition Rwandan Patriotic Front (FPR). In April 1994 French troops re-entered Rwanda to establish a 'safe humanitarian zone' for refugees fleeing the civil war. Although France declared its presence to be restricted to a transitional period prior to the arrival of UN peace-keeping forces, the FPR regarded its intervention as hostile, and accused France of using the operation secretly to transport alleged war criminals out of the country. In November 1996 the French Government rejected allegations that France had continued to supply arms to the Rwandan Government following the imposition, in May 1994, of a UN embargo on the delivery of military equipment to any party in the Rwandan conflict. In the same month France advocated strongly the dispatch of a multi-national force to Zaire, traditionally a close ally of France, to provide for the safe return of refugees to Rwanda, and to prevent the spread of political instability to neighbouring countries. In January 1998 new evidence in support of allegations that France had sold arms to Rwanda during the massacres in 1994 emerged. The Government again denied the accusations.

In September 1994, following the killing by Islamic terrorists of five French officials at the French embassy in Algiers, the French Government initiated an extensive security operation (under the code-name *Vigipirate*), the results of which included the detention and subsequent expulsion from France of a number of alleged Islamic fundamentalist activists. In December members of the French security forces killed four Islamic terrorists on board an Air France aircraft, which had been hijacked in Algiers and flown to Marseille. The following day four Catholic priests, three of them French citizens, were killed in Algeria, in apparent reprisal for the actions of the French security forces. Eight people were killed in the second half of 1995 in a series of bombings in Paris and Lyon, for which the Armed Islamic Group (GIA), an extremist Algerian terrorist organization, was widely believed to be responsible. Although a number of arrests followed, terrorist activity resumed in December 1996 when four people were killed and many injured in an explosion on a crowded commuter train in Paris. The *Vigipirate* security operation was immediately re-instated by the French Government. Although no organization claimed responsibility for the attack, the explosive device that the attackers used was similar to those used by the GIA in 1995, and it was speculated that the bombing might be in protest against the imminent trial in Paris of 30 young men of north African extraction who were accused of involvement in terrorist activities in Morocco in 1994. In a letter to President Chirac later in December 1996 the GIA warned that it would continue its terrorist campaign in France, unless the French Government undertook to sever ties with the Algerian Government. France has been accused by Islamic groups in Algeria of providing covert military assistance to the Algerian Government following the suspension of a general election in Algeria in 1992 (see chapter on Algeria). France continued to resist increasing pressure to intervene in the ongoing atrocities in Algeria during 1997 and early 1998.

Relations with the People's Republic of China (PRC) were severely prejudiced in 1993 by France's decision to sell armaments to China (Taiwan). The French consulate in Guangzhou was forced to close and the Chinese Government appeared to discriminate against French interests in the awarding of commercial contracts to foreign companies. In January 1994 France suspended further sales of military equipment to Taiwan and announced the renewal of normal working relations with the PRC. In April the French Prime Minister visited Beijing, and in July the President of the PRC signed a trade agreement in Paris.

France is a founder member of the EU and of NATO. In 1966 it withdrew from the integrated military structure of NATO, desiring a more self-determined defence policy, but remained a member of the alliance. In January 1988 France and the Federal Republic of Germany signed new agreements on defence and economic co-operation (including the formation of a joint military brigade) to commemorate the 25th anniversary of the Franco-German treaty of friendship. In September 1990 France announced plans to withdraw all of its 50,000 troops stationed in Germany over the next few years. In May 1992 France and Germany announced that they would establish a joint defence force of 50,000 troops, the 'Eurocorps', which was intended to provide a basis for a European army under the aegis of Western European Union (WEU, see p. 240) and which was to be operational by October 1995. The corps was also to be open to other WEU member countries. This development caused concern among some NATO member countries, particularly the USA and United Kingdom, who feared that it represented a fresh attempt (notably on the part of France, being, as it was, outside NATO's military structure) to undermine the Alliance's role in Europe. In January 1993, however, an agreement was signed between NATO and the French and German Governments, establishing formal links between the corps and NATO's military structure. In December 1995 it was announced that France would rejoin the military structure of NATO, although it would not initially become a full member of NATO's integrated military command and would retain control of its independent nuclear forces. France's re-entry into the integrated military command was delayed in 1996, following a dispute with the USA over command of the alliance troops in southern Europe (a division of the alliance which includes the US sixth fleet). France has repeatedly insisted that the division be under the command of a European officer, and the dispute has undermined efforts to restructure NATO.

Government

Under the 1958 Constitution, legislative power is held by the bicameral Parliament, comprising a Senate and a National Assembly. The Senate has 321 members (296 for metropolitan France, 13 for the overseas departments, 'collectivités territoriales' and territories, and 12 for French nationals abroad). Senators are elected for a nine-year term by an electoral college composed of the members of the National Assembly, delegates from the Councils of the Departments and delegates from the Municipal Councils. One-third of the Senate is renewable every three years. The National Assembly has 577 members, with 555 for metropolitan France and 22 for overseas departments, 'collectivités territoriales' and territories. Members of the Assembly are elected by universal adult suffrage, under a single-member constituency system of direct election, using a second ballot if the first ballot failed to produce an absolute majority for any one candidate. The Assembly's term is five years, subject to dissolution. Executive power is held by the President. Since 1962 the President has been directly elected by popular vote (using two ballots if necessary) for seven years. The President appoints a Council of Ministers, headed by the Prime Minister, which administers the country and is responsible to Parliament.

Metropolitan France comprises 21 administrative regions containing 96 departments. Under the decentralization law of March 1982, administrative and financial power in metropolitan France was transferred from the Préfets, who became Commissaires de la République, to locally-elected departmental assemblies (Conseils généraux) and regional assemblies (Conseils régionaux). The special status of a 'collectivité territoriale' was granted to Corsica, which has its own directly-elected legislative Assembly. There are four overseas departments (French Guiana, Guadeloupe, Martinique and Réunion), two overseas 'collectivités territoriales' (Mayotte and St Pierre and Miquelon) and four overseas territories (French Polynesia, the French Southern and Antarctic Territories, New Caledonia and the Wallis and Futuna Islands), all of which are integral parts of the French Republic (see p. 1370). Each overseas department is administered by an elected Conseil général and Conseil régional, each 'collectivité territoriale' by an appointed government commissioner, and each overseas territory by an appointed high commissioner.

Defence

French military policy is decided by the Supreme Defence Council. Military service is currently compulsory and lasts for 10 months, although proposals to create fully professional armed forces were submitted to the National Assembly in 1996. The cessation of conscription and decreased defence expenditure were expected to result in a reduction in the number of military personnel of some 25% by 2002. In August 1997 the total active armed forces numbered 380,820 (including 156,950 conscripts), including an army of 219,900, a navy of 63,300 and an air force of 83,420. In addition, there was a paramilitary gendarmerie of 92,300 (including 13,000 conscripts). Total reserves stood at 292,500 (army 195,500; navy 27,000; air force 70,000). Government expenditure on defence in 1996 amounted to 241,400m. francs. Defence expenditure was estimated at 190,900m. francs for 1997, and was projected at 185,000m. francs per year until 2002. Although a member of NATO, France withdrew from its integrated military organization in 1966, and possesses its own nuclear weapons. In 1995, however, it was announced that France was to rejoin NATO's defence committee, and in 1996 President Chirac declared France's intention to rejoin NATO's integrated military command.

Economic Affairs

In 1995, according to estimates by the World Bank, France's gross national product (GNP), measured at average 1993–95 prices, was US $1,451,051m., equivalent to $24,990 per head. During 1985–95, it was estimated, GNP per head expanded, in real terms, at an average annual rate of 1.5%. Over the same period, the population increased by an annual average of 0.5%. France's gross domestic product (GDP) increased, in real terms, by an annual average of 2.4% in 1980–90, and by 1.0% per year in 1990–95. Real GDP grew by 1.5% in 1996, by an estimated 2.4% in 1997, and was forecast to increase by 2.9% in 1998.

Agriculture (including forestry and fishing) contributed 2.5% of GDP, and engaged 4.7% of the employed labour force, in 1994. The principal crops are wheat, sugar beet, maize and barley. Livestock, dairy products and wine are also important. Agricultural production increased by an annual average of 2.0% in 1980–90, but declined by 1.1% per year in 1990–94.

Industry (including mining, manufacturing, construction and power) provided 27.6% of GDP, and employed 26.6% of the working population, in 1994. Industrial GDP, measured at constant prices, increased by an annual average of 1.1% during 1980–90, but declined by 1.0% in 1991, before increasing by 0.3% in 1992. Industrial production (excluding construction) declined by 3.8% in 1993, but rose by 3.7% in 1994 and by 1.6% in 1995.

Mining and quarrying contributed 0.5% of GDP in 1993, and employed 0.3% of the working population in 1994. Coal is the principal mineral produced, while petroleum and natural gas are also extracted. In addition, metallic minerals, including iron ore, copper and zinc, are mined. In real terms, the GDP of the mining sector declined at an average annual rate of 2.1% in 1980–89, but rose by 0.7% in 1990 and by 6.8% in 1991. It fell by 1.2% in 1992.

Manufacturing provided 20.5% of GDP in 1993, and employed 18.8% of the working population in 1994. Production in the manufacturing sector (excluding wine and handicrafts) increased at an average rate of 1.0% per year in 1980–90, declined in the early 1990s, remained almost constant in 1996 and grew by an estimated 3.5% in 1997. Measured by the value of output, the most important branches of manufacturing in 1994 were food products (accounting for 14.3% of the total), transport equipment (13.9%), industrial and other chemicals (10.0%), electrical machinery (8.5%), non-electric machinery (8.2%), metal products (6.0%) and metals (5.5%).

In 1994 nuclear power provided 75.2% of total electricity production, hydroelectric power 17.7% and thermal power 7.1%. Imports of mineral fuels comprised 6.7% of the value of total imports in 1995.

Services accounted for 69.9% of GDP, and employed 68.7% of the working population, in 1994. The combined GDP of all service sectors increased, in real terms, at an average rate of 3.0% per year in 1980–90, and by 1.5% in per year in 1990–94.

In 1996 France recorded a trade surplus of US $15,099m., and there was a surplus of $20,511m. on the current account of the balance of payments. In 1995 the principal source of imports (18.5%) was Germany, which was also the principal market for exports (17.7%). Other major trading partners were Italy (10.0% of imports; 9.7% of exports), Belgium and Luxembourg (9.0% of imports; 8.6% of exports), and the United Kingdom (8.0% of imports; 9.3% of exports). The EU as a whole provided 59.5% of imports in 1994 and took 60.6% of exports. The principal exports in 1995 were machinery and transport equipment, basic manufactures, chemicals and food and live animals. The principal imports were machinery and transport equipment, basic manufactures and miscellaneous manufactured articles.

The budget deficit for 1996 amounted to an estimated 295,000.4m. francs, equivalent to 4.2% of GDP. In 1997 the budget deficit was estimated at 3.8% at GDP and was forecast to be equivalent to some 4.5% of GDP in 1998. In 1997 gross state debt amounted to 58.9% of annual GDP. The average annual rate of inflation in 1985–95 was 2.7%. The annual rate of inflation averaged 1.8% in 1995, 1.7% in 1996 and decreased further, to 1.1%, in 1997. The average rate of unemployment decreased from 12.3% of the labour force in 1994 to 11.6% in 1995, but increased to 12.4% in 1996 and to 12.5% in late 1997.

France is a member of the European Union (see p. 152) and of the Organisation for Economic Co-operation and Development (see p. 208), and presides over the Franc Zone (see p. 181).

France is one of the world's leading industrial countries. After several years of expansion, the country experienced a recession in 1993, when real GDP declined by 1.3%. However, the economy moved back into growth in 1994, and GDP increased by an annual average of just over 2% in 1994–96. Nevertheless, unemployment remained high, at 12.5% of the labour force at the end of 1997. The Juppé Government introduced a number of austerity measures in 1995 and 1996, designed to prepare the French economy to satisfy the requirements of the Maastricht Treaty (see p. 158) for economic and monetary union (EMU). The subsequent administration of Lionel Jospin similarly attempted to restrict the budget deficit for 1998 to a level approximating the terms ('convergence criteria') of EMU, which stipulate a deficit no greater than 3% of GDP in order to qualify for the single-currency stage. The measures introduced included reductions in public spending (most notably in defence) and increased taxes for large companies (which were to be reduced progressively after 1998). However, forecasts predicted that the budget deficit would probably reach some 3.8% of GDP. The continued programme of privatization of a number of major state-owned corporations, initiated in 1993, was delayed, and in some cases suspended, by the Jospin administration. In October 1997, however, the Government announced the transfer of more than 30% of France Télécom to the private sector. Among the new Government's stated economic priorities was the reduction of the country's persistently high rate of unemployment, particularly among young people. Draft legislation approved in July 1997 aimed to create 150,000 new jobs by late 1998 and a further 200,000 by 2000 (at an estimated cost of 35,000m. francs). An additional 350,000 community service jobs were also to be created under a government scheme. Plans to reduce the duration of the working week from 39 to 35 hours by 2000, although harshly criticized by employers, were expected to increase the number of jobs available in the country by 11%.

Social Welfare

France has evolved a comprehensive system of social security, which is compulsory for all wage-earners and self-employed people. A national minimum hourly wage is in force, and is periodically adjusted in accordance with fluctuations in the cost of living. State insurance of wage-earners requires contributions from both employers and employees, and provides for sickness, unemployment, maternity, disability through industrial accident, and substantial allowances for large families. War veterans receive pensions and certain privileges, and widows the equivalent of three months' salary and pension. About 95% of all medical practitioners adhere to the state scheme. The patient pays directly for medical treatment and prescribed medicines, and then obtains reimbursement for all or part of the cost. Sickness benefits and pensions are related to the insured person's income, age and the length of time for which he or she has been insured. Plans for the reform of the state pension system and the encouragement of private pension schemes became law in 1994. Proposed budgetary expenditure by the central Government in 1995 included 61,781m. francs for social services and health (4.2% of total budgetary spending), although this was later revised to 64,500m. francs. Of total government expenditure (including disbursements by government-controlled social security funds) in 1992, about 487,700m. francs (15.5%) was for health, and a further 1,419,900m. francs (45.1%) for social security and welfare. The Caisse d'Amortissement de la Dette Sociale (CADES), a financial institution created in 1996, is responsible for eliminating the deficit in the social services sector (estimated at 120,000m. francs in 1994–95 and projected at 17,000m. francs for 1996). CADES is funded by a special income tax, levied since 1996. In 1993 France had 3,810 hospital establishments, with a total of 540,074 beds, equivalent to one for every 107 inhabitants. In 1993 there were 158,968 physicians registered in France.

Education

France is divided into 27 educational districts, called Académies, each responsible for the administration of education, from primary to higher levels, in its area. Education is compulsory and free for children aged six to 16 years. Primary education begins at six years of age and lasts for five years. At the age of 11 all pupils enter the first cycle of the Enseignement secondaire, with a four-year general course. At the age of 15 they may then proceed to the second cycle, choosing a course leading to the baccalauréat examination after three years or a course leading to vocational qualifications after two or three years, with commercial, administrative or industrial options. In 1963 junior classes in the Lycées were gradually abolished in favour of new junior comprehensives, called Collèges. Alongside the collèges and lycées, technical education is provided in the Lycées professionnels and the Lycées techniques. About 17% of children attend France's 10,000 private schools, most of which are administered by the Roman Catholic Church.

Educational reforms, introduced in 1980, aimed to decentralize the state school system: the school calendar now varies according to three zones, and the previously rigid and formal syllabus has been replaced by more flexibility and choice of curricula. Further decentralization measures included, from 1986, the transfer of financial responsibility for education to the local authorities.

The minimum qualification for entry to university faculties is the baccalauréat. There are three cycles of university education. The first level, the Diplôme d'études universitaires générales (DEUG), is reached after two years of study, and the first degree, the Licence, is obtained after three years. The master's degree (Maîtrise) is obtained after four years of study, while the doctorate requires six or seven years' study and the submission of a thesis. The prestigious Grandes Ecoles complement the universities; entry to them is by competitive examination, and they have traditionally supplied France's administrative élite. The 1968 reforms in higher education aimed to increase university autonomy and to render teaching methods less formal. Enrolment at schools in 1993 included 99% of children in the relevant age-group for primary education and 92% for secondary education. Expenditure on education by all levels of government in 1994 totalled 435,450m. francs (5.9% of GNP). Proposed budgetary expenditure on education by the central Government amounted to 304,381m. francs in 1995 (20.5% of total budgetary expenditure). Primary teachers are trained in Ecoles Normales. Secondary teachers must have been awarded either the Certificat d'Aptitude au Professorat d'Enseignement Général des Collèges (CAPEGC), the Certificat d'Aptitude au Professorat de l'Enseignement du Second Degré (CAPES) or the Agrégation.

Public Holidays

1998: 1 January (New Year's Day), 13 April (Easter Monday), 1 May (Labour Day), 8 May (Liberation Day), 21 May (Ascension Day), 1 June (Whit Monday), 14 July (National Day, Fall of the Bastille), 15 August (Assumption), 1 November (All Saints' Day), 11 November (Armistice Day), 25 December (Christmas Day).

1999: 1 January (New Year's Day), 5 April (Easter Monday), 1 May (Labour Day), 8 May (Liberation Day), 13 May (Ascension Day), 24 May (Whit Monday), 14 July (National Day, Fall of the Bastille), 15 August (Assumption), 1 November (All Saints' Day), 11 November (Armistice Day), 25 December (Christmas Day).

Weights and Measures

The metric system is in force.

Statistical Survey

Unless otherwise indicated, figures in this survey refer to metropolitan France, excluding Overseas Departments and Territories.
Source (unless otherwise stated): Institut national de la statistique et des études économiques, 18 boulevard Adolphe Pinard, 75675 Paris Cédex 14; tel. 1-45-17-50-50.

Area and Population

AREA, POPULATION AND DENSITY

Area (sq km)	543,965*
Population (census results, *de jure*)†	
4 March 1982	54,334,871
5 March 1990‡	
Males	27,553,788
Females	29,080,511
Total	56,634,299
Population (official estimates at mid-year)	
1994	57,899,702
1995	58,142,852
1996	58,375,000
Density (per sq km) at mid-1996	107.3

* 210,026 sq miles.

† Excluding professional soldiers and military personnel outside the country with no personal residence in France.

‡ Figures include double counting. The revised total is 56,615,155.

Population (official estimates at January): 58.47m. in 1997; 58.70m. in 1998.

NATIONALITY OF THE POPULATION
(numbers resident in France at 1990 census*)

Country of citizenship	Population	%
France	53,026,709	93.63
Algeria	619,923	1.09
Belgium	59,705	0.11
Germany	51,483	0.09
Italy	253,679	0.45
Morocco	584,708	1.03
Poland	46,283	0.08
Portugal	645,578	1.14
Spain	216,015	0.38
Tunisia	207,496	0.37
Turkey	201,480	0.36
Yugoslavia	51,697	0.09
Others	669,543	1.18
Total	56,634,299	100.00

* Figures include double counting. The revised total is 56,615,155.

REGIONS (estimated population at 1 January 1993)

	Area (sq km)	Population (rounded)	Density (per sq km)
Ile-de-France	12,012.3	10,904,000	907.7
Champagne–Ardenne	25,605.8	1,351,000	52.8
Picardie (Picardy)	19,399.5	1,847,000	95.2
Haute-Normandie	12,317.4	1,760,000	142.9
Centre	39,150.9	2,403,000	61.4
Basse-Normandie	17,589.3	1,404,000	79.8
Bourgogne (Burgundy)	31,582.0	1,614,000	51.1
Nord–Pas-de-Calais	12,414.1	3,985,000	321.0
Lorraine	23,547.4	2,295,000	97.5
Alsace	8,280.2	1,649,000	199.1
Franche-Comté	16,202.3	1,107,000	68.3
Pays de la Loire	32,081.8	3,112,000	97.0
Bretagne (Brittany)	27,207.9	2,828,000	103.9
Poitou–Charentes	25,809.5	1,617,000	62.7
Aquitaine	41,308.4	2,842,000	68.8
Midi–Pyrénées	45,347.9	2,471,000	54.5
Limousin	16,942.3	718,000	42.4
Rhône–Alpes	43,698.2	5,495,000	125.7
Auvergne	26,012.9	1,317,000	50.6
Languedoc–Roussillon	27,375.8	2,183,000	79.7
Provence–Alpes–Côte d'Azur	31,399.6	4,375,000	139.3
Corse (Corsica)	8,679.8	253,000	29.1
Total	543,965.4	57,530,000	105.8

PRINCIPAL TOWNS* (population at 1990 census)

Paris (capital)	2,152,423	Le Mans	145,502
Marseille (Marseilles)	800,550	Angers	141,404
Lyon (Lyons)	415,487	Clermont-Ferrand	136,181
Toulouse	358,688	Limoges	133,464
Nice	342,439	Amiens	131,872
Strasbourg	252,338	Tours	129,509
Nantes	244,995	Nîmes	128,471
Bordeaux	210,336	Aix-en-Provence	123,842
Montpellier	207,996	Metz	119,594
Rennes	199,396	Villeurbanne	116,872
Saint-Etienne	197,536	Besançon	113,828
Le Havre	195,854	Caen	112,846
Reims (Rheims)	180,620	Mulhouse	108,357
Lille	172,142	Perpignan	105,983
Toulon	167,619	Orléans	105,111
Grenoble	150,758	Rouen	102,723
Brest	147,956	Boulogne-Billancourt	101,743
Dijon	146,703		

* Figures refer to the population of communes.

BIRTHS, MARRIAGES AND DEATHS*

	Registered live births		Registered marriages		Registered deaths	
	Number	Rate (per 1,000)	Number	Rate (per 1,000)	Number	Rate (per 1,000)
1989	765,473	13.6	279,900	5.0	529,283	9.4
1990	762,407	13.4	287,099	5.1	526,201	9.3
1991	759,056	13.3	280,175	4.9	524,685	9.2
1992	743,658	13.0	271,427	4.7	521,530	9.1
1993	711,610	12.3	255,190	4.4	532,263	9.2
1994	710,993	12.3	253,746	4.4	519,965	9.0
1995†	729,000	12.5	254,000	4.4	529,000	9.1
1996†	734,000	12.6	n.a.	4.8	536,000	9.2

* Including data for national armed forces outside the country.

† Provisional figures.

1997 (provisional figures): 725,000 registered live births; 284,500 registered marriages; 534,000 registered deaths.

Expectation of life (years at birth, 1997, provisional figures): Males 74.2; Females 82.1.

ECONOMICALLY ACTIVE POPULATION*
(annual averages, '000 persons aged 15 years and over)

	1992	1993	1994
Agriculture, hunting, forestry and fishing	1,150.3	1,100.8	1,048.4
Mining and quarrying	72.0	69.6	65.8
Manufacturing	4,479.0	4,269.3	4,162.2
Electricity, gas and water	204.0	204.9	203.7
Construction	1,568.3	1,487.8	1,443.1
Trade, restaurants and hotels	3,715.2	3,680.5	3,715.7
Transport, storage and communications	1,418.4	1,403.1	1,397.0
Financing, insurance, real estate and business services	2,295.2	2,265.1	2,340.4
Community, social and personal services†	7,405.4	7,596.2	7,733.4
Total employed	22,307.6	22,078.2	22,109.7
Persons on compulsory military service	221.1	219.9	212.4
Unemployed	2,590.7	2,929.0	3,163.8
Total labour force	25,119.4	25,227.1	25,485.9

* Figures are provisional. The revised totals (in '000) are: Employed 22,306.0 in 1992, 22,052.7 in 1993, 22,043.8 in 1994; Persons on compulsory military service 225.0 in 1992; Unemployed 2,590.0 in 1992, 2,929.4 in 1993, 3,117.0 in 1994; Labour force 25,121.0 in 1992, 25,202.0 in 1993, 25,373.2 in 1994.

† Figures include regular members of the armed forces, officially estimated at 304,200 (males 286,000; females 18,200) in 1986.

Source: mainly ILO, *Yearbook of Labour Statistics*.

1995 (annual averages, '000 persons aged 15 years and over): Total employed 22,311.8; Persons on compulsory military service 206.6; Unemployed 2,950.2; Total labour force 25,468.6 (males 14,097.4, females 11,371.2).

Agriculture

PRINCIPAL CROPS ('000 metric tons)

	1994	1995	1996
Wheat	30,549	30,879	35,946
Rye	176	191	219
Barley	7,698	7,677	9,463
Oats	685	612	623
Maize*	12,943	12,784	14,449
Sorghum	263	249	340
Rice (paddy)	124	126	116
Sugar beet	29,084	30,571	30,720
Potatoes	5,496	5,839	6,462
Pulses	3,850	2,790	2,636
Soybeans	261	263	229
Sunflower seed	2,053	1,987	1,997
Rapeseed	1,772	2,789	2,904
Tobacco (leaves)	27	26	26
Artichokes	68	65	72
Cabbages	252	247	250†
Carrots	590	638	640†
Cauliflowers	522	539	531
Cucumbers and gherkins	142	147	150†
Melons	330	329	316
Onions (dry)	264	288	285
Garlic	55	50	47
Beans (green)	109	103	103†
Peas (green)	443	557	580
Tomatoes	800	811	805‡
Apples‡	2,683	2,516	2,455
Apricots	156	103	160
Grapes	6,945	7,213	7,213†
Peaches and nectarines	527	540	464
Pears‡	358	334	350
Plums	221	270	270†

* Figures refer to main, associated and catch crops.

† FAO estimate.

‡ Unofficial figure(s).

Source: FAO, *Production Yearbook*.

LIVESTOCK ('000 head, year ending 30 September)

	1994	1995	1996
Cattle	20,099	20,524	20,661
Pigs	14,291	14,593	14,800
Sheep	11,505	10,320	10,556
Goats	1,055	1,069	1,188
Horses	332	338	338*
Asses*	25	25	25
Mules	13	13	13*
Chickens (million)	217	219	221
Ducks (million)	20	20	20*
Turkeys (million)	33	36	37*

* FAO estimate(s).

Source: FAO, *Production Yearbook*.

LIVESTOCK PRODUCTS ('000 metric tons)

	1994	1995	1996
Beef and veal	1,627	1,640	1,686
Mutton and lamb	140	139	141
Goat meat	7	8	8
Pig meat	2,126	2,144	2,160
Horse meat	10	10	10*
Poultry meat	1,907	2,081	2,027
Other meat	294	290	294
Edible offals*	589	495	n.a.
Cows' milk	25,322	25,491	25,668†
Sheep's milk	211	228	218
Goats' milk	419	432	430
Butter	444	454	470†
Cheese	1,564	1,592	1,679
Honey	18	18*	18*
Hen eggs	982	1,025	1,018
Wool:			
greasy*	22	22	22
clean*	12	12	12
Cattle hides*	160	161	153
Sheepskins*	16	16	16

* FAO estimate(s).

† Unofficial figure.

Source: FAO, mainly *Production Yearbook*.

Forestry

ROUNDWOOD REMOVALS ('000 cubic metres, excluding bark)

	1992	1993	1994
Sawlogs, veneer logs and logs for sleepers	21,450	19,695	21,795
Pulpwood	10,600	15,219	16,728
Other industrial wood	534	594	640
Fuel wood*	10,448	10,454	10,454
Total	43,032	45,962	49,617

* FAO estimates.

Source: FAO, *Yearbook of Forest Products*.

SAWNWOOD PRODUCTION
('000 cubic metres, including railway sleepers)

	1992	1993	1994
Coniferous (softwood)	6,650	6,166	7,012
Broadleaved (hardwood)	3,838	2,966	3,164
Total	10,488	9,132	10,176

Source: FAO, *Yearbook of Forest Products*.

Fishing*

('000 metric tons, live weight)

	1993	1994	1995
Rainbow trout	45.8	47.5	48.9
Atlantic cod	16.4	15.0	14.4
Saithe (Pollock)	27.9	25.9	16.8
Whiting	25.3	28.9	24.5
European hake	16.3	16.3	12.3
Angler (Monk)	12.6	14.7	14.9
Atlantic herring	6.2	5.4	4.5
European pilchard (sardine)	22.2	20.5	13.4
European anchovy	26.7	22.7	11.3
Skipjack tuna	76.9	90.3	76.2
Yellowfin tuna	90.7	70.5	72.8
Bigeye tuna	19.1	18.4	15.6
Atlantic mackerel	12.9	14.7	12.5
Sharks, rays, skates, etc.	23.2	22.3	20.9
Other fishes (incl. unspecified)	144.3	148.9	136.8
Total fish	566.5	562.0	495.8
Crustaceans	23.0	22.6	20.5
Oysters	144.9	148.9	147.5
Blue mussel	57.1	52.3	56.2
Mediterranean mussel	15.5	16.8	16.9
Cuttlefishes and bobtail squids	14.0	12.1	14.8
Other molluscs	39.0	37.8	41.5
Other marine animals	0.4	0.3	0.2
Total catch	860.4	852.8	793.4
Inland waters	61.2	63.4	64.0
Mediterranean and Black Sea	75.3	74.0	67.1
Atlantic Ocean	629.1	617.5	563.6
Indian Ocean	94.8	97.8	98.7

* Figures exclude aquatic plants ('000 metric tons): 60.3 in 1993; 79.5 in 1994; 75.6 in 1995. Also excluded are corals and sponges.

Source: FAO, *Yearbook of Fishery Statistics*.

Mining

('000 metric tons, unless otherwise indicated)

	1992	1993	1994
Hard coal	9,478	8,576	7,538
Brown coal (incl. lignite)	1,578	1,672	1,501
Iron ore:			
gross weight	5,707	n.a.	2,418
metal content	1,697	798	697
Crude petroleum	2,866	2,752	2,769
Potash salts*	1,236	960	936
Salt (unrefined)	5,866	5,470	4,764
Zinc concentrates (metric tons)†	16,500	13,800	—
Natural gas (petajoules)	89.6	94.2	94.4

* Figures refer to recovered quantities of K_2O.

† Figures refer to the metal content of concentrates.

Source: mainly UN, *Industrial Commodity Statistics Yearbook*.

1995 ('000 metric tons): Iron ore (gross weight) 1,497 (metal content 433); Crude petroleum 2,503.

Industry

SELECTED PRODUCTS

('000 metric tons, unless otherwise indicated)

	1992	1993	1994
Margarine and other prepared fats	152.5	147.4	114.6
Wheat flour*	5,123	5,354	5,186
Raw sugar†	4,345	4,346	4,019
Wine ('000 hectolitres)	64,927	53,321	54,850
Beer ('000 hectolitres)	18,512	18,291	17,688
Cigarettes (million)	53,312	47,912	48,188
Cotton yarn—pure (metric tons)[1]	86,300	94,200	110,400
Woven cotton fabrics—pure and mixed (metric tons)	95,000	96,000	87,000
Wool yarn—pure and mixed (metric tons)	19,900	16,500	15,800
Woven woollen fabrics—pure and mixed (metric tons)	30,266	23,952	25,850
Non-cellulosic continuous filaments (metric tons)	51,000	47,700	63,100
Non-cellulosic discontinuous fibres (metric tons)	54,200	56,000	61,600
Woven fabrics of non-cellulosic (synthetic) fibres (metric tons)	102,047	8,088	14,028
Mechanical wood pulp	922	823	886
Chemical wood pulp‡	1,802	1,716	1,901
Newsprint	670	802	844
Other printing and writing paper	2,948	2,936	3,268
Other paper and paperboard	4,073	4,237	4,369
Synthetic rubber	498.6	486.4	518.4
Rubber tyres ('000)[2]	59,928	53,390	66,744
Sulphuric acid	2,871	2,357	2,227
Caustic soda (Sodium hydroxide)	1,476	1,473	1,561
Nitrogenous fertilizers (a)[3,4]	1,851	1,575	1,720
Phosphate fertilizers (b)[3]	1,069	1,217	936
Potash fertilizers (c)[3,4]	1,142	890	870
Liquefied petroleum gas[5]	2,530	2,694	2,488
Motor spirit (petrol)	18,015	17,966	17,543
Jet fuels	4,645	4,907	5,297
Kerosene	82	62	51
Distillate fuel oils	29,388	31,559	30,443
Residual fuel oil	12,456	12,637	10,668
Petroleum bitumen (asphalt)	3,215	3,142	3,348
Coke-oven coke	6,795	6,197	5,880
Cement	21,584	19,320	20,184
Pig-iron	12,264	11,880	12,444
Crude steel	18,190	17,313	18,242
Aluminium (unwrought):			
primary	414.3	424.5	481.5
secondary (incl. alloys)	222.4	202.8	227.4
Refined copper—unwrought (metric tons)	42,800	44,400	41,700
Lead (unwrought):			
primary	138.6	112.3	105.3
secondary	59.5	68.9	75.4
Zinc (unwrought):			
primary	304.7	309.8	293.0
secondary	14.1	13.6	29.3
Radio receivers ('000)	1,679	2,083	2,804
Television receivers ('000)	2,799	2,523	2,796
Merchant ships launched ('000 gross reg. tons)	82	240	172
Passenger motor cars ('000)	3,326	2,837	3,176
Lorries and vans ('000)	494.1	373.2	453.3
Electric energy (million kWh)	492,006	471,448	475,622

* Deliveries.

† Estimated production during crop year ending 30 September.

‡ Including semi-chemical pulp, but excluding dissolving grades.

1 Including tyre-cord yarn.

2 Tyres for road motor vehicles other than bicycles and motor cycles.

3 Production of fertilizers is in terms of plant nutrients: (a) nitrogen; (b) phosphoric acid; or (c) potassium oxide.

4 Figures refer to output during the 12 months ending 30 June of year stated.

5 Excluding production in natural gas processing plants ('000 metric tons): 229 in 1992; 228 in 1993; 154 in 1994.

Source: mainly UN, *Industrial Commodity Statistics Yearbook*.

Finance

CURRENCY AND EXCHANGE RATES

Monetary Units:

100 centimes = 1 French franc.

Sterling and Dollar Equivalents (30 September 1997)

£1 sterling = 9.583 francs;
US $1 = 5.932 francs;
1,000 French francs = £104.35 = $168.57.

Average Exchange Rate (francs per US $)

1994 5.5520
1995 4.9915
1996 5.1155

GENERAL BUDGET (estimates, million francs)

Revenue	1993	1994	1995*
Tax revenue	1,494,890	1,466,440	1,524,657
Income tax	309,100	296,700	303,555
Corporation tax	135,000	136,000	144,000
Value-added tax	646,008	647,000	673,224
Stamp duty, etc.†	404,782	79,700	83,400
Other taxes		307,040	320,478
Non-tax revenue	155,123	184,759	166,683
Sub-total	1,650,013	1,651,199	1,691,340
Tax relief and reimbursements	−238,696	−213,650	−220,365
Other deductions, e.g. EU	−237,473	−243,712	−245,154
Total	1,173,844	1,193,837	1,225,821

* Projected figures (at Sept. 1994).

† Including registration duties and tax on stock exchange transactions.

Expenditure	1994	1995*
Public authorities, general administration	333,362	336,790
Education	291,560	304,381
Culture	13,506	13,441
Social services and health	58,281	61,781
Employment	82,606	89,398
Agriculture and fisheries	28,420	28,901
Housing and town planning†	41,515	41,464
Transport, tourism and public works	83,280	84,634
Financial services	44,076	45,392
Industry, posts and telecommunications	30,379	28,132
Foreign affairs	14,699	15,143
Defence‡	242,558	243,445
Judiciary	21,266	22,122
Police	26,170	27,170
Research and development	27,920	27,991
Other purposes	115,929	113,129
Total	1,455,527	1,483,314

Note: The budgetary deficit for 1993 was revised to 315,650m. francs in December 1994.

* Projected figures (at Sept. 1994).

† Excluding extra-budgetary government financing.

‡ Including expenditure allocated for retired personnel.

Source: Ministère du Budget.

INTERNATIONAL RESERVES (US $ million at 31 December)*

	1994	1995	1996
Gold†	30,730	31,658	30,368
IMF special drawing rights	362	955	981
Reserve position in IMF	2,375	2,756	1,875
Foreign exchange	23,520	23,142	23,120
Total	56,987	58,511	56,344

* Excluding deposits made with the European Monetary Co-operation Fund.

† Valued at market-related prices.

Source: IMF, *International Financial Statistics*.

MONEY SUPPLY ('000 million francs at 31 December)

	1994	1995	1996
Currency outside banks	255	258	260
Demand deposits at banking institutions	1,415	1,557	1,548
Total money (incl. others)	1,673	1,819	1,812

Source: IMF, *International Financial Statistics.*

COST OF LIVING (Consumer Price Index for Urban Households, average of monthly figures; base: 1990 = 100)

	1993	1994	1995
Food (incl. beverages)	103.6	104.5	105.8
Fuel and light	103.8	103.4	103.6
Clothing and household linen	106.4	106.9	107.3
Rent	115.1	118.4	121.5
All items (incl. others)	107.9	109.7	111.6

Source: ILO, *Yearbook of Labour Statistics.*

1996: Food 107.1; All items 113.8 (Source: UN, *Monthly Bulletin of Statistics*).

NATIONAL ACCOUNTS

National Income and Product (million francs at current prices)

	1991	1992*	1993*
Compensation of employees	3,531,792	3,669,277	3,723,188
Operating surplus	1,513,219	1,572,768	1,572,457
Domestic factor incomes	5,045,011	5,242,045	5,295,645
Consumption of fixed capital	880,117	907,100	925,227
Gross domestic product (GDP) at factor cost	5,925,128	6,149,145	6,220,872
Indirect taxes	995,345	1,015,855	1,036,157
Less Subsidies	144,242	154,460	174,239
GDP in purchasers' values	6,776,231	7,010,540	7,082,790
Factor income received from abroad	329,004	345,525	394,368
Less Factor income paid abroad	367,291	402,655	449,683
Gross national product (GNP)	6,737,944	6,953,410	7,027,475
Less Consumption of fixed capital	880,117	907,100	925,227
National income in market prices	5,857,827	6,046,310	6,102,248
Other current transfers from abroad	171,448	166,376	180,637
Less Other current transfers paid abroad	193,977	195,086	208,844
National disposable income	5,835,298	6,017,600	6,074,041

* Figures are provisional. Revised totals (in '000 million francs) are: GDP in purchasers' values 6,999.6 in 1992, 7,077.1 in 1993; GNP 6,918.4 in 1992, 7,022.9 in 1993; National income 6,012.5 in 1992, 6,097.1 in 1993.

Source: mainly UN, *National Accounts Statistics.*

Expenditure on the Gross Domestic Product
('000 million francs at current prices)

	1994	1995	1996
Government final consumption expenditure	1,457.4	1,495.6	1,548.2
Private final consumption expenditure	4,442.3	4,586.6	4,769.4
Increase in stocks*	−3.2	23.7	−22.4
Gross fixed capital formation*	1,332.1	1,374.8	1,377.8
Total domestic expenditure	7,228.6	7,480.7	7,673.0
Exports of goods and services	1,684.1	1,803.0	1,885.9
Less Imports of goods and services	1,523.1	1,621.5	1,684.4
GDP in purchasers' values	7,389.7	7,662.2	7,874.5
GDP at constant 1990 prices	6,733.3	6,873.6	6,979.0

* Construction of non-residential buildings is included in 'Increase in stocks'.

Source: IMF, *International Financial Statistics.*

Gross Domestic Product by Economic Activity
(provisional, million francs at current prices)

	1991	1992	1993
Agriculture, hunting, forestry and fishing	204,959	198,222	165,587
Mining and quarrying	30,476	32,237	31,994
Manufacturing	1,407,648	1,430,849	1,400,791
Electricity, gas and water	153,193	165,272	176,357
Construction	358,171	364,538	363,974
Trade, restaurants and hotels	1,026,489	1,049,443	1,064,768
Transport, storage and communications	396,727	416,003	414,880
Finance, insurance, real estate and business services*	1,466,932	1,520,684	1,584,400
Government services†	1,076,279	1,145,098	1,206,414
Other community, social and personal services	387,469	414,298	435,101
Sub-total	6,508,343	6,736,644	6,844,266
Value-added tax and import duties	526,781	531,523	525,613
Less Imputed bank service charges	271,159	269,255	281,275
Total‡	6,776,231	7,010,540	7,082,790

* Including imputed rents of owner-occupied dwellings.
† Including private non-profit services to households.
‡ Including adjustments (million francs): 12,266 in 1991; 11,628 in 1992; −5,814 in 1993.

Source: UN, *National Accounts Statistics.*

BALANCE OF PAYMENTS (US $ million)*

	1994	1995	1996
Exports of goods f.o.b.	224,726	270,400	274,062
Imports of goods f.o.b.	−217,677	−259,225	−258,963
Trade balance	7,049	11,175	15,099
Exports of services	90,390	97,770	88,891
Imports of services	−71,103	−78,530	−72,087
Balance on goods and services	26,336	30,415	31,903
Other income received	110,034	130,033	128,417
Other income paid	−120,972	−137,479	−133,513
Balance on goods, services and income	15,398	22,969	26,808
Current transfers received	15,857	19,351	23,700
Current transfers paid	−24,222	−25,877	−29,996
Current balance	7,033	16,443	20,511
Capital account (net)	−4,641	−115	−155
Direct investment abroad	−22,801	−18,734	−26,547
Direct investment from abroad	16,628	23,735	20,068
Portfolio investment assets	−24,659	−22,901	−48,687
Portfolio investment liabilities	−30,109	9,700	−19,836
Other investment assets	26,316	−25,604	26,571
Other investment liabilities	30,689	13,320	23,004
Net errors and omissions	3,991	4,868	5,310
Overall balance	2,448	712	239

* Figures refer to transactions of metropolitan France, Monaco and the French Overseas Departments and Territories with the rest of the world.

Source: IMF, *International Financial Statistics.*

External Trade

Note: Figures refer to the trade of metropolitan France and Monaco with the rest of the world, excluding trade in war materials, goods exported under the off-shore procurement programme, war reparations and restitutions and the export of sea products direct from the high seas. The figures include trade in second-hand ships and aircraft, and the supply of stores and bunkers for foreign ships and aircraft.

PRINCIPAL COMMODITIES (distribution by SITC, million francs)

Imports c.i.f.	1993	1994	1995
Food and live animals	109,855.5	119,888	123,662
Meat and meat preparations	20,949.8	21,837	21,187
Fresh, chilled or frozen meat	18,626.1	19,505	18,685
Fish (not marine mammals), crustaceans, molluscs, etc., and preparations	14,169.3	15,155	15,907
Vegetables and fruit	27,774.6	30,216	31,609
Beverages and tobacco	13,920.1	15,142	16,263
Crude materials (inedible) except fuels	36,395.8	45,054	50,759
Mineral fuels, lubricants, etc. (incl. electric current)	101,132.5	97,087	92,574
Petroleum, petroleum products, etc.	76,084.6	72,586	68,560
Crude petroleum oils, etc.	50,610.4	48,630	48,011
Refined petroleum products	23,878.9	22,182	18,609
Gas (natural and manufactured)	18,353.5	18,276	18,107
Natural gas (whether or not liquefied)	16,430.7	16,269	16,227
Animal and vegetable oils, fats and waxes	3,990.8	4,784	5,325
Chemicals and related products	131,728.4	153,561	172,011
Organic chemicals	28,600.6	34,844	38,176
Plastics in primary forms	19,290.0	22,687	26,007
Basic manufactures	179,551.8	204,391	230,937
Paper, paperboard and manufactures	27,092.4	30,772	36,290
Paper and paperboard (not cut to size or shape)	19,234.2	21,908	25,673
Textile yarn, fabrics, etc.	34,264.7	36,716	37,575
Non-metallic mineral manufactures	21,219.3	22,445	23,486
Iron and steel	30,100.3	37,899	45,697
Non-ferrous metals	22,605.5	27,389	33,977
Other metal manufactures	26,545.4	29,692	33,200
Machinery and transport equipment	392,973.0	447,749	486,492
Power-generating machinery and equipment	34,945.3	39,277	34,199
Machinery specialized for particular industries	27,552.8	32,154	38,375
General industrial machinery, equipment and parts	50,157.7	56,170	64,241
Office machines and automatic data-processing equipment	52,988.1	60,068	66,225
Automatic data-processing machines and units	32,899.0	35,591	37,873
Parts and accessories for office machines, etc.	15,496.2	19,724	23,575
Telecommunications and sound equipment	26,629.1	29,243	32,165
Other electrical machinery, apparatus, etc.	60,740.3	75,085	86,504
Thermionic valves, tubes, etc.	17,931.4	20,868	25,969
Road vehicles and parts*	105,928.5	122,591	137,582
Passenger motor cars (excl. buses)	64,464.2	70,288	73,160
Motor vehicles for goods transport, etc.	11,630.7	18,940	27,232
Parts and accessories for cars, buses, lorries, etc.*	21,889.3	25,492	28,682
Other transport equipment and parts*	26,960.0	33,163	27,200
Aircraft, associated equipment and parts*	20,786.7	24,321	22,310
Miscellaneous manufactured articles	174,225.9	180,954	190,246
Furniture and parts	13,804.9	14,778	15,457
Clothing and accessories (excl. footwear)	49,315.5	50,711	51,723
Professional, scientific and controlling instruments, etc.	21,696.5	22,542	23,837
Photographic apparatus, optical goods, watches and clocks	14,595.5	15,240	16,014
Other commodities and transactions†	3,026.7	3,981	4,208
Total	1,146,800.4	1,272,591	1,372,478

* Excluding tyres, engines and electrical parts.
† Including items not classified according to kind (million francs): 196.3 in 1993; 272 in 1994; 261 in 1995.

Exports f.o.b.	1993	1994	1995
Food and live animals	145,434.7	144,883	154,935
Meat and meat preparations	21,333.6	22,711	23,043
Dairy products and birds' eggs	22,188.7	23,620	24,620
Cereals and cereal preparations	40,994.4	32,437	35,886
Wheat and meslin (unmilled)	17,472.1	11,091	14,755
Vegetables and fruit	16,885.7	17,894	18,549
Beverages and tobacco	38,050.0	40,904	41,816
Beverages	36,932.0	39,679	40,477
Alcoholic beverages	33,262.0	35,541	36,122
Crude materials (inedible) except fuels	28,270.7	32,792	35,636
Mineral fuels, lubricants, etc. (incl. electric current)	32,047.8	31,350	33,497
Animal and vegetable oils, fats and waxes	2,534.5	3,283	3,693
Chemicals and related products	167,897.9	187,256	210,278
Organic chemicals	33,792.8	38,808	45,055
Hydrocarbons and their derivatives	13,733.1	17,039	20,220
Inorganic chemicals	14,455.4	13,937	14,937
Medicinal and pharmaceutical products	26,961.1	30,358	34,264
Essential oils, perfume materials and cleansing preparations	30,893.8	34,843	37,701
Perfumery, cosmetics and toilet preparations (excl. soaps)	23,525.3	26,776	28,850
Plastics in primary forms	22,589.6	26,441	30,961
Basic manufactures	185,362.1	209,269	233,024
Rubber manufactures	17,019.8	18,777	19,365
Paper, paperboard and manufactures	22,542.8	26,682	31,460
Paper and paperboard (not cut to size or shape)	14,912.0	18,483	22,110
Textile yarn, fabrics, etc.	30,858.0	34,541	37,323
Non-metallic mineral manufactures	22,421.5	24,348	25,415
Iron and steel	41,521.9	46,782	52,704
Non-ferrous metals	18,568.2	21,401	25,306
Other metal manufactures	25,685.8	28,796	32,799
Machinery and transport equipment	450,085.1	509,257	562,948
Power-generating machinery and equipment	43,727.5	48,310	45,949
Internal combustion piston engines and parts	15,327.8	18,171	18,150
Machinery specialized for particular industries	30,420.4	35,522	39,579
General industrial machinery, equipment and parts	53,525.6	59,070	67,295
Office machines and automatic data-processing equipment	33,426.8	37,467	44,716
Automatic data-processing machines and units	19,019.0	21,574	28,524
Telecommunications and sound equipment	23,126.9	25,972	31,721
Other electrical machinery, apparatus, etc.	72,720.7	83,269	97,558
Switchgear, etc.	18,642.5	21,649	23,523
Road vehicles and parts*	129,212.2	147,547	156,656
Passenger motor cars (excl. buses)	69,748.8	76,365	75,959
Parts and accessories for cars, buses, lorries, etc.*	45,092.4	51,514	51,642
Other transport equipment and parts*	63,914.3	72,098	79,476

Exports f.o.b. — *continued*	1993	1994	1995
Aircraft, associated equipment and parts*	55,528.4	61,247	67,326
Miscellaneous manufactured articles	123,867.5	132,598	140,962
Clothing and accessories (excl. footwear)	26,172.7	27,681	28,364
Professional, scientific and controlling instruments, etc.	18,518.0	19,529	21,074
Other commodities and transactions†	3,122.7	2,950	2,869
Total	1,176,673.0	1,294,542	1,419,658

* Excluding tyres, engines and electrical parts.

† Including items not classified according to kind (million francs): 508.2 in 1993; 476 in 1994; 637 in 1995.

PRINCIPAL TRADING PARTNERS (million francs)*

Imports c.i.f.	1993	1994	1995
Austria	10,271	11,383	11,428
Belgium and Luxembourg	103,610	118,191	123,125
China, People's Republic	21,379	22,862	25,743
Denmark	10,354	11,419	12,269
Finland	7,594	9,133	10,567
Germany	203,197	227,605	253,789
Ireland	14,066	15,542	17,630
Italy	115,189	129,484	137,967
Japan	47,032	47,295	48,261
Morocco	10,879	11,859	12,952
Netherlands	59,445	64,007	74,015
Norway	15,176	17,301	18,926
Portugal	12,797	14,742	15,644
Russia	15,192	15,581	17,415
Saudi Arabia	15,132	15,420	12,788
Spain (excl. Canary Is.)	62,845	77,993	89,274
Sweden	15,964	17,194	20,484
Switzerland and Liechtenstein	28,203	31,841	35,419
United Kingdom	92,640	102,360	109,900
USA and Puerto Rico	99,967	108,605	106,628
Total (incl. others)	1,146,800	1,272,591	1,372,478

Exports f.o.b.	1993	1994	1995
Algeria	11,897	13,356	14,238
Austria	11,866	14,113	16,584
Belgium and Luxembourg	102,940	114,420	121,688
China, People's Republic	9,066	11,987	13,183
Denmark	9,557	11,454	12,698
Germany	204,591	222,529	250,707
Greece	9,462	9,335	10,818
Hong Kong	11,255	12,946	18,736
Italy	110,357	121,963	137,155
Japan	23,060	25,390	27,902
Morocco	11,391	12,039	12,918
Netherlands	56,845	60,364	65,747
Portugal	18,258	19,398	19,922
Spain (excl. Canary Is.)	78,054	92,346	103,402
Sweden	12,019	14,849	18,377
Switzerland and Liechtenstein	44,648	48,798	55,070
United Kingdom	111,336	128,721	131,509
USA and Puerto Rico	83,354	90,789	83,603
Total (incl. others)	1,176,673	1,294,542	1,419,658

* Imports by country of production; exports by country of last consignment.

Transport

RAILWAYS (traffic)

	1991	1992	1993
Paying passengers ('000 journeys)	837,000	830,000	823,000
Freight carried ('000 metric tons)	141,100	137,300	121,490
Passenger-km (million)	62,290	62,870	58,430
Freight ton-km (million)*	51,480	50,370	45,860

* Including passengers' baggage.

1994: Passenger-km (million) 58,900; Freight ton-km (million) 49,700.

1995: Passenger-km (million) 55,600; Freight ton-km (million) 49,000.

Source: mainly Société Nationale des Chemins de fer Français, Paris.

ROAD TRAFFIC ('000 motor vehicles in use at 31 December)

	1994	1995	1996
Passenger cars	24,900	25,100	25,500
Lorries and vans	4,881	4,926	4,976
Buses	78	79	82

Source: IRF, *World Road Statistics*.

INLAND WATERWAYS

	1992	1993	1994
Freight carried ('000 metric tons)	59,861	53,867	53,306
Freight ton-km (million)	6,911	5,950	5,607

Source: Voies navigables de France.

SHIPPING

Merchant Fleet (vessels registered at 30 June)

	Displacement ('000 gross reg. tons)		
	1994	1995	1996
Oil tankers	2,272	2,370	2,440
Total (incl. others)	4,002	4,080	4,163

Source: Direction de la Flotte de Commerce (Ministère de l'Equipement, du Logement, des Transports et du Tourisme).

Sea-borne Freight Traffic ('000 metric tons)

	1992	1993	1994
Goods loaded (excl. stores)	83,510	92,519	86,071
International	73,784	82,835	76,903
Coastwise	9,726	9,684	9,168
Goods unloaded (excl. fish)	218,856	211,853	217,406
International	207,701	200,082	204,628
Coastwise	11,155	11,771	12,778

Source: Ministère de l'Equipement, du Logement, des Transports et du Tourisme, Direction des Ports et de la Navigation Maritimes.

CIVIL AVIATION (revenue traffic on scheduled services)*

	1992	1993	1994
Kilometres flown (million)	441	471	511
Passengers carried ('000)	33,607	35,221	38,060
Passenger-km (million)	56,701	60,056	68,019
Total ton-km (million)	9,293	9,808	11,360

* Including data for airlines based in French Overseas Departments and Territories.

Source: UN, *Statistical Yearbook.*

Tourism

FOREIGN TOURIST ARRIVALS BY COUNTRY OF ORIGIN ('000)

	1994	1995	1996
Belgium and Luxembourg	6,549	7,307	7,375
Canada	560	n.a.	n.a.
Denmark	821	n.a.	n.a.
Germany	10,724	10,602	13,378
Italy	5,687	5,047	5,299
Japan	840	966	578
Netherlands	5,788	5,387	4,415
Portugal	644	n.a.	n.a.
Spain	4,175	3,870	2,759
Switzerland	3,285	3,111	3,737
United Kingdom and Ireland	12,293	11,173	9,926
USA	2,321	2,187	2,603
Total (incl. others)	61,312	60,110	62,406

Source: Ministère de l'Equipement, du Logement, des Transports et du Tourisme, Direction du Tourisme.

Net earnings from tourism (million francs): 60,742 (receipts 133,417, expenditure 72,675) in 1993; 60,542 (receipts 137,010, expenditure 76,468) in 1994.

Communications Media

	1993	1994	1995
Radio receivers ('000 in use)	51,200	51,450	52,000
Television receivers ('000 in use)	n.a.	34,100	34,250
Book production (titles)*	41,234	45,311	34,766
Telephones ('000 main lines in use)	30,900	31,600	n.a.
Mobile cellular telephones ('000 subscribers)	572	604	n.a.
Telefax stations ('000 in use)	1,000	n.a.	n.a.

* Including pamphlets (about 32% of all titles produced in 1984).

Sources: UN, *Statistical Yearbook*; UNESCO, *Statistical Yearbook.*

Daily newspapers (estimates, 1995): 80 titles (combined circulation 13,600,000 copies per issue).

Non-daily newspapers (1993): 322 titles (circulation 3,068,000 copies in 1991).

Other periodicals (1993): 2,683 titles (circulation 120,018,000 copies in 1991).

Education

(1994/95)

	Institutions	Teachers	Students
Pre-primary	18,989	106,297	2,530,856
Primary	41,244	216,962	4,071,599
Secondary*	11,212	473,673	6,003,797
Higher†:			
Universities	n.a.	46,196	1,395,103
Other	n.a.	6,467	688,129

* Including vocational education (1,703,765 students).

† Figures are for 1993/94.

Source: partly UNESCO, *Statistical Yearbook.*

Directory

The Constitution

The Constitution of the Fifth Republic was adopted by referendum on 28 September 1958 and promulgated on 6 October 1958.

PREAMBLE

The French people hereby solemnly proclaims its attachment to the Rights of Man and to the principles of national sovereignty as defined by the Declaration of 1789, confirmed and complemented by the Preamble of the Constitution of 1946.

By virtue of these principles and that of the free determination of peoples, the Republic hereby offers to the Overseas Territories that express the desire to adhere to them, new institutions based on the common ideal of liberty, equality and fraternity and conceived with a view to their democratic evolution.

Article 1. The Republic and the peoples of the Overseas Territories who, by an act of free determination, adopt the present Constitution thereby institute a Community.

The Community shall be based on the equality and the solidarity of the peoples composing it.

I. ON SOVEREIGNTY

Article 2. France shall be a Republic, indivisible, secular, democratic and social. It shall ensure the equality of all citizens before the law, without distinction of origin, race or religion. It shall respect all beliefs.

The national emblem shall be the tricolour flag, blue, white and red.

The national anthem shall be the 'Marseillaise'.

The motto of the Republic shall be 'Liberty, Equality, Fraternity'.

Its principle shall be government of the people, by the people, and for the people.

Article 3. National sovereignty belongs to the people, who shall exercise this sovereignty through their representatives and through the referendum.

No section of the people, nor any individual, may arrogate to themselves or himself the exercise thereof.

Suffrage may be direct or indirect under the conditions stipulated by the Constitution. It shall always be universal, equal and secret.

All French citizens of both sexes who have reached their majority and who enjoy civil and political rights may vote under the conditions to be determined by law.

Article 4. Political parties and groups are instrumental in the exercise of suffrage. They may form and carry on their activities freely. They must respect the principles of national sovereignty and of democracy.

II. THE PRESIDENT OF THE REPUBLIC*

Article 5. The President of the Republic shall see that the Constitution is respected. He shall ensure, by his arbitration, the regular functioning of the governmental authorities, as well as the continuity of the State.

He shall be the guarantor of national independence, of the integrity of the territory, and of respect for Community agreements and for treaties.

Article 6. (As amended by referendum of 28 October 1962.) The President of the Republic shall be elected for seven years by direct universal suffrage. The method of implementation of the present article shall be determined by an organic law.

Article 7. (As amended by referendum of 28 October 1962 and by legislation of 18 June 1976.) The President of the Republic shall be elected by an absolute majority of the votes cast. If such a majority is not obtained at the first ballot, a second ballot shall take place on the second following Sunday. Those who may stand for the second ballot shall be only the two candidates who, after the possible withdrawal of candidates with more votes, have gained the largest number of votes on the first ballot.

Voting shall begin at the summons of the Government. The election of the new President of the Republic shall take place not less than 20 days and not more than 35 days before the expiry of the powers of the President in office. In the event that the Presidency of the Republic has been vacated for any reason whatsoever, or impeded in its functioning as officially declared by the Constitutional Council, after the matter has been referred to it by the Government and which shall give its ruling by an absolute majority of its members, the functions of the President of the Republic, with the exception of those covered by Articles 11 and 12 hereunder, shall be temporarily exercised by the President of the Senate or, if the latter is in his turn unable to exercise his functions, by the Government.

In the case of vacancy or when the impediment is declared to be permanent by the Constitutional Council, the voting for the election of the new President shall take place, except in case of force majeure officially noted by the Constitutional Council, not less than 20 days and not more than 35 days after the beginning of the vacancy or of the declaration of the final nature of the impediment.

If, in the seven days preceding the latest date for the lodging of candidatures, one of the persons who, at least 30 days prior to that date, publicly announced his decision to be a candidate dies or is impeded, the Constitutional Council may decide to postpone the election.

If, before the first ballot, one of the candidates dies or is impeded, the Constitutional Council orders the postponement of the election.

In the event of the death or impediment, before any candidates have withdrawn, of one of the two candidates who received the greatest number of votes in the first ballot, the Constitutional Council shall declare that the electoral procedure must be repeated in full; the same shall apply in the event of the death or impediment of one of the two candidates standing for the second ballot.

All cases shall be referred to the Constitutional Council under the conditions laid down in paragraph 2 of article 61 below, or under those determined for the presentation of candidates by the organic law provided for in Article 6 above.

The Constitutional Council may extend the periods stipulated in paragraphs 3 and 5 above provided that polling shall not take place more than 35 days after the date of the decision of the Constitutional Council. If the implementation of the provisions of this paragraph results in the postponement of the election beyond the expiry of the powers of the President in office, the latter shall remain in office until his successor is proclaimed.

Articles 49 and 50 and Article 89 of the Constitution may not be put into application during the vacancy of the Presidency of the Republic or during the period between the declaration of the final nature of the impediment of the President of the Republic and the election of his successor.

Article 8. The President of the Republic shall appoint the Prime Minister. He shall terminate the functions of the Prime Minister when the latter presents the resignation of the Government.

At the suggestion of the Prime Minister, he shall appoint the other members of the Government and shall terminate their functions.

Article 9. The President of the Republic shall preside over the Council of Ministers.

Article 10. The President of the Republic shall promulgate laws within 15 days following the transmission to the Government of the finally adopted law.

He may, before the expiry of this time limit, ask Parliament for a reconsideration of the law or of certain of its articles. This reconsideration may not be refused.

Article 11. The President of the Republic, on the proposal of the government during [Parliamentary] sessions, or on joint motion of the two Assemblies published in the *Journal Officiel*, may submit to a referendum any bill dealing with the organization of the governmental authorities, entailing approval of a Community agreement, or providing for authorization to ratify a treaty that, without being contrary to the Constitution, might affect the functioning of the institutions.

When the referendum decides in favour of the bill, the President of the Republic shall promulgate it within the time limit stipulated in the preceding article.

Article 12. The President of the Republic may, after consultation with the Prime Minister and the Presidents of the Assemblies, declare the dissolution of the National Assembly.

A general election shall take place 20 days at the least and 40 days at the most after the dissolution.

The National Assembly shall convene by right on the second Thursday following its election. If this meeting takes place between the periods provided for ordinary sessions, a session shall, by right, be opened for a 15-day period.

There may be no further dissolution within a year following this election.

Article 13. The President of the Republic shall sign the ordinances and decrees decided upon in the Council of Ministers.

He shall make appointments to the civil and military posts of the State.

Councillors of State, the Grand Chancellor of the Legion of Honour, Ambassadors and Envoys Extraordinary, Master Councillors of the Audit Court, prefects, representatives of the Government in the Overseas Territories, general officers, rectors of academies [regional divisions of the public educational system] and directors of central administrations shall be appointed in meetings of the Council of Ministers.

An organic law shall determine the other posts to be filled by decision of the Council of Ministers, as well as the conditions under which the power of the President of the Republic to make appointments to office may be delegated by him to be exercised in his name.

Article 14. The President of the Republic shall accredit Ambassadors and Envoys Extraordinary to foreign powers; foreign Ambassadors and Envoys Extraordinary shall be accredited to him.

Article 15. The President of the Republic shall be commander of the armed forces. He shall preside over the higher councils and committees of national defence.

Article 16. When the institutions of the Republic, the independence of the nation, the integrity of its territory or the fulfilment of its international commitments are threatened in a grave and immediate manner and the regular functioning of the constitutional governmental authorities is interrupted, the President of the Republic shall take the measures required by these circumstances, after official consultation with the Prime Minister and the Presidents of the Assemblies, and the Constitutional Council.

He shall inform the nation of these measures in a message.

These measures must be prompted by the desire to ensure to the constitutional governmental authorities, in the shortest possible time, the means of accomplishing their mission. The Constitutional Council shall be consulted with regard to such measures.

Parliament shall meet by right.

The National Assembly may not be dissolved during the exercise of exceptional powers.

Article 17. The President of the Republic shall have the right of pardon.

Article 18. The President of the Republic shall communicate with the two Assemblies of Parliament by means of messages, which he shall cause to be read, and which shall not be the occasion for any debate.

Between sessions, the Parliament shall be convened especially to this end.

Article 19. Official decisions of the President of the Republic, other than those provided for under Articles 8 (first paragraph), 11, 12, 16, 18, 54, 56 and 61, shall be counter-signed by the Prime Minister and, where applicable, by the appropriate ministers.

* On 31 July 1995 legislation was enacted to permit the President to hold referendums on reforms affecting the economic and social policy of the nation and the regulation of public services.

III. THE GOVERNMENT

Article 20. The Government shall determine and conduct the policy of the nation.

It shall have at its disposal the administration and the armed forces.

It shall be responsible to the Parliament under the conditions and according to the procedures stipulated in Articles 49 and 50.

Article 21. The Prime Minister shall direct the operation of the Government. He shall be responsible for national defence. He shall ensure the execution of the laws. Subject to the provisions of Article 13, he shall have regulatory powers and shall make appointments to civil and military posts.

He may delegate certain of his powers to the ministers.

He shall replace, should the occasion arise, the President of the Republic as the Chairman of the councils and committees provided for under Article 15.

He may, in exceptional instances, replace him as the chairman of a meeting of the Council of Ministers by virtue of an explicit delegation and for a specific agenda.

Article 22. The official decisions of the Prime Minister shall be counter-signed, when circumstances so require, by the ministers responsible for their execution.

Article 23. The functions of Members of the Government shall be incompatible with the exercise of any parliamentary mandate, with the holding of any office, at the national level, in business, professional or labour organizations, and with any public employment or professional activity.

An organic law shall determine the conditions under which the holders of such mandates, functions or employments shall be replaced.

The replacement of the members of Parliament shall take place in accordance with the provisions of Article 25.

IV. THE PARLIAMENT

Article 24. The Parliament shall comprise the National Assembly and the Senate.

The deputies to the National Assembly shall be elected by direct suffrage.

The Senate shall be elected by indirect suffrage. It shall ensure the representation of the territorial units of the Republic. French nationals living outside France shall be represented in the Senate.

Article 25. An organic law shall determine the term for which each Assembly is elected, the number of its members, their emoluments, the conditions of eligibility, and the offices incompatible with membership of the Assemblies.

It shall likewise determine the conditions under which, in the case of a vacancy in either Assembly, persons shall be elected to replace the deputy or senator whose seat has been vacated until the holding of new complete or partial elections to the Assembly concerned.

Article 26. No Member of Parliament may be prosecuted, subjected to inquiry, arrested, detained or tried as a result of the opinions expressed or votes cast by him in the exercise of his functions.

No Member of Parliament may, during parliamentary session, be prosecuted or arrested for criminal or minor offences without the authorization of the Assembly of which he is a member except in the case of *flagrante delicto*.

When Parliament is not in session, no Member of Parliament may be arrested without the authorization of the Secretariat of the Assembly of which he is a member, except in the case of *flagrante delicto*, of authorized prosecution or of final conviction.

The detention or prosecution of a Member of Parliament shall be suspended if the assembly of which he is a member so demands.

Article 27. Any compulsory vote shall be null and void.

The right to vote of the members of Parliament shall be personal.

An organic law may, under exceptional circumstances, authorize the delegation of a vote. In this case, no member may be delegated more than one vote.

Article 28. (As amended by legislation of 31 July 1995.) Parliament shall convene by right in one ordinary session a year.

The session shall open on 2 October and last for not more than 120 days.

If 2 October is a public holiday, the session shall begin on the first working day thereafter.

Article 29. Parliament shall convene in extraordinary session at the request of the Prime Minister or of the majority of the members comprising the National Assembly, to consider a specific agenda.

When an extraordinary session is held at the request of the members of the National Assembly, the closure decree shall take effect as soon as the Parliament has exhausted the agenda for which it was called, and at the latest 12 days from the date of its meeting.

Only the Prime Minister may ask for a new session before the end of the month following the closure decree.

Article 30. Apart from cases in which Parliament meets by right, extraordinary sessions shall be opened and closed by decree of the President of the Republic.

Article 31. The members of the Government shall have access to the two Assemblies. They shall be heard when they so request.

They may call for the assistance of Commissioners of the Government.

Article 32. The President of the National Assembly shall be elected for the duration of the legislature. The President of the Senate shall be elected after each partial re-election [of the Senate].

Article 33. The meetings of the two Assemblies shall be public. An *in extenso* report of the debates shall be published in the *Journal Officiel*.

Each Assembly may sit in secret committee at the request of the Premier or of one-tenth of its members.

V. ON RELATIONS BETWEEN PARLIAMENT AND THE GOVERNMENT

Article 34. Laws shall be voted by Parliament.

Legislation shall establish the regulations concerning:

Civil rights and the fundamental guarantees granted to the citizens for the exercise of their public liberties; the obligations imposed by the national defence upon the person and property of citizens;

Nationality, status and legal capacity of persons; marriage contracts, inheritance and gifts;

Determination of crimes and misdemeanours as well as the penalties imposed therefor; criminal procedure; amnesty; the creation of new juridical systems and the status of magistrates;

The basis, the rate and the methods of collecting taxes of all types; the issue of currency.

Legislation likewise shall determine the regulations concerning:

The electoral system of the Parliamentary Assemblies and the local assemblies;

The establishment of categories of public institutions;

The fundamental guarantees granted to civil and military personnel employed by the State;

The nationalization of enterprises and the transfers of the property of enterprises from the public to the private sector.

Legislation shall determine the fundamental principles of:

The general organization of national defence;

The free administration of local communities, of their competencies and their resources;

Education;

Property rights, civil and commercial obligations;

Legislation pertaining to employment unions and social security.

The financial laws shall determine the financial resources and obligations of the State under the conditions and with the reservations to be provided for by an organic law.

Laws pertaining to national planning shall determine the objectives of the economic and social action of the State.

The provisions of the present article may be detailed and supplemented by an organic law.

Article 35. Parliament shall authorize the declaration of war.

Article 36. Martial law shall be decreed in a meeting of the Council of Ministers.

Its extension beyond 12 days may be authorized only by Parliament.

Article 37. Matters other than those that fall within the domain of law shall be of a regulatory character.

Legislative texts concerning these matters may be modified by decrees issued after consultation with the Council of State. Those legislative texts which shall be passed after the entry into force of the present Constitution shall be modified by decree only if the Constitutional Council has stated that they have a regulatory character as defined in the preceding paragraph.

Article 38. The Government may, in order to carry out its programme, ask Parliament for authorization to take through ordinances, during a limited period, measures that are normally within the domain of law.

The ordinances shall be enacted in meetings of Ministers after consultation with the Council of State. They shall come into force upon their publication but shall become null and void if the bill for their ratification is not submitted to Parliament before the date set by the enabling act.

At the expiry of the time limit referred to in the first paragraph of the present article, the ordinances may be modified only by the law in respect of those matters which are within the legislative domain.

Article 39. The Prime Minister and the Members of Parliament alike shall have the right to initiate legislation.

Government bills shall be discussed in the Council of Ministers after consultation with the Council of State and shall be filed with the secretariat of one of the two Assemblies. Finance bills shall be submitted first to the National Assembly.

Article 40. Private members' bills and amendments shall be inadmissible when their adoption would have as a consequence either a diminution of public financial resources or an increase in public expenditure.

Article 41. If it shall appear in the course of the legislative procedure that a Parliamentary bill or an amendment is not within the domain of law or is contrary to a delegation granted by virtue of Article 38, the Government may declare its inadmissibility.

In case of disagreement between the Government and the President of the Assembly concerned, the Constitutional Council, upon the request of one or the other, shall rule within a time limit of eight days.

Article 42. The discussion of bills shall pertain, in the first Assembly to which they have been referred, to the text presented by the Government.

An Assembly given a text passed by the other Assembly shall deliberate on the text that is transmitted to it.

Article 43. Government and private members' bills shall, at the request of the Government or of the Assembly concerned, be sent for study to committees especially designated for this purpose.

Government and private members' bills for which such a request has not been made shall be sent to one of the permanent committees, the number of which is limited to six in each Assembly.

Article 44. Members of Parliament and of the Government have the right of amendment.

After the opening of the debate, the Government may oppose the examination of any amendment which has not previously been submitted to committee.

If the Government so requests, the Assembly concerned shall decide, by a single vote, on all or part of the text under discussion, retaining only the amendments proposed or accepted by the Government.

Article 45. When, as a result of disagreement between the two Assemblies, it has been impossible to adopt a Government or private member's bill after two readings by each Assembly, or, if the Government has declared the matter urgent, after a single reading by each of them, the Prime Minister shall have the right to bring about a meeting of a joint committee composed of an equal number from both Assemblies charged with the task of proposing a text on the matters still under discussion.

The text elaborated by the joint committee may be submitted by the Government for approval of the two Assemblies. No amendment shall be admissible except by agreement with the Government.

If the joint committee does not succeed in adopting a common text, or if this text is not adopted under the conditions set forth in the preceding paragraph, the Government may, after a new reading by the National Assembly and by the Senate, ask the National Assembly to rule definitively. In this case, the National Assembly may reconsider either the text elaborated by the joint committee, or the last text voted by it, modified when circumstances so require by one or several of the amendments adopted by the Senate.

Article 46. The laws that the Constitution characterizes as organic shall be passed and amended under the following conditions:

A Government or private member's bill shall be submitted to the deliberation and to the vote of the first Assembly notified only at the expiration of a period of 15 days following its introduction;

The procedure of Article 45 shall be applicable. Nevertheless, lacking an agreement between the two Assemblies, the text may be adopted by the National Assembly on final reading only by an absolute majority of its members;

The organic laws relative to the Senate must be passed in the same manner by the two Assemblies;

The organic laws may be promulgated only after a declaration by the Constitutional Council on their constitutionality.

Article 47. The Parliament shall pass finance bills under the conditions to be stipulated by an organic law.

Should the National Assembly fail to reach a decision on first reading within a time limit of 40 days after a bill has been filed, the Government shall refer it to the Senate, which must rule within a time limit of 15 days. The procedure set forth in Article 45 shall then be followed.

Should Parliament fail to reach a decision within a time limit of 70 days, the provisions of the bill may be enforced by ordinance.

Should the finance bill establishing the resources and expenditures of a fiscal year not be filed in time for it to be promulgated before the beginning of that fiscal year, the Government shall urgently request Parliament for authorization to collect taxes and shall make available by decree the funds needed to meet the Government commitments already voted.

The time limits stipulated in the present article shall be suspended when the Parliament is not in session.

The Audit Court shall assist Parliament and the Government in supervising the implementation of the finance laws.

Article 48. The discussion of the bills tabled or agreed upon by the Government shall have priority on the agenda of the Assemblies in the order determined by the Government.

One meeting a week shall be reserved, by priority, for questions asked by Members of Parliament and for answers by the Government.

Article 49. The Prime Minister, after deliberation by the Council of Ministers, shall make the Government responsible, before the National Assembly, for its programme or, should the occasion arise, for a declaration of general policy.

The National Assembly may challenge the responsibility of the Government by a motion of censure. Such a motion is admissible only if it is signed by at least one-tenth of the members of the National Assembly. The vote may not take place before 48 hours after the motion has been filed. Only the votes that are favourable to a motion of censure shall be counted; the motion of censure may be adopted only by a majority of the members comprising the Assembly. Should the motion of censure be rejected, its signatories may not introduce another motion of censure during the same session, except in the case provided for in the paragraph below.

The Prime Minister may, after deliberation by the Council of Ministers, make the Government responsible before the National Assembly for the adoption of a bill. In this case, the text shall be considered as adopted unless a motion of censure, filed during the twenty-four hours that follow, is carried under the conditions provided for in the preceding paragraph.

The Prime Minister shall have the right to request the Senate for approval of a declaration of general policy.

Article 50. When the National Assembly adopts a motion of censure, or when it disapproves the programme or a declaration of general policy of the Government, the Prime Minister must hand the resignation of the Government to the President of the Republic.

Article 51. The closure of ordinary or extraordinary sessions shall by right be delayed, should the occasion arise, in order to permit the application of the provisions of Article 49.

VI. ON TREATIES AND INTERNATIONAL AGREEMENTS

Article 52. The President of the Republic shall negotiate and ratify treaties.

He shall be informed of all negotiations leading to the conclusion of an international agreement not subject to ratification.

Article 53. Peace treaties, commercial treaties, treaties or agreements relative to international organization, those that commit the finances of the State, those that modify provisions of a legislative nature, those relative to the status of persons, those that call for the cession, exchange or addition of territory may be ratified or approved only by a law.

They shall go into effect only after having been ratified or approved.

No cession, no exchange, or addition of territory shall be valid without the consent of the populations concerned.

Article 54. If the Constitutional Council, the matter having been referred to it by the President of the Republic, by the Prime Minister, or by the President of one or the other Assembly, shall declare that an international commitment contains a clause contrary to the Constitution, the authorization to ratify or approve this commitment may be given only after amendment of the Constitution.

Article 55. Treaties or agreements duly ratified or approved shall, upon their publication, have an authority superior to that of laws, subject, for each agreement or treaty, to its application by the other party.

VII. THE CONSTITUTIONAL COUNCIL

Article 56. The Constitutional Council shall consist of nine members, whose mandates shall last nine years and shall not be renewable. One-third of the membership of the Constitutional Council shall be renewed every three years. Three of its members shall be appointed by the President of the Republic, three by the President of the National Assembly, three by the President of the Senate.

In addition to the nine members provided for above, former Presidents of the Republic shall be members *ex officio* for life of the Constitutional Council.

The President shall be appointed by the President of the Republic. He shall have the deciding vote in case of a tie.

Article 57. The office of member of the Constitutional Council shall be incompatible with that of minister or Member of Parliament. Other incompatibilities shall be determined by an organic law.

Article 58. The Constitutional Council shall ensure the regularity of the election of the President of the Republic.

It shall examine complaints and shall announce the results of the vote.

Article 59. The Constitutional Council shall rule, in the case of disagreement, on the regularity of the election of deputies and senators.

Article 60. The Constitutional Council shall ensure the regularity of the referendum procedure and shall announce the results thereof.

Article 61. (As amended by legislation of 29 October 1974.) Organic laws, before their promulgation, and regulations of the parliamentary Assemblies, before they come into application, must be submitted to the Constitutional Council, which shall rule on their constitutionality.

To the same end, laws may be submitted to the Constitutional Council, before their promulgation, by the President of the Republic, the Prime Minister, the President of the National Assembly, the President of the Senate, or any 60 deputies or 60 senators.

In the cases provided for by the two preceding paragraphs, the Constitutional Council must make its ruling within a time limit of one month. Nevertheless, at the request of the Government, in case of urgency, this period shall be reduced to eight days.

In these same cases, referral to the Constitutional Council shall suspend the time limit for promulgation.

Article 62. A provision declared unconstitutional may not be promulgated or implemented.

The decisions of the Constitutional Council may not be appealed to any jurisdiction whatsoever. They shall be binding on the governmental authorities and on all administrative and juridical authorities.

Article 63. An organic law shall determine the rules of organization and functioning of the Constitutional Council, the procedure to be followed before it, and in particular of the periods of time allowed for laying disputes before it.

VIII. ON JUDICIAL AUTHORITY

Article 64. The President of the Republic shall be the guarantor of the independence of the judicial authority.

He shall be assisted by the High Council of the Judiciary.

An organic law shall determine the status of the judiciary.

Judges may not be removed from office.

Article 65. The High Council of the Judiciary shall be presided over by the President of the Republic. The Minister of Justice shall be its Vice-President *ex officio*. He may preside in place of the President of the Republic.

The High Council shall, in addition, include nine members appointed by the President of the Republic in conformity with the conditions to be determined by an organic law.

The High Council of the Judiciary shall present nominations for judges of the Court of Cassation and for First Presidents of courts of appeal. It shall give its opinion under the conditions to be determined by an organic law on proposals of the Minister of Justice relative to the nominations of the other judges. It shall be consulted on questions of pardon under conditions to be determined by an organic law.

The High Council of the Judiciary shall act as a disciplinary council for judges. In such cases, it shall be presided over by the First President of the Court of Cassation.

Article 66. No one may be arbitrarily detained.

The judicial authority, guardian of individual liberty, shall ensure the respect of this principle under the conditions stipulated by law.

IX. THE HIGH COURT OF JUSTICE

Article 67. A High Court of Justice shall be instituted.

It shall be composed, in equal number, of members elected, from among their membership, by the National Assembly and by the Senate after each general or partial election to these Assemblies. It shall elect its President from among its members.

An organic law shall determine the composition of the High Court, its rules, as well as the procedure to be applied before it.

Article 68. The President of the Republic shall not be held accountable for actions performed in the exercise of his office except in the case of high treason. He may be indicted only by the two Assemblies ruling by identical vote in open balloting and by an absolute majority of the members of said Assemblies. He shall be tried by the High Court of Justice.

The members of the Government shall be criminally liable for actions performed in the exercise of their office and rated as crimes or misdemeanours at the time they were committed. The procedure defined above shall be applied to them, as well as to their accomplices, in case of a conspiracy against the security of the State. In the cases provided for by the present paragraph, the High Court shall be bound by the definition of crimes and misdemeanours, as well as by the determination of penalties, as they are established by the criminal laws in force when the acts are committed.

[This article was amended in July 1993 to allow any person believing himself injured by a crime or misdemeanour committed by a member of the Government in the exercise of his functions to bring a complaint before a Commission of Requests.]

X. THE ECONOMIC AND SOCIAL COUNCIL

Article 69. The Economic and Social Council, at the referral of the Government, shall give its opinion on the Government bills, draft ordinances and decrees, as well as on the private members' bills submitted to it.

A member of the Economic and Social Council may be designated by the Council to present, before the Parliamentary Assemblies, the opinion of the Council on the Government or private members' bills that have been submitted to it.

Article 70. The Economic and Social Council may likewise be consulted by the Government on any problem of an economic or social character of interest to the Republic or to the Community. Any plan, or any bill dealing with a plan, of an economic or social character shall be submitted to it for advice.

Article 71. The composition of the Economic and Social Council and its rules of procedure shall be determined by an organic law.

XI. ON TERRITORIAL UNITS

Article 72. The territorial units of the Republic shall be the communes, the Departments, and the Overseas Territories. Any other territorial unit shall be created by law.

These units shall be free to govern themselves through elected councils and under the conditions stipulated by law.

In the Departments and the Territories, the Delegate of the Government shall be responsible for the national interests, for administrative supervision, and for seeing that the laws are respected.

Article 73. Measures of adjustment required by the particular situation of the Overseas Departments may be taken with regard to the legislative system and administrative organization of those Departments.

Article 74. The Overseas Territories of the Republic shall have a particular organization, taking account of their own interests within the general interests of the Republic. This organization shall be defined and modified by law after consultation with the Territorial Assembly concerned.

Article 75. Citizens of the Republic who do not have ordinary civil status, the only status referred to in Article 34, may keep their personal status as long as they have not renounced it.

Article 76. The Overseas Territories may retain their status within the Republic.

If they express the desire to do so by decision of their Territorial Assemblies taken within the time limit set in the first paragraph of Article 91, they shall become either Overseas Departments of the Republic or, organized into groups among themselves or singly, member States of the Community.

XII. ON THE COMMUNITY

Article 77. In the Community instituted by the present Constitution, the States shall enjoy autonomy; they shall administer themselves and, democratically and freely, manage their own affairs.

There shall be only one citizenship in the Community.

All citizens shall be equal before the law, whatever their origin, their race and their religion. They shall have the same duties.

Article 78. The Community shall have jurisdiction over foreign policy, defence, the monetary system, common economic and financial policy, as well as the policy on strategic raw materials.

In addition, except by special agreement, control of justice, higher education, the general organization of external and common transport, and telecommunications shall be within its jurisdiction.

Special agreements may establish other common jurisdictions or regulate the transfer of jurisdiction from the Community to one of its members.

Article 79. The member States shall benefit from the provisions of Article 77 as soon as they have exercised the choice provided for in Article 76.

Until the measures required for implementation of the present title go into force, matters within the common jurisdiction shall be regulated by the Republic.

Article 80. The President of the Republic shall preside over and represent the Community.

The Community shall have, as organs, an Executive Council, a Senate and a Court of Arbitration.

Article 81. The member States of the Community shall participate in the election of the President according to the conditions stipulated in Article 6.

The President of the Republic, in his capacity as President of the Community, shall be represented in each State of the Community.

Article 82. The Executive Council of the Community shall be presided over by the President of the Community. It shall consist of the Prime Minister of the Republic, the heads of Government of each of the member States of the Community, and the ministers responsible for the common affairs of the Community.

The Executive Council shall organize the co-operation of members of the Community at Government and administrative levels.

The organization and procedure of the Executive Council shall be determined by an organic law.

Article 83. The Senate of the Community shall be composed of delegates whom the Parliament of the Republic and the legislative assemblies of the other members of the Community shall choose from among their own membership. The number of delegates of each State shall be determined, taking into account its population and the responsibilities it assumes in the Community.

The Senate of the Community shall hold two sessions a year, which shall be opened and closed by the President of the Community and may not last more than one month each.

The Senate of the Community, upon referral by the President of the Community, shall deliberate on the common economic and financial policy, before laws in these matters are voted upon by the Parliament of the Republic, and, should circumstances so require, by the legislative assemblies of the other members of the Community.

The Senate of the Community shall examine the acts and treaties or international agreements, which are specified in Articles 35 and 53, and which commit the Community.

The Senate of the Community shall take enforceable decisions in the domains in which it has received delegation of power from the legislative assemblies of the members of the Community. These decisions shall be promulgated in the same form as the law in the territory of each of the States concerned.

An organic law shall determine the composition of the Senate and its rules of procedure.

Article 84. A Court of Arbitration of the Community shall rule on litigations occurring among members of the Community.

Its composition and its competence shall be determined by an organic law.

Article 85. By derogation from the procedure provided for in Article 89, the provisions of the present title that concern the functioning of the common institutions shall be amendable by identical laws passed by the Parliament of the Republic and by the Senate of the Community.

The provisions of the present title may also be revised by agreements concluded between all states of the Community: the new provisions are enforced in the conditions laid down by the Constitution of each state.

Article 86. (As amended by legislation of 4 June 1960.) A change of status of a member State of the Community may be requested, either by the Republic, or by a resolution of the legislative assembly of the State concerned confirmed by a local referendum, the organization and supervision of which shall be ensured by the institutions of the Community. The procedures governing this change shall be determined by an agreement approved by the Parliament of the Republic and the legislative assembly concerned.

Under the same conditions, a Member State of the Community may become independent. It shall thereby cease to belong to the Community.

A Member State of the Community may also, by means of agreement, become independent without thereby ceasing to belong to the Community.

An independent State which is not a member of the Community may, by means of agreements, adhere to the Community without ceasing to be independent.

The position of these States within the Community is determined by the agreements concluded for that purpose, in particular the agreements mentioned in the preceding paragraphs as well as, where applicable, the agreements provided for in the second paragraph of Article 85.

Article 87. The particular agreements made for the implementation of the present title shall be approved by the Parliament of the Republic and the legislative assembly concerned.

XIII. ON AGREEMENTS OF ASSOCIATION

Article 88. The Republic or the Community may make agreements with States that wish to associate themselves with the Community in order to develop their own civilizations.

XIV. ON AMENDMENT

Article 89. The initiative for amending the Constitution shall belong both to the President of the Republic on the proposal of the Prime Minister and to the Members of Parliament.

The Government or private member's bill for amendment must be passed by the two Assemblies in identical terms. The amendment shall become definitive after approval by a referendum.

Nevertheless, the proposed amendment shall not be submitted to a referendum when the President of the Republic decides to submit it to Parliament convened in Congress; in this case, the proposed amendment shall be approved only if it is accepted by a three-fifths majority of the votes cast. The Secretariat of the Congress shall be that of the National Assembly.

No amendment procedure may be undertaken or followed if it is prejudicial to the integrity of the territory.

The republican form of government shall not be the object of an amendment.

XV. TEMPORARY PROVISIONS

Article 90. The ordinary session of Parliament is suspended. The mandate of the members of the present National Assembly shall expire on the day that the Assembly elected under the present Constitution convenes.

Until this meeting, the Government alone shall have the authority to convene Parliament.

The mandate of the members of the Assembly of the French Union shall expire at the same time as the mandate of the members of the present National Assembly.

Article 91. The institutions of the Republic, provided for by the present Constitution, shall be established within four months counting from the time of its promulgation.

This period shall be extended to six months for the institutions of the Community.

The powers of the President of the Republic now in office shall expire only when the results of the election provided for in Articles 6 and 7 of the present Constitution are proclaimed.

The Member States of the Community shall participate in this first election under the conditions derived from their status at the date of the promulgation of the Constitution.

The established authorities shall continue in the exercise of their functions in these States according to the laws and regulations applicable when the Constitution goes into force, until the establishment of the authorities provided for by their new regimes.

Until its definitive constitution, the Senate shall consist of the present members of the Council of the Republic. The organic laws that shall determine the definitive constitution of the Senate must be passed before 31 July 1959.

The powers conferred on the Constitutional Council by Articles 58 and 59 of the Constitution shall be exercised, until the establishment of this Council, by a committee composed of the Vice-President of the Council of State, as Chairman, the First President of the Court of Cassation, and the First President of the Audit Court.

The peoples of the member States of the Community shall continue to be represented in Parliament until the entry into force of the measures necessary to the implementation of Chapter XII.

Article 92. The legislative measures necessary to the establishment of the institutions and, until they are established, to the functioning of the public powers, shall be taken in meetings of the Council of Ministers, after consultation with the Council of State, in the form of ordinances having the force of law.

During the time limit set in the first paragraph of Article 91, the Government shall be authorized to determine, by ordinances having the force of law and passed in the same way, the system of elections to the Assemblies provided for by the Constitution.

During the same period and under the same conditions, the Government may also adopt measures, in all domains, which it may deem necessary to the life of the nation, the protection of citizens or the safeguarding of liberties.

ELECTORAL LAW, JULY 1986

The 577 Deputies of the National Assembly are to be directly elected under the former single-member constituency system (in force before the implementation of a system of proportional representation imposed by the electoral law of 1985). Participating parties can nominate only one candidate and designate a reserve candidate, who can serve as a replacement if the elected Deputy is appointed a Minister or a member of the Constitutional Council, or is sent on a government assignment scheduled to last more than six months, or dies. A candidate must receive an absolute majority and at least one-quarter of registered votes in order to be elected to the National Assembly. If these conditions are not fulfilled, a second ballot will be held a week later, for voters to choose between all candidates receiving 12.5% of the total votes on the first ballot. The candidate who receives a simple majority of votes on the second ballot will then be elected. Candidates polling less than 5% of the votes will lose their deposit.

The Government

HEAD OF STATE

President: Jacques Chirac (took office 17 May 1995).

COUNCIL OF MINISTERS
(February 1998)

A coalition of the Parti Socialiste (PS), the Parti Communiste Français (PCF), the Parti Radical Socialiste (PRS), the Mouvement des Citoyens (MDC) and Les Verts (Green).

Prime Minister: Lionel Jospin (PS).

Minister of Labour and Social Affairs: Martine Aubry (PS).

Minister of Justice: Elisabeth Guigou (PS).

Minister of National Education, Research and Technology: Claude Allègre (PS).

Minister of Defence: Alain Richard (PS).

Minister of Public Works, Housing and Transport: Jean-Claude Gaysott (PCF).

Minister of Foreign Affairs: Hubert Védrine (PS).

Minister of the Interior: Jean-Pierre Chevènement (MDC).

Minister of the Economy, Finance and Industry: Dominique Strauss-Kahn (PS).

Minister of Relations with Parliament: Daniel Vaillant (PS).

Minister of Town and Country Planning and the Environment: Dominique Voynet (Green).

Minister of Culture and Communications and Government Spokesperson: Cathérine Trautmann (PS).

Minister of Agriculture and Fisheries: Louis Le Pensec (PS).

Minister of Youth and Sport: Marie-George Buffet (PCF).

Minister of the Civil Service, Administrative Reform and Decentralization: Emile Zuccarelli (PRS).

There were also two Ministers-Delegate and 10 Secretaries of State.

MINISTRIES

Office of the President: Palais de l'Elysée, 55–57 rue du Faubourg Saint Honoré, 75008 Paris; tel. 1-42-92-81-00; telex 650127; fax 1-47-42-24-65.

Office of the Prime Minister: Hôtel Matignon, 57 rue de Varenne, 75700 Paris; tel. 1-42-75-80-00; telex 200724; fax 1-42-75-75-04.

Ministry of Agriculture and Fisheries: 78 rue de Varenne, 75700 Paris; tel. 1-49-55-49-55; telex 205202; fax 1-49-55-40-39.

Ministry of the Budget: 139 rue de Bercy, 75572 Paris Cédex 12; tel. 1-40-04-04-04; fax 1-43-41-22-03.

Ministry of the Civil Service: 35 rue Saint Dominique, 75700 Paris; tel. 1-47-53-71-48; fax 1-47-05-93-32.

Ministry of Communications: 69 rue de Varenne, 75700 Paris; tel. 1-42-75-80-00; fax 1-42-75-87-93.

Ministry of Co-operation: 20 rue Monsieur, 75700 Paris; tel. 1-47-83-10-10; telex 202363; fax 1-43-06-97-40.

Ministry of Culture: 3 rue de Valois, 75001 Paris; tel. 1-40-15-80-00; telex 215134; fax 1-42-61-35-77.

Ministry of Defence: 14 rue Saint Dominique, 75700 Paris; tel. 1-42-19-30-11; telex 201375; fax 1-47-05-40-91.

Ministry of the Economy, Finance and Industry: 139 rue de Bercy, 75572 Paris Cédex 12; tel. 1-40-04-04-04; telex 217068; fax 1-43-43-75-97.

Ministry of Enterprises and Economic Development: 101 rue de Grenelle, 75700 Paris; tel. 1-43-19-24-24; fax 1-43-19-21-50.

Ministry of Foreign Affairs: 37 quai d'Orsay, 75700 Paris Cédex 07; tel. 1-43-17-53-53; telex 202329; fax 1-43-17-52-03.

Ministry of Higher Education, Research and Technology: 1 rue Descartes, 75005 Paris; tel. 1-46-34-35-35; fax 1-46-34-32-35.

Ministry of Industry, the Post Office and Telecommunications: 20 ave de Ségur, 75007 Paris; tel. 1-43-19-36-36; fax 1-44-11-60-80.

Ministry of the Interior: place Beauvau, 75800 Paris; tel. 1-49-27-49-27; telex 290922; fax 1-43-59-89-50.

Ministry of Justice: 13 place Vendôme, 75042 Paris Cédex 01; tel. 1-44-77-60-60; telex 211320; fax 1-44-77-70-20.

Ministry of Labour and Social Affairs: 127 rue de Grenelle, 75700 Paris; tel. 1-40-56-60-00; fax 1-40-56-67-60.

Ministry of National Education: 110 rue de Grenelle, 75700 Paris; tel. 1-49-55-10-10; fax 1-45-51-53-63.

Ministry of Overseas Departments and Territories: 27 rue Oudinot, 75358 Paris 07 SP; tel. 1-53-69-20-00; fax 1-43-06-60-30; internet http://www.outre-mer.gouv.fr.

Ministry of Public Works, Housing, Transport and Tourism: Grande Arche-La Défense, 92055 Paris La Défense Cédex; tel. 1-40-81-21-22; internet http://www.equipement.gouv.fr.

Ministry of Town and Country Planning and the Environment: 20 ave de Ségur, 75302 Paris Cédex 07; tel. 1-42-19-20-21.

Ministry of Youth and Sport: 78 rue Olivier de Serres, 75015 Paris; tel. 1-40-45-90-00; fax 1-42-50-42-49.

President and Legislature

PRESIDENT

Elections of 23 April and 7 May 1995

	First ballot	Second ballot
EDOUARD BALLADUR (Rassemblement pour la République)	5,658,796	—
JACQUES CHEMINADE (Fédération pour une nouvelle solidarité)	84,959	—
JACQUES CHIRAC (Rassemblement pour la République)	6,348,375	15,763,027
ROBERT HUE (Parti Communiste Français)	2,632,460	—
LIONEL JOSPIN (Parti Socialiste)	7,097,786	14,180,644
ARLETTE LAGUILLER (Lutte Ouvrière)	1,615,552	—
JEAN-MARIE LE PEN (Front National)	4,570,838	—
PHILIPPE DE VILLIERS (Mouvement pour la France)	1,443,186	—
DOMINIQUE VOYNET (Les Verts)	1,010,681	—

PARLEMENT
(Parliament)

Assemblée Nationale
(National Assembly)

President: LAURENT FABIUS.

General Election, 25 May and 1 June 1997

Party	% of votes cast in first ballot	% of votes cast in second ballot*	Seats
Parti Socialiste (PS)	23.53	38.05	241
Rassemblement pour la République (RPR)	15.70	22.82	134
Union pour la Démocratie Française (UDF)	14.22	20.77	108
Parti Communiste Français (PCF)	9.94	3.84	38
Parti Radical Socialiste (PRS)	1.45	2.19	12
Front National (FN)	14.94	5.60	1
Various ecologist candidates	6.81	1.62	7
Various right-wing candidates	6.70	2.45	14
Various left-wing candidates	5.32	2.55	21
Others	1.39	0.11	1
Total	100.00	100.00	577

* Held where no candidate had won the requisite overall majority in the first ballot, between candidates who had received at least 12.5% of the votes in that round.

Sénat
(Senate)

President: RENÉ MONORY.

Members of the Senate are indirectly elected for a term of nine years, with one-third of the seats renewable every three years.

After the most recent election, held on 24 September 1995, the Senate had 321 seats: 296 for metropolitan France; 13 for the overseas departments and territories; and 12 for French nationals abroad. The strength of the parties was as follows:

	Seats
Groupe du Rassemblement pour la République	94
Groupe socialiste	75
Groupe de l'Union centriste des Démocrates de Progrès	59
Groupe de l'Union des Républicains et des Indépendants	47
Groupe du Rassemblement démocratique et européen	24
Groupe communiste	15
Non-attached	7
Total	321

Political Organizations

Alliance Populaire: Paris; extreme right-wing; Pres. JEAN-FRANÇOIS TOUZÉ.

Alternative Rouge et Verte (AREV): 40 rue de Malte, 75011 Paris; tel. 1-43-57-44-80; f. 1993 to replace the Parti Socialiste Unifié (f. 1960); left-wing; Leaders MARTINE BULTOT, JEAN-PIERRE LEMAIRE, MARIE-FRANÇOISE PIROT, ROGER WINTERHALTER.

Centre National des Indépendants et Paysans (CNI): 146 rue de l'Université, 75007 Paris; tel. 1-40-62-63-64; fax 1-45-56-02-63; f. 1949; right-wing; Pres. JEAN PERRIN; Sec.-Gen. ANNICK DU ROSCOAT.

Front National (FN): 4 rue Vauguyon, 92210 Saint Cloud; tel. 1-41-12-10-18; fax 1-41-12-10-86; f. 1972; extreme right-wing nationalist; Pres. JEAN-MARIE LE PEN; Sec.-Gen. BRUNO GOLLNISCH.

Génération Ecologie: 73 ave Paul Doumer, 75016 Paris; tel. 1-45-03-82-82; fax 1-45-03-82-80; f. 1990; emphasis on environmental matters; Leader BRICE LALONDE.

Ligue Communiste Révolutionnaire (LCR): c/o Rouge, 2 rue Richard Lenoir, 93108 Montreuil; tel. 1-48-70-42-30; fax 1-48-59-23-28; f. 1974; Trotskyist; French section of the Fourth International; 1,500 mems (1996); Leader ALAIN KRIVINE.

Lutte Ouvrière (LO): BP 233, 75865 Paris Cédex 18; Trotskyist; Leaders ARLETTE LAGUILLER, F. DUBURG, J. MORAND.

Mouvement des Citoyens: Paris; sceptical of increased European integration; Leader JEAN-PIERRE CHEVÈNEMENT.

Mouvement des Démocrates: Paris; tel. 1-47-54-06-57; fax 1-47-63-27-58; f. 1974; Leader MICHEL JOBERT.

Mouvement Ecologiste Indépendent: Paris; f. 1994; emphasis on environmental matters; 3,000 mems; Pres. GENEVIÈVE ANDUÉZA; Nat. Sec. GÉRARD MONNIER-BESOMBES.

Mouvement pour la France: Paris; f. 1994; opposes terms of the Maastricht Treaty; Chair. PHILIPPE DE VILLIERS.

Mouvement des Réformateurs (MR): 7 rue de Villersexel, 75007 Paris; tel. 1-45-44-61-50; fax 1-45-44-91-90; f. 1992; centrist; formed by merger of Association des Démocrates, France Unie and Performance et Partage; Sec.-Gen. JEAN-PIERRE SOISSON.

Parti Communiste Français (PCF): 2 place du Colonel Fabien, 75940 Paris Cédex 19; tel. 1-40-40-12-12; fax 1-40-40-13-56; subscribed to the common programme of the United Left (with the Parti Socialiste) until 1977; aims to follow the democratic path to socialism and advocates an independent foreign policy; national bureau of 22 mems; Nat. Sec. ROBERT HUE.

Parti Radical Socialiste (PRS): 13 rue Duroc, 75007 Paris; tel. 1-45-66-67-68; fax 1-45-66-47-93; f. 1973 by fmr members of Parti Radical; present name since 1996; left-wing; Pres. JEAN-MICHEL BAYLET.

Parti Socialiste (PS): 10 rue de Solférino, 75333 Paris Cédex 07; tel. 1-45-56-77-00; fax 1-47-05-15-78; f. 1971; subscribed to the common programme of the United Left (with the Parti Communiste) until 1977; advocates solidarity, full employment and the eventual attainment of socialism through a mixed economy; 109,000 mems (1996); First Sec. FRANÇOIS HOLLANDE.

Rassemblement pour la République (RPR): 123 rue de Lille, 75007 Paris; tel. 1-49-55-63-00; telex 260820; fax 1-45-51-44-79; f. 1976 from the Gaullist party Union des Démocrates pour la République; has frequently formed electoral alliances with UDF (q.v.); 150,000 mems; Pres. PHILIPPE SÉGUIN; Sec.-Gen. JEAN-FRANÇOIS MANCEL.

Union pour la Démocratie Française (UDF): 12 rue François I, 75008 Paris; tel. 1-40-75-40-00; fax 1-40-75-40-10; formed in 1978 to unite for electoral purposes non-Gaullist 'majority' candidates; has frequently formed electoral alliances with RPR (q.v.); Chair. FRANÇOIS LÉOTARD; Sec.-Gen. PIERRE CALZAT.

Affiliated parties:

Force Démocrate (FD): 133 bis rue de l'Université, 75007 Paris; tel. 1-53-59-20-00; fax 1-53-59-20-59; f. 1976 as Centre des Démocrates Sociaux, renamed in 1995; Pres. FRANÇOIS BAYROU.

Parti Populaire pour la Démocratie Française (PPDF): 250 blvd Saint Germain, 75007 Paris; tel. 1-42-22-69-51; fax 1-42-22-59-49; f. 1965, present name since 1995; Leaders HERVÉ DE CHARETTE, JEAN-PIERRE RAFFARIN.

Parti Républicain (PR): 105 rue de l'Université, 75007 Paris; tel. 1-40-62-30-30; fax 1-45-55-92-76; formed May 1977 as a grouping of the Fédération Nationale des Républicains Indépendants (FNRI) and three smaller 'Giscardian' parties; Sec.-Gen. JOSÉ ROSSI.

Parti Radical: 1 place de Valois, 75001 Paris; tel. 1-42-61-56-32; fax 1-42-61-49-65; f. 1901; Pres. THIERRY CORNILLET; Sec.-Gen. AYMERI DE MONTESQUIOU.

Parti social-démocrate (PSD): 191 rue de l'Université, 75007 Paris; tel. 1-47-53-84-41; fax 1-47-05-73-53; f. 1973 as Mouvement des démocrates socialistes de France, name changed 1982; Pres. MAX LEJEUNE; Sec.-Gen. ANDRÉ SANTINI.

Les Verts: 107 ave Parmentier, 75011 Paris; tel. 1-43-55-10-01; fax 1-43-55-16-15; e-mail secretar@verts.imaginet.fr; f. 1984; ecologist party; Spokespersons DOMINIQUE VOYNET, YVES COCHET, MARIE-ANNE ISLER-BÉGUIN, GUY HASCOËT; National Sec. MARIE-FRANÇOISE MENDEZ.

Diplomatic Representation

EMBASSIES IN FRANCE

Afghanistan: 32 ave Raphaël, 75016 Paris; tel. 1-45-25-05-29; fax 1-45-24-46-87; Chargé d'affaires a.i.: DAOUD M. MIR.

Albania: 131 rue de la Pompe, 75116 Paris; tel. 1-45-53-51-32; telex 611534; fax 1-45-53-89-38; Ambassador: BESNIK MUSTAFAJ.

Algeria: 50 rue de Lisbonne, 75008 Paris; tel. 1-42-25-70-70; fax 1-42-25-10-25; Ambassador: HOCINE DJOUDI.

Andorra: 26 ave de l'Opéra, 75001 Paris; tel. 1-42-61-53-33; Ambassador: MERITXELL MATEU.

Angola: 19 ave Foch, 75116 Paris; tel. 1-45-01-58-20; telex 649847; fax 1-45-00-33-71; Ambassador: BOAVENTURA DA SILVA CARDOSO.

Argentina: 6 rue Cimarosa, 75116 Paris; tel. 1-44-05-27-00; fax 1-45-53-46-33; Ambassador: JUAN ARCHIBALDO LANUS.

Armenia: 9 rue Viète, 75017 Paris; tel. 1-42-12-98-01; Ambassador: VAHAN PAPAZIAN.

Australia: 4 rue Jean Rey, 75724 Paris Cédex 15; tel. 1-40-59-33-00; telex 202313; fax 1-40-59-33-10; Ambassador: JOHN SPENDER.

Austria: 6 rue Fabert, 75007 Paris; tel. 1-40-63-30-63; telex 200708; fax 1-45-55-63-65; Ambassador: FRANZ CESKA.

Azerbaijan: 209 rue de l'Université, 75007 Paris; tel. 1-44-18-60-20; Ambassador: ELÉONORA GOUSSEINOVA.

Bahrain: 3B place des Etats Unis, 75116 Paris; tel. 1-47-23-48-68; fax 1-47-20-55-75; Ambassador: Dr ALI MOHAMED FAKHRO.

Bangladesh: 5 sq. Pétrarque, 75116 Paris; tel. 1-47-04-94-35; telex 630868; fax 1-47-04-72-41; Ambassador: TUFAIL K. HAIDER.

Belarus: 38 blvd Suchet, 75016 Paris; tel. 1-44-14-69-79; fax 1-44-14-69-70; Ambassador: VLADIMIR SENKO.

Belgium: 9 rue de Tilsitt, 75017 Paris; tel. 1-44-09-39-39; telex 660484; fax 1-47-54-07-64; Ambassador: ALAIN RENS.

Benin: 87 ave Victor Hugo, 75116 Paris; tel. 1-45-00-98-82; telex 610110; fax 1-45-01-82-02; Ambassador: ANDRÉ-GUY OLOGOUDOU.

Bolivia: 12 ave Président Kennedy, 75116 Paris; tel. 1-42-24-93-44; telex 611879; fax 1-45-25-86-23; Ambassador: CARLOS ANTONIO CARRASCO.

Bosnia and Herzegovina: 174 rue de Courcelles, 75017 Paris; tel. 1-42-67-34-22; fax 1-40-53-85-22; Ambassador: NIKOLA KOVAČ.

Brazil: 34 cours Albert 1er, 75008 Paris; tel. 1-45-61-63-00; telex 650063; fax 1-42-89-03-45; e-mail service presse@bresil anidia.fr; Ambassador: MARCOS CASTRISTO DE AZAMBUJA.

Brunei: 4 rue Logelbach, 75017 Paris; tel. 1-42-67-49-47; fax 1-42-67-53-65; Ambassador: Pengiran Haji IDRISS.

Bulgaria: 1 ave Rapp, 75007 Paris; tel. 1-45-51-85-90; fax 1-45-51-18-68; Ambassador: STÉPHANE TAFRON.

Burkina Faso: 159 blvd Haussmann, 75008 Paris; tel. 1-43-59-90-63; telex 641870; fax 1-42-56-50-07; Ambassador: FILIPPE SAWADOGO.

Burundi: 24 rue Raynouard, 75116 Paris; tel. 1-45-20-60-61; telex 611463; fax 1-45-20-03-11; Ambassador: JEAN-BAPTISTE MBONYINGINGO.

Cambodia: 4 rue Adolphe Yvon, 75116 Paris; tel. 1-45-03-47-20; fax 1-45-03-47-40; Ambassador: HOR NAMHONG.

Cameroon: 73 rue d'Auteuil, 75116 Paris; tel. 1-47-43-98-33; telex 640087; fax 1-46-51-24-52; Ambassador: PASCAL BILOA TANG.

Canada: 35 ave Montaigne, 75008 Paris; tel. 1-44-43-29-00; fax 1-44-43-29-99; Ambassador: JACQUES ROY.

Cape Verde: 80 rue Jouffroy d'Abbans, 75017 Paris; tel. 1-42-12-73-50; Ambassador: RUI ALBERTO DE FIGUEIREDO SOARES.

Central African Republic: 30 rue des Perchamps, 75116 Paris; tel. 1-42-24-42-56; telex 611908; fax 1-42-88-98-95; Ambassador: JEAN POLOKO.

Chad: 65 rue des Belles Feuilles, 75116 Paris; tel. 1-45-53-36-75; telex 610629; fax 1-45-53-16-09; Ambassador: MAHAMAT ALI ABDALLAH NASSOUR.

Chile: 2 ave de la Motte Picquet, 75007 Paris; tel. 1-45-51-46-68; telex 260075; fax 1-45-51-13-33; Ambassador: JOSÉ MANUEL MORALES.

China, People's Republic: 11 ave George V, 75008 Paris; tel. 1-47-23-34-45; fax 1-47-20-24-22; Ambassador: CAI FANGBO.

Colombia: 22 rue de l'Elysée, 75008 Paris; tel. 1-42-65-46-08; telex 640935; fax 1-42-66-18-60; e-mail emcolombia@wanadoo.fr; Ambassador: RODRIGO PARDO GARCÍA PEÑA.

Comoros: 20 rue Marbeau, 75116 Paris; tel. 1-40-67-90-54; fax 1-40-67-72-96; Ambassador: SAID HASSAN SAID HACHIM.

Congo, Democratic Republic: 32 cours Albert 1er, 75008 Paris; tel. 1-42-25-57-50; telex 280661; fax 1-42-89-80-09; Ambassador: (vacant).

Congo, Republic : 37 bis rue Paul Valéry, 75116 Paris; tel. 1-45-00-60-57; telex 611954; Ambassador: PIERRE-MICHEL NGUIMBI.

Costa Rica: 78 ave Emile Zola, 75015 Paris; tel. 1-45-78-96-96; fax 1-45-78-99-66; Ambassador: EDGAR MOHS.

Côte d'Ivoire: 102 ave Raymond Poincaré, 75116 Paris; tel. 1-53-64-62-62; telex 611915; fax 1-45-00-47-97; Ambassador: JEAN-MARIE KALOU-GERVAIS.

Croatia: 39 ave Georges Mandel, 75116 Paris; tel. 1-53-70-02-80; fax 1-53-70-02-90; Ambassador: SMILJAN ŠIMAC.

Cuba: 16 rue de Presles, 75015 Paris; tel. 1-45-67-55-35; telex 200815; fax 1-45-66-80-92; Ambassador: RAÚL ROA KOURI.

Cyprus: 23 rue Galilée, 75116 Paris; tel. 1-47-20-86-28; fax 1-40-70-13-44; e-mail embrecyp@worldnet.fr; Ambassador: ANDRÉAS PIRISHIS.

Czech Republic: 15 ave Charles Floquet, 75007 Paris; tel. 1-40-65-13-00; telex 611032; fax 1-47-83-50-78; Ambassador: PETR LOM.

Denmark: 77 ave Marceau, 75116 Paris; tel. 1-44-31-21-21; telex 640445; fax 1-44-31-21-88; Ambassador: PETER PEDERSEN DYVIG.

Djibouti: 26 rue Emile Ménier, 75116 Paris; tel. 1-47-27-49-22; telex 643690; fax 1-45-53-50-53; Ambassador: DJAMA OMAR IDLEH.

Dominican Republic: 17 rue La Fontaine, 75116 Paris; tel. 1-40-50-64-97; fax 1-40-50-65-21; Ambassador: GUILLERMO PINA CONTRERAS.

Ecuador: 34 ave de Messine, 75008 Paris; tel. 1-45-61-10-21; telex 641333; fax 1-42-89-22-09; e-mail ambecuad@infonie.fr; Ambassador: JUAN CUEVA JARAMILLO.

Egypt: 56 ave d'Iéna, 75116 Paris; tel. 1-53-67-88-30; telex 611691; fax 1-47-23-06-43; Ambassador: ALY MAHER EL-SAYED.

El Salvador: 12 rue Galilée, 75116 Paris; tel. 1-47-20-42-02; fax 1-40-70-01-95; Ambassador: Ramiro Zepeda Roldan.

Equatorial Guinea: 6 rue Alfred de Vigny, 75008 Paris; tel. 1-47-66-44-33; fax 1-47-64-94-52; Ambassador: Lino Simo Ekua Avomo.

Estonia: 14 blvd Montmartre, 75009 Paris; tel. 1-48-01-00-22; fax 1-48-01-02-95; Ambassador: Andres Tomasberg.

Ethiopia: 35 ave Charles Floquet, 75007 Paris; tel. 1-47-83-83-95; telex 260008; fax 1-43-06-52-14; Ambassador: Mulugetta Etaffa.

Finland: 1 place de Finlande, 75007 Paris; tel. 1-44-18-19-20; telex 200054; fax 1-45-55-51-57; e-mail finlande@pratique.fr; Ambassador: Antti Hynninen.

Gabon: 26 bis ave Raphaël, 75116 Paris; tel. 1-42-24-79-60; telex 610146; fax 1-42-24-62-42; Ambassador: Honorine Dossou-Naki.

The Gambia: 117 rue St Lazare, 75008 Paris; tel. 1-42-94-09-30; telex 660503; fax 1-42-94-11-91; Ambassador: John P. Bojang.

Georgia: 104 ave Raymond Poincaré, 75116 Paris; tel. 1-45-02-16-16; Ambassador: Gotcha Tchogovadze.

Germany: 13–15 ave Franklin D. Roosevelt, 75008 Paris; tel. 1-53-83-45-75; fax 1-43-59-74-18; Ambassador: Dr Immo Stabreit.

Ghana: 8 Villa Saïd, 75116 Paris; tel. 1-45-00-09-50; telex 645084; fax 1-45-00-81-95; Ambassador: Harry Osei Blavo.

Greece: 17 rue Auguste Vacquerie, 75116 Paris; tel. 1-47-23-72-28; telex 612747; fax 1-47-23-73-85; Ambassador: Charalambos Korakas.

Guatemala: 73 rue de Courcelles, 75008 Paris; tel. 1-42-27-78-63; telex 650850; fax 1-47-54-02-06; Ambassador: Gloria Regina Montenegro Passarelli de Chirouze.

Guinea: 51 rue de la Faisanderie, 75116 Paris; tel. 1-47-04-81-48; telex 648497; fax 1-47-04-57-65; Ambassador: Ibrahima Sylla.

Guinea-Bissau: 94 rue Saint Lazare, 75009 Paris; tel. 1-45-26-18-51; fax 1-42-81-24-90; Ambassador: Fali Embalo.

Haiti: 10 rue Théodule Ribot, 75017 Paris; tel. 1-47-63-47-78; fax 1-42-27-02-05; Ambassador: Marc A. Trouillot.

Holy See: 10 ave du Président Wilson, 75116 Paris (Apostolic Nunciature); tel. 1-53-23-01-50; fax 1-47-23-65-44; e-mail noncapfr@worldnet.fr; Apostolic Nuncio: Most Rev. Mario Tagliaferri, Titular Archbishop of Formia.

Honduras: 8 rue Creveaux, 75116 Paris; tel. 1-47-55-86-45; fax 1-47-55-86-48; e-mail embhondu@worldnet.fr; Ambassador: Max Velasquez Díaz.

Hungary: 80 Avenue Foch, 75116 Paris; tel. 1-45-00-41-59; telex 610822; fax 1-45-01-66-00; Ambassador: Béla Szombati.

Iceland: 8 ave Kléber, 75116 Paris; tel. 1-44-17-32-85; fax 1-40-67-99-96; Ambassador: Sverrir Haukur Gunnlaugsson.

India: 15 rue Alfred Dehodencq, 75016 Paris; tel. 1-40-50-70-70; telex 64562; fax 1-40-50-09-96; e-mail culture@indembparis.zcc.net; Ambassador: Ranjit Sethi.

Indonesia: 47–49 rue Cortambert, 75116 Paris; tel. 1-45-03-07-60; telex 648031; fax 1-45-04-50-32; Ambassador: Satrio B. Joedono.

Iran: 4 ave d'Iéna, 75116 Paris; tel. 1-40-69-79-00; telex 645600; fax 1-40-70-01-57; Ambassador: Dr Hamid Reza Assefi.

Iraq: see Morocco.

Ireland: 12 ave Foch, 75116 Paris; tel. 1-44-17-67-00; fax 1-44-17-67-60; Ambassador: Patrick O'Connor.

Israel: 3 rue Rabelais, 75008 Paris; tel. 1-40-76-55-00; fax 1-40-76-55-55; Ambassador: Avi Pazner.

Italy: 51 rue de Varenne, 75007 Paris; tel. 1-45-44-38-90; telex 270827; fax 1-45-49-35-81; Ambassador: Sergio Vento.

Japan: 7 ave Hoche, 75008 Paris; tel. 1-48-88-62-00; fax 1-42-67-28-85; Ambassador: Koichiro Matsuura.

Jordan: 80 blvd Maurice Barrès, 92200 Neuilly-sur-Seine; tel. 1-46-24-51-38; telex 630084; fax 1-46-37-02-06; Ambassador: Al-Sharif Sharaf Fawaz.

Kazakhstan: 59 rue Pierre Charron, 75008 Paris; tel. 1-45-61-52-00; fax 1-45-61-52-01; Ambassador: Nourlan Danenov.

Kenya: 3 rue Cimarosa, 75116 Paris; tel. 1-45-53-35-00; telex 640950; fax 1-45-53-95-32; Ambassador: Steven A. Loyatum.

Korea, Republic: 125 rue de Grenelle, 75007 Paris; tel. 1-47-53-01-01; fax 1-47-53-71-49; Ambassador: Lee See-Young.

Kuwait: 2 rue de Lübeck, 75116 Paris; tel. 1-47-23-54-25; telex 620513; fax 1-47-20-33-59; Ambassador: Tarek Razzouqi.

Laos: 74 ave Raymond Poincaré, 75116 Paris; tel. 1-45-53-02-98; telex 610711; fax 1-47-57-27-89; Ambassador: Khamphanh Simmalavong.

Latvia: 14 blvd Montmartre, 75009 Paris; tel. 1-48-01-00-44; fax 1-48-01-03-71; Ambassador: Sandra Kalniete.

Lebanon: 3 villa Copernic, 75116 Paris; tel. 1-40-67-75-75; telex 641087; fax 1-40-67-16-42; Ambassador: Naji Raymond Abi Assi.

Liberia: 8 rue Jacques Bingen, 75017 Paris; tel. 1-47-63-58-55; telex 290288; fax 1-47-64-36-50; Ambassador: Aaron George.

Libya (People's Bureau): 2 rue Charles Lamoureux, 75116 Paris; tel. 1-47-04-71-60; telex 620643; fax 1-47-55-96-25; Sec. of People's Bureau: Dr Ali A. Treiki.

Lithuania: 14 blvd Montmartre, 75009 Paris; tel. 1-48-01-00-33; fax 1-48-01-03-31; e-mail navikas@emb.frmug.org; Ambassador: Richard Bačkis.

Luxembourg: 33 ave Rapp, 75007 Paris; tel. 1-45-55-13-37; telex 204711; fax 1-45-51-72-29; Ambassador: Paul Mertz.

Macedonia, former Yugoslav republic: 21 rue Sebastian Mercier, 75015 Paris; tel. 1-45-77-10-50; fax 1-45-77-14-84; Ambassador: Luan Starova.

Madagascar: 4 ave Raphaël, 75116 Paris; tel. 1-45-04-62-11; telex 645394; fax 1-45-03-34-54; Ambassador: Raymond Raoelina.

Malawi: 20 rue Euler, 75008 Paris; tel. 1-47-20-20-27; telex 642804; fax 1-47-23-62-48; Ambassador: Augustine W. Mnthambala.

Malaysia: 2 bis rue Bénouville, 75116 Paris; tel. 1-45-53-11-85; fax 1-47-27-34-60; Ambassador: Mohamed Haron.

Mali: 89 rue du Cherche-Midi, 75006 Paris; tel. 1-45-48-58-43; telex 260002; fax 1-45-48-55-34; Ambassador: Madina Ly-Tall.

Malta: 92 ave des Champs Elysées, 75008 Paris; tel. 1-45-62-68-16; fax 1-45-62-00-36; Ambassador: Vincent Camilleri.

Mauritania: 5 rue de Montévidéo, 75116 Paris; tel. 1-45-04-88-54; telex 620506; fax 1-40-72-82-96; Ambassador: Dah Ould Abdi.

Mauritius: 127 rue de Tocqueville, 75017 Paris; tel. 1-47-66-11-73; telex 644233; fax 1-40-53-02-91; e-mail ambparis.ilemaurice@francophonie.org; Ambassador: Marie-France Roussety.

Mexico: 9 rue de Longchamp, 75116 Paris; tel. 1-53-70-27-70; fax 1-47-55-65-29; Ambassador: Jorge Carpizo Macgregor.

Monaco: 22 blvd Suchet, 75116 Paris; tel. 1-45-04-74-54; telex 611088; fax 1-45-04-45-16; Ambassador: Christian Orsetti.

Mongolia: 5 ave Robert Schuman, 92100 Boulogne-Billancourt; tel. 1-46-05-28-12; telex 633339; fax 1-46-05-30-16; Ambassador: Khasbazaryn Bekhbat.

Morocco: 3–5 rue Le Tasse, 75116 Paris; tel. 1-45-20-69-35; telex 611025; fax 1-45-20-22-58; Ambassador: Mohamed Berrada.; Iraqi Interests Section: Head: Ahmad el-Azzawi.

Mozambique: 82 rue Laugier, 75017 Paris; tel. 1-47-64-91-32; telex 641527; fax 1-44-15-90-13; Ambassador: José Rui Mota do Amaral.

Myanmar: 60 rue de Courcelles, 75008 Paris; tel. 1-42-25-56-95; telex 642190; fax 1-42-56-49-41; Ambassador: U Nyunt Tin.

Namibia: 80 Avenue Foch, 75016 Paris; tel. 1-44-17-32-65; fax 1-44-17-32-73; Ambassador: Leonard Iipumbu.

Nepal: 45 bis rue des Acacias, 75017 Paris; tel. 1-46-22-48-67; fax 1-42-27-08-65; Ambassador: Keshav Raj Jha.

Netherlands: 7–9 rue Eblé, 75007 Paris; tel. 1-40-62-33-00; fax 1-40-62-34-56; Ambassador: Ronald van Beuge.

New Zealand: 7 ter rue Léonard de Vinci, 75116 Paris; tel. 1-45-00-24-11; fax 1-45-01-26-39; e-mail nzembpar@compuserve.com; Ambassador: Edward Richard Woods.

Nicaragua: 8 rue de Sfax, 75116 Paris; tel. 1-45-00-41-02; fax 1-45-00-96-81; Ambassador: (vacant).

Niger: 154 rue de Longchamp, 75116 Paris; tel. 1-45-04-80-60; telex 611080; fax 1-45-04-62-26; Ambassador: Mariama Hima.

Nigeria: 173 ave Victor Hugo, 75116 Paris; tel. 1-47-04-68-65; telex 620106; fax 1-47-04-47-54; Ambassador: Gabriel Olusanya.

Norway: 28 rue Bayard, 75008 Paris; tel. 1-53-67-04-00; fax 1-53-67-04-40; e-mail ambassade-paris@ud.dep.telemax.no; Ambassador: Rolf Trolle Andersen.

Oman: 50 ave d'Iéna, 75116 Paris; tel. 1-47-23-01-63; telex 643205; fax 1-47-23-77-10; Ambassador: Munir A. Makki.

Pakistan: 18 rue Lord Byron, 75008 Paris; tel. 1-45-62-23-32; telex 644000; fax 1-45-62-89-15; Ambassador: Saidulla Dehlavi.

Panama: 145 ave de Suffren, 75015 Paris; tel. 1-47-83-23-32; fax 1-45-67-99-43; e-mail panaemba@worldnet.fr; Ambassador: Arístides Royo.

Papua New Guinea: 25 ave George V, 75008 Paris; tel. 1-53-23-96-00; fax 1-53-23-96-09; Chargé d'affaires: Kappa Yamka.

Paraguay: 1 rue St Dominique, 75007 Paris; tel. 1-42-22-85-05; fax 1-42-22-83-57; Ambassador: Rubén Bareiro Saguier.

Peru: 50 ave Kléber, 75116 Paris; tel. 1-53-70-42-00; fax 1-47-55-98-30; e-mail perou@easynet.fr; Ambassador: María Luisa Federici Soto.

Philippines: 4 hameau de Boulainvilliers, 75116 Paris; tel. 1-44-14-57-00; telex 645283; fax 1-46-47-56-00; Ambassador: Rora Navarro-Tolentino.

Poland: 1–5 rue de Talleyrand, 75343 Paris Cédex 07; tel. 1-45-51-60-80; fax 1-45-55-72-02; e-mail 106033.3056@compuserve.com; Ambassador: Stefan Meller.

Portugal: 3 rue de Noisiel, 75116 Paris; tel. 1-47-27-35-29; telex 640045; fax 1-47-55-00-40; Ambassador: JOSÉ CÉSAR PAULOURO DAS NEVES.

Qatar: 57 quai d'Orsay, 75007 Paris; tel. 1-45-51-90-71; telex 270074; fax 1-45-51-77-07; Ambassador: ABDUL RAHMAN M. AL-KHULAIFI.

Romania: 5 rue de l'Exposition, 75007 Paris; tel. 1-40-62-22-05; fax 1-45-56-97-47; Ambassador: DAMITRU CIAUSU.

Russia: 40 blvd Lannes, 75116 Paris; tel. 1-45-04-05-50; telex 611761; fax 1-45-04-17-65; Ambassador: YURII RYZHOV.

Rwanda: 12 rue Jadin, 75017 Paris; tel. 1-42-27-36-31; fax 1-42-27-74-69; Chargé d'affaires a.i.: MODESTE RUTABAYIRU.

San Marino: 41 ave d'Iéna, 75116 Paris; tel. 1-47-23-77-32; fax 1-47-23-78-05; Ambassador: Countess ISA CORINALDI DE BENEDETTI.

Saudi Arabia: 5 ave Hoche, 75008 Paris; tel. 1-47-66-02-06; telex 641508; fax 1-44-40-25-76; Ambassador: FAISAL ABDULAZIZ ALHEGELAN.

Senegal: 14 ave Robert Schuman, 75007 Paris; tel. 1-47-05-39-45; telex 611563; fax 1-45-56-04-30; Ambassador: KÉBA BIRANE CISSÉ.

Seychelles: 51 ave Mozart, 75016 Paris; tel. 1-42-30-57-47; fax 1-42-30-57-40; Ambassador: CALLIXTE D'OFFAY.

Singapore: 12 ave Foch, 75116 Paris; tel. 1-45-00-33-61; telex 645994; fax 1-45-00-61-79; Ambassador: THAMBYNATHAN JASUDASEN.

Slovakia: 125 rue du Ranelagh, 75016 Paris; tel. 1-44-14-51-20; fax 1-42-88-76-53; Ambassador: VLADIMIR VALACH.

Slovenia: 21 rue Bouquet de Longchamp, 75116 Paris; tel. 1-47-55-65-90; fax 1-47-55-60-05; Ambassador: ANDREJ CAPUDER.

Somalia: 26 rue Dumont d'Urville, 75116 Paris; tel. 1-45-00-76-51; telex 611828; Ambassador: Said Hagi MUHAMMAD FARAH.

South Africa: 59 quai d'Orsay, 75343 Paris Cédex 07; tel. 1-45-55-92-37; fax 1-47-05-51-28; Ambassador: BARBARA JOYCE R. MASEKELA.

Spain: 22 ave Marceau, 75008 Paris; tel. 1-44-43-18-00; telex 651089; fax 1-47-20-56-69; Ambassador: CARLOS DE BENAVIDES Y SALAS.

Sri Lanka: 15 rue d'Astorg, 75008 Paris; tel. 1-42-66-35-01; telex 642337; fax 1-40-07-00-11; Ambassador: SUMITRA PERIES.

Sudan: 56 ave Montaigne, 75008 Paris; tel. 1-42-25-55-71; telex 660268; fax 1-54-63-66-73; Ambassador: EL TIGANI SALIH FIDAIL.

Sweden: 17 rue Barbet de Jouy, 75007 Paris; tel. 1-44-18-88-00; telex 204675; fax 1-44-18-88-40; e-mail ambsuede@clubinternet.fr; internet http://www.ambsuede.fr; Ambassador: ÖRJAN BERNER.

Switzerland: 142 rue de Grenelle, 75007 Paris; tel. 1-49-55-67-00; telex 270969; fax 1-45-51-34-77; Ambassador: BENEDIKT VON TSCHARNER.

Syria: 20 rue Vaneau, 75007 Paris; tel. 1-40-62-61-00; telex 250090; fax 1-47-05-92-73; Ambassador: ELIAS NEJMÉH.

Tanzania: 13 ave Raymond Poincaré, 75116 Paris; tel. 1-47-55-11-18; telex 643968; fax 1-47-66-29-73; Chargé d'affaires: M. KITOI.

Thailand: 8 rue Greuze, 75116 Paris; tel. 1-47-04-32-22; telex 611626; fax 1-47-55-67-13; Ambassador: TEJ BUNNAG.

Togo: 8 rue Alfred Roll, 75017 Paris; tel. 1-43-80-12-13; telex 651497; fax 1-43-80-91-71; Ambassador: KONDI CHARLES MADJOME AGBA.

Tunisia: 25 rue Barbet de Jouy, 75007 Paris; tel. 1-45-55-95-98; telex 200639; fax 1-45-56-02-64; Ambassador: MONGI BOUSNINA.

Turkey: 16 ave de Lamballe, 75016 Paris; tel. 1-45-24-52-24; telex 645326; fax 1-45-20-41-91; e-mail ambtrparis@cie.fr; Ambassador: TANSUG BLEDA.

Turkmenistan: 13 rue Picot, 75116 Paris; tel. 1-47-55-05-36; Ambassador: TCHARY G. NIIAZOV.

Uganda: 13 ave Raymond Poincaré, 75116 Paris; tel. 1-53-70-62-70; telex 630028; fax 1-53-70-85-15; Ambassador: DAVID KAZUNGU.

Ukraine: 21 ave de Saxe, 75007 Paris; tel. 1-43-06-07-37; fax 1-43-06-02-94; Ambassador: YURI KOCHUBEY.

United Arab Emirates: 3 rue de Lota, 75116 Paris; tel. 1-45-53-94-04; telex 620003; fax 1-47-55-61-04; Ambassador: ABDUL AZIZ N. R. AL-SHAMSI.

United Kingdom: 35 rue du Faubourg Saint Honoré, 75383 Paris Cédex 08; tel. 1-44-51-31-00; fax 1-44-51-32-88; Ambassador: Sir MICHAEL JAY.

USA: 2 ave Gabriel, 75382 Paris Cédex 08; tel. 1-43-12-22-22; telex 285319; fax 1-43-12-97-63; Ambassador: FELIX ROHATYN.

Uruguay: 15 rue Le Sueur, 75116 Paris; tel. 1-45-00-81-37; telex 645564; fax 1-45-01-25-17; Ambassador: HÉCTOR GROS ESPIELL.

Uzbekistan: 3 ave F. Roosevelt, 75008 Paris; tel. 1-53-83-80-70; Ambassador: TOKHIRJON MAMAJANOV.

Venezuela: 11 rue Copernic, 75116 Paris; tel. 1-45-53-29-98; telex 645683; fax 1-47-55-64-56; Ambassador: FRANCISCO KERDEL VEGAS.

Viet Nam: 62 rue Boileau, 75116 Paris; tel. 1-44-14-64-00; telex 613240; fax 1-45-24-39-48; Ambassador: NGUYÊN CHIÊN THANG.

Yemen: 25 rue Georges Bizet, 75116 Paris; tel. 1-47-23-61-76; telex 645231; fax 1-47-23-69-41; Ambassador: ABDULLAH AL-ERYANI.

Yugoslavia: 54 rue de la Faisanderie, 75116 Paris; tel. 1-40-72-24-24; telex 645846; fax 1-40-72-24-11; Ambassador: BOGDAN TRIFUNOVIĆ.

Zimbabwe: 5 rue de Tilsitt, 75008 Paris; tel. 1-53-81-90-10; telex 643505; fax 1-53-81-90-19; Ambassador: JOEY MAZORODZE BIMHA.

Judicial System

The Judiciary is independent of the Government. Judges of the Court of Cassation and the First President of the Court of Appeal are appointed by the executive from nominations of the High Council of the Judiciary.

Subordinate cases are heard by Tribunaux d'instance, of which there are 471, and more serious cases by Tribunaux de grande instance, of which there are 181. Parallel to these Tribunals are the Tribunaux de commerce, for commercial cases, composed of judges elected by traders and manufacturers among themselves. These do not exist in every district. Where there is no Tribunal de commerce, commercial disputes are judged by Tribunaux de grande instance.

The Conseils de Prud'hommes (Boards of Arbitration) consist of an equal number of workers or employees and employers ruling on the differences which arise over Contracts of Work.

The Tribunaux correctionnnels (Correctional Courts) for criminal cases correspond to the Tribunaux de grande instance for civil cases. They pronounce on all graver offences (délits), including those involving imprisonment. Offences committed by juveniles of under 18 years go before specialized tribunals for children.

From all these Tribunals appeal lies to the Cours d'appel (Courts of Appeal).

The Cours d'assises (Courts of Assize) have no regular sittings, but are called when necessary to try every important case, for example, murder. They are presided over by judges who are members of the Cours d'appel, and are composed of elected judges (jury). Their decision is final, except where shown to be wrong in law, and then recourse is had to the Cour de cassation (Court of Cassation). The Cour de cassation is not a supreme court of appeal but a higher authority for the proper application of the law. Its duty is to see that judgments are not contrary either to the letter or the spirit of the law; any judgment annulled by the Court involves the trying of the case anew by a court of the same category as that which made the original decision.

Plans for extensive reforms in the judicial system were announced in late 1997. The proposed reforms aimed to reduce political control of the Judiciary and to increase citizens' rights.

COUR DE CASSATION

Palais de Justice, 5 quai de l'Horloge, 75001 Paris; tel. 1-44-32-50-50; fax 1-44-32-78-28.

First President: PIERRE TRUCHÉ.

Presidents of Chambers: PIERRE BÉZARD (Chambre commerciale), JACQUES LEMONTEY (1ère Chambre civile), GÉRARD GÉLINEAU-LARRIVET (Chambre sociale), ROGER BEAUVOIS (3ème Chambre civile), IVAN ZAKINE (2ème Chambre civile).

Solicitor-General: JEAN-FRANÇOIS BURGELIN.

There are 85 Counsellors, one First Attorney-General and 22 Attorneys-General.

Chief Clerk of the Court: MARLENE TARDI.

Council of Advocates at Court of Cassation: Pres. JEAN BARTHÉLÉMY.

COUR D'APPEL DE PARIS

Palais de Justice, blvd du Palais, 75001 Paris; tel. 1-44-32-52-52.

First President: GUY CANIVET.

There are also 69 Presidents of Chambers.

Solicitor-General: ALEXANDRE BENMAKHLOUF.

There are also 121 Counsellors, 24 Attorneys-General and 38 Deputies.

TRIBUNAL DE GRANDE INSTANCE DE PARIS

Palais de Justice, blvd du Palais, 75001 Paris; fax 1-43-29-12-55.

President: JACQUELINE COHARD.

Solicitor of Republic: GABRIEL BESTARD.

TRIBUNAL DE COMMERCE DE PARIS

1 quai de Corse, 75181 Paris Cédex 04.

President: JEAN-PIERRE MATTEÏ.

TRIBUNAUX ADMINISTRATIFS

Certain cases arising between civil servants (when on duty) and the Government, or between any citizen and the Government are judged by special administrative courts.

The Tribunaux administratifs, of which there are 22, are situated in the capital of each area; the Conseil d'Etat (see below) has its seat in Paris.

TRIBUNAL DES CONFLITS

Decides whether cases shall be submitted to the ordinary or administrative courts.

President: The Minister of Justice.

Vice-President: PIERRE NICOLAI.

There are also four Counsellors of the Cour de cassation and three Counsellors of State.

COUR DES COMPTES

13 rue Cambon, 75100 Paris; tel. 1-42-98-54-69; fax 1-42-98-96-02.

An administrative tribunal (Audit Court) competent to judge the correctness of public accounts. It is the arbiter of common law of all public accounts laid before it. The judgments of the Court may be annulled by the Conseil d'Etat.

First President: FRANÇOIS LOGEROT.

Presidents: MICHEL DUVAL, JAMES CHARRIER, GEORGES DOMINJON, CHARLES RENARD, BERTRAND LABRUSSE, ROLAND MORIN, JACQUES GISCARD D'ESTAING, PIERRE LELONG, JEAN DRIOL, JACQUES MAGNET.

Solicitor-General: HÉLÈNE GISSEROT.

CHAMBRES RÉGIONALES DES COMPTES

In 1983 jurisdiction over the accounts of local administrations (Régions, Départements and Communes) and public institutions (hospitals, council housing, etc.) was transferred from the Cour des comptes to local Chambres régionales. The courts are autonomous but under the jurisdiction of the State. Appeals may be brought before the Cour des comptes.

CONSEIL D'ETAT

Palais-Royal, 75100 Paris; tel. 1-40-20-80-00; fax 1-40-20-83-72.

The Council of State is a council of the central power and an administrative tribunal, with 201 members in active service. As the consultative organ of the Government, it gives opinions in the legislative and administrative domain (interior, finance, public works and social sections). In administrative jurisdiction it has three functions: to judge in the first and last resort such cases as appeals against excess of power laid against official decrees or individuals; to judge appeals against judgments made by Tribunaux administratifs and resolutions of courts of litigation; and to annul decisions made by various specialized administrative authorities which adjudicate without appeal, such as the Cour des comptes.

President: The Prime Minister.

Vice-President: RENAUD DENOIX DE SAINT-MARC.

Presidents of Sections: NICOLE QUESTIAUX, ALAIN BACQUET, JEAN-MICHEL GALABERT, DIEUDONNÉ MANDELKERN, YVES GALMOT, GUY BRAIBANT, MICHEL COMBARNOUS, MICHEL BERNARD.

General Secretary: MARTINE DE BOISDEFFRE.

Religion

CHRISTIANITY

Conseil d'Eglises Chrétiennes en France: 80 rue de l'Abbé-Carton, 75014 Paris; tel. 1-45-42-00-39; fax 1-45-42-03-07; f. 1987; ecumenical organization comprising representatives from all Christian denominations to express opinions on social issues; 21 mems; Pres. Most Rev. LOUIS-MARIE BILLÉ, Pastor JACQUES STEWART, Most Rev. JÉRÉMIE CALIGIORGIS; Secs Pastor JEAN TARTIER, Fr GUY LOURMANDE, Fr MICHEL EVDOKIMOV.

The Roman Catholic Church

For ecclesiastical purposes, France comprises nine Apostolic Regions, together forming 19 archdioceses (of which two, Marseille and Strasbourg, are directly responsible to the Holy See), 93 dioceses (including one, Metz, directly responsible to the Holy See) and one Territorial Prelature. The Archbishop of Paris is also the Ordinary for Catholics of Oriental Rites. An estimated 81% of the population of France are adherents of the Roman Catholic Church.

Bishops' Conference: Conférence des Evêques de France, 106 rue du Bac, 75341 Paris Cédex 07; tel. 1-45-49-69-70; fax 1-45-48-13-39; e-mail cef@worldnet.fr; Pres. Most Rev. LOUIS-MARIE BILLÉ, Archbishop of Aix.

Latin Rite

Archbishop of Lyon and Primate of Gaul: (vacant), Archevêché, 1 place de Fourvière, 69321 Lyon Cédex 05; tel. 4-78-25-12-27; fax 4-78-36-06-00.

Archbishop of Aix: Most Rev. LOUIS-MARIE BILLÉ.

Archbishop of Albi: Most Rev. ROGER MEINDRE.

Archbishop of Auch: Most Rev. MAURICE FRÉCHARD.

Archbishop of Avignon: Most Rev. RAYMOND BOUCHEX.

Archbishop of Besançon: Most Rev. LUCIEN DALOZ.

Archbishop of Bordeaux: Cardinal PIERRE EYT.

Archbishop of Bourges: Most Rev. PIERRE PLATEAU.

Archbishop of Cambrai: Most Rev. JACQUES DELAPORTE.

Archbishop of Chambéry: Most Rev. CLAUDE FEIDT.

Archbishop of Marseille: Most Rev. BERNARD PANAFIEU.

Archbishop of Paris: Cardinal JEAN-MARIE LUSTIGER.

Archbishop of Reims: Most Rev. GÉRARD DEFOIS.

Archbishop of Rennes: Most Rev. JACQUES JULLIEN.

Archbishop of Rouen: Most Rev. JOSEPH DUVAL.

Archbishop of Sens: Most Rev. GEORGES GILSON.

Archbishop of Strasbourg: Most Rev. CHARLES-AMARIN BRAND.

Archbishop of Toulouse: Most Rev. EMILE MARCUS.

Archbishop of Tours: Most Rev. JEAN HONORÉ.

Armenian Rite

Bishop of Sainte-Croix-de-Paris: KRIKOR GHABROYAN, 10 bis rue Thouin, 75005 Paris; tel. 1-40-51-11-90; fax 1-40-51-11-99; 30,000 adherents (1989).

Ukrainian Rite

Apostolic Exarch of France: MICHEL HRYNCHYSHYN (Titular Bishop of Zygris), 186 blvd Saint-Germain, 75006 Paris; tel. 1-45-48-48-65; 16,000 adherents (1989).

Protestant Churches

There are some 950,000 Protestants in France.

Eglise Méthodiste: 3 rue Paul Verlaine, 30100 Alès; tel. 4-66-86-20-72; the total Methodist community was estimated at 2,900 mems in 1982.

Fédération Protestante de France: 47 rue de Clichy, 75311 Paris Cédex 09; tel. 1-44-53-47-00; fax 1-42-81-40-01; e-mail federation.-protestante@wanadoo.fr; f. 1905; Pres. Pastor JACQUES STEWART; Gen. Sec. Pastor CHRISTIAN SEYTRE.

The Federation comprises the following Churches:

Armée du Salut: 60 rue des Frères Flavien, 75020 Paris; tel. 1-43-62-25-00; fax 1-43-62-25-56; Pres. Col GEORGES MAILLER.

Communauté protestant évangélique de Vannes: 18 blvd Edouard Herriot, 56000 Vannes; tel. 4-94-47-16-75; Pres. Pastor JEAN-MARC THOBOIS.

Eglise apostolique (EA): 5 rue de l'Est, 94600 Choisy-le-Roi; tel. 1-48-92-17-27; fax 1-69-03-97-70; 2,800 mems; Pres. Pastor J. GERMAIN.

Eglise de la Confession d'Augsbourg d'Alsace et de Lorraine: 1 quai Saint Thomas, 67081 Strasbourg Cédex; tel. 3-88-25-90-05; fax 3-88-25-90-99; 218,000 mems; Pres. MICHEL HOEFFEL (until 31 August 1997), MARC LIENHARD (from 1 September); Gen. Secs Pastor BERNARD STURNY, B. ZIMPFER, D. BIRMELE.

Eglise de Dieu en France: 42 Grand Rue, 68230 Turckheim; tel. 3-89-27-02-78; 484 mems; Pres. Pastor EMMANUEL GUGLELMI.

Eglise évangélique luthérienne de France: 13 rue Godefroy, 75013 Paris; tel. 1-45-82-19-99; fax 1-44-24-36-18; 40,000 mems; Pres. JEAN-MICHEL STURM; Sec. LILIANE ISOUL.

Eglise évangélique de Rochefort: 42 Quéreux de la Laiterie, 17000 Rochefort; tel. 5-46-87-10-82; Pres. Pastor PIERRE ROCHAT.

Eglise réformée d'Alsace et de Lorraine: 1 quai St Thomas, 67081 Strasbourg Cédex; tel. 3-88-25-90-10; fax 3-88-25-90-80; 35,000 mems; Pres. Pastor ANTOINE PFEIFFER.

Eglise réformée de France: 47 rue de Clichy, 75311 Paris Cédex 09; tel. 1-48-74-90-92; fax 1-42-81-52-40; 350,000 mems; Pres. National Council Pastor MICHEL BERTRAND; Gen. Sec. Pastor MARC RICHALOT.

Fédération des Eglises évangéliques baptistes de France: 48 rue de Lille, 75007 Paris; tel. 1-42-61-13-96; fax 1-40-20-05-26; 6,310 mems; Pres. Pastor HENRI FRANTZ; Sec. Pastor JEAN-PIERRE DASSONVILLE.

Mission évangélique tzigane de France: 'Les Petites Brosses', 45500 Neuvoy; tel. 2-38-67-38-00; 70,000 mems; Pres. Pastor GEORGES MEYER.

Mission populaire évangélique de France: 47 rue de Clichy, 75311 Paris Cédex 09; tel. 1-48-74-98-58; fax 1-48-78-52-37; Pres. GEORGES KONONOVITCH; Gen. sec. Pastor JEAN-FRANÇOIS FABA.

Union d'Eglises chrétiennes évangéliques: 83 rue du Pontereau, 44300 Nantes; tel. 2-40-52-02-73; f. 1936; 400 mems; Pres. Pastor LAURENT BURKI.

Union des Eglises évangéliques de Réveil: 14 rue F. Buisson, 69680 Chassieu; tel. 4-78-49-51-77; fax 4-78-49-52-78; 970 mems; Pres. JEAN DEMOURDJIAN.

Union des Eglises évangeliques libres de France: 3 rue Germain Dardan, 92120 Montrouge; tel. 1-46-57-38-09; fax 1-47-35-06-48; Pres. Pastor CLAUDE BATY.

Union Nationale des Eglises réformées évangéliques indépendantes de France: 34 bis rue Florian, 30900 Nîmes; tel. 4-66-62-93-96; 13,000 mems; Pres. PAUL AIMÉ LANDES; Gen. Secs A. BERGESE, D. BERGESE.

The Orthodox Churches

There are about 200,000 Orthodox believers in France, of whom 100,000 are Russian Orthodox and 50,000 Greek Orthodox. There are 85 parishes and eight monasteries.

Administration of Russian Orthodox Churches in Europe (Jurisdiction of the Oecumenical Patriarchate): 12 rue Daru, 75008 Paris; tel. 1-46-22-38-91; Pres. Most Rev. SERGE, Archbishop of Russian Orthodox Churches in Europe.

Greek Orthodox Church: Cathedral of St Stéphane, 7 rue Georges Bizet, 75116 Paris; tel. 1-47-20-82-35; fax 1-47-20-83-15; Exarch Most Rev. JÉRÉMIE CALIGIORGIS, Greek Archbishop of France, Spain and Portugal.

The Anglican Communion

Within the Church of England, France forms part of the diocese of Gibraltar in Europe. The Bishop is resident in London.

Archdeacon of France: Ven. MARTIN DRAPER, 7 rue Auguste Vacquerie, 75116 Paris; tel. 1-47-20-22-51.

Other Christian Churches

Société Religieuse des Amis (Quakers) et Centre Quaker International: 114 rue de Vaugirard, 75006 Paris; tel. 1-45-48-74-23.

ISLAM

In numerical terms, Islam is the second most important religion in France; in 1993 there were about 3m. adherents, of whom more than 750,000 resided in the Marseille area. A High Council of Islam was founded in Paris in 1995.

Conseil Représentatif des Musulmans de France: c/o Paris Mosque, 2 place du Puits de l'Ermite, 75005 Paris; f. 1994; Pres. Dr DALIL BOUBAKEUR.

Fédération Nationale des Musulmans de France (FNMF): c/o Paris Mosque, 2 place du Puits de l'Ermite, 75005 Paris; f. 1985; 20 asscns; Pres. DANIEL YOUSSOF LECLERQ.

Institut Musulman de la Grande Mosquée de Paris: 2 place du Puits de l'Ermite, 75005 Paris; tel. 1-45-35-97-33; f. 1923; cultural, diplomatic, social, judicial and religious sections; research and information and commercial annexes; Dir Dr DALIL BOUBAKEUR.

JUDAISM

There are about 700,000 Jews in France.

Consistoire Central—Union des Communautés Juives de France: 19 rue Saint Georges, 75009 Paris; tel. 1-49-70-88-00; fax 1-42-81-03-66; f. 1808; 170 asscns; Chief Rabbi of France JOSEPH SITRUK; Pres. JEAN KAHN; Dir.-Gen. LÉON MASLIAH.

Consistoire Israélite de Paris (Jewish Consistorial Association of Paris): 17 rue Saint Georges, 75009 Paris; tel. 1-40-82-76-76; 40,000 mems; Pres. MOÏSE COHEN; Chief Rabbi ALAIN GOLDMANN; Sec.-Gen. SERGE GUEDJ.

BUDDHISM

World Federation of Buddhists, French Regional Centre: 98 chemin de la Calade, 06250 Mougins; Sec. Mme TEISAN PERUSAT STORK.

Association Zen Internationale: 175 rue Tolbiac, 75013 Paris; tel. 1-53-80-19-19; Pres. MICHEL BOVAY.

The Press

In 1993 there were nine national daily newspapers (published in Paris) and 66 provincial daily newspapers (together with 14 specialist dailies—financial, sport, medical, etc.). In the same year circulation figures were 779,031 for the Parisian press and 2,258,469 for the provincial press. In recent years sharply rising costs and falling advertising revenue have increased the difficulties caused by declining circulation; during 1991–94 sales of national daily newspapers declined by some 15%. The provincial press has proved more adept than the national press at dealing with the fall in revenue and rising costs. The best-selling provincial dailies now match the most popular Paris dailies for circulation and they have initiated various rationalization schemes.

In 1993 there were 570 weekly magazines (and 353 free weekly advertising magazines), and 1,152 monthly periodicals (including 34 free monthly advertising magazines).

The only major daily which acts as the organ of a political party is the Communist paper, *L'Humanité.* All others are owned by individual publishers or by the powerful groups which have developed round either a company or a single personality. The major groups are as follows:

Amaury Group: 25 ave Michelet, 93408 Saint Ouen Cédex; tel. 1-40-10-30-30; telex 234341; fax 1-40-11-15-26; owns *Le Parisien, Aujourd'hui en France,* the sports daily *L'Equipe*, the weeklies *L'Equipe Magazine* and *France-Football,* and the monthlies *Vélo* and *Tennis de France;* Man. Dir PHILIPPE AMAURY.

Bayard Presse: 3 rue Bayard, 75008 Paris; tel. 1-44-35-60-60; fax 1-44-35-61-61; Catholic press group; owns 91 publs worldwide (43 within France), incl. the national *La Croix, Pèlerin Magazine, Panorama, Notre Temps,* magazines for young people and the over 50s, and several specialized religious publications; Pres. BERNARD PORTE.

Emap (France): 43 rue du Colonel Pierre Avia, 75754 Paris Cédex 15; tel. 1-41-33-50-00; fax 1-41-33-57-19; formerly Editions Mondiales; owns several popular weekly magazines, incl. *Nous Deux, Studio, Télé-Star, Top Santé, Les Veillées des Chaumières, Télé-Poche, Auto Plus,* and also specialized magazines; Man. Dir KEVIN HAND.

Expansion Group: 25 rue Leblanc, 75842 Paris; tel. 1-40-60-40-60; f. 1967; owns a number of magazines, incl. *L'Expansion, L'Entreprise, Architecture d'Aujourd'hui, Harvard L'Expansion, Voyages, La Vie Française;* Chair. and Man. Dir JEAN-LOUIS SERVAN-SCHREIBER.

Filipacchi Group: Paris; tel. 1-40-74-70-00; controls a number of large-circulation magazines incl. *Paris-Match, Salut, 7 à Paris, OK!, Podium, Top 50, Newlook, Penthouse, Union, Echo des Savanes, Les Grands Ecrivains, Femme, Pariscope, Jazz Magazine, Lui, Les Grands Peintres, Les Grands Personnages, Jeune et Jolie, Fortune* and *Photo;* Pres. DANIEL FILIPACCHI.

Hachette Groupe Presse: 6 rue Ancelle, 92525 Neuilly-sur-Seine Cédex; tel. 1-40-88-60-00; telex 611462; fax 1-45-63-93-61; f. 1826; publs incl. *Le Journal du Dimanche, France-Dimanche, Elle, Télé 7 Jours, Parents, Le Provençal, Le Méridional, Var Matin, Les Dernières, Nouvelles d'Alsace*; Chair. JEAN-PIERRE MILET; Man. Dir DANIEL FILIPACCHI.

Socpresse (formerly Hersant Group): one of the largest of the provincial daily press groups; owns 20 dailies, numerous weeklies, fortnightlies and periodicals; dailies incl. *Le Progrès, Le Figaro, France-Soir, Le Dauphiné Libéré, Nord-Matin* and *Nord-Eclair*; Chair. and Man. Dir YVES DE CHAISEMARTIN.

DAILY PAPERS (PARIS)

La Croix: 3-5 rue Bayard, 75393 Paris Cédex 08; tel. 1-44-35-60-60; fax 1-44-35-60-01; f. 1883; Catholic; Dir BERNARD PORTE; Editor-in-Chief BRUNO FRAPPAT; circ. 98,233.

Les Echos: 46 rue la Boétie, 75381 Paris Cédex 08; tel. 1-49-53-65-65; fax 1-45-61-48-92; f. 1908; economic and financial; Chair. OLIVIER FLEUROT; Editor NICOLAS BEYTOUT; circ. 127,741.

L'Equipe: 4 rue Rouget-de-l'Isle, 92137 Issy-les-Moulineaux Cédex; tel. 1-40-93-20-20; telex 203004; fax 1-40-93-20-08; f. 1946; sport; Man. Dir PAUL ROUSSEL; Editorial Dir JÉRÔME BUREAU; circ. 377,098.

Le Figaro: 37 rue du Louvre, 75002 Paris; tel. 1-42-21-62-00; telex 211112; fax 1-42-21-64-05; e-mail hchateauneuf@lefigaro.fr; f. 1828; morning; news and literary; magazine on Saturdays; three weekly supplements; Editor-in-Chief FRANZ-OLIVIER GIESBERT; circ. 375,000.

France-Soir: 37 rue du Louvre, 75081 Paris Cédex 02; tel. 1-44-82-87-00; telex 210888; fax 1-44-82-88-45; f. 1941 as *Défense de la France,* present title 1944; Editor-in-Chief CLAUDE LAMBERT; circ. 184,000.

L'Humanité: 32 rue Jean Jaurès, 93528 Saint-Denis Cédex; tel. 1-49-22-72-72; telex 234915; fax 1-49-22-73-00; f. 1904 by Jean Jaurès; communist; morning; Dir PIERRE ZARKA; Editor-in-Chief CLAUDE CABANES; circ. 117,005.

International Herald Tribune: 181 ave Charles de Gaulle, 92521 Neuilly-sur-Seine Cédex; tel. 1-41-43-93-00; fax 1-41-43-93-93; e-mail iht@iht.com; f. 1887; English language; Co-Chairs KATHARINE GRAHAM, ARTHUR O. SULZBERGER; CEO PETER GOLDMARK; Exec. Editor MICHAEL GETLER; circ. 210,000.

Le Journal Officiel de la République Française: 26 rue Desaix, 75727 Paris Cédex 15; tel. 1-40-58-75-00; telex 201176; fax 1-45-79-17-84; f. 1870; official journal of the Government; publishes laws, decrees, parliamentary proceedings, and economic bulletins; Dir JEAN JACQUES PASCAL.

Libération: 11 rue Béranger, 75154 Paris Cédex 03; tel. 1-42-76-17-89; telex 217656; fax 1-42-72-94-93; f. 1973; 65%-owned by the

Chargeurs group from 1996; independent; Publr SERGE JULY; Editor JEAN-MICHEL HELVIG; circ. 195,000 (1989).

Le Monde: 21 bis rue Claude-Bernard, 75242 Paris Cédex 05; tel. 1-42-17-20-00; telex 206806; fax 1-42-17-21-21; f. 1944; liberal; independent; Man. Dir NOËL-JEAN BERGEROUX; Editor-in-Chief JEAN-MARIE COLOMBANI; monthly supplements *Le Monde Diplomatique, Le Monde de l'Education, Le Monde des Débats, Le Monde des Philatélistes, Dossiers et Documents* (irregular); circ. 368,856.

Le Parisien: 25 ave Michelet, 93408 Saint Ouen Cédex; tel. 1-40-10-30-30; fax 1-40-10-35-16; e-mail infoat@leparisien.fr; internet http://www.leparisien.fr; f. 1944; morning; sold in Paris area only; Man. Dir FABRICE NORA; Editor-in-Chief NOËL COUEDEL; circ. 457,244.

Aujourd'hui en France: 25 ave Michelet, 93408 Saint Ouen Cédex; tel. 1-40-10-30-30; fax 1-40-10-35-16; f. 1994; national version of *Le Parisien*; based in Paris but distributed nationally.

Le Quotidien du Médecin: 140 rue Jules Guesde, 92300 Levallois-Perret; tel. 1-41-40-75-00; fax 1-41-40-75-75; medical journal; Dir Dr MARIE CLAUDE TESSON MILLET; Editors-in-Chief LILIANE LAPLAINE, RENÉE CARTON, BRUNO KELLER, EMMANUEL DE VIEL; circ. 82,000.

Le Quotidien de Paris: Paris; tel. 1-47-30-78-00; fax 1-47-30-78-78; f. 1974, relaunched 1979; suspended in July 1994, relaunched in February 1995; circ. 75,000.

La Tribune: 42–46 rue Notre Dame des Victoires, 75002 Paris; tel. 1-40-13-13-13; fax 1-44-82-17-92; economic and financial; Chair. FABRICE LARUE; Man. Dir ELISABETH DESCOMBES.

SUNDAY PAPERS (PARIS)

France-Dimanche: 10 rue Thierry le Luron, 92592 Levallois-Perret Cédex; tel. 1-41-34-85-51; telex 611462; fax 1-41-34-85-81; f. 1946; Dir ANNE-MARIE CORRE; circ. 640,000.

Humanité-Dimanche: 32 rue Jean Jaurès, 93528 Saint Denis Cédex; tel. 1-49-22-72-72; telex 234915; fax 1-49-22-73-00; f. 1946; organ of the French Communist Party; Dir ROLAND LEROY; Editor MARTINE BULARD; circ. 360,000.

Le Journal du Dimanche: 149 rue Anatole France, 92534 Levallois-Perret Cédex; tel. 1-41-34-60-00; fax 1-41-34-70-76; e-mail jcave@hfp.fr; Dir ALAIN GENESTAR; Editor-in-Chief JEAN CAVÉ.

Le Nouveau Dimanche: Paris; f. 1995; Dir PATRICE GELOBTER; Editor JEAN-CYRILLE GODEFROY; circ. 10,000.

Votre Dimanche: Paris; f. 1995; Publr GILBERT CARON; circ. 15,000.

PRINCIPAL PROVINCIAL DAILY PAPERS

Amiens

Le Courrier Picard: 29 rue de la République, BP 1021, 80010 Amiens Cédex 01; tel. 3-22-82-60-00; fax 3-22-82-60-12; f. 1944; Chair., Man. Dir FRANÇOIS LACHAT; Editor-in-Chief FRANÇOIS PERRIER; circ. 82,739.

Angers

Le Courrier de l'Ouest: blvd Albert Blanchoin, BP 728, 49007 Angers Cédex 01; tel. 2-41-68-86-88; telex 720997; fax 2-41-68-13-27; f. 1944; Chair., Man. Dir CHRISTIAN COUSTAL; Editor-in-Chief JACQUES BOSSEAU; circ. 108,802.

Angoulême

La Charente Libre: BP 1025, 16001 Angoulême Cédex; tel. 5-45-94-16-00; fax 5-45-94-16-19; Chair. LOUIS-GUY GAYAN; Man. Dir MICHEL LÉPINAY; Editor-in-Chief JACQUES GUYON; circ. 40,496.

Auxerre

L'Yonne Républicaine: 8-12 ave Jean Moulin, 89025 Auxerre Cédex; tel. 3-86-49-52-00; fax 3-86-46-99-90; f. 1944; Gen. Man. J. F. COMPÉRAT; circ. 44,109.

Bordeaux

Sud-Ouest: 8 rue de Cheverus, 33094 Bordeaux Cédex; tel. 5-56-00-33-33; telex 570670; fax 5-56-44-64-41; f. 1944; independent; Chair., Man. Dir JEAN-FRANÇOIS LEMOINE; Editor-in-Chief JOËL AUBERT; circ. 359,282.

Chalon-sur-Saône

Le Journal de Saône-et-Loire: 9 rue des Tonneliers, BP 134, 71104 Chalon-sur-Saône; tel. 3-85-44-68-68; fax 3-85-93-02-96; f. 1826; Dir FRANÇOIS PRETET; circ. 46,021.

Chartres

L'Echo Républicain: 37 rue de Châteaudun, BP 189, 28000 Chartres; f. 1929; Chair., Man. Dir ALAIN GASCON; Sec.-Gen. EMMANUEL RAUX; circ. 35,000.

Clermont-Ferrand

La Montagne: 28 rue Morel Ladeuil, 63000 Clermont-Ferrand; tel. 4-73-17-17-17; fax 4-73-17-18-19; f. 1919; independent; Man. Dir JEAN-PIERRE CAILLARD; Editor-in-Chief PAUL SAIGNE; circ. 232,473.

Dijon

Le Bien Public: 7 blvd du Chanoine Kir, BP 550, 21015 Dijon Cédex; tel. 3-80-42-42-42; fax 3-80-42-42-73; f. 1850; Chair. ARNOULD THENARD; Dir-Gen. FRANÇOIS PRETET; Editors-in-Chief YVON MEZOU, MICHEL BEY; circ. 61,492.

Les Dépêches: 5 rue Pierre Palliot, BP 570, 21015 Dijon; tel. 3-80-42-16-16; f. 1936; Chair. XAVIER ELLIE; Man. Dir PIERRE VILLEZ; circ. 42,000.

Epinal

Liberté de l'Est: 44 quai des Bons Enfants, BP 273, 88001 Epinal Cédex; tel. 3-29-82-98-00; fax 3-29-82-30-57; f. 1945; Man. SERGE CLÉMENT; Editor-in-Chief JACQUES DALLÉ; circ. 31,319.

Grenoble

Le Dauphiné Libéré: Les Iles Cordées, 38913 Veurey Cédex; tel. 4-76-88-71-00; telex 320822; fax 4-76-88-70-96; f. 1945; Chair., Man. Dir DENIS HUERTAS; Editor-in-Chief HUBERT PERRIN; circ. weekdays 281,416, Sunday 397,282.

Lille

Nord-Matin: Lille; tel. 3-20-06-45-20; fax 3-20-82-83-63; Chair., Man. Dir MICHEL NOZIÈRE; circ. 76,896.

La Voix du Nord: 8 place du Général de Gaulle, BP 549, 59023 Lille Cédex; tel. 3-20-78-40-40; fax 3-20-78-42-44; f. 1944; Chair., Man. Dir JEAN-LOUIS PRÉVOST; Editor-in-Chief PHILIPPE CARON; circ. 356,903.

Limoges

L'Echo du Centre: 44 rue Rhin et Danube, BP 1582, 87022 Limoges Cédex 9; tel. 5-55-04-49-99; fax 5-55-04-49-86; f. 1943; five editions; Communist; Man. Dir CHRISTIAN AUDOUIN; Editor-in-Chief BERNARD CUNY; circ. 26,853.

Le Populaire du Centre: rue du Général Catroux, BP 541, 87011 Limoges Cédex; tel. 5-55-58-59-60; fax 5-55-58-59-79; f. 1905; Chair, Man. Dir JEAN-PIERRE CAILLARD; Editor-in-Chief SERGE JOFFRE; circ. 53,622.

Lyon

Le Progrès: 93 ave du Progrès, 69680 Chassieu; tel. 4-72-22-23-23; fax 4-78-90-52-40; f. 1859; Chair., Man. Dir XAVIER ELLIE; Editor-in-Chief JEAN LOUIS DOUSSON; circ. 299,047.

Le Mans

Le Maine Libre: 28–30 place de l'Eperon, BP 299, 72007 Le Mans Cédex; tel. 2-43-83-72-50; fax 2-43-83-72-59; Chair., Man. Dir GÉRARD CHOL; Editor-in-Chief RAYMOND MAUDET; circ. 54,891.

Marseille

La Marseillaise: 19 cours Honoré d'Estienne d'Orves, BP 1862, 13001 Marseille; tel. 4-91-57-75-00; fax 4-91-57-75-25; f. 1944; Communist; Man. Dir PAUL BIAGGINI; Editor-in-Chief ALAIN FABRE; circ. 78,900.

La Provence: 248 ave Roger Salengro, 13015 Marseille; tel. 4-91-84-45-45; fax 4-91-84-49-95; f. 1996 following merger of *Le Provençal* with *Le Méridional*; Chair., Man. Dir JEAN-PIERRE MILET; Editor-in-Chief LAURENT GILARDINO.

Metz

Le Républicain Lorrain: 3 rue Saint-Eloy, 57777 Metz Cédex 9; tel. 3-87-34-17-89; fax 3-87-33-28-18; f. 1919; independent; Chair. MARGUERITE PUHL-DEMANGE; Man. Dir MATHIEU PUHL; Editor-in-Chief JEAN CHARLES BOURDIER; circ. 184,861.

Montpellier

Midi-Libre: 'Le Mas de Grille', route de Sète, Saint Jean de Vedas, 34063 Montpellier Cédex 02; tel. 4-67-07-67-07; telex 480650; fax 4-67-07-68-13; f. 1944; Chair., Man. Dir CLAUDE BUJON; Editor-in-Chief ALAIN PLOMBAT; circ. 175,420.

Morlaix

Le Télégramme de Brest: 7 voie d'Accès au Port, BP 243, 29205 Morlaix Cédex; tel. 2-98-62-11-33; fax 2-98-88-76-65; e-mail telegramme@bretagneonline.tm.fr; internet http://www.bretagneonline.tm.fr; f. 1944; Chair., Man. Dir EDOUARD COUDURIER; Editor-in-Chief JEAN CLAUDE CASSENAC; circ. 194,112.

Mulhouse

L'Alsace: 25 ave du Président Kennedy, BP 1160, 68053 Mulhouse; tel. 3-89-32-70-00; fax 3-89-32-11-26; e-mail alsajou@nucleus.fr; f. 1944; Chair. RÉMY PFLIMLIN; Editor-in-Chief JEAN-MARIE HAEFFELLE; circ. 124,997.

Nancy

L'Est Républicain: rue Théophraste Renaudot, Nancy Houdemont, 54185 Heillecourt Cédex; tel. 3-83-59-80-54; fax 3-83-59-80-13; f.

1889; Chair., Man. Dir Gérard Lignac; Editor-in-Chief Pierre Taribo; circc. 230,922.

Nantes

Presse Océan: 7–8 allée Duguay Trouin, BP 1142, 44000 Nantes Cédex; tel. 2-40-44-24-00; fax 2-40-44-24-59; f. 1944; Chair. Jean-Claude Pierre; Editor-in-Chief Jean-Marie Gautier; circ. 77,931.

Nevers

Le Journal du Centre: 3 rue du Chemin de Fer, 58000 Nevers; tel. 3-86-71-45-00; fax 3-86-71-45-10; f. 1943; Man. Dir Jean-Pierre Caillard; Editor-in-Chief Philippe Vazeille; circ. 37,348.

Nice

Nice-Matin: 214 route de Grenoble, BP 4, 06290 Nice Cédex 3; tel. 4-93-18-28-38; fax 4-93-83-93-97; f. 1944; Chair., Man. Dir Gérard Bavastro; Editor-in-Chief Charles Buchet; circ. 243,831; also Corsican edition *Corse-Matin*.

Orléans

La République du Centre: rue de la Halte, 45770 Saran; tel. 2-38-78-79-80; fax 2-38-78-79-79; f. 1944; Chair., Man. Dir Jacques Camus; Editor-in-Chief Denis Leger; circ. 61,044.

Perpignan

L'Indépendant: Le Mas de la Garrigue, 2 ave Alfred Sauvy, 66605 Rivesaltes Cédex; tel. 4-68-64-88-88; fax 4-68-64-88-38; f. 1846; also **Indépendant-Dimanche** (Sunday); Dir-Gen. Dominique Pretet; circ. 82,110.

Reims

L'Union: 87 place Drouet d'Erlon, 51083 Reims Cédex; tel. 3-26-50-50-50; fax 3-26-50-51-69; f. 1944; Chair. Michel Nozière; Man. Dir Daniel Hutier; Editor-in-Chief Michel Grenouilloux; circ. 137,518.

Rennes

Ouest-France: 10 rue du Breil, 35051 Rennes Cédex 09; tel. 2-99-32-60-00; telex 730965; fax 2-99-32-60-25; f. 1944; Chair., Man. Dir François-Régis Hutin; Editor-in-Chief Didier Pillet; circ. 797,091.

Roubaix

Nord-Eclair: 15–21 rue du Caire, BP 58, 59052 Roubaix Cédex 1; tel. 3-20-75-92-56; fax 3-20-82-83-63; f. 1944; Chair., Man. Dir Michel Prouvot; Editor-in-Chief André Farine; circ. 96,661.

Rouen

Paris-Normandie: 19 place du Général de Gaulle, 76000 Rouen; tel. 2-35-14-56-56; fax 2-35-14-56-15; f. 1944; Chair., Man. Dir Philippe Hersant; Editor-in-Chief Dominique Raffin; circ. 104,327.

Strasbourg

Les Dernières Nouvelles d'Alsace: 17–21 rue de la Nuée Bleue, BP 406/R1, 67077 Strasbourg Cédex; tel. 3-88-21-55-00; telex 880445; fax 3-88-21-56-41; e-mail dnasug@sdu.fr; internet http://www.dna.fr; f. 1877; non-party; Chair., Man. Dir Gérard Lignac; Editor-in-Chief Alain Howiller; circ. 215,460.

Toulon

Var Matin: route de la Seyne, BP 116, 83196 Ollioules Cédex; tel. 4-94-06-91-91; telex 440691; fax 4-94-63-49-98; f. 1946; Chair. Jean-Pierre Milet; Man. Dir René Clau; Editor-in-Chief Daniel Cuxac; circ. 75,021.

Toulouse

Dépêche du Midi: ave Jean Baylet, 31095 Toulouse Cédex; tel. 5-62-11-33-00; fax 5-61-44-74-74; f. 1870; radical; Chair., Man. Dir Jean Michel Baylet; Editors-in-Chief Guy-Michel Empociello, Henri Amar; circ. 218,214.

Tours

La Nouvelle République du Centre-Ouest: 232 ave de Grammont, 37048 Tours Cédex; tel. 2-47-31-70-00; fax 2-47-31-70-70; f. 1944; non-party; Co-Chairs David Bohbot, Jacques Saint-Cricq; Editor-in-Chief Hervé Guéneron; circ. 259,606.

Troyes

L'Est-Eclair: 71 ave du Maréchal Leclerc, 10120 St André les Vergers; tel. 3-25-79-90-10; fax 3-25-79-58-54; f. 1945; Dir François Le Saché; circ. 33,000.

SELECTED PERIODICALS

General, Current Affairs and Politics

L'Action Française Hebdo: 10 rue Croix des Petits Champs, 75001 Paris; tel. 1-40-39-92-06; fax 1-40-26-31-63; f. 1947; weekly; monarchist; organ of L'Action Française; Dir Pierre Pujo.

Annales—Histoire, Sciences sociales: 54 blvd Raspail, 75006 Paris; tel. 1-49-54-23-77; fax 1-49-54-26-88; e-mail annales@ehess.fr; f. 1929; every 2 months.

L'Asie Magazine: Paris; monthly; f. 1997; Asian current affairs.

Armées d'Aujourd'hui: 14 rue St Dominique, 75997 Paris; 10 a year; military and technical; produced by the Service d'information et de relations publiques des armées (SIRPA); circ. 130,000.

L'Autre Journal: Paris; tel. 1-44-50-11-50; fax 1-42-61-04-09; f. 1984, fmrly *Nouvelles Littéraires*; monthly; literature, medicine, science, technology, news; Dir Alain Kruger; circ. 220,000.

Le Canard Enchaîné: 173 rue Saint Honoré, 75051 Paris Cédex 01; tel. 1-42-60-31-36; fax 1-42-27-97-87; f. 1915; weekly; political satire; Dir Michel Gaillard; circ. 520,000.

Courrier International: Paris; f. 1990; weekly; current affairs and political; Dir Hervé Lavergne; Editor-in-Chief Jean-Michel Boissier; circ. 87,000.

Le Crapouillot: 75008 Paris; tel. 1-47-42-21-72; fax 1-42-66-93-96; f. 1915; satire and humorous; Man. N. Dupaty; Publr, Editor Roland Gaucher.

Croissance: Le monde en développement: 163 blvd Malesherbes, 75017 Paris; tel. 1-48-88-46-00; telex 649333; fax 1-42-27-29-03; f. 1961 as *Croissance des Jeunes Nations*; monthly on developing nations; circ. 25,000.

Europe Outremer: Paris; tel. 1-46-47-78-44; f. 1923; monthly; Dir R. Taton; circ. 17,800.

L'Evénement du Jeudi: 2 rue Christine, 75280 Paris Cédex 06; tel. 1-43-54-84-80; telex 205802; fax 1-46-34-69-36; f. 1984; weekly; current affairs; Dir Jean-François Kahn; circ. 145,950.

L'Express: 61 ave Hoche, 75411 Paris Cédex 08; tel. 1-40-54-30-00; telex 650009; fax 1-42-67-72-93; f. 1953; weekly; Dir Christian Bregou; Editor-in-Chief Denis Jeambar; circ. 428,125.

Globe Hebdo: 73–77 rue Pascal, 75013 Paris; tel. 1-44-08-02-02; fax 1-44-08-02-49; weekly; current affairs; Dir Georges-Marc Benamou; Editors Stéphane Benamou, Robert Melcher.

L'Humanité Hebdo: 32 rue Jean Jaurès, 93528 Saint-Denis Cedex; tel. 1-49-22-72-72; fax 1-49-22-73-00.

Ici-Paris: Paris; tel. 1-49-53-49-53; telex 642970; fax 1-42-89-31-78; f. 1941; weekly; Dir Ghislain Le Leu; Editor Robert Madjar; circ. 372,386.

Lutte Ouvrière: BP 233, 75865 Paris Cédex 18; f. 1968; weekly; left-wing; Editor Michel Rodinson.

Marianne: 2 rue Christine, 75280 Paris Cédex 06; f. 1997; weekly; current affairs; Dir Jean-François Kahn.

Minute: 16–18 place de la Chappelle, 75018 Paris; tel. 1-40-05-10-91; fax 1-40-05-00-09; f. 1962; right-wing weekly; Chair. Gérald Pehciolelli; Editor Patrice Boizeau; circ. 75,000.

Le Nouvel Observateur: 10-12 place de la Bourse, 75081 Paris Cédex 02; tel. 1-40-28-34-34; telex 680729; fax 1-42-36-19-63; f. 1964; weekly; left-wing political and literary; Chair. Claude Perdriel; Dir Jean Daniel; circ. 432,433.

Paris-Match: 63 ave des Champs Elysées, 75008 Paris; tel. 1-40-74-70-00; telex 290294; fax 1-40-74-76-35; f. 1949; weekly; magazine of French and world affairs; Dir Roger Thérond; circ. 690,000.

Passages: 17 rue Simone Weil, 75013 Paris; tel. 1-45-86-30-02; fax 1-44-23-98-24; f. 1987; monthly; Jewish current affairs, humour and literary review; Dir Emile Malet; Editor Bernard Ullmann; circ. 75,000.

Le Peuple: 263 rue de Paris, Case 432, 93514 Montreuil Cédex; tel. 1-48-18-83-06; fax 1-48-59-28-31; e-mail lepeuple@cgt.fr; f. 1921; fortnightly; official organ of the Confédération Générale du Travail (trade union confederation); Dir Daniel Prada; Editor-in-Chief Marie-Laure Hergès.

Le Point: 74 ave du Maine, 75014 Paris; tel. 1-44-10-10-10; fax 1-43-21-43-24; f. 1972; weekly; politics and current affairs; Man. Dir Bernard Wouts; Editor-in-Chief Claude Imbert; circ. 310,000.

Point de Vue: 142 rue du Bac, 75007 Paris; tel. 1-44-39-11-11; fax 1-42-84-17-34; weekly; Dir and Editor Laure Boulay de la Meurthe; circ. 370,311.

Politique Internationale: 11 rue du Bois de Boulogne, 75116 Paris; tel. 1-45-00-15-26; fax 1-45-00-38-79; f. 1978; quarterly; Dir and Editor-in-Chief Patrick Wajsman.

Révolution: 15 rue Montmartre, 75001 Paris; tel. 1-42-33-61-26; fax 1-42-33-58-92; f. 1980; weekly; political and cultural; Dir Guy Hermier; Editor-in-Chief Jean-Paul Jouary.

Revue 'Défense Nationale': Ecole Militaire, 1 place Joffre, 75700 Paris; tel. 1-44-42-31-90; fax 1-44-42-31-89; f. 1939; monthly; publ. by Committee for Study of National Defence; military, economic, political and scientific problems; Chair. Gen. Philippe Vougny; Editor Adm. Jacques Hugon.

Revue des Deux Mondes: 216 blvd Saint Germain, 75007 Paris; tel. 1-42-84-22-28; fax 1-42-84-22-39; f. 1829; monthly; current affairs; Dir MARC LADREIT DE LACHARRIÈRE.

Rivarol: 1 Rue St Hauteville, 75010 Paris; tel. 1-44-83-06-31; fax 1-44-83-01-96; f. 1951; weekly; political, literary and satirical; Dir and Editor-in-Chief CAMILLE-MARIE GALIC; circ. 45,000.

Sélection du Reader's Digest: 212 blvd Saint Germain, 75007 Paris; tel. 1-46-74-84-84; telex 200882; monthly; Chair. DANIÈLE FRANCK; circ. 929,710.

La Vie: 163 blvd Malesherbes, 75017 Paris; tel. 1-48-88-46-00; fax 1-48-88-46-01; internet http://www.lavie.edi.fr/lavie; f. 1945; weekly; Catholic, general; Dir JEAN-CLAUDE PETIT; circ. 241,000.

The Arts

L'Architecture d'Aujourd'hui: Paris; tel. 1-47-63-12-11; telex 650242; f. 1930; publ. by Groupe Expansion; Editor-in-Chief FRANÇOIS CHASLIN; circ. 25,791.

Art et Décoration: 16–18 rue de l'Amiral Mouchez, 75686 Paris Cédex 14; tel. 1-45-65-48-48; f. 1897; 8 a year; Editor FLORENCE REMY; circ. 451,443.

Critique: 7 rue Bernard Palissy, 75006 Paris; tel. 1-45-44-23-16; fax 1-45-44-82-36; f. 1946; monthly; general review of French and foreign literature, philosophy, social sciences and history; Dir PHILIPPE ROGER; Editor ISABELLE CHAVE.

Diapason-Harmonie: 9–13 rue du Colonel Pierre Avia, 75754 Paris Cédex 15; tel. 1-46-62-20-00; fax 1-46-62-25-33; f. 1956; monthly; Pres. and Dir-Gen. CLAUDE POMMEREAU; Editor-in-Chief YVES PETIT DE VOIZE; circ. 70,000.

Ecrivain: Paris; f.1995; 6 a year; literature, history, philosophy, science; Dirs PIERRE BONCENNE, GÉRARD LARPENT.

Gazette des Beaux-Arts: 140 rue du Faubourg Saint Honoré, 75008 Paris; tel. 1-45-61-61-70; fax 1-45-61-61-71; f. 1859; monthly; the oldest review of the history of art; Dir DANIEL WILDENSTEIN.

Les Lettres Françaises: Ivry sur Seine; tel. 1-46-71-35-95; monthly arts magazines; Dir JEAN RISTAT.

Lire: 17 rue de l'Arrivée,75733 Paris Cédex 15; tel. 1-53-91-11-11; fax 1-53-91-11-04; monthly; literary review; Editor PIERRE ASSOULINE; circ. 110,000.

Livres-Hebdo: 35 rue Grégoire de Tours, 75006 Paris; tel. 1-44-41-28-00; fax 1-43-29-77-85; f. 1979; 46 a year; Dir JEAN-MARIE DOUBLET.

Livres de France: 35 rue Grégoire de Tours, 75006 Paris; tel. 1-44-41-28-00; fax 1-43-29-77-85; f. 1979; 11 a year; Dir JEAN-MARIE DOUBLET.

L'Oeil: 10 rue Guichard, 75116 Paris; tel. 1-45-25-85-60; fax 1-42-88-65-87; f. 1955; monthly; Editor-in-Chief SOLANGE THIERRY.

Magazine littéraire: Paris; f. 1966; monthly; literature; Editor-in-Chief JEAN-JACQUES BROCHIER; circ. 100,000.

Poétique: Editions du Seuil, 27 rue Jacob, 75261 Paris Cédex 06; tel. 1-40-46-50-50; telex 270024; fax 1-40-46-51-43; f. 1970; quarterly; literary review.

La Quinzaine Littéraire: 135 rue Saint-Martin, 75194, Paris Cédex 04; tel. 1-48-87-48-58; fax 1-48-87-13-01; f. 1966; fortnightly; Dir MAURICE NADEAU; circ. 40,000.

Les Temps Modernes: 4 rue Férou, 75006 Paris; tel. 1-43-29-08-47; fax 1-40-51-83-38; f. 1945 by J.-P. Sartre; monthly; literary review; publ. by Gallimard.

Economic and Financial

L'Expansion: 25 rue Leblanc, 75842 Paris Cédex 15; tel. 1-40-60-40-60; telex 205583; fax 1-40-60-41-22; f. 1967; fortnightly; economics and business; Dir JEAN BOISSONNAT; Editor JACQUES BARRAUX; circ. 200,565.

Marchés Tropicaux et Méditerranéens: 190 blvd Haussmann, 75008 Paris; tel. 1-44-95-99-50; telex 651131; f. 1945; weekly; analysis and information on Africa and the Indian Ocean and on tropical products; Pres. SERGE MARPAUD; Editor F. GAULME.

Le Nouvel Economiste: 10 rue Guynemer, 92130 Issy-les-Moulineaux; tel. 1-41-09-30-00; telex 648991; fax 1-41-09-31-00; f. 1975 by merger; weekly; Chair. GÉRALD DE ROQUEMAUREL; Dir JEAN-PIERRE SÉRÉNI; circ. 117,090.

L'Usine Nouvelle: 59 rue du Rocher, 75008 Paris; tel. 1-44-69-55-55; telex 640485; fax 1-43-87-42-65; f. 1945; weekly with monthly supplements; technical and industrial journal; Dir JEAN GLOAGUEN; circ. 60,000.

Valeurs Actuelles: 10 place du Général Catroux, 75858 Paris Cédex 17; tel. 1-40-54-11-00; fax 1-40-54-12-85; f. 1966; weekly; politics, economics, international affairs; Editor FRANÇOIS D'ORCIVAL; circ. 100,000.

La Vie Française: 14 blvd Poissonnière, 75308 Paris Cédex 09; tel. 1-53-24-40-40; fax 1-53-24-41-10; f. 1945; weekly; economics and finance; Publishing Dir CHRISTIAN BRÉGOU; Editorial Dir CLAUDE BAROUX; circ. 125,000.

History and Geography

Acta geographica: 184 blvd Saint Germain, 75006 Paris; tel. 1-45-48-54-62; fax 1-42-22-40-93; f. 1821; quarterly of the Geographical Society of Paris; Chair. JEAN BASTIÉ.

Annales de géographie: 5 rue Laromiguière, 75005 Paris; tel. 1-40-46-61-54; fax 1-40-46-62-21; f. 1891; every 2 months.

Cahiers de civilisation médiévale: 24 rue de la Chaine, 86022 Poitiers; tel. 5-49-45-45-63; fax 5-49-45-45-73; f. 1958; quarterly; Dir PIOTR SKUBISZEWSKI.

Historia-Historama: 25 blvd Malesherbes, 75008 Paris Cédex; tel. 1-44-51-01-01; fax 1-44-51-01-00; f. 1946; monthly; Dirs FRANÇOIS DE L'ESPEE, CHRISTIAN MELCHIOR-BONNET; circ. 104,097.

Kiosque: Paris; f. 1994; every 2 months; Dir YVES DAUDU; circ. 100,000.

Revue d'histoire diplomatique: 13 rue Soufflot, 75005 Paris; tel. 1-43-54-05-97; fax 1-46-34-07-60; f. 1887; quarterly; Dirs MAURICE VAISSE, GEORGES-HENRI SOUTOU.

Revue Historique: Archives Nationales, 60 rue des Francs Bourgeois, 75003 Paris; f. 1876; quarterly; Dirs JEAN FAVIER, RENÉ RÉMOND.

Revue de synthèse: Centre International de Synthèse, 12 rue Colbert, 75002 Paris; tel. 1-42-97-50-68; fax 1-42-97-46-46; e-mail synthese@filnet.fr; f. 1900; quarterly; Dir ERIC BRIAN.

Leisure

Cahiers du Cinéma: 9 passage de la Boule Blanche, 75012 Paris; tel. 1-43-43-92-20; telex 215092; fax 1-43-43-95-04; f. 1951; monthly; film reviews; Dir SERGE TOUBIANA; circ. 80,000.

Le Chasseur Français: 14 rue Jean Rey, 75015 Paris; tel. 1-42-73-01-23; fax 1-43-06-34-64; monthly; hunting and shooting; Dir DANIEL DIGNE; Editor PIERRE LANCRENON.

France-Football: 4 rue Rouget de Lisle, 92137 Issy-les-Moulineaux Cédex; tel. 1-40-93-20-20; telex 631653; fax 1-40-93-20-08; f. 1946; twice-weekly; owned by Amaury Group; Editor GÉRARD ERNAULT; circ. 230,000 (Tues.), 100,000 (Fri.).

Photo: 151 rue Anatole France, 92300 Levallois-Perret; tel. 1-41-34-73-27; telex 290294; fax 1-41-34-71-52; f. 1960; 10 a year; specialist photography magazine; circ. 191,908.

Télé-Magazine: 28 rue Jean Jaurès, 92800 Puteaux; tel. 1-47-62-60-00; telex 612797; fax 1-47-76-07-29; f. 1955; weekly; Dir JACQUES BURGAN; Editor MONIQUE GAUTHIER; circ. 418,967.

Télé-Poche: 9–13 rue du Colonel Pierre Avia, 75754 Paris Cédex 15; tel. 1-46-62-20-00; fax 1-46-62-23-89; f. 1966; weekly; television magazine; Pres., Dir-Gen. KEVIN HAND; Editor SERGE SEBBAH; circ. 1,800,000.

Télérama: 129 blvd Malesherbes, 75017 Paris; tel. 1-48-88-48-88; fax 1-47-64-02-04; f. 1972; weekly; radio, TV, film, literature and music; Dir PIERRE BÉRARD; circ. 599,912; also *Télérama Câble* (Dir CLAUDE SALES).

Télé 7 Jours: 2–6 rue Ancelle, 92525 Neuilly-sur-Seine Cédex; tel. 1-40-88-60-00; telex 611462; fax 1-40-88-61-44; f. 1960; weekly; television; Dir FRANÇOIS DIWO; Editor-in-Chief ALAIN LAVILLE; circ. 2,800,000.

Velo Magazine: 4 rue Rouget de Lisle, 92137 Issy-les-Moulineaux; tel. 1-40-93-20-20; fax 1-40-93-20-09; monthly; cycling.

Maritime

Le Droit Maritime Français: 190 blvd Haussmann, 75008 Paris; tel. 1-44-95-99-50; telex 651131; fax 1-42-89-08-72; f. 1949; monthly; maritime law; Editor STÉPHANE MIRIBEL.

Le Journal de la Marine Marchande et du Transport Multimodal: 190 blvd Haussmann, 75008 Paris; tel. 1-44-95-99-50; telex 290131; fax 1-42-89-08-72; f. 1919; weekly shipping publication; Pres. SERGE MARPAUD; Editor ALAIN GIRARD.

Nouveautés Techniques Maritimes: 190 blvd Haussmann, 75008 Paris; tel. 1-44-95-99-50; fax 1-49-53-90-16; f. 1950; monthly; international shipbuilding and harbours; Editor ALAIN GIRARD.

La Pêche Maritime: 190 blvd Haussmann, 75008 Paris; tel. 1-44-95-99-50; telex 651131; fax 1-42-89-08-72; f. 1919; every 2 months; fishing industry; Pres. SERGE MARPAUD; Editor-in-Chief BERNARD LAVAGNE.

Religion and Philosophy

L'Actualité Religieuse: 163 blvd Malesherbes, 75017 Paris; tel. 1-48-88-46-00; telex 649333; fax 1-42-27-04-19; f. 1983; Editor JEAN-PAUL GUETNY; circ. 35,000.

Etudes: 35 bis rue de Sèvres, 75006 Paris; tel. 1-44-39-48-48; fax 1-40-49-01-92; f. 1856; monthly; general interest; Editor JEAN-YVES CALVEZ.

France Catholique: BP 25, 78117 Châteaufort; tel. 1-39-56-80-00; fax 1-39-56-17-18; weekly; Dir ANNIE CHABADEL; circ. 20,000.

Pèlerin Magazine: 3 rue Bayard, 75008 Paris; tel. 1-44-35-60-60; fax 1-44-35-60-21; f. 1873; weekly; Dir BERNARD PORTE; Editor GÉRARD BARDY; circ. 344,974.

Prier: 163 blvd Malesherbes, 75017 Paris; tel. 1-48-88-46-00; telex 649333; fax 1-42-27-29-03; f. 1978; monthly; review of modern prayer and contemplation; circ. 62,611.

Revue des sciences philosophiques et théologiques: Librairie J. Vrin, 6 place de la Sorbonne, 75005 Paris; tel. 1-43-54-03-47; fax 1-43-54-48-18; f. 1907; quarterly.

Témoignage Chrétien: 49 rue du Faubourg Poissonnière, 75009 Paris; tel. 1-44-83-82-82; fax 1-44-83-82-88; f. 1941; weekly; Dirs PIERRE-LUC SEGUILLON, BERNARD GINISTY; circ. 52,000.

Tribune Juive: 29 rue du Faubourg Poissonière, 75009 Paris; tel. 1-45-23-19-20; fax 1-45-23-13-04; fortnightly; Jewish affairs; Dir YVES DERAI.

La Voix Protestante: 14 rue de Trévise, 75009 Paris; tel. 1-47-70-23-53; fax 1-48-01-09-13; monthly review of Protestant churches; Editor DIDIER WEIL.

Science and Technology

Action Auto-Moto: 1 rue du Colonel Pierre Avia, 75015 Paris; tel. 1-46-48-48-48; fax 1-46-48-49-90; e-mail automoto@francenet.fr; monthly; cars; Dir PAUL DUPUY; Editor-in-Chief JEAN SAVARY.

Annales de Chimie—Science des Matériaux: Editions Scientifiques et Médicales Elsevier, 141 rue de Javel, 75747 Paris Cédex 15; tel. 1-45-58-91-10; fax 1-45-58-94-19; e-mail acsm@girtcnrs.fr; f. 1789; 8 a year; chemistry and material science.

L'Argus de l'Automobile: 1 place Boieldieu, 75082 Paris Cédex 02; tel. 1-53-29-11-00; fax 1-49-27-09-50; internet http://www.argusanto.com; f. 1927; motoring weekly.

Astérisque: Montrouge; tel. 1-40-84-80-55; fax 1-40-84-80-52; f. 1973; monthly; mathematics; Dir L. SZPIRO; Sec. C. HÉTIER.

L'Astronomie: 3 rue Beethoven, 75016 Paris; tel. 1-42-24-13-74; fax 1-42-30-75-47; e-mail saf@calva.net; internet http://www.iap.fr/saf; f. 1887; monthly; publ. by Société Astronomique de France; Chair. ROGER FERLET.

L'Auto Journal: 43 rue du Colonel Pierre Avia, 75754 Paris; tel. 1-41-33-50-00; fax 1-41-33-57-04; fortnightly; cars; Editor-in-Chief MARC SCHLICKLIN.

Aviation Magazine International: 15–17 quai de l'Oise, 75019 Paris; tel. 1-42-02-40-41; telex 211678; f. 1950; fortnightly; circ. 30,000.

Biochimie: Collège de France, 11 place Marcellin Berthelot, 75231 Paris Cédex 05; tel. 1-44-27-13-41; fax 1-44-27-11-09; f. 1914; monthly; bio-chemistry; Editor-in-Chief Mme M. GRUNBERG-MANAGO.

Electronique pratique: 2-12 rue de Bellevue, 75940 Paris Cédex 19; tel. 1-44-84-84-84; fax 1-42-41-89-40; monthly; electronics; Editor BERNARD FIGHIERA.

Industries et techniques: 26 rue d'Oradour-sur-Glane, 75504 Paris Cédex 15; tel. 1-44-25-30-01; fax 1-45-58-15-19; monthly; Dir PAUL WAGNER.

Ingénieurs de l'Automobile: 15 rue du 19 Janvier, 92380 Garches; tel. 1-47-01-44-74; fax 1-47-01-48-25; e-mail ublcda@lcda.fr; internet http://www.lcda.fr; f. 1927; 8 a year; technical automobile review; Editor-in-Chief JEAN PIERRE GOSSELIN.

Matériaux et Techniques: 76 rue de Rivoli, 75004 Paris; tel. 1-42-78-52-20; fax 1-42-74-40-48; f. 1913; monthly; review of engineering research and progress on industrial materials; Editor-in-Chief R. DROUHIN.

Le Monde Informatique: Immeuble Lafayette, 2 place des Vosges, 92051 Paris La Défense Cédex 65; tel. 1-49-04-79-00; fax 1-49-04-79-04; weekly; information science; Editor FRANÇOIS MONTEL.

Le Moniteur des Travaux Publics et du Bâtiment: 17 rue d'Uzès, 75002 Paris; tel. 1-40-13-30-30; fax 1-40-41-94-95; e-mail redac@groupemoniteur.fr; f. 1903; weekly; construction; Chair. MARC-NOËL VIGIER; Editor-in-Chief NATHALIE SEYER; circ. 67,000.

Objectif Multi Media: 2-12 rue de Bellevue, 75940 Paris Cédex 19; tel. 1-44-84-84-62; fax 1-44-84-84-69; internet http://www.lehp.com; quarterly; computers, multi-media; Editor CLAUDE DUCROS.

Psychologie française: 2 rue de la Liberté, 93526 Saint Denis, Paris Cédex 02; tel. 1-49-40-67-94; fax 1-49-40-64-94; f. 1956; quarterly; review of the Société Française de Psychologie; Editor RODOLPHE GHIGLIONE.

La Revue Générale des Chemins de Fer: 19 rue d'Amsterdam, 75008, Paris; e-mail gauthier.villars.publisher@mail.sgip.fr; internet http://www.gauthiervillars.fr; f. 1878; monthly; Editor-in-Chief PIERRE DOGNETON; circ. 8,000.

Science et vie: 1 rue du Colonel Pierre Avia, 75015 Paris; tel. 1-46-48-48-48; telex 641866; fax 1-46-48-48-67; f. 1913; monthly; Pres. PAUL DUPUY; circ. 325,800.

Techniques et Equipements de Production: 59 rue du Rocher, 75008 Paris; tel. 1-44-69-52-00; fax 1-43-87-05-15; f. 1906 as *Machine Moderne*; monthly; technical magazine; Dir JACQUES-YVES DUQUENNOY; circ. 13,000.

Women's, Home and Fashion

Bonne Soirée: 3-5 rue Bayard, 75008 Paris; tel. 1-44-35-59-61; fax 1-44-35-60-37; f. 1922; weekly; Editor-in-Chief MARIE-HÉLÈNE ADLER; circ. 234,637.

Cosmopolitan: 11 bis rue Boissy d'Anglas, 75008 Paris; tel. 1-42-66-88-88; fax 1-42-66-85-56; Dir EVELYNE PROUVOST-BERRY; Editor JULIETTE BOISRIVEAUD.

Elle: 6 rue Ancelle, 92525 Neuilly-sur-Seine Cédex; tel. 1-40-88-60-00; telex 611462; fax 1-47-45-38-12; f. 1945; weekly; Dir ANN-MARIE PERIER; circ. 395,007.

Femme Actuelle: 73–75 rue La Condamine, 75854 Paris Cédex 17; tel. 1-42-94-67-67; fax 1-42-94-67-14; f. 1984; weekly; Editor MARYSE BONNET; circ. 2,100,000.

Femme Pratique: ZAC de Frégy, 77610 Fontenay Trésigny; tel. 1-64-25-21-93; fax 1-64-25-21-01; f. 1958; monthly; Dir MAX BENSOUSSON; circ. 380,000.

Le Journal de la Maison: 20 rue de Billancourt, BP 406, 92103 Boulogne-Billancourt Cédex; tel. 1-48-25-61-20; fax 1-48-25-69-61; monthly; home; Editor JEAN-FRANÇOIS REMY.

Marie-Claire: 10 blvd des Frères Voisin, 92792 Issy-les-Moulineaux; tel. 1-41-46-88-88; telex 240387; fax 1-41-46-86-86; f. 1954; monthly; Chair. EVELYNE PROUVOST-BERRY; Editor JACQUES GARAI; circ. 599,362.

Marie-Claire Maison: 10 blvd des Frères Voisin, 92792 Issy-les-Moulineaux; tel. 1-41-46-88-88; telex 240387; fax 1-41-46-86-86; f. 1967; monthly; home interest; Editor CAROLINE TINÉ; circ. 200,801.

Marie-France: 31 rue Bergère, 75009 Paris; tel. 1-48-01-31-31; fax 1-48-01-31-00; f. 1944; monthly; Editor CHARLOTTE SEELING; circ. 280,000.

Modes et travaux: 9-13 rue du Colonel Pierre Avia, 75754 Paris Cédex 15; tel. 1-46-62-20-50; fax 1-46-62-22-32; f. 1919; monthly; Editor HÉLÈNE TOKAY; circ. 1,500,000.

Notre Temps: 3–5 rue Bayard, 75393 Paris Cédex 08; tel. 1-44-35-60-60; fax 1-44-35-60-31; monthly; for retired people; Dir PATRICK DARDE; Editor REMY MICHEL.

Nous Deux: 9–13 rue du Colonel Pierre Avia, 75754 Paris Cédex 15; tel. 1-46-62-20-00; fax 1-46-62-24-65; f. 1947; weekly; Editor CATHERINE AUGER; circ. 823,397.

Parents: 6 rue Ancelle, 92525 Neuilly-sur-Seine Cédex; tel. 1-40-88-60-90; telex 611462; fax 1-40-88-70-79; magazine for parents; Dir MAGDA DARLET; circ. 367,571.

Questions de femmes: Paris; f. 1996; monthly; women's; Editor-in-Chief NATHALIE COTTIN.

Santé Magazine: 110 rue Marius Aufan, BP 318, 92304 Levallois Perret Cédex; tel. 1-41-49-41-49; fax 1-40-89-04-30; f. 1976; monthly; health; Editor ANDRÉ GIOVANNI.

Vogue: 56A rue du Faubourg Saint Honoré, 75008 Paris; tel. 1-53-43-60-00; fax 1-53-43-60-60; monthly; Publr GARDNER BELLANGER; Editor-in-Chief JOAN JULIET BUCK.

NEWS AGENCIES

In 1995 there were some 216 news agencies in France.

Agence France-Presse: 11–15 place de la Bourse, BP 20, 75061 Paris Cédex 02; tel. 1-40-41-46-46; telex 210064; fax 1-40-41-46-32; f. 1944; 24-hour service of world political, financial, sporting news, and photographs; 165 agencies and 2,000 correspondents all over the world; Chair. and Man. Dir JEAN MIOT.

Agence Parisienne de Presse: 18 rue Saint Fiacre, 75002 Paris; tel. 1-42-36-95-59; fax 1-42-33-83-24; f. 1949; Man. Dir MICHEL BURTON.

Infomedia M.C.: 43 rue Saint Augustin, 75002 Paris; tel. 1-47-42-14-33; fax 1-47-42-14-39; f. 1988; economic and financial news; Dir FRANÇOIS COUDURIER.

Foreign Bureaux

Agence Maghreb Arabe Presse (MAP) (Morocco): 4 place de la Concorde, 75008 Paris; tel. 1-42-65-40-45; fax 1-42-66-26-43; f. 1959; Correspondent MANSOUR MADANI.

Agencia EFE (Spain): 10 rue Saint-Marc, 75002 Paris; tel. 1-44-82-65-40; fax 1-40-39-91-78; e-mail agencia.efe.paris@wanadoo.fr; f. 1939; Delegate ANTONIO JAVALOYES.

Agenzia Nazionale Stampa Associata (ANSA) (Italy): 29 rue Tronchet, 75008 Paris; tel. 1-42-65-55-16; telex 290120; fax 1-42-65-12-11; Bureau Chief LUAN REXHA.

Associated Press (AP) (USA): 162 rue du Faubourg Saint Honoré, 75008 Paris; tel. 1-43-59-86-76; telex 651770; fax 1-40-74-00-45; Bureau Chief ABNER KATZMAN.

Deutsche Presse-Agentur (dpa) (Germany): 30 rue Saint Augustin, 75002 Paris; tel. 1-47-42-95-02; fax 1-47-42-51-75; Bureau Chief NORBERT HOYER.

Informatsionnoye Telegrafnoye Agentstvo Rossii—Telegrafnoye Agentstvo Suverennykh Stran (ITAR-TASS) (Russia): 27 ave Bosquet, 75007 Paris; tel. 1-44-11-31-80; fax 1-47-05-33-98; Correspondent ALEKSANDR KONDRASHOV.

Inter Press Service (Italy): Paris; tel. 1-42-21-14-19; telex 217511; Correspondent DANIEL GATTI.

Jiji Tsushin-sha (Japan): 27 blvd des Italiens, 75002 Paris; tel. 1-42-66-96-57; telex 660616; fax 1-42-66-96-61; Bureau Chief YUKIO YOSHINAGA.

Kyodo News Service (Japan): 19 rue Paul Lelong, 75002 Paris; tel. 1-42-60-13-16; telex 215516; fax 1-40-20-08-87; Bureau Chief NORIFUMI MORITOKI.

Magyar Távirati Iroda (MTI) (Hungary): 52 ave Mozart, 75016 Paris; Correspondent Dr LÁSZLÓ S. TÓTH.

Middle East News Agency (Egypt): 6 rue de la Michodière, 75002 Paris; tel. 1-47-42-16-03; telex 230011; fax 1-47-42-44-52; f. 1956; Dir MOHAMED EL-SHAMY.

Prensa Latina (Cuba): Paris; tel. 1-42-60-22-18; telex 213688; Bureau Chief RAMÓN MARTÍNEZ CRUZ.

Reuters (UK): 101 rue Réaumur, 75080 Paris Cédex 02; tel. 1-42-21-50-00; fax 1-40-26-69-70; Dir DANIEL FOGEL; Editor-in-Chief F. DURIAUD.

Rossiyskoye Informatsionnoye Agentstvo-Novosti (RIA-Novosti) (Russia): 14 place du Général Catroux, 75017 Paris; tel. 1-42-27-79-21; fax 1-43-80-96-83; Bureau Chief N. VIKHLAEV.

United Press International (UPI) (USA): 8 rue Choiseul, 75002 Paris; tel. 1-42-60-23-68; fax 1-42-60-30-98; Bureau Chief EDUARDO CUE.

Xinhua (New China) News Agency (People's Republic of China): 27–31 rue Médéric, 92110 Clichy-la-Garenne; tel. 1-42-70-67-37; fax 1-42-70-61-28; Bureau Chief GUIHE LIANG.

PRESS ASSOCIATIONS

Comité de Liaison de la Presse: 6 bis rue Gabriel Laumain, 75010 Paris; tel. 1-42-46-67-82; liaison organization for press, radio and cinema.

Fédération Française des Agences de Presse (FFAP): 32 rue de Laborde, 75008 Paris; tel. 1-42-93-42-57; fax 1-42-93-15-32; comprises five syndicates (news, photographs, television, general information and audiovisual) with a total membership of 109 agencies; Pres. DANIEL RENOUF; Dir JACQUES MORANDAT.

Fédération Nationale de la Presse Française: 7 rue de Madrid, 75376 Paris Cédex 08; tel. 1-44-90-43-90; fax 1-44-90-43-91; f. 1944; mems. Syndicat de la Presse Parisienne, Syndicat Professionnel de la Presse, Magazine et d'Opinion, Syndicat de la Presse Quotidienne Régionale, Syndicat des Quotidiens Départementaux, Fédération de la Presse Périodique Régionale, Fédération Nationale de la Presse d'Information Spécialisée; Chair. JACQUES SAINT CRICQ (acting); Dir-Gen. FRANÇOIS DEVEVEY; Gen. Sec. CHRISTIAN METGE.

Fédération Nationale de la Presse Hebdomadaire et Périodique: 9 rue Jean Mermoz, 75008 Paris; tel. 1-42-89-27-66; fax 1-42-89-31-05; asscn of the national periodical press.

Fédération Nationale de la Presse d'Information Spécialisée: 7 rue de Madrid, 75376 Paris Cédex 08; tel. 1-44-90-43-60; fax 1-44-90-43-72; CEO GÉRARD LACAPE.

Fédération de la Presse Périodique Régionale: 54 rue Taitbout, 75009 Paris; tel. 1-45-26-46-95; fax 1-45-26-48-32; f. 1978; mems Syndicat National de la Presse Hebdomadaire Régionale d'Information, Syndicat National des Publications Régionales, Syndicat de la Presse Judiciaire de Province; Chair. J. P. VITTU DE KERRAOUL.

Syndicat de la Presse Quotidienne Régionale: 17 place des Etats Unis, 75116 Paris; tel. 1-40-73-80-20; fax 1-47-20-48-94; f. 1986; regional dailies; Pres. JEAN-LOUIS PRÉVOST; Dir-Gen. JEAN VIANSSON-PONTÉ.

PRESS INSTITUTE

Institut Français de Presse et des Sciences de l'Information: 92 rue d'Assas, 75006 Paris; tel. 1-44-41-57-93; fax 1-44-41-57-04; e-mail ifp@ensiupaus2.fr; f. 1953; studies and teaches all aspects of communication and the media; maintains research and documentation centre; open to research workers, students, journalists; Dir RÉMY RIEFFEL.

Publishers

Editions Albin Michel: 22 rue Huyghens, 75680 Paris Cédex 14; tel. 1-42-79-10-00; telex 203379; fax 1-43-27-21-58; f. 1901; general, fiction, history, classics; Chair. and Man. Dir FRANCIS ESMÉNARD.

Editions Arthaud: 20 rue Monsieur le Prince, 75006 Paris; tel. 1-40-51-31-00; telex 205641; fax 1-43-29-21-48; f. 1873; arts, history, travel books, reference; Chair. CHARLES-HENRI FLAMMARION; Man. Dirs ALAIN FLAMMARION, JEAN-PIERRE ARBON.

Editions de l'Atelier/Editions Ouvrières: 12 ave Soeur Rosalie, 75013 Paris; tel. 1-44-08-95-15; fax 1-44-08-95-00; f. 1929; religious, educational, political and social, including labour movement; Man. Dir DANIEL PRIN.

Editions Aubier—Flammarion: 13 quai de Conti, 75006 Paris; tel. 1-40-51-31-00; fax 1-43-29-71-04; f. 1924; psychoanalysis, literature, philosophy, history and sociology; Man. Dir CHARLES-HENRI FLAMMARION.

J. B. Baillière: 46 rue la Boétie, 75008 Paris; tel. 1-49-53-69-00; fax 1-49-53-01-65; f. 1818; science, medicine and technical books; Man. Dir PHILIPPE LEDUC.

Editions Balland: 33 rue Saint André des Arts, 75006 Paris; tel. 1-43-25-74-40; fax 1-46-33-56-21; f. 1967; literature; Chair., Man. Dir JEAN-JACQUES AUGIER.

Bayard Editions—Centurion: 3 rue Bayard, 75393 Paris Cédex 08; tel. 1-44-35-60-60; fax 1-44-35-60-25; f. 1870; children's books, religion, human sciences; Man. Dir JEAN-CLAUDE DUBOST.

Beauchesne Editeur: 72 rue des Saints Pères, 75007 Paris; tel. 1-45-48-80-28; fax 1-42-22-59-79; f. 1900; scripture, religion and theology, philosophy, religious history, politics, encyclopaedias, periodicals.

Editions Belfond: 216 blvd Saint Germain, 75007 Paris; tel. 1-45-44-38-23; telex 260717; fax 1-45-44-98-04; f. 1963; fiction, poetry, documents, history, arts; Chair. JÉRÔME TALAMON; Man. Dir FABIENNE DELMOTE.

Berger-Levrault: 5 rue Auguste Comte, 75006 Paris; tel. 1-44-07-14-94; fax 1-44-07-15-25; f. 1976; fine arts, health, social and economic sciences, law; Chair. MARC FRIEDEL; Man. Dir BERNARD AJAC.

De Boccard, Edition-Diffusion: 11 rue de Médicis, 75006 Paris; tel. 1-43-26-00-37; fax 1-43-54-85-83; f. 1866; history, archaeology, religion, orientalism, medievalism; Man. Dir DOMINIQUE CHAULET.

Bordas: 17 rue Rémy Dumoncel, 75661 Paris Cédex 14; tel. 1-42-79-62-00; fax 1-43-22-85-18; f. 1946; encyclopaedias, dictionaries, history, geography, arts, children's and educational; Chair. and CEO PATRICE MAUBOURGUET.

Editions Bornemann: 15 rue de Tournon, 75006 Paris; tel. 1-40-87-40-28; fax 1-45-89-72-88; f. 1829; art, fiction, sports, nature, easy readers; Chair. and Man. Dir JACQUES HERSANT.

Bottin, SA: 31 cours de Juilliottes, 94706 Maisons-Alfort Cédex; tel. 1-49-81-56-56; telex 262407; fax 1-49-77-85-28; data bases, videotex, business directories; Chair. JEAN-FRANÇOIS MICHON.

Buchet-Chastel: 18 rue de Condé, 75006 Paris; tel. 1-44-32-05-60; fax 1-44-32-05-61; f. 1929; literature, music, crafts, religion, practical guides; Chair. PIERRE ZECH.

Calmann-Lévy, SA: 3 rue Auber, 75009 Paris; tel. 1-47-42-38-33; telex 290993; fax 1-47-42-77-81; f. 1836; French and foreign literature, history, social sciences, economics, sport, leisure; Chair. OLIVIER NORA.

Editions Casterman: 66 rue Bonaparte, 75006 Paris; tel. 1-40-51-28-00; fax 1-43-54-54-24; f. 1857; juvenile, comics, fiction, education, leisure, art; Chair. DIDIER PLATTEAU; Man. Dir SIMON CASTERMAN.

Les Editions du Cerf: 29 blvd de Latour Maubourg, 75340 Paris Cédex 07; tel. 1-44-18-12-12; fax 1-45-56-04-27; f. 1929; juvenile, religion, social science; Chair. MICHEL BON; Man. Dir NICOLAS SED.

Chiron (Editions): 40 rue de Seine, 75006 Paris; tel. 1-46-33-18-93; fax 1-43-25-61-56; f. 1907; technical, sport, education, fitness, health, dance, games; Chair. and Man. Dir DENYS FERRANDO-DURFORT.

Armand Colin Editeur: 103 blvd Saint Michel, 75240 Paris Cédex 05; tel. 1-46-34-12-19; telex 201269; fax 1-43-26-96-38; f. 1870; literature, fine arts, history, science, school and university textbooks; Chair. JÉRÔME TALAMON; Man. Dir CHRISTIAN BOUET.

Editions Complexe: 68 rue Mazarine, 75006 Paris; tel. 1-46-34-00-76; fax 1-43-26-73-81; f. 1971; literature, history, politics.

Editions Dalloz-Sirey: 35 rue Tournefort, 75240 Paris Cédex 05; tel. 1-40-51-54-54; telex 206446; fax 1-45-87-37-48; f. 1824; law, philosophy, political science, geography, history, business and economics; Chair. CHARLES VALLÉE; Man. Dir CHRISTIAN ROBLIN.

Dargaud: 6 rue Gager Gabillot, 75015 Paris; tel. 1-40-45-35-35; fax 1-42-50-11-30; f. 1943; juvenile, cartoons, comics, video, graphic novels; Chair. and Man. Dir CLAUDE DE SAINT-VINCENT.

La Découverte: 9 bis rue Abel Hovelacque, 75013 Paris; tel. 1-44-08-84-00; fax 1-44-08-84-19; e-mail decouverte@dial.oleane.com; f. 1959; economic, social and political science, literature, history; Man. Dir FRANÇOIS GÈZE.

Editions Denoël: 9 rue du Cherche-Midi, 75006 Paris; tel. 1-44-39-73-73; fax 1-44-39-73-60; f. 1929; general literature, science fiction, crime, history; Man. Dir HENRY MARCELLIN.

Editions Des Femmes Antoinette Fouque: 6 rue de Mézières, 75006 Paris; tel. 1-42-22-60-74; fax 1-42-22-62-73; f. 1973; mainly women authors; fiction, essays, art, history, politics, psychoanalysis, talking books; Dirs ANTOINETTE FOUQUE, MARIE-CLAUDE GRUMBACH.

Desclée De Brouwer: 76 bis rue des Saints Pères, 75007 Paris; tel. 1-45-49-61-92; fax 1-42-22-61-41; f. 1877; religion, philosophy, arts, human sciences; Chair. MICHEL HOUSSIN; Man. Dir ANDRÉ BOURGEOIS.

Diderot Editeur: 20 rue Notre Dame de Nazareth, 75003 Paris; tel. 1-48-04-91-45; f. 1995; science, fine arts, history of art and culture.

La Documentation Française: 29 quai Voltaire, 75344 Paris Cédex 07; tel. 1-40-15-70-00; telex 204826; fax 1-40-15-72-30; f. 1945; government publs; politics, law, economics, culture, science; Man. Dir JEAN JENGER.

Dunod Editeur: 5 rue Laromiguière, 75005 Paris Cédex; tel. 1-40-48-35-00; fax 1-40-46-81-11; internet http://www.dunod.com; f. 1800; scientific, technical, computer science, electronic, scientific journals; Chair. CHRISTOPHE BINNENDYCK.

Edisud: La Calade RN 7, 13090 Aix-en-Provence; tel. 4-42-21-61-44; fax 4-42-21-56-20; f. 1971; Dir CHARLY-YVES CHAUDOREILLE.

ESF Editeur: 17 rue Viète, 75017 Paris; tel. 1-44-15-62-00; fax 1-46-22-67-45; f. 1928; business, humanities, social sciences, law, communications, new technology; Chair. GÉRARD DIDIER; Man. Dir FRANÇOISE DAUZAT.

Eyrolles: 61 blvd Saint Germain, 75240 Paris Cédex 05; tel. 1-44-41-11-11; fax 1-44-41-11-44; f. 1918; science, technology, electronics, management, law; Man. Dirs SERGE EYROLLES, ALAIN-ROLAND KIRSCH, JEAN-PIERRE TISSIER.

Fayard: 75 rue des Saints Pères, 75278 Paris Cédex 06; tel. 1-45-49-82-00; fax 1-42-22-40-17; f. 1857; literature, biography, history, religion, essays, music; Chair. and Man. Dir CLAUDE DURAND.

Librairie Ernest Flammarion: 26 rue Racine, 75006 Paris; tel. 1-40-51-31-00; telex 205641; fax 1-43-29-76-44; f. 1875; general literature, art, human sciences, sport, children's books, medicine; Chair. CHARLES-HENRI FLAMMARION; Man. Dir JEAN-PIERRE ARBON.

Fleuve Noir: 12 ave d'Italie, 75013 Paris; tel. 1-44-16-05-00; fax 1-44-16-05-11; f. 1949 (Presses de la Cité); crime and science fiction; Chair. BERTRAND EVENO; Man. Dir MARTINE SOLIRENNE.

Les Editions Foucher: 128 rue de Rivoli, 75038 Paris Cédex 01; tel. 1-42-36-38-90; fax 1-45-08-18-38; f. 1936; science, economics, law, medicine text-books; Chair. and Man. Dir BERNARD FOULON.

Editions Gallimard: 5 rue Sébastien Bottin, 75007 Paris; tel. 1-49-54-42-00; telex 204121; fax 1-40-20-09-39; f. 1921; general fiction, literature, history, poetry, children's, philosophy; Chair. and Man. Dir ANTOINE GALLIMARD.

Editions Grasset et Fasquelle: 61 rue des Saints Pères, 75006 Paris; tel. 1-44-39-22-00; fax 1-42-22-64-18; f. 1907; contemporary literature, criticism, general fiction and children's books; Chair. and Man. Dir JEAN-CLAUDE FASQUELLE.

Groupe de la Cité International: 12 ave d'Italie, 75013 Paris; tel. 1-44-16-05-00; fax 1-44-16-09-40; f. 1942 as Presses de la Cité; renamed 1988; general fiction, history, paperbacks; group comprises Bordas, Dalloz-Sirey, Nathan, Larousse, Laffont, Garancière, Garnier, Plon, G.P. Rouge et Or, Solar, Perrin, Julliard, Presses Pocket, Editions Fleuve Noir, Messageries Centrales du Livre, Editions Christian Bourgeois, le Rocher, UGE 10/18, Olivier Orban, M. A.-Edition, OCI; Man. Dir DOMINIQUE DESMOTTES.

Groupe Fleurus-Mame: 11 rue Duguay Trouin, 75006 Paris; tel. 1-45-44-38-34; fax 1-45-49-93-92; arts, education, leisure; Chair. PIERRE PENET; Man. Dir PIERRE-MARIE DUMONT; also Fleurus Idées, Fleurus Enfants, Fleurus Essais, Fleurus Jeunesse, Fleurus Tardy, Critérion.

Librairie Gründ: 60 rue Mazarine, 75006 Paris; tel. 1-43-29-87-40; telex 204926; fax 1-43-29-49-86; f. 1880; art, natural history, children's books, guides; Chair. ALAIN GRÜND.

Hachette Livre: 83 ave Marceau, 75116 Paris; tel. 1-40-69-16-00; fax 1-47-23-01-92; f. 1826; group includes Hachette Education, Hachette Jeunesse, Hachette Littératures, Hachette Référence; Chair., Man. Dir JEAN-LOUIS LISIMACHIO.

L'Harmattan Edition: 7 rue de l'Ecole Polytechnique, 75005 Paris; tel. 1-43-54-79-10; fax 1-43-25-82-03; f. 1975; politics, human sciences, developing countries; Dir DENIS PRYEN.

Editions Hatier: 8 rue d'Assas, 75278 Paris Cédex 06; tel. 1-49-54-49-54; fax 1-40-49-00-45; f. 1880; children's books, fiction, history, science, nature guides; Chair. BERNARD FOULON.

Hermann: 293 rue Lecourbe, 75015 Paris; tel. 1-45-57-45-40; fax 1-40-60-12-93; f. 1870; sciences and art, humanities; Chair. PIERRE BERÈS.

I.D. Music, SA: 29 rue de Bitche, 92400 Courbevoie; tel. 1-41-88-98-98; fax 1-47-68-74-28; e-mail idmusic@easynet.fr; f. 1988; music; Dir PHILIPPE AGEON.

Editions Ibolya Virag: 2 rue de Cadix, 75015 Paris; tel. and fax 1-45-31-52-74; f. 1996; fiction, history; Dir IBOLYA VIRAG.

J'ai Lu: 84 rue de Grenelle, 75007 Paris; tel. 1-44-39-34-70; telex 202765; fax 1-45-44-65-52; f. 1958; fiction, paperbacks; subsidiary of Flammarion; Chair. CHARLES-HENRI FLAMMARION; Man. Dir FRÉDÉRIC MOREL.

Julliard: 24 ave Marceau, 75008 Paris; tel. 1-53-67-14-00; fax 1-53-67-14-14; f. 1931; general literature, biography, essays; Chair., Man. Dir BERNARD BARRAULT.

Jeanne Laffitte: 25 Cours d'Estienne d'Orves, BP 1903, 13225 Marseille Cédex 02; tel. 4-91-59-80-40; fax 4-91-54-25-64; f. 1972; art, geography, culture, medicine, history; Chair. and Man. Dir JEANNE LAFFITTE.

Editions Robert Laffont: 24 ave Marceau, 75831 Paris Cédex 08; tel. 1-53-67-14-00; fax 1-53-67-14-14; f. 1941; literature, history, art, translations; Publr ROBERT LAFFONT; Chair. BERNARD FIXOT.

Librairie Larousse, SA: 17 rue du Montparnasse, 75298 Paris Cédex 06; tel. 1-44-39-44-00; telex 250828; fax 1-44-39-43-43; f. 1852; general, specializing in dictionaries, illustrated books on scientific subjects, encyclopaedias, classics, textbooks and periodicals; Chair. and CEO BERTRAND EVENO.

Editions Jean-Claude Lattès: 17 rue Jacob, 75006 Paris; tel. 1-44-41-74-00; fax 1-43-25-30-47; f. 1968; general fiction and non-fiction, biography; Man. Dir ISABELLE LAFFONT.

Letouzey et Ané: 87 blvd Raspail, 75006 Paris; tel. 1-45-48-80-14; fax 1-45-49-03-43; f. 1885; theology, religion, archaeology, history, ecclesiastical encyclopaedias and dictionaries, biography; Man. Dir FLORENCE LETOUZEY.

LGDJ—Montchrestien: Paris; tel. 1-43-35-01-67; telex 203918; fax 1-43-20-07-42; f. 1836; law and economy; Chair. LIONEL GUÉRIN; Man. Dir NATHALIE JOUVEN.

LITEC: 27 place Dauphine, 75001 Paris; tel. 1-43-26-26-86; fax 1-43-54-52-09; f. 1927; law, economics, taxation; Chair. FRANÇOIS-RÉGIS THIAULT; Man. Dir MARINE DURIEUX D'HEMERY.

Le Livre de Poche: 43 quai de Grenelle, 75905 Paris Cédex 15; tel. 1-43-92-30-00; telex 204434; fax 1-43-92-35-90; *Le Livre de Poche* paperback series, general literature, dictionaries, encyclopaedias; f. 1953; Chair. DOMINIQUE GOUST.

Editions Magnard: 91 blvd Saint Germain, 75006 Paris; tel. 1-43-26-39-52; fax 1-46-33-96-04; f. 1941; children's and educational books; Man. Dir ISABELLE MAGNARD.

Masson Editeur: 120 blvd Saint Germain, 75006 Paris; tel. 1-40-46-60-00; telex 260946; fax 1-40-46-61-00; f. 1804; medicine and science, books and periodicals; publrs for various academies and societies; Chair. BERTRAND EVENO; Man. Dirs C. BINNENDYCK, J.-P. BAUDOUIN.

Mercure de France, SA: 26 rue de Condé, 75006 Paris; tel. 1-43-29-21-13; fax 1-43-54-49-91; f. 1894; general fiction, history, biography, sociology; Chair. and Man. Dir ANTOINE GALLIMARD; Editor ISABELLE GALLIMARD.

Les Editions de Minuit: 7 rue Bernard Palissy, 75006 Paris; tel. 1-44-39-39-20; fax 1-45-44-82-36; f. 1945; general literature; Chair. JÉRÔME LINDON; Man. Dir IRÈNE LINDON.

Nathan Education: 9 rue Méchain, 75014 Paris; tel. 1-45-87-50-00; fax 1-47-07-66-97; f. 1881; educational books for all levels; Chair. BERTRAND EVENO; Man. Dir JEAN-PAUL BAUDOIN.

Ouest-France: 13 rue du Breil, BP 6339, 35063 Rennes Cédex; tel. 2-99-32-58-27; fax 2-99-32-58-30; history, atlases, guides; Chair. FRANCOIS-XAVIER HUTIN; Man. Dir SERVANE BIGUAIS.

Editions Payot: 106 blvd Saint Germain, 75006 Paris; tel. 1-43-29-74-10; fax 1-43-25-68-45; f. 1917; literature, human sciences, philosophy; Chair. and Man. Dir JEAN-FRANÇOIS LAMUNIÈRE.

Perrin: 76 rue Bonaparte, 75284 Paris Cédex 06; tel. 1-44-41-35-00; fax 1-44-41-05-02; f. 1884; history, biography; Chair. OLIVIER ARBAN; Man. Dir XAVIER DE BARTILLAT.

A. et J. Picard: 82 rue Bonaparte, 75006 Paris; tel. 1-43-26-97-78; fax 1-43-26-42-64; f. 1869; archaeology, architecture, history of art, history, pre-history, auxiliary sciences, linguistics, musicological works, antiquarian books; Chair. and Man. Dir CHANTAL PASINI-PICARD.

Plon: 76 rue Bonaparte, 75284 Paris Cédex 06; tel. 1-44-41-35-00; fax 1-44-41-35-01; f. 1844; fiction, travel, history, anthropology, human sciences, biography.

Presses de Sciences Po: 44 rue du Four, 75006 Paris; tel. 1-44-39-39-60; fax 1-45-48-04-41; e-mail info@presses.sciences-po.fr; internet http://www.sciences-po.fr; f. 1975; history, politics, linguistics, economics, sociology; Dir BERTRAND BADIE.

Presses Universitaires de France: 108 blvd Saint Germain, 75279 Paris Cédex 06; tel. 1-46-34-12-01; telex 600474; fax 1-46-34-65-41; e-mail info@puf.com; f. 1921; philosophy, psychology, psychoanalysis, psychiatry, education, sociology, theology, history, geography, economics, law, linguistics, literature, science; Chair. MICHEL PRIGENT.

Presses Universitaires de Grenoble: BP 47, 38040 Grenoble Cédex 09; tel. 4-76-82-56-51; telex 980910; fax 4-76-82-78-35; f. 1972; psychology, law, economics, management, history, statistics, literature, medicine, science, politics; Man. Dirs CORINE DESBENOIT, JEAN BORNAREL, BARBARA MULLER.

Presses Universitaires de Nancy: 42–44 ave de la Libération, BP 33–47, 54014 Nancy Cédex; tel. 3-83-93-58-30; fax 3-83-93-58-39; f. 1976; literature, history, law, social sciences, politics; Chair., Man. Dir ALAIN TROGNON.

Privat, SA: 14 rue des Arts, 31068 Toulouse Cédex; tel. 5-61-22-07-51; fax 5-61-13-74-41; f. 1839; regional publs, history, social sciences, education; Man. Dirs JEAN LISSARRAGUE, PIERRE-ANDRÉ MICHEL.

Quillet Diffusion: 58 rue Jean Bleuzen, 92170 Vanves; tel. 1-40-95-21-93; fax 1-40-95-22-35; f. 1902; specializes in dictionaries and encyclopaedias; Chair. ETIENNE VENDROUX; Man. Dir JACQUES SOYER.

Editions du Seuil: 27 rue Jacob, 75261 Paris Cédex 06; tel. 1-40-46-50-50; fax 1-43-29-08-29; f. 1936; modern literature, fiction, illustrated books, non-fiction; Chair. and Man. Dir CLAUDE CHERKI.

Editions Signe: Eckbolsheim, Strasbourg; f. 1987; religion; Chair. and Man. Dir CHRISTIAN RIEHL.

Editions Stock: 23 rue du Sommerard, 75005 Paris; tel. 1-44-41-86-86; fax 1-43-25-98-62; f. 1710; literature (French and foreign), biography, human sciences, guides; Chair., Man. Dir CLAUDE DURAND.

Succès du Livre: 19–21 rue de l'Ancienne Comédie, 75006 Paris; tel. 1-43-29-82-82; fax 1-43-29-60-75; f. 1987; fiction, biography; Chair. JACQUES DOMAS.

Editions de la Table Ronde: 7 rue Corneille, 75006 Paris; tel. 1-43-26-03-95; fax 1-44-07-09-30; f. 1944; fiction, essays, religion, travel, theatre, youth; Man. Dir DENIS TILLINAC.

Editions Tallandier: 25 blvd Malesherbes, 75008 Paris Cédex 11; tel. 1-44-51-01-01; fax 1-44-51-01-00; history, reference, romance; Man. Dir FRANÇOIS DE L'ESPÉE.

Editions Vigot: 23 rue de l'Ecole de Médecine, 75006 Paris; tel. 1-43-29-54-50; fax 1-46-34-05-89; f. 1890; medicine, pharmacology, nature, veterinary science, sport; Chair. CHRISTIAN VIGOT; Man. Dir DANIEL VIGOT.

Librairie Philosophique J. Vrin: 6 place de la Sorbonne, 75005 Paris; tel. 1-43-54-03-47; fax 1-43-54-48-18; f. 1911; university textbooks, philosophy, education, science, law, religion; Chair. and Man. Dir A. PAULHAC-VRIN.

PUBLISHERS' AND BOOKSELLERS' ASSOCIATIONS

Cercle de la Librairie (Syndicat des Industries et Commerces du Livre): 35 rue Grégoire de Tours, 75006 Paris Cédex; tel. 1-44-41-28-00; fax 1-43-29-68-95; f. 1847; a syndicate of the book trade, grouping the principal asscns of publishers, booksellers and printers; Chair. CHARLES-HENRI FLAMMARION; Man. Dir JEAN-MARIE DOUBLET.

Chambre Syndicale des Editeurs de Musique de France: 215 rue du Faubourg Saint Honoré, 75008 Paris; tel. 1-53-83-84-50; fax 1-45-63-62-91; f. 1873; music publishers' asscn; Chair. JEAN-MANUEL MOBILLION DE SCARAND; Sec. THIERRY CHEVRIER DE CHOUDENS.

Chambre Syndicale de l'Edition Musicale (CSDEM): 62 rue Blanche, 75009 Paris; tel. 1-48-74-09-29; fax 1-42-81-19-87; f. 1978; music publishers; Chair. JEAN DAVOUST.

Fédération Française Syndicale de la Librairie: 49 rue de Châteaudun, 75009 Paris; tel. 1-42-82-00-03; fax 1-42-82-10-51; f. 1892; booksellers' asscn; 2,000 mems; Chair. JEAN LEGUÉ; Gen. Man. JEAN-BAPTISTE DAELMAN.

Syndicat National de l'Edition: 115 blvd Saint-Germain, 75006 Paris; tel. 1-44-41-40-50; fax 1-44-41-40-77; f. 1892; publishers' asscn; 550 mems; Chair. SERGE EYROLLES; Man. Dir JEAN SARZANA.

Syndicat National de la Librairie: 40 rue Grégoire de Tours, 75006 Paris; tel. 1-46-34-74-20; fax 1-44-07-14-73; booksellers' asscn; Pres. ALAIN DIART.

Broadcasting and Communications

TELECOMMUNICATIONS

France Télécom: 6 place d'Alleray, 75505 Paris Cédex 15; tel. 1-44-44-89-34; fax 1-48-42-32-64; telephone and telecommunications company; 30% transferred from state-ownership to the private sector in 1997; turnover 150,000m. francs (1997); Chair. MICHEL BON.

BROADCASTING

Conseil Supérieur de l'Audiovisuel (CSA): Tour Mirabeau, 39–43 quai André Citroën, 75739 Paris Cédex 15; tel. 1-40-58-38-00; telex 200365; fax 1-45-79-00-06; f. 1989 as replacement for the Commission Nationale de la Communication et des Libertés (CNCL); supervises all French broadcasting; awards licences to private radio and television stations, allocates cable networks and frequencies, appoints heads of state-owned radio and television companies, oversees telecommunications sectors, monitors programme standards; consists of nine members, appointed for six years: three nominated by the Pres. of the Republic; three by the Pres. of the National Assembly; and three by the Pres. of the Senate; Pres. HERVÉ BOURGES.

Institut National de l'Audiovisuel: 4 ave de l'Europe, 94366 Bry sur Marne Cédex; tel. 1-49-83-20-00; telex 262493; fax 1-49-83-25-84; e-mail brodowski@ina.fr; internet http://www.ina.fr; f. 1975; research and professional training in the field of broadcasting; radio and TV archives; Pres. JEAN-PIERRE TEYSSIER.

Télédiffusion de France (TDF), SA: 21–27 rue Barbès, BP 518, 92542 Montrouge Cédex; tel. 1-49-65-10-00; fax 1-46-57-48-50; f. 1975, partly privatized in 1987; responsible for broadcasting programmes produced by the production companies, for the organization and maintenance of the networks, for study and research into radio and television equipment; operates a cable television network; administrative council comprising 16 members, of which six are representatives of the State; Chair. BRUNO CHETAILLE.

Radio

State-controlled Radio

Public radio services are provided by three entities: Radio France for the domestic audience; Radio-Télévision Française d'Outre-Mer for the French overseas departments and territories; and Radio France International for foreign countries (and those of foreign origin in France).

Société Nationale de Radiodiffusion (Radio France): 116 ave du Président Kennedy, 75786 Paris Cédex 16; tel. 1-42-30-22-22; telex 200002; fax 1-42-30-14-88; f. 1975; planning and production of radio programmes; provides five national services, 49 local stations and two European services (see below); Chair. and Man. Dir MICHEL BOYON; Dir PATRICE DUHAMEL.

Radio France provides the following domestic radio services for a nationwide audience:

France Inter (general programmes, for entertainment and information);
France Culture;
France Info (continuous news and information);
France Musique;
Le Mouv' (music and general interest for young people).
Radio Bleue (for older people).

Radio France's local services comprise:

France Inter (39 decentralized local radio stations);
Réseau FIP (nine local stations);
Sorbonne Radio France (educational programmes broadcast six hours daily during university terms; Paris region).

Radio France's European services (broadcast by TDF1/TDF2 satellite) comprise:

Hector (mainly classical music);
France Culture Europe (cultural and information).

Radio France Internationale: 116 ave du Président Kennedy, BP 9516, 75786 Paris Cédex 16; tel. 1-42-30-12-12; fax 1-42-30-47-59; internet http://www.rfi.fr; broadcasts on medium wave and FM transmitters, mainly to Africa, Eastern Europe, North America, the Caribbean, South-East Asia and the Middle East, in French and 18 other languages; Pres. JEAN-PAUL CLUZEL; Dir-Gen. CHRISTIAN CHARPY; Dir MICHEL MEYER.

Société Nationale de Radio-Télévision Française d'Outre-Mer (RFO): 5 ave du Recteur Poincaré, 75016 Paris; tel. 1-42-15-71-00; fax 1-42-15-74-37; controls broadcasting in the French overseas territories; nine local stations providing two radio networks and two television channels, the latter broadcasting material from the state channels F2 and F3 and the private channel TFI (see below) as well as local programmes; Chair., Man. Dir JEAN-MARIE CAVADA.

Private Radio

In 1994 there were about 2,730 private radio stations, mostly local stations broadcasting on frequency modulation (FM) transmitters. In 1996 the largest private local radio stations were Europe 2, Fun Radio, Nostalgie, NRJ and Sky Rock. There were three private networks broadcasting general programmes to a nationwide audience (Europe 1, RMC—based in Monaco—and RTL) and seven nationwide private networks broadcasting mostly music.

Europe 1: 28 rue François 1er, 75008 Paris; tel. 1-47-23-19-19; fax 1-47-23-88-13; owned by Groupe Lagardère, which also owns Europe 2 and RFM; broadcasting on long wave and 99 FM frequencies; Chair. JACQUES LEHN; Man. Dir JEAN-PIERRE OZANNAT.

Radio Monte-Carlo (RMC): 12 rue Magellan, 75008 Paris; tel. 1-40-69-88-00; telex 610214; fax 1-40-69-88-55; broadcasting on long wave and 102 FM frequencies; Man. Dir JEAN-NOEL TASSEZ.

RTL: 22 rue Bayard, 75008 Paris; tel. 1-40-70-40-70; telex 280801; fax 1-40-70-42-72; broadcasting on long wave and 129 FM frequencies; Chair., Man. Dir JACQUES RIGAUD.

Television

State-controlled Television

France Télévision: 1 place Henri de France, 75015 Paris; tel. 1-44-31-60-00; fax 1-47-20-24-54; f. 1992 as supervisory authority for the two national public television networks (France 2 and France 3: see below); Chair. XAVIER GOUYOU-BEAUCHAMPS; Sec.-Gen. FRANÇOIS GUILBEAU.

Société Nationale de Télévision—France 2 (F2): 22 ave Montaigne, 75387 Paris Cédex 08; tel. 1-44-21-42-42; telex 642313; fax 1-44-21-51-45; f. 1975 as Antenne 2 (A2); general programmes for a nationwide audience; Dir-Gen. MICHÈLE PAPPALARDO.

Société Nationale de Programmes—France 3 (F3): 116 ave du Président Kennedy, 75790 Paris Cédex 16; tel. 1-42-30-13-13; telex 645720; fax 1-46-47-92-94; f. 1975 as France Régions 3 (FR3); general programmes for a nationwide audience (with a larger proportion of cultural and educational programmes than F2), and regional programmes transmitted from 13 regional stations; Dir-Gen. PHILIPPE LEVRIER.

La Sept-Arte et La Cinquième: 10–14 rue Horace Vernet, 92136 Issy-les-Moulineaux Cédex; tel. 1-41-46-55-55; f. 1994; merger with private television channel Arte scheduled in 1997; educational programmes; Pres. JÉRÔME CLÉMENT.

Television programmes for France's overseas departments and territories are provided by Radio-Télévision Française d'Outre-Mer (see under Radio).

Private Television

Canal Plus: 85–89 quai André Citroën, 75711 Paris Cédex 15; tel. 1-44-25-10-00; telex 201141; fax 1-44-25-12-34; f. 1984; 38.2% public ownership, 23.6% owned by Havas, 20.4% by Compagnie Générale des Eaux, and the remainder by other companies; coded programmes financed by audience subscription; uncoded programmes financed by advertising sold by Canal Plus; specializes in drama (including cinema films) and sport; launched a 'pay-per-view' service for sports events in 1996; Pres. PIERRE LESCURE.

Demain!: 85-89 quai André Citroën, 75711 Paris Cédex 15; f. 1997; owned by Canal Plus; information about employment for job-seekers; Dir-Gen.: MARTINE MAULÉON.

M6: 89 ave Charles de Gaulle, 92575 Neuilly-sur-Seine Cédex; tel. 1-41-92-66-66; telex 649781; fax 1-41-92-66-10; f. 1986 as TV6, reformed as M6 in 1987; 34% owned by Lyonnaise des Eaux, 40% by CLT, and smaller percentages by other shareholders; specializes in drama, music and magazines; Pres. JEAN DRUCKER; Dir-Gen. NICOLAS DE TAVERNOST.

Télévision Française 1 (TF1): 1 quai du Point du Jour, 92656 Boulogne Cédex; tel. 2-41-41-12-34; fax 2-41-41-28-40; f. 1975 as a state-owned channel, privatized 1987; 39% owned by Bouygues SA, 6% by Société Générale, and smaller percentages by other shareholders, including 1.9% by TF1 employees; general programmes; Pres. PATRICK LE LAY.

Satellite Television

In 1984 TV5 began broadcasting programmes relayed from French, Belgian and Swiss television stations by satellite. In the same year, the French Government reached an agreement with Luxembourg to finance jointly a communal direct-broadcasting satellite television system (TDF1). TDF1 was inaugurated in 1988, after a series of technical problems, and another satellite television system, TDF2 (financed by private investors), was launched in 1989. In 1993 the TDF1/TDF2 satellites were transmitting television programmes for Arte, Canal Plus and the MCM-Euromusique music channel, and radio programmes for Radio France (Hector and Victor). Two telecommunications satellites, Télécom 2A and Télécom 2B, were also transmitting programmes for the principal television channels. In 1995 the Astra, Eutelsat and Télécom satellites were transmitting to the majority of the 1.0m. households that were able to receive satellite television. In 1996, with the advent of digital television programming, three new satellites, Canal Satellite, Télévision par satellite and AB Sat, were launched.

Cable Television

By August 1995 there were 1,239,771 households subscribing to cable television in France. There were 11 specialized national channels (including Canal J for children, Ciné-Cinémas, providing cinema films, Planète, specializing in documentaries, and Eurosport France), and 21 local channels; 23 foreign channels also broadcast on the French cable network (subject to the CSA's regulations). The following are the principal operators of cable television:

Citécâble: 8 rue de Liège, 75009 Paris; tel. 1-40-82-91-97; fax 1-42-82-18-99; Chair. ALAIN COQUARD.

Communication–Développement: 6 place Abel Gance, 92652 Boulogne-Billancourt Cédex; tel. 1-49-94-45-11; fax 1-49-94-45-99; affiliated to Groupe Lyonnaise des Eaux.

Compagnie Générale de Vidéocommunication: 42 quai du Point du Jour, 92659 Boulogne-Billancourt Cédex; tel. 1-47-61-57-00; fax 1-47-61-57-95; affiliated to Groupe Générale des Eaux.

Eurocâble: 39 allée Gluck, BP 2519, 68058 Mulhouse Cédex; tel. 3-89-42-60-10; fax 3-89-42-98-22.

France Télécom (Service des Télécommunications de l'Image): 124 rue Réaumur, 75002 Paris; tel. 1-42-21-71-71; fax 1-40-39-86-25; Chair. MARCEL ROULET.

Lyonnaise Communications: 6 villa Thoréton, 75015 Paris; tel. 1-44-25-81-81; fax 1-44-25-81-40; f. 1986; affiliated to Groupe Lyonnaise des Eaux; Chair. CYRILLE DU PELOUX.

Réseaux Câblés de France: 92130 Issy-les-Moulineaux; tel. 1-46-48-77-77; fax 1-46-48-79-05; Chair., Man. Dir MICHEL GILLARD.

Vidéopole: 45 ave de Clichy, 75017 Paris; tel. 1-44-69-88-44; fax 1-44-69-88-40; Chair. PAUL GODIN; Man. Dir BERNARD TOURAINE.

Finance

(cap. = capital; p.u. = paid up; dep. = deposits; res = reserves; m. = million; brs = branches; amounts in French francs)

BANKING

Central Bank

Banque de France: 39 rue Croix des Petits Champs, BP 140-01, 75049 Paris; tel. 1-42-92-42-92; telex 220932; fax 1-42-96-04-23; f. 1800; cap. 3,000m., res 179,698.7m., dep. 72,182.0m., total assets 550,234.1m. (Dec. 1996); nationalized in 1946; became independent in 1994; acts as banker to the Treasury, issues bank notes, controls credit and money supply and administers France's gold and currency assets; in 1993 the National Assembly approved legislation to make the Banque de France an independent central bank, with a General Council to supervise activities and appoint the principal officials, and a nine-member monetary policy committee, independent of government control, to be in charge of French monetary policy; Gov. JEAN-CLAUDE TRICHET; Dep. Govs DENIS FERMAN, HERVÉ HANNOUN; 214 brs.

State Savings Bank

Caisse des depôts et consignations: 56 rue de Lille, 75356 Paris; tel. 1-40-49-56-78; telex 200055; fax 1-40-49-76-87; f. 1816; manages state savings system, holds widespread investments in industrial cos; dep. 639,834m., total assets 842,680m. (Dec. 1996); CEO ROBERT LION; Gen. Man. DANIEL LEBÈGUE; 1 br.

Commercial Banks

American Express Bank (France) SA: 11 rue Scribe, 75009 Paris Cédex 09; tel. 1-47-14-50-00; telex 290177; fax 1-42-68-17-17; f. 1957; cap. 310m., res 35.3m., dep. 1,889.3m. (Dec. 1995); Pres. PIERO GRANDI; Country Man. GORDON JOOST; 4 brs.

Banque Arabe et Internationale d'Investissement (BAII): 12 place Vendôme, 75001 Paris; tel. 1-47-03-23-45; telex 680330; fax 1-47-03-28-00; f. 1973; investment bank; cap. 650.8m., total assets 19,468.3m. (Dec. 1990); subsidiary of BAII Holdings, Luxembourg; Chair. ROBERT K. SURSOCK; Dir-Gen. PHILIPPE GASTON.

Banque Bruxelles Lambert France: Immeuble Kupka B, 16 rue Hoche, Cédex 96, 92906 Paris La Défense; tel. 1-41-26-70-00; telex 616794; fax 1-41-26-77-77; f. 1955 as Banque Louis-Dreyfus, name changed in 1990; cap. 2,000m., res 105.2m., dep. 17,677m. (Dec. 1996); Chair. JOHN GIELEN; Dir-Gen. GUY BENADIA; 1 br.

Banque CGER France: 21 blvd Malesherbes, BP 496, 75366 Paris Cédex 08; tel. 1-42-68-62-00; telex 650582; fax 1-42-66-35-30; f. 1933; present name adopted 1990; 98.9%-owned by ASLK–CGER Bank (Belgium); cap. 225m., res 97.2m., dep. 7,688.0m. (Dec. 1993); Chair. GILBERT MITTLER; Dir-Gen. JOSEPH DUPLICY.

Banque CGM—Caisse de Gestion Mobilière: 6 rue des Petit Pères, 75002 Paris Cédex 02; tel. 1-40-20-20-00; telex 220480; fax 1-42-86-90-05; f. 1929; cap. 84.1m., res 123.7m. (Dec. 1993), dep. 15,903.0m. (Dec. 1992); Chair., Dir-Gen. PHILIPPE DELIENNE.

Banque de Bretagne: 18 quai Duguay Trouin, 35084 Rennes Cédex; tel. 2-99-01-77-77; telex 730094; fax 2-99-01-75-00; f. 1909; cap. 325.7m., res 101.2m., dep. 6,492.4m. (Dec. 1996); Chair., Man. Dir CLAUDE WICKY; 70 brs.

Banque Colbert: 10–12 rue d'Anjou, 75008 Paris; tel. 1-40-07-40-40; telex 282897; fax 1-40-07-40-99; f. 1992 (fmrly Banque Financière Parisienne); cap. 451.5m., res 1,165.6m., dep. 18,786.3m. (Dec. 1993); Pres. and Chair. BERNARD THIOLON; Dir-Gen. MAURICE BELLET.

Banque Commerciale pour l'Europe du Nord (EUROBANK), SA: 79–81 blvd Haussmann, 75382 Paris Cédex 08; tel. 1-40-06-43-

21; telex 280200; fax 1-40-06-48-48; f. 1921; cap. 1,215.8m., res 179.9m., dep. 7,241.9m. (Dec. 1996); Pres. IOURI PONOMAREV; Chair. BERNARD DUPUY.

Banque Fédérative du Crédit Mutuel, SA: 34 rue du Wacken, BP 412, 67002 Strasbourg Cédex; tel. 3-88-14-88-14; telex 880034; fax 3-88-14-67-00; f. 1933; cap. 501.3m., res 3,264.5m., dep. 157,456.1m. (Dec. 1995); Chair. ETIENNE PFLIMLIN; CEO MICHEL LUCAS.

Banque de l'Economie—Crédit Mutuel: 34 rue du Wacken, BP 412, 67002 Strasbourg Cédex; tel. 3-88-14-88-14; telex 870350; fax 3-88-14-75-10; f. 1992; cap. 400m.; Chair. of Supervisory Bd ETIENNE PFLIMLIN; Chair. of Bd of Management BERNARD BARTELMANN; 33 brs.

Banque Française de Crédit Coopératif: 33 rue des Trois Fontanot, BP 211, 92002 Nanterre Cédex; tel. 1-47-24-85-00; telex 620496; fax 1-47-24-89-25; f. 1969; cap. 363.2m., res 117.4m., dep. 19,428.3m. (Dec. 1996); Pres., Gen. Man. JEAN-CLAUDE DETILLEUX; 54 brs.

Banque Française de l'Orient: 30 ave George V, 75008 Paris; tel. 1-49-52-18-32; telex 640822; fax 1-49-52-17-14; f. 1989 by merger; cap. 500.0m., res 362.4m., dep. 17,223.7m. (Dec. 1996); Chair. BERNARD VERNHES.

Banque La Henin: 16 rue de la Ville l'Evêque, 75008 Paris Cédex 08; tel. 1-44-51-20-20; telex 285741; fax 1-44-51-25-25; f. 1949; cap. 587m., res 520.1m., dep. 37,014.8m. (Dec. 1996); Chair., Man. Dir JÉRÔME MEYSSONNIER; Sec.-Gen. PHILIPPE DESPRAT.

Banque Hervet, SA: 127 ave Charles de Gaulle, 92200 Neuilly; tel. 1-46-40-90-00; telex 620466; fax 1-46-40-92-77; f. 1830; 55.4% state-owned; cap. 110.2m., res 951.9m., dep. 21,542.5m. (Dec. 1996); Chair., Man. Dir PATRICK CAREIL; Gen. Man. ALAIN CADIOU; 78 brs.

Banque Indosuez: 9 rue Louis Murat, 75371 Paris Cédex 08; tel. 1-44-20-20-20; telex 650409; fax 1-44-20-29-56; f. 1975; owned by Caisse Nationale de Crédit Agricole since 1996; cap. 3,684.9m., res 10,543.4m., dep. 325,445m. (Dec. 1995); Chair. CHRISTIAN MAURIN; Gen. Mans PHILIPPE GESLIN, PHILIPPE GUIRAL, ALAIN DE KORSAK; 14 brs.

Banque Intercontinentale Arabe: 67 ave Franklin D. Roosevelt, 75008 Paris; tel. 1-43-59-61-49; telex 640340; fax 1-42-89-09-59; f. 1975; cap. 550m., res 24.1m., dep. 1,667.8m. (Dec. 1996); Pres. MOHAMED BENHALIMA; Gen. Man. KHALIFA GANA.

Banque Internationale de Placement: 108 blvd Haussman, 75008 Paris; tel. 1-44-70-80-80; telex 660002; fax 1-42-93-03-30; f. 1979; cap. 193m., res 1,196.1m. (Dec. 1996); Chair. JEAN-LOUIS LAURENS; Gen. Mans JEAN-MICHEL MEPUIS, DOMINIQUE OULD FERHAT, PATRICK HÉNAFF.

Banque Nationale de Paris, SA: 16 blvd des Italiens, 75009 Paris; tel. 1-40-14-45-46; telex 280605; fax 1-40-14-69-55; f. 1966; under state control 1982, privatized 1993; cap. 5,186.0m., res 49,316.0m., dep. 1,516.7m. (Dec. 1996); Chair. MICHEL PÉBEREAU; Man. Dir BAUDOUIN PROT; 2,000 brs.

Banque Nationale de Paris Intercontinentale, SA: 1 rue Taitbout, 75009 Paris; tel. 1-40-14-22-11; telex 283419; fax 1-40-14-69-34; f. 1940; cap. 190.8m. (Dec. 1993), dep. 20,374m. (Dec. 1995); Chair. DANIEL LEBEGUE; CEO VINCENT DE ROUX; 166 brs.

Banque de Neuflize, Schlumberger, Mallet: 3 ave Hoche, 75410 Paris Cédex 08; tel. 1-47-66-61-11; telex 640653; fax 1-47-66-62-89; f. 1966; subsidiary of ABN AMRO Bank NV; cap. 672m., res 1,094m., dep. 30,285m. (Dec. 1996); Chair. Supervisory Bd ROGER PAPAZ; Chair. Man. Bd HENRI MOULARD; 18 brs.

Banque OBC—Odier Bungener Courvoisier, SA: 57 ave d'Iéna, BP 195, 75783 Paris Cédex 16; tel. 1-45-02-40-00; telex 645889; fax 1-45-00-77-79; f. 1960; cap. 211.3m., res 114.4m., dep. 6,915.2m. (Dec. 1996); Chair. and Man. Dir MAGGIEL SCALONGNE.

Banque Paribas: 3 rue d'Antin, 75002 Paris; tel. 1-42-98-12-34; telex 210041; fax 1-42-98-11-42; f. 1872; fmrly Banque de Paris et des Pays-Bas; cap. 5,651m., res 13,277m., dep. 1,042,277m. (Dec. 1996); Chair. ANDRÉ LEVY-LANG.

Banque Parisienne de Crédit: 56 rue de Châteaudun, 75009 Paris; tel. 1-42-80-68-68; telex 280179; fax 1-40-16-16-30; f. 1920; cap. 230.6m., res 803.4m., dep. 9,612.0m. (Dec. 1996); Chair. GUY CHARTIER; Gen. Man. FRANÇOIS GOULARD; 69 brs.

Banque du Phénix: 6 ave Kléber, 75116 Paris; tel. 1-44-17-21-00; telex 641411; fax 1-45-01-66-88; f. 1991 by merger; owned by ABN AMRO France from 1996; cap. 38.7m., res 0.8m., dep. 20,479.7m. (Dec. 1995); Pres. CHRISTIAN DE GOURNAY.

Banque Régionale de l'Ain, SA: 2 ave Alsace-Lorraine, 01001 Bourg en Bresse; tel. 4-74-32-50-00; telex 330431; fax 4-74-32-50-81; f. 1849; mem. of Crédit Industriel et Commercial Group; cap. 101.4m., res 294.4m., dep. 7,208.4m. (Dec. 1996); Chair., Man. Dir PAUL DEGUERRY; 50 brs.

Banque Régionale de l'Ouest, SA: 7 rue Gallois, BP 49, 41003 Blois Cédex; tel. 2-54-56-54-56; telex 750564; fax 2-54-56-54-00; f. 1913; mem. of Crédit Industriel et Commercial Group; cap. 207m., res 306.5m., dep. 14,402.7m. (Dec. 1996); Pres. JEAN-CLAUDE CAMUS; Gen. Man. ROBERT LE MOAL; 95 brs.

Banque Sanpaolo, SA: 52 ave Hoche, 75382 Paris Cédex 08; tel. 1-47-54-42-50; fax 1-40-54-14-02; f. 1871 as Banque Vernes et Commerciale de Paris, SA; cap. 2,100m., res 54.1m. (Dec. 1996); Pres. LANFRANCO VIVARELLI; Gen. Man. CLAUDIO FERRARI; 52 brs.

Banque Scalbert-Dupont: 33 ave le Corbusier, BP 567, 59023 Lille Cédex; tel. 3-20-12-64-64; telex 820680; fax 3-20-12-64-00; f. 1838; cap. 250m., res 897.9m., dep. 22,563.6m. (Dec. 1996); Chair. CLAUDE LAMOTTE; Gen. Man. JÉRÔME GUILLEMARD.

Banque Sudameris: 4 rue Meyerbeer, 75009 Paris; tel. 1-48-01-77-77; telex 283669; fax 1-48-01-79-90; f. 1910; cap. 627.7m., res 3,220.4m., dep. 49,405.2m. (Dec. 1996); active principally in South America; Chair. and Pres. ALBERTO ABELLI.

Banque Worms, SA: Tour Voltaire, 1 place des Degrés Cédex 58, 92059 Paris La Défense; tel. 1-49-07-50-50; telex 616023; fax 1-49-07-59-11; f. 1928; 100% subsidiary of Union des Assurances de Paris; cap. 2,100.0m., res 104.4m., dep. 37,181.9m. (Dec. 1996); Chair. HENRI DE CASTRIES; Gen. Man. MARC VUILLERMET; 18 brs.

Barclays Bank PLC: 21 rue Lafitte, 75002 Paris; tel. 1-44-79-79-79; telex 282700; fax 1-44-79-72-52; f. 1968; cap. 850m., res 278.2m., dep. 41,794.4m. (Dec. 1990); Gen. Man. CHRISTIAN MENARD; 71 brs and sub-brs.

BNP Finance: 9 blvd des Italiens, 75002 Paris; tel. 1-40-14-16-01; telex 281366; fax 1-40-14-16-80; f. 1980 as Banque Natiotrésorie; cap. 100m., res 456.0m., dep. 102,394.4m. (Dec. 1995); Chair PHILIPPE BORDENAVE; CEO PHILIPPE RAKOTOVAO.

BRED Banque Populaire: 18 quai de la Rapée, 75604 Paris Cédex 12; tel. 1-48-98-60-00; telex 214844; fax 1-40-04-71-57; f. 1919; fmrly Banque Régionale d'Escompte et de Dépôts; present name since 1994; cap. 1,250m., res 1,169.9m., dep. 130,554.6m. (Dec. 1996); Chair. MICHEL DE MOURGUES; 194 brs.

Caisse Centrale des Banques Populaires: 10–12 ave Winston Churchill, 94677 Charenton Le Pont Cédex; tel. 1-40-39-30-00; telex 210993; fax 1-40-39-39-49; f. 1921; the central banking institution of 30 co-operative regional Banques Populaires; cap. 1,608.2m., res 2,285.7m., dep. 176,237.1m. (Dec. 1996); Chair. JACQUES DELMAS-MARSALET; Gen. Man., CEO PAUL LORIOT.

Caisse d'Epargne Ile de France Paris: 19 rue du Louvre, 75001 Paris; tel. 1-40-41-30-31; telex 210503; fax 1-40-41-34-67; f. 1818; savings bank; cap. 2,021m., res 2,086m., dep. 98,717m. (Dec. 1995); Chair. BERNARD CONOLET; 301 brs.

Caisse Nationale de Crédit Agricole (CNCA), SA: 91–93 blvd Pasteur, 75015 Paris; tel. 1-43-23-52-02; fax 1-43-23-20-28; internet http://www.creditagricole.fr; f. 1920; central institution for co-operative banking group comprising 85 Caisses Regionales; emphasis on agribusiness; cap. 28,100m., total assets 477,300m. (Dec. 1996); Chair. YVES BARSALOU; CEO LUCIEN DOUROUX; 8,174 brs.

Compagnie Bancaire: 5 ave Kléber, 75116 Paris; tel. 1-45-25-25-25; telex 645750; fax 1-40-69-38-74; f. 1959; cap. 2,798m., res 16,446m., dep. 274,847m. (Dec. 1996); Chair. BERNARD MÜLLER.

Compagnie Financière du Crédit Mutuel de Bretagne: 29808 Brest Cédex 09; tel. 2-98-00-22-22; telex 941569; fax 2-98-00-27-24; f. 1960; cap. 1,548.1m., res 1,738.0m., dep. 67,369.9m. (Dec. 1996); Chair. YVES LE BAQUER; 282 brs.

CPR: 30 rue Saint Georges, 75312 Paris Cédex 09; tel. 1-45-96-20-00; telex 282511; fax 1-45-96-25-55; f. 1928 as Compagnie Parisienne de Réescompte; present name adopted 1989; discount bank; cap. 531.5m., res 1,923.5m., dep. 99,037.2m. (Dec. 1996); Chair. HENRI CUKIERMAN; Gen. Man. PHILIPPE DELIENNE; 2 brs.

Crédit Commercial de France (CCF), SA: 103 ave des Champs Elysées, 75008 Paris; tel. 1-40-70-70-40; telex 630300; fax 1-40-70-70-09; f. 1894; cap. 1,740.3m., res 9,821.6m., dep. 224,951.2m. (Dec 1995); Chair. and CEO CHARLES DE CROISSET; 184 brs.

Crédit Foncier de France, SA: 19 rue des Capucines, BP 65, 75050 Paris Cédex 01; tel. 1-42-44-80-00; telex 220349; fax 1-42-44-86-99; f. 1852; plans to dismantle the bank were announced in late 1996; cap. 3,771.0m., res 5,448.4m., dep. 293,619.1m. (Dec. 1996); Chair. JÉRÔME MEYSSONIER; 14 brs.

Crédit Industriel d'Alsace et de Lorraine (CIAL): 31 rue Jean Wenger-Valentin, 67000 Strasbourg; tel. 3-88-37-61-23; telex 890167; fax 3-88-37-71-81; f. 1919; cap. 145.2m., res 2,844.2m. dep. 78,056.6m. (Dec. 1996); Chair. JEAN WEBER; Gen. Man. GÉRARD OBRINGER; 154 brs and sub-brs.

Crédit Industriel et Commercial (CIC): 6 ave de Provence, 75452 Paris Cédex 09; tel. 1-45-96-96-96; telex 688314; fax 1-45-96-96-66; f. 1859; nationalized 1982; privatization plans suspended in 1996; cap. 1,609.8m., res 1,475.4m., dep. 89,484.4m. (Dec. 1996); Chair. GILLES GUITTON; Gen. Man. JEAN HUET; 120 brs.

Crédit Industriel de Normandie, SA: 15 place de la Pucelle d'Orléans, BP 3026, 76041 Rouen Cédex; tel. 2-35-08-64-00; telex 770950; fax 2-35-08-64-38; f. 1932; cap. 107.0m., res 115.1m., dep.

11,003.0m. (Dec. 1996); Chair. and Man. Dir JEAN DURAMÉ; 7 brs and 71 sub-brs.

Crédit Industriel de l'Ouest, SA: 2 ave Jean-Claude Bonduelle, 44000 Nantes; tel. 2-40-12-91-91; telex 700590; fax 2-40-12-92-07; f. 1957; cap. 237.1m., res 673.3m., dep. 32,660.8m. (Dec. 1996); Chair. BENOÎT DE LA SEIGLIÈRE; Man. Dir GÉRARD GOULET; 18 brs and 178 sub-brs.

Crédit Lyonnais, SA: 90 quai de Bercy, 75613 Paris Cédex 12; tel. 1-42-95-70-00; telex 615310; fax 1-42-95-11-96; f. 1863; 55.3% state-owned; privatization announced in 1993, but delayed, owing to financial difficulties; cap. 9,390m., res 16,011m., dep. 1,172,306m. (Dec. 1996); Chair. JEAN PEYRELEVADE; Gen. Man. MICHEL RENAULT; 2,100 brs.

Crédit du Nord, SA: 6–8 blvd Haussmann, 75009 Paris (administrative headquarters); tel. 1-40-22-40-22; telex 641379; fax 1-40-22-27-51; f. 1848; 61%-owned by Société Générale (q.v.) from 1997; cap. 1,076.2m., res 411.5m., dep. 94,454.6m. (Dec. 1994); Chair. of Supervisory Bd FRANÇOIS HENROT; Chair. of Management Bd PHILIPPE TOUSSAINT; 405 brs.

Lyonnaise de Banque, SA: 8 rue de la République, 69001 Lyon; tel. 4-78-92-02-12; telex 330532; fax 4-78-92-03-00; f. 1865 as Société Lyonnaise de Dépôts et de Crédit Industriel; cap. 1,000.0m., res 922.9m., dep. 50,688.0m. (Dec. 1996); Chair. DENIS SAMUEL LAJEUNESSE; Man. Dir MICHEL ANGE; 300 brs.

Midland Bank, SA: 20 bis ave Rapp, 75332 Paris Cédex 07; tel. 1-44-42-70-00; telex 648022; fax 1-44-42-77-77; f. 1978; cap. 475.6m., res 447.4m., dep. 16,723.7m. (Dec. 1990); Chair. R. J. MOSELEY.

Natexis Groupe: 45 rue Saint-Dominique, 75007 Paris; tel. 1-45-50-90-00; telex 206323; fax 1-45-55-89-58; f. 1996, as Groupe Crédit National BFCE, by merger of Crédit National and Banque Française du Commerce Extérieur; name changed in 1997; Chair. EMMANUEL RODOCANACHI; 31 brs.

SBT-BATIF: 34/36 ave de Friedland, 75008 Paris; tel. 1-47-54-80-00; telex 642349; fax 1-47-54-82-91; f. 1991 by merger; cap. 2,518m., res 11,885m., dep. 53,447m. (Dec. 1993); Chair. CLAUDE-ERIC PAQUIN; Man. Dir CLAUDE HAUVILLE.

Société de Banque Occidentale (SDBO): 8 rue de la Rochefoucauld, BP 302, 75425 Paris Cédex 09; tel. 1-49-95-70-00; telex 285159; fax 1-49-95-72-00; f. 1907; wholly-owned subsidiary of Crédit Lyonnais; cap. 515m., res 263.1m., dep. 19,688.5m. (Dec. 1993); Chair., Man. Dir PIERRE DOREL; 6 brs.

Société Bordelaise de Crédit Industriel et Commercial, SA: 42 cours du Chapeau Rouge, 33000 Bordeaux; tel. 5-56-56-10-00; telex 540914; fax 5-56-79-32-22; f. 1880; cap. 205m., res 53.4m., dep. 8,244.7m. (Dec. 1996); Chair. JEAN-PAUL ESCANDE; Man. Dir JEAN-PHILIPPE BRINET; 69 brs.

Société Générale, SA: Tour Société Générale, 92972 Paris La Défense; tel. 1-42-14-90-00; telex 210944; fax 1-40-98-20-99; f. 1864; cap. 18,997m., res 34,296m., dep. 1,418,016m. (Dec. 1996); Chair. MARC VIÉNOT; CEO DANIEL BOUTON; 2,000 brs.

Société Générale Alsacienne de Banque (SOGENAL): 8 rue du Dôme, 67003 Strasbourg Cédex; tel. 3-88-77-66-55; telex 870720; fax 3-88-77-60-09; f. 1881; cap. 376.2m., res 2,648.9m., dep. 67,485.3m. (Dec. 1996); Chair., Man. Dir HENRI LASSALLE; 110 brs.

Société Marseillaise de Crédit, SA: 75 rue Paradis, 13006 Marseille; tel. 4-91-13-33-33; telex 430232; fax 4-91-53-23-41; f. 1865; nationalized 1982; 100% state-owned, but scheduled for privatization; cap. 560.0m., res 259.2m., dep. 20,901.9m. (Dec. 1996); Chair., PATRICK CAREIL; CEO GENEVIÈVE GÓMEZ; 165 brs.

Société Nancéienne Varin-Bernier (SNVB): 4 place André Maginot, 54000 Nancy; tel. 3-83-34-50-00; telex 960205; fax 3-83-34-50-99; f. 1881; cap. 380.0m., res 797.7m., dep. 29,180.6m. (Dec. 1996); Chair. PHILIPPE VIDAL; Gen. Man. MICHEL MICHENKO; 138 brs.

Union de Banques à Paris, SA: 17–19 place Etienne Pernet, 75738 Paris Cédex 15; tel. 1-45-30-44-44; telex 206771; fax 1-45-30-44-77; f. 1935; cap. 331.3m., res 0.01m., dep. 8,724.3m. (Dec. 1996); Chair. and CEO RAYMOND BERT; 51 brs.

Union de Banques Arabes et Françaises (UBAF): 190 ave Charles de Gaulle, 92523 Neuilly Cédex; tel. 1-46-40-61-01; telex 610334; fax 1-47-38-13-88; f. 1970; cap. 1,492.0m., res 156.3m., dep. 14,190.8m. (Dec. 1996); Chair. Supervisory Bd MOHAMED SEQAT; Chair. Management Bd GUY DE JACQUELOT DU BOISROUVRAY.

Union Européenne de CIC: 4 rue Gaillon, BP 89, 75107 Paris Cédex 02; tel. 1-42-66-70-00; telex 210942; fax 1-42-66-78-90; f. 1990 by merger; cap. 6,626m., res 7,638m., dep. 507,176m. (Dec. 1996); Chair. PHILIPPE PONTET; CEO JEAN-JACQUES TAMBURINI; 1,318 brs.

Union Française de Banques (UFB LOCABAIL): 14 rue Louis Blériot, BP 229, 92503 Paris Cédex; tel. 1-41-42-60-60; telex 200015; fax 1-41-42-77-21; f. 1950; cap. and res 3,168m., dep. 24,545m. (Dec. 1996); Chair. FRANÇOIS DAMBRINE; Man. Dir JACQUES MALLET; 60 brs.

Via Banque: 10 rue Volney, BP 27, 75002 Paris; tel. 1-49-26-26-26; telex 220711; fax 1-49-26-29-99; f. 1974; cap. 533.2m., res 1,361.1m., dep. 12,798.0m. (Dec. 1996); Chair. ANDRÉ LAUNOIS; Gen. Man. ROLAND DE MONTLIVAULT.

Supervisory Body

Association Française des Etablissements de Crédit (AFEC): 36 rue Taitbout, 75009 Paris; tel. 1-48-24-34-34; fax 1-48-24-13-31; f. 1983; advises Government on monetary and credit policy and supervises the banking system; Pres. MICHEL FREYCHE; Gen. Man. ROBERT PELLETIER.

Banking Association

Association Française des Banques: 18 rue La Fayette, 75440 Paris Cédex 09; tel. 1-48-00-52-52; telex 660282; fax 1-42-46-76-40; f. 1941; 430 mems; Chair. MICHEL FREYCHE; Man. Dir PATRICE CAHART.

STOCK EXCHANGES

The Paris Stock Exchange (Bourse) was established in 1725. There are provincial exchanges at Bordeaux, Lille, Lyon, Marseille, Nancy and Nantes. During the 1980s the Paris Bourse underwent extensive changes and deregulation. Floor-based transactions were replaced by a nationwide electronic market, and a fully computerized clearing and settlement system, called Relit, was installed. The reforms also eliminated the obstacles that had previously kept brokerage business separate from other financial activities, and allowed member firms to open their capital to banks, insurance companies and other financial institutions. The Marché des Options Négociables de Paris (MONEP) opened in 1987, and forms part of the Paris Bourse, offering stock and index options. The Marché à Terme International de France (MATIF), founded in 1986, is the financial and commodities futures exchange and is independent of the Paris Bourse.

Société des Bourses Françaises (SBF)—Bourse de Paris: 39 rue Cambon, 75001 Paris; tel. 1-49-27-10-00; fax 1-49-27-14-33; Chair. JEAN-FRANÇOIS THÉODORE.

Stock Exchange Associations

Commission des Opérations de Bourse (COB): Tour Mirabeau, 39–43 quai André Citroën, 75015 Paris; tel. 1-40-58-65-65; internet http://www.cob.fr; f. 1967; 200 mems; Chair. MICHEL PRADA; CEO GÉRARD RAMEUX.

Fédération Nationale des Associations de Clubs d'Investissement: 39 rue Cambon, 75001 Paris; tel. 1-42-60-12-47; fax 1-42-60-10-14; f. 1961; advocates self-regulation, closer collaboration and responsible conduct in the securities industry.

INSURANCE

In 1995 there were some 577 insurance companies, including 140 offering life insurance; a list is given below of some of the more important companies.

Allianz Via Assurances: 2–4 ave du Général de Gaulle, 94220 Charenton le Pont; tel. 1-46-76-76-76; telex 262521; fax 1-46-76-76-13; part of Allianz group; Chair. ROBERTO GAVAZZI; Dirs-Gen. GÉRARD BOUCHER, PIERRE MARQUET.

Assurances Générales de France (AGF): 87 rue de Richelieu, 75060 Paris Cédex 02; tel. 1-44-86-20-00; telex 210697; fax 1-44-86-21-34; f. 1968 by merger; privatized in 1996; insurance and reinsurance; cap. 407m.; Chair. ANTOINE JEANCOURT-GALIGNANI;Man. Dirs JEAN DANIEL LE FRANC,YVES MANSION; JEAN-FRANÇOIS DEBROIS.

AXA/UAP: 23 ave de Matignon, 75008 Paris; tel. 1-40-75-57-59; fax 1-40-75-59-34; f. 1996 by merger of Groupe AXA and Union des Assurances de Paris; Chair. CLAUDE BÉBÉAR; Gen. Man. CLAUDE TENDIL.

AZUR Assurances: 7 ave Marcel Proust, 28032 Chartres Cédex; tel. 2-37-28-82-28; telex 760511; f. 1819; Chair. CHRISTIAN SASTRE.

Caisse Industrielle d'Assurance Mutuelle (CIAM): 95 rue d'Amsterdam, 75208 Paris Cédex 08; tel. 1-49-95-20-20; fax 1-49-95-20-00; f. 1891; Chair. ROBERT CAPITAIN; Gen. Man. HENRI DORON.

CNP Assurances: 4 place Raoul Dautry, 75015 Paris; tel. 1-42-18-88-88; fax 1-42-18-86-55; f. 1992 (fmrly public-sector co Caisse National de Prévoyance); 42.5% state-owned; 35% of state's shares to be sold in 1997; life insurance; Chair. PIERRE DARNIS.

Commercial Union France: 52 rue de la Victoire, 75009 Paris; tel. 1-42-80-75-75; fax 1-45-26-63-54; f. 1994; previously Groupe Victoire; Chair. BERNARD POTTIER.

La Concorde: 5 rue de Londres, 75456 Paris Cédex 09; tel. 1-55-32-30-00; telex 650734; fax 1-48-74-54-69; f. 1905; Chair. MARC GARNIER.

La France IARD: 7–9 blvd Haussmann, 75309 Paris Cédex 09; tel. 1-48-00-80-00; telex 660272; fax 1-42-46-17-04; f. 1837; Chair. THÉODORE GICQUEL.

Garantie Mutuelle des Fonctionnaires: 76 rue de Prony, 75857 Paris Cédex 17; tel. 1-47-54-10-10; telex 640377; fax 1-47-54-18-97; f. 1934; Chair. YVES CAZAUX; Gen. Man. CHRISTIAN SASTRE.

Groupe des Assurances Nationales (GAN): 2 rue Pillet Will, 75448 Paris Cédex 09; tel. 1-42-47-50-00; telex 280006; fax 1-42-47-67-66; f. 1820 (fire), 1830 (life), 1865 (accident), nationalized 1946, reorganized 1968; scheduled for privatization in early 1998; Chair. DIDIER PFEIFFER; Dir-Gen. THIERRY AULAGNON.

Groupement Français d'Assurances (GFA): 38 rue de Châteaudun, 75439 Paris Cédex 09; tel. 1-40-82-48-48; telex 660418; Chair. HERMANN VON TRESKOW; Dir-Gen. JEAN-MARC JACQUET.

Mutuelle Centrale d'Assurances (MCA): 65 rue de Monceau, 75008 Paris; tel. 1-49-95-79-79; fax 1-40-16-43-21; Chair. WIM JEAN DE ZEEUW.

Mutuelles du Mans Assurances: 19–21 rue Chanzy, 72030 Le Mans Cédex 9; tel. 2-43-41-72-72; telex 720764; fax 2-43-41-72-26; life and general insurance; f. 1828; Chair. JEAN CLAUDE JOLAIN; Gen. Man. RAYMOND FEKIK.

PFA Assurances: 92076 Paris La Défense Cédex 43; tel. 1-42-91-10-10; telex 615030; fax 1-42-91-12-20; Chair. JEAN-PHILIPPE THIERRY; Gen. Mans JEAN-FRANÇOIS LEMOUX, PATRICK THOUROT.

Société Anonyme Française de Réassurances (SAFR): 153 blvd de Courcelles, 75017 Paris Cédex 17; tel. 1-42-27-86-82; telex 650493; reinsurance; Chair. HERVÉ CACHIN.

Société Commerciale de Réassurance (SCOR): Immeuble SCOR, 1 ave du Président Wilson, 92074 Paris la Défense Cédex 09; tel. 1-46-98-70-00; telex 614151; fax 1-47-67-04-09; f. 1969; reinsurance; Chair. JACQUES BLONDEAU.

Société de Réassurance des Assurances Mutuelles Agricoles (SOREMA): 20 rue Washington, 75008 Paris; tel. 1-40-74-66-00; telex 640774; fax 1-45-63-25-47; f. 1978; reinsurance; Chair. and CEO J. BALIGAND; Man. Dir J. P. LASSERRE.

Insurance Associations

Fédération Française des Courtiers d'Assurances et de Réassurances: 91 rue Saint Lazare, 75009 Paris; tel. 1-48-74-19-12; fax 1-42-82-91-10; f. 1896; Chair. FRANÇOIS LE CORNER; c. 800 mems.

Fédération Française des Sociétés d'Assurances: 26 blvd Haussmann, 75311 Paris Cédex 09; tel. 1-42-47-90-00; fax 1-42-47-93-11; f. 1937; Chair. JEAN ARVIS; Gen. Man. PATRIK WERNER; Sec.-Gen. GILLES WOLKOWITSCH.

Fédération Nationale des Syndicats d'Agents Généraux d'Assurances de France: 104 rue Jouffroy d'Abbans, 75847 Paris Cédex 17; tel. 1-44-01-18-00; fax 1-46-22-76-29; Chair. JEAN-CLAUDE LECHANOINE.

Syndicat Français des Assureurs-Conseils: 14 rue de la Grange Batelière, 75009 Paris; tel. 1-45-23-25-26; fax 1-48-00-93-01; Chair. HERVÉ DE WAZIÈRES.

Trade and Industry

GOVERNMENT AGENCIES

Centre Français du Commerce Extérieur: 10 ave d'Iéna, 75783 Paris Cédex 16; tel. 1-40-73-30-00; telex 645412; fax 1-40-73-39-79; Pres. FRANÇOIS DOUBIN; Gen. Man. JEAN-DANIEL GARDÈRE.

Conseil National du Commerce: 53 ave Montaigne, 75008 Paris; tel. 1-42-25-01-25; fax 1-45-63-21-83; Chair. J. DERMAGNE.

Syndicat Général du Commerce et de l'Industrie—Union des Chambres Syndicales de France: 163 rue Saint Honoré, 75001 Paris; tel. 1-42-60-66-83; fax 1-42-61-23-18; Pres. HENRI GERMANY.

DEVELOPMENT ORGANIZATIONS

Agence Nationale pour la Création et le Développement des Nouvelles Entreprises: 14 rue Delambre, 75682 Paris Cédex 14; tel. 1-42-18-58-58; fax 1-42-18-58-00; e-mail ance@cal.fr.

Groupe IDI: 4 rue Ancelle, 92521 Neuilly-sur-Seine: tel. 1-47-47-71-17; telex 630006; fax 1-47-47-72-06; f. 1970 as Institut de Développement Industriel; provides venture capital, takes equity shares in small and medium-sized businesses; Chair. CHRISTIAN LANGLOIS MEURINNE.

CHAMBERS OF COMMERCE

There are Chambers of Commerce in all the larger towns for all the more important commodities produced or manufactured.

Assemblée des Chambres Françaises de Commerce et d'Industrie: 45 ave d'Iéna, 75116 Paris; tel. 1-40-69-37-00; telex 610396; Pres. GÉRARD TRÉMÈGE; Man. Dir MAUD BAILLY-TURCHI.

Chambre de Commerce et d'Industrie de Paris: 27 ave de Friedland, 75382 Paris Cédex 08; tel. 1-42-89-70-00; telex 650100; fax 1-42-89-72-86; f. 1803; 273,000 mems; Chair. HUBERT FLAHAULT; Man. Dir RAYMOND-FRANÇOIS LE BRIS.

INDUSTRIAL AND TRADE ASSOCIATIONS

Assemblée Permanente des Chambres d'Agriculture (APCA): 9 ave George V, 75008 Paris; tel. 1-53-57-10-10; telex 280720; fax 1-53-57-10-05; f. 1929; Chair. JEAN FRANÇOIS HERVIEU; Gen. Sec. MAURICE RIGAUD.

Association Nationale des Industries Agro-alimentaires (ANIA): 52 rue Faubourg Saint Honoré, 75008 Paris; tel. 1-42-66-40-14; telex 641784; f. 1971; food and agricultural produce; Chair. FRANCIS LEPATRE; 43 affiliated federations.

Centre des Jeunes Dirigeants d'Entreprise (CJD): 13 rue Duroc, 75007 Paris; tel. 1-47-83-42-28; telex 200298; fax 1-42-73-32-90; f. 1938; asscn for young entrepreneurs (under 45 years of age); Pres. DIDIER LIVIO; Sec.-Gen. YVES PINAUD; 2,500 mems.

Chambre Syndicale de l'Ameublement, Négoce de Paris et de l'Ile de France: 15 rue de la Cerisaie, 75004 Paris; tel. 1-42-72-13-79; fax 1-42-72-02-36; f. 1860; furnishing; Chair. NICOLE PHILIBERT; 407 mems.

Chambre Syndicale des Céramistes et Ateliers d'Art: 62 rue d'Hauteville, 75010 Paris; tel. 1-47-70-95-83; telex 660005; fax 1-47-70-10-54; f. 1937; ceramics and arts; Chair. M. LUBRANO; 1,200 mems.

Chambre Syndicale des Constructeurs de Navires: 47 rue de Monceau, 75008 Paris; tel. 1-53-89-52-01; fax 1-53-89-52-15; shipbuilding; Chair. ALAIN GRILL; Gen. Man. FABRICE THEOBALD.

Chambre Syndicale des Industries Transformatrices de Fibres Techniques: 10 rue de la Pépinière, 75008 Paris; tel. 1-45-22-12-34; fax 1-40-08-01-99; f. 1898; asbestos; Chair. CYRIL X. LATTY; 15 mems.

Comité Central de la Laine et des Fibres Associées (Groupement Général de l'Industrie et du Commerce Lainiers Français): BP 121, 37–39 rue de Neuilly, 92113 Clichy; tel. 1-47-56-31-41; fax 1-47-37-06-20; f. 1922; manufacture of wool and associated textiles; Chair. CAMILLE AMALRIC; Vice-Chairs ALAIN DALLE, OLIVIER TOULEMONDE, CHRISTIAN DEWAVRIN; 250 mems.

Comité Central des Armateurs de France: 47 rue de Monceau, 75008 Paris; tel. 1-53-89-52-52; fax 1-53-89-52-53; f. 1903; shipping; Pres. PHILIPPE D'ORSAY; Delegate-Gen. EDOUARD BERLET; 110 mems.

Comité des Constructeurs Français d'Automobiles: 2 rue de Presbourg, 75008 Paris; tel. 1-47-23-54-05; telex 610-446; fax 1-47-23-74-73; f. 1909; motor manufacturing; Chair. RAYMOND RAVENEL; 9 mems.

Comité National des Pêches Maritimes et des Elevages Marins: 51 rue Salvador Allende, 92027 Nanterre Cédex; tel. 1-47-75-01-01; fax 1-49-00-06-02; marine fisheries.

Comité Professionnel du Pétrole: Tour Corosa, 3 rue Eugène et Armand Peugeot, BP 282, 92505 Rueil-Malmaison Cédex; tel. 1-47-16-94-60; fax 1-47-08-10-57; petroleum industry.

Commissariat à l'Energie Atomique (CEA) (Atomic Energy Commission): 31-33 rue de la Fédération, 75752 Paris Cedex 15; tel. 1-40-56-10-00; telex 200671; fax 1-40-56-25-38; f. 1945; promotes the uses of nuclear energy in science, industry and national defence; involved in production of nuclear materials; reactor development; fundamental research; innovation and transfer of technologies; military applications; bio-technologies; robotics; electronics; new materials; radiological protection and nuclear safety; Gen. Administrator PHILIPPE ROUVILLOIS; High Commissioner JEAN TEILLAC; Sec.-Gen. EMMANUEL DURET.

Confédération des Commerçants-Détaillants de France: 21 rue du Château d'Eau, 75010 Paris; tel. 1-42-08-17-15; retailers; Chair. M. FOUCAULT.

Confédération des Industries Céramiques de France: 15 ave Victor Hugo, 75116 Paris; tel. 1-45-00-18-56; fax 1-45-00-47-56; f. 1937; ceramic industry; Chair. JACQUES RUSSEIL; Man. Dir FRANÇOIS DE LA TOUR; 144 mems, 9 affiliates.

Confédération Générale des Petites et Moyennes Entreprises: 10 Terrasse Bellini, 92806 Puteaux Cédex; tel. 1-47-62-73-73; telex 630358; fax 1-47-73-08-86; f. 1945; small and medium-sized enterprises; Chair. LUCIEN REBUFFEL; 3,500 affiliated asscns.

Fédération des Chambres Syndicales de l'Industrie du Verre: 3 rue la Boétie, 75008 Paris; tel. 1-42-65-60-02; f. 1874; glass industry; Chair. JEAN-NOËL CHEVREAU.

Fédération des Chambres Syndicales des Minerais, Minéraux Industriels et Métaux non-Ferreux: 30 ave de Messine, 75008 Paris; tel. 1-45-63-02-66; fax 1-45-63-61-54; f. 1945; minerals and non-ferrous metals; Chair. BERNARD PACHE; Delegate-Gen. G. JOURDAN; 16 affiliated syndicates.

Fédération des Exportateurs des Vins et Spiritueux de France: 95 rue de Monceau, 75008 Paris; tel. 1-45-22-75-73; fax 1-45-22-94-16; f. 1921; exporters of wines and spirits; Pres. PHILIPPE PASCAL; Delegate-Gen. LOUIS RÉGIS AFFRE; 450 mems.

Fédération Française de l'Acier: Immeuble Pacific, 11-13 Cours Valmy, 92070 Paris La Défense; tel. 1-41-25-58-00; fax 1-41-25-59-8; e-mail ffa@ffa.fr; f. 1945; steel-making; Chair. FRANCIS MER; Delegate-Gen. J.-C. GEORGES FRANÇOIS.

Fédération Française de la Bijouterie, Joaillerie, Orfèvrerie du Cadeau, Diamants, Pierres et Perles et Activités qui s'y

rattachent (BJOC): 58 rue du Louvre, 75002 Paris; tel. 1-42-33-61-33; fax 1-40-26-29-51; jewellery, gifts and tableware; Chair. DIDIER ROUX; 1,200 mems.

Fédération Française de l'Industrie Cotonnière: BP 121, 37–39 rue de Neuilly, 92113 Clichy Cédex; tel. 1-47-56-30-40; fax 1-47-56-30-49; f. 1902; cotton manufacturing; Chair. YVES DUBIEF; Vice-Chair. DENIS CHAIGNE; mems 71 (spinning), 153 (weaving).

Fédération Française du Négoce de Bois d'Oeuvre et Produits Dérivés: 251 blvd Pereire, 75852 Paris Cédex 17; tel. 1-45-72-55-50; fax 1-45-72-55-56; timber trade; Pres. ANDRÉ TALON; Dir-Gen. LIONEL THOMAS D'ANNEBAULT.

Fédération Française de la Tannerie-Mégisserie: 122 rue de Provence, 75008 Paris; tel. 1-45-22-96-45; telex 290785; fax 1-42-93-37-44; f. 1885; leather industry; 180 mems.

Fédération de l'Imprimerie et de la Communication Graphique: 68 blvd Saint Marcel, 75005 Paris; tel. 1-44-08-64-46; fax 1-43-36-09-51; printing; Pres. JACQUES SCHOR.

Fédération des Industries de la Parfumerie (France): 8 place du Général Catroux, 75017 Paris; tel. 1-44-15-83-83; telex 640583; fax 1-42-12-01-37; makers of perfume, cosmetics and toiletries.

Fédération des Industries Electriques et Electroniques (FIEE): 11–17 rue Hamelin, 75783 Paris Cédex 16; tel. 1-45-05-70-70; telex 611045; fax 1-45-53-03-93; f. 1925; electrical and electronics industries; Chair. HENRI STARCK; Delegate-Gen. JEAN-CLAUDE KARPELÈS; c. 1,000 mems.

Fédération des Industries Mécaniques: 39–41 rue Louis Blanc, 92400 Courbevoie; tel. 1-47-17-60-00; telex 616382; fax 1-47-17-64-99; e-mail fim@ceus.internet.fr; f. 1840; mechanical and metal-working; Chair. MARTINE CLÉMENT; Man. Dir MARC BAY.

Fédération des Industries Nautiques: Port de la Bourdonnais, 75007 Paris; tel. 1-45-55-10-49; telex 203963; fax 1-47-53-94-75; f. 1965; pleasure-boating; Chair. MICHEL RICHARD; Sec.-Gen. PIERRE-EDOUARD DE BOIGNE; 700 mems.

Fédération Nationale du Bâtiment: 33 ave Kléber, 75784 Paris Cédex 16; tel. 1-40-69-51-00; e-mail fnbbox@fnb.fr; f. 1906; building trade; Chair. ALAIN SIONNEAU; Dir-Gen. BERTRAND SABLIER; 55,000 mems.

Fédération Nationale du Bois: 1 place André Malraux, 75001 Paris; tel. 1-42-60-30-27; fax 1-42-60-58-94; timber and wood products; Chair. R. LESBATS; Dir PIERRE VERNERET; 2,000 mems.

Fédération Nationale de l'Industrie Hôtelière (FNIH): 22 rue d'Anjou, 75008 Paris; tel. 1-44-94-19-94; telex 640033; fax 1-42-65-16-21; Chair. JACQUES THÉ.

Fédération Nationale de l'Industrie Laitière: 140 blvd Haussmann, 75008 Paris; tel. 1-45-62-96-60; dairy products.

Fédération Nationale des Industries Électrométallurgiques, Électrochimiques et Connexes: 30 ave de Messine, 75008 Paris; tel. 1-45-61-06-63; fax 1-45-63-61-54; Chair. JACQUES GANI.

Fédération Nationale de la Musique: 62 rue Blanche, 75009 Paris; tel. 1-48-74-09-29; fax 1-42-81-19-87; f. 1964; includes Chambre Syndicale de la Facture Instrumentale, Syndicat National de l'Edition Phonographique and other groups; musical instruments, publications and recordings; Chair. PIERRE HENRY; Sec.-Gen. FRANÇOIS WELLEBROUCK.

Groupe Intersyndical de l'Industrie Nucléaire (GIIN): 15 rue Beaujon, 75008 Paris; tel. 1-42-67-30-68; telex 280900; f. 1959; aims to promote the interests of the French nuclear industry; over 200 member firms.

Groupement des Industries Françaises Aéronautiques et Spatiales (GIFAS): 4 rue Galilée, 75782 Paris Cédex 16; tel. 1-44-43-17-52; telex 645615; fax 1-40-70-91-41; aerospace industry; Pres. SERGE DASSAULT; Delegate-Gen. BERNARD NICOLAS.

Syndicat Général des Cuirs et Peaux Bruts: Bourse de Commerce, 2 rue de Viarmes, 75040 Paris Cédex 01; tel. 1-45-08-08-54; fax 1-40-39-97-31; f. 1977; untreated leather and hides; Chair. PIERRE DUBOIS; 60 mems.

Syndicat Général des Fabricants d'Huile et de Tourteaux de France: 118 ave Achille Peretti, 92200 Neuilly-sur-Seine; tel. 1-46-37-22-06; fax 1-46-37-15-60; f. 1928; edible oils; Pres. CHRISTIAN GODDE; Sec.-Gen. JEAN-CLAUDE BARSACQ.

Syndicat Général des Fabricants et Transformateurs de Pâtes, Papiers et Cartons de France: 154 blvd Haussmann, 75008 Paris; tel. 1-53-89-25-25; fax 1-53-89-25-26; f. 1864; paper, cardboard and cellulose; Chair. JEAN DERVAUX; Gen. Man. JEAN-FRANÇOIS HEMON-LAURENS; 500 firms affiliated.

Syndicat Général des Fondeurs de France: 45 rue Louis Blanc, 92400 Courbevoie; tel. 1-43-34-76-30; telex 640623; fax 1-43-34-76-31; e-mail sgff@wanadoo.fr; f. 1897; metal casting; Chair. FRANÇOIS DELACHAUX; Dir OLIVIER DUCRU.

Syndicat de l'Imprimerie et de la Communicatiòn Graphique de l'Ile-de-France: 8 rue de Berri, 75008 Paris; tel. 1-42-25-04-35; fax 1-42-25-04-32; f. 1991; printers' asscn; 700 mems; Chair. JOËL CARDINAL.

Syndicat National de l'Industrie Pharmaceutique (CSNIP): 88 rue de la Faisanderie, 75782 Paris Cédex 16; tel. 1-45-03-88-88; fax 1-45-04-47-71; pharmaceuticals; Chair. BERNARD MESURÉ.

Union des Armateurs à la Pêche de France: 59 rue des Mathurins, 75008 Paris; tel. 1-42-66-32-60; fax 1-47-42-91-12; f. 1945; fishing-vessels; Chair. JEAN-MARC LEGARREC; Vice-Pres Delegate A. PARRES.

Union des Fabricants de Porcelaine de Limoges: 7 bis rue du Général Cérez, 87000 Limoges; tel. 5-55-77-29-18; fax 5-55-77-36-81; porcelain manufacturing; Chair. MICHEL BERNARDAUD; Sec.-Gen. MARIE-THÉRÈSE PASQUET.

Union des Industries Chimiques: Cédex 5, 92080 Paris La Défense; tel. 1-47-78-50-00; f. 1860; chemical industry; Chair. J.-C. ACHILLE; Dir-Gen. C. MARTIN; 58 affiliated unions.

Union des Industries Métallurgiques et Minières: 56 ave de Wagram, 75017 Paris; tel. 1-40-54-20-20; fax 1-47-66-22-74; metallurgy and mining; Chair. ARNAUD LEENHARDT.

Union des Industries Textiles (Production): BP 249, 37 rue de Neuilly, 92113 Clichy Cédex; tel. 1-47-56-31-21; telex 615280; fax 1-47-30-25-28; f. 1901; Chair. GEORGES JOLLÈS; 2,500 mems.

Union Parisienne des Syndicats Patronaux de l'Imprimerie: 8 rue de Berri, 75008 Paris; tel. 1-42-25-04-35; fax 1-42-25-04-32; f. 1923; Chair. JACQUES NOULET.

EMPLOYERS' ORGANIZATIONS

Association des Grandes Entreprises Françaises (AGREF): 63 rue la Boétie, 75008 Paris; tel. 1-43-59-65-35; fax 1-43-59-81-17.

Centre des Jeunes Dirigeants d'Entreprise (CJD): 13 rue Duroc, 75007 Paris; tel. 1-47-83-42-28; fax 1-42-73-32-90.

Centre Français du Patronat Chrétien (CFPC): 25 rue Hamelin, 75016 Paris; tel. 1-45-53-31-59; fax 1-47-27-43-32; asscn of Christian employers.

Confédération Générale des Petites et Moyennes Entreprises (CGPME): 10 terrasse Bellini, 92806 Puteaux Cédex; tel. 1-47-62-73-73; fax 1-47-73-08-86; small and medium-sized cos.

Conseil National du Patronat Français (CNPF): 31 ave Pierre Ier de Serbie, 75784 Paris Cédex 16; tel. 1-40-69-44-44; fax 1-47-23-47-32; f. 1946; an employers' organization grouping 1.5m. companies from all sectors of activity; Pres. ERNEST-ANTOINE SEILLIÈRE DE LABORDE; Exec. Vice-Pres PIERRE BELLON, ARNAUD LEENHARDT, BRUNO LACROIX, MARTINE CLEMENT, DENIS KESSLER.

UTILITIES

Electricity

Alcatel Alsthom: 54 rue la Boétie, 75382 Paris Cedex 08; tel. 1-40-76-10-10; telex 651953; fax 1-40-76-14-00; f. 1898; energy, nuclear energy and electrical contracting (also involved in industrial process control, telecommunications and business systems, cables and batteries, transportation); 213,000 employees; Chair. PIERRE SUARD.

Charbonnages de France (CdF): Tour Albert 1er, 65 ave de Colmar, 92507 Rueil-Malmaison Cédex; tel. 1-47-52-35-00; telex 631450; fax 1-47-51-31-63; established under the Nationalization Act of 1946; responsible for coal mining, sales and research in metropolitan France; there are also engineering and informatics divisions; 15,010 employees; Chair. and Dir-Gen. PHILIPPE DE LADOUCETTE.

Electricité de France: 2 rue Louis Murat, 75008 Paris; tel. 1-40-42-53-33; telex 648676; established under the Electricity and Gas Industry Nationalization Act of 1946; responsible for generating and supplying electricity for distribution to consumers in metropolitan France; 120,000 employees; Chair. EDMOND ALPHANDÉRY; Man. Dir PIERRE DAURÈS.

Fédération Nationale des Producteurs Indépendants d'Electricité (EAF): 9 blvd Lannés, 75116 Paris; tel. 1-45-04-08-21; fax 1-45-04-51-99; association of producers and distributors of electricity; 800 mems; Pres. PIERRE DUMONS; Delegate-Gen. ANNE MARY ROUSSEL.

Gas

Gaz de France: 23 rue Philibert Delorme, 75840 Paris Cédex 17; tel. 1-47-54-20-20; telex 650483; fax 1-47-54-21-87; established under the Electricity and Gas Industry Nationalization Act of 1946; responsible for distribution of gas in metropolitan France; about 10% of gas was produced in France (Aquitaine) in 1993 and the rest imported from Algeria, the Netherlands, Norway and the territory constituting the former USSR; Chair. PIERRE GADONNEIX; Dir-Gen. JACQUES MAIRE.

Water

Compagnie Générale des Eaux: 52 rue d'Anjou, 75008 Paris; Chair. JEAN-MARIE MESSIER.

TRADE UNIONS

In late 1995 it was estimated that some 8% of the French labour force belonged to trade unions (compared with 18% in 1980).

There are three major trade union organizations:

Confédération Générale du Travail (CGT): Complexe Immobilier Intersyndical CGT, 263 rue de Paris, 93516 Montreuil Cédex; tel. 1-48-18-80-00; telex 235069; fax 1-49-88-18-57; e-mail internat@cgt.fr; f. 1895; National Congress is held every three years; Sec.-Gen. LOUIS VIANNET; 640,000 mems.

Affiliated unions:

Agroalimentaire et Forestière (FNAF): 263 rue de Paris, 93100 Montreuil Cédex; Sec.-Gen. FREDDY HUCK.

Bois Ameublement (Woodworkers): 263 rue de Paris, Case 414, 93514 Montreuil Cédex; tel. 1-48-18-81-61; fax 1-48-51-59-91; Sec.-Gen. HENRI SANCHEZ.

Cheminots (Railway Workers): 263 rue de Paris, 93100 Montreuil Cédex; Sec.-Gen. BERNARD THIBAULT.

Construction (Building): 263 rue de Paris, 93100 Montreuil Cédex; tel. 1-48-18-81-60; fax 1-48-59-10-37; Sec.-Gen. ROBERT BRUN.

Education, Recherche et Culture: 263 rue de Paris, Case 544, 93515 Montreuil Cédex; tel. 1-48-18-82-44; fax 1-49-88-07-43; Sec.-Gen. CHRISTIAN DUBOT.

Enseignements Techniques et Professionnels (Technical and Professional Teachers): 263 rue de Paris, 93100 Montreuil Cédex; Sec.-Gen. MICHÈLE BARACAT.

Equipement et l'Environnement: 263 rue de Paris, Case 543, 93515 Montreuil Cédex; tel. 1-48-18-82-81; fax 1-48-51-62-50; Sec.-Gen. DENIS GLASSON.

Fédération Nationale de l'Energie: 16 rue de Candale, 93507 Pantin Cédex; tel. 1-49-91-86-00; fax 1-49-91-87-40; f. 1905; Sec.-Gen. DENIS COHEN; 65,000 mems.

Finances: 263 rue de Paris, 93100 Montreuil Cédex; tel. 1-48-18-82-21; Sec.-Gen. PIERRETTE CROSEMARIE.

Fonctionnaires (Civil Servants): 263 rue de Paris, 93515 Montreuil Cédex; tel. 1-48-18-82-31; telex 218912; groups National Education, Finance, Technical and Administrative, Civil Servants, Police, etc.; mems about 70 national unions covered by six federations; Sec.-Gen. BERNARD LHUBERT.

Industries Chimiques (Chemical Industries): 263 rue de Paris, Case 429, 93514 Montreuil Cédex; tel. 1-48-18-80-36; fax 1-48-18-80-35; Sec.-Gen. GEORGES HERVO.

Industries du Livre du Papier et de la Communication (FILPAC) (Printing and Paper Products): 263 rue de Paris, Case 426, 93514 Montreuil Cédex; tel. 1-48-18-80-24; Sec.-Gen. MICHEL MULLER.

Ingénieurs, Cadres et Techniciens (Engineers, Managerial Staff and Technicians): 263 rue de Paris, Case 408, 93514 Montreuil Cédex; tel. 1-48-18-81-25; fax 1-48-51-64-57; f. 1963; Sec.-Gen. GÉRARD DELAHAYE.

Journalistes: 263 rue de Paris, Case 570, 93514 Montreuil Cédex; tel. 1-48-18-81-78; fax 1-48-51-58-08; Sec.-Gen. MICHEL DIARD.

Marine Marchande (Merchant Marine): Fédération des Officiers CGT, Cercle Franklin, Cours de la République, 76600 Le Havre; tel. 2-35-25-04-81; fax 2-35-24-23-77; Sec.-Gen. CHARLES NARELLI.

Fédération des Travailleurs de la Métallurgie (Metalworkers): 263 rue de Paris, 93514 Montreuil Cédex; tel. 1-48-18-21-02; fax 1-48-59-80-66; f. 1891; Sec.-Gen. JEAN-LOUIS FOURNIER.

Organismes Sociaux: 263 rue de Paris, 93100 Montreuil Cédex; tel. 1-48-18-83-56; fax 1-48-59-24-75; Sec.-Gen. PHILIPPE HOURCADE.

Personnels du Commerce, de la Distribution et des Services: 263 rue de Paris, Case 425, 93514 Montreuil Cédex; tel. 1-48-18-83-11; Sec.-Gen. JACQUELINE GARCIA.

Police: 263 rue de Paris, Case 550, 93514 Montreuil Cédex; tel. 1-48-18-81-85; fax 1-48-59-30-56; f. 1906; Sec.-Gen. PASCAL MARTINI.

Ports et Docks: 263 rue de Paris, 93100 Montreuil Cédex; Sec.-Gen. DANIEL LEFÈVRE.

Postes et Télécommunications: 263 rue de Paris, 93100 Montreuil Cédex; Sec.-Gen. MARYSE DUMAS.

Santé, Action Sociale, CGT (Health and Social Services): 263 rue de Montreuil, Case 538, 93515 Montreuil Cédex; tel. 1-48-18-20-70; fax 1-48-18-80-93; f. 1907; Sec.-Gen. JEAN-LUC GIBELIN.

Secteurs Financiers: 263 rue de Paris, 93515 Montreuil Cédex; tel. 1-48-18-83-40; fax 1-49-88-16-36; Sec.-Gen. JEAN DOMINIQUE SIMONPOLI.

Services Publics (Community Services): 263 rue de Paris, Case 547, 93515 Montreuil Cédex; tel. 1-48-18-83-74; fax 1-48-51-98-20; Sec.-Gen. VINCENT DEBEIR.

Sous-sol (Miners): 263 rue de Paris, Case 535, 93515 Montreuil Cédex; Sec.-Gen. JACKY BERNARD.

Spectacle, Audio-Visuel et Action Culturelle (Theatre, Media and Culture): 14-16 rue des Lilas, 75019 Paris; tel. 1-48-03-87-60; Sec.-Gen. JEAN VOIRIN.

Syndicats Maritimes (Seamen): 263 rue de Paris, Case 420, 93514 Montreuil Cédex; tel. 1-48-18-84-21; fax 1-48-51-59-21; Sec.-Gen. ROBERT BILLIEN.

Tabac et Allumettes (Tobacco and Matches): 263 rue de Paris, 93100 Montreuil Cédex; Sec.-Gen. BERTRAND PAGE.

THC (Textiles): 263 rue de Paris, 93100 Montreuil Cédex; Sec.-Gen. CHRISTIAN LAROSE.

Transports: 263 rue de Paris, 93100 Montreuil Cédex; Sec.-Gen. ALAIN RENAULT.

Travailleurs de l'Etat (State Employees): 263 rue de Paris, 93100 Montreuil Cédex; Sec.-Gen. JEAN LOUIS NAUDET.

Verre et Céramique (Glassworkers and Ceramics): 263 rue de Paris, Case 417, 93514 Montreuil Cédex; tel. 1-48-18-80-13; fax 1-48-18-80-11; Sec.-Gen. JACQUES BEAUVOIR.

Voyageurs-Représentants, Cadres et Techniciens de la Vente (Commercial Travellers): Bourse du Travail, 3 rue du Château d'eau, 75010 Paris; tel. 1-44-84-50-00; Sec.-Gen. ALAIN SERRE.

Force Ouvrière: 141 ave du Maine, 75680 Paris Cédex 14; tel. 1-40-52-82-00; telex 203405; fax 1-40-52-82-02; f. 1947 by breakaway from the more left-wing CGT (above); Force Ouvrière is a member of ICFTU and of the European Trade Union Confederation; Sec.-Gen. MARC BLONDEL; c. 1m. mems.

Affiliated federations:

Action Sociale: 7 passage Tenaille, 75680 Paris Cédex 14; tel. 1-40-52-85-80; fax 1-40-52-85-79; Sec. MICHEL PINAUD.

Administration Générale de l'État: 46 rue des Petites Ecuries, 75010 Paris; tel. 1-42-46-40-19; fax 1-42-46-19-57; f. 1948; Sec.-Gen. FRANCIS LAMARQUE; 20,000 mems.

Agriculture, Alimentation et Tabacs (Agriculture, Food and Tobacco): 7 passage Tenaille, 75680 Paris Cédex 14; tel. 1-40-52-85-10; fax 1-40-52-85-12; Sec.-Gen. GÉRARD FOSSÉ.

Bâtiment, Travaux Publics, Bois, Céramique, Papier Carton et Matériaux de Construction (Building, Public Works, Wood, Ceramics, Paper, Cardboard and Building Materials): 170 ave Parmentier, 75010 Paris; tel. 1-42-01-30-00; fax 1-42-39-50-44; Sec.-Gen. ALAIN EMILE.

Union des Cadres et Ingénieurs (UCI) (Engineers): 2 rue de la Michodière, 75002 Paris; tel. 1-47-42-39-69; fax 1-47-42-03-53; Sec.-Gen. HUBERT BOUCHET.

Cheminots (Railway Workers): 60 rue Vergniaud, 75640 Paris Cédex 13; tel. 1-45-80-22-98; fax 1-45-88-25-49; f. 1948; Sec.-Gen. JEAN-JACQUES CARMENTRAN; 14,000 mems.

Coiffeurs, Esthétique et Parfumerie (Hairdressers, Beauticians and Perfumery): 3 rue de la Croix Blanche, 18350 Nerondes; tel. 1-48-74-89-32; fax 1-48-74-81-26; Sec.-Gen. MICHEL BOURLON.

Cuirs, Textiles, Habillement (Leather, Textiles and Clothing): 7 passage Tenaille, 75680 Paris Cédex 14; tel. 1-40-52-83-00; fax 1-40-52-82-99; Sec.-Gen. JEAN-CLAUDE HUMEZ.

Défense, Industries de l'Armement et Secteurs Assimilés (Defence, Arms Manufacture and Related Industries): 46 rue des Petites Ecuries, 75010 Paris; tel. 1-42-46-00-05; fax 1-45-23-12-89; Sec.-Gen. ALBERT SPARFEL.

Employés et Cadres (Managerial Staff): 28 rue des Petits Hôtels, 75010 Paris; tel. 1-48-01-91-91; fax 1-48-01-91-92; Sec.-Gen. ROSE BOUTARIC.

Energie Electrique et Gaz (Gas and Electricity): 60 rue Vergniaud, 75640 Paris Cédex 13; tel. 1-44-16-86-20; fax 1-44-16-86-32; f. 1947; Sec.-Gen. GABRIEL GAUDY; 22,000 mems.

Enseignement, Culture et Formation Professionnelle (Teaching, Culture and Professional Training): 7 passage Tenaille, 75680 Paris Cédex 14; tel. 1-40-52-85-30; fax 1-40-52-85-35; Sec.-Gen. FRANÇOIS CHAINTRON; 50,000 mems.

Equipement, Transports et Services (Transport and Public Works): 46 rue des Petites Ecuries, 75010 Paris; tel. 1-42-46-36-63; telex 643115; fax 1-48-24-38-32; f. 1932; Sec.-Gen. YVES VEYRIER; 50,000 mems.

Finances: 46 rue des Petites Ecuries, 75010 Paris; tel. 1-42-46-75-20; fax 1-47-70-23-92; Sec. JACKY LESUEUR.

Fonctionnaires (Civil Servants): 46 rue des Petites Ecuries, 75010 Paris; tel. 1-44-83-65-55; fax 1-42-46-97-80; Sec. ROLAND GAILLARD.

Industries Chimiques (Chemical Industries): 60 rue Vergniaud, 75640 Paris Cédex 13; tel. 1-45-80-14-90; fax 1-45-80-08-03; f. 1948; Sec.-Gen. FRANÇOIS GRANDAZZI.

Livre (Printing Trades): 7 passage Tenaille, 75680 Paris Cédex 14; tel. 1-40-52-85-00; fax 1-40-52-85-01; Sec.-Gen. MAURICE ROSSAT.

Métaux (Metals): 9 rue Baudouin, 75013 Paris; tel. 1-45-82-01-00; fax 1-45-83-78-87; Sec.-Gen. MICHEL HUC.

Mineurs, Miniers et Similaires (Mine Workers): 7 passage Tenaille, 75680 Paris Cédex 14; tel. 1-40-52-85-50; fax 1-40-52-85-48; Sec.-Gen. ROLAND HOUP.

Personnels des Services des Départements et Régions (Local Public Services): 46 rue des Petites Ecuries, 75010 Paris; tel. 1-42-46-50-52; fax 1-47-70-26-06; Sec.-Gen. MICHÈLE SIMONNIN.

Pharmacie (Pharmacists): 7 passage Tenaille, 75680 Paris Cédex 14; tel. 1-40-52-85-60; fax 1-40-52-85-61; Sec.-Gen. BERNARD DEVY.

Police: 6 rue Albert Bayet, 75013 Paris; tel. 1-45-82-28-08; fax 1-45-82-64-24; f. 1948; Sec. CHRISTIAN THURIES; 11,000 mems.

Postes et Télécommunications (Posts and Telecommunications): 60 rue Vergniaud, 75640 Paris Cédex 13; tel. 1-40-78-31-50; telex 200644; fax 1-40-78-30-58; f. 1947; Sec.-Gen. JACQUES LEMERCIER.

Services Publics et de Santé (Health and Public Services): 153–155 rue de Rome, 75017 Paris; tel. 1-44-01-06-00; fax 1-42-27-21-40; f. 1947; Sec.-Gen. CAMILLE ORDRONNEAU; 130,000 mems.

Syndicats des Arts des Spectacles de l'Audiovisuel et de la Presse et de la Communication F.O. (FASAPFO) (Theatre and Cinema Performers, Press and Broadcasting): 2 rue de la Michodière, 75002 Paris; tel. 1-47-42-35-86; fax 1-47-42-39-45; Sec.-Gen. BERTRAND BLANC.

Transports: 7 passage Tenaille, 75680 Paris Cédex 14; tel. 1-40-52-85-45; fax 1-40-52-85-09; Sec. ROGER POLETTI.

Voyageurs-Représentants-Placiers (Commercial Travellers): 6–8 rue Albert-Bayet, 75015 Paris; tel. 1-45-82-28-28; fax 1-45-70-93-69; f. 1930; Sec. MICHEL BOUTELEUX.

Confédération Française Démocratique du Travail (CFDT): 4 blvd de la Villette, 75955 Paris Cédex 19; tel. 1-42-03-80-00; telex 240832; fax 1-42-03-81-44; e-mail conf.internationale@cfdt.fr; constituted in 1919 as Confédération Française des Travailleurs Chrétiens—CFTC, present title and constitution adopted in 1964; moderate; co-ordinates 2,200 trade unions, 102 departmental and overseas unions and 19 affiliated professional federations, all of which are autonomous. There are also 22 regional orgs; 701,000 mems (1997); affiliated to European Trade Union Confederation and to CISL; Sec.-Gen. NICOLE NOTAT; Nat. Secs JEAN-MARIE SPAETH, JEAN-RÉNÉ MASSON, JEAN-FRANÇOIS TROGRLIC.

Principal affiliated federations:

Agroalimentaire (FGA): 47/49 ave Simon Bolivar, 75950 Paris Cédex 19; tel. 1-53-38-12-12; fax 1-53-38-12-00; f. 1980; Sec.-Gen. ODILE BELLOUIN.

Banques (Fédération des Syndicats CFDT de Banques et Sociétés Financières) (Banking): 47/49 ave Simon Bolivar, 75950 Paris Cédex 19; tel. 1-44-52-71-20; fax 1-44-52-71-21; Sec.-Gen. BERNARD DUFIL.

Chimie-Energie (FCE-CFDT): 47/49 ave Simon Bolivar, 75950 Paris Cédex 19; tel. 1-44-84-86-00; fax 1-44-84-86-05; f. 1946; Sec.-Gen. JACQUES KHELIFF.

Communication et Culture (FTILAC): 47/49 ave Simon Bolivar, 75950 Paris Cédex 19; tel. 1-44-52-52-70; fax 1-42-02-59-74; Sec.-Gen. DANIÈLE RIVED.

Construction-Bois (FNCB): 47/49 ave Simon Bolivar, 75950 Paris Cédex 19; tel. 1-53-72-87-20; fax 1-53-72-87-21; f. 1934; Sec.-Gen. JOSEPH MURGIA.

Education Nationale (SGEN-CFDT) (National Education): 47/49 ave Simon Bolivar, 75950 Paris Cédex 19; tel. 1-40-03-37-00; fax 1-42-02-50-97; internet http://www.sgen-cfdt.org; f. 1937; Sec.-Gen. JEAN MICHEL BOULLIER.

Etablissements et Arsenaux de l'Etat: 47/49 ave Simon Bolivar, 75950 Paris Cédex 19; tel. 1-42-02-44-62; fax 1-42-02-08-81; Sec.-Gen. JEAN-PIERRE LE VELLY.

Finances et Affaires Economiques (Finance): 47/49 ave Simon Bolivar, 75950 Paris Cédex 19; tel. 1-53-72-73-00; fax 1-42-02-49-91; f. 1936; civil servants and workers within government financial departments; Sec.-Gen. PHILIPPE LECLEZIO.

Fonctionnaires et Assimilés (UFFA-CFDT) (Civil Servants): 47/49 ave Simon Bolivar, 75950 Paris Cédex 19; tel. 1-42-02-44-70; fax 1-42-02-38-77; f. 1932; Sec.-Gen. MICHEL PÉRIER.

Formation et Enseignement Privés (Non-State education): 47/49 ave Simon Bolivar, 75950 Paris Cédex 19; tel. 1-42-02-44-90; fax 1-40-40-99-14; Sec.-Gen. PHILIPPE LEPEU.

Habillement, Cuir et Textile (HACUITEX-CFDT): 47/49 ave Simon Bolivar, 75950 Paris Cédex 19; tel. 1-42-02-50-20; fax 1-42-01-02-98; f. 1963; Sec.-Gen. YVONNE DELEMOTTE.

Ingénieurs et Cadres (UCC-CFDT): 47 ave Simon Bolivar, 75950 Paris Cédex 19; tel. 1-42-02-44-43; fax 1-42-02-48-58; e-mail ucc-cfdt@ucc-cfdt.fr; Sec.-Gen. MARIE ODILE PAULET.

Justice: 47 ave Simon Bolivar, 75019 Paris; tel. 1-42-38-64-10; fax 1-42-38-18-15; Sec.-Gen. JEAN-MARIE LIGIER.

Mines et Métallurgie (Miners and Metal Workers): 47/49 ave Simon Bolivar, 75950 Paris Cédex 19; tel. 1-44-52-20-20; fax 1-44-52-20-52; Sec.-Gen. ROBERT BONNAND.

Personnel du Ministère de l'Intérieur et des Collectivités Locales (INTERCO-CFDT): 47/49 ave Simon Bolivar, 75950 Paris Cédex 19; tel. 1-40-40-85-50; telex 660154; fax 1-42-06-86-86; Sec.-Gen. ALEXIS GUÉNÉGO.

Protection Sociale, Travail, Emploi (Social Security): 47/49 ave Simon Bolivar, 75950 Paris Cédex 19; tel. 1-40-18-77-77; fax 1-40-18-77-79; Sec.-Gen. JEAN-LOUIS TARDIVAUN.

PTT (Post, Telegraph and Telephone Workers): 47/49 ave Simon Bolivar, 75950 Paris Cédex 19; tel. 1-42-02-43-03; telex 650346; fax 1-42-02-42-10; Sec.-Gen. MARIE-PIERRE LIBOUTET.

Santé et Services Sociaux (Hospital and Social Workers): 47/49 ave Simon Bolivar, 75950 Paris Cédex 19; tel. 1-40-40-85-00; fax 1-42-02-48-08; Sec.-Gen. FRANÇOIS CHEREQUE.

Services: 47/49 ave Simon Bolivar, 75950 Paris Cédex 19; tel. 1-42-02-50-48; telex 660154; fax 1-42-02-56-55; Sec.-Gen. RÉMY JOUAN.

Transports et Equipement: 47/49 ave Simon Bolivar, 75950 Paris Cédex 19; tel. 1-44-84-29-50; fax 1-42-02-49-96; f. 1977; Sec.-Gen. GÉRARD BALBASTRE.

Union Confédérale des Retraités (UCR): 47/49 ave Simon Bolivar, 75950 Paris Cédex 19; tel. 1-44-52-12-90; fax 1-42-02-34-51; Sec.-Gen. JACQUES SENSE.

Confédération Française de l'Encadrement (CGC): 30 rue de Gramont, 75002 Paris; tel. 1-44-55-77-77; telex 215116; fax 1-42-96-45-97; f. 1944; organizes managerial staff, professional staff and technicians; co-ordinates unions in every industry and sector; Chair. MARC VILBENOÎT; Sec.-Gen. CLAUDE CAMBUS; 300,000 mems.

Confédération Française des Travailleurs Chrétiens (CFTC): 13 rue des Ecluses Saint Martin, 75483 Paris Cédex 10; tel. 1-44-52-49-00; fax 1-44-52-49-18; f. 1919; present form in 1964 after majority CFTC became CFDT (see above); mem. European Trade Union Confederation; Chair. ALAIN DELEU; Gen. Sec. JACQUES VOISIN; 250,000 mems.

Confédération des Syndicats Libres (CSL) (formerly Confédération française du Travail): 37 rue Lucien Sampaix, 75010 Paris; tel. 1-55-26-12-12; telex 201390; fax 1-55-26-12-00; f. 1959; right-wing; Sec.-Gen. AUGUSTE BLANC; 250,000 mems.

Fédération de l'Education Nationale (FEN): 48 rue La Bruyère, 75440 Paris Cédex 09; tel. 1-42-85-71-01; telex 648356; fax 1-40-16-05-92; f. 1948; federation of teachers' unions; Sec.-Gen. JEAN-PAUL ROUX.

Fédération Nationale des Syndicats Autonomes: 19 blvd Sébastopol, 75001 Paris; f. 1952; groups unions in the private sector; Sec.-Gen. MICHEL-ANDRÉ TILLIÈRES.

Fédération Nationale des Syndicats d'Exploitants Agricoles (FNSEA) (National Federation of Farmers' Unions): 11 rue de la Baume, 75008 Paris; tel. 1-53-83-47-47; telex 660587; fax 1-53-83-48-48; f. 1946; divided into 92 departmental federations and 30,000 local unions; Chair. LUC GUYAU; Dir-Gen. YVES SALMON; 700,000 mems.

Fédération Syndicale Unitaire (FSU): Paris; f. 1993, following split in FEN (see above); federation of 18 teachers' unions; Sec.-Gen. MICHEL DESCHAMPS; 150,000 mems.

Syndicat National Unitaire des Instituteurs (SNUIPP): Paris; f. 1993; primary-school teachers; Secs-Gen. DANIEL LE BRET, DANIELLE CZALCZYNSKI, NICOLE GENEIX.

Transport

RAILWAYS

Most of the French railways are controlled by the Société Nationale des Chemins de fer Français (SNCF) which took over the activities of the five largest railway companies in 1937. In 1997 the Réseau Ferré National was created to manage track and infrastructure. The SNCF is divided into 23 régions (areas), all under the direction of a general headquarters in Paris. In 1993 the SNCF operated 32,579 km of track, of which 13,572 km were electrified. By 1995 total track length had been reduced to 32,200 km and was forecast to fall to 26,000 km by 2000. High-speed services (trains à grande vitesse—TGV) operate between Paris and Lyon (TGV Sud-Est), Paris and Bordeaux (TGV Atlantique) and Paris and Calais (TGV Nord). TGV Mediterranée, which will link Montpellier and Marseille with Lyon, was being electrified in 1996. The TGV network exceeded

1,200 km of track in late 1995. The Parisian transport system is controlled by a separate authority, the Régie Autonome des Transports Parisiens (RATP, see below). A number of small railways in the provinces are run by independent organizations. In 1994 a rail link between France and the United Kingdom was opened, including a tunnel under the English Channel (la Manche), from Calais to Folkestone. The rail link was constructed and operated by the Anglo-French Eurotunnel Consortium. In 1996 some 13m. passengers used the link, compared with 8m. in 1995. The Paris-Calais TGV line, via Lille, completed in 1993, is to form the main artery of a high-speed rail network serving Belgium, the Netherlands, Germany and France. In 1996 it was announced that the TGV network was to be extended to link Strasbourg with Paris.

Société Nationale des Chemins de fer Français (SNCF): 86–88 rue Saint Lazare, 75436 Paris Cédex 09; tel. 1-53-25-60-00; telex 290936; fax 1-53-25-61-08; f. 1937; formerly 51% state-owned, wholly nationalized 1983; 182,539 employees; Chair. LOUIS GALLOIS; Sec.-Gen. PIERRE FA.

Metropolitan Railways

Régie Autonome des Transports Parisiens (RATP): 54 quai de la Rapee, 75599 Paris Cédex 12; tel. 1-44-68-20-20; telex 200000; fax 1-44-68-31-60; f. 1948; state-owned; operates the Paris underground and suburban railways (totalling 325.6 km in 1995), and buses; Chair. and Dir-Gen. JEAN-PAUL BAILLY.

Three provincial cities also have underground railway systems: Marseille, Lyon and Lille. In 1996 it was announced that an underground railway system was to be built in Rennes.

ROADS

At 31 December 1996 there were 9,500 km of motorways (autoroutes). There were also 28,000 km of national roads (routes nationales), 355,000 km of secondary roads and 500,000 km of major local roads. In 1993 the Government announced its intention to construct a further 2,600 km of motorways by 2003.

Fédération Nationale des Transports Routiers (FNTR): 6 rue Paul Valéry, 75116 Paris; tel. 1-45-53-92-88; road transport; Chair. RENÉ PETIT.

INLAND WATERWAYS

In 1990 there were 8,500 km of navigable waterways, of which 1,647 km were accessible to craft of 3,000 tons. In 1995 it was announced that a company had been formed to construct a 230-km canal linking the Rivers Rhône and Rhine. The canal was scheduled to be completed by 2010 at a projected cost of 17,000m. francs.

Voies navigables de France: 175 rue Ludovic Boutleux, BP 820, 62408 Béthune Cédex; tel. 3-21-63-24-24; f. 1991; management and development of France's inland waterways.

SHIPPING

At 1 January 1997 the French merchant shipping fleet numbered 210 cargo-carrying vessels (excluding supply ships), with a total displacement of 4,085,748 gross tons (not including vessels of less than 100 tons, or the fishing fleet). Of this tonnage, 9.6% comprised passenger vessels, 32.8% cargo vessels and 57.6% petroleum carriers. In 1993 the principal ports, in terms of quantity of cargo, were Marseille, Le Havre and Dunkerque, and the principal passenger port was Calais. The six major seaports (Marseille, Le Havre, Dunkerque, Rouen, Nantes–Saint-Nazaire and Bordeaux) are operated by autonomous authorities, although the State retains supervisory powers.

Conseil National des Communautés Portuaires: 34 rue de la Fédération, 75015 Paris; tel. 1-40-81-71-04; f. 1987; central independent consultative and co-ordinating body for ports and port authorities; over 50 mems including 10 trade union mems; Pres. JACQUES DUPUYDAUBY; Sec.-Gen. M. DE ROCQUIGNY DU FAYEL.

Principal Shipping Companies

Note: Not all the vessels belonging to the companies listed below are registered under the French flag.

Bretagne-Angleterre-Irlande (BAI): Port du Bloscon, BP 72, 29688 Roscoff Cédex; tel. 2-98-29-28-00; telex 940360; fax 2-98-29-27-00; transport between France, Ireland, Spain and the United Kingdom; Chair. ALEXIS GOURVENNEC; Man. Dir CHRISTIAN MICHIELINI; displacement 85,021 grt.

CETRAMAR, Consortium Européen de Transports Maritimes: 87 ave de la Grande Armée, 75782 Paris Cédex 16; tel. 1-40-66-11-11; telex 645188; fax 1-45-00-23-97; tramping; Man. Dir ANDRÉ MAIRE; displacement 564,291 grt.

Compagnie de Navigation UIM: 93–95 rue de Provence, 75009 Paris; tel. 1-42-85-19-00; telex 290673; fax 1-45-26-13-02; Chair. MICHEL DUVAL; Man. Dir JEAN-YVES THOMAS.

Compagnie Générale Maritime: 22 quai Galliéni, 92158 Suresnes Cédex; tel. 1-46-25-70-00; telex 630387; fax 1-46-25-78-00; f. 1976 by merger; 99.9% state-owned (1995); privatization initiated in 1996; freight services to USA, Canada, West Indies, Central and South America, northern and eastern Europe, the Middle East, India, Australia, New Zealand, Indonesia and other Pacific and Indian Ocean areas; sales totalled 4,794m. Frs in 1994; Chair. PHILIPPE PONTET; Gen. Man. J. RIBIÈRE; displacement 653,405 grt.

Compagnie Maritime d'Affrètement: Immeuble le Mirabeau, 4 quai d'Arenc, 13002 Marseille; tel. 4-91-39-30-00; telex 401667; fax 4-91-39-30-95; Mediterranean, Middle East and Far East freight services; Chair. JACQUES R. SAADÉ; Man. Dir FARID T. SALEM; displacement 590,985 grt.

Compagnie Nationale de Navigation: 128 blvd Haussmann, 75008 Paris; tel. 1-53-04-20-00; telex 290673; fax 1-45-22-48-03; f. 1930 as Compagnie Navale Worms; merged with Compagnie Nationale de Navigation and Société Française de Transports Maritimes, and changed name to Compagnie Nationale de Navigation in 1986; holding co with subsidiaries: Société Française de Transports Pétroliers, Cie Morbihannaise et Nantaise de Navigation, Héli-Union, Worms Services Maritimes and other subsidiaries abroad; Chair. GILLES BOUTHILLIER; Man. Dir PIERRE DE DEMANDOLX; displacement 2,221,546 grt.

Esso SAF: 2 rue des Martinets, 92569 Rueil-Malmaison Cédex; tel. 1-47-10-60-00; telex 620031; fax 1-47-10-60-44; Chair., Man. Dir JEAN VERRÉ; Marine Man. PIERRE LANGE; 5 petroleum tankers, displacement 428,431 grt.

Louis-Dreyfus Armateurs (SNC): 87 ave de la Grande Armée, 75782 Paris Cédex 16; tel. 1-40-66-11-11; telex 645188; fax 1-45-00-23-97; gas and bulk carriers; CEO PHILIPPE POIRIER D'ANGÉ D'ORSAY; Man. Dir PHILIPPE LOUIS-DREYFUS.

MARFRET (Compagnie Maritime Marfret): 13 quai de la Joliette, 13002 Marseille; tel. 4-91-56-91-00; telex 440570; fax 4-91-56-91-01; Mediterranean, South American and northern Europe freight services; Chair. RAYMOND VIDIL; displacement 8,711 grt.

Mobil Oil Française: Tour Septentrion, 92081 Paris La Défense Cédex; tel. 1-41-45-42-41; fax 1-41-45-42-93; bulk petroleum transport; refining and marketing of petroleum products; Chair. CHRISTIAN SCHNEEBELI; displacement 281,489 grt.

SCAC Delmas-Vieljeux: Tour Delmas, 31–32 quai de Dion-Bouton, 92811 Puteaux Cédex; tel. 1-46-96-44-33; telex 616260; fax 1-46-96-44-22; f. 1964; world-wide cargo services; Chair. VINCENT BOLLORÉ; Pres. YVES BARRAQUAND; displacement 795,799 grt.

Société Européenne de Transport Maritime: 9 allées de Tourny, 33000 Bordeaux; tel. 5-56-00-00-56; telex 550455; fax 5-56-48-51-23; Man. Dirs GILLES BOUTHILLIER, FERNAND BOZZONI; displacement 53,261 grt.

Société Française de Transports Pétroliers: 128 blvd Haussmann, 75008 Paris; tel. 1-53-04-20-00; telex 290765; fax 1-53-04-20-14; long-distance petroleum transport; Chair., Man. Dir FRANÇOIS ARRADOU; displacement 236,907 grt.

Société Maritime BP: 8 rue des Gémaux, Cergy St Christophe, 95866 Cergy Pontoise Cédex; tel. 1-34-22-40-00; telex 608622; fax 1-34-22-47-65; oil tankers; Dir PHILIPPE VALOIS; displacement 259,082 grt.

Société Nationale Maritime Corse-Méditerranée: 61 blvd des Dames, BP 1963, 13226 Marseille Cédex 02; tel. 4-91-56-32-00; telex 440068; fax 4-91-56-34-94; passenger and roll on/roll off ferry services between France and Corsica, Sardinia, North Africa; Chairs CLAUDE ABRAHAM, G. MARAIS; Man. Dir BERNARD ANNE; displacement 141,454 grt.

Société Navale Caennaise: 24 rue Dumon d'Urville, 14000 Caen; tel. 2-31-72-54-00; telex 772452; fax 2-31-78-04-94; f. 1901; cargo services to Europe and West Africa; Chair., Man. Dir A. LABAT; displacement 59,680 grt.

Société Nouvelle d'Armement Transmanche (SNAT): 3 rue Ambroise-Paré, 75010 Paris; tel. 1-49-95-58-92; telex 280549; fax 1-48-74-62-37; vehicle and passenger services between France and the United Kingdom; Chair. MICHEL FÈVE; Man. Dir DIDIER BONNET; displacement 29,251 grt.

Société des Petroles Shell: 89 blvd Franklin Roosevelt, 92564 Rueil-Malmaison Cédex; tel. 1-47-14-71-00; telex 615013; fax 1-47-14-82-99; petroleum, chemicals and gas tankers; Chair., Man. Dir H. DU ROURET.

Société Services et Transports: route du Hoc Gonfreville-L'Orcher, 76700 Harfleur; tel. 2-35-24-72-00; telex 190634; fax 2-35-53-36-25; petroleum and gas transport, passenger transport; Chair. JEAN-MARC POYLO; Man. Dir JACQUES CHARVET; displacement 118,274 grt.

Total Transport Maritime: Tour Aurore, Place des Reflets, La Défense 10, 92800 Puteaux; tel. 1-41-35-52-00; telex 616258; fax 1-47-78-59-99; f. 1931; petroleum tankers; Chair. PHILIPPE GUÉRIN; displacement 273,542 grt.

Van Ommeren Tankers: 5 ave Percier, 75008 Paris; tel. 1-42-99-66-66; telex 650252; fax 1-45-63-87-82; oil product and chemical coastal tankers and tramping; Chair. FRANCIS VALLAT; Man. Dir PATRICK DECAVELE; displacement 251,000 grt.

CIVIL AVIATION

There are international airports at Orly, Roissy and Le Bourget (Paris), Bordeaux, Lille, Lyon, Marseille, Nice, Strasbourg and Toulouse.

Aéroports de Paris: 291 blvd de Raspail, 75675 Paris Cédex 14; tel. 1-43-35-70-00; telex 261333; fax 1-43-35-72-19; state authority in charge of Paris airports; in 1996 it was announced that a third airport was to be constructed in the Paris area, near Chartres, designed to be operational by 2005; Chair. JEAN FLEURY; Man. Dir JEAN-CLAUDE ALBOUY.

National Airlines

Air France: 45 rue de Paris, 95747 Roissy Cédex; tel. 1-41-56-78-00; fax 1-41-56-70-29; f. 1933; 99% state-owned; privatization plans abandoned in 1997; international, European and inter-continental services; flights to Africa, Americas, Middle and Far East and West Indies; sales totalled 56,200m. Frs in 1994; Chair. and Man. Dir (vacant); Dep. Man. Dirs PATRICE DURAND, MARC VÉRON.

Air France Europe: 1 ave du Maréchal Devaux, 91551 Paray Vieille Poste Cédex; tel. 1-46-75-12-12; telex 265952; fax 1-46-75-12-22; f. 1954; fmrly Air Inter; operates internal freight and passenger services; plans to merge with Air France in 1997 announced in 1996; Chair. (vacant); Man. Dir MARC VÉRON.

Private Airlines

Air Liberté: 3 rue du Pont des Halles, Rungis Cédex 94656; tel. 1-49-79-23-00; fax 1-46-86-50-95; f. 1987; operates international, regional and domestic passenger and cargo services; 70%-owned by British Airways, 30%-owned by Banque Rivaud; Chair. MARC ROCHET.

Air Littoral: Le Millénaire II, 417 rue Samuel Morse, 34961 Montpellier Cédex 2; tel. 4-67-20-67-20; telex 490601; fax 4-67-64-10-61; f. 1972; merged with Compagnie Aérienne du Languedoc in 1988; operates international, regional and domestic passenger and cargo services; Chair. MARC DUFOUR.

AOM French Airlines: 13-15 rue du Pont des Halles, Rungis Cédex; tel. 4-66-70-72-05; telex 233050; fax 4-66-70-04-13; f. 1992 by merger of Air Outre Mer and Minerve; services to the USA, West Indies and Far East; Chair. (vacant).

Brit Air: Aérodrome de Ploujean, BP 156, 29204 Morlaix; tel. 2-98-62-10-22; telex 940929; fax 2-98-62-77-66; f. 1973; international services to the United Kingdom, Spain, Germany and Belgium; Chair. XAVIER LECLERCQ.

Euralair International: Aéroport du Bourget, 93350 Paris; tel. 1-49-34-62-00; telex 230662; fax 1-49-34-63-00; f. 1964; international services to Europe and the Mediterranean region; Pres. ANTOINE DE SIZEMONT; Chair. ALEXANDRE COUVELAIRE.

Hex Air: Aéroport Le Puy, 43320 Loudes; tel. 4-72-08-62-28; telex 990534; fax 4-71-08-04-10; f. 1991; operates domestic scheduled and charter services; Pres. PIERRE BERNARD.

TAT European Airlines: 47 rue Christiaan Huygens, BP 7237, 37072 Tours Cédex 02; tel. 2-47-42-30-00; telex 750876; fax 2-47-54-29-50; f. 1968; fmrly Transport Aérien Transrégional; took over Air Alpes 1981; took over Air Alsace routes following its demise in 1982; wholly-owned by British Airways since 1996; regional charter services; Pres. RODOLPHE MARCHAIS; Chair. MARC ROCHET.

Airlines Associations

Chambre Syndicale du Transport Aérien (CSTA): 28 rue de Chateaudun, 75009 Paris; tel. 1-45-26-23-24; f. 1946 to represent French airlines at national level; Chair. XAVIER LECLERCQ; Delegate-Gen. JEAN-PIERRE LE GOFF; 13 mems.

Fédération Nationale de l'Aviation Marchande (FNAM): 28 rue de Chateaudun, 75009 Paris; tel. 1-45-26-23-24; f. 1991; Chair. XAVIER LECLERCQ; Delegate-Gen. JEAN-PIERRE LE GOFF.

Tourism

France attracts tourists from all over the world. Paris is famous for its boulevards, historic buildings, theatres, art treasures, fashion houses, restaurants and night clubs. The Mediterranean and Atlantic coasts and the French Alps are the most popular tourist resorts. Among other attractions are the many ancient towns, the châteaux of the Loire, the fishing villages of Brittany and Normandy, and spas and places of pilgrimage, such as Vichy and Lourdes. The theme park, Euro Disney, also attracts large numbers of tourists. There were 62,406,000 tourist arrivals in 1996, when estimated tourist receipts totalled US $28,200m. Most visitors are from the United Kingdom, Germany, Belgium, the Netherlands and Italy.

Ministère de l'Equipement, du Logement, des Transports et du Tourisme: Grande Arche La Défense, 92055 Paris La Défense Cédex; tel. 1-40-81-21-22.

Direction du Tourisme: 2 rue Linois, 75740 Paris Cédex 15; tel. 1-44-37-36-00; fax 1-44-37-36-36; Dir HUGUES PARANT.

Maison de la France: 8 ave de l'Opéra, 75001 Paris; tel. 1-42-96-10-23; telex 214260; fax 1-42-86-80-52; f. 1987; Pres. GILBERT TRIGANO.

Observatoire National du Tourisme: 2 rue Linois, 75015 Paris Cédex 15; tel. 1-44-37-36-49; fax 1-44-37-38-51; f. 1991; conducts studies and publishes information on all aspects of tourism in France; Pres. MAURICE BERNADET; Dir ALAIN MONFERRAND.

There are Regional Tourism Committees in the 23 regions and 4 overseas départements. There are more than 3,200 Offices de Tourisme and Syndicats d'Initiative (tourist offices operated by the local authorities) throughout France.

FRENCH OVERSEAS POSSESSIONS

Ministry of Overseas Departments and Territories: 27 rue Oudinot, 75358 Paris 07 SP, France; tel. 1-53-69-20-00; fax 1-43-06-60-30.

Minister of State responsible for Overseas Departments and Territories: JEAN-JACK QUEYRANNE.

The national flag of France, proportions three by two, with three equal vertical stripes, of blue, white and red, is used in the Overseas Possessions.

French Overseas Departments

The four Overseas Departments (départements d'outre-mer) are French Guiana, Guadeloupe, Martinique and Réunion. They are integral parts of the French Republic. Each Overseas Department is administered by a Prefect, appointed by the French Government, and the administrative structure is similar to that of the Departments of metropolitan France. Overseas Departments, however, have their own Courts of Appeal. In 1974 each of the Overseas Departments was granted the additional status of a Region (a unit devised for the purpose of economic and social planning, presided over by a Regional Council). Under the decentralization law of March 1982, the executive power of the Prefect in each Overseas Department was transferred to the locally-elected General Council. A proposal to replace the General Council and the indirectly-elected Regional Council by a single assembly was rejected by the French Constitutional Council in December 1982. As a compromise between autonomy and complete assimilation into France, the Regional Councils' responsibility for economic, social and cultural affairs was increased in 1983. In February of that year the first direct elections for the Regional Councils were held. The Overseas Departments continue to send elected representatives to the French National Assembly and to the Senate in Paris, and also to the European Parliament in Strasbourg.

FRENCH GUIANA

Introductory Survey

Location, Climate, Language, Religion, Capital

French Guiana (Guyane) lies on the north coast of South America, with Suriname to the west and Brazil to the south and east. The climate is humid, with a season of heavy rains from April to July and another short rainy season in December and January. Average temperature at sea-level is 27°C (85°F), with little seasonal variation. French is the official language, but a creole patois is also spoken. The majority of the population belong to the Roman Catholic Church, although other Christian churches are represented. The capital is Cayenne.

Recent History

French occupation commenced in the early 17th century. After brief periods of Dutch, English and Portuguese rule, the territory was finally confirmed as French in 1817. The colony steadily declined, after a short period of prosperity in the 1850s as a result of the discovery of gold in the basin of the Approuague river. French Guiana, including the notorious Devil's Island, was used as a penal colony and as a place of exile for convicts and political prisoners before the practice was halted in 1937. The colony became a Department of France in 1946.

French Guiana's reputation as an area of political and economic stagnation was dispelled by the growth of pro-independence sentiments, and the use of violence by a small minority, compounded by tensions between the Guyanais and large numbers of immigrant workers. In 1974 French Guiana was granted regional status, as part of France's governmental reorganization, thus acquiring greater economic autonomy. In that year, none the less, demonstrations against unemployment, the worsening economic situation and French government policy with regard to the Department led to the detention of leading trade unionists and pro-independence politicians. In 1975 the French Government announced plans to increase investment in French Guiana, but these were largely unsuccessful, owing partly to the problems of developing the interior (about 90% of the territory is covered by forest). Further industrial and political unrest in the late 1970s prompted the Parti Socialiste Guyanais (PSG), then the strongest political organization, to demand greater autonomy for the department. In 1980 there were several bomb attacks against 'colonialist' targets by an extremist group, Fo nou Libéré la Guyane. Reforms introduced by the French Socialist Government in 1982–83 devolved some power over local affairs to the new Regional Council. In May 1983 French Guiana was the target for bombings by the Alliance Révolutionnaire Caraïbe, an extremist independence movement based in Guadeloupe.

In the February 1983 elections to the Regional Council the left-wing parties gained a majority of votes, but not of seats, and the balance of power was held by the separatist Union des Travailleurs Guyanais (UTG), the political wing of which became the Parti National Populaire Guyanais (PNPG) in November 1985. At elections to the General Council held in March 1985, the PSG and left-wing independents secured 13 seats out of a total of 19.

For the general election to the French National Assembly in March 1986, French Guiana's representation was increased from one to two deputies. The incumbent PSG deputy was re-elected, the other seat being won by the Gaullist Rassemblement pour la République (RPR). At simultaneous elections to the Regional Council, the PSG increased its strength on the Council from 14 to 15 members, and Georges Othily of the PSG was re-elected President of the Council. The RPR won nine seats, and the centre-right Union pour la Démocratie Française (UDF) three, while the remaining four seats were secured by Action Démocratique Guyanaise.

Of the votes cast in the Department at the 1988 French presidential election, the incumbent François Mitterrand of the Parti Socialiste (PS) obtained 52% in the first round, and 60% in the second round—against Jacques Chirac of the RPR. In the legislative elections held in June, the RPR none the less retained a seat in the National Assembly. In September–October the left-wing parties won 14 of the 19 seats at elections to the General Council. In September 1989 Othily, the President of the Regional Council, was elected to take French Guiana's seat in the French Senate. Othily had recently been expelled from the PSG for having worked too closely with the opposition parties. However, he attracted support from those who regarded the party's domination of French Guiana as corrupt, and his victory over the incumbent senator, a PSG member, was believed to reflect the level of dissatisfaction within the party.

In September 1991 an agreement signed between the state Bureau d'études géologiques et minières and a South African mining group, providing for the joint exploitation of gold deposits in French Guiana, provoked opposition from the local political parties, who united in appealing to the central Government to reconsider its position, accusing the French of colonialism. A general strike was organized in the Department, and the two organizations withdrew from the agreement in October, citing the strength of local opposition to the project.

In March 1992 elections were held to both the General and Regional Councils. In the former, the PSG retained 10 seats, while other left-wing candidates took five seats. The PSG leader, Elie Castor, retained the presidency of the General Council. The party also won 16 seats in the Regional Council, and the PSG Secretary-General, Antoine Karam, was subsequently elected as the body's President, defeating Othily (whose party, the Forces Démocratiques Guyanaises, had secured 10 seats). In a referendum in September, 67.3% of voters in French Guiana approved ratification of the Treaty on European Union (see p. 158), although an abstention rate of 81.4% was recorded.

In October 1992 the Mouvement Syndical Unitaire organized demonstrations and a widely-observed general strike, to protest against France's perceived indifference to the Department's worsening economic crisis. The strike was terminated after one week, following the signing of an accord between the French Government and professional and trade union organizations. The agreement included provisions for the reduction of redundancies and for the financing of a programme of infrastructural improvements, as well as social and educational measures.

At the March 1993 elections to the French National Assembly Léon Bertrand of the RPR was re-elected in the Kourou, Saint-Laurent-du-Maroni constituency, taking 52.1% of the valid votes. Christiane Taubira-Delannon the founder of the independent left-wing Walawari movement and an outspoken critic of existing policies for the management of French Guiana's natural resources, was elected in the Cayenne, Macouria constituency (traditionally a PSG stronghold), winning 55.5% of the votes; she subsequently joined the République et liberté grouping in the National Assembly.

The PSG's representation in the General Council declined to eight seats following the March 1994 cantonal elections; none the less, one of its members, Stéphan Phinéra-Horth, was subsequently elected President of the Council (Elie Castor having left the party). Taubira-Delannon, defeated by Karam, failed to secure election, although another member of the Walawari movement did enter the Council. Taubira-Delannon was elected to the European Parliament in June, as a representative of the Energie radicale grouping—which secured the greatest percentage of the votes (36.3%) in the department, ahead of the government list and a combined list of the parties of the left of the four Overseas Departments. An abstention rate of 80.4% was recorded.

At the first round of voting in the 1995 presidential elections, on 23 April, there was a considerable increase in support in French Guiana for Chirac, who took 39.8% of the votes cast, at the expense of the candidate of the PS, Lionel Jospin, who received the support of 24.2% of voters. The level of support for Jean-Marie Le Pen, of the extreme right-wing Front National, almost doubled (to 8.1%), compared with that at the 1988 election. At the second round, on 7 May 1995, Chirac won 57.4% of the valid votes cast. The rate of participation by voters at this round was 48.0%. At municipal elections in June the PSG retained control of the Cayenne council, although with reduced support.

With effect from the beginning of 1996 the social security systems of the Overseas Departments were aligned with those of metropolitan France. In February of that year more than 300 representatives of the Overseas Departments' political, economic, trade union and professional organizations attended the National Assizes of Social Equality and Development, a meeting held in Paris at the instigation of Jean-Jacques de Peretti, the Minister-Delegate responsible for the Overseas Departments and Territories.

Beginning in late October 1996 a boycott of classes by secondary-school pupils, who were demanding improved conditions of study, escalated in the following month into a crisis that was regarded as exemplifying wider social tensions between the Department and metropolitan France. The refusal of the Prefect, Pierre Dartout, to receive schools' representatives prompted protests in Cayenne, which swiftly degenerated into rioting and looting, apparently as the protesters were joined by disaffected youths from deprived areas. Considerable material damage was caused to government and commercial property during two nights of violence. One pupil sustained gunshot wounds and several gendarmes were injured in clashes between rioters and security forces; a dead body was, moreover, subsequently discovered in a building that had been destroyed by fire. The central Government dispatched units of anti-riot police to assist the local security forces (reinforcements numbered about 200 by mid-November), and it was announced that de Peretti and the Minister of National Education, François Bayrou, would visit French Guiana: President Chirac was reported to have emphasized personally the need to pay particular attention to the problems at the root of the crisis. However, the conviction, shortly afterwards, of several people implicated in the rioting provoked further violent protests and clashes with security forces, and a one-day general strike in Cayenne, organized by the UTG, resulted in the closure of most businesses and government departments. The extent of the security forces' actions in suppressing the demonstrations was criticized both by those involved in the schools' protest and by local politicians, while the competence of the Department's administrators in their approach to the crisis was the focus of considerable scrutiny. Local officials, meanwhile, denounced the role in the violence not only of unemployed youths but also of separatist groups, alleging that the latter were seeking to exploit the crisis for their own ends. Differences also emerged between the Department's education inspector, Jean-Marcel Coteret, and the Rector of the Antilles-Guyane Academy, Michèle Rudler, as Coteret openly criticized Rudler for remaining in Martinique (the seat of the Academy) throughout the crisis. (Rudler had visited French Guiana shortly before the boycott of classes had begun, and was reported to have agreed to the pupils' demands, subject to confirmation that was reportedly never received in the Department.) Bayrou and de Peretti subsequently arrived in Cayenne to meet those involved in the crisis. Local administrators and schools' representatives had already reached agreement on the students' material demands, but, to considerable local acclaim, the ministers announced the establishment, effective from the beginning of 1997, of separate Academies for French Guiana, Guadeloupe and Martinique (a policy said to be strongly favoured by Chirac). The creation was also announced of additional primary educational facilities for some 3,000 children, and a programme was declared to improve academic standards in secondary schools. In all, the measures were to cost the French Government more than 500m. francs. The removal from his post of Coteret, in early December 1996, and the appointment of a new Prefect in early January 1997 (Dartout was transferred to an administrative post in metropolitan France) were perceived as indicative of the central Government's desire to assuage tensions in French Guiana.

Elie Castor died in France in June 1996; prior to his death he had been under investigation in connection with allegations including fraud and abuse of influence during his time in public office. In May 1997 further details of irregularities in the General Council's administration of French Guiana during Elie Castor's presidency were revealed in a letter from the Antilles–Guyane Chambre régionale des comptes (responsible for monitoring public finances in the region) to Phinéra-Horth, current President of the Council.

In mid-April 1997 violent incidents followed the arrest of five pro-independence activists suspected of setting fire to the home of the public prosecutor during the disturbances of November 1996. Five others, including leading members of the UTG and the PNPG, were subsequently detained in connection with the arson incident. The transfer of all ten detainees to Martinique (termed a deportation by separatist organizations) prompted further violent protests in Cayenne. Police reinforcements were dispatched by the central Government to help suppress the violence, as nine gendarmes reportedly received gunshot wounds during two nights of rioting. In late July one of the detainees, Jean-Victor Castor, a prominent member of the UTG and the pro-independence Mouvement pour la Décolonisation et l'Emancipation Sociale, who had been released the previous month, was rearrested and accused of assaulting a policeman during the April riots. Following the announcement, in early August, that Castor was to remain in custody, some 200 demonstrators clashed with riot police in Cayenne. Castor was released shortly afterwards, and in mid-September a further four separatists, who had been held on remand since April, were also released from prison.

In late May and early June 1997 Léon Bertrand, securing 63.3% of votes cast, and Christiane Taubira-Delannon, winning 64.8% of votes, were both re-elected to the French National Assembly in elections that were marked by a high rate of abstention. Candidates from pro-independence parties notably gained increased support, winning slightly more than 10% of the votes cast in both constituencies.

In 1986–87 French Guiana's relations with neighbouring Suriname deteriorated as increasing numbers of Surinamese refugees fled across the border to escape rebel uprisings in their own country. In late 1986 additional French troops were brought in to patrol the border, as a result of which the Surinamese Government accused the French Government of preparing an invasion of Suriname via French Guiana. It was also reported that Surinamese rebels were using French Guiana as a conduit for weapons and supplies. In 1989 there was an escalation in violent crime, which was generally attributed to the immigrant and refugee population. In August a 24-hour strike, in protest against the high rate of crime, was called by the Chamber of Commerce. The strike was widely supported by trade unions and business proprietors alike. In response to demands for more effective policing, the French Government dispatched 100 riot police from France as reinforcements for the Department's regular police. In 1992 the French Government implemented a programme under which all of the refugees from Suriname were to be repatriated by the end of September. By July of that year 2,500 of the 5,900 registered Surinamese refugees had accepted financial incentives from the French administration and returned to Suriname.

Government

France is represented in French Guiana by an appointed Prefect. There are two Councils with local powers: the General Council, with 19 members, and the Regional Council, with 31 members. Both are elected by universal adult suffrage for a period of six years. French Guiana elects two representatives to the French National Assembly in Paris, and sends one elected representative to the French Senate. French Guiana is also represented at the European Parliament.

Defence

At 1 August 1997 France maintained military forces of 3,600 with their headquarters in Cayenne.

Economic Affairs

In 1989, according to estimates by the UN, French Guiana's gross domestic product (GDP), measured at current prices, was US $266m., equivalent to $2,800 per head. Between 1980 and 1985, it was estimated, GDP increased, in real terms, at an average rate of 0.8% per year, and in 1985–89 the average annual growth rate increased to 3.6% per year. During 1980–86 GDP per head declined by 2.8% annually. GDP in 1992 was 7,976m. French francs, equivalent to 59,700 francs per head. Between 1985 and 1995, according to estimates by the World Bank, the population increased by an annual average of 5.4%.

Agriculture engaged about 11.4% of the employed labour force at the time of the 1990 census. The dominant activities are fisheries and forestry, although the contribution of the latter to export earnings has declined in recent years. In 1995 exports of fisheries products (particularly shrimps) provided 25.5% of total export earnings. The principal crops for local consumption are cassava, vegetables and rice, and sugar cane is grown for making rum. Rice, pineapples and citrus fruit are cultivated for export. Agricultural GDP increased by an annual average of 2.1% in 1980–85, and by 1.6% in 1985–89.

Industry, including mining, manufacturing, construction and power, engaged about 20.7% of the employed labour force in 1990. The mining sector is dominated by the extraction of gold, which involves small-scale alluvial operations as well as larger local and multinational mining concerns. Exploration activity intensified in the mid-1990s, and the proposed construction of a major new road into the interior of the Department was expected to encourage further development. Officially-recorded gold exports contributed 15.9% of total export earnings in 1995: actual production levels and sales are widely believed to be considerably higher than published levels. Crushed rock for the construction industry is the only other mineral extracted in significant quantities, although exploratory drilling of known diamond deposits began in 1995. Deposits of bauxite, columbo-tantalite and kaolin are also present.

There is little manufacturing activity, except for the processing of fisheries products (mainly shrimp-freezing) and the distillation of rum. Manufacturing GDP declined by an annual average of 10.6% in 1980–85, and by 1.8% per year in 1985–89.

French Guiana was heavily dependent on imported fuels for the generation of energy prior to the flooding of the Petit-Saut hydroelectric dam on the River Sinnamary, in 1994. Together with existing generating plants, the 116-MW dam was expected to satisfy the territory's electrical energy requirements for about 30 years. Imports of mineral fuels accounted for 5.3% of total imports in 1995.

The services sector engaged 67.9% of the employed labour force in 1990. The European Space Agency's satellite-launching centre at Kourou (established in 1964 and to be expanded during the 1990s) has provided a considerable stimulus to the economy, most notably the construction sectors. Some 1,100 people were employed at the centre in 1991. In 1996 15 satellites were launched from 10 *Ariane-4* rockets, although the explosion of the new *Ariane-5* rocket, in July of that year, delayed the centre's programme. In October 1997 the *Ariane-5* rocket was successfully launched, and was set to replace *Ariane-4* in 1999, pending the outcome of a further test launch. The tourist sector expanded during the 1980s, although its potential is limited by the lack of infrastructure away from the coast. In 1994 187,182 visitor arrivals were recorded.

In 1995 French Guiana recorded a trade deficit of US $625.1m. In 1995 the principal source of imports was France (which supplied 60.7% of total imports in that year); other major suppliers were Trinidad and Tobago and Italy. France was also the principal market for exports in that year (72.4%); other important purchasers were Guadeloupe and Martinique. The principal imports in 1995 were machinery and transport equipment, food and live animals, manufactured articles, chemicals, mineral fuels and lubricants, and beverages and tobacco. The principal exports were shrimps, gold, helicopters and parts, tools, rice, and road vehicles and parts.

In 1992 there was a combined deficit on the budgets of French Guiana's government authorities (state, regional, departmental and communal) of 974m. French francs. By September 1988 French Guiana's external debt had reached US $1,200m. The annual rate of inflation averaged 1.9% in 1990–96; consumer prices increased by an average of 0.8% in 1996. Unemployment in August 1996 was estimated at 21.7% of the total labour force. However, there is a shortage of skilled labour, offset partly by immigration.

As an integral part of France, French Guiana is a member of the European Union (EU—see p. 152). The French Overseas Departments were to receive a total of ECU 1,500m. from EU regional funds during 1994–2000.

Economic development in French Guiana has been hindered by the Department's location, poor infrastructure away from the coast and lack of a skilled indigenous labour force, although there is considerable potential for further growth in the fishing, forestry and tourism (notably 'eco-tourism') sectors. A particular concern in the 1990s is the rapid rise in the rate of unemployment, and youth unemployment and related social problems were widely interpreted as having contributed to the violence in Cayenne in late 1996 (see Recent History). French Guiana's geographical characteristics—large parts of the territory are accessible only by river—have resulted in difficulties in regulating key areas of the economy, such as gold-mining and forestry. Considerable concern has been expressed regarding the ecological consequences of such a lack of controls; moreover, the flooding of a large area of forest (some 340 sq km), as part of the Petit-Saut barrage project, has prompted disquiet among environmental groups, as has uncertainty regarding the ecological implications of the satellite-launching programme at Kourou. The budget deficit represents a significant obstacle to growth, while high demand for imported consumer goods (much of which is generated by relatively well-remunerated civil servants, who constitute about two-thirds of the working population) undermines progress in reducing the trade deficit.

Social Welfare

In 1997 there were two hospital complexes, a medical centre and three private clinics. In addition, each of the 22 communes has a health centre. There were 200 doctors, 32 dental surgeons and 31 midwives in 1991. The Institut Pasteur, in Cayenne, undertakes research into malaria and other tropical diseases. Welfare payments and the statutory minimum wage in the Overseas Departments are aligned with those of metropolitan France.

Education

Education is modelled on the French system, and is compulsory for 10 years between the ages of six and 16 years. Primary education begins at six years of age and lasts for five years. Secondary education, beginning at 11 years of age, lasts for up to seven years, comprising a first cycle of four years and a second of three years. Education at state schools (which accounted for more than 90% of total enrolment in 1992/93) is provided free of charge. Between 1980 and 1993 the number of children attending primary schools increased by more than 70%, and the number of pupils at secondary schools by 87%, although such expansion has placed considerable strain on existing facilities. Higher education in law, administration and French language and literature is provided by a branch of the Université Antilles-Guyane in Cayenne (the university as a whole had 15,810 enrolled students in the 1995/96 academic year), and one department of a technical institute opened at Kourou in 1988. There is also a teacher-training college and an agricultural college. Total government expenditure on education amounted to 851m. French francs in 1993. An Academy for French Guiana was established in January 1997. In 1982 the average rate of adult illiteracy was 17.0% (males 16.4%; females 17.7%).

Public Holidays

1998: 1 January (New Year's Day), 23–24 February (Lenten Carnival), 10–13 April (Easter), 1 May (Labour Day), 21 May (Ascension Day), 1 June (Whit Monday), 14 July (National Day), 11 November (Armistice Day), 25 December (Christmas Day).

1999: 1 January (New Year's Day), 15–16 February (Lenten Carnival), 2–5 April (Easter), 1 May (Labour Day), 13 May (Ascension Day), 24 May (Whit Monday), 14 July (National Day), 11 November (Armistice Day), 25 December (Christmas Day).

Weights and Measures

The metric system is in use.

Statistical Survey

Sources (unless otherwise stated): Institut national de la statistique et des études économiques, 1 rue Maillard-Dumesle, 97306 Cayenne; tel. 31-56-03; fax 30-87-89; Ministère des départements et territoires d'outre-mer, 27 rue Oudinot, 75358 Paris 07 SP; tel. 1-53-69-20-00; fax 1-43-06-60-30; internet http://www.outre-mer.gouv.fr.

AREA AND POPULATION

Area: 83,534 sq km (32,253 sq miles).

Population: 73,012 at census of 9 March 1982; 114,808 (males 59,798, females 55,010) at census of 15 March 1990; 144,000 (official estimate) at mid-1994.

Density (mid-1994): 1.7 per sq km.

Principal Towns (population at 1990 census): Cayenne (capital) 41,067; Kourou 13,873; Saint-Laurent-du-Maroni 13,616; Remire-Montjoly 11,709; Matoury 10,152.

Births, Marriages and Deaths (provisional figures, 1994): Registered live births 4,236 (birth rate 29.4 per 1,000); Registered marriages 614 (marriage rate 4.3 per 1,000); Registered deaths 565 (death rate 3.9 per 1,000).

Economically Active Population (persons aged 15 years and over, 1990 census): Agriculture, hunting, forestry and fishing 4,177; Industry and energy 3,130; Construction 4,440; Trade 3,152; Transport and telecommunications 1,857; Marketable services 7,352; Financial services 408; Non-marketable services 12,068; Total employed (excl. military personnel) 36,584. Unemployed 11,700. Total labour force 48,700.

AGRICULTURE, ETC.

Principal Crops (FAO estimates, '000 metric tons, 1996): Sugar cane 2; Cassava 18; Other roots and tubers 10; Rice (paddy) 26. Source: FAO, *Production Yearbook*.

Livestock (FAO estimates, '000 head, year ending September 1996): Cattle 8; Pigs 9; Sheep 3; Goats 1. Source: FAO, *Production Yearbook*.

Livestock Products (metric tons, unless otherwise indicated, 1995): Beef and veal 235; Pig meat 625; Mutton, lamb and goat meat 12; Poultry meat 495; Cow's milk (hl) 1,475; Eggs ('000) 8,465.

Forestry ('000 cu m, 1994): *Roundwood removals* (FAO estimates, excl. bark): Sawlogs, veneer logs and logs for sleepers 51; Other industrial wood 9; Fuel wood 72; Total 132. *Sawnwood production* (incl. railway sleepers): Total 15. Source: FAO, *Yearbook of Forest Products*.

Fishing (metric tons, live weight, 1995): Marine fishes 3,600; Shrimps and prawns 4,137; Total catch 7,737. Source: FAO, *Yearbook of Fishery Statistics*.

MINING

Production: Gold (metal content of ore, metric tons) 2.6 in 1996 (Source: Gold Fields Mineral Services Ltd, *Gold 1997*); Gravel and crushed stone, incl. sand ('000 metric tons) 400 in 1990 (Source: UN, *Industrial Commodity Statistics Yearbook*).

INDUSTRY

Production (1994): Rum 1,376 hl; Electric energy 446 million kWh (Source: UN, *Industrial Commodity Statistics Yearbook*).

FINANCE

Currency and Exchange Rates: 100 centimes = 1 French franc. *Sterling and Dollar Equivalents* (30 September 1997): £1 sterling = 9.583 francs; US $1 = 5.932 francs; 1,000 French francs = £104.35 = $168.57. *Average Exchange Rate* (French francs per US dollar): 5.5520 in 1994; 4.9915 in 1995; 5.1155 in 1996.

Budget (million French francs, 1992): *French Government:* Revenue 706; Expenditure 1,505. *Regional Government:* Revenue 558; Expenditure 666. *Departmental Government:* Revenue 998; Expenditure 803. *Communes:* Revenue 998; Expenditure 982.

Money Supply (million francs at 31 December 1995): Currency outside banks 3,964; Demand deposits at banks 1,444; Total money 5,408.

Cost of Living (Consumer Price Index for Cayenne; base: 1990 = 100): 108.9 in 1994; 110.9 in 1995; 111.8 in 1996. Source: UN, *Monthly Bulletin of Statistics*.

Expenditure on the Gross Domestic Product (million French francs at current prices, 1992): Government final consumption expenditure 2,780; Private final consumption expenditure 4,647; Increase in stocks 118; Gross fixed capital formation 2,457; *Total domestic expenditure* 10,002; Exports of goods and services 5,220; *Less* Imports of goods and services 7,246; *GDP in purchasers' values* 7,976.

EXTERNAL TRADE

Principal Commodities (US $ million, 1995): *Imports c.i.f.:* Food and live animals 104.3 (Meat and meat preparations 29.6, Dairy products and birds' eggs 15.6); Beverages and tobacco 39.0 (Beverages 34.3); Mineral fuels, lubricants, etc. 41.9 (Petroleum and petroleum products 40.5); Chemicals and related products 58.0 (Medicinal and pharmaceutical products 17.2); Basic manufactures 92.5; Machinery and transport equipment 330.0 (Power-generating machinery and equipment 27.0, General industrial machinery, equipment and parts 28.0, Office machines and automatic data-processing machines 22.2, Telecommunications and sound equipment 27.6, Road vehicles and parts 88.6, Other transport equipment 88.6); Miscellaneous manufactured articles 97.0 (Professional, scientific and controlling instruments, etc. 15.6); Total (incl. others) 783.3. *Exports f.o.b.:* Food and live animals 50.8 (Fresh, chilled or frozen fish 5.5, Crustaceans and molluscs 34.9, Rice 10.2); Basic manufactures 15.3 (Metal hand or machine tools 13.6); Machinery and transport equipment 52.1 (Telecommunications and sound equipment 3.2, Road vehicles and parts 9.5, Aircraft, associated equipment and parts 29.4); Miscellaneous manufactured articles 9.8 (Professional, scientific and controlling instruments, etc. 5.0. Non-military firearms 3.3); Non-monetary gold 25.1; Total (incl. others) 158.2. Source: UN, *International Trade Statistics Yearbook*.

Principal Trading Partners (US $ million, 1995): *Imports c.i.f.:* Belgium-Luxembourg 32.5; Brazil 8.4; France (incl. Monaco) 475.8; Germany 21.3; Italy 38.1; Japan 11.3; Netherlands 16.7; Trinidad and Tobago 40.2; United Kingdom 7.8; USA 26.2; Total (incl. others) 783.3. *Exports f.o.b.:* Belgium-Luxembourg 5.0; France (incl. Monaco) 96.4; Guadeloupe 13.3; Italy 4.2; Martinique 7.1; Spain 2.6; USA 1.7; Total (incl. others) 133.1 (excl. gold). Source: UN, *International Trade Statistics Yearbook*.

TRANSPORT

Road Traffic ('000 motor vehicles in use, 1993): Passenger cars 29.1; Commercial vehicles 10.6. Source: UN, *Statistical Yearbook*.

International Sea-borne Shipping (traffic, 1994): Vessels entered 333; Goods loaded 70,000 metric tons; Goods unloaded 530,000 metric tons.

Civil Aviation (1992): Freight carried 5,472 metric tons; Passengers carried 324,100.

TOURISM

Tourist Arrivals (1994): 187,182.

COMMUNICATIONS MEDIA

Radio Receivers ('000 in use) 90 in 1994; **Television Receivers** ('000 in use) 25 in 1994; **Telephones** ('000 main lines in use) 40 in 1994; **Telefax Stations** (number in use) 185 in 1990; **Daily Newspaper** 1 in 1994 (average circulation 2,000 copies). Sources: UNESCO, *Statistical Yearbook;* UN, *Statistical Yearbook*.

EDUCATION

Pre-primary (1994/95): 42 institutions (1993/94); 8,583 students.

Primary (1994/95): 78 institutions (1993/94); 16,449 students.

Secondary (1994/95): 15,034 students (12,731 general, 2,303 vocational).

Source: UNESCO, *Statistical Yearbook*.

Higher (1992): 427 students.

Directory

The Government

(January 1998)

Prefect: Dominique Vian.

President of the General Council: Stéphan Phinéra-Horth (PSG).

Deputies to the French National Assembly: Christiane Taubira-Delannon (Independent left), Léon Bertrand (RPR).

Representative to the French Senate: Georges Othily (FDG).

REGIONAL COUNCIL

Conseil Regional, 66 ave du Général de Gaulle, BP 7025, 97307 Cayenne Cédex; tel. 29-20-20; fax 31-95-22.

President: Antoine Karam (PSG).

Election, 22 March 1992

	Votes	%	Seats
PSG	8,626	39.55	16
FDG	5,090	23.34	10
RPR	1,273	5.84	2
Others	6,823	31.28	3
Total	21,812	100.00	31

Political Organizations

Action Démocratique Guyanaise (ADG): Cayenne; Leader André Lecante.

Forces Démocratiques Guyanaises (FDG): Cayenne; f. 1989 by a split in the PSG; Leader Georges Othily.

Mouvement pour la Décolonisation et l'Emancipation Sociale (MDES): pro-independence party; Sec.-Gen. Maurice Pindard.

Parti National Populaire Guyanais (PNPG): Cayenne; f. 1985; pro-independence party; Leader José Dorcy.

Parti Socialiste: Cayenne; tel. 37-81-33; local branch of the national party; Leader Pierre Ribardière.

Parti Socialiste Guyanais (PSG): 1 Cité Césaire, Cayenne; f. 1956; Sec.-Gen. Marie-Claude Verdan.

Rassemblement pour la République (RPR): Cayenne; tel. 31-66-60; f. 1946; local branch of the national party; Gaullist; Leader ROLAND HO-WEN-SZE.

Union pour la Démocratie Française (UDF): Cayenne; tel. 31-17-10; f. 1979; local branch of the national party; centre-right; Leader R. CHOW-CHINE.

Union Socialiste Démocratique (USD): Cayenne; Leader THÉODORE ROUMILLAC.

Walawari: Cayenne; left-wing; Leader CHRISTIANE TAUBIRA-DELANNON.

Judicial System

Courts of Appeal: see Judicial System, Martinique.

Tribunal de Grande Instance: Palais de Justice, 9 ave du Général de Gaulle, 97300 Cayenne; Pres. FRANÇOIS CRÉÉE.

Religion

CHRISTIANITY

The Roman Catholic Church

French Guiana comprises the single diocese of Cayenne, suffragan to the archdiocese of Fort-de-France, Martinique. At 31 December 1995 there were an estimated 120,000 adherents in French Guiana, representing some 80% of the total population. French Guiana participates in the Antilles Episcopal Conference, currently based in Port of Spain, Trinidad and Tobago.

Bishop of Cayenne: Rt Rev. FRANÇOIS-MARIE MORVAN, Evêché, 24 rue Madame-Payé, BP 378, 97328 Cayenne Cédex; tel. 31-01-18; fax 30-20-33.

The Anglican Communion

Within the Church in the Province of the West Indies, French Guiana forms part of the diocese of Guyana. The Bishop is resident in Georgetown, Guyana.

Other Churches

Assembly of God: 16 route La Madeleine, 97300 Cayenne; tel. 31-09-14; fax 35-23-05; Pres. JACQUES RHINO.

Church of Jesus Christ of Latter-day Saints (Mormons): chemin Constant Chlore, 97354 Rémire-Montjoly; tel. 30-55-92; Br. Pres. FRANÇOIS PRATIQUE, allée des Cigales, route de Montabo, 97300 Cayenne; tel. 31-21-86.

Quadrangular Gospel Church: 97300 Cayenne; tel. 37-84-81.

Seventh-day Adventist Church: Mission Adventiste, 39 rue Schoëlcher, 97300 Cayenne Cédex; tel. 30-30-64; fax 37-93-02.

The Jehovah's Witnesses are also represented.

The Press

France-Guyane: 88 bis ave du Général de Gaulle, 97300 Cayenne; tel. 29-85-86; fax 31-11-57; daily; Dir PHILIPPE HERSANT; circ. 5,500.

La Presse de Guyane: 26 rue du Lieutenant Brassé, BP 6012, 97300 Cayenne; tel. 29-59-90; 4 a week; Dir JOSÉPHINE LUCAS; circ. 1,000.

Broadcasting and Communications

BROADCASTING

Société Nationale de Radio-Télévision Française d'Outre-mer (RFO): 43 rue du Dr Devèze, BP 7013, 97305 Cayenne; tel. 29-99-00; fax 30-26-49; Radio-Guyane Inter: broadcasts 18 hours daily; Téléguyane: 2 channels, 32 hours weekly; Pres. JEAN-MARIE CAVADA; Dir JEAN-CLAUDE ARGENTIN.

Radio

Cayenne FM: 88 ave Général de Gaulle, BP 428, 97300 Cayenne; tel. 31-37-38; private radio station broadcasting 126 hours weekly.

Radio Nou Men: private station; broadcasts in Creole and Boni.

Radio Tout Moune: rue des Mandarines, 97300 Cayenne; tel. 31-80-74; fax 30-91-19; f. 1982; private station; broadcasts 24 hours a day; Pres. R. BATHILDE; Dir GUY SAINT-AIME.

Television

Antenne Créole: 31 ave Louis Pasteur, 97300 Cayenne; tel. 31-20-20; private television station.

Canal Plus Guyane: Cayenne; private 'coded' television station.

Finance

(cap. = capital; res = reserves; dep. = deposits; m. = million; brs = branches; amounts in French francs)

BANKING

Central Bank

Institut d'Emission des Départements d'Outre Mer (IEDOM): 8 rue Christophe Colomb, BP 6016, 97306 Cayenne Cédex; tel. 29-36-50; telex 910529; fax 30-02-76.

Commercial Banks

Banque Française Commerciale Antilles–Guyane (BFC Antilles–Guyane): 8 place des Palmistes, 97300 Cayenne (see section on Guadeloupe).

Banque Nationale de Paris—Guyane (BNP Guyane): 2 place Victor Schoëlcher, BP 35, 97300 Cayenne; tel. 39-63-00; telex 910522; fax 30-23-08; f. 1855; cap. 71.7m., res 100.0m., dep. 2,007m. (Dec. 1994); Chair. of Bd (Cayenne) VINCENT DE ROUX; 5 brs.

Crédit Populaire Guyanais: Caisse de Crédit Mutuel, 93 rue Lallouette, BP 818, 97338 Cayenne; tel. 30-15-23; fax 30-17-65.

Development Bank

Société financière pour le développement économique de la Guyane (SOFIDEG): PK 3, route de Baduel, BP 860, 97339 Cayenne Cédex; tel. 29-94-29; telex 910556; fax 30-60-44; f. 1982; Dir FRANÇOIS CHEVILLOTTE.

Trade and Industry

GOVERNMENT AGENCY

Direction Régionale de l'Industrie, de la Recherche et de l'Environnement (DRIRE): impasse Buzaré, BP 7001, 97307 Cayenne; tel. 30-00-06; fax 31-97-77; mining authority; responsible for assessing applications for and awarding exploration and exploitation rights; Regional Dir JEAN-CLAUDE BARA.

DEVELOPMENT ORGANIZATION

Caisse Française de Développement (CFD): Cayenne; tel. 31-41-33; telex 910570; fmrly Caisse Centrale de Coopération Economique, name changed 1992; Dir CLAUDE ALBINA.

CHAMBERS OF COMMERCE

Chambre de Commerce et d'Industrie de la Guyane: Hôtel Consulaire, place de l'Esplanade, BP 49, 97321 Cayenne Cédex; tel. 29-96-00; telex 910537; fax 29-96-34; Pres. JEAN-PIERRE PRÉVÔT.

Chambre de Métiers de Guyane: Jardin Botanique, blvd de la République, BP 176, 97324 Cayenne Cédex; tel. 30-21-80; Pres. RICHARD HO-A-SIM.

Jeune Chambre Economique de Cayenne: Cité A. Horth, route de Montabo, BP 683, Cayenne; tel. 31-62-99; fax 31-76-13; f. 1960; Pres. FRANCK VERSET.

EMPLOYERS' ORGANIZATIONS

Organisation des Producteurs Guyanais de Crevettes (OPG): Le Larivot, c/o GUYAPECHE, BP 413, 97310 Kourou; tel. 32-27-26; fax 32-19-18; shrimp producers' asscn and export business; Man. ROBERT COTONNEC.

Syndicat des Exploitants Forestiers et Scieurs de la Guyane (SEFSEG): CD 5, Quesnel, PK 29, 97313 Macouria; tel. 31-72-50; fax 30-08-27; f. 1987; asscn of 14 forestry developers (450 employees); timber processers; Man. M. POMIES.

Syndicat des Exportateurs de la Guyane: Z. I. de Dégrad-des-Cannes, 97354 Rémire-Montjoly; tel. 35-40-78; Pres. JEAN PATOZ.

Union Patronale de la Guyane (UPDG): c/o SOFIDEG, km 3 route de Baduel, BP 820, 97338 Cayenne Cédex; tel. 31-17-71; fax 30-32-13; Pres. ALAIN CHAUMET.

TRADE UNIONS

Centrale Démocratique des Travailleurs de la Guyane (CDTG): 113 rue Christophe Colomb, BP 383, Cayenne; tel. 31-02-32; Sec.-Gen. RENÉ SYDALZA.

Force Ouvrière (FO): 107 rue Barthélemy, Cayenne; Sec.-Gen. M. XAVERO.

SE/FEN (Syndicat des enseignants): 52 rue F. Arago, Cayenne; Sec.-Gen. GEORGINA JUDICK-PIED.

Union des Travailleurs Guyanais (UTG): 7 ave Ronjon, Cayenne; tel. 31-26-42; Sec.-Gen. PAUL CÉCILIEN.

Transport

RAILWAYS

There are no railways in French Guiana.

ROADS

In 1988 there were 1,137 km of roads in French Guiana, of which 371 km were main roads. Much of the network is concentrated along the coast, although proposals for a major new road into the interior of the Department were under consideration in late 1997.

SHIPPING

Dégrad-des-Cannes, on the estuary of the river Mahury, is the principal port, handling 80% of maritime traffic in 1989. There are other ports at Le Larivot, Saint-Laurent-du-Maroni and Kourou. Saint-Laurent is used primarily for the export of timber, and Larivot for fishing vessels. There are river ports on the Oyapock and on the Approuague. There is a ferry service across the Maroni river between Saint-Laurent and Albina, Suriname. The rivers provide the best means of access to the interior, although numerous rapids prevent navigation by large vessels.

Direction Départementale des Affaires Maritimes: 2 bis rue Mentel, BP 307, 97305 Cayenne Cédex; tel. 31-00-08; telex 910568; Dir Pierre-Yves Andrieux.

Somarig: Z. I. de Dégrad-des-Cannes, Remire, BP 81, 97322 Cayenne Cédex; tel. 35-42-00; telex 910528; fax 35-53-44; joint venture between the Compagnie Générale Maritime and Delmas; Dir Daniel Douret.

CIVIL AVIATION

Rochambeau International Airport, situated 17.5 km (11 miles) from Cayenne, is equipped to handle the largest jet aircraft. Access to remote inland areas is frequently by helicopter.

Air Guyane: Aéroport de Rochambeau, 97300 Matoury; tel. 35-65-55; operates internal services.

Guyane Aéro Services: Aéroport de Rochambeau, 97307 Matoury; tel. 35-65-55; telex 910619; f. 1980; fmrly Guyane Air Transport; Pres. Pierre Prévôt; Dir Patrick Lencloe.

Tourism

The main attractions are the natural beauty of the tropical scenery and the Amerindian villages of the interior. In 1994 there were 38 hotels with 1,311 rooms, and 187,182 tourist arrivals were recorded.

Comité du Tourisme de la Guyane: Pavillon du Tourisme, Jardin Botanique, 12 rue Lalouette, BP 801, 97338 Cayenne Cédex; tel. 29-65-00; fax 29-65-01.

Délégation Régionale au Tourisme pour la Guyane: BP 7008, 97307 Cayenne; tel. 31-01-04; fax 31-84-91.

Fédération des Offices de Tourisme et Syndicats de l'Initiative de la Guyane (FOTSIG): 12 rue Lalouette, 97300 Cayenne; tel. 30-96-29; fax 31-23-43; e-mail fotsig@nplus.gf; internet http://www.guyane.net.

GUADELOUPE

Introductory Survey

Location, Climate, Language, Religion, Capital

Guadeloupe is the most northerly of the Windward Islands group in the West Indies. Dominica lies to the south, and Antigua and Montserrat to the north-west. Guadeloupe is formed by two large islands, Grande-Terre and Basse-Terre, separated by a narrow sea channel (but linked by a bridge), with a smaller island, Marie-Galante, to the south-east, and another, La Désirade, to the east. There are also a number of small dependencies, mainly Saint-Barthélemy and the northern half of Saint-Martin (the remainder being part of the Netherlands Antilles), among the Leeward Islands. The climate is tropical, with an average temperature of 26°C (79°F), and a more humid and wet season between June and November. French is the official language, but a creole patois is widely spoken. The majority of the population profess Christianity, and belong to the Roman Catholic Church. The capital is the town of Basse-Terre; the other main town and the principal commercial centre is Pointe-à-Pitre, on Grande-Terre.

Recent History

Guadeloupe was first occupied by the French in 1635, and has remained French territory, apart from a number of brief occupations by the British in the 18th and early 19th centuries. It gained departmental status in 1946.

The deterioration of the economy and an increase in unemployment provoked industrial and political unrest during the 1960s and 1970s, including outbreaks of serious rioting in 1967. Pro-independence parties (which had rarely won more than 5% of the total vote at elections in Guadeloupe) resorted, in some cases, to violence as a means of expressing their opposition to the economic and political dominance of white, pro-French landowners and government officials. In 1980 and 1981 there was a series of bomb attacks on hotels, government offices and other targets by a group called the Groupe Libération Armée, and in 1983 and 1984 there were further bombings by a group styling itself the Alliance Révolutionnaire Caraïbe (ARC), which was also responsible for bomb attacks in French Guiana and Martinique at this time. The Government responded by outlawing the ARC and reinforcing the military and police presence throughout Guadeloupe. (The ARC merged with the Mouvement Populaire pour une Guadeloupe Indépendante—MPGI—in 1984). Further sporadic acts of violence continued into 1985, but in October of that year the ARC suspended its bombing campaign prior to the holding of legislative elections. A further series of bomb attacks began in November 1986, and in January 1988 responsibility for bomb explosions in various parts of the territory was claimed by a previously unknown pro-independence group, the Organisation Révolutionnaire Armée.

In 1974 Guadeloupe was granted the status of a Region, and an indirectly-elected Regional Council was formed. In direct elections to a new Regional Council in February 1983, held as a result of the recent decentralization reforms, the centre-right coalition succeeded in gaining a majority of the seats and control of the administration. In January 1984 Lucette Michaux-Chevry, the President of the General Council, formed a new conservative centre party, Le Parti de la Guadeloupe, which remained in alliance with the right-wing Rassemblement pour la République (RPR). However, at the elections for the General Council, held in March 1985, the left-wing combination of the Parti Socialiste (PS) and the Parti Communiste Guadeloupéen (PCG) gained a majority of seats on the enlarged (42-member) Council, and the PS leader, Dominique Larifla, was elected its President. In July demonstrations and a general strike, organized by pro-separatist activists in order to obtain the release of a leading member of the MPGI, quickly intensified into civil disorder and rioting in the main commercial centre, Pointe-à-Pitre.

For the March 1986 general election to the French National Assembly, Guadeloupe's representation was increased from three to four deputies. The local branches of the RPR and the centre-right Union pour la Démocratie Française (UDF), which had campaigned jointly at the 1981 general election and the 1983 regional elections, presented separate candidates. Ernest Moutoussamy and Frédéric Jalton, respectively the incumbent PCG and PS members of the Assembly, were re-elected, but the UDF deputy was not; the two remaining seats were won by RPR candidates (Michaux-Chevry and Henri Beaujean). In the concurrent elections for the 41 seats on the Regional Council, the two left-wing parties together won a majority of seats, increasing their combined strength from 20 to 22 members (PS 12, PCG 10). As a result, José Moustache of the RPR was replaced as President of the Council by Félix Proto of the PS. In September 1986 the publication of a report (prepared at Proto's request) criticizing the management of finances by the former RPR-UDF majority on the Regional Council, led by Moustache, caused disruption within the Council and had repercussions on the indirect elections for the two Guadeloupe members of the French Senate later in the month: there was a decline in support for centre-right candidates, and, as before, two left-wing Senators were elected (one from the PCG and one from the PS).

At the 1988 French presidential elections the incumbent President François Mitterrand of the PS received 55% of the votes cast in Guadeloupe in the first round, and 69% in the second round against Jacques Chirac of the RPR. At elections to the French National Assembly in June, Larifla (for the PS) defeated Beaujean, while the three other deputies to the National Assembly retained their seats.

In September–October the left-wing parties won 26 of the 42 seats at elections to the General Council, and Larifa was re-elected President of the Council.

In April 1989 the separatist Union Populaire pour la Libération de la Guadeloupe (UPLG) organized protests in Port Louis to demand the release of 'political prisoners', which led to violent clashes with the police. A number of activists of the now disbanded ARC (including its leader, Luc Reinette) staged a hunger strike while awaiting trial in Paris, accused in connection with politically-motivated offences in the Overseas Departments. In the following month the Comité Guadeloupéen de Soutien aux Prisonniers Politiques united 11 organizations in demonstrations against the Government. Demands included the release of the prisoners held in France, a rejection of the Single European Act (see p. 158) and the granting of a series of social demands. In June the French National Assembly approved legislation granting an amnesty for crimes that had taken place before July 1988, and that were intended to undermine the authority of the French Republic in the Overseas Departments. The agreement of those seeking greater independence in Guadeloupe to work within the democratic framework had gained parliamentary support for the amnesty. However, when the freed activists returned to Guadeloupe in July 1989, they urged increased confrontation with the authorities in order to achieve autonomous rule. In March 1990 the UPLG declared that it would henceforth participate in elections, and would seek associated status (rather than full independence) for Guadeloupe.

In March 1992 concurrent elections were held to the General and Regional Councils. Larifla was re-elected as President of the General Council, despite his refusal to contest as part of the local official PS list of candidates and his leadership of a group of 'dissident' PS members. (The division was not recognized at national level.) In the elections to the Regional Council the official PS list (headed by Jalton) secured nine seats and the dissident PS members seven. Former members of the PCG, who had formed a new organization, the Parti Progressiste Démocratique Guadeloupéen (PPDG) in September 1991, won five seats, compared with only three for the PCG. The RPR, the UDF and other right-wing candidates formed an electoral alliance, Objectif Guadeloupe, to contest the elections, together securing 15 of the 41 seats in the Regional Council. Jalton's refusal to reach an agreement with the dissident PS members prompted Larifla's list to support the presidential candidacy of Michaux-Chevry. Thus, despite an overall left-wing majority in the Regional Council, the right-wing Michaux-Chevry was elected as President with 21 votes. In December 1992, however, the French Conseil d'Etat declared the election to the Regional Council invalid, owing to the failure of Larifla's list to pay a deposit on each seat prior to the registration of its candidates. Seven other heads of lists, including Moutoussamy of the PPDG, were subsequently found to have submitted incomplete documents to the election commission, and (although malpractice was discounted) the electoral code necessitated that they be declared ineligible for election to the Regional Council for one year. Fresh elections took place in January 1994, at which Objectif Guadeloupe took 22 seats, while the PS and 'dissident' PS retained a total of only 10 seats.

In a referendum on 20 September 1992 67.5% of voters in Guadeloupe endorsed ratification of the Treaty on European Union (see p. 153), although an abstention rate of 83.4% was recorded. In November banana growers in Guadeloupe and Martinique suspended economic activity in their respective Departments by obstructing access to ports and airports and blocking roads, in protest at the threatened loss of special advantages under the Single European Act. Order was restored, however, following assurances that subsidies would be maintained and that products such as bananas (Guadeloupe's main export) would be protected under new proposals.

The persistence of divisions between the socialists was evident at the March 1993 elections to the French National Assembly. Michaux-Chevry of the RPR was re-elected, as were Moutoussamy (for the PPDG) and Jalton (representing the anti-Larifla faction of the PS). Larifla, meanwhile, was defeated by Edouard Chammougon, a candidate of the independent right who was elected (despite his implication in several corruption scandals—see below) with the assistance of votes in the second round of those socialists who resented Larifla's support for Michaux-Chevry in 1992. Michaux-Chevry was appointed to the position of Minister-Delegate, with responsibility for human rights and humanitarian action, in Edouard Balladur's centre-right coalition Government.

The left retained control of the General Council following cantonal elections in March 1994: Jalton's PS won eight seats, and the 'dissident' PS and PPDG six each. Larifla was subsequently re-elected President of the Council. At elections to the European Parliament in June, a combined list of parties of the left of the French Overseas Departments, including the PPDG (the list was headed by Moutoussamy), won the greatest share of the votes cast (37.2%) in Guadeloupe; an abstention rate of 85.4% was recorded.

Meanwhile, local political affairs were dominated by scandals involving prominent public figures. Twice during 1993 the Antilles-Guyane Chambre régionale des comptes—the body responsible for overseeing public finances in the region—rejected budget figures submitted by Guadeloupe's Regional Council, deeming that the Council's deficit projections were severely underestimated. In January 1994 an administrative tribunal in Basse-Terre ruled that Michaux-Chevry had been unjustified in dismissing (following the first rejection of the budget) the Regional Council's director of finances, who had submitted departmental accounts, as required by law, to the Chambre régional des comptes; this judgment was upheld at an appeal in Paris in April 1995. In January 1993 Chammougon, the Mayor of Baie-Mahault, was sentenced to three years' imprisonment, fined and deprived of his civic and civil rights for 10 years, following his conviction on corruption charges dating as far back as 1980. He remained at liberty pending an appeal and also, after March 1993, benefited from parliamentary immunity; the prison sentence was suspended and the fine lowered in November 1993, and in October 1994 a higher appeal reduced the deprivation of rights to five years. In September 1993 an investigation of alleged corruption among several of Chammougon's close associates resulted in the deputy's implication in further charges of 'passive corruption' and the abuse and misappropriation of public funds. Civil proceedings were also pending against him in respect of a bank loan disbursed in 1989 for a municipal construction contract in Baie-Mahault that was never undertaken. In November 1994 the French Constitutional Council revoked Chammougon's membership of the National Assembly, and the former deputy was subsequently detained briefly in Pointe-à-Pitre, in connection with the failure to honour a security of 1m. francs arising from an earlier detention. In January 1995 Chammougon's wife (elected in the previous month to replace him as Mayor of Baie-Mahault) was elected to succeed him in the General Council, although Léo Andy, the candidate of the 'dissident' PS, was elected to the vacant seat in the National Assembly, defeating (at the second round) the candidate supported by both Chammougon and Michaux-Chevry.

The rate of abstention in Guadeloupe (64.5%) at the first round of the 1995 presidential election, held on 23 April, was the highest recorded at a presidential contest since 1965. Chirac emerged as the leading candidate, with 38.2% of the valid votes cast, ahead of the PS candidate, Lionel Jospin, who took 35.1%. At the second round, on 7 May 1995, Jospin secured 55.1% of the votes, having benefited from the expressed support of all the parties of the left. The level of abstention at this round was 55.2%. At municipal elections in June, Michaux-Chevry became mayor of Basse-Terre, defeating the incumbent PPDG candidate. Jalton, who was supplanted as mayor of Les Abymes by a candidate of the 'dissident' PS, died in November. Michaux-Chevry and Larifla were elected to the Senate in September; the defeat of one of the incumbents, Henri Bangou of the PPDG, was attributed to the continuing divisions within the left. Philippe Chaulet of the RPR was subsequently elected to take Michaux-Chevry's seat in the National Assembly.

Hurricanes Luis and Marilyn struck the islands in September 1995, causing widespread devastation. The former, which resulted in at least two deaths, affected in particular Saint-Martin and Saint-Barthélemy, where a natural catastrophe was declared. The destruction on Saint-Martin of the dwellings of some 7,000 illegal immigrants (many of whom were Haitians employed for many years in the construction and tourist industries) was apparently used by the island's authorities as a pretext for the repatriation of the immigrants: the rebuilding of shanty towns was forbidden, and it was stated that, should an insufficient number fail to take advantage of incentives to leave the island, compulsory repatriations would ensue.

With effect from the beginning of 1996 the social security systems of the Overseas Departments were aligned with those of metropolitan France. In February delegates from Guadeloupe were among more than 300 representatives of the Overseas Departments' political, economic, trade union and professional organizations who attended a meeting in Paris, entitled the National Assizes of Social Equality and Development, held at the instigation of Jean-Jacques de Peretti, the Minister-Delegate responsible for the Overseas Departments and Territories.

At elections to the French National Assembly in late May and early June 1997, Moutoussamy, Andy and Chaulet all retained their seats, while Daniel Marsin, a candidate of the independent left, was elected in the constituency of Les Abymes, Pointe-à-Pitre. An abstention rate of 52.5% was recorded.

Government

France is represented in Guadeloupe by an appointed prefect. There are two councils with local powers: the 42-member General Council and the 41-member Regional Council. Both are elected by universal adult suffrage for a period of up to six years. Guadeloupe elects four deputies to the French National Assembly in Paris, and sends two indirectly-elected representatives to the Senate. The Department is also represented at the European Parliament.

Defence

At 1 August 1997 France maintained a military force of 5,000 in the Antilles, with its headquarters in Fort-de-France (Martinique).

Economic Affairs

In 1994, according to UN estimates, Guadeloupe's gross domestic product (GDP), measured at current prices, was US $3,362m., equivalent to $7,985 per head. During 1985–94 GDP increased, in real terms, at an average annual rate of 3.2%; GDP increased by 1.9% in 1994. Between 1985 and 1995, according to estimates by the World Bank, the population increased by an annual average of 1.8%.

Agriculture, hunting, forestry and fishing contributed 7.3% of GDP in 1991, and engaged an estimated 4.3% of the labour force in 1996. The principal cash crops are bananas and sugar cane; exports of the former provided 25.4% of total export earnings in 1995, while exports of raw sugar accounted for 11.5% of the total in that year. Yams, sweet potatoes and plantains are the chief subsistence crops. Fishing, mostly at an artisanal level, fulfilled about two-thirds of domestic requirements in the mid-1990s; shrimp-farming was developed during the 1980s. Agricultural GDP increased by an annual average of 4.9% in 1980–85, and by 3.9% per year in 1985–89.

The industrial sector (including manufacturing, construction and power) contributed 14.6% of GDP in 1991, and engaged about 20.1% of the employed labour force at the time of the 1990 census. The main manufacturing activity is food processing, particularly sugar production, rum distillation, and flour-milling. The sugar industry was in decline in the early 1990s, owing to deteriorating equipment and a reduction in the area planted with sugar cane (from 20,000 ha in 1980 to 16,000 ha in 1990). Industrial GDP increased by an annual average of 2.7% in 1980–85, and by 1.8% per year in 1985–89.

Of some 700,000 tons of petroleum imported annually, about one-third is used for the production of electricity. Efforts are currently being concentrated on the use of renewable energy resources—notably solar, geothermal and wind power—for energy production; there is also thought to be considerable potential for the use of sugar cane as a means of generating energy in Guadeloupe. Imports of mineral fuels accounted for 5.8% of total expenditure on imports in 1995.

The services sector engaged 72.8% of the employed labour force in 1990 and provided 78.1% of GDP in 1991. Tourism superseded sugar production in 1988 as the Department's principal source of income, and there is significant potential for the further development of the sector, particularly 'eco-tourism'. In 1994 tourist arrivals totalled 556,000, and receipts from tourism amounted to US $490m.

In 1995 Guadeloupe recorded a trade deficit of US $1,739.3m. In 1995 the principal source of imports (63.8%) was France, which was also the principal market for exports (65.8%). Martinique, which took 10.6% of exports in 1995, is also an important trading partner. The principal exports in 1995 were boats, bananas, raw sugar and rum. The principal imports in that year were machinery and transport equipment (mainly road vehicles), food and live animals, miscellaneous manufactured articles, basic manufactures and chemicals.

Guadeloupe's budget deficit was estimated by the metropolitan authorities to amount to some 800m. French francs (including arrears) in 1993. The annual rate of inflation averaged 2.2% in 1990–96; consumer prices increased by an average of 1.4% in 1996. Some 27.3% of the labour force were unemployed in August 1996.

As an integral part of France, Guadeloupe belongs to the European Union (EU—see p. 152). Guadeloupe and the other French Overseas Departments were to receive a total of ECU 1,500m. from EU regional funds in 1994–2000.

Economic growth in Guadeloupe has been restricted by certain inherent problems: its location; the fact that the domestic market is too narrow to stimulate the expansion of the manufacturing base; the lack of primary materials; and the inflated labour and service costs compared with those of neighbouring countries. Economic activity was severely disrupted in September 1989, when Hurricane Hugo struck the islands, causing widespread devastation. The French Government undertook to provide more than 2,000m. French francs for reconstruction, and additional aid for the modernization of the sugar industry. The banana-growing sector and the tourist industry, both of which were particularly adversely affected, had recovered well by the early 1990s. However, Hurricanes Luis and Marilyn, which struck in September 1995, caused severe infrastructural damage, destroyed banana plantations, hotels and public buildings, and threatened the 1996 sugar crop. A ruling by the World Trade Organization, in 1997, in favour of a complaint, brought by the USA and four Latin American countries, against the EU's banana import regime—which gives preferential access to imports from member states' overseas possessions and countries linked to the EU by the Lomé Convention—could threaten Guadeloupe's banana-growing sector.

Social Welfare

In 1997 there were seven hospital complexes (including one for psychiatric care), two local hospitals, a physiotherapy clinic and 16 private clinics. In addition, each of the 34 communes has a clinic. In 1990 there was a total of 3,278 hospital beds, of which 2,163 were in public institutions and 1,115 in private institutions. In that year there were 555 physicians, 175 pharmacists and 110 dentists working in Guadeloupe. The social security legislation of metropolitan France is applicable in Guadeloupe. With effect from 1 January 1996 welfare payments and the statutory minimum wage in the Overseas Departments were aligned with those of metropolitan France.

Education

The education system is similar to that of metropolitan France (see chapter on French Guiana). In 1996 secondary education was provided at 40 junior comprehensives, or collèges, 10 vocational lycées, 10 general and technological lycées and one agricultural lycée. A branch of the Université Antilles-Guyane, at Pointe-à-Pitre, has faculties of law, economics, sciences, medicine and Caribbean studies. The university as a whole had 15,810 enrolled students in the 1995/96 academic year. There is also a teacher training college. An Academy for Guadeloupe was established in January 1997. In 1982 the average rate of adult illiteracy was 10.0% (males 10.4%; females 9.6%).

Public Holidays

1998: 1 January (New Year's Day), 23–24 February (Lenten Carnival), 10–13 April (Easter), 1 May (Labour Day), 8 May (Victory Day), 21 May (Ascension Day), 1 June (Whit Monday), 14 July (National Day), 21 July (Victor Schoëlcher Day), 15 August (Assumption), 1 November (All Saints' Day), 11 November (Armistice Day), 25 December (Christmas Day).

1999: 1 January (New Year's Day), 15–16 February (Lenten Carnival), 2–5 April (Easter), 1 May (Labour Day), 8 May (Victory Day), 13 May (Ascension Day), 24 May (Whit Monday), 14 July (National Day), 21 July (Victor Schoëlcher Day), 15 August (Assumption), 1 November (All Saints' Day), 11 November (Armistice Day), 25 December (Christmas Day).

Weights and Measures

The metric system is in use.

Statistical Survey

Sources (unless otherwise stated): Institut national de la statistique et des études économiques, ave Paul Lacavé, BP 96, 97102 Basse-Terre; tel. 81-17-86; telex 919915; fax 81-07-15; Ministère des départements et territoires d'outre-mer, 27 rue Oudinot, 75700 Paris 07 SP; tel. 1-53-69-20-00; fax 1-43-06-60-30; internet http://www.outre-mer.gouv.fr.

AREA AND POPULATION

Area: 1,705 sq km (658.3 sq miles), incl. dependencies (La Désirade, Les Saintes, Marie-Galante, Saint-Barthélemy, Saint-Martin).

Population: 327,002 (males 160,112, females 166,890) at census of 9 March 1982; 387,034 (males 189,187, females 197,847) at census of 15 March 1990; 413,900 (official estimate) at mid-1994.

Density (mid-1994): 242.8 per sq km.

Principal Towns (population at 1990 census): Basse-Terre (capital) 14,003; Les Abymes 62,605; Saint-Martin 28,518; Pointe-à-Pitre 26,069; Le Gosier 20,688; Capesterre/Belle-Eau 19,012.

Births, Marriages and Deaths (provisional figures, 1994): Registered live births 7,248 (birth rate 17.5 per 1,000); Registered marriages 1,911 (marriage rate 4.6 per 1,000); Registered deaths 2,331 (death rate 5.6 per 1,000).

Expectation of Life (UN estimates, years at birth, 1990–95): 74.6 (males 71.7, females 78.0). Source: UN, *World Population Prospects: The 1994 Revision*.

Economically Active Population (persons aged 15 years and over, 1990 census): Agriculture, hunting, forestry and fishing 8,391; Industry 9,630; Construction and public works 13,967; Trade 15,020; Transport and telecommunications 6,950; Marketable services 26,533; Financial services 2,802; Non-marketable services 34,223; Total employed 117,516 (males 68,258, females 49,258); Unemployed 54,926 (males 25,691; females 29,235); Total labour force 172,442 (males 93,949, females 78,493).

AGRICULTURE, ETC.

Principal Crops (FAO estimates, '000 metric tons, 1996): Sweet potatoes 5; Yams 7; Cassava 2; Other roots and tubers 2; Vegetables 21; Melons and watermelons 4; Pineapples 4; Bananas 116; Plantains 6; Sugar cane 376. Source: FAO, *Production Yearbook*.

Livestock (FAO estimates, '000 head, year ending September 1996): Cattle 60; Goats 63; Pigs 14; Sheep 3. Source: FAO, *Production Yearbook*.

Livestock Products (FAO estimates, '000 metric tons, 1996): Beef and veal 3; Pig meat 1; Poultry meat 1; Hen eggs 2. Source: FAO, *Production Yearbook*.

Forestry: Roundwood removals (FAO estimate, '000 cu m, excl. bark, 1994): Total (fuel wood) 15. Source: FAO, *Yearbook of Forest Products*.

Fishing (metric tons, live weight): Total catch 8,640 in 1993; 8,826 in 1994; 9,530 in 1995. Source: FAO, *Yearbook of Fishery Statistics*. Production of shrimps by aquaculture: 52 metric tons (1988).

MINING

Production ('000 metric tons, 1994): Pozzolan 210.0. Source: UN, *Industrial Commodity Statistics Yearbook*.

INDUSTRY

Production (1994, '000 metric tons, unless otherwise indicated): Raw sugar 67; Cement 283; Electric energy (million kWh) 1,005. Source: UN, *Industrial Commodity Statistics Yearbook*. Rum (hl) 49,814 (1995).

FINANCE

Currency and Exchange Rates: French currency is used (see French Guiana).

Budget (million French francs): **State budget** (1990): Revenue 2,494; Expenditure 4,776. **Regional budget** (1989): Revenue 1,046; Expenditure 1,025. **Departmental budget** (1989): Revenue 1,617; Expenditure 1,748.

Money Supply (million francs at 31 December 1995): Currency outside banks 1,075; Demand deposits at banks 6,185; Total money 7,260.

Cost of Living (Consumer Price Index for urban areas; base: 1990 = 100): 110.1 in 1994; 112.4 in 1995; 114.0 in 1996. Source: UN, *Monthly Bulletin of Statistics*.

Expenditure on the Gross Domestic Product (million French francs at current prices, 1992): Government final consumption expenditure 5,385; Private final consumption expenditure 14,999; Increase in stocks 227; Gross fixed capital formation 5,004; *Total domestic expenditure* 25,615; Exports of goods and services 803; *Less* Imports of goods and services 8,447; *GDP in purchasers' values* 17,972.

EXTERNAL TRADE

Principal Commodities (US $ million, 1995): *Imports c.i.f.:* Food and live animals 302.8 (Meat and meat preparations 74.7, Dairy products and birds eggs 51.9, Cereals and cereal preparations 55.6, Vegetables and fruit 51.4); Beverages and tobacco 88.1 (Beverages 78.8); Mineral fuels, lubricants, etc. 110.7 (Petroleum, petroleum products, etc. 52.5, Gas, natural and manufactured 58.0); Chemicals and related products 172.8 (Medicinal and pharmaceutical products 78.1); Basic manufactures 259.5 (Paper, paperboard and manufactures 39.3); Machinery and transport equipment 607.0 (Office machines and automatic data-processing equipment 40.7, Telecommunications and sound equipment 43.0, Road vehicles and parts 217.7, Other transport equipment 100.0); Miscellaneous manufactured articles 282.6 (Furniture and parts 47.2, Clothing and accessories, excl. footwear, 52.6, Printed matter 39.5); Total (incl. others) 1,901.3. *Exports f.o.b.:* Food and live animals 74.5 (Cereals and cereal preparations 7.8, Bananas and plantains 41.1, Raw sugar 18.6); Beverages and tobacco 10.0 (Alcoholic beverages 8.3); Basic manufactures 7.2; Machinery and transport equipment 59.1 (Road vehicles and parts 3.5, Ships and boats 42.7); Miscellaneous manufactured articles 8.0; Total (incl. others) 162.0. Source: UN, *International Trade Statistics Yearbook*.

Principal Trading Partners (US $ million, 1995): *Imports c.i.f.:* Belgium-Luxembourg 31.3; Brazil 27.4; France (incl. Monaco) 1,213.9; Germany 60.8; Italy 65.0; Japan 41.6; Martinique 45.9; Netherlands 24.9; Spain 35.0; Trinidad and Tobago 70.3; United Kingdom 26.1; USA 62.4; Total (incl. others) 1,901.2. *Exports f.o.b.:* Bahamas 7.1; Belgium-Luxembourg 4.4; France (incl. Monaco) 106.6; French Guiana 3.5; Italy 7.3; Martinique 17.1; United Kingdom 3.6; USA 5.5; Total (incl. others) 161.9. Source: UN, *International Trade Statistics Yearbook*.

TRANSPORT

Road Traffic ('000 motor vehicles in use, 1993): Passenger cars 101.6; Commercial vehicles 37.5. Source: UN, *Statistical Yearbook*.

Shipping *Merchant Fleet* (vessels registered, '000 grt at 31 December 1992): Total displacement 6. Source: Lloyd's Register of Shipping. *International sea-borne traffic,* (1994): Vessels entered 6,838; Goods loaded 1,816,000 metric tons; Goods unloaded 6,661,000 metric tons; Passenger arrivals 995,000; Passenger departures 992,000.

Civil Aviation (commercial traffic, 1990): Number of flights 31,108; Passengers carried 1,466,100; Freight carried 13,500 metric tons.

TOURISM

Tourist Arrivals ('000): 341 in 1992; 453 in 1993; 556 in 1994.

Receipts from Tourism (US $ million): 269 in 1992; 370 in 1993; 490 in 1994.

Source: UN, *Statistical Yearbook*.

COMMUNICATIONS MEDIA

Radio Receivers ('000 in use) 96 in 1994; **Television Receivers** ('000 in use) 111 in 1994; **Telephones** ('000 main lines in use) 159 in 1994; **Telefax Stations** (number in use) 291 in 1990; **Mobile Cellular Telephones** (subscribers) 814 in 1990; **Daily Newspaper** 1 in 1994 (average circulation 35,000 copies). Sources: UNESCO, *Statistical Yearbook*; UN, *Statistical Yearbook*.

EDUCATION

Pre-primary (1993/94): 121 institutions; 760 teachers; 22,678 students (1994/95).

Primary (1992/93): 219 institutions; 1,920 teachers; 38,332 students (1994/95).

Secondary (1994/95): 3,467 teachers (1992/93); 41,656 general students (males 19,818, females 21,838), 9,243 vocational students (males 4,800, females 4,443). Source: UNESCO, *Statistical Yearbook*.

Higher (1993): 4,308 students (Université Antilles-Guyane).

Directory

The Government

(January 1998)

Prefect: JEAN FEDINI, Préfecture, Palais d'Orléans, rue Lardenoy, 97109 Basse-Terre Cédex; tel. 81-15-60; fax 81-84-97.

President of the General Council: DOMINIQUE LARIFLA ('dissident' PS), rue Lardenoy, 97100 Basse-Terre; tel. 81-99-99; fax 81-68-79.

President of the Economic and Social Committee: GUY FRÉDÉRIC.

Deputies to the French National Assembly: ERNEST MOUTOUSSAMY (PPDG), LÉO ANDY ('dissident' PS), PHILIPPE CHAULET (RPR), DANIEL MARSIN (Independent left).

Representatives to the French Senate: LUCETTE MICHAUX-CHEVRY (RPR), DOMINIQUE LARIFLA ('dissident' PS).

REGIONAL COUNCIL

rue Paul Lacavé, 97100 Basse-Terre; tel. 80-40-40; fax 81-34-19.

President: LUCETTE MICHAUX-CHEVRY.

Election, 22 March 1992*

	Votes	%	Seats
Objectif Guadeloupe†	35,590	29.27	15
PS	21,226	17.46	9
PS-Dissident	18,706	15.38	7
PPDG	13,108	10.78	5
PCG	7,096	5.83	3
UPLG	6,673	5.49	2
Others	19,190	15.78	—
Total	121,589	100.00	41

* On 4 December 1992 the French Conseil d'Etat annulled the results of the election. New elections were scheduled for January 1994, at which Objectif Guadeloupe increased its number of seats to 22, while the PS and the dissident PS only secured 10 seats.

† The RPR, the UDF and other right-wing candidates formed an electoral alliance, Objectif Guadeloupe, to contest the election.

Political Organizations

***Fédération de la Guadeloupe du Rassemblement pour la République (RPR):** Lotissement SIG, Ffrench, Sainte-Anne; Gaullist; Departmental Sec. ALDO BLAISE.

Fédération Guadeloupéenne du Parti Socialiste (PS): 801 Residence Collinette, Grand Camp, 97139 Les Abymes; tel. and fax

82-19-32; divided into two factions to contest the March 1992 and March 1993 elections; First Sec. GEORGES LOUISOR.
A 'dissident' faction of the party is led by DOMINIQUE LARIFLA.

***Fédération Guadeloupéenne de l'Union pour la Démocratie Française (UDF):** Pointe-à-Pitre; centrist; Pres. MARCEL ESDRAS.

Mouvement Populaire pour une Guadeloupe Indépendante (MPGI): Pointe-à-Pitre; f. 1982; merged with Alliance Révolutionnaire Caraïbe in 1984; extremist pro-independence party; Sec.-Gen. SIMONE FAISANS-RENAC.

Mouvement Socialiste Départmentaliste Guadeloupéen: Mairie de Morne-à-l'Eau, 97111 Morne-à-l'Eau; Sec.-Gen. ABDON SAMAN.

Parti Communiste Guadeloupéen (PCG): 119 rue Vatable, 97110 Pointe-à-Pitre; tel. 82-19-45; fax 83-69-90; f. 1944; Sec.-Gen. CHRISTIAN CÉLESTE.

Parti Progressiste Démocratique Guadeloupéen (PPDG): Pointe-à-Pitre; f. 1991; includes a breakaway group of PCG militants; Leaders HENRI BANGOU; DANIEL GENIES.

Union Populaire pour la Libération de la Guadeloupe (UPLG): Basse-Terre; f. 1978; favours increased autonomy for Guadeloupe; Sec.-Gen. LUCIEN PERRUTIN.

* The RPR, the UDF and other right-wing candidates allied to contest the 1992 elections to the Regional Council as Objectif Guadeloupe.

Judicial System

Cour d'Appel: Palais de Justice, 97100 Basse-Terre; tel. 80-63-36; telex 919890; fax 80-63-39; First Pres. B. BACOU; Procurator-Gen. MICHEL BRÉARD; two Tribunaux de Grande Instance, four Tribunaux d'Instance.

Religion

The majority of the population belong to the Roman Catholic Church.

CHRISTIANITY

The Roman Catholic Church

Guadeloupe comprises the single diocese of Basse-Terre, suffragan to the archdiocese of Fort-de-France, Martinique. At 31 December 1995 there were an estimated 390,674 adherents, representing some 95.8% of the total population. The Bishop participates in the Antilles Episcopal Conference, currently based in Port of Spain, Trinidad and Tobago.

Bishop of Basse-Terre: Rt Rev. ERNEST MESMIN LUCIEN CABO, Evêché, place Saint-François, BP 369, 97106 Basse-Terre Cédex; tel. 81-36-69; fax 81-98-23.

Other Denominations

Apostles of Infinite Love: Plaines, 97116 Pointe-Noire; tel. 98-01-19.

Mission Baptiste: 13 Résidence Dampierre, 97190 Le Gosier; tel. 84-30-04.

The Press

L'Etincelle: 119 rue Vatable, 97110 Pointe-à-Pitre; tel. 91-12-77; fax 83-69-90; f. 1944; weekly; organ of the PCG; Dir RAYMOND BARON; circ. 5,000.

France-Antilles: 1 rue Hincelin, BP 658, 97159 Pointe-à-Pitre; tel. 90-25-25; telex 919728; fax 91-78-31; daily; Dir CLAUDE PROVENÇAL; circ. 25,000.

Guadeloupe 2000: Résidence Massabielle, 97110 Pointe-à-Pitre; tel. 82-36-42; fax 91-52-57; fortnightly; right-wing extremist; Dir EDOUARD BOULOGNE; circ. 3,500.

Jakata: 18 rue Condé, 97110 Pointe-à-Pitre; f. 1977; fortnightly; Dir FRANTZ SUCCAB; circ. 6,000.

Match: 33 rue St John Perse, 97110 Pointe-à-Pitre; tel. 82-01-87; fortnightly; Dir CAMILLE JABBOUR; circ. 6,000.

Newsmagazine Guadeloupéen: Résidence Vatable, Bâtiment B, BP 1286, 97178 Pointe-à-Pitre; tel. 91-16-94; fax 82-22-38; f. 1994; fmrly *Magwa*; fortnightly; independent; Editor DANNICK ZANDRONIS; circ. 4,000.

Le Progrès social: rue Toussaint L'Ouverture, 97100 Basse-Terre; tel. 81-10-41; weekly; Dir JEAN-CLAUDE RODES; circ. 5,000.

TV Magazine Guadeloupe: 1 rue Paul Lacavé, BP 658, 97169 Pointe-à-Pitre; tel. 90-25-25; telex 919728; weekly.

NEWS AGENCIES

Agence Centrale Parisienne de Presse (ACP): Pointe-à-Pitre; tel. 82-14-76; telex 919728; fax 83-78-73; Rep. RENÉ CAZIMIR-JEANON.

Foreign Bureaux

Agencia EFE (Spain): BP 1016, 97178 Pointe-à-Pitre; Correspondent DANNICK ZANDRONIS.

United Press International (UPI) (USA): BP 658, 97159 Pointe-à-Pitre; Rep. STÉPHANE DELANNOY.

Broadcasting and Communications

BROADCASTING

Société Nationale de Radio-Télévision Française d'Outre-Mer (RFO): BP 402, 97163 Pointe-à-Pitre Cédex; tel. 93-96-96; fax 93-96-82; 24 hours radio and 24 hours television broadcast daily; Pres. JEAN-MARIE CAVADA; Dir JEAN-LOUIS BALAUDRAUD.

Radio

More than 30 private FM radio stations are in operation.

Radio Actif: Petit-Pérou, BP 3060, 97139 Les Abymes; tel. 26-68-47; fax 26-73-38; commercial; satellite link to Radio Monte-Carlo (Monaco and France).

Radio Caraïbes International (RCI): BP 1309, 97187 Point-à-Pitre Cédex; tel. 83-96-96; telex 19083; fax 83-96-97; two commercial stations broadcasting 24 hours daily; Dir OLIVIER GARON.

Radio Saint-Martin: Port de Marigot, 97150 Saint-Martin; commercial station broadcasting 94 hours weekly; Man. H. COOKS.

Television

In addition to RFO, four unauthorized private television stations were in operation in mid-1997: Archipel 4, Canal 10, TV Eclair and TCI Guadeloupe.

Finance

(cap. = capital; res = reserves; dep. = deposits; m. = million; brs = branches; amounts in French francs)

BANKING

Central Bank

Institut d'Emission des Départments d'Outre Mer: Pointe-à-Pitre.

Commercial Banks

Banque des Antilles Françaises: place de la Victoire, BP 696, 97171 Pointe-à-Pitre Cédex; tel. 26-80-07; telex 919866; fax 26-78-98; rue de Cours Nolivos, 97100 Basse-Terre; f. 1853; cap. 32.6m., res 42.9m., dep. 2,243.6m. (Dec. 1996); Chair. JACQUES GIRAULT; Gen. Man. JEAN TAUZIES.

Banque Française Commerciale Antilles-Guyane (BFC Antilles-Guyane): BP 13, 97151 Pointe-à-Pitre Cédex; tel. 89-64-00; telex 919764; fax 83-60-63; f. 1976 as branch of Banque Française Commerciale SA, separated 1984; Pres. PHILIPPE BRAULT; Chair. and CEO GERARD MORANDEAU.

Banque Nationale de Paris: place de la Rénovation, 97110 Pointe-à-Pitre; tel. 90-58-58; telex 919449; fax 90-04-07; Dir HENRI BETBEDER; 6 further brs in Guadeloupe.

Crédit Martiniquais: Angle des rues Paul Lacavé et Cités Unies, 97100 Pointe-à-Pitre; tel. 83-18-59; f. 1987 (see section on Martinique).

Société Générale de Banque aux Antilles (SGBA): 30 rue Frébault, BP 630, 97110 Pointe-à-Pitre; tel. 82-54-23; telex 919735; fax 83-57-83; f. 1979; Pres. JACQUES DE MALEVILLE; Gen. Man. HENRI GILLES; 6 brs in French West Indies.

INSURANCE

Mutuelle Antillaise d'Assurances, Société d'Assurances à forme mutuelle: 12 rue Gambetta, BP 409, 97110 Pointe-à-Pitre; tel. 83-23-32; telex 919945; fax 83-34-99; f. 1937; Dir-Gen. FÉLIX CHERDIEU D'ALEXIS; Man. A. ZOGG.

Foreign Companies

Some 30 of the principal European insurance companies are represented in Pointe-à-Pitre, and another six companies have offices in Basse-Terre.

Trade and Industry

DEVELOPMENT ORGANIZATIONS

Agence pour la Promotion des Investissements en Guadeloupe (APRIGA): BP 514, 97165 Pointe-à-Pitre; tel. 83-48-97; fax 82-07-09; f. 1979 as Agence pour la Promotion de l'Industrie de la Guadeloupe; Pres. PATRICK DOQUIN; Dir CHARLY BLONDEAU.

Caisse Française de Développement (CFD): Faubourg Frébault, BP 160, 97154 Pointe-à-Pitre; tel. 83-32-72; telex 919074; fmrly Caisse Centrale de Coopération Economique, name changed 1992.

Centre Technique Interprofessionnel de la Canne et du Sucre: Morne Epingle, Les Abymes, BP 397, 97162 Pointe-à-Pitre Cédex; tel. 82-94-70; fax 20-97-84; Pres. MICHEL MONTEIRO; Dir MICHEL MARCHAT.

CHAMBERS OF COMMERCE

Chambre de Commerce et d'Industrie de Pointe-à-Pitre: rue F. Eboué, BP 64, 97152 Pointe-à-Pitre Cédex; tel. 93-76-00; fax 90-21-87; Pres. FÉLIX CLAIREVILLE; Dir-Gen. JACQUES GARRETA.

Chambre de Commerce et d'Industrie de Basse-Terre: 6 rue Victor Hugues, 97100 Basse-Terre; tel. 81-16-56; telex 919781; fax 81-21-17; f. 1832; 24 mems; Pres. JEAN-JACQUES FAYEL; Sec.-Gen. JEAN-CLAUDE BAPTISTIDE.

Chambre Départementale d'Agriculture de la Guadeloupe: 23 rue Lardenoy, 97100 Basse-Terre; tel. 81-34-61; Pres. MAURICE RAMASSAMY; Dir FRANCK LOMBION.

Chambre de Métiers de la Guadeloupe: route de Choisy, BP 61, 97120 Sainte-Claude; tel. 80-23-33; fax 80-08-93.

EMPLOYERS' ORGANIZATIONS

Union Patronale de la Guadeloupe: Pointe-à-Pitre; Pres. LIONEL DE LAVIGNE.

Société d'Intérêt Collectif Agricole (Sica-Assobag): Desmarais, 97100 Basse-Terre; tel. 81-05-52; telex 919727; f. 1967; banana producers; Pres. FRANÇOIS LE METAYER; Dir JEAN-CLAUDE PETRELLUZZI.

Syndicat des Producteurs-Exportateurs de Sucre et de Rhum de la Guadeloupe et Dépendances: Zone Industrielle de la Pointe Jarry, 97122 Baie-Mahault, BP 2015, 97191 Pointe-à-Pitre; tel. 26-62-12; telex 919824; fax 26-86-76; f. 1937; 4 mems; Pres. AMÉDÉE HUYGHUES-DESPOINTES.

TRADE UNIONS

Confédération Générale du Travail de la Guadeloupe (CGTG): 4 cité Artisanale de Bergevin, BP 779, 97173 Pointe-à-Pitre Cédex; tel. 82-34-61; telex 919061; fax 91-04-00; f. 1961; Sec.-Gen. CLAUDE MORVAN; 5,000 mems.

Union Départementale de la Confédération Française des Travailleurs Chrétiens: BP 245, 97159 Pointe-à-Pitre; tel. 82-04-01; f. 1937; Sec.-Gen. PIERROT TAURUS; 3,500 mems.

Union Départementale des Syndicats CGT-FO: 59 rue Lamartine, 97110 Pointe-à-Pitre; Gen. Sec. FERDINAND QUILLIN; 1,500 mems.

Union Générale des Travailleurs de la Guadeloupe: rue Paul Lacavé, 97110 Pointe-à-Pitre; tel. 83-10-07; confederation of pro-independence trade unions; Sec.-Gen. GABY CLAVIER.

Union Interprofessionnelle de la Guadeloupe (UIG): Logement TEFT, Bergevin, 97181 Pointe-à-Pitre; tel. 83-16-50; affiliated to the Confédération Française Démocratique du Travail; Institut National de la Recherche Agronomique (INRA), Domaine de Duclos, 97170 Petit-Bourg; Sec.-Gen. A. MEPHON.

Transport

RAILWAYS

There are no railways in Guadeloupe.

ROADS

In 1990 there were 2,069 km of roads in Guadeloupe, of which 323 km were Routes Nationales.

SHIPPING

The major port is at Pointe-à-Pitre, and a new port for the export of bananas has been built at Basse-Terre.

Direction Départementale des Affaires Maritimes de la Guadeloupe: 1 Quai Layrle, BP 473, 97164 Pointe-à-Pitre Cédex; tel. 82-03-13; fax 90-07-33; Dir RENÉ GOALLO.

Port Autonome de la Guadeloupe: Gare Maritime, BP 485, 97165 Pointe-à-Pitre Cédex; tel. 91-63-13; telex 919710; fax 91-56-79; port authority; Gen. Man. JEAN CHARLES LE CLECH.

Compagnie Générale Maritime Antilles-Guyane: Zone Industrielle de la Pointe Jarry, BP 92, 97100 Baie-Mahault; tel. 26-72-39; telex 919880; fax 26-74-62.

Société Guadeloupéenne de Consignation et Manutention (SGCM): 8 rue de la Chapelle, BP 2360, 971001 Jarry Cédex; tel. 38-05-55; telex 919720; fax 26-95-39; f. 1994; shipping agents, stevedoring; Chair. LUC EMY; Gen. Man. ALAIN APPÉ.

CIVIL AVIATION

Raizet International Airport is situated 3 km (2 miles) from Pointe-à-Pitre and is equipped to handle jet-engined aircraft. There are smaller airports on the islands of Marie-Galante, La Désirade and Saint-Barthélémy.

Air Guadeloupe: Aéroport du Raizet, Immeuble Le Caducet, 97110 Abymes; tel. 91-53-44; telex 919008; fax 91-75-66; f. 1970; 46% owned by Département de Guadeloupe, 45% by Air France; operates inter-island and regional services, flights to Paris; 170 employees; Pres. FRANÇOIS PANEOLE.

Tourism

Guadeloupe is a popular tourist destination, especially for visitors from France and the USA. The main attractions are the beaches, the mountainous scenery and the unspoilt beauty of the island dependencies. In 1994 556,000 tourists visited Guadeloupe, and receipts from tourism totalled US $490m. In the mid-1990s there were 169 hotels, with some 7,550 rooms.

Delégation Régionale au Tourisme: 5 rue Victor Hugues, 97100 Basse-Terre; tel. 81-15-60; fax 81-94-82; Dir HUGUES JONNIAUX.

Office du Tourisme: 5 square de la Banque, POB 1099, 97110 Pointe-à-Pitre; tel. 82-09-30; telex 919715; fax 83-89-22; Dir-Gen. ERICK W. ROTIN; Pres. PHILIPPE CHAULET.

Syndicat d'Initiative de la Guadeloupe: Pointe-à-Pitre; Pres. Dr EDOUARD CHARTOL.

MARTINIQUE

Introductory Survey

Location, Climate, Language, Religion, Capital

Martinique is one of the Windward Islands in the West Indies, with Dominica to the north and Saint Lucia to the south. The island is dominated by the volcanic peak of Mont Pelée. The climate is tropical, but tempered by easterly and north-easterly breezes. The more humid and wet season runs from July to November, and the average temperature is 26°C (79°F). French is the official language, but a creole patois is widely spoken. The majority of the population profess Christianity and belong to the Roman Catholic Church. The capital is Fort-de-France.

Recent History

Martinique has been a French possession since 1635. The prosperity of the island was based on the sugar industry, which was devastated by the volcanic eruption of Mont Pelée in 1902. Martinique became a Department of France in 1946, when the Governor was replaced by a Prefect, and an elected General Council was created.

During the 1950s there was a growth of nationalist feeling, as expressed by Aimé Césaire's Parti Progressiste Martiniquais (PPM) and the Parti Communiste Martiniquais (PCM). However, economic power remained concentrated in the hands of the *békés* (descendants of white colonial settlers), who owned most of the agricultural land and controlled the lucrative import-export market. This provided little incentive for innovation or selfsufficiency, and fostered resentment against lingering colonial attitudes.

In 1974 Martinique, together with Guadeloupe and French Guiana, was given regional status as part of France's governmental reorganization. An indirectly-elected Regional Council was created, with some control over the local economy. In 1982 and 1983 the socialist Government of President François Mitterrand, which had pledged itself to decentralizing power in favour of the Overseas Departments, made further concessions towards autonomy by giving the local councils greater control over taxation, local police and the economy. At the first direct elections to the new Regional Council, held in February 1983, left-wing parties (the PPM, the PCM and the Fédération Socialiste de la Martinique—FSM) won 21 of the 41 seats. This success, and the election of Aimé Césaire as the Council's President, strengthened his influence against the pro-independence elements in his own party. (Full independence for Martinique attracted support from only a small minority of the population; the majority sought reforms that would bring greater autonomy, while retaining French control.) The Mouvement Indépendantiste Martiniquais (MIM), the most vocal of the separatist parties, fared badly in the elections, obtaining less than 3% of the total vote. In late 1983 and in 1984 Martinique became a target for bomb attacks by the outlawed Alliance Révolutionnaire Caraïbe, an extremist independence movement based in Guadeloupe. At elections to the enlarged General Council, held in March 1985, the left-wing parties increased their representation, but the centre-right coalition of the Union pour la Démocratie Française (UDF) and the Rassemblement pour la République (RPR) maintained their control of the administration.

For the general election to the French National Assembly in March 1986, Martinique's representation was increased from three to four deputies. Aimé Césaire (who had been returned to the French legislature at every election since the liberation of France) and a member of the FSM were elected from a unified list of left-wing candidates, while the RPR and the UDF (which had also presented a joint list) each won one seat. For the concurrent elections to the Regional Council the left-wing parties (including the PPM, the FSM and the PCM) won 21 of the 41 seats, and the RPR and the UDF together won the remaining seats. Aimé Césaire retained the presidency of the Council until June 1988, when he relinquished the post to Camille Darsières (the Secretary-General of the PPM). In September 1986 indirect elections were held for Martinique's two seats in the French Senate. As in the March elections, the left-wing parties united, and, as a consequence, Martinique acquired a left-wing senator for the first time since 1958, a PPM member, while the other successful candidate belonged to the UDF.

Following the recent trend in Martinique, the incumbent, François Mitterrand of the Parti Socialiste (PS), won a decisive majority of the island's votes (71% at the second round, contested against Jacques Chirac of the RPR) at the 1988 French presidential election. Left-wing candidates secured all four seats at elections to the French National Assembly in June. Furthermore, in September–October, for the first time in 40 years, the parties of the left achieved a majority at elections to the General Council, winning 23 of the 45 seats. Emile Maurice of the RPR was, none the less, elected President of the General Council for a seventh term.

In June 1990 the results of the 1986 election to the Regional Council were annulled because of a technicality, and another election was therefore held in October 1990. Pro-independence candidates won nearly 22% of the votes, and secured nine seats (of which seven were won by the MIM). The PPM, the FSM and the PCM again formed a joint electoral list, but won only 14 seats, and therefore lost their absolute majority on the Council; Camille Darsières was, however, re-elected to the presidency of the Council. The success of the pro-independence candidates was attributed to local apprehension concerning the implications of plans within the European Community (EC, known as the European Union—see p. 152—from November 1993) for a single market, which would, it was feared, expose Martinique's economy to excessive competition.

In March 1991 the civil service unions organized a general strike to coincide with a visit to Martinique by Mitterrand and the US President, George Bush. The strike, which was observed by 65% of civil servants, was in protest at proposed central government measures to reduce what were held to be excessive civil service benefits in the Overseas Departments and Territories.

At elections to the General Council in March 1992, left-wing parties secured 26 seats and right-wing organizations 19. Claude Lise, a PPM deputy to the French National Assembly, was elected President of the General Council. In concurrent elections to the Regional Council the RPR and the UDF, contesting the election as the Union pour la France (UPF), won 16 seats, the MIM (which contested the election under the title Patriotes Martiniquais) and the PPM secured nine seats each, and the PCM (under the title Pour une Martinique au Travail) and the FSM (as the Nouvelle Génération Socialiste) won four and three seats respectively. Following the withdrawal in his favour of three other left-wing candidates for the presidency, Emile Capgras of the PCM was finally elected President of the Regional Council: in the third round of the election Capgras and Pierre Petit of the RPR (the UPF candidate) both secured 16 votes, but Capgras was appointed President, on the grounds of his seniority in age.

In September 1992 72.3% of voters in Martinique approved ratification of the Treaty on European Union (see p. 158), although the abstention rate was 75.6%. In November of that year banana-growers in Guadeloupe and Martinique suspended economic activity in their respective Departments by obstructing access to ports and airports and blocking roads, in protest at the threatened loss of special advantages under the Single European Act. Order was restored after four days, however, following assurances that subsidies would be maintained and that certain products, such as bananas (one of Martinique's principal exports), would be protected under EC proposals.

At the March 1993 elections to the French National Assembly there was a marked swing in favour of the parties of the right: André Lesueur and Pierre Petit were elected to represent the RPR, while a third right-wing candidate, Anicet Turinay, campaigned successfully on behalf of the UPF. Aimé Césaire did not seek re-election, and was replaced at the National Assembly by Camille Darsières.

The composition of the General Council remained largely unchanged following cantonal elections in March 1994, at which the PPM retained 10 seats, the RPR seven and the UDF three; Claude Lise was subsequently re-elected President of the Council. At elections to the European Parliament in June, the government list secured the greatest proportion (36.6%) of the votes cast. A combined list of parties of the left of the four Overseas Departments (which included the PPM and the Parti Martiniquais Socialiste) took 20.2% of the votes. An abstention rate of 82.2% was recorded.

Beginning in mid-January 1995 a strike by bank workers in Martinique, in support of demands for increased pay and a revision of banking practices, caused widespread economic disruption, which was exacerbated as public- and private-sector trade unions took sympathetic industrial action in February. The strike—one of the longest ever experienced in Martinique—was ended in mid-March, when bank workers and employers reached an accommodation with regard to the workers' demands.

At the first round of voting in the 1995 presidential election, which took place on 23 April, Martinique was the only French overseas possession in which the candidate of the PS, Lionel Jospin, received the greatest proportion of the valid votes cast (34.4%). Jospin, supported by all the parties of the left, took 58.9% of the votes cast at the second round on 7 May, which was contested against Chirac (who had won 29.1% of the first-round votes). The rate of abstention by eligible voters was 59.4% at the first round and 51.2% at the second. At municipal elections in June the PPM retained control of Martinique's principal towns. In September Claude Lise was elected to the Senate, while the incumbent PPM representative, Rodolphe Désiré, was returned to office.

With effect from the beginning of 1996 the social security systems of the Overseas Departments were aligned with those of metropolitan France. In February delegates from Martinique were among more than 300 representatives of the Overseas Departments' political, economic, trade union and professional organizations who attended a meeting in Paris, entitled the National Assizes of Social Equality and Development, held at the instigation of Jean-Jacques de Peretti, the Minister-Delegate responsible for the Overseas Departments and Territories.

At elections to the French National Assembly in May and June 1997, Anciet Turinay and Pierre Petit, representing the RPR, were re-elected, together with Camille Darsières of the PPM. Alfred Marie-Jeanne, the First Secretary and a founding member of the MIM, was elected in the constituency of Le François, Le Robert (hitherto held by the RPR).

Government

France is represented in Martinique by an appointed prefect. There are two councils with local powers: the 45-member General Council and the 41-member Regional Council. Both are elected by universal adult suffrage for a period of up to six years. Martinique elects four deputies to the French National Assembly in Paris, and sends two indirectly-elected representatives to the Senate. The Department is also represented at the European Parliament.

Defence

At 1 August 1997 France maintained a military force of about 5,000 in the Antilles, with its headquarters in Fort-de-France.

Economic Affairs

In 1994, according to UN estimates, Martinique's gross domestic product (GDP), measured at current prices, was US $4,377m., equivalent to about $11,671 per head. During 1985–94, it was estimated, GDP increased, in real terms, at an average rate of 3.2% per year; GDP increased by 1.9% in 1994. During 1985–95, according to estimates by the World Bank, the population increased by an annual average of 1.1%.

Agriculture, hunting, forestry and fishing contributed 5.7% of GDP in 1991, and engaged an estimated 6.2% of the labour force in 1996. The principal cash crops are bananas (which accounted for 40.4% of export earnings in 1995), sugar cane (primarily for the production of rum), limes, melons and pineapples. Severe damage to banana plantations was caused by Cyclone Debbie in September 1994. The cultivation of cut flowers is also of some significance. Roots and tubers and vegetables are grown for local consumption. Fisheries, mostly at an artisanal level, provided about one-third of the domestic consumption of fish in 1989. Agricultural GDP increased by an annual average of 5.5% in 1980–85, although the growth rate slowed to an average of 1.6% per year in 1985–89.

The industrial sector (including mining, manufacturing, construction and power) contributed 15.3% of GDP in 1990, and engaged 17.3% of the employed labour force at that year's census. The most important manufacturing activities are petroleum refining (exports of refined petroleum products accounted for 17.2% of the value of total exports in 1995) and the processing of agricultural products—the production of rum being of particular significance. Exports of distilled alcoholic beverages provided 10.0% of export earnings in 1995. Martiniquais rum was accorded the designation of Appellation d'origine contrôlée (AOC) in 1996 (the first AOC to be designated outside metropolitan France). Other areas of activity include metals, cement, chemicals, plastics, wood, printing and textiles. Industrial GDP increased by an annual average of 3.4% in 1980–85, and by 2.6% per year in 1985–89.

Energy is derived principally from mineral fuels. Imports of mineral fuels (including crude petroleum destined for the island's refinery) accounted for 7.5% of the value of total imports in 1995.

The services sector engaged 75.1% of the employed labour force in 1990 and provided 78.8% of GDP in 1991. Tourism is a major activity on the island and one of the most important sources of foreign exchange. In 1995 929,000 tourists (including 428,000 cruise-ship passengers) visited the island. In 1994 earnings from the tourist industry totalled an estimated US $379m.

In 1995 Martinique recorded a trade deficit of US $1,727.9m. In 1995 the principal source of imports (62.8%) was France, which was also the principal market for exports (61.4%). Guadeloupe, Belgium-Luxembourg and the United Kingdom were also significant purchasers of Martinique's exports. The principal exports in 1995 were bananas and other fruit, refined petroleum products, machinery and transport equipment and rum. The principal imports were machinery and transport equipment (especially road vehicles), food and live animals, miscellaneous manufactured articles, basic manufactures, chemicals and mineral fuels.

Under the 1991 budget it was envisaged that revenue and expenditure would balance at 1,755m. French francs. In 1988 the French Government's expenditure on Martinique totalled 4,486m. French francs. The annual rate of inflation averaged 2.7% in 1990–96; consumer prices increased by an average of 1.4% in 1996. Some 27.8% of the labour force were unemployed in August 1996. In 1990 the level of emigration from the island was estimated at about 15,000 per year; most of the emigrants were under 25 years of age.

As an integral part of France, Martinique belongs to the European Union (EU—see p. 152). Martinique and the other French Overseas Departments were to receive a total of ECU 1,500m. from EU regional funds during 1994–2000.

Martinique's economic development has created a society that combines a relatively high standard of living with a weak economic base in agricultural and industrial production, as well as a chronic trade deficit. Levels of unemployment and emigration are high (in 1990 some 30% of Martiniquais nationals were resident in France), although the rate of growth of both these factors has slowed since the mid-1980s. The linking of wage levels to those of metropolitan France, despite the island's lower level of productivity, has increased labour costs and restricted development. A ruling by the World Trade Organization, in 1997, in favour of a complaint, brought by the USA and four Latin American countries, against the EU's banana import regime—which gives preferential access to imports from member states' overseas possessions and countries linked to the EU by the Lomé Convention—could adversely affect Martinique's banana-growing sector.

Social Welfare

Martinique has a system of social welfare similar to that of metropolitan France. With effect from 1 January 1996 welfare payments and the statutory minimum wage in the Overseas Departments were aligned with those of metropolitan France. In 1997 Martinique had a regional and university hospital complex, 13 general hospitals, five maternity hospitals and a hospital complex specializing in physiotherapy. In 1990 there were 623 physicians, 125 dentists and 174 pharmacists.

Education

The educational system is similar to that of metropolitan France (see chapter on French Guiana). Higher education in law, French language and literature, human sciences, economics, medicine and Creole studies is provided in Martinique by a branch of the Université Antilles-Guyane. The university as a whole had 15,810 enrolled students in the 1995/96 academic year. There are also two teacher-training institutes, and colleges of agriculture, fisheries, hotel management, nursing, midwifery and child care. Separate Academies for Martinique, French Guiana and Guadeloupe were established in January 1997, replacing the single Academy for the Antilles-Guyane (which was based in Fort-de-France). The average rate of adult illiteracy in 1982 was only 7.2% (males 8.0%; females 6.6%).

Public Holidays

1998: 1 January (New Year's Day), 23–24 February (Carnival), 25 February (Ash Wednesday), 10–13 April (Easter), 1 May (Labour Day), 8 May (Victory Day), 21 May (Ascension Day), 1 June (Whit Monday), 14 July (National Day), 15 August (Assumption), 1 November (All Saints' Day), 11 November (Armistice Day), 25 December (Christmas Day).

1999: 1 January (New Year's Day), 15–16 February (Carnival), 17 February (Ash Wednesday), 2–5 April (Easter), 1 May (Labour Day), 8 May (Victory Day), 13 May (Ascension Day), 24 May (Whit Monday), 14 July (National Day), 15 August (Assumption), 1 November (All Saints' Day), 11 November (Armistice Day), 25 December (Christmas Day).

Weights and Measures

The metric system is in use.

Statistical Survey

Sources (unless otherwise stated): Institut national de la statistique et des études économiques, Pointe de Jaham Schoëlcher, BP 605, 97261 Fort-de-France; tel. 60-73-73; fax 60-73-50; Ministère des départements et territoires d'outre-mer, 27 rue Oudinot, 75700 Paris 07 SP; tel. 1-53-69-20-00; fax 1-43-06-60-30; internet http://www.outre-mer.gouv.fr.

AREA AND POPULATION

Area: 1,100 sq km (424.7 sq miles).

Population: 326,717 (males 158,415, females 168,302) at census of 9 March 1982; 359,579 (males 173,878, females 185,701) at census of 15 March 1990; 381,200 (official estimate) at mid-1994.

Density (mid-1994): 346.5 per sq km.

Principal Towns (at 1990 census): Fort-de-France (capital) 100,080; Le Lamentin 30,028; Schoelcher 19,825; Sainte-Marie 19,682; Le Robert 17,713; Le François 16,925.

Births, Marriages and Deaths (provisional figures, 1994): Registered live births 5,718 (birth rate 15.0 per 1,000); Registered marriages 1,494 (marriage rate 3.9 per 1,000); Registered deaths 2,214 (death rate 5.8 per 1,000).

Expectation of Life (UN estimates, years at birth, 1990–95): 76.2 (males 72.9, females 79.4). Source: UN, *World Population Prospects: The 1994 Revision*.

Economically Active Population (persons aged 15 years and over, 1990 census): Agriculture, hunting, forestry and fishing 8,445; Industry 9,706; Construction and public works 9,298; Trade 13,965; Transport and telecommunications 6,673; Marketable services 23,537; Financial services 2,952; Non-marketable services 35,541; Total employed 110,117 (males 60,137, females 49,980); Unemployed 54,760 (males 26,416, females 28,344); Total labour force 164,877 (males 86,553, females 78,324).

AGRICULTURE, ETC.

Principal Crops (FAO estimates, '000 metric tons, 1996): Yams 7; Sweet potatoes 1; Other roots and tubers 14; Sugar cane 212; Bananas 210; Plantains 14; Pineapples 30; Melons 3; Oranges 1; Source: FAO, *Production Yearbook*.

Livestock (FAO estimates, '000 head, year ending September 1996): Cattle 30; Sheep 42; Pigs 33; Goats 22. Source: FAO, *Production Yearbook*.

Livestock Products (FAO estimates, '000 metric tons, 1996): Beef and veal 2; Pig meat 2; Poultry meat 1; Cows' milk 2; Hen eggs 2. Source: FAO, *Production Yearbook*.

Forestry: Roundwood removals (FAO estimates, '000 cu m, excluding bark, 1994): Sawlogs, veneer logs and logs for sleepers 2; Fuel wood 10; Total 12. Source: FAO, *Yearbook of Forest Products*.

Fishing (metric tons, live weight): Total catch 5,957 in 1993; 5,905 in 1994; 5,377 in 1995. Source: FAO, *Yearbook of Fishery Statistics*.

MINING

Production (1994, '000 metric tons): Pumice 130.0. Source: UN, *Industrial Commodity Statistics Yearbook*.

INDUSTRY

Production (1994, '000 metric tons, unless otherwise indicated): Pineapple juice 3.2; Canned or bottled pineapples 18.4; Raw sugar 7; Rum ('000 hl) 78; Motor spirit (petrol) 142 (estimate); Kerosene 128 (estimate); Gas-diesel (distillate fuel) oils 156 (estimate); Residual fuel oils 272 (estimate); Liquefied petroleum gas 20 (estimate); Lime 5 (estimate); Cement 231; Electric energy (million kWh) 903. Source: UN, *Industrial Commodity Statistics Yearbook*.

FINANCE

Currency and Exchange Rates: French currency is used (see French Guiana).

Budget (estimates, 1991): Revenue and expenditure to balance at 1,755 million francs.

Expenditure by Metropolitan France (1988): 4,486 million francs.

Money Supply (million francs at 31 December 1995): Currency outside banks 1,493; Demand deposits at banks 5,444; Total money 6,937.

Cost of Living (Consumer Price Index; base: 1990 = 100): 113.3 in 1994; 115.6 in 1995; 117.2 in 1996. Sources: ILO, *Yearbook of Labour Statistics*; UN, *Monthly Bulletin of Statistics*.

Expenditure on the Gross Domestic Product (million French francs at current prices, 1992): Government final consumption expenditure 6,390; Private final consumption expenditure 18,590; Increase in stocks –205; Gross fixed capital formation 5,212; *Total domestic expenditure* 29,987; Exports of goods and services 1,497; *Less* Imports of goods and services 19,390; *GDP in purchasers' values* 22,093.

EXTERNAL TRADE

Principal Commodities (US $ million, 1995): *Imports c.i.f.:* Food and live animals 319.6 (Meat and meat preparations 82.8, Dairy products and birds' eggs 53.6, Fish and fish preparations 38.6, Cereals and cereal preparations 45.6, Vegetables and fruit 49.1); Beverages and tobacco 52.0 (Beverages 45.0); Mineral fuels, lubricants, etc. 148.0 (Petroleum and petroleum products 146.2); Chemicals and related products 189.5 (Medicinal and pharmaceutical products 83.9); Basic manufactures 260.1 (Paper, paperboard and manufactures 45.1); Machinery and transport equipment 637.6 (Power-generating machinery and equipment 62.8, General industrial machinery, equipment and parts 83.2, Telecommunications and sound equipment 41.1, Road vehicles and parts 240.7, Ships and boats 50.3); Miscellaneous manufactured articles 288.5 (Furniture and parts 46.2, Clothing and accessories, excl. footwear 62.6); Total (incl. others) 1,969.8. *Exports f.o.b.:* Food and live animals 116.8 (Bananas and plantains 97.7); Beverages and tobacco 33.2 (Non-alcoholic beverages 8.9, Alcoholic beverages 24.2); Mineral fuels and lubricants 43.2 (Refined petroleum products 41.5); Chemicals and related products 5.2; Basic manufactures 5.2; Machinery and transport equipment 31.4 (Power-generating machinery and equipment 4.9, Ships and boats 18.8); Total (incl. others) 241.9. Source: UN, *International Trade Statistics Yearbook*.

Principal Trading Partners (US $ million, 1995): *Imports c.i.f.:* Belgium-Luxembourg 27.7; Brazil 21.7; Cameroon 28.3; France (incl. Monaco) 1,235.5; Gabon 23.3; Germany 64.3; Italy 73.4; Japan 43.7; Netherlands 26.9; Spain 21.8; Trinidad and Tobago 30.2; United Kingdom 38.0; USA 56.4; Total (incl. others) 1,968.7. *Exports f.o.b.:* Belgium-Luxembourg 20.7; France (incl. Monaco) 148.5; French Guiana 7.5; Guadeloupe 30.2; Saint Lucia 2.4; United Kingdom 16.9; USA 6.4; Total (incl. others) 241.9. Source: UN, *International Trade Statistics Yearbook*.

TRANSPORT

Road Traffic ('000 motor vehicles in use, 1993): Passenger cars 108.3; Commercial vehicles 32.2. Source: UN, *Statistical Yearbook*.

Shipping *Merchant Fleet* (vessels registered '000 grt at 31 December, 1992): 1. Source: Lloyd's Register of Shipping. *International Sea-borne Traffic* (1994): Vessels entered 2,996; Goods loaded 890,000 metric tons; Goods unloaded 1,817,000 metric tons; Passenger arrivals 532,000; Passenger departures 534,000.

Civil Aviation (1989): Passengers carried 1,317,100; Freight 16,148 metric tons; Mail 1,795 metric tons.

TOURISM

Tourist Arrivals (1995): 929,000 (Cruise-ship passengers 428,000).

Receipts from Tourism (US $ million): 282 in 1992; 332 in 1993; 379 in 1994. Source: UN, *Statistical Yearbook*.

COMMUNICATIONS MEDIA

Radio Receivers ('000 in use) 76 in 1994; **Television Receivers** ('000 in use) 51 in 1994; **Telephones** ('000 main lines in use) 155 in 1994; **Telefax Stations** (number in use) 690 in 1990; **Mobile Cellular Telephones** (subscribers) 802 in 1990; **Daily Newspaper** 1 in 1994 (average circulation 32,000 copies). Sources: UNESCO, *Statistical Yearbook;* UN, *Statistical Yearbook*.

EDUCATION

Pre-primary (1993/94): 84 institutions; 696 teachers; 21,475 students (1994/95).

Primary (1993/94): 190 institutions; 2,483 teachers; 33,917 students (1994/95).

Secondary (1994/95): 36,810 general students (males 17,819, females 18,991); 9,368 vocational students (males 5,101, females 4,267).

Source: UNESCO, *Statistical Yearbook.*

Higher (1996): 11,937 students (Université Antilles-Guyane).

Directory

The Government

(January 1998)

Prefect: JEAN-FRANÇOIS CORDET, Préfecture, 82 rue Victor Sévère, BP 647, 97262 Fort-de-France Cédex; tel. 63-18-61.

President of the General Council: CLAUDE LISE (PPM), Conseil Général de la Martinique, 20 ave des Caraïbes, BP 679, 97264 Fort-de-France Cédex; tel. 55-26-00; telex 912889; fax 73-59-32.

Deputies to the French National Assembly: ANICET TURINAY (RPR), PIERRE PETIT (RPR), CAMILLE DARSIÈRES (PPM), ALFRED MARIE-JEANNE (Independent).

Representatives to the French Senate: CLAUDE LISE (PPM), RODOLPHE DÉSIRÉ (PPM).

REGIONAL COUNCIL

Hôtel de Région, rue Gaston Deferre, 97262 Fort-de-France Cédex; tel. 59-63-00; telex 912041; fax 72-68-10

President: EMILE CAPGRAS (PCM).

Election, 22 March 1992

	Votes	%	Seats
Union pour la France (RPR-UDF)	30,776	25.92	16
Patriotes Martiniquais (MIM)	19,029	16.02	9
Parti Progressiste Martiniquais (PPM)	18,790	15.82	9
Pour une Martinique au Travail (PCM)	8,110	6.83	4
Nouvelle Génération Socialiste (FSM)	7,368	6.20	3
Others	34,681	29.20	—
Total	118,754	100.00	41

Political Organizations

***Fédération Socialiste de la Martinique (FSM):** Cité la Meynard, 97200 Fort-de-France; tel. 75-53-28; telex 912136; local branch of the **Parti Socialiste (PS)**; Sec.-Gen. JEAN CRUSOL.

Groupe Révolution Socialiste (GRS): 97200 Fort-de-France; tel. 70-36-49; f. 1973; Trotskyist; Leader GILBERT PAGO.

***Mouvement Indépendantiste Martiniquais (MIM):** Fort-de-France; f. 1978; pro-independence party; First Sec. ALFRED MARIE-JEANNE.

***Parti Communiste Martiniquais (PCM):** Fort-de-France; f. 1920; affiliated to French Communist Party until 1957; Leader ARMAND NICOLAS.

Parti Martiniquais Socialiste (PMS): Fort-de-France; Pres. LOUIS JOSEPH DOGUÉ; Sec. ERNEST WAN AJOUHU.

Parti Progressiste Martiniquais (PPM): Fort-de-France; tel. 71-86-83; f. 1957; left-wing; Pres. AIMÉ CÉSAIRE; Sec.-Gen. CAMILLE DARSIÈRES.

***Rassemblement pour la République (RPR):** 97205 Fort-de-France; Gaullist; Sec. STEPHEN BAGOE.

***Union pour la Démocratie Française (UDF):** Fort-de-France; centrist; Pres. JEAN MARAN.

* The RPR and the UDF allied to contest the 1992 regional elections as the Union pour la France (UPF); the MIM contested the election under the title Patriotes Martiniquais; the PCM under the title Pour une Martinique au Travail; and the FSM as the Nouvelle Génération Socialiste. At the 1993 elections to the French National Assembly two candidates of the right campaigned on behalf of the RPR, while two were listed as representatives of the UPF.

Judicial System

Cour d'Appel de Fort-de-France: Fort-de-France; tel. 70-62-62; telex 635213; highest court of appeal for Martinique and French Guiana; First Pres. CHRISTIAN AUDOUARD; Procurator-Gen. YVES CHARFENEL.

There are two Tribunaux de Grande Instance, at Fort-de-France and Cayenne (French Guiana), and three Tribunaux d'Instance (two in Fort-de-France and one in Cayenne).

Religion

The majority of the population belong to the Roman Catholic Church.

CHRISTIANITY

The Roman Catholic Church

Martinique comprises the single archdiocese of Fort-de-France, with an estimated 351,000 adherents (some 88.4% of the total population) at 31 December 1995. The Archbishop participates in the Antilles Episcopal Conference, currently based in Port of Spain, Trinidad and Tobago.

Archbishop of Fort-de-France: Most Rev. MAURICE MARIE-SAINTE, Archevêché, 5–7 rue du Révérend Père Pinchon, BP 586, 97207 Fort-de-France Cédex; tel. 63-70-70; fax 63-75-21.

Other Churches

Among the denominations active in Martinique are the Assembly of God, the Evangelical Church of the Nazarene and the Seventh-day Adventist Church.

The Press

Antilla: BP 46, Lamentin; tel. 75-48-68; fax 75-58-46; weekly; Dir ALFRED FORTUNE.

Aujourd'hui Dimanche: Presbytère de Bellevue, Fort-de-France; tel. 71-48-97; weekly; Dir Père GAUTHIER; circ. 12,000.

Carib Hebdo: 97200 Fort-de-France; f. 1989; Dir GISÈLE DE LA FARGUE.

Combat Ouvrier: Fort-de-France; weekly; Dir M. G. BEAUJOUR.

France-Antilles: place Stalingrad, 97200 Fort-de-France; tel. 59-08-83; fax 60-29-96; f. 1964; daily; Dir HENRI MERLE; circ. 30,000 (Martinique edition).

Information Caraïbe (ICAR): 18 allée des Perruches, 97200 Fort-de-France; tel. 64-37-40; weekly; Editor DANIEL COMPÈRE; circ. 1,500.

Justice: rue André Aliker, 97200 Fort-de-France; tel. 71-86-83; weekly; organ of the PPM; Dir G. THIMOTÉE; circ. 8,000.

Le Naif: voie no 7, route du Lamentin, Fort-de-France; weekly; Dir R. LAOUCHEZ.

Le Progressiste: Fort-de-France; weekly; organ of the PPM; Dir PAUL GABOURG; circ. 13,000.

Révolution Socialiste: BP 1031, 97200 Fort-de-France; tel. 70-36-49; f. 1973; weekly; organ of the GRS; Dir PHILIPPE PIERRE CHARLES; circ. 2,500.

Télé Sept Jours: rond-point du Vietnam Héroïque, 97200 Fort-de-France; tel. 63-75-49; weekly.

L'Union: Fort-de-France; weekly; Dir JEAN MARAN.

Broadcasting and Communications

BROADCASTING

Société Nationale de Radio-Télévision Française d'Outre-mer (RFO): La Clairère, BP 662, 97263 Fort-de-France; tel. 59-52-00; telex 912659; broadcasts 24 hours of radio programmes daily and 37 hours of television programmes weekly; Pres. JEAN-MARIE CAVADA; Dir CLAUDE RUBEN.

Radio

There are some 40 licensed private FM radio stations.

Radio Caraïbe International (RCI): 2 blvd de la Marne, 97200 Fort-de-France Cédex; tel. 63-98-70; telex 912579; fax 63-26-59; internet http://www.fwinet.com/rci.htm; commercial station broadcasting 24 hours daily; Dir YANN DUVAL.

Television

ATV Antilles Télévision: 28 rue Arawaks, 972000 Fort de France; tel. 75-44-44; fax 75-55-65; commercial station.

Canal Antilles: Centre Commerciale la Galléria, 97232 Le Lamentin; tel. 50-57-87; private commercial television station.

Finance

(cap. = capital; res = reserves; dep. = deposits; m. = million; brs = branches; amounts in French francs)

BANKING

Central Bank

Institut d'Emission des Départements d'Outre-Mer: Fort-de-France.

Major Commercial Banks

Banque des Antilles Françaises: 28–34 rue Lamartine, BP 582, 97207 Fort-de-France Cédex; tel. 73-93-44; telex 912636; fax 63-58-94; f. 1853; cap. 32.6m., res 42.9m., dep. 2,243.6m. (Dec. 1996); Chair. JACQUES GIRAULT.

Banque Nationale de Paris: 72 ave des Caraïbes, 97200 Fort-de-France; tel. 59-46-00; telex 912619; fax 63-71-42; Dir MICHEL MASSE; 8 further brs in Martinique.

Caisse Nationale d'Epargne et de Prévoyance: 82 rue Perrinon, 97200 Fort-de-France; telex 912435; Dir Mme M. E. ANDRE.

Caisse Régionale de Crédit Agricole Mutuel: 106 blvd Général de Gaulle, BP 583, 97207 Fort-de-France; tel. 55-39-55; telex 912657; fax 60-96-38; f. 1950; 9,500 mems; Pres. M. GABRIEL-REGIS; Dir MAURICE LAOUCHEZ; 28 brs.

Crédit Maritime Mutuel: 45 rue Victor Hugo, 97200 Fort-de-France; tel. 73-00-93; telex 912477.

Crédit Martiniquais: 17 rue de la Liberté, Fort-de-France; tel. 71-12-40; telex 912963; f. 1922; associated since 1987 with Chase Manhattan Bank (USA) and, since 1990, with Mutuelles du Mans Vie (France); cap. 156.8m. (1990); Administrator ALAIN DENNHARDT; 10 brs.

Société Générale de Banque aux Antilles: 19 rue de la Liberté, BP 408, 97200 Fort-de-France; tel. 71-69-83; telex 912545; f. 1979; cap. 15m.; Dir MICHEL SAMOUR.

Société Martiniquaise de Financement (SOMAFI): route de Sainte Thérèse, 97200 Fort-de-France; Dir JEAN MACHET.

INSURANCE

Cie Antillaise d'Assurances: 19 rue de la Liberté, 97205 Fort-de-France; tel. 73-04-50.

Caraïbe Assurances: 11 rue Victor Hugo, BP 210, 97202 Fort-de-France; tel. 63-92-29; telex 912096; fax 63-19-79.

Groupement Français d'Assurances Caraïbes (GFA Caraïbes): 46–48 rue Ernest Deproge, 97205 Fort-de-France; tel. 59-04-04; fax 73-19-72.

La Nationale (GAN): 30 blvd Général de Gaulle, BP 185, Fort-de-France; tel. 71-30-07; Reps MARCEL BOULLANGER, ROGER BOULLANGER.

La Protectrice: 97205 Fort-de-France; tel. 70-25-45; Rep. RENÉ MAXIMIN.

Le Secours: 74 ave Duparquet, 97200 Fort-de-France; tel. 70-03-79; Dir Y. ANGANI.

Trade and Industry

DEVELOPMENT ORGANIZATIONS

Agence pour le Développement Economique de la Martinique: 26 rue Lamartine, BP 803, 97244 Fort-de-France; tel. 73-45-81; telex 912946; fax 72-41-38; f. 1979; promotion of industry.

Bureau de l'Industrie de l'Artisanat: Préfecture, 97262 Fort-de-France; tel. 71-36-27; telex 029650; f. 1960; government agency; research, documentation and technical and administrative advice on investment in industry and tourism; Dir RAPHAËL FIRMIN.

Caisse Française de Développement (CFD): 12 blvd du Général de Gaulle, BP 804, 97244 Fort-de-France Cédex; tel. 59-44-73; telex 912313; fax 59-44-88; fmrly Caisse Centrale de Coopération Economique, name changed 1992; Dir JACQUES ALBUGUES; Regional Man. XAVIER BLANCHARD.

Société de Crédit pour le Développement de la Martinique (SODEMA): 12 blvd du Général de Gaulle, BP 575, 97242 Fort-de-France Cédex; tel. 72-87-72; telex 912402; fax 72-87-70; f. 1970; cap. 25m. frs; medium-and long-term finance; Dir-Gen. JACKIE BATHANY.

Société de Développement Régional Antilles-Guyane (SODERAG): 111–113 rue Ernest Deproge, BP 450, 97205 Fort-de-France Cédex; tel. 59-71-00; telex 912343; fax 63-38-88; Dir-Gen. FULVIO MAZZEO; Sec.-Gen. OLYMPE FRANCIL.

CHAMBERS OF COMMERCE

Chambre d'Agriculture: Place d'Armes, BP 312, 97286 Le Lamentin; tel. 51-75-75.

Chambre de Commerce et d'Industrie de la Martinique: 50–54 rue Ernest Deproge, BP 478, Fort-de-France; tel. 55-28-00; telex 912633; fax 60-66-68; f. 1907; Pres. JEAN-CLAUDE LUBIN; Dir-Gen. FERNAND LERYCHARD.

Chambre des Métiers de la Martinique: 2 rue du Temple, Morne Tartenson, BP 1194, 97200 Fort-de-France; tel. 71-32-22; fax 70-47-30; f. 1970; Pres. CHRISTIANE CAYOL; 8,000 mems.

EMPLOYERS' ORGANIZATIONS

Groupement de Producteurs d'Ananas de la Martinique: 97201 Fort-de-France; f. 1967; Pres. C. DE GRYSE.

Ordre des Médecins de la Martinique: 80 rue de la République, 97200 Fort-de-France; tel. 63-27-01; Pres. Dr René Legendri.

Ordre des Pharmaciens de la Martinique: BP 587, 97207 Fort-de-France Cédex.

Société Coopérative d'Intérêt Collectif Agricole Bananière de la Martinique (SICABAM): Domaine de Montgéralde, La Dillon, 97200 Fort-de-France; telex 912617; f. 1961; Pres. Alex Assier de Pompignan; Dir Gérard Bally; 1,000 mems.

Syndicat des Distilleries Agricoles: Fort-de-France; tel. 71-25-46.

Syndicat des Producteurs de Rhum Agricole: La Dillon, 97200 Fort-de-France.

Union Départementale des Coopératives Agricoles de la Martinique: Fort-de-France; Pres. M. Ursulet.

TRADE UNIONS

Centrale Démocratique Martiniquaise des Travailleurs: BP 21, 97201 Fort-de-France; Sec.-Gen. Line Beausoleil.

Confédération Générale du Travail de la Martinique (1936): Maison des Syndicats, porte no 14, Jardin Desclieux, 97200 Fort-de-France; tel. 60-45-21; f. 1936; affiliated to World Federation of Trade Unions; Sec.-Gen. Luc Bernabé; c. 12,000 mems.

Syndicat des Enseignants de la Martinique: Fort-de-France.

Union Départementale des Syndicats—FO: BP 1114, 97248 Fort-de-France Cédex; affiliated to International Confederation of Free Trade Unions; Sec.-Gen. Albert Sabel; c. 2,000 mems.

Transport

RAILWAYS

There are no railways in Martinique.

ROADS

There are 267 km of motorways and first-class roads, and 615 km of secondary roads.

SHIPPING

Direction des Concessions Services Portuaires: Quai de l'Hydro Base, BP 782, 97244 Fort-de-France Cédex; tel. 59-00-00; fax 71-35-73; port services management; Dir F. Thodiard.

Direction Départementale des Affaires Maritimes: blvd Chevalier de Sainte-Marthe, BP 620, 97261 Fort-de-France Cédex; tel. 71-90-05; fax 63-67-30; Dir François Nihoul.

Alcoa Steamship Co, Alpine Line, Agdwa Line, Delta Line, Raymond Witcomb Co, Moore MacCormack, Eastern Steamship Co: c/o Etablissements René Cottrell, Fort-de-France.

American President Lines: c/o Compagnie d'Agence Multiples Antillaise (CAMA), 44 rue Garnier Pages, 97205 Fort-de-France Cédex; tel. 71-31-00; fax 63-54-40.

Compagnie Générale Maritime Antilles-Guyane: 8 blvd Général de Gaulle, BP 503, 97241 Fort-de-France Cédex; tel. 55-32-03; telex 912049; fax 60-68-57; also represents other passenger and freight lines; Rep. Franck Beroard.

Compagnie de Navigation Mixte: Immeuble Rocade, La Dillon, BP 1023, 97209 Fort-de-France; Rep. R. M. Michaux.

CIVIL AVIATION

Martinique's international airport is at Le Lamentin, 6 km from Fort-de-France. A new terminal was inaugurated in July 1995.

Air Martinique (Compagnie Antillaise d'Affrètement Aérien—CAAA): Aéroport de Fort-de-France, 97232 Le Lamentin; tel. 51-08-09; telex 912048; fax 51-59-27; f. 1981; operates regional services; 102 employees; Chair. Guy Arore; Gen. Man. Michel Gouze.

Tourism

Martinique's tourist attractions are its beaches and coastal scenery, its mountainous interior, and the historic towns of Fort-de-France and Saint Pierre. In 1995 tourist arrivals totalled 929,000, including some 428,000 cruise-ship passengers. Tourist receipts in 1994 totalled an estimated US $379m., an increase of 14.2% compared with the previous year. In 1997 there were 101 hotels, with some 3,796 rooms.

Agence Régionale pour le Développement du Tourisme en Martinique: Anse Gouraud, 97233 Schoelcher; tel. 61-61-77; telex 912929; fax 61-22-72.

Chambre Syndicale des Hôtels de Tourisme de la Martinique: Entrée Montgéralde, Route de Chateauboeuf, Fort-de-France; tel. 70-27-80.

Délégation Régionale au Tourisme: 41 rue Gabriel Péri, 97200 Fort-de-France; tel. 63-18-61; Dir Gilbert Lecurieux.

Fédération Martiniquaise des Offices de Tourisme et Syndicats d'Initiative (FMOTSI): Maison du Tourisme Vert, 9 blvd du Général de Gaulle, BP 491, 97207 Fort-de-France Cédex; tel. 63-18-54; fax 70-17-61; f. 1984; Pres. Victor Grandin.

Office Départemental du Tourisme de la Martinique: 2 rue Ernest Desproges, 97200 Fort-de-France; tel. 63-79-60.

RÉUNION

Introductory Survey

Location, Climate, Language, Religion, Capital

Réunion is an island in the Indian Ocean, lying about 800 km (500 miles) east of Madagascar. The climate varies greatly according to altitude: at sea-level it is tropical, with average temperatures between 20°C (68°F) and 28°C (82°F), but in the uplands it is much cooler, with average temperatures between 8°C (46°F) and 19°C (66°F). Rainfall is abundant, averaging 4,714 mm annually in the uplands, and 686 mm at sea-level. The population is of mixed origin, including people of European, African, Indian and Chinese descent. The official language is French. A large majority of the population are Christians belonging to the Roman Catholic Church. The capital is Saint-Denis.

Recent History

Réunion was first occupied by France in 1642, and was ruled as a colony until 1946, when it received full departmental status. In 1974 it became an Overseas Department with the status of a region.

In June 1978 the liberation committee of the Organization of African Unity (OAU, see p. 215) adopted a report recommending measures to hasten the independence of the island, and condemned its occupation by a 'colonial power'. However, this view seemed to have little popular support in Réunion. Although the left-wing political parties on the island advocated increased autonomy (amounting to virtual self-government), few people were in favour of complete independence.

In 1982 the French Government proposed a decentralization scheme, envisaging the dissolution of the General and Regional Councils in the Overseas Departments and the creation in each department of a single assembly, to be elected on the basis of proportional representation. As a result of considerable opposition in Réunion and the other Overseas Departments, the Government was eventually forced to abandon the project. Revised legislation on decentralization in the Overseas Departments, however, was approved by the French National Assembly in December 1982. Elections to the Regional Council took place in Réunion in February 1983, when left-wing candidates won 50.77% of the votes cast.

In elections to the French National Assembly in March 1986, Réunion's representation was increased from three to five deputies. The Parti Communiste Réunionnais (PCR) won two seats, while the Union pour la Démocratie Française (UDF), the Rassemblement pour la République (RPR) and a newly-formed right-wing party, France-Réunion-Avenir (FRA), each secured one seat. In the concurrent elections to the Regional Council, an alliance between the RPR and the UDF obtained 18 of the 45 seats, while the PCR secured 13 and the FRA eight. The leader of the FRA, Pierre Lagourgue, was elected as President of the Regional Council.

In September 1986 the French Government's plan to introduce a programme of economic reforms provoked criticism from the left-wing parties, which demanded that the Overseas Departments be granted social equality with metropolitan France, through the standardization of social security payments and guaranteed minimum income. In October Paul Vergès, the Secretary-General of the PCR and a deputy to the French National Assembly, formally protested to the European Parliament in Strasbourg. In October 1987 Vergès and the other PCR deputy, Elie Hoarau, resigned from the National Assembly, in protest at the Government's proposals. (Two other members of the PCR subsequently assumed the vacated seats.)

In the second round of the French presidential election on 8 May 1988, François Mitterrand, the incumbent President and a candidate of the Parti Socialiste (PS), received 60.3% of the votes cast in Réunion, while Jacques Chirac, the RPR Prime Minister, obtained 39.7%. Mitterrand won an absolute majority of votes in all five electoral districts in Réunion, including the RPR stronghold of Saint-Denis. At elections to the French National Assembly in June, the PCR won two of the seats allocated to Réunion, while the UDF and the RPR (which contested the elections jointly as the Union du Rassemblement du Centre—URC), and the FRA each won one seat. (The RPR and FRA deputies later became independents, although they maintained strong links with the island's right-wing groups.) Relations between the PCR and the PS subsequently deteriorated, following mutual recriminations concerning their failure to co-operate in the general election. In July the PCR criticized the Socialist Government for continuing to allocate lower levels of benefits and revenue to the Overseas Departments, despite a pledge, made by President Mitterrand during a visit to Réunion in February of that year, to grant the Departments social equality with metropolitan France.

In the elections for the newly-enlarged 44-member General Council in September and October 1988, the PCR and the PS won nine and four seats respectively, while left-wing independent candidates obtained two seats. The UDF secured six seats and right-wing independent candidates 19, but the RPR, which had previously held 11 seats, won only four. Later in October, Eric Boyer, a right-wing independent candidate, was elected as President of the General Council. The results of the municipal elections in March 1989 represented a slight decline in support for the left-wing parties; for the first time since the 1940s, however, a PS candidate, Gilbert Annette, became mayor of Saint-Denis.

In September 1990, following the restructuring of the RPR under the new local leadership of Alain Defaud, several right-wing and centrist movements, including the UDF and the RPR, established an informal alliance, known as the Union pour la France (UPF), to contest the regional elections in 1992. During a visit to Réunion in November 1990 the French Minister for Overseas Departments and Territories, Louis Le Pensec, announced a series of proposed economic and social measures, in accordance with the pledges made by Mitterrand in 1988 regarding the promotion of economic development and social equality between the Overseas Departments and metropolitan France. However, the proposals were criticized as insufficient by right-wing groups and by the PCR. Following a meeting in Paris between Le Pensec and a delegation from Réunion, the adoption of a programme of social and economic measures was announced in April 1991.

In March 1990 violent protests took place in support of an unauthorized television service, Télé Free-DOM, following a decision by the French national broadcasting commission, the Conseil Supérieur de l'Audiovisuel (CSA), to award a broadcasting permit to a rival company. In February 1991 the seizure by the CSA of Télé Free-DOM's broadcasting transmitters prompted renewed demonstrations in Saint-Denis. Some 11 people were killed in ensuing riots, and the French Government dispatched police reinforcements to restore order. Le Pensec, who subsequently visited Réunion, ascribed the violence to widespread discontent with the island's social and economic conditions. A visit to Réunion in March by the French Prime Minister, Michel Rocard, precipitated further rioting. In the same month a commission of enquiry attributed the riots in February to the inflammatory nature of television programmes that had been broadcast by Télé Free-DOM in the weeks preceding the disturbances, and cited the station's director, Dr Camille Sudre, as responsible. However, the commission refuted allegations by right-wing and centrist politicians that the PCR had orchestrated the violence. Later in March President Mitterrand expressed concern over the outcome of the enquiry, and appealed to the CSA to reconsider its policy towards Télé Free-DOM. In April, however, the CSA, which intended to award a franchise for another private television station, indicated its continued opposition to Télé Free-DOM.

In March 1992 Annette expelled Sudre, who was one of the deputy mayors of Saint-Denis, from the majority coalition in the municipal council, after Sudre presented a list of independent candidates to contest the forthcoming regional elections. In the elections to the Regional Council, which took place on 22 March, Sudre's list of candidates (known as Free-DOM) secured 17 seats, while the UPF obtained 14 seats, the PCR nine seats and the PS five seats. In concurrent elections to the General Council (newly enlarged to 47 seats), right-wing independent candidates won 20 seats, although the number of PCR deputies increased to 12, and the number of PS deputies to six; Boyer retained the presidency of the Council. Following the elections, the Free-DOM list of candidates formed an alliance with the PCR, thereby obtaining a narrow majority of 26 of the 45 seats in the Regional Council. Under the terms of the agreement, Sudre was to assume the presidency of the Regional Council, and Paul Vergès the vice-presidency. Later in March Sudre was accordingly elected as President of the Regional Council by a majority of 27 votes, with the support of members of the PCR. Shortly afterwards, the UPF and the PS rejected an offer by Sudre that they join the Free-DOM–PCR alliance. The PS subsequently appealed against the results of the regional elections on the grounds of media bias; Sudre's privately-owned radio station, Radio Free-DOM, had campaigned on his behalf prior to the elections.

Following his election to the presidency of the Regional Council, Sudre announced that Télé Free-DOM was shortly to resume broadcasting. The CSA indicated, however, that it would continue to regard transmissions by Télé Free-DOM as illegal, and liable to judicial proceedings. Jean-Paul Virapoullé, a deputy to the French National Assembly, subsequently proposed the adoption of legislation that would legalize Télé Free-DOM and would provide for the establishment of an independent media sector on Réunion. In April 1992 Télé Free-DOM's transmitters were returned, and at the end of May a full broadcasting service was resumed (without the permission of the CSA).

In June 1992 a delegation from the Regional Council met President Mitterrand to submit proposals for economic reforms, in accordance with the aim of establishing parity between Réunion and metropolitan France. In early July, however, the French Government announced increases in social security benefits that were substantially less than had been expected, resulting in widespread discontent on the island. In September the PCR demanded that the electorate refuse to participate in the forthcoming French referendum on ratification of the Treaty on European Union (see p. 158), in protest at the alleged failure of the French Government to recognize the requirements of the Overseas Departments. At the referendum, which took place later that month, the ratification of the Treaty was approved by the voters of Réunion, although only 26.25% of the registered electorate voted.

At the end of September 1992 Boyer and the former President of the Regional Council, Pierre Lagourgue, were elected as representatives to the French Senate. (The RPR candidate, Paul Moreau, retained his seat.) In October the investigation of allegations that members of the General Council had misappropriated funds and obtained contracts by fraudulent means commenced. In December increasing discontent with deteriorating economic conditions on Réunion prompted violent rioting in Saint-Denis and in the town of Le Port.

In March 1993 Sudre announced that he was to contest Virapoullé's seat on behalf of the Free-DOM–PCR alliance in the forthcoming elections to the French National Assembly (despite opposition from a number of members of the PCR to the joint candidacy). However, at the elections, which took place later that month, Sudre was defeated by Virapoullé in the second round of voting, while another incumbent right-wing deputy, André Thien Ah Koon (who contested the elections on behalf of the UPF), also retained his seat. The PCR, the PS and the RPR each secured one of the remaining seats.

In May 1993 the French Conseil d'Etat declared the results of the regional elections in March 1992 to be invalid, and prohibited Sudre from engaging in political activity for a year, on the grounds that programmes broadcast by Radio Free-DOM prior to the elections constituted political propaganda. Sudre subsequently nominated his wife, Margie, to assume his candidacy in further elections to the Regional Council. In the elections, which took place on 20 June, the Free-DOM list of candidates, headed by Margie Sudre, secured 12 seats, while the UDF obtained 10 seats, the RPR eight seats, the PCR nine seats and the PS six seats. Margie Sudre was subsequently elected as President of the Regional Council, with the support of the nine PCR deputies and three dissident members of the PS, obtaining a total of 24 votes.

In April 1993 a number of prominent business executives were arrested in connection with the acquisition of contracts by fraudulent means; several senior politicians, including Boyer and Pierre Vergès (the mayor of Le Port and son of Paul Vergès), were also implicated in malpractice, following the investigation into their activities. Both Boyer and Pierre Vergès subsequently fled in order to evade arrest. In August Boyer, who had surrendered to the security forces, was formally charged with corruption and placed in detention. (Joseph Sinimalé, a member of the RPR, temporarily assumed the office of President of the General Council.) In the same month the Vice-President of the General Council, Cassam Moussa, was also arrested and charged with corruption.

In January 1994 Jules Raux, a deputy mayor of Saint-Denis who was also the local treasurer of the PS, was arrested on charges of corruption: it was alleged that both local and French enterprises had obtained contracts from the Saint-Denis municipality in exchange for a share in profits (which was apparently used, in part, to finance PS activities on the island). In February two municipal councillors from Saint-Denis were arrested on suspicion of involvement in the affair. In the same month a French citizen (who was believed to have connections with members of the Djibouti Government) was arrested on Réunion on charges of having transferred the funds that had been illegally obtained by the Saint-Denis municipality to enterprises in Djibouti. In March Annette, who was implicated in the affair, resigned as mayor of Saint-Denis, and was subsequently charged with corruption. Later that month Boyer and Moussa were convicted and sentenced to terms of imprisonment.

At elections to the General Council, which took place in late March 1994, the PCR retained 12 seats, while the number of PS deputies increased to 12 (despite adverse publicity attached to the PS as a result of the alleged corruption within the Saint-Denis municipality). The number of seats held by the RPR and UDF declined to five and 11 respectively (compared with six and 14 in the previous Council). The RPR and UDF subsequently attempted to negotiate an alliance with the PCR; however, the PCR and PS established a coalition (despite the long-standing differences between the two parties), thereby securing the support of 24 of the 47 seats in the General Council. On 4 April a member of the PS, Christophe Payet, was elected President of the General Council (obtaining 26 votes), defeating Sinimalé; the right-wing parties (which had held the presidency of the General Council for more than 40 years) boycotted the poll. The PS and PCR signed an agreement whereby the two parties were to control the administration of the General Council jointly, and indicated that centrist deputies might be allowed to join the alliance. In July, following a judicial appeal, Boyer's custodial sentence was reduced to a term of one year.

In November 1994 an official visit to Réunion by the French Prime Minister, Edouard Balladur (who intended to contest the French presidential election in early 1995), prompted strike action in protest at his opposition to the establishment of social equality between the Overseas Departments and metropolitan France. Jacques Chirac, who was the official presidential candidate of the RPR, visited the island in December; the organ of the PCR, *Témoignages* (which had criticized Balladur), declared its approval of Chirac's stated commitment to the issue of social equality. In the second round of the presidential election, which took place in May 1995, the socialist candidate, Lionel Jospin, secured 56% of votes cast on Réunion, while Chirac won 44% of the votes (although Chirac obtained the highest number of votes overall); the PCR and Free-DOM had urged their supporters not to vote for Balladur in the first round, owing to his opposition to the principle of social equality between the Overseas Departments and metropolitan France. Following Chirac's election to the French presidency, Margie Sudre was nominated Minister of State with responsibility for Francophone Affairs, prompting concern among right-wing organizations on Réunion. In municipal elections, which took place in June, the joint candidate of the PCR and the PS, Guy Etheve, was elected mayor of Saint-Louis, although the candidate of the RPR—UDF alliance, Marc-André Hoarau, submitted an official appeal against the results of the ballot; Elie Hoarau was re-elected mayor of Saint-Pierre.

In August 1995 Pierre Vergès was sentenced *in absentia* to a custodial term of 18 months; an appeal was rejected in July 1996. In September the mayor of Salazie, who was a member of the RPR, was also charged with corruption. In November 1995 Boyer lost an appeal against his 1994 conviction and was expelled from the French Senate.

With effect from the beginning of 1996 the social security systems of the Overseas Departments were aligned with those of metropolitan France. In February Alain Juppé, the French Prime Minister, invited more than 300 representatives from the Overseas Departments to Paris to participate in discussions on social equality and development; participants came from political parties, trade unions and other associations. The main issue uniting the political representatives from Réunion was the need to align the salaries of civil servants on the island with those in metropolitan France. Several trade unionists declared themselves willing to enter into negotiations, on the condition that only new recuits would be affected. The French Government remained undecided. President Chirac's visit to Réunion in March coincided with the 50th anniversary of France's establishment of Overseas Departments. The main issues that the President addressed during his visit were unemployment, the reinforcement of social policy, and equality with metropolitan France. Paul Vergès, joint candidate of the PCR and the PS, was elected to the French Senate on 14 April 1996, securing 51.9% of the votes cast. Fred K/Bidy won 40.0% of the votes, failing to retain Eric Boyer's seat for the RPR. In the by-election to replace Paul Vergès, which took place in September, Claude Hoarau, the PCR candidate, was elected with 55.98% of the votes cast, while Margie Sudre obtained 44.01%. A new majority alliance between Free-DOM, the RPR and the UDF was subsequently formed in the Regional Council, with the re-election of its 19-member permanent commission in October. In November Jean-Paul Virapoullé was re-elected mayor of Saint-André, following the annulment of the results of the election of June 1995 (which he had also won), although Claude Hoarau, the PCR candidate, questioned the legitimacy of electoral proceedings. Wilfried Bertile, the candidate for the PS, secured the highest number of votes in both the municipal and district elections of Saint-Philippe.

In October 1996 the trial of a number of politicians and business executives, who had been arrested in 1993–94 on charges of corruption, took place, after three years of investigations. Gilbert Annette and Jules Raux were convicted and, in December, received custodial sentences. Jacques de Châteauvieux, the Chairman of Groupe Sucreries de Bourbon (principally concerned with the production and exportation of sugar), was found guilty of bribing members of the commission responsible for issuing permits for the construction of supermarkets on the island, and also received a custodial term. Two senior executives from the French enterprise, Compagnie Générale des Eaux, were given suspended sentences, although the public prosecutor subsequently appealed for part of the sentences to be made custodial. Some 20 others were also found guilty of corruption. Pierre Vergès surrendered to the authorities in December and appeared before a magistrate in Saint-Pierre, where he was subsequently detained; in February 1997 he was released by the Court of Appeal. Also in December 1996 voting on the regional budget for 1997 was postponed three times, as a result of the abstention of eight Free-DOM councillors, led by the first Vice-President of the Regional Council, Jasmin Moutoussamy, who demanded the dismissal of Gilbert Payet, a Sub-Prefect and special adviser to Sudre, and greater delegation of power to the Vice-Presidents. They also objected to Sudre's alliance with the RPR-UDF majority. In late March 1997 the regional budget was eventually adopted, although Sudre and many right-wing councillors abstained from voting because of the opposition's insistence on a number of amendments, most significantly to the composition of the Council's permanent commission, in which it had no representation. Following the vote, Sudre suspended the session to allow for discussion between the political organizations. Also in March Joseph Sinimalé of the RPR was re-elected mayor of Saint-Paul, defeating Paul Vergès.

Meanwhile, civil servants and students protested violently against a French government proposal, made earlier in March 1997, to undertake reform of the civil service, including a reduction in the incomes of new recruits to bring them closer to those in metropolitan France. Senator Pierre Lagourgue was designated to mediate between the French Government and the civil servants' trade unions, but strike action and demonstrations continued into April, leading to violent clashes with the security forces.

Four left-wing candidates were successful in elections to the French National Assembly held in late May and early June 1997. Claude Hoarau (PCR) retained his seat and was joined by Huguette Bello and Elie Hoarau, also both from the PCR, and Michel Tamaya (PS), while André Thien Ah Koon, representing the RPR—UDF coalition, was re-elected.

In January 1986 France was admitted to the Indian Ocean Commission (IOC, see p. 261), owing to its sovereignty over Réunion. Réunion was given the right to host ministerial meetings of the IOC, but would not be allowed to occupy the presidency, owing to its status as a non-sovereign state.

Government

France is represented in Réunion by an appointed Prefect. There are two councils with local powers: the 47-member General Council and the 45-member Regional Council. Both are elected for up to six years by direct universal suffrage. Réunion sends five directly-elected deputies to the National Assembly in Paris and three indirectly-elected representatives to the Senate. The Department is also represented at the European Parliament.

Defence

Réunion is the headquarters of French military forces in the Indian Ocean. At 1 August 1997 there were 4,000 French troops stationed on Réunion and Mayotte.

Economic Affairs

Réunion's gross national product (GNP) per head in 1991 was estimated at 40,000 French francs. During 1985–95, according to World Bank estimates, Réunion's population increased at an average annual rate of 1.6%. In 1994 Réunion's gross domestic product (GDP) was estimated at 35,266m. French francs, equivalent to 54,431 francs per head. GDP increased, in real terms, by an annual average of 3.4% in 1988–94.

Agriculture (including hunting, forestry and fishing) contributed 3.7% of GDP in 1989. An estimated 4.7% of the economically active population were employed in the sector in 1996. The principal cash crops are sugar cane (sugar accounted for 64.1% of export earnings in 1996), maize, tobacco, vanilla, and geraniums and vetiver root, which are cultivated for the production of essential oils. Fishing and livestock production are also important to the economy. Agricultural production increased by 0.9% during 1988–95 (increasing by 0.7% in 1995).

Industry (including mining, manufacturing, construction and power) contributed 19.0% of GDP in 1989, and employed an estimated 13.7% of the working population in 1993. The principal branch of manufacturing is food-processing, particularly the production of sugar and rum. Other significant sectors include the fabrication of construction materials, mechanics, printing, metalwork, textiles and garments, and electronics.

There are no mineral resources on the island. Energy is derived from thermal and hydroelectric power. Imports of petroleum products comprised 5.6% of the value of total imports in 1996.

Services (including transport, communications, trade and finance) contributed 77.4% of GDP in 1989, and employed 71.7% of the working population in 1993. The public sector accounts for about one-half of employment in the services sector. Tourism is also significant; in 1996 347,000 tourists visited Réunion (an increase of 14.1% compared with 1995), and tourist revenue totalled 1,332m. French francs.

In 1996 Réunion recorded a trade deficit of 13,143.0m. French francs. The principal source of imports (65.6%) in that year was France; other major suppliers are Italy and Bahrain. France is also the principal market for exports (taking 70.9% of the total in 1996); other significant purchasers are Japan and Belgium-Luxembourg. The principal exports in 1995 were food products (particularly raw sugar) and machinery and transport equipment. The principal imports in that year were machinery and transport equipment (particularly road vehicles and parts), food products, miscellaneous manufactured articles, basic manufactures and chemical products.

In 1995 there was an estimated budgetary deficit of 9,244.5m. French francs. The annual rate of inflation averaged 2.8% in 1990–96; consumer prices increased by 1.9% in 1996. An estimated 39.5% of the labour force were unemployed in August 1996.

Réunion is represented by France in the Indian Ocean Commission (IOC, see p. 261). As an integral part of France, Réunion belongs to the European Union (EU—see p. 152).

Réunion has a relatively developed economy, but is dependent on financial aid from France. The economy has traditionally been based on agriculture, and is therefore vulnerable to poor climatic conditions. During the 1990s the production of sugar cane (which dominates this sector) has been adversely affected by increasing urbanization, which has resulted in a decline in agricultural land. During the period 1989–93 Réunion received aid from the EC, in order to adapt to the requirements of the single European Market, which became operational in 1993. In September 1992 the Regional Council introduced an economic development programme, which provided for the creation of an export free zone. In 1994 the Government indicated that it intended to give priority to the reduction of unemployment and announced a programme of economic and social development, which comprised measures to stimulate employment and to assist economic sectors that had been adversely affected by international competition. However, Réunion's rate of unemployment remained the highest of all the French Departments in 1997, with youth unemployment of particular concern. In November of that year the Government and the authorities on Réunion signed an agreement that was designed to create nearly 3,500 jobs for young people over a period of three years.

Social Welfare

At 1 January 1997 there were 1,218 physicians, 2,845 nurses and 294 dentists working on Réunion. In 1997 there were two general hospitals, four local hospitals, a hospital complex specialized in psychiatric care and nine private surgical clinics. The island had a total of 2,861 hospital beds at 1 January 1996. There is a system of social welfare similar to that of metropolitan France. With effect from 1 January 1996 welfare payments and the statutory minimum wage in the Overseas Departments were aligned with those of metropolitan France.

Education

Education is modelled on the French system, and is compulsory for 10 years between the ages of six and 16 years. Primary education begins at six years of age and lasts for five years. Secondary education, which begins at 11 years of age, lasts for up to seven years, comprising a first cycle of four years and a second of three years. For the academic year 1996/97 there were 44,464 pupils enrolled at 176 pre-primary schools, 74,953 at 350 primary schools, and 95,578 at 107 secondary schools (comprising 66 junior comprehensives, or collèges, and 41 lycées). There is a university, with several faculties, providing higher education in law, economics, politics, and French language and literature, and a teacher-training college. In 1982 the illiteracy rate among the population over 15 years of age averaged 21.4% (males 23.5%; females 19.5%).

Public Holidays

The principal holidays of metropolitan France are observed.

Weights and Measures

The metric system is in use.

Statistical Survey

Source (unless otherwise indicated): Institut National de la Statistique et des Etudes Economiques, Service Régional de la Réunion, 15 rue de l'Ecole, 97490 Sainte-Clotilde; tel. 29-51-57; fax 29-76-85.

AREA AND POPULATION

Area: 2,507 sq km (968 sq miles).

Population: 515,798 (males 252,997, females 262,801) at census of 9 March 1982; 597,828 (males 294,256, females 303,572) at census of 15 March 1990; 675,100 (official estimate) at 1 January 1997.

Density (1 January 1997): 269.3 per sq km.

Principal Towns (population at census of 15 March 1990): Saint-Denis (capital) 121,999; Saint-Paul 71,669; Saint-Pierre 58,846; Le Tampon 47,593.

Births and Deaths (1996): Registered live births 13,114 (birth rate 19.6 per 1,000); Registered deaths (provisional figure) 3,649 (death rate 5.4 per 1,000).

Economically Active Population (persons aged 15 years and over, 1990 census): Agriculture. hunting, forestry and fishing 11,141; Mining, manufacturing, electricity, gas and water 11,295; Construction 16,563; Wholesale and retail trade 17,902; Transport, storage and communications 7,250; Financing, insurance, real estate and business services 3,005; Other services (incl. activities not adequately defined) 79,097; Total employed 146,253 (males 90,526, females 55,727); Unemployed 86,108 (males 45,889, females 40,219); Total labour force 232,361 (males 136,415, females 95,946). Figures exclude persons on compulsory military service. Source: International Labour Office, *Yearbook of Labour Statistics*.

Mid-1996 (estimates in '000): Agriculture, etc. 12; Total labour force 267. Source: FAO, *Production Yearbook*.

AGRICULTURE, ETC.

Principal Crops (FAO estimates, '000 metric tons, 1996): Sugar cane 1,850; Raw sugar 233; Maize 18; Vegetables 57; Fruit 37. Source: FAO, *Production Yearbook*.

Livestock (FAO estimates, '000 head, year ending September 1996): Cattle 27; Pigs 95; Sheep 2; Goats 32; Chickens 8,000. Source: FAO, *Production Yearbook*.

Livestock Products (metric tons, unless otherwise indicated, 1995): Beef and veal 1,182; Pig meat 10,314; Mutton, lamb and goat meat 59; Poultry meat 15,620; Cow's milk (hl) 115,292; Eggs ('000) 76,113.

Forestry (FAO estimates, '000 cubic metres): Roundwood removals: 36 in 1992; 36 in 1993; 36 in 1994. Source: FAO, *Yearbook of Forest Products*.

Fishing (metric tons, live weight): Total catch 4,487 in 1994; 4,821 in 1995; 5,195 in 1996.

INDUSTRY

Production (metric tons, 1992): Oil of geranium 14.7; Oil of vetiver root 1.9; Tobacco 22.0; Vanilla 116.5; Ginger 95.0; Pimento 405.6; Rum (hl) 72,181 (1996); Electric energy (million kWh) 1,385.8 (1996).

FINANCE

Currency and Exchange Rates: French currency is used (see French Guiana).

Budget (million francs, 1995): *State Budget:* Revenue 6,009.0, Expenditure 13,426.5; *Regional Budget:* Revenue 2,165, Expenditure 2,162; *Departmental Budget:* Revenue 4,520, Expenditure 3,992. **1996** (million francs): *State Budget*: Revenue 6,646.6, Expenditure 14,331.5.

Money Supply (million francs at 31 December 1995): Currency outside banks 4,486; Demand deposits at banks 7,201; Total money 11,687.

Cost of Living (Consumer Price Index for urban areas, average of monthly figures; base: 1990 = 100): 113.5 in 1994; 115.5 in 1995; 117.7 in 1996. Source: UN, *Monthly Bulletin of Statistics*.

Expenditure on the Gross Domestic Product (provisional figures, million francs at current prices, 1994): Government final consumption expenditure 10,188; Private final consumption expenditure 27,514; Increase in stocks 38; Gross fixed capital formation 9,925; *Total domestic expenditure* 47,665; Exports of goods and services 1,015; *Less* Imports of goods and services 13,414; *GDP in purchasers' values* 35,266.

Gross Domestic Product by Economic Activity (million francs at current prices, 1989): Agriculture, hunting, forestry and fishing 918; Mining and manufacturing 2,089; Electricity, gas and water 1,156; Construction 1,479; Trade, restaurants and hotels 4,921;

Transport, storage and communications 1,233; Government services, 6,906; Other services 6,174; *Sub-total* 24,836; Import duties 1,036; Value-added tax 933; *Less* Imputed bank service charge 1,192; *Total* 25,613. Source: UN, *National Accounts Statistics*.

EXTERNAL TRADE

Principal Commodities (distribution by SITC, US $ million, 1995): *Imports c.i.f.:* Food and live animals 452.1 (Meat and meat preparations 100.7, Dairy products and birds' eggs 59.6, Cereals and cereal preparations 108.0, Vegetables and fruit 56.7); Beverages and tobacco 74.6 (Beverages 55.3); Mineral fuels, lubricants, etc. 128.2 (Petroleum, petroleum products, etc. 106.1); Chemicals and related products 283.0 (Medicinal and pharmaceutical products 138.6, Essential oils, perfume materials and cleansing preparations 57.0); Basic manufactures 414.6 (Paper, paperboard and manufactures 76.7, Non-metallic mineral manufactures 84.1, Iron and steel 68.1); Machinery and transport equipment 807.2 (Machinery specialized for particular industries 51.7, General industrial machinery, equipment and parts 99.2, Office machines and automatic data-processing equipment 59.9, Telecommunications and sound equipment 65.6, Other electrical machinery, apparatus, etc. 101.3, Road vehicles and parts 379.0); Miscellaneous manufactured articles 438.0 (Furniture and parts 72.4, Clothing and accessories, excl. footwear 98.3); Total (incl. others) 2,711.1. *Exports f.o.b.:* Food and live animals 156.1 (Fish, crustaceans and molluscs 16.5, Raw sugar 131.5); Beverages and tobacco 6.8 (Alcoholic beverages 6.2); Basic manufactures 6.3; Machinery and transport equipment 26.6 (Machinery specialized for particular industries 4.1, Road vehicles and parts 9.2); Miscellaneous manufactured articles 7.0; Total (incl. others) 208.7. Source: UN, *International Trade Statistics Yearbook*. **1996** (million francs): *Imports* 14,214.2; *Exports* 1,071.2 (Sugar 686.5).

Principal Trading Partners (US $ million, 1995): *Imports c.i.f.:* Bahrain 83.8; Belgium-Luxembourg 59.0; France (incl. Monaco) 1,797.9; Germany 76.0; Italy 95.6; Japan 57.3; Madagascar 27.5; Malaysia 26.4; Mauritius 26.6; Netherlands 30.0; Southern African Customs Union 70.3; Spain 42.6; Thailand 32.5; United Kingdom 39.3; Total (incl. others) 2,711.0. *Exports f.o.b.:* Belgium-Luxembourg 10.4; Comoros 9.9; France (incl. Monaco) 148.9; Japan 12.7; Madagascar 6.6; Mauritius 4.1; United Kingdom 4.2; Total (incl. others) 208.7. Source: UN, *International Trade Statistics Yearbook*.

TRANSPORT

Road Traffic (1 Jan. 1997): Motor vehicles in use 208,300.

Shipping: *Merchant Fleet* (total displacement at 31 December 1992): 21,000 grt (Source: UN, *Statistical Yearbook*); *Traffic* (1996): Vessels entered 626; Freight unloaded 2,168,600 metric tons; Freight loaded 426,100 metric tons; Passenger arrivals 6,740; Passenger departures 7,288.

Civil Aviation (1996): Passenger arrivals 629,665; Passenger departures 624,733; Freight unloaded 13,678 metric tons; Freight loaded 4,396 metric tons.

TOURISM

Tourist Arrivals (by country of residence, 1996): France 285,000, Mauritius 27,000, Madagascar 8,000, EU countries (excl. France) 9,000; Total (incl. others) 347,000.

Tourist Receipts (million francs): 907 in 1994; 1,116 in 1995; 1,332 in 1996.

COMMUNICATIONS MEDIA

Radio Receivers (1994): 158,000 in use. Source: UNESCO, *Statistical Yearbook*.

Television Receivers (1 Jan. 1993): 116,181 in use.

Telephones (main lines at 31 Dec. 1996): 225,851.

Telefax Stations (1991): 1,906 in use. Source: UN, *Statistical Yearbook*.

Mobile Cellular Telephones (1991): 2,735 subscribers. Source: UN, *Statistical Yearbook*.

Book Production (1992): 69 titles (50 books; 19 pamphlets). Source: UNESCO, *Statistical Yearbook*.

Daily Newspapers (1994): 3 (estimated average circulation 55,000 copies). Source: UNESCO, *Statistical Yearbook*.

Non-daily Newspapers (1988, estimates): 4 (average circulation 20,000 copies). Source: UNESCO, *Statistical Yearbook*.

EDUCATION

Pre-primary (1996/97): Schools 176; teachers 1,336 (1986); pupils 44,464.

Primary (1996/97): Schools 350; teachers 3,917 (1986); pupils 74,953.

Secondary (1996/97): Schools 107; teachers 6,259; pupils 95,578.

University: (1996/97): Teaching staff 242; students 8,745.

Directory

The Government

(January 1998)

Prefect: Robert Pommiès, Préfecture, Place du Barachois, 97405 Saint-Denis Cédex; tel. 40-77-77; fax 41-73-74.

President of the General Council: Christophe Payet, Hôtel du Département, 2 rue de la Source, 97400 Saint-Denis; tel. 90-30-30; fax 90-39-99.

President of the Economic and Social Committee: Tony Manglou.

Deputies to the French National Assembly: Huguette Bello (PCR), Claude Hoarau (PCR), Elie Hoarau (PCR), Michel Tamaya (PS), André Thien Ah Koon (UPF).

Representatives to the French Senate: Edmond Lauret (RPR), Pierre Lagourgue, Paul Vergès (PCR).

REGIONAL COUNCIL

Hôtel de la Région, ave René Cassin, Moufia BP 7190, 97719 Saint-Denis; tel. 48-70-00; telex 916040; fax 48-70-71.

President: Margie Sudre (Independent).

Election, 25 June 1993

Party	Seats
Free-DOM*	12
UDF	10
RPR	8
PCR	9
PS	6
Total	45

* List of independent candidates affiliated to Margie Sudre.

Political Organizations

Front National (FN): Saint-Denis; f. 1972; extreme right-wing; Leader Alix Morel.

Mouvement des Radicaux de Gauche (MRG): Saint-Denis; f. 1977; advocates full independence and an economy separate from, but assisted by, France; Pres. Jean-Marie Finck.

Mouvement pour l'Egalité, la Démocratie, le Développement et la Nature: affiliated to the PCR; advocates political unity; Leader René Payet.

Mouvement pour l'Indépendance de la Réunion (MIR): f. 1981 to succeed the fmr Mouvement pour la Libération de la Réunion; grouping of parties favouring autonomy.

Parti Communiste Réunionnais (PCR): 21 bis rue d l'Est, 97400 Saint-Denis; f. 1959; Pres. Paul Vergès; Sec.-Gen. Elie Hoarau.

Parti Socialiste (PS)–Fédération de la Réunion: Saint-Denis; tel. 21-77-95; telex 916445; left-wing; Sec.-Gen. Jean-Claude Fruteau.

Rassemblement des Démocrates pour l'Avenir de la Réunion (RADAR): Saint-Denis; f. 1981; centrist.

Rassemblement des Socialistes et des Démocrates (RSD): Saint-Denis; Sec.-Gen. Daniel Cadet.

***Rassemblement pour la République (RPR):** 6 bis blvd Vauban, BP 11, 97400 Saint-Denis; tel. 20-21-18; telex 916080; Gaullist; Pres. André Maurice Pihouée; Sec.-Gen. Tony Manglou.

***Union pour la Démocratie Française (UDF):** Saint-Denis; f. 1978; centrist; Sec.-Gen. Gilbert Gérard.

* The RPR and the UDF jointly contested the 1992 regional elections as the Union pour la France (UPF).

Judicial System

Cour d'Appel: Palais de Justice, 166 rue Juliette Dodu, 97488 Saint-Denis; tel. 40-58-58; telex 916149; fax 21-95-32; Pres. Jean Claude Carrié.

There are two **Tribunaux de Grande Instance**, one **Cour d'Assises**, four **Tribunaux d'Instance**, two **Tribunaux pour Enfants** and two **Conseils de Prud'hommes**.

Religion

A substantial majority of the population are adherents of the Roman Catholic Church. There is a small Muslim community.

CHRISTIANITY

The Roman Catholic Church

Réunion comprises a single diocese, directly responsible to the Holy See. At 31 December 1995 there were an estimated 574,000 adherents, equivalent to almost 90% of the population.

Bishop of Saint-Denis-de-La Réunion: Mgr GILBERT AUBRY, Evêché, 36 rue de Paris, BP 55, 97462 Saint-Denis; tel. 21-28-49; fax 41-77-15.

The Press

DAILIES

Journal de l'Ile de la Réunion: 42 rue Alexis de Villeneuve, BP 98, 97463 Saint-Denis Cédex; tel. 21-32-64; telex 916453; fax 41-09-77; f. 1956; Dir PHILIPPE BALOUKJY; circ. 26,000.

Quotidien de la Réunion: BP 303, 97712 Saint-Denis Messag Cédex 9; tel. 92-15-15; fax 28-43-60; f. 1976; Dir MAXIMIN CKANE KI CKUNE; circ. 30,000.

PERIODICALS

Al-Islam: Centre Islamique de la Réunion, BP 437, 97459 Saint-Pierre Cédex; tel. 25-45-43; fax 35-58-23; f. 1975; 4 a year; Dir SAÏD INGAR.

Cahiers de la Réunion et de l'Océan Indien: 24 blvd des Cocotiers, 97434 Saint-Gilles-les-Bains; monthly; Man. Dir CLAUDETTE SAINT-MARC.

L'Economie de la Réunion: c/o INSEE, 15 rue de l'Ecole, BP 13 Le Chaudron, 97408 Saint-Denis; tel. 48-89-00; fax 48-89-89; 6 a year; Dir RENÉ JEAN; Editor-in-Chief COLETTE PAVAGEAU.

L'Eglise à la Réunion: 18 rue Montreuil, 97469 Saint-Denis; tel. 41-56-90; Dir P. FRANÇOIS GLÉNAC.

L'Enjeu: Saint-Denis; tel. 21-75-76; fax 41-60-62; Dir BLANDINE ETRAYEN; Editor-in-Chief JEAN-CLAUDE VALLÉE; circ. 4,000.

Le Journal de la Nature: 97489 Saint-Denis; tel. 29-45-45; fax 29-00-90; Dir J. Y. CONAN.

Le Memento Industriel et Commercial Réunionnais: 80 rue Pasteur, 97400 Saint-Denis; tel. 21-94-12; fax 41-10-85; Dir CATHERINE LOUAPRE POTTIER; circ. 10,000.

974 Ouest: Montgaillard, 97400 Saint-Denis; monthly; Dir DENISE ELMA.

La Réunion Agricole: Chambre d'Agriculture, 24 rue de la Source, BP 134, 97463 Saint-Denis Cédex; tel. 21-25-88; fax 41-17-84; f. 1967; monthly; Dir JEAN-YVES MINATCHY; Chief Editor HERVÉ CAILLEAUX; circ. 8,000.

Télé 7 Jours Réunion: 6 rue Montyon, BP 405, 93200 Saint-Denis; weekly; Dir MICHEL MEKDOUD; circ. 25,000.

Témoignage Chrétien de la Réunion: 21 bis rue de l'Est, 97465 Saint-Denis; weekly; Dir RENÉ PAYET; circ. 2,000.

Témoignages: 21 bis rue de l'Est, BP 192, 97465 Saint-Denis; tel. 21-13-07; f. 1944; publ. of the PCR; weekly; Dir ELIE HOARAU; circ. 6,000.

Visu: 97712 Saint-Denis Cédex 9; tel. 90-20-60; fax 90-20-61; weekly; Editor-in-Chief J. J. AYAN; circ. 53,000.

Broadcasting and Communications

BROADCASTING

Société Nationale de Radio-Télévision Française d'Outre-Mer (RFO): 1 rue Jean Chatel, 97716 Saint-Denis Cédex; tel. 40-67-67; fax 21-64-84; internet http://www.rfo.fr; home radio and television relay services in French; operates two television channels; Chair. JEAN-MARIE CAVADA; Dir ALBERT-MAX BRIAND.

Radio

Radio Free-DOM: BP 666, 97473 Saint-Denis Cédex; tel. 41-51-51; fax 21-68-64; f. 1981; privately-owned radio station; Dir Dr CAMILLE SUDRE.

Television

Antenne Réunion: 33 rue des Vavangues, 97490 Sainte-Clotilde; tel. 48-28-28; fax 48-28-29; f. 1991; broadcasts 12 hours daily; Dir THIERRY NICHAUT.

Canal Réunion: 2D ave de Lattre de Tassigny, 97490 Sainte-Clotilde; tel. 21-16-17; fax 21-46-61; subscription television channel; broadcasts a minimum of 12 hours daily; Chair. DOMINIQUE FAGOT; Dir JEAN-BERNARD MOURIER.

TV-4: 8 chemin Fontbrune, 97400 Saint-Denis; tel. 52-73-73.

TV Sud: 10 rue Aristide Briand, 97430 Le Tampon; tel. 57-42-42; commenced broadcasting in Oct. 1993.

Other privately-owned television services include TVB, TVE, RTV, Télé-Réunion and TV-Run.

Finance

(cap. = capital; res = reserves; dep. = deposits; m. = million; brs = branches; amounts in French francs)

BANKING

Central Bank

Institut d'Emission des Départements d'Outre-Mer: 1 cité du Retiro, 75008 Paris, France; Office in Réunion: 4 rue de la Compagnie, 97487 Saint-Denis Cédex; tel. 21-18-96; telex 916176; fax 21-41-32; Dir YVES ESQUILAT.

Commercial Banks

Banque Française Commerciale Océan Indien (BFCOI): 60 rue Alexis de Villeneuve, BP 323, 97468 Saint-Denis Cédex; tel. 40-55-55; telex 916162; fax 40-54-55; Chair. PHILIPPE BRAULT; Dir PHILIPPE LAVIT D'HAUTEFORT; 8 brs.

Banque Nationale de Paris Intercontinentale: 67 rue Juliette Dodu, BP 113, 97463 Saint-Denis; tel. 40-30-30; telex 916133; fax 41-39-09; Chair. RENÉ THOMAS; Man. Dir JEAN-CLAUDE LALLEMANT; 11 brs.

Banque de la Réunion, SA: 27 rue Jean-Chatel, 97711 Saint-Denis Cédex; tel. 40-01-23; telex 916134; fax 40-00-61; f. 1849; affiliate of Crédit Lyonnais; cap.121.0m., res 345.7m., dep. 4,804.6m. (Dec. 1996); Pres. JACQUES BARILLET; Gen. Man. CHRISTIAN GODEFROY; 12 brs.

Caisse Régionale de Crédit Agricole Mutuel de la Réunion: parc Jean de Cambiaire, cité des Lauriers, BP 84, 97462 Saint-Denis Cédex; tel. 40-81-81; telex 916139; fax 40-81-40; f. 1949; affiliate of Caisse Nationale de Crédit Agricole; Chair. CHRISTIAN DE LA GIRODAY; Dir ERIC PRADEL.

Development Bank

Banque Populaire Fédérale de Développement: 33 rue Victor MacAuliffe, 97400 Saint-Denis; tel. 21-18-11; telex 916582; Dir OLIVIER DEVISME; 3 brs.

INSURANCE

More than 20 major European insurance companies are represented in Saint-Denis.

Trade and Industry

DEVELOPMENT ORGANIZATIONS

Association pour le Développement Industriel de la Réunion: 8 rue Philibert, BP 327, 97466 Saint-Denis Cédex; tel. 94-43-00; fax 94-43-09; f. 1975; 190 mems; Pres. GÉRARD DEBEUX.

Chambre d'Agriculture: 24 rue de la Source, BP 134, 97464 Saint-Denis Cédex; tel. 21-25-88; telex 916843; fax 21-06-17; Pres. JEAN-YVES MINATCHY; Dir FATMA BADAT.

Direction de l'Action Economique: Secrétariat Général pour les Affaires Economiques, ave de la Victoire, 97405 Saint-Denis; tel. 21-86-10; telex 916111.

Jeune Chambre Economique de Saint-Denis de la Réunion: 25 rue de Paris, BP 1151, 97483 Saint-Denis; f. 1963; 30 mems; Chair. JEAN-CHRISTOPHE DUVAL.

Société de Développement Economique de la Réunion—SODERE: 26 rue Labourdonnais, 97469 Saint-Denis; tel. 20-01-68; telex 916471; fax 20-05-07; f. 1964; Chair. RAYMOND VIVET; Man. Dir ALBERT TRIMAILLE.

CHAMBERS OF COMMERCE

Chambre de Commerce et d'Industrie de la Réunion: 5 bis rue de Paris, BP 120, 97463 Saint-Denis Cédex; tel. 94-20-00; telex 916278; fax 94-22-90; f. 1830; Pres. ROGER ROLAND.

Chambre de Métiers: 42 rue Jean Cocteau, 97490 Sainte-Clotilde; tel. 21-04-35; fax 21-68-33.

INDUSTRIAL AND TRADE ASSOCIATIONS

Syndicat des Exportateurs d'Huiles Essentielles, Plantes Aromatiques et Medicinales de Bourbon: Saint-Denis; tel. 20-10-23; exports oil of geranium, vetiver and vanilla; Pres. RICO PLOENIÈRES.

Syndicat des Fabricants de Sucre de la Réunion: BP 284, 97466 Saint-Denis Cédex; tel. 90-45-00; fax 41-24-13; Chair. XAVIER THIEBLIN.

Syndicat des Producteurs de Rhum de la Réunion: BP 284, 97466 Saint-Denis; tel. 90-45-00; fax 41-24-13; Chair. XAVIER THIEBLIN.

EMPLOYERS' ORGANIZATION

Syndicat Patronal du Bâtiment de la Réunion: BP 108, 97462 Saint-Denis Cédex; tel. 21-03-81; fax 21-55-07; Pres. P. PAVARD; Sec.-Gen. C. OZOUX.

TRADE UNIONS

Confédération Générale du Travail de la Réunion (CGTR): 144 rue du Général de Gaulle, BP 1132, 97482 Saint-Denis Cédex; Sec.-Gen. GEORGES MARIE LEPINAY.

Réunion also has its own sections of the major French trade union confederations, **Confédération Française Démocratique du Travail (CFDT), Force Ouvrière (FO), Confédération Française de l'Encadrement** and **Confédération Française des Travailleurs Chrétiens (CFTC)**.

Transport

ROADS

A route nationale circles the island, generally following the coast and linking the main towns. Another route nationale crosses the island from south-west to north-east linking Saint-Pierre and Saint-Benoît. In 1994 there were 370 km of routes nationales, 754 km of departmental roads and 1,630 km of other roads; 1,300 km of the roads were bituminized.

SHIPPING

In 1986 work was completed on the expansion of the Port de la Pointe des Galets, which was divided into the former port in the west and a new port in the east (the port Ouest and the port Est). In 1996 some 2.6m. tons of freight were loaded and discharged at the two ports.

Compagnie Générale Maritime (CGM): 3 rue Velásquez, BP 2007, 97822 Le Port Cédex; tel. 55-10-10; fax 43-23-04; agents for Mitsui OSK Lines; Dir HENRI FELCE.

Maritime Delmais-Vieljeux: BP 2006, 97822 Le Port Cédex; tel. 42-03-46; telex 916151; fax 43-72-06; Dir ARMAND BARUCH.

Réunion Maritime: f. 1991; consortium of 15 import cos; freight only.

Shipping Mediterranean Co: Le Port.

Société de Manutention et de Consignation Maritime (SOMACOM): BP 7, Le Port; agents for Scandinavian East Africa Line, Bank Line, Clan Line, Union Castle Mail Steamship Co and States Marine Lines.

Société Réunionnaise de Services Maritimes: 81 rue de St Paul, BP 2006, 97822 Le Port Cédex; tel. 42-03-46; telex 916170; fax 43-34-79; freight only; Man. DENIS LAURE.

CIVIL AVIATION

Réunion's international airport, Roland Garros-Gillot, is situated 14 km from Saint-Denis. A programme to develop the airport was completed in 1994, and in August 1997 work commenced on the extension of its terminal, at a cost of some 175m. French francs. A project to develop the Pierrefonds airfield, near Saint-Pierre, as an international airport, at an estimated cost of nearly 50m. French francs, was due for completion by the end of 1997.

Air Austral: BP 611, 97473 Saint-Denis; tel. 28-27-27; telex 916236; fax 29-28-95; f. 1975; subsidiary of Air France; scheduled services to Madagascar, South Africa, Mauritius and the Comoros; Chair G. ETHEVE; Gen. Man. Mme B. POPINEAU.

Air Outre-Mer: Saint-Denis; f. 1990; scheduled services to Paris; Chair. RENÉ MICAUD.

Tourism

Tourism is being extensively promoted. Réunion's attractions include spectacular scenery and a pleasant climate. In 1996 the island had 44 hotels with a total of 1,810 rooms. In that year a total of 347,000 tourists visited Réunion, and revenue from tourism totalled about 1,332m. French francs.

Comité du Tourisme de la Réunion: BP 615, 97472 Saint-Denis Cédex; tel. 21-00-41; telex 916068; fax 20-25-93; e-mail ctm@gvetali.fr; Pres. JASMIN MOUTOUSSAMY.

Délégation Régionale au Commerce, à l'Artisanat et au Tourisme: Préfecture de la Réunion, 97400 Saint-Denis; tel. 40-77-58; telex 916111; fax 40-77-01; Dir JEAN-FRANÇOIS DESROCHES.

Office du Tourisme: 48 rue Sainte-Marie, 97400 Saint-Denis; tel. 41-83-00; fax 21-37-76; Vice-Pres. YASMINA HATIA.

French Overseas Collectivités Territoriales

The two overseas Collectivités Territoriales are Mayotte and St Pierre and Miquelon. Their status is between that of an Overseas Department and that of an Overseas Territory. They are integral parts of the French Republic and are each administered by a Prefect, who is appointed by the French Government. The Prefect is assisted by an elected General Council. The Collectivités Territoriales are represented in the French National Assembly and in the Senate in Paris, and also in the European Parliament in Strasbourg.

MAYOTTE

Introductory Survey

Location, Climate, Language, Religion, Capital

Mayotte forms part of the Comoros archipelago, which lies between the island of Madagascar and the east coast of the African mainland. The territory comprises a main island, Mayotte (Mahoré), and a number of smaller islands. The climate is tropical, with temperatures averaging between 24°C and 27°C (75°F to 81°F) throughout the year. The official language is French, and Islam is the main religion. The capital is Dzaoudzi, which is connected to the island of Pamandzi by a causeway.

Recent History

Since the Comoros unilaterally declared independence in July 1975, Mayotte has been administered separately by France. The independent Comoran state claims sovereignty of Mayotte, and officially represents it in international organizations, including the UN. In December 1976 France introduced the special status of Collectivité Territoriale for the island. Following a coup in the Comoros in May 1978 (see p. 985), Mayotte rejected the new Government's proposal that it should rejoin the other islands under a federal system, and reaffirmed its intention of remaining linked to France. In December 1979 the French National Assembly approved legislation that extended Mayotte's special status for another five years, during which the islanders were to be consulted. In October 1984, however, the National Assembly further prolonged Mayotte's status, and the referendum on the island's future was postponed indefinitely. The UN General Assembly has adopted a number of resolutions in support of the sovereignty of the Comoros over the island. The main political party on Mayotte, the Mouvement Populaire Mahorais (MPM), demands full departmental status for the island, but France has been reluctant to grant this in view of Mayotte's lack of development.

At the general election to the French National Assembly in March 1986, Henry Jean-Baptiste, a member of the Centre des Démocrates Sociaux (CDS), which was affiliated to the Union pour la Démocratie Française (UDF), was elected as deputy for Mayotte. During a visit (the first by a French Prime Minister) to Mayotte in October, Jacques Chirac assured the islanders that they would remain French citizens for as long as they wished. Relations between the MPM and the French Government rapidly deteriorated after the Franco-African summit in November 1987, when Chirac expressed reservations concerning the elevation of Mayotte to the status of an Overseas Department (despite his announcement, in early 1986, that he shared the MPM's aim to upgrade Mayotte's status).

In the second round of the French presidential election, which took place on 8 May 1988, François Mitterrand, the incumbent President and the candidate of the Parti Socialiste (PS), received 50.3% of the votes cast on Mayotte, defeating Chirac, the candidate of the Rassemblement pour la République (RPR). At elections to the French National Assembly, which took place in June, Jean-Baptiste retained his seat. (Later that month, he joined the newly-formed centrist group in the French National Assembly, the Union du Centre—UDC.) In elections to the General Council in September and October, the MPM retained the majority of seats. In November the General Council demanded that the French Government introduce measures to restrict immigration to Mayotte from neighbouring islands, particularly from the Comoros.

Following the assassination of the Comoran President, Ahmed Abdallah, in November 1989, Mayotte was used as a strategic military base, where additional French troops were stationed in December, in preparation for possible military intervention. (The territory was similarly used in late 1990, prior to French participation in the multinational forces that opposed Iraq in the war in the Persian (Arabian) Gulf in early 1991.)

In 1989 and 1990 concern about the number of Comoran immigrants seeking employment on the island resulted in an increase in racial tension. In 1989 more than 150 Comoran refugees were prevented from landing on Mayotte by security forces. In mid-January 1990 demonstrators in the town of Mamoudzou protested against illegal immigration to the island. A paramilitary organization, known as Caiman, was subsequently formed in support of the expulsion of illegal immigrants, but was refused legal recognition by the authorities.

At elections to the General Council, which took place in March 1991, the MPM secured an additional three seats, although Younoussa Bamana, the President of the General Council and leader of the MPM, was defeated in his canton, Keni-Keli, by the RPR candidate. In April, however, Bamana secured the majority of votes cast in a partial election, which took place in the canton of Chicani, and was subsequently re-elected to the presidency of the General Council.

In late June 1991 a demonstration on the island of Pamandzi in protest at the relocation of a number of people as a result of the expansion of the airfield prevented an aircraft from Réunion from landing. Unrest among young people on Pamandzi culminated in violence in early July, when demonstrators attempted to set fire to the town hall. Clashes between demonstrators and security forces ensued, and the Prefect, Jean-Paul Costes, requested that police reinforcements be dispatched from Réunion to restore order. An organization of young islanders, the Association des Jeunes pour le Développement de Pamandzi (AJDP), accused the mayor of mismanagement and demanded his resignation. The demonstrations, which threatened to destabilize the MPM, were believed to reflect general dissatisfaction among young people on Mayotte (who comprised about 60% of the population) with the authorities. Later in July five members of the AJDP, who had taken part in the demonstration at the airfield in June, received custodial sentences.

In June 1992 increasing resentment resulted in further attacks against Comoran immigrants resident in Mayotte. In early September representatives of the MPM met the French Prime Minister, Pierre Bérégovoy, to request the reintroduction of entry visas to restrict immigration from the Comoros. Later that month the MPM organized a boycott (which was widely observed) of Mayotte's participation in the French referendum on the Treaty on European Union (see p. 158), in support of the provision of entry visas. In December Costes and a number of other prominent officials were charged in connection with the deaths of six people in domestic fires, which had been caused by dangerous fuel imported from Bahrain. In February 1993 a general strike, which was staged in support of claims for wage increases, culminated in protracted violent rioting. Security forces were subsequently dispatched from Réunion to restore order, while trade unions agreed to end the strike. Later that month Costes was replaced as Prefect.

At elections to the French National Assembly, which took place in March 1993, Jean-Baptiste was returned, securing 53.4% of votes cast, while the Secretary-General of the RPR, Mansour Kamardine, received 44.3% of the votes. Kamardine (who contested the elections as an independent candidate) subsequently accused Jean-Baptiste of illegally claiming the support of an electoral alliance of the RPR and the UDF, known as the Union pour la France, by forging the signatures of party officials on a document. Jean-Baptiste, however, denied the allegations, and began legal proceedings against Kamardine for calumny.

Elections to the General Council (which was enlarged from 17 to 19 members) took place in March 1994: the MPM retained 12 seats, while the RPR secured four seats, and independent candidates three seats. During an official visit to Mayotte in November, the French Prime Minister, Edouard Balladur, announced the reintroduction of entry visas as a requirement for Comoran nationals, and the adoption of a number of security measures, in an effort to reduce illegal immigration to the island. In January 1995 the reimposition of visa requirements prompted widespread protests on the Comoros; the Comoran Government suspended transport links between Mayotte and the Comoros in response to the measure. In the first round of the French presidential election in April, Balladur received the highest number of votes on Mayotte (although Chirac subsequently won the election).

Following a further coup attempt by mercenaries in the Comoros, which took place in September 1995 (see p. 988), the French Government dispatched additional troops to Mayotte, prior to staging a military intervention. In elections to the Senate in September, the incumbent MPM representative, Marcel Henry, was returned by a large majority. During a visit to Mayotte in October, the French Minister of Overseas Departments and Territories pledged that a referendum on the future status of the island would be conducted by 1999. In October 1996 he confirmed that two commissions, based in Paris and Mayotte, were preparing a consultation document, which would be presented in late 1997, and announced that the resulting referendum would take place before the end of the decade.

Partial elections to fill nine seats in the General Council were held in March 1997; the MPM secured three seats (losing two that it had previously held), the RPR won three seats, the local PS one seat, and independent right-wing candidates two seats. In elections to the French National Assembly Jean-Baptiste, representing the alliance of the UDF and the Force Démocrate (FD, formerly the CDS), defeated Kamardine, securing 51.7% of votes cast in the second round of voting, which took place at the beginning of June.

In July 1997 the relative prosperity of Mayotte was thought to have prompted separatist movements on the Comoran islands of Nzwani and Mwali to demand the restoration of French rule, and subsequently to declare their independence in August (see p. 989). In September, following an unsuccessful military intervention, mounted by the Comoran Government in an attempt to quell the insurrection, many of those injured in the fighting were taken to Mayotte for medical treatment.

(For further details of the recent history of the island, see the chapter on the Comoros, p. 985.)

Government

The French Government is represented in Mayotte by an appointed Prefect. There is a General Council, with 19 members, elected by universal adult suffrage. Mayotte elects one deputy to the French National Assembly, and one representative to the Senate. Mayotte is also represented at the European Parliament.

Defence

At 1 August 1997 there were 4,000 French troops stationed in Mayotte and Réunion.

Economic Affairs

Mayotte's gross domestic product (GDP) per head in 1991 was estimated at 4,050 French francs. Between the censuses of 1991 and 1997 the population of Mayotte increased by a total of 39.1%, according to provisional figures.

The economy is based almost entirely on agriculture. The principal export crops are ylang-ylang, vanilla, cinnamon, coconuts and coffee. Rice, cassava and maize are cultivated for domestic consumption. Livestock-rearing and fishing are also important activities. However, Mayotte imports large quantities of foodstuffs, which comprised 22% of the value of total imports in 1988.

Construction is the sole industrial sector. There are no mineral resources on the island. Imports of mineral products comprised 4.4%, and metals 10.5%, of the value of total imports in 1988.

In 1992 Mayotte recorded a trade deficit of 437.8m. French francs. The principal source of imports in 1992 was France (74%); other major suppliers were South Africa, Singapore and Thailand. France was also the principal market for exports (taking 70% of exports in that year); other significant purchasers were the Comoros and Réunion. The principal exports in 1994 were oil of ylang-ylang and vanilla. The principal imports in 1989 were foodstuffs, machinery, transport equipment and metals.

In 1986 Mayotte's external assets totalled 203.8m. French francs, and banking aid reached 6.3m. francs. In 1996 Mayotte's budget expenditure was 806m. French francs. Official debt was 435.7m. French francs at 31 December 1995. It was estimated that 38% of the labour force were unemployed in 1991.

Mayotte suffers from a high trade deficit, owing to its reliance on imports, and is largely dependent on French aid. From the late 1980s the French Government granted substantial aid to finance a number of construction projects, in an attempt to encourage the development of tourism on the island. Mayotte's remote location, however, continued to prove an impediment to the development of the tourist sector. A five-year Development Plan (1986–91) included measures to improve infrastructure and to increase investment in public works; the Plan was subsequently extended to the end of 1993. In April 1995 an economic and social development agreement was signed with the French Government for the period 1995–99. Later that year Mayotte received credit from France to finance further investment in infrastructure, particularly in the road network. As Mayotte's labour force has continued to increase, mostly owing to a high birth rate and continued illegal immigration, youth unemployment had caused particular concern. In 1997 it was estimated that approximately one-half of the unemployed population was under 25 years of age.

Social Welfare

Medical services on Mayotte are available free of charge. The island is divided into six sectors, each of which is allocated a doctor or medical worker. Mayotte has two hospitals, situated at Mamoudzou and at Dzaoudzi, which provide a total of 100 beds. In 1985 there were nine physicians and 51 qualified nurses working in Mayotte.

Education

Education is compulsory for children aged six to 16 years, and comprises five years' primary and five years' secondary schooling. In 1986 there were 28 primary schools on the island. In 1997 there were eight secondary schools, comprising seven collèges (junior comprehensives) and a lycée. In the same year 25,805 pre-primary and primary school pupils and 6,190 secondary school pupils were enrolled. Some vocational training is provided on Mayotte, and further technical training is available in Réunion. In December 1996 the Caisse Française de Développement provided 21.6m. French francs for the construction of pre-primary and primary schools.

Public Holidays

The principal holidays of metropolitan France are observed.

Statistical Survey

Source (unless otherwise indicated): Office of the Prefect, Government Commissioner, Dzaoudzi.

AREA AND POPULATION

Area: 374 sq km (144 sq miles).

Population: 67,167 (census of August 1985); 94,410 (census of August 1991); 131,320 (provisional, census of August 1997). *Principal towns* (population at 1985 census): Dzaoudzi (capital) 5,865, Mamoudzou 12,026, Pamandzi-Labattoir 4,106. *Dzaoudzi* (estimated population at 1991 census): 8,300.

Births and Deaths (1991): Birth rate 43.7 per 1,000; Death rate 6.0 per 1,000.

Source: Institut National de la Statistique et des Etudes Economiques.

AGRICULTURE, ETC.

Livestock (1990): Cattle 12,000; Sheep 3,000; Goats 15,000. Source: Secrétariat du Comité Monétaire de la Zone Franc, *La Zone Franc, Rapport 1990*.

Fishing (metric tons, live weight): Total catch 425 in 1993; 528 in 1994; 500 in 1995. Source: FAO, *Yearbook of Fishery Statistics*.

FINANCE

Currency and Exchange Rates: French currency is used (see French Guiana).

Budget (million francs): Total expenditure 632 (current 449, capital 183) in 1994; 703 (current 545, capital 158) in 1995; 806 (current 561, capital 245) in 1996. Source: Institut d'Emission d'Outre-Mer.

Money Supply (million French francs at 31 December 1995): Currency outside banks 898; Demand deposits 207; Total money 1,105. Source: Institut National de la Statistique et des Etudes Economiques.

EXTERNAL TRADE

Total Trade (million francs): *Imports:* 527 in 1993; 539 in 1994; 648 in 1995. *Exports:* 15 in 1993; 21 in 1994; 18 in 1995. Source: Institut National de la Statistique et des Etudes Economiques.

Principal Commodities ('000 francs, 1988): *Imports:* Foodstuffs 65,014; Machinery and appliances 61,097; Metals and metal products 31,061; Transport equipment 50,097; Total (incl. others) 294,981. *Exports:* Oil of ylang-ylang 8,188; Vanilla 1,810; Coffee (green) 178; Total (incl. others) 10,189. Figures exclude re-exports (42.9 million francs in 1988).

Principal Trading Partners ('000 francs): *Imports* (1988): France 193,984; Singapore 9,507; South Africa 26,854; Thailand 12,617; Total (incl. others) 294,981. *Exports* (1983): France 4,405.

Source: Secrétariat du Comité Monétaire de la Zone Franc, *La Zone Franc, Rapport 1988.*

TRANSPORT

Roads (1984): 93 km of main roads, of which 72 km are tarred, 137 km of local roads, of which 40 km are tarred, and 54 km of tracks unusable in the rainy season; 1,528 vehicles.

Civil Aviation (1984): *Arrivals:* 7,747 passengers, 120 metric tons of freight; *Departures:* 7,970 passengers, 41 metric tons of freight.

TOURISM

Tourist arrivals (1994): 24,464. Source: Ministère des Départements et Territoires d'Outre-Mer.

EDUCATION

Pre-primary and Primary (1997): 25,805 pupils.

Secondary (1997): 8 schools; 6,190 pupils.

Source: Ministère des Départements et Territoires d'Outre-Mer.

Directory

The Constitution

Under the status of Collectivité Territoriale, which was adopted in December 1976, Mayotte has an elected General Council, comprising 19 members, which assists the Prefect in the administration of the island. In 1984 a referendum on the future of Mayotte was postponed indefinitely.

The Government

Représentation du Gouvernement, Dzaoudzi, 97610 Mayotte; tel. 60-10-54.

(February 1998)

Prefect: PHILIPPE BOISADAM.

Secretary-General: JEAN-PIERRE LAFLAQUIÈRE.

Deputy to the French National Assembly: HENRY JEAN-BAPTISTE (UDF–Force Démocrate).

Representative to the French Senate: MARCEL HENRY (MPM).

GENERAL COUNCIL

Conseil Général, Mamoudzou, 97600 Mayotte; tel. 61-12-33.

The General Council comprises 19 members. At elections in March 1994, the Mouvement Populaire Mahorais (MPM) secured 12 seats, the Fédération de Mayotte du Rassemblement pour la République four seats, and independent candidates three seats. As a result of by-elections held in March 1997, the MPM holds eight seats, the Fédération de Mayotte du Rassemblement pour la République five seats, independent right-wing candidates five seats, and the Parti Socialiste one seat.

President of the General Council: YOUNOUSSA BAMANA.

Political Organizations

Fédération de Mayotte du Rassemblement pour la République: Dzaoudzi, 97610 Mayotte; local branch of the French (Gaullist) Rassemblement pour la République (RPR); Sec.-Gen. MANSOUR KAMARDINE.

Mouvement Populaire Mahorais (MPM): Dzaoudzi, 97610 Mayotte; seeks departmental status for Mayotte; Leader YOUNOUSSA BAMANA.

Parti pour le Rassemblement Démocratique des Mahorais (PRDM): Dzaoudzi, 97610 Mayotte; f. 1978; seeks unification with the Federal Islamic Republic of the Comoros; Leader DAROUÈCHE MAOULIDA.

Parti Socialiste: Dzaoudzi; local branch of the French party of the same name.

In 1990 the two major French right-wing political parties, the **Rassemblement pour la République (RPR)** and the **Union**

pour la Démocratie Française (UDF), formed an electoral alliance, the **Union pour la France (UPF)**.

Judicial System

Tribunal Supérieur d'Appel: Mamoudzou, 97600 Mayotte; tel. 61-12-65; fax 61-19-63; Pres. JEAN-BAPTISTE FLORI.

Procureur de la République: PATRICK BROSSIER.

Tribunal de Première Instance: Pres. ARLETTE MEALLONNIER-DUGUE.

Religion

Muslims comprise about 98% of the population. Most of the remainder are Christians, mainly Roman Catholics.

CHRISTIANITY

The Roman Catholic Church

Mayotte is within the jurisdiction of the Apostolic Administrator of the Comoros.

The Press

L'Insulaire: Immeuble Villa Bourhani, rue du Collège, BP 88, 97600 Mamoudzou; tel. 61-37-85; fax 61-37-86; weekly.

Le Kwezi: BP 243, 97600 Mamoudzou; tel. 61-16-52; fax 61-05-29; weekly.

Broadcasting and Communications

RADIO AND TELEVISION

Société Nationale de Radio-Télévision Française d'Outre-Mer (RFO): BP 103, Dzaoudzi, 97610 Mayotte; tel. 60-10-17; telex 915822; fax 60-18-52; f. 1977; govt-owned; radio broadcasts in French and Mahorian; television transmissions began in 1986; Pres. JEAN-MARIE CAVADA; Station Dir ROBERT XAVIER.

Finance

BANKS

Institut d'Emission d'Outre-Mer: BP 500, Mamoudzou, 97600 Mayotte; tel. 61-10-38; telex 915804; fax 61-05-02.

Banque Française Commerciale: Mamoudzou, 97600 Mayotte; br. at Dzaoudzi.

Transport

ROADS

The main road network totals approximately 93 km, of which 72 km are bituminized. There are 137 km of local roads, of which 40 km are tarred, and 54 km of minor tracks which are unusable during the rainy season.

SHIPPING

Coastal shipping is provided by locally-owned small craft. There is a deep-water port at Longoni.

CIVIL AVIATION

There is an airfield at Dzaoudzi, serving four-times weekly commercial flights to Réunion, twice-weekly services to Madagascar, Njazidja, Nzwani and Mwali, and a weekly service to Kenya.

Tourism

Tropical scenery provides the main tourist attraction. In 1994 the island had 11 hotels, providing a total of approximately 120 rooms. Mayotte received 24,464 tourists in that year.

Comité Territorial du Tourisme de Mayotte: rue de la Pompe, BP 1169, Mamoudzou, 97600 Mayotte; tel. 61-09-09; fax 61-03-46.

ST PIERRE AND MIQUELON

Introductory Survey

Location, Climate, Language, Religion, Capital

The territory of St Pierre and Miquelon (Iles Saint-Pierre-et-Miquelon) consists of a number of small islands which lie about 25 km (16 miles) from the southern coast of Newfoundland, Canada, in the North Atlantic Ocean. The principal islands are St Pierre, Miquelon (Grande Miquelon) and Langlade (Petite Miquelon)—the last two being linked by an isthmus of sand. Winters are cold, with temperatures falling to −20°C (−4°F), and summers are mild, with temperatures averaging between 10° and 20°C (50° and 68°F). The islands are particularly affected by fog in June and July. The language is French, and the majority of the population profess Christianity and belong to the Roman Catholic Church. The capital is Saint-Pierre, on the island of St Pierre.

Recent History

The islands of St Pierre and Miquelon are the remnants of the once extensive French possessions in North America. They were confirmed as French territory in 1816, and gained departmental status in July 1976. The departmentalization proved unpopular with many of the islanders, since it incorporated the territory's economy into that of the European Community (EC, now European Union, see p. 152), and was regarded as failing to take into account the islands' isolation and dependence on Canada for supplies and transport links. In March 1982 socialist and other left-wing candidates, campaigning for a change in the islands' status, were elected unopposed to all seats in the General Council. St Pierre and Miquelon was excluded from the Mitterrand administration's decentralization reforms, undertaken in 1982.

In 1976 Canada imposed an economic interest zone extending to 200 nautical miles (370 km) around its shores. Fearing the loss of traditional fishing areas and thus the loss of the livelihood of the fishermen of St Pierre, the French Government claimed a similar zone around the islands. Hopes of discovering valuable reserves of petroleum and natural gas in the area heightened the tension between France and Canada.

In December 1984 legislation was approved giving the islands the status of a Collectivité Territoriale with effect from 11 June 1985. This was intended to allow St Pierre and Miquelon to receive the investment and development aid suitable for its position, while allaying Canadian fears of EC exploitation of its offshore waters. Local representatives, however, remained apprehensive about the outcome of negotiations between the French and Canadian Governments to settle the dispute over coastal limits. (France continued to claim a 200-mile fishing and economic zone around St Pierre and Miquelon, while Canada wanted the islands to have only a 12-mile zone.) In January 1987 it was decided that the dispute should be submitted to international arbitration. Discussions began in March, and negotiations to determine quotas for France's catch of Atlantic cod over the period 1988–91 were to take place simultaneously. In the mean time, Canada and France agreed on an interim fishing accord, which would allow France to increase its cod quota. The discussions collapsed in October, however, and French trawlers were prohibited from fishing in Canadian waters. In February 1988 Albert Pen and Gérard Grignon, St Pierre's elected representatives to the French legislature, together with two members of the St Pierre administration and 17 sailors, were arrested for fishing in Canadian waters. This episode, and the arrest of a Canadian trawler captain in May for fishing in St Pierre's waters, led to an unsuccessful resumption of negotiations in September. In November the President of the Inter-American Development Bank was appointed as mediator in the dispute, and agreement was reached on fishing rights in March 1989, whereby France's annual quotas for Atlantic cod and other species were determined for the period until the end of 1991. (Further quotas were subsequently stipulated for the first nine months of 1992.) At the same time the Governments agreed upon the composition of an international arbitration tribunal which would delineate the disputed maritime boundaries and exclusive economic zones.

Meanwhile, in January 1989 two factory fishing ships from metropolitan France sailed to the area to catch the fish under agreed quotas, but there were protests by the islanders, who feared that damage might be caused to fishing stocks by the factory ships. After discussions with the French Prime Minister, it was agreed that one of the factory ships would return to France. In October 1990 the islanders protested to the Government concerning illegal fishing in their waters by a metropolitan-based company.

In July 1991 the international arbitration tribunal began its deliberations in New York, USA. The tribunal's ruling, issued in June 1992, was generally deemed to be favourable to Canada. France was allocated an exclusive economic zone around the territory totalling 2,537 square nautical miles (8,700 sq km), compared with its demand for more than 13,000 square nautical miles. The French authorities claimed that the sea area granted would be insufficient to sustain the islands' fishing community. Canadian and French officials met in Canada in the following month to negotiate new fishing quotas for the area off Newfoundland; however, the talks failed, and, in the absence of a new agreement, industrial fishing in the area was effectively halted until November 1994, when the Governments of the two countries signed an accord specifying new quotas for a period of 10 years. In the following month deputies in the French National Assembly expressed concern that the terms of the agreement would be detrimental to St Pierre and Miquelon's interests, although the Government asserted that the accord recognized the islanders' historic fishing rights in Canadian waters. Meanwhile, in January of that year St Pierre and Miquelon protested at what it alleged was an unauthorized entry into the islands' waters by Canadian coastguards (who had been attempting to intercept goods being smuggled from Saint-Pierre to Newfoundland), and appealed to France to intensify its efforts to protect the islands' territorial integrity.

At the March 1986 election to the French National Assembly the islands' incumbent deputy, Albert Pen of the Parti Socialiste (PS), was re-elected. Pen was also the sole candidate at the indirect election to choose the islands' representative in the French Senate in September. A fresh election for a deputy to the National Assembly was held in November, when Gérard Grignon, representing the centre-right Union pour la Démocratie Française (UDF), was elected. At the 1988 French presidential election Jacques Chirac of the right-wing Rassemblement pour la République (RPR) received 56% of the votes cast by the islanders in the second round, in May, against the successful PS incumbent, François Mitterrand. In June Grignon was re-elected to the National Assembly, taking 90.3% of the valid votes. In September–October, however, the parties of the left won a majority at elections to the General Council, securing 13 of the 19 seats.

In September 1992 64.2% of voters approved ratification of the Treaty on European Union (see p. 158), although only a small percentage of the electorate participated in the referendum. Grignon was re-elected to the National Assembly in March 1993; some 83% of the electorate participated in the poll. At the 1995 presidential election Chirac received the greatest proportion of the votes cast at the first round on 23 April (33.97%), and was the winning candidate at the second round on 7 May, taking 66.86% of the votes cast. The rate of abstention at the second round was 33.2%. At elections to the Senate in September, Pen was narrowly defeated at a second round of voting by Victor Reux of the RPR, since 1994 the Secretary of the islands' Economic and Social Council. Grignon was re-elected to the National Assembly at a second round of voting on 1 June 1997, with 52.34% of the votes cast.

Government

The French Government is represented in St Pierre by an appointed Prefect. There is a General Council, with 19 members (15 for St Pierre and four for Miquelon), elected by adult universal suffrage for a period of six years. St Pierre and Miquelon elects one deputy to the French National Assembly and one representative to the Senate in Paris.

Defence

France is responsible for the islands' defence.

Economic Affairs

The soil and climatic conditions of St Pierre and Miquelon do not favour agricultural production, which is mainly confined to smallholdings, except for market-gardening and the production of eggs and chickens.

The principal economic activity of the islands is traditionally fishing and related industries, which employed some 18.5% of the working population in 1996. However, the sector has been severely affected by disputes with Canada regarding territorial waters and fishing quotas. The absence of quotas in 1992–94 effectively halted industrial fishing, although a catch of 13,900 metric tons (comparable with levels in the late 1980s and early 1990s) was recorded in 1995. New arrangements are, however, regarded as being to the detriment of St Pierre and Miquelon, although there is some optimism regarding potential for the exploitation of shellfish, notably scallops, in the islands' waters.

Processing of fish provides the basis for industrial activity, which engages about 41% of the labour force. It is dominated by one major company, which produces frozen and salted fish, and fish meal for fodder. In 1988 the industry recorded a sharp decrease in production (to 3,710 metric tons), compared with preceding years; total production increased to 5,457 tons in 1990. Much of the fish processed is now imported. Electricity is generated by two thermal power stations, with a combined capacity of 23 MW.

The replenishment of ships' (mainly trawlers') supplies was formerly an important economic activity, but has now also been adversely affected by the downturn in the industrial fishing sector. During the late 1980s efforts were made to promote tourism, and the opening of the St Pierre–Montréal air route in 1987 led to an increase in air traffic. Tourist arrivals in 1996 were estimated at 11,958. The construction of a new airport capable of accommodating larger aircraft is expected further to improve transport links.

In 1995 St Pierre and Miquelon recorded a trade deficit of 316m. French francs; total exports were 55m. francs. Most trade is with Canada and France and other countries of the European Union. The only significant exports are fish and fish meal. The principal imports in 1994 were fuel, building supplies and food from Canada. Items such as clothing and other consumer goods are generally imported from France.

The annual rate of inflation averaged 6.3% in 1981–91, and consumer prices increased by an average of 2.1% per year between December 1991 and December 1996. Some 7.7% of the labour force were unemployed in 1989.

Given the decline of the fishing sector, the development of the port of Saint-Pierre and the expansion of tourism (particularly from Canada and the USA) are regarded by St Pierre and Miquelon as the principal means of maintaining economic progress. The islands will, none the less, remain highly dependent on budgetary assistance from the French central Government.

Social Welfare

In 1997 there was one hospital complex, which included a retirement home and a centre for the handicapped. Citizens of St Pierre and Miquelon benefit from similar social security provisions to those of metropolitan France.

Education

The education system is modelled on the French system, and education is compulsory for children between the ages of six and 16 years. In 1995 there were eight primary schools, three secondary schools (one of which is private and has a technical school annex) and one technical school.

Public Holidays

1998: 1 January (New Year's Day), 10–13 April (Easter), 1 May (Labour Day), 21 May (Ascension Day), 1 June (Whit Monday), 14 July (National Day), 11 November (Armistice Day), 25 December (Christmas Day).

1999: 1 January (New Year's Day), 2–5 April (Easter), 1 May (Labour Day), 13 May (Ascension Day), 24 May (Whit Monday), 14 July (National Day), 11 November (Armistice Day), 25 December (Christmas Day).

Weights and Measures

The metric system is in use.

Statistical Survey

Source: Préfecture, Place du Lieutenant-Colonel Pigeaud, BP 4200, 97500 Saint-Pierre; tel. 41-10-10; telex 914410; fax 41-25-46.

AREA AND POPULATION

Area: 242 sq km (93.4 sq miles): St Pierre 26 sq km; Miquelon-Langlade 216 sq km.

Population: 6,392 at census of 15 March 1990: Saint-Pierre 5,683, Miquelon-Langlade 709; 6,600 (estimate) at 31 December 1996.

Density (1996): 27.3 per sq km.

Births, Marriages and Deaths (1996): Live births 74; Marriages 29; Deaths 37.

Economically Active Population (1992): Fish and fish-processing 540; Construction 333; Transport 192; Dockers 44; Trade 409; Restaurants and hotels 154; Business services 417; Government employees 727; Activities not adequately defined 106; Total labour force 2,922.

FISHING

Total Catch (metric tons, live weight): 13,900 in 1995.

FINANCE

Currency and Exchange Rates: French currency is used (see French Guiana).

Expenditure by Metropolitan France (1995): 285 million francs.

Budget (estimates, million francs, 1996): Expenditure 271 (current 126; capital 145).

Money Supply (million francs at 31 December 1995): Currency outside banks 274; Demand deposits at banks 763; Total money 1,037.

Cost of Living (Consumer price index; base: 1981 = 100): 183.0 in 1989; 189.6 in 1990; 196.5 in 1991.

EXTERNAL TRADE

Total (million francs, 1995): *Imports:* 371; *Exports:* 55. Most trade is with Canada, France (imports), other countries of the European Union (exports) and the USA.

TRANSPORT

Road Traffic (1995): 3,386 motor vehicles in use.

Shipping (1995): Ships entered 884; Freight entered 20,400 metric tons.

Civil Aviation (1995): Passengers carried 30,128, Freight carried 109 metric tons.

TOURISM

Tourist Arrivals (estimate, 1996): 11,958.

COMMUNICATIONS MEDIA

Radio Receivers (estimate, '000 in use): 4.8 in 1995.

Television Receivers (estimate, '000 in use): 3.2 in 1995.

EDUCATION

Primary (1995): 8 institutions; 50 teachers (1987); 793 students.

Secondary (1995): 3 institutions; 55 teachers (1987); 549 students.

Technical (1995): 1 institution; 147 students.

Directory

The Government

(February 1998)

Prefect and President of the Economic and Social Council: RÉMI THUAU.

Deputy to the French National Assembly: GÉRARD GRIGNON (UDF).

Representative to the French Senate: VICTOR REUX (RPR).

GENERAL COUNCIL

Place de l'Eglise, 97500 Saint-Pierre; tel. 41-46-22; fax 41-22-97.

The General Council has 19 members (St Pierre 15, Miquelon four).

President of the General Council: BERNARD LESOAVEC.

Political Organizations

Centre des Démocrates Sociaux (CDS): 97500 Saint-Pierre.

Parti Socialiste (PS): 97500 Saint-Pierre; left-wing.

Rassemblement pour la République (RPR): BP 113, 97500 Saint-Pierre; tel. 41-35-73; fax 41-29-97; Gaullist.

Union pour la Démocratie Française (UDF): 97500 Saint-Pierre; centrist.

Judicial System

Tribunal Supérieur d'Appel: 97500 Saint-Pierre; tel. 41-56-71; fax 41-49-45; Pres. FRANÇOIS JALLIN.

Tribunal de Première Instance: 14 rue Emile Sasco, BP 4215, 97500 Saint-Pierre; tel. 41-47-26; fax 41-49-45; Presiding Magistrate PASCAL MATHIS.

Religion

Almost all of the inhabitants are adherents of the Roman Catholic Church.

CHRISTIANITY

The Roman Catholic Church

The islands form the Apostolic Vicariate of the Iles Saint-Pierre et Miquelon. At 31 December 1996 there were an estimated 6,300 adherents.

Vicar Apostolic: FRANÇOIS JOSEPH MAURER (Titular Bishop of Chimaera), Vicariat Apostolique, BP 4245, 97500 Saint-Pierre; tel. 41-20-35; fax 41-47-09.

The Press

L'Echo des Caps: Mairie de Saint-Pierre, 22 rue Raymond Poincaré, BP 4213, 97500 Saint-Pierre; tel. 41-41-01; fax 41-43-13; e-mail echohebd@cancom.net; f. 1982; weekly; circ. 2,500.

Recueil des Actes Administratifs: 4 rue du Général Leclerc, BP 4233, 97500 Saint-Pierre; tel. 41-24-50; fax 41-20-85; f. 1866; monthly; Dir E. DEROUET.

Trait d'Union: BP 113, 97500 Saint-Pierre; tel. 41-35-73; fax 41-29-97; six a year; organ of the RPR.

Le Vent de la Liberté: 36 rue Maréchal Foch, BP 1179, 97500 Saint-Pierre; tel. 41-42-19; fax 41-45-06; monthly; circ. 600.

Broadcasting and Communications

RADIO AND TELEVISION

Société Nationale de Radio-Télévision Française d'Outre-mer (RFO): BP 4227, 97500 Saint-Pierre; tel. 41-11-11; fax 41-22-19; broadcasts 24 hours of radio programmes daily and 175 hours of television programmes weekly on two channels; Pres. JEAN-MARIE CAVADA; Dir JEAN-MICHEL CAMBIANICA.

Radio Atlantique: 97500 Saint-Pierre; private; broadcasts 24 hours of radio programmes daily; Pres. and Dir PATRICK MELIN.

Finance

(cap. = capital, res = reserves, dep. = deposits; m. = million; amounts in French francs)

MAJOR BANKS

Banque des Iles Saint-Pierre-et-Miquelon: rue Jacques Cartier, 97500 Saint-Pierre; tel. 41-35-45; telex 914435; fax 41-25-31; f. 1889; cap. 23m., res 3.5m., dep. 252m. (Dec. 1996); Pres. and Gen. Man. BRUNO DE PAZZIS; Man. BERNARD DURDILLY.

Crédit Saint Pierrais: 20 place du Général de Gaulle, BP 4218, 97500 Saint-Pierre; tel. 41-22-49; telex 914429; fax 41-25-96; f. 1962; cap. 30.2m., res 9m., dep. 298m. (Dec. 1996); Pres. GUY SIMON; Man. PIERRE SPIETH.

PRINCIPAL INSURANCE COMPANIES

Mutuelle des Iles: 5 rue Maréchal Foch, BP 1112, 97500 Saint-Pierre; tel. 41-28-69; fax 41-51-13.

Paturel Assurances SARL, Agence PFA Athéna: 31 rue Maréchal Foch, BP 4288, 97500 Saint-Pierre; tel. 41-32-98; telex 914420; fax 41-51-65; Gen. Agent GUY PATUREL; Man. NATHALIE CLAIREAUX PATUREL.

Trade and Industry

CHAMBER OF COMMERCE

Chambre de Commerce, d'Industrie et de Métiers: 4 blvd Constant-Colmay, BP 4207, 97500 Saint-Pierre; tel. 41-45-12; fax 41-32-09; Pres. JEAN LEBAILLY.

TRADE UNIONS

Syndicat National de l'Enseignement Catholique (SNEC-CFTC): BP 1117, 97500 Saint-Pierre; tel. 41-37-19; affiliated to the Confédération Française des Travailleurs Chrétiens.

Union Interprofessionnelle CFDT—SPM: BP 4352, 97500 Saint-Pierre; tel. 41-23-20; fax 41-27-99; affiliated to the Confédération Française Démocratique du Travail; Sec.-Gen. PHILIPPE GUILLAUME.

Union Intersyndicale CGT de Saint-Pierre et Miquelon: 97500 Saint-Pierre; tel. 41-41-86; affiliated to the Confédération Générale du Travail; Sec.-Gen. RONALD MANET.

Union des Syndicats CGT-FO de Saint-Pierre et Miquelon; 15 rue Dr Dunan, BP 4241, 97500 Saint-Pierre; tel. 41-25-22; fax 41-46-55; affiliated to the Confédération Générale du Travail-Force Ouvrière; Sec.-Gen. MAX OLAISOLA.

Transport

SHIPPING

Packet boats and container services operate between Saint-Pierre, Halifax, Nova Scotia, and Boston, MA. The seaport at Saint-Pierre has three jetties and 1,200 metres of quays.

CIVIL AVIATION

There is an airport on St Pierre, served by airlines linking the territory with France and Canada. Construction of a new airport, able to accommodate larger aircraft and thus improve air links, was scheduled for completion in 1998.

Air Saint-Pierre: 18 rue Albert Briand, Saint-Pierre, BP 4225, 97500 Saint-Pierre; tel. 41-47-18; telex 914422; fax 41-23-36; f. 1964; connects the territory directly with Newfoundland, Nova Scotia and Québec; Pres. RÉMY L. BRIAND; Man. THIERRY BRIAND.

Tourism

There were an estimated 11,958 tourist arrivals in 1996.

Agence Régionale du Tourisme: 22 place du Général de Gaulle, BP 4274, 97500 Saint-Pierre; tel. 41-22-22; telex 914437; fax 41-33-55; f. 1959; Pres. BERNARD LESOAVEC; Dir JEAN-HUGUES DETCHEVERRY.

French Overseas Territories

The four Overseas Territories (territoires d'outre-mer) are French Polynesia, the French Southern and Antarctic Territories, New Caledonia, and the Wallis and Futuna Islands. They are integral parts of the French Republic. Each is administered by a High Commissioner or Chief Administrator, who is appointed by the French Government. Each permanently inhabited Territory also has a Territorial Assembly or Congress, elected by universal adult suffrage. Certain members of the Territorial Assembly or Congress sit in the French National Assembly and the Senate of the Republic in Paris. The Territories have varying degrees of internal autonomy.

FRENCH POLYNESIA

Introductory Survey

Location, Climate, Language, Religion, Flag, Capital

French Polynesia comprises several scattered groups of islands in the south Pacific Ocean, lying about two-thirds of the way between the Panama Canal and New Zealand. Its nearest neighbours are the Cook Islands, to the west, and the Line Islands (part of Kiribati), to the north-west. French Polynesia consists of the following island groups: the Windward Islands (Iles du Vent—including the islands of Tahiti and Moorea) and the Leeward Islands (Iles Sous le Vent—located about 160 km north-west of Tahiti) which, together, constitute the Society Archipelago; the Tuamotu Archipelago, which comprises 78 islands scattered east of the Society Archipelago in a line stretching north-west to south-east for about 1,500 km; the Gambier Islands, located 1,600 km south-east of Tahiti; the Austral Islands, lying 640 km south of Tahiti; and the Marquesas Archipelago, which lies 1,450 km north-east of Tahiti. There are 120 islands in all. The average monthly temperature throughout the year varies between 20°C (68°F) and 29°C (84°F), and most rainfall occurs between November and April, the average annual precipitation being 1,625 mm (64 ins). The official language is French, and Polynesian languages are spoken by the indigenous population. The principal religion is Christianity; about 55% of the population are Protestant and some 34% Roman Catholic. The official flag is the French tricolour. Subordinate to this, there is a territorial flag (proportions 3 by 2), comprising three horizontal stripes, of red, white (half the depth) and red, with, in the centre, the arms of French Polynesia, consisting of a representation in red of a native canoe, bearing a platform supporting five stylized persons, on a circular background (five wavy horizontal dark blue bands, surmounted by 10 golden sunrays). The capital is Papeete, on the island of Tahiti.

Recent History

Tahiti, the largest of the Society Islands, was declared a French protectorate in 1842, and became a colony in 1880. The other island groups were annexed during the last 20 years of the 19th century. The islands were governed from France under a decree of 1885 until 1957, when French Polynesia became an Overseas Territory, administered by a Governor in Papeete. A Territorial Assembly and a Council of Government were elected to advise the Governor.

Between May 1975 and May 1982 a majority in the Territorial Assembly sought independence for French Polynesia. Following pressure by Francis Sanford, leader of the largest autonomist party in the Assembly, a new Constitution for the Territory was negotiated with the French Government and approved by a newly-elected Assembly in 1977. Under the provisions of the new statute, France retained responsibility for foreign affairs, defence, monetary matters and justice, but the powers of the territorial Council of Government were increased, especially in the field of commerce. The French Governor was replaced by a High Commissioner, who was to preside over the Council of Government and was head of the administration, but had no vote. The Council's elected Vice-President, responsible for domestic affairs, was granted greater powers. An Economic, Social and Cultural Council, responsible for all development matters, was also created, and French Polynesia's economic zone was extended to 200 nautical miles (370 km) from the islands' coastline.

Following elections to the Territorial Assembly in May 1982, the Gaullist Tahoeraa Huiraatira, led by Gaston Flosse, which secured 13 of the 30 seats, formed successive ruling coalitions, first with the Ai'a Api party and in September with the Pupu Here Ai'a Te Nunaa Ia Ora party. Seeking greater (but not full) independence from France, especially in economic matters, elected representatives of the Assembly held discussions with the French Government in Paris in 1983, and in September 1984 a new statute was approved by the French National Assembly. This allowed the territorial Government greater powers, mainly in the sphere of commerce and development; the Council of Government was replaced by a Council of Ministers, whose President was to be elected from among the members of the Territorial Assembly. Flosse became the first President of the Council of Ministers.

At elections held in March 1986 the Tahoeraa Huiraatira gained the first outright majority to be achieved in the Territory, winning 24 of the 41 seats in the Territorial Assembly. Leaders of opposition parties subsequently expressed dissatisfaction with the election result, claiming that the Tahoeraa Huiraatira victory had been secured only as a result of the allocation of a disproportionately large number of seats in the Territorial Assembly to one of the five constituencies. The constituency at the centre of the dispute was that comprising the Mangareva and Tuamotu islands, where the two French army bases at Hao and Mururoa constituted a powerful body of support for Flosse and the Tahoeraa Huiraatira, which, in spite of winning a majority of seats, had obtained a minority of individual votes in the election (30,571, compared with the opposition parties' 43,771). At the concurrent elections for French Polynesia's two seats in the National Assembly in Paris, Flosse and Alexandre Léontieff, the candidates of the Rassemblement pour la République (RPR—to which Tahoeraa Huiraatira is affiliated), were elected, Flosse subsequently ceding his seat to Edouard Fritch. Later in March the French Prime Minister, Jacques Chirac, appointed Flosse to a post in the French Council of Ministers, assigning him the portfolio of Secretary of State for South Pacific Affairs.

In April 1986 Flosse was re-elected President of the Council of Ministers. However, he faced severe criticism from leaders of the opposition for his allegedly inefficient and extravagant use of public funds, and was accused, in particular, of corrupt electoral practice. Flosse resigned as President of the Territory's Council of Ministers in February 1987, and was replaced by Jacques Teuira.

Unrest among dock-workers led to serious rioting in October 1987 and the declaration of a state of emergency by the authorities. In December, amid growing discontent over his policies, Teuira resigned as President of the Council of Ministers, along with the seven remaining ministers (the three other ministers, including Léontieff, having resigned a few days previously). Léontieff, the leader of the Te Tiaraama party (a breakaway faction of the Tahoeraa Huiraatira), was elected President of the Council of Ministers by a new alliance of 28 of the Territorial Assembly's 41 members. Jean Juventin, the Mayor of Papeete and the leader of the Pupu Here Ai'a Te Nunaa Ia Ora, replaced Roger Doom as President of the Territorial Assembly.

In June 1988, in the elections to the French National Assembly, Léontieff retained his seat, while the other was secured by Emile Vernaudon, the leader of the Ai'a Api.

The Léontieff Government survived several challenges in the Territorial Assembly to its continuation in office during 1988 and 1989. Amendments to the Polynesian Constitution, which were approved by the French Parliament and enacted by July 1990, augmented the powers of the President of the Territorial Council of Ministers and increased the competence of the Territorial Assembly. In addition, five consultative Archipelago Councils were established, comprising Territorial and municipal elected representatives. The major purpose of these amendments was to clarify the areas of responsibility of the State, the Territory and the judiciary, which was considered particularly necessary following various disputes about the impending single market of the European Community (EC—now European Union, EU, see p. 152). In June 1989, in protest, 90% of the electorate had refused to vote in the elections to the European Parliament.

At territorial elections in March 1991 the Tahoeraa Huiraatira won 18 of the 41 seats. Flosse then formed a coalition with the Ai'a Api, thereby securing a majority of 23 seats in the Territorial Assembly. Vernaudon, leader of the Ai'a Api, was elected President of the Assembly shortly afterwards, with 37 votes, and Flosse was elected President of the Council of Ministers. In September Flosse announced the end of the coalition between his party and the Ai'a Api, accusing Vernaudon of disloyalty to the Government. This announcement was followed by the signing of a new alliance between the RPR and the Pupu Here Ai'a Te Nunaa Ia Ora led by Jean Juventin.

In April 1992 Flosse was found guilty of fraud (relating to an illegal sale of government land to a member of his family) and there were widespread demands for his resignation. In November Juventin and Léontieff were charged with 'passive' corruption, relating to the construction of a golf course by a Japanese company. In the following month the French Court of Appeal upheld the judgment against Flosse, who received a six-month, suspended prison sentence. The case provoked a demonstration by more than 3,000 people in January 1993, demanding the resignation of Flosse and Juventin. In September 1994 Flosse succeeded in having the conviction overturned, on a procedural issue, in a second court of appeal. In October 1997, however, Léontieff was found guilty of accepting substantial bribes in order to facilitate a business venture and was sentenced to three years in prison (half of which was to be suspended).

The approval by the Territorial Assembly in September 1994 of a new version of the fiscal law, the Contribution de Solidarité Territoriale (first introduced in July 1993), provoked widespread popular unrest and led to a six-day general strike and demonstrations by up to 10,000 people, who blocked the port and major roads around the capital. Protests continued into late October, following a series of unsuccessful negotiations between the Government and the principal labour organizations.

French presidential elections took place in April/May 1995. During the second round of voting in the Territory, the socialist candidate, Lionel Jospin, received 39% of the total votes, while the RPR candidate, Jacques Chirac, won 61%. (Chirac was elected to the presidency with 52.6% of votes cast throughout the republic.)

In November 1995 the Territorial Assembly adopted a draft statute of autonomy, which proposed the extension of the Territory's powers to areas such as fishing, mining and shipping rights, international transport and communications, broadcasting and the offshore economic zone. France, however, would retain full responsibility for defence, justice and security in the islands. Advocates of independence for French Polynesia criticized the statute for promising only relatively cosmetic changes, while failing to increase the democratic rights of the islanders. The statute was approved by the French National Assembly in December and came into force in April 1996.

At territorial elections held on 13 May 1996 the Gaullist Tahoeraa Huiraatira achieved an outright majority, although the principal pro-independence party, Tavini Huiraatira, made considerable gains throughout the Territory (largely owing to increased popular hostility towards France since the resumption of nuclear-weapons tests at Mururoa Atoll—see below). Tahoeraa Huiraatira secured 22 of the 41 seats in the Territorial Assembly, with 38.7% of total votes cast, while Tavini Huiraatira won 10 seats, with 24.8% of votes. Other anti-independence parties won a total of eight seats and an additional pro-independence grouping secured one seat. Flosse defeated the independence leader, Oscar Temaru, by 28 votes to 11 to remain as President of the Council of Ministers later in the month, and Justin Arapari was elected President of the Territorial Assembly.

At elections for French Polynesia's two seats in the French National Assembly in May 1997 Michel Buillard and Emile Vernaudon, both supporters of the RPR, were elected with 52% and 59% of total votes cast, respectively. However, the pro-independence leader, Oscar Temaru, was a strong contender for the western constituency seat, securing 42% of the vote. In August Temaru led a delegation in lobbying the South Pacific Forum to support the reinscription of French Polynesia on the UN Decolonization Committee list, prior to a meeting of the regional group in the Cook Islands

The testing of nuclear devices by the French Government began in 1966 at Mururoa Atoll, in the Tuamotu Archipelago. In 1983, in spite of strong protests by many Pacific nations, the Government indicated that tests would continue for a number of years. In October 1983 Australia, New Zealand and Papua New Guinea accepted a French invitation jointly to send scientists to inspect the test site. The team subsequently reported definite evidence of environmental damage, resulting from the underground explosions, which had caused subsidence by weakening the rock structure of the atoll. Significant levels of radioactivity were also detected.

A series of tests in May and June 1985, involving bigger explosions than hitherto, prompted a renewed display of opposition. In July the trawler *Rainbow Warrior*, the flagship of the anti-nuclear environmentalist group, Greenpeace, which was to have led a protest flotilla to Mururoa, was sunk in Auckland Harbour, New Zealand, in an explosion that killed one crew member. Two agents of the French secret service, the Direction générale de sécurité extérieure (DGSE), were subsequently convicted of manslaughter and imprisoned in New Zealand. In July 1986, however, they were transferred to Hao Atoll, in the Tuamoto Archipelago, after a ruling by the UN Secretary-General (acting as mediator), which effectively reduced the agents' sentences from 10 to three years' imprisonment, in return for a French payment of $NZ 7m. in compensation to the New Zealand Government. Relations between France and New Zealand deteriorated still further in 1987, when the French Prime Minister, Jacques Chirac, approved the removal of one of the prisoners to Paris, owing to illness. By the terms of the UN ruling, 'mutual consent' by both Governments was to be necessary for any such repatriation. An exchange of letters between the Prime Ministers of the two countries failed to resolve the issue, and in 1988 the other prisoner was also flown back to Paris after she became pregnant (see chapter on New Zealand for further details). In May 1991, during a visit to New Zealand, the French Prime Minister, Michel Rocard, formally apologized for the bombing of the *Rainbow Warrior*, which had hampered relations between the two countries since 1985. However, in July tension between France and the region was exacerbated by the French Government's decision to award a medal for 'distinguished service' to one of the agents convicted for his role in the bombing. Between 1975 and 1992 France performed 135 underground nuclear tests in the Territory.

In April 1992 the French Prime Minister, Pierre Bérégovoy, announced that nuclear tests would be suspended until the end of the year. Although the decision was welcomed throughout the South Pacific, concern was expressed in French Polynesia over the economic implications of the move, because of the Territory's dependence on income received from hosting the nuclear-test programme. Similarly, it was feared that unemployment resulting from the ban (some 1,500 people were employed at the test centre alone) would have a serious impact on the economy. A delegation of political leaders subsequently travelled to Paris to express its concerns, and in January 1993 accepted assistance worth 7,000m. francs CFP in compensation for lost revenue and in aid for development projects. Following the announcement of a new six-year defence plan by the French Government in early 1994, there was considerable speculation that tests would resume. As a result, the Australian Minister for Foreign Affairs sought assurance that the moratorium on testing would be maintained.

However, shortly after his election in May 1995, President Jacques Chirac announced that France would resume nuclear testing, with a programme of eight tests between September 1995 and May 1996. The decision provoked almost universal outrage in the international community, and was condemned for its apparent disregard for regional opinion, as well as for undermining the considerable progress made by Western nations towards a worldwide ban on nuclear testing. Scientists also expressed concern at the announcement; some believed that further explosions at Mururoa could lead to the collapse of the atoll, which had been weakened considerably by more than 130 blast cavities. Large-scale demonstrations and protest marches throughout the region were accompanied by boycotts of French products and the suspension of several trade and defence co-operation agreements. Opposition to the French Government intensified in July 1995, when French commandos violently seized *Rainbow Warrior II*, the flagship of the environmental group Greenpeace, and its crew, which had been protesting peacefully near the test site. Chirac continued to defy mounting pressure to reverse the decision from within the EU, from Japan and Russia, as well as from Australia, New Zealand and the South Pacific region. French Polynesia became the focus of world attention when the first test took place on 5 September 1995. The action attracted further statements of condemnation from Governments around the world, and provoked major demonstrations in many countries. In Tahiti hitherto peaceful protests soon developed into full-scale riots, as several thousand demonstrators, enraged by the French authorities' intransigent stance, rampaged through the capital, demanding an end to French rule. Faaa airport was closed, as protesters occupied the runway and destroyed adjacent buildings and vehicles. Meanwhile, violent clashes with police, and the burning of dozens of buildings in Papeete during the riots, left much of the capital in ruins. In response, the French Government drafted thousands of extra security personnel on to the island, to quell the unrest. In defiance of world opinion, a further five tests were carried out, the sixth and final one being conducted in January 1996. In early 1996 the French Government confirmed reports by a team of independent scientists that radioactive isotopes had leaked into the waters surrounding the atoll, but denied that they represented a threat to the environment. Scientists remained concerned, however, that the damaged rock structure of the atoll would continue to release toxic materials into the sea.

Further controversy surrounding the operations of the French authorities at the Mururoa test site arose in late 1997, following the publication of a report in Geneva by the World Council of Churches. The report claimed that up to 10% of the 10,000–15,000 staff employed at the test centre between 1963 and 1996 were under 18 years of age and that some 60% of these were under 16 years of age. The authorities in French Polynesia denied the allegations. Work to dismantle facilities at the test site began in 1997 and the installation was expected to have been removed by July 1998.

Government

The French Government is represented in French Polynesia by its High Commissioner to the Territory, and controls various important spheres of government, including defence, foreign diplomacy and justice. A local Territorial Assembly, with 41 members, is elected for a five-year term by universal adult suffrage. The Assembly may elect a President of an executive body, the Territorial Council of Ministers, who, in turn, submits a list of between six and 12 members of the Assembly to serve as ministers, for approval by the Assembly.

In addition, French Polynesia elects two deputies to the French National Assembly in Paris and one representative to the French Senate, all chosen on the basis of universal adult suffrage. French Polynesia is also represented at the European Parliament.

Defence

France has been testing nuclear weapons at Mururoa Atoll, in the Tuamotu Archipelago, since 1966 and was maintaining a force of 3,800 military personnel in the Territory in August 1997, as well as a gendarmerie of 350.

Economic Affairs

In 1994, according to UN estimates, French Polynesia's gross domestic product (GDP), measured at current prices, was US $4,216m., equivalent to $19,608 per head. During 1985–95 the population increased by an annual average of 2.7%.

Agriculture, forestry and fishing contributed only 4.7% of GDP in 1990, but provide most of French Polynesia's exports. The sector engaged 3.2% of the employed labour force in 1992. Coconuts are the principal cash crop, and in 1995 the estimated harvest was 86,000 metric tons. Vegetables, fruit (especially pineapples and citrus fruit), vanilla and coffee are also cultivated. Most commercial fishing, principally for tuna, is conducted, under licence, by Japanese and Korean fleets. Another important activity is the production of cultured black pearls, of which the quantity exported increased from 112 kg in 1984 to 833 kg in 1991. In 1997 the Territory exported some 5,200kg of black pearls, earning US $148m. (compared with US $93m. and US $139m. in 1995 and 1996 respectively), and during the mid-1990s was estimated to have produced more than 95% of the world's cultured black pearls.

Industry (comprising mining, manufacturing, construction and utilities) employed 16.0% of the working population in 1992, and provided 15.1% of GDP in 1990. There is a small manufacturing sector, which is heavily dependent on agriculture. Coconut oil and copra are produced, as are beer, dairy products and vanilla essence. Important deposits of phosphates and cobalt were discovered during the 1980s. The manufacturing sector (with mining and quarrying) engaged 5.1% of the employed labour force in 1992.

Hydrocarbon fuels are the main source of energy in the Territory, with the Papeete thermal power station providing about three-quarters of the electricity produced. Hydroelectric and solar energy also make a significant contribution to French Polynesia's domestic requirements. Hydroelectric power dams, with the capacity to generate the electricity requirements of 45% of Tahiti's population, have been constructed.

Tourism is the Territory's major industry. In 1990 the trade, restaurants and hotels sector contributed 22.7% of GDP, and in 1996 some 164,000 tourists visited French Polynesia, with an estimated 175,000 arrivals in the following year. French Polynesia's hotel capacity, which amounted to some 3,000 rooms in the mid-1990s, was expected to have doubled by 2001, as a result of several major construction projects initiated in 1997. Tourist arrivals to the islands declined significantly following the resumption of nuclear testing in September 1995, and specialist advisers were employed in 1996 in an attempt to reverse the damage caused to the industry. The services sectors engaged 80.8% of the employed labour force in 1992, and provided 80.3% of GDP in 1990.

In 1995 French Polynesia recorded a trade deficit of 73,835m. francs CFP. In 1994 the principal sources of imports were France (which provided 44.7% of total imports), the USA (13.9%), Australia (6.8%) and New Zealand (7.4%). The principal market for exports in that year was France (accounting for 32.7% of the total). The principal imports in that year included petroleum products (5.9% of the total). The principal commodity exports were cultured black pearls (providing 53.7% of total export revenue).

In 1994 there was an estimated territorial budgetary surplus of 648m. francs CFP. In 1993 expenditure by the French State in the Territory totalled 114,760m. francs CFP, 36% of which was on the military budget. The total external debt was estimated at US $390m. in 1992. The annual rate of inflation averaged 5.5% in 1980–94 but only 1.6% in 1994. A high unemployment rate (estimated at some 15% of the labour force in 1990) is exacerbated by the predominance of young people in the population.

French Polynesia forms part of the Franc Zone (see p. 181), and is a member of the Pacific Community (formerly the South Pacific Commission—see p. 232), which provides technical advice, training and assistance in economic, cultural and social development to countries in the region.

French Polynesia's traditional agriculture-based economy was distorted by the presence of large numbers of French military personnel (in connection with the nuclear-testing programme which began in 1966), stimulating employment in the construction industry and services at the expense of agriculture, and encouraging migration from the outer islands to Tahiti, where 75% of the population currently reside. These dramatic changes effectively transformed French Polynesia from a state of self-sufficiency to one of import dependency in less than a generation. The development of tourism had a similar effect. In the late 1980s some 80% of the Territory's food requirements had to be imported, while exports of vanilla and coffee, formerly important cash crops, were negligible, owing to a long-term decline in investment. An agreement for metropolitan France to provide the Territory with 28,300m. francs CFP annually between 1996 and 2006 was concluded in 1995 and took effect upon completion of the last series of nuclear tests in early 1996. It was hoped that the arrangement would enable French Polynesia to diversify its economic activities and thus enhance its potential for durable independence. In an attempt to increase revenue, the Territorial Government announced the introduction of a value-added tax from October 1997. This was intended to supplement revenue provided by the Contribution de Solidarité Territoriale, an income tax introduced in 1993.

As the Territory gradually achieves a greater degree of independence from metropolitan France, it is seeking closer ties with countries of Asia and the Pacific (particularly Australia, New Zealand, Japan, Taiwan and the Republic of Korea) in the hope of improving its poor export performance.

Social Welfare

In 1991 there were 34 hospitals in French Polynesia, with a total of 1,176 beds, and in that year there were 323 physicians working in the Territory. All medical services are provided free of charge for the inhabitants of French Polynesia. An estimated US $94m. was spent on social security services in the Territory in 1990.

Education

Education is compulsory for eight years between six and 14 years of age. It is free of charge for day pupils in government schools. Primary education, lasting six years, is financed by the territorial budget, while secondary and technical education are supported by state funds. In 1995/96 there were 59 kindergartens, with 16,049 children enrolled, and 170 primary schools, with 29,415 pupils. Secondary education is provided by both church and government schools. In 1992/93 there were 22,366 pupils at general secondary schools, while 3,730 secondary pupils were enrolled at vocational institutions in that year. The French University of the Pacific was established in French Polynesia in 1987. In 1993 the Papeete branch had 34 teachers and 892 students. Total government expenditure on education in the Territory was 1,894m. French francs in 1993.

Public Holidays

1998: 1 January (New Year's Day), 13 April (Easter Monday), 4 May (for Labour Day), 7 May (Liberation Day), 21 May (Ascension Day), 1 June (Whit Monday), 14 July (Fall of the Bastille), 11 November (Armistice Day), 25 December (Christmas Day).

1999: 1 January (New Year's Day), 5 April (Easter Monday), 3 May (for Labour Day), 8 May (Liberation Day), 13 May (Ascension Day), 24 May (Whit Monday), 14 July (Fall of the Bastille), 11 November (Armistice Day), 25 December (Christmas Day).

Weights and Measures

The metric system is in force.

Statistical Survey

Source (unless otherwise indicated): Institut Territorial de la Statistique, Immeuble Donald (2e étage), Angle rue Jeanne d'Arc et blvd Pomare, BP 395, Papeete; tel. 437196; telex 537; fax 427252.

AREA AND POPULATION

Area: Total 4,167 sq km (1,609 sq miles); Land area 3,521 sq km (1,359 sq miles).

Population: 166,753 (86,914 males, 79,839 females) at census of 15 October 1983; 188,814 (98,345 males, 90,469 females) at census of 6 September 1988; 219,521 at census of 3 September 1996.

Density (September 1996): 52.7 per sq km.

Ethnic Groups (1983 census): Polynesian 114,280; 'Demis' 23,625 (Polynesian-European 15,851, Polynesian-Chinese 6,356, Polynesian-Other races 1,418); European 19,320; Chinese 7,424; European-Chinese 494; Others 1,610; Total 166,753. *1988 census* ('000 persons): Polynesians and 'Demis' 156.3; Others 32.5.

Principal Towns (population at 1983 census): Papeete (capital) 23,496; Faaa 21,927; Pirae 12,023; Uturva 2,733. *1988 census:* Papeete 23,555.

Births, Marriages and Deaths (1996): Registered live births 4,683 (birth rate 21.0 per 1,000); (1994) Registered marriages 1,318 (marriage rate 6.2 per 1,000); Registered deaths 1,001 (death rate 4.5 per 1,000).

Expectation of Life (UN estimates, years at birth, 1990–95): 71.5 (males 69.5; females 73.7). Source: UN, *World Population Prospects: The 1994 Revision*.

Economically Active Population (persons aged 14 years and over, 1988 census): Agriculture, hunting, forestry and fishing 7,555; Mining and manufacturing 4,938; Electricity, gas and water 478; Construction 5,548; Trade, restaurants and hotels 10,304; Transport, storage and communications 2,780; Financing, insurance, real estate and business services 1,161; Community, social and personal services 21,525; Activities not adequately defined 9,717; Total employed 64,006 (males 41,651, females 22,355); Unemployed 11,387 (males 5,783, females 5,604); Total labour force 75,393 (males 47,434, females 27,959). Figures exclude persons on compulsory military service. Source: ILO, *Yearbook of Labour Statistics*.

AGRICULTURE, ETC.

Principal Crops (metric tons, 1995): Roots and tubers 13,000*; Vegetables and melons 6,000*; Pineapples 4,000*; Other fruit 3,000*; Coconuts 86,000*; Copra 11,000; Vanilla 39 (1990); Coffee 6 (1990).

* FAO estimate.

Livestock (FAO estimates, year ending September 1995): Cattle 7,000; Horses 2,000; Pigs 42,000; Goats 16,000; Sheep (1989) 2,000. Source: FAO, *Production Yearbook*.

Livestock Products (FAO estimates, metric tons, 1995): Cows' milk 2,000; Pig meat 1,000; Other meat 1,000; Hen eggs 1,250; Other eggs 85; Honey 50.

Fishing (metric tons, live weight): Total catch 8,082 in 1993; 8,832 in 1994; 8,824 (FAO estimate) in 1995. Source: FAO, *Yearbook of Fishery Statistics*.

INDUSTRY

Production: Coconut oil 5,366 metric tons (1994); Oilcake 4,477 metric tons (1987); Beer 129,000 hectolitres (1992); Printed cloth 200,000 m (1979); Japanese sandals 600,000 pairs (1979); Electric energy 335m. kWh (1994).

FINANCE

Currency and Exchange Rates: 100 centimes = 1 franc des Comptoirs français du Pacifique (franc CFP or Pacific franc). *Sterling, Dollar and French Franc Equivalents* (30 September 1997): £1 sterling = 174.23 francs CFP; US $1 = 107.86 francs CFP; 1 French franc = 18.182 francs CFP; 1,000 francs CFP = £5.739 = $9.271 = 55 French francs.

Territorial Budget (estimates, million francs CFP, 1994): *Revenue:* Current 64,858 (Indirect taxation 39,927). *Expenditure:* Current 64,210, Capital 30,058, Total 94,268.

French State Expenditure (million francs CFP, 1990): Civil budget 38,492 (Current 29,748, Pensions 6,689, Capital 2,055); Military budget 21,987 (Current 17,436, Capital 4,551); Total (incl. others) 63,877.

1993 (million francs CFP): Civil budget 73,642; Military budget 41,118; Total 114,760.

Money Supply (million French francs at 31 December 1995): Currency in circulation 6,597; Demand deposits 52,727; Total money 59,324. Source: Institut National de la Statistique et des Etudes Economiques.

Cost of Living (Consumer Price Index; base: 1988 = 100): 107.1 in 1993; 108.7 in 1994; 110.0 in 1995. Source: Institut National de la Statistique et des Etudes Economiques.

Gross Domestic Product (million francs CFP at current prices): 303,212 in 1991; 306,493 in 1992; 317,948 in 1993.

Expenditure on the Gross Domestic Product (million francs CFP at current prices, 1990): Government final consumption expenditure 120,207; Private final consumption expenditure 178,697; Increase in stocks 482; Gross fixed capital formation 63,033; *Total domestic expenditure* 362,419; Exports of goods and services 27,262; *Less* Imports of goods and services 91,926; *GDP in purchasers' values* 297,754. Source: UN, *National Accounts Statistics*.

Gross Domestic Product by Economic Activity (million francs CFP at current prices, 1990): Agriculture, forestry and fishing 13,849; Energy and water 4,957; Other manufacturing 21,648; Construction 18,294; Trade, restaurants and hotels 67,632; Transport, finance and social services 84,436; Government and other services 86,938; *GDP in purchasers' values* 297,754. Source: UN, *National Accounts Statistics*.

EXTERNAL TRADE

Principal Commodities (million francs CFP, 1994): *Imports c.i.f.:* Rice 439; Sugar 359; Hydraulic cement 882; Petroleum products 5,145; Total (incl. others) 87,866. *Exports f.o.b.:* Vanilla 86; Mother of pearl 254; Coconut oil 375; Cultured pearls 11,967; Total (incl. others) 22,288.

Principal Trading Partners (million francs CFP, 1994): *Imports:* Australia 5,998; France (metropolitan) 39,313; Germany 2,808; Japan 3,541; New Zealand 6,516; USA 12,254; Total (incl. others) 87,866. *Exports:* France (metropolitan) 7,292; New Caledonia 271; USA 1,875; Total (incl. others) 22,288. **1995** (million francs CFP): *Imports:* 91,384. *Exports:* 17,549.

Source: Institut National de la Statistique et des Etudes Economiques.

TRANSPORT

Road Traffic (1987): Total vehicles registered 54,979.

Shipping (1990): *International traffic:* Passengers carried 47,616; Freight handled 642,314 metric tons. *Domestic traffic:* Passengers carried 596,185; Freight handled 261,593 metric tons.

Civil Aviation (1994): *International traffic:* Passengers carried (incl. those in transit) 470,939; Freight handled 5,763 metric tons. *Domestic traffic:* Passengers carried 484,195; Freight handled 1,320 metric tons.

TOURISM

Visitors (excluding cruise passengers and excursionists): 123,534 in 1992; 147,847 in 1993; 166,086 in 1994.

COMMUNICATIONS MEDIA

Radio Receivers (1995): 122,000 in use*.

Television Receivers (1995): 38,000 in use*.

Telephones (1994): 47,000 main lines in use†.

Daily Newspapers (1995): 4; estimated circulation 24,000*.

* Source: UNESCO, *Statistical Yearbook*.

† Source: UN, *Statistical Yearbook*.

EDUCATION

Pre-primary (1995/96): 59 schools; 408 teachers; 16,049 pupils.

Primary (1995/96): 170 schools; 2,052 teachers; 29,415 pupils.

General Secondary (1992/93): 1,592 teachers; 22,366 pupils.

Vocational (1992): 316 teachers; 3,730 students.

Tertiary (1993): 34 teachers; 892 students.

Source: mainly UNESCO, *Statistical Yearbook*.

Directory

The Constitution

The constitutional system in French Polynesia is established under the aegis of the Constitution of the Fifth French Republic and specific laws of 1977, 1984 and 1990. The French Polynesia Statute 1984, the so-called 'internal autonomy statute', underwent amendment in a law of July 1990. A further extension of the Territory's powers under the statute was approved by the French National Assembly in December 1995.

French Polynesia is declared to be an autonomous Territory of the French Republic, of which it remains an integral part. The High Commissioner, appointed by the French Government, exercises the prerogatives of the State in matters relating to defence, foreign relations, the maintenance of law and order, communications and citizenship. The head of the local executive and the person who represents the Territory is the President of the Territorial Government, who is elected by the Territorial Assembly from among its own number. The Territorial President appoints and dismisses the Council of Ministers and has competence in international relations as they affect French Polynesia and its exclusive economic zone, and is in control of foreign investments and immigration. The Territorial Assembly, which has financial autonomy in budgetary affairs and legislative authority within the Territory, is elected for a term of up to five years on the basis of universal adult suffrage. There are 41 members: 22 elected by the people of the Windward Islands (Iles du Vent—Society Islands), eight by the Leeward Islands (Iles Sous le Vent—Society Islands), five by the Tuamotu Archipelago and the Gambier Islands and three each by the Austral Islands and by the Marquesas Archipelago. The Assembly elects a Permanent Commission of between seven and nine of its members, and itself meets for two ordinary sessions each year and upon the demand of the majority party, the Territorial President or the High Commissioner. Local government is conducted by the municipalities; there are five regional, consultative Archipelago Councils, comprised of all those elected to the Territorial Assembly and the municipalities by that region (the Councils represent the same areas as the five constituencies for the Territorial Assembly). There is an Economic, Social and Cultural Council (composed of representatives of professional groups, trade unions and other organizations and agencies which participate in the economic, social and cultural activities of the Territory), a Territorial Audit Office and a judicial system which includes a Court of the First Instance, a Court of Appeal and an Administrative Court. The Territory, as a part of the French Republic, also elects two deputies to the National Assembly and one member of the Senate, and has representation in the European Parliament.

The Government

(February 1998)

High Commissioner: Jean Aribaud (appointed November 1997).

Secretary-General: Anne Boquet.

COUNCIL OF MINISTERS

President: Gaston Flosse.

Vice-President and Minister for the Sea, Outer Island Development, Ports and Post and Telecommunications: Edouard Fritch.

Minister for the Economy, Economic Planning, Business and Energy: Georges Puchon.

Minister for Health and Research: Patrick Howell.

Minister for Social Welfare and the Family: Béatrice Vernaudon.

Minister for Transport (responsible for Relations with the Territorial Assembly and the Economic, Social and Cultural Council): Jacquie Graffe.

Minister for Public Works: Jonas Tahuaitu.

Minister for Housing, Town Planning, Urban Affairs and Revenue: Gaston Ton Sang.

Minister for Agriculture and Livestock: Patrick Bordet.

Minister for Finance (responsible for Administrative Reforms and the Implementation of the Pacte de Progrès): Patrick Peaucellier.

Minister for Culture, the Arts and Community Life: Angelino Bonno.

Minister for Education and Superior and Technical Training: Nicolas Sanquer.

Minister for Employment and Professional Training (responsible for Social Dialogue and Women's Affairs): Lucette Taero.

Minister for the Environment (responsible for Decentralization): Karl Meuel.

Minister for Youth, Sports and Local Government: Michel Buillard.

GOVERNMENT OFFICES

Office of the High Commissioner of the Republic: Bureau du Haut Commissaire, BP 115, Papeete; tel. 468686; fax 468689.

Office of the President of the Territorial Government: BP 2551, 98713 Papeete; tel. 543450; fax 419781.

Territorial Government of French Polynesia: BP 2551, Papeete; fax 419781; all ministries; Delegation in Paris: 28 blvd Saint-Germain, 75005 Paris, France; tel. 1-46-34-50-70; fax 1-40-46-09-76.

Economic, Social and Cultural Council: BP 1657, Papeete; tel. 416500; fax 419242; Representative to National Economic and Social Council Christian Vernaudon.

Legislature

ASSEMBLÉE TERRITORIALE

President: Justin Arapari.

Territorial Assembly: Assemblée Territoriale, BP 28, Papeete; tel. 540100; fax 416123.

Election, 13 May 1996

Party	Seats
Tahoeraa Huiraatira/RPR	22
Tavini Huiraatira	10
Ai'a Api	5
Fe'tia Api	1
Te Avei'a Mau	1
Te Henua Enata Kotoa	1
Alliance 2000	1
Total	41

PARLEMENT

Deputies to the French National Assembly: Emile Vernaudon (Ai'a Api/RPR), Michel Buillard (Tahoeraa Huiraatira/RPR).

Representative to the French Senate: Daniel Millaud (Union centriste des Démocrates de Progrès).

Political Organizations

Ai'a Api (New Land): BP 11055, Mahina, Tahiti; tel. 481135; f. 1982 after split in Te E'a Api; Leader Emile Vernaudon.

Alliance 2000: c/o Assemblée Territoriale, BP 28, Papeete; pro-independence grouping.

Fe'tia Api (New Star): c/o Assemblée Territoriale, BP 28, Papeete; Leader Boris Léontieff.

Ia Mana Te Nunaa: rue du Commandant Destrémau, BP 1223, Papeete; tel. 426699; f. 1976; advocates 'socialist independence'; Sec.-Gen. Jacques Drollet.

Pupu Here Ai'a Te Nunaa Ia Ora: BP 3195, Papeete; tel. 420766; f. 1965; advocates autonomy; 8,000 mems; Pres. (vacant).

Pupu Taina/Rassemblement des Libéraux: rue Cook, BP 169, Papeete; tel. 429880; f. 1976; seeks to retain close links with France; associated with the French Union pour la Démocratie Française (UDF); Leader Michel Law.

Taatiraa Polynesia: BP 2916, Papeete; tel. 437494; fax 422546; f. 1977; Federal Pres. Arthur Chung; Exec. Pres. Robert Tanseau.

Tahoeraa Huiraatira/Rassemblement pour la République—RPR: rue du Commandant Destrémeau, BP 471, Papeete; tel. 429898; telex 249; fax 437758; f. 1958; supports links with France, with internal autonomy; Pres. Gaston Flosse; Hon. Pres. Jacques Teuira.

Tavini Huiraatira/Front de Libération de la Polynésie (FLP): independence movement; anti-nuclear; Leader Oscar Temaru.

Te Avei'a Mau (True Path): c/o Assemblée Territoriale, BP 28, Papeete; Leader Tinomana Ebb.

Te Henua Enata Kotoa: c/o Assemblée Territoriale, BP 28, Papeete; Leader Lucien Kimitete.

Te Tiaraama: Papeete; f. 1987 by split from the RPR; Leader Alexandre Léontieff.

Judicial System

Court of Appeal: Cour d'Appel de Papeete, BP 101, Papeete; tel. 415500; fax 424416; Pres. Andrée Gervais de Lafond; Attorney-General Jack Gauthier.

Court of the First Instance: Tribunal de Première Instance de Papeete, BP 101, Papeete; tel. 415500; telex 454012; Pres. Jean-Louis Thiolet; Procurator Michel Marotte; Clerk of the Court Daniel Salmon.

Court of Administrative Law: Tribunal Administratif, BP 4522, Papeete; tel. 422482; telex 451724; Pres. Alfred Poupet; Cllrs Raoul Aureille, Hubert Lenoir, Marie-Christine Lubrano.

Religion

About 55% of the population are Protestant Christians.

CHRISTIANITY

Protestant Church

L'Eglise évangélique de Polynésie française (Etaretia Evaneria no Porinetia Farani): BP 113, Papeete; tel. 460600; fax 419357; f. 1884; autonomous since 1963; c. 95,000 mems; Pres. of Council Rev. Jacques Terai Ihorai; Sec.-Gen. Ralph Teinaore.

The Roman Catholic Church

French Polynesia comprises the archdiocese of Papeete and the suffragan diocese of Taiohae o Tefenuaenata (based in Nuku Hiva, Marquesas Is). At 31 December 1995 there were an estimated 89,186 adherents in the Territory, representing about 30% of the total population. The Archbishop and the Bishop participate in the Episcopal Conference of the Pacific, based in Fiji.

Archbishop of Papeete: Most Rev. Michel-Gaspard Coppenrath, Archevêché, BP 94, Vallée de la Mission, Papeete; tel. 420251; fax 424032.

Other Churches

There are small Sanito, Church of Jesus Christ of Latter-day Saints (Mormon), and Seventh-day Adventist missions.

The Press

La Dépêche de Tahiti: Société Océanienne de Communication, BP 50, Papeete; tel. 464343; fax 464350; f. 1964; daily; French; Editor-in-Chief Daniel Pardon; Dir-Gen. Amaury Dewaurin; circ. 15,000.

L'Echo de Tahiti-Nui: Papeete; tel. 439476; fax 439430; f. 1993; weekly; French; satirical, economic, social and cultural affairs; Editor Jérôme Jannot; Dir Bernard Mathis.

Les Nouvelles de Tahiti: place de la Cathédrale, BP 1757, Papeete; tel. 434445; fax 421800; f. 1956; daily; French; Editor I. N. Biré; Dir-Gen. Stéphane Antonin; Publr Philippe Hersant; circ. 18,500.

Le Semeur Tahitien: Papeete; f. 1909; bi-monthly; publ. by the Roman Catholic Church.

Tahiti Beach Press: BP 887, Papeete; tel. 426850; f. 1980; weekly; English; Publr G. Warti; circ. 3,000.

Tahiti Matin: place du Marché, BP 392, Papeete; tel. 481048; fax 481220; daily; Dir Pierre Marchesini.

Tahiti Pacifique Magazine: BP 368, Maharepa, Moorea; tel. and fax 563007; monthly; Editor Alex du Prel.

Tahiti Rama: Papeete; weekly.

Tahiti Today: BP 887, 98713 Papeete; tel. 426850; fax 423356; f. 1996; quarterly; Publr G. Warti; circ. 3,000.

La Tribune Polynésienne: place du Marché, BP 392, Papeete; tel. 481048; fax 481220; weekly; Dir Louis Bresson.

Ve'a Katorika: Papeete; f. 1909; monthly; publ. by the Roman Catholic Church.

Ve'a Porotetani: BP 113, Papeete; tel. 460623; fax 419357; f. 1921; monthly; French and Tahitian; publ. by the Evangelical Church; Editor Gilles Marsauche; Dir Ihorai Jacques; circ. 5,200.

Foreign Bureaux

Agence France-Presse (AFP): BP 629, Papeete; tel. 434445; fax 421800; Correspondent Denis Herrmann.

Associated Press (AP) (USA): BP 912, Papeete; tel. 437562; telex 537; Correspondent Al Prince.

Reuters (UK): BP 50, Papeete; tel. 464340; fax 464350; Correspondent Daniel Pardon.

Publishers

Haere Po No Tahiti: BP 1958, Papeete; fax 582333; f. 1981; travel, history, botany, linguistics and local interest.

Government Printer

Imprimerie Officielle: BP 117, 98713 Papeete; tel. 425067; fax 425261; f. 1851; printers, publrs; Dir Claudino Laurent.

Broadcasting and Communications

RADIO AND TELEVISION

Radio-Télé-Tahiti: 410 rue Dumont d'Urville, BP 125, Papeete; tel. 430551; telex 290; fax 413155; f. 1951 as Radio-Tahiti; television service began 1965; operated by Société Nationale de Radio-Télévision Française d'Outre-Mer (RFO), Paris; daily programmes in French and Tahitian; Dir C. Allouard; Head of Information P. Durand-Gaillard.

Radio Te Reo O Tefana: BP 13069, Punaauia; privately-owned; pro-independence; operates service in Society Islands and due to begin broadcasting in Tuamotu Islands in 1997.

Canal Plus Polynésie: Colline de Putiaoro, BP 20051, Papeete; tel. 540754; fax 540755; e-mail cpluspfd@mail.pf; Dir Christophe Lassagne.

In January 1994 a private company, Téléfenua, received authorization to transmit television programmes in seven communes. In the mid-1990s there were some 10 private radio stations in operation.

Finance

(cap. = capital; res = reserves; dep. = deposits; m. = million; brs = branches; amounts in CFP francs)

BANKING

Commercial Banks

Banque Paribas de Polynésie: BP 4479, Papeete; tel. 437100; fax 431329; f. 1985; 70% owned by Banque Paribas (France); cap. 506m. (Dec. 1996), dep. 1,000m. (Dec. 1991); Chair. Pierre Martinaud; Man. Dir F. du Peuty.

Banque de Polynésie SA: 355 blvd Pomare, BP 530, Papeete; tel. 466666; telex 230; fax 466664; f. 1973; 80% owned by Société Générale (France); cap. and res 2,167m. (Dec. 1992); Chair. Alain Bataille; Gen. Man. Jean-Maurice Beaux; 14 brs.

Banque de Tahiti SA: rue François Cardella, BP 1602, Papeete; tel. 427000; fax 423376; f. 1969; owned by Bank of Hawaii (USA—94%) and Crédit Lyonnais (France—3%); cap. 1,336m., res 3,806m., dep. 64,833m. (Dec. 1995); Pres. Charles Giordan; Exec. Vice-Pres. Michel Dupieux; 16 brs.

Banque SOCREDO—Société pour le Crédit et le Développement en Océanie: 115 rue Dumont d'Urville, BP 130, 98713 Papeete; tel. 415123; fax 433661; f. 1959; public body; affiliated to Banque Nationale de Paris (France); cap. 7,000m. (Dec. 1993), dep. 76,610m. (Dec. 1995); Pres. Jean Vernaudon; Dir Eric Pommier; 24 brs.

Westpac Banking Corporation (Australia): 2 place Notre-Dame, BP 120, Papeete; tel. 467979; telex 232; fax 431313; acquired operations of Banque Indosuez in French Polynesia in 1990; Gen. Man. Patrick Picard.

Trade and Industry

DEVELOPMENT ORGANIZATIONS

Conseil Economique, Social et Culturel de Polynésie Française: ave Bruat, BP 1657, Papeete; tel. 416500; fax 419242; Dir Willy Richmond.

Conseil Français de Développement (CFD): BP 578, Papeete; tel. 430486; telex 231; fax 434645; public body; development finance institute.

Service de l'Artisanat Traditionnel: BP 4451, Papeete; tel. 423225.

Service du Développement de l'Industrie et des Métiers: BP 20728, 98713 Papeete; tel. 533096; fax 412645; industry and small business development.

Société pour le Développement de l'Agriculture et de la Pêche: BP 1247, Papeete; tel. 836798; fax 856886; agriculture and marine industries.

SODEP—Société pour le Développement et l'Expansion du Pacifique: BP 4441, Papeete; tel. 429449; f. 1961 by consortium of banks and private interests; regional development and finance co.

CHAMBERS OF COMMERCE

Chambre de Commerce, d'Industrie, des Services et des Métiers de Polynésie Française: BP 118, Papeete; tel. 540700; fax 540701; f. 1880; 36 mems; Pres. Albert Le Caill.

Chambre d'Agriculture et d'Elevage (CAEP): route de l'Hippodrome, BP 5383, Pirae; tel. 425393; f. 1886; 10 mems; Pres. Sylvain Millaud.

Jeune Chambre Economique de Polynésie Française: BP 1640, Papeete; tel. 466231; fax 466287; Dir Hinano Jonque.

EMPLOYERS' ORGANIZATIONS

Chambre Syndicale des Entrepreneurs du Bâtiment et des Travaux Publics: BP 2218, Papeete; tel. 425309; fax 583349; Pres. BERNARD GALLOIS.

Conseil des Employeurs: Immeuble FARA, rue E. Ahnne, BP 972, Papeete; tel. 438898; fax 423237; f. 1983; Pres. GEORGES TRADINI; Sec.-Gen. ASTRID PASQUIER.

Fédération Générale de Commerce (FGC): rue Albert Leboucher, BP 1607, 98713 Papeete; tel. 429908; fax 422359; Pres. GILLES YAU.

Fédération Polynésienne de l'Agriculture et de l'Elevage: Papara, Tahiti; Pres. MICHEL LEHARTEL.

Syndicat des Importateurs et des Négociants: BP 1607, Papeete.

Union Interprofessionnelle du Tourisme de la Polynésie Française: BP 4560, Papeete; tel. 439114; f. 1973; 1,200 mems; Pres. PAUL MAETZ; Sec.-Gen. JEAN CORTEEL.

Union Patronale: BP 317, Papeete; tel. 420257; f. 1948; 63 mems; Pres. DIDIER CHONER.

TRADE UNIONS

A Tia I Mua: ave Georges Clemenceau, BP 4523, Papeete; tel. 436038; fax 450245; affiliated to CFDT (France); Pres. BRUNO SANDRAS.

Fédération des Syndicats de la Polynésie Française: BP 1136, Papeete; Pres. MARCEL AHINI.

Syndicat Territorial des Instituteurs et Institutrices de Polynésie: BP 3007, Papeete; Sec.-Gen. WILLY URIMA.

Union des Syndicats Affiliés des Travailleurs de Polynésie/Force Ouvrière-USATP/FO: BP 1201, Papeete; tel. 426049; fax 450635; Pres. COCO TERAIEFA CHANG; Sec.-Gen. PIERRE FRÉBAULT.

Union des Syndicats de l'Aéronautique: Papeete; Pres. JOSEPH CONROY.

Union des Travailleurs de Tahiti et des Iles: rue Albert Leboucher, BP 3366, Papeete; tel. 437369; Pres. JOHN TEFATUA-VAIHO.

Transport

ROADS

French Polynesia has 792 km of roads, of which about one-third are bitumen-surfaced and two-thirds stone-surfaced.

SHIPPING

The principal port is Papeete, on Tahiti.

Port Authority: Motu Uta, BP 9164, 98715 Papeete; tel. 505454; fax 421950; Harbour Master Capt. EDGAR BLOUIN; Port Man. BÉATRICE CHANSIN.

Agence Maritime Internationale de Tahiti: BP 274, Papeete; tel. 428972; telex 227; fax 432184; services to New Zealand, USA, Australia, American Samoa, Fiji, Europe.

Agence Tahiti Poroi: 23 ave du Prince Hinoi, BP 83, Papeete; tel. 435440; fax 435335; f. 1956; travel agents, tour operators.

CGM Tour du Monde SA: 80 rue du Général de Gaulle, BP 96, Papeete; tel. 420890; telex 259; fax 436806; shipowners and agents; freight services between Europe and many international ports; Dir HENRI C. FERRAND.

Compagnie Française Maritime de Tahiti: 2 rue de Commerce, Papeete; Man. M. GARBUTT.

Compagnie Maritime des Iles Sous le Vent: BP 9012, Papeete.

Compagnie Polynésienne de Transport Maritime: BP 220, Papeete; tel. 426240; fax 434889; Chair. SHAN NIM ENN; Man. Dir JEAN WONG.

Société de Navigation des Australes: BP 1890; Papeete; tel. 429367; fax 420609.

Société de Transport Insulaire Maritime (STIM): BP 635, Papeete; tel. 452324.

Société de Transport Maritime de Tuamotu: BP 11366, Mahina; tel. 422358; fax 430373.

CIVIL AVIATION

There is one international airport, Faaa airport, 6 km from Papeete, on Tahiti, and there are about 40 smaller airstrips. International services are operated by Air France, Qantas (Australia), Air New Zealand, UTA (France), LAN-Chile and Hawaiian Airlines (USA).

Air Moorea: BP 6019, Faaa; tel. 864100; fax 864269; f. 1968; operates internal services between Tahiti and Moorea Island and charter flights throughout the Territory; Pres. MARCEL GALENON; Dir-Gen. FRANÇOIS MARTIN.

Air Tahiti: blvd Pomare, BP 314, Papeete; tel. 864000; fax 864069; f. 1953, Air Polynésie 1970–87; inter-island services to 37 islands; Chair. CHRISTIAN VERNAUDON; Gen. Man. MARCEL GALENON.

Tourism

Tourism is an important and developed industry in French Polynesia, particularly on Tahiti, and 163,774 people visited the Territory in 1996, excluding cruise passengers and excursionists. In that year some 30% of arrivals were from France, 28% from the USA and 6% from Japan. There were a total of 3,075 hotel rooms in Tahiti in 1996, in which year the industry earned an estimated US $320m. Tourist arrivals declined dramatically following the resumption of nuclear testing in the Territory in September 1995.

GIE Tahiti Tourisme: Fare Manihini, blvd Pomare, BP 65, 98713 Papeete; tel. 505700; fax 436619; e-mail tahititourisme@mail.pf; internet http://www.tahititourisme.co; f. 1966 as autonomous public body, transformed into private corpn in 1993; tourist promotion; Man. Dir NELSON LEVY.

Service du Tourisme: Fare Manihini, blvd Pomare, BP 4527, Papeete; tel. 505700; fax 481275; govt dept; manages Special Fund for Tourist Development; Dir GÉRARD VANIZETTE.

Syndicat d'Initiative de la Polynésie Française: BP 326, Papeete; Pres. PIU BAMBRIDGE.

FRENCH SOUTHERN AND ANTARCTIC TERRITORIES

The French Southern and Antarctic Territories (Terres australes et antarctiques françaises) form an Overseas Territory but are administered under a special statute. The territory comprises Adélie Land, a narrow segment of the mainland of Antarctica together with a number of offshore islets, and three groups of sub-Antarctic islands (the Kerguelen and Crozet Archipelagos and St Paul and Amsterdam Islands) in the southern Indian Ocean.

Under the terms of legislation approved by the French Government on 6 August 1955, the French Southern and Antarctic Territories were placed under the authority of a chief administrator, who was responsible to the Ministry of Overseas Departments and Territories. The Chief Administrator is assisted by a consultative council, which meets at least twice annually. The Consultative Council is composed of seven members who are appointed for five years by the Ministers of Defence and of Overseas Departments and Territories (from among members of the Office of Scientific Research and from those who have participated in scientific missions in the sub-Antarctic islands and Adélie Land) and by the Minister of Research and Technology and the Minister of Equipment, Housing, Transport and the Sea.

In 1987 certain categories of vessels were allowed to register under the flag of the Kerguelen Archipelago, provided that 25% of their crew (including the captain and at least two officers) were French. These specifications were amended to 35% of the crew and at least four officers in April 1990. At 31 December 1997 there were 145 registered vessels.

In early January 1989 work on the construction of a 1,100-m airstrip in Adélie Land (which, the authorities asserted, would improve access to research facilities) was suspended, following clashes between construction workers and members of the international environmental protection group Greenpeace, who had occupied the site to protest against the project, which, they claimed, would involve the destruction of large penguin breeding colonies. The French authorities subsequently agreed to allow Greenpeace to conduct an independent assessment of the environmental impact of the airstrip, and work on the project resumed shortly afterwards. In February 1991 the French Government invited five environmental groups to visit the construction site. Four of these groups subsequently published a report detailing their findings and recommendations concerning the future use of the runway. The project was subsequently abandoned, however, following severe storm damage in 1994.

In January 1992 the French Government created a 'public interest group', the Institut Français pour la Recherche et la Technologie Polaires (IFRTP), to assume responsibility for the organization of scientific and research programmes in the French Southern and Antarctic Territories.

France is a signatory to the Antarctic Treaty (see p. 398).

Statistical Survey

Area (sq km): Kerguelen Archipelago 7,215, Crozet Archipelago 515, Amsterdam Island 85, St Paul Island 7, Adélie Land (Antarctica) 432,000.

Population (the population, comprising members of scientific missions, fluctuates according to season, being higher in the summer; the figures given are approximate): Kerguelen Archipelago, Port-aux-Français 64; Amsterdam Island at Martin de Viviès 20; Adélie Land at Base Dumont d'Urville 27; the Crozet Archipelago at Alfred-Faure (on Ile de la Possession) 17; St Paul Island is uninhabited. Total population (January 1997): 128.

Fishing (catch quotas in metric tons): Crayfish (spiny lobsters) in Amsterdam and St Paul: 340 (1995); fishing by French and foreign fleets in the Kerguelen Archipelago: 4,500 (1995).

Currency: French currency is used (see French Guiana).

Budget: Projected to balance at 111.0m. francs in 1997.

External Trade: Exports consist mainly of crayfish and other fish to France and Réunion. The Territories also derive revenue from the sale of postage stamps and other philatelic items.

Directory

Government: Chief Administrator PIERRE LISE; there is a central administration in Paris (34 rue des Renaudes, 75017 Paris, France; tel. (1) 40-53-46-51; telex 640980; fax (1) 47-66-91-23).

Consultative Council: Pres. JEAN-PIERRE CHARPENTIER.

Transport: An oceanographic and supply vessel, the *Marion Dufresne*, operated by the Institut Français pour la Recherche et la Technologie Polaires (IFRTP), provides regular links between Réunion and the sub-Antarctic islands. Another specialized vessel, the *Astrolabe*, calls five times a year at the Antarctic mainland.

Research Stations: There are meteorological stations and geophysical research stations on Kerguelen, Amsterdam, Adélie Land and Crozet.

NEW CALEDONIA

Introductory Survey

Location, Climate, Language, Religion, Capital

The Territory of New Caledonia comprises one large island and several smaller ones, lying in the south Pacific Ocean, about 1,500 km (930 miles) east of Queensland, Australia. The main island, New Caledonia (la Grande-Terre), is long and narrow, and has a total area of 16,750 sq km. Rugged mountains divide the west of the island from the east, and there is little flat land. The nearby Loyalty Islands, which are administratively part of the Territory, are 2,353 sq km in area, and a third group of islands, the uninhabited Chesterfield Islands, lies about 400 km north-west of the main island. The climate is generally a mild one, with an average temperature of about 23°C (73°F) and a rainy season between December and March. The average rainfall in the east of the main island is about 2,000 mm (80 ins) per year, and in the west about 1,000 mm (40 ins). French is the official language and the mother tongue of the Caldoches (French settlers); the indigenous Kanaks (Melanesians) also speak Melanesian languages. Other immigrants speak Polynesian and Asian languages. New Caledonians almost all profess Christianity; about 59% are Roman Catholics, and there is a substantial Protestant minority. The capital is Nouméa, on the main island.

Recent History

New Caledonia became a French possession in 1853, when the island was annexed as a dependency of Tahiti. In 1884 a separate administration was established, and in 1946 it became an Overseas Territory of the French Republic. Early European settlers on New Caledonia, supported by legislation, quickly assumed possession of Melanesian land, which provoked a number of rebellions by the indigenous Kanak (Melanesian) population.

In 1956 the first Territorial Assembly, with 30 members, was elected by universal adult suffrage, although the French Governor effectively retained control of the functions of government. New Caledonian demands for a measure of self-government were answered in December 1976 by a new statute, which gave the Council of Government, elected from the Territorial Assembly, responsibility for certain internal affairs. The post of Governor was replaced by that of French High Commissioner to the Territory. In 1978 the Kanak-supported, pro-independence parties obtained a majority of the posts in the Council of Government. In March 1979, however, the French Government dismissed the Council, following its failure to support a proposal for a 10-year 'contract' between France and New Caledonia, because the plan did not acknowledge the possibility of New Caledonian independence. The Territory was then placed under the direct authority of the High Commissioner. A general election was held in July, but a new electoral law, which affected mainly the pro-independence parties, ensured that minor parties were not represented in the Assembly. Two parties loyal to France together won 22 of the 36 seats.

Tension increased in September 1981 after the assassination of Pierre Declercq, the Secretary-General of the pro-independence party, Union Calédonienne (UC). In December of that year the French Government made proposals for change that included fiscal reform, equal access for all New Caledonians to positions of authority, land reforms, the wider distribution of mining revenue and the fostering of Kanak cultural institutions. To assist in effecting these reforms, the French Government simultaneously announced that it would rule by decree for a period of at least one year. In June 1982, accusing its partner in the ruling coalition of 'active resistance to evolution and change' in New Caledonia, the Fédération pour une Nouvelle Société Calédonienne (FNSC) joined with the opposition grouping, Front Indépendantiste (FI), to form a government which was more favourable to the proposed reforms.

In November 1983 the French Government proposed a five-year period of increased autonomy from July 1984 and a referendum in 1989 to determine New Caledonia's future. The statute was opposed in New Caledonia, both by parties in favour of earlier independence and by those against, and it was rejected by the Territorial Assembly in April 1984. However, the proposals were approved by the French National Assembly in September 1984. Under the provisions of the statute, the Territorial Council of Ministers was given responsibility for many internal matters of government, its President henceforth being an elected member instead of the French High Commissioner; a second legislative chamber, with the right to be consulted on development planning and budgetary issues, was created at the same time. All of the main parties seeking independence (except the Libération Kanak Socialiste (LKS) party, which left the FI) boycotted elections for the new Territorial Assembly in November 1984 and, following the dissolution of the FI, formed a new movement called the Front de Libération Nationale Kanak Socialiste (FLNKS). On 1 December, the FLNKS Congress established a 'provisional government', headed by Jean-Marie Tjibaou. The elections to the Territorial Assembly attracted only 50.1% of the electorate, and the anti-independence party Rassemblement pour la Calédonie dans la République (RPCR) won 34 of the 42 seats. An escalation of violence began in November, and in the following month 10 Kanaks were killed by security forces in the far north of the Territory.

In January 1985 Edgard Pisani, the new High Commissioner, announced a plan by which the Territory might become independent 'in association with' France on 1 January 1986, subject to the result of a referendum in July 1985. Kanak groups opposed the plan, insisting that the indigenous population be allowed to determine its own fate. A resurgence of violence followed the announcement of Pisani's plan, and a state of emergency was declared after Eloi Machoro, a leading member of the FLNKS, was killed by security forces.

In April 1985 the French Prime Minister, Laurent Fabius, put forward new proposals for the future of New Caledonia, whereby the referendum on independence was deferred until an unspecified date not later than the end of December 1987. Meanwhile, the Territory was to be divided into four regions, each to be governed by its own elected autonomous council, which would have extensive powers in the spheres of planning and development, education, health and social services, land rights, transport and housing. The elected members of all four councils together would serve as regional representatives in a Territorial Congress (to replace the Territorial Assembly).

The 'Fabius plan' was well received by the FLNKS, although the organization reaffirmed the ultimate goal of independence. It was also decided to maintain the 'provisional Government' under Tjibaou at least until the end of December 1985. The RPCR, however, condemned the plan, and the proposals were rejected by the predominantly anti-independence Territorial Assembly at the end of May. However, the necessary legislation was approved by the French National Assembly in July, and the Fabius plan came into force. The elections were held in September, and, as expected, only in the region around Nouméa, where the bulk of the population is non-Kanak, was an anti-independence majority recorded. However, the pro-independence Melanesians, in spite of their majorities in the three non-urban regions, would be in a minority in the Territorial Congress.

The FLNKS boycotted the general election to the French National Assembly in March 1986. Only about 50% of the eligible voters in New Caledonia participated in the election, at which the Territory's two seats in the Assembly were won by RPCR candidates. In May the French Council of Ministers approved a draft law providing for a referendum to be held in New Caledonia within 12 months, whereby voters would choose between independence and a further extension of regional autonomy. In December, in spite of strong French diplomatic opposition, the UN General Assembly voted to reinscribe New Caledonia on the UN list of non-self-governing territories, thereby affirming the population's right to self-determination.

The FLNKS decided to boycott the referendum on 13 September 1987, at which 48,611 votes were cast in favour of New Caledonia's continuation as part of the French Republic (98.3% of the total) and only 842 (1.7%) were cast in favour of independence. Of the registered electorate, almost 59% voted, a higher level of participation than was expected, although 90% of the electorate abstained in constituencies inhabited by a majority of Kanaks.

In October 1987 seven pro-French loyalists were acquitted on a charge of murdering 10 Kanak separatists in 1984. Tjibaou, who reacted to the ruling by declaring that his followers would have to abandon their stance of pacifism, and his deputy, Yeiwéné Yeiwéné, were indicted for 'incitement to violence'. In April 1988 four gendarmes were killed, and 27 held hostage in a cave, on the island of Ouvéa by supporters of the FLNKS. Two days later, Kanak separatists prevented about one-quarter of the Territory's polling stations from opening, when local elections, scheduled to coincide with the French presidential election, were held. The FLNKS boycotted the elections. Although 12 of the gendarmes taken hostage were subsequently released, six members of a French anti-terrorist squad were captured. French security forces immediately laid siege to the cave and, in the following month, made an assault upon it, leaving 19 Kanaks and two gendarmes dead. Following the siege, allegations that three Kanaks had been executed or left to die, after being arrested, led to an announcement by the new French Socialist Government that a judicial inquiry into the incident was to be opened.

At the elections to the French National Assembly in June 1988, both New Caledonian seats were retained by the RPCR. Michel Rocard, the new French Prime Minister, chaired negotiations, at the Hôtel Matignon (his official residence) in Paris, between Jacques Lafleur (leader of the RPCR) and Tjibaou, who agreed to transfer the administration of the Territory to Paris for 12 months. Under the provisions of the agreement (known as the Matignon Accord), the Territory was to be divided into three administrative Provinces prior to a territorial plebiscite on independence to be held in 1998. Only people resident in the Territory in 1988, and their direct descendants, would be allowed to vote in the plebiscite. The agreement also provided for a programme of economic development, training in public administration for Kanaks, and institutional reforms. The Matignon Accord was presented to the French electorate in a referendum, held on 6 November 1988, and approved by 80% of those voting (although an abstention rate of 63% of the electorate was recorded). The programme was approved by a 57% majority in New Caledonia, where the rate of abstention was 37%. In November, under the terms of the agreement, 51 separatists were released from prison, including 26 Kanaks implicated in the incident on Ouvéa.

In May 1989 the leaders of the FLNKS, Tjibaou and Yeiwéné, were murdered by separatist extremists, alleged to be associated with the Front Uni de Libération Kanak (FULK), a grouping which had until then formed part of the FLNKS, but which opposed the Matignon Accord on the grounds that it conceded too much to the European settlers. The assassinations were regarded as an attempt to disrupt the implementation of the Accord. Elections to the three Provincial Assemblies were nevertheless held, as scheduled, in June: the FLNKS won a majority of seats in the Province of the North and the Province of the Loyalty Islands, while the RPCR obtained a majority in the Province of the South, and also emerged as the dominant party in the Territorial Congress, with 27 of the 54 seats, while the FLNKS secured 19 seats.

The year of direct rule by France ended, as agreed, on 14 July 1989, when the Territorial Congress and Provincial Assemblies assumed the administrative functions allocated to them in the Matignon Accord (see below under Government). In November the French National Assembly approved an amnesty (as stipulated in the Matignon Accord) for all who had been involved in politically-motivated violence in New Caledonia before August 1988, despite strong opposition from the right-wing French parties.

In April 1991 the LKS announced its intention to withdraw from the Matignon Accord, accusing the French Government, as well as several Kanak political leaders, of seeking to undermine Kanak culture and tradition. The RPCR's policy of encouraging the immigration of skilled workers from mainland France and other European countries continued to be a source of conflict between the conservative coalition and the FLNKS. Racial tension itensified in early 1992, when riots in Nouméa by more than 100 Kanak youths resulted in the burning and destruction of the capital's principal commercial centre. Concern was expressed that increased levels of youth unemployment (particularly among the Melanesian community, many of whom migrate to Nouméa in search of work) would lead to further social instability.

At elections for the Representative to the French Senate in September 1992, the RPCR's candidate, Simon Loueckhote, narrowly defeated Rock Wamytan, the Vice-President of the FLNKS.

Debate concerning the political future of the Territory continued in 1994. In October the RPCR leader, Jacques Lafleur, proposed that New Caledonia abandon the planned 1998 referendum on self-determination, in favour of a 30-year agreement with France, similar to the Matignon Accord, but with provision for greater autonomy in judicial matters. The UC, however, rejected the proposal and, at the party's annual congress in November, its members reiterated their demand for a gradual transfer of power from France to New Caledonia, culminating in a return to sovereignty in 1998.

French presidential elections took place in April/May 1995. During the second round of voting in the Territory (in which only 35% of the electorate participated), the socialist candidate, Lionel Jospin, received 25.9% of the total votes, while the candidate of the Gaullist Rassemblement pour la République (RPR), Jacques Chirac, won 74.1%. (Chirac was elected to the presidency with 52.6% of votes cast throughout the republic.)

At provincial elections in July 1995 the RPCR remained the most successful party, although its dominance was reduced considerably. The FLNKS remained in control of the Provinces of the North and the Loyalty Islands, while the RPCR retained a large majority in the Province of the South. The RPCR retained an overall majority in the Territorial Congress, while the FLNKS remained the second largest party. Considerable gains were made by a newly-formed party led by a Nouméa businessman, Une Nouvelle-Calédonie pour Tous (NCPT), which secured seven seats in the Territorial Congress and seven seats in the Provincial Government of the South. An estimated 67% of the electorate participated in the elections. In the period following the elections, however, a political crisis arose as a result of the NCPT's decision to align itself with the FLNKS, leaving the RPCR with a minority of official positions in the congressional committees. Lafleur would not accept a situation in which the NCPT appeared to be the dominant party in Congress, and Pierre Frogier, the RPCR's President of Congress, refused to convene a congressional sitting under such circumstances. The deadlock was broken only when the FLNKS released a statement in October, reiterating the importance of the relationship between the FLNKS and the RPCR as signatories of the Matignon Accord, and proposing the allocation of congressional positions on a proportional basis.

Negotiations between the French Government and delegations from the FLNKS and the RPCR were held in Paris in late 1995. It was agreed that further discussions would take place in early 1996, involving representatives from numerous interest groups in the Territory, to examine the possibility of achieving a consensus solution on the future of the islands. Thus, the major political groups in New Caledonia sought to achieve a consensus solution on the Territory's future, which could be presented to the electorate for approval in the 1998 referendum. It was widely believed that this was preferable to a simple 'for' or 'against' vote on independence, which would necessarily polarize the electorate and create a confrontational political climate.

Intensive negotiations involving the RPCR, the FLNKS and the French Government took place throughout early 1996. However, in April Rock Wamytan (the recently-elected leader of the FLNKS) announced the withdrawal of his party from the discussions, in protest at the disclosure of confidential information regarding the talks to the French press. The FLNKS was also reported to be angry that France had apparently reneged on its promise to consider all available options for the Territory's political future by discounting the possibility of outright independence. The FLNKS subsequently announced that it would resume negotiations only in the presence of an independent and neutral mediator. The Prime Minister of Papua New Guinea, Sir Julius Chan, responded by offering to act as such a mediator. In July, however, the FLNKS accepted the French Government's offer to hold bilateral negotiations directly with the party, although without a mediator. The RPCR's exclusion from the discussions coincided with Jacques Lafleur's admission that he had been responsible for the disclosure of confidential material from the talks to the press in April. France's refusal to grant final approval for a large-scale nickel smelter project in the North Province (see Economic Affairs) until the achievement of consensus in the discussions on autonomy prompted accusations of blackmail from several sources within the Territory and fuelled suspicions that metropolitan France would seek to retain control of the islands' valuable mineral resources in any settlement on New Caledonia's future status. The issue proved to be a serious obstacle in the negotiations and resulted in the virtual cessation of discussions between the two sides during the remainder of 1996. The FLNKS argued that the smelter project should be administered by local interests, consistent with the process of reallocating responsibility for the economy from metropolitan France to the Territory as advocated in the Matignon Accord. Their demands were supported by widespread industrial action in the mining sector during late 1996.

In February 1997 the French Minister for Overseas Territories travelled to the Territory in an attempt to achieve an agreement between the locally-controlled Société Minière du Sud-Pacifique (SMSP) and the French-owned company, with numerous interests in the islands, Société Le Nickel (SLN). The minister failed to resolve the dispute during his visit; however, at the end of the month, in a complete reversal of its previous position, the French Government announced its decision to exclude SLN from the project. The decision provoked strong criticism from SLN and Eramet, the French mining conglomerate, of which SLN is a subsidiary, and attracted protests from shareholders and employees of the company. During March large-scale demonstrations were held by the UC and the trade union, USTKE, in support of the SMSP's acquisition of the smelter. Meanwhile, another trade union, USOENC (which represents a high proportion of SLN employees), organized a protest rally against the exclusion of SLN from the project. In mid-1997 the newly-elected French Government announced the appointment of Philippe Essig (a former head of the French national railway company) in the role of adviser and mediator in the dispute. The search for an agreement between SLN and the SMSP had become centred on the issue of access to nickel resources. Essig compiled a report on the matter, published in November 1997, which proposed the creation of an independent body to supervise the management of deposits, gradually ceding control to the operators once an agreement had been reached. Frustrated at SLN's seemingly intransigent position in the negotiations the FLNKS organized protests and blockades at all the company's major mining installations. Supporters of the pro-independence organization also restricted shipments of ore around the Territory. Consequently, four mines were forced to close, while a 25% reduction in working hours was imposed on 1,500 mine workers, prompting protests by SLN employees and demands from USOENC that the blockades be removed. In January 1998 Rock Wamytan urged the French Prime Minister, Lionel Jospin, to settle the dispute by the end of the month in order that official negotiations on the political future of the Territory, in preparation for the referendum, might begin. The position of the FLNKS had been somewhat undermined by the decision, in the previous month, of a breakaway group of pro-independence politicians (including prominent members of the UC, Palika, the UMP and the LKS) to begin negotiations on that subject with the RPCR. A draft agreement on the exchange of deposits was signed by SLN and the SMSP on 1 February.

Census figures published in late 1996 indicated a 10-fold increase in the immigration rate of Europeans to the Territory since the previous census of 1989. The fact that Kanaks comprised only 44.1% of the islands' total population, despite a relatively high birth rate, prompted demands that the French Government control immigration in order to secure more employment for local people. In late October the FLNKS organized a demonstration in Nouméa, attended by more than 5,000 people, to express concern at the continued high unemployment rate among the Kanak population.

Elections to the French National Assembly in May–June 1997 were boycotted by the pro-independence FLNKS and LKS, resulting in a relatively low participation rate among the electorate. Jacques Lafleur and Pierre Frogier, both candidates of the RPCR, were elected to represent the Territory.

Government

The French Government is represented in New Caledonia by its High Commissioner to the Territory, and controls a number of important spheres of government, including external relations, defence, justice, finance, external trade and secondary education. In July 1989 administrative reforms were introduced, as stipulated in the Matignon Accord (which had been approved by national referendum in November 1988). The Territory was divided into three Provinces (North, South and Loyalty Islands), each governed by an assembly, which is elected by direct universal suffrage. The members of the three Provincial Assemblies together form the Territorial Congress. Members are subject to re-election every six years. The responsibilities of the Territorial Congress include the Territory's budget and fiscal affairs, infrastructure and primary education, while the responsibilities of the Provincial Assemblies include local economic development, land reform and cultural affairs. These institutions were to remain in place until the holding, in 1998, of a territorial referendum on the question of self-determination for New Caledonia.

In addition, New Caledonia elects two deputies to the French National Assembly in Paris, one representative to the French Senate and one Economic and Social Councillor, all of whom are chosen on the basis of universal adult suffrage. The Territory is also represented at the European Parliament.

Defence

In August 1997 France was maintaining a force of 3,900 military personnel in New Caledonia, including a gendarmerie of 1,100.

Economic Affairs

In 1994, according to UN estimates, New Caledonia's gross domestic product (GDP), measured at current prices, totalled US $3,316m., equivalent to US $18,631 per head. During 1985–92, it was estimated, New Caledonia's GDP increased, in real terms, at an average annual rate of 6.7%. The Territory's population increased by an annual average of 2.0% in 1985–95.

Agriculture and fishing contributed only 2.0% of GDP in 1990, although 14% of the employed labour force were engaged in the sector in 1989. In 1995 only some 0.7% of total land area was used for arable purposes or permanent crops. Maize, yams, sweet potatoes and coconuts are the principal crops. Pumpkins also became an important export crop for the Japanese market in the mid-1990s. Livestock consists mainly of cattle and pigs. New Caledonia also began to export deer, principally to Thailand, in 1994. The main fisheries products are tuna (most of which is exported to Japan) and shrimps. Six farms produced a total of 632 metric tons of shrimps for export in 1993. Furthermore, a giant clam project was undertaken in 1996, as well as a prawn hatchery, which was established to supply two aquaculture farms in the North Province.

Industry (comprising mining, manufacturing, construction and utilities) provided 24.9% of GDP in 1990, and employed 19% of the working population in 1989. Mining employed only 1.6% of the working population in 1989, but it constitutes the most important industrial sector of New Caledonia's economy: in the mid-1990s mining and quarrying contributed an estimated 20% of GDP and provided at least 80% of total export earnings. The Territory possesses the world's largest known nickel deposits, accounting for about 30% of the world's known reserves, and is the world's largest producer of ferro-nickel. Sales of nickel accounted for 90.6% of export revenues in 1994. In 1995 Société Le Nickel (SLN) announced some $A500m. worth of new investment in its current operations and stated its aim to raise annual output of processed metal to 60,000 metric tons by 2000 (compared with 53,412 tons in 1996). Moreover, in 1996 proposals were announced for the establishment of a nickel smelter in the North Province (under a joint agreement with a Canadian company—see Recent History). The project, which was to cost an estimated US $1,060m., envisaged the construction of a deep-water port, international airport, power station and associated infrastructure, and was expected to provide 2,000 jobs. Chromium ore is also extracted, but the closure of the principal mine in August 1990 reduced output for that year to 11m. metric tons, compared with 114m. tons in 1989. In late 1997 an Australian company was granted permission to conduct exploratory drilling for gold, silver, copper, lead and zinc in the north of the main island.

The manufacturing sector, which provided 6.4% of GDP in 1990 and engaged 8.4% of the employed labour force in 1989, consists mainly of small and medium-sized enterprises, most of which are situated around the capital, Nouméa, producing building materials, furniture, salted fish, fruit juices and perishable foods.

Electrical energy is provided by thermal power stations (70.5% in 1992) and by hydroelectric plants. Mineral fuels accounted for 7.3% of total imports in 1992. In 1996 construction began on a plant producing wind-generated electricity near Nouméa, at a cost of US $7m., which was expected to provide some 6.5m. kWh of energy per year.

Despite considerable investment in tourism in the 1980s, the industry failed to experience the same expansion as in many Pacific islands. Tourist arrivals were seriously affected by political unrest and outbreaks of violence in mid-1988 between the Caldoches and Kanaks. Several luxury tourists resorts were under construction in the mid-1990s, in an attempt to attract more visitors to the islands, and by 1996 annual arrivals had increased to 91,121.

In 1996 there was a trade deficit of some US $465m. The principal imports in that year were mineral fuels, foodstuffs and machinery and transport equipment. France is the chief trading partner, providing 43.7% of imports and purchasing 27.7% of exports in 1994; other major trading partners in that year were Japan (27.1% of exports), Australia, Germany, New Zealand, Singapore and the USA.

The budget for 1991 envisaged revenue and expenditure of 3,345m. French francs; fiscal receipts were expected to contribute 2,607m. French francs, or 78% of budgetary revenue. The annual rate of inflation averaged 2.6% in 1985–94. Consumer prices increased by an average of 1.4% in 1995 and by 1.5% in 1996. Almost 16% of the labour force were unemployed at the time of the 1989 census.

New Caledonia forms part of the Franc Zone (see p. 181), is an associate member of the UN's Economic and Social Commission for Asia and the Pacific (ESCAP—see p. 27) and is a member, in its own right, of the Pacific Community (formerly the South Pacific Commission) — see p. 232).

During the 1980s New Caledonia's two principal sources of income, nickel production and tourism, were both affected by political unrest. Fluctuations in international prices for nickel also illustrated the disadvantages of relying on one commodity. The Matignon Accord, approved by referendum in 1988 (see Recent History), stipulated that a programme of economic development should be undertaken, with the aim of improving the economic conditions of the Kanak population and increasing their participation in the market economy and in public administration. However, in the late 1990s the indigenous population was still largely excluded from the economic and political administration of the Territory and a considerable proportion continued to experience economic hardship.

Social Welfare

In 1992 there were 1,301 hospital beds in New Caledonia, and in 1993 there were 334 physicians working in the Territory.

Education

Education is compulsory for 10 years between six and 16 years of age. Schools are operated by both the State and churches, under the supervision of the Department of Education. The French Government finances the state secondary system. Primary education begins at six years of age, and lasts for five years; secondary education, beginning at 11 years of age, comprises a first cycle of four years and a second, three-year cycle. In 1991 there were 80 pre-primary and 200 primary schools, and in 1990 there were 43 secondary schools, 31 vocational institutions and five institutions of higher education. Some students attend universities in France. Part of a regional university, the Université française du Pacifique, is based in New Caledonia. In 1989 the rate of adult illiteracy averaged 6.9% (males 6.0%, females 7.9%). According to UNESCO, total public expenditure on education in 1993 was 1,652m. French francs.

Public Holidays

1998: 1 January (New Year's Day), 13 April (Easter Monday), 4 May (for Labour Day), 8 May (Liberation Day), 21 May (Ascension Day), 1 June (Whit Monday), 14 July (Fall of the Bastille), 11 November (Armistice Day), 25 December (Christmas Day).

1999: 1 January (New Year's Day), 5 April (Easter Monday), 3 May (for Labour Day), 8 May (Liberation Day), 13 May (Ascension Day), 24 May (Whit Monday), 14 July (Fall of the Bastille), 11 November (Armistice Day), 25 December (Christmas Day).

Weights and Measures

The metric system is in force.

Statistical Survey

Source (unless otherwise stated): Institut Territorial de la Statistique et des Etudes Economiques, BP 823, Nouméa; tel. 275481; fax 288148.

AREA AND POPULATION

Area (sq km): New Caledonia island (Grande-Terre) 16,750; Loyalty Islands 1,981 (Lifou 1,150, Maré 650, Ouvéa 130); Total 19,103 (7,376 sq miles).

Population: 145,368 (males 74,285, females 71,083) at census of 15 April 1983; 164,173 (males 83,862, females 80,311) at census of 4 April 1989; 196,836 at census of 16 April 1996.

Density (April 1996): 10.3 per sq km.

Ethnic Groups (census of 1989): Melanesians 73,598; French and other Europeans 55,085; Wallisians and Futunians (Polynesian) 14,186; Indonesians 5,191; Tahitians (Polynesian) 4,750; Others 11,363.

Principal Town (1989): Nouméa (capital), population 65,110.

Births, Marriages and Deaths (1994): Registered live births 4,267 (birth rate 23.2 per 1,000); Registered marriages 898 (marriage rate 4.9 per 1,000); Registered deaths 1,060 (death rate 5.8 per 1,000).

Expectation of Life (UN estimates, years at birth, 1990–95): 72.1 (males 69.7; females 74.7). Source: UN, *World Population Prospects: The 1994 Revision*.

Economically Active Population (persons aged 14 years and over, 1989 census): Agriculture, hunting, forestry and fishing 7,763; Mining and quarrying 910; Manufacturing 4,668; Electricity, gas and water 576; Construction 4,476; Trade, restaurants and hotels 9,454; Transport, storage and communications 3,087; Financing, insurance, real estate and business services 2,475; Community, social and personal services 22,016 (incl. 2,500 members of the armed forces); Total employed 55,425 (males 34,905, females 20,520); Unemployed 10,520 (males 6,306, females 4,214); Total labour force 65,945 (males 41,211, females 24,734). Source: ILO, *Yearbook of Labour Statistics*.

AGRICULTURE, ETC.

Principal Crops (FAO estimates, '000 metric tons, 1995): Maize 1; Taro 2; Potatoes 4; Sweet potatoes 3; Yams 11; Cassava 3; Other roots and tubers 1; Coconuts 10; Vegetables and melons 3; Fruit 4. Source: FAO, *Production Yearbook*.

Livestock (FAO estimates, '000 head, year ending September 1995): Horses 12; Cattle 113; Pigs 39; Sheep 4; Goats 17; Chickens 1,000 (Source: FAO, *Production Yearbook*); Rabbits (1984) 5.3.

Livestock Products (FAO estimates, metric tons, 1995): Beef and veal 4,000; Pigmeat 1,000; Cows' milk 3,000; Hen eggs 1,400.

Forestry: Roundwood removals ('000 cubic metres): 6 in 1992; 4 in 1993; 5 in 1994. Source: FAO, *Yearbook of Forest Products*.

Fishing (metric tons, live weight): Total catch 3,479 in 1993; 4,050 in 1994; 4,000 (FAO estimate) in 1995. Source: FAO, *Yearbook of Fishery Statistics*.

MINING

Production ('000 metric tons): Nickel ore (metal content) 99.6 in 1992; 97.1 in 1993; 97.3 in 1994. Source: UN, *Industrial Commodity Statistics Yearbook*.

INDUSTRY

Production: Ferro-nickel and nickel matte 53,412 metric tons (1996); Electric energy 1,170m. kWh (1994).

FINANCE

Currency and Exchange Rates: see French Polynesia.

Budget (million French francs, 1991): *Expenditure*: Ordinary expenditure 2,862, Extraordinary expenditure 483, Total 3,345; *Revenue:* Fiscal receipts 2,607, Other 738, Total 3,345. Source: Secrétariat du Comité Monétaire de la Zone Franc.

Aid from France (US $ million): 308.7 in 1991; 354.5 in 1992; 392.6 in 1993. Source: UN, *Statistical Yearbook for Asia and the Pacific*.

Money Supply (million French francs at 31 December 1995): Currency in circulation 8,899; Demand deposits 53,554; Total money 62,453. Source: Institut National de la Statistique et des Etudes Economiques.

Cost of Living (Consumer Price Index for Nouméa; base: 1990 = 100): 112.5 in 1994; 114.1 in 1995; 115.8 in 1996. Source: UN, *Monthly Bulletin of Statistics*.

Gross Domestic Product (US $ million at current prices): 2,926 in 1992; 3,116 in 1993; 3,316 in 1994. Source: UN, *Statistical Yearbook*.

Expenditure on the Gross Domestic Product (million francs CFP at current prices, 1990): Government final consumption expenditure 81,645; Private final consumption expenditure 143,470; Increase in stocks –2,759; Gross fixed capital formation 61,074; *Total domestic expenditure* 283,430; Exports of goods and services 54,976; *Less* Imports of goods and services 88,567; *Sub-total* 249,839; Statistical discrepancy 588; *GDP in purchasers' values* 250,427. Source: UN, *National Accounts Statistics*.

Gross Domestic Product by Economic Activity (million francs CFP at current prices, 1990): Agriculture, forestry and fishing 5,032; Mining and quarrying 25,977; Manufacturing 15,933; Electricity, gas and water 6,357; Construction 14,151; Wholesale and retail trade 57,566; Transport, storage and communications 13,957; Government services 62,076; Other services (incl. restaurants and hotels) 46,699; Other producers 2,678; *GDP in purchasers' values* 250,427. Source: UN, *National Accounts Statistics.*

EXTERNAL TRADE

Principal Commodities (million francs, 1994): *Imports:* Rice 371, Sugar 367, Wine 1,060, Cement and clinker 438, Solid mineral fuels 685, Petroleum products 7,443; Total (incl. others) 87,306. *Exports:* Ferro-nickel 23,353; Nickel ore 6,833; Nickel matte 4,814; Total (incl. others) 36,209.

Principal Trading Partners (US $ '000, 1994): *Imports:* Australia 10,348; France (metropolitan) 38,148; Japan 4,175; New Zealand 4,947; Singapore 4,089; USA 3,984; Total (incl. others) 87,306. *Exports:* France (metropolitan) 10,029; Germany 2,746; Japan 9,800; USA 1,743; Total (incl. others) 36,209.

Source: Institut National de la Statistique et des Etudes Economiques.

TRANSPORT

Road Traffic (1993): Passenger cars in use 58,500; Commerical vehicles in use 22,600. Source: UN, *Statistical Yearbook.*

Shipping (1990): Vessels entered 536; Goods unloaded 930,000 metric tons, Goods loaded 1,040,000 metric tons. Source: mainly UN, *Monthly Bulletin of Statistics. Merchant Fleet* (vessels registered, '000 grt, at 31 December 1992): 14. Source UN, *Statistical Yearbook.*

Civil Aviation (La Tontouta airport, Nouméa, 1990): Passengers arriving 144,435, Passengers departing 143,539; Freight unloaded 4,975 metric tons, Freight loaded 1,993 metric tons.

TOURISM

Visitors: 85,103 in 1994; 86,289 in 1995; 91,121 in 1996.

COMMUNICATIONS MEDIA

Radio Receivers (1995): 102,000 in use*.

Television Receivers (1995): 49,000 in use*.

Telephones (1994): 42,000 main lines in use†.

Daily Newspapers (1995): 3; estimated circulation 23,000*.

* Source: UNESCO, *Statistical Yearbook.*

† Source: UN, *Statistical Yearbook.*

EDUCATION

Pre-primary (1991): 80 schools; 461 teachers; 12,776 pupils (1994).

Primary (1991): 200 schools; 1,096 teachers; 22,308 pupils (1994).

Secondary (1991): 74 schools (43 general, 31 vocational—1990); 1,669 teachers; 21,908 pupils (14,889 general, 7,019 vocational).

Higher (1990): 5 institutions; 66 teachers; 1,007 students.

Source: mainly UNESCO, *Statistical Yearbook.*

Directory

The Constitution

The constitutional system in New Caledonia and its dependencies is established under the Constitution of the Fifth French Republic and specific laws, the most recent of which were enacted in July 1989 in accordance with the terms agreed by the Matignon Accord. A referendum on the future of New Caledonia is to be conducted in 1998. The islands are declared to be an Overseas Territory of the French Republic, of which they remain an integral part. The High Commissioner is the representative of the State in the Territory and is appointed by the French Government. The High Commissioner is responsible for external relations, defence, law and order, finance and secondary education. The Territory is divided into three Provinces, of the South, the North and the Loyalty Islands. Each is governed by a Provincial Assembly, which is elected by direct universal suffrage and is responsible for local economic development, land reform and cultural affairs. Members of the Assemblies (32 for the South, 15 for the North and seven for the Loyalty Islands) are subject to re-election every six years. The members of the three Provincial Assemblies together form the Territorial Congress, which is responsible for the territorial budget and fiscal affairs, infrastructure and primary education. The Assemblies and the Congress each elect a President to lead them; the Presidents join the High Commissioner as part of the territorial executive. Provision is also made for the maintenance of Kanak tradition: there are eight custom regions, each with a Regional Consultative Custom Council. These eight Councils, with other appropriate authorities, are represented on the Territorial Custom Council, which is consulted by the Congress and the Government. Local government is conducted by 32 communes. The Territory also elects two deputies to the National Assembly in Paris, one Senator and one Economic and Social Councillor, all on the basis of universal adult suffrage. The Territory is represented in the European Parliament.

The Government

(February 1998)

High Commissioner: Dominique Bur (appointed 1995).

Secretary-General: Laurent Cayrel.

Deputy Secretary-General: Jacques Michaut.

GOVERNMENT OFFICES

Office of the High Commissioner: Haut-commissariat de la République en Nouvelle-Calédonie, BP C5, 98848 Nouméa Cédex; tel. 266300; fax 272828.

Territorial Government: Executif du Congrés: Haut-commissariat de la République en Nouvelle-Calédonie, BP C5, 98848 Nouméa Cédex; tel. 256000; fax 272828; *Congrés du Territoire:* BP 31, 98845 Nouméa Cédex; tel. 273129; fax 276219.

Government of the Province of the Loyalty Islands: Gouvernement Provincial des Iles Loyauté, BP 50, 98820 Wé, Lifou, Loyalty Islands; tel. 455100; fax 451440; e-mail loyalty@loyalty.nc.

Government of the Province of the North: Gouvernement Provincial du Nord, BP 41, 98860 Koné, Grande-Terre; tel. 477100; fax 355475.

Government of the Province of the South: Hôtel de la Province Sud, Rue des Artifices, BP 4142, 98846 Nouméa; tel. 258000; fax 274900.

Legislature

ASSEMBLÉES PROVINCIALES

The three provinces each elect an autonomous provincial assembly, which, in turn, elects the President of the respective Provincial Government. The Assembly of the Province of the North has 15 members, that of the Province of the South 32 members and that of the Province of the Loyalty Islands seven members.

Election, 9 July 1995 (results by province)

Party	North	South	Loyalty Islands
RPCR	2	18	2
FLNKS	6	3	3
Une Nouvelle-Calédonie pour Tous (NCPT)	—	7	—
Union Nationale pour l'Indépendance (UNI)	5	—	—
Rassemblement pour une Calédonie dans la France (RCF)	—	2	—
Front National (FN)	—	2	—
Développer Ensemble Pour Construire l'Avenir (DEPCA)	2	—	—
Front pour le Développement des Iles Loyauté (FDIL)	—	—	1
Libération Kanak Socialiste (LKS)	—	—	1

Province of the North: President Léopold Jorédié (FLNKS).

Province of the South: President Jacques Lafleur (RPCR).

Province of the Loyalty Islands: President Nidoïsh Naisseline (LKS).

CONGRÈS TERRITORIAL

The members of the three Provincial Assemblies sit together, in Nouméa, as the Territorial Congress. There are, therefore, 54 members in total.

President: Harold Martin (RPCR).

Election, 9 July 1995 (results for the Territory as a whole)

Party	Votes	%	Seats
RPCR	25,883	39.49	22
FLNKS	13,660	20.84	12
NCPT	8,380	12.79	7
UNI	7,017	10.71	5
DEPCA	2,479	3.78	2
FN	2,343	3.57	2
RCF	2,280	3.48	2
KA	1,987	3.03	1
FDIL	1,510	2.30	1
Total	65,539	100.00	54

PARLEMENT

Deputies to the French National Assembly: JACQUES LAFLEUR (RPCR), PIERRE FROGIER (RPCR).

Representative to the French Senate: SIMON LOUECKHOTE (RPCR).

Political Organizations

Calédonie Demain: Nouméa; right-wing; comprises former adherents of the RPCR and the Front National; Leader BERNARD MARANT.

Congrès Populaire du Peuple Kanak: f. 1992; including fmr mems of the pro-independence Front Uni de Libération Kanak; Leader YANN CÉLÉNÉ UREGEÏ.

Fédération pour une Nouvelle Société Calédonienne (FNSC): 8 rue Gagarine, Nouméa; tel. 252395; f. 1979; Leader JEAN-PIERRE AÏFA; favours a degree of internal autonomy for New Caledonia; a coalition of the following parties:

Mouvement Wallisien et Futunien: f. 1979; Pres. FINAU MELITO.

Parti Républicain Calédonien (PRC): f. 1979; Leader LIONEL CHERRIER.

Union Démocratique (UD): f. 1968; Leader GASTON MORLET.

Union Nouvelle Calédonienne (UNC): f. 1977; Leader JEAN-PIERRE AÏFA.

Front Calédonien (FC): extreme right-wing; Leader M. SARRAN.

Front de Libération Nationale Kanak Socialiste (FLNKS): Nouméa; tel. 272599; f. 1984 (following dissolution of Front Indépendantiste); pro-independence; Pres. ROCK WAMYTAN; a grouping of the following parties:

Parti de Libération Kanak (PALIKA): f. 1975; 5,000 mems; Leaders PAUL NÉAOUTYINE, ELIE POIGOUNE, RAPHAEL MAPOU.

Parti Socialiste Calédonien (PSC): f. 1975; Leader M. VIOLETTE.

Rassemblement Démocratique Océanien (RDO): Nouméa; f. 1994 by breakaway faction of UO; supports Kanak sovereignty; Pres. ALOISIO SAKO.

Union Calédonienne (UC): f. 1952; 11,000 mems; Pres. BERNARD LEPEU; Sec.-Gen. DANIEL YEIWÉNÉ.

Union Progressiste Mélanésienne (UPM): f. 1974 as the Union Progressiste Multiraciale; 2,300 mems; Pres. VICTOR TUTUGORO; Sec.-Gen. RENÉ POROU.

Front National (FN): Nouméa; extreme right-wing; Leader GUY GEORGE.

Génération Calédonienne: f. 1995; youth-based; aims to combat corruption in public life; Pres. JEAN RENAUD POSAP.

Libération Kanak Socialiste (LKS): Maré, Loyalty Islands; moderate, pro-independence; Leader NIDOÏSH NAISSELINE.

Rassemblement pour la Calédonie dans la République (RPCR): 8 ave Foch, BP 306, Nouméa; tel. 282620; f. 1977; affiliated to the metropolitan Rassemblement pour la République (RPR); in favour of retaining the status quo in New Caledonia; Leader JACQUES LAFLEUR; a coalition of the following parties:

Centre des Démocrates Sociaux (CDS): f. 1971; Leader JEAN LÈQUES.

Parti Républicain (PR): Leader PIERRE MARESCA.

Une Nouvelle-Calédonie pour Tous (NCPT): f. 1995; Leader DIDIER LEROUX.

Union Océanienne (UO): Nouméa; f. 1989 by breakaway faction of RPCR; represents people whose origin is in the French Overseas Territory of Wallis and Futuna; conservative; Leader MICHEL HEMA.

Other political organizations participating in the elections of July 1995 included: **Développer Ensemble pour Construire l'Avenir, Front pour le Développement des Iles Loyauté, Kanaky Avenir** and **Union Nationale pour l'Indépendance.**

Judicial System

Court of Appeal: Palais de Justice, BP F4, 98848 Nouméa; tel. 279350; fax 269185; First Pres. OLIVIER AIMOT; Procurator-Gen. GÉRARD NÉDELLEC.

Court of the First Instance: Nouméa; Pres. JEAN PRADAL; Procurator of the Republic JEAN-LOUIS CATEZ. From January 1990 two subsidiary courts, with resident magistrates, were established at Koné (Province of the North) and Wé (Province of the Loyalty Islands).

Custom Consultative Council: Conseil Coutumier Territorial, Nouméa; f. 1990; consulted by Govt on all matters affecting land and Kanak tradition; mems: 40 authorities from eight custom areas; Pres. BERGE KAWA; Vice-Pres. JOSEPH PIDJOT.

Religion

The majority of the population is Christian, with Roman Catholics comprising about 59% of the total in 1989. About 3% of the inhabitants are Muslims.

CHRISTIANITY

The Roman Catholic Church

The Territory comprises a single archdiocese, with an estimated 105,601 adherents in 1995. The Archbishop participates in the Catholic Bishops' Conference of the Pacific, based in Fiji.

Archbishop of Nouméa: Most Rev. MICHEL-MARIE-BERNARD CALVET, Archevêché, BP 3, 4 rue Mgr-Fraysse, 98845 Nouméa; tel. 265353; fax 265352.

The Anglican Communion

Within the Church of the Province of Melanesia, New Caledonia forms part of the diocese of Vanuatu (q.v.). The Archbishop of the Province is the Bishop of Central Melanesia (resident in Honiara, Solomon Islands).

Protestant Churches

Eglise évangélique en Nouvelle-Calédonie et aux Iles Loyauté: BP 277, Nouméa; f. 1960; Pres. Rev. SAILALI PASSA; Gen. Sec. Rev. TELL KASARHEROU.

Other churches active in the Territory include the Assembly of God, the Free Evangelical Church, the Presbyterian Church and the Tahitian Evangelical Church.

The Press

Agri-Info: BP 111, Nouméa; every 2 months; official publ. of the Chambre d'Agriculture; circ. 3,000.

L'Avenir Calédonien: 10 rue Gambetta, Nouméa; organ of the Union Calédonienne; Dir PAÏTA GABRIEL.

Eglise de Nouvelle-Calédonie: BP 3, 98845 Nouméa; fax 265352; f. 1976; monthly; official publ. of the Roman Catholic Church; circ. 450.

Les Nouvelles Calédoniennes: 41–43 rue de Sébastopol, BP 179, Nouméa; tel. 272584; fax 281627; f. 1971; daily; Publr PHILIPPE HERSANT; Dir BENOÎT LUIZET; Editor DIDIER FLEAUX; circ. 18,500.

Télé 7 Jours: route de Vélodome, BP 2080, 98846 Nouméa Cédex; tel. 284598; weekly.

NEWS AGENCY

Agence France-Presse (AFP): 15 rue Docteur Guégan, 98800 Nouméa; tel. 263033; fax 278699; Correspondent FRANCK MADOEUF.

Publishers

Editions d'Art Calédoniennes: 3 rue Guynemer, BP 1626, Nouméa; tel. 277633; fax 281526; art, reprints, travel.

Les Editions du Devenir: 7 rue Mascart, Rivière Salée, BP 4481, Nouméa; tel. 285752; telex 3045; magazines, politics, tourism.

Broadcasting and Communications

TELECOMMUNICATIONS

Offices des Postes et Télécommunications: rue Porcheron, Nouméa.

RADIO

Radiodiffusion Française d'Outre-mer (RFO): BP 332, Nouméa Cédex; tel. 275327; fax 281252; f. 1942; 24 hours of daily programmes in French; Dir WALLES KOTRA; Editor-in-Chief FRANCIS ORNY.

Radio Djiido: 29 rue du Maréchal Juin, BP 14359, 98803 Nouméa Cédex; tel. 253515; fax 272187; Dir OCTAVE TOPNA; Man. NICOLE WAIA.

NRJ Nouvelle-Calédonie: 41–43 rue Sebastopol, BP 179, Nouméa; tel. 272584; fax 281627.

Radio Rythme Bleu: BP 578, Nouméa; tel. 254646; fax 284928.

TELEVISION

Télé Nouméa: Société Nationale de Radiodiffusion Française d'Outre-mer, BP G3, Nouméa; tel. 274327; telex 3052; fax 281252; f. 1965; transmits 10 hours daily; Dir WALLES KOTRA.

Canal Calédonie: 8 rue de Verneilh, Nouméa.

Finance

(cap. = capital; res = reserves; dep. = deposits; m. = million; brs = branches; amounts in CFP francs unless otherwise stated)

BANKING

Bank of Hawaii—Nouvelle-Calédonie: 21–25 ave de la Victoire, BP L3, 98849 Nouméa Cédex; tel. 257400; telex 3091; fax 274147; e-mail proger@boh.nc; internet http://www.boh.nc; f. 1974; owned by Bank of Hawaii (USA—92%) and Crédit Lyonnais (France—3%); cap. 1,477.7m., res 23,215m., dep. 23,720m. (Dec. 1997); Pres. MIKE ORD; Gen. Man. DANIEL OZOUX; 6 brs.

Banque Nationale de Paris Nouvelle-Calédonie (France): 37 ave Henri Lafleur, BP K3, Nouméa Cédex; tel. 258400; telex 3022; fax 258459; f. 1969 as Banque Nationale de Paris; present name adopted in 1978; cap. 30.0m. French francs, res 159.0m. French francs, dep. 1,927.0m. French francs (Dec. 1994); Pres. GÉRARD LOHIER; Gen. Man. JEAN TABARIES; 10 brs.

Banque Paribas Pacifique (Nouvelle-Calédonie): 33 rue de l'Alma, BP J3, Nouméa; tel. 275181; telex 3086; fax 275619; f. 1971; cap. 1,000.0m., res 109.5m., dep. 21,626.0m. (Dec. 1995); Chair. PIERRE MARTINAUD; Gen. Man. FRANÇOIS DAUGE.

Société Générale Calédonienne de Banque: 56 ave de la Victoire, BP G2, Nouméa Cédex; tel. 272264; telex 3067; fax 276245; f. 1981; cap. 825.0m., res 1,679.3m., dep. 32,980.7m. (Dec. 1995); Pres. JEAN-LOUIS MATTEI; Gen. Man. JOËL BREDELET; 11 brs.

Westpac Banking Corporation (Australia): 44 rue Alma, BP G5, 98848 Nouméa Cédex; tel. 256300; telex 3023; fax 256306; acquired operations of Banque Indosuez in New Caledonia in 1990; Man. GILLES THERRY; 12 brs.

Trade and Industry

DEVELOPMENT ORGANIZATIONS

Agence de Développement Economique Calédonien (ADECAL): 15 rue Guynemer, BP 2384, 98846 Nouméa Cédex; tel. 249077; fax 249087; e-mail adecal@offratel.nc; promotes investment in the islands; Dirs YANN PITOLLET, BENOÎT RENGADE.

Agence de Développement Rural et d'Aménagement Foncier (ADRAF): 1 rue de la Somme, BP 4228, Nouméa; tel. 284242; fax 284322; f. 1986, reorganized 1989; acquisition and redistribution of land; Chair. DOMINIQUE BUR; Dir-Gen. GÉRARD VLADYSLAV.

Institut Calédonien de Participation: Nouméa; f. 1989 to finance development projects and encourage the Kanak population to participate in the market economy.

CHAMBERS OF COMMERCE

Chambre d'Agriculture: BP 111, Nouméa; tel. 272056; fax 284587; f. 1909; 35 mems; Pres. ANDRÉ MAZURIER.

Chambre de Commerce et d'Industrie: BP M3, 98849 Nouméa Cédex; tel. 272551; fax 278114; f. 1879; 20 mems; Pres. FRANCIS GUILLEMIN; Gen. Man. GEORGES GIOVANNELLI.

STATE-OWNED INDUSTRIES

Société Minière du Sud-Pacifique (SMSP): Nouméa; 71% owned by Province of the North, 24% owned by Institut Calédonien de Participation; nickel-mining co; subsidiaries: Compagnie Maritime Calédonienne (stevedoring), Nouméa Nickel, Nord Industrie Services, and tourism cos Compagnie d'Investissement Touristiques, Nord Tourisme, Société d'Exploitation Malabou, Société d'Exploitation Koulnoué; Man. Dir ANDRÉ DANG; CEO RAPHAËL PIDJOT.

Société Le Nickel (SLN): Doniambo; subsidiary of the French state-owned mining conglomerate Eramet; nickel mining, processing and sales co; CEO YVES RAMBAUD.

EMPLOYERS' ORGANIZATION

Fédération Patronale de Nouvelle-Calédonie et Dépendances: Immeuble Jules Ferry, 1 rue de la Somme, BP 466, 98845 Nouméa Cédex; tel. 273525; fax 274037; f. 1936; represents the leading companies of New Caledonia in the defence of professional interests, co-ordination, documentation and research in socio-economic fields; Pres. JEAN RÉMI BURAGLIO; Sec.-Gen. ANNIE BEUSTES.

TRADE UNIONS

Confédération Générale du Travail–Force Ouvrière (CGT-FO): BP 4773, Nouméa; tel. 274950; fax 278202; Sec.-Gen. ROBERT FORT.

Confédération des Travailleurs Calédoniens: Nouméa; Sec.-Gen. R. JOYEUX; grouped with:

Fédération des Fonctionnaires: Nouméa; Sec.-Gen. GILBERT NOUVEAU.

Syndicat Général des Collaborateurs des Industries de Nouvelle Calédonie: Sec.-Gen. H. CHAMPIN.

Union Syndicale des Travailleurs Kanak et des Exploités (USTKE): BP 4372, Nouméa; tel. 277210; fax 277687; Leader LOUIS KOTRA UREGEÏ.

Union des Syndicats des Ouvriers et Employés de Nouvelle-Calédonie (USOENC): BP 2534, Nouméa; tel. 259640; fax 278544; Sec.-Gen. GASTON HMEUN.

Union Territoriale Force Ouvrière: 13 rue Jules Ferry, BP 4773, 98847 Nouméa; tel. 274950; fax 278202; f. 1982; Sec.-Gen. ROBERT FORT.

Transport

ROADS

In 1983 there was a total of 5,980 km of roads on New Caledonia island; 766 km were bitumen-surfaced, 589 km unsealed, 1,618 km stone-surfaced and 2,523 km tracks in 1980. The outer islands had a total of 470 km of roads and tracks in 1980.

SHIPPING

Most traffic is through the port of Nouméa. Passenger and cargo services, linking Nouméa to other towns and islands, are regular and frequent. There are plans to develop Nepoui, in the Province of the North, as a deep-water port and industrial centre.

Port Autonome de la Nouvelle-Calédonie: BP 14, Nouméa; tel. 275966; telex 3138; fax 275490; Port Man. PHILIPPE LAFLEUR.

Compagnie Wallisienne de Navigation: BP 1080, Nouméa; tel. 287222; fax 287388; Chair. RICHARD E. PEQUIGNOT; Man. Dir JEAN-YVES BOILEAU.

CIVIL AVIATION

There is an international airport, Tontouta, 47 km from Nouméa, and an internal network, centred on Magenta airport, which provides air services linking Nouméa to other towns and islands. Air France operates a service three times a week between Nouméa and Tokyo, and Corsair and Air Outremer a twice-weekly flight, from Paris to Nouméa.

Air Calédonie: BP 212, Nouméa; tel. 252339; fax 254869; f. 1954; services throughout New Caledonia; 263,674 passengers carried in 1996; turnover US $20m. in 1996; Pres. CHARLES LAVOIX; Chair. ALAIN BALLEREAU.

Air Calédonie International (Aircalin): 8 rue Frédéric Surleau, BP 3736, 98846 Nouméa Cédex; tel. 265500; fax 272772; f. 1983; 62% owned by Territorial Govt; services to Sydney, Brisbane and Melbourne (Australia), Auckland (New Zealand), Nadi (Fiji), Papeete (French Polynesia), Uvea (Wallis and Futuna), Port Vila (Vanuatu); CEO CHARLES LAVOIX; Man. Dir ALAIN BALLEREAU.

Tourism

An investment programme was begun in 1985 with the aim of developing and promoting tourism. In 1996 there were 91,121 visitors to New Caledonia, of whom 30.3% came from France, 29.6% from Japan, 15.8% from Australia and 7.4% from New Zealand. The industry earned US $102m. in 1994.

New Caledonia Tourism: Immeuble Manhattan, 39–41 rue de Verdun, BP 688, Nouméa; tel. 272632; fax 274623; f. 1990; international promotion of tourism in New Caledonia; Chair. GABY BRIAULT; Dir JEAN-MICHEL FOUTREIN.

WALLIS AND FUTUNA ISLANDS

Introductory Survey

Location, Climate, Language, Religion, Capital

The Territory of Wallis and Futuna comprises two groups of islands: the Wallis Islands, including Wallis Island (also known as Uvea) and 22 islets on the surrounding reef, and, to the south-east, Futuna (or Hooru), comprising the two small islands of Futuna and Alofi. The islands are located north-east of Fiji and west of Samoa. Temperatures are generally between about 23°C (73°F) and 30°C (86°F), and there is a cyclone season between October and March. French and Wallisian (Uvean), the indigenous Polynesian language, are spoken in the Territory, and the entire population is nominally Roman Catholic. The capital is Mata-Utu, on Wallis Island.

Recent History

The Wallis and Futuna Islands were settled first by Polynesian peoples, Wallis from Tonga and Futuna from Samoa. Three kingdoms had emerged by 1842, when a French protectorate was proclaimed, coinciding with a similar proclamation in Tahiti (now French Polynesia). Protectorate status was formalized in 1887 for Wallis and in 1888 for the two kingdoms of Futuna, but domestic law remained in force. The islands were never formally annexed, and nor were French law or representative institutions introduced, although Wallis and Futuna were treated as a dependency of New Caledonia. In 1959 the traditional Kings and chiefs requested integration into the French Republic. The islands formally became an Overseas Territory in July 1961, following a referendum in December 1959, in which 94.4% of the electorate requested this status (almost all the opposition was in Futuna, which itself recorded dissent from only 22.2% of the voters; Wallis was unanimous in its acceptance).

Although there is no movement in Wallis and Futuna seeking secession of the Territory from France (in contrast with the situation in the other French Pacific Territories, French Polynesia and New Caledonia), the two Kings whose kingdoms share the island of Futuna requested in November 1983, through the Territorial Assembly, that the island groups of Wallis and Futuna become separate Overseas Territories of France, arguing that the administration and affairs of the Territory had become excessively concentrated on Uvea (Wallis Island).

At elections to the 20-member Territorial Assembly in March 1982, the Rassemblement pour la République (RPR) and its allies won 11 seats, while the remaining nine were secured by candidates belonging to, or associated with, the Union pour la Démocratie Française (UDF). Later that year one member of the Lua Kae Tahi, a group affiliated to the metropolitan UDF, defected to the RPR group. In November 1983, however, three of the 12 RPR members joined the Lua Kae Tahi, forming a new majority. In the subsequent election for President of the Territorial Assembly, this 11-strong block of UDF-associated members supported the ultimately successful candidate, Falakiko Gata, even though he had been elected to the Territorial Assembly in 1982 as a member of the RPR.

In April 1985 Falakiko Gata formed a new political party, the Union Populaire Locale (UPL), which was committed to giving priority to local, rather than metropolitan, issues. At a meeting with the French Prime Minister in Paris in June, Falakiko Gata reaffirmed that it was in the Territory's interests to remain French and not to seek independence.

In 1987 a dispute broke out between two families both laying claim to the throne of Sigave, one of the two kingdoms on the island of Futuna. The conflict arose following the deposition of the former King, Sagato Keletaona, and his succession by Sosepho Vanaï. The intervention of the island's administrative authorities, who attempted to ratify Vanaï's accession to the throne, was condemned by the Keletaona family as an interference in the normal course of local custom, according to which such disputes are traditionally settled by a fight between the protagonists.

At elections to the Territorial Assembly held in March 1987, the UDF (together with affiliated parties) and the RPR each won seven seats. However, by forming an alliance with the UPL, the RPR maintained its majority, and Falakiko Gata was subsequently re-elected President. In October Gérard Lambotte replaced Jacques Le Hénaff as the islands' Chief Administrator, and in July 1988 was himself replaced by Roger Dumec. At elections for the French National Assembly in June 1988, Benjamin Brial was re-elected Deputy. However, when the result was contested by an unsuccessful candidate, Kamilo Gata, the election was investigated by the French Constitutional Council and the result declared invalid, owing to electoral irregularities. When the election was held again in January 1989, Kamilo Gata was elected Deputy, obtaining 57.4% of total votes.

In August 1989 members of the RPR/UPL majority grouping in the Territorial Assembly, led by Clovis Logologofolau (who had replaced Falakiko Gata as President of the Assembly), accused the Chief Administrator, Dumec, of abusing his powers by excluding the traditional chiefs and the Assembly majority from decision-making. In September 1990 a new Chief Administrator, Robert Pommies, was appointed. At the same time, Philippe Deblonde was appointed acting Chief Administrator.

Statistical information, gathered in 1990, showed that the emigration rate of Wallis and Futuna islanders had risen to over 50%. In October of that year 13,705 people (of whom 97% were Wallisians and Futunians) lived in the Territory, while 14,186 were resident in New Caledonia. According to the results, a proportion of the islanders had chosen to emigrate to other French Overseas Possessions or to metropolitan France. The principal reason for the increase was thought to be the lack of employment opportunities in the islands.

At elections to the Territorial Assembly in March 1992 the newly-founded Taumu'a Lelei secured 11 seats, while the RPR won nine. The new Assembly was remarkable for being the first since 1964 in which the RPR did not hold a majority. At elections to the French National Assembly in March 1993, Kamilo Gata was re-elected Deputy, obtaining 52.4% of total votes cast to defeat Clovis Logologofolau. In the same month an earthquake on Futuna resulted in the death of five people and the destruction of many buildings and roads.

In June 1994 the Union Locale Force Ouvrière organized a general strike in protest at the increasing cost of living in the Territory and the allegedly inadequate education system. It was reported that demonstrations continued for several days, during which the Territorial Assembly building was damaged in an arson attack.

In October 1994 it was reported that the King of Sigave, Lafaele Malau, had been deposed by a unanimous decision of the kingdom's chiefs. The action followed the appointment of two customary leaders to represent the Futunian community in New Caledonia, which had led to unrest among the inhabitants of Sigave. He was succeeded by Esipio Takasi.

At elections to the Territorial Assembly in December 1994 the RPR secured 10 seats, while a coalition group, Union pour Wallis et Futuna, won seven, and independent candidates three. Mikaele Tauhavili was subsequently elected President of the Assembly.

The refusal by 10 of the 20 members of the Territorial Assembly to adopt budgetary proposals in January 1996, led to appeals for the dissolution of the Government by France and the organization of new elections. The budget (which, at US $20m., was some US $4.5m. smaller than the previous year) aroused opposition for its apparent lack of provision for development funds, particularly for the islands' nascent tourist industry.

Elections to the Territorial Assembly took place on 16 March 1997. A participation rate of 87.2% was recorded at the poll, in which RPR candidates secured 14 seats and left-wing candidates (including independents and members of various political groupings) won six seats. Victor Brial, a representative of the RPR, was elected President of the Territorial Assembly. At the second round of elections to the French National Assembly, on 1 June, Brial defeated Kamilo Gata, obtaining 3,241 votes (51.3% of the total).

Government

The Territory of Wallis and Futuna is administered by a representative of the French Government, the Chief Administrator, who is assisted by the Territorial Assembly. The Assembly has 20 members and is elected for a five-year term. The three traditional kingdoms, from which the Territory was formed, one on Wallis and two sharing Futuna, have equal rights, although the kings' powers are limited. In addition, the Territory elects one Deputy to the French National Assembly in Paris and one Representative to the French Senate. The islands are also represented at the European Parliament.

Economic Affairs

In 1994 it was estimated that Wallis and Futuna's gross national product (GNP) per head was equivalent to US $3,000. Most monetary income in the islands is derived from government employment and remittances sent home by islanders employed in New Caledonia. Coconut products (chiefly copra) and handicrafts are the only significant export commodities, which together earned 0.2m. francs CFP in export revenue in 1985. Yams, taro, bananas, cassava and other food crops are also cultivated. In late 1995 the South Pacific Commission, now the Pacific Community (of which Wallis and Futuna is a member—see p. 232), agreed to undertake a study into the possibility of cultivating taro and breadfruit as export crops. Imports, which are provided mainly by metropolitan France and New Caledonia, cost 1,350m. francs CFP in 1985 and consisted principally of raw materials, manufactured goods and petroleum products. Imports from New Zealand cost $NZ5.6m. in 1996. Mineral fuels are the main source of electrical energy, although it is hoped that hydroelectric power can be developed, especially on Futuna.

In 1985 the President of the Territorial Assembly informed the French Government that, in his opinion, the policies relating to agricultural and fisheries development since 1960 had failed completely. It was hoped that these areas of the economy could be improved through new administrative arrangements, whereby development funding would be channelled through traditional chiefs.

In December 1986 almost all the cultivated vegetation on the island of Futuna, notably the banana plantations, was destroyed by a cyclone. In response to the cyclone damage, the French Government announced, in February 1987, that it was to provide exceptional aid of 55m. French francs to alleviate the situation. No copra was exported in 1987, but export levels subsequently recovered. In August 1989 the French Prime Minister visited the islands, inaugurated a new earth station for satellite communications, and announced that additional funds were to be made available for the development of agriculture and fisheries. The fishing industry benefited from the success of a three-month project in late 1991 involving Fijian vessels operating in the Territory's exclusive fishing zone. The total catch was estimated at 170 metric tons in 1995, compared with 70 metric tons in 1991. The islands also benefited from an increase in building activity and public works in the early 1990s. Plans, under consideration in the mid-1990s, to develop a small tourist industry on the islands were prompted in part by the expectation that France was to reduce its financial assistance to the Territory.

Social Welfare

In 1990 there was one hospital on Wallis Island, with a total of 60 beds, and two health centres on Futuna Island, where a 21-bed hospital was under construction. In 1982 there were four physicians working in the islands.

Education

In 1987 there were 13 state-financed primary and lower-secondary schools in Wallis and Futuna, with a total of 4,622 pupils.

Public Holidays

1998: 1 January (New Year's Day), 13 April (Easter Monday), 4 May (for Labour Day), 8 May (Liberation Day), 21 May (Ascension Day), 1 June (Whit Monday), 14 July (Fall of the Bastille), 11 November (Armistice Day), 25 December (Christmas Day).

1999: 1 January (New Year's Day), 5 April (Easter Monday), 3 May (for Labour Day), 8 May (Liberation Day), 13 May (Ascension Day), 24 May (Whit Monday), 14 July (Fall of the Bastille), 11 November (Armistice Day), 25 December (Christmas Day).

Weights and Measures

The metric system is in force.

Statistical Survey

AREA AND POPULATION

Area (sq km): 274. *By island:* Uvea (Wallis Island) 60, Other Wallis Islands 99; Futuna Island 64, Alofi Island 51.

Population (census of 15 February 1983): 12,408: Wallis Islands 8,084, Futuna Island 4,324, Alofi Island uninhabited; (October 1990 census): 13,705 (males 6,829, females 6,876): Wallis Islands 8,973, Futuna Island 4,732 (Alo 2,860, Sigave 1,872); 14,186 Wallisians and Futunians resided in New Caledonia. Total population 15,000 (official estimate) at mid-1996.

Density (1996): 54.7 per sq km.

Principal Town: Mata-Utu (capital), population 815 at 1983 census.

AGRICULTURE, ETC.

Principal Crops (FAO estimates, '000 metric tons, 1995): Cassava 2; Yams 1; Taro 2; Other roots and tubers 1; Coconuts 2; Bananas 4; Other fruit 5; Vegetables and melons 1. Source: FAO, *Production Yearbook*.

Livestock (FAO estimates, '000 head, year ending September 1995): Pigs 25; Goats 7. Source: FAO, *Production Yearbook*.

Livestock Products (FAO estimates, metric tons, 1995): Hen eggs 33; Honey 11. Source: FAO, *Production Yearbook*.

Fishing (metric tons, live weight): 150 in 1993; 193 in 1994; 170 in 1995. Source: FAO, *Yearbook of Fishery Statistics*.

FINANCE

Currency and Exchange Rates: see French Polynesia.

Budget: US $24.5m. in 1995; US $20m. in 1996.

Aid from France (1982): 55,000,000 French francs.

Money Supply: (million French francs, 1995): Currency in circulation 273; Demand deposits 1,060; Total money 1,333. Source: Institut National de la Statistique et des Etudes Economiques.

EXTERNAL TRADE

1985 (francs CFP): *Imports:* 1,350m. *Exports:* 0.21m.

TRANSPORT

Shipping: *Merchant Fleet* (vessels registered, '000 grt, at 31 December 1996): 92.2. Source: Lloyd's Register of Shipping.

Civil Aviation (Uvea, 1980): aircraft arrivals and departures 581; freight handled 171 metric tons; passenger arrivals 4,555, passenger departures 4,300; mail loaded and unloaded 72 metric tons.

TOURISM

Visitors: 400 in 1985.

Hotels (1990): Number 3; Rooms 30.

COMMUNICATIONS MEDIA

Telephones (1994): 1,000 main lines in use.

Telefax Stations (1993): 90 in use.

Source: UN, *Statistical Yearbook*.

EDUCATION

Primary and Lower Secondary (1987): 13 state-financed schools, 4,622 pupils.

Directory

The Constitution

The Territory of the Wallis and Futuna Islands is administered according to a statute of 1961, and subsidiary legislation, under the Constitution of the Fifth Republic. The Statute declares the Wallis and Futuna Islands to be an Overseas Territory of the French Republic, of which it remains an integral part. The Statute established an administration, a Council of the Territory, a Territorial Assembly and national representation. The administrative, political and social evolution envisaged by, and enacted under, the Statute is intended to effect a smooth integration of the three customary kingdoms with the new institutions of the Territory. The Kings are assisted by ministers and the traditional chiefs. The Chief Administrator, appointed by the French Government, is the representative of the State in the Territory and is responsible for external affairs, defence, law and order, financial and educational affairs. The Chief Administrator is required to consult with the Council of the Territory, which has six members: three by right (the Kings of Wallis, Sigave and Alo) and three appointed by the Chief Administrator upon the advice of the Territorial Assembly. This Assembly assists in the administration of the Territory; there are 20 members elected on a common roll, on the basis of universal adult suffrage, for a term of up to five years. The Territorial Assembly elects, from among its own membership, a President to lead it. The Territory elects national representatives (one Deputy to the National Assembly, one Senator and one Economic and Social Councillor) and votes for representatives to the European Parliament in Strasbourg.

The Government

(February 1998)

Chief Administrator (Administrateur Supérieur): LÉON ALEXANDRE LEGRAND (appointed August 1994).

CONSEIL DU TERRITOIRE

Chair: Chief Administrator.

Members by Right: King of Wallis, King of Sigave, King of Alo.

Appointed Members: VITOLIO VAIVAIKAVA (Kalae Kivalu), ATOLOTO UHILA (Kulitea), LITA MULIAKAAKA.

GOVERNMENT OFFICE

Government Headquarters: Bureau de l'Administrateur Supérieur, Mata-Utu, Uvea, Wallis Islands, Wallis and Futuna (via Nouméa, New Caledonia); tel. 722727; telex 5074; fax 722324; all departments.

Legislature

ASSEMBLÉE TERRITORIALE

The Territorial Assembly has 20 members and is elected for a five-year term. The most recent general election took place on 16 March 1997, at which RPR candidates secured a total of 14 seats and various left-wing candidates (including independents) won six seats.

President: VICTOR BRIAL (RPR).

PARLEMENT

Deputy to the French National Assembly: VICTOR BRIAL (RPR).

Representative to the French Senate: SOSEFO MAKAPE PAPILIO (RPR).

The Kingdoms

WALLIS

(Capital: Mata-Utu on Uvea)

Lavelua, King of Wallis: TOMASI KULIMOETOKE.

Council of Ministers: Prime Minister (Kivalu) and five other ministers.

The Kingdom of Wallis is divided into three districts (Hihifo, Hihake, Mua), and its traditional hierarchy includes three district chiefs (Faipule) and 20 village chiefs (Pule).

SIGAVE

(Capital: Sigave on Futuna)

Tuisigave, King of Sigave: ESIPIO TAKASI.

Council of Ministers: five ministers, chaired by the King.

The Kingdom of Sigave is located in the north of the island of Futuna; there are five village chiefs.

ALO

(Capital: Alo on Futuna)

Tuigaifo, King of Alo: LOMANO MUSULAMU.

Council of Ministers: five ministers, chaired by the King.

The Kingdom of Alo comprises the southern part of the island of Futuna and the entire island of Alofi. There are seven village chiefs.

Political Organizations

Mouvement des Radicaux de Gauche (MRG): c/o Assemblée Territoriale, Mata-Utu, Uvea, Wallis Islands, Wallis and Futuna (via Nouméa, New Caledonia); left-wing.

Rassemblement pour la République (RPR): c/o Assemblée Territoriale, Mata-Utu, Uvea, Wallis Islands, Wallis and Futuna (via Nouméa, New Caledonia); Gaullist; Territorial Leader CLOVIS LOGOLOGOFOLAU.

Taumu'a Lelei (Bright Future): c/o Assemblée Territoriale, Mata-Utu, Uvea, Wallis Islands, Wallis and Futuna (via Nouméa, New Caledonia); f. 1992; Leader SOANE MANI UHILA.

Union Populaire Locale (UPL): c/o Assemblée Territoriale, Mata-Utu, Uvea, Wallis Islands, Wallis and Futuna (via Nouméa, New Caledonia); f. 1985; emphasizes importance of local issues; strongest in Futuna; Leader FALAKIKO GATA.

Union pour la Démocratie Française (UDF): c/o Assemblée Territoriale, Mata-Utu, Uvea, Wallis Islands, Wallis and Futuna (via Nouméa, New Caledonia); centrist; based on Uvean (Wallis) support.

Religion

Almost all of the inhabitants profess Christianity and are adherents of the Roman Catholic Church.

CHRISTIANITY

The Roman Catholic Church

The Territory comprises a single diocese, suffragan to the archdiocese of Nouméa (New Caledonia). The diocese estimated that the entire population were adherents, and that this totalled some 14,880 in number on 31 December 1995. The Bishop participates in the Catholic Bishops' Conference of the Pacific, currently based in Fiji.

Bishop of Wallis and Futuna: Mgr LOLESIO FUAHEA, Evêché, Lano, BP G6, Mata-Utu, Uvea, Wallis Islands, Wallis and Futuna (via Nouméa, New Caledonia); tel. 722932; fax 722783.

Broadcasting and Communications

RADIO AND TELEVISION

Radiodiffusion Française d'Outre-mer (RFO): RFO Wallis et Futuna, BP 102, 97911 Mata-Utu, Uvea, Wallis Islands, Wallis and Futuna (via Nouméa, New Caledonia); tel. 722020; fax 722346; transmitters at Mata-Utu (Uvea) and Alo (Futuna); programmes broadcast 24 hours daily in Uvean (Wallisian), Futunian and French; a television service on Uvea, transmitting for 12 hours daily in French, began operation in 1986; a television service on Futuna was inaugurated in December 1994; Man. JOSEPH BLASCO; Head of Information BERNARD JOYEUX.

Trade and Industry

TRADE UNION

Union Locale Force Ouvrière: BP 46, Mata-Utu, Uvea, Wallis Islands, Wallis and Futuna (via Nouméa, New Caledonia); tel. 721732; fax 721732; Sec.-Gen. MIKAELE TUI.

Transport

ROADS

Uvea has a few kilometres of road, one route circling the island, and there is also a road circling the island of Futuna; the only surfaced roads are in Mata-Utu.

SHIPPING

Mata-Utu serves as the seaport of Uvea and the Wallis Islands, while Sigave is the only port on Futuna.

Compagnie Wallisienne de Navigation (CWN): Kalaétoa, BP 72, Mata-Utu, Uvea, Wallis Islands, Wallis and Futuna (via Nouméa, New Caledonia); inter-island services and to Nouméa (New Caledonia), Port Vila (Vanuatu) and Brisbane (Australia); 1 vessel.

AMACAL (General Agent): POB 1080, Nouméa, New Caledonia; tel. 287222; fax 287388.

CIVIL AVIATION

There is an international airport in Hihifo district on Uvea, about 5 km from Mata-Utu. Air Calédonie (New Caledonia) operates three flights a week from Wallis to Futuna, and one flight a week from Wallis to Nouméa (New Caledonia); Air Calédonie International also serves Wallis and Futuna. The airport on Futuna is in the south-east, in the Kingdom of Alo.

Tourism

Tourism remains undeveloped. There are four small hotels and a guest-house on Uvea, Wallis Islands. In 1985 there were some 400 tourist visitors, in total, to the islands. There is no commercial accommodation for visitors on Futuna.

GABON

Introductory Survey

Location, Climate, Language, Religion, Flag, Capital

The Gabonese Republic is an equatorial country on the west coast of Africa, with Equatorial Guinea and Cameroon to the north and the Congo to the south and east. The climate is tropical, with an average annual temperature of 26°C (79°F) and an average annual rainfall of 2,490 mm (98 ins). The official language is French, but Fang (in the north) and Bantu dialects (in the south) are also widely spoken. About 60% of the population are Christians, mainly Roman Catholics. Most of the remainder follow animist beliefs. The national flag (proportions 4 by 3) has three equal horizontal stripes, of green, yellow and blue. The capital is Libreville.

Recent History

Formerly a province of French Equatorial Africa, Gabon was granted internal autonomy in November 1958, and proceeded to full independence on 17 August 1960 with Léon M'Ba, leader of the Bloc démocratique gabonais (BDG), as Head of State. He was elected President of the Republic in 1961. In February 1964 M'Ba was deposed in a military coup, but was reinstated after French military intervention. At elections in April the BDG secured a majority of seats in the National Assembly. During the next two years Gabon effectively became a one-party state: most opposition members of the Assembly joined the BDG, which contested the March 1967 elections unopposed. M'Ba died in November and was succeeded by the Vice-President, Albert-Bernard Bongo. In March 1968 Bongo announced the formal creation of a one-party state and a new ruling party, the Parti démocratique gabonais (PDG).

Gabon enjoyed political stability in the 1970s. Legislative and presidential elections took place in February 1973; all PDG candidates for the National Assembly, and Bongo, the sole candidate for the presidency, were elected with 99.56% of the votes cast. In September he announced his conversion to Islam, adopting the forename Omar. In April 1975 Bongo abolished the office of Vice-President, appointing Léon Mébiame to the new post of Prime Minister.

In December 1979 Bongo was re-elected for another seven-year term as President, securing 99.96% of the votes cast. Independent candidates were permitted to contest legislative elections held in February 1980; however, members of the PDG retained all seats in the National Assembly. In August 1981 Bongo relinquished the title of Head of Government (thereafter conferred upon the Prime Minister, Léon Mébiame) and his ministerial portfolios.

A moderate opposition group, the Mouvement de redressement national (MORENA), emerged in November 1981 and demanded the restoration of a multi-party system. However, Bongo maintained his commitment to one-party rule. In March 1985 PDG candidates obtained 99.5% of votes cast at elections to the National Assembly. In November 1986 Bongo was re-elected for a further seven-year term, with 99.97% of the vote. (A MORENA candidate who contested the election was prevented from conducting a campaign.)

In May 1989 the Chairman of MORENA, Fr Paul M'Ba Abessole, visited Gabon, and, after a meeting with Bongo, announced that he and many of his supporters (who in 1985 had formed a government-in-exile in Paris) would return to Gabon. In January 1990 representatives of MORENA announced that M'Ba Abessole had been dismissed from the leadership of the movement, following his declaration of support for the Government. M'Ba Abessole subsequently formed a breakaway faction, known as MORENA des bûcherons (renamed Rassemblement national des bûcherons in 1991 to avoid confusion with the rival MORENA—originels.).

A number of arrests took place in October 1989, following an alleged conspiracy to overthrow the Government. It was claimed that the plot had been instigated by Pierre Mamboundou, the leader of the Union du peuple gabonais (UPG, an opposition movement based in Paris). Further arrests were made in November, after the alleged discovery of a second plot to overthrow the Government.

In early 1990 a series of strikes and demonstrations by students and workers reflected increasing public discontent, following the imposition of economic austerity measures. In February a 'special commission for democracy' (which had been established by the PDG in January) submitted a report condemning Gabon's single-party political system. Bongo subsequently announced that extensive political reforms were to be introduced and proposed that the ruling party be replaced by a new organization, to be known as the Rassemblement social-démocrate gabonais (RSDG). However, strike action continued in a number of sectors, resulting in severe disruption.

In early March 1990 a joint session of the Central Committee of the PDG and the National Assembly ruled that legislative elections, which had been scheduled for April, be postponed to allow time for the Constitution to be amended. On 9 March the Political Bureau of the PDG announced that a multi-party system was to be introduced, under the supervision of the RSDG, at the end of a five-year transitional period. A national conference was convened in late March to determine the programme for the transfer to multi-party democracy. The conference (which was attended by representatives of more than 70 political organizations, as well as professional bodies and other special interest groups) rejected Bongo's proposals for a transitional period of political reform under the aegis of the RSDG, and demanded the immediate establishment of a multi-party system and the formation of a new government, which would hold office only until legislative elections could take place. Bongo acceded to the decisions of the conference, and in late April Casimir Oye Mba, the Governor of the Banque des états de l'Afrique centrale, was appointed Prime Minister of a transitional administration, which included several opposition members).

On 22 May 1990 the Central Committee of the PDG and the National Assembly approved constitutional changes that would facilitate the transition to a multi-party political system. The existing presidential mandate (effective until January 1994) was to be respected; thereafter, elections to the presidency would be contested by more than one candidate, and the tenure of office would be reduced to five years, renewable only once. At the same time, Bongo resigned as Secretary-General of the PDG, claiming that this role was now incompatible with his position as Head of State. In the same month, however, the death, in suspicious circumstances, of Joseph Rendjambe, the Secretary-General of the opposition Parti gabonais du progrès (PGP), provoked violent demonstrations in protest at Bongo's alleged complicity in the death. A national curfew was imposed in response to the increasing unrest, while French troops were briefly deployed in Gabon, to protect the interests of the 20,000 resident French nationals, and several hundred Europeans were evacuated. A state of emergency was imposed in Port-Gentil and its environs, and at least two deaths were reported after Gabonese security forces intervened to restore order. It was announced in early June that the French military reinforcements were to be withdrawn. The national curfew was ended in early July, although the state of emergency remained in force until mid-August in the area surrounding Port-Gentil.

Legislative elections were scheduled for 16 and 23 September 1990: however, only political parties which had registered during the national conference in March were allowed to present candidates. The first round of the elections was disrupted by violent protests by voters who claimed that electoral fraud was being practised, to the advantage of the PDG. Following allegations by opposition parties of widespread electoral malpractices, results in 32 constituencies were declared invalid, although the election of 58 candidates (of whom 36 were members of the PDG) was confirmed. The interim Government subsequently conceded that electoral irregularities had taken place, and further voting was postponed until 21 and 28 October. A commission, representing both the PDG and opposition parties, was established to supervise polling. At the elections the PDG won an overall majority in the 120-member National Assembly, with 62 seats, while opposition candidates secured 55 seats.

On 27 November 1990 the formation of a government of national unity, under Casimir Oye Mba, was announced. Sixteen posts were allocated to members of the PDG, while the remaining eight portfolios were distributed among members of five opposition parties. A new draft Constitution, which was promulgated on 22 December, endorsed reforms that had been included in the transitional Constitution, introduced in May. Further measures included the proposed establishment of an upper house, to be known as the Senate, which was to control the balance and regulation of power. A Constitutional Council was to replace the administrative chamber of the Supreme Court, and a National Communications Council was to be formed to ensure the impartial treatment of information by the state media.

The final composition of the National Assembly was determined in March 1991, when elections took place in five constituencies, where the results had been annulled, owing to alleged malpractice. Following the completion of the elections, the PDG held a total of 66 seats in the National Assembly, while various opposition groups held 54 seats. The two most prominent opposition movements, the PGP and the Rassemblement national des bûcherons (RNB), held 19 and 17 seats respectively.

In May 1991 six opposition parties formed an alliance, known as the Co-ordination de l'opposition démocratique (COD), in protest at the delay in the implementation of the new Constitution. The COD also demanded the appointment of a new Prime Minister, the abolition of certain institutions under the terms of the Constitution, and the liberalization of the state-controlled media. Following a general strike, organized by the COD, Bongo announced the resignation of the Council of Ministers, and declared that he was prepared to implement fully the new Constitution. He also claimed that, in accordance with the Constitution, several institutions, including the High Court of Justice, had been dissolved, and that a Constitutional Court and a National Communications Council had been established. However, opposition parties within the COD refused to be represented in a new government of national unity, of which Oye Mba was appointed as Prime Minister. Later that month opposition deputies who had taken part in the boycott of the National Assembly resumed parliamentary duties. On 22 June Oye Mba appointed a new coalition Government, in which 14 members of the previous Council of Ministers retained their portfolios. Members of MORENA–originels, the Union socialiste gabonaise (USG) and the Association pour le socialisme au Gabon (APSG) were also represented in the Government.

In February 1992 MORENA–originels, the USG and the Parti socialiste gabonais formed an alliance within the COD, known as the Forum africain pour la reconstruction (FAR). In the same month a general strike, which was organized by the RNB (without the support of other opposition groups), in an attempt to oblige the Government to comply with the demands presented by the COD, was only partially observed. Later in February the Government announced that a multi-party presidential election, would take place in December 1993; a population census was to be conducted prior to the election.

In mid-February 1992 a meeting of supporters of the RNB was violently suppressed by security forces. In the same month the university in Libreville was closed, and a ban on political gatherings and demonstrations was imposed, following protests by students against inadequate financing. Later in February the COD organized a one-day general strike in Port-Gentil (which was only partially observed), followed by a one-day campaign of civil disobedience which suspended economic activity in Port-Gentil and Libreville. At the end of February the Government reopened the university, and ended the ban on political gatherings and demonstrations. In March, however, the COD instigated a further one-day campaign of civil disobedience in Libreville, following the violent suppression of a demonstration by teachers who were demanding improvements in salaries and working conditions. In early April the PDG organized a pro-Government demonstration, in an attempt to gain public support.

In early July 1992 the National Assembly adopted a new electoral code (which had been submitted by the Government), despite protests by the FAR that the Government had failed to comply with the demands presented by the COD in October 1991. Later in July a motion of censure against the Government, proposed by opposition deputies in the National Assembly in response to the postponement of local government elections, was defeated. The Council of Ministers was reshuffled in August, and in December three members of the PDG, including a former minister, were expelled from the party, after establishing a faction, known as the Cercle des libéraux réformateurs (CLR).

Social unrest continued during the first half of 1993. In April security forces were dispatched to restore order, after protesters blockaded roads in central and southern Gabon, in support of demands for improved social infrastructure. In the same month Jules Bourdès-Ogouliguendé (who had resigned from the PDG in January) relinquished his post as President of the National Assembly, prior to standing as a candidate in the forthcoming presidential election. In July Bongo reorganized the Council of Ministers, following the resignation of the Minister of Labour, Employment, Professional Training and Human Resources, Simon Oyono Aba'a, who had been nominated as the presidential candidate of MORENA–originels. In September the Government established a commission to supervise the organization of the presidential election, which was scheduled for 5 December, and was to be followed by local government elections. In October Bongo announced that he was to contest the presidential election; by the end of that month 16 candidates had emerged, including the leader of the RNB, M'Ba Abessole, the leader of the PGP, Pierre-Louis Agondjo-Okawé, and the former Prime Minister, Léon Mébiame.

In early November 1993 five political associations, the PDG, the USG, the APSG, the CLR and the Parti de l'unité du peuple gabonais, agreed to support Bongo's candidacy in the presidential election, while eight opposition candidates established an informal alliance, known as the Convention des forces du changement. Later in the same month a number of demonstrations were staged by members of the opposition, in support of demands for the revision of the electoral register. Clashes between opposition and government supporters ensued, following opposition allegations that irregularities in the electoral register indicated deliberate malpractice on the part of the Government. In early December the Government agreed to revise the register in part, but rejected opposition demands that the election be postponed.

At the presidential election, which took place on 5 December 1993, Bongo was re-elected, winning 51.18% of votes cast, while M'Ba Abessole secured 26.51% of the votes. The official announcement of the results prompted rioting by opposition supporters, in which several foreign nationals were attacked (apparently as a result of dissatisfaction with international observers, who declared that no electoral irregularities had taken place). Five deaths were reported after security forces suppressed the unrest, and a national curfew and state of alert were subsequently imposed. M'Ba Abessole, however, claimed that he had won the election, and formed a High Council of the Republic, later redesignated as the High Council of Resistance (HCR), which included the majority of opposition presidential candidates, and a parallel government. Despite the reports by international observers that the elections had been conducted fairly, the opposition appealed to the Constitutional Court to annul the results, on the grounds that the Government had perpetrated electoral malpractice. In mid-December Bongo condemned M'Ba Abessole's formation of a parallel administration, and invited the other candidates who had contested the election to participate in a government of national consensus. As a result of the administrative confusion, local government elections, which were due to take place in late December, were postponed until March 1994. (In February 1994 they were further postponed, to August).

In early January 1994 the USA criticized Bongo's administration for alleged infringement of human rights, after three opposition leaders, including two presidential candidates, were prevented from leaving the country. Later that month the Constitutional Court ruled against the appeal by the opposition and endorsed the election results. On 22 January Bongo was officially inaugurated as President. In mid-February the national curfew and the state of alert, which had been in force since December 1993, were repealed, but later that month were reimposed, after a general strike, in support of demands for an increase in salaries to compensate for a devaluation of the CFA franc in January (see Economic Affairs), degenerated into violence. Security forces destroyed the transmitters of a radio station owned by the RNB (which had supported the strike), and attacked M'Ba Abessole's private residence, resulting in clashes with protesters. Strike action was suspended after four days, following negotiations between the Government and trade unions; nine people had been killed during that period, according to official figures (although the opposition claimed that a total of 38 had died). At the end of February 1994 the Minister of

State Control in charge of Parastatal Affairs resigned from the Government and from the PDG, owing to disagreement with the increasingly authoritarian stance adopted by Bongo.

In March 1994 Oye Mba resigned and dissolved the Council of Ministers. Later that month he was reappointed as Prime Minister, and, following the opposition's refusal to participate in a government of national unity, formed a 38-member administration, solely comprising representatives of the presidential majority (apart from one member of the PGP, who was expected to be expelled from that party). The size of the new Government, in view of the deterioration of the economy, prompted widespread criticism, and two of the newly-appointed ministers subsequently refused to assume their allocated posts, apparently owing to disagreement regarding the composition of the portfolios. In the same month the National Assembly approved a constitutional amendment that provided for the establishment of a Senate (which the opposition had resisted) and repealed legislation prohibiting unsuccessful presidential candidates from participating in the Government within a period of 18 months. In June opposition parties agreed to a further postponement of the local government elections, to early 1995. In August opposition parties announced that they were prepared to participate in a coalition government, on condition that it was installed as a transitional organ pending legislative elections. In September negotiations between the Government and opposition took place in Paris, under the auspices of the Organization of African Unity (OAU see p. 215), in order to resolve remaining differences concerning the results of the presidential election and the proposed formation of a government of national unity. In mid-September the RNB, which was attending the discussions, indicated that it would refuse to join a coalition government.

At the end of September 1994 an agreement was reached, as a result of the Paris meetings, whereby a transitional coalition government was to be installed, with local government elections scheduled to take place after a period of one year, followed by legislative elections six months later; the electoral code was to be revised and an independent electoral commission established, in an effort to ensure that the elections be conducted fairly. In early October Oye Mba resigned from office and dissolved the Council of Ministers. Shortly afterwards Bongo appointed Dr Paulin Obame-Nguema, a member of the PDG who had served in former administrations, as Prime Minister. Obame-Nguema subsequently formed a 27-member Council of Ministers, which included six opposition members. The composition of the new Government was, however, immediately criticized by the opposition, on the grounds that it was entitled to one-third of ministerial portfolios in proportion to the number of opposition deputies in the National Assembly; the HCR announced that the opposition would boycott the new administration, which, it claimed, was in violation of the Paris accord. Four opposition members consequently refused to accept the portfolios allocated to them, although two of these finally agreed to join the Government. (The portfolios that remained vacant were later assigned to a further two opposition members.) Following the inauguration of the Council of Ministers in early November, a motion expressing confidence in the new Prime Minister was adopted by 99 of 118 votes cast in the National Assembly. In the same month associates of Bongo established an informal grouping, known as the Mouvement des amis de Bongo.

In January 1995 controversy emerged over the extent of the authority vested in the National Assembly, after members of the HCR refused to participate in the drafting of the new electoral code until the Paris agreement was ratified. The Constitutional Court subsequently ruled that the National Assembly was not empowered, under the terms of the Constitution, to ratify the agreement. In early February, however, opposition deputies ended a boycott of the National Assembly, following a further ruling by the Constitutional Court that the National Assembly was entitled to act as a parliamentary body, pending the installation of a Senate after the legislative elections in 1996, but that the constitutional provisions adopted under the terms of the Paris accord would require endorsement by referendum. Following a declaration by the authorities that all illegal immigrants remaining in Gabon by mid-February would be arrested, some 55,000 foreign nationals left the country by the stipulated date. In April Bongo announced that a referendum to endorse the constitutional amendments would take place in June. In the same month, in accordance with the Paris accord, the Cabinet approved legislation providing for the release of prisoners detained on charges involving state security. Later in April Gabon withdrew its ambassador in Paris, in protest at reports by the French media regarding Bongo's alleged involvement with prostitutes; a number of demonstrations in support of Bongo took place in Libreville. Government efforts to prohibit two pro-opposition newspapers, which had published French press reports considered to be critical of Bongo, were rejected by the National Communications Council. At the national referendum (which had been postponed until 24 July), the constitutional amendments were approved by 96.5% of votes cast, with 63% of the electorate participating. In September 1995, following dissent within the UPG, Sébastien Mamboundou Mouyama, the Minister of Social Affairs and National Solidarity, was elected party Chairman, replacing Pierre Mamboundou. However, the latter subsequently regained the leadership of the UPG. (Mamboundou Mouyama formed a new political party, the Mouvement alternatif, in August 1996.)

During early 1996 opposition parties criticized the Government for delaying the implementation of the electoral timetable contained in the Paris accord. At the beginning of May, following a meeting attended by all the officially recognized political parties, Bongo agreed to establish a National Electoral Commission to formulate a timetable for local, legislative and senatorial elections, in consultation with all the official parties. It was also decided that access to state-controlled media and election funding should be equitably divided. On 20 May 1996 the National Assembly's mandate expired, and Obame-Nguema's Government resigned at the beginning of June, in accordance with the Paris accord. Bongo, however, rejected the resignation on the grounds that the Government should, before leaving office, organize the elections and finalize pending agreements with the IMF and the World Bank. At the beginning of October the National Electoral Commission adopted a timetable for legislative elections: the first round was to take place on 17 November, with a second round scheduled for 1 December. HCR representatives denounced the timetable, withdrew their participation from the commission and demanded the postponement of the local and legislative elections. In mid-October Pierre-Claver Maganga Moussavou, the leader of the PSD, was forced to resign from the Government, following his condemnation of the electoral timetable. The Chairman of the HCR claimed that the 'dismissal' was a violation of the Paris accord. Later that month a minor reshuffle of the Council of Ministers was effected. Meanwhile, the Government announced the suspension of salary payments for teachers, who had been on strike since 1 October in protest against the Government's suspension of their housing allowances. The teachers' unions subsequently announced their intention to seek legal redress.

Organizational problems disrupted the local elections, which were held on 20 October 1996, having been postponed twice previously; according to reports, only 15% of the electorate participated. The PDG gained control of the majority of the municipalities, although the PGP secured victory in Port-Gentil, while the RNB was successful in the north of the country. Elections in Fougamou (where voting had not taken place) and Libreville (where the results had been invalidated) were eventually rescheduled for 24 November, although the RNB demanded the validation of the original results. On 24 November the RNB secured 62 of the 98 seats available in Libreville; M'Ba Abessole was subsequently elected mayor.

Legislative elections were rescheduled on several occasions, owing to the delay in the release of the local election results and the failure to revise electoral registers in time. The first round of the elections took place on 15 December 1996, without major incidents. Later that month it was reported that the PDG had obtained 47 of the 55 seats that were decided in the first round of voting. The opposition disputed the results, and there were demands for protest marches and a boycott of the second round of voting. The PDG secured a substantial majority of the seats decided in the second round, which was held on 29 December, winning 84 seats, while the RNB obtained seven, the PGP six and independent candidates four, with the remaining 14 seats shared by the CLR, the UPG, the USG and others. Polling was unable to proceed for the five remaining seats, and results in a number of other constituencies were later annulled, owing to irregularities. (Following by-elections held in August 1997, during which five people were reportedly killed in violent incidents in north-east Gabon, the PDG held 88 seats, the PGP nine and the RNB five.) Guy Ndzouba Ndama was elected President of the new National Assembly. Following the legislative elections, the Prime Minister and his Council of Ministers resigned on 24 January 1997, in accordance with the terms of the Constitution. Obame-Nguema was reappointed Prime

Minister on 27 January, and a new Council of Ministers, dominated by members of the PDG, was announced on the following day. The PGP, the main opposition party represented in the National Assembly, had refused to participate in the new Government.

Elections to the new Senate took place on 26 January and 9 February 1997, with senators to be elected by members of municipal councils and departmental assemblies. The PDG won 53 of the Senate's 91 seats, while the RNB secured 20 seats, the PGP four, the Alliance démocratique et républicaine (ADERE) three, the CLR one, and the RDP one, with independent candidates obtaining nine seats. The results for a number of seats were annulled, however, and in subsequent by-elections, held later that year, the PDG increased its representation to 58 seats, while the RNB held 20 seats and the PGP four.

On 18 April 1997, at a congress of deputies and senators, constitutional amendments which extended the presidential term to seven years, provided for the creation of the post of Vice-President and formally designated the Senate as an upper chamber of a bicameral legislature were adopted, despite the protests of opposition leaders who objected to the creation of a vice-presidency and demanded that a referendum be held. The Vice-President was to deputize for the President when required, but was not to have any power of succession. In late May Didjob Divungui-di-N'Dingue, a senior member of the ADERE and a candidate in the 1993 presidential election, was appointed to the new position. Although officially part of the HCR, the ADERE had signed a number of local electoral agreements with other parties, including the PDG, prior to the legislative elections. In November opposition parties invited international organizations to oversee the forthcoming presidential election, due to be held in late 1998, for which the leader of the PSD, Maganga Moussavou, had already announced his candidature.

President Bongo has pursued a policy of close co-operation with France in the fields of economic and foreign affairs. Relations became strained in March 1997, however, when allegations that Bongo had been a beneficiary in an international fraud emerged, during a French judicial investigation into the affairs of the petroleum company Elf-Aquitaine. The Chairman of Elf-Gabon, André Tarallo, was temporarily detained, and bank accounts in Switzerland and the British Virgin Islands, said to contain Gabonese government funds, were blocked. In response, Bongo cancelled a visit to France and reportedly threatened to impose economic sanctions on French oil interests in Gabon. He insisted that the Elf enquiry was a matter for the French judiciary and was not the concern of Gabon. Tarallo, who had been replaced as chairman of Elf-Gabon, came under further investigation in November 1997.

Bongo has often acted as an intermediary in regional disputes, chairing the OAU *ad hoc* committee seeking to resolve the border dispute between Chad and Libya, and encouraging dialogue between Angola and the USA. In 1997 he mediated in civil conflicts in Zaire (now the Democratic Republic of the Congo), the Central African Republic and the Republic of the Congo. In July of that year the Government expressed concern at the large numbers of refugees arriving in Gabon and subsequently announced plans for repatriation.

In February 1996 the northern part of Gabon was quarantined in response to an outbreak of Ebola haemorrhagic fever, in which at least 13 people died, according to the World Health Organization (WHO). In April it was reported that the World Bank and the World Wide Fund for Nature were seeking to identify areas of equatorial forest for conservation, amid fears that increasing exploitation by logging companies would imperil the survival of indigenous plant and animal species. It was also feared that opening up the forest could lead to another outbreak of the Ebola virus, of which forest-dwelling fauna are believed to be carriers. In October a second outbreak claimed 14 lives in the north-east of the country, and by January 1997 a further 40 deaths had been reported.

Government

The Constitution of March 1991 provides for a multi-party system, and vests executive power in the President, who is directly elected by universal suffrage for a period of seven years. The President appoints the Prime Minister, who is Head of Government and who (in consultation with the President) appoints the Council of Ministers. The legislative organ is the National Assembly, comprising 120 members, who are elected by direct universal suffrage for a term of five years. Provision is made for the formation of an upper house. Elections to a 91-member Senate took place in January and February 1997. The independence of the judiciary is guaranteed by the Constitution. Gabon is divided into nine provinces, each under an appointed governor, and 37 prefectures.

Defence

At 1 August 1997 the army consisted of 3,200 men, the air force of 1,000 men, and the navy of an estimated 500 men. Paramilitary forces numbered 4,800 (including a gendarmerie of 2,000). Military service is voluntary. France maintains a military detachment of 600 in Gabon. The defence budget for 1997 was estimated at 67,000m. francs CFA.

Economic Affairs

In 1995, according to estimates by the World Bank, Gabon's gross national product (GNP), measured at average 1993–95 prices, was US $3,759m., equivalent to $3,490 per head. During 1985–95, it was estimated, GNP per head declined, in real terms, by 1.6% per year, while the population increased by an annual average of 2.9%. Gabon's gross domestic product (GDP) increased, in real terms, by an annual average of 0.6% in 1985–95. The IMF estimated real GDP growth at 3.1% in 1996.

Agriculture (including forestry and fishing) contributed an estimated 7.1% of GDP in 1996. About 44.3% of the labour force were employed in the agricultural sector in 1996. Cocoa, coffee, oil palm and rubber are cultivated for export. Gabon has yet to achieve self-sufficiency in staple crops: imports of foods accounted for an estimated 22.3% of the value of total imports in 1995. The principal subsistence crops are cassava, plantains and maize. The exploitation of Gabon's forests (which cover about 75% of the land area) is a principal economic activity. The forestry sector accounted for an estimated 2.7% of GDP in 1996, and engaged an estimated 15% of the working population in 1991. In 1995 okoumé timber accounted for an estimated 76% of all timber production. Although Gabon's territorial waters contain important fishing resources, their commercial exploitation is minimal. Agricultural GDP increased by an annual average of 0.3% in 1985–95. The IMF estimated a decline of 0.3% in agricultural GDP in 1996.

Industry (including mining, manufacturing, construction and power) contributed an estimated 54.6% of GDP in 1996. About 14.1% of the working population were employed in the sector in 1991. Industrial GDP increased by an annual average of 4.2% in 1985–95. The IMF estimated growth in industrial GDP at 2.2% in 1996.

Mining accounted for an estimated 43.6% of GDP in 1996 (of which 41.9% was contributed by the petroleum sector). In that year sales of petroleum and petroleum products provided an estimated 81.4% of export revenue. Gabon is among the world's foremost producers and exporters of manganese (which contributed an estimated 4.9% of export earnings in 1996). Significant deposits of uranium have been exploited since the late 1950s at Mounana, although operations are expected to cease by the year 2000. Major reserves of iron ore remain undeveloped, owing to the lack of appropriate transport facilities. Small amounts of gold are extracted, and the existence of many mineral deposits, including niobium (columbium), talc, barytes, phosphates, rare earths, titanium and cadmium, has also been confirmed.

The manufacturing sector contributed an estimated 6.0% of GDP in 1996. The principal activities are the refining of petroleum and the processing of other minerals, the preparation of timber and other agro-industrial processes. The chemicals industry is also significant. Manufacturing GDP increased by an annual average of 6.8% in 1985–95. The IMF estimated growth in manufacturing GDP at 8.5% in 1996.

Electrical energy is derived principally from hydroelectric installations (which accounted for more than 75% of total production in the mid-1980s). Imports of fuel and energy comprised an estimated 21.3% of the total value of imports in 1995.

Services engaged 18.8% of the economically active population in 1991 and provided an estimated 38.3% of GDP in 1996. According to the IMF, in real terms, the combined GDP of the service sectors increased at an average rate of 0.2% per year during 1991–95. Growth was estimated at 3.7% in 1996.

In 1995 Gabon recorded a visible trade surplus of US $1,744.4m., and there was a surplus of $99.8m. on the current account of the balance of payments. In 1994 the principal source of imports (39.8%) was France; other major sources were the USA, the United Kingdom and Germany. The principal market for exports in that year was the USA (49.9%); France was also an important purchaser. The principal exports in 1996 were petroleum and petroleum products, timber, manganese and uranium. The principal imports in 1994 were machinery and transport equipment, basic manufactures, food products and chemicals and related products.

In 1996 there was an estimated budgetary deficit of 46,500m. francs CFA (equivalent to 1.6% of GDP). Gabon's external debt totalled US $4,492m. at the end of 1995, of which $4,099m. was long-term public debt. In that year the cost of debt-servicing was equivalent to 15.8% of the value of exports of goods and services. In 1985–95 the average annual rate of inflation was 4.2%. The annual rate of inflation, which had been negligible prior to the 50% devaluation of the CFA franc in January 1994, increased to 36.1% in 1994, but had declined to 4.7% by 1996. The Government estimated about 20% of the labour force to be unemployed in 1996.

Gabon is a member of the Central African organs of the Franc Zone (see p. 181), and of the Communauté économique des états de l'Afrique centrale (CEEAC, see p. 260). In June 1996 Gabon, which had been a member of OPEC (see p. 227) since 1973, announced its withdrawal from the organization, with effect from the end of that year.

Gabon's potential for economic growth is based upon its considerable mineral and forestry resources. In the mid-1980s, however, the country's vulnerability to fluctuations in international prices and demand for its principal commodities precipitated a decline in export and budget revenue. By the early 1990s the country's economic and financial situation had deteriorated, owing to a decline in the international price for petroleum and the accumulation of debt arrears. Following the devaluation of the CFA franc by 50% in relation to the French franc in January 1994, a programme for economic recovery, which included the further restructuring of public-sector enterprises, was agreed with the IMF in March. In November 1995 the IMF approved a further three-year credit under an extended facility, in support of the Government's programme for 1995–98, which aimed to stimulate employment through economic diversification, to liberalize the regulatory framework and further to develop the non-petroleum sector; subsequent reviews have indicated that satisfactory progress has been made, although the level of unemployment remains high. By December 1995 all external debt arrears had been cleared, and a favourable rescheduling agreement was concluded with the 'Paris Club' of official creditors. In 1996 the Government adopted measures to begin the transfer of state-owned enterprises to the private sector. In 1997 the divestiture of Gabon's electricity and water services was the first major privatization project to be implemented.

Social Welfare

There is a national Fund for State Insurance, and a guaranteed minimum wage. In January 1985 Gabon had 28 hospitals, 87 medical centres and 312 dispensaries, with a total of 5,156 hospital beds. In 1984 there were 300 physicians in the country. Maternal and infant health is a major priority. The 1988 budget allocated 18,000m. francs CFA (10% of total administrative spending) to health expenditure.

Education

Education is officially compulsory for 10 years between six and 16 years of age: in 1993 89% of children in the relevant age-group attended primary and secondary schools (90% of boys; 88% of girls). Primary and secondary education is provided by state and mission schools. Primary education begins at the age of six and lasts for six years. Secondary education, beginning at 12 years of age, lasts for up to seven years, comprising a first cycle of four years and a second of three years. The Université Omar Bongo, at Libreville, had 2,741 students in 1986. The Université des Sciences et des Techniques de Masuku was opened in 1986, with an enrolment of 550 students. In 1995, according to estimates by UNESCO, adult illiteracy averaged 36.8% (males 26.3%; females 46.7%). The 1994 budget allocated 78,850m. francs CFA (19% of total administrative spending) to expenditure on education.

Public Holidays

1998: 1 January (New Year's Day), 30 January* (Id al-Fitr, end of Ramadan), 12 March (Anniversary of Renovation, foundation of the Parti démocratique gabonais), 8 April* (Id al-Adha, feast of the Sacrifice), 13 April (Easter Monday), 1 May (Labour Day), 1 June (Whit Monday), 7 July* (Mouloud, birth of Muhammad), 17 August (Anniversary of Independence), 1 November (All Saints' Day), 25 December (Christmas).

1999: 1 January (New Year's Day), 19 January* (Id al-Fitr, end of Ramadan), 12 March (Anniversary of Renovation, foundation of the Parti démocratique gabonais), 28 March* (Id al-Adha, feast of the Sacrifice), 5 April (Easter Monday), 1 May (Labour Day), 24 May (Whit Monday), 26 June (Mouloud, birth of Muhammad), 17 August (Anniversary of Independence), 1 November (All Saints' Day), 25 December (Christmas).

* These holidays are dependent on the Islamic lunar calendar and may vary by one or two days from the dates given.

Weights and Measures

The metric system is in official use.

Statistical Survey

Source (unless otherwise stated): Direction Générale de l'Economie, Ministère de la Planification, de l'Economie et de l'Administration Territoriale, Libreville.

Area and Population

AREA, POPULATION AND DENSITY

Area (sq km)	267,667*
Population (census results)	
8 October 1960–May 1961	448,564
31 July 1993 (provisional)	
Males	498,710
Females	513,000
Total	1,011,710
Density (per sq km) at 31 July 1993	3.8

* 103,347 sq miles.

REGIONS (1993 census)

Region	Area (sq km)	Population*	Density (per sq km)	Chief town
Estuaire	20,740	462,086	22.3	Libreville
Haut-Ogooué	36,547	102,387	2.8	Franceville
Moyen-Ogooué	18,535	41,827	2.3	Lambaréné
N'Gounié	37,750	77,871	2.1	Mouila
Nyanga	21,285	39,826	1.9	Tchibanga
Ogooué-Ivindo	46,075	48,847	1.1	Makokou
Ogooué-Lolo	25,380	42,783	2.1	Koula-Moutou
Ogooué-Maritime	22,890	98,299	4.3	Port-Gentil
Woleu-N'Tem	38,465	97,739	2.5	Oyem
Total	267,667	1,011,665	3.8	

* Excluding 45 persons in unspecified regions.

Source: UN, *Demographic Yearbook*.

PRINCIPAL TOWNS (population in 1988)

Libreville (capital)	352,000	Franceville	75,000
Port-Gentil	164,000		

BIRTHS AND DEATHS (UN estimates, annual averages)

	1980–85	1985–90	1990–95
Birth rate (per 1,000)	33.8	36.5	37.3
Death rate (per 1,000)	18.1	16.6	15.5

Expectation of life (UN estimates, years at birth, 1990–95): 53.5 (males 51.9; females 55.2).

Source: UN, *World Population Prospects: The 1994 Revision*.

ECONOMICALLY ACTIVE POPULATION
(estimates, '000 persons, 1991)

	Males	Females	Total
Agriculture, etc.	187	151	338
Industry	62	9	71
Services	69	26	95
Total labour force	318	186	504

Source: UN Economic Commission for Africa, *African Statistical Yearbook*.

Mid-1996 (estimates, '000 persons): Agriculture, etc. 227; Total 512.
Source: FAO, *Production Yearbook*.

Agriculture

PRINCIPAL CROPS ('000 metric tons)

	1994	1995	1996
Maize*	25	26	27
Cassava (Manioc)*	230	210	220
Yams*	120	120	120
Taro (Coco yam)*	64	64	65
Vegetables*	32	33	33
Bananas*	9	9	9
Plantains*	250	250	250
Cocoa beans†	1	1	1
Groundnuts (in shell)*	15	15	15
Sugar cane*	210	220	220

* FAO estimates. † Unofficial figures.

Source: FAO, *Production Yearbook*.

LIVESTOCK (FAO estimates, '000 head, year ending September)

	1994	1995	1996
Cattle	39	39	39
Pigs	165	165	165
Sheep	172	172	172
Goats	84	84	84

Poultry (FAO estimates, million): 3 in 1994; 3 in 1995; 3 in 1996.
Source: FAO, *Production Yearbook*.

LIVESTOCK PRODUCTS

1996 (FAO estimates, '000 metric tons): Meat 28; Hen eggs 2.
Source: FAO, *Production Yearbook*.

Forestry

ROUNDWOOD REMOVALS (FAO estimates, '000 cubic metres)

	1992	1993	1994
Sawlogs, veneer logs and logs for sleepers*	1,633	1,633	1,633
Fuel wood	2,657	2,734	2,812
Total	4,290	4,367	4,445

* Annual output assumed to be unchanged since 1990.

Source: FAO, *Yearbook of Forest Products*.

SAWNWOOD PRODUCTION
(FAO estimates, '000 cubic metres, incl. railway sleepers)

	1992	1993	1994
Total	32	32	32

Source: FAO, *Yearbook of Forest Products*.

Fishing

('000 metric tons, live weight)

	1993	1994	1995
Freshwater fishes*	2.5	2.5	2.5
Grunts, sweetlips, etc.	0.7	0.7	1.1
Bobo croaker	0.2	0.9	1.0
West African croakers	3.4	1.6	2.1
Dentex	0.8	0.5	0.8
Lesser African threadfin	1.6	1.0	1.9
Bonga shad	10.0*	10.0	11.8
Other marine fishes (incl. unspecified)	7.4*	6.5	5.8
Total fish	26.5	23.6	27.0
Southern pink shrimp	0.5	0.6	0.9
Other crustaceans and molluscs	0.1	0.1	0.2
Total catch	27.1	24.4	28.0

* FAO estimate(s).

Source: FAO, *Yearbook of Fishery Statistics*.

Mining

('000 metric tons, unless otherwise indicated)

	1992	1993	1994
Crude petroleum	15,368	15,068	15,823
Natural gas (petajoules)*	4	4	3
Uranium ore (metric tons)†	589	556	650
Manganese ore*†‡	718	595	663
Gold (kilograms)†‡	70	120	72

* Provisional or estimated figures.
† Figures refer to the metal content of ores.
‡ Data from the US Bureau of Mines.

Source: UN, *Industrial Commodity Statistics Yearbook*.

Industry

PETROLEUM PRODUCTS ('000 metric tons)

	1992	1993	1994
Liquefied petroleum gas*	7	8	8
Motor spirit (petrol)*	91	93	95
Kerosene*	78	80	85
Jet fuel*	65	68	70
Distillate fuel oils	227	218*	223*
Residual fuel oil	292	294*	295*
Bitumen (asphalt)*	1	1	1

* Provisional or estimated figure(s).

Source: UN, *Industrial Commodity Statistics Yearbook*.

SELECTED OTHER PRODUCTS
('000 metric tons, unless otherwise indicated)

	1990	1991	1992
Palm oil (crude)*†	5	5	n.a.
Flour	29	30	31
Beer ('000 hectolitres)	819	814	785
Soft drinks ('000 hectolitres)	413	439	410
Cement‡	116	117	116
Electric energy (million kWh)*	908	914	919

1993: Cement ('000 metric tons) 132‡; Electric energy (million kWh) 922*.

1994: Cement ('000 metric tons) 126‡; Electric energy (million kWh) 933*.

* Provisional or estimated figure(s).

† Data from the FAO.

‡ Data from the US Bureau of Mines.

Source: UN, *Industrial Commodity Statistics Yearbook*.

Plywood (FAO estimates, '000 cu metres): 80 in 1991; 80 in 1992; 80 in 1993 (Source: FAO, *Yearbook of Forest Products*).

Veneer sheets ('000 cu metres): 60 in 1991 (Unofficial figure); 60 in 1992 (FAO estimate); 60 in 1993 (FAO estimate) (Source: FAO, *Yearbook of Forest Products*).

Finance

CURRENCY AND EXCHANGE RATES

Monetary Units

100 centimes = 1 franc de la Coopération financière en Afrique centrale (CFA).

French Franc, Sterling and Dollar Equivalents (30 September 1997)
1 French franc = 100 francs CFA;
£1 sterling = 958.3 francs CFA;
US $1 = 593.2 francs CFA;
1,000 francs CFA = £1.044 = $1.686.

Average Exchange Rate (francs CFA per US $)
1994 555.20
1995 499.15
1996 511.55

Note: An exchange rate of 1 French franc = 50 francs CFA, established in 1948, remained in force until January 1994, when the CFA franc was devalued by 50%, with the exchange rate adjusted to 1 French franc = 100 francs CFA.

BUDGET ('000 million francs CFA)

Revenue*	1994	1995	1996
Petroleum revenue	324.9	442.4	530.2
Profits tax	151.2	252.1	311.9
Royalties	139.8	155.7	185.5
Production-sharing and assets	23.9	14.6	17.8
Dividends	10.0	20.0	15.0
Non-petroleum revenue	221.2	288.2	306.0
Tax revenue	210.5	277.7	293.9
Direct taxes	58.3	76.8	80.2
Company taxes	25.0	42.7	45.0
Individual taxes	33.4	34.1	35.2
Indirect taxes	58.5	61.7	43.0
Turnover taxes	45.0	51.6	29.4
Taxes on goods and services	13.5	10.1	13.6
Taxes on refined petroleum products	6.2	4.3	—
Taxes on international trade and transactions	87.2	128.7	147.8
Import duties	75.2	110.7	125.2
Export duties	12.0	18.0	22.6
Other revenue	17.2	21.0	35.0
Total	546.1	730.6	836.2

Expenditure	1994	1995	1996
Current expenditure	461.2	514.9	512.0
Wages and salaries	165.1	178.1	184.8
Other goods and services	113.8	112.9	132.4
Transfers and subsidies	26.0	23.0	21.6
Interest payments	156.3	201.0	173.1
Domestic	38.8	n.a.	n.a.
External	117.5	n.a.	n.a.
Capital expenditure	131.2	136.0	154.3
Domestically financed investment	89.9	n.a.	n.a.
Externally financed investment	41.3	n.a.	n.a.
Other expenditure	—	—	10.2
Sub-total	592.4	650.9	676.5
Adjustment for payment arrears	370.3	53.6	125.1
Total (cash basis)	962.7	704.5	801.6

* Excluding grants received ('000 million francs CFA): 8.4 in 1994.

Source: IMF, *Gabon—Statistical Annex* (July 1997).

INTERNATIONAL RESERVES (US $ million at 31 December)

	1994	1995	1996
Gold*	4.85	4.95	4.73
IMF special drawing rights	0.25	—	0.03
Reserve position in IMF	0.08	0.08	0.09
Foreign exchange	174.86	148.01	248.59
Total	180.04	153.04	253.45

* Valued at market-related prices.

Source: IMF, *International Financial Statistics*.

MONEY SUPPLY ('000 million francs CFA at 31 December)

	1994	1995	1996
Currency outside banks	76.93	100.69	110.88
Demand deposits at commercial and development banks	117.96	117.90	159.11
Total money (incl. others)	195.01	219.09	276.00

Source: IMF, *International Financial Statistics*.

COST OF LIVING
(Retail Price Index for African families in Libreville; base: 1991 = 100)

	1994	1995	1996
Food	111.3	120.2	128.3
All items	123.8	135.6	142.0

Source: UN, *Monthly Bulletin of Statistics*.

NATIONAL ACCOUNTS ('000 million francs CFA at current prices)

Expenditure on the Gross Domestic Product

	1994	1995	1996*
Government final consumption expenditure	278.9	291.0	317.2
Private final consumption expenditure	994.0	1,188.3	1,343.4
Increase in stocks	18.5	—	—
Gross fixed capital formation	490.3	541.7	587.0
Total domestic expenditure	1,781.7	2,021.1	2,247.7
Exports of goods and services	1,435.0	1,455.4	1,738.5
Less Imports of goods and services	890.0	922.1	1,068.4
GDP in purchasers' values	2,326.8	2,554.4	2,917.8

* Estimates.

Source: IMF, *Gabon—Statistical Annex* (July 1997).

Gross Domestic Product by Economic Activity

	1994	1995	1996*
Agriculture, livestock, hunting and fishing	115.5	118.8	123.4
Forestry	95.9	77.1	75.3
Petroleum exploitation and research	914.3	951.8	1,170.0
Other mining	49.1	47.6	48.9
Manufacturing	114.7	148.3	166.3
Electricity and water	34.2	39.1	40.3
Construction and public works	83.5	91.6	98.9
Trade	264.0	360.3	424.3
Transport	133.6	139.2	147.6
Financial services	14.8	14.2	14.9
Government services	222.1	232.5	245.3
Other services	209.8	223.2	237.5
GDP at factor cost	2,251.6	2,443.6	2,792.8
Import duties	75.2	110.7	125.0
GDP in purchasers' values	2,326.8	2,554.4	2,917.8

* Estimates.

Source: IMF, *Gabon—Statistical Annex* (July 1997).

BALANCE OF PAYMENTS (US $ million)

	1993	1994	1995
Exports of goods f.o.b.	2,326.2	2,365.3	2,642.9
Imports of goods f.o.b.	−845.1	−776.7	−898.5
Trade balance	1,481.1	1,588.6	1,744.4
Exports of services	311.1	219.6	272.9
Imports of services	−1,022.7	−826.7	−949.4
Balance on goods and services	769.5	981.4	1,067.8
Other income received	32.1	11.9	13.4
Other income paid	−658.3	−509.9	−783.5
Balance on goods, services and income	143.4	483.4	297.7
Current transfers received	48.0	18.7	4.4
Current transfers paid	−240.5	−184.8	−202.3
Current balance	−49.1	317.4	99.8
Direct investment abroad	−2.5	—	n.a.
Direct investment from abroad	−113.7	−99.6	−113.4
Other investment assets	−7.8	−258.6	−5.4
Other investment liabilities	−265.2	−386.7	−293.9
Net errors and omissions	−13.6	254.6	−108.2
Overall balance	−451.9	−173.0	−421.2

Source: IMF, *International Financial Statistics*.

External Trade

PRINCIPAL COMMODITIES

Imports c.i.f. (US $ million)	1993	1994
Food and live animals	131.5	105.8
Meat and meat preparations	34.8	32.0
Fresh, chilled or frozen meat	31.5	28.9
Fresh or frozen bovine meat	16.7	13.1
Dairy products and birds' eggs	16.1	10.7
Fish and fish preparations	15.4	8.7
Cereals and cereal preparations	35.5	32.3
Beverages and tobacco	17.7	15.5
Mineral fuels, lubricants, etc.	14.5	17.1
Petroleum, petroleum products, etc.	14.3	16.9
Refined petroleum products	14.2	16.8
Chemicals and related products	83.6	70.1
Medicinal and pharmaceutical products	30.7	18.4
Medicaments (incl. veterinary)	28.3	16.7
Basic manufactures	123.8	112.1
Paper, paperboard and manufactures	19.4	14.1
Iron and steel	30.9	27.2
Tubes, pipes and fittings	23.7	19.7
Machinery and transport equipment	316.4	314.3
Power-generating machinery and equipment	26.9	25.9
Machinery specialized for particular industries	21.0	46.4
Civil engineering and contractors' plant and equipment	12.1	30.9
General industrial machinery, equipment and parts	67.0	82.2
Pumps for liquids, etc.	10.7	14.1
Other pumps, centrifuges, etc.	14.6	18.5
Office machines and automatic data-processing equipment	15.2	12.3
Telecommunications and sound equipment	19.0	16.6
Other electrical machinery, apparatus, etc.	40.0	29.8
Switchgear, etc., and parts	15.3	9.1
Road vehicles and parts	68.7	57.6
Passenger motor cars (excl. buses)	30.8	18.6
Motor vehicles for goods transport, etc.	18.8	14.1
Goods vehicles (lorries and trucks)	17.7	13.2
Other transport equipment	57.8	42.8
Ships, boats and floating structures	50.8	37.9
Miscellaneous manufactured articles	77.9	62.3
Professional, scientific and controlling instruments, etc.	21.3	16.9
Measuring and controlling instruments	15.3	14.3
Total (incl. others)	774.9	707.5

Source: UN, *International Trade Statistics Yearbook*.

Exports ('000 million francs CFA)	1994	1995	1996*
Petroleum and petroleum products	1,019.2	1,055.3	1,295.1
Manganese	57.4	66.4	77.6
Timber	194.6	172.6	196.0
Uranium	16.0	15.5	13.2
Total (incl. others)	1,313.2	1,319.1	1,591.7

* Preliminary figures.

Source: IMF, *Gabon—Statistical Annex* (July 1997).

PRINCIPAL TRADING PARTNERS (US $ million)

Imports c.i.f.	1993	1994
Belgium-Luxembourg	22.5	24.5
Cameroon	6.3	12.0
Côte d'Ivoire	6.3	7.6
France (incl. Monaco)	370.4	281.4
Germany	27.8	39.7
Italy	24.3	29.6
Morocco	10.1	4.5
Netherlands	36.0	35.1
Panama	—	11.3
Spain	11.2	11.4
United Kingdom	29.4	45.1
USA	71.0	83.5
Total (incl. others)	774.9	707.5

Exports f.o.b.	1993	1994
Argentina	25.4	—
Canada	52.3	—
Chile	81.6	22.6
China, People's Republic	29.4	54.5
France (incl. Monaco)	505.6	361.6
Gibraltar	17.2	42.0
Korea, Republic	16.1	35.4
Morocco	14.5	76.2
Netherlands	2.9	89.0
Portugal	1.9	91.2
Singapore	17.1	40.6
Spain	32.9	92.5
United Kingdom	93.1	61.8
USA	1,388.2	1,192.9
Total (incl. others)	2,637.0	2,391.0

Source: UN, *International Trade Statistics Yearbook*.

Transport

RAILWAYS (traffic)

	1993	1994	1995*
Passengers carried ('000)	150.5	180.8	175.8
Freight carried ('000 metric tons)	2,402.8	2,548.1	3,012.9

* Estimates.

Source: IMF, *Gabon—Statistical Annex* (July 1997).

ROAD TRAFFIC (estimates, motor vehicles in use)

	1994	1995	1996
Passenger cars	22,310	24,000	24,750
Lorries and vans	14,850	15,840	16,490

Source: IRF, *World Road Statistics.*

INTERNATIONAL SEA-BORNE SHIPPING
(freight traffic, '000 metric tons)

	1988	1989	1990
Goods loaded	8,890	10,739	12,828
Goods unloaded	610	213	212

Source: UN, *Monthly Bulletin of Statistics.*

CIVIL AVIATION (traffic on scheduled services)

	1992	1993	1994
Kilometres flown (million)	6	6	6
Passengers carried ('000)	471	302	481
Passenger-kilometres (million)	536	570	719
Total ton-kilometres (million)	77	82	96

Source: UN, *Statistical Yearbook.*

Tourism

	1992	1993	1994
Tourist arrivals ('000)	133	115	103
Tourist receipts (US $ million)	5	4	5

Source: UN, *Statistical Yearbook.*

Communications Media

	1993	1994	1995
Radio receivers ('000 in use)	183	189	195
Television receivers ('000 in use)	48	49	51
Telephones ('000 main lines in use)	30	31	n.a.
Mobile cellular telephones (subscribers)	1,200	2,580	n.a.
Daily newspapers:			
Number	n.a.	1	2
Average circulation ('000 copies)	n.a.	20*	30*

* Provisional or estimated figure.

Telefax stations (1990): 191 in use.

Sources: UNESCO, *Statistical Yearbook*; UN, *Statistical Yearbook.*

Education

(1996)

	Institu-tions	Teachers	Pupils		
			Males	Females	Total
Pre-primary*	9	37	465	485	950
Primary	1,147	4,944	126,208	124,398	250,606
Secondary:					
General	88	1,107	31,318	28,863	60,181
Technical	5	181	5,521	1,033	6,554
Vocational	6	52	291	189	480
University level*	2	299	2,148	852	3,000
Other higher	n.a.	257†	1,033‡	315‡	1,348‡

* 1991/92 figures. † 1983/84 figure. ‡ 1986/87 figure.

Sources: Ministère de l'Education Nationale; UNESCO, *Statistical Yearbook.*

Directory

The Constitution

The Constitution of the Gabonese Republic was adopted on 14 March 1991. The main provisions are summarized below:

PREAMBLE

Upholds the rights of the individual, liberty of conscience and of the person, religious freedom and freedom of education. Sovereignty is vested in the people, who exercise it through their representatives or by means of referenda. There is direct, universal and secret suffrage.

HEAD OF STATE*

The President is elected by direct universal suffrage for a five-year term, renewable only once. The President is Head of State and of the Armed Forces. The President may, after consultation with his ministers and leaders of the National Assembly, order a referendum to be held. The President appoints the Prime Minister, who is Head of Government and who is accountable to the President. The President is the guarantor of national independence and territorial sovereignty.

EXECUTIVE POWER

Executive power is vested in the President and the Council of Ministers, who are appointed by the Prime Minister, in consultation with the President.

LEGISLATIVE POWER

The National Assembly is elected by direct universal suffrage for a five-year term. It may be dissolved or prorogued for up to 18 months by the President, after consultation with the Council of Ministers and President of the Assembly. The President may return a bill to the Assembly for a second reading, when it must be passed by a majority of two-thirds of the members. If the President dissolves the Assembly, elections must take place within 40 days.

The Constitution also provides for the establishment of an upper chamber (the Senate), to control the balance and regulation of power.

POLITICAL ORGANIZATIONS

Article 2 of the Constitution states that 'Political parties and associations contribute to the expression of universal suffrage. They are formed and exercise their activities freely, within the limits delineated by the laws and regulations. They must respect the principles of democracy, national sovereignty, public order and national unity'.

JUDICIAL POWER

The President guarantees the independence of the Judiciary and presides over the Conseil Supérieur de la Magistrature. Supreme judicial power is vested in the Supreme Court.

* A constitutional amendment, adopted by the legislature on 18 April 1997, extended the presidential term to seven years and provided for the creation of the post of Vice-President.

The Government

HEAD OF STATE

President: El Hadj OMAR (ALBERT-BERNARD) BONGO (took office 2 December 1967, elected 25 February 1973, re-elected December 1979, November 1986 and December 1993).

Vice-President: DIDJOB DIVUNGUI-DI-N'DINGUE.

COUNCIL OF MINISTERS
(February 1998)

Prime Minister: Dr PAULIN OBAME-NGUEMA.

Minister of State for Foreign Affairs and Co-operation: CASIMIR OYÉ MBA.

Minister of State for Equipment and Construction: ZACHARIE MYBOTO.

Minister of State for Justice and Keeper of the Seals: MARCEL ELOI RAHANDI CHAMBRIER.

Minister of State for Habitat, Housing, Urban Planning and Territorial Administration and Welfare: JEAN-FRANÇOIS NTOUTOUME-EMANE.

Minister of State for Labour, Human Resources and Professional Training: JEAN-RÉMY PENDY BOUYIKI.

Minister of State for Agriculture, Livestock and Rural Development: EMMANUEL ONDO METHOGO.

Minister of State for the Interior: ANTOINE MBOUMBOU MIYAKOU.

Minister of State for National Education and Women's Affairs: PAULETTE MISSAMBO.

Minister of Mining, Energy and Oil: PAUL TOUNGUI.

Minister of National Defence, Security and Immigration, in charge of Posts and Telecommunications: Gen. IDRISS NGARI.

Minister of Communications, Culture, the Arts and Mass Education: JACQUES ADIAHÉNOT.

Minister of Finance, the Economy, the Budget and Participation, in charge of Privatization: MARCEL DOUPAMBY MATOKA.

Minister of Commerce, Industry, Small and Medium-sized Enterprises and Industries and Handicrafts: MARTIN FIDÈLE MAGNAGA.

Minister of Water, Forestry and Reafforestation: ANDRÉ DIEUDONNÉ BERRE.

Minister of Planning, the Environment and Tourism: JEAN PING.

Minister of the Civil Service and Administrative Reform: PATRICE ZIENGUI.

Minister of Transport and Civil Aviation: Gen. ALBERT NDJAVÉ-NDJOY.

Minister of Social Affairs, National Solidarity and the Family: PIERRE-CLAVER ZENG EBOME.

Minister of Merchant Marine and Fishing: FÉLIX SIBY.

Minister of Youth, Sports and Leisure: ALEXANDRE SAMBAT.

Minister of Higher Education and Scientific Research: LAZARE DIGOMBÉ.

Minister of Relations with Parliament and the Assemblies and Spokesperson for the Government: ANDRÉ MBA OBAME.

Minister of Public Health and Population: FAUSTIN BOUKOUBI.

Minister Delegate to the Prime Minister: EMMANUEL AKOGHE MBA.

Minister Delegate to the Minister of State for Equipment and Construction: SENTUREL NGOMA MADOUNGOU.

Minister Delegate to the Minister of State for National Education and Women's Affairs: JEAN-PIERRE MENGWANG-ME-NGIEMA.

Minister Delegate to the Minister of State for Habitat, Housing, Urban Planning and Territorial Administration: ANDRÉ JULES NDJAMBE.

Minister Delegate in charge of the Budget: ANTOINE YALANZELE.

Minister Delegate in charge of Small and Medium-sized Enterprises and Industries: FABIEN OWONO ESSONO.

Minister Delegate to the Minister of Planning, the Environment and Tourism: ALFRED MABIKA.

Minister Delegate to the Minister of Public Health and Population: DANIEL ONA ONDO.

MINISTRIES

Office of the Prime Minister: BP 546, Libreville; tel. 77-89-81; telex 5409.

Ministry of Agriculture, Livestock and Rural Development: BP 551, Libreville; tel. 72-09-60; telex 5587.

Ministry of the Civil Service and Administrative Reform: BP 496; Libreville; tel. 76-38-86.

Ministry of Commerce, Industry, Small and Medium-sized Enterprises and Industries and Handicrafts: BP 3096, Libreville; tel. 74-59-21; telex 5347.

Ministry of Communications, Culture, the Arts and Mass Education: BP 2280; Libreville; tel. 76-61-83.

Ministry of Equipment and Construction: BP 49, Libreville; tel. 76-38-56; telex 5408; fax 74-80-92.

Ministry of Finance, the Economy, the Budget and Participation: BP 165, Libreville; tel. 76-12-10; telex 5238.

Ministry of Foreign Affairs and Co-operation: BP 2245, Libreville; tel. 73-94-65; telex 5255.

Ministry of Habitat, Housing, Urban Planning and Territorial Administration: Libreville.

Ministry of Higher Education and Scientific Research: BP 2217; Libreville; tel. 72-41-08.

Ministry of the Interior: BP 2110, Libreville; tel. 72-00-75.

Ministry of Justice: BP 547, Libreville; tel. 74-66-28.

Ministry of Labour, Human Resources and Professional Training: BP 4577, Libreville; tel. 74-32-18.

Ministry of Merchant Marine and Fishing: Libreville.

Ministry of Mining, Energy and Oil: BP 576, Libreville; tel. 77-22-39; telex 5629.

Ministry of National Defence, Security and Immigration: BP 13493, Libreville; tel. 77-86-94; telex 5453.

Ministry of National Education and Women's Affairs: BP 6, Libreville; tel. 76-13-01; fax 74-14-48.

Ministry of Planning, the Environment and Tourism: BP 178, Libreville; tel. 76-34-62; telex 5711.

Ministry of Public Health and Population: BP 50, Libreville; tel. 76-36-11; telex 5385.

Ministry of Relations with Parliament and the Assemblies: Libreville.

Ministry of Social Affairs, National Solidarity and the Family: BP 5684, Libreville; tel. 77-50-32.

Ministry of Transport and Civil Aviation: BP 803, Libreville; tel. 74-71-96; telex 5479; fax 77-33-31.

Ministry of Water, Forestry and Reafforestation: Libreville.

Ministry of Youth, Sports and Leisure: Libreville.

President and Legislature

PRESIDENT

Presidential Election, 5 December 1993

Candidate	% of votes
El Hadj OMAR (ALBERT-BERNARD) BONGO	51.18
Fr PAUL M'BA ABESSOLE	26.51
PIERRE-LOUIS AGONDJO-OKAWÉ	4.78
PIERRE-CLAVER MAGANGA MOUSSAVOU	3.64
JULES BOURDÈS-OGOULIGUENDÉ	3.38
ALEXANDRE SAMBAT	2.59
DIDJOB DIVUNGUI-DI-N'DINGUE	2.20
Prof. LÉON MBOYEBI	1.83
JEAN-PIERRE LEPANDOU	1.38
MARC SATURNIN NAN NGUEMA	0.86
SIMON OYONO ABA'A	0.83
ADRIEN NGUEMA ONDO	0.44
LÉON MÉBIAME	0.38
Total	100.00

ASSEMBLÉE NATIONALE

President: GUY NDZOUBA NDAMA.

Secretary-General: PIERRE NGUEMA-MVE.

General Election, 15 and 29 December 1996

Party	Seats
Parti démocratique gabonais (PDG)	84
Rassemblement national des bûcherons (RNB)	7
Parti gabonais du progrès (PGP)	6
Independents	4
Cercle des libéraux réformateurs (CLR)	3
Union du peuple gabonais (UPG)	2
Union socialiste gabonais (USG)	2
Others	7
Total	115*

* Voting was unable to proceed normally in five constituencies, and results in a number of other constituencies were later annulled. Following subsequent by-elections, the PDG held 88 seats, the PGP nine and the RNB five. Two seats still remained vacant at mid-February 1998.

SÉNAT

President: GEORGES RAWIRI.

Secretary-General: LOUIS SAMBA IGAMBA.

Election, 26 January and 9 February 1997*

Party	Seats
Parti démocratique gabonais (PDG)	53
Rassemblement national des bûcherons (RNB)	20
Independents	9
Parti gabonais du progrès (PGP)	4
Alliance démocratique et républicaine (ADERE)	3
Cercle des libéraux réformateurs (CLR)	1
Rassemblement pour la démocratie et le progrès (RDP)	1
Total	91

* By-elections were subsequently held following the annulment of a number of results. At mid-February 1998 the PDG held 58 seats, the RNB 19 and the PGP four.

Political Organizations

Constitutional amendments providing for the introduction of a multi-party system took effect in May 1990. Political associations in existence in early 1998 included:

Alliance démocratique et républicaine (ADERE).

Association pour le socialisme au Gabon (APSG).

Cercle des libéraux réformateurs (CLR): f. 1993 by breakaway faction of the PDG; Leader JEAN-BONIFACE ASSELE.

Cercle pour le renouveau et le progrès (CRP).

Congrès pour la démocratie et la justice.

Convention des forces du changement: f. 1993 as an informal alliance of eight opposition presidential candidates.

Coordination de l'opposition démocratique (COD): f. 1991 as an alliance of eight principal opposition parties; Chair. SÉBASTIEN MAMBOUNDOU MOUYAMA.

Forum africain pour la reconstruction (FAR): f. 1992; a factional alliance within the COD; Leader Prof. LÉON MBOYEBI; comprises three political parties:

Mouvement de redressement national (MORENA-originels): f. 1981 in Paris, France; Leader (vacant).

Parti socialiste gabonais (PSG): f. 1991; Leader Prof. LÉON MBOYEBI.

Union socialiste gabonais (USG): Leader Dr SERGE MBA BEKALE.

Front national (FN): f. 1991; Leader MARTIN EFAYONG.

Mouvement alternatif: f. 1996; Leader SÉBASTIEN MAMBOUNDOU MOUYAMA.

Mouvement pour la démocratie, le développement et la reconciliation nationale (Modern): Libreville; f. 1996; Leader GASTON MOZOGO OVONO.

Parti démocratique gabonais (PDG): BP 268, Libreville; tel. 70-31-21; fax 70-31-46; f. 1968; sole legal party 1968–90; Sec.-Gen. JACQUES ADIAHÉNOT.

Parti gabonais du centre indépendent (PGCI): Leader JEAN-PIERRE LEPANDOU.

Parti gabonais du progrès (PGP): f. 1990; Pres. PIERRE-LOUIS AGONDJO-OKAWÉ; Sec.-Gen. ANSELME NZOGHE.

Parti des libéraux démocrates (PLD): Leader MARC SATURNIN NAN NGUEMA.

Parti social-démocrate (PSD): f. 1991; Leader PIERRE-CLAVER MAGANGA MOUSSAVOU.

Parti de l'unité du peuple gabonais (PUP): Libreville; f. 1991; Leader LOUIS GASTON MAYILA.

Rassemblement des démocrates (RD): f. 1993.

Rassemblement pour la démocratie et le progrès (RDP): Pres. ALEXANDRE SAMBAT.

Rassemblement des Gaubis: Libreville; f. 1994; Leader MAX ANICET KOUMBA-MBADINGA.

Rassemblement des Gaullois: f. 1998.

Rassemblement national des bûcherons (RNB): f. 1990 as MORENA des bûcherons; Leader Fr PAUL M'BA ABESSOLE; Sec.-Gen. Prof. PIERRE-ANDRÉ KOMBILA.

Union pour la démocratie et le développement Mayumba (UDD).

Union démocratique et sociale (UDS): f. 1996; Leader HERVÉ OUSSAMANE.

Union nationale pour la démocratie et le développement (UNDD): f. 1993; supports President Bongo.

Union du peuple gabonais (UPG): f. 1989 in Paris, France; Leader PIERRE MAMBOUNDOU.

Diplomatic Representation

EMBASSIES IN GABON

Algeria: BP 4008, Libreville; tel. 73-23-18; telex 5313; fax 73-14-03; e-mail ambalgabon@tiggabon.com; Ambassador: ABDELHAMID CHEBCHOUB.

Angola: BP 4884, Libreville; tel. 73-04-26; telex 5565; Ambassador: BERNARDO DOMBELE M'BALA.

Argentina: BP 4065, Libreville; tel. 74-05-49; telex 5611; Ambassador: HUGO HURTUBEI.

Belgium: BP 4079, Libreville; tel. 73-29-92; telex 5273; Ambassador: PAUL DE WULF.

Brazil: BP 3899, Libreville; tel. 76-05-35; telex 5492; fax 74-03-43; Ambassador: JAIME VILLA-LOBOS.

Cameroon: BP 14001, Libreville; tel. 73-28-00; telex 5396; Chargé d'affaires a.i.: NYEMB NGUENE.

Canada: BP 4037, Libreville; tel. 74-34-64; telex 5527; Ambassador: JEAN NADEAU.

Central African Republic: Libreville; tel. 72-12-28; telex 5323; Ambassador: FRANÇOIS DIALLO.

China, People's Republic: BP 3914, Libreville; tel. 74-32-07; telex 5376; Ambassador: SUN ZHIRONG.

Congo, Democratic Republic: BP 2257, Libreville; tel. 74-32-53; telex 5335; Ambassador: KABANGI KAUMBU BULA.

Congo, Republic: BP 269, Libreville; tel. 73-29-06; telex 5541; Ambassador: PIERRE OBOU.

Côte d'Ivoire: BP 3861, Libreville; tel. 73-82-68; telex 5317; Ambassador: JEAN-OBEO COULIBALY.

Egypt: BP 4240, Libreville; tel. 73-25-38; telex 5425; fax 73-25-19; Ambassador: SALAH ZAKI.

Equatorial Guinea: BP 1462, Libreville; tel. 75-10-56; Ambassador: CRISANTOS NDONGO ABA MESSIAN.

France: blvd de l'Indépendance, BP 2125, Libreville; tel. 76-10-64; telex 5249; Ambassador: MICHEL LUNVEN.

Germany: blvd de l'Indépendance, BP 299, Libreville; tel. 76-01-88; telex 5248; fax 72-40-12; Ambassador: HORST K. RUDOLF.

Guinea: BP 4046, Libreville; tel. 73-85-09; Chargé d'affaires a.i.: MAMADI KOLY KOUROUMA.

Iran: BP 2158, Libreville; tel. 73-05-33; telex 5502; Ambassador: AHMAD SOBHAM.

Italy: Immeuble Personnaz et Gardin, rue de la Mairie, BP 2251, Libreville; tel. 74-28-92; telex 5287; fax 74-80-35; Ambassador: VITTORIO FUMO.

Japan: BP 3341, Libreville; tel. 73-22-97; telex 5428; fax 73-60-60; Ambassador: HIDEO KAKINUMA.

Korea, Republic: BP 2620, Libreville; tel. 73-40-00; telex 5356; fax 73-00-79; Ambassador: PARK CHANG-IL.

Lebanon: BP 3341, Libreville; tel. 73-96-45; telex 5547; Ambassador: MAMLOUK ABDELLATIF.

Mauritania: BP 3917, Libreville; tel. 74-31-65; telex 5570; Ambassador: El Hadj THIAM.

Morocco: BP 3983, Libreville; tel. 77-41-51; telex 5434; fax 77-41-50; Ambassador: MOHAMED GHALI TAZI.

Nigeria: BP 1191, Libreville; tel. 73-22-03; telex 5605; Ambassador: ISMEAL BAMIDELE MOHAMMED.

Philippines: BP 1198, Libreville; tel. 72-34-80; telex 5279; Chargé d'affaires a.i.: ARCADIO HERRERA.

Russia: BP 3963, Libreville; tel. 72-48-68; telex 5797; fax 72-48-70; Ambassador: YOURI LEYZARENKO.

São Tomé and Príncipe: BP 489, Libreville; tel. 72-09-94; telex 5557; Ambassador: JOSEPH FRET LAU CHONG.

Senegal: BP 3856, Libreville; tel. 77-42-67; telex 5332; Ambassador: OUMAR WELE.

South Africa: Immeuble les Arcades, 142 rue des Chavannes, BP 4063, Libreville; tel. 77-45-30; fax 77-45-36; Chargé d'affaires: HEINRICH LOTZE.

Spain: Immeuble Diamant, blvd de l'Indépendance, BP 2105, Libreville; tel. 72-12-64; telex 5258; fax 74-88-73; Ambassador: MIGUEL ANTONIO ARIAS ESTÉVEZ.

Togo: BP 14160, Libreville; tel. 73-29-04; telex 5490; Ambassador: AHLONKO KOFFI AQUEREBURU.

Tunisia: BP 3844, Libreville; tel. 73-28-41; Ambassador: EZZEDINE KERKENI.

USA: blvd de la Mer, BP 4000, Libreville; tel. 76-20-03; telex 5250; Ambassador: ELIZABETH RASPOLIC (designate).

Venezuela: BP 3859, Libreville; tel. 73-31-18; telex 5264; fax 73-30-67; Ambassador: VÍCTOR CROQUER-VEGA.

Yugoslavia: Libreville; tel. 73-30-05; telex 5329; Ambassador: ČEDOMIR STRBAC.

Judicial System

Supreme Court: BP 1043, Libreville; tel. 72-17-00; three chambers: judicial, administrative and accounts; Pres. BENJAMIN PAMBOU-KOMBILA.

Constitutional Court: Libreville; tel. 72-57-17; Pres. MARIE MADELEINE BORANSOUO.

Courts of Appeal: Libreville and Franceville.

Court of State Security: Libreville; 13 mems; Pres. FLORENTIN ANGO.

Conseil Supérieur de la Magistrature: Libreville; Pres. El Hadj OMAR BONGO; Vice-Pres. Pres. of the Supreme Court (ex officio).

There are also Tribunaux de Première Instance (County Courts) at Libreville, Franceville, Port-Gentil, Lambaréné, Mouila, Oyem, Koula-Moutou, Makokou and Tchibanga.

Religion

About 60% of Gabon's population are Christians, mainly adherents of the Roman Catholic Church. About 40% are animists, and fewer than 1% are Muslims.

CHRISTIANITY

The Roman Catholic Church

Gabon comprises one archdiocese and three dioceses. At 31 December 1995 the estimated number of adherents in the country was equivalent to 51.6% of the total population.

Bishops' Conference: Conférence Episcopale du Gabon, BP 209, Oyem; tel. 98-63-20; f. 1989; Pres. Rt Rev. BASILE MVÉ ENGONE, Bishop of Oyem.

Archbishop of Libreville: Most Rev. ANDRÉ-FERNAND ANGUILÉ, Archevêché, Sainte-Marie, BP 2146, Libreville; tel. 72-20-73.

Protestant Churches

Christian and Missionary Alliance: active in the south of the country; 16,000 mems.

Eglise Evangélique du Gabon: BP 10080, Libreville; tel. 72-41-92; f. 1842; independent since 1961; 120,000 mems; Pres. Pastor SAMUEL NANG ESSONO; Sec. Rev. EMILE NTETOME.

The Evangelical Church of South Gabon and the Evangelical Pentecostal Church are also active in Gabon.

The Press

Le Bûcheron: BP 6424, Libreville; official publ. of the Rassemblement national des bûcherons; Pres. PIERRE-ANDRÉ KOMBILA.

Bulletin Evangélique d'Information et de Presse: BP 80, Libreville; monthly; religious.

Bulletin Mensuel de la Chambre de Commerce, d'Agriculture, d'Industrie et des Mines: BP 2234, Libreville; tel. 72-20-64; telex 5554; fax 74-64-77; monthly.

Bulletin Mensuel de Statistique de la République Gabonaise: BP 179, Libreville; monthly; publ. by Direction Générale de l'Economie.

L'Economiste Gabonais: BP 3906, Libreville; quarterly; publ. by the Centre gabonais du commerce extérieur.

Gabon d'Aujourd'hui: BP 750, Libreville; weekly; publ. by the Ministry of Communications, Posts and Telecommunications.

Gabon Libre: BP 6439, Libreville; tel. 74-42-22; weekly; Dir DZIME EKANG; Editor RENÉ NZOVI.

Gabon-Matin: BP 168, Libreville; daily; publ. by Agence Gabonaise de Presse; Man. HILARION VENDANY; circ. 18,000.

La Griffe: BP 4928, Libreville; tel. 74-73-45; weekly; independent; satirical; Pres. JÉRÔME OKINDA; Editor NDJOUMBA MOUSSOCK.

Journal Officiel de la République Gabonaise: BP 563, Libreville; f. 1959; fortnightly; Man. EMMANUEL OBAMÉ.

Ngondo: BP 168, Libreville; monthly; publ. by Agence Gabonaise de Presse.

Le Progressiste: blvd Léon-M'Ba, Libreville; tel. 74-54-01; Dir BENOÎT MOUITY NZAMBA; Editor JACQUES MOURENDE-TSIOBA.

La Relance: Libreville; tel. 70-31-66; weekly; publ. of the Parti démocratique gabonais; Pres. JACQUES ADIAHÉNOT; Dir RENÉ NDEMEZO'O OBIANG.

Sept Jours: BP 213, Libreville; weekly.

L'Union: BP 3849, Libreville; tel. 73-21-84; telex 5305; fax 73-83-26; f. 1975; 75% state-owned; daily; official govt publication; Man. Dir ALBERT YANGARI; Editor NGOYO MOUSSAVOU; circ. 40,000.

NEWS AGENCIES

Agence Gabonaise de Presse (AGP): BP 168, Libreville; tel. 21-26; telex 5628.

Foreign Bureau

Agence France-Presse (AFP): Immeuble Sogapal, Les Filaos, BP 788, Libreville; tel. 76-14-36; telex 5239; fax 72-45-31; e-mail afp-libreville@tiggabon.com; Dir JEAN-PIERRE REJETE.

Publishers

Imprimerie Centrale d'Afrique (IMPRIGA): BP 154, Libreville; tel. 70-22-55; fax 70-05-19; f. 1973; Chair. ROBERT VIAL; Dir FRANCIS BOURQUIN.

Multipress Gabon: blvd Léon-M'Ba, BP 3875, Libreville; tel. 73-22-33; telex 5389; f. 1973; Chair. PAUL BORY.

Société Imprimerie de l'Ogooué (SIMO): BP 342, Port-Gentil; f. 1977; Man. Dir URBAIN NICOUE.

Société Nationale de Presse et d'Edition (SONAPRESSE): BP 3849, Libreville; tel. 73-21-84; telex 5391; f. 1975; Pres. and Man. Dir JOSEPH RENDJAMBE.

Broadcasting and Communications

TELECOMMUNICATIONS

Société des Télécommunications Internationales Gabonaises (TIG): BP 2261, Libreville; tel. 78-77-56; telex 5200; fax 74-19-09; f. 1971; cap. 3,000 m. francs CFA; 61% state-owned; study and development of international telecommunications systems; Man. Dir A. N'OUMA MWYUMALA.

RADIO

The national network, 'La Voix de la Rénovation', and a provincial network broadcast for 24 hours each day in French and local languages.

Africa No. 1: BP 1, Libreville; tel. 76-00-01; telex 5558; fax 74-21-33; f. 1980; 35% state-controlled; international commercial radio station; broadcasts began in 1981; daily programmes in French and English; Pres. LOUIS BARTHÉLEMY MAPANGOU; Mans MICHEL KOUMBANGOYE, PIERRE DEVOLUY.

Radiodiffusion-Télévision Gabonaise (RTG): BP 150, Libreville; tel. 73-20-25; telex 5342; f. 1959; state-controlled; Dir-Gen. JOHN JOSEPH MBOUROU; Dir of Radio PIERRE-NOËL BOTSIKABOBE.

Radio Fréquence 3: f. 1996.

Radio Génération Nouvelle: f. 1996; Dir JEAN-BONIFACE ASSELE.

Radio Mandarine: f. 1995.

Radio Soleil: f. 1995; affiliated to Rassemblement national des bûcherons.

Radio Unité: f. 1996.

TELEVISION

Radiodiffusion-Télévision Gabonaise (RTG): BP 150, Libreville; tel. 73-21-52; telex 5342; fax 73-21-53; f. 1959; state-controlled; Dir-Gen. JOHN JOSEPH MBOUROU; Dir of Television ROBERT ALOLI.

Télé-Africa: Libreville; tel. 76-20-33; private channel; daily broadcasts in French.

Télédiffusion du Gabon: f. 1995.

Finance

(cap. = capital; res = reserves; dep. = deposits; m. = million; brs = branches; amounts in francs CFA)

BANKING

Central Bank

Banque des Etats de l'Afrique Centrale (BEAC): BP 112, Libreville; tel. 76-13-52; telex 5215; fax 74-45-63; headquarters in Yaoundé, Cameroon; f. 1973 as central bank of issue for mem. states of the Customs and Economic Union of Central Africa (UDEAC); cap. 45,000.0m., res 169,492.2m. (June 1996); Gov. JEAN-FÉLIX MAMALEPOT; Dir in Gabon JEAN-PAUL LEYIMANGOYE; 3 brs.

Commercial Banks

Banque Gabonaise et Française Internationale: blvd de l'Indépendance, BP 2253, Libreville; tel. 76-01-37; telex 5265; fax 74-08-94; f. 1971 as Banque Paribas-Gabon; 39.6% state-owned; cap. 7,892.0m., res 17,846.1m., dep. 48,037.7m. (Dec. 1995); Chair. PATRICE OTHA; Dir-Gen. HENRI-CLAUDE OYIMA; br. at Port-Gentil.

Banque Internationale pour le Commerce et l'Industrie du Gabon, SA (BICIG): ave du Colonel Parant, BP 2241, Libreville; tel. 76-26-13; telex 5226; fax 74-64-10; f. 1973; 26.4% state-owned; cap. 7,000m. (Dec. 1994); Pres. GUY-ETIENNE MOUVAGHA-TCHIOBA; Man. Dir EMILE DOUMBA; 9 brs.

Banque Internationale pour le Gabon: Immeuble Concorde, blvd de l'Indépendance, BP 106, Libreville; tel. 76-26-26; telex 5221; fax 76-20-53.

Banque Populaire du Gabon 'La Populaire': blvd d'Indépendance, BP 6663, Libreville; tel. 72-86-88; telex 5264; fax 72-86-91; f. 1996; Pres. JEAN-MARCE EKOHNGYEMA; Dir-Gen. SAMSON NGOMO.

Crédit Foncier du Gabon: blvd de l'Indépendance, BP 3905, Libreville; tel. 72-47-45; telex 3905; fax 76-08-70; 75% state-owned; Pres. HENRI MINKO; Dir-Gen. EMMANUEL NTOUTOUME.

Union Gabonaise de Banque, SA (UGB): ave du Colonel Parant, BP 315, Libreville; tel. 77-70-00; telex 5232; fax 76-46-16; f. 1962; 25% state-owned; cap. 5,000.0m., res 10,107.4m., dep. 79,637.0m. (Dec. 1996); Pres. MICHEL ANCHOUEY; Man. Dir JEAN-CLAUDE DUBOIS; 6 brs.

Development Banks

Banque Gabonaise de Développement (BGD): rue Alfred Marche, BP 5, Libreville; tel. 76-24-29; telex 5430; fax 74-26-99; f. 1960; 69% state-owned; cap. 10,500m. (Dec. 1995); Pres. JEAN-BAPTISTE OBIANG ETOUGHE; Dir-Gen. RICHARD ONOUVIET; 3 brs.

Banque Nationale de Crédit Rural (BNCR): ave Bouet, BP 1120, Libreville; tel. 72-47-42; telex 5830; fax 74-05-07; f. 1986; 74% state-owned; cap. 1,350m. (Dec. 1992); Pres. GÉRARD MEYO M'EMANE; Man. Dir GEORGES ISSEMBE.

Société Gabonaise de Participation et de Développement (SOGAPAR): blvd de l'Indépendance, BP 2253, Libreville; tel. 73-23-26; telex 5265; fax 74-08-94; f. 1971; 38% state-owned; studies and promotes projects conducive to national economic development; cap. 2,063m. (Dec. 1995); Pres. DANIEL BEDIN; Man. Dir HENRI-CLAUDE OYIMA.

Société Nationale d'Investissement du Gabon (SONADIG): BP 479, Libreville; tel. 72-09-22; fax 74-81-70; f. 1968; state-owned; cap. 500m.; Pres. ANTOINE OYIEYE; Dir-Gen. MASSALA TSAMBA.

Financial Institution

Caisse Autonome d'Amortissement du Gabon: BP 912, Libreville; tel. 74-41-43; telex 5537; management of state funds; Dir-Gen. MAURICE EYAMBA TSIMAT.

INSURANCE

Agence Gabonaise d'Assurance et de Réassurance (AGAR): BP 1699, Libreville; tel. 74-02-22; fax 76-59-25; f. 1987; cap. 50m.; Man. Dir LOUIS GASTON MAYILA.

Assurances Générales Gabonaises (AGG): ave du Colonel Parant, BP 2148, Libreville; tel. 76-09-73; telex 5473; f. 1974; cap. 66.5m.; Co-Chair. JEAN DAVIN, JACQUES NOT.

Assureurs Conseils Franco-Africains du Gabon (ACFRA-GABON): BP 1116, Libreville; tel. 72-32-83; telex 5485; cap. 43.4m.; Chair. FRÉDÉRIC MARRON; Dir M. GARNIER.

Assureurs Conseils Gabonais-Faugère et Jutheau & Cie: Immeuble Shell-Gabon, rue de la Mairie, BP 2138, Libreville; tel. 72-04-36; telex 5435; fax 76-04-39; cap. 10m.; represents foreign insurance cos; Dir GÉRARD MILAN.

Groupement Gabonais d'Assurances et de Réassurances (GGAR): Immeuble les Horizons, blvd Triomphal Omar Bongo, BP 3949, Libreville; tel. 74-28-72; telex 5673; f. 1985; cap. 225m.; Chair. RASSAGUIZA AKEREY; Dir-Gen. DENISE OMBAGHO.

Mutuelle Gabonaise d'Assurances: ave du Colonel Parant, BP 2225, Libreville; tel. 72-13-91; telex 5240; Sec.-Gen. M. YENO-OLINGOT.

Omnium Gabonais d'Assurances et de Réassurances (OGAR): 546 blvd Triomphal Omar Bongo, BP 201, Libreville; tel. 76-15-96; telex 5505; fax 76-58-16; f. 1976; 10% state-owned; cap. 340m.; general; Pres. MARCEL DOUPAMBY-MATOKA; Man. Dir EDOUARD VALENTIN.

Société Nationale Gabonaise d'Assurances et de Réassurances (SONAGAR): ave du Colonel Parant, BP 3082, Libreville; tel. 76-28-97; telex 5366; f. 1974; owned by l'Union des Assurances de Paris (France); Dir-Gen. JEAN-LOUIS MESSAN.

SOGERCO-Gabon: BP 2102, Libreville; tel. 76-09-34; telex 5224; f. 1975; cap. 10m.; general; Dir M. RABEAU.

L'Union des Assurances du Gabon (UAG): ave du Colonel Parant, BP 2141, Libreville; tel. 74-34-34; telex 5404; fax 74-14-53; f. 1976; cap. 280.5m.; Chair. ALBERT ALEWINA CHAVIOT; Dir EKOMIE AFENE.

Trade and Industry

GOVERNMENT AGENCY

Conseil Economique et Social de la République Gabonaise: BP 1075, Libreville; tel. 76-26-68; comprises representatives from salaried workers, employers and Govt; commissions on economic, financial and social affairs and forestry and agriculture; Pres. LOUIS GASTON MAYILA.

DEVELOPMENT ORGANIZATIONS

Agence Nationale de Promotion de la Petite et Moyenne Entreprise (PROMO-GABON): BP 3939, Libreville; tel. 74-31-16; telex 000576; f. 1964; state-controlled; promotes and assists small and medium-sized industries; Pres. SIMON BOULAMATARI; Man. Dir JEAN-FIDÈLE OTANDO.

Caisse Française de Développement: BP 64, Libreville; tel. 74-33-74; telex 5362; fax 74-51-25; Dir ANTOINE BAUX.

Centre Gabonais de Commerce Extérieur (CGCE): BP 3906, Libreville; tel. 76-11-67; telex 5347; promotes foreign trade and investment in Gabon; Man. Dir MICHEL LESLIE TEALE.

Commerce et Développement (CODEV): BP 2142, Libreville; tel. 76-06-73; telex 5214; f. 1976; cap. 2,000m. francs CFA; 95% state-owned, proposed transfer to private ownership announced 1986; import and distribution of capital goods and food products; Chair. and Man. Dir JÉRÔME NGOUA-BEKALE.

Mission Française de Coopération: BP 2105, Libreville; tel. 76-10-56; telex 5249; fax 74-55-33; administers bilateral aid from France; Dir JEAN-CLAUDE QUIRIN.

Office Gabonais d'Amélioration et de Production de Viande (OGAPROV): BP 245, Moanda; tel. 66-12-67; f. 1971; development of private cattle farming; manages ranch at Lekedi-Sud; Pres. PAUL KOUNDA KIKI; Dir-Gen. VINCENT EYI-NGUI.

Palmiers et Hévéas du Gabon (PALMEVEAS): BP 75, Libreville; f. 1956; cap. 145m. francs CFA; state-owned; palm-oil development.

Société de Développement de l'Agriculture au Gabon (AGRO-GABON): BP 2248, Libreville; tel. 76-40-82; fax 76-44-72; f. 1976; cap. 2,788m. francs CFA; 92% state-owned; Man. Dir ANDRÉ PAUL-APANDINA.

Société de Développement de l'Hévéaculture (HEVEGAB): BP 316, Libreville; tel. 72-08-29; telex 5615; fax 72-08-30; f. 1981; cap. 5,500m. francs CFA; 99.9% state-owned; development of rubber plantations in the Mitzic, Bitam and Kango regions; Chair. FRANÇOIS OWONO-NGUEMA; Man. Dir RAYMOND NDONG-SIMA.

Société Gabonaise de Recherches et d'Exploitations Minières (SOGAREM): blvd de Nice, Libreville; state-owned; research and development of gold mining; Chair. ARSÈNE BOUNGUENZA; Man. Dir SERGE GASSITA.

Société Gabonaise de Recherches Pétrolières (GABOREP): BP 564, Libreville; tel. 75-06-40; telex 8268; fax 75-06-47; exploration and exploitation of hydrocarbons; Chair. HUBERT PERRODO; Man. Dir P. F. LECA.

Société Nationale de Développement des Cultures Industrielles (SONADECI): Libreville; tel. 76-33-97; telex 5362; f. 1978; cap. 600m. francs CFA; state-owned; agricultural development; Chair. PAUL KOUNDA KIKI; Man. Dir GEORGES BEKALÉ.

CHAMBER OF COMMERCE

Chambre de Commerce, d'Agriculture, d'Industrie et des Mines du Gabon: BP 2234, Libreville; tel. 72-20-64; telex 5554;

fax 74-64-77; f. 1935; regional offices at Port-Gentil and Franceville; Pres. JOACHIM BOUSSAMBA-MAPAGA; Sec.-Gen. DOMINIQUE MANDZA.

EMPLOYERS' ORGANIZATIONS

Confédération Patronale Gabonaise: BP 410, Libreville; tel. 76-02-43; fax 74-86-52; f. 1959; represents the principal industrial, mining, petroleum, public works, forestry, banking, insurance, commercial and shipping concerns; Pres. EMILE DOUMBA; Sec.-Gen. ERIC MESSERSCHMITT.

Conseil National du Patronat Gabonais (CNPG): Libreville; Pres. RAHANDI CHAMBRIER; Sec.-Gen. THOMAS FRANCK EYA'A.

Syndicat des Entreprises Minières du Gabon (SYNDIMINES): BP 260, Libreville; telex 5388; Pres. ANDRÉ BERRE; Sec.-Gen. SERGE GREGOIRE.

Syndicat des Importateurs Exportateurs du Gabon (SIMPEX): BP 1743, Libreville; Pres. ALBERT JEAN; Sec.-Gen. R. TYBERGHEIN.

Syndicat des Producteurs et Industriels du Bois du Gabon: BP 84, Libreville; tel. 72-26-11; fax 77-44-43; Pres. HERVÉ BOZEC.

Syndicat Professionnel des Usines de Sciages et Placages du Gabon: Port-Gentil; f. 1956; Pres. PIERRE BERRY.

Union des Représentations Automobiles et Industrielles (URAI): BP 1743, Libreville; Pres. M. MARTINENT; Sec. R. TYBERGHEIN.

Union Nationale du Patronat Syndical des Transports Urbains, Routiers et Fluviaux du Gabon (UNAPASYFTUROGA): BP 1025, Libreville; f. 1977; Pres. LAURENT BELLAL BIBANG-BI-EDZO; Sec.-Gen. MARTIN KOMBILA-MOMBO.

UTILITIES

Société d'Energie et d'Eau du Gabon (SEEG): BP 2187, Libreville; tel. 72-19-11; telex 5222; f. 1963; 51% owned by Compagnie Générale des Eaux (France) and Electricity Supply Board International (Ireland); controls 35 electricity generation and distribution centres and 32 water production and distribution centres.

TRADE UNIONS

Confédération Gabonaise des Syndicats Libres (CGSL): Libreville; Sec.-Gen. FRANCIS MAYOMBO.

Confédération Syndicale Gabonaise (COSYGA): BP 14017, Libreville; telex 5623; f. 1969, by the Govt, as a specialized organ of the PDG, to organize and educate workers, to contribute to social peace and economic development, and to protect the rights of trade unions; Gen. Sec. MARTIN ALLINI.

Transport

RAILWAYS

The construction of the Transgabonais railway, which comprises a section running from Owendo (the port of Libreville) to Booué (340 km) and a second section from Booué to Franceville (357 km), was completed in December 1986. By 1989 regular services were operating between Libreville and Franceville. More than 3m. metric tons of freight and 175,000 passengers were carried on the network in 1995. Plans to transfer ownership of the railways to the private sector were announced in 1996.

Office du Chemin de Fer Transgabonais (OCTRA): BP 2198, Libreville; tel. 70-24-78; telex 5307; fax 70-27-68; f. 1972; state-owned; Chair. ALEXANDRE AYO BARRO; Dir-Gen. FIRMIN GORRA.

ROADS

In 1996 there were an estimated 7,670 km of roads, including 30 km of motorways, 3,780 km of main roads and 2,420 km of secondary roads; about 8.2% of the road network was paved. In 1992 a seven-year project to surface some 1,400 km of road by the year 2000 was announced. In the same year a programme was initiated to construct a further 1,851 km of roads, at an estimated cost of some US $528m.

INLAND WATERWAYS

The principal river is the Ogooué, navigable from Port-Gentil to Ndjolé (310 km) and serving the towns of Lambaréné, Ndjolé and Sindara.

Compagnie de Navigation Intérieure (CNI): BP 3982, Libreville; tel. 72-39-28; fax 74-04-11; f. 1978; cap. 500m. francs CFA; state-owned; inland waterway transport; agencies at Port-Gentil, Mayumba and Lambaréné; Chair. JEAN-PIERRE MENGWANG ME NGYEMA; Dir-Gen. JEAN LOUIS POUNAH-NDJIMBI.

SHIPPING

The principal deep-water ports are Port-Gentil, which handles mainly petroleum exports, and Owendo, 15 km from Libreville, which services mainly barge traffic. The principal ports for timber are at Owendo, Mayumba and Nyanga, and there is a fishing port at Libreville. The construction of a deep-water port at Mayumba is planned. A new terminal for the export of minerals, at Owendo, was opened in 1988. In 1995 the merchant shipping fleet had a total displacement of 32,178 grt, compared with a displacement of 98,000 grt in 1985. In November 1997 the Islamic Development Bank granted a loan of 11,000m. francs CFA for the rehabilitation of Gabon's ports.

Compagnie de Manutention et de Chalandage d'Owendo (COMACO): BP 2131, Libreville; tel. 70-26-35; telex 5208; f. 1974; Pres. GEORGES RAWIRI; Dir in Libreville M. RAYMOND.

Office des Ports et Rades du Gabon (OPRAG): BP 1051, Libreville; tel. 70-00-48; telex 5319; fax 70-37-35; f. 1974; state-owned; national port authority; Pres. ALI BONGO; Dir-Gen. PHILIBERT ANDZEMBE.

SAGA Gabon: BP 518, Port-Gentil; tel. 55-54-00; telex 8205; fax 55-21-71; Chair. G. COGNON; Man. Dir J. C. SIMON.

Société Nationale d'Acconage et de Transit (SNAT): BP 3897, Libreville; tel. 70-04-04; telex 5420; fax 70-13-11; f. 1976; 51% state-owned; freight transport; Dir-Gen. CLAUDE AYO-IGUENDHA.

Société Nationale de Transports Maritimes (SONATRAM): BP 3841, Libreville; tel. 74-06-32; telex 5289; fax 74-59-67; f. 1976; relaunched 1995; 51% state-owned; river and ocean cargo transport; Man. Dir RAPHAEL MOARA WALLA.

Société du Port Minéralier d'Owendo: f. 1987; cap. 4,000m. francs CFA; majority holding by COMILOG; management of new terminal for minerals at Owendo.

SOCOPAO–Gabon: BP 4, Libreville; tel. 70-21-40; telex 5212; fax 70-02-76; f. 1963; freight transport and storage; Dir HENRI LECORDIER.

CIVIL AVIATION

There are international airports at Libreville, Port-Gentil and Franceville, 65 other public and 50 private airfields linked mostly with the forestry and petroleum industries.

Air Affaires Gabon: BP 3962, Libreville; tel. 73-25-13; telex 5360; fax 73-49-98; f. 1975; domestic passenger chartered and scheduled flights; Chair. RAYMOND BELLANGER; Dir-Gen. Commdr RENÉ MORVAN.

Air Service Gabon (ASG): BP 2232, Libreville; tel. 73-24-08; telex 5522; fax 73-60-69; f. 1965; charter flights; Chair. JÉRÔME OKINDA; Gen. Man. FRANCIS LASCOMBES.

Compagnie Nationale Air Gabon: BP 2206, Libreville; tel. 73-00-27; telex 5371; fax 73-11-56; f. 1951 as Cie Aérienne Gabonaise; began operating international services in 1977, following Gabon's withdrawal from Air Afrique (see under Côte d'Ivoire); 80% state-owned; internal and international cargo and passenger services; Chair. MARTIN BONGO; Dir-Gen. Commdr RENÉ MORVAN.

Société de Gestion de l'Aéroport de Libreville (ADL): BP 363, Libreville; tel. 73-62-44; fax 73-61-28; f. 1988; 26.5% state-owned; management of airport at Libreville; Pres. CHANTAL LIDJI BADINGA; Dir-Gen. PIERRE ANDRÉ COLLET.

Tourism

Tourist arrivals were estimated at 103,000 in 1994, while receipts from tourism totalled US $5m. The tourist sector is being extensively developed, with new hotels and associated projects and the promotion of national parks. In 1996 there were 74 hotels, with a total of 4,000 rooms.

Centre Gabonais de Promotion Touristique (GABONTOUR): BP 2085, Libreville; tel. 72-85-04; fax 72-85-03; e-mail gabontour@compuserve.com; f. 1988; Dir-Gen. JOSEPH ADJEMBIMANDE.

Office National Gabonais du Tourisme: BP 161, Libreville; tel. 72-21-82.

THE GAMBIA

Introductory Survey

Location, Climate, Language, Religion, Flag, Capital

The Republic of The Gambia is a narrow territory around the River Gambia on the west coast of Africa. The country has a short coastline on the Atlantic Ocean, but is otherwise surrounded by Senegal. The climate is tropical, with a rainy season from July to September. Away from the river swamps most of the terrain is covered by savanna bush. Average temperatures in Banjul range from 23°C (73°F) in January to 27°C (81°F) in July, while temperatures inland can exceed 40°C (104°F). English is the official language, while the principal vernacular languages are Mandinka, Fula and Wolof. About 85% of the inhabitants are Muslims; most of the remainder are Christians, and there are a small number of animists. The national flag (proportions 3 by 2) has red, blue and green horizontal stripes, with two narrow white stripes bordering the central blue band. The capital is Banjul (formerly called Bathurst).

Recent History

The Gambia was formerly a British dependency. It became a separate colony in 1888, having previously been administered with Sierra Leone. The principle of election was first introduced in the 1946 Constitution. Political parties were formed in the 1950s, and another Constitution was adopted in 1960. In April 1962 a constitutional amendment made provision for the office of Premier. Following legislative elections in May of that year, the leader of the People's Progressive Party (PPP), Dr (later Sir) Dawda Kairaba Jawara, was appointed to this post. Full internal self-government followed in October 1963. On 18 February 1965 The Gambia became an independent country within the Commonwealth, with Jawara as Prime Minister. The country became a republic on 24 April 1970, whereupon Sir Dawda Jawara took office as President. He was re-elected in 1972 and again in 1977, as a result of overwhelming PPP victories in legislative elections.

In October 1980, fearing military disaffection, the Government asked neighbouring Senegal to dispatch troops to The Gambia to assist in maintaining internal security (under the terms of a mutual defence pact). In July 1981, however, a coup was attempted while Jawara was visiting the United Kingdom. Left-wing rebels formed a National Revolutionary Council, and proclaimed their civilian leader, Kukoi Samba Sanyang, as Head of State. Senegalese troops again assisted in the suppression of the rebellion. About 1,000 people were arrested and more than 60 people were subsequently sentenced to death, although no executions took place. A state of emergency remained in force until February 1985. All those convicted of involvement in the insurrection had been released by early 1991.

The first presidential election by direct popular vote was held in May 1982. Jawara was re-elected, with 72% of the votes cast; he was opposed by the leader of the National Convention Party (NCP), Sherif Mustapha Dibba (who was in detention for his alleged involvement in the abortive coup). In the concurrent legislative elections the PPP won 27 of the 35 elective seats in the House of Representatives. At legislative elections in March 1987 the PPP took 31 of the 36 directly-elected seats in the House of Representatives. Three other parties presented candidates: the NCP (which won the remaining five elective seats) and two new groupings, the Gambia People's Party (GPP) and the People's Democratic Organization for Independence and Socialism (PDOIS). In the presidential election Jawara was re-elected with 59% of the votes cast, while Sherif Dibba (who had been acquitted and released from detention in June 1982) received 27% of the votes; Assan Musa Camara (the GPP leader and a former Vice-President) won 14%. Rumours of financial impropriety, corruption and the abuse of power at ministerial level persisted throughout the decade, and apparently prompted the dismissal of at least four government members between 1984 and 1990.

Plans were announced in August 1981 for a confederation of The Gambia and Senegal, to be called Senegambia. The confederal agreement came into effect on 1 February 1982; a Confederal Council of Ministers, headed by President Abdou Diouf of Senegal (with President Jawara as his deputy), held its inaugural meeting in January 1983, as did the 60-member Confederal Assembly. Agreements followed on co-ordination of foreign policy, communications, defence and security, but Senegal was critical of Jawara's reluctance to proceed towards full economic and political integration. In August 1989 Diouf announced that Senegalese troops were to be withdrawn from The Gambia, apparently in protest at a request by Jawara that The Gambia be accorded more power within the confederal agreement. The confederation was dissolved in the following month. The Gambia subsequently protested that the Senegalese authorities had introduced restrictions concerning customs duties and travel that were unfavourable to Gambian interests, and that supplies of important commodities were being prevented from entering The Gambia via Senegal. Tensions were exacerbated as Senegal accused The Gambia of harbouring rebels of the Mouvement des forces démocratiques de la Casamance (MFDC), an organization seeking independence for Casamance—which is virtually separated from the rest of Senegal by the enclave of The Gambia. Bilateral links remained strained until January 1991, when the two countries signed an agreement of friendship and co-operation. In September 1993, however, Senegal's unilateral decision to close the Gambian–Senegalese border, apparently to reduce smuggling, again strained relations.

The Commander of the National Gendarmerie and Army resigned in June 1991, following a brief rebellion in Banjul by soldiers who were demanding the payment of outstanding allowances; seven officers were subsequently dismissed. In July a Nigerian national was appointed Commander of the Gambian armed forces, and a defence co-operation agreement was signed by the two countries in early 1992. There was a similar short-lived protest in February 1992. Meanwhile, concern for national security had prompted the arrest, in October 1991, of several people, including the brother of Kukoi Samba Sanyang. This was followed in March 1992 by the arrest of seven people in response to a government announcement that a Libyan-backed rebel force, led by Kukoi Samba Sanyang, was preparing to invade The Gambia. (Sanyang had previously been linked to a coup plot uncovered by the authorities in early 1988.)

Despite an earlier announcement that he would not be seeking a sixth presidential mandate, Jawara was re-elected on 29 April 1992, receiving 58% of the votes cast. Again, Jawara's closest rival was Sherif Dibba, who took 22% of the votes cast; the other candidates were Assan Musa Camara, Dr Momodou Lamin Bojang (the leader of the People's Democratic Party—PDP) and Sidia Jatta of the PDOIS. In concurrent elections to the House of Representatives the PPP lost six seats but retained a clear majority, with 25 elected members. The NCP secured six seats, the GPP two and independent candidates the remaining three. In a cabinet reorganization in May Jawara relinquished the defence portfolio to Saihou Sabally, who had been transferred from the finance ministry to the hitherto largely ceremonial vice-presidency. The former Vice-President, Bakary B. Dabo, was named Minister of Finance and Economic Affairs. At the same time an amnesty was announced for members of the Marxist Movement for Justice in Africa—The Gambia (MOJA—G), although it was believed that Kukoi Samba Sanyang, rumoured to be linked to the group, was excluded from the clemency measures. In November Jawara ended a ban (in force since 1980) on MOJA—G and another Marxist organization, the Gambia Socialist Revolutionary Party. In April 1993 the House of Representatives approved the abolition of the death penalty: although a total of 87 death sentences had been imposed (mostly in cases of high treason) since independence, only one execution had taken place.

Jawara was deposed in an apparently abrupt but bloodless coup on 22 July 1994. Soldiers seized strategic positions, including the airport and power installations, and radio broadcasts were made announcing that Jawara had been overthrown by a group of young army officers, styling themselves the Armed Forces Provisional Ruling Council (AFPRC), led by Lt (later Capt.) Yahya Jammeh. Jawara and members of his entourage, including several government ministers, left The Gambia aboard a US navy vessel (which had been anchored off Banjul in preparation for manoeuvres with the Gambian fleet) and were initially granted asylum by the Senegalese Government. Jawara later took up permanent residence in the United Kingdom.

The five-member AFPRC suspended the Constitution and announced a ban on all political activity. The new regime undertook to eliminate the institutionalized corruption that it claimed had been fostered under Jawara, pledging a return to civilian rule once this had been accomplished, and also promised to recover state funds allegedly misappropriated by former public officials. Jammeh officially pronounced himself Head of State, and named a mixed civilian and military Government. (Two ministers were dismissed almost immediately, accused of colluding with the deposed regime.) Included in the Cabinet was Dabo, who had initially fled with Jawara but now returned to Banjul to resume the finance portfolio. Fafa Idriss M'bai (who as Minister of Justice in 1982–84 had been responsible for drafting anti-corruption legislation, but who had been forced to resign after having himself been implicated in allegations of financial impropriety) was designated Minister of Justice and Attorney-General. Those members of Jawara's Government who had been arrested following the coup were released shortly afterwards. The new authorities gave assurances that all members of the former regime would be welcome to return to The Gambia to participate in the reform programme, but warned that none would be exempt from the country's judicial processes. Purges of the armed forces and public institutions were implemented, and several of Jawara's former ministers were twice rearrested and briefly detained during September 1994, as part of investigations into state security and financial impropriety. In October Dabo was dismissed from the Government (after reportedly having opposed the AFPRC's arms procurement programme), and was replaced by Bala Garba Jahumpa.

The AFPRC's timetable for a transition to civilian rule, published in October 1994, envisaged a programme of reform culminating in the inauguration of new elected institutions, of what was to be designated the Second Republic, in December 1998. The length of the transition period prompted criticism both internationally and, within The Gambia, from prominent judicial, religious and trade union figures. In November 1994 it was announced that 10 former government ministers (reportedly including Dabo) would be tried on charges of corruption. Shortly afterwards it was revealed that a coup attempt, involving military officers who were said by the AFPRC to wish to install an entirely military regime, had been foiled. Some 50 soldiers, including the coup leaders, were reported to have been killed during the attempt and its suppression, and several arrests were made. Dabo, denying allegations of complicity, subsequently fled the country. Later in the month some of the police and army officers who had been detained since July were released.

The coup attempt prompted the Governments of the United Kingdom, Denmark and Sweden to issue warnings that their nationals should avoid travelling to The Gambia, and this advice had a devastating effect on the Gambian tourist industry in subsequent months. At the end of November 1994 Capt. Jammeh commissioned a National Consultative Committee (NCC) to make recommendations regarding a possible shortening of the period of transition to civilian rule. In January 1995 two members of the AFPRC (the Vice-President, Sana Sabally, and Sadibou Hydara, the Minister of the Interior), both of whom were said to be opposed to the NCC's recommendations for a curtailment of the transition period (the Committee proposed a return to civilian government in July 1996), were arrested, following an alleged attempt to seize power. M'bai, a principal instigator of the NCC, was dismissed from the Government in March 1995, and was subsequently arrested and charged with corruption. Jahumpa was at the same time transferred to the Ministry of Trade, Industry and Employment. However, his replacement as Minister of Finance, Ousman Koro Ceesay, was reported in June to have been killed in a motor accident, and Jahumpa thereafter resumed the finance portfolio. A new Minister of Works and Communications was appointed in September (the outgoing minister having been accused of failing to use available funds for the implementation of infrastructural projects), and a new Minister of Health and Social Welfare was named in November.

The death penalty was restored by government decree in August 1995, reportedly in response to a recent increase in the murder rate. In October Capt. Ebou Jallow, since January the official spokesman of the AFPRC, sought asylum in Senegal; he stated that he was seeking to overthrow Jammeh, accusing the regime of complicity in murder and arbitrary arrests. For its past, the AFPRC asserted that Jallow had embezzled funds from the Central Bank prior to his departure and that he was conspiring with Jawara. In November a government decree was issued conferring wide powers of arrest and detention on the Minister of the Interior: under its terms, the police were authorized to detain without trial for a period of up to three months any person considered to be a threat to state security. In December Sabally was sentenced by court martial to nine years' imprisonment for plotting to overthrow Jammeh. (Hydara was reported to have died of natural causes while in detention.) In January 1996 Jawara was charged *in absentia* with embezzlement, following investigations into the alleged diversion of proceeds from the sale of petroleum donated by Nigeria. During March–April 1996 the confiscation was ordered of the assets in The Gambia of Jawara and 11 former government members. In July the Minister of Health and Social Welfare was arrested and charged with the misappropriation of state funds.

Although the AFPRC expressed its commitment to freedom of expression, a ban on the publication of journals by political organizations was introduced shortly after the July 1994 *coup d'état*. What was regarded as the harassment of journalists in The Gambia provoked considerable international concern, as there were periodic incidents of the arrest of, or fines against, journalists, while several non-Gambian journalists were deported.

A Constitutional Review Commission was inaugurated in April 1995, and submitted its recommendations to Jammeh in November; the draft was published in early March 1996. Despite demands by organizations such as the European Union (EU) and the Commonwealth, as well as by individual countries that had previously been major donors to The Gambia (most notably the United Kingdom and the USA), for an early return to civilian rule, the AFPRC continued to assert that it would adhere to its revised timetable. In April it was announced that it would be impossible to complete the return to elected civilian government by July, and in May new dates were set for the presidential and legislative elections, which would now take place in September and December, respectively. Meanwhile, the draft Constitution would be submitted to a national referendum in August. Opponents of the AFPRC criticized provisions of the Constitution that, they alleged, had been formulated with the specific intention of facilitating Jammeh's election to the presidency (although the Head of State had frequently asserted that he would not seek election) and of giving political advantage to his supporters.

The constitutional referendum took place on 8 August 1996. The rate of participation was high (85.9%), and 70.4% of voters endorsed the new document. A presidential decree was issued in the following week reauthorizing party political activity. Shortly afterwards, however, it was announced that the PPP, the NCP and the GPP were to be prohibited from contesting the forthcoming presidential and parliamentary elections, as were all holders of executive office in the 30 years prior to July 1994. Thus, the only parties from the Jawara era authorized to contest the elections were the PDOIS and the PDP. The effective ban on participation in the restoration of elected institutions of all those associated with political life prior to the military takeover was strongly criticized by the Commonwealth and its Ministerial Action Group on the Harare Declaration (CMAG, see p. 127), which had hitherto made a significant contribution to the transition process. At the same time the AFPRC announced that, following consultations between the military authorities and the Provisional Independent Electoral Commission (PIEC), which had expressed concern that newly-authorized political organizations would have insufficient time to campaign for the elections, the presidential poll was to be postponed by two weeks, to 26 September 1996.

Jammeh did not formally announce his intention to contest the presidency until mid-August 1996. At the end of the month the establishment was reported of a political party supporting Jammeh, the Alliance for Patriotic Reorientation and Construction (APRC). In early September Jammeh announced his resignation from the army, in order to contest the presidency as a civilian, as required by the Constitution. The presidential election took place, as scheduled, on 26 September. Three people were reportedly killed, and more than 30 injured, in violence shortly before the poll. The earliest results of voting showed a victory for Jammeh; his nearest rival, Ousainou Darboe (leader of the United Democratic Party—UDP), meanwhile sought refuge at the residence of the Senegalese ambassador, where he remained until the end of the month. The official results, issued by the PIEC on 27 September, confirmed Jammeh's election as President, with 55.77% of the total votes cast, ahead of Darboe, with 35.84%, Hamat Bah of the National Reconciliation Party (NRP), with 5.52%, and Sidia Jatta of the PDOIS, with 2.87%. The rate of participation by voters was again high, especially in rural areas. However, observers, including CMAG, expressed doubts as to the credibility of the election results. The dissolution of the AFPRC was announced the same day. Jammeh was inaugurated as President on 18 October. In early November an unconditional amnesty was proclaimed for more than 40 political detainees, among them former government ministers detained since July 1994.

An attack took place in early November 1996 on an army camp at Farafenni, 100 km east of Banjul, as a result of which six people were killed and five injured. Shortly afterwards it was announced that the legislative elections, due to take place on 11 December, were to be postponed until 2 January 1997. All the registered parties presented candidates for the 45 elective seats in the new National Assembly. Voting took place as scheduled, and the Gambian authorities, opposition groups and most international observers expressed broad satisfaction at the conduct of the poll. As expected, the APRC won an overwhelming majority of the seats in the legislature. The final results, as issued by the PIEC, allocated 28 seats to Jammeh's party (additionally, the APRC had been unopposed in five constituencies), seven to the UDP, two to the NRP and one to the PDOIS; independent candidates took the two remaining seats. The overall rate of participation by voters (again higher in rural areas) was 73.2%. As Head of State, Jammeh was empowered by the Constitution to nominate four additional members of parliament, from whom the Speaker (and Deputy Speaker) would be chosen. The opening session of the National Assembly, on 16 January, accordingly elected Mustapha Wadda, previously Secretary-General of the APRC and Secretary at the Presidency, as Speaker. This session denoted the full entry into force of the Constitution and thus the inauguration of the Second Republic. A further 12 political detainees were released in early February. At the end of that month it was reported that the Commander of the Presidential Guard had been arrested, accused of circulating malicious tracts.

Under the new Constitution government ministers of cabinet rank were designated Secretaries of State, and the Government was reorganized to this effect in early March 1997. Later in the month Isatou Njie-Saidy, Secretary of State for Health, Social Welfare and Women's Affairs, was appointed Vice-President. However, most of the responsibilities hitherto associated with this post were transferred to the Secretary of State for the Office of the President, a position now held by Edward Singhateh: although Singhateh had succeeded Sabally as AFPRC Vice-President in early 1995, he was, under the terms of the new Constitution, too young (at 27) to assume the office of Vice-President. In mid-April 1997 the remaining four regional military governors were replaced by civilians. Among the new governors was Jawara's former head of police, who had been released from detention only two months previously.

Supporters of the new regime attributed the electoral success of Jammeh and the APRC to the popularity within The Gambia of the ambitious infrastructural projects undertaken since July 1994, citing in particular the construction of more new schools and hospitals than had been built in 30 years by the Jawara administration, as well as a new airport terminal and modernized port facilities, a television station, and the impending inauguration of a national university. However, Jammeh's critics condemned what they regarded as excessive expenditure on 'prestige' projects. Furthermore, in early February 1997 CMAG reiterated its earlier concerns regarding the exclusion of what it termed a 'significant element' of The Gambia's political class from the process of restoring government to elected civilian institutions.

In early April 1997 the trial began in camera of five alleged mercenaries suspected of involvement in the November 1996 attack on the Farafenni barracks. The accused apparently confirmed press reports at the time of the attack that they had formed part of a 40-strong commando group, trained in Libya and led by Kukoi Samba Sanyang, which had fought for Charles Taylor's National Patriotic Front of Liberia during the early 1990s. Four of the accused (three Gambians and one Senegalese national) were subsequently sentenced to death—the fifth defendant had died in detention in May 1997. In early October, however, the Supreme Court ruled that the convictions, on charges of treason, were not sustainable, and ordered that the four be retried on conspiracy charges. Meanwhile, the arrest of a further mercenary had been reported in mid-April; some 13 other suspects remained at large.

Responsibility for religious affairs was transferred from the Secretary of State for the Interior to the Secretary of State for Youth and Sports in early October 1997. In the previous month members of the Pakistani Ahmadi Islamic sect had left The Gambia (where they had been working for more than 20 years), accusing the incumbent Secretary of State, Momodou Bojang, of fomenting religious intolerance by describing the sect as 'infidels' and allowing Gambian Islamic leaders to deliver sermons hostile to the Ahmadi.

In July 1997 CMAG reiterated its previous concerns regarding the lack of a 'fully inclusive' political system in The Gambia, urging the immediate removal of the ban on political activities by certain parties and individuals; the group also sought demonstration of the Jammeh administration's expressed commitment to the observance of human rights and the rule of law, and appealed to the Government to investigate allegations of the harassment of members of the opposition. In September, none the less, CMAG reported signs of progress in the democratization process.

Jawara's overthrow, the suspension of constitutional government and the initial timetable for the restoration of civilian institutions were widely condemned by many of The Gambia's external creditors, and in the months that followed the coup the EU, the United Kingdom, the USA and Japan suspended much co-operation (although vital aid projects were generally to continue), while the Commonwealth was repeatedly critical of the AFPRC's actions. Advice issued by the Governments of the United Kingdom, Denmark and Sweden, following the November 1994 attempted coup, that their nationals should avoid travelling to The Gambia prompted protests by the Jammeh administration, which claimed that the political situation in The Gambia entailed no risk for tourists. (All three had withdrawn warnings to tourists by March 1995.) The loss of financial and military co-operation, as well as of tourist revenue (on which the economy is heavily reliant) was widely perceived as having in part prompted the revision of the transitional programme. The Gambia's international economic and political links were strengthened with the completion of the transition process. Jammeh attended the Commonwealth Heads of Government Meeting in Edinburgh, United Kingdom, in late October 1997, at which Commonwealth leaders welcomed CMAG's report regarding democratization in The Gambia.

Deprived of support by The Gambia's traditional aid donors and trading partners, the Jammeh administration sought new links. Diplomatic relations with Libya, severed in 1980, were restored in November 1994. Links with Taiwan, ended in 1974, were re-established in July 1995, whereupon that country was reported to have advanced substantial funding. The People's Republic of China subsequently severed relations with The Gambia. Close links were also forged with Cuba, Iran and Nigeria.

Despite the presence in Senegal of prominent opponents of the new regime, Jammeh also sought to improve relations with that country, and in January 1996 the two countries signed an agreement aimed at increasing bilateral trade and at minimizing cross-border smuggling. The agreement was signed on behalf of Senegal by Diouf, who was visiting The Gambia for the first time since Jawara's overthrow. A further agreement, concluded in April 1997, was designed to facilitate the trans-border movement of goods destined for re-export. In June the two countries agreed to take joint measures to combat insecurity, illegal immigration, arms-trafficking and drugs-smuggling. In the following month the MFDC strenuously denied involvement in a commando raid on a Gambian military post near the border, in which one soldier was killed and three injured.

Government

The Constitution of the Second Republic of The Gambia, which was approved in a national referendum on 8 August 1996, entered into full effect on 16 January 1997. Under its terms, the Head of State is the President of the Republic, who is directly elected by universal adult suffrage (the minimum age for voters is 18 years). No restriction is placed on the number of times a President may seek re-election. Legislative authority is vested in the National Assembly, comprising 45 members elected by direct suffrage and four members nominated by the President of the Republic. The President appoints government members, who are reponsible both to the Head of State and to the National Assembly.

Defence

In August 1997 the Gambian National Army comprised 800 men (including a marine unit of about 70 and a presidential guard) in active service. Military service has been mainly voluntary; however, the Constitution of the Second Republic, which entered into full effect in January 1997, makes provision for compulsory service. The defence budget for 1997/98 was estimated at D150m.

Economic Affairs

In 1995, according to estimates by the World Bank, The Gambia's gross national product (GNP), measured at average 1993–95 prices, was US $354m., equivalent to $320 per head. Between 1985 and 1994, it was estimated, GNP per head increased, in real terms, at an average annual rate of 0.5%. During 1985–95 the population increased by an annual average of 4.0%. The Gambia's gross domestic product (GDP) increased, in real terms, by an annual average of 2.4% in 1985–95; following a decline of 4.8% in 1994, the World Bank estimated GDP growth of 3.2% in 1995.

Agriculture (including forestry and fishing) contributed 27.5% of GDP in 1994. About 79.3% of the labour force were employed in the sector in 1996. The dominant agricultural activity is the cultivation of groundnuts. Exports of groundnuts and related products accounted for an estimated 50.1% of domestic export earnings in the financial year ending 30 June 1995; however, a significant proportion of the crop is frequently smuggled into Senegal. Cotton, citrus fruits, avocados and sesame seed are also cultivated for export. The principal staple crops are rice, millet, sorghum and maize, although The Gambia remains heavily dependent on imports of rice and other basic foodstuffs. The attainment of food self-sufficiency is a stated priority of the Jammeh Government. Fishing makes an important contribution both to the domestic food supply and to export earnings: exports of fish and fish products contributed an estimated 11.0% of the value of domestic exports in 1994/95. According to World Bank data, agricultural GDP increased by an annual average of 1.2% in 1985–95; growth in the sector's GDP was estimated at 2.6% in 1995 (compared with a decline of 1.1% in 1994).

Industry (including manufacturing, construction, mining and power) contributed 14.6% of GDP in 1994. About 4.2% of the labour force were employed in the sector at the time of the 1983 census. Industrial GDP increased by an annual average of 2.7% in 1985–95; industrial GDP fell by 11.9% in 1994, but increased by an estimated 4.9% in 1995.

The Gambia has no economically viable mineral resources, although seismic surveys have indicated the existence of deposits of petroleum. Manufacturing contributed 7.3% of GDP in 1994, and employed about 2.5% of the labour force in 1983. The sector is dominated by agro-industrial activities, most importantly the processing of groundnuts. Beverages and construction materials are also produced for the domestic market. Manufacturing GDP increased by an annual average of 2.8% in 1985–95; the sector's GDP declined by 2.8% in 1994, and by an estimated 1.9% in 1995.

The Gambia is highly reliant on imported energy. According to figures published by IMF, imports of petroleum products accounted for an estimated 11.1% of the value of imports for domestic use in 1994/95.

The services sector, according to World Bank data, contributed 57.8% of GDP in 1994. The tourist industry is of particular significance as a generator of foreign exchange. Tourism contributed about 10% of annual GDP in the early 1990s, and employed about one-third of workers in the formal sector at that time. The international response to the 1994 coup and its aftermath had a severe adverse impact on tourism to The Gambia, although a strong recovery was apparent by 1996. The Jammeh administration has expressed its intention further to exploit the country's potential as a transit point for regional trade and also as a centre for regional finance and telecommunications. Re-exports contributed an estimated 81.9% of the value of total merchandise exports in 1994/95, according to IMF figures. The GDP of the services sector increased by an annual average of 1.5% in 1990–95; following a decline of 6.8% in 1994, the World Bank estimated growth of 3.6% in 1995.

In 1996 The Gambia recorded a visible trade deficit of US $98.35m., while there was a deficit of $47.7m. on the current account of the balance of payments. In 1994 the principal source of imports was the People's Republic of China, which supplied an estimated 24.7% of total imports; other major sources were the Belgo-Luxembourg Economic Union (BLEU), the United Kingdom, Hong Kong and Senegal. The BLEU was the principal market for exports (an estimated 50.4%) in that year; other major purchasers were Japan and Guinea. The Gambia's principal domestic exports in 1994/95 were groundnuts and related products, cotton products and fish and fish products. The principal imports in 1993/94 were manufactured goods, food and live animals, machinery and transport equipment, mineral fuels and lubricants, beverages and tobacco, and chemicals.

In 1994/95 there was an estimated overall budget deficit of D150.4m. (equivalent to 4.4% of that year's GDP). The Gambia's total external debt was US $425.6m. at the end of 1995, of which $383.7m. was long-term public debt. In that year the cost of debt-servicing was equivalent to 14.0% of the value of exports of goods and services. The average annual rate of inflation was 13.7% in 1985–95; inflation, which had averaged only 1.7% in 1994, increased to 7.0% in 1995, but slowed again to average only 1.1% in 1996. The rate of unemployment was estimated at some 26% of the labour force in mid-1994.

The Gambia is a member of the Economic Community of West African States (ECOWAS, see p. 145), of The Gambia River Basin Development Organization (OMVG, see p. 261), of the African Groundnut Council (see p. 256), of the West Africa Rice Development Association (WARDA, see p. 258), and of the Permanent Inter-State Committee on Drought Control in the Sahel (CILSS, see p. 262).

Following the July 1994 *coup d'état*, the Jammeh Government expressed its desire to eliminate corruption in public life and to ensure the more equitable distribution of the benefits of economic growth. The administration's long-term aim, outlined in its ambitious *Vision 2020* document published in September 1996, setting targets for all sectors of the economy, for education, health care, welfare, the environment and public administration, is to achieve the status of a middle-income economy within 25 years. Initially, however, its economic aims were severely impeded by the suspension by principal donors of much financial co-operation; the dramatic decline in the number of tourists to The Gambia in the months following the military takeover caused considerable economic disruption, and the economy suffered from the loss of entrepôt trade (as a result both of the coup and of the 50% devaluation, in January 1994, of the CFA franc—the currency of Senegal and of several other countries of the region). The new regime none the less undertook numerous infrastructural, education and health care projects, assistance for which was apparently advanced by new partners, including Cuba, Libya and Taiwan. Meanwhile, domestic funding was facilitated by the collection of taxes outstanding from the Jawara era. Economic recovery from 1995 was in large part boosted by the recovery in the tourism sector. The return to government by elected civilian institutions, from early 1997, was expected to prompt a return to full support by the international economic community: the World Bank, notably, resumed co-operation in late 1997. Considerable efforts have also been made to attract new investors to The Gambia. However, a major obstacle to sustained growth in The Gambia remains the overwhelming dependence on the groundnut sector, which itself lags behind other sectors in terms of modernization and productivity; a 50% decline in the groundnut crop in 1996/97, to only 16,000 metric tons, was likely to undermine growth in other areas of the economy.

Social Welfare

At the end of 1980 there were 43 government physicians, 23 private practitioners and five dentists. There were four hospitals and a network of 12 health centres, 17 dispensaries and 68 maternity and child welfare clinics throughout the country. A major programme to improve health and social welfare facilities has been undertaken by the Jammeh administration. Among the schemes is a new hospital at Farafenni, under construction at a cost of US $65m.

Education

Primary education, beginning at seven years of age, is free but not compulsory and lasts for six years. Secondary education, from 13 years of age, comprises a first cycle of five years and a second, two-year cycle. In 1992/93 some 55% of children in the relevant age-group were enrolled at primary schools (64% of boys; 46% of girls), while secondary enrolment included only 18% of students aged between 13 and 19 (24% of boys; 12% of girls). According to UNESCO estimates, adult illiteracy in 1995 averaged 61.4% (males 47.2%; females 75.1%). The Jammeh administration has, since 1994, embarked on an ambitious project to improve educational facilities and levels of attendance and attainment. A particular aim has been to ameliorate access to schools for pupils in rural areas. Post-secondary education is available in teacher training, agriculture, health and technical subjects. Some 1,591 students were enrolled at tertiary establishments in 1994/95. The new University of The Gambia was scheduled for inauguration in three phases, beginning in October 1997. In 1977 The Gambia introduced Koranic studies at all stages of education, and many children attend Koranic schools (daara).

Expenditure on education by the central Government in 1991/92 was D78m. (12.9% of total government spending in that year).

Public Holidays

1998: 1 January (New Year's Day), 30 January* (Id al-Fitr, end of Ramadan), 18 February (Independence Day), 8 April* (Id al-Adha, Feast of the Sacrifice), 10–13 April (Easter), 1 May (Labour Day), 7 July* (Mouloud, Birth of the Prophet), 22 July (AFPRC Revolution Day), 15 August (Assumption), 25 December (Christmas).

1999: 1 January (New Year's Day), 19 January* (Id al-Fitr, end of Ramadan), 18 February (Independence Day), 28 March* (Id al-Adha, Feast of the Sacrifice), 2–5 April (Easter), 1 May (Labour Day), 26 June* (Mouloud, Birth of the Prophet), 22 July (AFPRC Revolution Day), 15 August (Assumption), 25 December (Christmas).

* These holidays are dependent on the Islamic lunar calendar and may vary by one or two days from the dates given.

Weights and Measures

Imperial weights and measures are used. Importers and traders also use the metric system.

Statistical Survey

Source (unless otherwise stated): Department of Information, 14 Hagan St, Banjul; tel. and fax 227230.

Area and Population

AREA, POPULATION AND DENSITY

Area (sq km)	11,295*
Population (census results)	
15 April 1983	
Total	687,817
15 April 1993†	
Males	514,530
Females	511,337
Total	1,025,867
Density (per sq km) at census of 1993	90.8

* 4,361 sq miles. † Provisional.

PRINCIPAL TOWNS (population at 1983 census)

Banjul (capital)	44,188	Farafenni	10,168
Serrekunda	68,433	Sukuta	7,227
Brikama	19,584	Gunjur	7,115
Bakau	19,309		

BIRTHS AND DEATHS (UN estimates, annual averages)

	1980–85	1985–90	1990–95
Birth rate (per 1,000)	48.2	46.5	43.7
Death rate (per 1,000)	23.1	20.7	18.8

Expectation of life (UN estimates, years at birth, 1990–95): 45.0 (males 43.4; females 46.6).

Source: UN, *World Population Prospects: The 1994 Revision*.

ECONOMICALLY ACTIVE POPULATION* (persons aged 10 years and over, 1983 census)

	Total
Agriculture, hunting, forestry and fishing	239,940
Quarrying	66
Manufacturing	8,144
Electricity, gas and water	1,233
Construction	4,373
Trade, restaurants and hotels	16,551
Transport, storage and communications	8,014
Public administration and defence	8,295
Education	4,737
Medical services	2,668
Personal and domestic services	6,553
Activities not adequately defined	25,044
Total	325,618†

* Figures exclude persons seeking work for the first time.
† Males 174,856; females 150,762.

Mid-1996 (estimates in '000): Agriculture, etc. 457; Total 576 (Source: FAO, *Production Yearbook*).

Agriculture

PRINCIPAL CROPS ('000 metric tons)

	1994	1995	1996
Millet	53	54	61
Sorghum	9	12	14
Rice (paddy)	20	19	20
Maize	13	14	10
Cassava (Manioc)*	6	6	6
Pulses*	4	4	4
Palm kernels*	2	2	2
Groundnuts (in shell)	81	75	46
Vegetables*	8	8	8
Fruits*	4	4	4
Cottonseed*	3	2	3

* FAO estimates.

Source: FAO, *Production Yearbook*.

LIVESTOCK ('000 head, year ending September)

	1994*	1995	1996
Cattle	308	314	323
Goats	216	218*	224
Sheep	157	158*	159
Pigs	14	14	14
Asses*	30	30	30
Horses*	16	16	16

Poultry (FAO estimates, million): 1 in 1994; 1 in 1995; 1 in 1996.

Source: FAO, *Production Yearbook*.

LIVESTOCK PRODUCTS (FAO estimates, '000 metric tons)

	1994	1995	1996
Beef and veal	3	3	3
Goat meat	1	1	1
Mutton and lamb	1	1	1
Poultry meat	1	1	1
Other meat	1	1	1
Cows' milk	6	7	7
Poultry eggs	1	1	1

Source: FAO, *Production Yearbook*.

Forestry

ROUNDWOOD REMOVALS
('000 cubic metres, excluding bark)

	1992*	1993	1994
Sawlogs, veneer logs and logs for sleepers	90	103	106
Other industrial wood	7	7	7
Fuel wood	1,016	1,078	1,096
Total	1,113	1,188	1,209

* FAO estimates.

Source: FAO, *Yearbook of Forest Products*.

Fishing

('000 metric tons, live weight)

	1993	1994	1995
Tilapias	1.1	1.0	1.1
Other freshwater fishes	1.4	1.4	1.5
Tonguefishes	0.2	0.2	0.9
Sea catfishes	0.4	0.3	0.8
Croakers and drums	1.2	0.5	1.4
Bonga shad	14.1	16.9	13.9
Other marine fishes (incl. unspecified)	1.5	1.3	2.6
Total fish	19.8	21.7	22.2
Southern pink shrimp	0.5	0.6	0.4
Other crustaceans and molluscs	0.1	0.1	0.5
Total catch	20.5	22.3	23.1
Inland waters	2.4	2.4	2.5
Atlantic Ocean	18.1	19.9	20.6

Source: FAO, *Yearbook of Fishery Statistics*.

Industry

SELECTED PRODUCTS

	1990	1991	1992
Salted, dried or smoked fish ('000 metric tons)*	0.7	0.5	0.5
Vegetable oils—unrefined ('000 metric tons)†	3	3	n.a.
Electric energy (million kWh)†	70	70	71

Electric energy (million kWh)†: 73 in 1993; 75 in 1994.

* Data from the FAO. † Provisional or estimated figures.

Source: UN, *Industrial Commodity Statistics Yearbook*.

Finance

CURRENCY AND EXCHANGE RATES

Monetary Units
100 butut = 1 dalasi (D).

Sterling and Dollar Equivalents (30 September 1997)
£1 sterling = 16.88 dalasi;
US $1 = 10.45 dalasi;
1,000 dalasi = £59.23 = $95.68.

Average Exchange Rate (dalasi per US $)
1994 9.576
1995 9.546
1996 9.789

BUDGET (million dalasi, year ending 30 June)

Revenue*	1992/93	1993/94	1994/95‡
Tax revenue	704.4	682.9	599.9
Direct taxes	122.9	126.0	135.8
Taxes on personal incomes	40.4	36.4	55.3
Taxes on corporate profits	76.6	80.6	73.7
Indirect taxes	581.5	556.9	464.1
Domestic taxes on goods and services	47.9	57.1	48.7
Domestic sales tax	46.5	54.7	36.8
Taxes on international trade	374.2	306.5	256.2
Customs duties	196.1	156.9	144.7
Sales tax on imports	178.1	149.1	109.8
Petroleum taxes	159.4	193.3	159.2
Duty	136.8	166.8	137.8
Sales tax	22.6	26.5	21.4
Other current revenue	61.9	84.2	65.7
Government services and charges	18.8	22.8	27.0
Interest on property	19.8	10.3	10.0
Central Bank profit	17.7	28.0	25.0
Capital revenue	0.6	4.0	3.7
Total	766.9	771.1	669.3

Expenditure†	1992/93	1993/94	1994/95‡
Current expenditure	570.7	613.3	613.4
Expenditure on goods and services	369.4	414.3	432.5
Personal emoluments, allowances and pensions	161.0	198.6	206.0
Other charges	208.4	215.7	226.5
Goods and services	128.3	133.5	142.5
Maintenance and equipment	49.0	65.0	45.2
Interest payments	117.9	133.9	128.6
Internal	72.7	84.9	77.3
External	45.2	49.2	51.3
Subsidies and current transfers	83.4	65.1	52.4
To non-profit institutions	54.4	44.9	29.7
Development expenditure	253.2	248.6	266.3
Unallocated expenditure	3.4	5.8	22.4
Total	827.3	867.7	902.2

* Excluding grants received (million dalasi): 123.3 in 1992/93; 126.5 in 1993/94; 67.8 in 1994/95.

† Excluding lending minus repayments (million dalasi): 12.1 in 1992/93; −5.7 in 1993/94; −14.7 in 1994/95.

‡ Estimates.

Source: IMF, *The Gambia—Recent Economic Developments* (December 1995).

INTERNATIONAL RESERVES (US $ million at 31 December)

	1994	1995	1996
IMF special drawing rights	0.26	0.13	0.29
Reserve position in IMF	2.17	2.21	2.14
Foreign exchange	95.59	103.81	99.71
Total	98.02	106.15	102.13

Source: IMF, *International Financial Statistics.*

MONEY SUPPLY (million dalasi at 31 December)

	1994	1995	1996
Currency outside banks	207.36	247.97	255.03
Demand deposits at commercial banks	200.17	223.50	198.46
Total money	407.53	471.47	453.49

Source: IMF, *International Financial Statistics.*

COST OF LIVING
(Consumer Price Index for Banjul and Kombo St Mary; base: 1990 = 100)

	1992	1993	1994
Food	117.6	127.7	126.2
Fuel and light	116.2	119.9	160.1
Clothing*	124.5	122.5	130.9
Rent	198.0	209.2	219.1
All items (incl. others)	118.9	126.6	128.8

* Including household linen.

Source: ILO, *Yearbook of Labour Statistics.*

1995: Food 137.1; All items 137.8.

1996: Food 138.6; All items 139.3.

Source: UN, *Monthly Bulletin of Statistics.*

NATIONAL ACCOUNTS
(million dalasi at current prices, year ending 30 June)

Expenditure on the Gross Domestic Product

	1992/93	1993/94	1994/95*
Government final consumption expenditure	576.1	613.9	615.5
Private final consumption expenditure	2,427.7	2,605.8	2,708.6
Increase in stocks / Gross fixed capital formation	677.9	626.6	557.1
Total domestic expenditure	3,681.7	3,846.3	3,881.2
Exports of goods and services	1,973.0	1,916.9	1,505.6
Less Imports of goods and services	2,426.0	2,352.1	1,949.7
GDP in purchasers' values	3,228.6	3,411.2	3,438.5†
GDP at constant 1976/77 prices	572.2	579.8	556.8

* Estimates.

† Including adjustment.

Gross Domestic Product by Economic Activity

	1991/92	1992/93	1993/94†
Agriculture, hunting, forestry and fishing	663.0	641.9	762.5
Manufacturing	166.4	188.3	191.7
Electricity and water	25.6	31.4	35.7
Construction	148.9	166.1	186.0
Trade, restaurants and hotels	647.0	738.4	635.2
Transport and communications	280.8	335.2	378.6
Business services and housing	171.8	194.9	228.1
Government services	196.9	227.3	262.3
Other services*	110.5	123.5	174.1
GDP at factor cost	2,410.9	2,647.1	2,854.3
Indirect taxes, *Less* Subsidies	536.7	581.5	556.9
GDP in purchasers' values	2,947.6	3,228.6	3,411.2

* Including banking and insurance, net of imputed bank service charges.

† Estimates.

Source: IMF, *The Gambia—Recent Economic Developments* (December 1995).

BALANCE OF PAYMENTS (US $ million, year ending 30 June).

	1994	1995	1996
Exports of goods f.o.b.	124.97	122.96	118.75
Imports of goods f.o.b.	−181.62	−162.53	−217.10
Trade balance	−56.65	−39.57	−98.35
Exports of services	90.47	53.71	101.21
Imports of services	−67.04	−69.25	−77.03
Balance on goods and services	−33.22	−55.11	−74.17
Other income received	4.87	4.37	6.01
Other income paid	−5.14	−9.58	−9.28
Balance on goods, services and income	−33.50	−60.32	−77.44
Current transfers received	45.85	55.81	35.10
Current transfers paid	−4.18	−3.68	−5.35
Current balance	8.17	−8.19	−47.70
Capital account (net)	—	—	8.52
Direct investment from abroad	9.81	7.78	10.80
Other investment assets	3.79	−3.66	5.62
Investment liabilities	19.54	20.65	42.18
Net errors and omissions	−35.12	−15.63	−4.94
Overall balance	6.19	0.95	14.47

Source: IMF, *International Financial Statistics.*

External Trade

PRINCIPAL COMMODITIES (SDR '000, year ending 30 June)

Imports c.i.f.	1991/92	1992/93	1993/94
Food and live animals	50,838	45,688	39,594
Beverages and tobacco	7,748	6,527	8,175
Raw materials	1,273	2,117	1,443
Mineral fuels, lubricants, etc.	19,223	14,641	9,618
Animal and vegetable oils	3,456	5,292	3,687
Chemicals	9,400	8,820	8,175
Manufactured goods classified by material	31,018	37,220	40,716
Machinery and transport equipment	26,457	41,101	37,671
Miscellaneous manufactured articles	12,385	13,585	10,099
Total (incl. others)	163,901	176,400	160,300

Exports f.o.b.*	1992/93	1993/94	1994/95†
Groundnuts and groundnut products	8,300	7,579	7,571
Fish and fish products	2,233	1,500	1,633
Cotton products	95	2,800	3,853
Total (incl. others)	13,695	13,962	14,900

* Excluding re-exports (SDR '000): 97,000 in 1992/93; 75,232 in 1993/94; 67,332 in 1994/95.

† Estimates.

Source: IMF, *The Gambia—Recent Economic Developments* (December 1995).

PRINCIPAL TRADING PARTNERS (percentage of trade)

Imports c.i.f.	1992	1993	1994*
Belgium-Luxembourg	5.7	7.9	10.1
China, People's Repub.	14.8	20.3	24.7
France (incl. Monaco)	6.2	7.9	4.2
Germany	4.2	3.9	4.6
Hong Kong	16.0	11.1	7.7
Italy	7.0	3.2	2.2
Japan	3.1	3.7	2.1
Netherlands	4.7	5.8	4.3
Senegal	1.9	2.9	5.4
Spain	1.6	1.1	0.8
Thailand	4.5	4.2	4.9
United Kingdom	10.1	10.3	8.5
USA	2.9	2.9	1.3

Exports f.o.b.	1992	1993	1994*
Belgium-Luxembourg	51.5	51.0	50.4
France (incl. Monaco)	0.5	0.6	2.6
Guinea	3.5	5.7	6.2
Italy	19.7	n.a.	n.a.
Japan	14.3	22.0	21.5
Senegal	n.a.	n.a.	n.a.
Spain	2.2	1.3	2.2
United Kingdom	2.1	5.0	3.6
USA	0.4	5.7	1.3

* Estimates.

Source: IMF, *The Gambia—Recent Economic Developments* (December 1995).

Transport

ROAD TRAFFIC (estimates, motor vehicles in use)

	1993	1994	1995
Passenger cars	6,860	7,840	8,000
Lorries and vans	7,120	8,010	8,280

Source: IRF, *World Road Statistics*.

SHIPPING

Merchant Fleet (registered at 31 December)

	1994	1995	1996
Number of vessels	9	6	6
Total displacement (grt)	2,512	1,490	1,490

Source: Lloyd's Register of Shipping, *World Fleet Statistics*.

International Sea-borne Freight Traffic (estimates, '000 metric tons)

	1991	1992	1993
Goods loaded	175	181	185
Goods unloaded	220	230	240

Source: UN Economic Commission for Africa, *African Statistical Yearbook*.

CIVIL AVIATION (traffic on scheduled services)

	1992	1993	1994
Kilometres flown (million)	1	1	1
Passengers carried ('000)	19	19	19
Passenger-km (million)	50	50	50
Total ton-km (million)	5	5	5

Source: UN, *Statistical Yearbook*.

Tourism

TOURIST ARRIVALS (air charter tourists, year ending 30 June)

	1992/93	1993/94	1994/95*
Total	63,940	89,997	38,000

* Estimate.

Source: IMF, *The Gambia—Recent Economic Developments* (December 1995).

Communications Media

	1992	1993	1994
Radio receivers ('000 in use)	155	169	176
Television receivers ('000 in use)	n.a.	n.a.	3
Daily newspapers	2	n.a.	2
Books published (first editions)*			
Titles	n.a.	n.a.	21
Copies ('000)	n.a.	n.a.	20

* Including pamphlets: 5 titles, 9,000 copies in 1994.

Telephones: ('000 main lines in use, excluding public call offices, year ending 31 March): 14 in 1992/93; 16 in 1993/94; 18 in 1994/95.

Telefax stations (number in use, year ending 31 March): 365 in 1992/93; 650 in 1993/94; 700 in 1994/95.

Mobile cellular telephones (subscribers, year ending 31 March): 204 in 1992/93; 400 in 1993/94; 810 in 1994/95.

Sources: UNESCO, *Statistical Yearbook*; UN, *Statistical Yearbook*.

Education

(1992/93, unless otherwise indicated)

	Teachers	Students		
		Males	Females	Total
Pre-primary*	408	n.a.	n.a.	13,118
Primary	3,193	56,948	40,314	97,262
Secondary	1,054	16,916	9,013	25,929

* 1991/92 figures.

Tertiary (1994/95): 155 teachers; 1,591 students (males 1,018, females 573).

Source: UNESCO, *Statistical Yearbook*.

Directory

The Constitution

Following the *coup d'état* of July 1994, the 1970 Constitution was suspended and the presidency and legislature, as defined therein, dissolved. A Constitutional Review Commission was inaugurated in April 1995. Its findings were submitted to the Armed Forces Provisional Ruling Council in November; the amended document was published in March 1996, and approved in a national referendum on 8 August. The new Constitution of the Second Republic of The Gambia entered into full effect on 16 January 1997.

The Constitution provides for the separation of the powers of the executive, legislative and judicial organs of state. The Head of State is the President of the Republic, who is directly elected by universal adult suffrage. No restriction is placed on the number of times a President may seek re-election. Legislative authority is vested in the National Assembly, comprising 45 members elected by direct universal suffrage and four members nominated by the President of the Republic. The Speaker and Deputy Speaker of the Assembly are elected, by the members of the legislature, from among the President's nominees. The Constitution upholds the principle of executive accountability to parliament. Thus, the Head of State appoints government members, but these are responsible both to the President and to the National Assembly. Ministers of cabinet rank take the title of Secretary of State. Committees of the Assembly have powers to inquire into the activities of ministers and of government departments, and into all matters of public importance.

In judicial affairs, the final court of appeal is the Supreme Court. Provision is made for a special criminal court to hear and determine all cases relating to the theft and misappropriation of public funds.

The Constitution provides for an Independent Electoral Commission, an Independent National Audit Office, an Office of the Ombudsman, a Lands Commission and a Public Service Commission, all of which are intended to ensure transparency, accountability and probity in public affairs.

The Constitution guarantees the rights of women, of children and of the disabled. Tribalism and other forms of sectarianism in politics are forbidden. Political activity may be suspended in the event of a state of national insecurity.

The Government

HEAD OF STATE

President: Capt. (retd) YAHYA A. J. J. JAMMEH (proclaimed Head of State 26 July 1994; elected President 26 September 1996).

Vice-President: ISATOU NJIE-SAIDY.

THE CABINET
(January 1998)

President: Capt. (retd) YAHYA A. J. J. JAMMEH.

Vice-President and Secretary of State for Health, Social Welfare and Women's Affairs: ISATOU NJIE-SAIDY.

Secretary of State for the Office of the President, responsible for the National Assembly, the Civil Service, Fisheries and Natural Resources: Capt. (retd) EDWARD SINGHATEH.

Secretary of State for Local Government and Lands: Capt. (retd) YANKUBA TOURAY.

Secretary of State for the Interior: Maj. (retd) MOMODOU BOJANG.

Secretary of State for Finance and Economic Affairs: DOMINIC MENDY.

Secretary of State for External Affairs: LAMINE SEDAT JOBE.

Secretary of State for Education: SATANG JAW.

Secretary of State for Tourism and Culture: SUSAN WAFFA-OGOOH.

Secretary of State for Agriculture: MUSA MBENGA.

Secretary of State for Works, Communications and Information: EBRIMA CEESAY.

Secretary of State for Trade, Industry and Employment: FAMARA JATTA.

Secretary of State for Youth, Sports and Religious Affairs: Capt. (retd) LAMIN BAJO.

MINISTRIES

Office of the President: State House, Banjul; tel. 223851; fax 227034.

Department of State for Agriculture and Natural Resources: The Quadrangle, Banjul; tel. 22147; fax 229546.

Department of State for Defence: Banjul.

Department of State for Education: Bedford Place Bldg, POB 989, Banjul; tel. 228522; telex 2264; fax 225066.

Department of State for External Affairs: 4 Marina Parade, Banjul; tel. 225654; telex 2351; fax 228060.

Department of State for Finance and Economic Affairs: The Quadrangle, Banjul; tel. 227221; fax 227954.

Department of State for Health, Social Welfare and Women's Affairs: The Quadrangle, Banjul; tel. 227872; telex 2357; fax 228505.

Department of State for the Interior: 71 Dobson St, Banjul; tel. 228611.

Department of State for Justice: Marina Parade, Banjul; tel. 228181.

Department of State for Local Government and Lands: The Quadrangle, Banjul; tel. 228291.

Department of State for Tourism and Culture: The Quadrangle, Banjul; tel. 228496; fax 227753.

Department of State for Trade, Industry and Employment: Central Bank Bldg, Banjul; tel. 228229; telex 2293.

Department of State for Works, Communication and Information: Half-Die, Banjul; tel. 228251.

Department of State for Youth, Sports and Religious Affairs: Bedford Place Bldg, POB 989, Banjul; tel. 228522; telex 2264; fax 225066.

President and Legislature

PRESIDENT

Presidential Election, 26 September 1996

Candidate	Votes	% of votes
YAHYA A. J. J. JAMMEH	220,011	55.77
OUSAINOU DARBOE	141,387	35.84
HAMAT N. K. BAH	21,759	5.52
SIDIA JATTA	11,337	2.87
Total	394,494	100.00

NATIONAL ASSEMBLY

Speaker: MUSTAPHA WADDA.

General Election, 2 January 1997

Party	Seats
Alliance for Patriotic Reorientation and Construction	33*
United Democratic Party	7
National Reconciliation Party	2
People's Democratic Organization for Independence and Socialism	1
Independents	2
Total	45†

* Including five seats taken in constituencies in which the party was unopposed.

† The President of the Republic is empowered by the Constitution to nominate four additional members of parliament.

Political Organizations

The ban on all political activity, imposed following the *coup d'état* of July 1994, was revoked in August 1996.

The following parties were authorized at this time:

Alliance for Patriotic Reorientation and Construction (APRC): Banjul; f. 1996; Chair. President YAHYA A. J. J. JAMMEH.

National Reconciliation Party (NRP): Banjul; f. 1996; Leader HAMAT N. K. BAH.

People's Democratic Organization for Independence and Socialism (PDOIS): Banjul; f. 1986; radical socialist; Leaders HALIFA SALLAH, SAM SARR, SIDIA JATTA.

People's Democratic Party (PDP): Bojang Kunda, Brikama, Kombo Central; tel. 84190; f. 1991; advocates promotion of agricultural self-sufficiency, mass education and infrastructural development; Pres. Dr MOMODOU LAMIN BOJANG; First Sec. JABEL SALLAH.

United Democratic Party (UDP): Banjul; f. 1996; Leader OUSAINOU DARBOE.

Note: The **Gambia People's Party,** of ASSAN MUSA CAMARA, the **National Convention Party,** of SHERIF MUSTAPHA DIBBA, and the **People's Progressive Party,** of fmr Pres. Sir DAWDA KAIRABA JAWARA, were banned from contesting the 1996 presidential election and the 1997 legislative elections.

Diplomatic Representation

EMBASSIES AND HIGH COMMISSIONS IN THE GAMBIA

China (Taiwan): Banjul; Ambassador FRANCIS CHUNG LEE.

Liberia: Banjul; Ambassador: JAMES MOLLY SCOTT.

Nigeria: Garba Jahumpa Ave, Banjul; tel. 95805; High Commissioner: MARK NNABUGWU EZE.

Senegal: 10 Nelson Mandela St, Banjul; tel. 227469; Ambassador: MOKTAR KÉBÉ.

Sierra Leone: 67 Hagan St, Banjul; tel. 228206; High Commissioner: AROUN BOHARE.

United Kingdom: 48 Atlantic Rd, Fajara, POB 507, Banjul; tel. 495133; fax 496134; e-mail bhc-gambia@dfid.gtnet.gov.uk; High Commissioner: TONY MILLSON.

USA: Kairaba Ave, Fajara, POB 19, Banjul; tel. 392856; fax 392475; Ambassador: GERALD W. SCOTT.

Judicial System

The judicial system of The Gambia is based on English Common Law and legislative enactments of the Republic's Parliament which include an Islamic Law Recognition Ordinance whereby an Islamic Court exercises jurisdiction in certain cases between, or exclusively affecting, Muslims.

The Constitution of the Second Republic guarantees the independence of the judiciary. The Supreme Court is defined as the final court of appeal. Provision is made for a special criminal court to hear and determine all cases relating to theft and misappropriation of public funds.

Supreme Court of The Gambia: Law Courts, Independence Drive, Banjul; tel. 227383; fax 228380; consists of the Chief Justice and puisne judges.

Chief Justice: BRAIMAH AMEN OMOSUN.

The Banjul Magistrates Court, the Kanifing Magistrates Court and the **Divisional Courts** are courts of summary jurisdiction presided over by a magistrate or in his absence by two or more lay justices of the peace. There are resident magistrates in all divisions. The magistrates have limited civil and criminal jurisdiction, and appeal lies from these courts to the Supreme Court.

Islamic Courts have jurisdiction in matters between, or exclusively affecting, Muslim Gambians and relating to civil status, marriage, succession, donations, testaments and guardianship. The Courts administer Islamic (Shari'a) Law. A cadi, or a cadi and two assessors, preside over and constitute an Islamic Court. Assessors of the Islamic Courts are Justices of the Peace of Islamic faith.

District Tribunals have appellate jurisdiction in cases touching on customs and traditions. Each court consists of three district tribunal members, one of whom is selected as president, and other court members from the area over which it has jurisdiction.

Attorney-General: FATOU BENSOUDA.

Religion

About 85% of the population are Muslims. The remainder are mainly Christians, and there are a few animists, mostly of the Jola and Karoninka ethnic groups.

ISLAM

Imam Ratib of Banjul: Alhaji ABDOULIE M. JOBE, King Fahd Bun Abdul Aziz Mosque, 39 Lancaster St, POB 562, Banjul; tel. 228094.

CHRISTIANITY

The Gambia Christian Council: POB 27, Banjul; tel. and fax 392092; telex 2290; f. 1966; six mems (churches and other Christian bodies); Chair. Rt Rev. SOLOMON TILEWA JOHNSON (Anglican Bishop of The Gambia); Sec.-Gen. HANNAH ACY PETERS.

The Anglican Communion

The diocese of The Gambia, which includes Senegal and Cape Verde, forms part of the Church of the Province of West Africa. The Metropolitan of the Province is the Archbishop of West Africa. There are about 1,500 adherents in The Gambia.

Bishop of The Gambia: Rt Rev. SOLOMON TILEWA JOHNSON, Bishopscourt, POB 51, Banjul; tel. 227405; fax 229495.

The Roman Catholic Church

The Gambia comprises a single diocese (Banjul), directly responsible to the Holy See. At 31 December 1995 there were an estimated 27,200 adherents of the Roman Catholic Church in the country. The diocese administers a development organization (Caritas, The Gambia), and runs 63 schools and training centres. The Bishop of Banjul is a member of the Inter-territorial Catholic Bishops' Conference of The Gambia, Liberia and Sierra Leone (based in Freetown, Sierra Leone).

Bishop of Banjul: Rt Rev. MICHAEL J. CLEARY, Bishop's House, POB 165, Banjul; tel. 393437; fax 390998.

Protestant Church

Methodist Church: POB 288, Banjul; f. 1821; tel. 227425; Chair. and Gen. Supt Rev. K. JOHN A. STEDMAN; Sec. Rev. TITUS K. A. PRATT.

The Press

Publication of newspapers and journals by political organizations was officially suspended following the July 1994 *coup d'état*. All publications were required to re-register in February 1996: those failing to do so were obliged to close.

The Daily Observer: PMB 131, Banjul; tel. 496608; fax 496878; f. 1992; daily; independent; Editor BABA GALLEH JALLOW.

Foroyaa (Freedom): Bundunka Kunda, POB 2306, Serrekunda; publ. by the PDOIS; Editors HALIFA SALLAH, SAM SARR, SIDIA JATTA.

The Gambia Daily: Dept of Information, 14 Hagan St, Banjul; tel. and fax 227230; f. 1994; govt organ; Editor ALIEU F. SAGNIA; circ. 500.

The Gambia Onward: 48 Grant St, Banjul; Editor RUDOLPH ALLEN.

The Gambian: 60 Lancaster St, Banjul; Editor NGAING THOMAS.

The Gambian Times: 21 OAU Blvd, POB 698, Banjul; tel. 445; f. 1981; fortnightly; publ. by the PPP; Editor MOMODOU GAYE.

The Nation: People's Press, 3 Boxbar Rd, POB 334, Banjul; fortnightly; Editor W. DIXON-COLLEY.

The Point: 2 Garba Jahumpa Rd, Fajara, Banjul; tel. 49-74-41; fax 49-74-42; f. 1991; 2 a week; Man. Editor DEYDA HYDARA; circ. 4,000.

The Toiler: 31 OAU Blvd, POB 698, Banjul; Editor PA MODOU FALL.

The Worker: 6 Albion Place, POB 508, Banjul; publ. by the Gambia Labour Union; Editor M. M. CEESAY.

NEWS AGENCIES

Gambia News Agency (GAMNA): Dept of Information, 14 Hagan St, Banjul; tel. and fax 227230; Dir EBRIMA COLE.

Foreign Bureau

Agence France-Presse (AFP): Banjul; tel. 497442; Correspondent DEYDA HYDARA.

Associated Press (USA), Inter Press Service (Italy) and Reuters (UK) are also represented in The Gambia.

Publisher

Government Printer: MacCarthy Sq., Banjul; tel. 227399; telex 2204.

Broadcasting and Communications

TELECOMMUNICATIONS

Gambia Telecommunications Company Ltd (GAMTEL): 3 Nelson Mandela St, POB 37, Banjul; tel. 229999; telex 2208; fax 227214; Man. Dir BAKARY K. NJIE.

RADIO AND TELEVISION

Gambia Television and Radio: Serrekunda Exchange Complex, Kairaba Ave, Serrekunda; tel. 374223; telex 2207; fax 374242; e-mail tsaidy1050@aol.com; f. 1962; non-commercial govt service of information, education and entertainment; radio broadcasts in English, Mandinka, Wolof, Fula, Jola, Serer and Serahuli; television broadcasts began in 1996; Dir TOMBONG SAIDY.

Radio 1 FM; Pipe Line Rd, POB 2700, Serrekunda, Fajara; tel. 394900; fax 394911; e-mail george.radio1@commit.gm; f. 1990; private station broadcasting FM music programmes to the Greater Banjul area; Dir GEORGE CHRISTENSEN.

Radio Syd: POB 279/280, Banjul; tel. and fax 226490; commercial station broadcasting mainly music; programmes in English, French, Spanish, Wolof, Mandinka, Fula, Jola and Serahuli; also tourist information in Swedish; Dir CONSTANCE WADNER ENHÖRNING.

Finance

(cap. = capital; res = reserves; dep. = deposits; m. = million; brs = branches; amounts in dalasi)

BANKING

Central Bank

Central Bank of The Gambia: 1–2 Ecowas Ave, Banjul; tel. 228103; telex 2218; fax 226969; f. 1971; bank of issue; cap. and res 4.0m., dep. 756.1m. (June 1994); Gov. MOMODOU CLARK BAJO; Gen. Man. J. A. BAYO.

Other Banks

Arab-Gambian Islamic Bank: Banjul; f. 1996, operations commenced 1997; Man. Dir MAMOUR JAGNE.

Continent Bank Ltd: 61 Ecowas Ave, PMB 142, Banjul; tel. 229961; telex 2257; fax 229711; f. 1990; privately-owned; cap. 4m. (June 1996); Chair. Dr MUHAMMAD NADAR BAYZID; Man. Dir Alhaji ALIEU NJIE

Meridien BIAO Bank Gambia Ltd: 3–4 Ecowas Ave, POB 1018, Banjul; tel. 225777; telex 2382; fax 225781; f. 1992; management assumed by Central Bank of The Gambia in 1995; cap. 20m. (Dec. 1994); Man. Dir ANTHONY C. GRANT; 3 brs.

Standard Chartered Bank Gambia Ltd: 8 Ecowas Ave, POB 259, Banjul; tel. 227744; telex 2210; fax 227714; f. 1978; 75% owned by Standard Chartered Bank Africa PLC (UK); cap. and res 44.0m., dep. 419.8m. (Dec. 1996), Chair. Dr PETER JOHN N'DOW; Man. Dir DAVID N. T. KUWANA; 3 brs.

INSURANCE

There were seven insurance companies operating in The Gambia at the end of 1997.

Capital Insurance Co Ltd: 22 Anglesea St, POB 485, Banjul; tel. 228544; telex 2320; fax 229219; f. 1986; Man. Dir JOSEPH C. FYE.

The Gambia National Insurance Co Ltd: 6 OAU Blvd, POB 750, Banjul; tel. 228412; telex 2268; f. 1979; Chair. BAI MATARR DRAMMEH.

Greater Alliance Insurance Co: 10 Nelson Mandela St, Banjul; tel. 227839; telex 2245; fax 226687; f. 1989.

Senegambia Insurance Co Ltd: 7 Nelson Mandela St, POB 880, Banjul; tel. 228866; telex 2314; fax 226820; f. 1984; Man. Dir Alhaji BABOU A. M. CEESAY; Gen. Man. PA ALASSAN JAGNE.

Insurance Association

Insurance Association of The Gambia: Banjul.

Trade and Industry

GOVERNMENT AGENCIES

National Environmental Agency (NEA): 5 Fitzgerald St, Banjul; tel. 228056; fax 229701.

National Investment Promotion Authority (NIPA): Independence Drive, Banjul; tel. 228332; telex 2230; fax 229220; f. 1994 to replace the National Investment Bd; CEO S. M. MBOGE.

National Trading Corpn of The Gambia Ltd (NTC): 1–3 Wellington St, POB 61, Banjul; tel. 228395; telex 2252; f. 1973; transfer pending to private-sector ownership; Chair. and Man. Dir MOMODOU CHAM; 15 brs.

CHAMBER OF COMMERCE

Gambia Chamber of Commerce and Industry: NTC Complex, Ecowas Ave, POB 33, Banjul; e-mail gcci@delphi.com; f. 1961; Pres. BAI NDONGO FALL; Chief Exec. KEBBA T. N'JAI.

UTILITIES

Utilities Holding Corporation (UHC): Independence Drive, POB 609, Banjul; telex 2302; fax 228260; fmrly The Gambia Utilities Corpn, privatized in 1993; distributes electricity and water; Man. Dir SHOLA JOINER.

CO-OPERATIVE

The Gambia Co-operative Union (GCU): Banjul; f. 1959; co-operative for groundnut producers; Gen. Man. LAMIN WILLY JAMMEH; 110,000 mems.

TRADE UNIONS

Gambia Labour Union: 6 Albion Place, POB 508, Banjul; tel. 641; f. 1935; 25,000 mems; Pres. B. B. KEBBEH; Gen. Sec. MOHAMED CEESAY.

Gambia Workers' Confederation: Banjul; f. 1958 as The Gambia Workers' Union, present name adopted in 1985; govt recognition withdrawn 1977–85; Sec.-Gen. PA MODOU FALL.

The Gambia Trades Union Congress: POB 307, Banjul; Sec.-Gen. SAM THORPE.

Transport

Gambia Public Transport Corporation: Factory St, Kanifing Industrial Estate, POB 801, Kanifing; tel. 392230; telex 2243; fax 392454; f. 1975; operates road transport and ferry services; Chair. KEKOTO B. S. MAANE; Man. Dir ISMAILLA CEESAY.

RAILWAYS

There are no railways in The Gambia.

ROADS

In 1996 there were an estimated 2,700 km of roads in The Gambia, of which 850 km were main roads, and 520 km were secondary roads. In that year only about 35% of the road network was paved. Some roads are impassable in the rainy season. The expansion and upgrading of the road network is planned, as part of the Jammeh administration's programme to improve The Gambia's transport infrastructure. Among intended schemes is the construction of a motorway along the coast, with the aid of a loan of US $8.5m. from Kuwait.

SHIPPING

The River Gambia is well suited to navigation. A weekly river service is maintained between Banjul and Basse, 390 km above Banjul, and a ferry connects Banjul with Barra. Small ocean-going vessels can reach Kaur, 190 km above Banjul, throughout the year. Facilities at the port pf Banjul have been modernized and expanded during the mid-1990s, with the aim of enhancing The Gambia's potential as a transit point for regional trade.

Gambia Ports Authority: Wellington St, POB 617, Banjul; tel. 227266; telex 2235; fax 227268.

The Gambia River Transport Co Ltd: 61 Wellington St, POB 215, Banjul; tel. 227664; river transport of groundnuts and general cargo; Man. Dir. LAMIN JUWARA; 200 employees.

The Gambia Shipping Agencies Ltd: Liberation Ave, Banjul; tel. 227518; telex 2202; fax 227929; shipping agents and forwarders; Man. NILS LANGGAARD SORENSEN; 30 employees.

CIVIL AVIATION

Banjul International Airport, at Yundum, 27 km from the capital, handled some 275,000 passengers and 3,000 metric tons of cargo in 1992. Construction of a new terminal, at a cost of some US $10m., was completed in late 1996. Facilities at Yundum have been upgraded by the US National Aeronautics and Space Administration (NASA), to enable the airport to serve as an emergency landing site for space shuttle vehicles.

Gambia International Airlines: Banjul International Airport, PMB, Banjul; tel. 472747; fax 472750; f. 1996; state-owned; sole handling agent at Banjul, sales agent; Man. Dir LAMIN K. MANJANG.

Tourism

Tourists are attracted by The Gambia's beaches and also by its abundant birdlife. A total of 89,997 air-charter tourists visited The Gambia in 1993/94, of whom 67.9% came from the United Kingdom and 7.5% from Sweden. Gross earnings from the sector were D241.5m. in 1992/93. A major expansion of tourism facilities was under way in the early 1990s. However, the withdrawal from The Gambia of many tour operators in the final months of 1994, in response to fears of political insecurity, resulted in a dramatic fall in tourist arrivals (to an estimated 38,000). Most operators resumed tours to The Gambia for the 1995/96 season. More than 100,000 visitors were expected in the 1997/98 season. An annual 'Roots Festival' was inaugurated in 1996, with the aim of attracting African-American visitors to The Gambia.

Department of State for Tourism and Culture: New Administrative Bldg, The Quadrangle, Banjul; tel. 228496; fax 227753; Dir of Tourism M. B. O. CHAM.

Hotel Owners' Association of The Gambia (HOAG): Banjul; Chair. SAMMY LAI MBOGE.

GEORGIA

Introductory Survey

Location, Climate, Language, Religion, Flag, Capital

Georgia (formerly the Georgian Soviet Socialist Republic and, between 1990 and 1995, the Republic of Georgia) is situated in west and central Transcaucasia, on the southern foothills of the Greater Caucasus mountain range. There is a frontier with Turkey to the south-west and a western coastline on the Black Sea. The northern frontier with the Russian Federation follows the axis of the Greater Caucasus, and includes borders with the Russian republics of Dagestan, Chechnya, Ingushetiya, North Ossetia (Osetiya), Kabardino-Balkariya and Karachai-Cherkessiya. To the south lies Armenia, and to the south-east is Azerbaijan. Georgia includes two autonomous republics (Abkhazia and Ajaria) and the autonomous region of South Ossetia. (In the late 1990s the status of these three territories was in dispute.) The Black Sea coast and the Rion plains have a warm, humid subtropical climate, with annual rainfall of more than 2,000 mm and average temperatures of 6°C (42°F) in January and 23°C (73° F) in July. Eastern Georgia has a more continental climate, with cold winters and hot, dry summers. The official language is Georgian (a member of the Caucasian language group), which is written in the Georgian script. Most of the population are adherents of Christianity; the principal denomination is the Georgian Orthodox Church. Islam is professed by Ajarians, Azerbaijanis, Kurds and some others. Most Ossetians in Georgia are Eastern Orthodox Christians, although their co-nationals in North Ossetia are mainly Sunni Muslims. There are also other Christian groups, and a small number of adherents of the Jewish faith (both European and Georgian Jews). The national flag (proportions 5 by 3) consists of a field of cornelian red, with a canton, divided into two equal horizontal stripes of black over white, in the upper hoist. The capital is Tbilisi.

Recent History

A powerful kingdom in medieval times, Georgia subsequently came under periods of foreign domination, becoming annexed by the Russian Empire during the 19th century. After the collapse of the Russian Empire in 1917, an independent Georgian state was established on 26 May 1918. Independent Georgia was ruled by a Menshevik Socialist Government and received recognition from the Bolshevik Government of Soviet Russia by treaty in May 1920. However, against the wishes of the Bolshevik leader, Lenin, Georgia was invaded by Bolshevik troops in early 1921, and a Georgian Soviet Socialist Republic (SSR) was proclaimed on 25 February of that year. In December 1922 it was absorbed into the Transcaucasian Soviet Federative Socialist Republic (TSFSR), which, on 22 December, became a founder member of the USSR. The Georgian SSR became a full union republic in 1936, when the TSFSR was disbanded.

During the 1930s Georgians suffered persecution under the Soviet leader, Stalin, himself an ethnic Georgian. The first victims had been opponents of Stalin during his time as a revolutionary leader in Georgia, but later the persecution became more indiscriminate. Most members of the Georgian leadership were dismissed after the death of Stalin in 1953. There was a further purge in 1972, when Eduard Shevardnadze became First Secretary of the Communist Party of Georgia (CPG) and attempted to remove officials who had been accused of corruption. Despite Soviet policy, Georgians retained a strong national identity. Opposition to a perceived policy of 'russification' was demonstrated in 1956, when anti-Russian riots were suppressed by security forces, and in 1978, when there were mass protests against the weakened status of the Georgian language in the new Constitution. Shevardnadze remained leader of the CPG until July 1985, when he became Minister of Foreign Affairs in the Government of the USSR.

The increased freedom of expression that followed the election of Mikhail Gorbachev as the Soviet leader in 1985 allowed the formation of unofficial groups, which campaigned on linguistic, environmental and ethnic issues. Such groups were prominent in organizing demonstrations in November 1988 against russification in Georgia. In February 1989 Abkhazians renewed a campaign, begun in the 1970s, for secession of their autonomous republic (in north-western Georgia) from the Georgian SSR (see below). Counter-demonstrations were staged in the capital, Tbilisi, by Georgians demanding that Georgia's territorial integrity be preserved. On the night of 8–9 April 1989 demonstrators in Tbilisi, who were demanding that Abkhazia remain within the republic and advocating the restoration of Georgian independence, were attacked by Soviet security forces using clubs and toxic gas. Sixteen people were killed, while many more were injured. Despite the resignation after the incident of state and party officials (including the First Secretary of the CPG, Jumber Patiashvili) and the announcement of an official investigation into the deaths, anti-Soviet sentiment and inter-ethnic conflict increased sharply in the republic.

Public outrage over the killings in April 1989 and the inreasing influence of unofficial groups forced the CPG to adapt its policies to retain some measure of popular support. In November the Georgian Supreme Soviet (legislature), which was dominated by CPG members, declared the supremacy of Georgian laws over all-Union (USSR) laws. In February 1990 the same body declared Georgia 'an annexed and occupied country', and in the following month Article Six of the Georgian Constitution, which ensured that the CPG retained a monopoly on power, was abolished. Pressure from the newly-established opposition parties forced the elections to the Georgian Supreme Soviet, which were scheduled for 25 March, to be postponed to allow time for a more liberal election law to be drafted. Legislation permitting full multi-party elections was finally adopted in August.

Despite the success of the opposition in influencing the position of the CPG, there were considerable differences between the many opposition parties. Attempts to create a united front for the independence movement were unsuccessful. In early 1990, however, many of the principal political parties united in the Round Table–Free Georgia coalition. This and other leading parties aimed to achieve independence by parliamentary means and were willing, in the mean time, to participate in elections to Soviet institutions such as the Georgian Supreme Soviet. Many of the more radical parties, however, united in the National Forum, headed by Giorgi Chanturia, which announced its intention to boycott the elections to the Supreme Soviet and, instead, to elect a rival parliament, the National Congress. The announcement of elections to the Congress, to be held on 30 September 1990 (thus pre-empting the elections to the Supreme Soviet, scheduled for late October), caused increased tension and acts of violence between parties of the two tendencies. The elections to the National Congress took place as scheduled, but only 51% of the electorate participated. Many parties did not present candidates, preferring to contest the elections to the Supreme Soviet.

In the elections to the Supreme Soviet, held on 28 October and 11 November 1990, the Round Table–Free Georgia coalition, under the leadership of Zviad Gamsakhurdia, received 64% of the votes cast, winning 155 seats in the 250-seat chamber. Fourteen political parties or coalitions were involved in the election campaign; all of them, including the CPG, were united in seeking Georgia's independence. The CPG won only 64 seats, while the remainder were won by the Georgian Popular Front (GPF), smaller coalitions and independents. The elections were boycotted by many non-ethnic Georgians, since parties limited to one area of the country were prevented from participating.

The new Supreme Soviet convened for the first time on 14 November 1990 and elected Gamsakhurdia as its Chairman. Two symbolic gestures of independence were adopted: the territory was henceforth to be called the Republic of Georgia, and the white, black and cornelian-coloured flag of independent Georgia was adopted as the official flag. Tengiz Sigua, also a member of the Round Table–Free Georgia coalition, was appointed Chairman of the Council of Ministers.

The new Supreme Soviet adopted several controversial laws at its first session, declaring illegal the conscription of Georgians into the Soviet armed forces. Many young men were reported to have joined nationalist paramilitary groups or were ready to join the National Guard (a *de facto* republican army), which the Supreme Soviet established on 30 January 1991.

The Georgian authorities officially boycotted the all-Union referendum on the future of the USSR, held in nine other Soviet republics, in March 1991, but polling stations were opened in the autonomous territories of South Ossetia and Abkhazia, and also in local military barracks. In South Ossetia 43,950 people took part in the referendum; of these, only nine voted against the preservation of the USSR. In Abkhazia almost the entire non-Georgian population voted to preserve the Union. The Georgian leadership refused to participate in the negotiations on a new union treaty. Instead, on 31 March, the Government conducted a referendum asking whether 'independence should be restored on the basis of the act of independence of 26 May 1918'. Of those eligible to vote, 95% participated in the referendum, 93% of whom voted for independence. On 9 April 1991 the Georgian Supreme Soviet approved a decree formally restoring Georgia's independence. Georgia thus became the first republic to secede from the USSR. Direct elections to the newly-established post of executive President, held in May, were won by Gamsakhurdia, who received 86.5% of the votes cast. Voting did not take place in South Ossetia or Abkhazia.

Despite the high level of popular support that Gamsakhurdia received from the electorate, there was considerable opposition from other politicians to what was perceived as an authoritarian style of rule. His actions during the failed Soviet coup attempt of August 1991 were also strongly criticized, and he initially refrained from publicly condemning the coup leaders. After the coup had collapsed, Gamsakhurdia's position became tenuous. Tengiz Kitovani, the leader of the National Guard (who was officially dismissed by Gamsakhurdia on 19 August, when the Soviet coup attempt began), announced that 15,000 of his men had remained loyal to him and were no longer subordinate to the President. Kitovani was joined in opposition to Gamsakhurdia by Tengiz Sigua, who had resigned as Chairman of the Council of Ministers in mid-August. In September 30 opposition parties united to demand the resignation of Gamsakhurdia and organized a series of anti-Government demonstrations. When opposition supporters occupied the television station in Tbilisi, several people were killed in clashes between Kitovani's troops and those forces still loyal to Gamsakhurdia.

Throughout October 1991 demonstrations by both supporters and opponents of Gamsakhurdia continued, but the strength of Gamsakhurdia's support among the rural and working-class population, his arrests of prominent opposition leaders and imposition of a state of emergency in Tbilisi, and his effective monopoly of the republican media, all weakened the position of the opposition. In December armed conflict broke out, as the opposition resorted to force to oust the President. Kitovani and Jaba Ioseliani, the leader of the paramilitary *Mkhedrioni* (Horsemen) group were joined by other opposition figures and increasing numbers of former Gamsakhurdia supporters. The fighting was mostly confined to central Tbilisi, around the parliament buildings, where Gamsakhurdia was besieged. More than 100 people were believed to have been killed. Gamsakhurdia and some of his supporters fled Georgia on 6 January 1992 (eventually taking refuge in southern Russia). A few days previously the opposition had declared Gamsakhurdia deposed and formed a Military Council, led by Kitovani and Ioseliani, which appointed Tengiz Sigua as acting Chairman of the Council of Ministers. The office of President was abolished, and the functions of Head of State were to be exercised by the Chairman of the Supreme Soviet.

In mid-January 1992 Sigua began the formation of a new Government, and also announced plans for significant economic reforms. An Interim Consultative Council, comprising representatives of all the major political groups, was established, in an attempt to create stability. (The Council did not include the CPG, which had been disbanded in August 1991.) In early March 1992 Eduard Shevardnadze returned to Georgia, and a State Council was created to replace the Military Council in legislative and executive matters. The State Council, of which Shevardnadze was designated Chairman, comprised 50 members, drawn from all the major political organizations, and included Sigua, Ioseliani and Kitovani. Shevardnadze succeeded in reconciling the various factions of the State Council, as well as the leaders of the two principal military bodies, the National Guard and the *Mkhedrioni*. The loyalty of these forces was essential to Shevardnadze in suppressing repeated attempts by Gamsakhurdia and his supporters in early 1992 to re-establish control. Further civil unrest ensued, especially in the western strongholds (including Abkhazia) of Gamsakhurdia's supporters (or 'Zviadists'), and curfews were imposed in Tbilisi and other towns. By April it was reported that government troops had re-established control in the rebellious areas. In July, however, one of Georgia's deputy premiers was taken hostage by 'Zviadists' in western Georgia. This was followed by the kidnapping of Roman Gventsadze, the Georgian Minister of Internal Affairs, and several other officials. In response, the State Council dispatched more than 3,000 National Guardsmen to Abkhazia, where the hostages were believed to be held, prompting armed resistance by Abkhazian militia. In mid-August three of the hostages, including Gventsadze, were released.

Elections to the Supreme Council (as the Supreme Soviet was now known) were held on 11 October 1992, against a background of intensified hostilities in Abkhazia and the threat of disruptive actions by the 'Zviadists'. In the event, however, the election was conducted peacefully, although it was boycotted in South Ossetia, Mengrelia and parts of Abkhazia. An estimated 75% of the total electorate participated. Of the more than 30 parties and alliances contesting the election, none succeeded in gaining a significant representation in the 235-seat legislature. The largest number of seats (a mere 29) was won by the centrist Peace bloc, which mainly comprised former communists as well as intellectuals. Of greater consequence, however, was the direct election of the legislature's Chairman—effectively a presidential role—which was held simultaneously. Shevardnadze was the sole candidate for the post, winning more than 95% of the total votes, thus obtaining the legitimate popular mandate that he had hitherto lacked.

The Supreme Council convened for the first time in early November 1992 and adopted a decree on state power, whereby supreme executive authority was vested in Shevardnadze as the Council's Chairman (or Head of State), in conjunction with the Council of Ministers, while the Supreme Council remained the highest legislative body. Shevardnadze was also elected Commander-in-Chief of the Georgian armed forces and Tengiz Sigua was re-elected Chairman of the Council of Ministers. One of the principal aims of the new Government was to create a unified army; an 11-member National Security and Defence Council was established for this purpose in early 1993. A comprehensive programme of economic reforms was also initiated.

Almost directly after his election, Shevardnadze was confronted by opposition from within his own administration. In response to rumours that Kitovani was plotting to overthrow him, Shevardnadze suspended the National Security and Defence Council in May 1993, also dismissing Kitovani from his post as Minister of Defence. In August the entire Council of Ministers tendered its resignation, following the legislature's rejection of the Council's proposed budget for 1993. In the following month Shevardnadze appointed a new Council of Ministers, which was headed by Otar Patsatsia, a former CPG official. Shevardnadze himself tendered his resignation as Head of State in mid-September, in response to accusations of dictatorial methods. However, crowds blockaded the parliament building, demanding his reinstatement, and the Supreme Council voted overwhelmingly to reject Shevardnadze's resignation.

By late September 1993 Georgia appeared ungovernable: confronted by growing political and economic crisis and military defeat in Abkhazia (see below), Shevardnadze's position was made more precarious by the reappearance of Gamsakhurdia and the 'Zviadists' in western Georgia. In early October the former President's forces captured the Black Sea port of Poti as well as the strategic town of Samtredia, blocking all rail traffic to Tbilisi. As the rebel forces advanced further eastwards, Shevardnadze persuaded the Supreme Council to agree to Georgia's immediate membership of the Commonwealth of Independent States (CIS, see p. 132), established in December 1991 by 11 former Soviet republics. In late October 1993 Russian troops were dispatched to Georgia, and by early November the 'Zviadists' had been entirely routed from the republic. In early January 1994 it was reported that Gamsakhurdia had died by his own hand, after having been surrounded by government troops in western Georgia.

Georgia's formal admittance to the CIS was delayed until early December 1993, when all of the member states finally granted their approval. Despite the restoration of some measure of stability in the republic, in November Shevardnadze extended the state of emergency (which had been declared in September) until early 1994. Shevardnadze also created his own party, the Citizens' Union of Georgia (CUG), formed from several existing parties. In February 1994 the *Mkhedrioni* group was transformed into a 'Rescue Corps', as part of the continuing process of creating a unified army.

Throughout 1994 Shevardnadze sought to curb the increasing level of organized crime and 'mafia' activity in the republic; however, the incidence of assassinations and other acts of political violence remained high, as rival paramilitary groups—often based on regional affiliations or loyalty to certain powerful figures—competed for influence. Shevardnadze's own administration was undermined by clan-based rivalries. Popular opposition to the regime escalated, and demonstrations against Shevardnadze were held at regular intervals. New opposition parties emerged: a National Liberation Front (NLF) was established by Sigua and Kitovani with the declared aim to restore Georgia's territorial integrity (i.e. regain Abkhazia); in June several small parties claiming to be successors to the CPG merged as the United Communist Party of Georgia (UCPG). Nevertheless, in May more than 30 political and public organizations, including leading opposition parties (such as the GPF and Giorgi Chanturia's National Democratic Party of Georgia, NDPG) signed a declaration 'of national unity and accord' in an attempt to bring stability to Georgian politics. In December, however, the wave of political violence culminated in the assassination of Chanturia. (A former member of the *Mkhedrioni* confessed to this murder in April 1997.) In the following month Kitovani led an armed convoy of some 350 NLF supporters towards Abkhazia in an apparent attempt to 'liberate' the region. The convoy was halted and disarmed by government security forces; Kitovani was arrested and the NLF was banned. Attempts to curtail the criminal activities of the numerous politico-military groups operating in Georgia culminated in May 1995, when the leading such group, Ioseliani's Rescue Corps, was ordered to surrender its arms; in July Ioseliani was reported to have established a political organization from elements of the *Mkhedrioni*.

In August 1995 the Supreme Council adopted Georgia's new Constitution, which had been prepared by a special constitutional commission. The document provided for a strong executive presidency and a 235-member unicameral Georgian Parliament. The Government was to be directly subordinate to the President, to whom it would act as an advisory body. The post of Prime Minister was abolished; the most senior position in the Government was henceforth to be that of the Minister of State, who was to co-ordinate the ministers' work and liaise with the President. The country (whose official title was changed from the Republic of Georgia to Georgia) was described as 'united and undivided'; however, the territorial status of Abkhazia and South Ossetia was not defined. It was stated that, following the eventual conclusion of political settlements in those regions, the Georgian Parliament would be transformed into a bicameral body (comprising a Council of the Republic and a Senate, the latter representing the various territorial units of Georgia).

The Constitution was due to be signed at an official ceremony on 29 August 1995. However, following an assassination attempt on Shevardnadze, the signing was postponed, eventually taking place on 17 October. Security forces began a large-scale search for the perpetrators, arresting many suspects, and the Minister of State Security, Igor Giorgadze, was dismissed for having failed to prevent the attack. Giorgadze was subsequently named by state prosecutors as the chief instigator of the plot, along with his deputy, Temur Khachishvili, and a leading member of the Rescue Corps, Gia Gelashvili. Warrants were issued for their arrest; however, the three men were believed to have fled to Russia. Shevardnadze announced the complete disbandment of the Rescue Corps, and in November Ioseliani was arrested, charged with complicity in the assassination attempt.

Direct elections to the restored post of President of Georgia were held on 5 November 1995. Shevardnadze won a convincing victory, receiving almost 75% of the total votes. His closest rival (with only 19%) was Jumber Patiashvili, the former First Secretary of the CPG. The election of the new Georgian Parliament was held simultaneously with the presidential election. A mixed system of voting was employed: 150 seats were to be filled by proportional representation of parties, while the remaining 85 deputies were to be elected by majority vote in single-member constituencies. The election was boycotted in Abkhazia and in parts of South Ossetia. Only three parties contesting the 150 proportional seats succeeded in gaining the 5% of the votes necessary for representation in the Parliament. Of these, Shevardnadze's CUG won the largest number of seats (90), followed by the NDPG (31) and the All-Georgian Union of Revival (AUR), chaired by Aslan Abashidze, the regional leader of Ajaria (25 seats). Only about one-half of the single-mandate seats were filled; however, following a further two rounds of voting, all 85 deputies were elected. These included 17 members of the CUG and 29 independent candidates, as well as 12 deputies from Abkhazia (elected in 1992), whose mandates were renewed. This produced a total of 231 parliamentarians (representing 11 parties); the CUG emerged with a total of 107 seats, but it was supported by many of the other parties that gained representation. Four seats remained vacant. Approximately 64% of the registered electorate was believed to have participated in the legislative elections.

The Georgian Parliament convened for the first time in late November 1995 and elected as its Chairman (Speaker) Zurab Zhvania, General Secretary of the CUG and a close associate of Shevardnadze. In early December Shevardnadze appointed Nikoloz Lekishvili, formerly Mayor of Tbilisi, as Minister of State. The remaining members of the Government were appointed later in the month. In January 1996, in accordance with the Constitution, a National Security Council was established as a consultative body dealing with issues relating to defence and security and the elimination of terrorism and corruption.

Meanwhile, in late 1995 criminal proceedings commenced in Tbilisi against Kitovani, in connection with the NLF's attempted raid on Abkhazia in early 1995 (see above). In May 1996 Ioseliani, the former leader of the *Mkhedrioni*, was convicted of complicity in the assassination attempt against Shevardnadze in August 1995, and in June 1996 supporters of former President Gamsakhurdia received lengthy prison sentences for their role in the civil war of 1993. Kitovani was convicted on charges of establishing an illegal armed formation in September 1996 and was sentenced to eight years' imprisonment. Further trials of 'Zviadists' on charges of treason and the preparation of terrorist acts commenced in March 1997. Also in that month nine opposition parties, which supported Gamsa-khurdia, formed the Front for the Reinstatement of Legitimate Power in Georgia.

In April 1997 the Minister of Finance, Davit Iakobidze, resigned, following criticism of his performance by Shevardnadze. Allegations that the Ministry of State Security had authorized the illegal tapping of senior journalists' telephones were confirmed in a closed session of the Georgian Parliament by the Procurator-General. While the Georgian legislature refrained from holding the Minister, Shota Kviraia, personally responsible, he nevertheless tendered his resignation in July. Moreover, opposition parties called for the resignation of the Ministers of Defence and of the Interior, on the grounds that there was documentary evidence of corruption within the Ministries. A review of the state security system was subsequently announced. Judicial and administrative reforms were also implemented, with the establishment of the Justice Council, which was formed to co-ordinate the appointment of members of the judiciary, and there was discussion in Parliament concerning the formation of organs of local government. A Civil Code, second in importance only to the Constitution, was adopted in June, and capital punishment was formally abolished.

On 9 February 1998 President Shevardnadze survived a second attempt on his life, when grenades were launched at his motorcade.

Following his return to Georgia in March 1992, Shevardnadze struggled to resolve the inter-ethnic tensions in Georgia's autonomous territories, which had intensified following the election of Gamsakhurdia's nationalist Government in 1990, and which led to serious armed conflict in South Ossetia and Abkhazia. Ossetia, whose original inhabitants are an East Iranian people, was divided into two parts under Stalin, North Ossetia falling under Russian jurisdiction and South Ossetia becoming an autonomous region of Georgia. At the census of 1979 ethnic Ossetians comprised 66% of the region's population. The longstanding Georgian animosity towards the Ossetians stems not only from ethnic differences but also from the Ossetians' traditional pro-Russian stance. The current dispute began in 1989, when Ossetian demands for greater autonomy and eventual reunification with North Ossetia (which would entail secession from Georgia and integration into the Russian Federation) led to violent clashes between local Georgians and Ossetians. Troops of the Soviet Ministry of Internal Affairs were dispatched to South Ossetia in January 1990, but in September the South Ossetian Supreme Soviet (legislature) proclaimed South Ossetia's independence and state sovereignty within the USSR. This decision was declared unconstitutional by the Georgian

Supreme Soviet, which in December formally abolished the region's autonomous status. Following renewed violence, the Georgian legislature declared a state of emergency in Tskhinvali, the South Ossetian capital.

In January 1991 the Soviet President, Mikhail Gorbachev, annulled both South Ossetia's declaration of independence and the Georgian Supreme Soviet's decision of December 1990. However, violence continued throughout 1991, with the resulting displacement of many thousands of refugees. There was a series of cease-fires, which were all almost immediately violated. In December the South Ossetian Supreme Soviet declared both a state of emergency and a general mobilization, in response to the Georgian Government's dispatch of troops to the region. In the same month the South Ossetian legislature adopted a second declaration of the region's independence, as well as a resolution in favour of its integration into the Russian Federation. These resolutions were overwhelmingly endorsed by South Ossetians at a referendum held in January 1992. While denouncing these developments, the new administration in Tbilisi (the Military Council) none the less declared its willingness to discuss the issue. However, hostilities continued in early 1992 between the rival factions, compounded by the intervention of Georgian government troops (which, by April, were attacking Tskhinvali). The situation was further complicated by the arrival of volunteer fighters from North Ossetia, in support of their South Ossetian neighbours. Negotiations held in May resulted in a temporary cease-fire. This, however, was violated by Georgian militia, who attacked a convoy of South Ossetian refugees, reportedly killing 36 people.

Negotiations between Shevardnadze and President Yeltsin of the Russian Federation in late June 1992, and their agreement to secure a lasting cease-fire, promised a peaceful solution to the conflict (in which more than 400 Georgians and 1,000 Ossetians had been killed since its outbreak in 1989). Peacekeeping monitors (comprising Georgians, Ossetians and Russians) were deployed in South Ossetia during July, with the simultaneous withdrawal of all armed forces from the region. The return of refugees to South Ossetia began in that month. However, although the cease-fire subsequently remained in force, no political settlement to the conflict was reached at talks held in 1993–94, and South Ossetia remained effectively a seceded territory. This delayed the repatriation of refugees: in early 1994 some 11,000 South Ossetians remained in North Ossetia, while some 7,000 ethnic Georgians had yet to return to their homes in South Ossetia. In July 1995 representatives from Georgia, Russia, North Ossetia and South Ossetia reopened talks, under the aegis of the Organization for Security and Co-operation in Europe (OSCE, see p. 212), on a political settlement. Negotiations continued in 1996 under the auspices of the OSCE. The South Ossetian leadership demanded recognition of the region's independence, rejecting proposals to grant South Ossetia the status of an autonomous republic within Georgia. However, a significant breakthrough was achieved in April, when a memorandum 'on strengthening mutual trust and security measures' was initialled in Tsikhinvali by the participants in the talks. The memorandum was signed in Moscow in the following month. A series of meetings was subsequently held between President Shevardnadze and Ludvig Chibirov, the Chairman of the South Ossetian legislature, to negotiate South Ossetia's political status. In September, however, the legislature of the separatist region approved an amendment to its Constitution to allow the introduction of a presidential government. Despite the Georgian leadership's declaration that the results of any election would be considered illegitimate, elections for the post of President of South Ossetia were held on 10 November, and were won by Chibirov. Shevardnadze, while criticizing the election, insisted that the search for a political settlement would continue.

At quadripartite negotiations, held at intervals throughout 1997, the principal issues discussed were the function of the peace-keeping forces deployed in South Ossetia (whose policing role was to be transferred to regional law-enforcement bodies), procedures for the return of refugees, and the revival of the region's economy. Talks held in Moscow in March confirmed the principle of Georgia's territorial integrity, while allowing a measure of self-determination for South Ossetia. In September, at a meeting between Shevardnadze and Chibirov, an agreement was signed on the return of refugees to South Ossetia, described as the main concern of the two sides.

The cease-fire that was declared in South Ossetia in mid-1992 coincided with a resurgence of violence in the Autonomous Republic of Abkhazia. As in South Ossetia, a movement for Abkhazian secession from Georgia had been revived in 1989. Abkhazians are a predominantly Muslim people, and their region had enjoyed virtual sovereignty within Georgia during the 1920s. However, in 1930 Abkhazia was made an autonomous republic, and, on Stalin's orders, large numbers of western Georgians were resettled in the region. As a result, by 1989 ethnic Abkhazians comprised only 18% of the area's population, while Georgians constituted the largest ethnic group (46%). The Georgian Government repeatedly rejected Abkhazian secessionist demands on these demographic grounds. The movement for Abkhazian independence was also fiercely resisted by the local Georgian population. In July 1989 there were violent clashes between ethnic Georgians and Abkhazians in Sukhumi, the republic's capital, resulting in 14 deaths. A state of emergency was imposed throughout Abkhazia, but troops did not succeed in preventing further inter-ethnic violence.

In August 1990 the Abkhazian Supreme Soviet voted to declare independence from Georgia. This declaration was pronounced invalid by the Georgian Supreme Soviet, and Georgians living in Abkhazia staged protests and began a rail blockade of Sukhumi. In late August Georgian deputies in the Abkhazian legislature succeeded in reversing the declaration of independence. Inter-ethnic unrest continued during late 1990 and in 1991. Following the overthrow of Zviad Gamsakhurdia, in January 1992, there was renewed unrest in Abkhazia, as large numbers of ethnic Georgians demonstrated in support of the former President. In July the Abkhazian legislature declared Abkhazia's sovereignty as the 'Republic of Abkhazia'.

A period of violent armed conflict began in Abkhazia in August 1992, when the Georgian Government dispatched some 3,000 members of the National Guard to the secessionist republic. It was claimed that the troops had been sent to release those senior officials who had been taken hostage by the 'Zviadists' and who were allegedly being held in Abkhazia (see above), but the covert reason for their deployment, it was believed, was to suppress the growing secessionist movement. Abkhazian militia launched a series of attacks against the Georgian troops, but failed to retain control of Sukhumi. The Chairman of the Abkhazian legislature and leader of the independence campaign, Vladislav Ardzinba, retreated north with his forces, establishing his base at Gudauta. The situation was complicated by the dispatch of Russian paratroopers to the region to protect Russian military bases.

Relations between Georgia and Russia became strained, following Georgian accusations that conservative elements within the Russian leadership and armed forces were supplying military equipment and personnel to the Abkhazians. In October 1992 the Abkhazians launched a successful counter-offensive, regaining control of all of northern Abkhazia, and reportedly killing hundreds of its ethnic Georgian inhabitants. Hostilities intensified in the first half of 1993, with the Georgian Government continuing to implicate Russia in the conflict. Peace talks were held at regular intervals, finally culminating in the signing of a provisional peace agreement, in July, by Georgian and Abkhazian leaders. The cease-fire held (albeit with minor violations) until mid-September, when the Abkhazians launched surprise attacks in parts of the region, capturing Sukhumi after 11 days of intense fighting. Shevardnadze, who had arrived in Sukhumi at the start of the offensive (vowing to remain until the town was securely under government control), was forced to flee by air, under heavy bombardment. By late September almost all Georgian forces had been expelled from Abkhazia, and the region was declared 'liberated'.

Several hundred people were believed to have been killed during the fighting, and more than 200,000 ethnic Georgians and others fled Abkhazia. Many thousands of the refugees were subsequently stranded, in freezing conditions, in the mountainous border region separating Abkhazia and Georgia, where large numbers perished. The situation in Abkhazia following the rout of the Georgian forces was reported to be close to anarchy, with atrocities allegedly being perpetrated against remaining ethnic Georgians and other nationalities by Abkhazians. Nevertheless, in early December 1993 Georgian and Abkhazian officials signed an eight-point 'memorandum of understanding' at UN-sponsored talks in Geneva. A small number of UN military personnel, part of the UN Observer Mission in Georgia (UNOMIG, see p. 54), were subsequently dispatched to Sukhumi in a peace-keeping capacity.

Outbreaks of violence continued in Abkhazia throughout 1994, despite the holding of peace talks (under UN and other auspices) at regular intervals. The fundamental disagreement between the Georgian and Abkhazian delegations concerned the future status of Abkhazia: Ardzinba demanded full independence (or confederal ties at the least) for Abkhazia, while the Georgian Government insisted on the preservation of Georgia's territorial integrity. However, hope for a peaceful solution was raised in April, when the two sides, meeting in Moscow, issued a statement approving the creation of a union in which Georgia and Abkhazia would enjoy equal status, a proposal that was subsequently rejected by the Georgian leadership. This was followed, in May, by the declaration of a full cease-fire (only statements or memorandums had been issued up to this point). Under the accord, a contingent of some 2,500 CIS (mainly Russian) peace-keepers were deployed in June, joining the (augmented) UN observer force in Abkhazia. Nevertheless, the peace-keeping presence was unable to prevent renewed hostilities.

In November 1994 the Abkhazian legislature adopted a new Constitution, which declared the 'Republic of Abkhazia' to be a sovereign state. Ardzinba was elected to the new post of 'President'. The declaration of sovereignty was condemned by the Georgian Government, and the peace negotiations were subsequently suspended. Protests were also voiced by the USA, Russia and the UN Security Council, all of which reaffirmed their recognition of Georgia's territorial integrity. Peace negotiations were resumed in 1995, despite periodic outbreaks of violence in Abkhazia. The Abkhaz legislature rejected Russian proposals for a future Georgian federation, in which Abkhazia would enjoy broad autonomy, insisting on a confederal structure of two sovereign units. In January 1996, at a summit meeting of CIS leaders in Moscow, it was agreed to implement Shevardnadze's request for economic sanctions to be imposed against Abkhazia until it consented to rejoin Georgia. In early 1996 tension increased over the issue of the CIS peace-keeping forces, whose mandate was due to expire in February. The Council of CIS Ministers of Foreign Affairs and the separatist Abkhaz negotiators dismissed Georgian proposals to modify the mandate of the peace-keepers (which would grant them additional powers, in particular policing duties, and the right to assist in the repatriation of refugees), but the Georgian legislature declared that it would not renew the mandate under its existing terms. In July the UN Security Council extended the mandate of the UNOMIG observers until January 1997 (when it was extended for a further six months). The CIS peacekeepers' mandate was extended in August 1996 until January 1997, and allowed for the peace-keepers to adopt measures to protect returning refugees.

On 23 November 1996 elections to the secessionist Abkhaz parliament, the People's Assembly, were held. The UN and the OSCE severely criticized the holding of the elections, while the Georgian legislature declared that the election results were invalid. President Shevardnadze organized a plebiscite among refugees from Abkhazia, to be held simultaneously with the elections; voters were asked whether they supported the holding of parliamentary elections in Abkhazia prior to the restoration of Georgia's territorial integrity and the repatriation of refugees, and it was reported that some 99% of refugees had taken part, of whom almost all had voted against the holding of the elections.

The mandate of the CIS peace-keeping forces in Abkhazia was the focus of much controversy in 1997. Members of the Abkhazeti faction in the Georgian Parliament staged a hunger strike in March, demanding the withdrawal of the CIS peace-keepers. However, at the CIS summit meeting later in that month the peace-keepers' mandate was extended until the end of July, and expanded to include the whole district of Gali, in order to facilitate the repatriation of refugees. The Abkhazian legislature claimed that the decision could not be implemented, since it required the approval of all parties in the conflict. Regular calls for the resumption of peace negotiations met with little success, and the diversion of Abkhazian long-distance telephone connections via Tbilisi, in April, coupled with the Abkhazian leadership's failure to achieve the lifting of economic sanctions against the region, further hampered the renewal of talks. Furthermore, in May the Georgian legislature approved a resolution, which stated that unless the decision adopted at the CIS summit meeting in March to expand the peace-keepers' mandate was implemented, the peace-keepers would be requested to withdraw, following the expiry of their mandate at the end of July. Ardzinba condemned the resolution, while opposing an expansion of the mandate, and warned of a resurgence of paramilitary violence, should the peace-keepers be required to leave. However, in June talks were held in Moscow between Ardzinba and the Georgian ambassador to Russia, and it was reported that agreement was reached on some issues.

Violent clashes took place in the Kodori Gorge region of Abkhazia in early July 1997, with 20 people reported killed. UN-sponsored peace talks were subsequently held in Geneva and, although no formal conclusion was reached, the two sides affirmed their commitment to resolving the conflict by peaceful means. The UN observers' mandate, which expired on 31 July, was renewed for a further six months. The status of the CIS peace-keepers remained undecided, since, upon the expiry of their mandate at the end of July, the Georgian National Security Council approved a resolution neither to request their immediate withdrawal, nor to demand an extension of their mandate. It was agreed to refer the issue to the forthcoming CIS summit meeting. Shevardnadze, meanwhile, advocated the replacement of the CIS forces with international peace-keeping troops.

Russian proposals for a settlement of the conflict, which provided for substantial autonomy for Abkhazia, while retaining Georgia's territorial integrity, were welcomed by Shevardnadze, but rejected by Ardzinba, who continued to demand equal status for Abkhazia within a confederation. In August 1997, for the first time since 1992, Ardzinba visited Georgia, together with the Russian Minister of Foreign Affairs, Yevgenii Primakov. Talks were held with Shevardnadze, and, although no political consensus was reached, a reaffirmation of both sides' commitment to a peaceful resolution of the conflict was made. At further talks in September 1997 progress was reportedly achieved on the conditions for the repatriation of refugees, although the political status of the region remained a subject of dispute.

At the CIS summit meeting held in October 1997, the mandate of the CIS peace-keepers was extended until 31 January 1998. Shevardnadze, while welcoming the decision, criticized the peace-keepers' failure to create the conditions necessary for the safe return of ethnic Georgian refugees. The refugees, and the Tbilisi-based official leadership of Abkhazia, continued to demand the withdrawal of the Russian forces, fearing an escalation of Russian military intervention in the republic. A partial lifting by Russia of the economic sanctions against Abkhazia was condemned by Shevardnadze. Meanwhile, UN-sponsored talks, which were due to have taken place in Geneva in mid-October 1997, were postponed at the request of the Abkhaz leadership. The talks were finally convened in mid-November, when a measure of progress in the search for a peaceful resolution of the conflict was achieved. A joint co-ordinating council was to be established, with the task of incorporating working groups to resolve the three main issues: a cessation of armed hostilities, the repatriation of refugees, and the settlement of economic and social issues. Representatives of the parties to the conflict, as well as Russian, UN and European Union delegates were to participate in the council. Shevardnadze's declaration that he would favour the use of force to establish peace in Abkhazia, should further peace talks fail, was criticized by Ardzinba, who warned that any deployment of international forces in Abkhazia would be viewed as an act of aggression. Shevardnadze, meanwhile, remained extremely critical of the effectiveness of the CIS peace-keepers.

The Autonomous Republic of Ajaria has proved to be the least troubled of Georgia's three autonomous territories. Despite being of ethnic Georgian origin, the Ajars, whose autonomous status was the result of a Soviet–Turkish Treaty of Friendship (1921), have retained a sense of separate identity, owing to their adherence to Islam. In recent years some Christian Georgians have considered the Muslim Ajars a threat to a unified Georgian nation. Tensions between Muslims and Christians increased in 1991, after the Georgian Supreme Soviet ruled as unconstitutional a law relating to elections to the Ajar Supreme Soviet, which restricted nominations for the forthcoming elections to permanent residents of Ajaria. In April there were several days of demonstrations in protest against proposals to abolish Ajar autonomy and against perceived 'christianization' of the Muslim population. Ajaria remained calm during the latter half of 1991 and during 1992, in an otherwise volatile region. In February 1993, however, there were reports of provocations against Russian troops in Ajaria by armed Ajar groups. Nevertheless, the situation remained stable during 1994. In February 1995 there was reported to have been an assassination attempt against Aslan Abashidze, the Chairman of the Ajar Supreme Council (regional leader), and against the commander of Russian military forces in Ajaria. Elections to the Supreme Council (legislature) of Ajaria were held on 22 September 1996, and the majority of seats were won by the Union of Revival party. Aslan Abashidze was re-elected Chairman of the Council. In December the deployment of armoured vehicles, allegedly from Russian military units, on the streets of Batumi, the republic's capital, led to tension between the Georgian authorities and the leadership of Ajaria. Abashidze denied rumours in the Georgian press that a state of emergency had been declared, and announced that the military units were carrying out deployment exercises. The Georgian leadership responded by issuing a statement declaring that it had full control of the situation, although it appeared unable to verify on whose orders the vehicles had been deployed.

Georgia was one of only four republics of the USSR not to join the CIS at its formation in December 1991. However, as civil and separatist conflicts threatened to destroy the country altogether, Shevardnadze was forced to reverse official Georgian policy on the CIS, and in late 1993 the republic was admitted to that body, including its collective security system. Georgia's relations with the Russian Federation were strained by developments in secessionist Abkhazia in 1992–93 and by Georgian accusations of Russian involvement. However, in February 1994 Georgia and Russia signed a 10-year treaty of friendship and co-operation. The treaty provided, *inter alia*, for the establishment of Russian military bases in Georgia to 'protect the security of the CIS'. Abkhazian and South Ossetian leaders opposed the treaty, claiming that Russian-Georgian military co-operation would lead to an escalation of tension in the region. Nationalist opposition forces in Georgia also opposed the strengthening of the republic's ties with Russia. In 1996 President Shevardnadze and the Georgian legislature threatened to close the Russian military bases, unless Russia adopted a firmer stance against the separatists in South Ossetia and Abkhazia. In 1997 Russia continued to participate in the search for a resolution of the Abkhaz conflict. Tension between Georgia and Russia increased, however, over the issue of the CIS peace-keepers and the partial lifting of economic sanctions against Abkhazia (see above). Furthermore, Georgia criticized its exclusion by Russia and Ukraine from decisions pertaining to the division of the former Black Sea Fleet.

Georgia sought to develop its international relations in the late 1990s. In April 1996, together with Armenia and Azerbaijan, it signed an agreement on partnership and co-operation with the European Union (EU, see p. 152), and in July it submitted a formal application to join the Council of Europe (see p. 140). An agreement on the sale of electricity to Turkey was concluded in February 1997, and measures on economic co-operation with Ukraine were also signed. Shevardnadze visited the USA in July, where US support was expressed for the proposed oil pipeline from the Caspian Sea to Turkey, via Georgian territory. The Georgian President also visited Greece and Italy. An agreement to extend the terms of repayment of Georgia's debt to Turkmenistan, which had accrued as a result of substantial imports of natural gas from that country, was concluded in late 1997.

Government

Under the Constitution of August 1995, the President of Georgia is Head of State and the head of the executive, and also Commander-in-Chief of the Armed Forces. The President is directly elected for a five-year term (and may not hold office for more than two consecutive terms). The Government (headed by the Minister of State), is accountable to the President, to whom it acts as an advisory body. The supreme legislative body is the unicameral 235-member Georgian Parliament, which is directly elected for four years. (The Constitution provides for a future bicameral Parliament, comprising a Council of the Republic and a Senate, following the eventual restoration of Georgia's territorial integrity.)

Defence

One of the principal objectives of the Government following independence in 1991 was to create a unified army from the various existing paramilitary and other groups. A National Security Council (headed by the President of Georgia) was established in early 1996 as a consultative body co-ordinating issues related to defence and security. Compulsory military service lasts for two years. In August 1997 total armed forces numbered some 33,200: 12,600 army, 2,000 navy, 3,000 air force, and 15,600 troops attached to the Ministry of Defence. There were also 8,500 Russian troops based in Georgia. In late 1993 Georgia joined the CIS and its collective security system. In March 1994 Georgia joined NATO's 'Partnership for Peace' programme of military co-operation (see p. 206). The 1998 budget allocated 82m. lari to defence.

Economic Affairs

In 1995, according to estimates by the World Bank, Georgia's gross national product (GNP), measured at average 1993–95 prices, was US $2,358m., equivalent to $440 per head. During 1985–95, it was estimated, GNP per head declined, in real terms, by an average annual rate of 17.0%. In the same period the population increased by an annual average of 0.2%. Georgia's gross domestic product (GDP) decreased, in real terms, by an average of 17.4% annually during 1985–95. Real GDP declined by 11.4% in 1994, but increased by 2.4% in 1995. Real GDP rose by 11.0% in 1996, and was estimated to have increased by 10.0% in 1997.

Agriculture contributed an estimated 38.0% of GDP in 1995 and in that year the sector (including forestry) provided 29.8% of employment. Georgia's exceedingly favourable climate allows the cultivation of subtropical crops, such as tea and citrus fruits. Non-citrus fruits (including wine grapes), flowers, tobacco and almonds are also cultivated, as are grain and sugar beet. The mountain pastures are used for sheep- and goat-farming. In 1996 private agricultural production provided more than 85% of total agricultural output. During 1985–95, according to the World Bank, agricultural GDP decreased, in real terms, by an annual average of 12.4%. In 1994 agricultural GDP declined by about 58%, compared with 1993, but in 1995 growth of 18% was recorded. Agricultural output increased by an estimated 11% in 1996.

Industry (including construction) contributed an estimated 18.5% of GDP in 1995, and provided 20.5% of employment in that year. The most significant parts of the sector are the agro-processing and energy industries. According to the World Bank, industrial GDP decreased, in real terms, by an annual average of 22.0% in 1985–95. In 1995 industrial GDP declined by 10%, but in 1996 the sector recorded growth of 7.7%.

The principal minerals extracted are coal, petroleum and manganese ore, but reserves of high-grade manganese ore are largely depleted. There are also deposits of coal, copper, gold and silver. Substantial natural gas deposits were discovered in 1994–96.

The manufacturing sector contributed an estimated 12.9% of GDP in 1995. The machinery and metal-working industries, traditionally the most important parts of the sector, were in decline in the late 1990s. According to the World Bank, manufacturing GDP decreased, in real terms, by an annual average of 21.3% in 1985–95. A decline of 3.2% was estimated for 1995.

Georgia has traditionally been highly dependent on imports of fuel and energy, in particular the import of natural gas from Turkmenistan, and crude petroleum from Russia. However, since 1993, when the prices of imported energy were raised to international market prices, there has been a significant reduction in the amount of fuel imported, leading to widespread energy shortages. The import of natural gas from Turkmenistan ceased in 1994. In mid-1996 the Georgian Government was negotiating with international organizations to construct some 200 hydroelectric power stations over the next 10 years. Imports of fuel and energy comprised an estimated 31.6% of total imports in 1995.

The services sector contributed 43.5% of GDP in 1995 and engaged 49.7% of the employed labour force. Trade is the leading activity of the sector and tourism is expected to expand. According to the World Bank, the GDP of the sector decreased, in real terms, by an average of 20.5% annually in 1985–95. However, in 1995 the sector was estimated to have grown by 5.3%. In 1996 trade increased by more than 8%, compared with 1995.

In 1995 Georgia recorded a visible trade deficit of US $338.8m., while there was a deficit of $218.5m. on the current account of the balance of payments. In 1995 Turkey was the principal source of imports (21.2% of total imports); other major sources were Russia, Azerbaijan and Turkmenistan. The principal market for exports in that year was Russia (30.4% of total exports); other important purchasers were Turkey, Armenia and Azerbaijan. The principal exports in 1995 were metal products, mineral products and vegetable products. The principal imports in that year were mineral products, foodstuffs and vegetable products.

In 1995 there was a budgetary deficit of 194.5m. lari (equivalent to 5.3% of GDP). At the end of 1995 Georgia's total external debt was US $1,189m., of which $988m. was long-term public debt. The annual rate of inflation averaged 1,816% during

1991–95. Consumer prices increased by an average annual rate of 15,606.5% in 1994 and by 162.7% in 1995. In 1996 the rate of increase declined to 39.4%. In the first 11 months of 1997 the rate of inflation was 6.5%. In September 1997 some 143,450 people were registered as unemployed. However, the actual number of people without work was believed to be much greater.

In 1992 Georgia became a member of the IMF and the World Bank, as well as joining the European Bank for Reconstruction and Development (EBRD, see p. 148). Georgia is also a member of the Black Sea Economic Co-operation group (see p. 260). In June 1996 Georgia was granted observer status at the World Trade Organization (WTO, see p. 244); an application for full membership followed shortly thereafter.

Georgia's economy was adversely affected not only by the collapse of the USSR in late 1991 but also, and even more critically, by the outbreak of three separate armed conflicts in the country. Apart from the resulting loss of life and infrastructural damage, supplies of fuel and basic commodities to the republic were severely disrupted. All sectors of the economy recorded a sharp decline in output, and many enterprises were either closed or operating below capacity. Georgia became increasingly dependent on international financial and humanitarian aid; at the same time the political instability in the republic discouraged investment by foreign companies. However, with the return of relative political stability in 1994, the Government embarked on a programme of comprehensive stabilization. By early 1998 the programme of structural reforms had achieved considerable success. The Government's adherence to strict financial policies, the liberalization of prices and a significant decline in the rate of inflation were accompanied by growth in all sectors. The establishment of a legal framework encouraged the expansion of private-sector economic activity, and by early 1998 almost all small-scale enterprises had been transferred to private ownership, while the privatization of medium- and large-scale enterprises had accelerated. Reform of the banking and energy sectors was under way in 1997 and measures to reduce the fiscal deficit by improving revenue collection were being implemented. Development of Georgia's oil pipeline and refining facilities, in conjunction with the exploitation of the Caspian oilfields by international consortia, was an indication of investor confidence in the progress of the economic reform programme. Unemployment and poverty, however, remained at critical levels, and in December 1996 it was reported that some 70% of the population were in receipt of incomes below the minimum subsistence level. The IMF, however, estimated this figure to be lower (25%–30%), owing to the fact that many people were in receipt of payment other than cash income.

Social Welfare

Georgia's social welfare system was enormously strained by the civil and separatist conflicts in the early 1990s, and radical reforms were subsequently implemented. Three extrabudgetary funds provide social welfare benefits: the Social Security Fund, established in 1991, which distributes old-age, invalidity and widows' pensions; the Employment Fund, also established in 1991, which provides unemployment, sickness and maternity benefits; and the Health Fund, established in 1995. The Government aimed to privatize most health care facilities by 1998. However, free medical care was to continue to be provided to the neediest sections of the population. In March 1997 some 287,000 refugees received assistance from the Government.

In 1993 there were 95 people per hospital bed and 182 people per physician. Total expenditure on social transfers amounted to 3.2% of GDP in 1996.

Education

Until the late 1980s the education system was an integrated part of the Soviet system. Considerable changes were made following the restoration of independence in 1991, including the ending of the teaching of ideologically-orientated subjects, and greater emphasis on Georgian language and history. Education is officially compulsory for nine years, between the ages of six and 14. Primary education begins at six years of age and lasts for four years. Secondary education, beginning at 10, lasts for a maximum of seven years, comprising a first cycle of five years and a second cycle of two years. In 1994 total enrolment at primary and secondary schools was equivalent to 80% of the school-age population (82% of males; 78% of females). Primary enrolment in that year was equivalent to 82% of the relevant age group, while the comparable ratio for secondary enrolment was 79%. In the 1994/95 academic year there were 3,139 secondary schools, with a total enrolment of 700,472 pupils; of these, 75.4% were taught in Georgian-language schools, while 3.9% were taught in Russian-language schools, 3.7% in Armenian-language schools, 6.1% in Azerbaijani-language schools, and 9.6% in mixed Georgian- and Russian-language schools. In 1993/94 89,361 students were enrolled at 23 institutions of higher education (including universities). In 1989, according to census results, only 1% of the adult population was illiterate. In 1995 it was estimated that the illiteracy rate had decreased to 0.5% of the adult population. Government expenditure on education in 1995 was 34.2m. lari (8.0% of total spending).

Public Holidays

1998: 6 January (Christmas), 17–20 April (Easter), 26 May (Independence Day), 31 December (New Year).

1999: 6 January (Christmas), 9–12 April (Easter), 26 May (Independence Day), 31 December (New Year).

Weights and Measures

The metric system is in force.

Statistical Survey

Principal sources: IMF, *Georgia—Economic Review* and *Georgia—Recent Economic Developments*; World Bank, *Statistical Handbook: States of the Former USSR.*

Area and Population

AREA, POPULATION AND DENSITY

Area (sq km)	69,700*
Population (census results)†	
17 January 1979	4,993,182
12 January 1989	
Males	2,562,040
Females	2,838,801
Total	5,400,841
Population (official estimates at 1 January)‡	
1993	5,395,700
1994	5,377,900
1995 (provisional)	5,368,700
Density (per sq km) at 1 January 1995	77.0

* 26,911 sq miles.

† Population is *de jure*. The *de facto* total at the 1989 census was 5,443,359.

‡ Figures include persons registered in Georgia but residing abroad. As a result of large-scale emigration from Georgia in the early 1990s, the population was estimated to have declined to about 4,600,000 by late 1994.

POPULATION BY NATIONALITY (1989 census result)

	%
Georgian	68.8
Armenian	9.0
Russian	7.4
Azerbaijani	5.1
Ossetian	3.2
Greek	1.9
Abkhazian	1.7
Others	2.9
Total	100.0

PRINCIPAL TOWNS
(estimated population at 1 January 1990)

Tbilisi (capital)	1,268,000	Batumi	137,000
Kutaisi	236,000	Sukhumi	122,000
Rustavi	160,000		

Source: UN, *Demographic Yearbook.*

BIRTHS, MARRIAGES AND DEATHS

	Registered live births		Registered marriages		Registered deaths	
	Number	Rate (per 1,000)	Number	Rate (per 1,000)	Number	Rate (per 1,000)
1987	94,595	17.9	39,157	7.4	46,332	8.8
1988	91,905	17.1	38,100	7.1	47,544	8.9
1989	91,138	16.7	38,288	7.0	47,077	8.6

Source: UN, *Demographic Yearbook*.

1990–95 (UN estimates, annual averages): Birth rate 15.9 per 1,000; Death rate 8.9 per 1,000 (Source: UN, *World Population Prospects: The 1994 Revision*).

Expectation of life (years at birth, 1989): 72.1 (males 68.1; females 75.7) (Source: Goskomstat USSR).

EMPLOYMENT (annual averages, '000 persons)*

	1993	1994	1995
Material sphere	1,201.2	1,203	1,169
Industry†	303.4	277	264
Construction	125.3	64	90
Agriculture	553.4	539	510
Forestry	9.0	6	6
Transport and communications	57.4	63	52
Trade and other services	152.7	254	257
Non-material sphere	590.6	547	561
Housing and municipal services	66.3	53	52
Science, research and development	40.6	36	36
Education, culture and arts	222.5	216	228
Health, social security and sports	155.8	155	160
Banking and financial institutions	12.4	10	10
Government	49.0	35	35
Other non-material services	44.3	42	40
Total	1,791.8	1,750	1,730

* Figures exclude employment in the informal sector, estimated to total about 750,000 persons at mid-1996.

† Comprising manufacturing (except printing and publishing), mining and quarrying, electricity, gas, water, logging and fishing.

Agriculture

PRINCIPAL CROPS ('000 metric tons)

	1994	1995	1996
Wheat	98	82	179
Barley	25	37	56
Maize	343	387	395
Potatoes	297	353	360
Sunflower seed	9	8	8
Cabbages	100	100*	90*
Tomatoes*	230	235	220
Cucumbers and gherkins	20	20*	25*
Onions (dry)	36	40*	35*
Carrots	5	5*	5*
Other vegetables	51	28	20
Watermelons†	800	800	750
Grapes	285	422	350
Sugar beet	9	14	n.a.
Apples	237	255	140*
Pears*	5	10	10
Peaches and nectarines*	7	13	7
Plums*	6	10	5
Citrus fruit	98	118	66*
Apricots*	8	12	7
Tea (made)	62	39	34
Tobacco (leaves)	2	1	1

* Unofficial figures.

† FAO estimates. Figures for watermelons include melons, pumpkins and squash.

Source: FAO, *Production Yearbook*.

LIVESTOCK ('000 head at 1 January)

	1994	1995	1996
Horses*	18	16	15
Cattle	944	974	980
Buffaloes*	20	20	20
Pigs	367	367	353
Sheep	950*	754	674
Goats	50*	39	51
Poultry (million)*	10	12	12

* FAO estimate(s).

Source: FAO, *Production Yearbook*.

LIVESTOCK PRODUCTS ('000 metric tons)

	1994	1995	1996
Beef and veal*	44	45	52
Mutton and lamb*	4	6	8
Pig meat*	45	51	60
Poultry meat*	19	22	29
Cows' milk	425	430	530
Cheese†	25	55	55
Hen eggs*	14	15	17

* Unofficial figures. † FAO estimates.

Source: FAO, *Production Yearbook*.

Fishing

(FAO estimates, metric tons, live weight)

	1993	1994	1995
Common carp	2,638	2,495	2,727
Cape horse mackerel	4,500	4,257	4,000
Other jack and horse mackerels	2,237	2,122	2,027
Round sardinella	3,350	3,168	3,030
European pilchard	11,440	10,820	10,350
European anchovy	6,604	3,209	3,586
Chub mackerel	1,170	1,107	1,060
Total catch (incl. others)	34,165	29,407	28,902
Inland waters	2,900	2,744	3,000
Mediterranean and Black Sea	4,665	1,500	1,902
Atlantic Ocean	26,600	25,163	24,000

Source: FAO, *Yearbook of Fishery Statistics*.

Mining

('000 metric tons, unless otherwise indicated)

	1993	1994*	1995*
Coal	82.2	44.5	42.7
Crude petroleum	88.2	66.9	42.7
Natural gas (million cu m)	21.8	11.4	3.3
Manganese ore	36.8	29.3	41.9

* Data for South Ossetia and Abkhazia are not included.

Industry

SELECTED PRODUCTS ('000 metric tons, unless otherwise indicated)

	1993	1994*	1995*
Margarine	2.3	0.1	0.1
Vegetable oil	0.5	0.0	0.0
Wine ('000 hectolitres)	1,042.5	436.3	412.3
Beer ('000 hectolitres)	120.4	64.8	67.1
Cigarettes (million)	3,600	3,300	1,900
Wool yarn	1.5	0.3	0.3
Cotton yarn	2.6	0.8	1.0
Cotton fabrics (million sq metres)	7.5	1.5	0.6
Woollen fabrics (million sq metres)	1.9	0.5	0.5
Footwear (million pairs)	1.0	0.2	0.1
Paper	0.3	0.1	n.a.
Synthetic resins and plastics	10.2	2.1	0.6
Chemical fibres and threads	8.0	0.9	0.2
Soap	1.4	1.1	n.a.
Motor spirit (petrol)	18.6	8.8	3.3
Distillate fuel oil (diesel fuel)	34.5	17.9	8.4
Residual fuel oil (mazout)	72.0	24.8	11.7
Building bricks (million)	22.8	9.1	6.4
Steel	221.7	121.2	88
Electric energy (million kWh)	9,748	7,039	7,100

* Data for South Ossetia and Abkhazia are not included.

Finance

CURRENCY AND EXCHANGE RATES

Monetary Units

100 tetri = 1 lari.

Sterling and Dollar Equivalents (31 December 1996)

£1 sterling = 2.180 lari;
US $1 = 1.274 lari;
100 lari = £45.87 = $78.49.

Average Exchange Rate (lari per US $)

1994 1.102
1995 1.288
1996 1.263

Note: On 25 September 1995 Georgia introduced the lari, replacing interim currency coupons at the rate of 1 lari = 1,000,000 coupons. From April 1993 the National Bank of Georgia had issued coupons in various denominations, to circulate alongside (and initially at par with) the Russian (formerly Soviet) rouble. Following the dissolution of the USSR in December 1991, Russia and several other former Soviet republics retained the rouble as their monetary unit. The average interbank market rate in 1992 was $1 = 222.1 roubles. From August 1993 coupons became Georgia's sole legal tender, but their value rapidly depreciated. The transfer from coupons to the lari lasted one week, and from 2 October 1995 the lari became the only permitted currency in Georgia. Some of the figures in this Survey are still in terms of coupons.

BUDGET (million lari)*

Revenue†	1994	1995	1996
Tax revenue	41.1	131.9	304.5
Taxes on income	3.4	20.9	44.5
Taxes on profits	11.6	28.6	37.9
Value-added tax	16.6	58.5	133.8
Customs duties	2.3	4.5	19.9
Other current revenue	7.6	16.9	50.0
Extrabudgetary revenue‡	9.4	41.2	111.2
Total	58.2	189.9	465.7

Expenditure§	1994	1995	1996
Current expenditure	296.2	319.2	736.4
Wages and salaries	11.0	59.5	103.7
Other goods and services	25.0	56.1	120.1
Subsidies and transfers	190.1	39.1	59.0
Interest payments	33.8	54.6	57.3
Other current expenditure	21.7	49.7	101.4
Unclassified expenditure	8.4	10.4	82.4
Extrabudgetary expenditure‖	6.2	49.9	103.8
Local government expenditure	22.6	70.1	108.7
Capital expenditure	4.0	38.8	68.9
Total	322.8	428.1	805.3

* Figures represent a consolidation of the State Budget (covering the central Government and local administrations) and extrabudgetary funds. Figures for 1996 are estimates, based on data for the first 11 months of 1996.

† Excluding grants received (million lari): 47.9 in 1994; 71.0 in 1995; 71.1 in 1996.

‡ Comprising the revenues of the Social Security Fund, the Employment Fund, the Health Fund, the Privatization Fund and the Road Fund (established in October 1995).

§ Excluding net lending (million lari): 10.2 in 1994; 27.3 in 1995; –8.9 in 1996.

‖ Including the payment of pensions and unemployment benefit.

INTERNATIONAL RESERVES (million lari at 31 December)

	1994	1995	1996
Gold	1.5	1.5	1.5
Foreign exchange	53.7	197.7	201.5

MONEY SUPPLY (million lari at 31 December)

	1994	1995	1996
Currency outside banks	21.1	131.4	185.6

COST OF LIVING (Consumer price index; base: December 1992 = 100)

	1994	1995	1996
All items	236,243.3	620,652.7	864,951.1

NATIONAL ACCOUNTS

Gross Domestic Product (million lari at current prices)

	1994	1995	1996
GDP in purchasers' values	1,373.2	3,694.0	4,557.8

Gross Domestic Product by Economic Activity (% of total)

	1993	1994	1995
Agriculture	67.7	28.7	38.0
Industry*	6.3	21.3	14.5
Construction	0.6	5.5	4.0
Transport and communications	3.4	8.8	4.3
Trade and catering	6.9	6.4	21.4
Other services	15.1	29.3	17.8
Total	100.0	100.0	100.0

* Principally mining, manufacturing, electricity, gas and water.

BALANCE OF PAYMENTS (US $ million)

	1993	1994	1995
Exports of goods f.o.b.	457.0	380.7	347.2
Imports of goods f.o.b.	-905.3	-745.7	-686.1
Trade balance	-448.3	-365.0	-338.8
Exports of services	72.7	102.0	121.8
Imports of services	-89.8	-149.5	-104.8
Balance on goods and services	-465.4	-412.5	-321.8
Other income received	0.4	0.3	1.0
Other income paid	-20.1	-35.7	-86.8
Balance on goods, services and income	-485.1	-447.9	-407.7
Current transfers (net)	131.2	170.0	189.2
Current balance	-353.9	-277.9	-218.5
Medium- and long-term borrowing (net)	381.7	-23.7	-169.4
Other capital (net) } Net errors and omissions }	-91.2	4.4	84.2
Overall balance	-63.4	-297.2	-303.7

External Trade

PRINCIPAL COMMODITIES (US $ million)

Imports f.o.b.	1993	1994	1995
Live animals and animal products	4.8	4.3	10.9
Vegetable products	4.9	4.2	24.5
Animal or vegetable fats, oil and waxes	5.5	3.9	10.5
Prepared foodstuffs, beverages, spirits, vinegar and tobacco	20.9	18.0	76.2
Mineral products	166.3	267.9	198.9
Products of the chemical or allied industries	5.2	2.8	9.9
Machinery (incl. electrical) and parts	6.8	10.1	18.5
Total (incl. others)	238.5	327.4	379.0

Exports f.o.b.	1993	1994	1995
Vegetable products	55.7	20.0	19.8
Prepared foodstuffs, beverages, spirits, vinegar and tobacco	22.8	11.6	19.2
Mineral products	20.1	14.6	21.2
Products of the chemical or allied industries	15.2	13.9	13.1
Plastics, rubber and articles thereof	1.7	3.7	1.8
Textiles and textile articles	15.5	13.6	5.2
Pearls, precious or semi-precious stones, precious metals and articles thereof	10.1	1.0	1.2
Base metals and articles thereof	66.8	48.4	56.4
Machinery (incl. electrical) and parts	8.1	18.1	7.5
Total (incl. others)	226.7	155.7	154.4

PRINCIPAL TRADING PARTNERS (US $ million)

Imports f.o.b.	1993	1994	1995
Armenia	4.7	1.0	11.2
Austria	1.6	0.3	12.0
Azerbaijan	2.5	21.9	43.2
Bulgaria	0.2	1.9	25.5
China, People's Republic	2.9	0.1	0.1
Czech Republic	3.9	0.1	0.4
France	6.9	0.3	1.5
Germany	1.6	4.3	10.1
Netherlands	6.2	0.8	4.4
Romania	0.0	3.0	28.2
Russia	9.7	24.7	49.3
Turkey	34.5	35.1	80.2
Turkmenistan	132.6	215.6	41.2
Ukraine	13.2	3.8	7.1
United Kingdom	4.1	0.3	10.7
USA	2.7	4.6	17.9
Total (incl. others)	238.5	327.4	378.9

Exports f.o.b.	1993	1994	1995
Armenia	10.2	12.9	18.9
Azerbaijan	14.8	14.7	12.7
Belarus	2.2	3.3	2.1
Bulgaria	3.4	0.1	5.7
Czech Republic	9.9	0.2	0.0
Italy	0.3	0.1	2.8
Kazakhstan	12.9	9.0	1.8
Russia	103.3	52.3	47.0
Switzerland	0.4	2.1	6.1
Turkey	21.9	23.6	34.9
Turkmenistan	12.4	15.5	6.9
Ukraine	12.7	6.1	5.7
USA	0.7	3.7	0.6
Uzbekistan	4.7	2.7	0.6
Total (incl. others)	226.7	155.7	154.4

Transport

RAILWAYS (traffic)

	1991	1992	1993
Passenger-km (million)	2,135	1,210	1,003
Freight net ton-km (million)	9,916	3,677	1,750

Source: UN, *Statistical Yearbook*.

ROAD TRAFFIC ('000 motor vehicles in use)

	1991	1992	1993
Passenger cars	479.0	479.0	468.8
Commercial vehicles	94.0	66.7	56.0

Source: UN, *Statistical Yearbook*.

SHIPPING

Merchant Fleet (registered at 31 December)

	1994	1995	1996
Number of vessels	98	85	84
Total displacement ('000 grt)	439.4	282.0	206.0

Source: Lloyd's Register of Shipping, *World Fleet Statistics*.

Communications Media

	1992	1993	1994
Telephones ('000 main lines in use)	573	571	526
Telefax stations (number in use)	n.a.	420	460

1994: Radio receivers ('000 in use): 3,000; Television receivers ('000 in use) 2,500; Book production* 314 titles and 1,131,000 copies.

* Includes pamphlets (53 titles and 75,000 copies in 1994).

Sources: UN, *Statistical Yearbook*; UNESCO, *Statistical Yearbook*.

Education

(1994/95)

	Institutions	Students
Kindergartens	1,621	80,200
Secondary schools	3,139	700,472
State secondary specialized schools*	76	30,153
Private secondary specialized schools	98	14,200
Vocational/technical schools	115	18,500
Higher schools (incl. universities)*	23	89,361

* 1993/94.

Teachers: 80,002 in secondary schools in 1994/95.

Source: Ministry of Education, Tbilisi.

Directory

The Constitution

A new Constitution was approved by the Georgian legislature on 24 August 1995; it entered into force on 17 October. The Constitution replaced the Decree on State Power of November 1992 (which had functioned as an interim basic law). The following is a summary of the Constitution's main provisions:

GENERAL PROVISIONS

Georgia is an independent, united and undivided state, as confirmed by the referendum conducted throughout the entire territory of the country (including Abkhazia and South Ossetia) on 31 March 1991, and in accordance with the Act on the Restoration of the State Independence of Georgia of 9 April 1991. The Georgian state is a democratic republic. Its territorial integrity and the inviolability of its state borders are confirmed by the republic's Constitution and laws.

All state power belongs to the people, who exercise this power through referendums, other forms of direct democracy, and through their elected representatives. The State recognizes and defends universally recognized human rights and freedoms. The official state language is Georgian; in Abkhazia both Georgian and Abkhazian are recognized as state languages. While the State recognizes the exceptional role played by the Georgian Orthodox Church in Georgian history, it declares the complete freedom of faith and religion as well as the independence of the Church from the State. The capital is Tbilisi.

FUNDAMENTAL HUMAN RIGHTS AND FREEDOMS

Georgian citizenship is acquired by birth and naturalization. A Georgian citizen may not concurrently be a citizen of another state. Every person is free by birth and equal before the law, irrespective of race, colour, language, sex, religion, political and other views, national, ethnic and social affiliation, origin and place of residence. Every person has the inviolable right to life, which is protected by law. Until its complete abolition, the death penalty may be pronounced only by the Georgian Supreme Court. No one may be subjected to torture or inhuman, cruel or humiliating treatment or punishment.

Freedom of speech, thought, conscience and faith are guaranteed. The mass media are free. Censorship is prohibited. The right to assemble publicly is guaranteed, as is the right to form public associations, including trade unions and political parties. Every citizen who has attained the age of 18 has the right to participate in referendums and elections of state and local administrative bodies.

THE GEORGIAN PARLIAMENT

The Georgian Parliament is the supreme representative body, implementing legislative power and determining the basic directions of the country's domestic and foreign policy. It controls the activities of the Government, within the limits prescribed by the Constitution, and it implements other powers.

Parliament is elected on the basis of universal, equal and direct suffrage by secret ballot, for a term of four years. It is composed of 235 members (150 elected according to the proportional system and 85 according to the majority system). Any citizen, who has attained the age of 25 years and has the right to vote, may be elected a member of Parliament. The instigation of criminal proceedings against a member of Parliament, and his/her detention or arrest, are only possible upon approval by Parliament. A member of Parliament does not have the right to hold any position in state service or to engage in entrepreneurial activities.

Parliament elects for the duration of its term of office its Chairman and Deputy Chairmen (including one Deputy Chairman each from deputies elected in Abkhazia and Ajaria). Members of Parliament may unite to form parliamentary factions. A faction may have no fewer than 10 members.

(Following the creation of the appropriate conditions throughout the territory of Georgia and the formation of bodies of local self-government, the Georgian Parliament will be composed of two chambers: the Council of the Republic and the Senate. The Council of the Republic will be composed of deputies elected according to the proportional system. The Senate will be composed of deputies elected in Abkhazia, Ajaria and other territorial units of Georgia, and five members appointed by the President of Georgia.)

THE PRESIDENT OF GEORGIA AND THE GOVERNMENT

The President of Georgia is Head of State and the head of executive power. The President directs and implements domestic and foreign policy, ensures the unity and territorial integrity of the country, and supervises the activities of state bodies in accordance with the Constitution. The President is the supreme representative of Georgia in foreign relations. He/she is elected on the basis of universal, equal and direct suffrage by secret ballot, for a period of five years. The President may not be elected for more than two consecutive terms. Any citizen of Georgia, who has the right to vote and who has attained the age of 35 years and has lived in Georgia for no less than 15 years, is eligible to be elected President.

The President of Georgia concludes international treaties and agreements and conducts negotiations with foreign states; with the consent of Parliament, appoints and dismisses Georgian ambassadors and other diplomatic representatives; receives the credentials of ambassadors and other diplomatic representatives of foreign states and international organizations; with the consent of Parliament, appoints members of the Government and Ministers; is empowered to remove Ministers from their posts; submits to Parliament the draft state budget, after agreeing upon its basic content with parliamentary committees; in the event of an armed attack on Georgia, declares a state of war, and concludes peace; during war or mass disorders, when the country's territorial integrity is threatened, or in the event of a *coup d'état* or an armed uprising, an ecological catastrophe or epidemic, or in other instances when the bodies of state power are deprived of the possibility of implementing their constitutional powers normally, declares a state of emergency; with the consent of Parliament, has the right to halt the activities of representative bodies of self-government or territorial units (if their activities create a threat to the sovereignty and territorial integrity of the country) as well as to halt state bodies in the exercise of their constitutional powers; signs and promulgates laws; decides questions of citizenship and of granting political asylum; grants pardons; schedules elections to Parliament and other representative bodies; has the right to revoke acts of executive bodies subordinate to him/her; is the Commander-in-Chief of the Armed Forces; appoints members of the National Security Council, chairs its meetings, and appoints and dismisses military commanders.

The President enjoys immunity. During his/her period in office, he/she may not be arrested, and no criminal proceedings may be instigated against him/her. In the event that the President violates the Constitution, betrays the State or commits other crimes, Parliament may remove him/her from office (with the approval of the Constitutional Court or the Supreme Court).

Members of the Government are accountable to the President. They do not have the right to hold other posts (except party posts), to engage in entrepreneurial activities or to receive a wage or any other permanent remuneration for any other activities. Members of the Government may be removed from their posts by an edict of the President or by Parliament. Ministries perform state management in specific spheres of state and public life. Each Ministry is headed by a Minister, who independently adopts decisions on questions within his/her sphere of jurisdiction.

JUDICIAL POWER

Judicial power is independent and is implemented only by the courts. Judges are independent in their activities and are subordinate only to the Constitution and the law. Court proceedings are held in public (except for certain specified instances). The decision of the court is delivered in public. Judges enjoy immunity. It is prohibited to instigate criminal proceedings against a judge or to detain or arrest him/her, without the consent of the Chairman of the Supreme Court.

The Constitutional Court is the legal body of constitutional control. It is composed of nine judges, three of whom are appointed by the President, three elected by Parliament, and three appointed by the Supreme Court. The term of office of members of the Constitutional Court is 10 years.

The Supreme Court supervises legal proceedings in general courts according to the established judicial procedure and, as the court of first instance, examines cases determined by law. On the recommendation of the President of Georgia, the Chairman and judges of the Supreme Court are elected by Parliament for a period of at least 10 years.

The Procurator's Office is an institution of judicial power that carries out criminal prosecution, supervises the preliminary investigation and the execution of a punishment, and supports the state prosecution. On the recommendation of the President of Georgia, the Procurator-General is appointed by Parliament for a term of five years. Lower-ranking procurators are appointed by the Procurator-General.

DEFENCE OF THE STATE

Georgia has armed forces to protect the independence, sovereignty and territorial integrity of the country, and also to fulfil international obligations. The President of Georgia approves the structure of the armed forces and Parliament ratifies their numerical strength, on the recommendation of the National Security Council. The National Security Council, which is headed by the President of Georgia, carries out military organizational development and the defence of the country.

The Government

HEAD OF STATE

President of Georgia: EDUARD SHEVARDNADZE (elected by direct popular vote 5 November 1995).

GOVERNMENT

(February 1998)

Minister of State: NIKOLOZ LEKISHVILI.

First Deputy Minister of State and Head of State Chancellery: PETRE MAMRADZE.

Minister of Agriculture and the Food Industry: BAKUR GULUA.

Head of the Committee for Refugee and Resettlement Issues: VALERI VASHAKIDZE.

Minister of Communications: PRIDON INJIA.

Minister for Control of State Property: AVTANDIL SILAGADZE.

Minister of Culture: VALERI ASATIANI.

Minister of Defence: Lt-Gen. VARDIKO NADIBAIDZE.

Minister of the Economy: VLADIMER PAPAVA.

Minister of Education: TAMAZ KVACHANTIRADZE.

Minister of the Environment: NINO CHKHOBADZE.

Minister of Finance: MIKHEIL CHKUASELI.

Minister of Foreign Affairs: IRAKLI MENAGHARISHVILI.

Minister of Fuel and Energy: DAVIT ZUBITASHVILI.

Minister of Health: AVTANDIL JORBENADZE.

Minister of Industry: TAMAZ AGLADZE.

Minister of Internal Affairs: KAKHA TARGAMADZE.

Minister of Justice: TEDO NINIDZE.

Minister of Labour and Social Security: TENGIZ GAZDELIANI.

Minister of State Security: JEMAL GAKHOKIDZE.

Minister of Trade and Foreign Economic Relations: KONSTANTIN ZALDASTANISHVILI.

Minister of Transport: Dr MERAB ADEISHVILI.

Minister of Urban Affairs and Construction: MERAB CHKHENKELI.

MINISTRIES

Office of the Government: 380018 Tbilisi, Ingorokva 7; tel. (32) 93-59-07; fax (32) 98-23-54.

Ministry of Agriculture and the Food Industry: 380023 Tbilisi, Kostava 41; tel. (32) 99-02-72; fax (32) 98-57-78.

Ministry of Communications: 380008 Tbilisi, Chitadze 2; tel. (32) 99-95-28; telex 212911; fax (32) 93-44-19.

Ministry for Control of State Property: Tbilisi, Chavchavadze 64; tel. (32) 29-48-75.

Ministry of Culture: 380008 Tbilisi, Rustaveli 37; tel. (32) 93-74-33; fax (32) 98-74-26.

Ministry of Defence: Tbilisi, Universitetis 2; tel. (32) 30-31-63; fax (32) 98-39-25.

Ministry of the Economy: 380008 Tbilisi, Chanturia 12; tel. (32) 23-09-25; fax (32) 98-27-43.

Ministry of Education: 380002 Tbilisi, Uznadze 52; tel. (32) 95-63-95; fax (32) 77-00-73.

Ministry of the Environment: Tbilisi, Kostava 68A; tel. (32) 23-06-64; fax (32) 98-34-25; e-mail irisi@gmep.kneta.ge.

Ministry of Finance: 380062 Tbilisi, Barnov 170; tel. (32) 22-68-05; fax (32) 29-23-68.

Ministry of Foreign Affairs: 380008 Tbilisi, Chitadze 4; tel. (32) 98-93-77; fax (32) 99-72-49.

Ministry of Fuel and Energy: 380007 Tbilisi, Lermontov 10; tel. (32) 99-60-98; fax (32) 93-35-42.

Ministry of Health: 380113 Tbilisi, K. Gamsakhurdia 30; tel. (32) 38-70-71; fax (32) 38-98-02.

Ministry of Industry: Tbilisi.

Ministry of Internal Affairs: 380014 Tbilisi, Didi Kheivnis 10; tel. (32) 99-62-33; fax (32) 98-65-32.

Ministry of Justice: Tbilisi, Chavchavadze 2; tel. (32) 98-92-52; fax (32) 99-02-25.

Ministry of Labour and Social Security: 380007 Tbilisi, Leonidze 7-2; tel. (32) 93-69-68; fax (32) 93-61-50.

Ministry of State Security: 380008 Tbilisi, 9 April St 2; tel. (32) 99-95-82; fax (32) 99-57-84.

Ministry of Trade and Foreign Economic Relations: Tbilisi, Kazbegi 142; tel. (32) 38-96-52; fax (32) 38-07-23.

Ministry of Transport: 380060 Tbilisi, Aleksandr Kazbegi 12; tel. (32) 93-28-46; fax (32) 93-91-45.

Ministry of Urban Affairs and Construction: 380113 Tbilisi, Vazha Pshavela 16; tel. (32) 37-42-76; fax (32) 36-31-02.

President and Legislature

PRESIDENT

Presidential Election, 5 November 1995

Candidates	Votes	%
EDUARD SHEVARDNADZE	1,589,909	74.94
JUMBER PATIASHVILI	414,303	19.53
AKAKI BAKRADZE	31,350	1.48
PANTELEIMON GIORGADZE	10,697	0.50
KARTLOS GHARIBASHVILI	10,023	0.47
ROIN LIPARTELIANI	7,948	0.37
Total*	2,121,510	100.00

* Including 57,280 spoilt voting papers (2.70% of the total).

GEORGIAN PARLIAMENT

(Sakartvelos Parlamenti)

Chairman: ZURAB ZHVANIA.

Deputy Chairmen: EDUARD SURMANIDZE, ELDAR SHENGELAIA, GIORGI KOBAKHIDZE, VAKHTANG KOLBAIA.

General Election, 5 and 19 November and 3 December 1995

Parties and blocs	Party lists: % of votes*	Party lists: Seats	Single-member constituency seats	Total seats
Citizens' Union of Georgia	23.71	90	17	107
National Democratic Party of Georgia	7.95	31	3	34
All-Georgian Union of Revival	6.84	25	6	31
Socialist Party of Georgia	3.79	0	4	4
'Progress' bloc	n.a.	0	4	4
'Tanadgoma' (Solidarity) bloc	n.a.	0	3	3
Union of Georgian Traditionalists	4.22	0	2	2
Reformers Union of Georgia—National Concord	2.89	0	2	2
United Republican Party	n.a.	0	1	1
State Justice Union	n.a.	0	1	1
Lemi organization	n.a.	0	1	1
Abkhazian deputies†	—	—	12	12
Independent candidates	—	—	29	29
Total	100.00	146	85	231‡

* In order to win seats, parties needed to obtain at least 5% of the total votes cast.

† Owing to the electoral boycott in the secessionist region of Abkhazia, the mandates of 12 deputies from Abkhazia (elected to the previous legislature in 1992) were renewed.

‡ Four of the 150 party seats remained unfilled.

In December 1995 it was reported that six factions had been formed within the Parliament: those of the Citizens' Union of Georgia, the National Democratic Party of Georgia and the All-Georgian Union of Revival, the Mazhoritari faction (uniting deputies elected by majority vote), the Imedi (Hope) faction, and the Abkhazeti faction (uniting deputies representing Abkhazia). A seventh faction, Mamuli (Fatherland), was registered in September 1997.

According to the Constitution of August 1995, the unicameral Georgian Parliament would be transformed into a bicameral body following the eventual restoration of Georgia's territorial integrity. The future Parliament would comprise a Council of the Republic and a Senate (the latter representing the various territorial units of the country).

Political Organizations

More than 50 parties and alliances contested the legislative election of 5 November 1995. The following are among the most prominent parties in Georgia:

Agrarian Party of Georgia: Tbilisi; f. 1994; Chair. ROIN LIPARTELIANI.

All-Georgian Union of Revival: Batumi, Gogebashvili 7; tel. (200) 76-500; f. 1992; 26,000 mems; Chair. ASLAN ABASHIDZE.

Citizens' Union of Georgia (CUG): Tbilisi, Marshal Gelovani 4; tel. (32) 38-47-87; f. 1993; 100,000 mems; Chair. EDUARD SHEVARDNADZE; Gen. Sec. ZURAB ZHVANIA.

Conservative–Monarchist Party: Tbilisi; Chair. TEIMURAZ ZHORZHOLIANI (sentenced to four years' imprisonment in June 1996 for possession of drugs and weapons).

Georgian Labour Party: f. 1997; main aim is the social protection of the population; 2,000 mems.

Georgian People's Party: Tbilisi; f. 1996 by dissident members of the National Democratic Party of Georgia.

Georgian Social Democratic Party: 380018 Tbilisi, Tskhra Aprilis 2; tel. (32) 99-95-50; fax (32) 98-73-89; f. 1893; ruling party 1918–21; re-established 1990; Chair. Prof. GURAM MUCHAIDZE.

Green Party of Georgia: Tbilisi; f. 1990.

Liberal Democratic Party: Tbilisi; Chair. MIKHEIL NANEISHVILI.

National Democratic Party of Georgia: 380008 Tbilisi, Rustaveli 21; tel. (32) 98-31-86; fax (32) 98-31-88; f. 1981; Leader IRINA SARISHVILI-CHANTURIA.

National Independence Party: Tbilisi; Chair. IRAKLI TSERETELI.

Revived Communist Party of Georgia: f. 1997; Chair. SHALVA BERIANIDZE.

Round Table—Free Georgia: Tbilisi, Dgebuadze 4; tel. (32) 95-48-20; f. 1990; opposition party uniting supporters of former President ZVIAD GAMSAKHURDIA.

Socialist Party of Georgia: Tbilisi, Leselidze 41; tel. (32) 98-33-67; f. 1995; Chair. TEMUR GAMTSEMLIDZE.

Union of Georgian Realists: f. 1997; aims to achieve political and economic stability in a united Georgia.

United Communist Party of Georgia: Tbilisi, Chodrishvili 45; tel. and fax (32) 95-32-16; f. 1994, uniting various successor parties to former Communist Party of Georgia; 128,000 mems (1995); First Sec. PANTELEIMON GIORGADZE.

United Republican Party: Tbilisi; f. 1995; absorbed Georgian Popular Front (f. 1989); Chair. NODAR NATADZE.

Diplomatic Representation

EMBASSIES IN GEORGIA

Armenia: Tbilisi, Tetelashvili 4; tel. (32) 95-17-23; fax (32) 99-01-26; Ambassador: LEVON KHACHATURIAN.

China, People's Republic: Tbilisi, Barnov 52; tel. (32) 99-80-11; Ambassador: LI JINGXIAN.

France: Tbilisi, Gogebashvili 15; tel. (32) 93-42-10; fax (32) 95-33-75; Ambassador: MIREILLE MUSSO.

Germany: 380012 Tbilisi, Davit Aghmashenebeli 166; tel. (32) 95-09-36; telex 212973; fax (32) 95-89-10; Ambassador: Dr NORBERT BAAS.

Holy See: 380086 Tbilisi, Dzhgenti 40; tel. (32) 94-13-05; Apostolic Nuncio: Most Rev. JEAN-PAUL GOBEL, Titular Archbishop of Galazia in Campania.

Iran: Tbilisi, Zovreti 16; tel. (32) 29-46-95; Ambassador: FEREYDUN HAQBIN.

Israel: 380012 Tbilisi, Davit Aghmashenebeli 61; tel. (32) 96-02-13; fax (32) 95-17-09; Ambassador: BARUKH BEN-NERIA.

Korea, Republic: Tbilisi; Ambassador: YI CHONG-PIN.

Russia: 380012 Tbilisi, Davit Aghmashenebeli 61; tel. (32) 95-16-04; fax (32) 95-52-33; Ambassador: FELIKS STANEVSKII.

Turkey: 380012 Tbilisi, Davit Aghmashenebeli 61; tel. (32) 95-20-14; telex 212997; fax (32) 95-18-10; Ambassador: TEFHIK OKYANUZ.

Ukraine: 380012 Tbilisi, Davit Aghmashenebeli 61; tel. and fax (32) 98-93-62; Ambassador: ANATOLIY KASIANENKO.

United Kingdom: 380003 Tbilisi, Metechi Palace Hotel; tel. (32) 95-54-97; fax (32) 00-10-65; Ambassador: RICHARD JENKINS.

USA: Tbilisi, Atoneli 25; tel. (32) 98-99-67; fax (32) 93-37-59; Ambassador: WILLIAM COURTNEY.

Judicial System

In late 1997 the 12-member Georgian Justice Council was established, to co-ordinate the appointment of judges and their activities. It comprises four members nominated by the President, four nominated by the Parliament and four nominated by the Supreme Court. Chair. MIKHEIL SAAKASHVILI.

Chairman of the Constitutional Court: AVTANDIL DEMETRASHVILI.

Chairman of the Supreme Court: MINDIA UGREKHELIDZE.

Procurator-General: JAMLET BABILASHVILI.

First Deputy Procurator-General: REVAZ KIPIANI.

Religion

CHRISTIANITY

The Georgian Orthodox Church

The Georgian Orthodox Church is divided into 15 dioceses, and includes not only Georgian parishes, but also several Russian and Greek Orthodox communities, which are under the jurisdiction of the Primate of the Georgian Orthodox Church. There are eight monasteries, a theological academy and a seminary.

Patriarchate: 380005 Tbilisi, Sioni 4; tel. (32) 72-27-18; Catholicos-Patriarch of All Georgia ILIYA II.

The Roman Catholic Church

The Apostolic Administrator of the Caucasus is the Apostolic Nuncio to Georgia, Armenia and Azerbaijan, who is resident in Tbilisi (see Diplomatic Representation, above).

ISLAM

There are Islamic communities among the Ajars, Abkhazians, Azerbaijanis, Kurds and some Ossetians. The country falls under the jurisdiction of the Muslim Board of Transcaucasia, based in Baku (Azerbaijan).

The Press

Department of the Press: 380008 Tbilisi, Jorjiashvili 12; tel. (32) 98-70-08; govt regulatory body; Dir V. RTSKHILADZE.

PRINCIPAL NEWSPAPERS

In Georgian, except where otherwise stated.

Akhalgazrda Iverieli (Young Iberian): Tbilisi, Kostava 14; tel. (32) 93-31-49; 3 a week; organ of the Georgian Parliament; Editor MERAB BALARJISHVILI.

Droni (Times): Tbilisi, Kostava 14; tel. (32) 99-56-54; Editor-in-Chief SOSO SIMONISHVILI.

Eri (Nation): Tbilisi; weekly; organ of the Georgian Parliament; Editor A. SILAGADZE.

Georgian Times: Tbilisi, Giorgi Tsabadze 6; tel. (32) 94-25-92; fax (32) 23-70-12; e-mail times@gtze.com.ge; f. 1993; bi-weekly; separate edns in Georgian and English; Editors-in-Chief ZAZA GACHECHILADZE (English edn), GOGA OKROPIRIDZE (Georgian edn).

Iberia Spektri (Iberian Spectrum): Tbilisi, Machabeli 11; tel. (32) 98-73-87; fax (32) 98-73-88; Editor IRAKLI GOTSIRIDZE.

Literaturuli Sakartvelo (Literary Georgia): Tbilisi, Gudiashvili Sq. 2; tel. (32) 99-84-04; weekly; organ of the Union of Writers of Georgia; Editor TAMAZ TSIVTSIVADZE.

Mamuli (Native Land): Tbilisi; fortnightly; organ of the Rustaveli Society; Editor T. CHANTURIA.

Respublika (Republic): 380096 Tbilisi, Kostava 14; tel. (32) 99-54-70; telex 212132; fax (32) 29-44-60; f. 1990; weekly; independent; Editor J. NINUA; circ. 40,000.

Rezonansi: Tbilisi, Davit Aghmashenebeli 89-24; tel. (32) 95-69-38; daily; Editor-in-Chief SHALVA MEGRELISHVILI.

Sakartvelo (Georgia): 380096 Tbilisi, Kostava 14; tel. (32) 99-92-26; 5 a week; organ of the Georgian Parliament; Editor (vacant).

Shvidi Dghe (Seven Days): Tbilisi, Davit Aghmashenebeli 89-24; tel. and fax (32) 95-40-76; f. 1991; weekly; Dir GELA GURGENIDZE; circ. 4,000.

Svobodnaya Gruziya (Free Georgia): Tbilisi, Rustaveli 42; tel. and fax (32) 93-17-06; in Russian; Editor-in-Chief APOLON SILAGADZE.

Tavisupali Sakartvelo (Free Georgia): 380008 Tbilisi, POB W227; tel. (32) 95-48-20; weekly; organ of Round Table—Free Georgia.

Vestnik Gruzii (Georgian Herald): Tbilisi; 5 a week; organ of the Georgian Parliament; in Russian; Editor V. KESHELAVA.

PRINCIPAL PERIODICALS

Alashara: 394981 Sukhumi, Government House, kor. 1; tel. (300) 2-35-40; organ of Abkhazian Writers' Organization of the Union of Writers of Georgia; in Abkhazian.

Dila (Morning): 380096 Tbilisi, Kostava 14; tel. (32) 99-41-30; f. 1904; monthly; illustrated; for 5–10-year-olds; Editor-in-Chief REVAZ INANISHVILI; circ. 168,000.

Drosha (Banner): Tbilisi; f. 1923; monthly; politics and fiction; Editor O. KINKLADZE.

Fidiyag: Tskhinvali, Kostava 3; tel. 2-22-65; organ of the South Ossetian Writers' Organization of the Union of Writers of Georgia; in Ossetian.

Khelovneba (Art): Tbilisi; f. 1953, fmrly *Sabchota Khelovneba* (Soviet Art); monthly; journal of the Ministry of Culture; Editor N. GURABANIDZE.

Kritika (Criticism): 380008 Tbilisi, Rustaveli 42; tel. (32) 93-22-85; f. 1972; every 2 months; publ. by Merani Publishing House; journal of the Union of Writers of Georgia; literature, miscellaneous; Editor V. KHARCHILAVA.

Literaturnaya Gruziya (Literary Georgia): 380008 Tbilisi, Kostava 5; tel. (32) 93-65-15; f. 1957; quarterly; journal of the Union of Writers of Georgia; politics, art and fiction; in Russian; Editor Z. ABZIANIDZE.

Metsniereba da Tekhnika (Science and Technology): 380060 Tbilisi; f. 1949; monthly; publ. by the Metsniereba Publishing House; journal of the Georgian Academy of Sciences; popular; Editor Z. TSILOSANI.

Mnatobi (Luminary): 380004 Tbilisi, Rustaveli 12; tel. (32) 93-55-11; f. 1924; monthly; journal of the Union of Writers of Georgia; fiction and politics; Editor A. SULAKAURI.

Nakaduli (Stream): Tbilisi, Kostava 14; tel. (32) 93-31-81; f. 1926; fmrly *Pioneri*; monthly; journal of the Ministry of Education; illustrated; for 10–15-year-olds; Editor V. GINCHARADZE; circ. 5,000.

Niangi (Crocodile): 380096 Tbilisi, Kostava 14; f. 1923; fortnightly; satirical; Editor Z. BOLKVADZE.

Politika (Politics): Tbilisi; theoretical, political, social sciences; Editor M. GOGUADZE.

Sakartvelos Kali (Georgian Woman): 380096 Tbilisi, Kostava 14; tel. (32) 99-98-71; f. 1957; popular, socio-political and literary; Editor-in-Chief NARGIZA MGELADZE; circ. 25,000.

Sakartvelos Metsnierebata Akedemiis Matsne (Herald of the Georgian Academy of Sciences, Biological Series): Tbilisi; f. 1975; once every two months; in Georgian, English and Russian; Editor-in-Chief VAZHA OKUJAVA.

Sakartvelos Metsnierebata Akedemiis Matsne (Herald of the Georgian Academy of Sciences, Chemical Series): Tbilisi; f. 1975; quarterly; in Georgian, English and Russian; Editor-in-Chief TEIMURAZ ANDRONIKASHVILI.

Sakartvelos Metsnierebata Akademiis Moambe (Bulletin of Georgian Academy of Sciences): 380008 Tbilisi, Rustaveli 52; tel. (32) 99-75-93; fax (32) 99-88-23; e-mail bulletin@presid.achet.ge; f. 1940; once every two months; in Georgian and English; Editor-in-Chief ALBERT TAVKHELIDZE.

Saunje (Treasure): 380007 Tbilisi, Dadiani 2; tel. (32) 72-47-31; f. 1974; 6 a year; organ of the Union of Writers of Georgia; foreign literature in translation; Editor S. NISHNIANIDZE.

Tsiskari (Dawn): 380007 Tbilisi, Dadiani 2; tel. (32) 99-85-81; f. 1957; monthly; organ of the Union of Writers of Georgia; fiction; Editor I. KEMERTELIDZE.

NEWS AGENCIES

BS Press: Tbilisi, Rustaveli 42; tel. (32) 93-51-20; fax (32) 93-13-02; Dir DEVI IMEDASHVILI.

Iberia: Tbilisi, Marjanishvili 5; tel. (32) 93-64-22; Dir KAKHA GAGLOSHVILI.

Iprinda: Tbilisi, Rustaveli 19; tel. (32) 99-03-77; fax (32) 98-73-65; Dir KETEVAN BOKHUA.

Kontakt: Tbilisi, Kostava 68; tel. (32) 36-04-79; fax (32) 22-18-45; Dir DIMITRI KIKVADZE.

Sakinform: 380008 Tbilisi, Rustaveli 42; tel. (32) 93-19-20; fax (32) 99-92-00; e-mail gha@lberiapac.ge; f. 1921; state information agency; Dir VAKHTANG ABASHIDZE.

Publishers

Ganatleba (Education): 380025 Tbilisi, Orjonikidze 50; f. 1957; educational, literature; Dir L. KHUNDADZE.

Georgian National Universal Encyclopaedia: Tbilisi, Tsereteli 1; Editor-in-Chief A. SAKVARELIDZE.

Khelovneba (Art): 380002 Tbilisi, Davit Aghmashenebeli 179; f. 1947; Dir N. JASHI.

Merani (Writer): 380008 Tbilisi, Rustaveli 42; tel. (32) 99-64-92; fax (32) 93-29-96; f. 1921; fiction; Dir G. GVERDTSITELI.

Metsniereba (Science): 380060 Tbilisi, Kutuzov 19; f. 1941; publishing house of the Georgian Academy of Sciences; Editor S. SHENGELIA.

Nakaduli (Stream): 380060 Tbilisi, Mshvidoba 28; f. 1938; books for children and youth; Dir V. CHELIDZE.

Publishing House of Tbilisi State University: 380079 Tbilisi, Chavchavadze 14; f. 1933; scientific and educational literature; Editor V. GAMKRELIDZE.

Sakartvelo (Georgia): 380002 Tbilisi, Marjanishvili 16; f. 1921; fmrly *Sabchota Sakartvelo* (Soviet Georgia); political, scientific and fiction; Dir D. GVINJILIA.

Broadcasting and Communications

RADIO

Georgian Radio: 380071 Tbilisi, Kostava 68; tel. (32) 36-83-62; telex 212106; fax (32) 36-86-65; govt controlled; broadcasts in Georgian and Russian, with regional services for Abkhazia, Ajaria and South Ossetia; foreign service in English and German; Dir VAKHTANG NANITASHVILI.

TELEVISION

Georgian Television: 380071 Tbilisi, Kostava 68; tel. (32) 36-22-94; fax (32) 36-23-19; two stations; relays from Russian television.

Finance

(cap. = capital; res = reserves; dep. = deposits; m. = million; brs = branches; amounts in lari, unless otherwise indicated)

BANKING

In August 1991 the Georgian Supreme Soviet adopted legislation which nationalized all branches of all-Union (USSR) banks in Georgia. Georgian branches of the USSR State Bank (Gosbank) were transferred to the National Bank of Georgia.

At the beginning of 1993 the Georgian banking system comprised the National Bank, five specialized state commercial banks (consisting of the domestic branches of the specialized banks of the former USSR) and 72 private commercial banks. However, of the last, only about one-half satisfied general legal provisions and only five properly complied with the paid-in capital requirement. As a result, in 1995 more than 50% of the commercial banks in Georgia (then numbering almost 230) were closed down. The remaining banks were to be audited by the National Bank to verify their commercial viability. In April 1995 three of the five specialized state commercial banks—Sakeksimbanki (Export-Import Bank), Industriabanki and Akhali Kartuli Banki (Savings Bank)—merged to form the United Georgian Bank. In 1996 the authorized capital requirement was raised to 5m. lari. At 31 December 1997 there were 53 commercial banks in Georgia.

Central Bank

National Bank of Georgia: 380005 Tbilisi, Leonidze 3-5; tel. (32) 99-65-05; telex 212952; fax (32) 99-98-85; f. 1991; total assets 930.0m. (October 1997); Pres. NODAR JAVAKHISHVILI.

Other Banks

Absolute Bank: 380027 Tbilisi, Ingorokva 8; tel. (32) 99-61-82; telex 212225; fax (32) 93-89-21; cap. 3.9m., dep. 13.1m. (Dec. 1997); Pres. I. DURLAND.

Agrobank: Tbilisi, Khasina 3; tel. (32) 93-46-29; f. 1991 as specialized state commercial bank; 63 brs.

Bank of Georgia: 380007 Tbilisi, Pushkin 3; tel. (32) 99-77-26; telex 212357; fax (32) 98-32-62; f. 1991 as Zhilsotsbank—Social Development Bank, one of five specialized state commercial banks; renamed as above 1994; universal joint-stock commercial bank; cap. 7.5m., dep. 20.3m. (Dec. 1997); Pres. VLADIMER PATEISHVILI; 36 brs.

Intellectbank: 380064 Tbilisi, Davit Aghmashenebeli 127; tel. (32) 23-70-83; telex 212157; fax (32) 23-70-82; cap. 3.3m., dep. 13.0m. (Dec. 1997); Gen. Dir D. VEPKHVADZE.

Ivertbank: Tbilisi, Rustaveli 27; tel. (32) 98-60-20; cap. 2.0m., dep. 7.9m. (Dec. 1997); Chair. O. TOKHADZE.

Rossisski Credit Kartu Bank: Tbilisi, Chavchavadze 39A; tel. (32) 23-35-74; cap. 14.1m., dep. 0.7m. (Dec. 1997); Chair. G. GOBECHIA.

TBC-Bank: 380079 Tbilisi, Chavchavadze 11; tel. (32) 22-06-61; telex 212904; fax (32) 22-04-06; cap. 4.5m., dep. 10.9m. (Dec. 1997); Gen. Dir V. BUTSKHRIKIDZE.

TbilComBank: 380007 Tbilisi, Dadiani 2; tel. (32) 98-85-92; f. 1990; cap. 3.5m., res 1.5m. (Dec. 1997); 10 brs.

Tbilcreditbank: 380002 Tbilisi, Davit Aghmashenebeli 79; tel. (32) 95-83-43; telex 212117; fax (32) 98-27-83; cap. 2.2m., dep. 6.9m. (Dec. 1997); Chair. T. JORJOLIANI.

Tbiluniversalbank: 380071 Tbilisi, Kostava 70; tel. (32) 99-82-92; telex 212234; fax (32) 98-61-68; cap. 1.3m., dep. 1.4m. (Dec. 1997); Gen. Dir T. GVALIA.

United Georgian Bank: 380008 Tbilisi, Uznadze 37; tel. (32) 95-60-98; telex 212346; fax (32) 95-60-85; f. 1995 by merger of three specialized state commercial banks; cap. 8.6m., res 2.8m., dep. 22.5m. (Dec. 1997); Gen. Dir A. INGOROKVA; 25 brs.

COMMODITY AND STOCK EXCHANGES

Caucasian Exchange: 380086 Tbilisi, Vazha Pshavela 72; tel. (32) 30-25-15; telex 212945; fax (32) 30-44-03; f. 1991; authorized cap. 80m. roubles; Chair. of Council AMIRAN KADAGISHVILI; includes:

Caucasian Commodity and Raw Materials Exchange.

Caucasian Stock Exchange.

INSURANCE

Caucasus Insurance Co: 380086 Tbilisi, Vazha Pshavela 72; tel. (32) 30-01-56; telex 212313; fax (32) 30-46-64; f. 1991; authorized cap. 50m. roubles; Chair. of Bd NUGZAR CHOKHELI.

Trade and Industry

GOVERNMENT AGENCY

State Property Management Agency: Tbilisi; f. 1992; responsible for divestment of state-owned enterprises.

CHAMBER OF COMMERCE

Chamber of Commerce and Industry of Georgia: 380079 Tbilisi, Chavchavadze 11; tel. (32) 23-00-45; telex 212183; fax (32) 23-57-60; brs in Sukhumi and Batumi; Chair. GURAM D. AKHVLEDIANI.

TRADE ASSOCIATION

Georgian Import Export (Gruzimpex): 380008 Tbilisi, Giorgiashvili 12; tel. (32) 99-70-90; telex 212191; fax (32) 99-73-13; Gen. Dir T. A. GOGOBERIDZE.

UTILITIES

Electricity

Gruzenergo: energy supplier.

Sakenergo: formerly state-owned energy supplier; in 1996 restructured into three cos (generation, transmission and distribution); transformation into joint-stock cos under way in 1997.

Sakenergogeneratsia: state power-generating co.

Gas

Gruztransgazprom: gas distribution co.

International Gas Corpn of Georgia: joint-stock co; Chair. ALEKSANDR GOTSIRIDZE.

TRADE UNIONS

Confederation of Trade Unions of Georgia: 380122 Tbilisi, Shartava 7; tel. (32) 38-29-95; fax (32) 22-46-63; f. 1995; comprises branch unions with a total membership of c. 1.4m.; Chair. IRAKLI TUGUSHI.

Transport

RAILWAYS

In 1995 Georgia's rail network (including the sections within the secessionist republic of Abkhazia) totalled approximately 1,600 km. However, some 500 km of track was reported to be in a poor state of repair, as a result of which the capacity of some sections of the network had fallen by more than 75% since 1990. The main rail links are with the Russian Federation, along the Black Sea coast, with Azerbaijan, with Armenia and with Iran. The Georgian–Armenian railway continues into eastern Turkey. However, various civil conflicts in the mid-1990s disrupted sections of the railway network. The separatist war in Abkhazia resulted in the severance of Georgia's rail connection with the Russian Federation. However, services to Moscow resumed in mid-1997, following a four-year interruption.

The first section of the Tbilisi Metro was opened in 1966; by 1994 the system comprised two lines with 20 stations, totalling 23 km in length.

Georgian Railways: 380012 Tbilisi, Tsaritsa Tamara 15; tel. (32) 95-25-27; f. 1992, following the dissolution of the former Soviet Railways; Chair. AKAKI CHKHAIDZE.

ROADS

In 1996 the total length of roads in use was an estimated 20,700 km (6,170 km of highways and 14,500 km of secondary roads), of which 93.5% were paved.

SHIPPING

There are international shipping services with Black Sea and Mediterranean ports. The main ports are at Batumi and Sukhumi.

Shipowning Company

Georgian Shipping Company: 384517 Batumi, Gogebashvili 60; tel. (200) 14-02-312; telex 412617; fax (200) 14-05-477; Pres. Capt. B. VARSHANIDZE.

CIVIL AVIATION

Orbi (Georgian Airlines): 380058 Tbilisi, Tbilisi Airport; tel. (32) 98-73-28; fax (32) 49-51-51; successor to the former Aeroflot division in Georgia; services to destinations in the CIS and the Middle East; CEO VASILI JAMILBASHI.

Tourism

Prior to the disintegration of the USSR, Georgia attracted some 1.5m. tourists annually (mainly from other parts of the Soviet Union), owing to its location on the Black Sea and its favourable climate. However, since the outbreak of civil conflict in the early 1990s in South Ossetia and Abkhazia, there has been an almost complete cessation in tourism. It was hoped that, with the restoration of law and order in Georgia following the signing of cease-fire agreements with the secessionist republics, tourist numbers would increase in the late 1990s.

GERMANY

Introductory Survey

Location, Climate, Language, Religion, Flag, Capital

The Federal Republic of Germany, which was formally established in October 1990 upon the unification of the Federal Republic of Germany (FRG, West Germany) and the German Democratic Republic (GDR, East Germany), lies in the heart of Europe. Its neighbours to the west are the Netherlands, Belgium, Luxembourg and France, to the south Switzerland and Austria, to the east the Czech Republic and Poland, and to the north Denmark. The climate is temperate, with an average annual temperature of 9°C (48°F), although there are considerable variations between the North German lowlands and the Bavarian Alps. The language is German. There is a small Sorbian-speaking minority (numbering about 100,000 people). About 35% of the population are Protestants and an estimated 34% are Roman Catholics. The national flag (proportions 5 by 3) consists of three equal horizontal stripes, of black, red and gold. The capital is Berlin. The provisional seat of government is Bonn. (In June 1991 the lower house and main legislative organ, the Bundestag, voted in favour of Berlin as the seat of the legislature and government, and in September 1996 the upper house, the Bundesrat, also voted to move to the capital. The transference of organs of government from Bonn to Berlin was to be completed by 2000. Eight Federal Ministries were to remain in Bonn.)

Recent History

Following the defeat of the Nazi regime and the ending of the Second World War in 1945, Germany was divided, according to the Berlin Agreement, into US, Soviet, British and French occupation zones. Berlin was similarly divided. The former German territories east of the Oder and Neisse rivers, with the city of Danzig (now Gdańsk), became part of Poland, while the northern part of East Prussia, around Königsberg (now Kaliningrad), was transferred to the USSR. After the failure of negotiations to establish a unified German administration, the US, French and British zones were integrated economically in 1948. In May 1949 a provisional Constitution, the Grundgesetz (Basic Law), came into effect in the three zones (except in Saarland, which was not reunited with the FRG until 1957), and federal elections were held in August. On 21 September 1949 a new German state, the Federal Republic of Germany (FRG), was established in the three Western zones. In October 1949 Soviet-occupied Eastern Germany declared itself the German Democratic Republic (GDR), with the Soviet zone of Berlin as its capital. This left the remainder of Berlin (West Berlin) as an enclave of the FRG within the territory of the GDR.

The FRG and GDR developed sharply divergent political and economic systems. The leaders of the GDR created a socialist state, based on the Soviet model. As early as 1945 large agricultural estates in eastern Germany were nationalized, followed in 1946 by major industrial concerns. Exclusive political control was exercised by the Sozialistische Einheitspartei Deutschlands (SED, Socialist Unity Party of Germany), which had been formed in April 1946 by the merger of the Communist Party of Germany and the branch of the Sozialdemokratische Partei Deutschlands (SPD, Social Democratic Party of Germany) in the Soviet zone. Other political parties in eastern Germany were under the strict control of the SED, and no political activity independent of the ruling party was permitted. In 1950 Walter Ulbricht was appointed Secretary-General (later restyled First Secretary) of the SED.

The transfer, as war reparations, of foodstuffs, livestock and industrial equipment to the USSR from eastern Germany had a devastating effect on the area's economy in the immediate post-war period. In June 1953 increasing political repression and severe food shortages led to uprisings and strikes, which were suppressed by Soviet troops. The continued failure of the GDR to match the remarkable economic recovery of the FRG prompted a growing number of refugees to cross from the GDR to the FRG (between 1949 and 1961 an estimated 2.5m. GDR citizens moved permanently to the FRG). Emigration was accelerated by the enforced collectivization of many farms in 1960, and in August 1961 the GDR authorities hastily constructed a guarded wall between East and West Berlin.

In May 1971 Ulbricht was succeeded as First Secretary of the SED by Erich Honecker. Ulbricht remained Chairman of the Council of State (Head of State), a post that he had held since 1960, until his death in August 1973. He was initially succeeded in this office by Willi Stoph, but in October 1976 Stoph returned to his previous post as Chairman of the Council of Ministers, and Honecker became Chairman of the Council of State. Under Honecker, despite some liberalization of relations with the FRG, there was little relaxation of repressive domestic policies. Honecker strongly opposed the political and economic reforms that began in the USSR and some other Eastern European countries in the mid-1980s.

The 1949 elections in the FRG resulted in victory for the conservative Christlich-Demokratische Union Deutschlands (CDU, Christian Democratic Union of Germany), together with its sister party in Bavaria, the Christlich-Soziale Union (CSU, Christian Social Union). The SPD was the largest opposition party. Dr Konrad Adenauer, the leader of the CDU, was elected Federal Chancellor by the Bundestag (Federal Assembly); Theodor Heuss became the first President of the Republic. Under Adenauer's chancellorship (which lasted until 1963) and the direction of Dr Ludwig Erhard, his Minister of Economics (and successor as Chancellor), the FRG rebuilt itself rapidly to become one of the most affluent and economically dynamic states in Europe, as well as an important strategic ally of other Western European states and the USA. The Paris Agreement of 1954 gave full sovereign status to the FRG from 5 May 1955, and also granted it membership of NATO.

The CDU/CSU ruled in coalition with the SPD from 1966 to 1969, under the chancellorship of Dr Kurt Kiesinger, but lost support at the 1969 general election, allowing the SPD to form a coalition Government with the Freie Demokratische Partei (FDP, Free Democratic Party), under the chancellorship of Willy Brandt, the SPD leader. Following elections in November 1972, the SPD became, for the first time, the largest party in the Bundestag. In May 1974, however, Brandt resigned as Chancellor, after the discovery that his personal assistant had been a clandestine agent of the GDR. He was succeeded by Helmut Schmidt of the SPD, hitherto the Minister of Finance. In the same month Walter Scheel, Brandt's Vice-Chancellor and Minister of Foreign Affairs, was elected President in place of Gustav Heinemann. A deteriorating economic situation was accompanied by a decline in the popularity of the Government and increasing tension between the coalition partners. In the general election of October 1976 the SPD lost its position as largest party in the Bundestag, but the SPD-FDP coalition retained a slender majority. In July 1979 Dr Karl Carstens of the CDU succeeded Scheel as President.

At the general election of October 1980 the SPD-FDP coalition secured a 45-seat majority in the Bundestag. However, over the next two years the coalition became increasingly unstable, with the partners divided on issues of nuclear power, defence and economic policy. In September 1982 the coalition finally collapsed when the two parties failed to agree on budgetary measures. In October the FDP formed a Government with the CDU/CSU, under the chancellorship of Dr Helmut Kohl, the leader of the CDU. This new partnership was consolidated by the results of the general election of March 1983, when the CDU/CSU substantially increased its share of the votes cast, obtaining 48.8% of the total, compared with 38.8% for the SPD, now led by Hans-Jochen Vogel. An environmentalist party, Die Grünen (The Greens), gained representation in the Bundestag for the first time.

In July 1984 Dr Richard von Weizsäcker of the CDU, the former Governing Mayor of West Berlin, became Federal President, succeeding Carstens. Despite domestic problems, the CDU/CSU-FDP coalition retained power after the general election of January 1987, with a reduced majority. Kohl was reappointed Chancellor by the Bundestag, although with substantially less support.

During the period 1949–69 the FRG, under the CDU/CSU, remained largely isolated from Eastern Europe, owing to the FRG Government's refusal to recognize the GDR as an independent state or to maintain diplomatic relations with any other states that recognized the GDR. When Willy Brandt of the SPD became Chancellor in 1969, he adopted a more conciliatory approach to relations with Eastern Europe and, in particular, towards the GDR, a policy which came to be known as Ostpolitik. In 1970 formal discussions were conducted between representatives of the GDR and the FRG for the first time, and there was a significant increase in diplomatic contacts between the FRG and the other countries of Eastern Europe. In 1970 treaties were signed with the USSR and Poland, in which the FRG formally renounced claims to the eastern territories of the Third Reich and recognized the 'Oder–Neisse Line' as the border between Germany (actually the GDR) and Poland. Further negotiations between the GDR and the FRG, following a quadripartite agreement on West Berlin in September 1971, clarified access rights to West Berlin and also allowed West Berliners to visit the GDR. In December 1972 the two German states signed a 'Basic Treaty', agreeing to develop normal, neighbourly relations with each other, to settle all differences without resort to force, and to respect each other's independence. The Treaty permitted both the FRG and the GDR to join the UN in September 1973, and allowed many Western countries to establish diplomatic relations with the GDR, although both German states continued to deny formal diplomatic recognition to each other.

In December 1981 the first official meeting took place between the two countries' leaders for 11 years, when Chancellor Schmidt of the FRG travelled to the GDR for discussions with Honecker. Inter-German relations deteriorated following the deployment, in late 1983, of US nuclear missiles in the FRG, and the subsequent siting of additional Soviet missiles in the GDR. Nevertheless, official contacts were maintained, and Honecker made his first visit to the FRG in September 1987.

Relations between the two German states were dramatically affected by political upheavals that occurred in the GDR in late 1989 and 1990. In the latter half of 1989 many thousands of disaffected GDR citizens emigrated illegally to the FRG, via Czechoslovakia, Poland and Hungary. The exodus was accelerated by the Hungarian Government's decision, in September 1989, to permit citizens of the GDR to leave Hungary without exit visas. Meanwhile, there was a growth in popular dissent within the GDR, led by Neues Forum (New Forum), an independent citizens' action group that had been established to encourage discussion of democratic reforms, justice and environmental issues.

In early October 1989, following official celebrations to commemorate the 40th anniversary of the foundation of the GDR, anti-Government demonstrations erupted in East Berlin and other large towns. Eventually, as the demonstrations attracted increasing popular support, intervention by the police ceased. (It was later reported that the SED Politburo had voted narrowly against the use of the armed forces to suppress the civil unrest.) In mid-October, as the political situation became more unsettled, Honecker resigned as General Secretary of the SED, Chairman of the Council of State and Chairman of the National Defence Council, ostensibly for reasons of ill health. He was replaced in all these posts by Egon Krenz, a senior member of the SED Politburo. Krenz immediately offered concessions to the opposition, initiating a dialogue with the members of Neues Forum (which was legalized in early November) and with church leaders. There was also a noticeable liberalization of the media, and an amnesty was announced for all persons who had been detained during the recent demonstrations and for those imprisoned for attempting to leave the country illegally. However, large demonstrations, to demand further reforms, continued in many towns throughout the GDR.

On 7 November 1989, in a further attempt to placate the demonstrators, the entire membership of the GDR Council of Ministers (including the Chairman, Willi Stoph) resigned. On the following day the SED Politburo also resigned. On 9 November restrictions on foreign travel for GDR citizens were ended, and all border crossings to the FRG were opened. During the weekend of 10–11 November an estimated 2m. GDR citizens crossed into West Berlin, and the GDR authorities began to dismantle sections of the wall dividing the city. Dr Hans Modrow, a leading member of the SED who was regarded as an advocate of greater reforms, was appointed Chairman of a new Council of Ministers. The new Government pledged to introduce comprehensive political and economic reforms and to hold free elections in 1990.

In early December 1989 the Volkskammer (the GDR's legislature) voted to remove provisions in the Constitution that protected the SED's status as the single ruling party. However, the mass demonstrations continued, prompted by revelations of corruption and personal enrichment by the former leadership and of abuses of power by the state security service (Staatssicherheitsdienst, known colloquially as the Stasi, which was subsequently disbanded). A special commission was established to investigate such charges, and former senior officials, including Honecker and Stoph, were expelled from the SED and placed under house arrest, pending legal proceedings. As the political situation became increasingly unstable, the entire membership of the SED Politburo and Central Committee, including Krenz, resigned, and both bodies, together with the post of General Secretary, were abolished. Shortly afterwards, Krenz also resigned as Chairman of the Council of State; he was replaced by Dr Manfred Gerlach, the Chairman of the Liberal-Demokratische Partei Deutschlands (LDPD, Liberal Democratic Party of Germany). Dr Gregor Gysi, a prominent defence lawyer who was sympathetic to the opposition, was elected to the new post of Chairman of the SED, restyled the Partei des Demokratischen Sozialismus (PDS, Party of Democratic Socialism) in February 1990.

In December 1989 and January 1990 all-party talks took place in the GDR, resulting in the formation, in early February, of a new administration, designated the Government of National Responsibility (still led by Modrow), to remain in office until elections were held. The GDR's first free legislative elections took place on 18 March 1990, with the participation of 93% of those eligible to vote. The East German CDU obtained 40.8% of the total votes cast, while the newly re-established East German SPD and the PDS secured 21.8% and 16.4% of the votes respectively. In April a coalition Government was formed, headed by Lothar de Maizière, leader of the CDU. Five parties were represented in the new Government: the CDU, the SPD, the Liga der Freien Demokraten (League of Free Democrats) and two smaller parties, the Deutsche Soziale Union (German Social Union), and Demokratische Aufschwung (Democratic Departure). The PDS was not invited to join the coalition.

As a result of the changes within the GDR and the subsequent free contact between Germans of east and west, the issue of possible unification of the two German states inevitably emerged. In November 1989 Chancellor Kohl proposed a plan for the eventual unification of the two countries by means of an interim confederal arrangement. In December Kohl made his first visit to the GDR, where he held discussions with the East German leadership. The two sides agreed to develop contacts at all levels and to establish joint economic, cultural and environmental commissions. However the GDR Government initially insisted that the GDR remain a sovereign, independent state. Nevertheless, in February 1990, in response to growing popular support among GDR citizens for unification, Modrow publicly advocated the establishment of a united Germany. Shortly afterwards, Kohl and Modrow met in Bonn, where they agreed to establish a joint commission to achieve full economic and monetary union between the GDR and the FRG. The new coalition Government of the GDR, formed in April 1990, pledged its determination to achieve German unification in the near future. In mid-May the legislatures of the GDR and the FRG approved the Treaty Between the FRG and the GDR Establishing a Monetary, Economic and Social Union; the Treaty came into effect on 1 July. Later in July the Volkskammer approved the re-establishment on GDR territory of the five Länder (states)—Brandenburg, Mecklenburg-Vorpommern (Mecklenburg-Western Pomerania), Sachsen (Saxony), Sachsen-Anhalt (Saxony-Anhalt) and Thüringen (Thuringia)—which had been abolished by the GDR Government in 1952 in favour of 14 Berzirke (districts). On 31 August the Treaty Between the FRG and the GDR on the Establishment of German Unity was signed in East Berlin by representatives of the two Governments. The treaty stipulated, *inter alia,* that the newly-restored Länder would accede to the FRG on 3 October 1990, and that the 23 boroughs of East and West Berlin would jointly form the Land (state) of Berlin.

Owing to the complex international status of the FRG and the GDR and the two countries' membership of opposing military alliances (respectively, NATO and the now-defunct Warsaw Pact), the process of German unification also included negotiations with other countries. In February 1990 representatives of

23 NATO and Warsaw Pact countries agreed to establish the so-called 'two-plus-four' talks (the FRG and the GDR, plus the four countries that had occupied Germany after the Second World War—France, the USSR, the United Kingdom and the USA) to discuss the external aspects of German unification. In June both German legislatures approved a resolution recognizing the inviolability of Poland's post-1945 borders, stressing that the eastern border of a future united Germany would remain along the Oder–Neisse line. In July, at bilateral talks in the USSR with Chancellor Kohl, the Soviet leader, Mikhail Gorbachev, agreed that a united Germany would be free to join whichever military alliance it wished, thus permitting Germany to remain a full member of NATO. The USSR also pledged to withdraw its armed forces (estimated at 370,000 in 1990) from GDR territory within four years, and it was agreed that a united Germany would reduce the strength of its armed forces to 370,000 within the same period. This agreement ensured a successful result to the 'two-plus-four' talks, which were concluded in September in Moscow, where the Treaty on the Final Settlement with Respect to Germany was signed. In late September the GDR withdrew from the Warsaw Pact.

On 1 October 1990 representatives of the four countries that had occupied Germany after the Second World War met in New York to sign a document in which Germany's full sovereignty was recognized. Finally, on 3 October, the two German states were formally unified. On the following day, at a session of the Bundestag (which had been expanded to permit the representation of former deputies of the GDR Volkskammer), five prominent politicians from the former GDR were sworn in as Ministers without Portfolio in the Federal Government.

Prior to unification, the CDU, the SPD and the FDP of the GDR had merged with their respective counterparts in the FRG to form three single parties. At state elections in the newly-acceded Länder, held on 14 October 1990, the CDU obtained an average of 41% of the total votes and won control of four Land legislatures, while the SPD received an average of 27% of the total votes and gained a majority only in Brandenburg. This surge of support for Chancellor Kohl and the CDU was confirmed by the results of the elections to the Bundestag on 2 December (the first all-German elections since 1933). The CDU (together with the CSU) won 43.8% of the total votes cast, and thus secured a total of 319 seats in the 662-member Bundestag. The SPD achieved its poorest result in a general election since 1957, receiving 33.5% of the votes and winning 239 seats in the legislature (a result attributed, in large part, to the party's cautious stance on unification). The FDP won 11% of the total votes, and consequently 79 seats in the Bundestag, its most successful result in legislative elections since 1961. Unexpectedly, the West German Grünen lost the 42 seats that they had previously held in the legislature, having failed to obtain the necessary 5% of the votes cast in the area formerly constituting the FRG. However, as a result of a special clause in the electoral law (adopted in October 1990, and valid only for the legislative elections of December 1990), which permitted representation in the Bundestag for parties of the former GDR that received at least 5% of the total votes cast in former GDR territory, the party's eastern German counterpart, in coalition with Bündnis 90 (Alliance 90), secured eight seats in the legislature. Under the same ruling, the PDS won 17 seats in the Bundestag (having received almost 10% of the total votes cast in the area formerly constituting the GDR). At state elections in Berlin, which were held simultaneously with the general election, the CDU won the largest share of the votes (40%), while the SPD received 30%. Both environmentalist parties (West and East) won seats, but the extreme right-wing Die Republikaner (Republicans) lost the 11 seats that they had won at elections in West Berlin in 1983.

Dr Kohl was formally re-elected to the post of Federal Chancellor in mid-January 1991, immediately after the formation of the new Federal Government. This comprised 20 members, but included only three politicians from the former GDR. The FDP's representation was increased from four to five ministers, reflecting the party's success in the recent legislative elections.

Investigations into the abuse of power by the administration of the former GDR, conducted during the early 1990s, prompted the dismissal or resignation from government posts of several former SED politicians. In January 1991 the German authorities temporarily suspended efforts to arrest Erich Honecker on charges of manslaughter (for complicity in the deaths of people who had been killed while attempting to escape from the GDR), owing to the severe ill health of the former GDR leader. In March it was announced that Honecker had been transferred, without the permission of the German authorities, to the USSR, and in December he took refuge in the Chilean embassy in Moscow.

One of the most serious problems confronting the Government immediately following unification was that of escalating unemployment in eastern Germany, as a result of the introduction of market-orientated reforms that were intended to integrate the economic system of the former GDR with that of the rest of the country. A substantial increase in the crime rate in eastern Germany was also recorded. A further disturbing social issue, particularly in the eastern Länder, was the resurgence of extreme right-wing and neo-Nazi groups, which were responsible for a series of brutal attacks against foreign workers and asylum-seekers. Moreover, there were also fears of a resurgence of political violence, following a series of terrorist acts culminating in the assassination, in April 1991, of Detlev Rohwedder, the executive head of the Treuhandanstalt (the trustee agency that had been established in March 1990 to supervise the privatization of state-owned enterprises in the former GDR). Responsibility for this and other attacks was claimed by the Rote Armee Fraktion (Red Army Faction), an organization which had perpetrated similar terrorist acts in the 1970s.

Increasing popular discontent with the Government's post-unification policies was reflected in successive victories for the SPD in Land elections in the first half of 1991, causing the SPD to regain its majority in the Bundesrat, which it had lost to the CDU/CSU-FDP coalition in October 1990.

In June 1991 the Bundestag voted in favour of Berlin as the future seat of the legislature and of government. It was envisaged that the transfer of organs of government from Bonn to Berlin would be completed by 2000, with the relocation of the Bundestag as the first priority. In July, however, the Bundesrat (Federal Council) voted to retain its seat in Bonn, and in December it was decided that eight Federal Ministries would also remain in Bonn. (In 1996, however, the Bundesrat reversed its decision to remain in Bonn, and voted to move to Berlin in 1999.)

At the beginning of January 1992 some 2m. Stasi files were opened to public scrutiny. In February Erich Mielke, the former head of the Stasi, was brought to trial on charges of murder, and in September Markus Wolf, the former head of East Germany's intelligence service, was charged with espionage, treason and corruption; both were subsequently found guilty and each was sentenced to six years' imprisonment. Meanwhile, Erich Honecker returned to Germany from Russia in July 1992. He was brought to trial in November, together with five other defendants (among them Mielke and Stoph), on charges of manslaughter and embezzlement. In April 1993, however, the charges against Honecker were suspended. (The former East German leader, who was terminally ill, had been allowed to leave for Chile in January of that year; he died in May 1994.) In May 1993 Hans Modrow was found guilty of electoral fraud at communal elections that had taken place in the former GDR in 1989; Modrow was subsequently sentenced to nine months' imprisonment (suspended).

The issue of asylum-seekers dominated domestic politics during the early 1990s. At Land elections which took place in April 1992, both the CDU and the SPD lost considerable support to right-wing extremist parties. In June the Bundestag approved controversial legislation that aimed to accelerate the processing of applications by refugees and introduced stricter rules for the granting of asylum. A six-week limit was imposed on the time that could be devoted to the consideration of each case, during which period applicants would be required to stay in special camps. Extreme nationalistic sentiment in some quarters began to pose a serious threat to law and order. In August 1992 neo-Nazi youths attacked refugee centres in more than 15 towns and bombed a memorial to the Holocaust (the Nazis' extermination of an estimated 6m. Jews) in Berlin. Sporadic attacks continued throughout Germany (though mainly in the east) in September and October. Several neo-Nazi vandals were arrested, but there was criticism of the lenient sentences imposed on those convicted. The murder in November of three Turkish immigrants in an arson attack in Mölln, Schleswig-Holstein, prompted the Government to ban several right-wing groups that were believed to have been responsible for co-ordinating attacks on foreigners. In December the main political parties reached agreement on the terms of a constitutional amendment to the law of asylum, and the new provisions, empowering immigration officials to refuse entry to economic migrants while still facilitating the granting of asylum to persons who were deemed to be political refugees, were approved by the Bundestag and the Bundesrat in May 1993. The Ministry of the Interior estimated that a record total of 438,191 people had sought asylum in Germany during 1992. By 1995, however, mainly as a result of the 1993 legislation, the number of applications had fallen to 127,937. During May 1993 the deaths of five Turkish women in an arson attack near Köln precipitated protest demonstrations throughout Germany and widespread condemnation in the international media.

In March 1992 Germany suspended sales of military equipment to Turkey, after the Government of that country admitted that armaments previously supplied by Germany had been used in actions to suppress Turkey's Kurdish minority. Revelations that tanks had been transferred to Turkey in late 1991, in contravention of a parliamentary ban on such shipments, obliged the Minister of Defence, Dr Gerhard Stoltenberg, to resign in March 1992. He was replaced by Volker Rühe, hitherto Secretary-General of the CDU. Further government changes were necessitated in May by the resignations of the Vice-Chancellor and Minister of Foreign Affairs, Hans-Dietrich Genscher (for reasons of ill health), and of Gerda Hasselfeldt, the Minister of Health. Genscher was replaced as Minister of Foreign Affairs by Dr Klaus Kinkel, while Jürgen Möllemann, the Minister of Economics, assumed the additional post of Vice-Chancellor. In January 1993, however, Möllemann was forced to resign from the Government, following disclosures that he had used his ministerial influence to promote the business interests of a relative. Dr Kinkel was subsequently promoted to the office of Vice-Chancellor.

The Kohl Government was further weakened by strike action in late April–early May 1992 by members of the country's largest public-sector union, the Gewerkschaft Öffentliche Dienste, Transport und Verkehr, who were demanding substantial pay increases. The strike (the first major industrial action in the sector since 1974) affected public transport services, refuse collection and hospital and postal services, and was accompanied by a number of short strikes by members of the large engineering and steelworkers' union, Industriegewerkschaft Metall.

In May 1993 accusations of professional misconduct prompted the resignations of Björn Engholm, the SPD leader and Minister-President of Schleswig-Holstein, Dr Max Streibl, the Bayern (Bavaria) Minister-President, and Dr Günther Krause, the Federal Minister of Transport.

In May 1994 the Bundesrat approved measures to impose stricter penalties on perpetrators of right-wing violence and on those who denied the existence of the Holocaust; further strong measures against nationalist extremists were adopted in September. In July 1994 Dr Roman Herzog of the CDU, the former President of the Constitutional Court, was sworn in as the new Federal President.

At a general election held in October 1994, the CDU/CSU-FDP coalition was re-elected; its majority in the Bundestag (enlarged to 672 seats) was, however, sharply reduced, from 134 to 10 seats. The CDU (with the CSU) won 41.4% of the votes and 294 seats, the SPD 36.4% of the votes and 252 seats, Bündnis 90 and the Grünen 7.3% of the votes and 50 seats, the FDP (which had lost representation at several Land parliament elections during 1994) 6.9% of the votes and 47 seats, and the PDS 4.4% of the votes and 30 seats. (The PDS secured 17.7% of the votes cast in the eastern Länder.) The right-wing extremist organizations did not attract strong support. In early November the ruling coalition negotiated a new political programme, with the creation of jobs a priority. Shortly afterwards Dr Kohl was formally re-elected as the Federal Chancellor, by a narrow margin of five votes.

In April 1995 the leaders of Berlin and Brandenburg signed an agreement which detailed the proposed amalgamation of the two Länder, dependent upon the approval of both state legislatures and of the two electorates. A regional referendum was held in early May 1996; 53.4% of those who voted in Berlin where in favour of the merger, while only 36.6% of the voters in Brandenburg supported the idea. The proposed amalgamation was, consequently, abandoned.

In May 1995 the Federal Constitutional Court ruled that alleged former East German spies should not be prosecuted by Federal courts regarding crimes that were committed against the Federal Republic on behalf of the former GDR prior to unification; consequently in October the 1992 conviction of Markus Wolf on espionage charges was overturned. In November 1996 the Federal Constitutional Court ruled that the legal principles of the FRG regarding human rights could be retroactively applied to actions carried out within the former GDR. Thus, in January 1997 Markus Wolf was charged with abduction, coercion and assault. In August Egon Krenz and two other former senior SED members were found guilty of the manslaughter and attempted manslaughter of people who had sought to flee the former GDR; all three were sentenced to terms of imprisonment. In the following month Krenz was released pending an appeal.

In the Land elections held in March 1996 in Baden-Württemberg, Rheinland-Pfalz and Schleswig-Holstein, the CDU increased its share of the vote by an average of 2%. This encouraged the Government to announce proposed stringent austerity measures in the following month, which were designed to help reduce Germany's budgetary deficit to the ceiling of 3% of GDP required to qualify for participation in European economic and monetary union (EMU) from 1999. These measures, the majority of which were approved by the Bundestag in June/July 1996, incorporated amendments to the social security system, which were strongly opposed by trade unions, including reductions in sick pay entitlement, unemployment benefit and pensions. In September legislation was passed to raise the age of retirement for both men and women to 65 by the year 2000, to facilitate the dismissal of employees of small businesses, and to reduce sick pay entitlement from 100% to 80% during the first six weeks of absence from work. These unpopular changes, combined with rising unemployment, prompted a series of strikes organized by leading trade unions. Meanwhile, there appeared to be increasing resistance both from certain political quarters and from the population at large to the exacting economic and social austerity measures required to meet the so-called 'convergence criteria' for participation in EMU.

From February 1997 unsuccessful negotiations took place between the ruling coalition and the opposition SPD concerning the possibility of producing a co-ordinated economic policy, in order that legislation central to the Government's economic reform programme should not be rejected by the SPD majority in the Bundesrat. During 1997 the opposition repeatedly blocked the progress of a package of taxation and pension reforms which had been devised by the Government with the aim of revitalizing the economy and facilitating job creation. However, in early October the Kohl administration did successfully introduce legislation to reduce the level of the 'solidarity tax' (levied during the 1990s in order to finance the reunification process). In January 1998 Kohl withdrew the contentious taxation and pension reform draft legislation for the duration of the current parliament, announcing that its implementation would be decided by voters at the general election which was scheduled for September 1998.

Tensions within the CDU/CSU–FDP coalition became apparent in 1997, mainly concerning the desirability and means of meeting the EMU 'convergence criteria' by 1999. Record levels of unemployment continued to cause concern, as well as an unexpectedly large deficit on the 1997 budget. In June an attempt by the Government to finance the deficit by means of a revaluation of the national gold reserves was strongly rebuffed by the Bundesbank. Despite these setbacks to the Kohl administration, the SPD received fewer votes than anticipated at an election to the Hamburg legislature in September. In the following month Kohl was officially selected as the CDU candidate for re-election to the chancellorship in September 1998. The SPD performed strongly at elections to the Niedersachsen Land parliament in March 1998, winning nearly one-half of the votes cast. It was subsequently announced that Gerhard Schröder, the Niedersachsen Minister-President, would be the SPD contender for election to the post of Federal Chancellor in September, representing a considerable challenge to Kohl.

The activities of extreme right-wing organizations appeared to increase in 1997, and during the latter half of the year a series of incidents were reported that suggested the infiltration of some sections of the armed forces by neo-Nazi interests.

In January 1998 three economists and a professor of law initiated a challenge at the Federal Constitutional Court to Germany's proposed participation in EMU, on the grounds that it would contravene the Government's constitutional duty to pursue sound monetary policy.

The orientation of Germany's foreign policy after unification broadly followed that of the pre-1990 FRG. The united Germany remained committed to a leading role in the European Community (EC—now European Union, EU), of which the FRG was a founding member, and NATO, while placing greater emphasis on defence co-operation with France. The country was also strongly committed to close relations with Eastern Europe, in particular with the USSR and, subsequently, its successor states. Relations between the FRG and the USSR had improved signficantly during the 1980s, culminating in the signing, in September 1990, of a Treaty on Good-Neighbourliness, Partnership and Co-operation. In April 1992 Germany and Russia agreed to a mutual cancellation of debts, and in December of the same year the two countries concluded an agreement whereby the Russian Government would grant autonomy to the 2.5m. ethnic Germans in the Volga region of Russia. In September 1996 the Land interior ministers agreed that the Länder could begin deporting some of the 320,000 refugees from Bosnia and Herzegovina who had been given temporary refuge in Germany. In October the German Government signed an agreement with the Federal Republic of Yugoslavia (FRY), providing for the return of about 135,000 Yugoslav refugees to the FRY over a three-year period (from the beginning of December). In January 1997, following more than a year of complex diplomatic negotiations, Dr Kohl and the Prime Minister of the Czech Republic, Václav Klaus, signed a joint declaration regretting past wrongs committed on both sides before, during and after the Second World War.

Following the Iraqi invasion and annexation of Kuwait in August 1990, the German Government expressed support for the deployment of US-led allied forces in the region of the Persian (Arabian) Gulf, and contributed substantial amounts of financial and technical aid to the effort to liberate Kuwait, although there were mass demonstrations against the allied action in many parts of Germany. Despite criticism from certain countries participating in the alliance, Germany did not contribute troops to the allied force, in accordance with a provision in the Grundgesetz that was widely interpreted as prohibiting intervention outside the area of NATO operations. In July 1992, however, the Government announced that it was to send a naval destroyer and reconnaissance aircraft to the Adriatic Sea to participate in the UN force monitoring the observance of UN sanctions on the Federal Republic of Yugoslavia (Serbia and Montenegro). This deployment was subsequently approved by the Bundestag. In April 1993 the Constitutional Court ruled that German forces could join the UN operation to enforce an air exclusion zone over Bosnia and Herzegovina. In mid-1993 Germany dispatched troops to assist the UN relief effort in Somalia. In May 1994 the Constitutional Court declared the participation of German military units in collective international defence and security operations, with the approval of the Bundestag in each instance, to be compatible with the Grundgesetz. In March 1997, while supervising the evacuation from Albania of citizens of western European states, German troops opened fire on hostile forces for the first time since 1945.

In May 1992 Germany and France reached agreement on the establishment of a combined defence corps, which, they envisaged, would provide the basis for a pan-European military force under the aegis of the Western European Union (WEU, see p. 240). The so-called Eurocorps became operational in November 1995.

In December 1992 the Bundestag ratified the Treaty on European Union, which had been approved by EC Heads of Government at Maastricht in December 1991 (see p. 158). At the same time the lower house approved an amendment to the Grundgesetz (negotiated in May 1992 with the Länder), whereby the state assemblies would be accorded greater involvement in the determination of German policy within the EC. The Bundesrat ratified the Maastricht Treaty later in December 1992.

Government

Germany is composed of 16 Länder (states), each Land having its own constitution, legislature and government.

The country has a parliamentary regime, with a bicameral legislature. The Upper House is the Bundesrat (Federal Council), with 69 seats. Each Land has between three and six seats, depending on the size of its population. The term of office of Bundesrat members varies in accordance with Land election dates. The Lower House, and the country's main legislative organ, is the Bundestag (Federal Assembly), with 672 deputies, who are elected for four years by universal adult suffrage (using a mixed system of proportional representation and direct voting).

Executive authority rests with the Federal Government, led by the Federal Chancellor, who is elected by an absolute majority of the Bundestag and appoints the other Ministers. The Federal President is elected by a Federal Convention (Bundesversammlung), which meets only for this purpose and consists of the Bundestag and an equal number of members elected by Land parliaments. The President is a constitutional Head of State with little influence on government.

Each Land has its own legislative assembly, with the right to enact laws except on matters which are the exclusive right of the Federal Government, such as defence, foreign affairs and finance. Education, police, culture and environmental protection are in the control of the Länder. Local responsibility for the execution of Federal and Land laws is undertaken by the city boroughs and counties.

Defence

Germany is a member of the North Atlantic Treaty Organisation (NATO—see p. 204). Military service is compulsory for a period of 10 months. In August 1997 Germany's armed forces totalled 347,100, including 152,560 conscripts. The strength of the army stood at 239,950, including 124,700 conscripts. The navy numbered 27,760 (including 5,460 conscripts), and there were 76,900 in the air force (22,400 conscripts). Defence expenditure for 1998 was projected at DM 46,700m.

At German unification, the National People's Army of the former GDR was dissolved, and 50,000 of its members were incorporated into the German Bundeswehr (armed forces). In accordance with a Soviet-German agreement, concluded in September 1990, the USSR withdrew its 370,000 troops from the territory of the former GDR during 1990–94, while Germany significantly reduced the total strength of its armed forces during the 1990s. In August 1997 the USA, the United Kingdom and France had approximately 115,285 troops stationed in Germany, while Belgium and the Netherlands maintained, respectively, forces of 2,000 and 3,000 men.

Economic Affairs

In 1995, according to estimates by the World Bank, Germany's gross national product (GNP), measured at average 1993–95 prices, was US $2,252,343m., equivalent to US $27,510 per head. During 1991–95, according to official estimates, GNP per head, measured in real terms, expanded at an average annual rate of 0.8%. Over the same period, the population increased by an annual average of 0.5%. Germany's gross domestic product (GDP) increased by an average of 1.4% annually during 1991–96. GDP grew by 1.4% in 1996 (1.3% in the region constituting the former FRG and 2.0% in the eastern Länder), and was estimated to have increased by 2.3% in 1997.

Agriculture (including forestry and fishing) employed 3.2% of the total working population in 1995 and provided 1.1% of Germany's gross domestic product (GDP) in 1996. The principal cash crops are potatoes, sugar beet, barley and wheat. Wine production is also important in western Germany.

Industry (including mining, power, manufacturing and construction) engaged 35.9% of the employed labour force in 1995, and contributed 33.4% of GDP in 1996.

The mining sector engaged 0.7% of the employed labour force in 1994 and contributed 0.5% of the GDP of the former FRG in 1993. The principal mining activities are the extraction of lignite (low-grade brown coal), hard coal and potash salts.

The manufacturing sector engaged 24.8% of the employed labour force in 1995 and provided 27.2% of the GDP of the former FRG in 1993. Measured by value of output, the principal branches of manufacturing in 1995 were transport equipment (accounting for 13.4% of the total), non-electric machinery (12.2%), chemical products (10.8%) and food products (10.5%). In 1993 Germany was the world's third largest producer, and second largest exporter, of passenger motor cars. Manufacturing production increased by 2.8% in 1995.

Petroleum accounts for nearly 40% of total energy consumption, while natural gas provides almost 22% of energy requirements, coal 14%, nuclear power 12% and lignite (primarily used in the eastern Länder) 11.5%. In 1996 imports of mineral fuels accounted for an estimated 7.9% of Germany's total imports.

Services engaged 60.9% of the employed labour force in 1995 and contributed 65.5% of GDP in 1996.

In 1996 Germany recorded a visible trade surplus of US $71,210m., while there was a deficit of $13,070m. on the current account of the balance of payments. More than half of Germany's total trade in that year was conducted with other countries of the European Union (EU—see p. 152). France is the most significant individual trading partner, supplying an estimated 10.6% of imports and purchasing an estimated 10.9% of exports in 1996. The principal imports in 1996 were road vehicles (10.2%), various categories of electrical machinery (6.9%), petroleum and petroleum products (5.4%), and clothing and accessories (also 5.4%). The principal exports were road vehicles (16.5%), non-electrical machinery, various categories of electrical machinery and metals and metal products (especially iron and steel).

The budgetary deficit for 1997 was projected at DM 69,300m. The annual rate of inflation averaged 1.5% in 1996 (1.4% in the west and 2.3% in the eastern Länder) and stood at 1.8% in the year to October 1997. An estimated 11.8% of the labour force were unemployed in November 1997 (the unemployment rate in the eastern Länder was 19.6%).

Germany is a member of the EU, including the European Monetary System (EMS—see p. 172), and of the Organisation for Economic Co-operation and Development (OECD—see p. 208).

By 1990, when German unification was achieved, the FRG was among the world's largest exporters, and its economy was one of the strongest in the world. By comparison, the GDR, following 40 years of Soviet-style command economy, was in a state of economic decline. Following economic, monetary and social union, which took place in July 1990, all economically relevant laws of the FRG were introduced in the GDR, and an extensive process of renewal was undertaken. During 1990–94 most of the 13,687 state-owned enterprises in the former GDR were transferred to private ownership; the majority were acquired by companies operating in the former FRG. In the period immediately following unification the economy was characterized by sustained growth in the west and a further sharp decline in industrial production in the east. From 1991–93, however, overall economic growth lost momentum, owing largely to a decline in orders from abroad (reflecting a world-wide economic recession). Moreover, an enormous increase in imports, attributable to a combination of high capacity utilization in Germany and vigorous domestic demand, severely depleted the visible trade surplus. Strong exports, a buoyant construction sector and increased capital spending improved economic growth during 1994. In 1995 and 1996, however, export growth slowed (owing to the damaging effect on Germany's international competitiveness of an appreciation in the value of the Deutsche Mark), which, combined with a sharp decline in the growth rate of the construction sector and restrained private consumption, resulted in a reduced rate of GDP growth. An increase in GDP growth was reported in 1997. However, record levels of unemployment were reached in that year. During the 1990s the adjustment to a market economy has precipitated a high level of unemployment in eastern Germany, while the stagnation in overall economic growth of the early 1990s contributed to an increase in the western German unemployment rate. In September 1996 the OECD warned that Germany's high levels of unemployment were due, in part, to a lack of flexibility in working practices and distorted tax and benefit incentives. Owing to high labour costs in Germany, many companies have relocated to neighbouring eastern European states. Although there continues to be a disparity between the economic conditions of the eastern and western Länder (at the end of 1997 GDP per head in the region constituting the former GDR was equivalent to only 57% of the level in the former FRG), favourable economic trends have emerged in eastern Germany: the region's GDP growth rate of 9.2% in 1994 was the highest of any part of the EU. The Government has aimed to reduce the budgetary deficit (which expanded rapidly, owing to the costs of unification), in order to satisfy the requirements stipulated by the EU for economic and monetary union (EMU) in 1999. The introduction of austerity measures to achieve this, including reductions in expenditure on social services, has been a feature of budgetary planning since the mid-1990s. A higher-than-anticipated budgetary deficit was forecast for 1997, owing partly to the high level of unemployment and associated social expenditure. An attempt by the Kohl administration in that year to revitalize the economy by means of a reduction in income and corporation tax rates and lower pension contributions was blocked by the opposition SPD (see Recent History). However, legislation was approved in October to reduce the level of the 'solidarity tax' (added to income and corporation tax during the 1990s in order to finance the reunification process) from 7.5% to 5.5%.

Social Welfare

Social legislation has established comprehensive insurance cover for sickness, accidents, retirement, disability and unemployment. The insurance schemes for disability, retirement and unemployment are compulsory for all employees. Insurance is administered by autonomous federal, regional and local organizations. Pensions are based on contributions paid; the amount is related to national average earnings and regularly adjusted. Health insurance pays for all medical attention. During the first six weeks of illness the employer is legally committed to pay 80% of the normal wage. Subsequent to this period, sickness insurance provides a benefit of 70% of the normal gross wage. Of total expenditure on social benefits (DM 1,106,200m. by the Federal Government, the Länder Governments, the municipalities, the private sector and social insurance institutions) in 1994, about DM 373,100m. (33.4%) was for health services, DM 433,700m. (39.2%) for old-age pensions and DM 125,000m. (11.3%) for employment initiatives and unemployment benefit.

In 1995 there were 2,325 hospitals in Germany, with a total of 609,123 beds.

Education

The Basic Law assigns the control of important sectors of the education system to the governments of the Länder. These do, however, co-operate quite closely to ensure a large degree of conformity in the system. Compulsory schooling begins at six years of age and continues for nine years (in some Länder for 10). Until the age of 18, all young people who do not continue to attend a full-time school must attend a part-time vocational school (Berufsschule). Primary education lasts four years and is provided free of charge. Attendance at the Grundschule (elementary school) is obligatory for all children, after which their education continues at one of four types of secondary school. Approximately one-third of this age-group attend the Hauptschule (general school) for five or six years, after which they may enter employment, but continue their education part-time for three years at a vocational school. Alternatively, pupils may attend the Realschule (intermediate school) for up to nine years, the Gymnasium (grammar school) for nine years, or the Gesamtschule (comprehensive school, not available in all parts of the country) for up to nine years. The Abitur (grammar school leaving certificate) is a necessary prerequisite for university education. In 1994 100% of the school-age population were enrolled at primary and secondary schools.

In 1994 total expenditure on education by the Federal Government, the Länder Governments and the municipalities amounted to DM 164,600m. (14.9% of total public expenditure).

Public Holidays

1998: 1 January (New Year's Day), 6 January (Epiphany)*, 10 April (Good Friday), 13 April (Easter Monday), 1 May (Labour Day), 21 May (Ascension Day), 1 June (Whit Monday), 11 June (Corpus Christi)*, 15 August (Assumption)*, 3 October (Day of Unity), 1 November (All Saints' Day)*, 25–26 December (Christmas).

1999: 1 January (New Year's Day), 6 January (Epiphany)*, 2 April (Good Friday), 5 April (Easter Monday), 1 May (Labour Day), 13 May (Ascension Day), 24 May (Whit Monday), 3 June (Corpus Christi)*, 15 August (Assumption)*, 3 October (Day of Unity), 1 November (All Saints' Day)*, 25–26 December (Christmas).

* Religious holidays observed in certain Länder only.

Weights and Measures

The metric system is in force.

Statistical Survey

Source (unless otherwise indicated): Statistisches Bundesamt, 65180 Wiesbaden; tel. (611) 752405; fax (611) 753330; internet http://www.statistikbund.de.

Area and Population

AREA, POPULATION AND DENSITY

Area (sq km)	357,022*
Population (official estimates at 31 December)	
1993	81,338,093
1994	81,538,603
1995	81,817,499†
Density (per sq km) at 31 December 1995	229.2

* 137,847 sq miles.

† Of the total (rounded to the nearest 100), 39,824,800 were males and 41,992,700 females.

STATES

	Area (sq km)	Population ('000) at 31 Dec. 1995	Density (per sq km)	Capital
Baden-Württemberg	35,753	10,319	289	Stuttgart
Bayern (Bavaria)	70,551	11,993	170	München
Berlin	891	3,471	3,897	Berlin
Brandenburg	29,479	2,542	86	Potsdam
Bremen	404	680	1,682	Bremen
Hamburg	755	1,708	2,262	Hamburg
Hessen (Hesse)	21,114	6,010	285	Wiesbaden
Mecklenburg-Vorpommern (Mecklenburg-Western Pomerania)	23,170	1,823	79	Schwerin
Niedersachsen (Lower Saxony)	47,611	7,780	163	Hannover
Nordrhein-Westfalen (North Rhine-Westphalia)	34,078	17,893	525	Düsseldorf
Rheinland-Pfalz (Rhineland-Palatinate)	19,847	3,978	200	Mainz
Saarland	2,570	1,084	422	Saarbrücken
Sachsen (Saxony)	18,413	4,567	248	Dresden
Sachsen-Anhalt (Saxony-Anhalt)	20,446	2,739	134	Magdeburg
Schleswig-Holstein	15,771	2,725	173	Kiel
Thüringen (Thuringia)	16,171	2,504	155	Erfurt
Total	357,022	81,817	229	—

PRINCIPAL TOWNS (estimated population at 30 June 1995)

Berlin (capital)*	3,470,200	Gelsenkirchen	291,800
Hamburg	1,706,800	Bonn*	291,700
München (Munich)	1,240,600	Halle an der Saale†	287,400
Köln (Cologne)	964,200	Karlsruhe	276,600
Frankfurt am Main	651,200	Chemnitz‡	271,400
		Wiesbaden	266,400
Essen	616,400	Mönchengladbach	266,000
Dortmund	600,000	Münster	264,500
Stuttgart	587,000	Magdeburg	263,000
Düsseldorf	571,900	Augsburg	261,000
Bremen	549,000	Braunschweig (Brunswick)	253,600
Duisburg	535,200	Krefeld	249,900
Hannover (Hanover)	524,600	Aachen (Aix-la-Chapelle)	247,400
Nürnberg (Nuremberg)	494,100	Kiel	247,300
Leipzig	478,200	Rostock	231,300
Dresden	472,900	Oberhausen	224,900
Bochum	400,500	Lübeck	216,900
Wuppertal	382,400	Hagen	212,700
Bielefeld	324,000	Erfurt	212,600
Mannheim	315,100	Kassel	201,400

* Berlin is the capital, while Bonn is the provisional seat of government.

† Including Halle-Neustadt.

‡ Chemnitz was renamed Karl-Marx-Stadt in 1953, but its former name was restored in 1990.

BIRTHS, MARRIAGES AND DEATHS

	Registered live births		Registered marriages		Registered deaths	
	Number	Rate (per 1,000)	Number	Rate (per 1,000)	Number	Rate (per 1,000)
1988	892,993	11.4	534,903	6.8	900,627	11.5
1989	880,459	11.2	529,597	6.7	903,441	11.5
1990	905,675	11.4	516,388	6.5	921,445	11.6
1991	830,019	10.4	454,291	5.7	911,245	11.4
1992	809,114	10.0	453,428	5.6	885,443	11.0
1993	798,447	9.8	442,605	5.5	897,270	11.1
1994	769,603	9.5	440,244	5.4	884,661	10.9
1995	765,221	9.4	430,534	5.3	884,588	10.8

Expectation of life (years at birth, 1993–95): Males 73.0; Females 79.5.

IMMIGRATION AND EMIGRATION

	1993	1994	1995
Immigrant arrivals	1,268,004	1,070,037	1,096,048
Emigrant departures	796,859	740,526	698,113

ECONOMICALLY ACTIVE POPULATION
(sample surveys, '000 persons aged 15 years and over)

	1992*	1993†	1994†
Agriculture, hunting, forestry and fishing	1,379	1,255	1,190
Mining and quarrying	352	307	265
Manufacturing	10,818	10,230	9,643
Electricity, gas and water	400	393	374
Construction	2,830	2,947	3,107
Trade, restaurants and hotels	5,355	5,306	5,383
Transport, storage and communications	2,257	2,219	2,169
Financing, insurance, real estate and business services	2,940	3,069	3,160
Community, social and personal services	10,610	10,654	10,784
Total employed	36,940	36,380	36,076
Unemployed	3,185	3,799	4,160
Total labour force	40,125	40,179	40,236
Males	23,045	23,088	23,038
Females	17,080	17,091	17,198

* May. † April.

April 1995 ('000 persons aged 15 years and over): Total employed 36,048; Unemployed 4,035; Total labour force 40,083 (males 22,929; females 17,154).

Source: ILO, *Yearbook of Labour Statistics*.

Agriculture

PRINCIPAL CROPS ('000 metric tons)

	1994	1995	1996
Wheat	16,481	17,763	18,922
Barley	10,903	11,819	12,074
Maize	2,446	2,395	2,913
Rye	3,451	4,521	4,214
Oats	1,663	1,420	1,606
Mixed grain	1,386	1,873	2,407
Potatoes	9,669	9,898	13,100
Dry broad beans	91	86	78
Sunflower seed*	311	137	114
Rapeseed	2,896	3,103	1,970
Cabbages	659	723	835
Cauliflowers	156	156	163
Cucumbers and gherkins	149	172	171
Onions (dry)	217	236	279
Green beans	38	44	49
Carrots	245	297	340
Grapes*	1,482†	1,375†	1,375‡
Sugar beets	24,211§	26,049	26,064§
Apples‖	880	573	878
Pears‖	39	40	37
Cherries‖	79	75	76
Plums‖	41	33	39
Strawberries‖	59	69	77
Currants*‡	170	170	170

* Source: FAO, *Production Yearbook*.
† Unofficial figure.
‡ FAO estimate(s).
§ Deliveries to sugar factories.
‖ Marketed production only.

LIVESTOCK ('000 head at December)

	1994	1995	1996
Horses	598.8	n.a.	652.4
Cattle	15,962.2	15,889.9	15,759.6
Pigs	24,698.1	24,466.2	24,405.1
Sheep	2,340.1	2,394.7	2,324.0
Goats*	89	89	90†
Chickens	101,139.0	n.a.	102,731.3
Geese	592.9	n.a.	641.2
Ducks	1,754.8	n.a.	2,059.8
Turkeys	6,391.1	n.a.	7,075.2

* Source: FAO, *Production Yearbook*.
† FAO estimate.

LIVESTOCK PRODUCTS ('000 metric tons)

	1994	1995	1996
Beef and veal	1,420	1,407	1,407*
Mutton and lamb	40	41	41*
Pig meat	3,604	3,602	3,700
Poultry meat	627	626	626
Edible offals*	385	n.a.	n.a.
Cows' milk	27,866	28,621	28,621
Goats' milk	25	25	25
Butter	461	486	478
Cheese	1,367	1,420	1,420
Hen eggs	843	836	836
Honey	22	24	24
Wool:			
greasy*	15	15	15
clean*	7	7	7
Cattle hides*	190	186	186

* FAO estimate(s). † Unofficial figure.

Source: FAO, mainly *Production Yearbook*.

Forestry

ROUNDWOOD REMOVALS
('000 cubic metres, excluding bark)

	1992	1993	1994
Sawlogs, veneer logs and logs for sleepers	16,400	17,522	21,073
Pulpwood	11,359	10,435	10,744
Other industrial wood	1,400	1,400	1,400
Fuel wood*	3,795	3,795	3,795
Total	32,954	33,152	37,012

* FAO estimates.

Source: FAO, *Yearbook of Forest Products*.

SAWNWOOD PRODUCTION
('000 cubic metres, including railway sleepers)

	1992	1993	1994
Coniferous (softwood)	11,866	10,358	12,365
Broadleaved (hardwood)	1,630	1,164	1,202
Total	13,496	11,522	13,567

Source: FAO, *Yearbook of Forest Products*.

Fishing

('000 metric tons, live weight)

	1993	1994	1995
Common carp	12.8	12.7	14.4
Rainbow trout	23.0	22.8	22.6
European plaice	7.0	5.8	6.5
Atlantic cod	18.6	22.1	31.9
Saithe (Pollock)	18.8	12.4	13.4
Atlantic redfishes	34.8	30.5	20.5
Atlantic horse mackerel	29.4	17.3	20.4
Atlantic herring	68.6	57.1	55.9
Atlantic mackerel	28.7	26.5	24.4
Other fishes	35.2	42.9	51.9
Total fish	276.8	250.0	261.9
Common shrimp	13.5	16.8	11.6
Blue mussel	24.7	4.9	17.8
Common cockle	1.3	1.0	6.6
Other aquatic animals	0.1	0.1	0.1
Total catch	316.4	272.8	298.0
Inland waters	49.3	48.5	62.1
Atlantic Ocean	267.1	224.3	236.0

Source: FAO, *Yearbook of Fishery Statistics*.

Mining

('000 metric tons, unless otherwise indicated)

	1994	1995	1996
Hard coal	54,344	53,564	48,197
Brown coal	207,131	192,700	187,180
Crude petroleum	2,936	2,959	2,849
Natural gas (petajoules)*	606.4	665.4	723.7
Potash salts (crude)	2,793†	n.a.	n.a.
Salt (unrefined)	5,526	7,059	8,525
Electricity (million kWh)	453,432	458,484	547,032

* Source: UN, *Monthly Bulletin of Statistics*.

† Figure refers to the K_2O content or equivalent of potash salts mined.

Industry

SELECTED PRODUCTS

('000 metric tons, unless otherwise indicated)

	1994	1995	1996
Margarine	648	656	657
Flour	3,651	3,721	3,851
Refined sugar	3,822	4,238	4,560
Beer ('000 hl)	116,265	111,875	108,938
Cigarettes (million)	222,791	201,070	193,279
Cotton yarn (pure and mixed)	30	97	97
Woven cotton fabrics ('000 sq metres)	n.a.	399,640	422,575
Carpets and rugs ('000 sq metres)	n.a.	181,405	173,797
Plywood	n.a.	456	454
Newsprint	1,428	1,771	1,711
Brown-coal briquettes	6,861	5,011	4,896
Pig-iron	29,923	n.a.	n.a.
Steel ingots	40,533	n.a.	n.a.
Motor spirit (petrol)	27,106	24,354	25,102
Diesel oil*	n.a.	44,756	46,256
Cement	40,217	37,480	35,845
Sulphuric acid	2,780	1,634	1,441
Nitrogenous fertilizers (N)	1,199	1,229	1,188
Artificial resins and plastics	11,307	10,313	10,001
Synthetic rubber	643	479	465
Soap	106	124	129
Aluminium (unwrought):			
Primary	n.a.	419	385
Secondary	n.a.	326	324
Refined lead (unwrought)	n.a.	202	142
Refined zinc (unwrought)	n.a.	345	352
Refined copper	n.a.	484	536
— continued	**1994**	**1995**	**1996**
Passenger cars and minibuses ('000)	3,497	4,503	4,702
Bicycles ('000)	2,951	2,631	2,277
Clocks, watches and non-electronic time-measuring instruments ('000)	18,688	19,336	19,350
Footwear ('000 pairs)†	46,085	38,102	34,401

* Including light heating oil.

† Excluding rubber and plastic footwear.

Finance

CURRENCY AND EXCHANGE RATES

Monetary Units

100 Pfennige = 1 Deutsche Mark (DM).

Sterling and Dollar Equivalents (30 September 1997)

£1 sterling = 2.853 DM;
US $1 = 1.766 DM;
100 DM = £35.05 = $56.62.

Average Exchange Rate (DM per US $)

1994 1.6228
1995 1.4331
1996 1.5048

BUDGET (million DM)*

Revenue	1994†	1995	1996
Current receipts	1,607,588	1,689,264	1,701,079
Taxes and similar revenue	1,390,458	1,455,302	1,470,761
Income from economic activity	39,109	37,670	35,603
Interest	19,086	20,393	18,766
Allocations and grants for current purposes	422,278	430,406	457,998
Other receipts	129,247	142,680	143,847
Less Deductible payments on the same level	392,590	397,187	425,896
Capital receipts	45,698	56,486	52,439
Sale of property	21,439	31,676	23,492
Loans and grants for investment	55,791	62,939	65,396
Repayment of loans	16,337	17,231	20,398
Public sector borrowing	1,764	1,662	2,198
Less Deductible payments on the same level	49,633	57,022	59,045
Total	1,653,286	1,745,750	1,753,518

Expenditure	1994†	1995	1996
Current expenditure	1,563,449	1,656,986	1,682,007
Personnel expenses	360,102	386,943	390,295
Goods and services	398,849	400,853	415,704
Interest	110,279	131,143	130,729
Allocations and grants for current purposes	1,086,809	1,135,234	1,171,175
Less Deductible payments on the same level	392,590	397,187	425,896
Capital expenditure	194,756	195,478	182,189
Construction	76,025	73,917	70,118
Purchase of property	22,983	22,089	21,867
Allocations and grants for investment	101,669	112,773	110,949
Loans	36,726	36,198	28,885
Sale of shares	4,903	5,663	7,405
Repayment expenses in the public sector	2,083	1,860	2,010
Less Deductible payments on the same level	49,633	57,022	59,045
Total	1,758,205	1,852,464	1,864,196

* Figures represent a consolidation of the accounts of all public authorities, including the Federal Government and state administrations.

† Figures for 1994 are not strictly comparable with subsequent years' figures.

INTERNATIONAL RESERVES (US $ million at 31 December)*

	1994	1995	1996
Gold†	8,839	9,550	8,805
IMF special drawing rights	1,114	2,001	1,907
Reserve position in IMF	4,030	5,210	5,468
Foreign exchange	72,219	77,794	75,803
Total	86,202	94,555	91,983

* Data on gold and foreign exchange holdings exclude deposits made with the European Monetary Co-operation Fund.

† National valuation.

Source: IMF, *International Financial Statistics.*

MONEY SUPPLY (million DM at 31 December)

	1994	1995	1996
Currency outside banks	225,900	237,464	246,810

COST OF LIVING

(Consumer Price Index for All Private Households; base: 1991 = 100)

	1994	1995	1996
Food	106.9	108.4	109.2
Clothes and shoes	106.8	107.7	108.5
Rent	128.1	133.4	137.9
Energy	105.6	104.9	103.3
Furniture, domestic appliances and other household expenses	107.8	109.3	110.2
Transport and communications	112.2	113.4	115.7
Health	110.8	112.7	115.0
Entertainment and culture	108.9	110.5	111.6
Personal expenses	119.3	122.5	123.3
All items	112.8	114.8	116.5

NATIONAL ACCOUNTS

(provisional, million DM at current prices)

National Income and Product

	1994	1995	1996
Compensation of employees	1,820,740	1,877,020	1,897,070
Operating surplus*	688,090	755,590	803,740
Domestic factor incomes	2,508,830	2,632,610	2,700,810
Consumption of fixed capital	435,790	452,970	464,790
Gross domestic product at factor cost	2,944,620	3,085,580	3,165,600
Indirect taxes	443,560	447,190	451,920
Less Subsidies	67,780	75,370	76,520
GDP in purchasers' values	3,320,400	3,457,400	3,541,000
Factor income from abroad	124,200	136,560	131,980
Less Factor income paid abroad	131,700	149,160	166,180
Gross national product	3,312,900	3,444,800	3,506,800
Less Consumption of fixed capital	435,790	452,970	464,790
National income in market prices	2,877,110	2,991,830	3,042,010
Other current transfers from abroad	23,320	24,890	27,030
Less Other current transfers paid abroad	83,130	81,700	80,300
National disposable income	2,817,300	2,935,020	2,988,740

* Obtained as a residual.

Expenditure on the Gross Domestic Product

	1994	1995	1996
Government final consumption expenditure	650,240	675,350	695,440
Private final consumption expenditure	1,902,860	1,974,680	2,039,140
Increase in stocks	16,370	27,710	17,020
Gross fixed capital formation	729,350	750,660	743,560
Total domestic expenditure	3,298,820	3,428,400	3,495,160
Exports of goods and services	758,590	817,160	859,700
Less Imports of goods and services	737,010	788,160	813,860
GDP in purchasers' values	3,320,400	3,457,400	3,541,000
GDP at constant 1991 prices	2,966,200	3,023,400	3,064,600

Gross Domestic Product by Economic Activity

	1994	1995	1996
Agriculture, forestry and fishing	36,050	35,830	37,150
Mining[1] Electricity, gas and water	89,630	89,180	82,420
Manufacturing[1, 2, 3]	808,280	833,130	843,810
Construction[2]	215,820	223,190	217,270
Wholesale and retail trade	283,130	290,860	294,820
Transport, storage and communications	175,700	182,570	176,680
Finance, insurance and dwellings[4]	436,630	464,240	497,570
Restaurants and hotels Community, social and personal services (excl. government)[3, 5]	689,580	737,160	783,490
Government services	371,050	381,860	387,040
Private households and non-profit organizations	88,840	94,670	99,730
Sub-total	3,194,710	3,332,690	3,419,980
Non-deductible sales tax	234,890	235,410	237,210
Import duties	30,150	31,090	31,080
Less Imputed bank service charges	139,350	141,790	147,270
GDP in purchasers' values	3,320,400	3,457,400	3,541,000

[1] Quarrying is included in manufacturing.

[2] Structural steel erection is included in manufacturing.

[3] Publishing is included in community, social and personal services.

[4] Including imputed rents of owner-occupied dwellings.

[5] Business services and real estate, except dwellings, are included in community, social and personal services.

BALANCE OF PAYMENTS (US $ million)*

	1994	1995	1996
Exports of goods f.o.b.	430,580	523,600	519,440
Imports of goods f.o.b.	−379,650	−458,520	−448,220
Trade balance	50,930	65,080	71,210
Exports of services	66,000	81,500	84,640
Imports of services	−105,890	−127,290	−128,060
Balance on goods and services	11,040	19,290	27,790
Other income received	68,040	84,270	76,800
Other income paid	−61,410	−86,050	−81,270
Balance on goods, services and income	17,670	17,520	23,320
Current transfers received	13,800	16,700	17,410
Current transfers paid	−52,700	−57,760	−53,810
Current balance	−21,230	−23,530	−13,070
Capital account (net)	150	−650	−20
Direct investment abroad	−17,180	−38,530	−27,790
Direct investment from abroad	1,680	11,960	−3,180
Portfolio investment assets	−53,990	−22,080	−38,150
Portfolio investment liabilities	23,060	59,100	90,680
Other investment assets	−740	−61,290	−66,330
Other investment liabilities	76,490	96,960	58,950
Net errors and omissions	−10,270	−14,710	−2,280
Overall balance	−2,040	7,220	−1,200

* Figures are rounded to the nearest $10 million.

Source: IMF, *International Financial Statistics.*

DEVELOPMENT AID (public and private development aid to developing countries and multilateral agencies, million DM)

	1993	1994	1995
Public development co-operation	11,505	11,057	10,787
Bilateral	7,473	6,720	6,903
Multilateral	4,032	4,337	3,884
Other public transactions	3,034	5,740	1,260
Bilateral	3,002	6,002	1,662
Multilateral	32	−261	−402
Private development aid	1,434	1,591	1,594
Other private transactions	9,449	20,438	16,808
Bilateral	8,054	20,144	16,384
Multilateral	1,395	295	424
Total	25,422	38,827	30,449

External Trade

Note: Figures include trade in second-hand ships, and stores and bunkers for foreign ships and aircraft. Imports exclude military supplies under the off-shore procurement programme and exports exclude war reparations and restitutions, except exports resulting from the Israel Reparations Agreement.

PRINCIPAL COMMODITIES
(distribution by SITC, million DM)

Imports c.i.f.	1994	1995	1996*
Food and live animals	52,371	54,504	53,916
Vegetables and fruit	17,919	18,570	18,782
Crude materials (inedible) except fuels	27,635	29,269	26,018
Mineral fuels, lubricants, etc.	43,163	41,189	52,817
Petroleum, petroleum products, etc.	31,109	28,365	36,427
Gas (natural and manufactured)	9,015	9,805	13,246
Chemicals and related products	54,999	60,742	59,384
Organic chemicals	12,969	14,120	13,570
Basic manufactures	100,247	112,325	100,043
Textile yarn, fabrics, etc.	17,769	17,865	17,125
Iron and steel	17,819	22,482	17,666
Non-ferrous metals	13,951	16,817	13,641
Other metal manufactures	14,874	16,017	15,540
Machinery and transport equipment	208,937	222,614	229,908
Power-generating machinery and equipment	13,087	14,094	16,404
General industrial machinery, equipment and parts	19,746	21,577	22,262
Office machines and automatic data-processing equipment	29,258	31,656	30,456
Telecommunications and sound equipment	17,947	17,518	17,532
Other electrical machinery, apparatus and appliances	40,976	46,734	46,106
Road vehicles (incl. air-cushion vehicles) and parts[1]	56,254	63,159	68,356
Other transport equipment	16,949	11,940	13,177
Miscellaneous manufactured articles	99,215	97,255	99,624
Articles of apparel and clothing accessories (excl. footwear)	36,768	35,175	36,220
Total (incl. others)[2]	616,955	664,234	669,060

* Provisional figures.
[1] Excluding tyres, engines and electrical parts.
[2] Including monetary gold and government imports. Also included are returns and replacements, not allocated to their appropriate headings.

Exports f.o.b.	1994	1995	1996*
Food and live animals	29,320	30,302	31,452
Chemicals and related products	92,829	99,467	101,564
Organic chemicals	19,013	20,793	20,253
Medicinal and pharmaceutical products	14,138	14,702	15,885
Plastics in primary forms	16,009	17,744	17,421
Basic manufactures	111,204	122,969	119,057
Paper, paperboard and manufactures	15,112	18,083	16,930
Textile yarn, fabrics, etc.	20,474	20,593	20,433
Iron and steel	22,089	25,415	22,982
Machinery and transport equipment	338,431	366,668	383,122
Power-generating machinery and equipment	19,990	20,608	23,950
Machinery specialized for particular industries	40,486	44,143	47,054
General industrial machinery and equipment	47,337	52,242	55,106
Office machines and automatic data-processing equipment	16,030	18,550	18,165
Telecommunications and sound equipment	14,799	15,987	17,458
Other electrical machinery, apparatus and appliances	53,427	61,001	61,099
Road vehicles (incl. air-cushion vehicles) and parts[1]	111,140	118,935	126,989
Other transport equipment	19,969	18,382	15,605
Miscellaneous manufactured articles	72,336	73,988	76,841
Professional scientific and controlling instruments, etc.	17,114	17,906	19,335
Total (incl. others)[2]	690,573	749,537	771,913

* Provisional figures.
[1] Excluding tyres, engines and electrical parts.
[2] Including monetary gold. Also included are returns and replacements, not allocated to their appropriate headings.

PRINCIPAL TRADING PARTNERS*
(million DM, including gold)

Imports c.i.f.	1994	1995	1996†
Austria	29,397.5	26,034.4	25,296.2
Belgium/Luxembourg.	38,048.5	43,965.4	42,140.7
China, People's Republic	15,399.9	15,989.2	17,917.3
Czech Republic/Slovakia	10,694.7	13,727.1	14,803.1
Denmark	11,503.4	12,784.8	11,985.9
France	68,330.2	73,085.9	71,034.6
Hungary	5,410.0	6,909.4	7,922.7
Ireland	6,865.0	8,437.7	7,454.8
Italy	51,830.3	56,824.9	55,009.5
Japan	34,143.8	35,411.5	34,097.8
Netherlands	51,652.1	58,175.6	57,481.8
Norway	10,341.1	10,807.0	13,598.4
Poland	10,126.0	12,413.1	12,181.8
Portugal.	5,570.0	7,005.8	7,920.2
Spain (excl. Canary Is)	17,307.4	20,837.3	21,796.1
Sweden	14,035.9	13,938.4	13,868.9
Switzerland	26,610.0	28,168.2	27,381.5
Taiwan	7,236.7	7,854.6	8,143.7
Turkey	7,237.8	7,954.5	8,445.2
USSR‡	16,027.6	16,963.4	18,622.7
United Kingdom	36,681.5	43,568.7	45,624.6
USA	44,679.2	45,289.3	48,980.3
Total (incl. others)	616,955.4	664,234.1	669,060.5

Exports f.o.b.	1994	1995	1996†
Austria	39,737.7	41,702.3	43,267.8
Belgium/Luxembourg	46,791.2	49,139.0	48,113.3
China, People's Republic	10,296.5	10,783.6	10,889.0
Czech Republic/Slovakia	11,678.7	14,903.5	17,533.2
Denmark	12,916.7	14,363.0	13,931.3
France	83,092.0	87,862.1	84,060.0
Italy	52,469.2	56,873.6	57,271.2
Japan	17,917.7	18,842.3	21,191.4
Korea, Republic	7,376.1	8,751.3	9,868.4
Netherlands	52,765.1	57,118.0	57,322.8
Poland	10,352.6	12,695.1	16,366.1
Spain (excl. Canary Is)	21,866.4	25,794.6	27,556.1
Sweden	15,322.1	18,399.1	18,443.0
Switzerland	37,064.7	39,680.5	37,793.2
Turkey	6,299.7	9,071.1	11,414.9
USSR‡	16,557.7	16,298.1	18,362.8
United Kingdom	55,395.2	61,912.1	61,671.2
USA	54,157.7	54,610.6	60,112.1
Total (incl. others)	690,572.7	749,536.9	771,913.4

* Imports by country of production; exports by country of consumption. The distribution by countries excludes stores and bunkers for ships and aircraft (million DM): Imports 201.0 in 1994, 629.9 in 1995, 712.3 in 1996; Exports 1,165.2 in 1994, 1,937.6 in 1995, 2,248.4 in 1996.

† Provisional figures.

‡ Figures refer to the member states of the former USSR.

Transport

FEDERAL RAILWAYS (traffic)

	1993	1994	1995
Passengers (million)	1,579	1,570	1,656
Passenger-km (million)	58,003	61,962	63,581
Freight net ton-km (million)	66,646	71,814	70,863

ROAD TRAFFIC
('000 licensed vehicles)

	1995	1996*	1997†
Passenger cars	40,404.3	40,987.5	41,045.2
Lorries	2,215.2	2,273.5	2,296.8
Buses	86.3	85.0	84.7
Motor cycles	2,267.4	2,470.5	2,534.2
Trailers	4,100.8	4,263.5	4,328.9

* At 1 July. † At 1 January.

SHIPPING

Inland Waterways

	1994	1995	1996
Freight ton-km (million)	61,772.2	n.a.	61,291.5

Merchant Fleet (registered at 31 December)

	1994	1995	1996
Number of vessels	1,200	1,146	1,101
Displacement ('000 grt)	5,696.1	5,626.2	5,842.1

Source: Lloyd's Register of Shipping, *World Fleet Statistics.*

Sea-borne Traffic*

	1993	1994	1996
Vessels entered ('000 net registered tons)†			
Domestic (coastwise)	18,585	18,390	18,532
International	221,741	223,363	251,500
Vessels cleared ('000 net registered tons)†			
Domestic	18,389	18,131	18,071
International	196,456	201,316	229,959
Freight unloaded ('000 metric tons)‡			
International	119,336	124,826	129,467
Freight loaded ('000 metric tons)‡			
International	57,537	64,975	69,137
Total domestic freight ('000 metric tons)	7,145	6,650	7,408

* Data for 1995 are not available.

† Loaded vessels only.

‡ Including transhipments.

CIVIL AVIATION (traffic on scheduled services)

	1992	1993	1994
Kilometres flown (million)	468	474	501
Passengers carried ('000)	25,578	29,363	30,964
Passenger-km (million)	48,965	52,941	56,903

Source: UN, *Statistical Yearbook.*

Tourism

FOREIGN TOURIST ARRIVALS ('000)*

Country of Residence	1994	1995	1996
Austria	566.4	592.8	611.5
Belgium and Luxembourg	589.0	543.4	633.8
Denmark	530.5	533.8	544.6
France	752.9	754.2	747.4
Italy	745.0	730.9	790.2
Japan	743.0	811.9	800.2
Netherlands	1,705.1	1,797.4	1,832.8
Poland	253.3	265.2	295.4
Spain	291.8	294.7	321.9
Sweden	593.4	551.3	574.3
Switzerland	751.9	801.4	816.7
United Kingdom	1,253.7	1,283.2	1,350.4
USA	1,509.1	1,535.9	1,588.2
Total (incl. others)	13,364.2	13,806.9	14,198.4

* Figures refer to arrivals at registered accommodation establishments.

Communications Media

	1993	1994	1995
Radio receivers ('000 in use)	72,000	76,000	77,000
Television receivers ('000 in use)	45,200	45,500	46,000
Telephones ('000 main lines in use)	36,900	39,200	n.a.
Telefax stations ('000 in use)	1,296	1,447	n.a.
Mobile cellular telephones ('000 subscribers)	1,768	2,501	n.a.
Book production: titles*	67,206	70,643	74,174
Daily newspapers:			
Number	n.a.	411	406
Average circulation ('000 copies)	n.a.	25,757	25,500†
Non-daily newspapers:			
Number	n.a.	n.a.	38†
Average circulation ('000 copies)	n.a.	n.a.	6,900†

* Including pamphlets. † Estimate.

Sources: UNESCO, *Statistical Yearbook*; UN, *Statistical Yearbook*.

Education

(1994)

	Teachers	Students ('000)
Pre-primary	7,357	87
Primary	174,182	3,603
Secondary:		
First stage	315,815	4,990
Second stage	61,677	692
Special	57,104	383
Higher:		
Non-university institutions	14,860*	420
Universities and equivalent institutions†	130,398*	1,300

* 1993 figures.

† Universities and other institutions of similar standing, including colleges of education, colleges of medicine, colleges of theology, and colleges of art and music.

Directory

The Constitution

The Basic Law (Grundgesetz), which came into force in the British, French and US Zones of Occupation in Germany (excluding Saarland) on 23 May 1949, was intended as a provisional Constitution to serve until a permanent one for Germany as a whole could be adopted. The Parliamentary Council which framed the Basic Law intended to continue the tradition of the Constitution of 1848–49, and to preserve some continuity with subsequent German constitutions (with Bismarck's Constitution of 1871, and with the Weimar Constitution of 1919), while avoiding the mistakes of the past. It contains 146 articles, divided into 11 sections, and is introduced by a short preamble.

With the accession of the five newly re-established eastern Länder and East Berlin to the Federal Republic of Germany on 3 October 1990, the Basic Law became the Constitution of the entire German nation.

The Basic Law has 182 articles, divided into 14 sections, and is introduced by a short preamble.

I. BASIC RIGHTS

The opening articles of the Constitution guarantee the dignity of man, the free development of his personality, the equality of all persons before the law, and freedom of faith and conscience. Men and women shall have equal rights, and no one shall suffer discrimination because of sex, descent, race, language, homeland and origin, faith or religion or political opinion.

No one may be compelled against his conscience to perform war service as a combatant (Article 4). All Germans have the right to assemble peacefully and unarmed and to form associations and societies. Everyone has the right freely to express and to disseminate his opinion through speech, writing or pictures. Freedom of the press and freedom of reporting by radio and motion pictures are guaranteed (Article 5). Censorship is not permitted.

The State shall protect marriage and the family, property and the right of inheritance. The care and upbringing of children is the natural right of parents. Illegitimate children shall be given the same conditions for their development and their position in society as legitimate children. Schools are under the supervision of the State. Religion forms part of the curriculum in the State schools, but parents have the right to decide whether the child shall receive religious instruction (Article 7).

A citizen's dwelling is inviolable; house searches may be made only by Court Order. No German may be deprived of his citizenship if he would thereby become stateless. The politically persecuted enjoy the right of asylum (Article 16).

II. THE FEDERATION AND THE LÄNDER

Article 20 describes the Federal Republic (Bundesrepublik Deutschland) as a democratic and social federal state. The colours of the Federal Republic are black-red-gold, the same as those of the Weimar Republic. Each Land within the Federal Republic has its own Constitution, which must, however, conform to the principles laid down in the Basic Law. All Länder, districts and parishes must have a representative assembly resulting from universal, direct, free, equal and secret elections (Article 28). The exercise of governmental powers is the concern of the Länder, in so far as the Basic Law does not otherwise prescribe. Where there is incompatibility, Federal Law overrides Land Law (Article 31). Every German has in each Land the same civil rights and duties.

Political parties may be freely formed in all the states of the Federal Republic, but their internal organization must conform to democratic principles, and they must publicly account for the sources of their funds. Parties which seek to impair or abolish the free and democratic basic order or to jeopardize the existence of the Federal Republic of Germany are unconstitutional (Article 21). So are activities tending to disturb the peaceful relations between nations, and, especially, preparations for aggressive war, but the Federation may join a system of mutual collective security in order to preserve peace (Articles 26 and 24). The rules of International Law shall form part of Federal Law and take precedence over it and create rights and duties directly for the inhabitants of the Federal territory (Article 25).

The territorial organization of the Federation may be restructured by Federal Law, subject to regional plebiscites and with due regard to regional, historical and cultural ties, economic expediency and the requirements of regional policy and planning.

III. THE BUNDESTAG

The Federal Assembly (Bundestag) is the Lower House. Its members are elected by the people in universal, free, equal, direct and secret elections, for a term of four years.* Any person who has reached the age of 18 is eligible to vote and any person who has reached the age of 18 is eligible for election (Article 38). A deputy may be arrested for a punishable offence only with the permission of the Bundestag, unless he be apprehended in the act or during the following day.

The Bundestag elects its President and draws up its Standing Orders. Most decisions of the House require a majority vote. Its meetings are public, but the public may be excluded by the decision of a two-thirds majority. Upon the motion of one-quarter of its members the Bundestag is obliged to set up an investigation committee.

IV. THE BUNDESRAT

The Federal Council (Bundesrat) is the Upper House, through which the Länder participate in the legislation and the administration of the Federation, and in matters relating to the European Union (see p. 152). The Bundesrat consists of members of the Land governments, which appoint and recall them (Article 51). Each Land has at least three votes; Länder with more than two million inhabitants have four, and those with more than six million inhabitants have five. Länder with more than seven million inhabitants have six votes. The votes of each Land may only be given as a block vote. The Bundesrat elects its President for one year. Its decisions are taken by simple majority vote. Meetings are public, but the public may be excluded. The members of the Federal Government have

* The elections of 1949 were conducted on the basis of direct election, with some elements of proportional representation. In January 1953 the draft of a new electoral law was completed by the Federal Government and was approved shortly before the dissolution. The new law represents a compromise between direct election and proportional representation, and is designed to prevent the excessive proliferation of parties in the Bundestag.

the right, and, on demand, the obligation, to participate in the debates of the Bundesrat.

V. THE FEDERAL PRESIDENT

The Federal President (Bundespräsident) is elected by the Federal Convention (Bundesversammlung), consisting of the members of the Bundestag and an equal number of members elected by the Land Parliaments (Article 54). Every German eligible to vote in elections for the Bundestag and over 40 years of age is eligible for election. The candidate who obtains an absolute majority of votes is elected, but if such majority is not achieved by any candidate in two ballots, whoever receives most votes in a further ballot becomes President. The President's term of office is five years. Immediate re-election is permitted only once. The Federal President must not be a member of the Government or of any legislative body or hold any salaried office. Orders and instructions of the President require the counter-signature of the Federal Chancellor or competent Minister, except for the appointment or dismissal of the Chancellor or the dissolution of the Bundestag.

The President represents the Federation in its international relations and accredits and receives envoys. The Bundestag or the Bundesrat may impeach the President before the Federal Constitutional Court on account of wilful violation of the Basic Law or of any other Federal Law (Article 61).

VI. THE FEDERAL GOVERNMENT

The Federal Government (Bundesregierung) consists of the Federal Chancellor (Bundeskanzler) and the Federal Ministers (Bundesminister). The Chancellor is elected by an absolute majority of the Bundestag on the proposal of the Federal President (Article 63). Ministers are appointed and dismissed by the President upon the proposal of the Chancellor. Neither he nor his Ministers may hold any other salaried office. The Chancellor determines general policy and assumes responsibility for it, but within these limits each Minister directs his department individually and on his own responsibility. The Bundestag may express its lack of confidence in the Chancellor only by electing a successor with the majority of its members; the President must then appoint the person elected (Article 67). If a motion of the Chancellor for a vote of confidence does not obtain the support of the majority of the Bundestag, the President may, upon the proposal of the Chancellor, dissolve the House within 21 days, unless it elects another Chancellor within this time (Article 68).

VII. THE LEGISLATION OF THE FEDERATION

The right of legislation lies with the Länder in so far as the Basic Law does not specifically accord legislative powers to the Federation. Distinction is made between fields within the exclusive legislative powers of the Federation and fields within concurrent legislative powers. In the field of concurrent legislation the Länder may legislate so long and so far as the Federation makes no use of its legislative right. The Federation has this right only in matters relating to the creation of equal living conditions throughout the country and in cases where the preservation of legal and economic unity is perceived to be in the national interest. Exclusive legislation of the Federation is strictly limited to such matters as foreign affairs, citizenship, migration, currency, copyrights, customs, railways, post and telecommunications. In most other fields, as enumerated (Article 74), concurrent legislation exists.

The legislative organ of the Federation is the Bundestag, to which Bills are introduced by the Government, by members of the Bundestag or by the Bundesrat (Article 76). After their adoption they must be submitted to the Bundesrat, which may demand, within three weeks, that a committee of members of both houses be convened to consider the Bill (Article 77). In so far as its express approval is not needed, the Bundesrat may veto a law within two weeks. This veto can be overruled by the Bundestag, with the approval of a majority of its members. When the Bill requires the consent of the Bundesrat, such an overruling may not take place.

An amendment of the Basic Law requires a majority of two-thirds in both houses, but an amendment affecting the division of the Federation into Länder and the basic principles contained in Articles 1 and 20 is inadmissible (Article 79).

VIII. THE EXECUTION OF FEDERAL LAWS AND THE FEDERAL ADMINISTRATION

The Länder execute Federal Laws as matters of their own concern in so far as the Basic Law does not otherwise determine. In doing so, they regulate the establishment of the authorities and the administrative procedure, but the Federal Government exercises supervision in order to ensure that the Länder execute Federal Laws in an appropriate manner. The Foreign Service, Federal finance, Federal railways, postal services, Federal waterways and shipping are matters of direct Federal administration.

In order to avert imminent danger to the existence of the democratic order, a Land may call in the police forces of other Länder; and if the Land in which the danger is imminent is itself not willing or able to fight the danger, the Federal Government may place the police in the Land, or the police forces in other Länder, under its instructions (Article 91).

IX. THE ADMINISTRATION OF JUSTICE

Judicial authority is vested in independent judges, who are subject only to the law and who may not be dismissed or transferred against their will (Article 97).

Justice is exercised by the Federal Constitutional Court, by the Supreme Federal Courts and by the Courts of the Länder. The Federal Constitutional Court decides on the interpretation of the Basic Law in cases of doubt, on the compatibility of Federal Law or Land Law with the Basic Law, and on disputes between the Federation and the Länder or between different Länder. Supreme Federal Courts are responsible for the spheres of ordinary, administrative, fiscal, labour and social jurisdiction. If a Supreme Federal Court intends to judge a point of law in contradiction to a previous decision of another Supreme Federal Court, it must refer the matter to a special senate of the Supreme Courts. Extraordinary courts are inadmissible.

The freedom of the individual may be restricted only on the basis of a law. No one may be prevented from appearing before his lawful judge (Article 101). Detained persons may be subjected neither to physical nor to mental ill-treatment. The police may hold no one in custody longer than the end of the day following the arrest without the decision of a court. Any person temporarily detained must be brought before a judge who must either issue a warrant of arrest or set him free, at the latest on the following day. A person enjoying the confidence of the detainee must be notified forthwith of any continued duration of a deprivation of liberty. An act may be punished only if it was punishable by law before the act was committed, and no one may be punished more than once for the same criminal act. A criminal act may not be punished by sentence of death.

X. FINANCE

The Federation has the exclusive power to legislate only on customs and fiscal monopolies; on most other taxes, especially on income, property and inheritance, it has concurrent power to legislate with the Länder (see VII above).

Customs, fiscal monopolies, excise taxes (with exception of the beer tax) and levies within the framework of the European Union are administered by Federal finance authorities, and the revenues thereof accrue to the Federation. The remaining taxes are administered, as a rule, by the Länder and the Gemeinden (communes) to which they accrue. Income tax, corporation tax and value-added tax are shared taxes, accruing jointly to the Federation and the Länder (after deduction of a proportion of income tax for the municipalities; Article 106). The Federation and the Länder shall be self-supporting and independent of each other in their fiscal administration (Article 109). In order to ensure the working efficiency of the Länder with low revenues and to equalize their differing burdens of expenditure, there exists a system of revenue sharing among the Länder; in addition, the Federation may make grants, out of its own funds, to the poorer Länder. All revenues and expenditures of the Federation must be estimated for each fiscal year and included in the budget, which must be established by law before the beginning of the fiscal year. Decisions of the Bundestag or the Bundesrat which increase the budget expenditure proposed by the Federal Government require its approval (Article 113).

XI. TRANSITIONAL AND CONCLUDING PROVISIONS

Articles 116–146 regulate a number of unrelated matters of detail, such as the relationship between the old Reich and the Federation. Article 143 contains divergences from the Basic Law, with regard to the newly-acceded Länder, as stipulated in the Unification Treaty.

The Government

(February 1998)

HEAD OF STATE

Federal President: Prof. Dr Roman Herzog (took office 1 July 1994).

THE FEDERAL GOVERNMENT

A coalition of the Christian Democratic Union (CDU)/Christian Social Union (CSU) and the Free Democratic Party (FDP).

Federal Chancellor: Dr Helmut Kohl (CDU).

Vice-Chancellor and Minister of Foreign Affairs: Dr Klaus Kinkel (FDP).

Minister for Special Tasks and Head of the Federal Chancellery: Friedrich Bohl (CDU).

Minister of the Interior: MANFRED KANTHER (CDU).

Minister of Justice: EDZARD SCHMIDT-JORTZIG (FDP).

Minister of Finance: Dr THEODOR WAIGEL (CSU).

Minister of Economics: Dr GÜNTHER REXRODT (FDP).

Minister of Food, Agriculture and Forestry: JOCHEN BORCHERT (CDU).

Minister of Labour and Social Affairs: Dr NORBERT BLÜM (CDU).

Minister of Defence: VOLKER RÜHE (CDU).

Minister of Family Affairs, Senior Citizens, Women and Youth: CLAUDIA NOLTE (CDU).

Minister of Health: HORST SEEHOFER (CSU).

Minister of Transport: MATTHIAS WISSMANN (CDU).

Minister of the Environment, Nature Conservation and Nuclear Safety: Dr ANGELA MERKEL (CDU).

Minister of Regional Planning and Urban Development: EDUARD OSWALD (CSU).

Minister of Education, Science, Research and Technology: JÜRGEN RÜTTGERS (CDU).

Minister of Economic Co-operation and Development: KARL-DIETER SPRANGER (CSU).

Secretary of State for Information: PETER HAUSMANN (CSU).

MINISTRIES

Office of the Federal President: 53113 Bonn, Kaiser-Friedrich-Str. 16; tel. (228) 2000; telex 886393; fax (228) 200200; internet http://www.bundespraesident.de.

Federal Chancellery: 53113 Bonn, Adenauerallee 139-141; tel. (228) 560; telex 886750; fax (228) 562357.

Press and Information Office of the Federal Government: 53113 Bonn, Welckerstr. 11, 53011 Bonn, Postfach 2160; tel. (228) 2080; telex 886741; fax (228) 2082555; internet http://www.government.de.

Ministry of Defence: 53003 Bonn, Hardthöhe, Postfach 1328; tel. (228) 121; telex 886575; fax (228) 125357; internet http://www.bundeswehr.de.

Ministry of Economic Co-operation and Development: 53113 Bonn, Friedrich-Ebert-Allee 40; tel. (228) 5350; telex 8869452; fax (228) 5353500; internet http://www.bundesregierung.de/bmz.

Ministry of Economics: 53123 Bonn, Villemombler Str. 76; tel. (228) 6150; telex 886747; fax (228) 6154436; e-mail buevo-ep-bonn@bonnl.bmwi.bund400.de; internet http://www.bmwi.de.

Ministry of Education, Science, Research and Technology: 53175 Bonn, Heinemannstr. 2; tel. (228) 570; fax (228) 573601; internet http://www.bmbf.de.

Ministry of the Environment: 53175 Bonn, Kennedyallee 5; tel. (228) 3050; telex 885790; fax (228) 3053225; internet http://www.bmu.de.

Ministry of Family Affairs, Senior Citizens, Women and Youth: 53123 Bonn, Rochusstr. 8–10; tel. (228) 9300; fax (228) 9302221; internet http://www.bmfsfj.de.

Ministry of Finance: 53117 Bonn, Graurheindorfer Str. 108; tel. (228) 6820; telex 886645; fax (228) 6824420; internet http://www.bundesfinanzministerium.de.

Ministry of Food, Agriculture and Forestry: 53123 Bonn, Rochusstr. 1; tel. (228) 5290; telex 886844; fax (228) 5294262; internet http://www.bml.de.

Ministry of Foreign Affairs: 53113 Bonn, Adenauerallee 99–103; tel. (228) 170; telex 886591; fax (228) 173402; internet http://www.auswaertigesamt.government.de.

Ministry of Health: 53121 Bonn, Am Propsthof 78A; tel. (228) 9410; fax (228) 9414900; internet http://www.bmgesundheit.de.

Ministry of the Interior: 53117 Bonn, Graurheindorfer Str. 198; tel. (228) 6811; telex 886896; fax (228) 6814665; internet http://www.bundesregierung.de.

Ministry of Justice: 53175 Bonn, Heinemannstr. 6; tel. (228) 580; fax (228) 584525; e-mail poststelle@bmj.bund400.de; internet http://www.bmj.bund.de.

Ministry of Labour and Social Affairs: 53123 Bonn, Rochusstr. 1, 53107 Bonn, Postfach 140280; tel. (228) 5270; telex 886641; fax (228) 527-2965; internet http://www.bma.de.

Ministry of Regional Planning, Building and Urban Development: 53179 Bonn, Deichmanns Aue 31-37; tel. (228) 3370; telex 885462; fax (228) 3373060; internet http://www.bmbau.bund.de.

Ministry of Transport: 53175 Bonn, Robert-Schumann-Platz 1; tel. (228) 3000; telex 885700; fax (228) 3003428; internet http://www.bmv.de.

Legislature

BUNDESTAG
(Federal Assembly)

President: Prof. Dr RITA SÜSSMUTH (CDU).

Vice-Presidents: HELMUT BECKER (SPD), DIETER JULIUS CRONENBERG (FDP), HANS KLEIN (CSU), RENATE SCHMIDT (SPD).

General Election, 16 October 1994

Parties and Groups	Votes*	%	Seats
Social Democratic Party (SPD)	17,141,319	36.4	252
Christian Democratic Union (CDU)	16,089,491	34.2	244
Christian Social Union (CSU)	3,427,128	7.3	50
Alliance 90/The Greens	3,423,091	7.3	49
Free Democratic Party (FDP)	3,257,864	6.9	47
Party of Democratic Socialism (PDS)	2,067,391	4.4	30
Republican Party	875,175	1.9	—
Others	823,117	1.7	—
Total	47,104,576	100.0	672

* Figures refer to valid second votes (i.e. for state party lists). Details of the numbers of valid first votes (for individual candidates) are not available.

BUNDESRAT
(Federal Council)

President: GERHARD SCHRÖDER (SPD).

The Bundesrat has 69 members. Each Land (state) has three, four, five or six votes, depending on the size of its population, and may send as many members to the sessions as it has votes. The head of government of each Land is automatically a member of the Bundesrat. Members of the Federal Government attend the sessions, which are held every two to three weeks.

Länder	Seats
Nordrhein-Westfalen (North Rhine-Westphalia)	6
Bayern (Bavaria)	6
Baden-Württemberg	6
Niedersachsen (Lower Saxony)	6
Hessen (Hesse)	4
Sachsen (Saxony)	5
Rheinland-Pfalz (Rhineland-Palatinate)	4
Berlin	4
Sachsen-Anhalt (Saxony-Anhalt)	4
Thüringen (Thuringia)	4
Brandenburg	4
Schleswig-Holstein	4
Mecklenburg-Vorpommern (Mecklenburg-Western Pomerania)	3
Hamburg	3
Saarland	3
Bremen	3

The Land Governments

The 16 Länder of Germany are autonomous but not sovereign states, enjoying a high degree of self-government and extensive legislative powers. Thirteen of the Länder have a Landesregierung (Government) and a Landtag (Assembly). The equivalent of the Landesregierung in Berlin, Bremen and Hamburg is the Senate. The equivalent of the Landtag is the House of Representatives in Berlin and the City Council in Bremen and Hamburg.

NORDRHEIN-WESTFALEN (NORTH RHINE-WESTPHALIA)

The present Constitution was adopted by the Assembly on 6 June 1950, and was endorsed by the electorate in the elections held on 18 June. The Government is presided over by the Minister-President who appoints his Ministers. It is currently formed from the majority SPD.

Minister-President: JOHANNES RAU (SPD).

The Assembly, elected on 14 May 1995, is composed as follows:

President of Assembly: ULRICH SCHMIDT (SPD).

Party	Seats
Social Democratic Party	108
Christian Democratic Union	89
Alliance 90/The Greens	24

The Land is divided into five governmental districts: Düsseldorf, Münster, Arnsberg, Detmold and Köln.

BAYERN (BAVARIA)

The Constitution of Bayern provides for a bicameral Assembly and a Constitutional Court. Provision is also made for referendums. The Minister-President is elected by the Assembly for four years. He appoints the Ministers and Secretaries of State with the consent of the Assembly. The Government is currently formed from the majority party (CSU).

Minister-President: Dr EDMUND STOIBER (CSU).

The composition of the Assembly, as a result of elections held on 25 September 1994, is as follows:

President of Assembly: JOHANN BÖHM (CSU).

Party	Seats
Christian Social Union	120
Social Democratic Party	70
Alliance 90/The Greens	14

The Senate, or second chamber, consists of 60 members, divided into 10 groups representing professional interests, e.g. agriculture, industry, trade, the professions and religious communities. Every two years one-third of the Senate is newly elected.

President of the Senate: Dr Dr WALTER SCHMITT GLAESER (CSU).

Bayern is divided into seven districts: Mittelfranken, Oberfranken, Unterfranken, Schwaben, Niederbayern, Oberpfalz and Oberbayern.

BADEN-WÜRTTEMBERG

The Constitution was adopted by the Assembly in Stuttgart on 11 November 1953 and came into force on 19 November. The Minister-President is elected by the Assembly. He appoints and dismisses his Ministers. The Government, which is responsible to the Assembly, is currently formed by the majority party (CDU).

Minister-President: ERWIN TEUFEL (CDU).

The composition of the Assembly, as the result of elections held on 24 March 1996, is as follows:

President of Assembly: Dr FRITZ HOPMEIER (CDU).

Party	Seats
Christian Democratic Union	69
Social Democratic Party	39
Republicans	14
Alliance 90/The Greens	19
Free Democratic Party	14

The Land is divided into four administrative districts: Stuttgart, Karlsruhe, Tübingen and Freiburg.

NIEDERSACHSEN (LOWER SAXONY)

The Constitution was adopted by the Assembly on 19 May 1993 and came into force on 1 June.

Minister-President: GERHARD SCHRÖDER (SPD).

As a result of elections held on 1 March 1998, the Assembly is composed as follows:

President of Assembly: HORST MILDE (SPD).

Party	Seats
Social Democratic Party	83
Christian Democratic Union	62
Alliance 90/The Greens	12

Niedersachsen is divided into four governmental districts: Braunschweig, Hannover, Lüneburg and Weser-Ems.

HESSEN (HESSE)

The Constitution of this Land dates from 1 December 1946. The Minister-President is elected by the Assembly and he appoints and dismisses his Ministers with its consent. The Assembly can force the resignation of the Government by a vote of no confidence. The Government is currently formed from a coalition of the SPD and The Greens.

Minister-President: HANS EICHEL (SPD).

The Assembly, elected on 19 February 1995, is composed as follows:

President of Assembly: KLAUS PETER MÖLLER (CDU).

Party	Seats
Christian Democratic Union	45
Social Democratic Party	44
Alliance 90/The Greens	13
Free Democratic Party	8

Hessen is divided into three governmental districts: Kassel, Gießen and Darmstadt.

SACHSEN (SAXONY)

The Government is currently formed by the majority party (CDU).

Minister-President: Prof. Dr KURT BIEDENKOPF (CDU).

The composition of the Assembly, as a result of elections held on 11 September 1994, is as follows:

President of Assembly: ERICH ILLTGEN (CDU).

Party	Seats
Christian Democratic Union	77
Social Democratic Party	22
Party of Democratic Socialism	21

RHEINLAND-PFALZ (RHINELAND-PALATINATE)

The three chief agencies of the Constitution of this Land are the Assembly, the Government and the Constitutional Court. The Minister-President is elected by the Assembly, with whose consent he appoints and dismisses his Ministers. The Government, which is dependent on the confidence of the Assembly, is currently composed of a coalition of the SPD and the FDP.

Minister-President: KURT BECK (SPD).

The members of the Assembly are elected according to a system of proportional representation. Its composition, as the result of elections held on 24 March 1996, is as follows:

President of Assembly: CHRISTOPH GRIMM.

Party	Seats
Social Democratic Party	43
Christian Democratic Union	41
Free Democratic Party	10
Alliance 90/The Greens	7

Rheinland-Pfalz is divided into three districts: Koblenz, Rheinhessen-Pfalz (Rheinhessen-Palatinate) and Trier.

BERLIN

The House of Representatives (Abgeordnetenhaus) is the legislative body, and has 206 members. The executive agency is the Senate, which is composed of the Governing Mayor (Regierender Bürgermeister), his deputy, and up to 10 Senators. The Governing Major is elected by a majority of the House of Representatives. The Senate is responsible to the House of Representatives and dependent on its confidence. The Senate is currently composed of a coalition of the CDU and the SPD.

Regierender Bürgermeister: EBERHARD DIEPGEN (CDU).

The composition of the House of Representatives, as the result of elections held on 22 October 1995, is as follows:

President of House of Representatives: Prof. Dr HERWIG HAASE (CDU).

Party	Seats
Christian Democratic Union	87
Social Democratic Party	55
Party of Democratic Socialism	34
Alliance 90/The Greens	30

SACHSEN-ANHALT (SAXONY-ANHALT)

The Government is currently formed from a coalition of the SPD and Alliance 90/The Greens.

Minister-President: Dr REINHARD HÖPPNER (SPD).

The composition of the Assembly, as a result of elections held on 26 June 1994, is as follows:

President of Assembly: Dr KLAUS KEITEL (CDU).

Party	Seats
Christian Democratic Union	37
Social Democratic Party	36
Party of Democratic Socialism	21
Alliance 90/The Greens	5

Sachsen-Anhalt is divided into three governmental districts: Magdeburg, Halle and Dessau.

THÜRINGEN (THURINGIA)

The Assembly Government is currently formed from a coalition of the CDU and the SPD.

Minister-President: BERNHARD VOGEL (CDU).

The composition of the Assembly, as a result of elections held on 16 October 1994, is as follows:

President of Assembly: MICHAEL PIETZSCH (CDU).

Party	Seats
Christian Democratic Union	42
Social Democratic Party	29
Party of Democratic Socialism	17

BRANDENBURG

The Government is currently formed by the majority party (SPD).

Minister-President: Dr MANFRED STOLPE (SPD).

The composition of the Assembly, as a result of elections held on 11 September 1994, is as follows:

President of Assembly: Dr KNOBLICH (SPD).

Party	Seats
Social Democratic Party	52
Christian Democratic Union	18
Party of Democratic Socialism	18

SCHLESWIG-HOLSTEIN

The Provisional Constitution was adopted by the Assembly on 13 December 1949. The Government consists of the Minister-President and the Ministers appointed by him. The Government is currently formed from a coalition of the SPD and Alliance 90/The Greens.

Minister-President: HEIDE SIMONIS (SPD).

The composition of the Assembly, as the result of elections held on 24 March 1996, is as follows:

President of Assembly: UTE ERDSIEK-RAVE (SPD).

Party	Seats
Social Democratic Party	33
Christian Democratic Union	30
Alliance 90/The Greens	6
Free Democratic Party	4
Südschleswigscher Wählerverband*	2

* Represents the Danish minority in Schleswig-Holstein.

MECKLENBURG-VORPOMMERN (MECKLENBURG-WESTERN POMERANIA)

The Constitution was adopted by the Assembly on 14 May 1993. The Government is currently formed from a coalition of the CDU and the SPD.

Minister-President: Dr BERNDT SEITE (CDU).

The composition of the Assembly, as a result of elections held on 16 October 1994, is as follows:

President of Assembly: RAINER PRACHTL (CDU).

Party	Seats
Christian Democratic Union	30
Social Democratic Party	23
Party of Democratic Socialism	18

HAMBURG

The Constitution of the Free and Hanseatic City of Hamburg was adopted in June 1952. The City Council (legislature) elects the members of the Senate (government), which in turn elects the President and his deputy from its own ranks. The President remains in office for one year, but may stand for re-election. The Senate is currently formed by a coalition of the SPD and Alliance 90/The Greens.

President of Senate and First Bürgermeister: ORTWIN RUNDE (SPD).

The City Council was elected on 21 September 1997, and is composed as follows:

President: UTE PAPE (SPD).

Party	Seats
Social Democratic Party	54
Christian Democratic Union	46
Alliance 90/The Greens	21

SAARLAND

Under the Constitution which came into force on 1 January 1957, Saarland was politically integrated into the FRG as a Land. It was economically integrated into the FRG in July 1959. The Minister-President is elected by the Assembly. The Government is currently formed by the SPD.

Minister-President: OSKAR LAFONTAINE (SPD).

The composition of the Assembly, as a result of elections held on 16 October 1994, is as follows:

President of the Assembly: HANS KASPER (SPD).

Party	Seats
Social Democratic Party	27
Christian Democratic Union	21
Alliance 90/The Greens	3

BREMEN

The Constitution of the Free Hanseatic City of Bremen was sanctioned by referendum of the people on 12 October 1947. The main constitutional organs are the City Council (legislature), the Senate (government) and the Constitutional Court. The Senate is the executive organ elected by the Council for the duration of its own tenure of office. The Senate elects from its own ranks two Mayors (Bürgermeister), one of whom becomes President of the Senate. Decisions of the Council are subject to the delaying veto of the Senate. The Senate is currently formed from a coalition of the SPD, the FDP and Alliance 90/The Greens.

First Bürgermeister and President of the Senate: HENNING SCHERF (SPD).

The City Council consists of 100 members elected for four years. The election of 14 May 1995 resulted in the following composition:

President of the City Council: BERNHARD MIETZ (CDU).

Party	Seats
Social Democratic Party	37
Christian Democratic Union	37
Alliance 90/The Greens	14
Work for Bremen*	12

* Arbeit für Bremen, local breakaway faction of the SPD.

Political Organizations

Bündnis 90/Die Grünen (Die Grünen) (Alliance 90/The Greens): 53113 Bonn, Baunscheidtstr. 1A; tel. (228) 91660; fax (228) 9166199; e-mail bgst@gruene.de; internet http://www.gruene.de; f. 1993 by merger of Bündnis 90 (f. 1990, as an electoral political assen of citizens' movements of the former GDR) and Die Grünen (f. 1980, largely comprised of the membership of the Grüne Aktion Zukunft, the Grüne Liste, Umweltschutz and the Aktionsgemeinschaft Unabhängiger Deutscher, also including groups of widely varying political views; essentially left-wing party programme includes ecological issues, democratization of society at all levels, social justice, comprehensive disarmament; Jt Speakers of Exec. GUNDA RÖSTEL, JÜRGEN TRITTIN; Parliamentary Leader JOSCHKA FISHER.

Christlich-Demokratische Union Deutschlands (in Bavaria: **Christlich-Soziale Union Deutschlands) (CDU/CSU)** (Christian Democratic and Christian Social Union):

CDU: 53113 Bonn, Konrad-Adenauer-Haus, Friedrich-Ebert-Allee 73–75; tel. (228) 5440; telex 886804; fax (228) 544216; internet http://www.cdu.de; f. 1945, became a federal party in 1950; stands for the united action between Catholics and Protestants for rebuilding German life on a Christian-Democratic basis, while guaranteeing private property and the freedom of the individual and for a 'free and equal Germany in a free, politically united and socially just Europe'; other objectives are to guarantee close ties with allies within NATO and the principle of self-determination; in Oct. 1990 incorporated the CDU of the former GDR; c. 640,000 mems (Aug. 1997); Chair. Dr HELMUT KOHL; Chair. of Parliamentary Party Dr WOLFGANG SCHÄUBLE; Sec.-Gen. PETER HINTZE.

CSU: 80335 München, Nymphenburger Str. 64; tel. (89) 12430; fax (89) 1243220; f. 1946; Christian Social party, aiming for a free market economy 'in the service of man's economic and intellectual freedom'; also combines national consciousness with support for a united Europe; 181,000 mems; Chair. Dr THEODOR WAIGEL; Sec.-Gen. Dr BERND R. PROTZNER.

Deutsche Kommunistische Partei (DKP) (German Communist Party): 45127 Essen, Hoffnungstr. 18; 7,000 mems (1998); Chair. HEINZ STEHR.

Freie Demokratische Partei (FDP) (Free Democratic Party): 53113 Bonn, Thomas-Dehler-Haus, Adenauerallee 266; tel. (228) 5470; fax (228) 547298; e-mail presse@fdp.mhs.compuserve.com; internet: http://www.fdp.de; f. 1948; represents democratic and social liberalism and makes the individual the focal point of the state and its laws and economy; in Aug. 1990 incorporated the three liberal parties of the former GDR—the Association of Free Democrats, the German Forum Party and the FDP; approx. 70,000 mems (Nov. 1997); Chair. Dr WOLFGANG GERHARDT; Deputy Chair. CORNELIA SCHMALZ-JACOBSEN, CORNELIA PIEPER, RAINER BRÜDERLE; Chair. in Bundestag Dr HERMAN OTTO SOLMS; Sec.-Gen. Dr GUIDO WESTERWELLE.

Nationaldemokratische Partei Deutschlands (NPD) (National Democratic Party of Germany): 70030 Stuttgart, Postfach 103528; tel. (711) 610605; fax (711) 611716; f. 1964; right-wing; 15,000 mems; youth organization Junge Nationaldemokraten (JN), 6,000 mems; Chair. UDO VOIGT.

Neues Forum (New Forum): 10117 Berlin, Friedrichstr. 165; tel. (2) 2292317; fax (2) 2291213; f. 1989 as a citizens' action group; played a prominent role in the democratic movement in the former GDR; Leaders KAROLIN SCHUBERT, MATTHIAS BÜCHNER, MICHAEL BONEHR.

Partei des Demokratischen Sozialismus (PDS) (Party of Democratic Socialism): 10178 Berlin, Kleine Alexanderstr. 28; tel. (30) 240090; fax (30) 24009425; e-mail pdspv@aol.com; the dominant political force in the former GDR until late 1989; formed in 1946 as the Socialist Unity Party (SED), as a result of a unification of the Social Democratic Party and the Communist Party in Eastern Germany; in Dec. 1989 renamed the SED-PDS; adopted present name in Feb. 1990; has renounced Stalinism, opposes fascism, right-wing extremism and xenophobia, advocates international disarmament and a socially- and ecologically-orientated market economy with public ownership of the means of production; 105,000 mems (Dec, 1997); Chair. Prof. Dr LOTHAR BISKY; Chair. of Parliamentary Party Dr GREGOR GYSI; Hon. Chair. Dr HANS MODROW.

Die Republikaner (REP) (Republican Party): f. 1983; approx. 25,000 mems; extreme right-wing; Chair. ROLF SCHLIERER.

Sozialdemokratische Partei Deutschlands (SPD) (Social Democratic Party of Germany): 53113 Bonn, Ollenhauerstr. 1; tel. (228) 5321; telex 2283620; fax (228) 532410; f. 1863; maintains that a vital democracy can be built only on the basis of social justice; advocates for the economy as much competition as possible, as much planning as necessary to protect the individual from uncontrolled economic interests; a positive attitude to national defence, while favouring controlled disarmament; rejects any political ties with Communism; in September 1990 incorporated the SPD of the former GDR; approx. 779,030 mems (Nov. 1997); Chair. OSKAR LAFONTAINE; Vice-Chair. and Chair. of Parliamentary Group RUDOLF SCHARPING; Deputy Chair. JOHANNES RAU, RENATE SCHMIDT, WOLFGANG THIERSE, H. WIECZOREK-ZEUL.

There are also numerous other small parties, none of them represented in the Bundestag, covering all shades of the political spectrum and various regional interests.

Diplomatic Representation

EMBASSIES IN GERMANY

Afghanistan: 53125 Bonn, Liebfrauenweg 1A; tel. (228) 251927; telex 885270; fax (228) 255310; Chargé d'affaires: HAFIZULLAH AYUBI.

Albania: 53173 Bonn, Dürenstr. 35–37; tel. (228) 351045; fax (228) 351048; Ambassador: XHEZAIR HYSEN ZAGANJORI.

Algeria: 53173 Bonn, Rheinallee 32–34; tel. (228) 82070; telex 885723; fax (228) 820744; Ambassador: MOHAMMED HANECHE.

Angola: 53111 Bonn, Kaiser-Karl-Ring 20C; tel. (228) 555708; telex 885775; fax (228) 690661; Ambassador: Dr JOÃO LANDOITE.

Argentina: 53113 Bonn, Adenauerallee 50–52; tel. (228) 2280143; fax (228) 214809; internet http://www.argentinischebotschaft.de; Ambassador: Dr CARLOS O. KELLER SARMIENTO.

Armenia: 53173 Bonn, Viktoriastr. 15; tel. (228) 3670089; fax (228) 3670077; Ambassador: Dr ASHOT VOSKANIAN.

Australia: 53175 Bonn, Godesberger Allee 107; tel. (228) 81030; fax (228) 376268; Ambassador: MAX HUGHES.

Austria: 53113 Bonn, Johanniterstr. 2; tel. (228) 530060; fax (228) 549040; Ambassador: Dr MARKUS LUTTEROTTI.

Azerbaijan: 53179 Bonn, Schloßallee 12; tel. (228) 9438917; fax (228) 858644; Ambassador: HUSSEIN-AGA M. SSADIGOV.

Bahrain: 53173 Bonn, Plittersdorfestr. 91; tel. (228) 957610; fax (228) 9576199; Ambassador: Dr AHMED ABBAS AHMED.

Bangladesh: 53173 Bonn, Bonner Str. 48; tel. (228) 352525; telex 885640; fax (228) 354142; Ambassador: SHAMSHER M. CHOWDHURY.

Belarus: 53113 Bonn, Fritz-Schäffer-Str. 20; tel. (228) 2011310; fax (228) 2011319; Ambassador: PJOTR BELJAJEW.

Belgium: 53113 Bonn, Kaiser-Friedrich-Str. 7; tel. (228) 201450; telex 886777; fax (228) 220857; Ambassador: BRUNO NÈVE DE MÉVERGNIES.

Benin: 53179 Bonn, Rüdigerstr. 10, 53132 Bonn, Postfach 200254; tel. (228) 943870; fax (228) 857192; Ambassador: CORNEILLE MEHISSOU.

Bolivia: 53179 Bonn, Konstantinstr. 16; tel. (228) 362038; fax (228) 355952; e-mail boliviabonn@t-online.de; Ambassador: ORLANDO DONOSO ARANDA.

Bosnia and Herzegovina: 53173 Bonn, St Augustinesstr. 21; tel. (228) 366101; fax (228) 365836; Ambassador: ENVER AJANOVIC.

Brazil: 53175 Bonn, Kennedyallee 74; tel. (228) 959230; telex 885471; fax (228) 373696; Ambassador: ROBERTO PINTO FERREIRA MAMERI ABDENUR.

Brunei: 53111 Bonn, Kaiser-Karl Ring 18; tel. (228) 672044; fax (228) 687329; Ambassador: MAHADI BIN Haji WASLI.

Bulgaria: 53173 Bonn, Auf der Hostert 6; tel. (228) 363061; fax (228) 358215; Ambassador: Dr STOYAN STALEV.

Burkina Faso: 53179 Bonn, Wendelstadtallee 18; tel. (228) 952970; telex 885508; fax (228) 9529720; e-mail embassy-burkina-faso@t-online.de; Ambassador: JEAN-BAPTISTE ILBOUDO.

Burundi: 53179 Bonn, Mainzerstr. 174; tel. (228) 345032; telex 885745; fax (228) 340148; Chargé d'affaires a.i.: BÉATRICE NYAMOYA.

Cambodia: 53343 Wachtberg, Grüner Weg 8; tel. (228) 328509; fax (228) 328572; Ambassador: CHHOEUNG CHAMROEUN.

Cameroon: 53173 Bonn, Rheinallee 76; tel. (228) 356038; fax (228) 359058; Ambassador: JEAN MELAGA.

Canada: 53113 Bonn, Friedrich-Wilhelm-Str. 18; tel. (228) 9680; fax (228) 91630; Ambassador: GAËTAN LAVERTU.

Cape Verde: 53113 Bonn, Fritz Schäfferstr. 5; tel. (228) 265002; fax (228) 265061; Ambassador: VICTOR ALFONSO G. FIDALGO.

Central African Republic: 53225 Bonn, Rheinaustr. 120; tel. (228) 233564; Ambassador: MARTIN-GÉRARD TEBITO.

Chad: 53173 Bonn, Basteistr. 80; tel. (228) 356026; telex 8869305; fax (228) 355887; Ambassador: LOSSIMIAN M'BAILAOU NAIMBAYE.

Chile: 53173 Bonn, Kronprinzenstr. 20; tel. (228) 955840; telex 885403; fax (228) 9558440; Ambassador: Dr ROBERTO CIFUENTES.

China, People's Republic: 53177 Bonn, Kurfürstenallee 12; tel. (228) 955970; fax (228) 361635; Ambassador: MEI ZHAORONG.

Colombia: 53113 Bonn, Friedrich-Wilhelm-Str. 35; tel. (228) 923700; fax (228) 9237037; Ambassador: JORGE JUAN BENDECK OLIVELLA.

Congo, Democratic Republic: 53177 Bonn, Im Meisengarten 133; tel. (228) 858160; telex 885511; fax (228) 340398; Ambassador: MABOLIA INENGO TRA BRATO.

Congo, Republic: 53173 Bonn, Rheinallee 45; tel. (228) 358355; fax (228) 358355; Chargé d'affaires a.i.: FERDINAND NGO-NGAKA.

Costa Rica: 53113 Bonn, Langenbachstr. 19; tel. (228) 540040; fax (228) 549053; e-mail 100730.1020@compuserve.com; Ambassador: EKHART PETERS.

Côte d'Ivoire: 53115 Bonn, Königstr. 93; tel. (228) 212098; telex 886524; fax (228) 217313; Ambassador: JEAN VINCENT ZINSOU.

Croatia: 53179 Bonn, Rolandstr. 45; tel. (228) 953420; fax (228) 335450; Ambassador: Prof. Dr ZORAN JASIC.

Cuba: 53175 Bonn, Kennedyallee 22–24; tel. (228) 3090; telex 885733; fax (228) 309244; Ambassador: OSCAR ISRAEL MARTÍNEZ CORDOVÉS.

Cyprus: 53173 Bonn, Kronprinzenstr. 58; tel. (228) 367980; fax (228) 353626; Ambassador: THEOPHILOS V. THEOPHILOU.

Czech Republic: 53127 Bonn, Ferdinandstr. 27; tel. (228) 9197110; fax (228) 9197281; e-mail bonn@embassy.mzv.cz; Chargé d'affaires: VLADISLAV LABUDEK.

Denmark: 53111 Bonn, Pfälzer Str. 14; tel. (228) 729910; fax (228) 7299131; e-mail botschaft@daenemark.org; Ambassador: Bent Haakonsen.

Dominican Republic: 53177 Bonn, Burgstr. 87; tel. (228) 364956; fax (228) 352576; Ambassador: Octavio Ramón Cáceres Michel.

Ecuador: 53173 Bonn, Koblenzer Str. 37; tel. (228) 352544; fax (228) 361765; Ambassador: Harry Klein.

Egypt: 53173 Bonn, Kronprinzenstr. 2; tel. (228) 956830; fax (228) 364304; Ambassador: Mohab Mokbel.

El Salvador: 53113 Bonn, Adenauerallee 238; tel. (228) 549914; fax (228) 549814; e-mail 75047,3040@compuserve.com; Ambassador: Dr José Saguer Saprissa.

Eritrea: 50968 Köln, Marktstr. 8; tel. (221) 373016; fax (221) 3404128; Ambassador: Dr Wolde Mariam Goytom.

Estonia: 53113 Bonn, Fritz-Schäffer-Str. 22; tel. (228) 914790; fax (228) 9147911; e-mail bonn@estebonn.estemb.de; Ambassador: Margus Laidre.

Ethiopia: 53113 Bonn, Brentanostr. 1; tel. (228) 233041; Ambassador: Dr Berhane Tensay.

Finland: 53173 Bonn, Friesdorfer Str. 1; tel. (228) 382980; fax (228) 3829857; internet http://www.finlandemb.de; Ambassador: Arto Mansala.

France: 53179 Bonn, An der Marienkapelle 3; tel. (228) 9556000; telex 885445; fax (228) 9556055; Ambassador: François Scheer.

Gabon: 53173 Bonn, Kronprinzenstr. 52; tel. (228) 359286; telex 885520; fax (228) 359195; Ambassador: Sylvestre Ratanga.

Georgia: 53177 Bonn, Am Kurpark 6; tel. (228) 957510; fax (228) 9575120; Ambassador: Konstantin Gabaschwili.

Ghana: 53173 Bonn, Rheinallee 58; tel. (228) 367960; fax (228) 363498; Ambassador: George R. Nipah.

Greece: 53179 Bonn, An der Marienkapelle 10; tel. (228) 83010; telex 885636; fax (228) 353284; Ambassador: Ioannis Bourloyannis-Tsangaridis.

Guatemala: 53173 Bonn, Zietenstr. 16; tel. (228) 351579; fax (228) 354940; e-mail embaguate-bonn@compuserve.com; Ambassador: Jorge Skinner-Klee.

Guinea: 53129 Bonn, Rochusweg 50; tel. (228) 231098; fax (228) 231097; Ambassador: Lamine Bolivogui.

Haiti: 53179 Bonn, Schlossallee 10; tel. (228) 857700; fax (228) 80228; Chargé d'affaires a.i.: Ernst Toussaint.

Holy See: 53175 Bonn, Turmstr. 29 (Apostolic Nunciature); tel. (228) 959010; telex 8869794; fax (228) 379180; Apostolic Nuncio: Mgr Giovanni Lasolo.

Honduras: 53173 Bonn, Ubierstr. 1; tel. (228) 356394; fax (228) 351981; Ambassador: Dr Ricardo Lagos Andino.

Hungary: 53175 Bonn, Turmstr. 30; tel. (228) 371112; fax (228) 371025; Ambassador: Dr Péter Balázs.

Iceland: 53173 Bonn, Kronprinzenstr. 6; tel. (228) 364021; e-mail icemb.bonn@utn.stir.is; internet http.//www.geysir.com/botschaft; telex 885690; fax (228) 361398; Ambassador: I. Sigfusson.

India: 53113 Bonn, Adenauerallee 262–264; tel. (228) 54050; telex 8869301; fax (228) 5405154; Ambassador: Satinder Kumar Lambah.

Indonesia: 53175 Bonn, Bernkasteler Str. 2; tel. (228) 382990; telex 886352; fax (228) 311393; Ambassador: Hartono Martodiredjo.

Iran: 53175 Bonn, Godesberger Allee 133–137; tel. (228) 81610; telex 885676; fax (228) 376154; Ambassador: Seyed Hossein Mousavian.

Iraq: 53173 Bonn, Dürenstr. 33; tel. (228) 950240; telex 8869471; fax (228) 9502430; Ambassador: Abdul Jabbar Omar Ghani.

Ireland: 53175 Bonn, Godesberger Allee 119; tel. (228) 959290; fax (228) 373500; Ambassador: Pádraig Murphy.

Israel: 53173 Bonn, Simrockallee 2; tel. (228) 9346500; fax (228) 9346555; e-mail botschaft@israel.de; Ambassador: Avi Primor.

Italy: 53173 Bonn, Karl-Finkelnburg-Str. 51; tel. (228) 822-0; telex 88550; fax (228) 822-169; Ambassador: Enzo Perlot.

Jamaica: 53177 Bonn, Am Kreuter 1; tel. (228) 354045; telex 885493; fax (228) 361890; Ambassador: Peter C. Black.

Japan: 53175 Bonn, Godesberger Allee 102–104; tel. (228) 81910; fax (228) 379399; Ambassador: Haruhiko Schibuya.

Jordan: 53173 Bonn, Beethovenallee 21; tel. (228) 357046; fax (228) 353951; Ambassador: Hussein Ahmad Hammami.

Kazakhstan: 53129 Bonn, Oberer Lindweg 2-4; tel (228) 923800; fax (228) 9238025; Ambassador: Erik Magsumovitch Asanbayev.

Kenya: 53177 Bonn, Villichgasse 17; tel. (228) 935800; telex 885570; fax (228) 9358050; Ambassador: Vincent John Ogutu-Obare.

Korea, Republic: 53113 Bonn, Adenauerallee 124; tel. (228) 267960; fax (228) 223943; Ambassador: Soon Young Hong.

Kuwait: 53175 Bonn, Godesberger Allee 77-81; tel. (228) 378081; fax (228) 378936; Ambassador: Abdulazeez A. al-Sharikh.

Kyrgyzstan: 53173 Bonn, Koblenzer Str. 62; tel. (228) 365230; fax (228) 365191; e-mail 101477.1160@compuserve.com; Ambassador: Omar Soultanov.

Laos: 53639 Königswinter, Am Lessing 6; tel. (223) 21501; fax (223) 3065; Ambassador: Done Somvorachit.

Latvia: 53113 Bonn, Adenauerallee 110; tel. (228) 264242; fax (228) 265840; Ambassador: Andris Kesteris.

Lebanon: 53173 Bonn, Rheinallee 27; tel. (228) 956800; fax (228) 357560; Ambassador: Salim Tabet.

Lesotho: 53175 Bonn, Godesberger Allee 50; tel. (228) 376868; telex 8869370; fax (228) 379947. Ambassador: Lebohang Nts'inyi.

Liberia: 53179 Bonn, Mainzerstr. 259; tel. (228) 340822; telex 886637; Chargé d'affaires a.i.: Ibrahim Nyei.

Libya: 53173 Bonn, Beethovenallee 12a; tel. (228) 820090; telex 885738; fax (228) 364260; Secretary of the People's Committee: Dr Omar Ali Shalbak.

Lithuania: 53115 Bonn, Argelanderstr. 108a; tel. (228) 914910; fax (228) 9149115; e-mail 0308911164-0001@t-online.de; Ambassador: Prof. Dr Zenonas Namivicius.

Luxembourg: 53113 Bonn, Adenauerallee 108; tel. (228) 214008; telex 886557; fax (228) 222920; Ambassador: Dr Julien Alex.

Macedonia, former Yugoslav republic: 53113 Bonn, Strässchens weg 6; tel. (228) 237744; fax (228) 237743; Ambassador: Dr Srgjan Kerim.

Madagascar: 53179 Bonn, Rolandstr. 48; tel. (228) 953590; fax (228) 334628; Chargé d'affaires a.i.: Jean-Pierre Totobesola.

Malawi: 53179 Bonn, Mainzer Str. 124; tel. (228) 943350; fax (228) 9433537; Ambassador: Geoffrey G. Chipungu.

Malaysia: 53175 Bonn, Mittelstr. 43; tel. (228) 308030; telex 885683; fax (228) 376584; Ambassador: Dato' Zainuddin Abdul Rahman.

Mali: 53173 Bonn, Basteistr. 86; tel. (228) 357048; fax (228) 361922; Ambassador: Ousmane Dembélé.

Malta: 53173 Bonn, Viktoriastr. 1; tel. (228) 363017; fax (228) 363019; Ambassador: Carmel J. Aquilina.

Mauritania: 53173 Bonn, Bonnerstr. 48; tel. (228) 364024; fax (228) 361788; Ambassador: Hamoud Ould Ely.

Mexico: 53113 Bonn, Adenauerallee 100; tel. (228) 914860; fax (228) 211113; Ambassador: Juan José Bremer Martino.

Moldova: 53113 Bonn, An der Elisabethkirche 24; tel. (228) 910940; fax (228) 910418; e-mail 113145.334@compuserve.com; Ambassador: Dr Aurelian Dánilá.

Monaco: 53113 Bonn, Zitelmannstr. 16; tel. (228) 232007; fax (228) 236282; Ambassador: Jean Herly.

Mongolia: 53844 Troisdorf-Sieglar, Siebengebirgsblick 4; tel. (2241) 402727; telex 885407; fax (2241) 47781; Ambassador: Luvsanjamts Udwal.

Morocco: 53175 Bonn, Gotenstr. 7–9; tel. (228) 367950; telex 885428; fax (228) 357894; Ambassador: Abderrahim Chawki.

Mozambique: 53113 Bonn, Adenauerallee 46a; tel. (228) 263921; telex 886405; fax (228) 213920; Ambassador: Manuel Tomás Lubisse.

Myanmar: 53113 Bonn, Schumann Str. 112; tel. (228) 210091; telex 8869560; fax (228) 219316; Ambassador: U Tun Ngwe.

Namibia: 53179 Bonn, Mainzer Str. 47; tel. (228) 346021; fax (228) 346025; Ambassador: Hinyangerwa P. Asheeke.

Nepal: 53179 Bonn, Im Hag 15; tel. (228) 343097; telex 8869297; fax (228) 856747; Ambassador: Dr Novel Kishore Rai.

Netherlands: 53113 Bonn, Strässchensweg 10; tel. (228) 53050; telex 886826; fax (228) 238621; e-mail nlgovbon@nlgovbon.bn .eunet.de; Ambassador: Peter van Walsum.

New Zealand: 53113 Bonn, Bonn-Center, HI 902, Bundeskanzlerplatz 2-10; tel. (228) 228070; fax (228) 221687; Ambassador: G. F. Thompson.

Nicaragua: 53179 Bonn, Konstantinstr. 41; tel. (228) 362505; fax 354001; Ambassador: Dr Ernesto J. Marín de la Rocha.

Niger: 53173 Bonn, Dürenstr. 9; tel. (228) 354814; telex 885572; fax (228) 363246; Ambassador: Abdou Garba.

Nigeria: 53177 Bonn, Goldbergweg 13; tel. (228) 322071; fax (228) 328088; Ambassador: A. A. Anopvechi.

Norway: 53175 Bonn, Mittelstr. 43; tel. (228) 819970; telex 885491; fax (228) 373498; Ambassador: Kjell Eliassen.

Oman: 53173 Bonn, Lindenallee 11; tel. (228) 357031; telex 885688; fax (228) 357045; Ambassador: Abdullah bin Mohammed al-Kharusi.

Pakistan: 53173 Bonn, Rheinallee 24; tel. (228) 95530; telex 885787; fax (228) 9553210; Ambassador: Gen. Asad Durrani.

Panama: 53173 Bonn, Lützowstr. 1; tel. (228) 361036; fax (228) 363558; Ambassador: Enrique Alberto Thayer.

Papua New Guinea: 53175 Bonn, Gotenstr. 163; tel. (228) 376855; fax (228) 375103; e-mail 106555.326@compuserve.com; Chargé d'affaires: P. Raka.

Paraguay: 53173 Bonn, Uhlandstr. 32; tel. (228) 356727; fax (228) 366663; Ambassador: Dr MARCOS MARTÍNEZ MENDIETA.

Peru: 53175 Bonn, Godesberger Allee 125; tel. (228) 373045; fax (228) 379475; Ambassador: Dr LUIS SILVA SANTISTEBAN.

Philippines: 53115 Bonn, Argelanderstr. 1; tel. (228) 267990; fax (228) 221968; Ambassador: ROMEO A. ARGUELLES.

Poland: 50968 Köln, Lindenallee 7; tel. (221) 937300; telex 8881040; fax (221) 343089; Ambassador: Dr ANDRZEJ BYRT.

Portugal: 53173 Bonn, Ubierstr. 78; tel. (228) 363011; telex 885577; fax (228) 352864; Ambassador: Dr LUIS M. P. ALONSO.

Qatar: 53177 Bonn, Brunnenallee 6; tel. (228) 957520; fax (228) 9575255; Ambassador: MOHAMED HASSAN AL-JABER.

Romania: 53117 Bonn, Legionsweg 14; tel. (228) 68380; fax (228) 680247; Ambassador: TUDOR DUNCA.

Russia: 53177 Bonn, Waldstr. 42; tel. (228) 312074; fax (228) 311563; e-mail botrus@t-online.de; Ambassador: SERGEI BORISOVICH KRYLOV.

Rwanda: 53173 Bonn, Beethovenallee 72; tel. (228) 355228; telex 885604; fax (228) 351922; Ambassador: BERNARD MAKUZA.

Saudi Arabia: 53175 Bonn, Godesberger Allee 40–42; tel. (228) 81090; telex 885442; fax (228) 375593; Ambassador: ABBAS FAIG GHAZZAWI.

Senegal: 53115 Bonn, Argelanderstr. 3; tel. (228) 218008; telex 8869644; fax (228) 217815; Ambassador: Gen. MOHAMADOU KEÏTA.

Sierra Leone: 53173 Bonn, Rheinallee 20; tel. (228) 352001; fax (228) 364269; Ambassador: UMARU BUNDU WURIE.

Singapore: 53175 Bonn, Südstr. 133; tel. (228) 951030; fax (228) 310527; e-mail sing.emb.bonn@t-online.de; Ambassador: WALTER WOON.

Slovakia: 53129 Bonn, August-Bier-Str. 31; tel. (228) 914550; fax (228) 9145538; e-mail sk.emb.bonn@t-online.de; Chargé d'affaires a.i.: MILAN MATLAK.

Slovenia: 53179 Bonn, Siegfriedstr. 28; tel. (228) 858031; fax (228) 858057; Ambassador: ALFONZ NABERŽNIK.

Somalia: 53173 Bonn, Hohenzollernstr. 12; tel. (228) 351643; telex 885724; Ambassador: Dr HASSAN ABSHIR FARAH.

South Africa: 53173 Bonn, Auf der Hostert 3; tel. (228) 82010; fax (228) 8201148; e-mail saebonn.consular@lg.elge.de; Ambassador: LINDIWE MABUZA.

Spain: 53115 Bonn, Schlossstr. 4; tel. (228) 217094; telex 886792; fax (228) 223405; Ambassador: JOSÉ PEDRO SEBASTIÁN DE ERICE.

Sri Lanka: 53111 Bonn, Noeggerathstr. 15; tel. (228) 698946; fax (228) 694988; Ambassador: G. WIJAYASIRI.

Sudan: 53177 Bonn, Koblenzer Str. 107; tel. (228) 933700; fax (228) 335115; Ambassador: Dr ACHOL DENG.

Sweden: 53113 Bonn, Allianzplatz, Haus I, Heussallee 2–10; tel. (228) 260020; telex 886667; fax (228) 223837; Ambassador: MATS HELLSTRÖM.

Switzerland: 53175 Bonn, Gotenstr. 156, 53153 Bonn, Postfach 260163; tel. (228) 810080; fax (228) 8100819; Ambassador: DIETER CHENAUX-REPOND.

Syria: 53175 Bonn, Andreas-Hermes-Str. 5; tel. (228) 819920; telex 885757; fax (228) 8199299; Ambassador: SULEYMAN HADDAD.

Tajikistan: 53225 Bonn, Hans-Böckler-Str. 3; tel. (228) 972950; fax (228) 9729555; Ambassador: AKBAR MIRZOYEV.

Tanzania: 53177 Bonn, Theaterplatz 26; tel. (228) 358051; telex 885569; fax (228) 358226; Ambassador: ANDREW M. DARAJA.

Thailand: 53173 Bonn, Ubierstr. 65; tel. (228) 956860; telex 885795; fax (228) 363702; Chargé d'affaires a.i.: Dr WARAWIT KANITHASEN.

Togo: 53173 Bonn, Beethovenallee 13; tel. (228) 355091; telex 885595; fax (228) 351639; Chargé d'affaires a.i.: DJISA AWOYO SENAYA.

Tunisia: 53175 Bonn, Godesberger Allee 103; tel. (228) 376981; telex 885477; fax (228) 374223; Ambassador: SLAHEDDINE BEN M'BAREK.

Turkey: 53179 Bonn, Ute Str. 47; tel. (228) 953830; telex 885521; fax 348877; Ambassador: VOLKAN VURAL.

Uganda: 53173 Bonn, Dürenstr. 44; tel. (228) 355027; telex 885578; fax (228) 351692; Ambassador: TIBAMANYA MWENE MUSHANGA.

Ukraine: 53424 Remagen, Rheinhöhenweg 101; tel. (228) 94180; fax (228) 941863; Ambassador: Dr ANATOLIY PONOMARENKO.

United Arab Emirates: 53113 Bonn, Erste Fährgasse 6; tel. (228) 267070; telex 885741; fax (228) 2670714; Ambassador: MOHAMMAD SULTAN ABDULLA AL-AWAIS.

United Kingdom: 53113 Bonn, Friedrich-Ebert-Allee 77; tel. (228) 91670; fax (228) 9167200; Ambassador: Sir PAUL LEVER.

USA: 53170 Bonn, Deichmanns Aue 29; tel. (228) 3391; telex 885452; fax (228) 3392663; Ambassador: JOHN C. KORNBLUM.

Uruguay: 53175 Bonn, Gotenstr. 1–3; tel. (228) 356570; telex 366036; fax (228) 361410; Ambassador: JUAN JOSÉ REAL.

Uzbekistan: 53177 Bonn, Deutschherrenstr. 7; tel. (228) 953570; fax (228) 9535799; Ambassador: ALISHER SHAIKHOV.

Venezuela: 53225 Bonn, Im Rheingarten 7; tel. (228) 400920; fax (228) 4009228; e-mail 100635.154@compuserve.com; Ambassador: ERIK BECKER BECKER.

Viet Nam: 53179 Bonn, Konstantinstr. 37; tel. (228) 357022; telex 8861122; fax (228) 351866; Ambassador: CHU TUAN CAP.

Yemen: 53113 Bonn, Adenauerallee 77; tel. (228) 220273; telex 885765; fax (228) 229364; Ambassador: ABDO OTHMAN MOHAMED.

Yugoslavia: 53179 Bonn, Schlossallee 5; tel. (228) 344051; fax (228) 344057; Ambassador: ZORAN JEREMIC.

Zambia: 53175 Bonn, Mittelstr. 39; tel. (228) 376813; telex 885511; fax (228) 379536; Ambassador: GWENDOLINE CHOMBA KONIE.

Zimbabwe: 53177 Bonn, Villichgasse 7; tel. (228) 356071; telex 885580; fax (228) 356309; Ambassador: Dr ELIJAH CHANAKIRA.

Judicial System

The Unification Treaty, signed by the FRG and the GDR in August 1990, provided for the extension of Federal Law to the territory formerly occupied by the GDR, and also stipulated certain exceptions where GDR Law was to remain valid.

Judges are not removable except by the decision of a court. Half of the judges of the Federal Constitutional Court are elected by the Bundestag and half by the Bundesrat. A committee for the selection of judges participates in the appointment of judges of the Superior Federal Courts.

FEDERAL CONSTITUTIONAL COURT

Bundesverfassungsgericht (Federal Constitutional Court): 76131 Karlsruhe, Schlossbezirk 3, 76006 Karlsruhe, Postfach 1771; tel. (721) 91010; telex 7826749; fax (721) 9101382.

President: Prof. Dr JUTTA LIMBACH.

Vice-President: Dr OTTO SEIDL.

Director: Dr KARL GEORG ZIERLEIN.

Judges of the First Senate: Prof. Dr DIETER GRIMM, Dr JÜRGEN KÜHLING, HELGA SEIBERT, RENATE JAEGER, Dr EVELYN HAAS, Dr DIETER HÖMIG, Prof. Dr UDO STEINER.

Judges of the Second Senate: Dr KARIN GRASSHOF, KONRAD KRUIS, Prof. Dr PAUL KIRCHOF, KLAUS WINTER, BERTOLD SOMMER, Dr HANS-JOACHIM JENTSCH, Prof. Dr WINFRIED HASSEMER.

SUPERIOR FEDERAL COURTS

Bundesgerichtshof (Federal Court of Justice): 76133 Karlsruhe, Herrenstr. 45A; tel. (721) 1590; telex 7825828; fax (721) 159830.

President: KARLMANN GEIß.

Vice-President: Prof. Dr HORST HAGEN.

Presidents of the Senate: Prof. Dr WILLI ERDMANN, VOLKER RÖHRICHT, Dr EBERHARD RINNE, Dr KARL BERNARD SCHMITZ, WERNER GROß, Dr ARNO LANG, Dr KATHARINA DEPPERT, Dr BERND PAULUSCH, RÜDGER ROGGE, HERBERT SCHIMANSKY, Dr FRIEDRICH BLUMENRÖHR, Dr GERHARD SCHÄFER, Dr BURKHARD JÄHNKE, KLAUS KUTZER, Dr LUTZ MEYER-GOßNER, HEINRICH WILHELM LAUFHÜTTE.

Federal Solicitor-General: KAY NEHM.

Federal Prosecutors: REINER SCHULTE, VOLKHARD WACHE, Dr HANS-JOACHIM KURTH.

Bundesverwaltungsgericht (Federal Administrative Court): 10623 Berlin, Hardenbergstr. 31, 10593 Berlin, Postfach 126060; tel. (30) 31971; fax (30) 3123021.

President: Dr EVERHARDT FRANSSEN.

Vice-President: Dr INGEBORG FRANKE.

Presidents of the Senate: ERICH BERMEL, WERNER MEYER, Dr NORBERT NIEHUES, FRIEDRICH SEEBASS, Dr WILHELM DIEFENBACH, Dr MANFRED KLEINVOGEL, Dr GÜNTER GAENTZSCH, HERBERT SEIDE, RÜDIGER ROTH, Dr HORST SÄCKER.

Bundesfinanzhof (Federal Financial Court): 81675 München, Ismaningerstr. 109, 81629 München, Postfach 860240; tel. (89) 92310; fax (89) 9231201.

President: Prof. Dr KLAUS OFFERHAUS.

Vice-President: Dr ALBERT BEERMANN.

Presidents of the Senate: Dr SIEGFRIED WIDMANN, Dr KLAUS EBLING, Dr REINHARD SUNDER-PLASSMANN, PETER HELLWIG, Dr HANS JOACHIM HERRMANN, Prof. Dr MANFRED GROH, Dr RUTH HOFMANN, Dr GEORG GRUBE.

Religion

CHRISTIANITY

Arbeitsgemeinschaft Christlicher Kirchen in Deutschland (Council of Christian Churches in Germany): 60487 Frankfurt a.M.,

Ludolfusstr. 2-4, 60446 Frankfurt a.M., Postfach 900617; tel. (69) 2470270; fax (69) 24702730; 18 affiliated Churches, including the Roman Catholic Church and the Greek Orthodox Metropoly.

The Roman Catholic Church

In December 1996 Germany comprised seven archdioceses and 20 dioceses. It is estimated that about 34% of the population are adherents of the Roman Catholic Church.

Bishops' Conference: Deutsche Bischofskonferenz, 53113 Bonn, Kaiserstr. 163; tel. (228) 1030; fax (228) 103299; Pres. Dr Dr KARL LEHMANN, Bishop of Mainz; Sec. Pater Dr HANS LANGENDÖRFER.

Archbishop of Bamberg: Dr KARL BRAUN, Obere Karolinenstr. 5, 96049 Bamberg, Postfach 120153; tel. (951) 50205; fax (951) 502212.

Archbishop of Berlin: Cardinal GEORG MAXIMILIAN STERZINSKY, 14057 Berlin, Wundtstr. 48–50; tel. (030) 326840; fax (030) 32684276.

Archbishop of Freiburg im Breisgau: Dr OSKAR SAIER, 79098 Freiburg i. Br., Herrenstr. 35; tel. (761) 21881; fax (761) 2188599.

Archbishop of Hamburg: Dr LUDWIG AVERKAMP, 20099 Hamburg, Danzigerstr. 52A; 20013 Hamburg, Postfach 106404; tel. (40) 248770; fax (40) 24877233.

Archbishop of Köln: Cardinal Dr JOACHIM MEISNER, Generalvikariat, 50668 Köln, Marzellenstr. 32; tel. (221) 16420; fax (221) 16421700.

Archbishop of München and Freising: Cardinal Dr FRIEDRICH WETTER, 80333 München, Rochhusstr. 5-7; 80079 München, Postfach 330360; tel. (89) 21370; fax (89) 2137585.

Archbishop of Paderborn: Dr JOHANNES JOACHIM DEGENHARDT, Erzbischöfliches Generalvikariat, 33098 Paderborn, Domplatz 3; tel. (5251) 1250; fax (5251) 125470.

Commissariat of German Bishops—Catholic Office: 53113 Bonn, Kaiser-Friedrich-Str. 9; tel. (228) 26940; fax (228) 261563; (represents the German Conference of Bishops before the Federal Govt on political issues); Leader Prälat PAUL BOCKLET.

Central Committee of German Catholics: 53175 Bonn, Hochkreuzallee 246; tel. (228) 382970; fax (228) 3829744; f. 1868; summarizes the activities of Catholic laymen and lay-organizations in Germany; Pres. Prof. Dr HANS JOACHIM MEYER; Gen. Sec. Dr FRIEDRICH KRONENBERG.

Evangelical (Protestant) Churches

About 35% of the population are members of the Evangelical Churches.

Evangelische Kirche in Deutschland (EKD) (Evangelical Church in Germany): 30419 Hannover, Herrenhäuser Str. 12; tel. (511) 27960; telex 923445; fax (511) 2796707; Berlin Office: 10117 Berlin, Auguststr. 80. The governing bodies of the EKD are its Synod of 120 clergy and lay members which meets at regular intervals, the Conference of member churches, and the Council, composed of 15 elected members; the EKD has an ecclesiastical secretariat of its own (the Evangelical Church Office), including a special office for foreign relations; Chair. of the Council Präses MANFRED KOCK, Dr KLAUS ENGELHARDT; Pres. of the Office VALENTIN SCHMIDT.

Synod of the EKD: 30419 Hannover, Herrenhäuser Str. 12; tel. (511) 2796114; fax (511) 2796707; Pres. Dr JÜRGEN SCHMUDE.

Deutscher Evangelischer Kirchentag (German Evangelical Church Assembly): 36037 Fulda, Magdeburgerstr. 59, 36004 Fulda, Postfach 480; tel. (661) 969500; fax (661) 9695090; e-mail fulda@kirchentag.de; Pres. BARBARA RINKE; Gen. Sec. Dr MARGOT KAESSMANN.

Churches and Federations within the EKD:

Arnoldshainer Konferenz: 10623 Berlin, Jebensstr. 3; tel. (30) 310010; fax (30) 31001200; f. 1967; a loose federation of the church governments of one Lutheran, two Reformed Territorial and all United Churches, aiming at greater co-operation between them; Chair. of Council Bischof Prof. Dr CHRISTIAN ZIPPERT.

Evangelische Kirche der Union (EKU) (Evangelical Church of the Union): 10623 Berlin, Chancellery, Jebensstr. 3; tel. (30) 310010; fax (30) 31001200; composed of Lutheran and Reformed elements; includes the Evangelical Churches of Anhalt, Berlin-Brandenburg, Silesian Oberlausitz, Pomerania, the Rhineland, Saxony and Westphalia; Chair. of Synod Präses MANFRED KOCK; Chair. of Council Bischof EDUARD BERGER; Pres. of Administration Dr WILHELM HÜFFMEIER.

Reformierter Bund (Reformed Alliance): 42109 Wuppertal, Vogelsangstr. 20; tel. (202) 755111; fax (202) 754202; f. 1884; unites the Reformed Territorial Churches and Congregations of Germany (with an estimated 2m. mems). The central body of the Reformed League is the 'Moderamen', the elected representation of the various Reformed Churches and Congregations; Moderator Rev. PETER BUKOWSKI; Gen. Sec. Rev. HERMANN SCHAEFER.

Vereinigte Evangelisch-Lutherische Kirche Deutschlands (VELKD) (The United Evangelical-Lutheran Church of Germany): 30177 Hannover, Richard-Wagner-Str. 26, 30634 Hannover, Postfach 510409; tel. (511) 62611; fax (511) 6261211; f. 1948; mems 11.2m.; a body uniting all but three of the Lutheran territorial Churches within the Evangelical Church in Germany; Presiding Bishop Landesbischof HORST HIRSCHLER (Hannover).

Affiliated to the EKD:

Bund Evangelisch-Reformierter Kirchen (Association of Evangelical Reformed Churches): 20095 Hamburg, Ferdinandstr. 21; tel. (40) 337260; Chair. Präses P. ROLF EHLENBRÖKER.

Herrnhuter Brüdergemeine or **Europäisch-Festländische Brüder-Unität** (Moravian Church): f. 1457; there are 25 congregations in Germany, Switzerland, Denmark, Sweden, Estonia and the Netherlands, with approximately 30,000 mems; Chair. Rev. HANS-BEAT MOTEL; (73087 Bad Boll, Badwasen 6; tel. (7164) 94210; fax (7164) 942199).

†**Evangelical Church in Baden:** 76133 Karlsruhe, Blumenstr. 1, 76010 Karlsruhe, Postfach 2269; tel. (721) 9175100; fax (721) 9175550; Landesbischof Prof. Dr KLAUS ENGELHARDT.

***Evangelical-Lutheran Church in Bayern:** 80332 München, Meiserstr. 13; tel. (89) 55950; telex 529674; fax (89) 559444; Landesbischof HERMANN VON LOEWENICH.

†**Evangelical Church in Berlin-Brandenburg:** 10555 Berlin, Bachstr. 1–2; tel. (30) 390910; fax (30) 39091375; Bischof Prof. Dr WOLFGANG HUBER.

Evangelical-Lutheran Church in Braunschweig: 38300 Wolfenbüttel Dietrich-Bonhoeffer-Str. 1; tel. (5331) 8020; fax (5331) 802707; Landesbischof CHRISTIAN KRAUSE.

†**Bremen Evangelical Church:** 28199 Bremen, Franziuseck 2–4, Postfach 106929; tel. (421) 55970; Pres. HEINZ HERMANN BRAUER.

***Evangelical-Lutheran Church of Hannover:** 30169 Hannover, Haarstr. 6; tel. (511) 800188; fax (511) 880438; Landesbischof D. HORST HIRSCHLER.

†**Evangelical Church in Hessen and Nassau:** 64276 Darmstadt, Paulusplatz 1; tel. (6151) 405284; fax (6151) 405441; Pres. Prof. Dr PETER SEINACKER.

†**Evangelical Church of Kurhessen-Waldeck:** 34131 Kassel-Wilhelmshöhe, Wilhelmshöher Allee 330, 34114 Kassel, Postfach 410260; tel. (561) 937801; fax (561) 9378400; e-mail Landeskirchen amt@ekkw.de; Bischof Prof. Dr CHRISTIAN ZIPPERT.

†**Church of Lippe:** 32756 Detmold, Leopoldstr. 27; tel. (5231) 97660; fax (5231) 976850; e-mail oealippe@t-online.de; Landessuperintendent GERRIT NOLTENSMEIER.

Evangelical-Lutheran Church of Mecklenburg: 19010 Schwerin, Münzstr. 8; tel. (385) 51850; fax (385) 5185170; Landesbischof HERMANN BESTE.

***Evangelical-Lutheran Church of North Elbe:** Bischof Dr HANS CHRISTIAN KNUTH (24837 Schleswig, Plessenstr. 5A; tel. (4621) 22056; fax (4621) 22194); Bischof KARL LUDWIG KOHLWAGE (23564 Lübeck, Bäckerstr. 3–5; tel. (451) 790201); Bishop MARIA JEPSEN (20457 Hamburg, Neue Burg 1; tel. (40) 373050); Pres. of North Elbian Church Administration Prof. Dr KLAUS BLASCHKE (24103 Kiel, Dänische Str. 21–23; tel. (431) 97955).

†**Evangelical-Reformed Church in North-West Germany:** 26789 Leer, Saarstr. 6; tel. (491) 91980; fax (491) 9198251; Moderator Rev. HINNERK SCHRÖDER; Synod Clerks Rev. WALTER HERRENBRÜCK, ERNST-JOACHIM PAGENSTECHER.

†**Evangelical-Lutheran Church in Oldenburg:** 26121 Oldenburg, Philosophenweg 1; tel. (441) 77010; fax (441) 7701299; e-mail ev.kirche.oldenburg@t-online.de; Bischof Dr WILHELM SIEVERS.

†**Evangelical Church of the Palatinate:** 67346 Speyer, Domplatz 5; tel. (6232) 6670; Pres. WERNER SCHRAMM.

†**Evangelical Church in the Rhineland:** 40476 Düsseldorf, Hans-Böckler-Str. 7, 40418 Düsseldorf, Postfach 320340; tel. (211) 45620; fax (211) 4562490; Pres. MANFRED KOCK.

Evangelical-Lutheran Church of Saxony: 01069 Dresden, Lukasstr. 6, 01013 Dresden, Postfach 320101; tel. (351) 46920; Landesbischof VOLKER KRESS.

***Evangelical-Lutheran Church of Schaumburg-Lippe:** 31675 Bückeburg, Herderstr. 27; tel. (5722) 9600; Landesbischof HEINRICH HERRMANNS.

Evangelical-Lutheran Church in Thuringia: 99817 Eisenach, Dr-Moritz-Mitzenheim Str. 2A; tel. (3691) 67899; e-mail landeskirch enamteisenach@compuserve.com; Landesbischof ROLAND HOFFMANN.

†**Evangelical Church of Westfalen:** 33602 Bielefeld, Altstädter Kirchplatz 5; tel. (521) 5940; fax (521) 594129; Präses MANFRED SORG.

†**Evangelical-Lutheran Church of Württemberg:** 70184 Stuttgart, Gänsheidestr. 4, Postfach 101342; tel. (711) 21490; fax (711) 2149236; e-mail renz@elk.wue.de; Landesbischof EBERHARDT RENZ.

(* Member of the VELKD; † member of the EKU)

Other Evangelical (Protestant) Churches

Arbeitsgemeinschaft Mennonitischer Gemeinden in Deutschland (Asscn of Mennonite Congregations in Germany): 22769 Hamburg, Mennonitenstr. 20; tel. (40) 857112; fax (40) 8507069; f. 1886, re-organized 1990; Chair. PETER FOTH.

Bund Evangelisch-Freikirchlicher Gemeinden (Union of Evangelical Free Church Congregations; Baptists): 61350 Bad Homburg v. d. H., Friedberger Str. 101; tel. (6172) 80040; fax (6172) 800436; f. 1849; Pres. WALTER ZESCHKY; Dirs HEINZ SAGER, Rev. ECKHARD SCHAEFER, Rev. MANFRED SULT.

Bund Freier evangelischer Gemeinden (Covenant of Free Evangelical Churches in Germany): 58452 Witten, Goltenkamp 4, 58426 Witten, Postfach 4005; tel. (2302) 9370; fax (2302) 93799; f. 1854; Pres. PETER STRAUCH; Administrator KLAUS KANWISCHER; 30,000 mems.

Christlicher Gemeinschafts-Verband Mülheim an der Ruhr (Pentecostal Church): 34305 Niedenstein, Hauptstr. 36, 34303 Niedenstein, Postfach 1109; tel. (5624) 775; fax (5624) 776; f. 1913.

Evangelisch-altreformierte Kirche von Niedersachsen (Evangelical Reformed Church of Lower Saxony): 49824 Laar, Hauptstr. 33; Sec. Rev. J.-F. FISCHER.

Evangelisch-methodistische Kirche (United Methodist Church): 60329 Frankfurt a.M., Wilhelm-Leuschner-Str. 8; tel. (69) 239373; fax (69) 239375; e-mail emk.kirchenkanzlei@t-online.de; f. 1968; Bishop Dr WALTER KLAIBER.

Gemeinschaft der Siebenten-Tags-Adventisten (Seventh-day Adventist Church): 73760 Ostfildern, Senefelderstr. 15, 73745 Ostfildern, Postfach 4260; tel. (711) 448190; fax (711) 4481960; e-mail 104474.1412@compuserve.com.

Heilsarmee in Deutschland (Salvation Army in Germany): 50677 Köln, Salierring 23–27; tel. (221) 208190; fax (221) 2081951; e-mail kriegsruf@t-online.de; f. 1886; Leader Col SIEGFRIED OLAUSEN.

Selbständige Evangelisch-Lutherische Kirche (Independent Evangelical-Lutheran Church): 30625 Hannover, Schopenhauerstr. 7; tel. (511) 557808; fax (511) 551588; e-mail selk@selk.de; f. 1972; Bishop Dr DIETHARDT ROTH; Exec. Sec. Rev. MICHAEL SCHÄTZEL.

Other Christian Churches

Alt-Katholische Kirche (Old Catholic Church): 53115 Bonn, Gregor-Mendel-Str. 28; tel. (228) 232285; fax (228) 238314; seceded from the Roman Catholic Church as a protest against the declaration of Papal infallibility in 1870; belongs to the Utrecht Union of Old Catholic Churches; in full communion with the Anglican Communion; Pres. Bischof JOACHIM VOBBE (Bonn); 28,000 mems.

Apostelamt Jesu Christi: 7500 Cottbus, Otto-Grotewohl-Str. 57; tel. 713297; Pres. WALDEMAR ROHDE.

Armenisch-Apostolische Orthodoxe Kirche in Deutschland: 50735 Köln, Allensteiner Str. 5; tel. (221) 7126223; fax (221) 7126267; Bishop KAREKIN BEKDJIAN.

Griechisch-Orthodoxe Metropolie von Deutschland (Greek Orthodox Metropoly of Germany): 53227 Bonn, Dietrich-Bonhoeffer-Str. 2, 53185 Bonn, Postfach 300555; tel. (228) 462041; fax (228) 464989.

Religiöse Gesellschaft der Freunde (Quäker) (Society of Friends): 1080 Berlin, Planckstr. 20; tel. 2082284; f. 1925; 350 mems; Sec. HANS-ULRICH TSCHIRNER.

Russische Orthodoxe Kirche—Berliner Diözese (Russian Orthodox Church): 10138 Berlin, Wildensteiner Str. 10, 10267 Berlin, Postfach 17; tel. (30) 5082024; fax (30) 5098153; Archbishop FEOFAN.

ISLAM

There are an estimated 2.6m. Muslims in Germany.

JUDAISM

The Jewish community in Germany numbered 61,203 in 1996.

Zentralrat der Juden in Deutschland (Central Council of Jews in Germany): 10117 Berlin, Oranienburger Str. 31; tel. (30) 2828714; fax (30) 2386607; 53173 Bonn, Rüngsdorfer Str. 6; tel. (228) 357023; fax (228) 361148; Pres. Board of Dirs IGNATZ BUBIS.

Jüdische Gemeinde zu Berlin (Jewish Community in Berlin): 10623 Berlin, Fasanenstr. 79–80; Pres. JERZY KANAL.

The Press

The German Press Council was founded in 1956 as a self-regulatory body, and is composed of publishers and journalists. It formulates guidelines and investigates complaints against the press.

In 1968 a government commission stipulated various limits on the proportions of circulation that any one publishing group should be allowed to control: (1) 40% of the total circulation of newspapers or 40% of the total circulation of magazines; (2) 20% of the total circulation of newspapers and magazines together; (3) 15% of the circulation in one field if the proportion owned in the other field is 40%.

The principal newspaper publishing groups are:

Axel Springer Group: 10969 Berlin, Kochstr. 50; tel. (30) 25910; fax (30) 25911909; and 20350 Hamburg, Axel-Springer-Platz 1; tel. (40) 3471; telex 403242; fax (40) 343180; the largest newspaper publishing group in continental Europe; includes five major dailies *(Die Welt, Hamburger Abendblatt, Bild-Zeitung, Berliner Morgenpost, BZ),* two Sunday papers *(Welt am Sonntag, Bild am Sonntag),* and radio, television, women's and family magazines; Chair. Supervisory Bd BERNHARD SERVATIUS.

Gruner und Jahr AG & Co Druck- und Verlagshaus: 25524 Itzehoe, Am Vossbarg, tel. (4821) 7771; fax (4821) 777449; and 20444 Hamburg; 20459 Hamburg, Am Baunwall 11; tel. (40) 37030; fax (40) 3703600; owns, amongst others, *Stern, Brigitte, Capital, Eltern, Schöner Wohnen, Hamburger Morgenpost.*

SüddeutscherVerlag GmbH: 80331 München, Sendlingerstr. 80; tel. (89) 21830; telex 523426; fax (89) 2183787; f. 1945; owns *Süddeutsche Zeitung*, special interest periodicals.

Jahreszeiten-Verlag GmbH: 22301 Hamburg, Possmoorweg 5; tel. (40) 27170; telex 213214; fax (40) 27172056; f. 1948; owns, amongst others, the periodicals *Für Sie* and *Petra*; Pres. THOMAS GANSKE.

Heinrich-Bauer-Verlag: 20095 Hamburg, Burchardstr. 11; tel. (40) 30190; fax (40) 30194081; and 81737 München, Charles-de-Gaulle-Str. 8; tel. (89) 678600; fax (89) 6702033; owns 29 popular illustrated magazines, including *Quick* (München), *Neue Revue* (Hamburg), *Praline, Neue Post, TV Horen + Sehen* and *Bravo*; Pres. HEINRICH BAUER.

Burda GmbH: 77652 Offenburg, Hauptstr. 130; tel. (781) 8401; telex 75280081; fax (781) 843064; f. 1908; publs incl. *Bunte, Burda Moden, Bild+Funk, Freundin, Meine Familie & ich* and *Schweriner Volkszeitung*; 10 Mans.

PRINCIPAL DAILIES

Aachen

Aachener Nachrichten: 52068 Aachen, Dresdner Str. 3, 52002 Aaachen, Postfach 110; tel. (241) 51010; telex 832365; fax (241) 5101399; f. 1872; Publrs Zeitungsverlag Aachen; Edited by Verlagsanstalt Cerfontaine GmbH & Co., 5100 Aachen, Theaterstr. 24–34; circ. 67,000.

Aachener Zeitung: 52068 Aachen, Dresdner Str. 3, Postfach 500110; tel. (241) 51010; telex 832851; fax (241) 5101396; f. 1946; Publrs Zeitungsverlag Aachen; Editor-in-Chief BERND MATHIEU; circ. 106,000.

Ansbach

Fränkische Landeszeitung: 91522 Ansbach, Nürnberger Str. 9–17, 91504 Ansbach, Postfach 1362; tel. (981) 95000; fax (981) 13961; Editors-in-Chief GERHARD EGETEMAYER, PETER M. SZYMANOWSKI; circ. 50,000.

Aschaffenburg

Main-Echo: 63741 Aschaffenburg a.M., Weichertstr. 20, Postfach 548; tel. (6021) 3960; telex 4188837; fax (6021) 396499; Editors HELMUT WEISS, Dr HELMUT TEUFEL; circ. 93,000.

Augsburg

Augsburger Allgemeine: 86167 Augsburg, Curt-Frenzel-Str. 2, 86133 Augsburg, Postfach 100054; tel. (821) 7770; telex 53837; fax (821) 704471; daily (Mon. to Sat.); Editors-in-Chief RAINER BONHORST, WINFRIED STRIEBEL; circ. 370,000.

Baden-Baden

Badisches Tagblatt: 76530 Baden-Baden, Stefanienstr. 1–3, 76481 Baden-Baden, Postfach 120; tel (7221) 215241; fax (7221) 215240; Editors-in-Chief HARALD BESINGER, VOLKER-BODO ZANGER; circ. 41,000.

Bamberg

Fränkischer Tag: 96050 Bamberg, Gutenbergstr. 1; tel. (951) 1880; fax (951) 188113; Publr Dr HELMUT JUNGBAUER; circ. 75,800.

Barchfeld

Südthüringer Zeitung: 36456 Barchfeld, Postfach 1225; tel. (36961) 4700; telex 628947; circ. 22,000.

Bautzen

Serbske Nowiny: 02625 Bautzen, Tuchmacher Str. 27; tel. (3591) 577232; (3591) 577243; evening; Sorbian language paper; Editor BENNO RÖTSCHKE; circ. 1,500.

Berlin

Berliner Kurier am Abend/... am Morgen: 10178 Berlin, Karl-Liebknecht-Str. 29; tel. (2) 2442403; telex 114854; fax (2) 2442274; evening; circ. 186,800.

Berliner Morgenpost: 10888 Berlin, Axel-Springer-Str. 65; tel. (30) 25910; telex 183508; fax (30) 2516071; e-mail redaktion@berlinermorgenpost.de; f. 1898; publ. by Ullstein GmbH; Editor-in-Chief PETER PHILIPPS; circ. 164,600 (Sun. 257,900).

Berliner Zeitung: 10178 Berlin, Karl-Liebknecht-Str. 29; tel. (2) 23279; fax (30) 23275533; f. 1945; morning; publ. by G&J-Berliner Zeitung Verlag; Editor DIETER SCHRÖDEN; circ. 230,300.

BZ (Berliner Zeitung): 10969 Berlin, Kochstr. 50; tel. (30) 25910; telex 183508; fax (30) 2516071; f. 1877; publ. by Ullstein Verlag GmbH & Co KG; Editor WOLFGANG KRYSZOHN; circ. 316,400.

Junge Welt: 1080 Berlin, Mauerstr. 39-40; tel. (2) 22330; telex 2443327; fax (2) 1302865; f. 1947; morning; Editor JENS KÖNIG; circ. 158,000.

Neues Deutschland: 10245 Berlin, Alt-Strolan 1–2; tel. (2) 293905; fax (2) 29390600; f. 1946; morning; independent; Editor WOLFGANG SPICKERMANN; circ. 74,200.

Der Tagesspiegel: 10785 Berlin, Potsdamer Str. 87, 10723 Berlin, Postfach 304330; tel. (30) 260090; telex 183773; fax (30) 26009332; f. 1945; circ. 130,200.

Die Welt: 10888 Berlin, Axel-Springer-Str. 65; tel. (30) 25910; fax (30) 25911929; f. 1946; publ. by Axel Springer Verlag; Editor Dr THOMAS LÖFFELHOLZ; circ. 215,000.

Bielefeld

Neue Westfälische: 33602 Bielefeld, Niedernstr. 21–27, 33502 Bielefeld, Postfach 100225; tel. (521) 5550; telex 932799; fax (521) 555348; f. 1967; Chief Editor REINER F. KIRST; circ. 219,850.

Westfalen-Blatt: 33611 Bielefeld, Südbrackstr. 14–18, 33531 Bielefeld, Postfach 8740; tel. (521) 5850; fax (521) 585370; f. 1946; Editor CARL-W. BUSSE; circ. 147,400.

Bonn

Bonner Rundschau: 53111 Bonn, Thomas-Mann-Str. 51–53, 53002 Bonn, Postfach 1248; tel. (228) 7210; fax (228) 721230; f. 1946; Publr HELMUT HEINEN; Editor-in-Chief DIETER BREUERS; circ. 23,700.

General-Anzeiger: 53100 Bonn, Justus-von-Liebig-Str. 15; tel. (228) 66880; telex 8869616; fax (228) 6688170; f. 1725; independent; Publrs HERMANN NEUSSER, HERMANN NEUSSER, Jr, MARTIN NEUSSER; EDITOR DR HELMUT HERLES; circ. 90,000.

Braunschweig

Braunschweiger Zeitung: 38114 Braunschweig, Hamburger Str. 277, 38022 Braunschweig, Postfach 3263; tel. (531) 39000; telex 952722; fax (531) 3900610; Editor Dr ARNOLD RABBOW; circ. 170,400.

Bremen

Bremer Nachrichten: 28195 Bremen, Martinistr. 43; 28078 Bremen, Postfach 107801; tel. (421) 36710; fax (421) 3379233; f. 1743; Publr HERBERT C. ORDEMANN; Editor DIETRICH IDE; circ. 44,000.

Weser-Kurier: 28195 Bremen, Martinistr. 43; 28078 Bremen, Postfach 107801; tel. (421) 36710; fax (421) 3379233; f. 1945; Publr HERBERT C. ORDEMANN; Editor VOLKER WEISE; circ. 185,000.

Bremerhaven

Nordsee-Zeitung: 27576 Bremerhaven 1, Hafenstr. 140; tel. (471) 5970; telex 238761; Chief Editor JÖRG JUNG; circ. 77,500.

Chemnitz

Freie Presse: 09111 Chemnitz, Brückenstr. 15, Postfach 261; tel. (371) 6560; telex 7233; fax (371) 643042; f. 1963; morning; Editor DIETER SOIKA; circ. 461,900.

Cottbus

Lausitzer Rundschau: 03050 Cottbus, Str. der Jugend 54; tel. (355) 4810; telex 379396; fax (355) 481245; independent; morning; Chief Officers BERND HARTMANN, J. FRIEDRICH ORTHS; circ. 190,000.

Darmstadt

Darmstädter Echo: 64295 Darmstadt, Holzhofallee 25–31, 64276 Darmstadt, Postfach 100155; tel. (6151) 3871; telex 419363; fax (6151) 387307; f. 1945; Publrs Dr HANS-PETER BACH, HORST BACH; Editor-in-Chief ROLAND HOF; circ. 87,300.

Dortmund

Ruhr-Nachrichten: 4600 Dortmund 1, Pressehaus, Westenhellweg 86–88, Postfach 105051; tel. (231) 18461; telex 822106; f. 1949; Editor FLORIAN LENSING-WOLFF; circ. 215,400.

Westfälische Rundschau: 44135 Dortmund, Brüderweg 9, 44047 Dortmund, Postfach 105067; tel. (201) 8040; fax (201) 8042841; Editor FRANK BÜNTE; circ. 250,000.

Dresden

Dresdner Morgenpost: 01067 Dresden, Ostra-Allee; tel. (51) 4864; telex 2291; fax (51) 4951116; circ. 126,700.

Dresdner Neueste Nachrichten/Union: 01097 Dresden, Hauptstr. 21; tel. (351) 8075210; fax (351) 8075212; morning; Editor-in-Chief PETER STEFAN HERBST; circ. 40,400.

Sächsische Zeitung: 01067 Dresden, Ostra-Allee 20, Haus der Presse; tel. (351) 48640; telex 329362; fax (351) 4952143; f. 1946; morning; Editor-in-Chief WOLFGANG SCHÜTZE; circ. 405,000.

Düsseldorf

Handelsblatt: 40213 Düsseldorf, Kasernenstr. 67; tel. (211) 8870; telex 8581815; fax (211) 329954; 5 a week; Publr DIETER VON HOLTZBRINCK; circ. 156,473.

Rheinische Post: 40196 Düsseldorf, Zülpicherstr. 10; tel. (211) 5050; telex 8581901; fax (211) 5047562; f. 1946; Editor ULRICH REITZ; circ. 349,200.

Westdeutsche Zeitung: 40212 Düsseldorf, Königsallee 27, 40002 Düsseldorf, Postfach 101132; tel. (211) 83820; fax (211) 83822225; Editor-in-Chief MICHAEL HARTMANN; Publr Dr M. GIRARDET; circ. 176,800.

Eisenach

Mitteldeutsche Allgemeine: 5900 Eisenach, Eisenbahnstr. 2; tel. 5237; circ. 18,000.

Thüringer Tagespost: 5900 Eisenach, A.-Puschkin-Str. 107-109; tel. 3082; fax 3084; circ. 80,000.

Erfurt

Thüringer Allgemeine: 99092 Erfurt, Gottstedter Landstr. 6; tel. (361) 2274; fax (361) 2275144; f. 1946; morning; Editor-in-Chief SERGEJ LOCHTHOFEN; circ. 330,000.

Essen

Neue Ruhr Zeitung: 45128 Essen, Friedrichstr. 34–38, Postfach 104161; tel. (201) 8040; telex 8575010; Editor-in-Chief Dr RICHARD KIESSLER; circ. 215,000.

Westdeutsche Allgemeine Zeitung: 45128 Essen, Friedrichstr. 34–38, Postfach 104161; tel. (201) 8040; telex 8575010; Editor RALF LEHMANN; circ. 650,000.

Frankfurt am Main

Frankfurter Allgemeine Zeitung: 60327 Frankfurt a.M., Hellerhofstr. 2–4, tel. (69) 75910; telex 41223; fax (69) 75911743; f. 1949; Editors JÜRGEN JESKE, Dr HUGO MÜLLER-VOGG, Dr GÜNTHER NONNENMACHER, Dr JOHANN GEORG REISSMÜLLER, Dr FRANK SCHIRRMACHER; circ. 400,200.

Frankfurter Neue Presse: 60327 Frankfurt a.M., Frankenallee 71–81, 60008 Frankfurt a.M., Postfach 100801; tel. (69) 75010; telex 411655; fax (69) 75014292; independent; Editor GERHARD MUMME; circ. 110,000.

Frankfurter Rundschau: 60313 Frankfurt a.M., Grosse Eschenheimer Str. 16–18; tel. (69) 21991; telex 411651; fax (69) 2199521; Editor RODERICH REIFENRATH; circ. 189,000.

Frankfurt an der Oder

Märkische Oderzeitung: 15230 Frankfurt a.d. Oder, Kellenspring 6; tel. (335) 55300; fax (335) 23214; morning; Editor CLAUS DETJEN; circ. 150,633.

Freiburg im Breisgau

Badische Zeitung: 79115 Freiburg i. Br., Pressehaus, Basler Str. 88; tel. (761) 4960; fax (761) 41098; f. 1946; Editor PETER CHRIST; circ. 174,300.

Gera

Ostthüringer Zeitung: 6500 Gera, De-Smit-Str. 18; tel. (70) 6120; telex 58227; fax (70) 51233; morning; Editor-in-Chief ULLRICH ERZIGKEIT; circ. 237,537.

Göttingen

Göttinger Tageblatt: 37079 Göttingen, Dransfelder Str. 1, 37009 Göttingen, Postfach 1953; tel. (551) 9011; telex 96800; fax (551) 901229; f. 1889; Man. Dir MANFRED DALLMANN; Editor-in-Chief HORST STEIN; circ. 50,200.

Hagen

Westfalenpost: 58097 Hagen, Schürmannstr. 4; tel. (2331) 9170; telex 823861; f. 1946; Chief Editor BODO ZAPP; circ. 160,000.

Halle

Hallesches Tageblatt: 06108 Halle, Gr. Brauhausstr. 16–17; tel. (46) 38396; telex 4359; fax (46) 28691; f. 1945; morning; Editor HARTWIG HOCHSTEIN; circ. 37,400.

Mitteldeutsche Zeitung: 4200 Halle, Str. der DSF 67; tel. (46) 8450; telex 4265; fax (46) 845351; f. 1946; morning; Editor Dr Hans-Dieter Krüger; circ. 425,000.

Hamburg

Bild–Zeitung: 20355 Hamburg, Axel-Springer-Platz 1; tel. (40) 34700; telex 2170010; fax (40) 345811; f. 1952; publ. by Axel Springer Verlag; Chief Editor Claus Larass; circ. 4,527,100.

Hamburger Abendblatt: 20355 Hamburg, Axel-Springer-Platz 1; tel. (40) 3471; telex 403242; fax (40) 343180; publ. by Axel Springer Verlag; Editor-in-Chief Klaus Korn; circ. 315,000 (Sat. 358,000).

Hamburger Morgenpost: 22763 Hamburg, Griegstr. 75, 22751 Hamburg; tel. (40) 8830303; fax (40) 88303349; e-mail iamedien@www.mopo.de; internet http://www.mopo.de; Editor Dr Matthias Döpfner; circ. 154,700.

Die Welt: 20355 Hamburg, Axel-Springer-Platz 1; tel. (40) 34700; fax (40) 345811; f. 1946; publ. by Axel Springer Verlag; Editor-in-Chief: Thomas Löeffelholz; circ. 203,340.

Hannover

Hannoversche Allgemeine Zeitung: 30559 Hannover, Bemeroder Str. 58; tel. (511) 5180; telex 92391115; fax (511) 513175; Editor Luise Madsack; circ. 269,600.

Heidelberg

Rhein-Neckar-Zeitung: 69117 Heidelberg, Hauptstr. 23, 69035 Heidelberg, Postfach 104560; tel. (6221) 5191; telex 461751; fax (6221) 519217; f. 1945; morning; Publrs Dr Ludwig Knorr, Winfried Knorr, Dr Dieter Schulze; circ. 104,600.

Heilbronn

Heilbronner Stimme: 74072 Heilbronn, Allee 2; tel. (7131) 6150; telex 728729; fax (7131) 615200; f. 1946; Editor-in-Chief Dr Wolfgang Bok; circ. 102,500.

Hof-Saale

Frankenpost: 95028 Hof, Poststr. 9–11, Postfach 1320; tel. (9281) 8160; telex 643601; fax (9281) 816283; e-mail fp-redaktion@-frankenpost.de; Publr Frankenpost Verlag GmbH; Editor-in-Chief Malte Buschbeck; circ 100,000.

Ingolstadt

Donaukurier: 85051 Ingolstadt, Stauffenbergstr. 2a; tel. (841) 96660; telex 55845; fax (841) 9666255; f. 1872; Publr and Dir Dr W. Reissmüller; circ. 84,700.

Karlsruhe

Badische Neueste Nachrichten: 7500 Karlsruhe 31, Linkenheimer Landstr. 133, Postfach 311168; tel. (721) 7890; telex 7826960; Publr and Editor Hans W. Baur; circ. 165,500.

Kassel

Hessische/Niedersächsische Allgemeine: 34121 Kassel, Frankfurter Str. 168, 34010 Kassel, Postfach 101009; tel. (561) 20300; fax (561) 2032406; f. 1959; independent; Editor-in-Chief Peter M. Zitzmann; circ. 189,200.

Kempten

Allgäuer Zeitung: 87435 Kempten, Kotternerstr. 64, 87401 Kempten, Postfach 1129; tel. (831) 2060; fax (831) 206354; f. 1968; Publrs Georg Fürst von Waldburg-Zeil, Günter Holland; Editor-in-Chief Markus Brehm; circ. 117,900.

Kiel

Kieler Nachrichten: 24103 Kiel, Fleethörn 1–7, 24100 Kiel, Postfach 1111; tel. (431) 9030; fax (431) 903935; Chief Editor Jürgen Heinemann; circ. 115,200.

Koblenz

Rhein-Zeitung: 56070 Koblenz, August-Horch-Str. 28, Postfach 1540; tel. (261) 89200; telex 862611; fax (261) 892476; Editor Martin Lohmann; circ. 246,100.

Köln

Express: 50667 Köln, Breite Str. 70, Postfach 100410; tel. (221) 2240; telex 8882965; f. 1964; Publr Alfred Neven Dumont; Editors Rainer M. Gefeller, Heinrich Jacob; circ. 370,000.

Kölner Stadt-Anzeiger: 50667 Köln, Breite Str. 70, 50450 Köln, Postfach 100410; tel. (221) 2240; telex 8881162; fax (221) 2242524; f. 1876; Publr Alfred Neven DuMont; Editor Dieter Jepsen-Föge; circ. 294,400.

Kölnische Rundschau: 50667 Köln, Stolkgasse 25–45, 50461 Köln, Postfach 102145; tel. (221) 16320; telex 8881267; fax (221) 1632491; f. 1946; Publr Helmut Heinen; Editor-in-Chief Dieter Breuers; circ. 155,100.

Konstanz

Südkurier: 78467 Konstanz, Max-Stromeyer-Str. 178, 78420 Konstanz, Presse- und Druckzentrum, Postfach 102001; tel. (7531) 9990; fax (7531) 26785; f. 1945; circ. 142,600.

Leipzig

Leipziger Volkszeitung: 04107 Leipzig, Peterssteinweg 3; tel. (41) 21810; telex 51495; fax (41) 310592; f. 1894; morning; Editor Bernd Radestock; circ. 320,700.

Leutkirch

Schwäbische Zeitung: 88299 Leutkirch, Rudolf-Roth-Str. 18, 88291 Leutkirch, Postfach 1145; tel. (7561) 800; telex 7321915; fax (7561) 80134; e-mail redaktion@svl.msh.de; f. 1945; Editor Joachim Umbach; circ. 191,100.

Lübeck

Lübecker Nachrichten: 23556 Lübeck, Herrenholz 10-12; tel. (451) 1440; telex 26801; fax (451) 1441022; f. 1945; Chief Editor Thomas Lubowski; circ. 117,800.

Ludwigshafen

Die Rheinpfalz: 67059 Ludwigshafen/Rhein, Amtsstr. 5–11, 67011 Ludwigshafen, Postfach 211147; tel. (621) 590201; telex 464822; fax (621) 5902546; Dir Dr Thomas Schaub; circ. 245,800.

Magdeburg

Magdeburger Volksstimme: 39104 Magdeburg, Bahnhofstr. 17; tel. (391) 59990; telex 351462; fax (391) 388400; f. 1890; morning; publ. by Magdeburger Verlags- und Druckhaus GmbH; Editor-in-Chief Dr Heinzgeorg Oette; circ. 316,900.

Mainz

Allgemeine Zeitung: 55116 Mainz, Grosse Bleiche 44–50, 55021 Mainz, Postfach 3120; tel. (6131) 1440; fax (6131) 144275; publ. by Rhein-Main-Presse; circ. 134,000.

Mannheim

Mannheimer Morgen: 68021 Mannheim, Postfach 102164; tel. (621) 39201; telex 462171; fax (621) 3921376; f. 1946; Publr R. von Schilling; Chief Editors Horst Roth, Horst-Dieter Schiele; circ. 86,200.

München

Abendzeitung: 80331 München, Sendlingerstr. 10; tel. (89) 23770; telex 528011; fax (89) 2377499; f. 1948; Publr Dr Johannes Friedmann; Editor-in-Chief Dr Uwe Zimmer; circ. 213,200.

Münchner Merkur: 80336 München, Paul-Heyse-Str. 2–4, Pressehaus; tel. (89) 53060; fax (89) 5306651; internet http://www.merkur-online.de; Publr Dr Dirk Ippen; Editor Peter Fischer; circ. 203,200.

Süddeutsche Zeitung: 80331 München, Sendlingerstr. 8, 80019 München, Postfach 201902; tel. (89) 21830; telex 523426; fax (89) 2183795; f. 1945; Editors-in-Chief Hans-Werner Kilz, Dr Gernot Sittner; circ. 401,900.

TZ: 80336 München, Paul-Heyse-Str. 2–4; tel. (89) 53060; fax (89) 5306640; f. 1968; Editor Werner Giers; circ. 154,600.

Münster

Münstersche Zeitung: 48143 Münster, Neubrückenstr. 8–11, 48030 Münster, Postfach 5560; tel. (251) 5920; fax (251) 592212; f. 1871; independent; Editor Dr Ralf Richard Koerner; circ. 42,500.

Westfälische Nachrichten: 48155 Münster, ZENO-Zeitungen, Soester Str. 13; tel. (251) 6900; telex 892830; fax (251) 690705; Chief Editor Jost Springensguth; circ. 125,900.

Neubrandenburg

Neubrandenburg Nordkurier: 17034 Neubrandenburg, Flurstr. 2; tel. (395) 45750; telex 381169; fax (395) 4575694.

Nürnberg

Nürnberger Nachrichten: 90402 Nürnberg, Marienstr. 9; tel. (911) 2160; fax (911) 2162326; f. 1945; Editor Felix Hartlieb; circ. 344,000.

Oberndorf-Neckar

Schwarzwälder Bote: 78722 Oberndorf-Neckar, Postfach 1380; tel. (7423) 780; fax (7423) 7873; circ. 104,300.

Oelde

Die Glocke: 59302 Oelde, Engelbert-Holterdorf-Str. 4–6; tel. (2522) 730; telex 89543; fax (2522) 73216; f. 1880; Editors Fried Gehring, Engelbert Holterdorf; circ. 65,500.

Offenbach

Offenbach-Post: 6050 Offenbach, Grosse Marktstr. 36–44, Postfach 164; tel. (69) 80630; telex 4152864; f. 1947; Publr Udo Bintz; circ. 53,200.

Oldenburg

Nordwest-Zeitung: 26121 Oldenburg, Peterstr. 28–34, 26015 Oldenburg, Postfach 2527; tel. (441) 998801; fax (441) 99882029; internet http://www.nwz-online.de; publ. by Druck- und Pressehaus GmbH; Editor ROLF SEELHEIM; circ. 130,000.

Osnabrück

Neue Osnabrücker Zeitung: 49074 Osnabrück, Breiter Gang 10–14 and Grosse Str. 17/19, 49032 Osnabrück, Postfach 4260; tel. (541) 3100; telex 94832; fax (541) 325696; f. 1967; Chief Editor F. SCHMEDT; circ. 179,700.

Passau

Passauer Neue Presse: 94032 Passau, Dr-Hans-Kapfinger-Str. 30; tel. (851) 8020; telex 57879; fax (851) 802256; f. 1946; Editor-in-Chief FRANZ XAVER HIRTREITER; circ. 162,900.

Potsdam

Märkische Allgemeine: 14473 Potsdam, Friedrich-Engels-Str. 24; tel. (331) 28400; telex 1533; fax (331) 2840301; f. 1990; morning; independent; Editor HANS-ULRICH KONRAD; circ. 220,400.

Regensburg

Mittelbayerische Zeitung: 93047 Regensburg, Margaretenstr. 4; tel. (941) 2070; fax (941) 207307; f. 1945; Editor PETER ESSER; circ. 135,000.

Rostock

Ostsee-Zeitung: 18055 Rostock, Richard-Wagner-Str. 1A; tel. (81) 3650; telex 398434; fax (81) 365244; f. 1952; independent; Editor GERD SPILKER; circ. 214,300.

Saarbrücken

Saarbrücker Zeitung: 66117 Saarbrücken, Gutenbergstr. 11–23; tel. (681) 5020; telex 4421262; fax (681) 5022500; f. 1761; Editors UWE JACOBSEN, RUDOLPH BERNHARD, GÜNTER KAMISSEK, FRANK REINERS; circ. 183,500.

Schwerin

Schweriner Volkszeitung: 19061 Schwerin, Gutenbergstr. 1; tel. (385) 63780; fax (385) 3975140; f. 1946; Editor CHRISTOPH HAMM; circ. 144,800.

Straubing

Straubinger Tagblatt: 94315 Straubing, Ludwigsplatz 30; tel. (9421) 9400; fax (9421) 940206; e-mail service@iolowa.de; f. 1860; morning; Chief Editor Dr HERMANN BALLE; circ. 140,000.

Stuttgart

Stuttgarter Nachrichten: 70567 Stuttgart, Plieninger Str. 150; 70039 Stuttgart, Postfach 104452; tel. (711) 72050; telex 7255395; fax (711) 7205747; f. 1946; Editor-in-Chief JÜRGEN OFFENBACH; circ. 59,300.

Stuttgarter Zeitung: 70567 Stuttgart, Plieninger Str. 150, 70049 Stuttgart, Postfach 106032; tel. (711) 72050; telex 7255384; fax (711) 7205516; f. 1945; Chief Editor Dr UWE VORKÖTTER; circ. 151,600.

Suhl

Freies Wort: 6000 Suhl, Wilhelm-Pieck-Str. 6; tel. (66) 5130; telex 62205; fax (66) 21400; morning; Editor GERD SCHWINGER; circ. 136,500.

Trier

Trierischer Volksfreund: 54290 Trier, Am Nikolaus-Koch-Platz 1–3, 54227 Trier, Postfach 3770; tel. (651) 71990; telex 472860; fax (651) 7199990; Chief Editor WALTER W. WEBER; circ. 100,000.

Ulm

Südwest Presse: 89073 Ulm, Frauenstr. 77; tel. (731) 1560; fax (731) 156308; circ. 107,800.

Weiden

Der Neue Tag: 92637 Weiden, Weigelstr. 16, 92603 Weiden, Postfach 1340; tel. (961) 850; telex 63880; fax (961) 44747; Editor-in-Chief HANS KLEMM; circ. 87,400.

Weimar

Thüringische Landeszeitung: 99423 Weimar, Marienstr. 14; tel. (3643) 206411; fax (3643) 206413; f. 1945; morning; Editor HANS HOFFMEISTER; circ. 62,000.

Wetzlar

Wetzlarer Neue Zeitung: 35578 Wetzlar, Elsa-Brandström-Str. 18, Postfach 2940; tel. (6441) 9590; telex 483883; fax (6441) 71684; f. 1945; Editor WULF EIGENDORF; circ. 75,000.

Wiesbaden

Wiesbadener Kurier: 65183 Wiesbaden, Langgasse 21, 65050 Wiesbaden, Postfach 6029; tel. (611) 3550; telex 4186841; fax (611) 355377; Chief Editor HILMAR BÖRSING; circ. 86,700.

Würzburg

Main-Post: 97084 Würzburg, Berner Str. 2; tel. (931) 60010; telex 68845; fax (931) 6001-242; f. 1883; independent; Publrs Dr RAINER ESSER, MANFRED WINTERBACH; Editors-in-Chief DAVID BRANDSTÄTTER, ANTON SAHLENDER; circ. 153,300.

SUNDAY AND WEEKLY PAPERS

Bayernkurier: 80636 München, Nymphenburger Str. 64; tel. (89) 120041; weekly; organ of the CSU; Chief Editor W. SCHARNAGL; circ. 156,300.

Bild am Sonntag: 20350 Hamburg, Axel-Springer-Platz 1; tel. (40) 34700; fax (40) 345811; f. 1956; Sunday; publ. by Axel Springer Verlag; Chief Editor MICHAEL H. SPRENG; circ. 2,737,086.

Deutsches Allgemeines Sonntagsblatt: 20149 Hamburg, Mittelweg 111; tel. (40) 414190; telex 212973; fax (40) 41419111; f. 1948; Friday; Dir ARND BRUMMER; circ. 97,592.

Frankfurter Allgemeine Sonntagszeitung: 60327 Frankfurt a.M., Hellerhofstr. 2-4; tel. (69) 75910; telex 41223; fax (69) 75911773; Sunday; Publr. Dr HUGO MÜLLER-VOGG; Editor-in-Chief CORNELIA VON WRANGEL; circ. 95,000.

Rheinischer Merkur: 53175 Bonn, Godesberger Allee 91; tel. (228) 8840; fax (228) 884199; f. 1946; weekly; Editor THOMAS KIELINGER; circ. 110,100.

Sonntag aktuell: 70567 Stuttgart, Plienigerstr. 150; tel. (711) 72050; fax (711) 7205930; Sunday; circ. 869,500.

Welt am Sonntag: 20355 Hamburg, Axel-Springer-Platz 1; tel. (40) 34700; telex 2170010; fax (40) 34724912; Sunday; publ. by Axel Springer Verlag; Editor MANFRED GEIST; circ. 374,900.

Wochenpost: 10969 Berlin, Ritterstr. 3; weekly; circ. 102,900.

Die Zeit: 200079 Hamburg; 20095 Hamburg, Speersort 1, Pressehaus; tel. (40) 32800; fax (40) 327111; f. 1946; weekly; Editor-in-Chief ROGER DE WECK; circ. 455,000.

SELECTED PERIODICALS

Agriculture

Agrar Praxis: 7022 Leinfelden-Echterdingen, Ernst-Mey-Str. 8; tel. (711) 7594423; telex 7255421; f. 1882; monthly; Editor-in-Chief KLAUS NIEHÖRSTER; circ. 60,250.

Agrarwirtschaft: 60326 Frankfurt a.M., Mainzer Landstr. 251; tel. (69) 759501; telex 4170335; fax (69) 75952999; f. 1952; 10 a year; agricultural management, market research and agricultural policy; publ. Verlag Alfred Strothe; Editor Prof. Dr BUCHHOLZ; circ. 1,150.

Bauernzeitung: 13355 Berlin, Brunnenstr. 128, 10108 Berlin, Postfach 318; tel. (30) 464060; fax (30) 46406205; e-mail verlags info@dt-bauernverlag.de; f. 1960; agricultural weekly; Editor RALF STEPHAN; circ. 40,000.

Bayerisches Landwirtschaftliches Wochenblatt: 80797 München, Lothstr. 29, 80703 München, Postfach 400320; e-mail redbaywo@t.online.de; f. 1810; weekly; organ of the Bayerischer Bauernverband; Editor-in-Chief JOHANNES URBAN; circ. 115,800.

Eisenbahn-Landwirt: 4300 Essen 11, Am Ellenbogen 12, Postfach 110664; tel. (201) 670525; f. 1918; monthly; Dir HANS HÜSKEN; circ. 120,000.

Das Landvolk: 30159 Hannover, Warmbüchenstr. 3; fax (511) 3670468; fortnightly; issued by Landbuch-Verlag GmbH; Chief Editor GÜNTHER MARTIN BEINE; circ. 98,000.

Die Landpost: 70599 Stuttgart, Wollgrasweg 31; tel. (711) 4586091; fax (711) 456603; f. 1945; weekly; agriculture and gardening; Editor ERICH REICH; circ. 60,000.

Art, Drama, Architecture and Music

AIT Architektur, Innenarchitektur, Technischer Ausbau: 70771 Leinfelden-Echterdingen, Fasanenweg 18; tel. (711) 7591286; fax (711) 7591267; e-mail ait-red@ait-online.de; internet http://www.ait-online.de; f. 1890; monthly; Editors Dr D. DANNER, F. DASSLER; circ. 16,000.

Die Kunst: 8000 München 90, Elisenstr. 3; telex 522745; f. 1885; monthly; arts and antiques; publ. by Karl Thiemig AG München; circ. 6,500.

Theater der Zeit: 10179 Berlin, Klosterstr. 68–70; tel. (30) 2423626; fax (30) 24722415; f. 1946; 6 a year; theatre, drama, opera, musical, children's theatre, puppet theatre, ballet; Editor MARTIN LINZER; circ. 8,000.

Theater heute: 10785 Berlin, Lützowplatz 7; tel. (30) 2544950; fax (30) 25449512; f. 1960; monthly; Editors BARBARA BURCKHARDT, Dr MICHAEL MERSCHMEIER, Prof. Dr HENNING RISCHBIETER, Dr FRANZ WILLE.

Economics, Finance and Industry

Absatzwirtschaft: 40213 Düsseldorf, Kasernenstr. 67, 40002 Düsseldorf, Postfach 101102; tel. (211) 8871422; fax (211) 8871420; f. 1958; monthly; journal for marketing; Dir UWE HOCH; Editor FRIEDHELM PÄLIKE; circ. 23,000.

atw—Internationale Zeitschrift für Kernenergie: 40002 Düsseldorf, Postfach 101102; tel. (211) 8871442; fax (211) 8871440; e-mail w.liebholz@vhb.de; f. 1956; monthly; technical, scientific and economic aspects of nuclear engineering and technology; Editors W.-M. LIEBHOLZ, Dr E. PASCHE; circ. 4,500.

Der Betrieb: 40123 Düsseldorf, Kasernenstr. 67, 40002 Düsseldorf, Postfach 101102; tel. (211) 8871451; telex 17211308; fax (211) 8871450; e-mail der-betrieb@vhb.de; weekly; business administration, revenue law, labour and social legislation; circ. 36,000.

Capital: Gruner und Jahr AG, 20444 Hamburg; tel. (40) 37032480; telex 219520; fax (40) 37035607; f. 1962; monthly; business magazine; circ. 295,440.

Creditreform: 40002 Düsseldorf, Kasernenstr. 67, Postfach 1102; tel. (211) 8871461; telex 17211308; fax (211) 8871463; f. 1879; Editor KLAUS-WERNER ERNST; circ. 124,870.

Finanzwirtschaft: 104010 Berlin, Am Friedrichshain 22; tel. (30) 42151237; telex 114566; fax (30) 42151332; 12 a year; finance and economics; circ. 4,818.

Getränketechnik, Zeitschrift für das technische Management: 8500 Nürnberg 1, Breite Gasse 58–60; tel. (911) 23830; telex 623081; fax (911) 204956; 6 a year; trade journal for the brewing and beverage industries; circ. 8,518.

HV-Journal Der Handelsvertreter und Handelsmakler: 60326 Frankfurt a.M., Mainzer-Land-Str. 251, 60019 Frankfurt a.M., Postfach 101937, Siegel-Verlag Otto Müller GmbH; tel. (69) 759506; fax (69) 75952850; f. 1949; fortnightly; Editor Dr ANDREAS PAFFHAUSEN; circ. 23,000.

Industrie-Anzeiger: 70746 Leinfelden-Echterdingen, Postfach 100252; f. 1879; weekly; Editor-in-Chief Dr R. LANGBEIN; circ. 52,000.

Management International Review: 65189 Wiesbaden, Abraham-Lincoln-Str. 46; tel. (611) 7878230; fax (611) 7878411; quarterly; issued by Gabler Verlag; English; Editor Prof. Dr K. MACHARZINA (Stuttgart-Hohenheim).

VDI Nachrichten: 40001 Düsseldorf, Postfach 101054, Heinrichstr. 24; tel. (211) 61880; telex 8587743; fax (211) 6188306; f. 1946; weekly; circ. 155,000.

Versicherungswirtschaft: 76137 Karlsruhe, Klosestr. 22; tel. (721) 35090; fax (721) 31833; e-mail rehnert@vvw.de; f. 1946; fortnightly; Editors KARL-HEINZ REHNERT, HUBERT CLEMENS; circ. 12,000.

Wirtschaftswoche: 40213 Düsseldorf, Kasernenstr. 67; tel. (211) 8770; fax (211) 133374; weekly; business; Publrs Dr HEIK AFHELDT, Dr RENATE MERKLEIN; Editor STEFAN BARON; circ. 163,000.

Education and Youth

Bravo: 81737 München, Charles-de-Gaulle-Str. 8; tel. (89) 6786700; fax (89) 6702033; weekly; for young people; circ. 1,659,360.

Deutsche Lehrerzeitung: 10117 Berlin, Lindenstr. 54B; tel. (2) 23809414; fax (2) 20183645; f. 1954; weekly for teachers; Editor RAINER WINKEL; circ. 22,000.

Erziehung und Wissenschaft: 45134 Essen, Goldammerweg 16; tel. (201) 843000; fax (201) 472590; e-mail info@stamm.de; f. 1948; monthly; Editor-in-Chief STEFFEN WELZEL; circ. 290,000.

Geographische Rundschau: 38104 Braunschweig, GeorgWestermann-Allee 66; tel. (531) 708385; telex 952841; fax (531) 708329; e-mail gr@westermann.de; f. 1949; monthly; Man. Editor REINER JUENGST; circ. 13,500.

PÄDAGOGIK: 69469 Weinheim, Werderstr. 10; tel. (40) 454595; fax (40) 4108564; f. 1949; monthly; Editor Prof. Dr J. BASTIAN; circ. 13,000.

Praxis Deutsch: 30917 Seelze, Postfach 100150; tel. (511) 40004139; fax (511) 40004219; e-mail redaktion.pd@friedrich-verlag.de; 6 a year; German language and literature; circ. 25,000.

Law

Deutsche Richterzeitung: 53173 Bonn, Seufertstr. 27; fax (228) 334723; f. 1909; monthly; circ. 11,000.

Juristenzeitung: 72074 Tübingen, Wilhelmstr. 18, 72010 Tübingen, Postfach 2040; tel. (7071) 95352; fax (7071) 51104; e-mail postmask@mohr.de; f. 1944; fortnightly; Editor HEIDE SCHAPKA; circ. 6,000.

Juristische Rundschau: 10785 Berlin, Genthiner Str. 13, 10728 Berlin, Postfach 303421; tel. (30) 260050; telex 184027; fax (30) 26005329; f. 1922; monthly; Editors-in-Chief Prof. Dr DIRK OLZEN, Prof. Dr HERBERT TRÖNDLE.

Neue Juristische Wochenschrift: 60325 Frankfurt a.M., Palmengartenstr. 14, and 80703 München, Wilhelmstr. 5–9; tel. (69) 7560910; fax (69) 75609149; f. 1947; weekly; 5 Editors; circ. 55,000.

Rabels Zeitschrift für ausländisches und internationales Privatrecht: 20148 Hamburg, Mittelweg 187; tel. (40) 41900263; fax (40) 41900288; f. 1927; quarterly; Editors JÜGEN BASEDOW, KLAUS J. HOPT, HEIN KÖTZ.

Versicherungsrecht: 76137 Karlsruhe, Klosestr. 22; tel. (721) 35090; fax (721) 31833; e-mail rehnert@vvw.de; f. 1950; 3 a month; Editors Prof. Dr EGON LORENZ, KARL-HEINZ REHNERT; circ. 8,800.

Zeitschrift für die gesamte Strafrechtswissenschaft: 10785 Berlin, Genthiner Str. 13, 10728 Berlin, Postfach 303421; tel. (30) 260050; telex 184027; fax (30) 26005329; f. 1881; quarterly; Editor-in-Chief Prof. Dr Dr HANS JOACHIM HIRSCH.

Politics, Literature, Current Affairs

Akzente: 81631 München, Kolbergerstr. 22; tel. (89) 998300; fax (89) 9827119; f. 1954; Editor MICHAEL KRÜGER.

Buch Aktuell: 44137 Dortmund, Königswall 21, 44018 Dortmund, Postfach 101852/62; tel. (231) 90560; fax (231) 9056110; e-mail post@harenberg.de; internet http://www.harenberg.de; 3 a year; Editor BODO HARENBERG; circ. 630,000.

Gegenwartskunde: Leske Verlag + Budrich GmbH, 51334 Leverkusen (Opladen), Postfach 300551; tel. (2171) 2079; fax (2171) 41209; e-mail lesbudpubl@aol.com; quarterly; economics, politics, education; Editors T. GRAMMES, H.-H. HARTWICH, B. SCHÄFERS, G. WEWER.

Internationale Politik: 53113 Bonn, Adenauerallee 131; tel. (228) 26750; fax (228) 2675173; e-mail mail@internationale-politik.bonn.com; f. 1946; monthly; journal of the German Society for Foreign Affairs; publ. by the Verlag für Internationale Politik GmbH, Bonn; Editor Prof. Dr WERNER WEIDENFELD; Exec. Editor Dr ANGELIKA VOLLE; circ. 6,000.

Merian, Hoffman und Campe Verlag: 20149 Hamburg, Harvestehuder Weg 42; tel. (40) 441880; telex 214259; fax (40) 44188310; f. 1948; monthly; every issue deals with a country or a city; Chief Editor VOLKER SKIERKA; circ. 170,000.

Merkur (Deutsche Zeitschrift für europäisches Denken): 80331 München, Pfisterstr. 10; tel. (89) 29163111; fax (89) 29163114; f. 1947; monthly; literary, political; Editors KARL HEINZ BOHRER, KURT SCHEEL; circ. 6,000.

Neue Deutsche Literatur: 10105 Berlin, Neue Promenade 6; tel. (30) 28394238; fax (30) 28394100; f. 1953; 6 a year; review of literature; Editor JÜRGEN ENGLER.

Die Neue Gesellschaft—Frankfurter Hefte: 53175 Bonn, Godesberger Allee 139; tel. (228) 883540; telex 885479; fax (228) 883539; f. 1946; monthly; cultural, political; Editors HOLGER BÖRNER, KLAUS HARPPRECHT, JOHANNES RAU, CAROLA STERN, HANS-JOCHEN VOGEL; circ. 11,000.

Neue Rundschau: 60553 Frankfurt a.M., Postfach 700355; tel. (69) 60620; fax (69) 6062326; f. 1890; quarterly; literature and essays; Editors MARTIN BAUER, HELMUT MAYER, UWE WITTSTOCK; circ. 6,000.

Sozialdemokrat Magazin: 5300 Bonn 2, Am Michaelshof 8; tel. (228) 361011; telex 885603; Publr Vorwärts Verlag GmbH; circ. 834,599.

Universitas: 70109 Stuttgart, Birkenwaldstr. 44, 70009 Stuttgart, Postfach 101061; tel. (711) 25820; fax (711) 2582290; f. 1946; monthly; scientific, literary and philosophical; Editor Dr CHRISTIAN ROTTA, Dr HARTMUT KUHLMANN; circ. 7,200.

VdK-Zeitung: 53175 Bonn, Wurzerstr. 4A; tel. (228) 820930; fax (228) 8209343; f. 1950; monthly; Publr Sozialverband VdK Deutschland eV; Editors JOACHIM FAUSTMANN, ULRICH LASCHET, GÜNTER NEUBERGER, Dr MARION LIENIG; circ. 1,000,000.

VdK-Zeitung, Bayern: 80799 München, Schellingstr. 31; tel. (89) 21170; fax (89) 2117280; e-mail info@vdk.de; f. 1948; monthly; Publr Sozialverband VdK Deutschland e.V.; Editor MICHAEL PAUSDER; circ. 1,100,000.

Welt des Buches: 10969 Berlin, Kochstr. 50; tel. (30) 25910; fax (30) 25911909; f. 1971; weekly; literary supplement of *Die Welt*.

Popular

Anna: 77652 Offenburg, Am Kestendamm 2; tel. (781) 8402; fax (781) 843207; f. 1974; knitting and needlecrafts; Editor AENNE BURDA.

Das Beste Readers Digest: 70049 Stuttgart, Postfach 106020; tel. (711) 66020; fax (711) 6602547; magazines, general, serialized and condensed books, music and video programmes; Man. Dir GERHARD FAISST; circ. 1,500,000.

Bild + Funk: 81925 München, Arabellastr. 23; tel. (89) 92500; telex 522043; radio and television weekly; Editor GÜNTER VAN WAASEN; circ. 1,040,829.

Brigitte: Gruner und Jahr AG, 20444 Hamburg; 20459 Hamburg, Am Baumwell 11; tel. (40) 37030; telex 219520; fax (40) 37035679; fortnightly; women's magazine; circ. 1,300,000.

Bunte: 81925 München, Arabellastr. 23; tel. (89) 92500; fax (89) 92503427; f. 1948; weekly family illustrated; circ. 850,000.

Burda Moden: 77652 Offenburg, Am Kestendamm 2; tel. (781) 8402; fax (781) 843319; e-mail vab@vabab.burda.com; f. 1949; monthly; fashion, beauty, cookery; circ. 2,000,000.

Deine Gesundheit: 1020 Berlin, Neue Grünstr. 18; tel. (2) 2700516; monthly; health and welfare; circ. 242,700.

Deutschland: 60008 Frankfurt a.M., Frankenallee 71–81, Postfach 10081; tel. (69) 75010; telex 411655; fax (69) 75014502; 6 a year; editions in German, Arabic, Chinese, English, French, Hungarian, Japanese, Polish, Portuguese, Romanian, Russian, Spanish, Turkish, Ukrainian; circ. 600,000.

Eltern: Gruner und Jahr AG, 20444 Hamburg; tel. (89) 41520; telex 529324; fax (89) 4152651; f. 1966; monthly; for parents; Editor NORBERT HINZE; circ. 645,000.

Eulenspiegel: 10243 Berlin, Franz-Mehring-Platz 1; tel. (30) 29784103; fax (30) 29782203; e-mail eule@eulenspiegel.b.uunet.de; internet http://www.bmp.de/eulenspiegel; political satirical and humorous monthly; Editors JÜRGEN NOWAK, HARTMUT BERLIN; circ. 130,000.

FF: 10117 Berlin, Mauerstr. 86-88; tel. (30) 231010; telex 302309; fax (30) 23101265; weekly; Editor ALFRED WAGNER; circ. 610,000.

Focus: 81925 München, Arabellastr. 23; tel. (89) 9250-0; fax (89) 9250-2026; f. 1993; weekly; political, general.

Frau aktuell: Düsseldorf, Adlerstr. 22; tel. (211) 36660; fax (211) 3666231; f. 1965; Editor THOMAS PFUNDTNER; circ. 450,000.

Frau im Spiegel: 22763 Hamburg, Griegstr. 75; tel. (40) 8830305; fax (40) 88303486; women's magazine; circ. 762,000.

Freundin: 81925 München, Arabellastr. 23; tel. (89) 92500; telex 522274; fax (89) 92503991; f. 1948; fortnightly for young women; Chief Editor EBERHARD HENSCHEL; circ. 745,556.

Funk Uhr: 20350 Hamburg, Axel-Springer-Platz 1; tel. (40) 3471; telex 403242; fax (40) 343180; radio and television weekly; publ. by Axel Springer Verlag; Editor IMRE KUSZTRICH; circ. 2,013,072.

Für Dich: 10178 Berlin, Karl-Liebknecht-Str. 29; tel. (2) 2440; telex 114854; fax (2) 2443327; f. 1962; women's weekly; Editors HANS EGGERT, Dr PETER PANKAU; circ. 350,000.

Für Sie: 22301 Hamburg, Possmoorweg 5; telex 213214; fax (40) 27172048; women's magazine; circ. 876,950.

Gong: 8500 Nürnberg, Innere Cramer-Klett-Str. 6; telex 9118134; f. 1948; radio and TV weekly; Editor BOB BORRINK; circ. 1,016,415.

Guter Rat!: 10178 Berlin, Mollstr. 1; tel. (30) 23876600; fax (30) 23876395; e-mail redaxtion@guter-rat.de; f. 1945; monthly consumer magazine; Editor-in-Chief Dr RAINER BIELING; circ. 260,000.

Heim und Welt: 3000 Hannover, Am Jungfernplan 3; tel. (511) 855757; telex 921158; fax (511) 854603; weekly; Editor H. G. BRÜNEMANN; circ. 300,000.

Hörzu: 20350 Hamburg, Axel-Springer-Platz 1, Postfach 304630; tel. (40) 3471; telex 217001210; f. 1946; radio and television; publ. by Axel Springer Verlag; Editor KLAUS STAMPFUSS; circ. 3,857,000.

Kicker-Sportmagazin: 90402 Nürnberg, Badstr. 4–6; tel. (911) 2160; f. 1946; sports weekly illustrated; publ. by Olympia Verlag; Man. Dirs DIETRICH PUSCHMANN, RAINER KUBE; circ. 349,131.

Das Magazin: 10119 Berlin, Brunnenstr. 4; tel. (30) 44337510; fax (30) 44337522; f. 1954; monthly; Editor MARTINA RELLIN; circ. 95,000.

Meine Familie & ich: 81925 München, Arabellastr. 23; tel. (89) 92500; fax (89) 92503030; circ. 620,000.

Neue Post: 20095 Hamburg, Burchardstr. 11, Postfach 100444; telex 2163770; weekly; circ. 1,728,750.

Neue Revue: 20095 Hamburg, Burchardstr. 11, Postfach 100406; tel. (40) 30190; telex 161821; fax (40) 338293; f. 1946; illustrated weekly; Editor-in-Chief RAINER PAHLKE; circ. 1,121,184.

Neue Welt: 4000 Düsseldorf 1, Adlerstr. 22; telex 8587669; f. 1932; weekly; Editors PETER PREISS, GÜNTHER GROTKAMP; circ. 499,885.

Pardon: 6000 Frankfurt a.M., Oberweg 157, Postfach 180426; f. 1962; satirical monthly; Editor HANS A. NIKEL; circ. 70,000.

Petra: Jahreszeiten-Verlag, 22301 Hamburg, Possmoorweg 1; telex 213214; monthly; circ. 496,305.

Praline: 20097 Hamburg, Hammerbrookstr. 5; fax (40) 24870190; weekly; women's magazine; circ. 569,300.

Schöner Wohnen: 20444 Hamburg; 20459 Hamburg, Am Baumwall 11; tel. (40) 37030; monthly; homes and gardens; Editor ANGELIKA JAHR; circ. 365,000.

7 Tage: 76485 Baden-Baden, Stadelhofer Str. 14, Postfach 940; telex 781410; f. 1843; weekly; Chief Editor PETER-MICHAEL VON MAYDELL; circ. 480,000.

Der Spiegel: 20457 Hamburg, Brandstwiete 19/Ost-West-Str.; tel. (40) 30070; fax (40) 30072247; f. 1947; weekly; political, general; Publr RUDOLF AUGSTEIN; Editor-in-Chief STEFAN AUST; circ. 1,100,000.

Stern: Gruner und Jahr AG, 20444 Hamburg; tel. (40) 37030; fax (40) 37035631; e-mail info@stern.de; internet http://www.stern.de; illustrated weekly; Publr and Editor-in-Chief Dr WERNER FUNK; circ. 1,406,400.

TV Hören+Sehen: 20095 Hamburg, Burchardstr. 11; tel. (40) 30194001; fax (40) 30194081; f. 1962; weekly; Chief Editor MARION HORN; circ. 2,936,670.

Wochenend: 20095 Hamburg, Burchardstr. 11; tel. (40) 30190; fax (40) 30194081; f. 1948; weekly; Editor GERD ROHLOF; circ. 668,278.

Wochenpost: 1086 Berlin, Mauerstr. 86-99; tel. (2) 2385084; fax (2) 2384617; f. 1953; weekly; Editor MATHIAS GREFFRATH; circ. 300,000.

Religion and Philosophy

Christ in der Gegenwart: 79104 Freiburg i. Br., Hermann-Herder-Str. 4; tel. (761) 2717276; fax (761) 2717520; f. 1948; weekly; Editor JOHANNES RÖSER; circ. 36,000.

Die Christliche Familie: 45239 Essen, Ruhrtalstr. 52–60; tel. (201) 8492411; f. 1885; weekly; Publr Dr ALBERT E. FISCHER; Editors ROBERT HIMMRICH, HELGA MECKNER, SABINE SANKE-WASSERMANN; circ. 45,000.

Der Dom: 33100 Paderborn, Karl-Schurz-Str. 26; tel. (5251) 1530; fax (5251) 153104; f. 1946; weekly; Catholic; Publr Bonifatius GmbH, Druck-Buch-Verlag; circ. 95,000.

Europa: 8000 München 5, Ickstattstr. 7, Postfach 140620; tel. (89) 2015505; telex 5215020; Publr VZV Zeitschriften-Verlags-GmbH; circ. 15,800.

Europa Magazin: 7000 Stuttgart 10, Landhausstr. 82, Postfach 104864; tel. (711) 268630; fax (711) 2686345; f. 1949; 6 a year.

Evangelischer Digest: 7000 Stuttgart 10, Landhausstr. 82, Postfach 104864; tel. (711) 268630; fax (711) 2686345; f. 1958; monthly; Publr Verlag Axel B. Trunkel; circ. 9,300.

Evangelische Theologie: 33311 Gütersloh, Postfach 450; f. 1934; 6 a year; Editor ULRICH LUZ; circ. 2,500.

Katholischer Digest: 7000 Stuttgart 10, Landhausstr. 82, Postfach 104864; tel. (711) 268630; fax (711) 2686345; f. 1949; monthly; Publr Verlag Axel B. Trunkel; circ. 28,900.

Katholisches Sonntagsblatt: 73760 Ostfildern, Senefelderstr. 12; tel. (711) 44060; telex 723556; fax (711) 4406101; f. 1848; weekly; Publr Schwabenverlag AG; circ. 90,000.

Die Kirche: 10117 Berlin, Ziegelstr. 30; tel. (30) 28303922; fax (30) 2829321; f. 1945; Protestant weekly; Editors-in-Chief GERHARD THOMAS, LUTZ BORGMANN; circ. 35,000.

Kirche und Leben: 48151 Münster, Antoniuskirchplatz 21, 48024 Münster, Postfach 4320; tel. (251) 535640; fax (251) 527370; f. 1945; weekly; Catholic; Chief Editor Dr GÜNTHER MEES; circ. 195,000.

Kirchenzeitung für das Erzbistum Köln: 50668 Köln, Ursulaplatz 1, 50460 Köln, Postfach 102041; tel. (221) 1619131; telex 8881128; fax (221) 1619216; weekly; Chief Editor Mgr ERICH LÄUFER; circ. 120,000.

Philosophisches Jahrbuch: 80539 München, Ludwig-Maximilians-Universität, Geschwister-Scholl-Platz 1; f. 1893; 2 a year; Editors Prof. Dr H. M. BAUMGARTNER, Prof. Dr A. HALDER, Prof. Dr K. JACOBI, Prof. Dr H. OTTMANN, Prof. Dr H. ROMBACH, Prof. Dr W. VOSSENKUHL.

Der Sonntagsbrief: 7000 Stuttgart 10, Landhausstr. 82, Postfach 104864; tel. (711) 268630; fax (711) 2686345; f. 1974; monthly; Publr AXEL B. TRUNKEL; circ. 81,400.

Standpunkt: 1190 Berlin, Fennstr. 16; tel. (2) 6350915; f. 1973; Protestant monthly; circ. 3,000.

Der Weg: 40032 Düsseldorf, Postfach 104153; tel. (211) 36101; telex 8582627; weekly; Protestant; Editor Dr MICHAEL SCHIBILSKY; circ. 50,000.

Weltbild: 86131 Augsburg, Steinerne Furt 67; tel. (821) 70048350; fax (821) 70048349; fortnightly; Catholic; Editor ALBERT HERCHENBACH; circ. 270,000.

Science, Medicine

Angewandte Chemie: 69451 Weinheim, Postfach 101161; tel. (6201) 606315; fax (6201) 602328; e-mail angewandte@miley-vch.de; f. 1888; fortnightly; circ. 4,000; international edition in English, f. 1962; circ. 3,000.

Ärztliche Praxis: 82116 Gräfelfing, Hans-Cornelius-Str. 4; tel. (89) 898170; fax (89) 89817195; 2 a week; Editor BURKHARD P. BIERSCHENCK; circ. 60,000.

Berichte der Bunsen-Gesellschaft für physikalische Chemie: VCH Verlagsgesellschaft mbH, 69451 Weinheim/Bergstr., Pappelallee 3, Postfach 101161; tel. (6201) 6060; telex 465516; f. 1894; monthly; Editors R. AHLRICHS, W. FREYLAND, M. KAPPES, P. C. SCHMIDT; circ. 2,300.

Chemie-Ingenieur-Technik: Wiley-VCH Verlagsgesellschaft mbH, 69451 Weinheim, Postfach 101161; tel. (6201) 606519; telex 465516; fax (6201) 606500; f. 1928; monthly; Editor R. PFEFFERKORN; circ. 7,807.

Der Chirurg: 69120 Heidelberg, Kirschnerstr. 1 (INF 110); tel. (6221) 402813; fax (6221) 402014; f. 1928; monthly; Editor Prof. Dr Ch. HERFARTH; circ. 7,200.

Deutsche Apotheker Zeitung: 70191 Stuttgart, Birkenwaldstr. 44, 70009 Stuttgart, Postfach 101061; tel. (711) 2582238; fax (711) 2582291; e-mail daz.daz@t-online.de; f. 1861; weekly; Editor PETER DITZEL; circ. 34,000.

Deutsche Medizinische Wochenschrift: 70469 Stuttgart, Rüdigerstr. 14; tel. (711) 8931232; fax (711) 8931298; f. 1875; weekly; Editor-in-Chief R. AUGUSTIN; circ. 40,000.

Deutsche Zahnärztliche Zeitschrift: 81679 München, Kolbergerstr. 22; tel. (89) 998300; fax (89) 984809; f. 1945; monthly; dental medicine; Editors Prof. Dr GEURTSEN, Prof. Dr TH. KERSCHBAUM, Dr G. MASCHINSKI; circ. 5,300.

Elektro-Anzeiger: 70771 Leinfelden-Echterdingen, Ernst-Mey-Str. 8; tel. (711) 7594279; fax (711) 7594221; f. 1948; monthly; Editor H. KLEWE; circ. 18,100.

Europa Chemie: 60329 Frankfurt a.M. 1, Karlstr. 21, tel. (69) 25561516; fax (69) 239564; f. 1949; industrial chemistry, the environment and economics; Editor-in-Chief Dr G. SCHRIMPF; circ. 4,000.

Geologische Rundschau: Geologische Vereinigung e.V., 56743 Mendig, Vulkanstr. 23; tel. (2652) 989360; fax (2652) 989361; e-mail geol.ver@t-online.de; f. 1910; quarterly; general, geological; Pres. Prof. Dr D. WELTE; circ. 2,400.

Handchirurgie, Mikrochirurgie, Plastische Chirurgie: 70469 Stuttgart, Rüdigerstr. 14, 70445 Stuttgart, Postfach 300504; tel. (711) 89310; telex 7252275; fax (711) 8931453; 6 a year; Editors Prof. Dr med. D. BUCK-GRAMCKO, Prof. Dr W. SCHNEIDER.

Historisches Jahrbuch: 7800 Freiburg i. Br., Hermann-Herder Str. 4; f. 1880; 2 vols a year; Editors Prof. Dr L. BOEHM, Prof. Dr R. A. MÜLLER.

Journal of Neurology: Axel Springer Verlag, 10969 Berlin, Kochstr. 50; tel. (30) 25910; fax (30) 25911909; f. 1891; official journal of the European Neurological Society; Editors-in-Chief Prof. A. COMPSTON, Prof. Dr K. POECK.

Kerntechnik: 85764 Oberschleissheim, Bundesamt für Strahlenschutz, Institut für Strahlenhygiene; Ingolstaedter Landstr. 1; tel. (89) 31603101; fax (89) 31603140; e-mail schmitt@bfs.de; f. 1958; publ. by Carl Hanser GmbH; 6 a year; independent journal on nuclear engineering, energy systems and radiation; Editor ANNE-MARIE SCHMITT-HANNIG; circ. 900.

Kosmos: 7000 Stuttgart 10, Neckarstr. 121, Postfach 106012; tel. (711) 26310; telex 7111193; fax (711) 2631107; f. 1904; monthly; popular nature journal; Editor Dr RAINER KÖTHE; circ. 80,000.

Mund-, Kiefer- und Gesichtschirurgie: 44892 Bochum, In der Schornau 23–25; tel. (234) 2993501; fax (234) 2993509; 7 a year; oral and maxillofacial surgery and oral pathology; Editor Prof. Dr Dr EGBERT MACHTEM.

Medizinische Klinik: 80337 München, Lindwurmstr. 95; tel. (89) 532920; fax (89) 53292100; f. 1904; monthly; Editor Dr HELGA SCHICHTL; circ. 10,000.

Nachrichten aus Chemie, Technik und Laboratorium: 69451 Weinheim, Postfach 101161; tel. (6201) 606318; fax (6201) 606203; f. 1953; monthly; journal of the German Chemical Society; Editors Prof. Dr HERMANN; G. HAUTHAL; circ. 28,000.

Naturwissenschaftliche Rundschau: 70191 Stuttgart, Birkenwaldstr. 44, 70009 Stuttgart, Postfach 101061; tel. (711) 25820; fax (711) 2582390; f. 1948; monthly; scientific; Editors HANS ROTTA, ROSWITHA SCHMID; circ. 7,600.

Planta medica: 70469 Stuttgart, Georg Thieme Verlag, Rüdigerstr. 14; 70451 Stuttgart, Postfach 301120; tel. (711) 89310; telex 7252275; fax (711) 8931298; f. 1952; every 2 months; journal of the Society of Medicinal Plant Research; Editor ADOLF NAHRSTEDT.

Radio Fernsehen Elektronik: 10407 Berlin, Am Friedrichshain 22; tel. (30) 42151313; fax (30) 42151208; f. 1952; monthly; practice and technology of consumer good electronics, multimedia, audio, video, broadcasting, TV; circ. 30,000.

Zahnärztliche Praxis: 82166 München-Gräfelfing, HansCornelius-Str. 4; tel. (89) 898170; telex 522451; fax (89) 853799; monthly; circ. 16,500.

Zeitschrift für Allgemeinmedizin: 70469 Stuttgart, Steiermärker Str. 3-5, 70445 Stuttgart, Postfach 300504; tel. (711) 89310; fax (711) 8931453; e-mail ruth.auschra@hippokrates.de; f. 1924; fortnightly; general and family medicine; publ. by Hippokrates Verlag GmbH; Editors Dr W. MAHRINGER, Dr U. MARSCH-ZIEGLER, Prof. Dr M. KOCHEN, Prof. Dr W. HARDINGHAUS, Dr H.-H. ABHOLZ; circ. 44,000.

Zeitschrift für Klinische Medizin (Das deutsche Gesundheitswesen): 1020 Berlin, Neue Grünstr. 18; fortnightly; for the medical profession.

Zeitschrift für Klinische Psychologie u. Psychotherapie: 33055 Paderborn, Jühenplatz am Rathaus, Postfach 2540; f. 1952; quarterly; Editor Prof. Dr F. PETERMANN.

Zeitschrift für Metallkunde: 70569 Stuttgart, Heisenbergstr. 5; tel. (711) 6861200; telex 7111576; fax (711) 6861255; f. 1911; monthly; metal research; Editors G. PETZOW, M. RÜHLE, P. P. SCHEPP.

Zeitschrift für Physik: 6900 Heidelberg 1, Philosophenweg 19; 16 a year.

Zeitschrift für Psychologie mit Zeitschrift für angewandte Psychologie: 04001 Leipzig, Postfach 100109; tel. (341) 9929200; fax (341) 9929209; internet http://www.psychologie.huberlin.de/psyzeit.html; f. 1890; 4 a year; psychology and applied psychology; Editors Prof. Dr F. KLIX, Prof. Dr W. HACKER, Prof. Dr E. VAN DER MEER, Dr M. ZIESSLER, Dr H. HAGENDORF, R. GRUHN; circ. 600.

Zentralblatt für Neurochirurgie: 40225 Düsseldorf, Heinrich-Heine-Universität, Moorenstr. 5; tel. (211) 8117928; fax (211) 316512; f. 1936; 4 a year; neuro-surgery, traumatology; Editor Prof. Dr W. J. BOCK; circ. 1,000.

NEWS AGENCIES

Allgemeiner Deutscher Nachrichtendienst GmbH (ADN): 1026 Berlin, Mollstr. 1; tel. (2) 2354415; telex 304270; fax (2) 2354474; f. 1946; fmrly the official news agency of the GDR; became independent 1989; bought by Effecten-Spiegel AG 1992; maintains seven branch offices in Germany; has eight offices, as well as additional correspondents, abroad; provides a daily news service and features in German; Man. Dir GÜNTER HUNDRO.

dpa Deutsche Presse-Agentur GmbH: 20148 Hamburg, Mittelweg 38; tel. (40) 41130; telex 212995; fax (40) 4113357; f. 1949; supplies all the daily newspapers, broadcasting stations and more than 1,000 further subscribers throughout Germany with its national and regional news services. English, Spanish, Arabic and German language news is also transmitted regularly to press agencies, newspapers, radio and television stations and ministries of information in about 100 countries; Dir Gen. Dr WALTER RICHTBERG; Editor-in-Chief Dr WILM HERLYN.

VWD: 65760 Eschborn, Niederurseler Allee 8–10; tel. (6196) 4050; fax (6196) 405303; economic and financial news.

Foreign Bureaux

Agence France-Presse (AFP): 53113 Bonn, Adenauerallee 266; tel. (228) 9172510; fax (228) 9172570; e-mail post@afp.de; internet http://www.afp.de; Mans N. C. WORTMANN, P. FEUILLY.

Agencia EFE (Spain): 53113 Bonn, Heussallee 2–10, Pressehaus II/12–14; tel. (228) 214058; telex 886556; fax (228) 224147; Bureau Chief GUILLERMO DÍAZ.

Agenzia Nazionale Stampa Associata (ANSA) (Italy): 53113 Bonn, Pressehaus 2, Heussallee 2/10; tel. (228) 214770; fax (228) 213980; Bureau Chief ALBERTO GINI; and 10623 Berlin, Savignyplatz 6; tel. (30) 3127745; fax (30) 3127747; Bureau Chief FLAMINIA BUSSOTTI.

Associated Press GmbH (AP) (USA): Frankfurt a.M, Moselstr. 27; tel. (69) 27130; telex 412118; fax (69) 251289; also in Hanover, Hamburg, Stuttgart, Wiesbaden, Saarbrücken, Bonn, Berlin, Munich, Düsseldorf, Dresden, Leipzig, Magdeburg, Schwerin and Erfurt; Man. STEPHEN H. MILLER.

Česká tisková kancelář (ČTK) (Czech Republic): 53113 Bonn, Heussallee 2–10, Pressehaus I/207; tel. (228) 215811; fax 214189; f. 1918; Correspondent FRANTIŠEK VACLAVIK.

Informatsionnoye Telegrafnoye Agentstvo Rossii-Telegrafnoye Agentstvo Suverennykh Stran (ITAR-TASS) (Russia): 53113 Bonn, Heussallee 2–10, Pressehaus I/133; tel. (228) 215665; telex 886472; fax (228) 210627.

Inter Press Service (IPS) (Italy): 53113 Bonn, Heussallee 2–10, Pressehaus II/205; tel. (228) 9145710; fax (228) 261205; Bureau Chief RAMESH JAURA.

Jiji Tsushin-sha (Japan): 20148 Hamburg, Mittelweg 38; tel. (40) 445553; fax (40) 456849.

Kyodo Tsushin (Japan): 53113 Bonn, Bonn-Center, Bundeskanzlerplatz 2-10; tel. (228) 225543; telex 886308; fax (228) 222198; Chief Correspondent KAKUYA OGATA.

Magyar Távirati Iroda (MTI) (Hungary): 53113 Bonn, Heussallee 2-10, Pressehaus I/202; tel. and fax (228) 210820; telex 8869652; Correspondent FERENC PACH.

Reuters (UK): 53113 Bonn, Bundeskanzlerplatz 2-10, Postfach 120324; tel. (228) 260970; telex 886677; fax (228) 26097125; Editor-in-Chief WOLFGANG WÄHNER-SCHMIDT; Chief Correspondent ROBERT MAHONEY.

United Press International (UPI) (USA): 53113 Bonn, Heussallee 2–10, Pressehaus II/224; tel. (228) 263787; Bureau Man. and Chief Correspondent PETER G. BILD.

Xinhua (New China) News Agency (People's Republic of China): 5300 Bonn 2, Lyngsbergstr. 33; tel. (228) 331845; telex 885531; fax (228) 331247; Chief Correspondent HU XUDONG.

RIA–Novosti (Russia) is also represented.

PRESS AND JOURNALISTS' ASSOCIATIONS

Bundesverband Deutscher Zeitungsverleger eV (German Newspaper Publishers' Association): 53175 Bonn, Riemenschneiderstr. 10, 53170 Bonn, Postfach 205002; tel. (228) 810040; fax (228) 8100415; there are 11 affiliated Land Asscns; Pres. WILHELM SANDMANN; Chief Sec. Dr VOLKER SCHULZE.

Deutscher Journalisten-Verband (German Journalists' Association): 53115 Bonn, Bennauerstr. 60; tel. (228) 22297180; telex 886567; fax (228) 214917; Chair. Dr HERMANN MEYN; Sec. HUBERT ENGEROFF; 16 Land Asscns.

Verband Deutscher Zeitschriftenverleger eV (Association of Publishers of Periodicals): 53177 Bonn, Winterstr. 50; tel. (228) 382030; fax (228) 3820345; there are seven affiliated Land Asscns; Pres. Dr WERNER HIPPE; Man. Dir GERRIT KLEIN.

Verein der Ausländischen Presse in der BRD (VAP) (Foreign Press Association): 53113 Bonn, Heussallee 2–10, Pressehaus I/35; tel. (228) 210885; fax (228) 219672; f. 1951; Chair. AHMET KÜLAHCI.

Publishers

The following is a selection of the most prominent German publishing firms.

ADAC Verlag GmbH: 81373 München, Am Westpark 8; tel. (89) 76760; fax (89) 76764621; f. 1958; guidebooks, legal brochures, maps, magazines ADAC-Motorwelt, Deutsches Autorecht; Man. Dir MANFRED M. ANGELE.

Ariston Verlag GmbH & Co KG: 81379 München, Boschetsrieder Str. 12; tel. (89) 7241034; fax (89) 7241718; f. 1964; medicine, psychology; Man. Dir FRANK AUERBACH.

Aufbau-Verlag GmbH: 10178 Berlin, Neue Promenade 6; tel. (30) 283940; fax (30) 28394100; e-mail info@aufbau-verlag.de; f. 1945; fiction, non-fiction, classical literature; Dirs PETER DEMPEWOLF, GOTTHARD ERLER, RENÉ STRIEN.

J.P. Bachem Verlag GmbH: 50668 Köln, Ursulaplatz 1; tel. (221) 16190; fax (221) 1619159; f. 1818; economics, social science, religion; Dirs Dr CLEMENS J. B. SANDMANN, LAMBERT BACHEM.

Bauverlag GmbH: 65396 Walluf, Am Klingenweg 4A; tel. (61213) 7000; fax (61213) 700122; f. 1929; civil engineering, architecture, environment, energy, etc.; Dirs OTTO GMEINER, REINER GROCHOWSKI.

Verlag C. H. Beck: 80801 München, Wilhelmstr. 9, 80703 München, Postfach 400340; tel. (89) 381890; telex 5215085; fax (89) 38189-398; f. 1763; law, science, theology, archaeology, philosophy, philology, history, politics, art, literature; Dirs Dr HANS DIETER BECK, WOLFGANG BECK.

Beltz Verlag: 6940 Weinheim, Am Hauptbahnhof 10, Postfach 100154; tel. (6201) 63071; telex 465500; fax (6201) 17464; f. 1841; textbooks; Man. Dir Dr MANFRED BELTZ-RÜBELMANN.

Bertelsmann Buch AG: 81673 München, Neumarkterstr. 18; tel. (89) 431890; fax (89) 4312837; f. 1994; general, reference; Man. Dirs FRANK WÖSSNER, S. KRÜMMER, B. v. MINCKWITZ, P. OLSON.

Bibliographisches Institut und F. A. Brockhaus GmbH: 6800 Mannheim 1, Dudenstr. 6, Postfach 100311; tel. (621) 390101; telex 462107; fax (621) 3901389; f. 1805; encyclopaedias, dictionaries, travel, natural sciences, memoirs, archaeology; Dirs HUBERTUS BROCKHAUS, CLAUS GREUNER, Dr MICHAEL WEGNER.

BLV Verlagsgesellschaft mbH: 80797 München, Lothstr. 29; tel. (89) 127050; telex 5215087; fax (89) 12705354; f. 1946; cookery, sports, gardening, riding, hunting, fishing, health, travel, adventure, technical books, nature; Man. Dirs HEINZ HARTMANN (books), HANS-PETER KLIEMANN (magazines).

Breitkopf & Härtel: 65195 Wiesbaden, Walkmühlstr. 52, Postfach 1707; tel. (611) 450080; fax (611) 4500859; f. 1719; music and music books; Dirs LIESELOTTE SIEVERS, GOTTFRIED MÖCKEL.

Brönner Verlag GmbH: 6000 Frankfurt a.M. 1, Stuttgarter Str. 18-24; tel. (69) 26000; telex 411964; fax (69) 2600223; art; Dirs KLAUS BREIDENSTEIN, HANS-JÜRGEN BREIDENSTEIN.

Verlag Bruckmann München: 80636 München, Nymphenburgerstr. 86; tel. (89) 125701; telex 523739; fax (89) 1257269; f.1858; books, calendars, video cassettes, magazines, fine art prints, original prints; Man. Dir Dr JÖRG D. STIEBNER.

Bund-Verlag GmbH: 5000 Köln 90, Hansestr. 63A; tel. (2203) 934758; telex 8873362; fax (2203) 934762; f. 1947; legal studies and commentaries, economics, politics, etc.; Man. Dir ERICH HENSLER.

Verlag Georg D. W. Callwey GmbH & Co: 81673 München, Streitfeldstr. 35; tel. (89) 4360050; fax (89) 43600513; e-mail rkonczak@callwey.de; internet http://www.callwey.de; f. 1884; cultural history, architecture, sculpture, painting, gardens, art restoration, crafts, do-it-yourself; Man. Dirs HELMUTH BAUR-CALLWEY, Dr VERONIKA BAUR-CALLWEY.

Carlsen Verlag GmbH: 22765 Hamburg, Völckersstr. 14–20, 22703 Hamburg, Postfach 500380; tel. (40) 3910090; telex 217879; fax (40) 39100962; f. 1953; children's and comic books; Dirs CARL-JOHAN BONNIER, TORSTEN LARSSON, KLAUS HUMANN, VIKTOR NIEMANN.

Cornelsen Verlag GmbH & Co: 14197 Berlin, Mecklenburgische Str. 53; tel. (30) 897850; fax (30) 89786299; internet http://www.cornelsen.de; f. 1946; school textbooks, educational software; Man. Dirs FRITZ VON BERNUTH, ALFRED GRÜNER, JÜRGEN L. PETER, Dr HANS WEYMAR.

Delius Klasing Verlag: 33602 Bielefeld, Siekerwall 21; tel. (521) 5590; fax (521) 559113; e-mail delius-klasing@t-online.de; f. 1911; yachting, motor boats, surfing, mountain biking, race biking, basketball, motor cars; Dir KONRAD DELIUS.

Deutsche Verlags-Anstalt GmbH: 7000 Stuttgart 1, Neckarstr. 121, Postfach 106012; tel. (711) 26310; fax (711) 2631292; f. 1831; general; Dir ULRICH FRANK-PLANITZ.

Deutscher Taschenbuch Verlag GmbH & Co KG (dtv): 80801 München, Friedrichstr. 1a, 80704 München, Postfach 400422; tel. (89) 381670; fax (89) 346428; f. 1961; general fiction, history, music, art, reference, children, general and social science, medicine, textbooks; Man. Dirs WOLFGANG BALK, Dr RÜDIGER SALAT.

Verlag Moritz Diesterweg: 60386 Frankfurt a.M., Wächtersbacherstr. 89; tel. (69) 420810; fax (69) 42081205; f. 1860; text books, economics, social sciences, sciences, pedagogics; Dirs RALF MEIER, KARL SLIPEK.

Droemersche Verlagsanstalt Th. Knaur Nachf GmbH & Co: 81679 München, Rauchstr. 9–11; tel. (89) 92710; fax (89) 9271168; f. 1901; general literature, non-fiction, art books, paperbacks; Man. Dirs PETER SCHAPER, Dr GÜNTHER FETZER.

DuMont Buchverlag GmbH & Co KG: 50672 Köln, Mittelstr. 12-14; tel. (221) 20530; fax (221) 2053281; f. 1956; archaeology, art, garden, travel, guidebooks, etc.; Publrs ERNST BRÜCHER, DANIEL BRÜCHER, Dr GOTTFRIED HONNEFELDER.

Econ Verlagsgruppe: 4000 Düsseldorf 30, Kaiserswertherstr. 282, Postfach 300321; tel. (211) 439060; telex 8587327; fax (211) 4390668; general fiction and non-fiction; Publr Dr HERO KIND; Man. Dir MICHAEL STAEHLER.

Eichborn Verlag: 6000 Frankfurt a.M. 1, Kaiserstr. 66; tel. (69) 2560030; fax (69) 25600330; f. 1980; literature non-fiction, historical science, humour, cartoons; Man. Dir VITO VON EICHBORN.

Europaverlag: 81679 München, Mauerkirchestr. 8; tel. (89) 9827790; fax (89) 98277950; fiction, non-fiction, poetry, biography and current events; Dirs GISELA ANNA STÜMPEL, WOLFGANG WEIDMANN.

Falk-Verlag GmbH: 21035 Hamburg, Im Gleisdreieck 5; tel. (40) 725990; fax (40) 72599200; f. 1945; maps, guidebooks, phrasebooks; Man. Dir Dr HELGE LINTZHÖFT.

Falken-Verlag GmbH: 65527 Niedernhausen, Schöne Aussicht 21; tel. (6127) 7020; fax (6127) 702133; f. 1923; health, gardening, humour, natural history, cooking, sports, etc.; Man. Dirs FRANK SICKER, MANFRED ABRAHAMSBERG.

Gustav Fischer Verlag GmbH: 07745 Jena, Villengang 2; tel. (3641) 27332; fax (3641) 22638; f. 1878; biological science, human and veterinary medicine; Dirs JOHANNA SCHLÜTER, BERND ROLLE, BERND VON BREITENBUCH, Dr WULF, D. V. LUCIUS.

S. Fischer Verlag GmbH: 60596 Frankfurt a.M., Hedderichstr. 114, 60553 Frankfurt a.M., Postfach 700355; tel. (69) 60620; fax (69) 6062319; f. 1886; general, paperbacks; Publr MONIKA SCHOELLER; Man. Dir Dr HUBERTUS SCHENKEL.

Franzis' Verlag GmbH: 85622 Feldkirchen, Dornacher Str. 3D; tel. (89) 991150; fax (89) 99115199; f. 1924; Gen. Man. Dr RÜDIGER HENNIGS.

Gräfe und Unzer Verlag GmbH: 81675 München, Grillparzer Str. 12; tel. (89) 419810; fax (89) 41981113; f. 1722; cookery, health, nature, travel; Man. Dirs FRANK WAGER, PETER NOTZ, CLAUDIA REITTER.

Walter de Gruyter & Co Verlag: 10785 Berlin, Genthiner Str. 13, 10728 Berlin, Postfach 303421; tel. (30) 260050; telex 184027; fax (30) 26005251; f. 1919; humanities and theology, law, science, medicine, mathematics, economics, data processing, general; Man. Dirs HANS-DIETER BRANDHOFF, Dr HANS-ROBERT CRAM.

Hallwag Verlag GmbH: 73760 Ostfildern, Brunnwiesenstr. 23, 73745 Ostfildern, Postfach 4266; tel. (711) 449840; fax (711) 44984-60; maps, travel guides, wine, other reference.

Carl Hanser Verlag: 81679 München, Kolbergerstr. 22; tel. (89) 998300; fax (89) 984809; f. 1928; modern literature, plastics, technology, chemistry, science, dentistry; Man. Dirs JOACHIM SPENCKER, WOLFGANG BEISLER, JÜRGEN HOSBACH, MICHAEL KRÜGER.

Harenberg Kommunikation Verlags- und Mediengesellschaft mbH & Co KG: 44137 Dortmund, Königswall 21, 44018 Dortmund,

Postfach 101852; tel. (231) 90560; fax (231) 9056110; e-mail post @harenberg.de; f. 1973; history, almanacs, encyclopaedias; Man. Dir BODO HARENBERG.

Rudolf Haufe Verlag GmbH & Co KG: 79102 Freiburg i. Br., Hindenburgstr. 64; tel. (761) 36830; telex 772442; fax (761) 3683195; e-mail online@haufe.de; internet http://www.haufe.de; f. 1934; business, law, finance, social science; Man. Dirs UWE RENALD MÜLLER, MARTIN LAQUA, HELMUTH HOPFNER.

Verlag Herder GmbH & Co KG: 79104 Freiburg i. Br., Hermann-Herder-Str. 4; tel. (761) 27170; fax (761) 2717520; e-mail vert rieb@herder.de; f. 1801; religion, philosophy, psychology, history, education, art, encyclopaedias, children's books, gift books, periodicals; Propr Dr H. HERDER.

Wilhelm Heyne Verlag: 80333 München, Türkenstr. 5-7; tel. (89) 286350; fax (89) 2800943; f. 1934; fiction, biography, history, cinema, etc.; Publr. ROLF HEYNE.

Hoffmann & Campe Verlag: 20149 Hamburg, Harvestehuderweg 42, 20139 Hamburg, Postfach 1304445; tel. (40) 441881; telex 214259; fax (40) 44188202; f. 1781; biography, fiction, history, economics, science, also magazine *Merian;* Man. Dirs LOTHAR MESSE, ULRICH MEIER.

Dr Alfred Hüthig Verlag GmbH: 6900 Heidelberg, Im Weiher 10; tel. (6221) 4890; telex 461727; fax (6221) 489279; f. 1925; chemistry, chemical engineering, metallurgy, dentistry, etc.

Axel Juncker-Verlag: 80711 München, Neusser Str. 3, Postfach 401120; tel. (89) 360960; fax (89) 36096222; f. 1902; dictionaries, phrase-books; Man. Dirs KARL ERNST TIELEBIER-LANGENSCHEIDT, ANDREAS LANGENSCHEIDT.

S. Karger GmbH: 7800 Freiburg, Lörracherstr. 16A; tel. (761) 452070; fax (761) 4520714; f. 1890; medicine, psychology, natural science; Man. Dir S. KARGER.

Gustav Kiepenheuer Verlag: 04103 Leipzig, Gerichtsweg 28; tel. (341) 9954600; fax (341) 9954620; f. 1909; fiction, non-fiction, cultural history; Chief Editor BIRGIT PETER.

Verlag Kiepenheuer & Witsch & Co: 5000 Köln 51, Rondorferstr. 5; tel. (221) 376850; telex 8881142; fax (221) 388595; f. 1948; general fiction, biography, history, sociology, politics; Man. Dir Dr REINHOLD NEVEN DU MONT.

Der Kinderbuchverlag GmbH: 10711 Berlin, Katharinenstr. 8; tel. (30) 8938840; fax (30) 89388420; f. 1949; children's books; Dir H. MEISINGER.

Ernst Klett Verlag: 7000 Stuttgart 1, Rötebühlstr. 77; tel. (711) 66720; telex 722225; fax (711) 6672800; f. 1844; secondary school and university textbooks (especially German as a foreign language), dictionaries, atlases, teaching aids; Dirs MICHAEL KLETT, ROLAND KLETT, Dr THOMAS KLETT.

Verlag W. Kohlhammer GmbH: 70565 Stuttgart, Hessbrühlstr. 69; tel. (711) 78630; fax (711) 7863263; f. 1866; periodicals, general textbooks; Man. Dirs Dr JÜRGEN GUTBROD, HANS-JOACHIM NAGEL.

Kösel-Verlag GmbH & Co: 80639 München, Flüggenstr. 2; tel. (89) 178010; fax (89) 1780111; f. 1593; philosophy, religion, psychology, esoteric, family and education; Dir Dr CHRISTOPH WILD.

Kreuz Verlag GmbH: 70565 Stuttgart, Breitwiesenstr. 30, Postfach 800669; tel. (711) 788030; fax (711) 7880310; f. 1983; theology, psychology, pedagogics; Man. Dir Dr JÜRGEN A. BACH.

Verlag der Kunst GmbH: 01309 Dresden, Glashütter Str. 55; tel. (351) 3100052; fax (351) 3105245; e-mail verlag-der-kunst.dd@ t-online.de; f. 1952; art books and reproductions; Dir ROGER N. GREENE.

Langenscheidt-Verlag: 10827 Berlin, Crellestr. 28–30; 80807 München, Neusser Str. 3, Postfach 401120; tel. (89) 360960; telex 183175; fax (89) 36096222; f. 1856; foreign languages, German for foreigners, dictionaries, textbooks, language guides, records, tapes, cassettes, video cassettes, software, electronic dictionaries; Man. Dirs KARL ERNST TIELEBIER-LANGENSCHEIDT, ANDREAS LANGENSCHEIDT.

Edition Leipzig GmbH: 04105 Leipzig, Jacobstr. 6, 04003 Leipzig, Postfach 340; tel. (341) 7736; fax (341) 295820.

Paul List Verlag KG: 8000 München 2, Goethestr. 43; tel. (89) 51480; telex 522405; fax (89) 5148185; f. 1894; general fiction, history, music, art, philosophy, religion, psychology, school books; Editorial Dir GERALD TRAGEISER.

Gustav Lübbe Verlag GmbH: 51469 Bergisch Gladbach, Scheidtbachstr. 23-25; tel. (2202) 1210; f. 1964; general fiction and non-fiction, biography, history, etc. Man. Dirs PETER MOLDEN, Dr PETER ROGGEN.

Hermann Luchterhand Verlag GmbH: 56564 Neuwied, Heddesdorfer Str. 31, 56513 Neuwied, Postfach 2352; tel. (2631) 8010; fax (2631) 801210; e-mail luchterhand@t-online.de; f. 1924; insurance, law, taxation, labour; Man. Dir N. W. A. DE GIER, J. LUCZAK.

Mairs Geographischer Verlag: 7302 Ostfildern 4, Marco-Polo-Zentrum, Postfach 3151; tel. (711) 45020; telex 721796; fax (711) 4502310; f. 1848; road maps, atlases, tourist guides; Man. Dir Dr VOLKMAR MAIR.

J. B. Metzlersche Verlagsbuchhandlung: 70028 Stuttgart, Kernerstr. 43, Postfach 103241; tel. (711) 229020; telex 7262891; fax (711) 2290290; literature, music, pedagogics, linguistics, history, economics, commerce, textbooks; Dir Dr BERND LUTZ.

Verlag Moderne Industrie AG: 86895 Landsberg, Justus-von-Liebig-Str. 1; tel. (8191) 1250; telex 527114; fax (8191) 125309; f. 1952; management, investment, technical; Man. Dir Dr REINHARD MÖSTL.

Morgenbuch Verlag GmbH: 1170 Berlin, Seelenbinderstr. 152; tel. (2) 6504151; telex 112629; f. 1958; belles-lettres, politics; Dir Dr WOLFGANG TENZLER.

Verlagsgesellschaft Rudolf Müller GmbH & Co KG: 50933 Köln, Stolbergerstr. 84; tel. (221) 54970; fax (221) 5497326; f. 1840; architecture, construction, engineering, education; Publrs CHRISTOPH MÜLLER, RUDOLF M. BLESER, GÜNTER SANDSCHEPER.

Verlag Friedrich Oetinger: 22397 Hamburg, Poppenbütteler Chaussee 53; tel. (40) 60790902; fax (40) 6072326; juvenile, illustrated books; Man. Dirs SILKE WEITENDORF, UWE WEITENDORF, THOMAS HUGGLE.

R. Oldenbourg Verlag GmbH: 81671 München, Rosenheimerstr. 145; tel. (89) 4904110; fax (89) 490411207; f. 1858; technology, science, history, textbooks, mathematics, economics, dictionaries, periodicals; Dirs Dr T. VON CORNIDES, Dr D. HOHM, WOLFGANG DICK, JOHANNES OLDENBOURG.

Orell Füssli & Parabel Verlag GmbH: 6200 Wiesbaden, Gaabstr. 6; tel. (6121) 401062; fax (6121) 408737; f. 1981; reference; Man. Dir RENATE SCHULZE.

Verlagsunion Erich Pabel—Arthur Moewig KG: 76437 Rastatt, Karlsruher Str. 31; tel. (7222) 130; telex 722259; fax (7222) 13301; Gen. Man. GERHARD STEDTFELD.

Verlag Paul Parey: 20095 Hamburg, Spitalerstr. 12; tel. (40) 339690; telex 2161391; fax (40) 33969198; f. 1848; biology, botany, zoology, ethology, veterinary science, laboratory animals science, food technology and control, agriculture, starch research and technology, brewing and distilling, forestry, horticulture, phytomedicine, plant and environment protection, water management, hunting, fishing, dogs, equitation; technical and scientific journals; Dirs Dr FRIEDRICH GEORGI, Dr RUDOLF GEORGI.

Manfred Pawlak Grossantiquariat und Verlagsgesellschaft mbH: 8036 Herrsching, Gachenau Str. 31; tel. (8152) 37070; telex 527724; fax (8152) 370748; f. 1949; history, art, general interest; Dir ULRIKE PAWLAK.

Pestalozzi-Verlag graphische Gesellschaft mbH; 8520 Erlangen, Am Pestalozziring 14; tel. (9131) 60600; telex 629766; fax (9131) 606078; f. 1844; children's books; Man. Dirs Dr REINHOLD WEIGAND, NORBERT FRANKE.

Piper Verlag GmbH: 80799 München, Georgenstr. 4, Postfach 430861; tel. (89) 3818010; fax (89) 338704; f. 1904; literature, philosophy, theology, psychology, natural sciences, political and social sciences, history, biographies, music; Dir VIKTOR NIEMANN.

Quell Verlag: 7000 Stuttgart 1, Furtbachstr. 12A, Postfach 897; tel. (711) 601000; f. 1830; Protestant literature; Dirs Dr WOLFGANG REISTER, WALTER WALDBAUER.

Ravensburger Buchverlag Otto Maier GmbH: 88212 Ravensburg, Marktstr. 22-26; tel. (751) 860; fax (751) 861289; e-mail info@ ravensburger.de; internet http://www.ravensburger.de; f. 1883; Man. Dirs Dr DETLEV LUX, KLAUS-JÜRGEN SCHIRMER.

Philipp Reclam jun. Verlag GmbH: 71254 Ditzingen bei Stuttgart, Siemensstr. 32; tel. (7156) 1630; fax (7156) 163197; e-mail werbung@reclam.de; f. 1828; literature, literary criticism, fiction, history of culture and literature, philosophy and religion, biography, fine arts, music; Acting Partner Dr DIETRICH BODE.

Rowohlt Taschenbuch Verlag GmbH: 21465 Reinbek bei Hamburg, Hamburgerstr. 17; tel. (40) 72721; telex 217854; fax (40) 7272319; f. 1908/1953; politics, science, fiction, translations of international literature; Dirs Dr HELMUT DÄHNE, NICOLAUS HANSEN.

K.G. Saur Verlag: 81373 München, Ortlerstr. 8, 81316 München, Postfach 701649; tel. (89) 769020; fax (89) 76902150; f. 1949; library science, reference, dictionaries, microfiches; brs in Providence, London, Paris, Bern, Melbourne and Leipzig; subsidiary of Reed Elsevier PLC, London, Amsterdam.

F.K. Schattauer Verlag GmbH: 70192 Stuttgart, Lenzhalde 3, 70040 Stuttgart, Postfach 104545; tel. (711) 229870; telex 177111402; fax (711) 2298750; f. 1949; medicine and related sciences; Publr DIETER BERGEMANN.

Scherz Verlag GmbH: 8000 München 19, Stievestr. 9; tel. (89) 172237; telex 5215282; fax (89) 174030; f. 1957; general fiction, history, politics, etc.; Man. Dir RUDOLF STREIT-SCHERZ.

Verlag Dr Otto Schmidt KG: 50968 Köln, Unter den Ulmen 96–98; tel. (221) 9373801; fax (221) 93738943; f. 1905; university textbooks, jurisprudence, tax law; Man. Dir K. P. WINTERS.

Egmont Franz Schneider Verlag GmbH: 80809 München, Schleißheimer Str. 267; tel. (89) 358116; fax (89) 35811755; e-mail postmaster@schneiderbuch.de; f. 1913; children's books; Publr Dr WOLFGANG REINHARD.

Schroedel Schulbuchverlag GmbH: 30519 Hannover, Hildesheimer Str. 202–206; tel. (511) 83880; fax (511) 8388343; f. 1982; school textbooks and educational software; Man. Dirs THOMAS BAUMANN, Dr WERNER KUGEL.

Springer-Verlag GmbH & Co KG: 14197 Berlin, Heidelberger Platz 3; tel. (30) 827870; telex 183319; fax (30) 8214091; f. 1842; medicine, biology, mathematics, physics, chemistry, psychology, engineering, geosciences, philosophy, law, economics; Proprs CLAUS MICHALETZ, Dr HANS-ULRICH DANIEL, Prof. Dr DIETRICH GÖTZE, BERNHARD LEWERICH.

Stollfuss Verlag Bonn GmbH & Co KG: 53115 Bonn, Dechenstr. 7; tel. (228) 7240; telex 8869477; fax (228) 659723; reference, fiscal law, economics, investment, etc.; Man. Dir WOLFGANG STOLLFUSS.

Suhrkamp Verlag KG: 60325 Frankfurt a.M., Suhrkamp Haus, Lindenstr. 29–35, 60019 Frankfurt a.M., Postfach 101945; tel. (69) 756010; fax (69) 75601522; f. 1950; modern German and foreign literature, philosophy, poetry; Dir Dr SIEGFRIED UNSELD.

Sybex Verlag GmbH: 40231 Düsseldorf, Erkratherstr. 345-349; tel. (211) 97390; fax (211) 9739199; f. 1981; computers; Man. Dirs HANS NOLDEN, RODNAY ZAKS.

Georg Thieme Verlag: 70469 Stuttgart, Rüdigerstr. 14, 70451 Stuttgart, Postfach 301120; tel. (711) 89310; telex 7252275; fax (711) 8931298; f. 1886; medicine and natural science; Man. Dirs Dr GÜNTHER HAUFF, ALBRECHT HAUFF.

K. Thienemanns Verlag: 70182 Stuttgart, Blumenstr. 36; tel. (711) 210550; fax (711) 2105539; f. 1849; picture books, children's books, juveniles; Dirs HANSJÖRG WEITBRECHT, GUNTER EHNI.

transpress Verlagsgesellschaft mbH: 13181 Berlin, Borkumstr. 2; tel. (30) 47805151; fax (30) 47805160; f. 1990; specialized literature on transport and marketing; Man. Dr HARALD BÖTTCHER.

Verlag Eugen Ulmer GmbH & Co: 70574 Stuttgart, Postfach 700561; tel. (711) 45070; telex 723634; fax (711) 4507120; e-mail info@ulmer.de; f. 1868; agriculture, horticulture, science, periodicals; Dir ROLAND ULMER.

Verlag Ullstein GmbH: 10969 Berlin, Charlottenstr. 13; tel. (30) 25913570; fax (30) 25913523; f. 1894; literature, art, music, theatre, contemporary history, biography; Pres. Dr JÜRGEN RICHTER.

Urban & Schwarzenberg GmbH: 8000 München 2, Landwehrstr. 61; tel. (89) 53830; fax (89) 5383221; f. 1866; medicine, natural sciences; Man. Dir MICHAEL URBAN.

VGS-Verlagsgesellschaft mbH & Co KG: 50667 Köln, Gertrudenstr. 30–36; tel. (221) 208110; fax (221) 2081166; e-mail 100340.1540@compuserve.com; internet http://www.vgs.de; f. 1970; fiction, hobbies, natural sciences, culture, popular culture, TV, history, etc.; Man. Dir Dr HEINZ GOLLHARDT.

Verlag Volk und Welt GmbH: 1086 Berlin, Glinkastr. 13-15; tel. (2) 2202851; Dir JÜRGEN GRUNER.

Weltbild Verlag GmbH: 86167 Augsburg, Steinerne Furt 67–72; tel. (821) 70040; fax (821) 7004279; f. 1949; religion, philosophy, fashion, heraldry, nature and environment, culture, history, photography, literature, health, travel.

Georg Westermann Verlag GmbH: 3300 Braunschweig, Georg-Westermann-Allee 66, Postfach 5367; tel. (531) 7080; telex 952841; fax (531) 796569; f. 1838; non-fiction, paperbacks, periodicals; Dir Dr JÜRGEN RICHTER.

Wiley-VCH Verlag: 69451 Weinheim, Pappelallee 3, Postfach 101161; tel. (6201) 6060; telex 465516; fax (6201) 6063288; e-mail info@wiley-vch.de; internet http://www.wiley-vch.de; f. 1921; natural sciences, especially chemistry, biotechnology, materials science, life sciences, information technology and physics, law, scientific software; Man. Dir Dr MANFRED ANTONI.

PRINCIPAL ASSOCIATION OF BOOK PUBLISHERS AND BOOKSELLERS

Börsenverein des Deutschen Buchhandels eV (German Publishers and Booksellers Association): 60311 Frankfurt a.M., Grosser Hirschgraben 17–21, 60004 Frankfurt a.M., Postfach 100442; tel. (69) 13060; fax (69) 1306201; f. 1825; Chair. GERHARD A. KURTZE; Man. Dir Dr HANS-KARL VON KUPSCH.

Broadcasting and Communications

TELECOMMUNICATIONS

Deutsche Telekom AG: Bonn; tel. (228) 1810.

BROADCASTING

Arbeitsgemeinschaft der öffentlich-rechtlichen Rundfunkanstalten der Bundesrepublik Deutschland (ARD) (Association of Public Law Broadcasting Organizations): 60320 Frankfurt a.M., Bertramstr. 8; tel. (69) 590607; telex 411127; fax (69) 1552075; f. 1950; Chair. Prof. Dr UDO REITER; the co-ordinating body of the following radio and television organizations: Bayerischer Rundfunk, Radio Bremen, Hessischer Rundfunk, Mitteldeutscher Rundfunk, Norddeutscher Rundfunk, Ostdeutscher Rundfunk Brandenburg, Saarländischer Rundfunk, Sender Freies Berlin, Süddeutscher Rundfunk, Südwestfunk, Westdeutscher Rundfunk, Deutsche Welle.

Bayerischer Rundfunk: 80300 München, Rundfunkplatz 1; tel. (89) 590001; telex 521070; fax (89) 59002375; Dir-Gen. Prof. ALBERT SCHARF; Chair. of Broadcasting Council Dr WILHELM FRITZ; Chair. of Administration Bd JOHANN BÖHM.

Radio Bremen: 28329 Bremen, Bürgermeister-Spitta-Allee 45; tel. (421) 2460; telex 245181; fax (421) 2461010; internet http://www.radiobremen.de; f. 1945; radio and television; Dir-Gen. KARL-HEINZ KLOSTERMEIER.

Deutsche Welle: 50968 Köln, Raderberggürtel 50; tel. (221) 3892500; fax (221) 3892510; e-mail deutsche.welle@dw.gmd.de; German short-wave radio and satellite television service; broadcasts daily in 40 languages for Europe and overseas; Dir-Gen. DIETER WEIRICH.

Deutschland Radio: 10825 Berlin, Hans Rosenthal Platz; tel. (30) 85030; Dir-Gen. ERNST ELLITZ.

Hessischer Rundfunk: 60320 Frankfurt a.M., Bertramstr. 8; tel. (69) 1551; telex 411127; fax (69) 1552900; Dir-Gen. Prof. Dr KLAUS BERG; Chair. Admin. Council GERT LÜTGERT; Chair. Broadcasting Council EDITH STRUMPF.

Mitteldeutscher Rundfunk: 04275 Leipzig, Kanstr. 71–73; tel. (341) 3000; fax (341) 3005544; f. 1992; Dir-Gen. Prof. Dr UDO REITER.

Norddeutscher Rundfunk: 20149 Hamburg, Rothenbaumchaussee 132; tel. (40) 41560; telex 2198910; fax (40) 447602; internet http://www.ndr.de; Dir-Gen. JOBST PLOG.

Ostdeutscher Rundfunk Brandenburg: 14482 Potsdam, August-Bebel-Str. 26-53; tel. (331) 7210; fax (331) 7213571; Dir-Gen. Prof. HANSJÜRGEN ROSENBAUER.

Saarländischer Rundfunk: 66100 Saarbrücken, Funkhaus Halberg; tel. (681) 6020; telex 4428977; fax (681) 6023874; f. 1952; Dir-Gen. FRITZ RAFF.

Sender Freies Berlin: 14057 Berlin, Masurenallee 8–14; tel. (30) 30310; fax (30) 3015062; internet http://www.sfb-berlin.de; Dir-Gen. Dr GÜNTHER VON LOJEWSKI; Chair. Broadcasting Council MARIANNE BRINCKMEIER; Dir of Radio JENS WENDLAND; Dir of TV HORST SCHÄTTLE.

Süddeutscher Rundfunk: 70190 Stuttgart, Neckarstr. 230, 70049 Stuttgart, Postfach 106040; tel. (711) 9290; telex 723456; fax (711) 9292600; f. 1924; Dir-Gen. HERMANN FÜNFGELD.

Südwestfunk: 76530 Baden-Baden, Hans-Bredow-Str.; tel. (7221) 920; fax (7221) 922010; Dir-Gen. PETER VOß.

Westdeutscher Rundfunk: 50667 Köln, Appellhofplatz 1; tel. (221) 2201; telex 8882575; fax (221) 2204800; Dir-Gen. FRITZ PLEITGEN.

Radio

Each of the members of ARD broadcasts 3–5 channels. There are also regional commercial radio stations.

Foreign Radio Stations

American Forces Network: 60320 Frankfurt a.M., Bertramstr. 6; tel. (69) 15688240; f. 1943; 19 affiliated stations world-wide; transmits three TV channels via satellite; Commanding Officer Col MITCHELL MAROVITZ; Programme Dir HERB GLOVER.

British Forces Broadcasting Service, Germany: 32049 Herford, Wentworth Barracks, Liststr.; tel. (5221) 98340; 12 VHF radio transmitters and 45 low-powered TV transmitters; Gen. Man. MARC TYLEY.

Radio Free Europe/Radio Liberty Inc: Oettingenstr. 67, 80538 München; tel. (89) 21020; fax (89) 21023322; a non-profit-making private corporation, operating under US management and funded by congressional grants supplied through the Board for International Broadcasting, which also oversees the operations of both stations; transmitter facilities in Spain, Portugal and Germany. Radio Free Europe broadcasts to Armenia, Azerbaijan, Belarus, Bulgaria, the Czech Republic, Estonia, Georgia, Kazakhstan, Kyrgyzstan, Latvia, Lithuania, Poland, Romania, Russia, Slovakia, Tajikistan, Turkmenistan, Ukraine and Uzbekistan. Pres. KEVIN KLOSE; Dir of Broadcasting ROBERT GILLETTE.

Voice of America (VOA Europe): 80539 München, Ludwigstr. 2; tel. (89) 286-91; telex 523737; fax (89) 2809210; f. 1985; broadcasts 24 hours daily in English on MW, FM and cable to parts of Europe and Asia in 46 languages; music, news and features on US life and culture; Dir European Operations CSABA T. CHIKES.

Television

There are three public service television channels. The autonomous regional broadcasting organizations combine to provide material for the First Programme which is produced by ARD. The Second Programme (Zweites Deutsches Fernsehen/ZDF) is completely separate and is controlled by a public corporation of all the Länder. It is partly financed by advertising. The Third Programme provides a cultural and educational service in the evenings only with contributions from several of the regional bodies. Commercial television channels also operate.

Zweites Deutsches Fernsehen (ZDF): 55100 Mainz, Postfach 4040; tel. (6131) 702050; fax (6131) 702052; f. 1961 by the Länder Govts as a second television channel; 104 main transmitters; Dir-Gen. Prof. DIETER STOLTE; Dir of Programmes OSWALD RING; Editor-in-Chief KLAUS BRESSER; Controller of International Affairs Dr GOTTFRIED LANGENSTEIN.

Finance

(cap. = capital; dep. = deposits; m. = million; res = reserves; brs = branches; amounts in Deutsche Marks)

The Deutsche Bundesbank, the central bank of Germany, consists of the central administration in Frankfurt am Main (considered to be the financial capital of the country) and 9 main offices (Landeszentralbanken) with over 200 branches. In carrying out its functions as determined by law the Bundesbank is independent of the Federal Government, but is required to support the Government's general economic policy. All other credit institutions are subject to governmental supervision through the Federal Banking Supervisory Office (Bundesaufsichtsamt für das Kreditwesen) in Berlin.

Banks outside the central banking system are divided into three groups: private commercial banks, credit institutions incorporated under public law and co-operative credit institutions. All these commercial banks are 'universal banks', conducting all kinds of customary banking business. There is no division of activities. As well as the commercial banks there are a number of specialist banks, such as private or public mortgage banks.

The group of private commercial banks includes all banks incorporated as a company limited by shares (Aktiengesellschaft—AG, Kommanditgesellschaft auf Aktien—KGaA) or as a private limited company (Gesellschaft mit beschränkter Haftung—GmbH) and those which are known as 'regional banks' because they do not usually function throughout Germany; and those banks which are established as sole proprietorships or partnerships and mostly have no branches outside their home town. The main business of all private commercial banks is short-term lending. The private bankers fulfil the most varied tasks within the banking system.

The public law credit institutions are the savings banks (Sparkassen) and the Landesbank-Girozentralen. The latter act as central banks and clearing houses on a national level for the savings banks. Laws governing the savings banks limit them to certain sectors—credits, investments and money transfers—and they concentrate on the areas of home financing, municipal investments and the trades. In December 1996 there were 607 savings banks and 13 Landesbank-Girozentralen in Germany.

The head institution of the co-operative system is the DG BANK Deutsche Genossenschaftsbank. In December 1996 there were three regional co-operative central banks and 2,510 local co-operative banks.

BANKS

The Central Banking System

Deutsche Bundesbank: 60431 Frankfurt a.M., Wilhelm-Epstein-Str. 14; tel. (69) 95661; telex 414431; fax (69) 5601071; internet http://www.bundesbank.de; f. 1957; issues bank notes, regulates note and coin circulation and supply of credit; safeguards internal and external value of Deutsche Mark; maintains main offices (Landeszentralbanken). The Bank advises on important monetary policy, and members of the Federal Govt may take part in the deliberations of the Central Bank Council but may not vote; Pres. Prof. Dr HANS TIETMEYER; Vice-Pres. JOHANN-WILHELM GADDUM.

Landeszentralbank in Baden-Württemberg: 70173 Stuttgart, Marstallstr. 3; tel. (711) 9440; telex 723512; fax (711) 9441390; Pres. Bd of Management Dr GUNTRAM PALM.

Landeszentralbank im Freistaat Bayern: 80539 München, Ludwigstr. 13; tel. (89) 28895; telex 524365; fax (89) 28893598; internet http://www.bundesbank.de/lzb-bayern; Pres. Bd of Management Dr FRANZ-CHRISTOPH ZEITLER.

Landeszentralbank in Berlin und Brandenburg: 10831 Berlin, Postfach 110160; tel. (30) 23870; fax (30) 23872500; Pres. Bd of Management KLAUS-DIETER KUEHBACHER.

Landeszentralbank in der Freien Hansestadt Bremen, in Niedersachsen und Sachsen-Anhalt: 28203 Bremen, Kohlhökerstr. 29; tel. (421) 32910; telex 244810; Pres. Bd of Management Prof. Dr HELMUT HESSE.

Landeszentralbank in der Freien und Hansestadt Hamburg, in Mecklenburg-Vorpommern und Schleswig-Holstein: 20459 Hamburg, Ost-West-Str. 73; tel. (40) 37070; telex 214554; fax (40) 37072205; Pres. Bd of Management Prof. Dr HANS-JÜRGEN KRUPP.

Landeszentralbank in Hessen: 60329 Frankfurt a.M., Taunusanlage 5; tel. (69) 23880; fax (69) 23882130; Pres. ERNST WELTEKE.

Landeszentralbank in Nordrhein-Westfalen: 40212 Düsseldorf, Berliner Allee 14; tel. (211) 8740; telex 8582774; Pres. Prof. Dr REIMUT JOCHIMSEN.

Landeszentralbank in Rheinland-Pfalz und im Saarland: 52122 Mainz, Hegelstr. 65; tel. (6131) 377-0; fax (6131) 381664; Pres. HANS-JÜRGEN KOEBNICK.

Landeszentralbank in den Freistaaten Sachsen und Thüringen: 04358 Leipzig, Postfach 901121; tel. (341) 8600; fax (341) 8602389.

Private Commercial Banks

In December 1996 331 private commercial banks were operating in Germany. The most prominent of these are listed below:

Baden-Württembergische Bank AG: 70173 Stuttgart, Kleiner Schlossplatz 11, 70049 Stuttgart, Postfach 106014; tel. (711) 1800; telex 721881; fax (711) 1801712; f. 1977 by merger of Badische Bank, Handelsbank Heilbronn and Württembergische Bank; cap. 180m., dep. 26,802m. (Dec. 1996); Chair. GERHARD MAYER-VORFELDER; 9 main brs, 50 brs.

Bankhaus Gebrüder Bethmann: 60311 Frankfurt a.M., Bethmannstr. 7–9, Postfach 100349; tel. (69) 21770; telex 411273; fax (69) 2177283; f. 1748; commercial and investment bank; cap. and res 75m., dep. 914m. (Dec. 1996); Partners WOLFGANG ABRESS, JOHN Frhr VON TWICKEL; 7 brs.

Bankhaus Max Flessa & Co: 97421 Schweinfurt, Luitpoldstr. 2–6; tel. (9721) 5310; telex 673304; fax (9721) 531231; f. 1924; cap. and res 62m., dep. 2,011m. (Dec. 1996); Partners HORST RITZMANN, Dr ERICH SACHS, MATHIAS RITZMANN, Dr GERD SACHS; 20 brs.

Bankhaus Hermann Lampe KG: 33602 Bielefeld, Alter Markt 3; tel. (521) 5820; telex 932866; fax (521) 175190; f. 1852; cap. 110m., res 90m., dep. 3,499m. (Dec. 1996); Partners R.-A. OETKER, Dr HORST ANNECKE, CHRISTIAN Graf VON BASSEWITZ, GERHARD KAPPELHOFF-WULFF.

Bayerische Hypotheken- und Wechsel-Bank AG (Hypo-Bank): 80333 München, Theatinerstr. 11; tel. (89) 92440; telex 528650; fax (89) 92442880; f. 1835; merger with Bayerische Vereinsbank AG pending; cap. 1,285m., res 7,171m., dep. 215,440m. (Dec. 1996); Chair. Supervisory Bd Dr KLAUS GÖTTE; Chair. Bd of Management Dr EBERHARD MARTINI; 489 brs.

Bayerische Vereinsbank AG: 80311 München, Kardinal-Faulhaber-Str. 1 and 14, Postfach 100101; tel. (89) 3780; telex 528610; fax (89) 37826415; f. 1869; merger with Bayerische Hypotheken- und Wechsel- Bank AG pending; cap. 1,323m., res 8,211m., dep. 376,854m. (Dec. 1996); 11 Mans; 774 brs.

Joh. Berenberg, Gossler & Co: 20354 Hamburg, Neuer Jungfernstieg 20; tel. (40) 350600; telex 215781; fax (40) 352132; f. 1590; cap. 150m., dep. 2,818m. (Dec. 1996); Chair. Dr CHRISTIAN WILDE.

Berliner Bank AG: 10890 Berlin, Hardenbergstr. 20; tel. (30) 31090; telex 182010; fax (30) 31092165; f. 1950; cap. 300m., res 1,971m., dep. 43,387m. (Dec. 1996); Chair. Supervisory Bd WOLFGANG STEINRIEDE.

Berliner Volksbank eG: 14057 Berlin, Kaiserdamm 86; tel. (30) 30630; fax (30) 30631550; f. 1860; cap. 320m., res 331m., dep. 12,690m. (Dec. 1996); Chair. H.-D. BLAESE.

BfG—Bank AG: 60283 Frankfurt a.M.; 60325 Frankfurt a.M., Mainzer Landstr. 16; tel. (69) 2580; telex 4122122; fax (69) 2587578; f. 1958; cap. and res 2,398m., dep. 47,259m. (Dec. 1996); Chair. KARL-HEINZ HÜLSMANN; 180 brs.

BHF-Bank AG: 60323 Frankfurt a.M., Bockenheimer Landstr. 10; tel. (69) 7180; telex 411026; fax (69) 7182296; e-mail debhffm@ibmmail.com; f. 1856; cap. 432m., res 2,645m., dep. 68,157m. (Dec. 1996); Mans R. FIEDLER, M. KRUSE, A. MÖCKEL, T. PADUCH, R. SCHARFF, D. SCHMID, L. Graf VON ZECH.

Chase Manhattan Bank AG: 60325 Frankfurt a.M., Ulmenstr. 30; tel. (69) 71581; telex 411625; fax (69) 71582209; f. 1947; cap. 253.5m., res 33m., dep. 5,046m. (Dec. 1996); Mems Bd RAINER GEBBE, GÜNTHER HIMPICH, THOMAS HOTT, SYLVIA SEIGNETTE.

Citibank AG: 6000 Frankfurt a.M. 1, Neue Mainzer Str. 75; tel. (69) 13660; telex 4189211; fax (69) 13661113; f. 1976; cap. 408m., res 74m., dep. 6,027m. (Dec. 1996); Chair. Supervisory Bd ERNST BRUTSCHE; 3 brs.

Citibank Privatkunden AG: 40213 Düsseldorf, Kasernenstr. 10; tel. (211) 89840; telex 8582758; fax (211) 8984222; f. 1926; cap. and res. 748m., dep. 14,500m. (Dec. 1996).

Commerzbank AG: 60261 Frankfurt a.M.; 60311 Frankfurt a.M., Neue Mainzer Str. 32-36, tel. (69) 13620; telex 4152530; fax (69) 285389; f. 1870; cap. 2,001m., res 10,354m., dep. 411,819m. (Dec. 1996); Chair. Supervisory Bd WALTER SIEPP; Chair. Bd of Management MARTIN KOHLHAUSSEN; 964 brs.

Crédit Suisse First Boston AG: 60308 Frankfurt a.M., Messeturm; tel. (69) 75380; fax (69) 75382444; f. 1996 by merger; cap. and res 329m., dep. 5,120m. (Dec. 1996); Chair. Supervisory Bd OSWALD J. GRÜBEL.

Deutsche Bank AG: Central Office: 60325 Frankfurt a.M., Taunusanlage 12; tel. (69) 91000; telex 417300; fax (69) 71504225; f. 1870; cap. 2,501m., res 26,289m., dep. 731,192m. (Dec. 1996); Chair. Supervisory Bd HILMAR KOPPER; CEO ROLF-ERNST BREUER; 1,133 brs.

Dresdner Bank AG: 60301 Frankfurt a.M.; 60329 Frankfurt a.M., Jürgen-Ponto-Platz 1; tel. (69) 2630; telex 415240; fax (69) 634004; f. 1872; dep. 512,228m. (Dec. 1996); Chair. Supervisory Bd ALFONS TITZRATH; 1,200 brs.

Dresdner Bank Lateinamerika AG: 20354 Hamburg, Neuer Jungfernstieg 16, 20305 Hamburg, Postfach 301246; tel. (40) 35950; fax (40) 35953314; f. 1906; fmrly Deutsch-Südamerikanische Bank AG; cap. 178m., res 332m., dep. 11,742m. (Dec. 1996); Chair. Bd of Management HELMUT FRÖHLICH.

DSL Bank Deutsche Siedlungs- und Landesrentenbank: 53175 Bonn, Kennedyallee 62-70; tel. (228) 8890; fax (228) 889624; internet http://www.dsl-bank.de; f. 1966; cap. 219m., res 681m., dep. 93,534m. (Dec. 1996); Spokesman Bd of Dirs STEFAN JÜTTE.

Landesgirokasse: 70144 Stuttgart, Königstrasse 3-5; (711) 1240; fax (711) 1244144; f. 1975; cap. and res 1,710m., dep. 34,245m. (Dec. 1996); CEO Dr W. ZÜGEL.

Marcard, Stein & Co: 20095 Hamburg, Ballindamm 36; tel. (40) 320990; telex 2165032; fax (40) 32099200; f. 1790; cap. 94.2m., dep. 516m. (Dec. 1996).

Merck, Finck & Co: 80333 München, Pacellistr. 16; tel. (89) 21040; telex 522303; fax (89) 299814; f. 1870; cap. 300m., dep. 3,601m. (Dec. 1996); Partners GERD SCHMITZ-MORKRAMER, UTZ-DIETER BOLSTORFF.

B. Metzler seel. Sohn & Co KGaA Bankers: 60311 Frankfurt a.M., Grosse Gallusstr. 18, 60015 Frankfurt a.M., Postfach 101548; tel. (69) 21040; telex 412724; fax (69) 281429; f. 1674; cap. and res 144m., dep. 699m. (Dec. 1996).

Oldenburgische Landesbank AG: 26122 Oldenburg, Stau 15-17; tel. (441) 2210; telex 25882; fax (441) 210310; f. 1868; cap. 107m., res 434m., dep. 12,046m. (Dec. 1996); Spokesman Bd of Management H.-D. GELLER.

Sal. Oppenheim Jr & Cie KGaA: 50667 Köln, Unter Sachsenhausen 4; tel. (221) 14501; telex 8882547; fax (221) 1451512; f. 1789; cap. 200m., res 885m., dep. 11,395m. (Dec. 1996); Chair. KARL OTTO PÖHL.

Schmidt Bank KGaA: 95030 Hof, Ernst-Reuter-Str. 119; tel. (9281) 6010; fax (9281) 601427; f. 1828; cap. 390m., dep. 8,302m. (Dec. 1996); Partners Dr KARL-GERHARD SCHMIDT, Dr HANS NUISSL; 132 brs.

SGZ-Bank: 60322 Frankfurt a.M., Bockenheimer Anlage 46; tel. (69) 71390; fax (69) 71391309; f. 1883; cap. 400m., res 1,993m., dep. 41,678m. (Dec. 1996); Chair. Bd of Management Dr U. BRIXNER.

Skandinaviska Enskilda Banken AG: 60313 Frankfurt a.M., Rahmhofstr. 2–4, 60019 Frankfurt a.M., Postfach 101957; tel. (69) 290210; telex 413413; fax (69) 284191; f. 1975; cap. 81.3m., res 58.9m., dep. 1,343m. (Dec. 1996); Chair. RUTGER BLENNOW; Man. Dirs WOLFGANG AZGELANDER, LARS TÖRNQUIST; 2 brs.

Société Générale S.A.: 60325 Frankfurt a.M., Mainzer Landstr. 36; tel. (69) 71740; telex 411029; fax (69) 7174196; f. 1886; cap. 241m., dep. 6,255m. (Dec. 1993); Chair. JACQUES PETER; 11 brs.

Trinkaus & Burkhardt KGaA: 40212 Düsseldorf, Königsallee 21–23; tel. (211) 9100; telex 8581490; fax (211) 910616; f. 1785; cap. 131m., res 539m., dep. 14,096m. (Dec. 1996); 5 partners; 7 brs.

Union Bank of Switzerland (Deutschland) AG: 60313 Frankfurt a.M., Bleichstr. 52, 60020 Frankfurt a.M., Postfach 102063; tel. (69) 13690; telex 412194; fax (69) 13691366; f. 1909; merchant bank; frmly Deutsche Länderbank AG; cap. 65m., res 281m., dep. 7,354m. (Dec. 1996); Chair. Supervisory Bd D. ROBINS.

Vereins- und Westbank AG: 20457 Hamburg, Alter Wall 22; tel. (40) 369201; telex 2151640; fax (40) 36922870; f. 1974 by merger; cap. 270m., res 975m., dep. 25,029m. (Dec. 1996); 210 brs.

Weberbank Berliner Industriebank KGaA: 14199 Berlin, Hohenzollerndamm 134; tel. (30) 897980; fax (30) 8243003; f. 1949; cap. 100m., res 242m., dep. 12,370m. (Dec. 1996); 4 brs.

Westfalenbank AG: 44787 Bochum, Huestr. 21–25; tel. (234) 6160; telex 825825; fax (234) 616400; f. 1921; cap. 97m., res 207m., dep. 6,605m. (Dec. 1996).

Public-Law Credit Institutions

Together with the private banks, the banks incorporated under public law (savings banks—Sparkassen—and their central clearing houses—Landesbank-Girozentralen) play a major role within the German banking system. In 1996 there were 607 savings banks and 13 central clearing houses, the latter of which comprised the following:

Bayerische Landesbank Girozentrale: 80333 München, Brienner Str. 20; tel. (89) 217101; telex 5286270; fax (89) 21713579; f. 1972; cap. 3,862m., res 5,085m., dep. 323,354m. (Dec. 1996); Chair. Bd of Management FRANZ NEUBAUER.

Bremer Landesbank Kreditanstalt Oldenburg: 28195 Bremen, Domshof 26; tel. (421) 3320; telex 2402234; fax (421) 3322299; e-mail kontakt@bremerlandesbank.de; internet http://bremerlandes bank.de; f. 1983; cap. 667m., res 555m., dep. 47,801m. (Dec. 1996); Chair. Dr PETER HASSKAMP.

Deutsche Girozentrale-Deutsche Kommunalbank: 60329 Frankfurt a.M., Taunusanlage 10, 60040 Frankfurt a.M., Postfach 110542; tel. (69) 26930; telex 414163; fax (69) 26932490; f. 1918; cap. 1,060m., res 400m., dep. 102,826m. (1996); Chair. Bd of Management ERNST-OTTO SANDVOSS.

Hamburgische Landesbank-Girozentrale: 20095 Hamburg, Gerhart-Hauptmann-Platz 50; tel. (40) 33330; telex 2145100; fax (40) 33332707; e-mail hamburglg@compuserve.com; internet http://www.hamburglg.de; f. 1938; cap. 781m., res 1,193m., dep. 94,070m. (Dec. 1996); Chair. WERNER SCHULZ; 4 brs.

L-Bank Landeskreditbank Baden-Württenberg: 76113 Karlsruhe, Schlossplatz 10-12; tel. (721) 1500; fax (721) 1501001; f. 1972; cap. 900m., res 3,285m., dep. 115,407m. (Dec. 1996); Chair. H. D. SAUER.

Landesbank Berlin Girozentrale: 10889 Berlin-Wilmersdorf, Bundesallee 171; tel. (30) 869801; fax (30) 8610786; f. 1818; cap. 1,651m., res 2,579m., dep. 161,177m. (Dec. 1996); Chair. Bd of Management U.-W. DECKEN.

Landesbank Hessen-Thüringen Girozentrale: 60311 Frankfurt a.M., Junghofstr. 18–26; tel. (69) 913201; telex 4152910; fax (69) 291517; cap. 819m., res 1,678m, dep. 152,176m. (Dec. 1996); Chair. WALTER SCHÄFER.

Landesbank Rheinland-Pfalz Girozentrale: 55098 Mainz, Grosse Bleiche 54–56; tel. (6131) 1301; telex 4187885; fax (6131) 132724; f. 1958; cap. 520m., res 730m., dep. 73,187m. (Dec. 1996); Chair. and CEO KLAUS G. ADAM.

Landesbank Saar Girozentrale: 66111 Saarbrücken, Ursulinenstr. 2; tel. (681) 300600; telex 17681986; fax (681) 3006202; f. 1941; cap. 120m., res 179m., dep. 15,029m. (Dec. 1995); Chair. WERNER KLUMPP.

Landesbank Schleswig-Holstein Girozentrale: 24103 Kiel, Martendsdamm 6; tel. (431) 90001; telex 292822; fax (431) 9002446; e-mail info@eb-kiel.de; f. 1917; cap. 430m., res 2,343m., dep. 95,144m. (Dec. 1996); Chair. Dr DIETRICH RÜMKER.

Norddeutsche Landesbank Girozentrale (NORD/LB): 30159 Hannover, Georgsplatz 1; tel. (511) 3610; telex 921620; fax (511) 3612502; f. 1970 by merger of several north German banks; cap. and res 5,104m., dep. 97,499m. (Dec. 1996); Chair. Dr MANFRED BODIN; 130 brs.

Südwestdeutsche Landesbank Girozentrale: 70173 Stuttgart, Am Hauptbahnhof 2; tel. (711) 1270; telex 725190; fax (711) 1273278; e-mail 106307.305@compuserve.com; f. 1916; cap. 1,307m., res 1,731m., dep. 196,257m. (Dec. 1996); Chair. WERNER SCHMIDT; Deputy Chair. Dr KARL HEIDENREICH; 14 brs.

Westdeutsche Landesbank Girozentrale: 40217 Düsseldorf, Herzogstr. 15, Postfach 1128; tel. (211) 82601; telex 8582605; fax (211) 8266119; f. 1969; cap. 2,315m., res 9,942m., dep. 431,880m. (Dec. 1996); Chair. FRIEDEL NEUBER.

Central Bank of Co-operative Banking System

DG BANK Deutsche Genossenschaftsbank: 60325 Frankfurt a.M., Am Platz der Republik; tel. (69) 744701; telex 412291; fax (69) 74471685; f. 1949; cap. and res 5,647m., dep. 299,824m. (Dec. 1996); Chair. Supervisory Bd WOLFGANG GRÜGER; Chair. Bd of Management Dr BERND THIEMANN; 39 brs.

DG BANK is a specialist wholesale bank and is the central institution in the German co-operative banking sector, which comprises 2,510 local co-operative banks, three regional central banks and a number of specialist financial institutions.

Specialist Banks

Although Germany is considered the model country for universal banking, banks which specialize in certain types of business are also extremely important. In December 1996 there were 52 specialist banks. A selection of the most prominent among these is given below:

Allgemeine Hypotheken Bank AG: 60325 Frankfurt a.M., Bockenheimer Landstr. 25, 60075 Frankfurt a.M., Postfach 170162; tel. (69) 71790; fax (69) 7179100; f. 1962; cap. 170m., res 468m., dep. 39,566m. (Dec. 1996); Pres. REINHARD WAGNER.

Bayerische Handelsbank AG: 80539 München, Von-der-Tann-Str. 2; tel. (89) 286270; fax (89) 28627304; f. 1869; cap. 82m., res 637m., dep. 39,207m. (Dec. 1996).

Berlin-Hannoversche Hypothekenbank AG: 10787 Berlin, Budapester Str. 1; tel. (30) 259990; fax (30) 25999131; f. 1995 by merger;

cap. 144m., res 1,778m., dep. 61,030m. (Dec. 1996); Chair. Supervisor Bd WOLFGANG STEINRIEDE.

Deutsche Hypothekenbank AG: 30159 Hannover, Georgsplatz 8; tel. (511) 30450; telex 921240; fax (511) 3045459; f. 1872; cap. 45m., res 350m., dep. 28,786m. (Dec. 1996); Pres. WOLFGANG STRUTZ; Man. Dirs JÜRGEN GRIEGER, WOLFGANG HOLLENDER, THOMAS Frhr VON TÜCHER; 11 brs.

Deutsche Hypothekenbank Frankfurt AG: 60065 Frankfurt a.M., Taunusanlage 9, Postfach 160265; tel. (69) 25480; fax (69) 2548113; f. 1862; cap. 121m., res 1,174m., dep. 78,286m. (Dec. 1996); Chair. BERNHARD WALTER.

Deutsche Pfandbrief- und Hypothekenbank AG: 65189 Wiesbaden, Paulinenstr. 15, 65011 Wiesbaden, Postfach 2169; tel. (611) 3480; fax (611) 3482549; f. 1922; cap. 180m., res 1,783m., dep. 130,075m. (Dec. 1996); Chair. Bd of Management Dr T. KÖPFLER.

Deutsche Postbank AG: 53113 Bonn, Friedrich-Ebert-Allee 122–126; tel. (228) 9200; fax (228) 9202818; f. 1990; cap. 800m., res 2,304m., dep. 100,936m. (Dec. 1996); Chair. Dr PETER BOENING.

Frankfurter Hypothekenbank Centralboden AG: 60311 Frankfurt a.M., Junghofstr. 5–7; tel. (69) 298980; telex 411608; fax (69) 288469; internet http://www.frankfurter-hypo.de; f. 1862; cap. 201m., res 2,086m. (Sept. 1997); Chair. Supervisory Bd Dr MICHAEL ENDRES; 24 brs.

IKB Deutsche Industriebank AG: 40474 Düsseldorf, Willhelm-Bötzkes-Str.1, 40002 Düsseldorf, Postfach 101118; tel. (211) 82210; fax (211) 82212559; internet http://www.ikb.de: f. 1949; cap. 440m., res 1,525m., dep. 41,943m. (Dec. 1997); Gen. Mans Dr E. GOTTSCHALK, J. NEUPEL, St. ORTSEIFEN, G.-J. V. PUTTKAMER, Dr A. V. TIPPELSKIRCH.

Kreditanstalt für Wiederaufbau (KFW): 60325 Frankfurt a.M., Palmengartenstr. 5-9, 60046 Frankfurt a.M., Postfach 111141; tel. (69) 74310; telex 4152560; fax (69) 74312944; f. 1948; cap. 1,000m., res 8,473m., dep. 220,392m. (Dec. 1996); Spokesman Bd of Management Dr GERT VOGT.

Lübecker Hypothekenbank AG: 23554 Lübeck, Schwartauer Allee 107-109; tel. (451) 45060; telex 26717; fax (451) 4506370; f. 1927; cap. 29m., res 362m., dep. 12,845m. (Dec. 1996); Chair. Dr ECKART VAN HOOVEN.

Münchener Hypothekenbank eG: 80036 München, Nussbaumstr. 12; tel. (89) 53870; telex 5213637; fax (89) 5387333; f. 1896; cap. 85m., res 297m., dep. 26,762m. (Dec. 1996); Chair. Dr HELMUT KAMM.

RHEINHYP Rheinische Hypothekenbank AG: 60311 Frankfurt a.M., Taunustor 3; tel. (69) 23820; telex 413203; fax (69) 2382244; f. 1871; cap. 125m., res 1,170m., dep. 74,367m. (Dec. 1996); Chair. MARTIN KOHLHAUSEN; 20 brs.

Süddeutsche Bodencreditbank AG: 80333 München, Ottostr. 21; tel. (89) 51120; telex 523554; fax (89) 5112365; f. 1871; cap. 72m., res 537m., dep. 29,190m. (Dec. 1996); Chair. Dr ALBRECHT SCHMIDT; 9 brs.

Bankers' Organizations

Bundesverband deutscher Banken (Association of German Banks): 50445 Köln, Postfach 100555; tel. (221) 16630; fax (221) 1663280; internet http://www.bdb.de; f. 1951; Pres. MARTIN KOHLHAUSEN.

Bundesverband der Deutschen Volksbanken und Raiffeisenbanken eV (Association of German Industrial and Agricultural Credit Co-operatives): 53113 Bonn, Heussallee 5, Postfach 120440; tel. (228) 5090; telex 886779; fax (228) 509201; f. 1971; Pres. WOLFGANG GRUEGER; 2,600 mems.

Bundsverband öffentlicher Banken Deutschlands eV (Association of German Public-Sector Banks): 53175 Bonn, Godesberger Allee 88; tel. (228) 81920: e-mail postmaster@voeb.de; internet http://www.voeb.de.

Deutscher Sparkassen- und Giroverband eV (German Savings Banks Association); 53113 Bonn, Simrockstr. 4, Postfach 1429; tel. (228) 2040; telex 886709; fax (228) 204250; Pres. Dr HORST KÖHLER.

STOCK EXCHANGES

Frankfurt am Main: Deutsche Börse AG, 60313 Frankfurt a.M., Börsenplatz 4; tel. (69) 21010; fax (69) 29977580; internet http://www.exchange.de; f. 1585 as Frankfurter Wertpapierbörse; 269 mems; Chair. Supervisory Bd ROLF BREUER; Chair. of Bd of Management Dr WERNER G. SEIFERT.

Berlin: Berliner Wertpapierbörse, 10623 Berlin, Fasanenstr. 85; tel. (30) 3110910; fax (30) 31109179; internet http://www.berliner boerse.de; f. 1685; 82 mems; Pres. LEOPOLD TRÖBINGER.

Bremen: Bremer Wertpapierbörse, 28195 Bremen, Obernstr. 2–12, 28007 Bremen, Postfach 100726; tel. (421) 321282; fax (421) 323123; 48 mems; Pres. HORST-GÜNTER LUCKE; Man. AXEL H. SCHUBERT.

Düsseldorf: Rheinisch-Westfälische Börse zu Düsseldorf, 40212 Düsseldorf, Ernst-Schneider-Platz 1, 40033 Düsseldorf, Postfach 104262; tel. (211) 13890; telex 8582600; fax (211) 133287; f. 1935; 110 mem. firms; Pres. HERBERT H. JACOBI; Man. WOLFGANG P. PETERHOFF.

Hamburg: Hanseatische Wertpapierbörse Hamburg, 20095 Hamburg, Schauenburgerstr. 49; tel. (40) 3613020; fax (40) 36130223; 109 mem. firms; Pres. UDO BANDOW.

Hannover: Niedersächsische Börse zu Hannover, 30159 Hannover, Rathenaustr. 2; tel. (511) 327661; fax (511) 324915; f. 1787; 81 mems; Chair. Pres. Rechtsanwalt Dr FRIEDRICH KERSTING; Chair. Dr DIRK HOFFMAN.

München: Bayerische Börse, 80333 München, Lenbachplatz 2a/1; tel. (89) 5490450; fax (89) 54904532; 101 mems; Chair. Council JOSEF F. WERTSCHULTE.

Stuttgart: Baden-Württembergische Wertpapierbörse zu Stuttgart, 70173 Stuttgart, Königstr. 28; tel. (711) 290183; fax (711) 2268119; f. 1861; 50 mems; Pres. Dr WOLFRAM FREUDENBERG; Man. Dir HANS-JOACHIM FEUERBACH.

INSURANCE

German law specifies that property and accident insurance may not be jointly underwritten with life, sickness, legal protection or credit insurance by the same company. Insurers are therefore obliged to establish separate companies to cover the different classes of insurance.

Aachener und Münchener Lebensversicherung AG: 52066 Aachen, Robert-Schuman-Str. 51; tel. (241) 600101; telex 832346; fax (241) 60015138; f. 1868; Chair. Dr WOLFGANG KASKE; Gen. Man. Dr MICHAEL KALKA.

Albingia Versicherungs-AG: 20095 Hamburg, Ballindamm 39; tel. (40) 30220; telex 2161774; fax (40) 30222585; e-mail infoa@albingia.de; internet http://www.albingia.de; f. 1901; Chair. Dr K. ASCHER; Gen. Man. V. BREMKAMP.

Allianz AG: 80802 München, Königinstr. 28, 80790 München; tel (89) 38000; fax (89) 349941; f. 1890; Chair. Supervisory Bd Dr KLAUS LIESEN; Chair. Bd of Mans Dr HENNING SCHULTE-NOELLE.

Allianz Lebensversicherungs-AG: 70178 Stuttgart, Reinsburgstr. 19; tel. (711) 6630; telex 723571; fax (711) 6632654; internet http://www.allianz-leben.de; f. 1922; Chair. Supervisory Bd Dr H. SCHULTE-NOELLE; Chair. Bd of Mans Dr G. RUPPRECHT.

Allianz Versicherungs AG: 80802 München; tel. (89) 38000; fax (89) 349941; e-mail medienzentrale@allian.de; f. 1985; Chair. Dr H. SCHULTE-NOELLE; Gen. Man. Dr R. HAGEMANN.

Colonia Krankenversicherung AG: 50592 Köln, Elsa-Brandström-Str. 10–12; tel. (221) 148125; fax (221) 14832602; f. 1962; Chair. CLAAS KLEYBOLDT. Gen. Man. Dr CARL HERMANN SCHLEIFFER.

Colonia Lebensversicherung AG: 50670 Köln, Gereonstr. 43–65, 50466 Köln, Postfach 102644; tel. (221) 148106; fax (221) 14822750; f. 1853; Chair. of Bd of Management Prof. Dr KURT WOLFSDORF.

Colonia Versicherung AG: 51067 Köln, Colonia-Allee 10–20, 51058 Köln, Postfach 805050; tel. (221) 148105; fax (221) 14822740; f. 1839; Chair. Supervisory Bd CLAAS KLEYBOLDT; Chair. Bd of Management KLAUS-DIETER LÄSSKER.

Continentale Krankenversicherung AG: 44047 Dortmund, Postfach 105032; tel. (231) 9190; telex 822515; fax (231) 9191799; f. 1926; Chair. F. LENSING-WOLFF; Gen. Man. Dr H. HOFFMANN.

Debeka Krankenversicherungsverein AG: 56058 Koblenz, Ferdinand-Sauerbruch-Str. 18; tel. (261) 4980; fax (261) 41402; f. 1905; Chair. P. KUVEPKAT; Gen. Man. P. GREISLER.

Deutsche Beamten-Lebensversicherungs-AG: 65178 Wiesbaden, Postfach 2109; tel. (611) 3630; fax (611) 363359; f. 1872; Chair. E. BOCK; Man. Dir H. FALK.

Deutsche Krankenversicherung AG: 50933 Köln, Aachener Str. 300, 50448 Köln, Postfach 100865; tel. (221) 5780; fax (221) 5783694; internet http://www.dkv.com; f. 1927; Chair. Dr HANS-JÜRGEN SCHINZLER; Gen. Man. Dr J. BOETIUS.

Deutscher Herold Lebensversicherungs-AG: 53004 Bonn, Postfach 1448; tel. (228) 26801; telex 886653; fax (228) 2683692; f. 1921; Chair. W. SOBOTA; Gen. Man. H. D. RITTERBEX.

Frankfurter Versicherungs-AG: Frankfurt a.M., Postfach 100201; tel. (69) 71261; telex 411376; fax (69) 728750; f. 1929; Chair. Dr R. HAGEMANN; Gen. Man. Dr KARL LUDWIG Frhr VON FREYBERG.

Gerling-Konzern Allgemeine Versicherungs-AG: 50448 Köln, Postfach 100808; tel. (221) 1441; telex 88110; fax (221) 1443319; f. 1918; Chair. Supervisory Bd Dr J. ZECH; Chair. Bd of Management T. REINECKE.

Gothaer Versicherungsbank Versicherungsverein AG: 50672 Köln, Kaiser-Wilhelm-Ring 23-25; tel. (221) 574600; fax (221) 5746103; f. 1820; Chair. Supervisory Bd Prof. A. W. KLEIN; Chair. Bd Management Dr WOLFGANG PEINER.

Haftpflicht-Unterstützungs-Kasse kraftfahrender Beamter Deutschlands AG in Coburg (HUK-Coburg): 96444 Coburg,

Bahnhofsplatz; tel. (9561) 960; fax (9561) 963636; internet http://www.huk.de; f. 1933; Chair. Prof. Dr E. HELTEN.

HDI Haftpflichtverband der Deutschen Industrie Versicherungsverein AG: 30633 Hannover, Postfach 510369; tel. (511) 6450; fax (511) 6454545; e-mail *21226#; f. 1903; Chair. Dr H.-J. FONK; Gen. Man. W.-D. BAUMGARTL.

Hamburg-Mannheimer Versicherungs-AG: 22297 Hamburg, Überseering 45; tel. (40) 63760; telex 2174600; fax (40) 63763302; merger with Victoria Versicherung AG pending; f. 1899; Chair. Dr H.-J. SCHINZLER; Gen. Man. D. NONHOFF.

Iduna Vereinigte Lebensversicherung AG für Handwerk, Handel und Gewerbe: 20309 Hamburg, Postfach 302761; tel. (40) 41240; f. 1914; Chair. H. BECKER; Gen. Man. G. KUTZ.

LVM-Versicherungen: 48126 Münster, Kolde-Ring 21, Postfach 6145; tel. (251) 7020; telex 892560; fax (251) 7021099; internet http://www.lvm.de; f. 1896; Chair. H. OSTROP; Gen. Man. G. KETTLER.

Nordstern Allgemeine Versicherungs-AG: 51067 Köln, Colonia-Allee 10–20, 51058 Köln, Postfach 805020; tel. (221) 148110; fax (221) 14822740; f. 1866; all classes of casualty and accident insurance in Germany and abroad; Chair. Supervisory Bd CLAAS KLEYBOLDT; Chair. Bd of Management KLAUS-DIETER LÄSSKER.

Nordstern Lebensversicherungs-AG: 50670 Köln, Gereonstr. 43–65, 50466 Köln, Postfach 102655; tel. (221) 148111; fax (221) 14822750; Chair. C. KLEYBOLDT; Gen. Man. Dr CARL HERMANN SCHLEIFER.

R+V Versicherungsgruppe: 65193 Wiesbaden, Taunusstr. 1; tel. (611) 5330; fax (611) 5334500; f. 1922; group consists of 9 cos incl. R+V Allgemeine Versicherung AG, R+V Lebensversicherung AG and R+V Krankenversicherung AG; Chair. Dr J. BRIXNER; Gen. Man. Dr J. FÖRTERER.

SIGNAL Krankenversicherung AG: 44139 Dortmund, Joseph-Scherer-Str. 44139; tel. (231) 1350; telex 822231; fax (231) 1354638; f. 1907; Chair. PAUL SCHNITKER; Gen. Man. H. FROMMKNECHT.

Vereinte Krankenversicherung AG: 81737 München, Fritz-Schäffer-Str. 9; tel. (89) 67850; telex 5215721; fax (89) 67856523; f. 1925; Chair. Dr G. RUPPRECHT; Gen. Man. Dr U. RUMM.

Victoria Versicherung AG: 40002 Düsseldorf, Postfach 101116; tel. (221) 4770; fax (211) 4772222; merger with Hamburg-Mannheimer Versicherungs-AG pending; f. 1904; Chair. Prof. Dr W. HILGER; Gen. Man. Dr E. JANNOTT.

Victoria Lebensversicherung AG: 40002 Düsseldorf, Postfach 101116; tel. (211) 4770; fax (211) 4772222; merger with Hamburg-Mannheimer Versicherungs-AG pending; f. 1929; Chair. Prof. Dr W. HILGER; Gen. Man. Dr E. JANNOTT.

Volksfürsorge Deutsche Lebensversicherung AG: 20043 Hamburg, Postfach 106420; tel. (40) 28650; telex 2112440; fax (40) 28653369; f. 1913; Chair. Dr WOLFGANG KASKE; Gen. Man. Dr H. JÄGER.

Württembergische AG Versicherungs-Beteiligungsgesellschaft; 70176 Stuttgart, Gutenbergstr. 30; tel. (711) 6620; telex 723553; fax (711) 6622520; e-mail ken@wuerttembergische.de; internet http://www. wuerttembergische.de; f. 1828; Chair. Supervisory Bd Dr G. BÜCHNER; Chair. Bd of Management G. MEHL.

Reinsurance

Bayerische Rückversicherung AG: 80538 München, Sederanger 4-6; tel. (89) 38440; telex 5215247; fax (89) 38442279; e-mail info@bayerischerueck.com; f. 1911; Chair. Dr G. BÜCHNER; Gen. Man. Dr S. LIPPE.

Deutsche Rückversicherung AG: 40476 Düsseldorf, Roßstr. 166, 40417 Düsseldorf, Postfach 320269; tel. (211) 455401; fax (211) 4554199; f. 1951; Chair. Dr G. SCHMIDT; Gen. Man. JÜRGEN REHMANN.

DARAG Deutsche Versicherungs- und Rückversicherungs-AG: 13086 Berlin, Gustav-Adolf-Str. 130, 13062 Berlin, Postfach 10; tel. (30) 477080; fax (30) 47708100; f. 1957, re-formed 1990; fire and non-life, technical, cargo transport, marine hull, liability, aviation insurance and reinsurance; Chair. KLAUS-DIETER LÄSSKER; Gen. Man. Dr INGO WELTHER.

ERC-Aachener Rückversicherungs-Gesellschaft AG: 52001 Aachen, Postfach 25; tel. (241) 93690; fax (241) 9369205; f. 1853; Chair. Supervisory Bd KAJ AHLMANN; Chair. Management Bd BERNHARD C. FINK.

ERC-Frankona Rückversicherungs-AG: 81675 München, Maria-Theresia-Str. 35, 81630 München, Postfach 860380; tel. (89) 92280; fax (89) 9228395; f. 1886; Chair. A. AHLMANN; Gen. Man. BERNARD C. FINK.

Gerling-Konzern Globale Rückversicherungs-AG: 50597 Köln, Postfach 101544; tel. (221) 1441; telex 88110; fax (221) 1443718; f. 1954; Chair. A. KRACHT; Gen. Man. N. STROHSCHEN.

Hamburger Internationale Rückversicherung AG: 25462 Rellingen, Halstenbekerweg 96A, 25452 Rellingen, Postfach 1161; tel. (4101) 4710; fax (4101) 471298; f. 1965; Chair. IVOR KIVERSTEIN; Gen. Man. R. SOLL.

Hannover Rückversicherungs-AG: 30625 Hannover, Karl-Wiechert-Allee 50, 30603 Hannover, Postfach 610369; tel. (511) 56040; telex 922599; fax (511) 5604188; f. 1966; Chair. Supervisory Bd W. BAUMGARTL; Chair. Management Bd W. ZELLER.

Kölnische Rückversicherungs-Gesellschaft AG: 50668 Köln, Theodor-Heuss-Ring 11, 50462 Köln, Postfach 102244; tel. (221) 97380; fax (221) 9738494; internet http://www.colognere.com; f. 1846; Chair. PETER LÜTKE-BORNEFELD.

Münchener Rückversicherungs-Gesellschaft AG: 80791 München; 80802 München, Königinstr. 107; tel. (89) 38910; telex 52152330; fax (89) 399056; internet http://www.munichre.com; f. 1880; all classes of reinsurance; Chair. ULRICH HARTMANN; Gen. Man. Dr HANS-JÜRGEN SCHINZLER.

R + V Versicherung-AG Reinsurance: 65193 Wiesbaden, Sonnenberger Str. 44; tel. (611) 533940; fax (611) 529610; f. 1935; all classes of reinsurance; Chair. W. GRÜGER; Gen. Man. Dr J. FÖRTERER.

Principal Insurance Association

Gesamtverband der Deutschen Versicherungswirtschaft eV: 10117 Berlin, Friedrichstr. 191-193; tel. (30) 20205000; fax (30) 20206000; f. 1948; affiliating one mem. asscn and 479 mem. cos; Pres. Dr BERND MICHAELS (Düsseldorf).

Trade and Industry

GOVERNMENT AGENCIES

Arbeitsgemeinschaft Aussenhandel der Deutschen Wirtschaft: 50968 Köln, Gustav-Heinemann-Ufer 84–88, 50941 Köln, Postfach 510548; tel. (221) 37080; telex 8882601; fax (221) 3708-730; Dir STEFAN WINTER.

Bundesstelle für Aussenhandelsinformation (Federal Foreign Trade Information Office): 50676 Köln, Agrippastr. 87-93, 50445 Köln, Postfach 100522; tel. (221) 20570; telex 8882735; fax (221) 2057-212; and Aussenstelle Berlin, Scharnhorststr. 36, 10115 Berlin; tel. (30) 2014-5201; fax (30) 2014-5204.

Bundesverband des Deutschen Gross- und Aussenhandels eV: 53113 Bonn, Bonner Talweg 57, 53003 Bonn, Postfach 1349; tel. (228) 260040; fax (228) 2600455; f. 1949; Dir-Gen. Dr PETER SPARY; 77 mem. asscns.

Hauptverband des Deutschen Einzelhandels eV: 50969 Köln, Gothaer Allee 2, 50520 Köln, Postfach 250425; tel. (221) 9365502; fax (221) 93655909; f. 1947; Chair. HERMANN FRANZEN; Exec. Dir HOLGER WENZEL.

Zentralverband Gewerblicher Verbundgruppen: 53119 Bonn, Vorgebirgsstr. 43; tel. (228) 985840; fax (228) 9858410; f. 1992; six dirs; c. 400 mems.

CHAMBERS OF COMMERCE

Deutscher Industrie- und Handelstag (Association of German Chambers of Industry and Commerce): 53113 Bonn, Adenauerallee 148; tel. (228) 1040; telex 886805; fax (228) 104158; Pres. Dipl. Ing. HANS PETER STIHL; Sec.-Gen. Dr FRANZ SCHOSER; affiliates 83 Chambers of Industry and Commerce.

There are Chambers of Industry and Commerce in all the principal towns and also fourteen regional associations including:

Arbeitsgemeinschaft Hessischer Industrie- und Handelskammern: 60313 Frankfurt a.M., Börsenplatz 4; tel. (69) 21970; telex 411255; fax (69) 2197424; Chair. Dr FRANK NIETHAMMER; Sec.-Gen. Dr WOLFGANG LINDSTAEDT; 12 mems.

Arbeitsgemeinschaft der Industrie- und Handelskammern in Mecklenburg-Vorpommern: 19053 Schwerin, Schlossstr. 17; tel. (385) 51030; fax (385) 5103136; e-mail info@schwerin.ihk.de; Pres. HANSHEINRICH LIESBERG.

Arbeitsgemeinschaft der Industrie- und Handelskammern Rheinland-Pfalz: 67059 Ludwigshafen, Ludwigsplatz 2-4, 67007 Ludwigshafen, Postfach 210744; tel. (621) 59040; fax (621) 5904288; Sec. Dr ANDREAS HERTING; four mems.

Arbeitsgemeinschaft der Industrie- und Handelskammern in Sachsen: 01241 Dresden, Niedersedlitzerstr. 63; tel. (351) 28020; fax (351) 2802280.

Arbeitsgemeinschaft Norddeutscher Industrie- und Handelskammern: 20457 Hamburg, Adolphsplatzl; tel. (40) 366382; Vice-Pres. Dr MARTIN WILLICH; Sec. Dr UWE CHRISTIANSEN.

Arbeitsgemeinschaft der Thuringer Industrie- und Handelskammern: 99099 Erfurt, Weimarische Str. 45; tel. (361) 34840; fax (361) 3484299; f. 1991; Pres. NIELS LUND CHRESTENSEN.

Baden-Württembergischer Industrie-und Handelskammertag: 70174 Stuttgart, Jägerstr. 30, 70020 Stuttgart, Postfach

102444; tel. (711) 20050; fax (711) 2005586; e-mail ihktbawü@stuttgart.ihk.de; Chair. HANS PETER STIHL.

Bayerischer Industrie- und Handelskammern: 80333 München, Max-Joseph-Str. 2; tel. (89) 51160; telex 523678; fax (89) 5116306; Pres. Dr-Ing. DIETER SOLTMANN; Sec. Gen. Dr REINHOLD DÖRFLER; 10 mems.

IHK-Vereinigung Schleswig-Holstein: 24103 Kiel, Lorentzendamm 24; tel. (431) 51940; fax (431) 5194231; e-mail ihk@kiel.ihk.de; Chair. Konsul Dr FRITZ SÜVERKRÜP; Sec. Ass. WOLF-RÜDIGER JANZEN; three mems.

Industrie- und Handelskammern Magdeburg: 39104 Magdeburg, Alter Markt 8, Postfach 1840; tel. (391) 56930; fax (391) 344391; f. 1825; Pres. Dr KLAUS HIECKMAN.

Industrie- und Handelskammern Potsdam: 14469 Potsdam, Grosse Weinmeisterstr. 59; tel. (331) 27860; fax (331) 2786111; e-mail ulmannpotsdam.ihk.de/potsdam; internet http://www.ihk.de/potsdam; f. 1990; Pres. Dr VICTOR STIMMING; CEO PETER EGENTER.

Vereinigung der Industrie- und Handelskammern in Nordrhein-Westfalen: 4000 Düsseldorf 1, Postfach 240120; tel. (211) 352091; telex 8582363; fax (211) 161072; Chair. Dr AENGENEYNDT; 16 mems.

Vereinigung der Niedersächsischen Industrie- und Handelskammern: 30175 Hannover, Schiffgraben 49, 30030 Hannover, Postfach 3029; tel. (511) 3107289; telex 922769; fax (511) 3107383; f. 1899; Pres. Dr KLAUS SCHUBERTH; Man. Dir Dr WILFRIED PREWO; seven mems.

INDUSTRIAL AND TRADE ASSOCIATIONS

Bundesverband der Deutschen Industrie eV (Federation of German Industry): 50968 Köln, Gustav-Heinemann-Ufer 84–88; tel. (221) 3708565; fax (221) 3708650; e-mail presse@bdi-online.de; Pres. HANS-OLAF HENKEL; Dir-Gen. Dr LUDOLF VON WARTENBERG; mems include some of the following asscns:

Arbeitsgemeinschaft Keramische Industrie eV (Ceramics): 95100 Selb, Schillerstr. 17, 95090 Selb, Postfach 1624; tel. (9287) 80844; fax (9287) 70492; Pres. WOLFGANG H. MOLITOR; Man. PETER FRISCHHOLZ.

Bundesverband Bekleidungsindustrie eV (Clothing): 50668 Köln, Mevissenstr. 15, 50449 Köln, Postfach 100955; tel. (221) 7744110; fax (221) 7744118; Pres. Dr FRITZ GOOST; Dirs-Gen. RAINER MAUER, FRIEDHELM N. SARTORIS.

Bundesverband der Deutschen Entsorgungswirtschaft (BDE) (Waste Disposal): 50968 Köln, Schönhauser Str. 3; tel. (221) 9347000; fax (221) 93470090; e-mail info@bde.org; internet http://www.bde.org; Pres. GERHARD SCHEELE; Dir-Gen. FRANK-RAINER BILLIGMANN.

Bundesverband der Deutschen Luft- und Raumfahrtindustrie eV (BDLI) (German Aerospace Industries Asscn): 53179 Bonn, Konstantinstr. 90; tel. (228) 849070; fax (228) 330778; internet http://www.bdli.de; f. 1952; Pres. Dr MANFRED BISCHOFF; Man. Dir Dr HANS EBERHARD BIRKE.

Bundesverband Druck eV (Printing): 65187 Wiesbaden, Biebricher Allee 79, 65008 Wiesbaden, Postfach 1869; tel. (611) 8030; fax (611) 803113; e-mail info@bvd-online.de; f. 1947; Pres. ALEXANDER SCHORSCH; Man. Dir Dr WALTER HESSE; 12 mem. asscns.

Bundesverband Glasindustrie und Mineralfaserindustrie eV (Glass): 40210 Düsseldorf, Stresemannstr. 26, 40008 Düsseldorf, Postfach 101753; tel. (211) 168940; fax (211) 1689427; Chair. KLAUS PETER RAMBOW; 6 mem. asscns.

Bundesverband Steine und Erden eV (Building): 60325 Frankfurt a.M., Friedrich-Ebert-Anlage 38, 60061 Frankfurt a.M., Postfach 150162; tel. (69) 7560820; fax (69) 75608212; f. 1948; Pres. Dr JÜRGEN LOSE; Chief Dir Dr WOLFGANG MACK.

Bundesvereinigung der Deutschen Ernährungsindustrie eV (Food): 53175 Bonn, Winkelsweg 2; tel. (228) 373041; fax (228) 376176; f. 1949; Chair. Dr PETER TRAUMANN; Chief Gen. Man. Dr MATTHIAS HORST; 33 branch-organizations.

Deutscher Giessereiverband (Foundries): 40237 Düsseldorf, Sohnstr. 70, 40100 Düsseldorf, Postfach 101961; tel. (211) 68710; fax (211) 6871333; e-mail dgvguss@t-online.de; internet http://www.dgv.de; Pres. HELMUT CHRISTMANN; Man. Dir Dr KLAUS URBAT.

Deutscher Hotel- und Gaststättenverband eV: 53173 Bonn, Kronprinzenstr. 46; tel. (228) 820080; fax (228) 8200846; f. 1949; Pres. Dr ERICH KAUB; Gen. Sec. CHRISTIAN EHLERS; over 95,000 mems.

Deutsche Verbundgesellschaft eV (Electricity): 69120 Heidelberg, Ziegelhäuser Landstr. 5; tel. (6221) 40370; fax (6221) 4037-71; Pres. Prof. Dr ERNST HAGENMEYER; Dir-Gen. Dr JÜRGEN SCHWARZ.

EBM Wirtschaftsverband (Metal Goods): 40474 Düsseldorf, Kaiserswerther Str. 135, 40427 Düsseldorf, Postfach 321230; tel. (211) 454930; fax (211) 4549369; Pres. GÜNTER BECKER; Gen. Man. ULRICH BÖSHAGEN.

Gemeinschaftsausschuss der Deutschen gewerblichen Wirtschaft (Joint Committee for German Industry and Commerce): 5000 Köln 51, Gustav-Heinemann-Ufer 84–88; tel. (221) 370800; fax (221) 3708730; f. 1950; a discussion forum for the principal industrial and commercial orgs; Pres. Dr TYLL NECKER; 16 mem. orgs, including:

Gesamtverband kunststoffverarbeitende Industrie eV (GKV) (Plastics): 60329 Frankfurt a.M., Am Hauptbahnhof 12; tel. (69) 271050; fax (69) 232799; f. 1949; Chair. NORBERT WAGNER; Sec.-Gen. JOACHIM TEN HAGEN; 950 mems.

Gesamtverband der Textilindustrie in der BRD (Gesamttextil) eV (Textiles): 65760 Eschborn, Frankfurter Str. 10–14, 65728 Eschborn, Postfach 5340; tel. (6196) 9660; fax (6196) 42170; internet http://www.gesamttextil.de; Dir-Gen. Dr WOLF R. BAUMANN.

Hauptverband der Deutschen Bauindustrie eV (Building): 65189 Wiesbaden, Abraham-Lincoln-Str. 30, 65019 Wiesbaden, Postfach 2966; tel. (611) 7720; fax (611) 772240; f. 1948; Pres. Dr OTHMAR FRANZ; Dir-Gen. MICHAEL KNIPPER; 23 mem. asscns.

Hauptverband der Deutschen Holz und Kunststoffe verarbeitenden Industrie und verwandter Industriezweige eV (HDH) (Woodwork): 53604 Bad-Honnef, Flutgraben 2; tel (2224) 93770; fax (2224) 937777; f. 1948; Pres. Dr H. OLAF GLUNZ; Man. Dir DIRK-UWE KLAAS; 30 mem. asscns.

Hauptverband der Papier, Pappe und Kunststoffe verarbeitenden Industrie eV (HPV) (Paper, Board and Plastic): 60489 Frankfurt a.M., Strubbergstr. 70; tel. (69) 9782810; fax (69) 97828130; f. 1948; 10 regional groups, 20 production groups; Pres. LUTZ BOEDER; Dir-Gen. Dr HORST KOHL; 1,300 mems.

Mineralölwirtschaftsverband eV (Petroleum): 20099 Hamburg, Steindamm 55; tel. (40) 248490; fax (40) 24849-253; e-mail mwv@mwv.de; f. 1946; Chair. WINFRIED P. VOGLER; Man. Dir Dr PETER SCHLÜTER.

Verband der Automobilindustrie eV (Motor Cars): 60325 Frankfurt a.M., Westendstr. 61, 60079 Frankfurt a.M., Postfach 170563; tel. (69) 975070; fax (69) 97507261; Pres. Dr BERND GOTTSCHALK.

Verband der Chemischen Industrie eV (Chemical Industry): 60329 Frankfurt a.M., Karlstr. 21; tel. (69) 25560; fax (69) 2556-1471; f. 1877; Pres. Dr JÜRGEN STRUBE; Dir-Gen. Dr WILFRIED SAHM; 1,500 mems.

Verband der Cigarettenindustrie (Cigarettes): 53227 Bonn, Königswinterer Str. 550; tel. (228) 449060; fax (228) 442582; Chair. LUDGER W. STABY; Dir-Gen. Dr ERNST BRÜCKNER.

Verband der Deutschen Feinmechanischen und Optischen Industrie eV (Optical and Precision Instruments): 50858 Köln, Kirchweg 2; tel. (221) 9486280; fax (221) 483428; f. 1949; Chair. RANDOLF RODENSTOCK; Dir HARALD RUSSEGGER.

Verband der Deutschen Schmuck- und Silberwarenindustrie: 75172 Pforzheim, Poststr. 1; tel. (7231) 33041; fax (7231) 355887; Pres. CARL-HEINRICH LÜTH; Man. Dir Dr ALFRED SCHNEIDER.

Verband Deutscher Maschinen- und Anlagenbau eV (VDMA) (Machinery and Plant Manufacture): 60528 Frankfurt a.M., Lyoner Str. 18, 60498 Frankfurt a.M., Postfach 710864; tel. (69) 66030; fax (69) 66031511; f. 1892; Pres. Dr MICHAEL ROGOWSKI; Gen. Man. Dr HANS-JÜRGEN ZECHLIN.

Verband Deutscher Papierfabriken eV (Paper): 53113 Bonn, Adenauerallee 55; tel. (228) 267050; fax (228) 2670562; Pres. HANS-MICHAEL GELLENKAMP; Dir-Gen. Dr PETER OTZEN.

Verband für Schiffbau und Meerestechnik eV (Shipbuilding): 20099 Hamburg, An der Alster 1; tel. (40) 246205; fax (40) 246287; e-mail vsm.e.v.@t-online.de; Pres. Dr HEINZ ACHE.

Verein der Zuckerindustrie (Sugar): 53115 Bonn, Am Hofgarten 8; tel. (228) 22850; fax (228) 2285100; f. 1850; Chair. Dr KLAUS KORN; Dir-Gen. Dr DIETER LANGENDORF.

Wirtschaftsverband der Deutschen Kautschukindustrie eV (W.d.K.) (Rubber): 60487 Frankfurt a.M., Zeppelinallee 69; tel. (69) 79360; fax (69) 7936150; f. 1894; Pres. Dr HAVERBECK; Gen. Man. KLAUS MOCKER; 92 mems.

Wirtschaftsverband Erdöl- und Erdgasgewinnung eV (Association of Crude Oil and Gas Producers): 30169 Hannover, Brühlstr. 9; tel. (511) 121720; fax (511) 1217210; e-mail weg@hannover@t-online.de; f. 1945; Pres. Dr KARL HEINZ GEISEL; Gen. Man. LOTHAR MÖLLER.

Wirtschaftsverband Stahlbau und Energietechnik (SET) (Steel and Energy): 40479 Düsseldorf, Sternstr. 36, 40419 Düsseldorf, Postfach 320420; tel. (211) 498700; fax (211) 4987036; Chair. S. MICHELFELDER; Dir-Gen. Dipl.-Ing. A. SCHUMACHER.

Wirtschaftsverband Stahlumformung eV (Steelworks): 58093 Hagen, Goldene Pforte 1, 58040 Hagen, Postfach 4009; tel. (2331) 9588-0; fax (2331) 51046; Pres. JÜRGEN R. THUMANN; Dir-Gen. Dipl.-Phys. HANS-DIETER OELKERS.

Centralvereinigung Deutscher Wirtschaftsverbände für Handelsvermittlung und Vertrieb: 50931 Köln, Geleniusstr. 1; tel. (221) 514043; fax (221) 525767; e-mail cdh.centralvereinigung@

t-online.de; internet http://www.cdh.de; Pres. ALBERT KLOCKMANN; Gen. Sec. Dr ANDREAS PAFFHAUSEN; 20,000 mems in all brs.

Wirtschaftsvereinigung Bergbau eV (Mining): 53113 Bonn, Zitelmannstr. 9–11, 53044 Bonn, Postfach 120280; tel. (228) 540020; fax (228) 5400235; Pres. FRIEDRICH H. ESSER; Gen. Man. KARL-ERNST KEGEL; 18 mem. asscns.

Wirtschaftsvereinigung Metalle eV (Metal): 40474 Düsseldorf, Am Bonneshof 5, 40045 Düsseldorf, Postfach 105463; tel. (211) 47960; fax (211) 4796400; e-mail wvmetalle@compuserve.com; Pres. JOCHEN SCHIRNER; Dir-Gen. JÜRGEN ULMER.

Wirtschaftsvereinigung Stahl (Steel): 40213 Düsseldorf, Breite Str. 69, 40045 Düsseldorf, Postfach 105464; tel. (211) 8290; fax (211) 829231; e-mail brüninghaus@stahl-online.de; Pres. Dr RUPRECHT VONDRAN; Dirs ALBRECHT KORMANN, GEORG MÜLLER.

Wirtschaftsvereinigung Ziehereien und Kaltwalzwerke eV (Metal): 40474 Düsseldorf, Drahthaus, Kaiserswerther Str. 137; tel. (211) 4564246; fax (211) 432154; Chair. JÜRGEN R. THUMANN; Gen. Man. GÜNTER MÜLLER.

Zentralverband des Deutschen Handwerks: 53113 Bonn, Haus des Deutschen Handwerks, Johanniterstr. 1; tel. (228) 5450; fax (228) 545205; f. 1949; Pres. HERIBERT SPÄTH; Gen. Sec. HANNS-EBERHARD SCHLEYER; 56 mem. chambers, 52 asscns.

Zentralverband Elektrotechnik- und Elektronikindustrie e V (ZVEI) (Electrical and Electronic Equipment): 60596 Frankfurt a.M., Stresemannallee 19, 60591 Frankfurt a.M., Postfach 701261; tel. (69) 63020; fax (69) 6302317; e-mail zvei@zvei.org; f. 1918; Chair. Dr VOLKER JUNG; Dirs Dr FRANZ-JOSEF WISSING, NORBERT KNAUP, INGO RÜSCH, Dr WERNER SCHMIDT; 1,300 mems.

EMPLOYERS' ORGANIZATION

Bundesvereinigung der Deutschen Arbeitgeberverbände (Confederation of German Employers' Associations): 50968 Köln, Postfach 510508; tel. (221) 37950; telex 8881466; fax (221) 3795-235; f. 1913; Pres. Dr DIETER HUNDT; Dirs Dr REINHARD GÖHNER, JÜRGEN HUSMANN, Dr JOSEF SIEGERS, Dr ROLF THÜSING; represents the professional and regional interests of German employers in the social policy field, affiliates 15 regional asscns, and 46 trade asscns, of which some are listed under industrial asscns (see above).

Affiliated associations:

Arbeitgeberkreis Gesamttextil im Gesamtverband der Textilindustrie in der Bundesrepublik Deutschland eV (General Textile Employers' Organization): 65760 Eschborn, Frankfurter Strasse 10–14; tel. (6196) 9660; fax (6196) 42170; Chair. LEOPOLD SCHOELLER; Dir Dr KLAUS SCHMIDT; 9 mem. asscns.

Arbeitgeberverband der Cigarettenindustrie (Employers' Association of Cigarette Manufacturers): 20149 Hamburg, Harvestehuder Weg 88; tel. (40) 445739; fax (40) 443039; f. 1949; Pres. Dr DORIS ANDRÉ; Dir LUTZ SANNIG.

Arbeitgeberverband der Deutschen Binnenschiffahrt eV (Employers' Association of German Inland Waterway Transport): 47119 Duisburg, Dammstr. 15–17; tel. (203) 8000631; fax (203) 8000621; Pres. Dr WOLFGANG HÖNEMANN; Dir G. DÜTEMEYER.

Arbeitgeberverband Deutscher Eisenbahnen eV (German Railway Employers' Association): 50677 Köln, Volksgartenstr. 54A; tel. (221) 9318450; fax (221) 93184588; Pres. KLAUS-DIETER BOLLHÖFER; Dir Dr HANS-PETER ACKMANN.

Arbeitgeberverband des Privaten Bankgewerbes eV (Private Banking Employers' Association): 50667 Köln, Andreaskloster 27-31; tel. (221) 131024; f. 1954; 164 mems; Pres. Dr HORST MÜLLER; Dir Dr KLAUS DUTTI.

Arbeitgeberverband der Versicherungsunternehmen in Deutschland (Employers' Association of Insurance Companies): 81925 München, Arabellastr. 29; tel. (89) 9220010; fax (89) 92200150; Pres. HANS SCHREIBER; Dir-Gen. Dr JÖRG MULLER-STEIN.

Bundesarbeitgeberverband Chemie eV (Federation of Employers' Associations in the Chemical Industry): 65189 Wiesbaden, Abraham-Lincoln-Str. 24, Postfach 1280; tel. (611) 778810; fax (611) 719010; Pres. PAUL COENEN; Dir HANS PAUL FREY; 13 mem. asscns.

Bundesvereinigung der Arbeitgeber im Bundesverband Bekleidungsindustrie eV (Confederation of Employers of the Clothing Industry): 50668 Köln, Mevissenstr. 15, 50449 Köln, Postfach 100955; tel. (221) 7744110; fax (221) 7744118; Pres. WILFRIED BRANDES; Dir RAINER MAUER; 12 mem. asscns.

Gesamtverband der Deutschen Land- und Forstwirtschaftlichen Arbeitgeberverbände eV (Federation of Agricultural and Forestry Employers' Associations): 53175 Bonn, Godesberger Allee 142–148; tel. (228) 8198248; fax (228) 8198204; Pres. WOLF VON BUCHWALDT; Sec. Dipl.-Volksw. Dipl.-Landw. MARTIN MALLACH.

Gesamtverband der metallindustriellen Arbeitgeberverbände eV (Federation of the Metal Trades Employers' Associations): 50677 Köln, Volksgartenstr. 54A; tel. (221) 33990; telex 8882583; fax (221) 3399233; e-mail info@gesamtmetall.de; Pres. Dr WERNER STUMPFE; 15 mem. asscns.

Vereinigung der Arbeitgeberverbände der Deutschen Papierindustrie eV (Federation of Employers' Associations of the German Paper Industry): 53113 Bonn, Adenauerallee 55; tel. (228) 2672810; fax (228) 215270; Pres. HEINRICH AUGUST SCHOELLER; Dir Ass. PETER KARTHÄUSER; 8 mem. asscns.

Vereinigung der Arbeitgeberverbände energie- und versorgungswirtschaftlicher Unternehmungen (Employers' Federation of Energy and Power Supply Enterprises): 30159 Hannover, Kurt Schumacher-Str. 24; tel. (511) 911090; fax (511) 9110940; f. 1962; Pres. Dr ULF LANGE; Dir GERHARD M. MEYER; 7 mem. asscns.

Regional employers' associations:

Landesvereinigung Baden-Württembergischer Arbeitgeberverbände eV: 70597 Stuttgart, Löffelstr. 22–24, 70574 Stuttgart, Postfach 700501; tel. (711) 76820; telex 723651; fax (711) 7651675; Pres. Dr DIETER HUNDT; Dir Dr ULRICH BROCKER; 44 mem. asscns.

Vereinigung der Arbeitgeberverbände in Bayern (Federation of Employers' Associations in Bavaria): 80333 München, Brienner Str. 7, 80200 München, Postfach 202061; tel. (89) 29079-0; fax (89) 222851; f. 1949; Pres. HUBERT STÄRKER; Dir KARL BAYER; 78 mem. asscns.

Vereinigung der Unternehmensverbände in Berlin und Brandenburg eV (Federation of Employers' Associations in Berlin and Brandenburg): 10625 Berlin, Am Schillertheater 2; tel. (30) 310050; fax (30) 31005120; Pres. ERICH GERARD; Dir Dr HARTMANN KLEINER; 70 mem. asscns.

Vereinigung der Unternehmensverbände im Lande Bremen eV (Federation of Employers' Associations in the Land of Bremen): 28195 Bremen, Schillerstr. 10; tel. (421) 368020; fax (421) 3680249; Pres. Dr MANFRED AHLSDORFF; Dir EBERHARD SCHODDE; 16 mem. asscns.

Landesvereinigung der Unternehmensverbände in Hamburg eV (Federation of Employers' Associations in Hamburg): 20148 Hamburg, Feldbrunnenstr. 56; tel. (40) 4140120; fax (40) 418004; Pres. Dr HELLMUT KRUSE; Gen. Man. JÜRGEN MEINEKE; 30 mem. asscns.

Vereinigung der Hessischen Unternehmerverbände eV (Federation of Employers' Associations in Hesse): 60439 Frankfurt a.M., Emil-von-Behring-Str. 4; tel. (69) 958080; fax (69) 95808126; f. 1947; Pres. Prof. DIETER WEIDEMANN; Dir and Sec. VOLKER FASBENDER; 50 mem. asscns.

Vereinigung der Unternehmensverbände für Mecklenburg-Vorpommern e.V. (Federation of Employers' Associations of Mecklenburg-West Pomerania): 19061 Schwerin, Eckdrift 93; tel. (385) 6356100; fax (385) 6356151; Pres. KLAUS HERING; Dir Dr THOMAS KLISCHAN; 22 mem. asscns.

Unternehmensverbände Niedersachsen eV (Federation of Employers' Associations in Lower Saxony): 30175 Hannover, Schiffgraben 36; tel. (511) 85050; telex 929912; fax (511) 8505268; Pres. Dr KURT EIGLMEIER; Dir GERNOT PREUSS; 60 mem. asscns.

Landesvereinigung der Arbeitgeberverbände Nordrhein-Westfalen eV (North Rhine-Westphalia Federation of Employers' Associations): 40474 Düsseldorf, Uerdingerstr. 58–62, 40406 Düsseldorf, Postfach 300643; tel. (211) 45730; fax (211) 4573209; Pres. Dr Ing. JOCHEN F. KIRCHHOFF; Dir Dr HANSJÖRG DÖPP; 82 mem. asscns.

Landesvereinigung Rheinland-Pfälzischer Unternehmerverbände eV (Federation of Employers' Associations in the Rhineland Palatinate): 55131 Mainz, Hölderlinstr. 1; tel. (6131) 5575-0; fax (6131) 557539; f. 1963; Pres. Dr EBERHARD SCHWARZ; Man. Dr CHRISTOPH STOLLENWERK; 14 mem. asscns.

Vereinigung der Saarländischen Unternehmensverbände (Federation of Employers' Associations in Saarland): 66119 Saarbrücken, Harthweg 15; tel. (681) 954340; telex 4421229; fax (681) 5847386; Pres. Dr WALTER KOCH; Dir Dr HEIKO JÜTTE; 19 mem. asscns.

Vereinigung der Arbeitgeberverbände in Sachsen e.V. (VAS) (Federation of Employers' Associations in Saxony): 01277 Dresden, Karcherallee 25A; tel. (351) 255930; fax (351) 2559378; Pres. HELMUT SEIDENSCHNUR; Dir RUDOLF W. BÜRGER; 26 mem. asscns.

Landesvereinigung der Arbeitgeber-und-Wirtschaftsverbände Sachsen-Anhalt e.V. (Provincial Federation of Employers' and Managers' Associations of Saxony-Anhalt): 39017 Magdeburg, Postfach 4249; tel. (391) 625450; fax (391) 6254570; Pres. Dr ROLF BROSE; Dir Dr JOCHEN STEINECKE; 18 mem. asscns.

Vereinigung der Schleswig-Holsteinischen Unternehmensverbände eV (Federation of Employers' Associations in Schleswig-Holstein): 24768 Rendsburg, Adolf-Steckel-Str. 17; tel. (4331) 14200; fax (4331) 142020; Pres. Prof. Dr HANS HEINRICH DRIFTMANN; Dir JÜRGEN MEINEKE; 36 mem. asscns.

Verband der Wirtschaft Thüringens e.V. (Association of Thuringian Management): 99094 Erfurt, Lossiusstr. 1, 99007 Erfurt, Postfach 329; tel. (361) 67590; fax (361) 6759222; Pres. Dipl. Ing. WALTER BOTSCHATZKI; Dir LOTAR SCHMIDT; 37 mem. asscns.

TRADE UNIONS

Following German unification in October 1990, the trade unions of the former GDR were absorbed into the member unions of the DGB (see below).

Deutscher Gewerkschaftsbund (DGB): 40476 Düsseldorf, Hans-Böckler-Str. 39, 40001 Düsseldorf, Postfach 101026; tel. (211) 43010; telex 8584822; fax (211) 4301471; f. 1949; Pres. DIETER SCHULTE; Vice-Pres. URSULA ENGELEN-KEFER.

The following unions, with a total of 8,972,672 members (December 1996), are affiliated to the DGB:

Industriegewerkschaft Bauen-Agrar-Umwelt (Building and Construction Trade): 60439 Frankfurt a.M., Olof-Palme-Str. 19; tel. (69) 957370; fax (69) 95737800; e-mail presse@igbau.de; Pres. KLAUS WIESEHÜGEL; 649,612 mems (Oct. 1995).

Industriegewerkschaft Bergbau und Energie (Mining and Energy): 44789 Bochum, Alte Hattingerstr. 19; tel. (49) 3190; telex 825809; fax (49) 319514; f. 1889; Pres. HANS BERGER; 390,000 mems (Dec. 1995).

Industriegewerkschaft Chemie- Papier- Keramik (Chemical, Paper and Ceramics): 30030 Hannover, Postfach 3047; tel. (511) 76310; fax (511) 7631713; Pres. HUBERTUS SCHMOLDT; 694,000 mems (Dec. 1996).

Gewerkschaft der Eisenbahner Deutschlands (Railwaymen): 60325 Frankfurt a.M., Beethovenstr. 12–16; tel. (69) 7536390; fax (69) 7536222; Pres. RUDI SCHÄFER; 423,163 mems (Dec. 1994).

Gewerkschaft Erziehung und Wissenschaft (Education and Sciences): 60489 Frankfurt a.M., Reifenbergerstr. 21; tel. (69) 78973-0; telex 412989; fax (69) 78973201; Pres. Dr DIETER WUNDER; 316,196 mems (Dec. 1994).

Gewerkschaft Handel, Banken und Versicherungen (Commerce, Banks and Insurance): 40472 Düsseldorf, Kanzlerstr. 8; tel. (211) 90400; fax (211) 9040888; f. 1973; Pres. MARGRET MÖNIG-RAANE; 500,000 mems (Dec. 1996).

Gewerkschaft Holz und Kunststoff (Wood and Plastic-work): 40227 Düsseldorf, Sonnenstr. 10; tel. (211) 77030; fax (211) 7703201; e-mail 106443.1070@compuserve.com; f. 1945; Pres. GISBERT SCHLEMMER; 160,000 mems (Dec. 1996).

Gewerkschaft Leder (Leather): 70174 Stuttgart, Willi-Bleicher-Str. 20; tel. (711) 295555; fax (711) 293345; Pres. WERNER DICK; 25,000 mems (Dec. 1994).

Industriegewerkschaft Medien (Media): 70174 Stuttgart, Friedrichstr. 15, 70020 Stuttgart, Postfach 102451; tel. (711) 20180; fax (711) 2018282; Pres. DETLEV HENSCHE; 215,155 mems. (Dec. 1994).

Industriegewerkschaft Metall (Metal Workers' Union): 60519 Frankfurt a.M., Lyoner Str. 32; tel. (69) 66930; telex 411115; fax (69) 66932843; Chair. KLAUS ZWICKEL; 2,752,226 mems (Dec. 1996).

Gewerkschaft Nahrung-Genuss-Gaststätten (Food, Delicacies and Catering): 22765 Hamburg, Haubachstr. 76; tel. (40) 380130; fax (40) 3892637; f. 1949; Pres. FRANZ-JOSEF MÖLLENBERG; 325,000 mems (Oct. 1995).

Gewerkschaft Öffentliche Dienste, Transport und Verkehr (Public Services and Transport Workers' Union): 70174 Stuttgart, Theodor-Heuss-Str. 2; tel. (711) 20970; fax (711) 2097462; Chair. HERBERT MAI; 1,650,000 mems (Dec. 1997).

Gewerkschaft der Polizei (Police Union): 40721 Hilden, Forststr. 3A; tel. (211) 71040; telex 8581968; fax (211) 7104222; f. 1950; Chair. HERMANN LUTZ; Sec. W. DICKE; 197,482 mems (Dec. 1994).

Deutsche Postgewerkschaft (Post and Telecommunications Union): 60528 Frankfurt a.M., Rhonestr. 2; tel. (69) 66950; telex 412112; fax (69) 666941; internet http://www.dpg-hv.de; Pres. KURT VAN HAAREN; 492,000 mems (Oct. 1995).

Gewerkschaft Textil-Bekleidung (Textiles and Clothing): 40476 Düsseldorf, Ross Str. 94; tel. (211) 43090; fax (211) 4309505; Pres. WILLI ARENS; 234,240 mems (Dec. 1994).

The following are the largest unions outside the DGB:

Deutsche Angestellten-Gewerkschaft (DAG) (Clerical, Technical and Administrative Workers): 20355 Hamburg, Karl-Muck-Platz 1; tel. (40) 3491501; telex 211642; fax (40) 34915400; f. 1945; Chair. ROLAND ISSEN; 501,009 mems (1996).

Deutscher Beamtenbund (Federation of Civil Servants): 53175 Bonn, Peter-Hensen-Str. 5-7; tel. (228) 8110; fax (228) 811171; internet http://www.dbb.de; f. 1918; Pres. ERHARD GEYER; 1.1m. mems (1997).

Transport

RAILWAYS

In 1995 the total length of track in Germany was 46,756 km.

Deutsche Bahn AG (German Railways): 60326 Frankfurt a.M., Stephensonstr. 1; tel. (69) 97330; telex 411124; fax (69) 97337500; 10365 Berlin, Ruschestr. 59; tel. (30) 2970; telex 30215311; fax (30) 29726130; f. 1994 following merger of Deutsche Bundesbahn and Deutsche Reichsbahn; state-owned (transfer to private-sector ownership pending); Pres. HEINZ DÜRR; Man. Dir Dr GÜNTHER SAẞMANNSHAUSEN.

Metropolitan Railways

Berliner Verkehrsbetriebe (Berlin Transport Authority): 10773 Berlin, Potsdamer Str. 188; tel. (30) 2561; fax (30) 2164186; f. 1929; operates approximately 140 km of underground railway; also runs tram and bus services; Dirs RUDIGER VORM WALDE, Dr HANS-HEINO DUBENKROPP, WILFRIED MEHNER, Dr JOACHIM NIKLAS.

Stadtwerke München, Werkbereich Verkehr: 80287 München, Einsteinstr. 28; tel. (89) 21911; fax (89) 21912155; underground (71 km), tramway (65 km), omnibus (448 km); Man. HERBERT KÖNIG.

Association

Verband Deutscher Verkehrsunternehmen (VDV) (Association of German Transport Authorities): 50672 Köln, Kamekestr. 37–39; tel. (221) 579790; fax (221) 514272; f. 1895; Pres. Dipl.-Ing. DIETER LUDWIG; Exec. Dir Prof. Dr GÜNTER GIRNAU.

ROADS

In January 1996 there were 641,860 km of classified roads, including 11,190 km of motorway, 41,700 km of other main roads and 86,717 km of secondary roads.

INLAND WATERWAYS

There are 7,467 km of navigable inland waterways, including the Main-Danube Canal, linking the North Sea and the Black Sea, which was opened in September 1992. Inland shipping accounts for about 20% of total freight traffic.

Abteilung Binnenschiffahrt und Wasserstrassen (Federal Ministry of Transport, Inland Waterways Dept): 53175 Bonn, Robert-Schuman-Platz 1; tel. (228) 3000; telex 885700; fax (228) 3003428; deals with construction, maintenance and administration of federal waterways and with national and international inland water transport.

Associations

Bundesverband der Deutschen Binnenschiffahrt eV: 47119 Duisburg, Dammstr. 15–17; tel. (203) 800060; fax (203) 8000621; f. 1948; central Inland Waterway Association to further the interests of operating firms; Pres. WILHEIM MÜNNING; 5 Mans.

Bundesverband Öffentlicher Binnenhäfen eV: 41460 Neuss, Hammer Landstr. 3; tel. (2131) 21624; fax (2131) 908282; Chair. KLAUS VAN LITH.

Bundesverband der selbstständigen Abteilung Binnenschiffahrt eV; 53175 Bonn, Hochkreuzallee 89; tel. (228) 318162; fax (228) 318163; Man. Dir ANDREA BECKSCHÄFER.

Deutsche Binnenreederei Binnenschiffahrt Spedition Logistik GmbH: 10245 Berlin, Alt Stralau 55–58; tel. (30) 29382200; fax (30) 29382201; f. 1993; Dir-Gen. HANS-WILHELM DÜNNER.

Hafenschiffahrtsverband Hamburg eV: 20457 Hamburg, Mattentwiete 2; tel. (40) 361280; fax (40) 36128292.

Verein für europäische Binnenschiffahrt und Wasserstrassen eV (VBW): 47119 Duisburg, Dammstr. 15–17; tel. (203) 8000627; fax (203) 8000621; represents all branches of the inland waterways; Pres. Prof. D. SCHRÖDER; CEO G. DÜTEMEYER.

SHIPPING

The principal seaports for freight are Bremen, Hamburg, Rostock-Überseehafen and Wilhelmshaven. Some important shipping companies are:

Argo Reederei Richard Adler & Söhne: 28075 Bremen, Postfach 107529; tel. (421) 363070; telex 245206; fax (421) 321575; Finland, UK; Propr MAX ADLER.

Aug. Bolten, Wm. Miller's Nachfolger GmbH & Co: 20457 Hamburg, Mattentwiete 8; tel. (40) 36011; fax (40) 3601423; tramp; Man. Dir DIETER OSTENDORF.

Bugsier- Reederei- und Bergungs-Gesellschaft mbH & Co: 20459 Hamburg, Johannisbollwerk 10, 20422 Hamburg, Postfach 112273; tel. (40) 311110; telex 214274; fax (40) 313693; salvage, towage, tugs, ocean-going heavy lift cranes, submersible pontoons, harbour tugs; Man. Dirs B. J. SCHUCHMANN, J. W. SCHUCHMANN, A. HUETTMANN.

Christian F. Ahrenkiel GmbH & Co. KG: 20099 Hamburg, An der Alster 45, Postfach 100220; tel. (40) 248380; telex 2195560; fax (40) 24838346; operators, shipowners and managers.

DAL Deutsche Afrika-Linien GmbH & Co: 22767 Hamburg, Palmaille 45; tel. (40) 380160; telex 2128970; fax (40) 38016663; Europe and South Africa; Man. Dirs H. von Rantzau, Dr E. von Rantzau.

Deutsche Seereederei Rostock GmbH: 18055 Rostock, Lange Str. 1a, Haus der Schiffahrt; tel. (381) 4580; telex 398298; fax (381) 4582215; container ships, general cargo ships, bulk carriers, cargo trailer ships, railway ferries, special tankers.

Döhle, Peter, Schiffahrts-KG (GmbH & Co): 22767 Hamburg, Palmaille 33, 22767 Hamburg, Postfach 500440; tel. (40) 381080; telex 214666; fax (40) 38108255; internet http://www.doehle.de; Man. Dir Jochen Döhle; shipbrokers, chartering agent, shipowners.

Egon Oldendorff: 2400 Lübeck, Fünfhausen 1; tel. (451) 15000; telex 26411; fax (451) 73522; Dirs H. Oldendorff, G. Arndt, W. Drabert, T. Weber, U. Bertheau.

Ernst Russ GmbH: 20354 Hamburg, Alsterufer 10; tel. (40) 414070; telex 21500955; fax (40) 41407111; f. 1893; worldwide.

F. Laeisz Schiffahrtsgesellschaft mbH & Co: 20457 Hamburg, Trostbrücke 1, 20411 Hamburg, Postfach 111111; tel. (40) 368080; fax (40) 364876; e-mail info@laeiszline.de; f. 1983; Dirs Nikolaus W. Schües, Gerhard Heyenga, H. Nikolaus Schües.

Fisser & v. Doornum GmbH & Co: 20148 Hamburg, Feldbrunnenstr. 43, Postfach 130365; tel. (40) 441860; telex 212671; fax (40) 4108050; f. 1879; tramp; Man. Dirs Christian Fisser, Dr Michael Fisser.

Hamburg-Südamerikanische Dampfschiffahrts-Gesellschaft Eggert & Amsinck: 2000 Hamburg 11, Ost-West-Str. 59, Hamburg-Süd-Haus; tel. (40) 37050; telex 21321699; fax (40) 3705400; worldwide service.

Hapag-Lloyd AG: 20095 Hamburg, Ballindamm 25; tel. (40) 30010; fax (40) 336432; f. 1970; North, Central and South America, Middle East, Asia, Australasia; Chair. Bernd Wrede; Dir Albrecht Metze.

John T. Essberger GmbH & Co: 22767 Hamburg, Palmaille 49, Postfach 500429; tel. (40) 380160; telex 2163553; fax (40) 38016579; f. 1924; Man. Dirs Dr E. von Rantzau, H. von Rantzau.

Oldenburg-Portugiesische Dampfschiffs-Rhederei GmbH & Co KG: 20459 Hamburg, Kajen 10, 20408 Hamburg, Postfach 110869; tel. (40) 361580; telex 211110; fax (40) 36158200; f. 1882; Spain, Portugal, Madeira, North Africa, Canary Islands; Man. Dirs G. Kempf, J. Bergmann.

Rhein-, Maas und See-Schiffahrtskontor GmbH: 47119 Duisburg, Krausstr. 1a; tel. (203) 8040; telex 855700; fax (203) 804-330; f. 1948.

Sloman Neptun Schiffahrts-AG: 28195 Bremen, Langenstr. 44, 28014 Bremen, Postfach 101469; tel. (421) 17630; telex 244421; fax (421) 1763-200; f. 1873; Scandinavia, North-western Europe, Mediterranean, North Africa; gas carriers; agencies, stevedoring; Mans Sven-Michael Edye, Dirk Lohmann.

Walther Möller & Co: 22767 Hamburg, Thedestr. 2; tel. (40) 3803910; telex 211523; fax (40) 38039199.

Shipping Organizations

Verband Deutscher Küstenschiffseigner (German Coastal Shipowners' Association): Hamburg-Altona; tel. (40) 313435; telex 214444; fax (40) 315925; f. 1896; Pres. Peter Th. Hausen; Man. Klaus Köster.

Verband Deutscher Reeder eV (German Shipowners' Association): 20354 Hamburg, Esplanade 6, 20317 Hamburg, Postfach 305580; tel. (40) 350970; fax (40) 35097211; Pres. Frank Leonhardt; Man. Dir Dr Bernd Kröger.

Zentralverband der Deutschen Seehafenbetriebe eV (Federal Association of German Seaport Operators): Hamburg; tel. (40) 311561; fax (40) 315714; f. 1932; Chair. Peter Dietrich; approx. 850 mems.

CIVIL AVIATION

The major international airports are at Berlin (East and West), Köln-Bonn, Dresden, Düsseldorf, Frankfurt, Hamburg, Hannover, Leipzig, München and Stuttgart.

Aero Lloyd Flugreisen Luftverkehrs-KG: 61440 Oberursel, Lessingstr. 7–9, Postfach 2029; tel. (6171) 6401; telex 4189372; fax (6171) 641129; f. 1981; charter services; Gen. Mans Reinhard Kipke, Dr W. Schneider; Wolfgang John.

Condor Flugdienst GmbH: 65440 Kelsterbach, Am Greunen Weg 3; tel. (6107) 9390; fax (6107) 939440; f. 1955, wholly-owned subsidiary of Lufthansa; charter and inclusive-tour services; Man. Dirs Dr Franz Schoiber, Dr Dietmar Kirchner, Rudolf von Oertzen.

Deutsche Lufthansa AG: 50679 Köln, Von-Gablenz-Str. 2–6; tel. (221) 8260; telex 8873531; fax (221) 8263818; f. 1953; extensive world-wide network; Chair. Exec. Bd Jürgen Weber; Chair. Supervisory Bd Dr Wolfgang Röller.

Germania Flug-GmbH: 51129 Köln, Flughafen; tel. (2203) 402375; fax (2203) 504490; f. 1978; charter and inclusive-tour services; Man. Dr Henrich Bischoff.

Hapag-Lloyd Flug-GmbH: 30062 Hannover, Flughafenstr. 10, Box 420240; tel. (511) 97270; telex 930136; fax (511) 9727494; f. 1972; charter and inclusive-tour services; Man. Dir Wolfgang Kurth.

LTU Lufttransport-Unternehmen GmbH & Co KG: 40474 Düsseldorf, Flughafen, Halle 8; tel. (211) 9418888; telex 8585573; fax (211) 9418881; f. 1955; charter and scheduled services; CEO Dr Heinz Westen.

Lufthansa Cargo Airlines GmbH: 65441 Kelsterbach, Langer Kornweg 34; tel. (6107) 777666; telex 4189142; fax (6107) 777881; f. 1993; wholly-owned subsidiary of Lufthansa; freight-charter domestic, Africa and world-wide; Man. Dirs Johannes-Henrich Irle, Wilhelm Althen.

Lufthansa Cityline GmbH: 65830 Kriftel, Am Holzweg 26; tel. (6192) 4070; fax (6192) 407466; scheduled services; Man. Dir Georg Steinbacher.

Tourism

Germany's tourist attractions include spas, summer and winter resorts, mountains, medieval towns and castles, and above all a variety of fascinating cities. The North and Baltic Sea coasts, the Rhine Valley, the Black Forest, the mountains of Thuringia, the Erzgebirge and Bavaria are the most popular areas. In 1996 there were 51,635 hotels and guesthouses in Germany, with 2,227,339 beds available for tourists. Overnight stays by foreign tourists totalled about 32,251,600 in 1996, when the total number of foreign visitors was 14,198,400.

Deutsche Zentrale für Tourismus eV (DZT) (German National Tourist Board): 60325 Frankfurt a.M., Beethovenstr. 69; tel. (69) 974640; fax (69) 751903; f. 1948; Dir Ursula Schörcher.

GHANA

Introductory Survey

Location, Climate, Language, Religion, Flag, Capital

The Republic of Ghana lies on the west coast of Africa, with Côte d'Ivoire to the west and Togo to the east. It is bordered by Burkina Faso to the north. The climate is tropical, with temperatures generally between 21°C and 32°C (70°–90°F) and average annual rainfall of 2,000 mm (80 ins) on the coast, decreasing inland. English is the official language, but there are eight major national languages. Many of the inhabitants follow traditional beliefs and customs. Christians comprise an estimated 42% of the population. The national flag (proportions 3 by 2) has three equal horizontal stripes, of red, yellow and green, with a five-pointed black star in the centre of the yellow stripe. The capital is Accra.

Recent History

Ghana was formed as the result of a UN-supervised plebiscite in May 1956, when the British-administered part of Togoland, a UN Trust Territory, voted to join the Gold Coast, a British colony, in an independent state. Ghana was duly granted independence, within the Commonwealth, on 6 March 1957, and thus became the first British dependency in sub-Saharan Africa to achieve independence under majority rule. Dr Kwame Nkrumah, the Prime Minister of the former Gold Coast since 1952, became Prime Minister of the new state. Ghana became a republic on 1 July 1960, with Nkrumah as President. In 1964 the country became a one-party state, in which the Convention People's Party, led by Nkrumah, was the sole authorized party. On 24 February 1966 Nkrumah, whose repressive policies and financial mismanagement had caused increasing resentment, was deposed by the army and police. The coup leaders established a governing National Liberation Council (NLC), led by Gen. Joseph Ankrah. In April 1969, following disputes within the ruling NLC, Ankrah was replaced by Brig. (later Lt-Gen.) Akwasi Afrifa, and a new Constitution, which established a non-executive presidency, was introduced. At legislative elections in August, the Progress Party (PP), led by Dr Kofi Busia, won 105 of the 140 seats in a new National Assembly. Busia was appointed Prime Minister, and the PP Government took office on 1 October. A three-man commission, formed by NLC members, assumed presidential power until 31 August 1970, when Edward Akufo-Addo was inaugurated as civilian President.

In reaction to increasing economic and political difficulties, the army seized power again in January 1972. The Constitution was abolished, and all political institutions were replaced by a National Redemption Council (NRC), under the chairmanship of Lt-Col (later Gen.) Ignatius Acheampong. In 1975 supreme legislative and administrative authority was transferred from the NRC to a Supreme Military Council, which was also led by Acheampong. In 1976 Acheampong announced plans for a return to civilian rule by June 1979, and the establishment of a provisional 'union government', which would comprise members of the armed forces, security forces and civilians. At a referendum, which took place in March 1978, the proposals were approved by 55.6% of votes cast. However, this result was largely discredited, and in July Acheampong's deputy, Lt-Gen. Frederick Akuffo, assumed power in a bloodless coup. Akuffo declared that the return to a popularly elected government would take place in 1979, as planned, and appointed a number of civilians to the NRC. The six-year ban on party politics was ended in January 1979, and 16 new parties were subsequently registered, in preparation for the elections in June.

In May 1979, however, junior military officers staged an unsuccessful coup attempt. The alleged leader of the conspirators, Flight-Lt Jerry Rawlings, was imprisoned, but was subsequently released by other officers. On 4 June he and his associates successfully seized power, amid popular acclaim, established the Armed Forces Revolutionary Council (AFRC), led by Rawlings, and introduced measures to eradicate corruption. Acheampong, Akuffo, Afrifa and six other senior officers were convicted on charges of corruption and executed.

The AFRC indicated that its assumption of power was temporary, and the elections took place in June 1979, as scheduled, although the return to civilian rule was postponed until September. The People's National Party (PNP) secured 71 of the 140 seats in the legislature and agreed to form a governing coalition with the United National Convention (UNC), which obtained 13 seats. The leader of the PNP, Dr Hilla Limann, was elected to the presidency, and was inaugurated on 24 September. In 1980 the UNC ended its alliance with the PNP, which subsequently retained a majority of only one seat in the legislature. In September 1981 the other parties represented in the legislature, including the UNC, amalgamated to form the All People's Party. In the same year public discontent was manifested in widespread strikes and riots.

On 31 December 1981 Rawlings again seized power in a military coup, and established a governing Provisional National Defence Council (PNDC), with himself as Chairman. The Council of State was abolished, the Constitution suspended, the legislature dissolved and political parties banned. In 1982 city and district councils were replaced by People's Defence Committees (PDCs), which were designed to allow popular participation in local government. In 1984 the PDCs were redesignated as Committees for the Defence of the Revolution (CDRs).

The PNDC's policies initially received strong support, but discontent with the regime and with the apparent ineffectiveness of its economic policies was reflected by a series of attempted military coups and widespread student unrest; between 1984 and 1987 some 34 people were executed for their alleged involvement in conspiracies to overthrow the Government. In August 1986 a former government minister and presidential candidate, Victor Owusu, was arrested for alleged subversion. In June 1987 it was announced that several people had been arrested and that weapons had been seized, following the discovery of a further conspiracy to overthrow the PNDC. In November the detention of a further seven people, including leaders of two opposition movements, the New Democratic Movement (NDM) and the Kwame Nkrumah Revolutionary Guards (KNRG), was authorized in the interests of national security.

In July 1987 the PNDC announced that elections for district assemblies, scheduled for mid-1987, were to be postponed until late 1988, and that the ban on political parties was to remain. By April 1988 more than 89% of the electorate had been registered to vote in the forthcoming elections. In that month there was an extensive government reshuffle, in which a new post to co-ordinate the work of the CDRs was created. During 1988 the number of districts was increased from 65 to 110, and in October districts were grouped within three electoral zones. Elections for the district assemblies in each zone were held in stages between December 1988 and February 1989. Although one-third of the 7,278 members of the district assemblies were appointed by the PNDC, the establishment of the assemblies was envisaged as the first stage in the development of a new political system of national democratic administration.

On 24 September 1989 a coup attempt was staged, led by a close associate of Rawlings, Maj. Courage Quashigah. Shortly afterwards Lt-Gen. Arnold Quainoo was dismissed as Commander of the Armed Forces, although he remained a member of the PNDC. (Rawlings himself assumed control of the armed forces until June 1990, when Maj.-Gen. Winston Mensah-Wood was appointed Commander.) In October 1989 five senior members of the security forces, including Quashigah, were arrested on charges of conspiring to assassinate Rawlings. The predominance of the Ewe ethnic group in government positions and other important posts, which had provoked discontent among other factions, was initially considered to be the cause of the revolt. In November, however, a board of inquiry, which investigated the allegations of treason, concluded that most of the conspirators were motivated by personal grievances and ambition. In January 1990 five more arrests were made in connection with the coup attempt. In August the human rights organization, Amnesty International, criticized the continued detention of Quashigah and six other members of the security forces, and claimed that they were imprisoned for political dissension.

In July 1990, in response to pressure from Western aid donors to introduce further democratic reforms, the PNDC announced that a National Commission for Democracy (NCD), under the chairmanship of Justice Daniel Annan (the Vice-Chairman of the PNDC), would organize a series of regional debates to consider Ghana's political and economic future. (Ten such debates took place between July and October 1992.) In August a newly-formed political organization, the Movement for Freedom and Justice (MFJ), criticized the NCD, claiming that it was too closely associated with the PNDC. The MFJ also demanded the abolition of legislation prohibiting political associations, the release of all political prisoners, the cessation of press censorship and the holding of a national referendum on the restoration of a multi-party system. In September the MFJ accused the PNDC of intimidation, after an inaugural meeting of the MFJ was suppressed by security forces. In October the PNDC pledged to accept the conclusions of any national consensus on future democracy in the country.

In December 1990 Rawlings announced proposals for the introduction of a constitution by the end of 1991; the PNDC was to consider recommendations presented by the NCD, and subsequently to convene a consultative body to determine constitutional reform. However, the MFJ, the Christian Council of Ghana and the Ghana Bar Association objected to the proposals, on the grounds that no definite schedule for political reform had been presented, and that no criteria had been established for the composition of the consultative body.

In March 1991 the NCD presented a report on the democratic process, which recommended the election of an executive President for a fixed term, the establishment of a legislature and the creation of the post of Prime Minister. Rawlings announced that the PNDC would consider the report and submit recommendations to a national consultative body later that year. In May, however, the PNDC endorsed the restoration of a multi-party system and approved the NCD's recommendations, although it was emphasized that the formation of political associations remained prohibited. The MFJ immediately disputed the veracity of the PNDC's announcement, causing the state-controlled press to accuse the MFJ of planning subversive activity. Later in May the Government announced the establishment of a 260-member Consultative Assembly, which was to present a draft constitution to the PNDC by the end of 1991. The new Constitution was subsequently to be submitted for endorsement by a national referendum. The Government appointed a nine-member committee of constitutional experts, who were to submit recommendations for a draft constitution to the Consultative Assembly by the end of July.

In June 1991 the Government reiterated denials that a number of political prisoners were detained in Ghana. In the same month the PNDC announced an amnesty for political exiles, which did not, however, include persons who were implicated in acts of subversion against the Government. In early August a newly-formed alliance of eleven opposition movements, human rights organizations and trade unions, including the MFJ, the NDM and the KNRG, known as the Co-ordinating Committee of Democratic Forces of Ghana, demanded that a constitutional conference be convened to determine a schedule for the transition to a democratic system. In the same month the committee of constitutional experts submitted a series of recommendations for constitutional reform, which included the establishment of a parliament and a council of state. It was proposed that the President, who would also be Commander-in-Chief of the Armed Forces, would be elected by universal suffrage for a four-year term of office, while the leader of the party which commanded a majority in the legislature would be appointed to the post of Prime Minister. However, the subsequent review of the draft Constitution by the Consultative Assembly was impeded by opposition demands for a boycott, on the grounds that the number of government representatives in the Assembly was too high. Later in August Rawlings announced that presidential and legislative elections were to take place in late 1992.

In early December 1991 Rawlings ordered the arrest of the Secretary-General of the MFJ, John Ndebugre, for allegedly failing to stand when the national anthem was played. Amnesty International subsequently reiterated claims that a number of prisoners in Ghana were detained for political dissension. In the same month the Government established an Interim National Electoral Commission (INEC), which was to be responsible for the demarcation of electoral regions and the supervision of elections and referendums. In January 1992 the Government extended the allocated period for the review of the draft Constitution to the end of March 1992. In March Rawlings announced a programme for transition to a multi-party system, which was to be completed on 7 January 1993. Later in March 1992 the Government granted an amnesty to 17 prisoners who had been convicted of subversion, including Quashigah.

At the end of March 1992 the Consultative Assembly approved the majority of the constitutional recommendations that had been submitted to the PNDC. However, the proposed creation of the post of Prime Minister was rejected by the Assembly; executive power was to be vested in the President, who would appoint a Vice-President. Opposition groups subsequently objected to a provision in the draft Constitution that members of the Government be exempt from prosecution for human rights violations allegedly committed during the PNDC's rule. At a national referendum on 28 April, however, the adoption of the draft Constitution was approved by 92% of votes cast, with 43.7% of the electorate voting.

On 18 May 1992 the Government introduced legislation permitting the formation of political associations (opposition groups had previously demanded that a multi-party system be adopted prior to the constitutional referendum); political parties were henceforth required to apply to the INEC for legal recognition. Under the terms of the legislation, however, emergent parties were not permitted to use names or slogans associated with 21 former political organizations that remained proscribed; in addition, individual monetary contributions to political parties were restricted. Later in May the High Court rejected an application for an injunction against the legislation by opposition leaders, who claimed that it was biased in favour of the PNDC. At the end of May it was reported that some 63 people had been killed in clashes between the Gonja and Nawuri ethnic groups in northern Ghana.

In June 1992 a number of political associations were established, many of which were identified with supporters of former President Nkrumah; six opposition movements, including the People's National Convention (PNC), led by ex-President Limann, were subsequently granted legal recognition. In the same month a coalition of pro-Government organizations, the National Democratic Congress (NDC), was formed to contest the forthcoming elections on behalf of the PNDC. However, an existing alliance of Rawlings' supporters, the Eagle Club, refused to join the NDC, and created its own political organization, the Eagle Party (later known as the EGLE—Every Ghanaian Living Everywhere—Party). In July Rawlings denied that he was associated with the Eagle Club, and rejected the EGLE Party's nomination as its candidate for the presidential election. In August the Government promulgated a new electoral code, which included a provision that in the event that no presidential candidate received more than 50% of votes cast the two candidates with the highest number of votes would contest a second round within 21 days. In September Rawlings officially retired from the air force (although he retained the post of Commander-in-Chief of the Armed Forces in his capacity as Head of State), in compliance with a stipulation in the new Constitution, and accepted a nomination to contest the presidential election as a candidate of the NDC. The NDC, the EGLE Party and the National Convention Party (NCP) subsequently formed a pro-Government electoral coalition, known as the Progressive Alliance.

In early October 1992 legislation that permitted indefinite detention without trial was repealed, in response to repeated protests by human rights organizations and opposition groups. However, new legislation, providing for the detention of individuals suspected of certain crimes for a period of up to 14 days was promulgated, and a special review court, which was empowered to extend the initial 14-day detention period, was established. Later in October the High Court dismissed an application by the MFJ for an injunction to prevent Rawlings from contesting the presidential election, on the grounds that he was not a Ghanaian national (his father was British), and that he remained accountable for charges of treason in connection with the coups that he had led.

In the presidential election, which took place on 3 November 1992, Rawlings secured 58.3% of votes cast, thereby obviating the necessity for a second round of voting. The four opposition parties that had presented candidates, the PNC, the New Patriotic Party (NPP), the National Independence Party (NIP) and the People's Heritage Party (PHP), claimed that there had been widespread electoral malpractice, although international observers maintained that the election had been conducted fairly (despite isolated irregularities). A curfew was subsequently imposed in Kumasi, in the district of Ashanti, following riots by supporters of the NPP in protest at the election results; a series of bombings in Tema and Accra were also attributed to members of the opposition. Later in November the NPP, the PNC, the NIP and the PHP withdrew from the forthcoming legislative elections (scheduled for 8 December), in protest at the Government's refusal to comply with their demands that a new electoral register be compiled and that allegations of misconduct during the presidential election be investigated. As a result, the legislative elections were postponed until 22 December (and subsequently by a further week) to allow time for the nomination of new candidates. In December the opposition claimed that many of its members had left Ghana, as a result of widespread intimidation by the Government. In the legislative elections, which duly took place on 29 December, the NDC secured 189 of the 200 seats in the Parliament, while the NCP obtained eight seats, the EGLE Party one seat and independent candidates the remaining two. (The NDC, the NCP and the EGLE Party were obliged to present separate candidates, following the withdrawal of the opposition parties.) According to official figures, however, only 29% of the electorate voted in the legislative elections.

On 7 January 1993 Rawlings was sworn in as President of what was designated the Fourth Republic, and the PNDC was officially dissolved; on the same day the new Parliament was inaugurated, and Justice Daniel Annan was elected as its Speaker. Later in January the NPP, the PNC, the NIP and the PHP formed an alliance, known as the Inter-party Co-ordinating Committee, and announced that they were to act as an official opposition to the Government, despite their lack of representation in the Parliament. At the end of January Rawlings began to submit nominations for members of the Council of Ministers and the Council of State for approval by the Parliament. However, he announced that members of the existing Government were to remain in office in an interim capacity, pending the appointment of a Council of Ministers and other officials. The opposition subsequently criticized the delay in the formation of a new government, and protested that the new Constitution did not permit members of the former PNDC to remain in office. In March the nomination of a number of ministers was approved by the Parliament. Later that month legislation was promulgated to exempt from prosecution perpetrators of offences that had been committed under the auspices of the former PNDC Government. Also in March two members of the opposition were convicted on charges of organizing the bombings in November 1992 and were sentenced to terms of imprisonment.

In April 1993 elections took place for the regional seats in the Council of State. In May a 17-member Council of Ministers, which included several ministers who had served in the former PNDC administration, was inaugurated. Substantial pledges of assistance for Ghana, made in July at a meeting of donor nations (under the aegis of the World Bank), indicated Western support for the new Government. In the same month the Supreme Court upheld a motion by the NPP that certain existing legislation was in contravention of the Constitution. In August the NPP (which, together with other principal opposition parties, had hitherto continued to contest the results of the presidential election) announced that it was prepared to recognize the legitimacy of the Government. In October the Minister of Justice, who (in his capacity as public prosecutor) had failed to win several trials in the Supreme Court, resigned after a state-owned newspaper questioned his competence. In November a 20-member National Security Council, chaired by the Vice-President, Kow Nkensen Arkaah, was inaugurated. In December the PHP, the NIP and a faction of the PNC, all of which comprised supporters of ex-President Nkrumah, merged to form a new organization, known as the People's Convention Party (PCP). In the same month, following a further appeal by the NPP, the Supreme Court ruled that the anniversary of the December 1981 coup should no longer be observed as a public holiday.

In February 1994 long-standing hostility between the Konkomba ethnic group, which originated in Togo, and the land-owning Nanumba intensified, following demands by the Konkomba for traditional status that would entitle them to own land; some 500 people were killed in clashes between the two factions in the Northern Region. The Government subsequently dispatched troops to restore order and imposed a state of emergency in seven districts for a period of three months. Nevertheless, skirmishes continued in the region, with several other ethnic groups becoming involved in the conflict, and it was reported that some 6,000 Konkomba had fled to Togo. In early March 12 people were killed at Tamale (the capital of the Northern Region), when security forces fired on demonstrators belonging to the Dagomba ethnic group, who had allegedly attacked a number of Konkomba.

In March 1994 a minor government reorganization was effected. Later that month elections to the District Assemblies took place (except in the seven districts subject to the state of emergency). Negotiations between representatives of the various ethnic groups involved in the conflict in the Northern Region were initiated in April, under the aegis of the Government. In the same month the authorities claimed that reported threats to kill Quashigah (the instigator of the coup attempt in 1989) and editors of two privately-owned newspapers were part of a conspiracy to destabilize the Government. In May a further minor reorganization of the Government took place. Meanwhile, the state of emergency in force in the Northern Region (where a total of 1,000 people had been killed, and a further 150,000 displaced) was extended for one month. In early June, however, the ethnic factions involved in the hostilities signed a peace agreement that provided for the imposition of an immediate cease-fire and renounced violence as a means of settling disputes over land-ownership. The Government subsequently announced that troops were to be permanently stationed in the Northern Region in order to prevent further conflict, and established a negotiating team which was to attempt to resolve the inter-ethnic differences. The state of emergency was extended for a further month in June, and again in July; in early August, however, the Government announced that order had been restored in the Northern Region, and officially ended the state of emergency.

In September 1994 five civilians, who had allegedly conspired to overthrow the Government, were charged with treason. In October two men were arrested by security forces, after attempting to transport armaments illicitly to the Northern Region; an increase in tension in the region was reflected by further arrests, in connection with violent incidents in which several people had been killed. Following a joint rally of the NPP, the PNC and the PCP in November, the parties announced that they would present a single candidate to contest the presidential election in 1996. Meanwhile, rumours emerged of ill-feeling between Rawlings and Arkaah. In January 1995 Arkaah officially refuted speculation that Rawlings was responsible for allegations, which had appeared in an independent newspaper, of an illicit relationship between Arkaah and a minor, and attributed blame to subversive elements. In the same month, however, the Government denied a reported statement by Arkaah that he had refused a request by Rawlings for his resignation.

In March 1995 the Government imposed a curfew in the Northern Region following renewed ethnic violence, in which about 100 people were killed. In April a joint commission, comprising prominent members of the Konkomba and Nanumba ethnic groups, was established, in an effort to resolve the conflict. Meanwhile, the imposition, in February, of value-added tax (VAT) under the budget for 1995 prompted widespread protests, while civil servants threatened to initiate strike action; a series of demonstrations, which was organized by a grouping of opposition leaders, Alliance for Change, culminated in May, when five people were killed in clashes between government supporters and protesters. (The Government subsequently agreed to suspend VAT.) Later in May the National Executive Committee of the NCP decided to withdraw the party from the government coalition, claiming that the NDC had dominated the alliance. However, Arkaah (a member of the NCP) subsequently announced that he was to retain the office of Vice-President on the grounds that his mandate remained valid. In July the long-serving Minister of Finance, Kwesi Botchwey, resigned (apparently in response to the failure of government efforts to impose VAT); a minor reorganization of the Council of Ministers ensued. At a by-election in the same month, the vacant seat was secured by a joint candidate of the PNC, NPP, NCP and PCP. In October the Chairman of the NCP resigned, following dissent within the party. In November the Commission on Human Rights and Administrative Justice (CHRAJ) commenced investigations into allegations of corruption on the part of government ministers and civil servants. In January 1996 an alleged incident in which Rawlings assaulted Arkaah during a meeting of the Council of Ministers prompted further speculation of animosity between the President and Vice-President; opposition parties subsequently demanded that Rawlings resign. In February three journalists were arraigned after publishing a report alleging the Government's complicity in a case of drugs-trafficking involving a Ghanaian diplomat based in Geneva, Switzerland. In the same month the NCP and PCP merged to form a single party, known as the Convention People's Party. Rawlings reshuffled his Council of Ministers in March. In late May a violent confrontation between two Muslim factions in Atebubu led to one death and severe damage to property.

In April 1996 presidential and parliamentary elections were scheduled for 10 December, although this was later changed to 7 December to meet constitutional requirements. Nominations of candidates were to take place in September. In May Kwame Pianim, prospective presidential candidate for the NPP, was disqualified from the elections on the grounds of his conviction for treason in 1982. In the same month it was announced that the Popular Party for Democracy and Development (PPDD), a group formed in 1992 by supporters of Nkrumah, was to merge with the PCP. The PPDD also announced its support for unity with the NPP. In June Thomas Appiah resigned for personal reasons as Chairman of the NCP and Vice-Chairman of the PCP. In July the NCP announced that it had removed Kow Nkensen Arkaah as its leader, following his selection as presidential candidate by the PCP. In August the NPP and PCP announced their formation of an electoral coalition, to be known as the Great Alliance; it was subsequently announced that John Kufuor, of the NPP, was to be the Great Alliance's presidential candidate, with Arkaah, of the PCP, as the candidate for the vice-presidency. The NCP stated that it would support the NDC in the forthcoming elections, while the PNC announced its intention to contest the elections alone; Edward Mahama was subsequently selected as the PNC's presidential candidate. In September Rawlings was nominated as the NDC's presidential candidate. By 18 September, the official deadline for the nomination of candidates, only the Progressive Alliance (the NDC, the EGLE party and the Democratic People's Party—DPP), the Great Alliance and the PNC had succeeded in having their nomination papers accepted. In early October the NCP, which, according to the National Electoral Commission, had not presented the appropriate papers, declared its intention to take legal action against the Commission to force it to accept the nomination of the party's candidates. In mid-October the Electoral Commission denied accusations that it had shown bias against the NCP. The selection of common candidates provoked a lengthy dispute between the NPP and the PCP, with the parties contradicting each other regarding previous agreements on the distribution of seats. In late October at least 20 people were wounded in clashes between NDC and NPP militant supporters in Tamale (in the north) and Kibi (in the north-east). In November a network of Domestic Election Observers, comprising 25 groups (including religious councils, the Trades Union Congress, and civil servants' and journalists' associations), was created to oversee the December elections. The resignation of the Minister of the Interior in October was followed, in November, by the resignations of the Minister of Trade and Industry and the Presidential Aide on Cocoa Affairs, following corruption allegations against them published in an interim report by the CHRAJ.

In the presidential election, which took place on 7 December 1996, Rawlings was re-elected by 57.2% of votes cast, while Kufuor secured 39.8% of the votes. In the parliamentary elections the NDC's representation was reduced to 133 seats, while the NPP won 60 seats, the PCP five and the PNC one seat. Voting was postponed in the constituency of Afigya Sekyere East, in Ashanti, because of a legal dispute concerning the eligibility of candidates. (The seat was subsequently won by the NPP in a by-election in June 1997.) Despite opposition claims of malpractice, international observers declared that the elections had been conducted fairly, and a high electoral turn-out of 76.8% was reported. Following the announcement of the election results, about 15 people were injured in clashes between NDC and opposition supporters in Bimbila, south-east of Tamale. Later in December Kofi Annan, the Ghanaian candidate, was elected to serve a five-year term as Secretary-General of the UN. At the end of that month the PCP announced that its electoral alliance with the NPP had broken down. On 7 January 1997 Rawlings was sworn in as President.

The lengthy process of appointing a new Council of Ministers resulted in a protracted dispute between the NDC and the opposition, prompting a series of parliamentary walk-outs by the NPP, which insisted that all ministerial appointees be approved by the parliamentary appointments committee prior to assuming their duties. In late February 1997 opposition parties filed a writ in the Supreme Court preventing Kwame Peprah, the reappointed Minister of Finance, from presenting the budget. Owing to the NDC's parliamentary majority, however, procedures were approved to allow those ministers who had been retained from the previous Government to avoid the vetting process. The majority of ministerial appointments were made during March and April, although a number of posts were not filled until June. In early June the Supreme Court ruled that all presidential nominees for ministerial positions had to be approved by Parliament, even if they had served in the previous Government. Following the ruling, the NPP withdrew from the chamber on several occasions when ministers attempted to address Parliament. The Government subsequently announced that ministers who had participated in the previous administration were prepared to undergo vetting procedures.

In early September 1997 it was reported that three people had been killed, and more than 1,000 displaced, in the Brong Ahafo Region, following ethnic skirmishes which had been prompted by a dispute over land-ownership. In December violent clashes between two Muslim sects resulted in severe damage to property in Wa, in the north-west of Ghana. In the following month four people were killed, and 26 injured, in an outbreak of violence between opposing Muslim factions in Wenchi, in the Brong Ahafo Region; 57 people were subsequently arrested.

Following a military coup in Burkina Faso in October 1987, which was condemned by the Ghanaian Government (relations between Rawlings and the deposed Burkinabè leader, Capt. Thomas Sankara, had been close), links between the two nations were temporarily strained, but improved following meetings between Rawlings and Capt. Blaise Compaoré, the Burkinabè leader, in early 1988. In December 1989, however, Ghana was accused by Burkina Faso of involvement in an attempt to overthrow the Burkinabè Government. In mid-January 1990 120 Ghanaians were deported from Burkina Faso without official explanation.

In 1986 relations between Ghana and Togo became strained, following subversive activity by Ghanaian dissidents based in Togo, and an attempted coup in Togo, which was allegedly initiated from Ghanaian territory. The common border between the two countries was closed in October, but was reopened by Togo in February 1987, and by Ghana in May. Between December 1988 and January 1989 more than 130 Ghanaians were deported from Togo, where they were alleged to be residing illegally. In October 1991 the Governments of Ghana and Togo signed an agreement on the free movement of goods and persons between the two countries. In October 1992, however, Ghana denied claims by the Togolese Government that it was implicated in subversive activity by Togolese dissidents based in Ghana. In November Rawlings formally protested to the Togolese Government, after five Ghanaians were killed by Togolese security forces on the border between the two countries.

In March 1993 the Rawlings administration denied allegations, made by the Togolese Government, of Ghanaian complicity in an armed attack on the residence of Togo's President. In January 1994 relations with Togo further deteriorated, following an attempt to overthrow the Togolese Government, which was said by the Togolese authorities to have been staged by armed dissidents based in Ghana. The Ghanaian Chargé d'affaires in Togo was arrested, and Togolese forces killed 12 Ghanaians and bombarded a customs post at Aflao and several villages near the border. Ghana, however, denied the accusations of involvement in the coup attempt, and threatened to retaliate against further acts of aggression. In May allegations by the Togolese Government that Ghana had been responsible (owing to lack of border security) for bomb attacks in Togo resulted in further tension between the two nations. In August the Togolese Government protested to Ghana, following an article in a privately-owned Ghanaian newspaper to the effect that Togolese rebels based in Ghana were preparing to launch an offensive to overthrow the Eyadéma administration. Later that year, however, relations between the two countries improved, and in November full diplomatic links were formally restored. In the following month Togo's border with Ghana (which had been closed in January 1994) was reopened. After discussions between Eyadéma and Rawlings in July 1995, an agreement was reached, providing for the reconstitution of the Ghana-Togo joint commission for economic, social and technical co-operation and the Ghana-Togo border demarcation commission. In August the Togolese Government denied involvement in the assassination of a political opponent who had taken refuge in Ghana. In February 1996 both Parliaments established friendship groups to examine ways of easing tensions. By the end of that year some 48,000 Togolese refugees were estimated to have received payment for voluntary repatriation.

During the conflict in Liberia, which commenced in December 1989 (see Liberia, Vol. II), Ghana contributed troops to the Monitoring Group (ECOMOG) of the Economic Community of West African States (ECOWAS, see p. 145). In August 1994 Rawlings, who in that month replaced President Nicéphore Soglo of Benin as Chairman of the ECOWAS Conference of Heads of State and Government, indicated that Ghana was to consider the withdrawal of troops from ECOMOG. However, it subsequently appeared that the Ghanaian contingent was to remain in ECOMOG until peace was achieved, while Rawlings (in his capacity as Chairman) mediated protracted negotiations between the warring Liberian factions. In May 1996 an ECOWAS meeting, to discuss the situation in Liberia, took place at Rawlings' insistence, following intense fighting in Monrovia, Liberia. Ghana granted temporary asylum to some 2,000 Liberian war refugees, but insisted that no more could be accepted in the future. By mid-1997, however, some 17,000 Liberian refugees had arrived in Ghana. In August Rawlings was the first foreign leader to visit Liberia following its return to civilian rule. Meanwhile, in June Ghana, together with Côte d'Ivoire, Guinea and Nigeria, became a member of the 'committee of four', which was established by ECOWAS to monitor the situation in Sierra Leone, following the staging of a military coup in the previous month; troops were dispatched to participate in a peace-keeping force deployed in that country.

Government

Under the terms of the Constitution, which was approved by national referendum on 28 April 1992, Ghana has a multi-party political system. Executive power is vested in the President, who is the Head of State and Commander-in-Chief of the Armed Forces. The President is elected by direct universal suffrage for a maximum of two four-year terms of office. Legislative power is vested in a 200-member unicameral Parliament, which is elected by direct universal suffrage for a four-year term. The President appoints a Vice-President, and nominates a Council of Ministers, subject to approval by the Parliament. The Constitution also provides for a 25-member Council of State, principally comprising regional representatives and presidential nominees, and a 20-member National Security Council, chaired by the Vice-President, which act as advisory bodies to the President.

Ghana has 10 regions, each headed by a Regional Minister, who is assisted by a regional co-ordinating council. The regions constitute 110 administrative districts, each with a District Assembly, which is headed by a District Chief Executive. Regional colleges, which comprise representatives selected by the District Assemblies and by regional Houses of Chiefs, elect a number of representatives to the Council of State.

Defence

At 1 August 1997 Ghana had total armed forces of 7,000 (army 5,000, navy 1,000 and air force 1,000) and a paramilitary presidential guard of an estimated 800. Budget estimates for 1997 allocated 275,000m. cedis to defence. The headquarters of the Defence Commission of the OAU is in Accra.

Economic Affairs

In 1995, according to estimates by the World Bank, Ghana's gross national product (GNP), measured at average 1993–95 prices, was US $6,719m., equivalent to $390 per head. During 1985–95, it was estimated, GNP per head increased, in real terms, at an average annual rate of 1.5%, while the population increased by an annual average of 3.0% over the same period. Ghana's gross domestic product (GDP) increased, in real terms, by an annual average of 4.4% in 1985–95; in 1995 GDP increased by an estimated 4.5%.

Agriculture (including forestry and fishing) contributed an estimated 44% of GDP in 1995. An estimated 55.3% of the labour force were employed in the sector in 1996. The principal cash crops are cocoa beans (Ghana being one of the world's leading producers, and exports of which accounted for 25.2% of total exports in 1995), coffee, bananas, oil palm, coconuts, limes, kola nuts and shea-nuts (karité nuts). Timber production is also important, with the forestry sector accounting for 4.2% of GDP and 13.3% of total export earnings in 1995. Fishing satisfies more than three-quarters of domestic requirements. During 1985–95, according to the World Bank, agricultural GDP increased by an annual average of 1.9%; in 1995 agricultural GDP increased by an estimated 4.2%.

Industry (including mining, manufacturing, construction and power) contributed an estimated 16.5% of GDP in 1995, and employed 12.8% of the working population in 1984. According to the World Bank, industrial GDP increased by an annual average of 5.4% in 1985–95, by 4.3% in 1994 and by an estimated 3.3% in 1995.

Mining contributed an estimated 1.7% of GDP in 1995, and employed 0.5% of the working population in 1984. Gold and diamonds are the major minerals exported, although Ghana also exploits large reserves of bauxite and manganese ore. According to the IMF, the GDP of the mining sector increased by an average of 7.5% per year in 1990–95, and by an estimated 5.5% in 1995.

Manufacturing contributed an estimated 9.4% of GDP in 1995, and employed 10.9% of the working population in 1984. The most important sectors are food processing, textiles, vehicles, cement, paper, chemicals and petroleum. According to the World Bank, manufacturing GDP increased by an annual average of 3.6% in 1985–95, and by an estimated 1.8% in 1995.

The Akosombo and Kpong hydroelectric plants supply 90% of Ghana's electricity; thermal power provides an alternative source of energy. The construction of a nuclear reactor at Kwabenya, near Accra, was completed in January 1995. Imports of mineral fuels comprised 10.7% of the total value of imports in 1995. Electricity is exported to Benin and Togo.

The services sector contributed an estimated 39.5% of GDP in 1995, and engaged 26.1% of the working population in 1984. According to the World Bank, the GDP of the services sector increased by an annual average of 7.5% in 1985–95, and by an estimated 5.0% in 1995.

In 1996 Ghana recorded a visible trade deficit of US $366.0m., while there was a deficit of $323.8m. on the current account of the balance of payments. In 1996 the principal source of imports was the United Kingdom (16.8%); other major sources were the USA, Germany, Nigeria and Japan. Switzerland was the principal market for exports (taking 27.9% of the total) in that year; other important purchasers were the United Kingdom, the Netherlands and Germany. The principal exports in 1995 were gold (which accounted for 45.2% of total export earnings), cocoa beans and timber. The principal imports in 1992 were machinery and transport equipment, mineral fuels, particularly crude petroleum, basic manufactures, chemicals, and food.

Ghana's overall budget surplus for 1995 was estimated at 70,900m. cedis (equivalent to 0.9% of GDP). Ghana's external debt totalled US $5,874m. at the end of 1995, of which $4,568m. was long-term public debt. In the same year the cost of debt-servicing was equivalent to 23.1% of exports of goods and services. In 1985–95 the average annual rate of inflation was 29.0%. In 1996 consumer prices increased by 46.6%. In 1995 some 41,000 people were registered as unemployed in Ghana.

Ghana is a member of the Economic Community of West African States (ECOWAS, see p. 145), of the International Cocoa Organization (ICCO, see p. 257) and of the International Coffee Organization (ICO, see p. 257).

Ghana's economy has been adversely affected by political instability and mismanagement. It is also vulnerable to unfavourable weather conditions and to fluctuations in international commodity prices. In 1983, in response to a rapid decline in the economy, the Government introduced an extensive programme of economic reform, under the aegis of the IMF and the World Bank. In the late 1980s substantial progress was achieved, but in 1992, during the transition to civilian rule, economic growth decelerated, owing to increased budgetary pressures and a decline in the international price of cocoa. In June 1993, however, international donors pledged substantial aid to finance a further stage in the reform programme, which involved the diversification of exports and the transfer of a number of state-owned enterprises to the private sector. In July 1995 the IMF approved further credit under a three-year enhanced structural adjustment facility in support of the Government's economic programme, but Ghana failed to achieve several stipulated targets in the first year. The divestiture programme, which had been accelerated in 1994, showed some success in attracting greater foreign investment. Efforts to reduce Ghana's dependence on gold and cocoa proved successful in 1996, when the value of non-traditional exports increased by more than 75%. In November 1997 international donors agreed to grant some US $1,600m. in aid for the period 1997–99, in support of further macroeconomic reform.

Social Welfare

The Government provides hospitals and medical care at nominal rates, and there is a government pension scheme. In 1992 government health facilities included 49 general hospitals and about 300 rural health clinics; religious missions operated 41 hospitals and 64 clinics, while there were an additional 400 private clinics. In that year there were about 800 physicians and 11,000 nurses working in the public sector, with about 300 physicians working in private practice. Budget estimates for 1995 allocated 79,551m. cedis for health services (4.7% of total government expenditure).

Education

Education is officially compulsory for nine years between the ages of six and 16. Primary education begins at the age of six and lasts for six years. Secondary education, beginning at the age of 12, lasts for a further six years, comprising two three-year cycles. Following three years of junior secondary education, pupils are examined to determine admission to senior secondary school courses, or to technical and vocational courses. In 1992 primary enrolment was equivalent to 76% of children in the relevant age-group (boys 83%; girls 70%), while the comparable ratio for secondary enrolment was 36% (boys 44%; girls 28%). It was estimated that 52,000 students were enrolled in higher education in 1992, with about 10,700 students attending the country's five universities. Tertiary institutions also included 38 teacher-training colleges, seven diploma-awarding colleges, 21 technical colleges and six polytechnics. Expenditure on education by the central Government in 1995 was estimated at 255,792m. cedis (15.1% of total spending). According to UNESCO estimates, the average rate of adult illiteracy in 1995 was 35.5% (males 24.1%; females 46.5%).

Public Holidays

1998: 1 January (New Year's Day), 6 March (Independence Day), 10–13 April (Easter), 1 May (Labour Day), 1 July (Republic Day), 1 December (National Farmers' Day), 25–26 December (Christmas).

1999: 1 January (New Year's Day), 6 March (Independence Day), 2–5 April (Easter), 1 May (Labour Day), 1 July (Republic Day), 1 December (National Farmers' Day), 25–26 December (Christmas).

Weights and Measures

The metric system is in force.

Statistical Survey

Source (except where otherwise stated): Central Bureau of Statistics, POB 1098, Accra; tel. (21) 66512.

Area and Population

AREA, POPULATION AND DENSITY

Area (sq km)	238,537*
Population (census results)	
1 March 1970	8,559,313
11 March 1984	
Males	6,063,848
Females	6,232,233
Total	12,296,081
Population (official estimate at mid-year)	
1991	15,400,000
Density (per sq km) at mid-1991	64.6

* 92,100 sq miles.

POPULATION BY REGION (1984 census)

Western	1,157,807
Central	1,142,335
Greater Accra	1,431,099
Eastern	1,680,890
Volta	1,211,907
Ashanti	2,090,100
Brong-Ahafo	1,206,608
Northern	1,164,583
Upper East	772,744
Upper West	438,008
Total	12,296,081

Principal ethnic groups (1991 estimates, percentage of total population): Akan 52.4, Mossi 15.8, Ewe 11.9, Ga-Adangme 7.8, Guan 11.9, Gurma 3.3%, Yoruba 1.3%.

PRINCIPAL TOWNS (population at 1984 census)

Accra (capital)	867,459	Takoradi	61,484
Kumasi	376,249	Cape Coast	57,224
Tamale	135,952	Sekondi	31,916
Tema	131,528		

BIRTHS AND DEATHS (UN estimates, annual averages)

	1980–85	1985–90	1990–95
Birth rate (per 1,000)	45.2	44.3	41.7
Death rate (per 1,000)	14.3	13.1	11.7

Expectation of life (UN estimates, years at birth, 1990–95): 56.0 (males 54.2; females 57.8).

Source: UN, *World Population Prospects: The 1994 Revision.*

ECONOMICALLY ACTIVE POPULATION (1984 census)

	Males	Females	Total
Agriculture, hunting, forestry and fishing	1,750,024	1,560,943	3,310,967
Mining and quarrying	24,906	1,922	26,828
Manufacturing	198,430	389,988	588,418
Electricity, gas and water	14,033	1,404	15,437
Construction	60,692	3,994	64,686
Trade, restaurants and hotels	111,540	680,607	792,147
Transport, storage and communications	117,806	5,000	122,806
Financing, insurance, real estate and business services	19,933	7,542	27,475
Community, social and personal services	339,665	134,051	473,716
Total employed	2,637,029	2,785,451	5,422,480
Unemployed	87,452	70,172	157,624
Total labour force	2,724,481	2,855,623	5,580,104

Source: ILO, *Yearbook of Labour Statistics*.

Mid-1996 (estimates in '000): Agriculture, etc. 4,618; Total 8,347 (Source: FAO, *Production Yearbook*).

Agriculture

PRINCIPAL CROPS ('000 metric tons)

	1994	1995	1996
Maize	940	1,042	1,000*
Millet	168	201	201*
Sorghum	324	390	390*
Rice (paddy)	162	202	202*
Sugar cane*	110	110	110
Cassava (Manioc)	6,025	6,899	6,899*
Yams	1,700	2,234	2,234*
Taro (Coco yam)	1,148	1,360	1,360*
Onions	24	25*	25*
Tomatoes	182	160*	160*
Green chillies and peppers*	169	170	170
Eggplants (Aubergines)*	6	6	6
Pulses*	20	20	20
Oranges*	50	50	50
Lemons and limes*	30	30	30
Mangoes*	4	4	4
Bananas*	4	4	4
Plantains	1,475	1,642	1,642*
Pineapples*	21	18	12
Palm kernels*	30	31	31
Groundnuts (in shell)	176	150*	150*
Coconuts	264	240*	240*
Copra*	10	10	10
Coffee (green)	3†	3*	3*
Cocoa beans†	309	400	340
Tobacco (leaves)*	2	2	2

* FAO estimate(s). † Unofficial figure(s).

Source: FAO, *Production Yearbook*.

LIVESTOCK ('000 head, year ending September)

	1994	1995	1996
Horses*	2	2	2
Asses*	13	13	13
Cattle	1,187	1,200*	1,200*
Pigs	419	440*	440*
Sheep	2,279	2,400*	2,400*
Goats	2,194	2,250*	2,250*

Poultry (million*): 13 in 1994; 13 in 1995; 13 in 1996.

* FAO estimate(s).

Source: FAO, *Production Yearbook*.

LIVESTOCK PRODUCTS (FAO estimates, '000 metric tons)

	1994	1995	1996
Beef and veal	20	21	21
Mutton and lamb	6	7	7
Goat meat	5	5	5
Pig meat	9	10	10
Poultry meat	12	12	12
Other meat	91	89	89
Cows' milk	24	24	24
Hen eggs	13	14	14
Cattle hides	3	3	3

Source: FAO, *Production Yearbook*.

Forestry

ROUNDWOOD REMOVALS ('000 cubic metres, excl. bark)

	1992	1993	1994
Sawlogs, veneer logs and logs for sleepers	1,170	1,682	1,800
Other industrial wood	130	150	150*
Fuel wood	19,512*	22,612	25,190
Total	20,812	24,444	27,140

* FAO estimate.

Source: FAO, *Yearbook of Forest Products*.

SAWNWOOD PRODUCTION ('000 cubic metres, incl. railway sleepers)

	1992	1993	1994
Coniferous (softwood)	—	29	54
Broadleaved (hardwood)	410	475	582
Total	410	504	636

Source: FAO, *Yearbook of Forest Products*.

Fishing

('000 metric tons, live weight)

	1993	1994	1995
Freshwater fishes	52.5	55.2	50.6
Bigeye grunt	11.9	18.2	14.8
Red pandora	7.9	5.6	4.5
Jack and horse mackerels	1.9	2.7	9.5
Sardinellas	111.1	89.9	95.1
European anchovy	81.4	60.5	65.5
Skipjack tuna	26.1	23.5	25.4
Yellowfin tuna	9.2	8.5	5.5
Chub mackerel	4.3	9.8	12.5
Other marine fishes (incl. unspecified)	66.1	58.0	55.5
Total catch (incl. others)	375.7	337.0	344.5
Inland waters	52.5	55.2	50.6
Atlantic Ocean	323.2	281.8	293.9

Source: FAO, *Yearbook of Fishery Statistics*.

Mining

('000 metric tons, unless otherwise indicated)

	1992	1993	1994
Gold (kilograms)*†	31,000	39,200	44,500
Manganese ore*†	106	115	108
Bauxite‡	338	424	426

* Figures refer to the metal content of ores.

† Data from the US Bureau of Mines.

‡ Data from *World Metal Statistics* (London).

Source: UN, *Industrial Commodity Statistics Yearbook*.

Diamonds ('000 carats): 584.5 (1992); 222.0 (1993) 371.1 (1994 estimate).

Source: IMF, *Ghana—Selected Issues and Statistical Annex* (August 1996).

Industry

SELECTED PRODUCTS ('000 metric tons, unless otherwise indicated)

	1992	1993	1994
Groundnut oil	13.0	13.5	25.0
Coconut oil	5.5	5.6	5.6
Palm oil	100.0	108.0	108.0
Palm kernel oil	10.1	10.1	9.8
Cigarettes (millions)*	2,100	n.a.	n.a.
Motor spirit (petrol)*	212	215	217
Kerosene*	123	125	126
Diesel and gas oil*	212	214	215
Cement†	1,020	1,200	1,350
Aluminium (unwrought)‡§	179.9	175.4	140.7
Electric energy (million kWh)*	6,152	6,154	6,167

* Provisional or estimated figures.

† Data from US Bureau of Mines.

‡ Primary metal only.

§ Data from *World Metal Statistics* (London).

Sources: FAO, *Quarterly Bulletin of Statistics;* UN, *Industrial Commodity Statistics Yearbook.*

Finance

CURRENCY AND EXCHANGE RATES

Monetary Units
100 pesewas = 1 new cedi.

Sterling and Dollar Equivalents (30 September 1997)
£1 sterling = 3,580.2 cedis;
US $1 = 2,216.3 cedis;
10,000 cedis = £2.793 = $4.512.

Average Exchange Rate (cedis per US $)
1994 956.71
1995 1,200.43
1996 1,637.23

GENERAL BUDGET (million new cedis)

Revenue*	1993	1994	1995†
Tax revenue	509,152	841,123	1,138,514
Taxes on income, profits and capital gains	110,299	170,497	275,000
Individual	44,317	62,330	80,783
Corporate	54,330	89,491	157,181
Other unallocated taxes on income	11,652	18,676	37,036
Domestic taxes on goods and services	222,868	309,008	363,550
General sales, turnover or value-added tax	31,248	49,761	69,579
Excises (excl. petroleum)	39,727	57,547	69,947
Petroleum revenue	151,893	201,700	224,024
Taxes on international trade and transactions	175,985	361,618	499,964
Import duties	140,237	215,461	342,751
Export duties	35,748	146,157	157,213
Non-tax revenue	148,429	389,949	552,277
Receipts from divestiture of state-owned enterprises	85,750	261,778	111,787
Total	657,581	1,231,072	1,690,791

Expenditure‡	1992	1993	1994
General public services	58,450	83,918	145,432
Defence	23,242	39,481	33,853
Public order and safety	21,479	30,838	73,544
Education	118,363	179,234	255,792
Health	39,450	56,639	79,551
Social security and welfare	34,630	57,752	40,776
Housing and community amenities	8,639	12,403	8,707
Other community and social services	7,026	10,087	20,558
Economic affairs and services	82,691	129,721	110,059
Agriculture, forestry, fishing and hunting	19,815	28,449	26,752
Mining, manufacturing and construction	7,682	11,029	8,344
Transport and communications	47,693	79,474	60,893
Road transport	42,639	72,218	17,667
Other purposes	77,738	162,648	316,232
Interest payments	61,004	134,778	230,485
Sub-total	471,708	762,721	1,084,504
Special efficiency payments§	27,106	50,805	63,999
Total	498,813	813,526	1,148,503
Current	400,364	694,272	960,850
Capital	98,449	119,254	187,653

* Excluding grants received (million new cedis): 66,629 in 1993; 49,483 in 1994; 93,785 (provisional) in 1995.
† Provisional.
‡ Excluding lending minus repayments (million new cedis): 11,877 in 1992; 8,029 in 1993; 8,259 in 1994.
§ Including provision for redeployment, retraining and relocation of public-sector employees.

1995 (provisional million new cedis): Total expenditure 1,697,893 (current 1,321,375, Capital 376,518), excluding net lending (15,804).

Source: IMF, *Ghana—Selected Issues and Statistical Annex* (August 1996).

INTERNATIONAL RESERVES (US $ million at 31 December)

	1994	1995	1996
Gold*	77.2	77.4	77.2
IMF special drawing rights	4.2	2.4	2.2
Reserve position in IMF	25.4	25.8	25.0
Foreign exchange	554.3	669.2	801.5
Total	661.1	774.9	905.9

* National valuation.

Source: IMF, *International Financial Statistics.*

MONEY SUPPLY ('000 million new cedis at 31 December)

	1994	1995	1996
Currency outside banks	368.80	546.34	723.99
Deposits of non-financial public enterprises	3.49	6.31	7.87
Demand deposits at deposit money banks	320.86	371.07	482.14
Total money (incl. others)	693.55	925.29	1,215.72

Source: IMF, *International Financial Statistics.*

COST OF LIVING (Consumer Price Index; base: 1990 = 100)

	1994	1995	1996
Food (incl. beverages)	189.2	306.9	416.7
All items (incl. others)	202.7	323.2	473.7

Source: UN, *Monthly Bulletin of Statistics.*

NATIONAL ACCOUNTS (at current prices)

National Income and Product ('000 million new cedis)

	1993	1994	1995
GDP in purchasers' values	3,674.9	4,950.4	7,418.0
Net factor income from abroad	−72.9	−106.1	−155.1
Gross national product	3,602.0	4,844.3	7,262.9
Less Consumption of fixed capital	230.3	287.9	359.8
National income in market prices	3,371.7	4,556.4	6,903.1

Source: IMF, *International Financial Statistics.*

Expenditure on the Gross Domestic Product ('000 million new cedis)

	1993	1994	1995
Government final consumption expenditure	559.6	703.5	921.7
Private final consumption expenditure	3,158.9	4,093.4	6,108.1
Increase in stocks	3.4	4.3	5.4
Gross fixed capital formation	578.4	737.3	1,028.1
Total domestic expenditure	4,300.3	5,538.5	8,063.3
Exports of goods and services	784.2	1,325.2	1,898.9
Less Imports of goods and services	1,409.7	1,913.4	2,544.2
GDP in purchasers' values	3,674.9	4,950.4	7,418.0
GDP at constant 1990 prices	2,332.6	2,421.5	2,530.3

Source: IMF, *International Financial Statistics.*

Gross Domestic Product by Economic Activity (million new cedis)

	1993	1994	1995*
Agriculture and livestock	1,674,386	1,942,650	2,906,613
Forestry and logging	161,910	207,420	316,239
Fishing	51,337	67,410	103,060
Mining and quarrying	75,031	103,710	131,809
Manufacturing	359,361	466,716	712,467
Electricity, gas and water	71,082	98,528	146,288
Construction	126,369	171,129	255,422
Trade, restaurant and hotels	750,314	995,660	1,512,750
Transport, storage and communications	169,808	228,172	474,803
Finance, insurance, real estate and business services	150,063	197,057	292,073
Other services	339,616	451,157	705,312
Sub-total	3,929,278	4,929,609	7,556,836
Import duties	75,031	93,370	131,023
Less Imputed bank service charge	55,286	72,600	110,692
GDP in purchasers' values	3,949,023	4,950,379	7,577,167

* Estimates.

Source: IMF, *Ghana—Selected Issues and Statistical Annex* (August 1996).

BALANCE OF PAYMENTS (US $ million)

	1994	1995	1996
Exports of goods f.o.b.	1,237.7	1,431.2	1,571.0
Imports of goods f.o.b.	–1,579.9	–1,687.8	–1,937.0
Trade balance	–342.2	–256.6	–366.0
Exports of services	147.5	150.6	156.8
Imports of services	–420.8	–432.6	–456.4
Balance on goods and services	–615.5	–538.6	–665.6
Other income received	11.8	13.7	23.5
Other income paid	–122.7	–142.9	–163.4
Balance on goods, services and income	–726.4	–667.8	–805.5
Current transfers received	487.3	538.9	497.9
Current transfers paid	–15.5	–15.7	–16.2
Current balance	–254.6	–144.6	–323.8
Capital account (net)	–1.0	–1.0	–1.0
Direct investment from abroad	233.0	106.5	120.0
Other investment assets	–119.6	–20.0	–179.4
Other investment liabilities	368.3	375.6	344.5
Net errors and omissions	–54.0	–60.0	19.3
Overall balance	172.1	256.5	–20.4

Source: IMF, *International Financial Statistics*.

External Trade

PRINCIPAL COMMODITIES

Imports (million new cedis)	1991	1992
Food and live animals	8,396	97,337
Rice	1,237	32,062
Crude materials (inedible) except fuels	12,748	41,447
Mineral fuels, lubricants, etc.	16,662	163,622
Crude petroleum	14,913	130,570
Petroleum products	608	21,750
Chemicals	8,211	104,369
Basic manufactures	16,830	130,124
Cement	2,448	33,800
Machinery and transport equipment	118,373	315,506
Passenger cars (excl. buses)	2,386	35,756
Lorries and trucks	4,145	44,421
Miscellaneous manufactured articles	6,257	75,788
Total (incl. others)	188,136	937,733

Source: UN Economic Commission for Africa, *African Statistical Yearbook*.

Exports (US $ million)	1993	1994	1995
Cocoa beans	250.5	295.0	361.1
Cocoa products	35.4	25.2	28.4
Timber and timber products	147.4	165.4	190.6
Gold	434.0	548.6	647.2
Electricity	69.1	56.4	53.0
Total (incl. others)	1,063.6	1,226.8	1,431.2

Source: IMF, *Ghana—Selected Issues and Statistical Annex* (August 1996).

PRINCIPAL TRADING PARTNERS (US $ million)

Imports	1996
China, People's Repub.	96.7
France	123.7
Germany	341.5
India	72.2
Italy	108.6
Japan	176.0
Netherlands	109.1
Nigeria	262.5
Spain	82.1
United Kingdom	453.2
USA	360.7
Total (incl. others)	2,693.3

Exports	1996
Belgium	32.3
France	60.5
Germany	142.6
Italy	44.8
Japan	58.4
Netherlands	165.3
Spain	31.3
Switzerland	486.3
United Kingdom	369.5
USA	49.2
Total (incl. others)	1,741.1

Source: Ministry of Trade and Industry.

Transport

RAILWAYS (traffic)

	1988	1989	1990
Passengers carried ('000)	3,259.4	2,890.4	1,896.8
Freight carried ('000 metric tons)	774.0	751.4	724.1
Passenger-km (million)	389.3	330.5	277.5
Net ton-km (million)	125.5	130.8	126.9

ROAD TRAFFIC ('000 motor vehicles in use at 31 December)

	1994	1995*	1996*
Passenger cars	90.0	90.0	90.0
Lorries and vans	44.7	45.0	45.0

* Estimates.

Source: International Road Federation, *World Road Statistics*..

SHIPPING

Merchant Fleet (registered at 31 December)

	1994	1995	1996
Number of vessels	164	172	195
Total displacement ('000 grt)	105.9	113.5	134.7

Source: Lloyd's Register of Shipping.

International Sea-borne Freight Traffic
(estimates, '000 metric tons)

	1991	1992	1993
Goods loaded	2,083	2,279	2,424
Goods unloaded	2,866	2,876	2,904

Source: UN Economic Commission for Africa, *African Statistical Yearbook.*

CIVIL AVIATION (traffic on scheduled services)

	1992	1993	1994
Kilometres flown (million)	5	4	5
Passengers carried ('000)	206	152	182
Passenger-km (million)	352	387	478
Total ton-km (million)	62	61	72

Source: UN, *Statistical Yearbook.*

Tourism

	1992	1993	1994
Tourist arrivals ('000)	213	257	248
Receipts from tourism (US $ million)	167	206	218

Source: UN, *Statistical Yearbook.*

1996: Tourist arrivals 300,000; Receipts from tourism US $248m. (Source: Ministry of Tourism).

Communications Media

	1993	1994	1995
Radio receivers ('000 in use)	n.a.	3,880	4,000
Television receivers ('000 in use)	n.a.	1,500	1,600
Telephones ('000 main lines in use)	49	50	n.a.
Telefax stations (number in use)	4,000	4,500	n.a.
Mobile cellular telephones (subscribers)	1,742	3,340	n.a.
Daily newspapers			
Number	n.a.	4	4
Average circulation ('000 copies)	n.a.	310*	310*

* Provisional or estimated figure.

Sources: UNESCO, *Statistical Yearbook*; UN, *Statistical Yearbook.*

Education

(1989/90, unless otherwise indicated)

	Institutions	Teachers	Students
Pre-primary	4,735	15,152	323,406
Primary[1]	11,064	72,925[2]	2,011,602
Secondary			
General (public only)	n.a.	39,903[3]	841,722[1]
Teacher training	38[4]	1,001	15,723
Vocational (public only)	20[5]	1,247	22,578[1]
University	3[5]	700[6]	9,609[3]

[1] 1991/92 figure(s).
[2] Provisional figure.
[3] 1990/91 figure.
[4] 1988 figure.
[5] 1988/89 figure.
[6] Excluding the University of Ghana.

Source: mainly UNESCO, *Statistical Yearbook.*

1992: *Primary* 10,623 institutions, 1,800,000 students (estimate); *Junior secondary* 5,136 institutions, 569,000 students (estimate); *Senior secondary* 404 institutions, 147,000 students (estimate); *Higher* 52,000 students.

Source: African Development Bank.

Directory

The Constitution

Under the terms of the Constitution of the Fourth Republic, which was approved by national referendum on 28 April 1992, Ghana has a multi-party political system. Executive power is vested in the President, who is Head of State and Commander-in-Chief of the Armed Forces. The President is elected by universal adult suffrage for a term of four years, and appoints a Vice-President. The duration of the President's tenure of office is limited to two four-year terms. It is also stipulated that, in the event that no presidential candidate receives more than 50% of votes cast, a new election between the two candidates with the highest number of votes is to take place within 21 days. Legislative power is vested in a 200-member unicameral Parliament, which is elected by direct adult suffrage for a four-year term. The Council of Ministers is appointed by the President, subject to approval by the Parliament. The Constitution also provides for a 25-member Council of State, principally comprising presidential nominees and regional representatives, and a 20-member National Security Council (chaired by the Vice-President), both of which act as advisory bodies to the President.

The Government

HEAD OF STATE

President and Commander-in-Chief of the Armed Forces: Flt-Lt (retd) JERRY JOHN RAWLINGS (assumed power as Chairman of Provisional National Defence Council 31 December 1981; elected President 3 November 1992; re-elected 7 December 1996).

Vice-President: Prof. JOHN EVANS ATTA MILLS.

COUNCIL OF MINISTERS
(February 1998)

Minister of Defence: Alhaji MAHAMA IDDRISU.

Minister of State: KOFI TOTOBI-QUAKYI.

Minister of Finance: RICHARD KWAME PEPRAH.

Minister of Parliamentary Affairs: J. H. OWUSU-ACHEAMPONG.

Minister of Foreign Affairs: VICTOR GBEHO.

Attorney-General and Minister of Justice: Dr OBED ASAMOAH.

Minister of Local Government: KWAMENA AHWOI.

Minister of Education: Dr CHRISTINE AMOAKO-NUAMAH.

Minister of the Interior: NII OKAIDJA ADAMAFIO.

Minister of Food and Agriculture: KWABENA ADJEI.

Minister of Health: Dr EUNICE BROOKMAN-AMISSAH.

Minister of Roads and Transport: EDWARD SALIA.

Minister of Tourism: MIKE GIZO.

Minister of Trade and Industry: JOHN FRANK ABU.

Minister of Youth and Sports: E. T. MENSAH.

Minister of Lands and Forestry: CLETUS AVOKA.

Minister of Works and Housing: ISAAC ADJEI-MENSAH.

Minister of Communications: EKWOW SPIO-GARBRAH.

Minister of Employment and Social Welfare: Alhaji MOHAMMED MUMUNI.

Minister of the Environment, Science and Technology: J. E. AFFUL.

Minister of Mines and Energy: FRED OHENE-KENA.

There are also three Ministers of State.

REGIONAL MINISTERS
(February 1998)

Ashanti: DANIEL OHENE AGYEKUM.

Brong Ahafo: DAVID OSEI-WUSU.

Central: KOJO YANKAH.

Eastern: PATIENCE ADDO.

Greater Accra: JOSHUA ALABI.

Northern: GILBERT IDDI.

Upper East: DONALD ADABRE.

Upper West: AMIDU SULEMANA.

Volta: Lt Col CHARLES K. AGBENAZA.

Western: ESTHER LILY NKANSAH.

MINISTRIES

Office of the President: POB 1627, Osu, Accra.

Ministry of Communications: POB M41, Accra; tel. (21) 228011; fax (21) 229786.

Ministry of Defence: Burma Camp, Accra; tel. (21) 777611; telex 2077; fax (21) 773951.

Ministry of Education: POB M45, Accra; tel. (21) 665421; fax (21) 664067.

Ministry of Employment and Social Welfare: POB M84, Accra; tel. (21) 665421; fax (21) 667251.

Ministry of the Environment, Science and Technology: POB M39, Accra; tel. (21) 662013; fax (21) 666828.

Ministry of Finance: POB M40, Accra; tel. (21) 665441; telex 2132; fax (21) 667069.

Ministry of Food and Agriculture: POB M37, Accra; tel. (21) 665421; fax (21) 663250.

Ministry of Foreign Affairs: POB M53, Accra; tel. (21) 664951; telex 2001; fax (21) 665363.

Ministry of Health: POB M44, Accra; tel. (21) 665421; fax (21) 663810.

Ministry of the Interior: POB M42, Accra; tel. (21) 665421; fax (21) 667450.

Ministry of Justice: POB M60, Accra.

Ministry of Lands and Forestry: POB M212, Accra; tel. (21) 665421; fax (21) 666801.

Ministry of Local Government: POB M50, Accra; tel. (21) 665421; fax (21) 661015.

Ministry of Mines and Energy: POB M212, Accra; tel. (21) 667151; fax (21) 668262.

Ministry of Parliamentary Affairs: Accra.

Ministry of Roads and Transport: POB M38, Accra; tel. (21) 665421; fax (21) 668340.

Ministry of Tourism: POB 4386, Accra; tel. (21) 666701; fax (21) 666182.

Ministry of Trade and Industry: POB M85, Accra; tel. (21) 665421; telex 2105; fax (21) 664115.

Ministry of Works and Housing: POB M43, Accra; tel. (21) 665421; fax (21) 663268.

Ministry of Youth and Sports: POB 1272, Accra; tel. (21) 665421; fax (21) 663927.

President and Legislature

PRESIDENT

Presidential Election, 7 December 1996

Candidates	% of votes
Flt-Lt (retd) JERRY RAWLINGS (NDC)	57.2
JOHN KUFUOR (Great Alliance*)	39.8
EDWARD MAHAMA (PNC)	3.0
Total	100

* An electoral coalition comprising the New Patriotic Party (NPP) and the People's Convention Party (PCP).

PARLIAMENT

Speaker: Justice DANIEL F. ANNAN.

Legislative Election, 7 December 1996

	Seats
National Democratic Congress (NDC)	133
New Patriotic Party (NPP)	60
People's Convention Party (PCP)	5
People's National Convention (PNC)	1
Total*	200

* Voting in one constituency was postponed. At a by-election in June 1997 the seat was won by the NPP.

COUNCIL OF STATE

Chairman: Alhaji MUMUNI BAWUMIA.

Political Organizations

Democratic People's Party (DPP): Accra; f. 1992; Chair. T. N. WARD-BREW.

EGLE (Every Ghanaian Living Everywhere) Party: Accra; pro-Govt alliance; Co-Chair. OWORAKU AMOFA, Capt. NII OKAI.

Ghana Democratic Republican Party (GDRP): Accra; f. 1992; Leader Dr KOFI AMOAH.

Great Consolidated People's Party (GCPP): Leader DAN LARTEY; Chair. E. B. MENSAH.

National Convention Party (NCP): Accra; f. 1992; Leader EBO TAIWAH.

National Democratic Congress (NDC): Tamale; f. 1992; pro-Govt alliance; Leader Flt-Lt (retd) JERRY JOHN RAWLINGS; Chair. Alhaji ISSIFU ALI; Sec.-Gen. Alhaji HUUDU YAHAYA.

New Patriotic Party (NPP): Accra; f. 1992 by supporters of the fmr Prime Minister, Dr Kofi Busia; Chair PETER ALA ADJETEY; Sec.-Gen. AGYENIM BOATENG.

People's Convention Party (PCP): Accra; f. Dec. 1993 by the National Independence Party, the People's Heritage Party and a faction of the People's National Convention; merged with Popular Party for Democracy and Development in 1996; Chair. K. DONKOR-AYIFLI; Sec.-Gen. SETH ABLOSO.

People's National Convention (PNC): Accra; f. 1992 by supporters of the fmr Pres., Dr Kwame Nkrumah; Leader E. MAHAMA.

Diplomatic Representation

EMBASSIES AND HIGH COMMISSIONS IN GHANA

Algeria: 82 Josif Broz Tito Ave, POB 2747, Accra; tel. (21) 776719; Ambassador: HAMID BOURKI.

Benin: 19 Volta St, Second Close, Airport Residential Area, POB 7871, Accra; tel. (21) 774860; Chargé d'affaires a.i.: L. TONOUKOUIN.

Brazil: 5 Volta St, Airport Residential Area, POB 2918, Accra; tel. (21) 774921; telex 2081; Ambassador: HELDER MARTINS DE MORAES.

Bulgaria: 3 Kakramadu Rd, East Cantonments, POB 3193, Accra; tel. (21) 772404; telex 2709; fax (21) 774231; Chargé d'affaires: GEORGE MITEV.

Burkina Faso: 772/3, Asylum Down, off Farrar Ave, POB 651, Accra; tel. (21) 221988; telex 2108; Ambassador: EMILE GOUBA.

Canada: No. 46, Independence Ave, POB 1639, Accra; tel. (21) 228555; telex 2024; fax (21) 773792; High Commissioner: J. R. SCHRAM.

China, People's Republic: No. 7, Agostinho Neto Rd, Airport Residential Area, POB 3356, Accra; tel. (21) 774527; Ambassador: ZHANG DEZHENG.

Côte d'Ivoire: 9 18th Lane, off Cantonments Rd, POB 3445, Christiansborg, Accra; tel. (21) 774611; telex 2131; Ambassador: KONAN NDA.

Cuba: 20 Amilcar Cabral Rd, Airport Residential Area, POB 9163 Airport, Accra; tel. (21) 775868; telex 2234; Ambassador: JUAN CARRETERO.

Czech Republic: C260/5, Kanda High Rd No. 2, POB 5226, Accra-North; tel. (21) 223540; fax (21) 225337; Ambassador: VLADIMIR KLIMA.

Denmark: 67 Dr Isert Rd, 8th Ave Extension, North Ridge, POB C596, Accra; tel. (21) 226972; telex 2746; fax (21) 228061; e-mail danemb@ighmail.com; Ambassador: BIRGIT STORGAARD MADSEN.

Egypt: 27 Fetreke St, Roman Ridge, Ambassadorial Estate, POB 2508, Accra; tel. (21) 776925; telex 2691; fax (21) 776795; Ambassador: MOHAMED EL-ZAYAT.

Ethiopia: 6 Adiembra Rd, East Cantonments, POB 1646, Accra; tel. (21) 775928; fax (21) 776807; Ambassador: Dr KUWANG TUTILAM.

France: 12th Rd, off Liberation Ave, POB 187, Accra; tel. (21) 774480; telex 2733; fax (21) 778321; Ambassador: DIDIER FERRAND.

Germany: Valdemosa Lodge, Plot No. 18, North Ridge Residential Area, 7th Ave Extension, POB 1757, Accra; tel. (21) 221311; telex 2025; fax (21) 221347; Ambassador: HANS-JOACHIM HELDT.

Guinea: 11 Osu Badu St, Dzorwulu, POB 5497, Accra-North; tel. (21) 777921; Ambassador: DORE DIALE DRUS.

Holy See: 8 Drake Ave, Airport Residential Area, POB 9675, Accra; tel. (21) 777759; fax (21) 774019; Apostolic Nuncio: Most Rev. ANDRÉ DUPUY, Titular Archbishop of Selsea.

Hungary: 14 West Cantonments, off Switchback Rd, POB 3072, Accra; tel. (21) 777234; telex 2543; Chargé d'affaires a.i.: IMRE SOSOVICSKA.

India: 12 Mankata Ave, Airport Residential Area, POB 3040, Accra; tel. (21) 777566; telex 2154; fax (21) 772176; High Commissioner: DILJIT SINGH PANNUN.

Iran: 12 Sir Arku Korsah St, Roman Ridge, POB 12673, Accra North; tel. (21) 777043; telex 2117; Ambassador: SHAMEDDIN KHAREGHANI.

Italy: Jawaharlal Nehru Rd, POB 140, Accra; tel. (21) 775621; telex 2039; Ambassador: MARIO FUGAZZOLA.

Japan: 8 Josif Broz Tito Ave, off Jawaharlal Nehru Ave, POB 1637, Accra; tel. (21) 775616; fax (21) 775951; Ambassador: AKIHISA TANAKA.

Korea, Democratic People's Republic: 139 Nortei Ababio Loop, Ambassadorial Estate, POB 13874, Accra; tel. (21) 777825; Ambassador: RI JAE SONG.

Korea, Republic: 3 Abokobi Rd, East Cantonments, POB 13700, Accra North; tel. (21) 776157; Ambassador: HWANG PU-HONG.

Lebanon: 864/1 Cantonments Rd, OSU, POB 562, Accra; tel. (21) 776727; telex 2118; Ambassador: Dr MOUNIR KHREICH.

Liberia: 10 West Cantonments, off Jawaharlal Nehru Rd, POB 895, Accra; tel. (21) 775641; telex 2071; Ambassador: T. BOYE NELSON.

Libya: 14 Sixth St, Airport Residential Area, POB 9665, Accra; tel. (21) 774820; telex 2179; Secretary of People's Bureau: Dr FATIMA MAGAME.

Mali: Agostino Neto Rd, Airport Residential Area, POB 1121, Accra; tel. (21) 666423; telex 2061; Ambassador: MUPHTAH AG HAIRY.

Netherlands: 89 Liberation Rd, Thomas Sankara Circle, POB 3248, Accra; tel. (21) 773644; telex 2128; fax (21) 773655; Ambassador: HELN C. R. M. PRINCEN.

Niger: 104/3 Independence Ave, POB 2685, Accra; tel. (21) 224962; Ambassador: OUMAROU YOUSSOUFOU.

Nigeria: Josif Broz Tito Ave, POB 1548, Accra; tel. (21) 776158; telex 2051; High Commissioner: T. A. OLU-OTUNLA.

Pakistan: 11 Ring Rd East, Danquah Circle, POB 1114, Accra; tel. (21) 776059; telex 2426; High Commissioner: Dr ABDUL KABIR.

Poland: 2 Akosombo St, Airport Residential Area, POB 2552, Accra; tel. (21) 775972; telex 2558; fax (21) 776108; Chargé d'affaires a.i.: KAZIMIERZ MAURER.

Romania: North Labone, Ward F, Block 6, House 262, POB 3735, Accra; tel. (21) 774076; telex 2027; Chargé d'affaires a.i.: GHEORGHE V. ILIE.

Russia: F856/1, Ring Rd East, POB 1634, Accra; tel. (21) 775611; Ambassador: (vacant).

Saudi Arabia: 10 Noi Fetreke St, Roman Ridge, Airport Residential Area, POB 670, Accra; tel. (21) 774311; telex 2407; Chargé d'affaires a.i.: ANWAR ABDUL FATTAH ABDRABBUH.

South Africa: Room 305, Golden Tulip Hotel, Liberation Road, POB 16033, Kia, Accra; tel. (21) 775360; fax (21) 775361; High Commissioner: JOSIAH MOTSOPE.

Spain: Airport Residential Area, Lamptey Ave Extension, POB 1218, Accra; tel. (21) 774004; telex 2680; fax (21) 776217; Ambassador: DIEGO MARÍA SÁNCHEZ BUSTAMANTE.

Switzerland: 9 Water Rd S.I., North Ridge Area, POB 359, Accra; tel. (21) 228125; telex 2197; fax (21) 223583; Ambassador: PIERRE MONOD.

Togo: Togo House, near Cantonments Circle, POB C120, Accra; tel. (21) 777950; telex 2166; fax (21) 777961; Ambassador: ASSIONGBOR FOLIVI.

United Kingdom: Osu Link, off Gamel Abdul Nasser Ave, POB 296, Accra; tel. (21) 221665; telex 2323; fax (21) 664652; High Commissioner: IAN W. MACKLEY.

USA: Ring Road East, POB 194, Accra; tel. (21) 775347; fax (21) 776008; Ambassador: EDWARD BAYNN.

Yugoslavia: 47 Senchi St, Airport Residential Area, POB 1629, Accra; tel. (21) 775761; Ambassador: LAZAR COVIĆ.

Judicial System

The civil law in force in Ghana is based on the Common Law, doctrines of equity and general statutes which were in force in England in 1874, as modified by subsequent Ordinances. Ghanaian customary law is, however, the basis of most personal, domestic and contractual relationships. Criminal Law is based on the Criminal Procedure Code, 1960, derived from English Criminal Law, and since amended. The Superior Court of Judicature comprises a Supreme Court, a Court of Appeal and a High Court of Justice; Inferior Courts include Circuit Courts, District Courts and such other Courts as may be designated by law.

Supreme Court: Consists of the Chief Justice and not fewer than four other Justices. It is the final court of appeal in Ghana and has jurisdiction in matters relating to the enforcement or interpretation of the Constitution.

Chief Justice: ISAAC KOBINA ABBAN.

Court of Appeal: Consists of the Chief Justice and not fewer than five Judges of the Court of Appeal. It has jurisdiction to hear and determine appeals from any judgment, decree or order of the High Court.

High Court: Comprises the Chief Justice and not fewer than 12 Justices of the High Court. It exercises original jurisdiction in all matters, civil and criminal, other than those for offences involving treason. Trial by jury is practised in criminal cases in Ghana and the Criminal Procedure Code, 1960, provides that all trials on indictment shall be by a jury or with the aid of Assessors.

Circuit Courts: Exercise original jurisdiction in civil matters where the amount involved does not exceed C100,000. They also have jurisdiction with regard to the guardianship and custody of infants, and original jurisdiction in all criminal cases, except offences where the maximum punishment is death or the offence of treason. They have appellate jurisdiction from decisions of any District Court situated within their respective circuits.

District Courts: To each magisterial district is assigned at least one District Magistrate who has original jurisdiction to try civil suits in which the amount involved does not exceed C50,000. District Magistrates also have jurisdiction to deal with all criminal cases, except first-degree felonies, and commit cases of a more serious nature to either the Circuit Court or the High Court. A Grade I District Court can impose a fine not exceeding C1,000 and sentences of imprisonment of up to two years and a Grade II District Court may impose a fine not exceeding C500 and a sentence of imprisonment of up to 12 months. A District Court has no appellate jurisdiction, except in rent matters under the Rent Act.

Juvenile Courts: Jurisdiction in cases involving persons under 17 years of age, except where the juvenile is charged jointly with an adult. The Courts comprise a Chairman, who must be either the District Magistrate or a lawyer, and not fewer than two other members appointed by the Chief Justice in consultation with the Judicial Council. The Juvenile Courts can make orders as to the protection and supervision of a neglected child and can negotiate with parents to secure the good behaviour of a child.

National Public Tribunal: Considers appeals from the Regional Public Tribunals. Its decisions are final and are not subject to any further appeal. The Tribunal consists of at least three members and not more than five, one of whom acts as Chairman.

Regional Public Tribunals: Hears criminal cases relating to prices, rent or exchange control, theft, fraud, forgery, corruption or any offence which may be referred to them by the Provisional National Defence Council.

Special Military Tribunal: Hears criminal cases involving members of the armed forces. It consists of between five and seven members.

Religion

At the 1960 census the distribution of religious groups was: Christians 42.8%, traditional religions 38.2%, Muslims 12.0%, unclassified 7.0%. Since August 1989 religious bodies have been required to register with the Religious Affairs Committee of the National Commission for Culture.

CHRISTIANITY

Christian Council of Ghana: POB 919, Accra; tel. (21) 776725; f. 1929; advisory body comprising 14 Protestant churches; Chair. (vacant); Gen. Sec. Rev. DAVID A. DARTEY.

The Anglican Communion

Anglicans in Ghana are adherents of the Church of the Province of West Africa, comprising 12 dioceses, of which seven are in Ghana. In early 1997 it was announced that the dioceses of Sunyani and Tamale had been separated.

Archbishop of the Province of West Africa and Bishop of Koforidua: Most Rev. ROBERT OKINE, POB 980, Koforidua; tel. (81) 2329.

Bishop of Accra: Rt Rev. JUSTICE O. AKROFI (designate), Bishopscourt, POB 8, Accra; tel. (21) 662292.

Bishop of Cape Coast: Rt Rev. KOBINA ADDUAH QUASHIE, Bishopscourt, POB 233, Cape Coast; tel. (42) 2502.

Bishop of Kumasi: Rt Rev. EDMUND YEBOAH, Bishop's House, POB 144, Kumasi; tel. (51) 4117.

Bishop of Sekondi: Rt Rev. THEOPHILUS ANNOBIL, POB 85, Sekondi; tel. (31) 6048.

Bishop of Sunyani and Tamale: Rt Rev. JOSEPH KOBINA DADSON, Bishop's House, POB 110, Tamale; tel. (71) 2018.

The Roman Catholic Church

Ghana comprises three archdioceses and 12 dioceses. At 31 December 1995 there were 2,109,240 adherents in the country, equivalent to 12.3% of the total population.

Ghana Bishops' Conference: National Catholic Secretariat, POB 9712, Airport, Accra; tel. (21) 500491; telex 2471; fax (21) 500493; f. 1960; Pres. Rt Rev. FRANCIS A. K. LODONU, Bishop of Ho.

Archbishop of Accra: Most Rev. DOMINIC ANDOH, Chancery Office, POB 247, Accra; tel. (21) 222728; fax (21) 231619.

Archbishop of Cape Coast: Most Rev. PETER K. APPIAH-TURKSON, Archbishop's House, POB 112, Cape Coast; tel. (42) 33471; fax (42) 33473.

Archbishop of Tamale: Most Rev. GREGORY EEBO KPIEBAYA, Gumbehini Rd, POB 42, Tamale; tel. (71) 2924; fax (71) 2425.

Other Christian Churches

African Methodist Episcopal Zion Church: Sekondi; Pres. Rev. Dr ZORMELO.

Christian Methodist Episcopal Church: POB 3906, Accra; Pres. Rev. YENN BATA.

Evangelical-Lutheran Church of Ghana: POB 197, Kaneshie; tel. (21) 223487; telex 2134; fax (21) 223353; Pres. Rt Rev. Dr PAUL KOFI FYNN; 21,700 mems.

Evangelical-Presbyterian Church: POB 18, Ho; tel. (91) 755; f. 1847; Moderator Rt Rev. D. A. KORANTENG; 295,000 mems.

Ghana Baptist Convention: POB 1979, Kumasi; tel. (51) 5215; f. 1963; Pres. Rev. FRED DEEGBE; Sec. Rev. FRANK ADAMS.

Mennonite Church: POB 5485, Accra; fax (21) 220589; f. 1957; Moderator Rev. Dr TEI-KWABLA; Sec. ISAAC K. QUARTEY; 4,800 mems.

Methodist Church of Ghana: Liberia Rd, POB 403, Accra; tel. (21) 228120; fax (21) 227008; Pres. Rt Rev. Dr SAMUEL ASANTE ANTWI; Sec. Rev. MACLEAN AGYIRI KUMI; 341,000 mems.

Presbyterian Church of Ghana: POB 1800, Accra; tel. (21) 662511; telex 2525; fax (21) 665594; f. 1828; Moderator Rt Rev. ANTHONY ANTWI BEEKO; Sec. Rev. Dr D. N. A. KPOBI; 422,500 mems.

Seventh-day Adventists: POB 1016, Accra; tel. (21) 223720; telex 2119; f. 1943; Pres. P. K. ASAREH; Sec. SETH A. LARYEA.

The African Methodist Episcopal Church, the F'Eden Church and the Society of Friends (Quakers) are also active in Ghana.

In June 1989 the activities of the Church of Jesus Christ of Latter-day Saints (Mormons) and the Jehovah's Witnesses were banned. These groups were deemed to have conducted themselves in a manner not conducive to public order.

ISLAM

There is a substantial Muslim population in the Northern Region. The majority are Malikees.

Chief Imam: Alhaji MUKITAR ABASS.

The Press

In 1992 a commission was established to regulate the media.

DAILY NEWSPAPERS

Daily Graphic: Graphic Rd, POB 742, Accra; tel. (21) 228911; fax (21) 669886; f. 1950; state-owned; Editor ELVIS ARYEH; circ. 100,000.

The Ghanaian Times: New Times Corpn, Ring Rd West, POB 2638, Accra; tel. (21) 228282; fax (21) 229398; f. 1958; state-owned; Editor CHRISTIAN AGGREY; circ. 40,000.

PERIODICALS

Weekly

Bombshell: Crossfire Publications , POB 376, Sakumono, Accra; tel. (21) 234750; fax (21) 233172; Editor BEN ASAMOAH.

Business and Financial Times: POB 2157, Accra; tel. and fax (21) 223334; e-mail b&ft@igh.com; Man. Editor JOHN HANSON; Editor HENRY ADDISON.

Catholic Standard: Accra.

Champion: POB 6828, Accra-North; tel. (21) 229079; Man. Dir MARK D. N. ADDY; Editor FRANK CAXTON WILLIAMS; circ. 300,000.

Christian Chronicle: Accra; English; Editor GEORGE NAYKENE.

The Democrat: Democrat Publications, POB 13605, Accra; tel. (21) 76804; Editor L. K. NYAHO.

Echo: POB 5288, Accra; f. 1968; Sun.; Man. Editor M. K. FRIMPONG; circ. 40,000.

Entertaining Eye: Kad Publications, POB 125, Darkuman-Accra; Editor NANA KWAKYE YIADOM; circ. 40,000.

Evening Digest: News Media Ltd, POB 7082, Accra; tel. (21) 221071; Editor P. K. ANANTITETTEH.

Evening News: POB 7505, Accra; tel. (21) 229416; Man. Editor OSEI POKU; circ. 30,000.

Experience: POB 5084, Accra-North; Editor ALFRED YAW POKU; circ. 50,000.

Free Press: Tommy Thompson Books Ltd, POB 6492, Accra; tel. (21) 225994; independent; English; Editor EBEN QUARCOO.

Ghana Life: Ghana Life Publications, POB 11337, Accra; tel. (21) 229835; Editor NIKKI BOA-AMPONSEM.

Ghana Palaver: Palaver Publications, POB 15744, Accra-North; tel. (21) 232495; Editor BRUCE QUANSAH.

Ghanaian Chronicle: General Portfolio Ltd, Private mail bag, Accra-North; tel. (21) 227789; fax (21) 775895; Editor EBO QUANSAH; circ. 60,000.

Ghanaian Dawn: Dawn Publications, POB 721, Mamprobi, Accra; Editor MABEL LINDSAY.

The Ghanaian Voice: Newstop Publications, POB 514, Mamprobi, Accra; Editor DAN K. ANSAH; circ. 100,000.

The Gossip: Gossip Publications, POB 5355, Accra-North; Editor C. A. ACHEAMPONG.

Graphic Sports: Graphic Rd, POB 742, Accra; tel. (21) 228911; state-owned; Editor JOE AGGREY; circ. 60,000.

The Guide: Western Publications Ltd, POB 8253, Accra-North; tel. (21) 232760; Editor KWEKU BAAKO Jnr.

The Independent: Accra.

The Mirror: Graphic Rd, POB 742, Accra; tel. (21) 228911; telex 2475; fax (21) 669886; f. 1953; state-owned; Sat.; Editor E. N. V. PROVENCAL; circ. 90,000.

The New Ghanaian: Tudu Publishing House, POB 751, Tamale; tel. (71) 22579; Editor RAZAK EL-ALAWA.

New Nation: POB 6828, Accra-North; Editor S. N. SASRAKU; circ. 300,000.

The Pioneer: Abura Printing Works Ltd, POB 325, Kumasi; tel. (51) 2204; f. 1939; Editor JOHNSON GYAMPOH; circ. 100,000.

Private Eye: Kad Life Books Channels, POB 125, Accra; tel. (21) 230684; Editor AWUKU AGYEMANG-DUAH.

Public Agenda: P. A. Communications, POB 5564, Accra-North; tel. (21) 238821; fax (21) 231687; e-mail isodec@ncs.com.gh; f. 1994; Editor YAO GRAHAM; circ. 12,000.

Sporting News: POB 5481, Accra-North; f. 1967; Man. Editor J. OPPONG-AGYARE.

The Standard: Standard Newspaper Magazines Ltd, POB 247, Accra; tel. (21) 228410; Editor BENEDICT ASSOROW; circ. 50,000.

Statesman: Kinesic Communications, POB 846, Accra; tel. and fax (21) 233242; official publ. of the New Patriotic Party; Editor HARUNNA ATTAH.

Voice: Accra.

The Weekend: Newstop Publications, POB 514, Mamprobi, Accra; tel. and fax (21) 226943; Editor EMMANUEL YARTEY; circ. 40,000.

Weekly Events: Clear Type Image Ltd, 29 Olympic Street (Enterprise House), Kokomlemle, POB 7634, Accra-North; tel. (21) 223085; Editor JORIS JORDAN DODOO.

Weekly Insight: Militant Publications Ltd, POB K272, Accra New Town, Accra; tel. (21) 660148; f. 1993; independent; English; Editor KWESI PRATT Jnr.

Weekly Spectator: New Times Corpn, Ring Road West, POB 2638, Accra; tel. (21) 228282; fax (21) 229398; state-owned; f. 1963; Sun.; Editor WILLIE DONKOR; circ. 165,000.

Other

Africa Flamingo: Airport Emporium Ltd, POB 9194, Accra; monthly; Editor FELIX AMANFU; circ. 50,000.

African Observer: POB 1171, Kaneshie, Accra; tel. (012) 231459; bi-monthly; Editor STEVE MALLORY.

African Woman: Ring Rd West, POB 1496, Accra; monthly.

Akwansosem: Ghana Information Services, POB 745, Accra; tel. (21) 228011; telex 2201; quarterly; in Akuapim Twi, Asanti Twi and Fante; Editor KATHLEEN OFOSU-APPIAH.

Armed Forces News: General Headquarters, Directorate of Public Relations, Burma Camp, Accra; tel. (21) 776111; f. 1966; quarterly; Editor Adotey Ankrah-Hoffman; circ. 4,000.

Boxing and Football Illustrated: POB 8392, Accra; f. 1976; monthly; Editor Nana O. Ampomah; circ. 10,000.

Business and Financial Concord: Sammy Tech Consult Enterprise, POB 5677, Accra-North; tel. (21) 232446; fortnightly; Editor Kwabena Richardson.

Chit Chat: POB 7043, Accra; monthly; Editor Rosemond Adu.

Christian Messenger: Presbyterian Book Depot Bldg, POB 3075, Accra; tel. and fax (21) 662415; telex 2525; f. 1883; English; also **The Presbyterian** (in Twi and Ga); quarterly; Editor G. B. K. Owusu; circ. 40,000.

Drum: POB 1197, Accra; monthly; general interest.

Ghana Enterprise: c/o Ghana National Chamber of Commerce, POB 2325, Accra; tel. (21) 662427; telex 2687; fax (21) 662210; f. 1961; quarterly; Editor J. B. K. Amanfu.

Ghana Journal of Science: Ghana Science Asscn, POB 7, Legon; monthly; Editor Dr A. K. Ahafia.

Ghana Manufacturer: c/o Asscn of Ghana Industries, POB 8624, Accra-North; tel. (21) 777283; e-mail agi@ighmail.com; f. 1974; quarterly; Editor (vacant); circ. 1,500.

Ghana Official News Bulletin: Information Services Dept, POB 745, Accra; English; political, economic, investment and cultural affairs.

Ideal Woman (Obaa Sima): POB 5737, Accra; tel. (21) 221399; f. 1971; fortnightly; Editor Kate Abbam.

Independent: Trans Afrika News Ltd, POB 4031, Accra; tel. (21) 661091; bi-weekly; Editor Kabral Blay-Amihere.

Insight and Opinion: POB 5446, Accra; quarterly; Editorial Sec. W. B. Ohene.

Legon Observer: POB 11, Legon; telex 2556; fax (21) 774338; f. 1966; publ. by Legon Society on National Affairs; fortnightly; Chair. J. A. Dadson; Editor Ebow Daniel.

Police News: Police HQ, Accra; monthly; Editor S. S. Appiah; circ. 20,000.

The Post: Ghana Information Services, POB 745, Accra; tel. (21) 228011; telex 2201; f. 1980; monthly; current affairs and analysis; circ. 25,000.

Radio and TV Times: Ghana Broadcasting Corpn, Broadcasting House, POB 1633, Accra; tel. (21) 221161; telex 2114; f. 1960; quarterly; Editor Sam Thompson; circ. 5,000.

The Scope: POB 8162, Tema; monthly; Editor Emmanuel Doe Ziorklui; circ. 10,000.

Students World: POB M18, Accra; tel. (21) 763622; telex 2171; fax (21) 778715; f. 1974; monthly; educational; Man. Editor Eric Ofei; circ. 10,000.

The Teacher: Ghana National Asscn of Teachers, POB 209, Accra; tel. (21) 221515; fax (21) 226286; f. 1931; quarterly; circ. 30,000.

Truth and Life: Gift Publications, POB 11337, Accra-North; monthly; Editor Pastor Kobena Charm.

The Watchman: Watchman Gospel Ministry, POB 4521, Accra; tel. (21) 220892; bi-monthly; Editor Divine Kumah.

NEWS AGENCIES

Ghana News Agency: POB 2118, Accra; tel. (21) 665136; telex 2400; fax 669840; e-mail ghnews@ncs.com.gh; f. 1957; Gen. Man. Sam B. Quaicoe; 10 regional offices and 110 district offices.

Foreign Bureaux

Associated Press (AP) (USA): POB 6172, Accra; Bureau Chief P. K. Cobbinah-Essem.

Xinhua (New China) News Agency (People's Republic of China): 2 Seventh St, Airport Residential Area, POB 3897, Accra; tel. (21) 772042; telex 2314.

Deutsche Presse-Agentur (Germany) and Reuters (UK) are also represented.

Publishers

Advent Press: POB 0102, Osu, Accra; tel. (21) 777861; telex 2119; f. 1937; Gen. Man. Emmanuel C. Tetteh.

Adwinsa Publications (Ghana) Ltd: Advance Press Bldg, 3rd Floor, School Rd, POB 92, Legoh Accra; tel. (21) 221654; f. 1977; general, educational; Man. Dir Kwabena Amponsah.

Afram Publications: 9 Ring Rd East, POB M18, Accra; tel. (21) 763622; telex 2171; fax (21) 778715; f. 1974; textbooks and general; Man. Dir Eric Ofei.

Africa Christian Press: POB 30, Achimota; tel. (21) 220271; fax (21) 668115; f. 1964; religious, biography, children's; Gen. Man. Richard A. B. Crabbe.

Asempa Publishers: POB 919, Accra; tel. (21) 233084; fax (21) 233130; e-mail asempa@ncs.com.gh; f. 1970; religion, social issues, African music, fiction, children's; Gen. Man. Rev. Emmanuel B. Bortey.

Baafour and Co: POB K189, Accra New Town; f. 1978; general; Man. B. Kese-Amankwaa.

Benibengor Book Agency: POB 40, Aboso; fiction, biography, children's and paperbacks; Man. Dir J. Benibengor Blay.

Black Mask Ltd: POB 7894, Accra North; tel. (21) 229968; f. 1979; textbooks, plays, novels, handicrafts; Man. Dir Yaw Owusu Asante.

Editorial and Publishing Services: POB 5743, Accra; general, reference; Man. Dir M. Danquah.

Educational Press and Manufacturers Ltd: POB 9184, Airport-Accra; tel. (21) 220395; f. 1975; textbooks, children's; Man. G. K. Kodua.

Encyclopaedia Africana Project: POB 2797, Accra; tel. (21) 776939; f. 1962; reference; Dir J. O. Vanderpuye.

Frank Publishing Ltd: POB M414, Accra; f. 1976; secondary school textbooks; Man. Dir Francis K. Dzokoto.

Ghana Publishing Corpn: PMB Tema; tel. (221) 2921; f. 1965; textbooks and general fiction and non-fiction; Man. Dir F. K. Nyarko.

Ghana Universities Press: POB 4219, Accra; tel. (21) 761051; f. 1962; scholarly and academic; Dir K. M. Ganu.

Goodbooks Publishing Co: POB 10416, Accra North; tel. (21) 665629; f. 1968; children's; Man. A. Asirifi.

Miracle Bookhouse: POB 7487, Accra North; tel. (21) 226684; f. 1977; general; Man. J. Appiah-Berko.

Moxon Paperbacks: POB M160, Accra; tel. (21) 665397; fax (21) 774358; f. 1967; travel and guide books, fiction and poetry, Africana; quarterly catalogue of Ghanaian books and periodicals in print; Man. Dir James Moxon.

Sedco Publishing Ltd: Sedco House, Tabon St, North Ridge, POB 2051, Accra; tel. (21) 221332; telex 2456; fax (21) 220107; f. 1975; educational; Man. Dir Courage K. Segbawu.

Sheffield Publishing Co: Accra; tel. (21) 667480; fax (21) 665960; f. 1970; religion, politics, economics, science, fiction; Publr Ronald Mensah.

Unimax Publishers Ltd: 42 Ring Rd South Industrial Area, POB 10722, Accra-North; tel. (21) 227443; telex 2515; fax (21) 225215; e-mail unimax@africanonline.com.gh; atlases, educational and children's; Dir Edward Addo.

Waterville Publishing House: POB 195, Accra; tel. (21) 663124; f. 1963; general fiction and non-fiction, textbooks, paperbacks, Africana; Man. Dir H. W. O. Okai.

Woeli Publishing Services: POB K601, Accra New Town; tel. and fax (21) 229294; f. 1984; children's, fiction, academic; Dir W. A. Dekutsey.

PUBLISHERS' ASSOCIATIONS

Ghana Book Development Council: POB M430, Accra; tel. (21) 229178; f. 1975; govt-financed agency; promotes and co-ordinates writing, production and distribution of books; Exec. Dir D. A. Nimako.

Ghana Book Publishers' Association: c/o Africa Christian Press, POB 430, Achimota; Sec. E. B. Bortey.

Private Newspaper Publishers' Association of Ghana (PRINPAG): POB 125, Darkuman, Accra; Gen. Sec. K. Agyemang Duah.

Broadcasting and Communications

TELECOMMUNICATIONS

Ghana Telecommunication Co Ltd: Posts and Telecommunications Bldg, Accra-North; tel. (21) 221001; telex 3010; fax (21) 667979; f. 1974 as Posts and Telecommunications Corporation; 30% transferred to the private sector in 1997; provides both internal and external postal and telecommunication services; Dir-Gen. Joseph Aggrey-Mensah; Man. Dir Adnan Rofiee.

BROADCASTING

There are internal radio broadcasts in English, Akan, Dagbani, Ewe, Ga, Hausa and Nzema, and an external service in English and French. There are three transmitting stations, with a number of relay stations. There is a total of eight main colour television transmitters. In 1995 36 private companies were granted authorization to operate radio and television networks. The Ghana Frequency Registration and Control Board gave approval for 10 new community radio stations in 1996.

Ghana Broadcasting Corporation: Broadcasting House, POB 1633, Accra; tel. (21) 221161; telex 2114; fax (21) 221153; f. 1935; Dir-Gen. Dr KOFI FRIMPONG; Dir of TV Prof. MARK DUODU; Dir of Radio CRIS TACKIE.

Finance

(cap. = capital; res = reserves; dep. = deposits; m. = million; brs = branches; amounts in cedis)

BANKING

Central Bank

Bank of Ghana: Thorpe Rd, POB 2674, Accra; tel. (21) 666902; telex 2052; fax (21) 662996; f. 1957; bank of issue; cap. 100,000m., res 18,351m., dep. 405,977m. (Dec. 1995); Chair. and Gov. KWABENA DUFFOUR.

State Banks

Agricultural Development Bank: Cedi House, Liberia Rd, POB 4191, Accra; tel. (21) 662758; telex 2295; fax (21) 662846; f. 1965; 65% state-owned; credit facilities for farmers and commercial banking; cap. and res 53,804m., dep. 109,074.8m. (Dec. 1996); Chair. NATHAN QUAO; Man. Dir P. A. KURANCHIE; 32 brs.

Bank for Housing and Construction (BHC): Okofoh House, 24 Kwame Nkrumah Ave, POB M1, Adabraka, Accra; tel. (21) 220033; telex 2559; fax (21) 229631; f. 1983; 50% state-owned; cap. 1,000m. (Dec. 1995); Chair. K. TWUM BOAFO; Man. Dir J. E. ABABIO.

Ghana Commercial Bank: POB 134, Accra; tel. (21) 664914; telex 2034; fax (21) 662168; f. 1953; 58% state-owned; cap. 20,000m., res 47,830m., dep. 359,253m. (Dec. 1995); Chair. S. K. APPEA; Man. Dir HELEN K. LOKKO; 145 brs.

Ghana Co-operative Bank Ltd: Kwame Nkrumah Ave, POB 5292, Accra-North; tel. (21) 663131; telex 2446; fax (21) 662359; f. 1970; 81% state-owned; cap. 2,913.7m. (Dec. 1994); Chair. GEORGE K. HAGAN; Man. Dir K. K. MENSAH; 21 brs.

National Investment Bank Ltd (NIB): 37 Kwame Nkrumah Ave, POB 3726, Accra; tel. (21) 669301; telex 2161; fax (21) 669307; f. 1963; 86.3% state-owned; provides long-term investment capital, jt venture promotion, consortium finance man. and commercial banking services; cap. 3,242.0m., dep. 51,798.3m. (Dec. 1995); Chair. JOHN K. RICHARDSON; Man. Dir STEVE DADZIE; 10 brs.

National Trust Holding Co: Dyson House, Kwame Nkrumah Ave, POB 9563, Airport, Accra; tel. (21) 229664; fax (21) 229975; e-mail nthc@ncs.com.gh; f. 1976 to finance Ghanaian acquisitions of indigenous cos; also assists in their development and expansion, and carries out stockbroking, portfolio man., underwriting, trusteeship business, corporate advisory services and real estate development; cap. 500m. (1996); Chair. JOANA FELICITY DICKSON; Man. Dir CHARLES PADDY SAWYERR.

Social Security Bank (SSB): POB 13119, Accra; tel. (21) 221726; telex 2209; fax (21) 668651; f. 1976; cap. 6,734.5m., dep. 277,309.1m. (Dec. 1996); Chair. HENRY DEI; Man. Dir PRYCE K. THOMPSON.

Trust Bank Ghana Ltd: 68 Kwame Nkrumah Ave, POB 1862, Accra; tel. (21) 665708; telex 2782; fax (21) 665710; f. 1996 to take over assets and liabilities of Meridien BIAO Bank Ghana Ltd; cap. 10.1m. (April 1996); Man. Dir DAVID C. JOHNSON.

Merchant Banks

CAL Merchant Bank Ltd: 45 Independence Ave, POB 14596, Accra; tel. (21) 221056; telex 2675; fax (21) 231913; f. 1990 as Continental Acceptances Ltd; cap. and res 2,754.4m., dep. 28,464.4m. (Dec. 1993); Chair. LOUIS CASELY-HAYFORD; Gen. Man. CLIFTON J. BEST.

Ecobank Ghana (EBG): 19 Seventh Ave, Ridge West, Accra; tel. (21) 231931; telex 2718; fax (21) 231934; f. 1989; 74.7% owned by Ecobank Transnational Inc (operating under the auspices of the Economic Community of West African States); cap. 6,500m., res 10,448m., dep. 162,429m. (Dec. 1996); Chair. JOHN SACKAH ADDO; Man. Dir J. N. AKA.

First Atlantic Merchant Bank Ltd: Atlantic Place, 1 Seventh Ave, Ridge West, POB C1620, Cantonments, Accra; tel. (21) 231433; telex 2915; fax (21) 231399; f. 1995; cap. 1,975.0m., res 91.6m., dep. 13,130.5m. (Dec. 1996); Chair. SAM JONAH; Man. Dir JUDE ARTHUR.

Merchant Bank (Ghana) Ltd: Merban House, 44 Kwame Nkrumah Ave, POB 401, Accra; tel. (21) 666331; telex 2191; fax (21) 667305; f. 1972; cap. 5,000m., res 16,056.7m., dep. 123,768.2m. (Dec. 1996); Chair. J. RICHARDSON; Man. Dir CHRIS N. NARTEY; 4 brs.

Foreign Banks

Barclays Bank of Ghana Ltd (UK): High St, POB 2949, Accra; tel. (21) 667629; telex 2721; fax (21) 667420; f. 1917; 40% state-owned; cap. 1,000.0m., res 34,579.0m., dep. 283,996.0m. (Dec. 1996); Chair. NANA WEREKO AMPEM; Man. Dir M. O. BRISTOW; 26 brs.

Standard Chartered Bank Ghana Ltd (UK): Standard Bank Bldg, High St, POB 768, Accra; tel. (21) 664591; telex 2671; fax (21) 667751; f. 1896; cap. 500m., res 40,556m., dep. 275,311m. (Dec. 1996); Chair. DAVID ANDOH; CEO VISHNU MOHAN; 28 brs.

STOCK EXCHANGE

Ghana Stock Exchange (GSE): Cedi House, 5th Floor, Liberia Rd, POB 1849, Accra; tel. (21) 669908; telex 2722; fax (21) 669913; e-mail stockex@ncs.com.gh; 52 mems; Dir YEBOA AMOA.

INSURANCE

Ghana Union Assurance Co Ltd: POB 1322, Accra; tel. (21) 664421; telex 2008; fax (21) 664988; f. 1973; Man. Dir KWADWO DUKU.

The Great African Insurance Co Ltd: POB 12349, Accra North; tel. (21) 227459; telex 3027; fax (21) 228905; f. 1980; Man. Dir KWASI AKOTO.

The State Insurance Corporation of Ghana: POB 2363, Accra; tel. (21) 666961; telex 2171; fax (21) 662205; f. 1962; state-owned; undertakes all classes of insurance; also engages in real estate and other investment; Man. Dir B. K. QUASHIE.

Social Security and National Insurance Trust: Pension House, POB M149, Accra; tel. (21) 667742; telex 2564; fax (21) 662226; f. 1972; covers over 650,000 contributors; Dir-Gen. HENRY G. DEI.

Vanguard Assurance Co Ltd: Insurance Hall, Derby House, Derby Ave, POB 1868, Accra; tel. (21) 666485; telex 2005; fax (21) 668610; f. 1974; general accident, marine, motor and life insurance; Man. Dir NANA AWUAH-DARKO AMPEM; 7 brs.

Several foreign insurance companies operate in Ghana.

Trade and Industry

GOVERNMENT AGENCIES

Divestiture Implementation Committee: F3515 Ring Road East, North Labone, Cantonments, POB C102, Accra; tel. (21) 772049; fax (21) 773126; e-mail dicgh@ncs.com.gh; f. 1988; Exec. Sec. EMMANUEL AGBODO.

Food Production Corporation: POB 1853, Accra; f. 1971; state corpn providing employment for youth in large scale farming enterprises; controls 76,900 ha of land (16,200 ha under cultivation); operates 87 food farms on a co-operative and self-supporting basis, and rears poultry and livestock.

Ghana Export Promotion Council: Republic House, POB M146, Accra; tel. (21) 228813; fax (21) 668263; f. 1974; Chair. and mems appointed by Ministry of Trade and Industry, Asscn of Ghana Industries, Customs, Excise and Preventive Services, Bank of Ghana, Ghana Commercial Bank, GIHOC Distilleries, Export Finance Co Ltd, Information Service Dept, Ghana Trade Fair Authority, Asscn of Ghanaian Exporters and Ministry of the Environment, Science and Technology; Exec. Sec. TAWIA AKYEA.

Ghana Food Distribution Corporation: POB 4245, Accra; tel. (21) 228428; f. 1971; buys, stores, preserves, distributes and retails foodstuffs through 10 regional centres; Man. Dir E. H. K. AMANKWA.

Ghana Free Zones Board: POB M47, Accra; tel. (21) 780532; telex 2951; fax (21) 780536; approves establishment of companies in export processing zones; Exec. Sec. GEORGE ABOAGYE.

Ghana Industrial Holding Corporation (GIHOC): POB 2784, Accra; tel. (21) 664998; telex 2109; f. 1967; controls and manages 26 state enterprises, including steel, paper, bricks, paint, pharmaceuticals, electronics, metals, canneries, distilleries and boat-building factories; also has three subsidiary cos and four jt ventures; managed since 1989 by an interim superintending secr.

Ghana Investment Promotion Centre: Central Ministerial Area, POB M193, Accra; tel. (21) 665125; telex 2229; fax (21) 663801; e-mail gipc@ncs.com.gh; f. 1981; negotiates new investments, approves projects, registers foreign capital and decides extent of govt participation.

Ghana National Trading Corporation (GNTC): POB 67, Accra; tel. (21) 664871; f. 1961; organizes exports and imports of selected commodities; over 500 retail outlets in 12 admin. dists.

Ghana Standards Board: c/o POB M245, Accra; tel. (21) 500065; telex 2545; fax (21) 500092; f. 1967; establishes and promulgates standards; promotes standardization, industrial efficiency and development and industrial welfare, health and safety; operates certification mark scheme; 403 mems; Dir Rev. Dr E. K. MARFO.

National Board for Small-scale Industries: Ministry of Trade and Industry, POB M85, Accra; f. 1985; promotes small and medium-scale industrial and commercial enterprises by providing credit, advisory services and training.

State Farms Corporation: Accra; undertakes agricultural projects in all regions but Upper Region; Man. Dir E. N. A. THOMPSON (acting).

State Housing Construction Co: POB 2753, Accra; f. 1982 by merger; oversees govt housing programme.

CHAMBER OF COMMERCE

Ghana National Chamber of Commerce: POB 2325, Accra; tel. (21) 662427; telex 2687; fax (21) 662210; f. 1961; promotes and protects industry and commerce, organizes trade fairs; 2,500 individual mems and 8 mem. chambers; Pres. ALEX AWUKU; Exec. Sec. JOHN B. K. AMANFU.

INDUSTRIAL AND TRADE ASSOCIATIONS

Best Fibres Development Board: POB 1992, Kumasi; f. 1970; promotes the commercial cultivation of best fibres and their processing, handling and grading.

Ghana Cocoa Board (COCOBOD): POB 933, Accra; tel. (21) 221212; telex 2082; fax (21) 667104; f. 1985; monopoly purchaser of cocoa until 1993; responsible for purchase, grading and export of cocoa, coffee and shea nuts; also encourages production and scientific research aimed at improving quality and yield of these crops; controls all exports of cocoa; CEO JOHN NEWMAN.

Grains and Legumes Development Board: POB 4000, Kumasi; tel. (51) 4231; f. 1970; state-controlled; promotes and develops production of cereals and leguminous vegetables.

The Indian Association of Ghana: POB 2891, Accra; tel. (21) 776227; f. 1939; Pres. ATMARAM GOKALDAS.

Institute of Marketing (IMG): POB 102, Accra; tel. (21) 226697; telex 2488; fax (21) 222171; f. 1981; reorg. 1989; seeks to enhance professional standards; Chair. ISHMAEL YAMSON; Pres. FRANK APPIAH.

Minerals Commission: 10 Sixth St, Airport Residential Area, Accra; tel. (21) 772783; telex 2545; fax (21) 773324; f. 1984; supervises, promotes and co-ordinates the minerals industry.

Timber Export Development Board: POB 515, Takoradi; tel. (31) 29216; telex 2189; f. 1985; promotes the sale and export of timber; CEO SAMUEL KWESI APPIAH.

EMPLOYERS' ORGANIZATION

Ghana Employers' Association: 122 Kojo Thompson Rd, POB 2616, Accra; tel. (21) 228455; fax (21) 228405; f. 1959; 400 mems; Pres. ISHMAEL E. YAMSON; Vice-Pres. ATO AMPIAH.

Affiliated Bodies

Association of Ghana Industries: Trade Fair Centre, POB 8624, Accra-North; tel. (21) 777283; telex 3027; fax (21) 773143; e-mail agi@ighmail.com; f. 1957; Pres. Dr Justice ATTA ADDISON; Exec. Sec. EDDIE IMBEAH-AMOAKUH.

Ghana Booksellers' Association: POB 10367, Accra-North; tel. (21) 773002; fax (21) 773242; Pres. SAMPSON BRAKO; Gen. Sec. FRED J. REIMMER.

The Ghana Chamber of Mines: 2nd Floor, Diamond House, POB 991, Accra; tel. (21) 665355; telex 2036; fax (21) 662926; f. 1928; Pres. PETER BRADFORD; Exec. Dir GEORGE M. OSEI (acting).

Ghana Electrical Contractors' Association: POB 1858, Accra.

Ghana National Association of Teachers: POB 209, Accra; tel. (21) 221515; fax (21) 226286; f. 1931; Pres. G. N. NAASO; Gen. Sec. PAUL OSEI-MENSAH.

Ghana National Contractors' Association: c/o J. T. Osei and Co, POB M11, Accra.

Ghana Timber Association (GTA): POB 246, Takoradi; f. 1952; promotes, protects and develops timber industry; Chair. TETTEH NANOR.

UTILITIES

Electricity

Electricity Corporation of Ghana (ECG): Electro-Volta House, POB 521, Accra; tel. (21) 664941; telex 2107; fax (21) 666262; Man. Dir JOHN HAGAN.

Ghana Atomic Energy Commission: POB 80, Legon/Accra; tel. (21) 400310; fax (21) 400807; f. 1963; promotes, develops and utilizes nuclear techniques; construction of a research reactor at Kwabenya, near Accra, which was begun in 1964, was completed in 1995; Chair. Prof. KWAME SARPONG.

Volta River Authority: POB M77, Accra; tel. (21) 664941; telex 2022; fax (21) 662610; f. 1965; controls the generation and distribution of electricity; CEO ERASMUS KALITSI.

Water

Ghana Water and Sewerage Corporation: POB M194, Accra; f. 1966 to provide, distribute and conserve water for public, domestic and industrial use, and to establish, operate and control sewerage systems.

CO-OPERATIVES

The co-operative movement in Ghana began in the 1920s through government initiative and supervision to ensure the production of high quality cocoa. In 1997 there were 11,154 registered co-operatives, grouped into four sectors: industrial, financial, agricultural and service.

Department of Co-operatives: POB M150, Accra; tel. (21) 666212; fax (21) 772789; f. 1944; govt-supervised body, responsible for registration, auditing and supervision of co-operative socs; Registrar R. BUACHIE-APHRAM.

Ghana Co-operatives Council Ltd: POB 4034, Accra; f. 1951; co-ordinates activities of all co-operative socs; comprises 15 nat. co-operative asscns and five central socs; Sec.-Gen. THOMAS ANDOH.

The 15 co-operative associations include the Ghana Co-operative Marketing Asscn Ltd, the Ghana Co-operative Credit Unions Asscn Ltd, the Ghana Co-operative Agricultural Producers and Marketing Asscn Ltd, and The Ghana Co-operative Consumers' Asscn Ltd.

TRADE UNIONS

Ghana Trades Union Congress (GTUC): Hall of Trade Unions, POB 701, Accra; tel. (21) 662568; fax (21) 667161; f. 1945; 17 affiliated unions; all activities of the GTUC were suspended in March 1982; Chair. Interim Man. Cttee E. K. ABOAGYE; Sec.-Gen. CHRISTIAN APPIAH-AGYEI.

Transport

State Transport Corporation: Accra; f. 1965; Man. Dir Lt-Col AKYEA-MENSAH.

RAILWAYS

Ghana has a railway network of 1,300 km, which connects Accra, Kumasi and Takoradi.

Ghana Railway Corporation: POB 251, Takoradi; tel. (31) 22181; telex 2297; fax (31) 23797; f. 1977; responsible for the operation and maintenance of all railways; Man. Dir. M. K. ARTHUR.

ROADS

In 1996 Ghana had an estimated total road network of 37,800 km, including 30 km of motorways, 5,230 km of main roads, and 9,620 km of secondary roads; some 24.1% of the road network was paved. A five-year Road Sector Expenditure Programme, costing US $259m., was initiated in 1995.

Ghana Highway Authority: POB 1641, Accra; tel. (21) 666591; telex 2359; fax (21) 665571; f. 1974 to plan, develop, classify and maintain roads and ferries; CEO B. L. T. SAKIBU.

SHIPPING

The two main ports are Tema (near Accra) and Takoradi, both of which are linked with Kumasi by rail. Facilities at both ports are to be upgraded in a US $365m. project, scheduled to commence in 1998. In 1996 some 6.7m. metric tons of goods were handled at the two ports.

Ghana Ports and Harbour Authority: holding company for the ports of Tema and Takoradi; Dir Gen. K. T. DOVLO.

Alpha (West Africa) Line Ltd: POB 451, Tema; telex 2184; operates regular cargo services to west Africa, the UK, the USA, the Far East and northern Europe; shipping agents; Man. Dir AHMED EDGAR COLLINGWOOD WILLIAMS.

Black Star Line Ltd: 4th Lane, Kuku Hill Osu, POB 248, Accra; tel. (21) 2888; telex 2019; fax (21) 2889; f. 1957; state-owned; transfer to private sector pending in 1997; operates passenger and cargo services to Europe, the UK, Canada, the USA, the Mediterranean and west Africa; shipping agents; Chair. MAGNUS ADDICO; Man. Dir Capt. V. N. ATTUQUAYEFIO.

Holland West-Afrika Lijn NV: POB 269, Accra; POB 216, Tema; and POB 18, Takoradi; cargo services to and from North America and the Far East; shipping agents.

Liner Agencies and Trading (Ghana) Ltd: POB 214, Tema; tel. (22) 202187; fax (22) 202189; international freight services; shipping agents; Dir J. OSSEI-YAW.

Remco Shipping Lines Ltd: POB 3898, Accra; tel. (21) 224609.

Scanship (Ghana) Ltd: CFAO Bldg, High St, POB 1705, Accra; tel. (21) 664314; telex 2181; shipping agents.

Association

Ghana Shippers' Council: Enterprise House, 5th Floor, opp. Barclay's Bank, High St, POB 1321, Accra; tel. (21) 666915; fax (21) 668768; e-mail shippers@ncs.com.gh; f. 1974; represents interests of c. 3,000 registered Ghanaian shippers; also provides cargo-handling and allied services; CEO M. T. ADDICO.

CIVIL AVIATION

The main international airport is at Kotoka (Accra). There are also airports at Takoradi, Kumasi, Sunyani, Tamale and Wa. The construction of a dedicated freight terminal at Kotoka Airport was completed in 1994.

Gemini Airlines Ltd: America House, POB 7328, Accra-North; tel. (21) 665785; f. 1974; operates weekly cargo flight between Accra and London; Dir V. Owusu; Gen. Man. P. F. Okine.

Ghana Airways Ltd.: Plot 9, Ghana Airways Avenue, Ghana Airways House, POB 1636, Accra; tel. (21) 773321; telex 2489; fax (21) 777078; f. 1958; state-owned; transfer to private sector pending in 1998; operates regional services and international routes to West African and European destinations, and to the USA and South Africa; Chair. Edward Salia; Chair. of Interim Management Committee E. L. Quartey.

Ghana Civil Aviation Authority: CEO Andy Mensah.

Tourism

Ghana's attractions include fine beaches, game reserves, traditional festivals, and old trading forts and castles. In 1996 a national tourism development plan (1996–2010) was initiated. According to the Ministry of Tourism, 300,000 tourists visited Ghana in 1996, with revenue from tourism totalling US $248m.

Ghana Tourist Board: POB 3106, Accra; tel. (21) 222153; telex 2714; fax (21) 231779; f. 1968; Exec. Dir Edmund Y. Ofosu-Yeboah.

Ghana Association of Tourist and Travel Agencies: Ramia House, Kojo Thompson Rd, POB 7140, Accra; tel. (21) 228933; Pres. Joseph K. Ankumah; Sec. Johnnie Moreaux.

Ghana Tourist Development Co Ltd: POB 8710, Accra; tel. (21) 776109; telex 2714; fax (21) 772093; f. 1974; develops tourist infrastructure, including hotels, restaurants and casinos; operates duty-free and diplomatic shops; Man. Dir Alfred Komladzei.

GREECE

Introductory Survey

Location, Climate, Language, Religion, Flag, Capital

The Hellenic Republic lies in south-eastern Europe. The country consists mainly of a mountainous peninsula between the Mediterranean Sea and the Aegean Sea, bounded to the north by Albania, Bulgaria and the former Yugoslav republic of Macedonia, and to the east by Turkey. To the south, east and west of the mainland lie numerous Greek islands, of which the largest is Crete. The climate is Mediterranean, with mild winters and hot summers. The language is Greek, of which there are two forms—the formal language (katharevoussa) and the language commonly spoken and taught in schools (demotiki). Almost all of the inhabitants profess Christianity, and the Greek Orthodox Church, to which about 97% of the population adhere, is the established religion. The national flag (proportions 3 by 2) displays nine equal horizontal stripes of blue and white, with a white cross throughout a square canton of blue at the upper hoist. The capital is Athens.

Recent History

The liberation of Greece from the German occupation (1941–44) was followed by a civil war which lasted until 1949. The Communist forces were defeated, and the constitutional monarchy re-established. King Konstantinos (Constantine) acceded to the throne on the death of his father, King Paul, in 1964. A succession of weak governments and conflicts between the King and his ministers, and an alleged conspiracy involving military personnel who supported the Centre Union Party, resulted in a coup, led by right-wing army officers, in April 1967. An attempted counter-coup, led by the King, failed, and he went into exile. Col. Georgios Papadopoulos emerged as the dominant personality in the new regime, becoming Prime Minister in December 1967 and Regent in March 1972. The regime produced nominally democratic constitutional proposals, but all political activity was banned and opponents of the regime were expelled from all positions of power or influence.

Following an abortive naval mutiny, Greece was declared a republic in June 1973; Papadopoulos was appointed President in July. Martial law was ended, and a civilian Cabinet was appointed in preparation for a general election to be held by the end of that year. A student uprising at the Athens Polytechnic in November was violently suppressed by the army, and another military coup overthrew Papadopoulos. Lt-Gen. Phaidon Ghizikis was appointed President, and a mainly civilian Cabinet, led by Adamantios Androutsopoulos, was installed, but effective power lay with a small group of officers and the military police under Brig.-Gen. Demetrios Ioannides. As a result of the failure of the military junta's attempt to overthrow President Makarios of Cyprus, and its inability to prevent the Turkish invasion of the island (see chapter on Cyprus), the Androutsopoulos Cabinet collapsed in July 1974. President Ghizikis summoned from exile a former Prime Minister, Konstantinos Karamanlis, who was invited to form a civilian Government of National Salvation. Martial law was ended, the press was released from state control, and political parties, including the Communists, were allowed to operate freely. A general election in November resulted in a decisive victory for Karamanlis's Nea Dimokratia (New Democracy—ND) party, which gained 54% of the votes cast and won 220 of the 300 parliamentary seats. A referendum in December rejected proposals for a return to constitutional monarchy, and in June 1975 a new republican Constitution, providing for a parliamentary democracy, was promulgated. In the same month Prof. Konstantinos Tsatsos, a former cabinet minister, was elected President by the Parliament (Vouli).

In the general election of November 1977 ND was re-elected with a reduced majority. In May 1980 Karamanlis was elected President and subsequently resigned the premiership and the leadership of ND. The new party leader, Georgios Rallis, was appointed Prime Minister. Rallis encountered considerable opposition from the increasingly popular Panellinion Socialistikon Kinema (Panhellenic Socialist Movement—PASOK). In the general election of October 1981 PASOK gained an absolute majority in Parliament. The PASOK leader, Andreas Papandreou, became Prime Minister of the first socialist Government in Greek history, which was initially committed to withdrawal from the then European Community (EC, now the European Union—EU—see p. 152), to removal of US military bases from Greek territory, and to implementing an extensive programme of domestic reform. By the end of 1982 the Government had extended the franchise, legalized civil marriage and divorce, and restructured the university system, although plans to 'socialize' industry were scaled down, following widespread opposition.

In March 1985 Papandreou unexpectedly withdrew support for President Karamanlis's candidature for a further five-year term in office. The Prime Minister planned to amend the 1975 Constitution, proposing to relieve the President of all executive power, making the Head of State's functions largely ceremonial. Karamanlis resigned in protest, and Parliament elected Christos Sartzetakis, a judge, as President, in a vote that was widely considered to be unconstitutional. A general election was held in June 1985 to enable the Government to secure support for the proposed constitutional changes. PASOK was returned to power, winning 161 seats in the 300-member Parliament; ND secured 126 seats. In October the Government introduced a stringent programme of economic austerity, provoking widespread industrial unrest, which continued throughout Greece in 1986. In March 1986, despite considerable opposition from ND, the Greek Parliament approved a series of constitutional amendments limiting the influence of the President, whose executive powers were transferred to the legislature (see The Constitution).

In May 1987, in response to numerous accusations made by ND of mismanagement and corruption on the part of the Government in the public sector, Papandreou sought and won a parliamentary vote of confidence in his Government. Opposition to the Government's economic austerity programme had continued in 1987, prompting further strikes and demonstrations, and in November Papandreou was forced to modify the programme. Despite a series of disruptive strikes by teachers and doctors in June 1988, a parliamentary motion expressing 'no confidence' in the Government was defeated. However, the Government suffered a serious reverse in November, when several leading members of the Cabinet were implicated in a major financial scandal involving the alleged embezzlement of large amounts of money from the Bank of Crete, and were forced to resign.

In January 1989 the Elliniki Aristera (Greek Left Party—EAR), led by Leonidas Kyrkos, formed an electoral alliance with the 'Exterior' faction of the Kommunistiko Komma Ellados (Communist Party of Greece—KKE), under the leadership of Charilaos Florakis, to create the Coalition of the Left and Progress (Synaspismos), commonly referred to as the Left Coalition. Throughout the first half of 1989 a number of disruptive strikes were organized in protest against the Government's continuing policies of economic austerity and to demand wage increases. In early March the Government survived a parliamentary motion of 'no confidence', which was introduced by ND.

At a general election in June 1989 ND won the largest proportion of votes cast, but failed to attain an overall majority in Parliament. Following the failure of both ND and subsequently PASOK to reach an agreement with the Left Coalition to form a coalition government, President Sartzetakis empowered Florakis and the Left Coalition to seek a coalition agreement. The Left Coalition unexpectedly agreed to form an interim administration with ND, on condition that the ND leader, Konstantinos Mitsotakis, renounce his claim to the premiership. Accordingly, Tzannis Tzannetakis, an ND deputy for Athens, was appointed Prime Minister in a new Cabinet, which included two Communist ministers. The unprecedented Conservative-Communist coalition announced its intention to govern for only three months, during which time it would aim to implement a *katharsis* (campaign of purification) of Greek politics. Accordingly, the administration resigned in early October, having initiated investigations into the involvement of officials of the former socialist Government, including Papandreou, in a number of scandals involving banking, armaments and financial transactions. The President of the Supreme Court, Yannis

Grivas, was subsequently appointed Prime Minister in an interim Cabinet composed of non-political personalities, which was to oversee the year's second general election. However, the result of the election, conducted in November, was again inconclusive (ND won 46% of the total votes, PASOK 41% and the Left Coalition 11%). The political crisis was temporarily resolved in mid-November, when ND, PASOK and the Left Coalition agreed to form a coalition that would administer the country pending the results of a further poll, to be conducted in April 1990. Xenofon Zolotas, a former Governor of the Bank of Greece, was appointed Prime Minister to lead the interim Cabinet. However, following a dispute over military promotions in February 1990, the Government collapsed, and the same non-political individuals who had overseen the November election were reinstated to govern until the general election. Attempts by Parliament in February and March 1990 to elect a head of state by the required majority were unsuccessful, owing largely to a decision taken by ND representatives to abstain from voting, following the refusal of their candidate, Karamanlis, to take part in the election. A general election, conducted in April, finally resolved the parliamentary deadlock. ND secured 150 seats in the 300-seat Parliament. Following the announcement of the results, Mitsotakis secured the support of Konstantinos Stefanopoulos, the leader (and the one elected parliamentary representative) of the Komma Dimokratikis Ananeosis (Party of Democratic Renewal—DIANA), thereby enabling him to form the first single-party Government since 1981. On 5 May 1990 Konstantinos Karamanlis took office as President for a five-year term, following his election by 153 of the 300 members of Parliament. Stefanopoulos formally rejoined ND in June.

The failure of the interim administrations to reach a consensus on comprehensive economic programmes, and the unpopularity of austerity measures introduced by the new Government, led to widespread industrial unrest. Throughout 1990 appeals by trade unions for 24- and 48-hour general strikes were regularly supported by more than 1m. workers, seriously disrupting public services and industry. Despite apparent public dissatisfaction with many policies instigated by the new administration, ND were successful in municipal elections held in October. In November reforms to the electoral law, which provided for a modified form of proportional representation in which a minimum of 3% of the national vote in a general election would be required by political parties wishing to appoint representatives to Parliament, were finally ratified. The new electoral system, which also incorporated procedural disincentives to the formation of political alliances to contest elections, encountered vehement opposition from left-wing parties, which considered the reforms to be unconstitutional.

In March 1991 Andreas Papandreou and three of his former ministers were brought to trial on charges of complicity in large-scale embezzlement from the Bank of Crete during their terms of office. Papandreou, who refused to attend court proceedings (on the grounds that his indictment had been politically motivated), was tried *in absentia* and without legal representation. In January 1992 Papandreou was acquitted of all charges, while two of his former ministers received minor sentences (the fourth defendant had died during the trial).

In August 1991 Mitsotakis effected a comprehensive reorganization of the Cabinet (including the removal of his daughter from the post of Under-Secretary to the Prime Minister), in response to public criticism of family involvement in politics. In April 1992 the Prime Minister successfully sought a vote of confidence from Parliament, following the dismissal of the Minister of Foreign Affairs, Antonis Samaras, and Mitsotakis's assumption of the portfolio in order to co-ordinate personally the Greek response to attempts by the former Yugoslav republic of Macedonia to achieve international recognition as the independent Republic of Macedonia (see below). As part of a cabinet reorganization effected in August (which included the controversial reappointment of the Prime Minister's daughter to her previous post), Michalis Papakonstantinou, an uncompromising defender of national territorial integrity, was allocated the foreign affairs portfolio. Ministerial disaffection with what was perceived as Mitsotakis's moderate stance regarding the former Yugoslav republic, and with the Government's policy of economic austerity, increased in late 1992, but was curtailed following the Prime Minister's dismissal and reorganization of the entire Cabinet in early December.

Widespread disruption to public transport followed a decision by Parliament, taken in August 1992, to authorize the privatization of public transport in Athens. A public-sector strike later in the month sought to demonstrate opposition to economic policy in general. Further unrest, prompted by parliamentary debate of proposed reforms to the social security system (including a signficant increase in employees' contributions and the raising of the pensionable age), culminated in three general strikes, in September, which were well supported by both private and public sectors. A new austerity budget for 1993, approved by Parliament in December 1992, provoked further industrial unrest during 1993. General strikes were staged in March, May and July by employees in both the private and public sectors, demonstrating opposition to the Government's commitment to privatization and wage restraint. A further one-day strike was organized by public-sector workers in August, in protest at the planned sale of the state telecommunications company.

In September 1993 two ND deputies resigned, in response to an appeal for support by Politiki Anixi (Political Spring—POLA), a party that had been established in July by Antonis Samaras. The consequent loss of Mitsotakis's one-seat majority in Parliament obliged him to offer the Government's resignation and to call an early general election. At the election, conducted on 10 October, PASOK obtained 46.9% of the total votes cast and 170 parliamentary seats, while ND received 39.3% of the votes and 111 seats, and POLA secured 4.9% of the votes and 10 seats. At the end of October Mitsotakis resigned as leader of ND.

Papandreou's victory in the general election provoked immediate concern among members of the EU, owing to the anti-European attitude that the PASOK leader had adopted during his previous tenure of office. In his first policy statement, however, Papandreou gave assurances of his commitment to European integration. The new Prime Minister also announced his intention to revoke the privatization programme, including the proposed sale of the state telecommunications company. In December 1993, following the presentation to Parliament of draft legislation for the renationalization of public transport in Athens, protesters blocking bus depots had to be dispersed by riot police, and one person was killed in the unrest. In May 1994 Papandreou, contrary to his post-election commitment, announced his intention to generate revenue by means of the sale of a minority share in the state telecommunications company. The sale was formally approved by Parliament in November, although it was then postponed, owing to depressed world markets. Following a reduction in electoral support for PASOK in elections for the European Parliament held in June (the party received 37.6% of the votes cast), Papandreou undertook a reorganization of the Cabinet. At local elections in October, PASOK retained control of the majority of local councils; however, its candidate for the mayoralty of Athens, Theodhoros Pangalos (who had resigned as Minister of Transport and Communications in September) was defeated by the ND candidate. The elections were marred by alleged irregularities concerning the administration of polling stations.

In January 1994 Parliament approved the establishment of a commission to investigate claims that Mitsotakis had authorized illegal monitoring of opposition leaders' telephone conversations during the 1990 election campaign, and in May recommended that he be tried for his alleged involvement. In September Parliament voted to charge Mitsotakis and his former Ministers of Industry and of Commerce and Finance with bribery, in relation to the sale of a state-owned cement company in 1992; in January 1995, however, Parliament supported a proposal by Papandreou to suspend the trial, which had been scheduled to begin later that month.

In March 1995 Stefanopoulos was elected President by 181 of the 300 members of Parliament, having failed to secure the required two-thirds' majority in two earlier rounds of voting. Stefanopoulos, a candidate jointly favoured by PASOK and POLA, took office on 10 March. Later in the month the Minister of Public Order, Stylianos Papathemelis, resigned, owing to his refusal to authorize the use of riot police to end a week-long protest by farmers who had blockaded major roads and railways. The action, which was in protest against new legislative measures to reduce tax evasion, was terminated at the end of March. From mid-1995 tensions within the governing PASOK party became increasingly evident. In August a deputy was expelled from the party as a result of his suggestion that the Prime Minister should resign and his public criticism of the considerable political influence and ambitions of Papandreou's wife, Dimitra Liani-Papandreou, who was appointed Chief of Staff in October 1993. In September 1995 a minor reorganization of the Cabinet was undertaken following the resignation of the Minister of Industry, Energy and Technology and of Commerce,

Konstantinos Simitis, citing interference in his policies by senior PASOK officials, mainly supporters of the party Secretary-General, Apostolos-Athanasios (Akis) Tsohatzopoulos (a close associate of Papandreou), who were opposed to extensive economic reform. Simitis, together with Theodhoros Pangalos, who had resigned from the party's executive committee earlier in the month, Vasiliki (Vasso) Papandreou, a former EU Commissioner (who refused to accept a place in the Cabinet in the reorganization) and Paraskevas Avgerinos, a former Minister of EU Affairs, constituted a group of 'dissident' PASOK deputies (referred to as the Group of Four) who urged the resignation of Papandreou, in view of his failing health, and further reforms to modernize the party. In November Papandreou was admitted to hospital suffering from pneumonia. His prime ministerial duties were assumed by Tsohatzopoulos, who had joined the Cabinet in September and was replaced as Secretary-General of PASOK in October. While Papandreou's condition remained critical throughout December, vigorous internal discussions ensued within PASOK regarding his successor. In January 1996 the opposition parties expressed their concern at the power vacuum in the country resulting from Papandreou's confinement. A parliamentary motion of 'no confidence' in the Government was defeated; however, senior PASOK members subsequently strengthened their resolve to settle the issue. On 15 January Papandreou submitted his resignation as Prime Minister, although he remained leader of PASOK. Three days later Simitis was elected to the premiership, having won the support of 86 of the 167 members of the PASOK parliamentary party (compared with 75 by his nearest opponent, Tsohatzopoulos) in a second round of voting. Simitis awarded Pangalos the foreign affairs portfolio but retained Tsohatzopoulos and Gerasimos Arsenis (another supporter of Papandreou who had also contested the leadership election) in the Cabinet in an attempt to unite the party. However, in most cases former Papandreou associates were replaced by pro-European ministers who supported Simitis's desire for economic reform. Almost immediately after taking office Simitis was confronted by a sharp escalation in hostilities with Turkey (see below). Following his acceptance of a US-brokered compromise to defuse the situation, Simitis was vigorously condemned by all opposition parties. In February the Prime Minister dismissed the Chief of Staff of the Greek Armed Forces, Adm. Christos Lyberis, owing to his disclosure of government deliberations concerning the use of military force against Turkey during the Aegean crisis. Later in that month, Simitis and Pangalos undertook a tour of European countries to generate support for the Greek stance in the territorial dispute. At the same time, relations with the Italian and Dutch Governments were reportedly strained owing to allegations by the Greek authorities that the military attachés of these two countries were involved in espionage activities. In March Greece requested that the personnel involved be replaced.

In March 1996 the delayed privatization of the state telecommunications company was initiated, with an offer of 8% of the company's equity. The share issue was reportedly over-subscribed, despite a public demonstration of opposition by company employees in February. Also in March legislation (adopted by the PASOK administration in April 1994) to renationalize property owned by the exiled monarch, King Konstantinos, and to remove his family's citizenship, was ruled by the Supreme Court to be unconstitutional; however, in June 1997 the Supreme Court upheld the 1994 law.

In June 1996 Andreas Papandreou died. At a PASOK Congress, held a few days later, Simitis was elected leader of the party, with 53.5% of the votes, defeating his closest rival, Akis Tsohatzopoulos, who represented the populist faction of the party. None the less, in August Simitis announced that an early general election was to be held (the legal requirement for an election not being until October 1997) in order to obtain a firm mandate for his Government to pursue the economic, fiscal and social reforms needed to achieve European economic and monetary union (EMU) targets, and for the Government's approach regarding foreign affairs. In the poll, which was held on 22 September, PASOK won 162 of the 300 parliamentary seats, with 41.5% of the votes cast, securing victory over the ND which, having conducted a populist campaign, including commitments of financial assistance to farmers and pensioners and a tougher foreign policy stance, took 108 seats (38.2%). Support for POLA declined substantially, and the party lost all 10 of the seats gained at the previous election. Key ministers in the new PASOK administration were retained from the outgoing Cabinet, in particular to ensure continuity in foreign policy and management of the economy (with the Minister of the National Economy, Ioannis Papantoniou, assuming, in addition, responsibility for the Ministry of Finance). Tsohatzopoulos replaced Arsenis at the Ministry of National Defence, although Arsenis was retained in the Cabinet as Minister of Education and Religious Affairs.

In September 1996, following the ND's defeat in the general election, Miltiades Evert resigned as party leader. In early October, however, Evert was re-elected to the position, securing 103 votes from the party's electoral college, compared with the 84 votes cast in favour of the former ND Minister of Education Georgios Souflias. In March 1997 Konstantinos Karamanlis (a nephew of the former President and ND party leader) was elected leader of the ND, securing 69% of the votes cast by delegates to a party congress, despite his lack of experience in government.

In November 1996 austerity measures in the 1997 budget, designed to ensure Greece's participation in EMU, provoked a 24-hour general strike observed by an estimated 3m. workers. On the same day farmers across the country began an indefinite blockade of major road and rail links, and of important border crossings with Bulgaria and Turkey. The action aimed to demonstrate strong opposition to the PASOK economic programme, particularly the withdrawal of some tax exemptions, and to highlight the farmers' demands for extra subsidies and debt rescheduling. In December a general strike, organized by the General Confederation of Labour to coincide with Parliament's consideration of the budget, was, again, strongly supported by public- and private-sector workers, but failed to prevent Parliament's approval of the budget.

Manifestations of labour unrest continued in early 1997 with individual strikes by seamen, teachers and other civil servants, and a general stoppage organized by trade unions in late January. Farmers also renewed their protests, which had been temporarily suspended in December 1996, by constructing a series of road blockades in central Greece. Despite increasing criticism from former supporters, both within and outside the parliamentary party, who accused him of abandoning PASOK's commitment to protecting low-income workers, Simitis continued to implement unpopular austerity policies in accordance with his commitment to meeting the convergence criteria of EMU. A further 24-hour general strike, in protest at pay and conditions, was widely observed in October 1997. In December Simitis expelled three deputies from PASOK's parliamentary group for voting against 1998 budget proposals, which were subsequently passed by a considerable margin by Parliament.

In June 1997 the Government's decision to adopt the EU's Schengen Convention (see p.168) on cross-border travel provoked protests from Greek Orthodox priests and adherents who objected, on religious grounds, to the use of a computerized police database accessible to all signatories of the agreement.

In November 1997 the Government adopted controversial legislation to reform local government, transforming 5,797 municipalities and townships into 1,033 local administrative areas in order to reduce bureaucracy and facilitate communications between local and central government.

In November 1997 a Greek court ruled that the German Government pay £20m. in reparations to a village whose residents were massacred by German forces during the Second World War. A German government spokesman announced that Germany had no intention of meeting this claim, as compensation for the German occupation had been paid in 1960.

Throughout 1991 numerous terrorist attacks against 'capitalist' (and particularly US) military and commercial targets in Greece were carried out by terrorist groups, including the 17 November Revolutionary Organization and, to a lesser extent, the 1 May Revolutionary Organization and the Revolutionary People's Struggle (ELA). In July 1992 the 17 November group claimed responsibility for an unsuccessful attempt to assassinate the Minister of Finance, in which a member of the public died. In December an ND deputy was shot and injured by the same group, in protest against alleged corruption within the Government, and against recent economic initiatives. Activity by terrorist groups, in particular the 17 November organization and the ELA, was evident throughout 1994, with attacks against foreign companies and other targets. In July the 17 November group claimed responsibility for the assassination of a Turkish diplomat. A series of measures to combat terrorism was announced by the Government in September, following a bomb attack on a police vehicle. In February 1996 an unsuccessful attack on the US Embassy in Athens was believed by police to have been perpetrated by 17 November activists. In May 1997 three suspected terrorists shot and killed a shipowner in Piraeus. In December a bomb was discovered outside the office of the Minister of Development, Vasso Papandreou. A similar device was placed outside the offices of a Canadian gold-mining company whose activities had provoked violent protests, leading to the imposition of martial law in two villages and the conviction of five village mayors, who received suspended sentences for incitement to riot. In January 1998 the police arrested more than 15 suspected members of the 'Fighting Guerrilla Faction', a left-wing group believed to be responsible for a number of recent bombings, including an attack on the offices of Alitalia, the Italian airline, in 1997.

Greece became a full member of the EC (now EU) in January 1981, having signed the treaty of accession in May 1979. Although originally critical of Greece's membership, the PASOK Government confined itself to seeking modification of the terms of accession, in order to take into account the under-developed Greek economy, and gave qualified assent to concessions proposed by the EC in April 1983. In July 1992 the Greek Parliament voted overwhelmingly to ratify the Treaty on European Union ('Maastricht Treaty'—see p. 158).

Following his accession to power in 1996, Simitis adopted a new approach in foreign relations, promoting Greece as a regional leader both politically and economically. In June 1997 Greece hosted a conference in Thessaloniki (Salonika) for ministers responsible for foreign affairs from Balkan states to discuss ways of improving regional co-operation and security. This was followed in November in Crete by the first summit of leaders of 'south-east European' countries, which was attended by representatives from Greece, Turkey, Albania, Bulgaria, the former Yugoslav republic of Macedonia, Romania, Yugoslavia, and Bosnia and Herzegovina. Agreement was reached to establish a standing secretariat to help resolve outstanding disputes between the countries.

Relations with Turkey have been characterized by long-standing disputes concerning Cyprus (q.v.) and sovereignty over the continental shelf beneath the Aegean Sea. The difficulties in relations with Turkey were exacerbated by the unilateral declaration of an 'independent' Turkish-Cypriot state in Cyprus in November 1983 (the 'Turkish Republic of Northern Cyprus—'TRNC', together with various minor sovereignty disputes over islands in the Aegean Sea, which led to Greece's withdrawal from military exercises of the North Atlantic Treaty Organization (NATO—see p. 204) in August 1984 and to a boycott of manoeuvres in subsequent years. In March 1987 a disagreement between Greece and Turkey over petroleum-prospecting rights in disputed areas of the Aegean Sea almost resulted in military conflict. In January 1988, however, the Greek and Turkish Prime Ministers, meeting in Davos, Switzerland, agreed that the two countries' premiers should meet annually in order to improve bilateral relations (the Davos meeting was the first formal contact between Greek and Turkish Heads of Government for 10 years), and that joint committees should be established to negotiate peaceful solutions to disputes. In May the Greek and Turkish Ministers of Foreign Affairs met in Athens and formally pledged to respect each other's sovereignty in the Aegean region. In June Turgut Özal became the first Turkish Prime Minister to visit Greece for 36 years. Relations with Turkey were, however, placed under renewed strain in January 1990, when violent clashes occurred in Komotini, Thrace, between Greeks and some 1,500 resident Turkish Muslims, and in October 1991, when the 17 November Revolutionary Organization claimed responsibility for the murder of the press attaché at the Turkish Embassy in Athens.

Relations between Greece and Turkey improved in 1993, with continued dialogue between the two countries and recognition of the need for greater co-operation. In 1994, however, the issue of the demarcation of territorial waters in the Aegean Sea re-emerged as a major source of tension between the two countries. Greece's right to extend its territorial waters from six to 12 nautical miles, as enshrined in the international Convention on the Law of the Sea (see p. 193), was strongly condemned by Turkey, which feared the loss of shipping access, via the Aegean Sea, to international waters. The Turkish Government insisted that any expansion of territorial waters on the part of Greece would be considered an act of aggression, to which Turkey would retaliate. The dispute intensified prior to the scheduled entry into force of the Convention, in mid-November, with both countries conducting concurrent military exercises in the Aegean. In early 1995 the Greek Government obstructed an agreement to establish a customs union between Turkey and the EU until, in March, it secured a defined agreement from the EU regarding a timetable for accession negotiations with Cyprus (as well as compensation arrangements for the Greek textile industry). The concern surrounding the international Convention on the Law of the Sea re-emerged in June, when the Greek Parliament ratified the treaty. The Greek Government was criticized by some opposition politicians for not immediately enforcing the Convention, while Turkey reiterated its stance and conducted further military exercises in the region. In early 1996 tensions between the two countries flared, owing to conflicting claims of sovereignty over Imia (Kardak), small uninhabited islands in the Aegean Sea. By late January Greek and Turkish military vessels were patrolling the islands and attempts were made to raise the respective national flags on the territory. The new PASOK administration, despite considerable criticism from ND, complied with a petition by the US Government to withdraw all military vessels and troops from the area and to remove the national flags, in order to end the threat of military action.

In late February 1996 opposition by the Greek Government delayed the implementation of a financial protocol of the EU–Turkey customs union, which was to provide assistance amounting to ECU 375m. Greece claimed that Turkey's aggressive action in the Aegean violated the terms of the customs union agreement. While the new Greek Prime Minister, Simitis, resolved to pursue a more constructive foreign policy stance towards Turkey, a series of incidents throughout 1996 involving alleged violations of Greek airspace by Turkish planes and confrontations between Greek and Turkish patrol vessels in the Aegean precluded any improvement in relations. In July Greece finally withdrew its opposition to Turkey's participation in an EU-Mediterranean assistance programme in response to a joint statement by EU Heads of Government urging an end to Turkey's 'hostile policy' towards Greece; however, the block on funds from the customs union agreement remained in effect. In August, following an escalation in intercommunal tension in Cyprus, Greece reassured the Greek Cypriot authorities of its full support, and the Greek armed forces were placed on full alert. In November Greece announced an extensive programme to modernize the Greek military infrastructure, which, it insisted, was necessary to counter the perceived threat of military action by Turkey, yet which contributed to international concern at the escalating militarization of the region. In early 1997 the situation in Cyprus remained tense, and both the Turkish and Greek Governments strongly reaffirmed their commitment to support the respective authorities on the island (following Turkish warnings of military reprisals if a decision by the Greek Cypriot Government to purchase an anti-aircraft missile system was implemented), while Greece continued to refuse to conduct bilateral discussions with Turkey over sovereignty rights in the Aegean.

In April 1997 the Greek Deputy Minister of Foreign Affairs, Georgios Papandreou, met his Turkish counterpart in Malta, under EU auspices, and it was agreed to establish two committees of independent experts who would communicate through the EU to explore ways of improving relations between the two countries. At a NATO summit in Madrid in July Simitis and the Turkish President, Süleyman Demirel, held direct talks (the first such meeting for three years), which led to an agreement, known as the Madrid declaration, in which they pledged not to use violence or the threat of violence in resolving the countries' bilateral disputes. However, relations remained strained, particularly concerning Greek support of Cyprus's application to the EU; Turkey threatened integration with the 'TRNC' should Cyprus be admitted to the organization. Further tension was caused by frequent alleged violations of Greek airspace by Turkish military aircraft, in particular the alleged harassment of an aircraft carrying the Greek Minister of Defence en route from Cyprus to Greece, following joint military exercises with Greek Cypriot forces. These incidents and a near-collision between Greek and Turkish warships in October threatened the agreement made in Madrid. In November, however, Simitis held a cordial meeting with the Turkish Prime Minister, Mesut Yılmaz, at which Simitis accepted an invitation to visit Ankara and it was agreed to explore confidence-building measures. Turkey, however, continued to advocate dialogue on all issues, whereas Greece reaffirmed its commitment to a gradual approach, insisting that Turkey accept international arbitration for disputes over sovereignty in the Aegean as a prerequisite both to official talks and to the lifting of Greece's veto on EU financial aid to Turkey. In November Greece threatened to oppose Turkey's participation in a planned EU enlargement conference in London, unless Turkey abandoned its attempts to prevent EU accession talks with Cyprus which were due to begin in April 1998, and threatened to veto the admission to the EU of all the south-east European countries if Cyprus were rejected.

At a NATO summit at the beginning of December 1997 an agreement was signed, under which Greece and Turkey would share control of military flights in the Aegean under NATO's new military command structure (although this agreement had yet to be endorsed by the political leaders of each country). Later that month, however, Turkey resumed its violations of Greek airspace over the Aegean. In late December Turkey expelled a Greek diplomat for engaging in intelligence-gathering operations and Greece responded with the retaliatory expulsion of a Turkish diplomat.

In August 1985 Greece and Albania reopened their borders, which had remained closed since 1940, and Greece formally annulled claims to North Epirus (southern Albania), where there is a sizeable Greek minority. In August 1987 the Greek Government put a formal end to a legal vestige of the Second World War by proclaiming that it no longer considered Greece to be at war with Albania. In April 1988 relations between Greece and Albania improved significantly when the two countries signed an agreement to promote trade between their border provinces. During the early 1990s, however, bilateral relations were severely strained by persisting concerns relating to the treatment of ethnic Greeks residing in Albania (numbering an estimated 300,000), the illegal immigration of several thousand Albanians seeking work opportunities or political asylum in Greece, and the efforts of the Greek Government to secure their return. In March 1996 President Stefanopoulos signed a treaty of friendship and co-operation with Albania's President Berisha. Several issues appeared to have been resolved, with Albania agreeing to provide Greek-language education in schools serving the ethnic Greek population and Greece declaring its willingness to issue temporary work permits for at least 150,000 seasonal workers from Albania. In May, at a meeting of the defence ministers of both countries, Greece agreed to support Albania's efforts to join NATO.

Following a revolt in southern Albania in March 1997, the Greek Government obtained guarantees from Albania for the security of the ethnic Greek population and negotiated with rebel leaders to ensure stability. Greece contributed 700 men to a multinational force led by Italy, which was established with a mandate to facilitate the distribution of humanitarian aid. Albanian banditry became a security problem in June and July, especially on the island of Corfu, where naval frigates clashed with Albanian pirates. In August Greece agreed to legitimize the status of hundreds of thousands of illegal Albanian immigrants by granting them temporary work permits in exchange for assistance from the Albanians in combating cross-border crime. Further border problems, including the shooting of an Albanian civilian by Greek guards, resulted in a further agreement in late October, which envisaged joint action in the border area to prevent illegal activity.

Attempts after 1991 by the former Yugoslav republic of Macedonia to achieve international recognition as an independent state were strenuously opposed by the Greek Government, which insisted that 'Macedonia' was a purely geographical term (delineating an area which included a large part of northern Greece) and expressed fears that the adoption of such a name could imply ambitions on the Greek province of Macedonia and might foster a false claim to future territorial expansion. In early 1993 the Greek administration withdrew its former objection to the use of the word 'Macedonia', and its derivatives, as part of a fuller name for the new republic. At the end of March the Greek Government accepted a UN proposal that the title 'the former Yugoslav republic of Macedonia' (FYRM) should be used temporarily and agreed to hold direct talks with the FYRM to consider confidence-building measures. In late 1993 the newly-elected PASOK Government strongly criticized recognition of the FYRM by several EU members, and, despite assurances that the Government would adopt a more conciliatory attitude, in February 1994 the Government condemned a decision by the USA (the final member of the UN Security Council to do so) to recognize the FYRM. At an emergency meeting in mid-February, the Cabinet agreed to prevent any movement of goods, other than humanitarian aid, into the FYRM via the northern Greek port of Thessaloniki. The initiative was widely criticized by the international community as effectively constituting an illegal trade embargo, and the EU ministers responsible for foreign affairs urged Greece to revoke the measures, which, it was determined, violated EU law. Intensive negotiations with the Greek authorities failed to resolve the issue, and in mid-April the European Commission commenced legal proceedings against Greece at the Court of Justice of the European Communities. An attempt by the European Commission to obtain an interim ban on the trade embargo (prior to a final ruling) was refused by the Court in June. In April 1995 a preliminary opinion of the Court determined that the embargo was not in breach of Greece's obligations under the Treaty of Rome (see p. 155); however, in June France, which had assumed the presidency of the EU, criticized the Greek action. In September the ministers responsible for foreign affairs of Greece and the FYRM, meeting in New York, under UN auspices, signed an interim accord to normalize relations between the two countries, which included recognition of the existing international border. Under the terms of the agreement, Greece was to grant access to the port facilities at Thessaloniki and to remove all obstructions to the cross-border movement of people and goods following a period of 30 days, during which the FYRM was to approve a new state flag (removing the symbolic Vergina sun). The measures were successfully implemented by mid-October; a few days later agreement was concluded on the establishment of liaison offices in the two countries' capitals. Negotiations were to be pursued regarding the issue of a permanent name for the FYRM, which would be acceptable to both sides. In March 1997 the Greek Minister of Foreign Affairs visited the FYRM for the first time since its independence from Yugoslava.

During the conflict in the former Yugoslavia, Greece pursued an active involvement in efforts to promote a peaceful political settlement in the region. In contrast to most of its European partners, Greece maintained close relations with the Government in Belgrade and advocated the removal of the UN-imposed trade embargo against Serbia and Montenegro. Greece's stance, which was shared notably by Bulgaria and Russia, contributed to a strengthening of relations between these countries. In April 1995 Greece, Bulgaria and Russia approved the construction of a pipeline to transport Russian petroleum from Burgas, in Bulgaria, to the Greek port of Alexandroupolis, although in mid-1997 plans had not been finalized, owing to uncertainty over Russian participation. In January a 530-km pipeline for the transportation of natural gas from Russia to Greece was reported to have been completed. In April 1996 Greece formally recognized the Federal Republic of Yugoslavia, and in October the Presidents of the two countries, meeting in Athens, announced their commitment to strengthening bilateral political and economic relations.

In July 1990 an eight-year defence co-operation agreement with the USA was signed by the ND Government (to replace a 1983 agreement, which had been extended at six-monthly intervals since its formal expiry in 1988), providing for the closure of two US military bases and the continuation of US annual military aid to Greece (at the level of US $345m. per year) as a form of rent for the two remaining bases, together with the provision of aircraft and naval destroyers worth $1,000m. in total. The agreement encountered domestic opposition from left-wing parties anxious to curtail US involvement in Greece, as well as opposition from the Turkish Government.

Government

Under the Constitution of June 1975, the President is Head of State and is elected by Parliament for a five-year term. The President appoints the Prime Minister and, upon his recommendation, the other members of the Cabinet. In March 1986 Parliament approved a series of constitutional amendments, divesting the President of his executive powers and transferring them to the legislature (see The Constitution). The unicameral Parliament has 300 members, directly elected by universal adult suffrage for four years. Greece comprises 10 regions, including Greater Athens, and is divided into 51 administrative divisions.

Defence

Greece returned to the military structure of NATO in October 1980, after an absence of six years. Military service is compulsory for all men between 18 and 40 years of age, and lasts 19–23 months. In 1978 women were given the right to volunteer for military service of 30–50 days' basic training and for specialized training. At 1 August 1997 the armed forces numbered 162,300, of whom 119,200 were conscripts, and consisted of an army of 116,000, a navy of 19,500 and an air force of 26,800; in addition, there was a gendarmerie of 26,500 and a National Guard of 35,000. Budget estimates for 1997 allocated 912,000m. drachmae to defence (7.1% of total expenditure).

Economic Affairs

In 1995, according to estimates by the World Bank, Greece's gross national product (GNP), measured at average 1993–95 prices, was US $85,885m., equivalent to $8,210 per head. During 1985–95, it was estimated, GNP per head increased, in real terms, by 1.2% per year. Over the same period the population grew by an annual average of 0.5%. Greece's gross domestic product (GDP) increased, in real terms, by an annual average of 1.1% in 1990–95. In 1996, according to official estimates, real GDP increased by 2.5%.

Agriculture (including hunting, forestry and fishing) contributed an estimated 14.2% of GDP in 1995 and engaged 20.4% of the employed labour force. The principal cash crops are fruit and vegetables (which, together, accounted for about 11.6% of total export earnings in 1995), cereals, sugar beet and tobacco. During 1990–94 agricultural GDP increased by an annual average of 3.1%.

Industry (including mining, manufacturing, power and construction) provided an estimated 23.8% of GDP in 1995 and engaged 23.2% of the employed labour force. During 1990–94 industrial GDP declined by an annual average of 0.8%.

Mining contributed an estimated 1.2% of GDP in 1995 and engaged 0.4% of the employed labour force. Mineral fuels and lubricants, iron and steel, and aluminium and aluminium alloys are the major mineral/metal exports. Lignite, magnesite, silver ore and marble are also mined. In addition, Greece has small reserves of uranium and natural gas.

Manufacturing provided an estimated 13.9% of GDP in 1995 and engaged 15.1% of the working population. The most important branches in 1990, measured by the gross value of output, were food products (accounting for 18.8% of the total), metals and metal products (12.4%), textiles (particularly cotton), petroleum refineries and machinery and transport equipment. During 1990–94 manufacturing GDP declined by an annual average of 1.7%.

Energy is derived principally from petroleum and lignite. Petroleum and petroleum products accounted for 6.9% of the total cost of imports in 1995. Greece is currently exploiting an offshore petroleum deposit in the north-eastern Aegean Sea. Hydroelectric and solar power resources are also being developed.

The services sector contributed an estimated 62.0% of GDP in 1995 and employed 56.4% of the working population. Tourism is an important source of foreign exchange in Greece. In 1994 visitor arrivals totalled 11.2m.; receipts from the tourist sector amounted to US $3,905m. in that year. In 1995 there was concern at a considerable decline in the number of foreign visitors to the country. During 1990–94 GDP from the services sector increased by an annual average of 0.6%.

In 1996 Greece recorded a visible trade deficit of US $15,505m., and there was a deficit of $4,554m. on the current account of the balance of payments. In 1995 the principal source of imports (17.3%) was Italy, closely followed by Germany (16.8%); other major sources were France, the Netherlands and the United Kingdom. The principal market for exports (21.0%) was Germany; other major purchasers were Italy, the United Kingdom and France. The Balkan countries are increasingly emerging as important trading partners. The principal exports in 1995 were clothing, fruit and vegetables, petroleum and petroleum products and olive oil. The principal imports were road vehicles and parts, petroleum and petroleum products, textiles and electrical machinery.

The 1997 budget proposals, which were announced in November 1996, forecast revenue of 10,416,000m. drachmae and expenditure of 12,775,000m. drachmae, thus envisaging a budget deficit of 2,359,000m. drachmae. Greece's total public external debt was US $34,174m. at the end of 1995, of which $30,737m. was medium- and long-term debt. In that year the cost of debt-servicing was equivalent to 33.6% of earnings from exports of goods and services. In 1985–96 the average annual rate of inflation was 14.9%; it stood at 8.9% in 1995 and declined to 8.2% in 1996. According to the OECD, an estimated 10.2% of the labour force were unemployed in 1996.

Greece is a member of the European Union (EU—see p. 152), the Organisation for Economic Co-operation and Development (OECD—see p. 208) and the Black Sea Economic Co-operation Group (see p. 260).

Greece's major economic problem is the persistence of the public-sector deficit, despite the implementation of various austerity measures in the late 1980s and early 1990s. (In early 1996 the total public debt amounted to 111.7% of GDP.) The priority of the Simitis Government was to ensure the admittance of Greece to full EU economic and monetary union (EMU) by 2001. The budget for 1998 envisaged further reductions in the rate of inflation from an estimated 4.7% in 1997 to 2.5% in 1998, and in the budget deficit from an estimated 4.4% of GDP in 1997 to 2.4% in 1998, with both thus achieving the EU target of 3%. In order to achieve those targets, the Government was to continue with its restructuring of the state sector and hoped to amend existing legislation to allow more than 25% of state enterprises to be privatized. The budget also proposed several new taxes, mostly affecting the business sector. Following a sharp rise in interest rates in early November, an effective 'freeze' on public-sector wages and pensions was announced in order to combat the resultant high debt-financing costs. Greece's fiscal reforms were, however, undermined by continued investment in its military infrastructure; an improvement in Greece's relations with Turkey was essential to ensure a reduction in Greece's massive defence expenditure. As a member of the EU, Greece was attempting to exploit its location in the Balkans to take advantage of the new markets of that region's emerging economies.

Social Welfare

There is a state social insurance scheme for wage-earners, while voluntary or staff insurances provide for salaried staff. Every citizen is entitled to an old-age pension and sickness benefit. In 1987 Greece had 454 hospital establishments, with a total of 51,745 beds (equivalent to one for every 193 inhabitants), and in the same year there were 31,628 physicians working in the country. Of total projected expenditure by the central Government in 1997, some 2,001,000m. drachmae (15.7%) was allocated to health, social welfare and insurance.

Education

Education is available free of charge at all levels, and is officially compulsory for all children between the ages of six and 15 years. Primary education begins at the age of six and lasts for six years. Secondary education, beginning at the age of 12, is generally for six years, divided into two equal cycles. In 1990 the total enrolment at primary and secondary schools was equivalent to 95% of the school-age population. Primary enrolment in that year included 98% of children in the relevant age-group (males 98%; females 98%), while the comparable ratio at secondary schools was 83%. In 1994 enrolment in tertiary education was equivalent to 38.7% of the relevant age-group (males 37.5%; females 38.7%). Between 1951 and 1981 the average rate of adult illiteracy declined from 72% to 10%. At the 1991 census the rate was only 4.8% (males 2.3%; females 7.0%). In 1997 projected budgetary expenditure on education was 1,159,000m. drachmae (9.1% of total expenditure).

The vernacular language (demotiki) has replaced the formal version (katharevoussa) in secondary education.

Public Holidays

1998: 1 January (New Year's Day), 6 January (Epiphany), 2 March (Clean Monday), 25 March (Independence Day), 17–20 April (Greek Orthodox Easter), 1 May (Labour Day), 8 June (Whit Monday), 15 August (Assumption of the Virgin Mary), 28 October ('Ochi' Day, anniversary of Greek defiance of Italy's 1940 ultimatum), 25–26 December (Christmas).

1999: 1 January (New Year's Day), 6 January (Epiphany), 22 February (Clean Monday), 25 March (Independence Day), 9–12 April (Greek Orthodox Easter), 1 May (Labour Day), 31 May (Whit Monday), 15 August (Assumption of the Virgin Mary), 28 October ('Ochi' Day, anniversary of Greek defiance of Italy's 1940 ultimatum), 25–26 December (Christmas).

Weights and Measures

The metric system is in force.

Statistical Survey

Source (unless otherwise stated): National Statistical Service of Greece, Odos Lykourgou 14–16, 101 66 Athens; tel. (1) 3249302; telex 216734; fax (1) 3222205.

Area and Population

AREA, POPULATION AND DENSITY

Area (sq km)	131,957*
Population (census results)†	
5 April 1981	9,740,417
17 March 1991	
Males	5,055,408
Females	5,204,492
Total	10,259,900
Population (official estimates at mid-year)	
1994	10,426,289
1995	10,454,019
1996 (provisional)	10,475,000
Density (per sq km) at mid-1996	79.4

* 50,949 sq miles.

† Including armed forces stationed abroad, but excluding foreign forces stationed in Greece.

PRINCIPAL TOWNS (population at 1991 census)

Athinai (Athens, the capital)	772,072	Iraklion	116,178
Thessaloniki (Salonika)	383,967	Larissa	113,090
Piraeus	182,671	Volos	77,192
Patras	153,344	Kavala	58,025
		Serres	50,390
		Canea	50,077

BIRTHS, MARRIAGES AND DEATHS

	Registered live births		Registered marriages		Registered deaths	
	Number	Rate (per 1,000)	Number	Rate (per 1,000)	Number	Rate (per 1,000)
1988	107,505	10.7	47,873	4.8	92,407	9.2
1989	101,657	10.1	61,884	6.1	92,720	9.2
1990	102,229	10.1	59,052	5.8	94,152	9.3
1991	102,620	10.0	65,568	6.4	95,498	9.3
1992	104,081	10.1	48,631	4.7	98,231	9.5
1993	101,799	9.8	62,195	6.0	97,419	9.4
1994	103,763	9.9	56,813	5.4	97,807	9.4
1995	101,495	9.7	63,987	6.1	100,158	9.6

Expectation of life (UN estimates, years at birth, 1990–95): 77.6 (males 75.0; females 80.1). Source: UN, *World Population Prospects: The 1994 Revision.*

ECONOMICALLY ACTIVE POPULATION (sample surveys, '000 persons aged 14 years and over, April–June)*

	1993	1994	1995
Agriculture, hunting, forestry and fishing	793.9	789.7	781.9
Mining and quarrying	19.3	15.6	15.6
Manufacturing	579.5	577.8	577.7
Electricity, gas and water	39.6	40.6	41.5
Construction and public works	261.4	261.2	252.3
Trade, restaurants and hotels	791.5	814.2	848.7
Transport, storage and communications	249.0	252.3	248.0
Finance, insurance, banking and business services	220.8	231.0	241.0
Other services	765.2	807.3	817.2
Total employed	3,720.2	3,789.6	3,823.8
Unemployed	398.2	403.8	424.7
Total labour force	4,118.4	4,193.4	4,248.5
Males	2,584.0	2,622.6	2,628.3
Females	1,534.4	1,570.8	1,620.2

* Including members of the regular armed forces, but excluding persons on compulsory military service.

Agriculture

PRINCIPAL CROPS ('000 metric tons)

	1994	1995	1996
Wheat	2,417	2,214	1,841
Rice (paddy)	188	206	220†
Barley	406	423	359
Maize	2,098	1,722	1,814
Rye	39	41	39
Oats	79	83	96
Potatoes	968	1,185	1,150*
Dry beans	24	24	22
Other pulses	20	19	19
Sunflower seed	29	33	32
Cottonseed†	580	670	659
Olives	1,933	1,730†	1,600*
Cabbages	286	275	280*
Tomatoes	2,017	1,798	1,990†
Cucumbers and gherkins	185	185*	185*
Aubergines	83	72†	72*
Green peppers	104	100*	100*
Onions (dry)	137	155†	140*
Watermelons	650	683†	600*
Melons	160	170†	170*
Grapes	1,235	1,169	1,169*
Sugar beet	2,564	2,610†	2,440†
Apples	346	345	290†
Pears	107	89†	90*
Peaches and nectarines	1,174	900†	1,040†
Oranges	932	935	850†
Lemons and limes	178	106	125†
Apricots	82	47	55†
Almonds	56	46	50*
Tobacco (leaves)	142	135	129
Cotton (lint)†	396	433	390

* FAO estimate. † Unofficial figure(s).

Source: FAO, *Production Yearbook.*

LIVESTOCK ('000 head, year ending 30 September)

	1994	1995	1996
Asses	103	100*	100*
Cattle	608	600	640
Goats	5,378	5,400*	5,450*
Horses	38	38*	38*
Mules	47	45*	45*
Pigs	1,143	1,121	1,070
Sheep	8,706	9,559†	9,500*

Poultry (million): 28 in 1994; 28* in 1995; 28* in 1996.

* FAO estimate. † Unofficial figure.

Source: FAO, *Production Yearbook*.

LIVESTOCK PRODUCTS ('000 metric tons)

	1994	1995	1996
Beef and veal	74	75	74*
Mutton and lamb	83	80	83*
Goat meat	47	48	48*
Pig meat	145	142	143*
Horse meat*	3	3	3
Poultry meat	149	147	149
Other meat	508	503	508
Cows' milk	737†	690†	690*
Sheep's milk	629†	670*	670*
Goats' milk	460†	460*	460*
Cheese	211	221	222*
Butter	5	5*	5*
Poultry eggs	125	126	126*
Honey	15	15	14*
Wool: greasy	10	10	10*
Wool: clean	5	5	6*
Cattle and buffalo hides	14	14	14
Sheepskins*	18	18	18
Goatskins*	11	11	11

* FAO estimate(s). † Unofficial figure.

Source: FAO, *Production Yearbook*.

Forestry

ROUNDWOOD REMOVALS ('000 cubic metres, excl. bark)

	1992	1993	1994*
Sawlogs, veneer logs and logs for sleepers	605	650	650
Pulpwood	410*	410*	410
Other industrial wood	200	200*	200
Fuel wood	1,637	1,519	1,519
Total	2,852	2,779	2,779

* FAO estimate(s).

Source: FAO, *Yearbook of Forest Products*.

SAWNWOOD PRODUCTION ('000 cubic metres)

	1992	1993*	1994*
Coniferous (softwood)	210	210	210
Broadleaved (hardwood)	127	127	127
Total	337	337	337

* FAO estimates.

Source: FAO, *Yearbook of Forest Products*.

Fishing

('000 metric tons, live weight)

	1993	1994	1995
Freshwater fishes	11.0	13.5	17.8
European seabass	7.9	7.4	10.1
Gilthead seabream	6.3	6.9	9.6
Bogue	12.4	14.6	6.8
Picarels	7.4	14.1	6.4
Mediterranean horse mackerel	8.3	11.3	8.3
European pilchard (sardine)	20.7	20.3	20.4
European anchovy	14.6	17.3	13.9
Chub mackerel	11.0	14.3	6.5
Total fish (incl. others)	160.5	186.7	158.8
Crustaceans	5.8	4.5	4.4
Mediterranean mussel	19.6	19.1	21.7
Other molluscs	13.2	13.1	13.3
Total catch	199.1	223.4	198.2
Inland waters	13.3	16.2	19.9
Atlantic Ocean	14.7	9.3	8.7
Mediterranean and Black Sea	171.1	197.9	169.6

Source: FAO, *Yearbook of Fishery Statistics*.

Mining

('000 metric tons, unless otherwise indicated)

	1992	1993	1994
Lignite	55,051	54,817	56,741
Crude petroleum	653	537	500
Iron ore*	610†	575†	550§
Bauxite	2,085	2,023	2,194‡
Zinc concentrates*‡	26.2	22.0	17.2
Lead concentrates*†	28.3	26.4	19.9
Silver ore*‡	61	59	45
Magnesite§	250	250	200
Kaolin (raw)	89	n.a.	n.a.
Salt (unrefined)	143	n.a.	n.a.
Marble ('000 cu m)	200	n.a.	n.a.
Natural gas (petajoules)	6	4	2

* Figures refer to the metal content of ores and concentrates.

† Estimate(s).

‡ Data from *World Metal Statistics*.

§ Data from the US Bureau of Mines.

Source: UN, *Industrial Commodity Statistics Yearbook*.

1995 ('000 metric tons): Lignite 56,553; Bauxite 2,200; Zinc concentrates 28.5; Lead concentrates 20.5; Magnesite 566.

1996 ('000 metric tons): Lignite 58,950; Bauxite 1,881; Zinc concentrates 13; Lead concentrates 11; Magnesite 210. (Source: *Mining Annual Review.*)

Industry

SELECTED PRODUCTS
('000 metric tons, unless otherwise indicated)

	1991	1992	1993
Edible fats	45	50	47
Olive oil (crude)	387	310	303
Raw sugar	262	320	354
Wine	231	247	187
Beer ('000 hectolitres)	3,772	4,025	4,088
Cigarettes (million)	27,700	33,948	29,437
Cotton yarn (pure)	120.4	103.6	106.0
Woven cotton fabrics—pure and mixed (metric tons)	29,843	24,941	29,994
Wool yarn—pure (metric tons)	4,590	5,307	7,847
Woven woollen fabrics—pure and mixed (metric tons)[1]	1,829	1,273	2,444
Yarn of artificial material (metric tons)	6,507	5,312	8,133
Fabrics of artificial fibres (metric tons)	1,025	849	1,206
Footwear—excl. rubber and plastic ('000 pairs)	10,712	9,264	8,622
Rubber footwear ('000 pairs)	119	277	150
Paper and paperboard	344	343	351

— *continued*	1991	1992	1993
Sulphuric acid	841	617	550
Hydrochloric acid (21° Bé)	43	32	34
Nitric acid (54% or 36.3° Bé)	421	441	250
Ammonia (anhydrous)	256	168	57
Caustic soda (Sodium hydroxide)	39	38	n.a.
Nitrogenous fertilizers (single)	293	306	411
Superphosphatic fertilizers (single)	144	55	n.a.
Polyvinyl chloride	78	79	76
Liquefied petroleum gas	404	414	380
Naphthas	247	n.a.	n.a.
Motor spirit (petrol)	2,991	3,572	3,457
Jet fuels	1,405	1,432	1,310
Distillate fuel oils	3,154	3,719	3,252
Residual fuel oils	4,588	4,774	4,519
Cement	13,151	12,761	12,612*
Crude steel (incl. alloys)	980	924	980*
Aluminium (unwrought)*	147.7	175.1	174.5
Refrigerators—household ('000)	85	n.a.	n.a.
Washing machines—household ('000)	53	47	n.a.
Television receivers ('000)	2	—	n.a.
Lorries (number)[2]	1,534	1,919	n.a.
Electric energy (million kWh)*	38,396	35,813	37,410

[1] After undergoing finishing processes.
[2] Assembled wholly or mainly from imported parts.
* UN figure(s). Source: UN, *Industrial Commodity Statistics Yearbook*.
1994 ('000 metric tons, unless otherwise indicated): Olive oil (crude) 375, Cement 12,636, Crude steel (incl. alloys) 852, Aluminium (unwrought) 141.6, Electric energy (million kWh) 40,623. Source: UN, *Industrial Commodity Statistics Yearbook*.

Finance

CURRENCY AND EXCHANGE RATES

Monetary Units

100 lepta (singular: lepton) = 1 drachma (plural: drachmae).

Sterling and Dollar Equivalents (30 September 1997)

£1 sterling = 450.6 drachmae;
US $1 = 278.9 drachmae;
1,000 drachmae = £2.219 = $3.585.

Average Exchange Rate (drachmae per US $)

1994 242.60
1995 231.66
1996 240.71

BUDGET ('000 million drachmae)*

Revenue	1995	1996†	1997‡
Ordinary budget	6,728	7,410	8,715
Tax revenue	5,968	6,610	7,804
Direct taxes	2,133	2,314	2,790
Personal income tax	861	1,017	1,233
Corporate income tax	460	522	630
Indirect taxes	3,835	4,297	5,014
Consumption taxes	1,460	1,636	1,907
Transaction taxes	2,262	2,544	2,970
Value-added tax	1,933	2,154	2,520
Stamp duty	194	217	255
Non-tax revenue	760	800	911
Capital receipts	423	376	481
Investment budget	345	567	817
Receipts from European Union	322	551	700
SAGAP§	713	875	884
Total	7,786	8,853	10,416

Expenditure	1995	1996†	1997‡
Defence	781	792	912
Education	862	978	1,159
Health, social welfare and insurance	1,558	1,711	2,001
Agriculture	994	1,240	1,274
Interest payments‖	3,126	3,291	3,253
Other purposes	3,233	3,716	4,177
Total‖	10,555	11,728	12,775
Ordinary budget	8,880	9,737	10,225
Investment budget	962	1,116	1,666
SAGAP§	713	875	884

* Figures refer to the budgetary transactions of the central Government, excluding the operations of social security funds and public entities (such as hospitals, educational institutions and government agencies) with individual budgets.
† Provisional.
‡ Projected.
§ Special Account for Guarantees of Agricultural Products.
‖ Excluding capitalized interest ('000 million drachmae): 211 in 1995; 179 (provisional) in 1996; 33 (projected) in 1997.
Source: IMF, *Greece—Selected Issues and Statistical Appendix* (October 1997).

INTERNATIONAL RESERVES (US $ million at 31 December)*

	1994	1995	1996
Gold†	850.9	871.7	833.2
IMF special drawing rights	0.3	—	0.6
Reserve position in IMF	166.0	169.0	163.5
Foreign exchange	14,321.6	14,611.0	17,337.3
Total	15,338.8	15,651.7	18,334.6

* Figures exclude deposits made with the European Monetary Institute.
† Gold reserves are valued at market-related prices.
Source: IMF, *International Financial Statistics*.

MONEY SUPPLY ('000 million drachmae at 31 December)

	1994	1995	1996
Currency outside banks	1,725.9	1,904.4	1,995.1
Private-sector deposits at Bank of Greece	315.4	366.7	460.4
Demand deposits at commercial banks	1,344.6	1,568.7	1,879.4
Total money	3,385.8	3,839.8	4,334.9

Source: IMF, *International Financial Statistics*.

COST OF LIVING (Consumer Price Index; base: 1990 = 100)

	1993	1994	1995*
Food	153.4	173.2	189.2
Fuel and light	157.3	168.7	180.8
Clothing	147.3	162.2	178.3
Rent	188.5	216.4	241.5
All items (incl. others)	158.4	175.7	192.0

* Provisional.
Source: ILO, *Yearbook of Labour Statistics*.
1995 (revised): All items 191.4.
1996: All items 207.1.
Source: IMF, *International Financial Statistics*.

NATIONAL ACCOUNTS

Expenditure on the Gross Domestic Product
('000 million drachmae at current prices)

	1994	1995	1996
Government final consumption expenditure	3,275.7	3,899.0	4,239.4
Private final consumption expenditure	17,770.1	19,733.5	21,882.0
Increase in stocks	252.9	270.1	305.0
Gross fixed capital formation	4,730.7	5,344.6	6,309.9
Total domestic expenditure	26,029.4	29,247.2	32,736.3
Exports of goods and services	3,987.6	4,360.5	4,646.9
Less Imports of goods and services	6,261.2	7,123.3	7,807.2
GDP in purchasers' values	23,755.8	26,484.4	29,576.0
GDP at constant 1990 prices	13,730.5	n.a.	n.a.

Source: IMF, *International Financial Statistics*.

Gross Domestic Product by Economic Activity
(million drachmae at current prices)

	1993*	1994*	1995†
Agriculture, hunting, forestry and fishing	1,982,789	2,387,102	2,538,766
Mining and quarrying	172,944	186,238	213,615
Manufacturing	2,219,730	2,399,528	2,483,098
Electricity, gas and water	376,599	405,221	433,992
Construction	945,501	1,008,850	1,102,673
Wholesale and retail trade	1,975,000	2,162,625	2,455,455
Transport, storage and communication	1,015,958	1,142,953	1,309,314
Finance, insurance and real estate‡	1,624,951	1,735,160	2,000,522
Public administration and defence	1,574,498	1,763,479	1,951,916
Other services	2,471,129	2,787,915	3,327,313
GDP at factor cost	14,359,099	15,979,071	17,816,664
Indirect taxes, *less* subsidies	2,401,253	2,885,338	3,306,000
GDP in purchasers' values	16,760,352	18,864,409	21,122,664

* Figures are provisional.
† Estimates.
‡ Including imputed rents of owner-occupied dwellings.

BALANCE OF PAYMENTS (US $ million)

	1994	1995	1996
Exports of goods f.o.b.	5,338	5,918	5,890
Imports of goods f.o.b.	−16,611	−20,343	−21,395
Trade balance	−11,273	−14,425	−15,505
Exports of services	9,213	9,605	9,348
Imports of services	−3,774	−4,368	−4,238
Balance on goods and services	−5,834	−9,188	−10,395
Other income received	1,099	1,312	1,156
Other income paid	−2,347	−2,996	−3,337
Balance on goods, services and income	−7,082	−10,872	−12,576
Current transfers received	6,964	8,039	8,053
Current transfers paid	−28	−31	−31
Current balance	−146	−2,864	−4,554
Direct investment from abroad	981	1,053	1,058
Other investment liabilities (net)	5,922	2,109	7,600
Net errors and omissions	−448	−321	111
Overall balance	6,309	−23	4,215

Source: IMF, *International Financial Statistics*.

External Trade

PRINCIPAL COMMODITIES (million drachmae)

Imports c.i.f.	1993	1994	1995
Food and live animals	567,058	669,298	788,453
Meat and meat preparations	178,132	199,689	219,261
Fresh, chilled or frozen meat	110,454	114,992	121,575
Dairy products and birds' eggs	125,587	146,739	146,382
Crude materials (inedible) except fuels	146,889	177,557	212,188
Mineral fuels, lubricants, etc.	535,679	509,226	434,296
Petroleum and petroleum products	516,688	489,780	412,565
Crude petroleum	383,910	355,903	308,132
Chemicals and related products	557,661	659,941	791,164
Plastic materials, etc.	117,353	138,065	182,536
Basic manufactures	834,445	970,650	1,192,863
Paper, paperboard and manufactures	110,041	128,577	182,213
Textile yarn, fabrics, etc.	221,725	251,918	268,316
Iron and steel	145,585	171,995	227,551
Machinery and transport equipment	1,775,985	1,484,534	1,648,678
Machinery specialized for particular industries	148,903	142,928	174,450
General industrial machinery	177,330	189,760	230,338
Telecommunications and sound equipment	162,340	173,646	161,166
Other electrical machinery, apparatus, etc.	188,271	204,095	218,696
Road vehicles and parts*	539,932	412,951	513,446
Other transport equipment*	391,112	179,082	130,349
Ships, boats and floating structures	329,188	146,292	99,547
Miscellaneous manufactured articles	495,764	590,916	783,017
Total (incl. others)	5,050,531	5,207,563	5,907,978

* Excluding tyres, engines and electrical parts.

Exports f.o.b.	1993	1994	1995
Food and live animals	382,714	457,698	460,193
Cereals and cereal preparations	61,907	78,506	49,389
Vegetables and fruit	230,408	271,778	294,659
Fresh or dried fruit and nuts (excl. oil nuts)	85,670	111,923	111,858
Preserved fruit and fruit preparations	70,777	72,578	57,738
Beverages and tobacco	121,235	125,256	142,647
Tobacco and manufactures	89,496	82,951	93,858
Unmanufactured tobacco	77,041	70,907	71,588
Crude materials (inedible) except fuels	111,558	145,752	180,244
Mineral fuels, lubricants, etc.	151,653	235,605	165,291
Petroleum and petroleum products	148,423	233,238	162,214
Refined petroleum products	134,502	226,102	150,242
Animal and vegetable oils, fats and waxes	69,233	83,641	140,354
Fixed vegetable oils and fats	69,067	83,453	141,562
Olive oil (crude, refined or purified)	64,293	79,470	133,152
Chemicals and related products	89,614	97,471	123,652
Basic manufactures	387,578	471,645	545,362
Textile yarn, fabrics, etc.	98,264	104,423	120,727
Textile yarn	48,889	51,109	61,448
Non-metallic mineral manufactures	81,639	106,991	97,900
Lime, cement, etc.	70,418	90,469	78,043
Iron and steel	55,094	76,397	89,332
Non-ferrous metals	81,039	101,645	138,684
Aluminium and aluminium alloys	59,385	78,242	101,132
Machinery and transport equipment	121,215	152,477	203,769
Miscellaneous manufactured articles	472,172	484,441	529,540
Clothing and accessories (excl. footwear)	406,347	404,901	433,616
Total (incl. others)	1,933,432	2,288,831	2,539,416

PRINCIPAL TRADING PARTNERS (million drachmae)*

Imports c.i.f.	1993	1994	1995
Austria	53,347	54,257	62,210
Belgium-Luxembourg	168,930	198,637	217,386
Bulgaria	45,453	77,069	n.a.
China, People's Republic	66,811	68,025	78,081
Denmark	68,726	75,492	86,836
France	398,504	419,640	488,019
Germany	854,475	853,414	993,860
Italy	707,466	866,499	1,024,901
Japan	343,756	199,034	158,073
Korea, Republic	102,192	45,627	79,490
Libya	80,463	68,264	36,556
Netherlands	334,920	388,466	416,130
Saudi Arabia	66,705	46,151	62,301
Spain	135,508	163,713	203,049
Sweden	63,868	83,961	87,981
Switzerland	96,372	96,282	101,902
USSR (former)	125,988	175,721	191,996
United Kingdom	307,081	323,668	390,071
USA	188,092	166,704	194,287
Total (incl. others)	5,050,531	5,207,563	5,907,978

Exports f.o.b.	1993	1994	1995
Austria	27,917	32,119	34,517
Belgium-Luxembourg	29,517	37,019	49,206
Bulgaria	69,531	100,223	103,618
Cyprus	60,410	74,098	74,735
France	119,616	121,618	138,477
Germany	458,984	480,754	561,314
Italy	255,982	314,925	357,899
Lebanon	23,432	41,734	1,092
Netherlands	48,353	56,649	69,125
Saudi Arabia	31,999	34,457	62,301
Spain	32,174	50,496	87,809
Switzerland	27,532	25,769	33,863
Turkey	34,029	33,500	51,223
USSR (former)	52,737	85,391	99,575
United Kingdom	110,301	133,493	154,732
USA	86,467	122,652	79,665
Total (incl. others)	1,933,432	2,288,831	2,539,416

* Imports by country of first consignment; exports by country of consumption.

Transport

RAILWAYS (estimated traffic)

	1993	1994	1995
Passenger-kilometres (million)	1,726	1,599	1,568
Net ton-kilometres (million)	523	324	306

ROAD TRAFFIC (motor vehicles in use at 31 December)

	1993	1994	1995
Passenger cars	1,958,544	2,074,091	2,204,761
Buses and coaches	23,206	23,540	24,600
Goods vehicles	808,291	849,033	877,475
Motorcycles	387,877	n.a.	476,017

Source: International Road Federation, *World Road Statistics*.

SHIPPING

Merchant fleet (at 1 July)

	1995		1996	
	Vessels	Gross reg. tons	Vessels	Gross reg. tons
Cargo boats	868	15,109,160	823	14,691,256
Passenger boats	514	1,005,232	521	1,028,624
Tankers	431	14,306,996	425	14,753,083
Others	348	104,606	340	101,738

Freight traffic

	1993	1994	1995
Vessels entered ('000 net reg. tons)	63,767	68,785	73,059
Goods loaded ('000 metric tons)*	18,467	21,087	21,940
Goods unloaded ('000 metric tons)*	32,429	33,048	38,573

* International sea-borne shipping.

CIVIL AVIATION

(domestic and foreign flights of Olympic Airways)

	1993	1994	1995
Kilometres flown ('000)	61,698	63,953	62,016
Passenger-kilometres ('000)	7,898,715	8,428,539	7,945,008
Freight ton-kilometres ('000)	127,010	134,997	117,338
Mail ton-kilometres ('000)	8,387	8,963	9,031

Tourism

	1992	1993	1994
Number of visitors*	9,756,012	9,913,267	11,230,854
Receipts (US $'000)	3,268,400	3,335,200	3,904,900

* Including cruise passengers: 424,652 in 1992; 500,444 in 1993; 588,912 in 1994.

1995: Tourist receipts US$4,135.8 million.

TOURISTS BY COUNTRY OF ORIGIN

(foreign citizens, excluding cruise passengers)

Country	1992	1993	1994
Austria	345,259	288,636	348,091
Belgium-Luxembourg	225,099	224,036	265,148
Denmark	281,235	253,622	318,885
France	542,222	554,644	618,565
Germany	1,944,704	2,069,379	2,404,628
Italy	622,619	625,509	722,652
Netherlands	546,187	510,872	556,593
Sweden	314,251	317,030	387,639
Switzerland	163,126	164,999	193,327
United Kingdom	2,154,850	2,191,347	2,418,628
USA	278,941	256,719	270,777
Yugoslavia (former)	93,413	191,792	279,301
Total (incl. others)	9,331,360	9,421,823	10,641,942

Communications Media

	1993	1994	1995
Radio receivers ('000 in use)	4,320	4,352	4,389
Television receivers ('000 in use)	2,100	2,184	2,223
Telephones ('000 main lines in use)	4,744	4,976	5,163
Telefax stations (number in use)	15,260	n.a.	n.a.
Mobile cellular telephones (subscribers)	48,000	167,000	n.a.
Daily newspapers			
Number	n.a.	168	n.a.
Average circulation ('000 copies)	n.a.	1,622	n.a.

Non-daily newspapers (number): 1,041 in 1988.
Periodicals (number): 800 in 1988.
Books (titles published): 4,066 in 1991.

Sources: National Statistical Service of Greece; UN, *Statistical Yearbook* and UNESCO, *Statistical Yearbook*.

Education

(1992/93)

	Institutions	Teachers	Students
Pre-primary	5,505	8,491	135,822
Primary	7,368	43,636	753,401
Secondary:			
General	3,029	51,655	719,856
Vocational	705	13,105	160,867
Higher:			
Universities	17	9,301	111,911
Technical	12	5,577	49,573
Vocational and ecclesiastical	40	542	3,530

Directory

The Constitution

A new Constitution for the Hellenic Republic came into force on 11 June 1975. The main provisions of this Constitution, as subsequently amended, are summarized below.

Greece shall be a parliamentary democracy with a President as Head of State. All powers are derived from the people and exist for the benefit of the people. The established religion is that of The Eastern Orthodox Church of Christ.

EXECUTIVE AND LEGISLATIVE

The President

In March 1986 a series of amendments to the Constitution was approved by a majority vote of Parliament, which relieved the President of his executive power and transferred such power to the legislature, thus confining the Head of State to a largely ceremonial role.

The President is elected by Parliament for a period of five years. The re-election of the same person shall be permitted only once. The President represents the State in relations with other nations, is Supreme Commander of the armed forces and may declare war and conclude treaties. The President shall appoint the Prime Minister and, on the Prime Minister's recommendation, the other members of the Government. The President shall convoke Parliament once every year and in extraordinary session whenever he deems it reasonable. In exceptional circumstances the President may preside over the Cabinet, convene the Council of the Republic, and suspend Parliament for a period not exceeding 30 days. In accordance with the amendment of March 1986, the President was deprived of the right to dismiss the Prime Minister, his power to call a referendum was limited, and the right to declare a state of emergency was transferred to Parliament. The President can now dissolve Parliament only if the resignation of two Governments in quick succession demonstrates the absence of political stability. If no party has a majority in Parliament, the President must offer an opportunity to form a government to the leader of each of the four biggest parties in turn, strictly following the order of their parliamentary strengths. If no party leader is able to form a government, the President may try to assemble an all-party government; failing that, the President must appoint a caretaker cabinet, led by a senior judge, to hold office until a fresh election takes place. The Constitution continues to reserve a substantial moderating role for the President, however, in that he retains the right to object to legislation and may request Parliament to reconsider it or to approve it with an enlarged majority.

The Government

The Government consists of the Cabinet which comprises the Prime Minister and Ministers. The Government determines and directs the general policy of the State in accordance with the Constitution and the laws. The Cabinet must enjoy the confidence of Parliament and may be removed by a vote of no confidence. The Prime Minister is to be the leader of the party with an absolute majority in Parliament, or, if no such party exists, the leader of the party with a relative majority.

The Council of the Republic

The Council of the Republic shall be composed of all former democratic Presidents, the Prime Minister, the leader of the Opposition and the parliamentary Prime Ministers of governments which have enjoyed the confidence of Parliament, presided over by the President. It shall meet when the largest parties are unable to form a government with the confidence of Parliament and may empower the President to appoint a Prime Minister who may or may not be a member of Parliament. The Council may also authorize the President to dissolve Parliament.

Parliament

Parliament is to be unicameral and composed of not fewer than 200 and not more than 300 deputies elected by direct, universal and secret ballot for a term of four years. Parliament shall elect its own President, or Speaker. It must meet once a year for a regular session of at least five months. Bills passed by Parliament must be ratified by the President and the President's veto can be nullified by an absolute majority of the total number of deputies. Parliament may impeach the President by a motion signed by one-third and passed by two-thirds of the total number of deputies. Parliament is also empowered to impeach present or former members of the Government. In these cases the defendant shall be brought before an *ad hoc* tribunal presided over by the President of the Supreme Court and composed of 12 judges. Certain legislative work, as specified in the Constitution, must be passed by Parliament in plenum, and Parliament cannot make a decision without an absolute majority of the members present, which under no circumstances shall be less than one-quarter of the total number of deputies. The Constitution provides for certain legislative powers to be exercised by not more than two Parliamentary Departments. Parliament may revise the Constitution in accordance with the procedure laid down in the Constitution.

THE JUDICIAL AUTHORITY

Justice is to be administered by courts of regular judges, who enjoy personal and functional independence. The President, after consultations with a judicial council, shall appoint the judges for life. The judges are subject only to the Constitution and the laws. Courts are divided into administrative, civil and penal and shall be organized by virtue of special laws. They must not apply laws which are contrary to the Constitution. The final jurisdiction in matters of judicial review rests with a Special Supreme Tribunal.

Certain laws, passed before the implementation of this Constitution and deemed not contrary to it, are to remain in force. Other specified laws, even if contrary to the Constitution, are to remain in force until repealed by further legislation.

INDIVIDUAL AND SPECIAL RIGHTS

All citizens are equal under the Constitution and before the law, having the same rights and obligations. No titles of nobility or distinction are to be conferred or recognized. All persons are to enjoy full protection of life, honour and freedom, irrespective of nationality, race, creed or political allegiance. Retrospective legislation is prohibited and no citizen may be punished without due process of law. Freedom of speech, of the Press, of association and of religion are guaranteed under the Constitution. All persons have the right to a free education, which the state has the duty to provide. Work is a right and all workers, irrespective of sex or other distinction, are entitled to equal remuneration for rendering services of equal value. The right of peaceful assembly, the right of a person to property and the freedom to form political parties are guaranteed under the Constitution. The exercise of the right to vote by all citizens over 18 years of age is obligatory. No person may exercise his rights and liberties contrary to the Constitution.

MOUNT ATHOS

The district of Mount Athos shall, in accordance with its ancient privileged status, be a self-governing part of the Greek State and its sovereignty shall remain unaffected.

The Government

HEAD OF STATE

President: Konstantinos Stefanopoulos (took office 10 March 1995).

THE CABINET
(February 1998)

Prime Minister: Konstantinos Simitis.

Minister of the Interior, Public Administration and Decentralization: Alexandros Papadopoulos.

Minister of National Defence: Apostolos-Athanasios Tsohatzopoulos.

Minister of Foreign Affairs: Theodhoros Pangalos.

Minister of the National Economy and of Finance: Ioannis Papantoniou.

Minister of Development: Vasiliki (Vasso) Papandreou.

Minister of the Environment, Town Planning and Public Works: Konstantinos Laliotis.

Minister of Education and Religious Affairs: Gerasimos Arsenis.

Minister of Agriculture: Stephanos Tzoumakas.

Minister of Labour and Social Security: Miltiades Papaioannou.

Minister of Health and Welfare: Konstantinos Geitonas.

Minister of Justice: Evangelos Yiannopoulos.

Minister of Culture: Evangelos Venizelos.

Minister of Merchant Marine: Stavros Soumakis.

Minister of Public Order: Georgios Romaios.

Minister of Macedonia and Thrace: Filipos Petsalnikos.

Minister of the Aegean: Elisabeth Papazoi.

Minister of Transport and Communications: Kharalambos Kastanidis.

Minister of Press and Mass Media: Dimitris Reppas.

MINISTRIES

Ministry to the Prime Minister: Leoforos Vassilissis Sophias 15, 106 74 Athens; tel. (1) 3393502; telex 214333; fax (1) 3393500.

Ministry of the Aegean: Leoforos Syngrou 49, 117 43 Athens; tel. (1) 9225240; fax (1) 9216204.

Ministry of Agriculture: Odos Acharnon 2–6, Athens; tel. (1) 5245587; telex 215308; fax (1) 5240475.

Ministry of Culture: Odos Bouboulinas 20, 106 82 Athens; tel. (1) 8201637; fax (1) 8201373.

Ministry of Development: Odos Mihalakopoulou 80, 115 28 Athens; tel. (1) 7708615; telex 215811; fax (1) 7788279.

Ministry of Education and Religious Affairs: Odos Metropoleos 15, 105 57 Athens; tel. (1) 3230461; telex 216059; fax (1) 3248264.

Ministry of the Environment, Town Planning and Public Works: Odos Amaliados 17, 115 23 Athens; tel. (1) 6431461; telex 216374; fax (1) 6432589.

Ministry of Finance: Odos Karageorgi Servias 10, 105 62 Athens; tel. (1) 8477116; telex 216373; fax (1) 3238657.

Ministry of Foreign Affairs: Odos Zalokosta 2, 106 71 Athens; tel. (1) 3610581; fax (1) 3624195.

Ministry of Health and Welfare: Odos Aristotelous 17, 104 33 Athens; tel. (1) 5232820; telex 21625; fax (1) 5231707.

Ministry of the Interior, Public Administration and Decentralization: Odos Stadiou 27, 101 83 Athens; tel. (1) 3223521; telex 215776; fax (1) 3233218.

Ministry of Justice: Odos Mesogeion 96, 115 27 Athens; tel. (1) 7751303; fax (1) 7759879.

Ministry of Labour and Social Security: Odos Pireos 40, 104 37 Athens; tel. (1) 5291111; telex 216608; fax (1) 5249805.

Ministry of Macedonia and Thrace: Odos Doikitirio, 546 30 Thessaloniki; tel. (31) 275588; fax (31) 235109.

Ministry of Merchant Marine: Odos Gregoriou Lambraki 150, Piraeus; tel. (1) 4121211; telex 211232; fax (1) 4134286.

Ministry of National Defence: Stratopedo Papagou, Holargos, Athens; tel. (1) 6465201; fax (1) 6465584.

Ministry of National Economy: Plateia Syntagmatos, 105 63 Athens; tel. (1) 3230931; fax (1) 3232218.

Ministry of Press and Mass Media: Odos Zalokosta 10, 106 71 Athens; tel. (1) 3630911; fax (1) 3609682.

Ministry of Public Order: P. Khanellopoulou 4, 101 77 Athens; tel. (1) 6928510; telex 216353; fax (1) 6921675.

Ministry of Transport and Communications: Odos Xenofontos 13, 101 91 Athens; tel. (1) 3251211; telex 216369; fax (1) 3239039.

Legislature

VOULI

President of Parliament: Apostolos Kaklamanis.

General Election, 22 September 1996.

	Seats	Percentage of Votes
Panhellenic Socialist Movement (PASOK)	162	41.5
New Democracy (ND)	108	38.2
Communist Party (KKE)	11	5.6
Coalition of the Left and Progress . .	10	5.1
Democratic Social Movement (DHKKI) .	9	4.4
Political Spring (POLA)	—	2.9
Others	—	2.3
Total	300	100.0

Political Organizations

Coalition of the Left and Progress (Synaspismos): Pl. Elefthrias 1, 10553 Athens; tel. (1) 3219472; fax (1) 3217003; f. 1989 as an alliance of the nine political groups comprising the Greek Left Party and the Communist Party of Greece ('of the Exterior'); in 1991 the hard-line conservative faction of the Communist Party withdrew from the alliance; however, the Coalition continued to command considerable support from the large reformist faction of the KKE; transformed into a single party in 1992; Pres. Nikos Konstantopoulos.

Communist Party of Greece (Kommunistiko Komma Ellados—KKE): Leoforos Iraklиou 145, Perissos, 142 31 Athens; tel. (1) 2523543; telex 225402; fax (1) 2511998; f. 1918; banned 1947, reappeared 1974; factions include the KKE—'Exterior'; Gen. Sec. Aleka Papariga.

Democratic Social Movement (DHKKI): Athens; f. 1995; leftist party; opposes further integration with the EU; Leader Dimitris Tsovalas.

Democratic Socialist Party (KODISO): Odos Mavromichali 9, 106 79 Athens; tel. (1) 3602716; fax (1) 3625901; f. March 1979 by former EDIK deputies; favours membership of the EU and political wing of NATO, decentralization and a mixed economy; Pres. Ch. Protopapas.

Greek National Political Union (EPEN): Odos Voukourestiou, 106 71 Athens; tel. (1) 3643760; fax (1) 8943100; f. 1984; right-wing; Leader Chryssanthos Dimitriadis.

Hellenic Liberal Party: Vissarionos 1, 106 72 Athens; tel. (1) 3606111; telex 214886; f. 1910; aims to revive political heritage of fmr Prime Minister, Eleftherios Venizelos; 6,500 mems; Pres. Nikitas Venizelos.

New Democracy Party (Nea Dimokratia—ND): Odos Rigillis 18, 106 74 Athens; tel. (1) 7290071; telex 210856; fax (1) 7214327; f. 1974 by Konstantinos Karamanlis; a broadly-based centre-right party which advocates social reform in the framework of a liberal economy; supports European integration and enlargement; led and completed Greece's accession into the EU; Leader Konstantinos Karamanlis; Dir-Gen. Ioannis Vartholomeos.

Panhellenic Socialist Movement (Panellinion Socialistikon Kinima—PASOK): Odos Charilaou Trikoupi 50, Athens; tel. (1) 3232049; telex 218763; f. 1974; incorporates Democratic Defence and Panhellenic Liberation Movement resistance organizations; supports social welfare, decentralization and self-management, aims at a Mediterranean socialist development through international co-operation; 500 local organizations, 30,000 mems; Leader Konstantinos Simitis; Sec.-Gen. Konstantinos Skandalides.

Political Spring (Politiki Anixi—POLA): Pandrosou 7, Athens; tel. (1) 3249429; f. 1993; centre-right party with nationalist approach to foreign policy, particularly regarding negotiations concerning the former Yugoslav republic of Macedonia; Leader ANTONIS SAMARAS.

Union of Democratic Centre Party (Enossi Dimokratikou Kentrou—EDIK): Odos Charilaou Trikoupi 18, 106 79 Athens; tel. (1) 3612792; fax (1) 3634412; f. 1974; democratic socialist party, merging Centre Union (f. 1961 by GEORGIOS PAPANDREOU) and New Political Forces (f. 1974 by Prof. IOANNIS PESMAZOGLOU and Prof. G. A. MANGAKIS); favours a united Europe; Chair. Prof. NEOKLIS SARRIS.

Other parties include the People's Militant Unity Party (f. 1985 by PASOK splinter group), the Progressive Party (f. 1979, right-wing), the (Maoist) Revolutionary Communist Party of Greece (EKKE), the Panhellenic Unaligned Party of Equality (PAKI, f. 1988; Leader KHARALAMBOS ALOMA TAMONTSIDES), Olympianism Party (pacifist, Leader GIORGIOS ZOE), and the left-wing United Socialist Alliance of Greece (ESPE, f. 1984).

Terrorist organizations include the left-wing 17 November Revolutionary Organization (f. 1975; opposed to Western capitalism and the continuing existence of US military bases in Greece), the 1 May Revolutionary Organization, the Revolutionary People's Struggle (ELA), People's Revolutionary Solidarity, the Anti-State Struggle group, the Christos Tsoutsouvis Revolutionary Organization and the Revolutionary Praxis.

Diplomatic Representation

EMBASSIES IN GREECE

Albania: Odos Karachristou 1, Kolonaki, 115 21 Athens; tel. (1) 7234412; telex 210351; fax (1) 7231972; Ambassador: HASTRIOT ROBO.

Algeria: Leoforos Vassileos Konstantinou 14, 116 35 Athens; tel. (1) 7264191; fax (1) 7018681; e-mail ambdzath@denet.gr; Ambassador: KAMEL HOUHOU.

Argentina: Leoforos Vassilissis Sofias 59, Athens; tel. (1) 7224753; telex 215218; fax (1) 7227568; Ambassador: JORGE DE BELAUSTEGUI.

Armenia: Leoforos Sygrou 159, 171 21 Athens; tel. and fax (1) 9345727; Ambassador: ARMAN KIRAKOSSIAN.

Australia: Odos Dimitriou Soutsou 37/Odos Tsoha, Athens; tel. (1) 6447303; telex 215815; Ambassador: R. S. MERRILLEES.

Austria: Leoforos Alexandras 26, 106 83 Athens; tel. (1) 8211036; telex 215938; Ambassador: Dr HANS SABADITSCH.

Belgium: Odos Sekeri 3, 106 71 Athens; tel. (1) 3617886; telex 216422; fax (1) 3604289; Ambassador: Viscount GEORGES VILAIN.

Brazil: Plateia Philikis Etairias 14, 106 73 Athens; tel. (1) 7213039; telex 216604; Ambassador: ALCIDES DA COSTA GUIMARÃES FILHO.

Bulgaria: Odos Stratigou Kallari 33A, Palaio Psychiko, 154 52 Athens; tel. (1) 6478105; fax (1) 6478130; Ambassador: BRANIMIR PETROV.

Canada: Odos Ioannou Ghennadiou 4, 115 21 Athens; tel. (1) 7254011; Ambassador: DEREK R. T. FRASER.

Chile: Leoforos Vasilissis Sofias 25, 106 74 Athens; tel. (1) 7252574; fax (1) 7252536; Ambassador: MANUEL ATRIA RAWLINS.

China, People's Republic: Odos Krinon 2A, Paleo Psychiko, 154 52 Athens; tel. (1) 6723282; telex 214383; fax (1) 6723819; Ambassador: YANG GUANGSHENG.

Congo, Democratic Republic: Athens; tel. (1) 7016171; telex 215994; telex 215994; Ambassador: BOMOLO LOKOKA.

Cuba: Odos Sofokleou 5, Filothei, 152 37 Athens; tel. (1) 6842807; fax (1) 6849590; Ambassador: ANA MARÍA GONZÁLEZ SUÁREZ.

Cyprus: Odos Herodotou 16, 106 75 Athens; tel. (1) 7232727; telex 215642; fax (1) 7231927; Ambassador: KHARALAMBOS CHRISTOFOROU.

Czech Republic: Odos Georgiou Seferis 6, Palaio Psychiko, 154 52 Athens; tel. (1) 6713755; fax (1) 6710675; Ambassador: VLADIMÍR ZAVÁZAL.

Denmark: Leoforos Vassilissis Sofias 11, 106 71 Athens; tel. (1) 3608315; telex 215586; fax (1) 3636163; Ambassador: THOMAS RECHNAGEL.

Egypt: Leoforos Vassilissis Sofias 3, 106 71 Athens; tel. (1) 3618612; fax (1) 3603538; Ambassador: SAMIR SEIF EL-YAZAL.

Estonia: Patriarchou Ioakeim 48, 106 76 Athens; tel. (1) 7229803; fax (1) 7229804; Chargé d'affaires a.i.: JÜRI ARUSOO.

Ethiopia: Athens; Ambassador: SAMUEL TEFERRA.

Finland: Odos Eratosthenous 1, 116 35 Athens; tel. (1) 7010444; Ambassador: ARTO TANNER.

France: Leoforos Vassilissis Sofias 7, 106 71 Athens; tel. (1) 3391000; fax (1) 3391009; Ambassador: BERNARD KESSEDJIAN.

Georgia: Odos Agiou Dimitriou 24, 154 52 Paleo Psihio, Athens; tel. (1) 6716737; fax (1) 6716722; Ambassador: ALEKSANDRE CHIKVAIDZE.

Germany: Odos Karaoli and Dimitriou 3, 106 75 Athens; tel. (1) 7285111; telex 215441; fax (1) 7251205; Ambassador: Dr FRIEDRICH REICHE.

Holy See: POB 65075; Odos Mavili 2, Palaio Psychiko, 154 52 Athens; tel. (1) 6743598; fax (1) 6742849; e-mail nunate@mail.otenet.gr; Apostolic Nuncio: Most Rev. PAUL FOUAD TABET, Titular Archbishop of Sinna.

Honduras: Leoforos Vassilissis Sofias 86, 115 28 Athens; tel. (1) 7775802; telex 241890; fax (1) 4221736; Chargé d'affaires a.i.: TEODOLINDA BANEGAS DE MAKRIS.

Hungary: Odos Kalvou 16, Palaio Psychiko, 154 52 Athens; tel. (1) 6725337; Ambassador: JÁNOS HERMAN.

India: Odos Kleanthous 3, 106 74 Athens; tel. (1) 7216227; telex 216171; fax (1) 7211252; Ambassador: AFTAB SETH.

Indonesia: Odos Papanastasidu 55, Palaio Psychiko, 154 52 Athens; tel. (1) 6712737; telex 215078.

Iran: Odos Kalari 16, Palaio Psychiko, Athens; tel. (1) 6471436; Ambassador: MAHDI KHANDAGH ABADI.

Iraq: Odos Mazaraki 4, Palaio Psychiko, Athens; tel. (1) 6715012; Ambassador: FETAH AL-KHEZREJI.

Ireland: Leoforos Vassileos Konstantinou 7, Athens; tel. (1) 7232771; telex 218111; fax (1) 7240217; Ambassador: EAMON RYAN.

Israel: Odos Marathonodromou 1, Palaio Psychiko, 154 52 Athens; tel. (1) 6719530; fax (1) 6479510; Ambassador: DAVID SASSON.

Italy: Odos Sekeri 2, 106 74 Athens; tel. (1) 3617260; telex 210575; fax (1) 3617330; Ambassador: ENRICO PIETROMARCHI.

Japan: 21st Floor, Athens A Tower, Leoforos Messoghion 2–4, Pirgas Athinon, 115 27 Athens; tel. (1) 7758101; telex 214460; fax (1) 7758206; Ambassador: KAZUO MATSUMOTO.

Jordan: Odos Panagi Zervou 30, Palaio Psychiko, 154 10 Athens; tel. (1) 6474161; telex 219366; fax (1) 6470578; Ambassador: AMJAD MAJALI.

Korea, Republic: Odos Eratosthenous 1, 116 35 Athens; tel. (1) 7012122; telex 216202; Ambassador: NAM KYUN PARK.

Kuwait: Odos Marathonodromou 27, Palaio Psychiko, 154 52 Athens; tel. (1) 6473593; telex 214890; fax (1) 6875875; Ambassador: ALI FAHED AL-ZAID.

Lebanon: Odos Maritou 25, Palaio Psychiko, 154 52 Athens; tel. (1) 6855873; telex 218572; fax (1) 6855612; Ambassador: ELIAS GHOSN.

Libya: Odos Vironos 13, Palaio Psychiko, 154 52 Athens; tel. (1) 6472120; Secretary of the People's Bureau: AYAD M. TAYARI.

Mexico: Plateia Philikis Etairias 14, 106 73 Athens; tel. (1) 7294780; fax (1) 724783; e-mail embamex2@compulink.gr; Ambassador: HUGO SALVADOR CAMPOS ICARDO.

Morocco: Odos Mousson 14, Palaio Psychiko, 154 52 Athens; tel. (1) 6744209; fax (1) 6749480; Ambassador: NOUREDDINE SEFIANI.

Netherlands: Leoforos Vassileos Konstantinou 5–7, 106 74 Athens; tel. (1) 7239701; telex 215971; fax (1) 7248900; Ambassador: H. WAGENMAKERS.

New Zealand: Xenias 24, 115 28 Athens; tel. (1) 7770686; fax (1) 7777390; Ambassador: JUDITH TROTTER.

Norway: Leoforos Vassilissis Konstantinou 7, 106 74 Athens; tel. (1) 7246173; telex 215109; fax (1) 7244989; e-mail norwemba@socrates.netplan.gr; Ambassador: ROLF TROLLE ANDERSEN.

Pakistan: Odos Loukianou 6, Kolonaki, 106 75 Athens; tel. (1) 7290122; telex 221016; fax (1) 7247231; Ambassador: AMIN JAN NAIM.

Panama: Odos Panedistimiou 42, 106 79 Athens; tel. (1) 3636121; fax (1) 3631089; Ambassador: PABLO GARRIDO ARAUZ.

Peru: Leoforos Vassilissis Sofias 105, Athens; tel. (1) 6411221; fax (1) 6411321; Ambassador: MARTÍN YRIGOYEN-YRIGOYEN.

Poland: Odos Chryssanthemon 22, Palaio Psychiko, 154 52 Athens; tel. (1) 6716917; Ambassador: JANUSZ LEWANDOWSKI.

Portugal: Odos Karneadou 44–46, 106 76 Athens; tel. (1) 7290096; telex 214903; fax (1) 7236784; Ambassador: CARLOS SIMÕES COELHO.

Romania: Odos Emmanuel Benaki 7, Palaio Psychiko, Athens; tel. (1) 6728875; telex 215301; fax (1) 6728883; Ambassador: DAN RĂDULESCU.

Russia: Odos Nikiforou Litra 28, Palaio Psychiko, Athens; tel. (1) 6725235; Ambassador: VALERY D. NIKOLAYENKO.

Saudi Arabia: Odos Marathonodromou 71, Palaio Psychiko, 154 52 Athens; tel. (1) 6716911; Ambassador: Sheikh ABDULLAH ABDUL-RAHMAN AL-MALHOOQ.

Slovakia: Odos Georgiou Seferis 4, Palaio Psychiko, 154 52 Athens; tel. (1) 6776757; fax (1) 6776760; Ambassador: JÁN VALKO.

South Africa: Leoforos Kifissias 60, 151 25 Athens; tel. (1) 6806645; fax (1) 6806640; Ambassador: DAVID JACOBS.

Spain: Leoforos Vassilissis Sofias 29, Athens; tel. (1) 7214885; telex 215860; Ambassador: JOSÉ CUENCA.

Sweden: Leoforos Vassileos Konstantinou 7, 106 74 Athens; tel. (1) 7290421; telex 215646; fax (1) 7229953; Ambassador: KRISTER KUMLIN.

Switzerland: Odos Iassiou 2, 115 21 Athens; tel. (1) 7230364; telex 216230; Ambassador: CHARLES STEINHÄUSLIN.

Syria: Odos Marathonodromou 79, Palaio Psychiko, Athens; tel. (1) 6725577; Ambassador: SHAHIN FARAH.

Thailand: Odos Taigetou 23, Palaio Psychiko, 154 52 Athens; tel. (1) 6717969; telex 225856; fax (1) 6479508; Ambassador: SUKHUM RASMIDATTA.

Tunisia: Odos Anthéon 2, Palaio Psychiko, 154 52 Athens; tel. (1) 6717590; telex 223786; fax (1) 6713432; Ambassador: YOUSSEF BEN HAHA.

Turkey: Odos Vassileos Gheorghiou B 8, 106 74 Athens; tel. (1) 7245915; telex 216334; fax (1) 7221778; Ambassador: HÜSEYİN ÇELEM.

United Kingdom: Odos Ploutarchou 1, 106 75 Athens; tel. (1) 7236211; telex 216440; fax (1) 7241872; Ambassador: Sir MICHAEL LLEWELLYN SMITH.

USA: Leoforos Vassilissis Sofias 91, 106 60 Athens; tel. (1) 7212951; telex 215548; fax (1) 7226724; Ambassador: NICHOLAS BURNS.

Uruguay: Odos Likavitou I G, 106 72 Athens; tel. (1) 3613549; Ambassador: ULYSSES PEREIRA REVERBEL.

Venezuela: Leoforos Vassilissis Sofias 112, Athens; tel. (1) 7708769; Ambassador: OLGA LUCILA CARMONA.

Yugoslavia: Leoforos Vassilissis Sofias 106, Athens; tel. (1) 7774344; Ambassador: (vacant).

Judicial System

The Constitution of 1975 provides for the establishment of a Special Supreme Tribunal. Other provisions in the Constitution provided for a reorganization of parts of the judicial system to be accomplished through legislation.

SUPREME ADMINISTRATIVE COURTS

Special Supreme Tribunal: Odos Patision 30, Athens; this court has final jurisdiction in matters of constitutionality.

Council of State: Odos Panepistimiou 47, 105 64 Athens; tel. (1) 3223830; fax (1) 3231154; the Council of State has appellate powers over acts of the administration and final rulings of administrative courts; has power to rule upon matters of judicial review of laws.

SUPREME JUDICIAL COURT

Supreme Court: Leoforos Alexandros 121, Athens; this is the supreme court in the State, having also appellate powers. It consists of six sections, four Civil and two Penal, and adjudicates in quorum; **President:** VASSILIS KOKKINOS.

COURTS OF APPEAL

These are 12 in number. They have jurisdiction in cases of Civil and Penal Law of second degree, and, in exceptional penal cases, of first degree.

COURTS OF FIRST INSTANCE

There are 59 Courts of First Instance with jurisdiction in cases of first degree, and in exceptional cases, of second degree. They function both as Courts of First Instance and as Criminal Courts. For serious crimes the Criminal Courts function with a jury.

In towns where Courts of First Instance sit there are also Juvenile Courts. Commercial Tribunals do not function in Greece, and all commercial cases are tried by ordinary courts of law. There are, however, Tax Courts in some towns.

OTHER COURTS

There are 360 Courts of the Justice of Peace throughout the country. There are 48 Magistrates' Courts (or simple Police Courts).

In all the above courts, except those of the Justice of Peace, there are District Attorneys. In Courts of the Justice of Peace the duties of District Attorney are performed by the Public Prosecutor.

Religion

CHRISTIANITY

The Eastern Orthodox Church

The Orthodox Church of Greece: Odos Ioannou Gennadiou 14, 115 21 Athens; tel. (1) 7218381; f. 1850; 78 dioceses, 8,335 priests, 84 bishops, 9,025,000 adherents (1985).

The Greek branch of the Holy Eastern Orthodox Church is the officially established religion of the country, to which nearly 97% of the population profess adherence. The administrative body of the Church is the Holy Synod of 12 members, elected by the bishops of the Hierarchy.

Primate of Greece: Archbishop SERAPHIM of Athens.

Within the Greek State there is also the semi-autonomous Church of Crete, composed of seven Metropolitans and the Holy Archbishopric of Crete. The Church is administered by a Synod consisting of the seven Metropolitans under the Presidency of the Archbishop; it is under the spiritual jurisdiction of the Oecumenical Patriarchate of Constantinople, which also maintains a degree of administrative control.

Archbishop of Crete: Archbishop TIMOTHEOS (whose See is in Heraklion).

There are also four Metropolitan Sees of the Dodecanese, which are spiritually and administratively dependent on the Oecumenical Patriarchate and, finally, the peninsula of Athos, which constitutes the region of the Holy Mountain (Mount Athos) and comprises 20 monasteries. These are dependent on the Oecumenical Patriarchate of Constantinople, but are autonomous and are safeguarded constitutionally.

The Roman Catholic Church

Latin Rite

Greece comprises four archdioceses (including two directly responsible to the Holy See), four dioceses and one Apostolic Vicariate. At December 1995 there were an estimated 51,550 adherents in the country.

Bishop's Conference: Conferentia Episcopalis Graeciae, Odos Homirou 9, 106 72 Athens; tel. (1) 3624311; fax (1) 3618632; f. 1967; Pres. Most Rev. NIKOLAOS FÓSKOLOS, Archbishop of Athens.

Archdiocese of Athens: Archbishopric, Odos Homirou 9, 106 72 Athens; tel. (1) 3624311; fax (1) 3618632; Archbishop Most Rev. NIKOLAOS FÓSKOLOS.

Archdiocese of Rhodes: Archbishopric, Odos I. Dragoumi 5A, 851 00 Rhodes; tel. (241) 21845; fax (241) 26688; Apostolic Administrator Most Rev. NIKOLAOS FÓSKOLOS (Archbishop of Athens).

Metropolitan Archdiocese of Corfu, Zante and Cefalonia: Archbishopric, 491 00 Kerkyra; tel. and fax (661) 30277; Archbishop Mgr ANTONIOS VARTHALITIS.

Metropolitan Archdiocese of Naxos, Andros, Tinos and Mykonos: Archbishopric, 842 00 Tinos (summer residence); tel. (283) 22382; fax (283) 24769; Naxos (winter residence); also responsible for the suffragan diocese of Chios; Archbishop Mgr NIKOLAOS PRINTESIS

Apostolic Vicariate of Salonika (Thessaloniki): Leoforos Vassilissis Olgas 120B, 546 45 Thessaloniki; tel. (31) 835780; Apostolic Administrator Archbishop Mgr VARTHALITIS of Corfu.

Byzantine Rite

Apostolic Exarchate for the Byzantine Rite in Greece: Odos Akarnon 246, 112 53 Athens; tel. (1) 8670170; fax (1) 8677039; 2 parishes (Athens and Jannitsa, Macedonia); 9 secular priests, 2,300 adherents (Dec. 1995); Exarch Apostolic Mgr ANARGHYROS PRINTESIS, Titular Bishop of Gratianopolis.

Armenian Rite

Exarchate for the Armenian Catholics in Greece: Odos René Piot 2, 117 44 Athens; tel. (1) 9014089; fax (1) 9012109; 650 adherents (Dec. 1995); Exarch Archpriest NICHAN KARAKEHEYAN.

Protestant Church

Greek Evangelical Church (Reformed): Odos Markon Botsari 24, 117 41 Athens; tel. (1) 9222684; f. 1858; comprises 30 organized churches; 5,000 adherents (1996); Moderator Rev. JOANNIS YPHANTIDES.

ISLAM

The law provides as religious head of the Muslims a Chief Mufti; the Muslims in Greece possess a number of mosques and schools.

JUDAISM

The Jewish population of Greece, estimated in 1943 at 75,000 people, was severely reduced as a result of the German occupation. In 1994 there were about 5,000 Jews in Greece.

Central Board of the Jewish Communities of Greece: Odos Sourmeli 2, 104 39 Athens; tel. (1) 8839953; telex 225110; fax (1) 8234488; f. 1945; officially recognized representative body of the communities of Greece; Pres. NISSIM MAÏS.

Jewish Community of Athens: Odos Melidoni 8, 105 53 Athens; tel. (1) 3252823; fax (1) 3220761; Rabbi JACOB D. ARAR.

Jewish Community of Larissa: Odos Kentavrou 27, Larissa; tel. (41) 220762; Rabbi ELIE SABETAI.

Jewish Community of Thessaloniki: Odos Tsimiski 24, 546 24 Thessaloniki; tel. (31) 275701; Pres. ANDREAS SEFIHA; Rabbi ITZHAK DAYAN.

The Press

Afternoon papers are more popular than morning ones; in 1990 about 73,644 papers were sold each morning and up to 784,474 each afternoon.

PRINCIPAL DAILY NEWSPAPERS

Morning papers are not published on Mondays, nor afternoon papers on Sundays.

Athens

Acropolis: Athens; f. 1881; morning; Independent-Conservative; Acropolis Publications SA; Publr G. LEVIDES; Dir MARNIS SKOUNDRIDAKIS; circ. 50,819.

Apogevmatini (The Afternoon): Odos Phidiou 12, 106 78 Athens; tel. (1) 6430011; telex 215733; fax (1) 3609876; f. 1956; independent; Publr GEORGIOS HATZIKONSTANTINOU; Editor P. KARAYANNIS; circ. 67,257.

Athens Daily Post: Odos Stadiou 57, Athens; tel. (1) 3249504; f. 1952; morning; English; Owner G. SKOURAS.

Athens News: Odos Christou Lada 3, 102 37 Athens; tel. (1) 3333161; fax (1) 3231384; e-mail athnews@dolnet.gr; internet http://www.dolnet.gr; f. 1952; morning; English; Publr JOHN HORN; circ. 7,000.

Athlitiki Icho (Athletics Echo): Odos Aristonos 5-7, 104 41 Athens; tel. (1) 5232201; fax (1) 5232433; f. 1945; morning; Editor K. GEORGALAS; circ. 40,000.

Avghi (Dawn): Odos Ag. Konstantiou 12, 104 31 Athens; tel. (1) 5231831; telex 222671; fax (1) 5231830; f. 1952; morning; independent newspaper of the left; Dir and Editor L. VOUTSAS; circ. 5,400.

Avriani (Tomorrow): Odos Dimitros 11, 177 78 Athens; tel. (1) 3424090; telex 218440; fax (1) 3452190; f. 1980; evening; Publr GEORGE KOURIS; circ. 51,317.

Dimokratikos Logos (Democratic Speech): Odos Dimitros 11, 177 78 Athens; tel. (1) 3424023; telex 218440; fax (1) 3452190; f. 1986; morning; Dir and Editor KOSTAS GERONIKOLOS; circ. 7,183.

Eleftheri Ora: Odos Akademias 32, 106 72 Athens; tel. (1) 3621868; fax (1) 3603258; f. 1981; evening; Editor G. MIHALOPOULOS; circ. 1,026.

Eleftheros Typos (Free Press): Iroos Matsi, Ano Kalamaki, Athens; tel. (1) 9942431; f. 1983; evening; Dir. and Editor CH. PASALARIS; circ. 167,186.

Eleftherotypia (Press Freedom): Odos Minoou 10–16, 117 43 Athens; tel. (1) 9296001; fax (1) 9028311; f. 1974; evening; Publr CHR. TEGOPOULOS; Dir S. FYNDANIDIS; circ. 115,000.

Estia (Vesta): Odos Anthimou Gazi 7, 105 61 Athens; tel. (1) 3230650; fax (1) 3220631; f. 1898; afternoon; Publr and Editor ADONIS K. KYROU; circ. 85,000.

Ethnos (Nation): Odos Benaki 152, Metamorfosi Chalandriou, 152 35 Athens; tel. (1) 6580640; telex 2104415; fax (1) 6396515; f. 1981; evening; Publr GEORGE BOBOLAS; Dir TH. KALOUDIS; circ. 84,735.

Express: Odos Halandriou 39, Paradissos Amaroussiou, 151 25 Athens; tel. (1) 6850200; telex 219746; fax (1) 6852202; f. 1963; morning, financial; Publr Hellenews Publications; Editor D. G. KALOFOLIAS; circ. 28,000.

Filathlos: Odos Dimitros 11, 177 78 Athens; tel. (1) 3424090; telex 218440; f. 1982; morning; Dir NICK KARAGIANNIDIS; Publr and Editor G. A. KOURIS; circ. 40,000.

Imerisia (Daily): Odos Geraniou 7A, 105 52 Athens; tel. (1) 5231195; fax (1) 5245839; f. 1947; morning; Dir N. TSAGANELIS; Editor A. MOTHONIOS; circ. 11,000.

Kathimerini (Every Day): Odos Sokrateous 57, Athens; tel. (1) 5231001; telex 226692; fax (1) 5247685; f. 1919; morning; Conservative; Editor A. KARKAYANNIS; circ. 34,085.

Kerdos (Profit): Leoforos Kifissias 178, Halandri, 152 31 Athens; tel. (1) 6473384; fax (1) 6472003; f. 1985; morning; Publr TH. LIAKOUNAKOS; Man. Editor SERAFIM KONSTANDINIDIS; circ. 18,000.

Messimvrini (Midday): Leoforos G. Averop 26–28, Perissos, 142 32 Athens; tel. (1) 2184000; fax (1) 2529059; f. 1980; evening; Publr and Dir PANOS LOUKAKOS; circ. 17,451.

Naftemboriki (Daily Journal): Odos Lenorman 205, 104 42 Athens; tel. (1) 5130605; telex 221354; fax (1) 5146013; f. 1923; morning; non-political journal of finance, commerce and shipping; Dir N. ATHANASSIADIS; circ. 35,000.

Niki (Victory): Odos Halkokodili 9, 106 77 Athens; tel. (1) 3303201; fax (1) 3303213; f. 1989; Editor MARIA LOUDAROU.

Onoma: Athens; Publr MAKIS PSOMIADIS.

Ora Gia Spor (Time for Sport): Athens; tel. (1) 9251200; fax (1) 9226167; f. 1991; sport; Editor EVANGELOS SEMBOS.

Rizospastis (Radical): Odos Irakliou 145, Perissos, 142 31 Athens; tel. (1) 2522002; telex 216156; fax (1) 2529480; f. 1974; morning; pro-Soviet Communist; Dir T. TSIGAS; Editor G. TRIKALINOS; circ. 28,740.

Ta Nea (News): Odos Christou Lada 3, 102 37 Athens; tel. (1) 3250611; telex 210608; fax (1) 3228797; f. 1944; liberal; evening; Dir L. KARAPANAYIOTIS; Editor CHRISTOS LAMBRAKIS; circ. 135,000.

Vradyni (Evening Press): Athens; tel. (1) 5231001; telex 215354; f. 1923; evening; right-wing; Gen. Man. H. ATHANASIADOU; circ. 71,914.

Patras

Peloponnesos: Maizonos 206, 262 22 Patras; tel. (61) 312530; fax (61) 312535; f. 1886; independent conservative; Publr and Editor S. DOUKAS; circ. 7,000.

Thessaloniki

Ellinikos Vorras (Greek North): Odos Grammou-Vitsi 19, 551 34 Thessaloniki; tel. (31) 416621; telex 412213; f. 1935; morning; Publr TESSA LEVANTIS; Dir N. MERGIOS; circ. 14,467.

Thessaloniki: Odos Monastiriou 85, 546 27 Thessaloniki; tel. (31) 521621; f. 1963; evening; Propr Publishing Co of Northern Greece SA; Dir LAZAROS HADJINAKOS; Editor KATERINA VELLIDI; circ. 36,040.

SELECTED PERIODICALS

Agora (Market): Leoforos Kifissias 178, Halandri, 151 31 Athens; tel. (1) 6473384; telex 225591; fax (1) 6477893; f. 1987; fortnightly; politics, finance; Dir ANT. KEFALAS; circ. 3,496.

Aktines: Odos Karytsi 14, 105 61 Athens; tel. (1) 3235023; f. 1938; monthly; current affairs, science, philosophy, arts; aims to promote a Christian civilization; Publr Christian Union; circ. 10,000.

Athèmes: Athens; monthly; French; cultural; Chief Editor EMMANUEL ADELY; circ. 5,000.

The Athenian: Tsatsou 4, 105 58 Athens; tel. (1) 3222802; fax (1) 3223052; e-mail the-athenian@hol.gr; internet http://www.hol.gr; f. 1974; monthly; English; Publr KONSTANTINOS GEROU; Editor SLOANE ELLIOTT; circ. 13,200.

Auto Express: Odos Halandriou 39, Halandri, 152 32 Athens; tel. (1) 6816906; telex 219746; fax (1) 6825858; Dir D. KALOFOLIAS; circ. 18,828.

Cosmopolitan: Leoforos Marathonas 14, Pallini, 153 00 Athens; tel. (1) 6667312; f. 1979; monthly; women's magazine; Publr P. ROKANAS; Dir K. KOSTOULIAS; circ. 39,471.

Deltion Diikiseos Epichiriseon Euro-Unial(Business Administration Bulletin Euro-Unial): Odos Rhigillis 26, 106 74; Athens; tel. (1) 7235736; telex 29006; fax (1) 7240000; monthly; Editor I. PAPAMICHALAKIS; circ. 26,000.

Demosiografiki (Journalism): Procopiou 7–9, 171 24 Athens; tel. (1) 9731338; fax (1) 3816738; e-mail beny@athena.compulink.gr; f. 1987; quarterly; Dir JOHN MENOÚNOS; circ. 4,000.

Ekonomicos Tachydromos (Financial Courier): Odos Christou Lada 3, 102 37 Athens; tel. (1) 3333555; telex 210608; fax (1) 3238740; f. 1926; weekly; Man. Editor DENIS ANTIPAS; circ. 20,000.

Ena (One): Athens; tel. (1) 3643821; telex 223220; f. 1983; weekly; Dir S. TSIHLIAS; circ. 34,124.

Epiloghi: Odos Stadiou 4, 105 64 Athens; tel. (1) 3238427; fax (1) 3235160; f. 1962; weekly; economics.

Greece's Weekly for Business and Finance: Athens; tel. (1) 7707280; telex 210899; weekly; English; finance; Dir V. KORONAKIS.

Gynaika (Women): Odos Fragoklissias 7, Marousi, 151 25 Athens; tel. (1) 6826680; telex 218063; fax (1) 6824730; f. 1950; fortnightly; fashion, beauty, handicrafts, cookery, social problems, fiction, knitting, embroidery; Publr ARIS TERZOPOULOS; SA; circ. 45,559.

Hellenews: Odos Halandriou 39, Marousi, 151 25 Athens; tel. (1) 6899400; telex 219746; fax (1) 6899430; weekly; English; finance and business; Publr Hellenews Publications; Editor J. M. GERMANOS.

Hellenic Business: Odos Ravine 12, 115 21 Athens; fax (1) 7217519; Greek and English; circ. 20,000.

Makedoniki Zoi (Macedonian Life): Odos Mitropoleos 70, 546 22 Thessaloniki; tel. (31) 277700; fax (31) 266908; monthly; Editor N. J. MERTZOS; circ. 70,000.

48 Ores (48 Hours): Leoforos Alexandras 19, 114 73 Athens; tel. (1) 6430313; fax (1) 6461361; weekly; Dir and Editor SP. KARATZAFERIS; circ. 9,127.

Pantheon: Odos Christou Lada 3, 102 37 Athens; tel. (1) 3230221; telex 215904; fax (1) 3228797; fortnightly; Publr and Dir N. THEOFANIDES; circ. 23,041.

Politika Themata: Odos Ypsilantou 25, 106 75 Athens; tel. (1) 7218421; weekly; Publr J. CHORN; Dir C. KYRKOS; circ. 2,544.

Pontiki (Mouse): Odos Massalias 10, 106 81 Athens; tel. (1) 3609531; weekly; humour; Dir and Editor K. PAPAIOANNOU.

Radiotileorash (Radio-TV): Odos Mourouzi 16, 106 74 Athens; tel. (1) 7224811; weekly; circ. 134,626.

Tachydromos (The Courier): Odos Christou Lada 3, 102 37 Athens; tel. (1) 3250810; telex 215904; fax (1) 3228797; f. 1953; weekly; illustrated magazine; Publr C. LAMBRAKIS SA; Dir P. TSIMAS; circ. 50,611.

Technika Chronika (Technical Times): Odos Karageorgi Servias 4, 105 62 Athens; tel. (1) 3234751; f. 1952; monthly; general edition on technical and economic subjects; Editor D. ROKOS; circ. 12,000.

Tilerama: Odos Voukourestiou 18, 106 71 Athens; tel. (1) 3607160; fax (1) 3607032; f. 1977; weekly; radio and television; circ. 189,406.

To Vima (Tribune): Odos Christou Lada 3, 102 37 Athens; tel. (1) 3333103; telex 215904; fax (1) 3239097; f. 1922; weekly; liberal; Dir and Editor STAVROS R. PSYCHARIS; circ. 250,000.

La Tribune héllenique: Athens; bimonthly; French; politics, economics; Dir THEODORE BENAKIS; circ. 3,000.

Viomichaniki Epitheorissis (Industrial Review): Odos Zalokosta 4, 106 71 Athens; tel. (1) 3627218; fax (1) 3626388; e-mail viomep@acci.gr; f. 1934; monthly; industrial and economic review; Publr A.C. VOVOLINI-LASKARIDIS; Editor D. KARAMANOS; circ. 25,000.

NEWS AGENCIES

Athenagence (ANA): Odos Pindarou 6, 106 71 Athens; tel. (1) 3639816; telex 215300; fax (1) 3644326; f. 1896; correspondents in leading capitals of the world and towns throughout Greece; Gen. Dir ANDREAS CHRISTODOULIDES.

Foreign Bureaux

Agence France-Presse (AFP): Athens; tel. (1) 3633388; telex 215595; Bureau Chief JEAN-PIERRE ALTIER.

Agencia EFE (Spain): Athens; tel. (1) 3635826; telex 219561; Bureau Chief D. MARÍA-LUISA RUBIO; Correspondent JUAN JOSÉ FERNÁNDEZ ELORRIAGA.

Agenzia Nazionale Stampa Associata (ANSA) (Italy): Odos Kanari, 106 71 Athens; tel. (1) 3605285; telex 221860; fax (1) 3635367; Correspondent CESARE RIZZOLI.

Associated Press (AP) (USA): Leoforos Amalias 52, 105 52 Athens; tel. (1) 3310802; fax (1) 3310804.

Athens News Agency: c/o ANA-36, Odos Toscha, 115 21 Athens; tel. (1) 6400560; telex 215300; fax (1) 6400581.

Deutsche Presse-Agentur (dpa) (Germany): Miniati 1, 116 36 Athens; tel. (1) 9247774; telex 215839; fax (1) 9222185; Correspondent HILDEGARD HÜLSENBECK.

Informatsionnoye Telegrafnoye Agentstvo Rossii—Telegrafnoye Agentstvo Suverennykh Stran (ITAR—TASS) (Russia): Odos Gizi 39, Palaio Psychiko, 15 452 Athens; tel. and fax (1) 6713069; telex 214836; Bureau Chief VLADIMIR V. MALYSHEV.

Reuters Hellas SA (UK): 7th Floor, Kolokotroni 1/Leoforos Stadiou, 105 62 Athens; tel. (1) 3647610; telex 215912; fax (1) 3604490; Man. Dir WILLIAM CAIRLEY.

Rossiyskoye Informatsionnoye Agentstvo—Novosti (RIA—Novosti) (Russia): Odos Irodotou 9, 138 Athens; tel. (1) 7291016; telex 219601; Bureau Chief BORIS KOROLYOV; Correspondent J. KURZIN.

Telegrafska Agencija Nova Jugoslavija (Tanjug) (Yugoslavia): Evrou 94–96, Ambelokipi, Athens; tel. (1) 7791545.

United Press International (UPI) (USA): Odos Akademias 23, 106 71 Athens; tel. (1) 3639198; telex 215572; fax (1) 3639654; Correspondent RALPH JOSEPH.

Xinhua (New China) News Agency (People's Republic of China): Odos Amarilidos 19, Palaio Psychiko, Athens; tel. (1) 6724997; telex 216235; Bureau Chief XIE CHENGHAO.

PRESS ASSOCIATIONS

Enosis Antapokriton Xenou Tipou (Foreign Press Association of Greece): Odos Akademias 23, 106 71 Athens; tel. (1) 3637318; fax (1) 3605035.

Enosis Syntakton Imerission Ephimeridon Athinon (Journalists' Union of Athens Daily Newspapers): Odos Akademias 20, 106 71 Athens; tel. (1) 3632601; telex 219467; fax (1) 3632608; f. 1914; Pres. DIMITRIOS MATHIOPOULOS; Gen. Sec. MANOLIS MATHIOUDAKIS; 1,400 mems.

Enosis Syntakton Periodikou Tipou (Journalists' Union of the Periodical Press): Odos Valaoritou 9, 106 71 Athens; tel. (1) 3636039; fax (1) 3644967; Pres. ATHENESE PAPANDROPOULOS; 600 mems.

Publishers

Agyra Publications: Kifisou 85, Egaleo, 122 41 Athens; tel. (1) 3455276; telex 210804; fax (1) 3474732; f. 1890; general; Man. Dir DIMITRIOS PAPADIMITRIOU.

Akritas: Odos Efessou 24, 171 21 Athens; tel. (1) 9334685; fax (1) 9311436; e-mail akritaspublications@ath.forthnet.gr; history, spirituality, children's books.

John Arsenidis Ekdotis: Odos Akademias 57, 106 79 Athens; tel. (1) 3629538; biography, literature, children's books, history, philosophy, social sciences; Man. Dir JOHN ARSENIDIS.

Bergadi Editions: Odos Mavromichali 4, Athens; tel. (1) 3614263; academic, children's books; Dir MICHAEL BERGADIS.

Boukoumanis Editions: Odos Mavromichali 1, 106 79 Athens; tel. (1) 3618502; fax (1) 3630669; f. 1967; history, politics, sociology, psychology, belles-lettres, educational, arts, children's books, ecology; Man. ELIAS BOUKOUMANIS.

Delfini: Odos Payepistimiou 58, 106 78 Athens; tel. (1) 3830955; fax (1) 3303175; general; Dir. P. STATHATOS.

Ekdotike Athenon, SA: Odos Omirou 11, 106 72 Athens; tel. (1) 3608911; fax (1) 3606157; f. 1961; history, archaeology, art; Man. Dirs GEORGE A. CHRISTOPOULOS, JOHN C. BASTIAS.

G. C. Eleftheroudakis, SA: Odos Panepistimiou 17, 105 64 Athens; tel. (1) 3314180; fax (1) 3239821; e-mail elebooks@netor.gr; f. 1915; general, technical and scientific; Man. Dir VIRGINIA ELEFTHEROUDAKIS-GREGOU.

Etairia Ellinikon Ekdoseon: Odos Akademias 84, 142 Athens; tel. (1) 3630282; fax (1) 3604986; f. 1958; fiction, academic, educational; Man. Dir STAVROS TAVOULARIS.

Gnosi: Odos Ippokratous 31, 106 80 Athens; tel. (1) 3620941; fax (1) 3605910; history, literature, art, children's books.

Denise Harvey: 340 05 Limmi, Evia; tel. (227) 31921; fax (227) 31154; f. 1972; modern Greek literature and poetry, belles-lettres, theology, translations, selected general list (English and Greek); Man. Dir DENISE HARVEY.

Hellenic Editions Co, SA: Odos Akademias 84, 106 78 Athens; tel. (1) 3607343; encyclopaedias; Editor-in-Chief J. ZAFIROPOULOS.

Hestia-I.D. Kollaros & Co, SA: Odos Solonos 60, 106 72 Athens; tel. (1) 3615077; fax (1) 3606759; f. 1885; literature, history, politics, architecture, philosophy, travel, religion, psychology, textbooks, general; Gen. Dir MARINA KARAITIDIS.

Kassandra M. Grigoris: Odos Solonos 71, 106 79 Athens; tel. (1) 3629684; f. 1967; Greek history, Byzantine archaeology, literature, theology; Man. Dir MICHEL GRIGORIS.

Kronos: Odos Egnatia 33, 546 26 Thessaloniki; tel. (31) 532077; fax (31) 538158; Dir TH. GIOTAS.

Nea Synora: Odos Solonos 94, 106 80 Athens; tel. (1) 3610589; fax (1) 3617791; general; Publr A. A. LIVANI.

Odos Panos: Odos Didotou 39, 106 08 Athens; tel. and fax (1) 3616782; poetry, drama, biography.

Papazissis Publishers: Nikitara 2, 106 78 Athens; tel. (1) 3622496; telex 219807; fax (1) 3609150; f. 1929; economics, politics, law, history, school books; Man. Dir VICTOR PAPAZISSIS.

Patakis Publications: Odos Valtetsiou 14, 106 80 Athens; tel. (1) 3638362; fax (1) 3628950; art, reference, literature, educational, philosophy, psychology, sociology, religion, music, children's books, educational toys, CD-Rom and audiobooks.

D. and B. Saliveros: Arkadias and Teftidos 1, Peristeri, Athens; f. 1893; general and religious books, maps, diaries and calendars; Chair. D. SALIVEROS.

John Sideris: Odos Stadiou 44, 105 64 Athens; tel. (1) 3229638; fax (1) 3245052; f. 1898; school textbooks, general; Man. J. SIDERIS.

J. G. Vassiliou: Odos Hippokratous 15, 106 79 Athens; tel. (1) 3623382; fax (1) 3623580; f. 1913; fiction, history, philosophy, dictionaries and children's books.

Government Publishing House

Government Printing House: Odos Kapodistriou 34, 104 32 Athens; tel. (1) 5248320.

PUBLISHERS' FEDERATIONS

Association of Publishers and Booksellers of Athens: Odos Themistokleus 73, 106 83 Athens; tel. (1) 3303268; fax (1) 3823222; Pres. DIMITRIS PANDELESKOS; Sec. PETROS GAITANOS.

Hellenic Federation of Publishers and Booksellers: Odos Themistokleus 73, 106 83 Athens; tel. (1) 3300924; fax (1) 3301617; f. 1961; Pres. GEORGE DARDANOS; Gen. Sec. STEFANOS VASILOPOULOS.

Broadcasting and Communications

TELECOMMUNICATIONS

National Telecommunications Commission (NTC): Leoforos Kifissias 60, 151 25 Athens; tel. (1) 6805040; fax (1) 6805049; regulatory body; Chair. A. LAMBRINOPOULOS.

Hellenic Telecommunications Organization (OTE): Leoforos Kifissias 99, 151 81 Athens; f. 1949; owned 80% by the Government, 20% by public shareholders; 5.3m. lines in service; Pres. DIMITRIS PAPOULIAS.

Cosmote: OTE subsidiary, 30%-owned by Telenor; mobile services; Man. Dir NIKOS MANASSIS.

Maritel: OTE subsidiary; marine telecommunications.

Panafon SA: Mobile telecommunications.

Telestet Hellas SA: 75%-owned by STET International; mobile network; Man. Dir GIACINTO CICCHESE.

RADIO

Elliniki Radiophonia Tileorassi (ERT, SA) (Greek Radio-Television): Leoforos Messoghion 482, 153 42 Athens; tel. (1) 6066000; fax (1) 6009325; e-mail ertir@hol.gr; state-controlled since 1938; Pres. and Man. PANAYOTIS PANAYOTOU.

Elliniki Radiophonia-ERA (Greek Radio): POB 60019, 153 42 Aghia Paraskevi, Athens; tel. (1) 6066814; fax (1) 6066029; Dir YANNIS TZANNETAKOS.

Macedonia Radio Station: Odos Angelaki 2, 546 32 Thessaloniki; tel. (31) 244979; fax (31) 236370.

TELEVISION

A television network of 17 transmitters is in operation. The State's monopoly of television broadcasting ended in 1990, and by 1998 there were 17 private broadcasters.

State stations

Elliniki Radiophonia Tileorassi (ERT, SA) (Greek Radio-Television): (see Radio).

Elliniki Tileorassi (Greek Television) **1 (ET1):** Leoforos Messoghion 432, 153 42 Aghia Paraskevi Attikis; tel. (1) 6395970; fax (1) 6392263; Dir-Gen. GEORGE STAMATELOPOULOS.

ET2: Leoforos Messoghion 136; 115 25 Athens; tel. (1) 7701911; fax (1) 7797776; Dir-Gen. PANAYOTIS PANAYOTOU.

ET3: Aggelaki 2, 546 21 Thessaloniki; tel. (31) 278784; fax (31) 236466; Dir-Gen. MICHALIS ALEXANDRIDIS.

Private stations

Antenna TV: Leoforos Kifissias 10-12, Maroussi, 151 25 Athens; tel. (1) 6842220; fax (1) 3890304.

Argo TV: Metamorphosseos 9, 551 32 Kalamaria, Thessaloniki; tel. (31) 351733; fax (31) 351739.

Channel Seven-X: Leoforos Kifissias 64, Athens; tel. (1) 68976042; fax (1) 6897608.

City Channel: Leoforos Kastoni 14, 41223 Larissa; tel. (41) 232839; fax (41) 232013.

Jeronimo Groovy TV: Ag konstantin 40, 151 24 Athens; tel. (1) 6896360; fax (1) 6896950.

Mega Channel: Odos Alamanas 10, Amarousin, 151 25 Athens; tel. (1) 689900014; fax (1) 6899016.

Neo Kanali SA: Pireos 9-11, 105 52 Athens; tel. (1) 5238230; fax (1) 5247325.

Serres TV: Nigritis 27, 62124 Serres.

Skai TV: Phalereos & Ethnarchou 2, Macaroiu, N. Phaliro.

Star Channel: Dimitras 37, 1178 Tayros, Athens; tel. (1) 3450626; fax (1) 3452190.

Tele City: Praxitelous 58, 17674 Athens; tel (1) 9429222; fax (1) 9413589.

Teletora: Lycabetous 17, 10672 Athens; tel. (1) 3617285; fax (1) 3638712.

Traki TV: Central Square, 67100 Xanthi; tel. (541) 20670; fax (541) 27368.

TRT: Odos Zachou 5, 38333 Volos; tel. (421) 30500; fax (421) 36888.

TV Macedonia: Nea Egnatia 222, 54642 Thessaloniki; tel. (31) 850512; fax (31) 850513.

TV Plus: Leoforos Syngrou 97, 117 45 Athens; tel. (1) 9028707; fax (1) 9028310.

TV-100: Odos Aggelaki 16, 54621 Thessaloniki; tel. (31) 265828; fax (31) 267532.

Finance

(cap. = capital; p.u. = paid up; res = reserves; dep. = deposits; dre = drachmae; m. = million; br. = branch)

BANKING

Central Bank

Bank of Greece: Leoforos E. Venizelos 21, 102 50 Athens; tel. (1) 3201111; telex 215102; fax (1) 3232239; e-mail bogsecr@ath.forthnet.gr; f. 1927; state bank of issue; cap. dre 13,905.4m., res dre 25,591.3m., dep. dre 9,675,144.7m. (Dec. 1996); Gov. LUKAS PAPADEMOS; 27 brs.

Commercial Banks

Agricultural Bank of Greece: Odos Panepistimiou 23, 105 64 Athens; tel. (1) 3230521; telex 222160; fax (1) 3234386; f. 1929; wholly-owned by State; cap. dre 153,546.0m., res dre 33,884.4m., dep. dre 3,145,209.2m. (Dec. 1995); Gov. and Chair. CHRISTOS PAPATHANISSOU; 44 brs.

Alpha Credit Bank: Odos Stadiou 40, 102 52 Athens; tel. (1) 3260000; telex 218691; fax (1) 3265438; e-mail secretariat@alpha.gr; internet http://www.alpha.gr; f. 1879, renamed 1972; cap. dre 52,800.0m., res dre 82,665.1m., dep. dre 2,509,671.7m. (Dec. 1996); Chair. and Gen. Man. YANNIS S. COSTOPOULOS; 199 brs.

Bank of Athens SA: Odos Santaroza 3, 105 64 Athens; tel. (1) 3212371; fax (1) 3254069; f. 1924, renamed Traders' Credit Bank 1952, renamed as above 1992; affiliated to the National Bank of Greece; cap. dre 1,928.0m., res dre 5,012.1m., dep. dre 98,147.0m. (Dec. 1996); Chair. and CEO CHUL KIM; Deputy Gen. Man. L. BALTATZIS; 24 brs.

Bank of Attica: Odos Omirou 23, 106 72 Athens; tel. (1) 3646910; telex 223344; fax (1) 3646115; f. 1925; affiliated to the Commercial Bank of Greece; cap. dre 2,309.5m., res dre 5,931.1m., dep. dre 99,193.4m. (Dec. 1996); Chair. CHRISTOS APOSTOLOPOULOS; 31 brs.

Bank of Central Greece: Odos Neapoleos and Looforos Kifissias 2, Maroussi, 151 23 Athens; tel. (1) 6885600; telex 222268; fax (1) 6856585; f. 1936 as local bank in Lamia, achieved national status in 1980; affiliated to the Agricultural Bank of Greece; cap. dre 9,842.5m., res dre 4,827.3m., dep. dre 121,131.5m. (Dec. 1996); Pres. CHRISTOS A. PAPATHANASSIOU; CEO GEORGE K. ZYGOYIANNIS; 23 brs.

Bank of Crete, SA: Odos Voukourestiou 22, 106 71 Athens; tel. (1) 3606511; telex 218633; fax (1) 3644832; f. 1924 (reformed 1973); scheduled for transfer to the private sector in 1998; cap. dre 41,874m., res dre 0.7m., dep. dre 325,433.5m. (Dec. 1996); Dir KOSTAS GEORGAKOPOULOS; 87 brs.

Commercial Bank of Greece: Odos Sophokleous 11, 102 35 Athens; tel. (1) 3284000; telex 216545; fax (1) 3212821; f. 1907; cap. dre 35,896.3m., res dre 149,339.9m., dep. dre 2,149,881.2m. (Dec. 1996); Chair. and Man. Dir KONSTANTINOS GEORGOUTSAKOS; Gen. Man. GEORGE MICHELIS; 342 brs.

Credit Lyonnais Grèce, SA: Leoforos Vassilissis Sofias 75, 115 21 Athens; tel. (1) 7250323; telex 210226; fax (1) 7210134; f. 1981 as Banque Franco-Hellenique de Commerce International et Maritime SA, renamed as above 1994; cap. dre 8,300m., res dre 5,075.7m., dep. dre 105,245.6m. (Dec. 1996); Pres. ALFRED BOUCKAERT; Man. Dir BAUDOUIN MERLET; 1 br.

Dorian Bank, SA: Odos Dorilaiou 10-12, 115 21 Athens; tel. (1) 6400740; telex 216027; fax (1) 3636095; f. 1990; cap. dre 5,000m., res dre 498.2m., dep. dre 48,860.4m. (Dec. 1996); Chair. ANTHONY MANTZAVINOS; 3 brs.

EFG Eurobank SA: Odos Othonos 8, 105 57 Athens; tel. (1) 3337000; telex 210975; fax (1) 3233866; f. 1990 as Euromerchant Bank SA (Eurobank), renamed as above 1997; cap. dre 16,500m., res dre 6,980m., dep. dre 263.327m. (Dec. 1996); Chair. GEORGE GONTIKAS; Man. Dir NIKOLAS NANOPOULOS; 5 brs.

Ergobank, SA: Kolokotroni and Voulis 3, 105 62 Athens; tel. (1) 3221345; telex 216140; fax (1) 3253308; f. 1975; cap. dre 15,275.2m., res dre 57,289.0m., dep. dre 860,830.5m. (Dec. 1996); Chair. Gen. X. C. NICKITAS; Man. Dir A. G. BIBAS; 116 brs.

European Popular Bank SA: Odos Panepistimiou 13, 105 64 Athens; tel. (1) 3313300; telex 210573; fax (1) 3243141; f. 1992; cap. dre 5,500m.; res dre 1,202.3m; dep. dre 68,599.4m. (Dec. 1995); Chair. KIKIS LAZARIDES; Dep. Gen. Man. CHRISTOS STYLANIDES; 9 brs.

General Hellenic Bank, SA: Odos Panepistimiou 9, 102 29 Athens; tel. (1) 33250300; telex 210692; fax (1) 3222271; f. 1937 as Bank of the Army Share Fund, renamed 1966; cap. dre 7,071.7m., res dre 7,284.5m., dep. dre 325,151.0m. (Dec. 1996); Chair. GEORGIOS P. DASKALAKIS; Gen. Man. N. BERETANOS; 92 brs.

Interbank of Greece SA: Leoforos Voutiagmenis 2-4, 117 43 Athens; tel. (1) 9292100; telex 220790; fax (1) 9292236; f. 1990; 95% stake acquired by Euromerchant Bank in July 1996; cap. dre 7,980m.; res dre 3,170m.; dep. dre 170,000m. (Dec. 1996); Chair. GEORGIOS GONTIKAS; Man Dir. BYRON BALLIS.

Investment Bank, SA: Odos Korai 1, 105 64 Athens; tel. (1) 3230214; telex 214239; fax (1) 3239653; f. 1962; cap. dre 2,107.3m., res dre 1,837.7m., dep. dre 23,148.1m. (Dec. 1989); Chair. KONSTANTINOS J. LEVANTIS.

Ionian and Popular Bank of Greece, SA: Odos Panepistimiou 45, 102 43 Athens; tel. (1) 3225501; telex 215269; fax (1) 3222882; f. 1958, by merger of Ionian Bank (f. 1839) and Banque Populaire (f. 1905); cap. dre 15,078.7m., res dre 71,665.8m., dep. dre

1,471,458.5m. (Dec. 1996); Gov. Haris Stamatopoulos; Gen. Man. Dimitrios Frangetis; 216 local brs, 2 overseas.

Macedonia Thrace Bank, SA: Odos Ionos Dragoumi 5, 546 25 Thessaloniki; tel. (31) 5238317; telex 418415; fax (31) 547323; f, 1979; cap. dre 5,507.1m., res dre 18,572.7m., dep. dre 370,990.3m. (Dec. 1996); Chair. and CEO Spyridon K. Kouniakis; 73 brs.

National Bank of Greece, SA: Odos Aeolou 86, 102 32 Athens; tel. (1) 3441000; telex 214931; fax (1) 3228187; f. 1841; cap. dre 87,914.4m., res dre 106,977.2m., dep. dre 7,893,024.8m. (Dec. 1996); Gov. Theodhoros Karatzas; 496 local brs, 35 overseas brs.

National Mortgage Bank of Greece: POB 3667, Odos Panepistimiou 40, 102 10 Athens; tel. (1) 3648311; telex 221177; fax (1) 3605130; f. 1927; cap. dre 16,524.0m., res dre 58,898.0m., dep. dre 1,804,671,7m. (Dec. 1995); Gov. Prof. Vassilios Th. Rapanos; 60 brs.

Piraeus Bank, SA: Leoforos Amalias 20, 105 57 Athens; tel. (1) 3335000; fax (1) 3335030; f. 1916; cap. dre 10,080m. res 10,633.9m., dep. dre 160,504.5m. (Dec. 1996); Chair. of Bd and Man. Dir Michael Sallas; 16 brs.

Xiosbank, SA: Leoforos Vassilissis Sofias 11, 106 71 Athens; tel. (1) 3288888; telex 220640; fax (1) 3244909; e-mail xiosbank@neter.gr; internet http://www.netor.gr/xiosbank/; f. 1990; cap. dre 6,290.2m., res dre 1,444.1m., dep. dre 174,815.9m. (Dec. 1996); Chair. Vardis I. Vardinoyannis; Gen. Man. Ioannis G. Pehlivanidis; 25 brs.

Development Banks

Hellenic Industrial Development Bank, SA: Leoforos Syngrou 87, 117 45 Athens; tel. (1) 9241425; telex 214246; fax (1) 9241513; f. 1964; state-owned limited liability banking company; the major Greek institution in the field of industrial investment; cap. dre 62,513.3m., res dre 75,993.3m., dep. dre 534,605.4m. (Dec. 1990); Gov. Eftychia Piper-Pylarinou; 11 brs.

National Investment Bank for Industrial Development, SA: Leoforos Amalias 12-14, 102 36 Athens; tel. (1) 3242651; telex 216113; fax (1) 3296211; f. 1963; cap. dre 8,156.2m., res dre 23,653.7m., dep. dre 58,950.0m. (Dec. 1996); long-term loans, equity participation, promotion of co-operation between Greek and foreign enterprises; Chair. Theodore Karatzas; Man. Dir Demetrios Pavlakis.

STOCK EXCHANGE

Athens Stock Exchange: Odos Sophokleous 10, 105 59 Athens; tel. (1) 3211301; telex 215820; fax (1) 3213938; f. 1876; Pres. Manolis Xanthakis; Vice-Pres. Elias Hadellis.

PRINCIPAL INSURANCE COMPANIES

Agrotiki Hellenic General Insurance Co: Leoforos Syngrou 163, 171 21 Athens; tel. (1) 9358613; telex 223004; fax (1) 9358924.

Alfa Insurance Co SA: Leoforos Kifissias 250–254, 152 31 Athens; tel. (1) 6742411; fax (1) 6741826; e-mail info@atheneos.com; f. 1977; Pres. D. Daskalopoulos; Man. Dir D. Atheneos; Gen. Man. P. Athineos.

Apollon Insurance Co: Leoforos Syngrou 39, 117 43 Athens; tel. (1) 9236362; fax (1) 9236916; f. 1976; Gen. Man. E. Pananidis.

Aspis Pronia General Insurance SA: Leoforos Kifissias 62, Maroussi, 151 25 Athens; tel. (1) 6898960; telex 215350; fax (1) 6898990; f. 1941; Pres. and CEO Paul Psomiades.

Astir: Odos Merlin 6, 106 71 Athens; tel. (1) 3604111; telex 215383; fax (1) 3633333; f. 1930; Gen. Man. B. Chardalias.

Atlantiki Enosis: Odos Messoghion 71, 115 26 Athens; tel. (1) 7799211; telex 216822; f. 1970; Gen. Man. N. Lapatas.

Cigna Insurance Co Hellas, SA: Odos Erythrou Stavrou 5, Maroussi, 151 23 Athens; tel. (1) 6817777; fax (1) 6846475; Gen. Man. Andreas Chourdakis.

Continental Hellas, SA: Athens; tel. (1) 9242459; telex 222746; fax (1) 9231572; f. 1942; incorporating Plioktitai SA; Man. Dir Spyros Alexandratos.

Dynamis, SA: Leoforos Syngrou 106, 117 41 Athens; tel. (1) 9227255; telex 216678; f. 1977; Man. Dir Nikolas Stamatopoulos.

Egnatia Co: Odos Fragon 1, 546 26 Thessaloniki; tel. (31) 523325; telex 0410772; fax (31) 523555; Rep. P. Migas.

Emporiki: Odos Philhellinon 6, 105 57 Athens; tel. (1) 3240093; telex 219218; fax (1) 3223835; f. 1940; Chair. Photis P. Kostopoulos; Exec. Dir Michael P. Psalidas.

Estia Insurance and Reinsurance Co, SA: Athens; tel. (1) 9425513; telex 215833; f. 1943; Chair. Alkiviadis Chionis; Gen. Man. Stavroula Vavas-Polychronopoulos.

Ethniki Hellenic General Insurance Co: Odos Karageorgi Servias 8, 102 10 Athens; tel. (1) 3222121; telex 215400; fax (1) 3236101; f. 1891; Gen. Man. L. Kokkinos.

Euromonde A.E.G.A.: Leoforos Syngrou 102, 117 41 Athens; tel. (1) 9226094; telex 218722; fax (1) 9227788; Rep. Panos Papayannopoulos.

Europa Insurance Co, SA: Leoforos Syngrou 44, 117 42 Athens; tel. (1) 9226077; telex 215268; fax (1) 9231961; Rep. N. Makropoulos.

Galaxias: Leoforos Syngrou 40–42, 117 42 Athens; tel. (1) 9241082; fax (1) 9241698; f. 1967; Gen. Man. I. Tsoupras.

Geniki Epagelmatiki: Odos Panepistimiou 56, 106 78 Athens; tel. (1) 3636910; fax (1) 3606848; f. 1967; Gen. Man. G. Giatrakos.

Gothaer Hellas, SA: Odos Michalakopoulou 174, 115 27 Athens; tel. (1) 7750801; telex 216420; fax (1) 7757094; Gen. Man. S. Galanis.

Hellas: Leoforos Kifissias 119, 151 24 Marousi; tel. (1) 6124286; telex 215226; fax (1) 8027189; f. 1973; Gen. Man. N. Adamantiadis.

Hellenic Reliance General Insurances, SA: Leoforos Kifissias 304, 152 32 Halandri; tel. (1) 6843733; fax (1) 6843734; f. 1990; Man. Dir S. F. Triantafyllakis.

Hellenobretanniki General Insurances, SA: Leoforos Messogion 2–4, 115 27 Athens; tel. (1) 7755301; telex 216448; fax (1) 7714768; f. 1988; Gen. Man. D. J. Paleologos.

Helvetia General Insurance Co: Odos Hermou 2, 105 63 Athens; tel. (1) 3252106; telex 216936; fax (1) 3231415; f. 1943; Gen. Man. J. Delendas.

Hermes: Odos Christou Lada 2, 105 61 Athens; tel. (1) 3225602; telex 216243; fax (1) 3223472; f. 1940; general insurance; Gen. Man. N. Negas.

Horizon Insurance Co, SA: Leoforos Amalias 26A, 105 57 Athens; tel. (1) 3227932; telex 216158; fax (1) 3225540; f. 1965; Gen. Mans Theodore Achis, Chr. Achis.

Hydrogios: Odos Lagoumigi 6, 176 71 Athens; tel. (1) 9234888; telex 219536; fax (1) 9247288; Gen. Man. A. Kaskarelis.

Ikonomiki: Odos Kapodistriou 38, 104 32 Athens; tel. (1) 5243374; telex 219809; fax (1) 5234962; f. 1968; Gen. Man. D. Nikolaidis.

Imperial Hellas, SA: Leoforos Syngrou 253, 171 22 Athens; tel. (1) 9426352; fax (1) 9426202; f. 1971; Gen. Man. Savvas Tzanis.

Interamerican Hellenic Life Insurance Co: Interamerican Plaza, Leoforos Kifissias 117, 151 80 Maroussi, Athens; tel. (1) 6191111; telex 214685; fax (1) 6191877; e-mail tzoumass@interamerican.gr; f. 1971; Pres. and Man. Dir Dimitri Kontominas.

Interamerican Property and Casualty Insurance Co: Leoforos Kifissias 117, 151 80 Maroussi, Athens; tel. (1) 6191111; telex 226177; fax (1) 8060820; e-mail tzoumass@interamerican.gr; f. 1974; Man. Dir C. Bertsias.

Ioniki: Odos Korai 1, 105 64 Athens; tel. (1) 3236901; f. 1939; Gen. Man. E. Dorkofiki.

Kykladiki: Leoforos Syngrou 80–88, 117 41 Athens; tel. (1) 9247664; telex 218560; fax (1) 9247344; f. 1919; Gen. Man. Pan. Katsikostas.

Laiki Insurance Company, SA: Leoforos Syngrou 135, 171 21 N. Smyrni; tel. (1) 9332911; telex 215403; fax (1) 9335949; f. 1942; Gen. Man. N. Mourtzoukos.

Lloyd Hellenique, SA: Odos Psaron 2 and Odos Agiou Konstantinou, 104 37 Athens; tel. (1) 5237168; telex 225397; f. 1942; Dir Dominique Prigent.

Messoghios: Leoforos Syngrou 165, 117 21 N. Smyrni; tel. (1) 9333162; telex 216259; fax (1) 9359590; f. 1942; Gen. Man. E. Tsaousis.

National Insurance Institution of Greece: Odos Agiou Konstantinou 6, 104 31 Athens; tel. (1) 5223300; telex 215338; fax (1) 5239754; Rep. J. Kyriakos.

Olympic-Victoria General Insurance Co, SA: Odos Tsimiski 21, 546 22 Thessaloniki; tel. (31) 239331; telex 415251; fax (31) 239264; f. 1972; Man. Dir Emmanouk Matthias.

Panellinios: Leoforos Syngrou 171, 171 21 Athens; tel. (1) 9352003; telex 223744; fax (1) 9352451; f. 1918; Gen. Man. A. Valyrakis.

Pegasus Insurance Co: Odos Stadiou 5, 105 62 Athens; tel. (1) 3227357; telex 214188; fax (1) 3246728; Gen. Man. M. Paraskakis.

Phoenix-General Insurance Co of Greece, SA: Odos Omirou 2, 105 64 Athens; tel. (1) 3295111; telex 215608; fax (1) 3239135; f. 1928; general insurance; Rep. G. Kotsalos.

Piraiki: Odos Georges 10, 106 77 Athens; tel. (1) 3624868; telex 225921; f. 1943; Dir Gen. K. Papageorgiou.

Poseidon: Odos Karaiskou 163, 185 35 Piraeus; tel. (1) 4522685; fax (1) 4184337; f. 1972; Gen. Man. Thanos J. Melakopides.

Promitheus: Odos 3rd September 84, 104 Athens; tel. (1) 8827085; f. 1941; Gen. Man. C. Ghonis.

Proodos: Leoforos Syngrou 196, 176 71 Kallithea; tel. (1) 9506911; fax (1) 9524493; f. 1941; Gen. Man. P. Kakalis.

Propontis–Merimna A.E.A.: Odos Agiou Konstantinou 6, 104 31 Athens; tel. (1) 5223300; telex 215338; fax (1) 5239754; f. 1917; Man. Dirs E. Bala-Hill, M. Artavanis.

Sideris Insurance Co, SA: Odos Lekka 3–5, 105 63 Athens; tel. (1) 3253932; telex 221496; fax (1) 3250931; Dir G. Sideris.

Syneteristiki: Odos Gennadiou 8 and Akademias 65, 106 78 Athens; tel. (1) 3642611; telex 210255; fax (1) 3626452; Gen. Man. D. Zorbas.

A large number of foreign insurance companies also operate in Greece.

Insurance Association

Association of Insurance Companies: Odos Xenophontos 10, 105 57 Athens; tel. (1) 3236733; fax (1) 3236563; 149 mems.

Trade and Industry

GOVERNMENT AGENCY

Industrial Reconstruction Organization: Athens; f. 1982; reconstruction and sale of Greek businesses under state receivership.

CHAMBERS OF COMMERCE

Athens Chamber of Commerce & Industry: Odos Akademias 7, 106 71 Athens; tel. (1) 3602411; telex 215707; fax (1) 3616464; f. 1919; Pres. John Papathanassiou; Sec.-Gen. Eleftherios Kourtalis; 37,500 mems.

Athens Chamber of Small and Medium-Sized Industries: Odos Akademias 18, 106 71 Athens; tel. (1) 3635313; telex 210976; fax (1) 3614726; f. 1940; Pres. G. Kyriopoulos; Sec.-Gen. Stergios Vassiliou; c. 60,000 mems.

Handicraft Chamber of Piraeus: Odos Karaiscou 111, 185 32 Piraeus; tel. (1) 4174152; f. 1925; Pres. Konstantinos Moscholios; Sec.-Gen. Pantelis Antoniadis; 18,500 mems.

Piraeus Chamber of Commerce & Industry: Odos Loudovikou 1, 185 31 Piraeus; tel. (1) 4177241; telex 212970; fax (1) 4178680; f. 1919; Pres. George Kassimatis; Sec.-Gen. Konstantinos Sarantopoulos.

Thessaloniki Chamber of Commerce and Industry: Odos Tsimiski 29, 546 24 Thessaloniki; tel. (31) 224438; telex 412115; fax (31) 230237; f. 1919; Pres. Pantelis Konstantinidis; Sec.-Gen. Emmanuel Vlachoyannis; 14,500 mems.

INDUSTRIAL AND TRADE ASSOCIATIONS

Association of Industries of Northern Greece: Morihovou 1, 546 35 Thessaloniki; tel. (31) 539817, telex 418310; fax (31) 546244; f. 1914; Pres. Nikolaos Efthimiades.

Federation of Greek Industries (SEV): Odos Xenophontos 5, 105 57 Athens; f. 1907; Pres. Jason Stratos; 950 mems.

Hellenic Cotton Board: Leoforos Syngrou 150, 176 71 Athens; tel. (1) 9225011; telex 214556; fax (1) 9249656; f. 1931; state organization; Pres. P. K. Mylonas.

Hellenic Organization of Small and Medium-size Industries and Handicrafts: Odos Xenias 16, 115 28 Athens; tel. (1) 7715002; telex 218819; fax (1) 7712237; Pres. Anna Diamandopoulou.

UTILITIES

Electricity

Public Power Corpn (DEH): Athens; f. 1950; generating capacity 9,372 MW; generation, transmission and distribution of electricity in Greece; Exec. Dep. Gen.-Man. Konstantinos Yotopoulos.

Gas

Public Gas Corpn (DEPA): Athens; owned by Public Petroleum Corpn (DEH); began gas imports 1997; initially for industrial use.

TRADE UNIONS

There are about 5,000 registered trade unions, grouped together in 82 federations and 86 workers' centres, which are affiliated to the Greek General Confederation of Labour (GSEE).

Greek General Confederation of Labour (GSEE): Odos Patission 69, Athens; tel. (1) 8834611; telex 226372; fax (1) 8229802; f. 1918; Pres. Christos Protopapas; Gen. Sec. Ioannis Theonas; 700,000 mems.

Pan-Hellenic Federation of Seamen's Unions (PNO): Livanos Bldg, Akti Miaouli 47–49, 185 36 Piraeus; tel. (1) 4292960; telex 212623; fax (1) 4293040; f. 1920; confederation of 14 marine unions; Pres. Yannis Chelas; Gen. Sec. John Halas.

Transport

RAILWAYS

Ilektriki Sidirodromi Athinon–Pireos (ISAP) (Athens–Piraeus Electric Railways): Odos Athinas 67, 105 52 Athens; tel. (1) 3248311; telex 219998; fax (1) 3223935; 26 km of electrified track; Gen. Dir Aristos Sp. Lazaris.

Organismos Sidirodromon Ellados (OSE) (Hellenic Railways Organization Ltd): Odos Karolou 1–3, 104 37 Athens; tel. (1) 5248395; telex 215187; fax (1) 5243290; f. 1971; state railways. Total length of track: 2,600 km (1995); Chair. Chr. Papageorgiou; Dir Gen. A. Lazaris.

A five-year programme to upgrade the Greek rail network was initiated in 1996, supported by dre 350m. from EU structural funds. The major undertaking was to electrify the 500 km Athens-Thessaloniki line and to extend services to the Bulgarian border. Construction of a 26.3 km electrified extension to the Athens Piraeus line, in order to provide a 3-line urban railway system for Athens, was scheduled to be completed by October 1998.

ROADS

In 1995 there were an estimated 116,440 km of roads in Greece. Of this total, an estimated 9,120 km were main roads, and 420 km were motorways.

INLAND WATERWAYS

There are no navigable rivers in Greece.

Corinth Canal: built 1893; over six km long, links the Corinthian and Saronic Gulfs. The Canal shortens the journey from the Adriatic to the Piraeus by 325 km; it is spanned by three single-span bridges, two for road and one for rail. The canal can be used by ships of a maximum draught of 22 ft and a width of 60 ft.

SHIPPING

In 1996 the Greek merchant fleet totalled 1,743 vessels amounting to 27,507,109 grt. Greece controls one of the largest merchant fleets in the world. The principal ports are Piraeus, Patras and Thessaloniki.

Union of Greek Shipowners: Akti Miaouli 85, 185 38 Piraeus; Pres. John Goumas.

Port Authorities

Port of Patras: Patras Port Authority, Central Port Office, Patras; tel. (61) 277622; telex 312184; Harbour Master Capt. Nikolas Rafailovits.

Port of Piraeus: Port of Piraeus Authority, Odos Merarchias 2, 185 35 Piraeus; tel. (1) 4520910; telex 212187; fax (1) 4520852; Gen. Man. Nikos Papadoganos; Harbour Master Capt. Emmanuel Peloponnesios.

Port of Thessaloniki: Thessaloniki Port Authority, 541 10 Thessaloniki; tel. (31) 530721; telex 412536; fax (31) 510500.

Among the largest shipping companies are:

Anangel Shipping Enterprises, SA: Akti Miaouli 25, 185 10 Piraeus; tel. (1) 4224500; telex 212567; fax (1) 4224819; Man. Dir J. Platsidakis.

Attika Shipping Co.: Odos Voucourestion 16, 10671 Athens; tel. (1) 3609631; fax (1) 3601439; Dir G. Priovolos.

Bilinder Marine Corpn, SA: POB 51303, Odos Diligianni 59, Kifissia, 145 62 Athens; tel. (1) 8080211; telex 215394; fax (1) 8016681; Gen. Man. V. Armogeni.

Ceres Hellenic Shipping Enterprises Ltd: Akti Miaouli 69, 185 37 Piraeus; tel. (1) 4591000; telex 212257; fax (1) 4180549; Dir Nick Fistes.

Chandris (Hellas) Inc: POB 80067, Akti Miaouli 95, 185 38 Piraeus; tel. (1) 4290300; telex 212218; fax (1) 4290256; Man. Dirs A. C. Piperas, M. G. Skordias.

Costamare Shipping Co, SA: Akti Miaouli 59, 185 36 Piraeus; tel. (1) 4293140; telex 211399; fax (1) 4292037; Man. Dir F. C. Konstantakopoulos; Dir K. V. Konstantakopoulos; Gen. Man. G. Th. Sardis.

European Navigation Inc: Odos Artemissiou 2 and Fleming Sq., 166 75 Athens; tel. (1) 8981581; telex 216428; fax (1) 8946777; Dir P. Karnessis.

Glafki (Hellas) Maritime Co: Odos Mitropoleos 3, 105 57 Athens; tel. (1) 3244991; telex 214655; fax (1) 3228944; Dirs M. Fragoulis, G. Panagiotou.

Golden Union Shipping Co, SA: Odos Aegales 8, 185 45 Piraeus; tel. (1) 4329900; telex 211190; fax (1) 4627933; Man. Dir Theodore Veniamis.

M. Koutlakis and Co Ltd: Makras Stoas 5, 185 31 Piraeus; tel. (1) 4129428; telex 211798; fax (1) 4178755; Dir M. Koutlakis.

Laskaridis Shipping Co Ltd: Odos Chimaras 5, Maroussi, 151 25 Athens; tel. (1) 6899090; telex 216040; fax (1) 6851011; Man. Dirs P. C. Laskaridis, A. C. Laskaridis.

Marmaras Navigation Ltd: Odos Filellinon 4–6, Okeanion Bldg, 185 36 Piraeus; tel. (1) 4294226; telex 211234; fax (1) 4294304; Dir D. Diamantides.

Minoan Lines Shipping SA: Odos Agiou Titiou 38, 712 02 Iraklion; tel. (81) 330301; telex 262239; fax (81) 330308; Chair. K. KLIRONOMOS.

Naftomar Shipping and Trading Co Ltd: Leoforos Alkyonidon 243, 166 73 Voula; tel. (1) 9670220; telex 21839; fax (1) 9670237; Man. Dir RIAD ZEIN.

Strintzis Lines Maritime S.A.: Odos Akti Possidonos 26, 185 31 Piraeus; (1) 4225000; fax (1) 4225265; Man. Dir G. STRINTZIS.

Thenamaris (Ships Management) Inc: Odos Athinas 16, Kavouri, 166 71 Athens; tel. (1) 8969111; telex 210468; fax (1) 8969653; Dir K. MARTINOS.

Tsakos Shipping and Trading, SA: Akti Miaouli 85, 185 38 Piraeus; tel. (1) 4290810; telex 212670; fax (1) 4290853; Dirs P. N. TSAKOS, E. SAROGLOU.

United Shipping and Trading Co of Greece, SA: Odos Iassonos 6, 185 37 Piraeus; tel. (1) 4283660; telex 213014; fax (1) 4283630; Dir CH. TSAKOS.

Varnima Corporation International, SA: Odos Irodou Attikou 12A, Maroussi, 151 24 Athens; tel. (1) 8093000; telex 210562; fax (1) 8093222. Gen. Man. S. V. SPANOUDAKIS.

CIVIL AVIATION

There are international airports at Athens, Thessaloniki, Alexandroupolis, Corfu, Lesbos, Andravida, Rhodes, Kos and Heraklion/Crete, and 24 domestic airports (of which 13 are authorized to receive international flights). Construction of a new international airport at Spata, some 25 km east of Athens, was finally approved in July 1995. The airport was expected to become operational in 2000, with a handling capacity of 16m. passengers per year.

Olympic Airways, SA: Leoforos Syngrou 96–100, 117 41 Athens; tel. (1) 9269111; telex 216488; fax (1) 9267154; f. 1957; 51% state-owned, 49% of shares offered for transfer to private ownership in 1990; domestic services linking principal cities and islands in Greece, and international services to Singapore, Thailand, South Africa and the USA, and throughout Europe and the Middle East; Chair. Prof. NICOLAOS BLESSIOS; CEO (vacant); Gen. Man. MILTIADES TSANGARAKIS.

Olympic Aviation: Leoforos Syngrou 96–100, 117 41 Athens; tel. (1) 9269111; telex 215824; fax (1) 9884059; wholly-owned subsidiary of Olympic Airways; independent operator of scheduled domestic and regional services; Chair. ALEXANDROS VLAHOGIANNIS; Vice-Chair. ELIAS MASSOUROS.

Tourism

The sunny climate, the natural beauty of the country and its great history and traditions attract tourists to Greece. There are numerous islands and many sites of archaeological interest. The number of tourists visiting Greece increased from 1m. in 1968 to 11.2m. in 1994. Receipts from tourism, which totalled US $120m. in 1968, reached $3,905m. in 1994.

Ellinikos Organismos Tourismou (EOT) (Greek National Tourist Organization): Odos Amerikis 2B, 105 64 Athens; tel. (1) 3223111; telex 215832; fax (1) 3252895; Pres. IOANNIS STEFANIDES; Vice-Pres. IOANNIS ROUBATIS.

GRENADA

Introductory Survey

Location, Climate, Language, Religion, Flag, Capital

Grenada, a mountainous, heavily-forested island, is the most southerly of the Windward Islands, in the West Indies. The country also includes some of the small islands known as the Grenadines, which lie to the north-east of Grenada. The most important of these are the low-lying island of Carriacou and its neighbour, Petit Martinique. The climate is semi-tropical, with an average annual temperature of 28°C (82°F) in the lowlands. Annual rainfall averages about 1,500 mm (60 ins) in the coastal area and 3,800 mm to 5,100 mm (150–200 ins) in mountain areas. Most of the rainfall occurs between June and December. The majority of the population speak English, although a French patois is sometimes spoken. According to the census of 1991, 82% of Grenada's population were of African descent, while 13% were of mixed ethnic origins. Most of the population profess Christianity, and the main denominations are Roman Catholicism (to which 53% of the population adhered at the time of the 1991 census) and Anglicanism (about 14% of the population). The national flag (proportions 2 by 1) consists of a diagonally-quartered rectangle (yellow in the upper and lower segments, green in the right and left ones) surrounded by a red border bearing six five-pointed yellow stars (three at the upper edge of the flag, and three at the lower edge). There is a red disc, containing a large five-pointed yellow star, in the centre, and a representation of a nutmeg (in yellow and red) on the green segment near the hoist. The capital is St George's.

Recent History

Grenada was initially colonized by the French but was captured by the British in 1762. British control was recognized in 1783 by the Treaty of Versailles. Grenada continued as a British colony until 1958, when it joined the Federation of the West Indies, remaining a member until the dissolution of the Federation in 1962. Full internal self-government and statehood in association with the United Kingdom were achieved in March 1967. During this period, the political life of Grenada was dominated by Eric Gairy, a local trade union leader, who in 1950 founded the Grenada United Labour Party (GULP), with the support of an associated trade union. In 1951 GULP won a majority of the elected seats on the Legislative Council, but in 1957 it was defeated by the Grenada National Party (GNP), led by Herbert Blaize. Gairy was Chief Minister in 1961–62 but was removed from office by the British, and the Constitution suspended, after allegations of corruption. In the subsequent elections the GNP gained a majority of the elected seats, and Blaize became Chief Minister again. Gairy became Premier after the elections of 1967 and again after those of 1972, which he contested chiefly on the issue of total independence. Grenada became independent, within the Commonwealth, on 7 February 1974, with Gairy as Prime Minister. Opposition to Gairy within the country was expressed in demonstrations and a general strike, and the formation by the three opposition parties of the People's Alliance, which contested the 1976 general elections and reduced GULP's majority in the Lower House. The alliance comprised the GNP, the United People's Party and the New Jewel Movement (NJM).

The rule of Sir Eric Gairy, as he became in June 1977, was regarded by the opposition as increasingly autocratic and corrupt, and on 13 March 1979 he was replaced in a bloodless coup by the leader of the left-wing NJM, Maurice Bishop. The new People's Revolutionary Government (PRG) suspended the 1974 Constitution and announced the imminent formation of a People's Consultative Assembly to draft a new constitution. Meanwhile, Grenada remained a monarchy, with the British Queen as Head of State, represented in Grenada by a Governor-General. During 1980–81 there was an increase in repression, against a background of mounting anti-Government violence and the PRG's fears of an invasion by US forces.

By mid-1982 relations with the USA, the United Kingdom and the more conservative members of the Caribbean Community and Common Market (CARICOM—see p. 119) were becoming increasingly strained: elections had not been arranged, restrictions against the privately-owned press had been imposed, many detainees were still awaiting trial, and Grenada was aligning more closely with Cuba and the USSR. Cuba was contributing funds and construction workers for the airport at Point Salines, a project which further strengthened the US Government's conviction that Grenada was to become a centre for Soviet manoeuvres in the area.

In March 1983 the armed forces were put on alert, in response to renewed fears that the USA was planning to invade. (The USA strenuously denied any such plans.) In June Bishop sought to improve relations with the USA, and announced the appointment of a commission to draft a new constitution. This attempt at conciliation was denounced by the more left-wing members of the PRG as an ideological betrayal. A power struggle developed between Bishop and his deputy, Bernard Coard, the Minister of Finance and Planning. In October Bishop was placed under house arrest, allegedly for his refusal to share power with Coard. The commander of the People's Revolutionary Army (PRA), Gen. Austin Hudson, subsequently announced that Bishop had been expelled from the NJM. On 19 October thousands of Bishop's supporters stormed the house, freed Bishop from imprisonment, and demonstrated outside the PRA headquarters. Violence ensued, with PRA forces firing into the crowd. Later in the day, Bishop, three of his ministers and two trade unionists were executed by the PRA. The Government was replaced by a 16-member Revolutionary Military Council (RMC), led by Gen. Austin and supported by Coard and one other minister. The remaining NJM ministers were arrested and imprisoned, and a total curfew was imposed.

Regional and international outrage at the assassination of Bishop, in addition to fears of a US military intervention, were so intense that after four days the RMC relaxed the curfew, reopened the airport and promised a return to civilian rule as soon as possible. However, the Organization of Eastern Caribbean States (OECS, see p. 122) resolved to intervene in an attempt to restore democratic order, and asked for assistance from the USA, which readily complied. (It is unclear whether the decision to intervene preceded or followed a request for help to the OECS by the Grenadian Governor-General, Sir Paul Scoon.) On 25 October 1983 some 1,900 US military personnel invaded the island, accompanied by 300 troops from Jamaica, Barbados and member countries of the OECS. Fighting continued for some days, and the USA gradually increased its troop strength, with further reinforcements waiting off shore with a US naval task force. The RMC's forces were defeated, while Coard, Austin and others who had been involved in the coup were detained.

On 9 November 1983 Scoon appointed a non-political interim Council to assume responsibility for the government of the country until elections could be held. Nicholas Brathwaite, a former Commonwealth official, was appointed Chairman of this Council in December. The 1974 Constitution was reinstated (with the exception that the country did not rejoin the East Caribbean Supreme Court), and an electoral commission was created. By mid-December the USA had withdrawn all its forces except 300 support troops, military police and technicians who were to assist the 430 members of Caribbean forces who remained on the island. A 550-member police force, trained by the USA and the United Kingdom, was established, including a paramilitary body that was to be the new defence contingent.

Several political parties that had operated clandestinely or from exile during the rule of the PRG re-emerged and announced their intention of contesting the elections for a new House of Representatives. Sir Eric Gairy returned to Grenada in January 1984 to lead GULP, but stated that he would not stand as a candidate himself. In May three former NJM ministers formed the Maurice Bishop Patriotic Movement (MBPM) to contest the elections. A number of centrist parties emerged or re-emerged, including Blaize's GNP. Fears that a divided opposition would allow GULP to win a majority of seats in the new House resulted in an agreement by several of these organizations, in August 1984, to form the New National Party (NNP), led by Blaize.

At the general election held in December 1984 the NNP achieved a convincing victory over its opponents by winning 14 of the 15 seats in the House of Representatives, with 59% of the popular votes. Both GULP (which won 36% of the votes cast) and the MBPM claimed that the poll had been fraudulent, and the one successful GULP candidate, Marcel Peters, initially refused to take his seat in protest. He subsequently accepted the seat, but was expelled from the party and formed the Grenada Democratic Labour Party (GDLP). Blaize became Prime Minister, and appointed a Cabinet. US and Caribbean troops remained in Grenada, at Blaize's request, until September 1985.

The trial before the Grenada High Court of 19 detainees (including Coard, his wife, Phyllis, and Gen. Austin), accused of murder and conspiracy against Bishop and six of his associates, opened in November 1984. However, repeated adjournments postponed the trial of 18 of the detainees until April 1986. One of the detainees agreed to give evidence for the State in return for a pardon. Eventually, verdicts on 196 charges of murder and conspiracy to murder were returned by the jury in December. Fourteen of the defendants were sentenced to death, three received prison sentences of between 30 and 45 years, and one was acquitted.

Differences between its component groupings gradually led to the disintegration of the NNP. In 1986 the parliamentary strength of the NNP was reduced to 12 seats, following the resignation of two members who subsequently formed the Democratic Labour Congress (DLC). In April 1987 the coalition collapsed when three more government members resigned. In July the three former ministers joined forces with the DLC and the GDLP to form a united opposition, with six seats in the House of Representatives, and in October they formally launched a new party, the National Democratic Congress (NDC), led by George Brizan, who had earlier been appointed parliamentary opposition leader. In January 1989 Brizan resigned as leader of the NDC in order to allow the election of Nicholas Brathwaite (head of the interim Government of 1983–84) to that post.

During 1988 and 1989 the actions of the Blaize Government, under provisions of the controversial Emergency Powers Act of 1987, gave rise to concerns both within the opposition and among regional neighbours. Deportation orders and bans were enforced by the administration against prominent left-wing politicians and journalists from the region, and a variety of books and journals were proscribed.

Meanwhile, a deterioration in Blaize's health coincided with a growing challenge to his administration from within the NNP during 1988. In January 1989 Blaize was replaced as leader of the ruling party by his cabinet colleague, Dr Keith Mitchell, although he remained Prime Minister. In July, however, following allegations of corruption by the NDC, Blaize announced the dismissal of Mitchell and the Chairman of the NNP, accusing them of violating the principles of cabinet government. Amid uncertainty as to whether the Blaize faction had formed a separate party, two more members of the Government resigned, thus reducing support for the Blaize Government to only five of the 15 members of the House of Representatives. Blaize did not officially announce the formation of a new party, the National Party (TNP), until the end of August, by which time he had advised the acting Governor-General to prorogue Parliament. (The Government thereby avoided being defeated in a motion of 'no confidence' and the prospect of a general election consequent upon the immediate dissolution of Parliament.) The term of the Parliament was due to expire at the end of December, and a general election had to be held within three months. However, Blaize died in mid-December, and the Governor-General appointed Ben Jones, Blaize's former deputy and the new leader of TNP, as Prime Minister. At the general election, which was held in March 1990, no party achieved an absolute majority in the House of Representatives. The NDC won seven of the 15 seats, GULP (which had held no seats in the previous Parliament) won four, while TNP won only two, as did the NNP. The NDC achieved a working majority in Parliament when one of GULP's successful candidates announced his defection to the NDC. Brathwaite subsequently became Prime Minister and appointed a new Cabinet.

In July 1991 the Court of Appeal upheld the original verdicts that had been imposed in 1986 on the defendants in the Bishop murder trial, and further pleas for clemency were rejected. Preparations for the imminent hanging of the 14, however, provoked overwhelming international outrage, and in August Brathwaite announced that the death sentences were to be commuted to terms of life imprisonment. His decision (which was contrary to prevailing public opinion on Grenada) was considered to have been influenced by intense pressure from politicians and human rights organizations not to administer the sentences, together with the detrimental effect that the executions may have had on the country's important tourist industry.

A series of strikes by public-sector and port workers during 1992 and 1993 caused considerable disruption, and prompted the approval by Parliament in mid-1993 of legislation aimed at restricting the right of trade unions to take industrial action.

Brathwaite resigned as leader of the NDC in September 1994; Brizan, now Minister of Agriculture, Trade and Industry, was successful in a subsequent leadership election, defeating the Attorney-General, Francis Alexis (who, like Brizan had been a founder member of the NDC following their resignation from the NNP Government in 1987). In February 1995 Brathwaite resigned as Prime Minister, and was succeeded by Brizan.

A general election on 20 June 1995 was contested by candidates from seven political parties, as well as independents. The NNP won 32.7% of total votes cast, securing eight of the 15 seats in the House of Representatives, while the NDC's representation was reduced to five seats. The remaining two seats were secured by GULP. Keith Mitchell, leader of the NNP, became Prime Minister and appointed a 12-member Cabinet. The NNP subsequently undertook negotiations with GULP in an attempt to strengthen its single-seat majority and to secure the two-thirds' majority support necessary to amend the Constitution. In July Alexis resigned as deputy leader of the NDC, alleging that an NDC member of Parliament had been unfairly treated by the party prior to the election. In November Alexis and three other former NDC members announced the formation of a new opposition group, the Democratic Labour Party (DLP).

The appointment in August 1996 of Daniel (later Sir Daniel) Williams to the position of Governor-General provoked considerable controversy because of Williams' connections with the NNP (he had been deputy leader of the party during the 1980s) and his previous role as a cabinet minister in the Government of Herbert Blaize. Despite assurances from Williams that he would execute his duties without political bias, opposition members expressed concern at his appointment and, in protest, staged a walk-out at his inauguration ceremony. Later in August Parliament approved a motion claiming that the Leader of the Opposition, Brizan, had been guilty of contempt of Parliament and disrespect to Queen Elizabeth II (as Head of State) by leading a protest against the inauguration of the new Governor-General; Brizan was duly suspended from the House of Representatives for one month.

An extensive cabinet reorganization in September 1996 included the appointment of a GULP member, Clarence Rapier, in recognition of the alliance between that party and the NNP. However, relations between the two parties became strained in November when Rapier was dismissed following an incident involving a British bar proprietor. The junior Minister of State for Agriculture, Forestry, Fisheries and Lands was subsequently admonished by Mitchell after he had voiced criticisms of the police force at a GULP rally in support of the dismissed minister.

Concern that the Government was attempting to restrict media freedoms was heightened during 1996, following a series of apparently politically-motivated personnel changes at the state-owned Grenada Broadcasting Corporation. Local and regional press associations criticized the appointment, in April, of a senior NNP official as chief news editor and the dismissal, in July, of four experienced journalists (for allegedly failing to report an event staged by the NNP). In January 1997 the Chairman of the corporation was similarly dismissed for failing to broadcast the budget debate in its entirety.

In late February 1997 Mitchell removed the Minister of Health, Housing and the Environment, Grace Duncan, from the post of Deputy Prime Minister, announcing the abolition of the deputy premiership. Earlier in the month Duncan had, with some of her constituency supporters, boycotted the NNP's annual convention, stating that she and the Prime Minister had minor grievances to resolve. Duncan stated that she would not resign from the Government, but was dismissed in mid-July for making what were termed 'vulgar' remarks about Mitchell and for disclosing confidential information about government affairs, as well as allegedly disseminating misinformation, to the media. The dismissed minister subsequently stated that she had warned Mitchell of an internal party plot to undermine his administration. Meanwhile, in May GULP joined with the NDC, TNP, DLP and MBPM to announce that they were to co-operate in opposing the Government on major national issues, accusing Mitchell of a lack of consultation and of 'growing dictatorship'. In the previous month an opposition motion of 'no confidence' in the Government had been rejected by the House of Representatives, as had a motion against the chamber's Speaker, Sir Curtis Strachan. At the end of June the establishment was announced of an eighth political party, the Grenada Progressive Party, led by Prescott Williams.

In March 1997 the Government's Mercy Committee rejected a request made by the Conference of Churches of Grenada for the release, on the grounds of their deteriorating physical and mental health, of Phyllis Coard and another of those serving terms of life imprisonment for the murder of Maurice Bishop. None the less, the Committee gave assurances that the detainees' medical requirements would receive attention, and that conditions at the prison where they were being held would be improved for all inmates. Also in March Mitchell announced plans for the establishment of a national commission to investigate the 1979–83 revolutionary period.

Sir Eric Gairy died on 23 August 1997, after a period of ill health. Clarence Rapier subsequently failed to obtain a court order authorizing him to co-ordinate preparations for a party convention to elect a new GULP leader.

As a member of the OECS, Grenada has been involved in discussions concerning the possible formation of a political union. In 1988 Grenada, Dominica, Saint Lucia and Saint Vincent and the Grenadines decided to proceed with their own plans for a political union. At a meeting held by representatives of the four countries in St George's in late 1990, it was agreed that a Windward Islands Regional Constituent Assembly (RCA) would be convened to discuss the economic and political feasibilities of creating a federation. In late 1992 members of Grenada's House of Representatives fully endorsed a continuation of progress towards political unity. In 1995 the newly-elected Mitchell Government expressed its commitment to increased political and economic integration between the four countries.

In May 1996 Grenada signed two treaties with the USA, relating to mutual legal assistance and extradition, as part of a regional campaign to combat drugs-trafficking. Improved relations with Cuba, which had been severely strained since 1983, resulted in offers of assistance with education, health and agriculture in Grenada in early 1997. Mitchell led a delegation to Cuba in April 1997; at the same time an aircraft of Cuba's national airline, carrying representatives of the Cuban Government, landed at Point Salines for the first time since the downfall of the revolution.

Government

Grenada has dominion status within the Commonwealth. The British monarch is Head of State and is represented locally by a Governor-General. Executive power is held by the Cabinet, led by the Prime Minister. Parliament comprises the Senate, made up of 13 Senators appointed by the Governor-General on the advice of the Prime Minister and the Leader of the Opposition, and the 15-member House of Representatives, elected by universal adult suffrage. The Cabinet is responsible to Parliament.

Defence

A regional security unit was formed in late 1983, modelled on the British police force and trained by British officers. A paramilitary element, known as the Special Service Unit and trained by US advisers, acts as the defence contingent and participates in the Regional Security System, a defence pact with other East Caribbean states.

Economic Affairs

In 1995, according to estimates by the World Bank, Grenada's gross national product (GNP), measured at average 1993–95 prices, was US $271m., equivalent to US $2,980 per head. In 1985–94, it was estimated, the country's GNP per head increased, in real terms, by an average of 3.9% annually. Over the same period Grenada's population increased at an average rate of 0.2% per year. Gross domestic product (GDP) increased, in real terms, by an annual average of 2.2% in 1992–96. Following a decline of 1.2% in 1993, GDP increased by 3.3% in 1994 and by 3.1% annually in 1995 and 1996; growth was estimated at 4.3% in 1997.

Agriculture (including forestry and fishing) contributed some 9.5% of GDP in 1996. The sector engaged 17.1% of the employed labour force in 1995. According to agricultural census figures, some 11,871 farmers were active in the country in 1995. Grenada, known as the Spice Island of the Caribbean, is the largest producer of nutmeg after Indonesia (which produces some 75% of the world's total), and in 1987 it supplied 23% of the world's nutmeg. In 1996, according to IMF data, sales of nutmeg and mace (the pungent red membrane around the nut) accounted for 26.4% of Grenada's domestic export earnings. The other principal cash crops are bananas and other fruit and cocoa. In 1996 a US company conducted a feasibility study into the development of large-scale vanilla cultivation on Grenada. Livestock production, for domestic consumption, is important on Carriacou. There are extensive timber reserves on the island of Grenada; forestry development is strictly controlled and involves a programme of reafforestation. Exports of fish contributed 16.3% of domestic export earnings in 1996. Agricultural GDP declined by an annual average of 2.2% in 1992–96. A decline in agricultural output of 3.4% in 1996 largely reflected poorer harvests of bananas and nutmeg.

Industry (mining, manufacturing, construction and utilities) provided 19.1% of GDP in 1996, and engaged 22.4% of the employed labour force in 1995. The mining sector accounted for only 0.5% of employment in 1995 and the same percentage of GDP in 1996. However, in that year a US company announced plans to conduct exploration for oil and gas deposits off the southern coast of Grenada. Manufacturing, which contributed 6.8% of GDP in 1996 and employed 7.6% of the working population in 1995, consists mainly of the processing of agricultural products and of cottage industries producing garments and spice-based items. A nutmeg oil distillation plant, which aimed to produce 30 metric tons of oil per year from 300 tons of defective nutmegs, commenced production in 1995. Exports of the oil earned some EC $2m. in that year. Rum is the only significant industrial export, but soft drinks, paints and varnishes, household paper products and the tyre-retreading industries are also important. Manufacturing GDP increased by an average of 1.8% per year in 1992–96; the sector's GDP increased by 7.7% in 1995, and by 5.8% in 1996. Overall, industrial GDP increased by an average of 4.1% annually in 1992–96.

Grenada is dependent upon imports for its energy requirements, and in 1996 mineral fuels, lubricants, etc. accounted for 9.9% of the total cost of imports.

The services sector contributed 71.4% of GDP in 1996. According to the IMF, the hotels and restaurants sector accounted for 7.7% of GDP in 1996. Tourist receipts were estimated to total some EC $161m. in 1996. Since 1984 the number of stop-over arrivals and cruise-ship visitors has more than doubled. Of total stop-over visitors (excluding non-resident Grenadians) in 1996, 33.3% were from the USA, 15.7% from Caribbean countries and 21.5% from the United Kingdom. In 1996 15.7% of all stop-over arrivals were Grenadians resident abroad. The GDP of the services sector increased by an annual average of 2.6% in 1992–96.

In 1996 Grenada recorded a visible trade deficit of EC $331m. and there was a deficit of EC $156m. on the current account of the balance of payments. In 1995 the principal source of imports was the USA, accounting for 41.1% of the total. The United Kingdom is the principal market for exports, taking 22.7% of the total in 1991. The United Kingdom also provided 13.8% of imports in 1991 (and 10.5% of imports in 1995). Trinidad and Tobago provided 20.2% of imports in 1995 and received 13.1% of Grenada's exports in 1991. The principal exports are agricultural, notably nutmeg. The principal imports in 1996 were foodstuffs, machinery and transport equipment, and basic manufactures. The trade deficit is partly offset by earnings from tourism, capital receipts and remittances from Grenadians working abroad.

For 1997 there was a projected current budgetary surplus of EC $8.3m., but an overall deficit of EC $29.9m. Grenada's total external debt was US $112.8m. at the end of 1995, of which US $98.4m. was long-term public debt. In 1993 (when the external debt totalled US $135.5m.) the cost of debt-servicing was equivalent to 6.5% of the value of exports of goods and services. The average annual rate of inflation was 2.7% in 1985–95, and consumer prices increased by 3.0% in 1995 and by 2.0% in 1996. According to government figures, an estimated 14% of the labour force were unemployed at the end of 1997.

Grenada is a member of CARICOM (see p. 119), and secured limited protection for some of its products when tariff barriers within the organization were removed in 1988. It is also a member of the Economic Commission for Latin America and the Caribbean (ECLAC, see p. 29), the Organization of American States (OAS, see p. 219), the Organization of Eastern Caribbean

States (OECS, see p. 122) and is a signatory of the Lomé Conventions between the African, Caribbean and Pacific (ACP) countries and the European Union (see p. 178).

Grenada's economy was severely disrupted by the political troubles and military intervention of the early 1980s. Economic policy subsequently concentrated on the repair and development of infrastructure. However, the Government has been hindered by its sizeable internal and external debts, particularly with the cessation of US budgetary support in 1987. Grenada's economy remains largely dependent upon agriculture, which is vulnerable to adverse weather conditions and infestation by pests. Furthermore, the economy's susceptibility to the fluctuations in international commodity prices was demonstrated in 1990, when the price of nutmeg on the world market decreased by 30%, following the breakdown of Grenada's cartel agreement with Indonesia (signed in 1987). The two countries have since concluded several informal agreements in an attempt to stabilize the world nutmeg market through closer co-operation. The need for further economic diversification has also recently been underscored by the potential loss of preferential access to European markets for banana producers of the ACP countries. The most promising and rapidly expanding sector of the Grenadian economy is tourism, and revenue from tourism increased by some 56% between 1992 and 1996. This growth in the tourism sector has, in turn, stimulated the construction sector, the GDP of which expanded by 11.5% in 1996. Some 5,000 new jobs were expected to be created in tourism and construction in 1998–99. In late 1997, announcing the budget for 1998, Prime Minister Keith Mitchell stated that the aim of his administration was to double Grenada's income per head by 2000, by means of enhanced public and private investment in all sectors. Meanwhile, some 95% of all taxpayers were effectively exempted from personal income tax obligations after April 1996, when the Government raised the income threshold for liability for this tax from EC $10,000 to $60,000 per year. Loss of revenue from personal income tax was to be offset by increases in customs service charges and the elimination of tax exemptions on consumption of electricity and telephone services; efforts to reduce tax evasion were also to be intensified. Growth in GDP of some 5% was forecast for 1998.

Social Welfare

There was no system of social security payments in Grenada prior to 1979. New initiatives launched in that year included the Youth for Reconstruction Programme, to provide basic paramedical services and assistance to the elderly and disabled, a national milk distribution programme and the establishment of community-directed day care centres. A National Insurance Scheme began in 1983, and in 1988 had a total investment portfolio of EC $58m. In 1996 there was one hospital bed for every 290 people and one physician per 1,253 inhabitants. There are six local health centres, all in the main towns. The Ministry of Health also finances free weekly clinics in each district. A mental hospital, destroyed by military action in 1983, was rebuilt with US financial aid. Projected budgetary expenditure on health was EC $27.5m. in 1997 (equivalent to 13.3% of total recurrent expenditure).

Education

Education is free and compulsory for children between the ages of five and 16 years. Primary education begins at five years of age and lasts for seven years. Secondary education, beginning at the age of 12, lasts for a further five years. In 1994 a total of 23,256 children received public primary education in 57 schools. There were 19 public secondary schools, with 7,260 pupils registered, in that year. Technical Centres have been established in St Patrick's, St David's and St John's, and the Grenada National College, the Mirabeau Agricultural School and the Teachers' Training College have been incorporated into the Technical and Vocational Institute in St George's. The Extra-Mural Department of the University of the West Indies has a branch in St George's. A School of Medicine has also been established at St George's and a School of Fishing at Victoria. Projected budgetary expenditure on education was EC $25m. in 1998 (equivalent to 11.5% of total recurrent expenditure).

Public Holidays

1998: 1 January (New Year's Day), 7 February (Independence Day), 10 April (Good Friday), 13 April (Easter Monday), 4 May (for Labour Day), 1 June (Whit Monday), 11 June (Corpus Christi), 3–4 August (Emancipation Holidays), 25 October (Thanksgiving Day), 25–26 December (Christmas).

1999: 1 January (New Year's Day), 7 February (Independence Day), 2 April (Good Friday), 5 April (Easter Monday), 1 May (Labour Day), 24 May (Whit Monday), 3 June (Corpus Christi), 2–3 August (Emancipation Holidays), 25 October (Thanksgiving Day), 25–26 December (Christmas).

Weights and Measures

The metric system is in use.

Statistical Survey

Source (unless otherwise stated): Central Statistical Office, Ministry of Finance, Lagoon Rd, St George's; tel. 440-2731; fax 440-4115.

AREA AND POPULATION

Area: 344.5 sq km (133.0 sq miles).

Population: 89,088 at census of 30 April 1981; 94,806 (males 46,637; females 48,169) at census of 1991 (excluding 537 persons in institutions and 33 persons in the foreign service); 98,600 (official estimate) at mid-1996.

Density (mid-1996): 286.2 per sq km.

Principal Town: St George's (capital), population 4,439 (1991 census).

Births and Deaths (provisional, 1996): Registered live births 2,096 (birth rate 21.3 per 1,000); Registered deaths 782 (death rate 7.9 per 1,000).

Expectation of Life (years at birth, 1996): 78.1.

Employment (employees only, 1995): Agriculture, hunting, forestry and fishing 4,223; Mining and quarrying 126; Manufacturing 1,881; Electricity, gas and water 350; Construction 3,168; Wholesale and retail trade 4,299; Restaurants and hotels 850; Transport, storage and communications 1,614; Financing, insurance, real estate and business services 866; Community, social and personal services 4,980; Other services 1,334; Activities not adequately defined 959; Total employed 24,650 (males 15,194; females 9,456).

AGRICULTURE, ETC.

Principal Crops (FAO estimates, '000 metric tons, 1996): Roots and tubers 4; Pulses 1; Coconuts 7; Vegetables 2; Sugar cane 7; Apples 1; Plums 1; Oranges 1; Grapefruit and pomelos 2; Other citrus fruits 1; Avocados 2; Mangoes 2; Bananas 9; Plantains 1; Other fruits 2; Cocoa beans 2. Source: FAO, *Production Yearbook*.

Official Estimates ('000 lb, 1996): Cocoa beans 4,235; Bananas 4,126; Nutmeg 4,588; Mace 260.

Livestock (FAO estimates, '000 head, year ending September 1996): Cattle 4; Pigs 5; Sheep 13; Goats 7; Asses 1. Source: FAO, *Production Yearbook*.

Livestock Products (FAO estimates, '000 metric tons, 1996): Meat 1; Cows' milk 1; Hen eggs 1. Source: FAO, *Production Yearbook*.

Fishing ('000 lb, live weight): Total catch 4,644.9 in 1993; 3,609.4 in 1994; 3,287.5 in 1995.

INDUSTRY

Production (1994): Rum 3,000 hectolitres; Beer 24,000 hectolitres; Wheat flour 7,000 metric tons; Cigarettes 15m.; Electric energy 87.5 million kWh (1995).

FINANCE

Currency and Exchange Rates: 100 cents = 1 Eastern Caribbean dollar (EC $). *Sterling and US Dollar Equivalents* (30 September

1997): £1 sterling = EC $4.362; US $1 = EC $2.700; EC $100 = £22.93 = US $37.04. *Exchange Rate:* Fixed at US $1 = EC $2.70 since July 1976.

Budget (provisional, EC $ million 1996): *Revenue:* Tax revenue 180.8 (Taxes on income and profits 33.5, Taxes on domestic goods and services 32.3, Taxes on international trade and transactions 109.5); Other current revenue 18.0; Capital revenue 0.3; Total 199.1, excluding grants received (29.5). *Expenditure:* Current expenditure 182.4 (Personal emoluments 97.9, Goods and services 31.6, Interest payments 18.2, Transfers and subsidies 34.6); Capital expenditure 68.6; Total 251.4.

1997 (projections, EC$ million): *Revenue:* Recurrent 208.9; *Expenditure:* Recurrent 206.5; Capital 141.7.

International Reserves (US $ million at 31 December 1996): IMF special drawing rights 0.06; Foreign exchange 35.67; Total 35.73. Source: IMF, *International Financial Statistics*.

Money Supply (EC $ million at 31 December 1996): Currency outside banks 53.18; Demand deposits at deposit money banks 95.26; Total money (incl. others) 148.46. Source: IMF, *International Financial Statistics*.

Cost of Living (Consumer Price Index; base: 1990 = 100): 112.4 in 1994; 115.8 in 1995; 118.1 in 1996. Source: IMF, *International Financial Statistics*.

Expenditure on the Gross Domestic Product (EC $ million at current prices, 1996): Government final consumption expenditure 134.5; Private final consumption expenditure 457.6; Gross capital formation 352.5; *Total domestic expenditure* 944.6; Exports of goods and services, *less* Imports of goods and services −138.5; *GDP in purchasers' values* 806.1. Source: IMF, *Grenada—Recent Economic Developments* (November 1997).

Gross Domestic Product by Economic Activity (EC $ million at constant prices, 1996): Agriculture, hunting, forestry and fishing 55.6; Mining and quarrying 2.7; Manufacturing 39.6; Electricity and water 26.9; Construction 42.0; Wholesale and retail trade 65.0; Restaurants and hotels 44.7; Transport and communications 132.6; Finance and insurance 49.4; Real estate 24.6; Government services 85.2; Other community, social and personal services 15.4; *Sub-total* 583.5; *Less* Imputed bank service charge 38.3; *GDP at factor cost* 545.2. Source: IMF, *Grenada—Recent Economic Developments* (November 1997).

Balance of Payments (EC $ million, 1996): Exports of goods f.o.b. 67.30; Imports of goods f.o.b. -398.25; *Trade balance* −330.95; Exports of services 288.06; Imports of services −123.37; *Balance on goods and services* −166.26; Other income received 11.68; Other income paid −54.10; *Balance on goods, services and income* −208.68; Current transfers received 63.30; Current transfers paid −11.05; *Current balance* −156.43; *Capital account (net)* 79.31; *Direct investment (net)* 48.34; *Portfolio investment (net)* −7.14; *Other investments (net)* 24.98; *Net errors and omissions* 11.54; *Overall balance* 0.60. Source: Eastern Caribbean Central Bank, *Balance of Payments 1997*.

EXTERNAL TRADE

Principal Commodities (US $ million, 1996): *Imports:* Food and live animals 36.4; Crude materials (inedible) except fuels 4.9; Mineral fuels, lubricants, etc. 15.1; Chemicals 12.2; Basic manufactures 29.0; Machinery and transport equipment 33.7; Miscellaneous manufactured articles 17.6; Total (incl. others) 152.2 (excl. unrecorded imports 13.4). *Exports:* Cocoa 2.6; Nutmeg 4.2; Bananas 0.6; Mace 1.0; Fresh fruit and vegetables 0.6; Fish 3.2; Clothing 1.4; Total (incl. others) 19.4 (excl. re-exports 1.6). Source: IMF, *Grenada—Recent Economic Developments* (November 1997).

Principal Trading Partners (EC $ million, 1991): *Imports c.i.f.:* Barbados 11.1; Canada 16.5; Japan 22.3; Trinidad and Tobago 50.3; United Kingdom 43.7; USA 98.9; Total (incl. others) 316.5. *Exports f.o.b.:* Belgium-Luxembourg 3.7; Canada 7.2; Germany 5.9; Netherlands 5.1; Trinidad and Tobago 7.1; United Kingdom 12.3; USA 7.7; Total (incl. others) 54.1.

1995 (EC $ million): *Imports c.i.f.:* Barbados 9.2; Canada 13.8; Japan 11.4; Trinidad and Tobago 70.7; United Kingdom 36.7; USA 143.7; Total (incl. others) 349.7.

TRANSPORT

Road Traffic (1991): Motor vehicles registered 8,262.

Shipping: *Merchant Fleet* (registered at 31 December 1996): 5 vessels (total displacement 887 grt). Source: Lloyd's Register of Shipping, *World Fleet Statistics. International Sea-borne Freight Traffic* (estimates, '000 metric tons, 1995): Goods loaded 21.3; Goods unloaded 193.0. *Ship Arrivals* (1991): 1,254. *Fishing vessels* (registered, 1987): 635.

Civil Aviation (aircraft arrivals, 1995): 11,310.

TOURISM

Visitor Arrivals: 317,645 in 1994; 369,346 in 1995; 386,013 (108,231 stop-overs, 266,982 cruise-ship passengers, 10,800 excursionists) in 1996.

Cruise-ship Calls: 448 in 1995.

Receipts from Tourism (EC $ million): 158.7 in 1994; 155.9 in 1995; 161.1 (147.1 from stop-overs, 13.2 from cruise-ship passengers) in 1996.

COMMUNICATIONS MEDIA

Radio Receivers (1995): 55,000 in use*.

Television Receivers (1995): 32,000 in use*.

Telephones (1994): 21,000 main lines in use†.

Telefax Stations (1992): 272 in use†.

Mobile Cellular Telephones (1994): 350 subscribers†.

Non-Daily Newspapers (1992): 2; circulation (estimate) 5,000*.

* Source: UNESCO, *Statistical Yearbook*.

† Source: UN, *Statistical Yearbook*.

EDUCATION

Pre-primary (1994): 74 schools; 158 teachers; 3,499 pupils.

Primary (1995): 57 schools; 849 teachers; 23,256 pupils.

Secondary (1995): 19 schools; 381 teachers; 7,260 pupils.

Higher (excluding figures for the Grenada Teachers' College, 1993): 66 teachers; 651 students.

Directory

The Constitution

The 1974 independence Constitution was suspended in March 1979, following the coup, and almost entirely restored between November 1983, after the overthrow of the Revolutionary Military Council, and the elections of December 1984. The main provisions of this Constitution are summarized below:

The Head of State is the British monarch, represented in Grenada by an appointed Governor-General. Legislative power is vested in the bicameral Parliament, comprising a Senate and a House of Representatives. The Senate consists of 13 Senators, seven of whom are appointed on the advice of the Prime Minister, three on the advice of the Leader of the Opposition and three on the advice of the Prime Minister after he has consulted interests which he considers Senators should be selected to represent. The Constitution does not specify the number of members of the House of Representatives, but the country consists of 15 single-member constituencies, for which representatives are elected for up to five years, on the basis of universal adult suffrage.

The Cabinet consists of a Prime Minister, who must be a member of the House of Representatives, and such other ministers as the Governor-General may appoint on the advice of the Prime Minister.

There is a Supreme Court and, in certain cases, a further appeal lies to Her Majesty in Council.

The Government

Head of State: HM Queen ELIZABETH II (succeeded to the throne 6 February 1952).

Governor-General: Sir DANIEL WILLIAMS (appointed 8 August 1996).

THE CABINET
(February 1998)

Prime Minister and Minister of Finance, External Affairs, Information and National Security: Dr KEITH MITCHELL.

Minister of Health, Housing and the Environment: Sen. ROGER RADIX.

Minister of Education: Sen. LAWRENCE JOSEPH.

Minister of Youth, Sports, Culture and Community Development: ADRIAN MITCHELL.

Minister of Agriculture, Forestry, Fisheries and Lands: MARK ISAACS.

Minister of Labour, Legal Affairs, Local Government, CARICOM Affairs and Political Unification: RAPHAEL FLETCHER.

Minister of Tourism and Civil Aviation: Sen. JOSLYN WHITEMAN.

Minister of Women's Affairs, Co-operatives and Social Security: LORRAINE WALDRON.

Minister of Communications, Works and Public Utilities: Sen. GREGORY BOWEN.

Minister of State for Finance: Sen. PATRICK BUBB.

Minister of State for Agriculture, Forestry, Fisheries and Lands: MICHAEL BAPTISTE.

Minister of State for Youth, Sports, Culture and Community Development: WILLIAM DEWSBURY.

Minister of State for Works: OLIVER ARCHIBALD.

MINISTRIES

All ministries are in St George's.

Office of the Governor-General: Government House, St George's; tel. 440-2401.

Office of the Prime Minister: The Carenage, St George's; tel. 440-2255; telex 3423; fax 440-4116.

Ministry of Agriculture, Forestry, Fisheries and Lands: Mt Wheldale, St George's; tel. 440-3078; fax 440-4191.

Ministry of Finance: Lagoon Rd, St George's; tel. 440-2731; fax 440-4115.

Legislature

PARLIAMENT

Houses of Parliament: Church St, St George's; tel. 440-2090; fax 440-4138.

Senate

President: Sen. Dr JOHN WATTS.

There are 13 appointed members.

House of Representatives

Speaker: Sir CURTIS STRACHAN.

General Election, 20 June 1995

	Votes	%	Seats
New National Party (NNP)	14,195	32.7	8
National Democratic Congress (NDC)	13,504	31.1	5
Grenada United Labour Party (GULP)	11,643	26.8	2
Others	4,063	9.4	–
Total	43,405	100.0	15

Political Organizations

Democratic Labour Party (DLP): St George's; f. 1995 by former member of the NDC; Leader Dr FRANCIS ALEXIS; Deputy Leader WAYNE FRANCIS.

Grenada Progressive Party: f. 1997; Leader PRESCOTT WILLIAMS.

Grenada United Labour Party (GULP): St George's; f. 1950; right-wing; Gen. Sec. JOSEPH MCGUIRE; Leader (vacant).

Maurice Bishop Patriotic Movement (MBPM): St George's; f. 1984 by former members of the New Jewel Movement; socialist; Leader TERRENCE MARRYSHOW.

National Democratic Congress (NDC): St George's; tel. 440-3769; f. 1987 by former members of the NNP and merger of Democratic Labour Congress and Grenada Democratic Labour Party; centrist; Chair. KENNY LALSINGH; Leader GEORGE BRIZAN.

The National Party (TNP): St George's; f. 1989 by Prime Minister Herbert Blaize and his supporters, following a split in the New National Party; Chair. GEORGE MCGUIRE; Leader BEN JONES.

New National Party (NNP): St George's; f. 1984; merger of Grenada Democratic Movement, Grenada National Party and National Democratic Party; centrist; Chair. LAWRENCE JOSEPH; Leader Dr KEITH MITCHELL; Dep. Leader GREGORY BOWEN.

United Republican Party (URP): St George's; f. 1993 by Grenadians residing in New York, USA; Leader ANTONIO LANGDON.

Diplomatic Representation

EMBASSIES AND HIGH COMMISSION IN GRENADA

China (Taiwan): Archibald Ave, POB 36, St George's; tel. 440-3054; Ambassador: HSU CHI-MING.

United Kingdom: British High Commission, 14 Church St, St George's; tel. 440-3222; fax 440-4939 (High Commissioner resident in Barbados).

Venezuela: Archibald Ave, POB 201, St George's; tel. 440-1721; fax 440-6657; Ambassador: TEOFILO LABRADOR.

Judicial System

Justice is administered by the West Indies Associated States Supreme Court, composed of a High Court of Justice and a Court of Appeal. The Court of Magisterial Appeals is presided over by the Chief Justice. The Itinerant Court of Appeal consists of three judges and sits three times a year; it hears appeals from the High Court and the Magistrates' Court. The Magistrates' Court administers summary jurisdiction.

In 1988 the OECS excluded the possibility of Grenada' s readmittance to the East Caribbean court system until after the conclusion of appeals by the defendants in the Maurice Bishop murder trial (see Recent History). Following the conclusion of the case in 1991, Parliament voted to rejoin the system, thus also restoring the right of appeal to the Privy Council in the United Kingdom.

Attorney-General: ERROL THOMAS.

Puisne Judges: STANLEY MOORE, LYLE K. ST PAUL.

Registrar of the Supreme Court: GAIL CHARLES (acting).

President of the Court of Appeal: Sir VINCENT FLOISSAC.

Office of the Attorney-General: St George's; tel. 440-2050.

Religion

CHRISTIANITY

The Roman Catholic Church

Grenada comprises a single diocese, suffragan to the archdiocese of Castries (Saint Lucia). The Bishop participates in the Antilles Episcopal Conference (based in Port of Spain, Trinidad and Tobago). At 31 December 1995 there were an estimated 53,721 adherents in the diocese.

Bishop of St George's in Grenada: Rt Rev. SYDNEY ANICETUS CHARLES, Bishop's House, Morne Jaloux, POB 375, St George's; tel. 443-5299; fax 443-5758.

The Anglican Communion

Anglicans in Grenada are adherents of the Church in the Province of the West Indies, and represented 14% of the population at the time of the 1991 census. The country forms part of the diocese of the Windward Islands (the Bishop, the Rt Rev. SEHON GOODRIDGE, resides in Kingstown, Saint Vincent).

Other Christian Churches

The Presbyterian, Methodist, Plymouth Brethren, Baptist, Salvation Army, Jehovah's Witness, Pentecostal (7.2% of the population in 1991) and Seventh-day Adventist (8.5%) faiths are also represented.

The Press

NEWSPAPERS

Bernacle: Tyrell St, St George's; tel. 440-5151; monthly; Editor IAN GEORGE.

Business Eye: Young St, St George's; tel. 440-3425.

Grenada Guardian: Upper Lucas St, St George's; tel. 444-3823; fax 444-2873; weekly; organ of GULP.

The Grenada Times: Market Hill, POB 622, St George's; tel. 440-1530; fax 440-4117; weekly; Editor JEROME MCBARNETT.

Grenada Today: St John's St, POB 142, St George's; tel. 440-4401; weekly; Editor GEORGE WORME.

Grenadian Front Line: Grenville St, St George's; tel. 440-9704.

The Grenadian Voice: Melville St, POB 3, St George's; tel. 440-1498; fax 440-4117; weekly; Editor LESLIE PIERRE.

Government Gazette: St George's; weekly; official.

The Informer: Market Hill, POB 622, St George's; tel. 440-1530; fax 440-4119; f. 1985; weekly; Editor CARLA BRIGGS; circ. 6,500.

PRESS ASSOCIATION

Press Association of Grenada: St George's; f. 1986; Pres. LESLIE PIERRE.

Inter Press Service (IPS) (Italy) is also represented.

Publishers

Anansi Publications: Hillsborough St, St George's; tel. 440-3713.

Grenada Publishers Ltd: Torchlight, Melville St, St George's; tel. 440-2305.

Warren Associates Publishing: POB 675, St George's; tel. 444-3930.

West Indian Publishing Co Ltd: Hillsborough St, St George's; tel. 440-2118; govt-owned.

Broadcasting and Communications

TELECOMMUNICATIONS

Grenada Telecommunications Ltd (Grentel): POB 119, St George's; tel. 444-2202; telex 3438; fax 444-4848; Gen. Man. NEVILLE CALLISTE.

BROADCASTING

Grenada Broadcasting Corporation: Observatory Rd, POB 535, St George's; tel. 440-3033; fax 440-4180; f. 1972; name changed in 1979, 1983, 1984 and 1991; govt-owned; Chair. JOSEPH CHARTER; Gen. Man. CECIL BENJAMIN.

Radio

Spice Capitol Radio FM 90: Springs, St George's; tel. 440-0162.

The Harbour Light of the Windwards: Carriacou; tel. and fax 443-7628; Station Man. RANDY CORNELIUS; Chief Engineer JOHN McPHERSON.

Grenada Broadcasting Corporation Television: Morne Jaloux, St. George's; tel. 444-5522; fax 444-5054; Programme Dir ANDRÉ JEROME.

Television

Television programmes from Trinidad and from Barbados can be received on the island.

Finance

(cap. = capital; res = reserves; dep. = deposits; amounts in Eastern Caribbean dollars)

The Eastern Caribbean Central Bank (see p. 122), based in Saint Christopher, is the central issuing and monetary authority for Grenada.

Eastern Caribbean Central Bank—Grenada Office: NIS Bldg, Melville St, St George's; tel. 440-3016; fax 440-6721.

BANKING

Grenada Bank of Commerce Ltd: Corner of Cross and Halifax Sts, POB 4, St George's; tel. 440-3521; telex 3467; fax 440-4153; f. 1983; cap. 7.4m., res 7.4m., dep. 124.0m. (Dec. 1993); Chair. BYRON CAMPBELL; Man. MORRIS MATHLIN.

Grenada Co-operative Bank Ltd: 8 Church St, POB 135, St George's; tel. 440-2111; f. 1932; Man. Dir and Sec. G. V. STEELE; brs in St Andrew's and St Patrick's.

Grenada Development Bank: Halifax St, St George's; tel. 440-2382; fax 440-6610; f. 1976, following merger; Chair. ARNOLD CRUICKSHANK; Man. LUCIA LIVINGSTON-ANDALL.

National Commercial Bank of Grenada Ltd: Corner of Halifax and Hillsborough Sts, POB 57, St George's; tel. 440-3566; telex 3413; fax 440-4140; f. 1979; 51% owned by Republic Bank of Trinidad and Tobago, 39% publicly-owned, 10% govt-owned; cap. 7.5m., res 3.8m., dep. 0.1m. (Sept. 1994); Gen. Man. MICHAEL B. ARCHIBALD; Dep. Gen. Man. DANIEL A. ROBERTS; 1 br.

Foreign Banks

Bank of Nova Scotia (Canada): Granby and Halifax Sts, POB 194, St George's; tel. 440-3274; telex 3452; fax 440-4173; Man. LAWRENCE AQUI; 3 brs.

Barclays Bank PLC (UK): Church and Halifax Sts, POB 37, St George's; tel. 440-3232; telex 3421; fax 440-4103; Man. G. C. COMISSIONG; 3 sub-brs in Carriacou, Grenville and Grand Anse.

Caribbean Commercial Bank (Trinidad and Tobago): St George's; 1 br.

INSURANCE

Several foreign insurance companies operate in Grenada and the other islands of the group. Principal locally-owned companies include the following:

Grenada Insurance and Finance Co Ltd: Young St, POB 139, St George's; tel. 440-3004.

Grenada Motor and General Insurance Co Ltd: Scott St, St George's; tel. 440-3379.

Grenadian General Insurance Co Ltd: Corner of Young and Scott Sts, POB 47, St George's; tel. 440-2434; fax 440-6618.

Trade and Industry

CHAMBERS OF COMMERCE

Grenada Chamber of Industry and Commerce, Inc: DeCaul Bldg, Mt Gay, POB 129, St George's; tel. 440-2937; fax 440-6627; e-mail gcic@carib.surf.com; f. 1921, incorporated 1947; 180 mems; Pres. DARYL BRATHWAITE; Exec. Dir CHRISTOPHER DERIGGS.

Grenada Manufacturing Council: POB 129, St George's; tel. 440-2937; fax 440-6627; f. 1991 to replace Grenada Manufacturers' Asscn; Chair. CHRISTOPHER DEALLIE.

INDUSTRIAL AND TRADE ASSOCIATIONS

Grenada Cocoa Association: Scott St, St George's; tel. 440-2933; telex 3444; fax 440-1470; f. 1987, following merger; changed from co-operative to shareholding structure in late 1996; Chair. LAWRENCE GRENADE; Gen. Man. CARL PHILLIPS (acting).

Grenada Co-operative Banana Society: Scott St, St George's; tel. 440-2486; fax 440-4199; f. 1955; a statutory body to control production and marketing of bananas.

Grenada Co-operative Nutmeg Association: POB 160, St George's; tel. 440-2117; telex 3454; fax 440-6602; f. 1947; processes and markets all the nutmeg and mace grown on the island; Chair. CLIFFORD ROBERTSON; Sec. ALFRED LOGIE.

Grenada Industrial Development Corporation: Frequente Industrial Park, St George's; tel. 444-1035; fax 444-4828; f. 1985; Chair. RUPERT AGOSTINI; Man. ANTHONY BOATSWAIN.

Marketing and National Importing Board: Young St, St George's; tel. 440-3191; fax 440-4152; f. 1974; govt-owned; imports basic food items, incl. sugar, rice and milk; Chair. AARON MOSES; Gen. Man. FITZROY JAMES.

EMPLOYERS' ORGANIZATION

Grenada Employers' Federation: Mt Gay, POB 129, St George's; tel. 440-1832.

There are several marketing and trading co-operatives, mainly in the agricultural sector.

UTILITIES

Public Utilities Commission: St George's.

Electricity

Grenada Electricity Services Ltd (Grenlec): POB 381, St George's; 90% privately-owned, 10% govt-owned; tel. 440-2097; fax 440-4106; Gen. Man. NIGEL D. WARDLE; Chair. G. ROBERT BLANCHARD.

TRADE UNIONS

Grenada Trade Union Council (GTUC): Green St, POB 405, St George's; tel 440-3733; Pres. C. ERIC PIERRE; Gen. Sec. CLARIS CHARLES.

Commercial and Industrial Workers' Union: Bains Alley, St George's; tel. 440-3423; 492 mems; Pres. A. DE BOURG.

Grenada Union of Teachers (GUT): Marine Villa, St George's; f. 1913; Pres. CLARIS CHARLES; 1,300 mems.

Seamen and Waterfront Workers' Union: The Carenage, POB 154, St George's; tel. 440-2573; f. 1952; Pres. ALBERT JULIEN; Gen. Sec. ERIC PIERRE; 350 mems.

Technical and Allied Workers' Union (TAWU): Green St, POB 405, St George's; tel. 440-2231; fax 440-5878; f. 1958; Pres. Sen. CHESTER HUMPHREY.

Bank and General Workers' Union (BGWU): St George's; tel. 440-3563; Pres. DEREK ALLARD.

Grenada Manual, Maritime and Intellectual Workers' Union (GMMIWU): St George's; Pres. (vacant); Vice-Pres. RAYMOND ANTHONY.

Grenada Media Workers' Association: St George's; Pres. RAY ROBERTS.

Public Workers' Union (PWU): POB 420, St George's; tel. 440-2203; f. 1931; Pres. LAURET CLARKSON; Exec. Sec. ALVIN ST JOHN.

Transport

RAILWAYS

There are no railways in Grenada.

ROADS

In 1991 there were approximately 1,127 km (700 miles) of roads, more than half of which were suitable for motor traffic. Public transport is provided by small private operators, with a system covering the entire country. In 1996 a concessionary loan worth some US $29m. was secured from the Government of Japan for a project to improve the road between St George's and St Andrew's.

SHIPPING

The main port is St George's, with accommodation for two ocean-going vessels of up to 500 ft. A number of shipping lines call at St George's. Grenville, on Grenada, and Hillsborough, on Carriacou, are used mostly by small craft.

Grenada Ports Authority: St George's; tel. 440-7678; telex 3418; fax 440-3418; e-mail grenport@caribsurf.com.

CIVIL AVIATION

The Point Salines International Airport, 10 km (6 miles) from St George's, was opened in October 1984, and has scheduled flights to most East Caribbean destinations, including Venezuela, and to the United Kingdom and North America. There is an airfield at Pearls, 30 km (18 miles) from St George's, and Lauriston Airport, on the island of Carriacou, offers regular scheduled services to Grenada, Saint Vincent and Palm Island (Grenadines of Saint Vincent).

Grenada is a shareholder in the regional airline, LIAT (see under Antigua and Barbuda). In 1987 Air Antilles (based in Saint Lucia) was designated as the national carrier.

Grenada Airports Authority: Point Salines Int. Airport, POB 385, St George's; f. 1985; tel. 444-4101; fax 444-4838.

Tourism

Grenada has the attractions of both white sandy beaches and a scenic, mountainous interior with an extensive rain forest. There are also sites of historical interest, and the capital, St George's, is a noted beauty spot. In 1996 there were 386,013 tourist arrivals, of which 266,982 were cruise-ship passengers, and tourism earned some EC $161m. There were approximately 1,670 hotel rooms in 1996. In 1997 a joint venture between the Government of Grenada and the Caribbean Development Bank to upgrade and market some 50 unprofitable hotels in Grenada was implemented. In addition, the Ministry of Tourism, in conjunction with the Board of Tourism and the Hotel Association, announced a 10-year development plan to increase hotel capacity from its present level to 2,500 rooms.

Grenada Board of Tourism: POB 293, St George's; tel. 440-2001; fax 440-6637; Chair. Sir PAUL SCOON; Dir of Tourism NIGEL GRAVESANDE.

Grenada Hotel Association: POB 440, St George's; tel. 444-1353; fax 444-4847; f. 1961; Pres. LEO GARBUTT; Exec. Dir RUSSELL ANTOINE.

GUATEMALA

Introductory Survey

Location, Climate, Language, Religion, Flag, Capital

The Republic of Guatemala lies in the Central American isthmus, bounded to the north and west by Mexico, with Honduras and Belize to the east and El Salvador to the south. It has a long coastline on the Pacific Ocean and a narrow outlet to the Caribbean Sea. The climate is tropical in the lowlands, with an average temperature of 28°C (83°F), and more temperate in the central highland area, with an average temperature of 20°C (68°F). The official language is Spanish, but more than 20 indigenous languages are also spoken. Almost all of the inhabitants profess Christianity: the majority are Roman Catholics, while about 20% are Protestants. The national flag (proportions 8 by 5) has three equal vertical stripes, of blue, white and blue, with the national coat of arms (depicting a quetzal, the 'bird of freedom', and a scroll, superimposed on crossed rifles and sabres, encircled by a wreath) in the centre of the white stripe. The capital is Guatemala City.

Recent History

Under Spanish colonial rule, Guatemala was part of the Viceroyalty of New Spain. Independence was obtained from Spain in 1821, from Mexico in 1824 and from the Federation of Central American States in 1838. Subsequent attempts to revive the Federation failed and, under a series of dictators, there was relative stability, tempered by periods of disruption. A programme of social reform was begun by Juan José Arévalo (President in 1944–50) and his successor, Col Jacobo Arbenz Guzmán, whose policy of land reform evoked strong opposition from landowners. In 1954 President Arbenz was overthrown in a coup led by Col Carlos Castillo Armas, who invaded the country with US assistance. Castillo became President but was assassinated in July 1957. The next elected President, Gen. Miguel Ydigoras Fuentes, took office in March 1958 and ruled until he was deposed in March 1963 by a military coup, led by Col Enrique Peralta Azurdia. He assumed full powers as Chief of Government, suspended the Constitution and dissolved the legislature. A Constituent Assembly, elected in 1964, introduced a new Constitution in 1965. Dr Julio César Méndez Montenegro was elected President in 1966, and in 1970 the candidate of the Movimiento de Liberación Nacional (MLN), Col (later Gen.) Carlos Araña Osorio, was elected President. Despite charges of fraud in the elections of March 1974, Gen. Kjell Laugerud García of the MLN took office as President in July.

President Laugerud sought to discourage extreme right-wing violence and claimed some success, although in September 1979 Amnesty International estimated the number of lives lost in political violence since 1970 at 50,000–60,000. In March 1978 Gen. Fernando Romeo Lucas García was elected President. The guerrilla movement increased in strength in 1980–1981, while the Government was accused of the murder and torture of civilians and, particularly, persecution of the country's indigenous Indian inhabitants, who comprise 60% of the population.

In the presidential and congressional elections of 7 March 1982, from which the left-wing parties were absent, the largest number of votes was awarded to the Government's candidate, Gen. Angel Aníbal Guevara, who was later confirmed as President by Congress. The other presidential candidates denounced the elections as fraudulent. Guevara was prevented from taking office in July by a coup on 23 March, in which a group of young right-wing military officers installed Gen. José Efraín Ríos Montt (a candidate in the 1974 presidential elections) as leader of a three-man junta. Congress was closed, and the Constitution and political parties suspended. In June Gen. Ríos Montt dissolved the junta and assumed the presidency. He attempted to fight corruption, reorganized the judicial system and disbanded the secret police. The number of violent deaths diminished. However, after initially gaining the support of the national university, the Roman Catholic Church and the labour unions and hoping to enter into dialogue with the guerrillas, who refused to respond to an amnesty declaration in June, President Ríos Montt declared a state of siege, and imposed censorship of the press, in July. In addition, the war against the guerrillas intensified, and a civil defence force of Indians was established. The efficiency and ruthlessness of the army increased. Whole villages were burnt, and many inhabitants killed, in order to deter the Indians from supporting the guerrillas. President Ríos Montt's increasingly corporatist policies alienated all groups, and his fragile hold on power was threatened in 1982 by several attempted coups, which he managed to forestall.

The US administration was eager to renew sales of armaments and the provision of economic and military aid to Guatemala, which had been suspended in 1977 as a result of serious violations of human rights. In January 1983 the US Government, satisfied that there had been a significant decrease in such violations during Gen. Ríos Montt's presidency, announced the resumption of arms sales to Guatemala. However, independent reports claimed that the situation had deteriorated, and revealed that 2,600 people had been killed during the first six months of President Ríos Montt's rule. An estimated 100,000 refugees fled to Mexico during early 1983, and relations between Guatemala and Mexico were strained, following further incursions into Mexican territory by Guatemalan security forces, which resulted in the deaths of several refugees. In March the army was implicated in the massacre of 300 Indian peasants at Nahulá, and there was a resurgence in the activity of both left- and right-wing 'death squads'. The President declared a 30-day amnesty for guerrillas and political exiles, and lifted the state of siege which had been imposed in July 1982. Furthermore, he announced the creation of an electoral tribunal to organize and oversee a proposed transfer from military rule to civilian government. In April the army launched a new offensive, which made significant gains against the guerrillas. In response, the Unidad Revolucionaria Nacional Guatemalteca (URNG), the main guerrilla grouping (formed in February 1982 in a new initiative seeking to end repression by the Government), announced a major change in tactics, which gave priority to attacks on economic targets instead of to direct confrontation with the army. The Government's pacification programme comprised three phases of aid programmes, combined with the saturation of the countryside by anti-guerrilla units. The 'guns and beans' policy provided food and medicine in exchange for recruitment to the Patrullas de Autodefensa Civil (PAC), a pro-Government peasant militia. (By 1985 these self-defence patrols numbered 900,000 men.) The 'roofs, bread and work' phase involved the development of 'model villages', and the 'Aid Programme for Areas in Conflict' was an ambitious rural development scheme.

By June 1983 opposition to the President was widespread, and several attempted coups were reported. On 29 June the air force and four army garrisons rebelled against the President. They demanded a return to constitutional rule and the dismissal of the President's advisers. Gen. Ríos Montt agreed to both demands but remained unconvincing on the issue of electoral reform. On 8 August Gen. Oscar Humberto Mejía Victores, the Minister of Defence, led a successful coup against President Ríos Montt.

The new President announced the abolition of the secret tribunals and ended press censorship. A 90-day amnesty for guerrillas was announced in October 1983. The amnesty was extended throughout 1984. Urban and rural terrorism continued to escalate, however, and in November 1983 the Government was accused of directing a campaign of kidnappings against the Roman Catholic Church. Following the murder in northern Guatemala of six workers from the US Agency for International Development, the US House of Representatives suspended the US $50m. in aid which President Reagan had requested for Guatemala in 1984. Israel continued to supply weapons to Guatemala, and Israeli military advisers were reported to be active in the country. In October 1983 Gen. Mejía Victores acted to strengthen his position after rumours of his unpopularity among high-ranking officers. Supporters of Gen. Ríos Montt were sent into exile, and in January 1984 new army reforms were introduced. In accordance with the President's assurance of electoral reform, elections for a Constituent Assembly were scheduled for July 1984. Contrary to public forecasts, the centre groups, including the newly formed Unión del Centro Nacional

(UCN), obtained the greatest number of votes at the election. Under the system of proportional representation, however, the right-wing coalition of the MLN and the Central Auténtica Nacionalista (CAN) together obtained a majority of seats in the Assembly. In August a directive board, composed of representatives from the three major political parties, began drafting a new constitution.

In 1984 the Government continued to develop its controversial strategy of 'model villages', which entailed the construction of new settlements in isolated locations for Indian communities. Relations with neighbouring Mexico deteriorated in 1984, following an attack in April on a Guatemalan refugee camp situated in Mexico, during which six people were killed. By August the Organización del Pueblo en Armas (ORPA) had emerged as the most active of the guerrilla groups, operating in San Marcos and Quezaltenango.

Guatemala's new Constitution was promulgated in May 1985. In June President Mejía Victores confirmed that elections for the presidency, the National Congress and 331 mayoralties would be held in November. Prior to the elections, there was a substantial increase in rebel activity and political assassinations by 'death squads'. However, the principal threat to internal security before the elections occurred in September, when violent protests, led by students and trade unionists, erupted in reaction to a series of price increases which had been authorized by the Government in August. During the protests, several people were reported to have been killed and hundreds of demonstrators were arrested.

Eight candidates participated in the presidential election in November 1985, but the main contest was between Jorge Carpio Nicolle, the candidate of the UCN, and Mario Vinicio Cerezo Arévalo, the candidate of the Partido Democracia Cristiana Guatemalteca (PDCG). As neither of the leading candidates obtained the requisite majority, a second round of voting was held in December, when Cerezo secured 68% of the votes cast. The PDCG formed the majority party in the new National Congress and won the largest proportion of mayoralties. Cerezo was believed to enjoy the support of the US administration, which increased its allocation of economic aid and resumed military aid to Guatemala, in support of the new civilian Government.

Immediately prior to the transfer of power in January 1986, the outgoing military Government decreed a general amnesty to encompass those suspected of involvement in abuses of human rights since March 1982. In February 1986, however, in an attempt to curb the continuing violence and to improve the country's bad record for the observance of human rights, the Department of Technical Investigations, which had been accused of numerous kidnappings and murders of citizens, was dissolved and replaced by a new criminal investigations unit. Cerezo's action was welcomed by the Grupo de Apoyo Mutuo (GAM), a grouping of the relatives of victims of repression, and by Amnesty International. Violence continued unabated, however, with 700 killings reported in the first six months of 1986 alone. President Cerezo claimed that not all murders were politically motivated, while his relations with the armed forces remained precarious. Meanwhile, the GAM attracted increasing support, and in August about 3,000 demonstrators took part in a protest to demand information on the fate of the thousands of *'desaparecidos'* ('disappeared'). In April 1987 the creation of a government commission to investigate disappearances was announced, and in May Amnesty International appealed to the President to fulfil his pledge to investigate abuses of human rights. Nevertheless, by mid-1988 there were frequent reports of torture and killings by right-wing 'death squads' as discontent with the Government's liberal policies increased. In September 1989 the Consejo Nacional de Desplazados de Guatemala (CONDEG) was created to represent the 1m. refugees who had fled their homes since 1980. A report to the UN Commission for Human Rights in January 1990 stated that killings and disappearances were on the increase and that almost 3,000 complaints of human rights abuses had been lodged in 1989.

In June 1987 Guatemala was the venue for a meeting of Central American Presidents to discuss a peace proposal for the region. The country was a signatory of the agreed peace plan, signed in Guatemala City in August by the Presidents of Costa Rica, El Salvador, Guatemala, Honduras and Nicaragua. Although the plan was principally concerned with the conflicts in Nicaragua and El Salvador, it also referred to the long-standing guerrilla war in Guatemala. Subsequently, a Commission of National Reconciliation (CNR) was formed in compliance with the terms of the accord. In October representatives of the Guatemalan Government and URNG guerrillas met in Spain to discuss the question of peace in Guatemala. Although the negotiations ended without agreement, the two sides did not exclude the possibility of holding further talks. In December it was announced that an extreme right-wing coup attempt against President Cerezo had been foiled. Right-wing pressure on the Government forced President Cerezo to postpone negotiations with the URNG, scheduled for March 1988. In May a further attempted coup, involving both civilians and members of the army, was foiled without incident, but led to a further postponement of negotiations with the URNG. Despite evident right-wing opposition to the policies of President Cerezo, the PDCG won 140 mayoralties out of 272 at municipal elections held in April. These were Guatemala's first elections in which voting was not compulsory, and, consequently, the level of participation was low (only an estimated 40% of the electorate). Despite his party's success, President Cerezo remained wary of discontent within the army. After another coup plot was discovered in July, President Cerezo rejected the URNG's proposal for a truce.

During 1989 the political situation in Guatemala became more unstable, as guerrilla activity by groups from both the right and the left intensified. In January a new leftist group emerged, the Comando Urbano Revolucionario, which joined the URNG guerrillas. Meanwhile, President Cerezo continued to refuse to negotiate with the URNG for as long as its members remained armed. In September the URNG made further proposals for negotiations, following the signing of the Tela Agreement (the Central American peace plan accord, see p. 1027), but the Guatemalan President adhered firmly to his conditions, and negotiations were again postponed.

In May 1989 a group of retired and active military officers attempted to stage a coup. However, the Government drew upon support within the army, and was able to foil the attempt without bloodshed. Nevertheless, there was growing discontent with government policies, as was reflected by a protracted strike by teachers in support of demands for increased pay. The strike, which began in late May, was supported by a series of one-day strikes by other public-sector workers. In August the dispute erupted into violent confrontations between demonstrators and the security forces; these ended when an agreement was finally reached later that month.

During August and September 1989 a secret right-wing military organization perpetrated a series of terrorist attacks in an attempt to destabilize the Government. At the same time, the ruling party was undergoing a political crisis, following its internal presidential primary elections in August. The PDCG's choice of presidential candidate had been split between Alfonso Cabrera Hidalgo, the party's Secretary-General and former Minister of Foreign Affairs, and René de León Schlotter, the leader of the party's left wing and Minister of Urban and Rural Development. The most likely compromise candidate, Danilo Barillas, had been assassinated a short while before the selection procedure, allegedly by the extreme right, which, by provoking disunity within the PDCG, hoped to give an advantage to its own candidates. In November the former military ruler, Gen. José Efraín Ríos Montt, presented his candidacy for the presidential election that was to take place one year later. He was supported by the moderate Partido Institucional Democrático (PID) and the Frente de Unidad Nacional (FUN).

During 1989 many political figures and labour leaders fled the country after receiving death threats from paramilitary groups. In December the Government launched a major counter-insurgency operation to combat an escalation in guerrilla activity. In the same month, President Cerezo accused the ruling party in El Salvador of supplying weapons to the right-wing death squads of Guatemala.

In August 1989 President Cerezo and the President of Mexico held a meeting, aimed at resolving the refugee problem and at establishing collaboration against drug-trafficking in the region. As Mexico had begun implementing measures to combat the problem of drug-trafficking within its borders, with some success, Guatemala was consequently developing as a new centre for heroin production and cocaine transhipments from Central America to the USA. In 1988 and 1989 the production of opium poppies had become widespread. Local efforts to confront the problem were largely ineffective, and a US $1m. programme dedicated mainly to the aerial spraying of poppy fields, financed by the USA, was hampered by ground-level retaliatory attacks.

Relations between Guatemala and the USA deteriorated considerably in 1990. In March the US ambassador was recalled, in protest at President Cerezo's continued failure to curb the growing incidence of violations of human rights in Guatemala. In June Michael Devine, a US citizen and long-standing resident of Guatemala, was discovered to have been murdered. In December the USA suspended US $2.8m. in military aid, owing to the Guatemalan Government's initial failure to bring the perpetrators to justice; six members of the security forces were later convicted of the murder.

Despite President Cerezo's promise to restrict the unlawful activities of the armed forces and right-wing death squads, the number of politically-motivated assassinations and 'disappearances' escalated in 1990. Among those murdered was a leader of the human rights organization GAM, Oscar Augusto Miranda.

In March 1990 the URNG and the CNR began discussions in Oslo, Norway, with a view to resolving the problem of reincorporating the armed movements into the country's political process. In June representatives of the CNR and of nine political parties, including the ruling PDCG, met for further talks with the URNG in Madrid, Spain. As a result of these negotiations, the URNG pledged not to disrupt the presidential and legislative elections scheduled for November, and agreed to participate in a constituent assembly to reform the Guatemalan Constitution.

In the period preceding the presidential, congressional and municipal elections of November 1990, Gen. José Efraín Ríos Montt secured considerable public support in his attempt to regain the presidency. However, in October he finally lost a protracted struggle with the courts, and his candidacy was declared invalid on constitutional grounds. Under the Constitution, anyone taking part in, or benefiting from, a military coup was disqualified from participating in elections. As none of the presidential candidates obtained an absolute majority in November, a second ballot took place on 6 January 1991, with voters choosing between the two leading candidates, Jorge Serrano Elías of the Movimiento de Acción Solidaria (MAS), a former member of the 1982 Ríos Montt Government, who secured the support of right-wing opinion which had backed Gen. Ríos Montt until his disqualification, and Jorge Carpio Nicolle of the UCN. Serrano received 68% of the votes cast. The MAS failed to secure a majority in Congress, however, winning only 18 of the 116 contested seats. In an effort to offset the imbalance in Congress, Serrano invited members of the Plan por el Adelantamiento Nacional (PAN) and the Partido Socialista Democrático (PSD) to participate in the formation of a coalition Government.

In April 1991 a fresh round of direct talks between the URNG and the Government was begun in Mexico City. The initial meeting, which was presided over by the President of the CNR, resulted in an agreement on negotiating procedures and an agenda for further talks with a view to ending the conflict. However, in an attempt to destabilize the Government's efforts at national reconciliation, members of the state security forces, believed to be acting independently of their superiors, launched a campaign of violence, directing death threats against leaders of trade unions and human rights organizations, and murdering a PSD politician. These actions indicated a clear division within the military between those favouring a negotiated settlement and those regarding the talks merely as a political platform for the rebels. The failure of further peace talks to produce any agreement prompted President Serrano to reshuffle the military high command in December, replacing the Minister of National Defence, Gen. Luis Mendoza, with the more moderate Gen. José Domingo García Samayoa, in an attempt to facilitate a settlement with the guerrillas.

Apparent attempts by the Government to exert control over the security forces, in an effort to combat human rights abuses in Guatemala, resulted in the unprecedented conviction and sentencing (for terms of imprisonment of between 10 and 15 years), in March 1991, of four policemen for the murder of a homeless street child. Owing to a legal technicality, the convictions were overturned. (However, following a retrial the four were convicted in April 1992 for terms of between 12 and 18 years.) In August 1991, in a further unprecedented move, seven military personnel were arrested by the army on suspicion of having murdered 11 peasants in the Department of Escuintla. In the same month the human rights group GAM secured a commitment from Congress to create a special commission to investigate past human rights abuses. In late 1991 the ombudsman, Ramiro de León Carpio, secured the resignation of the Director of the National Police, Col. Mario Enrique Paíz Bolanos, who was alleged to be responsible for the use of torture.

Renewed talks between the Government and the URNG, which took place in Mexico City in February 1992, focused on the issue of human rights guarantees, but ended without agreement. A further round of talks, held in August, led to concessions by the Government, which agreed to curb the expansion of the PAC. These self-defence patrols played a major role in the army's counter-insurgency campaign and were widely accused of human rights violations. The URNG, which maintained that *campesinos* (peasants) were forcibly enlisted into the PAC, included in its conditions for a peace agreement the immediate dissolution of the patrols. Under the August agreement, any newly-formed PAC would operate under the supervision of the office of the human rights ombudsman. In November the Government accepted renewed proposals by the URNG for the establishment of a commission on past human rights violations, but only on the pre-condition that the rebels sign a definitive peace accord. In January 1993 President Serrano announced his commitment to the negotiation and signing of a peace agreement with the URNG within 90 days. In the event that an agreement was not reached, Serrano pledged that a cease-fire would be implemented at the end of that period, provided that the URNG demonstrate its commitment to the peace process. In reply to Serrano's announcement, the URNG called for a 50% reduction in the size of the armed forces, and repeated demands for the immediate dissolution of the PAC and the dismissal of military officials implicated in human rights violations. The Government rejected these proposals; talks continued in February, however, but faltered in the following month, owing principally to government demands that the URNG disarm as a precondition to the implementation of procedures for the international verification of human rights in Guatemala. Negotiations were suspended in May, owing to the prevailing constitutional crisis (see below).

In June 1993 the URNG announced a unilateral cease-fire as a gesture of goodwill to the incoming President Ramiro de León Carpio. Government proposals announced in July, which aimed to involve all sectors of society in a Permanent Forum for Peace addressing social, economic and human rights problems independently of simultaneous cease-fire negotiations with the URNG, were rejected by the rebels. In August, in a concession to the URNG, de León announced the reform of the Estado Mayor Presidencial, a military body widely accused of human rights offences. However, in the following month the army announced that it would be resuming military operations against the rebels, which had been suspended in June. In October the Government presented a revised peace plan to the UN, providing for the creation of a Permanent Forum for Peace and renewed cease-fire negotiations with a view to an eventual amnesty for the URNG; the plan was, however, rejected by the rebels. Preliminary talks were finally resumed in Mexico in early January 1994.

In May 1992 fears of a possible military coup were raised by a series of bombings and bomb threats in the capital. The campaign was widely recognized as the activity of right-wing elements of the military and the private sector, which aimed to force the Government to abandon its plans to implement tax reforms and to cease negotiations with the URNG. In July the Minister of the Interior, Fernando Hurtado Prem, was forced to resign amidst allegations of police brutality. The decision followed the violent dispersal by anti-riot police of some 500 *campesinos* who had gathered outside the Palacio Nacional to demand the resolution of a land dispute.

In October 1992 the Government signed an accord for the return from Mexico of an estimated 40,000 Guatemalan refugees. The refugees were promised land, security guarantees and a three-year exemption from military service. The first group, numbering some 2,480, arrived in the capital in January 1993. The flow of refugees from Mexico was stimulated in early 1994 by large numbers fleeing the Amerindian uprising in the Mexican state of Chiapas (see Chapter on Mexico, Vol II). However, by the end of 1994 few returnees had received the land that had been promised to them in the accord of October 1992, and many had suffered attacks and intimidation by the security forces.

In May 1993 unrest at economic austerity measures escalated as public confidence in the Government declined. In that month a rally attended by some 10,000 people was staged in the capital to demand Serrano's resignation. With the MAS no longer able to effect a constructive alliance in Congress and the country's stability in jeopardy, on 25 May Serrano, with the support of the military, suspended parts of the Constitution and dissolved

Congress and the Supreme Court. A ban was imposed on the media and Serrano announced that he would rule by decree pending the drafting of a new constitution by a constituent assembly, which was to be elected within 60 days. In addition to civil unrest, Serrano cited widespread corruption (which, he alleged, permeated all state institutions) as the motive for his actions. The constitutional coup provoked almost unanimous international condemnation, with the USA immediately suspending in excess of US $30m. in aid. Such pressure, in addition to overwhelming domestic opposition, led the military to reappraise its position and, opting to effect a return to constitutional rule, it forced the resignation of Serrano, who relinquished his post on 1 June and subsequently fled to El Salvador. He was later granted political asylum in Panama. The Minister of National Defence, Gen. José Domingo García Samayoa, assumed control of the country, pending the election of a new president. An attempt by Vice-President Gustavo Adolfo Espina Salguero to assume the presidency was prevented by a legislative boycott of his ratification. He was later ruled ineligible for the post by the Constitutional Court.

On 3 June 1993 the entire Cabinet, excluding García and the Minister of the Interior, Francisco Perdomo Sandoval, resigned. On the same day the Attorney-General presented charges, including those of violation of the Constitution, abuse of authority and embezzlement, against Serrano, Espina and Perdomo, all of whom were reported to have left the country. On 5 June, following an order by the Constitutional Court, Congress reconvened and conducted elections for a new president. The Instancia Nacional de Consenso (INC), a broad coalition of political parties, business leaders and trade unions which had been instrumental in removing Serrano from office, proposed three candidates, of whom Ramiro de León Carpio, the former human rights ombudsman, was elected President in an uncontested second round of voting. He was inaugurated on the following day to complete the remainder of Serrano's term, which was due to end in January 1996. The USA subsequently restored its aid programme to Guatemala.

In late August 1993, as an initial measure in a campaign to eradicate corruption from state institutions and restore dwindling public confidence in his Government, de León requested the voluntary resignation of Congress and the Supreme Court. The request caused a serious division in the legislature, which separated into two main factions, the Gran Grupo Parlamentario (GGP), which included some 70 members of the MAS, UCN, PAN and the Frente Republicano Guatemalteco (FRG) and supported the dismissal of 16 deputies identified by the INC as corrupt, and a group of 38 deputies, including members of the PDCG and independents, who supported the voluntary resignation of all 116 deputies. In early September, following the suspension of a congressional session by the President of Congress, Fernando Lobo Dubón (a member of the PDCG), the GGP defied the decision and elected a new President of Congress. Although Lobo was temporarily reinstated by the Constitutional Court, the GGP threatened to boycott any further sessions convened by him. In order to resolve the deadlock, in late September de León requested the Supreme Electoral Tribunal to put the issue to a referendum on 28 November. However, in early November the Constitutional Court upheld a Supreme Court injunction of the previous month, suspending the referendum.

In mid-November 1993, following the mediatorial intervention of the Bishops' Conference of Guatemala, a compromise was reached between the Government and the legislature, involving a series of constitutional reforms which were summarily approved by Congress in order to be put to a referendum on 30 January 1994. The constitutional reforms were subsequently approved by the referendum, although fewer than 20% of the electorate participated in the voting, reflecting popular concern that more extensive reforms were necessary. The reforms took effect in early April, and fresh legislative elections were to be held in mid-August. The new Congress, which was to serve until 14 January 1996, was to appoint the members of a new Supreme Court, enlarged from nine to 13 justices. Other reforms included a reduction in the terms of office of the President, legislature and municipal authorities (from five to four years), and of the Supreme Court justices (from six to five years), and a reduction in the number of seats in Congress (from 116 to 90, although the Supreme Electoral Tribunal later set the number at 80). Also agreed were measures to prevent corruption in the legislature and judiciary.

In January 1994 preliminary talks, held in Mexico, between the Government and the URNG resulted in an agreement providing for a resumption of formal peace negotiations, to be based on the agenda agreed in Mexico in April 1991. In late March 1994 agreement was reached on a timetable aimed at achieving a definitive peace agreement by the end of the year. In addition, a general human rights agreement was signed, providing guarantees, including a government commitment to eliminate illegal security corps, strengthen national human rights institutions and cease obligatory military recruitment. Agreement was also reached on the establishment of a UN human rights mission to verify the implementation of the accord. Further talks in Oslo, Norway, resulted in the signing, in June, of agreements on the resettlement of people displaced by the civil war (estimated to number some 1m.), and on the establishment of a Commission for Historical Clarification (Comisión para el Esclarecimiento Histórico—CEH) to investigate human rights violations committed during the 33-year conflict. The CEH was to be formally established following the signing of a definitive peace accord. The role of the CEH, the creation of which was strongly opposed by the security forces, would be to report on past violations but would not extend to initiating legal proceedings against offenders.

In August 1994 the URNG withdrew from the peace negotiations and accused the Government of failing to observe the human rights provisions agreed in March. Guerrilla activity subsequently escalated in late August. Talks resumed in November, focusing on the issue of the identity and rights of Indian peoples. However, the talks remained deadlocked until February 1995, when a new timetable for negotiations, achieved with the mediation of the UN, was announced. The new agenda, which was formally agreed by the Government and the URNG in March, provided for a cease-fire agreement by June and the signing of a definitive peace accord in August. In March the issue of the identity and rights of indigenous peoples was finally resolved. The principal remaining issues to be discussed included agrarian and other socio-economic reform, the role of the armed forces, the resettlement of displaced people and the incorporation of URNG guerrillas into civilian life. However, talks continued beyond the agreed deadline for a definitive accord, and throughout 1995, without agreement on the substantive issues. In September, in an attempt to lend impetus to the peace process, the Government announced the demobilization of the approximately 24,000-strong paramilitary force, the Comisionados Militares. However, in the following month relations were strained when a military patrol carried out an attack on a resettlement area for refugees returning from Mexico in the department of Alta Verapaz, killing 11 inhabitants. The incident prompted the resignation of the Minister of National Defence, Gen. Mario René Enríquez Morales.

A series of strikes and organized protests by public-sector unions, in support of demands including salary increases of 40%, higher social expenditure and an end to the Government's privatization programme, ended in April 1994, following government concessions. In that month the climate of increasing violence and instability, characterized by attacks on legislators and foreign citizens, and by the assassination of the President of the Constitutional Court, Epaminondas González Dubón, prompted de León to place the army in charge of internal security.

At the legislative election held in August 1994 only some 20% of the electorate exercised their vote, again reflecting widespread scepticism at the extent to which the reforms instigated by de León would serve to rid Guatemalan institutions of corruption. Of the 80 seats in the new legislature (reduced from 116), the FRG secured 32, the PAN 24, the PDCG 13, the UCN seven, the MLN three and the Unión Democrática (UD) one. Despite winning the greatest number of seats, the FRG, led by Gen. (retd) José Efraín Ríos Montt, was excluded from the 12-member congressional directorate by an alliance of the PAN, PDCG, MLN and UD. However, in December the PDCG transferred its allegiance to the FRG and Ríos Montt was subsequently elected President of Congress. His inauguration in January 1995 provoked demonstrations by human rights organizations, which considered him responsible for the deaths of as many as 15,000 civilians as a result of counter-insurgency operations conducted during his period as *de facto* ruler in 1982–83.

In September 1994 the UN General Assembly formally announced the establishment of the Human Rights Verification Mission in Guatemala (MINUGUA), as envisaged in the March 1994 agreement between the Government and the URNG. The mission, which was to comprise 220 human rights observers, 60 police and 10 military officers, began arriving in November.

In October 1994 Congress elected the 13 members of the new Supreme Court. In the same month the umbrella union Unidad de Acción Sindical y Popular launched a series of strikes in protest at government economic policy, and in particular at the privatization programme and at redundancies in the public sector. In November, 10 days of public protest at increases in bus fares in the capital culminated in violent clashes between protestors and the security forces. Troops were deployed to restore order, and de León announced that the fare increases, which had been unilaterally imposed by the bus companies, would be reversed.

In January 1995 the Minister of the Interior, Danilo Parinello, was removed from office, following allegations implicating him in corrupt practices. He was replaced by Carlos Enrique Reynoso Gil.

In March 1995 Guatemala's record on human rights came under particular scrutiny. At the beginning of the month the USA announced that it had suspended all remaining military aid to the country, in protest at the Government's failure to investigate cases involving the murder or disappearance of US citizens in Guatemala. In mid-March MINUGUA issued its first report since beginning operations in November 1994. The document drew attention to human rights abuses perpetrated by the security forces and the PAC, and the Government's failure to investigate such incidents was once again condemned.

In June 1995 Ríos Montt formally requested registration as a candidate in the forthcoming presidential election, despite a constitutional provision precluding the candidacy of anyone who had previously come to power by means of a coup, as Ríos Montt had done in 1982 (see above). In August the Supreme Electoral Tribunal confirmed that Ríos Montt was not eligible to stand for election. In the same month the Supreme Court ruled that Ríos Montt should be suspended from his position as President of Congress for a period of four months, in order that he answer charges of abuse of authority and violation of the Constitution. The charges concerned an attempt by Ríos Montt and several other FRG members of Congress to impeach the magistrates of the Supreme Electoral Tribunal without first securing congressional approval.

The presidential and legislative elections on 12 November 1995 were notable for the return to the electoral process, for the first time for more than 40 years, of the left wing, which was represented by the Frente Democrático Nueva Guatemala (FDNG). In addition, the URNG, which had boycotted all previous elections, declared a unilateral cease-fire to coincide with the electoral campaign and urged people to exercise their vote. As no candidate received the necessary 50% of the votes to win the presidential election outright, the two leading candidates, Alvaro Enrique Arzú Irigoyen of the PAN and Alfonso Portillo of the FRG, were to contest a second round of voting. At the legislative election the PAN secured 43 of the total of 80 seats in Congress, the FRG won 21, the Alianza Nacional (AN) nine, the FDNG six, and the MLN obtained the remaining seat. At the second round of the presidential election, conducted on 7 January 1996, Arzú secured a narrow victory with 51.22% of the votes cast.

Shortly after assuming office on 14 January 1996, Arzú demonstrated his intention to curb the power of the military and to expedite the peace process by implementing a comprehensive reorganization of the military high command, replacing those officers who were not in favour of a negotiated peace settlement. In late February Arzú met the high command of the URNG in Mexico City, the first direct meeting between a Guatemalan president and the rebels since the early 1970s. In March Congress ratified the International Labour Organization's Convention on the rights of indigenous peoples. However, the document, which had been before Congress since 1992 and had encountered strong opposition from landed interests, had been amended by Congress, prompting protests by Indian organizations. On 20 March the URNG announced an indefinite unilateral cease-fire. Arzú responded immediately by ordering the armed forces to suspend counter-insurgency operations.

On 6 May 1996 the Government and the URNG signed an agreement on agrarian and socio-economic issues. The accord, which aimed to address the problem of widespread poverty by establishing a more efficient and equitable agrarian structure, provided for the introduction of a new agrarian bank (which would supply funds for *campesinos* to purchase property), the establishment of a land registry to define ownership and the introduction of a land tax. The Government also undertook to double expenditure on health and education over the next four years. As a consequence of the agreement, the URNG suspended its 'war-tax' (protection money extorted from landowners and businesses). In that month Congress approved legislation limiting the right of public-sector employees to strike. A demonstration by trade unions in protest at the legislation was dispersed by the security forces. In the following month Congress adopted legislation that made members of the armed forces accountable to civilian courts for all but strictly military crimes.

In September 1996 Arzú's campaign to eliminate corruption in the armed forces continued, with the dismissal and arrest of eight high-ranking officers who were charged with involvement in a contraband network. In the same month the Government and the URNG signed an agreement in Mexico City on the strengthening of civilian power and the role of the armed forces. Under the terms of the accord, all military and intelligence services were to be placed under the authority of the Government. The police force was to be reorganized, with the creation of a new National Civilian Police force (Policía Nacional Civil—to number at least 20,000 by the end of 1999), which would replace the existing units. The armed forces were to be reduced in size by one-third in 1997 and were to relinquish responsibility for internal security. Also confirmed in the accord was the abolition of the PAC (the demobilization of which had begun in August).

In November 1996 the Government announced that a definitive peace accord would be signed on 29 December. In early December the demobilization of the PAC, estimated to number some 202,000 members, was officially concluded. Later that month a general amnesty law was approved by Congress. Whilst the law did not exonerate former combatants for human rights violations, the rebels expressed concern that the amnesty was too extensive and that atrocities committed by the armed forces would go unpunished. Human rights groups announced plans to take legal action to have the law annulled.

On 29 December 1996 the Government and the URNG signed the definitive peace treaty in Guatemala City, bringing to an end some 36 years of civil war, during which an estimated 140,000 people had died. The demobilization of URNG guerrillas, estimated to number some 3,250, was to be supervised by MINUGUA. Earlier in the year the URNG had established a 44-member political council to prepare for the reconstitution of the organization as a broad-based political party.

In January 1997 some 1,000 members of the approximately 4,000-strong Policía Ambulante Militar (PMA—Mobile Military Police), which, under the terms of the peace treaty, was to be disbanded, barricaded themselves inside their headquarters in the capital in armed rebellion and demanded compensation of US $10,000 each for their imminent demobilization. During the course of the rebellion two senior officers of the armed forces involved in negotiating a settlement with the military police were taken hostage. However, after five days the rebels agreed to surrender their arms and seek a peaceful agreement.

In February 1997 the Commission for Historical Clarification was appointed. The commission was to begin operating in August for a period of 10 months. In March Congress approved legislation providing for the privatization of state-owned companies, prompting widespread protest by trade unionists. In late March the UN General Assembly renewed the mandate of MINUGUA for a further year to monitor the implementation of the peace treaty. The demobilization of the URNG, which began in March, was completed by early May.

In June 1997 the URNG registered as a political party in formation. That month the former guerrilla group elected a transitional leadership committee to conduct the transformation of the movement. In August the URNG held elections to a provisional executive committee, of which Ricardo Arnoldo Ramírez de León was appointed Secretary-General. The URNG had expressed its intention to seek an alliance with the FDNG, which held six seats in Congress.

In July 1997 Arzú dismissed the Minister of National Defence, Gen. Julio Arnoldo Balconi Turcios, who was replaced by Gen. Héctor Mario Barrios Celada. In that month the first contingent of 1,200 agents of the new National Civilian Police force began operating. In December the demobilization of the PMA was concluded. In accordance with the terms of the peace treaty, more than 15,000 members of the armed forces had been demobilized by the end of 1997.

Until the return to civilian government in 1986, Guatemala remained steadfast in its claims to the neighbouring territory of Belize, a former British dependency. In protest at the UK's decision to grant independence to Belize, in accordance with a UN General Assembly resolution of November 1980, Guatemala severed diplomatic relations with the UK. However, Guatemala's new Constitution, which took effect in January 1986, did not include Belize in its delineation of Guatemalan territory. In August consular links between Guatemala and the UK were restored. In December full diplomatic relations were resumed, and in 1987 a British Embassy was opened in Guatemala City. The removal of economic sanctions and trade restrictions from Belize in late 1986 opened the way to Guatemalan investment in that territory and to the possibility of joint development projects.

In May 1988 discussions were held in Miami, USA, between representatives of Guatemala, Belize and the UK. The participants decided to establish a permanent Joint Commission to formulate a draft treaty to resolve Guatemala's claims to Belize. In October the Commission announced the establishment of three subcommissions, to be responsible for drafting the treaty; the delimitation of the border; and the creation of a joint development zone, with the co-operation of the UK and the EC. Approval of the treaty was to be decided by referendums, to be held in both Guatemala and Belize.

In September 1991 Guatemala and Belize signed an accord under the terms of which Belize pledged to legislate to reduce its maritime boundaries and to allow Guatemala access to the Caribbean Sea and use of its port facilities. In return, President Serrano officially announced his country's recognition of Belize as an independent state and established diplomatic relations. The Belizean legislature approved the Maritime Areas Bill in January 1992. Serrano's decision to recognize Belize, made without consulting Congress and without holding a referendum, provoked protests from the opposition, who claimed that Serrano's actions were unconstitutional. In November 1992 Guatemala's Constitutional Court rejected a request by opposition deputies to declare Serrano's actions unconstitutional. In an address to the nation, Serrano subsequently confirmed that Guatemala maintained its territorial claim on Belize. At the end of November Congress voted to ratify Serrano's decision to recognize Belize.

In April 1993 Guatemala and Belize signed a non-aggression pact, affirming their intent to refrain from the threat or use of force against each other, and preventing either country from being used as a base for aggression against the other. Relations between the two countries were jeopardized in June, when Serrano was ousted from the presidency (see above). However, his successor subsequently announced that Guatemala would continue to respect Belize's independence. In July the Belizean Prime Minister, Manuel Esquivel, reportedly suspended the September 1991 accord, stating that it involved too many concessions on the part of Belize and that the issue should be put to a referendum. In September the UK announced that the British garrison, which had been stationed in Belize since the mid-1970s and numbered some 1,500 in June 1993, was to be withdrawn by October 1994.

In March 1994, in a letter to the UN Secretary-General, Guatemala formally reaffirmed its territorial claim to Belize, prompting the Belizean Minister of Foreign Affairs to seek talks with the British Government regarding assistance with national defence. Concern was also expressed by the Standing Committee of CARICOM Ministers of Foreign Affairs, which reaffirmed its support for Belizean sovereignty. In September 1996 the Ministers of Foreign Affairs of Guatemala and Belize conducted preliminary talks in New York, USA, concerning a resumption of negotiations on the territorial dispute. In August 1997 President Arzú ordered an increased military presence on the border with Belize following reports of incursions by Belizean troops into Guatemalan territory. In late 1997 Guatemala was considering Belizean proposals for a frontier treaty following the rejection by Belize of a Guatemalan proposition to seek international arbitration on the issue.

Government

Guatemala is a republic comprising 22 departments. Under the 1986 Constitution (revised in 1994), legislative power is vested in the unicameral National Congress, with 80 members elected for four years by universal adult suffrage. Of the total seats, 64 are filled by departmental representation and 16 according to national listing. Executive power is held by the President (also directly elected for four years), assisted by a Vice-President and an appointed Cabinet.

Defence

In August 1997 the armed forces totalled 40,700, of whom 38,500 were in the army, 1,500 in the navy (including 650 marines) and 700 in the air force. In addition, there were paramilitary forces of 9,800. Military service is by selective conscription for 30 months. In September 1996, as part of the ongoing peace process, the Government signed an agreement with the rebel URNG whereby the armed forces were to be placed under the control of the Government. Under the terms of the accord, the armed forces were reduced in number by one-third in 1997. This reduction included the disbanding of the Policía Ambulante Militar (Mobile Military Police), which was completed in late 1997. In addition, the accord provided for the abolition of the Patrullas de Autodefensa Civil (PAC), an anti-guerrilla peasant militia, which was estimated to number some 202,000. In early December 1996 the demobilization of the PAC was officially completed. Defence expenditure in 1997 was budgeted at US $93m.

Economic Affairs

In 1995, according to estimates by the World Bank, Guatemala's gross national product (GNP), measured at average 1993–95 prices, was US $14,255m., equivalent to $1,340 per head. During 1985–95, it was estimated, GNP per head increased, in real terms, at an average rate of 0.3% per year. Over the same period, the population increased by an annual average of 2.9%. Guatemala's gross domestic product (GDP) increased, in real terms, by an annual average of 3.6% in 1985–95 and by 3.0% in 1996.

Agriculture, including forestry and fishing, contributed an estimated 24.0% of GDP in 1996. In 1995 an estimated 58.1% of the working population were employed in this sector. The principal cash crops are coffee (which accounted for an estimated 20.5% of export earnings in 1996), sugar cane, bananas and cardamom. Exports of shrimps are also significant. During 1985–95, according to the World Bank, agricultural GDP increased, in real terms, by an annual average of 2.6%. Growth in agricultural GDP was an estimated 2.5% in 1996.

Industry, including mining, manufacturing, construction and power, contributed an estimated 19.7% of GDP in 1996. This sector employed 18.1% of the working population in 1995. According to the World Bank, industrial GDP increased by an annual average of 3.0% in 1985–95. Growth in industrial GDP was 3.3% in 1996.

Mining contributed an estimated 0.5% of GDP in 1996 and employed 0.1% of the working population in 1995. The most important mineral export is petroleum, although this accounted for only an estimated 2.7% of total export earnings in 1996. In addition, copper, antimony, lead, zinc and tungsten are mined on a small scale. There are also deposits of nickel, gold and silver.

Guatemala's industrial sector is the largest in Central America. Manufacturing contributed an estimated 14.0% of GDP in 1996, and employed 13.6% of the working population in 1995. The main branches of manufacturing, measured by gross value of output, are food-processing, textiles, plastic products, pharmaceuticals and industrial chemicals. According to the World Bank, manufacturing GDP increased by an annual average of 2.1% in 1985–95. Growth in manufacturing GDP was an estimated 1.9% in 1996.

Energy is derived principally from mineral fuels and, to a lesser extent, hydroelectric power. Guatemala is a marginal producer of petroleum, with an average output of about 25,000 b/d in 1997. Imports of petroleum comprised an estimated 4.1% of the value of total imports in 1996.

In 1996 the services sector contributed an estimated 56.3% of GDP, and in 1995 it employed 23.8% of the working population. According to the World Bank, the GDP of the services sector increased by an annual average of 3.5% in 1985–95. The GDP of the services sector increased by an estimated 3.2% in 1996.

In 1996 Guatemala recorded a visible trade deficit of US $643.4m., and there was a deficit of $451.5m. on the current account of the balance of payments. In 1995 the principal source of imports (44.9%) was the USA; other major suppliers were Mexico, El Salvador, Venezuela, Japan and Germany. The USA was also the principal market for exports (taking 31.3% of exports in that year); other significant purchasers were El Salvador, Honduras, Germany and Costa Rica. The main exports in 1996 were coffee, sugar, bananas, petroleum and cardamom. The principal imports were raw materials for industry, non-durable consumer goods, capital goods for industry, durable consumer goods and fuels and lubricants.

In 1996 there was a budgetary deficit of 269.7m. quetzales, equivalent to some 0.3% of GDP. At the end of 1995 Guatemala's total external debt stood at US $3,275m., of which $2,493m. was long-term public debt. In that year the cost of debt-servicing was equivalent to 10.6% of the total value of exports of goods and services. In 1985–95 the average annual rate of inflation was 18.1%. Consumer prices increased by an average of 11.1% in 1996 and by 8.1% in the year to August 1997. An estimated 13% of the labour force were unemployed in 1989.

Guatemala is a member of the Central American Common Market (CACM, see p. 122).

In 1991 the Government adopted a structural adjustment programme in order to address the serious fiscal imbalances and external debt problems that had characterized the previous decade. The resultant economic recovery enabled the Government to resume relations with international credit agencies and clear debt arrears. However, political uncertainties in mid-1993 led to a deterioration of the economic situation, with rising inflation and declining international reserves. In 1995 the political situation stabilized and the economy began to recover. Low tax revenue (which, at less than 8.0% of GDP, was the lowest in the region) was a major problem, forcing the Government to borrow heavily, keeping interest rates high, discouraging investment and impeding growth. In early 1995 the legislature approved a series of reforms to the tax system, which, in turn, facilitated a new stand-by agreement with the IMF. The signing of the peace accord in December 1996, which signalled the end of the civil conflict, improved Guatemala's economic prospects significantly. It was envisaged that expenditure of US $2,500m. would be required to implement the accord. In January 1997 international donors pledged $1,900m. in loans and donations towards the Government's reconstruction programme. However, the funding was contingent upon the Government significantly increasing tax revenues. In that month the rate of value-added tax (VAT) was increased from 7% to 10%; however, efforts to effect a restructuring of the tax administration, including the creation of a tax superintendency, met considerable opposition in Congress. By September only $114m. of the funding pledged in January had been disbursed, largely as a result of the Government's failure to implement tax reforms. Under an agreement with the IMF, the Government was committed to raising tax revenue to 12% of GDP by 1999.

Social Welfare

Social security is compulsory, and all employers with five or more workers are required to enrol with the State Institute of Social Security. Benefits are available to registered workers for industrial accidents, sickness, maternity, disability, widowhood and hospitalization. In 1978 Guatemala had 107 hospitals, with a total of 12,217 beds, and in 1984 there were 3,544 physicians working in the health service. In 1986 a vaccination programme to benefit more than 1m. children was announced, in a campaign to combat infant mortality. According to preliminary figures, in 1995 budgetary expenditure on health was 718.7m. quetzales (8.8% of total spending).

Education

Elementary education is free and, in urban areas, compulsory between seven and 14 years of age. Primary education begins at the age of seven and lasts for six years. Secondary education, beginning at 13 years of age, lasts for up to six years, comprising two cycles of three years each. In 1993 there were 4,553 pre-primary schools and 10,770 primary schools. In 1992 there were 2,308 secondary schools. In 1993 enrolment at primary schools was equivalent to 84% of children in the relevant age-group (boys 89%; girls 78%). The comparable figure for secondary education in that year was 24% (boys 25%; girls 23%). There are five universities. In 1981 a 'national literacy crusade' was launched by the Government, but in 1995, according to estimates by UNESCO, the average rate of adult illiteracy was 44.4% (males 37.5%; females 51.4%). According to preliminary figures, in 1995 budgetary expenditure on education was 1,351.8m. quetzales (16.5% of total spending).

Public Holidays

1998: 1 January (New Year's Day), 6 January (Epiphany), 10–13 April (Easter), 1 May (Labour Day), 30 June (Anniversary of the Revolution), 15 August (Assumption, Guatemala City only), 15 September (Independence Day), 12 October (Columbus Day), 20 October (Revolution Day), 1 November (All Saints' Day), 24–25 December (Christmas), 31 December (New Year's Eve).

1999: 1 January (New Year's Day), 6 January (Epiphany), 2–5 April (Easter), 1 May (Labour Day), 30 June (Anniversary of the Revolution), 15 August (Assumption, Guatemala City only), 15 September (Independence Day), 12 October (Columbus Day), 20 October (Revolution Day), 1 November (All Saints' Day), 24–25 December (Christmas), 31 December (New Year's Eve).

Weights and Measures

The metric system is in official use.

Statistical Survey

Sources (unless otherwise stated): Banco de Guatemala, 7a Avda 22-01, Zona 1, Apdo 365, Guatemala City; tel. 230-6222; telex 5231; fax 253-4035; Dirección General de Estadística, Edif. América 4°, 8a Calle 9-55, Zona 1, Guatemala City; tel. 22-6136.

Area and Population

AREA, POPULATION AND DENSITY

Area (sq km)	
Land	108,429
Inland water	460
Total	108,889*
Population (census results)†	
26 March 1981	
Males	3,015,826
Females	3,038,401
Total	6,054,227
17 April 1994	8,322,051
Population (official estimates at mid-year)	
1994	10,321,971
1995	10,621,226
1996	10,928,000
Density (per sq km) at mid-1996	100.4

* 42,042 sq miles.

† Excluding adjustments for underenumeration, estimated to have been 13.7% in 1981.

DEPARTMENTS (estimated population at mid-1995)

Alta Verapaz	670,815	Jutiapa	387,177
Baja Verapaz	205,481	Quezaltenango	623,571
Chimaltenango	385,856	Retalhuleu	268,996
Chiquimula	274,091	Sacatepéquez	202,243
El Petén	310,008	San Marcos	790,118
El Progreso	117,943	Santa Rosa	291,611
El Quiché	652,022	Sololá	274,356
Escuintla	610,322	Suchitepéquez	403,618
Guatemala	2,246,170	Totonicapán	333,634
Huehuetenango	816,376	Zacapa	174,450
Izabal	370,538		
Jalapa	211,830	**Total**	10,621,226

PRINCIPAL TOWNS (estimated population at mid-1995)

Guatemala City (capital)	1,167,495	Mazatenango	43,316
Quezaltenango	103,631	Retalhuleu	40,062
Escuintla	69,532	Puerto Barrios	39,379
		Chiquimula	33,028

BIRTHS, MARRIAGES AND DEATHS

	Registered live births		Registered marriages		Registered deaths	
	Number	Rate (per 1,000)	Number	Rate (per 1,000)	Number	Rate (per 1,000)
1987	324,784	38.5	44,440	5.3	66,703	7.9
1988	341,382	39.3	46,795	5.4	64,837	7.5
1989	345,184	38.6	45,736	5.1	64,515	7.2
1990	352,149	38.3	47,608	5.1	72,748	7.9
1991	359,904	38.0	48,254	5.1	72,896	7.7
1992	363,648	37.3	49,831	5.1	73,124	7.5
1993	370,138	36.9	46,789	4.7	73,870	7.4

Expectation of life (UN estimates, years at birth, 1990–95): 64.8 (males 62.4; females 67.3) (Source: UN, *World Population Prospects: The 1994 Revision*).

ECONOMICALLY ACTIVE POPULATION
(official estimates for 1995)

	Males	Females	Total
Agriculture, forestry, hunting and fishing	1,767,791	30,436	1,798,227
Mining and quarrying	3,052	43	3,095
Manufacturing	329,033	91,895	420,928
Construction	126,234	664	126,898
Electricity, gas, water and sanitary services	9,023	262	9,285
Commerce	155,122	70,818	225,940
Transport, storage and communications	75,563	1,814	77,377
Services	163,945	207,462	371,407
Activities not adequately described	48,408	13,493	61,901
Total	2,678,171	416,887	3,095,058

Agriculture

PRINCIPAL CROPS ('000 metric tons)

	1994	1995	1996
Sugar cane	11,862	13,780*	14,380*
Cotton (lint)	14	7	5
Maize	1,188	1,062	1,136
Rice	39	31	33
Dry beans	91	81	83
Wheat	26	24	23
Coffee	214	216	207
Bananas	638†	705†	677
Plantains	47†	35†	38*

* FAO estimate. † Unofficial figure.

Source: FAO, *Production Yearbook*.

LIVESTOCK ('000 head, year ending September)

	1994	1995	1996
Horses*	116	116	116
Cattle	2,300	2,293	2,291
Sheep	500	525	551
Pigs	796	889	950
Goats*	78	78	78

Chickens* (million): 19 in 1994; 20 in 1995; 21 in 1996.

* FAO estimates.

Source: FAO, *Production Yearbook*.

LIVESTOCK PRODUCTS ('000 metric tons)

	1994	1995	1996
Beef and veal	56	53	53†
Pig meat	14	15	16
Poultry meat	101	106	110†
Cheese*	12	12	12
Hen eggs*	70	74	74
Cattle hides*	9	9	9

* FAO estimates. † Unofficial figure.

Source: FAO, *Production Yearbook*.

Forestry

ROUNDWOOD REMOVALS ('000 cubic metres, excl. bark)

	1992*	1993	1994
Sawlogs, veneer logs and logs for sleepers*	111	665	695
Other industrial wood*	10	41	42
Fuel wood	11,142	15,385	15,818
Total	11,263	16,091	16,555

* FAO estimates.

Source: FAO, *Yearbook of Forest Products*.

SAWNWOOD PRODUCTION
('000 cubic metres, incl. railway sleepers)

	1992*	1993	1994
Coniferous (softwood)	60	239	249
Broadleaved (hardwood)	30	159	167
Total	90	398	416

* FAO estimates.

Source: FAO, *Yearbook of Forest Products*.

Fishing

(metric tons, live weight)

	1993	1994	1995
Total catch	10,868	11,602	11,927

Source: FAO, *Yearbook of Fishery Statistics*.

Mining

SELECTED PRODUCTS (metric tons, unless otherwise indicated)

	1992	1993	1994
Antimony ore	6,107	n.a.	494
Petroleum ('000 barrels)	2,050	2,507	2,647
Iron ore	4,080	5,919	3,498
Lead ore	52	20	9

1995: Petroleum 3,442,000 barrels (estimate).

Source: Ministry of Energy and Mines.

Industry

SELECTED PRODUCTS
('000 metric tons, unless otherwise indicated)

	1993	1994	1995
Cement	1,119	1,162	1,185
Sugar	1,047	1,114	1,275
Electricity (million kWh)	3,053	3,222	3,498*
Cigarettes (million)	1,786	1,739	n.a.

* Estimate.

Source: Ministry of Energy and Mines.

Finance

CURRENCY AND EXCHANGE RATES

Monetary Units
100 centavos = 1 quetzal.

Sterling and Dollar Equivalents (30 September 1997)
£1 sterling = 9.9177 quetzales;
US $1 = 6.1395 quetzales;
1,000 quetzales = £100.83 = $162.88.

Average Exchange Rate (quetzales per US dollar)
1994 5.7512
1995 5.8103
1996 6.0495

Note: The multiple exchange rate system, introduced in 1984, was abolished in 1991.

BUDGET (million quetzales)

Revenue	1993	1994	1995*
Tax revenue	5,026.5	5,054.7	6,671.9
Direct taxes	1,225.7	902.1	1,387.7
Corporate income tax	1,029.3	610.1	979.0
Personal income tax	153.1	234.8	376.8
Indirect taxes	3,800.8	4,152.6	5,284.2
Value-added tax	1,679.0	1,883.1	2,441.4
Excise tax	682.3	763.6	859.6
Stamp tax	152.3	162.6	191.2
Taxes on imports	1,133.9	1,182.8	1,557.9
Non-tax revenue	255.0	301.1	313.8
Current transfers	463.0	327.8	372.0
Total	5,744.5	5,683.6	7,357.7

Expenditure	1993	1994	1995*
General public services	1,596.1	1,518.0	2,319.5
Defence	684.6	806.2	842.8
Education	1,158.0	1,272.3	1,351.8
Health	623.5	701.5	718.7
Social security and welfare	515.9	514.9	599.8
Housing and community services	597.8	453.8	514.1
Social funds	192.5	351.8	395.8
Transportation and communications	544.7	587.1	806.0
Total (incl. others)	6,791.5	6,841.9	8,176.5

* Preliminary figures.

Source: IMF, *Guatemala—Statistical Appendix* (December 1996).

1996 (million quetzales): Revenue 8,605.1 (excl. grants 53.0); Expenditure 8,687.2 (excl. net lending 240.6) (Source: IMF, *International Financial Statistics*).

INTERNATIONAL RESERVES (US $ million at 31 December)

	1994	1995	1996
Gold*	8.8	8.9	8.9
IMF special drawing rights	16.6	15.8	14.6
Foreign exchange	846.5	686.2	855.1
Total	871.9	710.9	878.6

* Valued at US $42.22 per troy ounce.

Source: IMF, *International Financial Statistics*.

MONEY SUPPLY (million quetzales at 31 December)

	1994	1995	1996
Currency outside banks	3,714.6	4,018.9	4,179.1
Private sector deposits at Bank of Guatemala	22.8	24.5	25.8
Demand deposits at deposit money banks	3,336.2	3,728.4	4,617.5
Total money	7,073.6	7,771.8	8,822.4

Source: IMF, *International Financial Statistics*.

COST OF LIVING
(Consumer Price Index; base: March–April 1983 = 100)

	1994	1995	1996
Food and beverages	725.8	790.0	880.6
Domestic living expenses	516.7	580.7	628.0
Furniture, maintenance and equipment for the home	548.6	597.5	676.2
Clothing and footwear	546.9	572.1	608.8
Medical assistance	717.8	773.8	869.9
Education	672.1	757.1	892.5
Transport and communications	587.8	619.9	701.4
Reading and recreation	452.8	480.0	526.5
Others	606.1	642.5	713.8
All items	628.8	681.7	757.1

NATIONAL ACCOUNTS

Expenditure on the Gross Domestic Product
(million quetzales at current prices)

	1994	1995	1996
Government final consumption expenditure	4,468	4,692	5,099
Private final consumption expenditure	63,893	72,899	82,802
Increase in stocks	1,087	319	–936
Gross fixed capital formation	10,622	12,371	12,745
Total domestic expenditure	80,070	90,281	99,710
Exports of goods and services	13,173	16,390	16,886
Less Imports of goods and services	18,571	21,656	21,477
GDP in purchasers' values	74,669	85,016	95,119

Source: IMF, *International Financial Statistics*.

Gross Domestic Product by Economic Activity
(million quetzales at constant 1958 prices)

	1994	1995	1996*
Agriculture, hunting, forestry and fishing	975.2	1,010.0	1,035.2
Mining and quarrying	13.8	15.8	19.4
Manufacturing	571.4	589.9	601.1
Electricity, gas and water	115.8	125.7	137.0
Construction	83.0	90.4	91.2
Trade, restaurants and hotels	977.2	1,036.5	1,060.6
Transport, storage and communications	335.6	361.0	377.2
Finance, insurance and real estate	184.2	201.2	215.2
Ownership of dwellings	189.0	196.7	203.0
General government services	303.0	309.4	316.8
Other community, social and personal services	234.5	242.6	250.7
Total	3,982.7	4,179.2	4,307.4

* Preliminary figures.

BALANCE OF PAYMENTS (US $ million)

	1994	1995	1996
Exports of goods f.o.b.	1,550.1	2,157.5	2,236.9
Imports of goods f.o.b.	−2,546.6	−3,032.6	−2,880.3
Trade balance	−996.5	−875.1	−643.4
Exports of services	697.5	665.9	559.0
Imports of services	−644.9	−694.9	−659.7
Balance on goods and services	−943.9	−904.1	−744.1
Other income received	63.6	46.6	40.2
Other income paid	−193.6	−205.7	−270.1
Balance on goods, services and income	−1,073.9	−1,063.2	−974.0
Current transfers received	456.4	508.2	537.1
Current transfers paid	−7.8	−17.0	−14.6
Current balance	−625.3	−572.0	−451.5
Capital account (net)	—	61.6	65.0
Direct investment from abroad	65.2	75.2	76.9
Portfolio investment assets	−9.8	−22.2	−11.5
Portfolio investment liabilities	7.1	5.9	−4.5
Other investment assets	116.8	125.1	199.2
Other investment liabilities	475.9	310.8	412.2
Net errors and omissions	−23.6	−136.2	−71.7
Overall balance	6.3	−151.8	214.1

Source: IMF, *International Financial Statistics*.

External Trade

PRINCIPAL COMMODITIES (US $ million)

Imports c.i.f.	1994	1995	1996*
Consumer goods	828.3	925.5	877.9
Non-durable	556.5	607.0	626.6
Durable	271.8	318.5	251.3
Raw materials and intermediate products	1,046.6	1,245.6	1,150.2
Materials for agriculture	107.9	114.1	115.3
Materials for industry	832.6	1,131.5	1,034.9
Fuels and lubricants	200.5	172.6	201.7
Petroleum	106.1	114.0	128.0
Construction materials	78.3	83.0	94.8
Capital goods	623.5	748.7	690.6
Industry	405.3	477.2	470.9
Transport	192.2	235.6	186.0
Total (incl. others)	2,781.4	3,292.5	3,146.2

Exports f.o.b.	1994	1995*	1996*
Coffee (incl. soluble)	346.0	575.9	453.5
Bananas	119.5	145.9	162.2
Sugar	172.4	246.0	220.4
Petroleum	22.2	32.8	60.3
Cardamom	42.2	40.7	39.4
Total (incl. others)	1,550.1	2,155.5	2,213.3

* Preliminary figures.

Source: Banco de Guatemala.

PRINCIPAL TRADING PARTNERS (US $ million)

Imports c.i.f.	1993	1994	1995
Aruba	8.6	2.0	102.0
Brazil	56.7	48.4	50.8
Canada	32.2	28.9	50.3
Costa Rica	65.0	83.8	69.3
El Salvador	138.9	165.0	161.2
Germany	102.2	104.8	116.1
Honduras	27.6	37.6	53.3
Italy	46.2	39.5	36.9
Japan	138.0	100.6	121.2
Korea, Republic	20.2	22.5	34.8
Mexico	168.5	185.9	308.2
Netherlands	24.6	29.0	30.2
Netherlands Antilles	—	47.3	1.0
Panama	49.5	68.1	86.4
Russia	9.8	27.2	24.7
United Kingdom	37.2	34.6	39.5
USA	1,313.2	1,169.0	1,478.4
Venezuela	130.9	137.2	151.7
Total (incl. others)	2,667.6	2,647.2	3,292.4

Exports f.o.b.	1993	1994	1995
Belgium-Luxembourg	15.1	16.6	32.7
Canada	12.6	14.9	22.2
China, People's Republic	—	—	34.0
Costa Rica	95.5	97.6	101.0
El Salvador	191.2	229.0	268.9
France (incl. Monaco)	15.4	15.0	21.5
Germany	59.3	65.3	112.5
Honduras	77.0	87.0	124.8
Italy	14.5	18.4	23.3
Japan	23.3	38.8	53.5
Mexico	47.6	67.2	45.0
Netherlands	20.8	27.9	38.4
Nicaragua	54.6	61.3	71.0
Panama	28.5	32.7	37.0
Peru	16.4	17.9	28.6
Saudi Arabia	18.6	19.8	19.8
Sri Lanka	1.2	23.6	12.4
Sweden	5.4	10.3	25.6
United Kingdom	15.8	11.2	13.2
USA	510.6	483.4	605.8
Venezuela	4.1	29.5	37.8
Total (incl. others)	1,338.2	1,502.4	1,935.5

Source: UN, *International Trade Statistics Yearbook*.

Transport

RAILWAYS (traffic)

	1989	1990	1991
Passenger-km (million)	10,213	15,960	12,531
Freight ton-km (million)	51,546	44,134	47,233

Source: UN, *Statistical Yearbook*.

ROAD TRAFFIC ('000 motor vehicles in use)

	1992	1993	1994
Passenger cars	306.3	323.9	347.2
Commercial vehicles	73.6	70.4	70.6

Source: Ministry of Public Finance.

SHIPPING

Merchant Fleet (registered at 31 December)

	1994	1995	1996
Number of vessels	7	5	5
Total displacement ('000 grt)	1.4	0.8	0.8

Source: Lloyd's Register of Shipping, *World Fleet Statistics*.

International Sea-borne Freight Traffic ('000 metric tons)

	1992	1993	1994
Goods loaded	2,176	1,818	2,096
Goods unloaded	3,201	3,025	3,822

CIVIL AVIATION (traffic on scheduled services)

	1992	1993	1994
Kilometres flown (million)	6	6	6
Passengers carried ('000)	230	240	252
Passenger-km (million)	366	384	411
Total ton-km (million)	52	56	58

Source: UN, *Statistical Yearbook*.

Tourism

	1993	1994	1995
Tourist arrivals	561,917	537,374	585,000
Receipts (US $ million)	265.4	258.0	276.0

Source: Instituto Guatemalteco de Turismo (INGUAT).

Communications Media

	1992	1993	1994
Radio receivers ('000 in use)	400	400	400
Television receivers ('000 in use)	n.a.	n.a.	768
Daily newspapers: number	6	6	6
Telephones ('000 main lines in use)*	214	231	245
Telefax stations (number in use)*	4,000	6,000	10,000
Mobile cellular telephones (subscribers)*	2,141	2,990	10,460

* Source: UN, *Statistical Yearbook*.

Education

(1993)

	Institutions	Teachers	Students		
			Males	Females	Total
Pre-primary	4,553	7,708	100,316	92,745	193,061
Primary	10,770	44,220	756,373	637,548	1,393,921
Secondary	2,308*	20,942	178,013	156,370	334,383

* 1992 figure, preliminary.

1994: Primary students 1,449,981.

Source: Mainly UNESCO, *Statistical Yearbook*.

Directory

The Constitution*

In December 1984 the Constituent Assembly drafted a new Constitution (based on that of 1965), which was approved in May 1985 and came into effect in January 1986. Its main provisions are summarized below:

Guatemala has a republican representative democratic system of government and power is exercised equally by the legislative, executive and judicial bodies. The official language is Spanish. Suffrage is universal and secret, obligatory for those who can read and write and optional for those who are illiterate. The free formation and growth of political parties whose aims are democratic is guaranteed. There is no discrimination on grounds of race, colour, sex, religion, birth, economic or social position or political opinions.

The State will give protection to capital and private enterprise in order to develop sources of labour and stimulate creative activity.

Monopolies are forbidden and the State will limit any enterprise which might prejudice the development of the community. The right to social security is recognized and it shall be on a national, unitary, obligatory basis.

Constitutional guarantees may be suspended in certain circumstances for up to 30 days (unlimited in the case of war).

CONGRESS

Legislative power rests with Congress, which is made up of 116 deputies, 87 of whom are elected directly by the people through universal suffrage. The remaining 29 deputies are elected on the basis of proportional representation. Congress meets on 15 January each year and ordinary sessions last four months; extraordinary sessions can be called by the Permanent Commission or the Executive. All Congressional decisions must be taken by absolute majority of the members, except in special cases laid down by law. Deputies are elected for five years; they may be re-elected after a lapse of one session, but only once. Congress is responsible for all matters concerning the President and Vice-President and their execution of their offices; for all electoral matters; for all matters concerning the laws of the Republic; for approving the budget and decreeing taxes; for declaring war; for conferring honours, both civil and military; for fixing the coinage and the system of weights and measures; for approving, by two-thirds' majority, any international treaty or agreement affecting the law, sovereignty, financial status or security of the country.

PRESIDENT

The President is elected by universal suffrage, by absolute majority for a non-extendable period of five years. Re-election or prolongation of the presidential term of office are punishable by law. The President is responsible for national defence and security, fulfilling the Constitution, leading the armed forces, taking any necessary steps in time of national emergency, passing and executing laws, international policy, nominating and removing Ministers, officials and diplomats, co-ordinating the actions of Ministers of State. The Vice-President's duties include presiding over Congress and taking part in the discussions of the Council of Ministers.

ARMY

The Guatemalan Army is intended to maintain national independence, sovereignty and honour, territorial integrity and peace within the Republic. It is an indivisible, apolitical, non-deliberating body and is made up of land, sea and air forces.

LOCAL ADMINISTRATIVE DIVISIONS

For the purposes of administration the territory of the Republic is divided into Departments and these into Municipalities, but this division can be modified by Congress to suit interests and general development of the Nation without loss of municipal autonomy.

JUDICIARY

Justice is exercised exclusively by the Supreme Court of Justice and other tribunals. Administration of Justice is obligatory, free and independent of the other functions of State. The President of the Judiciary, judges and other officials are elected by Congress for six years. The Supreme Court of Justice is made up of at least seven judges. The President of the Judiciary is also President of the Supreme Court. The Supreme Court nominates all other judges. Under the Supreme Court come the Court of Appeal, the Administrative Disputes Tribunal, the Tribunal of Second Instance of Accounts, Jurisdiction Conflicts, First Instance and Military, the Extraordinary Tribunal of Protection. There is a Court of Constitutionality presided over by the President of the Supreme Court.

* A series of changes to the Constitution, which were approved by referendum on 30 January 1994 and concerned the election of a new Congress (to serve until 14 January 1996), the appointment of members of a new Supreme Court and the reduction in the term of office of the President, legislature and municipal authorities (from five to four years), and of Supreme Court justices (from six to five years), took effect in April 1994. In addition, the number of deputies in Congress was reduced from 116 to 80, of whom 64 are elected according to departmental representation and 16 by national listing.

Under the terms of an accord, signed with the URNG in September 1996, concerning civilian power and the role of the armed forces, the Government undertook to revise the Constitution to relieve the armed forces of responsibility for internal security. This role would be assumed by a new National Civilian Police force.

The Government

HEAD OF STATE

President: Alvaro Enrique Arzú Irigoyen (took office 14 January 1996).

Vice-President: Luis Flores Asturias.

CABINET
(February 1998)

Minister of Foreign Affairs: Eduardo Stein.

Minister of the Interior: Rodolfo Adrián Mendoza Rosales.

Minister of National Defence: Gen. Hector Mario Barrios Celada.

Minister of Economy: Juan Mauricio Wurmser Ordóñez.

Minister of Public Finance: José Alejandro Arévalo Alburez.

Minister of Public Health and Social Welfare: Marco Tulio Sosa Ramírez.

Minister of Communications, Transport and Public Works: Fritz García Gallout.

Minister of Agriculture, Livestock and Food: Mariano Ventura.

Minister of Education: Roberto Moreno Godoy.

Minister of Employment and Social Security: Héctor Cifuentes Mendoza.

Minister of Energy and Mines: Leonel Eliseo López Rodao.

Minister of Culture and Sport: Víctor Augusto Vela Mena.

MINISTRIES

Ministry of Agriculture, Livestock and Food: Palacio Nacional, 6a Calle y 7a Avda, Zona 1, Guatemala City; tel. 28-6696; fax 253-6807.

Ministry of Communications, Transport and Public Works: Palacio Nacional, 6a Calle y 7a Avda, Zona 1, Guatemala City; tel. 22-1212; fax 28-1613.

Ministry of Culture and Sport: 24a Calle 3-81, Zona 1, Guatemala City; tel. 230-0718; fax 230-0758.

Ministry of Economy: Palacio Nacional, 6a Calle y 7a Avda, Zona 1, Guatemala City.

Ministry of Education: Palacio Nacional, 6a Calle y 7a Avda, Zona 1, Guatemala City; tel. 22-0162; fax 253-7386.

Ministry of Employment and Social Security: Edif. NASA, 14 Calle 5–49, Zona 1, Guatemala City; tel. 230-1364; fax 251-3559.

Ministry of Energy and Mines: Diagonal 17, 29–78, Zona 11, Guatemala City; tel. 276-0679; fax 276-3175.

Ministry of Foreign Affairs: Palacio Nacional, 6a Calle y 7a Avda, Zona 1, Guatemala City; tel. 22-1212; fax 251-6745.

Ministry of the Interior: Palacio Nacional, 6a Calle y 7a Avda, Zona 1, Guatemala City; tel. 22-1212; fax 251-5368.

Ministry of National Defence: Palacio Nacional, 6a Calle y 7a Avda, Zona 1, Guatemala City; tel. 22-1212; telex 248368; fax 28-1613.

Ministry of Public Finance: Edif. de Fianzas, Centro Cívico, 8a Avda y Calle 21, Zona 1, Guatemala City; tel. 251-1380; telex 9702; fax 251-0987.

Ministry of Public Health and Social Welfare: Palacio Nacional, 6a Calle y 7a Avda, Zona 1, Guatemala City; tel. 22-1212; fax 22-2736.

President and Legislature

PRESIDENT

Election, 12 November 1995

	Percentage of votes cast
Alvaro Enrique Arzú Irigoyen (PAN)	36.55
Alfonso Portillo (FRG)	22.04
Fernando Andrade (AN)	12.94
Jorge González del Valle (FDNG)	7.71
Total (incl. others)	100.00

Since none of the 19 candidates achieved the required 50% of the votes necessary to win outright, a second round of voting was held on 7 January 1996. At this election Alvaro Enrique Arzú Irigoyen (PAN) received 51.22% of the valid votes cast, while Alfonso Portillo (FRG) won the remaining 48.78%.

CONGRESO NACIONAL

President: Arabella Castro.

Election, 12 November 1995

	Seats
Partido de Avanzada Nacional (PAN)	43
Frente Republicano Guatemalteco (FRG)	21
Alianza Nacional (AN)	9
Frente Democrático Nueva Guatemala (FDNG)	6
Movimiento de Liberación Nacional (MLN)	1
Total	80

Political Organizations

Acción Reconciliadora Democrática (ARDE): 4a Avda 14-53, Zona 1, Guatemala City; tel. 232-0591; fax 251-4076; centre-right; Sec.-Gen. Herlindo Alvarez del Cid.

Alianza Democrática: Guatemala City; f. 1983; centre party; Leader Leopoldo Urrutia.

Alianza Nacional (AN): electoral alliance comprising:

Partido Democracia Cristiana Guatemalteca (PDCG): Avda Elena 20-66, Zona 3, Guatemala City; tel. 28-4988; f. 1968; 130,000 mems; Sec.-Gen. Luis Alfonso Cabrera Hidalgo.

Partido Socialista Democrático (PSD): 12a Calle 10-37, Zona 1, 01001, Apdo 1279, Guatemala City; tel. 253-3219; fax 273-7036; f. 1978; Sec.-Gen. Sergio Alejandro Pérez Cruz.

Unión del Centro Nacional (UCN): 12a Calle 2-45, Zona 1, Guatemala City; tel. 253-6211; f. 1984; centre party; Sec.-Gen. Edmond Mulet.

Alianza Popular Cinco (AP5): 6a Avda 3-23, Zona 1, Guatemala City; tel. 231-6022; Sec.-Gen. Max Orlando Molina Narciso.

Central Auténtica Nacionalista (CAN): 15a Avda 4-31, Zona 1, Guatemala City; tel. 251-2992; f. 1980 from the CAO (Central Arañista Organizado); Leader Héctor Mayora Dawe; Sec.-Gen. Jorge Roberto Arana España.

Comité Guatemalteca de Unidad Patriota (CGUP): f. 1982; opposition coalition consisting of:

Frente Democrático Contra la Represión (FDCR): Leader Rafael García.

Frente Popular 31 de Enero (FP-31): f. 1980; left-wing amalgamation of student, peasant and trade union groups.

Desarrollo Integral Auténtico (DIA): 12a Calle 'A' 2-18, Zona 1, Guatemala City; Sec.-Gen. Francisco Rolando Morales Chávez.

Frente de Avance Nacional (FAN): 3a Calle 'A' 1-66, Zona 10, Guatemala City; tel. 231-8036; right-wing group; Sec.-Gen. Federico Abundio Maldonado Gularte.

Frente Cívico Democrático (FCD): Guatemala City; Leader Jorge González del Valle; formed electoral alliance with PDCG, January 1985.

Frente Demócrata Guatemalteco: Leader Clemente Marroquín Rojas.

Frente Democrático Nueva Guatemala (FDNG): left-wing faction of Partido Revolucionario; Leader Jorge González del Valle.

Frente Republicano Guatemalteco (FRG): 6a Avda 'A' 3-18, Zona 1, Guatemala City; tel. 250-1778; right-wing group; leader Gen. (retd) José Efraín Ríos Montt.

Frente de Unidad Nacional (FUN): 6a Avda 5-18, Zona 12, Guatemala City; tel. 271-4048; f. 1971; nationalist group; Leader Gabriel Girón Ortiz.

Fuerza Demócrata Popular: 11a Calle 4-13, Zona 1, Guatemala City; tel. 251-5496; f. 1983; democratic popular force; Sec. Lic. Francisco Reyes Ixcamey.

Fuerza Nueva: Leader Carlos Rafael Soto.

Movimiento de los Descamisados (MD): Avda J. R. Barrios L. 896 Sta Luisa, Zona 6, Guatemala City; Sec.-Gen. Enrique Morales Pérez.

Movimiento Humanista de Integración Demócrata: Guatemala City; f. 1983; Leader Victoriano Alvarez.

Movimiento de Liberación Nacional (MLN): 5a Calle 1–20, Zona 1, Guatemala City; tel. 22-6528; f. 1960; extreme right-wing; 95,000 mems; Leader Lic. Mario Sandóval Alarcón; Sec.-Gen. Edgar Antonio Figueroa Muñoz.

Movimiento 20 de Octubre: Leader Marco Antonio Villamar Contreras.

Pantinamit: f. 1977; represents interests of Indian population; Leader Fernando Tezahuic Tohón.

Partido de Avanzada Nacional (PAN): 6a Calle 7-70, Zona 9, Guatemala City; tel. 231-7431; Leader Alvaro Enrique Arzú Irigoyen; Gen. Sec. Héctor Cifuentes Mendoza.

Partido Demócrata Guatemalteco (PDG): 5a Calle 3-30, Zona 9, Guatemala City; tel. 231-2550; Sec.-Gen. Jorge Antonio Reyna Castillo.

Partido Institucional Democrático (PID): 2a Calle 10–73, Zona 1, Guatemala City; tel. 28-5412; f. 1965; 60,000 mems; moderate conservative; Sec.-Gen. Oscar Humberto Rivas García; Dir Donaldo Alvarez Ruiz.

Partido Liberal Progresista (PLP): Diagonal 16, 11-188, Zona 1, Quetzaltenango; Sec.-Gen. Ismael Muñoz Pérez.

Partido Petenero: Guatemala City; f. 1983; defends regional interests of El Petén.

Partido Progresista (PP): 1a Calle 6-77, Zona 2, Guatemala City; Sec.-Gen. José Ramón Fernández González.

Partido Reformador Guatemalteco (PREG): 3a Calle 9-59, Zona 1, Guatemala City; tel. 22-8759; Sec.-Gen. Miguel Angel Montepeque Contreras.

Partido Revolucionario de los Trabajadores Centro-americanos (PRTC): Guatemala City.

Partido Social Cristiano (PSC): P. Savoy, Of. 113, 8°, 8a Calle 9-41, Zona 1, Guatemala City; tel. 274-0577; f. 1983; Sec.-Gen. Alfonso Alonzo Barillas.

Partido de Unificación Anticomunista (PUA): Guatemala City; right-wing party; Leader Leonel Sisniega Otero.

Unión Democrática (UD): 10a Avda 11-27, Zona 1, Guatemala City; tel. 251-7687; Sec.-Gen. José Luis Chea Urruela.

Unidad Nacionalista Organizada (UNO): Calzada Aguilar Batres 17-14, Zona 11, Guatemala City; Sec.-Gen. Mario Roberto Armando Ponciano Castillo.

Unión Reformista Social (URS): 5a Calle 'A' 0-64, Zona 3, Guatemala City; Sec.-Gen. Marcos Emilio Recinos Alvarez.

In February 1982 the principal guerrilla groups unified to form the **Unidad Revolucionaria Nacional Guatemalteca (URNG)** (Guatemalan National Revolutionary Unity), which has links with the PSD. The political wing of the URNG was the **Representación Unitaria de la Oposición Guatemalteca (RUOG).** At the end of 1996 the URNG consisted of:

Ejército Guerrillero de los Pobres (EGP): f. 1972; draws main support from Indians of western highlands; works closely with the **Comité de Unidad Campesina (CUC)** (Committee of Peasant Unity) and radical Catholic groups; mems 4,000 armed, 12,000 unarmed; Commdr Ricardo Arnoldo Ramírez de León ('Roland Morán').

Fuerzas Armadas Rebeldes (FAR): formed early 1960s; originally military commission of CGTG; associated with the CNT and CONUS trade unions; based in Guatemala City, Chimaltenango and El Petén; Commdr Jorge Ismael Soto García ('Pablo Monsanto').

Organización del Pueblo en Armas (ORPA): f. 1979; military group active in San Marcos province; originally part of FAR; Commdr Rodrigo Asturias ('Gaspar Ilom').

Partido Guatemalteco del Trabajo (PGT): communist party; divided into three armed factions: PGT-Camarilla (began actively participating in war in 1981); PGT-Núcleo de Conducción y Dirección; PGT-Comisión Nuclear; Gen. Sec. Ricardo Rosales ('Carlos González').

In December 1996 the Government and the URNG signed a definitive peace treaty, bringing the 36-year conflict to an end. The demobilization of the URNG guerrillas began in March 1997 and was completed by early May. In June the URNG registered as a political party in formation. In August the movement held elections to a provisional executive committee, at which the following were appointed: Sec.-Gen. Ricardo Arnoldo Ramírez de León; Deputy Sec.-Gen. Jorge Ismael Soto García.

Diplomatic Representation

EMBASSIES IN GUATEMALA

Argentina: 2a Avda 11-04, Zona 10, Guatemala City; telex 5285; Ambassador: Dr Angel Fernando Girardi.

Austria: 6a Avda 20-25, Zona 10, Guatemala City; tel. 368-1134; telex 5224; fax 333-6180; Ambassador: Dr Daniel Krumholz.

Belgium: Avda de la Reforma 13-70, Zona 9, Apdo 687-A, Guatemala City; tel. 231-5608; telex 5137; Ambassador: Paul Vermeirsch.

Belize: Edif. El Reformador, Suite 803, 8°, Avda de la Reforma 1-50, Zona 9, Guatemala City; tel. 334-5531; fax 334-5536; Ambassador: Mike Mena.

Bolivia: 12a Avda 15-37, Zona 10, Guatemala City; Chargé d'affaires a.i.: Dr José Gabina Villanueva G.

Brazil: 18a Calle 2-22, Zona 14, Apdo 196-A, Guatemala City; tel. 337-0949; telex 5200; fax 337-3475; e-mail brasilgua@gua.gbm.net; Ambassador: Sérgio Damasceno Vieira.

Canada: Edyma Plaza, 13a Calle 8-44210, 8 Nivel, Guatemala City; tel. 233-6102; telex 5206; fax 233-6189; Ambassador: James Fox.

Chile: 13a Calle 7-85, Zona 10, Guatemala City; telex 6162; Ambassador: Silvio Salgado Ramírez.

China (Taiwan): 4a Avda 'A' 13–25, Zona 9, Apdo 1646, Guatemala City; tel. 239-0711; Ambassador: Mao Chi-hsien.

Colombia: Edif. Gemini 10, 12a Calle, 1a Avda, Zona 10, Guatemala City; tel. 232-0604; Ambassador: Laura Ochoa de Ardilla.

Costa Rica: Edif. Galerías Reforma, Of. 702, Avda de la Reforma 8-60, Zona 9, Guatemala City; tel. 232-1522; Ambassador: Luis E. Guardia Mora.

Dominican Republic: 7a Calle 'A' 4-28, Zona 10, Guatemala City; Ambassador: Pedro Pablo Alvarez Bonilla.

Ecuador: Of. 602, Avda de la Reforma 12-01, Zona 10, Guatemala City; tel. 231-2439; telex 6218; Ambassador: Diego Paredes-Peña.

Egypt: Avda de la Reforma 7-89, Zona 10, Guatemala City; tel. 231-5315; telex 5157; fax 232-6055; Ambassador: Mohamed Fadel Weheba.

El Salvador: 12a Calle 5-43, Zona 9, Guatemala City; tel. 262-9385; telex 5418; Ambassador: Agustín Martínez Varela.

France: Edif. Marbella, 16a Calle 4-53, Zona 10, Guatemala City; tel. 237-3639; telex 5963; Ambassador: Serge Pinot.

Germany: Edif. Plaza Marítima, 6a Avda 20-25, Zona 10, Guatemala City; tel. 337-0028; telex 5209; Ambassador: Dr Joachim Neukirch.

Holy See: 10a Calle 4-47, Zona 9, Guatemala City (Apostolic Nunciature); tel. 332-4274; fax 362-9541; Apostolic Nuncio: Most Rev. Giovanni Battista Morandini, Titular Archbishop of Numida.

Honduras: 16a Calle 8-27, Zona 10, Apdo 730-A, Guatemala City; tel. 237-3919; telex 5865; fax 233-4629; Ambassador: Guillermo Boquín V.

Israel: 13a Avda 14-07, Zona 10, Guatemala City; telex 5218; Ambassador: Jacques Yaacov Deckel.

Italy: 5a Avda 8-59, Zona 14, Guatemala City; tel. 333-4557; telex 5129; fax 337-0795; e-mail embitaly@guatenet.net.gt; Ambassador: Alessandro Serafini.

Japan: Ruta 6, Zona 4, Apdo 531, Guatemala City; tel. 331-9666; telex 5926; fax 331-5462; Ambassador: Hisato Murayama.

Korea, Republic: 15a Avda 24-51, Zona 13, Apdo 1649, Guatemala City; tel. 232-1578; telex 5369; fax 234-7037; Ambassador: Wung-Sik Kang.

Mexico: 16a Calle 0-51, Zona 14, Guatemala City; tel. 268-0769; telex 5961; Ambassador: Abraham Talavera López.

Nicaragua: 10a Avda 14-72, Zona 10, Guatemala City; telex 5653; Ambassador: Ricardo Zambrana.

Paraguay: 7a Avda 7-78, 8°, Zona 4, Guatemala City; tel. 334-2981; fax 331-5048.

Peru: 2a Avda 9-67, Zona 9, Guatemala City; Ambassador: Julio Florián Alegre.

Portugal: 5a Avda 12-60, Zona 9, Guatemala City; Ambassador: António Cabrita Matias.

Spain: 6a Calle 6-48, Zona 9, Guatemala City; tel. 334-3757; telex 5393; fax 332-2456; Ambassador: Víctor Luis Fagilde González.

Sweden: 8a Avda 15-07, Zona 10, Guatemala City; tel. 233-6536; telex 5916; fax 233-7607; Ambassador: Staffan Wrigstad.

Switzerland: 4a Calle 7-73, Zona 9, Apdo 1426, Guatemala City; tel. 234-0743; telex 5257; fax 231-8524; Ambassador: Willy Hold.

United Kingdom: Edif. Centro Financiero, Torre II, 7°, 7a Avda 5-10, Zona 4, Guatemala City; tel. 332-1601; telex 5686; fax 334-1904; Ambassador: Peter M. Newton.

USA: Avda de la Reforma 7-01, Zona 10, Guatemala City; tel. 231-1541; Ambassador: Donald J. Planty.

Uruguay: 20a Calle 8–00, Zona 10, Guatemala City; Chargé d'affaires: Héctor L. Pedetti A.

Venezuela: 8a Calle 0-56, Zona 9, Guatemala City; telex 5317; Ambassador: Dr Rogelio Rosas Gil.

Judicial System

Corte Suprema: Centro Cívico, 21a Calle y 7a Avda, Guatemala City; tel. 284323.

There are 13 members of the Supreme Court, appointed by the Congress.

President of the Supreme Court: Ricardo Alfonso Umaña Aragón.

Civil Courts of Appeal: 10 courts, 5 in Guatemala City, 2 in Quezaltenango, 1 each in Jalapa, Zacapa and Antigua. The two Labour Courts of Appeal are in Guatemala City.

Judges of the First Instance: 7 civil and 10 penal in Guatemala City, 2 civil each in Quezaltenango, Escuintla, Jutiapa and San Marcos, 1 civil in each of the 18 remaining Departments of the Republic.

Religion

Almost all of the inhabitants profess Christianity, with a majority belonging to the Roman Catholic Church. In recent years the Protestant Churches have attracted a growing number of converts.

CHRISTIANITY

The Roman Catholic Church

For ecclesiastical purposes, Guatemala comprises two archdioceses, 10 dioceses and the Apostolic Vicariates of El Petén and Izabal. At 31 December 1995 adherents represented about 86% of the total population.

Bishops' Conference: Conferencia Episcopal de Guatemala, Secretariado General del Episcopado, Km 15, Calzada Roosevelt 4-54, Zona 7, Mixco, Apdo 1698, Guatemala City; tel. 293-1831; fax 293-1834; f. 1973; Pres. Jorge Mario Avila del Aguila, Bishop of Jalapa.

Archbishop of Guatemala City: Próspero Peñados del Barrio, Arzobispado, 7a Avda 6-21, Zona 1, Apdo 723, Guatemala City; tel. 22-9601; fax 22-8384.

Archbishop of Los Altos, Quetzaltenango—Totonicapán: Víctor Hugo Martínez Contreras, Arzobispado, 11a Avda 6-27, Zona 1, Apdo 11, Quezaltenango; tel. (961) 2840; fax (961) 6049.

The Anglican Communion

Guatemala is a missionary diocese of Province IX of the Episcopal Church in the USA.

Bishop of Guatemala: Rt Rev. Armando Guerra Soria; Avda Castellana 40–06, Zona 8, Apdo 58-A, Guatemala City; tel. 272-0852; fax 272-0764; diocese founded 1967.

Protestant Churches

The Baptist Church: Convention of Baptist Churches of Guatemala, 12a Calle 9–54, Zona 1, Apdo 322, Guatemala City; tel. 22-4227; f. 1946; Pres. Lic. José Marroquín R.

Church of Jesus Christ of Latter-day Saints: 12a Calle 3–37, Zona 9, Guatemala City; 17 bishoprics, 9 chapels; Regional Rep. Guillermo Enrique Rittscher.

Lutheran Church: Consejo Nacional de Iglesias Luteranas, Apdo 1111, Guatemala City; tel. 22-3401; 3,077 mems; Pres. Rev. David Rodríguez U.

Presbyterian Church: Iglesia Evangélica Presbiteriana Central, 6a Avda 'A' 4–68, Zona 1, Apdo 655, Guatemala City; tel. 22-0791; f. 1882; 36,000 mems; Pastors: Rev. Juan René Girón T., Rev. Julio César Paz Portillo, Rev. José Ramiro Bolaños R.

Union Church: 12a Calle 7–37, Plazuela España, Zona 9, Apdo 150-A, Guatemala City; tel. 331-6904; f. 1943; Pastor: Brent C. Williams.

BAHÁ'Í FAITH

National Spiritual Assembly of the Bahá'ís: 3a Calle 4–54, Zona 1, Guatemala City; tel. 22-9673; fax 22-9673; mems resident in 464 localities; Sec. Marvin E. Alvarado E.

The Press

PRINCIPAL DAILIES

Diario de Centroamérica: 18a Calle 6–72, Zona 1, Guatemala City; tel. 22-4418; f. 1880; morning; official; Dir Luis Mendizábal; circ. 15,000.

El Gráfico: 14a Avda 9–18, Zona 1, Guatemala City; tel. 251-0021; fax 22-1832; f. 1963; morning; Dir Rodrigo Carpio; circ. 60,000.

La Hora: 9a Calle 'A' 1–56, Zona 1, Apdo 1593, Guatemala City; tel. 22-6864; telex 9259; fax 251-7084; f. 1944; evening; independent; Dir Oscar Marroquín Rojas; circ. 18,000.

Impacto: 9a Calle 'A' 1-56, Apdo 1593, Guatemala City; tel. 22-6864; telex 9259; fax 251-7084; daily.

Imparcial: 7a Calle 10-54, Zona 1, Guatemala City; tel. 251-4723; daily; circ. 25,000.

La Nación: 1a Avda 11-12, Guatemala City.

Prensa Libre: 13a Calle 9–31, Zona 1, Apdo 2063, Guatemala City; tel. 251-1830; telex 5566; fax 251-8768; f. 1951; morning; independent; Gen. Man. Edgar Contreras; Editor Miguel Conde; circ. 116,000.

Siglo Veintiuno: 7a Avda 11-63, Guatemala City; tel. 234-6216; fax 231-9145; f. 1990; morning; Editor-in-Chief Jorge Yee.

La Tarde: 14a Avda 4-33, Guatemala City.

PERIODICALS

AGA: 9a Calle 3–43, Zona 1, Guatemala City; monthly; agricultural.

Gerencia: 6a Avda 1-36, Zona 14, Guatemala City; tel. 332-9332; fax 332-9342; f. 1963; monthly; official organ of the Association of Guatemalan Managers; Editor Margarita Sologuren.

El Industrial: 6a Ruta 9-21, Zona 4, Guatemala City; monthly; official organ of the Chamber of Industry.

Inforpress Centroamericana: 9a Calle 'A' 3-56, Zona 1, Guatemala City; tel. 22-9432; fax 28-3859; f. 1972; weekly; Spanish; regional political and economic news and analysis; Dir Ariel de León.

Panorama Internacional: 13a Calle 8-44, Zona 9, Apdo 611-A, Guatemala City; tel. 233-6367; fax 233-6203; weekly; politics, economics, culture.

PRESS ASSOCIATIONS

Asociación de Periodistas de Guatemala (APG): 14a Calle 3-29, Zona 1, Guatemala City; tel. 232-1813; fax 238-2781; f. 1947; Pres. Julio Rafael Mendizábal Guzmán; Sec. Alvaro Enrique Palma Sandoval.

Cámara Guatemalteca de Periodismo (CGP): Guatemala City; Pres. Eduardo Díaz Reina.

Círculo Nacional de Prensa (CNP): Guatemala City; Pres. Israel Tobar Alvarado.

NEWS AGENCIES

Inforpress Centroamericana: 7a Avda 2-05, Zona 1, Guatemala City; tel. and fax 232-9034; f. 1972; independent news agency; publishes two weekly news bulletins, in English and Spanish.

Foreign Bureaux

ACAN-EFE (Central America): Edif. El Centro, 8°, Of. 8-21, 9a Calle y 7a Avda, Zona 1, Of. Guatemala City; tel. 251-9454; fax 251-9484: Man. Ana Carolina Alpírez A.

Agenzia Nazionale Stampa Associata (ANSA) (Italy): Torre Norte, Edif. Geminis 10, Of. 805, 12a Calle 1-25, Zona 10, Guatemala City; tel. 235-3039; telex 5251; Chief Alfonso Anzueto López.

Deutsche Presse-Agentur (dpa) (Germany): 5a Calle 4-30, Zona 1, Apdo 2333, Guatemala City; tel. 251-7505; telex 5227; fax 251-7505; Correspondent Julio César Anzueto.

Inter Press Service (IPS) (Italy): Edif. El Centro, 3°, Of. 13, 7a Avda 8-56, Zona 1, Guatemala City; tel. 253-8837; telex 9246; fax 251-4736; Correspondent George Rodríguez-Oteiza.

United Press International (UPI) (USA): 6a Calle 4-17, Zona 1, Guatemala City; tel. and fax 251-4258; Correspondent Amafredo Castellanos.

Publishers

Ediciones América: 12a Avda 14-55b, Zone 1, Guatemala City; tel. 251-4556; Man. Dir Rafael Escobar Argüello.

Ediciones Gama: 5a Avda 14-46, Zone 1, Guatemala City; tel. 234-2331; Man. Dir SARA MONZÓN DE ECHEVERRÍA.

Ediciones Legales 'Commercio e Industria': 12a Avda 14-78, Zone 1, Guatemala City; tel. 253-5725; Man. Dir LUIS EMILIO BARRIOS.

Editorial Impacto: Via 6, 3-14, Zone 4, Guatemala City; tel. 232-2887; Man. Dir IVÁN CARPIO.

Editorial del Ministerio de Educación: 15a Avda 3-22, Zona 1, Guatemala City.

Editorial Nueva Narrativa: Edificio El Patio, Of. 106, 7a Avda 7-07, Zona 4, Guatemala City; Man. Dir MAX ARAÚJO A.

Editorial Oscar de León Palacios: 6a Calle 'A' 10-12, Zone 11, Guatemala City; tel. 272-1636; educational texts; Man. Dir OSCAR DE LEÓN CASTILLO.

Editorial Palo de Hormigo: O Calle 16-40, Zone 15, Col. El Maestro, Guatemala City; tel. 269-2080; fax 231-5928; Man. Dir JUAN FERNANDO CIFUENTES.

Editorial Universitaria: Edif. de la Editorial Universitaria, Universidad de San Carlos de Guatemala, Ciudad Universitaria, Zona 12, Guatemala City; tel. 276-0790; literature, social sciences, health, pure and technical sciences, humanities, secondary and university educational textbooks; Editor IVANOVA ALVARADO DE ANCHETA.

Piedra Santa: 5a Calle 7-55, Zona 1, Guatemala City; tel. 232-9053; fax 232-9053; f. 1947; children's literature, text books; Man. Dir ORALIA DÍAZ DE PIEDRA SANTA.

Seminario de Integración Social Guatemalteco: 11a Calle 4-31, Zona 1, Guatemala City; tel. 22-9754; f. 1956; sociology, anthropology, social sciences, educational textbooks.

Broadcasting and Communications

TELECOMMUNICATIONS

Superintendencia de Telecomunicaciones de Guatemala: Edif. Murano Center, 16°, 14a Calle 3-51, Zona 10, Guatemala City; tel. 366-5880; fax 366-5890; e-mail supertel@sit.gob.gt; Superintendent MARIO ROBERTO PAZ.

Empresa Guatemalteca de Telecomunicaciones (Guatel): 7a Avda 12-39, Zona 1, Guatemala City; privatization pending in 1998; Dir ALFREDO GUZMÁN.

BROADCASTING

Dirección General de Radiodifusión y Televisión Nacional: Edif. Tipografía Nacional, 3°, 18 de Septiembre 6-72, Zona 1, Guatemala City; tel. 253-2539; f. 1931; government supervisory body; Dir-Gen. ENRIQUE ALBERTO HERNÁNDEZ ESCOBAR.

Radio

There are five government and six educational stations, including:

La Voz de Guatemala: 18a Calle 6-72, Zona 1, Guatemala City; tel. 253-2539; government station; Dir ARTURO SOTO ECHEVERRÍA.

Radio Cultural TGN: 4a Avda 30-09, Zona 3, Apdo 601, Guatemala City; tel. 471-4378; fax 440-0260; f. 1950; religious and cultural station; programmes in Spanish and English, Cakchiquel and Kekchí; Dir ESTEBAN SYWULKA; Man. A. WAYNE BERGER.

There are some 80 commercial stations, of which the most important are:

Emisoras Unidas de Guatemala: 4a Calle 6-84, Zona 13, Guatemala City; tel. 440-5133; fax 440-5159; f. 1964; Pres. JORGE EDGARDO ARCHILA MARROQUÍN; Vice-Pres. ROLANDO ARCHILA MARROQUÍN.

Radio Cinco Sesenta: 14a Calle 4-73, Zona 11, Guatemala City; Dir EDNA CASTILLO OBREGÓN.

Radio Continental: 15a Calle 3-45, Zona 1, Guatemala City; Dir ROBERTO VIZCAÍNO R.

Radio Nuevo Mundo: 6a Avda 10-45, Zona 1, Apdo 281, Guatemala City; Man. ALFREDO GONZÁLEZ G.

Radio Panamericana: 1a Avda 35-48, Zona 7, Guatemala City; Dir JAIME J. PANIAGUA.

La Voz de las Américas: 11a Calle 2-43, Zona 1, Guatemala City; Dir AUGUSTO LÓPEZ S.

Television

Canal 3—Radio-Televisión Guatemala, SA: 30a Avda 3-40, Zona 11, Apdo 1367, Guatemala City; tel. 292-2491; telex 5253; fax 294-7492; f. 1956; commercial station; Pres. Lic. MAX KESTLER FARNÉS; Vice-Pres. J. F. VILLANUEVA.

Canal 5—Televisión Cultural y Educativa, SA: 4a Calle 18-38, Zona 1, Guatemala City; tel. 253-1913; f. 1979; cultural and educational programmes; Dir ALFREDO HERRERA CABRERA.

Teleonce: 20a Calle 5-02, Zona 10, Guatemala City; tel. 268-2165; commercial; Dir A. MOURRA.

Televisiete, SA: 3a Calle 6-24, Zona 9, Apdo 1242, Guatemala City; tel. 26-2216; f. 1964; commercial station channel 7; Dir Dr J. VILLANUEVA P.

Trecevisión, SA: 3a Calle 10-70, Zona 10, Guatemala City; tel. 26-3266; telex 6070; commercial; Dir Ing. PEDRO MELGAR R.; Gen. Man. GILDA VALLADARES ORTIZ.

Finance

(cap. = capital; p.u. = paid up; res = reserves; dep. = deposits; m. = million; brs = branches; amounts in quetzales)

BANKING

Superintendencia de Bancos: 9a Avda 22-00, Zona 1, Apdo 2306, Guatemala City; tel. 232-0001; telex 5231; fax 232-5301; e-mail sibcos@guate.net; f. 1946; Superintendent ROBERTO A. GUTIÉRREZ NÁJERA.

Central Bank

Banco de Guatemala: 7a Avda 22-01, Zona 1, Apdo 365, Guatemala City; tel. 230-6222; telex 5231; fax 253-4035; f. 1946; guarantee fund 94.8m. (Sept. 1987); Pres. EDÍN VELÁSQUEZ; Man. JULIO ROBERTO SUÁREZ GUERRA; 8 brs.

State Commercial Bank

Crédito Hipotecario Nacional de Guatemala: 7a Avda 22-77, Zona 1, Apdo 242, Guatemala City; tel. 230-6562; telex 5192; fax 351-2692; f. 1930; government-owned; cap. p.u. 15m., res 10.7m., dep. 1.9m. (June 1988); Pres. Lic. RICARDO CONTRERAS CRUZ; Gen. Man. GABRIEL RODRIGO CASTELLANOS QUINTANILLA; 19 agencies.

Private Commercial Banks

Guatemala City

Banco Agrícola Mercantil, SA: 7a Avda 9-11, Zona 1, Guatemala City; tel. 232-1601; telex 5347; fax 251-0780; f. 1948; cap. 5m., res 56.7m., dep. 893.3m. (Dec. 1994); Man. ARMANDO GONZÁLEZ CAMPO; 2 brs, 8 agencies.

Banco del Agro, SA: 9a Calle 5-39, Zona 1, Apdo 1443, Guatemala City; tel. 251-4026; fax 232-4566; f. 1956; cap. 10.0m., res 19.4m., dep. 374.9m. (June 1991); Pres. JOSÉ MARÍA VALDÉS GARCÍA; Gen. Man. HÉCTOR ESTUARDO PIVARAL; 25 brs.

Banco del Café, SA: Avda de la Reforma 9-30, Zona 9, Apdo 831, Guatemala City; tel. 331-1311; telex 5123; fax 331-1418; f. 1978; cap. 17.5m., res 29.1m., dep. 874.0m. (Dec. 1994); Pres. EDUARDO MANUEL GONZÁLEZ RIVERA; Asst Gen. Man. INGO HABERLAND HAESLOOP.

Banco de la Construcción, SA: 12a Calle 4-17, Zona 1, Apdo 999, Guatemala City; tel. 230-6382; telex 5708; fax 230-6148; f. 1983; cap. 40.0m., dep. 336.6m. (Dec. 1993); Pres. MANUEL ENRIQUE MOLINA BARRERA; Exec. Man. EDIN HOMERO VELÁSQUEZ ESCOBEDO.

Banco del Ejército, SA: 5a Avda 6-06, Zona 1, Apdo 1797, Guatemala City; tel. 253-2146; telex 5574; fax 251-9105; f. 1972; cap. 18.5m., res 31.3m., dep. 311.8m. (Dec. 1996); Pres. Col GUIDO FERNANDO ABDALA PEÑAGOS; 14 brs.

Banco de Exportación, SA: Avda de la Reforma 11-49, Zona 10, Guatemala City; tel. 231-9861; telex 5896; fax 232-2879; f. 1985; cap. 71.8m., res 30.0m., dep. 731.3m. (Dec. 1993); Pres. Dr FRANCISCO MANSILLA CÓRDOVA; Man. Ing. RAFAEL VIEJO RODRÍGUEZ.

Banco Granai y Townson, SA: 7a Avda 1-86, Zona 4, Apdo 654, Guatemala City; tel. 331-2333; telex 5159; fax 332-9083; f. 1962; cap. 33.0m., res 37.5m., dep. 1,405.8m. (Dec. 1993); Pres. MARIO GRANAI ARÉVALO; Gen. Man. GERARDO TOWNSON RINCÓN; 40 brs.

Banco Industrial, SA (BAINSA): Edif. Centro Financiero, Torre 1, 7a Avda 5-10, Zona 4, Apdo 744, Guatemala City; tel. 234-5111; telex 5236; fax 232-1712; f. 1964 to promote industrial development; cap. and res 119.1m., dep. 1,709.7m. (June 1994); Pres. JUAN MIGUEL TORREBIARTE LANTZENDORFFER; Gen. Man. Lic. NORBERTO RODOLFO CASTELLANOS DÍAZ.

Banco Inmobilario, SA: 7a Avda 11-59, Zona 9, Apdo 1181, Guatemala City; tel. 332-1950; telex 5204; fax 332-2325; f. 1958; cap. 45.0m., res 6.2m., dep. 532.3m. (June 1992); Pres. EMILIO ANTONIO PERALTA PORTILLO. ; Man. MARCO ANTONIO OVANDO; 15 brs.

Banco Internacional, SA: 7a Avda 11-20, Zona 1, Apdo 2588, Guatemala City; tel. 353-8679; telex 4178; fax 232-7390; f. 1976; cap. 10.0m., res 4.5m., dep. 236.5m. (Dec. 1988); Pres. Lic. JORGE SKINNER-KLÉE; Gen. Man. JULIO VIELMAN PINEDA; 11 brs.

Banco Metropolitano, SA: 5a Avda 8-24, Zona 1, Apdo 2688, Guatemala City; tel. 325-3609; telex 5188; fax 28-4073; f. 1978; cap. 39.4m., res 9.4m., dep. 410.6m. (Dec. 1994); Pres. Ing. FRANCISCO ALVARADO MACDONALD; Man. EBERTO CÉSAR SIGÜENZA LÓPEZ.

Banco Promotor, SA: 10a Calle 6-47, Zona 1, Apdo 930, Guatemala City; tel. 251-2928; telex 9238; fax 251-3387; f. 1986; cap. 15.0m., dep. 174.0m. (June 1994); Pres. Lic. JULIO VALLADARES CASTILLO; Gen. Man. Lic. JOSÉ LUIS URÍZAR NORIEGA; 6 brs.

Banco del Quetzal, SA: Edif. Plaza El Roble, 7a Ave 6-26, Zona 9, Apdo 1001-A, Guatemala City; tel. 231-8333; telex 5893; fax 232-6937; f. 1984; cap. 37.4m., dep. 342.7m. (July 1994); Pres. Lic. MARIO ROBERTO LEAL PIVARAL; Gen. Man. ALFONSO VILLA DEVOTO.

Banco de los Trabajadores: 8a Avda 9-41, Zona 1, Apdo 1956, Guatemala City; tel. 22-4651; telex 9212; fax 251-8902; f. 1966; cap. 19.2m., dep. 61.4m. (June 1988); deals with loans for establishing and improving small industries as well as normal banking business; Pres. Lic. CÉSAR AMILCAR BÁRCENAS; Gen. Man. Lic. OSCAR H. ANDRADE ELIZONDO.

Quezaltenango

Banco de Occidente, SA: 7a Ave 11-15, Zona 1, Quezaltenango; tel. (961) 53-1333; telex 5455; fax (961) 30-0970; f. 1881; cap. 10.0m., res 118.9m., dep. 1,227.8m. (Dec. 1993); Pres. Dr LUIS BELTRANENA VALLADARES; Gen. Man. Ing. JOSÉ E. ASCOLI CÁCERES; 29 brs.

State Development Banks

Banco Nacional de Desarrollo Agrícola—BANDESA: 9a Calle 9-47, Zona 1, Apdo 350, Guatemala City; tel. 232-2641; telex 4122; fax 253-7927; f. 1971; cap. 10.5m., dep. 89.2m. (June 1988); agricultural development bank; Pres. Minister of Agriculture, Livestock and Food; Gen. Man. GUSTAVO ADOLFO LEAL CASTELLANOS.

Banco Nacional de la Vivienda—BANVI: 6a Avda 1-22, Zona 4, Apdo 2632, Guatemala City; tel. 332-5777; telex 5371; fax 236-6592; f. 1973; cap. 30.6m., res 25.7m., dep. 258.3m. (April 1989); Pres. JOAQUÍN MARTÍNEZ.

Finance Corporations

Corporación Financiera Nacional—CORFINA: 11a Avda 3-14, Zona 1, Guatemala City; tel. 253-4550; telex 5186; fax 22-5805; f. 1973; provides assistance for the development of industry, mining and tourism; cap. 34.3m., res 0.2m. (June 1988); Pres. Lic. SERGIO A. GONZÁLEZ NAVAS; Gen. Man. Lic. MARIO ARMANDO MARTÍNEZ ZAMORA.

Financiera Guatemalteca, SA—FIGSA: 1a Avda 11-50, Zona 10, Apdo 2460, Guatemala City; tel. 232-1423; telex 5896; fax 231-0873; f. 1962; investment agency; cap. 4.7m., res 1.2m. (June 1988); Pres. CARLOS GONZÁLEZ BARRIOS; Gen. Man. Ing. ROBERTO FERNÁNDEZ BOTRÁN.

Financiera Industrial y Agropecuaria, SA—FIASA: Plaza Continental, 3°, 6a Avda 9-08, Zona 9, Guatemala City; tel. 239-1951; telex 5958; fax 239-2089; f. 1968; private development bank; medium- and long-term loans to private industrial enterprises in Central America; cap. 2.5m., res 27.1m. (Dec. 1994); Pres. JORGE CASTILLO LOVE; Gen. Man. Lic. ALEJANDRO MEJÍA AVILA.

Financiera Industrial, SA (FISA): Centro Financiero, Torre 2, 7a Avda 5-10, Zona 4, Apdo 744, Guatemala City; tel. 232-1750; telex 5236; fax 231-1773; f. 1981; cap. 3m., res 6.2m. (Aug. 1991); Pres. CARLOS ARÍAS MASSELLI; Gen. Man. Lic. ELDER F. CALDERÓN REYES.

Financiera de Inversión, SA: 11a Calle 7-44, Zona 9, Guatemala City; tel. 332-4020; fax 332-4320; f. 1981; investment agency; cap. 15.0m. (June 1997); Pres. Lic. MARIO AUGUSTO PORRAS GONZÁLEZ; Gen. Man. Lic. JOSÉ ROLANDO PORRAS GONZÁLEZ.

Foreign Bank

Lloyds Bank PLC: Edif. Gran Vía, 6a Avda 9-51, Zona 9, Guatemala City; tel. 332-7580; telex 5263; fax 332-7641; f. 1959; cap. 13m., dep. 159.1m. (1990); Man. N. M. A. HUBBARD; 8 brs.

Banking Association

Asociación de Banqueros de Guatemala: Edif. Quinta Montúfar, 2°, 12a Calle 4-74, Zona 9, Guatemala City; tel. 231-8211; fax 231-9477; f. 1961; represents all state and private banks; Pres. Ing. RAFAEL VIEJO RODRÍGUEZ.

STOCK EXCHANGE

Guatemala Stock Exchange: 4a Calle 6-55, Zona 9, Guatemala City; tel. 234-2479; fax 231-4509; f. 1987; the exchange is commonly owned (one share per associate) and trades stocks from private companies, government bonds, letters of credit and other securities.

INSURANCE

National Companies

La Alianza, Cía Anglo-Centroamericana de Seguros, SA: Edif. Etisa, 6°, Plazuela España, Zona 9, Guatemala City; tel. 231-5473; telex 5551; fax 231-0023; f. 1968; Pres. F. ANTONIO GÁNDARA GARCÍA; Man. Ing. RUDY GÁNDARA MERKLE.

Aseguradora General, SA: 10a Calle 3-17, Zona 10, Guatemala City; tel. 332-5933; telex 5441; fax 334-2093; f. 1968; Pres. JUAN O. NIEMANN; Man. ENRIQUE NEUTZE A.

Aseguradora Guatemalteca, SA: 5a Avda 6-06, Zona 1, Guatemala City; tel. 251-9795; telex 5574; fax 234-2093; f. 1978; Pres. Gen. CARLOS E. PINEDA CARRANZA; Man. CÉSAR A. RUANO SANDOVAL.

Cía de Seguros Generales Granai & Townson, SA: 2a Ruta, 2-39, Zona 4, Guatemala City; tel. 334-1361; telex 5955; fax 332-2993; f. 1947; Pres. ERNESTO TOWNSON R.; Exec. Man. MARIO GRANAI FERNÁNDEZ.

Cía de Seguros Panamericana, SA: Avda de la Reforma 9-00, Zona 9, Guatemala City; tel. 232-5922; telex 5925; fax 231-5026; f. 1968; Pres. JOHN ROBERTS; Gen. Man. Lic. SALVADOR ORTEGA.

Cía de Seguros El Roble, SA: Torre 2, 7a Avda 5-10, Zona 4, Guatemala City; tel. 332-1702; telex 6094; fax 332-1629; f. 1973; Pres. FEDERICO KÖNG VIELMAN; Man. Ing. RICARDO ERALES CÓBAR.

Comercial Aseguradora Suizo-Americana, SA: 7a Avda 7-07, Zona 9, Apdo 132, Guatemala City; tel. 332-0666; fax 331-5495; f. 1946; Pres. WILLIAM BICKFORD B.; Gen. Man. MARIO AGUILAR.

Departamento de Seguros y Previsión del Crédito Hipotecario Nacional: 7a Avda 22-77, Zona 1, Centro Cívico, Guatemala City; tel. 250-0271; telex 6065; fax 253-8584; f. 1935; Pres. FABIÁN PIRA; Man. SERGIO DURINI.

Empresa Guatemalteca Cigna de Seguros, SA: Edif. Plaza Marítima 10, 6a Avda 20-25, Zona 10, Guatemala City; tel. 337-2285; telex 5204; fax 337-0121; f. 1951; Gen. Man. Lic. RICARDO ESTRADA DARDÓN.

La Seguridad de Centroamérica, SA: Avda de la Reforma 12-01, Zona 10, Guatemala City; tel. 231-7566; telex 5243; fax 231-7580; f. 1967; Pres. EDGARDO WAGNER D.; Vice-Pres. RICARDO CAU MARTÍNEZ.

Seguros de Occidente, SA: 7a Calle 'A' 7-14, Zona 9, Guatemala City; tel. 231-1222; telex 5605; fax 234-1413; f. 1979; Pres. Lic. PEDRO AGUIRRE; Gen. Man. CARLOS LAINFIESTA.

Seguros Universales, SA: 4a Calle 7-73, Zona 9, Apdo 1479, Guatemala City; tel. 234-0733; telex 6104; fax 232-3372; f. 1962; Pres. MARÍA AUGUSTA VALLS DE SICILIA.

Insurance Association

Asociación Guatemalteca de Instituciones de Seguros—AGIS: Edif. Torre Profesional I, Of. 411, 4°, 6a Avda 0-60, Zona 4, Guatemala City; tel. 235-1657; fax 235-2021; f. 1953; 12 mems; Pres. ENRIQUE NUETZE A.; Man. Lic. FERNANDO RODRÍGUEZ TREJO.

Trade and Industry

DEVELOPMENT ORGANIZATIONS

Comisión Nacional Petrolera: Diagonal 17, 29-78, Zona 11, Guatemala City; tel. 276-0680; telex 5516; fax 276-3175; f. 1983; awards petroleum exploration licences.

Consejo Nacional de Planificación Económica: 9a Calle 10-44, Zona 1, Guatemala City; tel. 251-4549; telex 533127; fax 253-3127; e-mail mrayo@ns.concyt.gob.gt; f. 1954; prepares and supervises the implementation of the national economic development plan; Sec.-Gen. MARIANO RAYO MUÑOZ.

Corporación Financiera Nacional—CORFINA: see under Finance.

Empresa Nacional de Fomento y Desarrollo Económico de El Petén (FYDEP): 11a Avda 'B' 32-46, Zona 5, Guatemala City; tel. 231-6834; telex 6178; f. 1959; attached to the Presidency; economic development agency for the Department of El Petén; Dir FRANCISCO ANGEL CASTELLANOS GÓNGORA.

Instituto de Fomento de Hipotecas Aseguradas (FHA): 6a Avda 0-60, Zona 4, Guatemala City; f. 1961; insured mortgage institution for the promotion of house construction; Pres. Lic. HOMERO AUGUSTO GONZÁLEZ BARILLAS; Man. Lic. JOSÉ SALVADOR SAMAYOA AGUILAR.

Instituto Nacional de Administración Pública (INAP): 5a Avda 12-65, Zona 9, Apto 2753, Guatemala City; tel. 26-6339; f. 1964; provides technical experts to assist all branches of the Government in administrative reform programmes; provides in-service training for local and central government staff; has research programmes in administration, sociology, politics and economics; provides postgraduate education in public administration; Gen. Man. Dr ARIEL RIVERA IRÍAS.

Instituto Nacional de Transformación Agraria (INTA): 14a Calle 7-14, Zona 1, Guatemala City; tel. 28-0975; f. 1962 to carry out agrarian reform; current programme includes development of the 'Faja Transversal del Norte'; Pres. Ing. NERY ORLANDO SAMAYOA; Vice-Pres Ing. SERGIO FRANCISCO MORALES-JUÁREZ, ROBERTO EDMUNDO QUIÑÓNEZ LÓPEZ.

CHAMBERS OF COMMERCE AND INDUSTRY

Comité Coordinador de Asociaciones Agrícolas, Comerciales, Industriales y Financieras (CACIF): Edif. Cámara de Industria de Guatemala, 6a Ruta 9-21, Zona 4, Guatemala City; tel. 231-0651; telex 6133; co-ordinates work on problems and organization of free enterprise; mems: 6 chambers; Pres. JORGE BRIZ; Sec.-Gen. RAFAEL POLA.

Cámara de Comercio de Guatemala: 10a Calle 3-80, Zona 1, Guatemala City; tel. 28-2681; telex 5478; fax 251-4197; f. 1894; Gen. Man. EDGARDO RUIZ.

Cámara de Industria de Guatemala: 6a Ruta 9-21, 12°, Zona 4, Apdo 214, Guatemala City; tel. 334-0850; telex 5402; fax 334-1090; f. 1958; Pres. JUAN JOSÉ URRUELA KONG; Gen. Man. CARLOS PERALTA.

INDUSTRIAL AND TRADE ASSOCIATIONS

Asociación de Azucareros de Guatemala—ASAZGUA: Edif. Tívoli Plaza, 6a Calle 6-38, Zona 9, Guatemala City; telex 5248; fax 231-8191; f. 1957; sugar producers' asscn; 19 mems; Gen. Man. Lic. ARMANDO BOESCHE.

Asociación de Exportadores de Café: 11a Calle 5-66, 3°, Zona 9, Guatemala City; telex 5368; coffee exporters' asscn; 37 mems; Pres. EDUARDO GONZÁLEZ RIVERA.

Asociación General de Agricultores: 9a Calle 3-43, Zona 1, Guatemala City; f. 1920; general farmers' asscn; 350 mems; Pres. DAVID ORDÓÑEZ; Man. PEDRO ARRIVILLAGA RADA.

Asociación Nacional de Avicultores—ANAVI: Edif. Galerías Reforma, Torre 2, 9°, Of. 904, Avda de la Reforma 8-60, Zona 9, Guatemala City; tel. 231-1381; telex 6215; fax 234-7576; f. 1964; national asscn of poultry farmers; 60 mems; Pres. Lic. FERNANDO ROJAS; Dir Dr MARIO A. MOTTA GONZÁLEZ.

Asociación Nacional de Fabricantes de Alcoholes y Licores (ANFAL): Km 16½, Carretera Roosevelt, Zona 10, Apdo 2065, Guatemala City; tel. 292-0430; telex 5565; f. 1947; distillers' asscn; Pres. FELIPE BOTRÁN MERINO; Man. Lic. JUAN GUILLERMO BORJA MOGOLLÓN.

Asociación Nacional del Café—Anacafé: Edif. Etisa, Plazuela España, Zona 9, Guatemala City; tel. 236-7180; telex 5915; fax 234-7023; f. 1960; national coffee asscn; Pres. Lic. MAX QUIRÍN.

Asociación de Agricultores Productores de Aceites Esenciales: 6a Calle 1-36, Zona 10, Apdo 272, Guatemala City; tel. 234-7255; telex 5316; f. 1948; essential oils producers' asscn; 40 mems; Pres. FRANCISCO RALDA; Gen. Man. CARLOS FLORES PAGAZA.

Cámara del Agro: 15a Calle 'A' 7-65, Zona 9, Guatemala City; tel. 26-1473; f. 1973; Man. CÉSAR BUSTAMANTE ARAÚZ.

Consejo Nacional del Algodón: 11a Calle 6-49, Zona 9, Guatemala City; tel. 234-8390; fax 234-8393; f. 1964; consultative body for cultivation and classification of cotton; 119 mems; Pres. ROBERTO MARTÍNEZ R.; Man. ALFREDO GIL SPILLARI.

Gremial de Huleros de Guatemala: Edif. Centroamericano, Of. 406, 7a Avda 7-78, Zona 4, Guatemala City; tel. 231-4917; telex 5114; f. 1970; rubber producers' guild; 125 mems; Pres. JOSÉ LUIS RALDA; Man. Lic. CÉSAR SOTO.

UTILITIES

Electricity

Empresa Eléctrica de Guatemala, SA: 6a Avda 8-14, Zona 1, Guatemala City; state electricity producer; scheduled for privatization; Pres. OSCAR MARTÍNEZ AMAYA.

Instituto Nacional de Electrificación: Edif. La Torre, 7a Avda 2-29, Zona 9, Guatemala City; tel. (2) 34-5711; telex 5324; fax (2) 34-5811; f. 1959; state agency for the generation and distribution of hydroelectric power; principal electricity producer; scheduled for privatization; Pres. GUILLERMO RODRÍGUEZ.

TRADE UNIONS

Frente Nacional Sindical (FNS) (National Trade Union Front): Guatemala City; f. 1968 to achieve united action in labour matters; affiliated are two confederations and 11 federations, which represent 97% of the country's trade unions and whose General Secretaries form the governing council of the FNS. The affiliated organizations include:

Comité Nacional de Unidad Sindical Guatemalteca—CONUS: Leader MIGUEL ANGEL SOLÍS; Sec.-Gen. GERÓNIMO LÓPEZ DÍAZ.

Confederación General de Sindicatos (General Trade Union Confederation): 18a Calle 5-50, Zona 1, Apdo 959, Guatemala City.

Confederación Nacional de Trabajadores (National Workers' Confederation): Guatemala City; Sec.-Gen. MIGUEL ANGEL ALBIZÚREZ.

Consejo Sindical de Guatemala (Guatemalan Trade Union Council): 18a Calle 5-50, Zona 1, Apdo 959, Guatemala City; f. 1955; admitted to ICFTU and ORIT; Gen. Sec. JAIME V. MONGE DONIS; 30,000 mems in 105 affiliated unions.

Federación Autónoma Sindical Guatemalteca (Guatemalan Autonomous Trade Union Federation): Guatemala City; Gen. Sec. MIGUEL ANGEL SOLÍS.

Federación de Obreros Textiles (Textile Workers' Federation): Edif. Briz, Of. 503, 6a Avda 14-33, Zona 1, Guatemala City; f. 1957; Sec.-Gen. FACUNDO PINEDA.

Federación de Trabajadores de Guatemala (FTG) (Guatemalan Workers' Federation): 5a Calle 4-33, Zona 1, Guatemala City; tel. 22-6515; Promoter ADRIAN RAMÍREZ.

A number of unions exist without a national centre, including the Union of Chicle and Wood Workers, the Union of Coca-Cola Workers and the Union of Workers of the Enterprise of the United Fruit Company.

Central General de Trabajadores de Guatemala (CGTG): 3a Avda 12-22, Zona 1, Guatemala City; tel. 232-9234; fax 251-3212; f. 1987; Sec.-Gen. JOSÉ E. PINZÓN SALAZAR.

Central Nacional de Trabajadores (CNT): 9a Avda 4-29, Zona 1, Apdo 2472, Guatemala City; f. 1972; cover all sections of commerce, industry and agriculture including the public sector; clandestine since June 1980; Sec.-Gen. JULIO CELSO DE LEÓN; 23,735 mems.

Unidad de Acción Sindical y Popular (UASP): f. 1988; broad coalition of leading labour and peasant organizations; includes:

Comité de la Unidad Campesina (CUC) (Committee of Peasants' Unity).

Confederación de Unidad Sindical de Trabajadores de Guatemala (CUSG): 5a Calle 4-33, Zona 1, Guatemala City; tel. 22-6515; f. 1983; Sec.-Gen. FRANCISCO ALFARO MIJANGOS.

Federación Nacional de Sindicatos de Trabajadores del Estado de Guatemala (Fenasteg): Sec. ARMANDO SÁNCHEZ.

Sindicato de Trabajadores de la Educación Guatemaltecos (STEG).

Sindicato de Trabajadores de la Industria de la Electricidad (STINDE).

Sindicato de Trabajadores del Instituto Guatemalteco de Seguro Social (STIGSS).

Unidad Sindical de Trabajadores de Guatemala (UNSITRAGUA).

Transport

RAILWAYS

Ferrocarriles de Guatemala—FEGUA: 9a Avda 18-03, Zona 1, Guatemala City; tel. 28-3030; telex 5342; fax 251-2006; f. 1968; government-owned; 782 km from Puerto Barrios and Santo Tomás de Castilla on the Atlantic coast to Tecún Umán on the Mexican border, via Zacapa, Guatemala City and Santa María. Branch lines: Santa María–San José; Las Cruces–Champerico. From Zacapa another line branches southward to Anguiatú, on the border with El Salvador; owns the ports of Barrios (Atlantic) and San José (Pacific); all lines were inoperative in early 1998, pending privatization; Administrator ANDRÉS PORRAS.

There are 102 km of plantation lines.

ROADS

In 1996 there were an estimated 13,100 km of roads, of which 3,616 km were paved. The Guatemalan section of the Pan-American highway is 518.7 km long and totally asphalted. The construction of a 1,500-km network of new highways, including a four-lane motorway from the capital to Palín Escuintla, began in 1981. A 44-km toll road linking Escuintla with San José was built, in the mid-1980s, at a cost of US $18m.

SHIPPING

Guatemala's major ports are Santo Tomás de Castilla and Puerto Quetzal.

Armadora Marítima Guatemalteca, SA: 14a Calle 8-14, Zona 1, Apdo 1008, Guatemala City; tel. 253-7243; telex 5214; fax 253-7464; cargo services; Pres. and Gen. Man. L. R. CORONADO CONDE.

Empresa Portuaria 'Quetzal': Edif. 74, 6°, 7a Avda 3-74, Zona 9, Guatemala City; tel. 231-4824; telex 6134; fax 234-8152; port and shipping co; Man. Ing. ARTURO CAZALI REYES.

Empresa Portuaria Nacional Santo Tomás de Castilla: Santo Tomás de Castilla 18013; tel. 948-3211.

Flota Mercante Gran Centroamericana, SA: Edif. Canella, 5°, 1a Calle 7-21, Zona 9, Guatemala City; tel. 231-6666; telex 5211; f. 1959; services from Europe (in association with WITASS), Gulf of Mexico, US Atlantic and East Coast Central American ports; Pres. R. S. RAMÍREZ; Gen. Man. J. E. A. MORALES.

Líneas Marítimas de Guatemala, SA: Edif. Plaza Marítima, 8°, 6a Avda 20-25, Zona 10, Guatemala City; tel. 237-0166; telex 5174; cargo services; Pres. J. R. MATHEAU ESCOBAR; Gen. Man. F. HERRERÍAS.

Several foreign lines link Guatemala with Europe, the Far East and North America.

CIVIL AVIATION

In 1982 a new international airport was completed at Santa Elena Petén.

Aerolíneas de Guatemala—AVIATECA: Avda Hincapié 12-22, Aeropuerto 'La Aurora', Zona 13, Guatemala City; tel. 231-8261; telex 5960; fax 231-7401; f. 1945; internal services and external services to the USA, Mexico, and within Central America; transferred to private ownership in 1989; Pres. Ing. JULIO OBOLS GOMES; Gen. Man. ENRIQUE BELTRONERA.

Aeroquetzal: Avda Hincapié y 18a Calle, Lado Sur, Aeropuerto 'La Aurora', Zona 13, Guatemala City; tel. 231-8282; telex 5676; fax 232-1491; scheduled domestic passenger and cargo services, and external services to Mexico.

Aerovías: Avda Hincapié 4 y 18a Calle, Aeropuerta 'La Aurora', Zona 13, Guatemala City; tel. 232-5686; telex 5010; fax 234-7470; operates scheduled and charter cargo services; Pres. FERNANDO ALFONSO CASTILLO R.; Vice-Pres. NELSON C. PUENTE.

Aviones Comerciales de Guatemala (Avcom): Avda Hincapié, Aeropuerto 'La Aurora', Zona 13, Guatemala City; tel. 231-5821; fax 232-4946; domestic charter passenger services.

Tourism

As a result of violence in the country, the annual total of tourist arrivals declined from 504,000, in 1979, when tourist receipts were US $201m., to 192,000, in 1984 (receipts $56.6m.). After 1985, however, the number of arrivals recovered and were recorded as 585,000 in 1995, when receipts were $276.0m.

Guatemala Tourist Commission: Centro Cívico, 7a Avda 1-17, Zona 4, Guatemala City; tel. (2) 31-1333; telex 5532; fax 231-8893; f. 1967; policy and planning council: 13 mems representing the public and private sectors; Pres. LAURA DE ESTRADA; Dir CLAUDIA ARENAS BIANCHI.

Asociación Guatemalteca de Agentes de Viajes (AGAV) (Guatemalan Association of Travel Agents): 6a Avda 8-41, Zona 9, Apdo 2735, Guatemala City; tel. 231-0320; telex 5127; Pres. MARÍA DEL CARMEN FERNÁNDEZ O.

GUINEA

Introductory Survey

Location, Climate, Language, Religion, Flag, Capital

The Republic of Guinea lies on the west coast of Africa, with Sierra Leone and Liberia to the south, Senegal and Guinea-Bissau to the north, and Mali and Côte d'Ivoire inland to the east. The climate on the coastal strip is hot and moist, with temperatures ranging from about 32°C (90°F) in the dry season to about 23°C (73°F) in the wet season (May–October). The interior is higher and cooler. The official language is French, but Soussou, Manika and six other national languages are widely spoken. Most of the inhabitants are Muslims, but some follow traditional animist beliefs. Around 2% are Roman Catholics. The national flag (proportions 3 by 2) consists of three equal vertical stripes, of red, yellow and green. The capital is Conakry.

Recent History

The Republic of Guinea (formerly French Guinea, part of French West Africa) achieved independence on 2 October 1958, after 95% of voters had rejected the Constitution of the Fifth Republic under which the French colonies became self-governing within the French Community. The new state was the object of punitive reprisals by the outgoing French authorities: all aid was withdrawn, and the administrative infrastructure destroyed. The Parti démocratique de Guinée—Rassemblement démocratique africain (PDG—RDA) became the basis for the construction of new institutions. Its leader, Ahmed Sekou Touré, became President, and the PDG—RDA the sole political party.

Sekou Touré, formerly a prominent trade unionist, pursued vigorous policies of socialist revolution, with emphasis on popular political participation. Opposition was ruthlessly crushed: by 1983 almost 2m. Guineans were estimated to have fled the country. Several attempts to destabilize the Sekou Touré regime were alleged during the 1960s, and an abortive invasion by Portuguese troops and Guinean exiles in 1970 prompted the execution of many of those (including several foreigners) who were convicted of involvement. Guinea's external relations, notably with Senegal and Côte d'Ivoire, subsequently deteriorated, and the country became virtually isolated. The Sekou Touré regime perpetuated rumours of a 'permanent conspiracy' by foreign powers to overthrow the Government, but from 1975 Guinea sought a political and economic *rapprochement* with its African neighbours, with France and with other Western powers.

All private trade was forbidden in 1975: transactions were conducted through official co-operatives under the supervision of an 'economic police'. In August 1977 demonstrations by women in Conakry, in protest against the abolition of the traditional market and the abuse of power by the 'economic police', provoked rioting in other towns, as a result of which three state governors were killed. Sekou Touré responded by disbanding the 'economic police' and allowing limited private trading to recommence in July 1979. Meanwhile, in November 1978 it was announced that the functions of the PDG—RDA and the State were to be merged, and the country was renamed the People's Revolutionary Republic of Guinea. There was, none the less, a general move away from rigid Marxism and a decline in relations with the USSR. In December Valéry Giscard d'Estaing made the first visit by a French President to independent Guinea, and plans for economic co-operation between the two countries were discussed.

At legislative elections in January 1980 voters endorsed the PDG—RDA's list of 210 candidates for a new Assemblée nationale (to replace the Assemblée législative elected in December 1974). In May 1982 Sekou Touré was returned unopposed to the presidency for a fourth seven-year term of office, reportedly receiving 100% of the votes cast. He made his first official visit to France in September of that year.

In January 1984 a plot to overthrow the Government was disclosed when a group of 20 mercenaries was arrested in southern Senegal. It was reported that thousands of Guineans were subsequently detained, accused of complicity in the affair. In March Sekou Touré died while undergoing surgery in the USA. On 3 April, before a permanent successor had been chosen by the ruling party, the armed forces seized power in a bloodless coup. A Comité militaire de redressement national (CMRN) was appointed, headed by Col (later Gen.) Lansana Conté, hitherto commander of the Boké region. The PDG—RDA and the legislature were dissolved, and the Constitution was suspended. The CMRN pledged to restore democracy and to respect human rights; some 250 political prisoners were released, and a relaxation of press restrictions was announced. The Prime Minister, Col Diarra Traoré, toured West African states to rally support from Guinea's neighbours. In May the country was renamed the Second Republic of Guinea, and in June Traoré visited Europe in an effort to attract foreign investment and to consolidate relations, particularly with France. By July an estimated 200,000 Guinean exiles had returned to the country.

Trials of former associates of Sekou Touré, most of whom had been detained since the coup, began in November 1984. In December President Conté assumed the posts of Head of Government and Minister of Defence; the post of Prime Minister was abolished, and Traoré was demoted to a lesser post. In July 1985 Traoré attempted to seize power while Conté was chairing a regional conference in Togo. Troops loyal to the President suppressed the revolt, during which 18 people were killed. Traoré was arrested, along with many members of his family and more than 200 suspected sympathizers. A series of attacks was subsequently aimed at the Malinke ethnic group, of which both Traoré and the late President Sekou Touré were members. (Conté's opponents have frequently claimed that the regime has unduly favoured his own Soussou ethnic group.) In May 1987 it was announced that 58 people, including nine former government ministers, had been sentenced to death, following secret trials of more than 200 Guineans detained either for crimes committed under Sekou Touré or in the aftermath of the July 1985 coup attempt. The announcement did little to allay suspicions of international observers (which were repeatedly denied by the Government) that many detainees had already been executed in the aftermath of the abortive coup, and in December 1987 Conté admitted publicly that Traoré had died in the hours following his arrest. In January 1988 an amnesty was announced for 67 political prisoners, including Sekou Touré's widow and son.

In October 1985 Conté began to implement radical economic reforms that the World Bank and IMF had demanded as preconditions for the provision of structural aid. In December the Council of Ministers was reorganized to include a majority of civilians. In January 1988 rioting in Conakry forced the Government to abandon proposals for sharp increases in retail prices of staple goods. Conté subsequently reorganized the Government, transferring two senior ministers to regional ministries.

In October 1988 Conté proposed the establishment of a committee to draft a new constitution. One year later he announced that, following the approval of the document (in a national referendum that was to take place during 1990), the CMRN would be replaced by a Comité transitoire de redressement national (CTRN). The CTRN would be composed of both civilian and military officials, and would oversee a transitional period of not more than five years, at the end of which civilian rule, with an executive and legislature directly elected in the context of a two-party system, would be established.

In December 1989 the Government denied allegations made by a prominent human rights organization, Amnesty International, of the solitary confinement and torture of six members of an unofficial opposition grouping, the Rassemblement populaire guinéen (RPG). In February 1990 an amnesty was announced for all political prisoners and exiles. In November Conté appealed to political exiles to return to Guinea. Shortly afterwards, however, three members of the RPG were given custodial sentences: one was convicted of forging official documents, while his co-defendants were found guilty of distributing banned newspapers.

The draft Constitution of what was to be known as the Third Republic was submitted for approval in a national referendum on 23 December 1990, and was endorsed by 98.7% of those who voted (some 97.4% of the electorate). The period of transition to civilian rule was thus instigated, and in February 1991 the 36-member CTRN was inaugurated, chaired by Conté. Shortly beforehand three close associates of Conté, who were now appointed to the CTRN, had left the Government (in accordance with the constitutional stipulation that membership of the CTRN was incompatible with ministerial status). The military maintained a strong presence in the Council of Ministers.

The RPG leader, Alpha Condé, returned to Guinea in May 1991, after a long period of exile in France and Senegal. Three arrests were made when a meeting of his supporters was dispersed by security forces, and a ban was subsequently imposed on unauthorized meetings and demonstrations. In June one person was killed when security forces opened fire on a group of demonstrators who had gathered outside the police headquarters in Conakry, to where Condé had been summoned in connection with the seizure, at the country's main airport, of a consignment of allegedly subversive materials. As many as 60 people were reported to have been arrested; Condé sought refuge in the Senegalese embassy, and was subsequently granted political asylum in Senegal. In October three people were killed during anti-Government riots in Kankan. In December the Conté administration refuted further allegations made by Amnesty International of violations of human rights in Guinea.

In October 1991 Conté announced that an 'organic law' authorizing the registration of an unlimited number of political parties would come into effect in April 1992, and that legislative elections, in the context of a full multi-party political system, would take place before the end of 1992. The new Constitution was promulgated on 23 December 1991, and in January 1992 Conté ceded the presidency of the CTRN (whose membership was, at the same time, reduced to 15), in conformity with the Constitution, which envisaged the separation of the powers of the executive and the legislature. In the following month a major reorganization of the Council of Ministers entailed the departure of most military officers and of those who had returned from exile after the 1984 coup (known as *Guinéens de l'extérieur*), as well as the abolition of resident regional ministries.

The 'organic law' entered into force on 3 April 1992, whereupon 17 political parties were legalized. Among these was the RPG, and Condé returned to Guinea in June. However, a lack of cohesion among opposition parties undermined attempts to persuade the Government to convene a national conference in advance of the electoral programme. Moreover, it was widely rumoured that the pro-Conté Parti pour l'unité et le progrès (PUP), established by prominent *Guinéens de l'extérieur*, was benefiting from state funds. Conté reportedly escaped an assassination attempt in October, when gunmen opened fire on the vehicle in which he was travelling. In early December the Government announced the indefinite postponement of the legislative elections, which had been scheduled for the end of that month, stating that procedures for compiling an electoral register and issuing identity cards to voters were incomplete. Subsequent indications that the legislative elections would not take place until after a presidential election caused resentment among the opposition, which had hoped to present a single candidate (from the party that had enjoyed the greatest success in the legislative elections) for the presidency. In May 1993 some 30,000 people participated in a demonstration in Conakry to demand that the legislative elections be organized, in advance of a presidential poll, as early as possible. As many as three people were reported to have been killed, and 50 injured, during the protest, at which witnesses claimed that PUP activists had assaulted demonstrators. In July opposition rallies took place in Conakry and in several other towns to demand the establishment of a transitional government of national unity and of an independent electoral commission.

During the second half of 1993 opposition parties made numerous attempts to forge alliances, with the aim of preventing a divided opposition vote from benefiting Conté and the PUP at the elections. However, the opposition remained essentially fragmented, and its authority in demanding concessions from the Conté regime was thus undermined. In September the Government imposed a ban on all street demonstrations, following violent incidents when police opened fire on demonstrators in Conakry, as a result of which, according to official figures, as many as 18 people were killed and almost 200 injured. In October, at the first meeting between Conté and opposition leaders since the legalization of political parties, it was reportedly agreed to establish an independent electoral commission, although Conté rejected demands for the establishment of a transitional government. Controversy subsequently arose regarding the composition of the electoral commission, and the opposition denounced the Government's decision to place the commission under the jurisdiction of the Minister of the Interior and Security.

In October 1993 the Supreme Court approved eight candidates for the presidential election, scheduled for 5 December. Among Conté's main rivals for the presidency were Condé, representing the RPG, together with Mamadou Boye Bâ of the Union pour la nouvelle République (UNR) and Siradiou Diallo of the Parti pour le renouveau et le progrès (PRP). Opposition candidates subsequently demanded that the election be postponed, citing irregularities in the compilation of electoral lists as well as delays in the issuing of voting cards and in the appointment of the electoral commission. Complaints were also made that the PUP was able to hold electoral rallies, while the opposition remained subject to the ban on street demonstrations. In late November the Government announced a two-week postponement of the presidential election, although the opposition judged this insufficient. The election proceeded on 19 December. At least four deaths were recorded in pre-election violence involving PUP supporters and opposition activists in Conakry and in the interior, and there were six deaths in Conakry on the day of the election; there was also unrest among Guinean communities elsewhere in Africa, when demonstrators destroyed polling stations at Guinean embassies, alleging electoral fraud.) Although several opposition candidates were reported to have withdrawn from the presidential contest prior to the election, the rate of participation by voters was high (78.5%, according to official figures), with supporters of all candidates voting. Preliminary results indicated that Conté had secured in excess of 50% of the votes cast, thus obviating the need for a second round of voting (the Constitution requires that the President be elected by an absolute majority of the votes). Opposition claims that the poll had been fraudulent and the result manipulated in favour of Conté intensified when the Supreme Court annulled the outcome of voting in the Kankan and Siguiri prefectures (in both of which the RPG leader had won more than 95% of the votes), owing to irregularities in the conduct of the polls. According to the official results of the election, confirmed by the Court in early January 1994, Conté was elected with 51.70% of the votes cast; Condé took 19.55% of the votes, Bâ 13.37% and Diallo 11.86%.

Conté, who had resigned from the army in order to contest the election as a civilian, was inaugurated as President on 29 January 1994. He identified as priorities for his presidency the strengthening of national security and the promotion of economic growth. A major restructuring of the Council of Ministers was implemented in August: several new ministries were created, with a particular emphasis on economic reform and the development of the primary sector.

In May 1994 Bâ announced his lack of confidence in the Guinean opposition, and asserted the UNR's intention to support Conté as the country's legitimately elected Head of State. However, relations between the Government and the opposition remained generally strained, and the RPG in particular alleged the harassment of its supporters by the security forces. The brief detention, in June, of eight senior armed forces officers, including the Deputy Chief of Staff of the air force, prompted rumours of a coup plot. The Government confirmed that several members of the military had participated in a 'political' meeting, in contravention of their terms of service, but denied the existence of any conspiracy. In September the Government admitted that it had authorized security forces to disperse an RPG rally in Kérouané, in eastern Guinea, although it refuted RPG assertions that attempts had been made to assassinate Condé. A ban on political rallies was ended in November; however, the Government emphasized that rallies should not be confused with street demonstrations. The announcement, shortly afterwards, that there would be no facilities abroad to allow expatriate Guineans to vote in the forthcoming legislative elections (following the disturbances at polling stations outside Guinea at the presidential election) provoked criticism by opposition parties and by members of the electoral commission, who stated that the disenfranchisement of Guineans abroad was in contravention of both the Constitution and the electoral code. The UNR condemned the policy and withdrew its support for Conté. Earlier in the year the Association guinéenne des droits de l'homme (AGDH) had alleged a recent increase in the ill-treatment of prisoners in Guinea, together with attempts by the authorities to deny basic rights and freedoms.

In December 1994 the Government announced new measures aimed at combating organized crime and other serious offences. As well as the creation of a special police unit to counter banditry, the enforcement of the death penalty was envisaged, together with stricter policies governing immigration and asylum for refugees—the Conté administration frequently attributed the increase in insecurity to the presence of large numbers of refugees (see below) in Guinea. There were, in addition, increasing indications of the Government's desire to restrict the influence of Islamic fundamentalism. In January 1996 human rights organizations expressed concern at the recent rejection of appeals against six death penalties.

Meanwhile, in February 1995 Conté readopted his military title. In March it was announced that the legislative elections would take place on 11 June. Parties of the so-called 'radical' opposition (principally the RPG, the PRP and the UNR) immediately denounced the timing of the election, suggesting that the authorities had chosen a date during the rainy season so as effectively to prevent many voters in rural areas from participating in the poll. Prior to the elections opposition leaders frequently alleged harassment of party activists and supporters by the security forces, claiming that efforts were being made to prevent campaigning in areas where support for the opposition was, or was likely to be, strong. They also denounced the use by the PUP of portraits of Conté on campaign posters and literature, protesting that the President was constitutionally required to distance himself from party politics.

At the elections a total of 846 candidates, from 21 parties, contested the 114 seats in the Assemblée nationale. As preliminary results indicated that the PUP had won an overwhelming majority in the legislature, the radical opposition protested that voting had been conducted fraudulently, stating that they would take no further part in the electoral process and that they would boycott the legislature. According to the final election results, which were published more than one week after the polls (and verified by the Supreme Court in July 1995, whereupon the Assemblée nationale officially superseded the CTRN), the PUP won 71 seats—having taken 30 of the 38 single-member constituencies and 41 of the 76 seats allocated by a system of national proportional representation. Eight other parties won representation, principal among them the RPG, which took 19 seats, the PRP and the UNR, both of which won nine seats. Some 63% of the registered electorate were reported to have voted. At municipal elections in late June the PUP won control of 20 of the country's 36 municipalities, while the RPG, the PRP and the UNR, which had presented a co-ordinated campaign, took 10. Once again, the opposition protested of electoral fraud. In July the three radical opposition parties joined forces with nine other organizations in the Coordination de l'opposition démocratique (Codem). Codem indicated its willingness to enter into a dialogue with the authorities; however, at a meeting between a representative of Codem and the Minister of the Interior, Alsény René Gomez, the latter rejected what Codem had presented as evidence of electoral fraud as not affecting the overall credibility of the results. The official inauguration of the Assemblée nationale, on 30 August, was, none the less, attended by representatives of all the elected parties. Boubacar Biro Diallo, of the PUP, was elected (unopposed) as the new parliament's Speaker; the PUP and its allies also took control of all other prominent posts in the legislature, despite previous indications that some would be allocated to parties of the opposition.

Addressing the armed forces in November 1995, Conté warned against civilian interference in, and the politicization of, the military. In early February 1996 elements of the military wishing to overthrow Conté's regime apparently took advantage of protests by soldiers in Conakry who were demanding increased pay and improved allowances. Disaffected soldiers seized control of the airport and offices of the state broadcasting service, and shelling around the presidential palace caused severe damage. Conté was reportedly seized as he attempted to flee the palace, and was held by rebels for some 15 hours until he made concessions including a doubling of salaries and immunity from prosecution for those involved in the mutiny. He also agreed to the demand that the Minister of Defence, Col Abdourahmane Diallo, be dismissed, subsequently assuming personal responsibility for defence. It was estimated that about 50 people (some of them civilians) were killed and at least 100 injured as rebels clashed with forces loyal to the Conté regime. In all, as many as 2,000 soldiers, including members of the Presidential Guard, were believed to have joined the rebellion. Despite Conté's undertaking that there would be no punitive action, several officers—reportedly among them some of those detained in June 1994—were arrested shortly afterwards, and both Conté and Gomez stated that any legal proceedings would be a matter for the judiciary. Armoured vehicles were deployed in the capital for some weeks after the rebellion, and there were concerns that some armed mutineers had failed to return to barracks following the suppression of the revolt. That there had been a coup attempt was only admitted by Conté almost three weeks after the mutiny. Shortly afterwards members of Codem withdrew from a parliamentary commission that had been established to investigate the circumstances surrounding the rebellion, apparently in protest at Conté's allusions to opposition links with anti-Government elements within the military.

The initial recommendations of the parliamentary commission included that there should be a complete depoliticization of the military, accompanied by the demilitarization of political life; the need to restore discipline within the armed forces was emphasized. Meanwhile, the opposition warned that avoidance of further insurrection could be guaranteed only by full observance of the agreement reached by Conté and the military during the rebellion. In late March 1996, none the less, it was announced that eight members of the military (four of them senior officers) had been charged with undermining state security in connection with the coup attempt. A reinforcement of security measures followed the assassination of the commander of the military camp where the February rebellion had begun (a high-ranking officer who was reportedly a close associate of Conté), apparently in reprisal against the charges. Calm was quickly restored, and Conté left his barracks for the first time since early February to meet President Alpha Oumar Konaré of Mali, who arrived in Conakry to discuss terms for the release into Guinean custody of one of the alleged perpetrators of the coup attempt, who had taken refuge in the Malian embassy. In the following month, however, Mali recalled its ambassador from Conakry, protesting that Guinean forces had stormed the embassy to arrest the officer. By mid-June some 42 members of the armed forces had reportedly been charged in connection with the coup plot. An international warrant had also been issued for the arrest of Cmmdr Joseph Gbago Zoumanigui, suspected of being a main conspirator, who was rumoured to have fled the country. In addition, in early April 10 people, some of them civilians, were said to have been detained in connection with the assassination of the army commander in the previous month.

The armed forces Chief of Staff and the military Governor of Conakry, both of whom had been regarded as close associates of Conté, were replaced in mid-April 1996, apparently in accordance with the President's expressed commitment to a restructuring of both the civilian and military administration. In early July Conté announced (for the first time under the Third Republic) the appointment of a Prime Minister. The premiership was assigned to an economist, Sidia Touré, who reportedly had no party affiliation. A comprehensive reorganization of the Government included the departure of Gomez and the division of the Ministry of the Interior into two separate departments (one responsible for territorial administration and decentralization, the other for security), as well as the appointment of a new Minister of Justice. Touré, who held dual Guinean-Ivorian citizenship (and who had apparently been appointed premier in accordance with an Ivorian-brokered agreement), responded to criticism by opposition leaders that there was no constitutional provision for the post of Prime Minister by stating that his appointment was in accordance with the article of the Constitution empowering the President of the Republic to appoint ministers and to delegate part of his functions. During early August 1996 40 of those detained in connection with the February mutiny were released from custody; charges remained against three suspects, including Zoumanigui.

The removal from office of Gomez was welcomed by opposition groups. However, one of his last actions as Minister of the Interior, authorizing the establishment of a foundation dedicated to the philosophy of Ahmed Sekou Touré, was particularly criticized by the Union des forces démocratiques de Guinée (UFD), which was active in representing the interests of victims of the Sekou Touré regime. The party had also condemned the rehabilitation of Sekou Touré and recent legislation granting full privileges to members of the former President's family as trivializing the crimes of his regime.

Touré announced that his Government's priorities were to be economic recovery and the combating of institutionalized corruption, with the aim of securing new assistance from the international financial community, and also of attracting increased foreign investment. The new Prime Minister assumed personal responsibility for the economy, and immediate measures were announced to reduce public expenditure by one-third. A commitment was made, none the less, to honour the salary increases for the military conceded by Conté in February 1996, and it was emphasized that, while public-sector salaries could not be substantially increased at this time, arrears would not be allowed to accumulate, since this could jeopardize social harmony.

In early November 1996 the RPG's headquarters in Conakry was ransacked and damaged by fire, apparently following clashes between supporters of Condé and a group of students. Four prominent members of the RPG were subsequently arrested, and in the following month Codem announced its intention to establish a militia, with the aim of resisting further arrests of opposition activists. In mid-January 1997 the Minister of Territorial Administration and Decentralization, Dorank Assifat Diasseny, stated that no political party had the right to establish an armed force, and emphasized that the law would be applied vigorously against those seeking to foster what he termed a spiral of violence in Guinea. The four RPG officials were sentenced to two years' imprisonment in mid-June, convicted of violence and causing injury to others.

A new financing programme was agreed with the IMF in January 1997. In the following month Touré relinquished control of the economy portfolio to his two ministers-delegate, who now became Minister of Planning and Co-operation and Minister of Economic Affairs and Finance. In May, in response to parliamentary appeals that the post of Prime Minister be accorded constitutional status, the Government asserted that for the Constitution to vest powers directly in an office of Prime Minister would result in political instability and confusion.

In June 1997 it was announced that a State Security Court was to be established to deal with matters of exceptional jurisdiction, and that its first task would be to try the alleged leaders of the 1996 mutiny. The establishment of the court provoked strong criticism both by the opposition parties and the Guinean lawyers' association, which expressed particular concern that there was no constitutional provision for such a court, and that its members were to be personally appointed by Conté (Commdr Sama Pannival Bangoura, the head of the Alpha Yaya barracks, was named as the court's President); the announcement that the mutiny trial was to be held in camera caused further disquiet. Furthermore, the political opposition again warned that Conté should beware of reneging on his earlier pledge that there would be no reprisals for those involved in the rebellion. Following the announcement of the trial, unidentified forces were reported to have raided the home of one of Conté's closest advisers, leaving behind a written warning that the President should not seek re-election in 1998. Rumours circulated, meanwhile, that Guinean dissidents were conspiring with rebels in neighbouring Sierra Leone and Liberia to overthrow Conté, and that Zoumanigui was attempting to recruit mercenaries for a planned invasion. In mid-March 1997 it was reported that three Belgian nationals had been arrested in connection with a coup plot, although the Belgian authorities stated that they had been detained following a commercial dispute. (The Belgians were later charged with the illegal possession of weapons, with customs fraud and with attempting to corrupt civil servants.) However, opposition parties asserted that the Conté regime itself was the source of the rumours; in July Jean-Marie Doré, the leader of the Union pour le progrès de Guinée (UPG, which had withdrawn from Codem in May 1996), stated that the only possible source of dissension might come from members of the military who were disenchanted at their conditions of service.

The political atmoshpere remained tense for the remainder of 1997. In September the PUP indicated its suspicions that a number of recent defections to its ranks by former members of Codem might represent an attempt by the opposition to infiltrate the presidential movement. Later in the month it was announced that an independent national electoral commission would not be constituted to supervise the forthcoming presidential election (due in December 1998), and that the Minister of Territorial Administration and Decentralization would take responsibility for the revision of the voters' register. In early October 1997 Doré announced his intention to represent the UPG in the presidential election. Later in the month the UFD leader, Alpha Ibrahim Sow, issued an open letter urging Conté, in the interests of preventing further instability, not to seek a renewed mandate. The Ministers of Security and of Planning and Co-operation left the Government shortly afterwards, as part of a reorganization of portfolios in which a new Minister of the Interior and Decentralization, Zaïnoul Abidine Sanoussi, was appointed. Diasseny was transferred to the higher education and scientific research portfolio, but one month later was appointed Minister of National Defence (thereby becoming the first civilian to hold this position since the 1984 *coup d'état*).

In its report for 1996/97, presented in mid-October 1997, the AGDH accused the Guinean security forces of daily atrocities, alleging the systematic ill-treatment of detainees. The association expressed particular concern at the continued detention of civilians related to the suspects in the 1996 mutiny, and at the detention without trial, in solitary confinement, of Liberian and Sierra Leonean nationals. The detention of the three Belgian nationals, with a Guinean associate, was similarly condemned. In early November 1997 it was revealed that 53 soldiers, detained since the mutiny, had in a joint letter to the Assemblée nationale alleged that they had been tortured following their arrest and complained of their conditions of confinement. The authors of the letter appealed, in the absence of an amnesty law, for the legislature to exert pressure on the judiciary to ensure a fair trial. In December, furthermore, Agence France-Presse reported that the same soldiers had alleged that many senior military officers remained in post despite their active or passive complicity in the mutiny. Among the officers identified by the detainees were the present and former chief of staff of the armed forces, as well as Sama Pannival Bangoura and his predecessor at the Alpha Yaya barracks. A total of 96 defendants were brought before the State Security Court in mid-February 1998, to answer charges related to the attempted coup two years earlier; hearings were immediately adjourned until the end of the month, after defence lawyers complained that they had had no access to their clients for the past four months. Reportedly among the defendants was the former Minister of Defence dismissed by Conté on the second day of the mutiny.

Relations with both the Government of France and with private French interests have strengthened considerably in recent years: official assistance from, and trade with, France is of great importance to the Guinean economy, as is French participation in the mining sector and in newly-privatized organizations. Guinea, a member of the Organization of the Islamic Conference (see p. 224), has also forged links with other Islamic states, notably signing several co-operation agreements with Iran in the mid-1990s. Links with the People's Republic of China are also close, and the Chinese Government provided funds for the construction of a new presidential palace following the unrest of early 1996.

In August 1990 Guinean armed forces were deployed along the border with Liberia, following a series of violent incursions by deserters from the Liberian army. Guinean army units also participated in ECOMOG, deployed in Liberia in that month (see the Economic Community of West African States—ECOWAS, p.146), and in April 1991 it was announced that a Guinean contingent was to be dispatched to Sierra Leone to assist that country in repelling violations of its territory by Charles Taylor's National Patriotic Front of Liberia (NPFL). In October 1992 the Guinean Government admitted for the first time that Liberian forces were being trained in Guinea; however, it was stated that those receiving instruction were not, as had been widely rumoured, members of the anti-NPFL United Liberation Movement of Liberia for Democracy (ULIMO), but that they were to constitute the first Liberian government forces following an eventual restoration of peace in that country. Although Guinea consistently denied support for ULIMO, it was admitted in March 1993 that, contrary to earlier indications, Liberian forces trained in Guinea (at the request of the Liberian interim Government) had already returned to Liberia. Efforts were undertaken from early 1994 to reinforce security along Guinea's borders, following recent incursions by both ULIMO and NPFL fighters. In July 1995 the Government issued a statement reaffirming Guinea's determination to ensure the defence of its territory and security of its population, and indicating that attacks by Liberian factions against border areas, which undermined Guinea's territorial integrity and national sovereignty, would not be tolerated.

Following the *coup d'état* in Sierra Leone in April 1992, ex-President Momoh of that country was granted asylum in Guinea, although the Conté administration expressed its wish to establish 'normal' relations with the new regime led by Capt. Valentine Strasser and announced that Guinean forces would remain in Sierra Leone. Strasser, like his predecessor, took refuge in Guinea after he was deposed in January 1996. None the less, close co-operation was developed with the new regime, and President Ahmed Tejan Kabbah made several visits to Guinea both before and after his election to the presidency in March of that year. Kabbah, in turn, fled to Guinea in May 1997, following the seizure of power in Sierra Leone by forces led by Maj. Johnny Paul Koroma. Military reinforcements were deployed to protect Guinea's border, and 1,500 Guinean troops were dispatched in support of the Nigerian-led force in Sierra Leone. Guinea joined other members of the international community in condemning the subversion of constitutional order in Sierra Leone, and, following an *ad hoc* conference of ECOWAS ministers of foreign affairs (convened in Conakry in late June), Guinea became a member of the "Committee of Four" (with Côte d'Ivoire, Ghana and Nigeria) charged with ensuring the implementation of decisions and recommendations pertaining to the situation in Sierra Leone. A conference communiqué appealed for international assistance for Guinea and other countries of the subregion affected by the influx of refugees as a result of the coup.

The conflicts in Liberia and Sierra Leone have resulted in the presence in Guinea of large numbers of refugees from both countries. In early 1995 the Conté Government warned of the likelihood of food shortages in border areas, and appealed for international assistance for its efforts to meet the refugees' basic needs. Guinea established a special commission at this time to monitor the refugee crisis. In December 1995, following the conclusion (in Abuja, Nigeria, in August) of a new peace accord for Liberia, it was reported that arrangements were being finalized for the repatriation of Liberian refugees, at a rate of 150 per week, from Guinea. Several thousand refugees were also reported to have crossed into Liberia in December, following the reopening of a border point that had been blocked by the NPFL since 1994. A population census conducted in Guinea at the end of 1996 enumerated some 640,000 refugees from Liberia and Sierra Leone.

Government

Under the terms of the Constitution promulgated on 23 December 1991, and amended by an 'organic law' of 3 April 1992, the President of the Republic, who is Head of State, is elected for five years by universal adult suffrage, in the context of a multi-party political system. Similarly elected is the 114-member Assemblée nationale, which holds legislative power. The President of the Republic is also Head of Government, and in this capacity appoints the other members of the Council of Ministers.

Local administration is based on eight provinces, each under the authority of an appointed Governor; the country is subdivided into 34 regions, including Conakry (which is divided into three communes).

Defence

In August 1997 Guinea's active armed forces totalled 9,700, comprising an army of 8,500, a navy of 400 and an air force of 800. Paramilitary forces comprised a Republican Guard of 1,600 and a 1,000-strong gendarmerie, as well as a reserve 'people's militia' of 7,000. Military service is compulsory (conscripts were estimated at some 7,500 in 1997) and lasts for two years. The defence budget for 1997 was estimated at 59,000m. FG.

Economic Affairs

In 1995, according to estimates by the World Bank, Guinea's gross national product (GNP), measured at average 1993–95 prices, was US $3,593m., equivalent to $550 per head. Between 1985 and 1993, it was estimated, GNP per head, in real terms, increased at an average annual rate of 1.3%. Over the period 1985–95 the population increased by an annual average of 2.8%. During 1985–95 Guinea's gross domestic product (GDP) increased, in real terms, at an average annual rate of 3.5%; the IMF estimated GDP growth at 4.4% in 1995, and at 4.5% in 1996.

Measured at constant 1989 prices, agriculture (including hunting, forestry and fishing) contributed an estimated 24.5% of GDP in 1995. About 84.8% of the labour force were employed in the agricultural sector in 1996. The principal cash crops are fruits, oil palm, groundnuts and coffee. Important staple crops include cassava, rice and other cereals and vegetables. The attainment of self-sufficiency in rice and other basic foodstuffs remains a priority: some 384,000 metric tons of cereals were imported into Guinea in 1994. The food supply is supplemented by the rearing of cattle and other livestock. The Government hoped to enhance the commercial viability of the country's substantial forest resources during the 1990s, while introducing measures to compensate for the earlier, excessive exploitation of timber in some regions. Guinea's territorial waters contain significant stocks of fish, and efforts to stimulate their development by Guinean interests were initiated in the late 1980s. During 1988–95 agricultural GDP increased by an estimated annual average of 4.2%; the IMF estimated growth of 3.5% in 1995.

Industry (including mining, manufacturing, construction and power) contributed an estimated 31.4% of GDP (at constant 1989 prices) in 1995. Less than 2% of the employed labour force were engaged in the industrial sector at the time of the 1983 census. Industrial GDP increased by an estimated annual average of 2.5% in 1988–95; growth was estimated by the IMF at 3.7% in 1995.

Measured at constant 1989 prices, mining contributed an estimated 19.2% of GDP in 1995. Only 0.7% of the employed labour force were engaged in extractive activities in 1983. Guinea is the world's foremost exporter of bauxite and the second largest producer of bauxite ore, possessing between one-quarter and one-third of known reserves of that mineral. In 1995 exports of bauxite and alumina provided an estimated 54.7% of export earnings. Gold and diamonds are also extracted: exports of these contributed, respectively, 15.0% and 7.7% of total export revenue in 1995. The eventual exploitation of valuable reserves of high-grade iron ore at Mt Nimba, near the border with Liberia, is envisaged. Of Guinea's other known mineral deposits, only granite is exploitable on a commercial scale. The GDP of the mining sector increased by an estimated annual average of 1.3% during 1988–95; growth in the sector was estimated by the IMF at 2.5% in 1995.

The manufacturing sector, estimated by the IMF to have contributed 4.7% of GDP (at constant 1989 prices) in 1995, remains largely undeveloped. In 1983 only 0.6% of the employed labour force were engaged in the manufacturing sector. An alumina smelter is in operation; other industrial companies are involved in import-substitution, including the processing of agricultural products and the manufacture of construction materials. During 1988–95 manufacturing GDP increased by an estimated annual average of 4.1%; expansion in the sector was estimated by the IMF at 3.1% in 1995.

Electricity generation is, at present, insufficient to meet demand, and power failures outside the mining and industrial sectors (in which the largest operators generate their own power supplies) have been frequent. However, Guinea possesses considerable hydroelectric potential. Construction of the major Garafiri dam project began in 1995, with production scheduled to commence in 1999; financing for a second project has not yet been secured, although the scheme, at Kaléta, is expected to be operational in 2002. In the mean time, some 600,000 metric tons of hydrocarbons are imported annually, and in 1995 imports of fuel and energy accounted for 11.9% of the value of total imports.

The services sector contributed an estimated 44.0% of GDP (at constant 1989 prices) in 1995. During 1988–95 the estimated average rate of growth in the sector's GDP was 4.4% per year. The IMF estimated growth of 5.2% in 1995.

In 1996 Guinea recorded a visible trade surplus of US $111.2m., while there was a deficit of $177.3m. on the current account of the balance of payments. Excluding trade with countries of the former USSR, the principal suppliers of imports in 1995 were France (which supplied 20.5% of the total) and Côte d'Ivoire (18.3%); other major suppliers were the USA, the Belgo-Luxembourg Economic Union (BLEU) and Hong Kong. The principal markets for exports in the same year were the BLEU and the USA (which took 15.8% and 15.6%, respectively, of the total); other major purchasers included Spain, Ireland, Brazil, France and Italy. The principal exports in 1995 were bauxite, gold, alumina, coffee and diamonds. The principal imports include manufactured goods, mineral fuels and foodstuffs.

In 1995 Guinea recorded an overall budget deficit of an estimated 151,300m. FG, equivalent to 4.2% of GDP in that year. The country's total external debt was US $3,242m. at the end of 1995, of which $2,975m. was long-term public debt. In that year the cost of debt-servicing was equivalent to 25.3% of the value of exports of goods and services. Annual inflation averaged 15.6% in 1987–95; consumer prices increased by an annual average of 5.4% in 1995, and by 3.2% in 1996.

Guinea is a member of the Economic Community of West African States (ECOWAS, see p. 145), of the Gambia River

Basin Development Organization (OMVG, see p. 261), of the International Coffee Organization (see p. 257), of the West Africa Rice Development Association (WARDA, see p. 258) and of the Mano River Union (see p. 262).

Guinea's potential for the attainment of wealth is substantial, owing to its valuable mineral deposits, water resources and generally favourable climate; however, the economy is over-dependent on revenue from bauxite reserves, the country's infrastructure is generally poor and its manufacturing base narrow. The presence in the country of large numbers of refugees has, furthermore, placed considerable strain on the country's resources. Since 1985 economic liberalization measures have been undertaken, as advocated by the IMF and the World Bank, and by the mid-1990s, despite earlier difficulties in implementing reforms, growth in overall GDP was considerable. A new mining code was introduced in 1995, with the particular aim of attracting further foreign investment, and it was hoped that much-needed infrastructural development would ensue. The IMF approved a new three-year Enhanced Structural Adjustment Facility in January 1997, in support of the Government's reform programme for 1997–99; it was aimed to achieve average growth of almost 5% per year over this period. Priority was to be given to the improvement of basic health services and primary education, and it was aimed to strengthen social security provisions. The Government of Sidia Touré has emphasized the need to maintain rigorous controls on government expenditure, notably on the public-sector payroll, and to eliminate administrative inefficiency and corruption. It was anticipated that the budget would remain in deficit for the remainder of the decade, emphasizing the need for new assistance and debt-relief by bilateral and private creditors. In the mean time, the preservation of political stability will be essential to the pursuit of the reform programme and to the maintenance of investor and donor confidence, but will depend largely on the Government's ability to minimize the adverse impact on the population of its adjustment measures.

Social Welfare

Wages are fixed according to the Government Labour Code. A maximum working week of 48 hours is in force for industrial workers. In 1988 there were 2,945 physicians, and there were 18,674 hospital beds. The extension of basic health care to low-income groups forms a significant element of the Government's structural adjustment efforts. Private medical care has been legally available since 1984.

Education

Education is provided free of charge at every level in state institutions. Primary education, which begins at seven years of age and lasts for six years, is officially compulsory. In 1993, however, enrolment at primary schools was equivalent to only 46% of children in the relevant age-group (boys 61%; girls 30%). As part of government plans to extend the provision of basic education, it was aimed to increase the rate of primary enrolment to 53% by 2000. Secondary education, from the age of 13, lasts for seven years, comprising a first cycle (collège) of four years and a second (lycée) of three years. Enrolment at secondary schools in 1993 was equivalent to only 12% of children in the appropriate age-group (boys 18%; girls 6%). There are universities at Conakry and Kankan, and other tertiary institutions at Maneah, Boké and Faranah. In 1993, according to the national literacy service, the average rate of adult illiteracy was 72% (males 61%; females 83%). Under a six-year transitional education plan, announced in June 1984, ideological education was eliminated and French was adopted as the language of instruction in schools. Teaching of the eight national languages was suspended, although the reintroduction of classes in certain national languages was under consideration in 1996. Private schools, which had been banned for 23 years under the Touré regime, were legalized in 1984. Government expenditure on education in 1993 was equivalent to 26% of total budget spending.

Public Holidays

1998: 1 January (New Year's Day), 30 January* (Id al-Fitr, end of Ramadan), 13 April (Easter Monday), 1 May (Labour Day), 7 July* (Mouloud, birth of Muhammad), 27 August (Anniversary of Women's Revolt), 28 September (Referendum Day), 2 October (Republic Day), 1 November (All Saints' Day), 22 November (Day of 1970 Invasion), 25 December (Christmas).

1999: 1 January (New Year's Day), 19 January* (Id al-Fitr, end of Ramadan), 5 April (Easter Monday), 1 May (Labour Day), 26 June* (Mouloud, birth of Muhammad), 27 August (Anniversary of Women's Revolt), 28 September (Referendum Day), 2 October (Republic Day), 1 November (All Saints' Day), 22 November (Day of 1970 Invasion), 25 December (Christmas).

* These holidays are determined by the Islamic lunar calendar and may vary by one or two days from the dates given.

Weights and Measures

The metric system is in force.

Statistical Survey

Source (unless otherwise stated): Service de la Statistique Générale, Conakry; tel. 44-21-48.

Area and Population

AREA, POPULATION AND DENSITY

Area (sq km)	245,857*
Population (census results)	
4–17 February 1983	4,533,240†
31 December 1996‡	
Males	3,496,150
Females	3,668,673
Total	7,164,823
Density (per sq km) at census of 1996	29.1

* 94,926 sq miles.

† Excluding adjustment for underenumeration.

‡ Provisional figure, including refugees from Liberia and Sierra Leone (estimated at 640,000).

PRINCIPAL TOWNS (population at December 1972)

Conakry (capital) 525,671 (later admitted to be overstated); Kankan 60,000.

BIRTHS AND DEATHS (UN estimates, annual averages)

	1980–85	1985–90	1990–95
Birth rate (per 1,000)	51.3	51.0	50.6
Death rate (per 1,000)	23.8	22.0	20.3

Expectation of life (UN estimates, years at birth, 1990–95): 44.5 (males 44.0; females 45.0).

Source: UN, *World Population Prospects: The 1994 Revision*.

ECONOMICALLY ACTIVE POPULATION
(persons aged 10 years and over, census of 1983, provisional)

	Males	Females	Total
Agriculture, hunting, forestry and fishing	856,971	566,644	1,423,615
Mining and quarrying	7,351	4,890	12,241
Manufacturing	6,758	4,493	11,251
Electricity, gas and water	1,601	1,604	3,205
Construction	5,475	3,640	9,115
Trade, restaurants and hotels	22,408	14,901	37,309
Transport, storage and communications	17,714	11,782	29,496
Finance, insurance, real estate and business services	2,136	1,420	3,556
Community, social and personal services	82,640	54,960	137,600
Activities not adequately defined*	101,450	54,229	155,679
Total labour force	1,104,504	718,563	1,823,067

* Includes 18,244 unemployed persons (not previously employed), whose distribution by sex is not available.

Source: ILO, *Yearbook of Labour Statistics*.

Mid-1996 (estimates in '000): Agriculture, etc. 3,066; Total labour force 3,614 (Source: FAO, *Production Yearbook*).

Agriculture

PRINCIPAL CROPS ('000 metric tons)

	1994	1995	1996
Maize	88	79	90
Millet	5	8	8
Sorghum	4	5	6
Rice (paddy)	532	631	668
Other cereals	133	102	92
Sweet potatoes	143	130*	130*
Cassava (Manioc)	512	601	440
Yams	114	95*	95*
Taro (Coco yam)*	32	26	26
Pulses*	60	60	60
Coconuts	5	18*	18*
Cottonseed	10*	8*	5
Cotton (lint)	7†	7*	6
Vegetables*	420	420	420
Sugar cane*	220	220	220
Citrus fruits*	230	230	230
Bananas	151	150*	150*
Plantains*	429	429	429
Mangoes	105	80*	76
Pineapples	67	67	67*
Other fruits*	36	37	38
Palm kernels	53	53*	52
Groundnuts (in shell)	128	132	139
Coffee (green)	30	28*	23
Cocoa beans	4*	4†	4†
Tobacco (leaves)*	2	2	2

* FAO estimate(s). † Unofficial figure.

Source: FAO, *Production Yearbook*.

LIVESTOCK ('000 head, year ending September)

	1994	1995	1996
Cattle	1,874	2,188	2,212
Sheep	487	610	618
Goats	587	751	760
Pigs	41	44	45
Horses*	2	2	2
Asses*	1	1	1

Poultry (million): 7* in 1994; 7 in 1995; 7* in 1996.

* FAO estimate(s).

Source: FAO, *Production Yearbook*.

LIVESTOCK PRODUCTS (FAO estimates, '000 metric tons)

	1994	1995	1996
Beef and veal	12	15	15
Poultry meat	2	2	2
Mutton and lamb	1	1	1
Goat meat	2	3	3
Other meat	5	4	4
Cows' milk	48	49	50
Goats' milk	4	5	5
Sheep's milk	2	2	2
Poultry eggs	7	7	7
Cattle hides	2	2	2

Source: FAO, *Production Yearbook*.

Forestry

ROUNDWOOD REMOVALS ('000 cubic metres, excluding bark)

	1992	1993	1994
Sawlogs, veneer logs and logs for sleepers	140	140*	140*
Other industrial wood*	426	440	453
Fuel wood	3,849	4,125	4,296
Total	4,415	4,705	4,889

* FAO estimate(s).

Source: FAO, *Yearbook of Forest Products*.

SAWNWOOD PRODUCTION
('000 cubic metres, including railway sleepers)

	1992	1993	1994
Total	63	65	72

Source: FAO, *Yearbook of Forest Products*.

Fishing

('000 metric tons, live weight)

	1993*	1994*	1995
Freshwater fishes	4.0	4.4	4.0*
Sea catfishes	3.0	3.1	4.4
Bobo croaker	2.5	2.6	3.7
Other croakers and drums	2.8	2.9	4.1
Porgies and seabreams	3.3	3.3	4.7
Mullets	1.2	1.3	1.8
Carangids	3.5	3.6	5.0
Sardinellas	3.7	3.8	5.3
Bonga shad	23.0	25.0	23.6
Other marine fishes (incl. unspecified)	13.0	14.4	12.2
Total catch	60.0	64.4	68.8*

* FAO estimate(s).

Mining

	1990	1991	1992
Bauxite ('000 metric tons)	15,341	14,862	13,625
Diamonds ('000 carats)*	127	97	95

Bauxite ('000 metric tons)*: 14,784 in 1993; 13,761 in 1994.

* Data from the US Bureau of Mines.

Source: UN, *Industrial Commodity Statistics Yearbook*.

Gold (Mineral content of ore, metric tons): 4.2 in 1992; 3.8 in 1993; 4.3 in 1994; 6.5 in 1995; 7.0 in 1996 (Source: Gold Fields Mineral Services Ltd, *Gold 1997*).

Industry

SELECTED PRODUCTS ('000 metric tons, unless otherwise indicated)

	1992	1993	1994
Raw sugar	16*	20	10†
Alumina (calcined equivalent)	661	656	n.a.
Electric energy (million kWh)‡	531	536	530

* Data from the FAO.
† Data from the International Sugar Organization.
‡ Provisional or estimated figure(s).

Source: UN, *Industrial Commodity Statistics Yearbook*.

Palm oil (unrefined): 40 in 1992; 40 (estimate) in 1993; 50 in 1994; 50 (estimate) in 1995; 55 in 1996 (Source: FAO, *Production Yearbook*).

Finance

CURRENCY AND EXCHANGE RATES

Monetary Units

100 centimes = 1 franc guinéen (FG or Guinean franc).

Sterling and Dollar Equivalents (30 September 1997)
£1 sterling = 1,835.3 Guinean francs;
US $1 = 1,136.1 Guinean francs;
10,000 Guinean francs = £5.449 = $8.802.

Average Exchange Rate (Guinean francs per US $)
1994 976.6
1995 991.4
1996 1,004.0

BUDGET ('000 million Guinean francs)

Revenue*	1993	1994	1995†
Mining-sector revenue	137.5	98.5	110.7
Profit taxes and dividends	17.6	8.7	1.4
Turnover taxes on Société des Bauxites de Kindia (SBK)	8.1	0.9	7.4
Special tax on mining products	105.8	87.1	100.2
Other revenue	214.1	244.8	290.8
Tax revenue	190.1	220.4	265.6
Taxes on income and profits	24.3	30.1	36.6
Personal	16.5	16.2	20.9
Corporate	3.8	8.7	10.7
Taxes on domestic production and trade	114.5	136.5	171.0
Turnover taxes	36.6	38.5	52.4
Excise surcharge	6.9	10.2	13.8
Petroleum excise tax	52.6	65.1	72.6
Taxes on international trade	51.2	53.8	58.0
Import duties	46.0	50.6	54.8
Total	351.6	343.3	401.5

Expenditure‡	1993	1994	1995†
Current expenditure	293.5	311.7	332.8
Wages and salaries	140.3	145.5	154.9
Other goods and services	80.6	76.5	73.1
Subsidies and transfers	31.1	37.3	52.2
Interest payments	41.5	52.4	52.5
Public investment programme	286.1	268.8	313.9
Domestically financed	45.6	38.8	51.2
Externaly financed	240.5	230.0	262.7
Sub-total	579.6	580.5	646.9
Adjustment for payments arrears §	−0.3	−19.2	52.1
Total (cash basis)	579.3	561.3	699.0

* Excluding grants received ('000 million Guinean francs): 112.7 in 1993; 117.5 in 1994; 146.3† in 1995.
† Estimate(s).
‡ Excluding lending minus repayments ('000 million Guinean francs): 0.2† in 1995.
§ Minus sign indicates an increase in arrears.

Source: IMF, *Guinea—Statistical Annex* (March 1997).

INTERNATIONAL RESERVES (US $ million at 31 December)

	1994	1995	1996
IMF special drawing rights	5.53	7.45	0.77
Reserve position in IMF	0.10	0.10	0.11
Foreign exchange	82.22	79.21	86.46
Total	87.85	86.76	87.34

Source: IMF, *International Financial Statistics*.

MONEY SUPPLY (million Guinean francs at 31 December)

	1994	1995	1996
Currency outside banks	154,748	167,144	154,420
Demand deposits at commercial banks	94,430	104,060	112,590
Total (incl. others)	252,582	274,125	273,465

Source: IMF, *International Financial Statistics*.

COST OF LIVING
(Consumer Price Index for Conakry; base: 1990 = 100)

	1992	1993	1994
Food	134.9	147.5	154.5
Fuel and light	144.9	144.5	148.8
Clothing	118.8	129.6	132.5
Rent	135.9	142.7	143.5
All items (incl. others)	139.5	149.4	155.6

Source: ILO, *Yearbook of Labour Statistics*.

1995: Food 166.8; All items 164.0.
1996: Food 169.2; All items 169.3.

Source: UN, *Monthly Bulletin of Statistics*.

NATIONAL ACCOUNTS

Expenditure on the Gross Domestic Product
('000 million Guinean francs at current prices)

	1993	1994	1995*
Government final consumption expenditure	292.4	289.2	306.5
Private final consumption expenditure	2,411.2	2,728.1	2,966.1
Increase in stocks Gross fixed capital formation	491.7	451.8	529.7
Total domestic expenditure	3,195.3	3,467.0	3,802.4
Exports of goods and services	681.1	656.5	791.1
Less Imports of goods and services	840.1	809.9	952.0
GDP in purchasers' values	3,036.3	3,315.6	3,641.5
GDP at constant 1989 prices	1,657.3	1,723.6	1,799.4

* Estimates.

Gross Domestic Product by Economic Activity
('000 million Guinean francs at constant 1989 prices)

	1993	1994	1995*
Agriculture, hunting, forestry and fishing	395.8	415.7	430.2
Mining and quarrying	322.2	328.6	336.8
Manufacturing	75.4	79.6	82.1
Electricity, gas and water	3.6	3.7	3.9
Construction	113.8	119.5	128.1
Trade	423.1	448.5	472.7
Transport	85.0	88.4	94.2
Administration	92.9	91.3	91.3
Other services	105.4	105.7	114.1
GDP at factor cost	1,617.2	1,681.0	1,753.4
Indirect taxes	40.1	42.6	46.0
GDP in purchasers' values	1,657.3	1,723.6	1,799.4

* Estimates.

Source: IMF, *Guinea—Statistical Annex* (March 1997).

BALANCE OF PAYMENTS (US $ million)

	1994	1995	1996
Exports of goods f.o.b.	515.7	582.8	636.5
Imports of goods f.o.b.	–685.4	–621.7	–525.3
Trade balance	–169.7	–39.0	111.2
Exports of services	152.9	117.5	124.1
Imports of services	–366.0	–392.3	–422.2
Balance on goods and services	–382.9	–313.9	–186.9
Other income received	6.5	12.9	12.8
Other income paid	–79.8	–97.5	–105.7
Balance on goods, services and income	–456.1	–398.5	–279.8
Current transfers received	280.6	258.3	137.8
Current transfers paid	–72.5	–79.3	–35.3
Current balance	–248.0	–219.5	–177.3
Direct investment abroad	—	—	–0.5
Direct investment from abroad	0.2	0.8	23.8
Other investment assets	–14.5	–73.7	–48.9
Other investment liabilities	98.5	182.2	44.0
Net errors and omissions	39.8	37.8	99.1
Overall balance	–124.1	–72.5	–59.9

Source: IMF, *International Financial Statistics*.

External Trade

PRINCIPAL COMMODITIES (US $ million)

Imports c.i.f.	1993	1994	1995†
Public sector	146.6	138.2	148.2
Food aid	5.6	5.4	0.0
Public investment programme	119.0	109.9	124.4
Central Government and public enterprises	22.0	22.9	23.8
Mining companies	217.9	152.6	185.3
Other private sector*	367.7	397.0	475.6
Petroleum products	33.1	33.8	38.6
Total	732.2	687.9	809.2

Exports f.o.b.	1993	1994	1995†
Bauxite	323.7	271.5	298.5
Alumina	108.9	103.4	110.3
Diamonds	70.0	40.2	57.8
Gold	72.1	83.5	112.2
Coffee	36.6	56.7	72.4
Fish	16.6	19.7	29.3
Total (incl. others)	665.0	625.9	747.5

* Including some public-enterprise imports.
† Estimates.

Source: IMF, *Guinea—Statistical Annex* (March 1997).

PRINCIPAL TRADING PARTNERS (percentage of trade)*

Imports f.o.b.	1993	1994	1995
Austria	0.3	1.5	1.6
Belgium-Luxembourg	6.2	7.4	6.2
Brazil	2.1	6.6	3.1
China, People's Repub.	4.4	3.9	3.5
Côte d'Ivoire	13.8	17.2	18.3
France (incl. Monaco)	19.7	20.1	20.5
Germany	2.7	4.1	3.0
Hong Kong	6.8	6.5	5.8
Italy	4.6	3.4	3.5
Japan	2.8	3.5	2.8
Morocco	0.9	0.9	1.4
Netherlands	4.4	3.9	4.3
Nigeria	2.3	2.6	2.5
Senegal	1.8	1.4	1.5
Singapore	4.2	0.0	0.7
Spain	3.9	3.6	3.2
Switzerland	0.3	1.0	0.9
Taiwan	1.0	1.1	0.9
United Kingdom	2.3	5.1	3.3
USA	8.3	7.3	8.4

Exports f.o.b.	1993	1994	1995
Belgium-Luxembourg	24.2	26.5	15.8
Brazil	4.8	4.7	6.7
Cameroon	4.2	3.9	4.1
Canada	0.9	2.0	1.4
China, People's Repub.	2.9	1.6	0.3
Côte d'Ivoire	1.1	1.3	1.6
France (incl. Monaco)	5.8	4.3	6.1
Germany	5.3	5.5	3.6
India	1.1	0.7	0.0
Ireland	9.8	9.1	10.7
Italy	3.3	3.3	5.0
Japan	0.6	1.1	2.0
Norway	1.2	1.1	1.1
Spain	10.1	9.1	11.2
USA	19.1	14.4	15.6

* Data are compiled on the basis of reporting by Guinea's trading partners. Non-reporting countries include, notably, the former USSR.

Source: IMF, *Guinea—Statistical Annex* (March 1997).

Transport

RAILWAYS (estimated traffic)

	1991	1992	1993
Freight ton-km (million)	660	680	710

Source: UN Economic Commission for Africa, *African Statistical Yearbook*.

ROAD TRAFFIC (estimates, motor vehicles in use)

	1994	1995	1996
Passenger cars	13,160	13,720	14,100
Lorries and vans	18,000	19,400	21,000

Source: IRF, *World Road Statistics*.

SHIPPING

Merchant Fleet (registered at 31 December)

	1994	1995	1996
Number of vessels	26	27	25
Total displacement ('000 grt)	8.1	6.9	6.7

Source: Lloyd's Register of Shipping, *World Fleet Statistics*.

International Sea-borne Freight Traffic
(estimates, '000 metric tons)

	1991	1992	1993
Goods loaded	13,670	14,920	16,760
Goods unloaded	717	722	734

Source: UN Economic Commission for Africa, *African Statistical Yearbook*.

CIVIL AVIATION (traffic on scheduled services)

	1992	1993	1994
Kilometres flown (million)	1	1	2
Passengers carried ('000)	23	24	45
Passenger-km (million)	33	35	33
Total ton-km (million)	4	4	4

Source: UN, *Statistical Yearbook*.

Communications Media

	1992	1993	1994
Radio receivers ('000 in use)	257	270	280
Television receivers ('000 in use)	43	48	50
Telephones ('000 main lines in use)	11	12	9
Telefax stations (number in use)	n.a.	n.a.	30
Mobile cellular telephones (subscribers)	n.a.	42	310

Newspapers: 1 daily (average circulation 13,000) in 1988; 1 non-daily (estimated average circulation 1,000) in 1990.

Sources: UNESCO, *Statistical Yearbook*; UN, *Statistical Yearbook*.

Education

(1993/94)

	Institu-tions	Teachers	Students		
			Males	Females	Total
Primary	2,849	9,718	317,654	154,138	471,792
Secondary					
General	252	3,632	82,015	26,444	108,459
Teacher training	8	188	805	763	1,568
Vocational	50	1,302	6,538	2,740	9,278
University	2	659	6,786	296	7,082
Other higher	3	221	833	48	881

Source: the former Ministère de l'Enseignement Pré-Universitaire et de la Formation Professionnelle, Conakry.

Directory

The Constitution

The Constitution (*Loi fondamentale*) of the Third Republic of Guinea was adopted in a national referendum on 23 December 1990 and promulgated on 23 December 1991. An 'organic law' of 3 April 1992, providing for the immediate establishment of an unlimited number of political parties, countermanded the Constitution's provision for the eventual establishment of a two-party political system. There was to be a five-year period of transition, overseen by a Comité transitoire de redressement national (CTRN), to civilian rule, at the end of which executive and legislative authority would be vested in organs of state elected by universal adult suffrage in the context of a multi-party political system.

The Constitution defines the clear separation of the powers of the executive, the legislature and the judiciary. The President of the Republic, who is Head of State, must be elected by an absolute majority of the votes cast, and a second round of voting is held should no candidate obtain such a majority at a first round. The President is Head of Government, and is empowered to appoint ministers and to delegate certain functions. The legislature is the 114-member Assemblée nationale. One-third of the assembly's members are elected as representatives of single-member constituencies, the remainder being appointed from national lists, according to a system of proportional representation.

The CTRN was dissolved following the legislative elections of June 1995.

The Government

HEAD OF STATE

President: Gen. Lansana Conté (took office 4 April 1984; elected 19 December 1993).

COUNCIL OF MINISTERS

(January 1998)

President of the Republic: Gen. Lansana Conté.

Prime Minister: Sidia Touré.

Minister of National Defence: Dorank Assifat Diasseny.

Minister of Foreign Affairs: Lamine Camara.

Minister of the Interior and Decentralization: Zaïnoul Abidine Sanoussi.

Minister of Justice and Keeper of the Seals: Maurice Zobelemou Togba.

Minister of Equipment, Transport, Public Works, the Environment and Telecommunications: Cellou Dalein Diallo.

Minister of Health: Kandjoura Drame.

Minister of Energy and Natural Resources: Fassiné Fofana.

Minister of Agriculture, Water and Forests: Jean-Paul Sarr.

Minister of Industrial Promotion and Trade: Mady Kaba Camara.

Minister of Communication and Culture: Alpha Ibrahima Mongo Diallo.

Minister of Town Planning and Housing: Ousmane Diallo.

Minister of Higher Education and Scientific Research: (vacant).

Minister of Pre-university Education: Germain Doualamou.

Minister of Employment and the Civil Service: Almamy Fode Sylla.

Minister of Fishing and Livestock: Boubacar Barry.

Minister of Security: Goureissy Condé.

Minister of Social Affairs, Women and Children: Daraba Saran.

General Secretary to the Presidency: Almamy Fode Sylla.

Minister of Planning and International Co-operation: Mamadou Cellou Diallo.

Minister of Tourism and Hotels: Kozo Zoumanigui.

Minister of Social Welfare, Woman and Children: Saran Daraba.

Minister of Youth, Sport and Civic Education: Doumba Diakité.

MINISTRIES

All ministries are in Conakry.

Office of the President: Conakry; tel. 44-11-47; telex 623.

Ministry of Agriculture, Water and Forests: BP 576, Conakry; tel. 44-19-66.

Ministry of Energy and Natural Resources: BP 295, Conakry; tel. 44-11-86; fax 41-49-13.

Ministry of Equipment, Transport, Public Works and Telecommunications: Conakry; tel. 44-41-00; telex 22377; fax 41-35-77.

Ministry of Foreign Affairs: Conakry; tel. 40-50-55; telex 634.

Ministry of Justice: Conakry; tel. 44-16-04.

Ministry of National Education: BP 2201, Conakry; tel. 41-34-41; telex 22331; fax 41-30-41.

President and Legislature

PRESIDENT

Election, 19 December 1993

Candidate	% of votes
LANSANA CONTÉ (PUP)	51.70
ALPHA CONDÉ (RPG)	19.55
MAMADOU BOYE BÂ (UNR)	13.37
SIRADIOU DIALLO (PRP)	11.86
FACINÉ TOURÉ (UNPG)*	1.40
MOHAMED MANSOUR KABA (Djama) ISMAËL MOHAMED GASSIM GUSHEIN (PDG—RDA) JEAN-MARIE DORÉ (UPG)	2.12
Total	100.00

* Union nationale pour la prospérité de la Guinée. See political organizations, below, for expansion of other acronyms.

ASSEMBLÉE NATIONALE

Speaker: BOUBACAR BIRO DIALLO.

General election, 11 June 1995

Party	Seats
PUP	71
RPG	19
PRP	9
UNR	9
UPG	2
Djama	1
PDG—AST	1
PDG—RDA	1
UNP	1
Total	114

Political Organizations

Following the military coup of April 1984, the country's sole political party, the Parti démocratique de Guinée–Rassemblement démocratique africain (PDG—RDA), was dissolved, and party political activity officially ceased until April 1992, when legislation providing for the existence of an unlimited number of political parties came into effect. The following parties won representation in the legislature at the 1995 elections:

Parti démocratique de Guinée—Ahmed Sekou Touré (PDG—AST): f. 1994, following split from PDG—RDA.

Parti démocratique de Guinée—Rassemblement démocratique africain (PDG—RDA): f. 1946, revived 1992; Leader El Hadj ISMAËL MOHAMED GASSIM GUSHEIN.

Parti Djama: Leader MOHAMED MANSOUR KABA.

Parti pour le renouveau et le progrès (PRP): Sec.-Gen. SIRADIOU DIALLO.

Parti de l'unité et du progrès (PUP): supports Pres. Conté; Sec.-Gen. ABOUBACAR SOMPAORÉ.

Rassemblement populaire guinéen (RPG): Leaders ALPHA CONDÉ, AHMED TIDIANE CISSÉ.

Union pour la nouvelle République (UNR): Sec.-Gen. MAMADOU BOYE BÂ.

Union pour le progrès de Guinée (UPG): Sec.-Gen. JEAN-MARIE DORÉ.

Union nationale pour le progrès (UNP): Leader PAUL LOUIS FABER.

Note: The **Coordination de l'opposition démocratique (Codem)** was established in July 1995, under the leadership of MAMADOU BOYE BÂ, as an alliance of 12 opposition groups. Other than the UNR, leading members include the PRP and the RPG. The UPG withdrew from the alliance in May 1996.

Diplomatic Representation

EMBASSIES IN GUINEA

Algeria: BP 1004, Conakry; tel. 44-15-03; Chargé d'affaires a.i.: BOUCHERIT NACEUR.

Canada: Corniche Sud, BP 99, Coleah, Conakry; tel. 46-23-95; e-mail cnaky@paris03.x400.gc.ca; Ambassador: DENIS BRIAND.

China, People's Republic: BP 714, Conakry; Ambassador: KONG MINGHUI.

Congo, Democratic Republic: BP 880, Conakry; telex 632; Ambassador: B. KALUBYE.

Côte d'Ivoire: Conakry; telex 2126; Chargé d'affaires a.i.: ATTA YACOUBA.

Cuba: BP 71, Conakry; Ambassador: LUIS DELGADO PÉREZ.

Egypt: BP 389, Conakry; Ambassador: HUSSEIN EL-NAZER.

France: Immeuble Chavanel, Babadi Hadiri, BP 373, Conakry; tel. 44-16-55; telex 600; Ambassador: CHRISTOPHE PHILIBERT.

Germany: BP 540, Conakry; tel. 41-15-06; telex 22479; fax 41-22-18; Ambassador: PIUS FISCHER.

Ghana: Immeuble Ex-Urbaine et la Seine, BP 732, Conakry; tel. 44-15-10; Ambassador: Air Vice-Marshal J. E. A. KOTEI.

Guinea-Bissau: BP 298, Conakry; Ambassador: ARAFAN ANSU CAMARA.

Iraq: Conakry; telex 2162; Chargé d'affaires a.i.: MUNIR CHIHAB AHMAD.

Italy: BP 84, Village Camayenne, Conakry; tel. 46-23-32; telex 636; Ambassador: FAUSTO MARIA PENNACCHIO.

Japan: Lanseboundji, Corniche Sud, Commune de Matam, BP 895, Conakry; tel. 41-36-07; fax 41-25-75; Ambassador: KEIICHI KITABAN.

Korea, Democratic People's Republic: BP 723, Conakry; Ambassador: HANG CHANG RYOL.

Liberia: BP 18, Conakry; telex 2105; Chargé d'affaires a.i.: ANTHONY ZEZO.

Libya: BP 1183, Conakry; telex 645; Chargé d'affaires a.i.: MUFTAH MADI.

Mali: Conakry; telex 2154; Ambassador: KIBILI DEMBA DIALLO.

Morocco: BP 193, Conakry; telex 22422; Ambassador: MOHAMED AYOUCH.

Nigeria: BP 54, Conakry; telex 633; Ambassador: PETER N. OYEDELE.

Romania: BP 348, Conakry; tel. 44-15-68; Ambassador: MARCEL MÀMULARU.

Russia: BP 329, Conakry; tel. 46-37-25; fax 41-27-77; Ambassador: IGOR I. STOUDENNIKOV.

Saudi Arabia: BP 611, Conakry; telex 2146; Chargé d'affaires a.i.: WAHEEB SHAIKHON.

Senegal: BP 842, Conakry; tel. and fax 44-44-13; Ambassador: MAKHILY GASSAMA.

Sierra Leone: BP 625, Conakry; Ambassador: Commdr MOHAMED DIABY.

Syria: BP 609, Conakry; tel. 46-13-20; Chargé d'affaires a.i.: BECHARA KHAROUF.

Tanzania: BP 189, Conakry; tel. 46-13-32; telex 2104; Ambassador: NORMAN KIONDO.

USA: rue KA 038, BP 603, Conakry; tel. 41-15-20; fax 41-15-22; Ambassador: TIBOR P. NAGY, Jr.

Yugoslavia: BP 1154, Conakry; Ambassador: DANILO MILIĆ.

Judicial System

The Constitution of the Third Republic embodies the principle of the independence of the judiciary, and delineates the competences of each component of the judicial system, including the Higher Magistrates' Council, the Supreme Court, the High Court of Justice and the Magistrature. A restructuring of the judicial system is being undertaken, with international financial and technical support, as part of the programme of structural adjustment.

Chief Justice of the Supreme Court: LAMINE SIDIME.

Director of Public Prosecutions: ANTOINE IBRAHIM DIALLO.

Note: A State Security Court was established in June 1997, with exceptional jurisdiction to try, 'in times of peace and war', crimes against the internal and external security of the State. Members of the court are appointed by the President of the Republic. There is no constitutional provision for the existence of such a tribunal.

President of the State Security Court: Commdr SAMA PANNIVAL BANGOURA.

Religion

It is estimated that 95% of the population are Muslims and 1.5% Christians.

ISLAM

Islamic League: Conakry; Sec.-Gen. El Hadj AHMED TIDIANE TRAORÉ.

CHRISTIANITY

The Anglican Communion

Anglicans in Guinea are adherents of the Church of the Province of West Africa, comprising 11 dioceses. The diocese of Guinea (formerly the Río Pongas), was established in August 1985 as the first French-speaking diocese in the Province.

Bishop of Guinea: (vacant), BP 1187, Conakry.

The Roman Catholic Church

Guinea comprises the archdiocese of Conakry and the dioceses of N'Zérékoré and Kankan. There were some 109,297 Roman Catholics in Guinea at 31 December 1995 (comprising about 1.7% of the total population).

Bishops' Conference: Conférence Episcopale de la Guinée, BP 2016, Conakry; tel. and fax 41-32-70; Pres. Most Rev. ROBERT SARAH, Archbishop of Conakry.

Archbishop of Conakry: Most Rev. ROBERT SARAH, Archevêché, BP 2016, Conakry; tel. and fax 41-32-70.

The Press

L'Evénement de Guinée: BP 796, Conakry; monthly; independent; Dir BOUBACAR SANKARELA DIALLO.

Fonike: BP 341, Conakry; sport and general; Dir IBRAHIMA KALIL DIARE.

Horoya (Liberty): BP 191, Conakry; weekly; Dir MOHAMED MOUNIR CAMARA.

Journal Officiel de Guinée: BP 156, Conakry; fortnightly; organ of the Govt.

Le Lynx: Conakry; f. 1992; daily; satirical; Editor SOULEYMAN DIALLO.

L'Observateur: Conakry; independent; Dir SEKOU KONE.

L'Oeil: Conakry; independent; weekly; Dir of Publishing ISMAËL BANGOURA.

NEWS AGENCIES

Agence Guinéenne de Presse: BP 1535, Conakry; tel. 46-54-14; telex 640; f. 1960; Man. Dir MOHAMED CONDÉ.

Foreign Bureaux

Rossiiskoye Informatsionnoye Agentstvo—Novosti (RIA—Novosti) (Russia): BP 414, Conakry; Dir VASILII ZUBKOV.

Agence France-Presse and Reuters (UK) are also represented in Guinea.

PRESS ASSOCIATION

Association Guinéenne des Editeurs de la Presse Indépendante (AGEPI): Conakry; f. 1991; an assen of independent newspaper publ; Chair. BOUBACAR SANKARELA DIALLO.

Publisher

Editions du Ministère de l'Education Nationale: Direction nationale de la recherche scientifique, BP 561, Conakry; tel. 44-19-50; telex 22331; f. 1959; general and educational; Dir Prof. KANTÉ KABINÉ.

Broadcasting and Communications

TELECOMMUNICATIONS

Guinea's telecommunications facilities were expanding rapidly in the second half of the 1990s. By the end of 1997 there were some 25,000 telephone lines. SOTELGUI (see below) was to issue mobile cellular telephones from November of that year.

Direction Nationale des Postes et Télécommunications: Conakry; tel. 41-40-97; telex 22107; fax 44-20-12; Dir. KOLY CAMARA.

Comité National de Coordination des Télécommunications (CNCT): BP 5000, Conakry; tel. 41-40-79; fax 41-20-28; Exec. Sec. SEKOU BANGOURA.

Société des Télécommunications de Guinée (SOTELGUI): Conakry; transferred to majority private ownership in 1996; 60% owned by Telkom Malaysia; Man. JEAN-BAPTISTE KANTARA.

RADIO AND TELEVISION

Radiodiffusion-Télévision Guinéenne (RTG): BP 391, Conakry; tel. 44-22-05; telex 22341; radio broadcasts in French, English, Créole-English, Portuguese, Arabic and local languages; television transmissions in French and local languages; Dir-Gen. JUSTIN MOREL.

The establishment of a network of rural radio stations is in progress.

Finance

(cap. = capital; res = reserves; m. = million; brs = branches; amounts in Guinean francs).

BANKING

Central Bank

Banque Centrale de la République de Guinée (BCRG): 12 blvd du Commerce, BP 692, Conakry; tel. 41-26-51; telex 22225; fax 41-48-98; f. 1960; bank of issue; Gov. IBRAHIMA CHERIF BAH; Dep. Gov. FODÉ SOUMAH.

Commercial Banks

Banque Internationale pour l'Afrique en Guinée (BIAG): blvd du Commerce, BP 1419, Conakry; tel. 41-42-65; telex 22180; fax 41-22-97; f. 1985; 19% state-owned; cap. and res 15,940m., total assets 28,616m. (Dec. 1995); provides 'offshore' banking services; Pres. El Hadj ABDOURAHMANE CHERIF HAIDARA; Man. Dir JACKY VASSEUR; 1 br.

Banque Internationale pour le Commerce et l'Industrie de la Guinée (BICI-GUI): ave de la République, BP 1484, Conakry; tel. 41-45-15; telex 22175; fax 41-39-62; f. 1985; 51% state-owned; cap. and res 12,145m., total assets 141,914m. (Dec. 1995); transfer to private ownership pending; Pres. IBRAHIMA SOUMAH; Man. Dir OLIVIER DE BELLEVILLE; 11 brs.

Banque Populaire Maroco-Guinéenne (BPMG): Immeuble SCIM, 5e ave Manquepas, Kaloum, BP 4400, Conakry; tel. 41-23-60; telex 22211; fax 41-32-61; f. 1991; 35% owned by Banque Centrale Populaire (Morocco), 20% state-owned, cap. and res 262m., total assets 21,774m. (Dec. 1996); Pres. BEN YALLA SYLLA; Man. Dir AMRANI SIDI MOHAMED; 3 brs.

Société Générale de Banques en Guinée: ave de la République, BP 1514, Conakry 1; tel. 41-17-41; telex 22212; fax 41-25-65; f. 1985; 34% owned by Société Générale (France); cap. and res 6,344m., total assets 88,964m. (Dec. 1995); Pres. ALAIN BATAILLE; Man. Dir JEAN-CLAUDE ROBERT.

Union Internationale de Banque en Guinée (UIBG): 5e blvd, angle 6e ave, centre ville, BP 324, Conakry; tel. 41-20-96; telex 23135; fax 41-42-77; f. 1987; 51% owned by Crédit Lyonnais (France); cap. and res 2,048.6m., total assets 40,523.9m. (Dec. 1995); Pres. ALPHA AMADOU DIALLO; Man. Dir MAURICE TRANCHANT.

Islamic Bank

Banque Islamique de Guinée: 6 ave de la République, BP 1247, Conakry; tel. 44-21-10; telex 22184; fax 41-50-71; f. 1983; 51% owned by Dar al-Maal al-Islami (DMI Trust); cap. and res 4,565m., total assets 16,449m. (Dec. 1995); Pres. ADERRAOUF BENESSAIAH; Man. Dir BENJELLOUN ABDELMAJID.

INSURANCE

Union Guinéenne d'Assurances et de Réassurances (UGAR): BP 179, Conakry; tel. 41-48-41; telex 23211; fax 41-17-11; f. 1989; 40% owned by AXA-UAP (France), 35% state-owned; cap. 2,000m.; Man. Dir RAPHAËL Y. TOURÉ.

Trade and Industry

GOVERNMENT AGENCY

Entreprise Nationale Import-Export (IMPORTEX): BP 152, Conakry; tel. 44-28-13; telex 625; state-owned import and export agency; Dir MAMADOU BOBO DIENG.

DEVELOPMENT ORGANIZATIONS

Caisse Française de Développement (CFD): Conakry; telex 780; fmrly Caisse Centrale de Coopération Economique, name changed 1992; Dir in Guinea GUY TERRACOL.

Centre de Promotion et de Développement Minier (CPDM): BP 295, Conakry; tel. 44-11-86; fax 41-49-13; f. 1995; promotes investment in mining sector; Dir ALKANY YANSANE.

Mission Française de Coopération: Conakry; administers bilateral aid; Dir in Guinea ANDRÉ BAILLEUL.

CHAMBERS OF COMMERCE

Chambre de Commerce, d'Industrie et d'Agriculture de Guinée: BP 545, Conakry; tel. 44-44-95; telex 609; f. 1985; Chair. Capt. THIANA DIALLO; 70 mems.

Chambre Economique de Guinée: BP 609, Conakry.

UTILITIES

Enterprise Nationale d'Electricité de Guinée (ENELGUI): BP 322, Conakry; tel. 41-42-43; fax 41-17-51; production and distribution of electricity; Man. Dir BOKARY SYLLA.

Société Guinéenne d'Electricité (SOGEL): Conakry; f. 1994; 49% state-owned, 51% held jtly by Hydro-Québec (Canada), Electricité de France and SAUR (France); intended to oversee production, transport and distribution of electricity.

Société Nationale des Eaux de Guinée (SONEG): BP 825, Conakry; tel. and fax 41-43-81; f. 1988; national water co.

TRADE UNION

Confédération des travailleurs de Guinée (CTG): BP 237, Conakry; f. 1984; Sec.-Gen. Dr MOHAMED SAMBA KÉBÉ.

Transport

RAILWAYS

There are 662 km of 1-m gauge track from Conakry to Kankan in the east of the country, crossing the Niger at Kouroussa. The line is to be upgraded over two years: the contract for the first phase was awarded to a Slovak company in early 1997. Three lines for the transport of bauxite link Sangaredi with the port of Kamsar in the west, via Boké, and Conakry with Kindia and Fria, a total of 383 km. In late 1996 the government of Iran announced its intention to construct a railway linking the Dabola-Tougué bauxite deposits with Conakry: the preliminary contract was secured by Slovak State Railways. Plans exist for the eventual use of a line linking the Nimba iron-ore deposits with the port of Buchanan in Liberia.

Office National des Chemins de Fer de Guinée (ONCFG): BP 589, Conakry; tel. 44-46-13; telex 22349; f. 1905; Man. Dir FOFANA M. KADIO.

Chemin de Fer de Boké: BP 523, Boké; operations commenced 1973.

Chemin de Fer Conakry–Fria: BP 334, Conakry; telex 22251; operations commenced 1960; Gen. Man. A. CAMARA.

Chemin de Fer de la Société des Bauxites de Kindia: BP 613, Conakry; tel. 41-38-28; telex 22148; operations commenced 1974; Gen. Man. K. KEITA.

ROADS

In 1996 there were an estimated 30,500 km of roads, including 4,300 km of main roads and 7,960 km of secondary roads; about 5,030 km of the road network were paved. An 895-km cross-country road links Conakry to Bamako, in Mali, and the main highway connecting Dakar (Senegal) to Abidjan (Côte d'Ivoire) also crosses Guinea. The road linking Conakry to Freetown (Sierra Leone) forms part of the Trans West African Highway, extending from Morocco to Nigeria.

La Guinéenne-Marocaine des Transports (GUIMAT): Conakry; f. 1989; owned jtly by Govt of Guinea and Hakkam (Morocco); operates national and regional transport services.

Société Générale des Transports de Guinée (SOGETRAG): Conakry; f. 1984; 63% state-owned; bus operator.

SHIPPING

Conakry and Kamsar are the international seaports. Conakry handled 4.4m. metric tons of foreign trade in 1994, while some 12m. tons of bauxite were transported to Kamsar for shipment.

Port Autonome de Conakry: BP 715, Conakry; tel. 44-27-37; telex 22276.

Port de Kamsar OFAB: Kamsar.

Société Navale Guinéenne (SNG): BP 522, Conakry; tel. 44-29-55; telex 22234; fax 41-39-70; f. 1968; state-owned; shipping agents; Dir-Gen. NOUNKÉ KEITA.

SOTRAMAR: Kamsar; f. 1971; exports bauxite from mines at Boké through port of Kamsar.

CIVIL AVIATION

There is an international airport at Conakry-Gbessia, and smaller airfields at Labé, Kankan and Faranah. In 1995 France agreed to provide some 27.6m. French francs in support of a project (costing 31m. francs) to improve facilities at Conakry.

Nouvelle Air Guinée: 6 ave de la République, BP 12, Conakry; tel. 44-46-02; telex 22349; f. 1960; transfer pending to one-third private ownership; regional and internal services; Dir-Gen. El Hadj NFA MOUSSA DIANE.

Société de Gestion et d'Exploitation de l'Aéroport de Conakry (SOGEAC): Conakry; f. 1987; manages Conakry-Gbessia international airport; 51% state-owned.

Tourism

A major tourism development project was announced in 1995, with the eventual aim of attracting some 100,000 visitors annually: 186 tourist sites are to be renovated, and access to them improved, and it is planned to increase the number of hotel beds from less than 800 to 25,000 by 1999.

Ministère du Tourisme et de l'Hôtellerie: square des Martyrs, BP 1304, Conakry; tel. 44-26-06; f. 1989.

GUINEA-BISSAU

Introductory Survey

Location, Climate, Language, Religion, Flag, Capital

The Republic of Guinea-Bissau lies on the west coast of Africa, with Senegal to the north and Guinea to the east and south. The climate is tropical, although maritime and Sahelian influences are felt. The average temperature is 20°C (68°F). The official language is Portuguese, of which the locally spoken form is Creole (Crioulo). Other dialects are also widely spoken. The principal religious beliefs are animism and Islam. There is a small minority of Roman Catholics and other Christian groups. The national flag (proportions 2 by 1) has two equal horizontal stripes, of yellow over light green, and a red vertical stripe, with a five-pointed black star at its centre, at the hoist. The capital is Bissau.

Recent History

Portuguese Guinea (Guiné) was colonized by Portugal in the 15th century. Nationalist activism began to emerge in the 1950s. Armed insurgency commenced in the early 1960s, and by 1972 the Partido Africano da Independência da Guiné e Cabo Verde (PAIGC) was in control of two-thirds of the country. The independence of the Republic of Guinea-Bissau was unilaterally proclaimed in September 1973, with Luiz Cabral (the brother of the founder of the PAIGC, Amílcar Cabral) as President of the State Council. Hostilities ceased following the military coup in Portugal in April 1974, and on 10 September Portugal recognized the independence of Guinea-Bissau under the leadership of Luiz Cabral.

The PAIGC regime introduced measures to establish a single-party socialist state. At elections in December 1976 and January 1977 voters chose regional councils from which a new National People's Assembly was later selected. In 1978 the Chief State Commissioner, Francisco Mendes, died; he was succeeded by Commander João Vieira, hitherto State Commissioner for the Armed Forces and President of the National People's Assembly.

The PAIGC initially supervised both Cape Verde and Guinea-Bissau, the Constitutions of each remaining separate but with a view to eventual unification. These arrangements were terminated in November 1980, when President Cabral was deposed in a coup organized by Vieira, who was installed as Chairman of the Council of the Revolution. Diplomatic relations between Guinea-Bissau and Cape Verde were restored after the release of Cabral from detention in 1982. In May 1982 President Vieira removed several left-wing ministers from the Government and appointed Vítor Saúde Maria, Vice-Chairman of the Council of the Revolution and former Minister of Foreign Affairs, as Prime Minister.

In 1983 Vieira established a commission to examine plans for the revision of the Constitution and the electoral code. In early March 1984 Vieira dismissed Saúde Maria from the premiership. Although his removal from office was attributed to his alleged involvement in a coup plot, it appeared that the principal reason for Saúde Maria's dismissal was his opposition to the proposed constitutional changes, which would accord more power to the President. (Several other senior party members were subsequently accused of colluding with Saúde Maria and were expelled from the PAIGC.) In late March Vieira formally assumed the role of Head of Government, and elections to regional councils took place. In May the National People's Assembly, which had been dissolved following the 1980 coup, was re-established, and the Council of the Revolution was replaced by a 15-member Council of State, selected from among the members of the Assembly. Vieira was subsequently elected as President of the Council of State and Head of State. The National People's Assembly immediately ratified the new Constitution, and formally abolished the position of Prime Minister.

In August 1985 Vieira iniatiated a campaign against corruption, during which many senior officials were dismissed or arrested. This campaign apparently provoked a military coup attempt in November, led by Col Paulo Correia, the First Vice-President of the Council of State, and other senior army officers. Six people who had been implicated in the coup attempt subsequently died in prison. At the trial of the 53 surviving defendants, which concluded in July 1986, 12 alleged plotters were sentenced to death and 41 imprisoned. Correia and five other defendants, were executed, but the other death sentences were commuted. During 1988 and 1989 a number of those convicted of involvement in the coup were pardoned, and by January 1990 all the remaining detainees who had been implicated in the plot had been released.

During the fourth PAIGC congress, held in November 1986, delegates endorsed proposals for the liberalization of the economy, and re-elected Vieira as Secretary-General of the PAIGC for a further four years. In February 1987 Vieira appointed Dr Vasco Cabral, hitherto Minister of Justice, as Permanent Secretary of the Central Committee of the PAIGC, in an attempt to reinforce party support for the programme of economic liberalization. Following the devaluation of the peso in May of that year, political tension increased, and the Vieira Government denied reports that 20 army officers had been arrested for conspiring against Vieira.

In February 1989 it was announced that the PAIGC had established a six-member national commission to revise the Constitution. Regional elections took place in early June, at which 95.8% of those who voted (about 50% of the registered electorate) endorsed the single PAIGC list. In mid-June the Regional Councils, in turn, elected the National People's Assembly, which subsequently elected the Council of State, of which Vieira was re-elected President. In January 1990 President Vieira announced the creation of two commissions to review, respectively, the programme and statutes of the PAIGC and the laws governing land ownership. In March an extensive government reshuffle took place, in which Dr Vasco Cabral was appointed Second Vice-President and given responsibility for social affairs. In November the First Vice-President, Col Iafai Camara, was placed under house arrest, accused of supplying weapons to Senegalese separatists.

In April 1990 President Vieira announced his approval, in principle, of the introduction of a multi-party political system. In October a draft programme for the transition to a multi-party system was discussed at a national conference in Bissau. In December the Central Committee of the PAIGC agreed to the adoption of a multi-party system, following a period of transition, and that a presidential election, involving an unspecified number of candidates, would be held in 1993. A further congress of the PAIGC was held in January 1991 to discuss the implementation of the new system and the authorization of political parties.

In May 1991 a series of constitutional amendments bringing a formal end to one-party rule were approved by the National People's Assembly, terminating the political monopoly of the PAIGC. In addition, all links between the PAIGC and the armed forces were severed, and the introduction of a free market economy was guaranteed. New legislation in October accorded greater freedom to the press and permitted the formation of new trade unions. In November the Frente Democrática (FD) became the first opposition party to obtain official registration.

At its congress, which took place in December 1991, the PAIGC undertook a restructuring of the party, in preparation for the forthcoming legislative elections, which, it was envisaged, would be held during 1992.

In December 1991 a major government reshuffle took place, in which the office of Prime Minister (which had been abolished in 1984) was restored. Carlos Correia was appointed to the post. Dr Vasco Cabral, who had been transferred to the Ministry of Justice in March, was removed from the Council of Ministers. In late 1991 and early 1992 three further opposition parties obtained legal status: the Resistência da Guiné-Bissau—Movimento Bah-Fatah (RGB—MB) (the party changed its name prior to legalization, from Resistência da Guiné-Bissau—Movimento Bafatá, because the Constitution prohibited political parties with names reflecting regional or ethnic identifications), led by Domingos Fernandes Gomes; the Frente Democrática Social (FDS), led by Rafael Barbosa; and the Partido Unido Social Democrático (PUSD), led by Vítor Saúde Maria. Following a split in the FDS, a further party, the Partido da Renovação Social (PRS), was established in January 1992 by the former

Vice-Chairman of the FDS, Koumba Yalla. In the same month four opposition parties—the PUSD, FDS, RGB—MB and the Partido da Convergência Democrática (PCD), led by Vítor Mandinga—agreed on the establishment of a 'democratic forum', whose demands included the dissolution of the political police, further constitutional changes, a revision of the press law, the creation of an electoral commission and an all-party consultation on the setting of election dates.

In March 1992 some 30,000 people attended an opposition demonstration in Bissau, the first such mass-meeting to be permitted by the Government. The demonstrators were protesting against alleged government corruption and violations of human rights by the security forces. Following a meeting in the same month of the PAIGC National Council, it was announced that presidential and legislative elections would take place on 15 November and 13 December, respectively.

In May 1992 a dissident group, known as the 'Group of 121', broke away from the PAIGC to form a new party, the Partido de Renovação e Desenvolvimento (PRD). The PRD advocated the establishment of a transitional government, pending elections, and the disbanding of the political police. In mid-May the leader of the RGB—MB, Domingos Fernandes Gomes, returned from exile in Portugal and, with the leaders of the FD, PCD, FDS and the PUSD, met Vieira to discuss further democratic reform.

In July 1992, following threats by the 'democratic forum' that it would form a parallel government and boycott elections if the PAIGC did not seek consensus with the opposition on electoral issues, the Government agreed to establish a multi-party national transition commission to organize and oversee the democratic process. In late July the leader of the Frente da Luta para a Libertação da Guiné (FLING), François Kankoila Mendy, returned from The Gambia after a 40-year exile. Two further opposition parties—the Partido Democrático do Progresso (PDP), led by Amine Michel Saad, and the Movimento para a Unidade e a Democracia (MUDE), led by Filinto Vaz Martins—were legalized in August.

In October 1992 Vieira conducted a major reshuffle of the Council of Ministers, removing eight ministers who had been in the Government since independence in 1974. Other changes included the creation of a new Ministry of Territorial Administration, replacing the three resident ministries for the provinces.

In early November 1992 the Government announced the postponement of presidential and legislative elections until March 1993. The delay arose from a disagreement concerning the sequence in which the two sets of elections should take place. Contrary to government plans, the opposition parties demanded that the legislative elections precede the presidential election. In late November six opposition parties, the FD, FDS, MUDE, PRD, PUSD and the RGB—MB, staged a demonstration in Bissau to protest at the Government's decision.

Legislation preparing for the transition to a multi-party democracy was approved by the National Assembly in February 1993, and in the following month a commission was appointed to supervise the forthcoming elections. However, reports in March of a coup attempt against the Government threatened to disrupt the transition to democracy. Initial reports indicated that Maj. Robalo de Pina, commander of the Forças de Intervenção Rápida (an élite guard responsible for presidential security), had been assassinated in what appeared to be an army rebellion, provoked by disaffection at poor standards of pay and living conditions. Some 50 people were arrested, including the leader of the PRD, João da Costa. Opposition politicians claimed that the incident had been contrived by the Government in an effort to discredit the opposition. Da Costa and nine other PRD detainees were released in June pending trial, but were forbidden to engage in political activity. In April public-sector unions organized a three-day general strike in support of demands for wage increases and payment of arrears. In May, following a further split in the FDS, a new political party, the Partido da Convenção Nacional (PCN), was formed. In July Vieira announced that multi-party elections would be held on 27 March 1994. In early August 1993 da Costa was rearrested for allegedly violating the conditions of his parole, prompting renewed accusations by opposition politicians that the Government's actions were politically motivated. Following a threatened boycott of the National Electoral Commission by the opposition, da Costa was conditionally released. He was subsequently tried, but was acquitted in February 1994.

One week before the designated date of 27 March 1994 for presidential and legislative elections, Vieira announced their postponement, owing to financial and technical difficulties. Voter registration for the postponed elections took place during 11–23 April. On 11 May it was announced that the elections would be held on 3 July, with a 21-day period of electoral campaigning to begin on 11 June. In early May six opposition parties, the FD, FDS, MUDE, PDP, PRD and the Liga Guineense de Protecção Ecológica (LIPE), formed a coalition, the União para a Mudança (UM). Later that month a further five opposition parties, the FLING, PRS, PUSD, RGB—MB and the Foro Cívico da Guiné (FCG), announced the establishment of an informal alliance within which each party reserved the right to present its own candidates in the elections.

The elections took place, as scheduled, on 3 July 1994, although voting was extended for two days, owing to logistical problems. The PAIGC secured a clear majority in the National People's Assembly, winning 62 of the total 100 seats, but the results of the presidential election were inconclusive, with Vieira winning 46.29% of the votes, while his nearest rival, Koumba Yalla of the PRS, secured 21.92% of the votes. As no candidate had obtained an absolute majority, a second round of polling, with voters choosing between the two leading candidates, was conducted on 7 August. Despite receiving the combined support of all the opposition parties, Yalla was narrowly defeated, securing 47.97% of the votes, compared with Vieira's 52.03%. Yalla subsequently contested the results of the election, accusing the PAIGC of electoral fraud and claiming that the state security police had conducted a campaign of intimidation against opposition supporters. Yalla's claims were, however, rejected, and on 20 August he accepted the results of the election while affirming that the PRS would not participate in the new Government. International observers later declared the elections to have been free and fair.

Vieira was inaugurated as President on 29 September 1994 and, following considerable delays owing to divisions within the PAIGC, finally appointed Manuel Saturnino da Costa (the Secretary-General of the PAIGC) as Prime Minister in late October. The Council of Ministers was appointed in November, comprising solely members of the PAIGC.

Strike action, commonplace in recent years (owing to a decline in living standards), continued under the new Government. In February 1995 the national teachers' union conducted a three-day strike in support of demands for wage increases and payment of salary arrears. In May, following a two-day general strike by members of the principal trade union, the União Nacional dos Trabalhadores da Guiné (UNTG), in the previous month, the Government conceded a 100% increase in the country's minimum wage.

In April 1995 the FD, FDS, MUDE, PDP and the PRD reconstituted the UM coalition, and elected João da Costa as President and Amine Saad as Secretary-General. The LIPE, which had two representatives in the legislature and was a member of the original UM coalition, did not join the new organization, which was granted legal status in November. In August legal status was granted to a new party, the Partido Social Democrático, which was formed by dissidents from the RGB—MB.

In October 1995 a demonstration, organized by the PRS, was conducted in protest at the deterioration in the country's economy. The protest received widespread support from opposition parties, as well as from the Guinea-Bissau Human Rights League (formed in 1992 under the leadership of a former Justice of the Supreme Court, Fernando Gomes). A similar protest was organized later that month by the RGB—MB. Also in October, following negotiations with the UNTG, the Government granted a further increase, of 50%, in the minimum wage. In early November 1996 government plans to join the Union économique et monétaire ouest-africaine (UEMOA, see p. 182) were rejected by the National People's Assembly. A report by the parliamentary economic and financial commission recommended a transition period of two years before joining the francophone regional organization. However, in late November, after receiving a plea from Vieira, the legislature approved a constitutional amendment authorizing the Government to seek membership of the UEMOA, which it duly attained in January 1997. Guinea-Bissau subsequently entered the Franc Zone on 2 May. The national currency was replaced, over a three-month transitional period, by the franc CFA, and the Banque centrale des états de l'Afrique de l'ouest (BCEAO) assumed the central banking functions of the Banco Central da Guiné-Bissau.

In May 1997, in order to address what Vieira described as a serious political crisis that was undermining the functioning of the State, da Costa was dismissed. Carlos Correia was subsequently appointed Prime Minister and took office in the following month, when a new 14-member Council of Ministers was inaugurated.

In August 1997 the UNTG conducted a four-day general strike in support of demands for public-sector salaries to be increased and aligned with those of other countries belonging to the Franc Zone. The union claimed that Guinea-Bissau's entry into the Franc Zone had precipitated a significant increase in inflation, and that the Government had failed to adopt measures to compensate for the impact of membership on living standards. The Government subsequently agreed to increase public-sector salaries by 50%, with effect from January 1998.

On 11 October 1997 Correia was dismissed, bringing to an end an institutional crisis that had lasted since his inauguration as Prime Minister in June. The legislative process had been obstructed by opposition deputies who claimed that, by omitting to consult those parties represented in the legislature on Correia's appointment, Vieira had acted unconstitutionally. In August the matter was referred to the Supreme Court, which ruled, in early October, that Vieira had indeed contravened the Constitution. Following consultations with party leaders, Vieira reappointed Correia on 13 October, with the full support of the main opposition parties.

Relations with Portugal deteriorated in October 1987, when six Portuguese vessels were seized for alleged illegal fishing in Guinea-Bissau's territorial waters. Portugal retaliated by suspending non-medical aid, but revoked its decision in early November, after the vessels were released. A few days later, however, the head of security at the embassy of Guinea-Bissau in Lisbon requested political asylum and disclosed the presence of explosive devices in the embassy, which, he alleged, were to be used to eliminate members of the then-exiled opposition movement, RGB—MB (see above). These allegations were vehemently denied by the Government of Guinea-Bissau. A four-day visit by the Portuguese Prime Minister, Aníbal Cavaco Silva, in March 1989 signified a distinct improvement in relations between the two countries. In July 1996 Vieira made a four-day official visit to Portugal, during which agreement was reached on improved bilateral relations, particularly in the area of defence. In the same month Guinea-Bissau was among the five lusophone African nations which, along with Brazil and Portugal, officially established the Comunidade dos Países de Língua Portuguesa (CPLP), a lusophone grouping intended to benefit each member state by means of joint co-operation in technical, cultural and social matters.

Relations with Cape Verde, which had deteriorated in the aftermath of the 1980 coup, improved during the following decade. In January 1988 the two countries signed a bilateral co-operation agreement.

In August 1989 a dispute arose between Guinea-Bissau and Senegal over the demarcation of maritime borders, which had been based on a 1960 agreement between the former colonial powers, Portugal and France. Guinea-Bissau began proceedings against Senegal in the International Court of Justice (ICJ) after rejecting an international arbitration tribunal's ruling in favour of Senegal. President Abdou Diouf of Senegal postponed a planned visit to Guinea-Bissau, although he met President Vieira in Dakar, the Senegalese capital, at the end of August. Guinea-Bissau requested direct negotiations with Senegal, and enlisted the aid of President Mubarak of Egypt, then the President of the Organization of African Unity (OAU), and President Soares of Portugal as mediators.

In January 1990 Guinea-Bissau again urged the OAU, Portugal and also France to help in achieving a peaceful solution to the dispute. Guinea-Bissau and Senegal came close to armed conflict in May 1990, following a Senegalese military incursion into Guinea-Bissau territory. The Senegalese detachment was subsequently withdrawn. In August some 300 nationals of Guinea-Bissau fled the Senegalese region of Casamance, following clashes between the Senegalese army and Casamance separatists. In September more than 1,600 Senegalese sought refuge in Guinea-Bissau, having fled the Casamance region. In November 1991 the ICJ ruled that the 1960 agreement, concluded between France and Portugal, regarding the demarcation of maritime borders between Guinea-Bissau and Senegal remained valid. In December 1992, in retaliation for the deaths of two Senegalese soldiers at the hands of Casamance separatists, the Senegalese air force and infantry bombarded alleged Casamance separatist bases in the São Domingos area of Guinea-Bissau. The reprisals resulted in the death of two civilians. In response, the Government of Guinea-Bissau protested to the Senegalese authorities against the violation of Guinea-Bissau's borders and air space, and denied Senegalese claims that it was providing support for the rebels. The Senegalese Government offered assurances that there would be no repetition of the incident. In January 1993 the number of Senegalese refugees in Guinea-Bissau was estimated to total 11,000. In March, in an apparent attempt to convince Senegal that it did not support the rebels, the Government handed over Abbé Augustin Diamacouné Senghor, one of the exiled leaders of the Casamance separatists, to the Senegalese authorities.

In October 1993 the Presidents of Guinea-Bissau and Senegal signed an agreement in Dakar, providing for the joint management and exploitation of the countries' maritime zones. Petroleum resources were to be divided, with Senegal receiving an 85% share and Guinea-Bissau the remaining 15%. Fishing resources were to be divided according to the determination of a joint management agency (formally empowered by Presidents Diouf and Vieira in June 1995). The agreement, which was renewable after a period of 20 years, was expected to put a definitive end to the countries' dispute over the demarcation of their common maritime borders. In December 1995 the legislature authorized the ratification of the October 1993 accord. In the previous month the ICJ announced that Guinea-Bissau had halted all proceedings regarding the border dispute with Senegal.

In February 1995 the Senegalese air force bombarded the village of Ponta Rosa in Guinea-Bissau, close to the border with Senegal. Despite an acknowledgement by the Senegalese authorities that the bombing had occurred as the result of an error, the Senegalese armed forces conducted a similar attack later in the same month, when the border village of Ingorezinho came under artillery fire. In March, in an attempt to achieve a *rapprochement* between the two countries, President Diouf visited Guinea-Bissau to provide a personal apology for the two recent incidents and to offer a commitment that Senegal would respect Guinea-Bissau's sovereignty. In September, following a meeting at Gabú, in Guinea-Bissau, between representatives of both Governments, agreement was reached to strengthen co-operation and establish regular dialogue concerning security on the countries' joint border. However, a further attack by the Senegalese air force in October prompted the legislature to form a commission of inquiry to investigate such border incidents. In November da Costa paid a three-day visit to Senegal, aimed at strengthening co-operation between the two countries. In June 1996 a meeting held at Kolda, in Senegal, between ministerial delegations from Guinea-Bissau and Senegal resulted in renewed commitments to improved collaboration on security.

Government

Under the terms of the 1984 Constitution (revised in 1991), Guinea-Bissau is a multi-party state, although the formation of parties on a tribal or geographical basis is prohibited. Legislative power is vested in the National People's Assembly, which comprises 100 members, elected by universal adult suffrage for a term of four years. Executive power is vested in the President of the Republic, who is Head of State and who governs with the assistance of an appointed Council of Ministers, led by the Prime Minister. The President is elected by universal adult suffrage for a term of five years.

Defence

In August 1997 the armed forces totalled 9,250 men (army 6,800, navy 350, air force 100 and paramilitary gendarmerie 2,000). Expenditure on defence in 1997 was budgeted at an estimated US $8m.

Economic Affairs

In 1995, according to estimates by the World Bank, Guinea-Bissau's gross national product (GNP), measured at average 1993–95 prices, was US $265m., equivalent to $250 per head. During 1985–95, it was estimated, GNP per head increased, in real terms, at an average rate of 1.8% per year. Over the same period the population increased by an annual average of 1.9%. According to the World Bank, Guinea-Bissau's gross domestic product (GDP) increased, in real terms, at an average annual rate of 3.8% in 1985–95. Real GDP rose by an estimated 4.2% in 1995 and by an estimated 5.5% in 1996.

Agriculture (including forestry and fishing) contributed 53.0% of GDP in 1996, according to IMF estimates. An estimated 84.1% of the labour force were employed in the sector in 1996. The main cash crops are cashew nuts (which accounted for 85.8% of export earnings in 1995), cotton and palm kernels. Other crops produced include rice, roots and tubers, groundnuts, maize, millet and sorghum. Livestock and timber production are also important. The fishing industry is developing rapidly; earnings from fishing exports and the sale of fishing licences now represent the country's second largest source of export revenue. According to the World Bank, agricultural GDP increased, in real terms, by an annual average of 5.4% in 1985–95. Agricultural production decreased by 3.6% in 1996.

Industry (including mining, manufacturing, construction and power) employed an estimated 4.1% of the economically active population at mid-1994 and provided an estimated 14.4% of GDP in 1996. According to the World Bank, industrial GDP declined, in real terms, by an annual average of 1.3% in 1985–95, but increased by an estimated 3.1% in 1995.

The mining sector is underdeveloped, although Guinea-Bissau possesses large reserves of bauxite and phosphates. Drilling of three offshore petroleum wells began in November 1989.

The sole branches of the manufacturing sector are food-processing, brewing and cotton-processing, while there are plans to develop fish- and timber-processing. According to World Bank estimates, manufacturing contributed 6.5% of GDP in 1995. In that year manufacturing GDP increased by an estimated 2.0%.

Energy is derived principally from thermal and hydroelectric power. Imports of petroleum and petroleum products comprised 11.5% of the value of total imports in 1995.

Services employed an estimated 19.4% of the economically active population at mid-1994 and provided an estimated 32.5% of GDP in 1996. According to the World Bank, the combined GDP of the service sectors increased, in real terms, at an average rate of 3.0% per year in 1985–95. It rose by 10.3% in 1994 and by an estimated 2.5% in 1995.

In 1995 Guinea-Bissau recorded a trade deficit of US $35.4m. and there was a deficit of $41.5m. on the current account of the balance of payments. In 1995 the principal source of imports was Portugal (36.9%); other major suppliers were the Netherlands, the People's Republic of China, Japan and Spain. In that year India was the principal market for exports (87.8%); other significant purchasers were Portugal, France and Spain. The principal exports in 1995 were cashew nuts, cotton and logs. The principal imports in that year were food and live animals, transport equipment, and petroleum and petroleum products.

In 1995 there was a budgetary deficit of 66,600m. Guinea pesos (including grants from abroad and net lending), equivalent to 1.5% of GDP. Guinea-Bissau's total external debt was US $894.0m. at the end of 1995, of which $848.6m. was long-term public debt. In that year the cost of debt-servicing was equivalent to 33.7% of the total value of exports of goods and services. In 1987–95 the average annual rate of inflation was 50.0%. Consumer prices increased by an average of 45.4% in 1995 and by 50.7% in 1996.

Guinea-Bissau is a member of the Economic Community of West African States (ECOWAS, see p. 145) and of the West African organs of the Franc Zone (see p. 181).

Guinea-Bissau is one of the world's poorest countries. Its economy is largely dependent on the traditional rural sector, which employs the vast majority of the labour force and produces primarily for subsistence. The economy is therefore extremely vulnerable to unfavourable weather conditions. In 1987 the Government introduced a structural adjustment programme, which included measures to restructure the public investment programme and liberalize trade. Since then Guinea-Bissau has evolved from a rigidly controlled command economy into a largely free-market economy. Measures to liberalize the price and exchange rate system have been successfully implemented, and progress has been made in reorganizing the outsized and inefficient public sector. The decentralization of banking activities began in 1989, and in 1990 a five-year project, financed by the International Development Association (an affiliate of the World Bank), was introduced to rehabilitate the country's infrastructure. Guinea-Bissau's economy remains very dependent on foreign financing, which accounts for more than 50% of budget revenue. Guinea-Bissau joined the Union économique et monétaire ouest-africaine in January 1997 and entered the Franc Zone on 2 May, when the Guinea peso was replaced by the franc CFA as the unit of currency. As part of a three-year Enhanced Structural Adjustment Facility agreed in 1995, the IMF provided US $6.5m. in support of the Government's programme for 1997/98. The programme aimed to achieve annual GDP growth of 5%, and a reduction in the annual rate of inflation to 10% in 1997 and 7% in 1998. It was envisaged that considerable reductions in customs exemptions and enhanced efforts to recover taxes and duties would contribute to an increase in public revenue.

Social Welfare

Medical services are limited, owing to a severe shortage of facilities.The Government aims to establish one regional hospital in each of the eight regions. In 1981 there were 1,532 hospital beds. At mid-1989 there were 129 physicians and 235 qualified nurses working in the country. Of total budgetary expenditure by the central Government in 1987, 2,638.0m. pesos (5.4%) was for health services, and a further 4,272.7m. pesos (8.8%) for social security and welfare. In 1987 the IDA approved a credit of US $4.2m. for a health project involving the reorganization of the Ministry of Public Health, the rehabilitation of 25 health centres and the provision of drugs and other facilities, in an attempt to improve the level of primary health care. In 1988 Denmark provided a loan to build 13 health centres. In January 1989 the Government announced that hospital treatment would no longer be provided free of charge. In October 1997 the African Development Fund granted Guinea-Bissau a loan of $13.9m. towards improvements in the health sector.

Education

Education is officially compulsory only for the period of primary schooling, which begins at seven years of age and lasts for six years. Secondary education, beginning at the age of 13, lasts for up to five years (a first cycle of three years and a second of two years). In 1988 the total enrolment at primary and secondary schools was equivalent to 38% of the school-age population (males 49%; females 27%). In that year enrolment at primary schools was equivalent to 60% of children in the relevant age-group (males 77%; females 42%), and the comparable figure for secondary schools was 7% (males 9%; females 4%). Expenditure on education by the central Government in 1989 was 5,051m. pesos (2.7% of total spending). In 1997 the IDA approved a credit of US $14.3m. for a project to expand and upgrade the education system. Mass literacy campaigns have been introduced: according to UNESCO estimates, the average rate of adult illiteracy in 1980 was 60.9% (males 46.6%; females 74.4%), but by 1995 the rate had declined to 45.1% (males 32.0%; females 57.5%). In January 1991 President Vieira announced plans for the establishment of the country's first university.

Public Holidays

1998: 1 January (New Year), 20 January (Death of Amílcar Cabral), 30 January* (Korité, end of Ramadan), 8 April* (Tabaski, Feast of the Sacrifice), 1 May (Labour Day), 3 August (Anniversary of the Killing of Pidjiguiti), 24 September (National Day), 14 November (Anniversary of the Movement of Readjustment), 25 December (Christmas Day).

1999: 1 January (New Year), 19 January* (Korité, end of Ramadan), 20 January (Death of Amílcar Cabral), 28 March* (Tabaski, Feast of the Sacrifice), 1 May (Labour Day), 3 August (Anniversary of the Killing of Pidjiguiti), 24 September (National Day), 14 November (Anniversary of the Movement of Readjustment), 25 December (Christmas Day).

* Religious holidays, which are dependent on the Islamic lunar calendar, may differ by one or two days from the dates shown.

Weights and Measures

The metric system is used.

Statistical Survey

Area and Population

AREA, POPULATION AND DENSITY

Area (sq km)	36,125*
Population (census results)	
16–30 April 1979	753,313
1 December 1991	
Males	476,210
Females	507,157
Total	983,367
Population (UN estimates at mid-year)†	
1994	1,050,000
1995	1,073,000
1996	1,096,000
Density (per sq km) at mid-1996	30.3

* 13,948 sq miles.
† Source: UN, *World Population Prospects: The 1994 Revision*. According to later revisions, the estimated mid-year totals were 1,069,000 in 1995 and 1,091,000 in 1996.

POPULATION BY REGION (1991 census)

Bafatá	143,377
Biombo	60,420
Bissau	197,610
Bolama/Bijagos	26,691
Cacheu	146,980
Gabú	134,971
Oio	156,084
Quinara	44,793
Tombali	72,441
Total	983,367

PRINCIPAL TOWNS (population at 1979 census)

Bissau (capital)	109,214	Catió	5,170
Bafatá	13,429	Cantchungo†	4,965
Gabú*	7,803	Farim	4,468
Mansôa	5,390		

* Formerly Nova Lamego. † Formerly Teixeira Pinto.

BIRTHS AND DEATHS (UN estimates, annual averages)

	1980–85	1985–90	1990–95
Birth rate (per 1,000)	43.3	42.9	42.7
Death rate (per 1,000)	24.7	23.0	21.3

Expectation of life (UN estimates, years at birth, 1990–95): 43.5 (males 41.9; females 45.1).

Source: UN, *World Population Prospects: The 1994 Revision*.

ECONOMICALLY ACTIVE POPULATION
('000 persons at mid-1994)

	Males	Females	Total
Agriculture, etc.	195	175	370
Industry	15	5	20
Services	80	14	94
Total	290	194	484

Source: UN Economic Commission for Africa, *African Statistical Yearbook*.

Mid-1996 (estimates in '000): Agriculture, etc. 435; Total 517 (Source: FAO, *Production Yearbook*).

Agriculture

PRINCIPAL CROPS ('000 metric tons)

	1994	1995	1996
Rice (paddy)	131	133	120*
Maize	14	15	9*
Millet	29	35	21*
Sorghum	14	16	22*
Roots and tubers*	62	61	60
Groundnuts (in shell)	18	18*	18*
Cottonseed	2	2*	2*
Coconuts*	25	25	25
Copra*	5	5	5
Palm Kernels*	8	8	8
Vegetables and melons*	20	20	20
Plantains*	30	29	29
Other fruits*	31	31	31
Sugar cane*	6	6	6
Cashew nuts*	35	35	35
Cotton (lint)*	1	1	1

* FAO estimate(s).

Source: FAO, *Production Yearbook*.

LIVESTOCK (FAO estimates, '000 head, year ending September)

	1994	1995	1996
Cattle	475	475	475
Pigs	310	310	310
Sheep	255	255	255
Goats	270	270	270

Source: FAO, *Production Yearbook*.

LIVESTOCK PRODUCTS (FAO estimates, '000 metric tons)

	1994	1995	1996
Beef and veal	4	4	4
Pig meat	10	10	10
Cows' milk	12	12	12
Goats' milk	3	3	3

Source: FAO, *Production Yearbook*.

Forestry

ROUNDWOOD REMOVALS
(FAO estimates, '000 cubic metres, excluding bark)

	1992	1993	1994
Sawlogs, veneer logs and logs for sleepers*	40	40	40
Other industrial wood	110	112	115
Fuel wood†	422	422	422
Total	572	574	577

* Assumed to be unchanged since 1971.
† Assumed to be unchanged since 1979.

Source: FAO, *Yearbook of Forest Products*.

SAWNWOOD PRODUCTION
(FAO estimates, '000 cubic metres, including railway sleepers)

	1992	1993	1994
Total*	16	16	16

* Assumed to be unchanged since 1971.

Source: FAO, *Yearbook of Forest Products*.

Fishing

(FAO estimates, '000 metric tons, live weight)

	1993	1994	1995
Inland waters	0.3	0.3	0.3
Atlantic Ocean	5.1	5.3	5.3
Total catch	5.4	5.6	5.6

Source: FAO, *Yearbook of Fishery Statistics*.

Industry

SELECTED PRODUCTS

	1993	1994	1995
Vegetable oils (million litres)	6.2	6.0	5.6
Electric energy (million kWh)	44.0	44.9	46.3

Source: IMF, *Guinea-Bissau—Statistical Appendix* (May 1997).

Finance

CURRENCY AND EXCHANGE RATES

Monetary Units

100 centimes = 1 franc de la Communauté financière africaine (CFA).

French Franc, Sterling and Dollar Equivalents
(30 September 1997)

1 French franc = 100 francs CFA;
£1 sterling = 958.3 francs CFA;
US $1 = 593.2 francs CFA
1,000 francs CFA = £1.044 = $1.686.

Average Exchange Rate (francs CFA per US $)

1994 555.20
1995 499.15
1996 511.55

Note: An exchange rate of 1 French franc = 50 francs CFA, established in 1948, remained in force until January 1994, when the CFA franc was devalued by 50%, with the exchange rate adjusted to 1 French franc = 100 francs CFA. Following Guinea-Bissau's admission in January 1997 to the Union économique et monétaire ouest-africaine, the country entered the Franc Zone on 2 May. As a result, the Guinea peso was replaced by the CFA franc, although the peso remained legal tender until 31 July. The new currency was introduced at an exchange rate of 1 franc CFA = 65 Guinea pesos. At 31 March 1997 the exchange rate in relation to US currency was $1 = 36,793.3 Guinea pesos. The average exchange rate (Guinea pesos per US $) was: 12,892 in 1994; 18,073 in 1995; 26,373 in 1996.

BUDGET (million Guinea pesos)

Revenue*	1993	1994	1995
Tax revenue	121,018	207,370	317,700
Income taxes	18,005	25,190	45,700
Business profits	9,223	11,823	28,000
Individuals	5,395	9,474	12,000
Consumption taxes	23,362	27,659	97,900
On imports	22,209	25,572	95,100
Taxes on international trade and transactions	73,535	134,625	159,000
Import duties	25,150	33,476	60,300
Export duties	17,987	57,463	25,900
Port service charges	30,398	43,685	72,800
Other taxes	6,116	19,897	14,700
Non-tax revenue	132,637	168,408	263,100
Fees and duties	114,643	151,300	228,100
Fishing licences	113,659	150,579	219,100
Privatization receipts	4,404	—	4,000
Total	253,654	375,778	580,800

Expenditure†	1993	1994	1995
Current expenditure	343,327	440,757	703,300
Wages and salaries	77,935	80,815	128,200
Goods and services	90,435	135,571	165,900
Transfers	37,540	60,513	103,300
Scheduled external interest payments	137,416	163,858	305,900
Capital expenditure	587,561	604,693	695,700
Total	930,888	1,045,450	1,399,000

* Excluding grants received ('000 million pesos): 404.1 in 1993; 443.3 in 1994; 747.9 in 1995.

† Excluding net lending ('000 million pesos): 37.0 in 1993; 17.8 in 1994; -3.7 in 1995.

Source: IMF, *Guinea-Bissau—Statistical Appendix* (May 1997).

CENTRAL BANK RESERVES (US $ million at 31 December)

	1994	1995	1996
IMF special drawing rights	—	0.01	0.01
Foreign exchange	8.15	13.95	11.82
Total	8.15	13.96	11.83

Source: IMF, *International Financial Statistics*.

MONEY SUPPLY (million francs CFA at 31 December)*

	1994	1995	1996
Currency outside banks	3,015	4,278	6,370
Demand deposits at deposit money banks	1,855	2,880	4,507
Total money (incl. others)	4,912	7,219	10,913

* Figures have been converted from original data in Guinea pesos, assuming an exchange rate of 1 franc CFA = 65 Guinea pesos, the conversion factor used for the introduction of the CFA franc when Guinea-Bissau joined the Franc Zone in May 1997.

Source: IMF, *International Financial Statistics*.

COST OF LIVING (Consumer Price Index; base: 1990 = 100)

	1994	1995	1996
Food, beverages and tobacco	455.9	662.7	998.9

Source: IMF, *International Financial Statistics*.

NATIONAL ACCOUNTS

Expenditure on the Gross Domestic Product*
(million francs CFA at current prices)

	1991	1992	1993
Government final consumption expenditure	1,764	2,509	3,277
Private final consumption expenditure	12,174	26,160	34,562
Gross capital formation	3,562	6,241	8,312
Total domestic expenditure	17,499	34,910	46,151
Exports of goods and services	1,886	1,923	4,502
Less Imports of goods and services	-6,231	-13,294	-14,257
GDP in purchasers' values	13,154	23,539	36,396
GDP at constant 1990 prices	8,083	8,309	8,559

* Figures have been converted from original data in Guinea pesos, assuming an exchange rate of 1 franc CFA = 65 Guinea pesos, the conversion factor used for the introduction of the CFA franc when Guinea-Bissau joined the Franc Zone in May 1997.

Source: IMF, *International Financial Statistics*.

Gross Domestic Product by Economic Activity
('000 million Guinea pesos at current prices)

	1992	1993	1994
Agriculture, hunting, forestry and fishing	751	1,262	1,587
Mining and quarrying; Manufacturing; Electricity, gas and water	163	231	330
Construction	125	150	124
Trade, restaurants and hotels	394	538	748
Transport, storage and communications	41	60	74
Finance, insurance, real estate, etc.; Community, social and personal services (excl. government)	14	19	25
Government services	72	103	116
GDP at factor cost	1,561	2,364	3,004

Source: IMF, *Guinea-Bissau—Statistical Appendix* (May 1997).

BALANCE OF PAYMENTS (US $ million)

	1993	1994	1995
Exports of goods f.o.b.	15.96	33.21	23.90
Imports of goods f.o.b.	-53.82	-53.80	-59.34
Trade balance	-37.86	-20.59	-35.44
Imports of services	-11.38	-24.50	-21.09
Balance on goods and services	-49.24	-45.09	-56.53
Other income paid	-28.98	-26.27	-15.02
Balance on goods, services and income	-78.22	-71.36	-71.55
Current transfers received	14.39	21.79	31.42
Current transfers paid	-1.65	-1.06	-1.32
Current balance	-65.48	-50.63	-41.45
Capital account (net)	36.58	44.42	49.20
Other investment liabilities	-13.55	-26.98	-25.60
Net errors and omissions	-15.98	-21.36	-25.53
Overall balance	-58.43	-54.55	-43.38

Source: IMF, *International Financial Statistics*.

External Trade

PRINCIPAL COMMODITIES (US $ million)

Imports c.i.f.	1993	1994	1995
Food and live animals	25.1	17.3	25.6
Rice	17.2	8.6	18.0
Oil	1.1	1.8	2.0
Dairy products	1.2	0.9	1.1
Beverages and tobacco	3.2	3.7	4.3
Other consumer goods	5.1	6.2	6.6
Clothing and footwear	0.6	1.5	1.1
Durable consumer goods	2.7	2.9	2.3
Non-durable consumer goods	1.8	1.9	3.2
Petroleum and petroleum products	3.2	6.3	8.3
Diesel fuel and gasoline	2.5	4.2	5.8
Construction materials	4.9	6.0	7.3
Transport equipment	8.9	14.5	8.4
Passenger vehicles	3.6	5.7	2.2
Freight vehicles	1.8	6.7	5.2
Vehicle parts	3.5	2.1	1.0
Electrical equipment and machinery	5.3	6.5	7.7
Total (incl. others)	61.5	65.2	71.9

Exports f.o.b.	1993	1994	1995
Cotton	0.7	1.1	1.3
Palm kernels	0.3	0.1	n.a.
Cashew nuts	13.0	31.0	20.5
Fish	0.5	0.1	—
Logs	0.9	0.3	1.2
Total (incl. others)	16.0	33.2	23.9

Source: IMF, *Guinea-Bissau—Statistical Appendix* (May 1997).

PRINCIPAL TRADING PARTNERS

Imports (million pesos)	1984
France	232.7
Germany, Fed. Repub.	213.7
Italy	110.4
Netherlands	215.6
Portugal	924.0
Senegal	362.0
Sweden	70.2
USSR	462.7
USA	192.4
Total (incl. others)	3,230.7

Source: Ministry of Planning, Bissau.

Exports (US $ '000)	1981
China, People's Repub.	1,496
France	1,376
Portugal	2,890
Senegal	1,122
Spain	4,058
Sweden	1,627
Switzerland	1,617
United Kingdom	1,211
Total (incl. others)	15,730

Source: UN, *International Trade Statistics Yearbook*.

Transport

ROAD TRAFFIC (motor vehicles in use, estimates)

	1993	1994	1995
Passenger cars	4,930	5,920	6,300
Commercial vehicles	3,700	4,650	4,900

Source: IRF, *World Road Statistics*.

INTERNATIONAL SEA-BORNE SHIPPING
(UN estimates, freight traffic, '000 metric tons)

	1991	1992	1993
Goods loaded	40	45	46
Goods unloaded	272	277	283

Source: UN Economic Commission for Africa, *African Statistical Yearbook*.

CIVIL AVIATION (traffic on scheduled services)

	1992	1993	1994
Kilometres flown (million)	1	1	1
Passengers carried ('000)	21	21	21
Passenger-km (million)	10	10	10
Total ton-km (million)	1	1	1

Source: UN, *Statistical Yearbook*.

Communications Media

	1992	1993	1994
Radio receivers ('000 in use)	40	41	42
Telephones ('000 main lines in use)	8	9	n.a.
Telefax stations (number in use)	300	380	n.a.
Daily newspapers:			
Number	1	n.a.	1
Average circulation ('000 copies)	6	n.a.	6

Sources: UNESCO, *Statistical Yearbook*; UN, *Statistical Yearbook*.

Education

(1988)

	Insti-tutions	Teachers	Students		
			Males	Females	Total
Pre-primary	5	43	384	370	754
Primary	632*	3,065*	50,744	28,291	79,035
Secondary:					
General	n.a.	617†	3,588	1,917	5,505
Teacher training	n.a.	33	137	39	176
Vocational	n.a.	74	593	56	649
Tertiary	n.a.	n.a.	380	24	404

* 1987 figures. † 1986 figure.

Source: UNESCO, *Statistical Yearbook*.

Directory

The Constitution

A new Constitution for the Republic of Guinea-Bissau was approved by the National People's Assembly on 16 May 1984 and amended in May 1991 and November 1996 (see below). The main provisions of the 1984 Constitution were:

Guinea-Bissau is an anti-colonialist and anti-imperialist Republic and a State of revolutionary national democracy, based on the people's participation in undertaking, controlling and directing public activities. The Partido Africano da Independência da Guiné e Cabo Verde (PAIGC) shall be the leading political force in society and in the State. The PAIGC shall define the general bases for policy in all fields.

The economy of Guinea-Bissau shall be organized on the principles of state direction and planning. The State shall control the country's foreign trade.

The representative bodies in the country are the National People's Assembly and the regional councils. Other state bodies draw their powers from these. The members of the regional councils shall be directly elected. Members of the councils must be more than 18 years of age. The National People's Assembly shall have 150 members, who are to be elected by the regional councils from among their own members. All members of the National People's Assembly must be over 21 years of age.

The National People's Assembly shall elect a 15-member Council of State, to which its powers are delegated between sessions of the Assembly. The Assembly also elects the President of the Council of State, who is also automatically Head of the Government and Commander-in-Chief of the Armed Forces. The Council of State will later elect two Vice-Presidents and a Secretary. The President and Vice-Presidents of the Council of State form part of the Government, as do Ministers, Secretaries of State and the Governor of the National Bank.

The Constitution can be revised at any time by the National People's Assembly on the initiative of the deputies themselves, or of the Council of State or the Government.

Note: Constitutional amendments providing for the operation of a multi-party political system were approved unanimously by the National People's Assembly in May 1991. The amendments stipulated that new parties seeking registration must obtain a minimum of 2,000 signatures, with at least 100 signatures from each of the nine provinces. (These provisions were adjusted in August to 1,000 and 50 signatures, respectively.) In addition, the amendments provided for the National People's Assembly (reduced to 100 members) to be elected by universal adult suffrage, for the termination of official links between the PAIGC and the armed forces, and for the operation of a free market economy. Multi-party elections took place in July 1994.

In November 1996 the legislature approved a constitutional amendment providing for Guinea-Bissau to seek membership of the Union économique et monétaire ouest-africaine and of the Franc Zone.

The Government

HEAD OF STATE

President of the Republic and Commander-in-Chief of the Armed Forces: Commdr JOÃO BERNARDO VIEIRA (assumed power 14 November 1980; elected President of the Council of State 16 May 1984, and re-elected 19 June 1989; elected President in multi-party elections 3 July and 7 August 1994).

COUNCIL OF MINISTERS
(February 1998)

Prime Minister: CARLOS CORREIA.

Minister of Defence: SAMBA LAMINE MANÈ.

Minister of Foreign Affairs and Co-operation: FERNANDO DELFIM DA SILVA.

Minister in the Presidency with Responsibility for Parliamentary Affairs and Information: MALAL SANE.

Minister of Economy and Finance: ISSUF SANHA.

Minister of the Interior: FRANCISCA PEREIRA.

Minister of Territorial Administration: NICANDRO PEREIRA BARRETO.

Minister of Rural Development, Natural Resources and the Environment: AVITO JOSÉ DA SILVA.

Minister of Equipment: JOÃO GOMES CARDOSO.

Minister of Social Affairs and the Advancement of Women: NHAREBAT N'GAIA N'TCHASO.

Minister of Public Health: BRANDÃO GOMES CO.

Minister of Justice and Labour: DANIEL FERREIRA.

Minister of National Education: ODETTE SEMEDO.

Minister of Veterans' Affairs: ARAFAN MANÈ.

Minister of Fishing: ARTUR AUGUSTRO DA SILVA.

There are seven Secretaries of State.

MINISTRIES

All ministries are in Bissau.

President and Legislature

PRESIDENT

Presidential Election, First Ballot, 3 July 1994

Candidate	Votes	% of Votes
João Bernardo Vieira (PAIGC)	142,577	46.29
Koumba Yalla (PRS)	67,518	21.92
Domingos Fernandes Gomes (RGB—MB)	53,277	17.30
Carlos Domingos Gomes (PCD)	15,575	5.06
François Kankoila Mendy (FLING)	8,655	2.81
Alhaje Bubacar Djaló (UM)	8,506	2.76
Vítor Saúde Maria (PUSD)	6,388	2.07
Antonieta Rosa Gomes (FCG)	5,509	1.79
Total	308,005	100.00

Second Ballot, 7 August 1994

Candidate	Votes	%
João Bernardo Vieira (PAIGC)	159,993	52.03
Koumba Yalla (PRS)	147,518	47.97
Total	307,511	100.00

NATIONAL PEOPLE'S ASSEMBLY

President: Malang Bacai Sanha.

General Election, 3 July 1994

	% of Votes	Seats
Partido Africano da Independência da Guiné e Cabo Verde (PAIGC)	46.0	62
Resistência da Guiné-Bissau—Movimento Bah-Fatah (RGB—MB)	19.2	19
Partido para a Renovação Social (PRS)	10.3	12
União para a Mudança (UM)	12.8	6
Frente da Luta para a Libertação da Guiné (FLING)	2.5	1
Partido da Convergência Democrática (PCD)	5.3	—
Partido Unido Social Democrático (PUSD)	2.9	—
Foro Cívico da Guiné (FCG)	0.2	—
Total (incl. others)	100.0	100

Political Organizations

Foro Cívico da Guiné (FCG): Bissau; Leader Antonieta Rosa Gomes.

Frente da Luta para a Libertação da Guiné (FLING): Bissau; f. 1962; officially registered in May 1992; Leader François Kankoila Mendy.

Liga Guineense de Protecção Ecológica (LIPE): Bairro Missirá 102, CP 1290, Bissau; tel. and fax 252309; f. 1991; ecology party; Pres. Alhaje Bubacar Djaló.

Partido Africano da Independência da Guiné e Cabo Verde (PAIGC): CP 106, Bissau; f. 1956; fmrly the ruling party in both Guinea-Bissau and Cape Verde; although Cape Verde withdrew from the PAIGC following the coup in Guinea-Bissau in Nov. 1980, Guinea-Bissau has retained the party name and initials; Pres. Commdr João Bernardo Vieira; Sec.-Gen. Manuel Saturnino da Costa.

Partido da Convergência Democrática (PCD): Bissau; Leader Vítor Mandinga.

Partido para a Renovação Social (PRS): Bissau; f. 1992 by breakaway faction of the FDS; officially registered in Oct. 1992; Leader Koumba Yalla.

Partido Social Democrático (PSD): Bissau; f. 1995 by breakaway faction of RGB—MB; Leader Joaquim Baldé; Sec.-Gen. Gaspar Fernandes.

Partido Unido Social Democrático (PUSD): Bissau; f. 1991; officially registered in Jan. 1992; Leader Vítor Saúde Maria.

Resistência da Guiné-Bissau—Movimento Bah-Fatah (RGB—MB): Bissau; f. 1986 in Lisbon, Portugal, as Resistência da Guiné-Bissau—Movimento Bafatá; adopted present name prior to official registration in Dec. 1991; maintains offices in Paris (France), Dakar (Senegal) and Praia (Cape Verde); Chair. Domingos Fernandes Gomes.

União para a Mudança (UM): Bissau; f. 1994 as coalition to contest presidential and legislative elections, re-formed April 1995; Pres. João da Costa (PRD); Sec.-Gen. Amine Michel Saad (PDP); comprises following parties:

Frente Democrática (FD): Bissau; f. 1991; officially registered in Nov. 1991; Pres. Canjura Injai; Sec.-Gen. Marcelino Batista.

Frente Democrática Social (FDS): Bissau; f. 1991; legalized in Dec. 1991; Leader Rafael Barbosa.

Movimento para a Unidade e a Democracia (MUDE): Bissau; officially registered in Aug. 1992; Leader Filinto Vaz Martins.

Partido Democrático do Progresso (PDP): Bissau; f. 1991; officially registered in Aug. 1992; Pres. of Nat. Council Amine Michel Saad.

Partido de Renovação e Desenvolvimento (PRD): Bissau; f. 1992 as the 'Group of 121' by PAIGC dissidents; officially registered in Oct. 1992; Leaders Manuel Rambout Barcelos, Agnelo Regala, João da Costa.

Diplomatic Representation

EMBASSIES IN GUINEA-BISSAU

Brazil: Rua São Tomé, Bissau; tel. 201327; telex 245; fax 201317; Ambassador: Luiz Fernando Nazareth.

China (Taiwan): Avda Amílcar Cabral 35, CP 66, Bissau; tel. 201501; fax 201466.

Cuba: Rua Joaquim N'Com 1, Bissau; tel. 213579; Ambassador: Diosdado Fernández González.

Egypt: Avda Omar Torrijos, Rua 15, CP 72, Bissau; tel. 213642; Ambassador: Mohamed Reda Farahat.

France: Avda 14 de Novembro, Bairro de Penha, Bissau; tel. 251031; fax 253142; Ambassador: François Chappellet.

Guinea: Rua 14, no. 9, CP 396, Bissau; tel. 212681; Ambassador: Mohamed Laminé Fodé.

Libya: Rua 16, CP 362, Bissau; tel. 212006; Representative: Dokali Ali Mustafa.

Portugal: Rua Cidade de Lisboa 6, Apdo 276, Bissau; tel. 201261; telex 248; fax 201269; Ambassador: Francisco Henriques da Silva.

Russia: Avda 14 de Novembro, Bissau; tel. 251036; fax 251050; Ambassador: Viktor M. Zelenov.

Senegal: Bissau; tel. 212636; Ambassador: Ahmed Tijane Kane.

USA: CP 297, 1067 Bissau; tel. 252273; fax 252282; Ambassador: Peggy Blackford.

Judicial System

Judges of the Supreme Court are appointed by the Conselho Superior da Magistratura.

President of the Supreme Court: Mamadu Saliu Djalo Pires.

Religion

About 54% of the population are animists, 38% are Muslims and 8% are Christians, mainly Roman Catholics.

CHRISTIANITY

The Roman Catholic Church

Guinea-Bissau comprises a single diocese, directly responsible to the Holy See. The Bishop participates in the Episcopal Conference of Senegal, Mauritania, Cape Verde and Guinea-Bissau, currently based in Senegal. At 31 December 1995 there were an estimated 125,637 adherents in the country.

Bishop of Bissau: Rt Rev. Settimio Arturo Ferrazzetta, CP 20, 1001 Bissau; tel. 251057; fax 251058.

The Press

Baguerra: Bissau; owned by the Partido da Convergência Democrática.

Banobero: Bissau; weekly; Dir Fernando Jorge Pereira.

Nô Pintcha: Bissau; daily; Dir Sra Cabral; circ. 6,000.

NEWS AGENCY

Agência Noticiosa da Guinea (ANG): CP 248, Bissau; tel. 212151; telex 96900.

Broadcasting and Communications

An experimental television service began transmissions in 1989. Regional radio stations were to be established at Bafatá, Cantchungo and Catió in 1990. In 1990 Radio Freedom, which broadcast on behalf of the PAIGC during Portuguese rule and had ceased operations in 1974, resumed transmissions.

Radiodifusão Nacional da República da Guiné-Bissau: CP 191, Bissau; govt-owned; broadcasts in Portuguese on short-wave, MW and FM; Dir FRANCISCO BARRETO.

Rádio Pidjiguiti: f. 1995; independent.

Finance

(cap. = capital; m. = million; brs = branches; amounts in Guinea pesos)

BANKING

The decentralization of banking activities began in 1989.

Central Bank

Banque Centrale des Etats de l'Afrique de l'Ouest (BCEAO): Avda Amílcar Cabral, CP 38, Bissau; tel. 212434; telex 241; fax 201305; headquarters in Dakar, Senegal; f. 1955; bank of issue and central bank for the member states of the Union économique et monétaire ouest-africaine (UEMOA); cap. and res 657,592m. (Dec. 1995); Gov. CHARLES KONAN BANNY.

Other Banks

Banco Internacional da Guiné-Bissau: Avda Amílcar Cabral, CP 74, Bissau; tel. 213662; telex 204; fax 201033; f. 1989; cap. 3,260m. (Dec. 1993); 26% state-owned, 25% by Guinea-Bissau enterprises and private interests, 49% by Crédito Predial Português (Portugal); Chair. FILINTO E. BARROS; Gen. Man. JOSÉ ANTÓNIO TAVARES DA CRUZ.

Banco Totta e Açores (Portugal): Rua 19 de Setembro 15, CP 618, Bissau; tel. 214794; fax 201591; Gen. Man. CARLOS MADEIRA.

Caixa de Crédito da Guiné: Bissau; govt savings and loan institution.

Caixa Económica Postal: Avda Amílcar Cabral, Bissau; tel. 212999; telex 979; postal savings institution.

STOCK EXCHANGE

Côte d'Ivoire's Bourse des Valeurs d'Abidjan was scheduled to become a regional stock exchange, serving the member states of the UEMOA.

INSURANCE

In 1979 it was announced that a single state-owned insurer was to replace the Portuguese company Ultramarina.

Trade and Industry

The Government has actively pursued a policy of small-scale industrialization to compensate for the almost total lack of manufacturing capacity. Following independence, it adopted a comprehensive programme of state control, and in 1976 acquired 80% of the capital of a Portuguese company, **Ultramarina**, a large firm specializing in a wide range of trading activities, including ship-repairing and agricultural processing. The Government also holds a major interest in the **CICER** brewery and has created a joint-venture company with the Portuguese concern **SACOR** to sell petroleum products. Since 1975 three fishing companies have been formed with foreign participation: **GUIALP** (with Algeria), **Estrela do Mar** (with the former USSR) and **SEMAPESCA** (with France; now bankrupt). In December 1976 **SOCOTRAM**, an enterprise for the sale and processing of timber, was inaugurated. It operates a factory in Bissau for the production of wooden tiles and co-ordinates sawmills and carpentry shops throughout the country. In 1979 the **Empresa de Automóveis da Guiné** opened a car-assembly plant at Bissau, capable of producing 500 vehicles per year. A plan to restructure several public enterprises was proceeding in the mid-1990s, as part of the Government's programme to attract private investment.

Empresa Nacional de Pesquisas e Exploração Petrolíferas e Mineiras (PETROMINAS): Rua Eduardo Mondlane 58, Bissau; tel. 212279; state-owned; regulates all prospecting for hydrocarbons and other minerals; Dir-Gen. ANTÓNIO CARDOSO.

CHAMBER OF COMMERCE

Associação Comercial, Industrial e Agrícola da Guiné-Bissau: Bissau; f. 1987.

TRADE UNION

União Nacional dos Trabalhadores da Guiné (UNTG): 13 Avda Ovai di Vievra, CP 98, Bissau; tel. 212094; telex 900; Sec.-Gen. MÁRIO MENDES CORREA.

Legislation permitting the formation of other trade unions was approved by the National People's Assembly in 1991.

Transport

RAILWAYS

There are no railways in Guinea-Bissau.

ROADS

In 1995, according to International Road Federation estimates, there were about 4,350 km of roads, of which 444 km were paved. A major road rehabilitation scheme is proceeding, and an international road, linking Guinea-Bissau with The Gambia and Senegal, is planned. In 1989 the Islamic Development Bank granted more than US $2m. towards the construction of a 111-km road linking north and south and a 206-km road between Guinea-Bissau and Guinea.

SHIPPING

Under a major port modernization project, the main port at Bissau was to be renovated and expanded, and four river ports were to be upgraded to enable barges to load and unload at low tide. The total cost of the project was estimated at US $47.4m., and finance was provided by the World Bank and Arab funds. In 1986 work began on a new river port at N'Pungda, which was to be partly funded by the Netherlands.

CIVIL AVIATION

There is an international airport at Bissau, which there are plans to expand, and 10 smaller airports serving the interior.

Transportes Aéreos da Guiné-Bissau (TAGB): Aeroporto Osvaldo Vieira, CP 111, Bissau; tel. 201277; telex 268; fax 251536; f. 1977; domestic services and flights to France, Portugal, the Canary Islands (Spain), Guinea and Senegal; Dir Capt. EDUARDO PINTO LOPES.

Tourism

Centro de Informação e Turismo: CP 294, Bissau; state tourism and information service.

GUYANA

Introductory Survey

Location, Climate, Language, Religion, Flag, Capital

The Co-operative Republic of Guyana lies on the north coast of South America, between Venezuela to the west and Suriname to the east, with Brazil to the south. The narrow coastal belt has a moderate climate with two wet seasons, from April to August and from November to January, alternating with two dry seasons. Inland, there are tropical forests and savannah, and the dry season lasts from September to May. The average annual temperature is 27°C (80°F), with average rainfall of 1,520 mm (60 ins) per year inland, rising to between 2,030 mm (80 ins) and 2,540 mm (100 ins) on the coast. English is the official language but Hindi, Urdu and Amerindian dialects are also spoken. The principal religions are Christianity (which is professed by about 50% of the population), Hinduism (about 33%) and Islam (less than 10%). The national flag (proportions 5 by 3 when flown on land, but 2 by 1 at sea) is green, with a white-bordered yellow triangle (apex at the edge of the fly) on which is superimposed a black-bordered red triangle (apex in the centre). The capital is Georgetown.

Recent History

Guyana was formerly British Guiana, a colony of the United Kingdom, formed in 1831 from territories finally ceded to Britain by the Dutch in 1814. A new Constitution, providing for universal adult suffrage, was introduced in 1953. The elections of April 1953 were won by the left-wing People's Progressive Party (PPP), led by Dr Cheddi Bharat Jagan. In October, however, the British Government, claiming that a communist dictatorship was threatened, suspended the Constitution. An interim administration was appointed. The PPP split in 1955, and in 1957 some former members founded a new party, the People's National Congress (PNC), under the leadership of Forbes Burnham. The PNC drew its support mainly from the African-descended population, while PPP support came largely from the (Asian-descended) 'East' Indian community.

A revised Constitution was introduced in December 1956 and fresh elections held in August 1957. The PPP won and Dr Jagan became Chief Minister. Another Constitution, providing for internal self-government, was adopted in July 1961. The PPP won the elections in August and Dr Jagan was appointed Premier in September. In the elections of December 1964, held under the system of proportional representation that had been introduced in the previous year, the PPP won the largest number of seats in the Legislative Assembly, but not a majority. A coalition Government was formed by the PNC and The United Force (TUF), with Burnham as Prime Minister. This coalition led the colony to independence, as Guyana, on 26 May 1966.

The PNC won elections in 1968 and in 1973, although the results of the latter, and every poll thenceforth until the defeat of the PNC in 1992, were disputed by the opposition parties. Guyana became a co-operative republic on 23 February 1970, and Arthur Chung was elected non-executive President in March. In 1976 the PPP, which had boycotted the National Assembly since 1973, offered the Government its 'critical support'. Following a referendum in July 1978 that gave the Assembly power to amend the Constitution, elections to the Assembly were postponed for 15 months. The legislature assumed the role of a constituent assembly, established in November 1978, to draft a new constitution. In October 1979 elections were postponed for a further year. In October 1980 Forbes Burnham declared himself executive President of Guyana, and a new Constitution was promulgated.

Internal opposition to the PNC Government had increased after the assassination in June 1980 of Dr Walter Rodney, leader of the Working People's Alliance (WPA). The Government was widely believed to have been involved in the incident; an official inquest into Rodney's death was finally ordered in November 1987, but in 1988 it produced a verdict, rejected by the opposition, of death by misadventure. (In 1995, following recommendations by a delegation from the International Commission of Jurists, the Government announced that a fresh inquiry would be conducted into the affair by an independent international commission.) All opposition parties except the PPP and TUF urged their supporters to boycott the December 1980 elections to the National Assembly. The PNC, under Burnham, received 77.7% of the votes, according to official results, and won 41 of the 53 elective seats, although allegations of substantial electoral malpractice were made, both within the country and by international observers. However, Burnham was declared President and was formally inaugurated in January 1981.

In 1981 arrests and trials of opposition leaders continued, and in 1982 the Government's relations with human rights groups, and especially the Christian churches, deteriorated further. Editors of opposition newspapers were threatened, political violence increased, and the Government was accused of interference in the legal process. Industrial unrest and public discontent continued in 1983, as Guyana's worsening economic situation increased opposition to the Government, and led to growing disaffection within the trade union movement and the PNC. There were more strikes in 1984, and in December Burnham announced some concessions, including a rise in the daily minimum wage (virtually the only increase since 1979).

Burnham died in August 1985 and was succeeded as President by Desmond Hoyte, hitherto the First Vice-President and Prime Minister. President Hoyte's former posts were assumed by Hamilton Green, previously the First Deputy Prime Minister. At a general election in December the PNC won 78% of the votes and 42 of the elective seats in the National Assembly. Desmond Hoyte was declared President-elect. Opposition groups, including the PPP and WPA, denounced the poll as fraudulent. In January 1986 five of the six opposition parties formed the Patriotic Coalition for Democracy (PCD).

During 1988 the opposition expressed fears about the independence of the judiciary. In February the Government, prompted by a ruling of the Court of Appeal (in 1987), enacted a constitutional amendment which rescinded the court's jurisdiction in matters of labour legislation, particularly with regard to the Government's obligation to consult with trade unions and other organizations concerning such legislation. In addition, the amendment established that any legislation to be enacted by the National Assembly, including retrospective legislation, could not be deemed invalid on the grounds of inconsistency with former constitutions. Moreover, in April Keith Massiah retired as Chancellor of Justice, but, within one day, he was appointed to the Cabinet as Attorney-General, thereby causing controversy both in Guyana and other countries in the region. The opposition also claimed that the Government's continued recourse to the laws of libel against its critics was an abuse of the legal system.

Social unrest and industrial disruption in 1988 continued to hamper government efforts to reform the economy. Furthermore, the severity of austerity measures contained in the budget of March 1989, which included a devaluation of the currency, caused a six-week strike in the sugar and bauxite industries. Although a programme of IMF assistance was agreed in April, the Government's difficulties in achieving its economic targets were compounded by widespread industrial unrest and the unexpected failure of a group of donor nations, co-ordinated by Canada, to provide sufficient aid.

In 1988 the Government suffered a further loss of control, following a division within the trade union movement. Seven unions withdrew from the Trades Union Congress (TUC) in September, alleging that elections for TUC officials were weighted in favour of PNC-approved candidates. The seven independent unions formed a separate congress, the Federation of Independent Trade Unions in Guyana (FITUG), in October. However, the Government refused to negotiate with the FITUG, accusing it of being politically motivated.

Outside the formal opposition of the political parties, the Government also experienced pressure from members of the Guyana Human Rights Association, business leaders and prominent citizens such as the Anglican and Roman Catholic bishops. This culminated, in January 1990, in the formation of a movement for legal and constitutional change, Guyanese Action for Reform and Democracy (Guard), which initiated a series of mass protest rallies, urging the Government to accelerate the process of democratic reform. To counter this civic movement, the PNC began mobilizing its own newly-established Committees to Re-elect the President (Creeps). Guard accused the Creeps of orchestrating violent clashes at Guard's rallies, and of fomenting racial unrest in the country in an attempt to regain support from the Afro-Guyanese population.

In October 1990 the former US President, Jimmy Carter, visited President Hoyte to discuss matters related to electoral reform. The most striking concessions made by the Government, as a result of these discussions, were agreements to perform a preliminary count of votes at polling stations (an opposition demand previously rejected by the PNC) and to compile a new electoral register. The original electors' list had provoked popular outrage when it was found to include the names of several thousand dead people, while omitting thousands of eligible voters. Carter stated, after his visit, that his Council for Freely-Elected Heads of Government would organize an observer mission to help to guarantee that the forthcoming elections would be free and fair. However, the date of the general election was postponed, following the approval of legislation by the PNC in January 1991, extending the term of office of the National Assembly by two months after its official dissolution date of 2 February 1991 (in accordance with constitutional provisions, the general election was due to take place by 31 March). In March a further two-month extension of the legislative term provoked the resignation of TUF and PPP members from the National Assembly (in addition to the WPA members, who had resigned a month earlier). Similar extensions followed in May and July, owing to alleged continuing problems relating to the reform of the electoral process, until, finally, the National Assembly was dissolved in late September. The publication of the revised electoral register in that month, however, revealed widespread inaccuracies, including the omission of an estimated 100,000 eligible voters. In November several opposition parties announced a boycott of the general election, which had been rescheduled for mid-December. However, on 28 November Hoyte declared a state of emergency in order to legitimize a further postponement of the election (which, according to the Constitution, was due to take place by 28 December). Legislation restoring the opposition seats in the National Assembly followed, and the Assembly was reconvened. In mid-December the state of emergency was extended until June 1992. A further revised electoral register was published in that month, and was finally approved by the Elections Commission in August. The election took place on 5 October and resulted in a narrow victory for the PPP in alliance with the CIVIC movement (a social and political movement of businessmen and professionals), which secured 32 of the 65 elective seats in the National Assembly (53.5% of the votes), while the PNC secured 31 (42.3% of the votes). The result, which signified an end to the PNC's 28-year period in government, provoked riots by the mainly Afro-Guyanese PNC supporters in Georgetown, in which two people were killed. International observers were, however, satisfied that the elections had been fairly conducted, and on 9 October Dr Cheddi Bharat Jagan took office as President. On the following day Jagan appointed Samuel Archibald Anthony Hinds, an industrialist who was not a member of the PPP, as Prime Minister.

Following a joint conference in September 1993, the unions belonging to the TUC and the FITUG agreed to reunify as the TUC. In May 1994 a strike, organized by four public-sector unions in support of demands for pay increases, causing considerable disruption, was ended after ten days when the Government agreed to a 35% increase in the minimum wage.

At municipal and local government elections held in August 1994, the first to be contested since 1970, the PPP/CIVIC alliance secured control of 49 of the 71 localities concerned. However, the important post of mayor of Georgetown was won by Hamilton Green, representing Good and Green Georgetown, a party founded specifically to contest the election in the capital. In December, Green, who was expelled from the PNC in 1993, announced the establishment of a new nationwide political movement entitled Good and Green Guyana (GGG).

In December 1994 the National Assembly approved a proposal, drafted by the PPP, for the creation of a select parliamentary committee to review the Constitution, with a view to adopting reforms prior to the next general election, due in 1997. However, the PNC, whose support would be required to gain the two-thirds' majority necessary for constitutional amendments, voted against the proposal, favouring instead the appointment of a constituent assembly.

In August 1995 a serious environmental incident resulted in the temporary closure of Omai Gold Mines Ltd (OGML). The company, which began production in the Omai District of Essequibo province in 1993, was responsible for an increase of some 400% in Guyana's gold production in subsequent years and was a considerable source of government revenue. Already Guyana's largest foreign investor, OGML, which was owned by the Canadian companies Cambior (65%) and Golden Star Resources (30%), with the remaining 5% held by the Government of Guyana, announced further investment plans in 1995, aimed at increasing production by 20%. However, in August 1995 a breach in a tailings pond (a reservoir where residue from the gold extraction process is stored) resulted in the spillage of some 3.5m. cu m of cyanide-tainted water, of which a large volume flowed into the Omai river, a tributory of the Essequibo river. Environmental warnings were issued to people living in the Essequibo region, and the National Assembly approved a resolution to close the mine for an indefinite period pending an inquiry into the incident. The Government promptly appointed a technical committee to conduct an investigation into the spillage. A commission of inquiry was set up to review OGML's operations and determine the conditions under which the mine would be permitted to resume production. In January 1996 the commission of inquiry submitted a report to the Government recommending that OGML be permitted to resume operations subject to the prior implementation of certain environmental safeguards. The report also emphasized the need for comprehensive legislation on environmental protection. OGML resumed mining operations in the following month.

In February 1996, amid growing public concern at an increase in criminal violence, Guyana resumed judicial executions with the hanging of a convicted murderer. The execution, the first for more than five years, provoked protest from human rights organizations.

Following the demise, in March 1997, of Dr Cheddi Bharat Jagan, he was succeeded as President, in accordance with the provisions of the Constitution, by the Prime Minister, Samuel Hinds. Hinds subsequently appointed Janet Jagan, the widow of the former President, to the post of Prime Minister. In April Donald Ramotar was elected to succeed the late Dr Jagan as General Secretary of the PPP. In September the PPP/CIVIC alliance formally adopted Janet Jagan as its presidential candidate for the forthcoming general election.

At the general election of 15 December 1997 delays in the verification of votes prompted protest by PNC supporters who accused the Government of electoral fraud. Eleven people were injured during clashes between demonstrators and the security forces. With some 90% of the votes counted the Chairman of the Elections Commission, Doudnauth Singh, declared that Janet Jagan had established an unassailable lead and on 19 December she was inaugurated as President. Singh's actions were strongly criticized as being premature by opposition parties, and the PNC expressed its intention to appeal to the High Court to have Jagan's appointment annulled. In the following days PNC supporters began a series of public demonstrations in protest at the alleged electoral fraud and at Jagan's appointment. On 31 December the final election results were declared. With two legislative seats remaining to be decided by the National Congress of Local Democratic Organs (see The Constitution), the PPP/CIVIC alliance secured 34 seats, the PNC won 26, and TUF, the Alliance for Guyana and the Guyana Democratic Party each obtained one seat.

In January 1998, in the light of continued unrest being fomented by opposition supporters, the Government accepted a proposal by private-sector leaders for an international audit of the election to be conducted. The PNC, however, rejected the proposal and demanded instead the holding of fresh elections. In mid-January, in rejection of an appeal by the PNC, the Chief Justice ruled that it was beyond the jurisdiction of the High Court to prohibit Jagan from exercising her presidential functions pending a judicial review of the election. The ruling provoked serious disturbances in Georgetown, which, in turn, prompted the Government to introduce a one-month ban on public assemblies and demonstrations in the capital. However, public protests by PNC supporters continued in defiance of the ban, resulting in confrontation with the security forces. Later that month the Government and the PNC reached an agreement to end the electoral dispute. The terms of the accord included provision for fresh elections to be held by 2000 and for the reform of the Constitution. In February the remaining two legislative seats were declared to have been won by the PPP/CIVIC alliance.

Guyana has border disputes with its neighbours, Venezuela and Suriname, although relations with Brazil have continued to improve through trade and military agreements. Suriname restored diplomatic representation in Guyana in 1979, however, and bilateral meetings were resumed at the end of the year. In 1983 relations improved further as a result of increased trade links between the countries.

In 1962 Venezuela renewed its claim to 130,000 sq km (50,000 sq miles) of land west of the Essequibo river (nearly two-thirds of Guyanese territory). The area was accorded to Guyana in 1899, but Venezuela based its claim on a papal bull of 1493, referring to Spanish colonial possessions. The Port of Spain Protocol of 1970 put the issue in abeyance until 1982. Guyana and Venezuela referred the dispute to the UN in 1983, and, after a series of UN efforts and a visit to Venezuela by President Hoyte, the two countries agreed to a mutually acceptable intermediary, suggested by the UN Secretary-General, in August 1989.

Guyana officially condemned the US-led invasion of Grenada in October 1983. This attitude, although popular in Guyana, led to a rapid deterioration in relations with the USA, which had already been adversely affected by the US Government's veto of anticipated loans to Guyana in September. Guyana's decision to dispense with seeking IMF financial support further compounded the country's increasing isolation among Western nations. To offset the fall in Western aid, Guyana sought to improve relations with socialist countries, such as Cuba, Libya, Yugoslavia and the Democratic People's Republic of Korea. After Hoyte became President, however, Guyana sought to improve its relations with the USA and other Western countries. During the early 1990s Hoyte committed Guyana to closer integration with the Caribbean Community and Common Market (CARICOM, see p. 119).

Government

Under the 1980 Constitution, legislative power is held by the unicameral National Assembly, with 65 members: 53 elected for five years by universal adult suffrage, on the basis of proportional representation, and 12 regional representatives. Executive power is held by the President, who leads the majority party in the Assembly and holds office for its duration. The President appoints and heads a Cabinet, which includes the Prime Minister, and may include Ministers who are not elected members of the Assembly. The Cabinet is collectively responsible to the National Assembly. Guyana comprises 10 regions, each having a regional democratic council which returns a representative to the National Assembly.

Defence

The armed forces are combined in a single service, the Combined Guyana Defence Force, consisting of some 1,600 men (of whom 1,400 were in the army, 100 were in the air force and some 100 in the navy) in August 1997. One-third of the combined forces are civilian personnel. A paramilitary force, the People's Militia, totalled 1,500. The defence budget for 1996 was $ G1,000m.

Economic Affairs

According to estimates by the World Bank, in 1995 Guyana's gross national product (GNP), measured at average 1993–95 prices, was US $493m. GNP per head, equivalent to $590 in 1995, was estimated to have increased at an average rate of 0.8% per year, in real terms, between 1985 and 1995. Over the same period, the population increased by an annual average of 0.6%. Guyana's gross domestic product (GDP) increased, in real terms, by an average of 2.2% per year during 1985–95, by 5.0% in 1995 and by an estimated 7.9% in 1996.

Agriculture (including forestry and fishing) provided 41.4% of GDP in 1995, according to preliminary figures, and employed an estimated 19.5% of the economically active population in 1996. The principal cash crops are sugar cane (sugar providing 26.0% of the value of total domestic exports in 1994) and rice (12.5%). The sugar industry alone accounted for 19.9% of GDP in 1995, according to preliminary figures and, it was estimated, employed about one-half of the agricultural labour force in 1988. Vegetables and fruit are also cultivated for the local market, and livestock-rearing is being developed. According to the World Bank, agricultural production increased by an annual average of 4.2% during 1985–95. Agricultural production rose by 2.5% in 1996.

Timber resources in Guyana are extensive and underdeveloped. According to FAO estimates, some 77% of the country's total land area consisted of forest and woodland in 1994. In 1994 timber shipments provided only 1.9% of total domestic exports. Although foreign investment in Guyana's largely undeveloped interior continues to be encouraged by the Government, the Guyana Natural Resources Agency expressed concern in late 1991 over the extent of the exploitation of the rainforest. The lease of substantial areas of forest to two foreign companies for timber production during 1991 provoked protests from environmentalists, as well as from Amerindian organizations, who stated that the leased areas of land were far greater than those reserved for the 40,000 Amerindian tribal people of Guyana. In 1994 timber production increased dramatically (by some 70%), compared with the previous year.

Fishing, which contributed an estimated 6.2% of GDP in 1995, is being developed. The sector's principal export is shrimps, and between 1987 and 1991 the value of the catch increased almost fourfold, to constitute 7.1% of domestic exports by the latter year.

Industry (including mining, manufacturing, engineering, construction and power) provided 32.3% of GDP in 1995, according to preliminary figures, and engaged 24.0% of the employed labour force at the time of the 1980 census. According to the World Bank, industrial GDP declined by an annual average of 0.8% in 1985–95, but increased by 4.6% in 1994, and by an estimated 0.3% in 1995.

Mining contributed an estimated 16.5% of GDP in 1995, and employed 4.8% of the total working population in 1980. Bauxite, which is used for the manufacture of aluminium, is one of Guyana's most valuable exports, and accounted for 17.7% of total domestic exports in 1994. The registered production of gold (accounting for 28.6% of domestic exports in 1994) has increased considerably since 1986, when the Government raised the price payable to miners in an effort to prevent smuggling (which costs the country an estimated $ G360m. annually). The output of gold increased by 66% in 1991, compared with 1990, and by a further 34% in 1992, to reach 79,582 troy ounces, which represented the highest level of recorded production since 1913. In 1993 a new gold-mine in the Omai District of Essequibo province began production, and its output was such that the country's overall production increased dramatically to 310,072 troy ounces in 1993 and to 358,835 troy ounces in 1994. Owing to the temporary closure of the mine, beginning in August 1995 and continuing into early 1996, production in 1995 was reduced considerably, before recovering to reach 372,000 troy ounces in 1996. Diamonds constitute the country's other main mineral resource. Production reached 36,800 carats in 1994, and was estimated to have increased to 52,400 carats in 1995. There are also some petroleum reserves. The GDP of the mining sector was estimated to have increased by an average of 12.0% per year in 1991–94, before declining in 1995 by 11.4%, owing to the temporary closure of Omai Gold Mines Ltd.

Manufacturing (including power) accounted for 11.5% of GDP in 1995, according to preliminary figures, and, according to the 1980 census, employed 14.4% of the total working population. The main activities are the processing of bauxite, sugar, rice and timber. Rum is an important manufacture (accounting for 1.1% of total domestic exports in 1991), and in the late 1980s pharmaceuticals became an increasingly important export industry. According to the World Bank, manufacturing GDP declined by an annual average of 6.7% in 1985–95, and by an estimated 8.9% in 1995.

Energy requirements are almost entirely met by imported hydrocarbon fuels. In 1994 fuels and lubricants constituted 26.8% of the total value of imports (mainly from Venezuela and Trinidad and Tobago). Preparations were undertaken in 1991 for Guyana and Suriname to launch a joint petroleum exploration programme on their mutual border.

The services sector contributed 26.3% of GDP in 1995, according to preliminary figures, and engaged 43.2% of the employed labour force in 1980. According to the World Bank, the GDP of the services sector increased by an average of 0.9% per year in 1985–95, and by 4.8% in 1995.

In 1995 Guyana recorded a visible trade deficit of US $40.8m. and a deficit of US $134.8m. on the current account of the balance of payments. In 1983 the principal source of imports was Trinidad and Tobago (30.0%), mainly on account of petroleum imports, and Venezuela also became an important trading partner during the 1980s. The USA and the United Kingdom are other important suppliers of imports. The United Kingdom is the principal market for exports (35.9% of total exports in

1989); the USA, Canada and Japan are also significant recipients. The principal exports are gold, sugar and bauxite, and the principal imports are fuels and lubricants and capital goods.

In 1995 the overall budget deficit was $ G5,108m. (equivalent to 5.8% of GDP). By the end of 1995 Guyana's external debt totalled US $2,105m., of which US $1,782m. was long-term public debt. The cost of debt-servicing in that year was equivalent to 17.0% of the value of exports of goods and services. The average annual rate of inflation in 1985–92 was 11.9%. The level declined to 8.2% in 1993, before rising to 16.1% in 1994 and then declining to 8.1% in 1995, and an estimated 4.5% in 1996. An estimated 13.5% of the labour force were unemployed in 1991, but Guyana's greater problem is a shortage of trained personnel, particularly in the managerial and technical fields. The emigration rate remains high, at an estimated 15,000 per year, and compounds the existing economic difficulties.

Guyana is a founder member of CARICOM (see p. 119). It is also a member of the UN Economic Commission for Latin America and the Caribbean (ECLAC, see p. 29) and of the International Sugar Organization (see p. 258).

In 1988, in response to serious economic decline, the Government introduced an extensive recovery programme of adjustment measures and structural reforms, directing policy away from state control towards a market-orientated economy. Measures introduced included a restructuring of the public sector, liberalization of the exchange and trade system, and the elimination of the majority of price controls and state subsidies. Funds made available under a three-year Enhanced Structural Adjustment Facility (ESAF), approved by the IMF in 1990, contributed to the considerable success of the recovery programme. However, Guyana still had considerable economic difficulties, owing to its inadequate social and economic infrastructure, a shortage of skilled labour and a large external debt. In 1994 the IMF approved a further three-year ESAF, totalling US $79m., to support the Government's economic programme. The principal objectives of this programme included the reform of the financial system, development of the infrastructure and the acceleration of the programme of privatization of state enterprises. In 1996 negotiations with the Paris Club of creditor nations and Trinidad and Tobago resulted in the cancellation of 67% of Guyana's bilateral debt with five creditor nations (a total reduction of US $395m., of which US $359m. was owed to Trinidad and Tobago). Negotiations continued with Paris Club creditors in 1997, including the United Kingdom, which subsequently cancelled US $126.6m. of Guyana's bilateral debt. In December the IMF and the World Bank agreed to support a further debt-reduction plan for Guyana under the Initiative for Heavily Indebted Poor Countries, which would facilitate the cancellation of a further US $253m. In 1996, in view of the continuing deterioration of power supplies, the Government announced the partial divestment of the Guyana Electricity Company. In early 1997 the IMF released the third tranche of funding under the ESAF in support of the Government's programme for that year. Objectives for 1997 included real GDP growth of 7% and a reduction in the annual rate of inflation to 4%.

Social Welfare

Improved water supplies, anti-tuberculosis campaigns and the control of malaria have steadily improved general health. A national insurance scheme, compulsory for most workers and employers, was established in 1969, and was subsequently extended to cover self-employed people. In 1989 there was one physician for every 3,360 inhabitants in the country. In 1981 Guyana had 29 hospitals and 149 health centres. Of total expenditure by the central Government in 1984, $ G51.5m. (3.7%) was for health, and a further $ G36.8m. (2.7%) for social security and welfare. In the government budget for 1995 $ G1,400m. was allocated to health.

Education

Education is officially compulsory, and is provided free of charge, for eight years between six and 14 years of age. Primary education begins at six years of age and lasts for at least six years. Secondary education, beginning at 12 years of age, lasts for up to seven years, comprising a first cycle of five years and a second cycle of two years. Enrolment at all primary and secondary schools in 1988 was equivalent to 82% of the school-age population (males 82%; females 82%). Secondary enrolment in that year was equivalent to an estimated 57% of children in the relevant age-group (boys 56%; girls 59%). There are also 15 technical, vocational, special and higher educational institutions. These include the University of Guyana in Georgetown and three teacher training colleges. In 1995, according to estimates by UNESCO, the average rate of adult illiteracy was only 1.9% (males 1.4%; females 2.5%), one of the lowest in the Western hemisphere. Expenditure on education by the central Government in 1990 was estimated at $ G542m., and represented 8.9% of total spending in 1989. In the government budget for 1995 $ G1,300m. was allocated to education.

Public Holidays

1998: 1 January (New Year's Day), 30 January* (Id al-Fitr, end of Ramadan), 23 February (Mashramani, Republic Day), 8 April* (Id al-Adha, feast of the Sacrifice), 10 April (Good Friday), 13 April (Easter Monday), 1 May (Labour Day), 29 June (Caribbean Day), 7 July* (Yum an-Nabi, birth of the Prophet), 3 August (Freedom Day), 25–26 December (Christmas).

1999: 1 January (New Year's Day), 19 January* (Id al-Fitr, end of Ramadan), 23 February (Mashramani, Republic Day), 28 March* (Id al-Adha, feast of the Sacrifice), 2 April (Good Friday), 5 April (Easter Monday), 1 May (Labour Day), 26 June* (Yum an-Nabi, birth of the Prophet), 28 June (Caribbean Day), 2 August (Freedom Day), 25–26 December (Christmas).

* These holidays are dependent on the Islamic lunar calendar and may vary by one or two days from the dates given.

In addition, the Hindu festivals of Holi Phagwah (usually in March) and Divali (October or November) are celebrated. These festivals are dependent on sightings of the moon and their precise date is not known until two months before they take place.

Weights and Measures

The metric system has been introduced.

Statistical Survey

Source (unless otherwise stated): Bank of Guyana, 1 Church St and Ave of the Republic, POB 1003, Georgetown; tel. (2) 63261; telex 2267; fax (2) 72965.

AREA AND POPULATION

Area: 214,969 sq km (83,000 sq miles).

Population: 758,619 (males 375,481, females 382,778) at census of 12 May 1980; 838,000 at mid-1996 (UN estimate).

Density (mid-1996): 3.9 per sq km.

Ethnic Groups (1980 census): 'East' Indians 389,760, Africans 231,330, Portuguese 2,975, Chinese 1,842, Amerindians 39,867, Mixed 83,763, Others 9,082; Total 758,619.

Capital: Georgetown, population 72,049 (metropolitan area 187,056) at mid-1976 (estimate).

Births and Deaths: Birth rate 29.1 per 1,000 in 1980–85, 27.0 per 1,000 in 1985–90, 25.1 per 1,000 in 1990–95; Crude death rate 8.7 per 1,000 in 1980–85, 7.8 per 1,000 in 1985–90, 7.1 per 1,000 in 1990–95. Source: UN, *World Population Prospects: The 1994 Revision*.

Expectation of Life (UN estimates, years at birth, 1990–95): 65.2 (males 62.4; females 68.0). Source: UN, *World Population Prospects: The 1994 Revision*.

Economically Active Population (persons between 15 and 65 years of age, 1980 census): Agriculture, forestry and fishing 48,603; Mining and quarrying 9,389; Manufacturing 27,939; Electricity, gas and water 2,772; Construction 6,574; Trade, restaurants and hotels 14,690; Transport, storage and communications 9,160; Financing, insurance, real estate and business services 2,878; Community, social and personal services 57,416; Activities not adequately defined

15,260; Total employed 194,681 (males 153,645; females 41,036); Unemployed 44,650 (males 26,439, females 18,211); Total labour force 239,331 (males 180,084, females 59,247). **June 1987** (sample survey, persons aged 15 years and over): Total labour force 270,074 (males 189,337, females 80,737).

AGRICULTURE, ETC.

Principal Crops (FAO estimates, '000 metric tons, 1996): Rice (paddy) 520; Maize 3; Roots and tubers 51; Coconuts 73; Sugar cane 3,340 (unofficial figure); Pulses 1; Vegetables 13; Oranges 7; Bananas 17; Plantains 21; Other fruit 15. Source: FAO, *Production Yearbook*.

Livestock (FAO estimates, '000 head, year ending September 1996): Cattle 190; Pigs 30; Sheep 130; Goats 79; Chickens 8,000. Source: FAO, *Production Yearbook*.

Livestock Products (FAO estimates, '000 metric tons, 1996): Beef and veal 4; Mutton and lamb 1; Pig meat 1; Poultry meat 8; Cows' milk 13; Hen eggs 5. Source: FAO, *Production Yearbook*.

Forestry (FAO estimates, '000 cubic metres, 1994): Roundwood removals: Sawlogs, veneer logs and logs for sleepers 151, Other industrial wood 15, Fuel wood 14, Total 180; Sawnwood production: Total 15. Source: FAO, *Yearbook of Forest Products*.

Fishing (metric tons, live weight): Total catch 44,163 in 1993; 46,417 in 1994; 46,000 in 1995 (FAO estimate). Source: FAO, *Yearbook of Fishery Statistics*.

MINING

Production (1994): Bauxite 1,933,900 metric tons; Gold 375,500 troy oz; Diamonds 36,800 metric carats. Source: IMF, *Guyana—Recent Economic Developments and Selected Issues* (November 1996).

INDUSTRY

Selected Products (1994): Raw sugar 257,000 metric tons; Rum 258,000 hectolitres; Beer 99,000 hectolitres; Cigarettes 314m.; Electric energy 242m. kWh. Sources: UN, *Industrial Commodity Statistics Yearbook*; IMF, *Guyana—Recent Economic Developments and Selected Issues* (November 1996).

FINANCE

Currency and Exchange Rates: 100 cents = 1 Guyana dollar ($ G). *Sterling and US Dollar Equivalents* (30 September 1997): £1 sterling = $ G230.60; US $1 = $ G142.75; $ G1,000 = £4.337 = US $7.005. *Average Exchange Rate:* ($ G per US $): 138.3 in 1994; 142.0 in 1995; 140.4 in 1996.

Budget ($ G million, 1995): *Revenue:* Tax revenue 27,650 (Income tax 10,749, Consumption tax 9,623, Taxes on international trade 4,113, Sugar levy 1,900); Other revenue 1,667; Total 29,317. *Expenditure:* Current expenditure 22,155 (Personnel emoluments 5,514, Other goods and services 5,476, Interest 8,909, Transfers 2,256); Capital expenditure 12,270; Total 34,425. Source: IMF, *Guyana—Recent Economic Developments and Selected Issues* (November 1996).

International Reserves (US $ million at 31 December 1996): IMF special drawing rights 0.11, Foreign exchange 329.57; Total 329.68. Source: IMF, *International Financial Statistics*.

Money Supply ($ G million at 31 December 1996): Currency outside banks 9,959, Demand deposits at commercial banks 7,565; Total money (including also private-sector deposits at the Bank of Guyana) 17,531. Source: IMF, *International Financial Statistics*.

Cost of Living (Urban Consumer Price Index; base: 1991 = 100): 137.9 in 1993; 156.7 in 1994; 188.1 in 1995. Source: ILO, *Yearbook of Labour Statistics*.

Expenditure on the Gross Domestic Product ($ G million at current prices, 1993): Government final consumption expenditure 8,529; Private final consumption expenditure 29,134; Gross fixed capital formation 30,745; Statistical discrepancy –68; *Total domestic expenditure* 68,340; Exports of goods and services 52,160; *Less* Imports of goods and services, 61,376; *GDP in purchasers' values* 59,124; *GDP at constant 1990 prices* 19,370. Source: IMF, *International Financial Statistics*.

Gross Domestic Product by Economic Activity (preliminary figures, $ G million at current factor cost, 1995): Agriculture 23,378; Forestry and fishing 7,009; Mining and quarrying 12,095; Manufacturing (incl. power) 8,467; Construction 3,098; Distribution 3,205; Transport and communication 3,742; Rented dwellings 2,798; Financial services 2,324; Other services 1,057; Government 6,187; GDP at factor cost 73,360; Indirect taxes, *less* subsidies 14,071; GDP at market prices 87,431. Source: IMF, *Guyana—Recent Economic Development and Selected Issues* (November 1996).

Balance of Payments (US $ million, 1995): Exports of goods f.o.b. 495.7; Imports of goods f.o.b. –536.5; *Trade balance* –40.8; Exports of services 133.5; Imports of services –171.8; *Balance on goods and services* –79.2; Other income received 12.2; Other income paid –129.9; *Balance on goods, services and income* –196.8; Current transfers received 67.4; Current transfers paid –5.3; *Current balance* –134.8; Capital account (net) 9.5; Direct investment from abroad 74.4; Portfolio investment liabilities 3.2; Other investment assets –8.9; Other investment liabilities 2.3; Net errors and omissions 11.2; *Overall balance* –43.0. Source; IMF, *International Financial Statistics*.

EXTERNAL TRADE

Principal Commodities (US $ million, 1994): *Imports c.i.f.*: Capital goods 110.4; Consumer goods 82.3; Fuel and lubricants 135.9; Other intermediate goods 124.4; Total (incl. others) 506.3. *Exports f.o.b.*: Bauxite 79; Sugar 116; Rice 56; Gold 128, Total (incl. others) 447 (excl. re-exports 16). Source: IMF, *Guyana—Recent Economic Developments and Selected Issues* (November 1996).

Principal Trading Partners (US $ million, 1983): *Imports:* Brazil 5.8; Canada 6.6; German Democratic Republic 1.6; Germany, Federal Republic 8.0; Jamaica 5.1; Japan 3.9; Netherlands 9.3; Trinidad and Tobago 73.8; United Kingdom 27.9; USA 53.4; Total (incl. others) 246.1. *Exports:* Barbados 5.2; Canada 24.0; France 18.7; German Democratic Republic 14.9; Germany, Federal Republic 4.9; Italy 6.0; Jamaica 5.3; Japan 30.2; Mexico 4.2; Spain 4.2; Trinidad and Tobago 48.8; United Kingdom 103.3; USA 65.4; Venezuela 18.7; Total (incl. others) 375.8. Source: UN, *International Trade Statistics Yearbook*.

1989 ($ G million): *Exports:* Canada 1,312.4; Japan 530.9; United Kingdom 3,659.9; USA 1,900.9; Total (incl. others) 10,207.7.

TRANSPORT

Road Traffic ('000 vehicles in use, 1993): Passenger cars 24.0; Commercial vehicles 9.0. Source: UN, *Statistical Yearbook*.

Shipping (international sea-borne freight traffic, estimates in '000 metric tons, 1990): Goods loaded 1,730; Goods unloaded 673. Source: UN, *Monthly Bulletin of Statistics*. *Merchant Fleet* (at 31 December 1996): Vessels 61; Displacement 16,209 grt. (Source: Lloyd's Register of Shipping, *World Fleet Statistics*).

Civil Aviation (traffic on scheduled services, 1994): Kilometres flown (million) 2; passengers carried ('000) 115; passenger-km (million) 224; total ton-km (million) 23. Source: UN, *Statistical Yearbook*.

TOURISM

Tourist Arrivals ('000): 75 in 1992; 107 in 1993; 113 in 1994.

Tourist Receipts (US $ million): 31 in 1992; 45 in 1993; 47 in 1994.

COMMUNICATIONS MEDIA

Radio Receivers (1994): 405,000 in use*.

Television Receivers (1994): 33,000 in use*.

Telephones (1994): 44,000 main lines in use†.

Telefax Stations (1990): 195 in use†.

Mobile Cellular Telephones (1994): 1,250 subscribers†.

Daily Newspapers (1994): 2; estimated circulation 80,000*.

Non-daily Newspapers (1988): 6 (estimate); estimated circulation 84,000*.

Book Production (1989): 46 titles (9 books, 37 pamphlets)*.

* Source: UNESCO, *Statistical Yearbook*.

† Source: UN, *Statistical Yearbook*.

EDUCATION

Pre-primary (1992): Institutions 372; Teachers 1,495; Students 29,678.

Primary (1988): Institutions 414; Teachers 4,010 (provisional figure); Students 118,015.

Secondary (1988, excluding vocational courses): Teachers (1985) 2,087; Students 72,096.

Higher (1993): Teachers 518; Students 8,257.

Source: UNESCO, *Statistical Yearbook*.

Directory

The Constitution

Guyana became a republic, within the Commonwealth, on 23 February 1970. A new Constitution was promulgated on 6 October 1980. Its main provisions are summarized below:

The Constitution declares the Co-operative Republic of Guyana to be an indivisible, secular, democratic sovereign state in the course of transition from capitalism to socialism. The bases of the political, economic and social system are political and economic independence, involvement of citizens and socio-economic groups, such as co-operatives and trade unions, in the decision-making processes of the State and in management, social ownership of the means of production, national economic planning and co-operativism as the principle of socialist transformation. Personal property, inheritance, the right to work, with equal pay for men and women engaged in equal work, free medical attention, free education and social benefits for old age and disability are guaranteed. Individual political rights are subject to the principles of national sovereignty and democracy, and freedom of expression to the State's duty to ensure fairness and balance in the dissemination of information to the public. Relations with other countries are guided by respect for human rights, territorial integrity and non-intervention.

THE PRESIDENT

The President is the supreme executive authority, Head of State and Commander-in-Chief of the armed forces, elected for a term of office, usually of five years' duration, with no limit on re-election. The successful presidential candidate is the nominee of the party with the largest number of votes in the legislative elections. The President may prorogue or dissolve the National Assembly (in the case of dissolution, fresh elections must be held immediately) and has discretionary powers to postpone elections for up to one year at a time for up to five years. The President may be removed from office on medical grounds, or for violation of the Constitution (with a two-thirds' majority vote of the Assembly), or for gross misconduct (with a three-quarters' majority vote of the Assembly if allegations are upheld by a tribunal).

The President appoints a First Vice-President and Prime Minister who must be an elected member of the National Assembly, and a Cabinet of Ministers, which may include non-elected members and is collectively responsible to the legislature. The President also appoints a Minority Leader, who is the elected member of the Assembly deemed by the President most able to command the support of the opposition.

THE LEGISLATURE

The legislative body is a unicameral National Assembly of 65 members; 53 members are elected by universal adult suffrage in a system of proportional representation, 10 members are elected by the 10 Regional Democratic Councils and two members are elected by the National Congress of Local Democratic Organs. The Assembly passes bills, which are then presented to the President, and may pass constitutional amendments.

LOCAL GOVERNMENT

Guyana is divided into 10 Regions, each having a Regional Democratic Council elected for a term of up to five years and four months, although it may be prematurely dissolved by the President. Local councillors elect from among themselves deputies to the National Congress of Democratic Organs. This Congress and the National Assembly together form the Supreme Congress of the People of Guyana, a deliberative body which may be summoned, dissolved or prorogued by the President and is automatically dissolved along with the National Assembly.

OTHER PROVISIONS

Impartial commissions exist for the judiciary, the public service and the police service. An Ombudsman is appointed, after consultation between the President and the Minority Leader, to hold office for four years.

Note: In 1990 and 1991 there were negotiations about political reforms between the Government and the opposition parties. The National Assembly then enacted constitutional amendments extending its term of office and otherwise providing for the compilation of a new electoral roll, in preparation for elections held in October 1992.

The Government

HEAD OF STATE

President: JANET JAGAN (appointed 19 December 1997).

CABINET

(February 1998)

Prime Minister and Minister of Public Works and Home Affairs: SAMUEL ARCHIBALD ANTHONY HINDS.

Minister of Agriculture: REEPU DAMAN PERSAUD.

Minister of Health and Labour: Dr HENRY BENFIELD JEFFREY.

Attorney-General and Minister of Legal Affairs: CHARLES RISHRAM RAMSON.

Minister of Finance: BHARATT JAGDEO.

Minister of Culture, Youth and Sports: GAIL TEIXEIRA.

Minister of Education: Rev. Dr DALE RAMNAUTH BISNAUTH.

Minister of Foreign Affairs: CLEMENT JAMES ROHEE.

Minister of Trade, Tourism and Industry: MICHAEL SHREE CHAN.

Minister of Local Government: HARRIPERSAUD NOKTA.

Minister of Information: MOSES VEERASAMMY NAGAMOOTOO.

Minister of Public Service Management in the Office of the President: GEORGE E. FUNG-ON.

Minister of Amerindian Affairs: F. VIBERT DE SOUZA.

Minister of Marine Resources: SATYADEOW SAWH.

Minister of Human Services and Social Security: INDRANIE CHANDRAPAL.

Minister of Transport and Hydraulics: ANTHONY XAVIER.

Minister in the Ministry of Local Government: CLINTON COLLYMORE.

Minister of Housing: SHAIK K. Z. BAKSH.

Head of Presidential Secretariat: Dr ROGER LUNCHEON.

MINISTRIES

Office of the President: New Garden St and South Rd, Georgetown; tel. (2) 51330; telex 2205; fax (2) 63395.

Office of Amerindian Affairs: see Ministry of Public Works, Communications and Regional Development.

Ministry of Agriculture: POB 1001, Regent and Vlissingen Rds, Georgetown; tel. (2) 61565; fax (2) 73638.

Ministry of Education: 26 Brickdam, Stabroek, POB 1014, Georgetown; tel. (2) 63094; fax (2) 58511.

Ministry of Finance: Main and Urquhart Sts, Georgetown; tel. (2) 71114; fax (2) 61284.

Ministry of Foreign Affairs: Takuba Lodge, 254 New Garden St and South Rd, Georgetown; tel. (2) 57404; telex 2220; fax (2) 59192.

Ministry of Health and Labour: Brickdam, Stabroek, Georgetown; tel. (2) 61560; fax (2) 56958.

Ministry of Home Affairs: 6 Brickdam, Stabroek, Georgetown; tel. (2) 57270; fax (2) 62740.

Ministry of Housing: Georgetown.

Ministry of Human Services and Social Security: Homestretch Ave, Georgetown; tel. (2) 66115; fax (2) 53477.

Ministry of Information: see Office of the President.

Ministry of Legal Affairs and Office of Attorney-General: 95 Carmichael St, Georgetown; tel. (2) 53607; fax (2) 50732.

Ministry of Local Government: De Winkle Bldgs, Fort St, Kingston, Georgetown; tel. (2) 58621.

Ministry of Marine Resources: Georgetown.

Ministry of Public Works: Wight's Lane, Kingston, Georgetown; tel. (2) 72365; fax (2) 56954.

Ministry of Trade, Tourism and Industry: 229 South Rd, Lacytown, Georgetown; tel. (2) 62505; telex 2288; fax (2) 54310.

Ministry of Transport and Hydraulics: Georgetown.

Legislature

NATIONAL ASSEMBLY

Speaker: Dr DEREK JAGAN.

Election, 15 December 1997

Party	No. of Seats Regional	National	Total
People's Progressive Party (PPP)–CIVIC	7	29	36
People's National Congress (PNC)	4	22	26
Alliance For Guyana (AFG)	—	1	1
The United Force (TUF)	—	1	1
Guyana Democratic Party (GDP)	1	—	1
Total	12	53	65

Under Guyana's system of proportional representation, the nominated candidate of the party receiving the most number of votes was elected to the presidency. In the 1997 elections the PPP (candidate, JANET JAGAN), which was in alliance with the CIVIC movement, won 48% of the votes cast, compared with 35% for the PNC (HUGH DESMOND HOYTE).

Political Organizations

Alliance For Guyana (AFG): Georgetown; f. 1997; electoral alliance comprising following two parties:

Guyana Labour Party (GLP): Georgetown; f. 1992 by members of Guyanese Action for Reform and Democracy (see below).

Working People's Alliance (WPA): Walter Rodney House, Lot 80, Croal St, Stabroek, Georgetown; tel. (2) 53679; originally popular pressure group, became political party 1979; independent Marxist; Collective Leadership: EUSI KWAYANA, Dr CLIVE THOMAS, Dr RUPERT ROOPNARINE, WAZIR MOHAMED.

Al Mujahidden Party: Georgetown; represents Muslim population; Leader HOOSAIN GANIE.

CIVIC: New Garden St, Georgetown; social/political movement of businessmen and professionals; allied to PPP; Leader SAMUEL ARCHIBALD ANTHONY HINDS.

Good and Green Guyana (GGG): Georgetown; f. 1994; embraces 'Good and Green Georgetown' (f. to contest municipal and local government elections of Aug. 1994); Leader HAMILTON GREEN.

Guyana Democratic Party (GDP): Georgetown; f. 1996; Leaders ASGAR ALLY, NANDA K. GOPAUL.

Guyana People's Party (GPP): Georgetown; f. 1996; Leader MAX MOHAMED.

Guyana Republican Party (GRP): Paprika East Bank, Essequibo; f. 1985; right-wing; Leader LESLIE PRINCE (resident in the USA).

National Republican Party (NRP): Georgetown; f. 1990 after a split with URP; right-wing; Leader ROBERT GANGADEEN.

Patriotic Coalition for Democracy (PCD): Georgetown; f. 1986 by five opposition parties; the PCD campaigns for an end to alleged electoral malpractices; principal offices, including the chair of the collective leadership, rotate among the parties; now comprises the following three parties:

Democratic Labour Movement (DLM): 34 Robb and King Sts, 4th Floor, Lacytown, POB 10930, Georgetown; f. 1983; democratic-nationalist; Pres. PAUL NEHRU TENNASSEE.

People's Democratic Movement (PDM): Stabroek House, 10 Croal St, Georgetown; tel. (2) 64707; fax (2) 63002; f. 1973; centrist; Leader LLEWELLYN JOHN.

People's Progressive Party (PPP): 41 Robb St, Georgetown; tel. (2) 72095; fax (2) 72096; f. 1950; Marxist-Leninist; Gen. Sec. DONALD RAMOTAR.

People's National Congress (PNC): Congress Place, Sophia, POB 10330, Georgetown; tel. (2) 57850; f. 1955 after a split with the PPP; Leader HUGH DESMOND HOYTE; Gen. Sec. ROBERT CORBIN.

Union of Guyanese International (UGI): Robb and Orange Walk, Bourda, Georgetown; capitalist; Leader LINDLEY GE BORDE.

The United Force (TUF): 96 Robb St, Bourda, Georgetown; tel. (2) 62596; f. 1960; right-wing; advocates rapid industrialization through govt partnership and private capital; Leader MANZOOR NADIR.

United Republican Party (URP): Georgetown; f. 1985; right-wing; advocates federal govt; Leader Dr LESLIE RAMSAMMY.

United Workers' Party (UWP): Regent St, Georgetown; f. 1991; Leader WINSTON PAYNE.

In January 1989 a civic movement named **Guyanese Action for Reform and Democracy (Guard)** (Leader NANDA K. GOPAUL) was formed, committed to campaigning for constitutional and legal reforms and revised electoral practices.

Diplomatic Representation

EMBASSIES AND HIGH COMMISSIONS IN GUYANA

Brazil: 308 Church St, Queenstown, POB 10489, Georgetown; tel. (2) 57970; telex 2246; fax (2) 69063; e-mail bragetown@solutions2000.net; Ambassador: CLAUDIO LYRA.

Canada: High and Young Sts, POB 10880, Georgetown; tel. (2) 72081; telex 2215; fax (2) 58380; High Commissioner: ALAN BOWKER.

China, People's Republic: 108 Duke St, Kingston, Georgetown; tel. (2) 71651; tel. (2) 2251; Ambassador: ZHANG YU.

Colombia: 306 Church and Peter Rose Sts, Queenstown, POB 10185, Georgetown; tel. (2) 71410; telex 2206; fax (2) 58198; e-mail embcolguy@solutions2000.net; Ambassador: Dr LUIS GUILLERMO MARTÍNEZ FERNÁNDEZ.

Cuba: 46 High St, Kingston, Georgetown; tel. (2) 66732; telex 2272; Ambassador: OMAR MENDOZA SOSA.

India: 10 Ave of the Republic, Georgetown; tel. (2) 63996; telex 3025; High Commissioner: PRAVIN LAL GOYAL.

Korea, Democratic People's Republic: 88 Premniranjan Place, Georgetown; tel. (2) 60266; telex 2228; Ambassador: CHON HYUN CHAN.

Russia: 3 Public Rd, Kitty, Georgetown; tel. (2) 69773; telex 2277; fax (2) 72975; Ambassador: MIKHAIL A. SOBOLEV.

Suriname: 304 Church St, POB 10508, Georgetown; tel. (2) 67844; telex 2282; Ambassador: MOHAMED HOESSEIN.

United Kingdom: 44 Main St, POB 10849, Georgetown; tel. (2) 65881; fax (2) 53555; High Commissioner: IAN WHITEHEAD.

USA: Duke and Young Sts, Georgetown; tel. (2) 54900; telex 2213; fax (2) 58497; Chargé d'affaires: HUGH SIMON.

Venezuela: 296 Thomas St, Georgetown; tel. (2) 61543; telex 2237; Ambassador: ENRIQUE PEINADO BARRIOS.

Judicial System

The Judicature of Guyana comprises the Supreme Court of Judicature, which consists of the Court of Appeal and the High Court (both of which are superior courts of record), and a number of Courts of Summary Jurisdiction.

The Court of Appeal, which came into operation in 1966, consists of the Chancellor as President, the Chief Justice, and such number of Justices of Appeal as may be prescribed by the National Assembly.

The High Court of the Supreme Court consists of the Chief Justice as President of the Court and Puisne Judges. Its jurisdiction is both original and appellate. It has criminal jurisdiction in matters brought before it on indictment. A person convicted by the Court has a right of appeal to the Guyana Court of Appeal. The High Court of the Supreme Court has unlimited jurisdiction in civil matters and exclusive jurisdiction in probate, divorce and admiralty and certain other matters. Under certain circumstances, appeal in civil matters lies either to the Full Court of the High Court of the Supreme Court, which is composed of not less than two judges, or to the Guyana Court of Appeal.

A magistrate has jurisdiction to determine claims where the amount involved does not exceed a certain sum of money, specified by law. Appeal lies to the Full Court.

Chancellor of Justice: CECIL KENNARD.

Chief Justice: DESIRÉE BERNARD.

Attorney-General: BERNARD DE SANTOS.

Religion

CHRISTIANITY

Guyana Council of Churches: 71 Murray St, Georgetown; tel. (2) 66610; f. 1967 by merger of the Christian Social Council (f. 1937) and the Evangelical Council (f. 1960); 15 mem. churches, 1 assoc. mem.; Chair. Rt Rev. RANDOLPH OSWALD GEORGE (Anglican Bishop of Guyana); Sec. MICHAEL MCCORMACK.

The Anglican Communion

Anglicans in Guyana are adherents of the Church in the Province of the West Indies, comprising eight dioceses. The Archbishop of the Province is the Bishop of the North Eastern Caribbean and Aruba, resident in St John's, Antigua. The diocese of Guyana also includes French Guiana and Suriname. In 1986 the estimated membership in the country was 125,000.

Bishop of Guyana: Rt Rev. RANDOLPH OSWALD GEORGE, Austin House, Georgetown; tel. (2) 64183; fax (2) 63353.

The Baptist Church

The Baptist Convention of Guyana: POB 10149, Georgetown; tel. (2) 60428; Chair. Rev. ERIC NARINE.

The Lutheran Church

The Lutheran Church in Guyana: 28–29 North and Alexander Sts, Lacytown, Georgetown; tel. (2) 64227; 14,147 mems; Pres. JAMES LOCHAN.

The Roman Catholic Church

Guyana comprises the single diocese of Georgetown, suffragan to the archdiocese of Port of Spain, Trinidad and Tobago. At 31 December 1995 adherents of the Roman Catholic Church comprised about 10.9% of the total population. The Bishop participates in the Antilles Episcopal Conference Secretariat, currently based in Port of Spain, Trinidad.

Bishop of Georgetown: G. BENEDICT SINGH, Bishop's House, 27 Brickdam, POB 10720, Stabroek, Georgetown; tel. (2) 64469; fax (2) 58519.

Other Christian Churches

Other denominations active in Guyana include the African Methodist Episcopal Church, the African Methodist Episcopal Zion Church, the Church of God, the Church of the Nazarene, the Ethiopian Orthodox Church, the Guyana Baptist Mission, the Guyana Congregational Union, the Guyana Presbyterian Church, the Hallelujah Church, the Methodist Church in the Caribbean and the Americas, the Moravian Church and the Presbytery of Guyana.

HINDUISM

Hindu Religious Centre: Maha Sabha, 162 Lamaha St, POB 10576, Georgetown; tel. (2) 57443; f. 1934; Hindus account for about one-third of the population; Pres. RAMRAJ JAGNANDAN; Gen. Sec. CHRISHNA PERSAUD.

ISLAM

The Central Islamic Organization of Guyana (CIOG): M.Y.O. Bldg, Woolford Ave, Thomas Lands, POB 10245, Georgetown; tel. (2) 58654; fax (2) 72475.

Guyana United Sad'r Islamic Anjuman: 157 Alexander St, Kitty, POB 10715, Georgetown; tel. (2) 69620; f. 1936; 120,000 mems; Pres. Haji A. H. RAHAMAN; Sec. YACOOB HUSSAIN.

The Press

DAILY

Guyana Chronicle: 2A Lama Ave, Bel Air Park, POB 11, Georgetown; tel. (2) 63243; fax (2) 75208; e-mail khan@guyana.net.gy; f. 1881; govt-owned; also produces weekly *Sunday Chronicle* (tel. (2) 63243); Editor-in-Chief SHARIEF KHAN; circ. 23,000 (weekdays), 43,000 (Sundays).

WEEKLIES AND PERIODICALS

The Catholic Standard: 293 Oronoque St, Queenstown, POB 10720, Georgetown; tel. (2) 61540; f. 1905; weekly; Editor COLIN SMITH; circ. 10,000.

Diocesan Magazine: 144 Almond and Oronoque Sts, Queenstown, Georgetown; quarterly.

Guyana Business: 156 Waterloo St, POB 10110, Georgetown; tel. (2) 56451; f. 1889; organ of the Georgetown Chamber of Commerce and Industry; quarterly; Editor C. D. KIRTON.

Guynews: 18 Brickdam, Stabroek, Georgetown; monthly.

Kaieteur News: 24 Saffon St, Charlestown; tel. (2) 58452; fax (2) 58473; f. 1994; independent weekly; Editor W. HENRY SKERRETT; circ. 30,000.

Labour Advocate: 61 Hadfield St, Werkenrust, Georgetown; weekly.

Mirror: Lot 8, Industrial Estate, Ruimveldt, Greater Georgetown; tel. (2) 62471; fax (2) 62472; owned by the New Guyana Co Ltd; Sundays and Wednesdays; Editor JANET JAGAN; circ. 25,000.

New Nation: Congress Place, Sophia, Georgetown; tel. (2) 68520; f. 1955; organ of the People's National Congress; weekly; Editor FRANCIS WILLIAMS; circ. 26,000.

The Official Gazette of Guyana: Guyana National Printers Ltd, Lot 1, Public Road, La Penitence; weekly; circ. 450.

Ratoon: Georgetown; monthly.

Stabroek News: 46–47 Robb St, Lacytown, Georgetown; tel. (2) 57473; fax (2) 54637; e-mail stabroeknews@stabroeknews.com; internet http://www.stabroeknews.com; f. 1986; daily; liberal independent; Editor-in-Chief DAVID DE CAIRES; circ. 18,500 (weekdays), 34,000 (Sundays).

Thunder: 41 Robb St, Georgetown; f. 1950; organ of the People's Progressive Party; quarterly; Editor RALPH RAMKARRAN; circ. 5,000.

NEWS AGENCY

Guyana Information Services: Office of the President, New Garden St and South Rd, Georgetown; tel. (2) 63389; fax (2) 64003; f. 1993; Dir MILTON DREPAUL.

Foreign Bureaux

Informatsionnoye Telegrafnoye Agentstvo Rossii—Telegrafnoye Agentstvo Suverennykh Stran (ITAR—TASS) (Russia): Georgetown; Correspondent ALEKSANDR KAMISHEV.

Inter Press Service (Italy): Georgetown; tel. (2) 53213; Correspondent BERT WILKINSON.

United Press International (UPI) (USA): Georgetown; tel. (2) 65153; Correspondent DESIRÉE HARPER.

Xinhua (New China) News Agency (People's Republic of China): 52 Brickdam, Stabroek, Georgetown; tel. (2) 69965; Correspondent CHEN JING.

Associated Press (USA) is also represented.

PRESS ASSOCIATION

Guyana Press Association: Georgetown; revived in 1990; Pres. ENRICO WOOLFORD.

Publisher

Guyana National Printers Ltd: 1 Public Rd, La Penitence, POB 10256, Greater Georgetown; tel. (2) 53623; telex 2212; f. 1939; govt-owned printers and publishers; 89.6% share offered for private ownership in 1996; Gen. Man. NOVEAR DEFREITAS.

Broadcasting and Communications

TELECOMMUNICATIONS

Guyana Telephones and Telegraph Company (GT & T): Georgetown; f. 1991; formerly state-owned Guyana Telecommunications Corpn; 80% ownership by Atlantic Tele-Network (USA); Gen. Man. ANAND PERSAUD.

RADIO

Guyana Broadcasting Corporation (GBC): Broadcasting House, 44 High St, POB 10760, Georgetown; tel. (2) 58734; fax (2) 58756; f. 1979; formed by merger of the Guyana Broadcasting Service and the Broadcasting Co Ltd (Radio Demerara) when the Government took over the assets of the latter; operates channels GBC 1 (Coastal Service) and GBC 2 (National Service); Gen. Man. M. FAZIL AZEEZ.

TELEVISION

Guyana Television Broadcasting Company: Homestretch Ave, Georgetown; tel. (2) 71566; fax (2) 71568; f. 1993; fmrly Guyana Television Corporation; govt-owned; limited service; Dir A. BREWSTER.

Two private stations relay US satellite television programmes.

Finance

(dep. = deposits; m. = million; brs = branches; amounts in Guyana dollars)

BANKING

Central Bank

Bank of Guyana: 1 Church St and Ave of the Republic, POB 1003, Georgetown; tel. (2) 63251; telex 2267; fax (2) 72965; f. 1965; cap. 4.3m., res 10,092.4m., dep. 114,227.9m. (Dec. 1996); central bank of note issue; Gov. ARCHIBALD L. MEREDITH; Dep. Gov. DOLLY S. SINGH.

Commercial Banks

Demerara Bank Ltd: 230 Camp and South Sts, Georgetown; tel. (2) 50610; telex 3060; fax (2) 50601; f. 1994; cap. 450m., res 31.3m., dep. 4,318.7m. (Sept. 1997); Chair. YESU PERSAUD; Man. AHMED M. KHAN.

Guyana Bank for Trade and Industry Ltd: 47-48 Water St, POB 10280, Georgetown; tel. (2) 68431; telex 3063; fax (2) 71612; e-mail gbti@solutions2000.net; f. 1990 by merger of Guyana Bank for Trade and Industry (frmly Barclays Bank) and Republic Bank (frmly Chase Manhattan Bank); Pres. and CEO PAUL GEER; 3 brs.

Guyana Co-operative Mortgage Finance Bank: 46 Main St, POB 1083, Georgetown; tel. (2) 68415; f. 1973; Man. Dir EDWARD RICHMOND.

Guyana National Co-operative Bank: 1 Lombard and Cornhill Sts, POB 10400, Georgetown; tel. (2) 57810; telex 2235; fax (2) 60231; f. 1970; merged with Guyana Co-operative Agricultural and

Industrial Development Bank in 1995; Gen. Man. ROSALIE A. ROBERTSON; 11 brs.

National Bank of Industry and Commerce: 38–40 Water St, POB 10440, Georgetown; tel. (2) 64091; telex 3044; fax (2) 72921; Man. Dir CONRAD PLUMMER; 5 brs.

Foreign Banks

Bank of Baroda (India): 10 Regent St and Ave of the Republic, POB 10768, Georgetown; tel. (2) 64005; telex 2243; fax (2) 51691; f. 1908; Chief Man. DIPANKAR MUKERJEE.

Bank of Nova Scotia (Canada): 104 Carmichael St, POB 10631; Georgetown; tel. (2) 59222; telex 3028; fax (2) 59309; Man. J. F. I. COOPER; 2 brs.

Citizens' Bank Ltd (Jamaica): 201 Camp and Charlotte Sts, Lacytown, Georgetown; tel. (2) 78252; fax (2) 78251; f. 1994; Chair. DENNIS LALOR.

INSURANCE

Demerara Mutual Life Assurance Society Ltd: Demerara Life Bldg, 61 Ave of the Republic, POB 10409, Georgetown; tel. (2) 58991; fax (2) 58288; f. 1891; Chair. RICHARD B. FIELDS; Gen. Man. EAWAN E. DEVONISH.

Guyana Co-operative Insurance Service: 47 Main St, Georgetown; tel. (2) 68421; telex 2255; f. 1976; 67% share offered for private ownership in 1996; Chair. G. A. LEE; Gen. Man. PAT BENDER.

Guyana and Trinidad Mutual Life Insurance Co Ltd: Lots 27–29, Robb and Hincks Sts, Georgetown; tel. (2) 57912; fax (2) 59397; f. 1925; Chair. HAROLD B. DAVIS; Man. Dir R. E. CHEONG; affiliated company: Guyana and Trinidad Mutual Fire Insurance Co Ltd.

Hand-in-Hand Mutual Fire and Life Group: 1–4 Avenue of the Republic, POB 10188, Georgetown; tel. (2) 51867; fax (2) 57519; f. 1865; fire and life insurance; Chair. J. A. CHIN; Gen. Man. K. A. EVELYN.

There are also several foreign insurance companies operating in Guyana.

Insurance Association

Insurance Association of Guyana: 54 Robb St, Bourda, POB 10741, Georgetown; tel. (2) 63514; f. 1968.

STOCK EXCHANGE

In July 1989 the Government announced that it intended to establish a national securities exchange, with a view to becoming a member of the proposed regional stock exchange.

Trade and Industry

GOVERNMENT AGENCIES

Guyana Agency for the Environment: Georgetown; tel. (2) 57523; fax (2) 57524; f. 1988; formulates, implements and monitors policies on the environment; Dir Dr WALTER CHIN.

Guyana Marketing Corporation: 87 Robb and Alexander Sts, Georgetown; tel. (2) 68255; fax (2) 68255; Chair. CHANDRABALLI BISHESWAR; Gen. Man. ROXANNE GREENIDGE (acting).

Guyana Public Communications Agency: Georgetown; tel. (2) 72025; f. 1989; Exec. Chair. KESTER ALVES.

DEVELOPMENT ORGANIZATIONS

Guyana Office for Investment (Go-Invest): 237 Camp St, Cummingsburg, Georgetown: tel. (2) 62434; fax (2) 61492; f. 1994 to replace Guyana Manufacturing and Industrial Development Agency (Guymida); provision of investment promotion service for foreign and local cos; Dir. IVOR MITCHELL.

State Planning Commission: 229 South St, Lacytown, Georgetown; tel. (2) 68093; fax (2) 72499; Chief Planning Officer CLYDE ROOPCHAND.

CHAMBER OF COMMERCE

Georgetown Chamber of Commerce and Industry: 156 Waterloo St, Cummingsburg, POB 10110, Georgetown; tel. (2) 63519; f. 1889; 122 mems; Pres. JOHN S. DEFREITAS; Chief Exec. G. C. FUNG-ON.

INDUSTRIAL AND TRADE ASSOCIATIONS

Bauxite Industry Development Company Ltd: 71 Main St, Georgetown; tel. (2) 57780; telex 2244; fax (2) 67413; f. 1976; Chair. J. I. F. BLACKMAN.

Guyana Rice Development Board: 117 Cowan St, Georgetown; tel. (2) 58717; fax (2) 56486; f. 1994 to assume operations of Guyana Rice Export Board and Guyana Rice Grading Centre; Chair. and CEO CHARLES KENNARD.

Livestock Development Co Ltd: 58 High St, Georgetown; tel. (2) 61601.

EMPLOYERS' ORGANIZATIONS

Consultative Association of Guyanese Industry Ltd: 78 Church and Carmichael Sts, POB 10730, Georgetown; tel. (2) 57170; f. 1962; 193 mems, 3 mem. asscns, 159 assoc. mems; Chair. DAVID KING; Exec. Dir DAVID YANKANA.

Forest Products Association of Guyana: 6 Croal St and Manget Place, Georgetown; tel. (2) 69848; f. 1944; 47 mems; Pres. L. J. P. WILLEMS; Exec. Officer WARREN PHOENIX.

Guyana Manufacturers' Association Ltd: 62 Main St, Cummingsburg, Georgetown; tel. (2) 74295; fax (2) 70670; f. 1967; 190 members; Pres. KIM KISSOON; Exec. Sec. TREVOR SHARPLES.

Guyana Rice Producers' Association: Lot 104, Regent St, Lacytown, Georgetown; tel. (2) 64411; f. 1946; c. 35,000 families; Pres. BUDRAM MAHADEO; Gen. Sec. FAZAL ALLY.

UTILITIES

Electricity

Guyana Electricity Corporation (GEC): Georgetown; tel. (2) 60569; privatization pending.

CO-OPERATIVE SOCIETIES

Chief Co-operatives Development Officer: Ministry of Labour, Human Services and Social Security, 1 Water and Cornhill Sts, Georgetown; tel. (2) 58644; fax (2) 53477; f. 1948; A. HENRY.

In October 1996 there were 1,324 registered co-operative societies, mainly savings clubs and agricultural credit societies, with a total membership of 95,950.

TRADE UNIONS

Trades Union Congress (TUC): Critchlow Labour College, Woolford Ave, Non-pareil Park, Georgetown; tel. (2) 61493; fax (2) 70254; f. 1940; national trade union body; 22 affiliated unions; merged with the Federation of Independent Trade Unions in Guyana in 1993; Pres. GORDON TODD; Gen. Sec. JOSEPH H. POLLYDORE.

Amalgamated Transport and General Workers' Union: 46 Urquhart St, Georgetown; tel. (2) 66243; Pres. RICHARD SAMUELS.

Clerical and Commercial Workers' Union (CCWU): Clerico House, 140 Quamina St, South Cummingsburg, POB 101045, Georgetown; tel. (2) 52822; Gen. Sec. BIRCHMORE PHILADELPHIA.

General Workers' Union: 106–107 Lamaha St, North Cummingsburg, Georgetown; tel. (2) 61185; f. 1954; terminated affiliation to People's National Congress in 1989; Pres. NORRIS WITTER; Gen. Sec. EDWIN JAMES; 3,000 mems.

Guyana Agricultural and General Workers' Union (GAWU): 104–106 Regent St, Lacytown, Georgetown; tel. (2) 72091; allied to the PPP; Gen. Sec. KOMAL CHAND; 20,000 mems.

Guyana Bauxite Supervisors' Union: Linden; Gen. Sec. LINCOLN LEWIS.

Guyana Labour Union: 198 Camp St, Georgetown; tel. (2) 63275; Pres.-Gen. HUGH DESMOND HOYTE; 6,000 mems.

Guyana Mine Workers' Union: 784 Determa St, Mackenzie, Linden; tel. (4) 3146; Pres. ASHTON ANGEL; Gen. Sec. CHRISTOPHER JAMES; 5,800 mems.

Guyana Postal and Telecommunication Workers' Union: 310 East St, POB 10352, Georgetown; tel. (2) 65255; Pres. SELWYN O. FELIX; Gen. Sec. ANJOU DANIELS.

Guyana Public Service Union (GPSU): 160 Regent Rd and New Garden St, Georgetown; tel. (2) 61770; founder mem. of the FITUG in 1988; withdrew in May 1989; Pres. PATRICK YARDE; Gen. Sec. RANDOLPH KIRTON; 11,600 mems.

National Association of Agricultural, Commercial and Industrial Employees: 64 High St, Kingston, Georgetown; tel. (2) 72301; f. 1946; Pres. B. KHUSIEL; c. 2,000 mems.

University of Guyana Workers' Union: Turkeyen, Georgetown; supports Working People's Alliance; Pres. Dr CLIVE THOMAS.

Transport

RAILWAY

There are no public railways in Guyana.

Linmine Railway: Mackenzie, Linden; tel. (4) 2484; fax (4) 2795; bauxite transport; 48 km of line, Itumi to Linden; Superintendent G. RUTHERFORD FELIX.

ROADS

The coastal strip has a well-developed road system. In 1996 there were an estimated 7,970 km (4,859 miles) of paved and good-weather roads and trails. Construction of a long-delayed road link between Guyana and Brazil commenced in 1989; however, the section of road linking Georgetown with Lethem, on the border with Brazil, was only half completed by mid-1996.

Guyana Transport Services Ltd: Nelson Mandela Ave, Industrial Site, Ruimveldt, Greater Georgetown; tel. (2) 58261; f. 1971; transferred to private ownership 1989; provides road haulage and bus services; Gen Man. R. VAN VELZEN.

SHIPPING

Guyana's principal ports are at Georgetown and New Amsterdam. A ferry service is operated between Guyana and Suriname. Communications with the interior are chiefly by river, although access is hindered by rapids and falls. There are 1,077 km (607 miles) of navigable rivers. The main rivers are the Mazaruni, the Potaro, the Essequibo, the Demerara and the Berbice.

Transport and Harbours Department: Battery Rd, Kingston, Georgetown; tel. (2) 59350; Gen. Man. IVOR B. ENGLISH; Harbour Master STEPHEN THOMAS.

Shipping Association of Georgetown: 28 Main and Holmes Sts, Georgetown; tel. (2) 62632; f. 1952; Chair. F. A. GRIFFITH; Sec. and Man. W. V. BRIDGEMOHAN; members:

Caribbean Molasses Co Ltd: 1–2 Water St, POB 10208, Georgetown; tel. (2) 69238; fax 71327; e-mail cmc@tateandlyle.com; exporters of molasses in bulk; Man. Dir I. C. HENDRIE.

Guyana National Industrial Corporation Inc.: 1–9 Lombard St, Charlestown, POB 10520, Georgetown; tel. (2) 60882; telex 2218; fax (2) 58526; metal foundry, ship building and repair, agents for Intermarine Inc., Telpha Mapson Shipping, Yamagin Corpn, Ni Transport Services Inc., Nissui Shipping Corpn, Japan Reefer Carrier Co. Ltd, Hoech-Ugland Auto Liners A/S; Man. Dir and CEO CLAUDE SAUL.

Guyana National Shipping Corporation Ltd: 5–9 Lombard St, La Penitence, POB 10988, Georgetown; tel. (2) 61732; telex 2232; fax (2) 53815; govt-owned; reps for Harrison Line, Mitsui OSL Lines, Nedlloyd Lines and Lloyd Agencies; Exec. Chair. V. FORTUNE; Man. Dir M. F. BASCOM.

John Fernandes Ltd: 24 Water St, POB 10211, Georgetown; tel. (2) 56294; fax (2) 61881; ship agents and stevedore contractors; reps for Europe West Indies Lines, Bernuth Lines, Carib Services Inc. and Yuwa Shipping Co. Ltd; Man. Dir C. J. FERNANDES.

CIVIL AVIATION

The main airport is Timehri International, 42 km (26 miles) from Georgetown. The more important settlements in the interior have airstrips.

Guyana Airways Corporation: 32 Main St, POB 10223, Georgetown; tel. (2) 68195; telex 2242; fax (2) 60032; f. 1939 as British Guiana Airways; renamed as above 1963; govt-owned; operates internal scheduled services and external services to the USA and Canada; Chair. R. RAMKARRAN; Man. Dir FAZEL KHAN.

There is a weekly flight, via Georgetown, from Caracas (Venezuela) to Port of Spain (Trinidad and Tobago) and Suriname.

Tourism

Despite the beautiful scenery in the interior of the country, Guyana has limited tourist facilities, and began encouraging tourism only in the late 1980s. Plans to promote Guyana as an eco-tourism destination were being pursued in the late-1990s. According to UN figures, the total number of visitors to Guyana in 1994 was 113,000, when tourism receipts totalled US $47m.

Tourism Association of Guyana: Georgetown; f. 1991; Dir TONY THORNE.

HAITI

Introductory Survey

Location, Climate, Language, Religion, Flag, Capital

The Republic of Haiti occupies the western part of the Caribbean island of Hispaniola (the Dominican Republic occupies the remaining two-thirds) and some smaller offshore islands. Cuba, to the west, is less than 80 km away. The climate is tropical but the mountains and fresh sea winds mitigate the heat. Temperatures vary little with the seasons, and the annual average in Port-au-Prince is about 27°C (80°F). The rainy season is from May to November. The official languages are French and Creole. About 75% of the population belong to the Roman Catholic Church, the country's official religion, and other Christian churches are also represented. The folk religion is voodoo, a fusion of beliefs originating in West Africa involving communication with the spirit-world through the medium of trance. The national flag (proportions variable) has two equal vertical stripes, of dark blue and red. The state flag (proportions 5 by 3) has, in addition, a white rectangular panel, containing the national coat of arms (a palm tree, surmounted by a Cap of Liberty and flanked by flags and cannons), in the centre. The capital is Port-au-Prince.

Recent History

Haiti was first colonized in 1659 by the French, who named the territory Saint-Domingue. French sovereignty was formally recognized by Spain in 1697. Following a period of internal unrest, a successful uprising, begun in 1794 by African-descended slaves, culminated in 1804 with the establishment of Haiti as an independent state, ruled by Jean-Jacques Dessalines, who proclaimed himself Emperor. Hostility between the negro population and the mulattos continued throughout the 19th century until, after increasing economic instability, the USA intervened militarily and supervised the government of the country from 1915 to 1934. Mulatto interests retained political ascendancy until 1946, when a negro President, Dumarsais Estimé, was installed following a military coup. Following the overthrow of two further administrations, Dr François Duvalier, a country physician, was elected President in 1957.

The Duvalier administration soon became a dictatorship, maintaining its authority by means of a notorious private army, popularly called the Tontons Macoutes (Creole for 'Bogeymen'), who used extortion and intimidation to crush all possible opposition to the President's rule. In 1964 Duvalier became President-for-Life, and at his death in April 1971 he was succeeded by his 19-year-old son and designated successor Jean-Claude Duvalier.

At elections held in February 1979 for the 58-seat National Assembly, 57 seats were won by the official government party, the Parti de l'Unité Nationale. The first municipal elections for 25 years, which took place in 1983, were overshadowed by allegations of electoral fraud and Duvalier's obstruction of opposition parties. No opposition candidates were permitted to contest the elections for the National Assembly held in February 1984.

In April 1985 Duvalier announced a programme of constitutional reforms, including the eventual appointment of a Prime Minister and the formation of political parties, subject to certain limiting conditions. In September Roger Lafontant, the minister most closely identified with the Government's acts of repression, was dismissed. However, protests organized by the Roman Catholic Church and other religious groups gained momentum, and further measures to curb continued disorder were adopted in January 1986. The university and schools were closed indefinitely, and radio stations were forbidden to report on current events. Duvalier imposed a state of siege and declared martial law.

In February 1986, following intensified public protests, Duvalier and his family fled from Haiti to exile in France, leaving a five-member National Council of Government (Conseil National Gouvernemental—CNG), led by the Chief of Staff of the army, Gen. Henri Namphy, to succeed him. The interim military-civilian Council announced the appointment of a new Cabinet. The National Assembly was dissolved, and the Constitution was suspended. Later in the month, the Tontons Macoutes were disbanded. Prisoners from Haiti's largest gaol were freed under a general amnesty.

However, after the initial euphoria following the downfall of Duvalier, renewed rioting occurred to protest against the inclusion in the new Government of known supporters of the former dictatorship. In March 1986 there was a cabinet reshuffle, following the resignations of three Duvalierist members of the CNG (only one of whom was replaced). The new three-member CNG comprised Gen. Namphy, Col (later Brig.-Gen.) Williams Régala (Minister of the Interior and National Defence) and Jacques François (then Minister of Finance).

In April 1986 Gen. Namphy announced a proposed timetable for elections to restore constitutional government by February 1988. The first of these elections, to select 41 people (from 101 candidates) who would form part of the 61-member Constituent Assembly which was to revise the Constitution, took place in October 1986. However, the level of participation at the election was only about 5%.

The new Constitution was approved by 99.8% of voters in a referendum held on 29 March 1987. An estimated 50% of the electorate voted. An independent Provisional Electoral Council (Conseil Electoral Provisoire—CEP) was appointed to supervise the presidential and legislative elections, which were scheduled for 29 November.

On 29 November 1987 the elections were cancelled three hours after voting had begun, owing to renewed violence and killings, for which former members of the Tontons Macoutes were believed to be responsible. The Government dissolved the CEP and took control of the electoral process. In December a new CEP was appointed by the Government, and elections were rescheduled for 17 January 1988. A former university professor, Leslie Manigat of the Rassemblement des Démocrates Nationaux Progressistes (RDNP), with 50.3% of the total votes cast, was declared the winner of the presidential election. Legislative and municipal elections were held concurrently. It was officially estimated that 35% of the electorate had voted in the elections, although opposition leaders claimed that only 5% had participated, and alleged that there had been extensive fraud and malpractice.

The Manigat Government took office in February 1988, but was overthrown by disaffected members of the army in June. Gen. Namphy, whom Manigat had attempted to replace as army Chief of Staff, assumed the presidency and appointed a Cabinet comprising members of the armed forces. The Constitution of 1987 was abrogated, and Duvalier's supporters returned to prominence, as did the Tontons Macoutes.

On 18 September 1988 Gen. Namphy was ousted in a coup, led by Brig.-Gen. Prosper Avril (who became President) and non-commissioned officers from the presidential guard, who advocated the introduction of radical reforms. In November an independent electoral body, the Collège Electoral d'Haïti (CEDA), was established to supervise future elections, to draft an electoral law and to ensure proper registration of voters.

In March 1989 President Avril partially restored the Constitution of 1987 and restated his intention to hold democratic elections. In the following month the Government survived two coup attempts by the Leopard Corps, the country's élite anti-subversion squadron, and the Dessalines battalion, based in Port-au-Prince. Both battalions were subsequently disbanded.

In September 1989 Avril published a timetable for elections that had been drafted by the CEP. It provided for local and regional elections to be held in April 1990, followed by national and legislative elections, in two rounds, in July and August. The presidential election, also in two rounds, was scheduled to take place in October and November 1990. (These arrangements were revised under the interim presidency of Ertha Pascal-Trouillot—see below.) In August 1989 the conservative former Minister of Finance, Marc Bazin, and the leader of the Parti Nationaliste Progressiste Révolutionnaire (PANPRA), Serge Gilles, established the Alliance Nationale pour la Démocratie et le Progrès (ANDP).

In early January 1990, during the President's absence abroad on official business, the Rassemblement National, a broadly-based opposition coalition including conservative and left-wing political organizations, initiated a series of strikes and demonstrations to protest against the Government's economic policies. On 20 January, following his return to Haiti, Avril imposed a 30-day state of siege and a series of restrictions on political activity. However, within a few days Avril was compelled to lift the state of siege and other emergency measures. At the same time it was announced that all political prisoners had been released.

Avril resigned as President in March 1990, in response to sustained popular and political opposition, together with diplomatic pressure from the USA. Before entering temporary exile in the USA, Avril ceded power to the Chief of the General Staff, Gen. Hérard Abraham, who subsequently transferred authority to Ertha Pascal-Trouillot, a member of the Supreme Court. As President of a civilian interim Government, Pascal-Trouillot shared power with a 19-member Council of State, whose principal function was to assist in preparations for the elections that were to be held later in the year. In May a new CEP, with responsibility for the organization and supervision of the forthcoming elections, was established.

In July 1990 two exiled members of the Duvalier regime, Roger Lafontant and Brig.-Gen. Williams Régala, returned to the country, despite the existence of a warrant for their arrest, which was ignored by the security forces. A strike was organized by political leaders and business executives, in support of demands for the arrest of the two Duvalierists, who were considered to represent a threat to the planned free elections. In September the CEP announced the postponement, until mid-December, of the elections, owing to a delay in the arrival of necessary funds and materials from donor countries. In November the CEP declared invalid the candidacies for the presidency of Lafontant, the representative of the newly-formed Union pour la Réconciliation Nationale, and of former President Manigat, who had been allowed to return from exile to contest the forthcoming presidential election as the candidate of the RDNP.

The presidential and legislative elections took place, as scheduled, on 16 December 1990. Preliminary results indicated an overwhelming victory in the presidential election for Fr Jean-Bertrand Aristide, a left-wing Roman Catholic priest representing the Front National pour le Changement et la Démocratie (FNCD), who secured some 67% of the votes cast. His closest rival was Marc Bazin, the candidate of the centre-right Mouvement pour l'Instauration de la Démocratie en Haïti (MIDH), who obtained about 14% of the poll. However, the results of the concurrent first round of legislative voting were less decisive. Aristide's FNCD won five of the 27 seats in the Senate, and 18 (of 83) seats in the Chamber of Deputies, while the ANDP secured 16 seats in the lower house. Seven other seats in the Chamber of Deputies were distributed among other political parties.

In early January 1991, one month before Aristide was due to be sworn in as President, a group of army officers, led by Roger Lafontant, seized control of the presidential palace, and forced Pascal-Trouillot to announce her resignation. However, the army remained loyal to the Government and arrested Lafontant and his associates.

A low turn-out in the second round of legislative voting, on 20 January 1991, was attributed to popular unease as a result of the recent coup attempt. The most successful party, the FNCD, won a further nine seats in the Chamber of Deputies, and an additional eight in the Senate, thereby failing to secure an overall majority in the two legislative chambers.

Aristide was inaugurated as President on 7 February 1991. The new Head of State subsequently initiated proceedings to secure the extradition from France of ex-President Duvalier to face charges involving the embezzlement of state funds, the abuse of power and the murder of his political opponents. Aristide also undertook the reform of the armed forces, as a result of which several senior officers were obliged to resign. In mid-February the new President nominated one of his close associates, René García Préval, as Prime Minister.

In April 1991 Ertha Pascal-Trouillot was arrested on charges of complicity in the attempted coup three months previously. She was initially released, pending the completion of investigations, and in September left the country. In June, confronted by growing public impatience at the Government's failure to control the economy, Aristide dismissed the Ministers of Trade and Industry and of Social Affairs. In early July, in an attempt to strengthen his control over an unruly and factionalized army, Aristide reorganized the senior level of the armed forces, replacing Gen. Hérard Abraham with Gen. (later Lt-Gen.) Raoul Cédras as Commander-in-Chief of the armed forces. In late July Roger Lafontant was found guilty of organizing the attempted coup of January 1991 and sentenced to life imprisonment. A further 21 conspirators received sentences ranging from 10 years to life imprisonment.

In August 1991 Préval suffered criticism by the legislature of his Government's policies and avoided a vote of 'no confidence' only when a mass demonstration by government supporters alarmed members of the legislature and caused the session to be abandoned. Parliamentary criticism of the Government centred on its reluctance to consult the legislature on the formation of its policies, and in particular on the dismissal of some 8,000 public-sector employees.

On 30 September 1991 a military junta, led by Gen. Cédras, overthrew the Government. Following diplomatic intervention by the USA, France and Venezuela, Aristide was allowed to go into exile. The coup received international condemnation, and an almost immediate economic embargo was imposed on Haiti by the Organization of American States (OAS, see p. 219). Many hundreds of people were reported to have been killed during the coup, including the imprisoned Roger Lafontant. On 7 October military units assembled 29 members of the legislature and coerced them into approving the appointment of Joseph Nerette as interim President, and several days later a new Cabinet was announced. The OAS, however, continued to recognize Aristide as the legitimate President.

During the following months the OAS attempted to negotiate a settlement. However, the two sides remained deadlocked over the conditions for Aristide's return, the main obstacles being Aristide's insistence that Cédras be imprisoned or exiled, and the legislature's demands for an immediate repeal of the OAS embargo and a general amnesty. In late February 1992 talks taking place under the supervision of the OAS in Washington, DC, between Aristide and members of a Haitian legislative delegation resulted in the signing of an agreement providing for the installation of René Théodore, leader of the Mouvement pour la Reconstruction Nationale, as Prime Minister, who was to govern in close consultation with the exiled Aristide and facilitate his return. Aristide undertook to respect all decisions taken by the legislature since the coup of September 1991, and agreed to a general amnesty for the police and armed forces. Prior to the meeting, Aristide had withdrawn a demand for the dismissal of Cédras as Commander-in-Chief of the armed forces (although he later renewed this demand). The economic embargo imposed by the OAS was to be revoked on ratification of the agreement by the legislature. However, in mid-March 1992 politicians who were opposed to the accord withdrew from a joint session of the Senate and the Chamber of Deputies, leaving it inquorate and unable to vote on the issue. Many politicians were reportedly coerced into abandoning the session by the threatening behaviour of troops who were present, and by earlier veiled threats made in a speech by interim President Nerette. In late March, following an appeal by Nerette, the Supreme Court declared the agreement null and void, on the grounds that it violated the Constitution by endangering the country's sovereignty. In response, the OAS requested its members to impose stricter economic sanctions against Haiti.

In late May 1992, following a tripartite summit meeting involving the legislature, the Government and the armed forces, an agreement providing for a 'consensus government' was ratified by the Senate. The agreement envisaged the appointment of a new Prime Minister and a multi-party government of national consensus to seek a solution to the political crisis and negotiate an end to the economic embargo. In early June the legislature, in the absence of the FNCD (which boycotted the sessions) approved the nomination of Marc Bazin, of the MIDH, to be Prime Minister. On 19 June Bazin took office, and Nerette resigned as President. Under the terms of the tripartite agreement, the presidency was left vacant, ostensibly to allow for Aristide's return, although commentators suggested that this was purely a political manoeuvre by the military-backed Government and that such an eventuality was unlikely. A Cabinet of 12 ministers and 13 state secretaries, comprising members of most major parties (with the significant exception of the FNCD), was installed, with the army retaining control of the interior and defence. The appointment of the new Government provoked world-wide condemnation, and the Vatican was the only state to give official recognition to the regime.

In July 1992 a 10-member 'presidential commission', headed by Fr Antoine Adrien, was appointed by Aristide to hold negotiations with what he termed the 'real forces' in Haiti, referring to the armed forces and the wealthy élite. In September, following a meeting in the USA between Adrien and the Minister of Foreign Affairs, François Benoît, the Government agreed to allow the presence of an 18-member OAS commission in Haiti to help to guarantee human rights, reduce violence and assess progress towards a resolution of the prevailing political crisis. In early February 1993 Bazin issued a communiqué stating that an agreement had been reached with the OAS and the UN on sending another international civil commission comprising some 200 representatives.

In April 1993 the joint envoy of the UN and the OAS, Dante Caputo, visited Haiti to present a series of proposals for the restoration of democratic rule in Haiti. These provided for the resignation of the military high command in return for a full amnesty for those involved in the coup of 1991, and for the establishment of a government of consensus and the eventual reinstatement of Aristide. A sum of US $1,000m. in economic aid was to become available once democracy was restored. However, the proposals were rejected by Cédras. In May 1993 a proposal to send a UN multilateral police force to oversee a period of transition pending Aristide's reinstatement was similarly rejected by Cédras as unconstitutional.

In early June 1993 the USA imposed sanctions against individuals and institutions viewed as supportive of the military regime, including the 'freezing' of assets held in the USA and the cancellation of US entry visas. Shortly afterwards Bazin resigned as Prime Minister. His position was believed to have become untenable following the refusal of several cabinet ministers to respect his demand for their resignation, and the withdrawal of the support in the legislature of the PANPRA—which deprived the Government of a parliamentary majority. In late June, following the imposition of a world-wide petroleum and arms embargo by the UN Security Council, Cédras agreed to attend talks with Aristide on Governor's Island, New York, under the auspices of the UN and the OAS. On 3 July the so-called Governor's Island peace accord was signed, delineating a 10-point agenda for Aristide's reinstatement. Under the terms of the accord the embargo was to be revoked following the installation of a new Prime Minister (to be appointed by Aristide), Cédras would retire and a new Commander-in-Chief of the armed forces would be appointed by Aristide, who would return to Haiti by 30 October. In mid-July the accord was approved by a meeting of Haiti's main political parties, and a six-month political 'truce' was agreed to facilitate the transition. Legislation providing for a series of political and institutional reforms, as required under the terms of the accord, was to be enacted, including provision for the transfer of the police force to civilian control.

In August 1993 the legislature ratified the appointment by Aristide of Robert Malval as Prime Minister. The UN Security Council subsequently suspended its petroleum and arms embargo. Malval was formally inaugurated by Aristide on 30 August in Washington. On 2 September Malval installed a 13-member Cabinet. In that month a concerted campaign of political violence and intimidation by police auxiliaries, known as 'attachés', threatened to undermine the Governor's Island accord. Demands made by Malval that the 'attachés' be disbanded were ignored by the chief of police, Col Joseph Michel François. With the upsurge of a Duvalierist tendency, largely embodied by the 'attachés', a new political party, the Front Revolutionnaire pour l'Avancement et le Progrès d'Haïti (FRAPH), was founded in opposition to any attempt to reinstate Aristide. In late September the UN Security Council approved a resolution providing for the immediate deployment of a lightly-armed United Nations Mission In Haiti (UNMIH, renamed United Nations Support Mission in Haiti in June 1996, and United Nations Transition Mission in Haiti in July 1997, see p. 55), comprising 1,267 members, to advise in the creation of a new police force and the modernization of the army.

In October 1993, in violation of the Governor's Island accord, Cédras and François refused to resign their posts, asserting that the terms of the amnesty offered by Aristide were not sufficiently broad. In that month the campaign of political violence by the 'attachés' escalated. A US vessel transporting members of the UNMIH was prevented from docking at Port-au-Prince, and its arrival prompted violent demonstrations of defiance by the 'attachés'. Several days later the Minister of Justice, Guy Malary, was assassinated. In response, the US Government ordered six warships into Haitian territorial waters to enforce the reimposed UN embargo. As a result of the instability, the UN/OAS international civil commission and other foreign government personnel were evacuated to the Dominican Republic.

In December 1993 Malval officially resigned as Prime Minister, although he remained in office pending the appointment of a successor. In discussions with the US Government held earlier in the month, Malval announced a new initiative for a National Salvation Conference, involving multi-sector negotiations (to include the military) on a return to democratic rule. However, Aristide rejected the proposals, proposing instead a National Reconciliation Conference, excluding the military, which took place in Miami, USA, in mid-January 1994. Following the military regime's failure to meet the revised UN deadline of 15 January to comply with the terms of the Governor's Island accord, in late January the USA unilaterally imposed further sanctions denying officers of the military regime access to assets held in the USA and cancelling their travel visas. In that month members of the UN/OAS international civil commission began to return to Haiti.

In early February 1994 a 13-member faction of the Senate—including eight members elected in January 1993 in partial legislative elections condemned as illegal by the USA and UN and widely regarded as an attempt by the military regime to legitimize its rule—appointed Bernard Sansaricq as President of the Senate. However the incumbent President of the Senate, Firmin Jean-Louis, did not relinquish his position and continued to be recognized by the international community. In mid-February Aristide rejected a peace plan drafted by the USA which envisaged the formation of a broad-based government as part of a compromise solution to the political crisis. Aristide refused to discuss the plan with a Haitian parliamentary delegation in Washington, demanding instead the implementation of the Governor's Island accord. In March a report by the UN/OAS international civil commission reflected a marked rise in the number of political killings perpetrated by paramilitary members of the FRAPH and by the 'attachés', with some 80 deaths recorded in the previous two-month period. In the same month Aristide rejected a further, revised, peace plan proposed by the USA on the grounds that it did not provide for the expulsion of the leaders of the military regime.

In April 1994, following intense pressure from members of the US Congress, the US Government abandoned its attempts to effect a compromise solution to the crisis in Haiti in favour of the implementation of more rigorous economic sanctions with a view to forcing the military regime to relinquish power. In late April the USA proposed a resolution to the UN Security Council endorsing the implementation of extended sanctions. On 6 May the UN Security Council approved a resolution introducing sanctions banning all international trade with Haiti, excluding food and medicine, reducing air links with the country and preventing members of the regime from gaining access to assets held outside Haiti. The new sanctions came into force on 22 May.

In early 1994 the 13-member faction of the Senate led by Bernard Sansaricq declared the presidency of the Republic vacant, invoking Article 149 of the Constitution which provides that, in case of prolonged absence by the Head of State, the position may be assumed by the President of the Court of Cassation. In May, with the support of the armed forces, the 13 senators and 30 members of the Chamber of Deputies—not a sufficient number to form a quorum—appointed the President of the Court of Cassation, Emile Jonassaint, provisional President of the Republic. Jonassaint subsequently appointed a new Cabinet. The appointment of the Jonassaint administration was denounced as illegal by the international community and by the outgoing acting Prime Minister, Robert Malval. Jonassaint's appointment also revealed a division within the three-man junta at the head of the military regime—namely Cédras, François and the Chief of Staff of the army, Brig.-Gen. Philippe Biamby. François reportedly opposed the move and did not attend the inauguration ceremony.

In June 1994 the USA unilaterally increased its sanctions against Haiti, banning all financial transactions, excluding humanitarian transfers, and extending the 'freeze' on assets held in the USA to all Haitians. In that month international air links with Haiti were further reduced.

In July 1994 the Haitian junta issued an order providing for the expulsion of the UN/OAS international civil commission. The order was immediately condemned by the UN Security Council, which duly determined to seek a rapid and definitive solution to the political situation in Haiti. The USA was reported to be making military preparations for a possible invasion of Haiti. On 31 July the UN Security Council passed a resolution authorizing 'all necessary means' to remove the military regime from power. The terms of the resolution also provided for a UN peace-keeping force to be deployed once stability had been achieved, to remain in Haiti until February 1996, when Aristide's presidential term expired. In August, following the failure of a peace mission by a UN envoy, the UN officially abandoned efforts to effect a peaceful solution to the crisis in Haiti. In the same month leaders of the Caribbean Community and Common Market (CARICOM, see p. 119) meeting in Jamaica agreed to support a US-led military invasion. Also in August, a contingent of UN monitors arrived in the Dominican Republic to observe the implementation of UN sanctions on that country's border with Haiti. An agreement between the UN and the Dominican Republic allowing for the deployment of the observer mission had been reached in early June following concern that the smuggling of goods, especially petroleum, on a large scale across the border was undermining the effectiveness of UN sanctions.

On 19 September 1994 a nominally multinational force comprised almost entirely of US troops began a peaceful occupation of Haiti. The occupation followed the diplomatic efforts of a mission led by former US President Carter which resulted in the drawing up of a compromise agreement on 18 September, thus narrowly avoiding a full-scale invasion. Under the terms of the agreement, the Haitian security forces were to co-operate with the multilateral force in effecting a transition to civilian rule. All sanctions were to be lifted and the military junta granted 'early and honourable retirement' following legislative approval of a general amnesty law, or by 15 October at the latest (the date when Aristide was to return from exile to resume his presidency). The agreement did not, however, require the junta's departure from Haiti, nor did it address the reform of the security forces. In response to the agreement, the joint envoy of the UN and the OAS, Dante Caputo, resigned from his position citing the absence of consultation as the reason for his departure; he was succeeded by Lakhdar Brahimi. In late September the legislature began a joint session to discuss the draft amnesty law. Those legislators elected illegally in January 1993 were replaced by legislators returning from exile in the USA. Following the occupation, acts of violence by the Haitian police against supporters of Aristide led to a modification of the rules of operation of the multinational force, allowing for intervention to curb the violence. Following this modification, a confrontation between Haitian police and US troops in Cap-Haïtien resulted in the death of 10 Haitian police.

In late September 1994 the UN Security Council approved a resolution ending all sanctions against Haiti with effect from the day after the return to Haiti of Aristide. The USA had already announced, on 26 September, the suspension of its unilateral sanctions, although the Haitian military's assets in the USA remained 'frozen'.

In early October 1994 Aristide signed a decree authorizing legislation, approved by the legislature that month, for the amnesty of those involved in the coup of September 1991. Cédras and Biamby promptly went into exile in Panama, whilst François was reported to have already fled to the Dominican Republic where he was granted asylum. Later that month the USA formally ended its 'freeze' on the assets of the Haitian military regime, estimated to be worth some US $79m. On 12 October Robert Malval resumed office as interim Prime Minister following the resignation of the Jonassaint administration. Aristide returned to Haiti on 15 October to resume his presidency and on 25 October appointed Smarck Michel as Prime Minister. In the same month Aristide appointed Gen. Jean-Claude Duperval provisional Commander-in-Chief of the armed forces and Gen. Bernardin Poisson Chief of Staff of the army, replacing Cédras and Biamby, respectively.

A new Cabinet, comprising mainly members of the pro-Aristide Organisation Politique Lavalas (OPL), was inaugurated on 8 November 1994, with several further appointments made later in that month. The Cabinet included five new ministries, of culture, public administration, the environment, women's affairs and rights, and the Ministry of the 10th Department, with responsibility for Haitians residing abroad. The government programme announced that month envisaged measures including the reform of the security forces and the separation of the police from the army, the decentralization of government, economic democratization and the restructuring of the public sector. In mid-November Gen. Poisson succeeded Gen. Duperval as Commander-in-Chief of the armed forces. Later that month the legislature approved the separation of the police from the army, by which time some 3,000 of the Haitian armed forces, selected as free from accusations of human rights abuses, had undergone a rapid training course under the supervision of US and Canadian instructors to form part of a 4,000-strong interim police force. The remaining 1,000 recruits were returned refugees who had been trained for the purpose while at the refugee camp at Guantánamo, Cuba (see below).

In December 1994 the formation of a new CEP, responsible for organizing and supervising the forthcoming legislative, local and municipal elections, was completed. However, due to procedural delays the elections were thought unlikely to be held until mid-1995, leaving a period of legislative inactivity, between the end of the current legislative term, ending in January 1995, and the inauguration of a new legislature, at a time when reform would be vital to the successful transition to peaceful civilian rule. In mid-December 1994 Aristide authorized the creation of a national commission of truth and justice to investigate past human rights violations, and ordered the reduction of the armed forces to 1,500 (from an estimated combined army and police force of 7,000–7,500). In the following month two commissions were established for the restructuring of the armed forces and the new civilian police force.

In January 1995 US military commanders certified that the situation in Haiti was sufficiently stable to enable the transfer of authority to the UN. On 30 January the UN Security Council adopted a resolution authorizing the deployment of a UN force of 6,000 troops and 900 civil police to succeed the incumbent multinational force. The UN force, entitled (like that deployed in 1993) the United Nations Mission in Haiti (UNMIH), was to be led by a US commander and include some 2,400 US troops. It was to be responsible for reducing the strength of the army and training both the army and the 4,000-strong (subsequently increased to 6,000) civilian police force, as well as maintaining the 'secure and stable' environment. In February it was announced that the legislative, local and municipal elections (including elections to 18 of the 27 seats in the Senate, all 83 seats in the Chamber of Deputies, 125 mayorships and 555 local councils) would be held on 4 June, with a second round of voting on 25 June. In February Aristide retired the 43 most senior-ranking officers in the armed forces, leaving Maj. Dany Toussaint as the officer of highest rank.

On 31 March 1995, against a background of increasing violence and criticism at the inadequacy of the interim police force, authority was officially transferred from the multinational force to the UNMIH. The security situation deteriorated further in April, prompting demonstrations in support of demands for the resignation of Michel. The protests also revealed widespread discontent at high prices, unemployment and the planned privatization of state enterprises. In that month the CEP announced a revision of the electoral timetable, postponing the elections until 25 June and 16 July, respectively. In late April Aristide announced that, following the election of the new legislature, he would seek a constitutional amendment providing for the abolition of the armed forces. (The armed forces were subsequently disbanded, although the constitutional amendment providing for their official abolition could not be approved until the end of the new legislative term.)

Owing to administrative failures and isolated incidents of violence and intimidation, voting at the first round of the legislative, local and municipal elections that were held on 25 June 1995 continued into the following day. Despite the extension, thousands of intending voters were unable to participate, and a further, complementary poll was to be scheduled. The widespread irregularities prompted several opposition parties to demand the annulment of the elections and the dissolution of the CEP, which many perceived as too closely associated with the OPL, the party with majority representation in the Government. The official election results, which were released in mid-July, indicated that all of the 21 seats so far decided had been won by the Plate-forme Politique Lavalas (PPL), a three-party electoral alliance comprising the OPL, the Mouvement d'Organisation du Pays and the Pati Louvri Baryè. The results were rejected by the majority of opposition parties, which announced a boycott of the electoral process. Continued criticism of the CEP by the opposition led to the resignation of the President of the CEP, Anselme Rémy, in late July.

In early August 1995 the FNCD, MIDH and PANPRA withdrew their respective representatives from the Government, in protest at the absence of a resolution to the electoral dispute. Jean-Claude Bajeux of the Comité National du Congrès des Movements Démocratiques (KONAKOM) resisted his party's demand that he resign, and, as the Minister of Culture, remained the sole opposition member in the Cabinet. On 13 August, following successive postponements, the complementary elections, for voters who had been denied the opportunity to vote on 25 June, were conducted in 21 districts. A further 17 seats were decided, all of which were won by the PPL. In late August the US Government presented a plan aimed at resolving the electoral dispute and salvaging the electoral process, which was widely perceived as discredited. The proposals, which included the annulment of the first round elections in many areas, were rejected by the CEP, which subsequently announced that the second round would be conducted on 17 September. The elections were held as scheduled, despite the boycott which was maintained by the main opposition parties, and resulted in further large gains for the PPL, which won 17 of the 18 contested seats in the 27-member Senate and 68 seats in the 83-member Chamber of Deputies. The remaining contested seats were won mainly by independent candidates.

In October 1995 Michel resigned as Prime Minister, as a result of opposition from Aristide and from within the Cabinet to his negotiations with the IMF and the World Bank concerning economic adjustment, and, in particular, to plans for the divestment of state enterprises. Michel was succeeded by the Minister of Foreign Affairs, Claudette Werleigh, who took office on 7 November, when a new Cabinet was also sworn in. Werleigh indicated that the new administration intended to retain control of strategic state enterprises and would seek a national debate on the issue of privatization.

In November 1995, despite extensive popular support for Aristide to continue in office for a further three years (to compensate for those years spent in exile), the President confirmed that he would leave office in February 1996. At a presidential election held on 17 December 1995, which was boycotted by all the main opposition parties except KONAKOM, the candidate endorsed by Aristide, René Préval (who had been Prime Minister between February and September 1991), was elected with some 87.9% of the votes cast. In December 1995 Aristide formally disbanded the interim police force, which had, since June, been in the process of being replaced by the new civilian police force. However, the decision by Aristide to assimilate some 1,500 remaining members of the interim force into the new force prompted protest from the USA, which suspended US $5m. in funding for the police training programme, claiming that the members of the interim force were 'politicized'. The funds were restored in January 1996, on condition that the screening of the new force (to eliminate 'undesirable elements') was strictly maintained. Préval was inaugurated as President on 7 February, and later that month the legislature approved the appointment of Rosny Smarth as Prime Minister. A new Cabinet was sworn in on 6 March. In late February the UN Security Council extended the mandate of the UNMIH peace-keeping force for a period of four months. US troops withdrew from the force, which was reduced to 1,200 troops and 300 civil police. Canada provided an additional 700 troops at its own expense to support the UNMIH. In late June the mandate was renewed, with effect from 1 July, for a period of five months with a further reduction, by 600 troops, in the strength of the peace-keeping force, which was renamed the United Nations Support Mission in Haiti (UNSMIH).

The months following the inauguration of the Smarth administration were marked by a high incidence of violence in the capital. Some seven members of the civilian police force were murdered over a three-month period, in what was interpreted by Préval as an attempt by anti-democratic forces to destabilize the Government. In mid-August 1996, against a background of unrest and general hostility towards government economic policy, in particular plans for the privatization of state enterprises which were approved by the legislature that month, a series of armed attacks were conducted against public buildings, including the parliament building and the central police headquarters. The attacks followed the arrest that month, at the headquarters of the right-wing Mobilisation pour le Développement National (MDN), of some 20 former officers of the armed forces who were accused of plotting against the Government. Earlier, violent action had been threatened by former soldiers demanding due payment of salary arrears and pensions. On 20 August, two leading members of the MDN were murdered by unidentified gunmen. Opposition politicians accused the Government of responsibility for the killings, which they interpreted as an act of retaliation against the former soldiers and their allies. Subsequently, US officials produced evidence implicating members of the presidential guard in the murders, and in mid-September, on the advice of the US Government, Préval dismissed the head of the presidential guard and initiated a reorganization of the unit, which was conducted with the assistance of some 30 US security agents who were sent to protect the President. Also in August the Government pledged to meet the demands of former soldiers for payment of salary arrears and pensions.

In November 1996, as a result of diverging interests within the PPL, Aristide officially established a new political party, La Fanmi Lavalas, which, it was anticipated, would promote his candidacy for the next presidential election. Aristide had openly expressed his opposition to Préval's adoption of economic policies proposed by the IMF, notably the privatization of state enterprises.

In early December 1996 the UN Security Council approved a final extension of the mandate of the UNSMIH until 31 May 1997 (with an option to extend it for a further two months, which was subsequently adopted). There continued to be serious and widespread concern regarding the ability of the Haitian civilian police force to maintain order once the UN force had withdrawn from the country. In late 1996 a series of strikes were conducted by employees in the education, health and transport sectors in support of salary demands and in protest at price rises and poor working conditions. Protest against the Government escalated in early 1997. In mid-January a general strike, in support of demands for the resignation of the Smarth administration and the reversal of the planned divestment of state enterprises, was called by grass-roots organizations, and received considerable support. In March the Government narrowly avoided losing a confidence motion in the legislature.

On 6 April 1997 partial legislative elections were held for nine of the 27 seats in the Senate and two seats in the Chamber of Deputies, as well as elections to local councils. The elections were boycotted by many opposition parties, and less than 10% of the electorate participated in the poll. Of the legislative seats contested only two, in the Senate, were decided, both of which were secured by candidates of the La Fanmi Lavalas. The OPL, the majority party in the governing coalition, alleged that members of the CEP had manipulated the election results in favour of Aristide's party, and demanded the resignation of the CEP, the annulment of the election results and the conduct of a fresh ballot. La Fanmi Lavalas maintained that the results should stand. Reports from OAS observers of the poll supported the claims of electoral irregularities, and, following strong international pressure the CEP postponed the second round of the elections, which were scheduled for 25 May, until mid-June. The OPL had announed that it would boycott the second round elections.

In the light of mounting popular opposition, on 9 June 1997 Smarth resigned from office, although he remained Prime Minister in a caretaker capacity pending the appointment of a replacement. Smarth criticized the CEP for failing to annul the results of the April elections and thus perpetuating the electoral impasse. That month the CEP announced the indefinite postponement of the second round of elections.

On 30 July 1997 the UN Security Council voted to retain a reduced mission in Haiti for a further four months. The UN Transition Mission in Haiti (UNTMIH) was to include 250 police and 50 soldiers. In that month Préval nominated Ericq Pierre to replace Smarth as Prime Minister. However, in the following month the Chamber of Deputies rejected his nomination. In the light of Préval's failure to nominate a candidate for Prime Minister who was acceptable to the legislature, on 20 October Smarth announced that he was to cease his role as caretaker Prime Minister and recommended that his Cabinet resign. Several ministers complied with this request and in late October Préval redesignated their portfolios to remaining cabinet members.

In early November 1997, in an effort to resolve the political crisis, Préval nominated Hervé Y. Denis, an economist and former Minister of Information, Culture and Co-ordination in the Government of Robert Malval, as Prime Minister. In addition, Préval announced the establishment of an electoral commission, comprising three independent legal experts, to resolve the electoral deadlock, and the resignation of six of the nine members of the CEP. The OPL, however, continued to demand the annulment of the April elections and the replacement of the entire CEP. In that month the UN Security Council voted to replace the UNTMIH with a 290-strong international police force to remain in Haiti for a further year. The Haitian civilian police force was still considered incapable of maintaining security unassisted. The UNTMIH departed from Haiti on schedule on 30 November.

The political crisis remained unresolved in February 1998. In January La Fanmi Lavalas had rejected a proposal by the OPL for the creation of a body to mediate in the legislature towards creating a working majority and thus facilitating the appointment of a new Prime Minister. Earlier in the month the legislature had formally notified Denis that he was not considered an appropriate candidate for Prime Minister. In February the Organisation Politique Lavalas (OPL) renamed itself the Organisation du Peuple en Lutte (OPL).

International relations, although improved after 1971, continued to be strained because of Haiti's unpopular political regimes and government corruption. Relations between Haiti and its neighbour on the island of Hispaniola, the Dominican Republic, have traditionally been tense because of the use of the border area by anti-Government guerrillas, smugglers and illegal emigrants, resulting in the periodic closure of the border. Relations between the Dominican Republic and Haiti deteriorated in mid-1991, following a unilateral decision by President Balaguer of the Dominican Republic to repatriate all illegal Haitian residents aged under 16 or over 60, thus placing a considerable burden on Haiti's resources. In March 1996, following an official visit to the Dominican Republic by Préval, the first by a Haitian President since 1935, a joint communiqué was issued establishing a bilateral commission to promote improved co-operation between the two countries. In February 1997, following a rash of repatriations of Haitian refugees from the Dominican Republic, a further communiqué was signed outlining new conditions for the process of repatriation.

Following the coup of 30 September 1991, the USA came under international criticism for its forced repatriation of Haitian refugees fleeing the repressive military regime. In mid-November, following an appeal by the Haitian Refugee Center in Miami, USA, a US federal judge in Florida ordered a temporary halt to the repatriation. More than 10,000 refugees were taken into custody by the US coastguard in the period following the coup, the majority of whom were transported to a specially provided camp at the US naval base at Guantánamo, Cuba. However, at the end of January 1992 the US Supreme Court annulled the federal judge's ruling, and repatriation resumed. While a small percentage of refugees were considered for political asylum, the US Government insisted that the majority were economic refugees and therefore not eligible for asylum in the USA. In late May President Bush issued an executive order providing for refugees who were intercepted at sea by the US coastguard to be repatriated immediately without any evaluation being made of their right to asylum. The decision, which was condemned by human rights groups as a violation of international law, was overturned in late July by an appeals court in New York. However, in early August the US Supreme Court suspended the decision of the appeals court, and the executive order stood pending a definitive ruling by the Supreme Court itself. In mid-August fears for the safety of repatriated Haitians were redoubled when Haitian security forces immediately detained some 150 refugees on their return. The policy of President Bush concerning Haitian immigration continued under the presidency of Bill Clinton, despite promises to the contrary made during his election campaign. In January 1993, in response to concern that his election victory might encourage a considerable increase in Haitians seeking refuge, Clinton urged them not to flee Haiti and promised renewed efforts to find a democratic solution to the crisis. In June 1993 the US Supreme Court ruled to uphold the executive order of May 1992, continued under the Clinton administration, which provided for the forcible repatriation of Haitian refugees intercepted at sea.

In April 1994 Aristide announced that he was to abrogate a treaty signed in 1981 under the terms of which the USA was authorized to forcibly repatriate Haitian refugees intercepted at sea. In May, following concerted pressure by US groups, including a 40-strong black caucus in the US Congress, the US Government reversed its policy regarding Haitian refugees, agreeing to resume hearings for all asylum applications—to be conducted at screening centres established later on the British dependent territory of the island of Grand Turk and off the shore of Jamaica. The new policy, which took effect on 17 June, prompted a renewed exodus of thousands of refugees forcing a further change of US policy in July under which refugees granted asylum were henceforth to be held indefinitely in 'safe havens' outside the USA. In that month, however, Panama withdrew an offer to receive 10,000 Haitian refugees, necessitating a concomitant increase in the capacity of refugee facilities at Guantánamo. The USA did, however, receive commitments from several Central and South American countries to receive small numbers of refugees for limited periods. In January 1995, following a failed attempt, which included financial incentives, to persuade Haitian refugees at Guantánamo to return voluntarily to Haiti, the US Government ordered the immediate forcible repatriation of nearly all Haitians at the camp. By mid-January their repatriation was virtually complete. In the same month a repatriation accord was signed with the Bahamas providing for the return of some 10,000 refugees to Haiti by the end of 1995.

Government

The Constitution, approved by referendum in March 1987, provided for a bicameral legislature, comprising a 77-member Chamber of Deputies (later enlarged to 83 members) and a 27-member Senate. The Chamber of Deputies was elected for a term of four years, while the Senate was elected for a term of six years with one-third renewed every two years. Both houses were elected by universal adult suffrage. Executive power was held by the President, who was elected by universal adult suffrage for a five-year term and could not stand for immediate re-election. The President selected a Prime Minister from the political party commanding a majority in the legislature. The Prime Minister chose a Cabinet in consultation with the President. However, the Constitution was interrupted by successive coups, in June and September 1988 and September 1991. A return to constitutional rule was finally effected in October 1994, following the intervention of a US-led multinational force and the reinstatement of the exiled President Aristide.

There are nine Départements, subdivided into arrondissements and communes.

Defence

In November 1994, following the return to civilian rule, measures providing for the separation of the armed forces from the police force were approved by the legislature. In December President Aristide ordered the reduction of the armed forces to 1,500. In that month two commissions were established for the restructuring of the armed forces and the formation of a new 4,000-strong civilian police force (later enlarged to 6,000). In 1995 the armed forces were effectively dissolved, although officially they remained in existence pending an amendment to the Constitution providing for their abolition. In early 1996 the legislature undertook to adopt such an amendment at the end of the legislative term. The security budget for 1997 was an estimated US $32m.

Economic Affairs

In 1995, according to estimates by the World Bank, Haiti's gross national product (GNP), measured at average 1993–95 prices, was US $1,777m., equivalent to $250 per head. During 1985–95, it was estimated, GNP per head declined, in real terms, by an average of 5.2% per year. Over the same period the population increased by an annual average of 2.0%. According to the World Bank, Haiti's gross domestic product (GDP) decreased, in real terms, by an annual average of 3.1% in 1985–95. Real GDP increased by 3.8% in 1995.

Agriculture (including hunting, forestry and fishing) contributed an estimated 42.2% of GDP in 1995, according to the World Bank. About 65.3% of the employed labour force were engaged in agricultural activities in 1996. The principal cash crop is coffee (which accounted for 16.6% of export earnings in 1994/95). The export of oils for cosmetics and pharmaceuticals is also important. The main food crops are sugar, bananas, maize, sweet potatoes and rice. During 1985–95, according to the World Bank, agricultural output increased by an annual average of 0.2%; production increased by an estimated 1.5% in 1996.

Industry (including mining, manufacturing, construction and power) contributed an estimated 12.8% of GDP in 1995, according to the World Bank. About 8.8% of the employed labour force were engaged in the sector in 1990. According to the World Bank, industrial GDP declined by an annual average of 9.1% in 1985–95; it fell by 31.5% in 1994, before increasing by an estimated 9.3% in 1995.

Mining contributed less than 0.1% of GDP in 1993/94. About 1% of the employed labour force were engaged in extractive activities in 1990. Marble, limestone and calcareous clay are mined. There are also unexploited copper, silver and gold deposits.

Manufacturing contributed an estimated 9.5% of GDP in 1995, according to the World Bank. About 6.5% of the employed labour force were engaged in the sector in 1990. The most important branches in 1987/88, measured by contribution to GDP, were food products, metal products and machinery, and textiles. According to the World Bank, manufacturing GDP decreased by an average of 7.6% per year in 1985–95, and by 33.3% in 1994, before increasing by an estimated 0.6% in 1995.

Energy is derived principally from local timber and charcoal. Imports of fuel products accounted for an estimated 14.8% of the value of merchandise imports in 1994/95.

The services sector contributed an estimated 45.0% of GDP in 1995, according to the World Bank, and engaged 22.8% of the employed labour force in 1990. According to the World Bank, the GDP of the services sector declined by an average of 3.3% per year in 1985–95, and by 11.0% in 1994, before increasing by an estimated 4.8% in 1995.

In 1995/96 Haiti recorded a visible trade deficit of US $416.1m., and there was a deficit of $137.7m. on the current account of the balance of payments. In 1991/92 the principal source of imports (45.7%) was the USA; other major suppliers were Japan, France and Canada. The USA was also the principal market for exports (53.1%) in that year; other significant purchasers were Italy, France and Belgium. The principal exports in 1994/95 were manufactured articles (53.8%) and coffee. The principal imports in that year were food and live animals (45.1%) and machinery and transport equipment.

In the financial year ending 30 September 1996 there was a budgetary deficit of 329.5m. gourdes (equivalent to 0.8% of GDP). At the end of 1995 Haiti's total external debt was US $806.8m., of which $751.8m. was long-term public debt. In that year the cost of debt-servicing was equivalent to 45.2% of the total value of exports of goods and services. The annual rate of inflation averaged 14.6% in 1985–95. Consumer prices increased by an annual average of 20.6% in 1996. Some 70% of the labour force were estimated to be unemployed in 1997.

Haiti is a member of the International Coffee Organization (see p. 257) and the Latin American Economic System (SELA, see p. 261). In July 1997 Haiti was granted admission to the Caribbean Community and Common Market (CARICOM, see p. 119), conditional upon the implementation of IMF-approved structural adjustment measures.

In terms of average income, Haiti is among the poorest countries in the Western hemisphere, and there is extreme inequality of wealth. The suspension of all non-humanitarian aid and the imposition of successive, and increasingly severe, economic sanctions by the international community, following the military coup of September 1991, had devastating effects on the Haitian economy, serving to exacerbate the extreme poverty endured by the majority of the population. Following the return to civilian rule in late 1994, sanctions were ended and preparations made for the release of aid and new loans. At a meeting of donor nations in Paris in late January 1995 measures were agreed for the implementation of an Emergency Economic Recovery Programme, including commitments for the disbursement of $660m. in aid and $240m. in supplementary credits over the following 15 months, subject to the conclusion of a stand-by agreement with the IMF. However, structural adjustment measures stipulated by the IMF, notably the divestment of public enterprises and the rationalization of the civil service, were not approved by the legislature until late 1996. As a result, the IMF approved a three-year credit of US $131m. under an Enhanced Structural Adjustment Facility, which, in turn, facilitated access to further multilateral development aid totalling in excess of $1,000m. However, a parliamentary dispute concerning partial legislative elections held in April 1997, in addition to concerted political opposition to the Government's adjustment programme, obstructed the implementation of the reforms, thus delaying the disbursement of the development aid. This, in turn, prevented the Government from delivering promised improvements in living standards, serving to increase widespread popular opposition to the Government's economic policy.

Social Welfare

Industrial and commercial workers are provided with free health care. In 1980 Haiti had 52 hospital establishments, with a total of only 3,964 beds, equivalent to one for every 1,264 inhabitants: the lowest level of provision in any country of the Western hemisphere. In 1984 there were 810 physicians working in the country. Public health received an allocation of 89.5m. gourdes in the Government's budget for 1984/85. Religious and other voluntary groups provide medical services in rural areas and in Port-au-Prince.

Education

Education is provided by the State, by the Roman Catholic Church and by other religious organizations, but many schools charge for tuition, books or uniforms. Teaching is based on the French model, and French is used as the language of instruction. Primary education, which normally begins at six years and lasts for six years, is officially compulsory. Secondary education usually begins at 12 years of age and lasts for a further six years, comprising two cycles of three years each. In 1990 primary enrolment included only 26% of children in the relevant age-group (25% of boys; 26% of girls). Enrolment at secondary schools in 1990 was equivalent to only 22% of children in the relevant age-group (22% of boys; 21% of girls). In 1985, according to estimates by UNESCO, the average rate of adult illiteracy was 62.4% (males 59.9%; females 64.7%), the highest national level in the Western hemisphere. The rate was even higher in rural areas (about 85%), where Creole is the popular language. Some basic adult education programmes, with instruction in Creole, were created in an attempt to redress the problem of adult illiteracy. By 1995, according to UNESCO estimates, the rate had fallen to 55.0% (males 52.0%; females 57.8%). Higher education is provided by 18 vocational training centres and 42 domestic science schools, and by the Université d'Etat d'Haïti, which has faculties of law, medicine, dentistry, science, agronomy, pharmacy, economic science, veterinary medicine and ethnology. Government expenditure on education in 1990 was 216m. gourdes, equivalent to 20.0% of total government expenditure.

Public Holidays

1998: 1 January (Independence Day), 2 January (Heroes of Independence), 23 February (Shrove Monday, half-day), 24 February (Shrove Tuesday), 10 April (Good Friday), 14 April (Pan-American Day), 1 May (Labour Day), 18 May (Flag Day), 22 May (National Sovereignty), 15 August (Assumption), 24 October (United Nations Day), 2 November (All Souls' Day, half-day), 18 November (Army Day and Commemoration of the Battle of Vertières), 5 December (Discovery Day), 25 December (Christmas Day).

1999: 1 January (Independence Day), 2 January (Heroes of Independence), 15 February (Shrove Monday, half-day), 16 February (Shrove Tuesday), 2 April (Good Friday) 14 April (Pan-American Day), 1 May (Labour Day), 18 May (Flag Day), 22 May (National Sovereignty), 15 August (Assumption), 24 October (United Nations Day), 2 November (All Souls' Day, half-day), 18 November (Army Day and Commemoration of the Battle of Vertières), 5 December (Discovery Day), 25 December (Christmas Day).

Weights and Measures

Officially the metric system is in force but many US measures are also used.

Statistical Survey

Sources (unless otherwise stated): Banque de la République d'Haïti, angle rue du Magasin d'État et rue des Miracles, Port-au-Prince; tel. 22-4700; telex 0394; fax 22-2607; Ministère des Finances, Port-au-Prince.

Area and Population

AREA, POPULATION AND DENSITY

Area (sq km)	27,750*
Population (census results)†	
31 August 1971	4,329,991
30 August 1982	
Males	2,448,370
Females	2,605,422
Total	5,053,792
Population (official estimates at mid-year)‡	
1994	7,041,000
1995	7,180,000
1996	7,336,000
Density (per sq km) at mid-1996	264.4

* 10,714 sq miles.
† Excluding adjustment for underenumeration.
‡ Provisional figures.

DEPARTMENTS (provisional population estimates, 1987)

Artibonite	789,019	North-West	320,632
Central	393,217	South	526,420
Grande-Anse	514,962	South-East	379,273
North	602,336	West	1,811,698
North-East	197,669	**Total**	5,535,226

PRINCIPAL TOWN

Port-au-Prince (capital), estimated population 690,168 at mid-1990.

BIRTHS AND DEATHS (UN estimates, annual averages)

	1980–85	1985–90	1990–95
Birth rate (per 1,000)	36.6	36.2	35.3
Death rate (per 1,000)	14.5	13.2	11.9

Expectation of life (UN estimates, years at birth, 1990–95): 56.6 (males 54.9; females 58.3).

Source: UN, *World Population Prospects: The 1994 Revision.*

ECONOMICALLY ACTIVE POPULATION
(official estimates, persons aged 10 years and over, mid-1990)

	Males	Females	Total
Agriculture, hunting, forestry and fishing	1,077,191	458,253	1,535,444
Mining and quarrying	11,959	12,053	24,012
Manufacturing	83,180	68,207	151,387
Electricity, gas and water	1,643	934	2,577
Construction	23,584	4,417	28,001
Trade, restaurants and hotels	81,632	271,338	352,970
Transport, storage and communications	17,856	2,835	20,691
Financing, insurance, real estate and business services	3,468	1,589	5,057
Community, social and personal services	81,897	73,450	155,347
Activities not adequately defined	33,695	30,280	63,975
Total employed	1,416,105	923,356	2,339,461
Unemployed	191,333	148,346	339,679
Total labour force	1,607,438	1,071,702	2,679,140

Source: ILO, *Yearbook of Labour Statistics.*

Agriculture

PRINCIPAL CROPS ('000 metric tons)

	1994*	1995*	1996
Rice (paddy)	105	100	96
Maize	210	190	204
Sweet potatoes	185	185	183
Dry beans	50	30	49
Sugar cane	1,300	1,200	1,200
Bananas	233	235	239
Coffee (green)	31	29	27
Cocoa beans	6	7	4

* FAO estimates.

Source: FAO, *Production Yearbook.*

LIVESTOCK
('000 head, year ending September)

	1994	1995	1996
Horses*	470	480	490
Mules*	80	80	80
Asses*	210	210	210
Cattle	1,234†	1,240*	1,246
Pigs	360†	430*	500
Sheep	180*	182*	184
Goats	1,560*	1,600*	1,657

Chickens (million): 6* in 1994; 6* in 1995; 6 in 1996.

* FAO estimate(s). † Unofficial figure.

Source: FAO, *Production Yearbook.*

LIVESTOCK PRODUCTS ('000 metric tons)

	1994	1995	1996
Beef and veal	28†	28*	29
Goat meat	6*	6*	6
Pig meat*	20	20	20
Horse meat*	5	5	5
Poultry meat*	9	9	10
Cows' milk	40*	38*	37
Goats' milk*	19	19	20
Hen eggs*	4	4	4
Cattle hides*	3	3	4

* FAO estimate(s). † Unofficial figure.

Source: FAO, *Production Yearbook.*

Forestry

ROUNDWOOD REMOVALS
(FAO estimates, '000 cubic metres, excl. bark)

	1992	1993	1994
Sawlogs, veneer logs and logs for sleepers*	224	224	224
Other industrial wood*	15	15	15
Fuel wood	5,812	5,932	6,054
Total	6,051	6,171	6,293

* Assumed to be unchanged since 1971.

Sawnwood production (FAO estimates, '000 cubic metres, including railway sleepers): 14 per year in 1977–94.

Source: FAO, *Yearbook of Forest Products.*

Fishing

(FAO estimates, '000 metric tons, live weight)

	1993	1994	1995
Freshwater fishes	0.6	0.5	0.5
Marine fishes	3.7	3.4	3.6
Caribbean spiny lobster	0.8	0.8	0.9
Inshore shrimps	0.1	0.1	0.2
Stromboid conchs	0.4	0.4	0.4
Total catch	5.6	5.2	5.5

Source: FAO, *Yearbook of Fishery Statistics.*

Mining

('000 metric tons, year ending 30 September)

	1985/86	1986/87
Limestone	217.5	246.4
Calcareous clay	42.1	35.2

Industry

SELECTED PRODUCTS ('000 metric tons, unless otherwise indicated—year ending 30 September)

	1990/91	1991/92	1992/93
Wheat flour	62.0	11.6	n.a.
Cigarettes (million)	1,101.9	953.4	1,004.9
Soap	50.9	35.1	35.9
Cement	211.0	106.4	22.3
Electric energy (million kWh)	491.2	358.8	420.8

1993/94: Cement ('000 metric tons) 228; Electric energy (million kWh) 362 (preliminary figure). (Source: UN, *Industrial Commodity Statistics Yearbook.*)

Finance

CURRENCY AND EXCHANGE RATES

Monetary Units

100 centimes = 1 gourde.

Sterling and Dollar Equivalents (30 September 1997)

£1 sterling = 27.38 gourdes;
US $1 = 16.95 gourdes;
1,000 gourdes = £36.52 = $59.00.

Average Exchange Rate (gourdes per US $)

1993	13.5
1994	14.6
1995	15.0

Note: The official rate of exchange was maintained at US $1 = 5 gourdes until September 1991, when the central bank ceased all operations at the official rate, thereby unifying the exchange system at the 'floating' free market rate.

BUDGET (million gourdes, year ending 30 September)

Revenue*	1992/93	1993/94	1994/95
Current receipts	927.1	647.2	2,276.9
Internal receipts	747.9	542.2	1,853.1
Income tax	151.1	159.1	247.2
Turnover tax	229.5	160.9	476.9
Excises	167.9	26.3	501.5
Other domestic receipts	199.4	195.9	627.5
Customs	179.2	105.0	423.8
Transfers from public enterprises	36.5	10.9	200.7
Total	963.6	662.6†	2,477.6

* Excluding grants received (million gourdes): 0.0 in 1992/93; 12.4 in 1993/94; 864.7 in 1994/95.
† Including adjustment.

Expenditure	1992/93	1993/94	1994/95
Current expenditure	1,440.1	1,270.2	3,213.4
Wages and salaries	1,119.7	1,167.4	1,414.8
Operations	320.4	102.8	1,798.6
Subsidies	34.6	25.7	292.8
Investment	62.2	122.0	352.4
Interest on public debt	1.2	38.0	247.9
External debt	–	–	190.2
Internal debt	1.2	38.0	57.7
Total	1,538.1	1,617.2*	4,106.5

* Including adjustment.

1995/96 (million gourdes): Total revenue 3,436.1, excluding grants (354.3); Total expenditure 4,119.9 (Source: IMF, *International Financial Statistics*).

INTERNATIONAL RESERVES (US $ million at 31 December)*

	1994	1995	1996
IMF special drawing rights	—	0.5	0.1
Reserve position in IMF	0.1	0.1	0.1
Foreign exchange	30.9	105.2	107.8
Total	30.9	105.8	107.9

* Excluding gold (valued at market-related prices, US $ million): 6.6 in 1989.

Source: IMF, *International Financial Statistics.*

MONEY SUPPLY (million gourdes at 31 December)

	1994	1995	1996
Currency outside banks	3,029.5	3,536.7	3,386.1
Demand deposits at commercial banks	1,578.0	2,372.7	2,211.1
Total money (incl. adjustment)	5,095.5	6,703.9	5,739.6

Source: IMF, *International Financial Statistics.*

COST OF LIVING

(Consumer Price Index, year ending 30 September; base: 1991 = 100)

	1991/92	1992/93	1993/94
Food	119.0	134.3	182.0
Clothing and footwear	114.4	134.0	186.4
Furnishings	117.8	154.7	190.1
Housing, heating and light	108.3	138.9	204.9
Services	112.5	137.5	226.7
All items	115.6	137.3	186.9

NATIONAL ACCOUNTS
(million gourdes, year ending 30 September)

Expenditure on the Gross Domestic Product (at current prices)

	1993/94	1994/95	1995/96
Final consumption expenditure	27,735	45,623	47,671
Increase in stocks Gross fixed capital formation	2,063	3,568	3,989
Total domestic expenditure	29,798	49,191	51,660
Exports of goods and services	2,729	4,269	5,271
Less Imports of goods and services	4,834	11,910	13,409
GDP in purchasers' values	27,693	41,550	43,523
GDP at constant 1989/90 prices	10,172	10,618	10,913

Source: IMF, *International Financial Statistics*.

Gross Domestic Product by Economic Activity
(at constant 1975/76 prices)

	1991/92*	1992/93†	1993/94†
Agriculture, hunting, forestry and fishing	1,731.6	1,593.5	1,464.3
Mining and quarrying	3.6	2.5	1.3
Manufacturing	569.9	534.3	392.4
Electricity, gas and water	31.0	34.1	18.4
Construction	201.3	140.9	70.4
Trade, restaurants and hotels	472.4	426.7	390.0
Transport, storage and communication	97.5	87.4	52.5
Government services	623.0	694.6	718.8
Finance, insurance, real estate and business services Other services	520.5	508.3	436.4
Sub-total	4,250.9	4,022.2	3,544.4
Import duties	102.7	103.8	38.1
GDP in purchasers' values	4,353.6	4,126.1	3,582.5

* Provisional figures. † Estimates.

BALANCE OF PAYMENTS
(US $ million, year ending 30 September)

	1993/94	1994/95	1995/96
Exports of goods f.o.b.	60.3	88.3	82.5
Imports of goods f.o.b.	−171.5	−517.2	−498.6
Trade balance	−111.2	−428.9	−416.1
Exports of services	6.7	104.1	109.1
Imports of services	−63.9	−284.5	−283.3
Balance on goods and services	−168.4	−609.3	−590.3
Other income paid	−11.2	−30.6	−9.9
Balance on goods, services and income	−179.6	−639.9	−600.2
Current transfers received	156.2	552.9	462.5
Current balance	−23.4	−87.1	−137.7
Direct investment from abroad	—	7.4	4.1
Other investment assets	−5.5	−11.2	−4.6
Other investment liabilities	−10.3	103.1	68.4
Net errors and omissions	−10.5	124.9	19.4
Overall balance	−49.7	137.1	−50.4

Source: IMF, *International Financial Statistics*.

External Trade

PRINCIPAL COMMODITIES
(US $ million, year ending 30 September)

Imports c.i.f.	1992/93	1993/94	1994/95
Food and live animals	196.6	99.4	217.0
Mineral fuels, lubricants, etc.	70.7	46.2	71.3
Machinery and transport equipment	21.5	7.7	95.1
Raw materials	4.0	2.5	22.7
Manufactured goods	8.3	7.6	68.3
Total (incl. others)	346.2	183.3	481.4

Exports f.o.b.	1992/93	1993/94	1994/95
Coffee	8.5	7.7	14.1
Sisal	1.4	1.1	4.8
Cocoa	1.7	1.0	1.9
Essential oils	0.4	2.2	7.2
Light manufactures	66.9	44.4	45.7
Total (incl. others)	81.6	57.4	85.0

Source: IMF, *Haiti—Statistical Annex* (December 1996).

PRINCIPAL TRADING PARTNERS*
(US $ million, year ending 30 September)

Imports c.i.f.	1989/90	1990/91	1991/92
Belgium	3.4	3.7	2.9
Canada	22.0	31.9	15.2
France	24.5	32.4	17.2
Germany, Federal Republic	14.6	19.2	10.0
Japan	23.6	31.2	17.7
Netherlands	11.2	13.9	8.7
United Kingdom	5.6	6.7	4.2
USA	153.1	203.2	126.7
Total (incl. others)	332.2	400.5	277.2

Exports f.o.b.†	1989/90	1990/91	1991/92
Belgium	15.9	19.5	6.0
Canada	4.5	4.7	2.3
France	17.4	21.6	6.1
Germany, Federal Republic	5.4	6.6	2.4
Italy	16.5	20.7	8.7
Japan	2.4	2.9	0.9
Netherlands	3.4	4.3	1.4
United Kingdom	2.3	2.3	0.7
USA	78.3	96.3	39.7
Total (incl. others)	163.7	198.7	74.7

* Provisional.
† Excluding re-exports.

Source: Administration Générale des Douanes.

Transport

ROAD TRAFFIC ('000 motor vehicles in use)

	1990*	1991†	1992†
Passenger cars	25.8	32.0	32.0
Commercial vehicles	9.6	21.0	21.0

* Provisional figures.
† Source: *World Automotive Market Report,* Auto and Truck International (Illinois).

Source: UN, *Statistical Yearbook*.

1996 ('000 motor vehicles in use, estimates): Passenger cars 32; Commercial vehicles 21. (Source: IRF, World Road Statistics.)

SHIPPING

Merchant Fleet (registered at 31 December)

	1994	1995	1996
Number of vessels	4	2	6
Total displacement ('000 grt)	0.9	0.4	1.0

Source: Lloyd's Register of Shipping, *World Fleet Statistics*.

International Sea-borne Freight Traffic ('000 metric tons)

	1988	1989	1990
Goods loaded	164	165	170
Goods unloaded	684	659	704

Source: UN, *Monthly Bulletin of Statistics*.

CIVIL AVIATION

International flights, 1989: Passengers arriving 293,905; Passengers departing 311,643.

Tourism

	1992	1993	1994
Tourist arrivals ('000)	90	77	70
Tourist receipts (US $ million)	38	78	46

Source: UN, *Statistical Yearbook*.

Communications Media

	1993	1994	1995
Radio receivers ('000 in use)	330	350	380
Television receivers ('000 in use)	33	34	35

Telephones: 45,000 main lines in use in 1993.
Daily newspapers: 4 in 1995* (average circulation 45,000* copies).
Book production: 271 titles published in 1989.
* Estimate.

Sources: UNESCO, *Statistical Yearbook*; UN, *Statistical Yearbook*.

Education

(1990/91)

	Schools	Teachers	Students		
			Males	Females	Total
Pre-primary	n.a.	n.a.	19,791	110,600	230,391
Primary	7,306	26,208*	288,313	267,120	555,433
Secondary					
General	n.a.	9,470	94,434	90,534	184,968
Teacher training†	n.a.	159	279	588	867
Vocational†	n.a.	n.a.	n.a.	n.a.	3,469
Tertiary					
University and equivalent institutions†	n.a.	479	3,195	1,276	4,471
Other institutions†	n.a.	175	1,468	349	1,817

* Includes teachers at the pre-primary level.
† 1985 figures.

Source: UNESCO, *Statistical Yearbook*.

Directory

The Constitution

The Constitution of the Republic of Haiti, which was approved by the electorate in a referendum held in March 1987, provided for a system of power-sharing between a President (who may not serve two consecutive five-year terms), a Prime Minister and a bicameral legislature. Prominent former supporters of ex-President Jean-Claude Duvalier were to be barred from elective office for 10 years. Authority was to be distributed regionally. The army and the police were no longer to be a combined force. The death penalty was abolished, and there was to be an independent judiciary. Official status was given to the Creole language spoken by Haitians and to the folk religion, voodoo. In June 1988 the Constitution was suspended by a military Government, which was installed after a *coup d'état*. There was a further coup, in September, and the Constitution was partially restored in March 1989. The military ruler, Brig.-Gen. Prosper Avril, fled in March 1990, and an interim President was installed, pending a presidential election, which took place in December 1990. Fr Jean-Bertrand Aristide was freely elected President, but was deposed in September 1991 by a military coup. In October a new President and Government were installed by the army, which claimed that it was acting in accordance with the Constitution. In June 1992 the presidency was declared to be vacant, but in May 1994 a pro-military faction of the Senate declared the head of the Supreme Court, Emile Jonassaint, provisional President. Following US mediation and threat of invasion, international peacekeeping forces (initially a nominally multinational force comprised almost entirely of US troops) began to arrive on the island on 19 September. Lt-Gen. Raoul Cédras, the Commander-in-Chief of the armed forces, resigned on 10 October, and Jonassaint resigned on the following day. On 15 October President Aristide returned to Haiti, to begin the restoration of constitutional government.

The Government

HEAD OF STATE

President: RENÉ GARCÍA PRÉVAL (assumed office on 7 February 1996).

CABINET
(February 1998)

Prime Minister: (vacant).

Minister of the Interior and of National Defence: JEAN MOLIÈRE.

Minister of Justice: PIERRE MAX ANTOINE.

Minister of National Education: JACQUES ÉDOUARD ALEXIS.

Minister of Planning and External Co-operation: JEAN-ÉRIC DÉRICE.

Minister of Social Affairs and of Women's Affairs and Rights, and Culture: PIERRE-DENIS AMÉDÉE.

Minister of Commerce and Industry: FRESNEL GERMAIN.

Minister of Foreign Affairs: FRITZ LONGCHAMPS.

Minister of the Economy and of Agriculture, Natural Resources and Rural Development: FRED JOSEPH.

Minister of Public Health: (vacant).

Minister of Public Works, Transport and Communications and of the Environment: JACQUES DORCÉAN.

Minister for Haitians Residing Abroad: PAUL DÉJEAN.

There are five secretaries of state.

MINISTRIES

Office of the President: Palais National, Port-au-Prince; tel. 22-4020; telex 0068.

Ministry of Agriculture, Natural Resources and Rural Development: Damien, Port-au-Prince; tel. 22-5672.

Ministry of Commerce and Industry: rue Légitime 8, Champ-de-Mars, Port-au-Prince; tel. 22-2499; fax 23-8402.

Ministry of Culture: Port-au-Prince; tel. 23-2382.

Ministry of the Economy: Palais des Ministères, Port-au-Prince; tel. 22-1628; telex 2027.

Ministry of the Environment: Haut de Turgeau 181, Port-au-Prince; tel. 45-7585; fax 45-7360.

Ministry of Foreign Affairs: blvd Harry S. Truman, Cité de l'Exposition, Port-au-Prince; tel. 22-1668; fax 23-8912.

Ministry for Haitians Residing Abroad: Port-au-Prince; tel. 45-7006; fax 45-3400.

Ministry of the Interior: Palais des Ministères, Port-au-Prince; tel. 23-5744; fax 23-5742.

Ministry of Justice: blvd Harry S. Truman, Cité de l'Exposition, Port-au-Prince; tel. 45-5658.

Ministry of National Defence: Palais des Ministères, Port-au-Prince; tel. 23-5744; fax 23-5742.

Ministry of National Education: rue Audain, Port-au-Prince; tel. 23-4716; fax 23-7887.

Ministry of Planning and External Co-operation: Port-au-Prince; tel. 22-4148; fax 23-4193.

Ministry of Public Health: Palais de Ministères, Port-au-Prince; tel. 23-1636; fax 22-4066.

Ministry of Public Works, Transport and Communications: Palais des Ministères, BP 2002, Port-au-Prince; tel. 22-3230; telex 0353; fax 23-4586.

Ministry of Social Affairs: rue de la Réunion, Port-au-Prince; tel. 22-7053.

Ministry of Women's Affairs and Rights: angle rue Geffrard et rue Piquant, Port-au-Prince; tel. 22-4768.

President and Legislature

PRESIDENT

Presidential election, 17 December 1995

Candidates	% of votes
RENÉ GARCÍA PRÉVAL (OPL)	87.9
LÉON JEUNE (Independent)	2.5
VICTOR BENOÎT (KONAKOM)	2.3
Total (incl. others)	100.0

LEGISLATURE

The general election that was conducted on 25 June and 17 September 1995 resulted in a legislature heavily dominated by the Plate-forme Politique Lavalas (PPL), a three-party electoral coalition comprising the Organisation Politique Lavalas (OPL, renamed the Organisation du Peuple en Lutte in 1998), the Mouvement d'Organisation du Pays (MOP) and the Pati Louvri Baryè (PLB). Its members won 17 of the 18 contested seats in the 27-member Senate, leaving only four opposition or independent members in the upper chamber. The PPL secured 68 seats in the 83-member Chamber of Deputies. The remaining 15 seats were obtained by independents or members of small opposition parties, including two members of the Front National pour le Changement et la Démocratie (FNCD) and one member each from the Comité National du Congrès des Mouvements Démocratiques (KONAKOM), the Mouvement Koumbite National (MKN), the Parti Nationaliste Progressiste Révolutionnaire (PANPRA) and the Rassemblement Démocratique Chrétien d'Haïti (RDCH). However, leaders of all these parties, except KONAKOM, disowned their deputies, having boycotted the election as 'fraudulent' (see Recent History).

Partial legislative elections to nine seats in the Senate and two seats in the Chamber of Deputies were held in April 1997. Of the seats contested, only two, in the Senate, were decided. Both of these were secured by a breakaway faction of the PPL, La Fanmi Lavalas, which was led by Jean-Bertrand Aristide. However, the poll was disputed by the OPL, which accused the Provincial Electoral Council of manipulating the results in Aristide's favour. The results were still in dispute in early 1998 and a second round of elections to decide the remaining seats had been postponed indefinitely.

Political Organizations

Alliance pour la Libération et l'Avancement d'Haïti (ALAH): BP 13350, Station de Delmas, Port-au-Prince; tel. 45-0446; fax 57-4804; f. 1975; Leader Senator REYNOLD GEORGES.

Comité pour la Libération Economique (CLE): f. 1996; Leader LÉON JEUNE.

Comité National du Congrès des Mouvements Démocratiques (KONAKOM): f. 1987; social democratic; Leader VICTOR BENOÎT.

La Fanmi Lavalas: f. 1996; Leader JEAN-BERTRAND ARISTIDE.

Front National pour le Changement et la Démocratie (FNCD): f. 1990; coalition of centre-left organizations; Leaders EVANS PAUL, TURNEB DELPÉ.

Mobilisation pour le Développement National (MDN): c/o CHISS, 33 rue Bonne Foi, BP 2497, Port-au-Prince; tel. 22-3829; f. 1986; Pres. HUBERT DE RONCERAY (resident in USA).

Mouvement Koumbite National (MKN): Leader VOLVICK RÉMY JOSEPH.

Mouvement pour l'Instauration de la Démocratie en Haïti (MIDH): 114 ave Jean Paul II, Port-au-Prince; tel. 45-8377; f. 1986; centre-right; Pres. MARC BAZIN.

Mouvement National Patriotique (MNP-28): Leader DÉJEAN BÉLIZAIRE.

Mouvement pour la Reconstruction Nationale (MRN): f. 1991; Pres. JACQUES RONY MODESTIN.

Parti Agricole et Industriel National (PAIN): f. 1956; Sec.-Gen. LOUIS DÉJOIE II.

Parti Démocratique Chrétien d'Haïti (PDCH): f. 1978; Christian Democrat party; Leader MARIE-FRANCE CLAUDE.

Parti Nationaliste Progressiste Révolutionnaire (PANPRA): f. 1986; social-democratic; mem. of Socialist International; Leader SERGE GILLES.

Plate-forme Politique Lavalas (PPL): three-party electoral alliance comprising:

- **Mouvement d'Organisation du Pays (MOP):** f. 1946; centre party; Leader JEAN MOLIÈRE.
- **Organisation du Peuple en Lutte (OPL):** f. 1991 as Organisation Politique Lavalas; name changed as above 1998; Leader GÉRARD PIERRE-CHARLES.
- **Pati Louvri Baryè (PLB):** Leader RENAUD BERNARDIN.

Rassemblement Démocratique Chrétien d'Haïti (RDCH): Leader EDDY VOLEL.

Rassemblement des Démocrates Nationaux Progressistes (RDNP): f. 1979; centre party; Sec.-Gen. LESLIE MANIGAT.

Rassemblement des Enfants Légitimes de la Table: f. 1996; pro-Aristide; Leaders GÉRARD BLOT, YVON ROSEMOND.

Diplomatic Representation

EMBASSIES IN HAITI

Argentina: 8 rue Mangones, Berthe, Pétionville, BP 1755, Port-au-Prince; tel. 57-5725; telex 0176; fax 57-8227; Ambassador: JOSÉ MARÍA BERRO MADERO.

Brazil: 37 rue Lamarre, Pétionville, BP 808, Port-au-Prince; tel. 56-6208; telex 0181; fax 56-6206; Ambassador: ANTÔNIO FERREIRA DA ROCHA.

Canada: 18 route de Delmas, Port-au-Prince; tel. 23-2358; telex 0069; fax 23-8720; Ambassador: FRANCIS FILLEUL.

Chile: 384 route de Delmas, entre rues 42 et 44, Port-au-Prince; Ambassador: LUCHO LARRAÍN CRUZ.

China (Taiwan): 2 rue Rivière, Port-au-Prince; Ambassador: CHIOU JONG-NAN.

Colombia: Complexe 384, No 7, route de Delmas, entre rues 42 et 44, Port-au-Prince; tel. 46-2599; fax 46-5595; Ambassador: GUILLERMO TRIANA AYALA.

Cuba: Port-au-Prince; Ambassador: OSCAR COET BLACKSTOCK.

Dominican Republic: Port-au-Prince; Ambassador: RAFAEL A NTONIO JULIÁN CEDANO.

Ecuador: BP 2531, Port-au-Prince; tel. 22-4576; telex 0195; Chargé d'affaires: ADOLFO ALVAREZ.

France: 51 place des Héros de l'Indépendance, Port-au-Prince; tel. 23-1002; telex 0049; fax 23-2898; Ambassador: PATRICK ROUSSEL.

Germany: 2 impasse Claudinette, Bois Moquette, Pétionville, BP 1147, Port-au-Prince; tel. 57-7280; telex 20072; fax 57-7280; Chargé d'affaires: BERND K. VIERKOETTER.

Holy See: rue Louis Pouget, Morne Calvaire, BP 326, Port-au-Prince; tel. 57-6308; fax 57-3411; Apostolic Nuncio: Most Rev. CHRISTOPHE PIERRE, Titular Archbishop of Gunela.

Japan: Villa Bella Vista 2, impasse Tulipe, Desprez, Port-au-Prince; tel. 45-3333; telex 0368; Ambassador: AOKI SATOSHI.

Mexico: Delmas 60, 2, BP 327, Port-au-Prince; tel. 57-8100; fax 57-6783; Ambassador: CARLOS FERRER.

Spain: 54 rue Pacot, State Liles, BP 386, Port-au-Prince; tel. 45-4410; fax 45-3901; Ambassador: PABLO SÁNCHEZ-TERÁN.

USA: 14 ave Marie-Jeanne, Port-au-Prince; tel. 22-5726; fax 23-8324; Ambassador: WILLIAM L. SWING.

Venezuela: blvd Harry S. Truman, Cité de l'Exposition, BP 2158, Port-au-Prince; tel. 22-0973; telex 0413; Ambassador: IRMA ANTONINI.

Judicial System

Law is based on the French Napoleonic Code, substantially modified during the presidency of François Duvalier.

Courts of Appeal and Civil Courts sit at Port-au-Prince and the three provincial capitals: Gonaïves, Cap Haïtien and Port de Paix. In principle each commune has a Magistrates' Court.

Court of Cassation: Port-au-Prince; Pres. CLAUSEL DESBROSSE.

Courts of Appeal. Civil Courts. Magistrates' Courts. Judges of the Supreme Courts and Courts of Appeal appointed by the President.

Religion

Roman Catholicism is the official religion, followed by approximately 75% of the population. The folk religion, which co-exists with official Christianity, is voodoo. There are various Protestant and other denominations.

CHRISTIANITY

The Roman Catholic Church

For ecclesiastical purposes, Haiti comprises two archdioceses and seven dioceses.

Bishops' Conference: Conférence Episcopale de Haïti, angle rues Piquant et Lamarre, BP 1572, Port-au-Prince; tel. 22-5194; fax 23-5318; f. 1977; Pres. Most Rev. FRANÇOIS GAYOT, Archbishop of Cap-Haïtien.

Archbishop of Cap-Haïtien: Most Rev. FRANÇOIS GAYOT, Archevêché, rue 19–20 H, CP 22, Cap-Haïtien; tel. 62-0071; fax 62-0593.

Archbishop of Port-au-Prince: Most Rev. FRANÇOIS-WOLFF LIGONDÉ, Archevêché, rue Dr Aubry, BP 538, Port-au-Prince; tel. 22-2043.

The Anglican Communion

Anglicans in Haiti fall under the jurisdiction of a missionary diocese of Province II of the Episcopal Church in the USA.

Bishop of Haiti: Rt Rev. JEAN ZACHE DURACIN, Eglise Episcopale d'Haïti, BP 1309, Port-au-Prince.

Protestant Churches

Baptist Convention: BP 20, Cap-Haïtien; tel. 62-0567; f. 1964; Pres. Rev. JEAN DÉLINSE.

Lutheran Church: Petite Place Cuzeau, BP 13147, Delmas, Port-au-Prince; tel. 46-3179; f. 1975; Minister BEN BICHOTTE.

Other denominations active in Haiti include Methodists and the Church of God 'Eben-Ezer'.

The Press

DAILIES

Le Matin: 88 rue du Quai, BP 367, Port-au-Prince; tel. 22-2040; f. 1908; French; independent; Dir FRANK MAGLOIRE; circ. 5,000.

Le Nouvelliste: 198 rue du Centre, BP 1316, Port-au-Prince; tel. 23-2114; fax 23-2313; f. 1898; evening; French; independent; Editor MAX CHAUVET; circ. 6,000.

PERIODICALS

Haïti en Marche: 72 rue Pavée, Port-au-Prince; tel. 22-7652; weekly; Editor MARCUS GARCIA.

Haïti Progrès: 11 rue Capois, Port-au-Prince; tel. 22-6513; weekly; Dir BEN DUPUY.

Haïti Observateur: 98 ave John Brown, Port-au-Prince; tel. 28-0782; weekly; Editor LEO JOSEPH.

Liberté: BP 13441, Delmas; tel. 45-7766; fax 45-7760; f. 1990; weekly; Dir JEAN-YVES URFIE; circ. 25,000.

Le Messager du Nord-Ouest: Port de Paix; weekly.

Le Moniteur: BP 214 bis, Port-au-Prince; tel. 22-1026; 2 a week; French; the official gazette; circ. 2,000.

Optique: French Institute, BP 1316, Port-au-Prince; monthly; arts.

Le Septentrion: Cap-Haïtien; weekly; independent; Editor NELSON BELL; circ. 2,000.

NEWS AGENCIES

Agence Haïtienne de Presse (AHP): Port-au-Prince; tel. 45-3839; fax 45-5836; Dir VENEL REMARAIS.

Foreign Bureaux

Agence France-Presse (AFP): 72 rue Pavée, BP 62, Port-au-Prince; tel. 22-3469; fax 22-3759; Bureau Chief DOMINIQUE LEVANTI.

Agencia EFE (Spain): Port-au-Prince; tel. 55-9517; Correspondent HEROLD JEAN-FRANÇOIS.

Associated Press (AP) (USA): BP 2443, Port-au-Prince; tel. 57-4240; Correspondent MIKE NORTON.

Inter Press Service (Italy): 16 rue Malval, Turgeau, BP 19046, Port-au-Prince; tel. 45-9393; fax 45-9292; e-mail ipshaiti@acn.com; Correspondent IVES-MARIE CHANEL.

Prensa Latina (Cuba): Port-au-Prince; tel. 46-5149; Correspondent JACQUELÍN TELEMAQUE.

United Press International (UPI) (USA): Port-au-Prince; tel. 23-6565; Correspondent ROOSEVELT JEAN-FRANÇOIS.

Publishers

Editions Caraïbes S.A.: 57, rue Pavée, BP 2013, Port-au-Prince; tel. 22-0032; Man. PIERRE J. ELIE.

Editions du Soleil: BP 2471, rue du Centre, Port-au-Prince; tel. 22-3147; telex 0001; education.

Maison Henri Deschamps—Les Entreprises Deschamps Frisch, SA: Grand rue, BP 164, Port-au-Prince; tel. 23-2215; telex 0533; fax 23-4975; f. 1898; education and literature; Man. Dir JACQUES DESCHAMPS, Jr.

Natal: Imprimerie, rue Barbancourt, Port-au-Prince; Dir ROBERT MALVAL.

Théodore: Imprimerie, rue Dantes Destouches, Port-au-Prince.

Broadcasting and Communications

TELECOMMUNICATIONS

Conseil National des Télécommunications (CONATEL): 16, ave Marie Jeanne, Cité de l'Exposition, BP 2002, Port-au-Prince; tel. 22-0300; telex 0353; fax 23-0579; f. 1969; govt communications licensing authority; Dir-Gen. SAMUEL DUBOIS.

Télécommunications d'Haïti (Téléco): Port-au-Prince; tel. 22-3300; telex 0189; scheduled for privatization; Dir-Gen. PIERRE LISSADE.

RADIO

Radio Antilles International: 175 rue du Centre, BP 2335, Port-au-Prince; tel. 23-0696; f. 1984; independent; Dir-Gen. JACQUES SAMPEUR.

Radio Cacique: 5 Bellevue, BP 1480, Port-au-Prince; tel. 45-2326; f. 1961; independent; Dir JEAN-CLAUDE CARRIÉ.

Radio Caraïbes: 23 ruelle Chavannes, Port-au-Prince; tel. 23-0644; f. 1973; independent; Dir JACQUES G. SIMEON.

Radio Galaxie: 17 rue Pavée, Port-au-Prince; independent; Dir YVES JEAN-BART.

Radio Haïti Inter: Delmas 66A, 522, en face de Delmas 91, BP 737, Port-au-Prince; tel. 57-3111; f. 1935; independent; Dir JEAN LEOPOLD DOMINIQUE.

Radio Lakansyel: 285 route de Delmas, Port-au-Prince; tel. 46-2020; independent; Dir ALEX SAINT-SURIN.

Radio Lumière: Côte-Plage 16, BP 1050, Port-au-Prince; f. 1959; tel. 34-0330; f. 1959; Protestant; independent; Dir ROBINSON JOSEPH.

Radio Magic Stéreo: Port-au-Prince; tel. 45-5404; independent; Dir FRITZ JOASSIN.

Radio Metropole: 18 Delmas 52, BP 1050, Port-au-Prince; tel. 49-2034; fax 49-2020; f. 1970; independent; Dir-Gen. RICHARD WIDMAIER.

Radio Nationale d'Haïti: rue du Magasin de l'Etat, BP 1143, Port-au-Prince; tel. 23-8441; govt-operated; Dir PIERRE RAYMOND DUMAS.

Radio Plus: 85 rue Pavée, BP 1174, Port-au-Prince; tel. 22-1588; independent; Dir LIONEL BÉNJAMIN.

Radio Port-au-Prince: Stade Sylvio Cator, BP 863, Port-au-Prince; f. 1979; independent; Dir GEORGE L. HÉRARD.

Radio Signal FM: 199A route de Delmas, Port-au-Prince; tel. 46-4633; fax 46-1987; f. 1991; independent; Dir MARIO VIAU.

Radio Soleil: BP 1362, Archevêché de Port-au-Prince; tel. 22-3062; fax 22-3516; f. 1978; Catholic; independent; educational; broadcasts in Creole and French; Dir Fr ARNOUX CHÉRY.

Radio Superstar: 38 rue Safran, Delmas 68, Port-au-Prince; tel. 57-7219; independent; Dir ALBERT CHANCY.

Radio Tropic FM: 6 ave John Brown, Port-au-Prince; tel. 23-6565; independent; Dir GUY JEAN.

TELEVISION

PVS Antenne 16: 137 rue Monseigneur Guilloux, Port-au-Prince; tel. and fax 22-1277; f. 1988; independent; Dir-Gen. RAYNALD DELERME.

Télé Haïti: blvd Harry S. Truman, BP 1126, Port-au-Prince; tel. 22-3887; fax 22-9140; f. 1959; independent; pay-cable station with 13 channels; in French, Spanish and English; Dir MARIE CHRISTINE BUSSENIUS.

Télévision Nationale d'Haïti: Delmas 33, BP 13400, Port-au-Prince; tel. 45-5456; telex 0414; govt-owned; cultural; 4 channels in Creole, French and Spanish; administered by four-mem. board; Dir DOMINIQUE CONSTANT.

Trans-America: ruelle Roger, Gonaïves; f. 1990; tel 74-0113; independent; Dir-Gen. HÉBERT PELISSIER.

TVA: rue Liberté, Gonaïves; independent; cable station with three channels; Dir-Gen. GÉRARD LUC JEAN-BAPTISTE.

Finance

(cap. = capital; m. = million; res = reserves; dep. = deposits; amounts in gourdes; brs = branches)

BANKING

Central Bank

Banque de la République d'Haïti: angle rues du Magasin de l'Etat et des Miracles, BP 1570, Port-au-Prince; tel. 99-1000; telex 0394; fax 22-2607; f. 1911; bank of issue; cap. and res 6.5m., dep. 204m. (May 1994); Pres. FRITZ JEAN; Gen. Dir ROLAND PIERRE.

Commercial Banks

Banque Commerciale d'Haïti: Champ de Mars, Port-au-Prince; tel. 22-3931.

Banque Nationale de Crédit: angle rues du Quai et des Miracles, BP 1320, Port-au-Prince; tel. 22-0800; telex 0215; f. 1979; cap. 25m., dep. 729.9m. (Sept. 1989); Pres. EDOUARD RACINE; Gen. Man. SOCRATE L. DEVIME.

Banque Populaire Haïtienne: angle rues des Miracles et du Centre, Port-au-Prince; tel. 22-1800; telex 0406; fax 22-4389; f. 1955; state-owned; cap. and res 84m., dep. 210m. (July 1994); Dir-Gen. REGINALD MONDÉSIR.

Banque de Promotion Commerciale et Industrielle SA (PROMOBANK): ave John Brown et rue Lamarre, BP 2323, Port-au-Prince; tel. 23-5800; telex 0371; fax 22-6720; f. 1974 as B.N.P. Haïti, name changed as above 1994; cap. 35.5m., res 8.0m., dep. 926.8m. (Dec. 1996); Pres. GILBERT BIGIO; Gen. Man. DANIEL SOUPPER.

Banque de l'Union Haïtienne: angle rues du Quai et Bonne Foi, BP 275, Port-au-Prince; tel. 23-0491; telex 0173; fax 23-2852; f. 1973; cap. 37.5m., res 19.8m., dep. 1,104.5m. (Sept. 1996); Pres. OSWALD J. BRANDT II, 7 brs.

Capital Bank: 149-151 rue des Miracles, BP 2464, Port-au-Prince; tel. 22-2830; fax 22-2898; frmly Banque de Crédit Immobilier, SA; Pres. BERNARD ROY; Gen. Man. LILIANE C. DOMINIQUE.

Sogebank, SA (Société Générale Haïtienne de Banque, SA): rue des Miracles, BP 1315, Port-au-Prince; tel. 22-4800; telex 0026; fax 22-5366; f. 1986; cap. 79.5m.; Pres. JEAN CLAUDE NADAL; Dir-Gen. CHARLES CLERMONT; 7 brs.

Sogebel: route de l'Aéroport, BP 2409, Port-au-Prince; tel. 49-0400; fax 23-8481; f. 1988; cap. 15.1m., dep. 249.9m.; Gen. Man. MARIE-THÉRÈSE CHAUVET; 2 brs.

Unibank: 94 place Geffard, Port-au-Prince; tel. 23-7545; fax 23-6712; f. 1993; res and dep. 507m. (July 1994).

Foreign Banks

Bank of Nova Scotia (Canada): 18 rue des Miracles, BP 686, Port-au-Prince; tel. 22-4461; telex 0155; fax 22-9340; Dir-Gen. CLAUDE E. MARCEL; Man. B. A. THEARD; 3 brs.

Banque Nationale de Paris (France): ave John Brown et rue Lamarre, Port-au-Prince; tel. 22-2300; telex 0191; fax 22-6720; Dir-Gen. MARCEL GARCÍA; 2 brs.

Citibank, NA (USA): 242 route de Delmas, BP 1688, Port-au-Prince; tel. 46-2600; telex 0124; fax 46-0985; Vice-Pres. GLADYS M. COUPET.

Development Bank

Banque Nationale de Développement Agricole: Port-au-Prince; tel. 22-1969; telex 0116; Dir-Gen. YVES LEREBOURS.

INSURANCE

National Companies

L'Atout Assurance, SA: 77 rue Lamarre, Port-au-Prince; tel. 23-9378; Dir JEAN EVEILLARD.

Compagnie d'Assurances d'Haïti, SA (CAH): étage Dynamic Entreprise, route de l'Aéroport, BP 1489, Port-au-Prince; tel. 46-0700; fax 46-0236; f. 1978; Pres. PHILIPPE R. ARMAND.

Excelsior Assurance, SA: rue 6, no 24, Port-au-Prince; tel. 45-8853; Dir-Gen. EMMANUEL SANON.

Générale d'Assurance, SA: Champ de Mars, Port-au-Prince; tel. 22-5465; telex 0434; fax 22-6502; f. 1985; Dir-Gen. ROLAND ACRA.

Haïti Sécurité Assurance, SA: rue des Miracles, BP 1754, Port-au-Prince; tel. 23-2118; Dir-Gen. WILLIAM PHIPPS.

International Assurance, SA (INASSA): angle rues des Miracles et Pétion, Port-au-Prince; tel. 22-1058; Dir-Gen. RAOUL MÉROVÉ-PIERRE.

Multi Assurances, SA: route de l'Aéroport, Port-au-Prince; tel. 46-0700; fax 46-0236; Dir-Gen. PHILIPPE ARMAND.

National Assurance, SA (NASSA): 153 rue des Miracles, BP 532, Port-au-Prince; tel. 23-1058; fax 23-1821; Dir-Gen. FRITZ DUPUY.

Office National d'Assurance Vieillesse (ONA): Champ de Mars, Port-au-Prince; tel. 22-1655; Dir-Gen. MARGARETH LAMUR.

Société de Commercialisation d'Assurance, SA (SOCOMAS): autoroute de Delmas, BP 636, Port-au-Prince; tel. 49-3090; Dir-Gen. JEAN DIDIER GARDÈRE.

Foreign Companies

Les Assurances Léger, SA (France): 40 rue Lamarre, BP 2120, Port-au-Prince; tel. 22-3451; fax 23-8634; Pres. GÉRARD N. LÉGER.

Cabinet d'Assurances Fritz de Catalogne (USA): angle rues du Peuple et des Miracles, BP 1644, Port-au-Prince; tel. 22-6695; fax 23-0827; Dir FRITZ DE CATALOGNE.

Capital Life Insurance Company Ltd (Bahamas): angle rues du Peuple et des Miracles, BP 1644, Port-au-Prince; tel. 22-6695; fax 23-0827; Agent FRITZ DE CATALOGNE.

Dupuy & Merové-Pierre (USA): angle rues des Miracles et Pétion 153, Port-au-Prince; tel. 23-1058; fax 23-1821; agents for Cigna International La Nationale d'Assurance SA; Dirs FRITZ DUPUY, RAOUL MÉROVÉ-PIERRE.

Groupement Français d'Assurances (France): autoroute de Delmas, Port-au-Prince; tel. 49-0433; telex 0426; fax 22-6677; Agent ALBERT A. DUFORT.

National Western Life Insurance (USA): 13 rue Pie XII, Cité de l'Exposition, Port-au-Prince; tel. 23-0734; Agent VORBE BARRAU DUPUY.

Preservatrices Foncières Assurances (France): angle rues du Magasin de l'Etat et Eden, Place Geffrard 266, étage Stecher, Port-au-Prince; tel. 22-4210; Agent PHILIPPE GATION.

Union des Assurances de Paris (UAP) (France): autoroute de Delmas, Port-au-Prince; tel. 23-7652; Agent YVES GARDÈRE.

Insurance Association

Association des Assureurs d'Haïti: c/o Les Assurances Léger, SA, 40 rue Lamarre, BP 2120, Port-au-Prince; tel. 23-2137; fax 23-8634; Dir GÉRARD N. LÉGER.

Trade and Industry

GOVERNMENT AGENCY

Centre de Promotion des Investissements et des Exportations Haïtiennes (PROMINEX): angle rue Lamarre et ave John Brown, Port-au-Prince; tel. 22-6381; Pres. CLAUDE LEVY.

DEVELOPMENT ORGANIZATIONS

Fonds de Développement Industriel (FDI): Immeuble PROMOBANK, 4e Étage, ave John Brown et rue Lamarre, BP 2597, Port-au-Prince; tel. 22-7852; fax 22-8301; f. 1981; Dir ROOSEVELT SAINT-DIC.

Société Financière Haïtienne de Développement, SA (SOFIHDES): 11 blvd Harry S. Truman, BP 1399, Port-au-Prince; tel. 22-8904; fax 22-8997; f. 1983; industrial and agro-industrial project financing, accounting, data processing, management consultancy; cap. 7.5m. (1989); Dir-Gen. FAUBERT GUSTAVE; 1 br.

CHAMBERS OF COMMERCE

Chambre de Commerce et d'Industrie d'Haïti (CCIH): blvd Harry S. Truman, Cité de l'Exposition, BP 982, Port-au-Prince; tel. 23-0786; fax 22-0281; f. 1895; Pres. FRITZ KENOL; Exec. Dir MICHAËLE BERROUET FIGNOLÉ.

Chambre de Commerce et d'Industrie Haïtiano-Américaine (HAMCHAM): c/o R. Tippenhauer, RHT Trading, route de l'Aéroport, Port-au-Prince; tel. 46-0485; fax 46-0589; f. 1979; Pres. GLADYS COUPET.

Chambre Franco-Haïtienne de Commerce et d'Industrie (CFHCI): Holiday Inn, rue Capois, Champ de Mars, Port-au-Prince; tel. 23-8404; telex 0356; fax 23-8131; f. 1987; Pres. PATRICK VICTOR; Sec. AXAN ABELLARD.

INDUSTRIAL AND TRADE ORGANIZATIONS

Association des Industries d'Haïti (ADIH): 199 route de Delmas, entre Delmas 31 et 33, étage Galerie 128, BP 2568, Port-au-Prince; tel. 46-4509; telex 0071; fax 46-2211; f. 1980; Pres. JEAN EDOUARD BAKER; Exec. Dir RAYMOND LAFONTANT, Jr.

Association Nationale des Distributeurs de Produits Pétroliers (ANADIPP): Centre Commercial Dubois, route de Delmas, Bureau 401, Port-au-Prince; tel. 46-1414; fax 22-8695; f. 1979; Pres. MAURICE LAFORTUNE.

Association Nationale des Importateurs et Distributeurs de Produits Pharmaceutiques (ANIDPP): c/o Maison Nadal, rue du Fort Per, Port-au-Prince; tel. 22-1418; fax 22-4767; Pres. BERNARD CRAAN.

Association des Producteurs Agricoles (APA): c/o Chambre de Commerce et d'Industrie d'Haïti, blvd Harry S. Truman, Cité de l'Exposition, BP 982, Port-au-Prince; tel. 23-0786; fax 22-0281; f. 1985; Pres. REYNOLD BONNEFIL.

Association des Producteurs Nationaux (APRONA): c/o Mosaïques Gardère, ave Hailé Sélassié, Port-au-Prince; tel. and fax 49-4433; Pres. FRANTZ GARDÈRE.

Association des Exportateurs de Café (ASDEC): c/o USMAN, ave Somoza/Delmas, BP B-65, Port-au-Prince; tel. 22-2627; fax 22-1394; Pres. FRITZ BRANDT.

UTILITIES

Electricity

Electricité d'Haïti: rue Dante Destouches, Port-au-Prince; tel. 22-4600; telex 0113; state energy utility company; Dir ROSEMOND PRADEL.

Péligre Hydroelectric Plant: Artibonite Valley.

Saut-Mathurine Hydroelectric Plant: Les Cayes.

TRADE UNIONS

Centrale Autonome des Travailleurs Haïtiens (CATH): 93 rue des Casernes, Port-au-Prince; tel. 22-4506; f. 1980; Sec. Gen. FIGNOLE SAINT-CYR.

Centrale des Travailleurs Haïtiens (CTH): f. 1989; Sec.-Gen. JEAN-CLAUDE LEBRUN.

Confédération Ouvriers Travailleurs Haïtiens (KOTA): 155 rue des Césars, Port-au-Prince.

Confédération Nationale des Educateurs Haïtiens (CNEH): rue Berne 21, Port-au-Prince; tel. 45-1552; fax 45-9536; f. 1986.

Fédération Haïtienne de Syndicats Chrétiens (FHSC): BP 416, Port-au-Prince; Pres. LÉONVIL LEBLANC.

Fédération des Ouvriers Syndiques (FOS): angle rues Dr Aubry et des Miracles 115, BP 371, Port-au-Prince; tel. 22-0035; f. 1984; Pres. JOSEPH J. SÉNAT.

Organisation Générale Indépendante des Travailleurs et Travailleuses d'Haïti (OGITH): 121, 2e étage, angle route Delmas et Delmas 11, Port-au-Prince; tel. 49-0575; f. 1988; Gen. Sec. JEAN-PHILIPPE GESNER.

Syndicat des Employés de l'EDH (SEEH): c/o EDH, rue Joseph Janvier, Port-au-Prince; tel. 22-3367.

Union Nationale des Ouvriers d'Haïti—UNOH: Delmas 11, 121 bis, Cité de l'Exposition, BP 3337, Port-au-Prince; f. 1951; Pres. MARCEL VINCENT; Sec.-Gen. FRITZNER ST VIL; 3,000 mems from 8 affiliated unions.

A number of unions are non-affiliated and without a national centre, including those organized on a company basis.

Transport

RAILWAYS

The only remaining railway was used to transport sugar cane, but it closed during the early 1990s, owing to the effects of the international trade sanctions against Haiti.

ROADS

In 1996, according to International Road Federation estimates, there were 4,160 km of roads, of which 24.3% was paved. All-weather roads from Port-au-Prince, to Cap-Haïtien, on the northern coast, and to Les Cayes, in the south, were completed by the 1980s, with finance from the World Bank. Another, connecting Port-au-Prince with the southern town of Jacmel, was built and financed by France.

SHIPPING

Many European and American shipping lines call at Haiti. The two principal ports are Port-au-Prince and Cap-Haïtien. There are also 12 minor ports.

Autorité Portuaire Nationale: rue 17, Cap-Haïtien; tel. 32-0625; telex 0303; Port Man. ALINDI ACHILLE.

CIVIL AVIATION

The international airport, situated 8 km outside Port-au-Prince, is the country's principal airport, and is served by many international airlines linking Haiti with the USA and other Caribbean islands. There is an airport at Cap-Haïtien, and smaller airfields at Jacmel, Jérémie, Les Cayes and Port-de-Paix.

Air Haïti: Aéroport International, Port-au-Prince; tel. 46-3311; f. 1969; began cargo charter operations 1970; scheduled cargo and mail services from Port-au-Prince to Cap-Haïtien, San Juan (Puerto Rico), Santo Domingo (Dominican Republic), Miami and New York (USA); Gen. Man. Mr GONZALES.

Caribintair: Aéroport International, Port-au-Prince; tel. 46-0778; scheduled domestic service and charter flights to Santo Domingo (Dominican Republic) and other Caribbean destinations.

Haiti Air Freight, SA: Aéroport International, CP 170, Port-au-Prince; tel. 46-2572; telex 0370; fax 46-0848; cargo carrier operating scheduled and charter services from Port-au-Prince and Cap-Haïtien to Miami (USA) and Puerto Rico.

Haïti Trans Air: Aéroport International, BP 2526, Port-au-Prince; tel. 46-0418; fax 38938; scheduled flights to Miami and New York (USA); Pres. CHARLES H. VOIGHT.

Tourism

Tourism was formerly Haiti's second largest source of foreign exchange. In 1985/86 the number of visitors totalled 208,092. As a result of subsequent political instability, the number of cruise ships visiting Haiti declined considerably, causing a sharp decline in the number of tourist arrivals; visitors to Haiti in 1993/94 totalled an estimated 70,000.

Secrétariat d'Etat au Tourisme: 8 rue Légitime, Port-au-Prince; tel. 23-5631; fax 23-5359; Secretary of State for Tourism MARYSE PÉNETTE.

Association Hotelière et Touristique d'Haïti: c/o Hôtel Montana, rue F. Cardozo, route de Pétionville, BP 2562, Port-au-Prince; tel. 57-1920; telex 0493; fax 57-6137; Pres. DOMINIQUE CARVONIS; Exec. Dir JOËLLE L. COUPAUD.

HONDURAS

Introductory Survey

Location, Climate, Language, Religion, Flag, Capital

The Republic of Honduras lies in the middle of the Central American isthmus. It has a long northern coastline on the Caribbean Sea and a narrow southern outlet to the Pacific Ocean. Its neighbours are Guatemala to the west, El Salvador to the south-west and Nicaragua to the south-east. The climate ranges from temperate in the mountainous regions to tropical in the coastal plains: temperatures in the interior range from 15°C (59°F) to 24°C (75°F), while temperatures in the coastal plains average about 30°C (86°F). There are two rainy seasons in upland areas, May–July and September–October. The national language is Spanish. Almost all of the inhabitants profess Christianity, and the overwhelming majority are adherents of the Roman Catholic Church. The national flag (proportions 2 by 1) has three horizontal stripes, of blue, white and blue, with five blue five-pointed stars, arranged in a diagonal cross, in the centre of the white stripe. The capital is Tegucigalpa.

Recent History

Honduras was ruled by Spain from the 16th century until 1821 and became a sovereign state in 1838. From 1939 the country was ruled as a dictatorship by Gen. Tiburcio Carías Andino, leader of the Partido Nacional (PN), who had been President since 1933. In 1949 Carías was succeeded as President by Juan Manuel Gálvez, also of the PN. In 1954 the leader of the Partido Liberal (PL), Dr José Ramón Villeda Morales, was elected President but was immediately deposed by Julio Lozano Díaz, himself overthrown by a military Junta in 1956. The Junta organized elections in 1957, when the PL secured a majority in Congress and Dr Villeda Morales was re-elected President. He was overthrown in 1963 by Col (later Gen.) Oswaldo López Arellano, the Minister of Defence, who, following elections held on the basis of a new Constitution, was appointed President in June 1965.

A presidential election in March 1971 was won by Dr Ramón Ernesto Cruz Uclés, the PN candidate. In December 1972, however, Cruz Uclés was deposed in a bloodless coup, led by former President López Arellano. In March 1974, at the instigation of the Supreme Council of the Armed Forces, President López Arellano was replaced as Commander-in-Chief of the Armed Forces by Col (later Gen.) Juan Melgar Castro, who was appointed President in April 1975. President Melgar Castro was forced to resign by the Supreme Council of the Armed Forces in August 1978, and was replaced by a military Junta. The Commander-in-Chief of the Armed Forces, Gen. Policarpo Paz García, assumed the role of Head of State, and the Junta promised that elections would take place.

Military rule was ended officially when, in April 1980, elections to a Constituent Assembly were held. The PL won 52% of the votes but was unable to assume power. Gen. Paz was appointed interim President for one year. At a general election in November 1981 the PL, led by Dr Roberto Suazo Córdova, gained an absolute majority in the National Assembly. Dr Suazo was sworn in as President in January 1982. However, real power lay in the hands of Col (later Gen.) Gustavo Alvarez Martínez, who was appointed Head of the Armed Forces in the same month. In November Gen. Alvarez became Commander-in-Chief of the Armed Forces, having brought about an amendment to the Constitution in that month, whereby the posts of President and Commander-in-Chief of the Armed Forces, which had been merged under the rule of the military Junta, were separated. During 1982 and 1983 Gen. Alvarez suppressed increasing political unrest by authorizing the arrests of trade union activists and left-wing sympathizers; 'death squads' were allegedly also used to eliminate 'subversive' elements of the population. In March 1984 Gen. Alvarez was deposed as Commander-in-Chief of the Armed Forces by a group of army officers.

At the November 1985 presidential election the leading candidate of the PN, Rafael Leonardo Callejas Romero, obtained 42% of the individual votes cast, but the leading candidate of the PL, José Simeón Azcona del Hoyo (who had obtained only 27% of the individual votes cast), was declared the winner because, in accordance with a new electoral law, the combined votes of the PL's candidates secured the requisite majority of 51% of the total votes cast.

In February 1988 a report by a human rights organization, Amnesty International, gave evidence of an increase in violations of human rights by the armed forces and by right-wing 'death squads'. In August of that year, and again in 1989, the Inter-American Court of Human Rights (an organ of the Organization of American States—OAS, see p. 219) found the Honduran Government guilty of the 'disappearances' of Honduran citizens between 1981 and 1984, and ordered that compensation be paid to the families involved. In January 1989 Gen. Alvarez was killed by left-wing guerrillas in Tegucigalpa. The PL gained a majority of seats in the National Assembly at legislative elections held in November, while Rafael Leonardo Callejas of the PN won the concurrent presidential election, receiving 51% of the votes cast. Callejas assumed office in January 1990. From early that year the new administration adopted severe measures of economic austerity, which provoked widespread social unrest.

In May 1991 units of the armed forces were implicated in the massacre of nine farmers during a dispute over land ownership. In the following month Amnesty International published a report alleging the mistreatment, torture and killing of detainees by members of the Honduran security forces, and the International Confederation of Free Trade Unions accused the security forces of complicity in the assassinations of several trade union organizers during 1990 and early 1991. In January 1992 the Government announced the creation of a special commission to investigate numerous accusations of corruption against government officials.

In March 1993, in response to increasing pressure by human rights organizations and criticism by the State Department of the USA, the Government established a special commission to investigate allegations of human rights violations by the armed forces and to evaluate the need for a reform of the security forces and the judiciary. In its report, the commission recommended the replacement of the armed forces' much-criticized secret counter-intelligence organization, the División Nacional de Investigaciones (DNI), with a body under civilian control. Other recommendations included the establishment of a fully independent Public Ministry office headed by a democratically-elected Attorney-General.

At presidential and legislative elections held in November 1993, Carlos Roberto Reina Idiaquez, the candidate of the PL, was elected President, winning 52% of the votes cast; Osvaldo Ramos Soto, the PN candidate, took 41% of the votes. The PL also obtained a clear majority in the National Assembly, with 71 seats, while the PN secured 55 seats and the Partido Innovación y Unidad—Social Democracia (PINU) won the remaining two seats. Legislation replacing the DNI with a new ministry, the Dirección de Investigación Criminal (DIC), was approved in December 1993. On taking office in January 1994 Reina, a former President of the Inter-American Court of Human Rights, expressed his commitment to the reform of the judicial system, which had failed to act effectively against those responsible for human rights violations. In addition he promised to redefine the role of the armed forces, reducing its size and sphere of influence. In that month, following the release by the National Commission for the Protection of Human Rights of a report incriminating the armed forces in the disappearance of 184 people in the previous decade, the head of the Commission, Leo Valladares Lanza, demanded the resignation of the Commander-in-Chief of the Armed Forces, Gen. Luis Alonso Discua Elvir. At the time of the disappearances Discua had been the Commander of Battalion 3-16, the army intelligence unit widely regarded as responsible for the murder of left-wing political activists. As a result of the report, the Supreme Court ordered an investigation of the allegations.

In April 1994 an apparent attempt to assassinate Reina was thwarted when one of three Nicaraguan hired assassins revealed the plot to the Honduran authorities. The Nicaraguans reportedly had been offered US $400,000 by a Honduran, Luis Hernández Sosa, to conduct the killing. Reina dismissed suggestions of a political motive for the attempt, attributing it instead to the work of criminals opposed to his efforts to suppress drug trafficking in Honduras. In that month demonstrations were organized in the capital in protest at the deterioration of living standards caused by the Government's economic austerity policies. Demonstrations also occurred in the department of Copán where peasant organizations blocked the Pan-American Highway in support of demands for Reina to honour election commitments to reduce the severity of the economic policies of the previous administration.

In May 1994 the National Assembly approved a proposal for a reform of the Constitution to abolish compulsory military service. Subject to finalization by the National Assembly in 1995, military service was to be voluntary from that year. Also approved was the transfer of the police from military to civilian control. In that month measures initiated by the Callejas administration for the establishment of a Public Ministry were officially completed. The new ministry was to be supervised by the DIC, which was inaugurated in January 1995. The DNI was officially disbanded in June 1994.

In July 1994, following protracted demonstrations in the capital, 4,000 members of indigenous organizations occupied the National Assembly building and succeeded in securing an agreement with the Government granting rights and social assistance to the country's indigenous community, including the creation of the first indigenous municipality in Yamaranguila, Intibucá. In that month leaders of the Roman Catholic Church warned of the possibility of serious social unrest should measures not to be taken to alleviate the growing poverty that had been exacerbated by the Government's austerity measures. The following months were characterized by growing social and political tension, including several bomb attacks. Concern was also raised by human rights organizations that the climate of instability was being fomented by the armed forces in an attempt to stem the rapid diminution of its powers. In August however, Reina conceded the temporary reintroduction of compulsory conscription in order to fill some 7,000 vacancies which the armed forces complained were impairing military efficiency. In the same month Reina ordered an investigation into charges of corruption and drug trafficking in the air force. Widespread concern at the possibility that growing tension between the Government and the armed forces might result in a military coup prompted Gen. Discua to issue a public statement denying any such intentions and reaffirming military support for the civilian authorities. In mid-August an increase in the incidence of crime and violent demonstrations resulting from the accumulating effect of austerity measures, a worsening energy crisis and food shortages, forced the Government to declare a state of national emergency and to deploy the armed forces to maintain order.

In November 1994 public-sector unions organized strikes in protest at low pay, poor working conditions and the Government's failure to honour earlier pay agreements. The disputes were resolved, however, following government promises of concessions, to be awarded once new loans had been disbursed to Honduras by international lending agencies. In late November corruption charges were filed by the public prosecutor's office against former President Callejas and 12 of his former ministers. Callejas dismissed the case as political persecution and threatened to take retaliatory legal action.

In April 1995 the National Assembly ratified the constitutional amendment abolishing compulsory military service. Sustained protests by members of indigenous organizations, in support of demands that the Government honour its commitments of July 1994 to the indigenous community, culminated in July 1995 in a 2,000-strong demonstration in the capital. The protests resulted in renewed pledges by the Government to provide social assistance and grant land titles to the indigenous population. In September the PL, PN, PINU and Partido Demócrata Cristiano de Honduras (PDCH) established the Consejo Nacional de Convergencia (National Convergence Council) in order to seek a consensus on political, social and economic issues.

In July 1995, in an unprecendented development in the Government's efforts to investigate past human rights violations, a civilian court issued indictments against 10 senior officers of the security services who had been involved in the activities of Battalion 3-16 during the 1980s. The charges concerned the kidnapping, torture and attempted murder in 1982 of six left-wing students. However, the officers refused to appear in court, invoking an amnesty granted in 1991 which, they claimed, afforded them immunity from prosecution. In October a warrant was issued for the arrest of several of the officers, who promptly went into hiding. In January 1996 the Supreme Court ruled that the officers were not entitled to protection under the 1991 amnesty law, overturning an earlier decision by the Court of Appeal. Information concerning the activities of Battalion 3-16, which had been financed and trained by the US Central Intelligence Agency, was being sought from the US Government by Valladares to support the prosecution of this and other human rights cases.

In January 1996 Col. Mario Raúl Hung Pacheco succeeded Gen. Discua as Commander-in-Chief of the Armed Forces, and was subsequently promoted to the rank of General. In the following month, in an apparent demonstration of his control over the military high command, Reina ignored the nominations for a new Minister of National Defence and Public Security proposed by Gen. Hung, appointing his own candidate instead. It was widely believed that this decision would further exacerbate discontent within the military at its diminishing influence within the country. In the following month a grenade was thrown into the grounds of the presidential residence, prompting speculation that the armed forces had been responsible for the attack.

In mid-1996 there was widespread protest at the Government's policies of wage restraint and the implementation of public-sector redundancies. Public-sector workers conducted strikes in support of demands for salary increases, a reform of the labour code and price controls. Following negotiations, the Government granted concessions, including payments totalling US $12.2m. in answer to salary demands.

In July 1996 the Human Rights Defence Committee (Codeh) claimed that the extrajudicial execution of five former military intelligence agents had occurred in recent months, and alleged that the killings were the responsibility of military officers who were attempting to prevent evidence of human rights violations from coming to light. Later that month four officers of the armed forces were arrested for allegedly conspiring to overthrow the Commander-in-Chief of the Armed Forces. Gen. Hung claimed, however, that the incident had been exaggerated and that it merely reflected the discontent within the ranks at low pay and reductions in the defence budget.

In early October 1996 a bomb exploded, without causing injury, at the parliament building in the capital. A further device was defused outside the headquarters of the PL. Responsibility for the attacks was claimed later that month by a previously unknown organization describing itself as 'Hambre' (Hunger), which claimed to be acting in response to recent rises in fuel prices. However, the President of Codeh, Ramón Custodio, expressed the popular suspicion that the attacks had been perpetrated by the armed forces in an attempt to pressurize the civilian authorities into reversing the decline in military influence in the country. In mid-October, Custodio's home in San Pedro Sula was the target of a grenade attack. A further such attack was conducted in early November on a central court building in Tegucigalpa, resulting in one fatality. In response, the Government deployed some 3,000 troops to patrol the capital and San Pedro Sula. An organization known as 'Justa C.' claimed responsibility for the attack and issued a communiqué threatening the lives of several judges involved in the investigation of cases concerning official corruption and human rights abuses by the armed forces.

In late October 1996 a judge ordered the arrest of an entire former Cabinet which had served during the Callejas administration. It was alleged that the politicians were implicated in the illicit trade of passport documents in 1993.

In early 1997 the legislature approved a constitutional reform providing for control of the police force to be transferred from the military to the civilian authorities. The Fuerza de Seguridad Pública, which had been under military control since 1963 and was widely suspected of perpetrating human rights abuses, was to be replaced by a new force, the Policía Nacional. The official transfer occurred in October.

In February 1997 demonstrations by thousands of public-sector employees, who were protesting in support of demands for salary increases, culminated in violent clashes between demonstrators and the security forces. As a result of sustained unrest the Government subsequently signed a social pact with labour leaders, which included commitments to increased social spending and price controls on basic goods. In May, following the killing of two ethnic minority leaders in the previous month, more than 3,000 members of the indigenous community conducted a march from the western departments of Copán and

Ocotepeque to the capital to protest outside the presidential palace. As a result Reina signed an agreement to conduct a full investigation into the killings and to accelerate the distribution of some 7,000 ha of land to the indigenous community. However, the killing of a further two ethnic minority leaders later that month led to accusations by human rights groups that attempts were being made to eliminate minority autonomous organizations.

During August 1997 attention was drawn to a serious crisis in the national prison system following a series of riots by prison inmates who were protesting at overcrowding and poor conditions. Several prisons were destroyed by fire and hundreds of inmates escaped.

In September 1997 Reina announced that in 1998 the post of Commander-in-Chief of the Armed Forces was to be abolished and its responsibilities assumed by the Minister of National Defence and Public Security. In the following month the National Assembly unanimously approved a constitutional amendment providing for the reduction of the legislature from 128 to 80 seats. In order to be adopted, the legislation would have to be ratified by the succeeding National Assembly, following the forthcoming general election.

At the general election held on 30 November 1997 Carlos Roberto Flores Facussé, the candidate of the ruling PL, was elected President, winning 52.7% of the votes cast; Alba Nora Gúnera de Melgar, the PN candidate, took 42.7% of the votes. The PL also obtained a majority in the National Assembly, with 67 seats, while the PN secured 55 seats, the PINU won three, the PDCH two and the left-wing Partido de Unificación Democrática obtained the remaining seat. In December Flores announced his intention to conduct a restructuring of the armed forces, incorporating the reform announced by Reina in September. Flores was inaugurated on 27 January 1998.

From the early 1980s former members of the Nicaraguan National Guard, regarded by the left-wing Sandinista Government of Nicaragua as counter-revolutionaries ('Contras'), established bases in Honduras, from which they conducted raids across the border between the two countries, allegedly with support from the Honduran armed forces. In 1983, when Honduran foreign policy was controlled by the pro-US Gen. Alvarez (the Commander-in-Chief of the Armed Forces), US involvement in Honduras increased substantially. In February 1983 the USA and Honduras initiated 'Big Pine', a series of joint military manoeuvres on Honduran territory; these exercises continued throughout the 1980s, thus enabling the USA to construct permanent military installations in Honduras. In return for considerable military assistance from the USA, the Honduran Government permitted US military aid to be supplied to the Contras based in Honduras.

Following the overthrow of Gen. Alvarez in March 1984, public opposition to the US military presence in Honduras increased, causing a temporary deterioration in relations between Honduras and the USA. In mid-1984 the Suazo Government indicated that it would review its policy of co-operation with the USA. In 1985 the USA declined to enter into a security pact with Honduras, but confirmed that it would take 'appropriate' measures to defend Honduras against any Communist aggression. In August of that year the Honduran Government announced that it would prevent the US Government from supplying further military aid to the Contras through Honduras. However, following a visit by President Azcona to the USA in 1986, the supply of aid was believed to have resumed.

In 1986 relations with Nicaragua deteriorated sharply, when Honduran troops were mobilized in an attempt to curb alleged border incursions by Nicaraguan government forces. In December, however, following revelations that the USA had secretly sold weapons to the Government of Iran and that the proceeds had been used to finance the activities of the Contra rebels, President Azcona requested the departure of the Contras from Honduras. Their presence in an area that had become known as 'Nueva Nicaragua' (New Nicaragua) was also adversely affecting the Honduran economy, as the region contained important coffee-growing land.

In August 1987 Honduras, Costa Rica, El Salvador, Guatemala and Nicaragua signed a Central American peace plan, known as the 'Esquipulas agreement', the crucial provisions of which were the implementation of simultaneous cease-fires in Nicaragua and El Salvador, a halt to foreign assistance to rebel groups, democratic reform in Nicaragua, a ban on the use of foreign territory as a base for attack, and the establishment of national reconciliation commissions in each of the Central American nations. However, the commitment of the Honduran Government to the accord appeared to be only partial. Claiming that it no longer permitted the Nicaraguan Contras to maintain bases on its territory, the Honduran Government opposed a clause in the agreement providing for the establishment of a committee to monitor the dismantling of Contra bases in Honduras.

In March 1988 several thousand US troops were temporarily deployed in Honduras, in response to an incursion into Honduran territory by the Nicaraguan army. Further violations of the border between Honduras and Nicaragua occurred during that year, as Nicaraguan troops forced at least 12,000 Contra rebels, based in the border area, into Honduras. In November President Azcona declared his opposition to the presence of the Contras in his country. In the following month it was announced that the International Court of Justice (ICJ) would consider an application that had been submitted by the Nicaraguan Government in 1986, in which Nicaragua contended that Honduras had breached international law by allowing the Contras to operate from its territory. In response, the Honduran Government threatened to withdraw support from the Esquipulas agreement.

In February 1989 a summit meeting of the five Central American Presidents was convened at Costa del Sol, El Salvador. An agreement was reached whereby the Nicaraguan Contra forces encamped in Honduras would demobilize, while President Ortega of Nicaragua guaranteed that free and fair elections would take place in his country by February 1990. At a further summit meeting, held in August at Tela, Honduras, the conditions for the demobilization of the Contras were expanded. The Honduran Government agreed to the establishment by the UN and the OAS of an international commission to oversee the voluntary repatriation or removal to a third country of the rebel forces by December 1989; in return, the Nicaraguan Government agreed to abandon the action that it had initiated against Honduras at the ICJ.

Despite the initiatives towards peace which emerged during 1989, the Contra rebels continued to launch attacks against Nicaraguan troops during the latter part of that year, maintaining their positions in Honduras beyond the December deadline. In February 1990, following national elections in Nicaragua, the outgoing President Ortega of Nicaragua ordered his forces to observe an immediate unilateral cease-fire with the Contras. Contra raids into Nicaragua continued during early 1990; however, the rebel units officially disbanded and left Honduras in June.

In June 1995 Honduras and Nicaragua signed an accord providing for the visible demarcation of each country's territorial waters in the Gulf of Fonseca, and the establishment of a joint naval patrol to police the area. The agreement followed frequent disputes concerning fishing rights in the Gulf, which occurred as a consequence of inefficient demarcation. In May a Nicaraguan naval patrol boat had seized Honduran fishing vessels which were alleged to have been operating illegally in Nicaraguan waters. An armed confrontation between naval units of both countries had ensued. Despite the June agreement, however, conflict continued, and the demarcation process was still only in its initial stages in early 1998.

A long-standing dispute between Honduras and El Salvador, regarding the demarcation of the two countries' common border and rival claims to three islands in the Gulf of Fonseca, caused hostilities to break out between the two countries in 1969. Although armed conflict soon subsided, the Honduran and Salvadorean Governments did not sign a peace treaty until 1980. In 1982 the Honduran armed forces were engaged against guerrilla forces in El Salvador, indicating an improvement in Honduran-Salvadorean relations. Honduran troops were also reportedly responsible for the deaths of several hundred Salvadorean refugees in Honduras during that year. In 1984 the Government of Honduras suspended the training of Salvadorean troops by Honduran-based US military advisers, pending agreement on the disputed territory. In 1986, however, the Governments of Honduras and El Salvador agreed that their conflicting territorial claims should be examined by the ICJ. During 1989 several border clashes occurred between Honduran and Salvadorean troops. In September 1992 the ICJ awarded Honduras sovereignty over some two-thirds of the disputed mainland territory and over one of the disputed islands in the Gulf of Fonseca. However, in subsequent years disputes continued to arise concerning the legal rights of those people resident in the reallocated territory, particularly with regard to land ownership. Following protracted negotiation, a convention governing the acquired rights and nationality of those people was finally signed by the Presidents of both countries in January 1998. An agreement was also signed providing for the demarcation of the countries' common border to be undertaken within one year.

In November 1991 the Presidents of Honduras and El Salvador signed an agreement to establish a free-trade zone on their common border, and subsequently to seek economic union. In May 1992 the Governments of Honduras, El Salvador and Guatemala agreed to promote trade and investment between the three countries. A further agreement, concluded by Honduras, El Salvador and Guatemala in October of that year, provided for the eventual establishment of a Central American political federation.

Government

Under the provisions of the Constitution approved by the National Assembly in 1982, the President is elected by a simple majority of the voters. The President holds executive power and has a single four-year mandate. Legislative power is vested in the National Assembly, with 128 members elected by universal adult suffrage for a term of four years. The country is divided into 18 local Departments.

In October 1997 the National Assembly approved a constitutional amendment providing for the reduction of the legislature from 128 to 80 members. In order to be adopted, the amendment would have to be ratified by the succeeding National Assembly, which was elected in November 1997.

Defence

Military service is voluntary. Active service lasts eight months, with subsequent reserve training. In August 1997 the armed forces totalled 18,800 men, of whom 16,000 were in the army, 1,000 in the navy and 1,800 in the air force. Paramilitary forces numbered 5,500 men. In 1997 government expenditure on defence was budgeted at 548m. lempiras. In 1990 US military aid to Honduras was almost halved, compared with the previous year, to US $20.2m. By 1993 annual assistance from the USA had been reduced to $2.7m. In mid-1997 some 53 US troops were based in Honduras.

Economic Affairs

In 1995, according to estimates by the World Bank, Honduras' gross national product (GNP), measured at average 1993–95 prices, was US $3,566m., equivalent to $600 per head. During 1985–95, it was estimated, GNP per head increased, in real terms, at an average annual rate of 0.2%. Over the same period the population increased by an annual average of 3.0%. Honduras' gross domestic product (GDP) increased, in real terms, by an annual average of 3.3% in 1985–96, and by 3.0% in 1996.

Agriculture (including hunting, forestry and fishing) contributed an estimated 21.7% of GDP and employed 42.6% of the economically active population in 1995. The principal cash crops are coffee and bananas (which contributed, respectively, an estimated 21.6% and 19.7% of all export earnings in 1996), while the main subsistence crops include maize, plantains, beans, rice, sugar cane and citrus fruit. Exports of shellfish make a significant contribution to foreign earnings (supplying 13.8% of all export earnings in 1996), and timber production is also important. During 1985–95, according to the World Bank, agricultural GDP increased by an annual average of 3.7%. Agricultural GDP increased by an estimated 2.7% in 1996.

Industry (including mining, manufacturing, construction and power) contributed an estimated 30.9% of GDP in 1996, and employed 19.4% of the working population in 1995. During 1985–95, according to the World Bank, industrial GDP increased by an annual average of 4.4%. Industrial GDP increased by an estimated 3.3% in 1996.

Mining contributed an estimated 1.9% of GDP in 1996, and employed 0.2% of the working population in 1995. Lead, zinc and silver are the major mineral exports. Gold, copper and low-grade iron ore are also mined. In addition, small quantities of petroleum derivatives are exported. The GDP of the mining sector increased by an average of 5.9% per year in 1990–95, and by an estimated 6.3% in 1996.

Manufacturing contributed an estimated 18.3% of GDP in 1996, and employed 11.8% of the working population in 1995. In 1994 the most important branches, measured by gross value of output, were food products (providing 38.2% of the total), beverages, apparel, chemical products and wood products. During 1985–95, according to the World Bank, manufacturing GDP increased by an annual average of 3.5%. Manufacturing GDP increased by an estimated 4.6% in 1996.

Energy production relies heavily upon imports of mineral fuels and lubricants (an estimated 13.6% of the value of total imports in 1996), although hydroelectric power is increasingly important and fuel wood remains a prime source of domestic energy.

The services sector contributed an estimated 47.4% of GDP in 1996, and engaged 37.9% of the working population in 1995. According to the World Bank, the GDP of the services sector increased by an average of 2.2% per year in 1985–95. Growth in the sector was an estimated 3.1% in 1996.

In 1995 Honduras recorded a visible trade deficit of US $141.4m., while there was a deficit of $200.9m. on the current account of the balance of payments. In 1995 the principal source of imports (42.8%) was the USA; other major suppliers were Guatemala, Japan, El Salvador and Germany. The USA was also the principal market for exports (54.2%) in that year; other significant purchasers were Germany, Belgium and the United Kingdom. The principal exports in 1996 were coffee, bananas and shellfish. The principal imports in 1996 were crude materials for industry, non-durable consumer goods, mineral fuels and lubricants, and capital goods for industry.

In 1996 there was an estimated budgetary deficit of 1,470.6m. lempiras (equivalent to 3.1% of GDP in that year). Honduras' external debt totalled US $4,567m. at the end of 1995, of which $3,979m. was long-term public debt. In that year the cost of debt-servicing was equivalent to 31.0% of the value of exports of goods and services. The annual rate of inflation averaged 15.2% in 1985–96. Consumer prices increased by an annual average of 23.8% in 1996. An estimated 40% of the labour force were unemployed in 1994.

Honduras is a member of the Central American Common Market (CACM, see p. 122).

In terms of average income, Honduras is among the poorest nations in the Western hemisphere, with some 80% of the population living below the poverty line. During the 1980s high levels of international economic aid, principally from the USA, masked the serious shortcomings of an economy based on extensive government intervention—which served to discourage investment in the private sector—and burdened with an outsized and inefficient public sector. Despite assistance from the IMF and an attendant change in policy in the early 1990s, the Government was unable to control a rapidly widening fiscal deficit. On assuming office in 1994, the Reina administration inherited a public-sector deficit equivalent to in excess of 10% of GDP, as well as depleted foreign reserves and a large foreign debt burden. In order to address these problems, the Government developed an economic adjustment programme for 1994–97. Measures outlined in the programme included reductions in public expenditure, tax reform and the continued privatization of state enterprises. The programme was to be supported by loans of as much as US $600m., principally from multilateral sources. In early 1997, following the failure of his administration to meet IMF-stipulated economic targets (in particular those concerning privatization, inflation and the budget deficit), Reina imposed a 15% reduction in budget expenditure for that year. In April agreement was reached with the IMF on a 'monitored' plan for 1997 which would release credits of up to $190m. Economic targets stipulated by the plan included real GDP growth of 4.5%, and reductions in the fiscal deficit, to 2.5% of GDP, and in the annual rate of inflation, to 16%. The agreement also facilitated negotiations with the Paris Club of official creditors with regard to the rescheduling of the $1,200m. debt owed to it by Honduras. The Government succeeded in reducing the annual rate of inflation to 12.8% in 1997, when real GDP growth was estimated at 4.5%. Of the principal privatization projects, the sale (of a 47% share) of the state telecommunications company was expected to occur in early 1998. However, the divestment of the heavily indebted state electricity company continued to be delayed.

Social Welfare

The state-run system of social security provides benefits for sickness, maternity, orphans, unemployment and accidents. It also provides family and old-age allowances. The Labour Code affords guarantees for employees. In 1991 the Government announced plans to transfer the provision of some social welfare services to the private sector. In 1984 Honduras had 2,800 physicians (6.6 per 10,000 inhabitants), 614 dentists and 6,300 nursing personnel. In 1995 there were 62 hospitals (of which

33 were private), 889 health centres and 5,682 hospital beds, cots and incubators. The 1995 budget allocated 1,071.5m. lempiras to the health sector.

Education

Primary education, beginning at seven years of age and lasting for six years, is officially compulsory and is provided free of charge. Secondary education, which is not compulsory, begins at the age of 13 and lasts for up to five years, comprising a first cycle of three years and a second of two years. On completion of the compulsory period of primary education, every person is required to teach at least two illiterate adults to read and write. In 1995, according to estimates by UNESCO, adult illiteracy averaged 27.3% (males 27.4%; females 27.3%). In 1993 the enrolment at primary schools included 90% of children in the relevant age-group (males 89%; females 91%), while enrolment at secondary schools in that year was equivalent to only 32% of children in the appropriate age-group. There are six universities, including the Autonomous National University in Tegucigalpa. For 1995 the education budget was 1,353m. lempiras (16.5% of total government expenditure).

Public Holidays

1998: 1 January (New Year's Day), 10–13 April (Easter), 14 April (Pan-American Day/Bastilla's Day), 1 May (Labour Day), 15 September (Independence Day), 3 October (Morazán Day), 12 October (Discovery Day), 21 October (Army Day), 25 December (Christmas).

1999: 1 January (New Year's Day), 2–5 April (Easter), 14 April (Pan-American Day/Bastilla's Day), 1 May (Labour Day), 15 September (Independence Day), 3 October (Morazán Day), 12 October (Discovery Day), 21 October (Army Day), 25 December (Christmas).

Weights and Measures

The metric system is in force, although some old Spanish measures are used, including: 25 libras = 1 arroba; 4 arrobas = 1 quintal (46 kg).

Statistical Survey

Source (unless otherwise stated): Department of Economic Studies, Banco Central de Honduras—BANTRAL, 6a y 7a Avda, 1a Calle, Apdo 3165, Tegucigalpa; tel. 337-2270; telex 1121; fax 337-1876.

Area and Population

AREA, POPULATION AND DENSITY

Area (sq km)	112,492*
Population (census results)†	
6 March 1974	2,656,948
May 1988	
Males	2,110,106
Females	2,138,455
Total	4,248,561
Population (official estimates at mid-year)	
1994	5,770,000
1995	5,953,000
1996	6,140,000
Density (per sq km) at mid-1996	54.6

* 43,433 sq miles.

† Excluding adjustments for underenumeration, estimated to have been 10% at the 1974 census.

PRINCIPAL TOWNS (estimated population, '000 at mid-1995)

Tegucigalpa (capital)	813.9	Siguatepeque	39.4
San Pedro Sula	383.9	Puerto Cortés	33.9
La Ceiba	89.2	Juticalpa	26.8
El Progreso	85.4	Tela	25.0
Choluteca	76.4	Santa Rosa de Copán	24.1
Comayagua	55.3		
Danlí	46.2		

BIRTHS AND DEATHS (UN estimates, annual averages)

	1980–85	1985–90	1990–95
Birth rate (per 1,000)	42.3	39.4	37.1
Death rate (per 1,000)	8.9	7.1	6.1

Expectation of life (UN estimates, years at birth, 1990–95): 67.7 (males 65.4; females 70.1).

Source: UN, *World Population Prospects: The 1994 Revision*.

ECONOMICALLY ACTIVE POPULATION ('000)

	1993	1994	1995
Agriculture, forestry, hunting and fishing	733.8	749.7	766.0
Mining and quarrying	4.2	4.2	4.2
Manufacturing	194.9	203.0	211.5
Construction	102.5	110.2	118.5
Electricity, gas, water and sanitary services	12.2	13.2	14.4
Transport, storage and communications	46.3	48.2	50.1
Wholesale and retail trade	174.2	183.9	194.0
Banking, insurance, etc.	32.0	34.3	36.7
Other services	352.7	376.0	400.8
Total	1,652.8	1,722.7	1,796.2

Agriculture

PRINCIPAL CROPS ('000 metric tons)

	1994	1995	1996
Rice (paddy)	28	35	41*
Maize	536	672	580*
Sorghum	53	63	68*
Dry beans	73	38	55
Sugar cane	3,078	3,139	3,237
Pineapples	86†	90†	269
Bananas	839	839	927
Plantains	189	190†	190†
Coffee (green)	126	126	131
Tobacco	9	5	5

* Unofficial figure. † FAO estimate.

Source: FAO, *Production Yearbook*.

LIVESTOCK ('000 head)

	1994	1995	1996
Cattle	2,286*	2,111	2,127
Pigs†	600	600	600
Horses and mules†	242	243	244

Poultry (million): 13† in 1994; 14† in 1995; 15† in 1996.

* Unofficial figure. † FAO estimate(s).

Source: FAO, *Production Yearbook*.

LIVESTOCK PRODUCTS ('000 metric tons)

	1994	1995	1996
Beef and veal*	45	23	25
Pig meat	14	14	15
Poultry meat	46	50	54
Cows' milk	424	444	529
Hen eggs	32*	34*	41

* FAO estimate(s).

Source: FAO, *Production Yearbook*.

Forestry

ROUNDWOOD REMOVALS ('000 cubic metres, excluding bark)

	1992	1993	1994*
Sawlogs, veneer logs and logs for sleepers	539	591	591
Other industrial wood*	19	19	19
Fuel wood*	5,377	5,538	5,702
Total	5,935	6,148	6,312

* FAO estimates.

Source: FAO, *Yearbook of Forest Products*.

SAWNWOOD PRODUCTION
('000 cubic metres, incl. railway sleepers)

	1992	1993	1994*
Coniferous (softwood)	403	359	359
Broadleaved (hardwood)	8*	5*	3
Total	411	364	362

* FAO estimate(s).

Source: FAO, *Yearbook of Forest Products*.

Fishing

(metric tons, live weight)

	1993	1994	1995
Freshwater fishes	303	232	339
Marine fishes	7,674	5,153	5,181
Marine crustaceans	12,835	12,414	13,889
Marine molluscs	5,659	4,763	4,924
Total catch	26,471	22,562	24,333

Source: FAO, *Yearbook of Fishery Statistics*.

Mining

(metal content)

	1991	1992	1993
Lead ('000 metric tons)	8.7	9.2	4.9
Zinc ('000 metric tons)	33.7	29.8	26.5
Silver (metric tons)*	43	35	24

Gold (kg): 1,700 in 1991 (Source: US Bureau of Mines).
Silver (metric tons)*: 25 in 1994; 27 in 1995; 33 in 1996.

* Source: The Silver Institute, *World Silver Survey*.

Industry

SELECTED PRODUCTS

	1993	1994	1995
Raw sugar ('000 quintales)	3,839	3,474	4,060
Cement ('000 bags of 42.5 kg)	21,961	23,519	23,413
Cigarettes ('000 packets of 20)	109,642	120,311	119,425
Matches ('000 boxes of 50)	67,640	83,437	95,888
Beer ('000 12 oz bottles)	235,436	217,835	236,252
Soft drinks ('000 12 oz bottles)	876,772	947,573	1,054,591
Wheat flour ('000 quintales)	2,284	2,277	2,161
Fabric ('000 yards)	14,259	11,286	12,731
Rum ('000 litres)	2,409	2,530	2,375
Other alcoholic drinks ('000 litres)	4,561	4,220	5,130
Vegetable oil ('000 lb)	33,730	21,623	16,887
Vegetable fat ('000 lb)	107,115	101,276	102,942

Finance

CURRENCY AND EXCHANGE RATES

Monetary Units

100 centavos = 1 lempira.

Sterling and Dollar Equivalents (30 September 1997)

£1 sterling = 21.141 lempiras;
US $1 = 13.087 lempiras;
1,000 lempiras = £47.30 = $76.41.

Average Exchange Rate (lempiras per US $)

1994 8.4088
1995 9.4710
1996 11.7053

BUDGET (million lempiras)

Revenue	1994	1995*	1996†
Current revenue	4,604.7	6,819.8	7,922.0
Taxes	4,282.3	6,100.4	6,972.6
Direct taxes	1,137.2	1,942.1	2,043.2
Income tax	1,058.5	1,848.7	1,909.1
Property tax	78.7	93.4	134.1
Indirect taxes	3,145.1	4,158.3	4,929.4
External transactions	1,294.5	1,605.3	1,803.1
Exports	109.6	175.9	97.5
Imports	1,184.9	1,429.4	1,705.6
Internal transactions	1,850.6	2,553.0	3,126.3
Non-tax revenue	177.3	526.5	692.2
Transfers	145.1	192.9	257.2
Other revenue (incl. capital revenue)	15.7	27.3	1.9
Total	4,620.4	6,847.1	7,923.9

Expenditure	1994	1995*	1996†
Current expenditure	4,773.3	5,879.5	7,534.8
Consumption expenditure	2,697.2	3,424.4	4,119.5
Interest	1,445.9	1,747.4	2,313.9
Internal debt	348.2	459.7	673.6
External debt	1,097.7	1,287.7	1,640.3
Transfers	630.2	707.7	1,101.4
Capital expenditure	1,878.0	2,611.3	1,859.7
Real investment	1,149.5	1,313.0	1,323.7
Transfers	458.2	726.7	691.4
Net lending	270.3	571.6	–155.4
Total	6,651.3	8,490.8	9,394.5

* Preliminary figures. † Estimates.

CENTRAL BANK RESERVES (US $ million at 31 December)

	1994	1995	1996
Gold	8.307	8.41	8.03
IMF special drawing rights	0.21	0.15	0.09
Foreign exchange	170.80	261.30	249.10
Total	179.31	269.86	257.22

Source: IMF, *International Financial Statistics.*

MONEY SUPPLY (million lempiras at 31 December)

	1994	1995	1996
Currency outside banks	1,995	2,111	2,630
Demand deposits at commercial banks	1,761	2,368	3,074
Total money (incl. others)	3,845	4,678	6,053

Source: IMF, *International Financial Statistics.*

COST OF LIVING (Consumer Price Index; base: 1978 = 100)

	1994	1995	1996
Food	559.7	718.1	895.4
Housing	483.2	633.5	783.7
Clothing	671.9	826.8	1,008.9
Health care	621.9	784.9	960.5
Personal care	465.5	605.6	751.3
Beverages and tobacco	740.8	914.1	1,120.4
Transport	366.6	612.1	791.4
Education, reading matter and recreation	610.3	830.3	1,014.9
All items	550.0	712.0	881.8

NATIONAL ACCOUNTS (million lempiras at current prices)

Expenditure on the Gross Domestic Product

	1994	1995	1996
Government final consumption expenditure	2,780	3,535	4,600
Private final consumption expenditure	18,301	23,803	30,404
Increase in stocks	2,751	2,842	3,400
Gross fixed capital formation	8,110	9,105	11,607
Total domestic expenditure	31,942	39,285	50,011
Exports of goods and services	11,311	16,280	22,616
Less Imports of goods and services	14,391	18,033	24,821
GDP in purchasers' values	28,862	37,532	47,806

Source: IMF, *International Financial Statistics.*

Gross Domestic Product by Economic Activity

	1994	1995*	1996†
Agriculture, hunting, forestry and fishing	6,030	7,026	8,853
Mining and quarrying	490	629	763
Manufacturing	4,275	5,818	7,455
Electricity, gas and water	939	1,778	2,223
Construction	1,479	1,944	2,148
Wholesale and retail trade	2,607	3,915	4,972
Transport, storage and communications	1,323	1,546	1,824
Finance, insurance and real estate	2,205	3,007	3,837
Owner-occupied dwellings	1,441	1,832	2,350
Public administration and defence	1,547	1,912	2,334
Other services	2,687	3,372	4,026
GDP at factor cost	25,023	32,779	40,785
Indirect taxes, *less* subsidies	3,839	4,818	6,167
GDP in purchasers' values	28,862	37,597	46,952

* Preliminary figures. † Estimates.

BALANCE OF PAYMENTS (US $ million)

	1993	1994	1995
Exports of goods f.o.b.	999.6	1,101.5	1,377.2
Imports of goods f.o.b.	–1,203.1	–1,351.1	–1,518.6
Trade balance	–203.5	–249.6	–141.4
Exports of services	223.9	242.4	257.6
Imports of services	–294.7	–311.0	–333.7
Balance on goods and services	–274.3	–318.2	–217.5
Other income received	16.6	24.0	32.3
Other income paid	–215.3	–238.1	–258.2
Balance on goods, services and income	–473.0	–532.3	–443.4
Current transfers received	165.5	190.2	243.7
Current transfers paid	–1.2	–1.2	–1.2
Current balance	–308.7	–343.3	–200.9
Direct investment from abroad	26.7	34.8	50.0
Other investment assets	–139.6	8.9	–12.8
Other investment liabilities	135.7	113.8	77.4
Net errors and omissions	–47.5	115.5	45.0
Overall balance	–333.4	–70.3	–41.3

Source: IMF, *International Financial Statistics.*

External Trade

PRINCIPAL COMMODITIES (US $ million)

Imports c.i.f.	1994	1995	1996*
Consumer goods	318.8	356.8	393.2
Non-durable	224.0	250.7	276.3
Durable	94.8	106.1	116.9
Crude materials and intermediate products	527.2	590.1	650.4
For agriculture	109.7	122.8	135.4
For industry	417.5	467.3	515.0
Mineral fuels and lubricants	190.6	221.6	246.2
Construction materials	44.8	50.1	55.3
Capital goods	350.7	392.5	432.6
For industry	194.2	217.4	239.6
For transport	141.8	158.7	174.9
Total (incl. others)	1,460.3	1,642.7	1,812.5

Exports f.o.b.	1994	1995	1996*
Bananas	155.1	214.2	254.6
Coffee	200.1	349.3	278.9
Shellfish	165.5	158.6	178.2
Meat	39.0	13.0	10.7
Wood	21.3	19.0	21.7
Melons	24.2	22.2	n.a.
Pineapples	19.7	19.8	n.a.
Lead and zinc	22.8	28.9	n.a.
Total (incl. others)	965.5	1,220.2	1,290.4

* Preliminary figures.

PRINCIPAL TRADING PARTNERS (US $ million)

Imports c.i.f.	1993	1994	1995
Belgium	8.1	20.5	22.2
Canada	14.1	13.4	14.5
Costa Rica	38.0	23.9	44.0
El Salvador	44.5	48.1	65.1
Germany	29.7	52.3	56.7
Guatemala	77.6	86.6	114.3
Italy	12.9	9.9	10.7
Japan	56.8	68.7	74.5
Mexico	35.6	43.7	47.4
Netherlands	11.8	21.8	23.6
Spain	7.4	26.7	29.0
USA	588.3	626.6	679.5
Total (incl. others)	1,259.4	1,410.3	1,587.6

Exports f.o.b.	1993	1994	1995
Belgium	55.6	41.6	52.4
Costa Rica	6.0	9.9	16.3
El Salvador	18.2	15.3	12.9
France	8.2	11.2	14.1
Germany	99.7	60.0	75.5
Guatemala	13.7	7.2	8.1
Italy	9.0	16.3	20.5
Japan	18.9	31.2	39.3
Netherlands	8.5	18.4	23.1
Nicaragua	13.5	14.8	16.2
Spain	16.7	30.8	38.8
United Kingdom	24.1	38.3	48.2
USA	432.2	470.4	592.3
Total (incl. others)	808.0	872.8	1,092.9

Transport

ROAD TRAFFIC (motor vehicles in use)

	1993	1994	1995
Passenger cars	67,777	72,233	81,439
Commercial vehicles	146,866	161,757	170,006
Motorcycles and bicycles	18,021	19,427	22,482

SHIPPING

Merchant Fleet (registered at 31 December)

	1994	1995	1996
Number of vessels	1,400	1,409	1,408
Total displacement ('000 grt)	1,206.3	1,206.0	1,197.8

Source: Lloyd's Register of Shipping, *World Fleet Statistics*.

International Sea-borne Freight Traffic ('000 metric tons)

	1988	1989	1990
Goods loaded	1,328	1,333	1,316
Goods unloaded	1,151	1,222	1,002

Source: UN, *Monthly Bulletin of Statistics*.

CIVIL AVIATION (traffic on scheduled services)

	1992	1993	1994
Kilometres flown (million)	5	4	5
Passengers carried ('000)	438	409	449
Passenger-km (million)	309	362	323
Total ton-km (million)	40	50	42

Source: UN, *Statistical Yearbook*.

Tourism

	1992	1993	1994
Tourist arrivals	157,569	222,234	232,680
Tourist receipts (US $ million)	31.8	32.0*	33.0*

Tourist arrivals: 237,985 in 1995.

* Source: UN, *Statistical Yearbook*.

Communications Media

	1993	1994	1995
Radio receivers ('000 in use)	2,175	2,240	2,310
Television receivers ('000 in use)	415	428	500
Telephones ('000 main lines in use)	117	131	161
Daily newspapers			
Number	n.a.	5	5*
Average circulation ('000 copies)	n.a.	240*	240*

* Estimate.

Sources: partly UN, *Statistical Yearbook*, and UNESCO, *Statistical Yearbook*.

Education

(1995)

	Institutions	Teachers	Students
Pre-primary	1,348	2,671	73,491
Primary	8,168	28,978	1,008,092
Secondary	661	12,480	184,589
University level	8	3,676	54,293

Directory

The Constitution

Following the elections of April 1980, the 1965 Constitution was revised. The new Constitution was approved by the National Assembly in November 1982, and amended in 1995. The following are some of its main provisions:

Honduras is constituted as a democratic Republic. All Hondurans over 18 years of age are citizens.

THE SUFFRAGE AND POLITICAL PARTIES

The vote is direct and secret. Any political party which proclaims or practises doctrines contrary to the democratic spirit is forbidden. A National Electoral Council will be set up at the end of each presidential term. Its general function will be to supervise all elections and to register political parties. A proportional system of voting will be adopted for the election of Municipal Corporations.

INDIVIDUAL RIGHTS AND GUARANTEES

The right to life is declared inviolable; the death penalty is abolished. The Constitution recognizes the right of habeas corpus and arrests may be made only by judicial order. Remand for interrogation may not last more than six days, and no-one may be held incommunicado for more than 24 hours. The Constitution recognizes the rights of free expression of thought and opinion, the free circulation of information, of peaceful, unarmed association, of free movement within and out of the country, of political asylum and of religious and educational freedom. Civil marriage and divorce are recognized.

WORKERS' WELFARE

All have a right to work. Day work shall not exceed eight hours per day or 44 hours per week; night work shall not exceed six hours per night or 36 hours per week. Equal pay shall be given for equal work. The legality of trade unions and the right to strike are recognized.

EDUCATION

The State is responsible for education, which shall be free, lay, and, in the primary stage, compulsory. Private education is liable to inspection and regulation by the State.

LEGISLATIVE POWER

Deputies are obliged to vote, for or against, on any measure at the discussion of which they are present. The National Assembly has power to grant amnesties to political prisoners; approve or disapprove of the actions of the Executive; declare part or the whole of the Republic subject to a state of siege; declare war; approve or withhold approval of treaties; withhold approval of the accounts of public expenditure when these exceed the sums fixed in the budget; decree, interpret, repeal and amend laws, and pass legislation fixing the rate of exchange or stabilizing the national currency. The National Assembly may suspend certain guarantees in all or part of the Republic for 60 days in the case of grave danger from civil or foreign war, epidemics or any other calamity. Deputies are elected in the proportion of one deputy and one substitute for every 35,000 inhabitants, or fraction over 15,000. Congress may amend the basis in the light of increasing population.

EXECUTIVE POWER

Executive power is exercised by the President of the Republic, who is elected for four years by a simple majority of the people. No President may serve more than one term.

JUDICIAL POWER

The Judiciary consists of the Supreme Court, the Courts of Appeal and various lesser tribunals. The nine judges and seven substitute judges of the Supreme Court are elected by the National Assembly for a period of four years. The Supreme Court is empowered to declare laws unconstitutional.

THE ARMED FORCES

The armed forces are declared by the Constitution to be essentially professional and non-political. The President exercises military power through a Commander-in-Chief who is designated for a period of three years by the National Assembly, and may be dismissed only by it by a two-thirds' majority.

LOCAL ADMINISTRATION

The country is divided into 18 Departments for purposes of local administration, and these are subdivided into autonomous Municipalities; the functions of local offices shall be only economic and administrative.

The Government

HEAD OF STATE

President: CARLOS ROBERTO FLORES FACUSSÉ (assumed office 27 January 1998).

CABINET
(February 1998)

Minister of the Interior and Justice: DELMER URBIZO PANTING.

Minister in the Office of the President: GUSTAVO ALFARO.

Minister of Foreign Affairs: JOSÉ FERNANDO MARTÍNEZ.

Minister of Industry, Commerce and Tourism: REGINALDO PANTING.

Minister of Finance: GABRIELA NÚÑEZ LÓPEZ.

Minister of National Defence and Public Security: Col CRISTÓBAL CORRALES CÁLIX.

Minister of Labour and Social Welfare: ANDRÉS VÍCTOR ARTILES.

Minister of Health: MARCO ANTONIO ROSA.

Minister of Public Education: ARÍSTIDES MEJÍA CASCO.

Minister of Public Works, Transport and Housing: TOMÁS R. LOZANO REYES.

Minister of Culture, Art and Sports: HERMÁN ALLAN PADGET.

Minister of Agriculture and Livestock: PEDRO ARTURO SEVILLA.

Minister of Natural Resources and Environment: ELVIN ERNESTO SANTOS.

Ministers without Portfolio: JORGE ARTURO REINA, NAHUM VALLADARES, PLUTARCO CASTELLANOS, ROBERTO LEIVA.

MINISTRIES

Office of the President: Palacio José Cecilio del Valle, Blvd Juan Pablo II, Tegucigalpa; tel. 32-6282; fax 31-0097.

Ministry of Agriculture and Livestock: Tegucigalpa.

Ministry of Culture, Art and Sports: Avda La Paz, Tegucigalpa; tel. 36-9738; fax 36-9532.

Ministry of Finance: 5a Avda, 3a Calle, Tegucigalpa; tel. 22-1278; fax 38-2309.

Ministry of Foreign Affairs: Centro Cívico Gubernamental, Tegucigalpa; tel. 34-3297; fax 34-1484.

Ministry of Health: 4a Avda, 3a Calle, Tegucigalpa; tel. 22-1386; fax 38-4141.

Ministry of Industry, Commerce and Tourism: Edif. Salame, 5a Avda, 4a Calle, Tegucigalpa; tel. 38-2025; fax 37-2836.

Ministry of the Interior and Justice: Palacio de los Ministerios, 2°, Tegucigalpa; tel. 22-8604; fax 37-1121.

Ministry of Labour and Social Welfare: 2a y 3a Avda, 7a Calle, Comayagüela, Tegucigalpa; tel. 22-8526; fax 22-3220.

Ministry of National Defence and Public Security: 5a Avda, 4a Calle, Tegucigalpa; tel. 22-8560; fax 38-0238.

Ministry of Natural Resources and Environment: Blvd Miraflores, Tegucigalpa; tel. 32-3141.

Ministry of Public Education: 1a Avda, 2a y 3a Calle, No 201, Comayagüela, Tegucigalpa; tel. 22-8517; fax 37-4312.

Ministry of Public Works, Transport and Housing: Barrio La Bolsa, Comayagüela, Tegucigalpa; tel. 33-7690; fax 25-2227.

President and Legislature

PRESIDENT

Election, 30 November 1997

Candidate	Votes cast	% of votes
CARLOS ROBERTO FLORES FACUSSÉ (PL)	1,039,567	52.70
ALBA NORA GÚNERA DE MELGAR (PN)	843,154	42.74
OLBAN F. VALLADARES (PINU)	41,463	2.10
ARTURO CORRALES ALVÁREZ (PDCH)	24,717	1.25
MATÍAS FUNES (PUD)	23.745	1.20
Total	1,972,646	100.00

ASAMBLEA NACIONAL

General Election, 30 November 1997

Party	Votes cast	% of votes	Seats
Partido Liberal (PL)	940,575	49.55	67
Partido Nacional (PN)	789,015	41.56	55
Partido Innovación y Unidad—Social Democracia (PINU)	78,495	4.13	3
Partido Demócrata Cristiano de Honduras (PDCH)	49,650	2.62	2
Partido de Unificación Democrática (PUD)	40,658	2.14	1
Total*	1,898,393	100.00	128

* There were, in addition, 108,635 blank votes and 55,431 spoiled votes.

Political Organizations

Asociación para el Progreso de Honduras (APROH): right-wing grouping of business interests and members of the armed forces; Vice-Pres. MIGUEL FACUSSÉ; Sec. OSWALDO RAMOS SOTO.

Francisco Morazán Frente Constitucional (FMFC): f. 1988; composed of labour, social, political and other organizations.

Frente Patriótico Hondureño (FPH): left-wing alliance comprising:

Partido de Acción Socialista de Honduras (PASOH): Leaders MARIO VIRGILIO CARAS, ROGELIO MARTÍNEZ REINA.

Partido Comunista de Honduras—Marxista-Leninista (PCH—ML): f. 1954; gained legal status 1981; linked with DNU; Leader RIGOBERTO PADILLA RUSH.

Partido Demócrata Cristiano de Honduras (PDCH): legally recognized in 1980; Pres. EFRAÍN DÍAZ ARRIVILLAGA; Leader Dr HERNÁN CORRALES PADILLA.

Partido Innovación y Unidad—Social Democracia (PINU): Apdo 105, Tegucigalpa; tel. 37-1357; f. 1970; legally recognized in 1978; Leader OLBAN F. VALLADARES.

Partido Liberal (PL): Tegucigalpa; tel. 32-0520; f. 1980; factions within the party include the Alianza Liberal del Pueblo, the Movimiento Florista (Leader CARLOS ROBERTO FLORES FACUSSÉ), and the Movimiento Liberal Democrático Revolucionario (Pres. JORGE ARTURO REINA); Pres. CARLOS ROBERTO FLORES FACUSSÉ; Sec.-Gen. ROBERTO MICHELETTI BAIN.

Partido Nacional (PN): Tegucigalpa; f. 1902; traditional right-wing party; internal opposition tendencies include Movimiento Democratizador Nacionalista (MODENA), Movimiento de Unidad y Cambio (MUC), Movimiento Nacional de Reivindicación Callejista (MONARCA) and Tendencia Nacionalista de Trabajo; Sec. MARIO AGUILAR GONZÁLEZ; Leader ELIAS ASFURA.

Partido de Unificación Democrática (PUD): f. 1993; left-wing coalition comprising Partido Revolucionario Hondureño, Partido Renovación Patriótica, Partido para la Transformación de Honduras and Partido Morazanista.

Unión Revolucionaria del Pueblo (URP): f. 1980 following split in Communist Party; peasant support.

The Dirección Nacional Unificada—Movimiento Revolucionario Hondureño (DNU—MRH) comprises the following guerrilla groups:

Fuerzas Populares Revolucionarias (FRP) Lorenzo Zelaya.

Frente Morazanista para la Liberación de Honduras (FMLH).

Froylan Turcios.

Movimiento Popular de Liberación Cinchonero (MPLC).

Movimiento de Unidad Revolucionaria (MUR).

Partido Revolucionario de los Trabajadores Centroamericanos de Honduras (PRTCH).

Other guerrilla forces include the **Alianza por Acción Anticomunista (AAA)** and the **Frente Popular de Liberación, Nueve de Mayo (FPL)**.

Diplomatic Representation

EMBASSIES IN HONDURAS

Argentina: Avda José María Medina 417, Col. Rubén Darío, Apdo 3208, Tegucigalpa; tel. 32-3376; telex 1120; fax 31-0376; Ambassador: ADRIÁN GUILLERMO MIRSON.

Brazil: Col. La Reforma, Calle La Salle 1309, Apdo 341, Tegucigalpa; tel. 36-5867; fax 36-5873; e-mail brastegu@hondudata.hn; Ambassador: RUBEM AMARAL Jr.

Chile: Edif. Interamericana frente Los Castaños, Blvd Morazán, Apdo 222, Tegucigalpa; telex 1195; fax 32-8853; Ambassador: GERMÁN CARRASCO.

China (Taiwan): Col. Lomas del Guijarro, Calle Eucaliptos 3750, Apdo 3433, Tegucigalpa; tel. 31-1484; telex 1383; e-mail giohon@datum.hn; Ambassador: CHING-YEN CHANG.

Colombia: Edif. Palmira, 4°, Col. Palmira, Apdo 468, Tegucigalpa; tel. 32-9709; fax 32-8133; Ambassador: GERMÁN RAMÍREZ BULLA.

Costa Rica: Residencial El Triángulo, Lomas del Guijarro, Apdo 512, Tegucigalpa; tel. 32-1768; telex 1154; fax 32-1876; Ambassador: MANUEL CARBALLO QUINTANA.

Dominican Republic: Col. La Granja 402, 4a Calle entre 4a y 5a Avda Comayagüela, Apdo 1460, Tegucigalpa; Ambassador: JUAN EMILIO CANÓ DE LA MOTA.

Ecuador: Col. Palmira, Avda Juan Lindo 122, Apdo 358, Tegucigalpa; tel. 36-5980; telex 1471; fax 36-6929; Ambassador: Dr JOSÉ IGNACIO JIJÓN FREILE.

El Salvador: Col. San Carlos, 2a Avda 219, Tegucigalpa; tel. 36-7344; fax 36-9403; Ambassador: Dr BYRON FERNANDO LARIOS LÓPEZ.

France: Col. Palmira, Avda Juan Lindo, Apdo 3441, Tegucigalpa; tel. 36-6800; telex 1180; fax 36-8051; Ambassador: GILLES VIDAL.

Germany: Edif. Paysen, 3°, Blvd Morazán, Apdo 3145, Tegucigalpa; tel. 32-3161; fax 32-9518; Ambassador: ANDREAS KULICK.

Guatemala: Col. Palmira, Avda Juan Lindo 313, Apdo 34-C, Tegucigalpa; tel. 32-5018; Ambassador: EUNICE LIMA.

Holy See: Palacio de la Nunciatura Apostólica, Col. Palmira 412, Apdo 324, Tegucigalpa; tel. 31-4381; fax 32-8280; Apostolic Nuncio: Most Rev. LUIGI CONTI, Titular Archbishop of Gratiana.

Israel: Edif. Palmira, Col. Palmira, Apdo 1187, Tegucigalpa; Ambassador: SHIMON AGOUR.

Italy: Col. Reforma 2062, Avda Principal, Apdo 317, Tegucigalpa; telex 1332; Ambassador: Dr MARIO ALBERTO MONTECALVO.

Japan: Col. Reforma, 2a Avda, Plaza del Guanacaste, Apdo 125-C, Tegucigalpa; telex 1141; Ambassador: KIICHI ITABASHI.

Mexico: Avda República del Brasil 2028, Apdo 769, Tegucigalpa; tel. 32-4039; telex 1143; fax 32-4224; Ambassador: MANUEL MARTÍNEZ DEL SOBRAL.

Nicaragua: Col. Tepeyac, Bloque M-1, Apdo 392, Tegucigalpa; tel. 32-7224; fax 31-1412; Ambassador: Dr NOEL RIVAS GASTEAZORO.

Panama: Edif. Palmira, Col. Palmira, Apdo 397, Tegucigalpa; tel. 31-5441; fax 31-5441; Ambassador: JULIO E. GÓMEZ AMADOR.

Peru: Col. Alameda, Villeda Morales 1902, Apdo 3171, Tegucigalpa; tel. 31-5261; fax 32-0145; Ambassador: JOSÉ ARTURO MONTOYA STUVA.

Spain: Col. Matamoros, Calle Santander 801, Apdo 3223, Tegucigalpa; tel. 36-6875; telex 1142; fax 36-8682; Ambassador: CARLOS GÓMEZ-MÚGICA SANZ.

United Kingdom: Edif. Palmira, 3°, Col. Palmira, Apdo 290, Tegucigalpa; tel. 32-0612; fax 32-5480; Ambassador: PETER R. HOLMES.

USA: Avda La Paz, Apdo 26-C, Tegucigalpa; tel. 32-3120; fax 32-0027; Ambassador: JAMES F. CREAGAN.

Uruguay: Edif. Palmira, 4°, Col. Palmira, Apdo 329, Tegucigalpa; Ambassador: ALFREDO MENINI TERRA.

Venezuela: Col. Rubén Darío, entre Avda Las Minitas y Avda Rubén Darío, Casa 2321, Tegucigalpa; telex 1238; Ambassador: JESÚS ELÍAS M.

Judicial System

Justice is administered by the Supreme Court (which has nine judges), five Courts of Appeal, and departmental courts which have their own local jurisdiction.

Tegucigalpa has two Courts of Appeal which have jurisdiction (1) in the department of Francisco Morazán, and (2) in the departments of Choluteca Valle, El Paraíso and Olancho.

The Appeal Court of San Pedro Sula has jurisdiction in the department of Cortés. That of Comayagua has jurisdiction in the departments of Comayagua, La Paz and Intibucá; that of Santa Bárbara in the departments of Santa Bárbara, Lempira and Copán.

Supreme Court: Edif. Palacio de Justicia, contiguo Col. Miraflores, Centro Cívico Gubernamental, Tegucigalpa; tel. 33-9208; fax 33-6784.

President of the Supreme Court of Justice: MIGUEL ANGEL RIVERA PORTILLO.

Attorney-General: EDMUNDO ORELLANA.

Religion

The majority of the population are Roman Catholics; the Constitution guarantees toleration to all forms of religious belief.

CHRISTIANITY

The Roman Catholic Church

Honduras comprises one archdiocese and six dioceses. At 31 December 1995 some 94% of the population were adherents.

Bishops' Conference: Conferencia Episcopal de Honduras, Apdo 847, Tegucigalpa; tel. 32-4043; fax 38-7838; e-mail ceh@sdnhon.org.hn; f. 1929; Pres. Most Rev. OSCAR ANDRÉS RODRÍGUEZ MARADIAGA, Archbishop of Tegucigalpa.

Archbishop of Tegucigalpa: Most Rev. OSCAR ANDRÉS RODRÍGUEZ MARADIAGA, Arzobispado, 3a-2a Avda 1113, Apdo 106, Tegucigalpa; tel. 37-0353; fax 22-2337.

The Anglican Communion

Honduras comprises a single missionary diocese, in Province IX of the Episcopal Church in the USA.

Bishop of Honduras: Rt Rev. LEOPOLD FRADE, Apdo 586, San Pedro Sula; tel. 56-6155; fax 56-6467.

The Baptist Church

Baptist Convention of Honduras: Apdo 868, Tegucigalpa; tel. and fax 38-3717; Pres. MISAEL MARRIAGA.

BAHÁ'Í FAITH

National Spiritual Assembly: Apdo 273, Tegucigalpa; tel. and fax 33-1182; mems resident in 667 localities.

The Press

DAILIES

El Faro Porteño: Puerto Cortés.

La Gaceta: Tegucigalpa; f. 1830; morning; official govt paper; Dir MARCIAL LAGOS; circ. 3,000.

El Heraldo: Avda los Próceres, Frente Instituto del Tórax, Tegucigalpa; f. 1979; morning; independent; Dir JOSÉ FRANCISCO MORALES CÁLIX; circ. 45,000.

La Prensa: 3a Avda No 34, Apdo 143, San Pedro Sula; f. 1964; independent; Pres. AMILCAR SANTAMARÍA; circ. 50,000.

El Tiempo: Altos del Centro Comercial Miramontes, Col. Miramontes, Tegucigalpa; tel. 31-0418; f. 1970; liberal; Dir MANUEL GAMERO; circ. 42,000.

El Tiempo: 7a Avda 6, Calle SO 55, Apdo 450, San Pedro Sula; f. 1970; left-of-centre; Dir EDMOND L. BOGRÁN; Editor MANUEL GAMERO; circ. 70,000.

La Tribuna: Apdo 1501, Tegucigalpa; f. 1977; morning; independent; Dir ADÁN ELVIR FLORES; Editor CARLOS ROBERTO FLORES FACUSSÉ; circ. 60,000.

PERIODICALS

Cambio Empresarial: Apdo 1111, Tegucigalpa; tel. 37-2853; fax 37-0480; monthly; economic, political, social; Editor JOAQUÍN MEDINA OVIEDO.

El Comercio: Cámara de Comercio e Industrias de Tegucigalpa, Blvd Centroamérica, Apdo 3444, Tegucigalpa; tel. 32-8210; fax 31-2049; f. 1970; monthly; commercial and industrial news; Exec. Dir JOSÉ ANÍBAL MADRID.

Cultura para Todos: San Pedro Sula; monthly.

Espectador: San Pedro Sula; weekly.

Extra: Tegucigalpa; tel. 37-2533; f. 1965; monthly; independent; current affairs; Editor VICENTE MACHADO VALLE.

Hablemos Claro: Edif. EXPAHSA, Blvd Suyapa, Tegucigalpa; tel. 32-8058; fax 32-9950; e-mail abrecha@hondutel.hn; f. 1990; weekly; Editor RODRIGO WONG ARÉVALO; circ. 10,000.

Hibueras: Apdo 955, Tegucigalpa; Dir RAÚL LANZA VALERIANO.

Presente: Tegucigalpa; monthly.

Revista Ideas: Tegucigalpa; 6 a year; women's interest.

Revista Prisma: Tegucigalpa; quarterly; cultural; Editor MARÍA LUISA CASTELLANOS.

Sucesos: Tegucigalpa; monthly.

Tribuna Sindical: Tegucigalpa; monthly.

PRESS ASSOCIATION

Asociación de Prensa Hondureña: 6a Calle (altos), Barrio Guanacaste, Apdo 893, Tegucigalpa; tel. 37-8345; f. 1930; Pres. MIGUEL OSMUNDO MEJA ERAZO.

FOREIGN NEWS AGENCIES

Agence France-Presse (AFP) (France): Tegucigalpa; Correspondent WINSTON CÁLIX.

Agencia EFE (Spain): Edif. Jiménez Castro, 5°, Of. 505, Tegucigalpa; tel. 22-0493; Bureau Chief ARMANDO ENRIQUE CERRATO CORTÉS.

Agenzia Nazionale Stampa Associata (ANSA) (Italy): Edif. La Plazuela, Barrio La Plazuela, Tegucigalpa; tel. 37-7701; telex 1353; Correspondent RAÚL MONCADA.

Deutsche Presse-Agentur (dpa) (Germany): Edif. Jiménez Castro, Of. 203, 4a Calle y 5a Avda, No 405, Apdo 3522, Tegucigalpa; tel. 37-8570; Correspondent WILFREDO GARCÍA CASTRO.

Inter Press Service (IPS) (Italy): Apdo 228, Tegucigalpa; tel. 32-5342; Correspondent JUAN RAMÓN DURÁN.

Reuters (United Kingdom): Edif. Palmira, frente Honduras Maya, 5°, Col. Palmira, Tegucigalpa; tel. 31-5329.

United Press International (UPI) (USA): c/o El Tiempo, Altos del Centro Comercial Miramontes, Col. Miramontes, Tegucigalpa; tel. 31-0418; Correspondent VILMA GLORIA ROSALES.

Publishers

Compañía Editora Nacional, SA: 5a Calle Oriente, No 410, Tegucigalpa.

Editora Cultural: 6a Avda Norte, 7a Calle, Comayagüela, Tegucigalpa.

Editorial Nuevo Continente: Tegucigalpa; tel. 22-5073; Dir LETICIA SILVA DE OYUELA.

Editorial Paulino Valladares, Carlota Vda de Valladares: 5a Avda, 5a y 6a Calle, Tegucigalpa.

Guaymuras: Apdo 1843, Tegucigalpa; tel. 37-5433; fax 38-4578; f. 1980; Dir ISOLDA ARITA MELZER; Admin. ROSENDO ANTÚNEZ.

Industria Editorial Lypsa: Apdo 167-C, Tegucigalpa; tel. 22-9775; Man. JOSÉ BENNATON.

Universidad Nacional Autónoma de Honduras: Blvd Suyapa, Tegucigalpa; tel. 31-4601; telex 1289; fax 31-4601; f. 1847.

Broadcasting and Communications

TELECOMMUNICATIONS

Comisión Nacional de Telecomunicaciones (Conatel): Apdo 15012, Tegucigalpa; tel. 21-3500; fax 21-3511; Pres. GILBERTO AQUINO; Exec. Sec. WALTER DAVID SANDOVAL.

Empresa Hondureña de Telecomunicaciones (Hondutel): Apdo 1794, Tegucigalpa; tel. 22-2041; telex 1343; fax 38-4206; Gen. Man. ARTURO MORALES FÚNEZ.

RADIO

Radio América: Apdo 259, Tegucigalpa; commercial station; tel. 32-7028; fax 31-2923; 13 relay stations; Dir-Gen. AMILCAR ZELAYA R.

Radio Nacional de Honduras: Apdo 403, Tegucigalpa; tel. 38-5478; telex 1147; f. 1976; official station, operated by the Govt; Dir MIGUEL RAFAEL ZAVALA.

La Voz de Centroamérica: 10a Avda Norte, 9a Calle, Apdo 120, San Pedro Sula; commercial station; tel. 52-7660; telex 5716; fax 57-3257; Gen. Man. NOEMI SIKAFFY.

La Voz de Honduras: Blvd Suyapa, Apdo 642, Tegucigalpa; commercial station; 23 relay stations; Gen. Man. NOEMI VALLADARES.

TELEVISION

Compañía Televisora Hondureña, SA: Blvd Suyapa, Apdo 734, Tegucigalpa; tel. 32-7835; telex 1126; fax 32-0097; f. 1959; main station Channel 5; nine relay stations; Gen. Man. JOSÉ RAFAEL FERRARI.

Corporación Centroamericana de Comunicaciones, SA de CV: 9a Calle, 10a Avda, No 64, Barrio Guamilito, Apdo 120, San Pedro Sula; tel. 52-7660; fax 57-3257; Pres. BLANCA SIKAFFY.

Telesistema Hondureño, SA: Apdo 642, Tegucigalpa; tel. 32-0710; telex 1126; f. 1967; main station Channel 3; four relay stations; Gen. Man. MANUEL VILLEDA TOLEDO; Asst Gen. Man. ANA MARÍA VILLEDA F.

Trecevisión: Apdo 393, Tegucigalpa; subscriber TV; one relay station in San Pedro Sula; Gen. Man. F. PON AGUILAR.

Voz y Imagen de Centro América: Apdo 120, San Pedro Sula; tel. 52-7660; fax 57-3257; Channels 9, 2 and 13; Pres. BLANCA SIKAFFY.

Finance

(cap. = capital; res = reserves; dep. = deposits;
m. = million; brs = branches;
amounts in lempiras unless otherwise stated)

BANKING

Central Bank

Banco Central de Honduras—BANTRAL: 6a y 7a Avda, 1a Calle, Apdo 3165, Tegucigalpa; tel. 337-2270; telex 1121; fax 337-

1876; f. 1950; bank of issue; cap. 63.7m., res 373.5m., dep. 4,762.2m. (Dec. 1992); Pres. EMÍN BARJUM MAHOMAR; Man. J. ERNESTO ANARIBA; 4 brs.

Commercial Banks

Banco de el Ahorro Hondureño, SA (BANCAHORRO): Avda Colón 711, Apdo 78-C, Tegucigalpa; tel. 22-5161; telex 1184; f. 1960; cap. and res US $5.3m., dep. $83.3m. (June 1984); Pres. and Gen. Man. FRANCISCO VILLARS; 8 brs.

Banco Atlántida, SA (BANCATLAN): Blvd Centroamérica, Plaza Bancatlán, Apdo 3164, Tegucigalpa; tel. 332-1742; telex 1106; fax 332-6120; f. 1913; cap. 164.7m., res 28.4m., dep. 2,264.3m. (Dec. 1996); Exec. Pres. GUILLERMO BUESO; First Vice-Pres. SALVADOR GÓMEZ A.; 18 brs.

Banco La Capitalizadora Hondureña, SA (BANCAHSA): 5a Avda, 5a Calle 508, Apdo 344, Tegucigalpa; tel. 37-1171; telex 1162; f. 1948; cap. and res US $16.3m., dep. $119.9m. (June 1995); Pres. and Gen. Man. JORGE ALBERTO ALVARADO; 52 brs.

Banco del Comercio, SA (BANCOMER): 6a Avda, Calle SO 1-2, Apdo 160, San Pedro Sula; tel. 54-3600; telex 5480; cap. and res US $6.5m., dep. $28.3m. (June 1984); Pres. RODOLFO CÓRDOBA PINEDA; 4 brs.

Banco Continental, SA (BANCON): Edif. Continental, 3a Avda 7, entre 2a y 3a Calle, Apdo 390, San Pedro Sula; tel. 50-2942; telex 5648; fax 50-2750; f. 1974; cap. 100m., res 14.3m., dep. 304.5m. (Dec. 1994); Pres. JAIME ROSENTHAL OLIVA; 6 brs.

Banco de las Fuerzas Armadas, SA (BANFFAA): Centro Comercial Los Castaños, Blvd Morazán, Apdo 877, Tegucigalpa; tel. 331-2051; telex 1245; fax 331-3825; f. 1979; cap. 10m., res 33.2m., dep. 428.1m. (Dec. 1992); Pres. LUIS ALONSO DISCUA ELVIR; Gen. Man. CARLOS RIVERA XATRUCH; 15 brs.

Banco de Honduras, SA: Edif. Midence-Soto, frente a Plaza Morazán, Apdo 3434, Tegucigalpa; tel. 337-1151; telex 1116; fax 222-3451; f. 1889; cap. and res 23.4m., dep. 190m. (Dec. 1994); Gen. Man. MARÍA LIDIA SOLANO; 3 brs.

Banco Mercantil, SA: Blvd Suyapa, frente a Emisoras Unidas, Apdo 116, Tegucigalpa; tel. 32-0006; telex 1260; fax 32-3137; Pres. JOSÉ LAMAS; Gen. Man. JACOBO ATALA.

Banco de Occidente, SA (BANCOCCI): Calle Centenario, Apdo 208, Santa Rosa de Copán; tel. 662-0159; telex 5533; fax 662-0692; f. 1951; cap. and res 69m., dep. 606m. (June 1994); Pres. and Gen. Man. JORGE BUESO ARIAS; Vice-Pres. EMILIO MEDINA R.; 6 brs.

Banco Sogerin, SA: 8a Avda, 1a Calle, Apdo 440, San Pedro Sula; tel. 553-3888; telex 5624; fax 557-2001; f. 1969; cap. and res 92.2m., dep. 544m. (Dec. 1995); Pres. and Gen. Man. EDMOND BOGRÁN A.; 23 brs.

Banco de los Trabajadores, SA (BANCOTRAB): 3a Avda, 13a Calle, Paseo El Obelisco, Comayagüela, Apdo 3246, Tegucigalpa; tel. 37-8723; telex 1202; f. 1967; cap. and res US $6.6m., dep. $43.1m. (Dec. 1992); Pres. ROLANDO DEL CID VELÁSQUEZ; 13 brs.

Development Banks

Banco Centroamericano de Integración Económica: Apdo 772, Tegucigalpa; tel. 37-2230; telex 1103; fax 37-0793; f. 1960 to finance the economic development of the Central American Common Market and its mem. countries; mems Costa Rica, El Salvador, Guatemala, Honduras, Nicaragua; cap. and res US $895.3m. (Dec. 1996); Exec. Pres. JOSÉ MANUEL PACAS CASTRO.

Banco Hondureño del Café, SA (BANHCAFE): 6a Avda 501, 5a Calle, Apdo 583, Tegucigalpa; tel. 332-8370; telex 1278; fax 332-8338; f. 1981 to help finance coffee production; owned principally by private coffee producers; cap. and res 44.4m., dep. 362.2m. (Dec. 1994); Pres. RAMÓN DAVID RIVERA; Gen. Man. CARLOS E. CANIZALES SOLANO; 2 brs.

Banco Municipal Autónomo (BANMA): 6a Avda, 6a Calle, Tegucigalpa; tel. 22-5963; fax 37-5187; f. 1963; cap. and res US $25.2m., dep. $1.4m. (June 1984); Pres. JUSTO PASTOR CALDERÓN; 2 brs.

Banco Nacional de Desarrollo Agrícola (BANADESA): 405 Avda Comayagüela, 13a Calle, Comayagüela, Apdo 212, Tegucigalpa; tel. 337-3802; telex 1105; fax 337-5187; f. 1980; govt development bank (transfer to private ownership pending); loans to agricultural sector; cap. 34.5m., res 42.7m., dep. 126.9m. (March 1993); Pres. GUSTAVO A. ZELAYA CHÁVEZ.; 34 brs.

Financiera Centroamericana, SA (FICENSA): Edif. FICENSA, Blvd Los Castaños, Apdo 1432, Tegucigalpa; tel. 38-1661; telex 1200; fax 38-1630; f. 1974; private org. providing finance for industry, commerce and transport; cap. and res US $5.1m., dep. $42.6m. (Dec. 1995); Pres. OSWALDO LÓPEZ ARELLANO; Gen. Man. ROQUE RIVERA RIBAS.

Financiera Nacional de la Vivienda—FINAVI: Apdo 1194, Tegucigalpa; f. 1975; housing development bank; cap. and res US $5.3m. (July 1984); Exec. Pres. Lic. ELMAR LIZARDO.

Foreign Bank

Lloyds Bank PLC: Edif. Europa, Col. San Carlos, Calle República de México, Avda Ramón Ernesto Cruz, Apdo 3136, Tegucigalpa; tel. 336-6864; telex 1117; fax 336-6417; Man. J. S. MAIR.

Banking Association

Asociación Hondureña de Instituciones Bancarias (AHIBA): Blvd Suyapa contiguo a CANNON, Apdo 1344, Tegucigalpa; tel. 35-6770; fax 39-0191; f. 1956; 22 mem. banks; Pres. JACOBO ATALA Z.; Exec. Sec. GUILLERMO MATAMOROS.

STOCK EXCHANGE

Bolsa de Valores de Honduras: Edif. Martínez Valenzuela, 1°, 2a Calle, 3a Avda, San Pedro Sula; tel. 53-4410; fax 53-4480; Gen. Man. GUSTAVO RAUDALES.

INSURANCE

American Home Assurance Co: Edif. Los Castaños, 4°, Blvd Morazán, Apdo 113-C, Tegucigalpa; tel. 32-3938; fax 32-8169; f. 1958; Man. O. REYNALDO RAMÍREZ C.

Aseguradora Hondureña, SA: Centro Comercial Plaza Miraflores, 3°, Col. Miraflores, Apdo 312, Tegucigalpa; tel. 32-2729; telex 1246; fax 31-0982; f. 1954; Pres. FRANÇOIS DE PEYRECAVE; Gen. Man. ALBERTO AGURCIA.

Compañía de Seguros El Ahorro Hondureño, SA: Edif. Trinidad, 5a Calle, 11a Avda, Apdo 3643, Tegucigalpa; tel. 37-8219; telex 1122; fax 37-4780; e-mail ahseguro@hondutel.hn; f. 1917; Pres. GONZALO CARÍAS PINEDA; Gen. Man. MARCELO PEDEMONTE DEL CASTILLO.

Interamericana de Seguros, SA: Col. Los Castaños, Apdo 593, Tegucigalpa; tel. 32-7614; telex 1362; fax 32-7762; f. 1957; Pres. CAMILO ATALA FARAJ; Gen. Man. LUIS ATALA FARAJ.

Pan American Life Insurance Co (PALIC): Edif. PALIC, Avda República de Chile 804, Tegucigalpa; tel. 32-8774; telex 1237; fax 32-3907; f. 1944; Gen. Man. FERNANDO RODRÍGUEZ.

Previsión y Seguros, SA: Edif. Maya, Col. Palmira, Apdo 770, Tegucigalpa; tel. 31-2127; telex 1392; fax 32-5215; f. 1982; Pres. Gen. HÉCTOR CASTRO CABUS; Gen. Man. P. M. ARTURO BOQUÍN OSEJO.

Seguros Atlántida: Edif. Sonisa, Costado Este Plaza Bancatlán, Tegucigalpa; tel. 32-4014; fax 32-3688; f. 1986; Pres. GUILLERMO BUESO; Gen. Man. JUAN MIGUEL ORELLANA.

Seguros Continental, SA: 3a Avda 2 y 3, 7a Calle, Apdo 320, San Pedro Sula; tel. 52-0880; telex 5561; fax 52-2750; f. 1968; Pres. JAIME ROSENTHAL OLIVA; Gen. Man. MARIO R. SOLÍS.

Seguros Crefisa: Edif. Banfinan, 6°, Avda Cervantes 602, Apdo 3774, Tegucigalpa; tel. 38-5799; fax 38-8064; f. 1993; Pres. OSWALDO LÓPEZ ARELLANO; Gen. Man. HÉCTOR EDGARDO CHAVARRÍA R.

Insurance Association

Cámara Hondureña de Aseguradores (CAHDA): Edif. Los Jarros, Blvd Morazán, Local 313, Apdo 3290, Tegucigalpa; tel. 39-0342; fax 32-6020; f. 1974; Man. JOSÉ LUIS MONCADA RODRÍGUEZ.

Trade and Industry

DEVELOPMENT ORGANIZATIONS

Consejo Hondureño de la Empresa Privada (COHEP): Col. Reforma, Calle Principal 2723, Apdo 3240, Tegucigalpa; f. 1968; comprises 23 private enterprises; Pres. JUAN ANTONIO BENDECK.

Corporación Financiera de Olancho: f. 1977 to co-ordinate and manage all financial aspects of the Olancho forests project; Pres. RAFAEL CALDERÓN LÓPEZ.

Corporación Hondureña de Desarrollo Forestal (COHDEFOR): Salida Carretera del Norte, Zona El Carrizal, Comayagüela; Apdo 1378, Tegucigalpa; tel. 22-8810; telex 1172; fax 22-2653; f. 1974; semi-autonomous org. exercising control and man. of the forestry industry; transfer of all sawmills to private ownership was proceeding in 1991; Gen. Man. PORFIRIO LOBO S.

Dirección General de Minas e Hidrocarburos (General Directorate of Mines and Hydrocarbons): Blvd Miraflores, Apdo 981, Tegucigalpa; tel. 32-7848; telex 1404; fax 32-7848; Dir-Gen. MIGUEL VILLEDA VILLELA.

Instituto Hondureño del Café—IHCAFE: Apdo 40-C, Tegucigalpa; tel. 37-3131; telex 1167; f. 1970; coffee devt programme; Gen. Man. FERNANDO D. MONTES M.

Instituto Hondureño de Mercadeo Agrícola (IHMA): Apdo 727, Tegucigalpa; tel. 35-3193; fax 35-5719; f. 1978; agricultural devt agency; Gen. Man. TULIO ROLANDO GIRÓN ROMERO.

Instituto Nacional Agrario (INA): Col. La Almeda, 4a Avda, entre 10a y 11a Calles, No 1009, Apdo 3391, Tegucigalpa; tel. 32-8400; telex 1218; fax 32-8398; agricultural devt programmes; Exec. Dir ANÍBAL DELGADO FIALLOS.

Secretaría Técnica del Consejo Superior de Planificación Económica (CONSUPLANE): Edif. Bancatlán, 3°, Comayagüela, Apdo 1327, Tegucigalpa; tel. 22-8738; telex 1222; f. 1965; nat. planning office; Exec. Sec. FRANCISCO FIGUEROA ZÚÑIGA.

CHAMBERS OF COMMERCE

Cámara de Comercio e Industrias de Cortés: 17a Avda, 10a y 12a Calle, Apdo 14, San Pedro Sula; tel. 53-0761; f. 1931; 812 mems; Pres. ROBERTO REYES SILVA; Dir LUIS FERNANDO RIVERA.

Cámara de Comercio e Industrias de Tegucigalpa: Blvd Centroamérica, Apdo 3444, Tegucigalpa; tel. 32-8110; fax 31-2049; Pres. EDUARDO FACUSSÉ HANDAL.

Federación de Cámaras de Comercio e Industrias de Honduras (FEDECAMARA): Edif. Castañito, 2°, Col. Los Castaños, Sur 6a Avda, Calle Jamaica, Apdo 3393, Tegucigalpa; tel. 32-6083; fax 32-1870; f. 1948; 1,200 mems; Pres. ROLIN ELI ESCOBER; Exec. Dir DELFINA MEDINA.

INDUSTRIAL AND TRADE ASSOCIATIONS

Asociación de Bananeros Independientes—ANBI (National Association of Independent Banana Producers): San Pedro Sula; tel. 22-7336; f. 1964; 62 mems; Pres. Ing. JORGE ALBERTO ALVARADO; Sec. CECILIO TRIMINIO TURCIOS.

Asociación Hondureña de Productores de Café (Coffee Producers' Association): 10a Avda, 6a Calle, Apdo 959, Tegucigalpa.

Asociación Nacional de Exportadores de Honduras (ANEXHON): Tegucigalpa; comprises 104 private enterprises; Pres. Dr RICHARD ZABLAH.

Asociación Nacional de Industriales (ANDI) (National Association of Manufacturers): Blvd Los Próceres 505, Apdo 20-C, Tegucigalpa; Pres. HÉCTOR BULNES; Exec. Sec. DORCAS DE GONZALES.

Asociación Nacional de Pequeños Industriales (ANPI) (National Association of Small Industries): Apdo 730, Tegucigalpa; Pres. JUAN RAFAEL CRUZ.

Federación Nacional de Agricultores y Ganaderos de Honduras (FENAGH) (Farmers and Livestock Breeders' Association): Tegucigalpa; tel. 31-1392; Pres. ROBERTO GALLARDO LARDIZÁBAL.

Federación Nacional de Cooperativas Cañeras (Fenacocal) (National Federation of Sugar Cane Co-operatives): Tegucigalpa.

UTILITIES

Electricity

Empresa Nacional de Energía Eléctrica—ENEE (National Electrical Energy Co): Apdo 99, Tegucigalpa; tel 22-2432; state-owned electricity co; scheduled for privatization; Man. SALOMÁN ORDÓÑEZ.

TRADE UNIONS

Asociación Nacional de Empleados Públicos de Honduras (ANDEPH) (National Association of Public Employees of Honduras): Plaza Los Dolores, Tegucigalpa; tel. 37-4393; Pres. OSCAR MARTÍNEZ.

Confederación de Trabajadores de Honduras—CTH (Workers' Confederation of Honduras): Edif. FARAJ, 5°, Avda Lempira, Barrio La Fuente, Apdo 720, Tegucigalpa; tel. 38-7859; fax 37-4243; f. 1964; affiliated to CTCA, ORIT, CIOSL, FIAET and ICFTU; Pres. JOSÉ ANGEL MEZA; Sec.-Gen. FRANCISCO GUERRERO NÚÑEZ; 200,000 mems; comprises the following federations:

Federación Central de Sindicatos Libres de Honduras (FECESITLIH) (Honduran Federation of Free Trade Unions): 1a Avda, 1a Calle 102, Apdo 621, Comayagüela, Tegucigalpa; tel. 37-5601; Pres. JOSÉ ANGEL MEZA.

Federación Sindical de Trabajadores Nacionales de Honduras (FESITRANH) (Honduran Federation of Farmworkers): 10a Avda, 11a Calle, Barrio Los Andes, San Pedro Sula; tel. 57-2539; f. 1957; Pres. MARIO QUINTANILLA.

Sindicato Nacional de Motoristas de Equipo Pesado de Honduras (SINAMEQUIPH) (National Union of HGV Drivers): Tegucigalpa; tel. 37-4243; Pres. ERASMO FLORES.

Central General de Trabajadores de Honduras (CGTH) (General Confederation of Labour of Honduras): Calle Real de Comayagüela, Apdo 1236, Tegucigalpa; tel. 37-4398; attached to Partido Demócrata Cristiano; Sec.-Gen. FELICITO AVILA.

Federación Auténtica Sindical de Honduras (FASH): 1a Avda, 11a Calle 1102, Comayagüela, Tegucigalpa.

Federación de Trabajadores del Sur (FETRASUR) (Federation of Southern Workers): Choluteca.

Federación Unitaria de Trabajadores de Honduras (FUTH): 2a Avda entre 11a y 12a Calle, Casa 1127, frente a BANCAFE, Apdo 1663, Comayagüela, Tegucigalpa; tel. 37-6349; f. 1981; linked to left-wing electoral alliance Frente Patriótico Hondureño; Pres. HÉCTOR HERNÁNDEZ FUENTES; 45,000 mems.

Frente de Unidad Nacional Campesino de Honduras (FUNACAMH): f. 1980; group of farming co-operatives and six main peasant unions as follows:

Asociación Nacional de Campesinos Hondureños (ANACH) (National Association of Honduran Farmworkers): 3a Avda, entre 9ª y 10ª Calle, Barrio Barandillas, San Pedro Sula; tel. 53-1884; f. 1962; affiliated to ORIT; Pres. ANTONIO JULÍN MÉNDEZ; 80,000 mems.

Federación de Cooperativas Agropecuarias de la Reforma Agraria de Honduras (FECORAH): Barrio Guanacaste, Casa 1702, Tegucigalpa; tel. 37-5391; Pres. JOSÉ NAHUM CÁLIX.

Frente Nacional de Campesinos Independientes de Honduras.

Unión Nacional de Campesinos (UNC) (National Union of Farmworkers): 1a Avda, Comayagüela, Tegucigalpa; tel. 38-2435; linked to CLAT; Pres. MARCIAL REYES CABALLERO; c. 25,000 mems.

Unión Nacional de Campesinos Auténticos de Honduras (UNCAH).

Unión Nacional de Cooperativas Populares de Honduras (UNACOOPH).

Transport

RAILWAYS

The railway network is confined to the north of the country and most lines are used for fruit cargo.

Ferrocarril Nacional de Honduras (National Railway of Honduras): 1a Avda entre 1a y 2a Calle, Apdo 496, San Pedro Sula; tel. 53-1879; fax 52-8001; f. 1870; govt-owned; 595 km of track; Gen. Man. N. TORRES RIVERA.

Tela Railroad Co: La Lima; tel. 56-2037; telex 8305.

Vaccaro Railway: La Ceiba; tel. 43-0511; fax 43-0091; fmrly operated by Standard Fruit Co.

ROADS

In 1996 there were an estimated 15,400 km of roads in Honduras, of which 3,126 km were paved. Some routes have been constructed by the Instituto Hondureño del Café and COHDEFOR in order to facilitate access to coffee plantations and forestry development areas.

Dirección General de Caminos: Tegucigalpa; highways board.

SHIPPING

Empresa Nacional Portuaria (National Port Authority): Apdo 18, Puerto Cortés; tel. 55-0192; fax 55-0968; f. 1965; has jurisdiction over all ports in Honduras (Puerto Cortés, Tela, La Ceiba, Trujillo/Castilla, Roatán, Amapala and San Lorenzo); a network of paved roads connects Puerto Cortés and San Lorenzo with the main cities of Honduras, and with the principal cities of Central America; Gen. Man. ROBERTO VALENZUELA SIMÓN.

There are several minor shipping companies. A number of foreign shipping lines call at Honduran ports.

CIVIL AVIATION

Local airlines in Honduras compensate for the deficiencies of road and rail transport, linking together small towns and inaccessible districts. There are four international airports.

Honduras Airways: Tegucigalpa; f. 1994; operates domestic flights and scheduled services to the USA.

Isleña Airlines: Avda San Isidro, frente al Parque Central, Apdo 402, La Ceiba; tel. 43-2683; fax 43-2632; domestic service and service to the Cayman Islands; Pres. and CEO ARTURO ALVARADO WOOD.

Líneas Aéreas Nacionales, SA (LANSA): Apdo 35, La Ceiba; f. 1971; scheduled services within Honduras and to Islas de Bahía; Gen. Man. OSCAR M. ELVIR.

Tourism

Tourists are attracted by the Mayan ruins, the fishing and boating facilities in Trujillo Bay and Lake Yojoa, near San Pedro Sula, and the beaches on the northern coast. Honduras received 237,985 tourists in 1995. In 1994 tourism receipts totalled US $33m.

Instituto Hondureño de Turismo: Edif. Centro Guanacaste, Barrio Guanacaste, Apdo 3261, Tegucigalpa; tel. 38-3975; fax 38-2102; f. 1972; dept of the Secretaría de Cultura y Turismo; Dir-Gen. RICARDO MARTÍNEZ.

HUNGARY

Introductory Survey

Location, Climate, Language, Religion, Flag, Capital

The Republic of Hungary (known as the Hungarian People's Republic between August 1949 and October 1989) lies in eastern Europe, bounded to the north by Slovakia, to the east by Ukraine and Romania, to the south by Yugoslavia (the Serbian province of Vojvodina) and Croatia, and to the west by Slovenia and Austria. Its climate is continental, with long, dry summers and severe winters. Temperatures in Budapest are generally between −3°C (27°F) and 28°C (82°F). The language is Hungarian (Magyar). There is a large Romany community (numbering between 500,000 and 700,000 people), and also Croat, German, Romanian, Serbian, Slovak, Slovene and Jewish minorities. Most of the inhabitants profess Christianity, and the largest single religious denomination is the Roman Catholic Church, representing about 65% of the population. Other Christian groups are the Calvinists (20%), the Lutheran Church (5%) and the Hungarian Orthodox Church. The national flag (proportions 3 by 2) consists of three equal horizontal stripes, of red, white and green. The capital is Budapest.

Recent History

Hungary allied itself with Nazi Germany before the Second World War and obtained additional territory when Czechoslovakia was partitioned in 1938 and 1939. Having sought to break the alliance in 1944, Hungary was occupied by German forces. In January 1945 Hungary was liberated by Soviet troops and signed an armistice, restoring the pre-1938 frontiers. It became a republic in February 1946. Meanwhile, land distribution, instituted in 1945, continued. Nationalization measures began in December 1946, despite opposition from the Roman Catholic Church under Cardinal József Mindszenty. In the 1947 elections the Communists became the largest single party, with 22.7% of the vote. By the end of that year the Communist Party had emerged as the leading political force. The Communists merged with the Social Democrats to form the Hungarian Workers' Party in June 1948. A People's Republic was established in August 1949.

Mátyás Rákosi became the leading figure as First Secretary of the Workers' Party. Opposition was subsequently removed by means of purges and political trials. Rákosi became Prime Minister in 1952 but, after the death of Stalin a year later, lost this post to the more moderate Imre Nagy, and a short period of liberalization followed. Rákosi, however, remained as First Secretary of the party, and in 1955 forced Nagy's resignation. András Hegedüs, sponsored by Rákosi, was appointed Prime Minister. Dissension between the Rákosi and Nagy factions increased in 1956; in July Rákosi was forced to resign but was replaced by a close associate, Ernő Gerő.

The consequent discontent provoked demonstrations against communist domination, and in October 1956 fighting broke out. Nagy was reinstated as Prime Minister, renounced membership of the Warsaw Pact and promised various other controversial reforms. In November Soviet troops, stationed in Hungary under the 1947 peace treaty, intervened, and the uprising was suppressed. A new Soviet-supported Government, led by János Kádár, was installed. Some 20,000 participants in the uprising were arrested, of whom 2,000 were subsequently executed, including Nagy and four associates, who were hanged in June 1958. Many opponents of the regime were deported to the USSR. Kádár, who was appointed the leader of the renamed Hungarian Socialist Workers' Party (HSWP), held the premiership until January 1958, and from September 1961 to July 1965.

The 13th HSWP Congress, held in March 1985, re-elected Kádár leader of the party, with the new title of General Secretary of the Central Committee. The Congress reaffirmed the party's commitment to the country's economic reforms, which had been introduced in 1968. Legislative elections in June 1985 were the first to be held under the revised electoral law, giving voters a wider choice of candidates under the system of mandatory multiple nominations. In June 1987 Pál Losonczi was replaced in the largely ceremonial post of President of the Presidential Council by Károly Németh, a leading member of the HSWP. Károly Grósz, a member of the Politburo, was appointed Chairman of the Council of Ministers.

In March 1988, on the 140th anniversary of the 1848 Hungarian uprising against Austrian rule, some 10,000 people took part in an unofficial march through the capital, Budapest, demanding freedom of the press, freedom of association and the introduction of genuine reforms. At a special ideological conference of the HSWP, held in May, major changes in party personnel and policy were approved. Kádár was replaced as General Secretary of the Central Committee by Károly Grósz. Kádár was promoted to the newly-created and purely ceremonial post of HSWP President, but lost his membership of the Politburo. About one-third of the members of the Central Committee (in particular, conservative associates of Kádár) were removed and replaced by younger politicians. The new Politburo included Rezső Nyers, who had been largely responsible for the economic reforms initiated in 1968, but who had been removed from the Politburo in 1975. Grósz declared his commitment to radical economic and political change, although he excluded the immediate possibility of a multi-party political system. In June 1988 Dr Brunó Ferenc Straub, who was not a member of the HSWP, was elected to the post of President of the Presidential Council, in succession to Károly Németh. In November Miklós Németh, a prominent member of the HSWP, replaced Grósz as Chairman of the Council of Ministers.

Following Grósz's appointment as leader of the HSWP, there was a relaxation of censorship laws, and independent political groups were formally established. In July 1988 the HSWP voted overwhelmingly in favour of an austere economic programme, designed to revitalize the economy within 10 years. In January 1989 the right to strike was fully legalized. In the same month the National Assembly enacted two laws guaranteeing the right to demonstrate freely and to form associations and political parties independent of the HSWP.

In February 1989 the HSWP agreed to support the transition to a multi-party system and also to abandon the clause in the Constitution upholding the party's leading role in society. In the following month an estimated 100,000 people took part in a peaceful anti-Government demonstration in Budapest, in support of demands for democracy, free elections, the withdrawal of Soviet troops from Hungary, and an official commemoration of the 1956 uprising and of the execution of Imre Nagy in 1958.

During 1989 there was increasing evidence of dissension within the HSWP between conservative and reformist members. (At least 100,000 members had tendered their resignation between late 1987 and early 1989). In April Grósz was re-elected General Secretary of the party, and the Politburo was replaced by a smaller body. In May the Council of Ministers declared its independence from the HSWP. In the same month Kádár was relieved of his post as President of the HSWP and of his membership of the Central Committee of the party, officially for health reasons. In June a radical restructuring of the HSWP was effected, following increasing dissatisfaction among members with Grósz's leadership: while Grósz remained as General Secretary of the party, the newly-elected Chairman, Rezső Nyers, effectively emerged as the party's leading figure.

In June 1989 discussions were initiated between the HSWP and representatives of opposition groups regarding the holding of multi-party elections, changes to the presidential structure, amendments to the Constitution, and economic reforms. Evidence of the opposition's increasing strength was provided at a provincial by-election in July, when a joint candidate of three main opposition groups, the centre-right Hungarian Democratic Forum (HDF), the liberal Alliance of Free Democrats (AFD) and the Federation of Young Democrats (FYD), defeated a candidate of the HSWP, thus becoming the first opposition deputy since 1947 to win representation in the legislature. Four of five further by-elections were won by opposition candidates in July–September 1989.

At the 14th HSWP Congress, held in October 1989, delegates voted to dissolve the party and to reconstitute it as the Hungarian Socialist Party (HSP). Nyers was elected Chairman of the

HSP. The HSP initially failed to attract a large membership, however, and in December HSWP activists declared that their party had not been dissolved, and that it still retained a membership of around 80,000. Gyula Thürmer was elected the HSWP President.

On 23 October 1989 (the anniversary of the 1956 uprising) the Republic of Hungary was proclaimed. In preparation the National Assembly approved fundamental amendments to the Constitution, including the removal of the clause guaranteeing one-party rule. A new electoral law was approved, and the Presidential Council was replaced by the post of President of the Republic. Mátyás Szűrös, the President of the National Assembly (Speaker), was named President of the Republic, on an interim basis.

Hungary's first free multi-party elections since 1945 were held, in two rounds, on 25 March and 8 April 1990. The elections were held under a mixed system of proportional and direct representation and were contested by a total of 28 parties and groups. The HDF received the largest share of the total votes (42.7%) and won 165 of the 386 seats in the National Assembly. The Independent Smallholders' Party (ISP, which advocated the restoration to its original owners of land collectivized after 1947) and the Christian Democratic People's Party (CDPP), both of which contested the second round of the election in alliance with the HDF, secured 43 and 21 seats, respectively. The AFD obtained the second largest proportion of the total votes (23.8%), winning 92 seats in the Assembly. The FYD, which was closely aligned with the AFD, obtained 21 seats. The HSP, with 8.5% of the votes, secured 33 seats in the legislature. The HSWP failed to secure the 4% of the votes required for representation.

A coalition Government was formed in May 1990, comprising members of the HDF (which held the majority of posts), together with members of the ISP, the CDPP and three independents. József Antall, the Chairman of the HDF, had earlier been elected to chair the new Council of Ministers. Among the declared aims of the new Government was to withdraw from the Warsaw Pact (the defence grouping of the Soviet bloc), to seek membership of the European Community (now European Union—EU—see p. 152), and to effect a full transition to a western-style market economy. In August Árpád Göncz, a writer and member of the AFD, was elected President of the Republic by an overwhelming majority of the legislature. In May Gyula Horn, the Minister of Foreign Affairs in the outgoing Government, had replaced Nyers as leader of the HSP.

At elections in September and October 1990, which were designed to replace the Soviet-style council system with a system of multi-party self-governing local bodies, a coalition of the AFD and the FYD won control of Budapest and many other cities, while in rural areas independent candidates gained an overwhelming majority of the votes. The governing coalition's poor result was attributed, in large part, to its failure to redress the recent sharp increase in the rates of inflation and unemployment.

In mid-1991 the National Assembly approved legislation to compensate the former owners of land and property that had been expropriated between 1939 and 1989. Legislation was approved by parliament in November that would allow prosecution for the crimes of murder and treason committed between 1944 and 1990. It was expected that, under the new law, former communist leaders might be brought to trial, in particular in connection with the suppression of the 1956 uprising. However, Göncz refused to give assent to the bill, and in March 1992 the Constitutional Court ruled that such retroactive legislation, which held individuals responsible for the crimes of the former communist regime, was inadmissible. Nevertheless, in May the National Assembly approved legislation to compensate for persons killed, imprisoned or deported, or whose property had been expropriated, for political reasons during the period 1939–89. Further legislation was approved in early 1993 allowing for prosecutions in connection with crimes committed under the communist regime.

In February 1992 the Chairman of the ISP, József Törgyán, announced that his party was withdrawing from the government coalition, in protest at what he claimed to be a lack of political influence. However, most of the ISP's deputies in the National Assembly refused to withdraw their support for the Government, thus causing a rift in the ISP. In April as many as 20,000 people were reported to have attended an anti-Government demonstration organized by Törgyán in Budapest. The split in the party was formalized in June, when party members who remained loyal to Antall suspended Törgyán as their Chairman, and elected László Horváth to chair what subsequently became the United Historic Smallholders' Party.

Meanwhile, in June 1992 a public disagreement arose between Antall and Göncz over alleged widespread interference by the Government in the state radio and television corporations and other branches of the mass media. During 1992–93 many senior media figures were either dismissed or tendered their resignation, and in October 1993 some 10,000 people demonstrated in Budapest to demand press freedom.

In September 1992 a demonstration by some 50,000 people in Budapest against extreme right-wing figures, including the Vice-Chairman of the HDF, István Csurka, reflected public concern at the increase in extreme right-wing sentiment in the country. The Government's failure to censure Csurka prompted widespread criticism. At an HDF congress in January 1993 Antall avoided a threatened revolt and possible split in the party by accepting the election of six right-wing extremists to the party's presidium. In May Lajos Für resigned from his position as Secretary-General of the HDF, claiming that he had not been able to maintain the unity of the party, which was divided between supporters of Csurka and centrists led by Antall. In July, however, Csurka was expelled from the HDF for his increasingly unacceptable views. (He subsequently founded the Hungarian Justice and Life Party—HJLP.) Antall died in December; he was succeeded as Prime Minister by Dr Péter Boross, an independent and hitherto the Minister of the Interior, who had acted as premier while Antall was receiving medical treatment. In February 1994 Für was elected Chairman of the HDF. In that month an investigation was initiated into alleged financial irregularities at the Ministry of Defence.

In March 1994 129 employees of Hungarian Radio were dismissed, ostensibly for economic reasons. Mass demonstrations were staged in Budapest in support of freedom of the press. There were widespread accusations that the Government sought to use the state radio service for propaganda purposes, since many of the dismissed employees had been known for their anti-Government views.

Legislative elections, which took place on 8 and 29 May 1994, resulted in a clear parliamentary majority for the HSP, which received 33.0% of the votes for regional party lists and won 209 of the National Assembly's 386 seats. The AFD won 19.8% of the votes and 70 seats, while the HDF won only 11.7% of the votes and 37 seats. The Independent Smallholders' and Peasants' Party (ISPP—formerly the ISP), the CDPP and the FYD won, repectively, 26, 22 and 20 seats. Csurka's HJLP attracted only 1.6% of the votes at the first round and did not proceed to the second. Horn announced that the HSP would be willing to form a Government with the AFD, and the two parties signed a coalition agreement (whereby the HSP was to control the majority of posts in the Council of Ministers, while the AFD would have right to veto government decisions) in late June. With 279 seats in the National Assembly, the coalition held the two-thirds' majority necessary to institute constitutional reforms. Horn was invested as Prime Minister in July. At municipal elections in December the HSP won 32.3% of the votes and the AFD 15.7%.

In June 1994 the Hungarian Radio employees were reinstated. In the following month, however, the directors of Hungarian Radio and Hungarian Television were dismissed, having been accused of favouring the former HDF administration. In October the Constitutional Court declared government interference in the media to be unlawful. In January 1995 László Bekesi, the HSP Minister of Finance, resigned, following disagreements with Horn regarding the economic reform programme. In the same month the Director of the State Property Agency was dismissed, following his alleged mismanagement of the privatization of state-owned hotels. In late February Dr Lajos Bokros of the HSP was designated Minister of Finance; at the same time Horn appointed Tamás Suchman, also of the HSP, to the newly-created post of Minister for Privatization, under the jurisdiction of the Ministry of Finance, as well as a new president of the central bank. New economic austerity measures, adopted in March, prompted strong domestic criticism; the ministers responsible for public health and for national security (both members of the HSP) resigned shortly after the programme was announced, and some 10,000 people joined a demonstration in Budapest to denounce the measures.

In early May 1995 the National Assembly approved legislation which was designed to accelerate the privatization process. On 19 June Göncz was re-elected President of the Republic by an overwhelming majority in the National Assembly. In late June the HSP Minister of Trade and Industry, who had voiced criticism of the privatization of parts of the energy sector, was dismissed; he was replaced by Imre Dunai, a technocrat with no party affiliation, at the end of the month. At the end of June the Constitutional Court ruled that elements of the austerity programme announced in March (specifically those relating to welfare provisions) were unconstitutional. Accordingly, in late July the National Assembly approved new adjustments, including increases in fuel prices and reductions in government expenditure, in an attempt to mitigate losses arising from the judgment. The Court reiterated its decision in a further ruling in September.

The implementation of the economic programme continued to cause dissent within the Government. The HSP Minister of Labour tendered her resignation in early October, in protest against the adverse social consequences of the austerity measures. In late November, following a ruling by the Constitutional Court against the validity of further provisions of the austerity programme, Bokros submitted his resignation, although this was rejected by Horn. The AFD Minister of Culture and Education announced his intention to leave the Government, in protest against reductions in expenditure on education. Earlier in November workers from the health and education sectors had staged mass demonstrations in Budapest, demanding substantial pay rises and increased investment in the sectors.

In mid-February 1996, shortly before he was due to present a further series of austerity measures, Bokros again tendered his resignation (which was accepted by Horn), citing a lack of support from other government members. A banker, Péter Medgyessy, who had been Deputy Chairman and Chairman of the Planning and Economic Committee in the administration of Miklós Németh, was appointed the new Minister of Finance. Medgyessy undertook to pursue the programme of austerity instigated by Bokros, although his approach to politically sensitive issues such as health and social security was expected to be less confrontational than that of his predecessor.

Division was reported in the HDF in early March 1996, following the election of Sándor Lezsák to the party leadership. Denouncing what they regarded as an increasingly nationalistic tendency within the party, a faction led by Iván Szabó (who had been Minister of Finance in the HDF Government) broke away to form a new organization, the Hungarian Democratic People's Party.

In August 1996 Imre Dunai resigned from the post of Minister of Industry and Trade, ostensibly on grounds of ill health; it was reported that he had opposed the proposed increases in fuel prices. Dunai was replaced by Tamás Suchman (who retained responsibility for the privatization portfolio). Later in August the Government announced that increases in fuel prices were to be postponed, pending a review of the energy industry by a committee of independent experts. (In January 1997 the Government finally increased fuel prices, although by far less than originally envisaged.)

In early October 1996 it emerged that the Hungarian Privatization and State Holding Company (ÁPV Rt—which had been formed in 1995 by the amalgamation of the State Property Agency and State Holding Company) had made payments for consultations to a lawyer who had not been formally contracted, in contravention of the body's internal regulations. The Government removed the directors of ÁPV Rt, after they were discovered to have endorsed the payments. Horn subsequently announced the dismissal of Suchman from the Government, on the grounds that, as Minister for Privatization, he was responsible for ÁPV Rt's violation of regulations. In early November the Minister of Public Welfare tendered his resignation, after claiming that the funds allocated to the public welfare sector in the draft budget for 1997 were insufficient to support the country's health service. (The social security and welfare budget that was finally approved was considerably higher than originally envisaged.) In December the Minister of Agriculture was replaced on the recommendation of Horn, who indicated that a reallocation of the portfolio was necessary for the preparation of an agricultural programme in accordance with EU requirements.

In January 1997 the HDF proposed a motion expressing 'no confidence' against Horn in the National Assembly, on the grounds that he was ultimately responsible for the unauthorized payments made by ÁPV Rt. In February a parliamentary investigative committee attributed responsibility to the Government for the irregularities. (In June eight officials were charged with fraud or mismanagement in connection with the operations of ÁPV Rt.)

In March 1997 the National Assembly adopted legislation providing for the return of assets that had been seized during the Second World War from victims of the Nazi holocaust to organizations representing the communities concerned. Later that month two members of the National Intelligence Bureau were dismissed, after it emerged that the service had conducted unauthorized investigations of several prominent HSP members (who were suspected of having connections with organized crime groups). The Minister responsible for National Security ordered an official inquiry, which subsequently confirmed that irregularities had taken place and recommended that the Government regulate the operations of national security organizations.

Following a NATO summit meeting, which took place in Madrid, Spain, in July 1997, Hungary was invited to enter into discussions regarding its application for membership of the organization; it was envisaged that Hungary (together with the Czech Republic and Poland) would be formally admitted to NATO by April 1999. In August 1997 the Government announced that a national referendum on the country's entry into NATO would be conducted on 16 November. Amendments to legislation regulating land ownership were also to be submitted to the electorate at the referendum (after opposition parties criticized government proposals that foreign purchasers be authorized to acquire arable land).

In September 1997 Horn rejected demands that he resign from office by a committee which had been established to investigate the past of senior politicians; the committee claimed that Horn had served with a paramilitary force which had restored communist power following the 1956 rebellion, and that he had suppressed political opposition through the security services. In early October the National Assembly approved the wording of proposals on foreign land ownership, which were to be submitted to the electorate at the consultative referendum. However, the Constitutional Court overruled the decision of the National Assembly, and favoured an alternative formation of the proposals, which had been presented by opposition parties with the support of a petition. (Under the terms of constitutional amendments, adopted in July, a referendum that had been initiated by a minimum of 200,000 eligible voters was to be given precedence to a government-proposed referendum.) Following concern that the continuing controversy would delay the holding of the referendum, however, Horn announced that the planned amendments to legislation on land ownership were to be abandoned, and that the referendum was to be conducted on the single issue of Hungary's proposed admission to NATO. In early November the National Assembly approved the removal from the referendum of the proposals on land ownership.

At the national referendum, which took place on 16 November 1997 as scheduled, Hungary's accession to NATO was approved by 85.3% of votes cast, with 49% of the electorate participating in the referendum. The National Election Committee ratified the results of the referendum (despite objections by a pacifist movement, which claimed that the low rate of voter participation invalidated the results of the referendum). In December the HDF established an electoral alliance with the Federation of Young Democrats—Hungarian Civic Party (which had been reconstituted from the FYD), whereby the two parties were to present joint candidates to contest the forthcoming legislative elections in 1998. Later in December the two parties reached an electoral co-operation agreement with the Hungarian Democratic People's Party (which had been formed in 1996 by former members of the HDF).

There has been considerable activism within Hungary by the country's ethnic minorities for the protection of their rights. In July 1993 the National Assembly adopted legislation guaranteeing the cultural, civil and political rights of 12 minority groups and prohibiting all forms of ethnic discrimination. Following the approval of this legislation, minority rights activists launched a new campaign to change Hungary's electoral law, with the aim of securing the direct representation of ethnic groups in the legislature. In the 1994 municipal elections, ethnic minorities were able to elect their own local ethnic authorities, with consultative roles on cultural and educational issues affecting the community. In April 1995 the Roma of Hungary elected their own governing body. The National Autonomous Authority of the Romany Minority (the first such body in the former Eastern bloc) was to be empowered to administer funds and deliberate issues affecting the Roma. All of its 53 seats were won by the Lungo Drom Alliance, led by Florian Farkas.

In February 1995 Hungary signed the Council of Europe's Convention on the Protection of National Minorities. However, an increase in overt nationalism among the parties of the right became an issue of considerable concern during the 1990s.

In the late 1980s the Hungarian Government made successive diplomatic efforts in an attempt to improve the treatment of the 1.7m. ethnic Hungarians in Romania. It also established reception camps for Romanian refugees arriving in Hungary in the late 1980s. In March 1990, following outbreaks of violence against ethnic Hungarians by Romanian nationalist activists, several hundred ethnic Hungarian refugees arrived in Hungary. In mid-1991 hundreds of ethnic Hungarians were evacuated from the Serbian province of Vojvodina, to escape the fighting there between Serbs and Croats. Large numbers of refugees from Bosnia and Herzegovina also fled to Hungary.

Hungary pursues an active foreign policy, and relations with many Western nations improved steadily from the late 1980s. In November 1990 Hungary was the first Eastern European country to become a member of the Council of Europe (see p. 140). Hungary's associate membership of the EU came into effect on 1 February 1994, and in April of that year Hungary became the first post-communist state to apply for full EU membership. In March 1996 Hungary was admitted to the Organisation for Economic Co-operation and Development (see p. 208).

Apart from issues arising from the presence of a large ethnic Hungarian minority in Slovakia (numbering almost 570,000 in late 1993), relations between Hungary and Slovakia have been strained by a dispute over the Gabčíkovo-Nagymaros hydroelectric project (a joint Hungarian-Czechoslovak scheme initiated in 1977), involving the diversion of a 222-km stretch of the River Danube and the construction of a twin-dam system. In May 1989 the Hungarian Government suspended work on the dam in response to pressure from environmentalists, and in November it announced that it was abandoning the project. Czechoslovakia decided, in July 1991, to proceed unilaterally with the project; the resumption of work, in February 1992, prompted the Hungarian Government to abrogate the 1977 treaty with effect from May 1992. In April 1993 the two countries agreed to refer the case to the International Court of Justice (ICJ) and to operate a temporary water-management scheme in the mean time.

In March 1995 (despite protests by nationalists within Hungary against concessions made by the Government) Horn and his Slovak counterpart, Vladimír Mečiar, signed a Treaty of Friendship and Co-operation in which the two countries undertook to guarantee the rights of ethnic minorities and recognized the inviolability of their joint border. However, its ratification was subsequently delayed owing to differing interpretations of its provisions with regard to the protection of national minorities. An amendment to the treaty, approved by the Slovak legislature in March 1996, rejected the concept of autonomy for the Hungarian minority in Slovakia, prompting protests from the Hungarian opposition. Nevertheless, the treaty came into effect in May, following its ratification by the Slovak President.

In August 1997 discussions between Horn and the Slovak Prime Minister, Vladimír Mečiar, resulted in an agreement that a joint committee be established to monitor the standard of human rights of ethnic Hungarians resident in Slovakia and the Slovak community in Hungary; however, there was subsequent dissent over the composition of the proposed committee. In September relations between Hungary and Slovakia became strained, after Horn rejected a suggestion by Mečiar that a voluntary repatriation programme for the respective ethnic communities in the two countries be initiated. The Slovak Government suspended ministerial discussions on the issue, in protest at Horn's failure to apologize for his response to Mečiar's proposal. Later in September the ICJ concluded proceedings regarding the dispute between Hungary and Slovakia over the Gabčíkovo-Nagymaros hydroelectric project, ruling that both countries had contravened international law: Hungary had breached the terms of the agreement by withdrawing from the project, while the former Czechoslovakia had continued work without the permission of the Hungarian Government. Both Hungary and Slovakia were required to pay compensation for damages incurred, and to resume negotiations regarding the further implementation of the agreement. Hungarian and Slovak delegations were subsequently established to conduct discussions on the ruling of the ICJ. At a summit meeting between the Governments of Hungary, Slovakia and Austria, which took place in Vienna, Austria, in mid-December, Horn and Mečiar agreed that the dispute would be resolved by early 1998. In January 1998 it was announced that some progress had been achieved in the continuing discussions between the Hungarian and Slovak delegations

In August 1996 Hungary and Romania finalized a bilateral treaty (which was formally signed in September), guaranteeing the inviolability of the joint border between the two countries and the rights of ethnic minorities. (However, the Hungarian opposition protested at the failure of the treaty to recognize the right to autonomy of the ethnic Hungarian community in Romania.) In February 1997 the Ministers of Defence of Hungary and Romania signed a co-operation agreement, providing for the protection and exchange of military secrets between the two countries, and the establishment of a joint military unit, which would be deployed in peace-keeping operations. In May President Göncz made an official visit to Romania (the first by a Hungarian Head of State).

From December 1995 US troops belonging to the NATO-controlled Implementation Force in Bosnia and Herzegovina (IFOR, see p. 206) were stationed at an air base at Taszar, in south-western Hungary; a second base was subsequently established at the southern town of Pécs. In May 1996 the Government indicated that it would be willing for US troops to remain in Hungary, following the withdrawal of peace-keeping forces from Bosnia and Herzegovina. Hungary contributed some 450 troops to IFOR in 1996, and continued to support its replacement Stabilization Force (SFOR, see p. 207). Hungary was to be admitted to NATO in 1999 (see above).

Government

Legislative power is held by the unicameral National Assembly (Országgyülés), comprising 386 members, who are elected for four years by universal adult suffrage under a mixed system of proportional and direct representation. The President of the Republic (Head of State) is elected by the National Assembly for a term of five years. The President, who is also Commander-in-Chief of the Armed Forces, may be re-elected for a second term. The Council of Ministers, the highest organ of state administration, is elected by the Assembly on the recommendation of the President. For local administrative purposes Hungary is divided into 19 counties and the capital city (with 22 districts). A 53-member National Autonomous Authority of the Romany Minority, elected in April 1995, is empowered to administer funds disbursed by the central Government.

Defence

Military service starts at the age of 18 years. The period of military service was reduced from one year to nine months in November 1997. The total regular forces in August 1997 numbered 49,100 (including 30,200 conscripts): army 31,600 and air force 17,500. Paramilitary forces comprised 12,000 border guards, as well as 2,100 members of the internal security forces. The 1995 defence budget totalled an estimated 77,100m. forint.

Economic Affairs

In 1995, according to estimates by the World Bank, Hungary's gross national product (GNP), measured at average 1993–95 prices, was US $42,129m., equivalent to $4,120 per head. During 1985–95, it was estimated, GNP per head declined, in real terms, at an average annual rate of 1.0%. Over the same period the population decreased by an annual average of 0.3%. Hungary's gross domestic product (GDP) declined, in real terms, by an average of 0.9% annually during 1985–95; real GDP growth was estimated at 1.5% in 1995.

Agriculture (including forestry and fishing) contributed an estimated 7.2% of GDP in 1995. About 8.3% of the employed labour force were engaged in the sector in 1996. The principal crops are wheat, maize, sugar beet, barley and potatoes. Viticulture is also important. During 1985–95, according to the World Bank, agricultural GDP declined by an annual average of 3.0%. In 1995, however, growth in agricultural GDP was estimated at 2.0%.

Industry (including mining, manufacturing, construction, and power) contributed an estimated 31.8% of GDP in 1995, and engaged 32.6% of the employed labour force in 1996. According to the World Bank, industrial GDP declined by an annual average of 2.3% in 1985–95. However, growth in industrial GDP was estimated at 3.4% in 1995.

Mining and quarrying accounted for only 0.4% of GDP in 1995, and engaged 0.9% of the employed labour force in 1996. Hungary's most important mineral resources are lignite, brown coal and natural gas. Petroleum, bauxite and hard coal are also exploited.

The manufacturing sector contributed an estimated 23.0% of GDP in 1995, and engaged 23.3% of the employed labour force in 1996. In 1993 the principal branches of the sector, in terms of their contribution to gross production, were food, beverages and tobacco, chemicals, petroleum and plastics, and engineering. According to the World Bank, manufacturing GDP increased by an annual average of 2.2% in 1985–95. Growth in manufacuring GDP was estimated at 4.0% in 1995.

In 1993 some 43% of Hungary's electricity supply was generated by nuclear power. Further supply is derived from coal, petroleum and natural gas. Mineral fuels represented 11.7% of the value of total imports in 1995.

The services sector has a significant role in the Hungarian economy, contributing an estimated 61.0% of GDP in 1995, and engaging 59.1% of the employed labour force in 1996. According to the World Bank, the GDP of the services sector increased by an average of 0.5% per year in 1985–95; growth in the sector was estimated at 0.6% in 1995. In 1996 it was estimated that the tourist sector contributed about 20% of GDP and 30% of export earnings.

In 1996 Hungary recorded a visible trade deficit of US $2,652m., and there was a deficit of $1,689m. on the current account of the balance of payments. In 1995 the principal source of imports (23.4%) was Germany; other major sources were Russia, Austria and Italy. Germany was also the principal market for exports in that year (28.6%); other important purchasers were Austria, Italy and Russia. The principal exports in 1995 were machinery and transport equipment, food and live animals (particularly meat and meat preparations), basic manufactures, miscellaneous manufactured articles (most notably clothing and accessories) and chemical products. The main imports in that year were machinery and transport equipment (most notably road vehicles and parts), basic manufactures (particularly textile yarn and fabrics), chemical products, mineral fuels (particularly petroleum and petroleum products) and miscellaneous manufactured articles.

Hungary's overall budget deficit for 1995 was estimated at 207,100m. forint. The country's total external debt at the end of 1995 was estimated to be US $31,248m., of which $23,572m. was long-term public debt. In that year the cost of debt-servicing was equivalent to 39.1% of exports of goods and services. The annual rate of inflation averaged 20.3% in 1985–96; consumer prices increased by an average of 23.5% in 1996. About 10.5% of the labour force were unemployed at the end of 1996.

Hungary is a member (as a 'Country of Operations') of the European Bank for Reconstruction and Development (EBRD, see p. 148). Hungary became an associate member of the European Union (EU, see p. 152) in February 1994, and subsequently applied for full EU membership. In March 1996 Hungary was admitted to the Organisation for Economic Co-operation and Development (OECD, see p. 208). Hungary's free-trade agreement with the European Free Trade Association (EFTA, see p. 150) took effect from October 1993.

The Hungarian Democratic Forum-led Government, formed in mid-1990, pledged to effect a full transition to a Western-style market economy, and to this end initiated a comprehensive programme of liberalization measures. However, the programme's implementation caused increasingly high levels of inflation and unemployment, a large external debt and a deficit on the current account of the balance of payments. In 1994 the new Hungarian Socialist Party administration announced a series of devaluations of the forint, a widening and acceleration of the privatization programme, and controversial reductions in expenditure on social security and welfare. In March 1996 the IMF approved a stand-by credit arrangement for Hungary, which, it was hoped, would increase foreign investor confidence in the economy. By the end of 1997 the Government's policy of fiscal discipline, in conjunction with rapid progress in the programme of large-scale privatization and progressive reductions in real income, had resulted in a decline in the public-sector deficit and the rate of inflation. The high level of foreign investment, with consequent increase in industrial output and exports, contributed to a strong overall growth in the economy. Further large-scale privatization was envisaged in 1998, while the World Bank approved a public-sector adjustment loan to support the Government's introduction of comprehensive pension reforms (as part of its policy of fiscal restraint). However, the continued implementation of planned social and economic reforms was dependent on the outcome of legislative elections, which were due to take place in May 1998.

Social Welfare

The national insurance scheme is based largely on non-state contributions. Employers and employees pay health insurance and pension contributions. The Health Insurance Act, passed in July 1992, made health insurance obligatory.

The implementation of the five-day working week was completed by 1985. There is a guaranteed minimum wage, and employment is non-discriminatory. A uniform system of retirement pensions was introduced in 1975: workers draw between 33% and 75% of their earnings, according to the number of years of service. Male workers are usually entitled to retirement pensions at the age of 60 and women at 55. In January 1989 unemployment benefit was introduced. There are also invalidity pensions, widows' pensions and orphans' allowances. Social insurance covers sickness benefits. Most medical consultation and treatment is free, although a small charge is generally made for medicines, and between 15% and 50% for medical appliances. In 1989 private medical practice was authorized. The social insurance scheme also covers maternity benefits. Women are entitled to 24 weeks' maternity leave on full pay. In 1996 there were an estimated 91,514 hospital beds in use in Hungary. Total public expenditure on health care amounted to 422,500m. forint (equivalent to 6.3% of GDP) in 1996. In 1998 the Government introduced comprehensive pension reforms, supported by the World Bank, whereby employees would be legally obliged to pay 25% of pension contributions to private pension schemes.

Education

Children under the age of three years attend crèches (bölcsődék), and those between the ages of three and six years attend kindergartens (óvodák). Education is compulsory between the ages of six and 16 years. Primary education begins at six years of age, with the basic school (általános iskola), and continues until the age of 14. In 1994 primary enrolment included 93% of children in the relevant age-group (males 92%; females 94%), while the comparable ratio for secondary education was 73% (males 71%; females 76%). In southern Hungary bilingual schools have been established to promote the languages of the national minorities. The majority of children continue with their education after 16 years of age. The most popular types of secondary school are the grammar school (gimnázium) and the secondary vocational school (szakközépiskola). The gimnázium provides a four-year course of mainly academic studies, although some vocational training does figure on the curriculum. The szakközépiskola offers full vocational training together with a general education, emphasis being laid on practical work. Apprentice training schools (szakmunkásképző intézetek) are attached to factories, agricultural co-operatives, etc., and lead to full trade qualifications. Further educational reform is being directed at revising the curricula and the method of assessing pupils. There are 77 higher institutes, including 11 universities and 19 technical universities. In 1994 an estimated 19.1% of the relevant age-group continued into tertiary education (males 17.6%; females 20.7%). Government expenditure on education in 1994 was 278,332m. forint (6.9% of total government spending).

Public Holidays

1998: 1 January (New Year's Day), 15 March (anniversary of 1848 uprising against Austrian rule), 13 April (Easter Monday), 1 May (Labour Day), 20 August (Constitution Day), 23 October (Day of the Proclamation of the Republic), 25–26 December (Christmas).

1999: 1 January (New Year's Day), 15 March (anniversary of 1848 uprising against Austrian rule), 5 April (Easter Monday), 1 May (Labour Day), 20 August (Constitution Day), 23 October (Day of the Proclamation of the Republic), 25–26 December (Christmas).

Weights and Measures

The metric system is in force.

Statistical Survey

Source (unless otherwise stated): Központi Statisztikai Hivatal (Hungarian Central Statistical Office), 1525 Budapest, Keleti Károly u. 5–7; tel. (1) 212-6212; telex 224308; fax (1) 212-6378.

Area and Population

AREA, POPULATION AND DENSITY

Area (sq km)	93,030*
Population (census results)	
1 January 1980	10,709,463
1 January 1990	
Males	4,984,904
Females	5,389,919
Total	10,374,823
Population (official estimates at 1 January)	
1994	10,276,968
1995	10,245,677
1996	10,212,300
Density (per sq km) at 1 January 1996	109.8

* 35,919 sq miles.

Languages (1990 census): Magyar (Hungarian) 98.5%; German 0.4%; Slovak 0.1%; Romany 0.5%; Croatian 0.2%; Romanian 0.1%.

ADMINISTRATIVE DIVISIONS (1 January 1996)

	Area (sq km)	Resident Population ('000)	Density (per sq km)	County Town (with population)
Counties:				
Bács-Kiskun	8,362	541	65	Kecskemét (105,058)
Baranya	4,487	409	91	Pécs (162,216)
Békés	5,631	403	72	Békéscsaba (65,039)
Borsod-Abaúj-Zemplén	7,247	746	103	Miskolc (180,005)
Csongrád	4,263	427	100	Szeged (167,170)
Fejér	4,373	426	97	Székesfehérvár (107,181)
Győr-Moson-Sopron	4,062	426	105	Győr (127,404)
Hajdú-Bihar	6,211	550	89	Debrecen (210,143)
Heves	3,637	328	90	Eger (59,308)
Jász-Nagykun-Szolnok	5,607	421	75	Szolnok (78,398)
Komárom-Esztergom	2,251	312	139	Tatabánya (72,510)
Nógrád	2,544	222	87	Salgótarján (45,832)
Pest	6,394	985	154	Budapest* (1,907,000)
Somogy	6,036	337	56	Kaposvár (68,485)
Szabolcs-Szatmár-Bereg	5,937	572	96	Nyíregyháza (113,136)
Tolna	3,704	249	67	Szekszárd (35,637)
Vas	3,336	272	82	Szombathely (83,425)
Veszprém	4,639	378	81	Veszprém (64,345)
Zala	3,784	301	80	Zalaegerszeg (61,678)
Capital City				
Budapest*	525	1,907	3,632	—
Total	93,030	10,212	110	—

* Budapest has separate County status. The area and population of the city are not included in the larger County (Pest) which it administers.

PRINCIPAL TOWNS (population at 1 January 1996)

Budapest (capital)	1,907,000	Nyíregyháza	113,136
Debrecen	210,143	Székesfehérvár	107,181
Miskolc	180,005	Kecskemét	105,058
Szeged	167,170	Szombathely	83,425
Pécs	162,216	Szolnok	78,398
Győr	127,404	Tatabánya	72,510

BIRTHS, MARRIAGES AND DEATHS

	Registered live births		Registered marriages		Registered deaths	
	Number	Rate (per 1,000)	Number	Rate (per 1,000)	Number	Rate (per 1,000)
1989	123,304	11.9	66,949	6.4	144,695	13.9
1990	125,679	12.1	66,405	6.4	145,660	14.1
1991	127,207	12.3	61,198	5.9	144,813	14.0
1992	121,724	11.8	57,005	5.5	148,781	14.4
1993	117,033	11.4	54,099	5.3	150,244	14.6
1994	115,598	11.3	54,114	5.3	146,889	14.3
1995	112,054	11.0	53,463	5.2	145,431	14.2
1996*	105,500	10.4	49,500	4.9	143,500	14.1

* Estimates.

Expectation of Life (years at birth, 1993): Males 64.5; females 73.8. Source: UN, *Demographic Yearbook*.

ECONOMICALLY ACTIVE POPULATION

(labour force surveys, '000 persons aged 15 years to 74 years)

	1994	1995	1996
Agriculture, hunting, forestry and fishing	327.6	295.1	302.4
Mining and quarrying	39.2	34.0	32.8
Manufacturing	888.8	850.2	850.9
Electricity, gas and water supply	108.3	96.6	88.7
Construction	201.0	217.3	217.7
Wholesale and retail trade; repair of motor vehicles, motorcycles, and personal and household goods	467.4	459.9	486.9
Hotels and restaurants	110.6	116.6	114.1
Transport, storage and communications	314.5	319.6	321.2
Financial intermediation	72.9	82.2	83.3
Real estate, renting and business activities	125.6	130.6	128.2
Public administration and defence; compulsory social security	320.2	318.1	306.6
Education	338.6	335.4	319.6
Health and social work	239.0	231.4	225.6
Other community, social and personal service activities	188.4	186.8	169.8
Private household with employed persons	1.2	1.0	
Extra-territorial organizations and bodies	7.6	3.5	
Activities not adequately defined	0.6	0.5	0.4
Total employed*	3,751.5	3,678.8	3,648.0
Unemployed	451.2	416.5	n.a.
Total labour force	4,202.7	4,095.3	n.a.
Males	n.a.	2,311.1	n.a.
Females	n.a.	1,784.2	n.a.

* Excluding persons on child care leave.

Source: mainly IMF, *Hungary—Statistical Appendix* (October 1997).

Agriculture

PRINCIPAL CROPS ('000 metric tons)

	1993	1994	1995
Wheat	3,021	4,874	4,600
Rice (paddy)	13	15	20*
Barley	1,138	1,558	1,408
Maize	4,044	4,761	4,597
Rye	113	193	166
Oats	96	131	139
Potatoes	1,057	946	1,150
Pulses	149	144	130*
Sunflower seed	682	667	777
Rapeseed	22	53	53*
Sugar beet	2,182	3,370	4,192
Grapes	607	614	570*
Apples	819	657	600†
Tobacco (leaves)	11	12	12*

* FAO estimate. † Unofficial figure.

Source: FAO, *Production Yearbook*.

LIVESTOCK ('000 head at December each year)

	1993	1994	1995
Cattle	999	910	928
Pigs	5,001	4,356	5,032
Sheep	1,252	947	977
Goats*	29†	36	52
Horses	71	81	71
Chickens	30,813	33,906	31,596
Ducks	1,304	1,806	1,287
Geese	876	1,385	1,111
Turkeys	836	1,285	1,665

* Source: FAO, *Production Yearbook*.
† Unofficial figure.

LIVESTOCK PRODUCTS (metric tons)

	1993	1994	1995
Beef and veal	59,000	36,000*	33,000*
Mutton and lamb	2,000	2,000*	2,000*
Pig meat*	674,000	606,000	580,000
Poultry meat	271,000	270,000	325,000
Edible offals*	32,000	28,000	27,000
Cows' milk	2,080,000	1,936,000	1,915,000
Sheep's milk	30,000	27,000	25,000
Goats' milk	9,000	9,000	9,000*
Butter	18,392	15,296	15,404
Cheese	85,494	77,496*	77,496*
Hen eggs	233,900	215,388	180,000*
Honey	15,873	16,236	16,236*
Wool:			
greasy	4,092	3,875	2,723
clean*	1,600	1,550	1,090
Cattle hides	6,545	4,000*	3,800*

* FAO estimate(s).

Source: FAO, *Production Yearbook*.

Forestry

ROUNDWOOD REMOVALS ('000 cu metres)

	1993	1994	1995
Industrial wood	2,271	2,274	2,386
Fuel wood	2,201	2,067	1,948
Total	4,472	4,341	4,334

SAWNWOOD PRODUCTION ('000 cu metres)

	1992	1993	1994
Coniferous (softwood)	149	122	87
Broadleaved (hardwood)	518	358	330
Total	667	480	417

Source: FAO, *Yearbook of Forest Products*.

Fishing

(metric tons, live weight)

	1993	1994	1995
Common carp	13,915	14,924	14,503
Other cyprinids	8,008	7,237	6,572
Other fishes	1,481	1,796	1,791
Total catch	23,404	23,957	22,866

Source: FAO, *Yearbook of Fishery Statistics*.

Mining

('000 metric tons, unless otherwise indicated)

	1993	1994	1995
Hard coal	942	n.a.	n.a.
Brown coal	6,598	6,158	4,299
Lignite	5,052	6,727	7,151
Crude petroleum	1,709	1,631	1,669
Bauxite	1,561	836	1,015
Natural gas (million cu metres)	5,011	5,564	5,404

Industry

SELECTED PRODUCTS ('000 metric tons, unless otherwise indicated)

	1993	1994	1995
Pig-iron	1,407	n.a.	n.a.
Crude steel	1,753	1,937	1,865
Rolled steel	1,871	2,083	2,132
Aluminium	27.9	n.a.	n.a.
Cement	2,533	2,793	2,875
Nitrogenous fertilizers*	164.8	n.a.	n.a.
Phosphatic fertilizers†	3.7	n.a.	n.a.
Refined sugar	392.9	439.3	479.7
Buses (number)	3,181	1,625	1,207
Cotton fabrics ('000 sq metres)	80,769	78,483	68,237
Leather footwear ('000 pairs)	11,777	11,666	11,401
Electric power (million kWh)	32,630	33,366	33,928
Woollen cloth ('000 sq metres)	5,559	4,119	2,982
Television receivers ('000)	204	272	274
Radio receivers ('000)	1	2	n.a.

* Production in terms of nitrogen.
† Production in terms of phosphoric acid.

Finance

CURRENCY AND EXCHANGE RATES

Monetary Units

100 fillér = 1 forint.

Sterling and Dollar Equivalents (30 September 1997)

£1 sterling = 316.09 forint;
US $1 = 195.67 forint;
1,000 forint = £3.164 = $5.111.

Average Exchange Rate (forint per US dollar)

1994 105.160
1995 125.681
1996 152.647

CENTRAL BUDGET (million forint)*

Revenue	1994	1995	1996†
Primary revenue	1,391,305	1,643,480	1,970,355
Payments of economic units	257,955	384,970	399,020
Profit taxes	75,978	90,991	110,876
Customs duties	148,796	247,885	247,171
Taxes on consumption	500,643	624,894	737,196
Value-added tax	336,371	423,954	515,080
Excises	164,271	200,940	222,116
Payments of households	263,397	314,120	419,663
Personal income tax‡	243,478	290,113	389,392
Central budgetary institutions	274,328	243,092	279,504
Revenues related to debt service	62,760	43,713	44,378
Other revenue	57,999	167,767	317,181
Interest receipts	4,099	15,466	100,091
Proceeds of privatization	31,000	150,000	211,880
Total	1,449,304	1,811,247	2,287,536

Expenditure	1994	1995	1996†
Primary expenditure	1,407,767	1,484,101	1,602,570
Subsidies to economic units	101,098	96,431	114,054
Agricultural subsidies	61,620	66,604	72,345
Consumers' price subsidy	27,047	32,505	44,948
Investment expenditures	73,223	108,247	118,433
Government investment projects	43,653	48,394	67,189
Housing grant	29,570	59,853	51,244
Social subsidies	210,022	204,922	213,085
Family allowances	144,900	137,892	132,100
Income supplement benefits	41,156	45,718	56,909
Central budgetary institutions	612,636	612,666	715,981
Transfers	347,260	373,205	397,523
Transfer to local governments	298,624	320,200	327,014
Transfers to extrabudgetary funds	37,410	31,674	4,385
Other expenditure	287,714	484,274	603,531
Transfers covering losses by National Bank of Hungary	—	—	58,100
Interest payments	287,714	484,274	545,431
Total	1,695,481	1,968,375	2,206,101

* Excluding the operations of social security funds, local governments and extrabudgetary funds.

† Figures are preliminary.

‡ After deduction of tax revenue transferred to local governments.

Source: Ministry of Finance, Budapest.

INTERNATIONAL RESERVES (US $ million at 31 December)

	1994	1995	1996
Gold*	42	43	37
IMF special drawing rights	2	1	—
Reserve position in IMF	82	83	81
Foreign exchange	6,727	11,968	9,714
Total	6,853	12,095	9,832

* National valuation.

Source: IMF, *International Financial Statistics.*

MONEY SUPPLY (million forint at 31 December)

	1993	1994	1995
Currency outside banks	371,200	410,700	444,500
Demand deposits at commercial and savings banks	512,400	553,900	580,100
Total money (incl. others)	901,900	973,900	1,030,500

Source: IMF, *International Financial Statistics.*

COST OF LIVING (Consumer Price Index; base: 1990 = 100)

	1993	1994	1995
Food	188.0	232.1	304.3
Fuel and light	311.8	348.3	522.5
Clothing	189.6	220.1	264.6
Rent	142.8	164.9	238.3
All items (incl. others)	203.4	241.6	309.7

Source: ILO, *Yearbook of Labour Statistics.*

1996: Food 356.9; All items 382.8 (Source: UN, *Monthly Bulletin of Statistics*).

NATIONAL ACCOUNTS ('000 million forint at current prices)

Expenditure on the Gross Domestic Product

	1993	1994	1995
Government final consumption expenditure	508.8	546.9	629.5
Private final consumption expenditure	2,632.1	3,152.0	3,714.9
Increase in stocks	26.9	68.0	279.7
Gross fixed capital formation	661.1	865.4	1,059.6
Total domestic expenditure	3,828.9	4,632.3	5,683.7
Exports of goods and services	937.0	1,262.9	1,914.8
Less Imports of goods and services	1,228.1	1,544.2	2,036.6
GDP in purchasers' values	3,537.8	4,351.0	5,561.9
GDP at constant 1990 prices	1,770.1	1,821.8	n.a.

Source: IMF, *International Financial Statistics.*

Gross Domestic Product by Economic Activity

	1993	1994	1995
Agriculture, hunting, forestry and fishing	206.1	262.3	351.1
Mining and quarrying	20.1	20.0	23.2
Manufacturing*	688.4	848.2	1,125.5
Electricity, gas and water†	115.9	125.3	166.9
Construction	167.4	201.5	238.7
Trade, restaurants and hotels	417.5	493.8	607.1
Transport, storage and communications	277.0	333.8	480.7
Finance, insurance, real estate and business services	557.8	770.2	904.7
Government services (incl. non-profit institutions)	562.6	702.5	817.4
Other community and social services	129.5	161.8	169.7
Sub-total	3,142.3	3,919.4	4,885.0
Net taxes on commodities	530.4	644.5	828.0
Less Imputed bank service charge	124.4	199.1	219.2
Total	3,548.3	4,364.8	5,493.8

* The activities of the Hungarian Oil and Gas Company are included in manufacturing.

† The operations of eight coal mining enterprises are included in electricity.

BALANCE OF PAYMENTS (US $ million)

	1994	1995	1996
Exports of goods f.o.b.	7,648	12,864	14,184
Imports of goods f.o.b.	–11,364	–15,297	–16,836
Trade balance	–3,716	–2,433	–2,652
Exports of services	3,117	4,271	5,004
Imports of services	–2,958	–3,629	–3,506
Balance on goods and services	–3,557	–1,791	–1,154
Other income received	676	798	1,202
Other income paid	–2,082	–2,602	–2,658
Balance on goods, services and income	–4,963	–3,595	–2,610
Current transfers received	2,871	3,575	2,332
Current transfers paid	–1,961	–2,515	–1,411
Current balance	–4,054	–2,535	–1,689
Capital account (net)	—	59	156
Direct investment abroad	–49	–43	4
Direct investment from abroad	1,144	4,519	1,982
Portfolio investment assets	6	–1	–18
Portfolio investment liabilities	2,458	2,213	–851
Other investment assets	362	88	–1,256
Other investment liabilities	–551	–199	–1,436
Net errors and omissions	209	1,298	1,864
Overall balance	–475	5,399	–1,244

Source: IMF, *International Financial Statistics*.

External Trade

PRINCIPAL COMMODITIES (distribution by SITC, million forint)

Imports c.i.f.	1993	1994	1995
Food and live animals	58,444	87,132	91,791
Animal feeding-stuff (excl. cereals)	14,416	17,553	23,380
Crude materials (inedible) except fuels	35,658	56,897	78,860
Cork and wood	8,658	11,866	17,377
Mineral fuels, lubricants, etc.	154,971	181,081	225,942
Coal, coke and briquettes	14,195	21,839	25,584
Petroleum, petroleum products, etc.	90,522	102,299	117,621
Gas (natural and manufactured)	44,619	51,772	74,988
Chemicals and related products	138,317	194,992	275,155
Organic chemicals	28,746	37,473	61,218
Inorganic chemicals	8,522	11,213	14,277
Artificial resins and plastic materials, etc.	9,997	15,289	23,274
Basic manufactures	212,069	304,908	445,902
Paper, paperboard and manufactures	29,762	44,069	64,053
Textile yarn, fabrics, etc.	60,472	79,961	111,166
Iron and steel	26,444	34,707	60,972
Non-ferrous metals	24,095	39,903	65,996
Other metal manufactures	30,313	45,456	61,628
Machinery and transport equipment	425,293	523,959	595,885
Machinery specialized for particular industries	41,023	58,236	64,654
Metalworking machinery	4,776	7,203	10,761
Road vehicles and parts (excl. tyres, engines and electrical parts)	80,657	114,916	113,799
Miscellaneous manufactured articles	128,948	173,996	205,571
Total (incl. others)	1,162,491	1,537,002	1,936,387

Exports f.o.b.	1993	1994	1995
Food and live animals	137,531	186,392	290,478
Live animals	11,172	13,836	16,236
Meat and meat preparations	51,959	63,833	87,708
Cereals and cereal preparations	10,848	21,411	74,217
Vegetables and fruit	40,694	60,936	72,780
Beverages and tobacco	18,785	22,425	39,208
Crude materials (inedible) except fuels	46,978	59,236	77,852

Exports f.o.b. — *continued*	1993	1994	1995
Mineral fuels, lubricants, etc.	33,220	44,942	51,834
Petroleum, petroleum products, etc.	30,895	40,880	46,865
Chemicals and related products	99,442	126,974	190,861
Organic chemicals	27,428	30,778	39,827
Medicinal and pharmaceutical products	22,991	28,312	36,078
Basic manufactures	132,251	186,873	281,573
Textile yarn, fabrics, etc.	18,440	27,519	36,107
Iron and steel	28,920	38,257	53,130
Non-ferrous metals	17,531	30,890	53,348
Machinery and transport equipment	197,331	288,673	415,432
Machinery specialized for particular industries	16,699	23,295	34,306
Telecommunications and sound equipment	22,182	37,718	54,725
Other electrical machinery, apparatus, etc.	55,827	88,818	158,086
Road vehicles and parts (excl. tyres, engines and electrical parts)	51,953	57,161	86,118
Miscellaneous manufactured articles	145,654	202,438	262,813
Clothing and accessories (excl. footwear)	74,076	104,498	130,009
Footwear	22,617	29,536	33,825
Professional, scientific and controlling instruments and apparatus	8,210	10,710	16,919
Total (incl. others)	819,915	1,128,695	1,621,991

PRINCIPAL TRADING PARTNERS (million forint)*

Imports c.i.f.	1993	1994	1995
Algeria	142	7	1,383
Austria	135,065	184,292	207,900
Belgium and Luxembourg	23,055	33,988	48,989
Brazil	11,427	14,637	17,630
Czech Republic and Slovakia	46,569	74,208	91,944
France	38,467	52,398	76,346
Germany	250,891	359,089	453,689
Italy	69,555	107,163	152,930
Japan	31,864	41,472	42,321
Netherlands	31,308	46,707	60,848
Poland	20,437	20,437	39,332
Romania	7,893	12,534	16,439
Russia	257,927†	183,697	229,299
Sweden	17,809	32,060	38,659
Switzerland and Liechtenstein	33,428	41,476	47,981
United Kingdom	29,609	61,128	59,587
USA	45,406	47,711	60,343
Yugoslavia (former)	12,457	n.a.	n.a.
Total (incl. others)	1,162,491	1,537,002	1,936,387

Exports f.o.b.	1993	1994	1995
Austria	82,614	122,760	163,554
Belgium and Luxembourg	15,002	22,208	34,386
Czech Republic and Slovakia	27,453	35,981	53,128
France	28,273	40,045	65,127
Germany	218,247	318,489	464,461
Iran	5,316	2,795	4,252
Italy	65,544	95,426	137,551
Japan	7,905	9,760	9,697
Netherlands	19,365	28,635	47,313
Poland	15,038	23,438	42,563
Romania	16,923	20,939	45,267
Russia	125,243†	84,856	104,440
Sweden	8,396	13,172	15,830
Switzerland and Liechtenstein	15,946	17,798	22,432
Turkey	8,768	3,405	6,659
United Kingdom	18,703	48,427	49,229
USA	34,629	45,403	52,016
Yugoslavia (former)	22,978	n.a.	n.a.
Total (incl. others)	819,915	1,128,695	1,621,991

* Imports by country of production; exports by country of last consignment.
† Figure refers to the former USSR.

Transport

RAILWAYS (traffic)

	1993	1994	1995
Passengers carried (million)	230.9	230.5	222.7
Passenger-kilometres (million)	9,077	9,140	9,040
Net ton-kilometres (million)	7,708	7,707	8,422

ROAD TRAFFIC (motor vehicles in use at 31 December)

	1994	1995	1996
Passenger cars	2,176,922	2,283,597	2,434,241
Buses and coaches	21,472	21,424	21,790
Goods vehicles	258,081	298,000	332,203
Motorcycles	157,327	157,000	157,500

Source: International Road Federation, *World Road Statistics*.

SHIPPING

Merchant Fleet (registered at 31 December)

	1994	1995	1996
Number of vessels	9	9	10
Total displacement ('000 grt)	45	45	50

Source: Lloyd's Register of Shipping, *World Fleet Statistics*.

Inland Waterways (traffic)

	1993	1994	1995
Freight carried ('000 metric tons)	1,731	1,739	2,279
Freight ton-km (million)	831	772	1,338

CIVIL AVIATION (traffic)

	1993	1994	1995
Kilometres flown	27,181,033	n.a.	n.a.
Passengers carried	1,273,000	1,605,000	1,625,000
Passenger-km ('000)	1,630,900	2,234,400	2,383,400
Cargo carried: metric tons	7,000	11,061	13,000
Cargo ton-km	11,083,000	22,200,000	35,700,000

Tourism

('000 arrivals)

	1993	1994	1995
Foreign tourists	22,804	21,425	20,690
Foreign visitors in transit	17,795	18,411	18,550
Total	40,599	39,836	39,240
Tourist receipts (US $ million)	1,182	1,428	1,724

TOURISTS BY COUNTRY OF ORIGIN
('000 arrivals, including visitors in transit)

	1993	1994	1995
Austria	5,741	6,111	5,438
Bulgaria	754	640	482
Czech Republic and Slovakia	3,058	3,448	4,138
Germany	4,140	4,134	3,949
Poland	755	676	582
Romania	6,699	5,206	4,360
USSR (former)	2,704	3,884	n.a.
Yugoslavia (former)	13,715	12,723	n.a.
Total (incl. others)	40,599	39,836	39,240

Communications Media

	1993	1994	1995
Radio receivers ('000 in use)*	6,300	6,350	6,500
Television receivers ('000 in use)*	4,360	4,360	4,375
Main telephone lines in use†	1,498,000	1,732,000	n.a.
Telefax stations in use†	25,460	n.a.	n.a.
Mobile cellular telephone subscribers†	45,712	143,000	n.a.
Book titles (including translations)*	9,170	10,108	9,314
Daily newspapers	41	27*	36*
Average daily circulation	2,215,000	2,321,000*	1,706,000*

* Source: UNESCO, *Statistical Yearbook*.
† Source: UN, *Statistical Yearbook*.

Education

(1994/95, unless otherwise indicated)

	Institutions	Teachers	Students: Males	Students: Females	Students: Total
Pre-primary	4,719	37,470	205,827	190,357	396,184
Primary	3,814	89,939	503,410	481,881	985,291
Secondary	1,578*	40,083*	262,030	261,038	523,068
Teacher training	n.a.	n.a.	30	1,276	1,306
Vocational	n.a.	n.a.	210,467	170,943	381,410
Higher:					
Universities, etc.	n.a.	13,550	45,315	48,642	93,957
Other	n.a.	5,553	27,811	32,892	60,703

* 1995 figure.

Source: mainly UNESCO, *Statistical Yearbook*.

Directory

The Constitution

A new Constitution was introduced on 18 August 1949, and the Hungarian People's Republic was established two days later. The Constitution was amended in April 1972 and December 1983. Further, radical amendments were made in October 1989. Shortly afterwards, the Republic of Hungary was proclaimed.

The following is a summary of the main provisions of the Constitution, as amended in October 1989.

GENERAL PROVISIONS

The Republic of Hungary is an independent, democratic constitutional state in which the values of civil democracy and democratic socialism prevail in equal measures. All power belongs to the people, which they exercise directly and through the elected representatives of popular sovereignty.

Political parties may, under observance of the Constitution, be freely formed and may freely operate in Hungary. Parties may not directly exercise public power. No party has the right to guide any state body. Trade unions and other organizations for the representation of interests safeguard and represent the interests of employees, members of co-operatives and entrepreneurs.

The State safeguards the people's freedom, the independence and territorial integrity of the country as well as the frontiers thereof, as established by international treaties. The Republic of Hungary rejects war as a means of settling disputes between nations and refrains from applying force against the independence or territorial integrity of other states, and from threats of violence.

The Hungarian legal system adopts the universally accepted rules of international law. The order of legislation is regulated by an Act of constitutional force.

The economy of Hungary is a market economy, availing itself also of the advantages of planning, with public and private ownership enjoying equal right and protection. Hungary recognizes and supports the right of undertaking and free competition, limitable only by an Act of constitutional force. State-owned enterprises and organs pursuing economic activities manage their affairs independently, in accordance with the mode and responsibility as provided by law.

The Republic of Hungary protects the institutions of marriage and the family. It provides for the indigent through extensive social measures, and recognizes and enforces the right of each citizen to a healthy environment.

GOVERNMENT

National Assembly

The highest organ of state authority in the Republic of Hungary is the National Assembly, which exercises all the rights deriving from the sovereignty of the people and determines the organization, direction and conditions of government. The National Assembly enacts the Constitution and laws, determines the state budget, decides the socio-economic plan, elects the President of the Republic and the Council of Ministers, directs the activities of ministries, decides upon declaring war and concluding peace and exercises the prerogative of amnesty.

The National Assembly is elected for a term of four years and members enjoy immunity from arrest and prosecution without parliamentary consent. It meets at least twice a year and is convened by the President of the Republic or by a written demand of the Council of Ministers or of one-fifth of the Assembly's members. It elects a President, Deputy Presidents and Recorders from among its own members, and it lays down its own rules of procedure and agenda. As a general rule, the sessions of the National Assembly are held in public.

The National Assembly has the right of legislation which can be initiated by the President of the Republic, the Council of Ministers or any committee or member of the National Assembly. Decisions are valid only if at least half of the members are present, and they require a simple majority. Constitutional changes require a two-thirds majority. Acts of the National Assembly are signed by the President of the Republic.

The National Assembly may pronounce its dissolution before the expiry of its term, and in the event of an emergency may prolong its mandate or may be reconvened after dissolution. A new National Assembly must be elected within three months of dissolution and convened within one month of polling day.

Members of the National Assembly are elected on the basis of universal, equal and direct suffrage by secret ballot, and they are accountable to their constituents, who may recall them. All citizens of 18 years and over have the right to vote, with the exception of those who are unsound of mind, and those who are deprived of their civil rights by a court of law.

President of the Republic

The President of the Republic is the Head of State of Hungary. He/she embodies the unity of the nation and supervises the democratic operation of the mechanism of State. The President is also the Commander-in-Chief of the Armed Forces. The President is elected by the National Assembly for a period of five years, and may be re-elected for a second term. Any citizen of Hungary qualified to vote, who has reached 35 years of age before the day of election, may be elected President.

The President may issue the writ for general or local elections, convene the National Assembly, initiate legislation, hold plebiscites, direct local government, conclude international treaties, appoint diplomatic representatives, ratify international treaties, appoint higher civil servants and officers of the armed forces, award orders and titles, and exercise the prerogative of mercy.

Council of Ministers

The highest organ of state administration is the Council of Ministers, responsible to the National Assembly and consisting of the Prime Minister and other Ministers who are elected by the National Assembly on the recommendation of the President of the Republic. The Council of Ministers directs the work of the ministries (listed in a special enactment) and ensures the enforcement of laws and the fulfilment of economic plans; it may issue decrees and annul or modify measures taken by any central or local organ of government.

Local Administration

The local organs of state power are the county, town, borough and town precinct councils, whose members are elected for a term of four years by the voters in each area. Local councils direct economic, social and cultural activities in their area, prepare local economic plans and budgets and supervise their fulfilment, enforce laws, supervise subordinate organs, maintain public order, protect public property and individual rights, and direct local economic enterprises. They may issue regulations and annul or modify those of subordinate councils. Local Councils are administered by an Executive Committee elected by and responsible to them.

JUDICATURE

Justice is administered by the Supreme Court of the Republic of Hungary, county and district courts. The Supreme Court exercises the right of supervising in principle the judicial activities and practice of all other courts.

All judicial offices are filled by election; Supreme Court, county and district court judges are all elected for an indefinite period; the President of the Supreme Court is elected by the National Assembly. All court hearings are public unless otherwise prescribed by law, and those accused are guaranteed the right of defence. An accused person must be considered innocent until proved guilty.

Public Prosecutor

The function of the Chief Public Prosecutor is to supervise the observance of the law. He is elected by the National Assembly, to whom he is responsible. The organization of public prosecution is under the control of the Chief Public Prosecutor, who appoints the public prosecutors.

RIGHTS AND DUTIES OF CITIZENS

The Republic of Hungary guarantees for its citizens the right to work and to remuneration, the right of rest and recreation, the right to care in old age, sickness or disability, the right to education, and equality before the law; women enjoy equal rights with men. Discrimination on grounds of sex, religion or nationality is a punishable offence. The State also ensures freedom of conscience, religious worship, speech, the press and assembly. The right of workers to organize themselves is stressed. The freedom of the individual, and the privacy of the home and of correspondence are inviolable. Freedom for creative work in the sciences and the arts is guaranteed.

The basic freedoms of all workers are guaranteed and foreign citizens enjoy the right of asylum.

Military service (with or without arms) and the defence of their country are the duties of all citizens.

The Government

HEAD OF STATE

President of the Republic: ÁRPÁD GÖNCZ (elected 3 August 1990; re-elected 19 June 1995).

COUNCIL OF MINISTERS

(February 1998)

A coalition of the Hungarian Socialist Party (HSP) and the Alliance of Free Democrats (AFD).

Prime Minister: GYULA HORN (HSP).

Deputy Prime Minister and Minister of the Interior: GÁBOR KUNCZE (AFD).

Minister of Agriculture: FRIGYES NAGY (HSP).

Minister of Defence: GYÖRGY KELETI (HSP).

Minister of Justice: Dr PÁL VASTAGH (HSP).

Minister of Industry and Trade: SZABOLCS FAZAKAS (Independent).

Minister for the Environment and Regional Protection: Dr FERENC BAJA (HSP).

Minister of Transport, Communications and Water Management: Dr KÁROLY LOTZ (AFD).

Minister of Foreign Affairs: LÁSZLÓ KOVÁCS (HSP).

Minister of Labour: PÉTER KISS (HSP).

Minister of Culture and Education: BÁLINT MAGYAR (AFD).

Minister of Public Welfare: Dr MIHÁLY KÖKÉNY (HSP).

Minister of Finance: PÉTER MEDGYESSY (HSP).

Minister without Portfolio responsible for National Security: ISTVÁN NIKOLITS (HSP).

Minister without Portfolio responsible for Privatization: JUDIT CASIHA (HSP).

MINISTRIES

Office of the Prime Minister: 1055 Budapest, Kossuth Lajos tér 1–3; tel. (1) 112-0600; telex 225547; fax (1) 153-3622.

Ministry of Agriculture: 1055 Budapest, Kossuth Lajos tér 11; tel. (1) 301-4000; telex 225445; fax (1) 301-4662.

Ministry of Culture and Education: 1055 Budapest, Szalay u. 10–14; tel. (1) 302-0600; telex 225935; fax (1) 302-3002.

Ministry of Defence: 1055 Budapest, Balaton u. 7–11; tel. (1) 132-2500; telex 225424; fax (1) 112-8246.

Ministry for the Environment and Regional Protection: 1011 Budapest, Fő u. 44–50, POB 351; tel. (1) 201-3843; fax (1) 201-2846.

Ministry of Finance: 1051 Budapest, József Nádor tér 2–4; tel. (1) 118-2066; telex 202763; fax (1) 327-2749.

Ministry of Foreign Affairs: 1027 Budapest, Bem rkp. 47; tel. (1) 156-8000; telex 225571; fax (1) 156-3801.

Ministry of Industry, Trade and Tourism: 1024 Budapest, Margit Körút 85; tel. (1) 175-0419; fax (1) 175-2419.

Ministry of the Interior: 1051 Budapest, József Attila u. 2–4; tel. (1) 112-1710; telex 225216; fax (1) 118-0667.

Ministry of Justice: 1055 Budapest, Szalay u. 16; tel. and fax (1) 131-8922.

Ministry of Labour: 1051 Budapest, Roosevelt tér 7–8; tel. (1) 132-2100; fax (1) 131-6399.

Ministry of Public Welfare: 1051 Budapest, Arany János u. 6–8; tel. (1) 332-3100; telex 224337; fax (1) 302-0925.

Ministry of Transport, Communications and Water Management: 1400 Budapest, Dob u. 75–81, POB 87; tel. (1) 122-6667; telex 225729; fax (1) 122-3429.

Legislature

ORSZÁGGYÜLÉS

(National Assembly)

President of the National Assembly: Dr ZOLTÁN GÁL.

Deputy Presidents: MÁRIA KORODI, AGNES MACZO NAGY, LÁSZLÓ SALAMON.

General election, 8 and 29 May 1994

	% of votes*	Seats
Hungarian Socialist Party (HSP)	32.96	209
Alliance of Free Democrats (AFD)	19.76	70
Hungarian Democratic Forum (HDF)	11.73	37
Independent Smallholders' and Peasants' Party (ISPP)	8.85	26
Christian Democratic People's Party (CDPP)	7.06	22
Federation of Young Democrats (FYD)	7.00	20
Agrarian Association	12.64	1
Liberal Civil Alliance—Entrepreneurs		1
Total	100.00	386

* Figures refer to votes for regional party lists, from which as many as 152 members of the Assembly are elected. At the 1994 election 125 members were elected from such lists. The remaining 27 seats were filled by reapportioned votes on national lists. A further 58 members were chosen from national lists, and 176 elected from single-member constituencies.

Political Organizations

Agrarian Association (Agrarszövetség): Budapest; Chair. TAMÁS NAGY.

Alliance of Free Democrats—AFD (Szabad Demokraták Szövetsége—SzDSz): 1051 Budapest, Mérleg u. 6; tel. (1) 117-6911; fax (1) 118-7944; f. 1988; 35,000 mems (1990); Chair. GÁBOR KUNCZE.

Christian Democratic People's Party—CDPP (Keresztény-demokrata Néppárt—KDNP): 1126 Budapest, Nagy Jenő u. 5; tel. (1) 175-0333; fax (1) 155-5772; e-mail kulugy@kdnp.hu; re-formed 1989; Chair. GYÖRGY GICZY.

Federation of Young Democrats—Hungarian Civic Party—FYD—HCP (FIDESz—Magyar Polgári Párt): 1062 Budapest, Lendvay u. 28 ; tel. (1) 269-5353; fax (1) 269-5343; f. 1988 as the Federation of Young Democrats; renamed April 1995; 10,000 mems; Leader VIKTOR ORBAN.

Green Party of Hungary: Budapest; Chair. ZOLTAN MEDVECZKY.

Hungarian Civic Co-operation Association (Magyar Polgari Egyuettmuekoedes Egyesuelet): Budapest; f. 1996; Chair. FERENC MADL; Gen. Sec. ZOLTÁN VESZELOVSZKI.

Hungarian Democratic Forum—HDF (Magyar Demokrata Fórum—MDF): 1027 Budapest, Bem tér 3, 1539 Budapest, POB 579; tel. (1) 212-2819; fax (1) 212-2856; f. 1988; 25,000 mems (Dec. 1995); Chair. SÁNDOR LEZSÁK.

Hungarian Democratic People's Party—HDPP (Magyar Demokrata Néppárt—MDN): Budapest; f. 1996 by former mems of HDF; moderate.

Hungarian Justice and Life Party—HJLP (Magyar Igazság és Élet Párt—MIEP): c/o Office of Deputies, 1357 Budapest, Széchenyi rakpart 19; tel. (1) 111-1400; fax (1) 132-8326; f. 1993; Chair. ISTVÁN CSURKA.

Hungarian Social Democratic Party—HSDP (Magyarországi Szocialdemokrata Párt—MSzDP): 1074 Budapest, Dohány u. 76, POB 1067; tel. and fax (1) 342-3547; f. 1890; absorbed by Communist Party in 1948; revived 1988; affiliated with the Social Democratic Youth Movement; 3,000 mems (Dec. 1997); Chair. LÁSZLÓ KAPOLYI.

Hungarian Socialist Party—HSP (Magyar Szocialista Párt—MSzP): 1081 Budapest, Köztársaság tér 26; tel. (1) 210-0046; fax (1) 210-0081; f. 1989 to replace the Hungarian Socialist Workers' Party; 40,000 mems (Jan. 1997); Chair. Dr GYULA HORN.

Hungarian Workers' Party—HWP (Magyar Munkáspárt—MMP): 1082 Budapest, Baross út 61; tel. (1) 334-2721; fax (1) 313-5423; e-mail 100324.2566Compuserve; f. 1956 as Hungarian Socialist Workers' Party; dissolved and replaced by Hungarian Socialist Party (see above) in 1989; re-formed in 1989 as Hungarian Socialist Workers' Party, name changed as above 1992; approx. 30,000 mems (Oct. 1992); Pres. Dr GYULA THÜRMER.

Independent Smallholders' and Peasants' Party—ISPP (Független Kisgazda-, Földmunkás- és Polgári Párt—FKgP): 1056 Budapest, Belgrád rkp. 24; tel. and fax (1) 1181-824; f. 1988 as the Independent Smallholders' Party; 60,000 mems; Chair. Dr JÓZSEF TÖRGYÁN.

Liberal Civic Alliance—Entrepreneurs' Party: Budapest; Chair. PETER ZWACK.

Lungo Drom Alliance: ethnic Roma party; Leader FLORIAN FARKAS.

Movement for Hungarian Unity: Budapest; f. 1995; nationalist; Pres. IMRE POZSGAY.

National Alliance for Hungary: Salgotarjan; f. 1995; nationalist.

Peace Party of Hungarian Gypsies (Magyar Ciganyok Bekepartja): Budapest; f. 1993; Leader ALBERT HORVÁTH.

United Historic Smallholders' Party—UHSP (Egyesült Kisgazdapárt—Történelmi Tagozat—EKgP–TT): Budapest; f. 1992 as the 'Historical Section' of the Independent Smallholders' Party (now the ISPP); renamed 1993; Chair. JÁNOS SZABÓ; Gen. Sec. ANTAL BELAFI.

World National People's Rule Party: Budapest; f. 1993; right-wing; Chair. ALBERT SZABÓ.

Diplomatic Representation

EMBASSIES IN HUNGARY

Afghanistan: 1021 Budapest, Budakeszi út 55D, P5, 111.2; tel. (1) 176-7742; telex 223504; Chargé d'affaires: SAYED IBRAHIM GAILANI.

Albania: 1068 Budapest, Bajza u. 26; tel. (1) 122-7251; Ambassador: ISUF BASHKURTI.

Algeria: 1014 Budapest, Dísz tér 6; tel. (1) 175-9884; telex 226916; Ambassador: BACHIR ROUIS.

Argentina: 1023 Budapest, Vérhalom u. 12-16B; tel. (1) 122-8467; telex 224128; Ambassador: GUILLERMO JORGE MCGOUGH.

Australia: 1126 Budapest, Királyhágó tér 8–9; tel. (1) 201-8899; fax (1) 201-9792; Ambassador: D. J. KINGSMILL.

Austria: 1068 Budapest, Benczúr u. 16; tel. (1) 269-6700; telex 224447; fax (1) 269-6702; Ambassador: Dr ERICH KUSSBACH.

Belgium: 1015 Budapest, Toldy Ferenc u. 13; tel. (1) 201-1571; telex 224664; fax (1) 175-1566; Ambassador: MICHEL CARLIER.

Brazil: 1118 Budapest, Somlói út 3; tel. (1) 166-6044; fax (1) 166-8156; Ambassador: IVAN VELLOSO DA SILVEIRA BATALHA.

Bulgaria: 1062 Budapest, Andrássy út 115; tel. (1) 322-0824; fax (1) 322-5215; Ambassador: CHRISTO HALATCHEV.

Cambodia: 1122 Budapest, Ráth György u. 48; tel. (1) 155-1128; fax (1) 155-1128; Ambassador: UNG SEAN.

Canada: 1121 Budapest, Budakeszi út 32; tel. and fax (1) 275-1210; Ambassador: RODNEY IRWIN.

Chile: 1061 Budapest, Józsefhegyi út 28-30; tel. (1) 212-0061; telex 202858; fax (1) 212-0059; Ambassador: LUCIO PARADA-DAGNINO.

China, People's Republic: 1068 Budapest, Benczúr u. 17; tel. (1) 122-4872; Ambassador: CHEN ZHILIU.

Colombia: 1025 Budapest, Józsefhegyi út 28-30 C7; tel. (1) 115-4425; telex 226013; fax (1) 201-2844; Ambassador: ALBERTO ESTEBAN ROJAS PUYO.

Costa Rica: Budapest; tel. (1) 1851-431; Ambassador: JORGE EDOARDO VILLAFRANCA NÚÑEZ.

Croatia: 1125 Budapest, Nógradi út 28B; tel. (1) 155-1522; fax (1) 175-4336; Ambassador: Dr ALEKSANDAR SOLC.

Cuba: 1026 Budapest, Haranguirag utca 7; Ambassador: CARLOS TREJO SOSA.

Czech Republic: 1064 Budapest, Rozsa utca 61; tel. (1) 351-0539; fax (1) 351-9189; e-mail budapest@embassy.mzv.cz; Ambassador: RICHARD PRAŽÁK.

Denmark: 1122 Budapest, Határőr út 37; tel. (1) 155-7320; telex 224137; fax (1) 175-3803; Ambassador: ERIK SKOV.

Ecuador: 1021 Budapest, Budakeszi út 55D; tel. (1) 200-8918; fax (1) 200-8682; e-mail mecuahun@mail.elender.hu; Chargé d'affaires: Dr CARLOS BORJA MARTÍNEZ.

Egypt: 1016 Budapest, Bérc u. 16; tel. (1) 166-8060; telex 225184; Ambassador: MAHMOUD ABOU ZEID.

Finland: 1118 Budapest, Kelenhegyi út 16A; tel. (1) 185-0700; telex 224710; fax (1) 185-0843; Ambassador: JAAKO KAURINKOSKI.

France: 1062 Budapest, Lendvay u. 27; tel. (1) 132-4980; telex 225143; fax (1) 111-8291; Ambassador: PAUL POUPADE.

Germany: 1143 Budapest, Stefánia út 101–103; tel. (1) 467-3500; fax (1) 467-3505; Ambassador: HASSO BUCHRUCKER.

Greece: 1063 Budapest, Szegfű u. 3; tel. (1) 122-8004; telex 224113; Ambassador: IOANNIS DRAKOULARAKOS.

Holy See: 1026 Budapest, Gyimes út 1–3; tel. (1) 155-8979; fax (1) 155-6987; Apostolic Nuncio: Most Rev. ANGELO ACERBI, Titular Archbishop of Zella.

India: 1025 Budapest, Búzavirág u. 14; tel. (1) 325-7742; fax (1) 325-7745; Ambassador: SATNAM JIT SINGH.

Indonesia: 1068 Budapest, Városligeti fasor 26; tel. (1) 342-8508; telex 225263; fax (1) 322-8669; Ambassador: HASSAN ABDULDJALIL.

Iran: 1062 Budapest, Délibáb u. 29; tel. (1) 251-3755; telex 224129; fax (1) 251-2271; Ambassador: Dr MORTEZA SAFFARI NATANZI.

Iraq: 1145 Budapest, Jávor u. 13; tel. (1) 122-6418; telex 226058; Ambassador: MOHAMMED GHANIM AL-ANAZ.

Israel: 1026 Budapest, Fullánk u. 8; tel. (1) 2000-781; fax (1) 2000-783; e-mail isremb@alarmix.hu; Ambassador: JOEL ALON.

Italy: 1143 Budapest, Stefánia út 95; tel. (1) 343-6065; telex 225294; fax (1) 343-6058; Ambassador: PIETRO ERCOLE AGO.

Japan: 1125 Budapest, Zalai út 7; tel. (1) 275-1275; telex 225048; fax (1) 275-1281; Ambassador: YOSHITOMO TANAKA.

Kazakhstan: 1025 Budapest, III ker., Kapi út 59; tel. (1) 275-1300; telex 612-2708; fax (1) 275-2092; Ambassador: TULEUTAI SULEIMENOV.

Korea, Republic: 1062 Budapest, Andrássy út 109; tel. (1) 351-1179; fax (1) 351-1182; Chargé d'affaires: LEE CHONG-MOO.

Libya: 1143 Budapest, Stefánia út 111; tel. (1) 122-6076; telex 226940; Head of People's Bureau: OMAR MUFTAH DALLAL.

Mexico: 1023 Budapest, Vérhalom u. 12–16; tel. (1) 115-0442; fax (1) 135-5148; Ambassador: LUCIANO JOUBLANC.

Mongolia: 1022 Budapest II, k. Bogár u. 14/C; tel. (1) 115-9625; telex 225666; fax (1) 135-9532; Ambassador: DERGELDALIYN DZAMBADZANCAN.

Morocco: 1026 Budapest, Törökvész Lejto 12A; tel. (1) 275-1467; telex 223580; fax (1) 275-1437; Ambassador: MOHAMED LOULICHKI.

Netherlands: 1022 Budapest, Fűge út 5–7; tel. (1) 326-5301; telex 225562; fax (1) 326-5978; Ambassador: E. F. NIEHE.

New Zealand: Budapest; tel. (1) 131-2144; fax (1) 131-0593; Chargé d'affaires: TAMÁS TAKATSY.

Norway: 1122 Budapest, Határőr út 35, POB 32; tel. (1) 155-1811; telex 225867; fax (1) 156-7928; Ambassador: TORMOD PETTER SVENNEVIG.

Peru: 1122 Budapest, Tóth Lörinc u. 5 ; tel. (1) 155-4019; fax (1) 155-1019; Ambassador: BERTHA VEGA PÉREZ.

Philippines: 1025 Budapest II, Jozsefhegyi út 28–30; tel. (1) 212-3897; fax (1) 212-2945; Ambassador: FRANKLIN M. EBDALIN.

Poland: 1068 Budapest, Városligeti fasor 16; tel. (1) 342-5566; fax (1) 351-1722; Ambassador: GRZEGORZ LUBCZYK.

Portugal: 1118 Budapest, Kelenhegyi út 46B; tel. (1) 185-342-5566; telex 226509; fax (1) 166-5148; Ambassador: Dr ANTÓNIO BAPTISTA MARTINS.

Romania: 1146 Budapest, Thököly út 72; tel. (1) 268-0271; telex 225847; fax (1) 268-0269; Ambassador: IOAN DONCA.

Russia: 1062 Budapest, Bajza u. 35; tel. (1) 132-0911; Ambassador: IVAN P. ABOIMOV.

Slovakia: 1143 Budapest, Stefánia út 22-24; tel. (1) 251-1700; fax (1) 251-1460; Ambassador: EVA MITROVA.

Slovenia: 1025 Budapest, Cseppkö u. 68; tel. (1) 325-9202; fax (1) 325-9187; Ambassador: FERENC HAJÓS.

Spain: 1067 Budapest, Eötvös u. 11B; tel. (1) 3429-992; telex 224130; fax (1) 3510-572; Ambassador: FERNANDO PERPIÑÁ-ROBERT.

Sweden: 1146 Budapest, Ajtósi Dürer sor 27A; tel. (1) 352-2804; telex 225647; fax (1) 352-2807; Ambassador: JAN LUNDVIK.

Switzerland: 1143 Budapest, Stefánia út 107; tel. (1) 343-9491; Ambassador: CLAUDIO CARATSCH.

Syria: 1026 Budapest, Harangvirág u. 3; tel. (1) 176-7186; telex 226605; Ambassador: (vacant).

Thailand: 1025 Budapest, Verecke út 79; tel. (1) 325-9892; telex 202706; fax (1) 325-9886; Ambassador: PRADAP PIBULSONGGRAM.

Tunisia: 1021 Budapest, Budakeszi út 55D; tel. (1) 200-8929; fax (1) 200-8931; Chargé d'affaires: MONCEF RIAHI.

Turkey: 1014 Budapest, Úri u. 45; tel. (1) 155-0737; Ambassador: BEDRETTIN TUNABAS.

Ukraine: 1125 Budapest, Nogradi 8; tel. (1) 155-2443; fax (1) 202-2287; Ambassador: DMYTRO TKACH.

United Kingdom: 1051 Budapest, Harmincad u. 6; tel. (1) 266-2888; telex 224527; fax (1) 266-0907; Ambassador: NIGEL THORPE.

USA: 1054 Budapest, Szabadság tér 12; tel. (1) 267-4400; telex 224222; fax (1) 269-9326; internet http://www.usis.hu; Ambassador: PETER F. TUFO.

Uruguay: 1023 Budapest 2, Vérhalom u. 12–16; tel. and fax (1) 326-0459; e-mail urupest@euroweb.hu; Ambassador: HOMERO DIEGO MARTÍNEZ LOWLOR.

Venezuela: 1023 Budapest, Vérhalom u. 12–16; tel. (1) 326-0460; telex 226666; fax (1) 326-0450; Ambassador: JORGE A. GONZÁLEZ.

Viet Nam: 1068 Budapest 2, Benczúr u. 18; tel. (1) 142-9943; Ambassador: TRAN VAN DAO.

Yemen: 1025 Budapest, Józsefhegyi út 28-30; tel. (1) 115-3844; Ambassador: (vacant).

Yugoslavia: 1068 Budapest, Dózsa György út 92B; tel. (1) 142-0566; fax (1) 251-1283; Chargé d'affaires: BRANISAL NOVAKOVIĆ.

Judicial System

The system of court procedure in Hungary is based on an Act that came into effect in 1953 and has since been updated frequently. The system of jurisdiction is based on the local courts (district courts in Budapest, city courts in other cities), labour courts, county courts (or the Metropolitan Court) and the Supreme Court. In the legal remedy system of two instances, appeals against the decisions of city and district courts can be lodged with the competent county court and the Metropolitan Court of Budapest respectively. Against the judgment of first instance of the latter, appeal is to be lodged with the Supreme Court. The Chief Public Prosecutor and the President of the Supreme Court have the right to submit a protest on legal grounds against the final judgment of any court.

By virtue of the 1973 Act, effective 1974 and modified in 1979, the procedure in criminal cases is differentiated for criminal offences and for criminal acts. In the first instance, criminal cases are tried, depending on their character, by a professional judge; where justified by the magnitude of the criminal act, by a council composed of three members, a professional judge and two lay assessors, while in major cases the court consists of five members, two professional judges and three lay assessors. In the Supreme Court, second instance cases are tried only by professional judges. The President of the Supreme Court is elected by the National Assembly. Judges are appointed by the President of the Republic for an indefinite period. Assessors are elected by the local municipal councils.

In the interest of ensuring legality and a uniform application of the law, the Supreme Court exercises a principled guidance over the jurisdiction of courts. In the Republic of Hungary judges are independent and subject only to the Law and other legal regulations.

The Minister of Justice supervises the general activities of courts. the Chief Public Prosecutor is elected by the National Assembly. The Chief Public Prosecutor and the Prosecutor's Office provide for the consistent prosecution of all acts violating or endangering the legal order of society, the safety and independence of the state, and for the protection of citizens.

The Prosecutors of the independent prosecuting organization exert supervision over the legality of investigations and the implementation of punishments, and assist with specific means in ensuring that legal regulations should be observed by state, economic and other organs and citizens, and they support the legality of court procedures and decisions.

President of the Supreme Court: PÁL SOLT.

Chief Public Prosecutor: KÁLMÁN GYÖRGYI.

Religion

CHRISTIANITY

Ecumenical Council of Churches in Hungary (Magyarországi Egyházak Ökumenikus Tanácsa): 1026 Budapest, Bimbó u. 127; tel. (1) 176-4847; fax (1) 176-1210; f. 1943; member churches: Baptist, Bulgarian Orthodox, Evangelical Lutheran, Hungarian Orthodox, Methodist, Reformed Church, Romanian Orthodox and Serbian Orthodox; Pres. Bishop Dr BÉLA HARMATI; Gen. Sec. Rev. Dr ZOLTÁN BÓNA.

The Roman Catholic Church

In 1994 Hungary comprised four archdioceses, nine dioceses (including one for Catholics of the Byzantine rite) and one territorial abbacy (directly responsible to the Holy See). At 31 December 1995 the Church had 6,295,325 adherents in Hungary.

Bishops' Conference: Magyar Katolikus Püspöki Konferenciája, 1071 Budapest, Városligeti fasor 45; tel. (1) 342-6959; fax (1) 342-6957; f. 1969; Pres. Dr ISTVÁN SEREGÉLY, Archbishop of Eger.

Latin Rite

Archbishop of Eger: Dr ISTVÁN SEREGÉLY, 3301 Eger, Széchenyi u. 1, POB 80; tel. (36) 313-259; fax (36) 320-508.

Archbishop of Esztergom-Budapest: Cardinal Dr LÁSZLÓ PASKAI, Primate of Hungary, 1014 Budapest, Uri u. 62; tel. (1) 202-5611; fax (1) 202-5458.

Archbishop of Kalocsa-Kecskemét: Dr LÁSZLÓ DANKÓ, 6301 Kalocsa, POB 29, Szentháromság tér 1; tel. (64) 362-166; fax (64) 362-667.

Archbishop of Veszprém: Dr JÓZSEF SZENDI, 8200 Veszprém, Vár u. 16; tel. (88) 426-088; fax (88) 426-287.

Byzantine Rite

Bishop of Hajdúdorog: SZILÁRD KERESZTES, 4401 Nyiregyháza, Bethlen u. 5, POB 60; tel. (42) 317-397; fax (42) 314-734; 253,000 adherents (Dec. 1992); the Bishop is also Apostolic Administrator of the Apostolic Exarchate of Miskolc, with an estimated 25,730 Catholics of the Byzantine rite (Dec. 1992).

Protestant Churches

Baptist Union of Hungary (Magyarországi Baptista Egyház): 1062 Budapest, Aradi u. 48; tel. (1) 332-2332; fax (1) 131-0194; f. 1846; 11,500 mems; Pres. Rev. MIHÁLY ALMÁSI; Gen.-Sec. Rev. KORNÉL GYŐRI.

Hungarian Methodist Church (Magyarországi Metodista Egyház): 1068 Budapest, Felsöerdösor 5; tel. (1) 322-4723; Superintendent Dr ISTVÁN CSERNÁK.

Lutheran Church in Hungary (Magyarországi Evangélikus Egyház): 1447 Budapest, POB 500; tel. (1) 117-6413; fax (1) 138-2302; 430,000 mems (1992); Presiding Bishop Dr BÉLA HARMATI; Gen. Sec. ZOLTÁN SZEMEREI.

Reformed Church in Hungary—Presbyterian (Magyarországi Református Egyház): 1146 Budapest, Abonyi u. 21; tel. (1) 343-7870; e-mail rch@mail.elender.hu; 2m. mems (1987); 1,306 churches; Pres. of Gen. Synod Bishop Dr GUSZTÁV BÖLCSKEI.

Unitarian Church in Hungary (Magyarországi Unitárius Egyház): 1055 Budapest V, Nagy Ignác u. 4; tel. (1) 111-2801; Bishop Rev. MARTIN BENCZE.

The Eastern Orthodox Church

Hungarian Orthodox Church (Magyar Orthodox Egyház): 1052 Budapest, Petőfi tér 2.1.2.; tel. (1) 118-4813; Administrator Archpriest Dr FERIZ BERKI.

Romanian Orthodox Church in Hungary (Magyarországi Román Ortodox Egyház): 5700 Gyula, Groza park 2; tel. (66) 61-281; Bishop PÁL ÁRDELEÁN.

Serbian Orthodox Diocese (Szerb Görögkeleti Egyházmegye): 2000 Szentendre, POB 22; Bishop Dr DANILO KRISTIC.

The Russian (6,000 mems) and Bulgarian Orthodox Churches are also represented.

BUDDHISM

Hungarian Buddhist Mission (Magyarországi Buddhista Misszió): 1386 Budapest, Postatiók 952; Rep. Dr LAJOS PRESSING.

Hungarian Zen Buddhist Community (Magyarországi Csan Buddhista Közösség): Budapest; Leader FÁRAD LOTFI.

ISLAM

There are about 3,000 Muslims in Hungary.

Hungarian Islamic Community (Magyar Iszlám Közösség): 1066 Budapest, Teréz krt 65; tel. (1) 177-7602; Leader Dr BALÁZS MIHÁLFFY.

JUDAISM

The Jewish community in Hungary is estimated to number between 100,000 and 120,000 people. Some 80% of Hungary's Jewish community resides in Budapest.

Federation of Jewish Communities in Hungary (Magyarországi Zsidó Hitközségek Szövetsége): 1075 Budapest, Sip u. 12, Budapesti Zsidó Hitközség (Jewish Community of Budapest); tel. (1) 342-1335; fax (1) 342-1790; 80,000 mems; 40 active synagogues; Orthodox and Conservative; Man. Dir GUSZTÁV ZOLTAI; Chief Rabbi of Hungary Dr JÓZSEF SCHWEITZER.

The Press

In 1995 there were 36 dailies with an average daily circulation of 1,706,000. Budapest dailies circulate nationally. The most popular are: *Népszabadság, Nemzeti Sport* and *Népszava. Népszabadság,* the most important daily, was formerly the central organ of the Hungarian Socialist Workers' Party, but is now independent. Most daily newspapers were partially foreign-owned.

PRINCIPAL DAILIES

Békéscsaba

Békés Megyei Hírlap (Békés County News): 5601 Békéscsaba, Munkácsy u. 4; tel. (66) 446-242; fax (66) 441-020; f. 1945; Editor-in-Chief ZOLTÁN ÁRPÁSI; circ. 49,000.

Budapest

Blikk: Budapest; f. 1994; colour tabloid.

Esti Hirlap (Evening Journal): 1962 Budapest, Blaha Lujza tér 3; tel. (1) 138-2399; telex 227040; fax (1) 138-4550; 40% foreign-owned; Editor-in-Chief DÉNES MAROS; circ. 70,000.

Kurír: Budapest; tel. (1) 111-2659; Editor-in-Chief GÁBOR SZÜCS.

Magyar Hirlap (Hungarian Journal): 1087 Budapest, Kerepesi út 29B; tel. (1) 210-0050; telex 224268; fax (1) 210-3737; f. 1968; 100% foreign-owned; Editor-in-Chief MÁTYÁS VINCE; circ. 75,000.

Magyar Nemzet (Hungarian Nation): 1073 Budapest, Erzsébet krt 9–11; tel. (1) 141-4320; telex 224269; 45% foreign-owned; Editor-in-Chief TIBOR PETHŐ; circ. 70,000.

Mai Nap (Today): 1087 Budapest, Könyves Kálmán krt 76; tel. (1) 210-1483; fax (1) 333-9153; e-mail mainap@mail.datanet.hu; f. 1988; Editor-in-Chief FERENC KÖSZEGI; circ.100,000.

NAPI Gazdaság (World Economy): 1135 Budapest, Csata u. 32; tel. (1) 270-4349; fax (1) 270-1117; Editor-in-Chief ADÁM DANKÓ; circ. 15,000.

Nemzeti Sport (National Sport): 1133 Budapest, Visegrádi u. 113-115; tel. (1) 138-4366; fax (1) 138-4248; Editor-in-Chief ZOLTÁN ÉNEKES; circ. 140,000.

Népszabadság (People's Freedom): 1960 Budapest, Bécsi út 122-124; tel. (1) 250-1680; telex 225551; fax (1) 168-2001; f. 1942; independent; Editor-in-Chief PÁL EÖTVÖS; circ. 316,000.

Népszava (Voice of the People): 1022 Budapest, Törökvész u. 30A; tel. (1) 202-7788; telex 224105; fax (1) 202-7798; f. 1873; Editor ANDRÁS KERESZTY; circ. 120,000.

Pest Megyei Hirlap (Pest County Journal): Budapest; tel. (1) 138-2399; Editor-in-Chief Dr ANDRÁS BÁRD; circ. 43,000.

Pesti Hirlap (Pest Journal): 1051 Budapest, Október 6 u. 8; tel. (1) 117-6162; fax (1) 117-6029; f. 1993; Editor-in-Chief ANDRÁS BENCSIK; circ. 50,000.

Üzlet (Business): Budapest; tel. (1) 111-8260; Editor-in-Chief IVÁN ÉRSEK.

Debrecen

Hajdú-Bihari Napló (Hajdú-Bihar Diary): 4024 Debrecen, Dósa nádor tér 10; tel. (52) 412-144; fax (52) 417-985; f. 1944; Editor-in-Chief ENDRE BAKÓ; circ. 60,000.

Dunaújváros

A Hirlap (The Journal): 2400 Dunaújváros, Városháza tér 1; tel. (25) 16-010; Editor-in-Chief CSABA D. KISS.

Eger

Heves Megyei Hirlap (Heves County Journal): 3301 Eger, Barkóczy u. 7; tel. (36) 13-644; Editor-in-Chief LEVENTE KAPOSI; circ. 33,000.

Győr

Kisalföld: 9022 Győr, Szt István út 51; tel. (96) 15-544; Editor-in-Chief Dr ANDOR KLOSS; circ. 95,000.

Kaposvár

Somogyi Hirlap (Somogy Journal): 7401 Kaposvár, Latinca Sándor u. 2A; tel. (82) 11-644; Editor-in-Chief Dr IMRE KERCZA; circ. 59,000.

Kecskemét

Petőfi Népe: 6000 Kecskemét, Szabadság tér 1A; tel. (76) 481-391; Editor-in-Chief Dr DÁNIEL LOVAS; circ. 60,000.

Miskolc

Déli Hirlap (Midday Journal): 3527 Miskolc, Bajcsy-Zsilinszky út 15; tel. (46) 42-694; Editor-in-Chief DEZSŐ BEKES; circ. 20,000.

Észak-Magyarország (Northern Hungary): 3527 Miskolc, Bajcsy-Zsilinszky út 15; tel. (46) 341-888; Editor-in-Chief LÁSZLÓ GÖRÖMBÖLYI; circ. 45,000.

Nyíregyháza

Kelet-Magyarország (Eastern Hungary): 4401 Nyíregyháza, Zrínyi u. 3–5; tel. (42) 11-277; Editor-in-Chief Dr SÁNDOR ANGYAL; circ. 80,000.

Pécs

Új Dunántúli Napló: 7601 Pécs, Hunyadi út 11; tel. (72) 15-000; Editor-in-Chief JENŐ LOMBOSI; circ. 84,000.

Salgótarján

Új Nógrád (New Nógrád): 3100 Salgótarján, Palócz Imre tér 4; tel. (32) 10-589; Editor-in-Chief LÁSZLÓ SULYOK; circ. 23,000.

Szeged

Délvilág (Southern World): 6740 Szeged, Tanácsköztársaság út 10; tel. (62) 14-911; Editor-in-Chief ISTVÁN NIKOLÉNYI; circ. 20,000.

Délmagyarország (Southern Hungary): 6740 Szeged, Stefánia 10; tel. (62) 481-281; Editor-in-Chief IMRE DLUSZTUS; circ. 70,000.

Székesfehérvár

Fejér Megyei Hirlap (Fejér County Journal): 8003 Székesfehérvár, Honvéd u. 8; tel. (22) 12-450; Editor-in-Chief JÁNOS A. SZABÓ; circ. 52,000.

Szekszárd

Tolna Megyei Népújság (Tolna News): 7100 Szekszárd, Liszt Ferenc tér 3; tel. (74) 16-211; Editor-in-Chief GYÖRGYNÉ KAMARÁS; circ. 32,000.

Szolnok

Új Néplap (New People's Paper): 5001 Szolnok, Kossuth tér 1, I. Irodaház; tel. (56) 42-211; Editor-in-Chief JÓZSEF HAJNAL; circ. 46,000.

Szombathely

Vas Népe (Vas People): 9700 Szombathely, Berzsenyi tér 2; tel. (94) 12-393; Editor-in-Chief SÁNDOR LENGYEL; circ. 65,000.

Vasvármegye: 9701 Szombathely, Honvéd tér 2; tel. (94) 12-356; Editor-in-Chief LÁSZLÓ BURKON.

Tatabánya

24 Óra (24 Hours): 2801 Tatabánya, Felszabadulás tér 4; tel. (34) 10-053; Editor-in-Chief GÁBOR GOMBKÖTŐ; circ. 43,000.

Veszprém

Napló (Diary): 8201 Veszprém, Szabadság tér 15; tel. (80) 27-444; Editor-in-Chief ELEMÉR BALOGH; circ. 58,000.

Zalaegerszeg

Zalai Hirlap (Zala Journal): 8901 Zalaegerszeg, Ady Endre u. 62; tel. (92) 12-575; Editor-in-Chief JÓZSEF TARSOLY; circ. 71,000.

WEEKLIES

Élet és Irodalom (Life and Literature): 1089 Budapest, Rezsö tér 15; tel. (1) 210-2157; fax (1) 269-9241; f. 1957; literary and political; Editor ZOLTÁN KOVÁCS; circ. 16,000.

Élet és Tudomány (Life and Science): 1088 Budapest, Bródy Sándor u 16; tel. and fax (1) 138-2472; f. 1946; popular science; Editor-in-Chief Dr HERCZEG JÁNOS; circ. 20,000.

Evangélikus Élet (Evangelical Life): 1085 Budapest, Üllői út. 24; tel. and fax (1) 117-1108; f. 1933; Evangelical–Lutheran Church newspaper; Editor MIHÁLY TÓTH-SZÖLLŐS; circ. 12,000.

Heti Világgazdaság (World Economics Weekly): 1126 Budapest 64, Németvölgy u. 1; tel. (1) 155-5411; telex 222556; f. 1979; Editor-in-Chief IVÁN LIPOVECZ; circ. 141,000.

Képes Újság (Illustrated News): 1085 Budapest, Gyulai Pál u. 14; tel. (1) 113-7660; f. 1960; Editor MIHALY KOVÁCS; circ. 400,000.

Ludas Matyi: Budapest; tel. (1) 133-5718; satirical; Editor JÓZSEF ÁRKUS; circ. 352,000.

L'udové Noviny (People's News): 1065 Budapest, Nagymező u. 49; tel. (1) 131-9184; in Slovak, for Slovaks in Hungary; Editor PÁL KONDÁCS; circ. 1,700.

Magyar Mezőgazdaság (Hungarian Agriculture): 1355 Budapest, Kossuth Lajos tér 11; tel. (1) 112-2433; telex 225445; f. 1946; Editor-in-Chief Dr KÁROLY FEHÉR; circ. 24,000.

Magyar Nők Lapja (Hungarian Women's Journal): 1022 Budapest, Törökvész út 30A; tel. and fax (1) 115-4037; telex 225554; f. 1949; Editor-in-Chief LILI ZÉTÉNYI; circ. 550,000.

Magyarország (Hungary): Budapest; tel. (1) 138-4644; telex 226351; f. 1964; news magazine; Editor DÉNES GYAPAY; circ. 200,000.

Narodne Novine (People's News): 1396 Budapest, POB 495; tel. (1) 112-4869; f. 1945; for Yugoslavs in Hungary; in Serbo-Croat and Slovene; Chief Editor MARKO MARKOVIĆ; circ. 2,800.

Neue Zeitung (New Paper): 1391 Budapest, Nagymező u. 49, POB 224; tel. (1) 332-6334; e-mail neueztg@mail.elender.hu; f. 1957; for Germans in Hungary; Editor JOHANN SCHUTH; circ. 4,500.

Rádió és Televízióújság (Radio and TV News): 1801 Budapest; tel. (1) 138-8114; fax (1) 138-7349; f. 1924; Editor MÁRTA BÓDAY; circ. 300,000.

Reform: 1443 Budapest, POB 222; tel. and fax (1) 122-4240; telex 223333; f. 1988; popular tabloid; 50% foreign-owned; Editor PÉTER TŐKE; circ. 300,000.

Reformátusok Lapja: 1395 Budapest, POB 424; tel. (1) 117-6809; fax (1) 117-8386; f. 1957; Reformed Church paper for the laity; Editor-in-Chief and Publr ATTILA P. KOMLÓS; circ. 30,000.

Szabad Föld (Free Earth): 1087 Budapest, Könyves Kálmán krt 76; tel. and fax (1) 133-6794; f. 1945; Editor GYULA ÉCK; circ. 720,000.

Szövetkezet (Co-operative): 1054 Budapest, Szabadság tér 14; tel. (1) 131-3132; National Council of Hungarian Consumer Co-operative Societies; Editor-in-Chief ATTILA KOVÁCS; circ. 85,000.

Tallózó: 1133 Budapest, Visegrádi u. 110-112; tel. and fax (1) 149-8707; f. 1989; news digest; Editor-in-Chief GYÖRGY ANDAI; circ. 35,000.

Tőzsde Kurir (Hungarian Stock Market Courier): Budapest; tel. (1) 122-3273; fax (1) 142-8356; business; Editor-in-Chief ISTVÁN GÁBOR BENEDEK.

Új Ember (New Man): 1053 Budapest, Kossuth Lajos u. 1; tel. (1) 117-3661; fax (1) 117-3471; f. 1945; religious weekly; Editor LÁSZLÓ RÓNAY; circ. 70,000.

Vasárnapi Hirek (Sunday News): 1117 Budapest, POB 364; tel. (1) 161-2456; telex 225944; fax (1) 161-0284; f. 1984; political; Editor Dr ZOLTÁN LŐKÖS; circ. 250,000.

OTHER PERIODICALS

(Published monthly unless otherwise indicated)

Állami Gazdaság (State Farming): General Direction of State Farming, 1054 Budapest, Akadémia u. 1–3; tel. (1) 112-4617; fax (1) 111-4877; f. 1946; Editor P. GÖRGÉNYI.

Beszeloe (The Speaker): 1364 Budapest, POB 143; tel. and fax (1) 302-1271; e-mail beszelo@mailc3.hu; culture and criticism; Editor-in-Chief ILONA KISS.

Business Partner Hungary: 1051 Budapest, Dorottya u. 6; tel. (1) 117-0850; telex 225646; fax (1) 118-6483; f. 1986; quarterly; Hungarian, German, French and English; economic journal published by Institute for Economic, Market Research and Informatics (KOPINT-DATORG).

Egyházi Krónika (Church Chronicle): 1052 Budapest, Petőfi tér 2.1.2; tel. (1) 118-4813; f. 1952; every 2 months; Eastern Orthodox Church journal; Editor Archpriest Dr FERIZ BERKI.

Elektrotechnika (Electrical Engineering): 1055 Budapest, Kossuth Lajos tér 6–8; tel. (1) 153-0117; telex 225792; fax (1) 153-4069; e-mail lernyei.mee@mtesz.hu; f. 1908; organ of Electrotechnical Association; Editor Dr JÁNOS BENCZE; circ. 3,000.

Élelmezési Ipar (Food Industry): 1372 Budapest, POB 433; tel. (1) 214-6691; fax (1) 214-6692; f. 1947; Scientific Society for Food Industry; Editor Dr ISTVÁN TÓTH-ZSIGA.

Energia és Atomtechnika (Energy and Nuclear Technology): 1055 Budapest, Kossuth Lajos tér 6–8; tel. (1) 153-2751; telex 225792; fax (1) 156-1215; f. 1947; every two months; Scientific Society for Energy Economy; Editor-in-Chief Dr G. BŐKI.

Energiagazdálkodás (Energy Economy): 1055 Budapest, Kossuth Lajos tér 6; tel. (1) 153-2751; fax (1) 153-3894; Scientific Society for Energetics; Editor Dr ANDOR ANESINI.

Ezermester (The Handyman): 1137 Budapest, Jászai tér 5; tel. (1) 132-1987; telex 226423; f. 1957; do-it-yourself magazine; Editor JÓZSEF PERÉNYI; circ. 50,000.

Foaia Noastra (Our Newspaper): 1055 Budapest, Bajcsy Zs. u. 78; every 2 weeks; for Romanians in Hungary; Editor SÁNDOR HOCOPÁN; circ. 1,500.

Forum: Budapest; f. 1989; periodical of the Hungarian Socialist Party; Editor-in-Chief ISTVÁN SZERDAHELYI.

Gép (Machinery): 1027 Budapest, Fő u. 68; tel. (1) 135-4175; telex 225792; fax (1) 153-0818; f. 1949; Scientific Society of Mechanical Engineering; Editor Dr KORNÉL LEHOFER.

Hírmagazin: 1106 Budapest, Maglódi u. 16; tel. (1) 261-6669; fax (1) 261-9004; monthly news magazine; Editor-in-Chief TIBOR BARTHA; circ. 4,000.

Hungarian Business Herald: Budapest; tel. and fax (1) 186-6143; f. 1970; quarterly review published in English and German by the Ministry of Industry and Trade; Editor-in-Chief Dr GERD BIRÓ; circ. 4,000.

The Hungarian Economy: 1135 Budapest; tel. (1) 118-6064; fax (1) 118-0524; quarterly published in English; Editor-in-Chief ANDRÁS HIRSCHLER.

Hungarian Travel Magazine: Budapest, Múzeum u. 11; tel. (1) 138-4643; quarterly in English and German; illustrated journal of the Tourist Board for visitors to Hungary; Man. Editor JÚLIA SZ. NAGY.

Ipar-Gazdaság (Industrial Economy): 1371 Budapest, POB 433; tel. (1) 202-1083; f. 1948; Editor Dr TAMÁS MÉSZÁROS; circ. 4,000.

Jogtudományi Közlöny (Law Gazette): 1535 Budapest, POB 773; 1015 Budapest, Donáti u. 35-45; tel. (1) 212-1185; fax (1) 212-1184; f. 1866; monthly; legal and administrative sciences; Editor-in-Chief Dr IMRE VÖRÖS; circ. 2,500.

Kortárs (Contemporary): 1062 Budapest, Bajza u. 18; tel. (1) 142-1168; literary gazette; Editor-in-Chief IMRE KIS PINTÉR; circ. 5,000.

Közgazdasági Szemle (Economic Review): 1112 Budapest, Budaörsi u. 43–45; tel. (1) 319-3165; fax (1) 319-3166; f. 1954; monthly; published by Cttee for Economic Sciences of Hungarian Academy of Sciences; Editor KATALIN SZABÓ; circ. 3,000.

Made in Hungary: 1426 Budapest, POB 3; economics and business magazine published in English by Hungarian News Agency (MTI); Editor GYÖRGY BLASITS.

Magyar Hirek (Hungarian News): 1068 Budapest, Benczúr u. 15; tel. (1) 122-5616; telex 22317; fax (1) 122-2421; every 2 weeks; illustrated magazine primarily for Hungarians living abroad; Editor GYÖRGY HALÁSZ; circ. 70,000.

Magyar Jog (Hungarian Law): 1054 Budapest, Szemere u. 10; tel. (1) 111-4880; fax (1) 111-4013; f. 1953; law; Editor-in-Chief Dr JÁNOS NÉMETH; circ. 2,200.

Magyar Közlöny (Official Gazette): 1055 Budapest, Bajcsy Zs. u. 78; tel. (1) 112-1236; Editor Dr ELEMÉR KISS; circ. 90,000.

Magyar Tudomány (Hungarian Science): Hungarian Academy of Sciences, 1051 Budapest, Nádor u. 7; tel. (1) 117-9524; fax (1) 117-9524; e-mail matud@ella.hu; multidisciplinary science review; Editors GYÖRGY ENYEDI, ÉVA CSATÓ, ZSUZSA SZENTGYORGYI.

Nagyvilág (The Great World): 1054 Budapest, Széchenyi u. 1; tel. (1) 132-1160; f. 1956; review of world literature; Editor LÁSZLÓ KÉRY; circ. 6,000.

New Hungarian Quarterly: Budapest; tel. (1) 175-6722; fax (1) 118-8297; f. 1960; illustrated quarterly in English; politics, economics, philosophy, education, culture, poems, short stories, etc.; Editor MIKLÓS VAJDA; circ. 3,500.

Pedagógusok Lapja (Teachers' Review): 1068 Budapest, Varosligeti fasor 10; tel. (1) 322-8464; f. 1945; published by the Hungarian Union of Teachers; Editor-in-Chief LÁSZLÓ THOMA; circ. 10,000.

Református Egyház (Reformed Church): 1146 Budapest, Abonyi u. 21; tel. (1) 343-7870; f. 1949; official journal of the Hungarian Reformed Church; Editor-in-Chief LAJOS TEGEZ; circ. 1,300.

Statisztikai Szemle (Statistical Review): 1525 Budapest, POB 51; tel. (1) 375-6528; f. 1923; Editor-in-Chief MÁRIA VISI LAKATOS; circ. 800.

Társadalmi Szemle (Social Science Review): 1114 Budapest, Villányi ut 11–13; tel. (1) 209-2323; fax (1) 166-7410; theoretical-political review; Editor MIHÁLY BIHARI; circ. 3,000.

Technika (Technology): 1027 Budapest, Fö u. 68; tel. (1) 201-7083; fax (1) 201-8564; f. 1957; official journal of the Hungarian Academy of Engineering; monthly in Hungarian, annually in English, German and Russian; Editor-in-Chief MARGIT WELLEK; circ. 15,000.

Turizmus (Tourism): 1088 Budapest, Múzeum u. 11; tel. (1) 138-4638; telex 225297; Editor ZSOLT SZEBENI; circ. 8,000.

Új Élet (New Life): 1075 Budapest, Síp u. 12; tel. (1) 322-2829; every 2 weeks; for Hungarian Jews; Editor Dr PETER KARDOS; circ. 5,000.

Új Technika (New Technology): Budapest; tel. (1) 155-7122; telex 226490; f. 1967; popular industrial quarterly; circ. 35,000.

Vigilia: 1364 Budapest, POB 48; tel. (1) 117-7246; fax (1) 117-7682; f. 1935; Catholic; Editor LÁSZLÓ LUKÁCS; circ. 4,000.

NEWS AGENCIES

Hungarian News Agency (Magyar Távirati Iroda—MTI): 1016 Budapest, Naphegy tér 8; tel. (1) 175-6722; telex 224371; fax (1) 175-3973; f. 1880; 19 brs in Hungary; 14 bureaux abroad; Dir-Gen. KÁROLY ALEXA.

Foreign Bureaux

Agence France-Presse (AFP): 1016 Budapest, Naphegy u. 29; tel. (1) 156-8416; telex 223831; fax (1) 201-9161; Correspondents JULIA BORBÉLY, ESZTER SZÁMADÓ.

Agenzia Nazionale Stampa Associata (ANSA) (Italy): Budapest; tel. (1) 135-2323; telex 224711; Bureau Chief GAETANO ALIMENTI.

Allgemeiner Deutscher Nachrichtendienst GmbH (ADN) (Germany): 1025 Budapest XIV, Szeréna út 54; tel. (1) 135-5352; telex 224675; Correspondent GERHARD KOWALSKI.

Associated Press (AP) (USA): 1122 Budapest, Maros u. 13; tel. (1) 156-9129; Correspondent ALEX BANDY.

Česká tisková kancelář (ČTK) (Czech Republic): 1118 Budapest, Iglói út 6B; tel. (1) 166-9833; telex 225367; Correspondent KOKES JAN.

Informatsionnoye Telegrafnoye Agentstvo Rossii—Telegrafnoye Agenstvo Suverennykh Stran (ITAR—TASS) (Russia): 1023 Budapest, Vérhalom u. 12–16; Correspondent YEVGENI POPOV.

Prensa Latina (Cuba): Budapest; tel. (1) 175-6722; telex 224800; Correspondent EDIT PAPP.

Reuters (United Kingdom): 1088 Budapest, Rákóczi út 1–3, East-West Business Centre; tel. (1) 266-2410; fax (1) 266-2030; Chief Correspondent MITYA NEW.

Rossiyskoye Informatsionnoye Agentstvo—Novosti (RIA—Novosti) (Russia): Budapest; tel. (1) 132-0594; telex 61224792; fax (1) 142-3325; Bureau Chief A. POPOV.

Tlačová agentúra Slovenskej republiky (TASR) (Slovakia): 1026 Budapest, Garas út 24B; tel. and fax (1) 135-1843; Bureau Chief PETER KLENKO.

Xinhua (New China) News Agency (People's Republic of China): 1021 Budapest, Budakeszi út 55D P/8; tel. (1) 176-7548; telex 225447; fax (1) 176-2571; Chief Correspondent ZHOU DONGYAO.

PRESS ASSOCIATIONS

Hungarian Newspaper Publishers' Association: 1034 Budapest, Bécsi ùt 122-124; tel. (1) 368-8674; fax (1) 388-6707; f. 1990; Gen. Sec. JÁNOS PETŐ; 40 mems.

National Association of Hungarian Journalists (Magyar Újságírók Országos Szövetsége—MUOSZ): 1062 Budapest, Andrássy út 101; tel. (1) 322-1699; fax (1) 322-1881; f. 1896; Gen. Sec. GÁBOR BENCSIK; 7,000 mems.

Publishers

PRINCIPAL PUBLISHING HOUSES

Akadémiai Kiadó: 1117 Budapest, Prielle Kornélia u. 19–35; tel. (1) 204-3978; fax (1) 204-3979; e-mail spj@akkrt.hu; f. 1828; humanities, social, natural and technical sciences, dictionaries, periodicals; Man. Dir PÉTER JÁNOS.

Corvina Kiadó Kft.: 1051 Budapest, Vörösmarty tér 1; tel. (1) 118-4347; fax (1) 118-4410; f. 1955; Hungarian works translated into foreign languages, art and educational books, fiction and non-fiction, tourist guides, cookery books and musicology; Man. Dir ISTVÁN BART.

EMB Music Publisher Ltd: Budapest tel. (1) 118-4228; fax (1) 138-2732; f. 1950; music publishing and books on musical subjects; Dir ISTVÁN HOMOLYA.

Európa Könyvkiadó: 1055 Budapest, Kossuth Lajos tér 13–15; tel. (1) 131-2700; fax (1) 131-4162; f. 1945; world literature translated into Hungarian; Man. LEVENTE OSZTOVITS.

Gondolat Könyvkiadó Vállalat: 1088 Budapest, Bródy Sándor u. 16; tel. (1) 138-3358; fax (1) 138-4540; f. 1957; popular scientific publications on natural and social sciences, art, encyclopaedic handbooks; Dir GYÖRGY FEHÉR.

Helikon Kiadó: 1053 Budapest, Papnövelde u. 8; tel. (1) 117-4865; telex 227100; fax (1) 117-4865; bibliophile books; Dir KATALIN BERGER.

Képzőművészeti Kiadó: 1148 Budapest, Kerepesi út 26; tel. (1) 251-1527; fax (1) 251-1527; fine arts; Man. Dr ZOLTÁN KEMENCZEI.

Kossuth Kiadó Rt.: 1043 Budapest, Csányi László u. 36; tel. (1) 370-0607; fax (1) 370-0602; e-mail piridr@kossuted.hu; f. 1944; social sciences, educational and philosophy publications, information technology books; Man. ANDRÁS SÁNDOR KOCSIS.

Közgazdasági és Jogi Könyvkiadó Rt: 1054 Budapest, Nagysándor József u. 6; tel. (1) 112-6430; fax (1) 111-3210; f. 1955; business, economics, law, sociology, psychology, tax, politics, education, dictionaries; Man. Dir. DAVID G. YOUNG.

Magvető Könyvkiadó: 1806 Budapest, POB 123; tel. (1) 302-2799; fax (1) 302-2800; e-mail magveto@mail.datanet.hu; f. 1955; literature; Dir. GÉZA MORCSÁNYI.

Medicina Könyvkiadó Rt: 1054 Budapest, Zoltan u. 8; tel. (1) 112-2650; fax (1) 112-2450; f. 1957; books on medicine, sport, tourism; Dir BORBÁLA FARKASVÖLGYI.

Mezőgazda Kiadó: 1165 Budapest, Koronafürt u. 44; tel. (1) 407-6575; fax (1) 407-7571; ecology, natural sciences, environmental protection, food industry; Man. Dr LAJOS LELKES.

Móra Ferenc Ifjúsági Kiadó Rt.: 1134 Budapest, Váci út 19; tel. (1) 267-1930; fax (1) 267-1922; f. 1950; youth and children's books; Man. Dr JÁNOS CS. TÓTH.

Műszaki Könyvkiadó: 1033 Budapest III, Szentendre út 89–93; tel. (1) 4395005; fax (1) 4395004; f. 1955; scientific and technical, vocational and general text books; Man. SÁNDOR BÉRCZI.

Nemzeti Tankönyvkiadó Rt. (National Textbook Publishing Company): 1143 Budapest, Szobránc u. 6-8; tel. and fax (1) 363-2423; e-mail ntk@mail.datanet.hu.; f. 1949; school and university textbooks, pedagogical literature and language books; Man. ISTVÁN ABRAHAM.

Népszava Lap-és Könyvkiadó Vállalat: 1553 Budapest, Rákóczi u. 54; tel. (1) 122-4810; National Confederation of Hungarian Trade Unions; Man. Dr JENŐ KISS.

Statiqum Kiadó és Nyomda Kft: 1033 Budapest, Kaszásdülő u. 2; tel. (1) 250-0311; telex 226699; fax (1) 168-8635; f. 1991; publications on statistics, system-management and computer science; Dir BENEDEK BELECZ.

Szépirodalmi Könyvkiadó: 1073 Budapest, Erzsébet krt 9–11; tel. (1) 122-1285; telex 226754; f. 1950; modern and classical Magyar literature; Man. SÁNDOR Z. SZALAI.

Zrinyi Kiadó: 1087 Budapest, Kerepesi u. 29B; tel. (1) 133-9165; military literature; Man. MÁTÉ ESZES.

CARTOGRAPHERS

Cartographia—Hungarian Company for Mapping: 1443 Budapest, POB 132; tel. and fax (1) 163-4639; telex 226218; f. 1954; Dir Dr ÁRPÁD PAPP-VÁRY.

Department of Lands and Mapping (Földügyi és Térképészeti Főosztály): 1055 Budapest, Kossuth Lajos tér 11; tel. (1) 331-3736; telex 225445; fax (1) 301-4691; e-mail geza.apagyief-m.x400gw.itb.hu.; f. 1967; Gen. Man. GÉZA APAGYI.

PUBLISHERS' ASSOCIATION

Hungarian Publishers' and Booksellers' Association (Magyar Könyvkiadók és Könyvterjesztők Egyesülése): Budapest; tel. (1) 118-4758; fax (1) 118-4581; f. 1878; most leading Hungarian publishers are members of the Association; Pres. ISTVÁN BART; Sec.-Gen. PÉTER ZENTAI.

WRITERS' UNION

Association of Hungarian Writers (Magyar Írószövetség): 1062 Budapest, Bajza u. 18; tel. (1) 322-8840; f. 1945; Pres. BÉLA POMOGÁTS.

Broadcasting and Communications

TELECOMMUNICATIONS

Matav: Budapest; telecommunications co; scheduled for privatization in 1998; CEO EMIL TOMKA.

RADIO

Hungarian Radio (Magyar Rádió): 1800 Budapest, Bródy Sándor u. 5–7; tel. (1) 138-8388; telex 225188; fax (1) 138-7004; f. 1924; stations: Radio Kossuth (Budapest), Radio Petőfi (Budapest), Radio Bartók (Budapest, mainly classical music); 6 regional studios; external broadcasts in English, German, Hungarian, Romanian, Russian, Slovak and Serbo-Croat; Chair., Bd of Trustees GYÖRGY GABOR; Pres. JÁNOS SZIRÁNYI.

Radio Danubius: f. 1986; commercial station; broadcasts news, music and information in Hungarian 24 hours a day; transmitting stations in Budapest, Lake Balaton region, Sopron, Szeged and Debrecen; Dir JÓZSEF LÁSZLÓ.

TELEVISION

Hungarian Television (Magyar Televízió): 1810 Budapest, Szabadság tér 17; tel. (1) 153-3200; telex 225568; fax (1) 153-4568; f. 1957; first channel, MTV 1, broadcasts 98 hours a week and the second channel, MTV 2, 83 hours a week, every day, mostly colour transmissions; 100 high-capacity relay stations; Chair., Bd of Trustees ANDRÁS KOVÁCS; Pres. LORANT HORVÁTH (acting).

Finance

(cap. = capital; res = reserves; dep. = deposits; m. = million; Ft = forint; brs = branches)

Under economic reforms, introduced in 1987, three banks were established to assume the commercial banking activities of the National Bank of Hungary: the Hungarian Credit Bank, the Commercial and Credit Bank and the Budapest Bank. The already existing Hungarian Foreign Trade Bank and the National Savings and Commercial Bank also became fully chartered financial institutions. In 1997 there were seven large commercial banks, the other two being the Central European International Bank (which until 1997 operated as an 'offshore' bank) and the Post Bank and Savings Bank Corporation; all of these institutions were in private ownership. At the end of 1996 there were a total of 33 commercial banks, of which 22 were foreign- or jointly-owned banks, and an additional nine specialized financial institutions. There were also 247 savings co-operatives.

Responsibility for bank supervision is divided between the National Bank of Hungary and the State Banking Supervision Agency. Under new legislation, introduced in January 1997, the supervision of the banking system was reorganized, and the supervisory responsibilities of the National Bank were restricted to areas relating to the operation of monetary policy and the foreign exchange system.

BANKING

Central Bank

National Bank of Hungary (Magyar Nemzeti Bank): 1850 Budapest, Szabadság tér 8–9; tel. (1) 302-3000; telex 225678; fax (1) 332-3913; f. 1924; cap. 10,000m. Ft, res 49,313m. Ft, dep. 4,501,351m. Ft (Dec. 1996); issue of banknotes; transacts international payments business; supervises banking system; Pres. GYÖRGY SURÁNYI; 23 brs.

Commercial Banks

Bank of Hungarian Savings Co-operatives Ltd (Magyar Takarékszövetkezeti Bank Rt): 1122 Budapest, Pethényi köz 10; 1064 Budapest, POB 62; tel. (1) 155-3122; fax (1) 156-2649; f. 1989; 87% owned by the state; cap. 10,199m. Ft, res 544m. Ft, dep. 33,742m. Ft (Dec. 1993); Pres. Dr JÓZSEF TÓTH; Gen. Man. Dr ZSOLT HERNÁDI; 21 brs.

BNP-Dresdner Bank Ltd: 1055 Budapest, Houvéd utca 20; tel. (1) 269-3131; telex 222260; fax (1) 269-3967; f. 1990; cap. 1,470m. Ft, res 1,082m. Ft, dep. 30,083m. Ft (Dec. 1995); Chair. PIET-JOCHEN ETZEL; Gen. Man. LÁSZLÓ MADARÁSZ.

Budapest Bank Ltd: 1052 Budapest, Deak F. u. 5; tel. (1) 269-2333; telex 226618; fax (1) 269-2417; f. 1987; cap. 19,736m. Ft, res

2,895m. Ft, dep. 174,135m. Ft (Dec. 1995); privatized in 1996; CEO BÉLA SINGLOVICS; 75 brs.

Central-European International Bank Ltd (CIB): 1027 Budapest, Medve út. 4–14; tel. (1) 212-1330; telex 224759; fax (1) 212-4200; f. 1979; merged with CIB Hungária Bank Rt in 1998; cap. US $80m., res. US $1,061m., dep. US $912m. (Dec. 1996); Chair. LUIGI VERCELLINI; Pres. and CEO GYÖRGY ZDEBORSKY.

Citibank Rt: 1051 Budapest, Szabadság tér 7; tel. (1) 374-5000; telex 227822; fax (1) 374-5100; f. 1985; cap. 4,308m. Ft, res 1,487m. Ft, dep. 73,959m. Ft (Dec. 1996); Gen. Man. RICHARD D. JACKSON.

Commercial and Credit Bank Ltd (Kereskedelmiés Hitelbank Rt): 1051 Budapest, Vigadó tér 1; tel. (1) 267-5000; telex 223200; fax (1) 266-9696; f. 1986; cap. 10,381m. Ft, res 5,726m. Ft, dep. 325,472m. Ft (Dec. 1996); 163 brs; privatized in early 1997; CEO JÁNOS ERÖS.

Commerzbank (Budapest) Rt: 1054 Budapest, Széchenyi rkp. 8; tel. (1) 269-4510; telex 202663; fax (1) 302-3933; f. 1993; cap. 2,400m. Ft, res 1,147m. Ft, dep. 66,769m. Ft (Dec, 1996); Chair. of Supervisory Bd K. P. MÜLLER.

Creditanstalt Rt: 1054 Budapest, Akadémia út 17; tel. (1) 269-0812; telex 223446; fax (1) 153-4959; f. 1990; commercial banking and foreign exchange services; owned by Creditanstalt-Bankverein (Austria); cap. 5,965m. Ft, res 2,965m. Ft, dep. 98,232m. Ft (Dec. 1996); Chair. ERICH HAMPEL; Man. Dir HAROLD EDLINGER-ZECHER; 11 brs.

Daewoo Bank (Hungary) Ltd: 1052 Budapest, Bajcsy Zsilinszicy 42-46; tel. (1) 328-5200; telex 225036; fax (1) 328-5218; f. 1989; cap. 3,554m. Ft, res 442m. Ft, dep. 31,705m. Ft (Dec. 1996); Pres. ELEMÉR TERTÁK; CEO PARK JONG SOO.

DUNA Investment and Commercial Bank Co Ltd (DUNA Befektetési és Forgalmi Bank Rt): 1054 Budapest, Báthory u. 12; tel. (1) 111-2696; telex 225595; fax (1) 131-3786; f. 1987 as Bank for Investment and Transactions; renamed Dunabank 1989; Government's 96% stake sold to ING (Netherlands) in 1996; cap. and res 74m. Ft, dep. 13,660m. Ft (Dec. 1994); Pres. KÁLMÁN DEBRECZENI; Gen. Man. TIBOR HORVÁTH; 13 brs.

European Commercial Bank Ltd (Európai Kereskedelmi Bank Rt—EKB): 1056 Budapest, Váci utca 81; tel. (1) 329-4856; telex 222190; fax (1) 328-4801; f. 1990; cap. 3,262m. Ft (Dec. 1996); Chair. and Chief Exec. ANDRÁS FELKAI; 6 brs.

General Banking and Trust Co. Ltd (Általános Értékforgalmi Bank Rt): 1055 Budapest, Marko u. 9; tel. (1) 269-1473; telex 223578; fax (1) 269-1442; f. 1922; 50% share owned by Gazprom Bank (of Russia); cap. 5,000m. Ft, res 133m. Ft, dep. 66,048m. Ft (Dec. 1996); Chair. MEDGET RAHIMKULOV; 8 brs.

Hanwha Bank: 1088 Budapest, Rákóczi út 1–3; tel. (1) 266-2713; telex 222173; fax (1) 266-5231; f. 1990 as Kulturbank Ltd; cap. 1,000m. Ft, res 13m. Ft, dep. 3,259m. Ft (Dec. 1995); CEO HOC JUNG JÚNG.

Hungarian Credit Bank Ltd (ABN AMRO—Magyar—Bank Rt): 1853 Budapest, Szabadság tér 5–6; tel. (1) 269-2122; fax (1) 269-2245; f. 1987; cap. 14,000m. (Dec. 1991); activities include venture financing, securities trading, real estate investments; 89 brs; privatized in 1996; Chair. and CEO Dr ISTVÁN TÖRÖCSKEI; 89 brs.

Hungarian Development Bank Ltd: 1051 Budapest, Nador út 31; tel. (1) 153-0222; telex 224701; fax (1) 153-0909; f. 1991 as an investment company; cap. 16,700m. Ft; res. 13,206m. Ft (Dec. 1995); Chair. Dr TAMÁS TÉTÉNYI.

Hungarian Foreign Trade Bank Ltd (Magyar Külkereskedelmi Bank Rt): 1821 Budapest, V. Vaci utca 38; tel. (1) 269-0922; telex 226941; fax (1) 269-0959; f. 1950; commercial banking; 55.7% owned by the Bayerische Landesbank Girozentrale; cap. 9,092m. Ft, res 21,121m. Ft, dep. 277,799m. Ft (Dec. 1996); 8 brs; Chair. and CEO TAMÁS ERDEI.

HYPO-Bank Hungaria Rt: 1065 Budapest, Nagymezö u.44; tel. (1) 269-0400; fax (1) 269-0399; Chair. WALTER MINDE.

Industrial Co-operative Commercial Banking House Ltd (Iparbankház Rt): 1052 Budapest, Gerlóczy u. 5; tel. (1) 117-6811; telex 223042; fax (1) 118-2209; f. 1984; cap. 2,171m. Ft, dep. 6,981m. Ft (Dec. 1994); 12 brs; Pres. GÁBOR SZABÓ; CEO TIBOR ROSTÁS.

ING Bank Rt: 1061 Budapest, Andrássy ut 9; tel. (1) 268-0140; telex 222419; fax (1) 269-6447; f. 1992 as NMB Bank; owned by ING Bank NV (Amsterdam); cap. 1,716m. Ft, res 3,150m. Ft, dep. 71,092m. Ft (Dec. 1996); Gen. Man. TIBOR E. REJTŐ.

Inter-Európa Bank Ltd: 1054 Budapest, Szabadság tér 15; tel. (1) 373-6000; fax (1) 269-2526; f. 1981 as INTERINVEST; associated mem. of San Paolo Group; cap. 2,807m. Ft, res 917m. Ft, dep. 58,564m. Ft (Dec. 1996); Chair. Dr LÁSZLÓ BÓDY; Man. Dir PIER FRANCO RUBATTO.

Konzumbank Ltd: 1124 Budapest, Apor Vilmos tér 25–26; tel. (1) 319-0270; telex 222525; fax (1) 319-0276; f. 1986; cap. 2,375m. Ft, res 1,377m. Ft, dep. 11,329m. Ft (Dec. 1995); Dir Dr ÉVA HEGEDÜS.

Mezőbank Joint-Stock Co: 1054 Budapest, Hold út 16; tel. (1) 153-1000; telex 227615; fax (1) 112-1216; f. 1987, merged with Agrobank 1996; 91% state-owned; cap. 3,436m. Ft, dep. 80,381m. Ft (Jan. 1996); Chair. PÉTER SZERDAHELYI.

National Savings and Commercial Bank Ltd—NSB Ltd (Országos Takarékpénztár és Kereskedelmi Bank Rt—OTP Rt): 1051 Budapest, Nádor u. 16; tel. (1) 153-1444; telex 224280; fax (1) 312-6858; f. 1949; cap. 28,000m. Ft, res 19,805m. Ft, dep. 1,138,454m. Ft (Dec. 1996); savings deposits, credits, foreign transactions; privatized in late 1996; 380 brs; Chair. and Chief Exec. Dr SÁNDOR CSÁNYI.

Post Bank and Savings Bank Corporation (Postabank és Takarékpénztár Rt): 1920 Budapest, József nádor tér 1; tel. (1) 118-0855; telex 223294; fax (1) 117-1369; f. 1988; cap. 16,450m. Ft, res 4,116m. Ft, dep. 342,098m. Ft (Dec. 1996); Chair. and CEO GÁBOR PRINCZ; 39 brs.

Raiffeisen Unicbank Rt: 1052 Budapest, Váci út 19–21; tel. (1) 266-3140; telex 223172; fax (1) 266-3140; f. 1986; cap. 7,000m. Ft, res 3,276m. Ft, dep. 85,572m. Ft (Dec. 1996); Chair. Prof. TAMÁS BÁCSKAI; Man. Dir Dr PÉTER FELCSUTI; 11 brs.

Specialized Financial Institutions

Corvinbank Industrial Development Bank Ltd (Corvinbank Ipari Fejlesztési Bank Rt): 1054 Budapest, Hold út 25; tel. (1) 132-0320; telex 227351; fax (1) 112-9552; f. 1984; cap. 3,202m. Ft; Pres. Dr TAMÁS BÁNFI; Chief Exec. Dr GYULA PÁZMÁNDI.

Hungarian Export-Import Bank Ltd (Magyar Export-Import Bank Rt): 1065 Budapest, Nagymező u. 44; tel. (1) 269-0580; fax (1) 269-4476; Pres. Dr KÁLMÁN MIZSEI; Gen. Man. Dr IVÁN NYÍRI.

Kvantum Investment Bank Ltd: 1117 Budapest, Budafoki út 79; tel. (1) 464-4085; fax (1) 161-3457; Pres. JÁNOS ERŐS; Gen. Man. LÁSZLÓ HAÁS.

Merkantil Bank Ltd: 1051 Budapest, József Attila u. 24; tel. (1) 118-2688; telex 202579; fax (1) 117-2331; f. 1988; affiliated to Commercial and Creditbank Ltd; cap. 1,100m. Ft; Chair. and Chief Exec. ÁDÁM KOLOSSVÁRY.

Opel Bank Hungary: 1027 Budapest, Kapás u. 11-15; tel. (1) 457-9110; Gen. Man. JARI ARJAVALTA.

Porsche Bank Hungaria AG.: 1139 Budapest, Fay u. 27; tel. (1) 270-5060; fax (1) 270-5068; Pres. Dr MIKLÓS SZŐKE.

Rákóczi Regional Development Bank Ltd (Rákóczi Regionális Fejlesztési Bank Rt): 3530 Miskolc, Mindszent tér 1; tel. (46) 412-711; fax (46) 411-294; Pres. Dr GYÖRGY PETRILLA; Gen. Man. ERIKA SZÜCS.

Other Financial Institution

Central Corporation of Banking Companies (Pénzintézeti Központ): 1093 Budapest, Lónyay u. 38; tel. (1) 117-1255; telex 223484; fax (1) 215-9963; f. 1916; banking, property, rights and interests, deposits, securities, and foreign exchange management; cap. 11,127m. Ft, res 3,548m. Ft, dep. 12,289m. Ft; Chair. and CEO PÉTER KIRÁLY; 3 brs.

STOCK EXCHANGE

Budapest Stock Exchange (Budapesti Értéktőzsde): 1052 Budapest, Deák Ferenc u. 5; tel. (1) 117-5226; fax (1) 118-1737; f. 1990; Pres. ZSIGMOND FÁRAI; CEO ZOLTÁN PACSI.

COMMODITY EXCHANGE

Budapest Commodity Exchange (Budapesti Árutőzsde): 1134 Budapest, Róbert Károly krt. 61–65; tel. (1) 465-6979; fax (1) 465-6981; Chair. SZERGEJ KERESZTESI.

INSURANCE

In July 1986 the state insurance enterprise was divided into two companies, one of which retained the name of the former Állami Biztosító. By 1995 13 insurance companies had been established.

Atlasz Travel Insurance Company (Atlasz Utazási Biztosító): 1052 Budapest, Deák F. u. 23; tel. (1) 118-1999; telex 226725; fax (1) 117-1529; f. 1988; cap. 1,000m. Ft; Gen. Man. GÁBOR DARVAS.

Garancia Insurance Company (Garancia Biztosító Rt): 1054 Budapest, Vadász u. 12; tel. (1) 269-2533; fax (1) 269-2549; f. 1988; cap. 4,050m. Ft; Gen. Man. and CEO Dr ZOLTÁN NAGY; 25 brs.

Hungária Insurance Company (Hungária Biztosító Rt): 1054 Budapest, Vadász u. 23–25; tel. (1) 301-6565; telex 222277; fax (1) 301-6100; f. 1986; handles international insurance, industrial and commercial insurance and motor-car, marine, life, household, accident and liability insurance; cap. 4,266m. Ft; Chair. and CEO Dr MIHÁLY PATAI.

State Insurance Company (AB-AEGON Általános Biztosító Rt): 1092 Budapest, Ráday u. 42–44; tel. (1) 218-1866; telex 224875; fax (1) 217-7065; f. 1949 as Állami Biztosító, reorganized 1986, present name since 1992; handles life and property insurance, insurance of agricultural plants, co-operatives, foreign insurance, etc.; Gen. Man. Dr GÁBOR KEPECS.

Trade and Industry

GOVERNMENT AGENCY

Hungarian Privatization and State Holding Company (ÁPV Rt): 1133 Budapest, Pozsonyi út 56; tel. (1) 269-8600; fax (1) 149-5745; e-mail apvrt@apvrt.hu; f. 1995 by merger of the State Property Agency and the State Holding Company; Chair. Dr TAMÁS MÉSZÁROS.

NATIONAL CHAMBERS OF COMMERCE AND AGRICULTURE

Hungarian Chamber of Agriculture (Magyar Agrárkamara): 1036 Budapest, Lajos u. 160-162; tel. (1) 168-6890; fax (1) 188-6554; Pres. MIKLÓS CSIKAI.

Hungarian Chamber of Commerce and Industry (Magyar Kereskedelmi és Iparkamara): 1372 Budapest V, POB 452; tel. (1) 153-3333; fax (1) 269-4628; e-mail mkik@mail.mkik.hu; f. 1850; central organization of the 20 Hungarian county chambers of commerce and industry; based on a system of compulsory membership; over 400,000 mems. Pres. LAJOS TOLNAY.

INDUSTRIAL AND TRADE ASSOCIATIONS

HUNICOOP Foreign Trade Company Ltd for Industrial Co-operation: 1367 Budapest 5, POB 111; tel. (1) 267-1477; fax (1) 267-1482; agency for foreign companies in Hungary, export and import.

Interco-operation Co Ltd for Trade Promotion: 1085 Budapest, POB 136; tel. (1) 118-9966; fax (1) 118-2161; establishment and carrying out of co-operation agreements, representation of foreign companies, brands, marketing and distribution, joint ventures and import-export deals.

UTILITIES

Electricity

Hungarian Electrical Trust (Magyar Villamos Muvek Rt—MVM Rt): 1251 Budapest, POB 34; 1011 Budapest, Vám u. 5–7; tel. (1) 201-5455; fax (1) 202-1246; Hungarian national electricity wholesaler and power-system controller; 6 distributers and 2 generation plants privatized in 1995; remaining 5 plants privatized in 1996; Chair. GYÖRGY HATVANI.

National Power Grid Company Ltd: 1054 Budapest, Szabadsajto út 5.

Paks Nuclear Plant Ltd (Paksi Atomeromu v Pav): 7031 Paks POB 71; tel. (75) 11222; fax (75) 155-1332; Plant Man. EMO PETZ; 3,698 employees.

Gas

Degaz—Delalfoldi Gazszolgaltato Rezvenytarsasag: 6724 Szeged, Pulcz u. 44; tel. (62) 472-572; fax (63) 324-943; public gas supply and services; 1,327 employees.

Hungarian Oil and Gas Company Ltd (MOL—Magyar Olaj és Gáziparirt Rt): 1111 Budapest, Október huszonharmadika u. 18; tel. (1) 209-0000; telex 224762; fax (1) 209-0095; f. 1991 by merger of part of the National Oil and Gas Trust and a technical development co; privatized in 1995, with the state retaining a majority stake; 19,648 employees.

CO-OPERATIVE ORGANIZATIONS

Hungarian Industrial Association (Magyar Iparszövetség—OKISz): 1146 Budapest, Thököly u. 58–60; tel. (1) 343-5570; fax (1) 343-5521; e-mail okisz@mail.elender.hu; internet http://www.okisz-info.hu; safeguards interests of over 2,000 member enterprises (all private); Pres. Dr CSABA SÜMEGHY.

National Co-operative Council (Országos Szövetkezeti Tanács—OSzT): 1054 Budapest, Szabadság tér 14; tel. (1) 312-7467; telex 224862; fax (1) 111-3647; f. 1968; Pres. Dr PÁL BARTUS; Sec. Dr JÓZSEF PÁL.

National Federation of Agricultural Co-operators and Producers (Mezőgazdasági Szövetkezők és Termelők Országos Szövetsege—MOSZ): 1054 Budapest, Akadémia u. 1–3; tel. and fax (1) 153-2552; f. 1990; frmly Termelő szövetkezetek Országos Tanácsa (TOT) (National Council of Agricultural Co-operatives); Pres. TAMÁS NAGY; Sec.-Gen. GÁBOR HORVÁTH; est. 1,300 member organizations.

National Federation of Consumer Co-operatives (Általános Fogyasztási Szövetkezetek Országos Szövetsége—ÁFEOSz): 1054 Budapest, Szabadság tér 14; tel. (1) 153-4222; telex 224862; fax (1) 111-3647; safeguards interests of Hungarian consumer co-operative societies; organizes co-operative wholesale activities; Pres. Dr PÁL BARTUS; 800,000 mems.

TRADE UNIONS

Since 1988, and particularly after the restructuring of the former Central Council of Hungarian Trade Unions (SzOT) as the National Confederation of Hungarian Trade Unions (MSzOSz) in 1990, several new union federations have been created. Several unions are affiliated to more than one federation, and others are completely independent.

Trade Union Federations

Association of Hungarian Free Trade Unions (Magyar Szabad Szakszervezetek Szövetsége): Budapest; f. 1994; 200,000 mems.

Autonomous Trade Union Confederation (Autonóm Szakszervezetek Svövetsége): 1068 Budapest, Benczúr út 45; tel. (1) 342-1776; Pres. LAJOS FŐCZE.

Principal affiliated unions include:

Federation of Hungarian Chemical Industry Workers' Unions (Magyar Vegyipari Dolgozók Szakszervezeti Szövetsége): 1068 Budapest, Benczúr út 45; tel. (1) 342-1778; telex 223420; fax (1) 342-9978; f. 1906; Pres. LAJOS FŐCZE; 42,000 mems.

Democratic League of Independent Trade Unions (Függelten Szakszervezetek Demokratikus Ligája—FSzDL): 1146 Budapest, Thököly út 156; tel. (1) 251-2300; fax (1) 251-2288; e-mail liga@visi-o.c3.hu; f. 1988; Pres. ISTVÁN GASKÓ; 98,000 mems.

Principal affiliated unions include:

Democratic Trade Union of Scientific Workers (Tudományos Dolgozók Demokratikus Szakszervezete—TDDSz): 1068 Budapest, Városligeti fasor 38; tel. (1) 142-8438; f. 1988; Chair. PÁL FORGÁCS.

Federation of Unions of Intellectual Workers (Értelmiségi Szakszervezeti Tömörülés—ÉSzT): 1068 Budapest, Városligeti fasor 10; tel. (1) 122-8456; Pres. Dr LÁSZLÓ KIS; Gen. Sec. Dr GÁBOR BÁNK.

Forum for the Co-operation of Trade Unions (Szakszervezetek Együttműködési Fóruma—SzEF): 1068 Budapest VIII, Puskin u. 4; tel. (1) 138-2651; fax (1) 118-7360; f. 1990; Pres. Dr. ENDRE SZABÓ.

Principal affiliated unions include:

Federation of Hungarian Public Service Employees' Unions (Közszolgálati Szakszervezetek Szövetsége): 1081 Budapest, Kiss Jozsef u. 8 II em; tel. (1) 313-5436; fax (1) 133-7223; f. 1945; Pres. PÉTER MICHALKO; Vice-Pres. Dr JUDIT BÁRDOS, Dr CSILLA NOVÁK.

National Confederation of Hungarian Trade Unions (Magyar Szakszervezetek Országos Szövetsége—MSzOSz): 1415 Budapest, VI. Dózsa György út 84B; tel. (1) 268-1495; telex 225861; fax (1) 342-1924; f. 1898, reorganized 1990; Pres. Dr SÁNDOR LÁSZLÓ; Dep. Pres. JANOS VAGO; 850,000 mems in 49 member organizations.

Principal affiliated unions include:

Commercial Employees' Trade Union (Kereskedelmi Alkalmazottak Szakszervezete): 1066 Budapest, Jókai u. 6; tel. (1) 131-8970; fax (1) 132-3382; f. 1900; Pres. Dr JÓZSEF SÁLING; 160,000 mems.

Confederation of Iron and Metallurgical Industry Workers' Unions (Vas- és Fémipari Dolgozók Szakszervezeti Szövetsége): 1086 Budapest, Magdolna u. 5–7; tel. (1) 210-2985; telex 224791; fax (1) 210-0116; f. 1877; Pres. LÁSZLÓ PASZTERNÁK; 220,000 mems.

Federation of Agricultural, Forestry and Water Conservancy Workers' Unions (Mezőgazdasági, Erdészeti és Vizgazdálkodási Dolgozók Szakszervezeti Szövetsége): 1066 Budapest, Jókai u. 2–4; tel. (1) 331-4550; telex 227535; fax (1) 331-4568; f. 1906; Pres. (vacant); Gen. Sec. ANDRÁS BERECZKY; 21,000 mems.

Federation of Building, Wood and Building Industry Workers' Unions (Építő-, Fa-és Épitőanyagipari Dolgozók Szakszervezeteinek Szövetsége): 1068 Budapest, Dózsa György út 84A; tel. (1) 122-9426; fax (1) 142-4395; f. 1906; Pres. JÁNOS NAGYMIHALY; Vice-Pres. ANTAL MIHALUSZ; 140,000 mems.

Federation of Chemical Workers' Unions of Hungary, Confederation Founding Section (Magyar Vegyipari Dolgozók Szakszervezeti Szövetsége, össz-szövetségi alapító tagozata): 1068 Budapest, Benczúr út 45; tel. (1) 342-1778; fax (1) 342-9975; Gen. Sec. GYÖRGY PASZTERNÁK; 12,000 mems.

Federation of Communal Service Workers' Unions (Kommunális Dalgozók Szakszervezete): 1068 Budapest, Benczur u. 43; tel. (1) 111-6950; Gen. Sec. ZSOLT PÉK; 28,000 mems.

Federation of Hungarian Artworkers' Unions (Müvészeti Szakszervezetek Szövetsége): 1068 Budapest, Városligeti fasor 38; tel. (1) 342-8927; fax (1) 342-8372; e-mail eji@mail.datanet.hu; f. 1957; Pres. LÁSZLÓ GYIMESI; 32,000 mems.

Federation of Local Industry and Municipal Workers' Unions (Helyiipari és Városgazdasági Dolgozók Szövetségének): 1068 Budapest, Benczúr u. 43; tel. (1) 111-6950; f. 1952; Pres. JÓZSEFNÉ SVEVER; Gen. Sec. PÁL BAKÁNYI; 281,073 mems.

Federation of Mineworkers' Unions (Bányaipari Dolgozók Szakszervezeti Szövetsége): 1068 Budapest, Városligeti fasor

46–48; tel. (1) 322-1226; telex 227499; fax (1) 342-1942; f. 1913; Pres. ANTAL SCHALKHAMMER; Vice-Pres. Dr. JÁNOS HORN; 80,000 mems.

Federation of Municipal Industries and Service Workers' Unions (Települési Ipari és Szolgáltatási Dolgozók Szakszervezete): 1068 Budapest, Benczur u. 43; tel. (1) 111-6950; Gen. Sec. ZOLTÁN SZIKSZAI; 20,000 mems.

Federation of Postal and Telecommunications Workers' Unions (Postai és Hirközlési Dolgozók Szakszervezeti Szövetsége): 1146 Budapest, Cházár András u. 13; tel. (1) 142-8777; fax (1) 121-4018; f. 1945; Pres. ENIKŐ HESZKY-GRICSER; 69,900 mems.

Federation of Transport Workers' Unions (Közlekedési Dolgozók Szakszervezeteinek Szövetségé): 1081 Budapest, Köztársaság tér 3; tel. (1) 113-9046; f. 1898; Pres. ISTVÁN TRENKA; 8,000 mems.

Hungarian Federation of Food Industry Workers' Unions (Magyar Élelmezésipari Dolgozók Szakszervezeteinek Szövetsége): 1068 Budapest, Városligeti fasor 44; tel. (1) 122-5880; fax (1) 142-8568; f. 1905; Pres. GYULA SÓKI; Gen. Sec. BÉLA VANEK; 226,243 mems.

Hungarian Graphical Workers' Union (Nyomdaipari Dolgozók Szakszervezete): 1085 Budapest, Kölcsey u. 2; tel. (1) 266-0065; fax (1) 266-0028; f. 1862; Pres. ANDRÁS BÁRSONY; Vice-Pres JÁNOS ACZÉL, EMIL SZELEI; 17,000 mems.

Hungarian Union of Teachers (Magyar Pedagógusok Szakszervezete): 1068 Budapest, Városligeti fasor 10; tel. (1) 122-8456; fax (1) 142-8122; f. 1945; Gen. Sec. ISTVÁNNÉ SZÖLLŐSI; 200,000 mems.

Hungarian Union of Textile Workers (Magyar Textilipari Dolgozók Szakszervezete): 1068 Budapest, Rippl-Rónai u. 2; tel. (1) 428-196; fax (1) 122-5414; f. 1905; Pres. (vacant); Gen. Sec. TAMÁS KELETI; 70,241 mems.

Textile Workers' Union (Textilipari Dolgozók Szakszervezete): 1068 Budapest, Rippl Rónai u. 2; tel. (1) 112-3868; fax (1) 342-8169; Gen. Sec. TAMÁS KELETI; 39,500 mems.

Union of Health Service Workers (Egészségügyben Dolgozók Szakszervezeteinek Szövetsége): 1051 Budapest, Nádor u. 32, POB 36; tel. (1) 110-645; f. 1945; Pres. Dr ZOLTÁN SZABÓ; Gen. Sec. Dr PÁLNÉ KÁLLAY; 280,536 mems.

Union of Leather Industry Workers (Bőripari Dolgozók Szakszervezete): 1062 Budapest, Bajza u. 24; tel. (1) 342-9970; f. 1868; Gen. Sec. TAMÁS LAJTOS; 12,000 mems.

Union of Clothing Workers (Ruházatipari Dolgozók Szakszervezete (): 1077 Budapest, Almássy tér 2; tel. (1) 342-3702; fax (1) 122-6717; f. 1892; Gen. Sec. TAMÁS WITTICH; 22,000 mems.

Union of Railway Workers (Vasutasok Szakszervezete): 1068 Budapest, Benczúr u. 41; tel. (1) 122-1895; telex 226819; fax (1) 122-8818; f. 1945; Pres. PÁL PAPP; Gen. Sec. FERENC KOSZORUS; 115,000 mems.

Transport

RAILWAYS

In 1991 the total rail network in Hungary amounted to 10,607 km. Some 231m. passengers were carried in 1993. There is an underground railway in Budapest, with a network of 23 km in 1989; in that year 296m. passengers were carried. In May 1996 it was announced that PHARE, the EU's programme for the economic reconstruction of Eastern Europe, would finance 25% of MAV's 100,000m. forint modernization project.

Hungarian State Railways Ltd (Magyar Államvasutak—MÁV): 1940 Budapest, Andrássy út 73–75; tel. (1) 322-0660; telex 224342; fax (1) 342-8596; f. 1868; transformed into joint-stock co in 1993; total network 7,600 km, including 2,214 km of electrified lines; Pres. ISTVÁN TÖMPE; Gen. Dir ISTVÁN SIPOS.

Railway of Győr–Sopron–Ebenfurt (Győr–Sopron–Ebenfurti-Vasut—Gysev-ROeEE): 9400 Sopron, Matyas Kiraly u. 19; Hungarian-Austrian-owned railway; 84 km in Hungary, 82 km in Austria, all electrified; transport of passengers and goods; Dir-Gen. Dr JÁNOS BERÉNYI.

ROADS

At the end of 1996 the road network totalled 158,633 km, including 420 km of motorways, 29,653 km of main or national roads and 52,683 km of secondary roads. There are extensive long-distance bus services. Road passenger and freight transport is provided by the state-owned Volán companies and by individual operators. In January 1996 a section of a 42-km motorway was opened between Győr and Hegyeshalom. The road was eventually to extend from Budapest to Vienna (Austria).

Hungarocamion: 1442 Budapest, POB 108; tel. (1) 257-3600; telex 225455; fax (1) 256-6755; international road freight transport company; 17 offices in Europe and the Middle East; fleet of 1,100 units for general and specialized cargo; Gen. Man. GABRIELLA SZAKÁL; 3,800 employees.

Centre of Volán Enterprises (Volán Vállalatok Központja): 1391 Budapest, Erzsébet krt 96, POB 221; tel. (1) 112-4290; telex 225177; centre of 25 Volán enterprises for inland and international road freight and passenger transport, forwarding, tourism; fleet of 17,000 lorries, incl. special tankers for fuel, refrigerators, trailers, 8,000 buses for regular passenger transport; 3 affiliates, offices and joint-ventures in Europe; Head ELEMER SASLICS.

SHIPPING AND INLAND WATERWAYS

At the end of 1994 the Hungarian river merchant fleet comprised 199 vessels, with a capacity totalling 223,718. At 31 December 1996 the ocean merchant fleet comprised 10 vessels, with a combined displacement of 50,209 grt.

Hungarian Shipping Co (MAHART—Magyar Hajózási Rt): 1366 Budapest, POB 58; tel. (1) 118-1880; telex 225258; fax (1) 138-2421; carries passenger traffic on the Danube and Lake Balaton; cargo services on the Danube and its tributaries, Lake Balaton, and also Mediterranean and ocean-going services; operates port of Budapest (container terminal, loading, storage, warehousing, handling and packaging services); ship-building and ship-repair services; Pres. Dir-Gen. ANDRÁS FÁY.

MAFRACHT International Shipping, Forwarding and Agency Ltd Co: 1364 Budapest 4, POB 105; tel. (1) 266-1208; telex 226128; fax (1) 266-1329; shipping agency.

CIVIL AVIATION

The Ferihegy international airport is 16 km from the centre of Budapest. Ferihegy-2 opened in 1985. Balatonkiliti airport, near Siófok in western Hungary, reopened to international traffic in 1989. Public internal air services resumed in May 1993, after an interval of 20 years, between Budapest and Nyíregyháza, Debrecen, Szeged, Pécs, Szombathely and Győr.

Air Traffic and Airport Administration (Légiforgalmi és Repülőtéri Igazgatóság): 1675 Budapest, POB 53; tel. (1) 291-8722; telex 227837; fax (1) 157-6982; f. 1973; controls civil air traffic and operates Ferihegy and Siófok Airports; Dir-Gen. TAMÁS ERDEI.

General Directorate of Civil Aviation (Légügyi Főigazgatóság): 1400 Budapest, Dob u. 75–81, POB 87; tel. (1) 342-2544; telex 225729; fax (1) 322-2848; controls civil aviation; Dir-Gen. ÖDÖN SKONDA.

Hungarian Airlines (Magyar Légiközlekedési Részvénytársaság—MALEV Rt): 1051 Budapest, Roosevelt tér 2, POB 122; tel. (1) 266-9033; telex 224954; fax (1) 266-2685; f. 1946; regular services from Budapest to Europe, North Africa, North America, Asia and the Middle East; Chair. ANDRÁS DERZSI; CEO SÁNDOR SZATHMÁRY.

LinAir Hungarian Regional Airlines: 1675 Budapest, POB 53; tel. (1) 296-7092; fax (1) 296-7891; f. 1994; regional carrier; Man. Dir TAMÁS KOVÁCS.

Tourism

Tourism has developed rapidly and is an important source of foreign exchange. Lake Balaton is the main holiday centre for boating, bathing and fishing. Hungary's cities have great historical and recreational attractions. The annual Budapest Spring Festival is held in March. Budapest has numerous swimming pools watered by thermal springs, which are equipped with modern physiotherapy facilities. In 1995 there were about 39.2m. foreign visitors (including 18.6m. visitors in transit). Revenue from tourism in that year totalled about US $1,724m.

Hungarian Travel Agency (IBUSZ—Idegenforgalmi, Beszerzési, Utazási és Szállítási Rt): 1364 Budapest, Ferenciek tér 5; tel. (1) 118-6866; telex 224976; fax (1) 117-7723; f. 1902; has 118 brs throughout Hungary; Gen. Man. Dr ERIKA SZEMENKÁR.

Ministry of Industry, Trade and Tourism: 1024 Budapest, Margit Körút 85; tel. (1) 175-0419; fax (1) 175-2419; Dir-Gen. GYÖRGY SZÉKELY.

ICELAND

Introductory Survey

Location, Climate, Language, Religion, Flag, Capital

The Republic of Iceland comprises one large island and numerous smaller ones, situated near the Arctic Circle in the North Atlantic Ocean. The main island lies about 300 km (190 miles) south-east of Greenland, about 1,000 km (620 miles) west of Norway and about 800 km (500 miles) north of Scotland. The Gulf Stream keeps Iceland warmer than might be expected, with average temperatures ranging from 10°C (50°F) in the summer to 1°C (34°F) in winter. Icelandic is the official language. Almost all of the inhabitants profess Christianity: the Evangelical Lutheran Church is the established church and embraces 90% of the population. The civil flag (proportions 25 by 18) displays a red cross, bordered with white, on a blue background, the upright of the cross being towards the hoist; the state flag (proportions 16 by 9) bears the same design, but has a truncated triangular area cut from the fly. The capital is Reykjavík.

Recent History

Iceland became independent on 17 June 1944, when the Convention that linked it with Denmark, under the Danish crown, was terminated. Iceland became a founder-member of the Nordic Council (see p. 200) in 1952, and has belonged to both NATO (see p. 204) and the Council of Europe (see p. 140) since 1949. Membership of the European Free Trade Association (EFTA, see p. 150) was formalized in 1970.

From 1959 to 1971 Iceland was governed by a coalition of the Independence Party (IP) and the Social Democratic Party (SDP). Following the general election of June 1971, Ólafur Jóhannesson, the leader of the Progressive Party (PP), formed a coalition Government with the left-wing People's Alliance (PA) and the Union of Liberals and Leftists. At elections held in June 1974 voters favoured right-wing parties, and in August the IP and the PP formed a coalition Government, led by the IP leader, Geir Hallgrímsson. Failure to address adequately economic difficulties, including escalating inflation, resulted in a decline in the coalition's popularity and prompted the Government's resignation in June 1978, following extensive election gains by the PA and the SDP. Disagreements over economic measures, and over the PA's advocacy of Icelandic withdrawal from NATO, led to two months of negotiations before a new government could be formed. In September 1978 Jóhannesson formed a coalition of the PP with the PA and the SDP, but this Government, after addressing immediate economic necessities, resigned in October 1979, when the SDP withdrew from the coalition. An interim administration was formed by Benedikt Gröndal, the SDP leader. The results of a general election, held in December, were inconclusive, and in February 1980 Gunnar Thoroddsen of the IP formed a coalition with the PA and the PP.

In June 1980 Vigdís Finnbogadóttir, a non-political candidate who was favoured by left-wing groups because of her opposition to the US military airbase at Keflavík, achieved a narrow victory in the election for the mainly ceremonial office of President. She took office on 1 August 1980, becoming the world's first popularly-elected female Head of State. The coalition Government lost its majority in the Lower House of the Althing in September 1982, and a general election took place in April 1983. The IP received the largest share (38.7%) of the votes, but two new parties, the Social Democratic Alliance (SDA) and the Women's Alliance (WA), together won almost 13% of the votes. A centre-right coalition was formed by the IP and the PP, with Steingrímur Hermannsson (the PP leader and former Minister of Fisheries and Communications) as Prime Minister, and the IP leader, Geir Hallgrímsson, as Minister for Foreign Affairs. In an attempt to halt the sharp increase in the rate of inflation, the Government discontinued the indexation of wages, extended existing wage agreements and devalued the króna in May 1983. Although these measures reduced inflation in 1984, there was considerable industrial unrest in 1984–85, as a result of which large increases in wages for public-sector employees and fishermen were secured. There was also a further devaluation of the króna. In June 1985, to forestall the threat of further strikes, private-sector employers secured a guarantee from the Icelandic Federation of Labour to refrain from industrial action.

A general election for an enlarged, 63-seat Althing was held in April 1987. Both parties of the outgoing coalition suffered losses: the IP's representation decreased from 24 to 18 seats, and the PP lost one of its 14 seats. The right-wing Citizens' Party (CP, which had been formed only one month earlier by Albert Guðmundsson, following his resignation from the Ministry of Energy and Industry and from the IP) won seven seats. Ten seats were won by the SDP, which included former members of the SDA, disbanded in 1986. A coalition of the IP, the PP and the SDP was formally constituted in July 1987. Thorsteinn Pálsson, the leader of the IP since November 1983 and the Minister of Finance in the outgoing Cabinet, was appointed Prime Minister.

In June 1988 President Vigdís Finnbogadóttir (who had begun a second term in office, unopposed, in August 1984) was elected for a third term, receiving more than 90% of the votes. This was the first occasion on which an incumbent President seeking re-election had been challenged. In August 1992 the President began a fourth term of office, her candidacy being unopposed.

In September 1988 the SDP and the PP withdrew from the Pálsson Government, following disagreements over economic policy. Later that month, the PP leader, Steingrímur Hermannsson, became Prime Minister in a centre-left coalition with the SDP and the PA. The new Government committed itself to a series of devaluations of the króna, and introduced austerity measures, with the aim of lowering the rate of inflation and stimulating the fishing industry.

Following the resignation of Albert Guðmundsson from the leadership of the CP in January 1989, relations between this party and the left improved, and in September a new Government, based on a coalition agreement between the PP, the SDP, the PA, the CP and the Association for Equality and Social Justice, was formed. Steingrímur Hermannsson, who remained as Prime Minister, affirmed that the new Government would not change its policies, emphasizing the need to reduce inflation and to stimulate economic growth, as well as reiterating an earlier declaration of the Althing that no nuclear weapons would be located in Iceland.

In March 1991 Davíð Oddsson, the mayor of Reykjavík, successfully challenged Thorsteinn Pálsson for the leadership of the IP. At a general election in April the IP (which had promised to reduce taxes to stimulate the economy) emerged as the largest single party, securing 26 seats (with 38.6% of the votes), mostly at the expense of the CP. Although the incumbent coalition would have retained an overall majority of seats, the SDP decided to withdraw from the coalition, chiefly as a result of the failure to reach agreement on Iceland's position in the discussions between EFTA and the EC with regard to the creation of a European Economic Area (EEA, see below). A new coalition Government was formed in late April by the IP and the SDP, with Oddsson as Prime Minister; the new administration promised economic liberalization and a strengthening of links with the USA and Europe (although no application for membership of the EC was envisaged), but was faced with a deteriorating economic situation (see below).

A general election was held on 8 April 1995. Although the IP secured the largest number of seats (25, with 37% of the votes), the SDP obtained only seven seats, three fewer than in the previous election. Later in the month a new coalition Government was formed, comprising the IP and the PP, with Oddsson continuing as Prime Minister, and Halldór Ásgrímsson, the leader of the PP, being named Minister of Foreign Affairs. Since both parties in the coalition opposed the Common Fisheries Policy of the European Union (EU, as the EC has been restyled), it was considered unlikely that Iceland would apply for full membership of the EU in the near future.

Following the decision by Vigdís Finnbogadóttir not to seek re-election as President in 1996, the principal candidates were Ólafur Ragnar Grímsson, a former leader of the PA (who had previously opposed Iceland's membership of NATO), Pétur Hafstein, a justice in the Supreme Court, and Guðrún Agnarsdóttir of the WA. In the election, held on 29 June 1996, Grímsson secured 41% of the votes cast, while Hafstein won 29% and Agnarsdóttir gained 26%. Grímsson duly took office as President in August.

In 1991 Iceland's Constitution was amended, ending the system whereby the Althing was divided into an Upper House (one-third of the members) and a Lower House.

The importance of fishing to Iceland's economy, and fears of excessive exploitation of the fishing grounds near Iceland by foreign fleets, caused the Icelandic Government to extend its territorial waters to 12 nautical miles (22 km) in 1964 and to 50 nautical miles (93 km) in September 1972. British opposition to these extensions resulted in two 'cod wars'. In October 1975 Iceland unilaterally introduced a fishing limit of 200 nautical miles (370 km), both as a conservation measure and to protect important Icelandic interests. The 1973 agreement on fishing limits between Iceland and the United Kingdom expired in November 1975, and failure to reach a new agreement led to the third and most serious 'cod war'. Casualties occurred, and in February 1976 Iceland temporarily severed diplomatic relations with the UK, the first diplomatic break between two NATO countries. In June the two countries reached an agreement, and in December the British trawler fleet withdrew from Icelandic waters. In June 1979 Iceland declared its exclusive rights to the 200-mile fishing zone. Following negotiations between the EC and EFTA on the creation of the EEA, an agreement was reached (in October 1991) allowing tariff-free access to the EC for 97% of Iceland's fisheries products by 1997, while Iceland was to allow EC vessels to catch 3,000 metric tons of fish per year in its waters, in return for some access to EC waters. The EEA agreement was ratified by the Althing in January 1993 and entered into force in January 1994.

In August 1993 a dispute developed between Iceland and Norway over fishing rights in an area of the Barents Sea fished by Iceland, over which Norway claimed jurisdiction. The dispute continued throughout 1994, and in June the Norwegian coastguards cut the nets of Icelandic trawlers fishing for cod in the disputed region. Iceland's case was weakened in January 1995, when Canada officially recognized Norway's sovereign rights over the disputed area (a fisheries protection zone extending 200 km around the Svalbard archipelago). A similar dispute arose in August 1996 between Iceland and Denmark over fishing rights in an area of the Atlantic Ocean between Iceland and Greenland (a self-governing province of Denmark). The Danish Government claimed that an agreement had been concluded in 1988 to allow fishing boats that were in possession of a licence issued in Greenland to operate in the area. Iceland, however, denied the existence of such an agreement, and announced that Danish boats would not be permitted to fish in the disputed area.

Iceland strongly criticized the moratorium on commercial whaling, imposed (for conservation purposes) by the International Whaling Commission (IWC, see p. 253) in 1986, and continued to catch limited numbers of whales for scientific purposes until 1989, when it halted whaling, following appeals by environmental organizations for an international boycott of Icelandic products. In 1991 Iceland announced its withdrawal from the IWC (with effect from June 1992), claiming that certain species of whales were not only too plentiful to be in danger of extinction, but were also threatening Iceland's stocks of cod and other fish. In 1994 a report, commissioned by the Government, recommended that limited hunting be resumed in the future.

In May 1985 the Althing unanimously approved a resolution declaring the country a 'nuclear-free zone', i.e. banning the entry of nuclear weapons.

Government

According to the Constitution, executive power is vested in the President (elected for four years by universal adult suffrage) and the Cabinet, consisting of the Prime Minister and other ministers appointed by the President. In practice, however, the President performs only nominally the functions ascribed in the Constitution to this office, and it is the Cabinet alone which holds real executive power. Legislative power is held jointly by the President and the unicameral Althing (Parliament), with 63 members elected by universal suffrage for four years (subject to dissolution by the President), using a mixed system of proportional representation. The Cabinet is responsible to the Althing. Iceland has seven administrative districts.

Defence

Apart from a 120-strong coastguard, Iceland has no defence forces of its own, but it is a member of NATO. There are units of US forces at Keflavík air base, which is used for observation of the North Atlantic Ocean, under a bilateral agreement made in 1951 between Iceland and the USA. The airfield at Keflavík is a base for the US airborne early warning system. In August 1997 a total of 2,520 US military personnel (navy 1,800, air force 629, marines 91) were stationed in Iceland, together with a 30-strong naval contingent from the Netherlands.

Economic Affairs

In 1995, according to estimates by the World Bank, Iceland's gross national product (GNP), measured at 1993–95 prices, was US $6,686m., equivalent to $24,950 per head. During 1985–95, it was estimated, GNP per head increased, in real terms, at an average annual rate of 0.3%. Over the same period the population increased by an annual average of 1.1%. Iceland's gross domestic product (GDP) increased, in real terms, by an average of 1.8% per year in 1982–92. However, real GDP declined by 3.3% in 1992, and rose by only 0.9% in 1993. Contrary to earlier forecasts, GDP increased by 3.7% in 1994. It rose by 1.0% in 1995 and by 5.2% in 1996.

Agriculture (including forestry and fishing) contributes some 12% of GDP. About 9.3% of the labour force were employed in the agricultural sector in 1996. The principal agricultural products are dairy produce and lamb, although these provided less than 1% of export earnings in 1996. Fisheries products accounted for 64.2% of total export earnings in 1996. During 1986–96 agricultural production declined by an estimated annual average of 2.3%. According to IMF estimates, agricultural GDP declined by 10.1% in 1991, in real terms, but had recovered sufficiently by 1993 to register real growth of 4.2%. Growth in the sector's GDP was estimated at 1.7% for 1995.

Industry (including mining, manufacturing, construction and power) contributed 30.2% of GDP in 1991. Some 25% of the labour force were employed in the industrial sector in 1995. Mining activity is negligible. During 1986–91 industrial production increased by 8%.

Manufacturing contributed 17.3% of GDP in 1991, and, together with mining and quarrying but excluding fish-processing, employed 17.9% of the labour force in 1995. The most important sectors, measured by gross value of output (excluding fish-processing, which dominates the sector), are the production of aluminium, diatomite, fertilizer, cement and ferro-silicon. Manufacturing GDP (including that contributed by fish-processing) declined by 4.2% in 1992, but recovered in 1993 and 1994 (when real growth of 5.9% was recorded, largely owing to increased fish-processing). Growth in the sector's GDP was estimated at 2.0% for 1995.

Iceland is potentially rich in hydroelectric and geothermal power, but both energy sources were significantly underexploited in 1996. In that year some 85% of homes were equipped with geothermal heating. Imports of mineral fuels and lubricants comprised 7.8% of the value of merchandise imports in 1996.

In 1996 Iceland recorded a visible trade surplus of 1,817m. krónur, but there was a deficit of 8,231m. krónur on the current account of the balance of payments. In 1996 the principal sources of imports were Norway (13.5%), Germany (10.9%) and the United Kingdom (10.2%); the principal market for exports was the United Kingdom (19.0%), followed by Germany (12.8%) and the USA (12.1%). In 1996 EU member countries provided 56.4% of Iceland's merchandise imports and took 62.1% of exports. The principal imports in 1996 were road vehicles, petroleum and petroleum products, industrial machinery and equipment, and electrical machinery, apparatus and appliances. The principal exports in the same year were marine products (including animal feeds), aluminium and ships.

In 1995 there was a budgetary deficit of 20,270m. krónur, equivalent to 4.5% of GDP. Iceland's net external debt was estimated at 226,218m. krónur at the end of 1996. The cost of debt-servicing was equivalent to 28.8% of export earnings in 1995. The annual rate of inflation averaged 9.7% in 1986–96; consumer prices increased by 1.6% in 1994, by 1.7% in 1995, and by 2.3% in 1996. In June 1997 some 3.8% of the total labour force were unemployed.

Iceland is a member of the Nordic Council (see p. 200), the Nordic Council of Ministers (see p. 201), the European Free Trade Association (EFTA, see p. 150) and the Organisation for Economic Co-operation and Development (OECD, see p. 208).

Iceland's dependence on its fisheries proved to be a disadvantage in the late 1980s and early 1990s, when catches were reduced in volume (by 22.5% in 1992/93 and by a further 25% in 1993/94) as a deliberate conservation measure, made necessary by a serious depletion of stocks, while lower prices were paid for exports of fish products. (Since 1994 the total annual catch has remained stable at about 1.5m.–2.0m. metric tons.) Iceland's other principal exports—aluminium and ferro-silicon—were also affected by weakness of demand and deteriorating terms of trade. To offset these problems, the króna was devalued by 6% in November 1992 and by 7.5% in June 1993. Real GNP increased by only 0.9% in 1993. However, an economic upturn, with low inflation and strong export growth, resulted in real GDP growth of 3.7% in 1994, 1.0% in 1995 and 5.2% in 1996. Real growth in GDP was forecast at 4.5% for 1997 and 3.5% for 1998. The annual report of the Central Bank of Iceland, published in November 1997, identified an improvement in general economic conditions proceeding from foreign investment in power-intensive industries and renewed interest in recovered fish stocks, but warned that the continuing vulnerability of the króna, growth in domestic demand and possible pressure on prices, arising from a wage agreement concluded with unions in March, meant that stricter monetary policy would have to be maintained if recurrent economic problems, particularly that of the fiscal deficit, were to be addressed successfully. An average rate of inflation of 2.2% was forecast for 1997.

Social Welfare

There is a comprehensive system of social security, providing a wide range of insurance benefits, including old-age pensions, family allowances, maternity grants, widows' pensions, etc. The scheme is mainly financed by the Government. Pensions and health insurance now apply to the whole population. Accident insurance applies to all wage and salary earners and self-employed persons—unless they request exemption—and unemployment insurance to the unions of skilled and unskilled workers and seamen in all towns and villages of over 300 inhabitants, as well as to several unions in villages of less than 300 inhabitants. In 1993 there were 779 physicians working in Iceland. In 1991 the country had 14 general hospitals, with about 1,000 short-term beds. In addition there are a number of long-term institutions with more than 2,000 beds. Of total expenditure by the central Government in 1995, 34,164m. krónur (23.3%) was for health, while a further 34,764m. krónur (23.7%) was for social security and welfare.

Education

Education is compulsory and free for eight years between seven and 15 years of age (primary and lower secondary levels). Secondary education begins at 16 years of age and lasts for four years. In 1994 89% of 16-year-olds were continuing their education at a secondary school. Iceland has two universities and 12 other institutions of higher learning. Expenditure on education by the central Government in 1995 was 17,423m. krónur, representing 11.9% of total spending. Local communities contribute about 20% of the cost of compulsory and secondary education.

Public Holidays

1998: 1 January (New Year's Day), 9 April (Maundy Thursday), 10 April (Good Friday), 13 April (Easter Monday), 21 May (Ascension Day), 1 June (Whit Monday), 17 June (National Day), 3 August (Bank Holiday), 24–26 December (Christmas), 31 December (New Year's Eve).

1999: 1 January (New Year's Day), 1 April (Maundy Thursday), 2 April (Good Friday), 5 April (Easter Monday), 13 May (Ascension Day), 24 May (Whit Monday), 17 June (National Day), 2 August (Bank Holiday), 24–26 December (Christmas), 31 December (New Year's Eve).

Weights and Measures

The metric system is in force.

Statistical Survey

Sources (unless otherwise stated): Statistical Bureau of Iceland, Skuggasund 3, 150 Reykjavík; tel. 5526699; National Economic Institute of Iceland, Reykjavík; tel. 5699500; Seðlabanki Íslands (Central Bank of Iceland), Kalkofnsvegur 1, 150 Reykjavík; tel. 5699600; telex 2020.

AREA AND POPULATION

Area: 103,000 sq km (39,769 sq miles).

Population: 204,578 at census of 1 December 1970; 269,735 (males 135,184; females 134,551) at 1 December 1996 (official estimate); 269,727 at 1 December 1996 (revised estimate).

Density (per sq km): 2.6 (1996).

Principal Town: Reykjavík (capital), estimated population 105,487 at 1 December 1996.

Births, Marriages and Deaths (1995): Live births 4,280 (birth rate 16.0 per 1,000); Marriage rate 4.6 per 1,000; Deaths 1,923 (death rate 7.2 per 1,000).

Expectation of Life (years at birth, 1996/97): Males 76.3; Females 80.8.

Employment (1995): Agriculture, forestry and fishing 13,500; Mining, quarrying and manufacturing 25,300; Construction 9,700; Trade, restaurants and hotels 23,700; Transport, storage and communications 9,200; Finance, real estate and business services 13,400; Public administration, education and health services 47,000; Total 141,800.

AGRICULTURE, ETC.

Principal Crops (metric tons, 1995): Potatoes 7,324; Turnips 328. **1996** (metric tons): Roots and tubers 7,000 (Source: FAO, *Production Yearbook*).

Livestock ('000 head, year ending September 1996): Cattle 73; Sheep 450; Horses 79 (FAO estimate); Pigs 42 (FAO estimate) (Source: FAO, *Production Yearbook*).

Livestock Products (metric tons, 1996): Mutton and lamb 8,131; Beef and veal 3,142; Pig meat 3,740; Milk 101,643; Wool (unwashed) 866 (1995); Sheepskins 1,820 (1995); Eggs 2,195 (1995).

Fishing ('000 metric tons, live weight, 1996): Atlantic cod 179.5; Haddock 55.1; Saithe 39.1; Atlantic redfishes 64.7; Capelin 1,176.9; Atlantic herring 263.3; Crustaceans 77.4; Total (incl. others) 1,989.9.

INDUSTRY

Selected Products ('000 metric tons, unless otherwise indicated, 1996): Frozen fish 134.3 (1995); Salted, dried or smoked fish 66.3 (1995); Cement (sales) 88.2; Ferro-silicon 68.0; Aluminium (unwrought) 103.9; Electric energy 5,113 million kWh.

FINANCE

Currency and Exchange Rates: 100 aurar (singular: eyrir) = 1 new Icelandic króna (plural: krónur). *Sterling and Dollar Equivalents* (30 September 1997): £1 sterling = 115.11 krónur; US $1 = 71.26 krónur; 1,000 krónur = £8.687 = $14.033. *Average Exchange Rate* (krónur per US $): 69.944 in 1994; 64.692 in 1995; 66.500 in 1996.

Budget (million krónur, 1995): *Revenue:* Direct taxes 68,040; Indirect taxes 82,373 (value-added tax 42,944, taxes on alcohol and tobacco 5,228, excise tax 14,071, import duties 2,220, other indirect taxes 17,910); Non-tax revenue 12,345; Total 162,757. *Expenditure* (excluding net lending): General administration 8,707; Education 22,060; Health and welfare 71,943 (Subsidies 9,492); Agriculture 7,425; Fisheries 1,394; Manufacturing 1,035; Power 1,440; Communications 13,623; Other purposes 51,370; Total 178,997. **1996:** Total revenue 176,600m. krónur; Total expenditure 185,200m. krónur.

International Reserves (US $ million at 31 December 1996): Gold 2.7; IMF special drawing rights 0; Reserve position in IMF 15.1; Foreign exchange 516.8; Total 534.8.

Money Supply (million krónur at 31 December 1996): Currency outside banks 5,442; Demand deposits at commercial and savings banks 37,029; Total money 42,471.

Cost of Living (consumer price index for Reykjavík; average of monthly figures; base: May 1988 = 100): 170.3 in 1994; 173.2 in 1995; 177.1 in 1996.

Gross Domestic Product in purchasers' values (million krónur at current prices): 435,063 in 1994; 451,637 in 1995; 484,348 in 1996.

Expenditure on the Gross Domestic Product (million krónur at current prices, 1996): Government final consumption expenditure 100,679; Private final consumption expenditure 296,840; Increase in stocks −1,036; Gross fixed capital formation 84,828; *Total domestic expenditure* 481,311; Exports of goods and services 176,761; *Less* Imports of goods and services 173,725; *Gross domestic product* 484,347.

Balance of Payments (US $ million, 1995): Exports of goods f.o.b. 1,804.0, Imports of goods f.o.b. −1,598.0, *Trade balance* 206.0; Exports of services 670.0, Imports of services −641.0, *Balance on goods and services* 235.0; Other income received 91.0, Other income paid −270.0, *Balance on goods, services and income* 56.0; Current transfers received 15.0, Current transfers paid −20.0, *Current balance* 51.0; Capital account (net) −1.0, Direct investment abroad −6.0, Direct investment from abroad 4.0, Portfolio investment assets −43.0, Portfolio investment liabilities −9.0, Other investment assets 25.5, Other investment liabilities 65.0, Net errors and omissions −82.0, *Overall balance* 4.0. Source: IMF, *International Financial Statistics*.

EXTERNAL TRADE

Principal Commodities (distribution by SITC, million krónur, 1996): *Imports c.i.f.:* Fish, crustaceans, molluscs and preparations thereof 2,801; Metalliferous ores and metal scrap 3,349; Petroleum and petroleum products 10,012; Medicinal and pharmaceutical products 3,293; Paper, paperboard and articles thereof 4,661; Textile yarn, etc. 3,585; Iron and steel 2,818; Machinery specialized for particular industries 4,457; General industrial machinery and equipment 8,334; Office machines and computers 4,776; Telecommunications equipment, etc. 4,260; Electrical machinery, apparatus and appliances 7,504; Road vehicles 10,511; Other transport equipment 6,863; Apparel and clothing accessories 5,337; Total (incl. others) 135,995. *Exports f.o.b.:* Fish, crustaceans, molluscs and preparations thereof 81,065; Animal feeds (excl. unmilled cereals) 10,255; Animal oils and fats 3,908; Iron and steel 3,835; Non-ferrous metals 12,109; Transport equipment 4,180; Total (incl. others) 126,304.

Principal Trading Partners (million krónur, country of consignment, 1996): *Imports c.i.f.:* Australia 3,364; Belgium 2,582; China, People's Republic 1,774; Denmark 11,358; Finland 2,241; France 4,457; Germany 14,802; Italy 4,374; Japan 5,456; Korea, Republic 1,514; Netherlands 8,117; Norway 18,396; Poland 2,661; Russia 3,373; Spain 2,356; Sweden 9,132; Switzerland 1,996; United Kingdom 13,874; USA 12,840; Total (incl. others) 135,995. *Exports f.o.b.:* Belgium 1,553; Canada 1,462; Denmark 9,094; France 8,443; Germany 16,229; Italy 2,403; Japan 12,370; Netherlands 4,522; Norway 4,687; Portugal 3,238; Spain 4,881; Sweden 1,621; Switzerland 2,493; Taiwan 1,973; United Kingdom 23,949; USA 15,322; Total (incl. others) 126,304.

TRANSPORT

Road Traffic (registered motor vehicles at 31 December 1996): Passenger cars 124,909; Buses and coaches 1,363; Goods vehicles 15,260. Source: International Road Federation, *World Road Statistics*.

Shipping: *Merchant fleet* (registered vessels, 31 December 1995): Fishing vessels 830 (displacement 183,651 grt); Passenger ships, tankers and other vessels 158 (displacement 78,420 grt). **1996:** 355 vessels amounting to 217,874 grt. (Source: Lloyd's Register of Shipping, *World Fleet Statistics*.) *International freight traffic* ('000 metric tons, 1994): Goods loaded 1,162; Goods unloaded 1,733.

Civil Aviation (scheduled external Icelandic traffic, '000, 1995): Kilometres flown 19,489, Passenger-kilometres 2,430,000, Cargo ton-kilometres 44,785, Mail ton-kilometres 5,460.

TOURISM

Foreign Visitors by Country of Origin (1995): Denmark 22,512, France 9,142, Germany 36,840, Norway 13,448, Sweden 19,027, UK 17,520, USA 28,633; Total (incl. others) 189,796.

Number of Tourists: 200,835 in 1996.

Receipts from Tourists: 20,755m. krónur in 1996.

COMMUNICATIONS MEDIA

Radio Receivers (1995): 101,000 licensed.

Television Receivers (1995): 97,000 licensed.

Telephones (1995): 148,700 in use.

Telefax Stations (1993): 4,100 in use. (Source: UN, *Statistical Yearbook*.)

Mobile Cellular Telephones (subscribers, 1994): 21,850. (Source: UN, *Statistical Yearbook*.)

Books (production, 1995): 1,522 titles (incl. new editions).

Daily Newspapers (1995): 5 (combined circulation 100,000 copies per issue).

EDUCATION

Institutions (1996): Pre-primary 281; Primary and secondary (lower level) 205; Secondary (higher level) 35; Tertiary (universities and colleges) 14.

Teachers (incl. part-time, 1996): Pre-primary 1,710; Primary and secondary (lower level) 3,549; Secondary (higher level) 1,454; Tertiary 508.

Students (1996): Pre-primary 8,650; Primary 29,082; Secondary (lower level) 13,130; Secondary (higher level) 17,970; Tertiary 7,972.

Source: Ministry of Culture and Education.

Directory

The Constitution

A new Constitution came into force on 17 June 1944, when Iceland declared its full independence. The main provisions of the Constitution are summarized below:

GOVERNMENT

The President is elected for four years by universal suffrage. All those qualified to vote who have reached the age of 35 years are eligible for the Presidency.

Legislative power is jointly vested in the Althing and the President. Executive power is exercised by the President and other governmental authorities in accordance with the Constitution and other laws of the land.

The President summons the Althing every year and determines when the session shall close. The President may adjourn meetings of the Althing but not for more than two weeks nor more than once a year. The President appoints the Ministers and presides over the State Council. The President may be dismissed only if a resolution supported by three-quarters of the Althing is approved by a plebiscite.

The President may dissolve the Althing. Elections must be held within two months and the Althing must reassemble within eight months.

The Althing is composed of 63 members, elected by eight proportionately represented constituencies for a period of four years. Substitute members are elected at the same time and in the same manner as Althing members. Until 1991 the Althing was divided into two houses, the Upper House (efri deild) and the Lower House (nedri deild); but sometimes both Houses worked together as a United Althing. The Upper House consisted of 21 of the members, whom the United Althing chose from among the representatives, the remaining 42 forming the Lower House. Each House and the United Althing elected its own Speaker. In 1991 the two houses were merged to form a unicameral Althing. The minimum voting age, both for local administrative bodies and for the Althing, is 18 years, and all citizens domiciled in Iceland may vote, provided they are considered morally and financially responsible.

Bills must be given three readings in the Althing and be approved by a simple majority before they are submitted to the President. If the President disapproves a bill, it nevertheless becomes valid but must be submitted to a plebiscite. Ministers are responsible to the Althing and may be impeached by that body, in which case they are tried by the Court of Impeachment.

LOCAL GOVERNMENT

For purposes of local government, the country is divided into Provinces, Districts and Municipalities. The eight Urban Municipalities are governed by Town Councils, which possess considerable autonomy. The Districts also have Councils and are further grouped together to form the Provinces, over each of which a centrally appointed Chief Official presides. The franchise for municipal purposes is universal above the age of 18 years, and elections are conducted on a basis of proportional representation.

The Government

HEAD OF STATE

President: ÓLAFUR RAGNAR GRÍMSSON (took office 1 August 1996).

THE CABINET
(February 1998)

A coalition of the Independence Party (IP) and the Progressive Party (PP).

Prime Minister and Minister of the Statistical Bureau of Iceland: DAVÍÐ ODDSSON (IP).

Minister of Foreign Affairs: HALLDÓR ÁSGRÍMSSON (PP).

Minister of Finance: FRIDRIK SOPHUSSON (IP).

Minister of Fisheries, Justice and Ecclesiastical Affairs: THORSTEINN PÁLSSON (IP).

Minister of Agriculture and the Environment: GUDMUNDUR BJARNASON (PP).

Minister of Commerce and Industry: FINNUR INGOLFSSON (PP).

Minister of Education: BJÖRN BJARNASON (IP).

Minister of Social Affairs: PÁLL PETURSSON (PP).

Minister of Communications: HALLDÓR BLÖNDAL (IP).

Minister of Health: INGIBJORG PALMADÓTTIR (PP).

MINISTRIES

Prime Minister's Office: Stjórnarráðshúsið v/Laekjartorg, 150 Reykjavík; tel. 5609400; fax 5624014.

Ministry of Agriculture: Sölvhólsgötu 7, 150 Reykjavík; tel. 5609750; fax 5521160; e-mail bjorn.sigurbjornsson@lan.styr.is.

Ministry of Communications: Hafnarhúsinu við Tryggvagötu, 150 Reykjavík; tel. 5609630; fax 5621702.

Ministry of Education, Science and Culture: Sölvhólsgata 4, 150 Reykjavík; tel. 5609500; fax 5623068.

Ministry for the Environment: Vonarstraeti 4, 150 Reykjavík; tel. 5609600; fax 5624566.

Ministry of Finance: Arnarhváli, 150 Reykjavík; tel. 5609200; fax 5628280.

Ministry of Fisheries: Skúlagata 4, 150 Reykjavík; tel. 5609670; fax 5621853.

Ministry for Foreign Affairs: Rauðarárstíg 25, 150 Reykjavík; tel. 5609900; fax 5622373; e-mail external@utn.stjr.is.

Ministry of Health: Laugavegi 116, 150 Reykjavík; tel. 5609700; fax 5519165.

Ministry of Industry and Commerce: Arnarhváli, 150 Reykjavík; tel. 5609070; telex 2092; fax 5621289.

Ministry of Justice and Ecclesiastical Affairs: Arnarhváli, 150 Reykjavík; tel. 5609010; telex 2224; fax 5527340; e-mail postur@dkm.stjr.ls.

Ministry of Social Affairs: Hafnarhúsinu við Tryggvagötu, 150 Reykjavík; tel. 5609100; fax 5524804; e-mail postur@fel.stjr.is.

President and Legislature

PRESIDENT

Presidential Election, 29 June 1996

	Number of votes cast	% of votes
ÓLAFUR RAGNAR GRÍMSSON	68,370	40.9
PÉTUR K. HAFSTEIN	48,863	29.2
GUÐRÚN AGNARSDÓTTIR	43,578	26.0
ÁSTTHÓR MAGNÚSSON	4,422	2.6

ALTHING

Speaker of the Althing: SALOME THORKELSDÓTTIR.

Secretary-General (Clerk) of the Althing: FRIDRIK ÓLAFSSON.

General Election, 8 April 1995

	% of votes	Seats
Independence Party	37.1	25
Progressive Party	23.3	15
People's Alliance	14.3	9
Social Democratic Party	11.4	7
Awakening of the Nation	7.2	4
Women's Alliance	4.9	3
Others	1.8	—
Total	100.0	63

Political Organizations

Althýdubandalag (People's Alliance—PA): Austurstraeti 10, 101 Reykjavík; tel. 5517500; fax 5517599; f. 1956 by amalgamation of a section of the Social Democratic Party and the Socialist Unity Party, reorganized as a socialist party 1968; twin goals of socialism and national independence; Chair. MARGRÉT FRÍMANNSDÓTTIR; Parliamentary Leader SVAVAR GESTSSON; Gen. Sec. HEIMIR MÁR PÉTURSSON.

Althýduflokkurinn (Social Democratic Party—SDP): Althýduhusid, Hverfisgata 8–10, 101 Reykjavík; tel. 5529244; fax 5629155; f. 1916 with a moderate socialist programme; emphasizes greater equality in the distribution of wealth and income; Chair. JÓN BALDVIN HANNIBALSSON; Parliamentary Leader ÖSSUR SKARPHÉDINSSON.

Framsóknarflokkurinn (Progressive Party—PP): Hverfisgata 33, POB 453, 121 Reykjavík; tel. 5624480; fax 5623325; e-mail framsokn @islandia.is; f. 1916 with a programme of social liberalism and co-operation; Chair. HALLDÓR ÁSGRÍMSSON; Parliamentary Leader VALGERÐUR SVERRISDÓTTIR; Sec.-Gen. EGILL HEIÐAR GÍSLASON.

Samtök um kvennalista (Women's Alliance—WA): Pósthússtraeti 7, 101 Reykjavík; tel. 5513725; fax 5527560; e-mail kvennalis tinn@centrum.is; f. 1983; a non-hierarchical feminist movement to promote the interests of women and children; parliamentary leadership rotates.

Sjálfstaedisflokkurinn (Independence Party—IP): Háaleitisbraut 1, 105 Reykjavík; tel. 5151700; fax 5151717; e-mail xd@xd.is; internet http://www.xd.is; f. 1929 by an amalgamation of the Conservative and Liberal Parties; its programme is social reform within the framework of private enterprise and the furtherance of national and individual independence; Leader DAVÍÐ ODDSSON.

Thjóðvaki (Awakening of the Nation): Hafnarstraeti 7, 101 Reykjavík; tel. 5528100; fax 5627060; f. 1994; founded by dissident mems of the SDP; Leader JÓHANNA SIGURÐARÓTTIR.

Diplomatic Representation

EMBASSIES IN ICELAND

China, People's Republic: Viðimelur 29, POB 580, Reykjavík; telex 2148; Chargé d'affaires: ZHAI SHIXIONG.

Denmark: Hverfisgata 29, 101 Reykjavík; tel. 5621230; telex 2008; fax 5623316; Ambassador: KLAUS OTTO KAPPEL.

Finland: Túngata 30, 101 Reykjavík; tel. 5100100; telex 2373; fax 5623880; e-mail finamb@itn.is; Ambassador: TOM SÖDERMAN.

France: Túngata 22, 101 Reykjavík; tel. 5517621; telex 2063; fax 5628177; Ambassador: ROBERT CANTONI.

Germany: Laufásvegur 31, POB 400, 121 Reykjavík; tel. 5519535; telex 2002; fax 5525699; Ambassador: Dr REINHART W. EHNI.

Norway: Fjólugata 17, Reykjavík; tel. 5513065; fax 5529553; Ambassador: KNUT TARALDSET.

Russia: Garðastraeti 33, Reykjavík; tel. 5515156; telex 2200; fax 5620633; Ambassador: YURII RECHETOV.

Sweden: Box 8136, 128 Reykjavík; tel. 5201230; fax 5201235; e-mail sveamb@itn.is; Ambassador: PAR KETTIS.

United Kingdom: Laufásvegur 31, POB 101, 121 Reykjavík; tel. 5505100; fax 5505105; Ambassador: JAMES MCCULLOCH.

USA: Laufásvegur 21, Reykjavík; tel. 5629100; fax 5629139; Ambassador: DAY OLIN MOUNT.

Judicial System

All cases are heard in Ordinary Courts except those specifically within the jurisdiction of Special Courts. The Ordinary Courts include both a lower division of urban and rural district courts presided over by the district magistrates, and the Supreme Court.

Justices of the Supreme Court are appointed by the President and cannot be dismissed except by the decision of a court. The Justices elect the Chief Justice for a period of two years.

SUPREME COURT

Dómhúsið v. Armarhól, 150 Reykjavík; tel. 5103030; fax 5623995.

Chief Justice: PÉTUR KR. HAFSTEIN.

Justices: ARNLJÓTUR BJÖRNSSON, GUÐRÚN ERLENDSDÓTTIR, GARÐAR GÍSLASON, GUNNLAUGUR CLAESSEN, HJÖRTUR TORFASON, HRAFN BRAGASON, MARKÚS SIGURBJÖRNSSON, HARALDUR HENRYSSON.

Religion

CHRISTIANITY

Protestant Churches

Tjodkirkja Islands: (Evangelical Lutheran Church of Iceland): Biskupsstofa, Laugavegur 31, 150 Reykjavík; tel. 5351500; fax

5513284; the national Church, endowed by the State; more than 90% of the population are members; Iceland forms one diocese, Reykjavík, with two suffragan sees; 284 parishes and 138 pastors; Bishop KARL SIGURBJÖRNSSON.

Fríkirkjan í Reykjavík (The Congregational Church in Reykjavík): POB 1671, 121 Reykjavík; tel. 5514579; fax 5624451; f. 1899; Free Lutheran denomination; 5,500 mems; Head CECIL HARALDSSON.

Óhádi söfnudurinn (Independent Congregation): Reykjavík; Free Lutheran denomination; 1,100 mems; Head Rev. THÓRSTEINN RAGNARSSON.

Seventh-day Adventists: Suðurhlið 36, 105 Reykjavík; tel. 5679260; fax 5689460.

The Roman Catholic Church

Iceland comprises a single diocese, directly responsible to the Holy See. At 31 December 1997 there were an estimated 2,950 adherents in the country (just over 1% of the total population).

Bishop of Reykjavík: Most Rev. Dr JÓHANNES M. GIJSEN, Hávallagötu 14, POB 489, 121 Reykjavík; tel. 5525388; fax 5623878.

The Press

PRINCIPAL DAILIES

Althýdubladid (The Labour Journal): Hverfisgata 8-10, 101 Reykjavík; tel. 5625566; fax 5629244; f. 1919; organ of the Social Democratic Party; Editor HRAFN JÖKULSSON; circ. 4,000.

DV (Dagblaðið): Thverholt 11, POB 5380, 105 Reykjavík; tel. 5505000; fax 5505020; f. 1981; independent; Editor JÓNAS KRISTJÁNSSON; circ. 44,000.

Dagur-Tíminn: Strandgata 31, POB 58, 600 Akureyri; tel. 4606100; fax 4627639; f. 1918, restructured 1996; organ of the Progressive Party; Editor STEFÁN JÓN HAFSTEIN.

Morgunblaðið (Morning News): Kringlan 1, POB 3040, 103 Reykjavík; tel. 5691100; fax 5691181; f. 1913; independent; Editors MATTHÍAS JOHANNESSEN, STYRMIR GUNNARSSON; circ. 53,000.

WEEKLIES

Austri: Tjarnarbraut 19, POB 173, 700 Egilsstaðir; tel. 4711984; e-mail austri@eldhorn.is; local newspaper; f. 1979; Editor JÓN KRISTJÁNSSON; circ. 2,000.

Einherji: Siglufjorður; organ of the Progressive Party.

Fiskifréttir: POB 8820, 128 Reykjavík; tel. 5155500; fax 5155599; f. 1983; weekly; for the fishing industry; Editor GUÐJÓN EINARSSON; circ. 6,000.

Helgarpósturinn (Weekend Post): Borgartúni 27, 101 Reykjavík; tel. 5522211; fax 5522311; f. 1994; independent; Editor PÁLL VILHJÁLMSSON; circ. 10,000.

Íslendingur-Ísafold (Icelander-Icecountry): Kaupangi v/Mýrarveg, 600 Akureyri; tel. 4621500; f. 1915; for North and East Iceland; Editor STEFÁN SIGTRYGGSSON.

Séð & Heyrt: Seljavegur 2, 101 Helsinki; tel. 5155652; fax 5155599; showbusiness and celebrities; Editors BJARNI BRYNJOLFSSON, KRISTJAN THORVALDSSON; circ. 23,000.

Siglfirðingur: Siglufjorður; organ of the Independence Party.

Skagablaðið: Skólabraut 21, 300 Akranesi; tel. 4314222; fax 4314122; f. 1984; local newspaper; Editor SIGURÐUR SVERRISSON; circ. 1,500.

Suðurnesjafréttir: Hafnargötu 28, 230 Keflavík; tel. 4213800; fax 4213802; f. 1992; local newspaper; Editors EMIL PÁLL JÓNSSON, HALLDÓR LEVI BJÖRNSSON; circ. 6,500.

Sunnlenska Fréttablaðið: Austurvegi 1, 800 Selfoss; tel. 4823074; fax 4823084; f. 1991; local newspaper; Editor BJARNI HARÐARSON; circ. 6,300.

Vestfirska Fréttablaðið: Fjarðastraeti 16, 400 Ísafjörður; tel. 4564011; fax 4565225; f. 1975; local newspaper; Editors HLYNUR THÓR MAGNÚSSON, GÍSLI HJARTARSON; circ. 2,000.

Vikublaðið (The Weekly Paper): Austurstraeti 10A, 101 Reykjavík; tel. 5528655; fax 5517599; f. 1992; organ of People's Alliance; Editor FRIÐRIK THÓR GUÐMUNDSSON; circ. 3,000-4,000.

Víkurblaðið: Heðinsbraut 1, 640 Húsavík; tel. 4641780; fax 4641399; f. 1979; local newspaper; Editor JÓHANNES SIGURJÓNSSON; circ. 1,300.

Víkurfréttir: Vallargata 15, 230 Keflavík; tel. 4214717; fax 4212777; f. 1983; local newspaper; Editor PÁLL KETILSSON; circ. 6,400.

OTHER PERIODICALS

Ægir: Glerárgötu 28, 600 Akureyri; tel. 4611541; fax 4611547; f. 1905; published by the Fisheries Association of Iceland in co-operation with Athygli ehf Publishing; monthly; Editors BJARNI KR. GRÍMSSON, JÓHANN ÓLAFUR HALLDÓRSSON; circ. 2,500.

Æskan og ABC (The Youth and ABC): Eiríksgötu 5, 101 Reykjavík; tel. 5510248; fax 5510248; f. 1897; 9 a year; children's magazine; Editor KARL HELGASON.

Atlantica: Höfðabakki 9, 112 Reykjavík; tel. 5675700; fax 5674066; 5 a year; in-flight magazine of Icelandair; Editor HARALDUR J. HAMAR.

AVS (Arkitektur, verktækni og skipulag): Garðastræti 17, 101 Reykjavík; tel. 5616577; fax 5616571; e-mail skipark@centrum.is; f. 1979; 4 a year; architecture and environment; Editor GESTUR ÓLAFSSON; circ. 6,000.

Bændablaðið: POB 7080, 127 Reykjavík; tel. 5630300; fax 5623058; e-mail ath@bl.bondi.is; f. 1995; fortnightly; organ of the Icelandic Agriculture Union; Editor ÁSKELL THÓRISSON; circ. 6,400.

Bíllinn: Myrargata 26, 101 Reykjavík; tel. 5526090; fax 5529490; f. 1982; 3–4 a year; cars and motoring equipment; Editor LEÓ M. JÓNSSON; circ. 4,000.

Bleikt og Blátt: Seljavegur 2, 101 Reykjavík; tel. 5155500; fax 5155599; f. 1989; 6 a year; sex education, communication between men and women; Editor DAVÍÐ THOR JÓNSSON; circ. 11,000.

Economic Statistics: Central Bank of Iceland, Kalkofnsvegur 1, 150 Reykjavík; tel. 5699600; telex 2020; fax 5699608; f. 1980; quarterly; published in English by the Central Bank; circ. 1,550.

Eiðfaxi: Ármúli 38, POB 8133, 128 Reykjavík; tel. 5882525; fax 5882528; e-mail eidfaxi@eidfaxi.is; internet http://www.eidfaxi.is; f. 1977; monthly; horse-breeding and horsemanship; Man. Dir GYÐA GERÐARSDÓTTIR; Editor JENS EINARSSON; circ. 7,000.

Fasteignablaðið: Sídumúli 10, 108 Reykjavík; tel. 5888844; fax 5888843; monthly; real estate; Editor DAVÍÐ JÓNSSON; circ. 60,000.

Fjármálatíðindi: Kalkofnsvegur 1, 150 Reykjavík; tel. 5699600; fax 5699608; 2 a year; economic journal published by the Central Bank; circ. 2,300.

Freyr, búnaðarblað: Baendahöllin við Hagatorg, POB 7080, 127 Reykjavík; tel. 5630300; fax 5623058; monthly; agriculture; Editor MATTHÍAS EGGERTSSON; circ. 2,300.

Frjáls Verslun (Free Trade): Borgartún 23, 105 Reykjavík; tel. 5617575; fax 5618646; f. 1939; 10 a year; business magazine; Editor JÓN G. HAUKSSON; circ. 6,000–9,000.

Gestgjafinn: Seljavegur 2, 101 Reykjavík; tel. 5155500; fax 5155599; e-mail gestgjafinn@frodi.is; f. 1981; 6 a year; food and drink; Editor RUT HELGADÓTTIR; circ. 15,000.

Hagtíðindi (Monthly Statistics): published by the Statistical Bureau of Iceland, Skuggasund 3, 150 Reykjavík; tel. 5609800; fax 5628865; f. 1914; monthly; Dir-Gen. SIGURBORG STEINGRÍMSDÓTTIR; circ. 2,000.

Hagtölur mánaðarins: Kalkofnsvegur 1, 150 Reykjavík; tel. 5699600; fax 5699608; monthly statistical bulletin published by the Central Bank; circ. 1,650.

Hár og Fegurð (Hair and Beauty Magazine): Skúlagata 54, 105 Reykjavík; tel. and fax 5628141; e-mail pmelsted@vortex.is; f. 1980; 3 a year; hair, beauty, fashion; Editor PÉTUR MELSTEÐ.

Heilbrigðismál: Skógarhlíð 8, 105 Reykjavík; tel. 5621414; fax 5621417; f. 1949; quarterly; public health; Editor JÓNAS RAGNARSSON; circ. 6,000.

Heima Er Bezt: Ármuli 23, 108 Reykjavík; tel. 5882400; fax 5888994; f. 1951; monthly; literary; Editor GUÐJÓN BALDVINSSON; circ. 3,500.

Heimsmynd: Aðalstræti 4, 101 Reykjavík; tel. 5622020; fax 5622029; f. 1986; 10 a year; general interest; Editor KARL BIRGISSON; circ. 8,000.

Hús og Híbýli: Seljavegur 2, 101 Reykjavík; tel. 5155500; fax 5155599; e-mail hogh@frodi-is; f. 1978; 8 a year; architecture, family and homes; Editor ELÍN ALBERTSDÓTTIR; circ. 11,000–13,000.

Húsfreyjan (The Housewife): Túngata 14, 101 Reykjavík; tel. 5517044; f. 1950; quarterly; the organ of the Federation of Icelandic Women's Societies; Editor HRAFNHILDUR VALGARÐS; circ. 4,000.

Iceland Review: Höfðabakka 9, 112 Reykjavík; tel. 5675700; fax 5674066; f. 1963; quarterly, in English; general; Editor HARALDUR J. HAMAR.

Innflutningur (Import): Héðinsgata 1-3, 105 Reykjavík; tel. 5813411; fax 5680211; f. 1991; 3–4 a year; Editor SÓLVEIG BALDURSDÓTTIR; circ. 5,000.

Ithróttablaðið: Seljavegur 2, 101 Reykjavík; tel. 5155500; fax 5155599; f. 1939; 6 a year; sport; Editor JÓHANN ARNASON; circ. 6,000.

Lisin að lifa: Hverfisgata 105, 101 Reykjavík; tel. 5528819; fax 5621896; f. 1986; 2 a year; for elderly people; Editor ODDNÝ BJÖRGVINSDÓTTIR; circ. 7,000.

Mannlíf: Seljavegur 2, 101 Reykjavík; tel. 5155555; fax 5155599; f. 1984; 10 a year; general interest; Editors GUÐRÚN KRISTJANSDÓTTIR, KARL TH. BIRGISSON; circ. 16,000.

Myndbönd mánaðarins (Videos of the Month): Ármúli 15, 108 Reykjavík; tel. 5811280; fax 5811286; f. 1993; monthly; Editor GUÐBERGUR ÍSLEIFSSON; circ. 26,000.

News from Iceland: Höfðabakki 9, POB 8576, 112 Reykjavík; tel. 5675700; telex 2121; fax 5674066; f. 1975; monthly; in English; Editor HARALDUR J. HAMAR.

Ný menntamál: Lágmúli 7, 108 Reykjavík; tel. 5531117; e-mail hannes@ismennt.is; f. 1983; quarterly; educational issues; Editor HANNES ÍSBERG; circ. 6,500.

Nýtt Líf: Seljavegur 2, 101 Reykjavík; tel. 5155660; fax 5155599; f. 1978; 10 a year; fashion; Editor GULLVEIG SÆMUNDSDÓTTIR; circ. 13,000–16,000.

Sjávarfréttir: POB 8820, 128 Reykjavík; tel. 5155500; fax 5155599; f. 1973; yearly; ship registry, statistics on Icelandic fisheries; Editor GUÐJÓN EINARSSON; circ. 5,500.

Skutull (Harpoon): Fjarðarstræti 2, 400 Isafjörður; tel. 4563948; fax 4565148; e-mail stapi@isholf.is; f. 1923; monthly; organ of the Social Democratic Party; Editor GÍSLI HJARTARSON.

Stúdentablaðið: Stúdentaheimili v/Hringbraut, 101 Reykjavík; tel. 5621080; fax 5621040; f. 1924; every three weeks; students' interests; Editor MAGNEA HRÖNN ÖRVARSDÓTTIR; circ. 6,000.

Sveitastjórnarmál: Háaleitisbraut 11, 128 Reykjavík; tel. 5813711; fax 5687866; f. 1941; 24 a year; publ. by the Asscn of Icelandic Municipalities: Editor UNNAR STEFÁNSSON; circ. 3,400.

Uppeldi: Bolholt 4, 105 Reykjavík; tel. 5680170; fax 5677215; f. 1988; quarterly; Editor KRISTÍN ELFA GUÐNADÓTTIR; circ. 10,000.

Úrval (Digest): Thverholt 11, 105 Reykjavík; tel. 5632700; fax 5632999; f. 1942; bi-monthly; Editor SIGURÐUR HREIÐARSSON; circ. 6,500.

Veiðimaðurinn (Hunter): Hédinshúsið, Seljavegur 2, 101 Reykjavík; tel. 5155500; fax 5155599; f. 1984; 3 a year; fishing and hunting; Editor GYLFI PÁLSSON; circ. 6,000.

Vera: Posthússtraeti 7, 101 Reykjavík; tel. 5522188; fax 5527560; f. 1982; 6 a year; feminist issues; Editor ELÍSABET THORGEIRSDÓTTIR; circ. 5,000.

Víkingur (Seaman): Borgartún 18, 105 Reykjavík; 10 a year; Editor SIGURJÓN VALDIMARSSON.

Vinnan (Work): Grensásvegur 16A, 108 Reykjavík; tel. 5813044; fax 5680093; e-mail arnar@gsi.is; 14 a year; f. 1943; publ. by Icelandic Federation of Labour; Editor ARNAR GUÐMUNDSSON: circ. 5,000.

NEWS AGENCIES

Foreign Bureaux

Agence France-Presse (AFP): Garðastræti 13, 101 Reykjavík; tel. 5510586; Correspondent GÉRARD LEMARQUIS.

United Press International (UPI) (USA): Reykjavík; tel. 5539816; telex 2121; Correspondent BERNARD SCUDDER.

PRESS ASSOCIATION

Samtök bæjar- og héraðsfréttablaða (Asscn of Local Newspapers): Bæjarhraun 16, 220 Hafnarfjörður; tel. 5651945; fax 5650745; represents 15 newspapers; Pres. FRÍÐA PROPPE.

Publishers

Bifröst: Gimli, Álftanesvegi, 101 Reykjavík; tel. 5659300; fax 5653520; f. 1988; spiritual, self-help; Dir GUÐMUNDUR EINARSSON.

Bókaútgáfa Æskunnar: Eiríksgata 5, 101 Reykjavík; tel. and fax 5510248; Editor KARL HELGASON.

Bókaútgáfan Bjartur: Braeðraborgarstígur 9, 101 Reykjavík; tel. 5621826; fax 5628360; f. 1989; contemporary fiction; Man. Dir SNAEBJÖRN ARNGRÍMSSON.

Bókaútgáfan Björk: Birkivöllum 30, 800 Selfoss; tel. 4821394; fax 4823894; f. 1941; children's; Man. ERLENDUR DANIELSSON.

Fjölvaútgáfan: Njorvasundi 15a, 104 Reykjavík; tel. 5688433; fax 5688142; f. 1966; general; Dir THORSTEINN THORARENSEN.

Forlagið: Laugavegi 18, 101 Reykjavík; tel. 5524240; fax 5623523; f. 1984; general; Dir. JÓHANN PÁLL VALDIMARSSON.

Frjáls fjölmiðlun: Thverholt 11, 105 Reykjavík; tel. 5505000; fax 5632999; f. 1981; fiction in translation, newspapers; Editor SIGURÐUR HREIÐARSSON.

Fródi Ltd: Seljavegur 2, 101 Reykjavík; tel. 5155500; fax 5155599; e-mail frodi@frodi.is; f. 1989; general magazines and books; Man. HALLDÓRA VIKTORSDÓTTIR.; Editor STEINAR LUÐVIKSSON.

Háskólaútgáfan (University Publishing): Háskóli Íslands v/Suðurgötu, 101 Reykjavík; tel. 5254003; fax 5521331; f. 1988; non-fiction, science, culture, history; Man. Dir JÖRUNDUR GUÐMUNDSSON.

Hið íslenska bókmenntafélag: Siðumúli 21, POB 8935, 128 Reykjavík; tel. 5889060; fax 5889095; e-mail hib@islandia.is; internet http://www.arctic.is/hib; f. 1816; general; Pres. SIGURÐUR LÍNDAL; Dir SVERRIR KRISTINSSON.

Hið íslenska Fornritafélag: Siðumúli 21, POB 8935, 128 Reykjavík; tel. 5889060; fax 5889095; e-mail hib@islandia.is; internet http://www.arctic.is/hib; f. 1928; Pres. J. NORDAL.

Hörpuútgáfan: Stekkjarholti 8-10, POB 25, 300 Akranes; tel. 4312860; fax 4313309; Dir BRAGI THORÐARSON.

Iðunn: POB 294, 121 Reykjavík; tel. 5528555; fax 5528380; general; f. 1945; Man. Dir JÓN KARLSSON.

Krydd í tilveruna: Bakkasel 10, 109 Reykjavík; tel. 5575444; fax 5575466; f. 1989; mainly cookery; Dir ANTON ÖRN KJAERNSTED.

Mál og menning (Literary Book Club): Síðumúli 7–9, 108 Reykjavík; tel. 5887755; fax 5623523; f. 1937; 10,000 mems; Man. THÓRHILDUR GARÐARSDÓTTIR; Editor HALLDÓR GUÐMUNDSSON.

Námsgagnastofnun (National Centre for Educational Materials): POB 5020, Reykjavík 125; tel. 5528088; telex 3000; fax 5624137; e-mail simi@nams.is; f. 1979; Dir (Publishing House) ÁSGEIR GUÐMUNDSSON.

Ormstunga: Austurströnd 3, 170 Seltjarnarnes; tel. 5610055; fax 5610025; f. 1994; Icelandic and foreign fiction; Dir GÍSLI MÁR GÍSLASON.

Örn og Örlygur: Dvergshöfði 27, 112 Reykjavík; tel. 5671777; fax 5671240; f. 1966; non-fiction, dictionaries; Man. Dir PÁLL BRAGI KRISTJÓNSSON.

Reykholt: POB 8950, 128 Reykjavík; tel. 5888821; fax 5888380; f. 1987; general; Dir REYNIR JÓHANNSSON.

Setberg: Freyjugata 14, 101 Reykjavík; tel. 5517667; fax 5526640; fiction, cookery, juvenile, picture books, activity books and children's books; Dir ARNBJÖRN KRISTINSSON.

Skálholtsútgáfan: Laugavegur 31, 101 Reykjavík; tel. 5621581; fax 5621595; f. 1981; non-fiction, Christian church; Man. Dir EDDA MÖLLER.

Skjaldborg Ltd: Ármúli 23, POB 8427, 108 Reykjavík; tel. 5882400; fax 5888994; general; Dir BJÖRN EIRÍKSSON.

Sögufélagið: Fischersund 3, 101 Reykjavík; tel. 5514620; non-fiction, history; Dir RAGNHEIÐUR THORLÁKSDÓTTIR.

Vaka-Helgafell Inc: Siðumúli 6, 108 Reykjavík; tel. 5503000; fax 5503033; general reference, fiction, non-fiction; Dir ÓLAFUR RAGNARSSON.

PUBLISHERS' ASSOCIATION

Félag íslenskra bókaútgefenda (Icelandic Publishers' Asscn): Suðurlandsbraut 4A, 108 Reykjavík; tel. 5538020; fax 5888668; f. 1889; Pres. ÓLAFUR RAGNARSSON; Man. VILBORG HARÐARDÓTTIR.

Broadcasting and Communications

TELECOMMUNICATIONS

Iceland Telecom Ltd: Austurvöllur, 150 Reykjavík; tel. 5506000; fax 5506009; e-mail arij@simi.is; administration and operation of telecommunications; also operation of Skyggnir, earth station for satellite telecommunications.

BROADCASTING

Ríkisútvarpið (Icelandic National Broadcasting Service): Broadcasting Centre, Efstaleiti 1, 150 Reykjavík; tel. 5153000; telex 2066; fax 5153010; f. 1930; Dir-Gen. MARKÚS ÖRN ANTONSSON; Chair. of Programme Board GUNNLAUGUR SÆVAR GUNNLAUGSSON.

Radio

Ríkisútvarpið: Radio Division, Efstaleiti 1, 150 Reykjavík; tel. 5153000; fax 5153010; f. 1930.

Programme 1 has two long-wave, three medium-wave and 77 FM transmitters broadcasting 127 hours a week; Head MARGRÉT ODDSDÓTTIR.

Programme 2 has 67 FM transmitters broadcasting 168 hours a week; Head SIGURÐUR G. TÓMASSON.

Aðalstöðin: Aflvakinn hf, Aðalstræti 16, 101 Reykjavík; tel. 5621520; fax 5620044; Head BALDVIN JÓNSSON.

Addís, Addís: Islenskar ævitýraferðir, Álftaland 17, 108 Reykjavík; tel. 5885555; broadcasts only in Reykjanesbær; Head ARNGRÍMUR HERMANNSSON.

Alfa-Omega: Evrópsk fjölmiðlun, Hlaðbae 11, 110 Reykjavík; tel. 5676111; Head EIRÍKUR SIGURBJÖRNSSON.

Brosið: Suðurnesjabrosið hf, Hafnargata 15, 230 Keflavík; tel. 4216300; fax 4216301; broadcasts only in Reykjanesbær; Head RAGNAR ÖRN STEFÁNSSON.

Bylgjan: Lynghάls 5, 110 Reykjavík; tel. 5156300; fax 5156830; privately-owned by Icelandic Broacasting Corpn.

FM 95,7: Útvarp FM hf, Álfabakka 8, 109 Reykjavík; tel. 5870900; fax 5870920; Head BJÖRN Á. ÁRNASON.

Klassík FM: Aflvakinn hf, Aðalstræti 16, 101 Reykjavík; ; tel. 5626033; fax 5620044; Head THORMÓÐUR JÓNSSON.

Lindin: Krókháls 4, 110 Reykjavík; tel. 5671030; e-mail lindin@ lindin.is; Head MICHAEL E. FITZGERALD.

Rás Fás: Fjölbrautarskóli Norðurlands vestra, 550 Sauðárkrókur; Head GUNNAR BÚASON.

Stjarnan: Islenska útvarpsfélagið-Fjölmiðlum hf, Lynghals 5, 110 Reykjavík; Head JÓN ÓLAFSSON.

Útvarp Hafnarfjörður: Köldukinn 2, 220 Hafnarfjörður; tel. 5651766; fax 5651796; broadcasts only in Hafnarfjörður; Head HALLDÓR ÁRNI SVEINSSON.

Útvarp Húsavík: Ketilsbraut 9, 640 Húsavík; tel 4642277; broadcasts only in Húsavík; Head EINAR BJÖRNSSON.

Útvarp Kántrýbær: Brimnes, 545 Skagaströnd; tel. 4522960; e-mail kantrybar@islandia.is; broadcasts only in Skagaströnd; Head HALLBJÖRN J. HJARTARSON.

Útvarp Vestmannaeyjar: Brekkugata 1, 900 Vestmannaeyjar; tel. 4811534; broadcasts only in Vestmannaeyjar; Head BJARNI JÓNASSON.

Xið: Aflvakinn hf, Aðalstræti 16, 101 Reykjavík; tel. 5626977; fax 5620044; Head THORMÓÐUR JÓNSSON.

Vila-Árna Útvarp: Skipholt 6, 355 Ólafsvík; tel. 4361334; fax 4361379; Head VILHELM ÁRNASON.

Television

Ríkisútvarpið—Sjónvarp (Icelandic National Broadcasting Service—Television): Laugavegur 176, 105 Reykjavík; tel. 5153900; telex 2035; fax 5153988; e-mail istv@ruv.is; f. 1966; covers 99% of the population; broadcasts daily, total 62 hours a week; Dir of Television BJARNI GUÐMUNDSSON.

Aksjón ehf: Kaupvangsstræti 23, 600 Akureyri; tel. 4612355; fax 4612356; broadcasts only in Akureyri; Head GÍSLI GUNNLAUGSSON.

Fjölsýn: Strandvegur 47, 900 Vestmannaeyjar; tel. 4811300; fax 4812643; e-mail siglt@eyjar.is; broadcasts only in Vestmannaeyjar; Head ÓMAR GUÐMUNDSSON.

Íslenska Útvarpsfélagið hf (Icelandic Broadcasting Corporation): Channel 2 and TV SYN; Lynghalsi 5, 110 Reykjavík; tel. 5156000; fax 5156830; f. 1986; privately-owned 'pay-TV' station; Pres. JÓN ÓLAFFSSON.

Norðurljós: Húsvísk fjölmiðlun hf, Héðinsbraut 1, 640 Húsavík; tel. 4641780; fax 4641785; broadcasts only in Húsavík; Head ÓMAR GUÐMUNDSSON.

Omega: Kristniboðskirkjan, POB 3340, 123 Reykjavík; tel. 5683131; broadcasts only in Reykjavík; religious; Head EIRÍKUR R. SIGURBJÖRNSSON.

S.j.ó.l: Sjónvarp Ólafsfjörður, Ólafsvegur 28, 625 Ólafsfjörður; tel 4662111; broadcasts only in Ólafsfjörður; Head SKÚLI PÁLSSON.

Sjónvarp Hafnarfjarðar: Hafnfirsk fjölmiðlun hf, Bæjarhraun 16, 220 Hafnarfjörður; tel. 5651796; broadcasts only in Hafnarfjörður; Head HALLDÓR ÁRNI SVEINSSON.

Stöð 3: Íslenska Sjónvarpið hf, Kringlan 7, 103 Reykjavík; tel. 5335600; fax 5335699; f. 1996; Head MAGNÚS KRISTJÁNSSON.

Villa Video: Skipholt 6, 335 Ólafsvík; tel. 4361563; fax 4361379; broadcasts only in Ólafsvík; Head VILHELM ÁRNASON.

The US Navy operates a radio station (24 hours a day), and a cable television service (80 hours a week), on the NATO base at Keflavík.

Finance

(cap. = capital; p.u. = paid up; res = reserves; dep. = deposits; m. = million; kr = krónur; brs = branches)

BANKING

Since the 1980s Iceland's banking and finance system has undergone substantial transformation. In 1989–90 the number of commercial banks was reduced from seven to three, by amalgamating four banks to form Íslandsbanki as the only remaining major commercial bank in private ownership. The 31 savings banks operate a commercial bank, Icebank, which functions as a central banking institution. In January 1995 full liberalization of foreign exchange regulations on the long-term movement of capital was realized. (The deregulation was undertaken to achieve compatibility with the internal market of the EU.) In 1995 the commercial banks made a combined profit of 709m. krónur (compared with 418m. krónur in 1994). In the same year the savings banks registered a profit of 560m. krónur (330m. krónur in 1994).

Central Bank

Seðlabanki Íslands (Central Bank of Iceland): Kalkofnsvegur 1, 150 Reykjavík; tel. 5699600; telex 2020; fax 5699605; e-mail sedlab anki@sedlabanki.is; f. 1961 to take over central banking activities of Landsbanki Íslands; cap. and res 13,742m. kr, dep. 32,846m. kr (1994); Chair. of Bd. of Govs BIRGIR ÍSL. GUNNARSSON.

Commercial Banks

Búnaðarbanki Íslands (Agricultural Bank of Iceland): Austurstraeti 5, 155 Reykjavík; tel. 5256000; telex 2383; fax 5256189; f. 1929; independent state-owned bank; cap. 4,184.4m. kr, dep. 47,156.8m. kr (Dec. 1996); Chair. PÁLMI JÓNSSON; Man. Dirs STEFÁN PÁLSSON, JÓN ADÓLF GUÐJÓNSSON, SÓLON R. SIGURÐSSON; 35 brs.

Íslandsbanki hf: Kirkjusandur, 155 Reykjavík; tel. 5608000; telex 2047; fax 5608522; f. 1990 by merger of four banks; cap. 3,879m. kr, res 797m. kr, dep. 62,111m. kr (Dec. 1996); Chair. KRISTJÁN RAGNARSSON; Group Man. Dir VALUR VALSSON; 32 brs.

Landsbanki Íslands (National Bank of Iceland): Austurstraeti 11, 101 Reykjavík; tel. 5606600; telex 2030; fax 5529882; f. 1885; state-owned; acquired Co-operative Bank (Samvinnubanki Íslands, f. 1962) in 1990; cap. and res 6,594m. kr, dep. 97,060m. (Dec. 1996); Man. Dirs BJÖRGVIN VILMUNDARSON (Chair. Man. Bd), HALLDÓR GUDBJARNARSON, SVERRIR HERMANNSSON; 60 brs.

Savings Bank

Icebank Ltd (Sparisjódabanki Íslands hf): Rauðarárstígur 27, POB 5220, 125 Reykjavík; tel. 5404000; telex 3157; fax 5404001; f. 1986; central bank of the 30 Icelandic savings banks and wholly owned by them; cap. and res 572.5m. kr, dep. 9,739.9m. kr (Dec. 1996); Chair. HALLGRÍMUR JÓNSSON; Man. Dir SIGURÐUR HAFSTEIN; 51 brs.

INSURANCE

Tryggingastofnun Ríkisins (State Social Security Institution): Laugavegi 114, 150 Reykjavík; tel. 5604400; fax 5624535; f. 1936; Man. Dir KARL STEINAR GUÐNASON; Chair. of Tryggingaráð (Social Security Board) BOLLI HÉÐINSSON.

Private Companies

Iceland Insurance Co Ltd: Ármúla 3, 108 Reykjavík; tel. 5605060; fax 5605100; e-mail info@vis.is; f. 1989; Chair. KJARTAN GUNNARSSON; Man. Dir AXEL GÍSLASON.

Íslensk Endurtrygging hf (Icelandic Reinsurance Co Ltd): Suðurlandsbraut 6, 108 Reykjavík; tel. 5331200; fax 5331201; f. 1939; cap. 404.0m. kr (1996); Gen. Man. BJARNI THORDARSON.

Samábyrgð Íslands á fiskiskipum (Icelandic Mutual Fishing Craft Insurance): Lágmúli 9, 108 Reykjavík; tel. 5681400; telex 3163; fax 5584645; f. 1909; Man. Dir PÁLL SIGURÐSSON.

Sjóvá-Almennar tryggingar hf (Marine-General Insurance Co): Kringlan 5, POB 3200, 123 Reykjavík; tel. 5692500; telex 2051; fax 5813718; f. 1988; all branches except life; share cap. 305m. kr, res 6,884m. kr; Chair. BENEDIKT SVEINSSON; Gen. Mans EINAR SVEINSSON, ÓLAFUR B. THORS.

Supervisory Authority

Vátryggingaeftirlitið: Suðurlandsbraut 6, 108 Reykjavík; tel. 5685188; fax 5685253; f. 1974; Man. Dir ERLENDUR LÁRUSSON.

Trade and Industry

GOVERNMENT AGENCIES

Orkustofnun (National Energy Authority): Grensásvegi 9, 108 Reykjavík; f. 1967; advises the Minister of Industry on matters concerning energy; studies Icelandic energy resources and energy uses.

Trade Council of Iceland: POB 1000, 121 Reykjavík; tel. 5114000; fax 5114040; provides information on Icelandic exporters and products; Man. Dir JÓN ÁSBERGSSON.

DEVELOPMENT ORGANIZATIONS

Iðnlánasjóður (Industrial Loan Fund): Ármúla 13A, 155 Reykjavík; tel. 5886400; fax 5886420; f. 1935; independent public entity; makes loans for investment in industry.

Iðn Thróunarsjóður (Industrial Development Fund): Kalkofnsvegur 1, 150 Reykjavík; tel. 5699990; telex 2020; fax 5629992; provides finance for industrial investment; grants medium-term and long-term loans to profitable companies.

CHAMBER OF COMMERCE

Verzlunarrád Íslands (Iceland Chamber of Commerce); Hús verslunarinnar, 103 Reykjavík; tel. 5886666; telex 2316; fax 5686564; e-mail mottaka@chamber.is; f. 1917; Chair. KOLBEINN KRISTINSSON; Gen. Sec. VILHJÁLMUR EGILSSON; 370 mems.

INDUSTRIAL AND TRADE ASSOCIATIONS

Fiskifélag Íslands (Fisheries Association): Reykjavík; tel. 5510500; fax 5527969; f. 1911; conducts technical and economic research and services for fishing vessels and for fishing industry, collecting statistics and data of fishing and fish industries; Man. BJARNI KR. GRÍMSSON.

Fiskveiðasjóður Íslands (Fisheries Investment Fund of Iceland): Suðurlandsbraut 4, 155 Reykjavík; tel. 5889100; fax 5689588; f. 1905; lends money for construction and purchase of fishing vessels, equipment and plant; financed by interest charges; loans granted 2,595m. kr (1993); Chair. BJÖRGVIN VILMUNDARSON; Man. Dir MÁR ELÍSSON.

Landssamband Íslenzkra Utvegsmanna (Fishing Vessel Owners' Federation): POB 893, Reykjavík; tel. 5529500; fax 5516056; f. 1939; Chair. K. RAGNARSSON; Man. KRISTJAN RAGNARSSON.

SÍF Ltd (Union of Icelandic Fish Producers Ltd): Fjarðargata 13–15, POB 20, 222 Hafnarfjörður; tel. 5508000; fax 5508001; e-mail sif@sif.is; f. 1932; exporting salted fish and fish products; Gen. Man. GUNNAR ÖRN KRISTJÁNSSON.

EMPLOYERS' ORGANIZATIONS

Samtök Iðnaðarins (Federation of Icelandic Industries—FII): Hallveigarstig 1, POB 1450, 121 Reykjavík; tel. 5115555; fax 5115566; f. 1993 by merger of Federation of Icelandic Industries (f. 1933), Federation of Icelandic Crafts and Industries (f. 1932) and four other employers' organizations; Chair. HARALDUR SUMARLIDASON; Gen. Man SVEINN HANNESSON; 2,500 mems.

Vinnuveitendasamband Íslands (Confederation of Icelandic Employers): Garðastraeti 41, POB 520, 121 Reykjavík; tel. 5115000; fax 5115050; e-mail jg@vsi.is; f. 1934; Chair. ÓLAFUR B. ÓLAFSSON; Man. Dir THORARINN V. THORARINSSON.

UTILITIES

Electricity

Landsvirkjun (National Power Company): Háaleitisbraut 68, 103 Reykjavík; f. 1965, generates, transmits, sells and distributes electric power wholesale to public distribution systems and industrial enterprises.

Orkubú Vestfjarda (Vestfjords Power Company): Stakkanesi 1, 400 Isafjördur; f. 1977; produces, distributes and sells electrical energy in the Vestfjords area; 70 employees.

Rafmagnsveitur Ríkisins—RARIK (State Electric Power Works): Langavegi 118, 105 Reykjavík; f. 1947; produces, distributes and sells electrical energy.

Water

Hitaveita Suðurnesja (Suðurnes Regional Heating Corpn): Brekkustíg 36, POB 225, 260 Nardvík; f. 1974; produces and distributes hot-water heating and electricity for the Suðurnes region; 70 employees (1992).

TRADE UNIONS

Althýðusamband Íslands (ASÍ) (Icelandic Federation of Labour): Grensásvegi 16A, POB 8720, 128 Reykjavík; tel. 5813044; fax 5680093; e-mail skrifst@asi.is; f. 1916; affiliated to ICFTU, the European Trade Union Confederation and the Council of Nordic Trade Unions; Chair. GRÉTAR THORSTEINSSON; Gen. Sec. ARI SKÚLASON; 65,000 mems.

Menningar- og Fraeðslusamband Althýðu (MFA) (Workers' Educational Association): Grensásveg 16A, 108 Reykjavík; tel. 5331818; fax 5331819; e-mail mfa@asi.is; Chair. THÓRUNN SVEINBJÖRNSDÓTTIR; Gen. Sec. SNORRI S. KONRÁÐSSON.

Bandalag Starfsmanna Ríkis og Baeja (BSRB) (Municipal and Government Employees' Association): Grettisgötu 89, 105 Reykjavík; tel. 5626688; fax 5629106; e-mail bsrb@tv.is; f. 1942; Chair. ÖGMUNDUR JÓNASSON; 16,855 mems.

Blaðamannafélag Íslands (Union of Icelandic Journalists): Síðumúla 23, Reykjavík; tel. 5539155; fax 5539177; f. 1897; Chair. LUDVÍK GEIRSSON; Sec. FRÍÐA BJÖRNSDÓTTIR; 400 mems.

Transport

RAILWAYS

There are no railways in Iceland.

ROADS

Much of the interior is uninhabited and the main road follows the coastline. Regular motor coach services link the main settlements. At 31 December 1996 Iceland had 10,530 km of roads, of which 4,070 km were main roads.

Bifreiðastöð Íslands hf (BSÍ) (Iceland Motor Coach Service): Umferðarmiðstöðinni, Vatnsmýrarveg 10, 101 Reykjavík; tel. 5522300; fax 5529973; f. 1936; 45 scheduled bus lines throughout Iceland; also operates sightseeing tours and excursions; Chair. ÓSKAR SIGURJÓNSSON; Man. Dir GUNNAR SVEINSSON.

SHIPPING

Heavy freight is carried by coastal shipping. The principal seaport for international shipping is Reykjavík.

Port Authority

Port of Reykyavík: Hafnarhusi, Tryggvagotu 17, 121 Reykyavík; tel. 5528211; fax 5528990; e-mail rhofn@centrum.is; Harbour Master HORDUR THORHALLSSON.

Principal Companies

Eimskip (Iceland Steamship Co): POB 220, Pósthússtraeti 2, 101 Reykjavík; tel. 5257000; telex 2022; fax 5257009; e-mail mottaka@eimskip.is; f. 1914 as Eimskipafélag Íslands; transportation service incl. liner trade, general and bulk cargo between Iceland and the UK, Scandinavia, the Baltic, the rest of Europe and the USA; also operates coastal services, warehousing and stevedores; Man. Dir HÖRÐUR SIGURGESTSSON.

Nesskip hf: Nesskip's House, Austurströnd 1, 170 Seltjarnarnes; tel. 5625055; telex 2256; fax 5612052; f. 1974; bulk cargo shipping services to the USA, Canada, Russia, Scandinavia, the Baltic countries and other parts of Europe; Chair. E. SVEINSSON; Man. Dir G. ÁSGEIRSSON.

Samskip hf: Holtabakki v/Holtaveg, 104 Reykjavík; tel. 5698300; telex 2101; fax 5698327; services to Europe, USA, and the Far East; Dir ÓLAFUR ÓLAFSSON.

CIVIL AVIATION

Air transport is particularly important to Iceland and is used both for the transport of people and to transport agricultural produce from remote districts. More than 90% of passenger traffic between Iceland and other countries is by air. There are regular air services between Reykjavík and outlying townships. There is an international airport at Keflavík, 47 km from Reykjavík.

Icelandair (Flugleiðir hf): Reykjavík Airport, 101 Reykjavík; tel. 5050300; telex 2021; fax 5050391; f. 1973 as the holding company for the two principal Icelandic airlines, Flugfélag Íslands (f. 1937) and Loftleiðir (f. 1944); in 1979 all licences, permits and authorizations previously held by Flugfélag Íslands and Loftleiðir were transferred to it; network centred in Reykjavík, to nine domestic airfields, and scheduled external services to more than 20 international destinations in northern Europe and the USA; Pres. and CEO SIGURÐUR HELGASON.

Tourism

Iceland's main attraction for tourists lies in the ruggedness of the interior, with its geysers and thermal springs. In 1996 there were 200,835 tourist arrivals, an increase of 5.8% compared with 1995. Receipts totalled 20,755m. krónur in 1996.

Iceland Tourist Board: Laekjargata 3, 101 Reykjavík; tel. 5527488; telex 3169; fax 5624749; Gen. Man. MAGNÚS ODDSSON.

INDIA

Introductory Survey

Location, Climate, Language, Religion, Flag, Capital

The Republic of India forms a natural sub-continent, with the Himalaya mountain range to the north. Two sections of the Indian Ocean—the Arabian Sea and the Bay of Bengal—lie to the west and east, respectively. India's neighbours are Tibet (the Xizang Autonomous Region of the People's Republic of China), Bhutan and Nepal to the north, Pakistan to the north-west and Myanmar (formerly Burma) to the north-east, while Bangladesh is surrounded by Indian territory except for a short frontier with Myanmar in the east. Near India's southern tip, across the Palk Strait, is Sri Lanka. India's climate ranges from temperate to tropical, with an average summer temperature on the plains of approximately 27°C (85°F). Annual rainfall varies widely, but the summer monsoon brings heavy rain over much of the country in June and July. The official language is Hindi, spoken by about 30% of the population. English is used as an associate language for many official purposes. The Indian Constitution also recognizes 17 regional languages, of which the most widely spoken are Telugu, Bengali, Marathi, Tamil, Urdu and Gujarati. In addition, many other local languages are used. According to the 1981 census, about 80% of the population are Hindus and 11% Muslims. There are also Christians, Sikhs, Buddhists, Jains and other minorities. The national flag (proportions 3 by 2) has three equal horizontal stripes, of saffron, white and green, with the Dharma Chakra (Wheel of the Law), in blue, in the centre of the white stripe. The capital is New Delhi.

Recent History

After a prolonged struggle against British colonial rule, India became independent, within the Commonwealth, on 15 August 1947. The United Kingdom's Indian Empire was partitioned, broadly on a religious basis, between India and Pakistan. The principal nationalist movement that had opposed British rule was the Indian National Congress (later known as the Congress Party). At independence the Congress leader, Jawaharlal Nehru, became India's first Prime Minister. Sectarian violence, the movement of 12m. refugees, the integration of the former princely states into the Indian federal structure and a territorial dispute with Pakistan over Kashmir presented major problems to the new Government.

India became independent as a dominion, with the British monarch as Head of State, represented by an appointed Governor-General. In November 1949, however, the Constituent Assembly approved a republican Constitution, providing for a president (with mainly ceremonial functions) as head of state. Accordingly, India became a republic on 26 January 1950, although remaining a member of the Commonwealth. France transferred sovereignty of Chandernagore to India in May 1950, and ceded its four remaining Indian settlements in 1954.

The lack of effective opposition to Congress policies expedited industrialization and social reform. In December 1961 Indian forces overran the Portuguese territories of Goa, Daman and Diu, which were immediately annexed by India. Border disputes with the People's Republic of China escalated into a brief military conflict in 1962. Nehru died in May 1964 and was succeeded by Lal Bahadur Shastri. India and Pakistan fought a second war over Kashmir in 1965. Following mediation by the USSR, Shastri and President Ayub Khan of Pakistan signed a joint declaration, aimed at a peaceful settlement of the Kashmir dispute, on 10 January 1966. Shastri died on the following day, however, and Nehru's daughter, Indira Gandhi, became Prime Minister.

Following the presidential election of August 1969, when two factions of Congress supported different candidates, the success of Indira Gandhi's candidate split the party. The Organization (Opposition) Congress, led by Morarji Desai, emerged in November, but at the next general election to the lower house of the legislature, the Lok Sabha (House of the People), held in March 1971, Indira Gandhi's wing of Congress won 350 of the 515 elective seats.

Border incidents led to a 12-day war with Pakistan in December 1971. The Indian army rapidly occupied East Pakistan, which India recognized as the independent state of Bangladesh. Indira Gandhi and President Zulfikar Ali Bhutto of Pakistan held a summit conference at Simla in June–July 1972, when the two leaders agreed that their respective forces should respect the cease-fire line in Kashmir, and that India and Pakistan should resolve their differences through bilateral negotiations or other peaceful means. In 1975 the former protectorate of Sikkim became the 22nd state of the Indian Union, leading to tensions in India's relations with Nepal.

A general election to the Lok Sabha was held in March 1977, when the number of elective seats was increased to 542. The election resulted in victory for the Janata (People's) Party, chaired by Morarji Desai, who became Prime Minister. The Janata Party and an allied party, the Congress for Democracy, together won 298 of the 540 seats where polling took place. Congress obtained 153 seats. In January 1978 Indira Gandhi became leader of a new breakaway political group, the Congress (Indira) Party, known as Congress (I).

In 1979 the Government's ineffectual approach to domestic problems provoked a wave of defections by Lok Sabha members of the Janata Party. Many joined Raj Narain, who formed a new party, the Lok Dal, the policies of which were based on secularism. Congress (I) lost its position as official opposition party after defections from its ranks to the then official Congress Party by members who objected to Indira Gandhi's authoritarianism. The resignation of Desai's Government in July was followed by the resignation from the Janata Party of Charan Singh, who became the leader of the Lok Dal and, shortly afterwards, Prime Minister in a coalition with both Congress parties. When Congress (I) withdrew its support, Singh's 24-day administration collapsed, and Parliament was dissolved. A general election to the Lok Sabha was held in January 1980. Congress (I) received 42.7% of the total votes and won an overwhelming majority (352) of the elective seats. The Janata Party won only 31 seats, while the Lok Dal won 41 seats. Indira Gandhi was reinstated as Prime Minister. Presidential rule was imposed in nine states, hitherto governed by opposition parties, in February. At elections to state assemblies in June, Congress (I) won majorities in eight of them.

By-elections in June 1981 for the Lok Sabha and state assemblies were notable because of the landslide victory that Rajiv Gandhi, the Prime Minister's son, obtained in the former constituency of his late brother (killed in an air crash in 1980) and because of the failure of the fragmented Janata Party to win any seats. In February 1983 Rajiv Gandhi became a General Secretary of Congress (I).

Indira Gandhi's Government faced serious problems, as disturbances in several states continued in 1982 and 1983, with violent protests against the presence of Bengali immigrants. Presidential rule in Assam was replaced by a Congress (I) government in February 1982, and further elections were held in Assam (and Meghalaya) in February 1983, amid scenes of intercommunal violence. Election defeats in Andhra Pradesh, Karnataka and Tripura represented a series of set-backs for Indira Gandhi. Disturbances occurred in Jammu and Kashmir during local elections in 1983 and 1984. Alleged police corruption and the resurgence of caste violence (notably in Bihar and Gujarat) caused further problems for the Government.

There was also unrest in the Sikh community of Punjab, despite the election to the Indian presidency in July 1982 of Giani Zail Singh, the first Sikh to hold the position. Demands were made for greater religious recognition, for the settlement of grievances over land and water rights, and over the sharing of the state capital at Chandigarh with Haryana; in addition, a minority called for the creation of a separate Sikh state ('Khalistan'). In October 1983 the state was brought under presidential rule. However, the violence continued, and followers of an extremist Sikh leader, Jarnail Singh Bhindranwale, established a terrorist stronghold inside the Golden Temple (the Sikh holy shrine) at Amritsar. The Government sent in troops to dislodge the terrorists and the assault resulted in the death of Bhindranwale and hundreds of his supporters, and serious damage to sacred buildings. A curfew was imposed, and army personnel blockaded Amritsar.

In October 1984 Indira Gandhi was assassinated by militant Sikh members of her personal guard. Her son, Rajiv Gandhi, was immediately sworn in as Prime Minister, despite his lack of previous ministerial experience. The widespread communal violence that erupted throughout India, resulting in more than 2,000 deaths, was curbed by the prompt action of the Government. Congress (I) achieved a decisive victory in elections to the Lok Sabha in December. Including the results of the January 1985 polling, the party received 49.2% of the total votes and won 403 of the 513 contested seats. Rajiv Gandhi pledged to continue the majority of his mother's policies. At the state assembly elections in March, however, Congress (I) performed less well than expected.

In February 1986 there were mass demonstrations and strikes throughout India in protest at government-imposed increases in the prices of basic commodities. The opposition parties united against Rajiv Gandhi's policies, and Congress (I) suffered considerable reversals in the indirect elections to the upper house of the legislature, the Rajya Sabha (Council of States) in March. In April Rajiv Gandhi expelled one senior member and suspended three others from Congress (I), in an attempt to purge the party of critics calling themselves 'Indira Gandhi loyalists'. In a major government reorganization the Prime Minister appointed Sikhs to two senior positions. Rajiv Gandhi survived an assassination attempt by three Sikhs in October.

In June 1986 Laldenga, the leader of the Mizo National Front (MNF), signed a peace agreement with Rajiv Gandhi, thus ending Mizoram's 25 years of rebellion. The accord granted Mizoram limited autonomy in the drafting of local laws, independent trade with neighbouring foreign countries and a general amnesty for all Mizo rebels. Laldenga led an interim coalition government until February 1987, when the MNF won an absolute majority at elections to the state assembly. In that month Mizoram and Arunachal Pradesh were officially admitted as the 23rd and 24th states of India, and in May the Union Territory of Goa became India's 25th state.

During 1987 Congress (I) experienced serious political setbacks. It sustained defeats in state elections in Kerala, West Bengal and Haryana. Political tensions were intensified by an open dispute between the Prime Minister and the outgoing President, Giani Zail Singh. Public concern was aroused by various accusations of corruption and financial irregularities made against senior figures in Congress (I). Notable among these scandals was the 'Bofors affair', in which large payments were allegedly made to Indian agents by a Swedish company in connection with its sales of munitions to the Indian Government. The Prime Minister denied any involvement, and a committee of inquiry subsequently exonerated him of any impropriety. Five ministers and one deputy minister resigned from the Government, among them the Minister of Defence, Vishwanath Pratap Singh, who was also, with three other senior politicians, expelled from Congress (I) for 'anti-party activities'. V.P. Singh soon emerged as the leader of the Congress (I) dissidents, and in October formed a new political group, the Jan Morcha (People's Front), advocating more radical social change.

In 1988 a more confrontational style was adopted by the central administration towards non-Congress (I) state governments. President's rule was imposed in Tamil Nadu, Nagaland and Mizoram in response to political instability. The opposition forces attained a degree of unity when four major centrist parties, the Indian National Congress (S), the Jan Morcha, the Janata Party and the Lok Dal, and three major regional parties formed a coalition National Front (Rashtriya Morcha), to oppose Congress (I) at the next election. Three of the four centrist parties formed a new political grouping, the Janata Dal (People's Party), which was to work in collaboration with the National Front. V.P. Singh, who was widely regarded as Rajiv Gandhi's closest rival, was elected President of the Janata Dal.

At the general election to the Lok Sabha held in November 1989 throughout the country, apart from Assam, Congress (I) lost its overall majority. Of the 525 contested seats, it won 193, the Janata Dal and its electoral allies in the National Front won 141 and three, respectively, and the right-wing Hindu nationalist Bharatiya Janata Party (BJP) won 88. On 2 December, after the National Front had been promised the support of the communist parties and the BJP, V.P. Singh was sworn in as the new Prime Minister. He appointed Devi Lal, the populist Chief Minister of Haryana and President of Lok Dal (B), as Deputy Prime Minister, and a Kashmiri Muslim, Mufti Mohammed Sayeed, as Minister of Home Affairs. This latter appointment was widely seen as a gesture of reconciliation to the country's Muslims and as reaffirmation of the Government's secular stance. A few weeks later V.P. Singh's Government won a vote of confidence in the Lok Sabha, despite the abstention of all the Congress (I) members. In January 1990 the Government ordered the mass resignation of all the state Governors; the President then appointed new ones. In February elections were held to 10 state assemblies, all formerly controlled by Congress (I). Congress (I) lost power in eight of the 10 assemblies and there was a notable increase in support for the BJP.

In July 1990 Devi Lal was dismissed from his post as Deputy Prime Minister, for nepotism, disloyalty and for making unsubstantiated accusations of corruption against ministerial colleagues. In August there were violent demonstrations in many northern Indian states against the Government's populist decision to implement the recommendations of the 10-year-old Mandal Commission and to raise the quota of government and public-sector jobs reserved for deprived sections of the population. In October the Supreme Court directed the Government to halt temporarily the implementation of the quota scheme, in an attempt to curb the caste violence.

In October 1990 the BJP withdrew its support for the National Front, following the arrest of its President, Lal Krishna Advani, as he led a controversial procession of Hindu devotees to the holy town of Ayodhya, in Uttar Pradesh, to begin the construction of a Hindu temple on the site of a disused ancient mosque. V.P. Singh accused the BJP leader of deliberately inciting intercommunal hatred by exhorting Hindu extremists to join him in illegally tearing down the mosque. Paramilitary troops were sent to Ayodhya, and thousands of Hindu activists were arrested, in an attempt to prevent a Muslim-Hindu confrontation. However, following repeated clashes between police and crowds, Hindu extremists stormed and slightly damaged the mosque and laid siege to it for several days.

In November 1990 one of the Prime Minister's leading rivals in the Janata Dal, Chandra Shekhar (with the support of Devi Lal), formed his own dissident faction, known as the Janata Dal (Socialist) or Janata Dal (S) (which merged with the Janata Party in April 1991 to become the Samajwadi Party). The Lok Sabha convened for a special session, at which the Government overwhelmingly lost a vote of confidence. V.P. Singh immediately resigned, and the President invited Rajiv Gandhi, as leader of the party holding the largest number of seats in the Lok Sabha, to form a new government. Rajiv Gandhi refused the offer, in favour of Chandra Shekhar. Although the strength of the Janata Dal (S) in the Lok Sabha comprised only about 60 deputies, Congress (I) had earlier offered it unconditional parliamentary support. On 10 November 1990 Chandra Shekhar was sworn in as Prime Minister. Devi Lal became Deputy Prime Minister and President of the Janata Dal (S). Shekhar won a vote of confidence in the Lok Sabha and a new Council of Ministers was appointed. Although Shekhar succeeded in initiating talks between the two sides in the Ayodhya dispute, violence between Hindus and Muslims increased throughout India in December.

In January 1991 the Prime Minister imposed direct rule in Tamil Nadu, claiming that this was necessitated by the increased activity of Sri Lankan Tamil militants in the state, which had led to the breakdown of law and order. In the resultant riots more than 1,000 arrests were made. The Government suffered a further set-back in February. Five members of the Council of Ministers were forced to resign when they lost their seats in the Lok Sabha for violating India's anti-defection laws: they had left the Janata Dal to join the Janata Dal (S). The fragility of the parliamentary alliance between the Janata Dal (S) and Congress (I) became apparent in March, when the Congress (I) deputies boycotted Parliament, following the revelation that Rajiv Gandhi's house had been kept under police surveillance. In an unexpected counter-move, Chandra Shekhar resigned, but accepted the President's request that he remain as head of an interim Government until the holding of a fresh general election.

As the general election, which was scheduled to take place over three days in late May 1991, approached, it seemed likely that no party would win an outright majority and that the political stalemate would continue. On 21 May, however, after the first day's polling had taken place, Rajiv Gandhi was assassinated, by members of the Tamil separatist group, the Liberation Tigers of Tamil Eelam (LTTE), while campaigning in Tamil Nadu. Consequently, the remaining elections were postponed until mid-June. The final result gave Congress (I) 227 of the 511 seats contested, the BJP, which almost doubled its share of the vote compared with its performance in the 1989 general election, won 119 seats, and the Janata Dal, the popularity of which had considerably declined, gained only 55 seats. P.V. Narasimha Rao, who had been elected as acting President of Congress (I) following Rajiv Gandhi's assassination, assumed the premiership and appointed a new Council of Ministers. The new Government's main priority on assuming power was to attempt to solve the country's severe economic crisis, caused by an enormous foreign debt, high inflation, a large deficit on the current account of the balance of payments, and an extreme shortage of foreign exchange reserves. The new Minister of Finance, Dr Manmohan Singh (an experienced economist and former Governor of the Reserve Bank of India), launched a far-reaching programme of economic liberalization and reform, including the dismantling of bureaucratic regulations and the encouragement of private and foreign investment. In late September the Government announced that it had decided to adopt the recommendations of the Mandal Commission that 27% of government jobs and institutional places be reserved for certain lower castes, in addition to the 22.5% already reserved for 'untouchable' castes and tribal people. (In November 1992 the Supreme Court ruled that non-Hindus, such as Christians and Sikhs, who were socially disadvantaged were also entitled to job reservations.)

After a brief reconciliatory period in the latter half of 1991, Rao's Government began to be faced with problems, both from opposition agitation and from within its own ranks. In January 1992 the BJP increased communal tension between Hindus and Muslims by hoisting the national flag on Republic Day in Srinagar, the capital of Kashmir (see below). In mid-1992 efforts were also made by the BJP to use the contentious issue of the Ayodhya site (the Ram Janmabhoomi/Babri Masjid—Hindu temple/Muslim mosque—dispute, see above) to embarrass the Government. In May the country was shocked by revelations of a major financial scandal involving the Bombay Stock Exchange. It was alleged that several members of the Council of Ministers were amongst the beneficiaries, allegations that prompted the resignation of the Minister of State for Commerce. In July, however, the Congress (I) candidate, Dr Shankar Dayal Sharma, was elected, with no serious opposition, to the presidency.

Following the collapse of talks in November 1992 between the Vishwa Hindu Parishad (VHP) (World Hindu Council) and the All India Babri Masjid Action Committee regarding the Ayodhya dispute, the VHP and the BJP appealed for volunteers to begin the construction of a Hindu temple on the site of the existing mosque on 6 December. As thousands of Hindu militants assembled in Ayodhya, large numbers of paramilitary troops were dispatched to the town in an attempt to avert any violence. Despite the presence of thousands of troops, however, the temple/mosque complex was stormed by the Hindu volunteers, who proceeded to tear down the remains of the ancient mosque. This highly inflammatory action provoked widespread communal violence throughout India (Bombay, or Mumbai as it was later renamed, being one of the worst-affected areas), which resulted in more than 1,200 deaths, and prompted worldwide condemnation, notably from the neighbouring Islamic states of Pakistan and Bangladesh, where violent anti-Hindu demonstrations were subsequently held. The central Government also strongly condemned the desecration and demolition of the holy building and pledged to rebuild it. The leaders of the BJP, including L. K. Advani and the party's President, Dr Murli Manohar Joshi, and the leaders of the VHP were arrested, the BJP Chief Minister of Uttar Pradesh resigned, the state legislature was dissolved and Uttar Pradesh was placed under President's rule. On 8 December the security forces took full control of Ayodhya, including the disputed complex, meeting with little resistance. A few days later the Government banned five communal organizations, including the VHP and two Muslim groups, on the grounds that they promoted disharmony among different religious communities. Throughout India stringent measures were taken by the security forces to suppress the Hindu/Muslim violence, which lasted for about one week. In mid-December the Government established a commission of inquiry into the events leading to the demolition of the mosque at Ayodhya. In an attempt to avert any further acts of Hindu militancy, the central Government dismissed the BJP administrations in Madhya Pradesh, Rajasthan and Himachal Pradesh and placed these three states under presidential rule. Narasimha Rao's various actions were given implicit approval when on 21 December a motion of no confidence presented by the BJP against the Government was defeated by 334 votes to 106 votes. In late December the Government announced plans to acquire all the disputed areas in Ayodhya. The acquired land would be made available to two trusts which would be responsible for the construction of a new Hindu temple and a new mosque and for the planned development of the site.

There was a resurgence in Hindu/Muslim violence in India's commercial centre, Mumbai, and in Ahmedabad in January 1993, however, necessitating the imposition of curfews and the dispatch of thousands of extra paramilitary troops to curb the serious unrest. In an apparent attempt to restore public confidence in the Government, Rao carried out an extensive reshuffle of the Council of Ministers in mid-January. Despite a government ban on communal rallies, thousands of Hindu militants attempted to converge on the centre of New Delhi to attend a mass rally organized by the BJP on 25 February. In an effort to prevent the proposed rally taking place, thousands of BJP activists were arrested throughout India and the crowds that did gather in the capital were dispersed by the security forces using batons and tear gas. On 12 March there were a number of bomb explosions in Mumbai, which caused about 250 casualties. The Government claimed that the explosions were linked with Pakistan intelligence agencies.

In July 1993 Narasimha Rao narrowly survived (by 14 votes) a vote of no confidence which was moved in the Lok Sabha by virtually all the opposition parties. The following month the Prime Minister suffered a blow to his political prestige when the Government was forced to abandon two proposed bills (aimed at the BJP, in particular), which would have banned political parties from using religious appeals in campaigns. However, in November in the state assembly elections in the four northern states where BJP state administrations had been dismissed by the central Government in December 1992 following the Ayodhya crisis, the BJP regained power in only one state, Rajasthan, while Congress (I) obtained outright majorities in Himachal Pradesh and Madhya Pradesh. These results appeared to highlight a definite decline in the popularity of the Hindu nationalist BJP. In December 1993 Congress (I)'s political standing was strengthened when a small faction of the Janata Dal led by Ajit Singh merged with the ruling party, thus giving the latter a parliamentary majority.

The following year, 1994, was, for the most part, a period of relative political stability. The extensive economic reforms continued to show positive results and Narasimha Rao's premiership appeared fairly secure, with the opposition suffering from fragmentation (particularly the Janata Dal) and with no serious challenges from within Congress (I) itself. In July and August, however, the opposition deputies boycotted parliamentary proceedings for three weeks in protest at what they regarded as lack of effective action following an official inquiry into the 1992 securities scandal in order to understate the involvement of Congress (I) ministers.

The popularity and strength of the ruling Congress (I) appeared to have declined considerably by the end of 1994, when the party suffered crushing defeats in elections to the state assemblies in Andhra Pradesh and Karnataka (former strongholds of Congress (I)); it was also defeated in state elections in Sikkim. In late December the Government's image was enhanced to some extent when three ministers were finally forced to resign over their alleged roles in corruption scandals (the Prime Minister had earlier been reluctant to dismiss them). Shortly afterwards, the Minister for Human Resource Development, Arjun Singh, who was widely viewed as Rao's main rival within Congress (I), resigned from his post, citing his dissatisfaction and frustration at the Government's perceived incompetence regarding corruption, the Bombay Stock Exchange scandal, the Ayodhya crisis and the investigation into Rajiv Gandhi's assassination. In late January 1995, with six crucially important state elections rapidly approaching, Rao attempted to quell increasing dissent within his Government and party by suspending Arjun Singh from the working committee of Congress (I) for 'anti-party activities'; in early February the rebel politician was expelled from the party for six years. In May Singh, together with Narain Dutt Tewari, recruited dissident members of Congress (I) in many states and formed a new breakaway party, known as the All India Indira Congress (Tewari); the party merged with Congress (I), however, in December 1996.

Congress (I) enjoyed mixed results in the state elections held in February/March 1995. In an apparent attempt to bolster his political standing, Rao reshuffled and enlarged the Council of Ministers in mid-September. In January 1996, however, accusations of corruption came to the fore in Indian politics when the Central Bureau of Investigation charged seven leading politicians, including L.K. Advani of the BJP, Devi Lal and Arjun Singh, and sought the prosecution of three Union ministers (who subsequently resigned) for allegedly accepting bribes of large amounts of money from a Delhi-based industrialist, Surendra Jain. The sheer scale of the scandal (known as the Hawala—illegal money transfer—case), with regard to the size of the sums involved and the number of people implicated, led to widespread public disillusionment with politicians in general. The BJP attempted to implicate Rao in the scandal by releasing a purported statement by Surendra Jain alleging that payments were made to the Prime Minister; these accusations were promptly denied by Rao. The Prime Minister was also faced with more serious and potentially more damaging difficulties concerning the prosecution, on charges of cheating and criminal conspiracy, of a flamboyant faith healer and 'godman', Chandraswami, who had been consulted by generations of political leaders, including Rao himself. At the end of January another high-ranking political figure, the President of the Janata Dal, S.R. Bommai, was implicated in the scandal; Bommai subsequently resigned from his post. In February Congress (I)'s hopes of retaining power in the forthcoming general election appeared increasingly fragile when three more ministers resigned from the Council of Ministers after their names had been linked to the Hawala case.

The results of the general election, which was held over three days at the end of April and early May 1996, gave no party or group an overall majority. The largest party in terms of seats was the BJP, which won 160 seats, and with the support of the Shiv Sena and other smaller allies could count on an overall legislative strength of 194 seats. Congress (I) gained 136 seats. The National Front (comprising the Janata Dal and its allies) and Left Front (representing the two major communist parties) together obtained 179 seats, with the remainder won by minor parties and independents. State elections held concurrently in a number of states generally confirmed the national trend. On 15 May, as soon as the electoral position was clear, the President asked the BJP under its new parliamentary leader, Atal Bihari Vajpayee, to form the new Government and to prove its majority within two weeks. Given the antagonism felt towards the BJP by the majority of other political parties, the latter proved impossible, and Vajpayee resigned on 28 May in anticipation of his Government's inevitable defeat in a parliamentary vote of confidence. In the mean time, the National and Left Fronts had merged to form an informal coalition known as the United Front (UF), which comprised a total of 13 parties, with the Janata Dal, the Samajwadi Party, the two communist parties and the regional Dravida Munnetra Kazhagam (DMK) and Telugu Desam as its major components. With Congress (I) prepared to lend external support, the UF was able to form a Government at the end of May. A former Chief Minister of Karnataka, H. D. Deve Gowda, was selected to lead the UF and the new Government. To hold the key finance portfolio the new Prime Minister chose Palaniappan Chidambaram, who had been Minister of State for Commerce under Narasimha Rao and a committed liberalizer. The other major portfolios were distributed on political grounds.

In September 1996 Narasimha Rao resigned from the leadership of Congress (I) after he was ordered to stand trial for his alleged involvement in the Chandraswami case; the party presidency was assumed by the veteran politician, Sitaram Kesri. Later that month separate charges of forgery and criminal conspiracy (dating back to the former Prime Minister's tenure of the external affairs ministry in the 1980s) were made against the beleaguered Rao. In December 1996 Rao resigned as Congress (I)'s parliamentary leader and was replaced in the following month by Sitaram Kesri.

At the end of March 1997 Deve Gowda was faced with a serious political crisis following Congress (I)'s withdrawal of parliamentary support for the UF Government. On 11 April the Prime Minister resigned following the defeat of the UF administration in a vote of confidence (by 158 votes to 292). A few days later Inder Kumar Gujral, the Minister of External Affairs in the outgoing Government, was chosen by the UF to replace Deve Gowda as leader of the coalition. On 22 April Gujral was sworn in as Prime Minister and appointed a new Council of Ministers. In May Sonia Gandhi, the widow of the former Prime Minister Rajiv Gandhi, joined Congress (I) as a 'primary member', and in the following month Sitaram Kesri was re-elected President of the party in Congress (I)'s first contested leadership poll since 1977. In late June 1997 the ruling coalition was faced with another high-level corruption case when the President of the Janata Dal and Chief Minister of Bihar, Laloo Prasad Yadav, was forced to resign from his posts prior to his arrest on several counts of conspiracy in an animal fodder scandal. Yadav subsequently formed a breakaway faction of his party, known as the Rashtriya Janata Dal, and Sharad Yadav was elected as the new President of the Janata Dal. In mid-July Kocheril Raman Narayanan was elected, almost unanimously, as India's new President; this appointment was particularly notable in that Narayanan was the first Indian President to originate from a Dalit (or 'untouchables') background. In late September former Prime Minister Narasimha Rao was charged in a Delhi court with corruption and criminal conspiracy. In the same month a five-year investigation into the destruction of the mosque at Ayodhya in 1992 led to charges of criminal conspiracy and incitement to riot being filed against senior BJP and religious leaders, including L. K. Advani and the leader of Shiv Sena, Balashaheb 'Bal' Thackeray.

The UF Government looked increasingly insecure in late November 1997 when Congress (I) threatened to withdraw its parliamentary support unless the Tamil Nadu-based DMK, which was alleged to be indirectly implicated in the 1991 assassination of Rajiv Gandhi, was expelled from the coalition. Prime Minister Gujral rejected Congress (I)'s demand, and was consequently forced to resign on 28 November when Congress (I) withdrew its support for the Government, as earlier threatened. This constituted the third government collapse in less than two years. In early December President Narayanan dissolved the Lok Sabha following the inability of both Congress (I) and the BJP to form an alternative coalition government. It was announced that Gujral would retain the premiership in an acting capacity pending the holding of a fresh general election in February/March 1998. During December 1997 Congress (I) suffered a series of internal splits and defections in at least six states. In an apparent attempt to halt the fragmentation of the ailing Congress (I), in late December Sonia Gandhi agreed to campaign on behalf of the party in the run-up to the general election. After a low-key start Sonia Gandhi gained in confidence and popularity during the campaign and attracted ever-larger crowds; she steadfastly refused, however, to stand for actual parliamentary office. Sonia Gandhi's deceased husband was, once again, in the forefront of political news at the end of January 1998, when 26 Tamil militants implicated in the murder of Rajiv Gandhi were sentenced to death by a court in Chennai (Madras). In the general election the BJP and its regional allies established themselves as the pre-eminent force in Indian politics. The BJP emerged as the largest party, with 178 of the 545 seats in the Lok Sabha, but failed to win an overall majority. Congress (I) gained 141 seats, and shortly after the election Sonia Gandhi replaced Sitaram Kesri as the party's President. On 15 March President Narayanan appointed the parliamentary leader of the BJP, Atal Bihari Vajpayee (who had briefly held the premiership in mid-1996), as Prime Minister and asked him to form a stable coalition government and to seek a legislative vote of confidence within the next 10 days (see Late Information).

Regional issues have always played and continue to play an important role in Indian political affairs. In 1986 the Gurkhas (of Nepalese stock) in West Bengal launched a campaign for a separate autonomous homeland in the Darjeeling region and the recognition of Nepali as an official language. The violent separatist campaign, led by the Gurkha National Liberation Front (GNLF), was prompted by the eviction of about 10,000 Nepalis from the state of Meghalaya, where the native residents feared that they were becoming outnumbered by immigrants. When violent disturbances and a general strike were organized by the GNLF in June 1987, the central Government agreed to hold tripartite talks with the GNLF's leader, Subhas Ghising, and the Chief Minister of West Bengal. The Prime Minister rejected the GNLF's demand for an autonomous Gurkha state, but Subhas Ghising agreed to the establishment of a semi-autonomous Darjeeling Hill Development Council. Under the formal peace agreement, the GNLF was to cease all agitation and to surrender weapons, while the state government was to release all GNLF detainees. The Government agreed to grant Indian citizenship to all Gurkhas born or domiciled in India. Elections to the Darjeeling Hill Development Council were held in November. The GNLF won 26 of the 28 elective seats (the 14 remaining members of the Council were to be nominated) and Subhas Ghising was elected Chairman of the Council. However, the GNLF continued to demand the establishment of a fully autonomous Gurkha state. In August 1992 a constitutional amendment providing for the recognition of Nepali as an official language was adopted.

In December 1985 an election for the state assembly in Assam was won by the Asom Gana Parishad (AGP) (Assam People's Council), a newly-formed local party. This followed the signing, in August, of an agreement between the central Government and two groups of Hindu activists, concluded after five years of sectarian violence, which limited the voting rights of immigrants (mainly Bangladeshis) to Assam. When the accord was announced, Bangladesh stated that it would not take back Bengali immigrants from Assam and denied that it had allowed illegal refugees to cross its borders into Assam. Another disaffected Indian tribal group, the Bodos of Assam, demanded a separate state of Bodoland within India. In February 1989 the Bodos, under the leadership of the All Bodo Students' Union (ABSU), intensifed their separatist campaign by organizing strikes, bombings and violent demonstrations. The central Government dispatched armed forces to the state. In August the ABSU agreed to hold peace talks with the state government and central government officials. The ABSU agreed to suspend its violent activities, while the Assam government agreed to suspend emergency security measures. The situation became more complicated in 1989, when a militant Maoist group, the United Liberation Front of Assam (ULFA), re-emerged. The ULFA demanded the outright secession of the whole of Assam from India. In 1990 the ULFA claimed responsibility for about 90 assassinations, abductions and bombings. In November, when the violence began to disrupt the state's tea industry, the central Government placed Assam under direct rule, dispatched troops to the state and outlawed the ULFA. By late December the unrest seemed to have been substantially quelled. In the state elections in 1991 the AGP was defeated, and a Congress (I) ministry took power. In September, following the breakdown of prolonged talks with the ULFA, the Government launched a new offensive against the ULFA guerrillas and declared the entire state a disturbed area. The ULFA suffered a serious setback in mid-1992 when a large number of its leading members surrendered to the authorities. Meanwhile, following the suspension of violence by the ABSU, the Bodo Security Force (BSF) assumed the leading role in the violent campaign for a separate state of Bodoland. The separatist campaign was intensified in 1992 with indiscriminate killings, abductions, bomb explosions and large-scale extortion. The BSF was outlawed by the central Government in November 1992. At a tripartite meeting attended by the Minister of State for Home Affairs, the Chief Minister of Assam and the President of the ABSU in Guwahati in February 1993, a memorandum was signed providing for the establishment of a 40-member Bodoland Autonomous Council, which would be responsible for the socio-economic and cultural affairs of the Bodo people. However, attacks leading to substantial loss of life were made by Bodo and ULFA activists in 1994–97 both on the security forces and on non-tribal groups in the area. In October 1997 the central Government banned an Assam militant organization, known as the Bodoland Liberation Tigers Front, for two years; according to the Government, the organization, which had been formed in 1993, was involved in extortion, kidnapping and violent activities. Elsewhere in north-eastern India, violence, both intertribal (particularly against ethnic Bengali settlers) and anti-Government, continued throughout 1997 in Tripura, Bihar, Mizoram, Manipur and Nagaland.

In September 1985 there was a temporary improvement in the unstable situation in Punjab when an election for the state assembly was held, following an agreement between the central Government and the main Sikh party, the Akali Dal. The election was peaceful and resulted in a victory for the Akali Dal, which assumed power after two years of presidential rule. Part of the 1985 agreement was the proposed transfer of Chandigarh, since 1966 the joint capital of Punjab and Haryana, to Punjab alone. In return, Haryana was to benefit from the completion of the Sutlej-Yamuna canal, to bring irrigation water from Punjab to the dry south of the state, and the transfer of several Hindi-speaking border villages from Punjab to Haryana. Four commissions were established to organize the transfer, but all failed, and by early 1998 the transfer had still not taken place. In January 1986 the Sikh extremists re-established a stronghold inside the Golden Temple complex at Amritsar and Hindu–Sikh violence continued throughout the year. In mid-1986 the extremists separated from the ruling moderate Akali Dal (Longowal) and formed several militant factions. In 1987 Rajiv Gandhi reimposed President's rule in Punjab. Despite the resumption of discussions between the Government and the moderate Sikh leaders, the violence continued. In November 1991 more than 50,000 extra troops were deployed in Punjab (bringing the total number of army, paramilitary and police forces in the state to about 200,000) as part of an intensification of operations against Sikh separatists in the run-up to the state elections and parliamentary by-elections which were held in mid-February 1992. Congress (I) won 12 of the 13 parliamentary seats in Punjab and gained an overall majority in the state legislature. The elections, which brought to an end five years of presidential rule, were, however, boycotted by the leading factions of the Akali Dal and attracted an extremely low turnout (only about 22% of the electorate). The Congress (I) state government that was formed under the leadership of Beant Singh, therefore, lacked any real credibility. Despite the continuing violence between the separatists and the security forces, the large turn-out in the municipal elections in September (the first in 13 years) afforded some hope that normality was returning to Punjab. Local council elections, held in January 1993 (the first in 10 years), also attracted a substantial turnout. The security situation improved steadily in the course of 1993 and political activity revived. In late August 1995, however, violence erupted in Punjab again when Beant Singh was killed, along with 12 other people, in a powerful car-bomb explosion detonated by suspected Sikh extremists in Chandigarh. This seemed to have been an isolated act of terrorism, however; the national elections in April/May 1996 were conducted smoothly in the Punjab, and gave the mainstream Akali Dal a convincing victory in the state's parliamentary constituencies. The incumbent Congress (I) administration was routed by an Akali Dal/BJP electoral alliance in state elections held in February 1997; in contrast to the 1992 state elections, turn-out was high, at around 69%.

In December 1986 India and Bangladesh signed an agreement on measures to prevent cross-border terrorism. In September 1988 a joint working committee was established to examine methods of averting the annual devastating floods in the Ganges delta. In late June 1992 the Indian Government, under the provisions of an accord signed with Bangladesh in 1974, formally leased the Tin Bigha Corridor (a small strip of land covering an area of only 1.5 ha) to Bangladesh for 999 years. India maintains sovereignty over the Corridor, but the lease gives Bangladesh access to its enclaves of Dahagram and Angarpota. The transfer of the Corridor occasioned protests from right-wing quarters in India, who have also made an issue over the presence in Delhi and other cities of illegal immigrants from Bangladesh and claim that the Bangladesh Government has done little to protect its Hindu minority. In December 1996 India signed an 'historic' treaty with Bangladesh, which was to be in force for 30 years, regarding the sharing of the Ganges waters.

Relations between India and Nepal deteriorated in 1989, when India decided not to renew the two treaties determining trade and transit, insisting that a common treaty covering both issues be negotiated. Nepal refused, stressing the importance of keeping the treaties separate on the grounds that Indo-Nepalese trade issues are negotiable, whereas the right of transit is a recognized right of land-locked countries. India responded by closing most of the transit points through which Nepal's trade is conducted. The dispute was aggravated by Nepal's acquisition of Chinese-made military equipment which, according to India, violated the Treaty of Peace and Friendship of 1950. However, in June 1990 India and Nepal signed an agreement restoring trade relations and reopening the transit points. Chandra Shekhar visited Kathmandu in February 1991 (the first official visit to Nepal by an Indian Prime Minister since 1977), shortly after it was announced that the first free elections in Nepal were to be held in May. In June 1997 the Indian Prime Minister, Inder Kumar Gujral, made a visit to Nepal and announced the opening of a transit route through north-east India between Nepal and Bangladesh. Gujral and the Nepalese Prime Minister, Lokendra Bahadur Chand, also agreed that there should be a review of the 1950 treaty between the two countries.

Relations with Pakistan had deteriorated in the late 1970s and early 1980s, owing to Pakistan's potential capability for the development of nuclear weapons and as a result of major US deliveries of armaments to Pakistan. The Indian Government believed that such deliveries would upset the balance of power in the region and precipitate an arms race. Pakistan's President, Gen. Mohammad Zia ul-Haq, visited India in 1985, when he and Rajiv Gandhi announced their mutual commitment not to attack each other's nuclear installations and to negotiate the sovereignty of the disputed Siachin glacier region in Kashmir. Pakistan continued to demand a settlement of the Kashmir problem in accordance with earlier UN resolutions, prescribing a plebiscite under the auspices of the UN in the two parts of the state, now divided between India and Pakistan. India argued that the problem should be settled in accordance with the Simla agreement of 1972, which required that all Indo-Pakistani disputes be resolved through bilateral negotiations. The Indian decision to construct a barrage on the River Jhelum in Jammu and Kashmir, in an alleged violation of the 1960 Indus Water Treaty, also created concern in Pakistan. In December 1988 Rajiv Gandhi visited Islamabad for discussions with Pakistan's Prime Minister, Benazir Bhutto. The resulting agreements included a formal pledge not to attack each other's nuclear installations. Relations reached a crisis in late 1989, when the outlawed Jammu and Kashmir Liberation Front (JKLF) and several other militant Muslim groups intensified their campaigns of civil unrest, strikes and terrorism, demanding an independent Kashmir or unification with Pakistan. The Indian Government sent in troops and placed the entire Srinagar valley under curfew. Pakistan denied India's claim that the militants were trained and armed in Pakistan-held Kashmir (known as Azad Kashmir). In January 1990 Jammu and Kashmir was placed under Governor's rule, and in July under President's rule. Tension was eased in December, following discussions between the Ministers of External Affairs of both countries. Violence between the Indian security forces and the militant groups, however, continued during 1991 and 1992. Throughout 1993 and in early 1994, the Government's approach to the Kashmir crisis was a combination of a tough military policy and generally fruitless attempts to engage in dialogue. In December 1994 Pakistan was successful in securing the passage of a resolution condemning reported human rights abuses by Indian security forces in Kashmir at the summit meeting of the Organization of the Islamic Conference (OIC, see p. 224) held in Casablanca, Morocco. (In the same month Pakistan's decision to close down its consulate in Mumbai, amid claims of Indian support for acts of terrorism in Karachi, provided a further indication of the growing rift between the two countries.) By 1996 the total death toll resulting from the disturbances in Jammu and Kashmir, including civilians, security force personnel and militants, was estimated at up to 20,000. The situation in Kashmir improved somewhat , however, when elections for the national parliamentary seats were held in the troubled state shortly after the general election in April/May 1996. There was a reasonably high turn-out, although there were widespread complaints that the security forces had pressurized voters into going to the polling stations. Following the successful holding of elections to the Lok Sabha, state elections were conducted in Jammu and Kashmir in September (the first to be held since 1987) and attracted a turn-out of more than 50%, despite being boycotted by the majority of the separatist groups and being dismissed as a sham by the Pakistani Government. The moderate Jammu and Kashmir National Conference, led by Dr Farooq Abdullah, won the majority of seats in the state assembly, and, on assuming power, immediately offered to instigate talks with the separatist leaders.

Meanwhile, in June 1994 the Indian army had begun to deploy a new missile, named the Prithvi, which has the capacity to reach most of Pakistan. While the 'arms race' between the two countries has continued, with claims on both sides concerning the other's missile programmes, talks (which had been suspended since 1994) were resumed in March 1997, both at official and at ministerial level. Of most significance were the negotiations between India and Parkistan's Foreign Secretaries, which took place in Islamabad in late June. These talks resulted in an agreement to establish a series of working parties to consider groups of issues, which were to be considered separately from each other. One such group of issues specifically related to Jammu and Kashmir. Little progress was made, however, in improving bilateral relations during a further round of high-level talks held in New Delhi in September. Tension increased at the end of the month when a large-scale outbreak of artillery exchanges along the Line of Control resulted in about 40 civilian deaths. The Indian Prime Minister and his Pakistani counterpart kept in contact using a new telephone 'hotline' in an attempt to prevent hostilities from escalating.

Since 1983 India's relations with Sri Lanka have been dominated by conflicts between the island's Sinhalese and Tamil communities, in which India has sought to arbitrate. In July 1987 Rajiv Gandhi and the Sri Lankan President, Junius Jayewardene, signed an accord aimed at settling the conflict. An Indian Peace-Keeping Force (IPKF) was dispatched to Sri Lanka but encountered considerable resistance from the Tamil separatist guerrillas. Following the gradual implementation of the peace accord, the IPKF troops completed their withdrawal at the end of March 1990. Violence flared up again, however, and the flow of Sri Lankan refugees into Tamil Nadu increased considerably. By late 1991 the number of Sri Lankans living in refugee camps in the southern Indian state was estimated at more than 200,000. The assassination of Rajiv Gandhi in May 1991, by members of the LTTE, completed India's disenchantment with the latter organization. Measures were subsequently taken by the state government in Tamil Nadu to suppress LTTE activity within the state, and also to begin the process of repatriating refugees. The repatriation programme (allegedly conducted on a voluntary basis) has proved a slow and difficult process. In May 1992 the LTTE was officially banned in India.

During 1981 there was an improvement in India's relations with the People's Republic of China. Both countries agreed to attempt to find an early solution to their Himalayan border dispute and to seek to normalize relations. China was displeased, however, when, in February 1987, Arunachal Pradesh was granted full statehood, and in that year both sides accused each other of troop concentrations on the disputed frontier and of border violations. A joint working group to negotiate the border dispute met in July 1989. The first meeting of the Sino-Indian joint group on trade was held in September and considerable progress was made in arranging for an expansion of commercial contacts. The joint working group for settlement of the border dispute met again in August 1990, and agreed to a mechanism whereby their military personnel were to meet periodically, to maintain peace in the border region. In February 1991 a major breakthrough occurred when a draft protocol for 1991/92, including the proposed resumption of border trade between the two countries for the first time in three decades, was signed. All six border posts had been closed since the brief border war in 1962. In December 1991 the Chinese Prime Minister, Li Peng, made an official visit to India (the first such visit to India by a Chinese Prime Minister for 31 years), during which a memorandum on the resumption of bilateral border trade was signed. Bilateral border trade was actually resumed between India and China in July 1992. At the fourth meeting of the joint group on trade, held in Beijing in January 1993, a protocol was signed by the two sides, agreeing to open more border posts for trade, to expand the scope of traded commodities and to encourage mutual investment in each other's countries. In December 1994 it was announced that India and China had agreed to hold joint military exercises in 1995 along the border in the Himalayan region of Ladakh. Sino-Indian relations were further strengthened as a result of a three-day visit to India conducted by the Chinese President, Jiang Zemin, in November 1996 (the first visit by a Chinese Head of State to India).

Prior to its disintegration in December 1991, the USSR was a major contributor of economic and military assistance to India. In early 1992 both Russia and Ukraine agreed to maintain arms supplies to India, and in February an Indo-Russian trade and payments protocol was signed. The President of Russia, Boris Yeltsin, made an official visit to India in January 1993, during which he signed an Indo-Russian Treaty of Friendship and Co-operation. In October 1996 India and Russia signed a defence co-operation agreement, and in December India signed a US $1,800m.-contract to purchase 40 fighter aircraft from Russia.

Following the collapse of India's long-time ally the USSR in December 1991, the Indian Government sought to strengthen its ties with the USA. In January 1992 discussions were held between Indian and US officials regarding military co-operation and ambitious joint defence projects. However, the USA remains concerned about the risks of nuclear proliferation in the South Asia region as a whole, and has yet to achieve a mutual understanding with India as regards this issue (India has repeatedly refused to sign the Nuclear Non-Proliferation Treaty). In addition, despite India's recent adoption of a programme of economic liberalization, conflicts over trade and related issues have arisen between the USA and India. During a visit to India by the US Secretary of Defense in January 1995, a 'landmark' agreement on defence and security co-operation was signed by the two countries.

In mid-1996, in a move that provoked widespread international condemnation, India decided not to be party to the Comprehensive Test Ban Treaty, which it had earlier supported, so long as the existing nuclear powers were unwilling to commit themselves to a strict timetable for full nuclear disarmament. This obdurate stance had been adopted and clarified by the Narasimha Rao Government, but was reaffirmed by the new United Front coalition administration, which came to power in May 1996.

Government

India is a federal republic. Legislative power is vested in Parliament, consisting of the President and two Houses. The Council of States (Rajya Sabha) has 245 members, most of whom are indirectly elected by the state assemblies for six years (one-third retiring every two years), the remainder being nominated by the President for six years. The House of the People (Lok Sabha) has 542 elected members, serving for five years (subject to dissolution). A small number of members of the Lok Sabha may be nominated by the President to represent the Anglo-Indian community, while the 542 members are directly elected by universal adult suffrage in single-member constituencies. The President is a constitutional Head of State, elected for five years by an electoral college comprising elected members of both Houses of Parliament and the state legislatures. The President exercises executive power on the advice of the Council of Ministers, which is responsible to Parliament. The President appoints the Prime Minister and, on the latter's recommendation, other ministers.

India contains 25 self-governing states, each with a Governor (appointed by the President for five years), a legislature (elected for five years) and a Council of Ministers headed by the Chief Minister. Bihar, Jammu and Kashmir, Karnataka, Maharashtra and Uttar Pradesh have bicameral legislatures, the other 20 state legislatures being unicameral. Each state has its own legislative, executive and judicial machinery, corresponding to that of the Indian Union. In the event of the failure of constitutional government in a state, presidential rule can be imposed by the Union. There are also six Union Territories and one National Capital Territory, administered by Lieutenant-Governors or Administrators, all of whom are appointed by the President. The Territories of Delhi and Pondicherry also have elected chief ministers and state assemblies.

Defence

At 1 August 1997 the total strength of India's armed forces was 1,145,000: an army of 980,000, a navy of 55,000 and an air force of 110,000. Active paramilitary forces totalled 1,088,000 men, including the 185,000-strong Border Security Force (based mainly in the troubled state of Jammu and Kashmir). Military service is voluntary, but, under the amended Constitution, it is the fundamental duty of every citizen to perform national service when called upon. The proposed defence budget for 1997/98 was estimated at Rs 356,200m. (equivalent to 15.3% of total expenditure).

Economic Affairs

In 1995, according to estimates by the World Bank, India's gross national product (GNP), measured at average 1993–95 prices, was US $319,660m., equivalent to $340 per head. During 1985–95, it was estimated, GNP per head increased, in real terms, at an average annual rate of 3.1%. Over the same period, the population increased by an annual average of 1.9%. India's gross domestic product (GDP) increased, in real terms, by an annual average of 5.1% in 1985–95. Real GDP growth, which had declined to an annual average of about 3.0% in 1991–93 (as a consequence of contractionary macroeconomic stabilization policies), recovered to reach 6.3% in 1994/95, 7.0% in 1995/96 and an estimated 6.8% in 1996/97.

Agriculture (including forestry and fishing) contributed an estimated 27.9% of GDP in 1995/96. About 61.2% of the economically active population were employed in agriculture in 1996. The principal cash crops are cotton (cotton fabrics accounted for an estimated 8.1% of total export earnings in 1995/96), tea, rice, spices and cashew nuts. Coffee and jute production are also important. The average annual growth rate in the output of the agriculture and allied sectors (such as dairy-farming and animal husbandry) was almost 4.0% during 1992–97; agricultural GDP increased by an estimated 5.7% in 1996/97.

Industry (including mining, manufacturing, power and construction) contributed an estimated 26.2% of GDP in 1995/96. About 19.4% of the working population were employed in the industrial sector in 1991. Industrial GDP increased by an annual average of 7.9% during 1992–97; the rate of growth of industrial production fell to less than 5% in 1996/97. In terms of output, India ranks among the 12 leading industrial nations in the world.

Mining contributed an estimated 2.0% of GDP in 1995/96, and employed 0.6% of the working population in 1991. Iron ore and cut diamonds are the major mineral exports. Coal, limestone, zinc and lead are also mined. In 1996 India was the third largest coal producer in the world after the People's Republic of China and the USA. Mining GDP increased by an estimated 8.1% in 1995/96.

Manufacturing contributed an estimated 15.8% of GDP in 1995/96, and employed 10.0% of the working population in 1991. The GDP of the manufacturing sector increased by an annual average of 8.9% during 1992–97, and by 8.0% in 1996/97. In 1992 the most important branches, measured by gross value of output, were food products (accounting for 15.1% of the total), iron and steel (11.2%), textiles (11.1%) and industrial chemicals (8.8%).

Thermal plants account for 74% of total power generation and hydroelectric plants (often dependent on monsoons) for 24%; the remaining 2% is contributed by nuclear power. Imports of mineral fuels, lubricants, etc. comprised 20.5% of the cost of total imports in 1995/96.

The services sector, which is dominated by the growing tourism industry, contributed an estimated 42.1% of GDP in 1995/96, and engaged 20.5% of the economically active population in 1991. The GDP of the services sector increased by an average of 5.7% per year in 1985-95.

In 1995 India recorded a trade deficit of US $6,719m., and there was a deficit of $5,563m. on the current account of the balance of payments. In 1995/96 the principal source of imports (10.5%) and the principal market for exports (17.4%) was the USA. Other major trading partners were Japan, the United Kingdom and Germany. The principal exports in 1995/95 were gems and jewellery, ready-made garments, engineering products, and cotton fabrics. The principal imports were mineral fuels and lubricants, non-electric machinery, pearls, precious and semi-precious stones, and electronic goods.

In the financial year ending 31 March 1997 there was a projected budgetary deficit of Rs 314,749m. In 1993 India secured from its Western aid consortium financial aid commitments totalling US $7,400m. for 1993/94. India's total external debt was $93,766m. at the end of 1995, of which $79,725m. was long-term public debt. In that year the cost of debt-servicing was equivalent to 28.2% of earnings from the exports of goods and services. The average annual rate of inflation was an estimated 10.2% in 1990–96; inflation was expected to fall to about 5%–6% in 1997/98. In rural India the number of people wholly unemployed comprise about 6% of the potential labour force for adult males, but the proportion is around 23% when account is taken of underemployment.

India is a member of the Asian Development Bank (ADB, see p. 110) and of the South Asian Association for Regional Co-operation (SAARC, see p. 263).

The Government of P. V. Narasimha Rao, which came to power in June 1991, recast the entire eighth Five-Year Plan and rescheduled it to cover the period 1992–97 (originally, it was scheduled to cover 1990–95). The main objectives of the Plan, however—namely, economic liberalization, reduction of unemployment and promotion of exports—remained the same. The Gulf crisis, following the invasion and annexation of Kuwait by Iraq in August 1990, and the subsequent outbreak of war between Iraq and the multinational forces in January 1991, had had an extremely adverse effect on the already fragile Indian economy. The price of petrol had risen substantially (a large proportion of India's imports of mineral fuels are provided by Gulf states), the rate of inflation had surged, the balance-of-payments situation had deteriorated, owing partly to the cessation of remittances from Indians working in the Gulf region, foreign debt had grown, foreign exchange reserves had severely depleted and the budget deficit had increased. In an attempt to resolve the economic crisis, a series of reforms was introduced in mid-1991, which were to be instigated with the help of a US $2,300m. stand-by credit from the IMF. The extensive reforms included the virtual abolition of the complex system of licensing in the industrial sector, measures to strengthen competition between the private sector and public enterprises, and a considerable liberalization of foreign investment. By early 1994 the radical economic reform programme had begun to yield positive results: foreign exchange reserves had risen to $13,000m. (by the end of 1994/95 they stood at about $21,000m.), exports had shown a considerable increase, and there had been modest and sustained growths in both the agricultural and industrial sectors. In 1993–94 the Government introduced considerable liberalization of the banking and financial sector, with licences being granted to new private banks and more foreign banks establishing themselves in India, and with the rupee being made fully convertible on the current account in August 1994. In early 1995 the World Bank finalized a $700m.-loan package to help reform India's state-owned banks. Foreign direct investment in the four years to June 1994 totalled Rs 39,430m., compared with just Rs 3,510m. in 1991, when the liberalization programme was begun. In December 1995 the members of SAARC took their first step towards creating a regional trade bloc by launching the SAARC Preferential Trading Arrangement (SAPTA), which provided for tariff reductions on specified items and commodities. India sustained its momentum of economic growth in 1996/97, with an estimated 6.8% rise in GDP (helped by a revival in agricultural output) and increases in domestic savings and investment rates. The 1997/98 budget, which was announced in February 1997, included reductions in personal and corporate taxation, as well as reduced import duties; foreign investors were to be permitted to take stakes of up to 30% in Indian companies (up from 24%); and poverty alleviation measures included greater support for irrigation and fertilizer subsidies and rural housing, and an increase in the provision of agricultural credit.

Social Welfare

Health programmes are primarily the responsibility of the state governments, but the Union Government provides finance for improvements in public health services. The structure of the health system is based on a network of primary health centres. In 1977 there were 5,372 such centres and 37,745 sub-centres in rural areas. In 1984 India had 297,228 physicians (3.9 per 10,000 population), 9,598 dentists, 170,870 nursing personnel and 258,445 midwifery personnel. In 1993 there were an estimated 1,364 people per hospital bed. Various national health programmes aim to combat leprosy, malaria, polio and tuberculosis. Smallpox was declared eradicated in 1977. The family planning programme was launched in 1952 and the emphasis now is on advice and education through Family Welfare Centres. Proposed budgetary expenditure on social services by the central Government in the financial year 1997/98 was 121,042.2m. rupees (4.6% of total government spending).

Education

Education is primarily the responsibility of the individual state governments. Elementary education for children between the ages of six and 14 years of age is theoretically compulsory in all states except Nagaland and Himachal Pradesh. There are facilities for free primary education (lower and upper stages) in all the states. Enrolment at the first level of education in 1995 was equivalent to 100% of children aged six to 10 years (110% of boys; 90% of girls). Secondary enrolment in 1995 was equivalent to 49% of those aged 11 to 17 (59% of boys; 38% of girls). India had a total of 204 universities and institutions with university status in 1994/95, and some 8,613 university and affiliated colleges. University enrolment was 6.1m. in 1996. In 1995, according to UNESCO estimates, the rate of adult illiteracy in India averaged 48.0% (males 34.5%; females 62.3%). Budgetary expenditure on education in 1995/96 was 23,800m. rupees (1.4% of total spending).

Public Holidays

The public holidays observed in India vary locally. The dates given below apply to Delhi. As religious feasts depend on astronomical observations, holidays are usually declared at the beginning of the year in which they will be observed. It is not possible, therefore, to indicate more than the month in which some of the following holidays will occur.

1998: 1 January (New Year's Day), 26 January (Republic Day), 30 January (Id al-Fitr, end of Ramadan), 13 March (Holi), 5 April (Ram Navami), 8 April (Id uz-Zuha, Feast of the Sacrifice), 9 April (Mahabir Jayanti), 10 April (Good Friday), 13 April (Easter Monday), 7 May (Muharram, Islamic New Year), 11 May (Buddha Purnima), 7 July (Birth of the Prophet), 14–15 August (Janmashtami), 15 August (Independence Day), 1 October (Dussehra), 2 October (Mahatma Gandhi's Birthday), 19 October (Diwali), 4 November (Guru Nanak Jayanti), 25–26 December (Christmas).

1999: 1 January (New Year's Day), 19 January (Id al-Fitr, end of Ramadan), 26 January (Republic Day), March (Holi), March/April (Ram Navami and Mahabir Jayanti), 28 March (Id uz-Zuha, Feast of the Sacrifice), 2 April (Good Friday), 5 April (Easter Monday), 17 April (Muharram, Islamic New Year), May (Buddha Purnima), 26 June (Birth of the Prophet), August (Janmashtami), 15 August (Independence Day), October/November (Dussehra, Diwali and Guru Nanak Jayanti), 2 October (Mahatma Gandhi's Birthday) 25–26 December (Christmas).

Weights and Measures

The metric system has been officially introduced. The imperial system is also still in use, as are traditional Indian weights and measures, including:

1 tola = 11.66 grams
1 seer = 933.1 grams
1 maund = 37.32 kg
1 lakh = (1,00,000) = 100,000
1 crore = (1,00,00,000) = 10,000,000

Statistical Survey

Source (unless otherwise stated): Central Statistical Organization, Ministry of Planning, Sardar Patel Bhavan, Parliament St, New Delhi 110 001; tel. (11) 3732150; fax (11) 3342384.

Area and Population

AREA, POPULATION AND DENSITY*

Area (sq km)	3,287,263†
Population (census results)	
1 March 1981‡	683,329,097
1 March 1991§	
Males	439,230,458
Females	407,072,230
Total	846,302,688
Population (official estimates on 1 March)	
1995	898,200,000
1996	916,000,000
1997	936,000,000
Density (per sq km) on 1 March 1997	284.7

* Including Sikkim (incorporated into India on 26 April 1975) and the Indian-held part of Jammu and Kashmir.

† 1,269,219 sq miles.

‡ Excluding adjustment for underenumeration, estimated at 1.7%.

§ Including estimates for the Indian-held part of Jammu and Kashmir.

Source: Registrar General of India.

STATES AND TERRITORIES

	Capital	Area (sq km)	Population March 1981	Population March 1991
States				
Andhra Pradesh	Hyderabad	275,045	53,551,026	66,508,008
Arunachal Pradesh[1]	Itanagar	83,743	631,839	864,558
Assam	Dispur	78,438	18,041,248	22,414,322
Bihar	Patna	173,877	69,914,734	86,374,465
Goa[5]	Panaji	3,702	1,007,749	1,169,793
Gujarat	Gandhinagar	196,024	34,085,799	41,309,582
Haryana	Chandigarh[2]	44,212	12,922,119	16,463,648
Himachal Pradesh	Simla	55,673	4,280,818	5,170,877
Jammu and Kashmir[3]	Srinagar	222,236	5,987,389	7,718,700*
Karnataka	Bangalore	191,791	37,135,714	44,977,201
Kerala	Thiruvananthapuram (Trivandrum)	38,863	25,453,680	29,098,518
Madhya Pradesh	Bhopal	443,446	52,178,844	66,181,170
Maharashtra	Mumbai (Bombay)	307,713	62,782,818	78,937,187
Manipur	Imphal	22,429	1,420,953	1,837,149
Meghalaya	Shillong	22,429	1,335,819	1,774,778
Mizoram[4]	Aizawl	21,081	493,757	689,756
Nagaland	Kohima	16,579	774,930	1,209,546
Orissa	Bhubaneswar	155,707	26,370,271	31,659,736
Punjab	Chandigarh[2]	50,362	16,788,915	20,281,969
Rajasthan	Jaipur	342,239	34,261,862	44,005,990
Sikkim	Gangtok	7,096	316,385	406,457
Tamil Nadu	Chennai (Madras)	130,058	48,408,077	55,858,946
Tripura	Agartala	10,486	2,053,058	2,757,205
Uttar Pradesh	Lucknow	294,411	110,862,512	139,112,287
West Bengal	Calcutta	88,752	54,580,647	68,077,965
Territories				
Andaman and Nicobar Islands	Port Blair	8,249	188,741	280,661
Chandigarh[2]	Chandigarh	114	451,610	642,015
Dadra and Nagar Haveli	Silvassa	491	103,676	138,477
Daman and Diu[5]	Daman	112	78,981	101,586
Delhi	Delhi	1,483	6,220,406	9,420,644
Lakshadweep	Kavaratti	32	40,249	51,707
Pondicherry	Pondicherry	492	604,471	807,785

* Estimate.

1 Arunachal Pradesh was granted statehood in February 1987.

2 Chandigarh forms a separate Union Territory, not within Haryana or Punjab. As part of a scheme for a transfer of territory between the two states, Chandigarh was due to be incorporated into Punjab on 26 January 1986, but the transfer has been postponed.

3 The area figure refers to the whole of Jammu and Kashmir State, of which 78,114 sq km (Azad Kashmir) is occupied by Pakistan. The population figures refer only to the Indian-held part of the territory.

4 Mizoram was granted statehood in February 1987.

5 Goa was granted statehood in May 1987. Daman and Diu remain a Union Territory.

Source: *Census of India*, 1981 and 1991.

PRINCIPAL TOWNS (population at 1991 census*)

Greater Mumbai (Bombay)	9,925,891	Rajkot	612,458
Delhi	7,206,704	Mysore	606,755
Calcutta	4,399,819	Solapur	604,215
Chennai (Madras)	3,841,396	Ranchi	599,306
Bangalore	3,302,296	Srinagar	594,775†
Hyderabad	3,145,939	Bareilly	590,661
Ahmedabad	2,954,526	Guwahati	584,342
Kanpur (Cawnpore)	1,879,420	Kochi (Cochin)	582,588
Nagpur	1,624,752	Aurangabad	573,272
Lucknow	1,619,115	Kota	537,371
Pune (Poona)	1,566,651	Pimpri-Chinchwad	517,083
Surat	1,505,872	Chandigarh	510,565
Jaipur (Jeypore)	1,458,183	Jalandhar	509,510
Indore	1,091,674	Gorakhpur	505,566
Bhopal	1,062,771	Aligarh	480,520
Vadodara (Baroda)	1,061,598	Jamshedpur	478,950
Ludhiana	1,042,740	Guntur	471,051
Kalyan	1,014,557	Kozhikode (Calicut)	456,618
Haora (Howrah)	950,435	Ghaziabad	454,156
Madurai	940,989	Warangal	447,653
Varanasi (Banaras)	932,399	Raipur	438,639
Patna	917,243	Moradabad	429,214
Agra	891,790	Durgapur	425,836
Coimbatore	816,321	Amravati	421,576
Allahabad	806,486	Bikaner	416,289
Thane (Thana)	803,389	Bhubaneswar	411,542
Jabalpur (Jubbulpore)	764,586	Kolhapur	406,370
Meerut	753,778	Cuttack	403,418
Visakhapatnam (Vizag)	752,037	Ajmer	402,700
Amritsar	708,835	Bhavnagar	402,338
Vijayawada (Vijayavada)	701,827	Bhilainagar	395,360
Thiruvananthapuram (Trivandrum)	699,872	Bhiwandi	392,214
Gwalior	690,765	Tiruchirapalli	387,223
Jodhpur	666,279	Saharanpur	374,945
Nashik	656,925	Ulhasnagar	369,077
Hubli-Dharwar	648,298	Salem	366,712
Faridabad Complex	617,717	Ujjain	362,633
		Jamnagar	350,544
		Bokaro Steel City	333,683
		Rajahmundry	324,881
		Bhatpara	315,976
		Jhansi	313,491
		New Mumbai (Bombay)	307,724

* Figures refer to the city proper in each case. For urban agglomerations, the following populations were recorded: Greater Mumbai (Bombay) 12,596,243; Calcutta 11,021,918; Delhi 8,419,084; Chennai (Madras) 5,421,985; Hyderabad 4,344,437; Bangalore 4,130,288; Ahmedabad 3,312,216; Pune (Poona) 2,493,987; Kanpur 2,029,889; Lucknow 1,669,204; Nagpur 1,664,006; Surat 1,518,950; Jaipur (Jeypore) 1,518,235; Kochi (Cochin) 1,140,605; Vadodara (Baroda) 1,126,824; Indore 1,109,056; Coimbatore 1,100,746; Patna 1,099,647; Madurai 1,085,914; Visakhapatnam (Vizag) 1,057,118; Varanasi (Banaras) 1,030,863; Agra 948,063; Jabalpur (Jubbulpore) 888,916; Meerut 849,799; Vijayawada (Vijayavada) 845,756; Allahabad 844,546; Thiruvananthapuram (Trivandrum) 826,225; Dhanbad 815,005; Kozhikode (Calicut) 801,190; Asansol 763,939; Jamshedpur 763,939; Nashik 725,341; Gwalior 717,780; Tiruchirapalli 711,862; Durg-Bhilainagar 685,474; Rajkot 654,490; Mysore 653,345; Solapur 620,846; Bareilly 617,350; Ranchi 614,795; Aurangabad 592,709; Salem 578,291; Chandigarh 575,829; Ghaziabad 511,759; Warangal 467,757; Kannur 463,962; Raipur 462,694; Moradabad 443,701; Cuttock 440,295; Mangalore 426,341; Kolhapur 418,538; Bhavnagar 405,225; Belgaum 402,412; Pondicherry 401,437; Rajahmundry 401,397.

† 1981 census figure.

Capital: New Delhi, population 301,297 at 1991 census.

BIRTHS AND DEATHS
(estimates, based on Sample Registration Scheme)

	1993/94	1994/95	1995/96
Birth rate (per 1,000)	28.5	28.7	28.3
Death rate (per 1,000)	9.2	9.3	9.0

Expectation of life (UN estimates, years at birth, 1990–95): 60.4 (males 60.3; females 60.4) (Source: UN, *World Population Prospects: The 1994 Revision.*)

ECONOMICALLY ACTIVE POPULATION
(1991 census, excluding Jammu and Kashmir)

	Males	Females	Total
Agriculture, hunting, forestry and fishing	139,361,719	51,979,110	191,340,829
Mining and quarrying	1,536,919	214,356	1,751,275
Manufacturing	23,969,433	4,702,046	28,671,479
Construction	5,122,468	420,737	5,543,205
Trade and commerce	19,862,725	1,433,612	21,296,337
Transport, storage and communications	7,810,126	207,620	8,017,746
Other services	23,995,194	5,316,428	29,311,622
Total	221,658,584	64,273,909	285,932,493

Agriculture

PRINCIPAL CROPS ('000 metric tons, year ending 30 June)

	1994/95	1995/96	1996/97*
Rice (milled)	81,810	79,620	79,630
Sorghum (Jowar)	8,970	9,550	10,980
Cat-tail millet (Bajra)	7,160	5,390	7,470
Maize	8,880	9,440	9,650
Finger millet (Ragi)	2,340	2,760	2,620
Small millets	800	820	820
Wheat	65,770	62,620	64,500
Barley	1,730	1,650	1,500
Total cereals	177,460	171,860	177,180
Chick-peas (Gram)	6,440	5,020	5,500
Pigeon-peas (Tur)	2,140	2,360	2,970
Dry beans, dry peas, lentils and other pulses	5,450	5,810	6,030
Total food grains	191,500	185,050	191,180
Groundnuts (in shell)	8,062	7,814	9,120
Sesame seed	587	552	690
Rapeseed and mustard	5,758	6,071	6,100
Linseed	323	308	300
Castor beans	845	781	800
Total edible oil seeds (incl. others)	21,337	22,428	24,110
Cotton lint†	11,890	13,090	14,300
Jute‡	8,000	7,740	7,890
Kenaf (Mesta)‡	1,000	1,150	1,300
Tea (made)	744	754	780
Sugar cane:			
production gur	27,600	28,300	27,340
production cane	275,540	282,950	273,350
Tobacco (leaves)	567	557	n.a.
Potatoes	17,400	19,240	n.a.

* Provisional.

† Production in '000 bales of 170 kg each.

‡ Production in '000 bales of 180 kg each.

Source: Directorate of Economics and Statistics, Ministry of Agriculture and Ministry of Commerce (for tea).

LIVESTOCK ('000 head, year ending September)

	1994	1995	1996
Cattle*	193,585	194,655	196,003
Sheep*	44,809	45,000	45,390
Goats*	118,347	119,242	120,270
Pigs†	11,780	11,900	11,900
Horses†	990	990	990
Asses†	1,600	1,600	1,600
Mules†	142	142	142
Buffaloes*	79,070	79,500	80,102
Camels†	1,520	1,520	1,520

* Unofficial figures. † FAO estimates.

Chickens (FAO estimates, million): 535 in 1994; 610 in 1995; 610 in 1996.

Source: FAO, *Production Yearbook*.

LIVESTOCK PRODUCTS ('000 metric tons)

	1994	1995	1996
Beef and veal†	1,292	1,292	1,292
Buffalo meat†	1,204	1,204	1,204
Mutton and lamb†	171	173	179
Goat meat†	470	474	490
Pig meat†	408	420	420
Poultry meat†	507	578	578
Cows' milk*	31,000	32,000	33,000
Buffaloes' milk*	30,110	30,565	31,990
Goats' milk*	1,890	1,935	2,010
Butter and ghee*	1,200	1,280	1,350
Hen eggs	1,446*	1,540*	1,540†
Wool:			
greasy	44	44†	44†
clean	29*	30†	30†
Cattle and buffalo hides (fresh)†	843	843	843
Sheepskins (fresh)†	39	40	40
Goatskins (fresh)†	121	122	122

* Unofficial figure(s). † FAO estimate(s).

Source: FAO, *Production Yearbook*.

Forestry

ROUNDWOOD REMOVALS (FAO estimates, '000 cu metres)

	1992	1993	1994
Sawlogs, veneer logs and logs for sleepers*	18,350	18,350	18,350
Pulpwood†	1,208	1,208	1,208
Other industrial wood	5,040	5,138	5,234
Fuel wood	259,233	264,210	269,187
Total	283,831	288,906	293,979

* Assumed to be unchanged since 1985.

† Assumed to be unchanged since 1978.

Source: FAO, *Yearbook of Forest Products*.

SAWNWOOD PRODUCTION
(FAO estimates, '000 cu metres, incl. railway sleepers)

	1983	1984	1985
Coniferous sawnwood	2,091	2,286	2,500
Broadleaved sawnwood	12,404	13,621	14,960
Total	14,495	15,907	17,460

1986–94: Annual production as in 1985 (FAO estimates).

Source: FAO, *Yearbook of Forest Products*.

Fishing

('000 metric tons, live weight)

	1993	1994	1995
Indian Ocean:			
Bombay-duck (Bummalo)	148.7	139.7	146.8
Sea catfishes	98.2	85.9	83.6
Croakers and drums	275.8	308.7	275.2
Indian oil-sardine (sardinella)	137.4	96.3	96.0
Anchovies	38.0	59.2	94.6
Hairtails and cutlassfishes	37.3	65.5	45.7
Indian mackerel	147.7	206.3	192.2
Total sea-fish (incl. others)	2,212.0	2,199.3	2,241.3
Crustaceans and molluscs	403.1	534.0	458.2
Total sea catch	2,615.1	2,733.3	2,699.5
Inland waters:			
Freshwater fishes	1,930.6	2,004.5	2,204.1
Total catch	4,545.7	4,737.8	4,903.6

Source: FAO, *Yearbook of Fishery Statistics*.

1996/97 (provisional, '000 metric tons, live weight): Total catch 5,140 (Marine 2,857; Inland 2,283) (Source: Department of Agriculture and Co-operation (Fisheries Division), Ministry of Agriculture).

Mining

('000 metric tons, unless otherwise indicated)

	1994/95	1995/96	1996/97
Coal	254,180	273,420	286,000
Lignite	19,332	22,152	23,000
Iron ore*	64,512	67,428	66,672
Manganese ore*	1,680	1,836	1,836
Bauxite	4,896	5,568	5,928
Chalk (Fireclay)	427	456	372
Kaolin (China clay)	732	831	685
Dolomite	3,372	3,720	3,252
Gypsum	1,646	2,195	2,096
Limestone	93,204	95,784	100,908
Crude petroleum	32,244	35,172	32,532
Sea salt	11,040	14,544	14,988
Chromium ore*	1,139	1,704	1,392
Phosphorite	1,097	1,308	1,346
Kyanite	4.6	9.6	6.0
Magnesite	336	345	372
Steatite	409	541	462
Copper ore*	4,768	4,740	3,900
Lead concentrates*	53.0	61.5	60.0
Zinc concentrates*	269	289	277
Mica—crude (metric tons)	2,400	2,400	2,400
Gold (kilograms)	2,373	2,036	2,712
Diamonds (carats)	25,512	29,928	31,848
Natural gas (million cu m)†	17,330	20,916	20,484

* Figures refer to gross weight. The estimated metal content is: Iron 63%; Manganese 40%; Chromium 30%; Copper 1.2%; Lead 70%; Zinc 60%.

† Figures refer to gas utilized.

‡ Provisional.

Source: Indian Bureau of Mines.

Industry

SELECTED PRODUCTS ('000 metric tons, unless otherwise indicated)

	1994/95	1995/96	1996/97
Refined sugar*	12,612	14,788	15,312
Cotton cloth (million metres)	16,930	17,310	20,200
Jute manufactures	1,188	1,193	1,145
Paper and paper board	3,172	3,544	3,847
Soda ash	1,452	1,465	1,486
Fertilizers	11,244	12,888	12,720
Petroleum products	52,836	55,332	59,004
Cement	63,720	67,716	73,296
Pig-iron (saleable)	2,880	2,431	2,977
Finished steel	13,628	14,533	17,912
Aluminium (metric tons)	480,864	527,000	508,368
Diesel engines (number)	1,765,860	1,988,376	1,981,896
Sewing machines (number)	99,336	128,297	108,456
Radio receivers (number)	209,760	116,160	47,400
Television receivers (number)	1,559,124	2,213,916	1,948,500
Electric fans (number)	6,480,000	7,320,000	7,920,000
Passenger cars and jeeps (number)	291,204	364,452	443,436
Passenger buses and trucks (number)	216,168	293,172	349,128
Motor cycles, mopeds and scooters (number)	2,188,932	2,588,004	2,823,384
Bicycles (number)	8,907,240	9,912,600	10,861,560

* Figures relate to crop year (beginning November) and are in respect of cane sugar only.

Finance

CURRENCY AND EXCHANGE RATES

Monetary Units

100 paise (singular: paisa) = 1 Indian rupee.

Sterling and Dollar Equivalents (30 September 1997)

£1 sterling = 58.43 rupees;
US $1 = 36.17 rupees;
1,000 Indian rupees = £17.11 = $27.65.

Average Exchange Rate (rupees per US $)

1994	31.374
1995	32.427
1996	35.433

BUDGET (million rupees, year ending 31 March)

Revenue	1995/96	1996/97*	1997/98†
Tax revenue	999,504.4	1,187,899.2	1,379,568.1
Customs	357,568.3	441,350.0	525,500.0
Union excise duties	401,872.5	461,900.0	522,000.0
Corporation tax	164,871.2	190,100.0	218,600.0
Income tax	43,159.0	53,135.6	60,094.2
Estate duty	3.9	10.0	10.0
Wealth tax	741.6	1,100.0	1,300.0
Gift tax	114.0	100.0	100.0
Expenditure tax	2,280.8	1,900.0	2,100.0
Interest tax	11,700.5	20,000.0	18,000.0
Taxes from Union Territories	2,241.1	2,203.6	2,363.9
Service tax	8,610.8	9,700.0	21,500.0
Other taxes	6,340.3	6,400.0	8,000.0
Non-tax revenue	686,208.2	795,637.2	931,187.7
Fiscal services	10,392.7	10,646.7	10,526.9
Interest receipts	184,186.0	219,450.0	240,920.0
Dividends and profits	53,063.0	65,154.6	95,130.0
General services	40,229.4	47,199.5	48,003.0
Social and community services	5,868.7	7,469.9	9,016.5
Economic services	378,651.9	431,157.2	513,944.1
Grants in aid and contributions	11,380.2	11,992.5	11,001.2
Non-tax revenue from Union Territories	2,436.3	2,445.7	2,646.0
Total (incl. others)	1,983,023.3	2,265,589.7	2,613,408.6

Expenditure	1995/96	1996/97*	1997/98†
General services	847,709.9	969,405.9	1,167,096.2
Organs of state	8,475.0	9,175.5	9,511.4
Fiscal services	22,874.5	23,121.1	23,270.5
Interest payments and debt-servicing	500,312.0	585,000.0	680,000.0
Administrative services	48,482.5	59,481.6	103,029.8
Pensions and miscellaneous general services	69,022.2	73,304.8	75,114.8
Defence services	198,543.7	219,322.9	276,169.7
Social services	71,070.3	91,151.4	121,042.2
Economic services	658,217.3	737,839.5	834,705.8
Agriculture and related activities	92,362.4	106,224.0	130,385.8
Rural development	56,290.6	44,245.5	52,944.3
Irrigation and flood control	1,635.8	2,135.5	2,239.0
Special areas programmes	7,869.8	8,042.7	8,372.8
Energy	12,686.2	15,904.1	16,146.8
Industry and minerals	62,541.0	81,987.3	77,759.2
Transport	239,091.3	261,842.3	298,147.9
Communications	119,022.7	141,134.9	167,557.6
Science, technology and the environment	18,762.4	22,341.3	25,984.0
General economic services	47,955.1	53,981.9	55,168.4
Grants in aid and contributions	398,394.9	458,604.6	482,160.0
Grants in aid to state governments	212,868.0	236,260.5	230,271.7
Grants in aid to Union Territories	2,903.8	3,986.1	3,245.1
Payment of states' share of Union excise duties	180,111.5	215,780.0	245,630.0
Technical and economic co-operation with other countries	2,396.9	2,578.0	3,013.2
Aid materials and equipment	114.7	—	—
Disbursements by Union Territories	7,630.9	8,588.3	8,404.4
Total	1,983,023.3	2,265,589.7	2,613,408.6

* Revised estimates. † Estimates.

Source: Government of India, Annual Budget Papers, 1997/98.

INTERNATIONAL RESERVES (US $ million at 31 December)

	1994	1995	1996
Gold*	3,355	3,669	3,614
IMF special drawing rights	2	139	122
Reserve position in IMF	310	316	306
Foreign exchange	19,386	17,467	19,742
Total	23,053	21,591	23,784

* National valuation (8,922 rupees per troy ounce in 1994; 10,100 rupees per ounce in 1995; 10,160 rupees per ounce in 1996).

Source: IMF, *International Financial Statistics*.

MONEY SUPPLY
(million rupees, last Friday of year ending 31 March)

	1994/95	1995/96	1996/97
Currency with the public	1,006,810	1,182,580	1,324,330
Demand deposits with banks	881,930	932,330	1,049,240
Other deposits with Reserve Bank	33,830	33,440	32,380
Total money	1,922,570	2,148,350	2,405,950

Source: Reserve Bank of India.

COST OF LIVING
(Consumer Price Index for Industrial Workers; base: 1990 = 100)

	1993	1994	1995
Food	138.7	155.0	173.3
Fuel and light	127.8	133.9	141.1
Clothing	129.6	144.1	162.5
Rent	121.4	128.6	136.3
All items (incl. others)	135.5	149.5	164.5

Source: ILO, *Yearbook of Labour Statistics*.

1996: Food 188.0; All items 179.6 (Source: UN, *Monthly Bulletin of Statistics*).

NATIONAL ACCOUNTS
('000 million rupees at current prices, year ending 31 March)

National Income and Product

	1993/94	1994/95	1995/96
Domestic factor incomes*	6,503.39	7,636.98	8,755.94
Consumption of fixed capital	815.52	946.42	1,101.93
Gross domestic product at factor cost	7,318.91	8,583.40	9,857.87
Indirect taxes	1,011.26	1,209.19	1,422.71
Less Subsidies	232.51	255.79	294.82
GDP in purchasers' values	8,097.66	9,536.80	10,985.76
Factor income from abroad / *Less* Factor income paid abroad	−123.43	−150.46	−180.24
Gross national product	7,974.23	9,386.34	10,805.52
Less Consumption of fixed capital	815.52	946.42	1,101.93
National income in market prices	7,158.71	8,439.92	9,703.59
Other current transfers from abroad / *Less* Other current transfers paid abroad	112.76	194.67	250.19
National disposable income	7,271.47	8,634.59	9,953.78

* Compensation of employees and the operating surplus of enterprises.

Expenditure on the Gross Domestic Product

	1993/94	1994/95	1995/96
Government final consumption expenditure	899.31	1,003.61	1,164.60
Private final consumption expenditure	4,933.80	5,642.53	6,397.00
Increase in stocks	4.77	148.14	172.20
Gross fixed capital formation	1,749.96	2,140.38	2,702.60
Total domestic expenditure	7,587.84	8,934.66	10,436.40
Exports of goods and services	861.10	n.a.	n.a.
Less Imports of goods and services	857.00	n.a.	n.a.
Statistical discrepancy	505.72	n.a.	n.a.
GDP in purchasers' values	8,097.66	9,536.80	10,985.80

Gross Domestic Product by Economic Activity
(provisional estimates, at current factor cost)

	1993/94	1994/95	1995/96
Agriculture	2,049.62	2,374.91	2,525.44
Forestry and logging	92.50	102.61	107.04
Fishing	75.34	103.34	115.04
Mining and quarrying	169.49	181.87	196.69
Manufacturing	1,234.77	1,938.00	1,560.15
Electricity, gas and water	188.87	230.53	262.53
Construction	412.12	484.33	565.88
Trade, restaurants and hotels	971.70	1,166.03	1,404.59
Transport, storage and communications	563.27	660.42	763.59
Banking and insurance	399.15	500.19	574.65
Real estate and business services	234.89	262.78	286.25
Public administration and defence	400.05	447.30	524.26
Other services	439.26	508.94	593.91
Total	7,231.03	8,583.40*	9,857.87*

* Including adjustment.

BALANCE OF PAYMENTS (US $ million)

	1993	1994	1995
Exports of goods f.o.b.	22,016	25,523	31,239
Imports of goods f.o.b.	−24,108	−29,673	−37,957
Trade balance	−2,093	−4,150	−6,719
Exports of services	5,107	6,038	6,775
Imports of services	−6,497	−8,200	−10,268
Balance on goods and services	−3,482	−6,312	−10,212
Other income received	375	821	1,486
Other income paid	−4,121	−4,370	−5,219
Balance on goods, services and income	−7,228	−9,861	−13,945
Current transfers received	5,375	8,208	8,410
Current transfers paid	−23	−23	−27
Current balance	−1,876	−1,676	−5,563
Direct investment abroad	—	−83	−117
Direct investment from abroad	550	973	2,144
Portfolio investment liabilities	1,369	5,491	1,590
Other investment assets	1,830	1,170	−1,179
Other investment liabilities	3,325	3,024	1,423
Net errors and omissions	−987	1,492	970
Overall balance	4,211	10,391	−733

Source: IMF, *International Financial Statistics*.

External Trade

PRINCIPAL COMMODITIES
(million rupees, year ending 31 March)

Imports c.i.f.	1993/94	1994/95	1995/96
Manufactured fertilizers	19,815.0	23,985.9	46,210.0
Metalliferous ores and metal scrap	13,875.0	23,489.6	27,510.1
Mineral fuels, lubricants, etc.	180,461.9	186,125.5	251,736.0
Organic chemicals	27,700.0	43,394.8	56,983.4
Inorganic chemicals	15,291.5	23,708.6	28,833.1
Artificial resins, plastic materials, etc.	13,628.0	19,034.9	26,874.6
Pearls, precious and semi-precious stones	82,632.1	51,169.7	70,446.7
Iron and steel	24,936.1	36,533.9	48,375.5
Non-ferrous metals	15,030.1	22,540.9	30,235.1
Non-electrical machinery	114,783.8	150,558.5	223,689.0
Transport equipment	39,847.2	34,966.8	36,966.6
Electronic goods	29,182.8	39,929.8	62,657.4
Total (incl. others)	731,010.1	899,706.6	1,226,781.3

Source: Ministry of Commerce.

Exports f.o.b.	1993/94	1994/95*	1995/96*
Marine products	25,520	35,370	33,810
Tea and maté	10,590	9,750	11,710
Oil cakes	23,240	17,980	23,490
Cotton fabrics	48,210	70,140	86,190
Ready-made garments	81,120	103,050	122,950
Carpets (hand-made)	14,230	13,860	14,060
Leather and leather manufactures	40,770	50,570	57,900
Gems and jewellery	125,330	141,310	176,450
Iron ore	13,747	12,970	17,210
Engineering products	84,590	94,800	120,580
Chemicals and related products	46,350	61,400	78,910
Petroleum products	12,478	13,090	15,180
Ores and minerals (excluding iron ore, mica and coal)	n.a.	16,960	20,850
Man-made textiles	n.a.	19,280	25,110
Electronic goods and computer software	n.a.	14,670	25,200
Total (incl. others)	697,510	826,740	1,063,530

* Figures are provisional.

Source: Ministry of Commerce.

PRINCIPAL TRADING PARTNERS
(million rupees, year ending 31 March)

Imports c.i.f.	1993/94	1994/95	1995/96*
Australia	20,680.2	28,734.5	34,180.0
Bahrain	17,092.5	21,789.6	28,770.0
Belgium	58,808.0	37,888.6	56,930.0
Brazil	3,929.2	17,220.3	8,730.0
Canada	7,356.9	8,335.0	12,750.0
France	18,602.6	19,330.3	28,120.0
Germany	56,153.7	68,670.3	105,200.0
Iran	11,904.6	16,845.9	20,010.0
Italy	16,859.4	23,266.5	35,600.0
Japan	47,442.8	64,050.6	82,540.0
Korea, Republic	17,705.5	19,765.7	27,590.0
Kuwait	35,324.4	46,477.0	65,900.0
Malaysia	7,837.6	15,387.8	30,200.0
Morocco	4,955.8	8,644.2	10,070.0
Netherlands	12,053.2	12,115.3	19,070.0
Nigeria	25,951.6	13,307.7	25,750.0
Russia	11,930.2	23,500.0	40,900.0
Saudi Arabia	48,355.4	49,282.1	67,730.0
Singapore	19,664.4	28,249.3	36,520.0
Switzerland	15,879.7	25,881.6	34,140.0
United Arab Emirates	31,461.7	48,137.9	53,740.0
United Kingdom	48,182.1	48,950.0	64,150.0
USA	85,837.0	91,236.1	129,160.0
Total (incl. others)	731,010.7	899,706.6	1,226,780.0

Exports f.o.b.	1993/94	1994/95*	1995/96*
Australia	7,690	10,880	12,570
Bangladesh	13,490	20,240	35,090
Belgium	26,440	31,040	37,480
Canada	7,150	8,380	10,220
France	15,822	18,280	24,990
Germany	48,280	54,880	66,140
Hong Kong	39,190	47,640	60,930
Italy	18,950	26,940	33,920
Japan	54,610	63,630	74,110
Korea, Republic	6,470	10,440	14,990
Malaysia	7,760	9,000	13,150
Netherlands	16,030	18,380	25,720
Russia	20,370	25,340	34,950
Saudi Arabia	16,020	13,680	16,130
Singapore	23,590	24,190	30,160
Spain	6,080	8,450	13,080
Switzerland	6,931	7,770	9,420
Taiwan	8,650	7,870	8,610
Thailand	11,210	12,770	15,820
United Arab Emirates	36,320	39,750	47,780
United Kingdom	43,260	53,050	67,260
USA	125,420	157,640	184,660
Total (incl. others)	697,510	826,740	1,063,530

* Figures are provisional.

Source: Ministry of Commerce.

Transport

RAILWAYS (million, year ending 31 March)

	1994/95	1995/96	1996/97
Passengers	3,924	3,983	4,134
Passenger-km	310,620	333,132	344,436
Freight (metric tons)	381.6	391.2	409.2
Freight (metric ton-km)	252,972	271,068	279,120

Source: Railway Board, Ministry of Railways.

ROAD TRAFFIC ('000 motor vehicles in use at 31 March)

	1994	1995	1996
Private cars, jeeps and taxis	3,569	3,841	4,189
Buses and coaches	392	423	449
Goods vehicles	1,691	1,794	1,785
Motor cycles and scooters	18,899	20,831	23,111
Others	3,109	3,406	4,024
Total	27,660	30,295	33,558

Source: Transport Research Division, Ministry of Surface Transport.

SHIPPING

Merchant Fleet (registered at 31 December)

	1994	1995	1996
Vessels	881	916	920
Displacement ('000 grt)	6,485.4	7,126.9	7,127.2

Source: Lloyd's Register of Shipping, *World Fleet Statistics*.

International Sea-Borne Traffic (year ending 31 March)

	1992/93	1993/94	1994/95
Vessels* ('000 net regd tons):			
Entered	30,108	28,092	39,617
Cleared	34,656	36,264	42,883
Freight† ('000 metric tons):			
Loaded	43,163	53,220	n.a.
Unloaded	73,569	75,000	n.a.

* Excluding minor and intermediate ports.

† Including bunkers.

Sources: Transport Research Division, Ministry of Surface Transport; Directorate General of Commercial Intelligence and Statistics.

CIVIL AVIATION (traffic)

	1994/95	1995/96	1996/97
Kilometres flown ('000)	115,200	124,932	122,220
Passenger-km ('000)	16,479,060	19,095,324	18,633,072
Freight ton-km ('000)	584,184	616,080	498,000
Mail ton-km ('000)	28,536	27,240	21,924

Source: Directorate General of Civil Aviation.

Tourism

FOREIGN VISITORS BY COUNTRY OF ORIGIN*

	1994	1995	1996
Australia	33,142	36,150	48,755
Canada	56,441	63,821	74,031
France	73,088	82,349	93,325
Germany	85,352	89,040	99,853
Iran	14,775	12,337	12,171
Italy	43,510	53,015	49,910
Japan	63,398	76,042	99,018
Malaysia	40,762	50,039	53,370
Netherlands	35,094	40,147	40,246
Saudi Arabia	15,524	16,252	17,688
Singapore	44,157	48,632	47,136
Sri Lanka	89,009	114,157	107,351
Switzerland	30,102	29,388	34,989
USSR/CIS	56,387	40,665	41,085
United Arab Emirates	30,503	19,749	21,401
United Kingdom	300,696	334,827	360,686
USA	176,482	203,345	228,829
Total (incl. others)	1,562,016	1,762,228	1,923,695

* Figures exclude nationals of Bangladesh and Pakistan. Including these, the total was 1,886,433 in 1994, 2,123,685 in 1995 and 2,287,860 in 1996.

Source: Ministry of Tourism and Civil Aviation.

Receipts from tourism (million rupees, year ending 31 March): 71,035 in 1994; 86,400 in 1995; 100,614 in 1996.

Communications Media

	1993	1994	1995
Television receivers (million)	36.5	37.0	47.0
Radio receivers (million)	72.0	74.0	75.5
Telefax stations ('000 in use)	45	50	n.a.
Daily newspapers	3,740	n.a.	4,236
Net circulation (million)	67.6	n.a.	n.a.

1992/93 (year ending 31 March): 6,796,700 telephones; 28,455 non-daily newspapers and other periodicals.
1993/94 (year ending 31 March): 8,025,600 telephones; 29,872 non-daily newspapers and other periodicals.
1994/95 (year ending 31 March): 9,795,300 telephones.
1995/96 (year ending 31 March): 11,978,000 telephones.
Sources: Ministry of Communications; Registrar of Newspapers for India; Ministry of Information and Broadcasting; UNESCO, *Statistical Yearbook*; UN, *Statistical Yearbook*.

Education

(1996/97)

	Institutions	Teachers	Students
Primary	598,354	1,789,733	110,393,406
Middle	176,772	1,195,845	41,064,849
Secondary (High school)	73,127	926,480	17,861,774
Higher secondary (New pattern)	25,045	615,880	6,412,716

Source: Planning, Monitoring and Statistics Division, Department of Education, Ministry of Human Resources Development.

Directory

The Constitution

The Constitution of India, adopted by the Constituent Assembly on 26 November 1949, was inaugurated on 26 January 1950. The Preamble declares that the People of India solemnly resolve to constitute a Sovereign Democratic Republic and to secure to all its citizens justice, liberty, equality and fraternity. There are 397 articles and nine schedules, which form a comprehensive document.

UNION OF STATES

The Union of India comprises 25 states, six Union Territories and one National Capital Territory. There are provisions for the formation and admission of new states.

The Constitution confers citizenship on a threefold basis of birth, descent, and residence. Provisions are made for refugees who have migrated from Pakistan and for persons of Indian origin residing abroad.

FUNDAMENTAL RIGHTS AND DIRECTIVE PRINCIPLES

The rights of the citizen contained in Part III of the Constitution are declared fundamental and enforceable in law. 'Untouchability' is abolished and its practice in any form is a punishable offence. The Directive Principles of State Policy provide a code intended to ensure promotion of the economic, social and educational welfare of the State in future legislation.

THE PRESIDENT

The President is the head of the Union, exercising all executive powers on the advice of the Council of Ministers responsible to Parliament. He is elected by an electoral college consisting of elected members of both Houses of Parliament and the Legislatures of the States. The President holds office for a term of five years and is eligible for re-election. He may be impeached for violation of the Constitution. The Vice-President is the ex officio Chairman of the Rajya Sabha and is elected by a joint sitting of both Houses of Parliament.

THE PARLIAMENT

The Parliament of the Union consists of the President and two Houses: the Rajya Sabha (Council of States) and the Lok Sabha (House of the People). The Rajya Sabha consists of 245 members, of whom a number are nominated by the President. One-third of its members retire every two years. Elections are indirect, each state's legislative quota being elected by the members of the state's legislative assembly. The Lok Sahba has 543 members elected by adult franchise; not more than 13 represent the Union Territories and National Capital Territory. Two members are nominated by the President to represent the Anglo-Indian community.

GOVERNMENT OF THE STATES

The governmental machinery of states closely resembles that of the Union. Each of these states has a governor at its head appointed by the President for a term of five years to exercise executive power on the advice of a council of ministers. The states' legislatures consist of the Governor and either one house (legislative assembly) or two houses (legislative assembly and legislative council). The term of the assembly is five years, but the council is not subject to dissolution.

LANGUAGE

The Constitution provides that the official language of the Union shall be Hindi. (The English language will continue to be an associate language for many official purposes.)

LEGISLATION—FEDERAL SYSTEM

The Constitution provides that bills, other than money bills, can be introduced in either House. To become law, they must be passed by both Houses and receive the assent of the President. In financial affairs, the authority of the Lower House is final. The various subjects of legislation are enumerated on three lists in the seventh schedule of the Constitution: the Union List, containing nearly 100 entries, including external affairs, defence, communications and atomic energy; the State List, containing 65 entries, including local government, police, public health, education; and the Concurrent List, with over 40 entries, including criminal law, marriage and divorce, labour welfare. The Constitution vests residuary authority in the Centre. All matters not enumerated in the Concurrent or State Lists will be deemed to be included in the Union List, and in the event of conflict between Union and State Law on any subject enumerated in the Concurrent List the Union Law will prevail. In time of emergency Parliament may even exercise powers otherwise exclusively vested in the states. Under Article 356, 'If the President on receipt of a report from the government of a state or otherwise is satisfied that a situation has arisen in which the Government of the state cannot be carried on in accordance with the provisions of this Constitution, the President may by Proclamation: (a) assume to himself all or any of the functions of the government of the state and all or any of the powers of the governor or any body or authority in the state other than the Legislature of the state; (b) declare that the powers of the Legislature of the state shall be exercisable by or under the authority of Parliament; (c) make such incidental provisions as appear to the President to be necessary': provided that none of the powers of a High Court be assumed by the President or suspended in any way. Unless such a Proclamation is approved by both Houses of Parliament, it ceases to operate after two months. A Proclamation so approved ceases to operate after six months, unless renewed by Parliament. Its renewal cannot be extended beyond a total period of three years. An independent judiciary exists to define and interpret the Constitution and to resolve constitutional disputes arising between states, or between a state and the Government of India.

OTHER PROVISIONS

Other Provisions of the Constitution deal with the administration of tribal areas, relations between the Union and states, inter-state trade and finance.

AMENDMENTS

The Constitution is flexible in character, and a simple process of amendment has been adopted. For amendment of provisions concerning the Supreme Courts and the High Courts, the distribution of legislative powers between the Union and the states, the representation of the states in Parliament, etc., the amendment must be passed by both Houses of Parliament and must further be ratified by the legislatures of not less than half the states. In other cases no reference to the state legislatures is necessary.

Numerous amendments were adopted in August 1975, following the declaration of a state of emergency in June. The Constitution (39th Amendment) Bill laid down that the President's reasons for proclaiming an emergency may not be challenged in any court. Under the Constitution (40th Amendment) Bill, 38 existing laws may not be challenged before any court on the ground of violation of fundamental rights. Thus detainees under the Maintenance of Internal Security Act could not be told the grounds of their detention and were forbidden bail and any claim to liberty through natural or common law. The Constitution (41st Amendment) Bill provided that the President, Prime Minister and state Governors should be immune from criminal prosecution for life and from civil prosecution during their term of office.

In November 1976 a 59-clause Constitution (42nd Amendment) Bill was approved by Parliament and came into force in January 1977. Some of the provisions of the Bill are that the Indian Democratic Republic shall be named a 'Democratic Secular and Socialist Republic'; that the President 'shall act in accordance with' the advice given to him by the Prime Minister and the Council of Ministers, and, acting at the Prime Minister's direction, shall be empowered for two years to amend the Constitution by executive order, in any way beneficial to the enforcement of the whole; that the term of the Lok Sabha and of the State Assemblies shall be extended from five to six years; that there shall be no limitation on the constituent power of Parliament to amend the Constitution, and that India's Supreme Court shall be barred from hearing petitions challenging constitutional amendments; that strikes shall be forbidden in the public services and the Union Government have the power to deploy police or other forces under its own superintendence and control in any state. Directive Principles are given precedence over Fundamental Rights: 10 basic duties of citizens are listed, including the duty to 'defend the country and render national service when called upon to do so'.

The Janata Party Government, which came into power in March 1977, promised to amend the Constitution during the year, so as to 'restore the balance between the people and Parliament, Parliament and the judiciary, the judiciary and the executive, the states and the centre, and the citizen and the Government that the founding fathers of the Constitution had worked out'. The Constitution (43rd Amendment) Bill, passed by Parliament in December 1977, the Constitution (44th Amendment) Bill, passed by Parliament in December 1977 and later redesignated the 43rd Amendment, and the Constitution (45th Amendment) Bill, passed by Parliament in December 1978 and later redesignated the 44th Amendment, reversed most of the changes enacted by the Constitution (42nd Amendment) Bill. The 44th Amendment is particularly detailed on emergency provisions: An emergency may not be proclaimed unless 'the security of India or any part of its territory was threatened by war or external aggression or by armed rebellion.' Its introduction must be approved by a two-thirds majority of Parliament within a month, and after six months the emergency may be continued only with the approval of Parliament. Among the provisions left unchanged after these Bills were a section subordinating Fundamental Rights to Directive Principles and a clause empowering the central Government to deploy armed forces under its control in any state without the state government's consent. In May 1980 the Indian Supreme Court repealed sections 4 and 55 of the 42nd Amendment Act, thus curtailing Parliament's power to enforce directive principles and to amend the Constitution. The death penalty was declared constitutionally valid.

The 53rd Amendment to the Constitution, approved by Parliament in August 1986, granted statehood to the Union Territory of Mizoram; the 55th Amendment, approved in December 1986, granted statehood to the Union Territory of Arunachal Pradesh; and the 57th Amendment, approved in May 1987, granted statehood to the Union Territory of Goa (Daman and Diu remain, however, as a Union Territory). The 59th Amendment, approved in March 1988, empowered the Government to impose a state of emergency in Punjab, on the grounds of internal disturbances. In December 1988 the minimum voting age was lowered from 21 to 18 years. The 71st Amendment, approved in August 1992, gave official language status to Nepali, Konkani and Manipuri.

THE PANCHAYAT RAJ SCHEME

This scheme is designed to decentralize the powers of the Union and State Governments. It is based on the Panchayat (Village Council) and the Gram Sabha (Village Parliament) and envisages the gradual transference of local government from state to local authority. Revenue and internal security will remain state responsibilities at present. By 1978 the scheme had been introduced in all the states except Meghalaya, Nagaland and 23 out of 31 districts in Bihar. The Panchayat operated in all the Union Territories except Lakshadweep, Mizoram (which became India's 23rd state in February 1987) and Pondicherry. The 72nd Amendment, approved in late 1992, provided for direct elections to the Panchayats, members of which were to have a tenure of five years.

The Government

President: Dr Kocheril Raman Narayanan (sworn in 25 July 1997).

Vice-President: Krishan Kant (sworn in 21 August 1997).

COUNCIL OF MINISTERS*
(February 1998)

A coalition of the Janata Dal (JD), the Tamil Maanila Congress (TMC), the Samajwadi Party (SP), the Dravida Munnetra Kazhagam (DMK), Telugu Desam (Naidu) (TD–N), the Communist Party of India (CPI), the Asom Gana Parishad (AGP), Congress (I), the Maharashtrawadi Gomantak Party (MGP) and Independents (Ind.).

Prime Minister and also in charge of the Ministries/Departments of External Affairs, Electronics, Ocean Development and Space, Health and Family Welfare, Planning and Programme Implementation, Personnel, Public Grievances and Pensions, and of Atomic Energy, as well as all other Ministries/Departments not allocated to any other Minister or Minister of State with Independent Charge: Inder Kumar Gujral (JD).

Minister of Finance and of Company Affairs: Palaniappan Chidambaram (TMC).

Minister of Defence: Mulayam Singh Yadav (SP).

Minister of Home Affairs: Indrajit Gupta (CPI).

Minister of Agriculture (excluding the Department of Animal Husbandry and Dairying): Chaturanan Mishra (CPI).

Minister of Information and Broadcasting: S. Jaipal Reddy.

Minister of Environment and Forests: Saifuddin Soz.

Minister of Railways: Ram Vilas Paswan (JD).

Minister of Human Resource Development: S. R. Bommai (JD).

Minister of Communications: Beni Prasad Varma (SP).

Minister of Industry: Murasoli Maran (DMK).

Minister of Food and of Civil Supplies, Consumer Affairs and Public Distribution: Devendra Prasad Yadav (JD).

Minister of Chemicals and Fertilizers: M. Arunachalam (TMC).

Minister of Welfare: Balwant Singh Ramoowalia (Ind.).

Minister of Civil Aviation: C. M. Ibrahim (JD).

Minister of Surface Transport: T. G. Venkataraman (DMK).

Minister of Rural Areas and Employment: K. Yarram Naidu (TD–N).

Minister of Parliamentary Affairs and of Tourism: Srikanta Kumar Jena (JD).

Minister of Steel and of Mines: Birendra Prasad Baishya (AGP).

Minister of Petroleum and Natural Gas: Janeshwar Mishra (SP).

Minister of Textiles: (vacant).

Ministers of State with Independent Charge

Minister of State for Coal: Kanti Singh (JD).

Minister of State for Non-Conventional Energy Sources: Jal Narayan Prashad Nishad (JD).

Minister of State for Commerce: Bolla Buli Ramaiah (TD–N).

Minister of State for the Department of Animal Husbandry and Dairying: Raghubans Prasad Singh (JD).

Minister of State for Law, Justice and Company Affairs (excluding Department of Company Affairs): Ramakant D. Khalap (MGP).

Minister of State for Water Resources: Shees Ram Ola (Congress–I).

Minister of State for Planning and Programme Implementation and for Science and Technology: Yogendra Kumar Alagh (Ind.).

Minister of State for Labour: M. P. Veerendra Kumar (JD).

Minister of State for Urban Affairs and Employment: Dr U. Venkateshwarlu (TD-N).

Minister of State for Food-Processing Industries: Dilip Kumar Ray (JD).

* Following the general election of February–March 1998, it was expected that a new Council of Ministers would be formed (see Late Information).

MINISTRIES

President's Office: Rashtrapati Bhavan, New Delhi 110 004; tel. (11) 3015321; telex 3166427; fax (11) 3017290.

Vice-President's Office: 6 Maulana Azad Rd, New Delhi 110 011; tel. (11) 3016344; fax (11) 3018124.

Prime Minister's Office: South Block, New Delhi 110 011; tel. (11) 3013040; telex 3161876; fax (11) 3016857.

Ministry of Agriculture: Krishi Bhavan, Dr Rajendra Prasad Rd, New Delhi 110 001; tel. (11) 3382651; telex 3165054; fax (11) 3386004.

Ministry of Atomic Energy: South Block, New Delhi 110 011; tel. (11) 3011773; telex 3166182; fax (11) 3013843.

Ministry of Chemicals and Fertilizers: Shastri Bhavan, New Delhi 110 001; tel. (11) 3383695; telex 3162455; fax (11) 3386222.

Ministry of Civil Aviation: Rajiv Gandhi Bhavan, Safdarjung Airport, New Delhi 110 023; tel. (11) 4610358; telex 3174148; fax (11) 4610354.

Ministry of Civil Supplies, Consumer Affairs and Public Distribution: Krishi Bhavan, New Delhi 110 001; tel. (11) 3384882; telex 3161962; fax (11) 3388302.

Ministry of Coal: Shastri Bhavan, Rafi Marg, New Delhi 110 001; tel. (11) 3384884; telex 3166660; fax (11) 3387738.

Ministry of Commerce: Udyog Bhavan, New Delhi 110 011; tel. (11) 3016664; telex 3163233; fax (11) 3014335.

Ministry of Communications: Sanchar Bhavan, 20 Asoka Rd, New Delhi 110 001; tel. (11) 3719898; telex 3161740; fax (11) 3782344.

Ministry of Defence: South Block, New Delhi 110 011; tel. (11) 3012380; telex 3162679.

Ministry of Electronics: Electronics Niketan, 6 CGO Complex, New Delhi 110 003; tel. (11) 4364041; telex 3165103; fax (11) 4363134.

Ministry of Environment and Forests: Paryavaran Bhavan, CGO Complex Phase II, Lodi Rd, New Delhi 110 003; tel. (11) 4360721; telex 3166185; fax (11) 4360678.

Ministry of External Affairs: South Block, New Delhi 110 011; tel. (11) 3012318; telex 3161880; fax (11) 3010700.

Ministry of Finance: North Block, New Delhi 110 001; tel. (11) 3012611; telex 3166175; fax (11) 3012477.

Ministry of Food: 45 Krishi Bhavan, New Delhi 110 001; tel. (11) 3383911; telex 3166505; fax (11) 3782213.

Ministry of Food-Processing Industries: Panchsheel Bhavan, Khelgaon Marg, New Delhi 110 049; tel. (11) 6493012; telex 3173162; fax (11) 6493228.

Ministry of Health and Family Welfare: Nirman Bhavan, New Delhi 110 011; tel. (11) 3018863; telex 3165413.

Ministry of Home Affairs: North Block, New Delhi 110 001; tel. (11) 3011989; telex 3166724; fax (11) 3015750.

Ministry of Human Resource Development: Shastri Bhavan, New Delhi 110 001; tel. (11) 3386995; telex 3161221; fax (11) 3384093.

Ministry of Industry: Udyog Bhavan, New Delhi 110 011; tel. (11) 3012433; telex 3166565; fax (11) 3011770.

Ministry of Information and Broadcasting: Shastri Bhavan, New Delhi 110 001; tel. (11) 3382639; telex 3166349; fax (11) 3383513.

Ministry of Labour: Shram Shakti Bhavan, Rafi Marg, New Delhi 110 001; tel. (11) 3710265; telex 3162056; fax (11) 3711708.

Ministry of Law, Justice and Company Affairs: Shastri Bhavan, Dr Rajendra Prasad Rd, New Delhi 110 001; tel. (11) 3384777; telex 3165428; fax (11) 3387259.

Ministry of Mines: Udyog Bhavan, New Delhi 110 011; tel. (11) 3385173; telex 3166601; fax (11) 3386402.

Ministry of Non-Conventional Energy Sources: Block 14, CGO Complex, New Delhi 110 003; tel. (11) 4361481; telex 3161653; fax (11) 4361298.

Ministry of Ocean Development: Block 12, CGO Complex, Lodi Rd, New Delhi 110 003; tel. (11) 4360874; telex 3161535; fax (11) 4360779.

Ministry of Parliamentary Affairs: Parliament House, New Delhi 110 001; tel. (11) 3017663; fax (11) 3017726.

Ministry of Personnel, Public Grievances and Pensions: North Block, New Delhi 110 001; tel. (11) 3014848; telex 3162826; fax (11) 3012432.

Ministry of Petroleum and Natural Gas: Shastri Bhavan, New Delhi 110 001; tel. (11) 3383501; telex 3166235; fax (11) 3384787.

Ministry of Planning and Programme Implementation: Sardar Patel Bhavan, Patel Chowk, New Delhi 110 001; tel. (11) 3732150; telex 3163195; fax (11) 3732067.

Ministry of Power: Shram Shakti Bhavan, New Delhi 110 001; tel. (11) 3710271; telex 3162720; fax (11) 3717519.

Ministry of Railways: Rail Bhavan, Raisina Rd, New Delhi 110 001; tel. (11) 3382531; fax (11) 3384481.

Ministry of Rural Areas and Employment: Krishi Bhavan, New Delhi 110 001; tel. (11) 3384467; telex 3166489; fax (11) 3782502.

Ministry of Science and Technology: Technology Bhavan, New Mehrauli Rd, New Delhi 110 016; tel. (11) 660068; telex 3173317; fax (11) 6863847.

Ministry of Steel: Udyog Bhavan, New Delhi 110 011; tel. (11) 3015912; telex 3161483; fax (11) 3013236.

Ministry of Surface Transport: Parivahan Bhavan, 1 Sansad Marg, New Delhi 110 001; tel. (11) 3714938; telex 3161157; fax (11) 3714324.

Ministry of Textiles: Udyog Bhavan, New Delhi 110 011; tel. (11) 3011769; telex 3162762; fax (11) 3013711.

Ministry of Tourism: Transport Bhavan, Parliament St, New Delhi 110 001; tel. (11) 3711995; telex 3166527; fax (11) 3710518.

Ministry of Urban Affairs and Employment: Nirman Bhavan, New Delhi 110 011; tel. (11) 3019377; telex 3163255; fax (11) 3014459.

Ministry of Water Resources: Shram Shakti Bhavan, Rafi Marg, New Delhi 110 001; tel. (11) 3710305; telex 3166568; fax (11) 3710253.

Ministry of Welfare: Shastri Bhavan, New Delhi 110 001; tel. (11) 3382683; telex 3166256; fax (11) 3384918.

Legislature

PARLIAMENT

Rajya Sabha

(Council of States)

Most of the members of the Rajya Sabha are indirectly elected by the State Assemblies for six years, with one-third retiring every two years. The remaining members are nominated by the President.

Chairman: KRISHAN KANT.

Deputy Chairman: NAJMA HEPPTULLAH.

Distribution of Seats, August 1997

Party	Seats
Congress (I)	88
Janata Dal	23
Communist (CPI—Marxist)	15
Telugu Desam	8
Bharatiya Janata Party	44
Samajwadi Party	7
Muslim League	2
Forward Bloc	2
All India Anna Dravida Munnetra Kazhagam	14
Communist (CPI)	6
Jammu and Kashmir National Conference (F)	3
Shiv Sena	4
Bahujan Samaj Party	3
Independents and others	13
Nominated	5
Vacant	8
Total	245

Lok Sabha

(House of the People)

Speaker: PURNO AGITOK SANGMA.

General Election, 16, 22 and 28 February and 7 March 1998

Party	Seats
Bharatiya Janata Party	178
Congress (I)	141
Communist (CPI—Marxist)	32
Samajwadi Party	20
All-India Anna Dravida Munnetra Kazhagam	18
Rashtriya Janata Dal	17
Telugu Desam	12
Samata Party	12
Communist (CPI)	9
Biju Janata Dal	9
Akali Dal	8
Trinamool Congress	7

General Election, 16, 22 and 28 February and 7 March 1998 — *continued*

Party	Seats
Shiv Sena	6
Dravida Munnetra Kazhagam	6
Janata Dal	6
Bahujan Samaj Party	5
Revolutionary Socialist Party	5
Republican Party of India	4
Pattali Makkal Katchi	4
Haryana Lok Dal	4
Lok Shakti	3
Tamil Maanila Congress	3
Marumalarchi Dravida Munnetra Kazhagam	3
All India Forward Bloc	2
Arunachal Congress	2
Indian Union Muslim League	2
Janata Party	1
Kerala Congress (M)	1
All-India Indira Congress	1
Independents and others	14
Nominated	2*
Vacant	8
Total	545

* Nominated by the President to represent the Anglo-Indian community.

State Governments

(March 1998)

ANDHRA PRADESH
(Capital—Hyderabad)

Governor: Dr Chakravarty Rangarajan.

Chief Minister: N. Chandrababu Naidu (Telugu Desam (Naidu)).

Legislative Assembly: 294 seats (Telugu Desam (Naidu) 206, Telugu Desam (NTR) 16, Congress—I 26, Communist—CPI—M 15, Communist—CPI 19, Bharatiya Janata Party 3, independents and others 9).

ARUNACHAL PRADESH
(Capital—Itanagar)

Governor: Mata Prasad.

Chief Minister: Gegong Apang (Congress—I).

Legislative Assembly: 60 seats (Congress—I 43, Janata Dal 3, Samajwadi Party 2, independents 12).

ASSAM
(Capital—Dispur)

Governor: Lt-Gen. (retd) S. K. Sinha.

Chief Minister: Prafulla Kumar Mohanta (Asom Gana Parishad).

Legislative Assembly: 126 seats (Asom Gana Parishad 59, Congress—I 34, Bharatiya Janata Party 4, Communist—CPI 3, independents and others 22, vacant 4).

BIHAR
(Capital—Patna)

Governor: Dr A. R. Kidwai.

Chief Minister: Rabri Devi (Rashtriya Janata Dal).

Legislative Assembly: 325 seats (Rashtriya Janata Dal 136, Janata Dal 29, Congress—I 29, Communist—CPI 26, Bharatiya Janata Party 43, Jharkhand Mukti Morcha (Soren) 16, Communist—CPI—M 6, Samata Party 8, Jharkhand Mukti Morcha (Mardi) 2, independents and others 30).

Legislative Council: 96 seats.

GOA
(Capital—Panaji)

Governor: T. R. Satish Chandran.

Chief Minister: Dr Wilfred D'Souza (Maharashtrawadi Gomantak Party).

Legislative Assembly: 40 seats (Congress—I 18, Maharashtrawadi Gomantak Party 12, Bharatiya Janata Party 4, United Goans Party 3, independents and others 3).

GUJARAT
(Capital—Gandhinagar)

Governor: Krishna Pal Singh.

Chief Minister: Keshubhai Patel (Bharatiya Janata Party).

Legislative Assembly: 182 seats (Bharatiya Janata Party 116, Rashtriya Janata Party 4, Congress—I 55, Janata Dal 3, independents and others 4).

HARYANA
(Capital—Chandigarh)

Governor: Mahabir Prasad.

Chief Minister: Bansi Lal (Haryana Vikas Party).

Legislative Assembly: 90 seats (Congress—I 9, Samata Party 24, Haryana Vikas Party 32, Bharatiya Janata Party 11, independents and others 13, vacant 1).

HIMACHAL PRADESH
(Capital—Simla)

Governor: V. S. Rama Devi.

Chief Minister: Vir Bhadra Singh (Congress—I).

Legislative Assembly: 68 seats (Congress—I 31, Bharatiya Janata Party 28, Himachal Vikas Congress 4, independents 1, vacant 4).

JAMMU AND KASHMIR
(Capitals—(Summer) Srinagar, (Winter) Jammu)

Governor: Gen. (retd) K. V. Krishna Rao.

Chief Minister: Dr Farooq Abdullah (Jammu and Kashmir National Conference).

Legislative Assembly: 87 seats (Jammu and Kashmir National Conference 55, Bharatiya Janata Party 8, Congress—I 7, Janata Dal 5, Bahujan Samaj Party 4, All India Indira Congress (Tewari) 1, Communist—CPI—M 1, Awami League 1, independents 2, others 3).

Legislative Council: 36 seats.

KARNATAKA
(Capital—Bangalore)

Governor: Khurshid Alam Khan.

Chief Minister: J. H. Patel (Janata Dal).

Legislative Assembly: 224 seats (Janata Dal 116, Congress—I 35, Bharatiya Janata Party 40, Rajya Ryota Sangh 10, independents and others 23).

Legislative Council: 75 seats.

KERALA
(Capital—Thiruvananthapuram)

Governor: Sukhdev Singh Kang.

Chief Minister: E. K. Nayanar (Communist—CPI—M).

Legislative Assembly: 140 seats (Communist—CPI—M 41, Communist—CPI 18, Congress—I 37, Muslim League 13, Kerala Congress (Joseph) 6, Kerala Congress (M) 5, Congress—S 3, Janata Dal 4, Revolutionary Socialist Party 5, independents and others 8).

MADHYA PRADESH
(Capital—Bhopal)

Governor: Mohammed Shafi Qureshi.

Chief Minister: Digvijay Singh (Congress—I).

Legislative Assembly: 320 seats (Congress—I 176, Bharatiya Janata Party 118, Bahujan Samaj Party 11, independent and others 15).

MAHARASHTRA
(Capital—Mumbai)

Governor: Dr P. C. Alexander.

Chief Minister: Manohar Joshi (Shiv Sena).

Legislative Assembly: 288 seats (Congress—I 81, Shiv Sena 73, Bharatiya Janata Party 65, Janata Dal 11, Peasants' and Workers' Party 6, independents and others 52).

Legislative Council: 78 seats.

MANIPUR
(Capital—Imphal)

Governor: Oudh Narain Srivastava.

Chief Minister: W. Nipamacha Singh (Congress—I).

Legislative Assembly: 60 seats (Congress—I 26, Manipur Peoples' Party 11, Manipur State Congress 23).

MEGHALAYA
(Capital—Shillong)

Governor: M. M. Jacob.

Chief Minister: B. B. Lyngdoh (United Democratic Party).

Legislative Assembly: 60 seats (Congress—I 25, United Democratic Party 20, Bharatiya Janata Party 3, People's Democratic

Movement 3, Hills State People's Democratic Party 3, independents and others 6).

MIZORAM
(Capital—Aizawl)

Governor: Dr ARUN PRASAD MUKHERJEE.

Chief Minister: LALTHANHAWLA (Congress—I).

Legislative Assembly: 40 seats (Mizo National Front 14, Congress—I 16, Mizo Janta Dal 8, others 2).

NAGALAND
(Capital—Kohima)

Governor: OM PRAKASH SHARMA.

Chief Minister: S. C. JAMIR (Congress—I).

Legislative Assembly: 60 seats (Congress—I 53, independents and others 10).

ORISSA
(Capital—Bhubaneswar)

Governor: GOPALA RAMANUJAM.

Chief Minister: JANAKI BALLAV PATNAIK (Congress—I).

Legislative Assembly: 147 seats (Congress—I 80, Janata Dal 16, Biju Janata Dal 30, Bharatiya Janata Party 9, Jharkhand Mukti Morcha 4, independents and others 8).

PUNJAB
(Capital—Chandigarh)

Governor: Lt-Gen. (retd) B. K. N. CHIBBER.

Chief Minister: PRAKASH SINGH BADAL (Shiromani Akali Dal).

Legislative Assembly: 117 seats (Shiromani Akali Dal 75, Congress—I 14, Bharatiya Janata Party 18, Communist—CPI 2, Akali Dal (Mann) 1, Bahujan Samaj Party 1, independents 6).

RAJASTHAN
(Capital—Jaipur)

Governor: BALI RAM BHAGAT.

Chief Minister: BHAIRON SINGH SHEKHAWAT (Bharatiya Janata Party).

Legislative Assembly: 200 seats (Bharatiya Janata Party 95, Congress—I 77, Janata Dal 6, independents and others 22).

SIKKIM
(Capital—Gangtok)

Governor: CHAUDHURY RANDHIR SINGH.

Chief Minister: PAWAN KUMAR CHAMLING (Sikkim Democratic Front).

Legislative Assembly: 32 seats (Sikkim Democratic Front 19, Sikkim Samgram Parishad 10, Congress—I 2, independents and others 1).

TAMIL NADU
(Capital—Chennai)

Governor: M. S. FATHIMA BEEVI.

Chief Minister: MUTHUVEL KARUNANIDHI (Dravida Munnetra Kazhagam).

Legislative Assembly: 234 seats (Dravida Munnetra Kazhagam 172, Tamil Maanila Congress 39, Communist—CPI 8, AIADMK 4, independents and others 11).

TRIPURA
(Capital—Agartala)

Governor: SIDDHESWAR PRASAD.

Chief Minister: MANIK SARKAR (Communist—CPI—M).

Legislative Assembly: 60 seats (Communist—CPI—M 38, Congress—I 13, Tripura Upajati Juba Samity 4, independents and others 5).

UTTAR PRADESH
(Capital—Lucknow)

Governor: MOHAMMED SHAFI QURESHI.

Chief Minister: KALYAN SINGH (Bharatiya Janata Party).

Legislative Assembly: 425 seats (Bharatiya Janata Party 176, Samajwadi Party 110, Bahujan Samaj Party 54, Congress—I 15, Loktantric Congress 22, Janatantric Bahujan Samaj Party 13, Janata Dal (R) 4, Janata Dal 3, Communist—CPI—M 4, Bharatiya Kisan Kamgar Party 8, independents and others 16).

Legislative Council: 108 seats.

WEST BENGAL
(Capital—Calcutta)

Governor: K. V. RAGHUNATH REDDY.

Chief Minister: JYOTI BASU (Communist—CPI—M).

Legislative Assembly: 294 seats (Communist—CPI—M 150, Congress—I 82, Forward Bloc 21, Revolutionary Socialist 18, Communist—CPI 6, others 17).

UNION TERRITORIES

Andaman and Nicobar Islands (Headquarters—Port Blair):
Lt-Gov.: RAJENDRA KUMARI BAJPAI.

Chandigarh (Headquarters—Chandigarh):
Administrator: B. K. N. CHHIBER.
Chandigarh was to be incorporated into Punjab state on 26 January 1986, but the transfer was postponed indefinitely.

Dadra and Nagar Haveli (Headquarters—Silvassa):
Administrator: S. P. AGGARWAL.

Daman and Diu (Headquarters—Daman):
Administrator: S. P. AGGARWAL.

Lakshadweep (Headquarters—Kavaratti):
Administrator: RAJEEV TALWAR.

Pondicherry (Capital—Pondicherry):
Lt-Gov.: Dr RAJENDRA KUMARI BAJPAI.
Chief Minister: R. V. JANAKIRAMAN (Dravida Munnetra Kazhagam).
Assembly: 33 seats (DMK 9, AIADMK (J) 2, AIADMK (T) 1, Congress—I 9, Tamil Maanila Congress 6, Communist—CPI 2, independent and others 3, vacant 1).

NATIONAL CAPITAL TERRITORY

Delhi (Headquarters—Delhi):
Lt-Gov.: TEJENDRA KHANNA.
Chief Minister: SAHIB SINGH VERMA (Bharatiya Janata Party).
Assembly: 70 seats (Bharatiya Janata Party 49, Congress—I 14, Janata Dal 4, independents and others 3).

Political Organizations

MAJOR NATIONAL POLITICAL ORGANIZATIONS

All India Congress Committee (I): 24 Akbar Rd, New Delhi 110 011; tel. (11) 3019080; f. 1978, as Indian National Congress (I), as a breakaway group under Indira Gandhi; Pres. SONIA GANDHI; Vice-Pres. JITENDRA PRASAD; Gen. Secs MADHAV RAO SCINDIA, TARIQ ANWAR, MEIRA KUMAR, OSCAR FERNANDES, R. K. DHAWAN.

Bharatiya Janata Party (BJP) (Indian People's Party): 11 Ashok Rd, New Delhi 110 001; tel. (11) 3382234; fax (11) 3782163; f. 1980 as a breakaway group from Janata Party; radical right-wing Hindu party; Pres. LAL KRISHNA ADVANI; Gen. Secs KUSHABHAU THAKRE, SUSHMA SWARAJ, PRAMOD MAHAJAN, M. V. NAIDU, K. N. GOVINDACHARYA; 10.5m. mems.

Communist Party of India (CPI): Ajoy Bhavan, Kotla Marg, New Delhi 110 002; tel. (11) 3235546; fax (11) 3235543; f. 1925; advocates the establishment of a socialist society led by the working class, and ultimately of a communist society; nine-mem. central secretariat; Gen. Sec. ARDHENDU BHUSHAN BARDHAN; 558,838 mems (1997).

Communist Party of India—Marxist (CPI—M): A. K. Gopalan Bhavan, 27–29 Bhai Vir Singh Marg, New Delhi 110 001; tel. (11) 3747435; telex 3165729; fax (11) 3747483; f. 1964 as pro-Beijing breakaway group from the CPI; declared its independence of Beijing in 1968 and is managed by a central committee of 71 mems and a politburo of 15 mems; Leaders JYOTI BASU, PRAKASH KARAT, SITARAM YECHURY, SOMNATH CHATTERJEE; Gen. Sec. HARKISHAN SINGH SURJEET; 631,171 mems (1994).

Indian National Congress (S): New Delhi; tel. (11) 3382478; f. 1981; aims include the establishment by peaceful means of a socialist, co-operative commonwealth; advocates govt control of large-scale industries and services, co-operativism in industry and agriculture, and a neutral foreign policy; 4m. mems; Pres. SARAT CHANDRA SINHA; Gen. Sec. KISHORE CHANDRA S. DEO.

Janata Dal (People's Party): 7 Jantar Mantar Rd, New Delhi 110 001; tel. (11) 3321833; f. 1988 as a merger of parties within the Rashtriya Morcha; advocates non-alignment, the eradication of poverty, unemployment and wide disparities in wealth, and the protection of minorities; 136-mem. National Executive; Pres. SHARAD YADAV; Sec.-Gen. Dr BAPU KALDATE.

Rashtriya Janata Dal (RJD) (National People's Party): New Delhi; f. 1997 as a breakaway group from Janata Dal; Leader LALOO PRASAD YADAV.

Samajwadi Party (Socialist Party): New Delhi; f. 1991 by the merger of the Janata Dal (S) and the Janata Party; National Pres. MULAYAM SINGH YADAV; Gen. Sec. AMAR SINGH.

MAJOR REGIONAL POLITICAL ORGANIZATIONS

Akali Dal: Baradan Shri Darbar Sahib, Amritsar; f. 1920; merged with Congress Party 1958–62; Sikh party composed of several factions both moderate and militant; seeks the establishment of an autonomous Sikh state of 'Khalistan'; Pres. (Shiromani Akali Dal) PRAKASH SINGH BADAL.

Akhil Bharat Hindu Mahasabha: Hindu Mahasabha Bhavan, Mandir Marg, New Delhi 110 001; tel. (11) 343105; f. 1915; seeks the establishment of a democratic Hindu state; Pres. SHIVE SARAN; Gen. Sec. DINESH CHANDRA TYAGI; 500,000 mems.

All-India Anna Dravida Munnetra Kazhagam (AIADMK) (All-India Anna Dravidian Progressive Asscn): Lloyd's Rd, Chennai 600 004; f. 1972; breakaway group from the DMK; Leaders C. JAYALALITHA JAYARAM, M. CHINNASWAMY.

All India Forward Bloc: 28 Gurdwara Rakabganj Rd, New Delhi 110 001; tel. (11) 3712260; f. 1940 by Netaji Subhash Chandra Bose; socialist aims, including nationalization of major industries, land reform and redistribution; Chair. ASHOK GHOSH; Gen. Sec. DEBABRATA BISWAS SEN; 900,000 mems.

Asom Gana Parishad (AGP) (Assam People's Council): Golaghat, Assam; f. 1985; draws support from the All-Assam Gana Sangram Parishad and the All-Assam Students' Union (Pres. KESHAB MAHANTA; Gen. Sec. ATUL BORA); advocates the unity of India in diversity and a united Assam; Pres. PRAFULLA KUMAR MOHANTA; a breakaway faction formed a new central exec. committee under PULAKESH BARUA in April 1991.

Bahujan Samaj Party (Majority Society Party): promotes the rights of the *Harijans* ('Untouchables') of India; Leader KANSHI RAM; Gen. Sec. Ms MAYAWATI.

Dravida Munnetra Kazhagam (DMK): Anna Arivalayam, Teynampet, Chennai 600 018; f. 1949; aims at full autonomy for states (primarily Tamil Nadu) within the Union, to establish regional languages as state languages and English as the official language pending the recognition of regional languages as official languages of the Union; Pres. MUTHUVEL KARUNANIDHI; Gen. Sec. K. ANBAZHAGAN; more than 4m. mems.

Jammu and Kashmir National Conference (JKNC): Mujahid Manzil, Srinagar 190 002; tel. 71500; fmrly All Jammu and Kashmir National Conference, f. 1931, renamed 1939, reactivated 1975; state-based party campaigning for internal autonomy and responsible self-govt; Leader Dr FAROOQ ABDULLAH; Pres. BASHIR AHMAD BHAT (acting); Gen. Sec. SHEIKH NAZIR AHMED; 1m. mems.

Peasants' and Workers' Party of India: Mahatma Phule Rd, Naigaum, Mumbai 400 014; f. 1949; Marxist; seeks to nationalize all basic industries, to promote industrialization, and to establish a unitary state with provincial boundaries drawn on a linguistic basis; Gen. Sec. DAJIBA DESAI; c. 10,000 mems.

Republican Party of India (RPI): Ensa Hutments, I Block, Azad Maidan, Fort, Mumbai 400 001; tel. (22) 2621888; main aim is to realize the aims and objects set out in the preamble to the 1950 Constitution; Pres. PRAKASH RAO AMBEDKAR; Gen. Sec. RAMDAS ATHAVALE; 100,000 mems.

Shiv Sena: Mumbai; f. 1966; militant Hindu group; Leader BALASHAHEB 'BAL' THACKERAY.

Tamil Maanila Congress: c/o Lok Sabha, New Delhi; Pres. G. K. MOOPANAR; Gen. Sec. PETER ALPHONS.

Telugu Desam (Telugu Nation): 3-5-910, Himayatnagar, Hyderabad 500 029; tel. (842) 237290; f. 1982; state-based party (Andhra Pradesh); campaigns against rural poverty and social prejudice; split into two factions—Telugu Desam (NTR) (Pres. LAKSHMI PARVATHI) and Telugu Desam (Naidu) (Pres. N. CHANDRABABU NAIDU)—in 1995.

Diplomatic Representation

EMBASSIES AND HIGH COMMISSIONS IN INDIA

Afghanistan: 5/50F Shanti Path, Chanakyapuri, New Delhi 110 021; tel. (11) 603331; telex 3172253; fax (11) 6875439; Chargé d'affaires: AHMAD WALI MASUD.

Algeria: B-3/61 Safdarjung Enclave, New Delhi 110 029; tel. (11) 6185057; telex 3172373; fax (11) 6185062; e-mail embalg @nda.vsnl.net.in; Ambassador: ABDELHAMID SENOUCI BEREKSI.

Angola: C-12 Anand Niketan, New Delhi 110 021; tel. (11) 6888592; fax (11) 6884839; Ambassador: ARMANDO MATEUS CADATE.

Argentina: B-8/9 Vasant Vihar, Paschmi Marg, New Delhi 110 057; tel. (11) 6141345; telex 3172011; fax (11) 6873172; Ambassador: ELDA B. SAMPIETRO.

Australia: 1/50-G Shanti Path, Chanakyapuri, New Delhi 110 021; tel. (11) 6888223; telex 3182001; fax (11) 6873172; High Commissioner: ROBERT LAURIE.

Austria: EP/13 Chandragupta Marg, Chanakyapuri, New Delhi 110 021; tel. (11) 6889050; fax (11) 6886929; e-mail aedelhi@ del2.vsnl.net.in; Ambassador: Dr KARL PETERLIK.

Bangladesh: 56 Ring Rd, Lajpat Nagar-III, New Delhi 110 024; tel. (11) 6834668; telex 317528; fax (11) 6839237; High Commissioner: C. M. SAFISHAMI.

Belgium: 50N, Plot 4, Shanti Path, Chanakyapuri, New Delhi 110 021; tel. (11) 6889204; telex 3182008; fax (11) 6885821; Ambassador: GUILLAUME METTEN.

Bhutan: Chandragupta Marg, Chanakyapuri, New Delhi 110 021; tel. (11) 6889807; telex 3162263; fax (11) 6876710; Ambassador: Dasho NADO RINCHHEN.

Brazil: 8 Aurangzeb Rd, New Delhi 110 011; tel. (11) 3017301; telex 3165277; fax (11) 3793684; e-mail brasindi@giasdl01.vsnl.net.in; Ambassador: LUIZ FILIPE DE MACEDO SOARES.

Brunei: A-42 Vasant Marg, Vasant Vihar, New Delhi 110 057; tel. (11) 6888341; fax (11) 6881808.

Bulgaria: 16/17 Chandragupta Marg, Chanakyapuri, New Delhi 110 021; tel. (11) 6115550; telex 3172049; fax (11) 6876190; Ambassador: DIMITAR ALEXIEV BOJILOV.

Cambodia: B-47 Soami Nagar, New Delhi 110 017; tel. (11) 6423782; fax (11) 6425363; Ambassador: SIM SUONG.

Canada: 7/8 Shanti Path, Chanakyapuri, New Delhi 110 021; tel. (11) 6876500; telex 3172363; fax (11) 6876579; High Commissioner: PETER F. WALKER.

Chile: R/7 Hauz Khas, New Delhi 110 016; tel. (11) 6850537; telex 3182094; fax (11) 6850231; Ambassador: ULDARICIO FIGUEROA.

China, People's Republic: 50D Shanti Path, Chanakyapuri, New Delhi 110 021; tel. (11) 6871585; fax (11) 6885486; Ambassador: ZHOU GANG.

Colombia: 82D Malcha Marg, Chanakyapuri, New Delhi 110 021; tel. (11) 3012771; telex 3162090; fax (11) 3792485; Ambassador: Dr CARMENZA JARAMILLO.

Congo, Democratic Republic: C-56 Panchsheel Enclave, New Delhi 110 017; tel. (11) 6222796; telex 3166275; fax (11) 6227226; Ambassador: BELTCHIKA-KALUBYE.

Croatia: 70 Ruig Rd, Lajpat Nagar-III, New Delhi 110 024; tel. (11) 6924761; fax (11) 6924763; Ambassador: Dr DRAGO STAMBUCK.

Cuba: 4 Munirka Marg, Vasant Vihar, New Delhi 110 057; tel. (11) 6883849; telex 3162167; fax (11) 6883846; Ambassador: OLGA CHIMERO TRIAS.

Cyprus: 106 Jor Bagh, New Delhi 110 003; tel. (11) 4697503; fax (11) 4628828; High Commissioner: REA YLORDAMLIA.

Czech Republic: 50M Niti Marg, Chanakyapuri, New Delhi 110 021; tel. (11) 6110205; fax (11) 6886221; e-mail newdelhi@ embassy.mzv.cz; Ambassador: IVAN JESTŘÁB.

Denmark: 11 Aurangzeb Rd, New Delhi 110 011; tel. (11) 3010900; telex 3166160; fax (11) 3792891; e-mail dembassy@ giasdl01.vsnl.net.in; Ambassador: BJARNE HENNEBERG SØRENSEN.

Egypt: 1/50M Niti Marg, Chanakyapuri, New Delhi 110 021; tel. (11) 6114096; telex 3172245; fax (11) 6885355; e-mail egypt@del2.vsnl.net.in; Ambassador: GILLANE ALLAM.

Ethiopia: 7/50G Satya Marg, Chanakyapuri, New Delhi 110 021; tel. (11) 6119513; telex 3172358; fax (11) 6875731; Ambassador: DESTA ERIFO.

Finland: E–3 Nyaya Marg, Chanakyapuri, New Delhi 110 021; tel. (11) 6115258; fax (11) 6886713; e-mail finemb@del2.vsnl.net.in; Ambassador: BENJAMIN BASSIN.

France: 2/50E Shanti Path, Chanakyapuri, New Delhi 110 021; tel. (11) 6118790; telex 3172351; fax (11) 6872305; Ambassador: CLAUDE BLANCHEMAISON.

Germany: 6 Block 50G, Shanti Path, Chanakyapuri, POB 613, New Delhi 110 021; tel. (11) 6871831; telex 3172177; fax (11) 6873117; Ambassador: Dr HEINRICH-DIETRICH DIECKMAN.

Ghana: 50–N Satya Marg, Chanakyapuri, New Delhi 110 021; tel. (11) 6883298; telex 3172484; fax (11) 6883202; High Commissioner: ANTHONY FORSON.

Greece: 16 Sundar Nagar, New Delhi 110 003; tel. (11) 4617800; telex 3165232; fax (11) 4601363; Ambassador: Y. A. ZEPOS.

Holy See: 50C Niti Marg, Chanakyapuri, New Delhi 110 021 (Apostolic Nunciature); tel. (11) 6889184; fax (11) 6874286; Pro-Nuncio: Most Rev. GEORGE ZUR, Titular Archbishop of Sesta.

Hungary: Plot 2, 50M Niti Marg, Chanakyapuri, New Delhi 110 021; tel. (11) 6114737; fax (11) 6886742; Ambassador: ANDRAS DALLOS.

Indonesia: 50A Chanakyapuri, New Delhi 110 021; tel. (11) 6118642; telex 3172375; fax (11) 6884402; Ambassador: GATOT SUWARDI.

Iran: 5 Barakhamba Road, New Delhi 110 001; tel. (11) 3329600; telex 3166421; fax (11) 3325493; Ambassador: MIR MAHMOUD-MOUSSAVI KHAMENEH.

Iraq: 169–171 Jor Bagh, New Delhi 110 003; tel. (11) 4618011; telex 3166253; fax (11) 4631547; Ambassador: Mohammed F. H. al-Haboubi.

Ireland: 13 Jor Bagh, New Delhi 110 003; tel. (11) 4626733; telex 3165546; fax (11) 4697053; Ambassador: James Flavin.

Israel: 3 Aurangzeb Rd, New Delhi 110 011; tel. (11) 3013238; fax (11) 3014298; Ambassador: Dr Yehoyada Haim.

Italy: 50E Chandragupta Marg, Chanakyapuri, New Delhi 110 021; tel. (11) 6114355; telex 3182089; fax (11) 6873889; Ambassador: Dr Gaetano Zucconi.

Japan: Plots 4–5, 50G Shanti Path, Chanakyapuri, New Delhi 110 021; tel. (11) 6876581; telex 3172364; fax (11) 6885587; Ambassador: Hiroshi Hirabayashi.

Jordan: 1/21 Shanti Niketan, New Delhi 110 021; tel. (11) 607628; telex 3172045; fax (11) 6883763; Ambassador: Hisham Muhaisen.

Kazakhstan: EP 16–17 Chandragupta Marg, Chanakyapuri, New Delhi 110 021; tel. (11) 6888252; fax (11) 6888464; Ambassador: Erbol R. Shaimardanov.

Kenya: E-66 Vasant Marg, Vasant Vihar, New Delhi 110 057; tel. (11) 6146537; telex 3172166; fax (11) 6146550; High Commissioner: Joshua K. Terer.

Korea, Democratic People's Republic: 42/44 Sundar Nagar, New Delhi 110 003; tel. (11) 4617140; telex 3165059; Ambassador: Pak Myong Gu.

Korea, Republic: 9 Chandragupta Marg, Chanakyapuri, POB 5416, New Delhi 110 021; tel. (11) 6885412; fax (11) 6884840; Ambassador: Choi Dae-Hwa.

Kuwait: 5A Shanti Path, Chanakyapuri, New Delhi 110 021; tel. (11) 600791; telex 3172211; fax (11) 6873516; Ambassador: Abdul al-Suleiman Othman al-Qinaie.

Kyrgyzstan: A 9/32 Vasant Vihar, New Delhi 110 057; tel. (11) 6871680; fax (11) 6880372.

Laos: E53 Panchshila Park, New Delhi 110 017; tel. (11) 6427447; telex 3170128; fax (11) 6225812; Ambassador: Ammone Singhavong.

Lebanon: 10 Sardar Patel Marg, Chanakyapuri, New Delhi 110 021; tel. (11) 3013174; telex 3161161; fax (11) 3015555; Ambassador: Michel Bitar.

Libya: 22 Golf Links, New Delhi 110 003; tel. (11) 4697717; telex 3165193; fax (11) 4633005; Secretary of People's Bureau: Omar Ahmad Jadollah al-Aukali.

Malaysia: 50M Satya Marg, Chanakyapuri, New Delhi 110 021; tel. (11) 601291; telex 3182056; fax (11) 6881538; High Commissioner: Wan Hussain Wan Mustapha.

Mauritius: 5 Kautilya Marg, Chanakyapuri, New Delhi 110 021; tel. (11) 3011112; telex 3166045; fax (11) 3019925; High Commissioner: Mohunlal Goburdhan.

Mexico: B-33 Friends Colony (West), New Delhi 110 065; tel. (11) 6932860; telex 3166121; fax (11) 6932864; Ambassador: Edmundo Font.

Mongolia: 34 Archbishop Makarios Marg, New Delhi 110 003; tel. (11) 4631728; fax (11) 4633240; Ambassador: Dashdavaagiin Chuluundorj.

Morocco: 33 Archbishop Makarios Marg, New Delhi 110 003; tel. (11) 4636920; telex 3166118; fax (11) 4636925; Ambassador: Mohammed Belmahi.

Myanmar: 3/50F Nyaya Marg, Chanakyapuri, New Delhi 110 021; tel. (11) 6889007; telex 3172224; fax (11) 6877942; Ambassador: U Wynn Lwin.

Namibia: D-6/24 Vasant Vihar, New Delhi 110 057; tel. (11) 6140389; fax (11) 6146120; High Commissioner: Joel Kaapanda.

Nepal: Barakhamba Rd, New Delhi 110 001; tel. (11) 3329969; telex 3166283; fax (11) 3326857; Ambassador: Lok Raj Baral.

Netherlands: 6/50F Shanti Path, Chanakyapuri, New Delhi 110 021; tel. (11) 6884951; telex 3182054; fax (11) 6884956; e-mail nlembas@giasdloi.vsnl.net.in; Ambassador: J. H. J. Jeurissen.

New Zealand: 50N Nyaya Marg, Chanakyapuri, New Delhi 110 021; tel. (11) 6883170; fax (11) 6872317; High Commissioner: Adrian Simcock.

Nigeria: 21 Olof Palme Marg, Vasant Vihar, New Delhi 110 057; tel. (11) 6876646; telex 3182068; fax (11) 6876641; High Commissioner: E. Ola Adefemiwa.

Norway: 50C Shanti Path, Chanakyapuri, New Delhi 110 021; tel. (11) 6873532; telex 3182071; fax (11) 6873814; Ambassador: Arne Walther.

Oman: 16 Olof Palme Marg, New Delhi 110 057; tel. (11) 6140215; telex 3172342; fax (11) 6876478; Ambassador: Salim Mohammed Salim al-Wahaibi.

Pakistan: 2/50G Shanti Path, Chanakyapuri, New Delhi 110 021; tel. (11) 600603; telex 3165270; fax (11) 6872339; High Commissioner: Ashraf Jehangir.

Peru: D-6/13C, Vasant Vihar, New Delhi 110 057; tel. (11) 6143937; telex 3182067; fax (11) 6876427; Ambassador: Carlos Higueras-Ramos.

Philippines: 50N Nyaya Marg, Chanakyapuri, New Delhi 110 021; tel. (11) 601120; telex 3172397; fax (11) 6876401; Ambassador: José P. del Rosario, Jr.

Poland: 5/50M Shanti Path, Chanakyapuri, New Delhi 110 021; tel. (11) 6889211; telex 3172192; fax (11) 6871914; Ambassador: Jan Krzysztof Mroziewicz.

Portugal: 13 Sundar Nagar, New Delhi 110 003; tel. (11) 4601262; telex 3174181; fax (11) 4601252; e-mail ccpindia@giasdl101.vsnl.net.in; Ambassador: Manuel Marcelo Curto.

Qatar: G-5 Anand Niketan, New Delhi 110 021; tel. (11) 6117241; telex 3172304; fax (11) 6886080; Ambassador: Mubarak Rashid M. al-Boainin.

Romania: A-52 Vasant Marg, Vasant Vihar, New Delhi 110 057; tel. (11) 6140447; fax (11) 6140611; Ambassador: Petre Mateescu.

Russia: Shanti Path, Chanakyapuri, New Delhi 110 021; tel. (11) 6873799; telex 3182016; fax (11) 6876823; Ambassador: Albert Sergeyevich Chernyshov.

Saudi Arabia: D-12, New Delhi South Extension Part II, New Delhi 110 049; tel. (11) 6442470; telex 3171397; fax (11) 6449423; Ambassador: Fouad Hasan Faki.

Senegal: 30 Paschimi Marg, Vasant Vihar, New Delhi 110 057; tel. (11) 6873720; telex 3172041; fax (11) 6875809; Ambassador: Ahmed el Mansour Diop.

Singapore: E-6 Chandragupta Marg, Chanakyapuri, New Delhi 110 021; tel. (11) 6885659; fax (11) 6886798; e-mail singhnd@giasdlol.vsnl.net.in; High Commissioner: Ong Keng Yong.

Slovakia: 50M Niti Marg, Chanakyapuri, New Delhi 110 021; tel. (11) 6889071; fax (11) 6877941; Ambassador: Marain Tomasik.

Somalia: A-17, Defence Colony, New Delhi 110 024; tel. (11) 4619559; Ambassador: Mohamed Osman Omar.

South Africa: B-18 Vasant Marg, Vasant Vihar, New Delhi 110 057; tel. (11) 6149411; fax (11) 6143605; High Commissioner: Jerry Matthews Matsila.

Spain: 12 Prithviraj Rd, New Delhi 110 011; tel. (11) 3792085; telex 3161488; fax (11) 3793375; Ambassador: Alvaro de Castilla.

Sri Lanka: 27 Kautilya Marg, Chanakyapuri, New Delhi 110 021; tel. (11) 3010201; telex 3161162; fax (11) 3015295; High Commissioner: Mangala Moonesinghe.

Sudan: Plot No. 3, Shanti Path, Chanakyapuri, New Delhi 110 021; tel. (11) 6873785; telex 3172347; fax (11) 6883758; Ambassador: Awed el Karim Fadlalla.

Sweden: Nyaya Marg, Chanakyapuri, New Delhi 110 021; tel. (11) 6875760; telex 3182023; fax (11) 6885401; Ambassador: K. G. Engstrom.

Switzerland: Nyaya Marg, Chanakyapuri, New Delhi 110 021; tel. (11) 6878372; telex 3172350; fax (11) 6873093; Ambassador: Guy Ducrey.

Syria: 28 Vasant Marg, Vasant Vihar, New Delhi 110 057; tel. (11) 6140285; telex 3172360; fax (11) 6873107; Chargé d'affaires: Ahmad Mansour.

Tanzania: 10/1 Sarv Priya Vihar, New Delhi 110 016; tel. (11) 6853046; telex 3173095; fax (11) 6968408; High Commissioner: Alfred C. Tandau.

Thailand: 56N Nyaya Marg, Chanakyapuri, New Delhi 110 021; tel. (11) 605679; fax (11) 6872029; Ambassador: Vichai Vannasin.

Trinidad and Tobago: 131 Jor Bagh, New Delhi 110 003; tel. (11) 4618186; telex 3162481; fax (11) 4624581; High Commissioner: Ousman Ali.

Tunisia: 23 Olof Palme Marg, Vasant Vihar, New Delhi 110 057; tel. (11) 6885346; telex 3172162; fax (11) 6885301; Ambassador: Mohamed el Hedi ben Redjeb.

Turkey: 50N Nyaya Marg, Chanakyapuri, New Delhi 110 021; tel. (11) 601921; telex 3172408; fax (11) 6881409; Ambassador: Sami C. Onaran.

Turkmenistan: 1/13 Shanti Niketan, New Delhi 110 021; tel. (11) 6118409; fax (11) 6118332; Ambassador: Ashir Ataev.

Uganda: B-3/26 Vasant Vihar, New Delhi 110 057; tel. (11) 6144413; telex 3172198; fax (11) 6144405; High Commissioner: Joseph Tomusange.

Ukraine: 176 Jor Bagh, New Delhi 110 003; tel. (11) 4616019; fax (11) 4616085; ; Ambassador: G. I. Khodorovsky.

United Arab Emirates: EP–12 Chandragupt Marg, New Delhi 110 021; tel. (11) 4670830; telex 3172325; fax (11) 6873272; Ambassador: Ahmed Abdullah al-Musally.

United Kingdom: Shanti Path, Chanakyapuri, New Delhi 110 021; tel. (11) 6872161; telex 3165125; fax (11) 6872882; High Commissioner: Sir David Gore-Booth.

USA: Shanti Path, Chanakyapuri, New Delhi 110 021; tel. (11) 6889033; telex 3182065; fax (11) 4190017; Ambassador: RICHARD F. CELESTE.

Venezuela: N-114 Panchshila Park, New Delhi 110 017; tel. (11) 6496535; fax (11) 6491686; Ambassador: JOCELYN HENRÍQUEZ-KING.

Viet Nam: 17 Kautilya Marg, Chanakyapuri, New Delhi 110 021; tel. (11) 3018059; fax (11) 3017714; Ambassador: MUNGUYE CHI VYU.

Yemen: B-70 Greater Kailash-I, New Delhi 110 048; tel. (11) 6414731; telex 3171436; fax (11) 6478728; Ambassador: AHMED ABDO-RAGIH.

Yugoslavia: 3/50G Niti Marg, Chanakyapuri, New Delhi 110 021; tel. (11) 6873661; telex 3172365; fax (11) 6885535; Chargé d'affaires: SVETOZAR TOMIĆ.

Zambia: F 8/22 Vasant Vihar, New Delhi 110 057; tel. (11) 6145862; telex 3166084; fax (11) 6147928; High Commissioner: S. K. MUBUKWANU.

Zimbabwe: B-8 Anand Niketan, New Delhi 110 021; tel. (11) 6885060; telex 3172289; fax (11) 6886073; High Commissioner: TIRIVAFI JOHN KANGAI.

Judicial System

THE SUPREME COURT

The Supreme Court, consisting of a Chief Justice and not more than 25 judges appointed by the President, exercises exclusive jurisdiction in any dispute between the Union and the states (although there are certain restrictions where an acceding state is involved). It has appellate jurisdiction over any judgment, decree or order of the High Court where that Court certifies that either a substantial question of law or the interpretation of the Constitution is involved.

Provision is made for the appointment by the Chief Justice of India of judges of High Courts as ad hoc judges at sittings of the Supreme Court for specified periods, and for the attendance of retired judges at sittings of the Supreme Court. The Supreme Court has advisory jurisdiction in respect of questions which may be referred to it by the President for opinion. The Supreme Court is also empowered to hear appeals against a sentence of death passed by a State High Court in reversal of an order of acquittal by a lower court, and in a case in which a High Court has granted a certificate of fitness.

The Supreme Court also hears appeals which are certified by High Courts to be fit for appeal, subject to rules made by the Court. Parliament may, by law, confer on the Supreme Court any further powers of appeal.

The judges hold office until the age of 65 years.

Supreme Court: New Delhi; tel. (11) 3388942; telex 3166023; fax (11) 3383792.

Chief Justice of India: MADAN MOHAN PUNCHHI.

Judges of the Supreme Court: S. P. BHARUCHA, Dr A. S. ANAND, SUDHAKAR PANDITRAO KURDUKAR, S. B. MAJMUDAR, SUJATA V. MANOHAR, GANENDRA NARAYAN RAY, S. RAJENDRA BABU, A. P. MISRA, G. B. PATTAN, SYED SHAH MOHAMMED QUADRI, SURESH CHANDRA AGRAWAL, KALLUPURACKAL T. THOMAS, MANOJ KUMAR MUKHERJEE, Dr GIRISH THAKORLAL NANAVATI, SAIYED SAGHIR AHAMAD, BHUPINDER NATH KIRPAL, NAMIDANNA JAGANNADHA RAO, VISHESHWAR NATH KHARE, DEVINDAR PRATAP WADHWA.

Attorney-General: ASHOK HARIBHAI DESAI.

HIGH COURTS

The High Courts are the Courts of Appeal from the lower courts, and their decisions are final except in cases where appeal lies to the Supreme Court.

LOWER COURTS

Provision is made in the Code of Criminal Procedure for the constitution of lower criminal courts called Courts of Session and Courts of Magistrates. The Courts of Session are competent to try all persons duly committed for trial, and inflict any punishment authorized by the law. The President and the local government concerned exercise the prerogative of mercy.

The constitution of inferior civil courts is determined by regulations within each state.

Religion

INDIAN FAITHS

Buddhism: The Buddhists in Ladakh (Jammu and Kashmir) are followers of the Dalai Lama. Head Lama of Ladakh: KAUSHAK SAKULA, Dalgate, Srinagar, Kashmir. In 1981 there were 4.72m. Buddhists in India, representing 0.70% of the population.

Hinduism: 549.8m. Hindus (1981 census), representing 80.25% of the population.

Islam: Muslims are divided into two main sects, Shi'as and Sunnis. Most of the Indian Muslims are Sunnis. At the 1981 census Islam had 75.4m. adherents (11% of the population).

Jainism: 3.2m. adherents (1981 census), 0.46% of the population.

Sikhism: 13.1m. Sikhs (comprising 1.91% of the population at the 1981 census), the majority living in the Punjab.

Zoroastrians: More than 120,000 Parsis practise the Zoroastrian religion.

CHRISTIANITY

National Council of Churches in India: Christian Council Lodge, Civil Lines, POB 205, Nagpur 440 001, Maharashtra; tel. (712) 531312; fax (712) 520554; f. 1914; mems: 26 reformed and three orthodox churches, 14 regional Christian councils, 13 All-India ecumenical orgs and seven related agencies; represents c. 8m. mems; Pres. Dr K. RAJARATNAM; Gen. Sec. Rev. Dr IPE JOSEPH.

Orthodox Churches

Malankara Orthodox Syrian Church: Catholicate Palace, Devalokam, Kottayam 686 038, Kerala; tel. 578500; c. 2.5m. mems (1995); 22 bishops, 21 dioceses, 1,340 parishes; Catholicos of the East and Malankara Metropolitan: HH BASELIUS MARTHOMA MATHEWS II; Asscn Sec. A. K. THOMAS.

Mar Thoma Syrian Church of Malabar: Mar Thoma Sabha Office, Poolatheen, Tiruvalla 689 101, Kerala; tel. (473) 630449; fax (473) 630327; c. 800,000 mems (1997); Metropolitan: Most Rev. Dr ALEXANDER MAR THOMA; Sec. Rev. A. C. KURIAN.

The Malankara Jacobite Syrian Orthodox Church is also represented.

Protestant Churches

Church of North India (CNI): CNI Bhavan, 16 Pandit Pant Marg, New Delhi 110 001; tel. (11) 3716513; fax (11) 3716901; f. 1970 by merger of the Church of India (fmrly known as the Church of India, Pakistan, Burma and Ceylon), the Council of the Baptist Churches in Northern India, the Methodist Church (British and Australasian Conferences), the United Church of Northern India (a union of Presbyterians and Congregationalists, f. 1924), the Church of the Brethren in India, and the Disciples of Christ; comprises 24 dioceses; c. 1.2m. mems (1996); Moderator Most Rev. DHIRENDRA K. MOHANTY, Bishop of Cuttack; Gen. Sec. Dr VIDYA SAGAR LALL.

Bishop of Agra: Rt Rev. MORRIS ANDREWS, Diocesan Office, St Paul's Church Compound, Church Rd, Civil Lines, Agra 282 002; tel. (562) 354845; fax (562) 350244; Sec. Rev. S. R. CUTTING.

Bishop of Bhopal: Rt Rev. M. B. SINGH, 11 Bombay-Agra Rd, Indore 452 001; tel. (731) 494342; Sec. Rev. I. D. MAGANJI.

Bishop of Calcutta: Rt Rev. Dr D. C. GORAI, Bishop's House, 51 Chowringhee Rd, Calcutta 700 071; tel. (33) 2425259; fax (33) 2426360; Sec. C. BISWAS.

Bishop of Chotanagpur: Rt Rev. Z. J. TEROM, Bishop's Lodge, Church Rd, Ranchi 834 001; tel. (651) 311181; fax (651) 314184; Sec. Rev. B. DEMTA.

Bishop of Delhi: Rt Rev. KARAM MASIH, Bishop's Office, 1 Church Lane, New Delhi 110 001; tel. (11) 3717471; Sec. Rev. PAUL SWARUP.

Bishop of Gujarat: Rt Rev. VINOD KUMAR MATHUSHELLAH MALAVIYA, Bishop's House, Ellis Bridge, Ahmedabad 380 006; tel. and fax (79) 6561950; Sec. Rev. WILSON A. BARIA.

Bishop of Mumbai: Rt Rev. Dr S. B. JOSHUA, St John's House, Duxbury Lane, Colaba, Mumbai 400 005; tel. (22) 2151439; Sec. Rev. PRAKASH D. PATOLE.

Bishop of Patna: Rt Rev. P. P. MARANDIH, Bishop's House, Christ Church Compound, Bhagalpur 812 001; tel. (641) 400033; fax (641) 400314; Sec. Rev. SIMON TUDU.

Church of South India (CSI): Cathedral Rd, POB 4906, Chennai 600 086; tel. (44) 471266; f. 1947 by merger of the Methodist Church in South India, the South India United Church (itself a union of churches in the Congregational and Presbyterian/Reformed traditions) and the four southern dioceses of the (Anglican) Church of India; comprises 21 dioceses (incl. one in Sri Lanka); c. 2.2m. mems (1988); Moderator Most Rev. V. P. DANDIN, Bishop in Karnataka North; Gen. Sec. Prof. GEORGE KOSHY.

Methodist Church in India: Methodist Centre, 21 YMCA Rd, Mumbai Central, Mumbai 400 008; tel. and fax (22) 3074137; f. 1856 as the Methodist Church in Southern Asia; 473,000 mems (1985); Gen. Sec. Rev. JAMES C. LAL.

Samavesam of Telugu Baptist Churches: C. A. M. Compound, Nellore 524 003, Andhra Pradesh; tel. (861) 24177; f. 1962; comprises 856 independent Baptist churches; 578,295 mems (1995); Gen. Sec. Rev. Dr R. DANAMAIAH.

United Evangelical Lutheran Churches in India: 1 First St, Haddows Rd, Chennai 600 006; tel. (44) 6421575; fax (44) 6421870; f. 1975; 11 constituent denominations: Andhra Evangelical Lutheran Church, Arcot Lutheran Church, Evangelical Lutheran Church in Madhya Pradesh, Gossner Evangelical Lutheran Church, India Evangelical Lutheran Church, Jeypore Evangelical Lutheran Church, Northern Evangelical Lutheran Church, North Western Gossner Evangelical Lutheran Church, South Andhra Lutheran Church, Good Samaritan Evangelical Lutheran Church and Tamil Evangelical Lutheran Church; c. 1.3m. mems; Pres. Rev. C. S. R. TOPNO; Exec. Sec. Rev. PRASANNA KUMARI SAMUEL.

Other denominations active in the country include the Assembly of the Presbyterian Church in North East India, the Bengal-Orissa-Bihar Baptist Convention (6,000 mems), the Chaldean Syrian Church of the East, the Convention of the Baptist Churches of Northern Circars, the Council of Baptist Churches of North East India, the Council of Baptist Churches of Northern India, the Hindustani Convent Church and the Mennonite Church in India.

The Roman Catholic Church

India comprises 23 archdioceses and 110 dioceses. These include four archdioceses and nine dioceses of the the Syro-Malabar rite, and one archdiocese and three dioceses of the Syro-Malankarese rite. The archdiocese of Goa and Daman, the seat of the Patriarch of the East Indies, is directly responsible to the Holy See. The remaining archdioceses are metropolitan sees. In early 1997 there were an estimated 16m. adherents in the country.

Catholic Bishops' Conference of India (CBCI): CBCI Centre, 1 Ashok Place, Goledakkhana, New Delhi 110 001; tel. (11) 3344470; fax (11) 3344695; f. 1944; Pres. Most Rev. JOSEPH MAR POWATHIL, Archbishop of Changanacherry; Sec.-Gen. Rt Rev. CHARLES SORENG, Bishop of Hazaribagh.

Latin Rite

Conference of Catholic Bishops of India—Latin Rite (CCBI—LR): CCBI Secretariat, Divya Deepti Sadan, 2nd Floor, 9–10 Bhai Vir Singh Marg, POB 680, New Delhi 110 001; tel. (11) 3364222; fax (11) 3364343; f. 1994; Pres. Most Rev. MARIANUS AROKIASAMY, Archbishop of Madurai.

Patriarch of the East Indies: Most Rev. RAUL NICOLAU GONSALVES (Archbishop of Goa and Daman), Paço Patriarcal, POB 216, Altinho, Panjim, Goa 403 001; tel. (832) 223353; fax (832) 224139.

Archbishop of Agra: Most Rev. CECIL DE SA, Cathedral House, Wazirpura Rd, Agra 282 003; tel. (562) 351318.

Archbishop of Bangalore: Most Rev. ALPHONSUS MATHIAS, Archbishop's House, 18 Miller's Rd, Bangalore 560 046; tel. (80) 3330438.

Archbishop of Bhopal: Most Rev. PASCHAL TOPNO, Archbishop's House, 33 Ahmedabad Palace Rd, Bhopal 462 001; tel. (755) 540829; fax (755) 544737.

Archbishop of Bombay (Mumbai): Most Rev. IVAN DIAS, Archbishop's House, 21 Nathalal Parekh Marg, Fort, Mumbai 400 001; tel. (22) 2021093; telex 113263; fax (22) 2853872.

Archbishop of Calcutta: Most Rev. HENRY SEBASTIAN D'SOUZA, Archbishop's House, 32 Park St, Calcutta 700 016; tel. (33) 2471960; fax (33) 2474666; e-mail archbishop@cal.indiax.com.

Archbishop of Chennai (Madras) and Mylapore: Most Rev. JAMES MASILAMONY ARUL DAS, Archbishop's House, 21 San Thome High Rd, Chennai 600 004; tel. (44) 4940833; fax (44) 4941999.

Archbishop of Cuttack-Bhubaneswar: Most Rev. RAPHAEL CHEENATH, Archbishop's House, Satya Nagar, Bhubaneswar 751 007; tel. (674) 402234; fax (674) 401817.

Archbishop of Delhi: Most Rev. ALAN DE LASTIC, Archbishop's House, Ashok Place, New Delhi 110 001; tel. (11) 3343457; fax (11) 37465675.

Archbishop of Guwahati: Most Rev. THOMAS MENAMPARAMPIL, Archbishop's House, POB 100, Guwahati 781 001; tel. (361) 547664; fax (361) 520588.

Archbishop of Hyderabad: Most Rev. SAMININI ARULAPPA, Archbishop's House, Sardar Patel Rd, Secunderabad 500 003; tel. (40) 805545.

Archbishop of Imphal: Most Rev. JOSEPH MITTATHANY, Archbishop's House, POB 35, Imphal 795 001; tel. (385) 221170.

Archbishop of Madurai: Most Rev. MARIANUS AROKIASAMY, Archbishop's House, K. Pudur, Madurai 625 007; tel. (452) 533330; fax (452) 536630.

Archbishop of Nagpur: Most Rev. LEOBARD D'SOUZA, Archbishop's House, 25 Kamptee Rd, Mohan Nagar, Nagpur 440 001; tel. (712) 533239; fax (712) 525090.

Archbishop of Pondicherry and Cuddalore: Most Rev. S. MICHAEL AUGUSTINE, Archbishop's House, POB 193, Pondicherry 605 001; tel. (413) 34748; fax (413) 39911.

Archbishop of Ranchi: Most Rev. TELESPHORE P. TOPPO, Archbishop's House, Purulia Rd, POB 5, Ranchi 834 001; tel. (651) 204728; fax (651) 304844.

Archbishop of Shillong: Most Rev. TARCISIUS RESTO PHANRANG, Archbishop's House, POB 37, Shillong 793 003; tel. and fax (364) 223355.

Archbishop of Verapoly: Most Rev. DANIEL ACHARUPARAMBIL, Latin Archbishop's House, POB 2581, Kochi 682 031; tel. (484) 372892; fax (484) 360911.

Syro-Malabar Rite

Apostolic Administrator of Ernakulam-Angamaly: Most Rev. VARKEY VITHAYATHIL, The Syro-Malabar Archiepiscopal Curia, Mount St Thomas, Bharath Matha College, POB 2580, Kochi 682 031; tel. (484) 352629; fax (484) 366028.

Archbishop of Changanacherry: Most Rev. JOSEPH MAR POWATHIL, Archbishop's House, POB 20, Changanacherry 686 101; tel. and fax (482) 420040.

Archbishop of Tellicherry: Most Rev. GEORGE VALIAMATTAM, Archbishop House, POB 70, Tellicherry 670 101; tel. (497) 231058.

Archbishop of Trichur: Most Rev. JACOB THOOMKUZHY, Archbishop's House, Trichur 680 005; tel. (487) 333325; fax (487) 333580.

Syro-Malankarese Rite

Archbishop of Thiruvananthapuram: Most Rev. CYRIL MAR BASELIOS MALANCHARUVIL, Archbishop's House, Pattom, Thiruvananthapuram 695 004; tel. (471) 541643; fax (471) 541635.

BAHÁ'Í FAITH

National Spiritual Assembly: Bahá'í House, 6 Canning Rd, POB 19, New Delhi 110 001; tel. (11) 3386458; fax (11) 3782178; c. 2m. mems; Sec.-Gen. R. N. SHAH; Exec. Sec. A. K. MERCHANT.

The Press

Freedom of the Press was guaranteed under the 1950 Constitution. In 1979 a Press Council was established (its predecessor was abolished in 1975), the function of which was to uphold the freedom of the press and maintain and improve journalistic standards.

The growth of a thriving press has been inhibited by cultural barriers caused by religious, social and linguistic differences. Consequently the English-language press, with its appeal to the educated middle-class urban readership throughout the states, has retained its dominance. The English-language metropolitan dailies are some of the widest circulating and most influential newspapers. The main Indian language dailies, by paying attention to rural affairs, cater for the increasingly literate non-anglophone provincial population. Most Indian-language papers have a relatively small circulation.

The majority of publications in India are under individual ownership (74% in 1995), and they claim a large part of the total circulation (49% in 1995). The most powerful groups, owned by joint stock companies, publish most of the large English dailies and frequently have considerable private commercial and industrial holdings. Four of the major groups are as follows:

Times of India Group (controlled by ASHOK JAIN and family): dailies: *The Times of India, Economic Times*, the Hindi *Navbharat Times*, the *Maharashtra Times* (Mumbai); periodicals: the English fortnightlies *Femina* and *Filmfare*.

Indian Express Group (controlled by the RAMNATH GOENKA family): publishes nine dailies including the *Indian Express*, the Marathi *Lokasatta*, the Tamil *Dinamani*, the Telugu *Andhra Prabha*, the Kannada *Kannada Prabha* and the English *Financial Express*; six periodicals including the English weeklies the *Indian Express* (Sunday edition), *Screen,* the Telugu *Andhra Prabha Illustrated Weekly* and the Tamil *Dinamani Kadir* (weekly).

Hindustan Times Group (controlled by the K. K. BIRLA family): dailies: the *Hindustan Times* (Delhi and Patna), *Pradeep* (Patna) and the Hindi *Hindustan* (Delhi and Patna); periodicals: the weekly *Overseas Hindustan Times* and the Hindi monthly *Nandan* and *Kadambini* (New Delhi).

Ananda Bazar Patrika Group (controlled by AVEEK SARKAR and family): dailies: the *Ananda Bazar Patrika* (Calcutta) and the English *The Telegraph*; periodicals include: the English weekly *Sunday*, the English fortnightlies *Sportsworld* and *Business World*, Bengali fortnightly *Desh*, Bengali monthly *Anandamela*, Bengali fortnightly *Anandalok* and the Bengali monthly *Sananda*.

PRINCIPAL DAILIES

Delhi (incl. New Delhi)

The Asian Age: 210 Surya Kiran, 19 Kasturba Gandhi Marg, New Delhi 110 001; tel. (11) 3712543; fax (11) 3755514; f. 1994; morning; English; also publ. from Bangalore, Mumbai, Calcutta and London; Editor-in-Chief M. J. AKBAR; circ. 47,200 (New Delhi and Mumbai).

Business Standard: Pratap Bhavan, 5 Bahadur Shah Zafar Marg, New Delhi 110 002; tel. (11) 3720202; fax (11) 3720201; morning;

English; also publ. from Calcutta and Mumbai; Editor T. N. NINAN; combined circ. 25,500.

Daily Milap: 8A Bahadur Shah Zafar Marg, New Delhi 110 002; tel. (11) 3317737; fax (11) 3319166; e-mail milap@delz.vsnl.net.in; f. 1923; Urdu; nationalist; Man. Editor PUNAM SURI; Chief Editor NAVIN SURI; circ. 29,106.

Daily Pratap: Pratap Bhawan, 5 Bahadur Shah Zafar Marg, New Delhi 110 002; tel. (11) 3317938; fax (11) 3318276; f. 1919; Urdu; Editor K. NARENDRA; circ. 26,700.

Delhi Mid Day: World Trade Tower, Barakhamba Lane, New Delhi 110 001; tel. (11) 3715581; fax (11) 3350491; f. 1989; Editor JOHN DAYAL.

The Economic Times: 7 Bahadur Shah Zafar Marg, New Delhi 110 002; tel. (11) 3312277; telex 3161339; fax (11) 3323346; f. 1961; English; also publ. from Calcutta, Ahmedabad, Bangalore, Hyderabad, Chennai and Mumbai; Editor (Delhi) ARINDAM SENGUPTA; combined circ. 342,100, circ. (Delhi) 100,700.

Financial Express: Bahadur Shah Zafar Marg, New Delhi 110 002; tel. (11) 3311111; telex 3165803; f. 1961; morning; English; also publ. from Ahmedabad (in Gujarati), Mumbai, Bangalore, Calcutta, Coimbatore, Kochi and Chennai; Exec. Editor R. JAGANNATHAN; combined circ. 30,100.

The Hindu: INS Bldg, Rafi Marg, New Delhi 110 001; tel. (11) 3715426; fax (11) 3718158; f.1878; morning; English; also publ. from Bangalore, Coimbatore, Hyderabad, Chennai, Madurai, Thiruvananthapuram and Visakhapatnam; Editor N. RAVI; combined circ. 651,500.

Hindustan: 18/20 Kasturba Gandhi Marg, New Delhi 110 001; tel. (11) 3318201; telex 3166310; fax (11) 3321189; f. 1936; morning; Hindi; also publ. from Patna; Exec. Editor ALOK MEHTA; circ. (Delhi) 105,300, (Patna) 264,100.

The Hindustan Times: 18/20 Kasturba Gandhi Marg, New Delhi 110 001; tel. (11) 3318201; telex 3166310; fax (11) 3321189; f. 1923; morning; English; also publ. from Patna and Lucknow; Editor V. N. NARAYANAN; circ. (Delhi) 523,200; combined circ. 552,300.

Indian Express: Bahadur Shah Zafar Marg, New Delhi 110 002; tel. (11) 3311111; telex 3165908; fax (11) 3716037; f. 1953; English; also publ. from Mumbai, Chandigarh, Vadodara, Coimbatore, Kochi, Pune, Bangalore, Ahmedabad, Chennai, Madurai, Kozhikode, Nagpur, Hyderabad, Vizianagaram and Vijayawada; Man. Editor VIVEK GOENKA; Chief Editor SHEKHAR GUPTA; combined circ. 555,500, circ. (New Delhi and Chandigarh) 113,300.

Janasatta: 9/10 Bahadur Shah Zafar Marg, New Delhi 110 002; f. 1983; Hindi; tel. (11) 3311111; telex 3165908; fax (11) 3310089; also publ. from Chandigarh, Calcutta and Mumbai; Editor-in-Chief PRABHASH JOSHI; circ. (New Delhi and Chandigarh) 70,000.

National Herald: Herald House, Bahadur Shah Zafar Marg, New Delhi 110 002; tel. (11) 3319014; telex 3165821; fax (11) 3313458; f. 1938; English; nationalist; also publ. from Lucknow; Editor-in-Chief K. V. S. RAMA SARMA; combined circ. 80,000.

Navbharat Times: 7 Bahadur Shah Zafar Marg, New Delhi 110 002; tel. (11) 3312277; telex 3161337; fax (11) 3323346; f. 1947; Hindi; also publ. from Mumbai, Jaipur and Patna; Editor VIDYANIWAS MISRA; combined circ. 388,200, circ. (Delhi) 259,100.

The Observer of Business and Politics: 'Vijaya', 17 Barakhamba Rd, New Delhi 110 001; tel. (11) 3713200; telex 3166893; fax (11) 3327065; f. 1990; Chair. of Editorial Board and Editor-in-Chief R. K. MISHRA.

The Pioneer: Link House, 3 Bahadur Shah Zafar Marg, New Delhi 110 002; tel. (11) 3755271; telex 3161297; fax (11) 3755275; e-mail pioneer@del2.vsnl.net.in; f. 1865; also publ. from Lucknow, Allahabad, Varanasi and Kanpur; Editor CHANDAN MITRA.

Punjab Kesari: Romesh Bhavan, 2 Printing Press Complex, nr Wazirpur DTC Depot, Ring Rd, Delhi 110 052; tel. (11) 7181133; fax (11) 7187700; Hindi; also publ. from Jalandhar and Ambala; Editor VIJAY KUMAR; Resident Editor ASHWINI KUMAR; circ. 302,765 (Delhi).

Rashtriya Sahara: Amba Deep, Kasturba Gandhi Marg, New Delhi 110 001; tel. (11) 3327727; fax (11) 3755317; morning; Hindi; also publ. from Lucknow; Resident Editor NISHIT JOSHI; cir. 93,700 (Delhi), 115,500 (Lucknow).

Sandhya Times: 7 Bahadur Shah Zafar Marg, New Delhi 110 002; tel (11) 3312277; telex 3161339; fax (11) 3323346; f. 1979; Hindi; evening; Editor SAT SONI; circ. 76,100.

The Statesman: Rajiv Gandhi Circus, New Delhi 110 001; tel. (11) 3315911; telex 3166324; fax (11) 3315295; f. 1875; English; also publ. from Calcutta; Editor-in-Chief C. R. IRANI; Resident Editor MANASH GHOSH; combined circ. 173,300.

The Times of India: 7 Bahadur Shah Zafar Marg, Delhi 110 002; tel. (11) 3312277; telex 3161337; fax (11) 3323346; f. 1838; English; also publ. from Mumbai, Bangalore, Ahmedabad, Lucknow and Patna; Chair. ASHOK JAIN; Editorial Adviser H. K. DUA; circ. (Delhi) 420,300, combined circ. 1,076,400.

Andhra Pradesh

Hyderabad

Deccan Chronicle: 36 Sarojini Devi Rd, Hyderabad 500 003; tel. (40) 7803930; telex 4256644; fax (40) 7805256; f. 1938; English; Editor-in-Chief M. J. AKBAR; Editor A. T. JAYANTI; circ. 115,700.

Eenadu: Somajiguda, Hyderabad 500 082; tel. (40) 3318181; telex 4256521; fax (40) 3318555; f. 1974; Telugu; also publ. from Tirupati, Anantapur, Suryapet, Nellore, Guntur, Rajahmundry, Visakhapatnam, Karimnagar and Vijayawada; Chief Editor RAMOJI RAO; combined circ. 665,000.

Newstime: 6-3-570 Somajiguda, Hyderabad 500 482; tel. (40) 318181; telex 4256521; fax (40) 318555; f. 1984; also publ. from Vijaywada and Visakhapatnam; Editor RAMOJI RAO; circ. 60,000.

Rahnuma-e-Deccan: 5-3-831, Goshamahal, Hyderabad 500 012; tel. (40) 4732225; fax (40) 4616991; f. 1949; morning; Urdu; independent; Gen. Man. MIR ALI HYDER HUSSAINI; Chief Editor SYED VICARUDDIN; circ. 20,000.

Siasat Daily: Jawaharlal Nehru Rd, Hyderabad 500 001; tel. (40) 4603666; fax (40) 4603188; f. 1949; morning; Urdu; Editor ZAHID ALI KHAN; circ. 44,939.

Vijayawada

Andhra Jyoti: Andhra Jyoti Bldg, POB 712, Vijayawada 520 010; tel. (866) 474532; telex 475217; f. 1960; Telugu; also publ. from Hyderabad, Visakhapatnam and Tirupati; Editor NANDURI RAMAMOHAN RAO; combined circ. 91,100.

Andhra Patrika: POB 534, Gandhinagar, Vijayawada 520 003; tel. (866) 61247; f. 1914; Telugu; also publ. from Hyderabad; Editor S. RADHAKRISHNA; combined circ. 134,000.

Andhra Prabha: 16-1-28, Kolandareddy Rd, Vijayawada 520 016; tel. (866) 61351; telex 475231; f. 1935; Telugu; also publ. from Bangalore, Hyderabad, Chennai and Vijianagram; Editor P. V. RAO; combined circ. 32,000.

Indian Express: George Oakes Building, Besant Rd, Vijayawada 520 003; English; also publ. from Bangalore, Chennai, Kochi, Coimbatore, Hyderabad, Vijianagram and Madurai; Man. Editor VIVEK GOENKA; Editor SHEKHAR GUPTA; combined circ. 299,500.

Assam

Guwahati

Asomiya Pratidin: Maniram Dewan Rd, Guwahati 781 003; tel. (361) 540420; fax (361) 522017; morning; Assamese; circ. 86,700.

Assam Tribune: Tribune Bldgs, Maniram Dewan Rd, Chandmari, Guwahati 781 003; tel. (361) 541357; telex 2352417; fax (361) 540594; f. 1939; English; Man. Dir and Editor P. G. BARUAH; circ. 44,000.

Dainik Asam: Tribune Bldgs, Maniram Dewan Rd, Chandmari, Guwahati 781 003; tel. (361) 541356; telex 2352417; fax (361) 541360; f. 1965; Assamese; Chief Editor KIRTINATH HAZARIKA; circ. 20,200.

Jorhat

Dainik Janambhumi: Nehru Park Rd, Jorhat 785 001; tel. (376) 320033; telex 287220; fax (376) 321713; f. 1972; Assamese; Editor DEVA KR. BORAH; circ. 32,200.

Bihar

Patna

Aryavarta: Mazharul Haque Path, Patna 800 001; tel. (612) 233015; fax (612) 222350; morning; Hindi; Editor HARISHANKAR DWIVEDI.

Hindustan Times: Buddha Marg, Patna 800 001; tel. (612) 223434; telex 22357; fax (612) 226120; f. 1918; morning; English; also publ. from New Delhi; Editor V. N. NARAYANAN; circ. 29,000.

Indian Nation: Mazharul Haque Path, Patna 800 001; tel. (612) 233015; fax (612) 222350; morning; English; Editor HARISHANKAR DWIVEDI.

The Times of India: Times House, Fraser Rd, Patna 800 001; tel. (612) 226301; telex 222242; fax (612) 233525; Exec. Editor GAUTAM ADHIKARI; circ. 31,700.

Ranchi

Ranchi Express: 55 Baralal St, Ranchi 834 001; tel. (651) 206320; fax (651) 203466; f. 1963; Hindi; Editor AJAY MAROO; circ. 67,600.

Goa

Panaji

Gomantak: Gomantak Bhavan, St Inez, Panaji, Goa 403 001; tel. (832) 223212; telex 194237; fax (832) 223213; f. 1962; morning; Marathi and English edns; Editor NARAYAN G. ATHAWALAY; circ. 16,600 (Marathi), 5,700 (English).

Navhind Times: Navhind Bhavan, Rua Ismail Gracias, POB 161, Panaji, Goa 403 001; tel. (832) 224033; telex 194217; fax (832) 224258; f. 1963; morning; English; Editor ARUN SINHA; circ. 25,983.

Gujarat

Ahmedabad

Gujarat Samachar: Gujarat Samachar Bhavan, Khanpur, Ahmedabad 380 001; tel. (79) 5504010; telex 1216642; fax (79) 5502000; f. 1930; morning; Gujarati; also publ. from Surat, Rajkot, Baroda, Mumbai and New York; Editor SHANTIBHAI SHAH; combined circ. 725,700.

Indian Express: Janasatta Bldg, Mirzapur Rd, Ahmedabad; tel. (79) 5507028; fax (79) 5507708; f. 1968; English; also publ. in 19 other towns throughout India; Man. Editor VIVEK GOENKA; Chief Editor SHEKHAR GUPTA; circ. (Ahmedabad and Vadodara) 36,020.

Lokasatta—Janasatta: Mirzapur Rd, POB 188, Ahmedabad 380 001; tel. (79) 5507307; telex 1216429; fax (79) 5507708; f. 1953; morning; Gujarati; also publ. from Rajkot and Vadodara; Man. Editor VIVEK GOENKA; combined circ. 32,965.

Sandesh: Sandesh Bhavan, Gheekanta Rd, Ahmedabad 380 001; tel. (79) 5624241; fax (79) 5624392; e-mail sandesh@adl.vsnl.net.in; f. 1923; Gujarati; also publ. from Baroda, Rajkot and Surat; Editor FALGUNBHAI C. PATEL; combined circ. 561,362.

The Times of India: 139 Ashram Rd, POB 4046, Ahmedabad 380 009; tel. (79) 6582151; fax (79) 6583758; f. 1968; English; also publ. from Mumbai, Delhi, Bangalore, Patna and Lucknow; Resident Editor KAMLENDRA KANWAR; circ. (Ahmedabad) 77,540.

Western Times: 'Western House', Marutnandan Complex, Madalpur, Ahmedabad 380 006; tel. (79) 6576037; fax (79) 6577421; f. 1967; English and Gujarati edns; also publ. (in Gujarati) in Mehsana, Surendranagar, Godhra, Charotar-Nadiad, Baroda and Bharuch; Man. Editor NIKUNJ PATEL; Editor RAMU PATEL; circ. (Ahmedabad) 17,000 (English), 25,000 (Gujarati); circ. 16,000 (Mehsana), 15,000 (Surendranagar), 18,500 (Godhra), 10,000 (Charotar-Nadiad).

Rajkot

Jai Hind: Jai Hind Press Bldg, Babubhai Shah Marg, POB 59, Rajkot 360 001; tel. (281) 40511; fax (281) 48677; f. 1948; morning and evening (in Rajkot as *Sanj Samachar*); Gujarati; also publ. from Ahmedabad; Editor Y. N. SHAH; combined circ. 82,800.

Phulchhab: Phulchhab Bhavan, Mahatma Gandhi Rd, POB 118, Rajkot 360 001; tel. (281) 44611; f. 1950; morning; Gujarati; Man. MANSUKH C. JOSHI; Editor HARSUKH M. SANGHANI; circ. 86,500.

Surat

Gujaratmitra and Gujaratdarpan: Gujaratmitra Bhavan, nr Old Civil Hospital, Sonifalia, Surat 395 003; tel. (261) 478703; telex 188261; fax (261) 478700; f. 1863; morning; Gujarati; Editor B. P. RESHAMWALA; circ. 79,767.

Jammu and Kashmir

Jammu

Himalayan Mail: Srinagar; f. 1996; English.

Kashmir Times: Residency Rd, Jammu 180 001; tel. (191) 543676; telex 377255; fax (191) 542029; f. 1955; morning; English; Editor VED BHASIN; circ. 67,500.

Srinagar

Srinagar Times: Badshah Bridge, Srinagar; f. 1969; Urdu; Editor GULAM MUHAMMAD SOFI; circ. 14,000.

Karnataka

Bangalore

Deccan Herald: 75 Mahatma Gandhi Rd, Bangalore 560 001; tel. (80) 5588999; telex 8452339; fax (80) 5587179; f. 1948; morning; English; also publ. from Hubli-Dharwar; Editor-in-Chief K. N. HARI KUMAR; combined circ. 179,800.

Indian Express: 1 Queen's Rd, Bangalore 560 001; tel. (80) 2256893; telex 8452957; fax (80) 2256617; f. 1965; English; also publ. from Kochi, Hyderabad, Chennai, Madurai, Vijayawada and Vizianagaram; Man. Editor VIVEK GOENKA; Editor SHEKHAR GUPTA; combined circ. 299,500.

Kannada Prabha: 1 Queen's Rd, Bangalore 560 001; tel. (80) 2256893; telex 8452597; fax (80) 2256617; Kannada; Editor Y. N. KRISHNAMURTHY; circ. 85,800.

Prajavani: 66 Mahatma Gandhi Rd, Bangalore 560 001; tel. (80) 588999; telex 8452339; fax (80) 586443; f. 1948; morning; Kannada; also publ. from Hubli-Dharwar; Editor-in-Chief K. N. HARIKUMAR; combined circ. 300,000.

Hubli-Dharwar

Samyukta Karnataka: Koppikar Rd, Hubli 580 020; tel. 64858; telex 865220; f. 1933; Kannada; also publ. from Bangalore; Man. Editor K. SHAMA RAO; combined circ. 143,700.

Manipal

Udayavani: Udayavani Bldg, Press Corner, Manipal 576 119; tel. (8252) 70845; fax (8252) 70563; f. 1970; Kannada; Editor T. SATISH U. PAI; circ. 126,800.

Kerala

Kottayam

Deepika: POB 7, Kottayam 686 001; tel. (481) 566706; telex 888203; fax (481) 567947; e-mail deepika@md2.vsnl.net.in; internet http://www.deepika.com; f. 1887; Malayalam; independent; also publ. from Kannur, Kochi, Thiruvananthapuram and Thrissur; Dir GEORGE JACOB; combined circ. 150,000.

Malayala Manorama: K. K. Rd, POB 26, Kottayam 686 001; tel. (481) 563646; telex 888201; fax (481) 565398; f. 1888; also publ. from Kozhikode, Thiruvananthapuram, Palakkad, Kanur, Kollom and Kochi; morning; Malayalam; Man. Dir and Editor MAMMEN MATHEW; Chief Editor K. M. MATHEW; combined circ. 880,900.

Kozhikode

Deshabhimani: 11/127 Convent Rd, Kozhikode 673 032; tel. (495) 77286; f. 1946; morning; Malayalam; publ. by the CPI—M; also publ. from Kochi and Thiruvananthapuram; Chief Editor S. RAMACHANDRAN PILLAI; combined circ. 135,800.

Mathrubhumi: Mathrubhumi Bldgs, K. P. Kesava Menon Rd, POB 46, Kozhikode 673 001; tel. (495) 366655; telex 804286; fax (495) 366656; f. 1923; Malayalam; Editor K. K. SREEDHARAN NAIR; also publ. from Thiruvananthapuram, Kannur, Thrissur, Kottayam and Kochi; combined circ. 654,100.

Thiruvananthapuram

Kerala Kaumudi: POB 77, Pettah, Thiruvananthapuram 695 024; tel. (471) 461050; telex 4356214; fax (471) 461985; f. 1911; Malayalam; also publ. from Kollam, Alappuzha, Kochi and Kozhikode; Editor-in-Chief M. S. MANI; combined circ. 132,300.

Thrissur

Express: POB 15, Trichur 680 001; tel. 25800; f. 1944; Malayalam; Editor K. BALAKRISHNAN; circ. 68,200.

Madhya Pradesh

Bhopal

Dainik Bhaskar: 6 Dwarka Sadan, Habibganj Rd, Bhopal 462 011; tel. (755) 551601; telex 705267; f. 1958; morning; Hindi; also publ. from Indore, Raipur, Jabalpur, Jhansi, Bhopal, Bilaspur, Satna and Gwalior; Chief Editor R. C. AGARWAL; circ. 67,900 (Bhopal), 33,200 (Gwalior), 18,100 (Bilaspur), 16,900 (Satna), 32,500 (Jabalpur).

Indore

Naidunia: 60/1 Babu Labhchand Chhajlani Marg, Indore 452 009; tel. (731) 763111; fax (731) 763120; e-mail naidunia@edi.com; internet http://www.naidunia.com; f. 1947; morning; Hindi; Chief Editor ABHAY CHHAJLANI; circ. 117,076.

Raipur

Deshbandhu: Deshbandhu Complex, Ramsagarpara Layout, Raipur 492 001; tel. (771) 534911; fax (771) 534955; Hindi; also publ. from Jabalpur, Satna, Bilaspur and Bhopal; Chief Editor LALIT SURJAN; circ. 47,600 (Raipur), 19,300 (Satna), 24,385 (Bhopal), 17,931 (Jabalpur), 27,100 (Bilaspur).

Maharashtra

Kolhapur

Pudhari: 2318, 'C' Ward, Kolhapur 416 002; tel. (231) 22251; fax (231) 22256; f. 1974; Marathi; Editor P. G. JADHAV; circ. 120,200.

Mumbai

Afternoon Despatch and Courier: 6 Nanabhai Lane, Fort, Mumbai 400 001; tel. (22) 2871616; fax (22) 2870371; evening; English; Editor BEHRAM CONTRACTOR; circ. 65,100.

The Daily: Asia Publishing House, Mody Bay Estate, Calicut St, Mumbai 400 038; tel. (22) 2653104; telex 1186146; fax (22) 2188236; f. 1981; Editor RAJIV BAJAJ; circ. 44,000.

The Economic Times: Times of India Bldg, Dr D. N. Rd, Mumbai 400 001; tel. (22) 2620271; telex 1182879; fax (22) 2616564; e-mail et-bom@economictimes.com; f 1961; also publ. from New Delhi, Calcutta, Ahmedabad, Hyderabad, Chennai and Bangalore; English; Editor DON MANUAL; combined circ. 342,100, circ. (Mumbai) 108,000.

Financial Express: Express Towers, Nariman Point, Mumbai 400 021; tel. (22) 2022627; fax (22) 2022139; e-mail iemumbai@express.indexp.co.in; f. 1961; morning; English; also publ. from New Delhi, Bangalore, Calcutta, Coimbatore, Kochi, Ahmedabad (Gujarati) and Chennai; Man. Editor VIVEK GOENKA; Exec. Editor R. JAGANNATHAN; combined circ. 50,000.

The Free Press Journal: Free Press House, 215 Free Press Journal Rd, Nariman Point, Mumbai 400 021; tel. (22) 2874566; telex

1182570; fax (22) 2874688; f. 1930; English; also publ. from Indore; Man. Editor G. L. Lakhotia; combined circ. 87,000.

Indian Express: Express Towers, Nariman Point, Mumbai 400 021; tel. (22) 2022627; telex 1182585; fax (22) 2022139; f. 1940; English; also publ. from Pune and Nagpur; Man. Editor Vivek Goenka; Chief Editor Shekhar Gupta; combined circ. 161,500.

Inquilab: 156 D. J. Dadajee Rd, Tardeo, Mumbai 400 034; tel. (22) 4942586; telex 1175624; fax (22) 4938734; f. 1938; morning; Urdu; Editor Haroon Rashid; circ. 24,500.

Janmabhoomi: Janmabhoomi Bhavan, Janmabhoomi Marg, Fort, Mumbai 400 001; tel. (22) 2870831; telex 1186859; fax (22) 2874097; f. 1934; evening; Gujarati; Propr Saurashtra Trust; Editor Ramesh Jadhav; circ. 55,500.

Lokasatta: Express Towers, Nariman Point, Mumbai 400 021; tel. (22) 2022627; telex 1182585; fax (22) 2022139; f. 1948; morning (incl. Sunday); Marathi; also publ. from Pune, Nagpur and Ahmednagar; Editor Dr Aroon Tikekar; combined circ. 338,100.

Maharashtra Times: Dr Dadabhai Naoroji Rd, POB 213, Mumbai 400 001; tel. (22) 2620271; telex 1182879; fax (22) 2620144; f. 1962; Marathi; Editor G. S. Talwalkar; circ. 186,900.

Mid-Day: 64 Sitaram Mills Compound, N. M. Joshi Marg, Lower Parel, Mumbai 400 011; tel. (22) 3054545; telex 1175931; fax (22) 3054536; f. 1979; daily and Sunday; English; Editor Ayaz Memon; circ. 110,600.

Mumbai Samachar: Red House, Syed Abdulla Brelvi Rd, Fort, Mumbai 400 001; tel. (22) 2045531; telex 1184237; fax (22) 2046642; f. 1822; morning and Sunday; Gujarati; political, social and commercial; Editor Jehan D. Daruwala; circ. 133,800.

Navakal: 13 Shenviwadi, Khadilkar Rd, Girgaun, Mumbai 400 004; tel. (22) 353585; f. 1923; Marathi; Editor N. Y. Khadilkar; circ. 314,800.

Navbharat Times: Dr Dadabhai Naoroji Rd, Mumbai 400 001; tel. (22) 2620382; telex 1173300; f. 1950; Hindi; also publ. from New Delhi, Jaipur, Patna and Lucknow; circ. (Mumbai) 129,100.

Navshakti: Free Press House, 215 Nariman Point, Mumbai 400 021; tel. (22) 2874566; telex 112570; f. 1932; Marathi; Editor D. B. Joshi; circ. 65,000.

Pravasi: Janmabhoomi Bhavan, Janmabhoomi Marg, Fort, Mumbai 400 001; tel. (22) 2870831; telex 1186859; fax (22) 2874097; f. 1979; morning; Gujarati; Propr Saurashtra Trust; Editor Ramesh Jadhav; circ. 27,700.

Sakal: Sakal Bhavan, Plot No. 42-B, Sector No. 11, CBD Belapur, Navi Mumbai 400 614; tel. (22) 7574327; fax (22) 7574280; f. 1970; daily; Marathi; also publ. from Pune, Nasik and Kolhapur; Editor Radhakrishna Narvekar; combined circ. 372,700.

The Times of India: The Times of India Bldg, Dr Dadabhai Naoroji Rd, Mumbai 400 001; tel. (22) 2620271; telex 1182699; fax (22) 2620144; f. 1838; morning; English; also publ. from Delhi, Ahmedabad, Bangalore, Patna and Lucknow; Exec. Editor Gautam Adhikari; circ. (Mumbai) 499,800; combined circ. 1,076,400.

Nagpur

Hitavada: Wardha Rd, Nagpur 440 012; tel. (712) 523155; telex 7157517; fax (712) 535093; f. 1911; morning; English; Editor V. Phanshikar; circ. 45,800.

Lokmat: Lokmat Bhavan, Wardha Rd, Nagpur 440 012; tel. (712) 523527; telex 7157210; fax (712) 526923; also publ. from Jalgaon, Ahmednagar, Solapur, Nasik and Aurangabad; Marathi; **Lokmat Samachar** (Hindi) publ. from Nagpur and Aurangabad; **Lokmat Times** (English) publ. from Nagpur and Aurangabad; Editor Vijay Darda; combined circ. 450,800.

Nagpur Times: 37 Farmland, Ramdaspeth, Nagpur 440 010; tel. (712) 535071; telex 715235; fax (712) 543782; f. 1933; English; Man. Editor Dr Shrikant Jichkar; circ. 51,000.

Nava Bharat: Nava Bharat Bhavan, Cotton Market, Nagpur 440 018; tel. (712) 726677; f. 1938; morning; Hindi; also publ. from Bhopal, Jabalpur, Bilaspur, Indore and Raipur; Editor-in-Chief R. G. Maheswari; combined circ. 341,400.

Tarun Bharat: 28 Farmland, Ramdaspeth, Nagpur 440 010; tel. (712) 525052; f. 1944; Marathi; independent; also publ. from Pune and Belgaum; Editor L. T. Joshi; circ. 105,700 (Nagpur and Belgaum).

Pune

Kesari: 568 Narayan Peth, Pune 411 030; tel. (212) 459250; fax (212) 451677; f. 1881; Marathi; also publ. from Solapur, Kolhapur, Ahmednagar and Sangli; Editor Arvind Vyankatesh Gokhale; combined circ. 100,000.

Sakal: 595 Budhwar Peth, Pune 411 002; tel. (212) 455500; telex 1457504; fax (212) 450583; f. 1932; daily; Marathi; also publ. from Mumbai, Nashik and Kolhapur; Chief Editor Vijay Kuwalekar; Man. Dir Pratap Pawar; combined circ. 400,000.

Orissa

Bhubaneswar

Dharitri: B-26, Industrial Estate, Bhubaneswar 751 010; tel. (674) 480101; fax (674) 480795; morning; Oriya; circ. 104,100.

Pragativadi: 178-B, Mancheswar Industrial Estate, Bhubaneswar 751 010; fax (674) 482636; morning; Oriya; circ. 92,400.

Cuttack

Prajatantra: Prajatantra Bldgs, Behari Baug, Cuttack 753 002; tel. (671) 603071; telex 676269; fax (671) 603063; f. 1947; Oriya; Editor Bhartruhari Mahtab; circ. 103,000.

Samaj: Gopabandhu Bhawan, Buxibazar, Cuttack 753 001; tel. (671) 20994; telex 676267; fax (671) 601044; f. 1919; Oriya; Editor R. N. Rath; circ. 121,800.

Punjab

Chandigarh

The Tribune: 29c Chandigarh 160 020; tel. (172) 655065; telex 3957285; fax (172) 657149; f. 1881; English, Hindi and Punjabi; Editor (all edns) Hari Jaisingh; Editor (Hindi edn) Vijay Saighal; Editor (Punjabi edn) G. S. Bhullar; circ. 210,073 (English), 75,068 (Hindi), 70,544 (Punjabi).

Jalandhar

Ajit: Ajit Bhavan, Nehru Garden Rd, Jalandhar 144 001; f. 1955; Punjabi; tel. 55960; telex 385265; Man. Editor S. Barjinder Singh; circ. 183,300.

Hind Samachar: Civil Lines, Jalandhar 144 001; tel. (181) 280104; telex 385221; fax (181) 280113; f. 1948; morning and Sunday; Urdu; also publ. from Ambala; Dir Arvind Chopra; Editor Vijay Kumar Chopra; combined circ. 44,619.

Jag Bani: Civil Lines, Jalandhar 144 001; tel. (181) 280104; telex 385221; fax (181) 280113; f. 1978; morning; Punjabi; Editor Vijay Kumar Chopra; circ. 125,227.

Punjab Kesari: Civil Lines, Jalandhar 144 001; tel. (181) 280113; telex 385221; fax (181) 280113; f. 1965; morning and Sunday; Hindi; also publ. from Delhi and Ambala; Editor Vijay Kumar Chopra; combined circ. 742,050.

Rajasthan

Jaipur

Rajasthan Patrika: Kesargarh, Jawahar Lal Nehru Marg, Jaipur 302 004; tel. (141) 561582; telex 3652435; fax (141) 566011; f. 1956; Hindi and English edn; Hindi edn also publ. from Jodhphur, Bikaner, Udaipur, Bangalore and Kota; Editor Moti Chand Kochar; combined circ. (Hindi) 603,909, (English) 3,104.

Rashtradoot: M.I. Rd, POB 30, Jaipur 302 001; tel. (141) 372634; fax (141) 373513; f. 1951; Hindi; also publ. from Kota and Bikaner; CEO Somesh Sharma; Chief Editor Rajesh Sharma; circ. 126,000 (Jaipur), 56,000 (Kota), 48,000 (Bikaner).

Tamil Nadu

Chennai (Madras)

Daily Thanthi: 46 E.V.K. Sampath Rd, POB 467, Chennai 600 007; tel. (44) 587731; telex 418101; fax (44) 580069; f. 1942; Tamil; also publ. from Bangalore, Coimbatore, Cuddalore, Erode, Madurai, Nagercoil, Salem, Tiruchi, Tirunelveli, Pondicherry and Vellore; Chief Gen. Man. R. Somasundaram; Editor R. Thiruvadi; combined circ. 452,200.

Dinakaran: 106/107 Kutchery Rd, Mylapore, POB 358, Chennai 600 004; tel. (44) 4941007; telex 4121126; fax (44) 4942602; f. 1977; Tamil; also publ. from Madurai, Tiruchirapalli, Vellore. Tirunelveli, Salem and Coimbatore; Man. Dir K. Kumaran; Editor K. Kesavan; combined circ. 324,742.

Dinamalar: 161 Anna Salai, Chennai 600 002; tel. (44) 8523715; f. 1951; Tamil; also publ. from Coimbatore, Erode, Madurai, Pondicherry, Tiruchirapalli, Tirunelveli and Vellore; Editor R. Krishnamoorthy; combined circ. 341,500.

Dinamani: Express Estates, Mount Rd, Chennai 600 002; tel. (44) 8520751; telex 418222; fax (44) 8524500; f. 1934; morning; Tamil; also publ. from Madurai, Coimbatore and Bangalore; Editor Ms Vasanthi; combined circ. 180,800.

Financial Express: Vasanthi Medical Center, 20 Pycrofts Garden Rd, Chennai 600 006; tel. (44) 8231112; telex 418222; fax (44) 8231489; morning; English; also publ. from Mumbai, Ahmedabad (in Gujarati), Bangalore, Coimbatore, Kochi, Calcutta and New Delhi; Man. Editor Vivek Goenka; Exec. Editor R. Jagannathan; combined circ. 30,100.

The Hindu: Kasturi Bldgs, 859/860 Anna Salai, Chennai 600 002; tel. (44) 8535067; telex 416655; fax (44) 8535325; f. 1878; morning; English; independent; also publ. from Bangalore, Coimbatore, New Delhi, Visakhapatnam, Hyderabad, Thiruvananthapuram and Madurai; Publr S. Rangarajan Editor N. Ravi; combined circ. 651,520.

The Hindu Business Line: 859/860 Anna Salai, Chennai 600 002; tel. (44) 8535067; telex 416655; fax (44) 8535325; f. 1994; morning; English; also publ. from Bangalore, Hyderabad, Madurai, Coimbatore, New Delhi, Visakhapatnam and Thiruvananthapuram; Publr S. RANGARAJAN; Editor N. RAM; combined circ. 33,000.

Indian Express: Express Estate, Mount Rd, Chennai 600 002; tel. (44) 8520751; telex 418222; fax (44) 8524500; also publ. from Delhi, Pune, Coimbatore, Mumbai, Chandigarh, Kochi, Bangalore, Baroda, Kozhikode, Thiruvananthapuram, Ahmedabad, Madurai, Hyderabad, Visakhapatnam, Bhubaneswar, Belgaum and Vijayawada; Man. Editor VIVEK GOENKA; Chief Editor SHEKHAR GUPTA; combined circ. 473,352.

Murasoli: 93 Kodambakkam High Rd, Chennai 600 034; tel. (44) 470044; f. 1960; organ of the DMK; Tamil; Editor S. SELVAM; circ. 54,000.

Tripura

Agartala

Dainik Sambad: 11 Jagannath Bari Rd, POB 2, Agartala 799 001; tel. (381) 226676; fax (381) 224845; f. 1966; Bengali; morning; Editor BHUPENDRA CHANDRA DATTA BHAUMIK.

Uttar Pradesh

Agra

Amar Ujala: Sikandra Rd, Agra 282 007; tel. (562) 361600; telex 565255; fax (562) 361602; f. 1948; Hindi; also publ. from Bareilly, Kanpur, Moradabad and Meerut; Editor AJAY K. AGARWAL; Dep. Gen. Man. L. K. SHRIMALI; circ. 109,400 (Agra), 64,600 (Bareilly), 28,100 (Moradabad), 125,500 (Meerut), 14,900 (Kanpur).

Allahabad

Amrita Prabhat: 10 Edmonstone Rd, Allahabad 211 001; tel. (532) 600654; f. 1977; Hindi; Editor TAMAL KANTI GHOSH; circ. 44,000.

Northern India Patrika: 10 Edmonstone Rd, Allahabad 211 001; tel. (532) 52665; f. 1959; English; Chief Editor TUSHAR KANTI GHOSH; Editor MANAS MUKUL DAS; circ. 46,000.

Kanpur

Dainik Jagran: 2 Sarvodaya Nagar, Kanpur 208 005; tel. (512) 216161; fax (512) 216972; f. 1942; Hindi; also publ. from Gorakhpur, Jhansi, Lucknow, Meerut, Agra, Varanasi (Allahabad), Bareilly and New Delhi; Editor NARENDRA MOHAN; combined circ. 642,300.

Vyapar Sandesh: 26/104 Birhana Rd, Kanpur 208 001; tel. (512) 352066; f. 1958; Hindi; commercial news and economic trends; Editor HARI SHANKAR SHARMA; circ. 17,000.

Lucknow

National Herald: 1 Bisheshwar North Rd, Lucknow 226 001; f. 1938 Lucknow, 1968 Delhi; English; Editor-in-Chief K. V. S. RAMA SHARMA.

The Pioneer: 20 Vidhan Sabha Marg, Lucknow 226 001; tel. (522) 220516; telex 5352468; fax (522) 220466; f. 1865; English; also publ. from New Delhi; Publr DIPAK MUKERJI; Editor CHANDAN MITRA; combined circ. 136,000.

Swatantra Bharat: 1st Floor, Suraj Deep Complex, 1 Jopling Rd, Lucknow 226 001; tel. (522) 275990; fax (522) 280956; e-mail sbharat@lw1.vsnl.net.in; f. 1947; Hindi; also publ. from Kanpur; Editor K. K. SRIVASTAVA; circ. 41,403 (Lucknow), 25,304 (Kanpur).

Varanasi

Aj: Aj Bhavan, Sant Kabir Rd, Kabirchaura, Varanasi 221 001; tel. (542) 323981; fax (542) 323988; f. 1920; Hindi; also publ. from Gorakhpur, Patna, Allahabad, Ranchi, Agra, Bareilly, Lucknow, Jamshedpur and Kanpur; Editor S. V. GUPTA; circ. 45,200 (Agra), 16,100 (Allahabad), 18,000 (Jamshedpur), 22,800 (Lucknow), 128,600 (Patna), 22,800 (Ranchi), 78,800 (Varanasi).

West Bengal

Calcutta

Aajkaal: 96 Raja Rammohan Sarani, Calcutta 700 009; tel. (33) 3509803; telex 217491; fax (33) 3500877; f. 1981; morning; Bengali; Chief Editor PRATAP K. ROY; circ. 148,200.

Ananda Bazar Patrika: 6 Prafulla Sarkar St, Calcutta 700 001; tel. (33) 278000; telex 215468; fax (33) 303240; f. 1922; morning; Bengali; Editor AVEEK SARKAR; circ. 476,600.

Banga Sambad: 7 Old Court House St, Calcutta 700 001; tel. (33) 207618; fax (33) 206663; f. 1991; Bengali; Editor S. C. TALUKDAR; circ. 36,895.

Bartaman: 76A Acharya J.C. Bose Rd, Calcutta 700 014; tel. (33) 2448208; telex 215458; fax (33) 2441215; f. 1984; Editor BARUN SENGUPTA; circ. 288,800.

Business Standard: Church Lane, Calcutta 700 001; tel. (33) 278000; telex 215468; fax (33) 2253241; f. 1975; morning; also publ. from New Delhi and Mumbai; English; Editor T. N. NINAN; circ. 18,700 (Calcutta and New Delhi).

Dakshin Banga Sambad: 7 Old Court House St, Calcutta 700 001; tel. (33) 207618; fax (33) 206663; f. 1991; Bengali; Editor S. C. TALUKDAR; circ. 36,123.

The Economic Times: 105/7A, S. N. Banerjee Rd, Calcutta 700 014; tel. (33) 294232; telex 215946; fax (33) 292400; English; also publ. from Ahmedabad, Delhi, Bangalore and Mumbai; circ. (Calcutta) 48,100.

Financial Express: 83 B. K. Pal Ave, Calcutta 700 005; morning; English; also publ. from Mumbai, Ahmedabad, Bangalore, Coimbatore, Kochi, Chennai and New Delhi; Man. Editor VIVEK GOENKA; Exec. Editor R. JAGANNATHAN; combined circ. 30,100.

Frontier News: 7 Old Court House St, Calcutta 700 001; tel. (33) 207618; fax (33) 206663; f. 1992; English; Editor S. C. TALUKDAR; circ. 26,720.

Ganashakti: 74A A. J. C. Bose Rd, Calcutta 700 016; tel. (33) 2458950; telex 215904; fax (33) 2456263; e-mail gansakti@giascl01.vsnl.net.in; f. 1967; morning; Bengali; Chief Editor ANIL BISWAS; circ. 112,130.

Himalchuli: 7 Old Court House St, Calcutta 700 001; tel. (33) 207618; fax (33) 206663; f. 1982; Nepali; Editor S. C. TALUKDAR; circ. 42,494.

Overland: Calcutta; f. 1991; morning; Editor AJIT KUMAR BHOWAL; circ. 122,000.

Paschim Banga Sambad: 33 Chittaranjan Ave, Calcutta 700 012; tel. (33) 262934; fax (33) 296548; f. 1992; Bengali; Editor S. C. TALUKDAR; circ. 46,056.

Sambad Pratidin: 20 Prafulla Sarkar St, Calcutta 700 072; tel. (33) 2445441; fax (33) 2445451; morning; Bengali; Editor SWAPAN SADHAN BASU; circ. 148,800.

Sandhya Aajkaal: 96 Raja Rammohan Sarani, Calcutta 700 009; tel. (33) 3509803; telex 217491; fax (33) 3500877; evening; Bengali; Chief Editor PRATAP K. ROY; circ. 20,000.

Sanmarg: 160C Chittaranjan Ave, Calcutta 700 007; tel. (33) 2413862; fax (33) 2415087; f. 1948; Hindi; Editor RAMAWTAR A. GUPTA; circ. 71,300.

The Statesman: Statesman House, 4 Chowringhee Sq., Calcutta 700 001; tel. (33) 271000; telex 214509; fax (33) 270118; f. 1875; morning; English; independent; also publ. from New Delhi; Editor-in-Chief C. R. IRANI; combined circ. 173,300.

The Telegraph: 6 Prafulla Sarkar St, Calcutta 700 001; tel. (33) 278000; telex 215468; fax (33) 303240; f. 1982; English; Editor AVEEK SARKAR; circ. 165,900.

Uttar Banga Sambad: 7 Old Court House St, Calcutta 700 001; tel. (33) 2206663; fax (33) 296548; f. 1980; Bengali; Editor S. C. TALUKDAR; circ. 92,705.

Vishwamitra: 74 Lenin Sarani, Calcutta 700 013; tel. (33) 2441139; fax (33) 2446393; f. 1916; morning; Hindi; commercial; also publ. from Mumbai; Editor PRAKASH CHANDRA AGRAWALLA; combined circ. 70,204.

SELECTED PERIODICALS

Delhi and New Delhi

Alive: Delhi Press Bldg, E-3, Jhandewala Estate, Rani Jhansi Rd, New Delhi 110 055; tel. (11) 526311; telex 3163053; fax (11) 7525020; f. 1940; monthly; English; political and cultural; Editor VISHWA NATH; circ. 20,000.

Bal Bharati: Patiala House, Publications Division, Ministry of Information and Broadcasting, Delhi; tel. (11) 387038; f. 1948; monthly; Hindi; for children; Editor SHIV KUMAR; circ. 30,000.

Bano: 13/14 Asaf Ali Rd, New Delhi 110 002; tel. (11) 732666; telex 3161601; fax (11) 736539; f. 1947; monthly; Urdu; women's interests; Editor SADIA DEHLVI; circ. 5,500.

Biswin Sadi: 3583 Netaji Subash Marg, Darya Ganj, POB 7013, New Delhi 110 002; tel. (11) 271637; f. 1937; monthly; Urdu; Editor Z. REHMAN NAYYAR; circ. 36,000.

Business Today: F 14/15 Indira Gandhi Place, New Delhi 110 001; tel. (11) 3315801; fax (11) 3316180; fortnightly; English, Editor ANAND P. RAMAN; circ. 122,700.

Careers Digest: 21 Shankar Market, Delhi 110 001; tel. (11) 44726; f. 1963; monthly; English; Editor O. P. VARMA; circ. 35,000.

Catholic India: CBCI Centre, 1 Ashok Place, Goldakkhana, New Delhi 110 001; tel. (11) 3344470; fax (11) 3364615; quarterly.

Champak: Delhi Press Bldg, E-3, Jhandewala Estate, Rani Jhansi Rd, New Delhi 110 055; tel. (11) 526097; telex 3163053; fax (11) 7525020; f. 1969; fortnightly (Hindi, English, Gujarati and Marathi edns); monthly (Kannada edn); children; Editor VISHWA NATH; combined circ. 136,500.

Children's World: Nehru House, 4 Bahadur Shah Zafar Marg, New Delhi 110 002; tel. (11) 3316970; fax (11) 3721090; f. 1968; monthly; English; Editor VAIJAYANTI TONPE; circ. 25,000.

Competition Refresher: 2767, Bright House, Daryaganj, New Delhi 110 002; tel. (11) 3282226; telex 3176101; fax (11) 3269227; f. 1984; monthly; English; Chief Editor D. S. PHULL; Publr and Man. Dir PRITAM SINGH BRIGHT; circ. 131,800.

Competition Success Review: 604 Prabhat Kiran Bldg, Rajendra Place, Delhi 110 008; tel. (11) 5712898; fax (11) 5754647; monthly; English; f. 1964; Editor S. K. SACHDEVA; circ. 242,200.

Computers Today: Marina Arcade, C-59 Connaught Circus, New Delhi 110 001; tel. (11) 3736233; fax (11) 3729506; f. 1984; Editor J. SRIHARI RAJU; circ. 54,700.

Cricket Samrat: L–1, Kanchan House, Najafgarh Rd, Commercial Complex, nr Milan Cinema, New Delhi 110 015; tel. (11) 5191175; fax (11) 5469581; f. 1978; monthly; Hindi; Editor ANAND DEWAN; circ. 76,300.

Employment News: Government of India, East Block IV, Level 7, R. K. Puram, New Delhi 110 066; tel. (11) 6875316; f. 1976; weekly; Hindi, Urdu and English edns; Gen. Man. and Chief Editor MAN MOHAN PARIMOO; Editor KRISHAN SARUP GAUTAM; combined circ. 507,000.

Film Mirror: 26F Indira Gandhi Place, New Delhi 110 001; tel. (11) 3312329; f. 1964; monthly; English; Editor HARBHAJAN SINGH; circ. 37,200.

Filmi Duniya: 16 Darya Ganj, New Delhi 110 002; tel. (11) 3278087; fax (11) 3279341; f. 1958; monthly; Hindi; Chief Editor NARENDRA KUMAR; circ. 137,008.

Filmi Kaliyan: 4675-B/21 Ansari Rd, New Delhi 110 002; tel. (11) 3272080; f. 1969; monthly; Hindi; cinema; Editor-in-Chief V. S. DEWAN; circ. 85,300.

Grih Shobha: Delhi Press Bldg, E-3 Jhandewala Estate, Rani Jhansi Rd, New Delhi 110 055; tel. (11) 526097; telex 3163053; fax (11) 7525020; f. 1979; monthly; Kannada, Marathi, Hindi and Gujarati edns; women's interests; Editor VISHWA NATH; circ. 119,300 (Kannada), 56,100 (Gujarati), 121,100 (Marathi), 318,500 (Hindi).

India Perspectives: Room 149B 'A' Wing, Shastri Bhavan, New Delhi 110 001; tel. (11) 3389471; f. 1988; Editor BHARAT BHUSHAN.

India Today: F 14/15, Indira Gandhi Place, New Delhi 110 001; tel. (11) 3315801; telex 3161245; fax (11) 3316180; f. 1975; English (weekly); Tamil, Telugu, Malayalam and Hindi (fortnightly); Editor AROON PURIE; circ. 410,900 (English), 285,400 (Hindi), 121,000 (Tamil), 112,035 (Malayalam), 99,500 (Telugu).

Indian Observer: 26F Indira Gandhi Chowk (Connaught Place), New Delhi 110 001; tel. (11) 3312329; f. 1964; fortnightly; English; Editor HARBHAJAN SINGH; circ. 33,800.

Indian Railways: 411 Rail Bhavan, Raisina Rd, New Delhi 110 001; tel. (11) 3383540; telex 3166061; fax (11) 3384481; f. 1956; monthly; English; publ. by the Ministry of Railways (Railway Board); Editor MANOHAR D. BANERJEE; circ. 12,000.

Intensive Agriculture: Ministry of Agriculture, Directorate of Extension, New Delhi 110 066; tel. (11) 600591; f. 1955; monthly; English; Editor SHUKLA HAZRA; circ. 15,000.

Journal of Industry and Trade: Ministry of Commerce, Delhi 110 011; tel. (11) 3016664; f. 1952; monthly; English; Man. Dir A. C. BANERJEE; circ. 2,000.

Junior Science Refresher: 2769, Bright House, Daryaganj, New Delhi 110 002; tel. (11) 3282227; telex 3176101; fax (11) 3269227; f. 1987; monthly; English; Chief Editor D. S. PHULL; Publr and Man. Dir PRITAM SINGH BRIGHT; circ. 81,200.

Kadambini: Hindustan Times House, Kasturba Gandhi Marg, New Delhi 110 001; tel. (11) 3318201; telex 3166327; fax (11) 3321189; f. 1960; monthly; Hindi; Editor RAJENDRA AWASTHY; circ. 90,000.

Krishak Samachar: Bharat Krishak Samaj, Dr Panjabrao Deshmukh Krishak Bhavan, A-1 Nizamuddin West, New Delhi 110 013; tel. (11) 619508; f. 1957; monthly; English and Hindi edns; agriculture; Editor K. PRABHAKAR REDDY; circ. (English) 12,000, (Hindi) 30,000.

Kurukshetra: Ministry of Rural Areas and Employment, Room No. 655/661, 'A' Wing, Nirman Bhavan, New Delhi 110 011; tel. (11) 3015014; telex 3166489; fax (11) 3386879; monthly; English; rural development; Editor G. SUDHEER; circ. 14,000.

Mainstream: 145/1D Shahpur Jat, 1st Floor, nr Asiad Village, New Delhi 110 049; English; weekly; politics and current affairs; Editor SUMIT CHAKRAVARTTY.

Mayapuri: A-5, Mayapuri Phase 1, New Delhi 110 064; tel. (11) 5141439; telex 3176125; fax (11) 5138596; f. 1974; weekly; Hindi; cinema; Editor A. P. BAJAJ; circ. 146,144.

Mukta: Delhi Press Bldg, E-3 Jhandewala Estate, Rani Jhansi Rd, New Delhi 110 055; tel. (11) 7526311; telex 3163053; fax (11) 7525020; f. 1961; monthly; Hindi; youth; Editor VISHWA NATH; circ. 20,213.

Nandan: Hindustan Times House, Kasturba Gandhi Marg, New Delhi 110 001; tel. (11) 3318201; telex 3166327; fax (11) 3321189; f. 1963; monthly; Hindi; Editor JAI PRAKASH BHARTI; circ. 199,700.

New Age: 15 Kotla Rd, Delhi 110 002; tel. (11) 3310762; telex 3165982; f. 1953; main organ of the Communist Party of India; weekly; English; Editor PAULY V. PARAKAL; circ. 215,000.

The North East Sun: 8B Bahadur Shah Zafar Marg, New Delhi 110 002; tel. (11) 3316722; fax (11) 3317947; f. 1977; fortnightly; English; Editor V. B. GUPTA; circ. 26,374.

Organiser: 29 Rani Jhansi Marg, New Delhi 110 055; tel. (11) 7526977; fax (11) 7514876; f. 1947; weekly; English; Editor SESHADRI CHARI; circ. 44,100.

Outlook: A13-10 Safdarjung Enclave, New Delhi 110 029; tel. (11) 6191421; fax (11) 6191420; f. 1995; weekly; Editor-in-Chief VINOD MEHTA; circ. 105,500.

Panchjanya: Sanskriti Bhavan, Deshbandhu Gupta Marg, Jhandewala, New Delhi 110 055; tel. (11) 524244; fax (11) 3558613; f. 1947; weekly; Hindi; general interest; nationalist; Chair. S. N. BANSAL; Editor TARUN VIJAY; circ. 62,300.

Proven Trade Contacts: POB 5730, New Delhi 110 055; tel. (11) 526402; fax (11) 7525666; f.1992; e-mail net@narang.com; monthly; medical/surgical trade promotion; circ. 10,000.

Punjabi Digest: 209 Hemkunt House, 6 Rajendra Place, POB 2549, New Delhi 110 008; tel. (11) 5715225; f. 1971; literary monthly; Gurmukhi; Chief Editor Sardar J. B. SINGH; circ. 89,100.

Rangbhumi: 5A/15 Ansari Rd, Darya Ganj, Delhi 110 002; tel. (11) 3274667; f. 1941; Hindi; films; Editor S. K. GUPTA; circ. 30,000.

Sainik Samachar: Block L-1, Church Rd, New Delhi 110 001; tel. (11) 3019668; f. 1909; pictorial weekly for India's armed forces; English, Hindi, Urdu, Tamil, Punjabi, Telugu, Marathi, Kannada, Gorkhali, Malayalam, Bengali, Assamese and Oriya edns; Editor-in-Chief BIBEKANANDA RAY; circ. 18,000.

Saras Salil: Delhi Press Bldg, E-3, Jhandewala Estate, Rani Jhansi Rd, New Delhi 110 055; tel. (11) 7526311; fax (11) 7525020; f. 1993; fortnightly; Hindi; Editor VISHWA NATH; circ. 724,900.

Sarita: Delhi Press Bldg, E-3, Jhandewala Estate, Rani Jhansi Rd, New Delhi 110 055; tel. (11) 7526311; telex 3163053; fax (11) 7525020; f. 1945; fortnightly; Hindi; family magazine; Editor VISHWA NATH; circ. 174,100.

Shama: 13/14 Asaf Ali Rd, New Delhi 110 002; tel. (11) 3231446; fax (11) 3235054; f. 1939; monthly; Urdu; art and literature; Editors M. YUNUS DEHLVI, IDREES DEHLVI, ILYAS DEHLVI; circ. 69,000.

Sher-i-Punjab: Hemkunt House, 6 Rajendra Place, New Delhi 110 008; tel. (11) 5715225; f. 1911; weekly news magazine; Chief Editor Sardar JANG BAHADUR SINGH; circ. 15,000.

Suman Saurabh: Delhi Press Bldg, E-3 Jhandewala Estate, Rani Jhansi Rd, New Delhi 110 055; tel. (11) 526097; telex 3163053; fax (11) 7525020; f. 1983; monthly; Hindi; youth; Editor VISHWA NATH; circ. 56,800.

The Sun: 8B Bahadur Shah Zafar Marg, POB 7164, New Delhi 110 002; tel. (11) 3316722; telex 3165931; fax (11) 3317947; f. 1977; fortnightly; English; Editor V. B. GUPTA; circ. 69,953.

The Sunday Observer: Vijaya, 17 Barakhamba Rd, New Delhi 110 001; tel. (11) 3713200; telex 3166893; fax (11) 3327065; f. 1981; weekly; English and Hindi edns; also publ. from Mumbai; Editor-in-Chief NIKHIL LAKSHMAN; combined circ. 72,400.

Sushama: 13/14 Asaf Ali Rd, New Delhi 110 002; tel. (11) 3231446; fax (11) 3235054; f. 1959; monthly; Hindi; art and literature; Editors IDREES DEHLVI, ILYAS DEHLVI, YUNUS DEHLVI; circ. 82,000.

Trade Union Record: 24 Canning Lane, New Delhi 110 001; tel. (11) 3387320; fax (11) 3386427; f. 1930; fortnightly; English and Hindi edns; Editor SANTOSH KUMAR.

Vigyan Pragati: PID Bldg, Dr K. S. Krishnan Marg, New Delhi 110 012; tel. (11) 5785647; telex 317741; fax (11) 5731353; f. 1952; monthly; Hindi; popular science; Editor DEEKSHA BIST; circ. 100,000.

Woman's Era: Delhi Press Bldg, E-3, Jhandewala Estate, Rani Jhansi Rd, New Delhi 110 055; tel. (11) 526097; telex 3163053; fax (11) 7525020; f. 1973; fortnightly; English; Editor VISHWA NATH; circ. 92,600.

Yojana: Yojana Bhavan, Parliament St, Delhi 110 001; tel. (11) 3710473; f. 1957; monthly; English, Tamil, Bengali, Marathi, Gujarati, Assamese, Malayalam, Telugu, Kannada, Punjabi, Urdu, Oriya and Hindi edns; Chief Editor N. N. SHARMA; circ. 100,000.

Andhra Pradesh

Hyderabad

Andhra Prabha Illustrated Weekly: 591 Lower Tank Bund Rd, Express Centre, Domalaguda, Hyderabad 500 029; tel. (40) 233586; f. 1952; weekly; Telugu; Editor POTTURI VENKATESWARA RAO; circ. 28,900.

Secunderabad

Andhra Bhoomi Sachitra Vara Patrika: 36 Sarojini Devi Rd, Secunderabad 500 003; tel. (842) 7802346; telex 4256644; fax (842) 7805256; f. 1977; weekly; Telugu; Editor T. VENKATRAM REDDY; circ. 57,000.

Vijayawada

Andhra Jyoti Sachitra Vara Patrika: Vijayawada 520 010; tel. (866) 474532; telex 475217; f. 1967; weekly; Telugu; Editor PURANAM SUBRAMANYA SARMA; circ. 39,300.

Bala Jyoti: Labbipet, Vijayawada 520 010; tel. (866) 474532; telex 475217; f. 1980; monthly; Telugu; Assoc. Editor A. SASIKANT SATAKARNI; circ. 14,342.

Jyoti Chitra: Andhra Jyoti Bldgs, Vijayawada 520 010; tel. (866) 474532; telex 475217; f. 1977; weekly; Telugu; Editor T. KUTUMBA RAO; circ. 34,800.

Swati Sapari Vara Patrika: Anil Bldgs, Suryaraopet, POB 339, Vijayawada 520 002; tel. (866) 431862; fax (866) 430433; f. 1984; weekly; Telugu; Editor VEMURI BALARAM; circ. 263,539.

Vanita Jyoti: Labbipet, POB 712, Vijayawada 520 010; tel. (866) 474532; telex 475217; f. 1978; monthly; Telugu; Asst Editor J. SATYANARAYANA; circ. 17,300.

Assam

Guwahati

Agradoot: Agradoot Bhavan, Dispur, Guwahati 781 006; tel. (361) 561923; fax (361) 560655; f. 1971; bi-weekly; Assamese; Editor K. S. DEKA; circ. 40,100.

Asam Bani: Tribune Bldg, Guwahati 781 003; tel. (361) 541356; telex 2352417; fax (361) 540594; f. 1955; weekly; Assamese; Editor DILIP CHANDAN; circ. 20,000.

Bihar

Patna

Anand Digest: Govind Mitra Rd, Patna 800 004; tel. (612) 656557; fax 225192; f. 1981; monthly; Hindi; family magazine; Editor Dr S. S. SINGH; circ. 37,800.

Balak: Govind Mitra Rd, POB 5, Patna 800 004; tel. (612) 650341; f. 1926; monthly; Hindi; children's; Editor S. R. SARAN; circ. 32,000.

Gujarat

Ahmedabad

Akhand Anand: Anand Bhavan, Relief Rd, POB 123, Ahmedabad 380 001; tel. (79) 357482; f. 1947; monthly; Gujarati; Pres. ANAND AMIN; Editor PRAKASH N. SHAH; circ. 10,000.

Chitralok: Gujarat Samachar Bhavan, Khanpur, POB 254, Ahmedabad 380 001; tel. (79) 5504010; telex 1216642; fax (79) 5502000; f. 1952; weekly; Gujarati; films; Man. Editor SHREYANS S. SHAH; circ. 20,000.

Sakhi: Sakhi Publications, Jai Hind Press Bldg, nr Gujarat Chamber, Ashram Rd, Navrangpura, Ahmedabad 380 009; tel. (79) 6581734; fax (79) 6587681; f. 1984; fortnightly; Gujarati; women's; Man. Editor NITA Y. SHAH; Editor Y. N. SHAH; circ. 10,000.

Shree: Gujarat Samachar Bhavan, Khanpur, Ahmedabad 380 001; tel. (79) 5504010; telex 1216642; fax (79) 5502000; f. 1964; weekly; Gujarati; women's; Editor SMRUTIBEN SHAH; circ. 20,000.

Stree: Sandesh Bhavan, Gheekanta, POB 151, Ahmedabad 380 001; tel. (79) 24243; telex 1216532; fax (79) 24392; f. 1962; weekly; Gujarati; Jt Editors RITABEN PATEL, LILABEN PATEL; circ. 70,900.

Zagmag: Gujarat Samachar Bhavan, Khanpur, Ahmedabad 380 001; tel. (79) 22821; telex 1216642; f. 1952; weekly; Gujarati; for children; Editor BAHUBALI S. SHAH; circ. 38,000.

Rajkot

Amruta: Jai Hind Publications, Jai Hind Press Bldg, Babubhai Shah Marg, Rajkot 360 001; tel. (281) 440513; fax (281) 448677; f. 1967; weekly; Gujarati; films; Editor Y. N. SHAH; circ. 27,000.

Niranjan: Jai Hind Publications, Jai Hind Press Bldg, Babubhai Shah Marg, Rajkot 360 001; tel. (281) 440517; fax (281) 448677; f. 1972; fortnightly; Gujarati; children's; Editor N. R. SHAH; circ. 15,000.

Parmarth: Jai Hind Publications, Jai Hind Press Bldg, Babubhai Shah Marg, Rajkot 360 001; tel. (281) 440511; fax (281) 448677; monthly; Gujarati; philosophy and religion; Editor Y. N. SHAH; circ. 30,000.

Phulwadi: Jai Hind Publications, Jai Hind Press Bldg, Babubhai Shah Marg, Rajkot 360 001; tel. (281) 440513; fax (281) 448677; f. 1967; weekly; Gujarati; for children; Editor Y. N. SHAH; circ. 27,000.

Karnataka

Bangalore

Mayura: 75 Mahatma Gandhi Rd, Bangalore 560 001; tel. (80) 5588999; telex 8452339; fax (80) 5587179; f. 1968; monthly; Kannada; Editor-in-Chief K. N. HARI KUMAR; circ. 60,200.

New Leader: 93 North Rd, St Mary's Town, Bangalore 560 005; f. 1887; weekly; English; Editor Rt Rev. HERMAN D'SOUZA; circ. 10,000.

Prajamata: North Anjaneya Temple Rd, Basavangudi, Bangalore 560 004; tel. (80) 602481; f. 1931; weekly; Kannada; news and current affairs; Chief Editor G. V. ANJI; circ. 28,377.

Sudha: 66 Mahatma Gandhi Rd, Bangalore 560 001; tel. (80) 5588999; telex 8452339; fax (80) 5587179; f. 1965; weekly; Kannada; Editor-in-Chief K. N. HARI KUMAR; circ. 140,600.

Manipal

Taranga: Udayavani Bldg, Press Corner, Manipal 576 119; tel. (8252) 70845; fax (8252) 70563; f. 1983; weekly; Kannada; Editor S. K. GULVADY; circ. 111,200.

Kerala

Kottayam

Balarama: MM Publications Ltd, POB 226, Erayilkadavu, Kottayam 686 001; tel. (481) 563721; telex 888201; fax (481) 564393; f. 1972; children's fortnightly; Malayalam; Chief Editor BINA PHILIP MATHEW; Senior Man. V. SAJEEV GEORGE; circ. 298,040.

Malayala Manorama: K. K. Rd, POB 26, Kottayam 686 001; tel. (481) 563646; telex 888201; fax (481) 562479; f. 1937; weekly; Malayalam; also publ. from Kozhikode; Man. Dir and Editor MAMMEN MATHEW; Chief Editor MAMMEN VARGHESE; combined circ. 1,072,300.

Manorajyam: Manorajyam Bldg, M. C. Rd, Kottayam 686 039; tel. (481) 61203; telex 888260; f. 1967; weekly; Malayalam; Publr R. KALYANARAMAN; circ. 50,900.

Vanitha: MM Publications Ltd, POB 226, Erayilkadavu, Kottayam 686 001; tel. (481) 563721; telex 888201; fax (481) 564393; f. 1975; women's fortnightly; Malayalam; Chief Editor Mrs K. M. MATHEW; Senior Man. V. SAJEEV GEORGE; circ. 355,216.

The Week: Malayala Manorama Co Ltd, K. K. Rd, POB 26, Kottayam 686 001; tel. (481) 563646; telex 888201; fax (481) 562479; f. 1982; weekly; English; current affairs; Chief Editor MAMMEN MATHEW; circ. 108,000.

Kozhikode

Grihalakshmi: Mathrubhumi Bldgs, K. P. Kesava Menon Rd, POB 46, Kozhikode 673 001; tel. and fax (495) 366655; telex 804286; f. 1979; monthly; Malayalam; Editor M. T. VASUDEVAN NAIR; circ. 89,100.

Mathrubhumi Illustrated Weekly: Mathrubhumi Bldgs, K. P. Kesava Menon Rd, POB 46, Kozhikode 673 001; tel. (495) 366655; telex 804286; fax (495) 56656; f. 1923; weekly; Malayalam; Editor M. T. VASUDEVAN NAIR; circ. 56,400.

Quilon

Karala Sabdam: Thevally, Quilon 691 009; tel. (474) 72403; telex 886296; fax (474) 740710; f. 1962; weekly; Malayalam; Man. Editor B. A. RAJAKRISHNAN; circ. 66,600.

Nana: Therally, Quilon 691 009; tel. 2403; telex 886296; weekly; Malayalam; Man. Editor B. A. RAJAKRISHNAN; circ. 50,500.

Thiruvananthapuram

Kalakaumudi: Kaumudi Bldgs, Pettah, Thiruvananthapuram 695 024; tel. (471) 443531; telex 435214; fax (471) 461985; e-mail sreeni@giasmd01.vsnl.net.in; f. 1975; weekly; Malayalam; Chief Editor M. S. MANI; Gen. Man. ABRAHAM EAPEN; circ. 73,000.

Vellinakshatram: Kaumudi Bldgs, Pettah, Thiruvananthapuram 695 024; tel. (471) 447870; telex 435214; fax (471) 461985; f. 1987; film weekly; Malayalam; Editor PRASAD LAKSHMANAN; Man. Editor SUKUMARAN MANI; circ. 55,000.

Madhya Pradesh

Bhopal

Krishak Jagat: 14 Indira Press Complex, M. P. Nagar, POB 3, Bhopal 462 001; tel. (755) 768452; fax (755) 510334; f. 1946; weekly; Hindi; agriculture; Chief Editor VIJAY KUMAR BONDRIYA; Editor SUNIL GANGRADE; circ. 51,436.

Maharashtra

Mumbai (Bombay)

Abhiyaan: Abhiyaan Press and Publications Ltd, 4A/B, Government Industrial Estate, Charkop, Kandivli (W), Mumbai 400 067; tel. (22) 8687515; fax (22) 8680991; f. 1986; weekly; Gujarati; Dir DILIP PATEL; Editor VINOD PANDYA; circ. 86,100.

Auto India: Nirmal, Nariman Point, Mumbai 400 021; tel. (22) 2024422; telex 1183557; fax (22) 2875671; f. 1994; monthly; Editor Hormazd Sorabjee; circ. 78,800.

Bhavan's Journal: Bharatiya Vidya Bhavan, Mumbai 400 007; tel. (22) 3634462; fax (22) 3630058; f. 1954; fortnightly; English; literary; Man. Editor J. H. Dave; Editor S. Ramakrishnan; circ. 25,000.

Blitz News Magazine: 17/17H Cawasji Patel St, Fort, Mumbai 400 001; tel. (22) 2040720; fax (22) 2047984; f. 1941; weekly; English; Editor-in-Chief R. K. Karanjia; combined circ. 419,000.

Bombay Samachar: Red House, Sayed Brelvi Rd, Mumbai 400 001; tel. (22) 2045531; telex 1184237; fax (22) 2046642; f. 1822; weekly; Gujarati; Editor Jehanbux D. Daruwala; circ. 151,600.

Business India: Nirmal, 14th Floor, Nariman Point, Mumbai 400 021; tel. (22) 2024422; fax (22) 2875671; f. 1978; fortnightly; English; Editor Omkar Goswami; circ. 97,600.

Business World: 25–28 Atlanta, 2nd Floor, Nariman Point, Mumbai 400 021; tel. (22) 2851352; fax (22) 2870310; f. 1980; fortnightly; English; Man. Editor Parthasarathi Swami; Exec. Editor P. G. Mathai; circ. 89,500.

Chitralekha: 62 Vaju Kotak Marg, Fort, Mumbai 400 001; tel. (22) 2614730; fax (22) 2615895; e-mail jee@bom2.vsnl.net.in; f. 1950 (Gujarati), f. 1989 (Marathi); weekly; Gujarati and Marathi; Editors Madhuri Kotak, Harkishan Mehta; circ. 275,183 (Gujarati), 103,684 (Marathi).

Cine Blitz Film Monthly: 17/17H Cawasji Patel St, Fort, Mumbai 400 001; tel. (22) 2044143; telex 1186801; fax (22) 2047984; f. 1974; English; Editor Rita K. Mehta; circ. 225,000.

Dalal Street: DSJ Communications Ltd, 105 Shreyas Bldg, New Link Rd, Andheri (W), Mumbai 400 057; tel. (22) 6293293; fax (22) 6291105; f. 1985; fortnightly; investment; Editor Pratap Padode.

Debonair: Maurya Publications (Pvt) Ltd, 20/21, Juhu Centaur Hotel, Juhu Tara Rd, POB 18292, Mumbai 400 049; tel. (22) 6116631; fax (22) 6152677; e-mail maurya@bom3.vsnl.net.in; f. 1972; monthly; English; Publr/Editor Randhir Khare; CEO S. G. Bhangaria; circ. 110,000.

Economic and Political Weekly: Hitkari House, 284 Shahid Bhagatsingh Rd, Mumbai 400 001; tel. (22) 2696073; fax (22) 2696072; e-mail admin@epw.ilbom.ernet.in; f. 1966; English; Editor Krishna Raj; circ. 132,800.

Femina: Times of India Bldg, Dr Dadabhai Naoroji Rd, Mumbai 400 001; tel. (22) 2620271; telex 1182699; fax (22) 2620985; f. 1959; fortnightly; English; Editor Sathya Saran; circ. 141,800.

Filmfare: Times of India Bldg, Dr Dadabhai Naoroji Rd, Mumbai 400 001; tel. (22) 2620271; telex 1182699; fax (22) 2620944; f. 1952; fortnightly; English; Editor Khalid Mohamed; circ. 157,800.

G: 62 Vaju Kotak Marg, Fort, Mumbai 400 001; tel. (22) 2614730; fax (22) 2615395; e-mail jee@bom2.vsnl.net.in; monthly; English; Editor Bhawna Somaya; circ. 60,574.

Gentleman: 1st Floor, Vinmar House, A-41, Rd No. 2, MIDC Andheri (East), Mumbai 400 093; tel. (22) 8205525; fax (22) 8205873; f. 1980; monthly; English; Editor Sambit Bal.

Indian PEN: Theosophy Hall, 40 New Marine Lines, Mumbai 400 020; tel. (22) 2032175; e-mail ambika.sirkar.gems.vsnl.net. in; f. 1934; quarterly; organ of Indian Centre of the International PEN; Editor Nissim Ezekiel.

Janmabhoomi Pravasi: Janmabhoomi Bhavan, Janmabhoomi Marg, Fort, Mumbai 400 001; tel. (22) 2870831; telex 1186859; fax (22) 2874097; f. 1939; weekly; Gujarati; Editor Harindra J. Dave; circ. 102,100.

JEE: 62 Vaju Kotak Marg, Fort, Mumbai 400 001; tel. (22) 2614730; fax (22) 2615895; e-mail jee@bom2.vsnl.net.in; fortnightly; Gujarati, Hindi and Marathi; Editor Madhuri Kotak; circ. 79,086 (Gujarati), 76,127 (Hindi), 34,257 (Marathi).

Meri Saheli: C–14 Royal Ind. Estate, 5–B Naigaum Cross Rd, Wadala, Mumbai 400 031; tel. (22) 4182797; fax (22) 4133610; f. 1987; monthly; Hindi; Editor Hema Malini; circ. 217,880.

Movie: Mahalaxmi Chambers, 5th Floor, 22 Bhulabhai Desai Rd, Mumbai 400 026; tel. (22) 4935636; telex 1186297; fax (22) 4938406; f. 1981; monthly; English; Editor Dinesh Raheja; circ. 70,700.

Onlooker: Free Press House, 215 Free Press Journal Marg, Nariman Point, Mumbai 400 021; tel. (22) 2874566; telex 112570; f. 1939; fortnightly; English; news magazine; Exec. Editor K. Srinivasan; circ. 61,000.

Reader's Digest: Orient House, Adi Marzban Path, Ballard Estate, Mumbai 400 001; tel. (22) 2617291; fax (22) 2613347; f. 1954; monthly; English; Publr and Editor-in-Chief Ashok Mahadevan; circ. 380,256 (English).

Savvy: Magna Publishing Co Ltd, Magna House, 100/E Old Prabhadevi Rd, Prabhadevi, Mumbai 400 025; tel. (22) 4362270; telex 1173288; fax (22) 4306523; f. 1984; monthly; English; Editor Usha Radhakrishnan; circ. 115,300.

Screen: D-2, Podar Chambers, Mathuradas Mill Compound, Ideal Industrial Estate, Lower Parel (W), Mumbai 400 013; tel. (22) 4946420; telex 1182276; fax (22) 4971697; f. 1951; film weekly; English; Editor Rauf Ahmed; circ. 90,000.

Shree: 40 Cawasji Patel St, Mumbai 400 023; tel. (22) 2044171; telex 1176844; fax (22) 2045068; f. 1967; weekly; Marathi; Editor Kamlesh D. Mehta; circ. 75,600.

Shreewarsha: 40 Cawasji Patel St, Mumbai 400 023; f. 1980; weekly; Hindi; Editor and Man. Dir R. M. Bhutta; circ. 50,000.

Society: Magna Publishing Co Ltd, Magna House, 100/E Old Prabhadevi Rd, Prabhadevi, Mumbai 400 025; tel. (22) 4362270; telex 1173288; fax (22) 4306523; f. 1979; monthly; English; Editor Lalitha Gopalan; circ. 83,900.

Star and Style: 20/21, Juhu Centaur Hotel, Juhu Tara Rd, POB 18292, Mumbai 400 049; tel. (22) 6116632; fax (22) 6152677; f. 1965; bimonthly; English; film; Publr/Editor Nishi Prem; circ. 60,000.

Stardust: Magna Publishing Co Ltd, Magna House, 100/E Old Prabhadevi Rd, Prabhadevi, Mumbai 400 025; tel. (22) 4362270; telex 1173288; fax (22) 4306523; f. 1985; monthly; English; Editor Omar Qureshi; circ. 308,600.

Vyapar: Janmabhoomi Bhavan, Janmabhoomi Marg, POB 321, Fort, Mumbai 400 001; tel. (22) 2870831; telex 1186859; fax (22) 2874097; f. 1949 (Gujarati), 1987 (Hindi); Gujarati (2 a week) and Hindi (weekly); commerce; Propr Saurashtra Trust; Editor Shashikant J. Vasani; circ. 31,800 (Gujarati), 18,900 (Hindi).

Yuvdarhsan: c/o Warsha Publications Pvt Ltd, Warsha House, 6 Zakaria Bunder Rd, Sewri, Mumbai 400 015; tel. (22) 441843; f. 1975; weekly; Gujarati; Editor and Man. Dir R. M. Bhutta; circ. 18,600.

Nagpur

All India Reporter: AIR Ltd, Congress Nagar, POB 209, Nagpur 440 012; tel. (712) 34321; f. 1914; monthly; English; law journal; Chief Editor V. R. Manohar; circ. 36,000.

Rajasthan

Jaipur

Balhans: Kesargarh, Jawahar Lal Nehru Marg, Jaipur 302 004; tel. (141) 561582; telex 3652435; fax (141) 566011; fortnightly; Hindi; circ. 90,664.

Itwari Patrika: Kesargarh, Jawahar Lal Nehru Marg, Jaipur 302 004; tel. (141) 561582; telex 3652435; fax (141) 566011; weekly; Hindi; circ. 27,780.

Rashtradoot Saptahik: HO, M.I. Rd, POB 30, Jaipur 302 001; tel. (141) 372634; fax (141) 373513; f. 1983; Hindi; also publ. from Kota and Bikaner; Chief Editor and Man. Editor Rajesh Sharma; CEO Somesh Sharma; combined circ. 167,500.

Tamil Nadu

Chennai (Madras)

Aishwarya: 325 N. S. K. Salai, Chennai 600 024; tel. (44) 422064; f. 1990; weekly; Tamil; general; Editor K. Natarajan; circ. 20,000.

Ambulimama: 188 N. S. K. Salai, Vadapalani, Chennai 600 026; f. 1947; monthly; Tamil; Editor Nagi Reddi; circ. 60,000.

Ambuli Ammavan: 188 N. S. K. Salai, Vadapalani, Chennai 600 026; f. 1970; children's monthly; Malayalam; Editor Nagi Reddi; circ. 10,000.

Ananda Vikatan: 757 Anna Salai, Chennai 600 002; tel. (44) 8524054; telex 417358; fax (44) 8523819; f. 1924; weekly; Tamil; Editor S. Balasubramanian; circ. 362,100.

Chandamama: 188 N. S. K. Salai, Vadapalani, Chennai 600 026; f. 1947; children's monthly; Hindi, Gujarati, Telugu, Kannada, English, Sanskrit, Bengali, Assamese; Editor Nagi Reddi; combined circ. 410,200.

Chandoba: 188 N. S. K. Salai, Vadapalani, Chennai 600 026; f. 1952; monthly; Marathi; Editor Nagi Reddi; circ. 92,000.

Devi: 727 Anna Salai, Chennai 600 006; tel. (44) 8521428; f. 1979; weekly; Tamil; Editor B. Ramachandra Adityan; circ. 134,800.

Dinamani Kadir: Express Estate, Mount Rd, Chennai 600 002; tel. (44) 8520751; telex 418222; fax (44) 8524500; weekly; Editor G. Kasturi Rangan (acting); circ. 55,000.

Frontline: Kasturi Bldgs, 859/860 Anna Salai, Chennai 600 002; tel. (44) 8535067; telex 416655; fax (44) 8535325; f. 1984; fortnightly; English; Publr S. Rangarajan; Editor N. Ram; circ. 65,200.

Hindu International Edition: 859/860 Anna Salai, Chennai 600 002; tel. (44) 8535067; telex 416655; fax (44) 8535325; f. 1975; weekly; English; Editor N. Ravi; circ. 4,760.

Jahnamamu (Oriya): 188 N. S. K. Salai, Vadapalani, Chennai 600 026; f. 1972; children's monthly; Editor Nagi Reddi; circ. 110,000.

Junior Post: 757 Anna Salai, Chennai 600 002; tel. (44) 8524054; telex 417358; fax (44) 8523819; f. 1988; weekly; Tamil; Editor S. Balasubramanian; circ. 35,000.

Junior Vikatan: 757 Anna Salai, Chennai 600 002; tel. (44) 8524054; telex 417358; fax (44) 8523819; f. 1983; 2 times a week; Tamil; Editor S. Balasubramanian; circ. 249,700.

Kalai Magal: POB 604, Chennai 600 004; tel. (44) 843099; f. 1932; monthly; Tamil; literary and cultural; Editor R. Narayanaswamy; circ. 13,300.

Kalkandu: 151 Purasawalkam High Rd, Chennai; f. 1948; weekly; Tamil; Editor Tamil Vanan; circ. 94,400.

Kalki: 47 Jawaharlal Nehru Rd, Ekkaduthangal, Chennai 600 097; tel. (44) 2345621; f. 1941; weekly; Tamil; literary and cultural; Editor Seetha Ravi; circ. 53,552.

Kumudam: 151 Purasawalkam High Rd, Chennai 600 010; tel. (44) 6422146; fax (44) 6425041; e-mail kumudam@giasmd0l.vsnl.net.in; f. 1947; weekly; Tamil; Editor Dr S. A. P. Jawahar Palaniappan; circ 495,000.

Kungumam: 93A Kodambakkam High Rd, Chennai 600 034; tel. (44) 8268177; f. 1978; weekly; Tamil; Editor Parasakthi; circ. 46,600.

Malaimathi: Chennai; f. 1958; weekly; Tamil; Editor P. S. Elango; circ. 56,100.

Muththaram: 93A Kogambakkam High Rd, Chennai 600 034; tel. (44) 476306; f. 1980; weekly; Tamil; Editor Sri Parasakthi; circ. 42,900.

Pesum Padam: 325 N. S. K. Salai, Chennai 600 024; tel. (44) 422064; f. 1942; monthly; Tamil; films; Man. Editor K. Natarajan; circ. 34,326.

Picturpost: 325 N. S. K. Salai, Chennai 600 024; tel. (44) 422064; f. 1943; monthly; English; films; Man. Editor K. Natarajan; circ. 11,000.

Rajam: 325 N. S. K. Salai, Chennai 600 024; tel. (44) 422064; f. 1986; monthly; Tamil; women's interests; Man. Dir and Editor K. Natarajan; circ. 32,677.

Rani Muthu: 1091 Periyar E.V.R. High Rd, Chennai 600 007; tel. (44) 5324771; f. 1969; monthly; Tamil; Editor A. Ma. Samy; circ. 111,200.

Rani Weekly: 1091 Periyar E.V.R. High Rd, Chennai 600 007; tel. (44) 5324771; telex 4124127; f. 1962; Tamil; Editor A. Ma. Samy; circ. 255,300.

Sportstar: Kasturi Bldgs, 859/860 Anna Salai, Chennai 600 002; tel. (44) 8535067; telex 416655; fax (44) 8535325; f. 1978; weekly; English; Publr S. Rangarajan; Editor N. Ram; circ. 72,900.

Thuglak: 46 Greenways Rd, Chennai 600 028; tel. (44) 4936913; fax (44) 4936915; f. 1970; weekly; Tamil; Editor Cho S. Ramaswamy; circ. 149,100.

Vellore

Madha Jothidam: 3 Arasamaram St, Vellore 632 004; f. 1949; monthly; Tamil; astrology; Editor and Publr A. K. Thulasiraman; circ. 8,000.

Uttar Pradesh

Allahabad

Alokpaat: Mitra Prakashan (Pvt) Ltd, 281 Muthiganj, Allahabad 211 003; tel. (532) 606693; telex 540280; fax (532) 601156; f. 1986; monthly; Bengali; Editor Aloke Mitra; circ. 33,700.

Jasoosi Duniya: 5 Kolhan Tola St, Allahabad; f. 1953; monthly; Urdu and Hindi edns; Editor S. Abbas Husainy; combined circ. 70,000.

Manohar Kahaniyan: Mitra Prakashan (Pvt) Ltd, 281 Muthiganj, Allahabad 211 003; tel. (532) 606693; telex 540280; fax (532) 601156; f. 1940; monthly; Hindi; Editor Aloke Mitra; circ. 301,200.

Manorama: Mitra Parkashan (Pvt) Ltd, 281 Muthiganj, Allahabad 211 003; tel. (532) 606694; telex 540280; fax (532) 606379; f. 1924 (Hindi), 1986 (Bengali); fortnightly (Hindi), monthly (Bengali); Editor Aloke Mitra; circ. 176,000 (Hindi), 33,000 (Bengali).

Maya: Mitra Prakashan (Pvt) Ltd, 281 Muthiganj, Allahabad 211 003; tel. (532) 606694; telex 540280; fax (532) 601156; f. 1929; fortnightly; Hindi; Editor Aloke Mitra; circ. 175,200.

Nutan Kahaniyan: 15 Sheo Charan Lal Rd, Allahabad 211 003; tel. (532) 400612; f. 1975; Hindi; monthly; Chief Editor K. K. Bhargava; circ. 167,500.

Satyakatha: Mitra Prakashan (Pvt) Ltd, 281 Muthiganj, Allahabad 211 003; tel (532) 606693; telex 540280; fax (532) 606379; f. 1974; monthly; Hindi; Editor Aloke Mitra; circ. 98,100.

Kanpur

Kanchan Prabha: Kanpur; f. 1974; Hindi; monthly; Man. Editor P. C. Gupta; Editor Y. M. Gupta; circ. 26,000.

West Bengal

Calcutta

All India Appointment Gazette: 7 Old Court House St, Calcutta 700 001; tel. (33) 2206663; fax (33) 296548; f. 1973; 2 a week; English; Editor S. C. Talukdar; circ. 145,113.

Anandalok: 6 Prafulla Sarkar St, Calcutta 700 001; tel. (33) 278000; telex 215468; f. 1975; fortnightly; Bengali; film; Editor Dulendra Bhowmik; circ. 56,200.

Anandamela: 6 Prafulla Sarkar St, Calcutta 700 001; tel. (33) 278000; telex 215468; f. 1975; monthly; Bengali; juvenile; Editor Debashis Bandopadhyay; circ. 52,900.

Capital: 1/2 Old Court House Corner, POB 14, Calcutta 700 001; tel. (33) 200099; telex 217172; f. 1888; fortnightly; English; financial; Editor S. Banerjee (acting); circ. 8,000.

Desh: 6 Prafulla Sarkar St, Calcutta 700 001; tel. (33) 274880; telex 215468; f. 1933; fortnightly; Bengali; literary; Editor Amitabha Choudhury; circ. 67,900.

Investment Preview: 7 Old Court House St, Calcutta 700 001; tel. (33) 2206663; fax (33) 296548; f. 1992; weekly; English; Editor S. C. Talukdar; circ. 53,845.

Khela: 96 Raja Rammohan Sarani, Calcutta 700 009; tel. (33) 3509803; telex 212216; f. 1981; weekly; Bengali; sports; Editor Asoke Dasgupta; circ. 13,500.

Naba Kallol: 11 Jhamapookur Lane, Calcutta 700 009; tel. (33) 354294; f. 1960; monthly; Bengali; Editor P. K. Mazumdar; circ. 32,600.

Neetee: 4 Sukhlal Johari Lane, Calcutta; f. 1955; weekly; English; Editor M. P. Poddar.

Prabuddha Bharata (Awakened India): 5 Dehi Entally Rd, Calcutta 700 014; tel. (33) 2440898; fax (33) 2450050; e-mail advaita@giascl01.vsnl.net.in; f. 1896; monthly; art, culture, religion and philosophy; Publr Swami Bodhasarananda; circ. 8,000.

Sananda: 6 Prafulla Sarkar St, Calcutta 700 001; tel. (33) 278000; telex 215468; f. 1986; fortnightly; Bengali; Editor Aparna Sen; circ. 81,800.

Saptahik Bartaman: 76A J. C. Bose Rd, Calcutta 700 014; tel. (33) 2448208; telex 215458; fax (33) 2441215; f. 1988; weekly; Bengali; Editor Barun Sengupta; circ. 84,400.

Screen: P-5, Kalakar St, Calcutta 700 070; f. 1960; weekly; Hindi; Editor M. P. Poddar; circ. 58,000.

Sportsworld: 6 Prafulla Sarkar St, Calcutta 700 001; tel. (33) 278000; telex 215468; fax (33) 303240; fortnightly; English; Editor Mansur Ali Khan Pataudi; circ. 15,400.

Statesman: Statesman House, 4 Chowringhee Sq., Calcutta 700 001; tel. (33) 271000; telex 215303; fax (33) 270118; f. 1875; overseas weekly; English; Editor-in-Chief C. R. Irani.

Suktara: 11 Jhamapooker Lane, Calcutta 700 009; tel. (33) 355294; f. 1948; monthly; Bengali; juvenile; Editor M. Majumdar; circ. 34,500.

Sunday: 6 Prafulla Sarkar St, Calcutta 700 001; tel. (33) 274880; telex 215468; f. 1973; weekly; English; Editor Vir Sanghvi; circ. 40,600.

NEWS AGENCIES

Press Trust of India Ltd: 4 Parliament St, New Delhi 110 001; tel. (11) 3716621; telex 3163393; fax (11) 3716527; f. 1947, re-established 1978; Chair. Shobhana Bhartia; Gen. Man. M. K. Razdan.

United News of India (UNI): 9 Rafi Marg, New Delhi 110 001; tel. (11) 3715898; telex 3166305; fax (11) 3716211; f. 1961; Indian language news in Hindi and Urdu; English wire service; World TV News Service (UNISCAN); photograph service; graphics service; special UNIFIN service covering banking; brs in 90 centres in India; Chair. Vivek Goenka; Gen. Man. and Chief Editor Virender Mohan.

Foreign Bureaux

Agence France-Presse (AFP): 204 Surya Kiran Bldg, 19 Kasturba Gandhi Marg, New Delhi 110 001; tel. (11) 3712831; telex 3165075; fax (11) 3311105; Bureau Chief Philippe Sauvagnargues.

Agencia EFE (Spain): 72 Jor Bagh, New Delhi 110 003; tel. (11) 4618092; fax (11) 4615013; Correspondent Isabel Calleja Solera.

Agenzia Nazionale Stampa Associata (ANSA) (Italy): 74 Friends Colony West, New Delhi 110 065; tel. (11) 6844674; telex 3165381; fax (11) 6847358; Bureau Chief Beniamino Natale.

Associated Press (AP) (USA): 6B Jor Bagh Lane, New Delhi 110 003; tel. (11) 4698775; telex 3174132; fax (11) 4616870; Bureau Chief Arthur Max.

Deutsche Presse-Agentur (dpa) (Germany): 39 Golf Links, New Delhi 110 003; tel. (11) 4617792; fax (11) 4635772; e-mail dpadelhi@del2.vsnl.net.in; Chief Rep. Annegret Ratzkowsky.

Informatsionnoye Telegrafnoye Agentstvo Rossii—Telegrafnoye Agentstvo Suverennykh Stran (ITAR—TASS) (Russia): E-5/4 Vasant Vihar, New Delhi 110 057; tel. (11) 6886232; telex 3166092; fax (11) 6876233; Bureau Chief Leonid Kotov.

Inter Press Service (IPS) (Italy): 49 (F.F.) Defence Colony Market, New Delhi 110 024; tel. (11) 4634154; fax (11) 4624725.

Islamic Republic News Agency (IRNA) (Iran): 11 Hemkunt Colony, New Delhi 110 048; tel. (11) 6446866; telex 3171378; fax (11) 6221529; Bureau Chief Mohd Sorournia.

Jiji Tsushin (Japan): Apt No. 1/B, 13 Paschimi Nagar, Vasant Vihar, New Delhi 110 057; tel. (11) 6879432; telex 3170138; fax (11) 6113578; Correspondent Masashi Okuyama.

Kyodo News Service (Japan): PTI Bldg, 1st Floor, 4 Parliament St, New Delhi 110 001; tel. (11) 3711954; telex 3165016; fax (11) 3718756; Bureau Chief Shingo Kiniwa.

Reuters (UK): 1 Kautilya Marg, Chanakyapuri, New Delhi 110 021; tel. (11) 3012024; telex 3166423; fax (11) 3014043; Bureau Chief John Owen Davies.

United Press International (UPI) (USA): 706, Sector 7B, Chandigarh 160 019; tel. (172) 772365; fax (172) 772366; e-mail nsnanda@ch1.vsnl.net.in; Bureau Chief Harbaksh Singh Nanda.

Xinhua (New China) News Agency (People's Republic of China): 50D, Shanti Path, Chanakyapuri, New Delhi 110 021; tel. (11) 601886; telex 3162250; Chief Li Guorong.

The following agencies are also represented: Associated Press of Pakistan, A. P. Dow Jones, Bloomberg Business News, Depthnews, Knight-Ridder Financial News and Viet Nam News Agency.

CO-ORDINATING BODIES

Press Information Bureau: Shastri Bhavan, Dr Rajendra Prasad Rd, New Delhi 110 001; tel. (11) 3383643; f. 1946 to co-ordinate press affairs for the govt; represents newspaper managements, journalists, news agencies, parliament; has power to examine journalists under oath and may censor objectionable material; Prin. Information Officer S. Narendra.

Registrar of Newspapers for India: Ministry of Information and Broadcasting, West Block 8, Wing 2, Ramakrishna Puram, New Delhi 110 066; tel. (11) 608788; f. 1956 as a statutory body to collect press statistics; maintains a register of all Indian newspapers; Registrar P. B. Ray.

PRESS ASSOCIATIONS

All-India Newspaper Editors' Conference: 36–37 Northend Complex, Rama Krishna Ashram Marg, New Delhi 110 001; tel. (11) 3364519; fax (11) 3716665; f. 1940; c. 400 mems; Pres. Vishwa Bandhu Gupta; Secs Manak Chopra, Bishamber Newar.

Editors' Guild of India: New Delhi; f. 1977; Pres. Vinod Mehta; Sec.-Gen. Sumit Chakravarty.

The Foreign Correspondents' Club of South Asia: AB-19 Mathura Rd, New Delhi 110 001; tel. (11) 3388535; 210 mems; Pres. Michael Drudge; Man. Kiran Kapur.

Indian Federation of Working Journalists: F-101, M.S. Apts, Kasturba Gandhi Marg, New Delhi 110 001; tel. (11) 3384956; fax (11) 3384650; f. 1950; 27,000 mems; Pres. K. Vikram Rao; Sec.-Gen. Parmanand Pandey.

Indian Languages Newspapers' Assen: Janmabhoomi Bhavan, Janmabhoomi Marg, POB 10029, Fort, Mumbai 400 001; tel. (22) 2870537; f. 1941; 249 mems; Pres. Uttamehandra Sharma; Hon. Gen. Secs Pradeep G. Deshpande, Ambekar Balkrishna Vasantrao, Lalit Shrimal.

Indian Newspaper Society: INS Bldgs, Rafi Marg, New Delhi 110 001; tel. (11) 3715401; telex 3166312; fax (11) 3723800; f. 1939; 723 mems; Pres. Vijay Darda; Sec.-Gen. P. K. Lahiri.

Indian Small and Medium Newspapers' Federation: New Delhi; Pres. Pushpa Pandya.

National Union of Journalists (India): 7 Jantar Mantar Rd, 2nd Floor, New Delhi 110 001; tel. (11) 3368610; fax (11) 3368723; f. 1972; 10,000 mems; Pres. Rajendra Prabhu; Sec.-Gen. Asim Kr. Mitra.

Press Institute of India: Sapru House Annexe, Barakhamba Rd, New Delhi 110 001; tel. (11) 3318066; fax (11) 3311975; e-mail presinst@sansad.nic.in; f. 1963; 29 mem. newspapers and other orgs; Chair. Naresh Mohan; Dir Ajit Bhattacharjea.

Publishers

Delhi and New Delhi

Affiliated East-West Press (Pvt) Ltd: G-1/16 Ansari Rd, Daryaganj, New Delhi 110 002; tel. (11) 3264180; fax (11) 3260538; textbooks and reference books; Dirs Sunny Malik, Kamal Malik.

All India Educational Supply Co: 17 Sri Ram Bldg, Jawahar Nagar, POB 2147, Delhi 110 007; tel. (11) 2914448; telex 3173133; fax (11) 6866588; f. 1944; maps, charts and teaching aids; CEO R. D. Aggarwal.

Allied Publishers Ltd: 13/14 Asaf Ali Rd, New Delhi 110 002; tel. (11) 3239001; telex 3162953; fax (11) 3235967; academic and general; Man. Dir S. M. Sachdev.

Amerind Publishing Co (Pvt) Ltd: Oxford Bldg, N-56 Connaught Circus, New Delhi 110 001; tel. (11) 3314957; fax (11) 3322639; f. 1970; offices at Calcutta, Mumbai and New York; scientific and technical; Dirs Mohan Primlani, Gulab Primlani.

Arnold Publishers (India) Pvt Ltd: AB/9 Safdarjung Enclave, 1st Floor, New Delhi 110 029; tel. (11) 6883422; fax (11) 6877571; literature and general; Man. Dir G. A. Vazirani.

Atma Ram and Sons: 1376 Kashmere Gate, POB 1429, Delhi 110 006; tel. (11) 2523082; f. 1909; scientific, technical, humanities, medical; Man. Dir S. Puri.

B.I. Publications Pvt Ltd: 13 Daryaganj, New Delhi 110 002; tel. (11) 3274443; telex 3163352; fax (11) 3261290; f. 1959; academic, general and professional; Man. Dir R. D. Bhagat.

B.R. Publishing Corpn: A-6, Nimri Commercial Centre, nr Bharat Nagar, Ashok Vihar, Phase-IV, Delhi 110 052; tel. (11) 7430113; fax (11) 7452453; a division of BRPC (India) Ltd; Man. Dir Praveen Mittal.

S. Chand and Co Ltd: Ram Nagar, POB 5733, New Delhi 110 055; tel. (11) 7772080; telex 3161310; fax (11) 7777446; f. 1917; educational and general in English and Hindi; also book exports and imports; Man. Dir Rajendra Kumar Gupta.

Children's Book House: A-4 Ring Rd, South Extension Part I, New Delhi 110 049; tel. (11) 4636030; fax (11) 4636011; f. 1952; educational and general; Dir R. S. Gupta.

Children's Book Trust: Nehru House, 4 Bahadur Shah Zafar Marg, New Delhi 110 002; tel. (11) 3316970; fax (11) 3721090; f. 1957; children's books in English and other Indian languages; Editor C. G. R. Kurup; Gen. Man. Ravi Shankar.

Clarion Books: G.T. Rd, Dilshad Garden, Delhi 110 095; tel. (11) 2297792; fax (11) 2282332; art books, Indology, environment; Dir Madhvi Malhotra.

Concept Publishing Co: A/15-16, Commercial Block, Mohan Garden, New Delhi 110 059; tel. (11) 5648039; fax (11) 5648053; f. 1975; geography, rural and urban development, education, sociology, economics, anthropology, agriculture, religion, history, law, philosophy, information sciences, ecology; Man. Dir Ashok Kumar Mittal; Man. Editor Arvind Kumar Mittal.

Eurasia Publishing House (Pvt) Ltd: Ram Nagar, New Delhi 110 055; tel (11) 7772080; telex 3161310; fax (11) 7777446; f. 1964; educational in English and Hindi; Man. Dir Rajendra Kumar Gupta.

Frank Bros and Co (Publishers) Ltd: 4675A Ansari Rd, 21 Daryaganj, New Delhi 110 002; tel. (11) 3263393; telex 3163419; fax (11) 8521660; e-mail frank@nda.vsnl.net.in; f. 1930; children's and educational books; Chair. R. C. Govil.

Global Business Press: GT Rd, 18–19 Dilshad Garden, Delhi 110 095; tel. (11) 2297792; fax (11) 2282332; business, management and computers; Dir Shekhar Malhotra.

Heritage Publishers: 32 Prakash Apartments, 5 Ansari Rd, Darya ganj, New Delhi 110 002; tel. (11) 3266258; fax (11) 3263050; e-mail chawla.heritag@axcess.net.in; f. 1973; social sciences, art and architecture, economics, commerce, literature; Propr and Dir B. R. Chawla.

Hind Pocket Books (Pvt) Ltd: 18–19 Dilshad Garden, Delhi 110 095; tel. (11) 2297792; fax (11) 2282332; f. 1958; fiction and non-fiction paperbacks in English, Hindi, Punjabi, Malayalam and Urdu; Chair Dinanath Malhotra; Exec. Dir Shekhar Malhotra.

Hindustan Publishing Corpn (India): 4805/24 Bharat Ram Rd, Daryaganj, Delhi 110 002; tel. (11) 3254401; fax (11) 6863511; e-mail hpcpd@nda.vsnl.net.in; archaeology, pure and applied sciences, geology, sociology, anthropology, economics; Man. Partner P. C. Kumar.

Inter-India Publications: D-17, Raja Garden, New Delhi 110 015; tel. (11) 5441120; f. 1977; academic and research works; Dir Mool Chand Mittal.

Kali for Women: B1/8 Hauz Khas, New Delhi 110 016; tel. (11) 6852530; fax (11) 6864497; women's studies, social sciences, humanities, general non-fiction, fiction, etc.; Heads of Organization Urvashi Butalia, Ritu Menon.

Lancers Books: POB 4236, New Delhi 110 048; tel. (11) 6414617; f. 1977; politics (with special emphasis on north-east India), defence; Propr S. Kumar.

Motilal Banarsidas Publishers (Pvt) Ltd: 41 U.A. Bungalow Rd, Jawahar Nagar, Delhi 110 007; tel. (11) 2911985; fax (11) 2930689; e-mail gloryindia@poboxes.com; f. 1903; Indology, in English and Sanskrit; Editorial Exec. N. P. Jain.

Munshiram Manoharlal Publishers Pvt Ltd: 54 Rani Jhansi Rd, POB 5715, New Delhi 110 055; tel. (11) 7771668; fax (11) 7512745; e-mail mrmlpub.mrml@axcess.net.in; f. 1952; Indian art, architecture, archaeology, religion, music, law, medicine, dance, dictionaries, history, politics, numismatics, philosophy, sociology, etc.; Publishing Dir Devendra Jain; Sales Dir Ashok Jain.

National Book Trust: A-5 Green Park, New Delhi 110 016; tel. (11) 664020; telex 3173034; fax (11) 6851795; f. 1957; autonomous organization established by the Ministry of Human Resources Development to produce and encourage the production of good literary works; Chair. Sumatheendra Nadig.

National Council of Educational Research and Training (NCERT): Sri Aurobindo Marg, New Delhi 110 016; tel. (11) 6851070; telex 3173024; fax (11) 6868419; f. 1961; school text books, teachers' guides, research monographs, journals, etc.; Dir Prof. A. K. Sharma.

Neeta Prakashan: A-4 Ring Rd, South Extension Part I, POB 3853, New Delhi 110 049; tel. (11) 4636020; fax (11) 4636011; educational; Man. Dir Shanti Devi Gupta.

New Age International Pvt Ltd: 4835/24 Ansari Rd, Daryaganj, New Delhi 110 002; tel. (11) 3278348; fax (11) 3267437; f. 1966; science, engineering, technology, management, humanities, social science; Dir A. R. Kundaji.

Oxford and IBH Publishing Co (Pvt) Ltd: 66 Janpath, New Delhi 110 001; tel. (11) 3324578; fax (11) 3322639; e-mail oxford@nda.vsnl.net.in; f. 1964; science, technology and reference in English; Dir Vijay Primlani; Man. Dir Mohan Primlani.

Oxford University Press: YMCA Library Bldg, 1st Floor, Jai Singh Rd, POB 43, New Delhi 110 001; tel. (11) 3273841; fax (11) 3277812; f. 1912; educational, scientific, medical, general and reference; Man. Dir Manzar Khan.

Penguin Books India (Pvt) Ltd: 210 Chiranjiv Tower, 43 Nehru Place, New Delhi 110 019; tel. (11) 6234248; fax (11) 6234250; e-mail penguin@del2.vsnl.net.in; f. 1987; Indian literature in English; Chair. Michael Lynton; Man. Dir Aveek Sarkar.

People's Publishing House (Pvt) Ltd: 5E Rani Jhansi Rd, New Delhi 110 055; tel. (11) 7524701; f. 1947; Marxism, Leninism, peasant movt; Dir Shameem Faizee.

Pitambar Publishing Co Pvt Ltd: 888 East Park Rd, Karol Bagh, New Delhi 110 005; tel. (11) 7770067; fax (11) 7776058; academic, children's books, text books and general; Man. Dir Anand Bhushan.

Prentice-Hall of India (Pvt) Ltd: M-97 Connaught Circus, New Delhi 110 001; tel. (11) 3321779; telex 3161808; fax (11) 3717179; f. 1963; university-level text and reference books; Man. Dir A. K. Ghosh.

Puneet Enterprises: D-9 Krishna Park, Deoli Rd, New Delhi 110 062; tel. (11) 3363685; f. 1977; school books; Dir Vimla Gupta.

Pustak Mahal: 10B Netaji Subhas Marg, Daryaganj, New Delhi 110 002; tel. (11) 3268292; telex 3178090; fax (11) 3280567; children's, general, computers, religious, encyclopaedia; Man. Dir Ram Avtar Gupta; Dir (Production) Vinod Kumar Gupta.

Radhakrishna Prakashan (Pvt) Ltd: 2/38 Ansari Rd, New Delhi 110 002; tel. (11) 3279351; f. 1968; Hindi; literary; Dir Ashok Maheswari.

Rajkamal Prakashan (Pvt) Ltd: 1B Netaji Subhas Marg, New Delhi 110 002; tel. (11) 3274463; f. 1946; Hindi; literary; also literary journal and monthly trade journal; Man. Dir Ashok Maheshwari.

Rajpal and Sons: 1590 Madrasa Rd, Kashmere Gate, Delhi 110 006; tel. (11) 2965483; fax (11) 2967791; f. 1891; humanities, social sciences, art, juvenile; Hindi; Chair Vishwanath Malhotra.

RIS (Research and Information System) Publications: Zone IV, Fourth Floor, India Habitat Centre, Lodhi Rd, New Delhi 110 003; tel. (11) 4617403; fax (11) 4628068; f. 1983; current and economic affairs involving non-aligned and developing countries; Dir Dr V. R. Panchamukhi.

Rupa & Co: 7/16 Makhanlal St, Ansari Rd, Daryaganj, POB 7017, New Delhi 110 002; tel. (11) 3278586; telex 3166641; fax (11) 3277294; f. 1936; Chief Exec. R. K. Mehra.

Sage Publications India Pvt Ltd: 32 M-Block Market, Greater Kailash-1, POB 4215, New Delhi 110 048; tel. (11) 6485884; fax (11) 6472426; social science, development studies, business and management studies; Man. Dir Tejeshwar Singh.

Sahitya Akademi: Rabindra Bhavan, 35 Ferozeshah Rd, New Delhi 110 001; tel. (11) 3386626; telex 3165445; fax (11) 3382428; f. 1956; bibliographies, translations, literary classics, etc.; Chair. U. R. Anantha Murthy; Sec. Dr K. Satchidanandan.

Scholar Publishing House (P) Ltd: 85 Model Basti, New Delhi 110 005; tel. (11) 7528303; fax (11) 7776565; e-mail scholar@del2.vsnl.net.in; f. 1968; educational; Man. Dir Y. P. Ranade.

Shiksha Bharati: Madrasa Rd, Kashmere Gate, Delhi 110 006; tel. (11) 2965483; fax (11) 2967791; f. 1955; textbooks, creative literature, popular science and juvenile in Hindi and English; Editor Meera Johri.

Sterling Publishers (Pvt) Ltd: L-10 Green Park Extension, New Delhi 110 016; tel. (11) 660904; fax (11) 6886646; e-mail sterlin.gprb@axcess.net.in; f. 1965; academic books on the humanities and social sciences, children's books, computer books, management books, paperbacks; Man. Dir S. K. Ghai; Gen. Man. A. J. Sehgal.

Tata McGraw-Hill Publishing Co Ltd: 7 West Patel Nagar, New Delhi 110 008; tel. (11) 5732918; fax (11) 5732306; f. 1970; engineering, sciences, management, humanities, social sciences; Chair. F. A. Mehta; Man. Dir Dr N. Subramanyam.

Technical and Commercial Book Co: 75 Gokhale Market, Tis Hazari, Delhi 110 054; tel. (11) 228315; telex 112651; f. 1913; technical; Propr D. N. Mehra; Man. Raman Mehra.

Vikas Publishing House (Pvt) Ltd: 576 Masjid Rd, Jangpura, New Delhi 110 014; tel. (11) 4315313; fax (11) 3276593; medicine, sciences, engineering, textbooks, academic, fiction, women's studies, children's books; Chair. and Man. Dir Chander M. Chawla.

A. H. Wheeler & Co Ltd: 411 Surya Kiran Bldg, 19 K. G. Marg, New Delhi 110 001; tel. (11) 3312629; fax (11) 3357798; e-mail wheeler.jeet@axcess.net.in; f. 1958; textbooks, reference books, computer science and information technology, electronics, management, telecommunications, social sciences, etc.; Exec. Pres. Alok Banerjee.

Calcutta

Academic Publishers: 12/1A Bankim Chatterjee St, POB 12341, Calcutta 700 073; tel. and fax (33) 2413702; f. 1958; textbooks; Man. Partner Dipankar Dhur.

Advaita Ashrama: 5 Dehi Entally Rd, Calcutta 700 014; tel. (33) 2440898; fax (33) 2450050; e-mail advaita@giascl01.vsnl.net.in; f. 1899; religion, philosophy, spiritualism, Vedanta; publication centre of Ramakrishna Math and Ramakrishna Mission; Publication Man. Swami Bodhasarananda.

Allied Book Agency: 18A Shyama Charan De St, Calcutta 700 073; tel. (33) 312594; general and academic; Dir B. Sarkar.

Ananda Publishers (Pvt) Ltd: 45 Beniatola Lane, Calcutta 700 009; tel. (33) 2414352; fax (33) 2253240; literature, general; Dir A. Sarkar; Gen. Man. D. N. Basu.

Assam Review Publishing Co: 29 Waterloo St, Calcutta 700 069; tel. (33) 2482251; f. 1926; publrs of *Tea Plantation Directory* and *Tea News*; Partners G. L. Banerjee, S. Banerjee.

Book Land (Pvt) Ltd: Calcutta; tel. (33) 2414158; economics, politics, history and general; Dir Subhankar Basu.

Chuckervertty, Chatterjee and Co Ltd: 15 College Sq., Calcutta 700 073; tel. (33) 2416425; Man. Dir Mala Mazumdar.

Eastern Law House (Pvt) Ltd: 54 Ganesh Chunder Ave, Calcutta 700 013; tel. (33) 274989; fax (33) 2150491; f. 1918; legal, commercial and accountancy; Dir Asok De; br. in New Delhi.

Firma KLM Private Ltd: 257B B. B. Ganguly St, Calcutta 700 012; tel. (33) 274391; fax (33) 276544; f. 1950; Indology, scholarly in English, Bengali, Sanskrit and Hindi; Man. Dir R. N. Mukerji.

Intertrade Publications (India) (Pvt) Ltd: 55 Gariahat Rd, POB 10210, Calcutta 700 019; tel. (33) 474872; f. 1954; economics, medicine, law, history and trade directories; Man. Dir Dr K. K. Roy.

A. Mukherjee and Co (Pvt) Ltd: 2 Bankim Chatterjee St, Calcutta 700 073; tel. (33) 311406; fax (33) 7448172; f. 1940; educational and general in Bengali and English; Man. Dir Rajeev Neogi.

Naya Prokash: 206 Bidhan Sarani, POB 11468, Calcutta 700 006; tel. (33) 2414709; fax (33) 209673; f. 1960; agriculture, horticulture, Indology, history, political science, defence studies; Senior Partner Barin Mitra.

New Era Publishing Co: 31 Gauri Bari Lane, Calcutta 700 004; f. 1944; Propr Dr P. N. Mitra; Man. S. K. Mitra.

W. Newman and Co Ltd: 3 Old Court House St, Calcutta 700 069; tel. (33) 2489436; f. 1854; general; Man. K. M. Bantia.

Punthi Pustak: 136/4B Bidhan Sarani, Calcutta 700 004; tel. (33) 558473; religion, history, philosophy; Propr S. K. Bhattacharya.

Renaissance Publishers (Pvt) Ltd: 15 Bankim Chatterjee St, Calcutta 700 012; f. 1949; politics, philosophy, history; Man. Dir J. C. Goswami.

Saraswati Library: 206 Bidhan Sarani, Calcutta 700 006; tel. (33) 345492; f. 1914; history, philosophy, religion, literature; Man. Partner B. Bhattacharjee.

M. C. Sarkar and Sons (Pvt) Ltd: 14 Bankim Chatterjee St, Calcutta 700 073; tel. (33) 312490; f. 1910; reference; Dirs Supriya Sarkar, Samit Sarkar.

Thacker's Press and Directories: Calcutta; industrial publs and directories; Chair. Juthika Roy; Dirs B. B. Roy, A. Bose.

Visva-Bharati: 6 Acharya Jagadish Bose Rd, Calcutta 700 017; tel. (33) 2479868; f. 1923; literature; Dir Ashoke Mukhopadhyay.

Chennai (Madras)

Higginbothams Ltd: 814 Anna Salai, POB 311, Chennai 600 002; tel. (44) 8521841; telex 417038; fax (44) 834590; f. 1844; general; Chair. and Man. Dir K. S. Subramanian; Exec. Dir (Operations) S. Chandrasekhar.

B. G. Paul and Co: 4 Francis Joseph St, Chennai; f. 1923; general, educational and oriental; Man. K. Nilakantan.

T. R. Publications Pvt Ltd: PMG Complex, 2nd Floor, 57 South Usman Rd, T. Nagar, Chennai 600 017; tel. (44) 4340765; telex 417603; fax (44) 4348837; Chief Exec. S. Geetha.

Mumbai (Bombay)

Allied Publishers Ltd: 15 J. N. Heredia Marg, Ballard Estate, Mumbai 400 001; tel. (22) 2617926; fax (22) 2617928; f. 1934; economics, medicine, politics, history, philosophy, science, mathematics and fiction; Man. Dir S. M. SACHDEV.

Bharatiya Vidya Bhavan: Munshi Sadan, Kulapati K. M. Munshi Marg, Mumbai 400 007; tel. (22) 3634462; fax (22) 3630058; f. 1938; art, literature, culture, philosophy, religion, history of India; various periodicals in English, Hindi, Sanskrit and Gujarati; Pres. C. SUBRAMANIAM; Sec.-Gen. S. RAMAKRISHNAN.

Blackie and Son (Pvt) Ltd: Blackie House, 103–105 Walchand Hirachand Marg, POB 381, Mumbai 400 001; tel. (22) 261410; f. 1901; educational, scientific and technical, general and juvenile; Man. Dir D. R. BHAGI.

Himalaya Publishing House: 'Ramdoot', Dr Bhalerao Marg (Kelewadi), Girgaon, Mumbai 400 004; tel. (22) 3863863; f. 1976; textbooks and research work; Dir MEENA PANDEY.

India Book House Ltd: 412 Tulsiani Chambers, Nariman Point, Mumbai 400 021; tel. (22) 2840626; fax (22) 2048163; e-mail padmini@bom2.vsnl.net.in; Man. Dir DEEPAK MIRCHANDANI.

International Book House (Pvt) Ltd: Indian Mercantile Mansions (Extension), Madame Cama Rd, Mumbai 400 001; tel. (22) 2021634; fax (22) 2851109; e-mail intbh@giasbm01.vsnl.net.in; f. 1941; general, educational, scientific and law; Man. Dir S. K. GUPTA; Exec. Dir SANJEEV GUPTA.

Jaico Publishing House: 127 Mahatma Gandhi Rd, opposite Mumbai University, Mumbai 400 023; tel. (22) 2676702; telex 1186398; fax (22) 2656412; e-mail jaicopub@giasbm01.vsnl.net.in; f. 1947; general paperbacks, management, computer and engineering books, etc.; imports scientific, medical, technical and educational books; Man. Dir ASHWIN J. SHAH.

Popular Prakashan (Pvt) Ltd: 35c Pandit Madan Mohan Malaviya Marg, Tardeo, Popular Press Bldg, opp. Roche, Mumbai 400 034; tel. (22) 4941656; fax (22) 4952627; f. 1968; sociology, biographies, religion, philosophy, fiction, arts, music, current affairs, medicine, history, politics and administration in English and Marathi; Man. Dir R. G. BHATKAL.

Somaiya Publications (Pvt) Ltd: 172 Mumbai Marathi Grantha Sangrahalaya Marg, Dadar, Mumbai 400 014; tel. (22) 4130230; telex 112723; fax (22) 2047297; f. 1967; economics, sociology, history, politics, mathematics, sciences, language, literature, education, psychology, religion, philosophy, logic; Chair. Dr S. K. SOMAIYA.

Taraporevala, Sons and Co (Pvt) Ltd D.B.: 210 Dr Dadabhai Naoroji Rd, Fort, Mumbai 400 001; tel. (22) 2071433; f. 1864; Indian art, culture, history, sociology, scientific, technical and general in English; Chief Exec. R. J. TARAPOREVALA.

N. M. Tripathi (Pvt) Ltd: 164 Shamaldas Gandhi Marg, Mumbai 400 002; tel. (22) 2013651; f. 1888; law and general in English and Gujarati; Chair. R. D. TRIPATHI; Man. Dir V. J. MAZMUDAR.

Other Towns

Bharat Bharti Prakashan: Western Kutchery Rd, Meerut 250 001; tel. 73748; f. 1952; textbooks; Man. Dir SURENDRA AGARWAL.

Bharati Bhawan: Thakurbari Rd, Kadamkuan, Patna 800 003; tel. (612) 671356; fax (612) 670010; e-mail bbpdpat@giasclo1.vsnl.net.in; f. 1942; educational and juvenile; Man. Partner SANJIB BOSE.

Bishen Singh Mahendra Pal Singh: 23A Connaught Place, POB 137, Dehra Dun 248 001; tel. (135) 655748; fax (135) 650107; e-mail bsmps@del2.vsnl.net.in; f. 1957; botany; Dir GAJENDRA SINGH.

Catholic Press: Ranchi 834 001, Bihar; f. 1928; books and periodicals; Dir WILLIAM TIGGA.

Chugh Publications: 2 Strachey Rd, POB 101, Allahabad; tel. (532) 623063; sociology, economics, history, general; Propr RAMESH KUMAR CHUGH.

Geetha Book House: K. R. Circle, Mysore 570 001; tel. (821) 33589; f. 1959; general; Dirs M. GOPALA KRISHNA, M. GURURAJA RAO.

Kalyani Publishers: 1/1 Rajinder Nagar, Civil Lines, Ludhiana, Punjab; tel. (161) 745756; fax (161) 745872; textbooks; Dir USHA RAJKUMAR.

Kitabistan: 30 Chak, Allahabad 211 003; tel. (532) 653219; f. 1932; general, agriculture, govt publs in English, Hindi, Urdu, Farsi and Arabic; Partners A. U. KHAN, SULTAN ZAMAN.

Krishna Prakashan Media (P) Ltd: (Unit) Goel Publishing House, 11 Shivaji Rd, Meerut 250 001; tel. (121) 642946; fax (121) 645855; textbooks; Man. Dir SATYENDRA KUMAR RASTOGI; Dirs B. K. RASTOGI, ANITA RASTOGI.

The Law Book Co (Pvt) Ltd: 18B Sardar Patel Marg, Civil Lines, POB 1004, Allahabad 211 001; tel. (532) 624905; fax (532) 420852; f. 1929; legal texts in English; Man. Dir L. R. BAGGA.

Macmillan India Ltd: 315/316 Raheja Chambers, 12 Museum Rd, Bangalore 560 001; tel. (80) 5587878; telex 8452615; fax (80) 5588713; school and university books in English; general; Pres. and Man. Dir RAJIV BERI.

Navajivan Publishing House: PO Navajivan, Ahmedabad 380 014; tel. (79) 7540635; f. 1919; Gandhiana and related social science; in English, Hindi and Gujarati; Man. Trustee JITENDRA DESAI.

Nem Chand and Bros: Civil Lines, Roorkee 247 667; tel. (1332) 72258; fax (1332) 73258; f. 1951; engineering textbooks and journals.

Orient Longman Ltd: 3-6-272 Himayat Nagar, Hyderabad 500 029; tel. (40) 240305; telex 4256803; fax (40) 240393; f. 1948; educational, technical, general and children's in English and almost all Indian languages; Chair. J. RAMESHWAR RAO.

Publication Bureau: Panjab University, Chandigarh 160 014; tel. (172) 541782; f. 1948; textbooks, academic and general; Man. H. R. GROVER.

Publication Bureau: Punjabi University, Patiala 147 002; tel. 822161; university-level text and reference books; Head of Bureau Dr HAZARA SINGH.

Ram Prasad and Sons: Hospital Rd, Agra 282 003; tel. (562) 73418; f. 1905; agricultural, arts, history, commerce, education, general, pure and applied science, economics, sociology; Dirs R. N., B. N. and Y. N. AGARWAL; Man. S. N. AGARWAL.

Upper India Publishing House (Pvt) Ltd: Aminabad, Lucknow 226 018; tel. (522) 42711; f. 1921; Indian history, religion, art and science; English and Hindi; Man. Dir S. BHARGAVA.

Government Publishing House

Publications Division: Ministry of Information and Broadcasting, Govt of India, Patiala House, New Delhi 110 001; tel. (11) 3387983; fax (11) 3386879; f. 1941; culture, art, literature, planning and development, general; also 21 periodicals in English and several Indian languages; Dir SURINDER KAUR.

PUBLISHERS' ASSOCIATIONS

Bombay Booksellers' and Publishers' Association: No. 25, 6th Floor, Bldg No. 3, Navjivan Commercial Premises Co-op Society Ltd, Dr Bhadkamkar Marg, Mumbai 400 008; tel. (22) 3088691; f. 1961; 400 mems; Pres. CHANDRA PAL GUPTA; Gen. Sec. SAMSON JHIRAD.

Delhi State Booksellers' and Publishers' Association: 3026/7H Ranjit Nagar, New Delhi 110 008; tel. (11) 5786769; fax (11) 5782748; f. 1943; 400 mems; Pres. Dr S. K. BHATIA; Sec. S. K. JAIN.

Federation of Educational Publishers in India: 19 Rani Jhansi Rd, New Delhi 110 055; tel. (11) 522697; f. 1987; 14 affiliated asscns; 145 mems; Pres. H. L. GUPTA; Sec.-Gen. O. P. SHASTRI.

Federation of Indian Publishers: Federation House, 18/1-C Institutional Area, nr JNU, New Delhi 110 067; tel. (11) 6964847; fax (11) 6864054; 15 affiliated asscns; 150 mems; Pres. VISHWA NATH; Hon. Gen. Sec. SHAKTI MALIK.

Akhil Bharatiya Hindi Prakashak Sangh: A-2/1, Krishan Nagar, Delhi 110 051; tel. (11) 2219398; f. 1954; 400 mems; Pres. KESHAVDEV SHARMA; Gen. Sec. ARUN KUMAR SHARMA.

All India Urdu Publishers' and Booksellers' Association: Delhi; tel. and fax (11) 3265480; f. 1988; 150 mems; Pres. Dr KHALIQ ANJUM; Gen. Sec. S. M. ZAFAR ALI.

Assam Publishers' Association: College Hostel Rd, Panbazar, Guwahati 780 001; tel. (361) 43995; Pres. K. N. DUTTA BARUAH; Sec. J. N. DUTTA BARUAH.

Booksellers' and Publishers' Association of South India: 8, II Floor, Sun Plaza, G. N. Chetty Rd, Chennai 600 006; 158 mems; Pres. S. CHANDRASEKAR; Sec. RAVI CHOPRA.

Gujarati Sahitya Prakashak Vikreta Mandal: Navajivan Trust, P.O. Navajivan, Ahmedabad 380 014; tel. (79) 7540635; 125 mems; Pres. JITENDRA DESAI; Sec. K. N. MADRASI.

Karnataka Publishers' Association: 88 Mysore Rd, Bangalore 560 018; tel. (80) 601638; Pres. Prof. H. R. DASEGOWDA; Sec. S. V. SRINIVASA RAO.

Kerala Publishers' and Booksellers' Association: Piaco Bldg, Jew St, Kochi 682 011; 30 mems; Pres. D. C. KIZHAKEMURI; Sec. E. K. SEKHAR.

Marathi Prakashak Parishad: Mehta Publishing House, Dhanashree Apartments, 1216 Sadashiv Peth, Pune 411 030; tel. (212) 476924; fax (212) 475462; 100 mems; Pres. ANIL MEHTA.

Orissa Publishers' and Booksellers' Association: Binodbihari, Cuttack 753 002; f. 1973–74; 280 mems; Pres. KRISHNA CHANDRA BEHERA; Sec. BHIKARI CHARAN MOHAPATRA.

Paschimbanga Prakasak Sabha: 206 Bidhan Sarani, Calcutta 700 061; tel. (33) 2410176; Pres. J. SEN; Gen. Sec. T. SAHA.

Publishers' Association of West Bengal: 6-B, Ramanath Mazumder St, Calcutta 700 009; tel. (33) 325580; 164 mems; Pres. MOHIT KUMAR BASU; Gen. Sec. SHANKARI BHUSAN NAYAK.

Publishers' and Booksellers' Association of Bengal: 93 Mahatma Gandhi Rd, Calcutta 700 007; tel. (33) 2411993; f. 1912; 4,500 mems; Pres. PRASOON BASU; Gen. Sec. CHITTA SINGHA ROY.

Punjabi Publishers' Association: Satnam Singh, Singh Brothers, Bazar Mai Sewan, Amritsar 143 006; tel. (183) 45787; Sec. SATNAM SINGH.

Vijayawada Publishers' Association: 27-1-68, Karl Marx Rd, Vijayawada 520 002; tel. (866) 74500; 41 mems; Pres. DUPATI VIJAY KUMAR; Sec. U. N. YOGI.

Federation of Publishers' and Booksellers' Associations in India: 4833/24 Govind Lane, 1st Floor, Ansari Rd, New Delhi 110 002; tel. (11) 3272845; 17 affiliated asscns; 706 mems; Pres. C. M. CHAWLA; Sec. S. C. SETHI.

Publishers' and Booksellers' Guild: 5A Bhawani Dutta Lane, Calcutta 700 073; tel. (33) 2413680; fax (33) 2450027; f. 1976; 40 mems; Pres. SABITENDRANATH ROY; Sec. ANIL ACHARYA.

UP Publishers' and Booksellers' Association: 111-A/243 Ashok Nagar, Kanpur 208 012; asscn for Uttar Pradesh state.

Broadcasting and Communications

TELECOMMUNICATIONS

ITI (Indian Telephone Industries) Ltd: 45/1 Magrath Rd, Bangalore 560 025; tel. (80) 5566366; fax (80) 5593188; f. 1948; cap. p.u. Rs880m., res and surplus Rs939m. (March 1997); mfrs of all types of telecommunication equipment, incl. telephones, automatic exchanges and long-distance transmission equipment; also produces optical fibre equipment and microwave equipment; will manufacture all ground communication equipment for the 22 earth stations of the Indian National Satellite; in conjunction with the Post and Telegraph Department, a newly designed 2,000-line exchange has been completed; Chair. and Man. Dir S. S. MOTIAL.

Mahanagar Telephone Nigam Ltd (MTNL): Jeevan Bharati Tower, 124 Connaught Circus, New Delhi 110 001; tel. (11) 3732212; fax (11) 3317344; f. 1986; 66% state-owned; owns and operates telephone networks in Mumbai and Delhi; sales Rs30,230m. (1995); Chair. A. K. CHOUDHRI; Man. Dir S. RAJAGOPALAN.

Videsh Sanchar Nigam Ltd (VSNL): M. G. Rd, Fort, Mumbai 400 001; tel. (22) 2624020; telex 1182429; fax (22) 2624027; e-mail helpdesk@giaspn01.vsnl.net.in; f. 1986; 85% state-owned; has had monopoly on international telecommunications services since April 1994; sales Rs44,730m. (1996); Chair. B. K. SYNGAL.

BROADCASTING

In August 1990 the Lok Sabha unanimously passed the Prasar Bharati Corporation Bill granting autonomy to the state-operated national radio and television networks. Implementation of the Bill was delayed, however, until September 1997.

Prasar Bharati Corpn: New Delhi; f. 1997 as an autonomous body to oversee state broadcasting; Chair. NIKHIL CHAKRAVARTTY; Chief Exec. S. S. GILL.

Radio

All India Radio (AIR): Akashvani Bhavan, Parliament St, New Delhi 110 001; tel. (11) 3710006; telex 3165585; fax (11) 3714061; broadcasting is controlled by the Ministry of Information and Broadcasting and is primarily govt-financed; operates a network of 187 stations and 297 transmitters (grouped into four zones— north, south, east and west), covering 97.3% of the population and about 90% of the total area of the country; Dir-Gen. O. P. KEJRIWAL.

The News Services Division of AIR, centralized in New Delhi, is one of the largest news organizations in the world. It has 41 regional news units, which broadcast 306 bulletins daily in 24 languages and 38 dialects. One hundred and three bulletins in 19 languages are broadcast in the Home Services, 138 regional bulletins in 72 languages and dialects, and 65 bulletins in 24 languages in the External Services.

Television

Doordarshan India (Television India): Mandi House, Doordarshan Bhavan, Copernicus Marg, New Delhi 110 001; tel. (11) 3387786; telex 3166143; f. 1976; broadcasting is controlled by the Ministry of Information and Broadcasting and is govt-financed; programmes: 280 hours weekly; 3 main channels—the National Channel, Metro Channel and DD3—(broadcasting mostly in Hindi) and 16 other channels; Dir-Gen. K. S. SARMA.

In December 1996 69% of the country's area and 86% of the population were covered by the TV network. There were 834 transmitters in operation in March 1996. By that year 41 programme production centres and nine relay centres had been established.

Satellite television was introduced in India by a Hong Kong company, Star TV, in 1991. By mid-1993 Star TV attracted an audience of about 18.8m. in India. In July 1992 the Government announced that it would permit broadcasting time to private companies on a second state channel (the Metro Channel) broadcast to major Indian cities. In August 1993 Doordarshan India launched five new satellite television channels; three of the channels were taken off the air, however, in February 1994 following the introduction of a new satellite television policy. Doordarshan International Channel commenced broadcasting (three hours daily) in March 1995; the service was extended to 18 hours daily in November 1996. In 1997 legislation was introduced to license private broadcasters and to impose a 49% limit on foreign ownership of television channels.

Finance

(cap. = capital; p.u. = paid up; res = reserves; dep. = deposits; m. = million; brs = branches; amounts in rupees)

BANKING

State Banks

Reserve Bank of India: Central Office, Shahid Bhagat Singh Rd, POB 10007, Mumbai 400 001; tel. (22) 2661602; telex 112318; fax (22) 2661784; e-mail rbiprd@giasbm01.vsnl.net.in; internet http://www.rbi.org.in; f. 1934; nationalized 1949; sole bank of issue; cap. p.u. 50m., res 65,000m., dep. 788, 178.0m. (June 1996); Gov. Dr BIMAL JALAN; 4 offices and 18 brs.

State Bank of India: Madame Cama Rd, POB 10121, Mumbai 400 021; tel. (22) 2022426; telex 112995; e-mail gm@mumbai.cobom.sbi.co.in; internet http://www.sbi.co.in; f. 1955; cap. p.u. 5,263m., dep. 1,107,011.7m. (March 1997); 7 associates, 7 domestic subsidiaries/affiliates, 3 foreign subsidiaries, 4 jt ventures abroad; Chair. M. S. VERMA; Man. Dirs O. P. SETIA, M. P. RADHAKRISHNAN; 8,888 brs (incl. 52 overseas brs and rep. offices in 33 countries).

State-owned Commercial Banks

Fourteen of India's major commercial banks were nationalized in 1969 and a further six in 1980. They are managed by 15-mem. boards of directors (two directors to be appointed by the central Government, one employee director, one representing employees who are not workmen, one representing depositors, three representing farmers, workers, artisans, etc., five representing persons with special knowledge or experience, one Reserve Bank of India official and one Government of India official). The Department of Banking of the Ministry of Finance controls all banking operations.

There were 62,849 branches of public-sector and other commercial banks at 31 March 1996.

Aggregate deposits of all scheduled commercial banks amounted to Rs 5,035,960m. in March 1997.

Allahabad Bank: 2 Netaji Subhas Rd, Calcutta 700 001; tel. (33) 2204735; telex 217547; fax (33) 2214048; f. 1865; nationalized 1969; cap. p.u. 2,467m., dep. 115,405.5m. (March 1997); Chair. and Man. Dir HARBHAJAN SINGH; Exec. Dir Dr S. SINGH; 1,855 brs.

Andhra Bank: Andhra Bank Bldgs, 5-9-11 Saifabad, Hyderabad 500 004; tel. (40) 230001; telex 4256283; fax (40) 240509; f. 1923; nationalized 1980; cap. p.u. 5,913m., dep. 70,910m. (March 1997); Chair. and Man. Dir G. NARAYANAN; Exec. Dir T. J. A. GANIGA; 974 brs.

Bank of Baroda: 3 Walchand Hirachand Marg, Ballard Pier, POB 10046, Mumbai 400 038; tel. (22) 2610341; telex 1183172; fax (22) 2615065; f. 1908; nationalized 1969; cap. p.u. 2,543.4m., dep. 321,567.8m. (March 1997); Chair. and Man. Dir K. KANNAN; Chief Exec. Dr A. C. SHAH; 2,488 brs (world-wide).

Bank of India: Express Towers, Nariman Point, POB 234, Mumbai 400 021; tel. (22) 2023020; telex 1182281; fax (22) 2022831; f. 1906; nationalized 1969; cap. p.u. 5,967.3m., dep. 319,726m. (March 1997); Chair. and Man. Dir M. C. BHIDE; 2,461 brs (world-wide).

Bank of Maharashtra: 'Lokmangal', 1501 Shivajinagar, Pune 411 005; tel. (212) 322731; telex 1457207; fax (212) 322581; f. 1935; nationalized 1969; cap. p.u. 7,487m., dep. 72,370m. (March 1997); Chair. and Man. Dir T. S. RAGHAVAN; Exec. Dir V. LEELADHAR; 1,147 brs.

Canara Bank: 112 Jayachamarajendra Rd, POB 6648, Bangalore 560 002; tel. (812) 2221581; telex 8458075; fax (812) 2222704; f. 1906; nationalized 1969; cap. p.u. 4,848m., dep. 314,450m. (March 1997); Chair. and Man. Dir T. R. SRIDHARAN; 2,262 brs.

Central Bank of India: Chandermukhi, Nariman Point, Mumbai 400 021; tel. (22) 2026428; telex 112909; fax (22) 2044336; f. 1911; nationalized 1969; cap. 18,054m., res 440m., dep. 230,510m. (March 1997); Chair. and Man. Dir S. DORESWAMY; Exec. Dir K. C. CHOWDHARY; 3,077 brs.

Corporation Bank: Mangaladevi Temple Rd, POB 88, Mangalore 575 001; tel. (824) 426416; telex 832321; fax (824) 442208; e-mail corp-man999@x.400nicgw.nic.in; f. 1906; nationalized 1980; cap. p.u. 820m., dep. 66,730m. (March 1997); Chair. and Man. Dir R. S. HUGAR; 521 brs.

Dena Bank: Maker Towers 'E', 10th Floor, Cuffe Parade, Colaba, POB 6058, Mumbai 400 005; tel. (22) 2189151; telex 1183567; fax (22) 2189046; f. 1938; nationalized 1969; cap. p.u. 2,068.2m., dep. 78,613m. (March 1997); Chair. and Man. Dir RAMESH MISHRA; 1,134 brs.

Indian Bank: 31 Rajaji Salai, POB 1866, Chennai 600 001; tel. (44) 5232939; telex 418307; fax (44) 5231285; f. 1907; nationalized 1969; cap. 6,540m., dep. 143,288.2m. (March 1997); Chair. and Man. Dir S. RAJAGOPAL; Gen. Man. S. ARUNACHALAM; 1,424 brs.

Indian Overseas Bank: 762 Anna Salai, POB 3765, Chennai 600 002; tel. (44) 8524145; telex 417374; fax (44) 8523395; f. 1937; nationalized 1969; cap. p.u. 13,336m., dep. 159,726m. (March 1997); Chair. and Man. Dir K. SUBRAMANIAN; 1,365 brs.

Oriental Bank of Commerce: Harsha Bhavan, E Block, Connaught Place, POB 329, New Delhi 110 001; tel. (11) 3323444; telex 3165462; fax (11) 3321514; f. 1943; nationalized 1980; cap. p.u. 1,925m., dep. 100,000m. (March 1997); Chair. and Man. Dir DALBIR SINGH; Exec. Dir V. S. THAKUR; 800 brs.

Punjab and Sind Bank: 21 Bank House, Rajendra Place, New Delhi 110 008; tel. (11) 5720849; telex 3166456; fax (11) 5751765; f. 1908; nationalized 1980; cap. 7,055.3m., dep. 63,795.6m. (March 1997); Chair. and Man. Dir SURINDER SINGH KOHLI; Exec. Dir S. S. KOHLI; 691 brs.

Punjab National Bank: 7 Bhikaiji Cama Place, Africa Ave, POB 6, New Delhi 110 066; tel. (11) 6102303; telex 3172193; fax (11) 6196514; f. 1895; nationalized 1969; merged with New Bank of India in 1993; cap. 3,505.7m., dep. 308,064m. (March 1997); Chair. and Man. Dir RASHID JILANI; 4,052 brs.

Syndicate Bank: POB 1, Manipal 576 119; tel. (8252) 71181; telex 82242; fax (8252) 70266; f. 1925; cap. 12,896m., dep. 149,460m. (March 1997); Chair. and Man. Dir Dr NAVINCHANDRA K. THINGALAYA; 1,613 brs.

UCO Bank: 10 Biplabi Trailokya Maharaj Sarani (Brabourne Rd), POB 2455, Calcutta 700 001; tel. (33) 2254120; telex 215019; fax (33) 2253986; f. 1943; nationalized 1969; cap. p.u. 10,350m., dep. 126,140m. (March 1997); Chair. and Man. Dir SHARDA SINGH; 1,800 brs.

Union Bank of India: Union Bank Bhavan, 239 Vidhan Bhavan Marg, Nariman Point, Mumbai 400 021; tel. (22) 2023060; telex 1184208; fax (22) 2025238; f. 1919; nationalized 1969; cap. 3,380m., dep. 200,050m. (March 1997); Chair. and Man. Dir A. T. PANNIR SELVAM; 2,030 brs.

United Bank of India: 16 Old Court House St, Calcutta 700 001; tel. (33) 2487471; telex 217387; fax (33) 2485852; f. 1950; nationalized 1969; cap. p.u. 5,780.0m., res and surplus 1,149.6m., dep. 103,460m. (March 1997); Chair. and Man. Dir BISWAJIT CHOUDHURI; 1,332 brs.

Vijaya Bank: 41/2 Mahatma Gandhi Rd, Bangalore 560 001; tel. (80) 5584066; telex 8452428; fax (80) 5582759; f. 1931; nationalized 1980; cap. p.u. 2,543m., dep. 68,270m. (March 1997); Chair. and Man. Dir K. C. CHOWDHARY; 835 brs.

Principal Private Banks

Bank of Madura Ltd: 'Karumuttu Nilayam', 758 Anna Salai, POB 5225, Chennai 600 002; tel. (44) 8523456; telex 418173; fax (44) 8523868; e-mail mdsaab34@giasmd01.vsnl.net.in; f. 1943; cap. p.u. 116m., dep. 19,308m. (March 1997); Chair. Dr K. M. THIAGARAJAN; Gen. Mans V. NACHIAPPAN, S. KATHIRESAN; 276 brs.

The Bank of Rajasthan Ltd: C-3 Sardar Patel Marg, Jaipur 302 001; tel. (141) 381222; telex 3652429; fax (141) 381123; f. 1943; cap. p.u. 179.4m., dep. 29,389.3m. (March 1997); Chair. D. B. SANGANI; Man. Dir I. SADA SHIV GUPTA; 322 brs.

Benares State Bank Ltd (BSB): Shvetabh Bhavan, 20–22A Sankat Mochan Marg, POB 29, Varanasi 221 005; tel. (542) 312681; telex 545233; f. 1948; Chair. S. R. N. GOSAIN; 92 brs.

Bharat Overseas Bank Ltd: Habeeb Towers, 756 Anna Salai, Chennai 600 002; tel. (44) 8525686; telex 417493; fax (44) 8524700; f. 1973; cap. 52.5m., res 475.9m., dep. 8,489.1m. (March 1997); Chair. S. SRINIVASAN; Dep. Gen. Man. T. N. SANTNANA KRISHNAN; 57 brs.

Bombay Mercantile Co-operative Bank Ltd: 78 Mohammed Ali Rd, Mumbai 400 003; tel. (22) 3425961; telex 1173727; fax (22) 3433385; f. 1939; cap. p.u. 285m., dep. 17,500m. (March 1997); Chair. EDULJI H. TUREL; Man. Dir SHAMIM KAZIM; 52 brs.

The Catholic Syrian Bank Ltd: St Mary's College Rd, POB 502, Trichur 680 020; tel. (487) 333020; telex 887210; fax (487) 333435; f. 1920; cap. 53.5m., res and surplus 213.4m., dep. 11,806.7m. (March 1995); Chair. and CEO A. SOLOMON; Gen. Man. JOHN J. ALAPATT; 267 brs.

Centurion Bank Ltd: 1201 Raheja Centre, Free Press Journal Marg, Nariman Point, Mumbai 400 021; tel. (22) 2047234; telex 1185402; fax (22) 2845860; f. 1995; cap. 1,012.5m., res 52.8m., dep. 10,961.2m. (March 1997); Pres. M. G. RAMAKRISHNA; Man. Dir and CEO ASHISH SEN.

City Union Bank Ltd: 149 TSR (Big) St, Kumbakonam 612 001; tel. (435) 32322; telex 467212; fax (435) 31746; f. 1904; cap. 44.4m., res and surplus 142.1m., dep. 5,014.5m. (March 1995); Chair. V. NARYANAN; Gen. Man. K. VENKATRAMAN; 99 brs.

The Federal Bank Ltd: Federal Towers, POB 103, Alwaye 683 101; tel. (484) 624061; telex 882205; fax (484) 622566; f. 1931; cap. 168.7m., res and surplus 2,045.6m., dep. 39,648.5m. (March 1996); Chair. K. NANDAN; Exec. Dir K. P. PADMAKUMAR; 358 brs.

Global Trust Bank Ltd: 303-48-3 Sardar Patel Rd, Secunderabad 500 003; tel. (40) 819333; fax (40) 816892; cap. p.u. 1,040m., dep. 22,793.4m. (March 1997); Chair. and Man. Dir RAMESH GELLI; 23 brs.

ICICI Banking Corpn Ltd: Zenith House, 3rd Floor, Keshav Rao Khade Marg, Mahalaxmi, Mumbai 400 034; tel. (22) 4975277; telex 1184342; fax (22) 4975295; f. 1994; cap. p.u. 1,650m., dep. 13,470m. (March 1997); Man. Dir P. V. MAIYA; 24 brs.

IndusInd Bank Ltd: IndusInd House, 425 Dadasaheb Bhadkamkar Marg, Lamington Rd, nr Opera House, Mumbai 400 004; tel. (22) 3859901; fax (22) 3859931; f. 1994; cap. p.u. 1,200m., res and surplus 1,594.7m., dep. 30,931.0m. (March 1997); Chair. P. K. KAUL; Man. Dir S. SOLOMON RAJ; 18 brs.

Jammu and Kashmir Bank Ltd: Zam Zam Bldg, Ram Bagh, Srinagar 190 015; tel. (194) 30730; telex 375224; fax (194) 30247; f. 1938; cap. p.u. 70m., dep 36,880m. (March 1997); Chair. and CEO M. Y. KHAN; 367 brs.

Karnataka Bank Ltd: POB 716, Kodialbail, Mangalore 575 003; tel. (824) 440751; telex 832280; fax (824) 441212; f. 1924; cap. p.u. 134.9m., dep. 25,106m. (March 1997); Chair. M. S. KRISHNA BHAT; 311 brs.

The Karur Vysya Bank Ltd: Erode Rd, POB 21, Karur 639 002; tel. (4324) 32520; fax (4324) 30202; f. 1916; cap. 60.0m., res and surplus 1,154.8m., dep. 17,006.7m. (March 1997); Chair. A. D. NAVANEETHAN; Sr Gen. Man. V. DEVARAJAN.

Lakshmi Vilas Bank Ltd: Kathaparai, Salem Rd, POB 2, Karur 639 006; tel. (4324) 33023; telex 456210; fax (4324) 33024; f. 1926; cap. 113.5m., res 510.0m., dep. 9,131.3m. (March 1996); Chair. G. V. RAO; Gen. Man. R. MUNISWAMY; 181 brs.

The Sangli Bank Ltd: Rajwada Chowk, POB 158, Sangli 416 416; tel. (233) 73611; telex 193211; fax (233) 77156; f. 1916; cap. p.u. 60.2m., dep. 7,303.6m. (March 1995); Chair. and CEO SURESH D. JOSHI; Gen. Man. Dr V. PRASANNA BHAT; 178 brs.

The South Indian Bank Ltd: SIB House, Thrissur 680 001, Kerala; tel. (487) 420020; telex 887203; fax (487) 442021; f. 1929; cap. 141.6m., res 641.4m., dep. 17,238.8m. (March 1996); Chair. MAURICE D'SOUZA; 349 brs.

Tamilnad Mercantile Bank Ltd: 57 Victoria Extension Rd, Tuticorin 628 002; tel. (461) 321932; telex 434242; fax (461) 322994; f. 1921 as Nadar Bank, name changed as above 1962; cap. 2.8m., res 1,028.4m., dep. 13,160.8m. (March 1997); Chair. K. N. V. NAYAR; 142 brs.

The United Western Bank Ltd: 172/4 Raviwar Peth, Shivaji Circle, POB 2, Satara 415 001; tel. (2162) 20517; telex 147212; fax (2162) 23374; f. 1936; cap. p.u. 299m., dep. 20,440m. (March 1997); Chair. and Chief Exec. P. N. JOSHI; Gen. Man. V. G. PALKAR; 203 brs.

The Vysya Bank Ltd: 72 St Marks Rd, Bangalore 560 001; tel. (80) 2272021; telex 8452314; fax (80) 2272220; f. 1930; cap. p.u. 146.4m., dep. 50,890m. (March 1997); Chair. K. RAMAMOORTHY; Sr Gen. Man. G. LAXMINARAYANA; 416 brs.

Foreign Banks

ABN AMRO Bank NV (Netherlands): 14 Veer Nariman Rd, Mumbai 400 023; tel. (22) 2042331; telex 1183246; Gen. Man. ROMESH SOPRI; 4 brs.

Abu Dhabi Commercial Bank Ltd (UAE): Rehmat Manzil, 75-B Veer Nariman Rd, Mumbai; tel. (22) 2830235; telex 1185481; fax (22) 2870686; Man. AHMED SALEH AL BANNA.

American Express Bank Ltd (USA): Dalamal Tower, First Floor, 211 Nariman Point, Mumbai 400 021; tel. (22) 233230; telex 1183808; fax (22) 2872968; Country Head JAMES VAUGHAN; 4 brs.

ANZ Grindlays Bank (UK): 90 Mahatma Gandhi Rd, POB 725, Mumbai 400 023; tel. (22) 271295; telex 1184792; fax (22) 2619903; Gen. Man. and CEO MEHLI M. MISTRI; 57 brs.

Banca Nazionale del Lavoro Spa (Italy): 67 Maker Chambers VI, 6th Floor, Nariman Point, Mumbai 400 021; tel. (22) 2047763; telex 1184053; fax (22) 2023482; Rep. L. S. AGARWAL.

Bank of America National Trust and Savings Association (USA): Hansalaya, 15 Barakhamba Rd, New Delhi 110 001; tel. (11)

3715565; fax (11) 3714754; Sr Vice-Pres. and Country Man. AMBI VENKATESWARAN; 4 brs.

Bank of Bahrain and Kuwait BSC: Jolly Maker Chambers II, Ground Floor, 225 Nariman Point, Mumbai 400 021; tel. (22) 2823698; telex 1185101; fax (22) 2044458; Gen. Man. and CEO K. S. KRISHNAKUMAR; 2 brs.

Bank of Ceylon: 1090 Poonamallee High Rd, Chennai 600 084; tel. (44) 6420972; Gen. Man. ROHINI NANYAKKARA.

Bank of Nova Scotia (Canada): Mittal Tower B, Nariman Point, Mumbai 400 021; tel. (22) 2832822; telex 1184284; fax (22) 2873125; Vice-Pres. and Man. BHASKAR DESAI; 2 brs.

Bank of Tokyo-Mitsubishi Ltd (Japan): Jeevan Prakash, Sir P. Mehta Rd, Mumbai 400 001; tel. (22) 2660564; telex 1182155; fax (22) 2661787; Regional Rep. for India and Gen. Man. KUNIHIKO NISHIHARA; 4 brs.

Banque Nationale de Paris (France): French Bank Bldg, 62 Homji St, Fort, POB 45, Mumbai 400 001; tel. (22) 2660844; telex 1182341; fax (22) 2665490; Chief Exec. HENRI QUINTARD; 5 brs.

Barclays Bank PLC (UK): 21–23 Maker Chambers VI, 2nd Floor, Nariman Point, Mumbai 400 021; tel. (22) 2044353; telex 1182073; fax (22) 2043238; CEO AJAY SONDHI; 2 brs.

British Bank of the Middle East (Hong Kong): 16 Veer Nariman Rd, Fort, POB 876, Mumbai 400 023; tel. (22) 2048203; telex 1185956; fax (22) 2046077; Man. D. GHANSHYAMDAS; 2 brs.

Chase Manhattan Bank NA: Maker Chambers VI, 7/F, Nariman Point, Mumbai 400 021; tel. (22) 2855666; telex 1182715; fax (22) 2027772; Vice-Pres. and CEO (India and South Asia operations) FRANS A. KOEK; 1 br.

Citibank, NA (USA): Sakhar Bhavan, 230 Backbay Reclamation, Nariman Point, Mumbai 400 021; tel. (22) 2025499; telex 1185379; CEO DAVID CONNER; 4 brs.

Commerzbank AG (Germany): Free Press House, 215 Free Press Journal Rd, Nariman Point, Mumbai 400 021; tel. (22) 2885510; fax (22) 2885524; Gen. Man. ASHOK TANKHA; 1 br.

Crédit Agricole Indosuez (France): Ramon House, 169 Backbay Reclamation, Mumbai 400 020; tel. (22) 2045104; fax (22) 2049108; Gen. Man. NIRENDU MAZUMDAR.

Crédit Lyonnais (France): Scindia House, 1st Floor, Narottam Morarjee Marg, Ballard Estate, Mumbai 400 038; tel. (22) 2612313; telex 1182628; fax (22) 2612603; Chief Exec. and Country Man. JEAN-YVES LE PAULMIER; 4 brs.

Deutsche Bank AG (Germany): Tulsiani Chambers, Nariman Point, POB 9995, Mumbai 400 021; tel. (22) 223262; telex 1184042; fax (22) 2045047; CEO HARKIRAT SINGH; 5 brs.

Development Bank of Singapore Ltd: Maker Chambers IV, 12th Floor, Nariman Point, Mumbai 400 021; tel. (22) 2826991; telex 1186176; fax (22) 2875602; 1 br.

Dresdner Bank (Germany): Hoechst House, Nariman Point, Mumbai 400 021; tel. (22) 2850009.

Fuji Bank Ltd (Japan): Maker Chambers III, 1st Floor, Jamnalal Bajaj Rd, Nariman Point, Mumbai 400 021; tel. (22) 2886638; telex 1181030; fax (22) 2886640; CEO (India) and Gen. Man. TATSUJI TAMAKA; 1 br.

Hongkong and Shanghai Banking Corpn Ltd (Hong Kong): 52-60 Mahatma Gandhi Rd, POB 128, Mumbai 400 001; tel. (22) 2674921; telex 1182223; fax (22) 2658309; CEO DYFRIG JOHN; 21 brs.

Mashreq Bank PSC (United Arab Emirates): Air-India Bldg, Nariman Point, Mumbai 400 021; tel. (22) 2026096; telex 1185936; fax (22) 2873305; CEO SUNEIL KUCCHAL.

Midland Bank (UK): 152 Maker Chamber No. IV, 14th Floor, 222 Nariman Point, Mumbai 400 021; tel. (22) 2024973; telex 1185478; fax (22) 2024954; Rep. JOHN W. RAE.

Oman International Bank S.A.O.G. (Oman): 201 Raheja Centre, Free Press Journal Marg, Nariman Point, Mumbai 400 021; tel. (22) 2837733; telex 1183165; fax (22) 2875626; Country Man. S. SEETHARAMAN; 2 brs.

Sanwa Bank Ltd (Japan): Mercantile House, Upper Ground Floor, 15 Kasturba Gandhi Marg, New Delhi 110 001; tel. (11) 3318008; telex 3162961; fax (11) 3315162; Gen. Man. KANZO MURAKAMI.

Société Générale (France): Maker Chambers IV, Bajaj Marg, Nariman Point, POB 11635, Mumbai 400 021; tel. (22) 2870909; telex 1182635; fax (22) 2045459; Gen. Man. R. KERNEIS; 4 brs.

Sonali Bank (Bangladesh): 15 Park St, Calcutta 700 016; tel. (33) 297998; telex 212727; Dep. Gen. Man. SIRAJUDDIN AHMED; 1 br.

Standard Chartered Bank (UK): New Excelsior Bldg, 4th Floor, A. K. Naik Marg, POB 1806, Mumbai 400 001; tel. (22) 2075409; telex 1184142; fax (22) 2072550; e-mail vkrishn@scbindia.mhs.compuserve.com; Chief Exec. S. MARTIN FISH; 24 brs.

State Bank of Mauritius Ltd: 101, Raheja Centre, 1st Floor, Free Press Journal Marg, Nariman Point, Mumbai 400 021; tel. (22) 2842965; telex 1182229; fax (22) 2842966; Gen. Man. and CEO P. THONDRAYEN; 2 brs.

Sumitomo Bank (Japan): 15/F Jolly Maker Chamber No. 2, 225 Nariman Point, Mumbai 400 021; tel. (22) 2880025; telex 1183072; fax (22) 2880026; CEO and Gen. Man. KOZO OTSUBO.

Union Bank of Switzerland: Mumbai.

Banking Organizations

Indian Banks' Association: Stadium House, 6th Floor, Block 3, Veer Nariman Rd, Churchgate, Mumbai 400 020; tel. (22) 2844999; telex 1182373; fax (22) 2835638; 163 mems; Chair. A. T. PANEERSELVAM; Sec. M. N. DANDEKAR.

Indian Institute of Bankers: 'The Arcade', World Trade Centre, 2nd Floor, East Wing, Cuffe Parade, Mumbai 400 005; tel. (22) 2187003; telex 1183524; fax (22) 2185147; f. 1928; 343,202 mems; Pres. Dr C. RANGARAJAN; Chief Sec. R. H. SARMA.

National Institute of Bank Management: N.I.B.M. Post Office, Kondhwe Khurd, Pune 411 048; tel. (212) 673080; telex 1457256; fax (212) 674478; e-mail librarian@nibm.ernet.in; f. 1969; Dir Dr A. VASUDEVAN.

DEVELOPMENT FINANCE ORGANIZATIONS

Agricultural Finance Corporation Ltd: Dhanraj Mahal, 1st Floor, Chhatrapati Shivaji Maharaj Marg, Mumbai 400 001; tel. (22) 2028924; fax (22) 2028966; e-mail afcl@bom2.vsnl.net.in; f. 1968 by a consortium of 35 public- and private-sector commercial banks to help increase the flow of investment and credit into agriculture and rural development projects; provides project consultancy services to commercial banks, Union and State govts, public-sector corpns, the World Bank, the ADB, FAO, the International Fund for Agricultural Development and other institutions and to individuals; undertakes techno-economic and investment surveys in agriculture and agro-industries etc.; 3 regional offices and 9 br. offices; cap. p.u. 100m., res and surplus 31.4m. (March 1996); Chair. Dr. P. V. SHENOI; Man. Dir SUBHASH WADHWA.

Credit Guarantee Corpn of India Ltd: Mittal Tower, Nariman Point, Mumbai 400 021; f. 1971; promoted by the Reserve Bank of India; guarantees loans and other credit facilities extended by (i) scheduled and non-scheduled commercial banks to small traders, farmers and self-employed persons and small borrowers under a differential interest rates scheme; (ii) scheduled and non-scheduled commercial banks and state financial corpns to small transport and business enterprises; (iii) scheduled commercial banks and certain state and central co-operative banks to service co-operative socs assisting their mems engaged in industrial activity; Chair. Dr R. K. HAZARI; Man. C. S. SUBRAMANIAM.

Export-Import Bank of India: Centre 1, Floor 21, World Trade Centre, Cuffe Parade, Mumbai 400 005; tel. (22) 2185272; fax (22) 2182572; e-mail eximcord@bom3.vsnl.net.in; f. 1982; cap. p.u. Rs 5,000m., res and surplus Rs 5,445m. (March 1997); offices in Bangalore, Calcutta, Chennai, New Delhi, Ahmedabad, Johannesburg, Budapest, Rome, Singapore and Washington, DC; Man. Dir Y. B. DESAI; Exec. Dir T. C. VENKAT SUBRAMANIAN.

Housing Development Finance Corpn Ltd: Ramon House, 169 Backbay Reclamation, Mumbai 400 020; tel. (22) 2820282; fax (22) 2046758; provides loans to individuals and corporate bodies; Chair. DEEPAK S. PAREKH.

Industrial Credit and Investment Corpn of India Ltd: 163 Backbay Reclamation, Mumbai 400 020; tel. (22) 2022535; telex 1183062; fax (22) 2046582; f. 1955 to assist industrial enterprises by providing finance in both rupee and foreign currencies in the form of long- or medium-term loans or equity participation, guaranteeing loans from other private investment sources, furnishing managerial, technological and administration advice to industry; also offers suppliers' and buyers' credit, export development capital, asset credit, technology finance, instalment sale and equipment leasing facilities, and infrastructure finance; zonal offices at Mumbai, Calcutta, Chennai, New Delhi, Vadodara, Pune, Bangalore, Hyderabad and Coimbatore; development office at Guwahati (Assam); equity share cap. 4,760m., res 39,000m. (March 1997); Chair. N. VAGHUL, Man. Dir and CEO K. V. KAMATH.

Industrial Development Bank of India (IDBI): IDBI Tower, Cuffe Parade, Colaba, Mumbai 400 005; tel. (22) 2189111; telex 1182193; fax (22) 2180411; f. 1964, reorg. 1976; India's premier financial institution for providing direct finance, refinance of industrial loans and bills, finance to large- and medium-sized industries, and for extending financial services, such as merchant banking and forex services, to the corporate sector; 5 regional offices and 26 br. offices; equity cap. p.u. 6,731m., res 65,540m. (March 1997); Chair. and Man. Dir SERAJUL HAQ KHAN; Dep. Gen. Man. N. R. SHENOY.

Small Industries Development Bank of India: 10/10 Madan Mohan Malviya Marg, Lucknow 226 001; tel. 274517; fax 274512; e-mail nimbalkar@ho1.sidbi.sprintsmx.ems.vsnl.net.in; wholly-owned subsidiary of Industrial Development Bank of India; cap.

p.u. 4,500m., res 8,060m. (March 1997); Chair. SERAJUL HAQ KHAN; Man. Dir Dr SAILENDRA NARAIN; 39 offices.

Industrial Finance Corpn of India Ltd: IFCI Tower, 61 Nehru Place, New Delhi 110 019; tel. (11) 6487444; telex 3170333; fax (11) 6488471; f. 1948 to provide medium- and long-term finance to cos and co-operative socs in India, engaged in manufacture, preservation or processing of goods, shipping, mining, hotels and power generation and distribution; promotes industrialization of less developed areas, and sponsors training in management techniques and development banking; cap. p.u. 3,536.2m., res 13,508.6m. (March 1997); Chair. P. S. GOPALAKRISHNAN; Exec. Dirs S. P. BANERJEE, H. C. SHARMA; 8 regional offices and 10 br. offices.

Industrial Investment Bank of India: 19 Netaji Subhas Rd, Calcutta 700 001; tel. (33) 2209941; fax (33) 2207182; Chair. and Man. Dir Dr G. GOSWAMI.

National Bank for Agriculture and Rural Development: Sterling Centre, Shivsagar Estate, Dr Annie Besant Rd, Worli, POB 6552, Mumbai 400 018; tel. (22) 4964396; telex 1173770; fax (22) 4931621; f. 1982 to provide credit for agricultural and rural development through commercial, co-operative and regional rural banks; cap. p.u. 5,000m., res 12,320m. (March 1995); held 50% each by the cen. Govt and the Reserve Bank; Chair. P. KOTAIAH; Man. Dir SAROJ K. KALIA; 17 regional offices, 10 sub-offices and 5 training establishments.

STOCK EXCHANGES

There are 23 stock exchanges (with a total of more than 6,250 listed companies) in India, including:

National Stock Exchange of India Ltd: Mahindra Towers, 1st Floor, Worli, Mumbai 400 018; tel. (22) 4960525; fax (22) 4935631; f. 1994; Pres. RAMCHANDRA PATIL.

Ahmedabad Share and Stock Brokers' Association: Manek Chowk, Ahmedabad 380 001; tel. (79) 347149; telex 1216789; fax (79) 340117; f. 1894; 299 mems; Pres. V. G. GAJJAR; Exec. Dir M. L. SONEJI.

Bangalore Stock Exchange Ltd: 51 Stock Exchange Towers, 1st Corss, J. C. Rd, Bangalore 560 027; tel. (812) 2995234; telex 8452874; fax (80) 2995242; 134 mems; Pres. K. ISHWARA BHAT; Exec. Dir Mr RAMACHANDRA.

Calcutta Stock Exchange Association Ltd: 7 Lyons Range, Calcutta 700 001; tel. (33) 2209366; telex 217414; fax (33) 2202514; f. 1908; 877 mems; Pres. DINESH KUMAR SINGHANIA; Exec. Dir BIDHAN MAJUMDAR.

Delhi Stock Exchange Association Ltd: 3 & 4/4B Asaf Ali Rd, New Delhi 110 002; tel. (11) 3379951; fax (11) 3326182; f. 1947; 379 mems; Pres. DEEPAK CHOWDHRY; Exec. Dir S. S. SODHI.

Ludhiana Stock Exchange Association Ltd: Feroze Gandhi Market, Ludhiana 141 008; tel. (161) 336151; fax (161) 404748; f. 1984; 284 mems; Pres. JASPAL SINGH; Sec. P. S. BATHLA.

Madras Stock Exchange Ltd: Exchange Bldg, 11 Second Line Beach, POB 183, Chennai 600 001; tel. (44) 5221071; telex 418059; fax (44) 5244897; f. 1937; 177 mems; Pres. S. RAMASUBRAMANIAN; Exec. Dir S. RAMANATHAN.

Mangalore Stock Exchange: Rama Bhavan Complex, 4th Floor, Kodialbail, Mangalore 575 003; tel. (824) 440581; telex 832374; fax (824) 440736; 146 mems; Pres. RAMESH RAI; Exec. Dir UMESH P. MASKERI.

Mumbai Stock Exchange: Phiroze Jeejeebhoy Towers, 25th Floor, Dalal St, Fort, Mumbai 400 001; tel. (22) 2655581; telex 1185925; fax (22) 2658121; e-mail bse@shakti.ncst.ernt.in; f. 1875; 629 mems; Pres. M. G. DAMANI; Exec. Dir. R. C. MATHUR.

Uttar Pradesh Stock Exchange Association Ltd: 14/113 Civil Lines, Kanpur 208 001; tel. (512) 293115; telex 325420; fax (512) 293175; 500 mems; Pres. R. K. TANDON; Exec. Dir Dr J. N. GUPTA.

The other recognized stock exchanges are: Hyderabad, Madhya Pradesh (Indore), Cochin, Pune, Guwahati, Jaipur, Bhubaneswar (Orissa), Coimbatore, Saurashtra, Meerut, Vadodara and Magadh (Patna).

INSURANCE

In January 1973 all Indian and foreign insurance companies were nationalized. The general insurance business in India is now transacted by only four companies, subsidiaries of the General Insurance Corpn of India.

General Insurance Corpn of India (GIC): 'Suraksha', 170 J. Tata Rd, Churchgate, Mumbai 400 020; tel. (22) 2833046; telex 1183833; fax (22) 2855423; f. 1973 by the reorg. of 107 private non-life insurance cos (incl. brs of foreign cos operating in the country) as the four subsidiaries listed below; Chair. K. C. MITTAL; Mans U. MAHESH RAO, D. SWAMINATHAN.

National Insurance Co Ltd: 3 Middleton St, Calcutta 700 071; tel. (33) 2472130; fax (33) 2402369; Chair. and Man. Dir A. N. PODDAR; 19 regional offices, 254 divisional offices and 690 branch offices.

New India Assurance Co Ltd: New India Assurance Bldg, 87 Mahatma Gandhi Rd, Fort, Mumbai 400 001; tel. (22) 2674617; fax (22) 2652811; f. 1919; cap. p.u. 400m., res 9,181m. (1995); Chair./Man. Dir DEBDATTA SENGUPTA; 21 regional offices, 315 divisional offices, 827 branch offices and 32 overseas offices.

The Oriental Insurance Co Ltd: Oriental House, A-25/27 Asaf Ali Rd, New Delhi 110 002; tel. (11) 3279221; telex 3162643; fax (11) 3263175; Chair. and Man. Dir M. V. PUROHIT.

United India Insurance Co Ltd: 24 Whites Rd, Chennai 600 014; tel. (44) 8520161; telex 418484; fax (44) 8525280; cap. and res 966m.; Chair. and Man. Dir S. K. KANWAR.

Life Insurance Corpn of India (LIC): 'Yogakshema', Jeevan Bima Marg, Mumbai 400 021; tel. (22) 2021383; telex 1182327; fax (22) 2020274; f. 1956; controls all life insurance business; Chair. G. KRISHNAMURTHY; 2,024 brs and three overseas offices.

Trade and Industry

GOVERNMENT AGENCIES AND DEVELOPMENT ORGANIZATIONS

Coal India Ltd: 10 Netaji Subhas Rd, Calcutta 700 001; tel. (33) 2209980; telex 217180; fax (33) 2483373; cen. govt holding co with eight subsidiaries; responsible for almost total (more than 90%) exploration for, planning and production of coal mines; owns 498 coal mines throughout India; marketing of coal and its products; cap. p.u. Rs63,163.6m. (March 1995), sales US $2,873.4m. (1995/96); Chair. P. K. SENGUPTA; 660,000 employees (1995).

Cotton Corpn of India Ltd: Air-India Bldg, 12th Floor, Nariman Point, Mumbai 400 021; tel. (22) 2024363; telex 1183463; fax (22) 2025130; f. 1970 as an agency in the public sector for the purchase, sale and distribution of home-produced cotton and imported cotton staple fibre; exports long staple cotton; cap. p.u. Rs230m., res and surplus Rs961m. (March 1995); Chair. and Man. Dir M. B. LAL.

Export Credit Guarantee Corpn of India Ltd: Express Towers, 10th Floor, Nariman Point, Mumbai 400 021; tel. (22) 2845472; telex 1183231; fax (22) 2045253; f. 1957 to insure for risks involved in exports on credit terms and to supplement credit facilities by issuing guarantees, etc.; cap. Rs500m., res Rs2,061.5m. (March 1996); Chair. and Man. Dir DEV MEHTA; 18 brs.

Fertilizer Corpn of India Ltd: 'Madhuban', 55 Nehru Place, New Delhi 110 019; tel. (11) 6413215; telex 3162797; fax (11) 6224311; f. 1961; fertilizer factories at Sindri (Bihar), Gorakhpur (Uttar Pradesh), Talcher (Orissa) and Ramagundam (Andhra Pradesh), producing nitrogenous and some industrial products; cap. Rs6,617m. (March 1996); Chair. and Man. Dir V. N. RAI.

Food Corpn of India: 16–20 Barakhamba Lane, New Delhi 110 001; tel. (11) 3316871; telex 3166234; fax (11) 3316873; f. 1965 to undertake trading in food grains on a commercial scale but within the framework of an overall govt policy; to provide farmers an assured price for their produce; to supply food grains to the consumer at reasonable prices; also purchases, stores, distributes and sells food grains and other foodstuffs and arranges imports and handling of food grains and fertilizers at the ports; distributes sugar in a number of states and has set up rice mills; cap. p.u. Rs12,799.8m. (March 1995), sales US $3,465.6m. (1995/96); Chair. B. NARASIMHAN; Man. Dir SARITA DAS; 65,131 employees.

Handicrafts and Handlooms Exports Corpn of India Ltd: Jawahar Vyapar Bhavan Annexe, 1 Tolstoy Marg, New Delhi 110 001; tel. (11) 3311086; fax (11) 3315351; f. 1958; govt undertaking dealing in export of handicrafts, handloom goods, ready-to-wear clothes, carpets and precious jewellery, while promoting exports and trade development; cap. p.u. Rs108.2m., res and surplus Rs19.1m. (March 1995); Chair. and Man. Dir R. K. MATHUR.

Housing and Urban Development Corpn Ltd: HUDCO Bhavan, India Habitat Centre, Lodhi Rd, New Delhi 110 003; tel. (11) 4648160; telex 3161037; fax (11) 4625308; f. 1970; to finance and undertake housing and urban development programmes including the establishment of new or satellite towns and building material industries; cap. p.u. Rs3,500m., res and surplus Rs4,992m. (March 1997); 21 brs; Chair. and Man. Dir V. SURESH; Sec. GOPAL KRISHAN.

India Trade Promotion Organisation (ITPO): Pragati Bhavan, Pragati Maidan, Lal Bahadur Shastri Marg, New Delhi 110 001; tel. (11) 3318143; telex 3161311; fax (11) 3318142; f. 1992 following merger; promotes selective development of exports of high quality products; arranges investment in export-orientated ventures undertaken by India with foreign collaboration; organizes trade fairs; operates Trade Information Centre; cap. p.u. Rs2.5m., res and surplus Rs931m. (March 1995); brs in Bangalore, Mumbai, Calcutta, Kanpur and Chennai, and in Frankfurt, New York, Tokyo and Dubai; Chair. and Man. Dir K. K. MATHUR.

Jute Corpn of India Ltd: 1 Shakespeare Sarani, Calcutta 700 071; tel. (33) 2428831; telex 217266; f. 1971; objects: (i) to undertake price support operations in respect of raw jute; (ii) to ensure remunerative prices to producers through efficient marketing; (iii) to operate a buffer stock to stabilize raw jute prices; (iv) to handle the import and export of raw jute; (v) to promote the export of jute goods; cap. p.u. Rs50m., (March 1995); Chair. and Man. Dir A. N. SANYAL.

Minerals and Metals Trading Corpn of India Ltd: Scope Complex, Core-1, 7 Institutional Areas, Lodi Rd, New Delhi 110 003; tel. (11) 4362200; telex 3161045; fax (11) 4360274; f. 1963; export of iron and manganese ore, ferro-manganese, finished stainless steel products, engineering, agricultural and marine products, textiles, leather items, chemicals and pharmaceuticals, mica, coal and other minor minerals; import of steel, non-ferrous metals, rough diamonds, fertilizers, etc. for supply to industrial units in the country; cap. p.u. Rs500m., res Rs5,896.7m. (March 1997); 9 regional offices and 16 sub-regional offices in India; foreign offices in Japan, the Republic of Korea, Jordan and Romania; Chair. and Man. Dir Dr B. B. MADHUKAR; 3,246 employees.

National Co-operative Development Corpn: 4 Siri Institutional Area, Hauz Khas, New Delhi 110 016; tel. (11) 667475; telex 3173020; fax (11) 6962370; f. 1963 to plan, promote and finance country-wide programmes through co-operative societies for the production, processing, marketing, storage, export and import of agricultural produce, foodstuffs and notified commodities; also programmes for the development of poultry, dairy, fish products, coir, handlooms, distribution of consumer articles in rural areas and minor forest produce in the co-operative sector; seven regional and eight deputy regional directorates; Pres. CHATURANAN MISHRA; Man. Dir J. P. SINGH.

National Industrial Development Corpn Ltd: Chanakya Bhavan, Africa Ave, New Delhi 110 021; tel. (11) 6492985; telex 3172252; fax (11) 6876166; f. 1954; consultative engineering, management and infrastructure services to cen. and state govts, public and private sector enterprises, the UN and overseas investors; cap. p.u. Rs17.8m. (March 1996); Chair. and Man. Dir S. K TIWARI.

National Mineral Development Corpn Ltd: Khanij Bhavan, 10-3-311/A Castle Hills, Masab Tank, POB 1352, Hyderabad 500 028; tel. (40) 3538713; telex 4256452; fax (40) 3538711; f. 1958; cen. govt undertaking; to exploit minerals (excluding coal, atomic minerals, lignite, petroleum and natural gas) in public sector; may buy, take on lease or otherwise acquire mines for prospecting, development and exploitation; iron ore mines at Bailadila-11C, Bailadila-14 and Bailadila-5 in Madhya Pradesh, and at Donimalai in Karnataka State; new 5m. metric ton iron ore mine under construction at Bailadila-10/11A; diamond mines at Panna in Madhya Pradesh; research and development laboratories and consultancy services covering all aspects of mineral exploitation at Hyderabad; investigates mineral projects; iron ore production in 1995/96 was 14.31m. metric tons, diamond production 29,447 carats; cap. p.u. Rs1,321.6m., res and surplus Rs4,505m. (March 1997); Chair. and Man. Dir P. R. TRIPATHI.

National Productivity Council: Utpadakta Bhavan, Lodi Rd, New Delhi 110 003; tel. (11) 4698878; fax (11) 4615002; f. 1958 to increase productivity and to improve quality by improved techniques which aim at efficient and proper utilization of available resources; autonomous body representing national orgs of employers and labour, govt ministries, professional orgs, local productivity councils, small-scale industries and other interests; 75 mems; Chair. P. G. MANKAD; Dir-Gen. S. S. SHARMA.

National Research Development Corpn: 20–22 Zamroodpur Community Centre, Kailash Colony Extension, New Delhi 110 048; tel. (11) 6417821; telex 3171358; fax (11) 6449401; f. 1953 to stimulate development and commercial exploitation of new inventions with financial and technical aid; finances development projects to set up demonstration units in collaboration with industry; exports technology; cap. p.u. Rs32m., res and surplus Rs24.3m. (March 1994); Man. Dir N. K. SHARMA.

National Seeds Corpn Ltd: Beej Bhavan, Pusa, New Delhi 110 012; tel. (11) 5712292; telex 3177305; fax (11) 5766462; f. 1963 to improve and develop the seed industry; cap. p.u. Rs206.2m., res and surplus Rs208.9m. (March 1994); Chair. and Man. Dir DEEPIKA PADDA.

The National Small Industries Corpn Ltd: NSIC Bhavan, Okhla Industrial Estate, New Delhi 110 020; tel. (11) 6837071; telex 3175131; fax (11) 6840901; f. 1955 to aid, advise, finance, protect and promote the interests of small industries; establishes and supplies machinery for small industries in other developing countries on turn-key basis; cap. p.u. Rs839.9m. (March 1995); all shares held by the Govt; Chair. and Man. Dir M. AHMED.

Projects and Equipment Corpn of India Ltd: 'Hansalaya', 15 Barakhamba Rd, New Delhi 110 001; tel. (11) 3316372; telex 3165256; fax (11) 3314797; f. 1971; export of engineering, industrial and railway equipment; undertakes turnkey and other projects and management consultancy abroad; countertrade, trading in agrocommodities, construction materials (steel, cement, clinkers, etc.) and fertilizers; cap. p.u. Rs15m., res and surplus Rs155.6m. (March 1995); Chair. and Man. Dir O. N. KAPUR.

Rehabilitation Industries Corpn Ltd: 25 Mirza Ghalib St, Calcutta 700 016; tel. (33) 2441181; telex 215926; f. 1959 to create employment opportunities through multi-product industries, ranging from consumer goods to engineering products and services, for refugees from Bangladesh and migrants from Pakistan, repatriates from Myanmar and Sri Lanka, and other immigrants of Indian extraction; cap. p.u. Rs47.6m. (March 1994); Chair. and Man. Dir B. D. GHOSH.

State Farms Corpn of India Ltd: Farm Bhavan, 14–15 Nehru Place, New Delhi 110 019; tel. (11) 6446903; fax (11) 6226898; f. 1969 to administer the central state farms; activities include the production of quality seeds of high-yielding varieties of wheat, paddy, maize, bajra and jowar; advises on soil conservation, reclamation and development of waste and forest land; consultancy services on farm mechanization; auth. cap. Rs241.9m., res and surplus Rs329.1m. (March 1995); Chair. K. BRAHMANANDA RAO NAIDU; Man. Dir MAHENDRA SINGH.

State Trading Corpn of India Ltd: Jawahar Vyapar Bhavan, Tolstoy Marg, New Delhi 110 001; tel. (11) 3313177; telex 3165292; fax (11) 3324823; f. 1956; govt undertaking dealing in exports and imports; cap. p.u. Rs300m., res and surplus Rs4,169m. (March 1997); 18 regional brs and 9 offices overseas; Chair. and Man. Dir S. M. DEWAN; 1,930 employees (1994).

Steel Authority of India Ltd (SAIL): Ispat Bhavan, Lodi Rd, POB 3049, New Delhi 110 003; tel. (11) 4690481; telex 3162689; fax (11) 4625051; e-mail corporate.delhi@sail.sprintrpg.ems.vsnl.net.in; f. 1973 to provide co-ordinated development of the steel industry in both the public and private sectors; steel plants at Bhilai, Bokaro, Durgapur, Rourkela; alloy and special steel plants at Durgapur and Salem; subsidiaries: Visvesvaraya Iron and Steel Ltd (Karnataka), Indian Iron and Steel Co (West Bengal), IISCO-Ujjain Pipe and Foundry Co Ltd (Madhya Pradesh) and Maharashtra Elektrosmelt Ltd; combined crude steel capacity is 12.5m. metric tons annually; equity cap. Rs41,304m., res and surplus Rs43,511m. (March 1997); Chair. ARVIND PANDE; 189,195 employees (1993).

Tea Board of India: 14 B. T. M. Sarani (Brabourne Rd), POB 2172, Calcutta 700 001; tel. (33) 251411; telex 214527; fax (33) 2251417; provides financial assistance to tea research stations; sponsors and finances independent research projects in universities and tech. institutions to supplement the work of tea research establishments; also promotes tea production and export; Chair. S. S. AHUJA.

CHAMBERS OF COMMERCE

Associated Chambers of Commerce and Industry of India (ASSOCHAM): 2nd Floor, Allahabad Bank Bldg, 17 Parliament St, New Delhi 110 001; tel. (11) 3360704; fax (11) 3734917; e-mail raghuraman@sansad.nic.in; internet http://www.assocham.org; f. 1920; a central org. of 350 chambers of commerce and industry and industrial asscns representing more than 85,000 cos throughout India; 6 promoter chambers, 125 ordinary mems, 35 patron mems and 430 corporate associates; Pres. L. LAKSHMAN; Sec.-Gen. V. RAGHURAMAN.

Federation of Indian Chambers of Commerce and Industry (FICCI): Federation House, Tansen Marg, New Delhi 110 001; tel. (11) 3738760; telex 3162521; fax (11) 3320714; f. 1927; 420 ordinary mems, 36 corporate mems, 1,120 assoc. mems, 173 cttee mems; Pres. KRISHAN KUMAR MODI; Sec.-Gen. Dr AMIT MITRA.

ICC India: Federation House, Tansen Marg, New Delhi 110 001; tel. (11) 3738760; telex 3162521; fax (11) 3320714; e-mail iccindia@del2.vsnl.net.in; f. 1929; 49 org. mems, 439 assoc. mems, 13 patron mems, 128 cttee mems; Pres. CHIRAYU R. AMIN; Exec. Dir G. D. AWASTHI.

Associated Chamber of Commerce and Industry of Uttar Pradesh: C–107, Indira Nagar, Lucknow 226 016; tel. (522) 384545; fax (522) 388423; 521 mems; Pres. NARENDRA MOHAN: Sec.-Gen. R. K. JAIN.

Bengal Chamber of Commerce and Industry: 6 Netaji Subhas Rd, Calcutta 700 001; tel. (33) 2208393; telex 217369; fax (33) 2201289; f. 1853; 242 mems; Pres. S. S. PRASAD; Sec. PRADIP DAS GUPTA.

Bengal National Chamber of Commerce and Industry: 23 R. N. Mukherjee Rd, Calcutta 700 001; tel. (33) 2482951; telex 212189; fax (33) 2487058; e-mail bncci@wb.nic.in; f. 1887; 500 mems, 35 affiliated industrial and trading asscns; Pres. DIPANKAR DUTTA GUPTA; Sec. SUNIL BANIK.

Bharat Chamber of Commerce: 28 Hemanta Basu Sarani, Calcutta 700 001; tel. (33) 208286; f. 1900; 645 mems; Pres. ANAND AGARWAL; Sec. B. S. SARKAR.

Bihar Chamber of Commerce: Khem Chand Chaudhary Marg, POB 71, Patna 800 001; tel. (612) 670535; fax (612) 659505; f. 1926;

900 ordinary mems, 100 org. mems, 3 life mems; Pres. D. P. LOHIA; Sec.-Gen. NISHEETH JAISWAL.

Bombay Chamber of Commerce and Industry: Mackinnon Mackenzie Bldg, 4 Shoorji Vallabhdas Rd, Ballard Estate, POB 473, Mumbai 400 001; tel. (22) 2614681; fax (22) 2621213; e-mail bccm@giasbm.01.vsnl.net.in; f. 1836; 824 ordinary mems, 544 assoc. mems, 74 hon.mems; Pres. R. K. PITAMBER; Exec. Dir L. A. D'SOUZA.

Calcutta Chamber of Commerce: 18H Park St, Stephen Court, Calcutta 700 071; tel. (33) 290758; fax (33) 298961; 450 mems; Pres. VINOD BAID; Sec. PRADIP SANCHETI.

Chamber of Commerce and Industry (Regd): Panjbakhtar Rd, Jammu; tel. (191) 543543; fax (191) 572257; 1,069 mems; Pres. RAM SAHAI; Sec. TARA CHAND GUPTA.

Cochin Chamber of Commerce and Industry: Bristow Rd, Willingdon Island, POB 503, Kochi 682 003; tel. (484) 668349; telex 8856493; fax (484) 668651; f. 1847; 177 mems; Pres. M. H. ASHRAFF; Sec. EAPEN KALAPURAKAL.

Council of EU Chambers of Commerce in India: 3rd Floor, Y.B. Chavan Centre, Gen. J. Bhosale Marg, Mumbai 400 021; tel. (22) 2854563; fax (22) 2854564; e-mail ceuc@bom3.vsnl.net.in; 240 mems; Pres. K. R. EHRNREICH; Exec. Dir B. P. GUNAJI.

Federation of Andhra Pradesh Chambers of Commerce and Industry: 11-6-841, Red Hills, POB 14, Hyderabad 500 004; tel. (40) 393658; telex 4256038; fax (40) 395083; f. 1917; 2,100 mems; Pres. NARENDER SURANA; Sec. K. NARAYANA RAO.

Federation of Karnataka Chambers of Commerce and Industry: Kempegowda Rd, Bangalore 560 009; tel. (80) 2262355; fax (80) 2251826; f. 1916; 2,800 mems; Pres. K. LAKSHMAN; Sec. C. MANOHAR.

Federation of Madhya Pradesh Chambers of Commerce and Industry: Udyog Bhavan, 129A Malviya Nagar, Bhopal 462 003; tel. (755) 551451; fax (755) 551451; f. 1975; 500 ordinary mems, 58 asscn mems; Pres. RANJIT VITHALDAS; Sec.-Gen. PRAFULLA MAHESHWARI.

Goa Chamber of Commerce: Goa Chamber Bldg, Rua de Ormuz, POB 59, Panjim 403 001; tel. (832) 224223; fax (832) 223420; f. 1908; more than 500 mems; Pres. DATTARAJ V. SALGAOCAR; Sec. O. L. DA LAPA-SOARES.

Gujarat Chamber of Commerce and Industry: Shri Ambica Mills, Gujarat Chamber Bldg, Ashram Rd, POB 4045, Ahmedabad 380 009; tel. (79) 6582301; fax (79) 6587992; f. 1949; 9,600 mems; Pres. SAMVEG A. LALBHAI; Sec.-Gen. I. N. KANIA.

Haryana Chamber of Commerce and Industry: 342B Model Town, Ambala City, Haryana.

Indian Chamber of Commerce: India Exchange, 4 India Exchange Place, Calcutta 700 001; tel. (33) 2203243; telex 217432; fax (33) 2204495; e-mail icc.icccal@vsnl.net.in; f. 1925; 238 ordinary mems, 53 assoc. mems, 8 corporate group mems, 14 affiliated asscns; Pres. ADITYA V. LODHA; Sec.-Gen. NAZEEB ARIF.

Indian Chamber of Commerce and Industry: Four Square House, 49 Community Centre, New Friends Colony, New Delhi 110 065; tel. (11) 6832155; telex 3161179; fax (11) 6840775; Pres. L. K. MODI; Hon. Sec. R. P. SWAMI.

Indian Merchants' Chamber: IMC Marg, Mumbai 400 020; tel. (22) 2046633; telex 1185195; fax (22) 2048508; f. 1907; 184 asscn mems, 2,020 mem. firms; Pres. RAM P. GANDHI; Sec. P. N. MOGRE.

Indo-American Chamber of Commerce: 1C Vulcan Insurance Bldg, Veer Nariman Rd, Mumbai 400 020; tel. (22) 2821413; fax (22) 2046141; e-mail iacc@giasbm01.vsnl.net.in; 2,000 mems; Pres. M. V. RAJESHWARA RAO: Sec.-Gen. SUBRAMANIAM AYYAR; 4 regional offices, 8 br. offices and 1 rep. office in USA.

Indo-French Chamber of Commerce and Industry: B-5 Venkatesh Chambers, Prescot Rd, Mumbai 400 001; tel. (22) 2064660; fax (22) 2064619; f. 1977; 435 mems; Pres. BINAY KUMAR; Exec. Dir JEAN DUCHÊNE.

Indo-German Chamber of Commerce: Maker Towers 'E', 1st Floor, Cuffe Parade, Mumbai 400 005; tel. (22) 2186131; fax (22) 2180523; e-mail igcc@giasbm01.vsnl.net.in; f. 1956; 6,000 mems; Pres. MANFRED KNOLL; Exec. Dir Dr G. KRUEGER.

Karnataka Chamber of Commerce and Industry: Karnataka Chamber Bldg, Hubli 580 020; tel. (836) 363102; fax (836) 360933; f. 1928; 2,300 mems; Pres. C. B. PATIL; Hon. Sec. MADAN DESAI.

Madhya Pradesh Chamber of Commerce and Industry: Chamber Bhavan, Sanatan Dharam Mandir Marg, Gwalior 474 009; tel. (751) 321691; fax (751) 323844; f. 1906; 1,600 mems; Pres. V. K. GANGWAL; Hon. Sec. VIRENDRA BAPNA.

Madras Chamber of Commerce and Industry: Karumuttu Centre, 498 Anna Salai, Chennai 600 035; tel. (44) 4349452; fax (44) 4349164; f. 1836; 254 mem. firms, 49 assoc., 13 affiliated, 11 honorary, 3 others; Pres. N. SRINIVASAN; Sec. R. SUBRAMANIAN.

Maharashtra Chamber of Commerce and Industry: Oricon House, 6th Floor, 12 K. Dubhash Marg, Fort, Mumbai 400 023; tel. (22) 2855859; fax (22) 2855861; f. 1927; 1,700 mems; Pres. ARAVIND M. KULKARNI; Sec.-Gen. S. S. PINGLE.

Mahratta Chamber of Commerce and Industries: Tilak Rd, POB 525, Pune 411 002; tel. (212) 540371; telex 1457333; fax (212) 547902; f. 1934; 2,000 mems; Pres. Dr R. J. RATHI; Sec.-Gen. NEELA KHANDGE.

Merchants' Chamber of Commerce: 15B Hemanta Basu Sarani, Calcutta 700 001; tel. (33) 2483123; fax (33) 2488657; f. 1901; 550 mems; Pres. S. S. BAGARIA; Exec. Dir R. K. SEN.

Merchants' Chamber of Uttar Pradesh: 14/76 Civil Lines, Kanpur 208 001; tel. (512) 291306; fax (512) 210238; f. 1932; 200 mems; Pres. N. K. JHAJHARIA; Sec. S. S. KANODIA.

North India Chamber of Commerce and Industry: 9 Gandhi Rd, Dehra Dun, Uttar Pradesh; tel. (935) 23479; f. 1967; 105 ordinary mems, 29 asscn mems, 7 mem. firms, 91 assoc. mems; Pres. DEV PANDHI; Hon. Sec. ASHOK K. NARANG.

Oriental Chamber of Commerce: 6A Dr Rajendra Prasad Sarani, Calcutta 700 001; tel. (33) 2203609; fax (33) 2259394; f. 1932; 256 ordinary mems, 4 assoc. mems; Pres. SK. ABDUL HANNAN; Sec. KAZI ABU ZOBER.

PHD Chamber of Commerce and Industry: PHD House, Thapar Floor, 4/2 Siri Institutional Area, opp. Asian Games Village, POB 130, New Delhi 110 016; tel. (11) 6863802; telex 3173058; fax (11) 6863135; f. 1905; 1,585 mems, 80 asscn mems; Pres. O. P. VAISH; Sec.-Gen. H. S. TANDON.

Rajasthan Chamber of Commerce and Industry: Rajasthan Chamber Bhavan, M.I. Rd, Jaipur 302 003; tel. (141) 565163; fax (141) 561419; 860 mems; Pres. S. K. MANSINGHKA; Hon. Sec.-Gen. K. L. JAIN.

Southern India Chamber of Commerce and Industry: Indian Chamber Bldgs 6, Esplanade, POB 1208, Chennai 600 108; tel. (44) 5342228; fax (44) 5341876; f. 1909; 1,000 mems; Pres. A. L. VADIVELU; Sec. J. PRASAD DAVIDS.

Upper India Chamber of Commerce: 14/113 Civil Lines, POB 63, Kanpur 208 001; tel. (512) 210684; fax (512) 210684; f. 1888; 128 mems; Pres. DILIP BHARGAVA; Sec. S. P. SRIVASTAVA.

Utkal Chamber of Commerce and Industry Ltd: Barabati Stadium, Cuttack 753 005; tel. (671) 601211; fax (671) 602059; f. 1964; 250 mems; Pres. JAGDISH LAL; Sec. KEDAR PATTNAIK.

Uttar Pradesh Chamber of Commerce: 15/197 Civil Lines, Kanpur 208 001; tel. 211696; f. 1914; 200 mems; Pres. Dr B. K. MODI; Sec. AFTAB SAMI.

INDUSTRIAL AND TRADE ASSOCIATIONS

Ahmedabad Textile Mills' Association: Ranchhodlal Marg, Navrangpura, POB 4056, Ahmedabad 380 009; tel. (272) 6582273; fax (272) 6588574; f. 1891; 29 mems; Pres. MAHESH J. SHAH; Prin. Sec. N. V. RANGNATHAN.

All India Federation of Master Printers: A-370, 2nd Floor, Defence Colony, New Delhi 110 024; tel. (11) 4601571; fax (11) 4601570; f. 1953; 41 affiliates, 700 mems; Pres. P. HANUMANTHA RAO; Hon. Gen. Sec. V. K. MALIK.

All India Manufacturers' Organization (AIMO): Jeevan Sahakar, 4th Floor, Sir P.M. Rd, Fort, Mumbai 400 001; tel. (22) 2661016; fax (22) 2660838; f. 1941; 800 mems; Pres. KAMALKUMAR R. DUJODWALA; Hon. Gen. Sec. SURESH DEORA.

All India Plastics Manufacturers' Association: AIPMA House, A-52, St No. 1, MIDC, Andheri (E), Mumbai 400 093; tel. (22) 8217324; fax (22) 8216390; e-mail aipma@bom2.vsnl.net.in; f. 1947; 2,300 mems; Pres. RAJIV B. TOLAT; Hon. Sec. N. S. MANI.

All India Shippers' Council: Federation House, Tansen Marg, New Delhi 110 001; tel. (11) 3738760; telex 3162521; fax (11) 3320714; f. 1967; 200 mems; Chair. RAMU S. DEORA; Sec. M. Y. REDDY.

Association of Indian Automobile Manufacturers: Core 4B, Zone IV, 5th Floor, India Habitat Centre, Lodhi Rd, New Delhi 110 003; tel. (11) 4647810; fax (11) 4648222; f. 1960; 29 mems; Pres. V. M. RAVAL; Exec. Dir RAJAT NANDI.

Association of Man-made Fibre Industry of India: Resham Bhavan, 78 Veer Nariman Rd, Mumbai 400 020; tel. (22) 2040009; telex 1183925; fax (22) 2049172; f. 1954; 9 mems; Pres. NIRBHAY JAIN; Sec.-Gen. D. H. VORA.

Automotive Component Manufacturers' Association of India: 203-205 Kirti Deep Bldg, Nangal Raya Business Centre, New Delhi 110 046; tel. (11) 5501669; fax (11) 5593189; e-mail acma@giasdl01.vsnl.net.in; 360 mems; Pres. K. MAHESH; Exec. Dir VISHNU MATHUR.

Automotive Tyre Manufacturers' Association: PHD House, opp. Asian Games Village, Siri Fort Institutional Area, New Delhi 110 016; tel. (11) 6851187; telex 3161762; fax (11) 6864799; e-mail atma@nda.vsnl.net.in; 10 mems; Chair. ONKAR S. KANWAR; Dir-Gen. D. RAVINDRAN.

Bharat Krishak Samaj (Farmers' Forum, India): Dr Panjabrao Deshmukh Krishak Bhavan, A-1 Nizamuddin West, New Delhi 110

013; tel. (11) 4619508; f. 1954; national farmers' org.; 5m. ordinary mems, 60,000 life mems; Chair. Dr BAL RAM JAKHAR; Exec. Chair./Gen. Sec. Dr KRISHAN BIR CHAUDHARY.

Bombay Metal Exchange Ltd: 88/90, Gulalwadi, Kika St, 1st Floor, Mumbai 400 004; tel. (22) 3750964; fax (22) 3732640; promotes trade and industry in non-ferrous metals; 484 mems; Pres. SHARAD SURENDRABHAI PARIKH; Sec. T. S. B. IYER.

Bombay Shroffs Association: 233-A Shaikh Memon St, Mumbai 400 002; tel. (22) 3425588; f. 1910; 505 mems; Pres. KAMLESH C. SHAH; Hon. Secs S. I. PARIKH, R. O. DHARIA.

Calcutta Baled Jute Association: Calcutta; tel. (33) 208393; telex 217369; f. 1892; 49 mems; Chair. PURANMULL KANKARIA; Sec. A. E. SCOLT.

Calcutta Flour Mills Association: 25/B Shakespeare Sarani, Calcutta 700 017; tel. (33) 2476723; fax (33) 2209748; f. 1932; 28 mems; Chair. D. N. JATIA; Hon. Sec. R. BHAGAT.

Calcutta Tea Traders' Association: 6 Netaji Subhas Rd, Calcutta 700 001; tel. (33) 2208393; telex 217369; fax (33) 2201289; f. 1886; 1,490 mems; Chair. G. BHALLA; Sec. J. KALYANA SUNDARAM.

Cement Manufacturers' Association: Vishnu Kiran Chambers, 2142-47 Gurudwara Rd, Karol Bagh, New Delhi 110 005; tel. (11) 5763206; telex 3177232; fax (11) 5738476; 57 mems; 128 major cement plants; Pres. N. S. SEKHSARIA; Sec.-Gen. R. PARTHA SARATHY.

Confederation of Indian Industry (CII): 23–26 Institutional Area, Lodi Rd, New Delhi 110 003; tel. (11) 4629994; fax (11) 4626149; f. 1974; 3,400 mem. cos, 97 (54 national, 43 regional) affiliated asscns; Pres. N. KUMAR; Dir-Gen. TARUN DAS.

East India Cotton Association Ltd: Cotton Exchange Bldg, 9th Floor, 175 Kalbadevi Rd, Marwari Bazar, Mumbai 400 002; tel. (22) 2014876; telex 1183152; fax (22) 2015578; f. 1921; 414 mems; Pres. SURESH A. KOTAK; Secs HEMANT MULKY, S. S. BARODIA.

Federation of Gujarat Industries: Federation Bldg, Sampatrao Colony, R. C. Dutt Rd, Baroda 390 007; tel. (265) 311101; fax (265) 339054; f. 1918; 450 mems; Pres. RAKESH AGRAWAL; Sec.-Gen. RANJANKUMAR D. MUSHI.

Federation of Indian Export Organisations: PHD House, 3rd Floor, Siri Institutional Area, Hauz Khas, opposite Asian Games Village, New Delhi 110 016; tel. (11) 6851310; telex 3173194; fax (11) 6863087; f. 1965; 3,500 mems; Pres. RAMU S. DEORA; Sec.-Gen. Dr R. K. DHAWAN.

The Fertiliser Association of India: 10 Shaheed Jit Singh Marg, New Delhi 110 067; tel. (11) 6517305; telex 3173056; fax (11) 6960052; f. 1955; 1,796 mems; Chair. P. R. SUNDARAVADIVELU; Dir-Gen. PRATAP NARAYAN.

Grain, Rice and Oilseeds Merchants' Association: Grainseeds House, 72/80 Yusef Meheralli Rd, Mumbai 400 003; tel. (22) 3754021; f. 1899; 1,000 mems; Pres. HIRJI NANJI KENIA.

Indian Chemical Manufacturers' Association: New Delhi; tel. (11) 3327421; f. 1938; 240 mems; Pres. ASHWIN C. SHROFF; Chief Exec. R. PARTHASARATHY.

Indian Drug Manufacturers' Association: 102B Poonam Chambers, Dr A. B. Rd, Worli, Mumbai 400 018; tel. (22) 4944624; fax (22) 4950723; e-mail idma@giasbm01.vsnl.net.in; 600 mems; Pres. Dr DINESH S. PATEL; Sec.-Gen. I. A. ALVA.

Indian Electrical and Electronics Manufacturers' Association: 501 Kakad Chambers, 132 Dr Annie Besant Rd, Worli, Mumbai 400 018; tel. (22) 4930532; fax (22) 4932705; e-mail ieemamum@giasbm01.vsnl.net.in; f. 1948; 400 mems; Pres. K. VASUDEVAN; Sec.-Gen. SUNIL P. MORE.

Indian Jute Mills Association: Royal Exchange, 6 Netaji Subhas Rd, Calcutta 700 001; tel. (33) 2209918; telex 217369; fax (33) 2205643; sponsors and operates export promotion, research and product development; regulates labour relations; 37 mems; Chair. G. M. SINGHVI; Exec. Dir S. K. BHATTACHARYA.

Indian Leather Industries Association: India Exchange, 4 India Exchange Place, 7th Floor, Calcutta 700 001; tel. (33) 2207763; telex 217432; fax (33) 2203973; 70 mems; Pres. S. S. KUMAR; Exec. Dir S. K. GUPTA.

Indian Machine Tool Manufacturers' Association: 17 Nangal Raya Commercial Complex, New Delhi 110 046; tel. (11) 5592814; fax (11) 5599882; e-mail imtma@del2.vsnl.net.in; 400 mems; Pres. C. R. SWAMINATHAN; Sec.-Gen. A. MUKHERJEE.

Indian Mining Association: 6 Netaji Subhas Rd, Calcutta 700 001; tel. (33) 263861; telex 217369; f. 1892; 50 mems; Sec. K. MUKERJEE.

Indian Mining Federation: 135 Biplabi Rash Behari Basu Rd, 2nd Floor, Calcutta 700 001; tel. (33) 2428975; f. 1913; 40 mems; Chair. V. K. ARORA; Sec. S. K. GHOSE.

Indian Motion Picture Producers' Association: IMPPA House, Dr Ambedkar Rd, Bandra (West), Mumbai 400 050; tel. (22) 6486344; fax (22) 6480757; f. 1938; 1,700 mems; Pres. SULTAN AHMED; Jt Sec. SHASHANK JARE.

Indian National Shipowners' Association: 22 Maker Tower, F, Cuffe Parade, Mumbai 400 005; tel. (22) 2182103; fax (22) 2182104; f. 1929; 30 mems; Pres. B. L. MEHTA; CEO B. V. NILKUND.

Indian Oil & Produce Exporters' Association: 78/79 Bajaj Bhavan, Nariman Point, Mumbai 400 021; tel. (22) 2023225; telex 1185637; fax (22) 2029236; f. 1956; 425 mems; Chair. MULRAJ J. TANNA; Sec. A. N. SUBRAMANIAN.

Indian Paper Mills Association: India Exchange, 8th Floor, India Exchange Place, Calcutta 700 001; tel. (33) 2203242; telex 217432; fax (33) 2204495; f. 1939; 37 mems; Pres. K. K. KHEMKA; Sec. B. GHOSH.

Indian Refractory Makers' Association: 5 Lala Lajpat Rai Sarani, 4th Floor, Calcutta 700 020; tel. (33) 2401901; telex 217369; fax (33) 2408357; e-mail irma@giasdl01.vsnl.net.in; 85 mems; Chair. M. V. MURUGAPPAN; Exec. Dir P. DAS GUPTA.

Indian Soap and Toiletries Makers' Association: 614 Raheja Centre, Free Press Journal Marg, Mumbai 400 021; tel. (22) 2824115; fax (22) 2853649; 43 mems; Pres. M. S. BANGA; Sec.-Gen. V. P. MENON.

Indian Sugar Mills Association: 'Sugar House', 39 Nehru Place, New Delhi 110 019; tel. (11) 6472554; telex 3162654; fax (11) 6472409; e-mail sugarmil@nda.vsnl.net.in; f. 1932; 191 mems; Pres. SHISHIR BAJAJ; Dir-Gen. S. L. JAIN.

Indian Tea Association: Royal Exchange, 6 Netaji Subhas Rd, Calcutta 700 001; tel. (33) 2208393; fax (33) 2434301; f. 1881; 63 mem. cos; 238 tea estates; Chair. V. K. GOENKA; Sec.-Gen. R. DAS.

Indian Woollen Mills' Federation: Churchgate Chambers, 7th Floor, 5 New Marine Lines, Mumbai 400 020; tel. (22) 2624372; fax (22) 2624675; f. 1963; 70 mems; Chair. R. K. KHANNA; Sec.-Gen. A. C. CHAUDHURI.

Industries and Commerce Association: ICO Association Rd, POB 70, Dhanbad 826 001; tel. (326) 303147; fax (326) 303787; f. 1933; 72 mems; Pres. UMESH CHAND; Sec. K. R. CHAKRAVARTY.

Jute Balers' Association: 12 India Exchange Place, Calcutta 700 001; tel. (33) 2201491; f. 1909; 300 mems; Chair. NATHMAL JHANWAR; Sec. SUJIT CHOUDHURY.

Maharashtra Motor Parts Dealers' Association: 13 Kala Bhavan, 3 Mathew Rd, Mumbai 400 004; tel. (22) 3614468; 372 mems; Pres. CHITTRANJAN A. SHAH; Sec. G. L. SHROFF.

Millowners' Association, Mumbai: Elphinstone Bldg, 10 Veer Nariman Rd, Fort, POB 95, Mumbai 400 001; tel. (22) 2040411; fax (22) 2832611; f. 1875; 36 mem. cos; Chair. NANDAN S. DAMANI; Sec.-Gen. V. Y. TAMHANE.

Mumbai Motor Merchants' Association Ltd: 304 Sukh Sagar, N. S. Patkar Marg, Mumbai 400 007; tel. (22) 8112769; 409 mems; Pres. S. TARLOCHAN SINGH ANAND; Gen. Sec. S. BHUPINDER SINGH SETHI.

Mumbai Textile Merchants' Mahajan: 250 Sheikh Memon St, Mumbai 400 002; tel. (22) 2065750; fax (22) 2000311; f. 1881; 1,900 mems; Pres. SURENDRA TULSIDAS SAVAI; Hon. Secs DHIRAJ KOTHARI, DINESH M. MEHTA.

Organisation of Pharmaceutical Producers of India (OPPI): Cook's Blg, 1st Floor, 324 Dr Dadabhoy Naoroji Rd, Fort, Mumbai 400 001; tel. (22) 2045509; fax (22) 2044705; 68 mems; Pres. D. BHADURY; Sec.-Gen. R. D. JOSHI.

Silk and Art Silk Mills' Association Ltd: 3rd Floor, SASMIRA, Sasmira Marg, Worli, Mumbai 400 025; tel. (22) 4945372; fax (22) 4938350; f. 1939; 170 mems; Chair. M. H. DOSHI; Sec. K. A. SAMUEL.

Southern India Mills' Association: Racecourse, Coimbatore 641 018, Tamil Nadu; tel. (422) 211391; telex 8558238; fax (422) 217160; f. 1933; 347 mems; Chair. B. K. PATODIA; Sec. P. R. SUBRAMANIAN.

Surgical Manufacturers and Traders' Association: 60 Darya Ganj, New Delhi 110 002; tel. (11) 3271027; Pres. RAVINDER GUPTA; Sec. PRADEEP CHAWLA.

United Planters' Association of Southern India (UPASI): Glenview, POB 11, Coonoor 643 101; tel. (423) 30270; fax (423) 32030; f. 1893; 1,164 mems; Pres. A. D. CHANDRASHEKAR; Sec.-Gen. N. RAMADURAI.

EMPLOYERS' ORGANIZATIONS

Council of Indian Employers: Federation House, Tansen Marg, New Delhi 110 001; tel. (11) 3319251; telex 3161768; fax (11) 3320714; f. 1956; Advisor M. K. GARG; comprises:

All India Organisation of Employers (AIOE): Federation House, Tansen Marg, New Delhi 110 001; tel. (11) 3738760; telex 3161768; fax (11) 3320714; f. 1932; 200 mems (incl. 120 associate mems); Pres. VINEET VIRMANI; Sec.-Gen. Dr AMIT MITRA.

Employers' Federation of India (EFI): Army and Navy Bldg, 148 Mahatma Gandhi Rd, Mumbai 400 023; tel. (22) 2844232; fax (22) 2843028; f. 1933; 28 asscn mems, 176 ordinary mems, 18 hon. mems; Pres. ARVIND R. DOSHI; Sec.-Gen. S. K. NANDA.

Standing Conference of Public Enterprises (SCOPE): SCOPE Complex, 1st Floor, Core No. 8, 7 Lodi Rd, New Delhi

110 003; tel. (11) 4360101; fax (11) 4361371; f. 1973; representative body of all central public enterprises in India; advises the Govt and public enterprises on matters of major policy and co-ordination; trade enquiries, regarding imports and exports of commodities, carried out on behalf of mems; 198 mems; Chair. Dr UDDESH KOHLI; Sec.-Gen. M. A. HAKEEM.

Employers' Association of Northern India: 14/113 Civil Lines, POB 344, Kanpur 208 001; tel. (512) 210513; f. 1937; 181 mems; Chair. Dr K. B. AGARWAL; Sec.-Gen. J. N. SRIVASTAVA.

Employers' Federation of Southern India: Karumuttu Centre, 1st Floor, 498 Anna Salai, Chennai 600 035; tel. (44) 4349452; fax (44) 4349164; f. 1920; 420 mems; Pres. C. VALLIAPPA; Sec. N. KANNAN.

UTILITIES

Electricity

Damodar Valley Corpn: DVC Towers, VIP Rd, Calcutta 700 054; tel. (33) 3340686; telex 214353; fax (33) 3349937; f. 1948; set up to administer the Damodar Valley Project, which aims at unified development of irrigation, flood control and power generation in West Bengal and Bihar; operates 9 power stations, incl. thermal, hydel and gas turbine; power generating capacity 2,551.5 MW (1997); Chair. BADAL SENGUPTA.

National Thermal Power Corporation Ltd: Core-7, SCOPE Complex, Lodi Rd, New Delhi 110 003; tel. (11) 4360100; fax (11) 4361018; operates super thermal power stations in seven states and gas power projects in four states; cap. p.u. Rs74,037.8m., res and surplus Rs87,409m. (March 1997); sales US $1,998.5m. (1995/96); Dir RAJENDRA SINGH; 24,000 employees.

Nuclear Power Corporation of India Ltd: Commerce Center-1, World Trade Centre, Cuffe Parade, Mumbai 400 005; tel. (22) 2182171; telex 1182510; fax (22) 2180109; cap. p.u. Rs23,990m., res and surplus Rs1,045.5m. (March 1995); Chair. Dr Y. S. R. PRASAD.

Gas

Gas Authority of India Ltd: 16 Bhikaji Cama Place, R. K. Puram, Delhi 110 066; tel. (11) 6172580; fax (11) 6185941; f. 1984; 90% state-owned; transports, processes and markets natural gas; constructing gas-based petrochemical complex; cap. Rs8,453.2m., res and surplus Rs8,144m. (March 1995); Chair. and Man. Dir C. R. PRASAD; 1,513 employees.

TRADE UNIONS

Indian National Trade Union Congress (INTUC): 4 Bhai Veer Singh Marg, New Delhi 110 001; tel. (11) 3747768; fax (11) 3364244; f. 1947; 3,796 affiliated unions with a total membership of 5,932,440; affiliated to ICFTU; 27 state brs and 29 nat. feds; Pres. G. SANJEEVA REDDY; Gen. Sec. SUBRATA MUKHERJEE.

Indian National Cement Workers' Federation: Mazdoor Karyalaya, Congress House, Mumbai 400 004; tel. (22) 3871809; fax (22) 3870981; 49,000 mems; 38 affiliated unions; Pres. H. N. TRIVEDI; Gen. Sec. N. NANJAPPAN.

Indian National Chemical Workers' Federation: Tel Rasayan Bhavan, Tilak Rd, Dadar, Mumbai 400 014; tel. (22) 4121742; fax (22) 4130950; 35,000 mems; Pres. RAJA KULKARNI; Gen. Sec. R. D. BHARADWAJ.

Indian National Electricity Workers' Federation: 392 Sector 21-B, Faridabad 121 001; tel. (129) 215089; fax (129) 215868; 294,384 mems; 140 affiliated unions; Pres. D. P. PATHAK; Gen. Sec. S. L. PASSEY.

Indian National Metal Workers' Federation: 35 K Rd, Jamshedpur 831 001; tel. (657) 431475; Pres. N. K. BHATT; Gen. Sec. S. GOPESHWAR.

Indian National Mineworkers' Federation: Imperial House, 13 Ganesh Chandra Ave, Calcutta 700 013; tel. (33) 260987; fax (33) 2159644; f. 1949; 351,454 mems in 139 affiliated unions; Pres. RAJENDRA P. SINGH; Gen. Sec. S. Q. ZAMA.

Indian National Paper Mill Workers' Federation: 6/B, LIGH, Barkatpura, Hyderabad 500 027; tel. (842) 7564706; Pres. G. SANJEEVA REDDY; Gen. Sec. R. CHANDRASEKHARAN.

Indian National Port and Dock Workers' Federation: 15 Coal Dock Rd, Calcutta 700 043; tel. (33) 455929; f. 1954; 18 affiliated unions; 81,000 mems; Pres. JANAKI MUKHERJEE; Gen. Sec. G. KALAN.

Indian National Sugar Mills Workers' Federation: A-176, Darulsafa Marg, Lucknow 226 001; tel. (522) 247638; 100 affiliated unions; 40,000 mems; Pres. ASHOK KUMAR SINGH; Gen. Sec. P. K. SHARMA.

Indian National Textile Workers' Federation: 27 Burjorji Bharucha Marg, Mumbai 400 023; tel. (22) 261577; f. 1948; 400 affiliated unions; 363,790 mems; Pres. P. L. SUBBIAH; Gen. Sec. H. J. NAIK.

Indian National Transport Workers' Federation: L/1, Hathital Colony, Jabalpur 482 001; tel. (761) 29210; 329 affiliated unions; 286,573 mems; Pres. D. B. PILWALKAR; Gen. Sec. K. S. VERMA.

National Federation of Petroleum Workers: Tel Rasayan Bhavan, Tilak Rd, Dadar, Mumbai 400 014; tel. (22) 4181742; fax (22) 4130950; f. 1959; 22,340 mems; Pres. RAJA KULKARNI; Gen. Sec. S. N. SURVE.

Bharatiya Mazdoor Sangh: Ram Naresh Bhavan, Tilak Gali, Pahar Ganj, New Delhi 110 055; tel. (11) 7524212; fax (11) 7520654; f. 1955; 3,507 affiliated unions with a total membership of 3,116,564 mems; 24 state brs; 28 nat. feds; Pres. RAMAN GIRDHAR SHAH; Gen. Sec. HASU BHAI DAVE.

Centre of Indian Trade Unions: 15 Talkatora Rd, New Delhi 110 001; tel. (11) 3714071; fax (11) 3355856; f. 1970; 1,775,220 mems; 21 state and union territory brs; 3,656 affiliated unions, 10 nat. federations; Pres. E. BALANANDAN; Gen. Sec. Dr M. K. PANDHE.

Assam Chah Karmachari Sangha: POB 13, Dibrugarh 786 001; tel. 20870; 13,553 mems; 20 brs; Pres. G. C. SARMAH; Gen. Sec. A. K. BHATTACHARYA.

All-India Trade Union Congress (AITUC): 24 Canning Lane, New Delhi 110 001; tel. (11) 3387320; fax (11) 3386427; e-mail ctuc-connect014@mcr1.poptel.org.uk; f. 1920; affiliated to WFTU; 3m. mems, 3,000 affiliated unions; 26 state brs, 10 national federations; Pres. J. CHITHARANJAN; Gen. Sec. K. L. MAHENDRA.

Major affiliated unions:

Annamalai Plantation Workers' Union: Valparai, Via Pollachi, Tamil Nadu; over 21,000 mems.

Zilla Cha Bagan Workers' Union: Mal, Jalpaiguri, West Bengal; 15,000 mems; Pres. NEHAR MUKHERJEE; Gen. Sec. BIMAL DAS GUPTA.

United Trades Union Congress (UTUC): 249 Bepin Behari Ganguly St, Calcutta 700 012; tel. (33) 275609; f. 1949; 584,523 mems from 413 affiliated unions; 10 state brs and 6 nat. feds; Pres. SUSHIL BHATTACHRJEE; Gen. Sec. S. R. SEN GUPTA.

Major affiliated unions:

All India Farm Labour Union: c/o UTUC Jakkanpur New Area, Patna 800 001, Bihar; c. 35,000 mems; Pres. MAHENDRA SINGH TIKAIT.

Bengal Provincial Chatkal Mazdoor Union: Calcutta; textile workers; 28,330 mems.

Hind Mazdoor Sabha (HMS): Hotel Sealord Bldg, 167 P. D'Mello Rd, Mumbai 400 038; tel. (22) 2612185; fax (22) 2622388; f. 1948; affiliated to ICFTU; 4.9m. mems from 2,816 affiliated unions; 18 state councils; 15 nat. industrial feds; Pres. MANOHAR KOTWAL; Gen. Sec. UMRAOMAL PUROHIT.

Major affiliated unions:

Colliery Mazdoor Congress (Coalminers' Union): Pres. MADHU DANDAVATE; Gen. Sec. JAYANTA PODDER.

Mumbai Port Trust Employees' Union: Pres. Dr SHANTI PATEL; Gen. Sec. S. K. SHETYE.

Oil and Natural Gas Commission Employees' Mazdoor Sabha: Shram Sadhana, Raopura, Baroda 390 001; tel. (265) 555094; fax (265) 420838; 8,400 mems; Pres. SANAT MEHTA; Gen. Sec. BABA KADAM.

South Central Railway Mazdoor Union: 7C Railway Bldg, Accounts Office Compound, Secunderabad 500 371; tel. (842) 821351; f. 1966; 84,150 mems; Pres. K. S. N. MURTHY; Gen. Sec. N. SUNDARESAN; 129 brs.

Transport and Dock Workers' Union: Gen. Sec. MANOHAR KOTWAL.

West Bengal Cha Mazdoor Sabha: Cha Shramik Bhavan, Jalpaiguri 735 101, West Bengal; tel. (3561) 23140; fax (3561) 22349; f. 1947; 45,000 mems; Pres. SRIRAM SINGH; Gen. Sec. SAMIR ROY.

Western Railway Employees' Union: Pres. JAGDISH AJMERA; Gen. Sec. UMRAOMAL PUROHIT.

Confederation of Central Government Employees and Workers: 4B/6 Ganga Ram Hospital Marg, New Delhi 110 060; tel. (11) 587804; 1.2m. mems; Pres. S. MADHUSUDAN; Sec.-Gen. S. K. VYAS.

Affiliated union:

National Federation of Post, Telephone and Telegraph Employees (NFPTTE): C-1/2 Baird Rd, New Delhi 110 001; tel. (11) 322545; f. 1954; 221,880 mems (est.); Pres. R. G. SHARMA; Gen. Sec. O. P. GUPTA.

All India Bank Employees' Association (AIBEA): 3B Lall Bazar St, 1st Floor, Calcutta 700 001; tel. (33) 2489371; telex 217424; fax

(33) 2486072; 24 state units, 710 affiliated unions, 500,000 mems; Pres. N. SAMPATH; Gen. Sec. TARAKESWAR CHAKRABORTI.

All India Defence Employees' Federation (AIDEF): Survey No. 81, Elphinstone Rd, Khadki, Pune 411 003; tel. (212) 318761; 350 affiliated unions; 400,000 mems; Pres. SAMUEL AUGUSTINE; Gen. Sec. D. LOBO.

All India Port and Dock Workers' Federation: 9 Second Line Beach, Chennai 600 001; tel. (44) 5224222; fax (44) 5225983; f. 1948; 100,000 mems in 34 affiliated unions; Pres. S. R. KULKARNI; Gen. Sec. S. C. C. ANTHONY PILLAI.

All India Railwaymen's Federation (AIRF): 4 State Entry Rd, New Delhi 110 055; tel. (11) 3343493; fax (11) 3363167; f. 1924; 1,036,706 mems; 16 affiliated unions; Pres. UMRAOMAL PUROHIT; Gen. Sec. J. P. CHAUBEY.

National Federation of Indian Railwaymen (NFIR): 3 Chelmsford Rd, New Delhi 110 055; tel. (11) 3734013; f. 1952; 20 affiliated unions; 907,485 mems (1997); Pres. MAHINDRA PRATAP; Gen. Sec. M. RAGHAVAIAH.

Transport

RAILWAYS

India's railway system is the largest in Asia and the fourth largest in the world. The total length of Indian railways in 1995/96 was 62,915 route-km. The Government exercises direct or indirect control over all railways through the Railway Board. India's largest railway construction project of the century, the 760-km Konkan railway line (which took seven years and almost US $1,000m. to build), was officially opened in January 1998.

A 16.45-km underground railway, which was expected to carry more than 1m. people daily, was completed in Calcutta in 1995.

Ministry of Railways (Railway Board): Rail Bhavan, Raisina Rd, New Delhi; tel. (11) 3384010; fax (11) 3381453; Chair. V. K. AGGARWAL.

Zonal Railways

The railways are grouped into 15 zones:

Central: Chhatrapati Shivaji Terminus (Victoria Terminus), Mumbai 400 001; tel. (22) 2621230; telex 1173819; fax (22) 2624555; Gen. Man. K. BALAKESARI.

East Central: Hajipur; tel. (6224) 74728; fax (6224) 74738; f. 1996; Gen. Man. V. D. GUPTA.

East Coast: Bhubaneswar; tel. (674) 440773; fax (674) 440753; f. 1996; Gen. Man. ASHOK KUMAR.

Eastern: 17 Netaji Subhas Rd, Calcutta 700 001; tel. (33) 2206811; fax (33) 2480370; Gen. Man. S. RAMANATHAN.

North Central: Allahabad; tel. and fax (532) 402935; f. 1996; Gen. Man. R. N. MALHOTRA.

North Eastern: Gorakhpur 273 012; tel. (551) 333041; fax (551) 333842; Gen. Man. S. N. PANDEY.

North Western: Jaipur; tel. (141) 360695; fax (141) 200322; Gen. Man. K. B. WARRIGAR.

Northeast Frontier: Maligaon, Guwahati 781 011; tel. (361) 570422; telex 2352336; fax (361) 571124; f. 1958; Gen. Man. SUBHASH MEHTA.

Northern: Baroda House, Kasturba Gandhi Marg, New Delhi 110 001; tel. (11) 3387227; fax (11) 3384503; Gen. Man. SUBHAS P. MEHTA.

South Central: Rail Nilayam, Secunderabad 500 371; tel. (40) 833150; fax (40) 833203; Gen. Man. N. C. SINHA.

South Eastern: Garden Reach Rd, Kidderpore, Calcutta 700 043; tel. (33) 4793532; fax (33) 4974913; Gen. Man. R. N. MALHOTRA.

South Western: Bangalore; tel. (80) 2205773; fax (80) 2282787; f. 1996; Gen. Man. K. BALAKESARI.

Southern: Park Town, Chennai 600 003; tel. (44) 5354141; fax (44) 5357805; Gen. Man. N. KRITHIVASAN.

West Central: Jabalpur; tel. (761) 320052; fax (761) 320280; f. 1996; Gen. Man. K. B. SANKARAN.

Western: Churchgate, Mumbai 400 020; tel. (22) 2038016; fax (22) 2017631; Gen. Man. (vacant).

ROADS

In 1995 the Government announced plans to construct seven new national highways covering almost 13,000 km. In December 1996 there were an estimated 2.06m. km of roads in India, 34,900 km of which were national highways. About 50.2% of the total road network was paved. In January 1997 the World Bank announced that it was to give India a loan of 10,000m. rupees for the repair and construction of national highways throughout the country.

Ministry of Surface Transport (Roads Wing): Transport Bhavan, 1 Parliament St, New Delhi 110 001; tel. (11) 3715159; telex 312448; responsible for the construction and maintenance of India's system of national highways, with a total length of 34,298 km in 1996, connecting the state capitals and major ports and linking with the highway systems of neighbouring countries. This system includes 78 national highways which constitute the main trunk roads of the country.

Border Roads Development Board: f. 1960 to accelerate the economic development of the north and north-eastern border areas; it has constructed and improved 24,553 km of roads and maintains about 16,720 km in the border areas (March 1995).

INLAND WATERWAYS

About 15,655 km of rivers are navigable by power-driven craft, and 3,490 km by large country boats. Services are mainly on the Ganga and Brahmaputra and their tributaries, the Godavari, the Mahanadi, the Narmada, the Tapti and the Krishna.

Central Inland Water Transport Corpn Ltd: 4 Fairlie Place, Calcutta 1; tel. (33) 2202321; telex 212779; fax (33) 4693250; f. 1967; inland water transport services in Bangladesh and the north-east Indian states; also shipbuilding and repairing, general engineering, dredging, lightering of ships and barge services; Chair. and Man. Dir P. P. GANGOPADHYAY.

SHIPPING

In December 1996 India was 14th on the list of principal merchant fleets of the world. At the end of 1996 the fleet had 920 vessels, with a total displacement of 7.13m. grt. There are some 55 shipping companies in India. The major ports are Calcutta, Haldia, Jawaharlal Nehru (at Nhava Sheva near Mumbai), Kandla, Kochi, Chennai, Mormugao, Mumbai, New Mangalore, Paradip (Paradeep), Tuticorin and Visakha (Visakhapatnam).

Calcutta

India Steamship Co Ltd: India Steamship House, 21 Hemanta Basu Sarani, POB 2090, Calcutta 700 001; tel. (33) 2481171; telex 212549; fax (33) 2488133; f. 1928; cargo services; Chair. K. K. BIRLA; Man. Dir L. M. S. RAJWAR; br in Delhi.

Surrendra Overseas Ltd: Apeejay House, 15 Park St, Calcutta 700 016; tel. (33) 2452371; telex 215627; fax (33) 2452372; cargo services; Chair. JIT PAUL.

Chennai (Madras)

South India Shipping Corpn Ltd: Chennai House, 7 Esplanade Rd, POB 234, Chennai 600 108; tel. (44) 5341441; telex 418299; fax (44) 5340948; Chair. J. H. TARAPORE; Man. Dir F. G. DASTUR.

Mumbai (Bombay)

Century Shipping Ltd: 12th Floor, Earnest House, 194 Nariman Point, Mumbai 400 021; tel. (22) 2022734; telex 1185283; fax (22) 2027274; Chair. B. K. BIRLA; Pres. N. M. JAIN.

Chowgule & Co (Pvt) Ltd: Bakhtawar, 3rd Floor, Nariman Point, POB 11596, Mumbai 400 021; tel. (22) 2026822; telex 1182409; fax (22) 2024845; f. 1963; Chair. VISHWASRAO DATTAJI CHOWGULE; Man. Dir SHIVAJIRAO DATTAJI CHOWGULE.

Essar Shipping Ltd: Essar House, 11 Keshavrao Khadye Marg, Mahalaxmi, Mumbai 400 034; tel. (22) 4950606; fax (22) 4950607; Chair. S. N. RUIA.

The Great Eastern Shipping Co Ltd: Ocean House, 81 Dr Dadabmoy Naoroji Rd, Fort, Mumbai 400 001; tel. (22) 2626033; telex 1186196; fax (22) 2626823; f. 1948; cargo services; Chair. and Man. Dir K. M. SHETH; Dep. Chair. S. J. MULJI; br. in New Delhi.

Scindia Steam Navigation Co Ltd: Scindia House, Narottam Morarjee Marg, Ballard Estate, Fort, Mumbai 400 001; tel. (22) 2618162; telex 1180060; fax (22) 2618160; f. 1919; cargo services; Chair. and Man. Dir K. VENUGOPAL.

Shipping Corpn of India Ltd: Shipping House, 245 Madame Cama Rd, Mumbai 400 021; tel. (22) 2026666; telex 1182314; fax (22) 2026905; f. 1961 as a govt undertaking; Chair. and Man. Dir P. K. SRIVASTAVA; brs in Calcutta, New Delhi, Chennai and London.

Tolani Ltd: 10A Bakhtawar, Nariman Point, Mumbai 400 021; tel. (22) 2026878; telex 1182751; fax (22) 2870697; Chair. and Man. Dir Dr N. P. TOLANI.

Varun Shipping Co Ltd: 3rd Floor, Laxmi Bldg, 6 Shoorji Vallabhdas Marg, Ballard Estate, Mumbai 400 001; tel. (22) 2658114; telex 1181008; fax (22) 2621723; f. 1971; Chair. DILIP D. KHATAU; Man. Dir ARUN MEHTA.

CIVIL AVIATION

There are five international airports and more than 100 other airports in India. In early 1995 there were plans to build 12 new airports, and facilities in New Delhi and Mumbai were being upgraded to meet increased demand.

Airports Authority of India: Rajiv Gandhi Bhavan, Safdarjung Airport, New Delhi 110 003; tel. (11) 4632950; telex 3174151; fax (11) 4632990; maintains the international airports; Chair. RANJAN CHATTERJEE.

Air-India: Air-India Bldg, Nariman Point, Mumbai 400 021; tel. (22) 2024142; telex 1178327; fax (22) 2024897; f. 1932 as Tata Airlines; renamed Air-India in 1946; in 1953 became a state corpn responsible for international flights; services to 47 online stations (incl. 2 cargo stations) and 84 offline offices throughout the world; Chair. P. C. SEN; Man. Dir MICHAEL MASCARENHAS.

East West Airlines: 18 New Kantwadi Rd, Bandra, Mumbai 400 050; tel. (22) 6436678; fax (22) 6431724; f. 1992; private co; services to 33 major domestic destinations; Chair. NASIR A. WAHID; Man. Dir (vacant).

Indian Airlines: Airlines House, 113 Gurudwara Rakabganj Rd, New Delhi 110 001; tel. (11) 3718951; telex 3166110; fax (11) 3711730; f. 1953; state corpn responsible for regional and domestic flights; merged with subsidiary, Vayudoot Ltd, in 1993; services to 58 cities throughout India and to 17 destinations in the Middle East and the Far East; Chair. and Man. Dir P. C. SEN.

Jet Airways (India) Ltd: S. M. Centre, Andheri-Kurla Rd, Andheri (East), Mumbai 400 059; tel. (22) 8505080; fax (22) 8501837; Chair. NARESH GOYAL; Exec. Dir SAROJ DATTA.

NEPC Airlines: G.R. Complex, 407 & 408 Anna Salai, Chennai 600 035; tel. (44) 4345538; telex 4123199; fax (44) 4344370; private co; Chair. and Man. Dir RAVI PRAKASH KHEMKA.

NEPC Skylines: UG 26A Somdatt Chambers 1, Bhikaji Cama Place, New Delhi 110 066; fmrly known as Damania Airways; name changed as above in 1995; subsidiary of NEPC Airlines; services to four domestic destinations; Chair. and Man. Dir PARVEZ C. DAMANIA.

Sahara India Airlines: 14 Kasturba Gandhi Marg, New Delhi 110 001; tel. (11) 3325851; fax (11) 3313037; private co; services to four domestic destinations; Man. Dir S. K. ROY.

UP Airways Ltd: A-2 Defence Colony, New Delhi; tel. (11) 4638201; fax (11) 4636584; private co; services to six domestic destinations.

Tourism

The tourist attractions of India include its scenery, its historic forts, palaces and temples, and its rich variety of wild life. Tourist infrastructure has recently been expanded by the provision of more luxury hotels and improved means of transport. In 1996 there were about 2.3m. foreign visitors to India, and revenue from tourism totalled 100,614m. rupees.

Department of Tourism of the Government of India: Ministry of Tourism, Transport Bhavan, Parliament St, New Delhi 110 001; tel. (11) 3717890; telex 3166527; fax (11) 3710518; formulates and administers govt policy for promotion of tourism; plans the organization and development of tourist facilities; operates tourist information offices in India and overseas; Dir-Gen. ASHOK PAHWA.

India Tourism Development Corpn Ltd: SCOPE Complex, Core 8, 6th Floor, 7 Lodi Rd, New Delhi 110 003; tel. (11) 4360303; telex 3174074; fax (11) 4360233; f. 1966; operates Ashok Group of hotels (largest hotel chain owner), resort accommodation, tourist transport services, duty-free shops and a travel agency and provides consultancy and management services; Chair. and Man. Dir ASHOK PRADHAN.

INDONESIA

Introductory Survey

Location, Climate, Language, Religion, Flag, Capital

The Republic of Indonesia consists of a group of about 17,500 islands (including rocks, reefs, sandbanks, etc.), lying between the mainland of South-East Asia and Australia. The archipelago is the largest in the world, and it stretches from the Malay peninsula to New Guinea. The principal islands are Java, Sumatra, Kalimantan (comprising more than two-thirds of the island of Borneo), Celebes (Sulawesi), Irian Jaya (West New Guinea), the Moluccas (Maluku) and Timor. Indonesia's only land frontiers are with Papua New Guinea, to the east of Irian Jaya, and with the Malaysian states of Sarawak and Sabah, which occupy northern Borneo. The climate is tropical, with an average annual temperature of 26°C (79°F) and heavy rainfall during most seasons. Rainfall averages 706 mm (28 ins) annually in Indonesia, although there are large variations throughout the archipelago; the heaviest annual rainfall (2,286 mm or 90 ins) is along the equatorial rain belt, which passes through Sumatra, Borneo and Celebes. The official language is Bahasa Indonesia (a form of Malay); there are an estimated 583 other languages and dialects spoken in the archipelago, including Javanese, Sundanese, Arabic and Chinese. An estimated 88% of the inhabitants profess adherence to Islam. About 10% of the population are Christians, while most of the remainder are either Hindus or Buddhists. The national flag (proportions 3 by 2) has two equal horizontal stripes, of red and white. The capital is Jakarta, on the island of Java.

Recent History

Indonesia was formerly the Netherlands East Indies, except for the former Portuguese colony of East Timor (see below). Dutch occupation began in the 17th century and gradually extended over the whole archipelago. Nationalist opposition to colonial rule began in the early 20th century. During the Second World War the territory was occupied by Japanese forces from March 1942. On 17 August 1945, three days after the Japanese surrender, a group of nationalists proclaimed the independence of Indonesia. The first President of the self-proclaimed republic was Dr Sukarno, a leader of the nationalist movement since the 1920s. The declaration of independence was not recognized by the Netherlands, which attempted to restore its pre-war control of the islands. After four years of intermittent warfare and negotiations between the Dutch authorities and the nationalists, agreement was reached on a formal transfer of power. On 27 December 1949 the United States of Indonesia became legally independent, with Sukarno continuing as President. Initially, the country had a federal Constitution which gave limited self-government to the 16 constituent regions. In August 1950, however, the federation was dissolved and the country became the unitary Republic of Indonesia. The 1949 independence agreement excluded West New Guinea (now Irian Jaya), which remained under Dutch control until October 1962; following a brief period of UN administration, however, it was transferred to Indonesia in May 1963.

Sukarno followed a policy of extreme nationalism, and his regime became increasingly dictatorial. His foreign policy was sympathetic to the People's Republic of China but, under his rule, Indonesia also played a leading role in the Non-aligned Movement (see p. 271). Inflation and widespread corruption eventually provoked opposition to Sukarno's regime; in September–October 1965 there was an abortive military coup, in which the Partai Komunis Indonesia (PKI—Indonesian Communist Party) was strongly implicated. A mass slaughter of alleged PKI members and supporters ensued. In March 1966 Sukarno was forced to transfer emergency executive powers to military commanders, led by Gen. Suharto, Chief of Staff of the Army, who outlawed the PKI. In February 1967 Sukarno transferred full power to Suharto. In March the Majelis Permusyawaratan Rakyat (MPR—People's Consultative Assembly) removed Sukarno from office and named Suharto acting President. He became Prime Minister in October 1967 and, following his election by the MPR, he was inaugurated as President in March 1968. In July 1971, in the first general election since 1955, the government-sponsored Sekretariat Bersama Golongan Karya (Joint Secretariat of Functional Groups), known as Golkar, won a majority of seats in the Dewan Perwakilan Rakyat (Dewan—House of Representatives). Suharto was re-elected to the presidency in March 1973.

Under Suharto's 'New Order', real power passed from the legislature and the Cabinet to a small group of army officers and to the Operation Command for the Restoration of Order and Security (Kopkamtib), the internal security organization. Left-wing movements were suppressed, and a liberal economic policy adopted. A general election in May 1977 gave Golkar a majority in the legislature, and Suharto was re-elected President (unopposed) in March 1978. Despite criticism of the Government (most notably a petition signed by 50 prominent citizens in 1980), Golkar won an increased majority in the elections in May 1982, although the campaign was marred by considerable violence. In March 1983 Suharto was re-elected, again unopposed, as President.

During 1984 Suharto's attempt to introduce legislation requiring all political, social and religious organizations to adopt *pancasila,* the five-point state philosophy (belief in a supreme being; humanitarianism; national unity; democracy by consensus; social justice), as their only ideology encountered opposition, particularly from the Petition of 50 (the signatories of the 1980 protest). Serious rioting and a series of bombings and arson attempts in and around Jakarta were allegedly instigated by Muslim opponents of the proposed legislation, and many Muslims were tried and sentenced to long terms of imprisonment. A law concerning mass organizations was enacted in June 1985, and all the political parties had accepted Pancasila by July. At the April 1987 general election, despite persistent international allegations of corruption and of abuses of human rights, particularly in East Timor (see below), Golkar won 299 of the 500 seats in the Dewan. Moreover, for the first time, the party achieved an overall majority of seats in each of Indonesia's 27 provinces.

In February 1988 new legislation reaffirmed the 'dual (i.e. military and socio-economic) function' of the Indonesian Armed Forces (ABRI). Shortly afterwards, Gen. Try Sutrisno (hitherto Chief of Staff of the Army) replaced Gen. L. B. (Benny) Murdani as Commander-in-Chief of the Armed Forces. In March Suharto was again re-elected unopposed as President. At the subsequent vice-presidential election, in a departure from previous procedure, Suharto did not recommend a candidate, but encouraged the MPR to choose one. However, Lt-Gen. (retd) Sudharmono, the Chairman of Golkar, and Dr Jailani Naro, the leader of the Partai Persatuan Pembangunan (PPP—United Development Party), were both nominated for the post, and Gen. Suharto was obliged to indicate his preference for Sudharmono before Naro withdrew his candidacy and Sudharmono was elected unopposed. ABRI disapproved of Sudharmono's appointment as, under his chairmanship of Golkar, there had been a shift away from military dominance in the grouping and he was suspected of having left-wing sympathies. In October Sudharmono resigned as Chairman of Golkar and was replaced by Gen. (retd) Wahono, who was acceptable both to ABRI and the developing bureaucratic élite.

In early 1989 tension arising from land disputes produced social unrest in three areas of Java and on the island of Sumbawa (east of Bali and Lombok), in Nusa Tenggara. The most serious incident took place in February in southern Sumatra, where between 30 and 100 people were killed as a result of clashes between the armed forces and dissenting villagers. The first student demonstrations since 1978 were held to protest against the Government's expropriation of land without sufficient indemnification for those subject to relocation. The armed forces did not attempt to suppress the student protests. This implicit criticism of the regime and discussions about democratization and reform had been encouraged by speculation over Suharto's successor, which had begun as a result of comments made by Suharto in the previous April. In early May 1989, however, Suharto warned officials to dismiss the topic of the succession and in September, when the Partai Demokrasi Indonesia (PDI—Indonesian Democratic Party) announced that it would support his candidacy, it appeared likely that he would seek election for a sixth term. In August 1990 a group of 58 prominent Indonesians, comprising many of the original Petition of 50, issued a public demand to Suharto to retire from the presidency at the end of his current term of office and to permit greater democracy in Indonesia.

During 1991, in response to the growing demand for political *keterbukaan* (openness), several new organizations were formed to promote freedom of expression and other democratic values. In late 1991 this assertiveness by political groupings was paralleled by a climate of labour unrest. During this period, arrests and the alleged intimidation of activists were instrumental in curbing expressions of dissent. In an attempt to control student unrest, political campaigns were banned on university campuses. In September Suharto removed several of the most outspoken members of Golkar from the list of candidates to contest the legislative elections, scheduled to take place on 9 June 1992.

The Government had, for some time, been seeking to win the support of the Muslim electorate in preparation for the presidential elections in 1993. In 1989 Suharto promoted legislation whereby decisions by Islamic courts no longer required confirmation by civil courts, and in December 1990 the President opened the symposium of the newly-formed Association of Indonesian Muslim Intellectuals (ICMI), an organization which united a broad spectrum of Islamic interests. In 1991 Suharto made his first pilgrimage to Mecca, acceded to Islamic demands for certain educational reforms and supported the establishment of an Islamic bank. ABRI was opposed to the establishment of ICMI because it regarded the polarization of politics by religion as a threat to stability. During 1990 the nature of ABRI's dual function had been queried from within the armed forces, with some support evinced for a lessening of its political role. However, pressure from ABRI was widely believed to have led to Suharto's gestures towards democratization.

In March 1992 Indonesia's largest Islamic organization, Nahdlatul Ulama (Council of Scholars), held the first large rally of its kind in Indonesia since 1966. Attendance at the gathering (which was ostensibly organized in support of the Constitution and the state ideology but was effectively a display of support for the organization) was limited to 200,000 by the Government. In February and April, however, meetings of the Democratic Forum (also led by the Chairman of Nahdlatul Ulama, Abdurrahman Wahid) were banned.

During the strictly-monitored four-week campaign period leading to elections for the Dewan, for local government bodies and for district councils, political parties were prohibited from addressing religious issues, the question of the dominant role of the ethnic Chinese community in the economy, or any subject that might present a threat to national unity. The opposition parties did, however, exploit the increasing public resentment about the rapidly-expanding businesses of Suharto's children (some of whom had been awarded monopoly rights, which hindered economic development). The Forum for the Purification of People's Sovereignty (formed in 1991) urged the voters to boycott the elections, in an effort to elicit reforms from the Government, and also criticized the extent of the President's powers. Members of the Petition of 50 also refused to vote.

On 9 June 1992 90.4% of the electorate participated in the election to the Dewan, which resulted in a further victory for Golkar (although its share of the votes declined to 68%, compared with 73% in 1987). Golkar secured 282 of the 400 elective seats, while 62 seats were won by the PPP (a gain of one seat compared with 1987) and 56 seats (compared with 40) by the PDI, which had mobilized almost 3m. supporters at a rally in Jakarta in the week prior to the election.

In October 1992 Suharto accepted nominations by Golkar, the PPP, the PDI and ABRI for a sixth term of office as President. His victory in the presidential election, due to take place in March 1993, was thus assured. Public attention then focused on the vice-presidency. Owing to the increasing public debate over ABRI's active involvement in political affairs and, in particular, concern over whether the appointment of 100 members of ABRI to the Dewan remained justifiable, it was deemed important that ABRI consolidate its position through the election to the vice-presidency of its own principal candidate, Sutrisno. Suharto, however, was rumoured to support the prospective candidacy of the Minister of State for Research and Technology, Prof. Dr Ir Bucharuddin Jusuf (B. J.) Habibie, an influential Muslim leader and the Chairman of ICMI. Other prominent contenders included Gen. Rudini (the Minister of Home Affairs) and Maj.-Gen. Wismoyo Arismunandar (the Commander of the Strategic Reserve Command—Kostrad—and Suharto's brother-in-law). In a manifestation of greater political openness, the merits of the prospective candidates were discussed in the local press. Sutrisno was subsequently endorsed as a vice-presidential candidate by the PDI, the PPP, ABRI and, finally, Golkar. At a meeting of the MPR on 10 and 11 March Suharto and Sutrisno were duly elected to the posts of President and Vice-President respectively.

Suharto's new Government, which was announced in mid-March 1993, comprised 22 new appointees in the 41-member Cabinet. ABRI representation was reduced from 11 to eight members and the influential Rudini and Murdani were excluded from the Cabinet. Those primarily responsible for the country's economic policy since 1988, Prof. Dr Johannes B. Sumarlin, Adrianus Mooy and Radius Prawiro (all western-educated Christians) were replaced, leaving only three Christians in the Cabinet; several members of ICMI were included in the new list, thus advancing the faction led by Habibie, who was unpopular with ABRI, partly owing to his interference in arms purchases. Suharto announced that the new Government would pursue the aim of greater democracy and openness; the immigration blacklist was swiftly reduced from 17,000 names to less than 9,000. In mid-1993 Suharto met a prominent member of the Petition of 50, revoked a travel ban on all dissidents and established a National Council on Human Rights.

In October 1993 at the party Congress the Minister of Information, Harmoko, became the first civilian to be elected to the chairmanship of Golkar. In an unprecedented move Suharto had openly endorsed Harmoko's candidacy; it was widely speculated that this was to prevent ABRI from supporting its own candidate and effectively denying the President a choice, as was the case in the election of Sutrisno to the vice-presidency. Also at the Congress Suharto's family entered active national politics; his son, Bambang Trihatmodjo, and daughter, Siti Hardijanti Rukmana (known as Mbak Tutut), who had both been appointed to the MPR in 1992, were elected to positions of responsibility within Golkar.

In July 1993 the incumbent Chairman of the PDI, Soerjadi, was re-elected to the post at a fractious party Congress. The Government invalidated the election of Soerjadi, who had incurred Suharto's displeasure by campaigning during the June 1992 elections for a limited presidential term of office, and appointed a 23-member 'caretaker board' pending new elections. An extraordinary Congress of the PDI ended inconclusively in early December owing to the unexpected candidacy for the chairmanship of Megawati Sukarnoputri, the daughter of former President Sukarno. Despite government pressure to elect Budi Hardjono, a senior party official, Megawati received overwhelming support from the participants of the Congress. The 'caretaker board' prevented a vote from taking place and the PDI delegates were dispersed at midnight as the government-issued licence to hold a congress expired. Later that month, amid accusations of official interference, the Government ordered the holding of a new PDI Congress, at which Megawati was elected Chairman.

In June 1993 the USA imposed a deadline of February 1994 for Indonesia to improve workers' rights or lose trade privileges under the Generalized System of Preferences. In an attempt to avoid sanctions, the Government adopted reforms to the only officially recognized trade union, the Serikat Pekerja Seluruh Indonesia (All Indonesia Workers' Union), introduced a substantial increase in the minimum wage and revoked the controversial 1986 Labour Law which allowed the intervention of the armed forces in labour disputes. Indonesia suffered a subsequent increase in industrial unrest as workers went on strike accusing employers of failing to pay the new minimum wage and demanding improved working conditions. In February 1994 the independent Serikat Buruh Sejahtera Indonesia (SBSI—Indonesian Prosperous Labour Union), which had had its application for registration formally rejected in June 1993, appealed for a one-hour national work stoppage. Two days prior to the strike the General Secretary of the SBSI, Muchtar Pakpahan, was arrested and charged with inciting hatred against the Government (although he was released in the following month). In April 1994 riots broke out in Medan, Sumatra, over workers' demands for improved factory conditions and the implementation of the new minimum wage, and rapidly degenerated into attacks on Chinese property and business executives. The attacks on Chinese companies reflected a widely-held perception that the ethnic Chinese had benefited disproportionately from the country's rapid economic growth. Three members of the

SBSI surrendered to the authorities in May and admitted to having organized the protest. Further strikes broke out later in the month in other parts of north Sumatra. In August Pakpahan was rearrested. He was given a three-year prison sentence in November for inciting labour unrest (which was later extended to four years). By that time, it was estimated that the majority of factories had complied with the provision of the new minimum wage.

In January 1995 it was announced by the armed forces that 300 members of the PDI were to be investigated for links to the 1965 coup attempt, following allegations that many members had relatives or contacts in the banned PKI. This apparent attempt to discredit the opposition grouping was followed in May by a ban on the presence of Megawati at the commemoration, in June, of the 25th anniversary of the death of her father, Sukarno, ostensibly because it might provoke outbreaks of violence but more probably because the occasion might have fostered support for the PDI.

Throughout 1995 the Indonesian authorities attempted to ascribe social unrest to communist subversion, asserting that a communist revival remained a threat to national security. In September the Chief of Staff of the Armed Forces named several prominent dissidents, including Muchtar Pakpahan (whose conviction for incitement had been overturned by the Supreme Court in that month), as members of 'formless organizations,' which, he claimed, infiltrated pressure groups to promote the resurgence of communism. In November 300 people were arrested in Java as subversives, who were allegedly using the tactics of the PKI.

In July 1995, in response to widespread condemnation of Indonesia's human rights violations, Suharto announced that three prisoners detained for their complicity in the 1965 coup attempt would be released to coincide with the 50th anniversary of independence in August. The administration also subsequently announced that the code ET (which stood for *Eks Tahanan Politik* — former political prisoner) was to be removed from identity papers following the anniversary. The measure affected about 1.3m. citizens, most of whom had been arrested following the 1965 coup attempt, but released without trial; ET status had subjected them to certain restrictions (for example, in employment) and to widespread discrimination. The Government also revoked legislation requiring a permit for political gatherings, although the security forces still had to be notified. This display of liberality was, however, tempered by a new campaign against press freedom and political dissent.

In October 1995 30 members of an extreme right-wing group, the Islamic State of Indonesia, were arrested in western Java for attempting to overthrow 'the unitary state of Indonesia'. There were fears that Suharto's apparent attempt to balance the influence of the armed forces with an emphasis on Islam would create religious disharmony. Critics blamed the ICMI-sponsored newspaper *Republika* and its magazine *Ummat* for fomenting religious passions, leading to outbreaks of violence. Social unrest was also caused, however, by a disparity in living standards; in January 1996 in Bandung, West Java, thousands took part in demonstrations against the disproportionately wealthy ethnic Chinese.

In December 1995 Suharto implemented an unprecedented mid-term cabinet reorganization, in which Prof. Dr Satrio Budiardjo Yudono was dismissed and the Ministry of Trade, over which he had presided, was merged with the Ministry of Industry. This dismissal of one of Habibie's protégés, the day before Habibie's re-election to the chairmanship of the increasingly powerful ICMI, was widely interpreted as a signal from Suharto for Habibie to restrain his political ambitions. The accusations of financial irregularities and nepotism levelled against the Minister of Communications, Haryanto Dhanutirto (also a close associate of Habibie), were similarly interpreted.

In early 1996 there were limited moves to create greater political freedom. In January the Government abolished permit requirements for political meetings (police permission was still necessary for public gatherings and demonstrations). In March a group of political activists established an Independent Election Monitoring Committee, which was immediately declared unconstitutional by the Government. In April the Government restored voting rights to 1,157,820 people who had been associated with the PKI, leaving a further 20,706 still ineligible to vote. The Government's increasing concern over potential opposition to Golkar in the 1997 elections, however, resulted in a return to more authoritarian practices. In May 1996 Sri Bintang Pamungkas, an outspoken member of the PPP expelled from the Dewan in March 1995, received a custodial sentence of 34 months for insulting Suharto; he remained free, however, pending an appeal. In the same month Pamungkas formed a new political organization, the Partai Uni Demokrasi Indonesia (PUDI—United Democratic Party of Indonesia), which ABRI and the Government refused to recognize. In December the High Court upheld the verdict against Pamungkas, who subsequently appealed to the Supreme Court.

In June 1996 the Government responded to the increasing popularity of Megawati's leadership of the PDI, and consequent potential threat to Golkar: government supporters within the PDI organized a party congress in the northern Sumatran town of Medan, which removed Megawati as leader of the party, and installed a former Chairman, Soerjadi. PDI members loyal to Megawati (who contested the legitimacy of the congress) organized demonstrations in her support throughout the country during July, and occupied the PDI headquarters in Jakarta. At the end of July members of Soerjadi's PDI faction and the armed forces acted to remove Megawati and her supporters forcibly from the PDI headquarters, prompting mass rioting in Jakarta. Violent clashes ensued between protesters and the security forces, in which five people were killed, 149 injured and 23 accounted missing, according to an official report (although the PDI claimed that the actual figures were higher). Sporadic rioting continued in the following days, during which security forces were instructed to shoot demonstrators on sight. Following the riots, the Government declared the minor, Marxist-influenced Partai Rakyat Demokrasi (PRD) to be responsible for the disturbances, and renewed its campaign against communism, claiming that the PRD was the PKI's successor. Among those arrested in connection with the riots were Budiman Sujatmiko, the Chairman of the PRD, and the trade union leader, Muchtar Pakpahan, whose trials commenced in December. In April 1997 Sujatmiko was convicted of subversion and sentenced to three years' imprisonment. Sujatmiko announced that he and four other PRD members who were also given custodial sentences would appeal against the verdict. In September the Government disbanded the PRD, declaring it to be a proscribed organization.

In an attempt to inhibit opposition efforts in the 1997 legislative elections, Suharto, in October 1996, ordered ABRI to suppress all political dissent. The Government's continued lack of commitment to its stated policy of political openness was demonstrated when, in November, it declared that it would take action against non-governmental organizations which violated Indonesian law and the *pancasila* ideology. In December the Dewan ratified legislation granting the Government extensive powers to revoke the broadcasting permits of private television and radio stations. In the same month a government decree banned mass rallies during the 1997 election campaign. In February 1997 the Government announced that all election campaign speeches, including those broadcast on television and radio, were to be vetted to ensure their adherence to the *pancasila*.

Repressive measures against Megawati's faction of the PDI continued; in September 1996 the Government declared Megawati's new party headquarters in eastern Jakarta to be illegal and it was closed by the military. Candidates nominated by Megawati's faction for the 1997 parliamentary elections were omitted from the final list of candidates in January 1997. In April thousands of supporters of Megawati rallied outside the Dewan to demand the right to contest the general election. In March Pamungkas was arrested for promoting a boycott of the legislative elections and two PUDI officials were also detained.

Prior to the general election, which was held on 29 May 1997, the Government permitted a campaign period of 25 days during which no two parties were permitted to campaign simultaneously in the same region. Despite these precautions and a heavy security presence, there was extensive localized pre-election violence. In the worst incident 125 people were killed when a shopping centre was set alight during clashes between supporters of Golkar and the PPP in the provincial capital of Kalimantan, Banjarmasin; more than 150 others were killed in various other incidents across the country. Following the election, riots in Madura, as a result of PPP claims that ballots had not been counted, resulted in an unprecedented repeat of voting at 86 polling stations on 4 June. The final results of the election, which continued to attract allegations of electoral fraud, revealed that Golkar had secured 74.3% of the vote (compared with 68.1% in 1992) giving it control of 325 seats, the PPP had won 89 seats while Soerjadi's PDI had secured only 11 seats (compared with 56 in 1992).

Social unrest, which had been widespread in 1996, continued throughout 1997, as a result of religious tension, income disparity between social and ethnic groups and the repercussions of the transmigration programme initiated in 1971. The worst violence began in West Kalimantan in December 1996 as indigenous Dayak tribesmen massacred hundreds of Madurese transmigrants following an attack by Muslim youths on local school girls. Despite a peace agreement in February 1997 fighting continued into March and thousands were displaced as they sought refuge from the attacks. In September six people died and there was extensive damage to property in two days of rioting which took place in Ujung Pandang, South Sulawesi, following the murder of a Muslim girl by an ethnic Chinese youth.

In June 1997 Harmoko was replaced as Minister of Information by the retiring Army Chief of Staff Gen. Raden Hartono and allocated a newly-created special affairs portfolio. In October Harmoko was also elected Speaker of the Dewan. Gen. Wiranto, the head of Kostrad, was appointed Army Chief of Staff and subsequently replaced Gen. Feisal as Commander-in-Chief of the Armed Forces in February 1998. Following four such military reorganizations in 1996, an extensive military reorganization took place in August 1997 in which commanders regarded as loyal to Suharto gained promotions.

In August 1997 the two principal Muslim leaders, Abdurrahman Wahid and Amien Rais, the leader of the second largest Islamic grouping, Muhammadiyah, were excluded from the list of 500 civilian and military appointees to the MPR. Amien Rais had been forced to resign from a board of experts in ICMI in February for publicly criticizing the controversial Freeport mine in Irian Jaya (see below).

Following a massive decline in the value of the Indonesian currency between August and October 1997, Suharto was forced to accept a rescue package from the International Monetary Fund (IMF) to restore confidence in the country's economy. However, Suharto subsequently failed to implement reforms required by the IMF that he feared would provoke social and political unrest and adversely affect his family and friends, who had long benefited from control of lucrative monopolies and tariff protection of their businesses. In December widespread rumours of Suharto's ill health provoked a further crisis of confidence in the Indonesian economy owing to continuing uncertainty concerning the succession to the presidency. At the end of the month an unprecedented gathering of Muslim leaders and intellectuals took place, including members of ICMI; the participants rejected Suharto's leadership and rallied around Amien Rais, who had already offered himself as a presidential candidate. Wahid, although absent from the meeting, subsequently joined Amien and Megawati (who had entered an informal alliance) in calling for Suharto's resignation. Megawati also, in a largely symbolic gesture since the President has to be a nominee of a party represented in the MPR, presented herself as a presidential candidate. In January 1998 Suharto, who was subject to unprecedented criticism for his mishandling of the economy and tolerance of corruption, delivered an unrealistic budget which failed to comply with IMF stipulations. A further rapid decline of the currency and massive price increases of staple foodstuffs ensued, causing incidents of rioting and then widespread buying and hoarding of basic commodities. Following meetings with foreign leaders and IMF representatives, Suharto was forced to announce a second budget in which he agreed to measures which, if implemented, would seriously harm the interests of his family and friends. At the end of January, however, despite opposition to his candidacy, Suharto declared his acceptance of Golkar's nomination for the presidency (announced in October) thus assuring his victory in the presidential election scheduled to be held on 10 March 1998. He indicated that of the 13 contenders for the vice-presidency he would support Habibie's candidacy, despite the minister's unpopularity with ABRI and his reputation for extravagant expenditure on high-technology projects. His failure to formally endorse a successor, however, continued to exacerbate political and economic turmoil.

At the presidential election (held, as scheduled, on 10 March 1998) Suharto was re-elected unopposed. Following his re-election, Suharto endorsed the nomination of Habibie as the new Vice-President.

In 1975 Portugal withdrew from its colony of East Timor. The territory's capital, Dili, was occupied by the forces of the left-wing Frente Revolucionária do Timor Leste Independente (Fretilin), which advocated independence for East Timor. To prevent Fretilin from gaining full control, Indonesian troops intervened and established a provisional government. In July 1976 East Timor was made the 27th province of Indonesia. Human rights organizations claim that as many as 200,000 people, from a total population of 650,000, may have been killed by the Indonesian armed forces during the annexation. In February 1983 the UN Commission on Human Rights adopted a resolution affirming East Timor's right to independence and self-determination, and in early 1998 the UN continued to withhold recognition of Indonesia's absorption of the territory. In September 1983, following a five-month cease-fire (during which government representatives negotiated with Fretilin), the armed forces launched a major new offensive. During 1984 conditions in East Timor deteriorated, with widespread hunger, disease and repression among civilians, and continuing battles between rebels and Indonesian troops. The rebels suffered a serious set-back in August 1985, when the Australian Government recognized Indonesia's incorporation of East Timor. In November 1988 Suharto visited East Timor, prior to announcing that travel restrictions (in force since the annexation in 1976) were to be withdrawn. The territory was opened to visitors in late December. In October 1989 the Pope visited East Timor, as part of a tour of Indonesia, and made a plea to the Government to halt violations of human rights. Following a mass conducted by the Pope in the provincial capital, Dili, anti-Government protesters clashed with security guards. In January 1990 a visit to East Timor by the US Ambassador to Indonesia prompted further protest demonstrations, which were violently suppressed by the armed forces. In October student protests led to the occupation of two schools by the armed forces and to the arrest, and alleged torture, of nearly 100 students. In November the Government rejected proposals by the military commander of Fretilin, José Alexandre (Xanana) Gusmão, for unconditional peace negotiations aimed at ending the armed struggle in East Timor.

In 1991 tension in East Timor increased in the run-up to a proposed visit by a Portuguese parliamentary delegation. Some Timorese alleged that the armed forces had initiated a campaign of intimidation to discourage demonstrations during the Portuguese visit. The mission, which was to have taken place in November, was postponed, owing to Indonesia's objection to the inclusion of an Australian journalist who was a prominent critic of Indonesia's policies in East Timor. In November the armed forces fired on a peaceful demonstration (believed to have been originally organized to coincide with the Portuguese visit) at the funeral of a separatist sympathizer in Dili. ABRI, which admitted killing 20 civilians, claimed that the attack was provoked by armed Fretilin activists. Independent observers and human rights groups refuted this and estimated the number of deaths at between 100 and 180. There were also subsequent allegations of the summary execution of as many as 100 witnesses. Under intense international pressure, Suharto established a National Investigation Commission. The impartiality of the Commission was challenged, however, on the grounds that it excluded non-governmental organizations, and Fretilin announced that it would boycott the investigation. Despite this, the Commission's findings received cautious foreign approbation, as they were mildly critical of ABRI and stated that 50 people had died, and 90 disappeared, in the massacre. The senior military officers in East Timor were replaced, and 14 members of the armed forces were tried by a military tribunal. The most severe penalty received by any of the soldiers involved was 18 months' imprisonment; this contrasted starkly with the sentences of convicted demonstrators, which ranged from five years' to life imprisonment.

In July 1992 Indonesia and Portugal agreed to resume discussions on East Timor under the auspices of the UN Secretary-General (although without a representative from Fretilin, which had indicated in May that it was prepared to take part in the negotiations). In August the UN General Assembly adopted its first resolution condemning Indonesia's violations of fundamental human rights in East Timor. In September the appointment of Abilio Soares as Governor of East Timor provoked widespread criticism in the province; although Soares was a native of East Timor, he was a leading advocate of the Indonesian occupation. In October the US Congress suspended defence training aid to Indonesia, in protest at the killing of separatist demonstrators in November 1991. In October 1992, prior to the anniversary of the massacre, Amnesty International reported that hundreds of suspected supporters of independence had been arrested and tortured to prevent a commemorative demonstration.

In late November 1992 Xanana Gusmão was arrested. He was subsequently taken to Jakarta, where he was to be tried in February 1993 on charges of subversion and illegal possession of firearms. Xanana Gusmão's detention provoked international concern, and his replacement as leader of Fretilin, António Gomes da Costa (Mau Huno—who was himself arrested in April), claimed that his predecessor had been tortured. Two weeks after his capture, Xanana Gusmão publicly recanted his opposition to Indonesian rule in East Timor and advised Fretilin members to surrender. It transpired, however, that he was only co-operating with the authorities in order to gain the opportunity to speak publicly at a later date. During his trial, he was prevented from reading a prepared statement; the document was, however, illicitly conveyed to the press and was widely disseminated. In May Xanana Gusmão was found guilty of rebellion, conspiracy, attempting to establish a separate state and illegal possession of arms, and was condemned to life imprisonment. The sentence was commuted to 20 years by Suharto in August. During the same month it was announced that all government combat forces were to be withdrawn from East Timor, leaving only troops involved in development projects. In September, however, the new acting leader of Fretilin, Konis Santana, declared that, contrary to announcements, the Indonesians were renewing their forces in East Timor and that killings and atrocities continued.

In December 1993 Xanana Gusmão managed to convey letters to the Portuguese Government and the International Commission of Jurists (see p. 275) demanding an annulment of his trial owing to the lack of impartiality of his defence lawyer. The Government subsequently banned Xanana Gusmão from receiving visitors. Also in December the first reconciliation talks took place in the United Kingdom between an Indonesian government official and a former leader of Timorese exiles opposed to Indonesia's occupation of East Timor. In January 1994 Indonesia announced to the UN Secretary-General's envoy that it would facilitate access to East Timor by human rights and UN organizations. In late May, however, a privately-organized human rights conference being held in the Philippines, entitled the Asia-Pacific Conference on East Timor, provoked diplomatic tension with the Indonesian Government, which had attempted to force the abandonment of the conference. The outcome of the conference was the establishment of an Asia-Pacific coalition on East Timor, which consisted mainly of non-governmental organizations active in the region.

In July 1994 the Indonesian authorities suppressed a demonstration in Dili, following weeks of increasing tension in the capital; at least three people were reportedly killed and an estimated 20 injured during the protest. In August it was reported that the armed forces had held talks with Xanana Gusmão, included in which was the possibility of holding a referendum under the auspices of the UN to determine the status of the disputed territory. A second round of reconciliation talks between Indonesian officials and East Timorese exiles was held between late September and early October in the United Kingdom, and was attended by a UN envoy, although the main East Timorese opposition groups opposed the discussions on the grounds that the participating East Timorese exiles were mostly in favour of Indonesian rule. The Indonesian Minister of Foreign Affairs, Ali Alatas, also held talks in October in New York, in the USA, with José Ramos Horta, the Secretary for International Relations of Fretilin, the first such talks to be officially recognized. At the beginning of November President Suharto agreed to hold talks with exiled East Timorese dissidents. The Government's increasingly conciliatory position on East Timor was, however, reported largely to be a superficial attempt to improve the country's human rights image prior to the holding of the Asia-Pacific Economic Co-operation (APEC—see p. 108) summit in Bogor, 60 km south of Jakarta, in mid-November. On 12 November, the third anniversary of the Dili massacre in 1991, 29 East Timorese protesters began an occupation of the US embassy in Jakarta, which coincided with the attendance of the US President, Bill Clinton, at the summit. The students demanded, unsuccessfully, a meeting with the visiting US Secretary of State and the release of Xanana Gusmão. They were eventually granted political asylum in Portugal and were shortly afterwards allowed by the Indonesian authorities to leave the embassy compound. Also in November riots involving more than 1,000 demonstrators broke out in Dili as delegates began arriving in Jakarta for the opening of the APEC summit. Further disturbances later in the month were blamed by the authorities on incitement by the Western media.

In January 1995 Alatas, the Portuguese Minister of Foreign Affairs and the UN Secretary-General met in Geneva, Switzerland, for the fifth round of talks on East Timor. Agreement was reached to convene a meeting between separatist and pro-integrationist Timorese activists under the auspices of the UN, called the All-Inclusive Intra-East Timorese Dialogue (AETD). The AETD, which was held in June 1995, March 1996 and October 1997, failed to achieve any conclusive progress. The sixth and seventh rounds of talks between the Portuguese and Indonesian ministers responsible for foreign affairs took place in July 1995 and January 1996, with little progress.

In September 1995 the worst rioting that year took place in protest against Indonesian Muslim immigrants, following an Indonesian prison official's alleged insult to Roman Catholicism. Mosques and Muslim businesses were burned, and some Muslims were forced to flee the island. Further riots erupted in October, in which rival groups of separatists and integrationists clashed on the streets. The Roman Catholic Apostolic Administrator in Dili, the Rt Rev. Carlos Filipe Ximines Belo, persuaded the rioters to return home following an agreement with ABRI; however, the agreement was subsequently broken by the armed forces, who arrested more than 250 alleged rioters. In November the fourth anniversary of the Dili massacre passed without incident, owing to unprecedentedly high security.

From September 1995 East Timorese activists began forcing entry into foreign embassies in Jakarta and appealing for political asylum. They were granted asylum by the Portuguese, who were still officially recognized by the UN as the administrative power in East Timor. The Indonesian Government permitted the asylum-seekers to leave, but denied that there was any persecution in East Timor. The culmination of the successful campaign was the storming in December of the Dutch and Russian embassies by 58 and 47 activists respectively. The demonstrators, some of whom were non-Timorese and belonged to a radical group called the People's Democratic Union, demanded unsuccessfully a meeting with the UN High Commissioner for Human Rights, José Ayala Lasso, who was visiting Indonesia and who, following a brief visit to East Timor, confirmed the occurrence of severe violations of human rights in the province. In 1996 several further groups of East Timorese sought asylum in foreign embassies; the majority of these were successful.

In February 1996 President Suharto and the Portuguese Prime Minister met in Bangkok (the first meeting on East Timor by heads of government). During the negotiations Portugal offered to re-establish diplomatic links in return for the release of Xanana Gusmão and the guarantee of human rights in East Timor. International awareness of East Timor was heightened in October, when Belo and José Ramos Horta were jointly awarded the Nobel Prize for Peace. The Indonesian Government, displeased with the Nobel committee's choice, declared that there would be no change in its policy on East Timor. Four days after the announcement of the award, Suharto visited East Timor for the first time for eight years; during the visit he inaugurated a statue of Christ as a symbol of reconciliation.

Following the announcement of the Nobel Peace Prize, Belo repeated demands that the Government conduct a referendum on autonomy in East Timor. In November 1996 he became involved in a controversy regarding an interview that he had given to a German periodical, *Der Spiegel*, which quoted several controversial remarks, allegedly made by Belo, about the treatment of the East Timorese people by the Indonesian Government and ABRI. Belo denied having made the remarks, but was requested to appear before a parliamentary commission in Jakarta to explain the matter. This controversy, and the temporary confiscation of Belo's passport by the Indonesian authorities (which threatened to prevent Belo's visit to Norway to receive the Nobel award), prompted five days of demonstrations in his support in Dili. The rallies were reportedly the largest since 1975, but were conducted peacefully.

The award of the Nobel Peace Prize to José Ramos Horta proved even more controversial. The Governor of East Timor accused Horta of ordering the torture and killing of East Timorese people. Horta himself declared that the award should have been made to Xanana Gusmão and invited the Indonesian Government to enter into serious negotiations on the future of East Timor. Horta was banned from visiting the Philippines for the duration of an APEC summit meeting which took place there in late 1996; this ban was subsequently extended.

In November 1996 the Indonesian Government withdrew permission for foreign journalists to visit East Timor, where they had planned to attend a press conference conducted by Belo. In December Horta and Belo attended the Nobel Prize ceremony in Oslo, Norway. On receiving the award, Belo emphasized his role as a spiritual, rather than a political, leader to the people of East Timor. Riots in Dili (following a gathering of Belo's supporters to welcome his return) resulted in the death of a member of ABRI; it was reported later in the month that at least one East Timorese citizen had been killed by the Indonesian authorities in a raid to capture those believed to be responsible for the soldier's death. (It was, however, generally recognized by non-governmental organizations working in East Timor that the Indonesian authorities had become more lenient about allowing demonstrations in 1996.)

Following an increase in clashes between resistance forces and ABRI prior to the general election, in June 1997 a military commander of Fretilin, David Alex, was apprehended by the Indonesian armed forces. His subsequent death in custody was highly controversial as resistance groups rejected the official explanation that he had been fatally injured in a clash with security forces and claimed that he had been tortured to death. Guerrilla activity subsequently intensified and in September at least seven Indonesian soldiers were killed in a clash with resistance forces. Further fighting took place in November and December.

In July 1997 the President of South Africa, Nelson Mandela, met Xanana Gusmão, with the approval of Suharto. Mandela subsequently announced that he had written to Suharto to request the prisoner's release. In September Mandela continued his attempts to mediate in the Timorese conflict by holding talks with Bishop Belo. In the same month the Foreign Minister, Alatas, reaffirmed that the Government would be prepared to consider Mandela's proposal that Xanana Gusmão be released if certain other conditions, such as the recognition by Portugal of Indonesia's sovereignty over East Timor, were met.

In early November 1997 the Australia–East Timor Association released a report cataloguing a number of human rights abuses perpetrated by members of the Indonesian armed forces against Timorese women; abuses cited in the report included enforced prostitution, rape and forced sterilization programmes. Also in November shots were fired when Indonesian troops stormed the campus of the University of East Timor in Dili following a vigil held by students to commemorate the massacre in Dili in 1991. According to reports, at least one student was killed in the incident, a number of others were injured and many were arrested. Belo accused the Indonesian security forces of having used 'excessive fprce' and this was confirmed by a report made by the Indonesian National Commission on Human Rights in early December. Also in December the Commission demanded the abolition of the country's anti-subversion legislation. In the same month two Timorese were sentenced to death under the legislation for their part in an ambush of election security officials earlier in the year, prompting threats of increased guerrilla activities by separatist forces. Also in December four Timorese were sentenced to 12 years' imprisonment for taking part in armed resistance operations.

In December 1997 Abilio Soares, who had been re-elected as Governor of East Timor in September, ordered the arrest of the leaders of the recently-formed Movement for the Reconciliation and Unity of the People of East Timor (MRUPT) which he declared to be a proscribed movement. In the same month a Timorese cultural and humanitarian foundation, the Peace and Democracy Foundation, was launched. The aim of the foundation, which had been created with funds from the Nobel Peace prize awarded to Belo and Horta, was stated to be the training of Timorese youths and the promotion and preservation of Timorese culture.

In January 1998 Horta attempted to exploit the Government's economic difficulties by urging Suharto to agree to a cease-fire and to co-operate with the UN in creating protection zones to ensure the safety of disarmed resistance fighters; the Government, however, failed to respond to his requests. In the same month it was announced that a Timorese resistance congress that was due to be held in Portugal in March was to be replaced by a national convention to ensure the participation of the União Democrática Timorense (UDT—Timorese Democratic Union). The convention was expected to elect a body to represent the Timorese and would also draft a constitutional charter to enshrine the people's rights.

In May 1977 there was a rebellion in Irian Jaya, said to have been organized by the Organisasi Papua Merdeka (OPM—Free Papua Movement), which seeks unification with Papua New Guinea. Fighting continued until December 1979, when Indonesia and Papua New Guinea finalized a new border administrative agreement. Since then, however, there have been frequent border incidents, and in early 1984 fighting broke out in Jayapura, the capital of Irian Jaya. As a result, about 10,000 refugees fled over the border into Papua New Guinea. In October 1984 Indonesia and Papua New Guinea signed a five-year agreement establishing a joint border security committee; by the end of 1985 Indonesians were continuing to cross into Papua New Guinea, but a limited number of repatriations took place in 1986. There was also concern among native Irian Jayans (who are of Melanesian origin) at the introduction of large numbers of Javanese into the province, under the Government's transmigration scheme. This was interpreted as an attempt to reduce the Melanesians to a minority and thus to stifle opposition. In 1986 it was announced that the Government intended to resettle 65m. people over 20 years, in spite of protests from human rights and conservation groups that the scheme would cause ecological damage and interfere with the rights of the native Irian Jayans. Relations with Papua New Guinea improved when the Prime Minister, Paias Wingti, visited Suharto in January 1988. However, a series of cross-border raids by the Indonesian armed forces in October and November, in an attempt to capture Melanesian separatists operating on the border, led to renewed tension between the two countries. Nevertheless, following a further round of bilateral discussions on border issues in July 1989, it was announced that Papua New Guinea would establish a consulate in Jayapura and that an Indonesian consulate would be opened in the border town of Vanimo. In October 1990 a renewal of the basic accord on border arrangements, signed by both Governments, included an agreement on the formation of a joint defence committee and formal commitment to share border intelligence. In March 1991 the leader of the OPM, Melkianus Salossa (who had been arrested in Papua New Guinea in May 1990 and deported to Indonesia), was sentenced to life imprisonment. In January 1992 Indonesia and Papua New Guinea signed an accord providing for greater co-operation on security issues. In May Indonesian troops crossed into Papua New Guinea to destroy an OPM camp at Wutung, prior to the legislative elections in Indonesia in June. In early September the two countries agreed to facilitate the passage of border trade, and in the following month the aforementioned Indonesian consulate was duly established in Vanimo. In October 1993 clashes were reported in Irian Jaya between government troops and separatist rebels; the armed forces were alleged to have killed 73 inhabitants of a neighbouring village. In late February 1994 it was reported that the OPM had proposed entering into peace talks with the Indonesian Government.

In April 1995 the Australian Council for Overseas Aid (ACFOA) alleged that 37 Irian Jayans had been killed by security forces near the Freeport copper and gold mine between June 1994 and February 1995. In August the ACFOA's claims were reiterated by non-governmental organizations who lodged a complaint with the National Commission on Human Rights in Jakarta about summary executions, arbitrary detentions and torture in the province between mid-1994 and mid-1995. In November 1995 four members of ABRI were arrested in an investiagion into the killing in May of 11 unarmed civilians at a prayer meeting. Also in November the Overseas Private Investment Corporation (a US government agency) cancelled political risk insurance valued at US $100m. for Freeport (a subsidiary of a US enterprise), citing environmental concerns. Freeport's perceived responsibility for the situation in Irian Jaya arose from its role as civil administrator in the area of the mine and also because the indigenous inhabitants' campaigns against Freeport's indiscriminate exploitation of natural resources in the area often resulted in their being killed by security forces as suspected members of the OPM.

In December 1995 clashes between Indonesian forces and the OPM intensified, forcing hundreds of refugees to cross into Papua New Guinea. In January 1996, in an attempt to raise awareness about their cause, the OPM kidnapped 26 hostages, including seven Europeans. The various claims that the OPM hoped to highlight included the fact that ABRI has been responsible for killing 43,000 indigenous inhabitants of Irian Jaya since

1977; the movement's demands included autonomy for Irian Jaya, the withdrawal of Indonesian troops and compensation for those killed. A number of the hostages were released by the OPM. In May, however, 11 hostages (including six Europeans) remained captive; following the rejection of a negotiated settlement by the OPM, an operation to effect their rescue was instigated by ABRI. During the operation eight OPM soldiers were killed; two Indonesian hostages were killed by their captors, while the other nine hostages were rescued in safety.

Four people were killed in riots in Jayapura in March 1996, which had been precipitated by the return of the remains of Thomas Wainggai (a resistance leader who had died while serving a 20-year custodial sentence for subversion) for burial. Riots near the Grasberg mine in the same month were the result of problems similar to those experienced by residents in the Freeport area: lack of benefits to the local community and environmental concerns. There were also tensions between the local Irianese, Indonesians from other provinces and commercial operators. In April Freeport agreed to allocate 1% of revenue over a period of 10 years to community development programmes for tribal groups living around the mine, and to tighten environmental safeguards. In October armed clashes between Indonesian troops and the OPM resulted in the death of a separatist.

Under Suharto, Indonesia's foreign policy has been one of non-alignment, although the country maintains close relations with the West. Indonesia is a member of the Association of South East Asian Nations (ASEAN, see p. 113) and supported that organization's opposition to Viet Nam's military presence in Cambodia. Indonesia played a prominent role in attempts to find a political solution to the situation in Cambodia (see p. 768). The Indonesian Minister of Foreign Affairs and his French counterpart were appointed Co-Chairmen of the Paris International Conference on Cambodia, which first met in August 1989. In 1997, following Second Prime Minister Hun Sen's assumption of sole power in Cambodia, Indonesia led ASEAN attempts to resolve the crisis.

In July 1985 Indonesia and the People's Republic of China signed a memorandum of understanding on the resumption of direct trade links, which had been suspended since 1967. In April 1988 the Indonesian Government indicated its readiness to re-establish full diplomatic relations with China, subject to an assurance that the latter would not seek to interfere in Indonesia's internal affairs; previously, Suharto had insisted that China acknowledge its alleged complicity in the 1965 attempted coup. Diplomatic relations were finally restored in August 1990, following an Indonesian undertaking to settle financial debts incurred with China by the Sukarno regime. In November Suharto visited China and Viet Nam (the first Indonesian leader to do so since 1964 and 1975 respectively). Suharto subsequently announced that former Indonesian communists living in exile would be permitted to return home, although they risked imprisonment. In 1995 the People's Republic of China extended claims to territorial waters within Indonesia's exclusive economic zone, consequently threatening Indonesia's natural gas resources, in particular those situated in the region of the Natuna Islands. An extensive Indonesian military exercise in September 1996, which concluded at the Natuna Islands, was perceived to be intended to demonstrate strength to China. Also in September as many as 50 Chinese fishing vessels were detained by Indonesia and later expelled.

In December 1989 Indonesia and Australia concluded a temporary agreement providing for joint exploration for petroleum and gas in the Timor Gap, which had been a disputed area since 1978. However, no permanent sea boundary was approved. In April 1990 the two countries restored defence co-operation links, following a four-year disruption. In April 1992 the new Australian Prime Minister, Paul Keating, travelled to Indonesia, honouring the country with the first official visit of his administration. The validity of the Timor Gap agreement was challenged by Portugal, which instituted proceedings at the International Court of Justice (ICJ), on the grounds that the agreement infringed Portuguese sovereignty and interests. In June 1995 the ICJ rejected the case on the grounds that it would affect a country that was not represented, as Indonesia does not recognize the ICJ's jurisdiction. In June 1993 the East Timorese resistance began proceedings in the High Court of Australia to overturn legislation confirming the Timor Gap agreement on the grounds that Australia was bound by international law, which did not recognize Indonesia's annexation of East Timor. In October 1996 a joint venture involving four companies announced plans to proceed with the first oilfield development in the Timor Gap. Keating visited Indonesia again in June 1994, during which visit agreement was reached on the holding of two-yearly joint government meetings. In September Vice-President Sutrisno became the first high-ranking Indonesian official to visit Australia since Suharto's last visit in 1975, and, in so doing, emphasized the strength of relations between the two countries.

In July 1995 Indonesia withdrew the nomination of Lt-Gen. Herman Mantiri, a former Chief of the General Staff, as ambassador to Australia, owing to widespread protests there concerning his defence of the actions of the Indonesian armed forces in the 1991 Dili massacre. The position was left vacant until the end of the year, when a career diplomat, Wiryono Sastrohandojo, was nominated for the post. Relations with Australia were also strained by Australia's decision to allow 18 East Timorese refugees to remain in the country following their arrival by boat in May (although they were not granted political asylum), by several incidents involving the burning of the Indonesian flag in Australian cities in protest at Indonesia's occupation of East Timor, and by Australia's decision to investigate claims of new evidence about the killing of six Australian journalists during the annexation of East Timor in 1975. (The Indonesian Government claimed that the journalists were killed in cross-fire, while eyewitnesses said that they were executed by Indonesian troops. In June 1996 an Australian government report concluded that the journalists had been killed by the Indonesian army.) However, despite these difficulties, in December 1995, following 18 months of secret negotiations, Indonesia signed a treaty with Australia to enhance defence links, committing the two countries to consultation in the event of a threat to security.

In September 1996 Indonesia and Australia reached an agreement (to be formally approved) on the delineation of their maritime boundaries. Later in the month Indonesia accepted the appointment of John McCarthy as the Australian ambassador, following protracted diplomatic disputes. Relations between Australia and Indonesia were also affected by the imposition in September of bans on Indonesian cargo and shipping by the Maritime Union of Australia, in protest at Indonesian repression and the arrest of Indonesian trade union leaders. In October, however, the Australia-Indonesia Development Area was created to develop economic links between the two countries, and in March 1997 Indonesia and Australia signed a treaty defining permanent maritime boundaries between the two countries, whilst retaining the Timor Gap agreement.

In October 1996 Indonesia and Malaysia agreed to submit disputed claims to the islands of Ligitan and Sipadan to the International Court of Justice. In December the Indonesian Government formed a special task force on the islands, in agreement with Malaysia, in order to obtain evidence supporting Indonesia's claim. In February 1997 Malaysia closed its border with Indonesia on the island of Borneo for one week, owing to increased racial tension and riots in West Kalimantan. In August the two countries agreed to postpose talks on the issue of the islands of Ligitan and Sipadan, pending a ruling by the International Court of Justice.

In March 1996 the USA ended a ban on military training for members of ABRI, which had been imposed after the Dili massacre in 1991. In early June 1977, however, it wa announced that President Suharto had cancelled Indonesia's participation in US military training programmes in response to the recent condemnation by the US House of Representatives of abuses of human rights committed by Indonesian armed forces in East Timor; the planned purchase by Indonesia of a number of US military aircraft was also cancelled.

In September 1994 a 220-strong medical detachment from the Indonesian army joined the UN Protection Force in Bosnia and Herzegovina (UNPROFOR), in the first mission of its kind to Europe. Indonesia's international standing was further enhanced when, in January 1995, it replaced Pakistan as the non-permanent Asian representative on the UN Security Council for a period of two years. In October 1997 Indonesia proposed that two permanent seats for the representation of Asia be established on the Council. In October 1994 Indonesia underscored its pivotal regional role through hosting its fifth informal meeting to resolve peacefully the dispute over the conflicting claims of six Asian countries to sovereignty over parts of the South China Sea, particularly the Spratly Islands. Moreover, in November the APEC summit took place in Bogor and was hosted by Suharto in his capacity as Chairman of APEC.

On 16 November 1994 the United Nations Convention on the Law of the Sea came into effect and immediately led to recognition of Indonesia's status as an archipelago and the country's sovereignty over all of the waters between its islands. Enforcement of the convention increased Indonesia's territorial waters by more than 3m. sq km.

In August 1995 Queen Beatrix of the Netherlands, the former colonial power in Indonesia, visited Indonesia (the first Dutch monarch to do so for 24 years) and spoke of her regret for the suffering caused by Dutch rule. Bilateral relations have been strained since 1992, when Indonesia rejected Dutch aid because it was linked to progress on human rights.

In September and October 1997 President Suharto apologized to neighbouring countries when thick smog, caused by fires started in land-clearance operations in southern Sumatra and central and south Kalimanta, affected Malaysia, Singapore and parts of the Philippines and Thailand.

Government

The highest authority of the State is the Majelis Permusyawaratan Rakyat (MPR—People's Consultative Assembly), with 1,000 members who serve for five years. The MPR includes 500 members of the Dewan Perwakilan Rakyat (House of Representatives), the country's legislative organ. The Dewan has 75 appointed members (from the Indonesian Armed Forces—ABRI) and 425 directly-elected representatives. The remaining 500 seats in the MPR are allocated to regional representatives, members of ABRI belonging to the Golongan Karya (Golkar—the governing group), and delegates of other organizations, selected in proportion to their elected seats in the Dewan. Executive power rests with the President, elected for five years by the MPR. He governs with the assistance of an appointed Cabinet, which is responsible to him.

There are 27 provinces (including the disputed territory of East Timor), and local government is through a three-tier system of provincial, regency and village assemblies. Each province is headed by a Governor, who is elected to a five-year term of office by the Provincial Assembly. Provincial Governors must be confirmed by the President, who also approves the election of the Governor of Jakarta, which is designated as a 'special district', as are Aceh and Yogyakarta.

Defence

In August 1997 the total strength of the armed forces was 284,000 men: army 220,000, navy an estimated 43,000 and air force 21,000. There were also paramilitary forces, comprising some 177,000 police and 1.5m. trainees of KAMRA (People's Security). Military service is selective and lasts for two years. Defence expenditure for 1997 was budgeted at 8,000,000m. rupiahs.

Economic Affairs

In 1995, according to estimates by the World Bank, Indonesia's gross national product (GNP), measured at average 1993–95 prices, was US $190,105m., equivalent to $980 per head. During 1985–95, it was estimated, GNP per head increased, in real terms, at an average rate of 6.0% per year. Over the same period the population grew by an annual average of 1.7%. Indonesia's gross domestic product (GDP) increased, in real terms, by an annual average of 7.1% in 1985–95; GDP increased by an estimated 7.6% in 1996.

Agriculture, forestry and fishing contributed an estimated 16.3% of GDP in 1996, and engaged 52.8% of the labour force in that year. Principal crops for domestic consumption were rice, cassava and maize. Once self-sufficient in rice, Indonesia was obliged to import supplies for five of the six years between 1991 and 1997. In 1995 Indonesia remained the second largest exporter of rubber (after Thailand) and palm oil (after Malaysia). Other principal cash crops were coffee, spices, tea, cocoa, tobacco and sugar cane. The fishing sector contributed an estimated 1.7% of GDP in 1996 . In 1994 an estimated 61.7% of Indonesia's land area was covered by tropical rain forests. In 1985 a ban on the export of logs was announced, although processed wood products remained a significant export commodity. In 1992 this ban was replaced by an export tax. During 1985–95, according to the World Bank, agricultural GDP increased by an estimated annual average of 3.4%; agricultural GDP growth declined to 0.5% in 1994, but increased to 4.2% in 1995. The GDP of the sector rose by an estimated 1.9% in 1996.

Industry (including mining, manufacturing, construction and power) engaged 15.7% of the employed labour force in 1993, and provided an estimated 42.7% of GDP in 1996. During 1985–95, according to the World Bank, industrial GDP increased by an annual average of 9.4%; industrial GDP increased by 10.5% in 1996.

Mining engaged only 1.1% of the employed labour force in 1995, but contributed an estimated 8.3% of GDP in 1996. Indonesia's principal mineral resource is petroleum, and the country remained the world's leading exporter of liquefied natural gas in 1994. In 1996 Indonesia produced 582.5m. barrels of crude petroleum and 3,164,016m. cu ft of natural gas. In 1992 Indonesia became the world's second largest producer of tin. Bauxite, nickel, copper, gold, silver and coal are also mined. During 1991–96 mining and quarrying GDP increased by an annual average of 4.9%.

Manufacturing contributed an estimated 25.2% of GDP in 1996, and engaged 13.3% of the employed labour force in 1995. Apart from petroleum refineries, the main branches of the sector (in terms of output) in 1994 were textiles (contributing 13.4% of the total), food products (13.1%), wood products (8.8%), transport equipment (8.5%) and tobacco (6.6%). According to the World Bank, manufacturing GDP increased by an estimated annual average of 10.9% in 1985–95; manufacturng GDP increased by 11.0% in 1996.

Indonesia used to be largely dependent on petroleum for its energy supplies, but during the 1980s it broadened its base to include gas, coal, hydroelectricity and geothermal energy. In 1992/93 oil-fired thermal plants accounted for 50% of the total electricity generated, coal 25% and hydropower 18%. Total generating capacity in that year was 10,267 MW. In 1993 the Government approved a permit for the construction of Indonesia's first nuclear power station, scheduled to begin in 1998; in 1997, however, plans for the construction of the power station were suspended indefinitely. In 1995 imports of fuel products comprised 8.6% of the value of merchandise imports.

Services (including trade, transport and communications, finance and tourism) provided an estimated 41.0% of GDP in 1996, and engaged 33.5% of the employed labour force in 1993. Tourism is one of the principal sources of foreign exchange; revenue from the 5.03m. visitors in 1996 totalled US $6,100m. In 1993 a total of 187.9m. metric tons of freight for international traffic were loaded and discharged in Indonesian ports. According to the World Bank, the GDP of the services sector expanded by an estimated annual average of 8.1% in 1985–95; services GDP increased by 7.5% in 1996.

In 1995 Indonesia recorded a visible trade surplus of US $5,710m. There was, however, a deficit of $7,023m. on the current account of the balance of payments in that year. In 1995 the principal source of imports (22.7%) and principal market for exports (27.1%) was Japan. Other major suppliers were the USA, Germany, the Republic of Korea, Singapore and Australia; other major purchasers were the USA, Singapore, the Republic of Korea, the People's Republic of China and Hong Kong. The principal exports in that year were petroleum and petroleum products, wood and wood products (particularly plywood), natural and manufactured gas, machinery and transport equipment, clothing and textiles. The principal imports were machinery, transport and electrical equipment, and chemical and mineral products.

In the financial year ending 31 March 1997 there was an estimated budgetary surplus of 5,502,000m. rupiahs (equivalent to 1.0% of GDP). Indonesia's total external debt totalled US $107,831m. at the end of 1995, of which $65,347m. was long-term public debt. In that year the cost of debt-servicing was equivalent to 30.9% of revenue from exports of goods and services. The annual rate of inflation averaged 8.4% in 1986–96. Consumer prices rose by an average of 9.4% in 1995 and 7.9% in 1996. In 1994 about 4.4% of the labour force were unemployed; in the same year the rate of underemployment (defined as those working less than 35 hours per week) was 39.9%.

Indonesia is a member of the Association of South East Asian Nations (ASEAN—see p. 113), which aims to accelerate economic progress in the region, and of the Organization of the Petroleum Exporting Countries (OPEC—see p. 227). As a member of ASEAN, Indonesia signed an accord in January 1992, pledging to establish a free trade zone, to be known as the ASEAN Free Trade Area (AFTA), within 15 years (subsequently reduced to 10 years), beginning in January 1993.

The rapid financial deregulation from 1988 onwards, which resulted in a massive increase in the number of banks and an unsustainable expansion of bank credit and offshore borrowing, increased Indonesia's vulnerability to the currency crisis which affected South-East Asia in the second half of 1997. In August the Government was forced to allow the flotation of the currency, which constituted an effective devaluation, causing widespread unemployment and hardship. A US $43,000m. IMF programme to restore confidence in the economy was agreed in October but Suharto failed to honour the conditions of the agreement, finally announcing a completely unrealistic budget in January 1998. The rupiah continued to decline rapidly against other currencies, notably the US dollar, the value of shares on the Jakarta Stock Exchange dropped sharply and the price of basic commodities increased rapidly. Later in January Suharto endorsed a second IMF agreement and budget, in which commitments were made to remove politically sensitive subsidies on fuel and electricity by April, to dismantle monopolies (including those in flour and cloves), which were often awarded through nepotism, and to halt costly infrastructure projects, including those involving Suharto's family. Despite these pledges, the rupiah continued to fall, partly as a result of political uncertainty, owing to Suharto's failure to nominate a credible successor. Despite the closure of 16 banks in October 1997, the banking system remained in disarray with trade financing virtually suspended. At the end of January 1998 Indonesia announced that it would extend state guarantees on all bank deposits and loans to try to prevent further capital flight and to encourage funds to return to the banking sector. There were also plans to address the problem of private foreign debt through the formation of a committee of Indonesian borrowers, which was to meet with international lenders and attempt to negotiate an acceptable repayment plan.

Social Welfare

Certain members of the population benefit from a state insurance scheme. Benefits include life insurance and old-age pensions. In addition, there are two social insurance schemes, administered by state corporations, providing pensions and industrial accident insurance. In 1992 Indonesia had 971 hospitals (with a total of 112,779 beds) and 6,224 public health centres. In the same year there were 25,135 physicians working in the country and 118,555 nurses and midwives. In the 1994/95 budget 2,011,000m. rupiahs, 3.3% of total expenditure, was allocated to health.

Education

Education is mainly under the control of the Ministry of Education and Culture, but the Ministry of Religious Affairs is in charge of Islamic religious schools at the primary level. In 1987 primary education, beginning at seven years of age and lasting for six years, was made compulsory. In 1993 it was announced that compulsory education was to be expanded to nine years. Secondary education begins at 13 years of age and lasts for six years, comprising two cycles of three years each. Primary enrolment in 1994 included 93.5% of children in the relevant age-group. In 1993 enrolment at secondary level was equivalent to 45% of the relevant population (males 49%; females 41%). In 1996 there were 91 state universities and 1,479 private universities. In 1992 enrolment at tertiary level was equivalent to 9.3% of the relevant population (males 11.1%; females 7.4%). In 1994/95 the Government spent 6,045,000m. rupiahs, representing 9.8% of total expenditure, on education. In 1995, according to UNESCO estimates, the average rate of adult illiteracy was 16.2% (males 10.4%; females 22.0%).

Public Holidays

1998: 1 January (New Year's Day), 30 January* (Id al-Fitr, end of Ramadan), 8 April* (Id al-Adha, Feast of the Sacrifice), 10 April (Good Friday), 28 April* (Muharram, Islamic New Year), 11 May (Vesak Day), 21 May (Ascension Day), 7 July* (Mouloud, Prophet Muhammad's Birthday), 17 August (Independence Day), 17 November* (Ascension of the Prophet Muhammad), 25 December (Christmas Day).

1999: 1 January (New Year's Day), 19 January* (Id al-Fitr, end of Ramadan), 28 March* (Id al-Adha, Feast of the Sacrifice), 2 April (Good Friday), 17 April* (Muharram, Islamic New Year), 13 May (Ascension Day), 30 May (Vesak Day), 26 June* (Mouloud, prophet Muhammad's Birthday), 17 August (Independence Day), 6 November* (Ascension of the Prophet Muhammad), 25 December (Christmas Day).

* These holidays are dependent on the Islamic lunar calendar and may vary by one or two days from the dates given.

Weights and Measures

The metric system is in force.

Statistical Survey

Source (unless otherwise stated): Central Bureau of Statistics, Jalan Dr Sutomo 8, Jakarta 10710; tel. (21) 363360; telex 45159; fax (21) 3857046.

Note: Unless otherwise stated, figures for the disputed former Portuguese territory of East Timor (annexed by Indonesia in July 1976) are not included in the tables.

Area and Population

AREA, POPULATION AND DENSITY

Area (sq km)	
Indonesia	1,904,443*
East Timor	14,874†
Population (census results)	
31 October 1980	
Indonesia	146,934,948
East Timor	555,350
31 October 1990	
Indonesia	
Males	89,076,606
Females	89,554,590
Total	178,631,196
East Timor	
Males	386,939
Females	360,811
Total	747,750
Population (official estimate at 31 December)	
Indonesia	
1994	191,390,500
1995	194,440,100
1996	197,483,200
East Timor	
1994	826,000
1995	843,100
1996	859,700
Density (per sq km) at 31 December 1996	
Indonesia	103.7
East Timor	57.8

* 735,310 sq miles. † 5,743 sq miles.

ISLANDS (estimated population at 31 December 1996)*

	Area (sq km)	Population	Density (per sq km)
Jawa (Java) and Madura	132,186	116,379,200	880.4
Sumatera (Sumatra)	473,481	41,840,700	88.4
Sulawesi (Celebes)	189,216	14,019,800	74.1
Kalimantan	539,460	10,807,900	20.0
Nusa Tenggara†	68,053	7,348,600	108.0
Bali	5,561	2,924,400	525.9
Maluku (Moluccas)	74,505	2,141,700	28.7
Irian Jaya	421,981	2,020,900	4.8
Indonesia	1,904,443	197,483,200	103.7
Timor Timur (East Timor)	14,874	859,700	57.8
Total	1,919,317	198,342,900	103.3

* Figures refer to provincial divisions, each based on a large island or group of islands but also including adjacent small islands.

† Comprising most of the Lesser Sunda Islands, principally Flores, Lombok, Sumba, Sumbawa and part of Timor.

PRINCIPAL TOWNS (estimated population at 31 December 1996)

Jakarta (capital)	9,341,400
Surabaya	2,743,400
Bandung	2,429,000
Medan	1,942,000
Palembang	1,394,300
Semarang	1,366,500
Ujung Pandang (Makassar)	1,121,300
Malang	775,900
Padang	739,500
Banjarmasin	544,700
Surakarta	518,600
Pontianak	459,100
Yogyakarta (Jogjakarta)	421,000

BIRTHS AND DEATHS (UN estimates, annual averages)

Indonesia (excl. East Timor)	1980–85	1985–90	1990–95
Birth rate (per 1,000)	32.4	28.4	24.7
Death rate (per 1,000)	11.2	9.4	8.4

East Timor	1980–85	1985–90	1990–95
Birth rate (per 1,000)	44.1	43.3	36.5
Death rate (per 1,000)	23.0	20.4	17.4

Expectation of life (UN estimates, years at birth, 1990–95): Indonesia (excl. East Timor) 62.7 (males 61.0; females 64.5); East Timor 45.0 (males 44.1; females 45.9).

Source: UN, *World Population Prospects: The 1994 Revision.*

Birth rate (per 1,000): 24.5 in 1993; 24.1 in 1994; 23.6 in 1995. Source: UN, *Statistical Yearbook for Asia and the Pacific.*

Death rate (per 1,000): 7.9 in 1993; 7.8 in 1994; 7.7 in 1995. Source: UN, *Statistical Yearbook for Asia and the Pacific.*

ECONOMICALLY ACTIVE POPULATION (ISIC Major Divisions, persons aged 10 years and over, survey of August 1993)*

Agriculture, hunting, forestry and fishing	40,071,850
Mining and quarrying	653,297
Manufacturing	8,784,295
Electricity, gas and water	171,566
Construction	2,810,360
Trade, restaurants and hotels	12,508,070
Transport, storage and communications	2,931,346
Financing, insurance, real estate and business services	564,969
Public services	10,566,410
Activities not adequately defined	138,379
Total employed	79,200,542
Unemployed	2,245,536
Total labour force	81,446,078

* Figures include East Timor, with a labour force of 341,887 (employed 336,490; unemployed 5,397).

Mid-1996 (estimates in '000): Agriculture, etc. 49,169; Total labour force 93,101 (source: FAO, *Production Yearbook*).

Agriculture

PRINCIPAL CROPS ('000 metric tons)

	1994	1995	1996
Rice (paddy)	46,642	49,744	51,165
Maize	6,869	8,246	8,925
Potatoes	877	1,002	1,002*
Sweet potatoes	1,845	2,171	2,424
Cassava (Manioc)	15,729	15,438	15,438*
Other roots and tubers	151	150	150*
Dry beans	850	810*	810*
Soybeans	1,565	1,689	1,968
Groundnuts (in shell)†	1,020	1,227	1,240
Coconuts*	13,516	13,058	13,058
Copra	1,171	1,070†	1,150†
Palm kernels†	945	1,075	1,115
Vegetables	5,514	5,567	5,783*
Bananas	2,614	2,600*	2,600*
Other fruit	4,627	4,830*	4,830*
Sugar cane	32,834	31,427	32,053
Coffee (green)	421	426	431
Tea (made)	136	155	169
Tobacco (leaves)	130	133	136
Natural rubber	1,499	1,535	1,578

* FAO estimate(s). † Unofficial figure(s).

Source: FAO, *Production Yearbook.*

LIVESTOCK ('000 head, year ending September)

	1994	1995	1996
Cattle	11,368	11,550	11,930
Sheep	6,741	7,169	7,684
Goats	12,770	13,309	14,323
Pigs	8,858	7,825	7,825
Horses†	714	720	727
Buffaloes	3,104	3,112	3,140

Chickens (million): 930 in 1994; 992 in 1995; 1,103† in 1996.
Ducks (million): 27† in 1994; 27† in 1995; 27† in 1996.

* FAO estimate. † Unofficial figure(s).

Source: FAO, *Production Yearbook.*

LIVESTOCK PRODUCTS ('000 metric tons)

	1994	1995	1996
Beef and veal	336	339	342
Buffalo meat	48	47	45
Mutton and lamb	43	45	47
Goat meat	57	61	66
Pig meat*	660	589	583
Poultry meat	815	869	955
Cows' milk	427	433	458
Sheep's milk*	78	81	84
Goats' milk*	192	192	192
Hen eggs	423	457	493
Other poultry eggs*	124	126	128
Wool (greasy)*	20	22	23
Cattle and buffalo hides*	55	55	55

Note: Figures for meat refer to inspected production only, i.e. from animals slaughtered under government supervision.

* FAO estimate(s).

Source: FAO, *Production Yearbook.*

Forestry

ROUNDWOOD REMOVALS
(FAO estimates, '000 cubic metres, excluding bark)

	1992	1993	1994
Sawlogs, veneer logs and logs for sleepers:			
Coniferous	333	333	333
Non-coniferous	35,275	35,254	34,619
Pulpwood	200	200	200
Other industrial wood	2,931	2,976	3,022
Fuel wood	144,392	146,704	148,916
Total	183,130	185,466	187,089

Source: FAO, *Yearbook of Forest Products*.

SAWNWOOD PRODUCTION
('000 cubic metres, including railway sleepers)

	1992	1993	1994
Coniferous (softwood)*	138	138	138
Broadleaved (hardwood)†	8,300	8,200	8,000
Total	8,438	8,338	8,138

* FAO estimates. † Unofficial figures.

Source: FAO, *Yearbook of Forest Products*.

Fishing

('000 metric tons, live weight)

	1993	1994	1995
Carps, barbels, etc.	200.0	216.8	218.1
Other freshwater fishes (incl. unspecified)	372.5	390.9	399.5
Milkfish	164.4	153.1	157.0
Other diadromous fishes	45.3	47.0	50.7
Scads	203.4	219.9	230.0
Goldstripe sardinella	152.6	166.5	174.8
Bali sardinella	122.0	128.2	137.0
'Stolephorus' anchovies	142.8	150.6	153.0
Skipjack tuna	147.3	157.7	174.6
Other tunas, bonitos, billfishes, etc.	314.0	349.5	368.0
Indian mackerels	173.9	194.9	200.0
Other marine fishes (incl. unspecified)	1,204.0	1,285.7	1,359.7
Total fish	3,242.1	3,460.6	3,622.3
Marine shrimps, prawns, etc.	300.7	319.7	336.4
Other crustaceans	29.2	31.7	36.0
Molluscs	81.2	96.0	111.1
Other aquatic animals	32.4	9.2	12.2
Total catch	3,685.4	3,917.2	4,118.0
Inland waters	770.3	802.6	821.4
Indian Ocean	616.7	632.9	676.1
Pacific Ocean	2,298.5	2,481.6	2,620.6

Crocodiles (number): 3,327 in 1993; 12,362 in 1994.

Corals (metric tons): 2,000* in 1993; 1,800* in 1994; 1,700* in 1995.

Aquatic plants ('000 metric tons): 118.4 in 1993; 110.4 in 1994; 117.2 in 1995.

* FAO estimate.

Source: FAO, *Yearbook of Fishery Statistics*.

Mining

(metric tons, unless otherwise indicated)

	1994	1995	1996
Crude petroleum ('000 barrels)	588,304	586,264	582,484
Natural gas (million cu ft)	2,941,622	2,999,229	3,164,016
Bauxite	1,342,402	899,035	841,976
Coal	31,012,115	38,311,879	47,339,000‡
Nickel ore*	2,311,510	2,513,394	3,426,867
Copper concentrate*	1,065,488	1,516,605	1,758,910
Tin ore (metal content)	30,610	38,378	51,024
Gold (kg)†	42,597	62,818	83,564
Silver (kg)†	107,026	265,212	255,404

* Figures refer to gross weight. The estimated metal content was: Nickel 3.1%; Copper 44%.

† Including gold and silver in copper concentrate.

‡ Data from UN, *Monthly Bulletin of Statistics*.

Source (unless otherwise indicated): Department of Mines and Energy, Jakarta.

Industry

SELECTED PRODUCTS ('000 metric tons, unless otherwise indicated)

	1992	1993	1994
Refined sugar	1,509	2,294	n.a.
Cigarettes (million)	156,422	171,828	n.a.
Veneer sheets ('000 cubic metres)	55*	55[1]	55[1]
Plywood ('000 cubic metres)*	10,100*	10,050*	10,000*
Newsprint	61	54	n.a.
Other printing and writing paper	735*	844[1]	992*
Other paper and paperboard	1,359*	1,561[1]	1,823*
Nitrogenous fertilizers (a)[2]	2,302	2,280	n.a.
Phosphatic fertilizers (b)[2]	948	1,179	n.a.
Jet fuel	661	576	740
Motor spirit (petrol)	5,005	5,330	5,529*
Naphthas	1,075	1,002	990*
Kerosene	6,396	6,197	6,605
Distillate fuel oils	12,360	12,800*	13,200
Residual fuel oils	10,820	10,900*	11,000*
Lubricating oils	241	224	227*
Liquefied petroleum gas	7,359	7,482	7,520*
Rubber tyres ('000)[3]	8,460	14,376	n.a.
Cement	14,048	19,610	21,912
Aluminium (unwrought)[4]	213.5	202.1	221.9[5]
Tin (unwrought, metric tons)[4,5]	35,900*	38,300*	39,000*
Radio receivers ('000)	2,863	3,882	n.a.
Television receivers ('000)	700	1,001	n.a.
Passenger motor cars ('000)[6]	39	72	n.a.
Electric energy (million kWh)*	54,940	58,888	61,370
Gas from gasworks (terajoules)*	10,288	12,025	13,100*

* Provisional or estimated production.

[1] Data from the FAO.

[2] Production in terms of (a) nitrogen or (b) phosphoric acid.

[3] For road motor vehicles, excluding bicycles and motorcyles.

[4] Primary metal production only.

[5] Data from *World Metal Statistics*.

[6] Vehicles assembled from imported parts.

Source: UN, *Industrial Commodity Statistics Yearbook*.

Palm oil ('000 metric tons): 3,162 in 1992; 3,421 in 1993; 4,008 in 1994; 4,480 in 1995; 4,998 in 1996. Source: FAO, *Production Yearbook* and *Quarterly Bulletin of Statistics*.

Raw sugar ('000 metric tons): 2,300 (unofficial figure) in 1992; 2,483 in 1993; 2,454 in 1994; 2,098 in 1995; 2,404 in 1996. Sources: FAO, *Production Yearbook* and *Quarterly Bulletin of Statistics*.

Finance

CURRENCY AND EXCHANGE RATES

Monetary Units

100 sen = 1 rupiah (Rp.).

Sterling and Dollar Equivalents (30 September 1997)

£1 sterling = 5,290.4 rupiahs;
US $1 = 3,275.0 rupiahs;
10,000 rupiahs = £1.890 = $3.053.

Average Exchange Rate (rupiahs per US $)

1994 2,160.8
1995 2,248.6
1996 2,342.3

BUDGET ('000 million rupiahs, year ending 31 March)*

Revenue†	1994/95	1995/96	1996/97‡
Tax revenue	62,338	72,828	78,241
Taxes on income, profits, etc.	32,895	37,077	45,368
Social security contributions	1,380	4,811	2,431
Domestic taxes on goods and services	23,382	26,762	26,701
General sales, turnover or VAT	18,335	18,519	20,393
Excises	3,153	3,593	4,217
Taxes on international trade	4,224	3,215	2,877
Import duties	4,093	3,029	2,807
Other current revenue	7,056	7,584	12,048
Entrepreneurial and property income	5,286	6,210	8,807
Administrative fees and charges, non-industrial and incidental sales	1,623	928	1,763
Capital revenue	8	15	9
Total	69,402	80,427	90,298

Expenditure§	1994/95	1995/96	1996/97‡
General public services	3,948	4,713	12,281
Defence	4,266	4,792	5,695
Public order and safety	1,260	1,912	2,299
Education	6,045	6,042	7,040
Health	2,011	1,723	1,962
Social security and welfare	3,259	4,153	5,643
Housing and community amenities	11,041	13,699	15,819
Recreational, cultural and religious affairs and services	1,448	1,610	1,862
Economic affairs and services	19,358	14,125	18,431
Agriculture, forestry, fishing and hunting	11,903	6,290	9,729
Transport and communications	5,230	5,086	5,720
Other purposes	9,230	9,612	6,932
Interest payments	7,565	7,130	6,426
Unallocable	—	4,342	—
Total	61,866	66,723	77,964
Current	31,722	36,037	46,150
Capital	30,144	30,686	31,814

* Figures represent a consolidation of the General Budget, the Investment Fund, the Reforestation Fund and three social security schemes.
† Excluding grants received ('000 million rupiahs): 67 in 1994/95.
‡ Figures are provisional.
§ Excluding lending minus repayments ('000 million rupiahs): 4,022 in 1994/95; 3,619 in 1995/96; 6,154 (provisional) in 1996/97.

Source: IMF, *Government Finance Statistics Yearbook*.

INTERNATIONAL RESERVES (US $ million at 31 December)

	1994	1995	1996
Gold*	1,067	1,079	1,030
IMF special drawing rights	—	1	2
Reserve position in IMF	312	401	429
Foreign exchange	11,820	13,306	17,820
Total	13,200	14,787	19,281

* Valued at market-related prices.

Source: IMF, *International Financial Statistics*.

MONEY SUPPLY ('000 million rupiahs at 31 December)

	1994	1995	1996
Currency outside banks	18,634	20,807	22,487
Demand deposits at deposit money banks	22,710	26,202	28,883
Total money (incl. others)	41,462	47,135	51,652

Source: IMF, *International Financial Statistics*.

COST OF LIVING (Consumer Price Index; base: 1990 = 100)

	1993	1994	1995
Food (incl. beverages)	124.5	137.9	156.3
All items (incl.others)	129.0	139.9	153.2

Source: ILO, *Yearbook of Labour Statistics*.

1996: All items 165.5 (Source: IMF, *International Financial Statistics*).

NATIONAL ACCOUNTS ('000 million rupiahs at current prices)

National Income and Product

	1990	1991	1992
Domestic factor incomes*	172,393	201,118	229,946
Consumption of fixed capital	9,784	11,380	13,045
Gross domestic product (GDP) at factor cost	182,177	212,498	242,991
Indirect taxes, *less* subsidies	13,420	15,004	17,795
GDP in purchasers' values	195,597	227,502	260,786
Net factor income from abroad	-9,614	-10,899	-12,213
Gross national product (GNP)	185,983	216,603	248,573
Less Consumption of fixed capital	9,784	11,380	13,045
National income in market prices	176,199	205,223	235,528

* Compensation of employees and the operating surplus of enterprises. The amount is obtained as a residual.

Source: UN, *National Accounts Statistics*.

Expenditure on the Gross Domestic Product

	1994	1995	1996
Government final consumption expenditure	31,014	35,584	40,695
Private final consumption expenditure	228,119	279,876	325,585
Gross capital formation	118,708	145,118	170,811
Total domestic expenditure	377,841	460,578	537,091
Exports of goods and services	101,332	119,593	137,533
Less Imports of goods and services	96,953	125,657	141,993
GDP in purchasers' values	382,220	454,514	532,631
GDP at constant 1990 prices	255,055	276,020	298,047

Source: IMF, *International Financial Statistics*.

Gross Domestic Product by Economic Activity

	1994	1995*	1996*
Agriculture, forestry and fishing	66,071	77,639	86,212
Mining and quarrying	33,507	38,045	43,893
Manufacturing	89,241	109,395	133,088
Electricity, gas and water	4,577	5,625	6,561
Construction	28,017	34,452	42,279
Trade, hotels and restaurants	63,859	75,874	88,451
Transport and communications	27,353	30,778	35,554
Finance and insurance	17,818	21,233	25,532
Dwellings and real estate	11,239	11,899	13,237
Government services	22,755	26,555	29,532
Other services	17,784	20,886	24,618
Total	382,220	452,381	528,956

* Provisional.

BALANCE OF PAYMENTS (US $ million)

	1993	1994	1995
Exports of goods f.o.b.	36,607	40,223	45,479
Imports of goods f.o.b.	−28,376	−32,322	−39,769
Trade balance	8,231	7,901	5,710
Exports of services	3,959	4,797	5,681
Imports of services	−9,846	−11,416	−13,475
Balance on goods and services	2,344	1,282	−2,084
Other income received	1,028	1,048	1,345
Other income paid	−6,015	−5,741	−7,123
Balance on goods, services and income	−2,643	−3,411	−7,862
Current transfers received	537	619	839
Current balance	−2,106	−2,792	−7,023
Direct investment abroad	−356	−609	−603
Direct investment from abroad	2,004	2,109	4,348
Portfolio investment liabilities	1,805	3,877	4,100
Other investment liabilities	2,179	−1,538	2,541
Net errors and omissions	−2,932	−263	−1,790
Overall balance	594	784	1,573

Source: IMF, *International Financial Statistics.*

External Trade

PRINCIPAL COMMODITIES (distribution by SITC, US $ million)

Imports c.i.f.	1993	1994	1995
Food and live animals	1,340.4	1,895.6	3,020.0
Cereals and cereal preparations	546.0	926.6	1,551.5
Crude materials (inedible) except fuels	2,423.6	2,723.7	3,624.0
Pulp and waste paper	479.0	614.2	882.3
Textile fibres and waste	797.7	948.2	1,244.7
Cotton	557.0	701.3	923.2
Raw cotton (excl. linters)	556.4	700.6	922.3
Mineral fuels, lubricants, etc.	2,202.4	2,487.6	3,094.9
Petroleum, petroleum products, etc.	2,170.2	2,461.8	3,045.1
Crude petroleum oils, etc.	917.2	1,073.2	1,317.6
Refined petroleum products	1,163.7	1,290.5	1,604.8
Gas oils	579.4	582.9	783.6
Chemicals and related products	3,961.5	4,757.3	6,130.2
Organic chemicals	1,207.4	1,609.7	2,327.9
Plastic materials, etc.	981.3	1,145.3	1,390.7
Products of polymerization, etc.	648.0	754.2	893.5
Basic manufactures	5,007.7	5,386.7	6,855.2
Textile yarn, fabrics, etc.	1,129.1	1,175.3	1,327.1
Iron and steel	1,669.2	1,684.1	2,451.0
Non-ferrous metals	519.4	643.6	1,018.7

Imports c.i.f. — *continued*	1993	1994	1995
Machinery and transport equipment	12,116.4	13,426.3	16,257.1
Power-generating machinery and equipment	1,616.8	1,752.0	1,827.6
Internal combustion piston engines and parts	439.1	717.8	855.6
Machinery specialized for particular industries	2,773.9	3,014.7	3,891.4
Textile and leather machinery	815.1	836.9	1,051.3
General industrial machinery, equipment and parts	2,348.0	2,393.0	3,059.2
Heating and cooling equipment and parts	656.0	643.1	838.1
Telecommunications and sound equipment	999.1	759.5	1,086.2
Other electrical machinery, apparatus, etc.	1,709.5	1,758.2	1,965.6
Switchgear, etc., and parts	571.2	557.2	559.3
Road vehicles and parts*	1,324.1	2,335.2	2,983.7
Parts and accessories for cars, buses, lorries, etc.*	702.0	1,532.5	1,843.2
Other transport equipment*	778.0	800.6	606.1
Miscellaneous manufactured articles	908.4	967.8	1,282.6
Total (incl. others)	27,279.6	28,327.8	40,628.7

* Excluding tyres, engines and electrical parts.

Source: UN, *International Trade Statistics Yearbook.*

Exports f.o.b.	1993	1994	1995
Food and live animals	2,921.2	3,550.7	3,579.9
Fish, crustaceans and molluscs	1,416.1	1,581.5	1,665.3
Crustaceans and molluscs (fresh, chilled, frozen or salted)	906.8	1,050.9	1,080.8
Coffee, tea, cocoa and spices	858.3	1,296.9	1,250.5
Crude materials (inedible) except fuels	2,553.7	3,235.4	5,033.6
Crude rubber (incl. synthetic and reclaimed)	980.3	1,274.6	1,965.4
Natural rubber and gums	979.1	1,273.1	1,963.9
Natural rubber (other than latex)	931.9	1,228.3	1,919.3
Metalliferous ores and metal scrap	899.2	1,148.2	1,883.5
Ores and concentrates of non-ferrous base metals	892.4	1,133.2	1,870.2
Copper ores and concentrates	694.6	857.6	1,537.4
Mineral fuels, lubricants, etc.	10,390.9	10,523.5	11,508.6
Coal, coke and briquettes	645.1	829.6	1,043.7
Coal, lignite and peat	642.1	819.3	1,033.2
Petroleum, petroleum products, etc.	5,693.1	6,004.7	6,442.9
Crude petroleum oils, etc.	4,778.4	5,071.6	5,145.7
Refined petroleum products	905.5	923.3	1,276.4
Kerosene and other medium oils	772.7	138.0	—
Gas (natural and manufactured)	4,052.7	3,689.1	4,022.0
Petroleum gases, etc., in the liquefied state	4,052.7	3,689.1	4,022.0
Animal and vegetable oils, fats and waxes	848.1	1,374.4	1,383.6
Fixed vegetable oils and fats	708.4	1,132.4	1,040.8
Fixed vegetable oils, fluid or solid, crude, refined or purified	690.4	1,115.4	1,034.7
Chemicals and related products	823.7	1,001.2	1,510.1
Basic manufactures	9,723.0	9,534.9	10,527.2
Wood and cork manufactures (excl. furniture)	5,129.7	4,832.4	4,662.5
Veneers, plywood, etc.	4,585.4	4,123.9	3,825.5
Plywood of wood sheets	4,221.0	3,716.4	3,462.0
Paper, paperboard, etc.	494.5	595.2	933.1
Textile yarn, fabrics, etc.	2,656.2	2,515.9	2,738.1
Woven fabrics of man-made fibres*	1,205.3	1,115.7	1,179.9
Machinery and transport equipment	2,205.0	3,044.7	3,823.5
Telecommunications and sound equipment	963.6	1,472.5	1,634.3

Exports f.o.b. — *continued*	1993	1994	1995
Miscellaneous manufactured articles	1,982.3	7,499.9	7,806.1
Clothing and accessories (excl. footwear)	3,558.9	3,272.9	3,451.8
Men's and boys' outer garments (excl. knitted goods)	841.3	823.6	727.9
Women's, girls' and infants' outer garments (excl. knitted goods)	1,002.5	860.6	887.7
Footwear	1,628.0	1,848.3	1,998.1
Footwear with leather soles	1,305.8	1,511.5	1,601.9
Total (incl. others)	36,822.8	40,053.4	45,418.0

* Excluding narrow or special fabrics.

Source: UN, *International Trade Statistics Yearbook*.

PRINCIPAL TRADING PARTNERS (US $ million)*

Imports c.i.f.	1993	1994	1995
Australia	1,399.4	1,542.0	2,015.5
Belgium/Luxembourg	339.8	292.0	401.1
Brazil	288.3	313.5	413.7
Canada	410.0	496.8	810.7
China, People's Republic	936.0	1,369.0	1,495.2
France	853.4	788.3	1,063.6
Germany	2,072.4	2,472.7	2,819.2
India	335.4	318.3	478.8
Iran	503.0	248.7	257.0
Italy	523.2	667.8	791.0
Japan	6,248.2	7,739.5	9,215.8
Korea, Republic	2,103.1	2,165.9	2,451.3
Malaysia	517.4	578.8	767.0
Netherlands	626.0	563.7	842.1
Russia	96.5	220.3	438.1
Singapore	1,793.3	1,877.1	2,367.5
Sweden	455.5	356.1	354.1
Switzerland	333.4	266.2	380.6
Thailand	235.3	406.2	737.1
United Kingdom	782.0	710.1	902.5
USA	3,253.8	3,585.6	4,750.9
Total (incl. others)	28,326.8	31,980.6	40,622.7

Exports f.o.b.	1993	1994	1995
Australia	773.7	705.4	915.2
Belgium/Luxembourg	365.7	409.3	538.7
China, People's Republic	1,249.5	1,321.7	1,741.7
France	499.9	426.1	519.8
Germany	1,167.9	1,263.4	1,381.6
Hong Kong	879.1	1,305.1	1,648.3
Italy	614.8	660.7	783.7
Japan	11,168.0	10,928.9	12,287.8
Korea, Republic	2,220.5	2,593.0	2,916.7
Malaysia	586.0	738.5	986.6
Netherlands	1,086.4	1,323.5	1,452.4
Philippines	285.0	365.0	590.3
Saudi Arabia	556.3	413.1	448.2
Singapore	3,231.5	4,026.6	3,732.3
Spain	332.7	453.9	534.6
Thailand	467.7	401.3	702.8
United Arab Emirates	490.3	522.6	519.1
United Kingdom	1,004.9	1,038.2	1,127.1
USA	5,229.8	5,828.6	6,321.7
Total (incl. others)	36,642.5	39,907.1	45,372.6

* Imports by country of production; exports by country of consumption. Figures exclude trade in gold.

Source: UN, *International Trade Statistics Yearbook*.

Transport

RAILWAYS (traffic)

	1991	1992	1993
Passengers embarked (million)	2,288	2,128	2,296
Passenger-km (million)	9,767.3	10,458.5	12,377.1
Freight loaded ('000 tons)	13,726	14,988	15,679
Freight ton-km (million)	3,470	3,779	3,955

ROAD TRAFFIC (motor vehicles registered at 31 December)

	1994	1995*	1996*
Passenger cars	1,890,340	2,030,000	2,204,000
Lorries and trucks	1,251,986	1,310,000	1,391,000
Buses and coaches	651,608	699,000	771,000
Motor cycles	8,134,903	8,680,000	9,382,000

* Estimates.

Source: International Road Federation, *World Road Statistics*.

SHIPPING

Merchant Fleet (registered at 31 December)

	1994	1995	1996
Number of vessels	2,136	2,196	2,348
Displacement ('000 grt)	2,678.3	2,770.5	2,972.6

Source: Lloyd's Register of Shipping, *World Fleet Statistics*.

Sea-borne Freight Traffic ('000 metric tons)

	1992	1993
International:		
Goods loaded	128,570.3	142,968.4
Goods unloaded	38,178.1	44,958.8
Domestic:		
Goods loaded	87,107.1	93,815.6
Goods unloaded	111,663.6	115,485.5

CIVIL AVIATION (traffic on scheduled services)

	1992	1993	1994
Kilometres flown (million)	192	218	215
Passengers carried ('000)	11,177	12,009	12,290
Passenger-km (million)	18,758	19,846	21,166
Total ton-km (million)	2,213	2,416	2,666

Source: UN, *Statistical Yearbook*.

Tourism

FOREIGN VISITORS BY COUNTRY OF ORIGIN
(excluding cruise passengers and excursionists)

	1992	1993	1994*
Australia	220,288	202,831	242,398
France	65,212	63,598	72,812
Germany	120,073	152,062	176,529
Italy	57,213	39,958	45,998
Japan	400,615	440,265	506,346
Korea, Republic	84,442	138,338	162,344
Malaysia	336,393	262,290	294,384
Netherlands/Belgium/Luxembourg	104,222	119,124	138,575
Singapore	776,904	1,007,460	1,114,234
Switzerland	35,821	36,934	42,411
Taiwan	220,316	367,792	441,961
United Kingdom	165,844	131,434	148,428
USA	131,361	127,594	150,832
Total (incl. others)	3,064,161	3,403,138	3,915,000

* Estimates.

1996: Total visitors 5,034,472. Source: Directorate-General of Tourism, Jakarta.

Receipts from tourism (US $ million): 3,278 in 1992; 3,988 in 1993; 4,785 in 1994 (Source: UN, *Statistical Yearbook*); 6,100 in 1996 (Source: Directorate-General of Tourism, Jakarta).

Communications Media

	1992	1993	1994
Television receivers ('000 in use)*	11,500	11,800	12,000
Radio receivers ('000 in use)*	28,100	28,300	28,800
Telephones ('000 main lines in use)†	1,652	1,909	2,521
Telefax stations (number in use)†	35,000	45,000	55,000
Mobile cellular telephones (subscribers)†	35,546	53,438	78,020
Book production: titles‡	6,303§	n.a.	n.a.
Daily newspapers:			
Number of titles	68	n.a.	56
Average circulation ('000)	4,591	n.a.	3,800*
Non-daily newspapers:			
Number of titles	92	n.a.	n.a.
Average circulation ('000)	3,501	n.a.	n.a.
Other periodicals:			
Number of titles	117	n.a.	n.a.
Average circulation ('000)	3,985	n.a.	n.a.

* Estimate(s).
† Source: UN, *Statistical Yearbook.*
‡ Including pamphlets (175 in 1992).
§ First editions only.

Source (unless otherwise indicated): UNESCO, *Statistical Yearbook.*

Education

(1995/96)

	Institutions	Teachers	Pupils and Students
Primary schools	174,414	1,312,208	29,447,974
General junior high schools	28,089	546,230	8,450,606
General senior high schools	10,981	246,928	3,027,462
Senior technical high schools	1,355	50,999	722,744
Senior home economics high schools	166	5,189	53,913
Senior economics high schools.	2,060	55,749	812,208
Other vocational schools	232	6,527	59,617
Universities	1,570	179,687	2,650,244

Source: Indonesian National Commission for UNESCO.

Directory

The Constitution

Indonesia had three provisional Constitutions: in August 1945, February 1950 and August 1950. In July 1959 the Constitution of 1945 was re-enacted by presidential decree. The General Elections Law of 1969 supplemented the 1945 Constitution, which has been adopted permanently by the Majelis Permusyawaratan Rakyat (MPR—People's Consultative Assembly). The following is a summary of its main provisions:

GENERAL PRINCIPLES

The 1945 Constitution consists of 37 articles, four transitional clauses and two additional provisions, and is preceded by a preamble. The preamble contains an indictment of all forms of colonialism, an account of Indonesia's struggle for independence, the declaration of that independence and a statement of fundamental aims and principles. Indonesia's National Independence, according to the text of the preamble, has the state form of a Republic, with sovereignty residing in the People, and is based upon five fundamental principles, the *pancasila*:

1. Belief in the One Supreme God.
2. Just and Civilized Humanity.
3. The Unity of Indonesia.
4. Democracy led by the wisdom of deliberations (*musyawarah*) and consensus among representatives.
5. Social Justice for all the people of Indonesia.

STATE ORGANS

Majelis Permusyawaratan Rakyat—MPR (People's Consultative Assembly)

Sovereignty is in the hands of the People and is exercised in full by the MPR as the embodiment of the whole Indonesian People. The MPR is the highest authority of the State, and is to be distinguished from the legislative body proper (Dewan Perwakilan Rakyat, see below), which is incorporated within the MPR. The MPR, with a total of 1,000 members, is composed of all members of the Dewan, augmented by delegates from the regions, members of political organizations (including members of the armed forces belonging to Golkar), and representatives of other groups. Elections to the MPR are held every five years. The MPR sits at least once every five years, and its primary competence is to determine the Constitution and the broad lines of the policy of the State and the Government. It also elects the President and Vice-President, who are responsible for implementing that policy. All decisions are taken unanimously in keeping with the traditions of *musyawarah*.

The President

The highest executive of the Government, the President, holds office for a term of five years and may be re-elected. As Mandatory of the MPR he must execute the policy of the State according to the Decrees determined by the MPR during its Fourth General and Special Sessions. In conducting the administration of the State, authority and responsibility are concentrated in the President. The Ministers of the State are his assistants and are responsible only to him.

Dewan Perwakilan Rakyat (House of Representatives)

The legislative branch of the State, the Dewan Perwakilan Rakyat, sits at least once a year. It has 500 members: 75 nominated by the President (from the armed forces) and 425 directly elected. Every statute requires the approval of the Dewan. Members of the Dewan have the right to submit draft bills which require ratification by the President, who has the right of veto. In times of emergency the President may enact ordinances which have the force of law, but such Ordinances must be ratified by the Dewan during the following session or be revoked.

Dewan Pertimbangan Agung—DPA (Supreme Advisory Council)

The DPA is an advisory body assisting the President who chooses its members from political parties, functional groups and groups of prominent persons.

Mahkamah Agung (Supreme Court)

The judicial branch of the State, the Supreme Court and the other courts of law are independent of the Executive in exercising their judicial powers.

Badan Pemeriksa Keuangan (State Audit Board)

Controls the accountability of public finance, enjoys investigatory powers and is independent of the Executive. Its findings are presented to the Dewan.

The Government

HEAD OF STATE

President: Gen. Haji MOHAMED SUHARTO (inaugurated 27 March 1968; re-elected March 1973, March 1978, March 1983, March 1988, 10 March 1993 and 10 March 1998).

Vice-President: Prof. Dr Ir BUCHARUDDIN JUSUF (B.J.) HABIBIE.

CABINET*

(February 1998)

Minister of Home Affairs: YOGIE S. MEMET.
Minister of Foreign Affairs: ALI ALATAS.
Minister of Defence and Security: Gen. EDI SUDRADJAT.
Minister of Justice: Haji UTOYO USMAN.
Minister of Information: Gen. RADEN HARTONO.
Minister of Finance: Drs MARIE MUHAMMAD.
Minister of Trade and Industry: Ir TUNKY ARIWIBOWO.
Minister of Agriculture: Dr Ir SYARIFUDDIN BAHARSJAH.

Minister of Mining and Energy: I. B. SUDJANA.

Minister of Forestry: Ir JAMALUDIN SURYOHADIKUSUMO.

Minister of Public Works: RADINAL MOCHTAR.

Minister of Tourism, Posts and Telecommunications: JOOP AVE.

Minister of Communications: Dr HARYANTO DHANUTIRTO.

Minister of Co-operatives and Small-scale Business: Drs SUBIAKTO TJAKRA WERDAJA.

Minister of Manpower: Drs ABDUL LATIEF.

Minister of Transmigration and Resettlement: Ir SISWONO YUDOHUSODO.

Minister of Education and Culture: Dr Ir WARDIMAN DJOJONEGORO.

Minister of Health: Prof. Dr SUYUDI.

Minister of Religious Affairs: Dr TARMIZI TAHIR.

Minister of Social Affairs: Dr ENDANG KUSUMA INTAN SUWENO.

Minister and State Secretary: Drs MURDIONO.

Minister of State and Cabinet Secretary: Drs SAADILAH MURSJID.

Minister of State for Special Affairs: Haji HARMOKO.

Minister of State for National Development Planning and Chairman of the National Planning Development Board (Bappenas): Ir Drs GINANDJAR KARTASASMITA.

Minister of State for Food Affairs and Chairman of the State Logistics Agency (BULOG): Prof. Dr IBRAHIM HASSAN.

Minister of State for Research and Technology, Chairman of the Agency for the Assessment and Application of Technology, and Head of the Strategic Industrial Board: Prof. Dr Ir BUCHARUDDIN JUSUF (B. J.) HABIBIE.

Minister of State for Population and Chairman of the National Family Planning Co-ordinating Board: Dr Haji HARYONO SUYONO.

Minister of State for Investment and Chairman of the Investment Co-ordinating Board: Ir SANYOTO SASTROWARDOYO.

Minister of State for Agrarian Reform and Chairman of the National Land Agency: Ir SONNY HARSONO.

Minister of State for Public Housing: Ir AKBAR TANJUNG.

Minister of State for Environment: Ir SARWONO KUSUMAATMADJA.

Minister of State for Women's Affairs: MIEN SUGANDHI.

Minister of State for Youth Affairs and Sports: HAYONO ISMAN.

Minister of State for Administrative Reform: T. B. SILALAHI.

Co-ordinating Minister for Economics, Finance and Industry and Development Supervision: Prof Dr SALEH AFIFF.

Co-ordinating Minister for Production and Distribution: Ir HARTARTO.

Co-ordinating Minister for Politics and Security: (vacant).

Co-ordinating Minister for People's Welfare: Ir AZWAR ANAS.

Officials with the rank of Minister of State:

Attorney-General: SINGGIH.

Governor of Bank Indonesia: SJAHRIL SABIRIN.

Commander-in-Chief of the Indonesian Armed Forces: Gen. WIRANTO.

* Following his re-election in March 1998, President Suharto appointed a new Cabinet (see Late Information).

MINISTRIES

Office of the President: Istana Merdeka, Jakarta; tel. (21) 331097.

Office of the Vice-President: Jalan Merdeka Selatan 6, Jakarta; tel. (21) 363539.

Office of the Attorney-General: Jalan Sultan Hasanuddin 1, Jakarta; tel. (21) 773557.

Office of the Cabinet Secretary: Jalan Veteran 18, Jakarta Pusat; tel. (21) 3810973.

Office of the Co-ordinating Minister for Economics, Finance and Industry and Development Supervision: Jalan Lapangan Banteng Timur 2–4, Jakarta 10710; tel. (21) 3849895.

Office of the Co-ordinating Minister for Politics and Security: Jalan Merdeka Barat 15, Jakarta 10110; tel. (21) 376004.

Office of the Co-ordinating Minister for People's Welfare: Jalan Merdeka Barat 3, Jakarta 10110; tel. (21) 3849845; fax (21) 3453055.

Office of the Co-ordinating Minister for Production and Distribution: Jalan Jenderal Gatot Subroto, Kav. 52-53, Jakarta 12950; tel. (21) 5251738; fax (21) 5252720.

Office of the Minister of State for Women's Affairs: Jalan Merdeka Barat 15, Jakarta 10110; tel. (21) 3805563; fax (21) 3805562.

Office of the State Secretary: Jalan Veteran No. 17, Jakarta 10110; tel. (21) 3849043; fax (21) 3452685.

Ministry of Administrative Reform: Jalan Veteran III/2, Jakarta Pusat; tel. (21) 3847028.

Ministry of Agrarian Reform: Jalan Sisingamangaraja 2, Kebayoran Baru, Jakarta 12014; tel. (21) 7393939.

Ministry of Agriculture: Jalan Harsono R.M. 3, Ragunan Pasar Minggu, Jakarta Selatan 12550; tel. (21) 7804086.

Ministry of Communications: Jalan Merdeka Barat 8, Jakarta 10110; tel. (21) 3455665; telex 46116; fax (21) 3451657.

Ministry of Co-operatives and Small-scale Business: Jalan H. R. Rasuna Said, Kav. 3–5, POB 177, Jakarta Selatan 12940; tel. (21) 5204366; telex 62843; fax (21) 5204383.

Ministry of Defence and Security: Jalan Merdeka Barat 13-14, Jakarta 10110; tel. (21) 3812028; fax (21) 3845178.

Ministry of Education and Culture: Jalan Jenderal Sudirman, Senayan, Jakarta Pusat; tel. (21) 5731618; fax (21) 5736870.

Ministry of the Environment: Kantor MENLH, Jalan D.I. Panjaitan, Kebon Nanas, Jakarta Timur; tel. (21) 8580067.

Ministry of Finance: Jalan Lapangan Banteng Timur 2-4, Jakarta 10710; tel. (21) 3808388; fax (21) 3808395.

Ministry of Food Affairs: Jalan Kuningan Timur Blok M 2/5, Jakarta Selatan 12950; tel. (21) 5250075; fax. (21) 5256855.

Ministry of Foreign Affairs: Jalan Taman Pejambon 6, Jakarta 10110; tel. (21) 3456014; fax (21) 3813517.

Ministry of Forestry: Gedung Manggala Wanabakti, Block 1, 4th Floor, Jalan Jenderal Gatot Subroto, Jakarta 10270; tel. (21) 5731820; fax (21) 5700226.

Ministry of Health: Jalan H. R. Rasuna Said, Block X5, Kav. 4-9, Jakarta 12950; tel. (21) 5201587; fax (21) 5201591.

Ministry of Home Affairs: Jalan Merdeka Utara 7, Jakarta Pusat 10110; tel. (21) 3842222.

Ministry of Information: Jalan Merdeka Barat 9, Jakarta 10110; tel. (21) 3846189.

Ministry of Investment: Jalan Gatot Subroto 44, Jakarta Selatan; tel. (21) 5250023.

Ministry of Justice: Jalan H. R. Rasuna Said, Kav. 6–7, Kuningan, Jakarta Pusat; tel. (21) 5252575.

Ministry of Manpower: Jalan Jenderal Gatot Subroto 51, Jakarta 12950; tel. (21) 5255685.

Ministry of Mining and Energy: Jalan Merdeka Selatan 18, Jakarta Pusat; tel. (21) 360232; fax (21) 3847461.

Ministry of National Development Planning: Jalan Taman Suropati 2, Jakarta Pusat 10310; tel. (21) 3849063; fax (21) 334779.

Ministry for Population: Jalan Letjenderal Haryono MT, Kav. 9–10 Cawang Jaktim, Jakarta.

Ministry of Public Housing: Jalan Kebon Sirih 31, Jakarta 10340; tel. (21) 333649; fax (21) 327430.

Ministry of Public Works: Jalan Pattimura 20, Kebayoran Baru, Jakarta Selatan 12110; tel. (21) 7262805; fax (21) 7260769.

Ministry of Religious Affairs: Jalan Lapangan Banteng Barat 3–4, Jakarta Pusat; tel. (21) 3811436; fax (21) 380836.

Ministry of Research and Technology: Gedung BPPT, 3rd Floor, Jalan M. H. Thamrin 8, Jakarta Pusat 10310; tel. (21) 324767.

Ministry of Social Affairs: Jalan Salemba Raya 28, Jakarta Pusat 10430; tel. (21) 3103781; fax (21) 3103783.

Ministry of Tourism, Posts and Telecommunications: Jalan Medan Merdeka Barat 16–19, Jakarta 10110; tel. (21) 3456705.

Ministry of Trade and Industry: Jalan Jenderal Gatot Subroto, Kav. 52–53, Jakarta Selatan; tel. (21) 5256458; fax (21) 5201606.

Ministry of Transmigration and Resettlement: Jalan Taman Makam Pahlawan No. 17, Jakarta Selatan; tel. (21) 7989924.

Ministry of Youth Affairs and Sports: Pusat Komunikasi Pemuda, Jalan Gerbang Pemuda 3, Senayan, Jakarta Pusat; tel. (21) 5738318; fax (21) 5738313.

OTHER GOVERNMENT BODIES

Supreme Advisory Council: Jalan Merdeka Utara 15, Jakarta; tel. (21) 362369; Chair. SUDOMO.

Supreme Audit Board: Jalan Gatot Subroto 31, Jakarta; tel. (21) 584081; Chair. J. B. SUMARLIN.

Legislature

MAJELIS PERMUSYAWARATAN RAKYAT—MPR

(People's Consultative Assembly)

Jalan Gatot Subroto 6, Jakarta; tel. (21) 5801322.

The Majelis Permusyawaratan Rakyat (MPR—People's Consultative Assembly) consists of the 500 members of the Dewan Perwakilan

Rakyat (House of Representatives) and 500 other appointees, including regional delegates, members of political organizations (including members of the Indonesian Armed Forces (ABRI) belonging to the Golongan Karya—Golkar), and representatives of other groups.

Speaker: Haji HARMOKO.

	Seats
Members of the Dewan Perwakilan Rakyat	500
Regional representatives*	147
Political organizations†	253
Others	100
Total	1,000

* To be a minimum of four, and a maximum of eight, representatives from each region.

† Including members of the Indonesian Armed Forces (ABRI) belonging to the Golongan Karya (Golkar). Organizations are represented on a proportional basis, according to the composition of the Dewan Perwakilan Rakyat.

Dewan Perwakilan Rakyat
(House of Representatives)

Jalan Gatot Subroto 16, Jakarta; tel. (21) 586833.

In mid-1997 the Dewan Perwakilan Rakyat comprised 500 members; of these, 425 were directly elected and 75 were nominated by the President from the armed forces.

Speaker: Haji HARMOKO.

General Election, 29 May 1997

	Votes	% of votes	Seats
Golongan Karya (Golkar)	84,187,907	74.51	325
Partai Persatuan Pembangunan	25,340,028	22.43	89
Partai Demokrasi Indonesia	3,463,225	3.07	11
Appointed members*	—	—	75
Total	112,991,160	100.00	500

* Members of the political wing of the Indonesian Armed Forces (ABRI).

Political Organizations

A presidential decree of January 1960 enables the President to dissolve any party whose membership does not cover one-quarter of Indonesia, or whose policies are at variance with the aims of the State.

Electoral legislation permits only the following three organizations to contest elections:

Golongan Karya (Golkar) (Functional Group): Jalan Anggrek Nelimurni, Jakarta 11480; tel. (21) 5302222; fax (21) 5303380; f. 1964; reorg. 1971; the governing alliance of groups representing farmers, fishermen and the professions; 35m. mems in 1993; Pres. and Chair. of Advisory Bd Gen. Haji MOHAMED SUHARTO; Chair. Haji HARMOKO; Sec.-Gen. Maj.-Gen. ARY MARDJONO.

Partai Demokrasi Indonesia (PDI) (Indonesian Democratic Party): Jalan Diponegoro 58, Jakarta 10310; tel. (21) 336331; f. 1973 by the merger of five nationalist and Christian parties; party leaders were replaced by government-supported appointees in mid-1996; Chair. SOERJADI; Sec.-Gen. BUTU HUTAPEA.

Partai Persatuan Pembangunan (PPP) (United Development Party): Jalan Diponegoro 60, Jakarta 10310; tel. (21) 336338; fax (21) 3908070; f. 1973 by the merger of four Islamic parties; Chair. ISMAEL HASSAN METAREUM; Sec.-Gen. TOSARI WIDJAJA.

Other officially unrecognized parties include:

Indonesian National Unity: Jakarta; f. 1995 by fmr mems of Sukarno's National Party; seeks full implementation of 1945 Constitution; Chair. SUPENI.

National Brotherhood Foundation: Jakarta; f. 1995; Chair. KHARIS SUHUD.

Partai Rakyat Demokrasi (PRD) (People's Democratic Party): Jakarta; Chair. BUDIMAN SUJATMIKO.

Partai Uni Demokrasi Indonesia (PUDI) (United Democratic Party of Indonesia): Jakarta; f. 1996; anti-Suharto; Chair. SRI BINTANG PAMUNGKAS.

Other groups with political influence include: **Nahdlatul Ulama** (Council of Scholars), largest Muslim organization, 30m. mems, Chair. ABDURRAHMAN WAHID; the **Muhammadiyah,** second largest Muslim organization, f. 1912, 28m. mems; Chair. AMIEN RAIS; **Syarikat Islam**; the **Ikatan Cendekiawan Muslim Indonesia (ICMI)** (Association of Indonesian Muslim Intellectuals), f. 1990 with government support, Chair. Prof. Dr Ir BUCHARUDDIN JUSUF (B.J.) HABIBIE; and **Masyumi Baru,** Sec.-Gen. RIDWAN SAIDI.

The following groups are in conflict with the Government:

Frente Revolucionária do Timor Leste Independente (Fretilin—Revolutionary Front for an Independent East Timor): based in East Timor; f. 1974; seeks independence for East (fmrly Portuguese) Timor; entered into alliance with the UDT in 1986; forces numbering 600-800 men; Sec. for International Relations JOSÉ RAMOS HORTA; Mil. Commdr and acting Leader KONIS SANTANA.

Movement for the Reconciliation and Unity of the People of East Timor (MRUPT): f. 1997; Chair. MANUEL VIEGAS CARRASCALÃO.

National Council of the Maubere (East Timorese) Resistance: front organization for the East Timorese resistance, incl. Fretilin; Chair. JOSÉ ALEXANDRE (XANANA) GUSMÃO; Leader JOSÉ RAMOS HORTA.

National Liberation Front Aceh Sumatra: based in Aceh; f. 1989; seeks independence from Indonesia.

Organisasi Papua Merdeka (OPM) (Free Papua Movement): based in Irian Jaya; f. 1963; seeks unification with Papua New Guinea; Chair. MOZES WEROR; Leader KELLY KWALIK.

União Democrática Timorense (UDT): (Timorese Democratic Union): based in Dili, East Timor; f. 1974; advocates self-determination for East Timor through a gradual process in which ties with Portugal would be maintained; allied itself with Fretilin in 1986; Pres. VINCENTE DA SILVA GUTERRES; Leader JOÃO CARRASCALÃO.

Diplomatic Representation

EMBASSIES IN INDONESIA

Afghanistan: Jalan Dr Kusuma Atmaja 15, Jakarta; tel. (21) 333169; Chargé d'affaires: ABDUL GHAFUR BAHER.

Algeria: Jalan H. R. Rasuna Said, Kav. 10-1, Kuningan, Jakarta 12950; tel. (21) 5254719; fax (21) 5254654; Ambassador: SOUFIANE MIMOUNI.

Argentina: Jalan Panarukan 17, Jakarta 10310; tel. (21) 338088; fax (21) 336148; Ambassador: GASPAR TABOADA.

Australia: Jalan H. R. Rasuna Said, Kav. C15-16, Jakarta 12940; tel. (21) 5227111; fax (21) 5227101; Ambassador: JOHN MCCARTHY.

Austria: Jalan Diponegoro 44, Jakarta 10310; tel. (21) 338101; telex 46387; fax (21) 3904927; e-mail auambjak@rad.net.id; Ambassador: Dr VIKTOR SEGALLA.

Bangladesh: Jalan Situbondo 12, Menteng, Jakarta Pusat; tel. (21) 321690; fax (21) 324850; Ambassador: Maj.-Gen. MOINUL HUSSEIN CHOWDHURY.

Belgium: Wisma BCA, 15th Floor, Jalan Jenderal Sudirman 22–23, Jakarta 12920; tel. (21) 5710510; telex 65211; fax (21) 5700676; Ambassador: MARC VAN RIJSSELBERGHE.

Brazil: Menara Mulia, Suite 1602, Jalan Jenderal Gatot Subroto, Kav. 9, Jakarta 12930; tel. (21) 3904056; telex 45657; fax (21) 3101374; Ambassador: JADIEL FERREIRA DE OLIVEIRA.

Brunei: Wisma BCA, 8th Floor, Jalan Jenderal Sudirman, Kav. 22–23, Jakarta Selatan 12920; tel. (21) 5712124; fax (21) 5712205; Ambassador: Dato' Paduka Haji AWANG YAHYA BIN Haji HARRIS.

Bulgaria: Jalan Imam Bonjol 34–36, Jakarta 10310; tel. (21) 4214049; telex 61106; fax (21) 3150526; Ambassador: GATYU GATEV.

Canada: Wisma Metropolitan I, 5th Floor, Jalan Jenderal Sudirman, Kav. 29, POB 8324/JKS, Jakarta 12084; tel. (21) 5250709; fax (21) 5712251; e-mail jkrta.gr@jkrta01.x400.gc.ca; Ambassador: GARY J. SMITH.

Chile: Bina Mulia Bldg, 7th Floor, Jalan H. R. Rasuna Said, Kav. 10, Kuningan, Jakarta 12950; tel. (21) 5201131; telex 62587; fax (21) 5201955; Ambassador: FERNANDO COUSIÑO.

China, People's Republic: Jalan Jenderal Sudirman 69, Jakarta; tel. (21) 714897; fax (21) 7207782; Ambassador: ZHOU GANG.

Colombia: Central Plaza Bldg, 16th Floor, Jalan Jenderal Sudirman, Kav. 48, Jakarta; tel. (21) 516446; fax (21) 5207717; Ambassador: LUIS FERNANDO ANGEL.

Croatia: Menara Mulia, Suite 2101, Jalan Gatot Subroto, Kav. 9–11, Jakarta 12930; tel. (21) 5257822; fax (21) 5204073; Ambassador: ZELJKO KIRINČIĆ.

Czech Republic: Jalan Gereja Theresia 20, POB 1319, Jakarta Pusat; tel. (21) 3904075; telex 69241; fax (21) 336282; Ambassador: JAROSLAV OLŠA.

Denmark: Bina Mulia Bldg I, 4th Floor, Jalan H. R. Rasuna Said, Kav. 10, Kuningan, Jakarta 12950; tel. (21) 5204350; telex 62123; fax (21) 5201962; e-mail dkembjak@dnet.net.id; Ambassador: MICHAEL STERNBERG.

Egypt: Jalan Teuku Umar 68, Jakarta 10350; tel. (21) 331141; fax (21) 3105073; Ambassador: AHMAD NABIL ELSALAWY.

Finland: Bina Mulia Bldg 1, 10th Floor, Jalan H. R. Rasuna Said, Kav. 10, Kuningan, Jakarta 12950; tel. (21) 5207408; telex 62128; fax (21) 5252033; Ambassador: HANNU HIMANEN.

France: Jalan M. H. Thamrin 20, Jakarta 10310; tel. (21) 3142807; telex 61439; fax (21) 3143338; Ambassador: GERARD CROS.

Germany: Jalan M. H. Thamrin 1, Jakarta 10310; tel. (21) 323908; telex 44333; fax (21) 3143338; Ambassador: WALTER LEWALTER.

Holy See: Jalan Merdeka Timur 18, POB 4227, Jakarta Pusat (Apostolic Nunciature); tel. (21) 3841142; fax (21) 3841143; Apostolic Pro-Nuncio: PIETRO SAMBI, Titular Archbishop of Belcastro.

Hungary: 36 Jalan H. R. Rasuna Said, Kav. X/3, Kuningan, Jakarta 12950; tel. (21) 5203459; fax (21) 5203461; Chargé d'affaires: ÁRPÁD KOVÁCS.

India: Jalan H. R. Rasuna Said, Kav. S/1, Kuningan, Jakarta 12950; tel. (21) 5204150; telex 60953; fax (21) 5204160; e-mail eoijkt@indo.net.id; Ambassador: S.T. DEVARE.

Iran: Jalan Hos Cokroaminoto 110, Menteng, Jakarta Pusat; tel. (21) 331391; telex 69015; fax (21) 3107860; Ambassador: SEYED MOHSEN NABAVI.

Iraq: Jalan Teuku Umar 38, Jakarta 10350; tel. (21) 4214067; telex 69186; fax (21) 4214066; Chargé d'affaires: MUSTAFA MUHAMMAD TAWFIQ.

Italy: Jalan Diponegoro 45, Jakarta 10310; tel. (21) 337445; telex 61546; fax (21) 337422; Ambassador: Dr MARIO BRANDO PENSA.

Japan: Jalan M. H. Thamrin 24, Jakarta 10350; tel. (21) 324308; telex 69182; fax (21) 325460; Ambassador: TAIZO WATANABE.

Jordan: Jalan Denpasar Raya, Blok A XIII, Kav. 1–2, Jakarta 12950; tel. (21) 5204400; fax (21) 5202447; Ambassador: LU'AY KHASHMAN.

Korea, Democratic People's Republic: Jalan H. R. Rasuna Said, Kav. X.5, Jakarta; tel. (21) 5210181; Ambassador: JO KYU IL.

Korea, Republic: Jalan Jenderal Gatot Subroto 57, Jakarta Selatan; tel. (21) 5201915; fax (21) 514159; Ambassador: YOUNG-SUP KIM.

Kuwait: Jalan Denpasar Raya, Blok A XII, Kuningan, Jakarta 12950; tel. (21) 5202477; fax (21) 5204359; Ambassador: JASEM M. J. AL-MUBARAKI.

Laos: Jalan Kintamani Raya C-15, 33 Kuningan Timur, Jakarta 12950; tel. (21) 5229602; fax (21) 5229601; Ambassador: LY SOUTHAVILAY.

Libya: Jalan Pekalongan 24, Jakarta; tel. (21) 335308; fax (21) 335726; Chargé d'affaires a.i.: TAJEDDIN A. JERBI.

Malaysia: Jalan H. R. Rasuna Said, Kav. X/6, Kuningan, Jakarta 12950; tel. (21) 5224947; fax (21) 5224974; Ambassador: Dato' ZAINAL ABIDIN BIN ALIAS.

Mexico: Menara Mulia, Suite 2306, Jalan Gatot Subroto, Kav. 9–11, Jakarta 12930; tel. (21) 5203980; fax (21) 5203978; Ambassador: SERGIO LEY-LÓPEZ.

Morocco: Suite 512, 5th Floor, South Tower, Kuningan Plaza, Jalan H. R. Rasuna Said C-11-14, Jakarta 12940; tel. (21) 5200773; fax (21) 5200586; Ambassador: HASSAN FASSI-FIHRI.

Myanmar: Jalan Haji Agus Salim 109, Jakarta Selatan; tel. (21) 320440; telex 61295; fax (21) 327204; Ambassador: U NYUNT TIN.

Netherlands: Jalan H. R. Rasuna Said, Kav. S/3, Kuningan, Jakarta 12950; tel. (21) 5251515; telex 62411; fax (21) 5700734; Ambassador: P. R. BROUWER.

New Zealand: Jalan Diponegoro 41, Menteng, POB 2439, Jakarta 10310; tel. (21) 330680; fax (21) 3153686; Ambassador: TIM GROSER.

Nigeria: 15 Jalan Imam Bonjol, POB 3649, Jakarta 10310; tel. (21) 327838; telex 61607; fax (21) 3908450; Ambassador: T. SOLURI.

Norway: Bina Mulia Bldg, 4th Floor, Jalan H. R. Rasuna Said, Kav. 10, Jakarta 12950; tel. (21) 5251990; telex 62127; fax (21) 5207365; Ambassador: JAN WESSEL HEGG.

Pakistan: Jalan Teuku Umar 50, Jakarta 10350; tel. (21) 350576; Ambassador: MATAHAR HUSEIN.

Papua New Guinea: Panin Bank Centre, 6th Floor, Jalan Jenderal Sudirman 1, Jakarta 10270; tel. (21) 7251218; fax (21) 7201012; Ambassador: ALAN I. OAISA.

Peru: Bina Mulia Bldg 2, 3rd Floor, Jalan H. R. Rasuna Said, Kav. 11, Kuningan, Jakarta 12950; tel. (21) 5201176; fax (21) 5201932; Ambassador: ELARD ESCALA.

Philippines: Jalan Imam Bonjol 6–8, Jakarta 10310; tel. (21) 3100334; fax (21) 3151167; Ambassador: EUSEBIO A. ABAQUIN.

Poland: Jalan Diponegoro 65, Menteng, Jakarta Pusat 10320; tel. (21) 3140509; fax (21) 327343; Ambassador: KSAWERY BURSKI.

Romania: Jalan Teuku Cik Ditiro 42A, Menteng, Jakarta Pusat; tel. (21) 3106240; telex 61208; fax (21) 3907759; Ambassador: DUMITRU TANCU.

Russia: Jalan H. R. Rasuna Said, Blok X/7, Kav 1–2, Jakarta; tel. (21) 5222912; Ambassador: NIKOLAI SOLOVIYEV.

Saudi Arabia: Jalan Imam Bonjol 3, Jakarta 10310; tel. (21) 3105499; fax (21) 4214046; Ambassador: ABDULLAH A. ALIM.

Singapore: Jalan H. R. Rasuna Said, Blok X/4, Kav. 2, Kuningan, Jakarta 12950; tel. (21) 5201489; telex 62213; fax (21) 5201486; Ambassador: EDWARD LEE.

Slovakia: Jalan Prof. Mohammed Yamin 29, POB 1368, Jakarta Pusat; tel. (21) 3101068; fax (21) 3101180; Ambassador: PETER AMBROVIC.

South Africa: Suite 705, Wisma GKBI, Jalan Jenderal Sudirman 28, POB 1329, Jakarta 10210; tel. (21) 5740660; fax (21) 5740661; Ambassador: S. B. KUBHEKA.

Spain: Jalan H. Agus Salim 61, Jakarta 10350; tel. (21) 335937; telex 161667; fax (21) 325996; Ambassador: ANTONIO SÁNCHEZ JARA.

Sri Lanka: Jalan Diponegoro 70, Jakarta 10320; tel. (21) 3161886; fax (21) 3107962; e-mail lankaemb@vision.net.id; Ambassador: RATNE DESHAPRIYA SENANAYAKE.

Sudan: Wisma Bank Dharmala, 7th Floor, Suite 01, Jalan Jenderal Sudirman, Kav. 28, Jakarta 12920; tel. (21) 5212075; fax (21) 5212077; e-mail Sudanijk@Centrin.net.id; Ambassador: HASSAN IBRAHIM GADELKARIM.

Sweden: Bina Mulia Bldg, 7th Floor, Jalan H. R. Rasuna Said, Kav. 10; POB 2824, Jakarta 10001; tel. (21) 5201551; telex 62714; fax (21) 5252652; Ambassador: MIKAEL LINDSTRÖM.

Switzerland: Jalan H. R. Rasuna Said X-3/2, Kuningan 12950 Jakarta Selatan; tel. (21) 516061; telex 44113; fax (21) 5202289; Ambassador: BERNARD FREYMOND.

Syria: Jalan Karang Asem I/8, Jakarta 12950; tel. (21) 515991; Ambassador: NADIM DOUAY.

Thailand: Jalan Imam Bonjol 74, Jakarta 10310; tel. (21) 3904052; fax (21) 3107469; Ambassador: SOMPHAND KOKILANON.

Tunisia: Wisma Dharmala Sakti, Jalan Jenderal Sudirman 32, Jakarta 10220; tel. (21) 5703432; fax (21) 5700016; Ambassador: MOHAMED GHERIB.

Turkey: Jalan H. R. Rasuna Said, Kav. 1, Kuningan, Jakarta 12950; tel. (21) 516258; telex 62506; fax (21) 5226056; Ambassador: SEVINÇ DALYANOĞLU.

United Arab Emirates: Jalan Singaraja Blok C-4 Kav. 16-17, Jakarta Selatan; tel. (21) 5206518; fax (21) 5206526; Chargé d'affaires: HAMAD SAEED LI'ZAABI.

United Kingdom: Jalan M. H. Thamrin 75, Jakarta 10310; tel. (21) 3156264; fax (21) 3154061; Ambassador: ROBIN CHRISTOPHER.

USA: Jalan Merdeka Selatan 5, Jakarta; tel. (21) 3442211; fax (21) 3862259; internet http://www.usembassyjakarta.org; Ambassador: J. STAPLETON ROY.

Venezuela: Central Plaza Bldg, 17th Floor, Jalan Jenderal Sudirman, Kav. 47, Jakarta 12930; tel. (21) 516885; fax (21) 512487; Ambassador: Dr JOSÉ ALEJANDRO SUÑÉ.

Viet Nam: Jalan Teuku Umar 25, Jakarta; tel. (21) 3100358; telex 45211; fax (21) 3100359; Ambassador: NGUYEN DANG QUANG.

Yemen: Jalan Yusuf Adiwinata 29, Jakarta; tel. (21) 3904074; fax (21) 4214946; Ambassador: ABDUL WAHAD FARAH.

Yugoslavia: Jalan Hos Cokroaminoto 109, Jakarta 10310; tel. (21) 333593; telex 45149; fax (21) 333613; Ambassador: VJEKOSLAV KOPRIVNJAK.

Judicial System

There is one codified criminal law for the whole of Indonesia. In December 1989 the Islamic Judicature Bill, giving wider powers to Shariah courts, was approved by the Dewan Perwakilan Rakyat (House of Representatives). The new law gave Muslim courts authority over civil matters, such as marriage. Muslims may still choose to appear before a secular court. Europeans are subject to the Code of Civil Law published in the State Gazette in 1847. Alien orientals (i.e. Arabs, Indians, etc.) and Chinese are subject to certain parts of the Code of Civil Law and the Code of Commerce. The work of codifying this law has started, but, in view of the great complexity and diversity of customary law, it may be expected to take a considerable time to achieve.

Supreme Court (Mahkamah Agung): Jalan Merdeka Utara 9–13, Jakarta 10110; tel. (21) 3843348; fax (21) 3811057; the final court of appeal.

Chief Justice: SARWATA.

High Courts in Jakarta, Surabaya, Medan, Ujungpandang (Makassar), Banda Aceh, Padang, Palembang, Bandung, Semarang, Banjarmasin, Menado, Denpasar, Ambon and Jayapura deal with appeals from the District Courts.

District Courts deal with marriage, divorce and reconciliation.

Religion

All citizens are required to state their religion. According to a survey in 1985, 86.9% of the population were Muslims, while 9.6% were Christians, 1.9% were Hindus, 1.0% were Buddhists and 0.6% professed adherence to tribal religions.

ISLAM

In 1993 nearly 90% of Indonesians were Muslims. Indonesia has the world's largest Islamic population.

Majelis Ulama Indonesia (MUI) (Indonesian Ulama Council): Komp. Masjid Istiqlal, Jalan Taman Wijaya Kesuma, Jakarta 10710; tel. (21) 3455471; fax (21) 3855412; Central Muslim organization; Chair. H. HASAN BASRI.

CHRISTIANITY

Persekutuan Gereja-Gereja di Indonesia (Communion of Churches in Indonesia): Jalan Salemba Raya 10, Jakarta 10430; tel. (21) 3908119; fax (21) 3150457; f. 1950; 70 mem. churches; Chair. Rev. Dr SULARSO SOPATER; Gen. Sec. Rev. Dr JOSEPH M. PATTIASINA.

The Roman Catholic Church

Indonesia (excluding East Timor) comprises eight archdioceses and 26 dioceses. At 31 December 1995 there were an estimated 5,380,457 adherents, representing 2.7% of the population.

Bishops' Conference: Konferensi Waligereja Indonesia (KWI), Jalan Cut Meutia 10, POB 3044, Jakarta 10002; tel. (21) 336422; fax (21) 3918527; e-mail kwi@parokinet.org; f. 1973; Pres. Rt Rev. JOSEPH SUWATAN, Bishop of Manado.

Archbishop of Ende: Most Rev. ABDON LONGINUS DA CUNHA, POB 210, Jalan Katedral 5, Ndona-Ende 86312, Flores; tel. (381) 21176; fax (381) 21606.

Archbishop of Jakarta: Cardinal JULIUS RIYADI DARMAATMADJA, Keuskupan Agung, Jalan Katedral 7, Jakarta 10710; tel. (21) 3813345; fax (21) 3855681.

Archbishop of Kupang: Most Rev. GREGORIUS MANTEIRO, Keuskupan Agung, Jalan Thamrin, Oepoi, Kupang 85111, Timor NTT; tel. and fax (391) 33331.

Archbishop of Medan: Most Rev. ALFRED GONTI PIUS DATUBARA, Jalan Imam Bonjol 39, POB 192, Medan 20152, Sumatra Utara; tel. (61) 516647; fax (61) 545745.

Archbishop of Merauke: Most Rev. JACOBUS DUIVENVOORDE, Keuskupan Agung, Jalan Mandala 30, Merauke 99602, Irian Jaya; tel. (971) 21011.

Archbishop of Pontianak: Most Rev. HIERONYMUS HERCULANUS BUMBUN, Keuskupan Agung, Jalan A. R. Hakin 92A, POB 1119, Pontianak 78001, Kalimantan Barat; tel. (561) 32382; fax (561) 38785.

Archbishop of Semarang: (vacant), Keuskupan Agung, Jalan Pandanaran 13, Semarang 50244; tel. (24) 312276; fax (24) 414741.

Archbishop of Ujung Pandang: Most Rev. JOHANNES LIKU ADA', Keuskupan Agung, Jalan Thamrin 5–7, Ujung Pandang 90111, Sulawesi Selatan; tel. (411) 315744; fax (411) 326674.

East Timor comprises the dioceses of Dili and Baucau, directly responsible to the Holy See. In 1996 the territory had an estimated 732,017 Roman Catholics (about 85% of the total population).

Bishop of Baucau: (vacant); Apostolic Administrator: Rt Rev. BASILIO DO NASCIMENTO MARTINS (Titular Bishop of Septimunicia).

Bishop of Dili: (vacant); Apostolic Administrator: Rt Rev. CARLOS FILIPE XIMINES BELO (Titular Bishop of Lorium), Uskupan Lecidere (Bidau), POB 10250, Dili 88010; tel. (390) 21331.

Other Christian Churches

Protestant Church in Indonesia (Gereja Protestan di Indonesia): Jalan Medan Merdeka Timur 10, Jakarta 10110; tel. (21) 3519003; consists of nine churches of Calvinistic tradition; 2,789,055 mems, 3,839 congregations, 1,963 pastors (1997); Chair. Rev. D. J. LUMENTA.

Numerous other Protestant communities exist throughout Indonesia, mainly organized on a local basis. The largest of these (1985 memberships) are: the Batak Protestant Christian Church (1,875,143); the Christian Church in Central Sulawesi (100,000); the Christian Evangelical Church in Minahasa (730,000); the Christian Protestant Church in Indonesia (210,924); the East Java Christian Church (123,850); the Evangelical Christian Church in West Irian (360,000); the Evangelical Christian Church of Sangir-Talaud (190,000); the Indonesian Christian Church/Huria Kristen Indonesia (316,525); the Javanese Christian Churches (121,500); the Kalimantan Evangelical Church (182,217); the Karo Batak Protestant Church (164,288); the Nias Protestant Christian Church (250,000); the Protestant Church in the Moluccas (575,000); the Protestant Evangelical Church in Timor (700,000); the Simalungun Protestant Christian Church (155,000); and the Toraja Church (250,000).

BUDDHISM

All-Indonesia Buddhist Association: Jakarta.

Indonesian Buddhist Council: Jakarta.

The Press

In August 1990 the Government announced that censorship of both the local and foreign press was to be relaxed and that the authorities would refrain from revoking the licences of newspapers that violated legislation governing the press. In practice, however, there was little change in the Government's policy towards the press. In June 1994 the Government revoked the publishing licences of three principal news magazines, *Tempo, Editor* and *DeTik*.

PRINCIPAL DAILIES

Bali

Harian Pagi Umum (Bali Post): Jalan Kepudang 67A, Denpasar 80232; f. 1948; daily (Indonesian edn), weekly (English edn); Editor K. NADHA; circ. 25,000.

Irian Jaya

Berita Karya: Jayapura.

Teropong: Jalan Halmahera, Jayapura.

Java

Angkatan Bersenjata: Jalan Merdeka Barat 2, Jakarta Pusat; tel. (21) 364568; fax (21) 366870.

Bandung Post: Jalan Lodaya 38A, Bandung 40264; tel. (22) 305124; fax (22) 302882; f. 1979; Chief Editor AHMAD SAELAN; Dir AHMAD JUSACC.

Berita Buana: Jalan Letjenderal S. Parman, Kav. 72, Slipi, Jakarta; tel. (21) 5487175; fax (21) 5491555; f. 1970; relaunched 1990; Indonesian; circ. 150,000.

Berita Yudha: Jalan Letjenderal Haryono MT22, Jakarta; tel. (21) 8298331; f. 1971; Indonesian; Editor SUNARDI; circ. 50,000.

Bisnis Indonesia: Jalan Letjenderal S. Parman, Kav. 12, Slipi, Jakarta; tel. (21) 5305869; fax (21) 5305868; f. 1985; Indonesian; Editor SUKAMDANI S. GITOSARDJONO; circ. 60,000.

Harian Indonesia (Indonesia Rze Pao): Jalan Toko Tiga Seberang 21, POB 4755, Jakarta Kota; tel. (21) 6295984; fax (21) 6297830; f. 1966; Chinese; Editor W. D. SUKISMAN; Dir HADI WIBOWO; circ. 42,000.

Harian Terbit: Jalan Pulogadung 15, Kawasan Industri Pulogadung, Jakarta 13920; tel. (21) 4602953; fax (21) 4602950; f. 1972; Indonesian; Editor H. R. S. HADIKAMAJAYA; circ. 125,000.

Harian Umum AB: CTC Bldg, 2nd Floor, Kramat Raya 94, Jakarta Pusat; f. 1965; official armed forces journal; Dir GOENARSO; Editor-in-Chief N. SOEPANGAT; circ. 80,000.

The Indonesia Times: Jalan Pulo Lentut 12, Jakarta Timur; tel. (21) 4611280; fax (21) 375012; f. 1974; English; Editor TRIBUANA SAID; circ. 35,000.

Indonesian Observer: Redtop Square, Block C-7, Jalan Pecenongan 72, Jakarta 10120; tel. (21) 3500155; fax (21) 3502417; f. 1955; English; independent; Editor (vacant); circ. 25,000.

Jakarta Post: Jalan Palmerah Selatan 15, Jakarta 10270; tel. (21) 5300476; fax (21) 5309066; f. 1983; English; Gen. Man. RAYMOND TORUAN; Chief Editor SUSANTO PUDJOMARTONO; circ. 50,000.

Jawa Pos: Jalan Kembang Jepun 167–169, Surabaya; tel. (31) 830774; telex 31988; fax (31) 830996; f. 1949; Indonesian; Chief Editor DAHLAN ISKAN; circ. 120,000.

Kedaulatan Rakyat: Jalan P. Mangkubumi 40–42, Yogyakarta; tel. (274) 65685; fax (274) 63125; f. 1945; Indonesian; independent; Editor IMAN SUTRISNO; circ. 50,000.

Kompas: Jalan Palmerah Selatan 26–28, Jakarta; tel. (21) 5483008; fax (21) 5305868; f. 1965; Indonesian; Editor Drs JAKOB OETAMA; circ. 523,453.

Media Indonesia: Komplex Pelta Kedoya, Jalan Pilar Mas Raya, Kav. A-3, Kedoya Selatan-Kebon Jeruk, Jakarta 11520; tel. (21) 5812087; telex 45431; fax (21) 5812086; f. 1989; fmrly Prioritas; Indonesian; Pres. Dir SURYA PALOH; circ. 251,517.

Merdeka: Jalan Atang. M. Sangaji 11, Tangerang 15125; tel. (21) 5556059; f. 1945; Indonesian; independent; Dir and Chief Editor B. M. DIAH; circ. 130,000.

Neraca: Jalan Jambrut 2–4, Jakarta; tel. (21) 323969; fax (21) 3101873.

Pelita (Torch): Saleti Bldg, 4th Floor, Jalan Letjenderal Haryono 1, Jakarta Selatan; tel. (21) 3901404; fax (21) 5706788; f. 1974; Indonesian; Muslim; Editor AKBAR TANJUNG; circ. 80,000.

Pewarta Surabaya: Jalan Karet 23, POB 85, Surabaya; f. 1905; Indonesian; Editor RADEN DJAROT SOEBIANTORO; circ. 10,000.

Pikiran Rakyat: Jalan Asia-Afrika 77, Bandung 40111; tel. (22) 51216; telex 28385; f. 1950; Indonesian; independent; Editor BRAM M. DARMAPRAWIRA; circ. 150,000.

Pos Kota: Jalan Gajah Mada 100, Jakarta 10130; tel. (21) 6290874; telex 41171; f. 1970; Indonesian; Editor H. SOFYAN LUBIS; circ. 500,000.

Republika: Jalan Warung Buncit Raya 37, Jakarta 12510; tel. (21) 7803747; fax (21) 7800420; f. 1993; organ of ICMI; Chief Editor PARNI HADI.

Sinar Pagi: Jalan Letjenderal Haryono MT22, Jakarta Selatan.

Suara Karya: Jalan Bangka II/2, Kebayoran Baru, Jakarta Selatan; tel. (21) 7991352; fax (21) 7995261; f. 1971; Indonesian; Editor SYAMSUL BASRI; circ. 100,000.

Suara Merdeka: Jalan Pandanaran 30, Semarang 50241; tel. (24) 412660; telex 22269; fax (24) 411116; f. 1950; Indonesian; Publr Ir BUDI SANTOSO; Editor SUWARNO; circ. 200,000.

Suara Pembaruan: Jalan Dewi Sartika 136/D, Cawang, Jakarta 13630; tel. (21) 8093208; telex 48202; fax (21) 8091652; f. 1987; licence revoked in 1986 as Sinar Harapan (Ray of Hope); Chief Editor ALBERT HASIBUAN.

Surabaya Post: Jalan Taman Ade Irma Nasution 1, Surayaba; tel. (31) 45394; telex 31158; fax (31) 519585; f. 1953; independent; Publr Mrs TUTY AZIS; Editor IMAM PUJONO; circ. 115,000.

Wawasan: Komplek Pertokoan Simpang Lima, Blok A 10, Semarang 50241; tel. (24) 314171; telex 22183; fax (24) 413001; f. 1986; Indonesian; Chief Editor SOETJIPTO; circ. 65,000.

Kalimantan

Banjarmasin Post: Jalan Haryono MT 54–143, Banjarmasin; tel. (511) 53266; telex 39155; fax (511) 53120; f. 1971; Indonesian; Chief Editor H. J. MENTAYA; circ. 50,000.

Gawi Manuntung: Jalan Pangeran Samudra 97B, Banjarmasin; f. 1972; Indonesian; Editor M. ALI SRI INDRADJAYA; circ. 5,000.

Harian Umum Akcaya: Jalan Veteran 1, Pontianak.

Lampung Post: Jalan Pangkal Pinang, Lampung.

Manuntung: Jalan Jenderal Sudirman RT XVI 82, Balikpapan 76144; tel. (542) 35359.

Maluku

Pos Maluku: Jalan Raya Pattimura 19, Ambon; tel. (911) 44614.

Suara Maluku: Komplex Perdagangan Mardikas, Block D3/11A, Ternate; tel. (911) 44590.

Sulawesi

Bulletin Sulut: Jalan Korengkeng 38, Lt II Manado, 95114, Sulawesi Utara.

Cahaya Siang: Jalan Kembang II 2, Manado, 95114, Sulawesi Utara; tel. (431) 61054; fax (431) 63393.

Manado Post: Jalan Yos Sudarso 73, Manado.

Pedoman Rakyat: Jalan H. A. Mappanyukki 28, Ujungpandang; f. 1947; independent; Editor M. BASIR; circ. 30,000.

Suluh Merdeka: Jalan Haryane MT, POB 1105, Manado, 95110.

Tegas: Jalan Mappanyukki 28, Ujung Pandang; tel. (411) 3960.

Sumatra

Analisa: Jalan Jenderal A. Yani 37–43, Medan; tel. (61) 326655; telex 51326; fax (61) 514031; f. 1972; Indonesian; Editor SOFFYAN; circ. 75,000.

Harian Haluan: Jalan Damar 59 C/F, Padang; f. 1948; Editor-in-Chief RIVAI MARLAUT; circ. 40,000.

Harian Umum Nasional Waspada: Jalan Brigjenderal 1 Katamso, Medan 20151; tel. (61) 550858; telex 51347; fax (61) 510025; f. 1947; Indonesian; Editor-in-Chief HAJJAH ANI IDRUS.

Mimbar Umum: Merah, Medan; tel. (61) 517807; telex 51905; f. 1947; Indonesian; independent; Editor MOHD LUD LUBIS; circ. 55,000.

Serambi Indonesia: Jalan T. Nyak Arief 159, Lampriek, Banda Aceh.

Sinar Indonesia Baru: Jalan Brigjenderal Katamso 66, Medan 20151; tel. (61) 512530; telex 51713; fax (61) 510150; f. 1970; Indonesian; Chief Editor G. M. PANGGABEAN; circ. 150,000.

Suara Rakyat Semesta: Jalan K.H. Ashari 52, Palembang; Indonesian; Editor DJADIL ABDULLAH; circ. 10,000.

Waspada: Jalan Jenderal Sudirman, cnr Jalan Brigjenderal Katamso 1, Medan 20151; tel. (61) 550858; telex 51347; fax (61) 510025; f. 1947; Indonesian; Chief Editor ANI IDRUS; circ. 60,000 (daily), 55,000 (Sunday).

PRINCIPAL PERIODICALS

Amanah: Jalan Garuda 69, Kemayoran, Jakarta; tel. (21) 410254; fortnightly; Muslim current affairs; Indonesian; Man. Dir MASKUN ISKANDAR; circ. 180,000.

Berita Negara: Jalan Pertjetakan Negara 21, Kotakpos 2111, Jakarta; tel. (21) 4207251; fax (21) 4207251; f. 1951; 2 a week; official gazette.

Bobo: PT Gramedia, Jalan Kebahagiaan 4-14, Jakarta 11140; tel. (21) 6297809; telex 41216; fax (21) 6390080; f. 1973; weekly; children's magazine; Editor TINEKE LATUMETEN; circ. 240,000.

Bola: Jalan Palmerah Selatan 3, Jakarta 10270; tel. (21) 5301926; fax (21) 5301952; 2 a week; Tuesday and Friday; sports magazine; Indonesian; Editor SUMOHADI MARSIS; circ. 715,000.

Buana Minggu: Jalan Tanah Abang Dua 33, Jakarta Pusat 10110; tel. (21) 364190; telex 46472; weekly; Sunday; Indonesian; Editor WINOTO PARARTHO; circ. 193,450.

Business News: Jalan H. Abdul Muis 70, Jakarta 10160; tel. (21) 3848207; fax (21) 3454280; f. 1956; 3 a week (Indonesian edn), 2 a week (English edn); Chief Editor SANJOTO SASTROMIHARDJO; circ. 15,000.

Citra: Gramedia Bldg, Unit 11, 5th Floor, Jalan Palmerah Selatan No. 24-26, Jakarta 10270; tel. (21) 5483008; fax (21) 5494035; f. 1990; weekly; TV and film programmes, music trends and celebrity news; circ. 239,000

Depthnews Indonesia: Jalan Jatinegara Barat III/6, Jakarta 13310; tel. (21) 8194994; fax (21) 8195501; f. 1972; weekly; publ. by Press Foundation of Indonesia; Editor SUMONO MUSTOFFA.

Dunia Wanita: Jalan Brigjenderal, Katamso 1, Medan; tel. (61) 520858; fax (61) 510025; f. 1949; fortnightly; Indonesian; women's magazine; Chief Editor Dr RAYATI SYAFRIN; circ. 10,000.

Economic Review: c/o Bank BNI, Strategic Planning Division, Jalan Jenderal Sudirman, Kav. 1, POB 2955, Jakarta 10220; tel. (21) 5711185; telex 65511; fax (21) 5728456; f. 1966; 6 a year; English.

Ekonomi Indonesia: Jalan Merdeka, Timur 11–12, Jakarta; tel. (21) 494458; monthly; English; economic journal; Editor Z. ACHMAD; circ. 20,000.

Eksekutif: Jalan R. S. Fatmawati 21, Jakarta 12410; tel. (21) 7502513; fax (21) 7502676.

Femina: Jalan H. R. Rasuna Said, Blok B, Kav. 32–33, Jakarta Selatan; tel. (21) 513816; telex 62338; fax (21) 513041; f. 1972; weekly; women's magazine; Publr SOFJAN ALISJAHBANA; Editor WIDARTI GUNAWAN; circ. 130,000.

Forum: Kebayoran Centre, 12A–14, Jalan Kebayoran Baru, Welbak, Jakarta 12240; tel. (21) 7255625; fax (21) 7255645.

Gadis Magazine: Jalan H. R. Rasuna Said, Blok B, Kav. 32–33, Jakarta 12910; tel. (21) 513816; telex 62338; fax (21) 513041; f. 1973; every 10 days; Indonesian; youth, women's interest; Editor PIA ALISJAHBANA; circ. 90,000.

Gatra: Wisma Kosgoro, 6th Floor, Jalan M. H. Thamrin 53, Jakarta 10350; tel. (21) 2303007; fax (21) 2302516; f. 1995 by former employees of *Tempo* (banned in 1994); Gen. Man. LUKMAN SETIAWAN.

Hai: Jalan Kebahagiaan 4-14, Jakarta 11140; tel. (21) 6297809; telex 41216; fax (21) 6390080; f. 1973; weekly; youth magazine; Editor ARSWENDO ATMOWILOTO; circ. 70,000.

Indonesia Business News: Wisma Bisnis Indonesia, Jalan Letjenderal S. Parman, Kav. 12, Slipi, Jakarta 11410; tel. (21) 5304016; fax (21) 5305868; English.

Indonesia Business Weekly: Jalan Letjenderal S. Parman, Kav. 12, Slipi, Jakarta 11410; tel. (21) 5304016; fax (21) 5305868; English; Editor TAUFIK DARUSMAN.

Indonesia Magazine: 20 Jalan Merdeka Barat, Jakarta; tel. (21) 352015; telex 46655; f. 1969; monthly; English; Chair. G. DWIPAYANA; Editor-in-Chief HADELY HASIBUAN; circ. 15,000.

Intisari (Digest): Jalan Palmerah Selatan 24, Jakarta 10270; tel. (21) 5483008; telex 41216; fax (21) 5494035; f. 1963; monthly; Indonesian; investment and trading; Editors IRAWATI, Drs J. OETAMA; circ. 141,000.

Jakarta Jakarta: Gramedia Bldg, Unit 11, 5th Floor, Jalan Palmerah Selatan No. 24–26, Jakarta 10270; tel. (21) 5483008; fax (21) 5494035; f. 1985; weekly; food, fun, fashion and celebrity news; circ. 70,000.

Keluarga: Jalan Sangaji 11, Jakarta; fortnightly; women's and family magazine; Editor S. DAHONO.

Majalah Ekonomis: POB 4195, Jakarta; monthly; English; business; Chief Editor S. ARIFIN HUTABARAT; circ. 20,000.

Majalah Kedokteran Indonesia (Journal of the Indonesian Medical Asscn): Jalan Kesehatan 111/29, Jakarta 11/16; f. 1951; monthly; Indonesian, English.

Manglé: Jalan Lodaya 19–21, 40262 Bandung; tel. (22) 303438; f. 1957; weekly; Sundanese; Chief Editor Drs OEJANG DARAJATOEN; circ. 74,000.

Matra: Grafity Pers, Kompleks Buncit Raya Permai, Kav. 1, Jalan Warung, POB 3476, Jakarta; tel. (21) 515952; telex 46777; f. 1986; monthly; men's magazine; general interest and current affairs; Editor-in-Chief (vacant); circ. 100,000.

Mimbar Kabinet Pembangunan: Jalan Merdeka-Barat 7, Jakarta; f. 1966; monthly; Indonesian; publ. by Dept of Information.

Mutiara: Jalan Dewi Sartika 136D, Cawang, Jakarta Timur; general interest; Publr H. G. RORIMPANDEY.

Nova: PT Gramedia, Jalan Kebahagiaan 4-14, Jakarta 11140; tel. (21) 6297809; telex 41216; fax (21) 6390080; weekly; Sunday; women's interest; Indonesian; Editor EVIE FADJARI; circ. 220,000.

Otomotif: Gramedia Bldg, Unit 11, 5th Floor, Jalan Palmerah Selatan No 24–26, Jakarta 10270; tel. (21) 5483008; fax (21) 5494035; f. 1990; weekly; automotive specialist tabloid; circ. 204,000.

Peraba: Bintaran Kidul 5, Yogyakarta; weekly; Indonesian and Javanese; Roman Catholic; Editor W. KARTOSOEHARSONO.

Pertani PT: Jalan Pasar Minggu, Kalibata, POB 247/KBY, Jakarta Selatan; tel. (21) 793108; telex 47249; f. 1974; monthly; Indonesian; agricultural; Pres. Dir Ir RUSLI YAHYA.

Rajawali: Jakarta; monthly; Indonesian; civil aviation and tourism; Dir R. A. J. LUMENTA; Man. Editor KARYONO ADHY.

Selecta: Kebon Kacang 29/4, Jakarta; fortnightly; illustrated; Editor SAMSUDIN LUBIS; circ. 80,000.

Simponi: Jakarta; f. 1994 by former employees of *DeTik* (banned in 1994).

Sinar Jaya: Jakarta Selatan; fortnightly; agriculture; Chief Editor Ir SURYONO PROJOPRANOTO.

Swasembada: Gedung Chandra Lt 2, Jalan M. H. Thamrin 20, Jakarta 10310; tel. (21) 3103316.

Tiara: Gramedia Bldg, Unit 11, 5th Floor, Jalan Palmerah Selatan No 24–26, Jakarta 10270; tel (21) 5483008; fax (21) 5494035; f. 1990; fortnightly; lifestyles, features and celebrity news; circ. 47,000.

Ummat: Jakarta; Islamic; sponsored by ICMI.

NEWS AGENCIES

Antara (Indonesian National News Agency): Wisma Antara, 19th and 20th Floors, 17 Jalan Merdeka Selatan, POB 1257, Jakarta 10110; tel. (21) 364768; telex 44305; fax (21) 3843052; f. 1937; 2,784 commercial, 11 radio, five television and 86 newspaper subscribers in 1994; 27 brs in Indonesia, seven overseas brs; nine bulletins in Indonesian and seven in English; monitoring service of stock exchanges world-wide; photo service; Man. Dir and Editor-in-Chief HANDJOJO NITIMIHARDJO.

Kantorberita Nasional Indonesia (KNI News Service): Jalan Jatinegara Barat III/6, Jakarta Timur 13310; tel. (21) 811003; fax (21) 8195501; f. 1966; independent national news agency; foreign and domestic news in Indonesian; Dir and Editor-in-Chief Drs SUMONO MUSTOFFA; Exec. Editor HARIM NURROCHADI.

In July 1993 the National Council of the Maubere (East Timorese) Resistance announced the establishment of the East Timorese News Agency (ETNA).

Foreign Bureaux

Agence France-Presse (AFP): Jalan Indramayu 18, Jakarta Pusat 10310; tel. (21) 3336082; fax (21) 3809186; Chief Correspondent PASCAL MALLET.

Agenzia Nazionale Stampa Associata (ANSA) (Italy): Jalan Petogogan 1 Go-2 No, 13 Kompleks RRI, Kebayoran Baru, Jakarta Selatan; tel. (21) 7391996; telex 47140; fax (21) 7392247; Correspondent HERYTNO PUJOWIDAGDO.

Associated Press (AP) (USA): Wisma Antara, 18th Floor, Suite 1806, 17 Jalan Merdeka Selatan, Jakarta 10110; tel. (21) 3813510; fax (21) 3457690; Correspondent GHAFUR FADYL.

Central News Agency Inc (CNA) (Taiwan): Jalan Gelong Baru Timur 1-13, Jakarta Barat; tel. and fax (21) 5600266; Bureau Chief WU PIN-CHIANG.

Informatsionnoye Telegrafnoye Agentstvo Rossii—Telegrafnoye Agentstvo Suverennykh Stran (ITAR—TASS) (Russia): Jalan Surabaya 7, Jakarta; tel. (21) 3844700; telex 69033; Correspondent ANDREY ALEKSANDROVICH BYCHKOV.

Inter Press Service (IPS) (Italy): Gedung Dewan Pers, 4th Floor, Jalan Kebon Sirih 34, Jakarta 10110; tel. (21) 3453131; fax (21) 3453175; Chief Correspondent ABDUL RAZAK.

Jiji Tsushin (Japan): Jalan Raya Bogor 109B, Jakarta; tel. (21) 8090509; Correspondent MARGA RAHARJA.

Kyodo Tsushin (Japan): Skyline Bldg, 11th Floor, Jalan M. H. Thamrin 9, Jakarta 10310; tel. (21) 345012; Correspondent MASAYUKI KITAMURA.

Reuters (United Kingdom): Wisma Antara, 6th Floor, Jalan Medan Merdeka Selatan 17, POB 2318, Jakarta 10110; tel. (21) 8346364; fax (21) 3448404; Bureau Chief IAN MACKENZIE.

United Press International (UPI) (USA): Wisma Antara, 14th Floor, Jalan Medan Merdeka Selatan 17, Jakarta; tel. (21) 341056; telex 44305; Bureau Chief JOHN HAIL.

Xinhua (New China) News Agency (People's Republic of China): Jakarta.

PRESS ASSOCIATIONS

Alliance of Independent Journalists (AJI): Jakarta; f. 1994; unofficial; aims to promote freedom of the press; Sec.-Gen. AHMAD TAUFIK.

Persatuan Wartawan Indonesia (Indonesian Journalists' Asscn): Gedung Dewan Pers, 4th Floor, Jalan Kebon Sirih 34, Jakarta 10110; tel. (21) 353131; fax (21) 353175; f. 1946; government-controlled; 5,041 mems (April 1991); Chair. TARMAN AGAM; Gen. Sec. H. SOFJAN LUBIS.

Serikat Penerbit Suratkabar (SPS) (Indonesian Newspaper Publishers' Asscn): Gedung Dewan Pers, 6th Floor, Jalan Kebon Sirih 34, Jakarta 10110; f. 1946; tel. (21) 359671; fax (21) 3862373; Chair. (vacant); Sec.-Gen. Drs A. BAGJO PURWANTHO.

Yayasan Pembina Pers Indonesia (Press Foundation of Indonesia): Jalan Jatinegara Barat III/6, Jakarta 13310; tel. (21) 8194994; f. 1967; Chair. SUGIARSO SUROYO, MOCHTAR LUBIS.

Publishers

Jakarta

Aries Lima/New Aqua Press PT: Jalan Rawagelan II/4, Jakarta Timur; tel. (21) 4897566; general and children's; Pres. TUTI SUNDARI AZMI.

Aya Media Pustaka PT: Wijaya Grand Centre C/2, Jalan Dharmawangsa III, Jakarta 12160; tel. (21) 7206903; telex 47477; fax (21) 7201401; children's; Dir Drs ARIANTO TUGIYO.

Balai Pustaka: Jalan Gunung Sari Raya 4, POB 1029, Jakarta 10710; tel. (21) 385573; telex 45905; fax (21) 3841714; f. 1917; children's, school textbooks, literary, scientific publs and periodicals; Dir Dr Ir WAHYUDI RUWIYANTO.

Bhratara Niaga Media PT: Jalan Oto Iskandardinata III/29F, Jakarta 13340; tel. (21) 8502050; fax (21) 8191858; f. 1986; fmrly Bhratara Karya Aksara; university and educational textbooks; Man. Dir AHMAD JAYUSMAN.

Bina Rena Pariwara PT: Jalan Kyai Maja 227 E/1, Jakarta 12120; tel. (21) 7261179; fax (21) 7208571; f. 1988; financial, social science, economic, Islamic, children's; Dir Dra YULIA HIMAWATI.

Bulan Bintang PT: Jalan Kramat Kwitang 1/8, Jakarta 10420; tel. (21) 3842883; f. 1954; Islamic, social science, natural and applied sciences, art; Pres. AMRAN ZAMZAMI; Man. Dir FAUZI AMELZ.

Bumi Aksara PT: Jalan Sawo Raya 18, Rawamanguu, Jakarta 13220; tel. (21) 4892714; f. 1990; university textbooks; Dir H. AMIR HAMZAH.

Cakrawala Cinta PT: Jalan Minyak I/12B, Duren Tiga, Jakarta 12760; tel. (21) 7990725; fax (21) 7982454; f. 1984; science; Dir Drs M. TORSINA.

Centre for Strategic and International Studies (CSIS): Jalan Tanah Abang III/23–27, Jakarta 10160; tel. (21) 3865532; fax (21) 3847517; f. 1971; political and social sciences; Dir Dr DAOED JOESOEF.

Cipta Adi Pustaka: Jalan Letjenderal Suprapto L20K, Cempaka Putih, Jakarta Pusat; tel. (21) 4241484; fax (21) 4208830; f. 1986; encyclopedias; Dir BUDI SANTOSO.

Dian Rakyat PT: Jalan Rawagelas I/4, Kaw. Industri P/Gadung, Jakarta; tel. (21) 4891809; f. 1966; general; Dir H. MOHAMMED AIS.

Djambatan PT: Jalan Wijaya I/39, Jakarta 12170; tel. (21) 7203199; fax (21) 7208562; f. 1954; children's, textbooks, social sciences, fiction; Dir ROSWITHA PAMOENTJAK SINGGIH.

Dunia Pustaka Jaya: Gedung Maya Indah, Jalan Kramat Raya 5K, Jakarta 10450; tel. (21) 3909284; f. 1971; fiction, religion, essays, poetry, drama, criticism, art, philosophy and children's; Man. A. RIVAI.

EGC CV: Jalan Agung Jaya III/2, Sunter Agung Podomoro, Jakarta 14350; tel. (21) 686351; fax (21) 684546; f. 1978; medical and public health, psychology; Dir ADJI DHARMA.

Elex Media Komputindo PT: Jalan Palmerah Selatan 22, Jakarta 10270; tel. (21) 5483008; fax (21) 5485574; f. 1985; computing and technology; Dir TEDDY SURIANTO.

Erlangga PT: Jalan H. Baping 100, Ciracas, Jakarta 13740; tel. (21) 8717006; fax (21) 8717011; f. 1952; secondary school and university textbooks; Man. Dir GUNAWAN HUTAURUK.

Gaya Favorit Press: Jalan H. R. Rasuna Said, Blok B, Kav. 32–33, Jakarta 12910; tel. (21) 5253816; telex 62338; fax (21) 5209366; f. 1971; fiction, popular science and children's; Vice-Pres. MIRTA KARTOHADIPRODJO; Man. Dir WIDARTI GUNAWAN.

Gema Insani Press: Jalan Kalibata Utara II/84, Jakarta 12740; tel. (21) 7998593; fax (21) 7984388; f. 1986; Islamic; Dir UMAR BASYARAHIL.

Ghalia Indonesia: Jalan Pramuka Raya 4, Jakarta 13140; tel. (21) 8581814; fax (21) 8580842; f. 1972; children's and general science, textbooks; Man. Dir LUKMAN SAAD.

Gramedia Widyasarana Indonesia: Jalan Palmerah Selatan 22, Lantai IV, POB 615, Jakarta 10270; tel. (21) 5483008; telex 46327; fax (21) 5486085; f. 1973; university textbooks, general non-fiction, children's and magazines; Gen. Man. ALFONS TARYADI.

Gunung Mulia PT: Jalan Kwitang 22–23, Jakarta 10420; tel. (21) 3901208; fax (21) 3901633; f. 1951; general, children's, Christian; Man. L. Z. RAPRAP.

Hidakarya Agung PT: Jalan Kebon Kosong F/74, Kemayoran, Jakarta Pusat; tel. (21) 411074; Dir MAHDIARTI MACHMUD.

Ichtiar: Jalan Majapahit 6, Jakarta Pusat; tel. (21) 341226; f. 1957; textbooks, law, social sciences, economics; Dir JOHN SEMERU.

Indira PT: Jalan Borobudur 20, Jakarta 10320; tel. (21) 882754; telex 48211; f. 1953; general science and children's; Man. Dir BAMBANG P. WAHYUDI.

Kinta CV: Jalan Kemanggisan Ilir V/110, Pal Merah, Jakarta Barat; tel. (21) 5494751; f. 1950; textbooks, social science, general; Man. Drs MOHAMAD SALEH.

LP 3 ES: Jalan Letjen. S. Patman, Jakarta 11420; tel. (21) 5674211; fax (21) 5683785; f. 1971; general; Dir ARSELAN HARAHAP.

Masagung Group: Gedung Idayu, Jalan Kwitang 13, POB 2260, Jakarta 10420; tel. (21) 3154890; fax (21) 3154889; f. 1986; general, religious, textbooks, science; Pres. H. ABDURRAHMAN MASAGUNG.

Midas Surya Grafindo PT: Jalan Kesehatan 54, Cijantung, Jakarta 13760; tel. (21) 8400414; fax (21) 8400270; f. 1984; children's; Dir Drs FRANS HENDRAWAN.

Mutiara Sumber Widya PT: Jalan Salemba Tengah 36–38, Jakarta 10440; tel. (21) 3908651; telex 46709; fax (21) 3160313; f. 1951; textbooks, Islamic, social sciences, general and children's; Pres. FADJRAA OEMAR.

Penebar Swadya PT: Jalan Gunung Sahari III/7, Jakarta Pusat; tel. (921) 4204402; fax (21) 4214821; agriculture, animal husbandry, fisheries; Dir Drs ANTHONIUS RIYANTO.

Penerbit Universitas Indonesia: Jalan Salemba Raya 4, Jakarta; tel. (21) 335373; f. 1969; science; Man. S. E. LEGOWO.

Pradnya Paramita PT: Jalan Bunga 8–8A, Matraman, Jakarta 13140; tel. (21) 8504944; f. 1973; children's, general, educational, technical and social science; Pres. Dir SOEHARDJO.

Pustaka Antara PT: Jalan Teluk Betung 55, Jakarta 10230; tel. (21) 326510; fax (21) 3141433; f. 1952; textbooks, political, Islamic, children's and general; Man. Dir AIDA JOESOEF AHMAD.

Pustaka Binaman Pressindo: Jalan Menteng Raya 9, Jakarta 10340; tel. (21) 2300313; fax (21) 2302051; f. 1981; management; Dir A. PEKERTI.

Pustaka Sinar Harapan PT: Jalan Dewi Sartika 136D, Jakarta 13630; tel. (21) 8093208; telex 48202; fax (21) 8091652; f. 1981; general science, fiction, comics, children's; Dir ARISTIDES KATOPPO.

Pustaka Utma Grafiti PT: Pusat Perdagangan Senen Blok II, Lantai II, Jakarta Pusat; tel. (21) 4520747; fax (21) 4520246; f. 1981; general science; Dir ZULKIFLY LUBIS.

Rajagrafindo Persada PT: Jalan Pelepah Hijau IV TN-1 14–15, Kelapa Gading Permai, Jakarta 14240; tel. (21) 4520951; fax (21) 4529409; f. 1980; general science and religion; Dir Drs ZUBAIDI.

Rineka Cipta PT: Blok B/5, Jalan Jenderal Sudirman, Kav. 36A, Bendungan Hilir, Jakarta 10210; tel. (21) 5737646; fax (21) 5711985; f. 1990 by merger of Aksara Baru (f. 1972) and Bina Aksara; general science and university texts; Dir Drs SUARDI.

Rosda Jayaputra PT: Jalan Kembang 4, Jakarta 10420; tel. (21) 3904984; fax (21) 3901703; f. 1981; general science; Dir H. ROZALI USMAN.

Sastra Hudaya: Jalan Kalasan 1, Jakarta Pusat; tel. (21) 882321; f. 1967; religious, textbooks, children's and general; Man. ADAM SALEH.

Tintamas Indonesia: Jalan Kramat Raya 60, Jakarta 10420; tel. and fax (21) 3107148; f. 1947; history, modern science and culture, especially Islamic; Man. Miss MARHAMAH DJAMBEK.

Tira Pustaka: Jalan Cemara Raya 1, Kav. 10D, Jaka Permai, Jaka Sampurna, Bekasi 17145; tel. (21) 8841276; telex 62612; fax (21) 8842736; f. 1977; translations, children's; Dir ROBERT B. WIDJAJA.

Widjaya: Jalan Pecenongan 48C, Jakarta Pusat; tel. (21) 363446; f. 1950; textbooks, children's, religious and general; Man. DIDI LUTHAN.

Yasaguna: Jalan Minangkabau 44, POB 422, Jakarta Selatan; tel. (21) 8290422; f. 1964; agricultural, children's, handicrafts; Dir HILMAN MADEWA.

Bandung

Alma'arif: Jalan Tamblong 48–50, Bandung; tel. (22) 4207177; f. 1949; textbooks, religious and general; Man. H. M. BAHARTHAH.

Alumni: Ir H. Juanda 54, Bandung 40163; tel. (22) 2501251; fax (22) 2503044; f. 1968; university and school textbooks; Dir EDDY DAMIAN.

Angkasa: Jalan Merdeka 6, POB 1353 BD, Bandung 40111; tel. (22) 4204795; telex 46709; fax (22) 439183; Dir H. FACHRI SAID.

Armico: Jalan Madurasa Utara 10, Bandung 40253; tel. (22) 443107; fax (22) 471972; f. 1980; school textbooks; Dir Ir ARSIL TANJUNG.

Binacipta: Jalan Ganesya 4, Bandung; tel. (22) 84319; f. 1967; textbooks, scientific and general; Dir Mrs R. BARDIN.

Citra Aditya Bakti PT: Jalan Geusanulun 17; Bandung 40115; tel. (22) 438251; f. 1985; general science; Dir Ir IWAN TANUATMADJA.

Diponegoro Publishing House: Jalan Mohammad Toha 44–46, Bandung 40252; tel. and fax (22) 5201215; f. 1963; Islamic, textbooks, fiction, non-fiction, general; Man. H. A. DAHLAN.

Epsilon Grup: Jalan Pasir Bogor Indah Q.10, Margacinta, Bandung 40287; tel. (22) 762505; f. 1985; school textbooks; Dir Drs BAHRUDIN.

Eresco PT: Jalan Sriwulan 26, Srimahi Baru, Bandung; tel. (22) 470977; f. 1957; scientific and general; Man. Drs ARFAN ROZALI.

Ganeca Exact Bandung: Jalan Kiaracondong 167, Bandung 40283; tel. (22) 701519; fax (22) 75329; f. 1982; school textbooks; Dir Ir KETUT SUARDHARA LINGGIH.

Mizan Pustaka PT: Jalan Yodkali 16, Bandung 40124; tel. (22) 700931; e-mail mizan@ibm.net; internet http://www.mizan.com/; f. 1983; Islamic and general books; Dir HAIDAR BAGIR.

Orba Sakti: Jalan Pandu Dalam 3/67, Bandung; tel. (22) 614718; Dir H. HASBULLOH.

Penerbit ITB: Jalan Ganesa 10, Bandung 40132; tel. and fax (22) 2504257; e-mail itbpress@melsa.net.id; f. 1971; academic books; Dir ADJAT SAKRI; Chief Editor SOFIA MANSOOR-NIKSOLIHIN.

Remaja Rosdakarya PT: Jalan Ciateul 34–36, POB 284, Bandung 40252; tel. (22) 500287; textbooks and children's fiction; Pres. ROZALI USMAN.

Sarana Panca Karyam PT: Jalan Kopo 633 KM 13/4, Bandung 40014; f. 1986; general; Dir WIMPY S. IBRAHIM.

Tarsito PT: Jalan Guntur 20, Bandung 40262; tel. (22) 304915; fax (22) 314630; academic; Dir T. SITORUS.

Flores

Nusa Indah: Jalan El Tari, Ende 86318, Flores; tel. (381) 21502; fax (381) 21645; f. 1970; religious and general; Dir HENRI DAROS.

Kudus

Menara Kudus: Jalan Menara 4, Kudus 59315; tel. (291) 37143; fax (291) 36474; f. 1958; Islamic; Man. CHILMAN NAJIB.

Medan

Hasmar: Jalan Letjenderal Haryono M.T. 1, POB 446, Medan 20231; tel. (61) 24181; f. 1962; primary school textbooks; Dir HASBULLAH LUBIS; Man. AMRAN SAID RANGKUTI.

Impola: Jalan Sisingamangaraja 104, Medan 20218; tel. (61) 23614; f. 1984; school textbooks; Dir. PAMILANG M. SITUMORANG.

Islamiyah: Jalan Sutomo 328–329, Kotakpos 11, Medan; tel. (61) 25426; f. 1954.

Madju: Jalan Sisingamangaraja Raja 25, Medan 20215; tel. (61) 711990; f. 1950; textbooks, children's and general; Pres. H. MOHAMED ARBIE; Man. Dir Drs ALFIAN ARBIE.

Masco: Jalan Sisingamangaraja 191, Medan 20218; tel. (61) 713375; f. 1992; school textbooks; Dir P. M. SITUMORANG.

Monora: Jalan Pandu 79, Medan 20212; tel. (61) 518885; f. 1968; school textbooks; Dir CHAIRIL ANWAR.

Semarang

Aneka Ilmu: Jalan Pleburan VIII/64; Semarang 50242; tel. (24) 310274; f. 1983; general and school textbooks; Dir H. SUWANTO.

Effhar COY PT: Jalan Dorang 7, Semarang; tel. (24) 511172; fax (24) 551540; f. 1976; gen. textbooks; Dir H. DARADJAT HARAHAP.

Intan Pariwara: Jalan Macanan, Ketandan, Klaten, Jawa-Tengah; tel. (272) 21641; school textbooks; Pres. SOETIKNO.

Mandira PT: Jalan M.T. Haryono 501, Semarang 50136; tel. (24) 316150; fax (24) 415092; f. 1962; Dir Ir A. HARIYANTO.

Mandira Jaya Abadi PT: Jalan Kartini 48, Semarang 50124; tel. (24) 519547; fax (24) 542189; f. 1981; Dir Ir A. HARIYANTO.

Toha Putra: Jalan Kauman 16, Semarang; tel. (24) 24871; f. 1962; Islamic; Dir HASAN TOHA PUTRA.

Solo

Pabelan PT: Jalan Raya Pajang, Kertasura KM 8, Solo 57162; tel. (271) 48811; fax (271) 41375; f. 1983; school textbooks; Dir AGUNG SASONGKO.

Tiga Serangkai PT: Jalan Dr Supomo 23, Solo; tel. (271) 4344; f. 1977; school textbooks; Dir ABDULLAH.

Surabaya

Airlangga University Press: Dharmahusada 47, Surabaya; tel. (31) 472719; academic; Dir Drs SOEDHARTO.

Assegaff: Jalan Panggung 136, Surabaya; tel. (31) 22971; f. 1951; Islamic, languages, primary school textbooks; Man. HASSAN ASSEGAFF.

Bina Ilmu PT: Jalan Tunjungan 53E, Surabaya 60275; tel. (31) 5323214; fax (31) 5315421; f. 1973; school textbooks, Islamic; Pres. ARIEFIN NOOR.

Bintang: Jalan Potroagung III/1A, Surabaya; tel. (31) 315941; school textbooks; Dir AGUS WINARNO.

Grip: Jalan Kawung 2, POB 129, Surabaya; tel. (31) 22564; f. 1958; textbooks and general; Man. Mrs SURIPTO.

Jaya Baya: Jalan Embong Malang 69H, POB 250, Surabaya 60001; tel. (31) 41169; f. 1945; religion, philosophy and ethics; Man. TADJIB ERMADI.

Karunia: Jalan Peneleh 18, Surabaya; tel. (31) 44120; f. 1970; textbooks and general; Man. HASAN ABDAN.

Marfiah: Jalan Kalibutuh 131, Surabaya; tel. (31) 46023; reference and primary school textbooks; Man. S. WAHYUDI.

Sinar Wijaya: Komplek Terminal Jembatan Merah, Stand C33-37, Surabaya; tel. (31) 270284; general; Dir DULRADJAK.

Ujungpandang

Bhakti Centra Baru PT: Jalan Jenderal Akhmad Yani 15, Ujungpandang 90174; tel. (411) 5192; telex 71156; fax (411) 7156; f. 1972; textbooks, Islamic and general; Man. Dir Drs H. M. YUSUF KALLA.

Yogyakarta

Andi Publishers: Jalan Beo 38–40, Yogyakarta 55281; tel. (274) 561881; fax (274) 588282; e-mail andi-pub@indo.net.id; f. 1980; Christian, computing, business and management; Dir J. H. GONDOWIJOYO.

BPFE PT: Jalan Gambiran 37, Yogyakarta 55161; tel. (274) 373760; fax (274) 380819; f. 1984; university textbooks; Dir Drs INDRIYO GITOSUDARMO.

Centhini Yayasan: Gg. Bekisar UH V/716 E–1, Yogyakarta 55161; tel. (274) 383148; f. 1984; Javanese Culture; Chair. H. KARKONO KAMAJAYA.

Gadjah Mada University Press: Jalan Grafika 1, Campus UGM, Bulaksumur, Yogyakarta 55281; tel. (274) 88688; fax (274) 61037; f. 1971; university textbooks; Dir Drs H. SUKAMTO.

Indonesia UP: Gg. Bekisar UH V/716 E–1, Yogyakarta 55161; tel. (274) 383148; f. 1950; general science; Dir H. KARKONO KAMAJAYA.

Kanisius Publr: Jalan Cempaka 9, Deresan, POB 1125, Yogyakarta 55281; tel. (274) 588783; fax (274) 563349; e-mail kanissrn@yogya.wasantara.net.id; f. 1922; children's, textbooks, Christian and general; Man. E. SURONO.

Kedaulatan Rakyat PT: Jalan P. Mangkubumi 40–42, Yogyakarta; tel. (274) 2163; telex 25176; Dir DRONO HARDJUSUWONGSO.

Penerbit Tiara Wacana Yogya: Jalan Kaliurang KM 7, 8 Kopen 16, Banteng, Yogyakarta 55581; tel. (274) 880683; fax (274) 880683; f. 1986; university textbooks and general science; Dir SITORESMI PRABUNINGRAT.

Government Publishing House

Balai Pustaka (State Publishing and Printing House): Jalan Dr Wahadin 1, Jakarta 10710; tel. (21) 3855742; telex 45905; history, anthropology, politics, philosophy, medical, arts and literature; Pres. Dir Dr ZAKARA IDRIS.

PUBLISHERS' ASSOCIATION

Ikatan Penerbit Indonesia (IKAPI) (Asscn of Indonesian Book Publishers): Jalan Kalipasir 32, Jakarta 10330; tel. (21) 3141907; fax (21) 3146050; f. 1950; 437 mems (Dec. 1996); Pres. ROZALI USMAN; Sec.-Gen. SETIA DHARMA MADJID.

Broadcasting and Communications

TELECOMMUNICATIONS

Directorate-General of Posts and Telecommunications (Postel): Gedung Depparpostel, Jalan Medan Merdeka Barat 17, Jakarta 10110; tel. (21) 3838349; telex 44407; fax (21) 3860754; Dir Gen. DJAKARIA PURAWIDJAJA; Dep. Dir. Gen. EMAN S. SUMANTRI.

PT Indosat (Persero) Tbk.: Jalan Medan Merdeka Barat 21, POB 2905, Jakarta 10110; tel. (21) 3869122; telex 44046; fax (21) 3848107; e-mail wp-sec@indosat.net.id; telecommunications; partially privatized in 1994; Chair. MUCHTRARUDIN SINGAR; Pres. TJAHJONO SOERJODIBROTO.

PT Satelit Palpa Indonesia (SATELINDO): Jalan Daan Mogot Km 11, Jakarta 11710; POB 1220, Jakarta 11012; tel. (21) 5451745; fax (21) 5451748; Gen. Man. IWAN KRISNADI.

PT Telekomunikasi Indonesia Tbk (PT Telekom): Corporate Office, Jalan Japati No. 1, Bandung 40133; tel. (22) 4521510; fax (22) 440313; internet http://www.telkom.co.id; domestic telecommunications monopoly; 27.5% of share capital was transfered to the private sector in 1995; Chair. DJAKARIA PURAWIDJAJA; Pres. SETYANTO P. SANTOSA.

RADIO

Directorate-General of Radio, Television and Film: Jalan Merdeka Barat 9, Jakarta 10110; Dep. Dir M. ARSYAD SUBIK.

Radio Republik Indonesia (RRI): Jalan Medan Merdeka Barat 4–5, Jakarta 10160; tel. (21) 3849091; telex 44349; fax (21) 367132; f. 1945; 49 stations; Dir ARSYAD SUBIK; Dep. Dirs FACHRUDDIN SOEKARNO (Overseas Service), ABDUL ROCHIM (Programming), SUKRI (Programme Development), SAZLI RAIS (Administration), CHAERUL ZEN (News).

Voice of Indonesia: Medan Merdeka Barat 4–5, POB 1157, Jakarta; (021) 366811; foreign service; daily broadcasts in Arabic, English, French, German, Bahasa Indonesia, Japanese, Bahasa Malaysia, Mandarin, Spanish and Thai.

TELEVISION

In March 1989 Indonesia's first private commercial television station began broadcasting to the Jakarta area. In 1996 there were five privately-owned television stations in operation.

PT Cakrawala Andalas Televisi (ANTEVE): Sentra Mulia, 18th Floor, Jalan Rasuna Said, Kav. X-6 No. 8, Jakarta 12940; tel. (21) 5222086; fax (21) 5222087; e-mail ancorcom@uninet.net.id; f. 1993; private channel; broadcasting to ten cities; Pres. Dir H.R. AGUNG LAKSONO; Gen. Man. CEO NENNY SOEMAWINATA.

Directorate-General of Radio, Television and Film: (see Radio).

Rajawali Citra Televisi Indonesia (RCTI): Jalan Raya Pejuangan, Kebon Jeruk, Jakarta 11000; tel. (21) 5303540; fax (21) 5493852; f. 1989; first private channel; 20-year licence; Pres. Dir M. S. RALIE SIREGAR; Vice-Pres. ALEX KUMARA.

PT Surya Citra Televisi (SCTV): Jalan Raya Darmo Permai III, Surabaya 60189; tel. (31) 714567; fax (31) 717273; f. 1990; private channel broadcasting nationally; Pres. Dir SLAMET SOEPOYO.

Televisi Pendidikan Indonesia (TPI): Jalan Pintu II—Taman Mini Indonesia Indah, Pondok Gede, Jakarta Timur 13810; tel. (21) 8412473; fax (21) 8412470; f. 1991; private channel funded by commercial advertising; Pres. Dir SITI HARDIJANTI RUKMANA.

Televisi Republik Indonesia (TVRI): TVRI Senayan, Jalan Gerbang Pemuda, Senayan, Jakarta; tel. (21) 5733135; telex 46154; fax (21) 5732408; f. 1962; state-controlled; Man. Dir AZIS HUSEIN.

Finance

(cap. = capital; auth. = authorized; p.u. = paid up; res = reserves; dep. = deposits; m. = million; brs = branches; amounts in rupiahs)

BANKING

Until 1988 the Indonesian banking sector was dominated by five state commercial banks, one state savings bank and one state development bank, although 112 other banks, with 1,640 branches, were in operation. Following the introduction of extensive financial-sector reforms in October 1988, licences were granted to 14 new foreign joint-venture banks, 26 commercial banks and about 250 secondary banks before the end of 1989. By September 1995 there were 200 commercial banks and 40 foreign and joint-venture banks. At the end of March 1995 total bank deposits stood at 167,123,000m. rupiahs.

Central Bank

Bank Indonesia: Jalan M. H. Thamrin 2, Jakarta 10010; tel. (21) 2310408; telex 44164; fax (21) 2311058; f. 1828; nationalized as central bank in 1953; cap. 2,070m., dep. 27,286m. (March 1996); Gov. SJAHRIL SABIRIN; 42 brs.

State Banks

In late December 1997 the Government announced that four of the state-owned banks—Bank Bumi Daya, Bank Dagang Negara, Bank

Ekspor Impor Indonesia and Bank Pembangunan Indonesia—were to merge before 31 July 1998, and were then scheduled to be transferred to the public sector by the year 2000; no name for the resultant new bank was announced, however.

Bank Bumi Daya (BBD) (Persero): Jalan Imam Bonjol 61, POB 1106, Jakarta 10011; tel. (21) 2301810; telex 61277; fax (21) 2301855; f. 1959; commercial and foreign exchange bank, specializes in credits to the plantation and forestry sectors; cap. 1,418,296m., res 16,681m., dep. 21,586,014m. (Dec. 1996); Pres. Dir IWAN R. PRAWIRANATA; Chair. UMAR M. SAID; 137 brs, 57 sub-brs.

PT Bank Dagang Negara (Persero): Jalan M. H. Thamrin 5, Jakarta 10340; POB 1338/JKT, Jakarta 10013; tel. (21) 2301107; telex 61622; fax (21) 2300618; f. 1857; nationalized as Bank Dagang Negara in 1960, name changed in 1992; auth. foreign exchange bank; specializes in credits to the mining sector; cap. 1,000,000m., res 143,971m., dep. 25,143,667m. (Dec. 1995); Pres. Dir SALAHUDDIN N. KAOY; 200 brs.

PT Bank Ekspor Impor Indonesia (Persero): Jalan Jenderal Gatot Subroto, Kav. 36–38, Jakarta 12930; tel. (21) 5263580; telex 60663; fax (21) 5265008; f. 1960; commercial and foreign exchange bank; specializes in credits for manufacture and export; cap. 1,000,000m., res 9,013m., dep. 22,123,277m. (Dec. 1996); Pres. KODRADI; 73 brs, 105 sub-brs, 3 overseas brs.

PT Bank Negara Indonesia (Persero): Jalan Jenderal Sudirman, Kav. 1, POB 2955, Jakarta 10001; tel. (21) 2511946; telex 65511; fax (21) 2511113; f. 1946; commercial bank; specializes in credits to the industrial sector; cap. 1,232,547m., res 15,539m., dep. 16,962,166m. (Dec. 1995); Pres. Dir WIDIODO SUKARMAN; 298 local brs, 6 overseas brs.

Bank Pembangunan Indonesia (Bapindo) (Persero): Jalan R. P. Soeroso 2–4, POB 1140, Jakarta 10011; tel. (21) 2301908; telex 61576; fax (21) 2300154; f. 1960; commercial bank; provides medium- and long-term investment loans to business enterprises; cap. 600,000m., dep. 11,459,149m. (Dec. 1993); Pres. ARBALI SUKANAL; 42 local brs, 3 overseas brs.

PT Bank Rakyat Indonesia (Persero): Jalan Jenderal Sudirman, Kav. 44–46, POB 94, Jakarta 10210; tel. (21) 2510244; telex 65259; fax (21) 2510303; f. 1895, present name since 1946; commercial and foreign exchange bank; specializing in agricultural smallholdings and rural development; scheduled for transfer to the public sector by the year 2000; cap. 1,000,000m., res 349,456m., dep. 19,450,207m. (Dec. 1995); Pres. and Dir DJOKOSANTOSO MOELJONO; 324 brs.

PT Bank Tabungan Negara (Persero): Jalan Gajah Mada 1, Jakarta 10130; tel. (21) 3856789; telex 67278; fax (21) 3856704; f. 1964; commercial bank; scheduled to be made a subsidiary of Bank Negara Indonesia in 1998; cap. 1,000,000m., res 32,566m., dep. 6,425,262m. (Dec. 1995); Pres. WIDIGDO SUKARMAN; 48 brs.

Commercial Banks

PT ANZ Panin Bank: Wisma BNI, 17th Floor, Jalan Jenderal Sudirman, Kav. 1, Jakarta 10220; tel. (21) 5750300; telex 65651; fax (21) 5705135; f. 1990 as Westpac Panin Bank; 85%-owned by the Australia and New Zealand Banking Group Ltd; cap. 50,000m., dep. 527,875m. (Dec. 1996); Pres. Dir ALBERT BURGIO.

PT Bank Arta Prima: Jalan Kopi 2, Jakarta 11230; tel. (21) 6900161; telex 42907; fax (21) 6911520; f. 1967 as Bank Arta Pusara; cap. 35,000m., dep. 439,122m. (Dec. 1994); Pres. SUDJANTORO; Chair. HEDIJANTO; 13 brs; 21 sub-brs.

Bank Artha Graha: Bank Artha Graha Tower, Jalan Jenderal Sudirman, Kav. 52–53, Jakarta 12920; tel. (21) 5152168; telex 45503; fax (21) 5152162; f. 1967; cap. 75,000m., dep. 340,344m. (Dec. 1993); Pres. Dir ANTON B. S. HUDYANA; Chair. T. B. SILALAHI; 10 brs; 12 sub-brs.

PT Bank Bali: Bank Bali Tower, Jalan Jenderal Sudirman, Kav. 27, Jakarta 12920; tel. (21) 5237899; telex 60856; fax (21) 2500811; f. 1954; cap. 340,340m., dep. 4,927,014m. (Dec. 1996); Chair. SUKANTA TANUDJAJA; Pres. RUDY RAMLI; 195 brs.

PT Bank Central Asia: Wisma BCA, 5th Floor, Jalan Jenderal Sudirman, Kav. 22–23, Jakarta 12920; tel. (21) 5711250; telex 65364; fax (21) 5701865; f. 1957; cap. 1,000,000m., res 8,075, dep. 31,161,393m. (Dec. 1996); Chair. SUDONO SALIM; Pres. Dir ABDULLAH ALI; 87 brs; 352 sub-brs.

PT Bank Central Dagang: Menara BCD, Jalan Jenderal Sudirman, Kav. 26, Jakarta 12920; tel. (21) 2506288; telex 60397; fax (21) 2506280; f. 1969; cap. 20,000m., res 533m., dep. 685,874m. (Dec. 1996); Chair. SAM HANDOYO; Pres. Dir HINDARTO HOVERT TANTULAR: 11 brs.

Bank Crédit Lyonnais Indonesia: Menara Mulia, Suite 2501, Jalan Jenderal Gatot Subroto, Kav. 9–11, Jakarta 12930; tel. (21) 2520234; fax (21) 2520123; f. 1989; cap. 50,000m., res 13,825m., dep. 447,626m. (Dec. 1994); Chair. INDRA WIDJAJA; Gen. Man. P. A. MUYL; 2 brs.

PT Bank Dagang Nasional Indonesia (Indonesian National Commercial Bank Ltd): Jalan Hayam Wuruk 8, POB 1097 DAK, Wisma Hayam Wuruk, Jakarta 10120; tel. (21) 2310530; telex 46656; fax (21) 3805761; f. 1945; cap. 822,006m., res 198m., dep. 12,047,798m. (Dec. 1996); Pres. Dir SJAMSU NURSALIM; Exec. Dir R. M. T. HARIANDJA; 176 local brs, 4 overseas brs.

PT Bank Danamon: Wisma Bank Danamon, Jalan Jenderal Sudirman, Kav. 45, Jakarta 12930; tel. (21) 5770551; fax (21) 5770704; f. 1956; cap. 1,120,189m., res 300,028m., dep. 17,587,267m. (Dec. 1996); Chair. USMAN ADMADJAYA; Pres. NINIE N. ADMADJAYA; 588 brs.

PT Bank Dharmala: Wisma Bank Dharmala, Jalan Jenderal Sudirman, Kav. 28, Jakarta 12920; tel. (21) 5212211; telex 60451; fax (21) 5212251; f. 1989 as PT Bank Dharmala Nugraha; cap. 180,000m., dep. 1,189,959m. (Dec. 1996); Pres. T. A. SUTANTO; Chair. SUYANTO GONDOKUSUMO; 22 brs.

PT Bank Duta: Jalan Kebon Sirih 12, POB 265 KBY, Jakarta 10110; tel. (21) 3800900; telex 48308; fax (21) 3801005; f. 1966; placed under the control of Bank Indonesia in September 1990, owing to 'improper foreign exchange dealings'; cap. 140,597m., res 4,832m., dep. 2,209,879m. (Dec. 1990); Chair. M. HASSAN; Pres. MUCHTAR MANDALA; 40 brs.

Bank Internasional Indonesia: Jalan M. H. Thamrin, Kav. 22 No. 51, Jakarta Pusat 10350; tel. (21) 2300888; fax (21) 330961; cap. 967,185m., res 7,290m., dep. 12,854,893m. (Dec. 1996); Chair. EKA TJIPTA WIDJAJA; Pres. Dir INDRA WIDJAJA; 190 brs.

PT Bank LTCB Central Asia: Bank Central Asia Bldg, Jalan Jenderal Sudirman, Kav. 22–23, Jakarta 12920; tel. (21) 5712562; fax (21) 5710639; f. 1989; 75%-owned by Long-Term Credit Bank of Japan Ltd; cap. 50,000m., dep. 51,718m. (Dec. 1996); Pres. SHUICHI TAKENAKA; 442 brs.

PT Bank Mashill Utama: Plaza Mashill, 1st–6th Floor, Jalan Jenderal Sudirman, Kav. 25, Jakarta 12920; tel. (21) 5221995; fax (21) 5221985; f. 1988; cap. 108,800m., res 3,300m., dep. 1,193,038m. (Dec. 1996); Chair. KARTA WIDJAJA; Pres. Dir A. T. WINDOE; 31 brs.

PT Bank Mayapada Internasional: Jalan Jenderal Sudirman, Kav. 2, Jakarta 10220; tel. (21) 2511588; telex 65019; fax (21) 2511539; f. 1989; cap. 50,000m., dep. 420,638m. (Dec. 1996); Chair. J. K. WONSONO; Pres. Dir HARYONO TJAHJARIJADI.

PT Bank Muamalat Indonesia (BMI): Arthaloka Bldg, Jalan Jenderal Sudirman 2, Jakarta 10220; tel. (21) 2511414; fax (21) 2511453; Indonesia's first Islamic bank; cap. 101,110m. (July 1997); Pres. Dir ZAINUL ARIFIN.

PT Bank Niaga: Graha Niaga, Jalan Jenderal Sudirman, Kav. 58, Jakarta 12190; tel. (21) 2505252; telex 60875; fax (21) 2505205; f. 1955; cap. 373,191m., res 6,113m., dep. 5,686,297m. (Dec. 1996); Pres. GUNARNI SOEWORO; Chair. SUMITRO DJOJOHADIKUSUMO; 63 brs.

Bank NISP: Jalan Gunung Sahari 38, Jakarta 10720; tel. (21) 6009037; fax (21) 6492264; f. 1941; cap. 62,500m., dep. 557,071m. (Sept. 1996); Pres. Dir PRAMUKTI SURJAUDAJA; 49 brs.

PT Bank Nusa International (Nusabank): Wisma Bakrie, Jalan H. R. Rasuna Said, Kav. B1, Jakarta 12920; tel. (21) 2525109; fax (21) 5201017; f. 1989; cap. 91,683m., dep. 901,022m. (Dec. 1996); Chair. Ir ABURIZAL BAKRIE; Pres. Dir Ir BANGUN SARWITO KUSMULJONO; 21 brs.

PT Bank Sakura Swadharma: Wisma BNI, 19th Floor, Jalan Jenderal Sudirman, Kav. 1, POB 1658 JKP, Jakarta 10001; tel. (21) 5701401; fax (21) 5701398; f. 1989 as PT Bank Mitsui Swadharma; 85%-owned by Sakura Bank Ltd; cap. 50,000m., dep. 110,781m. (Dec. 1995); Pres. KENJI IKEMOTO.

PT Bank Sumitomo Niaga: New Summitmas Bldg, 10th Floor, Jalan Jenderal Sudirman, Kav. 61–62, Jakarta 12069; tel. (21) 5227011; fax (21) 5227022; f. 1989; cap. 56,075m., dep. 353,978m. (Dec. 1995); Pres. YASUAKI MURA; 1 br.

Bank Surya: Bank Surya Bldg, Jalan M.H. Thamrin, Kav. 9, Jakarta Pusat; tel. (21) 2302933; telex 69006; fax (21) 3902470; f. 1969; cap. 111,000m., dep. 1,305,290m. (Dec. 1996); Chair. H. SUDWIKATMONO; Pres. Dir A. K. ARIAWAN; 13 local brs, 1 overseas br.

PT Bank Tiara Asia: Wisma Bank Tiara, Jalan M.T. Haryono, Kav. 16, Jakarta 12810; tel. (21) 8310210; fax (21) 8310250; f. 1989; cap. 185,000m., dep. 1,880,211m. (Dec. 1996); Chair. Haji RADEN PANDI MOHAMMED NOER; Pres. Dir IGNATIUS HERRY WIBOWO; 33 brs.

PT Bank Umum Nasional: Atrium Bunas Centre, Jalan Senen Raya 135, Jakarta 10110; tel. (21) 2312828; telex 67178; fax (21) 2312929; f. 1952; cap. 162,000m., res 43,989m., dep. 2,364,189m. (Dec. 1991); Chair. MOHAMMED HASSAN; Pres. Dir LEONARD TANUBRATA; 29 brs; 70 sub-brs.

PT Bank Universal: Atrium Bldg, Plaza Setiabudi, Jalan H. R. Rasuna Said, Jakarta 12920; tel. (21) 5210550; telex 60668; fax (21) 5210588; f. 1990; cap. 119,577m., dep. 2,931,073m. (Dec. 1996); Pres. Dir STEPHEN Z. SATYAHADI; Chair. Prof. SUMITRO DJOJOHADIKUSUMO; 60 brs.

PT Bank Utama: Jalan Pecenongan 84, POB 1471 Jakarta 10120; tel. (21) 3458103; telex 44693; fax (21) 3451617; f. 1974; fmrly

Overseas Express Bank; cap. 85,000m., res 16,039m., dep. 1,944,241m. (Dec. 1995); Chair. A. SUBOWO; Pres. Dir JANPIE SIAHAAN; 8 brs.

PT Fuji Bank International Indonesia: Ratu Plaza Office Tower, 2nd Floor, Jalan Jenderal Sudirman 9, Jakarta 10270; tel. (21) 7204477; fax (21) 7204480; f. 1989; cap. 100,000m., res 25,908m., dep. 969,978m. (Dec. 1996); Pres. Dir SHOJI KURITA.

PT Lippo Bank: Asia Tower Bldg, Jalan Diponegoro Raya, Lippo Village, Karawaci-Tangerang 15810; tel. (21) 5460333; telex 62455; fax (21) 5460718; f. 1948; cap. 585,603m., res 1,674m., dep. 8,713,590m. (Dec. 1996); Chair. MOCHTAR T. RIADY; Pres. Dir MARKUS PARMADI; 298 brs.

PT Pan Indonesia (Panin) Bank: Panin Bank Centre, Jalan Jenderal Sudirman, Senayan, Jakarta 10270; tel. (21) 2700545; telex 47394; fax (21) 2700340; f. 1971; cap. 371,495m., res 1,565m., dep. 3,749,091m. (Dec. 1996); Chair. M. SAMADIKUN HARDJODARSONO; Pres. H. ROSTIAN SJAMSUDIN; 100 brs, 2 overseas brs.

PT Prima Express Bank: Plaza Bapindo, Menara II, 6–7th Floor, Jalan Jenderal Sudirman, Kav. 54–55, Jakarta 12190; tel. (21) 5266767; telex 60690; fax (21) 5266787; e-mail primex@rad.net.id; f. 1956; cap. and res 93,687m., dep. 836,295m. (Nov. 1997); Pres. WIBOWO NGASERIN; Dir TRISNO HUSIN; 19 brs, 10 sub-brs.

PT Sanwa Indonesia Bank: Bank Bali Tower, 4th–5th Floor, Jalan Jenderal Sudirman, Kav. 27, Jakarta 12920; tel. (21) 2500401; fax (21) 2500410; f. 1989; Pres. Dir SHINYA ENDO; Chair. KANEO MUROMACHI.

PT Tamara Bank: Jalan Asemka 31, Jakarta 11110; tel. (21) 2600180; telex 42910; fax (21) 2600105; f. 1957; cap. 124,200m., res 11,200m., dep. 2,002,260m. (Dec. 1996); Chair. SOEMITRO; Pres. Dir SETIJONO PUDJOWARSITO; 64 brs.

PT United City Bank Tbk (Unibank): Midplaza Bldg, 7th Floor, Jalan Jenderal Sudirman, Kav. 10–11, Jakarta 10220; tel. (21) 5735750; fax (21) 5735751; f. 1967 as Bank Permata Sari; cap. 50,000m., res 9,989m., dep. 943,819m. (Dec. 1996); Chair. SUKANTO TANOTO; Pres. Dir ODANG KARIANA; 9 brs.

Foreign Banks

ABN AMRO Bank NV (Netherlands): Jalan Ir H. Juanda 23–24, POB 2950, Jakarta 10029; tel. (21) 2312777; telex 44124; fax (21) 2313222; Man. C. J. DE KONING.

Bangkok Bank Public Company Ltd (Thailand): Jalan M. H. Thamrin 3, Jakarta 10110; POB 4165, Jakarta 11041; tel. (21) 3808065; telex 46193; fax (21) 3853881; f. 1968; Gen. Man. SAKSITH TEJASAKULSIN.

Bank of America NT & SA (USA): Jakarta Stock Exchange Bldg, 22nd Floor, Tower 1, Jalan Jenderal Sudirman, Kav. 52–53, Jakarta 12190; POB 4931 JKTM, Jakarta 12049; tel. (21) 5151392; fax (21) 5151407; f. 1968; Sr Vice-Pres. and Country Man. FREDERICK CHIN.

Bank of Tokyo-Mitsubishi Ltd (Japan): Midplaza Bldg, 1st–3rd Floors, Jalan Jenderal Sudirman, Kav. 10–11, POB 2711, Jakarta 10220; tel. (21) 5706185; telex 62467; fax (21) 5731927; Gen. Man. HIDEYUKI ABE.

The Chase Manhattan Bank, NA (USA): Chase Plaza, Jalan Jenderal Sudirman, Kav. 21, POB 311/JKT, Jakarta 12920; tel. (21) 5782213; telex 62152; fax (21) 5780958; Vice-Pres. and Sr Officer PETER NICE.

Citibank, NA (USA): Landmark Bldg, Jalan Jenderal Sudirman 1, Jakarta 12910; tel. (21) 5782007; telex 44368; fax (21) 5789303; f. 1912; Vice-Pres JAMES F. HUNT, EDWIN GERUNGAN, ROBERT THORNTON.

Deutsche Bank, AG (Germany): Wisma Kosgoro, Jalan M. H. Thamrin 53, Jakarta 10350; POB 1135, Jakarta 10011; tel. (21) 331092; telex 61524; fax (21) 335252; Gen. Man. HEINZ POEHLSEN.

Hongkong and Shanghai Banking Corpn Ltd (Hong Kong): 1–4/F, World Trade Centre, Jalan Jenderal Sudirman, Kav. 29–31, Jakarta 12920; POB 2307, Jakarta 10023; tel. (21) 5211010; telex 60137; fax (21) 5211103; CEO P. C. L. HOLBERTON; 6 brs.

Standard Chartered Bank (United Kingdom): Wisma Standard Chartered Bank, Jalan Jenderal Sudirman, Kav. 33-A, Jakarta 10220; POB 57 JKWK, Jakarta, 10350; tel. (21) 2513333; telex 65599; fax (21) 5721234; Chief Exec. DAVID HAWKINS; 4 brs.

Banking Association

The Association of Indonesian National Private Commercial Banks (Perhimpunan Bank-Bank Umum Nasional Swasta—PERBANAS): Jalan Perbanas, Karet Kuningan, Setiabudi, Jakarta 12940; tel. (21) 5223038; fax (21) 5223037; f. 1952; 146 mems; Chair. A. SUBOWO; Sec.-Gen. LEONARD TANUBRATA.

STOCK EXCHANGES

At the end of June 1997 265 companies were listed on the Jakarta Stock Exchange and capitalization was 259,500,000m. rupiahs (US $105,900m.).

Bursa Paralel: PT Bursa Paralel Indonesia, Gedung Bursa, Jalan Medan Merdeka Selatan 14, Jakarta; tel. (21) 3810963; fax (21) 3810989; f. 1987.

Jakarta Stock Exchange (JSX): PT Bursa Efek Jakarta, Jakarta Stock Exchange Bldg, 4th Floor, Jalan Jenderal Sudirman, Kav. 52–53, Jakarta 12190; tel. (21) 5150515; fax (21) 5150330; PT Bursa Efek Jakarta, the managing firm of the JSX was transferred to the private sector in April 1992; 197 securities houses constitute the members and the shareholders of the exchange, each company owning one share; Pres. Dir D. CYRIL NOERHADI.

Surabaya Stock Exchange: PT Bursa Efek Surabaya, 5th Floor, Gedung Medan Pemuda, Jalan Pemuda 27–31, Surabaya 60271; tel. (31) 5310646; fax (31) 5319490; e-mail helpdesk@bes.co.id; f. 1989; Chair. ISAKAYOGA.

Regulatory Authority

Badan Pengawas Pasar Modal (BAPEPAM) (Capital Market Supervisory Agency): Jalan Medan Merdeka Selatan 14, Jakarta 10110; POB 1439; tel. (21) 365509; telex 45604; fax (21) 361460; Chair. BACELIUS RURU; Exec. Sec. M. IRSAN NASARUDIN.

INSURANCE

In June 1996 there were 161 insurance companies, comprising 98 non-life companies, 54 life companies, four reinsurance companies and five social insurance companies.

Insurance Supervisory Authority of Indonesia: Directorate of Financial Institutions, Ministry of Finance, Jalan Dr Wahidin, Jakarta 10710; tel. (21) 3451210; telex 46415; fax (21) 3849504; Dir SOPHAR L. TORUAN.

Selected Life Insurance Companies

PT Asuransi Allianz Aken Life: Summitmas II, 20th Floor, Jalan Jenderal Sudirman, Kav. 61–62, Jakarta 12190; tel. (21) 2526690; fax (21) 2526580; Pres. Dir PUTU SETIAWAN.

Asuransi Jiwa Bersama Bumiputera 1912: Wisma Bumiputera, Lt. 17–21, Jalan Jenderal Sudirman, Kav. 75, Jakarta 12910; tel. (21) 5703812; fax (21) 5712837; Pres. Drs H. SUGUARTO; Dir H. SURATNO HADISUWITO.

PT Asuransi Jiwa Buana Putra: Jalan Salemba Tengah 23, Jakarta Pusat; tel. (21) 3908835; telex 47600; fax (21) 3908810; f. 1974; Pres. SUBAGYO SUTJITRO; Dir H. M. FATHONI SUSILO.

PT Asuransi Jiwa Bumiputera John Hancock: Plaza Mashill, 7th Floor, Jalan Jenderal Sudirman, Kav. 25, Jakarta 12920; tel. (21) 5228857; fax (21) 5228819; e-mail iby@pacific.net.id; life insurance and pension schemes; CEO DAVID W. COTTRELL.

PT Asuransi Jiwa Central Asia Raya: Komp. Duta Merlin, Blok A 6–7, Jalan Gajah Mada 3–5, Jakarta 10130; tel. (21) 6338512; fax (21) 6346972; Man. Dir DJONNY WIGUNA.

PT Asuransi Jiwa Ikrar Abadi: Jalan Letjenderal S. Parman 108, POB 3562, Jakarta 11440; tel. (21) 591335; f. 1975; Pres. Dir HARRY HARMAIN DIAH.

PT Asuransi Jiwasraya: Jalan H. Juanda 34, POB 240, Jakarta 10120; tel. (21) 3845031; telex 45601; fax (21) 3862344; f. 1959; Dir H. R. SUDRADJAT DJAJAKUSUMAH.

PT Asuransi Jiwa 'Panin Putra': Jalan Pintu Besar Selatan 52A, Jakarta 11110; tel. (21) 672586; telex 63824; fax (21) 676354; f. 1974; Pres. Dir SUJONO SOEPENO; Chair. NUGROHO TJOKROWIRONO.

PT Asuransi Jiwa Pura Nusantara: Wisma Bank Dharnala, Lt. 20–21, Jalan Jenderal Sudirman, Jakarta 12920; tel. (21) 5211990; fax (21) 5212001; Dir MURNIATY KARTONO.

PT Asuransi Lippolife: Lippolife Bldg, 6th Floor, Jalan H.R. Rasuna Said, Kav. B10–11, Jakarta 12310; tel. (21) 516123; telex 62180; fax (21) 516096; f. 1983; general and life insurance.

PT Asuransi Panin Life: Panin Bank Plaza, 5th Floor, Jalan Palmerah Utara 52, Jakarta 11480; tel. (21) 5484870; fax (21) 5484570; Pres. NUGROHO TJOKROWIRONO; Dir SUJONO SUPENO.

Bumi Asih Jaya Life Insurance Co Ltd: Jalan Matraman Raya 165–167, Jakarta 13140; tel. (21) 8509850 telex 48282; fax (21) 8509669; f. 1967; Chair. D. S. SINAGA; Pres. K. M. SINAGA.

Bumiputera 1912 Mutual Life Insurance Co: Wisma Bumiputera, 18th–21st Floors, Jalan Jenderal Sudirman, Kav. 75, Jakarta 12910; tel. (21) 5782717; telex 44494; f. 1912; Pres. SUGIARTO.

Koperasi Asuransi Indonesia: Jalan Iskandarsyah I/26, Jakarta; tel. (21) 7207879; fax (21) 7207451; Dir H. J. V. SUGIMAN.

Selected Non-Life Insurance Companies

PT Asuransi Bina Dharma Arta: Wisma Dharmala Sakti, Lt. 8, Jalan Jenderal Sudirman, Kav. 32, Jakarta 10220; tel. (21) 5708157; fax (21) 5708166; Pres. SUYANTO GONDOKUSUMO; Dir SUHANDA WIRAATMADJA.

PT Asuransi Bintang: Jalan R. S. Fatmawati 32, Jakarta 12430; tel. (21) 7504872; telex 47600; fax (21) 7506197; internet http://

www.bintang.co.id; f. 1955; general insurance; Dirs ARIYANTI SULIYANTO, M. IQBAL, DJUNAIDI MAHARI.

PT Asuransi Buana Independen: Jalan Pintu Besar Selatan 78, Jakarta 11110; tel. (21) 6904331; fax (21) 6263005; Exec. Vice-Pres. SUSANTY PURNAMA.

PT Asuransi Central Asia: Komp. Duta Meolin, Blok A 4–5, Jalan Gajah Mada 3–5, Jakarta 10130; tel. (21) 373073; telex 46569; fax (21) 3848526; Pres. ANTHONY SALIM; Dir TEDDY HAILAMSAH.

PT Asuransi Danamon: Gedung Danamon Asuransi, Jalan H. R. Rasuna Said, Kav. C10, Jakarta 12920; tel. (21) 516512; fax (21) 516832; Chair. USMAN ADMADJAJA; Pres. Dir OTIS WUISAN.

PT Asuransi Dayin Mitra: Gateway Bldg, 1st Floor, Jalan Letjen. S. Parman, Kav. 91, Jakarta 11420; tel. (21) 5668237; fax (21) 5668382; f. 1982; general insurance; Man. Dir LARSOEN HAKER.

PT Asuransi Indrapura: Jakarta; tel. (21) 5703729; telex 62641; fax (21) 5705000; f. 1954; Presiding Dir ROBERT TEGUH.

PT Asuransi Jasa Indonesia: Jalan Letjenderal M. T. Haryono, Kav. 61, Jakarta 12780; tel. (21) 7994508; telex 47365; Pres. Dr Ir BAMBANG SUBIANTO; Dir AMIR IMAM POERO.

PT Asuransi Parolamas: Jalan Teluk Betung 56, Jakarta 10230; tel. (21) 3144032; fax (21) 3145152; Pres. TJUT RUKMA; Dir Drs SYARIFUDDIN HARAHAP.

PT Asuransi Ramayana: Jalan Kebon Sirih 49, Jakarta 10343; tel. (21) 337148; telex 61670; fax (21) 334825; f. 1956; Chair. R. G. DOERIAT; Pres. Dir F. WIDYASANTO.

PT Asuransi Tri Pakarta: Jalan Paletehan I/18, Jakarta 12160; tel. (21) 711850; fax (21) 7394748; Pres. Drs M. MAINGGOLAN; Dir HUSNI RUSTAM.

PT Asuransi Wahana Tata: Jalan H. R. Rasuna Said, Kav. 12, Jakarta 12920; tel. (21) 5203145; fax (21) 5203146; Chair. S. SUGIARSO; Pres. RUDY WANANDI.

PT Lloyd Indonesia: Jalan Tiang Bendera 34-1, Jakarta 11230; tel. (21) 677195; Dir JOHNY BASUKI.

Berdikari Insurance Company: Jalan Merdeka Barat 1, Jakarta 10002; tel. (21) 375048; fax (21) 370586; Pres. Maj.-Gen. BUSTANUL ARIFIN.

PT Maskapai Asuransi Indonesia (MAI): Jalan Sultan Hasanuddin 53–54, Kebayoran Baru, Jakarta 12160; tel. (21) 710708; telex 47290; fax (21) 7398497; Dir JAN F. H. NINKEULA.

PT Maskapai Asuransi Jasa Tania: Gedung Agro Bank, Lt. 4, Jalan Teuku Cik Ditiro 14, Jakarta 10350; tel. (21) 3101912; fax (21) 323089; Pres. H. R. SUTEDJIO; Dir Drs H. ABELLAH.

PT Maskapai Asuransi Timur Jauh: Jalan Medan Merdeka Barat 1, Jakarta Pusat; tel. (21) 370266; telex 44828; f. 1954; Pres. Dir BUSTANIL ARIFIN; Dirs V. H. KOLONDAM, SOEBAKTI HARSONO.

PT Pan Union Insurance: Panin Bank Plaza, Lt. 6, Jalan Palmerah Utara 52, Jakarta 11480; tel. (21) 5480669; fax (21) 5484087; Pres. MUMIN ALI GUNAWAN; Dir NIZARWAN HARAHAP.

PT Perusahaan Maskapai Asuransi Murni: Jalan Roa Malaka Selatan 21–23, Jakarta Barat; tel. (21) 679968; telex 42851; f. 1953; Dirs HASAN DAY, HOED IBRAHIM, R. SOEGIATNA PROBOPINILIH.

PT Pool Asuransi Indonesia: Blok A–IV Utara, Jalan Muara Karang Raya 293, Jakarta 14450; tel. (21) 6621946; fax (21) 6678021; f. 1958; Pres. BAMBANG GUNAWAN TANUJAYA; Dir TANDJUNG SUSANTO.

PT Tugu Pratama Indonesia: Wisma Tugu, Jalan H. R. Rasuna Said, Kav. C-8-9, Jakarta 12940; tel. (21) 8299575; telex 62809; fax (21) 8291170; f. 1981; general insurance; Chair. F. ABDA'OE; Pres. SONNI DWI HARSONO.

Joint Ventures

PT Asuransi AIU Indonesia: Jalan K. H. Hasyim Ashari 35, Jakarta 10130; tel. (21) 3865467; fax (21) 3865504; Pres. Dir PETER MEYER; Vice-Pres. NANI KAUDIN.

PT Asuransi Jayasraya: Jalan M. H. Thamrin 9, Jakarta; tel. (21) 324207; Dirs SUPARTONO, SADAO SUZUKI.

PT Asuransi Jiwa EKA Life: Wisma EKA Jiwa, 8th Floor, Jalan Mangga Dua Raya, Jakarta 10730; tel. (21) 6257808; fax (21) 6257837; e-mail ekalife@uninet.net.id; Chair RAMON G. MADRID; Pres. G. SULISTIYANTO.

PT Asuransi Mitsui Marine Indonesia: Menara Thamrin, 14th Floor, Jalan M. H. Thamrin, Kav. 3, Jakarta 10340; tel. (21) 2303432; fax (21) 2302930; Pres. Dir S. AOSHIMA; Vice-Pres. PUTU WIDNYANA.

PT Asuransi Royal Indrapura: Jakarta Stock Exchange Bldg, 29th Floor, Jalan Jenderal Sudirman, Kav. 52–53, Jakarta 12190; tel. (21) 5151222; telex 65137; fax (21) 5151771; Pres. Dir Ir MINTARTO HALIM; Man. Dir MORAY B. MARTIN.

Insurance Association

Dewan Asuransi Indonesia (Insurance Council of Indonesia): Jalan Majapahit 34, Blok V/29, Jakarta 10160; tel. (21) 363264; telex 44981; fax (21) 354307; f. 1957; Chair. MUNIR SIAMSOEDDIN; Gen. Sec. SOEDJIWO.

Trade and Industry

GOVERNMENT AGENCIES

Agency for the Assessment and Application of Technology (BPPT): Jalan M. H. Thamrin 8, Jakarta; tel. (21) 322302; Chair. Prof. Dr Ir BUCHARUDDIN JUSUF (B. J.) HABIBIE.

Agency for Strategic Industries (BPIS): Jakarta; f. 1989; co-ordinates for production of capital goods; Chair. Prof. Dr. Ir BUCHARUDDIN JUSUF (B. J.) HABIBIE; Vice-Chair. Ir GIRI S. HADIHARDJONO.

National Agency for Export Development (NAFED): Jalan Gajah Mada 8, Jakarta; tel. (21) 3841072; fax (21 3848380.

National Atomic Energy Agency (BATAN): Jalan K. H. Abd. Rohim, Jakarta; tel. (21) 511109; fax (21) 511110.

National Family Planning Co-ordinating Board (NFPCB): Jalan Permata No. 1, Halim Perdanakusumah, Jakarta Timur 13650; tel. (21) 8098018; Chair. Dr Haji HARYONO SUYONO.

State Logistics Agency (BULOG): Jalan Jenderal Gatot Subroto 49, Jakarta; tel. (21) 510075; Chair. Prof. Dr IBRAHIM HASSAN.

DEVELOPMENT ORGANIZATIONS

Badan Koordinasi Penanaman Modal (BKPM) (Investment Co-ordinating Board): Jalan Jenderal Gatot Subroto 44, POB 3186, Jakarta; tel. (21) 512008; telex 45651; fax (21) 514945; f. 1976; Chair. Ir SANYOTO SASTROWARDOYO.

Commercial Advisory Foundation in Indonesia (CAFI): Jalan Probolinggo 5, Jakarta 10350; tel. (21) 3156013; fax (21) 3156014; f. 1958; information, economic regulations bulletin, consultancy and translation services; Chair. JOYCE SOSROHADIKOESOEMO; Man. Dir LEILA RIDWAN SOSROHADIKOESOEMO.

National Planning Development Board (Bappenas): Jalan Tarnan Suropati 2, Jakarta 10310; tel. (21) 334811; telex 61333; fax (21) 3105374; formulates Indonesia's national economic development plans; Chair. Ir Drs GINANDJAR KARTASASMITA; Vice-Chair. Prof. Dr B. S. MULJANA.

CHAMBER OF COMMERCE

Kamar Dagang dan Industri Indonesia (KADIN) (Indonesian Chamber of Commerce and Industry): Chandra Bldg, 3rd–5th Floors, Jalan M. H. Thamrin 20, Jakarta 10350; tel. (21) 324000; telex 61262; fax (21) 3150241; f. 1969; 27 regional offices throughout Indonesia; Chair. Ir ABURIZAL BAKRIE; Sec.-Gen. Ir IMAN SUCIPTO UMAR.

INDUSTRIAL AND TRADE ASSOCIATIONS

Association of Indonesian Automotive Industries (GAIKINDO): Jalan H.O.S. Cokroaminoto 6, Jakarta 10350; tel. (21) 3102754; fax (21) 332100.

Association of Indonesian Beverage Industries (ASRIM): Jalan M. Ikhwan Mais 8, Jakarta Pusat; tel. (21) 3841222; fax (21) 3842294.

Association of Indonesian Coal Industries (ABBI): Perum Batu Bara Bldg, Jalan Supomo 10, Jakarta Selatan; tel. (21) 8295608.

Association of Indonesian Coffee Exporters (AEKI): Jalan R. P. Soeroso 20, Jakarta 10330; tel. (21) 3155054; fax (21) 3144115; Chair. OESMAN SOEDARGO.

Association of Indonesian Heavy Equipment Industries (HINABI): c/o PT Traktor Nusantara, Jalan Pulogadung 32, Jakarta 13930; tel. (21) 4703932; fax (21) 4713940.

Association of Indonesian Tea Producers (ATI): Jalan Sindangsirna 4, Bandung 40153; tel. (22) 2038966; fax (22) 231455.

Association of State-Owned Companies: CTC Bldg, Jalan Kramat Raya 94–96, Jakarta; tel. (21) 346071; telex 44208; co-ordinates the activities of state-owned enterprises; Pres. ODANG.

Clove Stock Management and Marketing Agency: Jakarta; Chair. HUTOMO MANDALA PUTRA.

Electric and Electronic Appliance Manufacturers' Association: Jalan Pangeran, Blok 20/A-1D, Jakarta; tel. (21) 6480059.

GINSI (Importers' Asscn of Indonesia): Bank Niaga Bldg, 1st Floor, Jalan M. H. Thamrin 55, Jakarta 10350; tel. (21) 3911057; fax (21) 3911060; f. 1956; 2,921 mems (1996); Chair. AMIRUDIN SAUD; Sec.-Gen. D. KADARSYAH.

Indonesian Cocoa Association (AKI): Jalan Brawijaya VII/5, Kebayoran Baru, Jakarta 12160; tel. (21) 771721; fax (21) 7203487.

Indonesian Cement Association: Graha Purnayudha, Jalan Jenderal Sudirman, Jakarta; tel. (21) 5207603; fax (21) 5207188.

Indonesian Exporters' Federation: Menara Sudirman, 8th Floor, Jalan Jenderal Sudirman, Kav. 60, Jakarta 12190; tel. (21) 5226522; telex 60966; fax (21) 5203303; Chair. HAMID IBRAHIM GANIE.

Indonesian Footwear Association (APRISINDO): Duta Merlin Bldg, Jalan Gajah Mada 3, Jakarta 10130; tel. (21) 6337702; fax (21) 6337706; Exec. Dir P. A. PATTINAMA.

Indonesian Furniture Industry and Handicraft Association (ASMINDO): Gedung Manggala Wanabakti Blok IV, 5th Floor, Room 501A–502A, Jalan Jenderal Gatot Subroto, Senayan Jakarta 10270; tel. (21) 5700249; fax (21) 5704619.

Indonesian Nutmeg Exporters' Association: Jalan Hayam Wuruk 103, Jakarta; tel. (21) 6297432.

Indonesian Palm Oil Producers' Association: Jalan Pulo Mas IIID/1, Jakarta; tel. (21) 4892635; Chair. NUKMAN NASUTION.

Indonesian Precious Metals Association: Jalan Wahid Hasyim 45, Jakarta; tel. (21) 3841771.

Indonesian Pulp and Paper Association: Jalan Cimandiri 6, Jakarta 10330; tel. (21) 326084; fax (21) 3140168.

Indonesian Textile Association (API): Panin Bank Centre, 3rd Floor, Jalan Jenderal Sudirman 1, Jakarta Pusat 10270; tel. (21) 7396094; telex 47228; fax (21) 7396341; f. 1974; Sec.-Gen. DANANG D. JOEDONAGORO.

Indonesian Tobacco Association: Jalan H. Agus Salim 85, Jakarta 10350; tel. (21) 3140627; telex 61517; fax (21) 325181; Pres. H. A. ISMAIL.

Masyarakat Perhutanan Indonesia (MPI) (Indonesian Forestry Community): Gedung Manggala Wanabakti, 9th Floor, Wing B/Blok IV, Jalan Jenderal Gatot Subroto, Jakarta Pusat 10270; tel. (21) 5733010; telex 46977; fax (21) 5732564; f. 1974; nine mems; Pres. M. HASAN.

National Board of Arbitration (BANI): Jalan Merdeka Timur 11, Jakarta; f. 1977; resolves company disputes; Chair. Prof. R. SUBEKTI.

Rubber Association of Indonesia (Gapkindo): Jalan Cideng Barat 62A, Jakarta; tel. (21) 3846813; fax (21) 3846811; Pres. SUTRISNO BUDIMAN.

Shippers' Council of Indonesia: Jalan Kramat Raya 4–6, Jakarta; Pres. R. S. PARTOKUSUMO.

UTILITIES

Electricity

PT Perusahaan Umum Listrick: Jalan Trunojoyo, Blok 1/35, Kebayaran Baru, Jakarta Selatan 12610; tel. (21) 7395522; fax (21) 7711330; state-owned electricity co; Pres. Dir Ir DJITENG MARSUDI.

Gas

Perusahaan Pertambangan Minyak dan Gas Bumi Negara (PERTAMINA): Jalan Merdeka Timur 1, Jakarta 10110; tel. (21) 3815111; telex 44152; fax (21) 363585; f. 1957; state-owned petroleum and natral gas mining enterprise; Pres. Dir FAISAL ABDA'OE.

PGN (Public Gas Corporation): Jakarta; monopoly of domestic gas distribution; Pres. Dir QOYUM TJANDRANEGARA.

CO-OPERATIVES

In July 1992 there were 38,361 co-operatives in Indonesia, with a total membership of 33,719,000.

Indonesian Co-operative Council: Jakarta; Pres. SRI EDY SWASONO.

TRADE UNIONS

Serikat Buruh Sejahtera Indonesia (SBSI) (Indonesian Prosperous Labour Union): Jakarta; f. 1992; includes some fmr SPSI activists; application for official registration rejected in June 1993; 250,000 mems; Gen. Sec. MUCHTAR PAKPAHAN.

Serikat Pekerja Seluruh Indonesia (SPSI) (All Indonesia Workers' Union): Gedung Chandra Lantai VI, Jalan M. H. Thamrin 20, Jakarta 10240; tel. (21) 323872; fax (21) 3107868; f. 1973, renamed 1985; sole officially recognized workers' organization; comprises 13 national industrial unions; 2.8m. mems in June 1992; Gen. Chair. IMAM SOEDARWO; Gen. Sec. H. BOMER PASARIBU.

Transport

Directorate General of Land Transport and Inland Waterways: Ministry of Communications, Jalan Medan Merdeka Barat 8, Jakarta 10110; tel. (21) 3456332; Dir-Gen. SOEJONO.

RAILWAYS

There are railways on Java, Madura and Sumatra, totalling 6,362 km (4,010 miles) in 1995, of which 110 km (68.4 miles) were electrified.

In 1995 a memorandum of understanding was signed by a consortium of European, Japanese and Indonesian companies for a subway system for Jakarta, which was expected to cost US $1,300m. and be completed in 2001.

Perusahan Umum Kereta Api (PERUMKA): Jalan Perintis Kermedekaan 1, Bandung 40117, Java; tel. (22) 430031; telex 28263; fax (22) 430062; six regional offices; transferred to the private sector in 1991; Chief Dir Drs ANWAR SUPRIADI.

ROADS

There is an adequate road network on Java, Sumatra, Sulawesi, Kalimantan, Bali and Madura, but on most of the other islands traffic is by jungle track or river boat. In 1996 the road network in Indonesia totalled an estimated 393,000 km. About 31,000 km were main roads and 56,900 km were secondary roads. About 178,800 km of the network were paved.

Directorate General of Highways: Ministry of Public Works, Jalan Pattimura 20, Kebayoran Baru, Jakarta Selatan 12110; tel. (21) 7262805; fax (21) 7260769; Dir-Gen. Ir SURYATIN SASTROMIJOYO.

SHIPPING

The Ministry of Communications controls 349 ports and harbours, of which the four main ports of Tanjung Priok (near Jakarta), Tanjung Perak (near Surabaya), Belawan (near Medan) and Ujung Pandang (in South Sulawesi) have been designated gateway ports for nearly all international shipping to deal with Indonesia's exports and are supported by 15 collector ports. Of the ports and harbours, 127 are classified as capable of handling ocean-going shipping.

Directorate General of Sea Communications: Ministry of Communications, Jalan Medan Merdeka Barat 8, Jakarta 10110; tel. (21) 3456332; telex 46117; Dir-Gen. SOENTORO.

Indonesian National Ship Owners' Association (INSA): Jalan Gunung Sahari 79, Jakarta Pusat; tel. (21) 414908; telex 49157; fax (21) 416388; Pres. H. HARTOTO HADIKUSUMO.

Shipping Companies

Indonesian Oriental Lines, PT Perusahaan Pelayaran Nusantara: Jalan Raya Pelabuhan Nusantara, POB 2062, Jakarta 10001; tel. (21) 494344; telex 44233; Pres. Dir A. J. SINGH.

PT Jakarta Lloyd: Jalan Agus Salim 28, Jakarta Pusat 10340; tel. (21) 331301; telex 44375; fax (21) 333514; f. 1950; services to USA, Europe, Japan, Australia and the Middle East; Pres. Dir Drs M. MUNTAQA.

PT Karana Line: Jalan Kali Besar Timur 30, POB 1081, Jakarta 11110; tel. (21) 6907381; telex 42727; fax (21) 6908365; Pres. Dir BAMBANG EDIYANTO.

PT Pelayaran Bahtera Adhiguna (Persero): Jalan Kalibesar Timur 10–12, POB 4313, Jakarta 11043; tel. (21) 6912613; telex 42854; fax (21) 6901450; f. 1971; Pres. H. DJAJASUDHARMA.

PT Pelayaran Nasional Indonesia (PELNI): Jalan Gajah Mada 14, Jakarta; tel. (21) 343307; telex 44301; fax (21) 4204144; state-owned; national shipping co; Pres. Dir M. H. UMAR.

PT Pelayaran Samudera Admiral Lines: Jalan Gunung Sahari 79–80, Jakarta 10610; POB 1476, Jakarta 10014; tel. (21) 4247908; telex 49122; fax (21) 4206267; e-mail admiral@uninet.net.id; Pres. SOERJADI SASTROMIHARDJO.

PT (Persero) Pann Multi Finance: Pann Bldg, Jalan Cikini IV/11, POB 3377, Jakarta 10330; tel. (21) 322003; telex 61580; fax (21) 322980; state-controlled; Pres. Dir W. NAYOAN; Dir HAMID HADIJAYA.

PT Perusahaan Pelayaran Gesuri Lloyd: Gesuri Lloyd Bldg, Jalan Tiang Bendera IV 45, Jakarta 11230; tel. (21) 6904000; telex 42043; fax (21) 6904190; f. 1963; Pres. FRANKIE NURIMBA.

PT Perusahaan Pelayaran Nusantara 'Nusa Tenggara': Kantor Pusat, Jalan Diponegoro 115 Atas, POB 69, Denpasar 80113, Bali; tel. (361) 27720; telex 35210; fax (361) 35402; Man. Dir KETUT DERESTHA.

PT Perusahaan Pelayaran Samudera 'Samudera Indonesia': Jalan Kali Besar Barat 43, POB 1244, Jakarta; tel. (21) 671093; telex 42753; fax (21) 674242; Chair. and Dir SOEDARPO SASTROSATOMO; Exec. Dir RANDY EFFENDI.

PT Perusahaan Pelayaran Samudera Trikora Lloyd: Jalan Malaka 1, Jakarta 11230; POB 4076, Jakarta 11001; tel. (21) 6907751; telex 42061; fax (21) 6907757; f. 1964; Pres. Dir GANESHA SOEGIHARTO; Man. Dir P. R. S. VAN HEEREN.

PT Perusahaan Pertambangan Minyak dan Gas Bumi Negara (PERTAMINA): Directorate for Shipping, Harbour and Communication, Jalan Yos Sudarso 32–34, POB 327, Tanjung Priok, Jakarta; tel. (21) 4301086; telex 44152; fax (21) 4301492; state-owned; tanker services; Pres. and Chair. Dr IBNU SUTOWO.

CIVIL AVIATION

The first stage of a new international airport, the Sukarno-Hatta Airport, at Cengkareng, near Jakarta, was opened in April 1985, to complement Halim Perdanakusuma Airport, which was to handle charter and general flights only. A new terminal was opened at Sukarno-Hatta in December 1991, vastly enlarging airport capacity. Construction of an international passenger terminal at the Frans Kaisepo Airport, in Irian Jaya, was completed in 1988. Other international airports include Ngurah Rai Airport at Denpasar (Bali), Polonia Airport in Medan (North Sumatra), Juanda Airport, near Surabaya (East Java), Sam Ratulangi Airport in Manado (North Sulawesi) and Hasanuddin Airport, near Ujung Pandang (South Sulawesi). There are a total of 72 airports, six of which are capable of accommodating wide-bodied aircraft. Domestic air services link the major cities, and international services are provided by the state airline, PT Garuda Indonesia, by its subsidiary, PT Merpati Nusantara Airlines, and by numerous foreign airlines. In December 1990 it was announced that private airlines equipped with jet-engined aircraft would be allowed to serve international routes.

In 1994 Indonesia had 26 domestic airlines, six of which offered scheduled passenger services.

Directorate-General of Air Communications: Jalan Arief Rahman Hakim 3, Jakarta 10340; tel. (21) 3914235; fax (21) 3914239; Dir-Gen. ZAINUDDIN SIKADO.

PT Bali International Air Service: Jalan Angkasa 1–3, POB 2965, Jakarta 10720; tel. (21) 6295388; telex 41247; fax (21) 6249183; f. 1970; private company; subsidiary of BOU; scheduled and charter services; Gen. Man. J. A. SUMENDAP.

PT Bouraq Indonesia Airlines (BOU): Jalan Angkasa 1–3, POB 2965, Jakarta 10720; tel. (21) 6295289; telex 41247; fax (21) 6298651; f. 1970; private company; scheduled regional and domestic passenger and cargo services linking Jakarta with points in Java, Borneo, Celebes, Bali, Timor and Tawau (Malaysia); Pres. J. A. SUMENDAP; Exec. Vice-Pres. G. B. RUNGKAT.

PT Garuda Indonesia: Garuda Indonesia Bldg, Jalan Merdeka Selatan 13, Jakarta 10110; tel. (21) 2311801; fax (21) 2311962; f. 1949; state airline; operates scheduled domestic, regional and international services to destinations in Europe, the USA, the Middle East, Australasia and the Far East; scheduled for privatization in 1998; Pres. SUPANDI.

PT Mandala Airlines: Jalan Garuda 76, POB 3706, Jakarta 10620; tel. (21) 4206646; telex 45425; fax (21) 4249494; f. 1969; privately-owned; scheduled regional and domestic passenger and cargo services; Pres. V. SUBAGEO; Vice-Pres. ZAIDUN BHAKTI.

PT Merpati Nusantara Airlines: Jalan Angkasa, Blok B 15 Kav. 2–3, Jakarta 10720; tel. (21) 6548888; telex 49154; fax (21) 6540620; f. 1962; subsidiary of PT Garuda Indonesia; domestic and regional services to Australia, Malaysia and Singapore; Pres. Dir FRANS H. SUMOLANG.

PT Sempati Air: Terminal Bldg, Ground Floor, Halim Perdanakusuma Airport, Jakarta 13610; tel. (21) 8011612; telex 46132; fax (21) 8094420; f. 1968; fmrly PT Sempati Air Transport; scheduled regional and domestic passenger and cargo services; Pres. Dir HASAN M. SOEDJONO.

Tourism

Indonesia's tourist industry is based mainly on the islands of Java, famous for its volcanic scenery and religious temples, and Bali, renowned for its scenery and Hindu-Buddhist temples and religious festivals. Lombok, Sumatra and Sulawesi are also increasingly popular. Domestic tourism within Indonesia has also increased significantly. In 1996 an estimated total of 5.03m. foreign tourists visited Indonesia, compared with 4.3m. in 1995. Foreign exchange earnings from tourism rose from US $5,210m. in 1995 to US $6,100m. in 1996.

Direktorat Jenderal Pariwisata (Directorate-General of Tourism): Jalan Merdeka Barat 16–19, Jakarta 10110; tel. (21) 3860822; fax (21) 3860828; f. 1957; Chair. ANDI MAPPI SAMMENG.

Indonesia Tourist Promotion Board: Bank Pacific Bldg, 4th Floor, Jalan Jenderal Sudirman, Jakarta; private body; promotes national and international tourism; Chair. TANRI ABENG; Vice-Chair. J. L. PARAPAK; Man. Dir WURYASTUTI SUNARIO.

IRAN

Introductory Survey

Location, Climate, Language, Religion, Flag, Capital

The Islamic Republic of Iran lies in western Asia, bordered by Azerbaijan and Turkmenistan to the north, by Turkey and Iraq to the west, by the Persian (Arabian) Gulf and the Gulf of Oman to the south, and by Pakistan and Afghanistan to the east. The climate is one of great extremes. Summer temperatures of more than 55°C (131°F) have been recorded, but in the winter the great altitude of much of the country results in temperatures of −18°C (0°F) and below. The principal language is Farsi (Persian), spoken by about 50% of the population. Turkic-speaking Azerbaijanis form about 27% of the population, and Kurds, Arabs, Balochis and Turkomans form less than 25%. The great majority of Persians and Azerbaijanis are Shi'i Muslims, while the other ethnic groups are mainly Sunni Muslims. There are also small minorities of Christians (mainly Armenians), Jews and Zoroastrians. The Bahá'í faith, which originated in Iran, has been severely persecuted. The national flag (proportions 7 by 4) comprises three unequal horizontal stripes, of green, white and red, with the emblem of the Islamic Republic of Iran (the stylized word Allah) centrally positioned in red, and the inscription 'Allaho Akbar' ('God is Great') written 11 times each in white Kufic script on the red and green stripes. The capital is Teheran.

Recent History

Iran, called Persia until 1935, was formerly a monarchy, ruled by a Shah (Emperor). In 1927 Reza Khan, a Cossack officer, seized power in a military coup, and was subsequently elected Shah, adopting the title Reza Shah Pahlavi. In 1941 British and Soviet forces occupied Iran, and the Shah (who favoured Nazi Germany) was forced to abdicate in favour of his son, Muhammad Reza Pahlavi. British and US forces left Iran in 1945, but Soviet forces remained in the north-west of the country (Azerbaijan province) until 1946. The United Kingdom retained considerable influence through the Anglo-Iranian Oil Co, which controlled much of Iran's extensive petroleum reserves. In March 1951, however, the Majlis (National Consultative Assembly) approved the nationalization of the petroleum industry, despite British and other Western opposition. The leading advocate of nationalization, Dr Muhammad Mussadeq, who became Prime Minister in May 1951, was deposed in August 1953 in a military *coup d'état*, engineered by the US and British intelligence services.

The Shah gradually increased his personal control of government following the coup, assuming dictatorial powers in 1963 with the so-called 'White Revolution'. Large estates were redistributed to small farmers, and women were granted the right to vote in elections, provoking opposition from landlords and the conservative Muslim clergy. In 1965 the Prime Minister, Hassan Ali Mansur, was assassinated, reportedly by a follower of the Ayatollah Ruhollah Khomeini, a Shi'ite Muslim fundamentalist religious leader strongly opposed to the Shah. (Khomeini had been deported in 1964 for his opposition activities, and was living in exile in Iraq.) Amir Abbas Hoveida held the office of Prime Minister until 1977.

Between 1965 and 1977 Iran enjoyed political stability and considerable economic growth, based on high petroleum revenues which were used to fund a high level of expenditure on armaments and infrastructure projects. From late 1977, however, public opposition to the regime increased dramatically, largely in response to a declining economy and the repressive nature of the Shah's rule. By late 1978 anti-Government demonstrations and strikes were widespread, involving both left-wing and liberal opponents of the Shah, as well as Islamist activists. The most effective opposition came from supporters of the Ayatollah Khomeini, now based in France.

The growing unrest forced the Shah to leave Iran in January 1979. Khomeini arrived in Teheran on 1 February and effectively took power 10 days later. A 15-member Islamic Revolutionary Council was formed to govern the country, in co-operation with a Provisional Government, and on 1 April Iran was declared an Islamic republic. Supreme authority was vested in the Wali Faqih, a religious leader (initially Khomeini) appointed by the Shi'ite clergy. An elected President was to be the chief executive. In January 1980 Abolhasan Bani-Sadr obtained some 75% of the votes cast at a presidential election, and was sworn in as President in the next month. Elections to a 270-member Majlis (National—later Islamic—Consultative Assembly) took place in two rounds in March and May. The Islamic Republican Party (IRP), which was identified with Khomeini and traditionalist Muslims, won some 60 seats, but subsequently gained considerable support among other deputies.

In November 1979 Iranian students seized 63 hostages in the US embassy in Teheran. The original purpose of the siege was in support of a demand for the return of the Shah (then in the USA) to Iran to face trial. The Shah died in Egypt in July 1980, by which time Iran had made other demands, notably for a US undertaking not to interfere in its affairs. Intense diplomatic activity finally resulted in the release of the 52 remaining hostages in January 1981.

The hostage crisis had forced the resignation of the moderate Provisional Government, and during 1980 it became clear that a rift was developing between President Bani-Sadr and his modernist allies, on the one hand, and the more traditional Muslim elements (led by the IRP), on the other. Clashes between supporters of the two groups escalated in June 1981 into intense fighting between members of the Mujahidin-e-Khalq (an Islamist guerrilla group that supported Bani-Sadr) and troops of the Revolutionary Guard Corps. The Majlis voted to impeach the President, and on 10 June he was dismissed by Khomeini. Bani-Sadr fled to France, as did the leader of the the Mujahidin, Massoud Rajavi.

A presidential election in July 1981 resulted in victory for the Prime Minister, Muhammad Ali Rajani. He was succeeded as Prime Minister by Muhammad Javar Bahunar. Meanwhile, conflict between the Mujahidin and government forces intensified, with an estimated 900 members of the guerrilla group being executed by mid-August. In late August both the President and Prime Minister were killed in a bomb attack. The Mujahidin were held responsible, and repression against them intensified. A further presidential election, held in October, was won by Hojatoleslam Ali Khamenei. Later in the same month Mir Hussein Moussavi was appointed Prime Minister.

Two ministers resigned and three more were dismissed in August 1983. The outgoing ministers were right-wing 'bazaaris', the merchant class, who opposed the programme of nationalization and land reform advocated by technocrats in the Government. Moussavi's attempts to implement such economic reforms were continually obstructed by the predominantly conservative, clerical Majlis. Elections to the second Majlis in April and May 1984 resulted in a clear win for the IRP. The elections were boycotted by the Nehzat-Azadi (Liberation Movement of Iran—the sole opposition party to have a degree of official recognition), led by Dr Mehdi Bazargan (who had been Prime Minister of the Provisional Government from February to November 1979), in protest at the allegedly undemocratic conditions prevailing in Iran. During 1985 there were reports of anti-Government demonstrations and rioting in several Iranian cities, including Teheran, precipitated by austere economic conditions and dissatisfaction with the conduct of the war with Iraq (see below).

Three candidates, including the incumbent, contested the August 1985 presidential election. The Council of Guardians (responsible for the supervision of elections) had rejected almost 50 others, among them Bazargan, who opposed the continuation of the war with Iraq. Ali Khamenei was elected President for a second four-year term, with 85.7% of the total votes cast. Despite opposition in the Majlis, Hussein Moussavi was reconfirmed as Prime Minister in October.

Political opposition to the regime was strongly suppressed. In February 1987 a report by the UN Human Rights Commission claimed that at least 7,000 executions of political opponents had been carried out by the Islamic regime between 1979 and 1985. Reports issued by a prominent human rights organization, Amnesty International, in 1989 and 1990, and by the UN in 1992, alleged that abuses of human rights remained widespread.

For most of the 1980s Iran's domestic and foreign policy was dominated by the war with Iraq. In September 1980, ostensibly to assert a claim of sovereignty over the disputed Shatt al-Arab waterway, Iraqi forces invaded Iran along a 500-km (300-mile) front, with the aim of achieving a rapid military victory. Iranian forces displayed strong resistance and a conflict of attrition developed. Iran began a counter-offensive in early 1982; by June it had forced Iraq to withdraw from Iranian territory, and by July Iranian troops had entered Iraq. In October 1983 Iran launched a series of offensives across its northern border with Iraq, thus threatening Iraq's only remaining outlet for petroleum exports, the Kirkuk pipeline. In response, Iraq intensified its aerial attacks on Iranian towns and on Iran's petroleum industry, centred on Kharg Island, in the Persian (Arabian) Gulf. In February and March 1984 a further Iranian offensive led to the capture of the marshlands around the man-made Majnoun Islands in southern Iraq, the site of extensive petroleum resources. In May Iraq began attacking tankers using the Kharg Island oil terminal, and Iran retaliated by attacking Saudi Arabian and Kuwaiti tankers in the Gulf. Sporadic attacks on shipping by both Iran and Iraq continued in subsequent months.

In March 1985 an estimated 50,000 Iranian troops were committed to a mass offensive on the southern front. The army crossed the Tigris river, and temporarily closed the Baghdad–Basra road. The troops were repelled by Iraqi forces with heavy casualties on both sides, and Iraq renewed aerial bombardment of Iranian cities. In April 1985 the UN Secretary-General, Javier Pérez de Cuéllar, visited both Teheran and Baghdad, in an attempt to establish a basis for peace negotiations, but achieved little success. Iran rejected Iraqi's terms for a cease-fire, insisting that only the removal of the Iraqi President Saddam Hussain, in conjunction with agreement by Iraq to pay war reparations, could bring an end to the hostilities.

Between August 1985 and January 1986 Iraq undertook some 60 air raids on the Kharg Island terminal, limiting Iran's ability to maintain a high level of petroleum shipments from the terminal. In February 1986 Iraq announced an expansion of the area of the Gulf from which it would try to exclude Iranian shipping. Attacks on tankers and other commercial vessels were increased by both sides in 1986, and Iran intensified its practice of intercepting merchant vessels in the Gulf and confiscating goods that it believed to be destined for Iraq.

In January 1986 Iraq claimed to have recaptured most of the Majnoun Islands. In February, in the Wal-Fajr (Dawn) 8 offensive, Iranian troops crossed the Shatt al-Arab waterway and occupied the disused Iraqi port of Faw and part of the surrounding Faw peninsula, thus threatening Iraq's only access to the Gulf. Although the difficulty of the terrain to the west prevented further Iranian advances, and the position on the Faw peninsula was not easily defensible, an Iraqi counter-offensive failed to dislodge an estimated 30,000 Iranian troops from in and around Faw. Iraqi forces were diverted by a second offensive by Iran into Iraqi Kurdistan, several hundred kilometres to the north. In May Iraq made its first armed incursion into Iran since 1982, occupying the area around Mehran; however, an Iranian counter-offensive had forced Iraqi forces to withdraw within two months. Also in May 1986 Iraqi aircraft raided Teheran for the first time since June 1985, initiating a new wave of reciprocal attacks on urban and industrial centres in Iran and Iraq, which continued into 1987. In late 1986 and early 1987 Iranian forces advanced to within 10 km of the Iraqi city of Basra, at the expense of heavy casualties; further offensives during 1987 failed to capture the city.

As the war continued, the USSR, several Western countries and most Arab states provided armaments and other means of support to Iraq, while Iran remained diplomatically isolated. In November 1986, however, it emerged that the USA, despite its active discouragement of the sale of armaments to Iran by other countries, had been conducting secret negotiations with the country since July 1985 and had made three shipments of weapons to Iran in late 1985 and 1986, allegedly in exchange for Iranian assistance in releasing US hostages detained by Shi'ite groups in Lebanon, and an Iranian undertaking to relinquish involvement in international terrorism.

During 1986–87 the protection of international shipping in the Gulf became the focus of world-wide attention, as Iran had begun to attack Kuwaiti shipping and neutral shipping using Kuwait, because of Kuwait's support for Iraq. In May 1987 the USA agreed to reregister 11 Kuwaiti tankers under the US flag, thus entitling them to US naval protection, and in August the United Kingdom and France dispatched minesweepers to the Gulf region, followed in September by vessels from the Netherlands, Belgium and Italy. Iraqi air attacks on tankers transporting Iranian petroleum, and Iranian reprisals against merchant shipping involved with Iraq, continued. On 20 July, meanwhile, the UN Security Council adopted Resolution 598, urging an immediate cease-fire, the withdrawal of military forces to international boundaries, and the co-operation of Iran and Iraq in mediation efforts to achieve a peace settlement.

Iraqi forces recaptured the Faw peninsula in April 1988, forcing Iranian forces to withdraw across the Shatt al-Arab waterway in May. In June Iraq recaptured Majnoun Island and the surrounding area. In July the *USS Vincennes* shot down an Iran Air Airbus over the Strait of Hormuz, having mistaken the airliner for an attacking fighter aircraft; all 290 passengers and crew were killed. In that month Iraqi troops crossed into Iranian territory for the first time since 1986, capturing the border town of Dehloran, and the last Iranian troops on Iraqi territory were dislodged. On 18 July Iran unexpectedly announced its unconditional acceptance of the UN Security Council's Resolution 598. A cease-fire came into effect on 20 August, and peace negotiations between Iran and Iraq began shortly afterwards in Geneva, Switzerland, under UN auspices. In the same month a UN Iran-Iraq Military Observer Group (UNIIMOG) was deployed in the region. The negotiations soon became deadlocked in disputes regarding the sovereignty of the Shatt al-Arab waterway, the exchange of prisoners of war, and the withdrawal of armed forces to within international boundaries. An initial exchange of prisoners took place in late November, but attempts to effect a comprehensive exchange quickly collapsed. Thus, the only element of Resolution 598 to have been successfully implemented remained the cease-fire.

Hopes of a comprehensive peace settlement were raised by a meeting of the Iranian and Iraqi Ministers of Foreign Affairs in Geneva in July 1990, but were swiftly overshadowed by Iraq's invasion of Kuwait in August. On 16 August Saddam Hussain sought an immediate, formal peace with Iran, accepting all the claims that Iran had pursued since the declaration of a cease-fire (including the reinstatement of the Algiers Agreement of 1975, dividing the Shatt al-Arab waterway). Although clearly motivated by expediency (Iraq began to redeploy troops from the border with Iran to Kuwait the following day), the concessions were welcomed by Iran. Exchanges of prisoners of war took place, and in September 1990 Iran and Iraq restored diplomatic relations. In February 1991 the withdrawal of all armed forces to internationally recognized boundaries was confirmed by UNIIMOG, whose mandate was terminated shortly afterwards.

Iran condemned Iraq's invasion of Kuwait, and observed the economic sanctions that the UN imposed on Iraq. However, it was unequivocal in its condemnation of the deployment of a multinational force for the liberation of Kuwait, and urged the withdrawal of all Western forces from the Gulf region. Relations between Iran and Iraq deteriorated after the conclusion of hostilities between Iraq and the multinational force in late February 1991. Iran protested strongly against the suppression of the Shi'a-led rebellion in southern and central Iraq, and the accompanying destruction of Shi'a shrines in the region, and renewed its demand for the resignation of Saddam Hussain. Iraq, in turn, accused Iran of supporting the rebellion. Thus, there was little further progress in implementing the terms of Resolution 598 until October 1993, when high-level talks were reported to have recommenced between Iran and Iraq on the exchange of remaining prisoners of war. In late September 1997 the Iranian authorities claimed that Iran had hitherto unilaterally released a total of 9,650 Iraqi prisoners of war, while Iraq had released no Iranians during the previous five years. At the end of November the Iraqi Government estimated that there were some 18,000 Iraqi prisoners of war registered in Iran, in addition to 'several thousands' not registered with the International Committee of the Red Cross. (See below for further details of relations between Iran and Iraq.)

The cease-fire of August 1988 in the Iran–Iraq War exacerbated existing tensions within the Iranian leadership. Elections to the Majlis in April and May 1988 had provided a stimulus to the 'reformers' in the Government (identified with Hashemi Rafsanjani, the Speaker of the Majlis, and Prime Minister Moussavi) by producing an assembly strongly representative of their views. (The elections were the Islamic Republic's first not to be contested by the IRP, which had been dissolved in 1987.) In June 1988 Rafsanjani was re-elected as Speaker and Moussavi was overwhelmingly endorsed as Prime Minister. In February 1989, however, Khomeini referred explicitly to a division in the Iranian leadership between 'reformers' (who sought Western participation in Iran's post-war reconstruction) and 'conservatives' (who opposed such involvement), and declared that he would never permit the 'reformers' to prevail. His intervention was reportedly prompted by the decision of Rafsanjani to contest the presidential election scheduled for mid-1989. In March and April prominent 'reformers' within the leadership, including Ayatollah Montazeri (who had been designated as successor to Ayatollah Khomeini by the Council of Experts in 1985), resigned. In early 1989 it was reported that the Council of Experts had established a five-member leadership council to designate a replacement for Montazeri as Khomeini's successor.

Ayatollah Khomeini died on 3 June 1989. In an emergency session on 4 June the Council of Experts elected President Khamenei to succeed Khomeini as Iran's spiritual leader (Wali Faqih). The presidential election, scheduled to take place on 18 August, was brought forward to 28 July, to be held simultaneously with a referendum on proposed amendments to the Constitution. By mid-July both 'conservatives' and 'reformers' within the leadership had apparently united in support of the candidacy of Rafsanjani for the presidency. Rafsanjani easily won the election (his only opponent was Abbas Sheibani, a former government minister widely regarded as a 'token' candidate), receiving 95.9% of the total votes cast, according to official figures. A similar proportion of voters approved the constitutional amendments, the most important of which was the abolition of the post of Prime Minister (and a consequent increase in power for the President).

Rafsanjani's new Government was regarded as a balanced coalition of 'conservatives', 'reformers' and technocrats, and its endorsement by the Majlis, in late August 1989, was viewed as a mandate for Rafsanjani to conduct a more conciliatory policy towards the West, despite the opposition of some 'conservative' elements. Popular protests against food shortages and high prices in early 1990 demonstrated the urgent need for economic reform. In October, with the support of Ayatollah Khamenei, Rafsanjani was able to prevent the election of many powerful 'conservatives' to the Council of Experts. Elections to the fourth Majlis were held in April and May 1992. Of those who applied to contest the elections, about one-third (mostly considered to be opponents of Rafsanjani) were disqualified by the Council of Guardians. Of the total number of newly-elected deputies, it was estimated that about 70% were supporters of, or likely to align themselves with, Rafsanjani, who thus emerged in a strengthened position with regard to his policies of reform. However, while the President appeared to have succeeded in marginalizing the 'conservatives', he remained constrained, not least by the fact that economic reform was lowering the standard of living of the traditional constituency of the Islamic regime, the urban lower classes. Meanwhile, the middle classes, supposedly one of the engines of reform, remained deeply distrustful of the regime. Serious rioting reported to have occurred in the cities of Arak, Shiraz, Khorramabad and Mashad in April and May 1992, was attributed by some observers to the Government's economic reform programme.

The extent to which Rafsanjani had lost popular support became clear when he stood for re-election to the presidency on 11 June 1993. Competing against three ostensibly 'token' candidates, Rafsanjani received 63.2% of the votes in a low electoral turn-out of 56%. Furthermore, the refusal of the Majlis, in August, to accept Rafsanjani's first nominee (Mohsen Nourbakhch) for the post of Minister of Economy and Finance was interpreted as criticism of recent economic management. (Nourbakhch was, however, subsequently appointed Vice-President in charge of Economic Affairs, and in October, Morteza Muhammadkhan was appointed Minister of Economic Affairs and Finance.)

An attempt was made on Rafsanjani's life at a rally in Teheran in February 1994. Responsibility for the attack was later claimed by the self-styled 'Free Officers of the Revolutionary Guards'. Later in the month the President was obliged to appoint a new Minister of Culture and Islamic Guidance after Ayatollah Khamenei approved the appointment of the incumbent minister, Ali Larijani, to replace the President's brother, Hashemi, as Director-General of the national broadcasting authority. Hashemi Rafsanjani had for several months been criticized by 'conservatives' within the Majlis for mismanagement and for encouraging immoral broadcasts. While President Rafsanjani denied that the dismissal of his brother reflected on him, it was perhaps significant that, shortly afterwards, he announced that he would not seek a constitutional amendment allowing him to serve a third term as President. Rafsanjani's opponents in the Majlis sought, meanwhile, to modify economic reforms proposed by the Government. In May the Government indicated that it would proceed more cautiously with a plan to reduce economic subsidies applied to basic commodities. In November the Majlis approved the Government's second five-year economic plan, having debated it for almost one year.

In April 1995 riots in Islamshahr, a suburb of Teheran, were interpreted as a protest against the Government's economic reform programme, which had led to shortages of some consumer goods during the previous 12 months. In August the official news agency cited members of the special commission for monitoring political parties as stating that political parties, associations and groups were free to conduct political activities in Iran on condition that they honoured the country's Constitution. It was subsequently reported, however, that Nehzat-Azadi had been refused formal registration as a political party, despite its hitherto quasi-legal status. Earlier in the month representatives of Nehzat-Azadi had criticized new electoral legislation that granted the Council of Guardians the power to approve election candidates. In December Iranian officials were reported to have indicated that future elections would be contested by political parties.

Legislative elections (to the fifth Majlis) in 1996 provided an important measure of the shifting balance of power between 'liberals' and 'conservatives' in Iranian politics. The first round of voting, on 8 March, produced results in some 140 of the total 270 seats. Candidates of the Servants of Iran's Construction, a pro-Rafsanjani faction formed to contest the elections, were reported to have won some 70% of the seats. However, the 'conservative' Society of Combatant Clergy, which enjoyed the unofficial patronage of Ayatollah Khamenei, claimed that its candidates had achieved an equally conclusive victory. After the second round of voting, on 19 April, unofficial sources suggested that the Society of Combatant Clergy would command the loyalty of 110–120 deputies in the new Majlis, and the Servants of Iran's Construction that of 90–100 deputies. Some 77% of Iran's approximately 32m.-strong electorate were reported to have participated in the first round of voting.

In October 1996 Majma-e Hezbollah, a faction in the Majlis formed by supporters of President Rafsanjani, formally proposed former Prime Minister Moussavi as a candidate in the presidential election that was to take place in 1997. Rafsanjani had, for his part, again publicly dismissed speculation that he would seek an amendment to the Constitution permitting him to serve a third term of office. In late October, however, Moussavi withdrew his candidature. It was reported that Ali Akbar Nateq Nouri, the Majlis Speaker since 1992, had been nominated for the presidential office in late October, and that his candidacy was supported by virtually all of the members of the Society of Combatant Clergy.

In March 1997 Rafsanjani was appointed Chairman of the Committee to Determine the Expediency of the Islamic Order (which arbitrates in disputes between the Majlis and the Council of Guardians) for a further five-year term, indicating that he would continue to play an influential role in political life upon the expiry of his presidential mandate. In early May the Council of Guardians approved four candidatures for the presidential election (a further 234 were rejected). Other than Nateq Nouri, the candidates were Sayed Muhammad Khatami (a presidential adviser and former Minister of Culture and Islamic Guidance), Muhammad Mohammadi Reyshari (a former Minister of Intelligence and Internal Security, Prosecutor-General and, of late, Khamenei's representative in *Hajj* and pilgrimage affairs) and Sayed Reza Zavarei (hitherto vice-president of the judiciary and a member of the Council of Guardians). Despite early expectations that the Majlis Speaker would secure an easy victory, Khatami emerged as a strong contender in the days prior to the election, which took place on 23 May. Regarded as a 'liberal' candidate, Khatami—supported by the Servants of Iran's Construction, as well as by intellectuals, by women's and youth groups and by the business classes—took some 69.1% of the total votes cast, ahead of Nateq Nouri, with 24.9%. The rate of participation by voters was in excess of 88%. (Nateq Nouri was re-elected Speaker of the Majlis at the beginning of June.)

Khatami was sworn in by Khamenei on 3 August 1997, and took the presidential oath of office before the Majlis the following day. The new President stated that it would be the responsibility of his administration to create a safe atmosphere for the clash of views, within the framework of regulations defined by Islam and the Constitution, and advocated the promotion of 'easy and transparent' relations between the people and the organs of State. Khatami emphasized his commitment to fostering sustained and balanced growth in the political, economic, cultural and educational spheres, and to the freedom of and respect for the individual and rights of the nation, in the context of the rule of law. In foreign affairs, the President undertook to promote the principle of mutual respect, but pledged that Iran would stand up to any power seeking to subjugate Iranian sovereignty. Despite some concern that 'conservatives' in the Majlis might oppose some of the more liberal members of Khatami's first Council of Ministers, which was presented for approval in mid-August, all the government nominees were endorsed by the assembly after several days' debate. Notable among the 'moderate' appointees were Ata'ollah Mohajerani (a former Vice-President) as Minister of Culture and Islamic Guidance, and Abdollah Nuri as Minister of the Interior (a post he had previously held in 1989–93). Kamal Kharrazi (hithero Iran's ambassador to the UN) replaced Ali Akbar Velayati as Minister of Foreign Affairs, while Qorbanali Dorri Najafabadi became Minister of Information. Upon taking office, Khatami had reappointed Hassan Habibi as First Vice-President. Six further Vice-Presidents were named later in the month, among them Hashemi Rafsanjani, who retained the post of Vice-President in Charge of Executive Affairs; Ma'sumeh Ebtekar, as Vice-President and Head of the Organization for the Protection of the Environment, was the first woman to be appointed to a government post of such seniority since the Islamic Revolution. In mid-October Khatami named former Prime Minister Moussavi as his senior adviser.

Although Khatami pledged his allegiance to Khamenei as Iran's spiritual leader, the new President's assumption of office appeared to revive long-standing rivalries among the senior clergy. The focus of opposition to Khamenei was seemingly Ayatollah Montazeri (Khomenei's designated successor prior to March 1989), who began openly to criticize Khamenei's authority and to demand that Khatami be allowed to govern without interference. In mid-November 1997 police used tear gas to disperse a violent demonstration in Qom by supporters of Khamenei, who had gathered to denounce Montazeri and one of his allies, Ayatollah Azari Qumi. Demonstrations in support of Khamenei persisted in Qom, Teheran and elsewhere for several days, until Khamenei urged an end to the protests; none the less, he demanded that Montazeri be tried for treason, and that all others who questioned his authority be prosecuted in accordance with the law. In mid-December the General Secretary of Nehzat-Azadi, Ibrahim Yazdi, who had reportedly met with Montazeri shortly before the latter had publicly criticized Khamenei, was detained for almost two weeks, on charges of desecrating religious sanctities, after he had signed an open letter to Khatami urging that Montazeri's rights be respected. Meanwhile, in late November the President appointed a new Committee for Ensuring and Supervising the Implementation of the Constitution.

A *rapprochement* with the West, pursued successfully during 1990 and 1991, was hindered by the continuing dispute over the British writer Salman Rushdie. In February 1989 Ayatollah Khomeini issued a *fatwa* (edict) imposing a death sentence against Rushdie for writing material offensive to Islam in his novel, *The Satanic Verses.* Khomeini's pronouncement resulted in a sharp deterioration in relations with the United Kingdom and other Western countries. High-level diplomatic contacts between members of the European Community (EC, now European Union—EU) and Iran were suspended, and in March Iran severed diplomatic relations with the United Kingdom. Although there was no change in Iran's policy towards Rushdie, a gradual thaw in relations with the West followed Rafsanjani's election to the presidency in August 1989, aided by Iranian assistance in obtaining the release of Western hostages held by pro-Iranian Shi'ite groups in Lebanon, and, in particular, by Iran's declaration of neutrality during the Gulf crisis of 1990–91. In September 1990, after the British Government accepted that *The Satanic Verses* had caused offence to Muslims and stated that it had no wish to insult Islam, Iran and the United Kingdom restored diplomatic relations. In October the EC revoked its ban on high-level diplomatic contacts with Iran, and subsequently announced plans to establish permanent representation in Teheran. In December 1992, however, EC leaders meeting in Edinburgh, United Kingdom, criticized alleged abuses of human rights in Iran and stated 'that Iran's arms procurement should not pose a threat to regional stability'. In August 1993 talks took place between the United Kingdom and Iran, with the aim of raising diplomatic links between the two countries to ambassadorial level.

In April 1994 Iran's relations with the United Kingdom again deteriorated after the British Government accused Iran of having links with the proscribed Irish Republican Army. In May the British Government ordered an Iranian official to leave the United Kingdom, and a British diplomat was subsequently expelled from Iran, amid allegations that representatives of the Iranian Government had forged correspondence, purporting to be from members of the British Government, designed to discredit the United Kingdom's foreign policy in the former Yugoslavia. In May 1995 a statement by the head of the Iranian judiciary appeared to indicate that Iran would not attempt to enforce the *fatwa* against Rushdie. In July, none the less, Norway announced the withdrawal of its ambassador from Iran because the death sentence on Rushdie remained unrevoked. In February 1997 the United Kingdom denounced the decision of the Qom-based 15 Khordad Foundation to increase a reward offered for the murder of Salman Rushdie as an 'outrageous infringement' of the author's rights. The British Government claimed that the 15 Khordad Foundation was not independent of the Iranian Government, and appealed to Rafsanjani to distance his Government from the Foundation. Negotiations with the United Kingdom and the EU regarding the *fatwa* were effectively suspended after April 1997, but were expected to resume following the return of EU ambassadors to Iran at the end of the year (see below). President Khatami's new Minister of Culture and Islamic Guidance, regarded as a relative moderate, confirmed previous indications that the Iranian Government would not seek any execution in connection with the *fatwa* against Rushdie, but emphasized that the edict could not be revoked by a government. In late October the British Government followed the USA (see below) in classifying Mujahidin-e-Khalq as a terrorist organization and stating that its members would be excluded from the United Kingdom.

Despite US pressure (see below), the EU has pursued with a policy of 'critical dialogue' with Iran. However, in March 1996 it threatened to reconsider this policy following alleged remarks by Rafsanjani welcoming the assassination of the Israeli Prime Minister, Itzhak Rabin. 'Critical dialogue' was suspended in April 1997, after a German court ruled that the Iranian authorities had ordered the assassination of four prominent members of the dissident Democratic Party of Iranian Kurdistan in Berlin in September 1992: testimonies at the trial had directly implicated senior members of the Iranian political and religious establishment in sanctioning the murders, and, moreover, had alleged that Iran's Minister of Information and Security, Ali Falahian, had attempted to influence the outcome of the case. (The trial found two defendants—an Iranian and a Lebanese national—guilty of murder, sentencing them to life imprisonment, and two others—both Lebanese nationals—of having been accessories to the killings.) Germany announced the withdrawal of its ambassador to Teheran and expelled four Iranian diplomats, and other EU members similarly withdrew their representatives. Although the Union's ministers responsible for foreign affairs swiftly agreed to a return of their ambassadors, Iran's reluctance to readmit the German envoy prevented the normalization of relations for several months. The appointment, in August 1997, of a new Minister of Foreign Affairs, as well as a new Minister of Information, in Khatami's first Council of Ministers apparently allowed some relaxation of tensions, and in November a compromise arrangement was finally reached allowing the readmission of all ambassadors from EU countries.

Relations with the USA have been subject to conflicting influences. Iran's influence in obtaining the release of Western hostages in Lebanon notably contrasted with its hostility towards the USA's perceived interference in the region in the aftermath of the 1990–91 crisis in the Gulf region, and towards the peace agreement concluded between Israel and the Palestine Liberation Organization in September 1993. The USA has alleged that Iran has embarked on a programme of military expansion, and it has expressed particular concern over the nature of nuclear co-operation between the People's Republic of China, India, Russia and Iran. In February 1992, however, the International Atomic Energy Agency (see p. 65) stated that there was no evidence of an Iranian nuclear weapons programme. During 1993 the USA sought to persuade its Western allies to reduce their levels of economic assistance to Iran. In May 1994 US pressure was evident when the World Bank announced that it would approve no new loans to Iran in the foreseeable future. In July bomb attacks against Jewish targets in London, United Kingdom, and Buenos Aires, Argentina, prompted the USA to accuse Iran—which it alleged to have been responsible for the attacks—of seeking to disrupt the Middle East peace process.

In early 1995, at the time of a final preparatory UN session before a conference on the extension of the Nuclear Non-Proliferation Treaty (NPT), the US, British and Israeli Governments revived concerns regarding Iran's nuclear weapons potential. For its part, Iran was reported to be seeking a more effective effort from the five principal nuclear powers to disarm further, and insisting that Israel should also sign the NPT. (However, the head of the Atomic Energy Organization of Iran subsequently suggested that Iran would remain a party to the NPT whether Israel signed it or not.) At the end of April US efforts to isolate Iran internationally culminated in the announcement of a complete ban on trade with Iran within 30 days: all US companies and their overseas subsidiaries would be prevented from investing in Iran, and from undertaking any trade with the country. The USA subsequently announced that US oil companies active in the Caucasus and in Central Asia would be allowed to participate in exchange deals with Iran in order to facilitate the marketing of petroleum from former Soviet states. In May Russia announced that it would henceforth separate the civilian and military components of an agreement to supply Iran with a nuclear reactor, to be constructed at Bushehr, and that it would not sell Iran gas centrifuge systems which might enable it to develop nuclear weapons.

In mid-1996 the US Congress approved legislation seeking to penalize companies operating in US markets that were investing US $40m. or more in energy projects in several prescribed countries, including Iran, which the US authorities deemed to be a sponsor of terrorism. Like the trade embargo imposed on Iran in 1995, however, these so-called secondary economic sanctions received little support from the international community. In late September 1997, notably, a consortium comprising French, Malaysian and Russian energy companies signed a contract with the Iranian National Oil Company to invest some $2,000m. in the development of natural gas in Iranian waters in the Persian Gulf.

Israel and the USA continued to express concerns during 1997 that Iran was developing ballistic missiles with Russian and Chinese assistance: Iran has maintained that it is not engaged in the development of weapons of mass destruction, while the Governments of Russia and the People's Republic of China have strenuously denied involvement in non-civilian nuclear projects. In September the US Vice-President announced that US and Russian investigators had concluded that Iran was engaged in a 'vigorous effort' to obtain technology for the manufacture of nuclear weapons and ballistic missiles capable of transporting them. Earlier in the month the Russian authorities had stated that they would be willing to allow the USA to monitor the Bushehr nuclear power plant. In October China announced an end to the sale of nuclear technology, as well as of conventional weaponry, to Iran. In November Iran became a signatory to the International Chemical Weapons Convention; under its terms, which prohibit the production and possession of chemical weapons, Iran became subject to mandatory international inspections. Earlier in the month it was reported that the USA had purchased fighter aircraft from Moldova, in order to prevent their sale to Iran.

Khatami's election to the Iranian presidency prompted speculation regarding prospects for an improvement in relations with the USA and with other Western countries. The dispatch of US naval vessels to the Gulf region in early October 1997 (see below) contrasted notably with the designation by the USA of the opposition Mujahidin-e-Khalq as one of 30 proscribed terrorist organizations. (Members of these groups would be denied visas for entry to the USA and would be banned from fund-raising on US territory.) In mid-December Khatami expressed his desire to engage in a 'thoughtful dialogue' with the American people. Clinton responded that he was encouraged by Khatami's remarks, and subsequently, in what was interpreted as a major concession, stated that the USA would not require Iran (or any other Islamic state) to modify its attitude towards the Middle East peace process. The cautious *rapprochement* continued in January 1998, when Khatami made a widely-publicized address on US cable news television, emphasizing the need to develop closer cultural links between Iran and the USA; that he did not urge direct political dialogue was generally interpreted as a compromise between 'moderates' in his administration and the regime's 'conservatives', most notably Khamenei, who had of late vociferously rejected the possibility of any normalization of relations with the USA.

Relations between Iran and Saudi Arabia have been characterized by mistrust since the Islamic Revolution of 1979. The death of 275 Iranian pilgrims in an incident at Mecca, the Islamic holy city in Saudi Arabia, in July 1987 further damaged relations, and Iran began a boycott of the *Hajj* (annual pilgrimage to Mecca). In March 1991 Iran re-established diplomatic relations with Saudi Arabia, facilitating an agreement which allowed 115,000 Iranian pilgrims to participate in the *Hajj* that year. Some improvement in relations, which had been particularly strained by suspicions of Iranian involvement in the bombing of a US military housing complex in Saudi Arabia in June 1996, was apparent during 1997. In March the Saudi Crown Prince, Abdullah ibn Adb al-Aziz as-Sa'ud, received Iran's then Minister of Foreign Affairs, Velayati. Later in the same month an agreement on bilateral aviation co-operation was signed, and in September Iran Air resumed scheduled flights to Saudi Arabia for the first time since 1979. The installation of the new Government in Iran, in August 1997, facilitated further *rapprochement,* and the new Minister of Foreign Affairs toured Saudi Arabia and the other members of the Co-operation Council for the Arab States of the Gulf (see p. 136) in November.

During the 1990–91 conflict over Kuwait, Iran began to improve its relations with Egypt, Tunisia, Jordan and the Gulf states. Iran sought to achieve a common stance with Syria over the Gulf crisis, and in 1991 it re-established diplomatic relations with Jordan, after an 11-year rift. In the aftermath of the Gulf crisis, however, Iran refused to countenance efforts, based on the Damascus Declaration of March 1991, to create a regional security structure in the Gulf from which it was itself excluded. In September 1994, at the UN Conference on Disarmament in Geneva, the Iranian Minister of Foreign Affairs proposed a security agreement for the Gulf and a ban on weapons of mass destruction in the region; and in October Rafsanjani assured the Gulf states that they faced no threat from Iran. In December 1995 the Iranian First Vice-President postponed a visit to Syria in protest at Syria's support for the United Arab Emirates (UAE) in its dispute with Iran (see below). However, both Syria and Iran subsequently emphasized the friendly nature of their relations.

Iran has perceived considerable political and economic advantage arising from its potential as a transit route for hydrocarbons from the former Soviet republics of Central Asia. However, while well-placed geopolitically, Iran is disadvantaged by the fact that the countries of Central Asia, with the exception of Azerbaijan, are Sunni Muslim, and, with the exception of Tajikistan, speak languages belonging to the Turkic group. Iran is seeking to strengthen its position in Central Asia through bilateral agreements as well as institutions such as the Teheran-based Economic Co-operation Organization (see p. 260). Iran, which has particularly close ethnic and linguistic ties with Tajikistan, hosted peace negotiations between the Tajik Government and its opponents in 1994–97. Several bilateral, cultural and economic co-operation agreements were signed in 1995–96. In September 1996, however, relations became strained after Tajik President Rahmonov accused Iran of assisting rebel forces opposed to his Government. In May 1997 the two countries concluded a defence co-operation agreement. Meanwhile, in October 1995 Iran, Armenia and Turkmenistan signed a memorandum on economic co-operation. In December 1997 a pipeline was inaugurated to transport natural gas from Turkmenistan to northern Iran. In December 1996 Iran and Russia concluded an extensive economic agreement.

Victories achieved by the Sunni fundamentalist Taliban in the Afghan civil war in September 1996 prompted Iran, which supported the Government of President Burhanuddin Rabbani, to express fears for its national security, and to accuse the USA of interference in Afghanistan's internal affairs. Iran has urged the parties to the Afghan conflict to seek a negotiated settlement. In June 1997 Taliban accused Iran of espionage and ordered the closure of the Iranian embassy in Kabul and the withdrawal of all Iranian diplomats. In retaliation Iran halted all trade across its land border with Afghanistan, prompting Taliban protests that the ban on trade was violating international law.

In April–May 1991 President Rafsanjani made an official visit to Turkey—the first such visit by an Iranian Head of State since 1975—where he publicly stated his agreement with Turkey's President Turgut Özal that a Kurdish state should not be established in northern Iraq. In early 1992, none the less, Turkey alleged that Iran was lending support to guerrillas from the Kurdish Workers' Party (KWP) engaged in hostilities with Turkish armed forces in south-east Turkey. Further deteriorations in Iran's relations with Turkey were reported in mid-1992, but in October the Turkish Prime Minister, Süleyman Demirel, made a visit to Teheran, as a result of which the two countries agreed to increase bilateral economic and political co-operation. In December 1993 Iran's First Vice-President, Hassan Habibi, visited Turkey, where he signed an agreement on security co-operation between Turkey and Iran. In March 1995 Iran criticized a military operation undertaken by the Turkish armed forces against KWP fighters in northern Iraq, fearing that the hostilities might spread to Iran. In July Iran was reported to have organized a month-long extension of a cease-fire between rival Kurdish groups in Iraqi Kurdistan, prompting Iraq to denounce Iranian interference in Iraqi internal affairs. In April 1996 new tensions arose in relations with Turkey after four Iranian diplomats were arrested in Turkey for alleged espionage; retaliatory expulsions of Turkish diplomats by Iran ensued, amid allegations of Iranian involvement in terrorist attacks in Turkey in the early 1990s. The installation of an Islamist-led Government in Turkey in mid-1996 reportedly facilitated closer bilateral relations; however, the extent of Iranian influence was frequently cited as having been a prime factor motivating the Turkish military's efforts to bring about the collapse, in June 1997, of the coalition. In the same month Iran became a founder member of the Istanbul-based Developing Eight (D-8, see p. 260) group of Islamic countries. Meanwhile, in February the Iranian ambassador to Turkey provoked a diplomatic crisis by advocating the introduction of Islamic law in Turkey. Criticism of the actions of the Turkish military by an Iranian consul-general later in that month resulted in both men being asked to leave the country. Iran responded by expelling two Turkish diplomats. However, both countries immediately undertook diplomatic initiatives to restore relations, and in March it was agreed, during a visit to Turkey by Iran's Minister of Foreign Affairs, that all bilateral agreements were to be pursued. In November it was reported that a renewed exchange of ambassadors was imminent.

In October 1996 Iran complained that it was receiving insufficient assistance from international agencies to meet the needs of the large number of Iraqi Kurds sheltering in Iranian refugee camps. In the same month Iran denied that its armed forces had had any part in recent fighting between supporters of the Patriotic Union of Kurdistan (PUK) and those of the Democratic Party of Kurdistan (DPK). Iraq renewed its accusation of Iranian interference in Iraqi affairs. In early September 1997 Iraq opened a border crossing with Iran, thereby permitting, for the first time since the outbreak of the Iran–Iraq War, Iranian pilgrims to visit Shi'ite Muslim shrines on its territory. At the end of the month, however, Iranian aircraft violated the air exclusion zone over southern Iraq in order to bomb two bases of the Mujahidin-e-Khalq in that country (prompting Iraqi aircraft also to enter the zone, in pursuit of the Iranian bombers). In an effort to dispel the increase in tension in the region, in early October the USA ordered an aircraft carrier and other vessels to proceed directly to the Persian Gulf. Vice-President Taha Yassin Ramadan of Iraq, attending the eighth Conference of the Organization of the Islamic Conference (OIC, see p. 224), which took place in Teheran in December 1997, was the most senior Iraqi official to visit Iran since 1979. Following the conference, President Khatami expressed the hope that problems between the two countries could be resolved 'through negotiation and understanding'.

In March 1992 Iran occupied those parts of the Abu Musa islands and the Greater and Lesser Tumbs that had remained under the control of Sharjah, in the UAE, since the original occupation in 1971. In September the League of Arab States (the Arab League, see p. 195) expressed its support for the UAE in the dispute over the islands, and negotiations between Iran and the UAE on this issue collapsed. In December 1994 the UAE announced its intention to refer the dispute to the International Court of Justice in the Hague, the Netherlands. In February 1995 Iran was reported to have deployed air defence systems on Abu Musa and the islands of the Greater and Lesser Tumbs, prompting the USA to warn of a potential threat to shipping. In November talks between Iran and the UAE aimed at establishing an agenda for ministerial-level negotiations on the disputed islands ended in failure. Relations deteriorated further in 1996, after Iran opened an airport on Abu Musa in March and a power station on Greater Tumb in April. In January and February 1997 the UAE protested that Iran was repeatedly violating the UAE's territorial waters. Talks in March were inconclusive, and in June the UAE protested to Iran and the UN at Iran's construction of a pier on Greater Tumb. Following a meeting with the UAE's Minister of Foreign Affairs at the time of the December 1997 OIC Summit, President Khatami emphasized his willingness to discuss bilteral issues directly with President Zayed bin Sultan an-Nayhan of the UAE. Although the latter was reported to be cautious about Iran's attempts at *rapprochement*, in the following month authorities in the UAE expressed the view that the UAE was willing to enter into negotiations. None the less, both countries continued to assert their sovereignty over the three areas.

The eighth Conference of the OIC, which took place in Teheran in December 1997, was attended by senior representatives of each of the organization's 55 member states. Addressing the conference, Khatami appeared conciliatory towards the West, and also urged more tolerance of dissent in Islamic societies among groups 'who keep within the framework of law and order'. Khamenei, none the less, vehemently denounced the West's military and cultural ambitions, particularly those of the USA and Israel. The divergent messages of Iran's political and spiritual leaders were widely interpreted by Western commentators as indicative of the continuing conflict between the country's 'moderate' and 'conservative' factions.

Government

Legislative power is vested in the Islamic Consultative Assembly (Majlis), with 270 members. The chief executive of the administration is the President. The Majlis and the President are both elected by universal adult suffrage for a term of four years. A 12-member Council of Guardians supervises elections and ensures that legislation is in accordance with the Constitution and with Islamic precepts. The Committee to Determine the Expediency of the Islamic Order, created in February 1988 and formally incorporated into the Constitution in July 1989, rules on legal and theological disputes between the Majlis and the Council of Guardians. The executive, legislative and judicial wings of state power are subject to the authority of the Wali Faqih (religious leader).

At the 1996 census Iran was divided into 26 provinces. The creation of the new province of Qazvin was approved by the Majlis in January 1997, and in June the Council of Ministers approved draft legislation to establish the province of Gorgan. Each province has an appointed Governor.

Defence

In August 1997 Iran's regular armed forces totalled an estimated 518,000 (army 350,000, Revolutionary Guard Corps (Pasdaran) about 120,000, navy 18,000, air force 30,000). There were 350,000 army reserves. There is a 24-month period of military service. Defence expenditure for 1997/98 was budgeted at IR 8,200,000m.

Economic Affairs

In 1992 Iran's gross national product (GNP) per head, at average 1990–92 prices, was estimated at US $2,230. According to World Bank estimates, GNP per head increased by an annual average of 0.5% in 1985–95. Over the same period the population increased by an average of 3.2% per year. According to official estimates, the country's gross domestic product (GDP), measured at factor cost, increased, in real terms, by an annual average of 6.8% between 1989/90 and 1994/95 (Iranian years ending 20 March). GDP increased by 2.7% in 1995/96, and by an estimated 4.3% in 1996/97.

Agriculture (including forestry and fishing) contributed an estimated 20.9% of GDP in 1996/97. About 23.0% of the employed labour force were engaged in agriculture at the time of the 1996 census. The principal cash crops are fresh and dried fruit and nuts, which accounted for about 13% of non-petroleum export earnings in 1994/95. The principal subsistence crops are wheat, barley, sugar beet and sugar cane. Production of mutton and lamb, beef and veal, and of poultry meat is also important. Agricultural GDP increased by an average of 5.6% per year between 1989/90 and 1994/95; growth in the sector's GDP was 2.3% in 1995/96, and was estimated at 3.5% in 1996/97.

Industry (including mining, manufacturing, construction and power) contributed an estimated 36.4% of GDP in 1996/97, and engaged 30.7% of the employed labour force at the 1996 census. During 1989/90–1994/95 industrial GDP increased by an annual average of 7.0%; growth was 3.4% in 1995/96, and was estimated at 4.2% in 1996/97.

Mining (including petroleum refining) contributed an estimated 16.5% of GDP in 1995/96, and engaged 0.8% of the working population in 1996. Metal ores are the major non-hydrocarbon mineral exports, and coal, magnesite and gypsum are also mined. The sector is dominated by petroleum and natural gas, which together contributed an estimated 15.5% of GDP in 1996/97. In January 1997 Iran's reserves of petroleum were estimated at 93,000m. barrels, sufficient to maintain the 1996 level of production for about 69 years. Iran's reserves of natural gas (21,000,000m. cu m in January 1997) are the second largest in the world, after those of Russia. The GDP of the mining sector increased by an annual average of 5.7% in 1989/90–1994/95; growth in 1995/96 was 1.0%.

Manufacturing (excluding petroleum refining) contributed 14.3% of GDP in 1995/96, and engaged 17.5% of the employed labour force in 1996. The most important sectors, in terms of value added, are textiles, food processing and transport equipment. The sector's GDP increased by an average of 7.8% per year in 1989/90–1994/95, and by an estimated 5.8% in 1995/96.

Principal sources of energy are natural gas and coal. Imports of mineral fuels and lubricants comprised 2.7% of the value of total imports in 1994/95.

The services sector contributed an estimated 42.7% of GDP in 1996/97, and engaged 44.5% of the employed labour force in 1996. During 1989/90–1994/95 the GDP of the services sector increased by an annual average of 7.5%; growth in the sector's GDP was 2.4% in 1995/96, and was estimated at 4.9% in 1996/97.

In the year ending March 1997 Iran recorded an estimated visible trade surplus of US $7,523m., and there was an estimated surplus of $5,361m. on the current account of the balance of payments. In 1994/95 the principal source of imports was Germany (which supplied 18.7% of total imports); other major suppliers were Italy, Japan, Belgium and the United Arab Emirates. The principal markets for exports in that year were Japan and the USA (which took, respectively, 15.1% and 13.9% of total exports; the United Kingdom and Germany were also important markets for Iranian exports. Other than petroleum and natural gas, Iran's principal exports in 1994/95 were carpets, fruit and nuts, and iron and steel. Exports of petroleum and gas comprised 82.3% of the value of total exports in 1995/96. The principal imports in 1994/95 were machinery and transport equipment, basic manufactures, food and live animals, and chemicals.

For the financial year ending 20 March 1996 Iran recorded a budget deficit estimated at IR 6,936,000m. Iran's total external debt was US $21,935m. at the end of 1995, of which $17,392m. was long-term public debt. In 1994 (when the external debt totalled $22,712m.) the cost of debt-servicing was equivalent to 21.6% of the value of exports of goods and services. The annual rate of inflation averaged 28.6% in 1990–95. Consumer prices increased by an average of 49.6% in 1995, and by 28.9% in 1996; inflation in the year to September 1997 was 17.5%. Some 10% of the total labour force were estimated to be unemployed in April 1997.

Iran is a member of the Organization of the Petroleum Exporting Countries (OPEC, see p. 227), of the Economic Co-operation Organization (ECO, see p. 260) and of the Developing Eight (D-8, see p. 260) group of Islamic countries.

Sayed Muhammad Khatami, who assumed the Iranian presidency in August 1997, has identified as weaknesses in the Iranian economy the Government's dependence on revenue from the petroleum sector, high rates of inflation and unemployment (although considerable success was achieved in curtailing the former in the mid-1990s), and disparities in the distribution of income. The new President has indicated the intention of his administration to reduce the role of the public sector in the economy (some 85% of economic activity is controlled by the State) and to foster increased foreign investment. Additional strain has, moreover, been placed on domestic resources by the presence in Iran of some 2m. refugees from Afghanistan and Iraq. A major priority is the increased development of Iran's reserves of natural gas, and the country is also seeking to exploit its potential as a principal transit point for the export of hydrocarbons from the Central Asian republics of the former USSR. These two factors have, moreover, limited the efficacy of US-led attempts to isolate Iran by means of economic sanctions (see Recent History). Thus, in September 1997 French, Malaysian and Russian energy companies, operating in consortium, signed a contract for the development of natural gas in Iranian waters, and in December a pipeline was inaugurated to transport natural gas from Turkmenistan to northern Iran; it was anticipated that the latter project could be extended to Turkey and eventually to western Europe. None the less, the success of the new political administration in implementing measures of economic liberalization appear, to a large extent, to be dependent on support from the deeply-entrenched 'conservative' elements of the Islamic regime, whose willingness to sanction any degree of Western-inspired reform remains in considerable doubt.

Social Welfare

Under Article 29 of the 1979 Constitution, the Government has a duty to provide every citizen with insurance benefits covering illness, unemployment and retirement. In 1995 Iran had 4,060 medical centres. In the same year there were 95,000 hospital beds. In 1987 there were 16,918 physicians working in the country. Of total budgeted expenditure by the central Government in the financial year 1996/97, IR 2,397,000m. (3.9%) was for health and nutrition, and a further IR 6,741,000m. (11.0%) was for other social services (excluding education).

Education

Education is officially compulsory for five years, between six and 10 years of age, but this has not been fully implemented in rural areas. Primary education, which is provided free of charge, begins at the age of six and lasts for five years. Secondary education, from the age of 11, lasts for up to seven years: a first cycle of three years and a second of four years. In 1994 the total enrolment at primary and secondary schools was equivalent to 84% of the school-age population (89% of boys; 78% of girls). In 1991 primary enrolment included 97% of children in the relevant age-group (100% of boys; 93% of girls). There are 36 universities, including 15 in Teheran. There were 867,748 students enrolled at Iran's universities and equivalent institutions in 1995/96. In 1994/95, according to official figures, the rate of illiteracy among the population aged six years and over was 22%. Expenditure on education by the central Government in the financial year 1996/97 was budgeted at IR 7,999,000m. (13.1% of total spending). Post-revolutionary policy has been to eliminate mixed-sex schools and to reduce instruction in art and music, while greater emphasis has been placed on agricultural and vocational programmes in higher education.

Public Holidays

The Iranian year 1377 runs from 21 March 1998 to 20 March 1999, and the year 1378 runs from 21 March 1999 to 20 March 2000.

1998: 30 January (Id al-Fitr, end of Ramadan), 11 February (National Day—Fall of the Shah), 20 March (Oil Nationalization Day), 21–24 March (Now Ruz, the Iranian New Year), 1 April (Islamic Republic Day), 2 April (Revolution Day), 8 April (Id al-Adha, feast of the Sacrifice), 7 May (Ashoura), 7 July (Mouloud, Birth of Muhammad), 14 July (Martyrdom of Imam Ali), 17 November (Leilat al-Meiraj, ascension of Muhammad).

1999: 19 January (Id al-Fitr, end of Ramadan), 11 February (National Day—Fall of the Shah), 20 March (Oil Nationalization Day), 21–24 March (Now Ruz, the Iranian New Year), 28 March (Id al-Adha, feast of the Sacrifice), 1 April (Islamic Republic Day), 2 April (Revolution Day), 26 April (Ashoura), 26 June (Mouloud, Birth of Muhammed), 14 July (Martyrdom of Imam Ali), 6 November (Leilat al-Meiraj, ascension of Muhammad).

Weights and Measures

The metric system is in force, but some traditional units are still in general use.

Statistical Survey

The Iranian year runs from 21 March to 20 March.

Source (except where otherwise stated): Statistical Centre of Iran, Dr Fatemi Ave, Cnr Rahiye Moayeri, Opposite Sazeman-e-Ab, Teheran 14144; tel. (21) 655061; telex 213233; fax (21) 653451.

Area and Population

AREA, POPULATION AND DENSITY

Area (sq km)	1,648,000*
Population (census results)†	
1 October 1991	55,837,163
25 October 1996	
Males	30,515,159
Females	29,540,329
Total	60,055,488
Density (per sq km) at October 1996	36.4

* 636,296 sq miles.
† Excluding adjustment for underenumeration.

PROVINCES (1996 census)*

Province (Ostan)	Population	Provincial capital
Tehran (Teheran)	11,176,139	Tehran (Teheran)
Markazi (Central)	1,228,812	Arak
Gilan	2,241,896	Rasht
Mazandaran	4,028,296	Sari
East Azarbayejan	3,325,540	Tabriz
West Azarbayejan	2,496,320	Orumiyeh
Bakhtaran (Kermanshah)	1,778,596	Bakhtaran
Khuzestan	3,746,772	Ahwaz
Fars	3,817,036	Shiraz
Kerman	2,004,328	Kerman
Khorasan	6,047,661	Mashad
Esfahan	3,923,355	Esfahan
Sistan and Baluchestan	1,722,579	Zahedan
Kordestan	1,346,383	Sanandaj
Hamadan	1,677,957	Hamadan
Chaharmahal and Bakhtiari	761,168	Shahr-e-Kord
Lorestan	1,584,434	Khorramabad
Ilam	487,886	Ilam
Kohgiluyeh and Boyerahmad	544,356	Yasuj
Bushehr	743,675	Bushehr
Zanjan	1,036,873	Zanjan
Semnan	501,447	Semnan
Yazd	750,769	Yazd
Hormozgan	1,062,155	Bandar-e-Abbas
Ardabil	1,168,011	Ardabil
Qom	853,044	Qom
Total	60,055,488	—

* On 1 January 1997 the legislature approved a law creating a new province, Qazvin (with its capital in the city of Qazvin). In June 1997 the Council of Ministers approved draft legislation to establish another new province, Gorgan (with its capital in the city of Gorgan), by dividing the existing province of Mazandaran.

PRINCIPAL TOWNS (population at 1996 census)

Tehran (Teheran, the capital)	6,758,845	Rasht	417,748
Mashad (Meshed)	1,887,405	Mehrshahr	413,299*
Esfahan (Isfahan)	1,266,072	Hamadan	401,281
Tabriz	1,191,043	Kerman	384,991
Shiraz	1,053,025	Arak	380,755
Karaj	940,968	Ardabil (Ardebil)	340,386
Ahwaz	804,980	Yazd	326,776
Qom	777,677	Qazvin	291,117
Bakhtaran (Kermanshah)	692,986	Zanjan	286,295
Orumiyeh	435,200	Sanandaj	277,808
Zahedan	419,518	Bandar-e-Abbas	273,578
		Khorramabad	272,815
		Eslamshahr (Islam Shahr)	265,450

* Estimated population at 1 October 1994 (Source: UN, *Demographic Yearbook*).

BIRTHS AND DEATHS (UN estimates, annual averages)

	1980–85	1985–90	1990–95
Birth rate (per 1,000)	46.1	41.4	35.5
Death rate (per 1,000)	10.4	8.1	6.7

Expectation of life (UN estimates, years at birth, 1990–95): 67.5 (males 67.0; females 68.0).

Source: UN, *World Population Prospects: The 1994 Revision.*

1991: Registered live births 1,885,649 (birth rate 33.8 per 1,000); Registered deaths 461,443 (death rate 8.3 per 1,000).
1994: Registered live births 1,304,255 (birth rate 21.9 per 1,000); Registered deaths 175,438 (death rate 2.9 per 1,000).
Note: Registration is incomplete.

ECONOMICALLY ACTIVE POPULATION
(persons aged 6 years and over, 1996 census)

	Males	Females	Total
Agriculture, hunting and forestry	3,024,380	294,156	3,318,536
Fishing	38,418	309	38,727
Mining and quarrying	115,185	4,699	119,884
Manufacturing	1,968,806	583,156	2,551,962
Electricity, gas and water supply	145,239	5,392	150,631
Construction	1,634,682	15,799	1,650,481
Wholesale and retail trade; repair of motor vehicles, motorcycles and personal and household goods	1,804,843	38,146	1,842,289
Hotels and restaurants	82,293	2,485	84,778
Transport, storage and communications	955,271	17,541	972,792
Financial intermediation	139,286	13,586	152,872
Real estate, renting and business activities	137,039	12,051	149,090
Public administration and defence; compulsory social security	1,519,449	98,651	1,618,100
Education	581,597	459,459	1,041,056
Health and social work	184,242	118,897	303,139
Other community, social and personal service activities	183,246	41,159	224,405
Private households with employed persons	57,037	4,933	61,970
Extra territorial organizations and bodies	660	220	880
Central departments and offices	30,389	2,563	32,952
Activities not adequately defined	204,808	52,220	257,028
Total employed	12,860,170	1,765,402	14,571,572

Agriculture

PRINCIPAL CROPS ('000 metric tons)

	1994	1995	1996
Wheat	10,870	11,228	11,200*
Rice (paddy)	2,259	2,301	2,300*
Barley	3,045	2,952	3,000†
Maize	512	545	600†
Potatoes	3,185	2,974	3,200*
Dry beans	110	129	140†
Chick-peas	299	355	360†
Lentils	160*	110†	110†
Soybeans	147	134†	134†
Cottonseed	232	314	307*
Cotton (lint)*	118	165	156
Tomatoes	2,088	2,403	2,150*
Pumpkins, squash and gourds†	215	220	220
Cucumber and gherkins	1,227	1,286	1,250†
Onions (dry)	1,112	1,130	1,200*
Other vegetables†	1,185	1,216	1,215
Watermelons†	2,580	2,650	2,650
Melons†	1,185	1,215	1,215
Grapes	1,893	1,846	1,900*
Dates	774	780	795*
Apples	2,008	1,824	2,000*
Pears†	179	184	184
Peaches and nectarines†	123	126	126
Plums†	133	137	137
Oranges	1,584	1,556	1,600
Tangerines, mandarins, clementines and satsumas	629	599	630
Lemons and limes	649	726	655
Other citrus fruits†	125	150	130
Apricots†	118	121	121
Other fruits and berries	1,456	1,495†	1,496†
Sugar cane	1,857	1,859	1,900†
Sugar beets	5,295	5,521	4,000†
Almonds†	67	69	69
Pistachios	195	239	282*
Walnuts†	66	68	68
Tea (made)	56	54	56*
Tobacco (leaves)	10	14	17†

* Unofficial figure(s). † FAO estimate(s).

Source: FAO, *Production Yearbook*.

LIVESTOCK ('000 head, year ending September)

	1994	1995	1996
Horses*	250	250	250
Mules†	137	137	137
Asses†	1,400	1,400	1,400
Cattle	8,202	8,347	8,492
Buffaloes	438	447	456
Camels	143	143	143
Sheep	50,285	50,889	51,499
Goats	25,757	25,757	25,757

Chickens (million): 186* in 1994; 186* in 1995; 202 in 1996.

† Unofficial figures. * FAO estimates.

Source: FAO, *Production Yearbook*.

LIVESTOCK PRODUCTS ('000 metric tons)

	1994	1995	1996
Beef and veal	276*	276*	277
Buffalo meat*	10	10	10
Mutton and lamb	254*	256*	280
Goat meat	101*	101*	100
Poultry meat	635	659	672
Other meat*	16	16	17
Cows' milk	3,126†	3,400*	3,809
Buffaloes' milk	121†	121*	160
Sheep's milk	541†	540*	438
Goats' milk	662†	668*	412
Cheese*	207	216	196
Butter*	104	112	119
Hen eggs	516	466	520
Honey*	8	8	8
Wool:			
greasy	50†	51†	51
clean	28*	28*	28
Cattle and buffalo hides*	40	40	40
Sheepskins*	48	48	53
Goatskins*	18	18	18

* FAO estimate(s). † Unofficial figure.

Source: FAO, *Production Yearbook*.

Forestry

ROUNDWOOD REMOVALS ('000 cubic metres, excl. bark)

	1992	1993	1994*
Sawlogs, veneer logs and logs for sleepers	324	412	412
Pulpwood	508	523	523
Other industrial wood*†	4,007	4,007	4,007
Fuel wood*	2,519	2,531	2,549
Total	7,358	7,473	7,491

* FAO estimates.

† Annual output assumed to be unchanged since 1974.

Source: FAO, *Yearbook of Forest Products*.

SAWNWOOD PRODUCTION

('000 cubic metres, incl. railway sleepers)

	1992	1993	1994
Total (all broadleaved)	187	170	170*

* FAO estimate.

Source: FAO, *Yearbook of Forest Products*.

Fishing

('000 metric tons, live weight)

	1993	1994	1995
Freshwater fishes	46.2	47.8	58.9
Diadromous fishes	45.6	64.4	53.4
Marine fishes	216.8	211.8	246.3
Marine crustaceans and molluscs	9.5	8.5	9.7
Total catch	318.1	332.4	368.3
Inland waters	96.9	115.0	117.3
Indian Ocean	221.2	217.4	251.0

Source: FAO, *Yearbook of Fishery Statistics*.

Production of caviar (metric tons, year ending 20 March): 281 in1988/89; 310 in 1989/90; 233 in 1990/91.

Mining

CRUDE PETROLEUM

(net production, '000 barrels per day, year ending 20 March)

	1988/89	1989/90	1990/91
Southern oilfields	2,454	2,716	2,987
Offshore oilfields	103	231	244
Doroud–Forouzan–Abouzar–Soroush	58	162	166
Salman–Rostam–Resalat	23	40	46
Sirri–Hendijan–Bahregan	22	29	32
Total	2,557	2,947	3,231

1991/92 ('000 barrels per day): Total production 3,366.
1992/93 ('000 barrels per day): Total production 3,484.
1993/94 ('000 barrels per day): Total production 3,609.
1994/95 ('000 barrels per day): Total production 3,603.
1995/96 ('000 barrels per day): Total production 3,600.
1996/97 ('000 barrels per day): Total production 3,595.

Source: Ministry of Oil.

NATURAL GAS (million cu metres, year ending 20 March)

	1993/94	1994/95	1995/96
Consumption (domestic)*	36,900	35,500	37,000
Flared	11,500	11,600	22,300
Exports	0	100	
Regional uses and wastes	0	7,700	
Total production	48,400	54,900	59,300

* Includes gas for household, commercial, industrial, generator and refinery consumption.

OTHER MINERALS ('000 metric tons, year ending 20 March)

	1992/93	1993/94	1994/95
Hard coal	970	980	n.a.
Iron ore*	2,350	2,137	n.a.
Copper ore*	105.0	86.6	117.9
Lead ore*	12.4	14.7	18.3
Zinc ore*	65.0	70.0	72.9
Manganese ore*	12.8	18.7	13.0
Chromium ore*	65	48	39
Magnesite	36.2	40.0	40.0
Fluorspar (Fluorite)	12.0	10.0	10.0
Barytes	181	105	100
Salt (unrefined)	1,110	720	900
Gypsum (crude)	8,720	8,800	8,430

* Figures refer to the metal content of ores.

Source: UN, *Industrial Commodity Statistics Yearbook*.

Industry

PETROLEUM PRODUCTS

(estimates, '000 metric tons, year ending 20 March)

	1991/92	1992/93	1993/94
Liquefied petroleum gas	2,320	3,300	3,600
Naphtha	300	400	300
Motor spirit (petrol)	5,900	6,200	6,100
Aviation gasoline	110	90	100
Kerosene	4,000	4,400	4,500
White spirit	250	300	300
Jet fuel	1,000	1,100	1,200
Distillate fuel oils	13,100	14,200	14,400
Residual fuel oils	13,900	14,300	14,100
Lubricating oils	1,000	1,100	1,100
Petroleum bitumen (asphalt)	2,100	2,200	2,100

Source: UN, *Industrial Commodity Statistics Yearbook*.

OTHER PRODUCTS (year ending 20 March)*

	1993/94	1994/95	1995/96
Refined sugar ('000 metric tons)	1,060	1,052	1,151
Cigarettes (million)	7,835	7,939	9,787
Paints ('000 metric tons)	46	36	32
Cement ('000 metric tons)	16,321	16,250	16,861
Refrigerators ('000)	789	629	636
Gas stoves ('000)	191	215	243
Telephone sets ('000)	288	218	161
Radios and recorders ('000)	174	138	33
Television receivers ('000)	502	360	250
Motor vehicles (assembled) ('000)	66	69	92
Footwear (million pairs)	23	19	17
Machine-made carpets ('000 sq m)	14,480	16,560	13,823

* Figures refer to production in large-scale manufacturing establishments with 50 workers or more.

Production of Electricity (million kWh, year ending 20 March): *Ministry of Energy:* 71,335 in 1993/94; 77,086 in 1994/95; 80,044 in 1995/96; 85,825 in 1996/97. *Private Sector:* 4,679 in 1993/94; 4,933 in 1994/95; 4,925 in 1995/96.

Finance

CURRENCY AND EXCHANGE RATES

Monetary Units

100 dinars = 1 Iranian rial (IR).

Sterling and Dollar Equivalents (30 September 1997)

£1 sterling = 2,833.3 rials;
US $1 = 1,753.9 rials;
10,000 Iranian rials = £3.529 = $5.701.

Average Exchange Rate (rials per US $)

1994 1,748.75
1995 1,747.93
1996 1,750.76

Note: In March 1993 the multiple exchange rate system was unified, and since then the exchange rate of the rial has been market-determined. The foregoing information refers to the base rate. There is also an export rate, set at a mid-point of US $ = 3,007.5 rials in May 1995.

BUDGET ('000 million rials, year ending 20 March)*

Revenue	1994/95	1995/96†	1996/97‡
Oil and gas revenues	23,908	29,431	32,982
Non-oil revenues	9,574	15,990	27,566
Taxation	5,491	7,312	10,744
Income and wealth taxes	3,854	5,648	6,468
Corporate taxes	2,398	3,296	4,298
Public corporations	829	1,065	1,705
Private corporations	1,570	2,231	2,593
Taxes on wages and salaries	480	902	460
Taxes on other income	645	967	1,190
Import taxes	1,284	1,250	3,640
Customs duties	731	793	2,209
Order registration fees	390	405	1,200
Non-tax revenues	2,274	4,831	11,569
Services and sales of goods	831	1,347	3,012
Other revenues§	1,443	3,484	8,557
Excises on petroleum products	—	788	1,845
Special revenues	1,809	3,847	5,253
Total	33,482	45,421	60,548

Expenditure	1994/95	1995/96‡	1996/97‡
General services	2,368	2,705	3,957
National defence	2,496	2,355	3,532
Social services	11,059	12,991	17,137
Education	5,533	6,015	7,999
Health and nutrition	2,448	2,087	2,397
Other social services	3,078	4,889	6,741
Economic services	11,103	16,346	14,752
Agriculture	1,421	1,497	1,101
Water resources	960	1,545	2,021
Petroleum, fuel and power	3,301	6,203	7,532
Transport and communication	1,670	1,795	3,067
Other economic services	3,751	5,306	1,031
Other expenditure and net lending§	1,860	5,417	13,711
Foreign exchange obligations	8,513	2,729	2,757
Special expenditure	1,809	3,847	5,253
Total	39,208	46,390	61,099
Current	30,164	31,615	40,370
Capital	9,044	14,775	20,729

* Figures refer to the consolidated accounts of the central Government, comprising the General Budget, the operations of the Social Insurance Organization and special (extrabudgetary) revenue and expenditure.

† Provisional figures.

‡ Forecasts. The provisional total (in '000 million rials) for expenditure in 1995/96 is 52,357 (current 39,205; capital 13,152).

§ Including operations of the Organization for Protection of Consumers and Producers, a central government unit with its own budget.

Source: Bank Markazi Jomhouri Islami Iran.

INTERNATIONAL RESERVES (US $ million at 31 December)*

	1993	1994	1995
Gold (national valuation)	229	242	252
IMF special drawing rights	144	143	134
Total	473	485	486

* Excluding reserves of foreign exchange, for which no figures are available since 1982 (when the value of reserves was US $5,287m.).

1996 (US $ million at 31 December): IMF special drawing rights 345.

Source: IMF, *International Financial Statistics.*

MONEY SUPPLY ('000 million rials at 20 December)

	1994	1995	1996
Currency outside banks	6,199	7,949	9,598
Non-financial public enterprises' deposits at Central Bank	1,604	2,020	2,639
Demand deposits at commercial banks	18,120	24,373	33,628
Total money	25,923	34,342	45,865

Source: IMF, *International Financial Statistics.*

COST OF LIVING (Consumer Price Index in urban areas, year ending 20 March; base: 1990/91 = 100)

	1993/94	1994/95	1995/96
Food, beverages and tobacco	197.0	270.7	434.0
Clothing	142.3	198.2	320.0
Housing, fuel and light	178.5	215.6	278.0
All items (incl. others)	184.4	249.3	372.4

1996/97 (base: 1995/96 = 100): All items 123.2.

Source: Bank Markazi Jomhouri Islami Iran.

NATIONAL ACCOUNTS

('000 million rials at current prices, year ending 20 March)

National Income and Product

	1993/94	1994/95	1995/96
Domestic factor incomes	79,241.6	110,383.4	152,726.3
Consumption of fixed capital	14,276.4	18,967.4	28,073.8
Gross domestic product (GDP) at factor cost	93,518.0	129,350.8	180,800.1
Indirect taxes *Less* Subsidies	91.9	−968.9	−1,925.1
GDP in purchasers' values	93,609.9	128,381.9	178,875.0
Factor income from abroad *Less* Factor income paid abroad	−2,485.3	−3,015.3	−1,809.4
Gross national product (GNP)	91,124.6	125,366.6	177,065.6
Less Consumption of fixed capital	14,276.4	18,967.4	28,073.8
National income in market prices	76,848.2	106,399.2	148,991.9

* Compensation of employees and the operating surplus of enterprises.

Expenditure on the Gross Domestic Product

	1993/94	1995/96	1996/97*
Government final consumption expenditure	16,176.7	23,053.5	31,283.2
Private final consumption expenditure	71,962.9	108,921.5	143,664.1
Increase in stocks†	1,265.3	−6,507.2	−13,202.9
Gross fixed capital formation	29,853.1	41,511.0	59,473.7
Total domestic expenditure	119,258.0	166,978.5	221,218.1
Exports of goods and services	31,909.1	36,747.3	11,523.6
Less Imports of goods services	22,785.2	24,850.8	
GDP in purchasers' values	128,381.9	178,875.0	232,741.7
GDP at constant 1982/83 prices	13,180.9	13,740.5	14,549.7

* Provisional figures.

† Including statistical discrepancy.

‡ Including adjustment for changes in terms of trade ('000 million rials): −1,704.2 in 1994/95.

Gross Domestic Product by Economic Activity (at factor cost)

	1993/94	1994/95	1995/96
Agriculture, hunting, forestry and fishing	19,446.1	27,272.8	40,091.0
Mining and quarrying*	16,990.0	25,069.3	29,952.2
Manufacturing*	12,681.6	17,725.5	25,877.2
Electricity, gas and water	1,079.0	1,321.6	2,430.4
Construction	3,134.3	4,428.8	6,386.3
Trade, restaurants and hotels	14,535.7	19,978.4	28,988.7
Transport, storage and communications	6,582.0	8,166.8	11,368.2
Finance, insurance, real estate and business services	9,698.0	12,273.0	17,053.5
Government services	8,576.0	11,689.1	15,686.8
Other services	1,754.3	2,420.9	3,706.4
Sub-total	94,477.0	130,346.2	181,540.7
Less Imputed bank service charge	959.0	995.4	740.6
Total	93,518.0	129,350.8	180,800.1

* Refining of petroleum is included in mining and excluded from manufacturing.

BALANCE OF PAYMENTS (US $ million, year ending 20 March)

	1994/95	1995/96	1996/97*
Exports of goods f.o.b.	19,434	18,360	22,496
Petroleum and gas	14,603	15,103	19,271
Non-petroleum and gas exports	4,831	3,257	3,225
Imports of goods f.o.b.	–12,617	–12,774	–14,973
Trade balance	6,817	5,586	7,523
Exports of services	438	593	–2,625
Imports of services	–3,226	–2,339	
Other income received	142	316	
Other income paid	–413	–794	
Balance on goods, services and income	3,758	3,362	4,898
Unrequited transfers (net)	1,198	–4	463
Current balance	4,956	3,358	5,361
Long-term capital (net)	10,488	1,457	–5,417
Short-term capital (net)	–10,909	–2,231	–262
Net errors and omissions	–3,614	284	2,664
Overall balance	921	2,868	2,346

* Estimates.

Sources: Bank Markazi Jomhouri Islami Iran; IMF, *International Financial Statistics.*

External Trade

PRINCIPAL COMMODITIES (US $ million, year ending 20 March)

Imports c.i.f.*	1992/93	1993/94	1994/95
Food and live animals	2,276	2,446	1,369
Cereals and cereal preparations	1,047	1,376	693
Sugar, sugar preparations and honey	308	167	251
Crude materials (inedible) except fuels	758	551	649
Mineral fuels, lubricants, etc.	406	83	324
Animal and vegetable oils and fats	300	431	392
Vegetable oils and fats	274	414	376
Chemicals	2,689	2,023	1,376
Chemical elements and compounds	524	405	306
Plastic materials, etc.	690	516	237
Basic manufactures	5,507	3,344	1,654
Paper, paperboard, etc.	395	249	256
Textile yarn, fabrics, etc.	637	343	224
Iron and steel	2,481	1,667	686
Machinery and transport equipment	16,498	10,036	5,525
Non-electric machinery	10,193	6,957	4,054
Electrical machinery, apparatus, etc.	2,913	1,780	834
Transport equipment	3,392	1,299	637
Miscellaneous manufactured articles	1,317	760	403
Scientific instruments, watches, etc.	883	564	316
Total (incl. others)	29,870	20,037	11,795

Source: Bank Markazi Jomhouri Islami Iran.

* Including registration fee, but excluding defence-related imports.

Exports f.o.b.*	1992/93	1993/94	1994/95
Agricultural and traditional goods	1,995.6	2,516.1	3,258.6
Carpets	1,105.6	1,384.0	2,132.9
Fruit (fresh and dried)	577.6	674.5	628.3
Animal skins and hides, and leather	78.0	115.0	134.6
Casings	30.0	32.0	36.7
Cumin	38.8	27.0	22.5
Others	165.6	283.6	303.6
Metal ores	21.2	39.0	55.9
Industrial manufactures	970.9	1,191.7	1,510.0
Chemical products	17.7	29.5	35.3
Shoes	22.7	11.6	36.9
Textile manufactures	55.6	36.5	96.1
Motor vehicles	79.6	20.4	24.1
Copper bars, sheets and wire	131.6	140.6	106.8
Domestic appliances and sanitary ware	205.1	167.0	137.6
Iron and steel	142.6	398.8	340.5
Others	316.0	387.3	732.7
Total	2,987.7	3,746.8	4,824.5

* Excluding exports of petroleum and gas (US $ million): 16,880 in 1992/93; 14,333 in 1993/94; 14,603 in 1994/95.

1995/96 (US $ million, year ending 20 March): Imports c.i.f. 12,208; Exports f.o.b. 3,251 (excl. petroleum and gas 15,103).

PETROLEUM EXPORTS ('000 barrels per day, year ending 20 March)

	1994/95	1995/96	1996/97
Crude petroleum	2,220*	2,290*	2,620†

* Excluding petroleum exported for refining or exchange ('000 barrels per day, year ending 20 March): 185 in 1994/95; 148 in 1995/96.

† Including refined petroleum products.

Source: Ministry of Oil.

PRINCIPAL TRADING PARTNERS
(US $ million, year ending 20 March)

Imports c.i.f.	1992/93	1993/94	1994/95
Argentina	433	363	287
Australia	235	402	260
Austria	558	394	228
Belgium	1,052	537	649
Brazil	400	342	176
Canada	600	273	293
France	814	663	479
Germany	6,939	3,997	2,209
Italy	2,869	1,939	1,008
Japan	3,639	2,341	894
Korea, Republic	669	469	320
Netherlands	666	374	263
Spain	313	155	136
Switzerland	760	525	212
Thailand	242	541	69
Turkey	661	408	274
United Arab Emirates	1,588	1,120	647
United Kingdom	1,668	1,007	544
Total (incl. others)	29,870	20,037	11,795

Exports f.o.b.	1992/93	1993/94	1994/95
Bahamas	162	485	—
Belgium	554	473	466
Bermuda	618	559	—
China, People's Republic	155	329	223
France	609	450	398
Germany	794	939	1,204
Greece	622	615	704
India	375	364	493
Italy	615	397	758
Japan	2,524	2,476	2,941
Korea, Republic	549	780	927
Poland	353	258	158
Singapore	450	542	702
Switzerland	1,272	927	552
Turkey	762	908	865
United Arab Emirates	336	352	780
United Kingdom	1,537	1,975	1,790
USA	2,116	1,409	2,707
Total (incl. others)	19,871	18,080	19,434

Source: IMF, *Islamic Republic of Iran—Statistical Appendix* (October 1996).

Transport

RAILWAYS (traffic)

	1994	1995	1996
Passenger-km (million)	6,479	7,294	7,044
Freight ton-km (million)	10,700	11,865	13,638

ROAD TRAFFIC (estimates, '000 motor vehicles in use)

	1994	1995	1996
Passenger cars	1,636	1,714	1,793
Lorries and vans	626	657	692

Source: International Road Federation, *World Road Statistics*.

SHIPPING

Merchant Fleet (registered at 31 December)

	1994	1995	1996
Number of vessels	429	424	414
Displacement ('000 grt)	3,803.3	2,902.4	3,566.8

Source: Lloyd's Register of Shipping, *World Fleet Statistics*.

International Sea-borne Freight Traffic
('000 metric tons)

	1994	1995	1996
Goods loaded	128,026	132,677	140,581
Crude petroleum and petroleum products	123,457	127,143	134,615
Goods unloaded	20,692	22,604	27,816
Petroleum products	6,949	7,240	7,855

CIVIL AVIATION (traffic on scheduled services)*

	1994	1995	1996
Passengers carried ('000)	5,441	5,809	5,889
Passenger-km (million)	5,055	5,384	5,840
Cargo ton-km (million)	515	547	643

* Figures refer only to traffic of Iran Air.

Tourism

	1992	1993	1994
Tourist arrivals ('000)	278.6	304.1	362.0
Tourist receipts (US $ million)	121	131	153

Source: UN, *Statistical Yearbook*.

Communications Media

	1993	1994	1995
Radio receivers ('000 in use)	14,730	15,550	15,580
Television receivers ('000 in use)	4,050	4,076	4,300
Telephones ('000 main lines in use)*	3,642	4,320	5,090
Telefax stations (number in use)*	25,000	30,000	n.a.
Mobile cellular telephones (subscribers)	n.a.	9,200	n.a.
Book production†:			
Titles	8,183	10,753	9,716
Copies ('000)	n.a.	n.a.	61,652
Daily newspapers	26	28	29
Non-daily newspapers	50‡	n.a.	n.a.
Other periodicals	411	403	623

* Twelve months ending March following the year stated.
† Including pamphlets (140 titles in 1994).
‡ Figure refers to 1990.

Sources: partly UNESCO, *Statistical Yearbook*; UN, *Statistical Yearbook*.

Education

(1994/95)

	Institutions	Teachers	Students
Pre-primary	2,715	6,151	141,728
Primary	61,889	305,380*	9,745,600
Secondary:			
General	n.a.	228,889	7,284,611
Teacher-training	n.a.	538	21,210
Vocational	n.a.	19,880	347,008
Higher:			
Universities, etc.	n.a.	n.a.	758,150
Distance-learning	n.a.	3,177	104,631
Others	n.a.	5,208	46,695

* Teachers in public education only.

1995/96: Higher education: Universities, etc. 42,782 teachers, 869,748 students; Distance-learning 3,635 teachers, 118,496 students; Others 6,395 teachers, 58,849 students.

Source: UNESCO, *Statistical Yearbook*.

Directory

The Constitution

A draft constitution for the Islamic Republic of Iran was published on 18 June 1979. It was submitted to a 'Council of Experts', elected by popular vote on 3 August 1979, to debate the various clauses and to propose amendments. The amended Constitution was approved by a referendum on 2–3 December 1979. A further 45 amendments to the Constitution were approved by a referendum on 28 July 1989.

The Constitution states that the form of government of Iran is that of an Islamic Republic, and that the spirituality and ethics of Islam are to be the basis for political, social and economic relations. Persians, Turks, Kurds, Arabs, Balochis, Turkomans and others will enjoy completely equal rights.

The Constitution provides for a President to act as chief executive. The President is elected by universal adult suffrage for a term of four years. Legislative power is held by the Majlis (Islamic Consultative Assembly), with 270 members who are similarly elected for a four-year term. Provision is made for the representation of Zoroastrians, Jews and Christians.

All legislation passed by the Islamic Consultative Assembly must be sent to the Council for the Protection of the Constitution (Article 94), which will ensure that it is in accordance with the Constitution and Islamic legislation. The Council for the Protection of the Constitution consists of six religious lawyers appointed by the Faqih (see below) and six lawyers appointed by the High Council of the Judiciary and approved by the Islamic Consultative Assembly. Articles 19–42 deal with the basic rights of individuals, and provide for equality of men and women before the law and for equal human, political, economic, social and cultural rights for both sexes.

The press is free, except in matters that are contrary to public morality or insult religious belief. The formation of religious, political and professional parties, associations and societies is free, provided they do not negate the principles of independence, freedom, sovereignty and national unity, or the basis of Islam.

The Constitution provides for a Wali Faqih (religious leader) who, in the absence of the Imam Mehdi (the hidden Twelfth Imam), carries the burden of leadership. The amendments to the Constitution that were approved in July 1989 increased the powers of the Presidency by abolishing the post of Prime Minister, formerly the Chief Executive of the Government.

The Government

WALI FAQIH (RELIGIOUS LEADER)

Ayatollah SAYED ALI KHAMENEI.

HEAD OF STATE

President: Hojatoleslam Dr SAYED MUHAMMAD KHATAMI (assumed office 3 August 1997).

Vice-President in charge of Executive Affairs: MUHAMMAD HASHEMI RAFSANJANI.

Vice-President in charge of Legal and Parliamentary Affairs: SAYED ABDOLVAHED MUSAVI-LARI.

Vice-President and Head of the Organization for the Protection of the Environment: MA'SUMEH EBTEKAR.

Vice-President and Head of the Plan and Budget Organization: MUHAMMAD ALI NAJAFI.

Vice-President and Head of the Physical Education Organization: SAYED MOSTAFA HASHEMI-TABA.

Vice-President and Secretary General of the Organization for Administrative and Employment Affairs: MUHAMMAD BAQERIAN.

COUNCIL OF MINISTERS
(February 1998)

Minister of Foreign Affairs: KAMAL KHARRAZI.

Minister of Education: HOSSEIN MOZAFAR.

Minister of Culture and Islamic Guidance: ATA'OLLAH MOHAJERANI.

Minister of Information: QORBANALI DORRI NAJAFABADI.

Minister of Commerce: MUHAMMAD SHARI'ATMADARI.

Minister of Health: MUHAMMAD FARHADI.

Minister of Posts, Telegraphs and Telephones: MUHAMMAD REZA AREF.

Minister of Justice: MUHAMMAD ISMAÏL SHOUSHTARI.

Minister of Defence and Logistics: ALI SHAMKHANI.

Minister of Roads and Transport: MAHMUD HOJJATI.

Minister of Industries: GHOLAMREZA SHAFE'I.

Minister of Higher Education: MOSTAFA MO'IN.

Minister of Mines and Metals: ESHAQ JAHANGIRI.

Minister of Labour and Social Affairs: HOSSEIN KAMALI.

Minister of the Interior: ABDOLLAH NURI.

Minister of Agriculture: ISA KALANTARI.

Minister of Housing and Urban Development: ALI ABD AL-ALIZADEH.

Minister of Energy: HABIBOLLAH BITARAF.

Minister of Oil: BIZAM NAMDAR-ZANGENEH.

Minister of Economic Affairs and Finance: HOSSEIN NAMAZI.

Minister of Construction Jihad: MUHAMMAD SA'IDI-KIA.

Minister of Co-operatives: MORTEZA HAJI.

MINISTRIES

All ministries are in Teheran.

Ministry of Mines and Metals: 248 Somayeh Ave, Teheran; tel. (21) 836051; telex 212718.

Ministry of Roads and Transport: 49 Taleghani Ave, Teheran; tel. (21) 661034; telex 213381.

President and Legislature

PRESIDENT

Election, 23 May 1997

Candidates	Votes	%
SAYED MUHAMMAD KHATAMI	20,088,338	69.1
ALI AKBAR NATEQ NOURI	7,233,568	24.9
SAYED REZA ZAVAREI	771,463	2.7
MUHAMMAD MUHAMMADI REYSHAHRI	742,599	2.6
Spoilt votes	240,994	0.8
Total	29,076,962	100.0

MAJLIS-E-SHURA E ISLAMI—ISLAMIC CONSULTATIVE ASSEMBLY

Voting in the first round of elections to the fifth Majlis took place on 8 March 1996. It was reported that 145 candidates had gained a sufficiently large proportion (at least one-third in single-member constituencies, or selection by at least one-third of voters in multi-member constituencies where electors cast multiple votes) of the total votes cast in their constituencies to take up seats in the 270-member Majlis. About 77% of the approximately 32m. eligible voters were reported to have participated in the first round of the election. A second round of voting to the 125 seats which remained unfilled took place on 19 April. In May the Council of Constitutional Guardians, charged with monitoring the elections, declared the results of polling in 19 constituencies to be null and void. By-elections to the 19 vacant seats were held in April 1997.

Speaker: ALI AKBAR NATEQ NOURI.

Deputy Speakers: Hojatoleslam HOSSEIN HASHEMIAN, ASADOLLAH BAYAT.

SHURA-YE ALI-YE AMNIYYAT-E MELLI—SUPREME COUNCIL FOR NATIONAL SECURITY

Formed in July 1989 to co-ordinate defence and national security policies, the political programme and intelligence reports, and social, cultural and economic activities related to defence and security. The Council is chaired by the President and includes two representatives of the Wali Faqih, the Head of the Judiciary, the Speaker of the Majlis, the Chief of Staff, the General Command of the Armed Forces, the Minister of Foreign Affairs, the Minister of the Interior, the Minister of Information and the Head of the Plan and Budget Organization.

MAJLIS-E KHOBREGAN—COUNCIL OF EXPERTS

Elections were held on 10 December 1982 to appoint a Council of Experts which was to choose an eventual successor to the Wali Faqih, then Ayatollah Khomeini, after his death. The Constitution provides for a three- or five-man body to assume the leadership of the country if there is no recognized successor on the death of the

Wali Faqih. The Council comprises 83 clerics. Elections to a second term of the Council were held on 8 October 1990.

Speaker: Ayatollah ALI MESHKINI.

First Deputy Speaker: Hojatoleslam ALI AKBAR HASHEMI RAFSANJANI.

Secretaries: Hojatoleslam HASSAN TAHERI-KHORRAMABADI, Ayatollah MUHAMMAD MOMEN-QOMI, Ayatollah IBRAHIM AMINI.

SHURA-E-NIGAHBAN—COUNCIL OF GUARDIANS

The Council of Guardians, composed of six qualified Muslim jurists appointed by Ayatollah Khomeini and six lay Muslim lawyers, appointed by the Majlis from among candidates nominated by the Head of the Judiciary, was established in 1980 to supervise elections and to examine legislation adopted by the Majlis, ensuring that it accords with the Constitution and with Islamic precepts.

Chairman: Ayatollah MUHAMMAD MUHAMMADI GUILANI.

SHURA-YE TASHKHIS-E MASLAHAT-E NEZAM—COMMITTEE TO DETERMINE THE EXPEDIENCY OF THE ISLAMIC ORDER

Formed in February 1988, by order of Ayatollah Khomeini, to arbitrate on legal and theological questions in legislation passed by the Majlis, in the event of a dispute between the latter and the supervisory Council of Guardians. Its permanent members, defined in March 1997, are Heads of the Legislative, Judiciary and Executive Powers, the jurist members of the Council of Guardians and the Minister or head of organization concerned with the pertinent arbitration.

Chairman: Hojatoleslam ALI AKBAR HASHEMI RAFSANJANI.

HEY'AT-E PEYGIRI-YE QANUN ASASI VA NEZARAT BAR AN—COMMITTEE FOR ENSURING AND SUPERVISING THE IMPLEMENTATION OF THE CONSTITUTION

Formed by President Khatami in November 1997; members are appointed for a four-year term.

Members: Dr GUDARZ EFTEKHAR-JAHROMI; MUHAMMAD ISMAÏL SHOUSHTARI; SAYED ABDOLVAHED MUSAVI-LARI; Dr HOSEYN MEHRPUR; Dr MUHAMMAD HOSEYN HASHEMI.

Political Organizations

The Islamic Republican Party (IRP) was founded in 1978 to bring about the Islamic Revolution under the leadership of AYATOLLAH KHOMEINI. After the Revolution the IRP became the ruling party in what was effectively a one-party state. In June 1987 AYATOLLAH KHOMEINI officially disbanded the IRP at the request of party leaders, who said that it had achieved its purpose and might only 'provide an excuse for discord and factionalism' if it were not dissolved. Of the parties listed below, only the Nehzat-Azadi (Liberation Movement of Iran) has been afforded a degree of official recognition and been allowed to participate in elections.

Ansar-e-Hizbollah: f. 1995; seeks to gain access to the political process for religious militants.

Democratic Party of Iranian Kurdistan: f. 1945; seeks autonomy for Kurdish area; mem. of the National Council of Resistance; 54,000 mems; Sec.-Gen. MUSTAPHA HASSANZADEH.

Fedayin-e-Khalq (Warriors of the People): urban Marxist guerrillas; Spokesman FARRAKH NEGAHDAR.

Fraksion-e Hezbollah: f. 1996 by deputies in the Majlis who had contested the 1996 legislative elections as a loose coalition known as the Society of Combatant Clergy; Leader ALI AKBAR HOSSAINI.

Hezb-e-Komunist Iran (Communist Party of Iran): f. 1979 on grounds that Tudeh Party was Moscow-controlled; Sec.-Gen. 'AZARYUN'.

Komala: f. 1969; Kurdish wing of the Communist Party of Iran; Marxist-Leninist; Leader IBRAHIM ALIZADEH.

Majma-e Hezbollah: f. 1996 by deputies in the Majlis who supported President Rafsanjani and who had contested the 1996 legislative elections as a loose coalition known as the Servants of Iran's Construction; Leader ABDOLLAH NOURI.

Mujahidin-e-Khalq (Holy Warriors of the People): Islamic guerrilla group; since June 1987 comprising the National Liberation Army; mem. of the National Council of Resistance; Leaders MASSOUD RAJAVI and MARYAM RAJAVI (in Baghdad, 1986–).

National Democratic Front: f. March 1979; Leader HEDAYATOLLAH MATINE-DAFTARI (in Paris, January 1982–).

National Front (Union of National Front Forces): comprises Iran Nationalist Party, Iranian Party, and Society of Iranian Students; Leader Dr KARIM SANJABI (in Paris, August 1978–).

Nehzat-Azadi (Liberation Movement of Iran): f. 1961; emphasis on basic human rights as defined by Islam; Gen. Sec. Dr IBRAHIM YAZDI; Principal Officers Prof. SAHABI, S. SADR, Dr SADR, Eng. SABAGHIAN, Eng. TAVASSOLI.

Pan-Iranist Party: extreme right-wing; calls for a Greater Persia; Leader Dr MOHSEN PEZESHKPOUR.

Sazmane Peykar dar Rahe Azadieh Tabaqe Kargar (Organization Struggling for the Freedom of the Working Class): Marxist-Leninist.

Tudeh Party (Communist): f. 1941; declared illegal 1949; came into open 1979, banned again April 1983; First Sec. Cen. Cttee ALI KHAVARI.

The National Council of Resistance (NCR) was formed in Paris in October 1981 by former President ABOLHASAN BANI-SADR and the Council's current leader, MASSOUD RAJAVI, the leader of the Mujahidin-e-Khalq in Iran. In 1984 the Council comprised 15 opposition groups, operating either clandestinely in Iran or from exile abroad. BANI-SADR left the Council in 1984 because of his objection to RAJAVI'S growing links with the Iraqi Government. The French Government asked RAJAVI to leave Paris in June 1986 and he is now based in Baghdad, Iraq. On 20 June 1987 RAJAVI, Secretary of the NCR, announced the formation of a National Liberation Army (10,000–15,000-strong) as the military wing of the Mujahidin-e-Khalq. There is also a National Movement of Iranian Resistance, based in Paris. Dissident members of the Tudeh Party founded the Democratic Party of the Iranian People in Paris in February 1988.

Diplomatic Representation

EMBASSIES IN IRAN

Afghanistan: Dr Beheshi Ave, Pompe Benzine, Corner of 4th St, Teheran; tel. (21) 627531; Ambassador: MOHAMMAD KHEIRKHAH.

Albania: Teheran; Ambassador: GILANI SHEHU.

Angola: Teheran; Ambassador: MANUEL BERNARDO DE SOUSA.

Argentina: 3rd Floor, 7 Argentina Sq., Teheran; tel. (21) 8718294; fax (21) 8712583; Chargé d'affaires: EDUARDO LIONEL DE'AUP.

Armenia: 1 Ostad Shahriar St, Corner of Razi, Jomhouri Islami Ave, Teheran 11337; tel. (21) 674833; fax (21) 670657; Ambassador: YAHAN BAIBOURDIAN.

Australia: POB 15875-4334, 13 23rd St, Khaled al-Islambuli Ave, Teheran 15138; tel. (21) 8724456; fax (21) 8720484; Ambassador: STUART HUME.

Austria: 3rd Floor, 78 Argentine Sq., Teheran; tel. (21) 8710753; fax (21) 8710778; Ambassador: Dr HELMUTH WERNER EHRLICH.

Azerbaijan: Teheran; Ambassador: ALIYAR FARLI.

Bahrain: 31 Khaled al-Islambuli Ave, Teheran; tel. (21) 682079; Ambassador: (vacant).

Bangladesh: POB 11365-3711, Gandhi Ave, 5th St, Building No. 14, Teheran; tel. (21) 8772979; fax (21) 8778295; Ambassador: MUAZZEM ALI.

Belgium: POB 11365-115, Fayazi Ave, Shabdiz Lane, 3 Babak St, Teheran 19659; tel. (21) 2009507; telex 2009554; Ambassador: CHRISTIAAN COURTOIS.

Brazil: Vanak Sq., Vanak Ave No. 58, Teheran 19964; tel. (21) 2265175; telex 212392; fax (21) 8883348; Ambassador: SERGIO TUTIKIAN.

Bulgaria: POB 11365-7451, Vali Asr Ave, Tavanir St, Nezami Ganjavi St, No. 82, Teheran; tel. (21) 685662; telex 212789; Ambassador: STEFAN POLENDAKOV.

Canada: POB 11365-4647, 57 Shahid Sarafraz St; tel. (21) 8732623; fax 8733202; Ambassador: MICHEL DE SALABERRY.

China, People's Republic: Pasdaran Ave, Golestan Ave 1, No. 53, Teheran; tel. (21) 245131; Ambassador: WANG SHIJIE.

Colombia: Teheran; Ambassador: RAFAEL CANAL SANDOVAL.

Congo, Democratic Republic: Teheran; tel. (21) 222199; Chargé d'affaires a.i.: N'DJATE ESELE SASA.

Cuba: Teheran; tel. (21) 685030; Ambassador: ENRIQUE TRUJILLO RAPALLO.

Czech Republic: POB 11365-4457, Mirza-ye Shirazi Ave, Ali Mirza Hassani St, No. 15, Teheran; tel. (21) 8716720; fax (21) 8717858; Chargé d'affaires: Eng. JIŘÍ DOLEŽAL.

Denmark: POB 19395-5358, 18 Dashti Ave, Teheran 19148; tel. (21) 261363; telex 212784; fax (21) 2030007; Ambassador: HUGO ØESTERGAARD-ANDERSEN.

Ethiopia: Teheran; Ambassador: MOHAMMED HASAN KAHIM.

Finland: POB 15115-619, Vali Asr Ave, Vanak Sq., Nilou St, Teheran; tel. (21) 8889151; telex 212930; fax (21) 8889107; Ambassador: A. KOISTINEN.

France: 85 ave Neauphle-le-Château, Teheran; tel. (21) 676005; Ambassador: HUBERT COLIN DE VERDIÈRE.

Gabon: Teheran; tel. (21) 823828; telex 215038; Ambassador: J. B. ESSONGUE.

Gambia: Teheran; Ambassador: OMAR JAH.

Georgia: POB 19575-379, Farmaniye, Teheran; tel. (21) 2295135; fax (21) 2295136; Ambassador: JIMSHER GIUNASHVILI.

Germany: POB 11365-179, 324 Ferdowsi Ave, Teheran; tel. 3114111; telex 212488; Ambassador: Dr HORST BÄCHMANN.

Ghana: Teheran; Ambassador: Mr AL-HASSAN.

Greece: POB 11365-8151, Africa Expressway (Ex. Jordan Ave), Esfandiar St No. 43, Teheran 19686; tel. (21) 2050533; Ambassador: DIMITRI TSIKOURIS.

Guinea: POB 11365-4716, Teheran; tel. (21) 7535744; fax (21) 7535743; Ambassador: MAMDGU SOALIOU SYLLA.

Holy See: Apostolic Nunciature, POB 11365-178, Razi Ave, No. 97, ave Neauphle-le-Château, Teheran; tel. (21) 6403574; fax (21) 6419442; Apostolic-Nuncio: Most Rev. ROMEO PANCIROLI, Titular Archbishop of Noba.

Hungary: POB 19395-6363, Africa Ave, 16 Arash Blvd, Teheran; tel. (21) 2057939; Ambassador: Dr ISTVAN TOLLI.

India: POB 11365-6573, Saba-e-Shomali Ave, No. 166, Teheran; tel. (21) 894554; telex 212858; Ambassador: S. K. ARORA.

Indonesia: POB 11365-4564, Ghaem Magham Farahani Ave, No. 210, Teheran; tel. (21) 626865; telex 212049; Ambassador: BAMBANG SUDARSONO.

Iraq: Vali Asr Ave, No. 494, Teheran.

Ireland: Mirdamad Blvd, 10 North Razan St, Teheran 19116; tel. (21) 2227672; telex 213865; fax (21) 2222731; Ambassador: THOMAS D. LYONS.

Italy: POB 11365-7863, 81 ave Neauphle-le-Château, Teheran; tel. (21) 6496955; telex 214171; fax (21) 6496961; Ambassador: LUDOVICO ORTONA.

Japan: POB 11365-814, Bucharest Ave, N.W. Corner of 5th St, Teheran; tel. (21) 623396; telex 212757; Ambassador: TSUNEO OYAKE.

Jordan: POB 19395-4666, No. 6, 2nd Alley, Shadavar St, Mahmoodieh Ave, Teheran; tel. (21) 291432; telex 226899; fax (21) 2007160; Ambassador YASIN ISTANBULI.

Kazakhstan: Darrus, Hedayat St, Masjed, No. 4, Teheran; tel (21) 2565933; telex 216877; fax (21) 2546400; Ambassador: MURZATAY ZHOLDASBEKOV.

Kenya: 60 Hormoz Satari St, Africa Ave, Teheran; tel. (21) 2270795; telex 213652; fax (21) 2270160; Ambassador: SALIM JUMA.

Korea, Democratic People's Republic: Fereshteh Ave, Sarvestan Ave, No. 11, Teheran; tel. (21) 298610; Ambassador: CHOE YONG RO.

Korea, Republic: 37 Bucharest Ave, Teheran; tel. (21) 8751125; telex 212693; fax (21) 8737917; Ambassador: JAE KYU KIM.

Kuwait: Dehkadeh Ave, 3–38 Sazman-Ab St, Teheran; tel. (21) 636712; Ambassador: ABDULLAH ABD AL-AZIZ AD-DUWAYKH.

Kyrgyzstan: Teheran.

Laos: Teheran; Ambassador: CHANPHENG SIHAPHOM.

Lebanon: Teheran; Ambassador: MOUNIR TALHOUK

Libya: Ostad Motahhari Ave, No. 163, Teheran; tel. (21) 859191; Sec.-Gen. Committee of People's Bureau: MAHDI AL-MABIRASH.

Malaysia: 72 Fereshteh Ave, Teheran; tel. (21) 2009275; fax (21) 2009143; Ambassador: MUHAMMAD KHALIS.

Mauritania: Teheran.

Mexico: POB 15875-4636, No. 24, Shabnam Alley, Africa Expressway, Teheran; tel. (21) 2225374; telex 216557; fax (21) 2225375; Ambassador: ANTONIO DUENAS PULIDO.

Mongolia: Teheran; Ambassador: L. KHASHOAT.

Morocco: Teheran; tel. (21) 2059707; fax (21) 2051872; Ambassador: MOHAMMAD AZAROUAL.

Mozambique: Teheran; Ambassador: MURADE ISAC MIGUIGY MURARGY.

Myanmar: Teheran; Ambassador: U SAW HLAING.

Namibia: Teheran; Ambassador: MWAILEPENI T. P. SHITILIFA.

Nepal: Teheran; Ambassador: Gen. ARJUN NARSING RONA.

Netherlands: POB 11365-138, Vali Asr Ave, Ostad Motahhari Ave, Sarbederan St, Jahansouz Alley, No. 36, Teheran; tel. (21) 896011; telex 212788; fax (21) 8892087; Ambassador: M. DAMME.

New Zealand: POB 11365-436, Mirza-e-Shirazi Ave, Kucheh Mirza Hassani, No. 29, Teheran; tel. (21) 8715061; fax (21) 8861715; Ambassador: JOHN DANIEL LUTTON RICHARDS.

Nigeria: POB 11365-7148, Khaled Islamboli Ave, 31st St, No. 9, Teheran; tel. (21) 684921; telex 213151; fax (21) 684936; Ambassador: ANO SANUSI.

Norway: POB 19395-5398, Pasdaran Ave, Kouhestan 8, Ekhtiarieh Shomali 412, Teheran; tel. (21) 2291333; telex 213009; fax (21) 2292776; Chargé d'affaires: CARL S. WIBYE.

Oman: POB 41-1586, Pasdaran Ave, Golestan 9, No. 5 and 7, Teheran; tel. (21) 286021; telex 212835; Chargé d'affaires a.i.: RASHID BIN MUBARAK BIN RASHID AL-ODWALI.

Pakistan: Dr Fatemi Ave, Jamshidabad Shomali, Mashal St, No. 1, Teheran; tel. (21) 934332; KHALID MAHMUD.

Panama: Teheran; Ambassador: G. MOVAGA.

Philippines: POB 19395-4797, 24 Golazin Blvd., Africa Ave, Zafaranieh, Teheran; tel. (21) 2055134; fax (21) 2057260; Ambassador HARON P. ALONTO.

Poland: Africa Expressway, Piruz St, No. 1/3, Teheran; tel. (21) 227262; Ambassador: STEFAN SZYMCZYKIEWICZ.

Portugal: Vali Asr Ave, Tavanir Ave, Nezami Ghanjavi Ave, No. 30, Teheran; tel. (21) 8772132; telex 212588; fax (21) 8777834; Ambassador: Dr MANUEL MARCELO CURTO.

Qatar: Africa Expressway, Golazin Ave, Parke Davar, No. 4, Teheran; tel. (21) 221255; telex 212375; Ambassador: ALI ABDULLAH ZAID AL-MAHMOOOD.

Romania: Fakhrabad Ave 12, Darvaze Shemiran, Teheran; tel. (21) 7509309; telex 212791; fax (21) 7509841; Ambassador: CRISTIAN TEODORESCU.

Russia: 39 ave Neauphle-le-Château, Teheran; tel. (21) 671163; Ambassador: KONSTANTIN SHUVALOV.

Saudi Arabia: 10 Saba Blvd, Africa Ave, Teheran; tel. (21) 2050081; fax (21) 2050083; Ambassador: ABD AL-LATIF ABDULLAH AL-MEIMANI.

Singapore: Teheran; Ambassador: GOPINATH PILLAI.

Slovakia: POB 11365-4451, No. 24, Babak Markazi St, Africa Ave, Teheran; tel. (21) 2271058; fax (21) 2271057; Chargé d'affaires a.i.: ALEXANDER BAJKAI.

Somalia: Shariati Ave, Soheyl Ave, No. 20, Teheran; tel. (21) 272034; Ambassador: ABDI SHIRE WARSAME.

South Africa: Teheran; Ambassador: MUSA MOOLLA.

Spain: Vali-Asr Ave, 76 Sarv St, Teheran; tel. (21) 8714575; telex 212980; fax (21) 8724581. Ambassador: GABRIEL BUSQUETS.

Sudan: Khaled Islambouli Ave, 23rd St, No. 10, Teheran; tel. (21) 628476; telex 213372; Ambassador: Dr ABDEL RAHANA MOHAMMED SAID.

Sweden: POB 19575-458, 2 Nastaran St, Teheran; tel. (21) 2296802; telex 212822; fax (21) 2286021; Ambassador: HANS ANDERSSON.

Switzerland: POB 19395-4683, 13/1 Boustan Ave, 19649 Teheran; tel. (21) 268227; fax 269448; Ambassador: RUDOLF WEIERSMÜLLER.

Syria: Africa Ave, 19 Iraj St, Teheran; tel. (21) 229032; Ambassador: AHMAD AL-HASSAN.

Tajikistan: Teheran.

Thailand: POB 11495-111, Baharestan Ave, Parc Amin ed-Doleh, No. 4, Teheran; tel. (21) 7531433; telex 214040; fax (21) 7532022; Ambassador: MAHADI WIMANA.

Tunisia: Teheran; Ambassador: Dr NOUREDDINE AL-HAMDANI.

Turkey: Ferdowsi Ave, No. 314, Teheran; tel. (21) 3115299; telex 213670; fax (21) 3117928; Ambassador: (vacant).

Turkmenistan: Teheran.

Ukraine: Hefez Avenue, Teheran 487; tel. (21) 675148; telex 112574; Chargé d'affaires: IVAN G. MAYDAN.

United Arab Emirates: Zafar Ave, No. 355–7, Teheran; tel. (21) 221333; telex 212697; Ambassador: AHMAD MOHAMMED BORHEIMAH.

United Kingdom: POB 11365-4474, 143 Ferdowsi Ave, Teheran 11344; tel. (21) 675011; fax (21) 678021; e-mail britemb@neda.net; Ambassador: (vacant).

Uruguay: 45 Shabnam Alley, Atefi Shargi St, Jordan Ave, Teheran; tel. (21) 2052030; Ambassador: MARCIAL BIRRIEL IGLESIAS.

Uzbekistan: Teheran.

Venezuela: POB 15875-4354, Bucharest Ave, 9th St, No. 31, Teheran; tel. (21) 625185; telex 213790; fax (21) 622840; Ambassador: Dr HERNÁN CALCURIAN.

Viet Nam: Teheran; Ambassador: VUXNAN ANG.

Yemen: Bucharest Ave, No. 26, Teheran; Chargé d'affaires a.i.: Dr AHMED MOHAMED ALI ABDULLAH.

Yugoslavia: POB 11365-118, Vali Asr Ave, Fereshteh Ave, Amir Teymour Alley, No. 12, 19659 Teheran; tel. (21) 2044126; telex 214235; fax (21) 2044978; Chargé d'affaires: STOJAN GLIGORIĆ.

Judicial System

In August 1982 the Supreme Court revoked all laws dating from the previous regime which did not conform with Islam. In October 1982 all courts set up prior to the Islamic Revolution were abolished.

In June 1987 Ayatollah Khomeini ordered the creation of clerical courts to try members of the clergy opposed to government policy. A new system of *qisas* (retribution) was established, placing the emphasis on speedy justice. Islamic codes of correction were introduced in 1983, including the dismembering of a hand for theft, flogging for fornication and violations of the strict code of dress for women, and stoning for adultery. In 1984 there was a total of 2,200 judges. The Supreme Court has 16 branches.

SUPREME COURT

Chief Justice: Hojatoleslam MUHAMMAD MUHAMMADI GUILANI.

Prosecutor-General: Hojatoleslam MORTEZA MOQTADAI.

Religion

According to the 1979 constitution, the official religion is Islam of the Ja'fari sect (Shi'ite), but other Islamic sects, including Zeydi, Hanafi, Maleki, Shafe'i and Hanbali, are valid and will be respected. Zoroastrians, Jews and Christians will be recognized as official religious minorities. According to the 1976 census, there were then 310,000 Christians (mainly Armenian), 80,000 Jews and 30,000 Zoroastrians.

ISLAM

The great majority of the Iranian people are Shi'a Muslims, but there is a minority of Sunni Muslims. Persians and Azerbaijanis are mainly Shi'i, while the other ethnic groups are mainly Sunni.

CHRISTIANITY

The Roman Catholic Church

At 31 December 1995 there were an estimated 12,850 adherents in Iran, comprising 6,250 of the Chaldean Rite, 2,600 of the Armenian Rite and 4,000 of the Latin Rite.

Armenian Rite

Bishop of Isfahan: Dr VARTAN TEKEYAN, Armenian Catholic Bishopric, Khiaban Ghazzali 22, Teheran; tel. (21) 677204; fax (21) 8715191.

Chaldean Rite

Archbishop of Ahwaz: HANNA ZORA, Archbishop's House, POB 61956, Naderi St, Ahwaz; tel. (61) 24890.

Archbishop of Teheran: YOUHANNAN SEMAAN ISSAYI, Archevêché, Forsat Ave 91, Teheran 15819; tel. (21) 8823549.

Archbishop of Urmia (Rezayeh) and Bishop of Salmas (Shahpour): THOMAS MERAM, Khalifagari Kaldani Katholiq, POB 338, Orumiyeh 57135; tel. (441) 22739.

Latin Rite

Archbishop of Isfahan: IGNAZIO BEDINI, Consolata Church, POB 11365-445, 75 Neauphle-le-Château Ave, Teheran; tel. (21) 673210.

The Anglican Communion

Anglicans in Iran are adherents of the Episcopal Church in Jerusalem and the Middle East, formally inaugurated in January 1976. The Rt Rev. HASSAN DEHQANI-TAFTI, the Bishop in Iran from 1961 to 1990, was President-Bishop of the Church from 1976 to 1986. He was succeeded by the Bishop of Jerusalem during 1986–96 and the Bishop of Egypt from 1996 onwards.

Bishop in Iran: Rt Rev. IRAJ KALIMI MOTTAHEDEH, St Luke's Church, Abbas-abad, POB 81465-135, Isfahan; tel. (31) 231435; diocese founded 1912.

Presbyterian Church

Synod of the Evangelical (Presbyterian) Church in Iran: Assyrian Evangelical Church, Khiaban-i Hanifnejad, Khiaban-i Aramanch, Teheran; Moderator Rev. ADEL NAKHOSTEEN.

ZOROASTRIANS

There are about 30,000 Zoroastrians, a remnant of a once widespread sect. Their religious leader is MOUBAD.

OTHER COMMUNITIES

Communities of Armenians, and somewhat smaller numbers of Jews (an estimated 30,000 in 1986), Assyrians, Greek Orthodox Christians, Uniates and Latin Christians are also found as officially recognized faiths. The Bahá'í faith, which originated in Iran, has about 300,000 Iranian adherents, although at least 10,000 are believed to have fled since 1979 in order to escape persecution. The Government banned all Bahá'í institutions in August 1983.

The Press

Teheran dominates the media, as many of the daily papers are published there, and the bi-weekly, weekly and less frequent publications in the provinces generally depend on the major metropolitan dailies as a source of news. A press law announced in August 1979 required all newspapers and magazines to be licensed and imposed penalties of imprisonment for insulting senior religious figures. Offences against the Act will be tried in the criminal courts. Under the Constitution the press is free, except in matters that are contrary to public morality, insult religious belief or slander the honour and reputation of individuals.

PRINCIPAL DAILIES

Abrar (Rightly Guided): 26 Shahid Denesh Kian Alley, Below Zartasht St, Valiassr Ave, Teheran; tel. (21) 8848270; fax (21) 8849200; f. 1985 after closure of *Azadegan* by order of the Prosecutor-General; morning; Farsi; circ. 75,000.

Alik: POB 11365-953, Jomhoori Islami Ave, Alik Alley, Teheran 11357; tel. (21) 676671; f. 1931; afternoon; political and literary; Armenian; Propr A. AJEMIAN; circ. 3,400.

Bahari Iran: Khayaban Khayham, Shiraz; tel. (71) 33738.

Ettela'at (Information): 11 Khayyam St, Teheran; tel. (21) 3281; telex 212336; fax (21) 311223; f. 1925; evening; Farsi; political and literary; owned and managed by Mostazafin Foundation from October 1979 until 1 January 1987, when it was placed under the direct supervision of Wilayat-e-Faqih (religious jurisprudence); Editor S. M. DOAEI; circ. 500,000.

Iran News: 41 Lida St, Valiassr Ave, North Vanak Sq, tel. (21) 8880231; telex 216966; fax (21) 8786475; Teheran; English.

Kayhan (Universe): Ferdowsi Ave, Teheran; tel. (21) 310251; telex 212467; f. 1941; evening; Farsi; political; also publishes *Kayhan International* (f. 1959; daily and weekly; English; Editor HOSSEIN RAGHFAR), *Kayhan Arabic* (f. 1980; daily and weekly; Arabic), *Kayhan Persian* (f. 1942; daily; Persian), *Kayhan Turkish* (f. 1984; monthly; Turkish), *Kayhan Havaie* (f. 1950; weekly for Iranians abroad; Farsi), *Kayhan Andishe* (World of Religion; f. 1985; 6 a year; Farsi), *Zan-e-Ruz* (Woman Today; f. 1964; weekly; Farsi), *Kayhan Varzeshi* (World of Sport; f. 1955; weekly; Farsi), *Kayhan Bacheha* (Children's World; f. 1956; weekly; Farsi), *Kayhan Farhangi* (World of Culture; f. 1984; monthly; Farsi); *Kayhan Yearbook* (yearly; Farsi); *Period of 40 Years, Kayhan* (series of books; Farsi); owned and managed by Mostazafin Foundation from October 1979 until 1 January 1987, when it was placed under the direct supervision of Wilayat-e-Faqih (religious jurisprudence); Chief Editor HOSSEIN SHARIATMADARI; circ. 350,000.

Khorassan: Meshed; Head Office: Khorassan Daily Newspapers, 14 Zohre St, Mobarezan Ave, Teheran; f. 1948; Propr MUHAMMAD SADEGH TEHERANIAN; circ. 40,000.

Rahnejat: Darvazeh Dowlat, Isfahan; political and social; Propr N. RAHNEJAT.

Ressallat (The Message): Teheran; organ of right-wing group of the same name; political, economic, social; Propr Ressallat Foundation; circ. 100,000.

Salam: 2 Reza Shahid Nayebi Alley, South Felestin St, Teheran; tel. (21) 6495831; telex 222959; fax (21) 6495835; f. 1991; Farsi; political, economic, social; Editor MUHAMMAD MUSAVI KHOIENI.

Teheran Times: 32 Bimeh Alley, Nejatullahi Ave, Teheran 15998; tel. (21) 8810293; telex 8809470; fax (21) 8808214; f. 1979; independent; English.

PRINCIPAL PERIODICALS

Acta Medica Iranica: Faculty of Medicine, Poursina St, Teheran Medical Sciences Univ., Teheran 14-174; tel. (21) 6112743; fax (21) 6404377; f. 1960; quarterly; English; under the supervision of the Research Vice-Associate (A. JAWADIAN) and the Editorial Board; Editor-in-Chief PARVIZ JABAL-AMELI (Dean, Faculty of Medicine); circ. 2,000.

Akhbar-e-Pezeshki: 86 Ghaem Magham Farahani Ave, Teheran; weekly; medical; Propr Dr T. FORUZIN.

Ashur: Ostad Motahhari Ave, 11-21 Kuhe Nour Ave, Teheran; tel. (21) 622117; f. 1969; Assyrian; monthly; Founder and Editor Dr W. BET-MANSOUR; circ. 8,000.

Auditor: 77 Ferdowsi Ave North, Teheran; quarterly; financial and managerial studies.

Ayandeh: POB 19575-583, Niyavaran, Teheran; tel. (21) 283254; fax (21) 6406426; monthly; Iranian literary, historical and book review journal; Editor Prof. IRAJ AFSHAR.

Bulletin of the National Film Archive of Iran: POB 5158, Baharestan Sq., Teheran 11365; tel. 311242; telex 214283; f. 1989; English periodical; Editor M. H. KHOSHNEVIS.

Daneshmand: POB 15875, Teheran; tel. (21) 8741323; f. 1963; monthly; scientific and technical magazine; Editor Dr AHMAD FARMAD.

Daneshkadeh Pezeshki: Faculty of Medicine, Teheran Medical Sciences University; tel. (21) 6112743; fax (21) 6404377; f. 1947; 10 a year; medical magazine; Propr Dr HASSAN AREFI; circ. 1,500.

Donaye Varzesh: Khayyam Ave, Ettela'at Bldg, Teheran; tel. (21) 3281; telex 212336; fax (21) 3115530; weekly; sport; Editor G. H. SHABANI; circ. 200,000.

Echo of Islam: POB 14155-3987, Teheran; monthly; English; published by the Foundation of Islamic Thought.

Ettela'at Elmi: 11 Khayyam Ave, Teheran; tel. (21) 3281; telex 212336; fax (21) 3115530; f. 1985; fortnightly; sciences; Editor Mrs GHASEMI; circ. 75,000.

Ettela'at Haftegi: 11 Khayyam Ave, Teheran; tel. (21) 3281; telex 212336; fax (21) 3115530; f. 1941; general weekly; Editor F. JAVADI; circ. 150,000.

Ettela'at Javanan: POB 11335-9365, 11144 Khayyam Ave, Teheran; tel. (21) 3281; telex 212336; fax (21) 3115530; f. 1966; weekly; youth; Editor M. J. RAFIZADEH; circ. 120,000.

Farhang-e-Iran Zamin: POB 19575-583, Niyavaran, Teheran; tel. (21) 283254; annual; Iranian studies; Editor Prof. IRAJ AFSHAR.

Film International: POB 11365-5875, Teheran; tel. (21) 6457480; fax (21) 6459971; f. 1993; quarterly in English; Editor B. RAHIMIAN; circ 20,000.

Iran Press Digest (Economic): POB 11365-5551, Hafiz Ave, 4 Kucheh Hurtab, Teheran; tel. (21) 668114; telex 212300; weekly; Editor J. BEHROUZ.

Iran Press Digest (Political): POB 11365-5551, Hafiz Ave, 4 Kucheh Hurtab, Teheran; tel. (21) 668114; telex 212300; weekly.

Iranian Cinema: POB 5158, Baharestan Sq., Teheran 11365; tel. 311242; f. 1985; annually; English; Editor B. REYPOUR.

Javaneh: POB 15875-1163, Motahhari Ave, Cnr Mofatteh St, Teheran; tel. (21) 839051; published by Soroush Press; quarterly.

Kayhan Bacheha (Children's World): Shahid Shahsheragi Ave, Teheran; tel. (21) 310251; telex 212467; f. 1956; weekly; Editor AMIR HOSSEIN FARDI; circ. 150,000.

Kayhan Varzeshi (World of Sport): Ferdowsi Ave, Teheran; tel. (21) 310251; telex 212467; f. 1955; weekly; Dir MAHMAD MONSETI; circ. 125,000.

Mahjubah: POB 14155-3897, Teheran; tel. (21) 890226; fax (21) 8758296; Islamic women's magazine; published by the Islamic Thought Foundation.

Majda: POB 14155-3695, 94 West Pirouzi St, Kooye Nasr, Teheran; tel. (21) 639591; telex 212918; fax (21) 639592; f. 1963; four a year; medical; journal of the Iranian Dental Association; Pres. Dr ALI YAZDANI.

Music Iran: 1029 Amiriye Ave, Teheran; f. 1951; monthly; Editor BAHMAN HIRBOD; circ. 7,000.

Negin: Vali Asr Ave, Adl St 52, Teheran; monthly; scientific and literary; Propr and Dir M. ENAYAT.

Pars: Alley Dezhban, Shiraz; f. 1941; irregular; Propr and Dir F. SHARGHI; circ. 10,000.

Salamate Fekr: M.20, Kharg St, Teheran; tel. (21) 223034; f. 1958; monthly; organ of the Mental Health Soc.; Editors Prof. E. TCHEHRAZI, ALI REZA SHAFAI.

Soroush: POB 15875-1163, Motahhari Ave, Corner Mofatteh St, Teheran; tel. (21) 830771; f. 1972; two monthly magazines in Farsi, one for children and one for adolescents; Editor MEHDI FIROOZAN.

Zan-e-Ruz (Woman Today): Ferdowsi Ave, Teheran; tel. (21) 301570; telex 216186; fax (21) 301569; f. 1964; weekly; women's; circ. over 60,000.

NEWS AGENCIES

Islamic Republic News Agency (IRNA): POB 764, 873 Vali Asr Ave, Teheran; tel. (21) 892050; telex 212827; fax (21) 895068; f. 1936; Man. Dir FEREYDOUN VERDINEZHAD.

Foreign Bureaux

Agence France-Presse (AFP): POB 15115-513, Office 207, 8 Vanak Ave, Vanak Sq., Teheran 19919; tel. (21) 8777509; fax (21) 8886289; Correspondent CHRISTOPHE DE ROQUEFEUIL.

Agenzia Nazionale Stampa Associata (ANSA) (Italy): Khiabane Shahid Bahonar (Niavaran) Kuche Mina No. 16, Teheran 19367; tel. (21) 276930; telex 213629; Chief of Bureau LUCIANO CAUSA.

Anatolian News Agency (Turkey): Teheran.

Informatsionnoye Telegrafnoye Agentstvo Rossuii—Telegrafnoye Agentstvo Suverennykh Stran (ITAR—TASS) (Russia): Kehyaban Hamid, Kouche Masoud 73, Teheran.

Kyodo Tsushin (Japan): No. 23, First Floor, Couche Kargozar, Couche Sharsaz Ave, Zafar, Teheran; tel. (21) 220448; telex 214058; Correspondent MASARU IMAI.

Novinska Agencija Tanjug (Yugoslavia): Teheran.

Reuters (UK): POB 15875-1193, Teheran; tel. (21) 847700; telex 212634.

Xinhua (New China) News Agency (People's Republic of China): 75 Golestan 2nd St, Pasdaran Ave, Teheran; tel. (21) 241852; telex 212399; Correspondent CHEN MING.

Publishers

Amir Kabir: Esteghlal Sq, Teheran; f. 1950; historical, social, literary and children's books; Dir H. ANWARY.

Ebn-e-Sina: Meydane 25 Shahrivar, Teheran; f. 1957; educational publishers and booksellers; Dir EBRAHIM RAMAZANI.

Eghbal Printing & Publishing Organization: 15 Booshehr St, Dr Shariati Ave, Teheran; tel. (21) 768113; f. 1903; Man. Dir DJAVAD EGHBAL.

Iran Chap Co: Khayyam Ave, Teheran; tel. (21) 3281; telex 212336; fax (21) 3115530; f. 1966; newspapers, books, magazines, book binding, colour printing and engraving; Man. Dir M. DOAEI.

Iran Exports Publication Co Ltd: POB 15815-3373, 27 Eftekhar St, Vali Asr Ave, Teheran 15956; tel. (21) 8801800; telex 215017; fax (21) 890547; f. 1987; business and trade.

Ketab Sara: Teheran; Chair. SADEGH SAMII.

Khayyam: Jomhoori Islami Ave, Teheran; Dir MOHAMMAD ALI TARAGHI.

Majlis Press: Ketab-Khane Majlis-e-Showraie Eslami No. 1, Baharistan Sq., Teheran 11564; tel. (21) 3124257; f. 1924; Dir ABD AL-HOSSEIN HAIERI; Ketab Khane Majlis-e-Showraie Eslami No. 2, Imam Khomeini Ave, Teheran 13174; tel. (21) 6462906; f. 1950; Dir ABD AL-HOSSEIN HAIERI.

Sahab Geographic and Drafting Institute: POB 11365-617, 30 Somayeh St, Hoquqi Crossroad, Dr Ali Shariati Ave, Teheran 16517; tel. (21) 7535670; telex 222584; fax (21) 7535876; maps, atlases, and books on geography, science, history and Islamic art; Founder and Pres. ABBAS A. SAHAB.

Scientific and Cultural Publications Co: Ministry of Culture and Higher Education, 64th St, Sayyed Jamal-ed-Din Asad Abadi Ave; tel. (21) 685457; f. 1974; Iranian and Islamic studies and scientific and cultural books; Pres. SAYED JAVAD AZHARS.

Teheran University Press: 16 Kargar Shomali Ave, Teheran; tel. (21) 632062; fax (21) 632063; f. 1944; university textbooks; Man. Dir ABBAS RASTGOU.

Broadcasting and Communications

TELECOMMUNICATIONS

Telecommunication Company of Iran (TCI): Dr Shariati Ave, Teheran; tel. (21) 864796; telex 212444; fax (21) 866023; Chair. and Man. Dir Dr SAYED ABDOLLAH MIRTAHERI.

BROADCASTING

Islamic Republic of Iran Broadcasting (IRIB): POB 19395-3333, Vali Asr Ave, Jame Jam St, Teheran; tel. (21) 21961; telex 2045056; fax (21) 213910; semi-autonomous government authority; non-commercial; operates five national television and three national radio channels, as well as local provincial radio stations throughout the country; Dir-Gen. ALI LARIJANI.

Radio

Radio Network 1 (Voice of the Islamic Republic of Iran): there are three national radio channels: Radio Networks 1 and 2 and Radio Quran, which broadcasts recitals of the Quran (Koran) and other programmes related to it; covers whole of Iran and reaches whole of Europe, the Central Asian republics of the CIS, whole of Asia, Africa and part of USA; medium-wave regional broadcasts in local languages; Arabic, Armenian, Assyrian, Azerbaijani, Balochi, Bandari, Dari, Farsi, Kurdish, Mazandarani, Pashtu, Turkoman, Turkish and Urdu; external broadcasts in English, French, German, Spanish, Turkish, Arabic, Kurdish, Urdu, Pashtu, Armenian, Bengali, Russian and special overseas programme in Farsi; 53 transmitters.

Television

Television (Vision of the Islamic Republic of Iran): 625-line, System B; Secam colour; two production centres in Teheran producing for two networks and 28 local TV stations.

Finance

(cap. = capital; res = reserves; dep. = deposits; brs = branches; m. = million; amounts in rials)

BANKING

Banks were nationalized in June 1979 and a revised commercial banking system was introduced consisting of nine banks (subsequently expanded to 10). Three banks were reorganized, two (Bank Tejarat and Bank Mellat) resulted from mergers of 22 existing small banks, three specialize in industry and agriculture and one, the Islamic Bank (now Islamic Economy Organization), set up in May 1979, was exempt from nationalization. The tenth bank, the Export Development Bank, specializes in the promotion of exports. A change-over to an Islamic banking system, with interest being replaced by a 4% commission on loans, began on 21 March 1984. All short- and medium-term private deposits and all bank loans and advances are subject to Islamic rules.

Although the number of foreign banks operating in Iran has fallen dramatically since the Revolution, some 30 are still represented.

Central Bank

Bank Markazi Jomhouri Islami Iran (Central Bank): POB 11365-8551, Ferdowsi Ave, Teheran; tel. (21) 3110231; telex 212359; fax (21) 390323; f. 1960; Bank Markazi Iran until Dec. 1983; central note-issuing bank of Iran, government banking; cap. 200,000m., res 180,180m., dep. 43,142,714m., total assets 71,713,749m. (March 1996); Gov. Dr MOHSEN NOURBAKHSH.

Commercial Banks

Bank Keshavarzi (Agricultural Bank): POB 14155-6395, 129 Patrice Lumumba Ave, Jalal al-Ahmad Expressway, Teheran; tel. and fax (21) 8252246; telex 212058; f. 1979 as merger of the Agricultural Development Bank of Iran and the Agricultural Co-operative Bank of Iran; state-owned; cap. 408,322m., dep. 1,751,733m. (March 1996); 1,565 brs; Man. Dir SAYED ALI MILANI HOSSEINI.

Bank Mellat (Nation's Bank): Shahid Fayazbakhsh Ave, Keshavarzi St, Teheran; tel. (21) 32491; telex 212619; fax (21) 8964111; f. 1980 as merger of the following: International Bank of Iran, Bank Bimeh Iran, Bank Dariush, Distributors' Co-operative Credit Bank, Iran Arab Bank, Bank Omran, Bank Pars, Bank of Teheran, Foreign Trade Bank of Iran, Bank Farhangian; state-owned; cap. 605,000m., dep. 8,693,000m., total assets 11,436,000m. (March 1995); 1,288 brs throughout Iran and 5 brs abroad; Chair. and Man. Dir M. ARAMINIA.

Bank Melli Iran (The National Bank of Iran): POB 11365-171, Ferdowsi Ave, Teheran; tel. (21) 3231; telex 212890; fax (21) 302813; f. 1928; state-owned; cap. 1,145,000m., res 18,475m., dep. 21,724,454m., total assets 33,700,185m. (March 1996); 2,509 brs throughout Iran, 24 brs abroad; Chair. and Man. Dir ASSADOLLAH AMIRASLANI.

Bank Refah Kargaran: POB 15714, 40 Shirazi St, Mollasadra Ave, Teheran; tel. (21) 8042926; fax (21) 8042926; f. 1960; state-owned; cap. 55,000m., dep. 1,278,224m. (March 1996); 461 brs throughout Iran; Man. Dir J. SABER KHIABANI.

Bank Saderat Iran (The Export Bank of Iran): POB 15745-631, Bank Saderat Tower, 43 Somayyeh Ave, Teheran; tel. (21) 836091; telex 212352; fax (21) 8839539; f. 1952, reorganized 1979; state-owned; cap. 948,000m., res. 5,876.8m., dep. 8,148,885.5m., total assets 12,338,588.3m. (March 1995); 3,288 brs in Iran, 21 foreign brs; Chair. and Man. Dir MUHAMMAD REZA MOGHADASSI.

Bank Sepah (Army Bank): POB 9569, Imam Khomeini Sq, Teheran; tel. (21) 3111091; telex 212462; fax (21) 3112138; f. 1925, reorganized 1979; state-owned; cap. 400,000m., res 2,605,667m., dep. 9,204,258m., total assets 10,356,288m. (March 1996); 1,194 brs throughout Iran and 5 brs abroad; Chair. and Man. Dir VALIOLLAH SAIF.

Bank Tejarat (Commercial Bank): POB 11365-5416, 130 Taleghani Ave, Nejatoullahie, Teheran 15994; tel. (21) 81041; telex 212077; fax (21) 8828215; f. 1979 as merger of the following: Irano-British Bank, Bank Etebarate Iran, The Bank of Iran and the Middle East, Mercantile Bank of Iran and Holland, Bank Barzagani Iran, Bank Iranshahr, Bank Sanaye Iran, Bank Shahriar, Iranians' Bank, Bank Kar, International Bank of Iran and Japan, Bank Russo-Iran; state-owned; cap. 571,120m., res 14,883m., dep. 12,211,491m., total assets 14,951,980m. (March 1996); 1,390 brs in Iran and 2 abroad; Man. Dir and Chair. A. R. KHATIB.

Islamic Economy Organization (formerly Islamic Bank of Iran): Ferdowsi Ave, Teheran; f. February 1980; cap. 2,000m.; provides interest-free loans and investment in small industry.

Development Banks

Bank Sanat va Madan (Bank of Industry and Mines): POB 15875-4456, 593 Hafiz Ave, Teheran; tel. (21) 893271; telex 212816; fax (21) 895052; f. 1979 as merger of the following: Industrial Credit Bank (ICB), Industrial and Mining Development Bank of Iran (IMDBI), Development and Investment Bank of Iran (DIBI), Iranian Bankers Investment Company (IBICO); cap. 1,280,000m., res 36,257m., total assets 2,447,396m. (1996); Man. Dir MOJTABA HARATI NIK.

Export Development Bank of Iran: POB 15875-5964, 129 Khaled Eslambouli St, Teheran 15139; tel. (21) 8716607; telex 226895; fax (21) 8716979; cap. 100,000m., res. 971m., dep. 223,611m., total assets 331,419m. (1995); 4 brs; Chair and Man. Dir Dr NOWROUZ KOHZADI.

Housing Bank

Bank Maskan (Housing Bank): Ferdowsi Ave, Teheran; tel. (21) 675021; telex 226871; f. 1980; state-owned; cap. 42,663.8m., dep. 221,153.4m., total assets 3,594,364m. (June 1985); provides mortgage and housing finance; 187 brs; Chair. and Man. Dir AHMAD FARSHCHIAN.

STOCK EXCHANGE

Teheran Stock Exchange: 228 Hafez Ave, Teheran 11389; tel. (21) 670155; telex 223282; fax (21) 672524; f. 1966; Sec.-Gen. AHMAD MIRMOTAHARI.

INSURANCE

The nationalization of insurance companies was announced in June 1979.

Bimeh Alborz (Alborz Insurance Co): POB 4489-15875, Alborz Bldg, 234 Sepahboad Garani Ave, Teheran; tel. (21) 8803777; fax (21) 8803771; f. 1959; state-owned insurance company; all types of insurance; Man. Dir ALI FATHALI.

Bimeh Asia (Asia Insurance Co): POB 1365-5366, Asia Insurance Bldg, 297-299 Taleghani Ave, Teheran; tel. (21) 836040; telex 213664; fax (21) 827196; all types of insurance; Man. Dir MASOUM ZAMIRI.

Bimeh Dana (Dana Insurance Co): 25 Fifteenth Ave, Gandi St, Teheran; tel. (21) 8770971; fax 8770812; life, personal accident and health insurance; Chair. and Man. Dir. ALI FARHANDI.

Bimeh Iran (Iran Insurance Co): POB 11365-9153, Saadi Ave, Teheran; tel. (21) 304026; telex 212782; fax (21) 313510; all types of insurance; Man. Dir ALI MOSAREZA.

Bimeh Markazi Iran (Central Insurance of Iran): POB 15875-4345, 149 Ayatollah Taleghani Ave, Teheran 15914; tel. (21) 6409912; telex 212888; fax (21) 6405729; supervises the insurance market and tariffs for new types of insurance cover; the sole state reinsurer for domestic insurance companies, which are obliged to reinsure 50% of their direct business in life insurance and 25% of business in non-life insurance with Bimeh Markazi Iran; Pres. ABDOL NASSER HEMMATI.

Trade and Industry

CHAMBER OF COMMERCE

Iran Chamber of Commerce, Industries and Mines: 254 Taleghani Ave, Teheran; tel. (21) 8846031; fax (21) 8825111; supervises the affiliated 32 Chambers in the provinces; Pres. ALINAQI KHAMOUSHI.

INDUSTRIAL AND TRADE ASSOCIATIONS

National Iranian Industries Organization (NIIO): POB 14155-3579, 133 Dr Fatemi Ave, Teheran; tel. (21) 656031-40; telex 214176; fax (21) 658070; f. 1979; owns 400 factories in Iran.

National Iranian Industries Organization Export Co (NECO): POB 14335-589, No. 8, 2nd St, Ahmad Ghasir Ave, Teheran 15944; tel. (21) 8733564; telex 212429; fax (21) 8732586.

STATE HYDROCARBONS COMPANIES

Iranian Offshore Oil Co (IOOC): POB 15875-4546, 339 Dr Beheshti Ave, Teheran; tel. (21) 8714102; telex 212707; fax (21) 8717420; wholly owned subsidiary of NIOC; f. 1980; development, exploitation and production of crude petroleum, natural gas and other hydrocarbons in all offshore areas of Iran in the Persian Gulf and the Caspian Sea; Chair. M. AGAZADEH; Dir S. A. JALILIAN.

National Iranian Gas Co (NIGC): Man. Dir MOHAMMAD ISMAIL KARACHIAN.

National Iranian Oil Co (NIOC): POB 1863, Taleghani Ave, Teheran; tel. (21) 6151; telex 212514; a state organization controlling all 'upstream' activities in the petroleum and natural gas industries; incorporated April 1951 on nationalization of petroleum industry to engage in all phases of petroleum operations; in February 1979 it was announced that, in future, Iran would sell petroleum direct to the petroleum companies, and in September 1979 the Ministry of Oil assumed control of the National Iranian Oil Company, and the Minister of Oil took over as Chairman and Managing Director; Chair. of Board and Gen. Man. Dir BIZHAN NAMDAR-ZANGENEH (Minister of Oil).

National Refining and Distribution Co (NRDC): f. 1992 to assume responsibility for refining, pipeline distribution, engineering, construction and research in the petroleum industry from the NIOC; Chair. and Man. Dir GHOLAMREZA AQAZADEH.

CO-OPERATIVES

Central Organization for Co-operatives of Iran: Teheran; in October 1985 there were 4,598 labour co-operatives, with a total membership of 703,814 and capital of 2,184.5m. rials, and 9,159 urban non-labour co-operatives, with a total membership of 262,118 and capital of 4,187.5m. rials.

Central Organization for Rural Co-operatives of Iran (CORC): Teheran; Man. Dir SAYED HASSAN MOTEVALLI-ZADEH.

The CORC was founded in 1963, and the Islamic Government of Iran has pledged that it will continue its educational, technical, commercial and credit assistance to rural co-operative societies and unions. At the end of the Iranian year 1363 (1984/85) there were 3,104 Rural Co-operative Societies with a total membership of 3,925,000 and share capital of 25,900m. rials. There were 181 Rural Co-operative Unions with 3,097 members and capital of 7,890m. rials.

Transport

RAILWAYS

Iranian Islamic Republic Railways: Shahid Kalantary Bldg, Railway Sq., Teheran 13185; tel. (21) 5641600; fax (21) 5650532; f. 1934; Man. Dir Eng. SADEGH AFSHAR; Vice-Pres. Sheikh ALIREZA MAHFOUZI (Admin. and Finance), Vice-Pres. FARROKH MOADELI (Technical and Infrastructure), Vice-Pres. HORMOZ GHOTBI (Operation and Traffic), Vice-Pres. Eng. MOHSAN POUR SEYED AGHAIE (Fleet Affairs).

The total length of main lines in the Iranian railway system, which is generally single-tracked, is 5,093 km (4,997 km of 1,435 mm gauge and 96 km of 1,676 mm gauge). The system includes the following main routes:

Trans-Iranian Railway runs 1,392 km from Bandar Turkman on the Caspian Sea in the north, through Teheran, and south to Bandar Imam Khomeini on the Persian Gulf.

Southern Line links Teheran to Khorramshahr via Qom, Arak, Dorood, Andimeshk and Ahwaz; 937 km.

Northern Line links Teheran to Gorgan via Garmsar, Firooz Kooh and Sari; 499 km.

Teheran–Kerman Line via Kashan, Yazd and Zarand; 1,106 km.

Teheran–Tabriz Line linking with the Azerbaijan Railway; 736 km.

Tabriz–Djulfa Electric Line: 146 km.

Garmsar–Meshed Line connects Teheran with Meshed via Semnan, Damghan, Shahrud and Nishabur; 812 km. A line is under construction to link Meshed with Sarakhs on the Turkmen border. A 768-km line linking Meshed with Bafq is also under construction.

Qom–Zahedan Line when completed will be an intercontinental line linking Europe and Turkey, through Iran, with India. Zahedan is situated 91.7 km west of the Balochistan frontier, and is the end of the Pakistani broad gauge railway. The section at present links Qom to Kerman via Kashan, Sistan, Yazd, Bafq and Zarand; 1,005 km. A branch line from Sistan was opened in 1971 via Isfahan to the steel mill at Zarrin Shahr; 112 km. A broad-gauge (1,976-mm) track connects Zahedan and Mirjaveh, on the border with Pakistan; 94 km.

Zahedan–Quetta (Pakistan) Line: 685km; not linked to national network.

Ahwaz–Bandar Khomeini Line connects Bandar Khomeini with the Trans-Iranian railway at Ahwaz; this line is due to be double-tracked; 112 km.

Azerbaijan Railway extends from Tabriz to Djulfa (146.5 km), meeting the Caucasian railways at the Azerbaijani frontier. Electrification works for this section have been completed and the electrified line was opened in April 1982. A standard gauge railway line (139 km) extends from Tabriz (via Sharaf–Khaneh) to the Turkish frontier at Razi.

Bandar Abbas–Bafq: construction of a 730-km double-track line to link Bandar Abbas and Bafq commenced in 1982. The first phase, linking Bafq to Sirjan (260 km), was opened in May 1990, and the second phase was opened in March 1995. The line provides access to the copper mines at Sarcheshmeh and the iron ore mines at Gole-Gohar.

Bafq–Chadormalou: a 130-km line connecting Bafq to the Chadormalou iron-ore mines is under construction.

Chadormalou–Tabas: a 220-km line is under construction.

Underground Railway

Teheran Urban and Suburban Railway Co: POB 4661, 37 Mir Emad St, Teheran 15875; tel. (21) 8740144; telex 215676; fax (21) 8740114; Chair. and Man. Dir MOHSEN HASHEMI: in May 1995 the Teheran Urban and Suburban Railway Co concluded agreements with three Chinese companies for the completion of the Teheran underground railway, on which work had originally commenced in 1978. It was reported that about 80% of the work on two lines (one, 34 km in length, running north to south, and a second, 20 km in length, running east to west) had been completed. Construction of a 121-km motorway began in January 1997. The road, which will run from Teheran to the Caspian Sea is funded privately, with expenses to be recouped through toll fees.

ROADS

In 1996 there were an estimated 162,000 km of roads, including 470 km of motorways, 22,900 km of highways, main or national roads and 43,500 km of secondary or regional roads; about 50% of the road network was paved. There is a paved highway (A1, 2,089 km) from Bazargan on the Turkish border to the Afghanistan border. The A2 highway runs 2,473 km from the Iraqi border to Mir Javeh on the Pakistan border.

Ministry of Roads and Transport: 49 Taleghani Ave, Teheran; tel. (21) 661034; telex 213381.

INLAND WATERWAYS

Principal waterways:

Lake Rezaiyeh (Lake Urmia) 80 km west of Tabriz in North-West Iran; and River Karun flowing south through the oilfields into the River Shatt al-Arab, thence to the head of the Persian Gulf near Abadan.

Lake Rezaiyeh: From Sharafkhaneh to Golmankhaneh there is a twice-weekly service of tugs and barges for transport of passengers and goods.

River Karun: Regular cargo service is operated by the Mesopotamia-Iran Corpn Ltd. Iranian firms also operate daily motor-boat services for passengers and goods.

SHIPPING

Persian Gulf: The main oil terminal is at Kharg Island. The principal commercial non-oil ports are Bandar Shahid Rajai (which was officially inaugurated in 1983 and handles 9m. of the 12m. tons of cargo passing annually through Iran's Persian Gulf ports), Bandar Khomeini, Bushehr, Bandar Abbas and Chah Bahar. A project to develop Bandar Abbas port, which predates the Islamic Revolution and was originally to cost IR 1,900,000m., is now in progress. Khorramshahr, Iran's biggest port, was put out of action in the war with Iraq, and Bushehr and Bandar Khomeini also sustained war damage, which has restricted their use. In August 1988 the Iranian news agency (IRNA) announced that Iran was to spend $200m. on the construction of six 'multi-purpose' ports on the Arabian and Caspian Seas, while ports which had been damaged in the war were to be repaired.

Caspian Sea: Principal port Bandar Anzali (formerly Bandar Pahlavi) and Bandar Nowshahr.

Ports and Shipping Organization: 751 Enghelab Ave, Teheran; tel. (21) 8809280; telex 212271; fax (21) 8804100; Man. Dir Eng. MUHAMMAD MADAD.

Principal Shipping Companies

Irano–Hind Shipping Co: POB 15875-4647, Sedaghat St, Valiassr Ave, Teheran; tel. (21) 2871184; telex 1182371; fax (21) 2057739; joint venture between the Islamic Republic of Iran and the Shipping Corpn of India; Chair. Capt. P. P. RADHAKRISHNAN.

Islamic Republic of Iran Shipping Lines (IRISL): POB 15875-4646, 675 North East Corner of Vali Asr Sq., Teheran; tel. (21) 8893801; telex 212286; fax (21) 889413; f. 1967; affiliated to the Ministry of Commerce Jan. 1980; liner services between the Persian (Arabian) Gulf and Europe, the Far East and South America and the Caspian Sea and Central Asia; Chair. and Man. Dir AHAD MOHAMMADI.

National Iranian Tanker Co: POB 16765-947, 67–8 Atefis St, Africa Ave, Teheran; tel. (21) 2229093; telex 213543; fax (21) 2223011; Chair. and Man. Dir MUHAMMAD SOURI.

CIVIL AVIATION

The two main international airports are Mehrabad (Teheran) and Abadan. An international airport was opened at Isfahan in July 1984 and the first international flight took place in March 1986. Work on a new international airport, 40 km south of Teheran, abandoned in 1979, resumed in the mid-1980s, and work on three others, at Tabas, Ardebil and Ilam was under way in mid-1990. The airports at Urumiyeh, Ahwaz, Bakhtaran, Sanandaz, Abadan, Hamadan and Shiraz were to be modernized and smaller ones constructed at Lar, Lamard, Rajsanjan, Barm, Kashan, Maragheh, Khoy, Sirjan and Abadeh. In early 1995 the Economic Co-operation Organization (ECO) agreed to establish a regional airline (Eco Air), based in Teheran. Construction of Imam Khomeini airport in

Teheran, anticipated to be one of the largest airports in the world, is due to begin in 1998.

Iran Air (Airline of the Islamic Republic of Iran): Iran Air Bldg, Mehrabad Airport, Teheran 13185-775; tel. (21) 979111; telex 212795; fax (21) 903248; f. 1962; serves the Middle East and Persian Gulf area, Europe, Asia and the Far East; Man. Dir AHMAD REZA KAZEMI.

Iran Asseman Airlines: POB 141748, Mehrabad Airport, Teheran 13145-1476; tel. (21) 6481498; telex 212575; fax (21) 6404318; f. after Islamic Revolution as result of merger of Air Taxi Co (f. 1958), Pars Air (f. 1969), Air Service Co (f. 1962) and Hoor Asseman; Man. Dir ALI ABEDZADEH; domestic routes and charter services.

Kish Air: POB 19395-4639, 215 Africa Highway, Teheran 19697; tel. (21) 8370856; telex 686630; fax (21) 2266630; f. 1991 under the auspices of the Kish Development Organization; serves Persian Gulf area, Teheran, Dubai, Frankfurt, London and Paris; Pres. A. GOLROUNIA.

Saha Airline: POB 13445-965, Teheran 13873; tel. (21) 6696200; fax (21) 6698016; f. 1990; weekly cargo service between Teheran and Singapore.

Tourism

Tourism has been adversely affected by political upheaval since the Revolution. Iran's chief attraction for tourists is its wealth of historical sites, notably Isfahan, Rasht, Tabriz, Susa and Persepolis. Some 362,000 international tourist arrivals were recorded in 1994, compared with 153,615 in 1990. Receipts from tourism in 1994 totalled US $153m. Tourism centres are currently administered by the State, through the Ministry of Culture and Islamic Guidance, although in late 1997 the ministry indicated its intention to transfer all tourism affairs to the private sector.

IRAQ

Introductory Survey

Location, Climate, Language, Religion, Flag, Capital

The Republic of Iraq is an almost land-locked state in western Asia, with a narrow outlet to the sea on the Persian (Arabian) Gulf. Its neighbours are Iran to the east, Turkey to the north, Syria and Jordan to the west, and Saudi Arabia and Kuwait to the south. The climate is extreme, with hot, dry summers, when temperatures may exceed 43°C (109°F), and cold winters, especially in the highlands. Summers are humid near the Persian Gulf. The official language is Arabic, spoken by about 80% of the population. About 15% speak Kurdish, while there is a small Turkoman-speaking minority. About 95% of the population are Muslims, of whom more than 50% belong to the Shi'i sect. However, the regime that came to power in 1968 has been dominated by members of the Sunni sect. The national flag (proportions 3 by 2) has three equal horizontal stripes, of red, white and black, with three five-pointed green stars on the central white stripe. The inscription 'Allahu Akhbar' ('God is Great') was added to the flag in January 1991. The capital is Baghdad.

Recent History

Iraq was formerly part of Turkey's Ottoman Empire. During the First World War (1914–18), when Turkey was allied with Germany, the territory was captured by British forces. In 1920 Iraq was placed under a League of Nations mandate, administered by the United Kingdom. In 1921 Amir Faisal ibn Hussain, a member of the Hashimi (Hashemite) dynasty of Arabia, was proclaimed King of Iraq, and his brother, Abdullah, was proclaimed Amir (Emir) of neighbouring Transjordan (later renamed Jordan), also administered by the United Kingdom under a League of Nations mandate. The two new monarchs were sons of Hussain (Hussein) ibn Ali, the Sharif of Mecca, who had proclaimed himself King of the Hijaz (now part of Saudi Arabia) in 1916. The British decision to nominate Hashemite princes to be rulers of Iraq and Transjordan was a reward for Hussain's co-operation in the wartime campaign against Turkey.

During its early years the new kingdom was faced with Kurdish revolts (1922–32) and with border disputes in the south. The leading personality in Iraqi political life under the monarchy was Gen. Nuri as-Said, who became Prime Minister in 1930 and held the office for seven terms, over a period of 28 years. He strongly supported Iraq's friendship with the United Kingdom and with the West in general. After prolonged negotiations, a 25-year Anglo-Iraqi Treaty of Alliance was signed in 1930. The British mandate ended on 3 October 1932, when Iraq became fully independent.

After the death of King Faisal I in 1933, the Iraqi monarchy remained pro-British in outlook, and in 1955 Iraq signed the Baghdad Pact, a British-inspired agreement on collective regional security. However, following the overthrow of King Faisal II (the grandson of King Faisal I) during a military revolution on 14 July 1958, which brought to power a left-wing nationalist regime headed by Brig. (later Lt-Gen.) Abd al-Karim Kassem, the 1925 Constitution was abolished, the legislature was dissolved, and in March 1959 Iraq withdrew from the Baghdad Pact (the last British air base being closed in the same year). Until his assassination in February 1963, during a coup by members of the armed forces, Kassem maintained a precarious and increasingly isolated position, opposed by Pan-Arabs, Kurds and other groups. The new Government of Col (later Field Marshal) Abd as-Salem Muhammad Aref was more pan-Arab in outlook and sought closer relations with the United Arab Republic (Egypt). Following his death in March 1966, President Aref was succeeded by his brother, Maj.-Gen. Abd ar-Rahman Muhammad Aref, who remained in power until his ouster by members of the Arab Renaissance (Baath) Socialist Party on 17 July 1968. Maj.-Gen. (later Field Marshal) Ahmad Hassan al-Bakr, a former Prime Minister, became President and Prime Minister, and supreme authority was vested in the Revolutionary Command Council (RCC), of which President al-Bakr was also Chairman.

Relations with the Syrian Government deteriorated after a younger generation of Baathists seized power in Syria in 1970. A bitter rivalry existed thereafter between Syrian and Iraqi Baathists. Relations with Syria improved in October 1978, when President Assad of Syria visited Baghdad. Plans were announced for eventual complete political and economic union of the two countries. On 16 July 1979 the Vice-Chairman of the RCC, Saddam Hussain, who had long exercised the real power in Iraq, replaced al-Bakr as Chairman, and as President of Iraq. A few days later, an attempted coup was reported and several members of the RCC were executed for their alleged part in the plot. The suspicion of Syrian implication in this affair resulted in the suspension of discussions concerning political union between Iraq and Syria, but economic co-operation continued.

During 1979 the Iraqi Communist Party broke away from the National Progressive Front (NPF), an alliance of Baathists, Kurdish groups and Communists, claiming that the Baathists were conducting a 'reign of terror'. In February 1980 Saddam Hussain announced a National Charter, reaffirming the principles of non-alignment. In June elections, the first since the 1958 revolution, were held for a 250-member, legislative National Assembly, followed in September by the first elections to a 50-member Kurdish Legislative Council in the Kurdish Autonomous Region.

Saddam Hussain retained his positions as Chairman of the RCC and Regional Secretary of the Baath Party, following its regional Congress in June 1982. A subsequent purge throughout the administration left him more firmly in control than before. Kurdish rebels became active in northern Iraq, occasionally supporting Iranian forces in Iran's war against Iraq (see below). Another threat was posed by the Supreme Council of the Islamic Revolution in Iraq (SCIRI), formed in Teheran in November 1982 by the exiled Shi'ite leader, Hojatoleslam Muhammad Baqir al-Hakim. An unsuccessful coup was believed to have taken place in Baghdad in October 1983, led by the recently dismissed head of intelligence, Barzan Takriti (the President's half-brother), and a number of senior army officers, who were later reported to have been executed. Iraq's Shi'ite community, however, was not attracted by the Islamic fundamentalism of Ayatollah Khomeini of Iran, remaining loyal to Iraq and its Sunni President, while the opposition of Iranian-backed terrorist groups (such as the Shi'ite fundamentalist Ad-Da'wa al-Islamiya group, which repeatedly attempted to assassinate Saddam Hussain) had no significant effect.

In the second-half of the 1980s Saddam Hussain consolidated his control over the country and sought to retain the loyalty of Iraq's Shi'ite community. In 1988, as a reward for its role in the war against Iran, the President announced a programme of political reforms, including the introduction of a multi-party system, and in January 1989 declared that these would be incorporated into a new permanent constitution. In April 1989 elections were held to the 250-seat National Assembly, in which a quarter of the candidates were members of the Baath Party and the remainder either independent or members of the NPF. More than 50% of the newly-elected deputies were reported to be Baath members. In July the National Assembly approved a new draft constitution, under the terms of which a 50-member Consultative Assembly was to be established; both institutions would assume the duties of the RCC, which would be abolished after a presidential election.

During the 1980s representatives of Iraq's 2.5m.–3m. Kurds demanded greater autonomy (despite the formation in 1970 of the Kurdish Autonomous Region, where they exercised limited powers of self-determination). Resources were repeatedly diverted from the war with Iran to control Kurdish rebellion in the north-east of the country. Saddam Hussain sought an accommodation with the Kurds, and a series of discussions began in December 1983, after a cease-fire had been agreed with Jalal Talibani, the leader of the main Kurdish opposition party in Iraq, the Patriotic Union of Kurdistan (PUK). These discussions did not include the other main Kurdish group, the Democratic Party of Kurdistan (DPK), led by Masoud Barzani. The collapse of negotiations in May 1984 frustrated hopes for a government of national unity, including the PUK and the Iraqi Communist Party. However, it was reported that Saddam Hussain persisted, informally, in trying to persuade the PUK to join the NPF. In January 1985 armed conflict was resumed in Kurdistan between PUK guerrillas and government troops. In February the PUK rejected the offer of an amnesty for President Saddam Hussain's political opponents, at home and abroad, and fighting continued, with Kurdish and Iranian forces repeatedly collaborating in raids against Iraqi military and industrial targets.

In February 1988 DPK and PUK guerrillas (assisted by Iranian forces) made inroads into government-controlled territory in Iraqi Kurdistan. In March the Iraqi Government retaliated by using chemical weapons against the Kurdish town of Halabja. In May the DPK and the PUK announced the formation of a coalition of six organizations to continue the struggle for Kurdish self-determination and to co-operate militarily with Iran. The cease-fire in the Iran-Iraq War in August allowed Iraq to divert more troops and equipment to Kurdistan, and to launch a new offensive to overrun guerrilla bases near the borders with Iran and Turkey, during which chemical weapons were allegedly used, forcing Kurdish civilians and fighters to escape across the borders. By mid-September there were reported to be more than 200,000 Kurdish refugees in Iran and Turkey. In that month, with its army effectively in control of the border with Turkey, the Iraqi Government offered a full amnesty to all Iraqi Kurds inside and outside the country, excluding only Jalal Talibani, the leader of the PUK. It also began to evacuate inhabitants of the Kurdish Autonomous Region to the interior of Iraq, as part of a plan to create a 30-km-wide uninhabited 'security zone' along the whole of Iraq's border with Iran and Turkey. Kurdish opposition groups, however, claimed that the evacuations were in fact forcible deportations of Kurds to areas more susceptible to government control. By October 1989, despite international censure of the evacuation programme, the 'security zone' was reported to be in place, prompting the PUK to announce a campaign of urban guerrilla warfare against the Government throughout Iraq. In September elections to the legislative council of the Kurdish Autonomous Region took place.

Relations with Iran, precarious for many years, developed into full-scale war in September 1980. The Algiers Agreement between Iran and Iraq, signed in 1975, had defined the southern border between the two countries as a line along the middle of the Shatt al-Arab waterway. In the ensuing years, however, Iraq had become increasingly dissatisfied with the 1975 agreement; and also desired the withdrawal of Iranian forces from Abu Musa and the Tumb islands, which Iran had occupied in 1971. The Iranian Revolution of 1979 exacerbated these grievances. Conflict soon developed over Arab demands for autonomy in Iran's Khuzestan region (named 'Arabistan' by Arabs), which Iran accused Iraq of encouraging. Iraq's Sunni leadership was suspicious of Shi'ite Iran, and feared that dissent might be provoked among its own Shi'ites, who formed more than 50% of the population. Border disputes occurred in the summer of 1980, and more extensive fighting began after Iran ignored Iraqi diplomatic efforts, demanding the withdrawal of Iranian forces from the border area of Zain ul-Qos in Diali province. Iraq maintained that this area should have been returned under the 1975 agreement. In September 1980 Iraq abrogated the agreement, and Iraqi forces advanced into Iran. Fierce Iranian resistance brought about a military deadlock, which lasted until the spring of 1982, when Iranian counter-offensives led to the retaking of the port of Khorramshahr in May and the withdrawal of Iraqi troops from the territory which they had taken in 1980. In July 1982 the Iranian army crossed into Iraq. (For a fuller account of the Iran-Iraq War (1980–88), see Iran, Recent History, p. 1721).

In 1984 the balance of military power in the continuing war with Iran moved in Iraq's favour, and its financial position improved, as the USA and the USSR, both officially neutral, provided aid. (Iraq and the USA re-established full diplomatic relations in November 1984, more than 17 years after they had been severed by Iraq following the Arab-Israeli war of 1967.) In April 1985 the UN Secretary-General, Javier Pérez de Cuéllar, visited both Teheran and Baghdad, in an attempt to establish a basis on which peace negotiations between Iran and Iraq could begin. Iraq insisted that it was interested only in a permanent cease-fire and immediate, direct negotiations with Iran; while Iran continued to demand the removal of Saddam Hussain, an Iraqi admission of responsibility for starting the war, and the payment of reparations.

In early 1988 Iraqi forces began to recapture land occupied by Iran, and in July they crossed into Iran for the first time since 1986. In the same month, Iran announced its unconditional acceptance of UN Security Council Resolution 598, and by August a cease-fire was in force, monitored by the UN Iran–Iraq Military Observer Group (UNIIMOG). However, negotiations on the full implementation of the Resolution made little progress until Iraq's invasion of Kuwait in August 1990 (see below), at which point Saddam Hussain abruptly sought a formal peace agreement with Iran, by accepting all the claims that Iran had pursued since the cease-fire, including the reinstatement of the Algiers Agreement of 1975, dividing the Shatt al-Arab. In September 1997 Iraq reopened its border with Iran, permitting, for the first time in 17 years, Iranian pilgrims to visit Shi'ite Muslim shrines. However, tensions arose later in the month after Iranian military forces attacked two bases of an Iraqi-based opposition group, the Mujahidin-e-Khalq. Consequently both Iranian and Iraqi forces violated the air-exclusion zone (see below). In response, the USA deployed an aircraft carrier and six other warships in the Persian (Arabian) Gulf in order to deter further unauthorized flights. In December it was announced that bilateral talks between the two countries were to be held in the near future. Later in the month the Iranian Ministry of Foreign Affairs announced that Iran would transport humanitarian aid from foreign countries to Iraq, in accordance with UN resolutions.

In mid-1990 the Iraqi Government criticized countries (principally Kuwait and the UAE) which had persistently produced petroleum in excess of the quotas imposed by OPEC. Iraq also accused Kuwait of violating the Iraqi border in order to secure petroleum resources, and suggested that Kuwait should waive Iraq's debt repayments. On the eve of an OPEC ministerial meeting, held in Geneva in July, Iraq mustered troops on its border with Kuwait. At the meeting, Kuwait and the UAE agreed to reduce their petroleum production, and it was decided that the minimum price of crude petroleum should be increased. Direct negotiations between Iraq and Kuwait began at the end of July, with the aim of resolving their disputes over territory and Iraqi debt. The discussions failed, however, and on 2 August Iraqi forces invaded Kuwait, taking control of the country and establishing a provisional 'free government'. On 8 August Iraq announced its formal annexation of Kuwait, claiming that its forces had entered Kuwait at the invitation of insurgents, who had overthrown the Kuwaiti Government.

The UN Security Council responded to Iraq's action by unanimously adopting, on the day of the invasion, Resolution 660, which demanded the immediate and unconditional withdrawal of Iraqi forces from Kuwait. Subsequent resolutions imposed mandatory economic sanctions against Iraq and occupied Kuwait, and declared Iraq's annexation of Kuwait to be null and void. On 7 August 1990, at the request of King Fahd of Saudi Arabia, the US Government dispatched troops and aircraft to Saudi Arabia, in order to secure that country's border with Kuwait against a possible Iraqi attack: other countries quickly lent their support to 'Operation Desert Shield', as it was known, and a multinational force was formed to defend Saudi Arabia.

At a meeting of the Arab League, on the day after the Iraqi invasion of Kuwait, 14 of the 21 members condemned the invasion and demanded an unconditional withdrawal by Iraq, and a week later 12 member states voted to send an Arab deterrent force to the Persian (Arabian) Gulf. However, there were widespread demonstrations of popular support for Iraq, notably among the Palestinian population of Jordan and in the Maghreb states. 'Operation Desert Shield', despite being endorsed by the UN, was perceived in parts of the Arab world and elsewhere as a US-led campaign to secure US interests in the Gulf region.

Diplomatic efforts to achieve a peaceful solution to the Gulf crisis all foundered on Iraq's refusal to withdraw its forces from Kuwait. Diplomacy was initially complicated by Iraq's detention of foreign citizens as hostages (keeping them in places of strategic importance in Iraq, in order to deter an attack), but by early December 1990 all had been released. In late November the UN Security Council adopted a resolution (No. 678) which permitted member states to use 'all necessary means' to enforce the withdrawal of Iraqi forces from Kuwait, if they had not left by 15 January 1991. 'Operation Desert Storm'—in effect, war with Iraq—began on the night of 16–17 January, with air attacks on Baghdad by the multinational force. The Iraqi air force offered little effective resistance, and by the end of January the allies had achieved supremacy in the air. In January and

February Iraq launched *Scud* missiles against Saudi Arabia and Israel, but failed to provoke Israel into retaliating, which would have disrupted the multinational force (since it would have been politically impossible for any Arab state to fight alongside Israel against Iraq). In February Iraq formally severed diplomatic relations with Egypt, France, Italy, Saudi Arabia, Syria, the United Kingdom and the USA. In that month two peace plans, proposed by the Government of the USSR, were accepted by Iraq, but rejected by its opponents, because the plans did not comply with the UN Security Council resolutions on unconditional withdrawal from Kuwait. During the night of 23–24 February the multinational force began a ground offensive for the liberation of Kuwait: Iraqi troops were quickly defeated, and surrendered in large numbers. A cease-fire was declared by the US Government on 28 February. Iraq agreed to renounce its claim to Kuwait, to release prisoners of war, and to comply with the relevant UN Security Council resolutions.

Within Iraq the war was followed by domestic unrest: in early March 1991 rebel forces, including Shi'ite Muslims and disaffected soldiers, were reported to have taken control of Basra and other southern cities, but the rebellion was soon crushed by troops loyal to Saddam Hussain. In the north, Kurdish separatists overran a large area of Kurdistan, and in late March it was reported that Kurdish rebels had gained control of Kirkuk. The various Kurdish factions appeared to have achieved greater unity of purpose through their alliance, in May 1988, in the Kurdistan Iraqi Front (KIF). Rather than seeking the creation of an independent Kurdish state, the KIF claimed that the objective of the northern insurrection was the full implementation of a 15-article peace plan which had been concluded between Kurdish leaders and the Iraqi Government in 1970.

Lacking military support from the UN-authorized multinational force, the Kurdish guerrillas were unable to resist the onslaught of the Iraqi armed forces, which were redeployed northwards as soon as they had crushed the uprising in southern Iraq. Fearing genocide, an estimated 1m.–2m. Kurds fled before the Iraqi army across the northern mountains into Turkey and Iran. By mid-June 1991 the UN and the Iraqi Government had negotiated a 'memorandum of understanding', whereby the UN was permitted to establish humanitarian centres ('safe havens' for the Kurdish population) on Iraqi territory for a period of six months. The 'memorandum of understanding' was subsequently extended.

In late April 1991 the leader of the PUK, Jalal Talibani, announced that President Saddam Hussain had agreed, in principle, to implement the provisions of the Kurdish peace plan of 1970. However, negotiations subsequently became deadlocked over the delineation of the Kurdish Autonomous Region, in which Kurdish groups wished the city of Kirkuk to be included. In late October, in the absence of any negotiated agreement on an 'autonomous Kurdistan', the Iraqi Government was reported to have withdrawn all services from the area, effectively subjecting it to an economic blockade. The KIF proceeded to organize elections to a 105-member Kurdish national assembly, and for a paramount Kurdish leader. The result of the elections to the Assembly, held on 19 May 1992 and in which virtually the whole of the estimated 1.1m.-strong electorate participated, was that the DPK and the PUK were entitled to an almost equal number of seats. None of the smaller Kurdish parties achieved representation, and the DPK and the PUK subsequently agreed to share equally the seats in the new Assembly. The election for an overall Kurdish leader was inconclusive, Masoud Barzani, the leader of the DPK receiving 47.5% of the votes cast; and Jalal Talibani, the leader of the PUK, 44.9%. A run-off election was to be held at a future date.

In March 1993 the Kurdish Cabinet that had been elected in July 1992 was dismissed by the Kurdish National Assembly for its failure effectively to deal with the crisis in the region. A new Cabinet was appointed at the end of April 1993. In late December armed conflict was reported to have taken place between fighters of the PUK and the Islamic League of Kurdistan (ILK), also known as the Islamic Movement of Iraqi Kurdistan (IMIK). The two parties were reported to have signed a peace agreement in February 1994, following mediation by the Iraqi National Congress (INC). More serious armed conflict, between fighters belonging to the PUK and the DPK, was reported in May to have led to the division of the northern Kurdish-controlled enclave into two zones. The two parties were reported to have concluded a peace agreement in early June, but fighting broke out again in August. In late November the PUK and the DPK were reported to have concluded another peace agreement, which provided for a census of the region and for the holding of elections in May 1995. A further outbreak of fighting in late December was succeeded by another short-lived peace agreement. In early January 1995 fighting broke out again, prompting Saddam Hussain to offer, on 16 January, to mediate in the dispute, and the United Kingdom to warn that the conflict might provide Iraq with a pretext to reassert control over the north. In March Turkish armed forces attacked bases of the Kurdish Workers' Party (PKK) in the Kurdish enclave. A further deployment of Turkish troops across the border with northern Iraq took place in July. In June the IMIK withdrew from the INC, and in July there was renewed fighing between PUK and DPK forces, prompting attempts to mediate by the USA and Iran. As a result of this resumption of factional hostilities, elections to the Kurdish National Assembly were postponed and the mandate of the existing Kurdish Legislative Council was extended for a further 12 months. Peace negotiations sponsored by the USA began in Dublin, Ireland, in August 1995, but collapsed in mid-September. Subsequent negotiations in Teheran, Iran, in October led to the signing of an agreement by the DPK and the PUK to hold elections to the Kurdish National Assembly in May 1996. US-sponsored negotiations between the two parties resumed in northern Iraq in November. The USA and Turkey were concerned at reports that the armed wing of the pro-Iranian SCIRI had begun to deploy inside the Kurdish enclave. Turkey continued to support the DPK in its attempt to expel PKK fighters from the Kurdish enclave. This support was believed to have encouraged the PUK to seek support from Iran.

In February 1996 Turkey and NATO agreed to continue 'Operation Provide Comfort' (an air surveillance programme under which US, British and French aircraft, based in Turkey, monitored the exclusion zone) in order to protect the Kurdish enclave in areas of Iraq north of latitude 36°N. (The operation had become controversial in Turkey, owing to the presence of PKK bases in the Kurdish enclave.) In early 1996 Jalal Talibani, the leader of the PUK, offered to participate in peace negotiations with the DPK, and to take part in new elections to the Kurdish National Assembly. Meanwhile, the USA continued to try to mediate an agreement between the DPK and the PUK on the demilitarization of Arbil. On 17 August continued hostilities between the DPK and the PUK escalated, the PUK contesting the DPK's monopoly of duties levied on Turkish traders. Further US-sponsored peace negotiations in late August were unsuccessful, and on 31 August the deployment of Iraqi armed forces inside the Kurdish area of northern Iraq provoked a new international crisis. Iraq claimed that the deployment had been made in response to a request for assistance by the DPK. (For consequences of the Iraqi intervention, see below.) In early September the DPK captured the towns of Degala, Koy Sinjaq and Sulaimaniya, thereby gaining control of all three Kurdish provinces. The Iraqi Government, meanwhile, announced the restoration of Iraqi sovereignty over Kurdistan and offered an amnesty to its Kurdish opponents. In late September the DPK formed a DPK-led coalition government comprising, among others, the IMIK, the Kurdistan Communist Party and representatives of the northern Assyrian and Turkoman communities. In mid-October PUK fighters were reported to have recaptured much of the terrain they had ceded to the DPK, and to be approaching the town of Arbil, having regained control of Sulaimaniya, and Halabja. The PUK claimed that it would not, however, attempt to recapture Arbil because the town remained under the protection of Iraqi armed forces. Offers by both the Iraqi and the Iranian Governments to mediate in the conflict between the PUK and the DPK were reported to have been rejected in favour of US diplomacy. A new round of US-sponsored peace talks commenced in Ankara, Turkey, in late October, during which a cease-fire was negotiated.

In December 1996 Turkey requested the termination of 'Operation Provide Comfort' and it was subsequently replaced by a new air surveillance programme, 'Northern Watch', which was conducted by British, Turkish and US forces. France did not participate, however, since 'Northern Watch' contained no provisions for the supply of humanitarian aid. In late December Turkish troops recommenced military manoeuvres in Kurdistan, and in May 1997 more than 10,000 Turkish troops entered the region, where they launched a major military offensive against PKK bases. The incursion was condemned by Iraq and by several other Arab states. The UN Secretary-General, Kofi Annan, demanded the withdrawal of Turkish troops from the area, expressing concern that their presence might obstruct the supply of food to the Kurdish enclave. In defiance of Annan's demand, more Turkish troops were deployed in Kurdistan in September, attacking PKK bases in the Zab, Gharadag, Shivi and Zakho regions. In mid-October the crisis appeared to subside and the withdrawal of Turkish troops commenced. However, later in the month Turkey resumed air attacks on PKK bases.

In March 1997 the DPK had withdrawn from the US-sponsored peace negotiations. Although the DPK and the PUK affirmed their commitment to the peace process, each party accused the other of violating the cease-fire. In early October Turkish, British and US representatives met the leaders of the two parties in an attempt to defuse the escalating tensions. Diplomatic efforts failed, however, and on 12 October the PUK launched its strongest military assault against the DPK for a year, effectively terminating the cease-fire. In response to the violence, Western diplomats convened with representatives from the PUK and the DPK in Ankara, Turkey, and mediated a 72-hour cease-fire, beginning on 17 October. The cease-fire was extended for a further 24 hours on 21 October. Fighting resumed later in the month, however, and the PUK accused Turkey of assisting the forces of the DPK, which claimed to have regained most of the territory that had been lost to the PUK during the recent hostilities. Turkey denied the PUK's claim, insisting that its military campaign was directed solely against the PKK. In November Turkey claimed that its armed forces had suppressed the PKK and announced plans to withdraw from Kurdistan. In December, however, the Iraqi Ministry of Foreign Affairs declared that some 20,000 Turkish troops remained in the region, and clashes between them and their PKK counterparts continued into early 1998.

Following Iraq's defeat by the US-led coalition forces, Saddam Hussain strengthened his control over the country by placing family members and his closest supporters in the most important government positions. In early September 1991 the Baath Party held its 10th Congress—the first such Congress since 1982—at which Saddam Hussain was re-elected Secretary-General of the Party's powerful Regional Command. Saddam Hussain attempted to bolster his domestic popularity through continued defiant rhetoric and confrontation with the UN over the dispatching of UN inspectors to monitor the elimination of Iraq's weapons of mass destruction, as stipulated by UN Security Council Resolution 687. A reshuffle of the Council of Ministers in early September 1993 was interpreted by opposition sources as a sign of a further decline in support for Saddam Hussain's regime.

In May 1994, facing a deepening economic crisis, Saddam Hussain himself assumed the post of Prime Minister in a reshuffle of the Council of Ministers. In January 1995 a comprehensive reorganization of military ranks took place, apparently as the result of an unsuccessful attempt to stage a military *coup d'état* in the same month. In March another attempted coup—organized this time by the former head of Iraqi military intelligence and supported by Kurdish insurgents in the north and Shi'ite rebels in the south—was reported to have been suppressed. A further reorganization of military personnel resulted in the appointment of a new Chief of the General Staff in April 1995. Reports of a substantial insurrection by the armed forces at the Abu Ghraid army base, near Baghdad, in mid-June were strongly denied by the Government. However, there was evidence to suggest that an uprising had been organized by members of the Sunni Dulaimi clan, with the support of the élite 14 July battalion of the Iraqi army. There was a minor reorganization of the Council of Ministers in late June, and in July a new Minister of Defence and a new Chief of the General Staff were appointed. In August further significant divisions within Saddam Hussain's power base became apparent following the defection to Jordan of two sons-in-law of the President (including the Minister of Industry and Minerals, Hussain Kamel) and their families. In an apparent attempt to re-establish domestic and international recognition of Saddam Hussain's mandate, a meeting of the RCC was convened on 7 September and an interim amendment of the Constitution was approved whereby the elected Chairman of the RCC would automatically assume the Presidency of the Republic, subject to the approval of the National Assembly and endorsement by national plebiscite. Saddam Hussain's candidature was duly approved by the National Assembly on 10 September. The referendum for which the amendment to the Constitution provided took place on 15 October and 99.96% of the votes cast in a turnout of 99.47% of the estimated 8m.-strong electorate were in favour of the President continuing in office. The international community, however, reacted with incredulity to this degree of support. In Iraq the result of the referendum was declared null and void in a statement issued by nine opposition groups. Further reorganizations of the Council of Ministers took place in November and December.

The deaths in Baghdad, on 23 February 1996, of the two sons-in-law of the President, Hussain and Saddam Kamel, who had defected to Jordan in August 1995, and returned, unexpectedly, to Iraq in February 1996, provoked international condemnation. While some Iraqi media reported that the two men had been killed by kinsmen seeking to restore their family's honour, outside of Iraq it was widely believed that the two men had been executed by the Iraqi intelligence services.

In December 1996 Saddam Hussain's son, Uday, survived an assassination attempt, but sustained serious injuries. Although both the Sunni Dulaimi clan and Ad-Da'wa al-Islamiya claimed responsibility for the attack, it was widely reported that the shooting was engineered by a former army officer whose uncle, Gen. Olmer al-Hazaa, had been executed in 1990 after denouncing the Iraqi regime. In late January 1997 Western newspapers reported that the Iraqi President had placed his wife under house arrest after she criticized him for failing to obtain adequate medical provisions for Uday. The President's family denied the claim. In March an Iraqi opposition source alleged that Saddam Hussain had ordered the execution of 197 prisoners in retaliation for Uday's injuries. In the previous month it had been reported that the President's other son, Qusai, had twice been targeted by assassins, but had escaped injury on both occasions.

The first elections to the Iraqi National Assembly since 1989 took place on 24 March 1996. Two hundred and twenty of the 250 seats in the Assembly were contested by 689 candidates, all of whom had received the prior approval of a government selection committee. (The remaining 30 seats were reserved for representatives of the Autonomous Regions of Arbil, D'hok and As-Sulaimaniya and were filled by presidential decree.) It was estimated that some 90% of Iraq's 8m.-strong electorate had participated in the elections. Groups opposed to the Government, such as the London-based INC, denounced the elections from abroad, demanding 'suffrage for all Iraqis' instead. In October the Minister of Culture and Information was replaced in the Council of Ministers and the Baath Party elected two new members to its Regional Command. In August 1997 Hamid Yusuf Hammadi was replaced as Minister of Culture and Information by Humam Abd al-Khaliq Abd al-Ghafur.

One consequence of the conflicts over Iraqi compliance with UN Security Council Resolution 687 (see above) was that there was no easing of the economic sanctions that were first imposed on Iraq on 6 August 1990, under the terms of Resolution 661. In May 1991 the UN Security Council decided to establish a compensation commission (UNCC) for victims of Iraqi aggression (both governments and individuals), to be financed by a levy (subsequently fixed at 30%) on Iraqi petroleum revenues. In August the UN Security Council adopted Resolution 706 (subsequently approved in Resolution 712 in September), proposing that Iraq should be allowed to sell petroleum worth up to US $1,600m. over a six-month period, the revenue from which would be paid into an escrow account controlled by the UN. Part of the sum thus realized was to be made available to Iraq for the purchase of food, medicines and supplies for essential civilian needs. Iraq rejected the terms proposed by the UN for the resumption of exports of petroleum, and in February 1992 withdrew from further negotiations. In April the UN reiterated its demand that Iraq should comply with the terms of Security Council Resolutions 706 and 712 before resuming petroleum exports. On 2 October the UN Security Council adopted Resolution 778, permitting it to confiscate up to $500m.-worth of oil-related Iraqi assets.

In response to renewed attacks by Iraqi government forces on southern Iraqi Shi'ite communities and on the inhabitants of Iraq's southern marshlands, on 26 August 1992 the US, British, French and Russian Governments announced their decision to establish a zone in southern Iraq, south of latitude 32°N, from which all Iraqi fixed-wing aircraft would be excluded. The UN Secretary-General subsequently indicated UN Security Council support for the measure. In late December 1992 a combat aircraft shot down an Iraqi fighter which had allegedly entered the exclusion zone, and subsequent Iraqi military activity within the exclusion zone provoked attacks by Western forces on targets in southern Iraq on 13 January 1993. A ban which the Iraqi Government had imposed on UN flights into the country was cited as a further justification for the attacks. Further air raids by Western forces on targets in northern and southern Iraq took place in late January. In late May, in response to the deployment of Iraqi armed forces close to the UN-authorized exclusion zone north of latitude 36°N, the USA warned Iraq that it might suffer military reprisals in the event of any incursion into the Kurdish-held north. In late June the USA launched an attack against intelligence headquarters in Baghdad, in retaliation for Iraq's role in an alleged conspiracy to assassinate former US President Bush in Kuwait in April. In early July Iraqi armed forces were reported to have renewed the Government's offensive against the inhabitants of the marshlands of southern Iraq, and the INC urged the UN Security Council to send emergency supplies of food and medicine to communities there. In September hundreds of inhabitants of Iraq's southern marshlands were reported to have been killed by government forces using chemical weapons.

Meanwhile, Iraq had continued to reject the terms of UN Security Council Resolution 715, which governed the long-term monitoring of its weapons programmes, and further sessions of negotiations between Iraq and the UN on the resumption of petroleum exports had ended inconclusively. In October 1993, however, the Government agreed to UN demands that it should release details of its weapons suppliers; and in late November it agreed to the provisions for weapons-monitoring contained in Resolution 715. However, it was clear by the end of December that neither the UN Security Council nor the US Government would be willing to allow even a partial easing of sanctions until Iraq had demonstrated a sustained commitment to the dismantling of its weapons systems. Moreover, the US Government insisted that Iraq must first also comply with all other relevant UN resolutions, recognize the newly-demarcated border with Kuwait and cease the repression of its Kurdish and southern Shi'ite communities.

From March 1994 the Iraqi Government engaged in a campaign of diplomacy to obtain the lifting of economic sanctions, and in mid-July the first signs emerged of a division within the UN Security Council regarding their continuation. Russia, France and the People's Republic of China were all in favour of acknowledging Iraq's increased co-operation with UN agencies, but were unable to obtain the agreement of the other permanent members of the Council. On 6 October 1994 the head of the UN Special Commission on Iraq (UNSCOM, responsible for inspecting the country's weapons) announced that a system for monitoring Iraqi defence industries was ready to begin operating. On the same day, however, there was a large movement of Iraqi forces towards the border with Kuwait, apparently to draw attention to Iraq's demands for swift action to ease the sanctions. On 10 October Iraq announced that it would withdraw its troops northward, and on 15 October the Security Council adopted a resolution (No. 949) demanding that the withdrawal of all Iraqi forces recently transferred to southern Iraq be completed immediately; and stipulating that Iraq must not 'utilize its military or any other forces in a hostile or provocative manner to threaten its neighbours or the UN operations in Iraq'. On 10 November the Iraqi National Assembly voted to recognize Kuwait within the border defined by the UN in April 1992.

On 7 January 1995 the UN Secretary-General offered to resume dialogue with Iraq on a partial lifting of the economic sanctions. On 12 January the UN Security Council renewed the sanctions in force against Iraq for a further 60 days, although France and Russia were reported to have argued within the Security Council for a partial lifting of sanctions, provided that Iraq co-operated fully with the UN weapons-monitoring programme. The UN sanctions in force against Iraq were renewed for a further 60 days in March. In April the Iraqi Government rejected as a violation of its sovereignty a revised UN proposal (contained in Security Council Resolution 986) for the partial resumption of exports of Iraqi petroleum. Iraqi attempts to secure an end to the sanctions had suffered a serious reversal in February when the head of the UNSCOM announced that the Iraqi authorities had failed satisfactorily to account for material used in the manufacture of biological weapons, known to have been imported by Iraq in 1988. Further concerns regarding the use of these stockpiles were expressed by the UNSCOM in April, May and June. After a further renewal of the economic sanctions in early July, the Iraqi Minister of Foreign Affairs, Muhammad Saeed as-Sahaf insisted that the UNSCOM should complete its report and promote an end to the sanctions by the end of August if it wished to avoid the complete cessation of co-operation from the Iraqi authorities. By mid-August, however, the Government had adopted a more conciliatory stance, and it was reported that crucial new information regarding Iraq's military programme had been made available to the UN's officers. Sanctions were renewed for a further 60 days in early November.

In late January 1996 it was announced that talks between the UN and Iraq on the sale of Iraqi petroleum (on the basis of Resolution 986) were to recommence. On 20 May Iraq accepted the UN's terms governing a resumption of crude petroleum sales. At the insistence of the USA and the United Kingdom, the terms stipulated that Iraq should not be involved in the distribution to the Kurdish governorates of humanitarian aid purchased with funds realized. The memorandum of understanding signed by Iraq and the UN, with reference to UN Resolution 986, permitted Iraq to sell some 700,000 barrels per day (b/d) of petroleum over a period of six months, after which the UN would review the situation before deciding whether sales should continue for a further six months. Of every US $1,000m. realized through the sales, $300m. would be paid into the UN reparations fund; $30m.–$50m. would contribute to the costs of UN operations in Iraq; and $130m.–$150m. would go towards funding the UN's humanitarian operations in Iraq's Kurdish governorates. Remaining revenues would be used for the purchase and distribution, under close UN supervision, of humanitarian goods in Iraq. While Iraq heralded the signing of the memorandum of understanding as the beginning of the dismantlement of the economic sanctions imposed on it since August 1990, the position of the UN, as detailed in resolutions of the Security Council, remained that the embargo on sales of Iraqi petroleum would not be fully lifted until the UNSCOM was satisfied that all of the country's weapons of mass destruction had been accounted for and disposed of.

In March 1996 the UN renewed the sanctions in force against Iraq for a further period of 60 days. The head of the UNSCOM had reported to the Security Council his concern that Iraq might still be engaged in the development of prohibited weapons systems, and might be concealing biological missile warheads from the UN inspectorate. Incidents of non-co-operation between the Iraqi authorities and UN weapons inspection teams were reported in March, June and July. In July the UN sanctions committee announced procedures governing renewed sales of Iraqi petroleum. However, these terms had to be approved by all 15 members of the UN Security Council and their endorsement was delayed by the USA's insistence that they should include more stringent monitoring. A revised version finally received unanimous approval on 7 August. At the beginning of September, however, the implementation of Resolution 986 was postponed indefinitely in response to the deployment of Iraqi armed forces inside the Kurdish 'safe haven' in northern Iraq, where they assisted the forces of the DPK in assaults on the PUK-held Kurdish towns of Arbil and Sulaimaniya. Other retaliatory measures included US missile attacks on targets in southern Iraq, and the extension of the southern air exclusion zone from latitude 32°N to latitude 33°N in order to incorporate some parts of surburban Baghdad. The threat of further retaliatory US action subsided on 13 September when Iraq announced that it would suspend attacks on allied aircraft enforcing the air exclusion zones. There was, in any case, little support among the international community for further US retaliation, and the USA itself appeared not to wish to provoke further confrontation. In April 1997 Iraqi helicopters violated the southern air exclusion zone in order to transport a group of allegedly infirm Iraqi pilgrims to Iraq's border with Saudi Arabia. The US denounced the mission but did not enforce any punitive measures.

At the beginning of October 1996 the UNSCOM rejected Iraq's 'full, final and complete disclosures on its weapons programmes'. At about the same time the US Treasury was reported to have granted its approval for the opening of an escrow account with the New York branch of the Banque Nationale de Paris, but the implementation of Resolution 986 was now dependent on the satisfaction of the UN Secretary-General with stability in northern Iraq and the approval by the UN sanctions committee of a formula fixing the price of Iraqi crude petroleum to be sold. At the beginning of November the UN Security Council renewed the economic sanctions in force against Iraq for a further period of 60 days. In February 1997 Iraq permitted the UN to inspect key parts of missile engines outside the country. Despite signs of renewed co-operation, in April the head of the UNSCOM reiterated concerns that Iraq was not fully co-operating with its weapons inspectors. Relations between Iraq and the UNSCOM deteriorated in mid-June after the Security Council accused Iraq of obstructing UN inspectors' flights over Iraqi territory. Later in the month Iraq denied the UNSCOM access to three military sites. The UN reported renewed co-operation by Iraq in July, following the inauguration of Richard Butler as the new chairman of the UNSCOM. Relations deteriorated in October, however, after Butler submitted his initial report to the UN Security Council, claiming that, although some progress had been made in inspecting Iraqi missiles, Iraq had failed to produce a credible account of its biological, chemical and nuclear warfare programmes and was continuing to hinder the UNSCOM's work. Subsequently, within the UN Security Council, the USA and the UK proposed a resolution to prohibit Iraqi officials considered to be responsible for obstructing weapons inspections from leaving the country. France and Russia objected to the draft resolution but approved a revised version to impose a travel ban on Iraqi officials in April 1998 should non-co-operation with the UNSCOM continue. At the same time sanctions against Iraq were renewed for a further 60 days.

In late October 1997 the RCC criticized the high proportion of UNSCOM personnel supplied by the USA, claiming that they were opposed to the lifting of sanctions. Iraq demanded that all such personnel should leave the country by 5 November. This deadline was extended by one week, however, in order to allow a UN mission to travel to Baghdad in an attempt to resolve the dispute. Negotiations proved unsuccessful and therefore the UN Security Council unanimously adopted a resolution (No. 1137) which immediately activated the travel ban proposed earlier. The resolution also stipulated that Iraq should retract its decision to expel US personnel and stated that further Iraqi intransigence regarding weapons inspections would result in the suspension of the 60-day sanctions review until April 1998 and, furthermore, possibly provoke military action. Nevertheless, Iraq refused to rescind its decision and US weapons inspectors were forced to leave the country on 13 November. In response to the escalating crisis, both the USA and the UK ordered military reinforcements into the region, with both Kuwait and Bahrain reluctantly allowing warplanes to be deployed on their territory. Tensions appeared to ease on 19 November after the Iraqi deputy Prime Minister, Tareq Aziz, met the Russian Minister of Foreign Affairs, Yevgenii Primakov, who affirmed that Russia would continue to urge the lifting of economic sanctions, provided that Iraq complied with Resolution 1137. Following this assurance, UNSCOM weapons inspectors were permitted to return to Iraq on 21 November. Renewed Iraqi co-operation with the UNSCOM was short-lived, however: shortly after the inspectors' return, Iraqi officials refused to allow the UNSCOM the unconditional access to areas designated as presidential palaces which it sought. In mid-December Richard Butler, accompanied by commissioners from the UK, France and Russia, held talks in Baghdad with Tareq Aziz. Although Aziz expressed satisfaction at the presence of representatives of countries other than the USA, no progress was achieved. In response to the impasse, the US Secretary of Defense, William Cohen, reiterated the threat of military action in order to force Saddam Hussain to capitulate to UN demands, a move which was condemned by Russia. On 12 January 1998 Iraq prohibited inspections by a former US marine officer, Scott Ritter, claiming that he was spying for the US Central Intelligence Agency (CIA). Frustrated at Iraq's continued perceived intransigence, on 16 January the UK dispatched another aircraft carrier to the Gulf region. In response, Iraq reported that it had enlisted one million of its nationals for military training in order to counter any possible offensives. On 19 January Richard Butler returned to Iraq, where he agreed to Russian requests to introduce outside experts into technical talks regarding the weapons inspections, scheduled to commence in February, thereby diluting the presence of US personnel. In spite of this concession, Iraq maintained a policy of non-co-operation with the UNSCOM. In response, the US Secretary of State, Madeleine Albright, warned that the time for diplomacy was fast expiring and embarked on an intensive diplomatic mission in Europe and the Middle East in order to gain support for possible military action against Iraq. The US Secretary of State subsequently announced that Egypt, Jordan, Kuwait, Bahrain, Saudi Arabia and Israel were prepared for a military response. France, the People's Republic of China and Russia opposed the use of force. The apparently increased likelihood of air strikes against Iraq prompted Russia's Deputy Minister of Foreign Affairs, Viktor Posuvalyuk, to hold extensive talks with Iraqi officials in Baghdad in late January and early February. The USA did not consider that Russia had achieved a breakthrough and began to make preparations to evacuate 450 UN staff to secure hotels. However, the Russian President, Boris Yeltsin, maintained that progress was indeed being made and threatened that Russia would veto any Security Council resolutions authorizing military attacks on Iraq. The extent of Russian opposition to military force became evident on 4 February, after Yeltsin warned that US military strikes could have serious international repercussions. Indeed, and despite Albright's earlier claims, it became apparent that there was little support among the Gulf states for military action. Only Kuwait announced its approval of force if diplomatic efforts should fail, while Saudi Arabia and Bahrain refused to authorize military attacks from their territories. Meanwhile, senior representatives from the Arab League, Russia, Turkey and France met on 3 February, in Baghdad, in an attempt to defuse the crisis. In mid-February the five permanent members of the UN Security Council approved a compromise formula, which proposed that a special group of diplomats, appointed by the UN Secretary-General in consultation with experts from the UNSCOM and the International Atomic Energy Agency (IAEA), would be allowed unconditional and unrestricted access to presidential palaces. On 20 February Kofi Annan travelled to Baghdad in order to discuss the compromise. Iraq accepted the proposal and, on 24 February, a new agreement was signed by Tareq Aziz and Kofi Annan, thus averting the immediate threat of military action. Despite the apparent breakthrough, both the USA and the UK remained cautious and urged the UN Security Council to adopt a resolution advocating the use of force should Iraq breach the agreement. On 2 March the UN Security Council unanimously approved a resolution warning of extreme consequences, but not immediate use of force, if the agreement was reneged upon by Iraq.

Exports of Iraqi crude petroleum, under the terms of Resolution 986, recommenced on 10 December 1996, and the following day, according to Turkish officials, Iraq was pumping 350,000 b/d of crude petroleum through the Kirkuk-Yumurtalik pipeline. By 7 January 1997 the UN was reported to have approved more than 20 contracts for the sale of Iraqi petroleum. The first supplies of food purchased with the revenues from these sales arrived in Iraq in March 1997, resulting in an increase in basic food rations. In the same month the UNCC announced that current revenues accrued from sales of petroleum had enabled Iraq to pay US $144m.-worth of reparations to some 57,363 claimants. In June the 'oil-for-food' agreement was extended for a further six months, but Iraq suspended its petroleum exports shortly after the extension was announced, protesting that it had not received sufficient humanitarian aid from the UN. Iraq submitted a new distribution plan, and, in mid-August, after the UN had approved it, exports of petroleum recommenced. However, owing to the previous interruption of exports, the UN Security Council modified the terms of the original 'oil-for-food' agreement, permitting Iraq an extra 30 days to sell its first tranche of oil but contracting the time limit for sales of the second tranche of oil by 30 days. On 4 December the UN renewed the sales agreement for another six months, but the following day exports were again halted at Iraq's request. Iraq once again criticized the UN for inefficient delivery of humanitarian supplies and drafted another revised distribution plan. In late December the Iraqi Government announced that the inadequacy of food supplies under the UN programme had forced it to reduce rations of certain basic food items, including baby-milk. The USA denounced the decision, accusing Iraq of delaying the UN's approval of food contracts. In January 1998 exports of petroleum resumed, following the UN's approval of the new distribution plan. In February the UN Security Council raised the maximum permitted revenue from exports of petroleum to $5,200m. in the six months to 31 July, of which Iraq would be permitted to spend some $3,550m. on humanitarian goods. The remaining $1,650m. would be used to finance reparations and UN operations in the country. The new export entitlement was to be implemented immediately after Iraq and the UN had agreed to a revised distribution programme.

From mid-1992 onwards there were signs of increased co-operation between the various Iraqi opposition groups, based both in exile and in Iraqi Kurdistan. In June delegates from more than 30 Iraqi opposition groups attended a conference, organized by the INC, in Vienna. The conference was reported to have elected an 87-member assembly and a 17-member executive committee. On 23 September representatives of Iraqi opposition groups assembled at Salahuddin, in Kurdish-controlled northern Iraq. All of the different factions in opposition to Saddam Hussain's regime were reported to have participated in this conference, at the conclusion of which it was agreed to create a 174-member assembly in which religious groups would hold 35% of the seats; Kurdish groups 25%; and Arab nationalists 40%. On 27 October a conference of those opposition factions belonging to the INC and the SCIRI (see Directory) commenced in Salahuddin. The conference concluded with the election of a 25-member executive committee and a three-member presidential council.

In May 1997 Syria and Iraq secured some US $20m.-worth of trade agreements, marking a restoration of economic relations. The following month the border between the two countries, closed in 1980, was reopened. In late November Tareq Aziz made the first visit to Syria by a senior Iraqi official since 1980. Despite renewed trade co-operation, Syria emphasized its reluctance to re-establish full diplomatic relations with Iraq, owing to current tensions in the Gulf (see above). Relations between Jordan and Iraq deteriorated in December after Iraqi security forces intercepted a letter from a Jordanian source to an Iraqi general containing details of an anti-Iraq plot. In retaliation, Saddam Hussain ordered the execution of four Jordanian students whose crimes would normally have incurred a fine. The Iraqi general was executed some two weeks later. Tensions increased in January 1998 when Iraq's chargé d'affaires to Jordan, Hikmat al-Hajou, and seven other Iraqis were killed in the Jordanian town of Rabla. Following the murders, four Iraqi diplomats were prohibited from crossing the border and the Jordanian authorities instructed officials at air, sea, and land frontiers to interrogate and, if necessary, detain all Iraqis attempting to leave the country. In what was regarded as a reconciliation attempt, President Saddam Hussain announced shortly after the murders that all Jordanian prisoners awaiting trial in Iraq would be released.

Government

Power rests with the President and a Revolutionary Command Council (RCC), which in early 1996 comprised eight members (including the Chairman and Vice-Chairman). Considerable influence is exercised by the Iraq Regional Command of the Baath Party, while the routine administration of the country is undertaken by an appointed Council of Ministers. Legislative responsibility is shared between the RCC and the National Assembly, with 250 members elected by universal adult suffrage for four years. The country is divided into 18 governorates (including three Autonomous Regions). A Kurdish Autonomous Region was created in 1970, and elections to a 50-member Kurdish Legislative Council were held for the first time in September 1980.

Defence

Military service is compulsory for all men at the age of 18 years, and lasts between 18 months and two years, extendable in wartime. In August 1997 the armed forces totalled an estimated 387,500 regular members; the army had an estimated total strength of 350,000 (including an estimated 100,000 active reserves); the air force had a strength of 35,000, and the navy an estimated 2,500. Defence expenditure in 1996 was estimated at US $1,300m.

Economic Affairs

In 1996, according to estimates by the *Middle East Economic Digest* of London, Iraq's gross domestic product (GDP), measured in current prices, was US $11,500m., equivalent to about $596 per head. According to the same source, GDP declined by about 15% in 1996, compared with 1995. Over the period 1985–95, the population increased by an annual average of 2.7%, according to estimates by the World Bank.

Agriculture (including forestry and fishing) contributed 26.1% of GDP in 1991. Some 10.7% of the labour force were employed in agriculture in 1996. Dates are the principal cash crop. Other crops include wheat, barley, maize, sugar beet and cane, and melons. Production of eggs and poultry meat is also important. During 1986–96 agricultural production declined by an annual average of 1.2%.

Industry (including mining, manufacturing, construction and power) employed 18.3% of the labour force in 1987 and provided 10.3% of GDP in 1991.

Mining (including production of crude petroleum and gas) contributed only 0.6% of GDP in 1991. The sector employed 1.2% of the labour force in 1987. The principal mineral exports are crude petroleum and petroleum products, sulphur and phosphate-based fertilizers. In addition, Iraq has substantial reserves of natural gas.

Manufacturing contributed 5.5% of GDP in 1991, and employed 7.1% of the labour force in 1987. Measured by the value of output, chemical, petroleum, coal, rubber and plastic products accounted for 35.2% of manufacturing activity in 1986. Other important branches of the sector in that year were food products (providing 15.8% of manufacturing output), non-metallic mineral products (12.6%) and textiles (6.1%).

Energy is derived principally from hydroelectric power, and there is also an oil-fired power station.

All banks were nationalized until 1991, when private banking was permitted. Banks are few in number in comparison with other Arab countries.

In 1996, according to the *Middle East Economic Digest*, Iraq recorded a trade surplus of US $300m. In that year, according to the same source, the current account of the balance of payments was estimated to be in balance. In 1989 the principal source of imports was the USA, which was also the principal market for exports. Other major trading partners were the Federal Republic of Germany, Turkey, the United Kingdom, Italy and France. Crude petroleum was by far the most important export (before the imposition of economic sanctions—see below), accounting for more than 98% of total export earnings over the period 1980–89. Dates are the second most important export commodity. According to the IMF, the value of Iraq's imports in 1995 was 191m. Iraqi dinars, compared with 154.9m. Iraqi dinars in 1994 and 165.6m. Iraqi dinars in 1993.

In a six-month emergency reconstruction budget, announced in mid-1991, planned expenditure in the general consolidated budget was reduced from 14,596m. Iraqi dinars to 13,876m. Iraqi dinars, while investment budget expenditure was reduced from 2,340m. Iraqi dinars to 1,660m. Iraqi dinars. The Iraqi Government estimated that, at 1 January 1991, its total external debt stood at 13,118m. Iraqi dinars (US $42,320m.); and that the servicing of the debt over the period 1991–95 would cost 23,388m. Iraqi dinars ($75,450m.). These estimates did not, however, take into account loans made to Iraq during the Iran-Iraq War by Saudi Arabia and Kuwait. The annual rate of inflation averaged 11.0% in 1979–87, rising to 21.4% in 1988, but in the aftermath of Iraq's catastrophic adventure into Kuwait (see Recent History) figures of that order became meaningless. *The Middle East Economic Digest* estimated that in 1996 the average rate of inflation was 450%.

Iraq is a member of the Arab Fund for Economic and Social Development (see p. 259), the Council of Arab Economic Unity (p. 139), the Islamic Development Bank (p. 194), the Organization of Arab Petroleum Exporting Countries (p. 223), the Organization of the Petroleum Exporting Countries (p. 227), the Arab Co-operation Council (p. 259) and the Arab Monetary Fund (p. 259).

According to an official UN report (compiled in mid-March 1991), Iraq's war with the multinational force 'wrought near apocalyptic results on the economic infrastructure', relegating Iraq to a 'pre-industrial age but with all the disabilities of post-industrial dependency on an intensive use of energy and technology'. The damage to the infrastructure has been reflected in every sector. The failure of irrigation and drainage systems, owing to lack of fuel and spare parts, caused the 1992 grain harvest to decline to an estimated 1.25m. metric tons, about one-third of the amount harvested in 1990. In 1996, however, total grain production was estimated to have recovered to 95% of the 1990 level. Owing to economic sanctions (see below), farmers have been unable to obtain pesticides and fertilizers, and poor harvests have become the norm. Reduced production of animal feed has resulted in a significant decrease in livestock products; according to a report compiled by US and UN sources, domestic production of meat, milk and eggs during 1993–96 was less than 50% of output levels recorded in 1990. Prior to the war with the multinational force, Iraq imported some 70% of its food supplies at an annual cost of $1,100m. In late 1994 the Government was reported to be spending some $700m. annually on food, and the strain of this expense, in the continued absence of any significant revenues, was reflected in the decision, announced in September, to halve the basic ration issued to all Iraqis. Even prior to this measure, rations were estimated to meet only 70% of basic needs, and malnutrition was widespread. Unrest resulting from huge increases in the price of basic commodities and the collapse of the Iraqi dinar has been checked only by draconian security measures. In mid-1997 a survey conducted by UNICEF, the World Food Programme and Iraq's Ministry of Health reported that 27% of Iraqi children under five years of age were suffering from malnutrition. In September the Minister of Health, Umeed Madhat Mubarak, claimed that the sanctions had dramatically increased the mortality rate of Iraqi citizens: deaths of children under five years of age had increased from an average of 506 per month in the pre-war years to 6,500 per month following the imposition of sanctions. Likewise, the death rate of those over five years of age had increased from 1,600 per month before the sanctions to 8,000 per month in the period after their implementation.

In the immediate aftermath of the war with the multinational force, all of Iraq's electrically-powered installations were reported to have ceased functioning, as a result of the destruction of power plants, etc. By late 1991 a drastic decline in industrial output had been observed, with further hundreds of industrial projects having ceased, owing to the continued trade embargo, and a consequent steep rise in unemployment.

In August 1990, the UN imposed mandatory economic sanctions on Iraq, and exports of crude and refined petroleum ceased. The Government's post-war reconstruction efforts subsequently concentrated on repairing damage to facilities for the production of crude petroleum. In late 1991 the Government claimed that crude petroleum production capacity had been restored to 2m. barrels per day (b/d), and that of petroleum exports to 1.25m. b/d. In February 1992, however, petroleum refining capacity had reportedly attained only 3% of its pre-war level. Revenues accruing to Iraq through the 'oil-for-food' sales (permitted since early December 1996 in accordance with UN Security Council Resolution 986, see Recent History) are governed by stringent restrictions and clearly do not mark the beginning of an economic recovery. Under the terms of Resolution 986, for instance, Iraq is permitted to sell $2,000m.-worth of petroleum over a six-month period. However, only about $1,200m. is available to the Iraqi Government, exclusively for the purchase of humanitarian goods, under the supervision of the UN. The 'oil-for-food' agreement was extended by six months in June 1997 and again in December. In February 1998 the UN Security Council increased the maximum permitted revenue from exports of petroleum to $5,200m. in the six months to 31 July. Revenues accrued within the first three months of the 'oil-for-food' programme enabled the UN Compensation Commission (UNCC), established in 1991, to make some $144m.-worth of reparations payments to some 57,363 claimants who had suffered financially owing to Iraq's invasion of Kuwait. Such payments, in conjunction with compensation for damage to petroleum facilities and indemnities to foreign workers forced to leave Kuwait were expected to increase Iraq's total external debt to $200,000m. from its estimated pre-war level of $75,000m.

Social Welfare

A limited Social Security Scheme was introduced in 1957 and extended in 1976. Benefits are given for old age, sickness, unemployment, maternity, marriage and death. Health services are provided free of charge. Many of the new health facilities that were scheduled under the 1981–85 Five-Year Plan were completed in spite of the war with Iran. More than US $1,500m. was spent on building more than 30 new hospitals, providing about 11,500 beds. By the end of 1986, as a result of these additions, Iraq had 228 hospital establishments, with a total of 32,166 beds. There were reportedly 9,442 physicians working in the country in 1987. Owing to the impact of sanctions, Iraq lacks funds to pay for adequate medical provisions. In September 1997 the Minister of Health, Umeed Madhat Mubarak, announced that hospitals could operate at only 30% of capacity.

Education

Education is free, and primary education, beginning at six years of age and lasting for six years, has been made compulsory in an effort to reduce illiteracy. In 1995 an estimated 42% of Iraqi adults were illiterate. Enrolment at primary schools of children in the relevant age-group reached 100% in 1978, but the proportion had fallen to 91% by 1993. Secondary education begins at 12 years of age and lasts for up to six years, divided into two cycles of three years each. An estimated 44% of children in the appropriate age-group attended secondary schools in 1993. There are 47 teacher-training institutes, 19 technical institutes and eight universities. In the 1991/92 academic year 46,250 students were reported to have enrolled in courses of higher education.

Public Holidays

1998: 1 January (New Year's Day), 6 January (Army Day), 30 January* (Id al-Fitr, end of Ramadan), 8 February (14 Ramadan Revolution, anniversary of the 1963 coup), 8 April* (Id al-Adha, Feast of the Sacrifice), 28 April* (Islamic New Year), 7 May* (Ashoura), 7 July* (Mouloud, Birth of Muhammad), 14 July (Republic Day, anniversary of the 1968 coup), 17 November* (Leilat al-Meiraj, ascension of Muhammad).

1999: 1 January (New Year's Day), 6 January (Army Day), 19 January* (Id al-Fitr, end of Ramadan), 8 February (14 Ramadan Revolution, anniversary of the 1963 coup), 28 March* (Id al-Adha, Feast of the Sacrifice), 17 April* (Islamic New Year), 26 April* (Ashoura), 26 June* (Mouloud, Birth of Muhammad), 14 July (Republic Day, anniversary of the 1968 coup), 6 November* (Leilat al-Meiraj, ascension of Muhammad).

* These holidays are dependent on the Islamic lunar calendar and may vary by one or two days from the dates given.

Weights and Measures

The metric system is in force. Local measurements are also used, e.g. 1 meshara or dunum = 2,500 sq metres (0.62 acre).

Statistical Survey

Source (unless otherwise indicated): Central Statistical Organization, Ministry of Planning, Karradat Mariam, ash-Shawaf Sq., Baghdad; tel. (1) 537-0071; telex 212218.

Area and Population

AREA, POPULATION AND DENSITY*

Area (sq km)	438,317†
Population (census results)	
17 October 1987	16,335,199
17 October 1997	
Males	10,940,764
Females	11,077,219
Total	22,017,983
Density (per sq km) in October 1997	50.2

* No account has been taken of the reduction in the area of Iraq as a result of the adjustment to the border with Kuwait that came into force on 15 January 1993.

† 169,235 sq miles. This figure includes 924 sq km (357 sq miles) of territorial waters but excludes the Neutral Zone, of which Iraq's share is 3,522 sq km (1,360 sq miles). The Zone lies between Iraq and Saudi Arabia, and is administered jointly by the two countries. Nomads move freely through it but there are no permanent inhabitants.

GOVERNORATES (population at 1987 census)

	Area* (sq km)	Population	Density (per sq km)
Nineveh	37,698	1,479,430	39.2
Salah ad-Din	29,004	726,138	25.0
At-Ta'meem	10,391	601,219	57.9
Diala	19,292	961,073	49.8
Baghdad	5,159	3,841,268	744.6
Al-Anbar	137,723	820,690	6.0
Babylon	5,258	1,109,574	211.0
Karbala	5,034	469,282	93.2
An-Najaf	27,844	590,078	21.2
Al-Qadisiya	8,507	559,805	65.8
Al-Muthanna	51,029	315,816	6.2
Thi-Qar	13,626	921,066	67.6
Wasit	17,308	564,670	32.6
Maysan	14,103	487,448	34.6
Al-Basrah (Basra)	19,070	872,176	45.7
Autonomous Regions:			
D'hok	6,120	293,304	47.9
Irbil (Arbil)	14,471	770,439	53.2
As-Sulaimaniya	15,756	951,723	60.4
Total	437,393	16,335,199	37.3

* Excluding territorial waters (924 sq km).

PRINCIPAL TOWNS (estimated population, 1970)

Baghdad (capital)	1,984,142	An-Najaf	147,855
Al-Basrah (Basra)	333,684	Al-Hillah (Hilla)	103,544
Al-Mawsil (Mosul)	310,313	As-Sulaimaniya	103,091
Kirkuk	191,294	Irbil (Arbil)	101,779

BIRTHS AND DEATHS (UN estimates, annual averages)

	1980–85	1985–90	1990–95
Birth rate (per 1,000)	41.0	40.3	38.1
Death rate (per 1,000)	8.4	7.2	6.7

Source: UN, *World Population Prospects: The 1994 Revision.*

Registered live births (1992) 502,415 (birth rate 26.4 per 1,000); Registered deaths (1990) 76,683 (death rate 4.4 per 1,000). Note: Registration is incomplete.

Expectation of life (official estimates, years at birth, 1990): males 77.43; females 78.22.

ECONOMICALLY ACTIVE POPULATION*
(persons aged 7 years and over, 1987 census)

	Males	Females	Total
Agriculture, forestry and fishing	422,265	70,741	493,006
Mining and quarrying	40,439	4,698	45,137
Manufacturing	228,242	38,719	266,961
Electricity, gas and water	31,786	4,450	36,236
Construction	332,645	8,541	341,186
Trade, restaurants and hotels	191,116	24,489	215,605
Transport, storage and communications	212,116	12,155	224,271
Financing, insurance, real estate and business services	16,204	10,811	27,015
Community, social and personal services	1,721,748	233,068	1,954,816
Activities not adequately defined	146,616	18,232	167,848
Total labour force	3,346,177	425,904	3,772,081

* Figures exclude persons seeking work for the first time, totalling 184,264 (males 149,938, females 34,326), but include other unemployed persons.

Source: ILO, *Yearbook of Labour Statistics.*

Agriculture

PRINCIPAL CROPS ('000 metric tons)

	1994	1995	1996
Wheat	1,342	1,050	1,000
Rice (paddy)	383	403*	270*
Barley	971	700†	500†
Maize	128	90*	85†
Potatoes	418	420†	380†
Dry broad beans†	19	18	18
Sunflower seed	56	63*	55†
Sesame seed*	14	14	13
Olives†	14	13	12
Cabbages†	22	23	21
Tomatoes	863	870†	800†
Cauliflower†	36	36	34
Pumpkins, etc.†	61	62	60
Cucumbers†	340	345	340
Aubergines†	155	160	150
Green peppers†	31	32	30
Onions (dry)	70	75†	70†
Carrots†	10	11	10
Other vegetables	738	758†	747
Watermelons†	460	450	450
Melons†	220	220	225
Grapes	282	280†	300†
Dates	576	600†	550†
Sugar cane†	63	60	58
Apples	86	90†	80†
Peaches and nectarines†	25	26	25
Plums†	31	32	30
Oranges	315	318†	310†
Tangerines, etc.	45	45†	40†
Lemons and limes†	16	17	16
Apricots†	31	32	30
Other fruits and berries	93	95†	93†
Tobacco (leaves)†	2	3	2
Cottonseed†	19	18	18
Cotton (lint)†	10	9	9

* Unofficial figure(s). † FAO estimate(s).

Source: FAO, *Production Yearbook.*

LIVESTOCK (FAO estimates, '000 head, year ending September)

	1994	1995	1996
Horses	20	20	20
Mules	12	12	12
Asses	148	146	145
Cattle	1,050	1,030	1,000
Buffaloes	85	80	75
Camels	13	13	13
Sheep	5,150	5,100	5,000
Goats	600	500	350

Poultry (FAO estimates, million): 42 in 1994; 42 in 1995; 42 in 1996.

Source: FAO, *Production Yearbook*.

LIVESTOCK PRODUCTS (FAO estimates, '000 metric tons)

	1994	1995	1996
Beef and veal	29	28	28
Buffalo meat	10	10	10
Mutton and lamb	15	15	14
Goat meat	3	3	3
Poultry meat	110	110	110
Cows' milk	210	205	200
Buffalo milk	20	20	19
Sheep's milk	110	105	100
Goats' milk	32	25	18
Cheese	20	19	17
Butter	5	5	5
Hen eggs	41	40	40
Wool:			
greasy	17	16	15
clean	9	8	8
Cattle and buffalo hides	4	4	4
Sheepskins	3	3	3
Goatskins	1	1	n.a.

Source: FAO, *Production Yearbook*.

Forestry

ROUNDWOOD REMOVALS
(FAO estimates, '000 cubic metres, excl. bark)

	1992	1993	1994
Sawlogs, veneer logs and logs for sleepers*	20	20	20
Other industrial wood*	30	30	30
Fuel wood	105	105	105
Total	155	155	155

* Figures assumed to be unchanged since 1980.

Sawnwood production ('000 cubic metres, incl. railway sleepers): 8 per year (FAO estimates) in 1980–94.

Source: FAO, *Yearbook of Forest Products*.

Fishing

(FAO estimates, '000 metric tons, live weight)

	1993	1994	1995
Inland waters	19.0	18.0	18.6
Indian Ocean	4.5	4.0	4.0
Total catch	23.5	22.0	22.6

Source: FAO, *Yearbook of Fishery Statistics*.

Mining

('000 metric tons, unless otherwise indicated)

	1992	1993	1994
Crude petroleum	25,840	32,298	36,666
Natural gas (petajoules)	89	99	124
Native sulphur*	500	600	600
Natural phosphates	600	800	1,000
Salt (unrefined)	402	n.a.	n.a.
Gypsum (crude)*	380	450	450

* Estimates by the US Bureau of Mines.

Source: UN, *Industrial Commodity Statistics Yearbook*.

Industry

SELECTED PRODUCTS
('000 metric tons, unless otherwise indicated)

	1992	1993	1994
Cigarettes (million)	5,794	n.a.	n.a.
Cement	2,453	n.a.	n.a.
Liquefied petroleum gas*†	402	1,086	1,100
Naphtha	600	500	500
Motor spirit (petrol)	2,856	2,960*	2,970*
Kerosene	890	1,100	1,120
Jet fuel	826	910	1,110
Distillate fuel oils	6,694	6,800*	6,880*
Residual fuel oils	8,754	8,880*	9,000*
Lubricating oils*	200	200	200
Paraffin wax*	70	80	100
Petroleum bitumen (asphalt)*	400	410	420
Electric energy (million kWh)*	25,300	26,300	27,060

* Estimated production.

† Includes estimated production ('000 metric tons) from natural gas plants: 2 in 1992; 486 in 1993; 500 in 1994; and from petroleum refineries: 400 in 1992; 600 in 1993; 600 in 1994.

Footwear (excluding rubber): 4,087,000 pairs in 1992.

Source: UN, *Industrial Commodity Statistics Yearbook*.

Finance

CURRENCY AND EXCHANGE RATES

Monetary Units

1,000 fils = 20 dirhams = 1 Iraqi dinar (ID).

Sterling and Dollar Equivalents (30 September 1997)

£1 sterling = 502.16 fils;
US $1 = 310.86 fils;
100 Iraqi dinars = £199.14 = $321.69.

Exchange Rate

From February 1973 to October 1982 the Iraqi dinar was valued at US $3.3862. Since October 1982 it has been valued at $3.2169. The dinar's average value in 1982 was $3.3513. The aforementioned data refer to the official exchange rate. There is, in addition, a special rate for exports and also a free-market rate. The unofficial exchange rate was $1 = 1,200 dinars in May 1997.

BUDGET ESTIMATES (ID million)

Revenue	1981	1982
Ordinary	5,025.0	8,740.0
Economic development plan	6,742.8	7,700.0
Autonomous government agencies	7,667.8	n.a.
Total	19,434.9	n.a.

Petroleum revenues (estimates, US $ million): 9,198 in 1981; 10,250 in 1982; 9,650 in 1983; 10,000 in 1984; 11,900 in 1985; 6,813 in 1986; 11,300 in 1987.

Expenditure	1981	1982
Ordinary	5,025.0	8,740.0
Economic development plan	6,742.0	7,700.0
Autonomous government agencies	7,982.4	n.a.
Total	19,750.2	n.a.

1991 (ID million): General consolidated state budget expenditure 13,876; Investment budget expenditure 1,660.

CENTRAL BANK RESERVES (US $ million at 31 December)

	1975	1976	1977
Gold	168.0	166.7	176.1
IMF special drawing rights	26.9	32.5	41.5
Reserve position in IMF	31.9	31.7	33.4
Foreign exchange	2,500.5	4,369.8	6,744.7
Total	2,727.3	4,600.7	6,995.7

IMF special drawing rights (US $ million at 31 December): 132.3 in 1981; 81.9 in 1982; 9.0 in 1983; 0.1 in 1984; 7.2 in 1987.
Reserve position in IMF (US $ million at 31 December): 130.3 in 1981; 123.5 in 1982.

Note: No figures for gold or foreign exchange have been available since 1977.

Source: IMF, *International Financial Statistics.*

COST OF LIVING (Consumer Price Index; base: 1990 = 100)

	1991*
Food	363.9
Fuel and light	135.4
Clothing	251.1
Rent	107.0
All items (incl. others)	286.5

* May to December only.

Source: ILO, *Yearbook of Labour Statistics.*

NATIONAL ACCOUNTS (ID million at current prices)

National Income and Product

	1989	1990	1991
Compensation of employees	6,705.2	7,855.4	8,989.9
Operating surplus	11,866.0	12,936.6	10,405.2
Domestic factor incomes	18,571.2	20,792.0	19,395.1
Consumption of fixed capital	1,836.7	2,056.3	1,918.2
Gross domestic product (GDP) at factor cost	20,407.9	22,848.3	21,313.3
Indirect taxes	1,035.0	1,024.8	485.6
Less Subsidies	417.1	576.3	1,859.2
GDP in purchasers' values	21,025.8	23,296.8	19,939.7
Net factor income from the rest of the world	−704.3	−773.9	−650.5
Gross national product	20,321.5	22,522.9	19,289.2
Less Consumption of fixed capital	1,836.7	2,056.3	1,918.2
National income in market prices	18,484.8	20,466.6	17,371.0
Net current transfers from abroad	−149.3	−49.3	−122.8
National disposable income	18,335.5	20,417.3	17,248.2

Source: UN, *National Accounts Statistics.*

Expenditure on the Gross Domestic Product

	1989	1990	1991
Government final consumption expenditure	5,990.1	6,142.0	7,033.3
Private final consumption expenditure	11,232.4	11,760.5	9,611.1
Increase in stocks	−2,317.5	−976.9	−520.0
Gross fixed capital formation	6,305.5	6,220.0	3,289.1
Total domestic expenditure	21,210.5	23,145.6	20,453.5
Exports of goods and services	4,482.6	4,305.4	547.8
Less Imports of goods and services	4,667.3	4,154.2	1,061.6
GDP in purchasers' values	21,025.8	23,296.8	19,939.7

Source: UN, *National Accounts Statistics.*

Gross Domestic Product by Economic Activity (at factor cost)

	1989	1990	1991
Agriculture, hunting, forestry and fishing	3,346.1	4,613.3	6,047.0
Mining and quarrying	3,894.8	3,330.6	149.4
Manufacturing	2,694.2	2,058.7	1,273.9
Electricity, gas and water*	269.0	247.5	162.4
Construction	1,417.8	1,693.2	812.4
Trade, restaurants and hotels*	2,376.4	3,454.7	3,608.2
Transport, storage and communications	1,533.3	2,103.9	2,645.9
Finance, insurance and real estate†	2,384.8	2,781.2	3,150.4
Government services	3,599.1	3,823.5	4,845.7
Other services	305.0	292.2	489.8
Sub-total	21,820.5	24,398.8	23,185.1
Less Imputed bank service charge	1,412.6	1,550.5	1,871.8
Total	20,407.9	22,848.3	21,313.3
GDP at constant 1975 prices	6,491.8	6,492.9	2,199.8

* Gas distribution is included in trade.

† Including imputed rents of owner-occupied dwellings.

Source: UN, *National Accounts Statistics.*

External Trade

PRINCIPAL COMMODITIES (ID million)

Imports c.i.f.	1976	1977*	1978
Food and live animals	159.6	154.0	134.5
Cereals and cereal preparations	70.0	79.9	74.9
Sugar, sugar preparations and honey	37.2	24.1	10.2
Crude materials (inedible) except fuels	33.7	20.5	25.1
Chemicals	58.5	47.4	58.7
Basic manufactures	293.3	236.7	285.2
Textile yarn, fabrics, etc.	44.3	69.4	72.7
Iron and steel	127.5	44.3	73.2
Machinery and transport equipment	557.4	625.8	667.4
Non-electric machinery	285.4	352.5	368.1
Electrical machinery, apparatus, etc.	106.9	120.2	160.5
Transport equipment	165.2	153.1	138.8
Miscellaneous manufactured articles	33.2	49.4	51.7
Total (incl. others)	1,150.9	1,151.3	1,244.1

* Figures are provisional. Revised total is ID 1,323.2 million.

Total imports (official estimates, ID million): 1,738.9 in 1979; 2,208.1 in 1980; 2,333.8 in 1981.
Total imports (IMF estimates, ID million): 6,013.0 in 1981; 6,309.0 in 1982; 3,086.2 in 1983; 3,032.4 in 1984; 3,285.7 in 1985; 2,773.0 in 1986; 2,268.7 in 1987; 2,888.8 in 1988; 3,077.1 in 1989; 2,028.5 in 1990; 131.5 in 1991; 187.3 in 1992; 165.6 in 1993; 154.9 in 1994; 191.3 in 1995; 70.5 in 1996 (Source: IMF, *International Financial Statistics*).

Total exports (ID million): 5,614.6 (crude petroleum 5,571.9) in 1977; 6,422.7 (crude petroleum 6,360.5) in 1978; 12,522.0 (crude petroleum 12,480.0) in 1979.

Exports of crude petroleum (estimates, ID million): 15,321.3 in 1980; 6,089.6 in 1981; 5,982.4 in 1982; 5,954.8 in 1983; 6,937.0 in 1984; 8,142.5 in 1985; 5,126.2 in 1986; 6,988.9 in 1987; 7,245.8 in 1988.

Source: IMF, *International Financial Statistics*.

PRINCIPAL TRADING PARTNERS (US $ million)

Imports c.i.f.	1988	1989	1990
Australia	153.4	196.2	108.7
Austria	n.a.	1.1	50.9
Belgium and Luxembourg	57.6	68.2	68.3
Brazil	346.0	416.4	139.5
Canada	169.9	225.1	150.4
China, People's Republic	99.2	148.0	157.9
France	278.0	410.4	278.3
Germany	322.3	459.6	389.4
India	32.3	65.2	57.5
Indonesia	38.9	122.7	104.9
Ireland	150.4	144.9	31.6
Italy	129.6	285.1	194.0
Japan	533.0	621.1	397.2
Jordan	164.3	210.0	220.3
Korea, Republic	98.5	123.9	149.4
Netherlands	111.6	102.6	93.8
Romania	113.3	91.1	30.1
Saudi Arabia	37.2	96.5	62.5
Spain	43.4	129.0	40.5
Sri Lanka	50.1	33.5	52.3
Sweden	63.0	40.6	64.8
Switzerland	65.7	94.4	126.6
Thailand	22.3	59.2	68.9
Turkey	874.7	408.9	196.0
USSR	70.7	75.7	77.9
United Kingdom	394.6	448.5	322.1
USA	979.3	1,001.7	658.4
Yugoslavia	154.5	182.0	123.1
Total (incl. others)	5,960.0	6,956.2	4,833.9

Exports f.o.b.	1988	1989	1990*
Belgium and Luxembourg	147.5	249.6	n.a.
Brazil	1,002.8	1,197.2	n.a.
France	517.4	623.9	0.8
Germany	122.0	76.9	1.7
Greece	192.5	189.4	0.3
India	293.0	438.8	14.7
Italy	687.1	549.7	10.6
Japan	712.1	117.1	0.1
Jordan	28.4	25.2	101.6
Netherlands	152.9	532.3	0.2
Portugal	120.8	125.8	n.a.
Spain	370.0	575.7	0.7
Turkey	1,052.6	1,331.0	83.5
USSR	835.7	1,331.7	8.9
United Kingdom	293.1	167.0	4.4
USA	1,458.9	2,290.8	0.2
Yugoslavia	425.4	342.0	10.4
Total (incl. others)	10,268.3	12,333.7	392.0

* Excluding exports of most petroleum products.

Source: UN, *International Trade Statistics Yearbook*.

Transport

RAILWAYS (traffic)

	1992	1993	1996*
Passenger-km (million)	926	1,566	1,169
Freight ton-km (million)	1,141	1,649	931

* Figures for 1994 and 1995 unavailable.

Source: Railway Gazette International, *Railway Directory*.

ROAD TRAFFIC (estimates, motor vehicles in use at 31 December)

	1993
Passenger cars	672,000
Goods vehicles*	368,000

* Including vans.

Source: International Road Federation, *World Road Statistics*.

SHIPPING

Merchant Fleet (registered at 31 December)

	1994	1995	1996
Number of vessels	117	114	113
Total displacement ('000 grt)	884.7	857.8	856.9

Source: Lloyd's Register of Shipping, *World Fleet Statistics*.

CIVIL AVIATION (revenue traffic on scheduled services)

	1991	1992	1994*
Kilometres flown (million)	0	0	0
Passengers carried ('000)	28	53	31
Passenger-km (million)	17	35	20
Freight ton-km (million)	0	3	2

* Figures for 1993 unavailable.

Source: UN, *Statistical Yearbook*.

Tourism

	1992	1993	1994
Tourist arrivals ('000)*	504	400	330
Tourist receipts (US $ million)	20	15	12

* Including same-day visitors.

Source: UN, *Statistical Yearbook*.

Communications Media

	1993	1994	1995
Radio receivers ('000 in use)	4,225	4,335	4,500
Television receivers ('000 in use)	1,450	1,500	1,600
Daily newspapers	n.a.	4*	4†

* Combined average circulation 532,000 copies per issue.

† Estimate.

Non-daily newspapers: 12 in 1988.

Source: UNESCO, *Statistical Yearbook*.

Telephones ('000 main lines in use): 674 in 1987; 678 in 1988; 675 (estimate) in 1989 (Source: UN, *Statistical Yearbook*).

Education

	Teachers		Pupils/Students	
	1990	1992*	1990	1992*
Pre-primary	4,908	4,778	86,508	90,836
Primary	134,081	131,271	3,328,212	2,857,467
Secondary:				
General	44,772	48,496	1,023,710	992,617
Teacher training	n.a.	1,303	n.a.	22,018
Vocational	n.a.	9,318	n.a.	130,303

* Figures for 1991 are unavailable.

Schools: Pre-primary: 646 in 1990; 578 in 1992. Primary: 8,917 in 1990; 8,003 in 1992.

Higher education (1988): Teachers 11,072; Students 209,818.

1994: Pre-primary: 576 schools; 4,972 teachers; 93,028 pupils.

Source: UNESCO, *Statistical Yearbook*.

Directory

The Constitution

The following are the principal features of the Provisional Constitution, issued on 22 September 1968:

The Iraqi Republic is a popular democratic and sovereign state. Islam is the state religion.

The political economy of the State is founded on socialism.

The State will protect liberty of religion, freedom of speech and opinion. Public meetings are permitted under the law. All discrimination based on race, religion or language is forbidden. There shall be freedom of the Press, and the right to form societies and trade unions in conformity with the law is guaranteed.

The Iraqi people is composed of two main nationalities: Arabs and Kurds. The Constitution confirms the nationalistic rights of the Kurdish people and the legitimate rights of all other minorities within the framework of Iraqi unity.

The highest authority in the country is the Council of Command of the Revolution (or Revolutionary Command Council—RCC), which will promulgate laws until the election of a National Assembly. The Council exercises its prerogatives and powers by a two-thirds majority.

Two amendments to the Constitution were announced in November 1969. The President, already Chief of State and Head of the Government, also became the official Supreme Commander of the Armed Forces and President of the RCC. Membership of the latter body was to increase from five to a larger number at the President's discretion.

Earlier, a Presidential decree replaced the 14 local government districts by 16 governorates, each headed by a governor with wide powers. In April 1976 Tikrit (Salah ad-Din) and Karbala became separate governorates, bringing the number of governorates to 18, although three of these are designated Autonomous Regions.

The 15-article statement which aimed to end the Kurdish war was issued on 11 March 1970. In accordance with this statement, a form of autonomy was offered to the Kurds in March 1974, but some of the Kurds rejected the offer and fresh fighting broke out. The new Provisional Constitution was announced in July 1970. Two amendments were introduced in 1973 and 1974, the 1974 amendment stating that 'the area whose majority of population is Kurdish shall enjoy autonomy in accordance with what is defined by the Law'.

The President and Vice-President are elected by a two-thirds majority of the Council. The President, Vice-President and members of the Council will be responsible to the Council. Vice-Presidents and Ministers will be responsible to the President.

Details of a new, permanent Constitution were announced in March 1989. The principal innovations proposed in the permanent Constitution, which was approved by the National Assembly in July 1990, were the abolition of the RCC, following a presidential election, and the assumption of its duties by a 50-member Consultative Assembly and the existing National Assembly; and the incorporation of the freedom to form political parties. The new, permanent Constitution is to be submitted to a popular referendum for approval.

In September 1995 an interim constitutional amendment was endorsed by the RCC whereby the elected Chairman of the RCC will assume the Presidency of the Republic subject to the approval of the National Assembly and endorsement by national referendum.

In July 1973 President Bakr announced a National Charter as a first step towards establishing the Progressive National Front. A National Assembly and People's Councils are features of the Charter. A law to create a 250-member National Assembly and a 50-member Kurdish Legislative Council was adopted on 16 March 1980, and the two Assemblies were elected in June and September 1980 respectively.

The Government

HEAD OF STATE

President: SADDAM HUSSAIN (assumed power 16 July 1979; according to official results, at a national referendum conducted on 15 October 1995, 99.96% of Iraq's 8.4m. electorate recorded its endorsement of President Saddam Hussain's continuance in office for a further seven years).

Vice-Presidents: TAHA YASSIN RAMADAN, TAHA MOHI ED-DIN MARUF.

REVOLUTIONARY COMMAND COUNCIL

Chairman: SADDAM HUSSAIN.

Vice-Chairman: TAHA YASSIN RAMADAN.

Other Members:

IZZAT IBRAHIM
TAREQ AZIZ
Gen. SULTAN HASHIM AHMAD
MUHAMMAD HAMZAH AZ-ZUBAYDI
TAHA MOHI ED-DIN MARUF
SA'ADOUN HAMMADI MAZBAN KHADR HADI

COUNCIL OF MINISTERS
(February 1998)

Prime Minister: SADDAM HUSSAIN.

Deputy Prime Ministers: TAREQ AZIZ, TAHA YASSIN RAMADAN, MUHAMMAD HAMZAH AZ-ZUBAYDI.

Minister of the Interior: MUHAMMAD ZIMAN ABD AL-RAZZAQ.

Minister of Defence: Gen. SULTAN HASHIM AHMAD.

Minister of Foreign Affairs: MUHAMMAD SAEED AS-SAHAF.

Minister of Finance: HIKMAT MIZBAN IBRAHIM.

Minister of Agriculture: ABDULLAH HAMEED MAHMOUD SALEH.

Minister of Culture and Information: HUMAM ABD AL-KHALIQ ABD AL-GHAFUR.

Minister of Justice: SHABIB AL-MALKI.

Minister of Irrigation: MAHMOUD DIYAB AL-AHMAD.

Minister of Industry and Minerals: (vacant).

Minister of Oil: AMIR MUHAMMAD RASHID.

Minister of Education: FAHD SALIM ASH-SHAKRAH.

Minister of Health: UMEED MADHAT MUBARAK.

Minister of Labour and Social Affairs: LATIF NUSAYYIF JASIM.

Minister of Planning: SAMAL MAJID FARAJ.

Minister of Higher Education and Scientific Research: ABD AL-JABBAR TAWFIQ MUHAMMAD.

Minister of Housing and Construction: MAAN ABDULLAH SARSAM.

Minister of Transport and Communications: Dr AHMAD MURTADA AHMAD KHALIL.

Minister of Awqaf (Religious Endowments) and Religious Affairs: Dr ABD AL-MUNIM AHMAD SALIH.

Minister of Trade: MUHAMMAD MAHDI SALIH.

Minister of State for Military Affairs: Gen. ABD AL-JABBAR KHALIL ASH-SHANSHAL.

Ministers of State: ARSHAD MUHAMMAD AHMAD MUHAMMAD AZ-ZIBARI, ABD AL-WAHHAB UMAR MIRZA AL-ATRUSHI.

Presidential Advisers: WATBAN IBRAHIM AL-HASSAN, SAFA HADI JAWAD, ABD AS-SATTAR AHMAD AL-MAINI, ABD AL-WAHHAB ABDULLAH AS-SABBAGH, ABDULLAH FADEL-ABBAS, AMER HAMMADI AS-SAADI HATIM AL-AZAWI, NIZAR JUMAH ALI AL-QASIR.

MINISTRIES

Office of the President: Presidential Palace, Karradat Mariam, Baghdad.

Ministry of Agriculture and Irrigation: Khulafa St, Khullani Sq., Baghdad; tel. (1) 887-3251; telex 212222.

Ministry of Awqaf (Religious Endowments) and Religious Affairs: North Gate, St opposite College of Engineering, Baghdad; tel. (1) 888-9561; telex 212785.

Ministry of Culture and Information: Nr an-Nusoor Sq., fmrly Qasr as-Salaam Bldg, Baghdad; tel. (1) 551-4333; telex 212800.

Ministry of Defence: North Gate, Baghdad; tel. (1) 888-9071; telex 212202.

Ministry of Education: POB 258, Baghdad; tel. (1) 886-0000; telex 2259.

Ministry of Finance: Khulafa St, Nr ar-Russafi Sq., Baghdad; tel. (1) 887-4871; telex 212459.

Ministry of Foreign Affairs: Opposite State Org. for Roads and Bridges, Karradat Mariam, Baghdad; tel. (1) 537-0091; telex 212201.

Ministry of Health, Labour and Social Affairs: Khulafa St, Khullani Sq., Baghdad; tel. (1) 887-1881; telex 212621.

Ministry of Industry and Minerals: Nidhal St, Nr Sa'adoun Petrol Station, Baghdad; tel. (1) 887-2006; telex 212205.

Ministry of Local Government: Karradat Mariam, Baghdad; tel. (1) 537-0031; telex 212568.

Ministry of Oil: POB 6178, al-Mansour, Baghdad; tel. (1) 443-0749; telex 212216.

Ministry of Planning: Karradat Mariam, ash-Shawaf Sq., Baghdad; tel. (1) 537-0071; telex 212218.

Ministry of Trade: Khulafa St, Khullani Sq., Baghdad; tel. (1) 887-2682; telex 212206.

Ministry of Transport and Communications: Nr Martyr's Monument, Karradat Dakhil, Baghdad; tel. (1) 776-6041; telex 212020.

KURDISH AUTONOMOUS REGION

Executive Council: Chair. MUHAMMAD AMIN MUHAMMAD (acting).

Legislative Council: Chair. AHMAD ABD AL-QADIR AN-NAQSHABANDI.

In May 1992, in the absence of a negotiated autonomy agreement with the Iraqi Government, the KIF (see below) organized elections to a 105-member Kurdish National Assembly. The DPK and the PUK were the only parties to achieve representation in the new Assembly and subsequently agreed to share seats equally between them. Elections held at the same time as those to the National Assembly, to choose an overall Kurdish leader, were inconclusive and were to be held again at a later date.

Legislature

NATIONAL ASSEMBLY

No form of National Assembly existed in Iraq between the 1958 revolution, which overthrew the monarchy, and June 1980. (The existing provisional Constitution, introduced in 1968, contains provisions for the election of an assembly at a date to be determined by the Government. The members of the Assembly are to be elected from all political, social and economic sectors of the Iraqi people.) In December 1979 the RCC invited political, trade union and popular organizations to debate a draft law providing for the creation of a 250-member National Assembly (elected from 56 constituencies) and a 50-member Kurdish Legislative Council, both to be elected by direct, free and secret ballot. Elections for the first National Assembly took place on 20 June 1980, and for the Kurdish Legislative Council on 11 September 1980, 13 August 1986 and 9 September 1989. The Assembly was dominated by members of the ruling Baath Party.

Elections for the fourth National Assembly were held on 24 March 1996. Some 689 candidates contested 220 of the Assembly's 250 seats, while the remaining 30 seats (reserved for representatives of the Autonomous Regions of Arbil, D'hok and As-Sulaimaniya) were filled by presidential decree. According to official sources, 93.5% of Iraq's 8m.-strong electorate participated in the elections.

Chairman: Dr SA'ADOUN HAMMADI.

Chairman of the Kurdish Legislative Council: AHMAD ABD AL-QADIR AN-NAQSHABANDI.

Political Organizations

National Progressive Front: Baghdad; f. July 1973, when Arab Baath Socialist Party and Iraqi Communist Party signed a joint manifesto agreeing to establish a comprehensive progressive national and nationalistic front. In 1975 representatives of Kurdish parties and organizations and other national and independent forces joined the Front; the Iraqi Communist Party left the National Progressive Front in mid-March 1979; Sec.-Gen. NAIM HADDAD (Baath).

Arab Baath Socialist Party: POB 6012, al-Mansour, Baghdad; revolutionary Arab socialist movement founded in Damascus in 1947; has ruled Iraq since July 1968, and between July 1973 and March 1979 in alliance with the Iraqi Communist Party in the National Progressive Front; founder MICHEL AFLAQ; Regional Command Sec.-Gen. SADDAM HUSSAIN; Deputy Regional Command Sec.-Gen. IZZAT IBRAHIM; mems. of Regional Command: TAHA YASSIN RAMADAN, TAREQ AZIZ, MUHAMMAD HAMZAH AZ-ZUBAYDI, ABD AL-GHANI ABD AL-GHAFUR, SA'ADOUN HAMMADI MAZBAN KHADR HADI, ALI HASSAN AL-MAJID, KAMIL YASSIN RASHID, MUHAMMAD ZIMAM ABD AR-RAZZAQ, MUHAMMAD YOUNIS AL-AHMAD, KHADER ABD AL-AZIZ HUSSAIN, ABD AR-RAHMAN AHMAD ABD AR-RAHMAN, NOURI FAISAL SHAHIR, MIZHER MATNI AL-AWWAD, FAWZI KHALAF, LATIF NUSAYYIF JASIM, ADEL ADBULLAH MEHDI; approx. 100,000 mems.

Kurdistan Revolutionary Party: f. 1972; succeeded Democratic Kurdistan Party; admitted to National Progressive Front 1974; Sec.-Gen. ABD AS-SATTAR TAHER SHAREF.

There are several illegal opposition groups, including:

Ad-Da'wa al-Islamiya (Voice of Islam): f. 1968; based in Teheran; mem. of the Supreme Council of the Islamic Revolution in Iraq (see below); guerrilla group; Leader Sheikh AL-ASSEFIE.

Iraqi Communist Party: Baghdad: f. 1934; became legally recognized in July 1973 on formation of National Progressive Front; left National Progressive Front March 1979; proscribed as a result of its support for Iran during the Iran–Iraq War; First Sec. AZIZ MUHAMMAD.

Umma (Nation) Party: f. 1982; opposes Saddam Hussain's regime; Leader SAAD SALEH JABR.

There is also a breakaway element of the Arab Baath Socialist Party represented on the Iraqi National Joint Action Cttee (see below); the Democratic Gathering (Leader SALEH DOUBLAH); the Iraqi Socialist Party (ISP; Leader Gen. HASSAN AN-NAQUIB); the Democratic Party of Kurdistan (DPK; f. 1946; Leader MASOUD BARZANI); the Patriotic Union of Kurdistan (PUK; f. 1975; Leader JALAL TALIBANI); the Socialist Party of Kurdistan (SPK; f. 1975; Leader RASSOUL MARMAND); the United Socialist Party of Kurdistan (USPK; Leader MAHMOUD OSMAN), a breakaway group from the PUK; the Kurdistan People's Democratic Party (KPDP; Leader SAMI ABD AR-RAHMAN); the Kurdish Workers' Party (PKK); the Islamic League of Kurdistan (ILK, also known as the Islamic Movement of Iraqi Kurdistan (IMIK)); the Kurdish Hezbollah (Party of God; f. 1985; Leader Sheikh MUHAMMAD KALED), a breakaway group from the DPK and a member of the Supreme Council of the Islamic Revolution in Iraq (SCIRI), which is based in Teheran under the leadership of the exiled Iraqi Shi'ite leader, Hojatoleslam MUHAMMAD BAQIR AL-HAKIM, and has a military wing, the Badr Brigade; the Iraqi National Accord (INA); and Hizb al-Watan or Homeland Party (Leader MISHAAN AL-JUBOURI).

Various alliances of political and religious groups have been formed to oppose the regime of Saddam Hussain in recent years. They include the Kurdistan Iraqi Front (KIF; f. 1988), an alliance of the DPK, the PUK, the SPK, the KPDP and other, smaller Kurdish groups; the Iraqi National Joint Action Cttee, formed in Damascus in 1990 and grouping together the SCIRI, the four principal Kurdish parties belonging to the KIF, Ad-Da'wa al-Islamiya, the Movement of the Iraqi Mujahidin (based in Teheran; Leaders Hojatoleslam MUHAMMAD BAQIR AL-HAKIM and SAID MUHAMMAD AL-HAIDARI), the Islamic Movement in Iraq (Shi'ite group based in Teheran; Leader Sheikh MUHAMMAD MAHDI AL-KALISI), Jund al-Imam (Imam Soldiers; Shi'ite; Leader ABU ZAID), the Islamic Action Organization (based in Teheran; Leader Sheikh TAQI MODARESSI), the Islamic Alliance (based in Saudi Arabia; Sunni; Leader ABU YASSER AL-

ALOUSI), the Independent Group, the Iraqi Socialist Party, the Arab Socialist Movement, the Nasserite Unionist Gathering and the National Reconciliation Group. There is also the London-based Iraqi National Congress (INC; Presidential Council: MASOUD BARZANI, Gen. HASSAN AN-NAQUIB, MUHAMMAD BAHR AL-OLOUM), which has sought to unite the various factions of the opposition and in November 1992 organized a conference in Iraqi Kurdistan, at which a 25-member executive committee and a three-member presidential council were elected. In September 1992 the KPDP, the SPK and the Kurdish Democratic Independence Party were reported to have merged to form the Kurdistan Unity Party (KUP).

Diplomatic Representation

EMBASSIES IN IRAQ

Afghanistan: Maghrib St, ad-Difa'ie, 27/1/12 Waziriya, Baghdad; tel. (1) 5560331; Ambassador: ABD AR-RASHID WASEQ.

Albania: Baghdad; Ambassador: GYLANI SHEHU.

Algeria: ash-Shawaf Sq., Karradat Mariam, Baghdad; tel. (1) 537-2181; Ambassador: AL-ARABI SI AL-HASSAN.

Argentina: POB 2443, Hay al-Jamia District 915, St 24, No. 142, Baghdad; tel. (1) 776-8140; telex 213500; Ambassador: GERÓNIMO CORTES-FUNES.

Australia: POB 661, Masba 39B/35, Baghdad; tel. (1) 719-3434; telex 212148; Ambassador: P. LLOYD.

Austria: POB 294, Hay Babel 929/2/5 Aqaba bin Nafi's Sq., Masbah, Baghdad; tel. (1) 719-9033; telex 212383; Ambassador: Dr ERWIN MATSCH.

Bahrain: POB 27117, al-Mansour, Hay al-Watanabi, Mahalla 605, Zuqaq 7, House 4/1/44, Baghdad; tel. (1) 5423656; telex 213364; Ambassador: ABD AR-RAHMAN AL-FADHIL.

Bangladesh: 75/17/929 Hay Babel, Baghdad; tel. (1) 7196367; telex 2370; Ambassador: MUFLEH R. OSMARRY.

Belgium: Hay Babel 929/27/25, Baghdad; tel. (1) 719-8297; telex 212450; Ambassador: MARC VAN RYSSELBERGHE.

Brazil: 609/16 al-Mansour, Houses 62/62–1, Baghdad; tel. (1) 5411365; telex 2240; Ambassador: MAURO SERGIO CONTO.

Bulgaria: POB 28022, Ameriya, New Diplomatic Quarter, Baghdad; tel. (1) 556-8197; Ambassador: ASSEN ZLATANOV.

Canada: 47/1/7 al-Mansour, Baghdad; tel. (1) 542-1459; telex 212486; Ambassador: DAVID KARSGAARD.

Central African Republic: 208/406 az-Zawra, Harthiya, Baghdad; tel. (1) 551-6520; Chargé d'affaires: RENÉ BISSAYO.

Chad: POB 8037, 97/4/4 Karradat Mariam, Baghdad; tel. (1) 537-6160; Ambassador: MAHAMAT DJIBER AHNOUR.

China, People's Republic: New Embassy Area, International Airport Rd, Baghdad; tel. (1) 556-2740; telex 212195; Ambassador: SUN BIGAN.

Cuba: St 7, District 929 Hay Babel, al-Masba Arrasat al-Hindi; tel. 719-5177; telex 212389; Ambassador: JUAN ALDAMA LUGONES.

Czech Republic: Dijlaschool St, No. 37, Mansour, Baghdad; tel. (1) 5424868; telex 213543; fax (1) 5430275.

Denmark: POB 2001, Zuqaq No. 34, Mahalla 902, Hay al-Wahda, House No. 18/1, Alwiyah, Baghdad; tel. (1) 719-3058; telex 212490; Ambassador: TORBEN G. DITHMER.

Djibouti: POB 6223, al-Mansour, Baghdad; tel. (1) 551-3805; Ambassador: ABSEIA BOOH ABDULLA.

Finland: POB 2041, Alwiyah, Baghdad; tel. (1) 776 6271; telex 212454; Ambassador: (vacant).

Germany: Zuqaq 2, Mahalla 929, Hay Babel (Masbah Square), Baghdad; tel. (1) 719-2037; telex 212262; fax (1) 7180340; Ambassador: Dr RICHARD ELLERKMANN.

Greece: 63/3/913 Hay al-Jamia, al-Jadiriya, Baghdad; tel. (1) 776-6572; telex 212479; Ambassador: EPAMINONDAS PEYOS.

Holy See: POB 2090, as-Sa'adoun St 904/2/46, Baghdad (Apostolic Nunciature); tel. (1) 719-5183; fax (1) 719-6520; Apostolic Nuncio: Most Rev. GIUSEPPE LAZZAROTTO, Titular Archbishop of Numana.

Hungary: POB 2065, Abu Nuwas St, az-Zuwiya, Baghdad; tel. (1) 776-5000; telex 212293; Ambassador: TAMÁS VARGA; also represents Italian interests.

India: POB 4114, Zuqaq 25, Mahalla 306, Baghdad; tel. (1) 422-5438; telex 212248; Ambassador: ARIF QAMARAIN.

Indonesia: 906/2/77 Hay al-Wahda, Baghdad; tel. (1) 719-8677; telex 2517; Ambassador: A. A. MURTADHO.

Iran: Karradat Mariam, Baghdad; Ambassador: (vacant).

Ireland: 913/28/101 Hay al-Jamia, Baghdad; tel. (1) 7768661; Ambassador: PATRICK MCCABE.

Japan: 929/17/70 Hay Babel, Masba, Baghdad; tel. (1) 719-5156; telex 212241; fax (1) 7196186; Ambassador: TAIZO NAKAMARA.

Jordan: POB 6314, House No. 1, St 12, District 609, al-Mansour, Baghdad; tel. (1) 541-2892; telex 2805; Ambassador: HILMI LOZI.

Korea, Republic: 915/22/278 Hay al-Jamia, Baghdad; tel. (1) 7765496; Ambassador: BONG RHUEM CHEI.

Libya: Baghdad; Head of the Libyan People's Bureau: ABBAS AHMAD AL-MASSRATI (acting).

Malaysia: 6/14/929 Hay Babel, Baghdad; tel. (1) 7762622; telex 2452; Ambassador: K. N. NADARAJAH.

Malta: 2/1 Zuqaq 49, Mahalla 503, Hay an-Nil, Baghdad; tel. (1) 7725032; Chargé d'affaires a.i.: NADER SALEM RIZZO.

Mauritania: al-Mansour, Baghdad; tel. (1) 551-8261; Ambassador: MUHAMMAD YEHYA WALAD AHMAD AL-HADI.

Mexico: 601/11/45 al-Mansour, Baghdad; tel. (1) 719-8039; telex 2582; Chargé d'affaires: VÍCTOR M. DELGADO.

Morocco: POB 6039, Hay al-Mansour, Baghdad; tel. (1) 552-1779; Ambassador: ABOLESLAM ZENINED.

Netherlands: POB 2064, 29/35/915 Jadiriya, Baghdad; tel. (1) 776-7616; telex 212276; Ambassador: Dr N. VAN DAM.

New Zealand: POB 2350, 2D/19 az-Zuwiya, Jadiriya, Baghdad; tel. (1) 776-8177; telex 212433; Ambassador: (vacant).

Nigeria: POB 5933, 2/3/603 Mutanabi, al-Mansour, Baghdad; tel. (1) 5421750; telex 212474; Ambassador: A. G. ABDULLAHI.

Oman: POB 6180, 213/36/15 al-Harthiya, Baghdad; tel. (1) 551-8198; telex 212480; Ambassador: KHALIFA BIN ABDULLA BIN SALIM AL-HOMAIDI.

Pakistan: 14/7/609 al-Mansour, Baghdad; tel. (1) 541-5120; Ambassador: KHALID MAHMOUD.

Philippines: Hay Babel, Baghdad; tel. (1) 719-3228; telex 3463; Ambassador: AKMAD A. SAKKAN.

Poland: POB 2051, 30 Zuqaq 13, Mahalla 931, Hay Babel, Baghdad; tel. (1) 719-0296; Ambassador: KRZYSZTOF SLOMINSKI.

Portugal: POB 2123, 66/11 al-Karada ash-Sharqiya, Hay Babel, Sector 925, St 25, No. 79, Alwiya, Baghdad; tel. (1) 718-7524; telex 212716; Ambassador: (vacant).

Qatar: 152/406 Harthiya, Hay al-Kindi, Baghdad; tel. (1) 551-2186; telex 2391; Ambassador: MUHAMMAD RASHID KHALIFA AL-KHALIFA.

Romania: Arassat al-Hindia, Hay Babel, Zuqaq 31, Mahalla 929, No 452/A, Baghdad; tel. (1) 7762860; telex 2268; Ambassador: IONEL MIHAIL CETATEANU.

Russia: 4/5/605 al-Mutanabi, Baghdad; tel. (1) 541-4749; Ambassador: VIKTOR J. MININ.

Senegal: 569/5/10, Hay al-Mansour Baghdad; tel. (1) 5420806; Ambassador: DOUDOU DIOP.

Slovakia: POB 238, Jamiyah St, No. 94, Jadiriyah, Baghdad; tel. (1) 7767367; telex 214068.

Somalia: 603/1/5 al-Mansour, Baghdad; tel. (1) 551-0088; Ambassador: ISSA ALI MOHAMMED.

Spain: POB 2072, ar-Riyad Quarter, District 908, Street No. 1, No. 21, Alwiya, Baghdad; tel. (1) 719-2852; telex 212239; Ambassador: JUAN LÓPEZ DE CHICHERI.

Sri Lanka: POB 1094, 07/80/904 Hay al-Wahda, Baghdad; tel. (1) 719-3040; Ambassador: N. NAVARATNARAJAH.

Sudan: 38/15/601 al-Imarat, Baghdad; tel. (1) 542-4889; Ambassador: ALI ADAM MUHAMMAD AHMAD.

Sweden: 15/41/103 Hay an-Nidhal, Baghdad; tel. (1) 719-5361; telex 212352; Ambassador: HENRIK AMNEUS.

Switzerland: POB 2107, Hay Babel, House No. 41/5/929, Baghdad; tel. (1) 719-3091; telex 212243; Ambassador: HANS-RUDOLF HOFFMANN.

Thailand: POB 6062, 1/4/609, al-Mansour, Baghdad; tel. (1) 5418798; telex 213345; Ambassador: CHEUY SUETRONG.

Tunisia: POB 6057, Mansour 34/2/4, Baghdad; tel. (1) 551-7786; Ambassador: LARBI HANTOUS.

Turkey: POB 14001, 2/8 Waziriya, Baghdad; tel. (1) 422-2768; telex 214145; Ambassador: SÖNMEZ KÖKSAL.

Uganda: 41/1/609 al-Mansour, Baghdad; tel. (1) 551-3594; Ambassador: SWAIB M. MUSOKE.

United Arab Emirates: al-Mansour, 50 al-Mansour Main St, Baghdad; tel. (1) 551-7026; telex 2285; Ambassador: HILAL SA'ID HILAL AZ-ZU'ABI.

Venezuela: al-Mansour, House No. 12/79/601, Baghdad; tel. (1) 552-0965; telex 2173; Ambassador: FREDDY RAFAEL ALVAREZ YANES.

Viet Nam: 29/611 Hay al-Andalus, Baghdad; tel. (1) 551-1388; Ambassador: TRAN KY LONG.

Yemen: Jadiriya 923/28/29, Baghdad; tel. (1) 776-0647; Ambassador: MOHAMMED ABDULLAH ASH-SHAMI.

Yugoslavia: POB 2061, 16/35/923 Hay Babel, Jadiriya, Baghdad; tel. (1) 776-7887; telex 213521; fax (1) 217-1069; Chargé d'affaires a.i.: JOVAN KOSTIĆ.

Judicial System

Courts in Iraq consist of the following: The Court of Cassation, Courts of Appeal, First Instance Courts, Peace Courts, Courts of Sessions, *Shari'a* Courts and Penal Courts.

The Court of Cassation: This is the highest judicial bench of all the Civil Courts; it sits in Baghdad, and consists of the President and a number of vice-presidents and not fewer than 15 permanent judges, delegated judges and reporters as necessity requires. There are four bodies in the Court of Cassation, these are: (*a*) the General body, (*b*) Civil and Commercial body, (*c*) Personal Status body, (*d*) the Penal body.

Courts of Appeal: The country is divided into five Districts of Appeal: Baghdad, Mosul, Basra, Hilla, and Kirkuk, each with its Court of Appeal consisting of a president, vice-presidents and not fewer than three members, who consider the objections against the decisions issued by the First Instance Courts of first grade.

Courts of First Instance: These courts are of two kinds: Limited and Unlimited in jurisdiction.

Limited Courts deal with Civil and Commercial suits, the value of which is 500 Iraqi dinars and less; and suits, the value of which cannot be defined, and which are subject to fixed fees. Limited Courts consider these suits in the final stage and they are subject to Cassation.

Unlimited Courts consider the Civil and Commercial suits irrespective of their value, and suits the value of which exceeds 500 Iraqi dinars with first grade subject to appeal.

First Instance Courts consist of one judge in the centre of each *Liwa*, some *Qadhas* and *Nahiyas*, as the Minister of Justice judges necessary.

Courts of Sessions: There is in every District of Appeal a Court of Sessions which consists of three judges under the presidency of the President of the Court of Appeal or one of his vice-presidents. It considers the penal suits prescribed by Penal Proceedings Law and other laws. More than one Court of Sessions may be established in one District of Appeal by notification issued by the Minister of Justice mentioning therein its headquarters, jurisdiction and the manner of its establishment.

Shari'a Courts: A *Shari'a* Court is established wherever there is a First Instance Court; the Muslim judge of the First Instance Court may be a *Qadhi* to the *Shari'a* Court if a special *Qadhi* has not been appointed thereto. The *Shari'a* Court considers matters of personal status and religious matters in accordance with the provisions of the law supplement to the Civil and Commercial Proceedings Law.

Penal Courts: A Penal Court of first grade is established in every First Instance Court. The judge of the First Instance Court is considered as penal judge unless a special judge is appointed thereto. More than one Penal Court may be established to consider the suits prescribed by the Penal Proceedings Law and other laws.

One or more Investigation Court may be established in the centre of each *Liwa* and a judge is appointed thereto. They may be established in the centres of *Qadhas* and *Nahiyas* by order of the Minister of Justice. The judge carries out the investigation in accordance with the provisions of Penal Proceedings Law and the other laws.

There is in every First Instance Court a department for the execution of judgments presided over by the Judge of First Instance if a special president is not appointed thereto. It carries out its duties in accordance with the provisions of Execution Law.

Religion

ISLAM

About 95% of the population are Muslims, more than 50% of whom are Shi'ite. The Arabs of northern Iraq, the Bedouins, the Kurds, the Turkomans and some of the inhabitants of Baghdad and Basra are mainly of the Sunni sect, while the remaining Arabs south of the Diyali belong to the Shi'i sect.

CHRISTIANITY

There are Christian communities in all the principal towns of Iraq, but their principal villages lie mostly in the Mosul district. The Christians of Iraq comprise three groups: (*a*) the free Churches, including the Nestorian, Gregorian and Syrian Orthodox; (*b*) the churches known as Uniate, since they are in union with the Roman Catholic Church, including the Armenian Uniates, Syrian Uniates and Chaldeans; (*c*) mixed bodies of Protestant converts, New Chaldeans and Orthodox Armenians.

The Assyrian Church

Assyrian Christians, an ancient sect having sympathies with Nestorian beliefs, were forced to leave their mountainous homeland in northern Kurdistan in the early part of the 20th century. The estimated 550,000 members of the Apostolic Catholic Assyrian Church of the East are now exiles, mainly in Iraq, Syria, Lebanon and the USA. Their leader is the Catholicos Patriarch, His Holiness MAR DINKHA IV.

The Orthodox Churches

Armenian Apostolic Church: Bishop AVAK ASADOURIAN, Primate of the Armenian Diocese of Iraq, POB 2280, Younis as-Saba'awi Sq., Baghdad; tel. (1) 885-1853; fax (1) 885-1857; nine churches (four in Baghdad); 18,000 adherents, mainly in Baghdad.

Syrian Orthodox Church: about 12,000 adherents in Iraq.

The Greek Orthodox Church is also represented in Iraq.

The Roman Catholic Church

Armenian Rite

At 31 December 1995 the archdiocese of Baghdad contained an estimated 2,200 adherents.

Archbishop of Baghdad: Most Rev. PAUL COUSSA, Archevêché Arménien Catholique, Karrada Sharkiya, POB 2344, Baghdad; tel. (1) 719-1827.

Chaldean Rite

Iraq comprises the patriarchate of Babylon, five archdioceses (including the patriarchal see of Baghdad) and five dioceses (all of which are suffragan to the patriarchate). Altogether, the Patriarch has jurisdiction over 21 archdioceses and dioceses in Iraq, Egypt, Iran, Lebanon, Syria, Turkey and the USA, and the Patriarchal Vicariate of Jerusalem. At 31 December 1995 there were an estimated 214,009 Chaldean Catholics in Iraq (including 150,500 in the archdiocese of Baghdad).

Patriarch of Babylon of the Chaldeans: His Beatitude RAPHAËL I BIDAWID, POB 6112, Patriarcat Chaldéen Catholique, Baghdad; tel. (1) 887-9604; fax (1) 884-9967.

Archbishop of Arbil: (vacant), Archevêché Catholique Chaldéen, Ainkawa, Arbil; tel. (665) 526681.

Archbishop of Baghdad: the Patriarch of Babylon (see above).

Archbishop of Basra: Most Rev. DJIBRAIL KASSAB, Archevêché Chaldéen, POB 217, Ahsar-Basra; tel. (40) 210323.

Archbishop of Kirkuk: Most Rev. ANDRÉ SANA, Archevêché Chaldéen, Kirkuk; tel. (50) 213978.

Archbishop of Mosul: Most Rev. GEORGES GARMO, Archevêché Chaldéen, Mayassa, Mosul; tel. (60) 762149.

Latin Rite

The archdiocese of Baghdad, directly responsible to the Holy See, contained an estimated 3,000 adherents at 31 December 1995.

Archbishop of Baghdad: Most Rev. PAUL DAHDAH, Archevêché Latin, Hay al-Wahda—Mahalla 904, rue 8, Imm. 44, POB 35130, Baghdad; tel. (1) 719-9537; fax (1) 717-2471.

Melkite Rite

The Greek-Melkite Patriarch of Antioch (MAXIMOS V HAKIM) is resident in Damascus, Syria.

Patriarchal Exarchate of Iraq: Rue Asfar, Karrada Sharkiya, Baghdad; tel. (1) 719-1082; 600 adherents (31 December 1995); Exarch Patriarchal: Archimandrite NICOLAS DAGHER.

Syrian Rite

Iraq comprises two archdioceses, containing an estimated 51,700 adherents at 31 December 1995.

Archbishop of Baghdad: Most Rev. ATHANASE MATTI SHABA MATOKA, Archevêché Syrien Catholique, Baghdad; tel. (1) 719-1850; fax (1) 719-0168.

Archbishop of Mosul: Most Rev. CYRILLE EMMANUEL BENNI, Archevêché Syrien Catholique, Mosul; tel. (60) 762160.

The Anglican Communion

Within the Episcopal Church in Jerusalem and the Middle East, Iraq forms part of the diocese of Cyprus and the Gulf. Expatriate congregations in Iraq meet at St George's Church, Baghdad (Hon. Sec. GRAHAM SPURGEON). The Bishop in Cyprus and the Gulf is resident in Cyprus.

JUDAISM

Unofficial estimates assess the present size of the Jewish community at 2,500, almost all residing in Baghdad.

OTHERS

About 30,000 Yazidis and a smaller number of Turkomans, Sabeans and Shebeks reside in Iraq.

Sabean Community: 20,000 adherents; Head Sheikh DAKHIL, Nasiriyah; Mandeans, mostly in Nasiriyah.

Yazidis: 30,000 adherents; Leader TASHIN BAIK, Ainsifni.

The Press

DAILIES

Al-Baath ar-Riyadhi: Baghdad; sports; Propr and Editor UDAI SADDAM HUSSAIN.

Babil (Babylon): Baghdad; f. 1991; Propr and Editor UDAI SADDAM HUSSAIN.

Baghdad Observer: POB 624, Karantina, Baghdad; f. 1967; tel. (1) 416-9341; telex 212984; English; state-sponsored; Editor-in-Chief NAJI AL-HADITHI; circ. 22,000.

Al-Iraq: POB 5717, Baghdad; f. 1976; Kurdish; formerly *Al-Ta'akhi*; organ of the National Progressive Front; Editor-in-Chief SALAHUDIN SAEED; circ. 30,000.

Al-Jumhuriya (The Republic): POB 491, Waziriya, Baghdad; f. 1963, refounded 1967; Arabic; Editor-in-Chief SAMI MAHDI; circ. 150,000.

Al-Qadisiya: Baghdad; organ of the army.

Ar-Riyadhi (Sportsman): POB 58, Jadid Hassan Pasha, Baghdad; f. 1971; Arabic; published by Ministry of Youth; circ. 30,000.

Tariq ash-Sha'ab (People's Path): as-Sa'adoun St, Baghdad; Arabic; organ of the Iraqi Communist Party; Editor ABD AR-RAZZAK AS-SAFI.

Ath-Thawra (Revolution): POB 2009, Aqaba bin Nafi's Square, Baghdad; tel. (1) 719-6161; f. 1968; Arabic; organ of Baath Party; Editor-in-Chief HAMEED SAEED; circ. 250,000.

WEEKLIES

Alif Baa (Alphabet): POB 491, Karantina, Baghdad; tel. (1) 416-9341; telex 212984; fax (1) 416-1875; Arabic; Editor-in-Chief KAMIL ASH-SHARQI; circ. 150,000.

Al-Idaa'a wal-Television (Radio and Television): Iraqi Broadcasting and Television Establishment, Karradat Mariam, Baghdad; tel. (1) 537-1161; telex 212246; radio and television programmes and articles; Arabic; Editor-in-Chief KAMIL HAMDI ASH-SHARQI; circ. 40,000.

Majallati: Children's Culture House, POB 8041, Baghdad; telex 212228; Arabic; children's newspaper; Editor-in-Chief FAROUQ SALLOUM; circ. 35,000.

Ar-Rased (The Observer): Baghdad; Arabic; general.

Sabaa Nisan: Baghdad; f. 1976; Arabic; organ of the General Union of the Youth of Iraq.

Sawt al-Fallah (Voice of the Peasant): Karradat Mariam, Baghdad; f. 1968; Arabic; organ of the General Union of Farmers Societies; circ. 40,000.

Waee ul-Ummal (The Workers' Consciousness): Headquarters of General Federation of Trade Unions in Iraq, POB 2307, Gialani St, Senak, Baghdad; Arabic; Iraq Trades Union organ; Chief Editor KHALID MAHMOUD HUSSEIN; circ. 25,000.

PERIODICALS

Afaq Arabiya (Arab Horizons): POB 2009, Aqaba bin Nafi's Sq., Baghdad; monthly; Arabic; literary and political; Editor-in-Chief Dr MOHSIN J. AL-MUSAWI.

Al-Aqlam (Pens): POB 4032, Adamiya, Baghdad; tel. (1) 443-3644; telex 214135; f. 1964; publ. by the Ministry of Culture and Information; monthly; Arabic; literary; Editor-in-Chief Dr ALI J. AL-ALLAQ; circ. 7,000.

Bagdad: Dar al-Ma'mun for Translation and Publishing, POB 24015, Karradat Mariam, Baghdad; tel. (1) 538-3171; telex 212984; fortnightly; French; cultural and political.

Al-Funoon al-Ida'iya (Fields of Broadcasting): Cultural Affairs House, Karradat Mariam, Baghdad; quarterly; Arabic; supervised by Broadcasting and TV Training Institute; engineering and technical; Chief Editor MUHAMMAD AL-JAZA'RI.

Gilgamesh: Dar al-Ma'mun for Translation and Publishing, POB 24015, Karradat Mariam, Baghdad; tel. (1) 538-3171; telex 212984; quarterly; English; cultural.

Hurras al-Watan: Baghdad; Arabic.

L'Iraq Aujourd'hui: POB 2009, Aqaba bin Nafi's Sq, Baghdad; f. 1976; bi-monthly; French; cultural and political; Editor NADJI AL-HADITHI; circ. 12,000.

Iraq Oil News: POB 6178, al-Mansour, Baghdad; tel. (1) 541-0031; telex 2216; f. 1973; monthly; English; publ. by the Information and Public Relations Div. of the Ministry of Oil.

The Journal of the Faculty of Medicine: College of Medicine, University of Baghdad, Jadiriya, Baghdad; tel. (1) 93091; f. 1935; quarterly; Arabic and English; medical and technical; Editor Prof. YOUSUF D. AN-NAAMAN.

Majallat al-Majma' al-'Ilmi al-'Iraqi (Iraqi Academy Journal): Iraqi Academy, Waziriyah, Baghdad; f. 1947; quarterly; Arabic; scholarly magazine on Arabic Islamic culture; Gen. Sec. Dr NURI HAMMOUDI AL-QAISI.

Majallat ath-Thawra az-Ziraia (Magazine of Iraq Agriculture): Baghdad; quarterly; Arabic; agricultural; published by the Ministry of Agriculture and Irrigation.

Al-Maskukat (Coins): State Organization of Antiquities and Heritage, Karkh, Salihiya St, Baghdad; tel. (1) 537-6121; f. 1969; annually; the journal of numismatics in Iraq; Chair. of Ed. Board Dr MUAYAD SA'ID DAMERJI.

Al-Masrah wal-Cinema: Iraqi Broadcasting, Television and Cinema Establishment, Salihiya, Baghdad; monthly; Arabic; artistic, theatrical and cinema.

Al-Mawrid: POB 2009, Aqaba bin Nafi's Sq, Baghdad; f. 1971; monthly; Arabic; cultural.

Al-Mu'allem al-Jadid: Ministry of Education, al-Imam al-A'dham St, A'dhamaiya, Nr Antar Sq., Baghdad; tel. (1) 422-2594; telex 212259; f. 1935; quarterly; Arabic; educational, social, and general; Editor in Chief KHALIL I. HAMASH; circ. 190,000.

An-Naft wal-Aalam (Oil and the World): Ministry of Oil, POB 6178, Baghdad; f. 1973; monthly; Arabic; Editor-in-Chief USAMA ABD AR-RAZZAQ HAMMADI AL-HITHI (Minister of Oil).

Sawt at-Talaba (The Voice of Students): al-Maghreb St, Waziriyah, Baghdad; f. 1968; monthly; Arabic; organ of National Union of Iraqi Students; circ. 25,000.

As-Sina'a (Industry): POB 5665, Baghdad; every 2 months; Arabic and English; publ. by Ministry of Industry and Minerals; Editor-in-Chief ABD AL-QADER ABD AL-LATIF; circ. 16,000.

Sumer: State Organization of Antiquities and Heritage, Karkh, Salihiya St, Baghdad; tel. (1) 537-6121; f. 1945; annually; archaeological, historical journal; Chair. of Ed. Board Dr MUAYAD SA'ID DAMERJI.

Ath-Thaqafa (Culture): Place at-Tahrir, Baghdad; f. 1970; monthly; Arabic; cultural; Editor-in-Chief SALAH KHALIS; circ. 5,000.

Ath-Thaquafa al-Jadida (The New Culture): Baghdad; f. 1969; monthly; pro-Communist; Editor-in-Chief SAFA AL-HAFIZ; circ. 3,000.

At-Turath ash-Sha'abi (Popular Heritage): POB 2009, Aqaba bin Nafi's Sq., Baghdad; monthly; Arabic; specializes in Iraqi and Arabic folklore; Editor-in-Chief LUTFI AL-KHOURI; circ. 15,000.

Al-Waqai al-Iraqiya (Official Gazette of Republic of Iraq): Ministry of Justice, Baghdad; f. 1922; Arabic and English weekly editions; circ. Arabic 10,500, English 700; Dir HASHIM N. JAAFER.

PRESS ORGANIZATIONS

The General Federation of Journalists: POB 6017, Baghdad; tel. (1) 541-3993.

Iraqi Journalists' Union: POB 14101, Baghdad; tel. (1) 537-0762.

NEWS AGENCIES

Iraqi News Agency (INA): POB 3084, 28 Nissan Complex—Baghdad, Sadoun; tel. (1) 8863024; telex 212267; f. 1959; Dir-Gen. UDAI EL-TAIE.

Foreign Bureaux

Agence France-Presse (AFP): POB 190, Apt 761-91-97, Baghdad; tel. (1) 551-4333; Correspondent FAROUQ CHOUKRI.

Agenzia Nazionale Stampa Associata (ANSA) (Italy): POB 5602, Baghdad; tel. (1) 776-2558; Correspondent SALAH H. NASRAWI.

Associated Press (AP) (USA): Hay al-Khadra 629, Zuqaq No. 23, Baghdad; tel. (1) 555-9041; telex 213324; Correspondent SALAH H. NASRAWI.

Deutsche Presse-Agentur (dpa) (Germany): POB 5699, Baghdad; Correspondent NAJHAT KOTANI.

Informatsionnoye Telegrafnoye Agentstvo Rossii—Telegrafnoye Agentstvo Suverennykh Stran (ITAR—TASS) (Russia): 67 Street 52, Alwiya, Baghdad; Correspondent ANDREI OSTALSKY.

Reuters (UK): House No. 8, Zuqaq 75, Mahalla 903, Hay al-Karada, Baghdad; tel. (1) 719-1843; telex 213777; Correspondent SUBHY HADDAD.

Xinhua (New China) News Agency (People's Republic of China): al-Mansour, Adrus District, 611 Small District, 5 Lane No. 8, Baghdad; tel. (1) 541-8904; telex 213253; Correspondent ZHU SHAOHUA.

Publishers

National House for Publishing, Distribution and Advertising: Ministry of Culture and Information, POB 624, al-Jumhuriya St, Baghdad; tel. (1) 425-1846; telex 2392; f. 1972; publishes books on politics, economics, education, agriculture, sociology, commerce and science in Arabic and other Middle Eastern languages; sole importer and distributor of newspapers, magazines, periodicals and books; controls all advertising activities, inside Iraq as well as outside; Dir-Gen. M. A. ASKAR.

Afaq Arabiya Publishing House: POB 4032, Adamiya, Baghdad; tel. (1) 443-6044; telex 214135; fax (1) 4448760; publisher of literary monthlies, *Al-Aqlam* and *Afaq Arabiya*, periodicals, *Foreign Culture, Art, Folklore,* and cultural books; Chair. Dr MOHSIN AL-MUSAWI.

Dar al-Ma'mun for Translation and Publishing: POB 24015, Karradat Mariam, Baghdad; tel. (1) 538-3171; telex 212984; publisher of newspapers and magazines including: the *Baghdad Observer* (daily newspaper), *Bagdad* (monthly magazine), *Gilgamesh* (quarterly magazine).

Al-Hurriyah Printing Establishment: Karantina, Sarrafia, Baghdad; tel. (1) 69721; telex 212228; f. 1970; largest printing and publishing establishment in Iraq; state-owned; controls *Al-Jumhuriyah* (see below).

Al-Jamaheer Press House: POB 491, Sarrafia, Baghdad; tel. (1) 416-9341; telex 212363; fax (1) 416-1875; f. 1963; publisher of a number of newspapers and magazines, *Al-Jumhuriyah, Baghdad Observer, Alif Baa, Yord Weekly*; Pres. SAAD QASSEM HAMMOUDI.

Al-Ma'arif Ltd: Mutanabi St, Baghdad; f. 1929; publishes periodicals and books in Arabic, Kurdish, Turkish, French and English.

Al-Muthanna Library: Mutanabi St, Baghdad; f. 1936; booksellers and publishers of books in Arabic and oriental languages; Man. ANAS K. AR-RAJAB.

An-Nahdah: Mutanabi St, Baghdad; politics, Arab affairs.

Kurdish Culture Publishing House: Baghdad; f. 1976; attached to the Ministry of Culture and Information.

Ath-Thawra Printing and Publishing House: POB 2009, Aqaba bin Nafi's Sq., Baghdad; tel. (1) 719-6161; telex 212215; f. 1970; state-owned; Chair. TAREQ AZIZ.

Thnayan Printing House: Baghdad.

Broadcasting and Communications

TELECOMMUNICATIONS

Iraqi Telecommunications and Posts: POB 2450, Karrada Dakhil, Baghdad; tel. (1) 718-0400; telex 212002; fax (1) 718-2125; Dir-Gen. Eng. MEZHER M. HASAN.

BROADCASTING

State Enterprise for Communications and Post: f. 1987 from State Org. for Post, Telegraph and Telephones, and its subsidiaries.

State Organization for Broadcasting and Television: Broadcasting and Television Bldg, Salihiya, Karkh, Baghdad; tel. (1) 537-1161; telex 212246.

Iraqi Broadcasting and Television Establishment: Salihiya, Baghdad; tel. (1) 884-4412; telex 212246; fax (1) 541-0480; f. 1936; radio broadcasts began 1936; home service broadcasts in Arabic, Kurdish, Syriac and Turkoman; foreign service in French, German, English, Russian, Azeri, Hebrew and Spanish; there are 16 medium-wave and 30 short-wave transmitters; Dir-Gen. SABAH YASEEN.

Radio

Idaa'a Baghdad (Radio Baghdad): f.1936; 22 hours daily.

Idaa'a Sawt al-Jamahir: f. 1970; 24 hours.

Other stations include **Idaa'a al-Kurdia, Idaa'a al-Farisiya** (Persian).

Radio Iraq International: POB 8145, Baghdad.

Television

Baghdad Television: Ministry of Culture and Information, Iraqi Broadcasting and Television Establishment, Salihiya, Karkh, Baghdad; tel. (1) 537-1151; telex 212446; f. 1956; government station operating daily on two channels for 9 hours and 8 hours respectively; Dir-Gen. Dr MAJID AHMAD AS-SAMARRIE.

Kirkuk Television: f. 1967; government station; 6 hours daily.

Mosul Television: f. 1968; government station; 6 hours daily.

Basra Television: f. 1968; government station; 6 hours daily.

Missan Television: f. 1974; government station; 6 hours daily.

Kurdish Television: f. 1974; government station; 8 hours daily.

There are 18 other TV stations operating in the Iraqi provinces.

Finance

(cap. = capital; p.u. = paid up; dep. = deposits; res = reserves; brs = branches; m. = million; amounts in Iraqi dinars)

All banks and insurance companies, including all foreign companies, were nationalized in July 1964. The assets of foreign companies were taken over by the State. In May 1991 the Government announced its decision to end the State's monopoly in banking, and by mid-1992 three private banks had commenced operations.

BANKING

Central Bank

Central Bank of Iraq: POB 64, Rashid St, Baghdad; tel. (1) 886-5171; telex 212558; f. 1947 as National Bank of Iraq; name changed as above 1956; has the sole right of note issue; cap. and res 125m. (Sept. 1988); Gov. SUBHI N. FRANKOOL; brs in Mosul and Basra.

Nationalized Commercial Banks

Rafidain Bank: New Banks St, Baghdad; tel. (1) 415-8001; telex 2211; f. 1941; state-owned; cap. 500m., res 1,379.7m., dep. 213,284.4m., total assets 234,444.2m. (Dec. 1995); Pres. DHIA HABIB AL-KHAYYOON; 152 brs in Iraq, 9 brs abroad.

Rashid Bank: 7177 Haifa St, Baghdad; tel. (1) 5239123; telex 214357; f. 1988; state-owned; cap. 200m., res 209.1m., dep. 53,377.1m., total assets 61,005.9m. (Dec. 1994); Chair. and Gen. Man. SAMI SALEH ADH-DHAMIN; 133 brs.

Private Commercial Banks

Baghdad Bank: POB 64, Rashid St, Baghdad; tel. (1) 7175007; fax (1) 7173487; f. 1992; cap. 100m.; Chair. HASSAN AN-NAJAFI.

Dula Bank: f. 1991; cap. 100m.

Iraqi Commercial Bank SA: POB 5639, 902/14/13 Al-Wahda St, Baghdad; tel. (1) 707-0049, telex 213305; fax (1) 718-4312; f. 1991; cap. 150m.; Chair. SHAWQI AL-KUBAISI.

Specialized Banks

Al-Ahli Bank for Agricultural Investment and Financing: Al-Huria Sq., Al-Ahh, Baghdad.

Agricultural Co-operative Bank of Iraq: POB 2024, Rashid St, Baghdad; tel. (1) 886-4768; fax (1) 886-5047; f. 1936; state-owned; cap. p.u. 295.7m., res 14m., dep 10.5., total assets 351.6m. (Dec. 1988); Dir-Gen. HDIYA H. AL-KHAYOUN; 32 brs.

Industrial Bank of Iraq: POB 5825, as-Sinak, Baghdad; tel. (1) 887-2181; telex 2224; fax (1) 888-3047; f. 1940; state-owned; cap. p.u. 59.7m., dep. 77.9m. (Dec. 1988); Dir-Gen. BASSIMA ABD AL-HADDI ADH-DHAHIR; 5 brs.

Iraqi Bank for Investment SA: POB 3724, 102/91/24 Hay as-Sadoon, Alwiya, Baghdad; tel. (1) 719-5401.

Iraqi Islamic Bank SA: POB 940, Al-Kahiay, Bab Al-Muathem, Baghdad; tel. (1) 414-0694; telex 213890.

Iraqi Middle East Bank for Investment: POB 10379, Bldg 65 Hay Babel, 929 Arasat al-Hindiay, Baghdad; tel. (1) 717-3745.

Real Estate Bank of Iraq: POB 8118, 29/222 Haifa St, Baghdad; tel. (1) 885-3212; telex 5880; f. 1949; state-owned; gives loans to assist the building industry; cap. p.u. 800m., res 11m., total assets 2,593.6m. (Dec. 1988); acquired the Co-operative Bank in 1970; Dir-Gen. ABD AR-RAZZAQ AZIZ; 18 brs.

Socialist Bank: f. 1991; state-owned; gives interest-free loans to civil servants and soldiers who obtained more than three decorations in the Iran–Iraq War; cap. 500m.; Dir-Gen. ISSAM HAWISH.

INSURANCE

Iraqi Life Insurance Co: POB 989, Aqaba bin Nafi's Sq, Khalid bin al-Waleed St, Baghdad; tel. (1) 7192184; telex 213818; f. 1959; state-owned; Chair. and Gen. Man. ABD AL-KHALIQ RAUF KHALIL.

Iraq Reinsurance Co: POB 297, Aqaba bin Nafi's Sq., Khalid bin al-Waleed St, Baghdad; tel. (1) 719-5131; telex 214407; fax (1) 791497; f. 1960; state-owned; transacts reinsurance business on the international market; total assets 93.2m. (1985); Chair. and Gen. Man. K. M. AL-MUDARIES.

National Insurance Co: POB 248, Al-Khullani St, Baghdad; tel. (1) 886-0730; telex 2397; f. 1950; cap. p.u. 20m.; state monopoly for general business and life insurance; Chair. and Gen. Man. MOWAFAQ H. RIDHA.

STOCK EXCHANGE

Capital Market Authority: Baghdad; Chair. MUHAMMAD HASSAN FAG EN-NOUR.

Trade and Industry

CHAMBERS OF COMMERCE

Federation of Iraqi Chambers of Commerce: Mustansir St, Baghdad; tel. (1) 888-6111; f. 1969; all Iraqi Chambers of Commerce are affiliated to the Federation; Chair. ABD AL-MOHSEN A. ABU ALKAHIL; Sec.-Gen. FUAD H. ABD AL-HADI.

INDUSTRIAL AND TRADE ASSOCIATIONS

In 1987 and 1988, as part of a programme of economic and administrative reform, to increase efficiency and productivity in industry and agriculture, many of the state organizations previously responsible for various industries were abolished or merged, and new state enterprises or mixed-sector national companies were established to replace them.

Military Industries Commission (MIC): Baghdad; attached to the Ministry of Defence; Chair. ABD AT-TAWAB ABDULLAH MULLAH HAWAISH.

State enterprises include the following:

Iraqi State Enterprise for Cement: f. 1987 by merger of central and southern state cement enterprises.

National Co for Chemical and Plastics Industries: Dir-Gen. RAJA BAYYATI.

The Rafidain Co for Building Dams: f. 1987 to replace the State Org. for Dams.

State Enterprise for Battery Manufacture: f. 1987; Dir-Gen. ADEL ABBOUD.

State Enterprise for Construction Industries: f. 1987 by merger of state orgs for gypsum, asbestos, and the plastic and concrete industries.

State Enterprise for Cotton Industries: f. 1988 by merger of State Org. for Cotton Textiles and Knitting, and the Mosul State Org. for Textiles.

State Enterprise for Drinks and Mineral Water: f. 1987 by merger of enterprises responsible for soft and alcoholic drinks.

State Enterprise for the Fertilizer Industries: f. by merger of Basra-based and central fertilizer enterprises.

State Enterprise for Import and Export: f. 1987 to replace the five state organizations responsible to the Ministry of Trade for productive commodities, consumer commodities, grain and food products, exports and imports.

State Enterprise for Leather Industries: f. 1987; Dir-Gen. MUHAMMAD ABD AL-MAJID.

State Enterprise for Sugar Beet: f. 1987 by merger of sugar enterprises in Mosul and Sulaimaniya.

State Enterprise for Textiles: f. 1987 to replace the enterprise for textiles in Baghdad, and the enterprise for plastic sacks in Tikrit.

State Enterprise for Tobacco and Cigarettes.

State Enterprise for Woollen Industries: f. by merger of state orgs for textiles and woollen textiles and Arbil-based enterprise for woollen textiles and women's clothing.

AGRICULTURAL ORGANIZATIONS

The following bodies are responsible to the Ministry of Agriculture and Irrigation:

State Agricultural Enterprise in Dujaila.

State Enterprise for Agricultural Supplies: Dir-Gen. MUHAMMAD KHAIRI.

State Enterprise for Developing Animal Wealth.

State Enterprise for Fodder.

State Enterprise for Grain Trading and Processing: Dir-Gen. ZUHAIR ABD AR-RAHMAN.

State Enterprise for Poultry (Central and Southern Areas).

State Enterprise for Poultry (Northern Area).

State Enterprise for Sea Fisheries: POB 260, Basra; telex 7011; Baghdad office: POB 3296, Baghdad; tel. (1) 92023; telex 212223; fleet of 3 fish factory ships, 2 fish carriers, 1 fishing boat.

PEASANT SOCIETIES

General Federation of Peasant Societies: Baghdad; f. 1959; has 734 affiliated Peasant Societies.

EMPLOYERS' ORGANIZATION

Iraqi Federation of Industries: Iraqi Federation of Industries Bldg, al-Khullani Sq., Baghdad; f. 1956; 6,000 mems; Pres. HATAM ABD AR-RASHID.

UTILITIES

Electricity

State Enterprise for Generation and Transmission of Electricity: f. 1987 from State Org. for Major Electrical Projects.

PETROLEUM AND GAS

Ministry of Oil: POB 6178, al-Mansour City, Baghdad; tel. (1) 551-0031; telex 212216; solely responsible until mid-1989 for petroleum sector and activities relevant to it; since mid-1989 these responsibilities have been shared with the Technical Corpn for Special Projects of the Ministry of Industry and Military Industrialization (Ministry of Industry and Minerals from July 1991); the Ministry was merged with INOC in 1987; the state organizations responsible to the ministry for petroleum refining and gas processing, for the distribution of petroleum products, for training personnel in the petroleum industry, and for gas were simultaneously abolished, and those for northern and southern petroleum, for petroleum equipment, for petroleum and gas exploration, for petroleum tankers, and for petroleum projects were converted into companies, as part of a plan to reorganize the petroleum industry and make it more efficient; Minister of Oil AMIR MUHAMMAD RASHID.

Iraq National Oil Co (INOC): POB 476, al-Khullani Sq., Baghdad; tel. (1) 887-1115; telex 212204; f. in 1964 to operate the petroleum industry at home and abroad; when Iraq nationalized its petroleum industry, structural changes took place in INOC, and it became solely responsible for exploration, production, transportation and marketing of Iraqi crude petroleum and petroleum products. INOC was merged with the Ministry of Oil in 1987, and the functions of some of the organizations under its control were transferred to newly-created ministerial departments or to companies responsible to the ministry.

Iraqi Oil Drilling Co: f. 1990.

Iraqi Oil Tankers Co: POB 37, Basra; tel. (40) 319990; telex 207007; fmrly the State Establishment for Oil Tankers; re-formed as a company in 1987; responsible to the Ministry of Oil for operating a fleet of 17 oil tankers; Chair. MUHAMMAD A. MUHAMMAD.

National Co for Distribution of Oil Products and Gas: POB 3, Rashid St, South Gate, Baghdad; tel. (1) 888-9911; telex 212247; fmrly a state organization; re-formed as a company in 1987; fleet of 6 tankers; Dir-Gen. ALI H. IJAM.

National Co for Manufacturing Oil Equipment: fmrly a state organization; re-formed as a company in 1987.

National Co for Oil and Gas Exploration: INOC Building, POB 476, al-Khullani Sq, Baghdad; fmrly the State Establishment for Oil and Gas Exploration; re-formed as a company in 1987; responsible for exploration and operations in difficult terrain such as marshes, swamps, deserts, valleys and in mountainous regions; Dir-Gen. RADHWAN AS-SAADI.

Northern Petroleum Co (NPC): POB 1, at-Ta'meem Governorate; f. 1987 by the merger of the fmr Northern and Central petroleum organizations to carry out petroleum operations in northern Iraq; Dir-Gen. GHAZI SABIR ALI.

Southern Petroleum Co (SPC): POB 240, Basra; fmrly the Southern Petroleum Organization; re-formed as the SPC in 1987 to undertake petroleum operations in southern Iraq; Dir-Gen. ASRI SALIH (acting).

State Co for Oil Marketing (SCOM): Man.-Dir ZEIN SADDAM AT-TAKRITI.

State Co for Oil Projects (SCOP): POB 198, Oil Compound, Baghdad; tel. (1) 774-1310; telex 212230; fmrly the State Org. for Oil Projects; re-formed as a company in 1987; responsible for construction of petroleum projects, mostly inside Iraq through direct execution, and also for design supervision of the projects and contracting with foreign enterprises, etc.; Dir-Gen. FALIH AL-KHAYYAT.

State Enterprise for Oil and Gas Industrialization in the South: f. 1988 by merger of enterprises responsible for the gas industry and petroleum refining in the south.

State Enterprise for Petrochemical Industries.

State Establishment for Oil Refining in the Central Area: Dir-Gen. KAMIL AL-FATLI.

State Establishment for Oil Refining in the North: Dir-Gen. TAHA HAMOUD.

State Establishment for Pipelines: Dir-Gen. SABAH ALI JOUMAH.

TRADE UNIONS

General Federation of Trade Unions of Iraq (GFTU): POB 3049, Tahrir Sq, Rashid St, Baghdad; tel. (1) 887-0810; telex 212457; f. 1959; incorporates six vocational trade unions and 18 local trade union federations in the governorates of Iraq; the number of workers in industry is 536,245, in agriculture 150,967 (excluding peasants) and in other services 476,621 (1986); GFTU is a member of the International Confederation of Arab Trade Unions and of the World Federation of Trade Unions; Pres. FADHIL MAHMOUD GHAREB.

Union of Teachers: Al-Mansour, Baghdad; Pres. Dr ISSA SALMAN HAMID.

Union of Palestinian Workers in Iraq: Baghdad; Sec.-Gen. SAMI ASH-SHAWISH.

There are also unions of doctors, pharmacologists, jurists, artists, and a General Federation of Iraqi Women (Chair. MANAL YOUNIS).

Transport

RAILWAYS

The metre-gauge line runs from Baghdad, through Khanaqin and Kirkuk, to Arbil. The standard gauge line covers the length of the country, from Rabia, on the Syrian border, via Mosul, to Baghdad (534 km), and from Baghdad to Basra and Umm Qasr (608 km), on the Arabian Gulf. A 404-km standard-gauge line linking Baghdad to Husaibah, near the Iraqi-Syrian frontier, was completed in 1983. The 638-km line from Baghdad, via al-Qaim (on the Syrian border), to Akashat, and the 252-km Kirkuk–Baiji–Haditha line, which was designed to serve industrial projects along its route, were opened in 1986. The 150-km line linking the Akashat phosphate mines and the fertilizer complex at al-Qaim was formally opened in January 1986 but had already been in use for two years. Lines totalling some 2,400 km were planned at the beginning of the 1980s, but by 1988 only 800 km had been constructed. All standard-gauge trains are now hauled by diesel-electric locomotives, and all narrow-gauge (one-metre) line has been replaced by standard gauge (1,435 mm). As well as the internal service, there is a regular international service between Baghdad and İstanbul. A rapid transit transport system is to be established in Baghdad, with work to be undertaken as part of the 1987–2001 development plan for the city.

Responsibility for all railways, other than the former Iraq Republic Railways (see below), and for the design and construction of new railways, which was formerly the province of the New Railways Implementation Authority, was transferred to the newly created State Enterprise for Implementation of Transport and Communications Projects.

State Enterprise for Iraqi Railways: Baghdad Central Station Bldg, Damascus Sq., Baghdad; tel. (1) 543-4404; telex 212272; fax (1) 884-0480; fmrly the Iraqi Republic Railways, under the supervision of State Org. for Iraqi Railways; re-formed as a State Enterprise in 1987, under the Ministry of Transport and Communications; total length of track (1996): 2,029 km, consisting of 1,496 km of standard gauge, 533 km of one-metre gauge; Dir-Gen. Dr YOUSIF ABDUL WAHID JASSIM.

New Railways Implementation Authority: POB 17040, al-Hurriya, Baghdad; tel. (1) 537-0021; telex 2906; f. to design and construct railways to augment the standard-gauge network and to replace the metre-gauge network; Sec.-Gen. R. A. AL-UMARI.

ROADS

At the end of 1996, according to the International Road Federation, there was an estimated total road network of 47,400 km, of which approximately 40,760 km were paved.

The most important roads are: Baghdad–Mosul–Tel Kotchuk (Syrian border), 521 km; Baghdad–Kirkuk–Arbil–Mosul-Zakho (border with Turkey), 544 km; Kirkuk–Sulaimaniya, 160 km; Baghdad–Hilla–Diwaniya–Nasiriya–Basra, 586 km; Baghdad–Kut-Nasirya, 186 km; Baghdad–Ramadi–Rurba (border with Syria), 555 km; Baghdad–Kut–Umara–Basra–Safwan (border with Kuwait), 660 km; Baghdad–Baqaba–Kanikien (border with Iran). Most sections of the six-lane 1,264-km international Express Highway, linking Safwan (on the Kuwaiti border) with the Jordanian and Syrian borders, had been completed by June 1990. Studies have been completed for a second, 525-km Express Highway, linking Baghdad and Zakho on the Turkish border. The estimated cost of the project is more than US $4,500m. and is likely to preclude its implementation in the immediate future. An elaborate network of roads was constructed behind the war front with Iran in order to facilitate the movement of troops and supplies during the 1980–88 conflict.

Iraqi Land Transport Co: Baghdad; f. 1988 to replace State Organization for Land Transport; fleet of more than 1,000 large trucks; Dir Gen. AYSAR AS-SAFI.

Joint Land Transport Co: Baghdad; joint venture between Iraq and Jordan; operates a fleet of some 750 trucks.

State Enterprise for Implementation of Expressways: f. 1987; Dir-Gen. FAIZ MUHAMMAD SAID.

State Enterprise for Roads and Bridges: POB 917, Karradat Mariam, Karkh, Baghdad; tel. (1) 32141; telex 212282; responsible for road and bridge construction projects to the Ministry of Housing and Construction.

SHIPPING

The ports of Basra and Umm Qasr are usually the commercial gateway of Iraq. They are connected by various ocean routes with all parts of the world, and constitute the natural distributing centre for overseas supplies. The Iraqi State Enterprise for Maritime Transport maintains a regular service between Basra, the Gulf and north European ports. There is also a port at Khor az-Zubair, which came into use during 1979.

At Basra there is accommodation for 12 vessels at the Maqal Wharves and accommodation for seven vessels at the buoys. There is one silo berth and two berths for petroleum products at Muftia and one berth for fertilizer products at Abu Flus. There is room for eight vessels at Umm Qasr. There are deep-water tanker terminals at Khor al-Amaya and Faw for three and four vessels respectively. The latter port, however, was abandoned during the early part of the Iran–Iraq War.

For the inland waterways, which are now under the control of the General Establishment for Iraqi Ports, there are 1,036 registered river craft, 48 motor vessels and 105 motor boats.

General Establishment for Iraqi Ports: Maqal, Basra; tel. (40) 413211; telex 207008; f. 1987, when State Org. for Iraqi Ports was abolished; Dir-Gen. ABD AR-RAZZAQ ABD AL-WAHAB.

State Enterprise for Iraqi Water Transport: POB 23016, Airport St, al-Furat Quarter, Baghdad; telex 212565; f. 1987 when State Org. for Iraqi Water Transport was abolished; responsible for the planning, supervision and control of six nat. water transportation enterprises, incl.:

State Enterprise for Maritime Transport (Iraqi Line): POB 13038, al-Jadiriya al-Hurriya Ave, Baghdad; tel. (1) 776-3201; telex 212565; Basra office: 14 July St, POB 766, Basra; tel. 210206; telex 207052; f. 1952; Dir-Gen. JABER Q. HASSAN; Operations Man. M. A. ALI.

Shipping Company

Arab Bridge Maritime Navigation Co: Aqaba, Jordan; tel. (03) 316307; telex 62354; fax (03) 316313; f. 1987; joint venture by Egypt, Iraq and Jordan to improve economic co-operation; an expansion of the company that established a ferry link between the ports of Aqaba, Jordan, and Nuweibeh, Egypt, in 1985; cap. US $6m.; Chair. NABEEH AL-ABWAH.

CIVIL AVIATION

There are international airports near Baghdad, at Bamerni, and at Basra. A new airport, Saddam International, is under construction at Baghdad. Internal flights connect Baghdad to Basra and Mosul. Civilian, as well as military, airports sustained heavy damage during the war with the multinational force in 1991. Basra airport reopened in May 1991.

National Co for Civil Aviation Services: al-Mansour, Baghdad; tel. (1) 551-9443; telex 212662; f. 1987 following the abolition of the State Organization for Civil Aviation; responsible for the provision of aircraft, and for airport and passenger services.

Iraqi Airways Co: Saddam International Airport, Baghdad; tel. (1) 887-2400; telex 213453; fax (1) 887-5808; f. 1948; Dir-Gen. NOUR ED-DIN AS-SAFI HAMMADI; formerly Iraqi Airways, prior to privatization in September 1988; operates limited domestic services.

Tourism

The Directorate-General for Tourism was abolished in 1988 and the various bodies under it and the services that it administered were offered for sale or lease to the private sector. The directorate was responsible for 21 summer resorts in the north, and for hotels and tourist villages throughout the country. These were to be offered on renewable leases of 25 years or sold outright. In 1994 an estimated 330,000 tourists visited Iraq. Tourist receipts in that year were estimated at US $12m.

IRELAND

Introductory Survey

Location, Climate, Language, Religion, Flag, Capital

The Republic of Ireland consists of 26 of the 32 counties which comprise the island of Ireland. The remaining six counties, in the north-east, form Northern Ireland, which is part of the United Kingdom. Ireland lies in the Atlantic Ocean, about 80 km (50 miles) west of Great Britain. The climate is mild and equable, with temperatures generally between 0°C (32°F) and 21°C (70°F). Irish is the official first language, but its use as a vernacular is now restricted to certain areas, collectively known as the Gaeltacht, mainly in the west of Ireland. English is universally spoken. Official documents are printed in English and Irish. Almost all of the inhabitants profess Christianity: about 95% are Roman Catholics and 5% Protestants. The national flag (proportions 2 by 1) consists of three equal vertical stripes, of green, white and orange. The capital is Dublin.

Recent History

The whole of Ireland was formerly part of the United Kingdom. In 1920 the island was partitioned, the six north-eastern counties remaining part of the United Kingdom, with their own government. In 1922 the 26 southern counties achieved dominion status, under the British Crown, as the Irish Free State. The dissolution of all remaining links with Great Britain culminated in 1937 in the adoption, by plebiscite, of a new constitution, which gave the Irish Free State full sovereignty within the Commonwealth. Formal ties with the Commonwealth were ended in 1949, when the 26 southern counties became a republic. The partition of Ireland remained a contentious issue, and in 1969 a clandestine organization, calling itself the Provisional Irish Republican Army (IRA—see Northern Ireland, Vol. II), initiated a violent campaign to achieve reunification.

In the general election of February 1973, the Fianna Fáil (FF) party, which had held office, with only two interruptions, since 1932, was defeated. Jack Lynch, who had been Prime Minister since 1966, resigned, and Liam Cosgrave formed a coalition between his own party, Fine Gael (FG), and the Labour Party (LP). The Irish Government remained committed to power-sharing in the six counties, but opposed any British military withdrawal from Northern Ireland (see Northern Ireland, Vol. II).

Following the assassination of the British Ambassador to Ireland by the Provisional IRA in July 1976, the Irish Government introduced stronger measures against terrorism. FF won the general election of June 1977 and Jack Lynch again became Prime Minister. In December 1979 Lynch resigned as Prime Minister and was succeeded by Charles Haughey. In June 1981, following an early general election, Dr Garret FitzGerald, a former Minister for Foreign Affairs, became Prime Minister in a coalition government between his own party, FG, and the LP. However, the rejection by the Dáil of the coalition's budget proposals precipitated a further general election in February 1982. Haughey was returned to power, with the support of three members of the Workers' Party (WP) and two independents. The worsening economic situation, however, made the FF Government increasingly unpopular, and in November Haughey lost the support of the independents over proposed reductions in public expenditure. In the subsequent general election FF failed to gain an overall majority, and in December FitzGerald took office as Prime Minister in a coalition with the LP.

During 1986 FitzGerald's coalition lost popular support, partly due to the formation of a new party, the Progressive Democrats (PD), by disaffected members of FF. In early June a controversial government proposal to end a 60-year constitutional ban on divorce was defeated by national referendum, and shortly afterwards, as a result of a series of defections, the coalition lost its parliamentary majority. In January 1987 the LP refused to support FG's budget proposals envisaging reductions in planned public expenditure, and the coalition collapsed. FF, led by Charles Haughey, won 81 of the 166 seats in the Dáil at the general election held in February. FF formed a minority government, which initially retained popular support, despite instituting a programme of unprecedented economic austerity.

In May 1989, following the Government's sixth parliamentary defeat over a minor policy issue, Haughey called a general election for 15 June, to coincide with elections to the European Parliament. FG and the PD subsequently concluded an electoral pact to oppose FF. Although the Haughey administration had achieved significant economic improvements, severe reductions in public expenditure and continuing problems of unemployment and emigration adversely affected FF's electoral support, and it obtained only 77 of the 166 seats in the Dáil, while FG won 55 seats and the PD six seats. The LP and the WP both made significant gains.

At the end of June 1989 the Dáil reconvened to elect the Prime Minister. The PD voted in favour of Alan Dukes, the leader of FG, in accordance with their pre-election pact, and Haughey was defeated by 86 votes to 78. Dukes and Dick Spring, the leader of the LP, also failed to be elected. Haughey was forced to resign (on the insistence of the opposition parties, who claimed that his remaining as Prime Minister would be unconstitutional), although continuing to lead an interim administration. After nearly four weeks of negotiations, however, FF formed an 'alliance' with the PD and included two of the latter's members in a new cabinet. In mid-July 1989 Haughey became Prime Minister in an FF–PD coalition.

In October 1990 Brian Lenihan, the Deputy Prime Minister and Minister for Defence, was accused of having approached the President in an attempt to avert a general election following the collapse in 1982 of the FG–LP coalition. Lenihan denied the accusation, despite the subsequent release of tape-recordings in which he was heard to refer to the alleged incident. The opposition parties proposed a motion of 'no confidence' in Lenihan and the Government. The PD demanded Lenihan's resignation in return for its continued support. Following the resultant dismissal of Lenihan, the coalition Government defeated the no-confidence motion by 83 votes to 80. Lenihan was retained as the FF candidate in the forthcoming presidential election, which took place in November 1990, but was defeated by Mary Robinson, an independent candidate supported by the LP and the WP. Robinson, a liberal lawyer who specialized in issues of human rights, took office as President in December. Following FG's poor performance in the presidential election, Alan Dukes resigned the party leadership and was replaced by the party's deputy leader, John Bruton.

In October 1991 the Government, whose popularity had been adversely affected by economic recession, won a vote of confidence in the Dáil by 84 votes to 81. The motion of 'no confidence' had been introduced following a series of financial scandals involving public officials. Although members of FF were critical of Haughey's management of these affairs, which resulted in the resignation of five senior executives of state-owned and -subsidized enterprises, they were reluctant to precipitate a general election, owing to the party's decline in popularity. The narrow government victory was secured with the support of the PD, following an agreement between FF and the PD on a programme of tax reforms (which were implemented in the 1992 budget). In November 1991, however, a group of FF deputies proposed a motion demanding Haughey's removal as leader of the party. Albert Reynolds, the Minister for Finance and a former close associate of Haughey, and Padraig Flynn, the Minister for the Environment, announced their intention of supporting the motion, and were immediately dismissed from office. In the event the attempt to depose Haughey was defeated by a substantial majority of the FF parliamentary grouping.

In January 1992 a former Minister for Justice, Seán Doherty, alleged that, contrary to Haughey's previous denials, the Prime Minister had been aware of the secret monitoring, in 1982, of the telephone conversations of two journalists perceived to be critical of the Government. The PD made its continued support of the Government (without which a general election would have been necessary) conditional on Haughey's resignation. In February Reynolds was elected as leader of FF and assumed the office of Prime Minister, following Haughey's resignation. Reynolds extensively reshuffled the Cabinet, but retained the two representatives of the PD, in an attempt to preserve the coalition Government.

In June 1992 the leader of the PD, Desmond O'Malley, criticized Reynolds' conduct as Minister for Industry and Commerce in a parliamentary inquiry, which had been established in June 1991 to investigate allegations of fraud and political favouritism in the beef industry during 1987–88. In October 1992, in his testimony to the inquiry, the Prime Minister accused O'Malley of dishonesty. Following Reynolds' refusal to withdraw the allegations, in early November the PD left the coalition, and the Government was defeated on the following day in a motion of 'no confidence', proposed in the Dáil by the LP. It was subsequently announced that a general election was to take place on 25 November, concurrently with three constitutional referendums on abortion. Economic issues dominated the general election campaign. FF suffered a substantial loss of support, securing 68 of the 166 seats in the Dáil and 39% of the votes cast (compared with 77 seats and 44% of the votes in 1989). FG also obtained a reduced number of seats (45, compared with 55 in 1989). In contrast, the LP attracted substantial support, more than doubling its number of seats (33, compared with 15 in 1989), while the PD increased its representation from six seats in 1989 to 10. In the concurrent referendums on abortion two of the proposals (on the right to seek an abortion in another EC state and the right to information on abortion services abroad) were approved by about two-thirds of the votes cast. The third proposal—on the substantive issue of abortion, permitting the operation only in cases where the life (not merely the health) of the mother was threatened—was rejected, also by a two-thirds majority.

Since no party had secured an overall majority in the general election, an extended period of consultations ensued, during which the four major parties negotiated on the composition of a governing coalition. In early January 1993 FF and the LP reached agreement on a joint policy programme, which included plans for the establishment of a IR£250m. job creation fund and the introduction of legislative proposals, originating from the LP, for increases in spending on health and education. The FF–LP coalition Government took office on 12 January. Albert Reynolds retained the premiership, while Dick Spring received the foreign affairs portfolio, as well as the post of Deputy Prime Minister. Labour members of the Dáil were given five further ministerial portfolios, including those for the newly-created Departments of Enterprise and Employment, and of Equality and Law Reform. In June the Government began the introduction of a number of important social reforms. The Dáil approved legislation to provide for the legalized sale of prophylactics, despite opposition from the Roman Catholic Church, and decriminalized homosexual acts between consenting adults over the age of 17 years. Legislation was approved in March 1995 to give effect to the decision of the 1992 referendum to allow the distribution of information on foreign abortion services. However, other controversial social issues, in particular the legalization of divorce, remained unresolved.

In June 1994 elections were held for local councils and for the European Parliament, together with by-elections for two vacant seats, formerly held by FF, in the Dáil. These seats were won by FG and the Democratic Left (DL), and both FF and the LP, sustained significant losses in the local council polls. FF, however, increased its representation in the European Parliament by one seat to seven (of a total of 15) seats, and, reflecting an increasing national concern with environmental issues, the Green Party obtained two seats.

In November 1994 serious differences arose within the coalition Government over the insistence by FF that the Attorney-General, Harry Whelehan, be appointed to a senior vacancy that had arisen in the High Court. Although such promotions accorded with past precedent, Whelehan's conservative record on social issues, particularly in relation to abortion, was unacceptable to the LP, whose specific objection to Whelehan's appointment was based on his alleged obstruction, as Attorney-General, of the processing of an extradition warrant for a Roman Catholic priest sought by the authorities in Northern Ireland on charges of the sexual abuse of children. (During the seven months taken to process the extradition request, the accused had returned voluntarily to Northern Ireland, where he was tried and imprisoned.) It was alleged by the LP that the transfer of Whelehan to the presidency of the High Court was intended by FF to protect him from public accountability for his conduct as Attorney-General. However, Reynolds and the FF members of the Cabinet approved the appointment in the absence of the LP ministers.

On 15 November 1994 Reynolds admitted to the Dáil that there was no satisfactory explanation for the delay in processing the extradition warrant, but denied that the matter affected the suitability of Whelehan for judicial office. On the following day, after consultations with the new Attorney-General, Reynolds conceded that there had been unnecessary delays in the extradition procedure, and that Whelehan's promotion had been ill-advised. Spring, however, accused Reynolds of having earlier deliberately withheld information, and Whelehan of having lied. The LP withdrew from the coalition, and on the following day the Government resigned. Reynolds, while remaining as Prime Minister of a 'caretaker' Government, relinquished the FF leadership on 19 November and was succeeded by the Minister for Finance, Bertie Ahern. Whelehan, meanwhile, resigned as President of the High Court.

The desire of all the major political parties to avoid immediate general elections led to protracted efforts to form a new coalition administration. Discussions between Spring and Ahern, however, failed to produce an agreement, and, following extensive negotiations between the LP and other parties, a new coalition, led by John Bruton of FG, and with Spring again the Deputy Prime Minister and Minister for Foreign Affairs, took office on 15 December 1994. A third coalition partner, the DL, obtained the social welfare portfolio. The new Government stressed its strong commitment to the continuation of efforts to secure a permanent peace settlement in Northern Ireland (see below).

The coalition Government experienced few apparent internal stresses during 1995. In May, however, the Minister for Defence and for the Marine, Hugh Coveney, resigned following allegations of an attempt by him to obtain a state consultancy contract for his former business interests. In January 1996 the DL expressed disquiet at proposals by FG to reduce the payment of unemployment benefit to school-leavers. In November 1995 a referendum on the termination of the constitutional ban on divorce (which had been heavily defeated in 1986) resulted in a narrow majority (50.3% to 49.7%) in favour of legalizing the dissolution of marriage. The proposal was supported by all the major political parties, but strongly opposed by the Roman Catholic Church. The outcome of the referendum was the subject of an unsuccessful legal challenge in the Supreme Court in 1996, and the first divorce under the revised constitutional arrangements was granted in January 1997 (although legislation to implement the reform did not come into effect until February).

In June 1996 a journalist who had been investigating organized criminal activities for a national newspaper was shot dead in Dublin. The murder of Veronica Guerin focused national concern on an escalation of organized drugs-related crime in Ireland and prompted widespread criticism of the Government for having failed to implement adequate restraints to uphold law and order. The Government subsequently announced proposals to tighten the law on bail and to curtail the right of silence of people suspected of drugs-trafficking, and endorsed legislative measures, proposed by FF, to enable the courts to freeze personal assets thought to have been illegally obtained, for a period of up to five years. A constitutional referendum, on proposals to permit courts to refuse bail in certain circumstances to defendants in criminal proceedings, was conducted in November. These changes, which were supported by all of the main political parties, were approved in a low turn-out (29% of eligible voters). Earlier in November the Justice Minister, Nora Owen, was severely criticized by opposition parties following an incident in which 16 suspected terrorists appeared before the Central Criminal Court in front of a judge who was no longer eligible to consider cases assigned to that Court, forcing the temporary release of the prisoners and a judicial review of their detention. In an emergency parliamentary debate, a motion of 'no confidence' in Owen and the Government was defeated by 79 votes to 70.

At the end of November 1996 the Minister for Transport, Energy and Communications, Michael Lowry, resigned following allegations that he had received personal financial gifts from an Irish business executive, Ben Dunne. Alan Dukes was named as Lowry's successor. During 1997 an inquiry into other political donations by Dunne, chaired by Justice Brian McCracken, revealed that payments totalling some IR£1.3m. had been made to the former Irish Prime Minister, Charles Haughey, during his term in office. Haughey later admitted the allegations, although insisting that he had no knowledge of the donations until he resigned his premiership; however, McCracken's report, published in August, condemned Haughey's earlier misleading evidence given to the tribunal and recommended further legal investigation. The Government, at that time led by Bertie Ahern of FF following a general election (see below), endorsed the results of the inquiry and agreed to establish a new tribunal to investigate further payments made to politicians and the sources of specific 'offshore' bank accounts that had been used by Haughey.

In May 1997 Prime Minister Bruton called a general election, relying on strong economic growth figures and the negative impact of allegations concerning financial donations to former FF leader Charles Haughey to secure victory for FG's coalition with the LP and DL, despite public opinion polls revealing a significant shortfall in support for the Government over the opposition FF. In the election, which was conducted on 6 June, none of the main political parties secured an overall majority in the Dáil. FG increased its representation from 45 seats to 54, having won 27.9% of the first-preference votes cast, while FF secured 77 seats with 39.3% of the votes. Support for the LP, however, declined substantially and the party won just 17 seats (compared with 33 in the 1992 parliament). Sinn Féin won its first ever seat in the Dáil at the election. John Bruton conceded that he could not form a majority coalition administration, and Bertie Ahern, the FF leader, undertook to form a new government, in alliance with the PD, which had won four parliamentary seats, and with the support of independents. A new administration, with Ahern as Prime Minister, was formally approved in the Dáil at the end of June. Mary Harney of the PD was appointed as Deputy Prime Minister, the first woman ever to hold that position, while the other Cabinet positions were taken by FF.

In early October 1997 the Minister for Foreign Affairs, Ray Burke, resigned, owing to allegations of political favours granted in return for financial gifts (received in 1989) and the improper sale of Irish passports to Saudi Arabian business executives. In the resulting Cabinet reorganization David Andrews was awarded the foreign affairs portfolio and Michael Smith was appointed as Andrews's successor, responsible for defence and European affairs.

In September 1997 President Robinson resigned her position in order to assume her new functions as the United Nations High Commissioner for Human Rights. All the main parties put forward candidates to contest the ensuing presidential election; however, internal divisions within FF were revealed following the failure of Albert Reynolds, the former Prime Minister, to secure that party's nomination. Controversy arose during the election campaign when private documents were supplied to a newspaper, with the intention of undermining support for the FF candidate, Dr Mary McAleese, by emphasizing her sympathies with the republican movement. A former FG political adviser was later arrested in connection with the leaked information. In the election, conducted on 30 October, McAleese won 45.2% of the first-preference votes cast, compared with 29.3% for Mary Banotti of FG. McAleese was inaugurated on 11 November, and became the country's first President to be from Northern Ireland.

In early November 1997 the LP leader, Dick Spring, resigned, owing to his party's poor electoral performances. He was replaced by Ruairí Quinn, who had been Minister for Finance in the previous FG-LP administration.

Regular discussions between the British and Irish heads of government, initiated in May 1980, led to the formation in November 1981 of an Anglo-Irish Intergovernmental Council, intended to meet at ministerial and official levels. Consultations between the United Kingdom and Ireland on the future of Northern Ireland resulted in November 1985 in the signing of the Anglo-Irish Agreement. The Agreement provided for regular participation in Northern Ireland affairs by the Irish Government on political, legal, security and cross-border matters. The involvement of the Government of Ireland was to be through an Intergovernmental Conference. The Agreement maintained that no change in the status of Northern Ireland would be made without the assent of the majority of its population. The terms of the Agreement were approved by both the Irish and the British Parliaments, despite strong opposition by many Protestants in Northern Ireland.

Under the provisions of the Anglo-Irish Agreement, the Irish Government pledged co-operation in the implementation of new measures to improve cross-border security, in order to suppress IRA operations. It also promised to participate in the European Convention on the Suppression of Terrorism, which it signed in February 1986 and ratified in December 1987, when legislation amending the 1965 Extradition Act came into effect. In the same month the Government introduced controversial measures (without consulting the British Government) granting the Irish Attorney-General the right to approve or reject warrants for extradition of suspected IRA terrorists to the United Kingdom. In January 1988, however, the Irish Supreme Court ruled that members of the IRA could not be protected from extradition to Northern Ireland on the grounds that their offences were politically motivated. In December, however, the Irish Attorney-General refused to grant the extradition of an alleged terrorist who had been repatriated to Ireland in November, following a similar refusal by the Belgian authorities. The Irish decision was based on allegations that the accused man would not receive a fair trial in the United Kingdom because publicity had prejudiced his case.

Relations between the Irish and British Governments in 1988 were also strained when Irish confidence in the impartiality of the British legal system was severely undermined by proposed legislation to combat terrorism in Northern Ireland and by the decision, in January, not to prosecute members of the Royal Ulster Constabulary (RUC) allegedly implicated in a policy of shooting terrorist suspects, without attempting to apprehend them, in Northern Ireland in 1982. Difficult relations with the United Kingdom did not, however, present a threat to the Anglo-Irish Agreement, and the co-ordination between the Garda Síochána (Irish police force) and the RUC, established under the agreement, resulted in an unprecedentedly high level of co-operation on cross-border security. In February 1989 a permanent joint consultative assembly, comprising 25 British and 25 Irish MPs, was established. The representatives were selected in October. The assembly's meetings, the first of which began in February 1990, were to take place twice a year, alternately in Dublin and London.

In July 1990 an IRA member who had been charged with terrorist offences in the United Kingdom, lost his appeal against extradition in the High Court in Dublin. It was the first case to be considered under the 1987 Extradition Act, based on the European Convention on the Suppression of Terrorism. In November the Supreme Court upheld the ruling, and the alleged terrorist, Desmond Ellis, was extradited to stand trial in the United Kingdom. In November 1991 the Supreme Court upheld the extradition to the United Kingdom of an IRA member convicted of murder, who had escaped from detention in Belfast. At the same time, however, the Supreme Court overturned an order for extradition to the United Kingdom of two other IRA members who had similarly escaped, ruling that their convictions of possession of non-automatic fire-arms did not constitute an extraditable offence. This prompted assurances from the Minister of Justice that this omission in the legislation on extradition would be rectified. The Irish Government, however, also requested changes in British legislation to ensure that defendants could be tried in the United Kindom only for the offences for which they had been extradited. In January 1994 the Irish Cabinet approved draft legislation to remove the argument of 'political offence', and subsequent exemption from extradition, to persons charged with the use or possession of non-automatic weapons.

In January 1990 the British Secretary of State for Northern Ireland, Peter Brooke, launched an initiative to convene meetings between representatives from the major political parties in Northern Ireland, and the British and Irish Governments, to discuss devolution in Northern Ireland. In response to demands from Northern Ireland's Unionist parties, the Irish and British Governments publicly stated that they were prepared to consider an alternative to the Anglo-Irish Agreement. In March the Irish Supreme Court rejected an attempt by Ulster Unionists to have the Anglo-Irish Agreement declared contrary to Ireland's Constitution, which claims jurisdiction over Northern Ireland. In May the Unionists agreed to hold direct discussions with the Irish Government, a concession previously withheld because it lent credence to the Irish claim to a right to be involved in Northern Ireland's affairs. Disagreement remained, however, on the timing and conditions of Ireland's entry to the talks. Following extensive negotiations (see Northern Ireland, Vol. II), discussions between the Northern Ireland parties, which were a prelude to the inclusion of the Irish Government, commenced in June 1991. In early July, however, Brooke announced that the talks were to be discontinued, with no substantive progress having been made. This resulted from the Unionists' refusal to continue negotiations if the meeting of the Anglo-Irish Conference scheduled for July took place. The Irish and British Governments were both unwilling to postpone the Conference. In September Brooke announced an attempt to revive discussions on Northern Ireland, and in January 1992 presented an amended plan for negotiations (see Northern Ireland, Vol. II).

In February 1992 President Robinson met Brooke in Belfast, thus becoming the first Irish Head of State to visit Northern Ireland in an official capacity. However, the Lord Mayor of Belfast refused to meet Robinson, objecting to Ireland's constitutional claim to the six counties that form Northern Ireland. In May 1993 President Robinson undertook an unofficial visit to Britain, during the course of which a private meeting took place with the Queen. In the following month, during a visit by the President to Belfast, a brief meeting with Gerry Adams, the leader of Sinn Féin (the political wing of the IRA), was strongly opposed by the British Government and by Unionist politicians. An official visit to Britain by President Robinson took place in June 1996.

In April 1992 confidential discussions between the four major parties in Northern Ireland recommenced. No agreement was reached on the principal issue of devolved government for the province, but in mid-June the Unionists agreed, for the first time, to a meeting to discuss the agenda for the second element of the talks, which were to involve the Irish Government in the process for the first time. The second stage of negotiations formally began in early June, and in late July the talks were adjourned until September. The Irish and British Governments agreed on an agenda for the third element of the negotiating process in early July, comprising the discussion of the future of the Anglo-Irish Agreement (although this remained unaddressed, owing to the subsequent failure of the second stage of the talks). When the second stage of talks reopened in early September in Belfast, the principal point of contention was the Unionists' demand that Ireland hold a referendum on Articles 2 and 3 of its Constitution, which lay claim to the territory of Northern Ireland. Ireland was unwilling to make such a concession except as part of an overall settlement. The Democratic Unionist Party (DUP) left the talks over this issue and boycotted the meeting in Dublin that was held later in the month. The Ulster Unionist Party (UUP), however, attended the meeting: the first official Unionist deputation to visit the Republic since 1922. At the end of September, following a statement from Reynolds suggesting that the constitutional articles were not negotiable, the DUP returned to the talks to confront the Irish delegation. With no progress made on this question, nor the subject of Ireland's role in the administration of Northern Ireland, the negotiations formally ended in early November, and the Anglo-Irish Conference resumed.

In January 1993 the British Secretary of State for Northern Ireland, Sir Patrick Mayhew, challenged the incoming FF–LP Irish Government to review the controversial articles of the Constitution, in order to give a new impetus to the stalled negotiating process. Dick Spring, the new Minister for Foreign Affairs, expressed the opinion that constitutional changes were necessary, although he gave no outright commitment to undertake such measures. The first meeting of the Anglo-Irish Conference with the new Irish administration was convened in February. Unionist leaders, however, refused to participate in the negotiations, which made little progress. In July the Irish Government suggested that a political settlement for Northern Ireland be imposed if the Unionist parties maintained their boycott of the negotiating process; this proposal, however, was rejected by the British Government.

In September 1993 the British and Irish Governments agreed to renew efforts to recommence negotiations. A further meeting of the Anglo-Irish Conference, that had been scheduled for the end of October, was cancelled following the explosion of an IRA bomb in a loyalist district of Belfast, killing 10 people. The Irish Government condemned the close relationship of Sinn Féin to those responsible for the attack and distanced itself from a peace initiative which the Sinn Féin leader, Gerry Adams, had negotiated with the leader of Northern Ireland's Social Democratic and Labour Party (SDLP), John Hume.

At the end of October 1993 Albert Reynolds and John Major issued a joint statement setting out the principles on which future negotiations were to be based. The statement emphasized the precondition that Sinn Féin permanently renounce violence before being admitted to the negotiations. In mid-December the Prime Ministers made a joint declaration, known as the 'Downing Street Declaration', which provided a specific framework for a peace settlement. The Declaration referred to the possibility of a united Ireland and accepted the legitimacy of self-determination, but insisted on majority consent within Northern Ireland. While the Sinn Féin and Unionist parties considered their response to the Declaration, Reynolds received both groups' conditional support for his proposal to establish a 'Forum for Peace and Reconciliation', which was to encourage both sides to end violent action. In January 1994, in an apparently conciliatory approach to Sinn Féin's repeated requests for a 'clarification' of the Declaration, Spring and Mayhew agreed to expand on this theme in public speeches, but declined to participate in direct meetings with Sinn Féin. In the following month, despite the increasing impatience of the Irish Government for a definitive response by Sinn Féin, Reynolds informed Mayhew that substantive negotiations could not proceed without the participation of Sinn Féin. In January 1994 the Irish Cabinet relaxed a ban (that had operated since 1976) forbidding the broadcast of interviews and speeches by persons deemed to be paramilitary supporters.

During early 1994 the Government actively pursued discussions aimed at establishing a framework, in accordance with the 'Downing Street Declaration', for a comprehensive political settlement in Northern Ireland, although the involvement of the Irish Government continued to be opposed by Northern Ireland loyalists. In April the IRA declared a temporary ceasefire over the Easter period, although its operations were subsequently resumed. Subsequent negotiations culminated in an announcement on 31 August by the IRA that it had ceased all military operations. This was followed in October by a similar suspension on the part of its counterpart loyalist organizations, providing new impetus to hopes of an eventual permanent settlement. In late 1994 and early 1995 the Irish authorities granted early release to more than 15 prisoners convicted of IRA terrorist offences. Despite misgivings that the political crisis during November and early December 1994 (see above) might impede the progress of inter-governmental talks, consultations were effectively maintained, resulting in the publication, in February 1995, of a 'Joint Framework' document, in which the Irish Government undertook to support the withdrawal of the Republic's constitutional claim to jurisdiction over Northern Ireland. The document's proposals, which included detailed arrangements for cross-border institutions and economic programmes which would operate on an all-island basis (see Northern Ireland, Vol. II), were stated by the British Government to be intended to provide a basis for public discussion and not as a definitive statement of government policy.

During 1995 the Irish Government expressed its increasing concern at the delay in initiating substantive all-party negotiations on the formulation of a permanent settlement of the conflict in Northern Ireland. The insistence of the British Government that the IRA decommission its weapons as a precondition to such talks received strong support from the Unionists, but was denounced by Sinn Féin as a 'delaying tactic', and was also opposed by the SDLP and the Irish Government. In June 1995 Sinn Féin issued a warning that the peace process was 'losing momentum', and in the following month Bruton and Hume, with the support of Adams, appealed for the urgent initiation of all-party talks. The Irish Government, meanwhile, had continued its programme of the early release of certain IRA prisoners, freeing four in April 1995 and a further 12 in July. Joint proposals in August by the British and Irish Governments for the formation of an international panel to consider the merits of decommissioning paramilitary weaponry in Northern Ireland received the full support of the US Government; President Clinton additionally urged the British authorities to accelerate their programme of releases of IRA prisoners, and requested the IRA to negotiate on the question of decommissioning weapons. Clinton reinforced these proposals in meetings with political leaders during a visit in November/December to Dublin and Northern Ireland. The international panel, under the chairmanship of George Mitchell (a former US Senator and close political associate of President Clinton), began work in December, in a series of private meetings with representatives of the contending political interests. Its findings, announced in January 1996, recommended that the decommissioning of arms should take place in parallel with all-party talks, and that their destruction should be monitored by an independent commission. The report additionally called on all groups to renounce violence and commit themselves to peaceful and democratic means. The British and Irish Governments accepted the recommendations of the report, but new controversy arose over proposals by the

British Cabinet to hold elections for a Northern Ireland assembly which was to provide the framework for all-party negotiations. Although broadly acceptable to Unionist interests, this plan was rejected outright by the SDLP and Sinn Féin, and declared unacceptable by the Irish Government.

In February 1996, following a bomb explosion in London, the IRA announced that the cease-fire had been terminated. The British and Irish Governments, however, reiterated their determination to persevere with their aim to achieve a permanent resolution of the Northern Ireland issue. Official contacts with Sinn Féin were suspended by both governments, pending acceptable assurances that the IRA had discontinued all violence. It was announced at the end of February that plans were proceeding for an all-party meeting in June, at which Sinn Féin representation would be conditional on the restoration of the IRA cease-fire and on the willingness of Sinn Féin to participate in negotiations on the decommissioning of weapons. The multi-party meetings, which commenced in June without Sinn Féin participation, were overshadowed in July by violent confrontations in Northern Ireland between the RUC and nationalists opposed to the routing of loyalist parades through predominantly nationalist districts. The Irish Government formally protested to the British Government over the conduct of the RUC, both in failing to re-route the processions and in its methods of suppressing the ensuing public disorders. The FG–LP coalition Government, however, maintained its support of British government policy in relation to the terms under which Sinn Féin would be admitted to the peace negotiations, although it called for a more flexible response to any eventual IRA cease-fire announcement. The multi-party talks were suspended in March 1997, pending the outcome of a general election in the United Kingdom. In May a meeting of Bruton with the newly-elected British Prime Minister, Anthony (Tony) Blair, and the new Secretary of State for Northern Ireland, Dr Marjorie Mowlam, generated speculation that significant progress could be achieved in furthering a political agreement. In June the two Governments announced a new initiative to proceed with the decommissioning of paramilitary weapons, on the basis of the Mitchell report, at the same time as pursuing political negotiations for a constitutional settlement. In early July the newly-elected Irish Prime Minister, Bertie Ahern, confirmed his commitment to the peace initiative during a meeting with Blair in London, and declared his support for the efforts of the British administration to prevent violence during the sectarian marching season in Northern Ireland. On 19 July the IRA announced a restoration of its cease-fire. A few days later the Irish and British Governments issued a joint statement that all-party negotiations would commence in mid-September with the participation of Sinn Féin. At the same time, however, the Unionist parties rejected the measures for weapons decommissioning that had been formulated by the two Governments. At the end of July the Irish Government restored official contacts with Sinn Féin and resumed the policy of considering convicted IRA activists for early release from prison.

In September 1997 Sinn Féin endorsed the so-called Mitchell principles, which committed participants in the negotiations to accepting the outcome of the peace process and renouncing violence as a means of punishment or resolving problems, providing for the party's participation in all-party talks when they resumed in the middle of that month. However, the Unionist parties failed to attend the opening session of the talks, owing partly to a statement by the IRA undermining Sinn Féin's endorsement of the Mitchell principles. A procedural agreement to pursue negotiations in parallel with the decommissioning of weapons (which was to be undertaken by a separate commission, led by Gen. John de Chastelain of Canada) was signed by all the main parties later in September. Substantive negotiations commenced in October; however, the UUP withdrew from discussions concerning relations between Northern Ireland and Ireland on the issue of Ireland's constitutional claim to the six counties. The new Irish Minister for Foreign Affairs, David Andrews, confirmed that the constitutional Articles would be discussed during the talks but could not commit the Government to repealing them in advance of a final settlement or a popular referendum. In November Ahern met the UUP leader, David Trimble, to strengthen relations between the two sides and facilitate progress in the negotiations. The all-party talks were adjourned in mid-December without agreement on an agenda for the next session of discussions. At the end of that month the murder of a convicted loyalist activist by republican prisoners prompted a resumption of violence throughout Northern Ireland. None the less, the two Governments pursued efforts to ensure the future of the peace process, and in mid-January 1998 published a document outlining a framework for negotiations and specified that they hoped to achieve a settlement by May. The so-called Propositions on Heads of Agreement provided for 'balanced constitutional change' by both Governments and incorporated proposals for a Northern Ireland assembly, a joint north-south council and an inter-governmental Council of the Isles, that was to comprise representatives of the British and Irish Governments and of the assemblies in Northern Ireland, Scotland and Wales, under the framework of a new British-Irish Agreement. The document refrained from specifying whether the north-south organ was to have executive powers, as favoured by Sinn Féin and the SDLP, or advisory responsibilities, insisted upon by the Unionist parties. The issue was under consideration at multi-party talks held in London at the end of January. Prior to the meeting, the two Governments resolved temporarily to expel the Ulster Democratic Party from the talks, owing to its close relationship with a loyalist faction that had violated the cease-fire and admitted to the murder of three Catholic Northern Ireland citizens since the start of the year. In February Sinn Féin was suspended from the talks for a two-week period, following RUC claims that the IRA was responsible for two recent murders committed in Belfast.

Ireland became a member of the European Community (EC, now the European Union—see p. 152) in 1973. In May 1987 the country affirmed its commitment to the EC when, in a referendum, 69.9% of Irish voters supported adherence to the Single European Act, which provided for closer economic and political co-operation between EC member-states (including the creation of a single Community market by 1993). In December 1991, during the EC summit conference at Maastricht, in the Netherlands, Ireland agreed to the the far-reaching Treaty on European Union (see p. 158). Ireland secured a special provision within the Treaty (which was signed by all parties in February 1992), guaranteeing that Ireland's constitutional position on abortion would be unaffected by any future EC legislation. The four major political parties in Ireland united in support of the ratification of the Treaty prior to a referendum on the issue, which took place in June. Despite opposition, from both pro- and anti-abortion campaigners, to the special provision within the Treaty and the threat to Ireland's neutrality inherent in the document's proposals for a common defence policy, ratification of the Treaty was endorsed by 68.7% of the votes cast (57.3% of the electorate participated in the referendum).

Government

Legislative power is vested in the bicameral National Parliament, comprising the Senate (with restricted powers) and the House of Representatives. The Senate (Seanad Éireann) has 60 members, including 11 nominated by the Prime Minister (Taoiseach) and 49 indirectly elected for five years. The House of Representatives (Dáil Éireann) has 166 members (Teachtaí Dála), elected by universal adult suffrage for five years (subject to dissolution) by means of the single transferable vote, a form of proportional representation.

The President (Uachtarán) is the constitutional Head of State, elected by direct popular vote for seven years. Executive power is effectively held by the Cabinet, led by the Prime Minister, who is appointed by the President on the nomination of the Dáil. The President appoints other Ministers on the nomination of the Prime Minister with the previous approval of the Dáil. The Cabinet is responsible to the Dáil.

Defence

At 1 August 1997 the regular armed forces totalled 12,700. The army comprised 10,500, the navy 1,100 and the air force 1,100. There was also a reserve of 15,640. Defence was allocated IR£503m. in the 1997 budget, and a projected IR£560m. in the 1998 budget. Military service is voluntary.

Economic Affairs

In 1995, according to estimates by the World Bank, Ireland's gross national product (GNP), measured at average 1993–95 prices, was US $52,765m., equivalent to $14,710 per head. During 1985–95, it was estimated, GNP per head increased, in real terms, at an average rate of 5.2% per year. Over the same period, the population increased by an annual average of 0.1%. Ireland's gross domestic product (GDP) increased, in real terms, by an annual average of 4.7% in 1990–95. GDP rose by 6.5% in 1994, by 10.3% in 1995 and by an estimated 7.2% in 1996.

Agriculture (including forestry and fishing) contributed 7.2% of GDP (at factor cost) in 1996. An estimated 10.0% of the working population were employed in the sector in 1997. Beef and dairy production, which in 1994 accounted for an estimated 3.9% and 3.4% of total exports respectively, dominate Irish agriculture. Principal crops include barley, sugar beet, potatoes and wheat. Agricultural GDP increased by an annual average of 1.2% during 1980–90, by 6.0% in 1992, 2.7% in 1993 and by 5.1% in 1994.

Industry (comprising mining, manufacturing, construction and utilities) provided 36.5% of GDP in 1996, and employed an estimated 28.8% of the working population in 1997.

Mining (including quarrying and turf production) provided employment to 0.4% of the working population in 1997. Ireland possesses substantial deposits of lead-zinc ore and recoverable peat, both of which are exploited. Natural gas, mainly from the Kinsale field, and small quantities of coal are also extracted. Offshore reserves of petroleum have been located and several licences awarded to foreign-owned enterprises to undertake further exploration. During 1980–90 mining production decreased by an annual average of 1.7%.

Manufacturing was estimated to employ 20.3% of the working population in 1997. The manufacturing sector comprises many high-technology, largely foreign-owned, capital-intensive enterprises. The electronics industry accounted for 26.1% of the value of exports in 1994. During 1980–90 manufacturing production (excluding petroleum refineries) increased by an annual average of 7.0%.

Energy is derived principally from gas, which provided 54% of total requirements in 1984, while petroleum provided 20%, peat 18%, hydroelectric power 7% and coal 1%. In 1996 imports of mineral fuels were 3.7% (by value) of total merchandise imports.

Service industries (including commerce, finance, transport and communications, and public administration) contributed an estimated 56.3% of GDP in 1996 and employed 61.1% of the working population in 1997. The financial sector is of increasing importance to Ireland. An International Financial Services Centre in Dublin was opened in 1990; by June 1997 more than 300 companies were participating in the Centre, many of which were foreign concerns attracted by tax concessions offered by the Irish Government. Tourism is one of the principal sources of foreign exchange. The estimated revenue from the tourism and travel sector amounted to some IR£1,543m. in 1996.

In 1996, according to IMF statistics, Ireland recorded a visible trade surplus of US $15,194m. and there was a surplus of $1,402m. on the current account of the balance of payments. In that year the principal source of imports (34.8%) was the United Kingdom, which was also the principal market for exports (24.6%). Other major trading partners were the USA, Germany and France. In 1996 principal imports included office equipment and other electrical machinery, chemical products and other manufactured items. Principal exports included electronic goods, chemicals and beef and dairy products.

In 1998 it was projected that there would be a budgetary deficit of IR£301m. As a result of a decrease in debt-servicing costs and a high level of tax receipts, the 1997 budget recorded a surplus of IR£106m. At the end of 1996 Ireland's total national debt was estimated to be IR£29,912m., and in that year the cost of servicing the debt amounted to an estimated IR£2,560m. In 1994 the ratio of debt interest to GNP was 2.4%. The annual rate of inflation averaged 3.3% in 1984–93. The rate increased from 2.3% in 1994 to 2.5% in 1995, but declined to 1.7% in 1996. An estimated 11.6% of the labour force were unemployed in 1996, compared with 12.3% in the previous year and 14.3% in 1994.

Ireland became a member of the European Community (EC) (see European Union, EU, p. 152) in 1973, and of the EC's Exchange Rate Mechanism (ERM) in 1979.

In 1991–92, the Irish economy was affected by recessionary trends, particularly in its principal market, the United Kingdom. The crisis in the ERM during the latter half of 1992, during which the United Kingdom withdrew from the mechanism, threatened the value of the punt within the system and had a serious impact on Irish industry. The Central Bank of Ireland was forced to raise interest rates to protect the punt, and in January 1993 the Government was obliged to devalue the Irish currency by 10%. The Government has subsequently undertaken adjustments to the value of the currency as necessary, in order to secure its position within the ERM. During 1997 economic commentators speculated as to whether a devaluation of the punt would be implemented before its entry into European Economic and Monetary Union (EMU). Government policies to offer financial incentives to foreign-owned enterprises, together with the attractions of a skilled and relatively low-cost labour force, resulted in a substantial increase in direct foreign investment in the mid-1990s and a steady expansion of the Irish economy, particularly in the financial services and electronic manufacturing industries. However, there was concern that the large number of people employed in foreign-owned enterprises rendered the economy vulnerable to external influences. In addition, the rate of unemployment remained high, owing to the persisting structural problem of long-term unemployed workers. In December 1996 the Government, trade unions and industrial and agricultural organizations agreed a new centralized wage policy for the period 1997–99 (the so-called 'Partnership 2000 for Inclusion, Employment and Competitiveness'), which aimed to promote sustainable and non-inflationary economic growth. Accordingly, the Government's budget proposals for 1998 provided for a series of reductions in both corporate and personal rates of taxation and increased social welfare payments. The budget envisaged that the rate of inflation would be maintained at below 2% and that the government debt would be reduced to below 60% of GDP by 2000, thus ensuring that Ireland meet the entry requirements of EMU.

Social Welfare

Social welfare benefits in Ireland may be grouped broadly in three categories: contributory (social) insurance payments, which are made on the basis of pay-related social insurance contributions; non-contributory (social assistance) payments, which are made on the basis of claimants' satisfying the criteria of a means test; and universal services, such as child benefit and free travel. Child benefit is payable to all households for each child.

Social insurance is compulsory for both employees and the self-employed. The social insurance scheme provides for orphans' benefits, widows', retirement and old-age pensions; unemployment, disability, maternity, invalidity, death grants and occupational injury, dental and optical benefits. The cost of the social insurance scheme is shared by the employer, the employee, the self-employed and the State. Varying rates of social insurance are payable, and the rate payable determines the range of benefits available. Private-sector employees contribute the highest rate and have cover for all benefits; the contributions of the self-employed provide funds for old age, and survivors' benefits and orphans' contributory allowance; permanent and pensionable employees in the state sector have cover mainly for widows'/widowers' (contributory) pensions, orphans' (contributory) allowance and limited occupational injury benefits.

People of inadequate means who are not entitled to benefit under these contributory schemes may receive non-contributory pensions or other benefits from the State or other public funds. These benefits include one-parent family payments, old-age and blindness pensions, carers' allowance, orphans' (non-contributory) pension, supplementary welfare allowance, unemployment assistance and family income supplement. The central Government's budgetary expenditure on social welfare services in 1997 was IR£4,523m. (equivalent to 32.3% of total expenditure).

Health services are provided by eight health boards, administered by the Department of Health. There are two categories of entitlement, with people on low incomes qualifying for the full range of health services free of charge, and people on higher incomes qualifying for fewer free services.

Drugs and medicines are available free of charge to all people suffering from specified long-term ailments. Hospital in-patient and out-patient services are free of charge to all children under 16 years of age, suffering from specified long-term ailments. Immunization and diagnostic services, as well as hospital services, are free of charge to everyone suffering from an infectious disease. A maintenance allowance is also payable in certain cases. The central Government's budgetary expenditure on health was IR£2,657m. in 1997 (18.0% of total spending). In addition, there are various community welfare services for the chronically sick, the elderly, the disabled and families under stress. In 1995 Ireland had 104 publicly-funded hospitals, with a total of 13,557 beds. In 1995 there were 8,233 physicians resident in the country.

Education

The State in Ireland has constitutional responsibility for the national education system. Irish schools are owned, not by the

State, but by community groups, traditionally religious groups. It is in general an aided system: the State does not itself operate the schools (with a few minor exceptions) but assists other bodies, usually religious, to do so.

Education in Ireland is compulsory for nine years between six and 15 years of age. Primary education may begin at the age of four and lasts for eight years. Aided primary schools account for the education of 98.5% of children in the primary sector, who attend until the age of 12, when they transfer to a post-primary school.

Post-primary education lasts for up to six years, comprising a junior cycle of three years and a senior cycle of two or three years. The Junior Certificate examination is taken after three years in post-primary (second-level) education. In senior cycle there is an optional one-year Transition Year Programme, followed by a two-year course leading to the Leaving Certificate at 17 or 18. In 1995/96 there were 445 secondary schools and a further 246 vocational schools, providing primary school leavers with a general course which is similar to that for pupils in secondary schools, but with a greater emphasis on non-academic subjects. In 1995/96 there were 16 state comprehensive schools, offering academic and technical subjects, structured to the needs, abilities and interests of the pupils, and leading to examinations for the Transition Year Option or the Leaving Certificate. The 61 community schools offer a similar curriculum. They were originally intended to replace existing vocational and secondary schools in rural areas, but have also been established in new city areas. By 1997 some 92% of 16-year-olds were participating in full-time, post-compulsory education.

Eight technology colleges and 11 regional technical colleges provide a range of craft, technical, professional and other courses. The majority of courses lead to academic awards granted by the National Council for Educational Awards at Certificate, diploma, degree and postgraduate levels. In addition, pupils who have completed second-level education may pursue studies within that sector, mainly in Post-Leaving Certificate courses.

The gaining of certain successes in the Leaving Certificate examination qualifies for entrance to the four universities: the University of Dublin (Trinity College); the National University of Ireland (comprising the University Colleges of Cork, Dublin and Galway); and the Dublin City University and the University of Limerick (former National Institutes of Higher Education, which obtained university status in 1989). Universities and technology colleges and institutes are self-governing, although they receive annual state grants; the teacher-training colleges are privately managed but financed by the State. Undergraduate tuition fees are free to students, and government-funded Student Support Schemes help to promote access to tertiary education through the payment of means-tested maintenance grants.

In the 1997 budget IR£2,332m. (equivalent to 15.8% of total expenditure) was allocated to education.

Public Holidays

1998: 1 January (New Year), 17 March (St Patrick's Day), 10 April (Good Friday), 13 April (Easter Monday), 4 May (May Day Holiday), 1 June (June Bank Holiday), 3 August (August Bank Holiday), 26 October (October Bank Holiday), 25–28 December (Christmas).

1999: 1 January (New Year), 17 March (St Patrick's Day), 2 April (Good Friday), 5 April (Easter Monday), 3 May (May Day Holiday), 7 June (June Bank Holiday), 2 August (August Bank Holiday), 25 October (October Bank Holiday), 25–26 December (Christmas).

Weights and Measures

The metric system of weights and measures is the primary system in force, but the imperial system is still used in a number of limited activities.

Statistical Survey

Source (unless otherwise stated): Central Statistics Office, Skehard Rd, Cork; tel. (21) 359000; fax (21) 359090; e-mail information@cso.ie; internet http://www.cso.ie.

Area and Population

AREA, POPULATION AND DENSITY

Area (sq km)	70,273*
Population (census results)	
21 April 1991	3,525,719
28 April 1996	
Males	1,800,232
Females	1,825,855
Total	3,626,087
Density (per sq km) at April 1996	51.6

* 27,133 sq miles.

PROVINCES (1996 census)

	Area (sq km)	Population	Density (per sq km)
Connaught	17,711	433,231	24.5
Leinster	19,801	1,924,702	97.2
Munster	24,674	1,033,903	41.9
Ulster (part)	8,088	234,251	29.0
Total	70,273	3,626,087	51.6

PRINCIPAL TOWNS
(population, including suburbs or environs, at 1996 census)

Dublin (capital)*	952,700	Galway	57,400
Cork	180,000	Waterford	44,200
Limerick	79,100		

* Greater Dublin area, including Dún Laoghaire (population 55,540 in 1991).

BIRTHS, MARRIAGES AND DEATHS (rates per 1,000)

	Birth rate	Marriage rate	Death rate
1989	14.8	5.2	9.1
1990	15.1	5.1	9.0
1991	15.0	4.9	8.9
1992	14.4	4.7	8.7
1993	13.8	4.7	9.0
1994	13.5	4.6	8.6
1995	13.5	4.4	8.8
1996	13.9	4.5	8.7

Expectation of life (UN estimates, years at birth, 1990–95): 75.3 (males 72.6, females 78.1) (Source: UN, *World Population Prospects: The 1994 Revision*).

ECONOMICALLY ACTIVE POPULATION
(estimates, '000 persons, excluding unemployed)

	1995	1996	1997
Agriculture, forestry and fishing	143	138	134
Mining, quarrying and turf production	6	5	6
Manufacturing	248	250	271
Construction	83	87	97
Electricity, gas and water	13	14	12
Commerce, insurance and finance	262	275	281
Transport, communications and storage	76	81	84
Public administration and defence	73	77	74
Other economic activities	345	371	379
Total	1,248	1,297	1,338

Agriculture

PRINCIPAL CROPS ('000 metric tons)

	1994	1995	1996
Wheat	572	583	771
Oats	128	129	146
Barley	910	1,084	1,225
Potatoes	642	618	733
Sugar beet	1,390	1,547	1,485*

* Provisional figure.

LIVESTOCK ('000 head)

	1995	1996	1997
Cattle	7,122	7,423	7,625
Sheep	8,370	7,934	8,210
Pigs	1,542	1,665	n.a.

LIVESTOCK PRODUCTS ('000 metric tons)

	1994	1995	1996
Beef and veal	444	477	535
Mutton and lamb	94	89	90
Pig meat	216	212	211
Poultry meat	102	115	120
Cows' milk	5,338	5,346	5,351
Butter	140	154	154
Cheese	93	80	97
Dry milk (excl. whey)	161	140	152
Hen eggs	34.1	35.1	29.9
Cattle hides*	57	61	64
Sheepskins*	20	19	20

* FAO estimates.

Forestry

ROUNDWOOD REMOVALS ('000 cubic metres, excluding bark)

	1995	1996	1997
Sawlogs, veneer logs and logs for sleepers	1,397	1,490	1,389
Pulpwood	720	711	679
Fuel wood	25	23	15
Total	2,142	2,224	2,083

SAWNWOOD PRODUCTION ('000 cubic metres, including railway sleepers)

	1992	1993	1994
Coniferous (softwood)	560	622	699
Broadleaved (hardwood)	15	15	10
Total	575	637	709

Source: FAO, *Yearbook of Forest Products*.

1997: Coniferous production ('000 cubic metres): 653.

Fishing

SEA FISH (landings in metric tons)

	1994	1995	1996
European plaice	1,469	1,590	1,679
Atlantic cod	4,984	5,650	8,001
Haddock	2,860	3,417	4,462
Megrim	2,875	3,839	3,507
Whiting	8,735	11,262	10,340
Dogfish	3,624	4,112	3,265
Atlantic herring	51,006	46,643	71,953
Atlantic mackerel	86,274	78,534	49,966
Horse mackerel	85,804	178,356	127,876
Total fish (incl. others)	263,628	351,681	303,803
Crabs	6,875	7,689	6,153
Norway lobster (Dublin Bay prawn)	5,310	7,241	5,178
Mussels	3,616	6,667	5,628
Total shellfish (incl. others*)	25,296	32,318	28,513
Total catch	288,924	383,999	332,316

* Excludes oysters, clams and farmed mussels.

INLAND FISH (catch in metric tons)

	1994	1995	1996
Atlantic salmon	816	790	688
European eel	150	137	150

Mining

('000 metric tons, unless otherwise indicated)

	1995	1996	1997
Natural gas (terajoules)	106,285	102,934	90,685
Lead*	46.1	45.2	45.4
Zinc*	184.1	164.2	199.5
Silver (kilograms)*	13,683	14,706	12,911

* Figures refer to the metal content of ores mined.

Peat ('000 metric tons, excluding peat for horticultural use): 4,767 in 1992; 3,288 in 1993.

Industry

SELECTED PRODUCTS
(provisional, '000 metric tons, unless otherwise indicated)

	1989	1990	1991
Flour	161	n.a.	n.a.
Margarine	25	23	25
Cigarettes (million)	6,161	6,218	6,377
Wool yarn	8.6*	n.a.	n.a.
Woven woollen fabrics (million sq m)	1.8	1.3	0.9
Footwear ('000 pairs)	1,913	1,415	946
Nitrogenous fertilizers†	252.0	296.7	279.0
Motor spirit (petrol)	340	340	332
Distillate fuel oils	532	618	707
Residual fuel oils	508	621	640
Electric energy (million kWh)	13,640	14,325	14,990

* Source: UN, *Industrial Commodity Statistics Yearbook*.

† Source: FAO, *Quarterly Bulletin of Statistics*. Figures are in terms of nitrogen and refer to estimated production during the 12 months ending 30 June of the year stated.

1995: Margarine 17,000 metric tons, Woven woollen fabric 700,000 sq. m, Electric energy 17,556m. kWh.

1996: Margarine 14,000 metric tons, Woven woollen fabric 900,000 sq. m, Electric energy 18,935m. kWh.

1997: Margarine 12,600 metric tons, Electric energy 19,579 kWh.

Finance

CURRENCY AND EXCHANGE RATES

Monetary Units:

100 pence (singular: penny) = 1 Irish pound (IR£ or punt).

Sterling and Dollar Equivalents (30 September 1997)

£1 sterling = IR£1.1099;
US $1 = 68.70 pence;
IR£100 = £90.10 sterling = $145.55.

Average Exchange Rate (US $ per Irish pound)

1994	1.4978
1995	1.6038
1996	1.6006

BUDGET (IR£ million)

Revenue	1996	1997	1998*
Tax revenue	12,520	14,274	15,167
Customs	159	180	176
Excise	2,320	2,507	2,659
Capital taxes	178	225	198
Income tax	4,562	5,218	5,522
Corporation tax	1,426	1,699	1,926
Motor vehicle duties	258	100	—
Stamp duties	336	429	467
Value-added tax	3,105	3,718	4,017
Employment and training levy	164	189	193
Non-tax revenue	434	345	330
Total	12,954	14,619	15,497

Expenditure	1996	1997	1998*
Debt service	2,360	2,711	2,625
Agriculture, fisheries and forestry	668	659	632
Defence	456	503	560
Justice (incl. police)	649	722	736
Education	2,088	2,332	2,347
Social welfare	4,380	4,550	4,771
Health	2,333	2,657	2,894
Industry and labour	527	579	614
Total (incl. others)	13,469	14,725	15,196

* Projections.

GOLD RESERVES AND CURRENCY IN CIRCULATION
(IR£ million at 31 December)

	1995	1996	1997*
Official gold reserves	87.7	77.0	70.0
Coin and bank notes in circulation	2,091.6	2,286.7	2,365.0

* At November 1997.

COST OF LIVING
(Consumer Price Index; base: November 1968 = 100)

	1995	1996	1997
Food	874.6	908.4	975.9
Alcoholic drink	1,154.2	1,184.1	1,213.9
Tobacco	1,175.5	1,235.4	1,282.4
Clothing and footwear	665.1	658.1	610.7
Fuel and light	1,132.6	1,151.6	1,150.6
Housing	678.2	677.5	699.2
Durable household goods	672.5	678.9	679.4
Other goods	1,067.8	1,093.7	1,107.4
Transport	1,185.7	1,213.3	1,247.9
Services and related expenditure	1,293.0	1,307.8	1,328.8
All items	978.5	995.1	1,009.4

NATIONAL ACCOUNTS (IR£ million at current prices)

National Income and Product

	1994	1995	1996
Gross domestic product at factor cost	30,881	34,260	37,748
Net factor income from the rest of the world*	–3,575	–4,508	–5,121
Gross national product at factor cost	27,306	29,752	32,626
Less Consumption of fixed capital	3,488	3,848	4,303
Net national product at factor cost	23,818	25,904	28,323
of which:			
Compensation of employees	17,091	18,341	19,700
Other domestic income	6,726	7,563	8,623
Indirect taxes, less subsidies	3,964	4,377	4,356
Net national product at market prices	27,782	30,281	32,679
Consumption of fixed capital	3,488	3,848	4,303
Gross national product at market prices	31,269	34,129	36,983
Less Net factor income from the rest of the world*	–3,575	–4,508	–5,121
Gross domestic product at market prices	34,844	38,638	42,104
Balance of exports and imports of goods and services*	–3,418	–4,468	–4,629
Available resources	31,426	34,170	37,475
of which:			
Private consumption expenditure	20,400	21,695	23,318
Government consumption expenditure	5,579	5,949	6,244
Gross fixed capital formation	5,575	6,349	7,524
Increase in stocks	–128	177	389

* Excludes transfers between Ireland and the rest of the world.

Gross Domestic Product by Economic Activity (at factor cost)

	1994	1995	1996
Agriculture, forestry and fishing	2,669	2,845	2,858
Mining, manufacturing, electricity, gas, water and construction	11,407	13,304	14,480
Public administration and defence	1,714	1,752	1,931
Transport, communications and trade	5,147	5,721	6,749
Other services	11,437	12,409	13,648
Sub-total	32,374	36,031	39,666
Adjustment for financial services	–1,493	–1,770	–1,919
Total	30,881	34,261	37,747

BALANCE OF PAYMENTS (US $ million)

	1994	1995	1996
Exports of goods f.o.b.	33,642	44,423	48,500
Imports of goods f.o.b.	-24,275	-30,866	-33,306
Trade balance	9,366	13,557	15,194
Exports of services	4,319	5,017	5,563
Imports of services	-8,452	-11,303	-13,260
Balance on goods and services	5,233	7,270	7,497
Other income received	3,513	5,110	5,576
Other income paid	-8,919	-12,435	-13,855
Balance on goods, services and income	-173	-55	-782
Current transfers received	2,850	3,009	3,535
Current transfers paid	-1,100	-1,233	-1,351
Current balance	1,577	1,721	1,402
Capital account (net)	387	817	785
Direct investment abroad	-438	-820	-727
Direct investment from abroad	838	1,447	2,456
Portfolio investment assets	-1,019	-1,056	-183
Portfolio investment liabilities	-379	771	982
Other investment assets	-4,483	-16,572	-22,099
Other investment liabilities	1,519	16,197	16,691
Net errors and omissions	1,823	-167	640
Overall balance	-176	2,339	-52

Source: IMF, *International Financial Statistics*.

External Trade

PRINCIPAL COMMODITIES (distribution by SITC, IR£ million)

Imports c.i.f.	1994	1995	1996
Food and live animals	1,409.9	1,475.3	1,544.1
Crude materials (inedible) except fuels	398.2	408.6	406.9
Mineral fuels, lubricants, etc.	661.2	670.2	823.7
Petroleum, petroleum products, etc.	531.4	541.9	682.3
Chemicals and related products	2,237.3	2,636.6	2,762.8
Organic chemicals	516.1	678.3	646.8
Medicinal and pharmaceutical products	392.5	464.7	463.2
Artificial resins and plastic materials, etc.	262.1	335.1	305.6
Basic manufactures	2,018.4	2,374.3	2,419.9
Paper, paperboard, etc.	425.3	540.9	512.7
Textile yarn, fabrics, etc.	371.1	392.8	398.2
Machinery and transport equipment	6,715.8	8,826.2	9,448.4
Machinery specialized for particular industries	475.2	506.8	628.2
General industrial machinery, equipment and parts	425.1	481.4	553.4
Office machines and automatic data-processing equipment	2,274.0	3,524.0	3,842.8
Parts and accessories for office machines, etc.	1,081.0	1,763.8	1,606.9
Telecommunications and sound equipment	362.1	418.8	587.7
Other electrical machinery, apparatus, etc.	1,809.9	2,269.7	2,050.5
Road vehicles and parts (excl. tyres, engines and electrical parts)	853.5	931.1	1,214.5
Passenger motor cars (excl. buses)	528.7	579.9	810.1
Miscellaneous manufactured articles	2,134.7	2,424.8	2,859.2
Clothing and accessories (excl. footwear)	527.0	562.6	632.1
Total (incl. others)*	17,283.4	20,619.1	22,476.9

* Including transactions not classified by commodity.

Exports f.o.b.	1994	1995	1996
Food and live animals	4,276.3	4,850.0	4,142.7
Meat and meat preparations	1,214.7	1,252.1	1,082.1
Fresh, chilled or frozen meat	1,076.3	1,101.2	922.7
Dairy products and birds' eggs	767.0	994.1	757.2
Crude materials (inedible) except fuels	546.4	564.2	556.6
Chemicals and related products	4,756.0	5,272.5	6,726.8
Organic chemicals	2,432.1	2,649.5	3,163.5
Organo-inorganic and heterocyclic compounds	1,902.6	2,038.5	2,551.3
Heterocyclic compounds (incl. nucleic acids)	1,613.1	1,699.5	2,128.7
Basic manufactures	1,267.7	1,351.2	1,357.4
Machinery and transport equipment	6,972.5	9,597.8	10,552.9
Office machines and automatic data-processing equipment	4,138.3	5,853.7	6,426.8
Automatic data-processing machines and units	2,509.2	3,532.4	3,938.3
Electrical machinery, apparatus, etc.	1,899.4	2,679.1	2,941.6
Miscellaneous manufactured articles	3,295.1	4,326.9	4,600.2
Professional, scientific and controlling instruments and apparatus	472.0	540.1	763.0
Total (incl. others)*	22,753.4	27,824.7	30,351.6

* Including transactions not classified by commodity.

PRINCIPAL TRADING PARTNERS (IR£ million)*

Imports c.i.f.	1994	1995	1996
Belgium/Luxembourg	232.8	256.6	291.6
France	656.0	786.2	876.5
Germany	1,218.4	1,459.1	1,526.2
Italy	380.9	405.2	461.6
Japan	823.8	1,062.9	1,206.8
Malaysia	196.1	330.9	336.6
Netherlands	482.3	606.4	671.6
Norway	249.7	278.9	275.6
Singapore	368.9	807.8	988.3
Sweden	246.8	227.1	303.0
United Kingdom	6,314.4	7,296.4	7,814.7
USA	3,156.4	3,628.7	3,459.5
Total (incl. others)	17,283.4	20,619.1	22,476.9

Exports f.o.b.	1994	1995	1996
Belgium/Luxembourg	895.8	1,239.5	1,443.0
Canada	212.6	204.2	247.2
Denmark	220.8	353.1	387.5
France	2,095.3	2,621.3	2,498.2
Germany	3,222.4	4,038.0	3,929.9
Italy	895.8	1,072.5	1,099.4
Japan	715.7	815.0	860.6
Netherlands	1,275.5	1,935.6	2,041.8
Norway	248.0	294.4	336.0
Spain	529.6	679.0	700.0
Sweden	462.8	546.0	547.7
Switzerland	444.3	493.7	561.0
United Kingdom	6,390.9	7,099.4	7,464.5
USA	1,903.9	2,269.6	2,816.3
Total (incl. others)	22,753.4	27,824.7	30,351.6

* Imports by country of origin; exports by country of final destination.

Transport

RAILWAYS (traffic, '000)

	1994	1995	1996
Passengers carried	25,813	27,124	27,930
Passenger train-km	9,585	9,966	11,052
Freight tonnage	3,015	3,179	3,130
Freight train-km	4,124	4,417	4,335

ROAD TRAFFIC (licensed motor vehicles at 31 December)

	1994	1995	1996
Passenger cars	939,022	990,384	1,057,383
Lorries and vans	135,809	141,785	146,601
Buses and coaches	11,910	13,368	14,754
Motorcycles and mopeds	23,632	23,452	23,847

SHIPPING

Merchant Fleet (registered at 31 December)

	1994	1995	1996
Number of vessels	170	163	164
Total displacement (grt)	190,311	213,364	218,990

Source: Lloyd's Register of Shipping, *World Fleet Statistics*.

Sea-borne Freight Traffic ('000 net tons)*

	1994	1995	1996
Displacement	37,896†	44,799	54,602

* Figures refer to vessels engaged in both international and coastal trade.
† '000 net registered tons.

CIVIL AVIATION

	1994	1995	1996
Passengers carried ('000)	9,316	10,568	11,956
Freight (incl. mail) carried (tons)	104,263	124,144	146,681
Total aircraft movements	199,653	204,850	228,167
scheduled	113,011	120,884	136,667
non-scheduled	86,642	83,966	91,500

Tourism

FOREIGN TOURIST ARRIVALS BY ORIGIN ('000)*

	1994	1995	1996
Great Britain	2,087	2,365	2,698
France	230	232	261
Germany	258	310	333
Netherlands	79	92	108
Other continental Europe	403	450	462
USA	436	574	643
Canada	38	43	60
Other areas	150	190	174
Total	3,681	4,256	4,739

* Excluding visitors from Northern Ireland and excursionists.

Communications Media

	1995	1996	1997
Television licences*	952,589	972,069	989,651
Telephone lines	1,262,242	1,341,719	1,426,518
Daily newspapers	6	6	6

* Sales of licences.

Radio receivers (1995): 3.1m. in domestic use.

Television receivers (1995): 1.5m. in domestic use.

Book production (1985): 2,679 titles (including 2,051 pamphlets).

Education

(1995/96)

	Institutions	Teachers	Students (full-time)
National schools*	3,317	21,052	478,692
Secondary schools	445	12,736†	223,605
Vocational schools	246	5,229†	94,809
Comprehensive schools	16	565†	9,127
Community schools	61	2,357†	42,324
Teacher (primary) training colleges	3	15	388
Regional technical colleges‡	11	1,655	27,573
Technology colleges‡	8	700	10,557
Universities and institutes	10	2,518	55,850

* National schools are state-aided primary schools.
† Full-time teachers only.
‡ Third-level pupils only.

Directory

The Constitution

The Constitution took effect on 29 December 1937. Ireland became a republic on 18 April 1949. The following is a summary of the Constitution's main provisions:

TITLE OF THE STATE

The title of the State is Éire or, in the English language, Ireland.

NATIONAL STATUS

The Constitution declares that Ireland is a sovereign, independent, democratic State. It affirms the inalienable, indefeasible and sovereign right of the Irish nation to choose its own form of government, to determine its relations with other nations, and to develop its life, political, economic and cultural, in accordance with its own genius and traditions.

The Constitution applies to the whole of Ireland, but, pending the re-integration of the national territory, the laws enacted by the Parliament established by the Constitution have the same area and extent of application as those of the Irish Free State.

THE PRESIDENT

At the head of the State is the President, elected by direct suffrage, who holds office for a period of seven years. The President, on the advice of the Government or its head, summons and dissolves Parliament, signs and promulgates laws and appoints judges; on the nomination of the Dáil, the President appoints the Prime Minister and, on the nomination of the Prime Minister with the previous approval of the Dáil, the President appoints the other members of the Government. The supreme command of the Defence Forces is vested in the President, its exercise being regulated by law.

In addition, the President has the power to refer certain Bills to the Supreme Court for decision on the question of their constitutionality; and also, at the instance of a prescribed proportion of the members of both Houses of Parliament, to refer certain Bills to the people for decision at a referendum.

The President, in the exercise and performance of certain of his or her constitutional powers and functions, has the aid and advice of a Council of State.

PARLIAMENT

The Oireachtas, or National Parliament, consists of the President and two Houses, viz. a House of Representatives called Dáil Éireann, and a Senate, called Seanad Éireann. The Dáil consists of 166 members, who are elected for a five-year term by adult suffrage on the system of proportional representation by means of the single, transferable vote. Of the 60 members of the Senate, 11 are nominated by the Prime Minister, six are elected by the universities, and 43 are elected from five panels of candidates established on a vocational basis, representing: national language and culture, literature, art, education and such professional interests as may be defined by law for the purpose of this panel; agriculture and allied interests, and fisheries; labour, whether organized or unorganized; industry and commerce, including banking, finance, accountancy, engineering and architecture; and public administration and social services, including voluntary social activities.

A maximum period of 90 days is afforded to the Senate for the consideration or amendment of Bills sent to that House by the Dáil, but the Senate has no power to veto legislation.

EXECUTIVE

The Executive Power of the State is exercised by the Government, which is responsible to the Dáil and consists of not fewer than seven and not more than 15 members. The head of the Government is the Prime Minister.

FUNDAMENTAL RIGHTS

The State recognizes the family as the natural, primary and fundamental unit group of Society, possessing inalienable and imprescriptible rights antecedent and superior to all positive law. It acknowledges the right to life of the unborn and, with due regard to the equal right to life of the mother, guarantees in its laws to defend and vindicate that right. It acknowledges the right and duty of parents to provide for the education of their children, and, with due regard to that right, undertakes to provide free education. It pledges itself also to guard with special care the institution of marriage.

The Constitution contains special provision for the recognition and protection of the fundamental rights of citizens, such as personal liberty, free expression of opinion, peaceable assembly, and the formation of associations and unions.

Freedom of conscience and the free practice and profession of religion are, subject to public order and morality, guaranteed to every citizen. No religion may be endowed or subjected to discriminatory disability. Since December 1972, when a referendum was taken on the issue, the Catholic Church has no longer enjoyed a special, privileged position.

SOCIAL POLICY

Certain principles of social policy intended for the general guidance of Parliament, but not cognizable by the courts, are set forth in the Constitution. Among their objects are the direction of the policy of the State towards securing the distribution of property so as to subserve the common good, the regulation of credit so as to serve the welfare of the people as a whole, the establishment of families in economic security on the land, and the right to an adequate means of livelihood for all citizens.

The State pledges itself to safeguard the interests, and to contribute where necessary to the support, of the infirm, the widow, the orphan and the aged, and shall endeavour to ensure that citizens shall not be forced by economic necessity to enter occupations unsuited to their sex, age or strength.

AMENDMENT OF THE CONSTITUTION

No amendment to the Constitution can be effected except by the decision of the people given at a referendum.

The Government

HEAD OF STATE

Uachtarán (President): Dr Mary McAleese (assumed office 11 November 1997).

THE CABINET
(February 1998)

A coalition of Fianna Fáil (FF) and the Progressive Democrats (PD).

Taoiseach (Prime Minister): Bertie Ahern (FF).

Tánaiste (Deputy Prime Minister) and Minister for Enterprise, Trade and Employment: Mary Harney (PD).

Minister for the Marine and Natural Resources: Michael J. Woods (FF).

Minister for Foreign Affairs: David Andrews (FF).

Minister for Public Enterprise: Mary O'Rourke (FF).

Minister for Defence: Michael Smith (FF).

Minister for Agriculture and Food: Joe Walsh (FF).

Minister for Finance: Charles McCreevy (FF).

Minister for Health and Children: Brian Cowen (FF).

Minister for the Environment and Local Government: Noel Dempsey (FF).

Minister for Social, Community and Family Affairs: Dermot Ahern (FF).

Minister for Arts, Heritage, Gaeltacht and the Islands: Síle de Valera (FF).

Minister for Justice, Equality and Law Reform: John O'Donoghue (FF).

Minister for Tourism, Sport and Recreation: James McDaid (FF).

Minister for Education: Micheál Martin (FF).

MINISTRIES

Office of the President: Áras an Uachtaráin, Phoenix Park, Dublin 8; tel. (1) 6772815; fax (1) 6710529; e-mail webmaster@aras.irlgov.ie.

Department of the Taoiseach: Government Bldgs, Upper Merrion St, Dublin 2; tel. (1) 6224888; fax (1) 6789791.

Office of the Tánaiste: Government Bldgs, Upper Merrion St, Dublin 2; tel. (1) 6621000; fax (1) 6760273.

Department of Agriculture and Food: Kildare St, Dublin 2; tel. (1) 6072000; telex 93607; fax (1) 6616263; e-mail infodaff@indigo.ie; internet http://www.irlgov.ie/daff.

Department of Arts, Heritage, Gaeltacht and the Islands: Dún Aimhirgin, 43–49 Mespil Rd, Dublin 4; tel. (1) 6670788; fax (1) 6670827; e-mail eolas@ealga.irlgov.ie.

Department of Defence: Coláiste Caoimhín, Mobhí Rd, Dublin 9; tel. (1) 8042000; fax (1) 8377993.

Department of Education: Marlborough St, Dublin 1; tel. (1) 8734700; fax (1) 8729553.

Department of Enterprise, Trade and Employment: Kildare St, Dublin 2; tel. (1) 6614444; telex 93478; fax (1) 6762654.

Department of the Environment and Local Government: Custom House, Dublin 1; tel. (1) 6793377; telex 3152; fax (1) 8742710; e-mail press-office@environ.irlgov.ie.

Department of Finance: Government Bldgs, Upper Merrion St, Dublin 2; tel. (1) 6767571; telex 30357; fax (1) 6789936; e-mail webmaster@finance.irlgov.ie.

Department of Foreign Affairs: 80 St Stephen's Green, Dublin 2; tel. (1) 4780822; fax (1) 4781484.

Department of Health and Children: Hawkins House, Hawkins St, Dublin 2; tel. (1) 6714711; fax (1) 6711947.

Department of Justice, Equality and Law Reform: 72–76 St Stephen's Green, Dublin 2; tel. (1) 6028202; fax 6615461.

Department of the Marine and Natural Resources: Leeson Lane, Dublin 2; tel. (1) 6785444; telex 91798; fax (1) 6618214.

Department for Public Enterprise: 44 Kildare St, Dublin 2; tel. (1) 6707444; fax (1) 6709633.

Department of Social, Community and Family Affairs: Áras Mhic Dhiarmada, Store St, Dublin 1; tel. (1) 8748444; fax (1) 7043868.

Department of Tourism, Sport and Recreation: Kildare St, Dublin 2; tel. (1) 6621444; telex 93418; fax (1) 6611201; internet http://www.irlgov.ie/dtt.

Legislature

OIREACHTAS (PARLIAMENT)

Parliament comprises two Houses—Dáil Éireann (House of Representatives), with 166 members (Teachtaí Dála), elected for a five-year term by universal adult suffrage, and Seanad Éireann (Senate), with 60 members serving a five-year term, of whom 11 are nominated by the Taoiseach (Prime Minister) and 49 elected (six by the universities and 43 from specially constituted panels).

Dáil Éireann

Speaker: SÉAMUS PATTISON.

General Election, 6 June 1997

Party	Votes*	% of votes*	Seats
Fianna Fáil	703,682	39.33	77
Fine Gael	499,936	27.95	54
Labour Party	186,044	10.40	17
Progressive Democrats	83,765	4.68	4
Democratic Left	44,901	2.51	4
Others	270,657	15.13	10
Total	1,788,985	100.00	166

* The election was conducted by means of the single transferable vote. Figures refer to first-preference votes.

Seanad Éireann

Speaker: BRIAN MULLOLY.

Election, August 1997 (11 non-affiliated members nominated)

Party	Seats at election
Fianna Fáil	29
Fine Gael	16
Labour	4
Progressive Democrats	4
Others	7

Political Organizations

Christian Solidarity Party: 54A Booterstown Ave, Co Dublin; tel. (1) 2880273; fax (1) 2880420; Pres. and Leader Dr GERARD CASEY; Nat. Sec. PATRICK SMYTH.

Comhaontas Glas (The Green Party): 5A Upper Fownes St, Dublin 2; tel. (1) 6790012; fax (1) 6797168; e-mail greenpar@iol.ie; internet http://www.iol.ie/resource/green/index.htm; fmrly The Ecology Party; advocates a humane, ecological society, freedom of information and political decentralization; Nat. Co-ordinator MARY BOWERS.

Communist Party of Ireland: James Connolly House, 43 East Essex St, Dublin 2; tel. and fax (1) 6711943; f. 1933; advocates a united, socialist, independent Ireland; Chair. EUGENE MCCARTAN; Gen. Sec. JAMES STEWART.

Democratic Left: 69 Middle Abbey St, Dublin 1; tel. (1) 8729550; fax (1) 8729238; e-mail dlhead@indigo.ie; f. 1992; democratic socialist; Leader PROINSIAS DE ROSSA; Gen. Sec. JOHN GALLAGHER.

Fianna Fáil (The Republican Party): 13 Upper Mount St, Dublin 2; tel. (1) 6761551; fax (1) 6785690; e-mail fiannafáil@iol.ie; f. 1926; centrist; Pres. and Leader BERTIE AHERN; Gen. Sec. MARTIN MACKEN.

Fine Gael (United Ireland Party): 51 Upper Mount St, Dublin 2; tel. (1) 6761573; fax (1) 6625046; e-mail finegael@finegael.com; f. 1933; centrist; Pres. and Leader JOHN BRUTON; Gen. Sec. JIM MILEY.

The Labour Party: 17 Ely Place, Dublin 2; tel. (1) 6612615; fax (1) 6612640; f. 1912; Leader RUAIRÍ QUINN; Gen. Sec. RAYMOND KAVANAGH.

Muintir na hÉireann Party: 58 The Palms, Roebuck Rd, Dublin 14; tel. and fax (1) 2831484; e-mail muintir@indigo.ie; f. 1995; Christian conservative; Leader RICHARD GREENE.

Progressive Democrats: 25 South Frederick St, Dublin 2; tel. (1) 6794399; fax (1) 6794757; f. 1985 by fmr mems of Fianna Fáil; conservative; Leader MARY HARNEY.

Sinn Féin ('Ourselves Alone'): 44 Parnell Sq., Dublin 1; tel. (1) 8726100; fax (1) 8733411; e-mail sinnféin@iol.ie; internet http://www.serve.com/rm/sinnfein; f. 1905; advocates the termination of British rule in Northern Ireland; seeks the establishment of a democratic socialist republic in a reunified Ireland; Pres. GERRY ADAMS.

The Workers' Party: 23 Hill St, Dublin 1; tel. (1) 8740716; fax (1) 8748702; f. 1905; fmrly Sinn Féin The Workers' Party; aims to establish a unitary socialist state on the island of Ireland; Pres. TOM FRENCH; Gen. Sec. PAT QUEARNEY.

Diplomatic Representation

EMBASSIES IN IRELAND

Argentina: 15 Ailesbury Drive, Dublin 4; tel. (1) 2691546; telex 90564; fax (1) 2600404; e-mail argembsy@indigo.ie; Ambassador: ALBERTO E. HAM.

Australia: Fitzwilton House, 2nd Floor, Wilton Terrace, Dublin 2; tel. (1) 6761517; fax (1) 6685266; Ambassador: EDWARD J. STEVENS.

Austria: 15 Ailesbury Court, 93 Ailesbury Rd, Dublin 4; tel. (1) 2694577; fax (1) 2830860; e-mail austroam@iol.ie; Ambassador: Dr MICHAEL BREISKY.

Belgium: 2 Shrewsbury Rd, Dublin 4; tel. (1) 2692082; fax (1) 2838488; Ambassador: LOUIS FOBE.

Brazil: Europa House, Harcourt St, Dublin 2; tel. (1) 4756000; fax (1) 4751341; Ambassador: CARLOS A. BETTENCOURT BUENO.

Bulgaria: 22 Burlington Rd, Dublin 4; tel. (1) 6603293; fax (1) 6603915; bgemb@tinet.ie; Chargé d'affaires a.i.: PETER POPTCHEV.

Canada: 65–68 St Stephen's Green, Dublin 2; tel. (1) 4781988; fax (1) 4781285; e-mail cdnembsy@iol.ie; Ambassador: MICHAEL B. PHILLIPS.

China, People's Republic: 40 Ailesbury Rd, Dublin 4; tel: (1) 2691707; telex 30626; fax (1) 2839938; Ambassador: FAN HUIJUAN.

Czech Republic: 57 Northumberland Rd, Ballsbridge, Dublin 4; tel. (1) 6681135; fax (1) 6681660; Ambassador: Dr LUBOŠ NOVÝ.

Denmark: 121–122 St Stephen's Green, Dublin 2; tel. (1) 4756404; fax (1) 4784536; e-mail embdane@iol.ie; Ambassador: ULRIK FEDERSPIEL.

Egypt: 12 Clyde Rd, Dublin 4; tel. (1) 6606566; telex 33202; fax (1) 6683745; Ambassador: HASSAN SALEM.

Estonia: 24 Merlyn Park, Dublin 4; tel. (1) 2691552; fax (1) 2695119; e-mail jseilenthal@um.ie; Chargé d'affaires a.i.: JÜRI SEILENTHAL.

Finland: Russell House, Stokes Place, St Stephen's Green, Dublin 2; tel. (1) 4781344; fax (1) 4783727; Ambassador: TIMO JALKANEN.

France: 36 Ailesbury Rd, Ballsbridge, Dublin 4; tel. (1) 2601666; fax (1) 2830178; Ambassador: HENRI BENOÎT DE COIGNAC.

Germany: 31 Trimleston Ave, Booterstown, Blackrock, Co Dublin; tel. (1) 2693011; fax (1) 2693946; Ambassador: HORST PAKOWSKI.

Greece: 1 Upper Pembroke St, Dublin 2; tel. (1) 6767254; telex 30878; fax (1) 6618892; Ambassador: MARIA ZOGRAFOU.

Holy See: 183 Navan Rd, Dublin 7 (Apostolic Nunciature); tel. (1) 8380577; fax (1) 8380276; e-mail nuncio@tinet.ie; Apostolic Nuncio: Most Rev. LUCIANO STORERO, Titular Archbishop of Tigimma.

Hungary: 2 Fitzwilliam Place, Dublin 2; tel. (1) 6612902; fax (1) 6612880; Ambassador: LÁSZLÓ MOHAI.

India: 6 Leeson Park, Dublin 6; tel. (1) 4970843; fax (1) 4978074; Ambassador: H. C. S. DHODY.

Iran: 72 Mount Merrion Ave, Blackrock, Co Dublin; tel. (1) 2880252; telex 90336; fax (1) 2834246; Ambassador: HOSSEIN AMIN-RAD.

Israel: 122 Pembroke Rd, Dublin 4; tel. (1) 6680303; fax (1) 6680418; Ambassador: ZVI GABAY.

Italy: 63–65 Northumberland Rd, Dublin 4; tel. (1) 6601744; telex 93950; fax (1) 6682759; Ambassador: Dr FERDINANDO ZEZZA.

Japan: Nutley Bldg, Merrion Centre, Nutley Lane, Dublin 4; tel. (1) 2694244; fax (1) 2838726; Ambassador: TAKANORI KAZUHARA.

Korea, Republic: Clyde House, 15 Clyde Rd, POB 2101, Dublin 4; tel. (1) 6608800; fax (1) 6608716; Ambassador: SUK HYUN KIM.

Mexico: 43 Ailesbury Rd, Dublin 4; tel. (1) 2600699; fax (1) 2600411; e-mail embasmex@indigo.ie; Ambassador: DANIEL DULTZIN DUBIN.

Morocco: 53 Raglan Rd, Dublin 4; tel. (1) 6609449; fax (1) 6609468; Ambassador: ABDESLAM TADLAOUI.

Netherlands: 160 Merrion Rd, Dublin 4; tel. (1) 2693444; fax (1) 2839690; Ambassador: LOUIS PETER VAN VLIET.

Nigeria: 56 Leeson Park, Dublin 6; tel. (1) 6604366; telex 24163; fax (1) 6604092; Ambassador: ELIAS NATHAN.

Norway: 34 Molesworth St, Dublin 2; tel. (1) 6621800; fax (1) 6621890; Ambassador: HELGE VINDENES.

Poland: 5 Ailesbury Rd, Dublin 4; tel. (1) 2830855; fax (1) 2698309; Ambassador: (vacant).

Portugal: Knocksinna House, Knocksinna, Foxrock, Dublin 18; tel. (1) 2894416; telex 30777; fax (1) 2892849; Ambassador: MANUEL LOPES DA COSTA.

Romania: 47 Ailesbury Rd, Dublin 4; tel. (1) 2692852; fax (1) 2692122; e-mail romemb@iol.ie; Ambassador: Dr ELENA ZAMFIRESCU.

Russia: 186 Orwell Rd, Dublin 14; tel. (1) 4922048; telex 33622; fax (1) 4923525; Ambassador: NIKOLAI IVANOVICH KOZYREV.

Slovakia: 18 Hampton Cres., St Helen's Wood, Booterstown Ave, Co Dublin; tel. and fax (1) 2834958; Chargé d'affaires a.i.: MANUEL KORČEK.

South Africa: Alexander House, Earlsfort Terrace, Dublin 2; tel. (1) 6615553; fax (1) 6615590; e-mail saembdub@iol.ie; Ambassador: PIERRE DIETRICHSEN.

Spain: 17A Merlyn Park, Dublin 4; tel. (1) 2691640; fax (1) 2691854; Ambassador: JOSÉ MARÍA SANZ PASTOR.

Sweden: Sun Alliance House, 13–17 Dawson St, Dublin 2; tel. (1) 6715822; telex 93341; fax (1) 6796718; Ambassador: PETER OSVALD.

Switzerland: 6 Ailesbury Rd, Dublin 4; tel. (1) 2692515; fax (1) 2830344; e-mail 100634.3625@compuserve.com; Ambassador: WILLY HOLD.

Turkey: 11 Clyde Rd, Dublin 4; tel. (1) 6685240; fax (1) 6685014; e-mail turkemb@iol.ie; Ambassador: N. MURAT ERSAVCI.

United Kingdom: 29 Merrion Rd, Dublin 4; tel. (1) 2053700; fax (1) 2053885; Ambassador: VERONICA E. SUTHERLAND.

USA: 42 Elgin Rd, Dublin 4; tel. (1) 6687122; fax (1) 6689946; Ambassador: JEAN KENNEDY SMITH.

Judicial System

Justice is administered in public by judges appointed by the President on the advice of the Government. The judges of all courts are completely independent in the exercise of their judicial functions. The jurisdiction and organization of the courts are dealt with in the Courts (Establishment and Constitution) Act, 1961, and the Courts (Supplemental Provisions) Acts, 1961 to 1981.

Attorney-General: DAVID BYRNE.

SUPREME COURT

The Supreme Court: Four Courts, Dublin 7; tel. (1) 8725555; consisting of the Chief Justice and seven other judges, has appellate jurisdiction from all decisions of the High Court. The President of Ireland may, after consultation with the Council of State, refer a bill which has been passed by both Houses of the Oireachtas (other than a money bill or certain others), to the Supreme Court to establish whether it or any other provisions thereof are repugnant to the Constitution.

Chief Justice: LIAM HAMILTON.

Judges:

HUGH O'FLAHERTY, SUSAN GAGEBY DENHAM, DONAL BARRINGTON, RONAN KEANE, FRANCIS MURPHY, KEVIN LYNCH, HENRY BARRON.

COURT OF CRIMINAL APPEAL

The Court of Criminal Appeal, consisting of the Chief Justice or an ordinary judge of the Supreme Court and two judges of the High Court, deals with appeals by persons convicted on indictment, where leave to appeal has been granted. The Court has jurisdiction to review a conviction or sentence on the basis of an alleged miscarriage of justice. The Director of Public Prosecutions may appeal against an unduly lenient sentence. The decision of the Court of Criminal Appeal is final unless the Court or Attorney-General or the Director of Public Prosecutions certifies that a point of law involved should, in the public interest, be taken to the Supreme Court.

HIGH COURT

The High Court, consisting of the President of the High Court and 21 ordinary judges, has full original jurisdiction in, and power to determine, all matters and questions whether of law or fact, civil or criminal. The High Court on circuit acts as an appeal court from the Circuit Court. The Central Criminal Court sits as directed by the President of the High Court to try criminal cases outside the jurisdiction of the Circuit Court. The duty of acting as the Central Criminal Court is assigned, for the time being, to a judge of the High Court.

President: FREDERICK MORRIS.

Judges:

MELLA CARROLL, ROBERT BARR, RICHARD JOHNSON, VIVIAN LAVAN, PAUL CARNEY, FEARGUS FLOOD, DECLAN BUDD, HUGH GEOGHEGAN, DERMOT KINLEN, BRIAN MCCRACKEN, MARY LAFFOY, PETER SHANLEY, MICHAEL MORIARTY, PETER KELLY, CATHERINE MCGUINNESS, THOMAS G. SMYTH, DIARMUID O'DONOVAN, PHILIP O'SULLIVAN, KEVIN C. O'HIGGINS, JOHN QUIRKE.

CIRCUIT AND DISTRICT COURTS

The civil jurisdiction of the Circuit Court is limited to IR£30,000 in contract and tort and in actions founded on hire-purchase and credit-sale agreements and to a rateable value of IR£200 in equity, and in probate and administration, but where the parties consent the jurisdiction is unlimited. In criminal matters the Court has jurisdiction in all cases except murder, rape, treason, piracy and allied offences. One circuit judge is permanently assigned to each circuit outside Dublin and five to the Dublin circuit. In addition there is one permanently unassigned judge. The Circuit Court acts as an appeal court from the District Court, which has a summary jurisdiction in a large number of criminal cases where the offence is not of a serious nature. In civil matters the District Court has jurisdiction in contract and tort (except slander, libel, seduction, slander of title, malicious prosecution and false imprisonment) where the claim does not exceed IR£5,000 and in actions founded on hire-purchase and credit-sale agreements.

All criminal cases except those dealt with summarily by a justice in the District Court are tried by a judge and a jury of 12 members. Juries are also used in some civil cases in the High Court. In a criminal case 10 members of the jury may, in certain circumstances, agree on a verdict, and in a civil case the agreement of nine members is sufficient.

Religion

CHRISTIANITY

The organization of the churches takes no account of the partition of Ireland into two separate political entities; both the Republic of Ireland and Northern Ireland are subject to a unified ecclesiastical jurisdiction. The Roman Catholic Primate of All Ireland and the Church of Ireland (Protestant Episcopalian) Primate of All Ireland have their seats in Northern Ireland, at Armagh, and the headquarters of the Presbyterian Church in Ireland is at Belfast, Northern Ireland.

In 1996 the Roman Catholic population of Ireland was estimated to be 3,919,568. In 1997 there were 297,205 adherents to the Presbyterian Church and 58,659 to the Methodist Church. In 1991 there were 371,150 adherents to the Church of Ireland.

Irish Council of Churches: Inter-Church Centre, 48 Elmwood Ave, Belfast, BT9 6AZ, Northern Ireland; tel. (1232) 663145; fax (1232) 381737; e-mail icpep@unite.co.uk; internet http://www.unite.co.uk/customers/icpep; f. 1922 (present name adopted 1966); nine mem. churches; Pres. Rev. D. NESBITT (Presbyterian Church in Ireland); Gen. Sec. Dr R. D. STEVENS.

The Roman Catholic Church

Ireland (including Northern Ireland) comprises four archdioceses and 22 dioceses.

Archbishop of Armagh and Primate of All Ireland: Most Rev. SEÁN BRADY, Ara Coeli, Cathedral Rd, Armagh, BT61 7QY, Northern Ireland; tel. (1861) 522045; fax (1861) 526182.

Archbishop of Cashel and Emly: Most Rev. DERMOT CLIFFORD, Archbishop's House, Thurles, Co Tipperary; tel. (504) 21512; fax (504) 22680.

Archbishop of Dublin and Primate of Ireland: Most Rev. DESMOND CONNELL, Archbishop's House, Drumcondra, Dublin 9; tel. (1) 8373732; fax (1) 8369796.

Archbishop of Tuam: Most Rev. MICHAEL NEARY, Archbishop's House, St Jarlath's, Tuam, Co Galway; tel. (93) 24166; fax (93) 28070.

Numerous Roman Catholic religious orders are strongly established in the country. These play an important role, particularly in the spheres of education, health and social welfare.

Church of Ireland

(The Anglican Communion)

Ireland (including Northern Ireland) comprises two archdioceses and 10 dioceses.

Central Office of the Church of Ireland: Church of Ireland House, Church Ave, Dublin 6; tel. (1) 4978422; fax (1) 4978821; e-mail rcbdub@iol.ie; 370,000 mems (1993); Chief Officer and Sec. to the Representative Church Body R. H. SHERWOOD.

Archbishop of Armagh and Primate of All Ireland and Metropolitan: Most Rev. Lord EAMES, The See House, Cathedral Close, Armagh, BT61 7EE, Northern Ireland; tel. (1861) 527144; fax (1861) 527823.

Archbishop of Dublin and Primate of Ireland and Metropolitan: Most Rev. WALTON N. F. EMPEY, The See House, 17 Temple Rd, Milltown, Dublin 6; tel. (1) 4977849; fax (1) 4976355.

Other Christian Churches

Baptist Union of Ireland: 117 Lisburn Rd, Belfast, BT9 7AF, Northern Ireland; tel. (1232) 663108; fax (1232) 663616; Pres. JOHN WOOLSEY; Sec. Pastor W. COLVILLE (acting).

Church of Jesus Christ of Latter-day Saints (Mormon): The Willows, Glasnevin, Dublin 11; tel. (1) 8306899; fax (1) 8304638.

Greek Orthodox Church in Britain and Ireland: 38 Ardmore Crescent, Dublin 5; Very Rev. IRENEU CRACIUN.

Lutheran Church in Ireland: Lutherhaus, 24 Adelaide Rd, Dublin 2; tel. (1) 6766548; Pastor Rev. FRITZ-GERT MAYER.

Methodist Church in Ireland: 1 Fountainville Ave, Belfast, BT9 6AN, Northern Ireland; tel. (1232) 324554; fax (1232) 239467; e-mail mci@iol.ie; Sec. Rev. EDMUND T. I. MAWHINNEY.

Moravian Church in Ireland: 158 Finaghy Rd South, Belfast, BT10 0DH, Northern Ireland; tel. (1232) 619755; f. 1749; Chair. of Conf. Rev. L. BROADBENT.

Non-Subscribing Presbyterian Church of Ireland: 102 Carrickfergus Rd, Larne, Co Antrim, Northern Ireland; tel. (1574) 272600; Clerk to Gen. Synod Rev. Dr JOHN W. NELSON.

Presbyterian Church in Ireland: Church House, Fisherwick Place, Belfast, BT1 6DW, Northern Ireland; tel. (1232) 322284; fax (1232) 236609; Moderator of Gen. Assembly Rt Rev. Dr S. HUTCHINSON (until June 1998); Clerk of Assembly and Gen. Sec. Rev. D. POOTS (acting).

The Religious Society of Friends: Swanbrook House, Bloomfield Ave, Morehampton Rd, Dublin 4; tel. (1) 6683684; Registrar VALERIE O'BRIEN.

Salvation Army: POB 2098, 114 Marlborough St, Dublin 1; tel. (1) 8740987; fax (1) 8747478; Public Relations Officer Maj. DAVID GAUTON.

BAHÁ'Í FAITH

National Spiritual Assembly: 24 Burlington Rd, Dublin 4; tel. (1) 6683150; fax (1) 6689632; e-mail nsairl@iol.ie.

ISLAM

The Muslim population of the Republic of Ireland was enumerated at 3,875 in the 1991 census. The number of adherents was estimated to total 9,000 in 1996, inclusive of Northern Ireland.

Islamic Foundation of Ireland: 19 Roebuck Rd, Clonskeagh, Dublin 14; tel. (1) 2603740; fax (1) 2603708; Imam YAHYA MUHAMMAD AL-HUSSEIN.

JUDAISM

The Jewish community was estimated to number 1,200 in 1996.

Chief Rabbi: Very Rev. Dr GAVIN BRODER, Herzog House, Zion Rd, Dublin 6; tel. (1) 4923751; fax (1) 4924680.

The Press

A significant feature of the Irish press is the number of weekly newspapers published in provincial centres.

DAILIES

Cork

Evening Echo: Academy St, Cork; tel. (21) 272722; telex 6014; fax 275112; f. 1892; Editor BRIAN FEENEY; circ. 27,000.

Examiner: Academy St, POB 21, Cork; tel. (21) 272722; telex 6014; fax 275112; e-mail features@examiner.ie; f. 1841; Editor BRIAN LOONEY; circ. 52,000.

Dublin

Evening Herald: Independent House, 90 Middle Abbey St, Dublin 1; tel. (1) 8731666; telex 33472; fax (1) 8731787; e-mail herald.letters@independent.ie; f. 1891; Editor PAUL DRURY; circ. 115,000.

Irish Independent: Independent House, 90 Middle Abbey St, Dublin 1; tel. (1) 7055333; fax (1) 8720304; f. 1905; Editor VINCENT DOYLE; circ. 158,000.

The Irish Times: 10–16 D'Olier St, POB 74, Dublin 2; tel. (1) 6792022; telex 93639; fax (1) 6793910; e-mail itemail@irish-times.com; f. 1859; Editor CONOR BRADY; circ. 105,000.

The Star: Star House, 62A Terenure Rd North, Dublin 6; tel. (1) 4901228; fax (1) 4902193; Editor GERARD O'REAGAN; circ. 85,000.

PRINCIPAL WEEKLY NEWSPAPERS

An Phoblacht/Republican News: 58 Parnell Sq., Dublin 1; tel. (1) 8733611; fax (1) 8733074; f. 1970; Editor BRIAN CAMPBELL; circ. 28,000.

Anglo-Celt: Anglo-Celt Pl., Cavan; tel. (49) 31100; fax (49) 32280; f. 1846; Fri.; Editor J. F. O'HANLON; circ. 16,000.

Argus: Park St, Dundalk, Co Louth; tel. (42) 31500; fax (42) 31643; f. 1835; Thurs.; Editor KEVIN MULLIGAN; circ. 9,300.

Clare Champion: Barrack St, Ennis, Co Clare; tel. (65) 28105; fax (65) 20374; e-mail jgalvin@clarechampion.ie; internet http://www.clarechampion.ie; f. 1903; Thurs.; Editor GERRY COLLINSON; circ. 20,000.

Connacht Tribune: 15 Market St, Galway; tel. (91) 567251; fax (91) 567970; f. 1909; Fri.; Editor J. CUNNINGHAM; circ. 29,000.

Connaught Telegraph: Ellison St, Castlebar, Co Mayo; tel. (94) 21711; fax (94) 24007; e-mail conntel@iol.ie; f. 1828; Wed.; Editor TOM GILLESPIE; circ. 16,000.

Donegal Democrat: Donegal Rd, Ballyshannon, Co Donegal; tel. (72) 51201; fax (72) 51945; f. 1919; Fri.; Editor JOHN BROMLEY; circ. 18,000.

Drogheda Independent: 9 Shop St, Drogheda, Co Louth; tel. (41) 38658; fax (41) 34271; f. 1884; Thurs.; Editor PAUL MURPHY; circ. 14,000.

Dundalk Democrat: 3 Earl St, Dundalk, Co Louth; tel. (42) 34058; fax (42) 31399; f. 1849; Sat.; Editor PETER E. KAVANAGH; circ. 16,000.

Dungarvan Leader and Southern Democrat: 78 O'Connell St, Dungarvan, Co Waterford; tel. and fax (58) 41205; Wed.; Editor COLM J. NAGLE; circ. 13,000.

Dungarvan Observer and Munster Industrial Advocate: Shandon, Dungarvan, Co Waterford; tel. (58) 41205; fax (58) 41559; Editor JAMES A. LYNCH; circ. 11,000.

Echo and South Leinster Advertiser: Mill Park Rd, Enniscorthy, Co Wexford; tel. (54) 33231; fax (54) 33506; f. 1902; Wed.; Editor JAMES GAHAN; circ. 22,000.

The Guardian: The People Newspapers Ltd, Court St, Enniscorthy, Co Wexford; tel. (54) 33833; f. 1881; Fri.; Man. Dir MICHAEL ROCHE; circ. 36,000.

Iris Oifigiuil (Dublin Gazette): 4–5 Harcourt Rd, Dublin 2; tel. (1) 6613111; fax (1) 4752760; f. 1922; 2 a week; official govt bulletin; Publs Man. BRIAN O'CONNELL.

The Kerryman/The Corkman: Clash Industrial Estate, Tralee, Co Kerry; tel. (66) 21666; fax (66) 21608; f. 1904; Thurs.; Editor GERARD COLLERAN; circ. 34,500.

Kilkenny People: 34 High St, Kilkenny; tel. (56) 21015; fax (56) 21414; e-mail k.people@iol.ie; f. 1892; weekly; Editor JOHN KERRY KEANE; circ. 17,000.

Leinster Express: Dublin Rd, Portlaoise, Co Laois; tel. (502) 21666; fax (502) 20491; e-mail lexpress@indigo.ie; f. 1831; weekly; Man. Editor TEDDY FENNELLY; circ. 18,500.

Leinster Leader: 19 South Main St, Naas, Co Kildare; tel. (45) 897302; fax (45) 897647; f. 1880; Wed.; Editor VICKY WELLER; circ. 15,000.

Leitrim Observer: St George's Terrace, Carrick-on-Shannon, Co Leitrim; tel. (78) 20025; fax (78) 20112; f. 1889; Wed.; Editor ANTHONY HICKEY; circ. 10,000.

Limerick Chronicle: 54 O'Connell St, Limerick; tel. (61) 315233; fax (61) 314804; f. 1766; Tues.; Editor BRENDAN HALLIGAN; circ. 7,000.

Limerick Leader: 54 O'Connell St, Limerick; tel. (61) 315233; fax (61) 314804; f. 1889; 4 a week; Editor BRENDAN HALLIGAN; circ. 26,000 (weekend edn).

Limerick Post: Town Hall, Rutland St, Limerick; tel. (61) 413322; fax (61) 417684; e-mail lpost@iol.ie; f. 1986; Thurs.; Editor BILLY RYAN; circ. 31,000.

Longford Leader: Market Sq., Longford; tel. (43) 45241; fax (43) 41489; e-mail info@longford-leader.ie; f. 1897; Wed.; Editor EUGENE MCGEE; circ. 25,000.

Longford News: Earl St, Longford; tel. (43) 45627; fax (43) 41549; Wed.; Editor PAUL HEALY; circ. 24,000.

Mayo News: The Fairgreen, Westport, Co Mayo; tel. (98) 25311; fax (98) 26108; f. 1892; Wed.; Man. Editor SEÁN STAUNTON; circ. 35,000.

Meath Chronicle and Cavan and Westmeath Herald: 12 Market Sq., Navan, Co Meath; tel. (46) 21442; fax (46) 23565; f. 1897; Sat.; Editor KEN DAVIS; circ. 20,000.

Midland Tribune: Emmet St, Birr, Co Offaly; tel. (509) 20003; fax (509) 20588; e-mail midtrib@iol.ie; f. 1881; Wed.; Editor JOHN O'CALLAGHAN; circ. 16,000.

The Munster Express: 37 The Quay and 1–3 Hanover St, Waterford; tel. (51) 872141; fax (51) 873452; f. 1859; 2 a week; Editor K. J. WALSH; circ. 19,000.

Nationalist and Leinster Times: 42 Tullow St, Carlow; tel. (503) 31731; fax (503) 31442; e-mail nltnews@tinet.ie; f. 1883; weekly; Editor E. COFFEY; circ. 17,000.

Nationalist Newspaper: Queen St, Clonmel, Co Tipperary; tel. (52) 22211; fax (52) 25248; f. 1890; Thurs.; Editor TOM CORR; circ. 15,000.

The Northern Standard: The Diamond, Monaghan; tel. (47) 81867; fax (47) 84070; f. 1839; Fri.; Editor MARTIN SMYTH; circ. 15,000.

Offaly Express: Bridge St, Tullamore, Co Offaly; tel. (506) 21744; fax (506) 51930; e-mail lexpress@indigo.ie; weekly; Editor TEDDY FENNELLY; circ. 18,000 (with Leinster Express).

Roscommon Champion: Abbey St, Roscommon; tel. (903) 25051; fax (903) 25053; f. 1927; weekly; Editor PAUL HEALY; circ. 10,000.

Roscommon Herald: Boyle, Co Roscommon; tel. (79) 62622; fax (79) 62926; e-mail roherald@indigo.ie; f. 1859; weekly; Editor CHRISTINA MCHUGH; circ. 17,000.

Sligo Champion: Wine St, Sligo; tel. (71) 69222; fax (71) 69040; e-mail sales@sligochampion.ie; f. 1836; Wed.; Editor S. FINN; circ. 15,000.

Southern Star: Skibbereen, Co Cork; tel. (28) 21200; fax (28) 21071; f. 1889; Sat.; Editor LIAM O'REGAN; circ. 16,000.

Sunday Business Post: 27–30 Merchant's Quay, Dublin 8; tel. (1) 6799777; fax (1) 6796496; e-mail sbpost@iol.ie; Editor DAMIEN KIBERD; circ. 42,000.

Sunday Independent: Independent House, 90 Middle Abbey St, Dublin 1; tel. (1) 8731333; telex 33472; fax (1) 8721587; f. 1905; Editor AENGUS FANNING; circ. 334,000.

Sunday Tribune: 15 Lower Baggot St, Dublin 2; tel. (1) 6615555; fax (1) 6615302; e-mail stribune@indigo.ie; f. 1980; Editor MATT COOPER; circ. 84,000.

Sunday World: Newspaper House, 18 Rathfarnham Rd, Terenure, Dublin 6; tel. (1) 4901980; telex 24886; fax (1) 4901838; f. 1973; Editor COLM MACGINTY; circ. 304,000.

Tipperary Star: Friar St, Thurles, Co Tipperary; tel. (504) 21122; fax (504) 21110; e-mail info@tipperarystar.ie; internet http://www.tipperarystar.ie; f. 1909; Wed.; Editor MICHAEL DUNDON; circ. 10,000.

Tuam Herald: Dublin Rd, Tuam, Co Galway; tel. (93) 24183; fax (93) 24478; e-mail tuamhrld@iol.ie; f. 1837; Wed.; Editor DAVID BURKE; circ. 11,000.

Tullamore Tribune: Church St, Tullamore, Co Offaly; tel. (506) 21152; fax (506) 21927; e-mail midtrib@iol.ie; f. 1978; Wed.; Editor G. J. SCULLY; circ. 10,000.

Waterford News & Star: 25 Michael St, Waterford; tel. (51) 74951; fax (51) 55281; f. 1848; Thurs.; Editor P. DOYLE; circ. 16,000.

Western People: Francis St, Ballina, Co Mayo; tel. (96) 21188; fax (96) 70208; e-mail wpeople@iol.ie; internet http://www.mayo-ireland.ie/wpeople.htm; f. 1883; Tues.; Editor TERENCE REILLY; circ. 24,000.

Westmeath Examiner: 19 Dominick St, Mullingar, Co Westmeath; tel. (44) 48426; fax (44) 40640; f. 1882; weekly; Editor NICHOLAS J. NALLY; circ. 13,000.

Wicklow People: Main St, Wicklow; tel. (404) 67198; fax (404) 69937; f. 1883; Thurs.; Editor EOIN QUINN.

SELECTED PERIODICALS

Afloat Magazine: 2 Lower Glenageary Rd, Dún Laoghaire, Co Dublin; tel. (1) 2846161; fax (1) 2846192; e-mail afloat@indigo.ie; monthly; boating; Man. Editor DAVID O'BRIEN; circ. 10,000.

Banking Ireland: 50 Fitzwilliam Sq., Dublin 2; tel. (1) 6764587; fax (1) 6619781; f. 1898; quarterly; journal of the Inst. of Bankers in Ireland; Editor GERRY LAWLOR; circ. 15,500.

Business and Exporting: Tara House, Tara St, Dublin 2; tel. (1) 6713500; fax (1) 6713074; f. 1994; monthly; Publr NEIL WHORISKEY.

Business & Finance: 50 Fitzwilliam Sq., Dublin 2; tel. (1) 6764587; fax (1) 6619781; e-mail belenos@tinet.ie; f. 1964; weekly; Man. Editor JOHN MCGEE; circ. 11,000.

History Ireland: POB 695, James's St PO, Dublin 8; tel. (1) 4535730; fax (1) 4533234; e-mail history.ireland@infonet.ie; quarterly; Jt Editors HIRAM MORGAN, TOMMY GRAHAM.

Hot Press: 13 Trinity St, Dublin 2; tel. (1) 6795077; fax (1) 6795097; fortnightly; music, leisure, current affairs; Editor NIALL STOKES; circ. 21,000.

In Dublin: 3–7 Camden Place, Dublin 2; tel. (1) 4784322; fax (1) 4781055; f. 1976; fortnightly; listings and reviews of entertainments, restaurants; also news and current affairs; Editor DECLAN BURKE; circ. 16,000.

Industry and Commerce: Tara House, Tara St, Dublin 2; tel. (1) 6713500; fax (1) 6713074; monthly; Publr NEIL WHORISKEY; circ. 7,000.

Ireland's Own: North Main St, Wexford; tel. (53) 22155; f. 1902; weekly; family interest; Editors GERRY BREEN, MARGARET GALVIN; circ. 50,000.

The Irish Catholic: 55 Lower Gardiner St, Dublin 1; tel. (1) 8555619; fax (1) 8364805; e-mail icn@indigo.ie; weekly; Editor DAVID QUINN; circ. 30,000.

Irish Computer: 66 Patrick St, Dún Laoghaire, Co Dublin; tel. (1) 2847777; fax (1) 2847584; f. 1977; monthly; Editor DECLAN MCCOLGAN; circ. 7,000.

Irish Doctor: Tara House, Tara St, Dublin 2; tel. (1) 6713500; fax (1) 6713074; f. 1987; monthly; Editor Dr PAUL CARSON; circ. 6,000.

Irish Farmers' Journal: Irish Farm Centre, Bluebell, Dublin 12; tel. (1) 4501166; fax (1) 4520876; f. 1948; weekly; Editor MATTHEW DEMPSEY; circ. 75,000.

Irish Field: 11–15 D'Olier St, POB 711, Dublin 2; tel. (1) 6792022; fax (1) 6793029; f. 1870; e-mail irish-field@irish-times.ie; weekly; horse-racing, show-jumping and breeding; Man. Editor VALENTINE LAMB; circ. 11,000.

Irish Historical Studies: c/o Dept of Modern History, Trinity College, College Green, Dublin 2; tel. (1) 6081020; 2 a year; Editors Dr CIARAN BRADY, Dr KEITH JEFFERY.

Irish Journal of Medical Science: Royal Academy of Medicine in Ireland, 6 Kildare St, Dublin 2; tel. (1) 6767650; fax (1) 6611684; e-mail secretary@rami.iol.ie; f. 1832; quarterly; organ of the Royal Academy of Medicine; Editor THOMAS F. GOREY.

Irish Law Times (including Irish Law Log): Round Hall Sweet & Maxwell, Brehon House, 4 Upper Ormond Quay, Dublin 7; tel. (1) 8730101; fax (1) 8720078; f. 1983; 20 a year; Editor RAYMOND BYRNE.

Irish Medical Journal: 10 Fitzwilliam Place, Dublin 2; tel. (1) 6767273; fax (1) 6622818; e-mail imj@imo.ie; internet http://www.imj.ie; 10 a year; journal of the Irish Medical Org.; Editor Dr JOHN MURPHY; circ. 6,000.

The Irish Skipper: Taney Hall, Eglinton Terrace, Dublin 14; tel. (1) 2960000; fax (1) 2960383; e-mail newmedia@macpub.iol.ie; monthly; journal of the fishing industry; Man. Editor FIACC O'BROLCHAIN.

Irish University Review: Rm J210, University College, Belfield, Dublin 4; fax (1) 7061174; 2 a year; literature, history, fine arts, politics, cultural studies; Editor ANTHONY ROCHE.

Management: 52 Glasthule Rd, Sandycove, Co Dublin; tel. (1) 2800000; fax (1) 2801818; f. 1954; monthly; Editor SANDRA O'CONNELL; circ. 9,000.

Motoring Life: Cyndale Enterprises Ltd, 48 North Great George's St, Dublin 1; tel. (1) 8780444; f. 1946; monthly; Editor FERGAL HERBERT; circ. 10,000.

PC Live!: Prospect House, 1 Prospect Rd, Dublin 9; tel. (1) 8303455; fax (1) 8300888; e-mail pclive@scope.ie; internet http://www.infolive.ie; monthly; computers and the internet; Editor JOHN COLLINS; circ. 16,000.

Phoenix: 44 Lower Baggot St, Dublin 2; tel. (1) 6611062; fax (1) 6624532; e-mail goldhawk@indigo.ie; f. 1983; fortnightly; news and comment; Editor PADDY PRENDIVILLE; circ. 19,000.

RTE Guide: Radio Telefís Éireann, Donnybrook, Dublin 4; tel. (1) 2083111; fax (1) 2083085; weekly; programmes of the Irish broadcasting service; Editor HEATHER PARSONS; circ. 175,000.

Sportsworld: 48 North Great George's St, Dublin 1; tel. (1) 8780444; monthly; Editor DAVID GUINEY; circ. 23,000.

Studies: 35 Lower Leeson St, Dublin 2; tel. (1) 6766785; fax (1) 6762984; fax (1) 6762984; f. 1912; quarterly review of letters, history, religious and social questions; Editor Fr NOEL BARBER.

U Magazine: 2 Clanwilliam Court, Lower Mount St, Dublin 2; tel. (1) 6623158; fax (1) 6628719; f. 1979; monthly; Editor ANNETTE O'MEARA; circ. 24,000.

Woman's Way: 2 Clanwilliam Court, Lower Mount St, Dublin 2; tel. (1) 6623158; fax (1) 6628719; f. 1963; weekly; Editor CELINE NAUGHTON; circ. 67,000.

The Word: Divine Word Missionaries, Donamon, Roscommon, tel. and fax (903) 62608; f. 1953; monthly; Catholic general interest; Editor Rev. THOMAS CAHILL; circ. 32,000.

NEWS AGENCIES

Ireland International News Agency: 51 Wellington Quay, Dublin 2; tel. (1) 6712442; fax (1) 6796586; e-mail iina@indigo.ie; Chair. TOM MCPHAIL; Man. Dir DIARMAID MACDERMOTT.

Foreign Bureaux

Agenzia Nazionale Stampa Associata (ANSA) (Italy): 56 Greenfield Park, Knocklyon, Dublin 24; tel. and fax (1) 4941389; Bureau Chief ENZO FARINELLA.

Reuters Ireland: Kestrel House, Clanwilliam Place, Lower Mount St, Dublin 2; tel. (1) 6613377; fax (1) 6769783; Chief Correspondent ANDREW HILL.

Rossiyskoye Informationnoye Agentstvo—Novosti (RIA—Novosti) (Russia) and Informationsionnye Telegrafnoye Agentsvo Rossii–Telegrafnoye Agentsvo Suverennykh Stran (ITAR–TASS) are also represented.

PRESS ORGANIZATIONS

National Newspapers of Ireland: Clyde Lodge, 15 Clyde Rd, Dublin 4; tel. (1) 6689099; fax (1) 6689872; e-mail nni@nemo.gels.com; Chair. LOUIS O'NEILL; Co-ordinating Dir FRANK CULLEN.

Provincial Newspapers Association of Ireland: Sheridan House, 33 Parkgate St, Dublin 8; tel. (1) 6793679; fax (1) 6779144; e-mail Karen@rnan.ie; internet http://www.rnan.ie/rnan; f. 1917; 37 mems; Pres. JACK DAVIS; CEO NEVILLE GALLOWAY.

Publishers

Anvil Books Ltd: 45 Palmerston Rd, Dublin 6; tel (1) 4973628; fax (1) 4968263; f. 1964; Irish history and biography, folklore, children's fiction (8 years and above); Dirs R. DARDIS, M. DARDIS.

Basement Press: 29 Upper Mount St, Dublin 2; tel. (1) 6616128; fax (1) 6616176; general; Publr RÓISÍN CONROY.

Boole Press Ltd: Olympia House, 61–63 Dame St, Dublin 2; tel. (1) 6797655; fax (1) 6792469; e-mail 73173.1245@compuserve.com; f. 1979; scientific, technical, medical, scholarly; Man. Dir P. MCKEEVER.

Butterworth Ireland Ltd: 26 Upper Ormond Quay, Dublin 7; tel. (1) 8731555; fax (1) 8731876; e-mail ircustomer@butterworths.co.uk; taxation and law; Chair. S. STOUT.

Comhairle Bhéaloideas Éireann (Folklore of Ireland Council): c/o Folklore Dept, University College, Belfield, Dublin 4; tel. (1) 693244; Editor Prof. BO ALMQVIST.

Cork University Press: Crawford Business Park, Crosses Green, Cork; tel. (21) 902980; fax (21) 315329; e-mail corkunip@ucc.ie; internet http://www.ucc.ie/corkunip; f. 1925; academic; Man. Dir SARA WILBOURNE.

Dominican Publications: 42 Parnell Sq., Dublin 1; tel. (1) 8731355; fax (1) 8731760; e-mail dompubs@iol.ie; f. 1897; religious affairs in Ireland and the developing world, pastoral-liturgical aids; Man. Rev. AUSTIN FLANNERY.

Dundalgan Press (W. Tempest) Ltd: Francis St, Dundalk, Co Louth; tel. (42) 34013; fax (42) 32351; f. 1859; history and biography; Man. Dir GERARD GORMLEY.

C. J. Fallon: POB 1054, Lucan Rd, Palmerstown, Dublin 20; tel. (1) 6265777; fax (1) 6268225; f. 1927; educational; Man. Dir H. J. MCNICHOLAS.

Four Courts Press: Fumbally Lane, Dublin 8; tel. (1) 4534668; fax (1) 4534672; e-mail info@four-courts-press.ie; f. 1974; philosophy, theology, Celtic and Medieval studies, art, literature, modern history; Dirs MICHAEL ADAMS, MARTIN HEALY, GERARD O'FLAHERTY.

Gallery Press: Loughcrew, Oldcastle, Co Meath; tel. and fax (49) 41779; e-mail gallery@indigo.ie; f. 1970; poetry, plays, prose by Irish authors; Editor PETER FALLON.

Gill and Macmillan Ltd: Goldenbridge, Inchicore, Dublin 8; tel. (1) 4531005; fax (1) 4541688; f. 1968; literature, biography, history, mind, body and spirit, social sciences, theology, philosophy and textbooks; Man. Dir M. H. GILL.

Goldsmith Press: Newbridge, Co Kildare; tel. (45) 433613; fax (45) 434648; f. 1972; poetry, Irish art, plays, foreign language, general; Dirs DESMOND EGAN, VIVIENNE ABBOTT.

Irish Academic Press: 44 Northumberland Rd, Dublin 4; tel. (1) 6688244; fax (1) 6601610; e-mail info@iap.ie; f. 1974; academic, mainly history and Irish studies; Dirs FRANK CASS, MICHAEL ZAIDNER.

Lilliput Press: 62/63 Sitric Rd, Arbour Hill, Dublin 7; tel. (1) 6711647; fax (1) 6711233; e-mail lilliput@indigo.ie; internet http://indigo.ie/~lilliput; ecology and environment, literary criticism, biography, Irish history, general; Publr ANTONY FARRELL.

Mentor Publications: 43 Furze Rd, Sandyford Industrial Estate, Dublin 18; tel. (1) 2952112; fax (1) 2952114; educational, games, toys; Man. Dir DANIEL MCCARTHY.

Mercier Press Ltd: 5 French Church St, POB 5, Cork; tel. (21) 275040; fax (21) 274969; f. 1946; Irish folklore, history, literature, art, politics, humour, music, religious; Chair. GEORGE EATON; Man. Dir JOHN SPILLANE.

O'Brien Educational Ltd: 20 Victoria Rd, Dublin 6; tel. (1) 4923333; fax (1) 4922777; e-mail books@obrien.ie; internet http://www.obrien.ie; f. 1974; biography, reference, children's, reference; Man. Dir MICHAEL O'BRIEN.

Poolbeg Press Ltd: 123 Baldoyle Industrial Estate, Dublin 13; tel. (1) 8321477; fax (1) 8321430; e-mail poolbeg@iol.ie; f. 1976; general, poetry, politics, children's; Man. Dir PHILIP MACDERMOTT.

Round Hall Sweet & Maxwell: Brehon House, 4 Upper Ormond Quay, Dublin 7; tel. (1) 8730101; fax (1) 8720078; law books and journals; Dir ELEANOR MCGARRY.

Royal Irish Academy: 19 Dawson St, Dublin 2; tel. (1) 6762570; fax (1) 6762346; e-mail admin@ria.ie; f. 1785; humanities and sciences; Exec. Sec. PATRICK BUCKLEY.

Sáirséal-Ó Marcaigh: 13 Bóthar Chríoch Mhór, Dublin 11; tel. and fax (1) 8378914; books in Irish; Dirs AINGEAL Ó MARCAIGH, CAOIMHÍN Ó MARCAIGH.

Sporting Books: 4 Sycamore Rd, Mount Merrion, Co Dublin; tel. (1) 2887914; fax (1) 2885779; sports; Publr RAYMOND SMITH.

Town House/Country House: Trinity House, Charleston Rd, Dublin 6; tel. (1) 4972399; fax (1) 4970927; e-mail books@townhouse.ie; fiction, biography, art, environmental, general; Dirs TREASA COADY, JIM COADY.

Veritas Publications: 7–8 Lower Abbey St, Dublin 1; tel. (1) 8788177; fax (1) 8786507; f. 1900; religious and educational; Dir Rev. SEAN MELODY.

Wolfhound Press: 68 Mountjoy Sq., Dublin 1; tel. (1) 8740354; fax (1) 8720207; f. 1974; literature, biography, art, children's, fiction, history; Publr SÉAMUS CASHMAN.

Woodtown Music Publications Ltd: Teach an Dáma, Stráid an Dáma, Dublin 2; tel. and fax (1) 6793664; f. 1966; original works by Irish composers; Chair. GARECH DE BRÚN.

Government Publishing House

Stationery Office: Government Supplies Agency, 4–5 Harcourt Rd, Dublin 2; tel. (1) 6613111; fax (1) 4780645.

PUBLISHERS' ASSOCIATION

Irish Book Publishers' Association: The Irish Writers' Centre, 19 Parnell Sq., Dublin 1; tel. (1) 8729090; fax (1) 8722035; f. 1970; 54 mems; Pres. MICHAEL GILL; Admin. ORLA MARTIN.

Broadcasting and Communications

TELECOMMUNICATIONS

Office of the Director of Telecommunications Regulation: Abbey Court, Irish Life Centre, Lower Abbey St, Dublin 1; tel. (1) 8049600; fax (1) 8049680; f. 1997 as the regulatory authority for Ireland's telecommunication sector. Issues licences to service providers; manages the interconnection of telecommunications networks; approves equipment and oversees national telephone numbering; Dir ETAIN DOYLE.

Cable and Wireless Ltd: 1 Airton Rd, Dublin 24; tel. (1) 4040333; fax (1) 4040339; independent telecommunications services provider; supplies telecommunications equipment including video-conferencing systems and paging devices; Man. Dir EDDIE BRENNAN; Gen. Man. PAT MACGRATH.

ESAT Telecom: private telecommunication company. Chief Exec. DENIS O'BRIEN.

Stentor Plc: Dublin; provides telecommunications services.

Telecom Éireann: St Stephen's Green West, Dublin 2; tel. (1) 6714444; fax (1) 6716916; e-mail press-office@telecom.ie; internet http://www.telecom.ie; f. 1984; nationalized body responsible for the provision of national and international telecommunications services, including mobile services. Chair. RONALD J. BOLGER; CEO ALFIE KANE.

Telecom Internet: Merrion House, Merrion Rd, Dublin 4; tel. (1) 2692222; fax (1) 2692077; e-mail info@tinet.ie; internet http://tinet.ie; f. 1996 to provide internet services to both business and private customers; Marketing Man. DAVE HUGHES.

EIRCELL: a subsidiary of Telecom Éireann, providing national mobile telecommunications services.

BROADCASTING

The Radio and Television Act of 1988 provided for the establishment of an independent television station, an independent national radio service and a series of local radio stations (see below).

Radio Telefís Éireann (RTE): Donnybrook, Dublin 4; tel. (1) 2083111; telex 93700; fax (1) 2083080; national broadcasting corpn, f. 1960; operates two television channels and three radio networks; also operates the Irish language radio station, Raidió na Gaeltachta; financed by net licence revenue and sale of advertising time; governed by Authority of nine mems, appointed by the Govt; Chair. of Authority Prof. FARREL CORCORAN; Dir-Gen. BOB COLLINS; Dir of Programmes (Television) LIAM MILLER; Dir of Programmes (Radio) KEVIN HEALY.

The Independent Radio and Television Commission (IRTC): Marine House, Clanwilliam Place, Dublin 2; tel (1) 6760966; fax (1) 6760948; f. 1988; established by the Govt to ensure the creation, development and monitoring of independent broadcasting in Ireland; operations are financed by levies paid by franchised stations; Chair. NIALL STOKES; CEO MICHAEL O'KEEFFE.

Broadcasting Complaints Commission: POB 913, Dublin 2, tel. (1) 6767571; f. 1997; responsible for acting upon complaints relating to material broadcast by RTE and local radio stations; Chair. RAY MURPHY.

Radio

RTE broadcasts on three networks, Radio 1 (classical music), 2FM (popular music), with FM3 MUSIC sharing the same frequency as Raidió na Gaeltachta (see below). RTE operates a local radio station in Cork, which broadcasts 30 hours per week. Advertising on RTE stations is restricted to 10% of transmission time. By December 1995 21 local radio stations were operating under the supervision of the Independent Radio and Television Commission, in addition to one community/special interest station and one Irish language station. During 1995 a total of 11 community and community interest radio stations commenced operation on an 18-month trial basis. A new national independent radio station, Radio Ireland, commenced operation in March 1997.

Radio Ireland: Radio Ireland House, 124 Upper Abbey St, Dublin 1, tel. (1) 8049000; fax (1) 8049099; e-mail engineering@radioireland.ie; Chair. JOHN MCCOLGAN.

Raidió na Gaeltachta: Casla, Connemara, Co Galway; tel. (91) 506677; fax (91) 506666; f. 1972; broadcasts a minimum of 80 hours per week in Irish language; financed by RTE; Controller PÓL O GALLCHÓIR.

Ireland Radio News: 8 Upper Mount St, Dublin 2; tel. (1) 6708989; fax (1) 6708968; provides news service to independent local radio stations under contract from the IRTC; Chair. and CEO DENIS O'BRIEN.

Television

Reception of both RTE-1 and of Network 2 from nine main transmitters is available country-wide. Advertising is limited to 10% of transmission time. Regular RTE television transmissions: 148 hours a week. An Irish-language television service, Teilifis na Gaeilige, began transmissions in November 1996.

Finance

(cap. = capital; p.u. = paid up; res = reserves; dep. = deposits; m. = million; brs = branches; amounts in Irish pounds unless otherwise stated)

BANKING

Bank Ceannais na hÉireann (Central Bank of Ireland): POB 559, Dame St, Dublin 2; tel. (1) 6716666; telex 31041; fax (1) 6716561; f. 1942; bank of issue; cap. and res 946.5m., dep. 2,162.3m. (Dec. 1996); Gov. MAURICE O'CONNELL; Dir-Gen. Dr PÁDRAIG MCGOWAN.

Principal Banks

ACCBANK PLC: ACC House, Upper Hatch St, Dublin 2; tel. (1) 4780644; telex 93512; fax (1) 4780723; e-mail info@accbank.ie; f. 1927; state-owned; provides banking services to personal customers, small businesses, farmers and corporate entities; total assets 2,054m. (Dec. 1997); Chair. G. JOYCE; CEO J. MCCLOSKEY; 50 brs.

AIB Capital Markets PLC: AIB International Centre, IFSC, Dublin 1; tel. (1) 8740222; telex 93680; fax (1) 8741610; f. 1966; merchant banking and investment management; cap. p.u. 8m., dep. 1,105m. (Dec. 1997); Chair. and Man. Dir MICHAEL D. BUCKLEY.

AIB Group: POB 452, Bankcentre, Ballsbridge, Dublin 4; tel. (1) 6600311; telex 96380; fax (1) 6682508; f. 1966; fmrly Allied Irish Banks PLC; cap. and res 1,280.8m., dep. 20,665.2m. (Dec. 1996); Chair. LOCHLANN QUINN; CEO THOMAS P. MULCAHY; 900 brs and offices.

Anglo Irish Bank Corporation PLC: 18–21 St Stephen's Green, Dublin 2; tel. (1) 6760141; telex 30264; fax (1) 6618408; f. 1964; cap. and res 89.8m., dep. 2,083.0m. (Sept. 1996); Chair. A. G. MURPHY; CEO SEAN FITZPATRICK.

Ansbacher Bankers Ltd: 18–21 St Stephen's Green, Dublin 2; tel. (1) 6613699; telex 93241; fax (1) 6618408; f. 1950; cap. and res 12.4m., dep. 174m. (Dec. 1994); Chair. A. G. MURPHY.

Bank of Ireland Asset Management: 26 Fitzwilliam Place, Dublin 2; tel. (1) 6616433; fax (1) 6616688; f. 1966; merchant banking and investment management; auth. cap. 10m.; CEO WILLIAM R. COTTER.

Bank of Ireland Group: Lower Baggot St, Dublin 2; tel. (1) 6615933; telex 93836; fax (1) 6615675; f. 1783; cap. and res 606.8m., dep. 14,520.8m. (March 1996); Gov. H. E. KILROY; CEO MAURICE KEANE; 358 brs.

Banque Nationale de Paris: 5 George's Dock, Dublin 1; tel. (1) 6125000; telex 90641; fax (1) 6125001; e-mail bnp@indigo.ie; dep. 700m. (1994); Chair. G. DECOURCELLE; Gen. Man. MICHEL DE VIBRAYE.

Barclays Bank PLC: 47/48 St Stephen's Green, Dublin 2; tel. (1) 6611777; telex 30427; fax (1) 6623141; total assets 569m. (Dec. 1996); Country Dir PAUL SHOVLIN.

Chase Manhattan Bank (Ireland) PLC: Chase Manhattan House, International Financial Services Centre, Dublin 1; tel. (1) 612300; telex 93644; fax (1) 6123131; cap. and res US $22m., dep. US $176.1m. (Dec. 1995); Man. Dir FRANK GAYNOR.

Dresdner Bank (Ireland) PLC: La Touche House, International Financial Services Centre, Dublin 1; tel. (1) 6701444; telex 91867; fax (1) 6701414; f. 1995; commercial; subsidiary of Dresdner Bank (AG), Germany; total assets US $4,772.7m. (Dec. 1996); Chair. Dr ERNST-MORITZ LIPP.

Equity Bank Ltd: Canada House, 65–68 St Stephen's Green, Dublin 2; tel. (1) 4083500; telex 32343; fax (1) 4753220; f. 1965; forms part of the Bank of Scotland Group; cap. and res 12.8m., dep. 259.0m. (Feb. 1997); Chair. JOHN MCGILLIGAN; Chief Exec. MARK DUFFY.

Guinness and Mahon (Ireland) Ltd: 4 Earlsfort Terrace, Dublin 2; tel. (1) 7095200; telex 93667; fax (1) 7095210; f. 1836; cap. and res 5.7m., dep. 69.3m. (Dec. 1996); Chair. P. ROY DOUGLAS; Man. Dir PETER G. LEDBETTER.

ICC Bank PLC: 72–74 Harcourt St, Dublin 2; tel. (1) 4755700; telex 93220; fax (1) 6717797; e-mail info@icc.ie; f. 1933; state-owned; industrial and commercial financing; cap. and res 97.1m., dep. 1,406.6m. (Oct. 1997); Chair. P. FLYNN; Man. Dir MICHAEL QUINN; 6 brs.

Irish Intercontinental Bank Ltd: 91 Merrion Sq., Dublin 2; tel. (1) 6619744; telex 33322; fax (1) 6785034; f. 1973; subsidiary of Kredietbank NV, Belgium; merchant banking; cap. and res 107.2m., dep. 2,196.5m. (Dec. 1996); Chair. PATRICK MCEVOY; CEO EDWARD A. MARAH.

Lombard & Ulster Banking Ltd: Ulster Bank Group Centre, George's Quay, Dublin 2; tel. (1) 6085000; telex 91521; fax (1) 6085001; f. 1971; subsidiary of Ulster Bank Ltd; cap. p.u. 2.8m. (Dec. 1996); Chair. M. RAFFERTY; CEO P. A. MCARDLE; 13 brs.

National Irish Bank: 7/8 Wilton Terrace, Dublin 2; tel. (1) 6785066; telex 93347; fax (1) 6785269; f. 1986; subsidiary of National Australia Bank Ltd; cap. and res 84m., dep. 1,347.4m. (Sept. 1997); Chair. A. J. SPAIN; CEO GRAHAME SAVAGE; 60 brs.

Pfizer International Bank Europe: La Touche House, International Financial Services Centre, Dublin 1; tel. (1) 6700277; telex 93016; fax (1) 6700466; f. 1985; cap. and res 420.4m., dep. 76.8m. (Nov. 1996); Pres. FRANK E. SALERNO; Man. Dir B. M. SENIOR.

Rabobank Ireland Plc: George's Dock House, International Financial Services Centre, Dublin 1; tel. (1) 6076100; fax (1) 6701724; f. 1994; corporate and investment banking; owned by Rabobank Nederland; cap. and res 759m., dep. 9,503.7m. (Dec. 1996); Chair. WOUTER J. KOLFF; Gen. Man. RUURD WEULEN KRANENBERG.

Rheinhyp Bank Europe Plc: POB 4343, West Block Bldg, International Financial Services Centre, Dublin 1; tel. (1) 6781281; telex 500-32332; fax (1) 8290255; f. 1994 as RHEINHYP Europe Plc, name changed in 1995; total assets US $721.5m. (Dec. 1996); Chair. Dr KARSTEN VON KÖLLER; Man. Dir HUBERT BUHLER.

SGZ-Bank Ireland Plc: POB 4270, West Block Bldg, International Financial Services Centre, Dublin 1; tel. (1) 6700715; fax (1) 8290298; f. 1994 as SGZ (Ireland) Plc, name changed in 1995; total assets US $1,319m. (Dec. 1996); Gen. Mans JOHANNES HAAS, ANDREAS NEUGEBAUER.

Smurfit Paribas Bank Ltd: 94 St Stephen's Green, Dublin 2; tel. (1) 4756238; telex 90951; fax (1) 4783435; f. 1983; merchant banking; cap. and res 22.9m., dep. 151.3m. (Dec. 1995); Chair. IVOR KENNY; CEO GERALD CURRID.

Ulster Bank Ltd: 33 College Green, Dublin 2; tel. (1) 6777623; telex 93638; fax (1) 6775035; subsidiary of National Westminster Bank PLC (United Kingdom); cap. and res 116.9m., dep. 6,757.4m. (Dec. 1996); Chair. Sir GEORGE QUIGLEY; CEO R. D. KELLS; 201 brs.

Ulster Bank Markets Ltd: Ulster Bank Group Centre, George's Quay, Dublin 2; tel. (1) 6084000; telex 93638; fax (1) 6084288; f. 1973; subsidiary of Ulster Bank Ltd; total assets 3,786.3m. (Nov. 1996); Chair. MARTIN RAFFERTY; CEO PATRICK M. MCMAHON.

Woodchester Crédit Lyonnais Bank Ltd: Woodchester House, Golden Lane, Dublin 8; tel. (1) 4780000; telex 93243; fax (1) 4756681; f. 1972; merchant banking; cap. and res 34m., dep. 501.1m. (Dec. 1994); Chair. CRAIG MCKINNEY; 11 brs.

Savings Banks

An Post Savings and Investments: College House, Townsend St, Dublin 2; tel. (1) 7057200; telex 33444; fax (1) 7057292; internet http://www.anpost.ie; f. 1861; dep. 3,040m. (Dec. 1994); Dir TERRY REYNOLDS; 1,356 brs.

TSB Bank: Block 3, Harcourt Centre, Harcourt Rd, Dublin 2; tel. (1) 6790444; telex 93345; fax (1) 6790811; f. 1992; total assets 1,427m. (Oct. 1996); Chair. DERMOT WHELAN; CEO HARRY LORTON; 77 brs.

Banking Associations

The Institute of Bankers in Ireland: Nassau House, Nassau St, Dublin 2; tel. (1) 6793311; fax (1) 6793504; e-mail instbank@indigo.ie; f. 1898; 15,000 mems; Pres. TOM MULCAHY; CEO PATRICK J. ROCK.

Irish Bankers' Federation: Nassau House, Nassau St, Dublin 2; tel. (1) 6715311; fax (1) 6796680; e-mail ibf@ibf.ie; more than 50 mems; Pres. PHILIP HALPIN; Dir-Gen. JAMES A. BARDON.

Irish Banks' Information Service: Nassau House, Nassau St, Dublin 2; tel. (1) 6715299; fax (1) 6796680; e-mail ibis@ibisis.iol.ie; Chair. KEVIN KELLY; Man. FELIX O'REGAN.

STOCK EXCHANGE

The Irish Stock Exchange: 28 Anglesea St, Dublin 2; tel. (1) 6778808; telex 93437; fax (1) 6776045; f. 1799 as the Dublin Stock Exchange; amalgamated in 1973 with the United Kingdom stock exchanges to form The International Stock Exchange of the United Kingdom and the Republic of Ireland; separated from The International Stock Exchange in 1995; operates independently under the supervision of the Central Bank of Ireland; Chair. G. B. SCANLAN; CEO TOM HEALY; 99 mems.

INSURANCE

Principal Companies

Canada Life Assurance (Ireland) Ltd: Canada Life House, Temple Rd, Blackrock, Co Dublin; tel. (1) 2832377; fax (1) 2832036; f. 1903; Man. Dir D. A. GALLAGHER.

Cornhill Insurance PLC: Russell Court, St Stephen's Green, Dublin 2; tel. (1) 4025200; fax (1) 4025251; Man. B. J. GLASCOTT.

Eagle Star Insurance Co (Ireland) Ltd: Eagle Star House, Frascati Rd, Co Dublin; tel. (1) 2831301; fax (1) 2831578; f. 1950; Man. Dir M. J. BRENNAN.

Guardian PMPA Insurance Ltd: Wolfe Tone House, Wolfe Tone St, Dublin 1; tel. (1) 8721000; fax (1) 8721633; f. 1967; CEO G. P. N. HEALY.

Hansard Europe Ltd: POB 43, Enterprise House, Frascati Rd, Blackrock, Co Dublin; tel. (1) 2781488; fax (1) 2781499.

Hibernian Group PLC: Haddington Rd, Dublin 4; tel. (1) 6078000; fax (1) 6608730; f. 1908; life and general; Chair. J. CULLITON; CEO A. D. DALY.

Irish Life PLC: Irish Life Centre, Lower Abbey St, Dublin 1; tel. (1) 7042000; telex 32562; fax (1) 7041903; f. 1939; financial services; Chair. CONOR MCCARTHY; Man. Dir DAVID WENT.

Irish National Insurance Co PLC: 5–9 South Frederick St, Dublin 2; tel. (1) 6776881; telex 30460; fax (1) 6776161; f. 1919; subsidiary of Eagle Star Insurance; Man. Dir IAN C. STUART.

Irish Public Bodies Mutual Insurances Ltd: 12 Lower Mount St, Dublin 2; tel. (1) 6778000; fax (1) 6779558; f. 1926; fire and accident; Chair. J. LODGE; Gen. Man. BRENDAN DOYLE.

Lifetime Assurance Co Ltd: Lifetime House, Lower Baggot St, Dublin 2; tel. (1) 7039500; fax (1) 6620811; f. 1987; life; Chair. H. J. BYRNE; Man. Dir R. KEENAN.

New Ireland Assurance Co PLC: 11–12 Dawson St, Dublin 2; tel. (1) 6717077; telex 90692; fax (1) 6797313; f. 1924; Chair. and Man. Dir JOHN F. CASEY.

Norwich Union Life Insurance (Ireland) Ltd and **Norwich Union General Insurance (Ireland) Ltd:** 60–63 Dawson St, Dublin 2; tel. (1) 6717181; fax (1) 6710678; f. 1816; Group Chief Exec. VINCENT SHERIDAN.

Royal & SunAlliance: 13–17 Dawson St, Dublin 2; tel. (1) 6771851; fax (1) 6717625; Gen. Man. H. F. A. WANN.

Standard Life Assurance Co: 90 St Stephen's Green, Dublin 2; tel. (1) 4757411; fax (1) 4780262; f. 1834; life assurance, pensions, investments and annuities; Gen. Man. ALAN S. ASHE.

Zurich Insurance Co: Europa House, Harcourt St, Dublin 2; tel. (1) 4750300; fax (1) 4750263; property, liability, motor; Man. R. IRVINE.

Insurance Associations

Insurance Institute of Ireland: 39 Molesworth St, Dublin 2; tel. (1) 6772582; fax (1) 6772621; f. 1885; Pres. EDDIE SHAW; CEO DENIS HEVEY; 4,000 mems.

Irish Brokers' Association: 87 Merrion Sq., Dublin 2; tel. (1) 6613067; fax (1) 6619955; Pres. RICHARD ENDERSEN; 600 mems.

Irish Insurance Federation: Insurance House, 39 Molesworth St, Dublin 2; tel. (1) 6761820; fax (1) 6761943; e-mail fed@iif.ie; Pres. KEVIN MURPHY; CEO MICHAEL KEMP.

Trade and Industry

GOVERNMENT AGENCIES

An Post (The Post Office): General Post Office, Dublin 1; tel. (1) 7057000; fax (1) 8723553; e-mail press-office@anpost.ie; internet http://www.anpost.ie; f. 1984; provides national postal, savings and agency services through c. 2,000 outlets; Chair. STEPHEN O'CONNOR; CEO JOHN HYNES.

FÁS—Foras Áiseanna Saothair (Training and Employment Authority): 27–33 Upper Baggot St, Dublin 4; tel. (1) 6070500; fax (1) 6070600; f. 1988; responsible for the provision of training schemes and employment programmes; supports co-operative and community enterprise; offers an industrial advisory service; priority is given to the long-term and youth unemployed; Chair. CHRIS KIRWAN; Dir-Gen. JOHN J. LYNCH.

FORFÁS: Wilton Park House, Wilton Place, Dublin 2; tel. (1) 6073000; fax (1) 6073030; e-mail forfas@forfas.ie; internet http://www.forfas.ie; f. 1993 to provide advice and to co-ordinate national industrial and technological policy; co-ordinates Forbairt (see below); Chair. TOM TONER; Chief Exec. JOHN TRAVERS.

National Economic and Social Council—NESC: Upper Castle Yard, Dublin Castle, Dublin 2; tel. (1) 6713155; fax (1) 6713589; e-mail info@nesc.ie; f. 1973; provides advice and promotes the discussion of measures to improve the national economy and social justice; Dir SEAN O'HEIGEARTAIGH.

DEVELOPMENT ORGANIZATIONS

An Bord Tráchtála (Irish Trade Board): Merrion Hall, Strand Rd, Sandymount, Dublin 4; tel. (1) 2066000; fax (1) 2066400; internet http://www.irish-trade.ie; f. 1991; assists Irish firms to establish sustainable markets in Ireland and abroad; 23 overseas offices; Chair. SEÁN MURRAY; CEO OLIVER TATTAN.

Forbairt: Wilton Park House, Wilton Place, Dublin 2; tel. (1) 8082000; fax (1) 8082020; f. 1993; state-sponsored organization responsible for encouraging technological development of Irish industry; Chair. EILEEN O'MARA WALSH; CEO DAN FLINTER.

Industrial Development Agency (IDA Ireland): Wilton Park House, Wilton Place, Dublin 2; tel. (1) 6034000; fax (1) 6034040; f. 1993; state-sponsored organization responsible for the encouragement of foreign investment in Irish industrial development; administers financial incentive schemes; 19 overseas offices; Chair. DENIS HANRAHAN; CEO KIERAN MCGOWAN.

Irish Productivity Centre: IPC House, 42–47 Lower Mount St, Dublin 2; tel. (1) 6623233; fax (1) 6623300; aims to increase industrial productivity in Ireland; its council is composed of representatives from the Irish Business and Employers' Confed. and the Irish Congress of Trade Unions in equal numbers; offers consultancy services and practical assistance to Irish cos; Chair. J. HOEY; CEO TOM MCGUINNESS.

Teagasc (Agriculture and Food Development Authority): 19 Sandymount Ave, Dublin 4; tel. (1) 6688188; fax (1) 6688023; f. 1988; provides advisory, research, educational and training services to agri-food industries; Chair. DAN BROWNE; Nat. Dir Dr LIAM DOWNEY.

CHAMBERS OF COMMERCE

The Chambers of Commerce of Ireland: 22 Merrion Sq., Dublin 2; tel. (1) 6612888; fax (1) 6612811; e-mail chambers@iol.ie; f. 1923; represents c. 9,000 businesses and 39 direct corporate mems; Pres. TONY KEHOE; Chief Exec. SIMON NUGENT.

Cork Chamber of Commerce: Fitzgerald House, Summerhill North, Cork; tel. (21) 509044; fax (21) 508568; f. 1951; Pres. CONOR DOYLE; Chief Exec. MICHAEL GEARY.

Dublin Chamber of Commerce: 7 Clare St, Dublin 2; tel. (1) 6614111; fax (1) 6766043; e-mail info@dubchamber.ie; internet http://www.dubchamber.ie; f. 1783; Pres. JOHN MCNALLY.

INDUSTRIAL AND TRADE ASSOCIATIONS

Construction Industry Federation: Construction House, Canal Rd, Dublin 6; tel. (1) 4977487; fax (1) 4966953; e-mail cif@indigo.ie; 23 asscns representing 2,300 mems; Pres. KEVIN KELLY; Dir-Gen. LIAM B. KELLEHER.

Irish Creamery Milk Suppliers' Association (ICMSA): John Feely House, 15 Upper Mallow St, Limerick; tel. (61) 314677; fax (61) 315737; e-mail icmsa@tinet.ie; f. 1950; Pres. FRANK ALLEN; Gen. Sec. DONAL MURPHY.

Irish Farmers' Association (IFA): Irish Farm Centre, Bluebell, Dublin 12; tel. (1) 4500266; fax (1) 4551043; e-mail ifapress@indigo.ie; Pres. TOM PARLON; Gen. Sec. MICHAEL BERKEREY.

Irish Fishermen's Organisation Ltd: Cumberland House, Fenian St, Dublin 2; tel. (1) 6612400; fax (1) 6612424; f. 1974; Chair. J. V. MADDOCK; Sec.-Gen. J. F. DOYLE.

Irish Grain and Feed Association: 18 Herbert St, Dublin 2; tel. (1) 6760680; fax (1) 6616774; e-mail igfa@cereal.iol.ie; Pres. R. HARNEY; Dir S. A. FUNGE.

EMPLOYERS' ORGANIZATIONS

Irish Business and Employers Confederation (IBEC): Confederation House, 84–86 Lower Baggot St, Dublin 2; tel. (1) 6601011; fax (1) 6601717; f. 1993; represents c. 7,000 cos and orgs; Pres. TONY BARRY; Dir-Gen. JOHN DUNNE.

Irish Exporters Association: Holbrook House, Holles St, Dublin 2; tel. (1) 6612182; fax (1) 6612315; e-mail iea@exporters.itw.ie; Pres. MATT MURPHY; CEO COLUM MACDONNELL.

UTILITIES

Electricity

Electricity Supply Board: Lower Fitzwilliam St, Dublin 2; tel. (1) 6765831; fax (1) 6760727; internet http://www.esb.ie; f. 1927, reorg. 1988; operates 24 generating stations and manages the transmission and distribution of Ireland's electricity; Chair. W. M. MCCANN; CEO K. O'HARA.

Gas

Bord Gáis Éireann (BGE) (The Irish Gas Board): POB 51, Inchera, Little Island, Co Cork; tel. (21) 509199; telex 75087; fax (21) 353487; f. 1976; natural gas transmission and distribution; Chair. M. N. CONLON; CEO PHILIP CRONIN.

CO-OPERATIVE ORGANIZATIONS

Irish Co-operative Organisation Society Ltd: 84 Merrion Sq., Dublin 2; tel. (1) 6764783; fax (1) 6624502; f. 1894 to co-ordinate the co-operative movement; three operating divisions; offices in Dublin, Cork, Sligo and Brussels, Belgium; Pres. MICHAEL O'DWYER; Dir-Gen. JOHN TYRRELL; mems: 130 co-operatives representing c. 175,000 farmers.

Irish Dairy Board: Grattan House, Lower Mount St, Dublin 2; tel. (1) 6619599; fax (1) 6612778; e-mail idb@idb.ie; f. 1961, reorg. 1973 as a famers' co-operative; principal exporter of Irish dairy products; Chair. THOMAS CLEARY; Man. Dir NOEL CAWLEY.

TRADE UNIONS

Central Organization

Irish Congress of Trade Unions (ICTU): 19 Raglan Rd, Dublin 4; tel. (1) 6680641; fax (1) 6609027; e-mail raglan@ictu.iol.ie; internet http://www.iol.ie/ictu; f. 1894; represents 690,140 workers in 66 affiliated unions in the Republic and Northern Ireland (Jan. 1998); Gen. Sec. PETER CASSELLS.

Principal Trade Unions Affiliated to the ICTU

*__Amalgamated Engineering and Electrical Union, AEU Section:__ 26–34 Antrim Rd, Belfast, Northern Ireland, BT15 2AA; tel. (1232) 743271; f. 1992 by merger; Irish Rep. E. MILLER; 27,000 mems (1997).

*__Amalgamated Transport and General Workers' Union:__ Transport House, 102 High St, Belfast, Northern Ireland, BT1 2DL; tel. (1232) 232381; telex 747202; fax (1232) 734602; Irish Dist. Sec. M. O'REILLY; 53,500 mems (1997).

Association of Higher Civil and Public Servants: 4 Warner's Lane, Dartmouth Rd, Dublin 6; tel. (1) 6686077; fax (1) 6680380; e-mail info@ahcps.ie; Gen. Sec. S. Ó RIORDÁIN; 2,000 mems (1997).

Association of Secondary Teachers, Ireland (ASTI): ASTI House, Winetavern St, Dublin 8; tel. (1) 6719144; fax (1) 6719280; Gen. Sec. C. LENNON; 15,200 mems (1997).

Automobile, General Engineering and Mechanical Operatives' Union: 22 North Frederick St, Dublin 1; tel. (1) 8744233; Gen. Sec. LAURENCE DOYLE; 2,200 mems (1997).

Building and Allied Trades' Union: Arus Hibernia, 13 Blessington St, Dublin 7; tel. (1) 8301911; fax (1) 8304869; Gen. Sec. PATRICK O'SHAUGHNESSY; 8,000 mems (1997).

Civil and Public Service Union: 72 Lower Leeson St, Dublin 2; tel. (1) 6765394; Gen. Sec. JOHN O'DOWD; 12,000 mems (1997).

Communication Managers' Union: 577 North Circular Rd, Dublin 1; tel. (1) 8363232; Gen. Sec. A. HOURIGAN; 1,000 mems (1997).

Communications Workers' Union: 575 North Circular Rd, Dublin 1; tel. (1) 8366388; fax (1) 8365582; f. 1922; Gen. Sec. CON SCANLON; 19,600 mems (1996).

Electricity Supply Board Officers' Association: 43 East James's Place, Lower Baggot St, Dublin 2; tel. (1) 6767444; fax (1) 6789226; f. 1959; Gen. Sec. WILLIE CREMINS; 2,300 mems (1997).

Federated Union of Government Employees: 32 Parnell Sq., Dublin 1; tel. (1) 8787057; 1,300 mems (1997).

*__Graphical, Paper and Media Union:__ 107 Clonskeagh Rd, Dublin 6; tel. (1) 2697788; fax (1) 2839977; Irish Rep. E. A. KIRKPATRICK; 6,700 mems (1997).

Irish Bank Officials' Association: 93 St Stephen's Green, Dublin 2; tel. (1) 4755908; Gen. Sec. CIARAN RYAN; 15,600 mems (1998).

Irish Medical Organization: 10 Fitzwilliam Place, Dublin 2; tel. (1) 6767273; fax (1) 6612758; e-mail imo@iol.ie; CEO GEORGE MCNEICE; 3,000 mems (1997).

Irish Municipal, Public and Civil Trade Union (IMPACT): Nerney's Court, Dublin 1; tel. (1) 8745588; fax (1) 8728715; e-mail impact@iol.ie; f. 1991; Gen. Sec. PETER MCLOONE; 33,000 mems (1997).

Irish National Teachers' Organization: 35 Parnell Sq., Dublin 1; tel. (1) 8722533; fax (1) 8722462; e-mail info@into.ie; f. 1868; Gen. Sec. J. O'TOOLE; 26,000 mems (1997).

Irish Nurses' Organization: 11 Fitzwilliam Place, Dublin 2; tel. (1) 6760137; fax (1) 6610466; e-mail admin@ino.ie; Gen. Sec. P. J. MADDEN; 21,843 mems (1998).

Irish Print Union: 35 Lower Gardiner St, Dublin 1; tel. (1) 8747320; Gen. Sec. O. CURRAN; 2,500 mems (1997).

*__Manufacturing, Science and Finance (MSF) Union:__ 15 Merrion Sq., Dublin 2; tel. (1) 6761213; Nat. Sec. J. TIERNEY; 31,000 mems (1997).

Marine, Port and General Workers' Union: 14 Gardiner Place, Dublin 1; tel. (1) 8726566; fax (1) 8740327; Gen. Sec. MICHAEL HAYES; 3,000 mems (1997).

*__National Union of Journalists (Irish Executive Council):__ Liberty Hall, 9th Floor, Dublin 1; tel. (1) 8748694; fax (1) 8749250; Irish Rep. E. RONAYNE; 3,800 mems (1997).

Prison Officers' Association: 18 Merrion Sq., Dublin 2; tel. (1) 6625495; Gen. Sec. D. MCGRATH; 2,300 mems (1997).

Public Service Executive Union: 30 Merrion Sq., Dublin 2; tel. (1) 6767271; fax (1) 6615777; e-mail pseu@iol.ie; f. 1890; Gen. Sec. D. MURPHY; 7,000 mems (1997).

Services, Industrial Professional and Technical Union (SIPTU): Liberty Hall, Dublin 1; tel. (1) 8749731; fax (1) 8749368; f. 1990; Gen. Pres. JAMES SOMERS; Gen. Sec. WILLIAM A. ATTLEY; 218,000 mems (1998).

Teachers' Union of Ireland: 73 Orwell Rd, Dublin 6; tel. (1) 4922588; fax (1) 4922953; e-mail tui@aonad.iol.ie; internet http://www.tui.ie; f. 1955; Gen. Sec. JAMES DORNEY; 10,100 mems (1997).

Technical, Engineering and Electrical Union: 5 Cavendish Row, Dublin 1; tel. (1) 8747047; fax (1) 8747048; f. 1992; Gen. Sec. FRANK O'REILLY; 26,000 mems (1997).

*__Transport Salaried Staffs' Association:__ Nerney's Court, off Temple St, Dublin 1; tel. (1) 8743467; fax (1) 8745662; f. 1897; Sec. RODGER HANNON; 2,000 mems (1997).

*__Union of Construction, Allied Trades and Technicians:__ 56 Parnell Sq. West, Dublin 1; tel. (1) 8731599; Regional Sec. JIM MOORE; 12,000 mems (1997).

Union of Retail, Bar and Administrative Workers (MANDATE): O'Lehane House, 9 Cavendish Row, Dublin 1; tel. (1) 8746321; fax (1) 8729581; f. 1994; Gen. Sec. OWEN NULTY; 31,300 mems (1997).

*These unions have their head office in the United Kingdom. Membership figures relate jointly to the Republic of Ireland and Northern Ireland.

Unions not Affiliated to the ICTU

Institute of Journalists (Irish Region): EETPU Section, 5 Whitefriars, Aungier St, Dublin 2; tel. (1) 4784141; fax (1) 4750131; Chair. (Ireland) JAMES WIMS.

National Bus and Rail Union: 54 Parnell Sq., Dublin 1; tel. (1) 8730411; fax (1) 8730137; Gen. Sec. PETER BUNTING.

Transport

Coras Iompair Éireann (CIE) (The Irish Transport Co): Heuston Station, Dublin 8; tel. (1) 6771871; fax (1) 7032276; f. 1945, reorg. 1986; state corpn operating rail and road transport services; three operating cos: Iarnród Éireann (Irish Rail), Bus Éireann (Irish Bus) and Bus Atha Cliath (Dublin Bus); Chair. BRIAN A. JOYCE; CEO MICHAEL P. MCDONNELL.

RAILWAYS

In 1996 there were 1,872 km of track, of which 37 km were electrified. Railway services are operated by Iarnród Éireann.

Iarnród Éireann (Irish Rail): Connolly Station, Dublin 1; tel. (1) 8363333; fax (1) 8364760; f. 1987; division of CIE; Chair. MICHAEL P. MCDONNELL; CEO JOE MEAGHER.

INLAND WATERWAYS

The Grand and Royal Canals and the canal link into the Barrow Navigation system are controlled by CIE. The Grand Canal and Barrow are open to navigation by pleasure craft, and the rehabilitation and restoration of the Royal Canal is proceeding. The River Shannon, which is navigable from Limerick to Lough Allen, includes stretches of the Boyle, Suck, Camlin, and Inny Rivers, the Erne Navigation, and the Shannon-Erne Waterway. The total length of Irish navigable waterways is about 700 km. A further 10 km of the Suck and Boyle Rivers were due to be opened to navigation in 1998/99.

ROADS

At 31 December 1996 there were an estimated 92,500 km of roads, of which 5,270 km were main roads. About 94% of all roads were surfaced.

National Roads Authority: St Martin's House, Waterloo Rd, Dublin 4; tel. (1) 6602511; fax (1) 6680009; f. 1994; responsible for the planning, supervision and maintenance of nat. road network; Chair. LIAM CONNELLAN; CEO MICHAEL TOBIN.

SHIPPING

The principal sea ports are Dublin, Dún Laoghaire, Cork, Waterford, Rosslare, Limerick, Foynes, Galway, New Ross, Drogheda, Dundalk, Fenit and Whiddy Island.

Arklow Shipping Ltd: North Quay, Arklow, Co Wicklow; tel. (402) 39901; telex 80461; Man. Dir JAMES TYRELL; 9 carriers.

Dublin Shipping Ltd: Shrewsbury House, Cabinteely, Dublin 18; Chair. D. R. HUSSEY; Man. Dir P. H. MOONEY; 5 tankers.

Irish Continental Group PLC: Ferryport, Alexandra Rd, Dublin 1; tel. (1) 8552222; fax (1) 8552270; controls Irish Ferries, operating passenger vehicle and roll-on/roll-off freight ferry services between Ireland, the United Kingdom and continental Europe; Chair. T. TONER; Man. Dir E. ROTHWELL.

Irish Ferries: Ferryport, North Wall, Dublin 1; tel. (1) 8788077; telex 32549; fax (1) 8788490; drive-on/drive-off car ferry and roll-on/roll-off freight services between Dublin and Holyhead, and Rosslare and Pembroke; roll-on/roll-off freight service between Dublin and Liverpool; groupage and roll-on/roll-off from all parts of Britain to and from Ireland; unit load freight service between Dublin and Cork, and Le Havre, Rotterdam and Antwerp; agents in Ireland for Compagnie Maritime d'Affrètement (France); 6 vessels and other vessels on charter.

Stena Line: Ferry Terminal, Dún Laoghaire Harbour, Co Dublin; tel. (1) 2047700; fax (1) 2047620; services between Dún Laoghaire and Holyhead including high-speed catamaran, Rosslare and Fishguard, Belfast and Stranraer, passengers, drive-on/drive-off car ferry, roll-on/roll-off freight services.

Associations

Irish Chamber of Shipping: 5 Clanwilliam Sq., Grand Canal Quay, Dublin 2; tel. (1) 6618211; fax (1) 6618270; Pres. Capt. F. ALLEN; Dir B. W. KERR.

Irish Ship Agents' Association: 26 Harbour Row, Cobh, Co Cork; tel. (21) 813180; fax (21) 811849; Pres. ROY CONWAY; Sec. Lt-Commdr LIAM SMITH.

CIVIL AVIATION

There are international airports at Shannon, Dublin, Cork and Knock (Horan International), but only Shannon and Knock are used for transatlantic flights. The national airline is Aer Lingus.

Aer Rianta (Irish Airports Authority): Dublin Airport, Dublin; tel. (1) 8444900; telex 32169; fax (1) 8444534; state-controlled; responsible for the management and development of Dublin, Shannon and Cork airports; also operates seven hotels in Ireland and manages duty-free retail shops in several overseas locations; Chair. NOEL HANLON; CEO DEREK KEOGH.

Airlines

Aer Lingus Group PLC: Dublin Airport, Dublin; tel. (1) 7052222; telex 31404; fax (1) 7053832; internet http://www.aerlingus.ie; f. 1936, reorg. 1993; state-owned; domestic and international scheduled services; Chair. BERNIE CAHILL; CEO GARY MCGANN.

Aer Turas Teoranta: Corballis Park, Dublin Airport, Dublin; tel. (1) 8444131; telex 33393; fax (1) 8446049; f. 1962; world-wide cargo and passenger charter services; Chair. J. J. HARNETT; CEO P. J. COUSINS.

Ryanair: Dublin Airport, Dublin; tel. (1) 8444400; telex 33588; fax (1) 8444401; f. 1985; scheduled and charter passenger services; Chair. DAVID BONDERMAN; CEO MICHAEL O'LEARY.

Tourism

Intensive marketing campaigns have been undertaken in recent years to develop new markets for Irish tourism. In addition to many sites of historic and cultural interest, the country has numerous areas of natural beauty, notably the Killarney Lakes and the west coast. In 1997 a total of 5.03m. foreign tourists (excluding residents of Northern Ireland and excursionists) visited the Republic.

Bord Fáilte Éireann (Irish Tourist Board): Baggot St Bridge, Dublin 2; tel. (1) 6024000; fax (1) 6024100; e-mail user@irishtouristboard.ie; f. 1955; Chair. MARK MORTELL; Dir-Gen. MATT MCNULTY.

Dublin Regional Tourism Authority Ltd: Suffolk St, Dublin 2; tel. (1) 6057700; fax (1) 6057757; Chair. MICHAEL FLOOD; CEO FRANK MAGEE.

Irish Tourist Industry Confederation: Alliance House, Adelaide St, Dún Laoghaire, Co Dublin; tel. (1) 2844222; fax (1) 2804218; represents all major commercial tourism interests; Chair. DAVID BUNWORTH; CEO BRENDAN LEAHY.

Irish Travel Agents' Association: Heaton House, 3rd Floor, 32 South William St, Dublin 2; tel. (1) 6794089; fax (1) 6794179; f. 1971; 340 mems; Pres. P. J. BRENNAN; CEO BRENDAN MORAN.

ISRAEL

Introductory Survey

Location, Climate, Language, Religion, Flag, Capital

The State of Israel lies in western Asia, occupying a narrow strip of territory on the eastern shore of the Mediterranean Sea. The country also has a narrow outlet to the Red Sea at the northern tip of the Gulf of Aqaba. All of Israel's land frontiers are with Arab countries, the longest being with Egypt to the west and with Jordan to the east. Lebanon lies to the north, and Syria to the north-east. The climate is Mediterranean, with hot, dry summers, when the maximum temperature in Jerusalem is generally between 30°C and 35°C (86°F to 95°F), and mild, rainy winters, with a minimum temperature in Jerusalem of about 5°C (41°F). The climate is sub-tropical on the coast but more extreme in the Negev Desert, in the south, and near the shores of the Dead Sea (a lake on the Israeli-Jordanian frontier), where the summer temperature may exceed 50°C (122°F). The official language of Israel is Hebrew, spoken by about two-thirds of the population, including most Jews. About 15% of Israeli residents, including Muslim Arabs, speak Arabic (which is also the language spoken by the inhabitants of the Occupied Territories, and the semi-autonomous areas in the West Bank and Gaza), while many European languages are also spoken. About 81% of the population profess adherence to Judaism, the officially recognized religion of Israel, while about 14% are Muslims. The national flag (proportions 250 by 173) has a white background, with a six-pointed blue star composed of two overlapping triangles (the 'Shield of David') between two horizontal blue stripes near the upper and lower edges. The Israeli Government has designated the city of Jerusalem (part of which is Jordanian territory annexed by Israel in 1967) as the country's capital, but this is not recognized by the UN, and most foreign governments maintain their embassies in Tel-Aviv.

Recent History

The Zionist movement, launched in Europe in the 19th century, aimed at the re-establishment of an autonomous community of Jews in their historical homeland of Palestine (the 'Promised Land'). The growth of Zionism was partly due to the insecurity that was felt by Jewish minorities in many European countries as a result of racial and religious hostility, known as anti-semitism, which included discrimination, persecution and even massacre.

Palestine, for long inhabited by Arabs, became a part of Turkey's Ottoman Empire in the 16th century. During the First World War the Arabs under Ottoman rule rebelled. Palestine was occupied by British forces in 1917–18, when the Turks withdrew. In November 1917 the British Foreign Secretary, Arthur Balfour, declared British support for the establishment of a Jewish national home in Palestine, on condition that the rights of 'the existing non-Jewish communities' there were safeguarded. The Balfour Declaration, as it is known, was confirmed by the governments of other countries then at war with Turkey.

British occupation of Palestine continued after the war, when the Ottoman Empire was dissolved. In 1920 the territory was formally placed under British administration by a League of Nations mandate, which incorporated the Balfour Declaration. British rule in Palestine was hampered by the conflict between the declared obligations to the Jews and the rival claims of the indigenous Arab majority. In accordance with the mandate, Jewish settlers were admitted to Palestine (whose population in 1919 was almost entirely Arab), but only on the basis of limited annual quotas. Serious anti-Jewish rioting by Arabs occurred in 1921 and 1929. Attempts to restrict immigration led to Jewish-sponsored riots in 1933. The extreme persecution of Jews by Nazi Germany caused an increase in the flow of Jewish immigrants, both legal and illegal, but this intensified the unrest in Palestine. In 1937 a British proposal to establish separate Jewish and Arab states, while retaining a British-mandated area, was accepted by most of the Zionists but rejected by the Arabs, and by the end of that year the conflict between the two communities had developed into open warfare. A British scheme offering eventual independence for a bi-communal Palestinian state was postponed because of the Second World War (1939–45). During the war the Nazis caused the deaths of an estimated 6m. Jews in central and eastern Europe, more than one-third of the world's total Jewish population. The enormity of this massacre, known as the Holocaust, greatly increased international sympathy for Jewish claims to a homeland in Palestine.

After the war, there was strong opposition by Palestinian Jews to continued British occupation. Numerous terrorist attacks were made by Jewish groups against British targets. In November 1947 the UN approved a plan for the partition of Palestine into two states, one Jewish (covering about 56% of the area) and one Arab. The plan was, however, rejected by Arab states and by the leadership of the Palestinian Arabs. Meanwhile, the conflict between the two communities in Palestine escalated into full-scale war.

On 14 May 1948 the United Kingdom terminated its Palestine mandate, and Jewish leaders immediately proclaimed the State of Israel, with David Ben-Gurion as Prime Minister. Although the new nation had no agreed frontiers, it quickly received wide international recognition. Neighbouring Arab states sent forces into Palestine in an attempt to crush Israel. Fighting continued until January 1949. The cease-fire agreements left Israel in control of 75% of Palestine, including West Jerusalem. The *de facto* territory of Israel was thus nearly one-third greater than the area that had been assigned to the Jewish state under the UN partition plan. Most of the remainder of Palestine was controlled by Jordanian forces. This area, known as the West Bank (or, to Israelis, as Judaea and Samaria), was annexed by Jordan in December 1949 and fully incorporated in April 1950. No independent Arab state was established in Palestine, and the independence of Israel was not recognized by any Arab government until 1980.

When the British mandate ended, the Jewish population of Palestine was about 650,000 (or 40% of the total). With the establishment of Israel, the new state encouraged further Jewish immigration. The Law of Return, adopted in July 1950, established a right of immigration for all Jews. The rapid influx of Jewish settlers enabled Israel to consolidate its specifically Jewish character. Many former Arab residents of Palestine had become refugees in neighbouring countries, mainly Jordan and Lebanon. About 400,000 Arabs had evacuated their homes prior to May 1948, and another 400,000 fled subsequently. In 1964 some exiled Palestinian Arabs formed the Palestine Liberation Organization (PLO), with the aim, at that time, of overthrowing Israel.

In July 1956 the Egyptian Government announced the nationalization of the company that operated the Suez Canal. In response, Israel launched an attack on Egypt in October, occupying the Gaza Strip (part of Palestine under Egyptian occupation since 1949) and the Sinai Peninsula. After pressure from the UN and the USA, Israeli forces evacuated these areas in 1957, when a UN Emergency Force (UNEF) was established in Sinai. In 1967 the United Arab Republic (Egypt) secured the withdrawal of UNEF from its territory. Egyptian forces immediately reoccupied the garrison at Sharm esh-Sheikh, near the southern tip of Sinai, and closed the Straits of Tiran to Israeli shipping, effectively blockading the Israeli port of Eilat. In retaliation, Israel attacked Egypt and other Arab countries. Israeli forces quickly overcame opposition and made substantial territorial gains. The Six-Day War, as it is known, left Israel in possession of all Jerusalem, the West Bank area of Jordan, the Sinai Peninsula in Egypt, the Gaza Strip and the Golan Heights in Syria. East Jerusalem was almost immediately integrated into the State of Israel, while the other conquered areas were regarded as Occupied Territories.

Ben-Gurion resigned in June 1963 and was succeeded by Levi Eshkol. Three of the parties in the ruling coalition merged to form the Israel Labour Party in 1968. On the death of Eshkol in 1969, Golda Meir was elected Prime Minister. A cease-fire between Egypt and Israel was arranged in August 1970, but other Arab states and Palestinian Arab guerrilla (mainly PLO) groups continued hostilities. Another war between the Arab states and Israel broke out on 6 October 1973, coinciding with Yom Kippur (the Day of Atonement), the holiest day of the

Jewish year. In simultaneous attacks on Israeli-held territory, Egyptian forces crossed the Suez Canal and reoccupied part of Sinai, while Syrian troops launched an offensive on the Golan Heights. Having successfully countered these advances, Israel made cease-fire agreements with Egypt and Syria on 24 October.

Gen. Itzhak Rabin succeeded Golda Meir as Prime Minister of a Labour Alignment coalition in 1974. In May 1977 the Labour Alignment was defeated in a general election, and the Likud (Consolidation) bloc, led by Menachem Begin of the Herut (Freedom) Party, formed a Government with the support of minority parties.

In November 1977 President Anwar Sadat of Egypt visited Israel, indicating tacit recognition of the State of Israel. In September 1978 President Carter of the USA, President Sadat and Prime Minister Begin met at Camp David, in the USA, and concluded two agreements. The first was a 'framework for peace in the Middle East', providing for autonomy for the West Bank and Gaza Strip after a transitional period of five years, and the second was a 'framework for the conclusion of a peace treaty between Egypt and Israel'. In February 1980 Egypt was the first Arab country to grant diplomatic recognition to Israel. (Israel's phased withdrawal from Sinai was completed in April 1982.) The approval, in 1980, of legislation which stated explicitly that Jerusalem should be for ever the undivided capital of Israel, and Israel's formal annexation of the Golan Heights in 1981, subsequently inhibited prospects of agreement on Palestinian autonomy.

In June 1982 Israeli forces launched 'Operation Peace for Galilee', advanced through Lebanon and surrounded West Beirut, trapping 6,000 PLO fighters. Egypt withdrew its ambassador from Tel-Aviv in protest. Diplomatic efforts resulted in the evacuation of 14,000–15,000 PLO and Syrian fighters from Beirut to various Arab countries. In September a massacre took place in Beirut in the Palestinian refugee camps of Sabra and Chatila. The Israeli Government conducted an inquiry, which blamed Lebanese Phalangists for the killings, but concluded that Israel's leaders were indirectly responsible through negligence. Gen. Ariel Sharon was forced to resign as Minister of Defence. Talks between Israel and Lebanon culminated in the signing of an agreement, in May 1983, declaring an end to hostilities and envisaging the withdrawal of all foreign forces from Lebanon within three months. Syria rejected this, leaving some 30,000 troops and 7,000 PLO men in the north-east of Lebanon, and Israel consequently refused to withdraw from the south.

The Government's prestige had been damaged by the Beirut massacre and by a capitulation to wage demands by the country's doctors. In August 1983 Itzhak Shamir succeeded Begin as leader of the Likud bloc and Prime Minister. Economic problems troubled the Government during the second half of 1983, and the Labour Party forced a general election in 1984. Neither the Labour Alignment nor Likud could form a viable coalition government, so President Chaim Herzog invited the Labour leader, Shimon Peres, to form a government of national unity with Likud.

Responsibility for policing the occupied southern area of Lebanon fell increasingly on the Israeli-controlled 'South Lebanon Army' (SLA). The Israeli Government completed a withdrawal in June 1985, leaving a 10km–20km buffer zone on the Lebanese side of the border, controlled by the SLA. During 1986 rocket attacks on settlements in northern Israel were resumed by Palestinian guerrillas. Israel responded with air attacks on Palestinian targets in southern Lebanon. In the late 1980s support increased among Lebanese Muslims for the Shi'ite fundamentalist Hezbollah (Party of God), which intensified resistance to the Israeli-controlled SLA with attacks on positions within the buffer zone. The conflict escalated following the abduction, in July 1989, of Sheikh Abd al-Karim Obeid, a local Shi'a Muslim leader, by Israeli agents; and again in February 1992, after the assassination by the Israeli air force of Sheikh Abbas Moussawi, the Secretary-General of Hezbollah.

From 1984 onwards, numerous attempts were made to find a solution to the most urgent problem in the Middle East—the desire of Palestinians for an independent state. There was virtual deadlock because the PLO would not recognize Israel's right to exist, and Israel refused to participate in direct talks with the PLO, which it regarded as a terrorist organization. Repeated proposals by King Hussein of Jordan for an international peace conference were rejected by Israel, on the grounds that the PLO would be represented at it. In December 1987 demonstrations and civil disobedience against Israeli rule in the Gaza Strip intensified and spread to the other Occupied Territories. The uprising (*intifada*) was apparently a spontaneous expression of frustration at occupation and depressed living conditions. Israeli attempts to crush the uprising were condemned by world opinion for their severity.

In July 1988 King Hussein abrogated Jordan's legal and administrative responsibilities in the West Bank, cancelled the Jordanian programme of investment there, and declared that he would no longer represent the Palestinians in any international conference on the Palestinian question. This undermined Israel's Palestine policy, and strengthened the PLO's negotiating position. In November the PLO declared an independent Palestinian State (notionally the West Bank and Gaza Strip), and endorsed UN Security Council Resolution 242 (adopted in 1967), thereby implicitly granting recognition to Israel. In December Yasser Arafat, the Chairman of the PLO, stated explicitly that 'the Palestine National Council accepted two States, a Palestinian State and a Jewish State, Israel'. He presented a peace initiative, including proposals for the convening of an international conference under UN auspices, the establishment of a UN peace-keeping force to supervise Israeli withdrawal from the Occupied Territories, and a comprehensive settlement based on UN Security Council Resolutions 242 (1967) and 338 (1973). The USA refused to accept the PLO proposals, alleging ambiguities, but it did open a dialogue with the PLO. Israel's Prime Minister Shamir, however, would not negotiate, distrusting the PLO's undertaking to abandon violence. Instead, he appeared to favour the introduction of limited self-rule for the Palestinians of the West Bank and Gaza Strip, as outlined in the 1978 Camp David accords. Intense international pressure for the convening of a Middle East peace conference developed, with the USA and the USSR increasing efforts to bring Israel and the PLO to negotiations.

At the general election in November 1988, as in 1984, neither Likud nor Labour secured enough seats in the Knesset (Assembly) to form a coalition with groups of smaller parties. Eventually, another Government of national unity was formed, under the Likud leader, Itzhak Shamir, with Shimon Peres as Deputy Prime Minister and Minister of Finance. In the coalition accord no mention was made of an international Middle East peace conference, nor were any new proposals advanced for solving the Arab-Israeli conflict.

In April 1989 Shamir presented a peace proposal which included a reaffirmation by Egypt, Israel and the USA of the Camp David accords, and plans for the holding of free democratic elections in the West Bank and Gaza for Palestinian delegates who could negotiate self-rule under Israeli authority. The PLO did not consider that elections could establish the basis for a political settlement. In September President Mubarak of Egypt invited Israeli clarification of Shamir's election plans, and offered to convene an Israeli-Palestinian meeting in Cairo. This was rejected by the Likud ministers, on the grounds that they did not want direct contact with PLO delegates. In November Israel provisionally accepted a proposal by the US Secretary of State, James Baker, for a preliminary meeting to discuss the holding of elections in the West Bank and Gaza, on condition that Israel would not be required to negotiate with PLO delegates, and that the talks would concern only Israel's election proposals. However, the PLO continued to demand a direct role in talks with Israel, and the Baker initiative foundered.

The fragile Likud-Labour coalition was endangered in early 1990 by disputes and dismissals, and in March the Knesset adopted a motion of 'no confidence' in Prime Minister Shamir. Shimon Peres was invited to form a new coalition government, but was unsuccessful. After several months of political bargaining, Itzhak Shamir was able to form a new Government in June, and in a policy document he emphasized the right of Jews to settle in all parts of 'Greater Israel'; his opposition to the creation of an independent Palestinian state; and his refusal to negotiate with the PLO, indeed with any Palestinians other than those resident in the Occupied Territories (excluding East Jerusalem). The new Government, having won a vote of confidence in the Knesset, was a narrow, right-wing coalition of Likud and five small parties, with three independent members of the Knesset.

In March 1990 the US President, George Bush, opposed the granting to Israel of a US $400m.-loan for the housing of Soviet Jewish immigrants because Israel would not guarantee to refrain from constructing new settlements in the Occupied Territories. Violence erupted throughout Israel and the Occupied Territories in May. The USA demanded that the PLO should condemn the violence; when it refused, the USA suspended its dialogue with the PLO, and vetoed a UN Security Council resolution urging that international observers be dispatched to the Occupied Territories. In June Shamir invited President Assad of Syria to peace negotiations, and the UN Secretary-General's special envoy, Jean-Claude Aimé, also visited Israel for discussions. However, Shamir rejected US proposals for direct talks between Israeli and Palestinian delegations.

Iraq's invasion of Kuwait in August 1990 led to an improvement in US-Israeli relations, because it was vital, if a coalition of Western and Arab powers opposed to Iraq were to be maintained, that Israel did not become actively involved in the conflict. In October Israeli police shot and killed some 17 Palestinians on the Temple Mount in Jerusalem, after they had clashed with Jewish worshippers there. Intense international pressure on the UN to respond to this outrage resulted in a Security Council vote to send a mission to investigate the killings, but Israel would not co-operate. Israel did agree to discussions with a UN emissary, but the USA resisted UN attempts to hold an international conference, fearing that this could be construed as a concession to Iraq's charge that Israel's presence in the Occupied Territories was equivalent to Iraq's occupation of Kuwait.

Attacks on Israel by Iraqi *Scud* missiles in January 1991 threatened the integrity of the multinational force which had begun hostilities against Iraq. US diplomacy, and the installation in Israel of US air defence systems, averted an immediate Israeli response. In reaction to widespread support for President Saddam Hussain of Iraq by Palestinians, the Israeli Government's attitude hardened. In February Shamir again rejected proposals for an international peace conference, and promoted his own peace plan, formulated in 1989 (see above), as the only starting-point for any peace dialogue.

Intense diplomatic efforts, undertaken from mid-March 1991 by the US Secretary of State, James Baker, had secured, by early August, the agreement of the Israeli, Syrian, Egyptian, Jordanian and Lebanese Governments, and of Palestinian representatives, to attend a regional peace conference for which the terms of reference would be a comprehensive peace settlement based on UN Security Council Resolutions 242 and 338. The initial, 'symbolic' session of the conference was held in Madrid, Spain, in October 1991. After this, the negotiations soon become deadlocked over procedural issues. Israeli delegations, wary of making any gesture which might be construed as recognition of Palestinian independence, repeatedly questioned the status of the Palestinian-Jordanian delegation and the right of the Palestinian component to participate separately in negotiations; while Israel's refusal to halt the construction of new settlements in the Occupied Territories continually jeopardized the peace process. Israel's intransigence over the settlement issue further damaged its relations with the USA. As early as May 1991 the US Secretary of State, James Baker, had identified this issue as the main obstacle to US efforts to achieve a Middle Eastern peace settlement. In February 1992, immediately prior to the fourth session of the peace negotiations, Baker demanded a complete halt to Israeli settlement in the Occupied Territories as a condition for the granting of US $10,000m. in US-guaranteed loans for the housing of Jewish immigrants from the former USSR.

While the Israeli Government's refusal to halt the construction of new settlements was regarded as provocative by all the other parties to the peace conference, and by the US Government, the right-wing minority members of Israel's governing coalition, which opposed any Israeli participation in the peace conference at all, threatened to withdraw from the coalition if funds were not made available for the settlement programme. In December 1991 the Government's majority in the 120-seat Knesset was reduced when the Minister of Agriculture, Rafael Eitan (a member of the right-wing, nationalist Tzomet Party), resigned his portfolio in protest at the Prime Minister's opposition to electoral reform; and in mid-January 1992 the majority was lost entirely when two other right-wing, nationalist political parties, Moledet and Tehiya (which together held five seats in the Knesset), withdrew from the coalition. Their withdrawal was a deliberate attempt to obstruct the third session of the Middle East peace conference in Moscow, Russia, where delegates had begun to address the granting of transitional autonomy to Palestinians in the West Bank and Gaza Strip. A general election was subsequently scheduled to be held in June, and Itzhak Shamir remained the head of a minority Government. In late February Shamir retained the leadership of the Likud, receiving 46.4% of the votes cast at a party convention. At the same time, Itzhak Rabin, a former Israeli Prime Minister, was elected Chairman of the Labour Party, replacing Shimon Peres.

A fifth round of bilateral negotiations, between Israeli, Syrian, Lebanese and Palestinian-Jordanian delegations, was held in Washington, DC, USA, at the end of April 1992. In this latest session of the peace conference procedural issues were reported to have been resolved, and, in its talks with the Palestinian component of the Palestinian-Jordanian delegation, the Israeli delegation presented proposals for the holding of municipal elections in the West Bank and Gaza Strip; and for the transfer of control of health amenities there to Palestinian authorities. The Palestinian delegation did not reject the proposals outright, although they fell far short of the Palestinians' ambition for full legislative control of the Occupied Territories. No progress was made in the meetings between Israeli and Syrian delegations to discuss the principal dispute between Israel and Syria—Israel's continued occupation of the Golan Heights.

In May 1992 the first multilateral negotiations between the parties to the Middle East peace conference commenced, as had been arranged at the third session of bilateral talks in Moscow in January. However, these negotiations were boycotted by Syria and Lebanon, which argued that they were futile until progress had been made in the bilateral negotiations. Various combinations of delegations attended meetings convened to discuss regional economic co-operation; regional arms control; the question of Palestinian refugees; water resources; and environmental issues. Israel boycotted the meetings on Palestinian refugees and regional economic development after the USA approved Palestinian proposals to allow exiles (i.e. non-residents of the Occupied Territories) to be included in the Palestinian delegations to these two meetings.

In the general election, held on 23 June 1992, the Labour Party won 44 seats in the Knesset, and Likud 32. Meretz—an alliance of Ratz (Civil Rights and Peace Movement), Shinui and the United Workers' Party, which had won 12 seats in the Knesset—formally confirmed its willingness to form a coalition government with the Labour Party on 24 June. However, even with the support of the two Arab parties—the Democratic Arab Party and Hadash—which together had won five seats in the Knesset, such a coalition would have enjoyed a majority of only two votes over the so-called 'right bloc' (Likud, Tzomet, Moledet and Tehiya) and the religious parties which had allied themselves with Likud in the previous Knesset. Formally invited to form a government on 28 June, the Labour leader, Itzhak Rabin, was accordingly obliged to solicit support among the religious parties. On 13 July Rabin was able to present a new Government for approval by the Knesset. The new coalition, an alliance of Labour, Meretz and the ultra-orthodox Jewish party, Shas, had a total of 62 seats in the 120-seat Knesset; and also enjoyed the unspoken support of five deputies from the two Arab parties.

Most international observers regarded the formation of a new, Labour-led coalition Government as having improved the prospects of the Middle East peace process, especially when, in July, it indicated a more flexible position on the issue of Jewish settlements in the Occupied Territories than its predecessor. However, at the conclusion of a sixth round of bilateral negotiations between Israeli, Syrian, Lebanese and Palestinian-Jordanian delegations in late September it was reported that no tangible progress had been achieved.

In early October 1992, in a clear gesture of support for the new Government, the USA granted Israel the US $10,000m. in US-guaranteed loans for the housing of immigrants that it had previously withheld, owing to Israel's housing construction programme in the Occupied Territories. In late October a seventh round of bilateral negotiations between the parties to the Middle East peace conference commenced in Washington, DC, USA. The negotiations were adjourned, pending the conclusion of the US presidential election, but multilateral negotiations on regional economic co-operation, in which an Israeli delegation participated, took place in Paris, France, at the end of October. The seventh round of bilateral negotiations resumed in early November, but, again, no tangible progress was achieved. It was generally accepted that the peace process would be suspended until US President-elect Clinton formally took office in January 1993. Multilateral negotiations on the issue of refugees took place in Ottawa, Canada, on 11–12 November.

In spite of the hopes that had been expressed for the prospects of the peace process since the election of the Labour-led Israeli Government, the months of October and November 1992 were marked by violent clashes between Palestinians and members of the Israeli security forces in the Occupied Territories. At the end of November it was reported that, since 1987, 959 Palestinians, 543 alleged Palestinian 'collaborators' and 103 Israelis had died in the Palestinian *intifada*.

In early December 1992 an eighth round of bilateral negotiations between Israeli and Arab delegations commenced in Washington, DC, USA. However, the talks were quickly overtaken by events in the Occupied Territories, which led to the withdrawal of the Arab delegations. On 16 December, in response to the deaths in the Occupied Territories of five members of the Israeli security forces, and to the abduction and murder by the Islamic Resistance Movement (Hamas) of an Israeli border policeman, the Government ordered the deportation to Lebanon of 413 alleged Palestinian supporters of Hamas. Owing to the Lebanese Government's refusal to co-operate in this action, the deportees were stranded in the territory between Israel's self-declared southern Lebanese security zone and Lebanon proper.

The deportations caused international outrage, and intense diplomatic pressure was placed on Israel to revoke the deportation order. On 18 December 1992 the UN Security Council unanimously approved a resolution (No. 799) condemning the deportations and demanding the return of the deportees to Israel. At the end of December, however, the Israeli Government announced that only 10 of the deportees had been unjustifiably expelled and could return to Israel. The remainder would continue in exile. The future of the Middle East peace process, meanwhile, remained in doubt. The Palestinian delegation to the eighth round of bilateral negotiations had indicated that it would not resume negotiations until all of the deportees had been allowed to return to Israel, and the PLO formally expressed the same position in mid-January 1993. At the beginning of February the Israeli Government was reported to have indicated its willingness to allow some 100 of the deportees to return to Israel, but insisted that the remainder should serve a period of exile lasting at least until the end of 1993. On 5 February the ninth round of bilateral negotiations in the Middle East peace conference was formally suspended, but later in the month the UN Security Council was reported to have welcomed the Israeli Government's decision to permit 100 of the deportees to return to Israel, and to be ready to take no further action over the issue. Palestinians party to the peace negotiations, however, insisted that UN Security Council Resolution 799 should be implemented in full before a Palestinian delegation would resume negotiations.

During March 1993 the number of violent confrontations between Palestinians and the Israeli security forces in the Occupied Territories—especially in the Gaza Strip—increased to such an extent that, at the end of the month, the Government responded by sealing off the West Bank and the Gaza Strip indefinitely. Also in late March the Knesset elected Ezer Weizman, the leader of the Yahad political party, to replace Chaim Herzog as President of Israel in May 1993; and Binyamin Netanyahu was elected leader of the opposition Likud in place of Itzhak Shamir.

On 27 April 1993 the ninth round of bilateral negotiations in the Middle East peace process, which had been formally suspended in February, resumed in Washington, DC, USA. It was reported that the Palestinian delegation had only agreed to attend the ninth round of talks under pressure to do so from Arab governments, and after Israel had agreed to allow Faisal Husseini, the nominal leader of the Palestinian delegation, to participate in the talks. (Israel had previously refused to grant this concession because Husseini was a resident of East Jerusalem, the status of which Israel regarded as distinct from that of the West Bank, the Gaza Strip and the Golan Heights.) Israel was also reported to have agreed that it would not, in future, resort to deportations as a punitive measure, and to have restated, together with the USA, its commitment to UN Security Council Resolutions 242 and 338 as the terms of reference for the peace process. However, as previously, the ninth round of bilateral talks achieved no progress on substantive issues.

In mid-May 1993 Ezer Weizman formally assumed the presidency of Israel. At the end of the month a minor reshuffle of the Cabinet averted the defection of the ultra-orthodox Jewish party, Shas, from the governing coalition.

A tenth round of bilateral negotiations, held in Washington, DC, USA, on 15 June–1 July 1993, concluded in deadlock, having achieved no progress on a statement of principles concerning Palestinian self-rule in the Occupied Territories, which was now regarded as the key element in the Middle East peace process. However, it was reported that a committee had been established in an attempt to facilitate progress on this issue. By the same token, there was no progress on the issues of contention between the Israeli delegation and its Syrian, Lebanese and Jordanian counterparts.

In late July 1993 Israeli armed forces mounted the most intensive air and artillery attacks on targets in Lebanon since 'Operation Peace for Galilee' in 1982. The offensive was in retaliation for attacks by Hezbollah fighters on settlements in northern Israel, and provoked widespread international criticism for the high number of civilian casualties that it caused and for the threat that it posed to the Middle East peace process. The eleventh round of bilateral negotiations, which commenced in Washington on 31 August, was, in fact, eclipsed by a major, unexpected breakthrough in negotiations between Israel and the PLO, which culminated in the signing, on 13 September, of a declaration of principles on Palestinian self-rule in the Occupied Territories. The agreement, which entailed mutual recognition by Israel and the PLO, had been elaborated during a series of secret negotiations mediated by Norwegian diplomacy. The Declaration of Principles established a detailed timetable for Israel's disengagement from the Occupied Territories and stipulated that a permanent settlement of the Palestinian question should be in place by December 1998. From 13 October 1993 Palestinian authorities were to assume responsibility for education and culture, health, social welfare, direct taxation and tourism in the Gaza Strip and the Jericho area of the West Bank, and a transitional period of Palestinian self-rule was to begin on 13 December 1993.

While it was welcomed as a major breakthrough in the Middle East peace process, the Declaration of Principles was nevertheless regarded as only a tentative first step towards the resolution of the region's conflicts that could be threatened from many directions. Although the Israeli Prime Minister was able to obtain the ratification of the Declaration of Principles, and of Israel's recognition of the PLO, by the Knesset on 23 September 1993, there was widespread opposition to it from right-wing Israeli political groups. By the same token, the conclusion of the agreement aggravated divisions within the PLO and the wider Palestinian liberation movement. Within the PLO some senior officials, hitherto loyal to Yasser Arafat's leadership, now declared their opposition to him, while dissident groups, such as the Democratic Front for the Liberation of Palestine (DFLP), denounced the Declaration of Principles as treason.

The reaction to the Declaration of Principles by the other Arab Governments engaged in peace negotiations with Israel was mixed. King Hussein welcomed the agreement between Israel and the PLO, and Jordan immediately agreed an agenda for direct negotiations with Israel, which was also ratified by the Knesset on 23 September 1993. Lebanon, however, feared that the divisions that the Declaration of Principles had provoked within the Palestinian movement might in future lead to renewed conflict on Lebanese territory. It remained unclear, too, whether Syria—which neither condemned nor welcomed the Declaration of Principles—would continue to support those Palestinian groups opposed to the PLO's position.

In mid-September 1993 the resignation of Arye Deri as Minister of the Interior, following allegations of corruption, provoked the resignation of other members of Shas from the Cabinet, reducing the governing coalition to an alliance between the Labour Party and Meretz; and the Government's majority in the Knesset to only two. Protracted negotiations between the Labour Party and Shas failed to achieve the return of Shas to the governing coalition, and were eventually superseded by an agreement with Yi'ud, a breakaway group from the Tzomet Party, formed in early 1994, which allowed it to join the Government. Yi'ud signed a coalition agreement in July 1994, but did not formally join the Government until December, after the High Court of Justice had ruled that to do so did not contravene the country's anti-defection legislation.

In early October 1993 Itzhak Rabin and Yasser Arafat held their first meeting in the context of the Declaration of Principles in Cairo, Egypt, where they agreed to begin talks on the implementation of the Declaration of Principles on 13 October, and to establish general liaison, technical, economic and regional co-operation committees.

On 13 October 1993 the PLO-Israeli joint liaison committee met for the first time, the delegations to it headed, respectively, by Mahmoud Abbas and by Shimon Peres, the Israeli Minister of Foreign Affairs. It was agreed that the committee should meet at regular, short intervals to monitor the implementation of the Declaration of Principles. The technical committee also held three meetings during October in the Egyptian coastal resort of Taba. Its task was to establish the precise details of Israel's military withdrawal from the Gaza Strip and Jericho, which, under the terms of the Declaration of Principles, was scheduled to take place between 13 December 1993 and 13 April 1994. Also in October the Central Council of the PLO formally approved the Declaration of Principles by a large majority.

At the beginning of October 1993 talks took place in Washington, DC, USA, between Crown Prince Hassan of Jordan and Shimon Peres. Despite reports of subsequent secret negotiations, King Hussein of Jordan insisted, during visits to Egypt and Syria in November, that Jordan would not conclude a separate peace agreement with Israel.

As had been feared, it proved impossible satisfactorily to negotiate the details of Israel's military withdrawal from the Gaza Strip and Jericho by 13 December 1993. This failure cast doubt on the whole of the September agreement between Israel and the PLO. The main cause of the failure was the issue of security arrangements for border crossings between the Gaza Strip and Jericho and Jordan and Egypt.

Following meetings between the US Secretary of State, Warren Christopher, and President Assad of Syria and the Syrian Minister of Foreign Affairs in Damascus in early December 1993, Syria announced its willingness to resume bilateral negotiations with Israel in early 1994. Syrian Jews wishing to leave Syria were also to be granted exit visas. In early January 1994, before a meeting between US President Clinton and Syria's President Assad took place, Israel appeared to indicate, tentatively, that it might be prepared to execute a full withdrawal from the Golan Heights in return for a comprehensive peace agreement with Syria. On 17 January it was reported that the Government would put the issue to a referendum before making such a withdrawal. This was interpreted as an attempt by the Government to deflect in advance any pressure for a swift move towards a peace agreement with Syria which might emerge at the forthcoming summit meeting between the US and Syrian Presidents. Bilateral negotiations between Israeli and Syrian delegations resumed in Washington, DC, USA, on 24 January, after a four-month hiatus.

On 9 February 1994 Israel and the PLO appeared to achieve a breakthrough in their stalled negotiations when they signed an agreement to share control of the two future international border crossings. It was reported that security arrangements for Jewish settlers in the Gaza Strip had also been decided: three access routes to Jewish settlements there were to remain under Israeli control. However, the boundaries of the Jericho enclave remained undefined. Further talks began on 14 February to address the issues of the implementation of the first stage of Palestinian autonomy in the Gaza Strip and the Jericho area; the size, structure and jurisdiction of a future Palestinian police force; control of sea and air space; and the delineation of the Jericho enclave.

In late April 1994 Israel and the PLO signed an agreement concerning economic relations between Israel and the autonomous Palestinian entity during the five-year period leading to self-rule. At the end of the month it was reported that the US Secretary of State had submitted to President Assad of Syria Israel's proposals regarding a withdrawal from the occupied Golan Heights in exchange for a full peace agreement with Syria.

On 4 May 1994 in Cairo, Egypt, Israel and the PLO signed an agreement which set forth detailed arrangements for Palestinian self-rule in Gaza and Jericho. The agreement provided for Israel's military withdrawal from the Gaza Strip and Jericho, and for the deployment there of a 9,000-strong Palestinian police force. A nominated Palestine National Authority (PNA) was to assume the responsibilities of the Israeli military administration in Gaza and Jericho, although Israeli authorities were to retain control in matters of external security and foreign affairs. It was also announced that elections for a Palestinian Council, which, under the terms of the Declaration of Principles, were to have taken place in Gaza and the West Bank in July 1994, had been postponed until October. Israel's military withdrawal from Gaza and Jericho was reported to have been completed on 13 May, and on 17 May the PLO formally assumed control of the Israeli Civil Administration's departments in Gaza and Jericho. On 18 May Yasser Arafat held talks with Israel's Minister of Foreign Affairs, Shimon Peres, regarding future negotiations on the extension of Palestinian self-rule in the West Bank. On 26–28 May an incomplete PNA held its inaugural meeting in Tunis, Tunisia, setting out a political programme and distributing ministerial portfolios. It had originally been Arafat's intention to appoint 24 members to the PNA (12 from within the Occupied Territories and 12 from the Palestinian diaspora). In the event, some of his chosen appointees refused to serve on the PNA—reflecting the extent of divisions within the mainstream Palestinian movement regarding the terms of the peace with Israel—and only 20 members assembled in Tunis. The PNA held its first meeting in Gaza in late June.

On 1 July 1994 Yasser Arafat returned to Gaza City, a homecoming that had far more symbolic than practical significance. Negotiations continued with Israel on the extension of Palestinian authority and the redeployment of Israeli armed forces in the West Bank, and on the holding of Palestinian elections. In late July Israel and Jordan signed a joint declaration that formally ended the state of war between them and further defined the arrangements for future negotiations between the two sides. In late August Israel and the PLO signed an agreement which extended the authority of the PNA to include education, health, tourism, social welfare and taxation.

At the beginning of September 1994 Morocco became the second Arab state to establish diplomatic relations with Israel, albeit at a low level. Tunisia established diplomatic relations with Israel the following day. On 8 September Itzhak Rabin announced the details of a plan for a partial withdrawal of Israeli armed forces from the occupied Golan Heights, after which a three-year trial period of Israeli-Syrian 'normalization' would ensue. The proposals were rejected by President Assad of Syria; however, he did state his willingness, in an address to the Syrian People's Assembly on 10 September, to work towards peace with Israel.

A conference of international donors, sponsored by the World Bank, in Paris, France, on 8–9 September 1994 collapsed almost immediately owing to an Israeli-Palestinian dispute over Palestinian investment plans to fund projects in East Jerusalem. According to Israel, such plans would have compromised negotiations on the final status of Jerusalem which, under the terms of the Declaration of Principles, were not due to begin before May 1996. On 13 September Yasser Arafat and the Israeli Minister of Foreign affairs met in Oslo, Norway, and negotiated a 15-point agreement whose aim was to accelerate economic aid to the PNA. On 25 September Arafat and Rabin met at the Erez crossing point between Gaza and Israel to discuss the future Palestinian elections in the Gaza Strip and the West Bank. The PLO was reported to wish to elect a 100-member Palestinian Council, while Israel insisted that its size should be restricted to 25 members. It was agreed to meet again in October to negotiate a compromise, Israel having rejected Arafat's proposal to hold the elections on 1 November 1994 as unrealistic. At the same time, Arafat agreed to 'take all measures' to prevent attacks on Israeli targets by opponents of the Declaration of Principles.

One of the reasons for the growing crisis in the negotiations between Israel and the PLO was the revival of the controversial issue of Jewish settlements in the West Bank. On 26 September Itzhak Rabin approved a plan to construct some 1,000 new housing units at a Jewish settlement some 3 km inside the West Bank in an apparent reversal of the freeze he had imposed on new constructions in 1992 in return for US loan guarantees. The PLO claimed that this decision contravened both the letter and the spirit of the Declaration of Principles. On 29 September King Hussein of Jordan and Itzhak Rabin held talks in Aqaba with the aim of devising a timetable for a full Israeli-Jordanian peace treaty. On 30 September the six members of the GCC announced their decision to lift the subsidiary elements of the Arab economic boycott of Israel.

On 9 October 1994 Hamas claimed responsibility for an attack in Jerusalem in which an Israeli soldier and a Palestinian civilian died. On the same day another Israeli soldier was kidnapped by Hamas fighters near Tel-Aviv, who subsequently demanded the release from Israeli jails of the Hamas leader, Sheikh Ahmad Yassin, and other Palestinian prisoners in exchange for his life. Despite Palestinian action to detain some 300 Hamas members in the Gaza Strip, the kidnapped soldier was killed in the West Bank on 14 October. On 19 October an attack by a Hamas suicide bomber in Tel-Aviv, in which 22 people died, prompted Israel to close its borders with the West Bank and the Gaza Strip for an indefinite period the following day. On 26 October Israel and Jordan signed a formal peace treaty, fixing the border between the two countries and providing for normal relations between them. The peace treaty was criticized by the Syrian Government, all elements of Palestinian opinion and by some Islamists in Jordan. On 27 October US President Clinton visited President Assad of Syria in Damascus in an attempt to break the deadlock in peace negotiations between Israel and Syria.

On 2 November 1994 a member of Islamic Jihad was killed in a car bomb attack in Gaza. The attack was blamed on the Israeli security forces by many Palestinians who opposed the Declaration of Principles. On 11 November three Israeli soldiers were killed in a suicide bomb attack near a Jewish settlement in the Gaza Strip. Islamic Jihad claimed responsibility for the attack, which it said had been to avenge the death of its member on 2 November. On 9 November the EU signed an agreement to provide the PNA $125m. in loans and grants for development projects. On 18 November some 12 Palestinians were reported to have been killed in fighting between the Palestinian police force and supporters of Hamas and Islamic Jihad in the Gaza Strip. On the following day further violence in the Gaza Strip led to the death of two Palestinians and an Israeli soldier.

It became clear in December 1994 that Israel's concern about security would inevitably continue to delay the redeployment of its armed forces in the West Bank and the holding of Palestinian elections. In the middle of the month Rabin stated that the elections would either have to take place in the continued presence of Israeli armed forces, or be postponed for a year. At the end of the month it was reported that there had been a 10% increase in the number of Jewish settlers in the occupied West Bank during 1994. High-level military contacts between Israel and Syria were also reported to have taken place late in the month.

Perhaps the most serious blow yet to the peace negotiations between Israel and the PLO was the suicide bomb attack at Beit Lid in Israel on 22 January 1995, in which 21 Jews—mostly Israeli soldiers— died and more than 60 were injured. Islamic Jihad claimed responsibility for the attack, in response to which the Government again closed Israel's borders with the Gaza Strip and the West Bank and postponed the planned release of some 5,500 Palestinian prisoners.

At the beginning of February 1995 an emergency meeting of the leaders of Egypt, Israel, Jordan and the PLO was held in Cairo with the aim of lending support to the troubled peace process. A communiqué issued at the conclusion of the summit meeting condemned acts of terror and violence; and expressed support for the Declaration of Principles and the wider peace process. On 9 February Israeli armed forces completed their withdrawal from Jordanian territories, in accordance with the peace treaty concluded by the two countries in October 1994. On 12 February US President Clinton held a meeting with the Israeli and the Egyptian Ministers of Foreign Affairs and the Palestinian (PNA) Minister of Planning and Economic Co-operation, Nabil Shaath, in Washington, DC. Shimon Peres, the Israeli Minister of Foreign Affairs, was reported to have stated, after the meeting, that any further expansion of Palestinian self-rule in the West Bank was conditional upon real progress by the PNA in suppressing terrorism. On 21 February Rabin appointed ministers, in an acting capacity, to two portfolios which had been reserved for the Shas religious party. Shas had announced at the beginning of the month that, owing to its fears regarding Jewish security and the peace process, it would not rejoin the coalition Government.

In early March 1995 Yasser Arafat and the Israeli Minister of Foreign Affairs met in Gaza for talks. At the conclusion of the meeting it was announced that 1 July 1995 had been adopted as the date by which an agreement on the expansion of Palestinian self-rule in the West Bank should be concluded. In mid-March it was announced that Israel and Syria had agreed to resume peace negotiations, talks between the two countries having been suspended since February 1994. Speculation that a breakthrough in the talks between Israel and Syria might shortly be achieved was subdued, however, in late April, when the Syrian Vice-President made it clear that Syria was not about to renounce its demand that Israel should withdraw from the Golan Heights to the border pertaining before the June 1967 war.

In early April 1995 two suicide bomb attacks in the Gaza Strip killed seven Israeli soldiers and wounded more than 50 people. Hamas and Islamic Jihad claimed responsibility for the attacks, in the aftermath of which the Palestinian police force was reported to have arrested as many as 300 members of the two groups. On 24 May Syria and Israel were reported to have concluded a 'framework understanding on security arrangements', which would facilitate negotiations on security issues. At the end of the month Shimon Peres made public the Government's position with regard to the talks with Syria. Israel, he stated, had proposed that its forces should withdraw from the Golan Heights over a four-year period. Syria, however, had insisted that the withdrawal should be effected over 18 months.

In early June 1995 the Minister of Justice, David Libai, was appointed acting Minister of the Interior in place of Uzi Baram, who retained the tourism portfolio. The Likud party appeared to suffer a serious division in the same month, when one of its most prominent members, David Levy, announced that he was forming a new party to contest the legislative elections scheduled for 1996. The division was reportedly the result of Levy's opposition to new selection procedures for general election candidates, which Likud had formally adopted on 5 June. Levy's new political movement, Gesher, was formally inaugurated on 18 June, although Levy himself remained a member of Likud.

Despite intensive efforts to achieve a breakthrough, it proved impossible to conclude an agreement on the expansion of Palestinian self-rule in the West Bank by the target date of 1 July 1995. The principal obstacles to an agreement were the question of to where, exactly, Israeli troops in the West Bank would redeploy; and the precise nature of security arrangements to be made for the approximately 130,000 Jewish settlers who were to remain in the West Bank.

On 21 August 1995 a suicide bomb attack on a bus in Jerusalem killed six people. Hamas claimed responsibility for the attack, which brought the number of deaths in bombings over the previous 16 months to 77.

It was not until 28 September 1995 that the Israeli-Palestinian Interim Agreement on the West Bank and the Gaza Strip was finally signed by Israel and the PLO. Its main provisions were the withdrawal of Israeli armed forces from a further six West Bank towns (Nablus, Ramallah, Jenin, Tulkaram, Kakilya and Bethlehem) and a partial redeployment away from the town of Hebron; national Palestinian legislative elections to an 82-member Palestinian Council, and for a Palestinian Executive President; and the release, in three phases, of Palestinian prisoners detained by Israel. In anticipation of a violent reaction against the Interim Agreement by so-called 'rejectionist' groups within the West Bank and the Gaza Strip, Israel immediately announced the closure of its borders with the Gaza Strip and the West Bank. Meanwhile, right-wing elements within Israel denounced the agreement because they believed that too much had been conceded to the Palestinians. In mid-October Israeli armed forces launched an intensive military operation in southern Lebanon after a bomb attack by Hezbollah had caused the death of six Israeli soldiers on 16 October.

On 4 November 1995 the Israeli Prime Minister, Itzhak Rabin, was assassinated in Tel-Aviv by a Jewish law student who opposed the peace process, in particular the Israeli withdrawal from the West Bank. The assassination caused a further marginalization of those on the extreme right wing of Israeli politics who had advocated violence as a means of halting the implementation of the Declaration of Principles on Palestinian Self-Rule, and provoked criticism of Likud, which, it was widely felt, had not sufficiently distanced itself from such extremist elements. Following the assassination, Shimon Peres, hitherto the Minister of Foreign Affairs, became acting Prime Minister. On 15 November, with the agreement of the opposition Likud, Peres was invited to form a new government. On 21 November the leaders of the outgoing coalition parties—Labour, Meretz and Yi'ud—signed a new coalition agreement, and Peres announced a new Cabinet, which was formally approved by the Knesset on the following day.

In spite of the assassination, Israeli armed forces completed their withdrawal from the town of Jenin, in the West Bank, on 13 November, and during December they withdrew from Tulkaram, Nablus, Kakilya, Bethlehem and Ramallah. With regard to Hebron, Israel and the PNA signed an agreement transferring jurisdiction in some 17 areas of civilian affairs from Israel to the PNA. In early December Shimon Peres and Yasser Arafat held talks at the Erez border point between Israel and the Gaza Strip for the first time since the assassination of Itzhak Rabin. Peres confirmed at the talks that Israel would release some 1,000 Palestinian prisoners before the Palestinian legislative and presidential elections scheduled for January 1996.

Peace negotiations between Israel and Syria resumed in late December 1995 in Maryland, USA, and a second round of US-mediated talks took place there in early January 1996. In February the Prime Minister announced that elections to the Knesset and—for the first time—the direct election of the Prime Minister would take place as soon as electoral legislation allowed—in late May 1996. There was speculation that car-bomb attacks carried out by Hamas in Jerusalem and Ashkelon in late February, in which at least 25 people were killed, might increase support for Likud at the forthcoming elections and improve the prospects of Binyamin Netanyahu, the Likud leader, in the direct election for the Prime Minister.

On 10 January 1996 King Hussein of Jordan began a public visit to Tel-Aviv, during the course of which Israel and Jordan signed a number of agreements relating to the normalization of economic and cultural relations. Palestinian legislative and presidential elections were held in late January and in the normal course of events Palestinian and Israeli negotiators would, on their completion, have initiated the final stage of the peace process, addressing such issues as Jerusalem, the rights of Palestinian refugees, the status of Jewish settlements in the Palestinian Autonomous Areas and the extent of that autonomy. In late February and early March, however, suicide bomb attacks in Jerusalem, Ashkelon and Tel-Aviv caused the death of more than 50 Israelis and led to a further suspension of the peace process. Following the attacks in Jerusalem and Ashkelon, Israel ordered the indefinite closure of the West Bank and the Gaza Strip and demanded that the Palestinian authorities should suppress the activities of Hamas and Islamic Jihad in the areas under their control. It was unclear, however, whether either of these groups was responsible for the bomb attacks. A hitherto unknown group, the 'Yahya Ayyash Units', claimed responsibility for the first attacks on 25 February, which were apparently carried out to avenge the assassination—allegedly by Israeli agents—of a leading member (Yahya Ayyash) of Hamas in January 1996. Yasser Arafat, now the elected Palestinian President, condemned the bombings and in late February more than 200 members of Hamas were reported to have been detained by the Palestinian security forces.

The two suicide bomb attacks carried out at the beginning of March 1996 (for which the 'Yahya Ayyash Units' again claimed responsibility) led Israel to impose even more stringent security measures. Among other things Israel asserted the right of its armed forces to enter the areas under Palestinian jurisdiction when its security was at stake. The Palestinian authorities were reported to have held emergency talks with the leadership of Hamas and Islamic Jihad and to have outlawed their armed wings and other, unspecified Palestinian paramilitary groups.

The suicide bomb attacks also affected the talks taking place between Israeli and Syrian negotiating teams in the USA. Following the second attacks in March 1996 the Israeli team returned to Israel. On 18 March Peres revealed that peace negotiations with Syria had effectively been suspended because Syria had refused to condemn the bombings in precisely the way the USA had indicated that it should; and to give an assurance that it would not sponsor terrorist activities. Syria claimed that it did condemn terrorism in all forms, but drew a distinction between terrorism and legitimate resistance to occupation. Syria and Lebanon both declined an invitation to attend a summit meeting, held in the Egyptian town of Sharm esh-Sheikh on 13 March, at which some 27 heads of state expressed their support for the Middle East peace process and pledged to redouble their efforts to combat terrorism.

In early April 1996 Israel and Turkey signed a number of military co-operation agreements, one of which provided for the establishment of a joint organization for research and strategy. Syria condemned the agreement as a threat to its own security and to that of all Arab and Islamic countries. A visit by Peres to Oman and Qatar at the beginning of the month resulted in an agreement between Israel and Qatar to increase co-operation in trade.

Israel welcomed the decision of the Palestinian National Council in late April 1996 to amend the Palestinian Covenant (the constitution of the Palestinian resistance movement), thereby removing all of its clauses which demanded the destruction of Israel. Indeed, the Israeli Government had demanded that the Covenant be amended by 7 May 1996 as a precondition for its participation in the final stage of peace negotiations with the PLO.

In the months following the assassination of Itzhak Rabin the victory of the Labour Party and the Labour leader, Shimon Peres, in the legislative and prime ministerial elections held on 29 May 1996 was widely regarded as a foregone conclusion. Most significantly the US Administration appeared to exclude the possibility of any other outcome, even after the suicide bomb attacks during February and March 1996 led to increased support—expressed in opinion polls—for Likud and other right-wing political groups. In fact, no party gained an outright majority of the 120 seats in the new Knesset, but the Likud leader, Benyamin Netanyahu, gained a marginal victory over Shimon Peres in the direct election of the Prime Minister in which they were the only candidates. Prior to the legislative election a formal alliance between Likud, the Tzomet Party and Gesher (a new party formed in February 1996) had been announced. The success of the religious parties, Shas and the National Religious Party—even though they probably gained seats at the expense of the Likud-led alliance—was the key factor in determining that the new Government would be formed by Likud. Some 79.7% of the 3.9m.-strong Israeli electorate were reported to have participated in the elections.

The election of a new, Likud-led Israeli Government appeared to have grave implications for the future of the peace negotiations between Israel and the Palestinian authorities since, during the election campaign, the Likud alliance had explicitly stated that it would never agree to the establishment of a Palestinian state and even, at times, seemed to indicate that it was prepared to renege on some aspects of agreements which Israel had already concluded with the Palestinians. On 31 May 1996 the Palestinian Council of Ministers (formed after the Palestinian legislative elections in January 1996) and the Executive Committee of the PLO held a joint meeting in Gaza and urged the new Israeli Government about to be formed to implement all agreements which had already been concluded and to commence the final stage of the peace negotiations.

Prime Minister Netanyahu commenced negotiations to form a cabinet on 2 June 1996, and on 16 and 17 June signed a series of agreements between the Likud alliance and Shas, the National Religious Party, Israeli B'Aliyah, United Torah Judaism and the Third Way to incorporate their representatives into a coalition which would command the support of 66 deputies in the 120-member Knesset. In addition, Moledet agreed to support the Government, but did not formally enter the coalition. On 18 June the new Government received the approval of the Knesset and presented a summary of policies it would pursue in office. This excluded the possibility of granting Palestinian statehood or, with regard to Syria, of relinquishing *de facto* sovereignty of the occupied Golan Heights.

On 21–23 June 1996, in response to Likud's electoral victory, a summit meeting of the leaders of all Arab countries with the exception of Iraq was convened in Cairo. The meeting issued a final communiqué in which the participants reiterated Israel's withdrawal from all occupied territories (including East Jerusalem) as a basic requirement for a comprehensive Middle Eastern peace settlement.

By late August 1996 Palestinian frustration at what were regarded as deliberate attempts by the new Israeli Government to slow down the peace process was increasingly evident. In June it was reported that Prime Minister Netanyahu had postponed further discussion of the withdrawal of Israeli armed forces from the West Bank town of Hebron—where they remained in order to provide security for a community of some 400 Jewish settlers. An agreement for their withdrawal by 20 March 1996 had been concluded with the Palestinian authorities, but had been suspended by Shimon Peres following the suicide bomb attacks in February and March. Furthermore, Netanyahu had refused to meet the Palestinian President and had stated that he would never do so. In July the intransigent nature of the new Government was underlined by the incorporation into the Cabinet of Ariel Sharon—who had played a leading role in the creation and expansion of controversial Jewish settlements in the West Bank—although his appointment as Minister of Infrastructure was made only after the Minister of Foreign Affairs had forced it by threatening to resign, thus endangering Likud's alliance with Gesher. The PNA organized a short general strike at the end of the month in protest at the refusal of the Israeli authorities to allow Palestinian Muslims to participate in Friday prayers at the Al-Aqsa mosque in Jerusalem and also at a government decision to construct more housing units at existing Jewish settlements in the West Bank. On 4 September Netanyahu and Arafat did meet, for the first time, at the Erez crossing point between Israel and Gaza, and at a press conference they confirmed their commitment to the interim agreement and their determination to implement it. Reports persisted, however, that

Israel was seeking to modify some of the agreements concluded within its framework.

In mid-September 1996, at a meeting of the Arab League member states, the Syrian Minister of Foreign Affairs stated that the Arab states represented there had agreed in future to link relations with Israel to progress made in the peace process. Shortly afterwards it was announced that the Israeli Ministry of Defence had approved plans to construct some 1,800 new housing units at existing Jewish settlements in the West Bank. By late September many observers agreed that the new Israeli Government had effectively halted the peace process by either abandoning or postponing many of the commitments which it had inherited from its predecessor. There had been no indication of when even the discussion of the withdrawal of Israeli armed forces from Hebron would begin, even though agreements had been signed in the past which stipulated that the final stage of the peace negotiations with the Palestinians should be under way. On 25 September violent confrontations began between members of the Palestinian security forces, Palestinian civilians and members of the Israeli armed forces in which at least 50 Palestinians and 18 Israelis were killed and hundreds wounded. The West Bank town of Ramallah was the initial point of confrontation and the cause of the disturbances was attributed to the decision of the Israeli Government to open the north end of the Hasmonean tunnel which ran beneath the Al-Aqsa mosque in East Jerusalem. Most observers, however, viewed the violent confrontations as the inevitable culmination of Palestinian anger at the Israeli Government's apparent determination not to abide by some of the agreements it had signed with the Palestinian authorities. There was speculation that the violence marked the beginning of a new Palestinian *intifada* and signalled the end of the peace process. The Israeli military authorities declared a state of emergency in the Gaza Strip and the West Bank and threatened military intervention to suppress the disturbances. A special session of the UN Security Council was convened and intense international diplomacy led to the holding of a crisis summit meeting in Washington, DC, hosted by US President Clinton and attended by Binyamin Netanyahu, Yasser Arafat and King Hussein of Jordan. The meeting reportedly achieved nothing, but on 6 October it was announced that, following further US mediation, Israel had agreed to resume negotiations on the partial withdrawal of its armed forces from Hebron. On 7 October, at the opening of the winter session of the Knesset, Netanyahu stated that once the question of the redeployment from Hebron had been settled Israel would reopen its borders with the West Bank and the Gaza Strip—which had remained closed since February 1996—and move quickly towards seeking a final settlement with the Palestinians.

In mid-January 1997 Israel and the PNA finally concluded an agreement on the withdrawal of Israeli armed forces from Hebron. The principal terms of the agreement, which had been negotiated with the help of US diplomacy, were that Israeli armed forces should withdraw from 80% of the town of Hebron within 10 days, and that the first of three subsequent withdrawals from the West Bank should take place six weeks after the signing of the agreement and the remaining two by August 1998. With regard to security arrangements for Jewish settlers in central Hebron, Palestinian police patrols would be armed only with pistols in areas close to the Jewish enclaves, while joint Israeli/Palestinian patrols would secure the heights above the enclaves. The 'final status' negotiations on borders, the Jerusalem issue, Jewish settlements and Palestinian refugees—arguably the most intractable elements of the entire Arab-Israeli dispute—were to commence within two months of the signing of the agreement on Hebron. As guarantor of the agreement, the USA undertook to obtain the release of some Palestinian prisoners, and to ensure that Israel continued to engage in negotiations on a Palestinian airport in the Gaza Strip and on safe passage between the West Bank and the Gaza Strip for Palestinians. The USA also undertook to ensure that the Palestinians would continue to combat terrorism, complete the revision of the Palestinian Covenant and consider Israeli requests to extradite Palestinians suspected of involvement in attacks in Israel.

The conclusion of the agreement on the withdrawal of Israeli armed forces from Hebron marked the first significant progress in the peace process since Netanyahu's election as Prime Minister in May 1996. Negotiations with Syria, however, remained suspended. In late January 1997 Netanyahu urged Syria to exert pressure on Hezbollah to cease hostilities in Israel's self-declared security zone in southern Lebanon. In February, however, he denied speculation that Israel was considering a unilateral withdrawal from the Lebanese security zone. Such speculation had intensified as a result of the death, in a helicopter accident, of 73 Israeli soldiers travelling to southern Lebanon, which had prompted renewed questioning of the usefulness of deploying Israeli armed forces there.

In February 1997 the progress achieved through the agreement on Hebron was threatened when Israel announced that it was to proceed with the construction of 6,500 housing units at Har Homa in East Jerusalem. In response the UN Security Council submitted two resolutions in March, urging Israel to reconsider its construction plans. The USA vetoed the resolutions, however. Tensions escalated during March after Israel unilaterally decided to withdraw its armed forces from only 9% of the West Bank. Yasser Arafat denounced the decision and King Hussein of Jordan accused Netanyahu of intentionally destroying the peace process. Increasing anti-Israeli sentiment reportedly motivated a Jordanian soldier to murder seven Israeli schoolgirls in Nayarim, an enclave between Israel and Jordan, on 13 March. Israeli intransigence over the Har Homa settlement prompted Palestinians to abandon the 'final status' talks, scheduled to begin on 17 March, and on the following day construction at the site began. Riots among Palestinians erupted immediately. On 21 March Hamas carried out a bomb attack in Tel-Aviv, killing four and wounding more than 60 people. In response the Israeli Government ordered the closure of Israeli borders with the West Bank and the Gaza Strip. In late March the League of Arab States voted to resume its economic boycott of Israel, suspend moves to establish diplomatic relations, and withdraw from multilateral peace talks. (Jordan, the PNA and Egypt were excluded from the legislation, owing to their binding bilateral agreements with Israel.) Meanwhile in New York, Arab states continued to petition the UN General Assembly to appeal for a halt to the Har Homa development.

On 7 April 1997 Netanyahu met with US President Clinton in Washington, DC, and insisted that he would not suspend the programme of construction. Rioting occurred in Hebron the following day after a Palestinian was allegedly murdered by Jewish settlers. The disturbances subsided at the end of the month and, consequently, the borders with the Gaza Strip and the West Bank were reopened.

The latest crisis in Israeli-Palestinian relations coincided with domestic problems for the Government. In April 1997 police investigators recommended that the Prime Minister be charged with fraud and breach of trust for his appointment, in January, of Roni Bar-On, as Attorney-General. Bar-On resigned within 12 hours of his appointment after it was alleged that his promotion had been made in order to facilitate a plea bargain for Aryeh Der'i, leader of the orthodox Shas party, who was facing separate corruption charges. It was suggested that, in return for Bar-On's appointment, Der'i had pledged Shas party support for the Cabinet's decision regarding the withdrawal from Hebron. In early May Der'i was indicted for obstruction of justice, but charges against Netanyahu were dropped owing to lack of evidence. However, the Prime Minister's authority was further undermined by the subsequent resignation of the Minister of Finance, Dan Meridor; meanwhile Limor Livnat resigned as Cabinet Spokeswoman (although she continued as Minister of Communications). The Government's problems were compounded during May by the escalation of a long-standing dispute between orthodox and progressive Jewish communities regarding religious conversions. Meanwhile, in November Israel and the Vatican signed a memorandum to recognize the legal status of Catholic organizations in Israel.

In May 1997 the Palestinian Minister of Justice, Furayh Abu Middayn, announced that the PNA would sentence to death any Palestinian found guilty of selling land to Jews. The legislation provoked a spate of unlawful killings: within one month three Arab land dealers were reportedly executed without trial by a newly-established vigilante group called the 'Guardians of the Holy Land.' In May the USA's chief peace process negotiator, Dennis Ross, failed to achieve any progress towards a resumption of peace talks after a nine-day mediation attempt.

In mid-June 1997 the US House of Representatives voted in favour of recognizing Jerusalem as the undivided capital of Israel and of transferring the US embassy there, from Tel-Aviv. The decision coincided with violent clashes between Palestinian civilians and Israeli troops in both Gaza and Hebron. Meanwhile, Yasser Arafat, fearing Israeli reoccupation of Hebron, assigned 200 police officers to patrol the area in order to address the crisis. Although the police presence appeared to have a positive effect, four Palestinian officers were arrested by Israeli police outside Nablus on suspicion of conspiring to attack Israeli targets. At the same time the Palestinian police force discovered large stocks of ammunition in the West Bank, allegedly belonging to Hamas.

In June 1997 Ehud Barak, a former cabinet minister and chief of the army, won the Labour Party leadership election (to replace Shimon Peres), securing 51% of the votes. Yosi Beilin, Shloma Ben Ami, and Ephraim Sne won 18%, 14% and 6% of the votes respectively. On 9 July the Knesset approved the appointment of Michael Eitan as Minister of Science, following the resignation of Binyamin Begin. Yaacov Ne'eman was appointed as Minister of Finance.

In July 1997 a series of meetings between US Under-Secretary of State, Thomas Pickering, and officials from Israel and Palestine secured an agreement to resume peace talks the following month. However, on 30 July, the eve of a visit to Israel by Dennis Ross in order to reactivate the negotiations, two Hamas suicide bombers killed 14 civilians and wounded more than 150 others in Jerusalem. Ross consequently cancelled his visit and Israel immediately suspended payment of tax revenues to the PNA and closed the Gaza Strip and the West Bank. Prime Minister Netanyahu insisted that the restrictions would remain until the Palestinians demonstrated a commitment to combat terrorism.

On 18 August 1997 Israel released 30% of some US $50m. of tax revenues owed to the Palestinians. In late August Yasser Arafat convened a two-day forum during which he publicly embraced Hamas leaders and urged them, together with Islamic Jihad, to unite with the Palestinian people against Israeli policies. On 26 August Hamas rejected an Israeli request for them to suspend their attacks against Israel. Although Israel relaxed its closure of the West Bank and the Gaza Strip on 1 September, restrictions were reimposed three days later after a triple suicide bombing took place in West Jerusalem, killing eight people (including the bombers) and wounding more than 150 others. The security crisis cast doubt on the viability of a planned visit by Madeleine Albright, US Secretary of State, who was to tour the Middle East during 10–15 September, primarily to discuss substantive political issues in connection with the peace process. However, Albright's visit was positively received, and in mid-September Israel released further Palestinian assets and lifted the internal closure of the West Bank, while the Palestinians announced the closure of 17 institutions affiliated to Hamas. Renewed diplomatic activity ensued on 8 October, when the Israeli Prime Minister and Yasser Arafat met for the first time in eight months. The following day Israel announced plans to release further clearances to the PNA and to reopen the Israeli-Palestinian borders. Despite signs of progress in relations, Israel failed to participate in a second round of negotiations, scheduled for mid-October, to accelerate the 'final status' talks. In spite of US pressure, Netanyahu stated in late October that further redeployments would not take place until Palestinians made further efforts to combat terrorism.

Meanwhile, relations between Jordan and Israel deteriorated. On 25 September members of the Israeli intelligence force, Mossad, attempted to assassinate a Hamas leader, Khalid Mish'al, in Amman. King Hussein of Jordan threatened to sever diplomatic relations with Israel unless an antidote to the poison used in the assassination attempt was immediately dispatched. The attackers had carried forged Canadian passports, and Canada withdrew its ambassador to Israel in protest. An antidote was provided and, in an attempt to restore relations, intensive diplomatic negotiations took place between Netanyahu, Crown Prince Hassan of Jordan and US officials. As a result of talks, several agreements regarding the release of prisoners were made: on 1 October Israel released the founder of Hamas, Sheikh Ahmad Yassin, in return for the release by Jordan of two Mossad agents arrested in connection with the attack on Mish'al. A further 12 Mossad agents had been expelled by the Jordanian authorities by 12 October following the release of 23 Jordanian and 50 Palestinian prisoners by Israel.

Bilateral negotiations between Israel and Palestinian negotiators resumed in early November 1997. Israel offered to decelerate its construction of Jewish settlements in return for Palestinian approval of a plan to delay further redeployments of Israeli troops from the West Bank. At the same time, the Israeli Government announced plans to build 900 new housing units in the area, frustrating both the USA and PNA. The virtual stalemate in the peace process prompted several Arab states to boycott the Middle East and North Africa conference, held in Doha, Qatar, on 16–18 November. Separate peace talks, held between Madeleine Albright, Netanyahu and Arafat in mid-November, were inconclusive. Albright urged Israel to present plans for a significant withdrawal from the West Bank in the near future. On 30 November the Israeli Cabinet agreed in principle to a partial withdrawal from the West Bank, but specified neither its timing nor its scale.

In November 1997 a crisis erupted within Netanyahu's coalition after the Likud party endorsed a proposal to reform the electoral system. Candidates standing for election to the Knesset were to be chosen by the party's 2,700-strong Central Committee rather than the 200,000 registered members of the party. The decision provoked outrage amongst several of the other coalition parties who believed that the reform would simply strengthen Netanyahu's power. According to Israeli press reports, several coalition members planned to form a party to defeat the Government. In an attempt to restore the fractious coalition, Netanyahu retracted the plan, stating that the issue of electoral reform would be subjected to a referendum. In December a further dispute within the coalition arose over the issue of troop redeployments. Owing to conflicting opinions within the Cabinet, Netanyahu failed to produce a conclusive redeployment plan to present at talks with Madeleine Albright in Paris, France, on 17 December. On 10 December the Government blocked PNA officials from conducting a census in East Jerusalem. Despite the impasse, Israeli and Palestinian officials demonstrated their commitment to peace by signing a security memorandum on 17 December. Evidence of further divisions within the coalition emerged at the end of the month owing to the forthcoming 1998 budget vote, effectively a demonstration of confidence in the Prime Minister. In order to muster the necessary support, Netanyahu granted concessions to various parties, in particular to right-wing members of the coalition. These included such financial rewards as increased funding for construction on the West Bank and for Orthodox schools. Opposition parties claimed that the Prime Minister had bribed coalition members in order to remain in power. David Levy, the leader of Gesher, also denounced the budget, claiming it to be an infringement of social principles; and on 4 January Gesher withdrew from the Government, attributing the departure to dissatisfaction with the budget and with slow rate of progress in the peace talks. The withdrawal of Gesher left Netanyahu with a majority of 61–59 and prompted speculation about the Government's imminent collapse. However, the following day the budget was approved by a 58–52 majority. Plans to form a government of national unity for a period of six months, proposed by Shimon Peres, were rejected after the former Labour leader failed to secure enough support from party members.

On 12 January 1998 Netanyahu survived a vote of no-confidence. Nevertheless, the Prime Minister remained in a precarious position, and his vulnerability was exploited by coalition members; several parties threatened to leave the Government if their demands for troop redeployment were not met. Since right-wing members opposed redeployment and moderates advocated a withdrawal, Netanyahu was left with the challenge of satisfying all members of the coalition in order to remain in power, while, at the same time, fulfilling Israel's obligations to the Declaration of Principles. Recognizing Netanyahu's difficulty, the USA stated that it would not allow the political crisis to hinder the peace process and again urged the Prime Minister to present plans for redeployment to President Clinton in Washington, DC, on 20 January.

On 13 January 1998 Netanyahu announced that he would not make any further decisions regarding the peace process until the Palestinians had demonstrated further efforts to combat terrorism, reduced their security forces from 40,000 to 24,000 and amended their Constitution to recognize Israel's right to exist. The announcement was condemned by the PNA, which claimed that it had actively attempted to reduce terrorist activity.

On 20 January 1998 Netanyahu failed to present a plan of redeployment in talks with US President Clinton. However, the Israeli Prime Minister expressed an interest in a US proposal to withdraw troops from at least 10% of the land in several stages. Arafat rejected the suggestion in talks with Clinton on 22 January, stating that he would rather resign than capitulate to US pressure to accept Israel's demands. In response to the continuing stalemate, US Secretary of State Madeleine Albright reportedly told Netanyahu in early February that the USA was considering abandoning its mediation attempts unless Israel adopted a more conciliatory attitude towards the peace process.

Renewed hostilities erupted in northern Israel in August 1997 after Hezbollah launched a rocket attack on civilians living in the Israeli town of Kiryat Shmona. The attack, made in retaliation for attacks by Israeli commandos in which five Hezbollah members were killed, prompted further air strikes by Israel in southern Lebanon. Violence escalated and on 18 August the SLA shelled the Lebanese port of Sidon, killing at least six and wounding more than 30 civilians. Israeli denials of responsibility, claiming that the attack was the sole initiative of the SLA, were rejected by Hezbollah. On 5 September 12 Israeli marines, who were allegedly planning to assassinate Shi'ite leaders, were killed in the village of Insariyeh, south of Sidon, reportedly by the joint forces of Hezbollah and Amal, and Lebanese soldiers. The death toll was the highest to occur in a single incident since 1985, when Israeli troops withdrew to the buffer zone. Consequently the Israeli Government faced increasing pressure to withdraw from southern Lebanon. Such pressure was countered by a warning by the SLA commander, Gen. Antoine Lahad, that the SLA would possibly attack retreating Israeli forces.

Government

Supreme authority in Israel rests with the Knesset (Assembly), with 120 members elected by universal suffrage for four years (subject to dissolution), on the basis of proportional representation. The President, a constitutional Head of State, is elected by the Knesset for five years. Executive power lies with the Cabinet, led by a directly-elected Prime Minister. The Cabinet takes office after receiving a vote of confidence in the Knesset, to which it is responsible. Ministers are usually members of the Knesset, but non-members may be appointed.

The country is divided into six administrative districts. Local authorities are elected at the same time as elections to the Knesset. There are 31 municipalities (including two Arab towns), 115 local councils (46 Arab and Druze) and 49 regional councils (one Arab) comprising representatives of 700 villages.

Defence

The Israel Defence Forces consist of a small nucleus of commissioned and non-commissioned regular officers, a contingent enlisted for national service, and a large reserve. Men are enlisted for 36 months of military service, and women for 21 months. Military service is compulsory for Jews and Druzes, but voluntary for Christians, Circassians and Muslims. Total regular armed forces numbered 175,000 (including 138,500 conscripts) in August 1996, and full mobilization to 605,000 can be quickly achieved with reserves of 430,000. The armed forces are divided into an army of 134,000, a navy estimated at 9,000 and an air force of 32,000. The defence budget for 1997 was 22,000m. new shekels (US $6,600m.).

Economic Affairs

In 1995, according to estimates by the World Bank, Israel's gross national product (GNP), measured at average 1993–95 prices, was US $87,875m., equivalent to $15,920 per head. During 1985–95, it was estimated, GNP per head increased, in real terms, at an average rate of 2.5% per year. Over the same period, the population increased by an annual average of 2.7%. Israel's gross domestic product (GDP) increased, in real terms, by an annual average of 3.5% in 1980–90 and 6.4% in 1990–95.

Agriculture (including hunting, forestry and fishing) contributed 4.2% of the GDP of the business sector in 1994, and in 1996 employed 2.5% of the working population, the majority of whom lived in large co-operatives (*kibbutzim*), of which there were 267 in 1995, or co-operative smallholder villages (*moshavim*), of which there were 411 at December 1995. Israel is largely self-sufficient in foodstuffs. Citrus fruits constitute the main export crop. Other important crops are vegetables (particularly potatoes and tomatoes), wheat, melons and apples. Poultry, livestock and fish production are also important. Agricultural output increased at an average annual rate of less than 0.5% in 1985–95.

Industry (manufacturing and mining) contributed 29% of the GDP of the business sector in 1994, and employed 20.1% of the working population in 1996. The State plays a major role in all sectors of industry, and there is a significant co-operative sector. Industrial production increased by an average 5.9% annually in 1988–95.

The mining and quarrying sector employed about 0.3% of the working population in 1994. There were some 33 producing oil wells in 1995, and some natural gas is produced. Potash, bromides, magnesium and other salts are mined. Israel is the world's largest exporter of bromine. There are also proven reserves of 20m. metric tons of low-grade copper ore, and gold, in potentially commercial quantities, was discovered in 1988.

Manufacturing employed 20.9% of the working population in 1994. The principal branches of manufacturing, measured by gross revenue, in 1992 were food products, beverages and tobacco (accounting for 18.7% of the total), electrical machinery (15.6%), chemical, petroleum and coal products (11.6%), metal products (9.7%) and transport equipment (5.6%). Diamond polishing is also an important activity. In 1980–90 manufacturing production increased, on average, by 2.8% each year.

Construction contributed 9.1% of the GDP of the business sector in 1994, and in 1996 the sector employed 7.4% of the working population.

The power sector (water and electricity) contributed 4% of the GDP of the business sector in 1994. In 1996 the sector employed about 1% of the working population. Energy is derived principally from imported petroleum and petroleum products. Imports of mineral fuels comprised 6.1% of the total value of imports in 1994.

Tourism is an important source of revenue. In 1996 2.1m. tourists visited Israel. Receipts from the tourist sector totalled US $2,771m. in that year.

The Israeli banking system is highly developed. The subsidiaries of the three major Israeli bank-groups are represented in many parts of the world.

In 1996 Israel recorded a visible trade deficit of US $8,069m., and there was a deficit of $6,298m. on the current account of the balance of payments. In 1994 the principal source of imports was the USA, which was also the principal market for exports. Other major trading partners are the United Kingdom, Germany, Belgium, Italy, Japan and Switzerland. The principal exports in 1994 were worked diamonds, machinery and parts, chemical products, and clothing. The principal imports were machinery and parts, rough diamonds, chemicals and related products, crude petroleum and petroleum products and vehicles. In 1994 trade, services and finance contributed 41.3% of the GDP of the business sector.

The budget for 1995 set revenue and expenditure to balance at 149,393m. new shekels. Government revenue each year normally includes some US $3,000m. in economic and military aid from the USA. At 31 December 1995 Israel's gross foreign debt amounted to $45,189m., of which $23,251m. was government debt. In that year the cost of debt-servicing was $5,150m., equivalent to 17.9% of revenue from exports of goods and services. During 1990–95 consumer prices rose by an annual average rate of 12.8%. At the end of 1995 the unemployment rate stood at 6.9%.

The most significant factor affecting the Israeli economy in the 1990s has been the large number of Jewish immigrants arriving in the country from the former USSR. Among other things, large-scale immigration has led to a substantial increase in the population, additional flexibility in the labour market and greater opportunity for investment. GDP has been boosted by growth in construction, especially the residential sector. However, it is unclear whether high growth can be maintained into the medium term. Economic problems that the Government has not yet brought entirely under control include a huge trade deficit and a high—though manageable—rate of inflation. The Government is committed to an extensive programme of privatization and to welfare reform. These policies were the focus of several general strikes during 1997 which caused widespread disruption within Israel.

The bulk of Israel's foreign trade is with the USA and members of the EU. The progress that had been achieved in the Middle East peace process had led to some improvement in relations with other Middle Eastern states, notably Jordan and the member states of the Gulf Co-operation Council. However, in March 1997 the members of the League of Arab States voted to restore their economic boycott of Israel as a result of Israel's decision to build a settlement in East Jerusalem. A comprehensive peace settlement might in future alter the pattern of Israeli foreign trade, but this will not occur before the 21st century.

Social Welfare

There is a highly advanced system of social welfare. Under the National Insurance Law, the State provides retirement pensions, benefits for industrial injury and maternity, and allowances for large families. The Histadrut (General Federation of Labour), to which about 85% of all Jewish workers in Israel belong, provides sickness benefits and medical care. The Ministry of Social Welfare provides for general assistance, relief grants, child care and other social services. In 1983 Israel had 11,895 physicians, equivalent to one for every 339 inhabitants, one of the best doctor-patient ratios in the world. In 1992 there were 209 hospitals (of which 79 were private) and 30,695 beds. Of total budgetary expenditure by the central Government in 1995, 2,470m. new shekels (1.7%) was allocated to the Ministry of Health, and a further 15,826m. new shekels (10.6%) was given to the Ministry of Labour and Social Welfare.

Education

Israel has high standards of literacy and educational services. Free compulsory education is provided for all children between five and 15 years of age. Primary education is provided for all children between five and 10 years of age. There is also secondary, vocational and agricultural education. Post-primary education is also free, and it lasts six years, comprising two cycles of three years. Enrolment at primary and secondary schools in 1993 was equivalent to 96% of children aged six to 17. There are six universities, one institute of technology and one institute of science (the Weizmann Institute), which incorporates a graduate school of science. In 1995 budgetary expenditure on education, culture and sports, by the central Government was 17,046m. new shekels (11.4% of total spending).

Public Holidays

The Sabbath starts at sunset on Friday and ends at nightfall on Saturday. The Jewish year 5759 begins on 21 September 1998, and the year 5760 on 11 September 1999.

1998: 11–17 April (Passover—public holidays on first and last days of festival), 30 April (Independence Day), 31 May (Shavuot), 21–22 September (Rosh Hashanah, Jewish New Year), 30 September (Yom Kippur), 5–11 October (Succot).

1999: 1–7 April (Passover, see 1998), 21 April (Independence Day), 21 May (Shavuot), 11–12 September (Rosh Hashanah, Jewish New Year), 20 September (Yom Kippur), 25 September–1 October (Succot).

(The Jewish festivals and fast days commence in the evening of the dates given.)

Islamic holidays are observed by Muslim Arabs, and Christian holidays by the Christian Arab community.

Weights and Measures

The metric system is in force.

1 dunum = 1,000 sq metres.

Statistical Survey

Source: Central Bureau of Statistics, POB 13015, Hakirya, Romema, Jerusalem 91130; tel. 2-553553; fax 2-553325.

Area and Population

AREA, POPULATION AND DENSITY

Area (sq km)	
Land	21,501
Inland water	445
Total	21,946*
Population (*de jure*; census results)†	
20 May 1972	3,147,683
4 June 1983	
Males	2,011,590
Females	2,026,030
Total	4,037,620
Population (*de jure*; official estimates at 31 December)†	
1994	5,471,500
1995	5,609,100
1996	5,759,400
Density (per sq km) at 31 December 1996	262.4

* 8,473.4 sq miles. Area includes East Jerusalem, annexed by Israel in June 1967, and the Golan sub-district (1,176 sq km), annexed by Israel in December 1981.

† Including the population of East Jerusalem and Israeli residents in certain other areas under Israeli military occupation since June 1967. Beginning in 1981, figures also include non-Jews in the Golan sub-district, an Israeli-occupied area of Syrian territory. Census results exclude adjustment for underenumeration.

ADMINISTERED TERRITORIES*

	Area (sq km)	Estimated population (31 December 1993)
Golan	1,176	29,000
Judaea and Samaria	5,879	1,084,400‡
Gaza Area†	378	748,900‡
Total	7,433	1,862,300

The area figures in this table refer to 1 October 1973. No later figures are available.

* The area and population of the Administered Territories have changed as a result of the October 1973 war.

† Not including El-Arish and Sinai which, as of April 1979 and April 1982 respectively, were returned to Egypt.

‡ Excluding Israelis in Jewish localities. The population in this category at 31 December 1993 totalled 111,600 in Judaea and Samaria, and 4,800 in the Gaza Area.

POPULATION BY RELIGION (estimates, 31 December 1994)

	Number	%
Jews	4,441,100	81.17
Muslims	781,500	14.28
Christians	157,300	2.87
Druze and others	91,700	1.68
Total	5,471,500	100.00

PRINCIPAL TOWNS (estimated population at 31 December 1994)

Jerusalem (capital)	578,800*	Beersheba	147,900
Tel-Aviv—Jaffa	355,200	Netanya	144,900
Haifa	246,700	Bat Yam	142,300
Holon	163,700	Bene Beraq	127,100
Rishon LeZiyyon	160,200	Ramat Gan	122,200
Petach-Tikva	152,000		

* Including East Jerusalem, annexed in June 1967.

BIRTHS, MARRIAGES AND DEATHS*

	Registered live births		Registered marriages		Registered deaths	
	Number	Rate (per 1,000)	Number	Rate (per 1,000)	Number	Rate (per 1,000)
1988	100,454	22.6	31,218	7.0	29,176	6.6
1989	100,757	22.3	32,303	7.1	28,600	6.3
1990	103,349	22.2	31,746	6.8	28,734	6.2
1991	105,725	21.4	32,291	6.5	31,266	6.3
1992	110,062	21.5	32,769	6.4	33,327	6.5
1993	112,330	21.3	34,344	6.5	33,000	6.3
1994	114,543	21.2	n.a.	n.a.	33,535	6.2
1995	116,412	21.0	n.a.	n.a.	35,117	6.3

* Including East Jerusalem.

Expectation of life (years at birth, 1993): Males 75.3; Females 79.1 (Source: UN, *Demographic Yearbook.*)

IMMIGRATION*

	1992	1993	1994
Immigrants:			
on immigrant visas	70,580	68,624	69,226
on tourist visas†	5,825	7,650	9,930
Potential immigrants:			
on potential immigrant visas	103	91	36
on tourist visas†	522	440	652
Total	77,057	76,805	79,844

* Excluding immigrating citizens (2,868 in 1992; 3,467 in 1993; 3,315 in 1994) and Israeli residents returning from abroad.
† Figures refer to tourists who changed their status to immigrants or potential immigrants.

ECONOMICALLY ACTIVE POPULATION (annual averages, '000 persons aged 15 years and over, excluding armed forces)*

	1994	1995	1996
Agriculture, forestry and fishing	62.3	57.2	51.0
Mining and quarrying	5.7	404.6	405.1
Manufacturing	390.4		
Electricity and water	20.3	19.1	18.5
Construction	118.0	140.9	150.0
Trade, restaurants and hotels	280.8	244.6	n.a.
Transport, storage and communications	109.0	115.0	124.3
Financing and business services	206.4	224.3	n.a.
Public and community services	667.3	515.5	520.6
Personal and other services		125.3	125.1
Activities not adequately defined	11.2	n.a.	n.a.
Total employed	1,871.4	1,967.9	2,012.8
Unemployed	158.3	133.0	144.0
Total civilian labour force	2,029.7	2,100.9	2,156.8
Males	1,162.0	n.a.	n.a.
Females	867.7	n.a.	n.a.

* Figures are estimated independently, so the totals may not be the sum of the component parts.

Agriculture

PRINCIPAL CROPS ('000 metric tons)

	1994	1995	1996
Wheat	103	180	150
Barley	1	7	7*
Potatoes	272	281	280*
Groundnuts (in shell)	24	24	24*
Cottonseed	55	70	70*
Olives	27	37	37*
Cabbages	76	69	69*
Tomatoes	430	504	504*
Pumpkins, squash and gourds*	34	34	34
Cucumbers*	85	85	85
Peppers (green)*	55	55	55
Onions (dry)	67	100	100*
Carrots	88	71	71*
Watermelons*	125	125	125
Melons*	90	90	90
Grapes	80	86	86*
Apples	86	134	134*
Peaches*	59	59	59
Oranges	357	381	381*
Tangerines, mandarins, clementines and satsumas	100	130	130*
Lemons and limes	26	27	27*
Grapefruit	338	404	404*
Avocados*	50	50	50
Bananas	90	105	105*
Strawberries*	13	13	13
Cotton (lint)	31	43	43*

* FAO estimate(s).

Source: FAO, *Production Yearbook*.

LIVESTOCK ('000 head, year ending September)

	1994	1995	1996*
Cattle	368	379	379
Pigs	113*	109*	105
Sheep	339	352	352
Goats	96	91	90
Poultry	27,000*	27,000*	27,000

* FAO estimate(s).

Source: FAO, *Production Yearbook*.

LIVESTOCK PRODUCTS ('000 metric tons)

	1994	1995	1996
Beef and veal	37	37*	37*
Mutton and lamb*	5	5	5
Pig meat*	8	8	8
Poultry meat	227	227*	227*
Cows' milk	1,073	1,136	1,136*
Sheep's milk	17	17	17*
Goats' milk	13	12	12*
Cheese*	86	86	86
Butter	5	4	4*
Hen eggs	117	102†	98†
Honey	2	2	2*

* FAO estimate(s). † Unofficial figure.

Source: FAO, *Production Yearbook*.

Forestry

ROUNDWOOD REMOVALS
(FAO estimates, '000 cubic metres, excl. bark)

	1992	1993	1994
Sawlogs, veneer logs and logs for sleepers	36	36	36
Pulpwood	32	32	32
Other industrial wood	32	32	32
Fuel wood	13	13	13
Total	113	113	113

Source: FAO, *Yearbook of Forest Products*.

Fishing

(metric tons, live weight)

	1993	1994	1995
Inland waters	15,579	17,159	17,410
Mediterranean and Black Sea	3,387	3,295	3,154
Indian Ocean	80	—	—
Total catch	19,046	20,454	20,564

Source: FAO, *Yearbook of Fishery Statistics*.

Mining

	1992	1993	1994
Crude petroleum (million litres)	7.8	5.9	4.5
Natural gas (million cu m)	23	24	21.3
Phosphate rock ('000 metric tons)	2,372	2,662	2,779
Potash ('000 metric tons)	2,086	2,139	2,073

Industry

SELECTED PRODUCTS
('000 metric tons, unless otherwise stated)

	1992	1993	1994
Refined vegetable oils (metric tons)	56,463	57,558	45,447
Margarine	35.1	33.8	24.7
Wine ('000 litres)	12,373	12,733	n.a.
Beer ('000 litres)	51,078	58,681	50,750
Cigarettes (metric tons)	5,742	5,525	5,638
Newsprint (metric tons)	0	247	0
Writing and printing paper (metric tons)	66,334	65,426	65,790
Other paper (metric tons)	32,368	30,446	28,985
Cardboard (metric tons)	92,072	95,108	103,142
Rubber tyres ('000)	892	854	966
Ammonia (metric tons)	41,072	n.a.	n.a.
Ammonium sulphate (metric tons)	12,444	n.a.	n.a.
Sulphuric acid	138	n.a.	n.a.
Chlorine (metric tons)	33,912	35,241	37,555
Caustic soda (metric tons)	29,459	29,851	32,765
Polyethylene (metric tons)	128,739	144,147	126,979
Paints (metric tons)	58,963	57,429	53,260
Cement	3,960	4,536	4,800
Commercial vehicles (number)	852	836	1,260
Electricity (million kWh)	24,731	26,042	28,327

Finance

CURRENCY AND EXCHANGE RATES

Monetary Units

100 agorot (singular: agora) = 1 new sheqel (plural: sheqalim) or shekel.

Sterling and Dollar Equivalents (30 September 1997)

£1 sterling = 5.649 new shekels;
US $1 = 3.497 new shekels;
100 new shekels = £17.70 = $28.60.

Average Exchange Rate (new shekels per US $)

1994 3.0111
1995 3.0113
1996 3.1917

Note: The new shekel, worth 1,000 of the former units, was introduced on 1 January 1986.

CENTRAL GOVERNMENT BUDGET
(estimates, million new shekels)

Revenue	1993	1994	1995
Ordinary budget	73,546	88,983	109,485
Income tax and property tax	27,553	30,550	40,600
Customs and excise	1,691	1,600	1,450
Purchase tax	5,552	6,724	7,600
Employers' tax	517	700	730
Value added tax	17,730	21,088	25,290
Other taxes	6,141	8,085	10,820
Interest	1,374	1,892	2,080
Transfer from development budget	10,157	14,548	17,065
Other receipts	2,831	3,796	3,850
Development budget	31,763	39,498	39,908
Foreign loans	13,480	16,820	18,564
Internal loans	17,434	26,039	25,471
Transfer to ordinary budget	–10,157	–14,338	–17,065
Other receipts	11,006	10,977	12,938
Total	105,309	128,481	149,393

Expenditure*	1993	1994	1995
Ordinary account	73,547	88,983	109,485
Ministry of Finance	609	686	860
Ministry of Defence	19,164	20,546	25,297
Ministry of Health	1,390	1,808	2,470
Ministry of Education, Culture and Sports	9,267	12,575	17,046
Ministry of Police	1,638	1,887	2,597
Ministry of Labour and Social Welfare	11,153	13,823	15,826
Other ministries†	5,491	5,847	7,297
Interest	14,193	16,342	19,712
Pensions and compensations	1,614	2,026	2,676
Transfers to local authorities	1,498	1,657	2,750
Subsidies	3,472	3,130	3,960
Reserves	–	3,134	3,172
Other expenditures	4,058	5,522	5,822
Development budget	31,763	39,498	39,908
Agriculture	1,932	17	19
Industry, trade and tourism	373	451	617
Housing	4,688	3,890	4,123
Public buildings	1,083	941	1,003
Development of energy resources	5	—	—
Debt repayment	17,559	28,690	26,304
Other expenditures	6,123	5,509	7,842
Total	105,309	128,481	149,393

* Does not include the entire defence budget.

† Includes the President, Prime Minister, State Comptroller and the Knesset.

CENTRAL BANK RESERVES (US $ million at 31 December)

	1994	1995	1996
Gold*	0.4	0.5	0.4
IMF special drawing rights	0.4	0.6	1.4
Foreign exchange	6,792.0	8,118.7	11,413.2
Total	6,792.8	8,119.8	11,415.0

* Valued at SDR 35 per troy ounce.

Source: IMF, *International Financial Statistics.*

MONEY SUPPLY (million new shekels at 31 December)

	1994	1995	1996
Currency outside banks	5,467	6,731	7,772
Demand deposits at deposit money banks	8,946	9,870	12,227
Total money (incl. others)	14,523	16,716	n.a.

Source: IMF, *International Financial Statistics.*

COST OF LIVING
(Consumer Price Index, annual averages; base: 1990 = 100)

	1993	1994	1995
Food	135.0	150.3	161.1
Fuel and light	145.9	157.9	176.7
Clothing	125.6	131.3	140.7
Rent	188.2	232.6	265.7
All items (incl. others)	147.8	166.1	182.7

Source: ILO, *Yearbook of Labour Statistics.*

1996: Food 176.6; All items 203.4 (Source: UN, *Monthly Bulletin of Statistics).*

NATIONAL ACCOUNTS (million new shekels at current prices)

National Income and Product (provisional)

	1991	1992	1993
Compensation of employees	69,327	82,703	96,448
Operating surplus	29,153	34,601	38,220
Domestic factor incomes	98,480	117,304	134,668
Consumption of fixed capital	19,307	22,407	26,908
Gross domestic product at factor cost	117,787	139,711	161,576
Indirect taxes	28,483	35,202	38,922
Less Subsidies	3,799	4,901	4,701
GDP in purchasers' values	142,471	170,012	195,797
Factor income received from abroad	4,050	3,785	3,407
Less Factor income paid abroad	7,722	8,726	8,657
Gross national product	138,799	165,071	190,547
Less Consumption of fixed capital	19,307	22,407	26,908
National income in market prices	119,492	142,664	163,639
Other current transfers received from abroad	15,194	17,277	19,567
Less Other current transfers paid abroad	540	719	1,002
National disposable income	134,146	159,222	182,204

Source: UN, *National Accounts Statistics*.

Expenditure on the Gross Domestic Product

	1994	1995	1996
Government final consumption expenditure	61,790	77,695	90,774
Private final consumption expenditure	142,768	161,831	187,831
Increase in stocks	1,071	3,408	2,547
Gross fixed capital formation	52,014	61,393	70,634
Total domestic expenditure	257,643	304,327	351,786
Exports of goods and services	73,292	82,919	93,660
Less Imports of goods and services	107,750	126,074	141,634
GDP in purchasers' values	223,185	261,173	303,812
GDP at constant 1990 prices	132,016	141,328	147,628

Source: IMF, *International Financial Statistics*.

Net Domestic Product by Economic Activity (at factor cost)

	1991	1992	1993
Agriculture, hunting, forestry and fishing	2,648	3,312	3,197
Manufacturing, mining and quarrying	19,917	24,698	29,007
Electricity, gas and water	1,561	1,943	2,263
Construction	7,762	9,549	9,678
Wholesale and retail trade, restaurants and hotels	10,485	12,987	15,581
Transport, storage and communications	7,385	9,129	10,238
Finance, insurance, real estate and business services	24,513	29,421	34,906
Government services	22,875	26,438	30,482
Other community, social and personal services	4,069	4,893	5,683
Statistical discrepancy	581	520	474
Sub-total	101,796	122,890	141,509
Less Imputed bank service charge	4,988	5,273	5,480
Other adjustments (incl. errors and omissions)	1,671	−314	−1,362
Total	98,479	117,303	134,667

Source: UN, *National Accounts Statistics*.

BALANCE OF PAYMENTS (US $ million)

	1994	1995	1996
Exports of goods f.o.b.	16,783	19,146	20,418
Imports of goods f.o.b.	−22,745	−26,840	−28,487
Trade balance	−5,963	−7,694	−8,069
Exports of services	6,649	7,826	8,004
Imports of services	−8,284	−9,392	−10,080
Balance on goods and services	−7,598	−9,261	−10,145
Other income received	1,194	1,855	1,884
Other income paid	−2,924	−3,732	−4,375
Balance on goods, services and income	−9,328	−11,138	−12,636
Current transfers received	5,968	6,107	6,600
Current transfers paid	−229	−251	−262
Current balance	−3,589	−5,282	−6,298
Capital account (net)	1,254	1,408	1,537
Direct investment abroad	−735	−671	−762
Direct investment from abroad	442	1,525	2,016
Portfolio investment assets	−267	118	136
Portfolio investment liabilities	2,796	1,309	2,281
Other investment assets	−1,699	−556	1,217
Other investment liabilities	1,080	2,138	1,098
Net errors and omissions	786	1,260	2,219
Overall balance	69	1,250	3,443

Source: IMF, *International Financial Statistics*.

External Trade

PRINCIPAL COMMODITIES (US $ million)

Imports c.i.f.*	1992	1993	1994
Food and live animals	1,041.1	1,086.0	1,299.2
Crude materials (inedible) except fuels	567.2	552.9	599.3
Mineral fuels, lubricants, etc.	1,464.5	1,521.5	1,439.1
Petroleum, petroleum products, etc.	1,460.9	1,517.5	1,434.5
Crude petroleum oils, etc.	1,327.1	1,349.3	1,242.0
Chemicals and related products	1,753.0	1,848.6	2,056.4
Organic chemicals	394.8	442.9	496.3
Plastic materials, etc.	446.1	442.7	477.7
Basic manufactures	6,010.8	6,555.7	7,544.7
Textile yarn, fabrics, etc.	632.5	692.2	744.2
Non-metallic mineral manufactures	3,502.3	3,952.4	4,602.7
Pearls, precious and semi-precious stone, unworked or worked	3,124.2	3,578.2	4,152.4
Diamonds (excl. sorted industrial diamonds), unmounted	3,078.1	3,541.6	4,124.7
Diamonds, rough, sorted and simply worked	2,586.9	2,997.4	3,485.1
Diamonds, cut, etc., unmounted	491.2	544.2	639.7
Iron and steel	551.2	580.8	607.4
Machinery and transport equipment	5,981.1	6,706.9	8,228.3
Machinery specialized for particular industries	660.7	779.9	893.8
General industrial machinery, equipment and parts	773.5	838.0	994.3
Office machines and automatic data-processing equipment	556.2	620.9	743.7
Telecommunications and sound equipment	421.8	531.7	680.8
Other electrical machinery, apparatus, etc.	1,179.8	1,406.1	1,762.6
Switchgear, parts, etc.	312.6	395.2	513.7
Transistors, valves, etc.	292.8	392.4	502.0
Road vehicles and parts†	1,673.0	1,753.2	2,177.1
Passenger cars, excl. buses	1,049.2	1,003.9	1,257.8
Motor vehicles for goods transport and special purposes	351.5	454.0	588.4
Goods vehicles	329.9	432.0	532.3
Other transport equipment and parts	323.5	370.1	532.7
Aircraft, associated equipment and parts†	151.0	296.9	503.8
Miscellaneous manufactured articles	1,406.5	1,661.6	1,948.2
Total (incl. others)	18,813.6	20,517.7	23,778.9

* Figures exclude military goods. Total imports (in US $ million) were: 20,261 in 1992; 22,623 in 1993; 25,237 in 1994 (Source: IMF, *International Financial Statistics*).

Exports f.o.b.	1992	1993	1994
Food and live animals	788.4	792.2	809.9
Vegetables and fruit	560.9	516.6	516.2
Crude materials (inedible) except fuels	423.3	403.1	469.3
Chemicals and related products	1,759.0	2,079.3	2,316.9
Organic chemicals	495.0	566.8	625.7
Inorganic chemicals	269.3	290.4	281.7
Manufactured fertilizers	296.3	238.1	288.1
Basic manufactures	4,664.0	5,036.7	6,046.4
Textile yarn, fabrics, etc.	334.0	326.7	350.4
Non-metallic mineral manufactures	3,756.6	4,142.7	5,019.0
Pearls, precious and semi-precious stones, unworked or worked	3,730.0	4,113.8	4,967.6
Diamonds (excl. sorted industrial diamonds), unmounted	3,655.3	4,040.1	4,892.2
Diamonds, rough, sorted and simply worked	445.0	398.2	524.6
Diamonds, cut, etc., unmounted	3,210.3	3,642.0	4,367.2
Machinery and transport equipment	3,589.6	4,603.4	5,182.7
Machinery specialized for particular industries	769.3	1,305.7	1,382.3
Printing and bookbinding machinery and parts	304.3	376.3	411.3
Machinery, apparatus and accessories for type-setting, etc.	253.5	319.4	260.1
General industrial machinery, equipment and parts	460.2	461.0	549.8
Office machines and automatic data-processing equipment	436.0	590.7	525.2
Telecommunications and sound equipment	694.2	906.3	1,197.9
Other electrical machinery, apparatus, etc.	743.8	807.6	965.3
Transistors, valves, etc.	335.3	385.5	407.3
Electronic microcircuits	318.7	366.5	397.6
Road vehicles and other transport equipment and parts	350.6	382.5	422.8
Aircraft, associated equipment and parts†	294.1	340.9	355.9
Miscellaneous manufactured articles	1,742.1	1,772.5	1,961.4
Clothing (excl. footwear)	593.6	571.0	627.4
Professional, scientific and controlling instruments, etc.	270.7	278.3	321.9
Jewellery, goldsmiths' and silversmiths' wares, etc.	390.7	419.3	413.2
Jewellery of gold, silver or platinum-group metals (excl. watches and watch cases) and goldsmiths' or silversmiths' wares, incl. set gems	388.9	417.2	408.2
Articles of jewellery and parts, of precious metal or rolled precious metal	387.1	400.0	379.7
Total (incl. others)	13,082.3	14,825.3	16,934.0

† Excluding tyres, engines and electrical parts.

Source: UN, *International Trade Statistics Yearbook*.

PRINCIPAL TRADING PARTNERS (US $ million)

Imports (excl. military goods)	1992	1993	1994
Belgium-Luxembourg	2,391.0	2,503.2	3,038.4
France	844.7	857.6	1,058.0
Germany	2,246.9	2,132.2	2,467.5
Hong Kong	183.5	248.8	281.1
Italy	1,307.9	1,495.7	1,848.1
Japan	998.2	1,047.7	963.6
Korea, Republic	102.6	137.9	282.4
Netherlands	615.7	700.5	789.2
Southern African Customs Union	261.5	244.0	234.9
Spain	203.8	208.5	398.0
Sweden	206.4	286.2	326.7
Switzerland-Liechtenstein	1,265.6	1,432.0	1,447.8
United Kingdom	1,459.0	1,730.4	2,004.7
USA	3,229.5	3,634.5	4,256.3

Exports	1992	1993	1994
Australia	115.6	134.7	180.4
Belgium-Luxembourg	650.4	797.5	910.4
France	620.5	576.1	584.0
Germany	762.7	786.6	850.3
Hong Kong	666.4	722.5	843.8
India	127.5	228.3	361.9
Italy	459.6	437.3	505.2
Japan	689.1	769.0	989.4
Netherlands	553.8	554.0	633.1
Philippines	109.9	187.1	207.9
Russia	67.2	118.5	192.5
Spain	242.8	199.2	236.3
Switzerland-Liechtenstein	231.1	271.9	346.9
Thailand	91.1	146.7	248.9
United Kingdom	1,004.9	815.9	848.9
USA	3,995.8	4,621.7	5,262.4

Transport

RAILWAYS (traffic)

	1993	1994	1995
Freight ton-km (million)	1,072	1,079	1,176
Passenger-km (million)	215	238	267

ROAD TRAFFIC (vehicles in use)

	1994	1995	1996
Passenger cars	1,057,522	1,121,730	1,184,765
Buses and coaches	10,429	10,794	11,214
Lorries and vans	246,824	261,799	277,880
Motorcycles and mopeds	58,323	64,695	69,011

Source: International Road Federation, *World Road Statistics*.

SHIPPING

Merchant Fleet (registered at 31 December)

	1994	1995	1996
Number of vessels	57	55	54
Displacement ('000 grt)	645.7	598.7	678.9

Source: Lloyd's Register of Shipping, *World Fleet Statistics*.

International Sea-borne Freight Traffic* ('000 metric tons)

	1994	1995	1996
Goods loaded	11,675	10,880	10,680
Goods unloaded	22,929	27,370	25,900

* Excluding petroleum.

CIVIL AVIATION (El Al revenue flights only, '000)

	1992	1993	1994
Kilometres flown	51,064	55,416	60,634
Revenue passenger-km	8,492,000	8,949,000	9,925,000
Mail (tons)	1,353	1,206	1,246

Tourism

	1994	1995	1996
Tourist arrivals	1,838,700	2,214,646	2,100,051
Tourist receipts (U $ million)	2,266	2,784	2,771

Communications Media

	1993	1994	1995
Radio receivers ('000 in use)	2,510	2,610	2,700
Television receivers ('000 in use)	1,430	1,500	1,600
Telephones ('000 main lines in use)	1,958	2,138	n.a.
Telefax stations (number in use)	80,000	n.a.	n.a.
Mobile cellular telephones (subscribers)	64,484	140,000	n.a.
Daily newspapers	n.a.	34	34*

* Estimate.

Book production (1992): 4,608 titles; 9,368,000 copies.

Non-daily newspapers (1988): 80.

Other periodicals (1985): 807.

Sources: UNESCO, *Statistical Yearbook*, and UN, *Statistical Yearbook*.

Education

(1994/95)

	Schools	Pupils	Teachers
Jewish			
Kindergarten	n.a.	287,500	n.a.
Primary schools	1,323	539,270	45,132
Intermediate schools	354	142,664	17,829
Secondary schools	603	242,363	32,041
Vocational schools	304	105,226	n.a.
Agricultural schools	23	6,840	n.a.
Teacher training colleges	n.a.	18,830	n.a.
Others (handicapped)	209	12,946	4,028
Arab			
Kindergarten	n.a.	25,500	n.a.
Primary schools	324	146,557	8,639
Intermediate schools	95	39,653	2,840
Secondary schools	98	42,032	3,468
Vocational schools	51	9,835	n.a.
Agricultural schools	2	161	n.a.
Teacher training colleges	n.a.	1,193	n.a.
Others (handicapped)	40	2,228	484

Directory

The Constitution

There is no written constitution. In June 1950 the Knesset voted to adopt a state constitution by evolution over an unspecified period. A number of laws, including the Law of Return (1950), the Nationality Law (1952), the State President (Tenure) Law (1952), the Education Law (1953) and the 'Yad-va-Shem' Memorial Law (1953), are considered as incorporated into the state Constitution. Other constitutional laws are: The Law and Administration Ordinance (1948), the Knesset Election Law (1951), the Law of Equal Rights for Women (1951), the Judges Act (1953), the National Service and National Insurance Acts (1953), and the Basic Law (The Knesset) (1958). The provisions of constitutional legislation that affect the main organs of government are summarized below:

THE PRESIDENT

The President is elected by the Knesset for a maximum of two five-year terms.

Ten or more Knesset members may propose a candidate for the Presidency.

Voting will be by secret ballot.

The President may not leave the country without the consent of the Government.

The President may resign by submitting his resignation in writing to the Speaker.

The President may be relieved of his duties by the Knesset for misdemeanour.

The Knesset is entitled to decide by a two-thirds majority that the President is too incapacitated owing to ill health to fulfil his duties permanently.

The Speaker of the Knesset will act for the President when the President leaves the country, or when he cannot perform his duties owing to ill health.

THE KNESSET

The Knesset is the parliament of the state. There are 120 members.

It is elected by general, national, direct, equal, secret and proportional elections.

Every Israeli national of 18 years or over shall have the right to vote in elections to the Knesset unless a court has deprived him of that right by virtue of any law.

Every Israeli national of 21 and over shall have the right to be elected to the Knesset unless a court has deprived him of that right by virtue of any law.

The following shall not be candidates: the President of the state; the two Chief Rabbis; a judge (shofet) in office; a judge (dayan) of a religious court; the State Comptroller; the Chief of the General Staff of the Defence Army of Israel; rabbis and ministers of other religions in office; senior state employees and senior army officers of such ranks and in such functions as shall be determined by law.

The term of office of the Knesset shall be four years.

The elections to the Knesset shall take place on the third Tuesday of the month of Cheshven in the year in which the tenure of the outgoing Knesset ends.

Election day shall be a day of rest, but transport and other public services shall function normally.

Results of the elections shall be published within 14 days.

The Knesset shall elect from among its members a Chairman and Vice-Chairman.

The Knesset shall elect from among its members permanent committees, and may elect committees for specific matters.

The Knesset may appoint commissions of inquiry to investigate matters designated by the Knesset.

The Knesset shall hold two sessions a year; one of them shall open within four weeks after the Feast of the Tabernacles, the other within four weeks after Independence Day; the aggregate duration of the two sessions shall not be less than eight months.

The outgoing Knesset shall continue to hold office until the convening of the incoming Knesset.

The members of the Knesset shall receive a remuneration as provided by law.

THE GOVERNMENT

The Government shall tender its resignation to the President immediately after his election, but shall continue with its duties until the formation of a new government. After consultation with representatives of the parties in the Knesset, the President shall charge one of the members with the formation of a government. The Government shall be composed of a Prime Minister (directly elected from May 1996) and a number of ministers from among the Knesset members or from outside the Knesset. After it has been chosen, the Government shall appear before the Knesset and shall be considered as formed after having received a vote of confidence. Within seven days of receiving a vote of confidence, the Prime Minister and the other ministers shall swear allegiance to the State of Israel and its Laws and undertake to carry out the decisions of the Knesset.

The Government

HEAD OF STATE

President: Ezer Weizman (took office 13 May 1993).

THE CABINET

(February 1998)

Prime Minister, Minister of Housing and Construction and of Foreign Affairs: Binyamin Netanyahu (elected 29 May 1996) (Likud).

Deputy Prime Minister, Minister of Agriculture and Rural Development and Minister of the Environment: Rafael Eitan (Tzomet).

Deputy Prime Minister and Minister of Tourism: Moshe Katzav (Likud).

Minister of the Interior: Eli Suissa (Shas).

Minister of Trade and Industry: Natan Sharansky (Israel B'Aliyah).

Minister of Finance: Yaacov Ne'eman (Likud).

Minister of Defence: Itzhak Mordechai (Likud).

Minister of Communications: Limor Livnat (Likud).

Minister of Transport and Energy, of Education, Culture and Sport, and of Religious Affairs: Itzhak Levi (NRP).

Minister of Justice: Tzachi Hanegbi (Likud).

Minister of Health: Yehoshua Matza (Likud).

Minister of Science: Michael Eitan (Likud).

Minister of Immigrant Absorption: Yuli Edelstein (Israel B'Aliyah).

Minister of National Infrastructure: Ariel Sharon (Likud).

Minister of Labour and Welfare: Eliyahu Ishai (Shas).

Minister of Internal Security: Avigdor Kahalani (Third Way).

MINISTRIES

Office of the Prime Minister: POB 187, 3 Rehov Kaplan, Kiryat Ben-Gurion, Jerusalem 91919; tel. 2-6705555; fax 2-6512631.

Ministry of Agriculture: POB 7011, 12 Arania St, Kiryat Ben-Gurion, Tel-Aviv 61070; tel. 3-6971444; fax 3-6967891.

Ministry of Communications: 23 Jaffa St, Jerusalem 91999; tel. 2-6706320; fax 2-6706372.

Ministry of Defence: Kaplan St, Hakirya, Tel-Aviv 67659; tel. 3-5692010; telex 32147; fax 3-6916940.

Ministry of Economy and Planning: POB 13169, 3 Rehov Kaplan, Kiryat Ben-Gurion, Jerusalem 91131; tel. 2-6705111; fax 2-6536101.

Ministry of Education, Culture and Sport: POB 292, 34 Shivtei Israel St, Jerusalem 91911; tel. 2-5603700; fax 2-5603706; e-mail yairlevin@netvision.net.il.

Ministry of Energy and Infrastructure: POB 13106, 234 Jaffa St, Jerusalem 91130; tel. 2-316111; fax 2-381444.

Ministry of the Environment: POB 34033, 5 Kanfei Nesharim St, Givat Shaul, Jerusalem 95464; tel. 2-6553777; telex 25629; fax 2-6535934.

Ministry of Finance: POB 13191, 1 Rehov Kaplan, Kiryat Ben-Gurion, Jerusalem 91008; tel. 2-5317111; telex 25216; fax 2-5637891.

Ministry of Foreign Affairs: Hakirya, Romema, Jerusalem 91950; tel. 2-5303111; fax 2-5303506.

Ministry of Health: POB 1176, 2 Ben-Tabai St, Jerusalem 91010; tel. 2-6705705; telex 26138; fax 2-6796491.

Ministry of Housing and Construction: POB 18110, Kiryat Hamemshala (East), Jerusalem 91180; tel. 2-5825501; fax 2-5811904.

Ministry of Immigrant Absorption: POB 13061, 13 Rehov Kaplan, Kiryat Ben-Gurion, Jerusalem 91006; tel. 2-6752696; fax 2-5618138.

Ministry of the Interior: POB 6158, 2 Rehov Kaplan, Kiryat Ben-Gurion, Jerusalem 91061; tel. 2-6701411; fax 2-6701628.

Ministry of Internal Security: POB 18182, Kiryat Hamemshala, Jerusalem 91181; tel. 2-5308003; fax 2-5847872.

Ministry of Justice: 29 Rehov Salahadin, Jerusalem 91010; tel. 2-6708511; fax 2-6708714.

Ministry of Labour and Social Welfare: POB 915, 2 Rehov Kaplan, Kiryat Ben-Gurion, Jerusalem 91008; tel. 2-6752311; fax 2-6752803.

Ministry of National Infrastructure: POB 13106, 234 Jaffa St, Jerusalem 91130; tel. 2-5316111; fax 2-5380855; also responsible for **Israel Lands Administration:** 6 Shamai St, Jerusalem 94631; tel. 2-5208422; fax 2-5234960.

Ministry of Police: POB 18182, Bldg No. 3, Sheikh Jarrah, Kiryat Hamemshala (East), Jerusalem 91181; tel. 2-308088; fax 2-826770.

Ministry of Religious Affairs: POB 13059, 236 Jaffa St, Jerusalem 91130; tel. 2-5311175; fax 2-5311183.

Ministry of Science: POB 18195, Kiryat Hamemshala, Hamizrachit, Government Offices, Bldg 3, Jerusalem 91181; tel. 2-5825222; fax 2-5825725; e-mail nps@most.gov.il.

Ministry of Tourism: POB 1018, 24 Rehov King George, Jerusalem 91009; tel. 2-6754811; fax 2-6253407.

Ministry of Trade and Industry: POB 299, 30 Rehov Agron, Jerusalem 91002; tel. 2-6220339; fax 2-6259274.

Ministry of Transport: Klal Bldg, 97 Jaffa St, Jerusalem 91000; tel. 2-5319211; fax 2-5319693.

Legislature

KNESSET

Speaker: DAN TICHON.

General Election, 29 May 1996

Party	Seats
Labour	34
Likud-Tzomet-Gesher	32
Shas	10
National Religious Party	9
Meretz (an alliance of Ratz, Shinui and the United Workers' Party)	9
Israel B'Aliyah	7
Hadash	5
United Torah Judaism	4
The Third Way	4
United Arab List	4
Moledet	2
Total	120

According to Israel's General Election Committee, 79.7% of the 3.9m.-strong electorate participated in the legislative elections which were held on 29 May 1996. Likud, the Tzomet Party and Gesher announced a formal electoral alliance prior to voting. In 1996, for the first time, the position of Prime Minister became elective and voting to select the leader of the government took place at the same time as that to return deputies to the Knesset. In the election of the Prime Minister the leader of Likud, Binyamin Netanyahu, received 50.5% (1,501,023) of the total number of valid votes cast while Shimon Peres, the leader of the Labour Party, received 49.5% (1,471,566). Almost 5% of the votes cast in the election of the Prime Minister were reported to have been spoiled.

Political Organizations

Agudat Israel: POB 513, Jerusalem; tel. 2-385251; fax 2-385145; orthodox Jewish party; stands for strict observance of Jewish religious law; Leaders AVRAHAM SHAPIRO, MENACHEM PORUSH.

Agudat Israel World Organization (AIWO): POB 326, Hacherut Sq., Jerusalem 91002; tel. 2-5384357; f. 1912 at Congress of Orthodox Jewry, Kattowitz, Germany (now Katowice, Poland), to help solve the problems facing Jewish people all over the world; more than 500,000 mems in 25 countries; Pres. Rabbi Dr I. LEWIN (New York); Chair. Rabbi J. M. ABRAMOWITZ (Jerusalem), Rabbi M. SHERER (New York); Gen. Sec. ABRAHAM HIRSCH (Jerusalem).

Council for Peace and Security: f. 1988 by four retd Israeli generals: Maj.-Gen. AHARON YARIV, Maj.-Gen. ORI ORR, Brig.-Gen. YORAM AGMON and Brig.-Gen. EPHRAIM SNEH; MOSHE AMIRAV of Centre Party a founder mem.; aims: an Israeli withdrawal from the Occupied Territories in return for a peace treaty with the Arab nations.

Degel Hatora: 103 Rehov Beit Vegan, Jerusalem; tel. 2-418167; fax 2-438105; f. 1988 as breakaway from Agudat Israel; orthodox Western Jews; Chair. AVRAHAM RAVITZ.

Democratic Arab Party (DAP): Nazareth; tel. 06-560937; f. 1988; aims: to unify Arab political forces so as to influence Palestinian and Israeli policy; international recognition of the Palestinian people's right to self-determination; the withdrawal of Israel from all territories occupied in 1967, including East Jerusalem; the DAP also aims to achieve full civil equality between Arab and Jewish citizens of Israel, to eliminate discrimination and improve the social, economic and political conditions of the Arab minority in Israel; Chair. ABD AL-WAHAB DARAWSHAH.

Gesher (Bridge): f. 1996; Leader DAVID LEVY.

Gush Emunim (Bloc of the Faithful): f. 1967; engaged in unauthorized establishment of Jewish settlements in the Occupied Territories; Leader Rabbi MOSHE LEVINGER.

Hadash (Democratic Front for Peace and Equality): POB 26205, 3 Rehov Hashikma, Tel-Aviv; tel. 3-827492; descended from the Socialist Workers' Party of Palestine (f. 1919); renamed Communist Party of Palestine 1921, Communist Party of Israel (Maki) 1948; pro-Soviet anti-Zionist group formed New Communist Party of Israel (Rakah) 1965; Jewish Arab membership; aims for a socialist system in Israel, a lasting peace between Israel and the Arab countries and the Palestinian Arab people, favours full implementation of UN Security Council Resolutions 242 and 338, Israeli withdrawal from all Arab territories occupied since 1967, formation of a Palestinian Arab state in the West Bank and Gaza Strip, recognition of national rights of state of Israel and Palestine people, democratic rights and defence of working class interests, and demands an end to discrimination against Arab minority in Israel and against oriental Jewish communities; Sec.-Gen. MEIR VILNER.

Israel B'Aliyah: f. 1995; campaigns for immigrants' rights; Leader NATAN SHARANSKY.

Israel Labour Party: 110 Ha'yarkon St, Tel-Aviv 61032; tel. 3-5209222; fax 3-5271744; f. 1968 as a merger of the three Labour groups, Mapai, Rafi and Achdut Ha'avoda; a Zionist democratic socialist party; Chair. EHUD BARAK.

Kahane Chai (Kahane Lives): POB 5379, 111 Agripas St, Jerusalem; tel. 2-231081; f. 1977 as 'Kach' (Thus); right-wing religious nationalist party; advocates creation of a Torah state and expulsion of all Arabs from Israel and the annexation of the Occupied Territories; Leader Rabbi BINYAMIN ZEEV KAHANE.

Likud (Consolidation): 38 Rehov King George, Tel-Aviv 61231; tel. 3-5630666; fax 3-5282901; f. September 1973; is a parliamentary bloc of Herut (Freedom; f. 1948; Leader ITZHAK SHAMIR; Sec.-Gen. MOSHE ARENS), the Liberal Party of Israel (f. 1961; Chair. AVRAHAM SHARIR), Laam (For the Nation) (f. 1976; fmrly led by YIGAEL HURWITZ, who left the coalition to form his own party, Ometz, before the 1984 general election), Ahdut (a one-man faction, HILLEL SEIDEL), Tami (f. 1981; represents the interests of Sephardic Jews; Leader AHARON UZAN), which joined Likud in June 1987, and an independent faction (f. 1990; Leader ITZHAK MODAI), which formed the nucleus of a new Party for the Advancement of the Zionist Idea; Herut and the Liberal Party formally merged in August 1988 to form the Likud-National Liberal Movement; aims: territorial integrity (advocates retention of all the territory of post-1922 mandatory Palestine); absorption of newcomers; a social order based on freedom and justice, elimination of poverty and want; development of an economy that will ensure a decent standard of living; improvement of the environment and the quality of life; Leader of Likud BINYAMIN NETANYAHU.

Meretz (Vitality): an alliance of Ratz, Shinui and the United Workers' Party; stands for civil rights, electoral reform, welfarism, Palestinian self-determination, separation of religion from the state and a halt to settlement in the Occupied Territories; Leader YOSSI SARID.

Moledet (Homeland): 14 Rehov Yehuda Halevi, Tel-Aviv; tel. 3-654580; f. 1988; right-wing nationalist party; aims: the expulsion ('transfer') of the 1.5m. Palestinians living in the West Bank and Gaza Strip; united with Tehiya—Zionist Revival Movement (see below) in June 1994 as the Moledet—the Eretz Israel Faithful and the Tehiya; Leader Gen. RECHAVAM ZE'EVI.

Movement for the Advancement of the Zionist Idea (MAZI): f. 1990 as breakaway group of Likud; Leader ITZHAK MODAI.

National Religious Party (NRP): 12 Sarei Israel St, Jerusalem tel. 2-377277; fax 2-377757; f. 1902; as the Mizrachi Organization within the Zionist Movement; present name adopted in 1956; stands for strict adherence to Jewish religion and tradition, and strives to achieve the application of religious precepts of Judaism in everyday life; it is also endeavouring to establish the Constitution of Israel on Jewish religious law (the Torah); 126,000 mems; Leader (vacant); Sec.-Gen. ZEVULUN ORLEV.

New Liberal Party: Tel-Aviv; f. 1987 as a merger of three groups: Shinui-Movement for Change (f. 1974 and restored 1978, when Democratic Movement for Change split into two parties; centrist; Leader AMNON RUBINSTEIN), the Centre Liberal Party (f. 1986 by members of the Liberal Party of Israel; Leader ITZHAK BERMAN), and the Independent Liberal Party (f. 1965 by seven Liberal Party of Israel Knesset mems, after the formation of the Herut Movement and Liberal Party of Israel bloc; 20,000 mems; Chair. MOSHE KOL; Gen. Sec. NISSIM ELIAD); Leaders AMNON RUBINSTEIN, ITZHAK BERMAN and MOSHE KOL.

Poale Agudat Israel: f. 1924; working-class Orthodox Judaist party; Leader Dr KALMAN KAHANE.

Political Zionist Opposition (Ometz): f. 1982; one-man party, YIGAEL HURWITZ.

Progressive List for Peace: 5 Simtat Lane, Nes Tziona, Tel-Aviv; tel. 3-662457; fax 3-659474; f. 1984; Jewish-Arab; advocates recognition of the PLO and the establishment of a Palestinian state in the West Bank and the Gaza Strip; Leader MUHAMMAD MI'ARI.

Ratz (Civil Rights and Peace Movement): 21 Tchernihovsky St, Tel-Aviv 63291; tel. 3-5254847; fax 3-5255008; f. 1973; concerned with human and civil rights, opposes discrimination on basis of religion, gender or ethnic identification and advocates a peace settlement with the Arab countries and the Palestinians; Leader Mrs SHULAMIT ALONI.

Religious Zionism Party (Matzad): Tel-Aviv; f. 1983; breakaway group from the National Religious Party; also known as Morasha (Heritage); Leader Rabbi HAIM DRUCKMAN.

Shas (Sephardic Torah Guardians): Beit Abodi, Rehov Hahida, Bene Beraq; tel. 3-579776; f. 1984 by splinter groups from Agudat Israel; ultra-orthodox Jewish party; Spiritual Leader Rabbi ELIEZER SHACH.

Shinui (Centre Party): 10 Ha-Arbaa St, Tel-Aviv 64739; tel. 3-5620118; fax 3-5620139; f. 1974 as a new liberal party; combines a moderate foreign policy with a free-market economic philosophy. Leader AVRAHAM PORAZ.

Tehiya—Zionist Revival Movement: POB 355, 34 Rehov Hahaluts, Jerusalem; tel. 2-259385; f. 1979; aims: Israeli sovereignty over Judaea, Samaria, Gaza; extensive settlement programme; economic independence; uniting of religious and non-religious camps; opposes Camp David accords; united with Moledet in June 1994 (see above); Leaders GERSHON SHAFAT, GEULA COHEN, ELYAQIM HAEZNI, DAMI DAYAN.

Third Way: f. 1995; Leader AVIGDOR KAHALANI.

Tzomet Party: 22 Rehov Huberman, Tel-Aviv; tel. 3-204444; f. 1988; right-wing nationalist party; breakaway group from Tehiya party; Leader RAFAEL EITAN.

United Arab List: Arab party affiliated to Labour Party.

United Torah Judaism: electoral list of four minor ultra-orthodox parties (Moria, Degel Hatora, Poale Agudat Israel, Agudat Israel) formed, prior to 1992 election, to overcome the increase in election threshold from 1% to 1.5% and help to counter the rising influence of the secular Russian vote; Spiritual Leader Rabbi ELIEZER SHACH.

United Workers' Party (Mapam): POB 1777, 4 Rehov Itamar Ben-Avi, Tel-Aviv 61016; tel. 3-6972111; fax 3-6910504; f. 1948; left-wing socialist-Zionist Jewish-Arab party; grouped in Labour-Mapam Alignment with Israel Labour Party from January 1969 until Sept. 1984 when it withdrew in protest over Labour's formation of a Government with Likud; member of the Socialist International; 77,000 mems; Chair. CHANAN EREZ; Sec.-Gen. VICTOR BLIT.

Yahad (Together): f. 1984; advocates a peace settlement with the Arab peoples and the Palestinians; joined the Labour Party parliamentary bloc in January 1987.

Yi'ud: f. 1994; breakaway group from the Tzomet Party.

Diplomatic Representation

EMBASSIES IN ISRAEL

Argentina: 22nd Floor, Diamond Tower, 3A Jabolinsky Rd, Ramat Gan, Tel-Aviv 63571; tel. 3-5759173; fax 3-5759178; Ambassador: JOSÉ MARÍA V. OTEGUI.

Australia: Beit Europa, 4th Floor, 37 Shaul Hamelech Blvd, Tel-Aviv 64928; tel. 3-6950451; telex 33777; fax 3-6968404; Ambassador: IAN WILCOCK.

Austria: POB 11095, 11 Rehov Herman Cohen, Tel-Aviv 61110; tel. 3-5246186; telex 33435; fax 3-5244039; Ambassador: Dr HERBERT KRÖLL.

Belarus: 2 Rehov Kaufman, Tel-Aviv 68012; tel. 3-5102236; fax 3-5102235; Ambassador: MIKHAIL FARFEL.

Belgium: 266 Rehov Hayarkon, Tel-Aviv 63504; tel. 3-6054164; telex 342211; fax 3-5465345; Ambassador: MARK GELEYN.

Bolivia: 7A Rehov Hashalom, Mevasseret Zion 90805; tel. 2-335195; fax 2-335196; Ambassador: Dr MARIO VELARDE DORADO.

Brazil: 2 Rehov Kaplan, Beit Yachin, 8th Floor, Tel-Aviv 64734; tel. 3-6919292; telex 33752; fax 3-6916060; Ambassador: (vacant).

Bulgaria: 9th Floor, 124 Ibn Gvirol, Tel-Aviv 62038; tel. 3-5241751; fax 3-5241798; Ambassador: SVETLOMIR BAEV.

Cameroon: POB 50252, Dan Panorama Hotel, 10 Rehov Kaufman, Tel-Aviv 61500; tel. and fax 3-5190011; Chargé d'affaires a.i.: ETONNDI ESSOMBA.

Canada: 220 Rehov Hayarkon, Tel-Aviv 63405; tel. 3-5272929; fax 3-5272333; Ambassador: (vacant).

Chile: 7 Havakook St, Tel-Aviv 63505; tel. 3-6020130; telex 342189; fax 3-6020133; e-mail echileil@inter.net.il; Ambassador: JOSÉ RODRÍGUEZ ELIZONDO.

China, People's Republic: Tel-Aviv: Ambassador: LIN ZHEN.

Colombia: 52 Rehov Pinkas, Apt 26, Tel-Aviv 62261; tel. 3-449616; telex 342165; Chargé d'affaires a.i.: Dr EUFRACIO MORALES.

Congo, Democratic Republic: Apt 5, 60 Hei Be'Iyar, Kikar Hamedina, Tel-Aviv 62198; tel. 3-452681; telex 371239; Ambassador: Gen. ELUKI MONGA AUNDU.

Costa Rica: 13 Rehov Diskin, Apt 1, Kiryat Wolfson, Jerusalem 92473; tel. 2-5666197; telex 33533; fax 2-5632591; e-mail emcri@netmedia.net.il; Ambassador: MANUEL ENRIQUE LÓPEZ-TRIGO.

Côte d'Ivoire: POB 14371, Kikar Hamédina, 14 Hei Be'Iyar, Tel-Aviv 62093; tel. 3-6963727; telex 341143; fax 3-6968888; Ambassador: LÉON HOUADJA KACOU.

Czech Republic: POB 16361, 23 Rehov Zeitlin, Tel-Aviv 61664; tel. 3-6918282; fax 3-6918286; Ambassador GIŘI SCHNEIDER.

Denmark: POB 21080, 23 Rehov Bnei Moshe, Tel-Aviv 61210; tel. 3-5442144; telex 33514; fax 3-5465502; Ambassador: CARSTEN STAUR.

Dominican Republic: 4 Sderot Shaul Hamelech, Apt 81, Tel-Aviv 64733; tel. 3-6957580; fax 3-6962032; Ambassador: JOSÉ BATLLE-NICOLÁS.

Ecuador: POB 30, Room 211, 'Asia House', 4 Rehov Weizman, Tel-Aviv 64239; tel. 3-258764; telex 342179; fax 3-269437; Ambassador: PAULINA GARCÍA DE LARREA.

Egypt: 54 Rehov Bazel, Tel-Aviv 62744; tel. 3-5464151; telex 361289; fax 3-5441615; Ambassador: MUHAMMAD ABD AL-AZIZ BASSIOUNI.

El Salvador: POB 4005, Jerusalem 91039; tel. 2-5633575; fax 2-5638528; e-mail embasal@inter.net.il; Ambassador: RAFAEL A. ALFARO-PINEDA.

Ethiopia: Dan Panorama Hotel, 10 Rehov Kaufman, Tel-Aviv 61500; tel. 3-519019; Chargé d'affaires a.i.: Dr TESHOME TEKLU.

Finland: POB 20013, 8th Floor, Beit Eliahu, 2 Rehov Ibn Gvirol, Tel-Aviv 64077; tel. 3-6950527; fax 3-6966311; e-mail sanomat.tel@formi.fi; Ambassador: PASI PATOKALLIO.

France: 112 Tayeleth Herbert Samuel, Tel-Aviv 63572; tel. 3-5245371; telex 33662; fax 3-5249294; e-mail ambafran@actcom.co.il; Ambassador: JEAN-NOËL DE BOUILLANE DE LACOSTE.

Germany: POB 16038, 19th Floor, 3 Rehov Daniel Frisch, Tel-Aviv 61160; tel 03-6931313; telex 33621; fax 3-6969217; Ambassador: THEODOR WALLAN.

Greece: 47 Bodenheimer St, Tel-Aviv 62008; tel. 3-6055461; telex 341227; fax 3-6054374; Ambassador: Dr SOTIRIOS VAROUXAKIS.

Guatemala: 74 Rehov Hei Be'Iyar, Apt 6, Tel-Aviv 62198; tel. 3-5467372; Ambassador: JULIO ROBERTO PALOMO SILVA.

Haiti: 16 Rehov Bar Giora, Tel-Aviv 64336; tel. 3-280285; Ambassador: FRANCK M. JOSEPH.

Holy See: POB 150, 1 Netiv Hamazalot, Old Jaffa 68037; tel. 3-6835658; fax 3-6835659; Apostolic Nuncio: Mgr ANDREA CORDERO LANZA DI MONTEZEMELO, Titular Archbishop of Tuscania.

Honduras: 46 Rehov Hei Be'Iyar, Apt 3, Kikar Hamedina, Tel-Aviv 62093; tel. 3-5469506; fax 3-5469505; e-mail Honduras@netvision.net.il; Ambassador: FRANCISCO LÓPEZ REYES.

Hungary: 18 Rehov Pinkas, Tel-Aviv 62661; tel. 3-5466860; fax 3-5468968; Ambassador: Dr ISTVÁN CSEJTEI.

India: 4 Rehov Koifman, Tel-Aviv; tel. 3-5101431; telex 371583; fax 3-5101434; Ambassador: SHIVSHANKAR MENON.

Italy: 'Asia House', 4 Rehov Weizman, Tel-Aviv 64239; tel. 3-6948428; telex 342664; fax 3-6964223; Ambassador: PIER LUIGI RACHELE.

Japan: 'Asia House', 4 Rehov Weizman, Tel-Aviv 64239; tel. 3-6957292; telex 242202; fax 3-6910516; Ambassador: YUKATA KAWASHIMA.

Jordan: 12 Rehov Abba Hillel, Ramat-Gan, Tel-Aviv 52506; tel. 3-7517722; fax 3-7517713; Ambassador: MARWAN MUASHER.

Latvia: 52 Pinkas St, Apt 51, Tel-Aviv 62261; tel. 3-54624; fax 3-5444372; Ambassador: IVARS SILĀRS.

Liberia: 6 Shimon Frug, Ramat-Gan, Tel-Aviv 524282; tel. 3-728525; telex 361637; Ambassador: Maj. SAMUEL B. PEARSON, Jr.

Lithuania: Suite 1404, POB 23920, Dizengoff 50, Tel-Aviv 61231; tel. 3-5288514; fax 3-5257265; Ambassador: ROMAS JONAS MISIUNAS.

Mexico: 3 Rehov Bograshov, Tel-Aviv 63808; tel. 3-5230367; telex 32352; fax 3-5237399; e-mail embamex@netvision.net.il; Ambassador: JORGE ALBERTO LOZOYA.

Myanmar: 26 Rehov Hayarkon, Tel-Aviv 68011; tel. 3-5170760; telex 371504; fax 3-5171440; Ambassador: U KYAW MYINT.

Netherlands: 'Asia House', 4 Rehov Weizman, Tel-Aviv 64239; tel. 3-6957377; telex 342180; fax 3-6957370; Ambassador: CHRISTIAAN M. J. KRÖNER.

Nigeria: POB 3339, 34 Gordon St, Tel-Aviv 61030; tel. 3-5222144; fax 3-5237886; Ambassador: I. C. OLISEMEKA.

Norway: 40 Rehov Hei Be'Iyar, Tel-Aviv, Tel-Aviv 63506; tel. 3-5442030; telex 33417; fax 3-5442034; Ambassador: SVEN ERIK SVEDMAN.

Panama: 10 Rehov Hei Be'Iyar, Kikar Hamedina, Tel-Aviv 62998; tel. 3-6960849; fax 3-6910045; Ambassador: Prof. PAULINO C. ROMERO.

Peru: 52 Rehov Pinkas, Apt 31, 8th Floor, Tel-Aviv 62261; tel. 3-5442081; telex 371351; fax 3-5465532; Ambassador: JORGE TORRES.

Philippines: POB 50085, 13th Floor, Textile Centre Bldg, 2 Rehov Kaufmann, Tel-Aviv 68012; tel. 3-5175263; telex 32104; fax 3-5102229; Ambassador: ROSALINDA DE PERIO-SANTOS.

Poland: 16 Rehov Soutine, Tel-Aviv; tel. 3-5240186; telex 371765; fax 3-5237806; Ambassador: Chargé d'affaires a.i.: ZBIGNIEW ŻELAZOWSKI.

Portugal: 4 Rehov Weizman, Tel-Aviv; tel. 3-6956373; Ambassador: PAULO COUTO BARBOSA.

Romania: 24 Rehov Adam Hacohen, Tel-Aviv 64585; tel. 3-5230066; Ambassador: Dr RADU HOMESCU.

Russia: 120 Rehov Hayarkon, Tel-Aviv 63573; tel. 3-5226733; fax 3-5226713; Ambassador: MIKHAIL BOGDANOV.

Slovakia: POB 6459, Tel-Aviv 61064; tel. 3-5440066; fax 3-5440069; Ambassador Dr FRANTIŠEK DLHOPOLČEK.

South Africa: POB 7138, 16th Floor, Top Tower, 50 Dizengoff St, Tel-Aviv 61071; tel. 3-5252566; fax 3-5253230; Ambassador: FRANK LAND.

Spain: Dubnov Tower, 3 Rehov Daniel Frisch, 16th Floor, Tel-Aviv 64731; tel. 3-6965218; fax 3-6965217; Ambassador: FERMÍN ZELADA JURADO.

Sweden: 'Asia House', 4 Rehov Weizman, Tel-Aviv 64239; tel. 3-6958111; telex 33650; fax 3-6958116; Ambassador: CARL-MAGNUS HYLTENIUS.

Switzerland: 228 Rehov Hayarkon, Tel-Aviv 63405; tel. 3-5464455; telex 342237; fax 3-5464408; Ambassador: GASPARD BODMER.

Togo: POB 50222, Beit Hatassianim, 29 Rehov Hamered, Tel-Aviv 68125; tel. 3-652206; Ambassador: KOFFI-MAWUENAM KOWOUVI.

Turkey: 202 Rehov Hayarkon, Tel-Aviv 63405; tel. 3-35241101; fax 3-35240499; Ambassador: BARLAS ÖZENER.

Ukraine: 12 Stricker St, Tel-Aviv 62006; tel. 3-6040242; fax 3-6042512; Ambassador: ALEKSANDR IVANOVYCH MAYDANNYK.

United Kingdom: 192 Rehov Hayarkon, Tel-Aviv 63405; tel. 3-5249171; fax 3-5243313; Ambassador: DAVID GEOFFREY MANNING.

USA: 71 Rehov Hayarkon, Tel-Aviv 63903; tel. 3-5197575; telex 33376; fax 3-5173227; Ambassador: EDWARD WALKER.

Uruguay: 52 Rehov Pinkas, Apt. 10, 2nd Floor, Tel-Aviv 62261; tel. 3-440411; telex 342669; Ambassador: ANÍBAL DÍAZ MONDINO.

Venezuela: Textile Center, 2 Rehov Kaufmann, 16th Floor, Tel-Aviv 61500; tel. 3-5176287; telex 342172; fax 3-5176210; Ambassador: FREDDY ALVAREZ.

Yugoslavia: Iderot Shaul Hamelech 8, Tel-Aviv 64733; tel. 3-6938412; fax 3-6938411; Charge d'affaires a.i.: MIRKO STEFANOVIĆ.

Zambia: Tel-Aviv.

The Jewish Agency for Israel

POB 92, Jerusalem 91000; tel. 2-202222; fax 2-202303.

Organization: The governing bodies are the Assembly which determines basic policy, the Board of Governors which sets policy for the Agency between Assembly meetings and the Executive responsible for the day-to-day running of the Agency.

Chairman of Executive: AVRAHAM BURG.

Chairman of Board of Governors: CHARLES H. GOODMAN.

Director-General: MOSHE NATIV.

Secretary-General: HOWARD WEISBAND.

Functions: According to the Agreement of 1971, the Jewish Agency undertakes the immigration and absorption of immigrants in Israel, including absorption in agricultural settlement and immigrant housing; social welfare and health services in connection with immigrants; education, youth care and training; neighbourhood rehabilitation through project renewal.

Budget (1993): US $500m.

Judicial System

The law of Israel is composed of the enactments of the Knesset and, to a lesser extent, of the acts, orders-in-council and ordinances that remain from the period of the British Mandate in Palestine (1922–48). The pre-1948 law has largely been replaced, amended or reorganized, in the interests of codification, by Israeli legislation. This legislation generally follows a pattern which is very similar to that operating in England and the USA.

Attorney-General: ELYAQIM RUBENSTEIN.

CIVIL COURTS

The Supreme Court: Sha'arei Mishpat St, Kiryat David Ben-Gurion, Jerusalem 91950; tel. 2-6759666; fax 2-6759648. This is the highest judicial authority in the state. It has jurisdiction as an Appellate Court over appeals from the District Courts in all matters, both civil and criminal (sitting as a Court of Civil Appeal or as a Court of Criminal Appeal). In addition it is a Court of First Instance (sitting as the High Court of Justice) in actions against governmental authorities, and in matters in which it considers it necessary to grant relief in the interests of justice and which are not within the jurisdiction of any other court or tribunal. The High Court's exclusive power to issue orders in the nature of *habeas corpus, mandamus*, prohibition and *certiorari* enables the court to review the legality of and redress grievances against acts of administrative authorities of all kinds and religious tribunals.

President of the Supreme Court: AHARON BARAK.

Deputy-President of the Supreme Court: SH. LEVIN.

Justices of the Supreme Court: Y. KEDMI, Mrs D. BEINISCH, Y. TURKEL, M. CHESHIN, E. GOLDBERG, Mrs T. STRASBERG-COHEN, T. OR, E. MAZZA, Y. ENGLARD, Mrs D. DORNER, Y. ZAMIR, Y. GOLDBERG.

Registrars: Judge ORIT EPHAL-GABAI, Judge MICHAL AGMON.

The District Courts: There are five District Courts (Jerusalem, Tel-Aviv, Haifa, Beersheba, Nazareth). They have residual jurisdiction as Courts of First Instance over all civil and criminal matters not within the jurisdiction of a Magistrates' Court, all matters not within the exclusive jurisdiction of any other tribunal, and matters within the concurrent jurisdiction of any other tribunal so long as such tribunal does not deal with them. In addition, the District Courts have appellate jurisdiction over appeals from judgments and decisions of Magistrates' Courts and judgments of Municipal Courts and various administrative tribunals.

Magistrates' Courts: There are 29 Magistrates' Courts, having criminal jurisdiction to try contraventions, misdemeanours and certain felonies, and civil jurisdiction to try actions concerning possession or use of immovable property, or the partition thereof whatever may be the value of the subject matter of the action, and other civil claims not exceeding one million new shekels.

Labour Courts: Established in 1969. Regional Labour Courts in Jerusalem, Tel-Aviv, Haifa, Beersheba and Nazareth, composed of judges and representatives of the public. A National Labour Court in Jerusalem, presided over by Judge M. Goldberg. The Courts have jurisdiction over all matters arising out of the relationship between employer and employee or parties to a collective labour agreement, and matters concerning the National Insurance Law and the Labour Law and Rules.

RELIGIOUS COURTS

The Religious Courts are the courts of the recognized religious communities. They have jurisdiction over certain defined matters of personal status concerning members of their respective communities. Where any action of personal status involves persons of different religious communities the President of the Supreme Court decides which Court will decide the matter. Whenever a question arises as to whether or not a case is one of personal status within the exclusive jurisdiction of a Religious Court, the matter must be referred to a Special Tribunal composed of two Justices of the Supreme Court and the President of the highest court of the religious community concerned in Israel. The judgments of the Religious Courts are executed by the process and offices of the Civil Courts. Neither these Courts nor the Civil Courts have jurisdiction to dissolve the marriage of a foreign subject.

Jewish Rabbinical Courts: These Courts have exclusive jurisdiction over matters of marriage and divorce of Jews in Israel who are Israeli citizens or residents. In all other matters of personal status they have concurrent jurisdiction with the District Courts.

Muslim Religious Courts: These Courts have exclusive jurisdiction over matters of marriage and divorce of Muslims who are not foreigners, or who are foreigners subject by their national law to the jurisdiction of Muslim Religious Courts in such matters. In all other matters of personal status they have concurrent jurisdiction with the District Courts.

Christian Religious Courts: The Courts of the recognized Christian communities have exclusive jurisdiction over matters of marriage and divorce of members of their communities who are not foreigners. In all other matters of personal status they have concurrent jurisdiction with the District Courts.

Druze Courts: These Courts, established in 1963, have exclusive jurisdiction over matters of marriage and divorce of Druze in Israel, who are Israeli citizens or residents, and concurrent jurisdiction with the District Courts over all other matters of personal status of Druze.

Religion

JUDAISM

Judaism, the religion of the Jews, is the faith of the majority of Israel's inhabitants. On 31 December 1994 Judaism's adherents totalled 4,441,100, equivalent to 81.17% of the country's population. Its basis is a belief in an ethical monotheism.

There are two main Jewish communities: the Ashkenazim and the Sephardim. The former are the Jews from Eastern, Central, or Northern Europe, while the latter originate from the Balkan countries, North Africa and the Middle East.

There is also a community of about 10,000 Falashas (Ethiopian Jews) who have been airlifted to Israel at various times since the fall of Emperor Haile Selassie in 1974.

The supreme religious authority is vested in the Chief Rabbinate, which consists of the Ashkenazi and Sephardi Chief Rabbis and the Supreme Rabbinical Council. It makes decisions on interpretation of the Jewish law, and supervises the Rabbinical Courts. There are 8 regional Rabbinical Courts, and a Rabbinical Court of Appeal presided over by the two Chief Rabbis.

According to the Rabbinical Courts Jurisdiction Law of 1953, marriage and divorce among Jews in Israel are exclusively within the jurisdiction of the Rabbinical Courts. Provided that all the parties concerned agree, other matters of personal status can also be decided by the Rabbinical Courts.

There are 195 Religious Councils, which maintain religious services and supply religious needs, and about 405 religious committees with similar functions in smaller settlements. Their expenses are borne jointly by the State and the local authorities. The Religious Councils are under the administrative control of the Ministry of Religious Affairs. In all matters of religion, the Religious Councils are subject to the authority of the Chief Rabbinate. There are 365 officially appointed rabbis. The total number of synagogues is about 7,000, most of which are organized within the framework of the Union of Israel Synagogues.

Head of the Ashkenazi Community: The Chief Rabbi ISRAEL MEIR LAU.

Head of the Sephardic Community: Jerusalem; tel. 2-244785; The Chief Rabbi ELIAHU BAKSHI-DORON.

Two Jewish sects still loyal to their distinctive customs are:

The Karaites, a sect which recognizes only the Jewish written law and not the oral law of the Mishna and Talmud. The community of about 12,000, many of whom live in or near Ramla, has been augmented by immigration from Egypt.

The Samaritans, an ancient sect mentioned in 2 Kings xvii, 24. They recognize only the Torah. The community in Israel numbers about 500; about half of them live in Holon, where a Samaritan synagogue has been built, and the remainder, including the High Priest, live in Nablus, near Mt Gerizim, which is sacred to the Samaritans.

ISLAM

The Muslims in Israel are mainly Sunnis, and are divided among the four rites of the Sunni sect of Islam: the Shafe'i, the Hanbali, the Hanafi and the Maliki. Before June 1967 they numbered approx. 175,000; in 1971, approx. 343,900. On 31 December 1994 the total Muslim population of Israel was 781,500.

Mufti of Jerusalem: POB 19859, Jerusalem; tel. 2-283528; Sheikh ABD AL-QADIR ABIDIN (also Chair. Supreme Muslim Council for Jerusalem). The Palestine National Authority also claims the right to appoint the Mufti of Jerusalem and has named Sheikh AKRAM SA'ID SABRI as its choice.

There was also a total of 91,700 Druzes in Israel at 31 December 1994.

CHRISTIANITY

The total Christian population of Israel (including East Jerusalem) at 31 December 1994 was 161,000.

United Christian Council in Israel: POB 116, Jerusalem 91000; tel. 9-432832; fax 9-432081; f. 1956; 24 mems (churches and other bodies); Chair. TOM HOCUTT.

The Roman Catholic Church

Armenian Rite

The Armenian Catholic Patriarch of Cilicia is resident in Beirut, Lebanon.

Patriarchal Exarchate of Jerusalem: POB 19546, Via Dolorosa 41, Third and Fourth Stations of the Cross, Jerusalem; tel. 2-284262; fax 2-272123; f. 1885; Exarch Patriarchal ANTREAS BEDOGHOLIAN.

Chaldean Rite

The Chaldean Patriarch of Babylon is resident in Baghdad, Iraq.

Patriarchal Exarchate of Jerusalem: Chaldean Patriarchal Vicariate, Saad and Said Quarter, Nablus Rd, Jerusalem; Exarch Patriarchal Mgr PAUL COLLIN.

Latin Rite

The Patriarchate of Jerusalem covers Palestine, Jordan and Cyprus. At 31 December 1995 there were an estimated 70,000 adherents.

Bishops' Conference: Conférence des Evêques Latins dans les Régions Arabes, Patriarcat Latin, POB 14152, Jerusalem; tel. 2-292323; f. 1967; Pres. His Beatitude MICHEL SABBAH; Patriarch of Jerusalem.

Patriarchate of Jerusalem: Patriarcat Latin, POB 14152, Jerusalem; tel. 2-6282323; fax 2-6271652; e-mail latinpatr@isdn.co.il; Patriarch: His Beatitude MICHEL SABBAH; Vicar General for Israel: Mgr PETER MARCUZZO (Titular Bishop of Gaba), Vicariat Patriarcal Latin, Nazareth; tel. 6-6554075; fax 6-6452416.

Maronite Rite

The Maronite community, under the jurisdiction of the Maronite Patriarch of Antioch (resident in Lebanon), has about 7,500 members.

Patriarchal Exarchate of Jerusalem: Vicariat Maronite, 25 Maronite St, Jerusalem; tel. 2-6282158; fax 2-6272821; Exarch Patriarchal Mgr PAUL NABIL SAYAH (also the Archbishop of Haifa and the Holy Land).

Melkite Rite

The Greek-Melkite Patriarch of Antioch (Maximos V Hakim) is resident in Damascus, Syria.

Patriarchal Vicariate of Jerusalem: Vicariat Patriarcal Grec-Melkite Catholique, POB 14130, Porte de Jafa, Jerusalem 91141; tel. 2-6282023; fax 2-6286652; about 3,100 adherents (1995); Vicars Patriarchal Mgr HILARION CAPUCCI (Titular Archbishop of Caesarea in Palestine), Mgr LUTFI LAHAM (Titular Archbishop of Tarsus).

Archbishop of Akka (Acre): Most Rev. MAXIMOS SALLOUM, Archevêché Grec-Catholique, POB 279, 33 Hagefen St, Haifa; tel. 04-8523114; 45,000 adherents at 31 December 1995.

Syrian Rite

The Syrian Catholic Patriarch of Antioch is resident in Beirut, Lebanon.

Patriarchal Exarchate of Jerusalem: Vicariat Patriarcal Syrien Catholique, POB 19787, Chaldean St No. 6, Nablus Road, Jerusalem 91190; tel. 2-282657; fax 2-284217; 700 adherents in Palestine and Jordan (Dec. 1995); Exarch Patriarchal Mgr PIERRE ABD AL-AHAD.

The Armenian Apostolic (Orthodox) Church

Patriarch of Jerusalem: TORKOM MANOOGIAN, St James's Cathedral, Jerusalem; tel. 2-6264853; fax 2-6264862 .

The Greek Orthodox Church

The Patriarchate of Jerusalem contains an estimated 260,000 adherents in Israel, the Israeli-occupied territories, Jordan, Kuwait, the United Arab Emirates and Saudi Arabia.

Patriarch of Jerusalem: DIODOROS I, POB 19632-633, Greek Orthodox Patriarchate St, Old City, Jerusalem; tel. 2-6264853; fax 2-6264268.

The Anglican Communion

Episcopal Church in Jerusalem and the Middle East: POB 1248, St George's Close, Jerusalem; tel. 2-271670; fax (2) 273847; President-Bishop The Most Rev. SAMIR KAFITY, Bishop in Jerusalem.

Other Christian Churches

Other denominations include the Coptic Orthodox Church (700 members), the Russian Orthodox Church, the Ethiopian Orthodox Church, the Romanian Orthodox Church, the Lutheran Church and the Church of Scotland.

The Press

Tel-Aviv is the main publishing centre. Largely for economic reasons, there has developed no local press away from the main cities; hence all papers regard themselves as national. Friday editions, issued on Sabbath eve, are increased to as much as twice the normal size by special weekend supplements, and experience a considerable rise in circulation. No newspapers appear on Saturday.

Most of the daily papers are in Hebrew, and others appear in Arabic, English, French, Polish, Yiddish, Hungarian and German. The total daily circulation is 500,000–600,000 copies, or 21 papers per hundred people, although most citizens read more than one daily paper.

Most Hebrew morning dailies have strong political or religious affiliations. *Al-Hamishmar* is affiliated to Mapam, *Hatzofeh* to the National Religious Party—World Mizrachi. *Davar* is the long-established organ of the Histadrut. Most newspapers depend on subsidies from political parties, religious organizations or public funds. The limiting effect on freedom of commentary entailed by this party press system has provoked repeated criticism. There are around 400 other newspapers and magazines including some 50 weekly and 150 fortnightly; over 250 of them are in Hebrew, the remainder in 11 other languages.

The most influential and respected dailies, for both quality of news coverage and commentary, are *Ha'aretz* and the trade union paper, *Davar*, which frequently has articles by government figures. These are the most widely read of the morning papers, exceeded only by the popular afternoon press, *Ma'ariv* and *Yedioth Aharonoth*. The *Jerusalem Post* gives detailed and sound news coverage in English.

The Israeli Press Council (Chair. ITZHAK ZAMIR), established in 1963, deals with matters of common interest to the Press such as drafting the code of professional ethics which is binding on all journalists.

The Daily Newspaper Publishers' Association represents publishers in negotiations with official and public bodies, negotiates contracts with employees and purchases and distributes newsprint.

DAILIES

Al Anba (The News): POB 428, 37 Hillel St, Jerusalem; f. 1968 circ. 10,000.

Davar Rishon: POB 199, 45 Sheinkin St, Tel-Aviv; tel. 3-5286141; telex 33807; fax 3-6294783; f. 1925; morning; Hebrew; official organ of the General Federation of Labour (Histadrut); Editor RON BEN YSHAI; circ. 39,000; there are also weekly magazine editions.

Globes: 127 Igal Alon St, Tel-Aviv 67443; tel. 3-6979797; fax 3-6917573; e-mail shimoni@globes.co.il; f. 1983; evening; business, economics; Editor H. GOLAN; circ. 36,000.

Ha'aretz (The Land): POB 233, 21 Salman Schocken St, Tel-Aviv 61001; tel. 3-5121212; fax 3-6810012; f. 1918; morning; Hebrew; liberal, independent; Editor HANOCH MARMARI; circ. 65,000 (weekdays), 75,000 (weekends).

Hadashot (The News): 108 Yigal Alon St, Tel-Aviv; 3-5120555; fax 3-5623084; late morning; Hebrew.

Hamodia (The Informer): POB 1306, Yehuda Hamackabbi 3, Jerusalem; fax 2-539108; morning; Hebrew; organ of Agudat Israel; Editors M. A. DRUCK, H. M. KNOPF; circ. 15,000.

Hatzofeh (The Watchman): 66 Hamasger St, Tel-Aviv; tel. 3-5622951; fax 3-5621502; f. 1938; morning; Hebrew; organ of the National Religious Party; Editor M. ISHON; circ. 16,000.

Israel Nachrichten (News of Israel): 49 Tschlenow St, Tel-Aviv 66048; tel. 3-5372059; fax 3-6877142; f. 1974; morning; German; Editor ALICE SCHWARZ-GARDOS; circ. 20,000.

Israelski Far Tribuna: 113 Givat Herzl St, Tel-Aviv; tel. 3-3700; f. 1952; Bulgarian; circ. 6,000.

Al-Ittihad (Unity): POB 104, Haifa; tel. 4-511296; fax 4-511297; f. 1944; Arabic; organ of the Israeli Communist Party (Maki); Chief Editor NAZIR MJALLI ZUBIEDAT.

The Jerusalem Post: POB 81, Romema, 91000, Jerusalem; tel. 2-531566; fax 2-5387408; e-mail jpedt@jpost.co.il; f. 1932; morning; English; independent; Pres. and Pblr NORMAN SPECTOR; Editor JEFF BORAK; circ. 30,000 (weekdays), 50,000 (weekend edition); there is also a weekly international edition, circ. 70,000, and a weekly French-language edition, circ. 7,500.

Le Journal d'Israel: POB 28330, 26 Agra St, Tel-Aviv; f. 1971; French; independent; Chief Editor J. RABIN; circ. 10,000; also overseas weekly selection; circ. 15,000.

Letzte Nyess (Late News): POB 28034, 52 Harakevet St, Tel-Aviv; f. 1949; morning; Yiddish; Editor S. HIMMELFARB; circ. 23,000.

Ma'ariv (Evening Prayer): 2 Carlebach St, Tel-Aviv 61200; tel. 3-5632111; telex 33735; fax 3-5610614; f. 1948; mid-morning; Hebrew; independent; published by Modiin Publishing House; Editor OFFER NIMRODI; circ. daily 160,000, weekend 270,000.

Mabat: 8 Toshia St, Tel-Aviv 67218; tel. 3-5627711; fax 3-5627719; f. 1971; morning; economic and social; Editor S. YARKONI; circ. 7,000.

Nasha Strana (Our Country): 52 Harakeret St, Tel-Aviv 67770; tel. 3-370011; fax 3-5371921; f. 1970; morning; Russian; Editor S. HIMMELFARB; circ. 35,000.

Al-Quds (Jerusalem) POB 19788, Jerusalem; tel. 2-284061; fax 2-282475; f. 1968; circ. 40,000.

Uj Kelet: 49 Tchlenor St, Tel-Aviv; tel. 3-5371395; fax 3-377142; f. 1918; morning; Hungarian; independent; Editor D. DRORY; circ. 20,000.

Viata Noastra: 49 Tchlenor St, Tel-Aviv; tel. 3-5372059; fax 3-377142; f. 1950; morning; Romanian; Editor ISEF ROTEM; circ. 30,000.

Yated Ne'eman: POB 328, Bnei Brak; tel. 3-5709171; fax 3-5709181; f. 1986; morning; religious; Editors Y. ROTH and N.GROSSMAN; circ. 25,000.

Yedioth Ahronoth (The Latest News): 2 Yehuda and Noah Mozes St, Tel-Aviv 61000; tel. 3-6972222; telex 33847; fax 3-6953950; f. 1939; evening; independent; Editor-in-Chief MOSHE VARDI; circ. 300,000, Friday 600,000.

WEEKLIES AND FORTNIGHTLIES

Bama'alah: 120 Kibbutz Gabuyot St, Tel-Aviv; tel. 3-6814488; fax 3-6816852; Hebrew; journal of the young Histadrut Movement; Editor ODED BAR-MEIR.

Bamahane (In the Camp): Military POB 1013, Tel-Aviv; f. 1948; military, illustrated weekly of the Israel Armed Forces; Hebrew; Editor-in-Chief YOSSEF ESHKOL; circ. 70,000.

Davar Hashavua (The Weekly Word): 45 Shenkin St, Tel-Aviv; tel. 2-286141; f. 1946; weekly; Hebrew; popular illustrated; published by Histadrut, General Federation of Labour; Editor TUVIA MENDELSON; circ. 43,000.

Ethgar (The Challenge): 75 Einstein St, Tel-Aviv; twice weekly; Hebrew; Editor NATHAN YALIN-MOR.

Gesher (The Bridge): Jerusalem; fortnightly; Hebrew; Editor ZIAD ABU ZAYAD.

Glasul Populurui: Tel-Aviv; weekly of the Communist Party of Israel; Romanian; Editor MEIR SEMO.

Haolam Hazeh (This World): POB 136, 3 Gordon St, Tel-Aviv 61001; tel. 3-5376804; fax 3-5376811; f. 1937; weekly; independent; illustrated news magazine; Editor-in-Chief RAFFI GINAT.

Harefuah (Medicine): Twin Towers No. 2, 35 Jabotinsky St, Ramat-Gan, Tel-Aviv; tel. 3-6100444; fax 3-5751616; f. 1920; fortnightly journal of the Israeli Medical Association; Hebrew with English summaries; Editor Y. ROTEM; circ. 12,000.

Hotam: Al-Hamishmar House, Choma U'Migdal St, Tel-Aviv; Hebrew.

Al-Hurriya (Freedom): 38 King George St, Tel-Aviv; Arabic weekly of the Herut Party.

Illustrirte Weltwoch: Tel-Aviv; f. 1956; weekly; Yiddish; Editor M. KARPINOVITZ.

Jerusalem Post International Edition: POB 81, Romema, Jerusalem 91000; tel. 2-5315666; fax 2-5389527; e-mail jpedt@jpost.co.il; f. 1959; weekly; English; overseas edition of the *Jerusalem Post* (q.v.); circ. 70,000 to 106 countries.

The Jerusalem Times: POB 20185, Jerusalem; tel. 2-6264883; fax 2-6264975; e-mail tjt@palnet.com; f. 1994; weekly; Arabic and English; Editor SAMI KAMAL.

Kol Ha'am (Voice of the People): Tel-Aviv; f. 1947; Hebrew; organ of the Communist Party of Israel; Editor B. BALTI.

Laisha (For Women): POB 28122, 35 Bnei Brak St, Tel-Aviv 67132; tel. 3-638-6969; fax 3-638-6922; f. 1946; Hebrew; women's magazine; Editor ZVI ELGAT.

Ma'ariv Lanoar: 2 Carlebach St, Tel-Aviv 67132; tel. 3-5632111; fax 3-5632030; f. 1957; weekly for youth; Hebrew; Editor AVI MORGENSTERN; circ. 100,000.

MB (Mitteilungsblatt): POB 1480, Tel-Aviv 61014; tel. 3-5164461; fax 3-5164435; f. 1932; German monthly journal of the Irgun Olei Merkas Europa (The Association of Immigrants from Central Europe); Editor Prof. PAUL ALSBERG.

Otiot: Beit Orot, Hordes Post, Jerusalem 95908; tel. 2-895097; fax 2-895196; f. 1987; weekly for children; English; Editor URI AUERBACH.

People and Computers Weekly: POB 11616, 64 Pinsker St, Tel-Aviv 11616; tel. 3-295145; telex 341667; fax 3-295144; weekly; Hebrew; information technology; circ. 6,000.

Reshumot: Ministry of Justice, Jerusalem; f. 1948; Hebrew, Arabic and English; official government gazette.

Sada at-Tarbia (The Echo of Education): published by the Histadrut and Teachers' Association, POB 2306, Rehovot; f. 1952; fortnightly; Arabic; educational; Editor TUVIA SHAMOSH.

OTHER PERIODICALS

Ariel: the Israel Review of Arts and Letters: Cultural and Scientific Relations Division, Ministry for Foreign Affairs, Jerusalem; Distributor: Youval Tal Ltd, POB 2160, Jerusalem 91021; tel. 2-6248897; fax 2-6245434; Editorial Office: 214 Jaffa Road, Jerusalem 91130; tel. 2-5381515; fax 2-538062; f. 1962; quarterly review of all aspects of culture in Israel; regular edns in English, Spanish, French, German, Arabic and Russian; occasional edns in other languages; Editor ASHER WEILL; Asst Editor ALOMA HALTER; circ. 35,000.

Asakim Vekalkala (Business and Economics): POB 20027, 84 Hashmonaim St, Tel-Aviv 61200; tel. 3-5631010; telex 33484; fax 3-5619025; monthly; Hebrew; Editor ZVI AMIT.

Avoda Urevacha Ubituach Leumi: POB 915, Jerusalem; f. 1949; monthly review of the Ministry of Labour and Social Affairs, and the National Insurance Institute, Jerusalem; Hebrew; Chief Editor AVNER MICHAELI; Editor MICHAEL KLODOVSKY; circ. 2,500.

Bitaon Heyl Ha'avir (Air Force Magazine): Doar Zwai 01560, Zahal; tel. 3-5693886; fax 3-5695806; f. 1948; bi-monthly; Hebrew; Man. Editor D. MOLAD; Editor-in-Chief MERAV HALPERIN; circ. 30,000.

Al-Bushra (Good News): POB 6088, Haifa; f. 1935; monthly; Arabic; organ of the Ahmadiyya movement; Editor FALAHUD DIN O'DEH.

Business Diary: 37 Hanamal St, Haifa; f. 1947; weekly; English, Hebrew; shipping movements, import licences, stock exchange listings, business failures, etc.; Editor G. ALON.

Challenge: POB 41199, Jaffa 61411; tel. and fax 2-6792270; internet http://members.aol.com/challng/index.html; f. 1989; magazine on the Israeli–Palestinian conflict, published by Hanitzotz Publishing House; bi-monthly in English; circ. 1,000; Editor RONI BEN EFRAT.

Christian News from Israel: 30 Jaffa Rd, Jerusalem; f. 1949; half-yearly; English, French, Spanish; issued by the Ministry of Religious Affairs; Editor SHALOM BEN-ZAKKAI; circ. 10,000.

Di Goldene Keyt: 30 Weizmann St, Tel-Aviv; f. 1949; literary quarterly; Yiddish; published by the Histadrut; Man. Editor MOSHE MILLIS; Editor A. SUTZKEVER.

Divrei Haknesset: c/o The Knesset, Jerusalem; f. 1949; Hebrew; records of the proceedings of the Knesset; published by the Government Printer, Jerusalem; Editor DVORA AVIVI (acting); circ. 350.

The Easy Way to do Business with Israel: POB 20027, Tel-Aviv; published by Federation of Israeli Chambers of Commerce; Editor Y. SHOSTAK.

Eitanim (Popular Medicine): POB 16250, Merkez Kupat Holim, Tel-Aviv 62098; f. 1948; Hebrew; monthly; circ. 20,000.

Family Physician: POB 16250, 101 Arlosoroff St, Tel-Aviv 62098; tel. 3-433388; fax 3-433474; f. 1970; published three times per year in Hebrew and English; scientific articles on family medicine, community medicine, health care and general practice; Editor Prof. MAX POLLIACK.

Folk un Zion: POB 7053, Tel-Aviv 61070; tel. 3-5423317; f. 1950; bi-monthly; current events relating to Israel and World Jewry; circ. 3,000; Editor MOSHE KALCHHEIM.

Frei Israel: POB 8512, Tel-Aviv; progressive monthly; published by Asscn for Popular Culture; Yiddish.

Gazit: POB 4190, 8 Zvi Brook St, Tel-Aviv; f. 1932; monthly; Hebrew and English; art, literature; Publisher G. TALPHIR.

Hameshek Hahaklai: 21 Melchett St, Tel-Aviv; f. 1929; Hebrew; agricultural; Editor ISRAEL INBARI.

Hamizrah Hehadash (The New East): Israel Oriental Society, The Hebrew University, Mount Scopus, Jerusalem 91905; tel. 2-5883633; f. 1949; annual of the Israel Oriental Society; Middle Eastern, Asian and African Affairs; Hebrew with English summary; Editor HAIM GERBER; circ. 1,500–2,000.

Hamionai (The Hotelier): POB 11586, Tel-Aviv; f. 1962; monthly of the Israel Hotel Asscn; Hebrew and English; Editor Z. PELTZ.

Hapraklit: POB 14152, 8 Wilson St, Tel-Aviv 61141; tel. 3-5614695; fax 3-561476; f. 1943; quarterly; Hebrew; published by the Israel Bar Asscn; Editor-in-Chief A. POLONSKI; Editor ARNAN GAVRIELI; circ. 9,000.

Hassadeh: POB 40044, 8 Shaul Hamelech Blvd, Tel-Aviv 61400; tel. 3-6929018; fax 3-6929979; f. 1920; monthly; review of Israeli agriculture; English; Publr GUY KLUG; circ. 10,000.

Hed Hagan: 8 Ben Saruk St, Tel-Aviv 62969; tel. 3-6922958; f. 1935; Hebrew; educational; Editor Mrs ZIVA PEDAHZUR; circ. 8,400.

Hed Hahinukh: 8 Ben Saruk St, Tel-Aviv 62969; tel. 3-5432911; fax 3-5432928; f. 1926; monthly; Hebrew; educational; published by the Israeli Teachers' Union; Editor DALIA LACHMAN; circ. 40,000.

Israel Economist: POB 7052, 6 Hazanowitz St, Jerusalem 91070; tel. 2-234131; fax 2-246569; f. 1945; monthly; English; independent; political and economic; Editor BEN MOLLOV; Publisher ISRAEL KELMAN; also publishes *Keeping Posted* (diplomatic magazine), *Mazel and Brucha* (jewellers' magazine); annuals: *Travel Agents' Manual, Electronics, International Conventions in Israel, Arkia, In Flight,* various hotel magazines.

Israel Environment Bulletin: Ministry of the Environment, POB 34033, Jerusalem 95464; tel. 2-6553777; telex 25629; fax 2-6535934; f. 1973; Editor SHOSHANA GABBAY; circ. 3,000.

Israel Export and Trade Journal: POB 11586, Tel-Aviv; f. 1949; monthly; English; commercial and economic; published by Israel Periodicals Co Ltd; Man. Dir ZALMAN PELTZ.

Israel Journal of Mathematics: POB 7695, Jerusalem 91076; tel. 2-6586656; fax 2-5633370; f. 1951; monthly, four vols of three issues per year; published by Magnes Press; Editor Prof. G. KALAI.

Israel Journal of Medical Sciences: 2 Etzel St, French Hill, 97853 Jerusalem; tel. 2-5817727; fax 2-5815722; f. 1965; monthly; Editor-in-Chief Dr M. PRYWES; circ. 5,500.

Israel Journal of Psychiatry and Related Sciences: Gefen Publishing House Ltd, POB 36004, Jerusalem 91360; tel. 2-5380247; fax 2-5388423; e-mail isragefen@netmedia.net.il; f. 1963; quarterly; Editor-in-Chief Dr DAVID GREENBERG.

Israel Journal of Veterinary Medicine: POB 3076, Rishon Le-Zion 75130; tel. 9-7419929; fax 9-7431778; f. 1943; quarterly of the Israel Veterinary Medical Asscn; formerly *Refuah Veterinarith*; Editors G. SIMON, I. GLAS.

Israel Scene: World Zionist Org., POB 92, Jerusalem 91920; tel. 2-527156; telex 26436; fax 2-533542; f. 1980; monthly; English; Zionist; cir. 50,000.

Israel-South Africa Trade Journal: POB 11587, Tel-Aviv; f. 1973; bi-monthly; English; commercial and economic; published by Israel Publications Corpn Ltd; Man. Dir Z. PELTZ.

Israels Aussenhandel: POB 11586, Tel-Aviv 61114; tel. 3-5280215; telex 341118; f. 1967; monthly; German; commercial; published by Israel Periodicals Co Ltd; Editor PELTZ NOEMI; Man. Dir ZALMAN PELTZ.

Al-Jadid (The New): POB 104, Haifa; f. 1951; literary monthly; Arabic; Editor SALEM JUBRAN; circ. 5,000.

Journal d'Analyse Mathématique: f. 1955; 2 vols per year; published by Magnes Press; Editor Prof. L. ZALCMAN.

Kalkalan: POB 7052, 8 Akiva St, Jerusalem; f. 1952; monthly; independent; Hebrew commercial and economic; Editor J. KOLLEK.

Kibbutz Trends: Yad Tabenkin, Ramat Efal 52960; tel. 3-5344458; fax 3-5346376; e-mail yadtab@actcom.co.il; quarterly; English language journal on Kibbutz; Editors RUTH LACEY, IDIT PAZ, NEIL HARRIS; circ. 1,500.

Labour in Israel: 93 Arlosorof St, Tel-Aviv 62098; tel. 3-6921111; telex 342488; fax 3-6969906; quarterly; English, French, German and Spanish; bulletin of the Histadrut (General Federation of Labour in Israel); circ. 28,000.

Leshonenu: Academy of the Hebrew Language, POB 3449, Jerusalem 91034; tel. 2-5632242; fax 2-5617065; f. 1929; 4 a year; for the study of the Hebrew language and cognate subjects; Editor J. BLAU.

Leshonenu La'am: Academy of the Hebrew Language, POB 3449, Jerusalem 91034; tel. 2-5632242; fax 2-5617065; f. 1945; 4 a year; popular Hebrew philology; Editors C. E. COHEN, D. TALSHIR, Y. OFER.

Ma'arachot (Campaigns): POB 7026, Hakirya, 3 Mendler St, Tel-Aviv 61070; tel. 3-5694343; f. 1939; military and political bi-monthly; Hebrew; periodical of Israel Defence Force; Editors EVIATHAR BEN-ZEDEFF, Lt Col RACHEL ROJANSKI.

Ma'ariv Lanoar: POB 20020, 2 Carlebach St, Tel-Aviv; tel. 3-5632111; fax 3-5610614; f. 1957; children's weekly; circ. 100,000.

Magallati (My Magazine): POB 28049, Tel-Aviv; tel. 3-371438; f. 1960; bi-monthly children's magazine; circ. 3,000.

Melaha Vetaassiya (Trade and Industry): POB 11587, Tel-Aviv; f. 1969; bi-monthly review of the Union of Artisans and Small Manufacturers of Israel; Hebrew; Man. Dir Z. PELTZ; circ. 8,500.

M'Lakha V'ta Asiya (Israel Industry): POB 11587, 40 Rembrandt St, Tel-Aviv; monthly; circ. 8,500.

Molad: POB 1165, Jerusalem 91010; f. 1948; annual; Hebrew; independent political and literary periodical; published by Miph'ale Molad Ltd; Editor EPHRAIM BROIDO.

Monthly Bulletin of Statistics: Israel Central Bureau of Statistics, POB 13015, Jerusalem 91130; tel. 2-6521340; fax 2-6553400; f. 1949.

Foreign Trade Statistics: f. 1950; Hebrew and English; appears annually, 2 vols; imports/exports.

Foreign Trade Statistics Quarterly: f. 1950; Hebrew and English.

Tourism and Hotel Services Statistics Quarterly: f. 1973; Hebrew and English.

Price Statistics Monthly: f. 1959; Hebrew.

Transport Statistics Quarterly: f. 1974; Hebrew and English.

Agricultural Statistics Quarterly: f. 1970; Hebrew and English.

New Statistical Projects and Publications in Israel: f. 1970; quarterly; Hebrew and English.

Moznaim (Balance): POB 7098, Tel-Aviv; tel. 3-6953256; fax 3-6919681; f. 1929; monthly; Hebrew; literature and culture; Editor ASHER REICH; circ. 2,500.

Nekuda: Hebrew; organ of the Jewish settlers of the West Bank and Gaza Strip.

New Outlook: 9 Gordon St, Tel-Aviv 63458; tel. 3-5236496; fax 3-5232252; f. 1957; bi-monthly; Israeli and Middle Eastern Affairs; dedicated to the quest for Arab-Israeli peace; Editor-in-Chief CHAIM SHUR; Senior Editor DAN LEON; circ. 10,000.

People and Computers Israel: POB 11616, 13 Yad Harutzim St, Tel-Aviv 11616; tel. 3-295145; telex 341667; fax 3-295144; monthly; Hebrew; information technology; cir. 9,500.

Proche-Orient Chrétien: POB 19079, Jerusalem 91190; tel. 2-6283285; fax 2-6280764; e-mail mafrproc@jrol.com; f. 1951; quarterly on churches and religion in the Middle East; circ. 1,000.

Quarterly Review of the Israel Medical Asscn (Mif'al Haverut Hutz—World Fellowship of the Israel Medical Asscn): POB 33289, 39 Shaul Hamelech Blvd, Tel-Aviv 61332; tel. (3) 6955521; fax 3-6956103; quarterly; English; Editor-in-Chief YEHUDA SHOENFELD.

The Sea: POB 33706, Hane'emanim 8, Haifa; tel. 04-529818; every six months; published by Israel Maritime League; review of marine problems; Pres. M. POMROCK; Chief Editor M. LITOVSKI; circ. 5,000.

Shituf (Co-operation): POB 7151, 24 Ha'arba St, Tel-Aviv; f. 1948; bi-monthly; Hebrew; economic, social and co-operative problems in Israel; published by the Central Union of Industrial, Transport and Service Co-operative Societies; Editor L. LOSH; circ. 12,000.

Shivuk (Marketing): POB 20027, Tel-Aviv 61200; tel. 3-5612444; fax 3-5612614; monthly; Hebrew; publ. by Federation of Israeli Chambers of Commerce; Editor SARA LIPKIN.

Sinai: POB 642, Jerusalem; tel. 2-526231; f. 1937; Hebrew; Torah science and literature; Editor Dr YITZCHAK RAPHAEL.

Sindibad: POB 28049, Tel-Aviv; f. 1970; children's monthly; Arabic; Man. JOSEPH ELIAHOU; Editor WALID HUSSEIN; circ. 8,000.

At-Ta'awun (Co-operation): POB 303, 93 Arlosoroff St, Tel-Aviv 62098; tel. 3-431813; telex 342488; fax 3-267368; f. 1961; Arabic; published by the Arab Workers' Dept of the Histadrut; co-operatives irregular; Editor ZVI HAIK.

Terra Santa: POB 14038, Jaffa Gate, Jerusalem 91140; tel. 2-6272692; fax 2-6286417; e-mail cicbarat@netmedia.net.il; f. 1921; every two months; published by the Custody of the Holy Land (the official custodians of the Holy Shrines); Italian, Spanish, French, English and Arabic editions published in Jerusalem, by the Franciscan Printing Press, German edition in Munich, Maltese edition in Valletta.

Tmuroth: POB 23076, 48 Hamelech George St, Tel-Aviv; f. 1960; monthly; Hebrew; organ of the Liberal Labour Movement; Editor S. MEIRI.

WIZO Review: Women's International Zionist Organization, 38 Sderot David Hamelech Blvd, Tel-Aviv 64237; tel. 3-6923805; fax 3-6958267; f. 1947; English edition (quarterly), Spanish and German editions (two a year); Editor HILLEL SCHENKER; circ. 20,000.

Zion: POB 4179, Jerusalem 91041; tel. 2-5637171; fax 2-5662135; f. 1935; quarterly; published by the Historical Society of Israel; Hebrew, with English summaries; research in Jewish history; Editors R. I. COHEN, A. OPPENHEIMER, Y. KAPLAN; circ. 1,000.

Zraim: POB 40027, 7 Dubnov St, Tel-Aviv; tel. 3-691745; fax 3-6953199; f. 1953; Hebrew; journal of the Bnei Akiva (Youth of Tora Va-avoda) Movement; Editor URI AUERBACH.

Zrakor: Haifa; f. 1947; monthly; Hebrew; news digest, trade, finance, economics, shipping; Editor G. ALON.

The following are all published by Laser Pages Publishing Ltd of Israel, POB 50257, 40/18 Levi Eshkol Blvd, Jerusalem 97665; tel. 2-829770; fax 2-818782.

Israel Journal of Chemistry: f. 1951; quarterly; Editor Prof. H. LEVANON.

Israel Journal of Earth Sciences: f. 1951; quarterly; Editors Dr Y. BARTOV, Y. KOLODNY.

Israel Journal of Plant Sciences: f. 1994; quarterly; Editor Prof. A. M. MAYER.

Israel Journal of Zoology: f. 1951; quarterly; Editor Prof. D. GRAUER.

Lada'at (Science for Youth): f. 1971; Hebrew; ten issues per vol.; Editor Dr M. ALMAGOR.

Mada (Science): POB 801, 8A Horkanya St, Jerusalem 91007; tel. 2-783203; fax 2-783784; f. 1955; popular scientific bi-monthly in Hebrew; Editor-in-Chief Dr YACHIN UNNA; circ. 10,000.

PRESS ASSOCIATIONS

Daily Newspaper Publishers' Asscn of Israel: POB 51202, 74 Petach Tikva Rd, Tel-Aviv 61200; fax 3-5617938; safeguards professional interests and maintains standards, supplies newsprint to dailies; negotiates with trade unions, etc.; mems all daily papers; affiliated to International Federation of Newspaper Publishers; Pres. SHABTAI HIMMELFARB; Gen. Sec. BETZALEL EYAL.

Foreign Press Asscn: Govt. Press Office Bldg, 9 Rehov Itamar Ben Avi, Tel-Aviv; tel. 3-6916143; fax 3-6961548; Chair. NICOLAS B. TATRO.

Israel Press Asscn: Sokolov House, 4 Kaplan St, Tel-Aviv.

NEWS AGENCIES

Jewish Telegraphic Agency (JTA): Israel Bureau, Jerusalem Post Bldg, Romema, Jerusalem; Dir DAVID LANDAU.

ITIM, News Agency of the Associated Israel Press: 10 Tiomkin St, Tel-Aviv; f. 1950; co-operative news agency; Dir and Editor ALTER WELNER.

Palestine Press Service: Salah ad-Din St, East Jerusalem; Proprs IBRAHIM QARA'EEN, Mrs RAYMONDA TAWIL; only Arab news agency in the Occupied Territories.

Foreign Bureaux

Agence France-Presse: POB 1507, 17th Floor, Migdal Haïr Tower, 34 Ben Yehuda St, Jerusalem 91014; tel. 2-242005; telex 26401; fax 2-6793623; Correspondent SAMY KETZ.

Agencia EFE (Spain): POB 37190, 18 Hilel St, Jerusalem 91371; tel. 2-6242038; fax 2-6242056; Correspondent ELÍAS-SAMUEL SCHERBACOVSKY.

Agenzia Nazionale Stampa Associata (ANSA) (Italy): 30 Dizengoff St, Tel-Aviv 64332; tel. 3-6299319; fax 3-5250302; Bureau Chief FURIO MORRONI; c/o Associated Press, Jerusalem 92233 (see below); tel. 2-250571; fax 2-258656; Correspondent GIORGIO RACCAH.

Associated Press (AP) (USA): POB 20220, 30 Ibn Gavirol St, Tel-Aviv 61201; tel. 3-262283; telex 341411; POB 1625, 18 Shlomzion Hamalcha, Jerusalem; tel. 2-224632; telex 25258; Chief of Bureau NICHOLAS TATRO.

Deutsche Presse-Agentur (dpa) (Germany): 30 Ibn Gvirol St, Tel-Aviv 64078; tel. 3-6959007; fax 3-6969594; e-mail dpatlv@trendline.co.il; Correspondents Dr HEINZ-RUDOLF OTHMERDING, ANDY GOLDBERG.

Jiji Tsushin-Sha (Japan): 9 Schmuel Hanagld, Jerusalem 94592; tel. 2-232553; fax 2-232402; Correspondent HIROKAZU OIKAWA.

Kyodo News Service (Japan): 19 Lessin St, Tel-Aviv 62997; tel. 3-6958185; telex 361568; fax 3-6917478; Correspondent HAJIME OZAKI.

Reuters (UK): 38 Hamasger St, Tel-Aviv 67211; tel. 3-5372211; telex 361567; fax 3-5374241; Jerusalem Capital Studios (JCS) 206 Jaffa Road, Jerusalem 91131; tel. 2-5370502; fax 2-374241; Chief of Bureau PAUL HOLMES.

United Press International (UPI) (USA): 138 Petah Tikva Rd, Tel-Aviv; Bureau Man. BROOKE W. KROEGER; Bureau Man. in Jerusalem LOUIS TOSCANO.

Informatsionnoye Telegrafnoye Agentstvo Rossii—Telegrafnoye Agentstvo Suverennykh Stran (ITAR—TASS) (Russia) is also represented.

Publishers

Achiasaf Ltd: POB 4810, 13 Yosef Hanassi St, Tel-Aviv 65236; tel. 3-5283339; fax 3-5286705; f. 1933; general; Man. Dir MATAN ACHIASAF.

Am Hassefer Ltd: 9 Bialik St, Tel-Aviv; tel. 3-53040; f. 1955; Man. Dir DOV LIPETZ.

'Am Oved' Ltd: POB 470, 22 Mazah St, POB 470, Tel-Aviv; tel. 3-6291526; fax 3-6298911; f. 1942; fiction, non-fiction, reference books, school and university textbooks, children's books, poetry, classics, science fiction; Man. Dir AHARON KRAUS.

Amichai Publishing House Ltd: 5 Yosef Hanassi St, Tel-Aviv 65236; tel. 3-284990; f. 1948; fiction, general science, linguistics, languages, arts; Dir YITZHAK ORON.

Arabic Publishing House: POB 28049, 17A Hagra St, Tel-Aviv; tel. 3-371438; f. 1960; established by the Histadrut (trade union) organization; periodicals and books; Dir JOSEPH ELIAHOU.

Ariel Publishing House: POB 3328, 28 Nayadot St, Pisgat Ze'ev, Jerusalem 91033; tel. 2-524414; fax 2-436164; f. 1976; history, geology, religion, geography; CEO ELY SCHILLER.

Bitan Publishers Ltd: 50 Yeshayahu St, Tel-Aviv 62494; tel. 3-5189033; fax 3-5189037; f. 1965; aeronautics, aviation, biography, child development, fiction, educational, literature and literary criticism, mysteries, leisure, travel, women's studies; Man. A. BITAN.

Boostan Publishing House: 36 Moshav, Ben Shemen 73115; tel. 3-221821; fax 3-221299; f. 1969; education, fiction, poetry, biography, history, medicine, psychology, psychiatry; Man. Dir MORDECHAI BOOSTAN.

Carta, The Israel Map and Publishing Co Ltd: POB 2500, 18 Ha'uman St, Industrial Area Talpiot, Jerusalem 91024; tel. 2-6783355; fax 2-6782373; e-mail cartaben@netvision.net.il; f. 1958; the principal cartographic publisher; Pres. and CEO SHAY HAUSMAN.

Dvir Publishing Co Ltd: POB 22383, 32 Schocken St, Tel-Aviv; tel. 3-6812244; fax 3-6826138; f. 1924; literature, science, art, education; Publrs O. ZMORA, A. BITAN.

Encyclopedia Publishing Co: 29 Jabotinski St, Jerusalem; tel. 2-5664568; f. 1947; Hebrew Encyclopedia and other encyclopaedias; Chair. ALEXANDER PELI.

Rodney Franklin Agency: POB 37727, 5 Karl Netter St, Tel-Aviv 61376; tel. 3-5600724; fax 3-5600479; e-mail rodney@actcom.co.il; exclusive representative of various British and USA publishers; Dir RODNEY FRANKLIN.

Gazit: POB 4190, 8 Zvi Brook St, Tel-Aviv; tel. 3-53730; art publishers; Editor GABRIEL TALPHIR.

Gefen Publishing House Ltd: 7 Ariel St, Jerusalem 91360; tel. 2-5380247; fax 2-5388423; e-mail isragefen@netmedia.net.il; f. 1981; art, religion, archaeology, English as a second language, fiction, history, arts, linguistics, law, medicine, military, science, poetry, psychology, psychiatry, theology, food and drink; CEO MURRAY S. GREENFIELD.

Gvanim Publishing House: POB 11138, 29 Bar-Kochba St, Tel-Aviv; tel. 3-5283648; fax 3-5283648; f. 1992; poetry, belles lettres, fiction; Man. Dir MARITZA ROSMAN.

Hakibbutz Hameuchad Publishing House Ltd: POB 16040, 27 Sutin St, Tel-Aviv 64684; tel. 3-5452228; fax 3- 5230022; f. 1940; general; Dir UZI SHAVIT.

Hanitzotz A-Sharara Publishing House: POB 41199, Jaffa 61411; tel. 3-6839145; fax 3-6839148; 'progressive' booklets and publications in Arabic, Hebrew and English.

Hod-Ami: 6 Hareuveni St, Herzliya 46160; tel. 9-9564716; fax 9-9571582; e-mail hodami@netvision.net.il; f. 1984; computer science; Man. Dir ITZHAK AMIHUD.

Intermedia Audio, Video and Book Publishing Ltd: 20 Hashmal St, Tel-Aviv 61367; tel. 3-5608501; fax 3-5608513; business, education, English as a second language, journalism, health, nutrition, mathematics, medicine, nursing, dentistry, self-help; Man. Dir ARIE FRIED.

Israeli Music Publications Ltd: POB 7681, 25 Keren Hayesod St, Jerusalem 91076; tel. 2-6251370; fax 2-6241378; f. 1949; books on music and musical works; Dir of Music Publications SERGEY KHANUKAEV.

Izre'el Publishing House Ltd: 76 Dizengoff St, Tel-Aviv; tel. 3-285350; f. 1933; Man. ALEXANDER IZRE'EL.

The Jerusalem Publishing House Ltd: POB 7147, 39 Tchernechovski St, Jerusalem 91071; tel. 2-5636511; fax 2-5634266; f. 1967; biblical research, history, encyclopaedias, archaeology, arts of the Holy Land, cookbooks, guide books, economics, politics; Dir SHLOMO S. GAFNI; Man. Editor RACHEL GILON.

Jewish History Publications (Israel 1961) Ltd: POB 1232, 29 Jabotinski St, Jerusalem; tel. 2-5632310; f. 1961; encyclopaedias, World History of the Jewish People series; Chair. ALEXANDER PELI; Editor-in-Chief Prof. J. PRAWER.

Karni Publishers Ltd: POB 22383, 32 Schocken St, Tel-Aviv 61223; tel. 3-6812244; fax 3-6826138; f. 1951; children's and educational books; Publrs O. ZMORA.

Keter Publishing House Ltd: POB 7145, Givat Shaul B, Jerusalem 91071; tel. 2-6557822; fax 2-536811; e-mail heter01@netvision .net.il; f. 1959; original and translated works of fiction, encyclopaedias, non-fiction, guide books and children's books; publishing imprints: Israel Program for Scientific Translations, Keter Books, Encyclopedia Judaica; Man. Dir YIPTACH DEKEL.

Kinneret Publishing House: 10 Habanai St, Holom 58850; tel. 3-5582252; fax 3-5582255; f. 1980; child development and care, cookery, dance, educational, humour, non-fiction, music, home-care, psychology, psychiatry, travel; Man. Dir YORAM ROS.

Kiryat Sefer: 15 Arlosoroff St, Jerusalem; tel. 2-521141; f. 1933; concordances, dictionaries, textbooks, maps, scientific books; Dir AVRAHAM SIVAN.

Ma'ariv Book Guild Ltd: 3 Rehov Hilazon, Ramat-Gan 52522; tel. 3-5752020; fax 3-7525906; f. 1954 as Sifriat-Ma'ariv Ltd; Man. Dir IZCHAK KFIR; Editor-in-Chief ARYEH NIR.

Magnes Press: The Hebrew University, POB 7695, Jerusalem 91076; tel. 2-5660341; telex 25391; fax 2-5633370; f. 1929; biblical studies, Judaica, and all academic fields; Dir DAN BENOVICI.

Rubin Mass Ltd: POB 990, 7 Ha-Ayin- Het St, Jerusalem 91000; tel. 2-6277863; fax 2-6277864; e-mail rmass@inter.net.il; f. 1927; Hebraica, Judaica, export of all Israeli publications; Dir OREN MASS.

Massada Press Ltd: Jabotinsky 29, Jerusalem 92141; tel. 2-5632310; f. 1932; biography, history, education, cookery, psychology, psychiatry, philosophy, religion, science, social sciences, sociology; Chair. and CEO ALEXANDER PELI.

Ministry of Defence Publishing House: 107 Ha' Hashmonaim St, Tel-Aviv 67133; tel. 3-5655900; fax 3-5655994; f. 1939; military literature, Judaism, history and geography of Israel; Dir JOSEPH PERLOVITZ.

M. Mizrachi Publishing House: 106 Allenby Rd, Tel-Aviv; tel. 3-621492; fax 3-5660274; f. 1960; children's books, novels; Dir MEIR MIZRACHI.

Mosad Harav Kook: POB 642, Jerusalem; tel. 2-526231; f. 1937; editions of classical works, Torah and Jewish studies; Dir Rabbi M. KATZENELENBOGEN.

Otsar Hamoreh: POB 303, 8 Ben Saruk, Tel-Aviv; tel. 3-260211; f. 1951; educational.

Alexander Peli Jerusalem Publishing Co Ltd: POB 1232, 29 Jabotinsky St, Jerusalem; tel. 2-5632310; f. 1977; encyclopaedias, Judaica, history, the arts, educational material; Chair. ALEXANDER PELI.

Schocken Publishing House Ltd: POB 2316, 24 Nathan Yelin Mor St, Tel-Aviv 67015; tel. 3-5610130; fax 3-5622668; f. 1938; general; Dir Mrs RACHELI EDELMAN.

Shikmona Publishing Co Ltd: POB 7145, Givat Shaul B, Jerusalem 91071; tel. 2-6557822; fax 2-536811; e-mail ketera@netvision .net.il; f. 1965; Zionism, archaeology, art, guide-books, fiction and non-fiction; Man. Dir YIPTACH DEKEL.

Sifriat Poalim Ltd: Gate 3, 24 Kibbutz Galuiot St, Tel-Aviv 68166; tel. 3-5183143; fax 3-5183191; f. 1939; general literature; Gen. Man. NATHAN SHAHAM.

Sinai Publishing Co: 72 Allenby St, Tel-Aviv 65172; tel. 3-663672; f. 1853; Hebrew books and religious articles; Dir MOSHE SCHLESINGER.

Steinhart-Katzir: POB 16540, Tel-Aviv 61164; tel. 3-6997561; fax 3-6997562; e-mail steinhartkatzir@compuserve.com; f. 1991; travel.

Tehrikover Publishers Ltd: 12 Hasharon St, Tel-Aviv 66185; tel. 3-370621; fax 3-374729; education, psychology, economics, psychiatry, literature, literary criticism, essays, history geography, criminology, art, languages, management; Man. Editor S. TCHERIKOVER.

Tel-Aviv Books: MAP House, 18 Tchernikhovski St, Tel-Aviv 61560; tel. 3-6203252; fax 3-5257725; e-mail map@netvision.net.il; f. 1985; history; specializes in maps; Man. Dir DANI TRACZ; Editor-in-Chief MOULI MELTZER.

World Zionist Organization Torah Education Dept: POB 10615, Jerusalem 91104; tel. 2-6759232; fax 2-6759230; f. 1945; education, Jewish philosophy, studies in the Bible, children's books published in Hebrew, English, French, Spanish, German, Swedish and Portuguese.

Yachdav United Publishers Co Ltd: POB 20123, 29 Carlebach St, Tel-Aviv; tel. 3-5614121; fax 3-5611996; f. 1960; educational; Chair. EPHRAIM BEN-DOR; Exec. Dir AMNON BEN-SHMUEL.

Yavneh Publishing House Ltd: 4 Mazeh St, Tel-Aviv 65213; tel. 3-6297856; telex 35770; fax 3-6293638; f. 1932; general; Dir AVSHALOM ORENSTEIN.

Yeda Lakol Publications Ltd: POB 1232, 29 Jabotinsky St, Jerusalem; tel. 2-5632310; f. 1961; encyclopaedias, Judaica, the arts, educational material, children's books; Chair. ALEXANDER PELI.

Yedioth Ahronoth Books: POB 37744, 5 Mikunis St, Tel-Aviv 61376; tel. 3-374889; telex 33847; fax 3-5377820; f. 1952; non-fiction, Jewish religion, health, music, dance, fiction, education; Man. Dir ISRAEL SHALEV; Editor-in-Chief JON FEDER.

S. Zack and Co: 2 King George St, Jerusalem 94229; tel. 2-6257819; fax 2-6252493; f. c. 1930; fiction, science, philosophy, Judaism, children's books, educational and reference books, dictionaries; Dir MICHAEL ZACK.

PUBLISHERS' ASSOCIATION

Israel Book Publishers Association: POB 20123, 29 Carlebach St, Tel-Aviv 67132; tel. 3-5614121; fax 3-5611996; f. 1939; mems: 84 publishing firms; Chair. SHAI HAUSMAN; Man. Dir AMNON BEN-SHMUEL.

Broadcasting and Communications

TELECOMMUNICATIONS

Barak I.T.C.: Sival Industrial Park, 15 Harnelacha St, Rosh Hnáyin 48091; fax 3-9001023.

Bezeq, The Israel Telecommunication Corpn Ltd: POB 1088, 15 Hazvi St, Jerusalem 91010; tel. 2-5395333; telex 25225; fax 2-5378184; Pres. ISAAC KAUL.

RADIO

Israel Broadcasting Authority (IBA) (Radio): POB 28080, Jerusalem; tel. 2-240124; telex 26488; fax 2-257034; f. 1948; station in Jerusalem with additional studios in Tel-Aviv and Haifa. IBA broadcasts six programmes for local and overseas listeners on medium, shortwave and VHF/FM in 16 languages; Hebrew, Arabic, English, Yiddish, Ladino, Romanian, Hungarian, Moghrabi, Persian, French, Russian, Bucharian, Georgian, Portuguese, Spanish and Amharic; Chair. MICHA YINON; Dir-Gen. URI PORAT; Dir of Radio (vacant); Dir External Services VICTOR GRAJEWSKY.

Galei Zahal: MPOB 01005, Zahal; tel. 3-814888; fax 3-814697; f. 1950; Israeli defence forces broadcasting station, Tel-Aviv, with studios in Jerusalem; broadcasts music, news and other programmes on medium-wave and FM stereo, 24-hour in Hebrew; Dir MOSHE SHLENSKY; Dir of Engineering G. KERNER.

Kol Israel (The Voice of Israel): POB 1082, 21 Heleni Hamalka, Jerusalem 91010; tel. 2-248715; telex 25263; fax 2-253282; internet http://www-artificia.com/html/news.cgi; broadcasts music, news, and multilingual programmes for immigrants in Hebrew, Arabic, French and English on medium wave and FM stereo; Dir and Prog. Dir AMNON NADAV.

TELEVISION

Israel Broadcasting Authority (IBA): POB 7139, Jerusalem 91071; tel. 2-5301333; fax 2-292944; broadcasts began in 1968; station in Jerusalem with additional studios in Tel-Aviv; one colour network (VHF with UHF available in all areas); one satelite channel; broadcasts in Hebrew, Arabic and English; Dir-Gen URI PORAT; Dir of Television YAIR STERN; Dir of Engineering RAFI YEOSHUA.

Israel Educational Television: Ministry of Education and Culture, 14 Klausner St, Tel-Aviv; tel. 3-6415270; fax 3-6427091; f. 1966 by Hanadiv (Rothschild Memorial Group) as Instructional Television Trust; began transmission in 1966; school programmes form an integral part of the syllabus in a wide range of subjects; also adult education; Gen. Man. AHUVA FAINMESSE; Dir of Engineering S. KASIF.

In 1986 the Government approved the establishment of a commercial radio and television network to be run in competition with the state system.

Finance

(cap. = capital; p.u. = paid up; dep. = deposits; m. = million; res = reserves; brs = branches)

BANKING

Central Bank

Bank of Israel: POB 780, Bank of Israel Bldg, Kiryat Ben-Gurion, Jerusalem 91007; tel. 2-6552211; telex 25214; fax 2-6528805; e-mail webmaster@bankisrael.gov.il; f. 1954 as the Central Bank of the State of Israel; cap. 60m. new shekels, res 10m. new shekels, dep. 41,449m. new shekels (Dec. 1996); Gov. Prof. JACOB A. FRENKEL; 2 brs.

Principal Israeli Banks

American Israel Bank Ltd: 28A Rothschild Blvd, Tel-Aviv 61013; tel. 3-5647070; telex 341217; fax 3-5647114; f. 1933; subsidiary of Bank Hapoalim BM; total assets 3,330.5m. new shekels, dep. 3,064.1m. new shekels (Dec. 1996); Chair. Y. ELINAV; 18 brs.

Bank Hapoalim BM: POB 27, 50 Rothschild Blvd, Tel-Aviv 66883; tel. 3-5673333; telex 342342; fax 3-5607028; e-mail international@bnhp.co.il; f. 1921 as the Workers' Bank, name changed as above 1961; total assets 155,807m. new shekels, dep. 129,746m. new shekels (Dec. 1996); Chair. Bd of Man. and CEO AMIRAM SIVAN; 366 brs in Israel and abroad.

Bank Leumi le-Israel BM: POB 2, 24–32 Yehuda Halevi St, Tel-Aviv 65546; tel. 3-5148111; telex 33586; fax 3-5661872; f. 1902 as Anglo-Palestine Co; renamed Anglo-Palestine Bank 1930; reincorporated as above 1951; total assets 112,673m. new shekels, dep. 104,428m. new shekels (Dec. 1996); Chair. EITAN RAFF; Pres. and CEO GALIA MAOR; 242 brs.

Euro-Trade Bank Ltd: POB 37318, 41 Rothschild Blvd, Tel-Aviv 66883; tel. 3-5643838; telex 371530; fax 3-5602483; f. 1953; total assets 166,650m. new shekels, dep. 127,357m. new shekels (Dec. 1996); Chair. REUVEN KOKOLEVITZ; Man. Dir MENAHEM WEBER.

First International Bank of Israel Ltd: POB 29036, Shalom Mayer Tower, 9 Ahad Ha'am St, Tel-Aviv 65251; tel. 3-5196111; telex 341252; fax 3-5100316; f. 1972 as a result of a merger between The Foreign Trade Bank Ltd and Export Bank Ltd; total assets 32,035m. new shekels, cap. 22,486m. new shekels, dep. 25,435m. new shekels (Dec. 1996); Chair. YIGAL ARNON; Man. Dir SHLOMO PIOTRKOWSKY; 77 brs.

Industrial Development Bank of Israel Ltd: POB 33580, 2 Dafna St, Tel-Aviv 61334; tel. 3-6972727; telex 033646; fax 3-6972893; f. 1957; total assets 9,718.4m. new shekels (Dec. 1996); Chair. SHLOMO BOROCHEV; Gen. Man. YEHOSHUA ICHILOV.

Israel Continental Bank Ltd: POB 37406, 65 Rothschild Blvd, Tel-Aviv 61373; tel. 3-5641616; telex 341447; fax 3-200399; f. 1974; capital held jointly by Bank Hapoalim BM (63%) and Bank für Gemeinwirtschaft AG (37%); cap. and res 148.3m. new shekels, dep. 821.9m. new shekels (Dec. 1996); Chair. A. SIVAN; Man. Dir P. HOREV; 3 brs.

Israel Discount Bank Ltd: 27-31 Yehuda Halevi St, Tel-Aviv 65136; tel. 3-5145555; telex 33724; fax 3-5145346; e-mail intidb@netvision.net.il; f. 1935; cap p.u. 93m. new shekels, dep. 73,571m. new shekels (Sept. 1997); Chair. ARIE MIENTKAVICH; Pres. and CEO AVRAHAM ASHERI; some 168 brs in Israel and abroad.

Israel General Bank Ltd: POB 677, 38 Rothschild Blvd, Tel-Aviv 61006; tel. 3-5645645; telex 33515; fax 3-5645210; f. 1934 as Palestine Credit Utility Bank Ltd, name changed as above 1964; total assets 2,883.2m. new shekels, dep. 2,620.4m. new shekels (Dec. 1996); Chair. Baron EDMOND DE ROTHSCHILD; Man. Dir ELIEZER YONES; 3 brs.

Leumi Industrial Development Bank Ltd: POB 2, 35 Yehuda Halevi St, Tel-Aviv 65136; tel. 3-5149945; telex 33586; fax 3-5149897; f. 1944; subsidiary of Bank Leumi le-Israel BM; cap. and res 73m. new shekels (Dec. 1996); Chair. B. NAVEH; Gen. Man. M. ZIV.

Maritime Bank of Israel Ltd: POB 29373, 35 Ahad Ha'am St, Tel-Aviv 65202; tel. 3-5642222; telex 33507; fax 3-5642323; f. 1962; total assets 838.8m. new shekels, dep. 505.1m. new shekels (Sept. 1997); Chair. SHIMON TOPOR.

Mercantile Bank of Israel Ltd: POB 512, 24 Rothschild Blvd, Tel-Aviv; tel. 3-5607541; telex 341344; fax 3-5607949; f. as Barclays Discount Bank Ltd in 1971 by Barclays Bank International Ltd and Israel Discount Bank Ltd to incorporate Israel brs of Barclays; Israel Discount Bank Ltd became the sole owner in February 1993; total assets 334.3m. new shekels, dep. 297.8m. new shekels (Dec. 1995); Gen. Man. LEON GERSHON.

Union Bank of Israel Ltd: POB 2428, 6–8 Ahuzat Bayit St, Tel-Aviv 65143; tel. 3-5191276; telex 033493; fax 3-5191606; f. 1951; total assets 10,283m. new shekels, dep. 10,011m. new shekels (Dec. 1996); Chair. D. FRIEDMANN; 27 brs.

United Mizrahi Bank Ltd: POB 309, 13 Rothschild Blvd, Tel-Aviv 61002; tel. 3-5679211; telex 03-33625; fax 3-5604780; f. 1923 as Mizrahi Bank Ltd; 1969 absorbed Hapoel Hamizrahi Bank Ltd and name changed as above; total assets 47,243.3m. new shekels, dep. 45,203.6m. new shekels (Dec. 1996); Chair. DAVID BRODET; Gen. Man. VICTOR MEDINA; 114 brs.

Mortgage Banks

Discount Mortgage Bank Ltd: 16–18 Simtat Beit Hashoeva, Tel-Aviv 65814; tel. 3-7107333; fax 3-5661704; f. 1959; subsidiary of Israel Discount Bank Ltd; cap. p.u. 1.3m. new shekels, res 380.4m. new shekels (Dec. 1996); Chair. G. LAHAV; Jt Gen. Mans M. ELDAR, J. SHEMESH.

First International Mortgage Bank Ltd.: 39 Montefiore St, Tel-Aviv 65201; tel. 3-5643311; fax 3-5643321; f. 1922 as the Mortgage and Savings Bank, name changed as above 1996; subsidiary of First International Bank of Israel Ltd; cap. and res 334m. shekels (Dec. 1996); Chair. S. PIOTRKOWSKY; Man. Dir P. HAMO; 50 brs.

Leumi Mortgage Bank Ltd: POB 69, 31–37 Montefiore St, Tel-Aviv 65201; tel. 3-5648444; fax 3-5648334; f. 1921; subsidiary of Bank Leumi le-Israel BM; total assets 18,234.2m. new shekels (Dec. 1996); Chair. A. ZELDMAN; Gen. Man. B. AVITAL.

Mishkan-Hapoalim Mortgage Bank Ltd: POB 1610, 2 Ibn Gvirol St, Tel-Aviv 64077; tel. 3-6970505; fax 3-6959662; f. 1950; subsidiary of Bank Hapoalim BM; total assets 8,289m. new shekels, dep. 10,268.3m. new shekels (Dec. 1993); Chair. M. OLENIK; Man. Dir A. KROIZER; 131 brs.

Tefahot, Israel Mortgage Bank Ltd: POB 93, 9 Heleni Hamalka St, Jerusalem 91902; tel. 2-6755222; fax 2-6755344; f. 1945; subsidiary of United Mizrahi Bank Ltd; cap. and res 667m. new shekels, total assets 15,057m. new shekels (Sept. 1994); Chair. C. KUBERSKY; Man. Dir URI WÜRZBURGER; 60 brs.

STOCK EXCHANGE

Tel-Aviv Stock Exchange: POB 29060, 54 Ahad Ha'am St, Tel-Aviv 65202; tel. 3-5677411; fax 3-5105379; e-mail spokesperson@tase.co.il; internet http://www.tase.co.il; f. 1953; Chair. Prof. YAIR E. ORGLER; Gen. Man. SAUL BRONFELD.

INSURANCE

The Israel Insurance Asscn lists 35 companies, a selection of which are listed below; not all companies are members of the association.

Ararat Insurance Co Ltd: Ararat House, 13 Montefiore St, Tel-Aviv 65164; tel. 3-640888; telex 341484; f. 1949; Co-Chair. AHARON DOVRAT, PHILIP ZUCKERMAN; Gen. Man. PINCHAS COHEN.

Aryeh Insurance Co of Israel Ltd: 9 Ahad Ha'am St, Tel-Aviv 65251; tel. 3-5141777; telex 342125; fax 3-5179337; f. 1948; Chair. ELIEZER KAPLAN.

Clal Insurance Co Ltd: POB 326, 42 Rothschild Blvd, Tel-Aviv 61002; tel. 3-627711; telex 341701; fax 3-622666; f. 1962; Man. Dir RIMON BEN-SHAOUL.

Hassneh Insurance Co of Israel Ltd: POB 805, 115 Allenby St, Tel-Aviv 61007; tel. 3-5649111; telex 341105; f. 1924; Man. Dir M. MICHAEL MILLER.

Israel Phoenix Assurance Co Ltd: 30 Levontin St, Tel-Aviv 65116; tel. 3-5670111; telex 341199; fax 3-5601242; f. 1949; Chair. of Board JOSEPH D. HACKMEY; Man. Dir Dr ITAMAR BOROWITZ.

Maoz Insurance Co Ltd: Tel-Aviv; f. 1945; formerly Binyan Insurance Co Ltd; Chair. B. YEKUTIELI.

Menorah Insurance Co Ltd: Menorah House, 73 Rothschild Blvd, Tel-Aviv 65786; tel. 3-5260771; telex 341433; fax 3-5618288; f. 1935; Gen.-Man. SHABTAI ENGEL.

Migdal Insurance Co Ltd: POB 37633, 26 Sa'adiya Ga'on St, Tel-Aviv 61375; tel. 3-5637637; telex 32361; part of Bank Leumi Group; f. 1934; Chair. S. GROFMAN; CEO U. LEVY.

Palglass Palestine Plate Glass Insurance Co Ltd: Tel-Aviv 65541; f. 1934; Gen. Man. AKIVA ZALZMAN.

Sahar Israel Insurance Co Ltd: POB 26222, Sahar House, 23 Ben-Yehuda St, Tel-Aviv 63806; tel. 3-5140311; telex 33759; f. 1949; Chair. G. HAMBURGER.

Samson Insurance Co Ltd: POB 33678, Avgad Bldg, 5 Jabotinski Rd, Ramat-Gan 52520, Tel-Aviv; tel. 3-7521616; fax 3-7516644; f. 1933; Chair. E. BEN-AMRAM; Gen. Man. GIORA SAGI.

Sela Insurance Co Ltd: 53 Rothschild Blvd, Tel-Aviv 65124; tel. 3-61028; telex 35744; f. 1938; Man. Dir E. SHANI.

Shiloah Co Ltd: 2 Pinsker St, Tel-Aviv 63322; f. 1933; Gen. Man. Dr S. BAMIRAH; Man. Mme BAMIRAH.

Yardenia Insurance Co Ltd: 22 Maze St, Tel-Aviv 65213; f. 1948; Man. Dir H. LEBANON.

Zion Insurance Co Ltd: POB 1425, 41–45 Rothschild Blvd, Tel-Aviv 61013; f. 1935; Chair. A. R. TAIBER.

Trade and Industry

CHAMBERS OF COMMERCE

Federation of Israeli Chambers of Commerce: POB 20027, 84 Hahashmonaim St, Tel-Aviv 67011; tel. 3-5631010; telex 33484; fax 3-5619025; co-ordinates the Tel-Aviv, Jerusalem, Haifa and Beersheba Chambers of Commerce; Pres. DAN GILLERMAN.

Jerusalem Chamber of Commerce: POB 2083, 10 Hillel St, Jerusalem 91020; tel. 2-6254333; fax 2-6254335; f. 1908; c. 300 mems; Pres. JOSEPH PERLMAN.

Haifa Chamber of Commerce and Industry (Haifa and District): POB 33176, 53 Haatzmaut Rd, Haifa 31331; tel. 4-8626364; fax 4-8645428; f. 1921; 700 mems; Pres. S. GANTZ; Man. Dir C. WINNYKAMIN.

Chamber of Commerce, Tel-Aviv-Jaffa: POB 20027, 84 Hahashmonaim St, Tel-Aviv 61200; tel. 3-5631010 telex 33484; fax 3-5619025; f. 1919; 1,800 mems; Pres. DAN GILLERMAN.

Federation of Bi-National Chambers of Commerce and Industry with and in Israel: 76 Ibn Gvirol St, Tel-Aviv; tel. 3-264790; telex 342315; fax 3-221783; federates: Israel-America Chamber of Commerce and Industry; Israel-British Chamber of Commerce; Australia-Israel Chambers of Commerce; Chamber of Commerce and Industry Israel-Asia; Chamber of Commerce Israel-Belgique-Luxembourg; Canada-Israel Chamber of Commerce and Industry; Israel-Denmark Chamber of Commerce; Chambre de Commerce Israel-France; Chamber of Commerce and Industry Israel-Germany; Camera di Commercio Israeli-Italia; Israel-Japan Chamber of Commerce; Israel-Latin America, Spain and Portugal Chamber of Commerce; Netherlands-Israel Chamber of Commerce; Israel-Yugoslavia Chamber of Commerce; Israel-Greece Chamber of Commerce; Israel-Bulgaria Chamber of Commerce; Israel-Ireland Chamber of Commerce; Handelskammer Israel-Schweiz; Israel-South Africa Chamber of Commerce; Israel-Sweden Chamber of Commerce; Israel-Hungary Chamber of Commerce; Israel-Romania Chamber of Commerce; Israel-Russia Chamber of Commerce; Israel-Poland Chamber of Commerce; also incorporates Bi-National Chamber of Commerce existing in 20 foreign countries with Israel; Chair. J. ZIV; Vice-Chair. BEZALEL BLEI.

Israel-British Chamber of Commerce: POB 4610, 65 Allenby Road, Tel-Aviv 61046; tel. 3-5252232; telex 342315; fax 3-6203032; e-mail isbrit@netvision.net.il; f. 1951; 350 mems; Chair. AMNON DOTAN; Exec. Dir FELIX KIPPER.

INDUSTRIAL AND TRADE ASSOCIATIONS

Agricultural Export Co (AGREXCO): Tel-Aviv; state-owned agricultural marketing organization; Dir-Gen. AMOTZ AMIAD.

The Agricultural Union: Tchlenov 20, Tel-Aviv; consists of more than 50 agricultural settlements and is connected with marketing and supplying organizations, and Bahan Ltd, controllers and auditors.

Central Union of Artisans and Small Manufacturers: POB 4041, Tel-Aviv 61040; f. 1907; has a membership of more than 40,000 divided into 70 groups according to trade; the union is led by a 17-man Presidium; Chair. JACOB FRANK; Sec. ITZHAK HASSON; 30 brs.

Citrus Marketing Board: POB 80, Beit Dagan 50250; tel. 3-9683811; fax 3-9683838; f. 1942; the central co-ordinating body of citrus growers and exporters in Israel; represents the citrus industry in international organizations; licenses private exporters; controls the quality of fruit; has responsibility for Jaffa trademarks; mounts advertising and promotion campaigns for Jaffa citrus fruit worldwide; carries out, research into and development of new varieties of citrus fruit, and 'environmentally friendly' fruit; Chair. D. KRITCHMAN; Gen. Man. M. DAVIDSON.

Farmers' Union of Israel: POB 209, 8 Kaplan St, Tel-Aviv; tel. 3-69502227; fax 3-6918228; f. 1913; membership of 7,000 independent farmers, citrus and winegrape growers; Pres. PESACH GRUPPER; Dir-Gen. SHLOMO REISMAN.

Fruit Board of Israel: POB 20117, 119 Rehov Hahashmonaim, Tel-Aviv 61200; tel. 3-5612929; fax 3-5614672; Dir-Gen. SHALOM BLAYER.

General Asscn of Merchants in Israel: 6 Rothschild Blvd, Tel-Aviv; the organization of retail traders; has a membership of 30,000 in 60 brs.

Israel Cotton Production and Marketing Board Ltd: POB 384, Herzlia B'46103; tel. 3-9509491; telex 32120; fax 3-9509159.

Israel Diamond Exchange Ltd: POB 3222, Ramat-Gan, Tel-Aviv; tel. 3-5760211; fax 3-5750652; f. 1937; production, export, import and finance facilities; net exports (1997) US $4,101m.; Pres. ITZHAK FOREM.

Israel Export Institute: POB 50084, 29 Rehov Hamered, Tel-Aviv 68125; tel. 3-5142830; fax 3-5142902; Dir-Gen. AMIR HAYEK.

Israel Journalists' Asscn Ltd: 4 Kaplan St, Tel-Aviv; tel. 3-256141; Sec. YONA SHIMSHI.

Kibbutz Industries Asscn: 8 Rehov Shaul Hamelech, Tel-Aviv 64733; tel. 3-6955413; fax 3-6951464; e-mail luz@netvision.net.il; liaison office for marketing and export of the goods produced by Israel's kibbutzim; Pres. MICHA HERTZ.

Manufacturers' Asscn of Israel: POB 50022, Industry House, 29 Hamered St, Tel-Aviv 61500; tel. 3-5198787; fax 3-5162026; 1,700 mem.-enterprises employing nearly 85% of industrial workers in Israel; Pres. DAN PROPPER.

The Histadrut

Hahistadrut Haklalit shel Haovdim Beeretz Israel (General Federation of Labour in Israel): 93 Arlosoroff St, Tel-Aviv 62098; tel. 3-6921111; telex 342488; fax 3-6969906; f. 1920; publs *Labour in Israel* (quarterly) in English, French, Spanish and German.

The General Federation of Labour in Israel, usually known as the Histadrut, is the largest voluntary organization in Israel, and the most important economic body in the state. It is open to all workers, including the self-employed, members of co-operatives and of the liberal professions, as well as housewives, students, pensioners and the unemployed. Members of two small religious labour organizations, Histadrut Hapoel Hamizrahi and Histadrut Poalei Agudat Israel, also belong to the trade union section and social services of the Histadrut, which thus extend to *c.* 85% of all workers. Dues—between 3.6% and 5.8% of wages—cover all its trade union, health insurance and social service activities. The Histadrut engages in four main fields of activity: trade union organization (with some 50 affiliated trade unions and 65 local labour councils operating throughout the country); social services (including a comprehensive health insurance scheme 'Kupat Holim', pension and welfare funds, etc.); educational and cultural activities (vocational schools, workers' colleges, theatre and dance groups, sports clubs, youth movement); and economic development (undertaken by Hevrat Ovdim (Labour Economy), which includes industrial enterprises partially or wholly owned by the Histadrut, agricultural and transport co-operatives, workers' bank, insurance company, publishing house etc.). A women's organization, Na'amat, which also belongs to the Histadrut, operates nursery homes and kindergartens, provides vocational education and promotes legislation for the protection and benefit of working women. The Histadrut publishes its own daily newspaper, *Davar,* in Hebrew. The Histadrut is a member of the ICFTU and its affiliated trade secretariats, APRO, ICA and various international professional organizations.

Secretary-General: HAIM RAMON.

ORGANIZATION

In 1989 the Histadrut had a membership of 1,630,000. In addition some 110,000 young people under 18 years of age belong to the

Organization of Working and Student Youth, a direct affiliate of the Histadrut.

All members take part in elections to the Histadrut Convention (Veida), which elects the General Council (Moetsa) and the Executive Committee (Vaad Hapoel). The latter elects the 41-member Executive Bureau (Vaada Merakezet), which is responsible for day-to-day implementation of policy. The Executive Committee also elects the Secretary-General, who acts as its chairman as well as head of the organization as a whole and chairman of the Executive Bureau. Nearly all political parties are represented on the Histadrut Executive Committee.

The Executive Committee has the following departments: Trade Union, Organization and Labour Councils, Education and Culture, Social Security, Industrial Democracy, Students, Youth and Sports, Consumer Protection, Administration, Finance and International.

TRADE UNION ACTIVITIES

Collective agreements with employers fix wage scales, which are linked with the retail price index; provide for social benefits, including paid sick leave and employers' contributions to sick and pension and provident funds; and regulate dismissals. Dismissal compensation is regulated by law. The Histadrut actively promotes productivity through labour management boards and the National Productivity Institute, and supports incentive pay schemes. There are some 50 trade unions affiliated to the Histadrut.

There are unions for the following groups: clerical workers, building workers, teachers, engineers, agricultural workers, technicians, textile workers, printing workers, diamond workers, metal workers, food and bakery workers, wood workers, government employees, seamen, nurses, civilian employees of the armed forces, actors, musicians and variety artists, social workers, watchmen, cinema technicians, institutional and school staffs, pharmacy employees, medical laboratory workers, X-ray technicians, physiotherapists, social scientists, microbiologists, psychologists, salaried lawyers, pharmacists, physicians, occupational therapists, truck and taxi drivers, hotel and restaurant workers, workers in Histadrut-owned industry, garment, shoe and leather workers, plastic and rubber workers, editors of periodicals, painters and sculptors and industrial workers.

Histadrut Trade Union Department: Dir Haim Haberfeld.

ECONOMIC ACTIVITIES AND SOCIAL SERVICES

These include Hevrat Haovdim (Economic Sector, literally, 'the Workers' Company', employing 260,000 workers in 1983), Kupat Holim (the Sick Fund, covering almost 77% of Israel's population), seven pension funds, and NA'AMAT (women's organization which runs nursery homes and kindergartens, organizes vocational education and promotes legislation for the protection and benefit of working women).

Other Trade Unions

General Federation of West Bank Trade Unions: Sec.-Gen. Shaher Saad.

Histadrut Haovdim Haleumit (National Labour Federation): 23 Sprintzak St, Tel-Aviv 64738; tel. 3-6958351; fax 3-6961753; f. 1934; 170,000 mems; Chair. Hirshzon Abraham.

Histadrut Hapoel Hamizrahi (National Religious Workers' Party): 166 Even Gavirol St, Tel-Aviv 62023; tel. 3-5442151; fax 3-5468942; 150,000 mems in 85 settlements and 15 kibbutzim; Sec.-Gen. Eliezer Abtabi.

Histadrut Poale Agudat Israel (Agudat Israel Workers' Organization): POB 11044, 64 Frishman St, Tel-Aviv; tel. 3-5242126; fax 3-5230689; has 33,000 members in 16 settlements and 8 educational insts.

Transport

RAILWAYS

Freight traffic consists mainly of grain, phosphates, potash, containers, petroleum and building materials. Rail service serves Haifa and Ashdod ports on the Mediterranean Sea, while a combined rail-road service extends to Eilat port on the Red Sea. Passenger services operate between the main towns: Nahariya, Haifa, Tel-Aviv and Jerusalem. In 1988 the National Ports Authority assumed responsibility for the rail system.

Israel Railways: POB 18085, Central Station, Tel-Aviv 61180; tel. 3-6937401; telex 46570; fax 3-6937480; the total length of main line is 530 km and there are 170 km of branch line; gauge 1,435 mm; Gen. Man. Ehud Hadar.

Underground Railway

Haifa Underground Funicular Railway: 122 Hanassi Ave, Haifa 34633; tel. 04-376861; fax 04-376875; opened 1959; 2 km in operation; Man. Avi Tellem.

ROADS

In 1996 there were 15,065 km of paved roads, of which 56 km were motorways, 4,745 km highways, main or national roads and 10,064 km other roads.

Ministry of National Infrastructure: POB 13198, Public Works Dept, Jerusalem; tel. 2-277211; fax 2-823532.

SHIPPING

At 31 December 1996 Israel's merchant fleet consisted of 54 vessels amounting to 218,990 grt.

Haifa and Ashdod are the main ports in Israel. The former is a natural harbour, enclosed by two main breakwaters and dredged to 45 ft below mean sea-level. In 1965 the deep water port was completed at Ashdod which had a capacity of about 8.6m. tons in 1988.

The port of Eilat is Israel's gate to the Red Sea. It is a natural harbour, operated from a wharf. Another port, to the south of the original one, started operating in 1965. Gaza port fulfils the needs of the Gaza Strip.

The Israel Ports and Railways Authority: POB 20121, Maya Building, 74 Petach Tikva Rd, Tel-Aviv 61201; tel. 3-5657000; fax 3-5121048; f. 1961; to plan, build, develop, administer, maintain and operate the ports and railways. In 1988/89 investment plans amounted to US $68m. for the development budget in Haifa, Ashdod and Eilat ports. Cargo traffic April 1989–March 1990 amounted to 16.2m. tons (oil excluded); Chair. Arthur Israelovichi; Dir-Gen. Shoresh Lever.

ZIM Israel Navigation Co Ltd: POB 1723, 7–9 Pal-Yam Ave, Haifa 31000; tel. 04-8652111; telex 46501; fax 04-8652956; f. 1945; runs cargo and container services in the Mediterranean and to northern Europe, North, South and Central America, the Far East, Africa and Australia; operates 79 ships (including 6 general cargo ships, 23 container ships, 7 multipurpose ships, 1 bulk carrier and 1 pure car carrier); total cargo carried: more than 11.2m. metric tons in 1995; Chair. (vacant); Acting Pres. and CEO Dr Y. Sebba.

CIVIL AVIATION

Israel Airports Authority: Ben-Gurion International Airport, Tel-Aviv; tel. 3-9710576; telex 381050; fax 3-9721722; Dir-Gen. Avi Kostelitz.

El Al Israel Airlines Ltd: POB 41, Ben-Gurion International Airport, Tel-Aviv 70100; tel. 3-9716111; telex 381007; fax 3-9716040; f. 1948; daily services to most capitals of Europe; over 20 flights weekly to New York; services to the USA, Canada, China, Egypt, India, Kenya, South Africa, Thailand and Turkey; Pres. Joel Feldschuh.

Arkia Israeli Airlines Ltd: POB 39301, Sde-Dov Airport, Tel-Aviv 61392; tel. 3-6902222; telex 341749; fax 3-6991390; f. 1980 through merger of Kanaf-Arkia Airlines and Aviation Services; scheduled passenger services linking Tel-Aviv, Jerusalem, Haifa, Eilat, Rosh Pina and Masada; charter services to European destinations; Chair. Y. Arnon; Pres. and CEO Prof. Israel Borovich.

Tourism

In 1996 some 1,919,604 foreign tourists visited Israel.

Ministry of Tourism: POB 1018, 24 King George St, Jerusalem 91000; tel. 2-6754811; fax 2-6250890; Minister of Tourism Moshe Katzav; Dir-Gen. David Litvak.

Israeli-Occupied Territories and Emerging Palestinian Autonomous Areas

Introductory Survey

THE WEST BANK AND GAZA STRIP

Location, Climate, Flag, Capital

The West Bank (Judaea and Samaria) covers an area of 5,879 sq km (2,270 sq miles) and can be divided into three major sub-regions: the Mount Hebron massif, approximately 45 km long by 20 km wide, the peaks of which rise to between 700 m and 1,000 m above sea-level; the Jerusalem mountains, which extend to the northernmost point of the Hebron-Bethlehem massif; and the Mount Samaria hills, the central section of which—the Nablus mountains—reaches heights of up to 800 m before descending to the northern, Jenin hills, of between 300 m and 400 m. The eastern border of the West Bank is bounded by the valley of the River Jordan, leading to the Dead Sea (part of the Syrian-African rift valley), into which the River Jordan drains. The latter is 400 m below sea-level. Precipitation ranges between 600 mm and 800 mm on the massif and 200 mm in the Jordan Valley; 36% of the area is classified as cultivable land, 32% grazing land, 27% desert or rocky ground and 5% natural forest. Apart from the urban centres of Bethlehem and Hebron to the south, the majority of the Palestinian population is concentrated in the northern districts around Ramallah, Nablus, Jenin and Tulkaram. In November 1988 the Palestine National Council (PNC) proclaimed Jerusalem as the capital of the newly-declared independent State of Palestine. In fact, West Jerusalem has been the capital of the State of Israel since 1950. In 1967 East Jerusalem was formally annexed by Israel and is regarded as part of Israel by the Israeli authorities although the annexation has never been recognized by the UN. Under the terms of the Declaration of Principles on Palestinian Self-Rule concluded by Israel and the Palestinian component of the Jordanian-Palestinian delegation to the Middle East peace conference in September 1993, negotiations on the final status of the city are scheduled to begin not later than the beginning of the third year of the five-year transitional period following the completion of Israel's withdrawal from the Gaza Strip and the Jericho area.

The Gaza Strip, lying beside the Mediterranean Sea and the border with Egypt, is approximately 45 km long by 8 km wide at its widest point. Crossed only by two shallow valleys, the 378 sq km area is otherwise almost entirely flat, and has no surface water. Annual average rainfall is 300 mm. Gaza City is the main population centre.

The Palestinian flag (proportions 2:1) has three equal, horizontal stripes of black, white and green, with a red triangle the base of which corresponds to the hoist.

Administration

Until the end of the 1948 Arab-Israeli War, the West Bank formed part of the British Mandate of Palestine, before becoming part of the Hashemite Kingdom of Jordan under the Armistice Agreement of 1949. It remained under Jordanian sovereignty, despite Israeli occupation in 1967, until King Hussein of Jordan formally relinquished legal and administrative control on 31 July 1988. Under Israeli military occupation the West Bank was administered by a military government, which divided the territory into seven sub-districts. The Civil Administration, as it later became known, did not extend its jurisdiction to the many Israeli settlements which were established under the Israeli occupation; settlements remained subject to the Israeli legal and administrative system. By 1992 approximately 67% of the West Bank was under direct Israeli control, either resulting from settlement building (believed to have covered some 10% of the total area of the West Bank) on what has become Israeli 'state land', or through areas being declared closed military areas. Palestinians were believed to be in control of less than 5% of the total area of the West Bank.

An administrative province under the British Mandate of Palestine, Gaza was transferred to Egypt after the 1949 armistice and remained under Egyptian administration until June 1967, when it was invaded and occupied by Israel. Following Israeli occupation the Gaza Strip, like the West Bank, became an 'administered territory'. Until the provisions of the Declaration of Principles on Palestinian Self-Rule began to take effect, the management of day-to-day affairs was the responsibility of the area's Israeli military commander. Neither Israeli laws nor governmental and public bodies—including the Supreme Court—could review or alter the orders of the military command to any great extent. By 1993 it was estimated that approximately 50% of the land area was under Israeli control, either through Jewish settlements having been established or through areas being closed by the military.

In accordance with the Declaration of Principles on Palestinian Self-Rule of September 1993, and the Cairo Agreement on the Gaza Strip and Jericho, the PLO assumed control of the Jericho Area of the West Bank and of the Gaza Strip on 17 May 1994. In November and December 1995, under the terms of the Israeli-Palestinian Interim Agreement on the West Bank and the Gaza Strip signed by Israel and the PLO on 28 September, Israeli armed forces withdrew from the West Bank towns of Nablus, Ramallah, Jenin, Tulkaram, Kalkilya and Bethlehem. In late December the PLO assumed responsibility in some 17 areas of civil administration in the town of Hebron. In all of these localities the PLO's jurisdiction is exercised through the Palestinian Legislative Council elected in January 1996. In the 400 surrounding villages the PLO will eventually assume full responsibility for civil affairs, but the Israeli armed forces will retain freedom of movement to act against potential hostilities there. In Hebron Israel effected a partial redeployment of its armed forces in January 1997, but retains responsibility for the security of some 400 Jewish settlers occupying some 15% of the town. Responsibility for security in the rest of Hebron passed to the Palestinian police force, but Israel retains responsibility for security on access roads. It has been agreed (under the Interim Agreement of September 1995) that Israel will retain control over a large area of the West Bank (including Jewish settlements, rural areas, military installations and the majority of junctions between Palestinian roads and roads used by Israeli troops and settlers) until July 1997. Following the first phase of the redeployment and the holding, on its completion, of elections to a Palestinian legislative council and for a Palestinian executive president, Israel was to carry out a second phase of redeployment from rural areas, to be completed by July 1997. The Israeli occupation will be maintained in Jewish settlements, military installations, East Jerusalem and the Jewish settlements around Jerusalem until a final settlement of the Palestinian question, scheduled for May 1999. Subsequent postponements, and negotiations within the context of the Oslo peace process resulted in a new timetable for redeployment which envisaged two phases, subsequent to the Hebron withdrawal, to be completed by October 1997 and August 1998. By March 1997, however, conflicting interpretations of the extent of both the phased and total final redeployment (90% of the West Bank according to the Palestinians; less than 50% according to the Israelis) seemed certain to frustrate hopes that the new timetable would be adhered to. This seemingly intractable situation was compounded, in the same month, by the Israeli Government's decision to recommence construction of Jewish settlements in East Jerusalem, and by the subsequent resurgence in terrorist activity in mid–late 1997, which consequently paralysed the redeployment issue. In late November, a month after diplomatic activity resumed, the Israeli Government agreed to a partial withdrawal from the West Bank but stated neither the extent nor the timing of the redeployment. Palestinian proposals for a withdrawal from 30% of the West Bank were rejected by Israel, which reportedly planned to relinquish between 6% and 8%.

In late April 1997 Yasser Arafat's audit office announced the misappropriation by PNA ministers of $326m. of public funds. Khalid al-Quidram, the General Prosecutor of the PNA, who promptly resigned following the accusations, was reportedly placed under house arrest in early June. At the end of July a parliamentary committee, appointed by Arafat to conduct an inquiry into the affair, concluded that the Cabinet should be dissolved and some members put on trial: half of the ministers were allegedly implicated. In early August the Cabinet submitted its resignation to Yasser Arafat, which was duly accepted in December. However, the Cabinet was to remain in a provisional capacity until a new Government was formed in early 1998.

Demography and Economic Affairs

In 1996, according to estimates by the IMF, the gross national product (GNP) of the West Bank and the Gaza Strip, measured at current prices, was US $3,438m., equivalent to $1,346 per head. During 1993–96, it was estimated, GNP per head declined, in real terms, at an average annual rate of 6.7%. Over the same period, the population was estimated to have increased by an average annual rate of 4.0%. The region's gross domestic product (GDP) increased, in real terms, by 10.8% in 1994 and by an estimated 3.3% in 1995, but declined by 1.6% in 1996.

According to the Israeli Central Bureau of Statistics, agriculture (including hunting, forestry and fishing) contributed 16.1%–16.7% of GDP in the West Bank and 15.5%–15.9% of GDP in the Gaza Strip, and in 1996 employed 17% of the total labour force in the Territories, whilst 10.3% of the Gaza Strip's and West Bank's total labour force working in Israel were employed in agriculture in 1992. Olives, citrus fruits, vegetables and potatoes are all important crops, and the livestock sector is also significant. In spite of small increases in production in recent years, amongst other constraints, expansion in the West Bank and Gaza Strip is severely limited by problems with irrigation. The proportion of irrigated land in the West Bank is estimated to be less than 5%, compared with 45% within Israel. Of the total annual average water consumption by Palestinians of 115m. cu m, approximately 100m. cu m is for use in agriculture. The imbalance in allocation of this resource is reflected in figures for 1990, which show that the West Bank Palestinian population was allocated 137m. cu m by the Israeli authorities, compared with an allocation of 160m. cu m for 30 Israeli agricultural settlements and a population of approximately 100,000 settlers. In the Gaza Strip irrigation of the important citrus crop has been affected by rising salinity in the ground-water supply. In Central Gaza ground-water salinity levels are three times as high as the World Health Organization's recommended safety level. The area also suffers from a water deficit. Estimated annually at approximately 50m. cu m, the water deficit could reach 150m. cu m by 2000. The fishing industry, formerly one of the Gaza Strip's most profitable industries, has been severely constricted by Israeli military control over the area in which Palestinian boats may fish, including the prohibition of any fishing beyond a 19-mile radius established by the Israeli authorities.

According to Israel's Central Bureau of Statistics, industry (manufacturing, quarrying and mining) contributed an estimated 6.3%–6.6% of GDP in the West Bank and 12.5%–12.8% of GDP in the Gaza Strip in 1991. In 1996 the sector employed 17% of the labour force working in the West Bank and the Gaza Strip. In 1992 7% of West Bank Palestinians working in Israel were employed in industry, whilst an estimated 4.3% of Gaza Strip Palestinians employed in Israel were working in the sector. In 1991 construction in the Gaza Strip contributed 17.2%-17.6% of GDP. An estimated 75.4% of the Gazan labour force working in Israel were employed in construction in 1992, whilst 73.7% of West Bank Palestinians employed in Israel worked in the sector.

In 1991 public and community services (including electricity and water services) contributed 10.5%–10.9% of GDP in the West Bank and possibly as much as 50% of GDP in the Gaza Strip. In that year 5.4% of the Gazan labour force were employed in service industries, whilst service industries may have employed as many as 13.8% of those West Bank Palestinians employed in Israel. In 1996 the sector employed 30% of the total labour force working in the two Territories.

Despite concerted attempts during the Palestinian *intifada* to escape from Israeli economic domination, the relationship of the economy of the Gaza Strip and West Bank is still one of dependence. Israel remains by far the largest market for goods and services from the West Bank. Trade with Israel represents some 75% of exports from, and 87% of imports to, the Territories. Israel is also a significant employer of the burgeoning Palestinian labour force, although the proportion of the West Bank and Gazan labour force employed in Israel decreased from 17.0% in 1993 to an estimated 4.6% in 1996; meanwhile, the West Bank and Gazan unemployment rate increased from 18% in 1993 to an estimated 34% in 1996. Prior to the *intifada*, in 1987, the West Bank recorded a balance-of-trade deficit with Israel of $420.2m.; the value of exports to Israel amounted to $160.5m., compared with imports worth $580.7m. During 1988–90 the export of goods and services from the West Bank fell at an average annual rate of 16%, and the overall trade deficit was aggravated by the 1990/91 crisis in the Persian (Arabian) Gulf region, when the closure of borders and reduced demand affected the export of agricultural goods and manufactures to Arab markets. In 1992 the Gaza Strip recorded a trade deficit with Israel of $264.7m. (exports $63.8m., imports $328.5m.). In its trade with all countries the Gaza Strip recorded a deficit of $286.9m. (exports $79.3m., imports $366.2m.) in 1992. The value of Gazan exports to Jordan in 1992 amounted to $11.9m., while that of imports from Jordan was negligible. In its trade with all other countries, the Gaza Strip recorded a deficit of $34.1m. (exports $3.6m., imports $37.7m.) in 1992. In 1996 the West Bank and Gaza Strip recorded a visible trade deficit of an estimated $1,179m., and a deficit of $708m. on the current account of the balance of payments. During that year the value of exports to Israel was estimated to $278m., whilst the value of imports in the private sector amounted to an estimated $1,350m. In January 1998 Israel opened up its borders in accordance with the 1994 economic agreement signed with the PLO, allowing Palestinians to export various items of agricultural produce to Israel.

Attempts by the Palestinians in the early years of the *intifada* to disengage from the Israeli economy through the boycott of taxes levied by the Israeli authorities provoked a severe response. By the end of 1989, after two years of boycotts during which revenues for Israel declined by one-third, forced collections by the military authorities and intensive 'tax raids' had almost re-established the pre-1988 tax collection level. Israeli tax collection policy, as a form of collective punishment and a means of asserting Israeli control, caused a decline in the standard of living, constrained business expansion and reduced the personal savings of Palestinians in the territory. However, perhaps the strongest link with the Israeli economy, and the one which has proved the most difficult to break, is the employment that Palestinians find within the 'Green Line', which provides many families with their livelihoods. In 1992 some 35% of the West Bank's and 45% of the Gazan labour force was employed in Israel, mainly in unskilled and semi-skilled occupations—especially in the construction industry. In 1993, following a series of attacks on Jews within Israel, the Israeli Prime Minister, Itzhak Rabin, ordered the closure of Israel's borders with the West Bank and the Gaza Strip, preventing an estimated 70,000 West Bank and some 50,000 Gazan Palestinians from travelling to work. Palestinian leaders claim that some $1.6m. in income was lost as a result of the closure. Significantly, controls on cross-border movement were relaxed only after considerable pressure from Israeli employers; the 'reserve labour force' of 100,000 or so unemployed Israelis had been reluctant to do the Palestinians' work, which is often of a low-paid, menial nature. Israel's borders with the West Bank and the Gaza Strip were again closed in late 1994, following further attacks on Jews within Israel. Suicide bomb attacks on Jewish targets by agents of the Islamic Resistance Movement (Hamas) and of other so-called 'rejectionist organizations' led to further such closures at various times in 1995–97. The border policy of the Israeli authorities is thus one of the most important factors affecting the Palestinian economy: some 25% of Palestinian GNP is derived from remittances from Palestinians employed in Israel. In 1996 the Gaza Strip's and West Bank's budget deficit was estimated at $112m. (equivalent to 3.5% of GDP). Consumer prices increased at an annual average of 12.3% in 1991–94 and increased by an estimated 10.8% in 1995 and an estimated 7.9% in 1996. Unemployment in the Territories increased from 19.1% in 1991 to an estimated 34.2% in 1996, owing to intermittent closure of the Territories.

Following the signing of the Declaration of Principles on Palestinian Self-Rule in the Occupied Territories in September 1993, hopes were raised in the West Bank that future economic reconstruction would be financed from abroad. A World Bank report on the Occupied Territories estimated that a 10-year programme to construct essential infrastructure and social facilities would cost $3,000m. The PLO, with a more ambitious Palestine Development Programme (PDP), estimated that the reconstruction of the Palestinian economy during 1994–2000 would cost $11,600m. The planners expected $2,000m. to come from domestic savings, and the remainder from external donors; however, it was unclear how much of the total would be allocated to the West Bank if the plan were to be implemented. Following the signing of the Declaration of Principles in 1993, international donors pledged to invest some $2,900m. in the Gaza Strip and the West Bank. However, only $1,348m. of the $2,490m. pledged between 1994 and 1996 actually reached the Palestinian authorities owing to the vicissitudes of the peace process and to donors' concerns about the accountability of the Palestinian institutions involved. In December 1997 following a meeting, held under the auspices of the World Bank, of the Consultative Group of donors (to the Palestinian authorities), a three-year economic development plan, costing some $2,600m., was approved. The scheme aimed to rehabilitate the national economy and reduce Palestinian dependence on Israel. The plan's most substantial investments were to be made in infrastructure projects, including improvement of irrigation, road construction, and waste disposal. Private-sector projects, including agriculture and tourism, would also receive funds. The donor countries committed some $750m.-worth of aid for 1998, which would help finance the initial year of the development plan.

The IMF anticipated an improvement in the economy of the West Bank and Gaza Strip in 1997, following a period of stabilization towards the end of 1996 (growth of 8% was predicted). A short closure of the Occupied Territories in March did not appear to have serious implications for economic development and the average number of Palestinian workers entering Israel had increased from 22,000 in 1996 to 37,000 by mid-1997. Hopes for economic growth were frustrated in August after Israeli sanctions were reimposed on the West Bank and Gaza Strip (see p. 1790) including the partial suspension of payment of tax revenues which were to total some $50m. A month after the closures, losses in the West Bank and Gaza Strip were reported to total $31.1m., and export revenue had decreased by $29.9m. It was feared that the sanctions would be a distinct disincentive to investors, thereby threatening economic prospects for the Territories in the long term.

In January 1998 the PNA drafted a budget for the period 1998–2000, totalling $3,600m. The budget, expected to be completely financed by donor countries, was to allocate $1,690m. to infrastructure projects, $856m. to the public sector, $604m. to manufacturing and $304m. to private institutions.

Social Welfare

According to a study by the World Bank, programmes operated by the United Nations Relief and Works Agency for Palestine Refugees in the Near East (UNRWA) form the basis of the social welfare system in the West Bank and the Gaza Strip, since about one-half of the population there are registered refugees. A number of these programmes are directed at particularly vulnerable groups, such as the aged and the physically disabled. Palestinians working for Israeli employers are required to participate in Israel's national social security scheme. However, taxes deducted from Palestinian workers finance only very limited benefits to Palestinians as residency in Israel is a requirement to qualify for most Israeli schemes. Jordanian employment law applies to workers in the West Bank, whilst Egyptian employment law applies in the Gaza Strip. The Egyptian law regulates the conditions of work, including a minimum wage for employees and the maximum hours of work. However, neither law provides for pension rights, old-age insurance, survivor benefits, compensation for work-related disabilities, health insurance or family benefits.

Health services in the West Bank and the Gaza Strip are provided by the Israeli Civil Administration (whose jurisdiction in the Jericho Area has been transferred to the Palestine National Authority), the UNRWA, private voluntary organizations and private, profit-seeking organizations. Institutions operated by the Israeli Civil Administration in the West Bank derive from Jordanian systems whilst those operated in the Gaza Strip come from the Egyptian health care system. Until 1974, when a government health insurance scheme was introduced, residents of the West Bank were entitled to free health care from these facilities. Now only members of the government health insurance scheme may receive comprehensive care at government facilities without charge. Prenatal care and preventive services are provided by the Civil Administration free of charge to all children under the age of three years. The UNRWA provides basic health care free of charge to some 940,000 registered refugees in the West Bank and the Gaza Strip. It also reimburses refugees for 60% of the cost of hospital treatment obtained outside the UNRWA system. In 1991 the UNRWA spent about US $8m. on health programmes in the West Bank and $12m. on those in the Gaza Strip. According to the World Bank, the cost in 1991 of providing health care to the residents of the West Bank and the Gaza Strip represented about 7% of GNP, or about 9% of GDP. Israeli government health care services in the West Bank and the Gaza Strip were provided at 14 hospitals and 165 primary health care centres in 1990. The UNRWA provides its services through a network of 33 health centres in the West Bank where some 61 physicians care for about 400,000 refugees. The UNRWA also operates feeding centres, dental clinics, maternity centres and a 34-bed hospital. Nine health centres in the Gaza Strip provide UNWRA services. There are 82 physicians serving more than 500,000 refugees. Two government hospitals in the Gaza Strip are used to provide secondary care. In the West Bank and the Gaza Strip more than 700 physicians (about one-third of all physicians practising there) work at clinics in the voluntary and for-profit sectors.

THE GOLAN HEIGHTS

Location, Climate

The Golan Heights, a mountainous plateau which formed most of Syria's Quneitra Province (1,710 sq km) and parts of Dera'a Province, was occupied by Israel after the 1967 Arab-Israeli War. Following the Disengagement Agreement of 1974, Israel continued to occupy some 70% of the territory (1,176 sq km), valued for its strategic position and abundant water resources (the headwaters of the River Jordan have their source on the slopes of Mount Hermon). The average height of the Golan is approximately 1,200 m above sea-level in the northern region and about 300 m above sea-level in the southern region, near Lake Tiberias (the Sea of Galilee). Rainfall ranges from about 1,000 mm per year in the north to less than 600 mm per year in the southern region.

Administration

Prior to the Israeli occupation, the Golan Heights were incorporated by Syria into a provincial administration of which the city of Quneitra, with a population at the time of 27,378, was capital. The disengagement agreement that was mediated in 1974 by the US Secretary of State, Henry Kissinger, after the 1973 Arab-Israeli War, provided for the withdrawal of Israeli forces from Quneitra. Before they withdrew, however, Israeli army engineers destroyed the city. In December 1981 the Israeli Knesset enacted the Golan Annexation Law, whereby Israeli civilian legislation was extended to the territory of Golan, now under the administrative jurisdiction of the Commissioner for the Northern District of Israel. The Arab-Druze community of the Golan immediately responded by declaring a three-day strike and appealed to the UN Secretary-General to force Israel to rescind the annexation decision. At the seventh round of multilateral talks between Israeli and Arab delegations in Washington in August 1992, the Israeli Government of Itzhak Rabin for the first time accepted that UN Security Council Resolution 242, adopted in 1967, applied to the Golan Heights. The withdrawal of Israel from the Golan Heights is one of President Assad of Syria's primary objectives in any future peace agreement with Israel.

Demography and Economic Affairs

As a consequence of the Israeli occupation, an estimated 93% of the ethnically diverse Syrian population of 147,613, distributed across 163 villages and towns and 108 individual farms, was expelled. The majority were Arab Sunni Muslims, but the population also included Alawite and Druze minorities and also some Circassians, Turcomen, Armenians and Kurds. Approximately 9,000 Palestinian refugees from the 1948 Arab-Israeli War also inhabited the area. At the time of the occupation, the Golan was a predominantly agricultural province, 64% of the labour force of which was employed in agriculture. Only one-fifth of the population resided in the administrative centres. By 1991 the Golan Heights had a Jewish population of approximately 12,000, living in 21 Jewish settlements (four new settlements had been created by the end of 1992), and a predominantly Druze population of approximately 16,000 living in the only six remaining villages, of which Majd ash-Shams is by far the largest. The Golan Heights have remained predominantly an agricultural area, and, although large numbers of the Druze population now work in Israeli industry in Eilat, Tel-Aviv and Jerusalem, the indigenous economy relies almost solely on the cultivation of apples, for which the area is famous. The apple orchards benefit from a unique combination of fertile soils, abundance of water and a conducive climate.

EAST JERUSALEM

Location, Climate

Greater Jerusalem includes Israeli West Jerusalem (99% Jewish), the Old City and Mount of Olives, East Jerusalem (the Palestinian residential and commercial centre), Arab villages declared to be part of Jerusalem by Israel in 1967 and Jewish neighbourhoods constructed since 1967, either on land expropriated from Arab villages or in areas requisitioned as 'government land'. Although the area of the Greater Jerusalem district is 627 sq km, the Old City of Jerusalem covers just 1 sq km.

Administration

Until the 1967 Arab-Israeli War, Jerusalem had been divided into the new city of West Jerusalem—captured by Jewish forces in 1948—and the old city, East Jerusalem, which was part of Jordan. Israel's victory in 1967, however, reunited the city under Israeli control. Two weeks after the fighting had stopped, on 28 June, Israeli law was applied to East Jerusalem and the municipal boundaries were extended by 45 km (28 miles). Jerusalem had been, in effect, annexed. Israeli officials, however, still refer to the 'reunification' of Jerusalem.

Demography and Economic Affairs

In June 1993 the deputy mayor of Jerusalem, Avraham Kahila, declared that the city now 'had a majority of Jews', based on population projections which estimated the Jewish population at 158,000 and the Arab population at 155,000. This was a significant moment for the Israeli administration, as this had been a long-term objective. Immediately prior to the June 1967 Arab-Israeli War, East Jerusalem and its Arab environs had an Arab population of approximately 70,000, and a small Jewish population in the old Jewish quarter of the city. By contrast, Israeli West Jerusalem had a Jewish population of 196,000. As a result of this population imbalance, in the Greater Jerusalem district as a whole the Jewish population was in the majority even prior to the occupation of the whole city in 1967. Israeli policy following the occupation of East Jerusalem and the West Bank consisted of encircling the eastern sector of the city with Jewish settlements. In contrast to the more politically sensitive siting of Jewish settlements in the old Arab quarter of Jerusalem, the Government of Itzhak Rabin concentrated on the outer circle of settlement building. Greater Jerusalem has been reported to have a Jewish majority of 73%.

The Old City, within the walls of which are found the ancient quarters of the Jews, Christians, Muslims and Armenians, has a population of approximately 25,500 Arabs and 2,600 Jews. In addition, there are some 600 recent Jewish settlers in the Arab quarter.

Many imaginative plans have been submitted with the aim of finding a solution to the problem of sharing Jerusalem between Arabs and Jews, including the proposal that the city be placed under international trusteeship, under the auspices of the UN. However, to make the implementation of such plans an administrative as well as a political quagmire, the Israeli administration, after occupying the whole city in June 1967, began creating 'facts on the ground'.

Immediately following the occupation, all electricity, water and telephone grids in West Jerusalem were extended to the east. Roads were widened and cleared, and the Arab population immediately in front of the 'Wailing Wall' was forcibly evicted. Arabs living in East Jerusalem became 'permanent residents' and could apply for Israeli citizenship if they wished (in contrast to Arabs in the West Bank and Gaza Strip). However, few chose to do so. None the less, issued with identity cards (excluding the estimated 25,000 Arabs from the West Bank and Gaza Strip living illegally in the city), the Arab residents were taxed by the Israeli authorities, and their businesses and banks became subject to Israeli laws and business regulations. Now controlling approximately one-half of all land in East Jerusalem and the surrounding Palestinian villages (previously communally, or privately, owned by Palestinians), the Israeli authorities allowed Arabs to construct buildings on only 10%–15% of the land in the city; and East Jerusalem's commercial district has been limited to three streets. The Palestinian economy was quite seriously affected by the drop in tourism during the *intifada* and by curfews, enforced tax collections and confiscations of property exercised by the Israeli authorities.

Directory

Administration

PALESTINE NATIONAL AUTHORITY*

(February 1998)

Appointed in May 1994, the Palestine National Authority (PNA) has assumed some of the civil responsibilities formerly exercised by the Israeli Civil Administration in the Gaza Strip and the Jericho Area of the West Bank.

CABINET

(February 1998)

Minister of Civil Affairs: JAMIL AT-TARIFI (Fatah).

Minister of the Interior: AHMAD TAMIMI (Fatah).

Minister of Planning and International Co-operation: NABIL SHAATH (Fatah).

Minister of Finance: MUHAMMAD ZOHDI AN-NASHASHIBI (Independent).

Minister of Justice: FURAYH ABU MIDDAYN (Fatah).

Minister of Sports and Youth: (vacant).

Minister of Culture, Arts and Information: YASSER ABD AR-RABBUH (Democratic Party).

Minister of Awqaf (Religious Endowments): HASSAN TAHBOOB (Independent).

Minister of Local Authorities: Dr SAEB URAYQAT (Fatah).

Minister of Social Affairs: INTISAR AL-WASIR (Fatah).

Minister of Housing: ABD AR-RAHMAN HAMAD (Fatah).

Minister of Telecommunications: IMAD AL-FALLOULI (Islamist).

Minister of Public Works: AZZAM AL-AHMAD (Fatah).

Minister of Supply: ABU ALI SHAHEEN (Fatah).

Minister of Health: RIYAD AZ-ZAANOUN (Fatah).

Minister of Education: YASSER AMR (Fatah).

Minister of Higher Education: HANAN ASHRAWI (Independent).

Minister of Transport: ALI AL-KAWASMEH (Fatah).

Minister of Economy and Commerce: MAHER AL-MASRI (Fatah).

Minister of Industry: BASHIR AL-BARGHOUTHI (Ex-Communist).

Minister of Labour: Dr SAMIR GHOUSHA (PFLP).

Minister of Tourism: ELIAS FURAYZ (Independent).

Minister of Agriculture: ABDUL JAWAD SALEH (Independent).

Minister with Responsibility for Jerusalem Affairs: FAISAL HUSSEINI (Fatah).

General Secretary to the Cabinet: AHMAD ABD AR-RAHMAN (Fatah).

Advisers with ministerial rank: ABDULLAH HOURANI (Refugee Affairs, Independent), ABD AL-AZIZ al-Hajj AHMAD (Ministry of Health, Independent), ABD AL-HAFIDH AL-ASHHAB (Palestine People's Party).

MINISTRIES

Ministry of Civil Affairs: Ramallah; tel. (2) 2-9987336; fax 2-9987334.

Ministry of Planning and International Co-operation: Ramallah; tel. 2-5747045; fax 2-5747046; Gaza; tel. 7-829260; fax 7-824090.

Ministry of Finance: Ramallah; tel. 2-9985881; fax 2-9985880; Gaza; tel. 7-863994; fax 7-820696.

Ministry of the Interior: Gaza; tel. 7-824670; fax 7-862500.

Ministry of Justice: Gaza; tel. 7-822231; fax 7-867109.

Ministry of Sports and Youth: Ramallah; tel. 2-9985981; fax 2-9985991.

Ministry of Culture, Arts and Information: Ramallah; tel. 2-9986205; fax 2-9986204.

Ministry of Awqaf (Religious Endowments): Ramallah; tel. and fax 2-9986410.

Ministry of Local Government: Jericho; tel. 2-9922619; fax 2-9921240.

Ministry of Social Affairs: Ramallah; tel. 2-9986181; fax 2-9955723.

Ministry of Housing: Gaza; tel. 2-822233; fax 2-822235.

Ministry of Telecommunications: Ramallah; tel. 2-9986555; fax 2-9986556.

Ministry of Public Works: Gaza; tel. 7-865900; fax 7-868475; e-mail mopgaza@palnet.com.

Ministry of Supply: Gaza; tel. 7-824324; fax 7-868475.

Ministry of Health: Nablus; tel. 9-829173; fax 9-869809; e-mail pnamoh@palnet.com.

Ministry of Education: Ramallah; tel. 2-9985555; fax 2-9985559.

Ministry of Higher Education: Gaza; tel. 7-829211.

Ministry of Transport: Ramallah; tel. 2-9986947; fax 2-9986943.

Ministry of Economy and Commerce: Gaza; tel. 7-9982370; fax 7-5449032.

Ministry of Industry: Gaza; tel. and fax 7-5749032.

Ministry of Labour: Ramallah; tel. 2-9985607; fax 2-9986496.

Ministry of Tourism and Antiquities: POB 534, Bethlehem; tel. 2-741581; fax 2-743753.

Ministry of Agriculture: Ramallah; tel. 2-9986502; fax 2-9987422.

President

President: YASSER ARAFAT (took office 12 February 1996).

The first election for a Palestinian Executive President was contested on 20 January 1996 by two candidates: Yasser Arafat and Samiha Khalil. Arafat received 88.1% of the votes cast and Samiha Khalil 9.3%. The remaining 2.6% of the votes cast were spoilt.

Legislature

PALESTINIAN LEGISLATIVE COUNCIL

General Election, 20 January 1996

Party	Seats
Fatah	55
Independent Fatah	7
Independent Islamic	4
Independent Christian	3
Independent	15
Samaritan	1
Other	1
Total	86*

* The total number of seats in the Palestinian Legislative Council—including one which is automatically reserved for the Palestinian President—is 89. The results of voting in two constituencies—one in Gaza City and one in North Gaza—were unavailable in early March 1996.

The first Palestinian legislative elections took place in 16 multi-member constituencies—including East Jerusalem—on 20 January 1996. Some 75% of the estimated 1m. eligible Palestinian voters were reported to have participated in the elections. During the approach to the elections European Union observers criticized the election commission appointed by Yasser Arafat—and, indeed, Arafat himself—for late alterations to electoral procedure, which, it was felt, might prejudice the prospects of some candidates at the forthcoming polls. Some irregularities were reported to have occurred while voting took place, but these were not regarded as sufficiently serious to compromise the final outcome. The elections were officially boycotted by all sections of the so-called Palestinian rejectionist opposition, including Hamas and Islamic Jihad, although Hamas did endorse a list of 'approved' candidates for those voters who chose not to boycott the elections. All deputies elected to the Legislative Council automatically became members of the Palestine National Council, the existing 483 members of which were subsequently permitted to return from exile by the Israeli authorities, in order, among other things, to consider amendments to the Palestinian National Charter, which has in many ways been superseded by the agreements concluded between Israel and the PLO since September 1993.

Speaker: AHMED QURAY.

Political Organizations

Palestine Liberation Organization (PLO): Hammam ash-Shaat, Tunis, Tunisia; since the conclusion of the Cairo Agreement on the Gaza Strip and Jericho, signed by the PLO and Israel on 4 May 1994, the PLO has been in the process of transferring its administrative infrastructure and its officers from Tunis to the Gaza Strip, where its headquarters are in Gaza City; f. 1964; the supreme organ of the PLO is the Palestine National Council (PNC), while the Palestine Executive Committee deals with day-to-day business. Fatah (the Palestine National Liberation Movement) joined the PNC in 1968, and all the guerrilla organizations joined the Council in 1969; Chairman: YASSER ARAFAT.

The most important guerrilla organizations are:

Fatah (The Palestine National Liberation Movement): f. 1957; the largest single Palestinian movement, embraces a coalition of varying views from conservative to radical; leader YASSER ARAFAT; Sec.-Gen. FAROUK KADDOUMI; Central Cttee (elected by Fatah's 530-member Congress, 31 May 1980): YASSER ARAFAT, SALAH KHALAF, FAROUK KADDOUMI, MAHMOUD ABBAS, KHALID AL-HASSAN, HAYIL ABD AL-HAMID, MUHAMMAD GHUNAIM, SALIM AZ-ZA'NUN, RAFIQ AN-NATSHAH, HANI AL-HASAN.

Popular Front for the Liberation of Palestine (PFLP): Box 12144, Damascus, Syria; f. 1967; Marxist-Leninist; publ. *Democratic Palestine* (monthly, in English); Leader: GEORGE HABASH; in 1994 the PFLP announced the formation of the Democratic National Action Front (DNAF), which it described as an open political, popular forum, an extension of the PFLP.

Democratic Front for the Liberation of Palestine (DFLP): Damascus, Syria; Marxist; split from the PFLP in 1969; Leader: NAIF HAWATMEH.

Arab Liberation Front (ALF): f. 1969; Iraqi-backed; Leader: MAHMOUD ISMAIL.

Palestine Popular Struggle Front (PPSF): f. 1967; Sec.-Gen. SAMIR GHOUSHA.

Palestine People's Party: formerly Palestine Communist Party, admitted to the PNC at its 18th session in 1987; Sec.-Gen. SULEIMAN NAJJAB.

Palestine Liberation Front (PLF): split from PFLP-GC in April 1977; the PLF split into two factions at the end of 1983, both of which retained the name PLF; one faction (leader 'ABU ABBAS') based in Tunis and Baghdad and remaining nominally loyal to Yasser Arafat; the other faction belonging to the anti-Arafat National Salvation Front and having offices in Damascus, Syria, and Libya. A third group derived from the PLF was reported to have been formed by its Central Cttee Secretary, Abd al-Fattah Ghanim, in June 1986. At the 18th session of the PNC, a programme for the unification of the PLF was announced, with Talaat Yaqoub (died November 1988) named as Secretary-General and 'Abu Abbas' appointed to the PLO Executive Committee, while unification talks were held. The merging of the two factions was announced in June 1987, with 'Abu Abbas' becoming Deputy Secretary-General.

Palestinian Popular Forces Party: f. 1977; Sec.-Gen. Dr ADNAN ABU NAJILAH.

The anti-Arafat **National Salvation Front** includes the following organizations:

Popular Front for the Liberation of Palestine-General Command (PFLP-GC): Damascus, Syria; split from the PFLP; pro-Syrian; Leader: AHMAD JIBRIL.

Saiqa (Vanguard of the Popular Liberation War): f. 1967; Syrian-backed; Leader: ISSAM AL-QADI.

Palestine Revolutionary Communist Party: Damascus; Sec.-Gen.: ARBI AWAD.

Alliance of Palestinian Forces: f. 1994; 10 members representing the PFLP, the DFLP, the PLF, the PPSF, the Palestine Revolutionary Communist Party and the PFLP-GC; opposes the Declaration of Principles on Palestinian Self-Rule signed by Israel and the PLO (Fatah) in September 1993, and subsequent agreements concluded within its framework. The **Fatah Revolutionary Council**, headed by Sabri Khalil al-Banna, alias 'Abu Nidal', split from Fatah in 1973. Its headquarters were formerly in Baghdad, Iraq, but the office was closed down and its staff expelled from the country by the Iraqi authorities in November 1983 and a new base was established in Damascus, Syria, in December. Al-Banna was readmitted to Iraq in 1984, having fled Syria. With 'Abu Musa' (whose rebel Fatah group is called **Al-Intifada**, or 'Uprising'), 'Abu Nidal' formed a joint rebel Fatah command in February 1985, and both had offices in Damascus until June 1987, when those of 'Abu Nidal' were closed by the Syrian Government. In 1989 the Fatah Revolutionary Council was reported to have disintegrated, and in June 1990 forces loyal to Abu Nidal surrendered to Fatah forces at the Rashidiyeh Palestinian refugee camp near Tyre, northern Lebanon.

The Islamic fundamentalist organizations, Islamic Jihad (Gen. Sec. RAMADAN ABDALLAH SHALLAH) and the Islamic Resistance Movement (Hamas; Spiritual Leader Sheikh AHMAD YASSIN, imprisoned in Israel since 1989), are also active in the Gaza Strip and the West Bank, where they began to play an increasingly prominent role in the *intifada* during 1989. Like the organizations represented in the Alliance of Palestinian Forces, they are strongly opposed to the Declaration of Principles on Palestinian Self-Rule. The formation of the Right Movement for Championing the Palestinian People's Sons by former members of Hamas was announced in April 1995. The Movement, based in Gaza City, was reported to support the PNA.

Diplomatic Representation

Countries with which the PLO maintains diplomatic relations include:

Afghanistan, Albania, Algeria, Angola, Austria, Bahrain, Bangladesh, Benin, Bhutan, Botswana, Brunei, Bulgaria, Burkina Faso, Burundi, Cambodia, Cameroon, Cape Verde, Central African Republic, Chad, China (People's Rep.), Comoros, Congo (Dem. Rep.), Congo (Rep.), Cuba, Cyprus, Czechoslovakia (former), Djibouti, Egypt, Equatorial Guinea, Ethiopia, Gabon, Gambia, Ghana, Guinea, Guinea-Bissau, Hungary, India, Indonesia, Iran, Iraq, Jordan, Korea (Dem. People's Rep.), Kuwait, Laos, Lebanon, Libya, Madagascar, Malaysia, Maldives, Mali, Malta, Mauritania, Mauritius, Mongolia, Morocco, Mozambique, Nepal, Nicaragua, Niger, Nigeria, Norway, Oman, Pakistan, Philippines, Poland, Qatar, Romania, Russia, Rwanda, São Tomé and Príncipe, Saudi Arabia, Senegal, Seychelles, Sierra Leone, Somalia, Sri Lanka, Sudan, Swaziland, Sweden, Tanzania, Togo, Tunisia, Turkey, Uganda, United Arab Emirates, Vanuatu, the Vatican City, Viet Nam, Yemen, Yugoslavia, Zambia, Zimbabwe.

The following states, while they do not recognize the State of Palestine, allow the PLO to maintain a regional office: Belgium, Brazil, France, Germany, Greece, Italy, Japan, the Netherlands, Portugal, Spain, Switzerland, the United Kingdom.

A Palestinian passport has been available for residents of the Gaza Strip and the Jericho area only since April 1995. In September 1995 the passport was recognized by 29 states, including: Algeria, Bahrain, Bulgaria, China (People's Rep.), Cyprus, Egypt, France, Germany, Greece, India, Israel, Jordan, Malta, Morocco, the Netherlands, Pakistan, Qatar, Romania, Saudi Arabia, South Africa, Spain, Sweden, Switzerland, Tunisia, Turkey, the United Arab Emirates, the United Kingdom and the USA.

Judicial System

In the Gaza Strip and the West Bank towns of Jericho, Nablus, Ramallah, Jenin, Tulkaram, Kalkilya, Bethlehem and Hebron, the PNA has assumed limited jurisdiction with regard to civil affairs. However, the situation is confused owing to the various, sometimes conflicting legal systems which have operated in the territories occupied by Israel in 1967: Israeli military and civilian law; Jordanian law; and acts, orders-in-council and ordinances that remain from the period of the British Mandate in Palestine. Religious and military courts have been established under the auspices of the PNA. In February 1995 the PNA established a Higher State Security Court in Gaza to decide on security crimes both inside and outside the PNA's area of jurisdiction; and to implement all valid Palestinian laws, regulations, rules and orders in accordance with Article 69 of the Constitutional Law of the Gaza Strip of 5 March 1962.

General Prosecutor of the PNA: FAYIZ ABU RAHMA.

The Press

NEWSPAPERS

Filastin ath-Thawra (Palestine Revolution): normally published in Beirut, but resumed publication from Cyprus in November 1982; weekly newspaper of the PLO.

Al-Hadaf: organ of the PFLP; weekly.

Al-Haria (Liberation): organ of the DFLP.

Al-Hayat al-Jadidah: West Bank; f. 1994; weekly; Editor NADIL AMR.

Al-Istiqal: Gaza City; organ of the Islamic Jihad; weekly.

Al-Watan: Gaza City; supports Hamas; weekly.

PERIODICALS

Filastin (Palestine): Gaza City; f. 1994; weekly.

Shu'un Filastiniya (Palestine Affairs): POB 5614, 92 Gr. Afxentiou St, Nicosia, Cyprus; tel. 461140; telex 4706; monthly.

NEWS AGENCY

Wikalat Anbaa' Filastiniya (WAFA, Palestine News Agency): formerly in Beirut, but resumed activities in Cyprus and Tunis, November 1982; official PLO news agency; Editor ZIAD ABD AL-FATTAH.

Broadcasting and Communications

Palestinian Broadcasting Corpn: Dir-Gen. RADWAN ABU AYYASH.

Sawt Filastin (Voice of Palestine): c/o Police HQ, Jericho; tel. (2) 921220; official radio station of the PLO; broadcasts in Arabic from Jericho; Dir. RADWAN ABU HAYASH.

Finance

(cap. = capital; dep. = deposits; brs = branches; m. = million)

BANKING

PALESTINE MONETARY AUTHORITY

It is intended to develop the Palestine Monetary Authority (PMA) into the Central Bank of Palestine. In July 1995 the PMA began to license, inspect and supervise the Palestinian and foreign commercial banks operating in the Gaza Strip and the Jericho enclave in the West Bank at that time. In December 1995 the PMA assumed responsibility for 13 banks in the Palestinian autonomous areas over which the Central Bank of Israel had hitherto exercised control. The number of bank branches was reported to total 50, including those of three Israeli banks. Deposits in the Palestinian banking system (including those in Palestinian localities outside the jurisdiction of the PNA) totalled about $1,000m. in July 1995. Three currencies circulate in the Palestinian economy—the Jordanian dinar, the Israeli new shekel and the US dollar. The PMA, which is seeking a reserve base of $10m. from donors, currently has no right of issue. According to the PMA, bank deposits in Gaza and the West Bank rose by 47% in 1996, to $1,722m., compared with $1,174m. in 1995. Gov. FOUAD BESEISO.

Investment Banks

Arab Palestine Investment Bank: f. 1996; Arab Bank of Jordan has a 51% share; cap. p.u. US $15m.

Palestine Investment Bank: POB 4045, Omar al-Mukhtar St, Gaza City; tel. (7) 822105; fax (7) 822107; f. 1995 by the PNA; some shareholders based in Jordan and the Gulf states; cap. p.u. US $20m.; provides full commercial and investment banking services throughout the Gaza Strip and the West Bank; 3 brs.

Foreign Banks

Arab Bank plc (Jordan): Regional Management: POB 1476, Ramallah; tel. (2) 9954816; fax (2) 9954815; dep. of some US $800m. held by 12 brs in the West Bank and the Gaza Strip at Sep. 1996; Regional Man. SHUKRI BISHARA.

INSURANCE

A very small insurance industry exists in the West Bank.

Arab Insurance Establishment Co (AIEC): Nablus; Man. Dir IBRAHIM ABD AL-HADI.

DEVELOPMENT FINANCE ORGANIZATION

Palestinian Council for Economic Development and Reconstruction: Gov. NABIL SHAATH.

Trade and Industry

CHAMBERS OF COMMERCE

Tulkaram Chamber of Commerce: Tulkaram; tel. 9-671010; fax 9-675623; e-mail tulkarem@netvision.net.il; f. 1945.

TRADE AND INDUSTRIAL ORGANIZATIONS

Union of Industrialists: Gaza.

Transport

CIVIL AVIATION

Palestinian Civil Aviation Authority (PCAA): Gaza International Airport, Gaza; intends to operate services between Gaza and Egypt, Jordan, Cyprus, Turkey, Saudi Arabia, the Gulf States and the United Kingdom through its subsidiary, Palestinian Airlines; Palestinian Airlines currently operates a limited service from Port Said, Egypt, pending the conclusion of an agreement with the Israeli authorities which would allow it to use Gaza International Airport; Chair. and Dir-Gen. FAYEZ ZAIDAN.

ITALY

Introductory Survey

Location, Climate, Language, Religion, Flag, Capital

The Italian Republic comprises a peninsula, extending from southern Europe into the Mediterranean Sea, and a number of adjacent islands. The two principal islands are Sicily, to the south-west, and Sardinia, to the west. The Alps form a natural boundary to the north, where the bordering countries are France to the north-west, Switzerland and Austria to the north and Slovenia to the north-east. The climate is temperate in the north and Mediterranean in the south, with mild winters and long, dry summers. The average temperature in Rome is 7.4°C (45.3°F) in January and 25.7°C (78.3°F) in July. The principal language is Italian. German and Ladin are spoken in the Alto Adige region on the Austrian border, and French in the Valle d'Aosta region (bordering France and Switzerland), while in southern Italy there are Greek-speaking and Albanian minorities. A language related to Catalan is spoken in north-western Sardinia. Almost all of the inhabitants profess Christianity: more than 90% are adherents of the Roman Catholic Church. There is freedom of expression for other Christian denominations and for non-Christian religions. The national flag (proportions 3 by 2) has three equal vertical stripes, of green, white and red. The capital is Rome.

Recent History

The Kingdom of Italy, under the House of Savoy, was proclaimed in 1861 and the country was unified in 1870. Italy subsequently acquired an overseas empire, comprising the African colonies of Eritrea, Italian Somaliland and Libya. Benito Mussolini, leader of the Fascist Party, became Prime Minister in October 1922 and assumed dictatorial powers in 1925–26. Relations between the Italian State and the Roman Catholic Church, a subject of bitter controversy since Italy's unification, were codified in 1929 by a series of agreements, including the Lateran Treaty, which recognized the sovereignty of the State of the Vatican City (q.v.), a small enclave within the city of Rome, under the jurisdiction of the Pope. Under Mussolini, Italian forces occupied Ethiopia in 1935–36 and Albania in 1939. Italy supported the fascist forces in the Spanish Civil War of 1936–39, and from June 1940 supported Nazi Germany in the Second World War. In 1943, however, as forces from the allied powers invaded Italy, the fascist regime collapsed. In July of that year King Victor Emmanuel III dismissed Mussolini, and the Fascist Party was dissolved.

In April 1945 German forces in Italy surrendered and Mussolini was killed. In June 1946, following a referendum, the monarchy was abolished and Italy became a republic. Until 1963 the Partito della Democrazia Cristiana (DC—Christian Democratic Party) held power unchallenged, while industry expanded rapidly, supported by capital from the USA. By the early 1960s, however, public discontent was increasing, largely owing to low wage rates and a lack of social reform. In the general election of 1963 the Partito Comunista Italiano (PCI—Italian Communist Party), together with other parties of the extreme right and left, made considerable gains at the expense of the DC. During the next decade there was a rapid succession of mainly coalition Governments, involving the DC and one or more of the other major non-communist parties.

Aldo Moro's coalition Government of the DC and the Partito Repubblicano Italiano (PRI—Italian Republican Party), formed in November 1974, resigned in January 1976, following the withdrawal of support by the Partito Socialista Italiano (PSI—Italian Socialist Party). After the failure of a minority DC administration, general elections to both legislative chambers took place in June, at which the PCI won 228 seats in the 630-member Chamber of Deputies. The DC remained the largest party, but could no longer govern against PCI opposition in the legislature. However, the DC continued to insist on excluding the PCI from power, and in July formed a minority Government, with Giulio Andreotti as Prime Minister. He relied on the continuing abstention of PCI deputies to introduce severe austerity measures, in response to the economic crisis. In January 1978 the minority Government was forced to resign, owing to pressure from the PCI, which wanted more active participation in government (since July 1977 the PCI had been allowed to participate in policy-making but had no direct role in government). In March, however, Andreotti formed a new, almost identical Government, with PCI support. In May of the same year Aldo Moro, the former Prime Minister, was murdered by the Brigate Rosse (Red Brigades), a terrorist group. In the following month the President, Giovanni Leone, resigned as a result of allegations of corruption. In July Alessandro Pertini was inaugurated as the first socialist President of the Republic.

The Andreotti administration collapsed in January 1979, when the PCI withdrew from the official parliamentary majority. A new coalition Government, formed by Andreotti in March, lasted only 10 days before being defeated on a vote of no confidence. At elections in June the PCI's share of the votes cast for the Chamber of Deputies declined to 30.4%, and it returned to the role of opposition.

In August 1979 Francesco Cossiga, a former Minister of the Interior, formed a minority 'government of truce', composed of the DC, the Partito Liberale Italiano (PLI—Italian Liberal Party) and the Partito Socialista Democratico Italiano (PSDI—Italian Social Democratic Party), relying on the abstention of the PSI to remain in office. However, the new Government was continually thwarted by obstructionism in Parliament. In April 1980 Cossiga formed a majority coalition, comprising members of the DC, the PRI and the PSI. The deliberate exclusion of the PCI from the Government led to an open campaign by its deputies in the legislature to force the resignation of the new coalition. In September the Government resigned after losing a vote on its economic programme. In October Arnaldo Forlani, the Chairman of the DC, assembled a coalition Government, which included members of the DC, PSI, PRI and PSDI, but the new Government's integrity was damaged by a series of allegations of corruption. In May 1981 the Government was forced to resign, after it became known that more than 1,000 of Italy's foremost establishment figures belonged to a secret masonic lodge named P-2 ('Propaganda Due'), which had extensive criminal connections both in Italy and abroad. The lodge was linked with many political and financial scandals and with right-wing terrorism, culminating in mid-1982 with the collapse of one of Italy's leading banks, Banco Ambrosiano, and the death of its President, Roberto Calvi. In January 1989 a Milan court ruled that Calvi had been murdered, and in April it was announced that Licio Gelli, the former head of P-2, and 34 other people were to be tried on charges related to the Banco Ambrosiano bankruptcy. In March 1991 it was announced that Carlo De Benedetti, one of Italy's most prominent financiers, had been charged with fraudulent bankruptcy in connection with the collapse of the bank. In April 1992, along with more than 30 other defendants, both De Benedetti and Gelli were convicted on charges relating to the bank scandal.

In June 1981 Senator Giovanni Spadolini, leader of the PRI, formed a coalition Government comprising members of the PSI, PRI, DC, PSDI and PLI, thus becoming the first non-DC Prime Minister since 1946. In November 1982, however, Spadolini resigned, following a dispute over economic policy. Amintore Fanfani, a former DC Prime Minister, formed a new coalition Government in December, from members of the PSI, DC, PSDI and PLI. This administration lasted until April 1983, when the PSI withdrew its support. A general election was held in June, at which the DC lost considerable support, winning only 32.9% of the votes for the Chamber of Deputies. The PSI increased its share of the votes to 11.4%, and its leader, Bettino Craxi, was subsequently appointed the first socialist Prime Minister of Italy. He led a five-party coalition which was committed to reducing the budget deficit and implementing economic reforms. There was strong opposition to some of the Government's anti-inflation measures, particularly a government decree, imposed in February 1984, to reduce automatic index-linked wage increases. However, in a referendum on the decree, held in June 1985, 54.3% of votes cast were in support of the Government's policy.

In July 1985 Cossiga succeeded Alessandro Pertini as President of the Republic. In June 1986 the Government lost a vote of confidence in the Chamber of Deputies, thus bringing to an end Italy's longest administration (1,060 days) since the Second World War. Craxi resigned, and President Cossiga nominated a former Prime Minister, Giulio Andreotti (a member of the DC), to attempt to form a new government. However, the refusal of other parties to support Andreotti led to Craxi's return to power in July, on condition that he transfer the premiership to a DC member in March 1987.

Craxi duly submitted his resignation, and that of his Government, in March 1987, but, following the failure of first Andreotti, and then Nilde Jotti, of the PCI, to form a government, President Cossiga requested Craxi to attempt to revive his outgoing administration. However, members of the DC resigned from his Government, in protest against PSI proposals to hold referendums on nuclear issues and judicial reforms. The bitter rivalry between the DC and the PSI ended two further attempts to form a coalition, and a general election was held in June. The DC obtained 34.3% of the votes cast, and the PSI increased its share to 14.3%. The PCI, however, suffered its worst post-war electoral result, winning only 26.6% of the votes, thereby losing 21 seats in the Chamber of Deputies. The Federazione dei Verdi (Green Party) received 2.5% of the votes and entered the Chamber for the first time, occupying 13 seats.

Following the election, Giovanni Goria, a DC member and the former Minister of the Treasury, became Prime Minister, heading a five-party coalition Government. By the end of 1987, however, the Government had lost considerable support, following a series of strikes and other economic problems. Goria offered his resignation in November 1987 (following the withdrawal of the PLI from the coalition) and again in February 1988, but it was rejected both times by President Cossiga. Goria finally resigned in March 1988, as a result of opposition to the Government's decision to resume construction of the Montalto di Castro nuclear power station (suspended in 1987 because of public concern over environmental risks). After five weeks of inter-party talks, Ciriaco De Mita, the Secretary-General of the DC, formed a coalition Government with the same five parties that had served in Goria's administration. In May the Government's decision to grant a measure of autonomy to the Alto Adige region (known as Südtirol to its German-speaking inhabitants), on the north-eastern border with Austria, prompted a series of bombings, perpetrated by German-speaking extremists in the region. At provincial elections held in the Alto Adige region in November, the Movimento Sociale Italiano-Destra Nazionale (MSI-DN, Italian Social Movement-National Right), a neo-fascist group, almost doubled its share of the votes, thus replacing the DC as the largest Italian-language grouping in the region.

In early May 1989 an estimated 16m. workers, led by the three major trade unions, participated in a general strike to protest against a proposal to introduce health service charges. A few days later, severe criticism of De Mita's premiership by Craxi led to the collapse of the coalition Government, after 13 months in power. In June President Cossiga nominated De Mita to form a new government, but in early July De Mita announced that he had been unsuccessful. Cossiga then requested Andreotti to attempt to form a coalition, and in late July the coalition partners of the outgoing Government agreed to form a new administration, with Andreotti as Prime Minister (for the sixth time). The PSI also secured gains, with Gianni De Michelis appointed as the first socialist Minister of Foreign Affairs for many years, while Craxi's deputy, Claudio Martelli, became the Deputy Prime Minister. A further decline in support for the PCI, apparently as a result of the crisis facing communism in Eastern Europe and the suppression of the pro-democracy movement in the People's Republic of China, was revealed at both municipal elections and elections to the European Parliament in May and June respectively. At the municipal elections, the PSI gained a greater share of the votes than the PCI for the first time in 40 years.

In February 1990, as a result of an internal party dispute, De Mita resigned from the presidency of the DC. Supporters of De Mita, who together constituted a left-wing alliance within the DC, also withdrew from party posts, but pledged their continued support for the Andreotti Government. However, the cohesion of the coalition Government was threatened in early 1990 by the response of the PRI to a decree (issued in late 1989 by Claudio Martelli, the socialist Deputy Prime Minister) that aimed, for the first time, to impose restrictions on immigration levels. The PRI demanded more stringent legislation, but the Government's proposals received parliamentary approval in late February 1990.

At local government elections held in May 1990, the DC secured 33.6% of the votes cast, and the PSI won 15%. The PCI saw a further decline in its popularity, winning the support of just 24% of voters. The most significant gains were made by the Lega Nord (Northern League), a grouping of regionalist parties which denounced the 'southern hegemony' of the central Government. One such league, the Lega Lombarda, won almost 20% of the votes cast in the Lombardy region, while the Lega Nord secured 5.6% of the overall national vote.

In early November 1990 it was made known that the existence of a secret defence organization, code-named 'Operation Gladio', had recently been discovered. The Gladio network had been established in the late 1950s by the US Central Intelligence Agency (CIA), in co-operation with the North Atlantic Treaty Organisation (NATO—see p. 204), to plan for a counter-rebellion in the event of an invasion by forces of the Warsaw Pact, or to counter the rise to power of a domestic communist movement. Links were alleged between members of Gladio and the right-wing P-2 movement, and there were further allegations that the network had been involved in acts of terrorism in the early 1980s. In late November 1990 it was announced that Gladio had been formally dissolved, but the issue continued to damage the reputation of President Cossiga, who had admitted that, as an official in the Ministry of Defence in the late 1960s, he had been involved in the administration of the Gladio network. It was also alleged that, during the same period, he had been involved in a conspiracy to tamper with evidence that implicated senior intelligence officers in a plot to thwart the political ambitions of the PCI.

In response to the collapse of communist regimes in Eastern Europe in the late 1980s, the PCI began a process of internal reform. In November 1989 the PCI Central Committee renounced the party's communist identity and began a process of transforming the PCI into a mass social democratic party. In late January and early February 1991 the final Congress of the PCI took place in Rimini, where delegates voted to rename the party the Partito Democratico della Sinistra (PDS—Democratic Party of the Left). A minority of members of the former PCI refused to join the PDS, and in May they formed a communist party, Rifondazione Comunista (RC—Reconstructed Communism).

In March 1991 Italy experienced yet another political crisis, following demands by Craxi, the PSI leader, for the formation of a new government. He alleged that the current Government had failed to implement policies relating to the management of public finances, institutional reforms, effective measures to combat organized crime, and the development of Italy's international role. Despite Andreotti's attempts to preserve government unity, the PSI continued to express dissatisfaction with the Government, and, consequently, Andreotti resigned as Prime Minister. However, in April, following DC party approval, President Cossiga appointed Andreotti to form a new Government. The new administration (the 50th in Italy since the Second World War) initially comprised the same five coalition partners, but, before the Government was sworn in, the three PRI members withdrew, dissatisfied with the portfolios that they had been allocated. The new Government, now a four-party coalition (the DC, PSI, PSDI and PLI), nevertheless received a parliamentary vote of confidence.

At local elections held in May 1991 the DC and the PSI slightly increased their share of votes, mostly at the expense of the PDS. The elections demonstrated the weakness of the neo-fascist MSI-DN: the right-wing vote had apparently been transferred to the new separatist 'leagues', such as the Lega Nord.

In September 1991, apparently in response to widespread nationalist fervour in parts of Eastern Europe, German-speaking separatists from the Alto Adige region made demands for greater autonomy from Italy. In the same month the Union Valdôtaine, the nationalist party governing the Aosta Valley (on the borders of France and Switzerland), announced that it was planning a referendum on secession. Demands for greater autonomy were also made in Sardinia, following a resurgence of activism by militant separatists there. The growing influence of the Lega Lombarda was demonstrated at municipal elections in the important industrial city of Brescia (in Lombardy) in November, when the Lega Lombarda narrowly defeated the DC, hitherto the governing party in the city. (In January 1992 the Italian Government, in an attempt to end a long-standing dispute with Austria over the Alto Adige area, agreed to grant further autonomy to the region.)

In June 1991 a referendum was held to determine whether the voting system used for parliamentary and local elections should be reformed, in an attempt to prevent electoral malpractice and, in particular, interference by the Mafia and similar illegal organizations. The proposal to simplify the complex existing system of proportional representation received the support of 95.6% of participants in the referendum. It was estimated that 62.5% of the electorate had voted, despite the efforts of the PSI to persuade them to boycott the referendum, on the grounds that the reforms would limit the voters' choice of candidates. A new anti-Mafia political party, La Rete (Network), took part in elections to the Sicilian Assembly, also held in June, and obtained some 8% of the votes cast.

At a meeting in August 1991 between the Prime Minister and the leaders of the other coalition parties, it was agreed that the Government would adopt a series of measures with the aim of reducing public expenditure, including a controversial reform of the Italian pensions system. They also agreed not to hold a general election until the first half of 1992. In February 1992 President Cossiga dissolved the legislature and announced that the election would take place on 5 April. The election campaign was marred by the murder of Salvatore Lima, an associate of Andreotti (see below). At the election the DC suffered a setback, its support being reduced to less than 30% of votes cast. The PDS won 16.1% of votes cast for the Chamber of Deputies (a sharp decline compared with the PCI's result in 1987), while the PSI received 13.6%. The Lega Nord, led by Umberto Bossi, performed well in northern Italy, as did La Rete in the south. The results of local polls later in the year confirmed the decline in support for the major parties.

Following the general election, the Prime Minister announced his resignation. Although his mandate did not expire until July 1992, President Cossiga also resigned. Initial attempts to replace the President were unsuccessful, but in late May Cossiga was succeeded by Oscar Luigi Scalfaro the newly-elected President of the Chamber of Deputies. At the end of June a former law professor, Giuliano Amato of the PSI, was appointed Prime Minister. The new Council of Ministers comprised mainly members of the PSI and DC, with the remaining portfolios being allocated to the PSDI, PLI and non-party politicians. The incoming coalition was thus composed of the same four parties as the previous Government. The new administration was committed to economic reform. Its programme of drastic reductions in public expenditure, however, led to large-scale anti-Government protests. In October almost 60 people were injured during clashes between trade unionists and the police.

In October 1992 Mario Segni, a DC deputy, formed the Alleanza Democratica (Democratic Alliance) to encourage support for his proposals for constitutional reform of the electoral system by referendum. He was subsequently elected to the parliamentary constitutional reform commission (*Bicamerale*), which had been established in September under De Mita (who was replaced as President of the DC by Rosa Russo Jervolino). Owing to the commission's failure to achieve a consensus, however, in January 1993 the Constitutional Court ruled that referendums on electoral and other reforms (which were among proposals sponsored by Mario Segni) should take place later that year. Segni subsequently resigned from the commission.

Meanwhile, the extent of a corruption scandal, which had originated in Milan in early 1992, continued to widen. It was alleged that politicians (mainly of the PSI and DC) and government officials had accepted bribes in exchange for the awarding of large public contracts. Hundreds were questioned in connection with the affair. Among those accused of corruption was Gianni De Michelis, the senior PSI official and former Minister of Foreign Affairs. The Government's credibility was seriously undermined in February 1993, when the Minister of Justice, Claudio Martelli of the PSI, was obliged to resign, following his placement under formal investigation for alleged complicity in the collapse in 1982 of Banco Ambrosiano. Shortly afterwards Craxi resigned as Secretary-General of the PSI although he continued to deny accusations of fraud. (He was replaced by Giorgio Benvenuto, the former General Secretary of the trade union, Unione Italiana del Lavoro, and the Director-General of the Ministry of Finance.) The Prime Minister's difficulties were compounded at the end of the month, when the Ministers of Finance and of Health resigned, again following accusations of corruption. However, the Government survived two confidence motions during February. Public disillusionment was further increased upon the resignation of the PRI leader and former minister, Giorgio La Malfa, as a result of allegations of irregularities in party financing. La Malfa had previously been admired for his apparent integrity and for his stance against corruption. In March five DC politicians, including Andreotti, were subject to investigation of their alleged links with the Mafia. The Government position became increasingly untenable, but President Scalfaro appealed to Amato to remain in office until the referendums on constitutional reform had taken place. Later in March the Ministers of Finance and of Agriculture were forced to resign, following accusations of corruption.

On 18 and 19 April 1993 referendums were held throughout Italy on a number of proposed changes to the Constitution, including an amendment providing for the election by majority vote of 75% of the 315 elective seats in the Senate (the remainder would be elected under a system of proportional representation); the ending of state funding of political parties; and the establishment of an environmental regulator. These amendments were approved by a large majority of the 77% of voters who participated in the referendum, reflecting the considerable public disillusionment with the existing political system. (In August Parliament approved a similar system for elections to the Chamber of Deputies.) On 22 April Amato resigned as Prime Minister, and Carlo Azeglio Ciampi was subsequently invited by President Scalfaro to form a new Government. Ciampi, hitherto Governor of the Bank of Italy, was the first non-parliamentarian to be appointed to the position. He stated that the priority of his Government, chosen without consultation with party leaders, was the implementation of electoral reform and the resolution of the country's economic problems by means of a programme of privatization and the reduction of the budget deficit. The new notional coalition comprised the four parties of the outgoing administration but also included the PDS, the PRI and the Federazione dei Verdi. However, the PDS and the Federazione dei Verdi immediately withdrew their ministers from the coalition following the new Government's refusal to lift Craxi's parliamentary immunity from prosecution, although they subsequently continued to support Ciampi's Government. In August the Chamber of Deputies voted to allow Craxi to be investigated by magistrates on four charges of corruption. In May bomb attacks in Rome and Florence raised fears of a campaign by anti-democratic forces to destabilize the country. In the same month the Senate approved the removal of parliamentary immunity from Andreotti to allow investigations into his alleged association with the Mafia; his arrest, however, remained prohibited. On the same day the Chamber of Deputies voted overwhelmingly to abolish parliamentary immunity in cases of corruption and serious crime.

Giorgio Benvenuto resigned as Secretary-General of the PSI in May 1993, owing to the party's opposition to his proposals for reform. He was replaced by another trade unionist, Ottaviano del Turco. The PLI also elected a new party leader, Raffaele Costa, the Minister of Transport, in that month, following the arrest of the former Secretary-General, Renato Altissimo, on corruption charges in March. Investigations were initiated into the activities of the former DC Prime Minister, Arnaldo Forlani, in April. In May corruption investigations extended beyond the ranks of the former parties of the ruling coalition, to encompass politicians of the PDS and PRI, as arrests of leading political and business figures multiplied. At the end of the month demonstrations were held throughout the country to protest at financial corruption and the involvement of politicians in organized crime.

Municipal elections, which took place in a number of Italian cities in June 1993, confirmed the advance of the new parties, La Rete and the federalist Lega Nord (which was victorious in Milan), at the expense of their more established rivals. Of the latter only the PDS maintained its support, and even made some gains in the north and centre of the country.

In September 1993 Diego Curto, head of Milan's commercial court, became the first member of the judiciary to be investigated in connection with Italy's corruption scandals. A senior member of the PDS was also arrested and charged with receiving a bribe from a construction company, as the financial affairs of the former PCI became the focus of scrutiny. At the end of the month Andreotti was charged with having provided the Sicilian Mafia with political protection in exchange for votes in Sicily and complicity in the murder of an investigative journalist who had allegedly discovered evidence linking Andreotti with the Mafia. The trial began in October 1995 and was still in progress in early 1998. In August 1997 Prodi expressed his disbelief at the accusations and Dini also questioned whether the accusations had been politically motivated. In October a principal prosecution witness was arrested following allegations that he continued to be involved in Mafia activities. In November 1993 Giuseppe Leoni, a senator and founding member of the Lega Nord, resigned after a judicial inquiry was initiated into the illegal funding of his electoral campaign. Leoni was the first official of the federalist league to be subject to an investigation.

In October 1993 the Minister of Defence, Fabio Fabbri, suspended the head of the élite Rapid Intervention Force, Gen. Franco Monticone, following the publication of an account of his prominent role in a coup attempt that was envisaged for early 1994 and his involvement with the activities of a terrorist grouping, the Armed Phalange, which was responsible for several terrorist attacks in 1993. The army's member of the Joint Chiefs of Staff, Gen. Goffredo Canino, subsequently resigned. In the same month it was announced that the civilian and military intelligence services would be merged into a single organization directly responsible to the Prime Minister, owing to increasing evidence of the intelligence services' involvement in terrorism and organized crime. A further restructuring of the intelligence services was announced in July 1994.

In November 1993 President Scalfaro received widespread support following allegations that he had accepted monthly payments from a secret fund of the civilian intelligence service when he was Minister of the Interior in 1983–87. It was speculated that the accusations were designed to undermine the President's pivotal role in the process of reform in Italy.

In January 1994 Ciampi offered his resignation to President Scalfaro following a parliamentary debate which exposed deep divisions over the timing of a general election. On 16 January Scalfaro dissolved Parliament but requested Ciampi to remain in office, with full powers, until the forthcoming legislative elections. These elections, organized under the newly-introduced electoral system, were scheduled to take place at the end of March 1994. In late January Silvio Berlusconi, the principal shareholder in and former manager of Fininvest, Italy's third-largest private business group (including three television networks, a publishing company and one of Italy's leading football clubs, AC Milan), announced the formation of a right-wing organization, Forza Italia (Come on, Italy!), to contest the elections. The liberal wing of the DC, which was now entirely discredited by corruption scandals, relaunched itself as the centrist Partito Popolare Italiano (PPI—Italian People's Party). Prior to the elections, parties of the left, right and centre sought to form alliances capable of gaining a majority in the Chamber of Deputies. At the beginning of February seven parties, including the PDS, RC, the Federazione dei Verdi and La Rete, formed an electoral grouping, I Progressisti (the Progressives). Subsequently an electoral coalition, the Polo per le Libertà e del Buon Governo (hereafter referred to as the Polo per le Libertà—known in English as the Freedom Alliance), was formed by the Lega Nord, Forza Italia and the Alleanza Nazionale (AN—a new party led by Gianfranco Fini and incorporating members of the neo-fascist MSI-DN), under the leadership of Berlusconi. The centre-right electoral alliance, Patto per l'Italia (National Pact), comprised Mario Segni's Patto Segni and the new PPI. The election campaign intensified against a background of judicial investigations and mutual accusations of media bias and malpractice. During the period preceding the elections Silvio Berlusconi's popularity increased notably, despite the arrest of a number of senior Fininvest executives (including his brother) on suspicion of financial malpractice, and a police search of Forza Italia's campaign offices four days prior to polling.

At the legislative elections, held as scheduled on 27 and 28 March 1994, the Polo per le Libertà won an outright majority in the Chamber of Deputies, obtaining 366 of the 630 seats, and were only three seats short of an outright majority in the elections to the Senate, winning 156 of the 315 seats. The Progressisti gained 213 seats in the Chamber of Deputies and 122 seats in the Senate, while the Patto per l'Italia won a disappointing 46 and 31 seats respectively. In spite of the success of Berlusconi's alliance, major differences existed between the parties in the right-wing electoral grouping, and it remained an openly precarious coalition. Berlusconi selected his own candidates from the alliance for the usually impartial posts of President of the Chamber of Deputies and President of the Senate, using the threat of calling new elections to ensure that they were elected in the second round of voting. On 27 April Berlusconi was invited by President Scalfaro to form a Government; Berlusconi announced that he would employ measures to reduce the state deficit, increase employment, promote investment, simplify the tax system and intensify efforts to defeat organized crime. He also declared that a committee of three impartial legal and judicial specialists would be formed to guard against his potential conflict of interest as Prime Minister and main shareholder in the powerful Fininvest group. The new 28-member Council of Ministers, announced in May, included five members of the AN, two of whom were members of the neo-fascist MSI-DN. The appointment of neo-fascists to the Government caused alarm in the European Parliament, where, in an attempt to dissuade Berlusconi from making such appointments, a resolution had been passed a week earlier demanding that Italy respect democratic values. In addition, Berlusconi was criticized for appointing Roberto Maroni of the Lega Nord as Minister of the Interior. Berlusconi's popularity increased, however, and Forza Italia won 30.6% of the votes at elections to the European Parliament held in mid-June. The PDS won only 19.1% of the votes (compared with 27.6% in 1989), and its leader, Achille Occhetto, resigned. (Massimo D'Alema was elected as the new General Secretary in July.)

In July 1994 Berlusconi provoked widespread criticism when, despite his own personal interest in 80% of Italian commercial television networks, he suggested that it was anomalous for a state broadcasting company to contradict the political views of the Government. Later in the month the board of the state-owned RAI broadcasting company resigned following a government decree which introduced a clause increasing government control over the appointment of its directors.

Investigations into corruption continued in 1994, and in July Craxi and the former Minister of Justice, Claudio Martelli, were both sentenced to eight-and-a-half years' imprisonment for fraudulent bankruptcy in relation to the collapse of the Banco Ambrosiano in 1982. Craxi was sentenced *in absentia*, allegedly too ill to return from his holiday home in Tunisia. Thirty-two politicians and business figures, including the former Prime Minister, Forlani, also stood trial on charges of illegal party financing and fraud. In the same month an emergency decree was issued by Berlusconi abolishing pre-trial preventive detention of bribery and corruption suspects as the number of detainees had escalated since the corruption investigations began in February 1992. The decree was rescinded, however, following public protest and the resignation of the magistrates in Milan in charge of anti-corruption cases. The magistrates withdrew their resignations two days later. (In August 1995 the Chamber of Deputies approved an amendment to legislation on preventive detention, limiting its use to those under investigation for crimes punishable by sentences of more than four years' imprisonment, effectively impeding the detention of corruption suspects, who could receive a maximum sentence of three years in prison.) Shortly afterwards two Fininvest employees were arrested on charges of bribing the finance police, 23 of whose senior members were also taken into custody. The arrests and the dispute over media control rekindled concern about Berlusconi's continued involvement in Fininvest and his unresolved conflict of financial and political interests.

In August 1994 the crisis of confidence in the Government intensified and government-sponsored broadcasts which sought to improve the image of the Prime Minister were prohibited. In September Berlusconi met with leaders of the main trade union confederations in an unsuccessful attempt to avert a general strike in October in protest at the proposed reform of the pension system contained in the draft budget for 1995. As many as 3m. people subsequently participated in 90 demonstrations across the country during the four-hour strike. Following rumours of an impending corruption investigation of Berlusconi, Fininvest offices in Milan were searched by police in connection with bribery allegations and violations of anti-monopoly legislation. Italy's largest post-Second World War rally, involving some 1.5m. people, was held in Rome in November in a further protest at the Government's budget proposals. Berlusconi was forced to retract most of the controversial pension reforms incorporated in the draft budget and reintroduce them in a bill in order to avert another strike planned for December. In November, during a UN conference on combating transnational crime which Berlusconi was hosting in Naples, he was formally notified that he was under investigation for bribery.

In early December 1994 Antonio Di Pietro, the most high-profile of the magistrates in Milan and one of the most popular public figures in Italy, resigned from his post in protest at increasing government interference in the work of the judiciary in Milan. The failure of the Prime Minister to resolve his conflict of interests, together with the growing tension between the

Government and the judiciary, undermined the integrity of the Government and precipitated the disintegration of the coalition. The Government finally collapsed on 22 December following the resignation of Berlusconi to avoid probable defeat in three votes of no confidence proposed by the Lega Nord and opposition parties. Berlusconi remained as head of the caretaker administration and appealed for early elections, aware that his popularity remained largely intact. Almost all the other parties, however, favoured a broadly-based transitional coalition to allow for electoral reform and the imposition of more stringent controls on media ownership.

In January 1995 Lamberto Dini, the Minister of the Treasury and a former Director-General of the Bank of Italy, was invited to form an interim Government. Dini appointed a Council of Ministers comprised of technocrats, and pledged to hold elections once he had implemented a programme to improve public finances, reform the state pension system, introduce new regional electoral laws, and establish controls on media ownership and its use during electoral campaigns. Dini secured parliamentary approval for legislation reforming regional electoral procedures in February and for a supplementary budget in March, largely through recourse to parliamentary votes of confidence.

New political alliances emerged in 1995 in preparation for legislative elections. In January the MSI-DN was officially disbanded and most of its members were absorbed in the AN. The AN leader, Gianfranco Fini, distanced the party from its neofascist past, denouncing racism and anti-Semitism, in an attempt to widen support. The PSI had been dissolved in November 1994 and reformed as the Socialisti Italiani (Italian Socialists), under the leadership of Enrico Bosselli. In February 1995 Prof. Romano Prodi, a respected business executive and a former head of the Istituto per la Ricostruzione Industriale (IRI), the state industrial and banking holding, offered to lead the centre-left parties to challenge Berlusconi in the coming elections. In the same month Rocco Buttiglione, leader of the centrist PPI, won the support of the majority of his party to seek an alliance with Berlusconi (the more left-wing members of the party abstained from the vote). The PPI effectively split in March, following a meeting of the party's national executive, at which the alliance with Berlusconi was rejected and demands were made for the resignation of its leader. In mid-March, despite Buttiglione's refusal to tender his resignation, the PPI national executive elected Gerardo Bianco as its Secretary-General. (In January 1997 Franco Marini was elected to replace Bianco.) In July 1995 Buttiglione founded the Cristiani Democratici Uniti, a centre-right party, which absorbed the disaffected members of the PPI. In the same month the PDS formally endorsed Prodi as leader of the centre-left electoral alliance, subsequently named L'Ulivo (The Olive Tree). Divisions within the Lega Nord also emerged, and in February a breakaway group was formed under the leadership of Roberto Maroni, who was in favour of forming an alliance with Berlusconi.

The political career of Berlusconi was again threatened in March 1995, when it was formally announced that he was to be subject to further investigation on charges of financial irregularities. Moreover, in the following month Berlusconi's electoral alliance, the Polo per le Libertà, was defeated by the centre-left parties in nine of the 15 regional elections, despite obtaining 40.7% of the votes cast (compared with 40.5% won by parties of the centre-left). The PDS won the largest share of the votes (24.6%), followed by Forza Italia (22.4%) and the AN (14.1%). Both Berlusconi and Fini subsequently withdrew their demands for a general election to be held in June, because of their apparent decline in popularity. In May, after a second round of provincial and municipal elections, it was confirmed that 48 of the 54 posts for provincial Presidents were won by candidates from the centre-left parties; the Lega Nord and the Polo per le Libertà won three seats each.

In June 1995 some 57% of the electorate participated in 12 referendums held on issues including media ownership, trade union and electoral reform, retailing and crime. Significantly, the majority of the voters who participated in the referendums on media ownership approved the retention of laws permitting an individual to own more than one commercial television channel and preserving the existing monopoly on television advertising. The results of these referendums (which enhanced Berlusconi's dominance in the media) confirmed the former Prime Minister's continuing popularity, despite the judicial investigations into his financial affairs. In July, none the less, Berlusconi announced his intention to sell 20% of his media concern Mediaset (a subsidiary of Fininvest). In another referendum the majority of voters supported the partial privatization of the state-owned RAI broadcasting company, control of which had become increasingly contentious since the resignation of its board of directors in mid-1994 (see above). In the remaining referendums one of the most important results was the endorsement of proposed reforms to trade unions, restricting the unions' power of representation and effectively reducing the dominance of the three largest trade union federations.

In July 1995 Dini again successfully sought recourse to parliamentary votes of confidence to secure the approval of pension reforms that had been agreed with trade union leaders in May. In August the pension reform programme received parliamentary approval. However, Dini's premiership was threatened in October when the Minister of Justice, Filippo Mancuso, refused to resign from the Council of Ministers following the approval in the Senate by an overwhelming majority of a motion of no confidence in him which had been prompted by his allegedly ruthless vendetta against anti-corruption magistrates in Milan. Since Dini was constitutionally unable to remove a minister from office without submitting the Government's resignation, Scalfaro intervened and revoked Mancuso's mandate, appointing Dini as interim Minister of Justice. Dini's administration remained precarious, however, and shortly afterwards Berlusconi allied himself with Mancuso and proposed a motion of no confidence in the Government, claiming the support of the RC. The Government narrowly defeated the motion, after having forged an agreement with the RC whereby their deputies abstained from the vote on condition that Dini resign as Prime Minister by the end of the year.

In November 1995 Dini secured parliamentary approval for the draft budget for 1996, despite initial opposition from the Lega Nord, which had made its support of the budget conditional on the Government's approval of new measures against illegal immigrants. (The Government had in fact approved a controversial decree restricting immigration and imposing harsh sanctions on illegal immigrants as the budget debate began; however, the decree's contents were made public only after the budget debate had concluded.) At the end of the month the Chamber of Deputies approved legislation regulating political parties' access to RAI, the state broadcasting concern, and increasing the membership of its board from five to nine.

On 30 December 1995 Dini submitted his resignation to the President, a week after the Senate gave its final approval to the 1996 budget. President Scalfaro rejected the resignation, however, and asked Dini to continue in a caretaker capacity until a parliamentary debate were held to resolve the political crisis and determine the future of the Government. Although Scalfaro indicated his preference for Dini's continuation in office, in January 1996 the AN tabled a resolution demanding Dini's resignation, which it was likely to win with the support of parties from the extreme left. On 12 January, therefore, Scalfaro was obliged to accept Dini's second resignation, which he submitted prior to the vote; Dini remained as head of the caretaker administration. The political parties reached a general agreement to work towards constitutional reform (including changes to the electoral system and, possibly, the direct election of the Prime Minister) prior to a general election, in order to strengthen Italy's fragile democracy. It was also feared that a general election might threaten Italy's presidency of the European Union (EU—see p. 152), which was to extend from January to June. On 2 February the President nominated Antonio Maccanico, a bureaucrat and a former Chairman of Italy's powerful merchant bank, Mediobanca, as Prime Minister-designate. However, in mid-February Maccanico announced that he had been unable to form a Government. On 16 February Scalfaro dissolved Parliament and asked Dini to remain as interim Prime Minister until a general election in April 1996.

At the legislative elections, held on 21 April 1996, Romano Prodi's Ulivo alliance (dominated by the PDS, but also including the PPI and Dini's newly-formed centrist party, Rinnovamento Italiano—Italian Renewal) narrowly defeated the Polo per le Libertà, securing 284 of the 630 seats in the Chamber of Deputies and 157 of the 315 elective seats in the Senate; the Polo per le Libertà won 246 seats in the Chamber of Deputies and 116 seats in the Senate. Both the Lega Nord and the RC, which chose not to ally themselves with any grouping, increased their parliamentary representation, respectively obtaining 59 and 35 seats in the Chamber of Deputies and 27 and 10 seats in the Senate. In mid-May President Scalfaro invited Prodi to form a government; Prodi announced his intention to introduce educational and constitutional reforms, reduce unemployment, address the contentious issue of media ownership and persevere with a policy of economic austerity. Massimo D'Alema, the influential PDS General Secretary, elected not to serve in the 21-member Council of Ministers; however, his second-in-command, Walter Veltroni, was appointed Deputy Prime Minister. In late May Prodi assumed full powers, following votes of confidence in the Chamber of Deputies and in the Senate. Although the RC agreed to support the Government in the vote of confidence in the Chamber of Deputies, its Secretary-General, Fausto Bertinotti, emphasized that his party could express only 'conditional confidence' in the new administration, and in subsequent months he successfully forced the Government to accede to many RC demands (notably on budget proposals) in return for providing crucial parliamentary support.

In September 1996 the Government encountered severe criticism, both from right-wing elements within the Ulivo alliance and from the opposition, when it presented an austere budget for 1997, which was notably dependent on tax increases and averse to reductions in public expenditure. It was widely believed that the Government's reluctance to reduce expenditure was motivated primarily by its desire to maintain the support of the RC, upon whose tactical support it depended to secure a parliamentary majority. In November Berlusconi successfully exploited middle-class antipathy towards the Government's tax proposals (and in so doing enhanced his own credibility) by organizing a demonstration in Rome, which was attended by more than 500,000 people. (In June, Berlusconi's position had been weakened when Forza Italia suffered losses in the election to the regional council in Sicily, securing only 17.1% of the votes, compared with 32.2% at the general election.) Although bitter arguments ensued over economic policy, the budget was approved by the Chamber of Deputies in mid-November, and by the Senate in the following month.

The Prodi administration also experienced difficulty in reaching political consensus over constitutional reform. In July 1996, after lengthy negotiations, the Government reportedly reached agreement with the Polo per le Libertà on the establishment of a bicameral commission charged with advising Parliament on constitutional revision. Although Berlusconi had favoured the creation of a constituent assembly (elected by proportional representation), he was apparently prepared to persuade his alliance to accept the proposed commission in order to protect his media interests. In mid-July the Government had presented draft legislation on media reform that, appearing to adopt a lenient interpretation of the Constitutional Court's ruling, would allow Berlusconi's Mediaset media concern to convert one of its three television channels to cable or satellite (or else reduce its share of the terrestrial audience) rather than to divest it. The draft legislation also envisaged the establishment of a telecoms and media regulator, while the RAI broadcasting group would be obliged to convert one of its channels to a regional network. However, the reforms failed to receive parliamentary approval prior to the date set by the Constitutional Court (late August), and, in the absence of new legislation, the Court ruled that its proposal to limit the proportion of television companies held by any one group from 25% to 20% would take effect. It consequently announced that it would block the transmission of one of Mediaset's channels as of 22 December. In early December Massimo D'Alema, who had increasingly been acknowledged as the principal strategist in the Government, successfully exploited Berlusconi's vulnerability with regard to both media legislation and to the judicial investigations into his affairs (see below). D'Alema secured the temporary postponement (until 30 May 1997 at the earliest) of the Constitutional Court's decision to enforce its broadcasting ruling, and, in addition, suggested that the Government might support the introduction of judicial reforms which could result in extensive plea-bargaining in corruption cases. In return, Berlusconi agreed to collaborate with the Government and support the rapid conversion of numerous decrees into law. (In September the Constitutional Court had ruled that the widespread practice of renewing decrees without substantially altering their content was illegal; it declared that decrees issued by the Prodi administration, as well as those inherited from previous Governments, would no longer be renewable.) In January 1997 the continuing co-operation of the Polo per le Libertà enabled the Senate to approve the creation of a 70-member bicameral commission on constitutional reform, with D'Alema as its elected President. In June the commission presented its recommendations which included a directly-elected President, a reduction in the size of the Chamber of Deputies and the Senate and greater regional financial autonomy. Referendum procedures were also to be amended following the invalidation of seven referendums due to low participation in May.

In February 1997 at the first congress of the PDS, D'Alema, who was re-elected as the party's General Secretary, provoked anger amongst his left-wing supporters, most notably the trade union federation, the Confederazione Generale Italiana del Lavoro (CGIL), by a speech advocating radical restructuring of the welfare system, further pension reform and co-operation on constitutional reform and EMU membership. In early March President Scalfaro took the unusual step of summoning senior government ministers to discuss the problems of unemployment. Later that month trade unions organized a rally which was attended by 150,000 demonstrators, in protest at the Government's failure to implement a job-creation accord signed in September 1996. A supplementary budget announced in March provoked protests owing to the unpopularity of austerity measures designed to help achieve the convergence criteria of the EMU. In April a parliamentary budget commission voted against the supplementary budget and the Government was forced to resort to a confidence vote to gain parliamentary approval for the budget.

Partial local elections in April 1997 were marred by two bomb attacks by extremist groupings. The RC made significant gains in the elections, mostly at the expense of the Lega Nord, while the two main coalition groupings retained their positions.

In early April 1997 the Government's decision to lead a 5,000-strong multinational force (comprising up to 2,500 Italians) in Albania to ease the security situation in that country provoked serious opposition within Parliament. Following negotiations, the motion was passed, but the RC had voted against it (and therefore the Government) thus ending the Government's parliamentary majority; as a result, Prodi was forced to call a confidence vote in which the RC returned its support to the Government.

In October 1997 the RC announced that it would oppose the 1998 budget thus leaving the Government without a legislative majority. Following the failure of negotiations in which the Secretary-General of the RC, Fausto Bertinotti, demanded policy changes in exchange for their continued support, Prodi offered his resignation to Scalfaro. He remained as caretaker Prime Minister, however, and continued attempts to resolve the issue with Scalfaro and Bertinotti. A one-year political pact was subsequently announced, which included significant concessions from Bertinotti, who agreed to the adoption of measures to secure EMU membership, while Prodi was forced to compromise on pension reform. Scalfaro declared his rejection of Prodi's resignation and Prodi subsequently won a parliamentary vote of confidence. In partial local elections held in November, the L'Ulivo increased its support at the expense of the centre-right. L'Ulivo's victory was interpreted as an endorsement of Prodi's policies.

Meanwhile, in May 1996 Umberto Bossi of the Lega Nord announced the formation of an 11-member 'Government of the Independent Republic of Padania' (a territory comprising the regions of Liguria, Emilia-Romagna, Lombardy, Piedmont and the Veneto). The concept of the creation of a 'Republic of Padania' was generally regarded with scepticism, although many inhabitants of the northern regions were in favour of greater local autonomy. At local elections, which took place in June, the Lega Nord's share of the vote declined in the strategic cities of Pavia and Lodi, and it came third in mayoral elections in Mantua (the designated capital of 'Padania'). In September Bossi's credibility was damaged further by the expulsion from the party of Irene Pivetti (a highly-regarded Lega Nord member and former President of the Chamber of Deputies) for publicly supporting a less extreme policy of local autonomy. In addition, a well-publicized rally in Venice to mark the formal independence of 'Padania' was attended by only 50,000 people, compared with some 150,000 people who participated in an anti-secession demonstration held concurrently in Milan. Shortly afterwards Bossi was placed under investigation, and his offices were searched for anti-constitutional material.

At the Lega Nord party congress in February 1997 Bossi advocated consensual secession and in May the Lega Nord organized a referendum to determine the level of popular support for 'Padania'. Despite media reports that participation levels had been low, Bossi claimed that 5m. had voted, of whom 99% supported an independent 'Republic of Padania'. In local elections in April, however, the Lega Nord had suffered a sharp decline in support, losing control of Gorizia, Pavia and Mantua, the self-styled capital of the 'Republic of Padania'. In September 15,000 secessionists demonstrated in Venice in support of the 'Republic of Padania'. However, later that month anti-secession rallies attracted hundreds of thousands of supporters in Milan and Venice. In October elections to a 200-seat constituent assembly in the 'Republic of Padania', organized by the Lega Nord, were contested by 63 parties. The assembly held its first session in November. In January 1998 Bossi received a one-year suspended prison sentence for inciting criminal acts during a party meeting in 1995. He was to stand trial again in March 1998 on similar charges.

In May 1997 eight demonstrators were arrested after they had occupied the bell tower in St Mark's Square in Venice to promote their demands for the restoration of the former Venetian republic; they were sentenced to six years' imprisonment in July.

Investigations into corruption and bribery continued during 1995 and early 1996, resulting in the arrest and trial of numerous senior politicians and business executives. In July 1995 two international warrants were issued for the arrest of Craxi, and when he failed to return to Italy he was formally declared a fugitive from justice. In October anti-corruption magistrates in Milan issued arrest warrants for 20 army officers who had allegedly received bribes for contracts. (It was estimated that as many as 2,500 military personnel were subsequently subject to investigation on charges of corruption.) In late October, at the end of a trial concerning the illegal funding of political parties, all 22 defendants were convicted, including former Prime Ministers Craxi (*in absentia*) and Arnaldo Forlani, who were sentenced to four years' and 28 months' imprisonment respectively; Umberto Bossi received a suspended sentence. The most highly-publicized investigations, however, centred on Berlusconi and his political and business associates. In July it was announced that 22 people connected with Publitalia (the advertising subsidiary of Fininvest) would stand trial on charges of false accounting. In January 1996 Berlusconi, along with his brother Paolo (who in December had been convicted on a separate bribery charge and sentenced to 16 months' imprisonment) and nine others, went on trial in Milan charged with either giving or receiving bribes between 1989 and 1991. In January 1997 the trial was declared invalid, following the resignation of the presiding judge who had been accused of bias; a new trial began in February. In December Berlusconi was found guilty, although an initial prison sentence was quashed and a fine imposed. Later that month Berlusconi and Cesare Previti, a former Minister of Defence and a lawyer for Fininvest, were ordered to stand trial on charges relating to allegations that they had accumulated funds with the intention of bribing judges. Berlusconi also faced charges of making illicit payments, via Fininvest, to Craxi and the PSI in 1991, and of maintaining links with the Sicilian Mafia. Meanwhile the former magistrate, Antonio Di Pietro, countered a series of allegations that he had abused his position within the judiciary to extort favours and had been personally responsible for discrediting Berlusconi in an attempt to further his own political ambitions. In March 1996, after a court in Brescia dismissed charges against Di Pietro, Berlusconi's brother, Paolo, and Cesare Previti were placed under investigation for allegedly attempting to discredit him. (However, in January 1997 they were acquitted.) Although Di Pietro had been appointed Minister of Public Works in May 1996, by November he had resigned from the post, in protest at renewed investigations into his affairs. In December the Court of Review ruled that raids on Di Pietro's home and offices by the Finance Police (suspected of seeking vengeance on Di Pietro for his earlier investigations into their affairs) were 'unjustified and illegitimate'. In November 1997 Di Pietro was elected to the Senate as a PDS candidate in a by-election. In November 1996 Romano Prodi was himself placed under investigation for alleged abuse of office while head of the state holding company, IRI, during 1993–94; the Prime Minister dismissed the allegations and pledged to co-operate fully with the inquiry.

Despite mass trials of Mafia suspects in 1987 and 1988 (a total of 468 defendants were convicted), the Italian Government continued to experience problems in dealing with organized crime. At a further trial in April 1989, 42 mafiosi were convicted, but 82 defendants were acquitted, including the head of the Sicilian Mafia's governing 'commission', Michele Greco. In 1990 acts of violence escalated, with some 2,000 people reported to have been killed by the Mafia and similar organizations during that year. In September the Government announced measures that were intended to strengthen the powers of the police and judiciary in their efforts to combat organized crime. In March 1991 inter-clan rivalry for territorial monopoly of Taurianova, Calabria, resulted in an outbreak of retributive murders. In May President Cossiga partially revoked the powers of the Vice-President of the Consiglio Superiore delle Magistratura (the governing body of the judicial system) as a rebuke for the judiciary's failure to quell the criminal activities of the Mafia.

In March 1992 Salvatore Lima, a Sicilian politician and member of the European Parliament, was murdered. The assassination of Giovanni Falcone, a prominent anti-Mafia judge, in May, followed by that of his colleague, Paolo Borsellino, in July, provoked renewed public outrage. In August the powers of the police and of the judiciary were strengthened, in a fresh attempt to combat the Mafia. During 1992 hundreds of suspects were detained. In January 1993 the capture of Salvatore Riina, the alleged head of the Sicilian Mafia who had eluded the security forces for more than 20 years, was regarded as a significant success in the Government's campaign against organized crime. In the following month Rosetta Cutolo, leader of a faction of the Camorra (the Neapolitan Mafia), was also arrested. In 1993 the judiciary mounted a campaign to seize Mafia funds. In the course of the year several suspects, alleged to be leading figures in the world of organized crime, were arrested. Among these were Paolo Benedetto, regarded as the leader of the Mafia in Catania, Giuseppe Pulvirenti, alleged to be another principal figure of the Mafia in Eastern Sicily, and Michele Zaza, the alleged head of the Neapolitan Camorra. In March 1994 the Governments of Italy and France pledged to increase co-operation in the sharing of intelligence to combat Mafia activities, and in October a similar agreement was signed with Russia to fight organized crime and drugs-trafficking. A renewed campaign against the Mafia in June resulted in the arrests of 125 suspects in Messina, Sicily. In March Riina was sentenced to life imprisonment for the seventh time for his part in the murder of four people in the 1980s. A sudden increase in Mafia-related violence in Sicily during March was largely attributed to attempts to intimidate potential informers. Numerous alleged mafiosi were arrested in the following months, including Leoluca Bagarella, the alleged head of the Sicilian Mafia, in June, and some 150 suspected members of the Calabrian Mafia in July. In November Francesco Musotto, a senior politician in Palermo and an ally of Berlusconi, was arrested and charged with assisting high-ranking members of the Sicilian Mafia to evade capture over a four-year period. In January 1996 Marcello Dell'Utri, a leading Forza Italia politician, was reported to be subject to investigation on charges of links with the Mafia. (In December Dell'Utri received a custodial sentence of three years for the falsification of invoices and financial fraud while Chairman and Managing Director of Berlusconi's company, Publitalia.) Following the arrests of a number of senior mafiosi in 1996, in March 1997 more than 70 alleged members of the Mafia were arrested in Sicily and later that month a further 70 suspected members of the Calabrian Mafia were detained. In July troops were dispatched to Naples to help the security forces, owing to violent territorial disputes between rival Mafia groups. In September 24 influential members of the Mafia including Salvatore Riina and Pietro Aglieri (who had been arrested in June) were sentenced to life imprisonment for their part in the murder of the prominent judge, Giovanni Falcone.

Italy's foreign policy has traditionally been governed by its firm commitment to Europe, notably through its membership of the European Community (EC—renamed EU in 1993) and NATO. The Maastricht Treaty on European Union (see p. 158) was ratified by the Italian legislature in October 1992. Italy assumed the presidency of the EU in January 1996 for a six-month period.

In March 1991 some 24,000 Albanian refugees arrived at Italian ports, fleeing from economic hardship and political repression in their homeland. The refugees were temporarily housed in camps, and economic aid was offered to Albania by the Italian Government in an attempt to persuade the Albanian authorities to prevent further refugees from leaving. In August, however, there was a further influx of Albanian refugees, many of whom were forcibly repatriated without delay. The Italian Government criticized the lack of aid provided to Albania by other EC countries to deter the exodus.

In July 1991, following the escalation of hostilities in the neighbouring Yugoslav republic of Slovenia, the Italian Government temporarily deployed military personnel in the north-east of Italy and reinforced border posts in the region. Italy gave firm support to the EC's efforts to find a peaceful solution to the Yugoslav crisis. In January 1992 President Cossiga became the first European Head of State to visit Croatia and Slovenia since the former Yugoslav republics' recognition as independent states by the EC. In May the Italian Government was obliged to declare a state of emergency, following an influx of thousands of refugees from Bosnia and Herzegovina. Italy urged the EC to contribute towards the cost of sheltering the refugees. In May 1995 a contingent of some 500 troops was deployed along Italy's south-eastern coast in an attempt to halt a sudden influx of illegal immigrants, primarily from Albania and Montenegro. It was estimated that as many as 10,000 foreign nationals had entered Italy illegally via this route during the previous six months. Controversial legislation was approved in November restricting immigration and imposing harsh sanctions on illegal immigrants. As a result of the deteriorating political situation within Albania, large numbers of refugees arrived in Italy throughout 1997 and in March a state of emergency was declared for three months. In late March an estimated 80 refugees died following a collision between their ship and an Italian navy vessel which was later accused of having rammed the refugee ship, an accusation it strongly denied. Following a visit by Prodi, an Italian-led multinational peace-keeping force, known as Operation Alba, was deployed in Albania in April, with a mandate to facilitate the distribution of humanitarian aid. In June Italy was forced to recall two successive ambassadors to Albania following comments they were alleged to have made regarding the Albanian political situation. At the end of July, at an international conference in Rome, it was decided that Italian security aid to Albania would continue after the withdrawal of the international force and that co-operation on border control would be extended until October. At the end of August it was announced that the repatriation of refugees would be delayed until November. In October it was agreed to establish a joint office to combat organized crime and in December Italy and Albania signed an aid agreement.

Following Italy's accession to the EU's Schengen agreement on cross-border travel (see p. 168) in late October 1997, large numbers of refugees, mainly Turkish and Iraqi Kurds, began arriving in southern Italy provoking concern from Italy's EU partners. These concerns were partially alleviated by the initial approval, in November, of a bill designed to facilitate the deportation of illegal immigrants. However, the concerns resurfaced in January 1998, following comments by President Scalfaro, who proclaimed that Italy had an 'open arms' policy towards refugees.

In June 1997 the Government announced the creation of a commission to investigate claims that members of an Italian paratroop regiment attached to the UN peace mission in Somalia (UNOSOM) had tortured, sexually assaulted and murdered unarmed Somalis. The commission issued a report in August which declared that the abuses had taken place but were not widespread. Later that month the inquiry was reopened following allegations by a former member of the regiment that senior figures had been aware of the misconduct and that an investigative journalist had uncovered proof of their involvement prior to her murder in Somalia in March 1993.

In December 1997 the RC questioned the need for the continuing presence of US military bases in Italy. This issue was highlighted in early February when a low-flying US military jet cut through an overhead cable-car wire at a ski resort in the Dolomites causing 20 deaths. An emergency parliamentary debate was called to discuss the future of such bases.

The victory of Berlusconi's right-wing alliance in the general election in March 1994 was met with unease by the European Parliament due to the neo-fascist element of the grouping. In May Italy was refused a place on the international 'Contact Group' formed to facilitate a cease-fire in Bosnia and Herzegovina, following alleged statements by AN members reviving claims to territories of the former Yugoslavia. In September 1995 Italy protested at its continuing exclusion from the 'Contact Group' by refusing a US request to station fighter aircraft on its territory. Italy's Minister of Foreign Affairs announced that all NATO requests for logistical support in the former Yugoslavia would henceforth be considered on an individual basis. In November, following the signing of a peace accord by the leaders of the former Yugoslavia, the Italian Government agreed to dispatch troops for peace-keeping operations in Bosnia and Herzegovina and other disputed areas of the former Yugoslavia.

In July 1994 relations between Italy and Slovenia deteriorated following a threat by the Italian Government to veto Slovenian membership of the EU if some form of non-monetary compensation were not given to the ethnic Italians who were dispossessed when Slovenia (then part of the former Yugoslavia) was awarded the Italian territory of Istria as part of the post-1945 peace settlement. Slovenia subsequently conceded that legislation would be amended to allow foreign nationals to acquire property in Slovenia, and in March 1995 the Italian Government withdrew its veto on Slovenian negotiations to become a member of the EU.

In November 1995 relations between Italy and France were strained when the French President, Jacques Chirac, cancelled a meeting with the Prime Minister, Dini, in protest at Italy's support for a UN resolution condemning the nuclear tests carried out by France in the South Pacific. In January 1996 Dini met the French Prime Minister, Alain Juppé, in Paris, and good relations were restored between the two countries. In 1997 a Franco-Italian summit was held in Paris, France, at which an accord on working conditions was signed.

Government

Under the 1948 Constitution, legislative power was held by the bicameral Parliament, elected by universal suffrage for five years (subject to dissolution) on the basis of proportional representation. A referendum held in April 1993 supported the amendment of the Constitution to provide for the election of 75% of the members of the Senate by a simple plurality and the remainder under a system of proportional representation, and provided for further electoral reform. In August Parliament approved a similar system for elections to the Chamber of Deputies. The Senate has 315 elected members (seats allocated on a regional basis) and 10 life Senators. The Chamber of Deputies has 630 members. The minimum voting age is 25 years for the Senate and 18 years for the Chamber. The two houses have equal power.

The President of the Republic is a constitutional Head of State elected for seven years by an electoral college comprising both Houses of Parliament and 58 regional representatives. Executive power is exercised by the Council of Ministers. The Head of State appoints the President of the Council (Prime Minister) and, on the latter's recommendation, other ministers. The Council is responsible to Parliament.

The country is divided into 20 regions, of which five (Sicily, Sardinia, Trentino-Alto Adige, Friuli-Venezia Giulia and Valle d'Aosta) enjoy a special status. There is a large degree of regional autonomy. Each region has a regional council elected every five years by universal suffrage and a Giunta regionale responsible to the regional council. The regional council is a legislative assembly, while the Giunta holds executive power. The regions are subdivided into a total of 95 provinces.

In June 1997 a parliamentary commission on constitutional reform, which had been established in January, announced its recommendations, which included: a directly-elected President for a six-year term with overall control of foreign and defence policy; a reduction of the Chamber of Deputies from 630 to 400 members and of the Senate from 315 to 200 members; greater financial autonomy for the regional councils; and a second round of voting for seats allocated on the basis of a simple plurality. The commission's recommendations required approval by both the Chamber of Deputies and the Senate prior to endorsement at a national referendum.

Defence

Italy has been a member of the North Atlantic Treaty Organisation (NATO—see p. 204) since 1949. In August 1997 it maintained armed forces totalling 325,150 (conscripts numbered an estimated 163,800), including an army of 188,300, a navy of 44,000 and an air force of 63,600. There were also paramilitary forces numbering 255,700 men (including 113,200 Carabinieri). Military service lasts 10 months in all the services. The 1997 state budget allocated 31,100,000m. lire to defence.

Economic Affairs

In 1995, according to estimates by the World Bank, Italy's gross national product (GNP), measured at average 1993–95 prices, was US $1,088,085m., equivalent to $19,020 per head. During 1985–95, it was estimated, GNP per head increased, in real terms, at an average annual rate of 1.7%. Over the same period the population increased by an annual average of 0.1%. Italy's gross domestic product (GDP) increased, in real terms, by an annual average of 2.2% in 1980–93. Real GDP increased by 2.2% in 1994, by 3% in 1995, and by 0.8% in 1996.

Agriculture (including forestry and fishing) contributed 2.9% of GDP in 1996. In 1997 about 6.8% of the employed labour force were engaged in the agricultural sector. The principal crops are sugar beet, grapes, wheat, maize and tomatoes. Italy is a leading producer and exporter of wine. The total catch of fish (including crustaceans and molluscs) was about 559,800 metric tons in 1996. In 1985–93 agricultural output increased by an annual average of 0.2%; production declined by 0.03% in 1994.

Industry (including mining, manufacturing, construction and power) contributed 31.5% of GDP in 1996. Some 32.0% of the employed labour force were engaged in industrial activities in 1997. The State has traditionally played a major role in the development of heavy industry. In 1980–90 industrial GDP increased by an annual average of 1.7%. Industrial output increased by 5.3% in 1995. Production decreased by 3.1% in the year to December 1996.

The major product of the mining sector is petroleum, followed by rocksalt, feldspar and aplite, and lignite. Italy also has reserves of bentonite, lead and zinc. Reserves of epithermal gold in Sardinia were discovered in 1996.

Manufacturing contributed about 20% of GDP in the early 1990s, according to World Bank estimates. About 22.7% of the employed labour force were engaged in mining and manufacturing (excluding the energy sector) in 1997. The most important branches of manufacturing in the late 1980s, measured by gross value of output, were machinery and transport equipment, textiles and clothing, and food products. In 1980–90 manufacturing production increased by an annual average of 1.1%.

More than 80% of energy requirements are imported. In 1988 58% of requirements were derived from petroleum; coal-fired electricity generating stations provided 14.6%, natural gas-fired stations provided 12.6%, and nuclear power stations provided 4.6%. In late 1996 plans were announced for the construction of an integrated gasification and combined cycle power plant. In 1994 imports of mineral fuels and lubricants accounted for 8.2% of the value of total imports.

Services engaged 61.2% of the employed labour force in 1997 and accounted for 65.6% of GDP in 1996. According to the World Bank, the combined GDP of the services sector increased, in real terms, at an estimated average rate of 2.7% per year during 1980–90. Tourism is an important source of income, and in 1996 a total of 56.3m. foreigners visited Italy. Tourist receipts totalled 46,249,264m. lire in the same year. There were 1.7m. hotel beds at December 1994.

In 1996 Italy recorded a visible trade surplus of US $60,821m., and a surplus of $41,040m. on the current account of the balance of payments. In 1995 the principal source of imports (19.5%) was Germany, which was also the principal market for exports (18.7%). Other major trading partners in that year were France, the United Kingdom and the USA. In that year Italy's fellow members of the European Union (EU—see p. 269) purchased 61.7% of its exports. The principal exports in 1995 were machinery and transport equipment, clothing and footwear, basic manufactures, and chemicals and related products. The principal imports were machinery and transport equipment, basic manufactures, chemicals and related products, and food and live animals.

The budgetary deficit for 1995 was equivalent to 7.4% of annual GDP, while the 1996 budget proposals aimed to reduce the deficit to 5.9% of annual GDP. In 1996 Italy's total accumulated government debt was equivalent to 123% of annual GDP. The annual rate of inflation averaged 5.3% in 1985–95; it averaged 5.3% in 1995, 3.9% in 1996 and 2.6% in 1997. As a percentage of the total labour force, unemployment was 12.4% in 1997.

Italy is a member of the EU, the Organisation for Economic Co-operation and Development (OECD, p. 208) and the Central European Initiative (p. 269).

During the late 1980s Italy enjoyed sustained economic growth and strong industrial output. However, high levels of government expenditure on social services and industry, which for many years were not equalled by revenue and taxation, produced a large public-sector deficit. There are also long-term structural problems, principally the underdevelopment of the southern part of the country, a low level of agricultural productivity, and heavy dependence on imported energy supplies. International confidence in the lira was periodically undermined during 1992–95 by corruption scandals and political instability in Italy, and the lira lost as much as 30% of its value against other European currencies following its withdrawal, in September 1992, from the European Exchange Rate Mechanism (ERM, see p. 172) and subsequent devaluation. Since mid-1995, with the announcement by the Dini Government of a macroeconomic programme for 1996-98, government economic policy had been directed towards meeting the economic convergence criteria stipulated by the Maastricht Treaty for Economic and Monetary Union (EMU). As a result of the high level of public debt (123% of GDP in 1996), the divestment of state enterprises remained a priority. During 1995 and 1996, a total of 29% of the Ente Nazionale Idrocarburi (ENI) was privatized, and in 1997, Telecom Italia, the state telecommunications operator, and the Milan stock exchange were wholly privatized, along with parts of the banking sector. Following the implementation of austerity measures in 1996, re-entry of the lira in the ERM was achieved in November of that year. The Prodi Government continued to work towards membership of the EMU in 1998, with the announcement of a three-year economic strategy in May 1997. Preliminary figures for 1997 showed that both the government deficit and inflation met the EMU convergence criteria, and although the 1998 budget introduced reductions in expenditure which would help to maintain low deficits, welfare reform, necessary for long-term progress, remained largely unaddressed following the government crisis provoked by opposition to the budget (see Recent History).

Social Welfare

Italy has a comprehensive system of social benefits covering unemployment and disability as well as retirement pensions and family allowances. These benefits are all provided by the social security system (Istituto Nazionale della Previdenza Sociale). There is also an industrial injuries scheme, operated by the Istituto Nazionale per l'Assicurazione contro gli Infortuni sul Lavoro. Government expenditure on pensions in 1995 represented 13% of GDP. Legislation approved in August 1995 allowed for the separation of state pensions from all other social security payments and introduced a contributions-based pension with a minimum retirement age of 52 years, rising gradually to 57 years by 2008 (with 35 and 40 years' contributions respectively).

A comprehensive national health service, aiming to provide free medical care for all citizens, was introduced in 1980. However, minimum charges are still made for essential medicines, medical examinations and hospital treatment. All workers are eligible for benefits under a unified national medical insurance scheme. In 1986 Italy had 1,752 hospital establishments, with a total of 450,377 beds: equivalent to one for every 79 inhabitants. In 1992 there were 296,385 physicians working in Italy (5.2 per 1,000 head of population). In 1992 the state budget allocated 91,624,000m. lire to health. In 1988 expenditure on social security and welfare by the central Government (including social security funds) was 191,883,000m. lire (38.0% of total government spending).

Education

Education is free and compulsory between the ages of six and 13 years. The curricula of all Italian schools are standardized by the Ministry of Education. After primary school, for children aged six to 10 years, the pupil enters the lower secondary school (scuola media unificata). An examination at the end of three years leads to a lower secondary school certificate, which gives access to all higher secondary schools. Pupils wishing to enter a classical lycée (liceo classico) must also pass an examination in Latin.

Higher secondary education is provided by classical, artistic and scientific lycées, training schools for elementary teachers and technical and vocational institutes (industrial, commercial, nautical, etc.). After five years at a lycée, the student sits an examination for the higher secondary school certificate (maturità), which allows automatic entry into any university faculty. Special four-year courses are provided at the teachers' training schools and the diploma obtained permits entry to a special university faculty of education, the magistero, and a few other faculties. The technical institutes provide practical courses which prepare students for a specialized university faculty.

In 1993 the total enrolment at primary and secondary schools was equivalent to 87% of the school-age population (males 87%; females 87%). Primary enrolment in that year was equivalent to 98% of all children in the relevant age-group (males 95%; females 96%), while the comparable ratio for secondary enrolment was 81% (males 81%; females 82%). In 1995 the average rate of adult illiteracy was estimated at 1.9% (males 1.4%; females 2.4%).

University courses last for a minimum of four years. Study allowances are awarded to students according to their means and merit. In 1992 government expenditure on education (including higher education) was 80,268,000m. lire (equivalent to 5.4% of GNP).

Public Holidays

1998: 1 January (New Year's Day), 6 January (Epiphany), 13 April (Easter Monday), 25 April (Liberation Day), 1 May (Labour Day), 15 August (Assumption), 1 November (All Saints' Day), 5 November (National Unity Day), 8 December (Immaculate Conception), 25 December (Christmas Day), 26 December (St Stephen).

1999: 1 January (New Year's Day), 6 January (Epiphany), 5 April (Easter Monday), 25 April (Liberation Day), 1 May (Labour Day), 15 August (Assumption), 1 November (All Saints' Day), 5 November (National Unity Day), 8 December (Immaculate Conception), 25 December (Christmas Day), 26 December (St Stephen).

There are also numerous local public holidays, held on the feast day of the patron saint of each town.

Weights and Measures

The metric system is in force.

Statistical Survey

Source (unless otherwise stated): Istituto Nazionale di Statistica, Via Cesare Balbo 16, 00184 Rome; tel. (6) 46731; telex 610338; fax (6) 46733598.

Area and Population

AREA, POPULATION AND DENSITY

Area (sq km)	301,323*
Population (census results)	
25 October 1981	
Males	27,506,354
Females	29,050,557
Total	56,556,911
20 October 1991	56,778,031
Population (official estimates at mid-year)	
1994	57,203,534
1995	57,300,000†
1996	57,380,000†
Density (per sq km) at mid-1996	190.4

* 116,341 sq miles. † Provisional.

REGIONS (31 December 1993)

Region	Area (sq km)	Population	Regional capital	Population of capital
Abruzzo	10,795	1,262,948	L'Aquila	67,825
Basilicata	9,992	611,155	Potenza	65,713
Calabria	15,080	2,079,588	Catanzaro	96,886
Campania	13,595	5,708,657	Napoli (Naples)	1,061,583
Emilia-Romagna	22,123	3,924,348	Bologna	394,969
Friuli-Venezia Giulia	7,844	1,193,217	Trieste	226,707
Lazio	17,227	5,185,316	Roma (Rome)	2,687,881
Liguria	5,420	1,662,658	Genova (Genoa)	659,754
Lombardia (Lombardy)	23,872	8,901,023	Milano (Milan)	1,334,171
Marche	9,694	1,438,223	Ancona	100,597
Molise	4,438	331,494	Campobasso	51,318
Piemonte (Piedmont)	25,399	4,306,565	Torino (Turin)	945,551
Puglia	19,362	4,065,603	Bari	338,949
Sardegna (Sardinia)	24,090	1,657,375	Cagliari	178,063
Sicilia (Sicily)	25,707	5,025,280	Palermo	694,749
Toscana (Tuscany)	22,993	3,528,225	Firenze (Florence)	392,800
Trentino-Alto Adige	13,607	903,598	Bolzano (Bozen)*	97,924
			Trento (Trent, Trient)*	103,063
Umbria	8,456	819,172	Perugia	147,489
Valle d'Aosta	3,264	118,239	Aosta	35,767
Veneto	18,364	4,415,309	Venezia (Venice)	306,439

* Joint regional capitals.

PRINCIPAL TOWNS (population at 31 December 1996)

Roma (Rome, the capital)	2,645,322	Foggia	156,301
Milano (Milan)	1,303,925	Perugia	153,326
Napoli (Naples)	1,045,874	Salerno	143,751
Torino (Turin)	919,612	Ravenna	137,337
Palermo	687,855	Reggio nell' Emilia	137,242
Genova (Genoa)	653,529	Ferrara	134,297
Bologna	385,136	Rimini	129,596
Firenze (Florence)	380,058	Siracusa (Syracuse)	127,224
Catania	341,455	Sassari	121,412
Bari	335,410	Monza	119,197
Venezia (Venice)	296,422	Pescara	117,957
Messina	262,224	Bergamo	117,193
Verona	254,520	Latina	111,679
Trieste	221,551	Terni	108,432
Padova (Padua)	212,542	Vicenza	108,281
Taranto	211,660	Forlí	107,827
Brescia	189,767	Trento (Trent, Trient)	103,474
Reggio di Calabria	180,034	Novara	102,408
Modena	175,124	Lecce	99,763
Cagliari	174,175	Piacenza	99,665
Prato	168,892	Ancona	99,453
Parma	167,504	La Spezia	97,712
Livorno (Leghorn)	163,950	Torre del Greco	97,438

BIRTHS, MARRIAGES AND DEATHS

	Registered live births		Registered marriages		Registered deaths	
	Number	Rate (per 1,000)	Number	Rate (per 1,000)	Number	Rate (per 1,000)
1988	569,698	10.0	318,296	5.6	539,426	9.5
1989	560,688	9.9	321,272	5.7	531,853	9.4
1990	569,255	10.0	319,711	5.6	543,708	9.6
1991	562,787	9.9	312,061	5.5	553,833	9.8
1992	560,768	9.9	303,785	5.3	541,418	9.5
1993	538,168	9.4	292,632	5.1	543,433	9.5
1994	527,406	9.2	285,112	5.0	548,081	9.6
1995*	526,064	9.2	n.a.	n.a.	555,203	9.7
1996*	531,364	9.3	n.a.	n.a.	550,431	9.6

* Source: UN, *Population and Vital Statistics Report*

Expectation of life (years at birth, 1992): Males 73.8; Females 80.4. (Source: UN, *Demographic Yearbook*).

EMIGRATION

Destination	1993	1994	1995
Belgium	2,693	3,845	2,177
France	4,476	5,181	3,371
Germany	17,203	21,407	10,816
Switzerland	9,762	10,449	4,560
United Kingdom	2,418	3,515	2,787
Other European countries	7,692	6,380	6,780
Argentina	1,852	1,936	1,592
Brazil	594	636	641
Canada	975	1,082	693
USA	4,418	4,135	3,043
Venezuela	707	632	433
Oceania	963	866	692
Other countries	7,529	5,484	5,718
Total	61,282	65,548	43,303

ECONOMICALLY ACTIVE POPULATION*
(annual averages, '000 persons aged 15 years and over)

	1995	1996	1997
Agriculture, forestry, hunting and fishing	1,489	1,400	1,370
Energy and water	292	273	276
Industrial transformations†	4,534	4,566	4,550
Construction	1,607	1,592	1,586
Trade, restaurants and hotels	4,220	4,275	4,229
Transport, storage and communications	1,059	1,082	1,092
Financing, insurance, real estate and business services	1,598	1,690	1,753
Community, social and personal services	5,143	5,159	5,188
Total employed	19,942	20,037	20,044
Persons seeking work for the first time	1,454	1,496	1,521
Other unemployed	1,339	1,318	1,326
Total labour force	22,734	22,851	22,891
Males	14,244	14,236	14,206
Females	8,490	8,615	8,685

* Figures exclude permanent members of institutional households (134,031 in 1991) and persons on compulsory military service (218,000 in 1995; 213,750 in 1996; 230,000 in 1997).

† Mining and manufacturing, excluding energy.

Agriculture

PRINCIPAL CROPS ('000 metric tons)

	1994	1995	1996
Wheat	8,251	7,946	8,191
Rice (paddy)	1,361	1,321	1,424
Barley	1,467	1,387	1,405
Maize	7,483	8,454	8,712
Oats	355	301	580
Potatoes	2,021	2,081	2,120
Dry beans	28	24	24*
Dry broad beans	101	104	97
Soybeans (Soya beans)	720	732	742
Olives	2,640	3,288	3,000*
Cabbages	480	451	451*
Artichokes	534	517	517*
Tomatoes	5,130	5,156	5,156*
Cauliflowers	476	487	487*
Pumpkins, squash and gourds	334	286	286*
Aubergines (Egg-plants)	305	234	234*
Onions (dry)	441	442	442*
Green beans	215	158	158*
Green peas	136	130	130*
Carrots	442	396	396*
Watermelons	594	611	611*
Melons	426	372	372*
Grapes	9,323	8,470	9,000*
Sugar beet	12,629	13,188	12,125
Apples	2,233	1,940	1,940*
Pears	929	937	937*
Peaches and nectarines	1,790	1,689	1,689*
Oranges	1,809	1,597	1,597*
Lemons and limes	552	545	545*
Almonds (in the shell)	90	91	91*
Tobacco	121	124	104

* FAO estimate.

Source: FAO, *Production Yearbook*.

LIVESTOCK ('000 head, year ending September)

	1994	1995	1996
Horses	323	324	324*
Mules	17	16	16*
Asses	33	27†	27*
Cattle	7,459	7,164	7,018
Buffaloes	101	108	110
Pigs	8,348	8,023	7,964
Sheep	10,461	10,682	10,531
Goats	1,378	1,448	1,457

Chickens: (FAO estimates, million, year ending September): 130 in 1994; 133 in 1995; 130 in 1996.

Turkeys (FAO estimates, million, year ending September): 23 in 1994; 22 in 1995; 22 in 1996.

* FAO estimate. † Unofficial figure.

Source: FAO, *Production Yearbook*.

LIVESTOCK PRODUCTS ('000 metric tons)

	1994	1995	1996
Beef and veal	1,171	1,180	1,185
Mutton and lamb	75	73	73*
Goat meat	4	4	4*
Pig meat	1,369	1,346	1,430
Horse meat	58	56	56*
Poultry meat	1,087	1,091†	1,091*
Other meat	231	233	233
Cows' milk	10,674	10,674*	10,674*
Buffaloes' milk	79	79*	79*
Sheep's milk	800	800*	800*
Goats' milk	137	137*	137*
Butter	93	95†	94*
Cheese	905	899	899
Hen eggs	696	721†	680
Wool: greasy	13	12	12*

* FAO estimate. † Unofficial figure.

Source: FAO, *Production Yearbook*.

Forestry

ROUNDWOOD REMOVALS ('000 cubic metres, excl. bark)

	1992	1993	1994
Sawlogs, veneer logs and logs for sleepers	1,941	2,224	2,180
Pulpwood	1,612	1,619	1,320
Other industrial wood	872	1,115	984
Fuel wood	4,898	4,764	5,547
Total	9,323	9,722	10,031

Source: FAO, *Yearbook of Forest Products.*

SAWNWOOD PRODUCTION
('000 cubic metres, incl. railway sleepers)

	1992	1993	1994
Coniferous (softwood)	800	800	808
Broadleaved (hardwood)	1,023	900	1,000
Total	1,823	1,700	1,808

Source: FAO, *Yearbook of Forest Products.*

Fishing

('000 metric tons, live weight)

	1994	1995	1996
Freshwater fishes	11.6	12.2	12.0
Rainbow trout	38.2	40.3	40.7
Common sole	12.5	6.1	3.6
European hake	36.3	38.1	30.7
Porgies and seabreams	33.6	17.3	14.1
Surmullets (Red mullets)	12.6	9.4	11.3
European pilchard (sardine)	29.7	36.8	42.1
European anchovy	30.8	42.7	40.5
Other fishes (incl. unspecified)	122.6	122.3	99.4
Total fish	327.9	325.2	294.4
Shrimps, prawns, etc.	14.2	10.6	9.3
Other crustaceans	12.0	13.8	14.9
Mediterranean mussel	92.7	116.4	122.2
Striped venus	19.3	32.6	36.7
Carpet shells	54.9	65.8	40.3
Cuttlefishes	16.3	12.5	9.0
Squids	15.5	11.0	10.5
Octopuses	15.4	12.5	11.3
Other molluscs	7.3	13.3	11.2
Other aquatic invertebrates	0.6	—	—
Total catch	576.0	613.7	559.8
Inland waters	57.6*	n.a.	n.a.
Mediterranean and Black Sea	460.3*	n.a.	n.a.
Atlantic Ocean	49.4*	n.a.	n.a.
Indian Ocean	8.7*	n.a.	n.a.

* Source: FAO, *Yearbook of Fishery Statistics.*

Mining

('000 metric tons)

	1994	1995	1996
Lead concentrates*	20.4	22.7	20.3
Zinc concentrates*	40.9	43.7	20.1
Barytes	57.9	44.4	42.8
Fluorspar	77.9	124.7	126.7
Pyrites	258.4	n.a.	n.a.
Petroleum	4,897.9	5,208.0	5,369.0
Asphalt and bituminous rock	9.0	9.3	9.6
Lignite	509.2	352.3	192.9

* Figures refer to gross weight of ores and concentrates. The metal content (in '000 metric tons) was: Lead 12.7 in 1994, 14.0 in 1995; Zinc 21.3 in 1994, 22.7 in 1995.

Industry

SELECTED PRODUCTS
('000 metric tons, unless otherwise indicated)

	1994	1995	1996
Wine ('000 hectolitres)	59,280	56,200	60,000
Pig iron	11,160.9	11,677.7	10,324.3
Steel	25,933.7	27,771.1	24,284.9
Rolled iron	23,509.0	24,825.3	22,431.0
Other iron and steel-finished manufactures	879.6	1,032.4	982.3
Iron alloys and *spiegel-eisen* special pig irons	121	145	n.a.
Fuel oil	18,408.1	17,281.3	16,828.9
Synthetic ammonia	612.5	592.2	524.6
Sulphuric acid at 50° Bé	1,975.5	2,161.8	2,214.0
Synthetic organic dyes	24.2	23.0	23.7
Tanning materials	35.5	33.2	30.3
Caustic soda	952.9	922.1	875.7
Cotton yarn	262.5	260.1	262.0
Natural methane gas (million cu m)	20,341.4	20,383.5	20,047.5
Passenger motor cars ('000)	1,340.5	1,422.3	1,318.0
Lorries (Trucks) ('000)	194.1	245.7	227.6
Hydroelectric power (million kWh)*	47,731	41,907	47,072
Thermoelectric power (million kWh)*	173,071	187,904	184,921

* Net production.

Finance

CURRENCY AND EXCHANGE RATES

Monetary Units

100 centèsimi (singular: centèsimo) = 1 Italian lira (plural: lire).

Sterling and Dollar Equivalents (30 September 1997)

£1 sterling = 2,787.6 lire;
US $1 = 1,725.65 lire;
10,000 lire = £3.587 = $5.795.

Average Exchange Rate (lire per US $)

1994 1,612.4
1995 1,628.9
1996 1,542.9

STATE BUDGET ('000 million lire)*

Revenue†	1992	1993	1994
Taxation	585,541	637,198	630,952
Taxes on income, profits, etc.	220,801	250,124	237,806
Social security contributions	170,688	196,876	192,520
Domestic taxes on goods and services	179,165	174,260	184,185
Value-added tax	86,408	89,213	107,675
Excises	47,269	45,432	47,941
Other current revenue	17,181	18,036	18,363
Entrepreneurial and property income	12,563	12,176	11,988
Capital revenue	1,481	100	2,986
Unclassified receipts‡	19,912	9,061	12,619
Total	624,115	664,395	664,920

Expenditure§	1992	1993	1994
Current expenditure	731,010	777,005	787,905
Expenditure on goods and services	118,071	123,310	122,760
Wages and salaries	90,894	92,264	91,735
Interest payments	171,355	185,492	181,560
Subsidies and other current transfers	438,393	465,183	480,526
Unclassified items	3,191	3,020	3,059
Capital expenditure	51,152	45,804	30,919
Acquisition of fixed capital assets	15,649	15,482	5,429
Capital transfers	34,982	29,560	25,274
Domestic	34,763	29,306	25,028
Unclassified items	521	762	216
Total	782,162	822,809	818,824

* Figures represent the consolidated operations of the Central Government, comprising the General Account Budget and the budgets of three autonomous agencies and 12 social security institutions. Data exclude the accounts of the Deposit and Loan Fund and miscellaneous extrabudgetary agencies.

† Excluding grants received ('000 million lire): 3,091 in 1992; 10,653 in 1993; 3,430 in 1994.

‡ Including adjustment.

§ Excluding lending minus repayments ('000 million lire): 8,669 in 1992; 12,574 in 1993; 22,027 in 1994.

Source: IMF, *Government Finance Statistics Yearbook*.

INTERNATIONAL RESERVES (US $ million at 31 December)*

	1994	1995	1996
Gold†	26,342	25,570	25,369
IMF special drawing rights	125	—	29
Reserve position in IMF	2,033	1,963	1,855
Foreign exchange	30,107	32,942	44,064
Total	58,607	60,475	71,317

* Excluding deposits made with the European Monetary Co-operation Fund.

† Valued at market-related prices.

Source: IMF, *International Financial Statistics*.

MONEY SUPPLY ('000 million lire at 31 December)

	1994	1995	1996
Currency outside banks	96,050	98,180	100,110
Demand deposits at commercial banks	471,380	471,060	498,870
Checking deposits at Post Office	7,640	6,850	3,100
Total money	575,070	576,090	602,080

Source: IMF, *International Financial Statistics*.

COST OF LIVING (Consumer Price Index; base: 1990 = 100)

	1992	1993	1994
Food	111.9	114.4	118.4
Fuel and light	113.3	118.2	123.0
Clothing	110.9	115.1	118.8
Rent	112.9	121.0	131.6
All items (incl. others)	111.7	116.7	121.4

1995: All items: 127.7.

Source: ILO, *Yearbook of Labour Statistics*.

NATIONAL ACCOUNTS ('000 million lire at current prices)

National Income and Product

	1994	1995	1996
Compensation of employees	698,174	727,779	768,358
Operating surplus	572,440	637,567	676,120
Domestic factor incomes	1,270,614	1,365,346	1,444,478
Consumption of fixed capital	203,398	219,629	231,781
Gross domestic product (GDP) at factor cost	1,474,012	1,584,975	1,676,259
Indirect taxes	204,154	221,181	234,685
Less Subsidies	39,500	35,138	37,450
GDP in purchasers' values	1,638,666	1,771,018	1,873,494
Factor income received from abroad	46,355	55,657	59,574
Less Factor income paid abroad	73,697	81,526	83,790
Gross national product	1,611,324	1,745,149	1,849,278
Less Consumption of fixed capital	203,398	219,629	231,781
National income in market prices	1,407,926	1,525,520	1,617,497
Other current transfers from abroad	19,774	21,455	22,109
Less Other current transfers paid abroad	31,072	29,173	33,659
National disposable income	1,396,628	1,517,802	1,605,947

Expenditure on the Gross Domestic Product

	1994	1995	1996
Government final consumption expenditure	284,475	289,924	310,823
Private final consumption expenditure	1,029,231	1,107,423	1,165,352
Increase in stocks	9,695	15,267	1,158
Gross fixed capital formation	272,813	306,181	319,165
Total domestic expenditure	1,596,214	1,718,795	1,796,498
Exports of goods and services	361,600	444,747	452,277
Less Imports of goods and services	319,148	392,524	375,281
GDP in purchasers' values	1,638,666	1,771,018	1,873,494
GDP at constant 1990 prices	1,346,267	1,385,830	1,395,408

Gross Domestic Product by Economic Activity

	1994	1995	1996
Agriculture, forestry, hunting and fishing	47,527	50,843	53,302
Energy and water	95,920	103,575	107,174
Industrial transformations*	331,792	366,359	382,228
Construction	84,721	88,310	92,943
Trade, restaurants and hotels†	301,889	327,928	345,357
Transport, storage and communications	105,342	113,958	118,754
Other private services	428,610	466,415	502,037
Government services	203,439	209,229	225,873
Other producers	16,394	17,923	19,022
Sub-total	1,615,634	1,774,540	1,846,690
Import duties	95,839	104,924	107,994
Less Imputed bank service charge	72,807	78,446	81,190
GDP in purchasers' values	1,638,666	1,771,018	1,873,494

* Mining and manufacturing, excluding energy.
† Including repair services.

BALANCE OF PAYMENTS (US $ million)

	1994	1995	1996
Exports of goods f.o.b.	191,421	233,998	250,843
Imports of goods f.o.b.	−155,827	−189,240	−190,021
Trade balance	35,595	44,758	60,821
Exports of services	56,841	65,736	69,910
Imports of services	−55,427	−65,106	−67,445
Balance on goods and services	37,009	45,388	63,286
Other income received	28,599	34,168	40,142
Other income paid	−45,306	−49,817	−55,108
Balance on goods, services and income	20,302	29,739	48,319
Current transfers received	12,275	14,291	14,297
Current transfers paid	−19,366	−18,986	−21,576
Current balance	13,211	25,134	41,040
Capital account (net)	1,028	1,671	67
Direct investment abroad	−5,638	−6,925	−6,049
Direct investment from abroad	2,163	4,878	3,523
Portfolio investment assets	−19,207	−2,704	−23,893
Portfolio investment liabilities	25,408	38,652	81,413
Other investment assets	−15,932	−32,130	−73,370
Other investment liabilities	−1,002	−4,660	10,893
Net errors and omissions	1,544	−21,114	−21,717
Overall balance	1,575	2,804	11,907

Source: IMF, *International Financial Statistics*.

External Trade

Note: Data refer to the trade of Italy (excluding the communes of Livigno and Campione) and San Marino, with which Italy maintains a customs union. The figures include trade in second-hand ships, and stores and bunkers for foreign ships and aircraft, but exclude manufactured gas, surplus military equipment, war reparations and repayments and gift parcels by post. Also excluded are imports of military goods and exports of fish landed abroad directly from Italian vessels.

PRINCIPAL COMMODITIES (distribution by SITC, US $ million)

Imports c.i.f.	1993	1994	1995
Food and live animals	16,277.9	17,220.1	19,380.2
Meat and meat preparations	3,478.2	3,551.7	3,691.6
Fresh, chilled or frozen meat	3,325.3	3,389.4	3,518.1
Crude materials (inedible) except fuels	10,313.2	12,909.3	15,552.0
Mineral fuels and lubricants	13,810.8	13,730.2	15,060.6
Petroleum and petroleum products	12,634.5	12,515.8	13,436.1
Crude petroleum	8,872.7	8,584.4	9,103.3
Refined petroleum products	3,482.0	3,618.2	3,947.1
Chemicals and related products	18,081.0	21,041.2	25,993.9
Organic chemicals	4,532.5	5,454.3	6,800.0
Medicinal and pharmaceutical products	3,227.7	3,262.5	3,902.5
Artificial resins and plastic materials, and cellulose esters and ethers	4,279.0	5,330.7	7,256.1
Products of polymerization etc.	2,986.0	3,759.1	5,071.9
Basic manufactures	22,162.6	28,412.3	37,232.2
Textile yarn, fabrics, etc.	4,653.0	6,004.4	6,861.1
Iron and steel	4,577.3	6,205.3	9,558.5
Non-ferrous metals	3,259.4	4,304.2	6,122.9
Machinery and transport equipment	41,980.6	47,332.2	59,736.7
Machinery specialized for particular industries	2,897.7	3,170.1	4,459.2
General industrial machinery and equipment	4,598.0	5,373.4	7,191.9
Office machines and automatic data-processing equipment	5,089.8	5,373.9	6,743.5
Telecommunications and sound recording and reproducing apparatus and equipment	2,983.1	3,571.3	4,246.1
Other electrical machinery, apparatus, etc.	7,642.7	9,491.6	11,689.2
Transistors, valves, etc	2,763.8	3,682.0	4,390.3
Road vehicles and parts	13,572.5	14,908.9	18,825.5
Passenger motor cars (excl. buses)	9,977.6	10,728.3	13,299.2
Miscellaneous manufactured articles	14,286.4	15,661.9	18,355.5
Clothing and accessories (excl. footwear)	3,587.7	3,972.9	4,659.0
Special transactions and commodities not classified according to kind	4,391.8	4,256.1	5,123.1
Gold, non-monetary (excluding gold ores and concentrates)	3,862.7	4,173.4	4,317.7
Total (incl. others)	147,817.5	167,975.1	204,099.2

Exports f.o.b.	1993	1994	1995
Food and live animals	8,941.0	9,691.7	11,226.3
Fruit and vegetables	3,746.9	4,195.4	4,835.7
Mineral fuels, lubricants, etc.	3,697.0	3,052.1	2,932.6
Petroleum products	3,616.1	2,981.1	2,851.7
Refined petroleum products	3,511.3	2,872.0	2,755.2
Chemicals and related products	11,817.4	13,649.5	17,430.8
Artificial resins and plastic materials, and cellulose esters and ethers	3,222.4	3,915.9	5,271.9
Basic manufactures	37,691.7	43,399.6	52,881.5
Textile yarn, fabrics, etc.	9,481.2	10,874.8	12,809.2
Non-metallic mineral manufactures	6,455.7	7,485.9	8,744.6
Iron and steel	6,207.4	6,753.9	8,496.3
Other manufactures of metals	6,413.9	7,296.3	8,999.5
Machinery and transport equipment	61,763.1	69,730.6	86,706.2
Machinery specialized for particular industries	12,167.5	13,353.8	16,140.5
General industrial machinery and equipment	13,336.3	15,049.9	18,659.1
Non-electric machine parts and accessories	3,885.9	4,374.2	5,200.3
Office machines and automatic data-processing equipment	4,174.9	4,365.3	5,285.9
Electrical machinery, apparatus, etc. (excl. telecommunications and sound equipment)	9,840.6	11,593.5	14,039.2
Domestic electrical equipment	3,624.5	4,296.9	5,131.1
Road vehicles and parts	11,587.9	14,339.4	19,058.3
Passenger motor cars (excl. buses)	4,627.7	5,897.3	8,017.0
Motor vehicle parts and accessories	3,878.6	4,429.0	6,053.0

Exports f.o.b. — *continued*	1993	1994	1995
Miscellaneous manufactured articles	38,748.3	43,632.3	51,839.1
Furniture and parts thereof	5,797.4	6,735.4	8,365.5
Clothing and accessories (excl. footwear)	11,163.3	12,528.2	14,178.4
Outer garments and other articles, knitted or crocheted, not elastic nor rubberized	3,585.1	3,740.8	3,969.2
Footwear	5,743.1	6,465.4	7,304.5
Leather footwear	4,944.2	5,620.8	6,392.2
Jewellery, goldsmiths' and silversmiths' wares, etc.	4,207.3	4,297.5	4,745.7
Total (incl. others)	168,511.2	190,004.7	231,346.4

Source: UN, *International Trade Statistics Yearbook*.

PRINCIPAL TRADING PARTNERS (US $ million)*

Imports c.i.f.	1993	1994	1995
Algeria	1,935.5	1,627.0	2,289.3
Austria	3,269.7	3,761.1	4,705.2
Belgium-Luxembourg	6,884.7	7,968.5	9,758.5
Brazil	1,512.4	1,847.8	2,012.3
China, People's Republic	2,593.7	3,128.3	3,920.4
Denmark	1,522.6	1,660.8	1,869.9
France	20,108.4	22,751.9	28,293.8
Germany, Federal Republic	28,533.8	32,218.6	38,881.4
Japan	3,811.1	3,959.0	4,490.0
Libya	3,333.8	3,360.1	3,742.6
Netherlands	8,416.8	9,591.1	11,228.8
Russia	3,875.6	4,731.2	5,204.3
Saudi Arabia	1,720.0	1,481.5	1,581.8
Spain	4,949.7	6,511.9	8,008.0
Sweden	1,806.0	2,104.8	2,778.2
Switzerland	5,935.4	6,302.8	7,490.1
United Kingdom	8,610.0	10,214.7	12,287.4
USA	7,672.8	7,751.1	9,846.5
Total (incl. others)	143,954.8	163,801.6	199,781.5

Exports f.o.b.	1993	1994	1995
Austria	4,201.2	4,670.3	5,486.3
Belgium-Luxembourg	5,017.6	5,667.1	6,636.5
Brazil	1,080.9	1,845.9	3,170.6
China, People's Republic	2,468.6	2,285.6	2,695.5
France	22,127.3	24,844.4	30,015.2
Germany, Federal Republic	32,809.1	36,113.5	43,246.0
Greece	2,987.0	3,404.1	4,355.8
Hong Kong	2,509.0	3,139.4	3,905.2
Japan	3,201.8	4,054.2	5,346.2
Netherlands	4,739.3	5,440.5	6,824.0
Poland	1,501.1	1,769.3	2,514.4
Portugal	2,254.3	2,560.4	3,211.0
Russia	1,717.8	2,172.9	2,869.3
Saudi Arabia	2,024.7	1,556.2	1,524.2
Spain	7,368.2	8,919.3	11,312.6
Switzerland	6,591.1	7,138.6	8,743.5
Turkey	2,658.0	1,911.5	3,233.6
United Kingdom	10,701.7	12,303.1	14,269.7
USA	13,034.6	14,742.5	16,900.3
Total (incl. others)	168,363.3	189,913.3	231,265.9

* Imports by country of production; exports by country of consumption.

Source: UN, *International Trade Statistics Yearbook*.

Transport

STATE RAILWAYS (traffic)

	1994	1995	1996
Passenger journeys ('000)	455,000	462,500	468,300
Passenger-km (million)	48,900	49,700	50,300
Freight ton-km (million)	22,564	24,081	23,369

ROAD TRAFFIC (estimates, vehicles in use at 31 December)

	1994	1995	1996
Passenger motor cars	30,870,000	31,700,000	32,789,000
Buses and coaches	78,000	77,220	78,000
Goods vehicles	4,410,000	5,050,000	5,719,000

Source: International Road Federation, *World Road Statistics*.

SHIPPING

Merchant Fleet (registered at 31 December)

	1994	1995	1996
Number of vessels	1,434	1,397	1,348
Displacement ('000 grt)	6,818	6,699	6,594

Source: Lloyd's Register of Shipping, *World Fleet Statistics*.

Sea-borne Freight Traffic (international and coastwise)

	1990	1991	1992
Vessels entered ('000 nrt)	380,203	421,022	396,385
Vessels cleared ('000 nrt)	380,051	421,022	396,385
Goods loaded ('000 metric tons)	109,232	116,631	110,573
Goods unloaded ('000 metric tons)	295,766	313,745	291,933

CIVIL AVIATION (traffic on scheduled services)

	1992	1993	1994*
Kilometres flown (million)	233	242	248
Passengers carried ('000)	21,630	21,722	22,933
Passenger-km (million)	28,609	29,634	31,738
Freight ton-km (million)	1,270	1,335	n.a.

* Source: UN, *Statistical Yearbook*.

Tourism

	1994	1995	1996
Foreign tourist arrivals*	51,814,449	55,706,188	56,300,496
Amount spent (million lire)	38,307,122	44,717,611	46,249,264

* Including excursionists and cruise passengers. Arrivals at accommodation establishments were 21,025,353 in 1993; 24,757,062 in 1994; 27,993,388 in 1995.

Number of hotel beds: 1,722,977 in 1992; 1,720,637 in 1993; 1,718,442 in 1994.

TOURIST ARRIVALS BY COUNTRY OF ORIGIN
(including excursionists)

	1994	1995	1996
Austria	4,650,340	5,962,422	6,147,073
Belgium	676,985	778,176	670,122
France	8,057,960	8,405,889	9,303,490
Germany	8,301,869	8,806,197	8,752,281
Netherlands	1,032,759	1,145,502	933,549
Switzerland	8,657,703	8,982,815	8,374,527
United Kingdom	1,802,515	1,688,530	1,659,319
USA	1,292,062	1,384,006	1,309,113
Yugoslavia (former)	7,911,891	8,703,774	9,461,235
Total (incl. others)	51,814,449	55,706,188	56,300,496

Communications Media

	1992	1993	1994
Telephone subscriptions	23,708,388	24,166,572	24,542,000
Telefax stations (number in use)	201,000	202,000	n.a.
Mobile cellular telephones (subscribers)	783,000	1,207,000	2,239,740
Radio receivers ('000 in use)	45,734	45,800	45,850
Television receivers ('000 in use)	24,350	24,500	25,000
Book production (titles)	29,351	30,110	32,673
Daily newspapers:			
Number of titles	78	79	74
Average circulation ('000)	6,068	6,366	5,985
Non-daily newspapers:			
Number of titles	230	n.a.	231
Average circulation ('000)	1,277	n.a.	1,428

Source: mainly UNESCO, *Statistical Yearbook*.

Education

(1995/96)

	Schools	Teachers	Students
Pre-primary	26,249	121,520	1,573,308
Primary	20,442	289,055	2,825,838
Secondary:			
Scuola Media	9,278	214,861	1,907,024
Secondaria Superiore	7,888	313,001	2,661,760
of which:			
Technical	2,966	139,392	1,113,794
Vocational	1,690	68,957	507,125
Teacher training	762	22,317	200,305
Art Licei	312	13,481	93,429
Classical, linguistic and scientific Licei	2,158	68,854	747,107
Higher*	56	34,724	1,660,747

* Data refer to the 1994/95 academic year.

Source: Ministry of Education.

Directory

The Constitution*

The Constitution of the Italian Republic was approved by the Constituent Assembly on 22 December 1947 and came into force on 1 January 1948 (and was amended in April 1993). The fundamental principles are declared in Articles 1–12, as follows:

Italy is a democratic republic based on the labour of the people.

The Republic recognizes and guarantees as inviolable the rights of its citizens, either as individuals or in a community, and it expects, in return, devotion to duty and the fulfilment of political, economic and social obligations.

All citizens shall enjoy equal status and shall be regarded as equal before the law, without distinction of sex, race, language or religion, and without regard to the political opinions which they may hold or their personal or social standing.

It shall be the function of the Republic to remove the economic and social inequalities which, by restricting the liberty of the individual, impede the full development of the human personality, thereby reducing the effective participation of the citizen in the political, economic and social life of the country.

The Republic recognizes the right of all citizens to work and shall do all in its power to give effect to this right.

The Republic, while remaining one and indivisible, shall recognize and promote local autonomy, fostering the greatest possible decentralization in those services which are administered by the State, and subordinating legislative methods and principles to the exigencies of decentralized and autonomous areas.

The State and the Catholic Church shall be sovereign and independent, each in its own sphere. Their relations shall be governed by the Lateran Pact ('Patti Lateranensi'), and any modification in the pact agreed upon by both parties shall not necessitate any revision of the Constitution.

All religious denominations shall have equal liberty before the law, denominations other than the Catholic having the right to worship according to their beliefs, in so far as they do not conflict with the common law of the country.

The Republic shall do all in its power to promote the development of culture and scientific and technical research. It shall also protect and preserve the countryside and the historical and artistic monuments which are the inheritance of the nation.

The juridical system of the Italian Republic shall be in conformity with the generally recognized practice of international law. The legal rights of foreigners in the country shall be regulated by law in accordance with international practice.

Any citizen of a foreign country who is deprived of democratic liberty such as is guaranteed under the Italian Constitution, has the right of asylum within the territory of the Republic in accordance with the terms of the law, and his extradition for political offences will not be granted.

Italy repudiates war as an instrument of offence against the liberty of other nations and as a means of resolving international disputes. Italy accepts, under parity with other nations, the limitations of sovereignty necessary for the preservation of peace and justice between nations. To that end, it will support and promote international organizations.

The Constitution is further divided into Parts I and II, in which are set forth respectively the rights and responsibilities of the citizen and the administration of the Republic.

PART ONE

Civic Clauses

Section I (Articles 13–28). The liberty of the individual is inviolable and no form of detention, restriction or inspection is permitted unless it be for juridical purposes and in accordance with the provisions of the law. The domicile of a person is likewise inviolable and shall be immune from forced inspection or sequestration, except according to the provisions of the law. Furthermore, all citizens shall be free to move wheresoever they will throughout the country, and may leave it and return to it without let or hindrance. Right of public meeting, if peaceful and without arms, is guaranteed. Secret organizations of a directly or indirectly political or military nature are, however, prohibited.

Freedom in the practice of religious faith is guaranteed.

The Constitution further guarantees complete freedom of thought, speech and writing, and lays down that the Press shall be entirely free from all control or censorship. No person may be deprived of civic or legal rights on political grounds.

The death penalty is not allowed under the Constitution except in case of martial law. The accused shall be considered 'not guilty' until he is otherwise proven. All punishment shall be consistent with humanitarian practice and shall be directed towards the re-education of the criminal.

Ethical and Social Clauses

Section II (Articles 29–34). The Republic regards the family as the fundamental basis of society and considers the parents to be responsible for the maintenance, instruction and education of the children. The Republic shall provide economic assistance for the family, with special regard to large families, and shall make provision for maternity, infancy and youth, subject always to the liberty and freedom of choice of the individuals as envisaged under the law.

Education, the arts and science shall be free, the function of the State being merely to indicate the general lines of instruction. Private entities and individuals shall have the right to conduct educational institutions without assistance from the State, but such non-state institutions must ensure to their pupils liberty and instruction equal to that in the state schools. Institutions of higher culture, universities and academies shall be autonomous within the limitations prescribed by the law.

Education is available to all and is free and obligatory for at least eight years. Higher education for students of proven merit shall be aided by scholarships and other allowances made by the Republic.

Economic Clauses

Section III (Articles 35–47). The Republic shall safeguard the right to work in all its aspects, and shall promote agreement and co-operation with international organizations in matters pertaining to the regulation of labour and the rights of workers. The rights of Italian workers abroad shall be protected.

All workers shall be entitled to remuneration proportionate to the quantity and quality of their work, and in any case shall be ensured of sufficient to provide freedom and a dignified standard of life for themselves and their families.

The maximum working hours shall be fixed by law, and the worker shall be entitled to a weekly day of rest and an annual holiday of nine days with pay.

Women shall have the same rights and, for equal work, the same remuneration as men. Conditions of work shall be regulated by their special family requirements and the needs of mother and child. The work of minors shall be specially protected.

All citizens have the right to sickness, unemployment and disability maintenance.

Liberty to organize in trade unions is guaranteed and any union may register as a legal entity, provided it is organized on a democratic basis. The right to strike is admitted within the limitations of the relevant legislation.

Private enterprise is permitted in so far as it does not run counter to the well-being of society nor constitute a danger to security, freedom and human dignity.

Ownership of private property is permitted and guaranteed within the limitations laid down by the law regarding the acquisition, extent and enjoyment of private property. Inheritance and testamentary bequests shall be regulated by law.

Limitation is placed by law on private ownership of land and on its use, with a view to its best exploitation for the benefit of the community.

The Republic recognizes the value of mutual co-operation and the right of the workers to participate in management.

The Republic shall encourage all forms of saving, by house purchase, by co-operative ownership and by investment in the public utility undertakings of the country.

Political Clauses

Section IV (Articles 48–54). The electorate comprises all citizens, both men and women, who have attained their majority. Voting is free, equal and secret, and its exercise is a civic duty. All citizens have the right to associate freely together in political parties, and may also petition the Chambers to legislate as may be deemed necessary.

All citizens of both sexes may hold public office on equal terms.

Defence of one's country is a sacred duty of the citizen, and military service is obligatory within the limits prescribed by law. Its fulfilment shall in no way prejudice the position of the worker nor hinder the exercise of political rights. The organization of the armed forces shall be imbued with the spirit of democracy.

All citizens must contribute to the public expenditure, in proportion to their capacity.

All citizens must be loyal to the Republic and observe the terms of the law and the Constitution.

PART TWO

Sections I, II and III (Articles 55–100). These sections are devoted to a detailed exposition of the Legislature and legislative procedure of the Republic.

Parliament shall comprise two Chambers, namely the Chamber of Deputies (Camera dei Deputati) and the Senate of the Republic (Senato).

The Chamber of Deputies is elected by direct universal suffrage, the number of Deputies being 630. All voters who on the day of the elections are 25 years of age, may be elected Deputies.

Three-quarters of the seats are allocated on the basis of a simple plurality and the remaining one-quarter by proportional representation.

The Senate of the Republic is elected on a regional basis, the number of eligible Senators being 315. No region shall have fewer than seven Senators. Valle d'Aosta has only one Senator.

Three-quarters of the seats are allocated on the basis of a simple plurality and the remaining one-quarter by proportional representation.

The Chamber of Deputies and the Senate of the Republic are elected for five years.

The term of each House cannot be extended except by law and only in the case of war.

Members of Parliament shall receive remuneration fixed by law.

The President of the Republic must be a citizen of at least fifty years of age and in full enjoyment of all civic and political rights. The person shall be elected for a period of seven years (Articles 84–85).

The Government shall consist of the President of the Council and the Ministers who themselves shall form the Council. The President of the Council, or Prime Minister, shall be nominated by the President of the Republic, who shall also appoint the ministers on the recommendation of the Prime Minister (Article 92).

Section IV (Articles 101–113). Sets forth the judicial system and procedure.

Section V (Articles 114–133). Deals with the division of the Republic into regions, provinces and communes, and sets forth the limits and extent of autonomy enjoyed by the regions. Under Article 131 the regions are enumerated as follows:

Piemonte (Piedmont)	Marche
Lombardia (Lombardy)	Lazio
Veneto	Abruzzo
Liguria	Molise
Emilia-Romagna	Campania
Toscana (Tuscany)	Puglia
Umbria	Basilicata
Calabria	Trentino-Alto Adige†
Sicilia (Sicily)†	Friuli-Venezia Giulia†
Sardegna (Sardinia)†	Valle d'Aosta†

The final articles provide for the establishment of the Corte Costituzionale to deal with constitutional questions and any revisions which may be found necessary after the Constitution has come into operation.

* In June 1997 a parliamentary commission on constitutional reform, which had been established in January, announced its recommendations which included: a directly-elected President for a six-year term with responsibility for foreign and defence policy; a reduction of the Chamber of Deputies from 630 to 400 members and of the Senate from 315 to 200 members; greater financial autonomy for the regions; and a second round of voting for seats allocated on the basis of a simple plurality. The recommendations required approval by both the Chamber of Deputies and the Senate prior to endorsement at a national referendum.

† These five regions have a wider form of autonomy based on constitutional legislation specially adapted to their regional characteristics (Article 116). Each region shall be administered by a Regional Council, in which is vested the legislative power and which may make suggestions for legislation to the Chambers, and the Giunta regionale which holds the executive power (Article 121).

The Government

(January 1998)

HEAD OF STATE

President of the Republic: OSCAR LUIGI SCALFARO (inaugurated 28 May 1992).

COUNCIL OF MINISTERS

A coalition of the Partito Democratico della Sinistra (PDS), the Partito Popolare Italiano (PPI), the Rinnovamento Italiano (RI), the Federazione dei Verdi (FV), the Unione Democratica (UD) and Independents (Ind.).

Prime Minister: Prof. ROMANO PRODI (PPI).

Deputy Prime Minister and Minister of Cultural Heritage and Sport: WALTER VELTRONI (PDS).

Minister of Foreign Affairs: Prof. LAMBERTO DINI (RI).

Minister of the Interior: GIORGIO NAPOLITANO (PDS).

Minister of Justice: GIOVANNI MARIA FLICK (Ind.).

Minister of the Treasury and of the Budget: CARLO AZEGLIO CIAMPI (Ind.).

Minister of Finance: VICENZO VISCO (PDS).

Minister of Defence: BENIAMINO ANDREATTA (PPI).

Minister of Education and Research: LUIGI BERLINGUER (PDS).

Minister of Public Works: PAOLO COSTA (Ind.).

Minister of Agriculture: MICHELE PINTO (PPI).

Minister of Transport: CLAUDIO BURLANDO (PDS).

Minister of Post and Telecommunications: ANTONIO MACCANICO (UD).

Minister of Industry and Tourism: PIERLUIGI BERSANI (PDS).

Minister of Employment and Social Welfare: TIZIANO TREU (RI).

Minister of Foreign Trade: AUGUSTO FANTOZZI (RI).

Minister of Health: ROSI BINDI (PPI).

Minister of the Environment: EDO RONCHI (FV).

Ministers without Portfolio:

Family and Social Affairs: LIVIA TURCO (PDS).

Equal Opportunities: ANNA FINOCCHIARO (PDS).

Public Administration and Regional Affairs: FRANCO BASSANINI (PDS).

MINISTRIES

Office of the President: Palazzo del Quirinale, 00187 Rome; tel. (6) 46991; telex 611440.

Office of the Prime Minister: Palazzo Chigi, Piazza Colonna 370, 00187 Rome; tel. (6) 67791; telex 613199; fax (6) 6783998.

Ministry of Agriculture: Via XX Settembre, 00187 Rome; tel. (6) 46651; fax (6) 4742314.

Ministry of Cultural Heritage and Sport: Via del Collegio Romano 27, 00186 Rome; tel. (6) 67231; telex 621407; fax (6) 6793156.

Ministry of Defence: Via XX Settembre 8, 00187 Rome; tel. (6) 4882126; telex 611438; fax (6) 4747775.

Ministry of Education: Viale Trastevere 76A, 00153 Rome; tel. (6) 58491; telex 613181; fax (6) 5803381.

Ministry of Employment and Social Welfare: Via Flavia 6, 00187 Rome; tel. (6) 4683; telex 626144; fax (6) 47887174.

Ministry of the Environment: Piazza Venezia 11, 00187 Rome; tel. (6) 70361; fax (6) 6790130.

Ministry of the Family and Social Affairs: Via Veneto 56, 00187 Rome; tel. (6) 4820172; fax (6) 4821207.

Ministry of Finance: Viale America 242, 00144 Rome; tel. (6) 59648826; telex 614460; fax (6) 5910993.

Ministry of Foreign Affairs: Piazzale della Farnesina 1, 00194 Rome; tel. (6) 36911; telex 610611; fax (6) 3236210.

Ministry of Foreign Trade: Viale America 341, 00144 Rome; tel. (6) 59931; telex 610083; fax (6) 59647531.

Ministry of Health: Viale dell'Industria 20, 00144 Rome; tel. (6) 59941; fax (6) 59647749.

Ministry of Industry and Tourism: Via Vittorio Veneto 33, 00187 Rome; tel. (6) 47051; telex 622550; fax (6) 47052215.

Ministry of the Interior: Piazzale del Viminale, 00184 Rome; tel. (6) 46671; fax (6) 4825792.

Ministry of Justice: Via Arenula 71, 00186 Rome; tel. (6) 68851; telex 623072; fax (6) 6875419.

Ministry of Post and Telecommunications: Viale Europa, 00144 Rome; tel. (6) 59581; fax (6) 59582236.

Ministry of Public Administration: Palazzo Vidoni, Corso Vittorio Emanuele 116, 00186 Rome; tel. (6) 680031.

Ministry of Public Works: Piazza Porta Pia 1, 00198 Rome; tel. (6) 84821; fax (6) 867187.

Ministry of Transport: Piazza della Croce Rossa 1, 00161 Rome; tel. (6) 84901; telex 613111; fax (6) 8415693.

Ministry of the Treasury and of the Budget: Via XX Settembre 97, 00187 Rome; tel. (6) 59931; fax (6) 5913751.

Ministry of Universities and Scientific Research: Piazza J. F. Kennedy 20, 00144 Rome; tel. (6) 59911; fax (6) 59912967.

Legislature

PARLAMENTO
(Parliament)

Senato
(Senate)

President: NICOLA MANCINO.

General Election, 21 April 1996

Parties/Alliances	Percentage of votes for seats elected by proportional representation*	Total seats
L'Ulivo†	41.2	157
Polo per le Libertà‡	37.3	116
Lega Nord	10.4	27
Rifondazione Comunista (RC)	2.9	10
Liste Autonomiste§	1.8	3
Fiamma	2.3	1
Lista Pannella-Sgarbi	1.6	1
Socialisti Italiani (SI)	0.9	—
Others	1.6	—
Total	100.0	315‖

* Figures refer to seats elected by proportional representation (25% of the total); percentages for the remaining 75% of seats, elected by majority vote, are not available.

† Centre-left alliance comprising the Partito Democratico della Sinistra (PDS), the Partito Popolare Italiano (PPI), the Südtiroler Volkspartei (SVP), the Partito Repubblicano Italiano (PRI), the Unione Democratica (UD), the Lista Romano Prodi, the Rinnovamento Italiano (RI) and the Federazione dei Verdi (FV).

‡ Centre-right grouping including Forza Italia, the Alleanza Nazionale (AN), the Centro Cristiano Democratico (CCD) and the Cristiani Democratici Uniti (CDU).

§ Autonomous (regionalist) lists.

‖ In addition to the 315 elected members, there are 10 life members.

Camera dei Deputati
(Chamber of Deputies)

President: LUCIANO VIOLANTE.

General Election, 21 April 1996

Parties/Alliances	Percentage of votes for seats elected by proportional representation*	Total seats
L'Ulivo	34.8	284
Partito Democratico della Sinistra (PDS)	21.1	—
Partito Popolare Italiano (PPI), Lista Romano Prodi	6.8	—
Rinnovamento Italiano (RI)	4.3	—
Federazione dei Verdi (FV)	2.5	—
Others	0.1	
Polo per le Libertà e del Buon Governo	44.0	246
Forza Italia	20.6	—
Alleanza Nazionale (AN)	15.7	—
Centro Cristiano Democratico (CCD), Cristiani Democratici Uniti (CDU)	5.8	—
Others	1.9	—
Lega Nord	10.1	59
Rifondazione Comunista (RC)	8.6	35
Others	2.5	6
Total	100.0	630

* Figures refer to seats elected by proportional representation (25% of the total); percentages for the remaining 75% of seats, elected by majority vote, are not available.

Political Organizations

Alleanza Nazionale (AN) (National Alliance): Via della Scrofa 39, 00186 Rome; tel. (6) 68803014; fax (6) 6548256; f. 1994; in early 1995 absorbed the neo-fascist Movimento Sociale Italiano-Destra Nazionale (MSI-DN, f. 1946); Sec.-Gen. GIANFRANCO FINI; 400,000 mems.

Centro Cristiano Democratico (CCD) (Christian-Democratic Centre): Via dei Due Macelli 66, Rome; tel. (6) 69791001; fax (6) 6795940; e-mail direzione@ccd.it; advocates centre-right policies; Pres. CLEMENTE MASTELLA.

Cristiani Democratici Uniti (CDU) (United Christian Democrats): Rome; f. 1995 after split with Partito Popolare Italiano; advocates centre-right policies; Sec.-Gen. ROCCO BUTTIGLIONE.

Federazione dei Verdi (Green Party): Rome; tel. (6) 4957383; f. 1987; advocates environmentalist and anti-nuclear policies; branch of the European Green movement; Leader LUIGI MANCONI.

Fiamma (Torch): Rome; f. 1996; electoral alliance incorporating former mems of neo-fascist Movimento Sociale Italiano-Destra Nazionale.

Forza Italia (Come on, Italy!): Via dell'Umiltà 48, 00187 Rome; tel. (6) 67311; fax (6) 69941315; f. 1993; advocates principles of market economy; Leader SILVIO BERLUSCONI.

Lega Nord (Northern League): Milan; tel. (2) 6070379; fax (2) 66802766; f. 1991; advocates federalism and transfer of control of resources to regional govts; in 1996 declared the 'Independent Republic of Padania'; opposes immigration; a breakaway faction led by ROBERTO MARONI was formed in early 1995; Sec. UMBERTO BOSSI.

Partito Democratico della Sinistra (PDS) (Democratic Party of the Left): Via delle Botteghe Oscure 4, 00186 Rome; tel. (6) 67111; fax (6) 6792085; f. 1921 as the Partito Comunista Italiano (PCI) (Italian Communist Party); name changed 1991; advocates a democratic and libertarian society; Gen. Sec. MASSIMO D'ALEMA; approx. 1.4m. mems.

Partito Liberale Italiano (PLI) (Liberal Party): Via Frattina, 00187 Rome; tel. (6) 6796951; f. 1848 by Cavour, its chief aim is the realization of the principle of freedom in all public and private matters; Sec.-Gen. RAFFAELE COSTA; 153,000 mems.

Partito Popolare Italiano (PPI) (Italian People's Party): Central Office: Piazza del Gesù 46, 00186 Rome; tel. (6) 699591; fax (6) 6792304; f. 1994 as the successor to the Partito della Democrazia Cristiana (DC) (Christian Democrat Party; f. 1943); while extending its appeal to voters of all classes, the party attempts to maintain a centre position; Pres. GERARDO BIANCO; Sec.-Gen. FRANCO MARINI.

Partito Radicale (PR) (Radical Party): Via di Torre Argentina 76, 00186 Rome; tel. (6) 689791; telex 610495; fax (6) 68805396; campaigns on civil rights issues; Leader MARCO PANNELLA; 42,463 mems.

Partito Repubblicano Italiano (PRI) (Republican Party): Piazza dei Caprettari 70, 00186 Rome; tel. (6) 6834037; f. 1897; followers of the principles of Mazzini (social justice in a modern free society) and modern liberalism; Pres. BRUNO VISENTINI; 110,000 mems.

Partito Socialista Democratico Italiano (PSDI) (Italian Social Democrat Party): Piazza di Spagna 35, 00187 Rome; tel. (6) 67271; fax (6) 6841984; f. 1969 after breaking away from the former United Socialist Party, of which it had been part since 1966; composed of former Social Democrats and stands to the right of the SI; Pres. ANTONIO CARIGLIA; Sec. Prof. CARLO VIZZINI; 200,000 mems.

Patto Segni (Segni's Pact): Largo del Nazareno, 00187 Rome; f. 1993; liberal party, advocating principles of market economy; Leader MARIO SEGNI.

Polo per le Libertà e del Buon Governo (Freedom Alliance): Rome; f. 1994; centre-right alliance; including Forza Italia, the Alleanza Nazionale, the Centro Cristiano Democratico and the Cristiani Democratici Uniti; Leader SILVIO BERLUSCONI.

La Rete (The Network): Rome; f. 1991; anti-Mafia party; Leader LEOLUCA ORLANDO.

Rifondazione Comunista (RC) (Reconstructed Communism): Viale del Policlinico 131, 00163 Rome; tel. (6) 441821; fax (6) 44239490; f. 1991 by former members of the Partito Comunista Italiano (Italian Communist Party); Pres. ARMANDO COSSUTA; Sec.-Gen. FAUSTO BERTINOTTI.

Rinnovamento Italiano (Italian Renewal): Rome; f. 1996; centrist; Leader Prof. LAMBERTO DINI.

Socialisti Italiani (SI) (Italian Socialists): Via del Corso 476, 00186 Rome; tel. (6) 67781; telex 616300; f. 1892 as Partito Socialista Italiano (PSI); in 1921 a group broke away to found the Partito Comunista Italiano (Italian Communist Party); a further rift in 1947 led to the foundation of the Italian Social Democratic Party; in 1966 merged with the Social Democratic Party to form the United Socialist Party, but in 1969 the Social Democrats broke away; name changed as above 1994; centre-left; it adheres to the Socialist International and believes that socialism is inseparable from democracy and individual freedom; Sec.-Gen. ENRICO BOSSELLI.

Südtiroler Volkspartei (SVP) (South Tyrol People's Party): Brennerstrasse 7a, 39100 Bozen/Bolzano; tel. (471) 974484; fax (471) 981473; regional party of the German and Ladin-speaking people in the South Tyrol; Pres. SIEGFRIED BRUGGER; Gen. Sec. HARTMANN GALLMETZER.

L'Ulivo (The Olive Tree): Rome; f. 1995; centre-left alliance comprising the Partito Democratico della Sinistra, the Partito Popolare Italiano, the Südtiroler Volkspartei, the Unione Democratica, the Lista Romano Prodi, the Rinnovamento Italiano and the Federazione dei Verdi; Leader Prof. ROMANO PRODI.

Unione Democratica (UD) (Democratic Union): Via del Corso, 00187 Rome; f. 1996; moderate; centre-left; Leader ANTONIO MACCANICO.

There are also numerous small political parties, including the following: **Union Valdôtaine** (regional party for the French minority in the Valle d'Aosta); **Partito Sardo d'Azione** (Sardinian autonomy party); **Democrazia Proletaria** (left-wing); and **Lotta Continua** (left-wing).

Diplomatic Representation

EMBASSIES IN ITALY

Afghanistan: Via Nomentana, 120, 00161 Rome; tel. (6) 8611009; fax (6) 86322939; Ambassador: (vacant).

Albania: Via Asmara 9, 00198 Rome; tel. (6) 86218214; telex 614169; fax (6) 86216005; Ambassador: PANDELI DHIMITER PASKO.

Algeria: Via Barnaba Oriani 26, 00197; Rome; tel. (6) 80687620; telex 624171; fax (6) 8083436; Ambassador: HOCINE MEGHAR.

Angola: Via Filippo Bernardini 21, 00165 Rome; tel. (6) 39366902; telex 614505; fax (6) 634960; Ambassador: ANTERO ALBERTO EVERDOSA ABREU.

Argentina: Piazza dell'Esquilino 2, 00185 Rome; tel. (6) 4742551; telex 610386; fax (6) 4819787; Ambassador: (vacant).

Armenia: Via dei Colli della Farnesina 174, 00194 Rome; tel. (6) 3296638; fax (6) 3297763; Chargé d'affaires a.i.: GAGHIK BAGHDASSARIAN.

Australia: Via Alessandria 215, 00198 Rome; tel. (6) 852721; telex 610165; fax (6) 85272300; Ambassador: RORY STEELE.

Austria: Via G.B. Pergolesi 3, 00198 Rome; tel. (6) 8558241; telex 610139; fax (6) 8543286; Ambassador: Dr EMIL STAFFELMAYR.

Bangladesh: Via Antonio Bertoloni 14, 00197 Rome; tel. (6) 8083595; telex 620595; fax (6) 8084853; Ambassador: KHURSHID HAMID.

Belarus: Via della Giuliana 1B, 00195 Rome; tel. (6) 41268; fax (6) 24634.

Belgium: Via dei Monti Parioli 49, 00197 Rome; tel. (6) 3609511; telex 622514; fax (6) 3226935; Ambassador: ANDRÉ ONKELINX.

Bolivia: Via Brenta 2A, 00198 Rome; tel. (6) 8841001; telex 620221; fax (6) 8840740; Ambassador: MOIRA PAZ ESTENSSORO.

Bosnia and Herzegovina: Via Ginnio Bazzani 3, 00195 Rome; tel. (6) 3728509; fax (6) 3728526; Ambassador: VLATKO KRALJEVIĆ.

Brazil: Palazzo Pamphili, Piazza Navona 14, 00186 Rome; tel. (6) 683981; telex 610099; fax (6) 6867858; Ambassador: PAULO PIRES DO RIO.

Bulgaria: Via Pietro P. Rubens 21, 00197 Rome; tel. (6) 3224640; telex 610234; fax (6) 3226122; Ambassador: DIMITAR LASAROV.

Burkina Faso: Via Alessandria 26, 00198 Rome; tel. (6) 44250052; telex 624815; fax (6) 44250042; Ambassador: BEATRICE DAMIBA.

Burundi: Corso d'Italia 83, 00198 Rome; tel. (6) 8543995; telex 620143; fax (6) 8557343; Ambassador: JEAN-BAPTISTE MBONYINGINGO.

Cameroon: Via Siracusa 4-6, 00161 Rome; tel. (6) 44291285; telex 626873; fax (6) 44291323; Ambassador: MICHAEL TABONG KIMA.

Canada: Via G. B. de Rossi 27, 00161 Rome; tel. (6) 445981; fax (6) 44598750; Ambassador: JEREMY K. B. KINSMAN.

Cape Verde: Via Giosuè Carducci 4, 00187 Rome; tel. (6) 4744678; fax (6) 4744643; Ambassador: HORÁCIO CONSTANTINO DA SILVA SOARES.

Chile: Via Po 23, 00198 Rome; tel. (6) 8841433; fax (6) 8841452; e-mail echileit@flashnet.it; Ambassador: ALVARO BRIONES.

China, People's Republic: Via Bruxelles 56, 00198 Rome; tel. (6) 8848186; telex 622051; fax (6) 85352891; Ambassador: WU MINGLIAN.

Colombia: Via Giuseppe Pisanelli 4, 00196 Rome; tel. (6) 3612131; telex 611266; fax (6) 3225798; Ambassador: ALBERTO ZALAMEA COSTA.

Congo, Democratic Republic: Via Tuscolana 979, 00174 Rome; tel. (6) 7480240; Chargé d'affaires a.i. KAZADI MULUMBA.

Congo, Republic: Via Modena 50, 00184 Rome; tel. (6) 4746216; telex 626645; fax (6) 4826311; Ambassador: GRÉGOIRE MOUBÉRI.

Costa Rica: Via B. Eustachio 22, 00161 Rome; tel. (6) 44251046; fax (6) 44251048; Ambassador: RUBÉN HERNÁNDEZ.

Côte d'Ivoire: Via Lazzaro Spallanzani 4–6, 00161 Rome; tel. (6) 4402673; telex 610396; fax (6) 4402619; Ambassador: KOUASSI E. A. NOUAMA.

Croatia: Via L. Bodio 74-76, 00191 Rome; tel. 36307650; fax (6) 36303405; Ambassador: DAVORIN RUDOLF.

Cuba: Via Licinia 7, 00153 Rome; tel. (6) 5755984; telex 610677; fax (6) 5745445; Ambassador: MARIO RODRÍGUEZ MARTÍNEZ.

Cyprus: Via Francesco Denza 15, 00197 Rome; tel. (6) 8088365; fax (6) 8088338; Ambassador: MYRNA Y. KLEOPAS.

Czech Republic: Via dei Gracchi 322, 00192 Rome; tel. (6) 3244459; fax (6) 3244466; Ambassador: MARTIN STROPNICKÝ.

Denmark: Via dei Monti Parioli 50, 00197 Rome; tel. (6) 3200441; telex 624696; fax (6) 3610290; e-mail ambadane@iol.it; Ambassador: HENRIK RÉE IVERSEN.

Dominica: Via Laurentina 767, 00143 Rome; tel. (6) 5010643; fax (6) 5010643; Ambassador: HANNELORE BENJAMIN.

Dominican Republic: Via Domenico Chelini 10, 00197 Rome; tel. (6) 8074665; fax (6) 8074791; Ambassador: M. ALFREDO LEBRON PUMAROL.

Ecuador: Via Guido d'Arezzo 14, 00198 Rome; tel. (6) 8541784; telex 613256; fax (6) 85354434; Ambassador: MARCELO FERNANDEZ DE CORDOBA PONCE.

Egypt: 119 Roma Villa Savoia, Via Salaria 267, 00199 Rome; tel. (6) 8417420; telex 616339; fax (6) 8554424; Ambassador: NEHAD IBRAHIM ABD AL-LATIF.

El Salvador: Via Castellini 13, 00197 Rome; tel. (6) 8076605; telex 626229; fax (6) 8079726; Ambassador: ROBERTO ARTURO CASTRILLO HIDALGO.

Eritrea: Via Boncompagni 16B, 00187 Rome; tel. (6) 42741293; fax (6) 42741293; Ambassador: PIETROS FESSAHAZION.

Estonia: Via Po 2A, 00198 Rome; tel. (6) 8417595; fax (6) 8550192; e-mail saatkand@rooma.vm.ee; Chargé d'affaires a.i.: (vacant).

Ethiopia: Via Andrea Vesalio 16-18, 00161 Rome; tel. (6) 4402602; fax (6) 5040546; Ambassador: HALIMA MOHAMMED.

Finland: Via Lisbona 3, 00198 Rome; tel. (6) 852231; telex 625600; fax (6) 8540362; e-mail ambasciata.di.finlandia@interbusiness.it; Ambassador: DIETER VITZTHUM.

France: Piazza Farnese 67, 00186 Rome; tel. (6) 686011; telex 610093; fax (6) 68601360; Ambassador: JEAN-BERNARD MÉRIMÉE.

Gabon: Via del Pozzetto 122, 00187 Rome; tel. (6) 6990016; telex 626493; fax (6) 6990094; Ambassador: MARCEL IBINGA-MAGWANGU.

Georgia: Palazzo Pierret, Piazza di Spagna 20, 00187 Rome; tel. (6) 9941972; fax (6) 9941942; Ambassador: BEGI TAVARTKILADZE.

Germany: Via Po 25c, 00198 Rome; tel. (6) 884741; telex 610179; fax (6) 8547956; Ambassador: Dr DIETER KASTRUP.

Ghana: Via Ostriana 4, 00199 Rome; tel. (6) 86217191; telex 610270; fax (6) 86325762; Ambassador: AANAA NAMUA ENIN.

Greece: Via Mercadente 36, 00198 Rome; tel. (6) 8549630; telex 610416; fax (6) 8415927; e-mail gremroma@mbox.vol.it; Ambassador: ALEXANDROS SANDIS.

Guatemala: Via dei Colli della Farnesina 128, 00194 Rome; tel. (6) 36307392; Ambassador: ISMAEL PENEDO SOLÉ.

Guinea: Via Adelaide Ristori 9/13, 00197 Rome; tel. (6) 8078989; telex 611487; fax (6) 8075569; Ambassador: MAMADOU BAMBOUN KABA.

Haiti: 1st floor, Via Ottaviano 32, 00192 Rome; tel. (6) 39723362; fax (6) 33269214; Chargé d'affaires a.i.: JEAN-WALNARD DORNEVAL.

Holy See: Via Po 27–29, 00198 Rome; tel. (6) 8546287; fax (6) 8549725; Apostolic Nuncio: Cardinal FRANCESCO COLASUONNO.

Honduras: Via Giambattista Vico 40, 00196 Rome; tel. (6) 3207236; fax (6) 3207236; Ambassador: (vacant).

Hungary: Via dei Villini 14, 00161 Rome; tel. (6) 44230567; fax (6) 4403270; Ambassador: ATTILA GECSE.

India: Via XX Settembre 5, 00187 Rome; tel. (6) 4884642; telex 611274; fax (6) 4819539; Chargé d'affaires a.i.: BUTSHIKAN SINGH.

Indonesia: Via Campania 55, 00187 Rome; tel. (6) 4825951; telex 620087; fax (6) 4880280; Ambassador: WITJAKSANA SOEGARDA.

Iran: Via della Camilluccia 651, 00135 Rome; tel. (6) 3294294; telex 611337; fax (6) 36303757; Ambassador: SEYED MAJID HEDAYAT ZADEH.

Ireland: Piazza di Campitelli 3, 00186 Rome; tel. (6) 6979121; telex 626030; fax (6) 6792354; Ambassador: JOSEPH SMALL.

Israel: Via M. Mercati 14, 00197 Rome; tel. (6) 36198500; fax (6) 36198555; Ambassador: YEHUDA MILLO.

Japan: Via Quintino Sella 60, 00187 Rome; tel. (6) 487991; telex 610063; fax (6) 4873316; Ambassador: HIROMOTO SEKI.

Jordan: Via G. Marchi 1B, 00161 Rome; tel. (6) 86205303; telex 626097; fax (6) 8606122; Ambassador: SAMIR MASARWEH.

Kazakhstan: Piazza Farnese 101, 00186 Rome; tel. (6) 68808640; fax (6) 68891360; Ambassador: OLZHAS SULEYMENOV.

Kenya: Via Archimede 164, 00197 Rome; tel. (6) 8082717; telex 626537; fax (6) 8082707; Chargé d'affaires a.i.: ALICE OGWEL MANYALA.

Korea, Republic: Via Barnaba Oriani 30, 00197 Rome; tel. (6) 8088769; telex 610182; fax (6) 80687794; Ambassador: DOO BYONG SHIN.

Kuwait: Via Archimede 124, 00197 Rome; tel. (6) 8078415; telex 620426; fax (6) 8076651; Ambassador: QASIM O. AL YAGOUT.

Latvia: Via Boncompagni 16, 00187 Rome; tel. (6) 42817100; fax (6) 42815682; Chargé d'affaires a.i.: JURIS ANDARIŅŠ.

Lebanon: Via Giacomino Carissimi 38, 00198 Rome; tel. (6) 8557119; telex 622476; fax (6) 8411794; Ambassador: YAHYA MAHMASSANI.

Lesotho: Via Serchio 8, 00198 Rome; tel. (6) 8542496; telex 610053; fax (6) 8542527; Ambassador: MOOROSI VERNET RADITAPOLE.

Liberia: Via F. Canara 31, 00196 Rome; tel. (6) 3220497; telex 612569; fax (6) 3220062; Ambassador: FANNIE BROWNELL-ALLEN.

Libya: Via Nomentana 365, 00162 Rome; tel. (6) 86320951; telex 611114; fax (6) 86205473; Ambassador: ARAFA ABD AS-SALAM SALH.

Lithuania: Viale di Villa Grazioli 9, 00198 Rome; tel. (6) 8559052; fax (6) 8559053 Ambassador: ROMANAS PODAGĖLIS.

Luxembourg: Via S. Croce in Gerusalemme 90, 00185 Rome; tel. (6) 77201177; telex 622532; fax (6) 77201055; Ambassador: JEAN HOSTERT.

Macedonia, former Yugoslav republic: Viale Bruxelles 73-75, 00198 Rome; tel. (6) 84241109; fax (6) 84241113; Ambassador: VIKTOR GABER.

Madagascar: Via Riccardo Zandonai 84A, 00194 Rome; tel. (6) 36307797; telex 622526; fax (6) 3294306; Chargé d'affaires a.i.: RAPHAËL RABE.

Malaysia: Via Nomentana 297, 00162 Rome; tel. (6) 8415764; telex 611035; fax (6) 8555040; Ambassador: R. VENGADESAN.

Malta: Lungotevere Marzio 12, 00186 Rome; tel. (6) 6879990; fax (6) 6892687; Ambassador: HENRY C. DE GABRIELE.

Mauritania: Via Giovanni Paisiello 26, 00198 Rome; tel. (6) 85351530; fax (6) 85351441; Ambassador: MELANINE OULD MOCTAR NECHE.

Mexico: Via Lazzaro Spallanzani 16, 00161 Rome; tel. (6) 4404400; telex 625279; fax (6) 4403876; Ambassador: MARIO MOYA PALENCIA.

Monaco: Via Bertoloni 36, 00161 Rome: tel. (6) 4402524; fax (6) 8077692; fax (6) 4402695; Ambassador: ZINE EL ABIDINE SEBTI.

Morocco: Via Lazzaro Spallanzani 8, 00161 Rome; tel. (6) 4402524; telex 620854; fax (6) 4402695; Ambassador: ZINE EL ABIDINE SEBTI.

Mozambique: Via Filippo Corridoni 14, 00195 Rome; tel. (6) 37514852; fax (6) 37514699; Ambassador: AMADEU PAULO SAMUEL DA CONCEIÇÃO.

Myanmar: Via Bellini 20, 00198 Rome; tel. (6) 8549374; telex 625103; fax (6) 8413167; Ambassador: KHIN NYEIN.

Netherlands: Via Michele Mercati 8, 00197 Rome; tel. (6) 3221141; telex 3221440; fax (6) 3221440; Ambassador: C. R. VAN BEUGE.

New Zealand: Via Zara 28, 00198 Rome; tel. (6) 4402928; fax (6) 4402984; Ambassador: JUDITH CATHERINE TROTTER.

Nicaragua: Via Brescia 16, 00198 Rome; tel. (6) 8413471; fax (6) 8841695; Ambassador: HUMBERTO CARRIÓN.

Niger: Via Antonio Baiamonti 10, 00195 Rome; tel. (6) 3729013; telex 626290; Ambassador: ADAMOU SEYKOU.

Nigeria: Via Orazio 14–18, 00193 Rome; tel. (6) 6896243; telex 610666; fax (6) 6832528; Chargé d'affaires a.i.: THOMPSON SUNDAY OLUFUNSO OLUMOKO.

Norway: Via delle Terme Deciane 7, 00153 Rome; tel. (6) 5755833; telex 610585; fax (6) 5742115; Ambassador: GEIR GRUNG.

Oman: Via della Camilluccia 625, 00135 Rome; tel. (6) 36300517; telex 612524; fax (6) 3296802; Ambassador: SAID KHALIFA MUHAMMAD AL-BUSAIDI.

Pakistan: Via della Camilluccia 682, 00135 Rome; tel. (6) 36301775; telex 622083; fax (6) 36301936; Chargé d'affaires a.i.: ATHAR MAHMOOD.

Panama: Via del Vignola 39, 00196 Rome; tel. (6) 3619587; telex 622670; fax (6) 3211692; Ambassador: EDGAR E. AMEGLIO.

Paraguay: Via Salaria 237B, 00198 Rome; tel. (6) 8848150; fax (6) 8558739; Ambassador: OSCAR CABELLO SARUBBI.

Peru: Via Po 22, 00198 Rome; tel. (6) 8417265; fax (6) 85354447; e-mail amb.peru@agora.stm.it; Ambassador: ANA MARÍA DEUSTUA.

Philippines: Via San Valentino 12–14, 00197 Rome; tel. (6) 8083530; telex 612104; fax (6) 8084219; Ambassador: SERGIO A. BARRERA.

Poland: Via Pietro Paolo Rubens 20, 00197 Rome; tel. (6) 3224455; fax (6) 3217895; Ambassador: MACIEJ GORSKI.

Portugal: Viale Liegi 21-23, 00198 Rome; tel. (6) 844801; telex 612304; fax (6) 8542262; Ambassador: JOÃO DIOGO NUNES BARATA.

Qatar: Via Antonio Bosio 14, 00161 Rome; tel. (6) 44249450; fax (6) 44245273; Ambassador: AHMED ALI AHMED AL-ANSARI.

Romania: Via Nicolò Tartaglia 36, 00197 Rome; tel. (6) 8084529; telex 610249; fax (6) 8084995; Ambassador: CONSTANTIN MIHAIL GRIGORIE.

Russia: Via Gaeta 5, 00185 Rome; tel. (6) 4941680; telex 611286; fax (6) 491031; Ambassador: VALERY FIODOROVICH KENIAIKINE.

San Marino: Via Eleonora Duse 35, 00197 Rome; tel. (6) 8084567; fax (6) 8070072; Ambassador: BARBARA PARA.

Saudi Arabia: Via G. B. Pergolesi 9, 00198 Rome; tel. (6) 844851; telex 613115; fax (6) 8557633; Ambassador: MUHAMMAD BIN NAWAF BIN ABD AL-AZIZ AS-SAUD.

Senegal: Via Giulia 66, 00186 Rome; tel. (6) 6872381; telex 612522; fax (6) 6865212; Ambassador: MAME BALLA SY.

Slovakia: Via dei Colli della Farnesina 144, 00194 Rome; tel. (6) 36308741; fax (6) 36308617; Ambassador: RUDOLF ZELENAY.

Slovenia: Via Leonardo Pisano 10, 00197 Rome; tel. (6) 8081075; fax (6) 8081471; Ambassador: PETER ANDREJ BEKEŠ.

Somalia: Via dei Villini 9–11, 00161 Rome; tel. (6) 44251184; telex 613123; Ambassador: MUHAMMAD MUHAMOUD ABDULLAH.

South Africa: Via Tanaro 14, 00198 Rome; tel. (6) 852541; fax (6) 85254300; e-mail sae@flashnet.it; Ambassador: K. N. GINWALA.

Spain: Palazzo Borghese, Largo Fontenella Borghese 19, 00186 Rome; tel. (6) 6878172; telex 626126; fax (6) 6872256; Ambassador: JUAN PRAT COLL.

Sri Lanka: Via Giuseppe Cuboni 6-8, 00197 Rome; tel. (6) 3224162; telex 612602; fax (6) 3224193; Ambassador: UPATISSA PETHIYAGODA.

Sudan: Via Lazzaro Spallanzani 24, 00161 Rome; tel. (6) 4403609; telex 610302; fax (6) 4402358; Ambassador: MAHDI MUSTAFA EL HADI.

Sweden: CP 7201, 00100 Rome; Piazza Rio de Janeiro 3, 00161 Rome; tel. (6) 441941; fax (6) 44194760; Ambassador: TORSTEN ÖRN.

Switzerland: Via Barnaba Oriani 61; 00197 Rome; tel. (6) 809571; telex 610304; fax (6) 8088510; Ambassador: DANTE MARTINELLI.

Syria: Piazza dell' Ara Coeli, 00186 Rome; tel. (6) 6797791; telex 613083; fax (6) 6794989; Chargé d'affaires a.i.: NAJDI ALJAZZAR.

Tanzania: Via Ombrone 3, 00198 Rome; tel. (6) 8411830; telex 612286; fax (6) 8411827; Chargé d'affaires a.i.: JOSEPH KONG'ONHELI MHELLA.

Thailand: Via Nomentana 132, 00162 Rome; tel. (6) 86204381; telex 616297; fax (6) 86208399; e-mail thai.em.rome@pn.itnet.it; Ambassador designate: SOMBOON SANGIAMBUT.

Tunisia: Via Asmara 7, 00199 Rome; tel. (6) 8603060; telex 610190; fax (6) 86218204; Chargé d'affaires a.i.: ABD AR-RAHMAN BEN MANSOUR.

Turkey: Via Palestro 28, 00185 Rome; tel. (6) 4469933; fax (6) 4941526; Ambassador: UMUR ARIK.

Uganda: Via Ennio Quirino Visconti 8, 00193 Rome; tel. (6) 3225220; fax (6) 3203174; Ambassador: VINCENT KIRABOKYAMARIA.

Ukraine: Via Guido d'Arezzo 9, 00198 Rome; tel. (6) 8412630; fax (6) 8547539; Ambassador: ANATOLI KOSTYANTINOVICH OREL.

United Arab Emirates: Via della Camilluccia 551, 00135 Rome; tel. (6) 36306100; telex 622671; fax (6) 36306155; Ambassador: MUHAMMAD MUSABBAH KHALFAN AS-SUNEIDI.

United Kingdom: Via XX Settembre 80A, 00187 Rome; tel. (6) 4825551; telex 626119; fax (6) 4873324; Ambassador: THOMAS RICHARDSON.

USA: Via Vittorio Veneto 119A, 00187 Rome; tel. (6) 46741; telex 622322; fax (6) 46742356; Ambassador: THOMAS FOGLIETTA.

Uruguay: Via Vittorio Veneto 183, 00187 Rome; tel. (6) 4821776; telex 611201; fax (6) 4823695; Ambassador: CARLOS BRUGNINI.

Venezuela: Via Nicolò Tartaglia 11, 00197 Rome; tel. (6) 8079464; telex 610361; fax (6) 8084410; Ambassador: FERNANDO GERBASI.

Viet Nam: Via Clitunno 34-36, 00198 Rome; tel. (6) 8543223; telex 610121; fax (6) 8548501; Chargé d'affaires a.i.: DANG-KHANH THOAI.

Yemen Arab Republic: Viale Regina Margherita 1, 00198 Rome; tel. (6) 8416711; telex 621447; fax (6) 8416801; Ambassador: MUHAMMAD ABDULLAH ELWAZIR.

Yugoslavia: Via dei Monti Parioli 20, 00197 Rome; tel. (6) 3200796; telex 616303; fax (6) 3200868; Ambassador: MIODRAG LEKIC.

Zimbabwe: Via Virgilio 8, 00193 Rome; tel. (6) 68807781; telex 520178; fax (6) 68308324; Ambassador: STUART HAROLD COMBERBACH.

Judicial System

The Constitutional Court was established in 1956 and is an autonomous constitutional body, standing apart from the judicial system. Its most important function is to pronounce on the constitutionality of legislation both subsequent and prior to the present Constitution of 1948. It also judges accusations brought against the President of the Republic or ministers.

At the base of the system of penal jurisdiction are the Preture (District Courts), where offences carrying a sentence of up to four years' imprisonment are tried. Above the Preture are the Tribunali (Tribunals) and the Corti di Assise presso i Tribunali (Assize Courts attached to the Tribunals), where graver offences are dealt with. From these courts appeal lies to the Corti d'Appello (Courts of Appeal) and the parallel Corti di Assise d'Appello (Assize Courts of Appeal). Final appeal may be made, on juridical grounds only, to the Corte Suprema di Cassazione.

Civil cases may be taken in the first instance to the Giudici Conciliatori (Justices of the Peace), Preture or Tribunali, according to the economic value of the case. Appeal from the Giudici Conciliatori lies to the Preture, from the Preture to the Tribunali, from the Tribunali to the Corti d'Appello, and finally, as in penal justice, to the Corte Suprema di Cassazione on juridical grounds only.

Special divisions for cases concerning labour relations are attached to civil courts. Cases concerned with the public service and its employees are tried by Tribunali Amministrativi Regionali and the Consiglio di Stato. Juvenile courts have criminal and civil jurisdiction.

A new penal code was introduced in late 1989.

Consiglio Superiore della Magistratura (CSM): Piazza dell' Indipendenza 6, 00185 Rome; f. 1958; tel. (6) 444911; supervisory body of judicial system; 33 mems.

President: The President of the Republic.

CONSTITUTIONAL COURT

Corte Costituzionale: Palazzo della Consulta, Piazza del Quirinale 41, 00187 Rome; tel. (6) 46981; consists of 15 judges, one-third appointed by the President of the Republic, one-third elected by Parliament in joint session, one-third by the ordinary and administrative supreme courts.

President: RENATO GRANATA.

ADMINISTRATIVE COURTS

Consiglio di Stato: Palazzo Spada, Piazza Capo di Ferro 13, 00186 Rome; tel. (6) 67771; established in accordance with Article 10 of the Constitution; has both consultative and judicial functions.

President: GIORGIO CRISCO.

Corte dei Conti: Via Baiamonti 25, Rome; tel. (6) 48951, and Via Barberini 38, Rome; functions as the court of public auditors for the state.

President: GIUSEPPE CARBONE.

SUPREME COURT OF APPEAL

Corte Suprema di Cassazione: Palazzo di Giustizia, 00100 Rome; tel. (6) 686001; telex 626069; fax (6) 6874170; supreme court of civil and criminal appeal.

First President: ANTONIO BRANCACCIO.

Religion

More than 90% of the population of Italy are adherents of the Roman Catholic Church. Under the terms of the Concordat formally ratified in June 1985, Roman Catholicism was no longer to be the state religion, compulsory religious instruction in schools was abolished and state financial contributions reduced. The Vatican City's sovereign rights as an independent state, under the terms of the Lateran Treaty of 1929, were not affected.

Several Protestant churches also exist in Italy, with a total membership of about 50,000. There is a small Jewish community, and in 1987 an agreement between the state and Jewish representatives recognized certain rights for the Jewish community, including the right to observe religious festivals on Saturdays by not attending school or work.

CHRISTIANITY

The Roman Catholic Church

For ecclesiastical purposes, Italy comprises the Papal See of Rome, the Patriarchate of Venice, 58 archdioceses (including six directly responsible to the Holy See), 157 dioceses (including seven within the jurisdiction of the Pope, as Archbishop of the Roman Province, and 17 directly responsible to the Holy See), two territorial prelatures (including one directly responsible to the Holy See) and seven territorial abbacies (including four directly responsible to the Holy See). Almost all adherents follow the Latin rite, but there are two dioceses and one abbacy (all directly responsible to the Holy See) for Catholics of the Italo-Albanian (Byzantine) rite.

Bishops' Conference: Conferenza Episcopale Italiana, Circonvallazione Aurelia 50, 00165 Rome; tel. (6) 663981; fax (6) 6623037; f. 1985; Pres. HE Cardinal CAMILLO RUINI, Vicar-General of Rome.

Primate of Italy, Archbishop and Metropolitan of the Roman Province and Bishop of Rome: His Holiness Pope JOHN PAUL II.

Patriarch of Venice: HE Cardinal MARCO CÉ.

Archbishops:

Acerenza: Most Rev. MICHELE SCANDIFFIO.
Amalfi-Cava de' Tirreni: Most Rev. BENIAMINO DE PALMA.
Ancona-Osimo: Most Rev. FRANCO FESTORAZZI.
Bari-Bitonto: Most Rev. ANDREA MARIANO MAGRASSI.
Benevento: Most Rev. SERAFINO SPROVIERI.
Bologna: HE Cardinal GIACOMO BIFFI.
Brindisi-Ostuni: Most Rev. SETTIMIO TODISCO.
Cagliari: Most Rev. OTTORINO PIETRO ALBERTI.
Camerino-San Severino Marche: (vacant).

Campobasso-Boiano: Most Rev. Ettore Di Filippo.
Capua: Most Rev. Luigi Diligenza.
Catania: Most Rev. Luigi Bommarito.
Catanzaro-Squillace: Most Rev. Antonio Cantisani.
Chieti-Vasto: Most Rev. Edoardo Menichelli.
Cosenza-Bisignano: Most Rev. Dino Trabalzini.
Crotone-Santa Severina: Most Rev. Giuseppe Agostino.
Fermo: Most Rev. Cleto Bellucci.
Ferrara-Comacchio: Most Rev. Carlo Caffarra.
Florence: HE Cardinal Silvano Piovanelli.
Foggia-Bovino: Most Rev. Giuseppe Casale.
Gaeta: Most Rev. Vincenzo Maria Farano.
Genoa: HE Cardinal Dionigi Tettamanzi.
Gorizia: Most Rev. Antonio Vitale Bommarco.
Lanciano-Ortona: Most Rev. Enzio D'Antonio.
L'Aquila: Most Rev. Mario Peressin.
Lecce: Most Rev. Cosmo Francesco Ruppi.
Lucca: Most Rev. Bruno Tommasi.
Manfredonia-Vieste: Most Rev. Vincenzo D'Addario.
Matera-Irsina: Most Rev. Antonio Ciliberti.
Messina-Lipari-Santa Lucia del Mela: Most Rev. Ignazio Cannavò.
Milan: HE Cardinal Carlo Maria Martini.
Modena-Nonantola: Most Rev. Benito Cocchi.
Monreale: (vacant).
Naples: HE Cardinal Michele Giordano.
Oristano: Most Rev. Pier Giuliano Tiddia.
Otranto: Most Rev. Francesco Cacucci.
Palermo: HE Cardinal Salvatore De Giorgi.
Perugia-Città della Pieve: Most Rev. Giuseppe Chiaretti.
Pescara-Penne: Most Rev. Francesco Cuccarese.
Pisa: Most Rev. Alessandro Plotti.
Potenza-Muro Lucano-Marsico Nuovo: Most Rev. Ennio Appignanese.
Ravenna-Cervia: Most Rev. Luigi Amaducci.
Reggio Calabria-Bova: Most Rev. Vittorio Luigi Mondello.
Rossano-Cariati: Most Rev. Andrea Cassone.
Salerno-Campagna-Acerno: Most Rev. Gerardo Pierro.
Sant' Angelo dei Lombardi-Conza-Nusco-Bisaccia: Most Rev. Mario Milano.
Sassari: Most Rev. Salvatore Isgró.
Siena-Colle di Val d'Elsa-Montalcino: Most Rev. Gaetano Bonicelli.
Sorrento-Castellammare di Stabia: Most Rev. Felice Cece.
Spoleto-Norcia: Most Rev. Riccardo Fontana.
Syracuse: Most Rev. Giuseppe Costanzo.
Taranto: Most Rev. Benigno Luigi Papa.
Trani-Barletta-Bisceglie: Most Rev. Carmelo Cassati.
Trento: Most Rev. Giovanni Maria Sartori.
Turin: HE Cardinal Giovanni Saldarini.
Udine: Most Rev. Alfredo Battisti.
Urbino-Urbania-Sant' Angelo in Vado: Most Rev. Ugo Donato Bianchi.
Vercelli: Most Rev. Enrico Masseroni.

Azione Cattolica Italiana (ACI) (Catholic Action): Via della Conciliazione 1, 00193 Rome; tel. (6) 6868751; fax (6) 68802088; in Italy there are numerous apostolic lay organizations, prominent among which is Italian Catholic Action, which has a total membership of 1m.; National Presidency is the supreme executive body and co-ordinator of the different branches of Catholic Action; Pres. Avv. Giuseppe Gervasio; Sec.-Gen. Aureliano Inglesi.

Protestant Churches

Federazione delle Chiese Evangeliche in Italia (Federation of the Protestant Churches in Italy): Via Firenze 38, 00184 Rome; tel. (6) 4825120; fax (6) 4828728; e-mail fed.evangelica@agora.stm.it; the Federation was formed in 1967; total mems more than 50,000; Pres. Pastor Domenico Tomasetto; Sec. Luca Maria Negro; includes the following organizations:

Chiesa Apostolica Italiana

Chiesa Apostolica Pentecostale

Chiesa Evangelica Luterana in Italia (Lutheran Church): Via Toscana 7, 00187 Rome; tel. (6) 4880394; fax (6) 4874506; Dean Hartmut Diekmann; 20,100 mems.

Chiesa Evangelica Metodista in Italia (Evangelical Methodist Church): Via Firenze 38, 00184 Rome; tel. (6) 4743695; f. 1861; Pres. Pastor Valdo Benecchi; 4,000 mems.

Comunione delle Chiese Cristiane Libere

Comunità Ecumenica di Ispra-Varese

Comunità Evangelica di Confessione Elvetica

Fiumi di Vita

Missione Cristiana

Tavola Valdese (Waldensian Church): Via Firenze 38, 00184 Rome; tel. (6) 4745537; fax (6) 47885308; e-mail tvmode@tin.it; Moderator Gianni Rostan; Sec.-Treas. Rosella Panzironi; 22,000 mems.

Unione Cristiana Evangelica Battista d'Italia (Italian Baptist Union): Piazza San Lorenzo in Lucina 35, 00186 Rome; tel. (6) 6876124; fax (6) 6876185; f. 1873; Pres. Dott. Renato Maiocchi; Admin. Sec. Aldo Casonato; 5,000 mems.

Associated Organizations

Salvation Army (Esercito della Salvezza): Via degli Apuli 39, 00185 Rome; tel. (6) 4462614; fax (6) 490078; Officer Commanding for Italy Maj. David Armistead; 15 regional centres.

Seventh-day Adventists: Lungotevere Michelangelo 7, 00192 Rome; tel. (6) 3609591; fax (6) 36095952; e-mail uicca@avventisti.org; internet http://www.avventisti.org; f. 1929; represents 90 communities in Italy and Malta; Supt Vincenzo Mazza; Sec. Daniele Benini.

JUDAISM

The number of Jews was estimated at 35,000 in 1992.

Union of Italian Jewish Communities: Lungotevere Sanzio 9, 00153 Rome; tel. (6) 5803667; fax (6) 5899569; f. 1930; represents 21 Jewish communities in Italy; Pres. Tullia Zevi; Chief Rabbi of Rome Dott. Elio Toaff.

Rabbinical Council: Chief Rabbi Dott. Elio R. Toaff (Via Catalana 1a, Rome), Rabbi Dott. Giuseppe Laras (Via Guastalla 19, Milan), Rabbi Dott. Elia Richetti (Via Guastalla 19, Milan).

BAHÁ'Í FAITH

Assemblea Spirituale Nazionale: Via della Fontanella 4, 00187 Rome; tel. (6) 3225037; fax (6) 3611536; e-mail nsa.italy@agot-a.stm.it; mems resident in 270 localities.

The Press

Relative to the size of Italy's population, the number of daily newspapers is rather small (74 in 1994). The average total circulation of daily newspapers in 1994 was 5,985,000 copies per issue; sales in the north and centre of the country accounted for 80% of this figure, and those in the south for 20%.

Rome and Milan are the main press centres. The most important national dailies are *Corriere della Sera* in Milan and Rome and *La Repubblica* in Rome, followed by Turin's *La Stampa, Il Sole 24 Ore* in Milan, the economic and financial newspaper with the highest circulation in Europe, *Il Messaggero* in Rome, *Il Resto del Carlino* in Bologna, *La Nazione* in Florence, and *Il Giornale* and *Il Giorno*, which circulate mainly in the north.

In 1993 there were about 10,000 periodical titles, with a combined annual circulation of some 4,036m. Many illustrated weekly papers and magazines maintain very high levels of circulation, with *TV Sorrisi e Canzoni* and *Famiglia Cristiana* enjoying the highest figures. Other very popular general-interest weeklies are *Gente* and *Oggi*. Among the serious and influential magazines are *Panorama* and *L'Espresso*.

PRINCIPAL DAILIES

Ancona

Corriere Adriatico: Via Berti 20, 60100 Ancona; tel. (71) 4581; fax (71) 42980; f. 1860; Dir Dott. Paolo Biagi; circ. 29,349.

Bari

La Gazzetta del Mezzogiorno: Viale Scipione l'Africano 264, 70124 Bari; tel. (80) 5470400; telex 810844; fax (80) 270437; f. 1928; independent; Man. Dir Lino Patruno; circ. 82,398.

Bergamo

L'Eco di Bergamo: Viale Papa Giovanni XXIII 118, 24121 Bergamo; tel. (35) 386111; fax (35) 225785; f. 1880; Catholic; Man. Dr Sergio Borsi; circ 72,111.

Bologna

Il Resto del Carlino: Via Enrico Mattei 106, 40138 Bologna; tel. (51) 536111; telex 510037; fax 6570099; f. 1885; independent; Dir Marco Leonelli; circ. 232,866.

Bolzano/Bozen

Alto Adige: Lungotalvera S. Quirino 26, 39100 Bozen; tel. (471) 904111; f. 1945; independent; Dir Franco de Battaglia; circ. 53,674.

Dolomiten: Weinbergweg 7, 39100 Bozen; tel. (471) 925111; fax 925440; e-mail dolomiten@E-athesia.it; internet http://www.athesia.it/; f. 1926; independent; German language; Dir Dr Toni Ebner; circ. 56,500.

Brescia

Bresciaoggi Nuovo: Via Eritrea 20, 25126 Brescia; tel. (30) 22941; fax (30) 2294229; f. 1974; Dir Mino Allione; circ. 18,500.

Il Giornale di Brescia: Via Solferino 22, 25121 Brescia; tel. (30) 37901; telex 303165; fax (30) 292226; f. 1945; Editor GIAN BATTISTA LANZANI; Man. Dir FRANCESCO PASSERINI GLAZEL; circ. 72,301.

Cagliari

L'Unione Sarda: Viale Regina Elena 14, 09124 Cagliari; tel. (70) 60131; f. 1889; independent; Dir ANTONANGELO LIORI; circ. 81,810.

Catania

La Sicilia: Viale Odorico da Pordenone 50, 95126 Catania; tel. (95) 330544; telex 911321; fax (95) 253316; f. 1945; independent; Dir Dott. MARIO CIANCIO SANFILIPPO; circ. 87,942.

Como

La Provincia di Como: Via Anzani 52, 22100 Como; tel. (31) 31211; f. 1892; independent; Dir LUIGI DARIO; circ. 49,711.

Cremona

La Provincia di Cremona: Via delle Industrie 2, 26100 Cremona; tel. (372) 4981; fax (372) 28487; f. 1946; independent; Pres. MARIO MAESTRONI; Man. Editor ROBERTO GELMINI; circ. 26,777.

Ferrara

La Nuova Ferrara: Viale Cavour 129, 44100 Ferrara; tel. (532) 200777; fax (532) 47689; f. 1989; independent; Man. Dir ENRICO PIRONDINI; circ. 11,886.

Florence

La Nazione: Via Ferdinando Paolieri 2, 50121 Florence; tel. (55) 24851; f. 1859; independent; Dir RICCARDO BERTI; circ. 258,794.

Genoa

L'Avvisatore Marittimo: Viale Sauli 39, 16121 Genoa; tel. (10) 562929; fax (10) 566415; f. 1925; shipping and financial; Editor SANDRO GRIMALDI; circ. 2,400.

Corriere Mercantile: Via Archimede 169, 16142 Genoa; tel. (10) 517851; fax (10) 504148; f. 1824; political and financial; independent; Editor MIMMO ANGELI; circ. 17,000.

Il Secolo XIX: Via Varese 2, 16122 Genoa; tel. (10) 53881; f. 1886; independent; Dir GAETANO RIZZUTO; circ. 181,617.

Lecce

Quotidiano di Lecce/Brindisi/Taranto: Viale degli Studenti (Palazzo Casto), 73100 Lecce; tel. (832) 300897; f. 1979; Man. Editor VITTORIO BRUNO STAMERRA; circ. 26,502.

Leghorn/Livorno

Il Tirreno: Viale Alfieri 9, 57124 Livorno; tel. (586) 401141; fax (586) 416671; f. 1978; independent; Editor ENNIO SIMEONE; circ. 130,000.

Mantua

Gazzetta di Mantova: Via Fratelli Bandiera 32, 46100 Mantua; tel. (376) 303270; f. 1664; independent; Man. Editor SERGIO BARALDI; circ. 42,684.

Messina

Gazzetta del Sud: Uberto Bonino 15C, 98100 Messina; tel. (90) 2261; f. 1952; independent; Dir NINO CALARCO; circ. 92,722.

Milan

Avvenire: Via Mauro Macchi 61, 20124 Milan; tel. (2) 67801; telex 325096; f. 1968; Catholic; Man. Dir DINO BOFFO; circ. 131,500.

Corriere della Sera: Via Solferino 28, 20121 Milan; tel. (2) 6339; telex 310031; fax (2) 290009668; f. 1876; independent; contains weekly supplement, *Sette*; Dir PAOLO MIELI; circ. 720,239.

La Gazzetta dello Sport: Via Solferino 28, 20121 Milan; tel. (2) 6353; telex 321697; fax (2) 29009668; f. 1896; sport; Dir CANDIDO CANNAVÒ; circ. 426,000.

Il Giornale: Via Gaetano Negri 4, 20123 Milan; tel. (2) 85661; telex 333279; fax (2) 8566327; f. 1974; independent, controlled by staff; Editor MARIO CERVI; circ. 210,000.

Il Giorno: Piazza Cavour 2, 20121 Milan; tel. (2) 77681; telex 330390; Man. Dir ENZO CATANIA; circ. 255,377.

Il Sole 24 Ore: Via Paolo Lomazzo 52, 20154 Milan; tel. (2) 31031; telex 331325; fax (2) 312055; f. 1865; financial, political, economic; Dir ERNESTO AUCI; circ. 340,000.

Il Telegiornale: Milan; f. 1995; television; Dir GIGI VESIGNA; circ. 500,000.

Modena

Nuova Gazzetta di Modena: Via del Taglio 22, 41100 Modena; tel. (59) 247311; Dir ANTONIO MASCOLO; circ. 14,710.

Naples

Il Giornale di Napoli: San Giovanni Porzio 4, 80143 Naples; tel. (81) 7642040; fax (81) 5628105; f. 1985; Editor EMIDIO NOVI; circ. 11,000.

Il Mattino: Via Chiatamone 65, 80121 Naples; tel. (81) 7947111; f. 1892, reformed 1950; independent; Dir PAOLO GRALDI; circ. 207,040.

Padua

Il Mattino di Padova: Via Pelizzo 3, 35128 Padua; tel. (49) 8292611; f. 1978; Dir ALBERTO STATERA; circ. 37,252.

Palermo

Giornale di Sicilia: Via Lincoln 21, 90133 Palermo; tel. (91) 6165355; telex 911088; f. 1860; independent; Dir ANTONIO ARDIZZONE; circ. 89,880.

Parma

Gazzetta di Parma: Via Emilio Casa 5/A, 43100 Parma; tel. (521) 2251; fax (521) 285515; f. 1735; Pres. ACHILLE BORRINI; Dir BRUNO ROSSI; circ. 59,710.

Pavia

La Provincia Pavese: Viale Canton Ticino 16–18, 27100 Pavia; tel. (382) 434511; fax (382) 473875; e-mail staff@laprovincia.pv.it; f. 1870; independent; Editor FRANCO MANZITTI; circ. 33,793.

Perugia

Corriere dell' Umbria: Via Pievaiola km 5.8, 06132 Perugia; tel. (75) 52731; fax (75) 5273264; f. 1983; independent; Editor SEBASTIANO BOTTA; circ. 23,000.

Pescara

Il Centro: Corso Vittorio Emanuele 372, 65122 Pescara; tel. (85) 20521; fax (85) 4214568; f. 1986; independent; Editor PIER VITTORIO BUFFA; circ. 38,655.

Piacenza

Libertà: Via Benedettine 68, 29100 Piacenza; tel. (523) 393939; fax (523) 26396; f. 1883; Dir ERNESTO LEONE; circ. 37,445.

Reggio Emilia

Gazzetta di Reggio: Via Sessi 1, 42100 Reggio Emilia; tel. (552) 501511; fax (522) 454279; f. 1860; Dir UMBERTO BONAFINI; circ. 19,563.

Rome

Corriere dello Sport: Piazza Indipendenza 11B, 00185 Rome, tel. (6) 49921; telex 614472; fax (6) 4992690; f. 1924; 13 regional editions; Editor ITALO UCI; circ. 270,307.

Il Fiorino: Via Parigi 11, 00185 Rome; tel. (6) 47490; f. 1969; business; Editor LUIGI D'AMATO; circ. 4,500.

Il Giornale d'Italia: Via Parigi 11, 00185 Rome; tel. (6) 47490; Dir LUIGI D'AMATO; circ. 25,000.

Il Manifesto: Via Tomacelli 146, 00186 Rome; tel. (6) 6867029; fax (6) 6892600; f. 1971; splinter communist; Man. Editor VALENTINO PARLATO; circ. 55,000.

Il Messaggero: Via del Tritone 152, 00187 Rome; tel. (6) 47201; fax (6) 4720300; f. 1878; independent; Editor GIULIO ANSELMI; circ. 260,000.

L'Opinione: Via del Leone 13, 00186 Rome; tel. (6) 6861172; fax (6) 6832659; f. 1977; independent; Man. Editor ARTURO DIACONALE; circ. 5,000.

Ore 12 Il Globo: Via Alfana 39, 00191 Rome; tel. (6) 3331418; fax (6) 333199; financial; independent; Dir ENZO CARETTI; circ. 2,000.

Il Popolo: Piazza delle 5 Lune 113, 00186 Rome; tel. (6) 68251; fax (6) 6893724; telex 613276; f. 1944; organ of the PPI; Editor SERGIO MATTARELLA; circ. 6,000.

La Repubblica: Piazza Indipendenza 11B, 00185 Rome; tel. (6) 49821; telex 620660; fax (6) 49822923; f. 1976; left-wing; Publr Editoriale L'Espresso; Editor-in-Chief EZIO MAURO; circ. 662,000.

Il Secolo d'Italia: Via della Scrofa 43, 00187 Rome; tel. (6) 6833987; fax (6) 6861598; f. 1951; organ of the AN; Editor GENNARO MALGIERI; circ. 15,000.

Il Tempo: Piazza Colonna 366, 00187 Rome; tel. (6) 675881; telex 614087; f. 1944; right-wing; Editor GIOVANNI MOTTOLA; circ. 100,000.

L'Unità: Via dei Due Macelli 23/13, 00187 Rome; tel. (6) 699961; telex 613461; fax (6) 69996217; f. 1924; Dir MINO FUCCILLO; circ. 137,000.

La Voce Repubblicana: Piazza dei Capprettari 70, 00186 Rome; tel. (6) 68300802; fax (6) 6542990; f. 1921; organ of the PRI; Dir GIORGIO LA MALFA; circ. 18,000.

Sassari

La Nuova Sardegna: Via Porcellana 9, 07100 Sassari; tel. (79) 222400; fax (79) 236246; f. 1892; independent; Editor LIVIO LIUZZI; circ. 65,000.

Taranto

Corriere del Giorno di Puglia e Lucania: Piazza Dante 5, Zona 'Bestat', 74100 Taranto; tel. (99) 3591; f. 1947; Dir CLEMENTE SELVAGGIO; circ. 3,500.

Trent

L'Adige: Via Missioni Africane 17, 38100 Trent; tel. (461) 886111; fax (461) 886262; f. 1945; independent; Dir GIAMPAOLO VISETTI; circ. 25,450.

Treviso

La Tribuna di Treviso: Corso del Popolo 44, 31100 Treviso; tel. (422) 410001; fax (422) 579212; f. 1978; independent; Dir ALBERTO STATERA; circ. 25,641.

Trieste

Il Piccolo (Giornale di Trieste): Via Guido Reni 1, 34122 Trieste; tel. (40) 3733111; fax (40) 3733312; e-mail piccolo@ilpiccolo.it; internet http://www.ilpiccolo.it; f. 1881; independent; Dir MARIO QUAIA; circ. 52,544.

Primorski Dnevnik: Via dei Montecchi 6, 34137 Trieste; tel. (40) 7796600; fax (40) 772418; e-mail redakcija@primorski.it; f. 1945; Slovene; Editor-in-Chief BOJAN BREZIGAR; circ. 10,000.

Turin

La Stampa: Via Marenco 32, 10126 Turin; tel. (11) 65681; telex 221121; f. 1868; independent; Dir PAOLO PALOSCHI; circ. 500,000.

Tuttosport: Corso Svizzera 185, 10147 Turin; tel. (11) 77731; telex 224230; f. 1945; sport; Dir FRANCO COLOMBO; circ. 102,000.

Udine

Messaggero Veneto: Viale Palmanova 290, 33100 Udine; tel. (432) 5271; telex 450449; f. 1946; Editor SERGIO GERVASUTTI; circ. 60,309.

Varese

La Prealpina: Viale Tamagno 13, 21100 Varese; tel. (332) 264000; f. 1888; Dir GIGI GERVASUTTI; circ. 38,000.

Venice

Il Gazzettino: Via Torino 110, 30175 Venezia-Mestre; tel. (41) 665111; telex 410682; fax (41) 665386; f. 1887; independent; Dir GIULIO GIUSTINIANI; circ. 139,000.

La Nuova Venezia: Via Verdi 30/32, Castello, 5620 Rialto, 30175 Venice; tel. (41) 2403011; Dir ALBERTO STATERA; circ. 13,000.

Verona

L'Arena: Viale del Lavoro 11, 37036 S. Martino Buon Albergo, Verona; tel. (45) 8094000; telex 481815; fax (45) 994527; f. 1866; independent; Man. Dir Ing. ALESSANDRO ZELGER; circ. 67,746.

Vicenza

Il Giornale di Vicenza: Viale S. Lazzaro 89, 36100 Vicenza; tel. (444) 564533; f. 1946; Editor MINO ALLIONE; circ. 47,000.

SELECTED PERIODICALS

Fine Arts

Casabella: Via Trentacoste 7, 20134 Milan; tel. (2) 215631; fax (2) 21563260; e-mail casabella@mondadori.it; f. 1938; 10 a year; architecture and interior design; Editor FRANCESCO DAL CO ; circ. 43,000.

Domus: Via A. Grandi 5/7, 20089 Rozzano, Milan; tel. (2) 824721; fax (2) 82472386; e-mail domus@edidomus.it; internet http://www.edidomus.it; f. 1928; 11 a year; architecture, interior design and art; Editor FRANÇOIS BURKHARDT; circ. 53,000.

Il Fotografo: Via Rivoltana 8, 20090 Segrate, Milan; tel. (2) 75421; monthly; photography; Dir GIORGIO COPPIN.

Graphicus: Via Morgari 36/B, 10125 Turin; tel. (11) 6690577; fax (11) 6689200; f. 1911; 10 a year; printing and graphic arts; Dir ANGELO DRAGONE; Editor LUCIANO LOVERA; circ. 6,800.

L'Illustrazione Italiana: Via Nino Bixio 30, 20129 Milan; tel. (2) 2043941; fax (2) 2046507; f. 1873; quarterly; fine arts; Editor MASSIMO CAPRARA.

Interni: Via Trentacoste 7, 20134 Milan; tel. (2) 215631; telex 350523; fax (2) 26410847; monthly; interior decoration and design; Editor ANTONELLA BOISI; circ. 60,000.

Lotus international: Via Trentacoste 7, 20134 Milan; tel. (2) 21563240; telex 350523; fax (2) 26410847; f. 1963; quarterly; architecture, town-planning; Editor PIERLUIGI NICOLIN.

Rivista Italiana di Musicologia: Leo S. Olschki, Viuzzo del Pozzetto, 50126 Florence; tel. (55) 6530684; fax (55) 6530214; f. 1966; every 6 months; musicology; Editor MARCELLO CONATI.

Il Saggiatore Musicale: Leo S. Olschki, Viuzzo del Pozzetto, 50126 Florence; tel. (55) 6530684; fax (55) 6530214; f. 1994; twice a year; musicology.

Storia dell'Arte: Viale Carso 46, 00195 Rome; tel. (361) 3729220; fax 3251055; f. 1969; quarterly; art history; Dirs MAURIZIO CALVESI, ORESTE FERRARI, ANGIOLA M. ROMANINI: circ. 1,200.

Studi Musicali: Leo S. Olschki, Viuzzo del Pozzetto, 50126 Florence; tel. (55) 6530684; fax (55) 6530214; f. 1972; twice a year; musicology; Dir N. PIRROTTA.

General, Literary and Political

Archivio Storico Italiano: Leo S. Olschki, Viuzzo del Pozzetto, 50126 Florence; tel. (55) 6530684; fax (55) 6530214; f. 1842; quarterly; history; Editor EMILIO CRISTIANI.

Belfagor: POB 66, 50100 Florence; tel. (55) 6530684; fax (55) 6530214; f. 1946; every 2 months; historical and literary criticism; Editor CARLO FERDINANDO RUSSO; circ. 2,500.

La Bibliofilia: Leo S. Olschki, Viuzzo del Pozzetto, 50126 Florence; tel. (55) 6530684; fax (55) 6530214; f. 1899; every 4 months; bibliography, history of printing; Editor LUIGI BALSAMO.

Civitas: Via Tirso 92, 00198 Rome; tel. (6) 865651; f. 1919; monthly; magazine of political studies; Dir PAOLO EMILIO TAVIANI.

Critica Letteraria: Via Stazio 15, 80123 Naples; f. 1973; quarterly; literary criticism; Editor P. GIANNANTONIO; circ. 3,000.

Critica Marxista: Via dei Polacchi 41, 00186 Rome; tel. (6) 6789680; f. 1962; 6 a year; Dir ALDO ZANARDO.

La Discussione: Piazzale Luigi Sturzo 31, 00144 Rome; tel. (6) 5901353; f. 1953; weekly; supports PPI; Dir PIERLUIGI MAGNASCHI; circ. 50,000.

Epoca: Arnoldo Mondadori Editore SpA, Via Marconi 27, 20090 Segrate, Milan; tel. (2) 7542; telex 310119; f. 1950; illustrated; topical weekly; Dir CARLO ROGNONI; circ. 211,000.

L'Espresso: Via Po 12, 00198 Rome; tel. (6) 84781; telex 610629; weekly; independent left; political; illustrated; Editor CLAUDIO RINALDI; circ. 406,000.

Famiglia Cristiana: Via Giotto 36, 20145 Milan; tel. (2) 48071; telex 332232; fax (2) 48008247; f. 1931; weekly; Catholic; illustrated; Dir LEONARDO ZEGA; circ. 1,053,240.

Francofonia: Leo S. Olschki, Viuzzo del Pozzetto, 50126 Florence; tel. (55) 6530684; fax (55) 6530214; f. 1981; twice a year; French language; Dir L. PETRONI.

Gazzetta del Lunedì: Via Archimede 169, 16142 Genoa; tel. (10) 53691; f. 1945; weekly; political; Dir MIMMO ANGELI; circ. 83,315.

Gente: Viale Sarca 235, 20126 Milan; tel. (2) 27751; f. 1957; weekly; illustrated political, cultural and current events; Editor Dott. RENDINI; circ. 789,906.

Giornale della Libreria: Viale Vittorio Veneto 24, 20124 Milan; tel. (2) 29006965; fax (2) 654624; f. 1888; monthly; organ of the Associazione Italiana Editori; bibliographical; Editor FEDERICO MOTTA.

Il Giornale del Mezzogiorno: Via Messina 31, 00198 Rome; tel. (6) 8443151; telex 621401; fax (6) 8417595; f. 1946; weekly; politics, economics; Dir VITO BLANCO.

Lettere Italiane: Leo S. Olschki, POB 66, 50100 Florence; tel. (55) 6530684; fax (55) 6530214; f. 1949; quarterly; literary; Dirs VITTORE BRANCA, CARLO OSSOLA.

Liberale: Rome; f. 1995; monthly; political; circ. 15,000.

Mondo Economico: Via Paolo Lomazzo 51, 20154 Milan; tel. (2) 331211; fax (2) 316905; f. 1948; weekly; economics; business, finance; Editor ENRICO SASSOON; circ. 85,752.

Il Mulino: Strada Maggiore 37, 40125 Bologna; tel. (51) 222419; fax (51) 256034; e-mail mulino@fox.cib.unibo.it; f. 1951; every 2 months; culture and politics; Editor ALESSANDRO CAVALLI.

Nuovi Argomenti: Via Sicilia 136, 00187 Rome; tel. (6) 47497376; f. 1953; quarterly; Liberal; Editor ENZO SICILIANO.

Oggi: Gruppo Rizzoli, Corso Garibaldi 86, 20121 Milan; tel. (2) 665941; f. 1945; weekly; topical, literary; illustrated; Dir WILLY MOLCO; circ. 727,965.

Panorama: Arnoldo Mondadori Editore SpA, Via Marconi 27, 20090 Segrate, Milan; tel. (2) 7542; fax (2) 75422769; f. 1962; weekly; current affairs; Editor ANDREA MONTI; circ. 540,000.

Il Pensiero Politico: Leo S. Olschki, Viuzzo del Pozzetto, 50126 Florence, tel. (55) 6530684; fax (55) 6530214; f. 1968; every 4 months; political and social history; Editor SALVO MASTELLONE.

Il Ponte: Viale A. Giacomini 8, 50132 Florence; tel. (55) 473964; f. 1945; monthly; politics, art and literature; Publr Vallecchi Editore SpA; Editor MARCELLO ROSSI.

Rassegna Storica Toscana: Leo S. Olschki, Viuzzo del Pozzetto, 50126 Florence; tel. (55) 6530684; fax (55) 6530214; f. 1955; twice a year; Tuscan history.

Rivista di Storia della Filosofia: Via Albricci 9, 20122 Milan; tel. (2) 8052538; f. 1946; quarterly; philosophy.

Scuola e Didattica: Via L. Cadorna 11, 25186 Brescia; tel. (30) 29931; 19 a year; education; Editor GIUSEPPE VICO.

Selezione dal Reader's Digest: Via Alserio 10, 20173 Milan; tel. (2) 69871; fax (2) 66800070; monthly; Editor-in-Chief CLAUDIO PINA (acting); 521,432.

Tempo: Via S. Valeria 5, 20100 Milan; f. 1938; topical illustrated weekly; Dir CARLO GREGORETTI; circ. 230,000.

Visto: Via Rizzoli 4, 20132 Milan; tel. (2) 2588; telex 312119; fax (2) 25843683; f. 1989; illustrated weekly review; Editor-in-Chief MARCELLO MINERBI; circ. 342,850.

Zett-Volksbole: Weinbergweg 7, 39100 Bozen; tel. (471) 200400; fax (471) 200462; f. 1989; German language; circ. 31,200.

Religion

Città di Vita: Piazza Santa Croce 16, 50122 Florence; tel. (55) 242783; f. 1946; every 2 months; cultural review of religious research in theology, art and science; Dir P. M. GIUSEPPE ROSITO; circ. 2,000.

La Civiltà Cattolica: Via di Porta Pinciana 1, 00187 Rome; tel. (6) 6979201; fax (6) 69792022; f. 1850; fortnightly; Catholic; Editor GIAN PAOLO SALVINI.

Il Fuoco: Via Giacinto Carini 28, 00152 Rome; tel. (6) 5810969; every 2 months; art, literature, science, philosophy, psychology, theology; Dir PASQUALE MAGNI.

Humanitas: Via G. Rosa 71, 25121 Brescia; tel. (30) 46451; fax (30) 2400605; f. 1946; every 2 months; religion, philosophy, science, politics, history, sociology, literature, etc.; Dir STEFANO MINELLI.

Protestantesimo: Via Pietro Cossa 42, 00193 Rome; tel. (6) 3210789; fax (6) 3201040; f. 1946; quarterly; theology and current problems, book reviews; Prof. SERGIO ROSTAGNO.

La Rivista del Clero Italiano: Largo Gemelli 1, 20123 Milan; tel. (2) 72342370; telex 321033; fax (2) 72342260; f. 1920; monthly; Dir BRUNO MAGGIONI.

Rivista di Storia della Chiesa in Italia: c/o Herder Editrice e Libreria, Piazza Montecitorio 117–120, 00187 Rome; f. 1947; 2 a year; Editor MICHELE MACCARONE.

Rivista di Storia e Letteratura Religiosa: Leo S. Olschki, Viuzzo del Pozzetto, 50126 Florence; tel. (55) 6530684; fax (55) 6530214; f. 1965; every 4 months; religious history and literature; Dir FRANCO BOLGIANI.

Science and Technology

L'Automobile: Viale Regina Margherita 290, 00198 Rome; tel. (6) 441121; fax (6) 44231160; e-mail lea.srl@iol.it; f. 1945; monthly; motor mechanics, tourism; Dir CARLO LUNA; circ. 1,083,210.

Gazzetta Medica Italiana-Archivio per le Scienze Mediche: Corso Bramante 83–85, 10126 Turin; tel. (11) 678282; 6 a year; medical science; Dir ALBERTO OLIARO; circ. 2,900.

Meccanica: Piazza Leonardo da Vinci 32, 20133 Milan; tel. (2) 23994209; telex 333467; quarterly; Journal of Italian Association of Theoretical and Applied Mechanics; Editor Prof. GIULIANO AUGUSTI.

Il Medico d'Italia: Rome; tel. (6) 36000710; fax (6) 6876739; weekly; medical science; Editor-in-Chief Dott. ANDREA SERMONTI.

Minerva Medica: Corso Bramante 83–85, 10126 Turin; tel. (11) 678282; fax (11) 3121736; 10 a year, medical science; Dir ALBERTO OLIARO; circ. 4,900.

Monti e Boschi: Via Emilia Levante 31/2, 40139 Bologna; tel. (51) 492211; internet http://www.agriline.it/edagri; f. 1949; 2 a month; ecology and forestry; Pubr Edagricole; Editor UMBERTO BAGNARESI; circ. 16,700.

Motor: Piazza Antonio Mancini 4G, 00196 Rome; tel. (6) 3233195; fax (6) 3233309; f. 1942; monthly; motor mechanics; Dir S. FAVIA DEL CORE; circ. 12,500.

Nuncius: Leo S. Olschki, Viuzzo del Pozzetto, 50126 Florence; tel. (55) 6530684; fax (55) 6530214; f. 1976; twice a year; history of science; Dir P. GALLUZZI.

Physis–Rivista Internazionale di Storia della Scienza: Istituto della Enciclopedia Italiana, Piazza dell'Enciclopedia Italiana 4, 00186 Rome; tel. (6) 68985350; fax (6) 68985367; f. 1959; 3 a year; history of science; Editors V. CAPPELLETTI, G. CIMINO.

La Rivista dei Combustibili: Viale De Gasperi 3, 20097 S. Donato Milanese; tel. (2) 510031; telex 321622; fax (2) 514286; f. 1947; monthly; fuels review; Dir Dott. P. CARDILLO; circ. 2,000.

Rivista Geografica Italiana: Via Curtatone 1, 50123 Florence; tel. (55) 2710445; fax (55) 2710424; f. 1894; quarterly geographical review; Editor PAOLO DOCCIOLI.

Women's Publications

Amica: Via Rizzoli 2, 20132 Milan; tel. (2) 2588; telex 310031; f. 1962; weekly; Editor G. MAZZETTI; circ. 196,244.

Anna: Via Civitavecchia 102, Milan; tel. (2) 25843213; telex 312119; f. 1932; weekly; Editor M. VENTURI; circ. 549,227.

Confidenze: Arnoldo Mondadori Editore SpA, Via Mondadori, 20090 Segrate, Milan; tel. (2) 75421; telex 320457; fax (2) 75422806; f. 1946; weekly; Dir GIORDANA MASOTTO; circ. 303,178.

Gioia: Viale Sarca 235, 20126 Milan; f. 1938; weekly; Editor SILVANA GIACOBINI; circ. 432,326.

Grazia: Arnoldo Mondadori Editore SpA, Via Marconi 27, 20090 Segrate, Milan; tel. (2) 75422390; fax (2) 75422515; f. 1938; weekly; Dir CARLA VANNI; circ. 377,804.

Intimità della Famiglia: Via Borgogna 5, 20122 Milan; tel. (2) 781051; weekly; published by Cino del Duca; Dir G. GALLUZZO; circ. 424,946.

Vogue Italia: Piazza Castello 27, 20121 Milan; tel. (2) 85611; telex 313454; fax (2) 870686; monthly; Editor FRANCA SOZZANI; circ. 73,773.

Miscellaneous

Annali della Scuola Normale Superiore di Pisa: Scuola Normale Superiore, Pisa; tel. (50) 509111; telex 590548; fax (50) 563513; f. 1871; quarterly; mathematics, philosophy, philology, history, literature; Editor (Mathematics) Prof. EDOARDO VESENTINI; Editor (literature and philosophy) Prof. GIUSEPPE NENCI; circ. 1,300.

Atlante: Via G. Gozzi 1A, 20129 Milan; tel. (2) 700231; fax (2) 70100319; monthly; published by Istituto Geografico de Agostini Rizzoli Periodici (Milano); travel, art, geography, ethnology, archaeology; Dir Dott. MASSIMO MORELLO.

Comunità Mediterranea: Lungotevere Flaminio 34, 00196 Rome; quarterly; legal; Editor ENRICO NOUNÈ.

Cooperazione Educativa: La Nuova Italia, Via dei Piceni 16, 00185 Rome; tel. (6) 4457228; fax (6) 4460386; f. 1952; monthly; education; Dir MIRELLA GRIEG.

Il Maestro: Clivo Monte del Gallo 48, 00165 Rome; tel. (6) 634651; fax (6) 39375903; f. 1945; monthly; Catholic teachers' magazine; Dir MARIANGELA PRIORESCHI; circ. 40,000.

Quattroruote: Via A. Grandi 5/7, 20089 Rozzano, Milan; tel. (2) 824721; fax (2) 57500416; f. 1956; motoring; monthly; Editor MAURO COPPINI; circ. 662,000.

NEWS AGENCIES

Agenzia Giornalistica Italia (AGI): Via Nomentana 92, 00161 Rome; tel. (6) 84361; telex 610512; fax (6) 8416072; owned by ENI, a state-owned energy conglomerate; Editor FRANCO ANGRISANI.

Agenzia Nazionale Stampa Associata (ANSA): Via della Dataria 94, 00187 Rome; tel. (6) 6774310; telex 610242; fax (6) 6782408; f. 1945; 22 regional offices in Italy and 90 brs all over the world; service in Italian, Spanish, French, English; Pres. UMBERTO CUTTICA; Man. Dir and Gen. Man. ALFREDO ROMA; Chief Editor BRUNO CASELLI.

Inter Press Service (IPS): Via Panisperna 207, 00184 Rome; tel. (6) 485692; telex 610574; fax (6) 4817877; e-mail romadir@ips.org; internet http//www.ips.org; f. 1964; international daily news agency; Dir-Gen. ROBERTO SAVIO.

Foreign Bureaux

Agencia EFE (Spain): Via dei Canestrari 5, 00186 Rome; tel. (6) 6548802; telex 612323; fax (6) 6874918; Bureau Chief NEMESIO RODRÍGUEZ.

Agence France-Presse (AFP): Piazza Santi-Apostoli 66, 00187 Rome; tel. (6) 6793588; telex 613303; fax (6) 6793623; Bureau Chief XAVIER BARON.

Associated Press (AP) (USA): Piazza Grazioli 5, 00186 Rome; tel. (6) 6789936; telex 610196; Bureau Chief DENNIS F. REDMONT.

Česká tisková kancelář (ČTK) (Czech Republic): Via di Vigna Stelluti 150/13, 00191 Rome; tel. (6) 3270777; telex 43625664.

Deutsche Presse-Agentur (dpa) (Germany): Via della Mercede 55, Int. 15, 00187 Rome; tel. (6) 6789810; fax (6) 6841598; Bureau Chief LÁSZLÓ TRANKOVITS.

Informatsionnoye Telegrafnoye Agentstvo Rossii—Telegrafnoye Agentstvo Suverennykh Stran (ITAR—TASS) (Russia): Viale dell'Umanesimo 172, 00144 Rome; tel. (6) 5912882; fax (6) 5925711; e-mail latyzeva@hotmail.com; Correspondent SERGEI BATYREV.

Kyodo Tsushin (Japan): Rome, tel. (6) 8440709; telex 680840; Bureau Chief KATSUO UEDA.

Magyar Távirati Iroda (MTI) (Hungary): Villino 22, Capena, Castello di Sorano, 00060 Rome; tel. (6) 8441309; Correspondent ISTVÁN GÓZON.

Reuters (United Kingdom): Via della Cordonata 7, 00187 Rome; tel. (6) 6782501; telex 620602; fax (6) 6794248.

United Press International (UPI) (USA): Via della Mercede 55, 00187 Rome; tel. (6) 6795747; telex 624580; fax (6) 6781540; Correspondent CHARLES RIDLEY.

Xinhua (New China) News Agency (People's Republic of China): Via Bruxelles 59, 00198 Rome; tel. (6) 865028; telex 612208; fax (6) 8450575; Bureau Chief HUANG CHANGRUI.

CNA (Taiwan) and Jiji Tsushin (Japan) are also represented.

PRESS ASSOCIATIONS

Associazione della Stampa Estera in Italia: Via della Mercede 55, 00187 Rome; tel. (6) 6786005; foreign correspondents' asscn; Pres. DENNIS REDMONT; Sec. SANTIAGO FERNÁNDEZ ARDANAZ.

Federazione Italiana Editori Giornali (FIEG): Via Piemonte 64, 00187 Rome; tel. (6) 4881683; fax (6) 4871109; e-mail fiegroma@iol.it; f. 1950; association of newspaper publishers; Pres. MARIO CIANCIO SANFILIPPO; Dir-Gen. SEBASTIANO SORTINO; 268 mems.

Federazione Nazionale della Stampa Italiana: Corso Vittorio Emanuele 349, 00186 Rome; tel. (6) 6833879; fax (6) 6871444; f. 1877; 17 affiliated unions; Pres. GILBERTO EVANGELISTI; Nat. Sec. GIORGIO SANTERINI; 16,000 mems.

Unione Stampa Periodica Italiana (USPI): Viale Bardanzellu 95, 00155 Rome; tel. (6) 4071388; fax (6) 4066859; Pres. Avv. DARIO DI GRAVIO; Sec.-Gen. GIAN DOMENICO ZUCCALÀ; 4,500 mems.

Publishers

There are more than 300 major publishing houses and many smaller ones.

Bologna

Edizioni Calderini: Via Emilia Levante 31/2, 40139 Bologna; tel. (51) 492211; fax (51) 490200; e-mail commerciale@calderini.it; internet http://www.calderini.it; f. 1960; art, sport, electronics, mechanics, university and school textbooks, travel guides, nursing, architecture; Man. Dir ALBERTO PERDISA.

Nuova Casa Editrice Licinio Cappelli GEM SrL: Via Farini 14, 40124 Bologna; tel. (51) 239060; fax (51) 239286; f. 1848; medical science, history, politics, literature, textbooks; Chair. and Man. Dir MARIO MUSSO.

Edagricole–Edizioni Agricole: Via Emilia Levante 31, 40139 Bologna; tel. (51) 492211; fax (51) 490200; e-mail commerciale@calderini.it; internet http://www.agriline.it; f. 1935; agriculture, veterinary science, gardening, biology, textbooks, directories; Man. Dir ALBERTO PERDISA.

Malipiero Editore SpA: Via Liguria 8–10, CP 788, 40100 Bologna; tel. (51) 792111; telex 510260; fax (51) 792356; f. 1969; albums and books for children and young people, dictionaries, pocket dictionaries, stamp albums, etc.; Chair. LAURA PANINI; Man. Dir Dott. ENRICO BERARDI.

Società Editrice Il Mulino: Strada Maggiore 37, 40125 Bologna; tel. (51) 256011; fax (51) 256034; f. 1954; politics, history, philosophy, social sciences, linguistics, literary criticism, law, music, theatre, psychology, economics, journals; Gen. Man. GIOVANNI EVANGELISTI.

Zanichelli Editore SpA: Via Irnerio 34, 40126 Bologna; tel. (51) 293111; fax (51) 249782; e-mail zanichelli@zanichelli.it; internet http://www.zanichelli.it; f. 1859; educational, history, literature, philosophy, mathematics, science, technical books, law, psychology, architecture, reference books, dictionaries, atlases, earth sciences, linguistics, medicine, economics, etc.; Chair. and Gen. Man. FEDERICO ENRIQUES; Vice-Chair. and Man. Dir LORENZO ENRIQUES.

Brescia

Editrice La Scuola SpA: Via Cadorna 11, Brescia; tel. (30) 29931; fax (30) 2993299; f. 1904; educational magazines, educational textbooks, audiovisual aids and toys; Chair. Dott. Ing. LUCIANO SILVERI; Man. Dir Rag. GIUSEPPE COVONE.

Busto Arsizio

Bramante Editrice: Busto Arsizio; tel. (331) 620324; fax (331) 322052; f. 1958; art, history, encyclopaedias, natural sciences, interior decoration, arms and armour, music; Chair. Dott. GUIDO CERIOTTI.

Florence

Casa Editrice Bonechi: Via dei Cairoli 18B, 50131 Florence; tel. (55) 576841; telex 571323; fax (55) 5000766; e-mail bonechi@bonechi.it; internet http://www.bonechi.it; f. 1973; art, travel, reference; Man. Dir GIAMPAOLO BONECHI; Gen. Man. GIUSEPPE MASTROMARTINO.

Cremonese: Borgo Santa Croce 17, 50122 Florence; tel. (55) 2476371; fax (55) 2476372; f. 1929; history, reference, engineering, science, textbooks, architecture, mathematics, aviation; Chair. ALBERTO STIANTI.

Giunti Barbera Editore; Via Boloquese 165, 50139 Florence; tel. (55) 66791; telex 571438; f. 1839; art, psychology, literature, science, law; Dir Dott. SERGIO GIUNTI.

Le Monnier: Via A. Meucci 2, 50015 Grassina, Florence; tel. (55) 64910; fax (55) 643983; e-mail monnier@mbox.vol.it; f. 1836; academic and cultural books, textbooks, dictionaries; Man. Dirs Dott. VANNI PAOLETTI, Dott. GUGLIELMO PAOLETTI, Dott. SIMONE PAOLETTI.

La Nuova Italia Editrice SpA: Via Ernesto Codignola 1, 50018 Florence; tel. (55) 75901; fax (55) 7590208; f. 1926; biography, psychology, philosophy, philology, education, history, politics, belles-lettres, art, music and science; Man. Dirs FEDERICO CODIGNOLA, ACHILLE GERLI.

Casa Editrice Leo S. Olschki: CP 66, 50100 Florence; tel. (55) 6530684; fax (55) 6530214; f. 1886; reference, periodicals, textbooks, humanities; Man. ALESSANDRO OLSCHKI.

Adriano Salani Editore Srl: Via del Giglio 15, 50123 Florence; tel. (55) 283645; fax (55) 289288; f. 1988; fiction, children's books; Editor MARIAGRAZIA MAZZITELLI.

Edizioni Remo Sandron: Via L.C. Farini 10, 50121 Florence; tel. (55) 245231; f. 1839; textbooks; Pres. E. MULINACCI.

Vallecchi Editore SpA: Via Il Prato 21, 50123 Florence; tel. (55) 290765; fax (55) 293477; f. 1913; art, fiction, literature, essays, media; Pres. PIERO SUSMEL.

Genoa

Casa Editrice Marietti SpA: Via Piandilucco 7, 16155 Genoa; tel. (10) 6984226; fax (10) 667092; f. 1820; liturgy, theology, fiction, history, politics, literature, philosophy, art, children's books; Editor CARLA VILLATA.

Milan

Adelphi Edizioni SpA: Via S. Giovanni sul Muro 14, 20121 Milan; tel. (2) 72000975; fax (2) 89010337; f. 1962; classics, philosophy, biography, music, art, psychology, religion and fiction; Pres. GIUSEPPE LUCIANO FOÀ; Man. Dir ROBERTO CALASSO.

Editrice Ancora: Via G. B. Niccolini 8, 20154 Milan; tel. (2) 3456081; fax (2) 3456086; editrice@ancora-libri.it; f. 1934; religious, educational; Dir GILBERTO ZINI.

Franco Angeli Srl: Viale Monza 106, CP 17130, 20127 Milan; tel. (2) 2827651; fax (2) 2891515; f. 1956; general; Man. Dir FRANCO ANGELI.

Silvio Berlusconi Editore SpA: Corso Europa 5/7, 20122 Milan; tel. (2) 77941; fax (2) 76001488; television and light entertainment magazines; Chair. SILVIO BERLUSCONI.

Gruppo Editoriale Fabbri SpA: Via Mecenate 91, 20138 Milan; tel. (2) 50951; telex 311321; fax (2) 5065361; f. 1947; juveniles, education, textbooks, reference, literature, maps and encyclopaedia series, art books; Chair. GIOVANNI GIOVANNINI; Man. Dir Dott. GIANNI VALLARDI; Gen. Man. Dott. GIOVANNI UNGARELLI.

Bompiani: Via Mecenate 91, 20138 Milan; tel. (2) 50951; telex 311321; f. 1929; modern literature, biographies, theatre, science, art, history, classics, dictionaries, pocket books; Dir MARIO ANDREOSE.

Sonzogno: Via Mecenate 91, 20138 Milan; tel (2) 50951; telex 311321; f. 1861; fiction, non-fiction, illustrated, manuals; Dir MARIO ANDREOSE.

Feltrinelli SpA: Via Andegari 6, 20121 Milan; tel. (2) 808346; f. 1954; fiction, juvenile, science, technology, textbooks, poetry, art, music, history, literature, political science, philosophy, reprint editions of periodicals; Chair. INGE FELTRINELLI; Man. Dir GIUSEPPE ANTONINI.

Garzanti Editore: Via Newton 18A, 20148 Milan; tel. (2) 487941; telex 325218; fax (2) 48794292; f. 1938; literature, poetry, science, art, history, politics, encyclopaedias, dictionaries, scholastic and children's books; Chair. GIOVANNI MERLINI; Gen. Man. FRANCESCO RAMPINI.

Casa Editrice Libraria Ulrico Hoepli: Via Hoepli 5, 20121 Milan; tel. (2) 864871; fax (2) 8052886; f. 1870; grammars, art, technical, scientific and school books, encyclopaedias; Chair. ULRICO HOEPLI; Man. Dir GIANNI HOEPLI.

Longanesi e C. SpA: Corso Italia 13, 20122 Milan; tel. (2) 8692142; telex 353273; fax (2) 72000306; f. 1946; art, history, philosophy, fiction; Pres. S. PASSIGLI; Man. Dir M. SPAGNOL.

Massimo: Viale Bacchiglione 20/A, 20139 Milan; tel. (2) 55210800; fax (2) 55211315; f. 1950; fiction, biography, history, social science, philosophy, pedagogy, theology, school texts; Chair. CESARE CRESPI.

Arnoldo Mondadori Editore: Via Mondadori, 20090 Segrate, Milan; tel. (2) 75421; telex 320457; fax (2) 75422302; f. 1907; literature, fiction, essays, politics, science, music, art, religion, philosophy, encyclopaedias, children's books, magazines; Chair. LEONARDO MONDADORI; Man. Dir MAURIZIO COSTA.

Gruppo Ugo Mursia Editore SpA: Via Tadino 29, 20124, Milan; tel. (2) 29403030; fax (2) 29525557; e-mail mursiami@tin.it; f. 1955; general fiction and non-fiction, textbooks, reference, art, history, nautical books, philosophy, biography, sports, children's books; Gen. Man. FIORENZA MURSA.

Etas Srl: Via Mecenate 89, 20138 Milan; tel. (2) 580841; telex 331342; fax (2) 5060294; technical periodicals and books; Man. Dir Dott. GIORGIO ORSI.

Rcs Rizzoli: Via Mercenate 91, 20138 Milan; tel. 50950; fax (2) 58012040; f. 1929; newspapers, magazines and books; Dir-Gen. GIOVANNI UNGARELLI; Man. Dir GIORGIO FATTORI.

Riccardo Ricciardi Editore SpA: c/o Arnoldo Mondadori Editore, Via Mondadori 1, 20090 Segrate, Milan; tel. (2) 75421; f. 1907; classics, philology, history, literature; Gen. Man. GIAN ARTURO FERRARI.

Casa Ricordi SpA: Via Berchet 2, 20121 Milan; tel. (2) 88812206; telex 310177; (2) 88812212; f. 1808; academic, art, music; Chair. GIANNI BABINI; Man. Dir MIMMA GUASTONI.

Rusconi Libri Srl: Viale Sarca 235, 20126 Milan; tel. (2) 66191; telex 312233; fax (2) 66192758; f. 1969; non-fiction including history, biography, music, philosophy, archaeology, religion, needlecraft, embroidery and art; Pres. ALBERTO RUSCONI; Editorial Dir ALBERTO CONFORTI.

Edizioni San Paolo: Piazza Soncino 5, 20092 Cinisello Balsamo—Milan; tel. (2) 6600621; fax (2) 66015332; f. 1914; religious; Gen. Man. ANTONIO TARZIA.

L'Editrice Scientifica: Milan; tel. (2) 8390274; f. 1949; university publications in chemistry and medicine; Dirs Dotts. LEONARDA and GUIDO GUADAGNI.

Edizioni Scolastiche Bruno Mondadori: Via Archimede 23, 20129 Milan; tel. (2) 762151; fax (2) 76215278; f. 1946; textbooks and educational books; Chair. ROBERTA MONDADORI; Man. Dir ROBERTO GULLI; Gen. Man. AGOSTINO CATTANEO.

SEDES SpA-Ghisetti e Corvi Editori: Corso Concordia 7, 20129 Milan; tel. (2) 76006232; fax (2) 76009468; e-mail sedes.spa@gpa.it; internet http://www.sedes.gpa.it; f. 1937; educational textbooks.

Selezione dal Reader's Digest SpA: Via Alserio 10, 20173 Milan; tel. (2) 69871; fax (2) 6987401; f. 1948; educational, reference, general interest; Man. Dir CHARLES J. LOBKOWICZ.

Sugarco Edizioni Srl: Via E. Fermi 9, 21040 Carnago; tel. (331) 985511; fax (331) 985385; f. 1957; fiction, biography, history, philosophy, guidebooks, Italian classics; Chair. Prof. SERGIO CIGADA; Gen. Man. OLIVIERO CIGADA.

Casa Editrice Luigi Trevisini: Via Tito Livio 12, 20137 Milan; tel. (2) 5450704; fax (2) 55195782; f. 1849; school textbooks; Dirs LUIGI TREVISINI, GIUSEPPINA TREVISINI.

Vita e Pensiero: Largo A. Gemelli 1, 20123 Milan; tel. (2) 72342335; fax (2) 72342260; f. 1918; publisher to the Catholic University of the Sacred Heart; cultural, scientific books and magazines.

Naples

Casa Editrice Libraria Idelson Liviana Srl: Via Alcide De Gasperi 55, 80133 Naples; tel. (81) 5524733; fax 5518295; f. 1908; medicine, psychology, biology; CEO GUIDO GNOCCHI.

Liguori Editore Srl: Via Posillipo 394, 80123 Naples; tel. (81) 7206111; fax (81) 7206244; f. 1949; linguistics, mathematics, engineering, economics, law, history, philosophy, sociology; Man. Dir Dott. ROLANDO LIGUORI.

Gaetano Macchiaroli Editore: Via Michetti 11, 80127, Naples; tel. (81) 5783129; fax (81) 5780568; archaeology, classical studies, history, philosophy, political science.

Novara

Instituto Geografico De Agostini-Novara: Via Giovanni da Verrazano 15, 28100 Novara; tel. (321) 4241; telex 200290; fax (321) 471286; geography, maps, encyclopaedias, dictionaries, art, literature, textbooks, science; Chair. MARCO BOROLI; CEO MARCO DRAGO.

Padua

CEDAM—Casa Editrice Dr A. Milani: Via Jappelli 5/6, 35121 Padua; tel. (49) 656677; fax (49) 8752900; f. 1902; law, economics, political and social sciences, engineering, science, medicine, literature, philosophy, textbooks; Dirs ANTONIO MILANI, CARLO PORTA.

Libreria Editrice Gregoriana: Via Roma 82, 35122 Padua; tel. (49) 661033; f. 1922; *Lexicon Totius Latinitatis*, religion, philosophy, psychology, social studies; Dir DON GIANCARLO MINOZZI.

Libreria Editrice Internazionale Zannoni e Figlio: Corso Garibaldi 14, 35122 Padua; tel. (49) 44170; f. 1919; medicine, technical books, scholastic books, miscellaneous; Dir GIULIANA ZANNONI.

Piccin Nuova Libraria SpA: Via Altinate 107, 35121 Padua; tel. (49) 655566; fax (49) 8750693; f. 1980; scientific and medical textbooks and journals; Man. Dir Dott. MASSIMO PICCIN.

Valmartina Editore: Padua; tel. (49) 8710195; fax (49) 8710261; foreign languages, guide books; Pres. Rag. LUIGI VECCHIA; Gen. Man. Dott. GIORGIO RACCIS.

Rome

Armando Armando Editore Srl: Viale Trastevere 236, 00153 Rome; tel. (6) 5806420; fax (6) 5818564; e-mail armando@pelomar.it; internet http://www.armando.it; philosophy, psychology, social sciences, languages, ecology, education; Man. Dir ENRICO JACOMETTI.

Edizioni Borla Srl: Via delle Fornaci 50, 00165 Rome; tel. (6) 6381618; fax (6) 6376620; f. 1863; religion, philosophy, psychoanalysis, ethnology, literature, novels for teenagers; Man. Dir VINCENZO D'AGOSTINO.

Edizioni d'Arte di Carlo E. Bestetti & C. Sas: Via di San Giacomo 18, 00187 Rome; tel. (6) 6790174; f. 1947; art, architecture, industry; Man. Dir CARLO BESTETTI.

Ausonia: Rome; tel. (6) 595959; f. 1919; textbooks; Pres. E. LUCCHINI; Gen. Man. G. LUCCHINI.

AVE (Anonima Veritas Editrice): Via Aurelia 481, 00165 Rome; tel. (6) 6633041; fax (6) 6620207; f. 1935; theology, sociology, pedagogy, psychology, essays, learned journals, religious textbooks; Man. Dir ANTONIO SANTANGELO.

Vito Bianco Editore: Via Messina 31, 00198 Rome; tel. (6) 8443151; telex 621401; fax (6) 8417595; various, especially marine publications; Chair. Dott. VITO BIANCO.

Bulzoni Editore—Le edizioni universitarie d'Italia: Via dei Liburni 14, 00185 Rome; tel. (6) 4455207; fax (6) 4450355; f. 1969; science, arts, fiction, textbooks; Man. Dir MARIO BULZONI.

E. Calzono: Via del Collegio Romano 9, Rome; f. 1872; art, archaeology, philosophy, science, religion, economics; Dir Dott. RICCARDO GAMBERINI MONGENET.

Editrice Ciranna: Rome; tel. (773) 250746; fax (773) 250746; f. 1940; school textbooks; Man. Dir LIDIA FABIANO.

Armando Curcio Editore SpA: Via IV Novembre, 00187 Rome; tel. (6) 699971; fax (6) 69997247; f. 1954; encyclopaedias, classics, history, music, science, reference, geography, art, video series; Chair. Dott. MARIO SCHIMBERNI; Man. Dir Dott. MATILDE BERNABEI.

Edizioni Europa: Via G.B. Martini 6, 00198 Rome; tel. (6) 8449124; f. 1944; essays, literature, art, history, politics, music, economics; Chair. Prof. PIER FAUSTO PALUMBO.

Hermes Edizioni Srl: Via Flaminia 109, 00196 Rome; tel. (6) 3201656; fax (6) 3223540; f. 1979; alternative medicine, astrology, nature, dietetics, sports; Gen. Man. GIOVANNI CANONICO.

Giuseppe Laterza e Figli SpA: Via di Villa Sacchetti 17, 00197 Rome; tel. (6) 3218393; fax (6) 3223853; f. 1885; belles lettres, biography, reference, religion, art, classics, history, economics, philosophy, social science; Man. Dir VITO LATERZA; Editorial Dirs ALESSANDRO LATERZA, GIUSEPPE LATERZA.

Edizioni Lavoro: Via G.M. Lancisi 25, 00161 Rome; tel. (6) 44251174; fax (6) 44251177; f. 1982; history, politics, political philosophy, sociology, African literature; Chair. PAOLO FELTRIN; Man. Dir MARIO BERTIN.

Guida Monaci SpA: Via Vitorchiano 107, 00189 Rome; tel. (6) 3331333; fax (6) 3335555; f. 1870; commercial and industrial, financial, administrative and medical directories; Dir Ing. GIANCARLO ZAPPONINI.

Fratelli Palombi Srl: Via dei Gracchi 181-185, 00192 Rome; tel. (6) 3214150; fax (6) 3214752; f. 1914; history, art, etc. of Rome; Man. Dir Dott. MARIO PALOMBI.

Jandi Sapi Editori Srl: Via Crescenzio 62, 00193 Rome; tel. (6) 68805515; fax (6) 6832612; f. 1941; industrial and legal publications, art books; Dir Dott. CHIARA BASSANINI.

Angelo Signorelli: Via Falconieri 84, 00152 Rome; tel. (6) 5314942; fax (6) 531492; f. 1912; science, general literature, textbooks; Man. Dirs GIORGIO SIGNORELLI, GILBERTA ALPA.

Società Editrice Dante Alighieri Srl: Via Timavo 3, 00195 Rome; tel. (6) 3725870; fax (6) 37514807; f. 1928; school textbooks, science and general culture; Pres. and Man. Dir SILVANO SPINELLI.

Edizioni Studium: Via Cassiodoro 14, 00193 Rome; tel. (6) 6865846; fax (6) 6875456; f. 1927; philosophy, literature, sociology, pedagogy, religion, economics, law, science, history, psychology; periodical *Studium*.

Stresa

Edizioni Rosminiane Sodalitas Sas: Centro Internazionale di Studi Rosminiani, Corso Umberto I 15, 28049 Stresa; tel. (323) 30091; fax (323) 31623; f. 1925; philosophy, theology, *Rivista Rosminiana* (quarterly); Dir Prof. PIER PAOLO OTTONELLO.

Trent

G.B. Monauni: Trent; tel. (461) 21445; f. 1725; art, archaeology, ethnology, folklore, science, history; Man. Dir Dott. G. B. MONAUNI.

Turin

Editrice L'Artist Modern: Via Garibaldi 59, 10121 Turin; tel. (11) 541371; f. 1901; art; Dir. F. NELVA.

Bollati Boringhieri Editore: Corso Vittorio Emanuele II 86, 10121 Turin; tel. (11) 5611951; fax (11) 543024; f. 1957; psychology, social and human sciences, fiction and classical literature; Chair. ROMILDA BOLLATI.

Giulio Einaudi Editore SpA; Via Umberto Biancamano 2, CP 245, 10121 Turin; tel. (11) 56561; telex 220334; fax (11) 542903; f. 1933; fiction, classics, general; Chair. GIULIO EINAUDI; Gen. Man. VITTORIO BO.

Giorgio Giappichelli Editore Srl: Via Po 21, 10124 Turin; tel. (11) 8127623; f. 1921; university publications on law, economics, politics and sociology.

Lattes S. e C. Editori SpA: Via Confienza 6, 10121 Turin; f. 1893; tel. (11) 5625335; fax (11) 5625070; technical, textbooks; Pres. MARIO LATTES.

Levrotto e Bella, Libreria Editrice Universitaria: Corso Vittorio Emanuele II 26, 10123 Turin; tel. (11) 8121205; fax (11) 8124025; f. 1911; university textbooks; Man. Dir Dott. ELISABETTA GUALINI.

Loescher: Via Vittorio Amedeo II 18, 10121 Turin; tel. (11) 5654111; fax (11) 5625822; f. 1867; school textbooks, general literature, academic books; Chair. LORENZO ENRIQUES.

Edizioni Minerva Medica: Corso Bramante 83–85, 10126 Turin; tel. (11) 678282; fax (11) 674502; medical books and journals; Pres. ALBERTO OLIARO.

Petrini Editore: Strada del Portone 177, 10095 Grugliasco; tel. (11) 3158711; f. 1872; school textbooks; Dir GUIDO CARRARA.

Rosenberg & Sellier: Via Andrea Doria 14, 10123 Turin; tel. (11) 8127808; fax (11) 8127820; f. 1883; philology, social sciences, philosophy, linguistics, dictionaries, scientific journals; Chair. and Man. Dir UGO GIANNI ROSENBERG.

Società Editrice Internazionale SpA (SEI): Corso Regina Margherita 176, 10152 Turin; tel. (11) 52271; fax (11) 5211320; f. 1908; textbooks, fiction, art, literature, philosophy, children's books, etc.; Publishing Man. Prof. GIUSEPPE COSTA.

Unione Tipografico-Editrice Torinese (UTET): Corso Raffaello 28, 10125 Turin; tel. (11) 65291; telex 225553; fax (11) 6529369; e-mail utet@utet.com; f. 1791; university and specialized editions on history, geography, art, literature, economics, law, sciences, encyclopaedias, dictionaries, etc.; Pres. Dott. GIANNI MERLINI.

Venice

Alfieri Edizioni d'Arte: San Marco 1991, Cannaregio 6099, 30124 Venice; tel. (41) 5223323; f. 1939; modern art, Venetian art, architecture, periodicals; Chair. GIORGIO FANTONI; Gen. Man. MASSIMO VITTA ZELMAN.

Marsilio Editori: Marittima, Fabbricato 205, 30135 Venice; tel. (41) 5227822; fax (41) 5238352; f. 1961; fiction, non-fiction, history of art, catalogues, cartography; Man. Dirs Dott. EMANUELA BASSETTI, Prof. CESARE DE MICHELIS, Dott. RITA VIVIAN.

Verona

Bertani Editore Srl: Via Interr. Acqua Morta 31, 37129 Verona; tel. (45) 8011345; fax (45) 8350402; f. 1973; politics, literature, anthropology, sociology, theatre, cinema, geography, humanities, history of Verona, psychology, cultural journals; Man. Dir MARIO QUARANTA; Editorial Dir GIORGIO BERTANI.

Arnoldo Mondadori Editore: Via Arnoldo Mondadori 15, 37131 Verona; tel. (45) 934602; telex 480071; fax (45) 934566; f. 1912; children and young adults' books; Man. Dir. MARGHERITA FORESTAN.

Vicenza

Neri Pozza Editore SpA: Contrà Oratorio dei Servi 19–21, 36100 Vicenza; tel. (444) 320787; fax (444) 324613; f. 1946; art, fiction, history, politics; Pres. MINO ALLIONE; Dir ANGELO COLLA.

Government Publishing House

Istituto Poligrafico e Zecca dello Stato: Piazza Verdi 10, 00198 Rome; tel. (6) 85081; telex 611008; fax (6) 85082517; f. 1928; art, literary, scientific, technical books and reproductions; Chair. Dott. GIOVANNI RUGGERI; Gen. Dir ALFREDO MAGGI.

PUBLISHERS' ASSOCIATION

Associazione Italiana Editori: Via delle Erbe 2, 20121 Milan; tel. (2) 86463091; fax (2) 89010863; f. 1869; Via Crescenzio 19, 00193 Rome; tel. (6) 8806298; fax (6) 6872426; Pres. FEDERICO MOTTA; Dir IVAN CECCHINI.

Broadcasting and Communications

A joint regulatory authority for broadcasting and telecommunications was established in 1997 with Enzo Cheli as its Chairman.

TELECOMMUNICATIONS

Telecom Italia SpA: Via San Dalmazzo 15, 10122 Turin; tel. (11) 55141; telex 610647; Italy's leading telecommunications operator; merged with Società Finanzia à Telefonica SpA (STET) in 1997; privatized in 1997; Chair. GIAN MARIO ROSSIGNOLO; Man. Dir VITO GAMBERALE.

Telecom Italia Mobile SpA (TIM): Via Bertola 34; Turin; f. 1995 after split from Telecom Italia SpA; Italy's leading mobile telecommunications operator; Chair. VITTORIO DI STEFANO.

RADIO

In April 1975 legislation was adopted to ensure the political independence of Radiotelevisione Italiana (RAI). The state monopoly on broadcasting was abolished in 1976; more than 2,100 private local radio stations had begun broadcasting by 1995.

Radiotelevisione Italiana (RAI): Viale Mazzini 14, 00195 Rome; tel. (6) 38781; telex 614432; fax (6) 3226070; internet http://www.rai.it; f. 1924; a public share capital company; programmes comprise the national programme (general), Second Programme (recreational), Third Programme (educational); there are also regional programmes in Italian and in the languages of ethnic minorities; the foreign and overseas service (Radio Ronia) broadcasts in 27 languages; Pres. ROBERTO ZACCARIA; Gen. Man. FRANCO ISEPPI.

Rundfunk Anstalt Südtirol (RAS): Europaallee 164/A, 39100 Bozen; tel. (471) 202933; fax (471) 200378; f. 1975; relays television and radio broadcasts from Germany, Austria and Switzerland to the population of South Tyrol; Pres. HELMUTH HENDRICH; Man. Dir KLAUS GRUBER.

TELEVISION

Sixteen private stations have nationwide networks. IN 1995 there were about 900 privately-operated television stations, msotly offering a local service.

Radiotelevisione Italiana (RAI): Viale Mazzini 14, 00195 Rome; tel. (6) 38781; telex 614432; fax (6) 3226070; internet http://www.rai.it; f. 1924; operates three channels, RAI Uno, RAI Due and RAI Tre; also broadcasts local programmes in Italian and in German for the Alto Adige; Pres. ENZO SICILIANO; Gen. Man. FRANCO ISEPPI.

Rundfunk Anstalt Südtirol (RAS): (see Radio).

Finance

(cap. = capital; p.u. = paid up; res = reserves; dep. = deposits; m. = million; brs = branches; amounts in lire)

In 1997 there were more than 1,000 banks in Italy. Many banking companies are state-controlled, including the majority of the large banks. There are more than 100 private banks, and a large number of co-operative and savings banks (*banche popolari, casse di risparmio, casse rurali*) of widely ranging size and importance. In addition, there are 90 specialized credit institutions which provide medium- and long-term finance, together with other services outside the scope of the banks.

BANKING

Central Bank

Banca d'Italia: Via Nazionale 91, 00184 Rome; tel. (6) 47921; telex 630045; fax (6) 47922983; f. 1893; cap. 300m., res 10,791,700m., dep. 155,445,823m. (Dec. 1996); since 1926 the Bank has had the sole right to issue notes in Italy; Gov. ANTONIO FAZIO; Dir-Gen. VINCENZO DESARIO; 99 brs.

Major Commercial Banks

Banca Agricola Mantovana Scarl: Corso Vittorio Emanuele 30, 46100 Mantua; tel. (376) 3311; telex 304265; fax (376) 331261; f. 1871; cap. 446,345m., res 749,614m., dep. 9,138,917m. (Dec. 1996); Chair. PIERMARIA PACCHIONI; Gen. Man. MARIO PETRONI; 169 brs.

Banca Antoniana-Popolare Veneta Scarl: Via Verdi 13–15, 35122 Padua; tel. (49) 839111; telex 432047; fax (49) 839695; f. 1893; July 1996 merged with Banca Popolare di Verona Scarl; cap. 484,182m., res 1,072,630m., dep. 15,592,066m. (Dec. 1996); Pres. Dott. DINO MARCHIORELLO; Gen. Man. Dott. SILVANO PONTELLO; 277 brs.

Banca Carige SpA (Cassa di Risparmio di Genova e Imperia): Via Cassa di Risparmio 15, 16123 Genoa; tel. (10) 5792041; telex 270089; fax (10) 280013; f. 1846; cap. 1,376,828m., res 182,646m., dep. 14,344,049m. (Dec. 1996); Chair. Prof. FAUSTO CUOCOLO; Gen. Man. Dott. GIOVANNI BERNESCHI; 226 brs.

Banca Cassa di Risparmio di Torino SpA: Via XX Settembre 31, 10121 Turin; tel. (11) 6621; telex 212278; fax (11) 638203; f. 1827; savings bank; cap. 1,000,000m., res 1,593,128m., dep. 34,996,498m. (Dec. 1996); Chair. Prof. ENRICO FILIPPI; Gen. Man. Dott. GIORGIO GIOVANDO; 380 brs.

Banca Commerciale Italiana SpA—COMIT: Piazza della Scala 6, 20121 Milan; tel. (2) 88501; telex 532465; fax (2) 88503026; f. 1894; state holding (54%) sold to private interests in 1994; cap. 1,794,759m., res 6,104,254m., dep. 121,371,043m. (Dec. 1996); Chair. LUIGI FAUSTI; Vice-Chair. GIANFRANCO GUTTY; 991 brs.

Banca delle Marche SpA: Via Alessandro Ghislieri 6, 60035 Jesi; tel. (731) 5391; telex 560053; fax (731) 539328; f. 1994; cap. 665,960m., res. 324,168m., dep. 9,867,098m. (Dec. 1996); Chair. Dott. ALFREDO CESARINI; Gen. Man. CAMILLO PIAZZA SPESSA; 218 brs.

Banca Monte dei Paschi di Siena SpA: Piazza Salimbeni 3, 53100 Siena; tel. (577) 294111; telex 572346; fax (577) 294313; f. 1472; joint stock company; cap. 2,008,574m., res 4,074,447m., dep. 83,107,458m. (Dec. 1996); Chair. LUIGI SPAVENTA; CEO and Gen. Man. DIVO GRONCHI; 773 brs.

Banca Nazionale dell'Agricoltura SpA: Via Salaria 231, 00199 Rome; tel. (6) 85881; telex 625330; fax (6) 85883396; f. 1921; merged with Banco di Roma 1995; cap. 342,000m., res 646,045m., dep. 32,945,895m. (Dec. 1996); Chair. Dott. PAOLO ACCORINTI; Man. Dir Dott. GUSTAVO GRECO; 275 brs, including brs abroad.

Banca Nazionale del Lavoro SpA: Via Vittorio Veneto 119, 00187 Rome; tel. (6) 47021; telex 621030; fax (6) 47027298; f. 1913; cap. 2,119,492m., res 6,753,029m., dep. 124,420,687m. (Dec. 1996); Chair. MARIO SARCINELLI; Man. D. CROFF; 652 brs incl. 9 overseas brs.

Banca Popolare Commercio e Industria Scarl: POB 10167, Via della Moscova 33, 20121 Milan; tel. (2) 62751; telex 310276; fax (2) 6275640; f. 1888; cap. 202,720m., res 467,998m., dep. 7,470,517m. (Dec. 1996); Chair. GIUSEPPE VIGORELLI; Man. Dir GIUSEPPE GRASSANO; 95 brs.

Banca Popolare dell' Emilia Romagna Scrl, Gruppo Bancario Banca Popolare dell'Emilia Romagna: Via San Carlo 8/20, 41100 Modena; tel. (59) 202111; telex 510031; fax (59) 220537; f. 1867; cap. 62,358m., res 1,204,628m., dep. 15,750,549m. (Dec. 1996); Chair. Avv. PIER LUIGI COLIZZI; Gen. Man. Dott. GUIDO LEONI; 192 brs.

Banca Popolare dell' Etruria e del Lazio: POB 282, Corso Italia, 52100 Arezzo; tel. (575) 3071; telex 574047; fax (575) 307228; f. 1882; cap. 117,615m., res 404,923m., dep. 5,995,604m. (Dec. 1995); Chair. ELIO FARALLI; Gen. Man. ALESSANDRO REDI; 132 brs and agencies.

Banca Popolare di Bergamo-Credito Varesino Scarl: Piazza Vittorio Veneto 8, 24122 Bergamo; tel. (35) 392111; telex 305158; fax (35) 221417; e-mail info@bpb.it; f. 1869; co-operative bank; cap. 415,004m., res 1,376,418m., dep. 26,291,570m. (June 1997); Chair. E. ZANETTI; Gen. Man. G. FRIGERI; 313 brs.

Banca Popolare di Brescia Scarl: Via Leonardo da Vinci 74, 25122 Brescia; tel. (30) 39931; telex 301313; fax (30) 396313; f. 1983; cap. 349,997m., res 185,050m., dep. 9,983,182m. (Dec. 1996); Chair. GIACOMO FRANCESCHETTI; Gen. Man. BRUNO SONZOGNI; 69 brs.

Banca Popolare di Lodi: Via Cavour 40–42, 20075 Lodi; tel. (371) 5951; telex 321367; fax (371) 424173; f. 1864; cap. 225,266m., res 482,892m., dep. 8,195,109m. (Dec. 1996); Chair. GIOVANNI BENEVENTO; Gen. Man. ANGELO MAZZA; 135 brs.

Banca Popolare di Milano Scarl: Piazza F. Meda 4, 20121 Milan; tel. (2) 77001; telex 353356; fax (2) 77002156; f. 1865; cap. 1,121,489m., res 1,060,286m., dep. 29,994,423m. (Dec. 1996); Pres. PAOLO BASSI; Gen. Man. ERNESTO PAOLILLO; 288 brs.

Banca Popolare di Novara Scarl: Via Carlo Negroni 12, 28100 Novara; tel. (321) 662111; telex 200371; fax (321) 662100; f. 1871; co-operative bank; cap. 847,717m., res 876,294m., dep. 32,221,995m. (Dec. 1996); Chair. SIRO LOMBARDINI; Man. Dirs LUIGI CAPUANO, ALBERTO COSTANTINI; 516 brs and agencies.

Banca Popolare di Sondrio Scarl: Piazza Garibaldi 16, 23100 Sondrio; tel. (342) 528111; telex 311174; fax (342) 528204; f. 1871; cap. 137,566m., res 490,695m., dep. 6,950,636m. (Dec. 1996); Chair. and CEO PIERO MELAZZINI; 107 brs.

Banca Popolare di Verona Scarl: Piazza Nogara 2, 37100 Verona; tel. (45) 8675111; telex 480019; fax (45) 8675474; f. 1867; cap. 149,763m., res 2,136,749m., dep. 23,446,735m. (Dec. 1996); Pres. Prof. GIORGIO ZANOTTO; Gen. Man. and CEO ALDO CIVASCHI; 320 brs and agencies.

Banca Popolare Vicentina Scparl: Via Battaglione Framarin 18, 36100 Vicenza; tel. (444) 339111; telex 481194; fax (444) 320149; f. 1866; fmrly Banca Popolare di Vicenza; cap. 124,952m., res 1,033,381m., dep. 5,805,529m. (Dec. 1996); Chair. GIANNI ZONIN; Gen. Man. PIERO SANTELLI; 117 brs and agencies.

Banca Regionale Europea Spa: Via Monte di Pietà 7, 20121 Milan; tel. (2) 721211; telex 310568; fax (2) 865413; cap. 850,000m., res 227,456m., dep. 8,839,690m. (Dec. 1995); Chair. OSCAR CASNICI; CEO PIERO BERTOLOTTO; 220 brs.

Banca di Roma: Via Marco Minghetti 17, 00187 Rome; tel. (6) 54451; telex 616184; fax (6) 54453154; f. 1992 by merger; cap. 1,675,000m., res 8,725,800m., dep. 126,848,900m. (Dec. 1996); Chair. CESARE GERONZI; Vice-Chair. PIETRO CIUCCI; 1,260 local brs, 19 overseas brs.

Banca San Paolo di Brescia SpA: POB 346, Corso Martiri della Libertà 13, 25100 Brescia; tel. (30) 29921; telex 300010; fax (30) 2992734; f. 1888; cap. 135,000m., res 571,400m., dep. 9,430,625m. (Dec. 1996); Chair. Dott. GINO TROMBI; CEO Dott. ALBERTO VALDEMBRI; 145 brs.

Banca Toscana SpA: Via Leone Pancaldo 4, 50127 Florence; tel. (55) 43911; telex 570084; fax (55) 4360061; f. 1904; cap. 294,400m., res 1,229,346m., dep. 22,866,659m. (Dec. 1996); Pres. FABIO MERUSI; Man. Dir GIUSEPPE MAZZINI; 300 brs.

Banco Ambrosiano Veneto SpA: Piazza Paolo Ferrari 10, 20121 Milan; tel. (2) 85941; telex 312087; fax (2) 85947326; f. 1925; cap. 725,779m., res 1,545,445m., dep. 35,680,000m. (Dec. 1996); Chair. CORRADO PASSERA; Man. Dir Dott. CARLO SALVATORI; 650 brs.

Banco di Napoli SpA: Via Toledo 177–178, 80132 Naples; tel. (81) 7911111; telex 720530; fax (81) 5801390; f. 1539; chartered public institution; 60% of ordinary share capital to be sold in 1997; cap. 2,411,836m., res. 295,923m., dep. 56,926,092m. (Dec. 1996); Chair. Prof. CARLO PACE; CEO Prof. FREDERICO PEPE; 757 brs.

Banco di Sardegna SpA: Viale Umberto 36, 07100 Sassari; tel. (79) 226000; telex 790049; fax (79) 226015; f. 1953; public credit institution; cap. 206,611m., res 1,047,398m., dep. 17,640,313m. (Dec. 1996); Chair. Prof. LORENZO IDDA; Gen. Man. FLAVIO BOVO; 183 brs.

Banco di Sicilia SpA: Via Generale Magliocco 1, 90141 Palermo; tel. (91) 6081111; telex 910050; fax (91) 6085051; f. 1860; cap. 619,792m., res 736,981m., dep. 37,977,418m. (Dec. 1996); Chair. GUSTAVO VISENTINI; Gen. Man. and CEO CESARE CALETTI; 391 brs.

CAB SpA: Via Cefalonia 62, 25175 Brescia; tel. (30) 24331; telex 301558; fax (30) 2433802; f. 1883; cap. 133,478m., res 901,600m., dep. 11,407,306m. (Dec. 1995); Chair. ALBERTO FOLONARI; Gen. Man. BRUNO DEGRANDI; 200 brs.

Cariverona Banca SpA (Cassa di Risparmio di Verona, Vicenza, Belluno e Ancona SpA): Via G. Garibaldi 2, 37121 Verona; tel. (45) 8081111; telex 480056; fax (45) 8033679; f. 1825; cap. 1,773,721m., res 1,703,575m., dep. 28,608,930m. (Dec. 1996); Chair. PAOLO BIASI; Gen. Man. GIUSEPPE MAZZARELLO; 382 brs.

Cassa di Risparmio di Firenze SpA: Via Bufalini 4/6, 50122 Florence; tel. (55) 26121; telex 572391; fax (55) 679986; f. 1829; cap. 1,000,000m., res 349,393m., dep. 16,494,049m. (Dec. 1996); Chair. and Pres. AURELIANO BENEDETTI; Gen. Man. PAOLO CAMPAIOLI; 230 brs.

Cassa di Risparmio di Padova e Rovigo SpA: POB 1088, Via Trieste 57/59, 35121 Padua; tel. (49) 8228111; telex 430645; fax (49) 8229750; f. 1822; cap. 534,666m., res 1,155,011m., dep. 15,809,498m. (Dec. 1996); Pres. ORAZIO ROSSI; Gen. Man. PIO BUSSOLOTTO; 197 brs.

Cassa di Risparmio di Parma e Piacenza SpA: Via Università 1, 43100 Parma; tel. (521) 912111; telex 530420; fax (521) 912976; f. 1860; cap. 1,168,033m., res 457,571m., dep. 21,554,613m. (Dec. 1996); Chair. Dott. LUCIANO SILINGARDI; Gen. Man. FABRIZIO AMPOLLINI; 300 brs.

Cassa di Risparmio delle Provincie Lombarde SpA (CARIPLO): Via Monte di Pietà 8, 20121 Milan; tel. (2) 88661; telex 313010; fax (2) 88663250; f. 1823; cap. 3,500,000m., res 6,361,000m., dep. 163,216,000m. (Dec. 1996); Chair. SANDRO MOLINARI; 729 brs and agencies.

Cassa di Risparmio in Bologna SpA: Via Farini 22, 40124 Bologna; tel. (51) 6454111; telex 510282; fax (51) 6454366; f. 1837; cap. 1,196,029m., res 798,267m., dep. 19,145,810m. (Dec. 1996); Chair. GIANGUIDO S. MORSIANI; Gen. Man. LEONE SIBANI; 134 brs.

Credito Bergamasco SpA: Largo Porta Nuova 2, 24122 Bergamo; tel. (35) 393111; telex 300147; fax (35) 393144; f. 1891; cap. 308,634m., res 558,048m., dep. 10,877,854m. (Dec. 1996); Pres. CESARE ZONCA; Gen. Man. GIORGIO BRAMBILLA; 168 brs.

Credito Emiliano SpA: Via Emilia S. Pietro 4, 42100 Reggio-Emilia; tel. (522) 4501; telex 530305; fax (522) 433969; f. 1910; cap. 313,947m., res 365,274m., dep. 8,770,949m. (Dec. 1996); Pres. GIORGIO FERRARI; Man. Dir FRANCO BIZZOCCHI; 202 brs.

Credito Italiano SpA: Piazza Cordusio, 20123 Milan; tel. (2) 88621; telex 310103; fax (2) 88623034; e-mail info@credit.it; f. 1870; cap. 1,439,955m. (Dec. 1997), res 4,285,752m., dep. 86,618,453m. (Dec. 1996); Chair. LUCIO RONDELLI; Dep. Chair. EGIDIO G. BRUNO; CEO ALESSANDRO PROFUMO: 973 brs.

Deutsche Bank SpA: Via Borgogna 8, 20122 Milan; tel. (2) 77951; telex 311350; fax (2) 40242636; f. 1918 as Banca dell'Italia Meridionale; in 1923 name changed to Banca d'America e d'Italia SpA, and to above in 1994; cap. 595,921m., res 1,023,638m., dep. 36,157,581m. (Dec. 1996); Man. Dir GIANNI TESTONI; 261 brs.

Istituto Bancario San Paolo di Torino SpA: Piazza San Carlo 156, 10121 Turin; tel. (11) 5551; telex 212040; fax (11) 5556401; f. 1563; cap. 8,159,929m., res 1,408,224m., dep. 179,564,921m. (Dec. 1996); Chair. Prof. GIANNI ZANDANO; Man. Dir LUIGI MARANZIANA; 1,200 brs.

Mediocredito Centrale SpA: Via Piemonte 51, 00187 Rome; tel. (6) 47911; telex 621699; f. 1952; state-owned; cap. 2,081,942m., res

241,907m., dep. 7,657,398m. (Dec. 1996); Pres. GIANFRANCO IMPERATORI; Man. Dir GIORGIO TELLINI.

ROLO BANCA 1473 SpA: POB 775, Via Zamboni 20, 40126 Bologna; tel. (51) 6408111; telex 510131; fax (51) 6408377; f. 1896 as Piccolo Credito Romagnolo; cap. 334,672m., res 3,025,653m., dep. 50,270,653m. (Dec. 1996); Pres. ARISTIDE CANOSANI; Gen. Man. CESARE FARSETTI; 344 brs.

Sicilcassa SpA: Via Filippo Cordova 76, 90143 Palermo; tel. (91) 6291111; telex 910029; fax (91) 6292550; f. 1861 as Cassa Centrale di Risparmio VE per le Province Siciliane; cap. 496,946m., res 413,549m., dep. 12,370,168m. (Dec. 1995); Pres. ANTONIO CASSELLA; CEO LUCIANO BRIZZI; 242 brs.

FINANCIAL INSTITUTIONS

CENTROBANCA (Banca Centrale di Credito Popolare) SpA: Corso Europa 20, 20122 Milan; tel. (2) 77811; telex 320387; fax (2) 784372; f. 1946; cap. 200,000m., res 572,814m., dep. 14,046,587m. (Dec. 1996); central organization for medium- and long-term operations of Banche Popolari (co-operative banks) throughout Italy; Chair. EMILIO ZANETTI; Gen. Man. GIAN GIACOMO FAVERIO.

CREDIOP SpA: Via XX Setembre 30, 00187 Rome; tel. (6) 47711; telex 611020; fax (6) 4771595; f. 1919; newly-incorporated 1996; cap. 872,500m., res 71m., dep. 29,481,263m. (Dec. 1996); Pres. ANTONIO PEDONE; Man. Dir MAURO CICCHINE.

EFIBANCA—Ente Finanzario Interbancario SpA: Via Po 28/32, 00198 Rome; tel. (6) 85991; telex 621503; f. 1939; cap. 316,113m., res 455,267m., dep. 14,302,007m. (Dec. 1996); Chair. MARIO SARCINELLI; Gen. Man. VALERIO LATTANZI; 8 brs.

INTERBANCA (Banca per Finanziamenti a Medio e Lungo Termine SpA): Corso Venezia 56, 20121 Milan; tel. (2) 77311; telex 320458; fax (2) 784321; f. 1961; cap. 68,467m., res 370,638m., dep. 9,115,155m. (Dec. 1994); Chair. ANTONIO CEOLA; Gen. Man. MARIO GABRIELE.

Istituto Centrale delle Banche di Credito Cooperativo (ICCREA SpA): Via Torino 146, 00184 Rome; tel. (6) 47161; telex 620120; fax (6) 4747155; f. 1963; cap. 320,000m., res 2,800m., dep. 11,035,281m. (Dec. 1996); Pres. GIORGIO CLEMENTI; Gen. Man. ALFREDO NERI; 4 brs.

Istituto di Credito delle Casse di Risparmio Italiane SpA (ICCRI): Via San Basilio 15, 00187 Rome; tel. (6) 47151; telex 626115; fax (6) 47153579; f. 1919; cap. 231,000m., res 920,532m., dep. 15,589,393m. (Dec. 1996); Pres. Prof. ENRICO FILIPPI; Gen. Man. Dott. PAOLO GNES.

Istituto Mobiliare Italiano SpA (IMI): Viale dell'Arte 25, 00144 Rome; tel. (6) 59591; telex 610256; fax (6) 59593888; f. 1931; majority of state holding sold to private investors in February 1994; provides medium- and long-term credit; cap. 3,000,000m., res 3,590,510m., dep. 64,692,466m. (Dec. 1996); Chair. Dott. LUIGI ARCUTI; Dir-Gen. Dott. RAINER MASERA; 8 brs.

Mediobanca—Banca di Credito Finanziario SpA: Via Filodrammatici 10, 20121 Milan; tel. (2) 88291; telex 311093; fax (2) 8829367; f. 1946; deals in all medium- and long-term credit transactions; accepts medium-term time deposits, etc.; cap. 476,000m., res 3,355,908m., dep. 30,221,111m. (June 1997); Chair. FRANCESCO CINGANO; Man. Dir VINCENZO MARANGHI.

BANKERS' ORGANIZATIONS

Associazione Bancaria Italiana: Piazza del Gesù 49, 00186 Rome; tel. (6) 67671; telex 622107; fax (6) 6767457; Via della Posta 3, 20123 Milan; tel. (2) 86450695; telex 324195; fax (2) 878684; f. 1919; Pres. Prof. TANCREDI BIANCHI; Gen. Man. Dott. GIUSEPPE ZADRA; membership (1,032 mems) is comprised of the following institutions: banks authorized to gather savings from the general public and exercise credit business as well as to perform other financial activities; brs and representative offices of foreign banks; asscns of banks or financial intermediaries; financial intermediaries engaging in one or more of the activities subject to mutual recognition under the Second Banking Directive or other financial activities subject to public prudential supervison.

Associazione Italiana fra le Casse di Risparmio Italiane: Viale di Villa Grazioli 23, 00198 Rome; tel. (6) 855621; telex 622033; fax (6) 8540192; f. 1912; Chair. Dott. ROBERTO MAZZOTTA; Gen. Man. Dott. PIER GIULIO COTTINI.

Associazione fra gli Istituti Regionale Di Mediocredito: Piazza della Marina 1, 00196 Rome; tel. (6) 3225150; telex 620311; fax (6) 3225135; Pres. Prof. ANGELO CALOIA; Gen. Man. Dott. ANTONIO DE VITO.

Associazione Italiana per il Factoring: Via Cerva 9, 20122 Milan; tel. (2) 76020127; fax (2) 76020159; Pres. Avv. GIORGIO BONDIOLI; Sec.-Gen. Prof. ALESSANDRO CARRETTA.

Associazione Nazionale Aziende Ordinarie di Credito—ASSBANK: Via Domenichino 5, 20149 Milan; tel. (2) 48010278; telex 334355; fax (2) 48010137; Pres. Dott. Prof. TANCREDI BIANCHI; Dir-Gen. Dott. EDMONDO FONTANA.

Associazione Nazionale fra le Banche Popolari: Via Nazionale 230, 00184 Rome; tel. (6) 4884444; Pres. Dott. ANICETO VITTORIO RANIERI; Dir-Gen. Dott. GIORGIO CARDUCCI.

Associazione Nazionale fra gli Istituti di Credito Agrario (ANICA): Via A. Bertoloni 3, 00197 Rome; tel. (6) 8077506; telex 622129; fax (6) 8077506; f. 1946; Pres. Prof. GIUSEPPE GUERRIERI; Sec.-Gen. Dott. ERNESTO DE MEDIO.

Associazione Sindacale fra le Aziende del Credito—ASSICREDITO: Via G. Paisiello 5, 00198 Rome; tel. (6) 854591; f. 1947; Dir Dott. GIUSEPPE CAPO.

Associazione Italiana delle Società Edenti Digestione Mobiliare ed Immobiliare: Via In Lucina 12, 00186 Rome; tel. (6) 6893203; telex 630274; fax (6) 6893262; Pres. Prof. GUSTAVO VISENTINI; Sec. Gen. Prof. GUIDO CAMMARANO.

Associazione Italiana Leasing—ASSILEA: Piazza di Priscilla 4, 00199 Rome; tel. (6) 86211271; fax (6) 86211214; e-mail assilea@uni.net; internet http://www.uni.net/assilea; Pres. Dott. ANTONIO DATTOLO.

STOCK EXCHANGE

Commissione Nazionale per le Società e la Borsa (CONSOB) (Commission for Companies and the Stock Exchange): Via Isonzo 19, 00198 Rome; tel. (6) 84771; telex 612434; f. 1974; regulatory control over cos quoted on stock exchanges, convertible bonds, unlisted securities, insider trading, all forms of public saving except bank deposits and mutual funds; Chair. TOMMASO PADOA SCHIOPPA; there are 10 stock exchanges, of which the following are the most important:

Genoa: Borsa Valori, Via G. Boccardo 1, Genoa; tel. (10) 590920; f. 1855; Pres. LUCIANO GAMBAROTTA.

Italian Stock Exchange/Italian Derivatives Market: Piazza degli Affari 6, 20123 Milan; tel. (2) 72426202; telex 321430; fax (2) 72004333; Pres. Prof. FRANCESCO CESARINI; Dir-Gen. BENITO BOSCHETTO.

Naples: Borsa Valori, Palazzo Borsa, Piazza Bovio, Naples; tel. (81) 269151; Pres. GIORGIO FOCAS.

Rome: Borsa Valori, Via dei Burro 147, 00186 Rome; tel. (6) 6792701; f. 1821; Pres. ALBERTO BORTI.

Turin: Borsa Valori, Via San Francesco da Paola 28, Turin; tel. (11) 547743; telex 220614; fax (11) 5612193; f. 1850; Pres. Dott. FRANCO CELLINO.

INSURANCE

L'Abeille SpA: Via Leopardi 15, 20123 Milan; tel. (2) 480841; telex 316029; fax (2) 48084331; f. 1956; cap. 8,211m. (Dec. 1990); Chair. and Man. Dir Dott. PIERRE MERCIER.

Alleanza Assicurazioni SpA: Viale Luigi Sturzo 35, 20154 Milan; tel. (2) 62961; telex 331303; fax (2) 653718; e-mail info@alleanzaassicurazioni.it; f. 1898; life insurance; subsidiary of Assicurazioni Generali (q.v.); cap. 367,827m. (Dec. 1997); Chair. Dott. ALFONSO DESIATA; Gen. Mans Dott. ROBERTO PENNISI, Rag. FRANCO VIEZZOLI.

Allianz Pace, Assicurazioni e Riassicurazioni SpA: Piazza Cavour 5, 20121 Milan; tel. (2) 62421; telex 311636; fax (2) 6572684; f. 1919; cap. 15,000m. (Dec. 1990); Chair. Dott. RAFFAELE DURANTE; Man. Dir Dott. LUCIANO DALLA COSTA.

Assicuratrice Edile SpA: Via A. De Togni 2, 20123 Milan; tel. (2) 480411; telex 334697; fax (2) 48041292; f. 1960; cap. 16,000m. (Dec. 1996); Chair. JACQUES BRUNIER; Man. Dir GIAMPIERO SVEVO.

Assicurazioni Generali SpA: Piazza Duca degli Abruzzi 2, 34132 Trieste; tel. (40) 6711; telex 460190; fax (40) 671600; f. 1831; cap. 1,603,250m. (1994); Chair. ANTOINE BERNHEIM.

Le Assicurazioni d'Italia (ASSITALIA) SpA: Corso d'Italia 33, 00198 Rome; tel. (6) 84831; telex 611051; fax (6) 84833142; f. 1923; cap. 150,000m. (Dec. 1990); Pres. Avv. PIER LUIGI CASSIETTI; Gen. Man. Prof. Avv. VINCENZO MUNGARI.

Aurora Assicurazioni SpA: Via R. Montecuccoli 20, 20147 Milan; tel. (2) 41441; telex 312562; fax (2) 48300451; f. 1947; cap. 50,000m. (Dec. 1990); Chair. Avv. EMILIO DUSI; Gen. Man. Dott. GIACOMO NURRA.

Ausonia Assicurazioni SpA: Palazzo Ausonia, Milanofiori, 20089 Rozzano, Milan; tel. (2) 824731; telex 321225; fax (2) 8240641; f. 1907; cap. 296,302m. (Dec. 1990); Chair. Dott. GAETANO LAZZATI; Man. Dir Dott. GIORGIO LANZ.

Compagnia Assicuratrice Unipol SpA: Via Stalingrado 45, 40128 Bologna; tel. (51) 6097111; telex 510674; fax (51) 375349; f. 1961; cap. 257,622m. (Dec. 1997); Chair. GIOVANNI CONSORTE; Vice-Chair. IVANO SACCHETTI.

Compagnia Latina di Assicurazioni SpA: Strada 6, Palazzo A, 20090 Assago, (M1), Milanofiori; tel. (2) 824731; telex 310083; fax (2) 8240644; f. 1958; cap. 58,367m. (Dec. 1990); Chair. Prof. LUIGI SPAVENTA; Man. Dir Dott. GIORGIO LANZ.

Compagnie Riunite di Assicurazione (CRA): Via Consolata 3, 10122 Turin; tel. (11) 57741; telex 212597; fax (11) 4369161; f. 1935; cap. 40,000m. (Dec. 1990); Chair. CHARLES FRANÇOIS WALCKENAER; Man. Dir Dott. MARIO PASCUCCI.

L'Edera SpA: Piazzale de Matthaeis 41, 03100 Frosinone; tel. (775) 872579; telex 626152; fax (775) 873052; f. 1960; cap. 1,000m. (Dec. 1990); Pres. Avv. GIUSEPPE TODINI; Man. Dir Dott. GIUSEPPE ZEPPIERI.

FATA (Fondo Assicurativo Tra Agricoltori) SpA: Via Urbana 169/A, 00184 Rome; tel. (6) 47651; telex 620838; fax (6) 4871187; f. 1927; cap. 20,000m. (Dec. 1990); Chair. GIANCARLO BUSCARINI; Man. Dir FRANCO RIZZI.

LA FENICE RI. SpA—Compagnia di Riassicurazioni: Piazza de Ferrari 1, 16121 Genoa; tel. (10) 55291; telex 271297; fax (10) 5529450; cap. 50,000m. (Dec. 1992); Chair. Dott. FRANCO VIDA.

La Fiduciaria: Via A. Finelli 8, 40126 Bologna; tel. (51) 6307011; telex 511491; fax (51) 243030; f. 1970; cap. 11,508m. (June 1992); Chair. JEAN PAUL GALBRUN; Man. Dir Dott. Ing. SERGIO BEDINI.

Firs Italiana di Assicurazioni SpA: Via Adelmo Niccolai 24, 00155 Rome; tel. (6) 406911; telex 620185; fax (6) 4061459; f. 1965; cap. 36,120m. (Dec. 1990); Chair. Avv. CARLO BALESTRA; Man. Dir Dott. JEAN FESTEAU.

La Fondiaria Assicurazioni SpA: Piazza della Libertà 6, 50129 Florence; tel. (55) 47941; telex 570430; fax (55) 476026; f. 1879; cap. 390,160m. (1996); Pres. ALBERTO PECCI; Gen. Man. AMATO LUIGI MOLINARI.

Intercontinentale Assicurazioni SpA: Via di Priscilla 101, 00199 Rome; tel. (6) 83001; telex 611155; fax (6) 8319903; f. 1961; cap. 100,000m. (Dec. 1990); Chair. WALTER GEISER; Man. Dir Dott. ENNIO BAIOCCHI.

Istituto Nazionale delle Assicurazioni SpA (INA): Via Sallustiana 51, 00187 Rome; tel. (6) 47221; telex 610336; fax (6) 47224559; f. 1912; Chair. Dott. SERGIO SIGLIENTI; Man. Dirs LINO BENASSI, Dott. GIANCARLO GIANNINI, Dott. ROBERTO PONTREMOLI.

ITAS, Istituto Trentino-Alto Adige per Assicurazioni: Via Mantova 67, 38100 Trent; tel. (461) 982112; telex 400884; fax (461) 980297; f. 1821; cap. 60,000m. (Dec. 1996); Chair. Dott. EDO BENEDETTI; Gen. Man. Dott. ETTORE LOMBARDO.

Lavoro e Sicurtà SpA: Piazza Erculea 13–15, 20122 Milan; tel. (2) 85751; fax (2) 72021420; f. 1963; cap. 20,000m. (Dec. 1990); Chair. ENZO ZENI; Man. Dir ENRICO ORLANDO.

Lloyd Adriatico SpA: Largo Ugo Irneri 1, 34143 Trieste; tel. (40) 77811; telex 460350; fax (40) 7781311; f. 1936; cap. 60,000m. (Dec. 1990); Chair. and Man. Dir Dott. SANDRO SALVATI; Vice-Chair. Dott. ROBERTO GAVAZZI.

Lloyd Italico Assicurazioni SpA: Via Fieschi 9, 16121 Genoa; tel. (10) 53801; telex 270555; fax (10) 592856; f. 1983; cap. 61,500m. (Dec. 1990); Pres. KENNETH DESMOND SINFIELD; Man. Dir Dott. BRUNO MONDINI.

MAA Assicurazioni Auto e Rischi Diversi SpA: Via Tonale 26, 20125 Milan; tel. (2) 69791; telex 334397; fax (2) 6071965; f. 1952; cap. 66,500m. (Dec. 1990); Pres. Dott. Ing. ENRICO BONZANO.

Minerva Assicurazioni SpA: Via Quadrio 17, 20154 Milan; tel. (2) 290321; telex 321284; fax (2) 29032200; f. 1943; cap. 15,600m. (April 1991); Chair. PETER ECKERT; Man. Dir ADOLFO BERTANI.

La Nationale Assicurazioni SpA: Piazza del Porto di Ripetta 1, 00186 Rome; tel. (6) 682801; telex 611032; fax (6) 6834089; f. 1962; cap. 30,000m. (1992); Pres. JEAN PAUL GALBRUN; Vice-Pres. PIER UGO ANDREINI.

Norditalia Assicurazioni SpA: Viale Certosa 222, 20156 Milan; tel. (2) 30761; telex 331345; fax (2) 3086125; f. 1963; cap. 165,300m. (Dec. 1997); Pres. Ing. OLIVIERO TAROLLI; Man. Dir Dott. FERDINANDO MENCONI.

La Previdente Assicurazioni SpA: Via Copernico 38, 20125 Milan; tel. (2) 69561; telex 330488; fax (2) 6889995; f. 1917; cap. 25,000m. (Dec. 1990); Chair. ALFONSO SCARPA; Man. Dir Dott. CARLO GALEAZZI.

RAS-Riunione Adriatica di Sicurtà: Corso Italia 23, 20122 Milan; tel. (2) 72161; telex 320065; f. 1838; cap. 217,000m., res 1,932,599m. (Dec. 1991); Chair. and Man. Dir Dott. UMBERTO ZANNI.

SAI—Società Assicuratrice Industriale SpA: Corso Galileo Galilei 12, 10126 Turin; tel. (11) 65621; telex 212080; fax (11) 6562685; f. 1921; cap. 165,000m. (Dec. 1990); Chair. Dott. Ing. SALVATORE LIGRESTI; Gen. Man. Dott. GIORGIO BRINATTI.

SARA Assicurazioni SpA: Via Po 20, 00198 Rome; tel. (6) 84751; telex 614526; fax (6) 8475223; f. 1924; cap. 60,750m. (June 1994); Chair. ROSARIO ALESSI; Gen. Man. Dott. MARCO ROCCA.

Savoia: Via S. Vigilio 1, 20142 Milan; tel. (2) 84421; telex 311270; fax (2) 8442388; cap. 24,000m. (Dec. 1990); Chair. Dott. ERWIN ZIMMERMANN; Gen. Man. Dott. GIORGIO OPPEZZI.

Società Cattolica di Assicurazione: Lungadige Cangrande 16, 37126 Verona; tel. (45) 8391111; telex 480482; fax (45) 8391112; f. 1896; cap. 78,150m. (June 1994); Chair. Ing. GIULIO BISOFFI; Gen. Man. Dott. EZIO PAOLO REGGIA.

Società Italiana Cauzioni SpA (SIC): Via Crescenzio 12, 00193 Rome; tel. (6) 688121; telex 611050; fax (6) 6874418; f. 1948; cap. 30,000m. (June 1993); Chair. ERNESTO JUTZI; Man. Dir GIANLUIGI BOCCIA.

Società Reale Mutua di Assicurazioni: Via Corte d'Appello 11, 10122 Turin; tel. (11) 431111; telex 215105; fax (11) 4367290; f. 1828; total assets 5,303,773m. (1994); Chair. LEONE FONTANA; Gen. Man. ITI MIHALICH.

Toro Assicurazioni SpA: Via Arcivescovado 16, 10121 Turin; tel. (11) 57331; telex 221567; fax (11) 543587; f. 1833; cap. 122,700m. (Dec. 1990); Chair. Dott. UMBERTO AGNELLI; Man. Dir Rag. FRANCESCO TORRI.

Unione Italiana di Riassicurazione SpA: Via dei Giuochi Istmici 40, 00194 Rome; tel. (6) 323931; telex 610348; fax (6) 36303398; f. 1922; cap. 100,000m. (Dec. 1990); Chair. Avv. LORENZO PALLESI.

Unione Subalpina di Assicurazioni SpA: Via Alfieri 22, 10121 Turin; tel. (11) 55121; telex 221201; fax (11) 549756; f. 1928; cap. 9,187.5m. (Dec. 1990); Chair. Avv. VITTORIO BADINI CONFALONIERI; Man. Dir Dott. ROBERTO GAVAZZI.

Universo Assicurazioni SpA: Via del Pilastro 52, 40127 Bologna; tel. (51) 6371111; telex 511170; fax (51) 6371401; f. 1972; cap. 62,500m. (Dec. 1990); Chair. Dott. GIUSEPPE SOLINAS; Gen. Man. Dott. GIORGIO DI GIANSANTE.

Vittoria Assicurazioni SpA: Via Caldera 21, 20153 Milan; tel. (2) 77901; telex 331030; fax (2) 780329; f. 1921; cap. 30,000m. (Dec. 1990); Chair. Prof. LUIGI GUATRI; Man. Dir Dott. GIUSEPPE DE' CHIARA.

INSURANCE ASSOCIATION

Associazione Nazionale fra le Imprese Assicuratrici (ANIA): Piazza S. Babila 1, 20122 Milan; tel. (2) 77641; telex 333288; fax (2) 780870; f. 1944; Chair. Dott. ENRICO TONELLI; 216 mems.

Trade and Industry

GOVERNMENT AGENCY

Istituto Nazionale per il Commercio Estero (ICE) (National Institute for Foreign Trade): Via Liszt 21, 00144 Rome; tel. (6) 59921; fax (6) 59926899; e-mail ice@ice.it; f. 1919; govt agency for the promotion of foreign trade; Chair. and CEO Prof. FABRIZIO ONIDA.

CHAMBERS OF COMMERCE

Unione Italiana delle Camere di Commercio, Industria, Artigianato e Agricoltura (Italian Union of Chambers of Commerce, Industry, Crafts and Agriculture): Piazza Sallustio 21, 00187 Rome; tel. (6) 47041; telex 622327; f. 1954 to promote the development of chambers of commerce, industry, trade and agriculture; Pres. DANILO LONGHI; Sec.-Gen. Dott. GIUSEPPE CERRONI.

INDUSTRIAL AND TRADE ASSOCIATIONS

Confederazione Generale dell'Industria Italiana—CONFINDUSTRIA (General Confederation of Italian Industry): Viale dell'Astronomia 30, EUR, 00144 Rome; tel. (6) 59031; telex 611393; fax (6) 5903684; f. 1919, re-established 1944; mems: 106 territorial asscns and 108 branch asscns, totalling 109,000 firms and 4.2m. employees; office in Brussels; Pres. GIORGIO FOSSA; Dir-Gen. Dott. INNOCENZO CIPOLLETTA.

Principal Affiliated Organizations

Associazione degli Industriali della Birra e del Malto (Brewers): Viale di Val Fiorita 90, 00144 Rome; tel. (6) 54393210; fax (6) 5912910; Pres. Dott. RUDI PERONI; Dir Dott. DANIELE ROSSI.

Associazione Industrie Aerospaziali (AIA) (Aerospace Industries Asscn): Via Nazionale 200, 00184 Rome; tel. (6) 4880247; telex 622250; fax (6) 4827476; f. 1947; Pres. Ing. FAUSTO CERETI.

Associazione Industrie Siderurgiche Italiane—ASSIDER (Iron and Steel Industries): Via XX Settembre 1, 00187 Rome; tel. (6) 463867; f. 1946; Pres. Ing. ADAMO ADAMI; Dir-Gen. Dott. GIANCARLO LONGHI; 140 mems.

Associazione Italiana Industriali Abbigliamento e Maglieria (Clothing and Knitwear Manufacturers): Viale Sarca 223, 20126 Milan; tel. (2) 66103391; telex 333594; fax (2) 66103670; e-mail info@modaindustria.it; internet http://www.modaindustria.it; f. 1945; produces weekly, fortnightly and annual periodicals; Pres. VITTORIO GIULINI.

Associazione Italiana Industrie Prodotti Alimentari (AIIPA) (Food Manufacturers): Corso di Porta Nuova 34, 20121 Milan; tel. (2) 654184; fax (2) 654822; f. 1946; Pres. EMILIO LAVAZZA; Dir Dott. GIOVANNI FRANCO CRIPPA; 300 mems.

Associazione Italiana Tecnico Economica del Cemento (AITEC) (Cement): Via di S. Teresa 23, 00198 Rome; tel. (6) 8554714; fax (6) 8416176; Viale Milanofiori, Strada 1, Pal. F2, 20090 Milan; f. 1959; Pres. Dott. Ing. SANDRO BUZZI.

Associazione Mineraria Italiana (Mining): Via delle Tre Madonne 20, 00197 Rome; tel. (6) 8073045; fax (6) 8073385; f. 1144; Pres. Ing. GUGLIELMO MOSCATO; Dir-Gen. Dott. FRANCESCO SAVERIO GUIDI; 150 mems.

Associazione Nazionale Calzaturifici Italiani (ANCI) (Footwear Manufacturers): Via Dogana 1, 20123 Milan; tel. (2) 809721; telex 320018; fax (2) 72020112; f. 1945; Pres. NATALINO PANCALDI; Dir LEONARDO SOANA.

Associazione Nazionale Costruttori Edili (ANCE) (Builders): Via Guattani 16, 00161 Rome; tel. (6) 84881; fax (6) 44232832; e-mail info@ance.it; f. 1946; Pres. VICO VALASSI; Man. Dir CARLO FERRONI; mems: 19,000 firms in 101 provincial and 20 regional asscns.

Associazione Nazionale delle Fonderie—ASSOFOND (Foundries): Via Copernico 54, 20090 Trezzano Sul Naviglio; tel. (2) 48400967; telex 326344; fax (2) 48401282; f. 1948; Pres. EUGENIO COLOMBO.

Associazione Nazionale dell'Industria Farmaceutica—FARMINDUSTRIA (Pharmaceutical Industry): Piazza di Pietra 34, 00186 Rome; tel. (6) 675801; telex 614281; fax (6) 6786494; f. 1978; Pres. Dott. FEDERICO NAZZARI; Dir Dott. IVAN CAVICCHI; 208 mem. firms.

Associazione Nazionale fra Industrie Automobilistiche (ANFIA) (Motor Vehicle Industries): Corso Galileo Ferraris 61, 10128 Turin; tel. (11) 5546511; fax (11) 545986; f. 1912; Pres. Ing. PIERO FUSARO; Dir-Gen. Dott. EMILIO DI CAMILLO; 229 mems.

Associazione Nazionale Industrie Elettrotecniche ed Elettroniche (ANIE) (Electrotechnic and Electronic Industries): Via Algardi 2, 20148 Milan; tel. (2) 32641; telex 321616; fax (2) 3264212; Pres. RAFFAELE PALIERI; Sec.-Gen. CLAUDIO GATTI.

Associazione Nazionale Italiana Industrie Grafiche, Cartotecniche e Trasformatrici (Printing, Paper-Making and Processing Industries): Piazza Conciliazione 1, 20123 Milan; tel. (2) 4981051; fax (2) 4816947; f. 1946; Pres. Rag. ALBERTO GAJANI; Gen. Man. Dott. GIANCARLO LONGHI; 1,200 mems.

Federazione delle Associazioni Nazionali dell'Industria Meccanica Varia ed Affine (ANIMA) (Federation of Italian Mechanical and Engineering Industry Associations): Via L. Battistotti Sassi 11/B, 20133 Milan; tel. (2) 73971; telex 310392; fax (2) 7397316; f. 1945; Pres. LUIGI CAZZANIGA; Sec.-Gen. Dott. Ing. ENRICO MALCOVATI; 1,500 mems.

Federazione Italiana delle Industrie delle Acque Minerali, delle Terme e delle Bevande Analcooliche (Mineral Water and Non-Alcoholic Beverage Industries): Via Sicilia 186, 00187 Rome; tel. (6) 4557251; telex 626063; f. 1919; Pres. Dott. CARLO VIOLATI; Dir Dott. CARMELO CALLIPO.

Federazione Italiana Industriali Produttori Esportatori ed Importatori di Vini, Acquaviti, Liquori, Sciroppi, Aceti ed Affini—FEDERVINI (Producers, Importers and Exporters of Wines, Brandies, Liqueurs, Syrups, Vinegars and Allied Products): Via Mentana 2B, 00185 Rome; tel. (6) 4941630; telex 626436; fax (6) 4941566; f. 1921; Pres. LUIGI ROSSI DI MONTELERA; Dir-Gen. FEDERICO CASTELLUCCI.

Federazione Nazionale dell'Industria Chimica—FEDERCHIMICA (Chemical Industry): Via Accademia 33, 20131 Milan; tel. (2) 268101; fax (2) 26810310; Viale Pasteur 10, 00144 Rome; tel. (6) 5920873; fax (6) 5920836; f. 1945; Pres. Dott. BENITO BENEDINI; Dir-Gen. Dott. GUIDO VENTURINI.

Unione Industriali Pastai Italiani—UNIPI (Pasta Manufacturers): Via Po 102, 00198 Rome; tel. (6) 8543291; fax (6) 8415132; e-mail unipi@foodarea.it; Pres. Dott. GIUSEPPE MENCONI; Dir RAFFAELLO RAGAGLINI.

Unione Nazionale Cantieri e Industrie Nautiche ed Affini (UCINA) (Shipyard and Nautical Industries): Piazzale Kennedy 1, 16129 Genoa; tel. (10) 3751111; fax (10) 5531104; Pres. MARIO GIUSFREDI; Sec.-Gen. ANDREA GASPARRI.

Unione Petrolifera (Petroleum Industries): Via Giorgione 129, 00147 Rome; tel. (6) 59602939; telex 626568; fax (6) 59602924; f. 1948; Pres. Dott. GIAN MARCO MORATTI; Dir-Gen. Ing. BRUNO DATTILO; 40 mems.

Others

Associazione Nazionale Comuni Italiani (ANCI): Via dei Prefetti 46, 00186 Rome; tel. (6) 680091; telex 621313; fax (6) 6873547; Pres. Avv. ENZO BIANCO; Sec.-Gen. Dott. FABIO MELILLI.

Associazione Nazionale fra i Concessionari del Servizio di Riscossione dei Tributi (ASCOTRIBUTI) (Services relating to Collection of Payments): Via Parigi 11, 00185 Rome; tel. (6) 485764; fax (6) 4828184; Pres. Prof. AUGUSTO FANTOZZI; Dir-Gen. Dott. GERARDO CHIRO.

Associazione Sindacale Intersind: Piazza della Repubblica 59, 00185 Rome; tel. (6) 476791; f. 1960; represents manufacturing and service cos; Pres. Dott. AGOSTINO PACI; Dir-Gen. Dott. PIETRO VARALDO.

Associazione Sindacale per le Aziende Petrochimiche e Collegate a Partecipazione Statale (State-controlled Petrochemical Cos): Via Due Macelli 66, 00187 Rome; tel. (6) 67341; telex 310246; fax (6) 6734242; f. 1960; draws up labour and union contracts and represents the cos in legal matters; Pres. Avv. GUIDO FANTONI; Vice-Pres. and Dir-Gen. Dott. MODESTINO FUSCO.

Associazione fra le Società Italiane per Azioni—ASSONIME (Limited Cos): Piazza Venezia 11, 00187 Rome; tel. (6) 6784413; telex 613381; fax (6) 6790487; f. 1911; Pres. Dott. UMBERTO ZANNI; Dir-Gen. Dott. ALDO CARDARELLI.

Confederazione Generale della Agricoltura Italiana (General Agricultural): Corso Vittorio Emanuele 101, 00186 Rome; tel. (6) 68521; telex 612533; fax (6) 6878686; e-mail immco@mail.confagricoltura.it; f. 1945; Pres. Dott. AUGUSTO BOCCHINI; Dir-Gen. ARCANGELO MAFRICI.

Confederazione Generale Italiana del Commercio, del Turismo e dei Servizi—CONFCOMMERCIO (Commerce and Tourism): Piazza G.G. Belli 2, 00153 Rome; tel. (6) 58661; telex 614217; fax (6) 5809425; f. 1946; Pres. Dott. FRANCESCO COLUCCI; Sec.-Gen. Dott. LUIGI TRIGONA; 125 national and 97 territorial asscns affiliated.

Confederazione Italiana della Piccola e Media Industria—CONFAPI (Small and Medium Industry): Via della Colonna Antonina 52, 00186 Rome; tel. (6) 6991530; fax (6) 6791488; f. 1947; Pres. LUCIANO BOLZONI; Dir-Gen. Dott. SANDRO NACCARELLI; 55,000 mems.

Confederazione Italiana della Proprietà Edilizia—CONFEDILIZIA (Property and Building): Via Borgognona 47, 00187 Rome; tel. (6) 6793489; fax (6) 6793447; Pres. Avv. CORRADO SFORZA FOGLIANI; Sec.-Gen. Dott. MARCO BERTONCINI.

Delegazione Sindacale Industriale Autonoma della Valle d'Aosta (Autonomous Industrial Delegation of the Valle d'Aosta): Via G. Elter 6, 11100 Aosta; Pres. Dott. ETTORE FORTUNA; Sec. Dott. ROBERTO ANSALDO.

Federazione Associazioni Industriali (Industrial Asscns): Via Petitti 16, 20149 Milan; tel. (2) 326721; fax (2) 33003819; Pres. Dott. DINO FENZI; Dir-Gen. Dott. UMBERTO MALTAGLIATI.

Federazione delle Associazioni Italiane Alberghi e Turismo—FEDERALBERGHI (Hotels and Tourism): Via Toscana 1, 00187 Rome; tel. (6) 42741151; fax (6) 42871197; f. 1950; Pres. AMATO RAMONDETTI; Gen. Man. ALESSANDRO CIANELLA; 30,000 mems.

Federazione Italiana della Pubblicità (FIP) (Advertisers): Milan; tel. (2) 865262; Pres. GIANFRANCO MAI; Sec.-Gen. MARIO CORNELIO.

Unione Nazionale Aziende Autoproduttrici e Consumatrici di Energia Elettrica—UNAPACE (Concerns producing and consuming their own Electrical Power): Via Paraguay 2, 00198 Rome; tel. (6) 8554602; fax (6) 8417749; f. 1946; Pres. Prof. GIUSEPPE GATTI; Dir-Gen. FRANCESCO DE LUCA.

UTILITIES

Electricity

Ente Nazionale Idrocarburi (ENI): Piazzale Enrico Mattei 1, 00144 Rome; tel. (6) 59001; telex 610082; state-owned energy corpn with interests including energy (AGIP group), chemicals (Enimont), mining and metallurgy (SAMIN), engineering and financial services; transferred 29% of assets to private ownership by 1996; Pres. Ing. LUIGI MEANTI; Man. Dir Dott. FRANCO BERNABÈ.

Ente Nazionale per l'Energia Elettrica (ENEL): Via Giovanni Battista Martini 3, 00198 Rome; tel. (6) 85091; telex 610518; fax (6) 85092162; f. 1962 to generate and distribute electrical power throughout various areas of the country and to work in conjunction with the Ministry of Industry; scheduled for privatization in 1998; Chair. CHICO TESTA; CEO FRANCO TATO.

Gas

Snam: Rome; subsidiary of ENI; primary supplier of natural gas in Italy.

TRADE UNIONS

There are three main federations of Italian trade unions, CGIL, CISL and UIL, all of which have close ties with political parties. The CGIL was formerly dominated by the Partito Comunista Italiano (Italian Communist Party, now the Partito Democratico della Sinistra—Democratic Party of the Left), the CISL has links with the Partito Popolare Italiano (Italian Popular Party, formerly Partito della Democrazia Cristiana (Christian Democrat Party) and the UIL is associated with the socialists.

National Federations

Confederazione Autonomi Sindacati Artigiani (CASA): V. Flaminio Ponzio 2, 00153 Rome; tel. (6) 5758081; f. 1958; federation of artisans' unions and regional and provincial asscns; Pres. GIUSEPPE GUARINO; Sec.-Gen. GIACOMO BASSO.

Confederazione Generale Italiana dell' Artigianato—CONFARTIGIANATO (Artisans): Via di S. Giovanni in Laterano 152, 00184 Rome; tel. (6) 703741; telex 616261; fax (6) 70452188; f. 1945; independent; 170 mem. unions; 600,000 associate enterprises; Pres. IVANO SPALANZANI.

Confederazione Generale Italiana del Lavoro (CGIL) (General Union of Italian Workers): Corso d'Italia 25, 00198 Rome; tel. (6) 84761; telex 623083; f. 1944; federation of 17 unions; Gen. Sec. SERGIO COFFERATI; 5,247,201 mems.

Confederazione Italiana Dirigenti di Azienda (CIDA): Via Nazionale 75, 00184 Rome; tel. (6) 4818551; federation of six managers' unions; Pres. Dott. FAUSTO D'ELIA; Sec.-Gen. RAFFAELE CIABATTINI.

Confederazione Italiana dei Professionisti e Artisti (CIPA) (Artists and Professional People): Via S. Nicola da Tolentino 21, 00187 Rome; tel. (6) 461849; federation of 19 unions; Pres. Rag. SERGIO SPLENDORI.

Confederazione Italiana dei Sindacati Autonomi Lavoratori (CISAL): Viale Giulio Cesare 21, 00192 Rome; tel. (6) 3207941; fax (6) 3212521; f. 1957; no international affiliations; federation of 72 unions; Gen. Sec. GAETANO CERIOLI; 1,500,000 mems.

Confederazione Italiana Sindacati Lavoratori (CISL): Via Po 21, 00198 Rome; tel. (6) 84731; telex 614045; fax (6) 8413782; f. 1950; affiliated to the International Confederation of Free Trade Unions and the European Trade Union Confederation; federation of 17 unions; Sec.-Gen. SERGIO D'ANTONI; 3,800,000 mems.

Confederazione Italiana Sindacati Nazionali Lavoratori—CISNAL: Via P. Amedeo 42, 00185 Rome; tel. (6) 4824202; fax (6) 4882266; f. 1950; upholds traditions of national syndicalism; federation of 64 unions, 77 provincial unions; Gen. Sec. MAURO NOBILIA; 2,137,979 mems.

Confederazione Nazionale dell' Artigianato e delle Piccole Imprese (CNA): Via G. A. Guattani 13, 00161 Rome; tel. (6) 441881; fax (6) 44249518; provincial asscns; Pres. FILIPPO MINOTTI; Gen. Sec. Dott. GIAN CARLO SANGALLI.

Federazione fra le Associazioni e i Sindacati Nazionali dei Quadri Direttivi dell'amministrazione dello Stato—DIRSTAT: Via Ezio 12, 00192 Rome; tel. (6) 3211535; fax (6) 3212690; f. 1948; federation of 33 unions and asscns of civil service executives and officers; Sec.-Gen. EDUARDO MAZZONE; Treas. Dott. V. DONATO.

Unione Italiana del Lavoro (UIL): Via Lucullo 6, 00187 Rome; tel. (6) 47531; fax (6) 4753208; f. 1950; Socialist, Social Democrat and Republican; affiliated to the International Confederation of Free Trade Unions and European Trade Union Confederation; 35 national trade union federations and 95 provincial union councils; Gen. Sec. PIETRO LARIZZA; 1,709,502 mems.

Principal Unions

Banking and Insurance

Federazione Autonoma Bancari Italiana (FABI) (Bank, Tax and Finance Workers): Via Tevere 46, 00198 Rome; tel. (6) 8415751; fax (6) 8559220; f. 1948; independent; Sec.-Gen. GIANFRANCO STEFFANI; 69,000 mems.

Federazione Autonoma Lavoratori Casse di Risparmio Italiane (FALCRI) (Savings Banks Workers): Via Mercato 5, Milan; tel. (2) 86460536; Via Carducci 4, Rome; Sec.-Gen. DAVIDE CATTANEO.

Federazione Italiana Bancari e Assicuratori (FIBA): Via Modena 5, 00184 Rome; tel. (6) 4741245; fax (6) 4746136; affiliated to the CISL; Gen. Sec. SERGIO AMMANNATI; 58,980 mems.

Federazione Italiana Sindacale Lavoratori Assicurazioni Credito (Employees of Credit Institutions): Via Vicenza 5A, 00184 Rome; tel. (6) 4958261; affiliated to the CGIL; Sec. NICOLETTA ROCCHI; 60,000 mems.

Federazione Nazionale Assicuratori—FNA (Insurance Workers): Via Vincenzo Monti 25, Milan; Via Val Montebello 104, Rome; independent; Pres. LUIGI FERAZZI; Sec.-Gen. EZIO MARTONE.

Unione Italiana Lavoratori Assicurazioni—UILAS (Assurance Co Workers): Via Piemonte 39A, Rome; affiliated to the UIL; National Sec. GUGLIELMO BRONZI; 13,000 mems.

Building and Building Materials

Federazione Autonoma Italiana Lavoratori Cemento, Legno, Edilizia ed Affini (FAILCLEA) (Workers in Cement, Wood, Construction and Related Industries): Milan; affiliated to the CISAL; Sec. ENZO BOZZI.

Federazione Lavoratori delle Costruzioni (FLC): includes the following three organizations:

Federazione Italiana Lavoratori delle Costruzioni a Affini (FILCA) (Building Industries' Workers): Via dei Mille 23, Rome; tel. (6) 497801; f. 1955; affiliated to the CISL; Sec.-Gen. CARLO MITRA; 194,493 mems.

Federazione Nazionale Lavoratori Edili Affini e del Legno (FeNEAL) (Builders and Woodworkers): Via dei Mille 23, Rome; affiliated to the UIL and the FLC; Sec.-Gen. GIANCARLO SERAFINI; 135,000 mems.

Federazione Italiana Lavoratori del Legno, Edili ed Affini (FILLEA) (Wood-workers, Construction Workers and Allied Trades): Via dei Mille 23, 00184 Rome; tel. (6) 497801; affiliated to the CGIL; Sec. ANNIO BRESCHI; 434,154 mems.

Chemical, Mining and Allied Industries

Federazione Unitaria Lavoratori Chimici (FULC) (Chemical and Allied Workers): Via Bolzano 16, Rome; tel. (6) 855651; fax (6) 8412206; affiliated to the CGIL, CISL and UIL; Secs.-Gen. FRANCO CHIRIACO, ARNALDO MARIANI, DOMENICO VIOLA; 450,000 mems.

Unione Italiana Lavoratori Miniere e Cave (Mine Workers): Rome; independent; National Sec. BACCI LUCIANO; 16,000 mems.

Clothing and Textiles

Federazione Italiana Lavoratori Tessili Abbigliamento, Calzaturieri (FILTEA) (Textile and Clothing Workers and Shoe Manufacturers): Via Leopoldo Serra 31, 00153 Rome; tel. (6) 5811380; fax (6) 5803182; f. 1966; affiliated to the CGIL; Gen. Sec. AGOSTINO MEGALE; 150,000 mems.

Federazione Italiana dei Lavoratori Tessili e Abbigliamento (FILTA-CISL): Via Goito 39, 00185 Rome; tel. (6) 4270041; fax (6) 492544; affiliated to the CISL; Gen. Sec. AUGUSTA RESTELLI; 125,084 mems.

Engineering and Metallurgy

Confederazione Sindacale Italiana Libere Professioni—CONSILP (Liberal Professions): Via Leopoldo Traversi 40, 00154 Rome; Sec.-Gen. Dott. UBALDO PROCACCINI.

Federazione Architetti—FEDERARCHITETTI (Architects): Piazza Sallustio 24, 00187 Rome; Pres. Dott. Arch. GIANCARLO CAMPIOLI; Sec.-Gen. Dott. Arch. NICOLA D'ERRICO.

Federazione Impiegati Operai Metallurgici (FIOM—CGIL) (Metalworkers): Corso Trieste 36, 00198 Rome; tel. (6) 852621; fax (6) 85303079; e-mail fiom@cgil.it; internet http://www.cgil.it/fiom; f. 1902; affiliated to the CGIL; Sec. CLAUDIO SABATTINI; 400,000 mems.

Federazione Italiana Metalmeccanici (FIM) (Metal Mechanic Workers): Corso Trieste 36, 00198 Rome; tel. (6) 84711; fax (6) 8471305; affiliated to the CISL; Sec. Gen. GIANNI ITALIA; 277,789 mems.

Sindacato Nazionale Ingegneri Liberi Professionisti Italiana (SNILPI) (Liberal Professionals-Engineers): Via Salaria 292, 00199 Rome; Pres. Dott. Ing. LUIGI LUCHERINI; Sec.-Gen. Dott. Ing. GIUSEPPE MILONE.

Unione Italiana Lavoratori Metallurgici (UILM) (Metalworkers): Corso Trieste 36, 00198 Rome; tel. (6) 85262214; fax (6) 85262203; f. 1950; affiliated to the UIL; Sec.-Gen. LUIGI ANGELETTI; 139,000 mems.

Food and Agriculture

Confederazione Generale dell' Agricoltura Italiana—CONFAGRICOLTURA (Farmers): Corso Vittorio Emanuele 101, 00186 Rome; tel. (6) 68521; telex 612533; fax (6) 6861726; Pres. Dott. AUGUSTO BOCCHINI.

Confederazione Italiana Coltivatori (Farmers): Via Mariano Fortuny 20, 00196 Rome; tel. (6) 3227008; fax (6) 3208364; independent; Pres. GIUSEPPE AVOLIO; Vice-Pres. MASSIMO BELLOTTI.

Confederazione Nazionale Coltivatori Diretti—CONACOLTIVATORI (Small-holders): Via XXIV Maggio 43, 00187 Rome; tel. (6) 46821; telex 6751055; independent; Pres. Sen. ARCANGELO LOBIANCO; Sec. Dott. PIETRO GNISCI.

Federazione Italiana Salariati Braccianti Agricoli e Maestranze Specializzate (FISBA) (Permanent Unskilled and Skilled Agricultural Workers): Via Tevere 20, 00198 Rome; tel. (6) 8415455; f. 1950; Sec. ALBINO GORINI; 347,265 mems.

Federazione Lavoratori dell' Agroindustria (Workers in the Agricultural Industry): Via Leopoldo Serra 31, 00153 Rome; tel. (6) 585611; fax (6) 5880585; f. 1988; affiliated to the CGIL; Sec.-Gen. GIANFRANCO BENZI; 438,000 mems.

Federazione Nazionale Braccianti, Salariati, Tecnici,—FEDERBRACCIANTI (Agricultural Workers): Rome; tel. (6) 461760; affiliated to the CGIL; Sec. ANDREA GIANFAGNA; 600,000 mems.

Federazione Unitaria Lavoratori Prodotti Industrie Alimentari (Workers in the Manufactured Food Industry): Rome; affiliated to the CISL and the IUF; Sec. Dott. E. CREA; 40,000 mems.

Unione Coltivatori Italiana (UCI) (Farmers): Via in Lucina 10, 00186 Rome; tel. (6) 6871043; Pres. VINCENZO PANDOVINO.

Unione Generale Coltivatori (UGC): Via Tevere 44, 00198 Rome; tel. (6) 8552383; fax (6) 8553891; affiliated to the CISL; Pres. GAVINO DERUDA; 151,625 mems.

Unione Italiana Lavoratori Agroalimentari (UILA-UIL) (Food Workers): Via Savoia 80, 00198 Rome; tel. (6) 85301610; fax (6) 85303253; affiliated to the UIL; Sec. STEFANO MANTEGAZZA.

Unione Italiana Mezzadri e Coltivatori Diretti—UIMEC (Land Workers): Via Tirso 26, 00198 Rome; tel. (6) 8418044; fax (6) 8413968; affiliated to the UIL; Sec. FURIO VENARUCCI; 100,000 mems.

Medical

Federazione Italiana Sindacati Ospedalieri—FISOS (Hospital Workers' Unions): Via Salaria 89, 00198 Rome; tel. (6) 8414815; affiliated to the CISL; Sec.-Gen. GIACOMO MUSCOLINO; 150,501 mems.

Sindacato Nazionale Medici (SNM) (Doctors): Rome; affiliated to the CISNAL; Sec. VINCENZO AGAMENNONE.

Papermaking, Printing and Publishing

Federazione Italiana Lavoratori del Libro—FEDERLIBRO: Rome; tel. (6) 318202; affiliated to the CISL; Gen. Sec. GIUSEPPE SURRENTI; 35,000 mems.

Federazione Italiana Lavoratori Poligrafici e Cartai (Printing Workers and Papermakers): Via Piemonte 39, 00186 Rome; affiliated to the CGIL; Sec.-Gen. GIORGIO COLZI; 80,000 mems.

Public Services

Federazione Autonoma Italiana Lavoratori Elettrici (FAILE) (Electrical Workers): Via Cavour 310, Rome; Sec. ANGELO ISERNIA.

Federazione della Funzione Pubblica (FP): Via Rovereto 11, 00198 Rome; tel. (6) 869578; affiliated to the CISL; Sec. Gen. DARIO PAPPUCIA; 244,835 mems.

Federazione Italiana Lavoratori Esattoriali (Tax Collectors): Via A. Poliziano 80, 00184 Rome; tel. (6) 732246; affiliated to the UIL; Sec. LUCIANO PARODI.

Federazione Italiana Lavoratori Statali (State Employees): Via Livenza 7, 00198 Rome; tel. (6) 8547570; fax (6) 8546238; affiliated to the CISL; Gen. Sec. MAURINO LEDDA; 50,085 mems.

Federazione Italiana dei Servizi e degli Enti Locali (Services and Local Government Employees): Via Lancisi 25, Rome; tel. (6) 44230010; fax (6) 44230114; f. 1950; affiliated to the CISL; Sec. GIANNI BUSNELLO; 170,000 mems.

Federazione Lavoratori Aziende Elettriche Italiane (FLAEI) (Workers in Italian Electrical Undertakings): Via Salaria 83, 00198 Rome; tel. (6) 8552352; fax (6) 8548458; f. 1948; affiliated to the CISL; Sec. ARSENIO CAROSI; 32,000 mems.

Federazione Nazionale Dipendenti Enti Locali (Employees of Local Authorities): Via Principe Amadeo 42, 00185 Rome; tel. (6) 4824202; affiliated to the CISNAL; Sec. GUIDO ANDERSON.

Federazione Nazionale Dipendenti Enti Pubblici—UILDEP (Public Employees): Via Lucullo 6, Rome; f. 1962; affiliated to the UIL; Gen. Sec. GIAMPIETRO SESTINI; 30,000 mems.

Federazione Nazionale Lavoratori Funzione Pubblica: Via Leopoldo Serra 31, 00153 Rome; tel. (6) 585441; fax (6) 5836970; affiliated to the CGIL and Public Services International; Sec.-Gen. PAOLO NEROZZI.

Federazione Nazionale Lavoratori Energia (Gas, Water and Electricity): Via Piemonte 32, 00187 Rome; tel. (6) 4746153; affiliated to the CGIL; Sec. ANDREA AMARO; 72,000 mems.

Unione Italiana Lavoratori Pubblico Impiego (UILPI) (Public Office Workers): Via Lucullo 6, 00187 Rome; tel. (6) 49731; fax (6) 4973208; affiliated to the UIL; Sec. GIANCARLO FONTANELLI; 238,000 mems.

Unione Italiana Lavoratori Servizi Pubblici (Public Services Workers): Via Nizza 33, 00198 Rome; tel. (6) 865303; f. 1958; affiliated to the UIL; Sec. GIUSEPPE AUGIERI; 15,500 mems.

Unione Nazionale Dipendenti Enti Locali—UNDEL (Local Authority Employees): Via Po 162, 00198 Rome; tel. (6) 852340; affiliated to the UIL; Gen. Sec. FABRIZIO LUCARINI; 85,000 mems.

Teachers

Federazione Italiana Scuola Università e Ricerca (University Teachers): Via S. Croce in Gerusalemme 107, 00185 Rome; tel. (6) 757941; affiliated to the CISL; Gen. Secs GIORGIO ALESSANDRINI, PIETRO TALAMO; 184,235 mems.

Sindacato Nazionale Autonomo Lavoratori della Scuola (SNALS): Via Leopoldo Serra 5, 00153 Rome; tel. (6) 5898741; f. 1976; grouping of all independent teachers' unions; National Sec. NINO GALLOTTA.

Sindacato Nazionale Scuola Elementare (Elementary School Teachers): Via Santa Croce in Gerusalemme 91, 00185 Rome; tel. (6) 7597362; fax (6) 70475110; f. 1944; affiliated to the CISL; Sec.-Gen. RENATO D'ANGIO; 124,000 mems.

Tourism and Entertainments

Federazione Informazione e Spettacolo (FIS) (Actors, Artists and Media Workers): Via XX Settembre 40, 00187 Rome; tel. (6) 4888121; fax (6) 48881211; affiliated to the CISL; Gen. Sec. FULVIO GIACOMASSI; 43,388 mems.

Federazione Italiana Lavoratori Commercio Albergo Mensa e Servizi—FILCAMS (Hotel and Catering Workers): Via Leopoldo Serra 31, 00153 Rome; tel. (6) 5885102; fax (6) 5885323; f. 1960; affiliated to the CGIL; Sec.-Gen. ALDO AMORETTI; 189,000 mems.

Federazione Italiana Lavoratori Informazione e Spettacolo (FILIS) (Media and Entertainment Workers): Piazza Sallustio 24, 00187 Rome; tel. (6) 4814177; fax (6) 4824325; f. 1981; affiliated to the CGIL; Gen. Sec. MASSIMO BORDINI.

Federazione Italiana Personale Aviazione Civile (Aviation Employees): Via Ostiense 224, Rome; affiliated to the CGIL; Sec. PIERRO TORINO.

Federazione Italiana Sindacati Addetti Servizi Commerciali Affini e del Turismo (FISASCAT-CISL) (Commercial and Tourist Unions): Via Livenza 7, 00198 Rome; tel. (6) 8541042; fax (6) 8558057; Sec.-Gen. GIANNI BARATTA; 116,000 mems.

Unione Italiana Lavoratori Turismo Commercio e Servizi (UILTuCS): Via Nizza 59, 00198 Rome; tel. (6) 8550104; fax (6) 8844947; f. 1977; affiliated to the UIL; Gen. Sec. RAFFAELE VANNI; 140,000 mems.

Transport and Telecommunications

Federazione Italiana Dipendenti Aziende Telecomunicazioni (FIDAT) (Employees of Telecommunications Undertakings): Via Po 102, 00198 Rome; tel. (6) 855651; affiliated to the CGIL; Sec. GIANFRANCO TESTI; 12,000 mems.

Federazione Italiana Lavoratori Trasporti e Ausiliari del Traffico (FILTAT) (Transport and Associated Workers): Rome; tel. (6) 8448640; affiliated to the CISL; Sec. PIETRO LOMBARDI; 60,000 mems.

Federazione Italiana dei Postelegrafonici (Postal, Telegraph and Telephone Workers): Via Cavour 185, 00187 Rome; tel. (6) 461321; affiliated to the CGIL; Sec. GIUSEPPE MASTRACCHI; 35,000 mems.

Federazione Italiana Trasporti Settore Marittimi (Italian Maritime): Via Boncompagni 19, 00187 Rome; tel. (6) 4689216; fax (6) 4825233; affiliated to the International Transport Workers' Federation; Gen. Sec. REMODI FIORE.

Federazione Nazionale Autoferrotranvieri Internavigatori (FNAI) (Bus, Railway and Tram Workers): Rome; tel. (6) 483783; affiliated to the UIL; Sec. BRUNO MONOSILIO.

Federazione Italiana Sindacati dei Trasporti (FILT): Via G. B. Morgagni 27, 00198 Rome; tel. (6) 89961; affiliated to the CGIL; Sec. PAOLO BRUTTI.

Federazione Italiana Trasporti (FIT): Via Boncompagni 19, 00187 Rome; tel. (6) 4689235; fax (6) 4825404; f. 1950; affiliated to the CISL; National Sec. LUIGI VAGLICA; 40,000 mems.

Federazione Nazionale Lavoratori Auto-Ferrotramvieri e Internavigatori—FENLAI: Rome; affiliated to the CISL; Gen. Sec. LAURO MORRA; 28,091 mems.

Federazione Poste e Telecomunicazioni (FPT): Via dell'Esquilino 38, 00185 Rome; tel. (6) 4820264; f. 1981; affiliated to the CISL; Sec.-Gen. GIOVANNI IALONGO; 60,000 mems.

Federazione dei Sindacati Dipendenti Aziende di Navigazione—FEDERSINDAN: Via Tevere 48, Rome; independent; Sec.-Gen. Dott. GIUSEPPE AURICCHIO.

Sindacato Italiano Lavoratori Uffici Locali ed Agenzie Postelegrafoniche (Post and Telegraph Workers): Via dell'Esquilino 38, 00185 Rome; affiliated to the CISL; Gen. Sec. SALVATORE VILLA; 93,140 mems.

UILTRASPORTI: Via Salaria 44, 00198 Rome; tel. (6) 852511; fax (6) 85350501; affiliated to the UIL; Sec. RAFFAELE LIGUORI.

Unione Italiana Lavoratori Trasporti Ausiliari Traffico e Portuali (UILTATEP) (Transport and Associated Workers): Via Palestro 78, 00185 Rome; tel. (6) 4950698; f. 1950; affiliated to the UIL; Sec.-Gen. RAFFAELE LIGOURI; 134,280 mems.

Unione Italiana Marittimi (UIM) (Seamen): Rome; tel. (6) 422800; affiliated to the UIL; Nat. Sec. GIORGIO MARANGONI; 12,500 mems.

Miscellaneous

Federazione Italiana Agenti Rappresentanti Viaggiatori-Piazzisti 'Fiarvep' (Commercial Travellers and Representatives): Corso Porta Vittoria 43, Milan; affiliated to the CGIL; Sec. LIONELLO GIANNINI.

Federazione Nazionale Pensionati (FNP) (Pensioners): Via Alessandria 26, 00198 Rome; tel. (6) 8415670; fax (6) 8417565; f. 1952; affiliated to the CISL; Sec. GIANFRANCO CHIAPELLA; 1,180,000 mems.

Sindacato Pensionati Italiani (Pensioners): Via Frentani 4A, 00185 Rome; tel. (6) 444811; fax (6) 4440941; f. 1948; affiliated to the CGIL; Gen. Sec. RAFFAELE MINELLI; 2,876,463 mems.

Co-operative Unions

Confederazione Cooperative Italiane—CONFCOOPERATIVE: Borgo S. Spirito 78, 00193 Rome; tel. (6) 680001; telex 622465; fax (6) 6868595; f. 1945; federation of co-operative unions; Pres. LUIGI MARINO; Sec.-Gen. VINCENZO MANNINO.

Associazione Generale delle Cooperative Italiane (AGCI): Viale Somalia 164, 00199 Rome; tel. (6) 8313753; telex 622285; f. 1952; Pres. RENATO ASCARI RACCAGNI; Sec.-Gen. GINO MARINONI.

Lega Nazionale delle Cooperative e Mutue (National League of Co-operative and Friendly Societies): Via Guattani 9, 00161 Rome; tel. (6) 844391; fax (6) 84439406; f. 1886; 9 affiliated unions; Pres. IVANO BARBERINI.

Transport

Direzione Generale della Motorizzazione Civile e del Trasporti in Concessione: Via Giuseppe Caraci 36, 00157 Rome; tel. (6) 41581; fax (6) 41582211; controls road transport and traffic, and public transport services (railways operated by private cos, motor-buses, trolley-buses, funicular railways and inland waterways); Dir-Gen. Dott. GIORGIO BERRUTI.

RAILWAYS

The majority of Italian lines are controlled by an independent state-owned corporation. In 1993 the total length of the network was 15,942 km, of which 10,030 km were electrified. Apart from the state railway system there are 27 local and municipal railway companies, many of whose lines are narrow gauge. There are metro systems in Rome, Milan and Naples; a metro system is also planned for Turin. A high-speed service is planned on the following routes: Rome–Milan–Turin, Naples–Rome and Milan–Venice. In July 1991 TAV, a semi-private company for the creation of a high-speed train network, was established. Work on the following lines was to be completed by 1999: Turin–Milan–Naples, Milan–Venice and Milan–Genoa.

Ferrovie dello Stato SpA: Piazza della Croce Rossa 1, 00161 Rome; tel. (6) 84903758; telex 622345; fax (6) 84905186; Pres. G. CRISCI; Man. Dir GIANCARLO CIMOLI.

ROADS

In 1995 there were an estimated 314,360 km of roads in Italy, including 46,500 km of major roads, 117,000 km of secondary roads and 8,860 km of motorway. All the *autostrade* (motorways) are toll roads except for the one between Salerno and Reggio Calabria and motorways in Sicily. By law ANAS is responsible for the planning, construction and management of the motorway network. Plans were announced in 1996 for the privatization of the motorway network and for the construction of a bridge linking Sicily to the Italian mainland. The 13-km Mount Frejus highway tunnel, linking Italy and France through the Alps, opened in 1980.

Azienda Nazionale Autonoma delle Strade (ANAS) (National Autonomous Road Corpn): Via Monzambano 10, 00185 Rome; tel. (6) 44461; f. 1928; responsible for the administration of state roads and their improvement and extension; Pres. MARIO CONSTANTINI.

SHIPPING

In 1996 the Italian merchant fleet (1,348 vessels) had a displacement of 6,594,302 grt.

Direzione Generale della Marina Mercantile: Via dell' Arte 16, 00144 Rome.

Genoa

Costa Armatori SpA (Linea C): Via Gabriele D'Annunzio 2, 16100 Genoa; tel. (10) 54831; telex 270068; passenger and cargo service; Mediterranean–North, Central and South America; Caribbean cruises; Chair. NICOLA COSTA.

Franconia Srl: Via XX Settembre 37-11, 16121 Genoa; tel. (10) 818851; telex 270017; Chair. FRIGERIO BRUNO; Man. Dir EMANUELE RAVANO.

'Garibaldi' Società Cooperativa di Navigazione Srl: Piazza Dante 8, 16121 Genoa; tel. (10) 581635; telex 270548; fax (10) 5702386; f. 1918; tanker and cargo services; Pres. GIAN FRANCO VIALE.

Industriale Marittima SpA: Genoa; tramp; Man. Dir A. PORTA FIGARI.

'Italia di Navigazione' SpA: Torre WTC, Via de Marini 1, Genoa; tel. (10) 24021; telex 270032; fax (10) 2402445; f. 1932; freight services to Mediterranean, North, South and Central America and South Pacific; to be privatized 1998; Chair. LUCIO DE GIACOMO; Man. Dir EUGENIO GALLO.

Messina, Ignazio and C. SpA: Via G. d'Annunzio 91, 16121 Genoa; tel. (10) 53961; telex 270450; services to Arabian Gulf, Nigeria, North, East, South and West Africa, Libya and Near East, Red Sea, Malta, Europe; Chair. I. MESSINA.

Navigazione Alta Italia, SpA: Via Corsica 19, 16128 Genoa; tel. (10) 56331; telex 270181; f. 1906; worldwide dry and bulk cargo; Chair. and Man. Dir SEBASTIANO CAMELI; Gen. Man. ROMANO GUGLIELMINI.

Sidermar di Navigazione SpA: Via XX Settembre 41, Genoa; tel. (10) 56341; telex 270412; fax (10) 589149; f. 1956; cargo; Chair. Dott. DARIO DEL BUONO; Man. Dir Dott. CARLO CIONI.

Naples

Garolla Fratelli SpA: Pontile Falvio Giola 45, 80133 Naples; tel. (81) 5534477; telex 710256; Chair. R. GAROLLA; Dirs F. GAROLLA, C. GAROLLA.

Fratelli Grimaldi Armatori: Via M. Campodisola 13, 80133 Naples; tel. (81) 205466; telex 710058; passenger, cargo, containers and tramp to Europe, Middle East, South, Central and North America; Dirs M. GRIMALDI, G. GRIMALDI, A. GRIMALDI, U. GRIMALDI.

Tirrenia di Navigazione SpA: Head Office: Palazzo Sirignano, Rione Sirignano 2, 80121 Naples; tel. (81) 7201111; telex 710028; fax (81) 7201441; Man. Dir and Dir-Gen. FRANCO PECORINI.

Palermo

Sicilia Regionale Marittima SpA—SIREMAR: Via Principe di Belmonte, 90139 Palermo; tel. (91) 582688; telex 910135; fax (91) 582267; ferry services; Pres. Dott GIUSEPPE RAVERA; Man. Dir CARLO COSTA.

Sicula Oceanicas SA—SIOSA: Via Mariano Stabile 179, 90139 Palermo; tel. (91) 217939; telex 910098; f. 1941; cruises, passenger and cargo; Italy to North Europe, South, Central, North America; Dir G. GRIMALDI.

Rome

D'Amico Fratelli, Armatori, SpA: Via Liguria 36, 00187 Rome; tel. (6) 4671; telex 614545; dry cargo and tankers; Dirs GIUSEPPE D'AMICO, VITTORIO D'AMICO.

D'Amico Società di Navigazione SpA: Corso d'Italia 35B, 00198 Rome; tel. (6) 8841061; telex 611118; fax (6) 8553943; f. 1954; liner and tanker trade; Mans ANTONIO D'AMICO, CESARE D'AMICO, PAOLO D'AMICO.

Linee Marittime dell'Adriatico SpA: Via del Nuoto 11, 00194 Rome; tel. (6) 3272312; telex 611034.

Trieste

Fratelli Cosulich SpA: Piazza S. Antonio 4, 34122 Trieste; tel. (40) 631353; telex 460018; fax (40) 630844; f. 1854; shipowners and shipping agents; domestic network and cargo to Near East, Red Sea, Hong Kong, Singapore, New York and Zürich; Chair. and Man. Dir GEROLIMICH COSULICH.

Lloyd Triestino di Navigazione SpA: Palazzo del Lloyd Triestino, Piazza dell'Unità d'Italia 1, 34121 Trieste; tel. (40) 7785; telex 460321; fax (40) 7785424; f. 1836; cargo services by container, roll on/roll off and conventional vessels to Africa, Australasia and Far East; to be privatized 1998; Pres. Dott. ROBERTO JUCCI; Dir-Gen. Ing. TOMMASO RICCI.

Other Towns

Adriatica di Navigazione SpA: Zattere 1411, CP 705, 30123 Venice; tel. (41) 781611; telex 410045; fax (41) 781894; f. 1937; passenger services from Italy to Greece, Albania and Croatia; Pres. ORONZO GIANNUZZI; Man. Dir PAOLO CHENDA.

Snam SpA: Piazza Vanoni 1, San Donato Milanese, POB 12060, 20097 Milan; tel. (2) 5201; telex 310246; f. 1941; purchase, transport and sale of natural gas, transport of crude petroleum and petroleum products by means of pipeline and tanker fleet; Pres. Ing. PIO PIGORINI; Vice-Pres. and Man. Dir Ing. LUIGI MEANTI.

SHIPPING ASSOCIATION

Confederazione Italiana Armatori—CONFITARMA: Piazza S. Apostoli 66, 00187 Rome; tel. (6) 6991261; telex 626135; fax (6)

6789473; f. 1901; shipowners' asscn; Pres. PAOLO CLERICI; Dir-Gen. LUIGI PERISSICH; 140 mems.

CIVIL AVIATION

National Airline

Alitalia (Linee Aeree Italiane): Viale Alissandro Marchetti 111, 00148 Rome; tel. (6) 7092780; telex 656211; fax (6) 7093065; f. 1946; state-owned airline; international services throughout Europe and to Africa, North and South America, the Middle East, the Far East and Australia; Chair. FAUSTO CERETI; CEO DOMENICO CEMPELLA.

Other Airlines

Aero Trasporti Italiani SpA (ATI): Plazzo ATI, Aeroporto Capodichino, 80144 Naples; tel. (81) 7091111; telex 7110055; fax (81) 7092212; f. 1963; subsidiary of Alitalia; operates scheduled domestic services and services and charter flights to the Middle East, North Africa and Canary Islands and within Europe; Chair. Prof. CARLO BERNINI; Man. Dir GAETANO GALIA.

Air Europe: Corso Sempione 15A, Gallarte; tel. (331) 722111; telex 315050; fax (331) 783895; f. 1988; international charter flights; Man. Dir ANTONELLO ISABELLA.

Air One: Via Sardegna 14, 00187; Rome ; tel. (6) 478761; fax (6) 4885913; f. 1983 as Aliadratica; adopted current name in 1995; private co; domestic flights; Chair GIOVANNI SEBASTIANI; Pres. CARLO TOTO.

Azzurra Air: Bergamo; f. 1996; scheduled European flights.

Meridiana SpA: Zona Industriale A, 07026 Olbia, Sardinia; tel. (789) 52600; fax (789) 23661; f. 1963; scheduled and charter services throughout Italy and Europe; Pres. and Man. Dir FRANCO TRIVI.

Tourism

A great number of tourists are attracted to Italy by its Alpine and Mediterranean scenery, sunny climate, Roman archaeological remains, medieval and Baroque churches, Renaissance towns and palaces, paintings and sculpture and famous opera houses. Each of the 95 provinces has a Board of Tourism; there are also about 300 Aziende Autonome di Cura, Soggiorno e Turismo, with information about tourist accommodation and health treatment, and about 2,000 Pro Loco Associations concerned with local amenities. In 1996 a total of 56.3m. foreign visitors (including excursionists) arrived in Italy; tourist receipts totalled 46,249,264m. lire in that year.

Dipartimento del Turismo: Presidenza del Consiglio dei Ministri, Via della Ferratella in Laterano 51, 00184 Rome; tel. (6) 77321; telex 616400; fax (6) 7001992; Dir-Gen. Dott. STEFANO LANDI.

Ente Nazionale Italiano per il Turismo (ENIT) (National Tourist Board): Via Marghera 2, 00185 Rome; tel. (6) 49711; telex 680123; fax (6) 4963379; f. 1919; Chair. AMEDEO OTTAVIANI; Dir-Gen. PIERGIORGIO TOGNI.

JAMAICA

Introductory Survey

Location, Climate, Language, Religion, Flag, Capital

Jamaica is the third largest island in the Caribbean Sea, lying 145 km (90 miles) to the south of Cuba and 160 km (100 miles) to the south-west of Haiti. The climate varies with altitude, being tropical at sea-level and temperate in the mountain areas. The average annual temperature is 27°C (80°F) and mean annual rainfall is 198 cm (78 ins). The official language is English, although a local patois is widely spoken. The majority of the population belong to Christian denominations, the Church of God being the most numerous. The national flag (proportions 2 by 1) consists of a diagonal yellow cross on a background of black (hoist and fly) and green (above and below). The capital is Kingston.

Recent History

Jamaica became a British colony in 1655. Slaves, transported from Africa to work on the sugar plantations, formed the basis of the island's economy until the abolition of slavery in 1834. Plans for independence were made in the 1940s. Internal self-government was introduced in 1959, and full independence, within the Commonwealth, was achieved on 6 August 1962. Jamaica formed part of the West Indies Federation between 1958 and 1961, when it seceded, following a referendum. The Federation was dissolved in May 1962.

The two dominant political figures after the Second World War were the late Sir Alexander Bustamante, leader of the Jamaica Labour Party (JLP), who retired as Prime Minister in 1967, and Norman Manley, a former Premier and leader of the People's National Party (PNP), who died in 1969. The JLP won the elections of 1962 and 1967 but, under the premiership of Hugh Shearer, it lost the elections of February 1972 to the PNP, led by Michael Manley, the son of Norman Manley. Michael Manley advocated democratic socialism and his Government put great emphasis on social reform and economic independence.

The early 1970s were marked by escalating street violence and crime, with gang warfare rife in the slum areas of Kingston. More than 160 people were killed in the first half of 1976, and in June the Government declared a state of emergency (which remained in force until June 1977). Despite the unrest, high unemployment and severe economic stagnation, the PNP was returned to power in December 1976 with an increased majority. By January 1979, however, there was again widespread political unrest, and violent demonstrations signalled growing discontent with the Manley administration.

In February 1980, in the context of a worsening economic crisis, Manley rejected the stipulation of the IMF that economic austerity measures be undertaken, as a condition of its making further loans to Jamaica. He called a general election to seek support for his economic policies and his decision to end dependence on the IMF. The electoral campaign was one of the most violent in Jamaica's history. In the October election the JLP received about 57% of the total votes and won 51 of the 60 seats in the House of Representatives. Edward Seaga, the leader of the JLP, became Prime Minister; he supported closer political and economic links with the USA and the promotion of free enterprise. Seaga severed diplomatic relations with Cuba in October 1981, and secured valuable US financial support for the economy. Negotiations on IMF assistance were resumed.

In November 1983, before the completion of a new electoral roll, Seaga announced that an election would take place in mid-December. Only four days were allowed for the nomination of candidates, and the PNP, unable to present candidates at such short notice, refused to participate and declared the elections void. The JLP, opposed in only six constituencies (by independent candidates), won all 60 seats in the House of Representatives and formed a one-party legislature.

Devaluations of the Jamaican dollar and the withdrawal of food subsidies provoked demonstrations and sporadic violence in 1984, as the prices of foodstuffs and energy increased by between 50% and 100%. Despite government attempts to offset the effects of these economic austerity measures, imposed at the instigation of the IMF, unemployment, together with the consequences of illicit trading in drugs, contributed to a rise in the incidence of crime and violence, especially in Kingston. In 1985 another increase in fuel prices precipitated further violent demonstrations in the capital and industrial unrest in the public sector. In May 1986 Seaga defied recommendations by the IMF and other aid agencies, and introduced an expansionary budget for 1986/87, in an attempt to stimulate economic growth.

Municipal elections took place in July 1986, having been postponed three times. The PNP obtained control of 11 of the 13 municipalities in which polling took place, winning 57% of the total votes. A significant increase in drugs-related violence in mid-1987 prompted the Government to announce more severe punishments for drugs-related offences.

In September 1988 Jamaica was struck by 'Hurricane Gilbert', the most damaging storm in the country's recorded history. More than 100,000 homes were destroyed, while the economy, particularly the agriculture sector, was severely disrupted. Seaga's successful efforts to secure international aid won him some initial support, but this soon declined, particularly following controversy over the alleged preferential allocation of relief resources to JLP supporters.

After a brief, and relatively peaceful, campaign, a general election took place in February 1989. The PNP received about 56% of the votes cast, thereby securing 45 of the 60 seats in the House of Representatives. Michael Manley, who had developed a more moderate image during his years in opposition, again became Prime Minister. The Government conceded the necessity for a devaluation of the Jamaican dollar, which was announced in October. Unusually for Jamaican politics, the two main parties achieved a limited consensus on the pursuit of an economic policy of austerity, despite its unpopularity. There was also agreement that further action should be taken against the drugs trade. The Government was particularly anxious to prevent the use of Jamaican shipping and aviation for the smuggling of illegal drugs, and demanded further security measures, despite the consequent impediment to normal trade movements.

At local elections in March 1990, the PNP won control of 12 of the 13 local councils, obtaining some 60% of the votes cast. During 1990 there was disagreement within the opposition JLP: five MPs criticized Seaga's alleged autocratic leadership, and were banned by him from standing as JLP candidates at the next general election. New economic adjustment measures (including another devaluation of the Jamaican dollar), were adopted in January, in order to secure another IMF stand-by arrangement. In June a five-year economic development plan was announced, as part of the Government's programme of deregulation and reform. However, the cost of living continued to rise, prompting industrial unrest in late 1991.

In December 1991 controversy surrounding the waiving of taxes worth some US $30m. that were owed to Jamaica by an international petroleum company, Shell, resulted in the resignation of Horace Clarke, the Minister of Mining and Energy, and Percival Patterson, the Deputy Prime Minister, amid opposition allegations of corruption and misconduct. Patterson requested not to be included in the new Cabinet (which was reorganized following the scandal), but remained as Chairman of the PNP. In March 1992 Manley announced his resignation, owing to ill health, from the premiership and from the presidency of the PNP. Patterson was subsequently elected as Manley's successor by members of the PNP, and was appointed Prime Minister at the end of the month.

During 1992 there was a marked increase in violent crime, much of which appeared to be politically motivated. Speculation that the Government would organize an early general election intensified in the first few months of 1993, following reports that public support for the JLP had diminished considerably. Patterson's PNP duly secured 52 of the 60 seats in the House of Representatives at a general election contested on 30 March 1993. The scale of the PNP victory was widely attributed to the success of Patterson's populist overtures to the island's majority population of African origin, and a perceived shift in political influence away from the capital, traditionally a power base of the JLP (which won the remaining eight seats). In April Patterson announced plans to reform and modernize the electoral system. However, allegations of electoral malpractice and demands by the JLP for an official inquiry into suspected procedural abuses were rejected by the PNP, prompting the JLP to boycott the official opening of Parliament later in the month. By February 1994 attempts at electoral reform had been undermined by the resignation of the Chairman of the Electoral Advisory Committee (EAC), and by the failure of the EAC to appoint a new Director of Elections. Demands for constitutional and electoral reform continued, and the JLP repeatedly accused the Government of seeking to delay progress towards any such reforms. Proposals drafted in late 1994 recommended the establishment of a permanent electoral commission to supervise elections, the publication of a revised register of voters every six months, and rules governing political campaigning and the nomination of candidates. An electronic voter registration system was installed in 1996 and new electoral rolls were completed in late 1997.

Industrial relations deteriorated in 1994, with a series of strikes by public-sector workers demanding substantial wage increases. Meanwhile, the country's poor economic performance (particularly its high inflation rate and increasing trade deficit) compounded widespread dissatisfaction with the Government. A major reorganization of cabinet portfolios, in which three ministers were dismissed, was effected in January 1995. There was further industrial unrest in 1995, as workers in both the public and private sectors argued for large pay increases to compensate for high rates of inflation. Industrial production was badly affected by strikes at some of the country's bauxite refineries. The Government was widely criticized for a perceived lack of response to a growth in violent crime in Kingston in June, in which seven people were killed in one week. In July troops were deployed in the capital in an attempt to control the problem.

In early 1995 widespread dissatisfaction with the leadership of Edward Seaga of the JLP was reported among party members. However, Seaga survived an attempt to remove him as leader of the party in March, and in September the party leadership dismissed the main critics of Seaga as prospective parliamentary candidates for the JLP. In October Bruce Golding, who had resigned as Chairman of the JLP in February after disagreements with Seaga, announced the formation of a political party, the National Democratic Movement (NDM). The NDM, which aimed to achieve constitutional reform, including the introduction of an elected, executive president, gathered support from former members of both the JLP and the PNP. The creation of the party was strongly criticized by Seaga, who claimed that it would lead to political instability in Jamaica.

In an effort to stabilize the economy, and, in particular, to address the problem of continuing industrial unrest, in 1996 the Government sought the agreement of a 'social contract' with trade unions and the private sector. In return for a commitment to increase its efforts to reduce inflation, the Government hoped to secure an undertaking from the labour organizations to moderate their wage demands. In July the Government implemented a 60% increase in the minimum wage. However, efforts to establish a 'social contract' continued to be frustrated during 1997 owing to trade union intransigence concerning demands for salary increases.

A significant rise in violent crime in 1996 was partly attributed to political tension between militants of rival parties, notably between supporters of the NDM and those of the JLP, and also to the increasing activities of organized gangs, especially those involved in drugs trafficking. In October the Government presented for parliamentary approval a security plan, which included provision for the establishment of a special unit to address the problem of organized crime and for increases in police recruitment and training.

A general election was held on 18 December 1997, at which the PNP won 56% of the votes cast and 50 of the 60 seats in the House of Representatives. The JLP obtained 39% of the votes and secured 10 seats, but the NDM, which won 5% of the votes, failed to gain parliamentary representation. It was estimated that 67% of the electorate participated in the election. Patterson, who was subsequently sworn in as Prime Minister for a third consecutive term, appointed a new Cabinet in January 1998 and announced plans for Jamaica to become a republic within five years; it remained unclear whether the proposal would be subject to referendum.

A decision reached in November 1993 by the Judicial Committee of the Privy Council in the United Kingdom (in its capacity as the final court of appeal for the Jamaican legal system) to commute to life imprisonment the death sentences imposed on two Jamaicans in 1979, in recognition of their prolonged suffering in anticipation of execution, threw doubt on the legal position of many similarly-sentenced prisoners in Jamaica and other Caribbean Commonwealth countries, given the recommendation of the Judicial Committee that all executions not effected within five years of sentencing should be subject to review, with a recommendation for commutation. In September 1994 the Prime Minister announced plans to replace the Privy Council as the final court of appeal with a Caribbean Court of Appeal. In late 1997 the Government announced that as of January 1998 Jamaica would withdraw from a UN treaty which had hitherto allowed prisoners sentenced to death to appeal for a review by the UN Commission on Human Rights.

Relations between Jamaica and the USA have been hampered by persistent demands by the USA for the eradication of Jamaica's marijuana crop. In May 1997, after months of negotiation, the two countries concluded a counter-narcotics agreement, permitting US drug enforcement agents to pursue suspected drugs-traffickers in Jamaican airspace and territorial waters. Diplomatic relations with Cuba were resumed in mid-1990, and in February 1994 the two countries agreed a maritime border delimitation treaty. Relations with Cuba were consolidated further during a visit to that country in mid-1997 by Prime Minister Patterson.

Government

The Head of State is the British monarch, who is represented locally by the Governor-General, who is appointed on the recommendation of the Prime Minister. The Governor-General acts, in almost all matters, on the advice of the Cabinet.

Legislative power is vested in the bicameral Parliament: the Senate, with 21 appointed members, and the House of Representatives, with 60 elected members. Thirteen members of the Senate are appointed by the Governor-General on the advice of the Prime Minister and eight on the advice of the Leader of the Opposition. Members of the House are elected by universal adult suffrage for five years (subject to dissolution). Executive power lies with the Cabinet. The Governor-General appoints the Prime Minister and, on the latter's recommendation, other ministers. The Cabinet is responsible to Parliament.

Defence

In August 1997 the Jamaica Defence Force consisted of 3,320 men on active service, including an army of 3,000, a coastguard of 150 and an air wing of 170 men. There are reserves of some 870. Defence expenditure in 1997 was budgeted at J $1,000m.

Economic Affairs

In 1995, according to estimates by the World Bank, Jamaica's gross national product (GNP), measured at average 1993–95 prices, was US $3,803m., equivalent to US $1,510 per head. During 1985–95 GNP per head was estimated to have increased, in real terms, by an average of 3.7% per year. Over the same period, the population increased by an annual average of 0.9%. According to the World Bank, Jamaica's gross domestic product (GDP) increased, in real terms, by an annual average of 4.1% in 1985–95; GDP growth was 0.8% in 1994 and 1.0% in 1995, although in 1996 GDP declined by 1.7%.

Agriculture (including forestry and fishing) contributed an estimated 7.7% of GDP in 1996, and engaged an estimated 22.9% of the economically active population. The principal cash crops are sugar cane (sugar accounted for an estimated 7.9% of total export earnings in 1996/97), bananas, citrus fruit, coffee and cocoa. The cultivation of vegetables, fruit and rice is being encouraged, in an attempt to reduce imports and diversify agricultural exports. Goats, cattle and pigs are the principal livestock. According to the World Bank, agricultural GDP increased by an annual average of 3.1% in 1985–95, and by an estimated 7.5% in 1995.

Industry (including mining, manufacturing, public utilities and construction) contributed an estimated 33.8% of GDP in 1996, and engaged 20.2% of the employed labour force. According to the World Bank, industrial GDP increased at an average rate of 4.3% per year in 1985–95. There was no discernible growth in the sector in 1995.

Mining and quarrying contributed an estimated 5.5% of GDP in 1996, but engaged only 0.7% of the employed labour force. Mining is the principal productive sector of the economy, and in 1996/97 bauxite and its derivative, alumina (aluminium oxide), accounted for an estimated 49.1% of total export earnings. Bauxite, of which Jamaica is one of the world's leading producers, is the major mineral mined, but there are also reserves of marble, gypsum, limestone, silica and clay.

Manufacturing contributed an estimated 15.6% of GDP in 1996, and engaged some 10.3% of the employed labour force. Much of the activity in the sector is dependent upon the processing of agricultural products and bauxite. Food, beverages and tobacco together accounted for some 70% of industrial output in 1988, mainly for domestic use. Petroleum-refining is also important. The export of garments, mainly to the USA, became increasingly important during the 1980s, providing an estimated 17.0% of total export earnings in 1996/97. According to the World Bank, manufacturing GDP increased by an annual average of 1.8% during 1985–95, but declined by an estimated 1.0% in 1995.

Energy is derived principally from imported hydrocarbon fuels. Most of Jamaica's petroleum requirements are fulfilled by imports from Venezuela and Mexico. Imports of mineral fuels and lubricants accounted for an estimated 15.6% of the total value of merchandise imports in 1996/97.

The services sector contributed an estimated 58.5% of GDP in 1996, and engaged some 56.8% of the employed labour force. The principal earner of foreign exchange is tourism. Tourist arrivals exceeded 1m. for the first time in 1987 and totalled an estimated 1.75m. in 1996/97. The largest proportion of tourists is from the USA (75.4% in 1996). Earnings from tourism reached an estimated US $1,130m. in 1996/97. According to the World Bank, the GDP of the services sector increased by an annual average of 4.6% in 1985–95, and by an estimated 0.6% in 1995.

In 1995 Jamaica recorded a visible trade deficit of US $813.2m., and there was a deficit of US $245.2m. on the current account of the balance of payments. In 1995 the principal source of imports (50.5%) was the USA. Other major suppliers in that year were the European Union, Trinidad and Tobago, and Japan. In that year the USA was also the principal market for exports (36.5%), while the United Kingdom, Canada and Norway were among other important purchasers. The principal exports are bauxite and alumina, garments, sugar, rum and bananas. The principal imports in 1996/97 were raw materials, consumer goods (including food), capital goods (notably machinery and transport equipment) and mineral fuels. Between 1987 and 1989 domestic production of hemp (marijuana) and the use of the island as a transit centre for other illegal drugs from Latin America were believed to have generated more revenue than the country's legitimate exports.

For the financial year ending 31 March 1997 the Government announced recurrent expenditure of J $61,059m. and capital expenditure of J $38,796m. An overall budgetary deficit of J $3,500m. was projected for 1993/94. Total external debt in 1995 was US $4,270m., of which US $3,409m. was long-term public debt. In that year the cost of debt-servicing was equivalent to 17.9% of the value of exports of goods and services, and in the budget for 1996/97 some 44% of total expenditure was allocated to debt-servicing. The average annual rate of inflation was 26.8% in 1986–96, and stood at 26.4% in 1996. Some 16.2% of the labour force were unemployed in 1996.

Jamaica is a founding member of the Caribbean Community and Common Market (CARICOM—see p. 119) and of the Inter-American Development Bank (see p. 183).

During the 1980s and early 1990s the development of Jamaica's economy was hampered by a persistent trade deficit, a shortage of foreign exchange, and a high level of external indebtedness. Attempts at economic reform, on which assistance from the IMF was conditional, entailed credit restrictions, devaluations of the currency, and limits on government expenditure; these measures resulted in economic expansion in the late 1980s, but also caused hardship for the poorer Jamaicans. Further measures of economic liberalization, implemented in the early 1990s, included the privatization of some government services, tax reforms and a lessening of restrictions on investment by non-resident Jamaicans. In 1994 and 1995, despite the Government's strict fiscal and monetary policies, Jamaica continued to experience high levels of inflation, prompting demands for greater pay increases by workers, and resulting in frequent work stoppages and industrial unrest. During 1995 and 1996 the Government initiated legislation to strengthen banking regulation and supervision, and introduced a wide-ranging tax administration reform programme, while the divestment of the state petroleum refinery in 1996 resulted in receipts of US $68m. In early 1997 the Government announced measures to subsidize the garment industry in order to counteract the effects of increasing competition from Mexico, which enjoys preferential access to the US market. Later in the year a land reform programme was initiated, which was expected to alleviate conditions for the rural poor. Meanwhile, large increases in the production of bauxite and alumina in the late 1990s continued to be offset by weak international market prices.

Social Welfare

Social welfare is undertaken by the Government. The Social Development Commission arranges and co-ordinates social welfare in the villages. Contributory national insurance and housing trust schemes are administered by the Government. Government expenditure on social security and welfare services during the financial year 1996/97 was estimated to be some J $600.6m. In 1996 Jamaica had 24 public hospitals and 371 health centres. In 1992 there were 397 physicians and some 11,000 nurses working in the country. In the 1996/97 revised budget, projected expenditure on health was J $6.6m., representing 5.8% of total budgetary expenditure.

Education

Primary education is compulsory in certain districts, and free education is ensured. The education system (which begins at six years of age) consists of a primary cycle of six years, followed by two secondary cycles of three and four years respectively. In 1996 enrolment ratios at pre-primary, primary and secondary schools were 83.0%, 93.0% and 83.0% of children in the relevant age-group, respectively. In 1990 an estimated 1.6% of the adult population had received no schooling, and it was estimated that in 1995 some 15% of the adult population were illiterate (males 19.2%; females 10.9%). Higher education is provided by technical colleges and by the University of the West Indies, which has five faculties situated at its Mona campus in Kingston. Government expenditure on education during the financial year 1997/98 was estimated to be some J $16,400m., representing about 15% of total budgetary expenditure.

Public Holidays

1998: 1 January (New Year's Day), 25 February (Ash Wednesday), 10 April (Good Friday), 13 April (Easter Monday), 23 May (National Labour Day), 1 August (Emancipation Day), 6 August (Independence Day), 19 October (National Heroes' Day), 25–26 December (Christmas).

1999: 1 January (New Year's Day), 17 February (Ash Wednesday), 2 April (Good Friday), 5 April (Easter Monday), 23 May (National Labour Day), 1 August (Emancipation Day), 6 August (Independence Day), 18 October (National Heroes' Day), 25–26 December (Christmas).

Weights and Measures

Both the imperial and the metric systems are in use.

Statistical Survey

Sources (unless otherwise stated): Planning Institute of Jamaica, 39–43 Barbados Ave, Kingston 5, Jamaica; tel. 926-1480; telex 3529; fax 926-4670; Jamaica Information Service, 58A Half Way Tree Rd, Kingston 10, Jamaica; tel. 926-3741; telex 2393; fax 926-6715.

Area and Population

AREA, POPULATION AND DENSITY

Area (sq km)	10,991*
Population (census results)	
8 June 1982	
Males	1,079,640
Females	1,125,867
Total	2,205,507
8 April 1991 (provisional)	2,366,067
Population (official estimates at mid-year)	
1993	2,411,000
1994	2,496,000
1995	2,530,000
Density (per sq km) at mid-1995	230.2

* 4,243.6 sq miles.

PARISHES

	Area (sq miles)	Population* (at 1991 census)	Parish capitals (with population at 1982 census)
Kingston	8.406	643,801	Kingston M.A. (524,638)
St Andrew	166.308		
St Thomas	286.800	84,266	Morant Bay (8,823)
Portland	314.347	76,067	Port Antonio (12,285)
St Mary	235.745	107,993	Port Maria (7,508)
St Ann	468.213	149,015	St Ann's Bay (9,058)
Trelawny	337.651	71,646	Falmouth (6,713)
St James	229.728	156,152	Montego Bay (70,265)
Hanover	173.855	65,958	Lucea (6,652)
Westmoreland	311.604	128,213	Savanna La Mar (14,912)
St Elizabeth	468.085	144,118	Black River (3,601)
Manchester	320.482	164,979	Mandeville (34,502)
Clarendon	461.864	212,324	May Pen (40,962)
St Catherine	460.396	361,535	Spanish Town (89,097)
Total	4,243.484†	2,366,067	—

* Provisional census results. The revised total is 2,374,193.
† Revised total 4,411 sq miles (11,424 sq km).

BIRTHS, MARRIAGES AND DEATHS*

	Registered live births		Registered marriages		Registered deaths	
	Number	Rate (per 1,000)	Number	Rate (per 1,000)	Number	Rate (per 1,000)
1987	52,300	22.2	10,536	4.5	12,400	5.3
1988	53,623	21.9	10,429	4.4	12,167	5.0
1989	59,104	24.9	11,145	4.7	14,315	6.0
1990	59,606	24.7	13,037	5.4	12,174	5.0
1991	59,879	25.3	13,254	5.6	13,319	5.6
1992	56,276	23.5	13,042	5.6	13,225	5.5
1993	n.a.	n.a.	n.a.	n.a.	13,927	5.8
1994†	59,235	23.7	15,171	6.1	13,503	5.4

* Data are tabulated by year of registration rather than by year of occurrence.
† Provisional.

Source: partly UN, *Demographic Yearbook*.

Expectation of life (UN estimates, years at birth, 1990–95): 73.6 (males 71.4; females 75.8) (Source: UN, *World Population Prospects: The 1994 Revision*).

ECONOMICALLY ACTIVE POPULATION*
(sample surveys, '000 persons aged 14 years and over)

	1994	1995†	1996‡
Agriculture, forestry and fishing	217.7	220.2	219.9
Mining and quarrying	6.2	6.7	6.4
Manufacturing	95.0	105.5	99.1
Electricity, gas and water	5.3	6.6	7.1
Construction	67.5	76.3	81.1
Trade, restaurants and hotels	194.8	199.8	197.7
Transport, storage and communications	39.2	45.3	49.0
Financing, insurance, real estate and business services	47.8	53.1	54.8
Community, social and personal services	237.6	246.4	242.8
Activities not adequately defined	12.9	0.8	0.6
Total employed	923.8	960.5	958.3
Unemployed	166.1	189.1	185.3
Total labour force	1,089.9	1,149.6	1,143.6

* Average of April and October.
† Preliminary figures.
‡ Estimates.

Source: IMF, *Jamaica—Statistical Annex* (October 1997).

Agriculture

PRINCIPAL CROPS ('000 metric tons)

	1994	1995	1996
Sweet potatoes	29	31	33
Cassava	19	17	17*
Yams	234	240	240*
Other roots and tubers	48	58	56
Coconuts*	115	115	115
Pumpkins, squash and gourds	40	42	42*
Other vegetables and melons	36	41	49
Sugar cane	2,450	2,326	2,624
Oranges*	72	72	72
Lemons and limes*	24	24	24
Grapefruit and pomelo*	42	42	42
Bananas*	120	130	130
Plantains	35	35	35*
Other fruit	119	114	117
Coffee (green)	2†	3†	3*
Cocoa beans	3	3	1
Tobacco (leaves)*	2	2	2

* FAO estimate(s). † Unofficial figure.

Source: FAO, *Production Yearbook*.

LIVESTOCK (FAO estimates, '000 head, year ending September)

	1994	1995	1996
Horses	4	4	4
Mules	10	10	10
Asses	23	23	23
Cattle	440	450	420
Pigs	200	200	180
Sheep	1	1	2
Goats	440	440	440

Poultry (FAO estimates, million): 8 in 1994; 7 in 1995; 8 in 1996.

Source: FAO, *Production Yearbook*.

LIVESTOCK PRODUCTS ('000 metric tons)

	1994	1995	1996
Beef and veal	16	17	16
Goat meat*	2	2	2
Pig meat	7	7*	7
Poultry meat	44	40	43†
Cows' milk*	53	53	53
Poultry eggs*	28	28	28

* FAO estimate(s). † Unofficial figure.

Source: FAO, *Production Yearbook*.

Forestry

ROUNDWOOD REMOVALS ('000 cubic metres, excl. bark)

	1992	1993	1994
Sawlogs, veneer logs and logs for sleepers	96	80	64
Other industrial wood	1	1	1
Fuelwood	512	462	412
Total	609	544	477

Source: FAO, *Yearbook of Forest Products*.

SAWNWOOD PRODUCTION ('000 cubic metres, incl. railway sleepers)

	1992	1993	1994
Total	27	24	20

Source: FAO, *Yearbook of Forest Products*.

Fishing

(FAO estimates, '000 metric tons, live weight)

	1993	1994	1995
Total catch	13.0	13.5	13.6

Source: FAO, *Yearbook of Fishery Statistics*.

Mining

('000 metric tons)

	1992	1993	1994
Bauxite*	11,370	11,200	11,760
Alumina	2,930	2,895	3,320

* Dried equivalent of crude ore.

Crude gypsum ('000 metric tons): 100 in 1992; 109 in 1993; 164 in 1994 (Source: UN, *Industrial Commodity Statistics Yearbook*).

Industry

SELECTED PRODUCTS ('000 metric tons, unless otherwise indicated)

	1992	1993	1994
Margarine and lard	8.4	6.3	7.3
Wheat flour	145	110	147
Sugar	228	219	224
Animal foodstuffs	206	224	206
Rum ('000 hectolitres)	162	206	211
Beer ('000 hectolitres)	828	786	760
Soft drinks ('000 hectolitres)	520	486	557
Cigars (million)	7	9	n.a.
Cigarettes (million)	1,299	1,224	1,273
Jet fuels*	60	55	50
Motor gasoline—Petrol	173	95	116
Kerosene*	70	65	70
Distillate fuel oils	224	155	177
Residual fuel oils	650	344	387
Lubricating oils	10	8	8
Rubber tyres ('000)	308	359	331
Quicklime†	179	151	170
Cement	480	441	445
Electric energy (million kWh)	2,199	3,791	3,927*

* Provisional or estimated figure(s).

† Estimates from the US Bureau of Mines, incl. other types of lime.

Source: UN, *Industrial Commodity Statistics Yearbook*.

Finance

CURRENCY AND EXCHANGE RATES

Monetary Units

100 cents = 1 Jamaican dollar (J $).

Sterling and US Dollar Equivalents (30 September 1997)

£1 sterling = J $58.08;
US $1 = J $35.95;
J $1,000 = £17.22 = US $27.81.

Average Exchange Rate (J $ per US $)

1994 33.086
1995 35.142
1996 37.120

BUDGET (J $ million, year ending 31 March)*

Revenue†	1994/95	1995/96	1996/97‡
Tax revenue	38,071	50,262	55,191
Taxes on income and profits	15,377	18,888	21,646
Taxes on production and consumption	12,323	15,469	17,139
Taxes on international trade	9,925	15,428	16,006
Bauxite levy	2,374	2,795	2,798
Other current revenue	1,930	3,585	3,310
Capital revenue	877	700	727
Total	43,253	57,342	62,026

Expenditure§	1994/95	1995/96	1996/97‡
Current expenditure	34,455	44,442	64,225
Wages and salaries	11,143	15,806	24,043
Other goods and services	3,900	5,157	12,902
Pensions	968	1,222	
Other current transfers	3,429	4,286	
Interest payments	15,015	17,971	27,280
Capital expenditure	5,177	11,201	13,498
Unallocated expenditure (net)	–535	–926	330
Total	39,097	54,717	78,052

* Figures refer to budgetary transactions of the central Government, excluding the operations of the National Insurance Fund and other government units with individual budgets.

† Excluding grants received (J $ million): 1,343 in 1994/95; 1,181 in 1995/96; 1,060‡ in 1996/97.

‡ Preliminary.

§ Excluding net lending (J $ million): 705 in 1994/95.

Source: IMF, *Jamaica—Statistical Annex* (October 1997).

INTERNATIONAL RESERVES (US $ million, at 31 December)

	1994	1995	1996
IMF special drawing rights	—	0.5	0.1
Foreign exchange	735.9	680.8	879.9
Total	735.9	681.3	880.0

Source: IMF, *International Financial Statistics.*

MONEY SUPPLY (J $ million at 31 December)

	1994	1995	1996
Currency outside banks	7,118	9,516	10,760
Demand deposits at commercial banks	14,134	19,804	22,788
Total money	21,252	29,320	33,548

Source: IMF, *International Financial Statistics.*

COST OF LIVING (Consumer Price Index; base: January 1988 = 100)

	1994	1995*	1996†
Food (incl. beverages)	700.3	842.7	1,045.7
Fuel and household supplies	564.8	645.0	941.5
Clothing (incl. footwear)	640.5	752.7	946.3
Rent and household operation	486.3	576.1	686.5
All items (incl. others)	635.6	762.2	963.4

* Preliminary † Estimates.

Source: IMF, *Jamaica—Statistical Annex* (October 1997).

NATIONAL ACCOUNTS (J $ million at current prices)

Expenditure on the Gross Domestic Product

	1992	1993	1994
Government final consumption expenditure	7,692	13,614	17,515
Private final consumption expenditure	45,911	66,954	89,477
Increase in stocks	202	726	326
Gross fixed capital formation	23,953	33,781	43,499
Total domestic expenditure	77,758	115,075	150,817
Exports of goods and services	50,552	57,834	81,957
Less Imports of goods and services	−51,319	−67,883	−92,374
GDP in purchasers' values	76,992	105,027	140,400
GDP at constant 1990 prices	31,204	31,645	31,882

Source: IMF, *International Financial Statistics.*

Gross Domestic Product by Economic Activity

	1994	1995*	1996†
Agriculture, forestry and fishing	11,926	15,318	16,870
Mining and quarrying	9,435	11,712	11,915
Manufacturing	24,313	28,871	34,001
Electricity and water	2,839	3,634	4,239
Construction	15,555	21,187	23,598
Wholesale and retail trade	30,292	38,420	45,812
Hotels, restaurants and clubs	2,559	3,234	3,746
Transport, storage and communication	11,056	13,689	21,623
Finance, insurance, real estate and business services	18,012	22,562	28,022
Producers of government services	10,717	15,171	23,053
Household and private non-profit services	819	1,084	1,341
Other community, social and personal services	2,460	3,228	4,229
Sub-total	139,982	178,109	218,449
Value-added tax	10,345	14,397	16,965
Less Imputed bank service charge	10,672	12,820	16,311
GDP in purchasers' values	139,655	179,686	219,103

* Preliminary. †Estimates.

Source: IMF, *Jamaica—Statistical Annex* (October 1997).

BALANCE OF PAYMENTS (US $ million)

	1993	1994	1995
Exports of goods f.o.b.	1,105.4	1,551.0	1,792.7
Imports of goods f.o.b.	−1,920.5	−2,064.8	−2,605.9
Trade balance	−815.1	−513.8	−813.2
Exports of services	1,260.7	1,272.4	1,387.8
Imports of services	−823.5	−905.2	−1,034.3
Balance on goods and services	−377.9	−146.6	−459.7
Other income received	117.0	104.6	146.6
Other income paid	−312.9	−398.7	−466.7
Balance on goods, services and income	−573.8	−440.7	−779.8
Current transfers received	415.9	498.4	597.2
Current transfers paid	−26.1	−40.8	−62.6
Current balance	−184.0	16.9	−245.2
Capital account (net)	−12.9	14.7	37.1
Direct investment from abroad	77.9	116.8	166.7
Other investment assets	1.1	127.1	—
Other investment liabilities	178.1	80.8	34.7
Net errors and omissions	49.7	12.9	36.1
Overall balance	109.9	369.2	29.4

Source: IMF, *International Financial Statistics.*

External Trade

PRINCIPAL COMMODITIES (distributed by SITC, US $ '000)

Imports c.i.f.	1989	1990	1991
Food and live animals	290,831	231,568	184,023
Dairy products and birds' eggs	54,056	38,767	35,651
Cereals and cereal preparations	102,854	93,795	55,367
Crude materials (inedible) except fuels	47,186	45,901	51,913
Mineral fuels, lubricants, etc.	266,543	380,152	325,020
Petroleum, petroleum products etc.	259,011	360,647	311,750
Crude petroleum oils, etc.	13	2	128,197
Refined petroleum products	257,262	358,958	181,577
Fuel oils	173,505	244,525	—
Chemicals and related products	219,887	225,774	219,707
Inorganic chemicals	71,652	88,345	84,570
Inorganic chemical elements, oxides and halogen salts	58,845	74,806	66,331
Plastic materials, etc.	44,704	36,848	34,087
Basic manufactures	384,746	295,603	294,612
Paper, paperboard and manufactures	69,809	57,366	58,342
Paper and paperboard	54,205	38,949	40,542
Textile yarn, fabrics, etc.	69,129	60,632	50,782
Iron and steel	79,045	43,670	43,467
Other metal manufactures	67,890	58,216	66,752
Machinery and transport equipment	399,806	488,949	394,399
General industrial machinery, equipment and parts	80,315	88,426	78,708
Electrical machinery, apparatus and appliances, etc.	60,170	73,130	53,216
Road vehicles	111,778	111,529	142,042
Miscellaneous manufactured articles	184,953	178,639	182,546
Clothing and accessories	90,224	87,203	90,147
Total (incl. others)	1,864,807	1,918,798	1,700,666

Exports f.o.b.	1989	1990	1991
Food and live animals	141,631	178,571	198,861
Vegetables and fruit	40,438	62,365	65,625
Fruit and nuts (not incl. oil nuts), fresh or dried	22,802	41,461	46,165
Bananas (incl. plantains)	19,345	35,552	39,979
Sugar, sugar preparations and honey	65,279	75,291	87,335
Sugar and honey	64,850	74,940	87,004
Sugars, beet and cane, raw, solid	64,839	73,666	87,002
Beverages and tobacco	35,510	36,916	32,347
Beverages	28,462	30,003	26,776
Alcoholic beverages	28,080	29,374	25,998
Spirits, liqueurs and other spirituous beverages	21,347	22,256	20,108
Crude materials (inedible) except fuels	597,422	736,513	662,015
Metalliferous ores and metal scrap	586,803	730,165	657,241
Ores and concentrates of base metals	585,924	728,267	656,030
Aluminium ores and concentrates (incl. alumina)	585,924	728,267	656,013
Aluminium ores and concentrates	111,028	102,973	113,054
Alumina (aluminium oxide)	474,896	625,294	542,959
Chemicals and related products	24,479	24,575	22,918
Machinery and transport equipment	32,075	30,361	25,740
Miscellaneous manufactured articles	128,221	99,345	102,432
Clothing and accessories	111,430	83,196	86,177
Under garments, knitted or crocheted	50,817	33,997	51,794
Total (incl. others)	997,492	1,143,298	1,074,302

Source: UN, *International Trade Statistics Yearbook*.

PRINCIPAL TRADING PARTNERS (US $ million)

Imports c.i.f.	1993	1994	1995
Canada	89	83	99
CARICOM	115	149	240
Trinidad and Tobago	80	121	203
European Union	286	293	297
United Kingdom	95	96	113
Japan	182	133	185
Netherlands Antilles	50	29	19
USA	1,093	1,145	1,399
Venezuela	91	70	57
Total (incl. others)	2,189	2,177	2,773

Exports f.o.b.	1993	1994	1995
Canada	107	148	154
CARICOM	60	58	60
Trinidad and Tobago	22	21	21
European Union	274	287	411
United Kingdom	148	164	192
Japan	19	16	27
Norway	97	102	109
USA	419	440	522
Total (incl. others)	1,075	1,219	1,430

Source: IMF, *Jamaica—Statistical Annex* (October 1997).

Transport

RAILWAYS (traffic)

	1988	1989	1990
Passenger-km ('000)	36,146	37,995	n.a.
Freight ton-km ('000)	115,076	28,609	1,931

Source: Jamaica Railway Corporation.

ROAD TRAFFIC (vehicles passing road fitness test in fiscal year)

	1988/89	1990/91*	1991/92
Motor cars	63,126	68,473	77,840
Trucks, tractors and buses	26,885	28,212	29,771
Motorcycles	8,181	7,597	8,675
Trailers	665	1,126	1,112

* Figures for 1989/90 were unavailable.

Source: Island Traffic Authority.

SHIPPING

Merchant Fleet (registered at 31 December)

	1994	1995	1996
Number of vessels	11	11	11
Total displacement ('000 grt)	7.4	9.3	9.3

Source: Lloyd's Register of Shipping, *World Fleet Statistics*.

International Sea-borne Freight Traffic (estimates, '000 metric tons)

	1989	1990	1991
Goods loaded	7,711	8,354	8,802
Goods unloaded	5,167	5,380	5,285

Source: Port Authority of Jamaica.

CIVIL AVIATION (traffic on scheduled services)

	1992	1993	1994
Kilometres flown (million)	12	13	13
Passengers carried ('000)	983	1,038	1,011
Passenger-km (million)	1,460	1,488	1,430
Total ton-km (million)	151	155	150

Source: UN, *Statistical Yearbook*.

Tourism

(year ending 31 March)

	1994/95	1995/96	1996/97*
Visitor arrivals ('000)	1,541	1,667	1,751
Stop-overs	973	1,044	1,056
Cruise-ship passengers and armed forces	568	623	695
Tourist expenditure (US $ million)	972	1,086	1,130

* Preliminary figures.

Source: IMF, *Jamaica—Statistical Annex* (October 1997).

Hotel rooms (1995): 29,376.

Communications Media

(units in use, unless otherwise indicated)

	1992	1993	1994
Radio receivers ('000)	1,040	1,045	1,060
Television receivers ('000)	330	340	345
Telephones (main lines in use, '000)*	167	208	251
Telefax stations (number in use)*	1,567	n.a.	n.a.
Mobile cellular telephones (subscribers)*	7,910	18,640	26,110
Daily newspapers (number)	3	n.a.	3
Circulation (estimates, '000)	160	n.a.	160

* Year beginning 1 April.

Source: mainly UNESCO, *Statistical Yearbook*.

Education

(1992/93)

	Institutions	Teachers	Students
Pre-primary	1,668*	4,158†‡	114,427†‡
Primary	192†	8,315‡	333,104‡
Secondary	141§	10,931	235,071
Tertiary	14§	395*	15,891*
University	1	395*	6,284*

* Figure for 1991/92.

† Figure for 1990/91.

‡ Public sector only.

§ Figure for 1984.

Source: mainly UNESCO, *Statistical Yearbook*.

Directory

The Constitution

The Constitution came into force at the independence of Jamaica on 6 August 1962. Amendments to the Constitution are enacted by Parliament, but certain entrenched provisions require ratification by a two-thirds majority in both chambers of the legislature, and some (such as a change of the head of state) require the additional approval of a national referendum.

HEAD OF STATE

The Head of State is the British monarch, who is locally represented by a Governor-General, appointed on the recommendation of the Jamaican Prime Minister.

THE LEGISLATURE

The Senate or Upper House consists of 21 Senators of whom 13 will be appointed by the Governor-General on the advice of the Prime Minister and eight by the Governor-General on the advice of the Leader of the Opposition. (Legislation enacted in 1984 provided for eight independent Senators to be appointed, after consultations with the Prime Minister, in the eventuality of there being no Leader of the Opposition.)

The House of Representatives consists of 60 elected members called Members of Parliament.

A person is qualified for appointment to the Senate or for election to the House of Representatives if he or she is a citizen of Jamaica or other Commonwealth country, of the age of 21 or more and has been ordinarily resident in Jamaica for the immediately preceding 12 months.

THE PRIVY COUNCIL

The Privy Council consists of six members appointed by the Governor-General after consultation with the Prime Minister, of whom at least two are persons who hold or who have held public office. The functions of the Council are to advise the Governor-General on the exercise of the Royal Prerogative of Mercy and on appeals on disciplinary matters from the three Service Commissions.

THE EXECUTIVE

The Prime Minister is appointed from the House of Representatives by the Governor-General as the person who, in the Governor-General's judgement, is best able to command the support of the majority of the members of that House.

The Leader of the Opposition is appointed by the Governor-General as the member of the House of Representatives who, in the Governor-General's judgement, is best able to command the support of the majority of those members of the House who do not support the Government.

The Cabinet consists of the Prime Minister and not fewer than 11 other ministers, not more than four of whom may sit in the Senate. The members of the Cabinet are appointed by the Governor-General on the advice of the Prime Minister.

THE JUDICATURE

The Judicature consists of a Supreme Court, a Court of Appeal and minor courts. Judicial matters, notably advice to the Governor-General on appointments, are considered by a Judicial Service Commission, the Chairman of which is the Chief Justice, members being the President of the Court of Appeal, the Chairman of the Public Service Commission and three others.

CITIZENSHIP

All persons born in Jamaica after independence automatically acquire Jamaican citizenship and there is also provision for the acquisition of citizenship by persons born outside Jamaica of Jamaican parents. Persons born in Jamaica (or persons born outside Jamaica of Jamaican parents) before independence who immediately prior to independence were citizens of the United Kingdom and colonies also automatically become citizens of Jamaica.

Appropriate provision is made which permits persons who do not automatically become citizens of Jamaica to be registered as such.

FUNDAMENTAL RIGHTS AND FREEDOMS

The Constitution includes provisions safeguarding the fundamental freedoms of the individual, irrespective of race, place of origin, political opinions, colour, creed or sex, subject only to respect for the rights and freedoms of others and for the public interest. The fundamental freedoms include the rights of life, liberty, security of the person and protection from arbitrary arrest or restriction of movement, the enjoyment of property and the protection of the law, freedom of conscience, of expression and of peaceful assembly and association, and respect for private and family life.

The Government

Head of State: HM Queen ELIZABETH II (succeeded to the throne 6 February 1952).

Governor-General: Sir HOWARD FELIX HANLAN COOKE (appointed 1 August 1991).

PRIVY COUNCIL OF JAMAICA

Dr VERNON LINDO, EWART FORREST, G. OWEN, W. H. SWABY, Dr DOUGLAS FLETCHER.

CABINET

(February 1998)

Prime Minister and Minister of Defence: PERCIVAL J. PATTERSON.

Deputy Prime Minister and Minister of Foreign Affairs and Foreign Trade: SEYMOUR MULLINGS.

Minister of Finance and Planning: Dr OMAR DAVIES.

Minister of the Environment and Housing: EASTON DOUGLAS.

Minister of Labour, Social Welfare and Sport: PORTIA SIMPSON.

Minister of Local Government, Youth and Community Development: ARNOLD BERTRAM.

Minister of National Security and Justice: K. D. KNIGHT.

Minister of Agriculture: ROGER CLARKE.

Minister of Industry and Investment: Dr PAUL ROBERTSON.

Minister of Mining and Energy: ROBERT PICKERSGILL.

Minister of Health: JOHN JUNOR.

Minister of Education and Culture: BURCHELL WHITEMAN.

Minister of Transport and Works: Dr PETER PHILLIPS.

Minister of Water: Dr KARL BLYTHE.

Minister of Commerce and Technology: PHILLIP PAULWELL.

Minister in the Office of the Prime Minister (responsible for tourism): FRANCIS TULLOCH.

Minister without Portfolio: MAXINE HENRY-WILSON.

MINISTRIES

Office of the Governor-General: King's House, Hope Rd, Kingston 10; tel. 927-6424.

Office of the Prime Minister: 1 Devon Rd, POB 272, Kingston 10; tel. 927-9941; telex 2398; fax 929-0005.

Ministry of Agriculture: Hope Gardens, Kingston 6; tel. 927-1731; fax 927-1904.

Ministry of Commerce and Technology: 36 Trafalgar Rd, Kingston 10.

Ministry of Education and Culture: 2 National Heroes Circle, Kingston 4; tel. 922-1400; fax 967-1837.

Ministry of the Environment and Housing: 2 Hagley Park Rd, Kingston 10; tel. 926-1590; fax 929-2591.

Ministry of Finance and Planning: 30 National Heroes Circle, Kingston 4; tel. 922-8600; telex 2447; fax 922-8804.

Ministry of Foreign Affairs and Foreign Trade: 21 Dominica Drive, POB 624, Kingston 5; tel. 926-4220; telex 2114; fax 929-5112.

Ministry of Health: 10 Caledonia Ave, Kingston 5; tel. 926-9220; fax 926-3857.

Ministry of Industry and Investment: PCJ Bldg, 36 Trafalgar Rd, Kingston 5; tel. 929-8990; fax 929-8196.

Ministry of Labour, Social Welfare and Sport: 1F North St, POB 10, Kingston; tel. 922-9500; fax 922-6902.

Ministry of Local Government, Youth and Community Development: 140 Maxfield Ave, Kingston 10; tel. 926-3210; fax 960-0725.

Ministry of Mining and Energy: PCJ Bldg, 36 Trafalgar Rd, Kingston 10; tel. 926-9170; fax 926-2835.

Ministry of National Security and Justice: 12 Ocean Blvd, Kingston Mall, Kingston 10; tel. 922-0080; fax 922-6950 (Justice), 922-6028 (National Security).

Ministry of Transport and Works: PCJ Bldg, 36 Trafalgar Rd, Kingston 10.

Ministry of Water: 36 Trafalgar Rd, Kingston 10.

Legislature

PARLIAMENT

Houses of Parliament: Gordon House, Duke St, Kingston; tel. 922-0200.

Senate

President: SYRINGA MARSHALL-BURNETT.

The Senate has 20 other members.

House of Representatives

Speaker: VIOLET NIELSON.

General Election, 18 December 1997

	Votes cast	Seats
People's National Party (PNP)	441,739	50
Jamaica Labour Party (JLP)	312,471	10
National Democratic Movement (NDM)	38,430	—
Total	792,640	60

Political Organizations

African Comprehensive Party (ACP): Kingston; f. 1988 as political branch of a Rastafarian sect, the Royal Ethiopian Judah Coptic church; opposes IMF and 'capitalist banking system'; advocates legalizing the use of marijuana for religious purposes; Leader ABUNA STEDWICK WHYTE.

Jamaica Labour Party (JLP): 20 Belmont Rd, Kingston 5; f. 1943 as political wing of the Bustamante Industrial Trade Union; supports free enterprise in a mixed economy and close co-operation with the USA; Leader EDWARD SEAGA; Gen. Sec. EDMUND BARTLETT.

National Democratic Movement (NDM): Kingston; f. 1995; advocates a clear separation of powers between the central executive and elected representatives; supports private investment and a market economy; Leader BRUCE GOLDING.

People's National Party (PNP): 89 Old Hope Rd, Kingston 5; tel. 978-1337; fax 927-4389; f. 1938; socialist principles; affiliated with the National Workers' Union; Leader PERCIVAL J. PATTERSON; Gen. Sec. MAXINE HENRY-WILSON.

Diplomatic Representation

EMBASSIES AND HIGH COMMISSIONS IN JAMAICA

Argentina: Dyoll Bldg, 40 Knutsford Blvd, Kingston 5; tel. 926-5588; fax 926-0580; e-mail embargen@kasnet.com; Ambassador: ALFREDO ALCORTA.

Brazil: PCMB Bldg, 3rd Floor, 64 Knutsford Blvd, Kingston 5; tel. 929-8607; fax 929-1259; e-mail brasking@infochan.com; Ambassador: SÉRGIO ARRUDA.

Canada: 30 Knutsford Blvd, POB 1500, Kingston 5; tel. 926-1500; telex 2130; e-mail gavin.stewart@knstn01.x400.gc.ca; High Commissioner: GAVIN STEWART.

Chile: 1 Holborn Rd, Kingston 10; tel. 968-0260; Ambassador: JAIME JANA.

China, People's Republic: 8 Seaview Ave, Kingston 10; tel. 927-0850; telex 2202; Ambassador: YU MINGSHENG.

Colombia: Victoria Mutual Bldg, 3rd Floor, 53 Knutsford Blvd, Kingston 5; tel. 929-1702; fax 929-1701; Ambassador: RICARDO VARGAS TAYLOR.

Costa Rica: Belvedere House, Beverly Drive, Kingston 5; tel. 927-5988; fax 978-3946; e-mail pepitico@toj.com; Ambassador: JÓSE DE J. CONEJO AMADOR.

Cuba: 9 Trafalgar Rd, Kingston 5; tel. 978-0931; telex 3710; fax 978-5372; Ambassador: DARÍO DE URRA.

France: 13 Hillcrest Ave, POB 93, Kingston 6; Ambassador: PIERRE ARIOLA.

Germany: 10 Waterloo Rd, POB 444, Kingston 10; tel. 926-6728; telex 2146; fax 929-8282; Ambassador: ADOLF EDERER.

Haiti: 2 Monroe Rd, Kingston 6; tel. 927-7595; Chargé d'affaires: ANDRÉ L. DORTONNE.

India: 4 Retreat Ave, POB 446, Kingston 6; tel. 927-0486; fax 978-2801; High Commissioner: V. B. SONI.

Italy: 10 Rovan Drive, Kingston 6; tel. 978-1273; fax 978-0675; Ambassador: RAMIRO RUGGIERO.

Japan: The Atrium, 32 Trafalgar Rd, Kingston 10; tel. 929-3338; fax 968-1373; Ambassador: S. MOTOI OKUBO.

Korea, Republic: Pan Jamaican Bldg, 2nd Floor, 60 Knutsford Blvd, Kingston 5; tel. 929-3035; Ambassador: SUK-HYUN KIM.

Mexico: PCJ Bldg, 36 Trafalgar Rd, Kingston 10; tel. 926-4242; telex 2255; Ambassador: LUIS ORTÍZ MONASTERIO CASTELLANOS.

Netherlands: Victoria Mutual Bldg, 53 Knutsford Blvd, Kingston 5; tel. 926-2026; telex 2177; fax 926-1248; Ambassador: E. W. P. KLIPP.

Nigeria: 5 Waterloo Rd, Kingston 10; tel. 926-6400; telex 2443; fax 968-7371; High Commissioner: EMMANUEL UGOCHUKWU.

Panama: Suite B-4, 1 Braemar Ave, Kingston 10; tel. and fax 978-1953; Chargé d'affaires: ERNESTO LOZANO LÓPEZ.

Russia: 22 Norbrook Drive, Kingston 8; tel. 924-1048; telex 2216; Ambassador: (vacant).

Spain: 25 Dominica Drive, 10th Floor, Kingston 5; tel. 929-6710; telex 2364; Ambassador: FERNANDO DE LA SERNA INCIARTE.

Trinidad and Tobago: Pan Jamaican Bldg, 3rd Floor, 60 Knutsford Blvd, Kingston 5; tel. 926-5730; fax 926-5801; e-mail t&thckgn@infochan.com; High Commissioner: PEARL WILSON.

United Kingdom: 28 Trafalgar Rd, POB 575, Kingston 10; tel. 926-9050; fax 929-7869; e-mail bhcjamaica@toj.com; High Commissioner: A. RICHARD THOMAS.

USA: Mutual Life Centre, 2 Oxford Rd, Kingston 5; tel. 929-4850; Ambassador: STANLEY L. MCLELLAND.

Venezuela: Petroleum Corpn of Jamaica Bldg, 3rd Floor, 36 Trafalgar Rd, Kingston 10; tel. 926-5510; telex 2179; fax 926-7442; Chargé d'affaires a.i.: NÉSTOR CASTELLANOS.

Judicial System

The Judicial System is based on English common law and practice. Final appeal is to the Judicial Committee of the Privy Council in the United Kingdom, although in September 1994 the Jamaican Government announced plans to establish a Caribbean Court of Appeal to fulfil this function.

Justice is administered by the Privy Council, Court of Appeal, Supreme Court (which includes the Revenue Court and the Gun

Court), Resident Magistrates' Court (which includes the Traffic Court), two Family Courts and the Courts of Petty Sessions.

Judicial Service Commission: Office of the Services Commissions, 63–67 Knutsford Blvd, Kingston 5; advises the Governor-General on judicial appointments, etc.; chaired by the Chief Justice.

Attorney-General: ARNOLD J. NICHOLSON.

SUPREME COURT

POB 491, Kingston; tel. 922-8300.

Chief Justice: LENSLEY WOLFE.

Senior Puisne Judge: C. F. B. ORR.

Master: Z. R. MCCALLA.

Registrar: M. L. MCINTOSH.

COURT OF APPEAL

POB 629, Kingston; tel. 922-8300.

President: R. CARL RATTRAY.

Registrar: G. P. LEVERS.

Religion

CHRISTIANITY

There are more than 100 Christian denominations active in Jamaica. According to the 1982 census, the largest religious bodies were the Church of God, Baptists, Anglicans and Seventh-day Adventists. Other denominations include the Methodist and Congregational Churches, the Ethiopian Orthodox Church, the Disciples of Christ, the Moravian Church, the Salvation Army and the Society of Friends (Quakers).

Jamaica Council of Churches: 14 South Ave, POB 30, Kingston 10; tel. 926-0974; f. 1941; 11 member churches and seven agencies; Pres. Rev. OLIVER DALEY; Gen. Sec. CYNTHIA CLAIR.

The Anglican Communion

Anglicans in Jamaica are adherents of the Church in the Province of the West Indies, comprising eight dioceses. The Archbishop of the Province is the Bishop of the North East Caribbean and Aruba. The Bishop of Jamaica, whose jurisdiction also includes Grand Cayman (in the Cayman Islands), is assisted by three suffragan Bishops (of Kingston, Mandeville and Montego Bay). The 1982 census recorded 154,548 Anglicans.

Bishop of Jamaica: Rt Rev. NEVILLE WORDSWORTH DE SOUZA, Church House, 2 Caledonia Ave, Kingston 5; tel. 926-6609; fax 968-0618.

The Roman Catholic Church

Jamaica comprises the archdiocese of Kingston in Jamaica (also including the Cayman Islands), and the dioceses of Montego Bay and Mandeville. At 31 December 1995 the estimated total of adherents in Jamaica and the Cayman Islands was 111,385, representing about 5% of the total population. The Archbishop and Bishops participate in the Antilles Episcopal Conference (currently based in Port of Spain, Trinidad and Tobago).

Archbishop of Kingston in Jamaica: Most Rev. EDGERTON ROLAND CLARKE, Archbishop's Residence, 21 Hopefield Ave, POB 43, Kingston 6; tel. 927-9915; fax 927-4487.

Other Christian Churches

Assembly of God: Evangel Temple, 3 Friendship Park Rd, Kingston 3; tel. 928-2728; Pastor WILSON.

Baptist Union: 6 Hope Rd, Kingston 10; tel. 926-1395; fax 968-7832; Pres. Rev. Dr HECKFORD SHARPE; Gen. Sec. Rev. TREVOR EDWARDS.

Church of God in Jamaica: 35A Hope Rd, Kingston 10; tel. 927-8128; 400,379 adherents (1982 census).

First Church of Christ, Scientist: 17 National Heroes Circle, C.S.O., Kingston 4.

Methodist Church (Jamaica District): 143 Constant Spring Rd, POB 892, Kingston 8; tel. and fax 924-2560; f. 1789; 18,284 mems; Chair. Rev. BRUCE B. SWAPP; Synod Sec. Rev. GILBERT G. BOWEN.

Moravian Church in Jamaica: 3 Hector St, POB 8369, Kingston 5; tel. 928-1861; f. 1754; 35,000 mems; Pres. Rev. STANLEY G. CLARKE.

Seventh-day Adventist Church: 56 James St, Kingston; tel. 922-7440; f. 1901; 150,722 adherents (1982 census); Pastor Rev. E. H. THOMAS.

United Church in Jamaica and the Cayman Islands: 12 Carlton Cres., POB 359, Kingston 10; tel. 926-8734; fax 929-0826; f. 1965 by merger of the Congregational Union of Jamaica (f. 1877) and the Presbyterian Church of Jamaica and Grand Cayman to become United Church of Jamaica and Grand Cayman; merged with Disciples of Christ in Jamaica in 1992 when name changed as above; 20,000 mems; Gen. Sec. Rev. MAITLAND EVANS.

RASTAFARIANISM

Rastafarianism is an important influence in Jamaican culture. The cult is derived from Christianity and a belief in the divinity of Ras (Prince) Tafari Makonnen (later Emperor Haile Selassie) of Ethiopia. It advocates racial equality and non-violence, but causes controversy by the use of 'ganja' (marijuana) as a sacrament. The 1982 census recorded 14,249 Rastafarians (0.7% of the total population). Although the religion is largely unorganized, there are some denominations.

Royal Ethiopian Judah Coptic Church: Kingston; not officially incorporated, on account of its alleged use of marijuana; Leader ABUNA S. WHYTE.

BAHÁ'Í FAITH

National Spiritual Assembly: 208 Mountain View Ave, Kingston 6; tel. 927-7051; fax 978-2344; incorporated in 1970; 6,300 mems resident in 368 localities.

ISLAM

At the 1982 census there were 2,238 Muslims.

JUDAISM

The 1991 census recorded 250 Jews.

United Congregation of Israelites: 92 Duke St, Kingston; tel. 927-7948; fax 978-6240; f. 1655; c. 250 mems; Spiritual Leader and Sec. ERNEST H. DE SOUZA; Pres. WALLACE R. CAMPBELL.

The Press

DAILIES

Daily Gleaner: 7 North St, POB 40, Kingston; tel. 922-3400; telex 2319; fax 922-2058; e-mail ads@jamaica-gleaner.com; internet http://www.jamaica-gleaner.com; f. 1834; morning; independent; Chair. and Man. Dir OLIVER CLARKE; Editor-in-Chief WYVOLYN GAGER; circ. 44,000.

Daily Star: 7 North St, POB 40, Kingston; tel. 922-3400; evening; Editor LEIGHTON LEVY; circ. 49,500.

Jamaica Herald: 29 Molynes Rd, Kingston 10; tel. 968-7721; fax 968-7722; Man. Editor FRANKLIN MCKNIGHT.

Jamaica Observer: Kingston; internet http:www.jamaicaobserver.com; f. 1993; Chair. GORDON 'BUTCH' STEWART; CEO Dr GEORGE T. PHILLIP.

PERIODICALS

Caribbean Challenge: 55 Church St, POB 186, Kingston; tel. 922-5636; f. 1957; monthly; Editor JOHN KEANE; circ. 18,000.

Caribbean Shipping: Creative Communications Inc, 20 West Kings House Rd, Kingston 10; tel. 968-7279; fax 926-2217; 2 a year.

Catholic Opinion: 21 Hopefield Ave, POB 43, Kingston 6; tel. 927-9915; fax 927-0140; monthly; religious.

Children's Own: 7 North St, POB 40, Kingston; weekly during term time; circ. 122,000.

The Enquirer: Kingston; tel. 922-3952.

Government Gazette: POB 487, Kingston; f. 1868; Govt Printer RALPH BELL; circ. 1,350.

Jamaica Churchman: 2 Caledonia Ave, Kingston 5; tel. 926-6608; quarterly; Editor BARBARA GLOUDON; circ. 7,000.

Jamaica Journal: 4 Camp Rd, Kingston 4; tel. 929-4048; fax 926-8817; f. 1967; 3 a year; literary, historical and cultural review; publ. by Instit. of Jamaica Publs Ltd; Man. Dir PATRICIA ROBERTS; Editor LEETA HEARNE.

Jamaica Weekly Gleaner: 7 North St, POB 40, Kingston; tel. 922-3400; weekly; overseas; Chair. and Man. Dir OLIVER CLARKE; circ. 13,599.

New Kingston Times: Kingston; tel. 929-4595.

Sunday Gleaner: 7 North St, POB 40, Kingston; tel. 922-3400; weekly; Editor-in-Chief WYVOLYN GAGER; circ. 100,000.

Sunday Herald: 86 Hagley Park Rd, Kingston 10; tel. 901-5022; fax 937-7313; f. 1997; weekly; Editor FRANKLYN MCKNIGHT; circ. 20,000.

Swing: 102 East St, Kingston; f. 1968; monthly; entertainment and culture; Editor ANDELL FORGIE; circ. 12,000.

The Vacationer: POB 614, Montego Bay; tel. 952-6006; f. 1987; monthly; Man. Editor EVELYN L. ROBINSON; circ. 8,000.

The Visitor Vacation Guide: 82 Barnett St, POB 1258, Montego Bay; tel. 952-5253; fax 952-6513; weekly; Editor LLOYD B. SMITH.

Weekend Star: 7 North St, POB 40, Kingston; tel. 922-3400; weekly; Editor LOLITA TRACEY-LONG; circ. 100,000.

The Western Mirror: 82 Barnett St, POB 1258, Montego Bay; tel. 952-5253; fax 952-6513; f. 1980; 2 a week; Man. Dir and Editor Lloyd B. Smith; circ. 16,000.

West Indian Medical Journal: Faculty of Medical Sciences, University of the West Indies, Kingston 7; tel. 927-1214; fax 927-2556; f. 1951; quarterly; Editor-in-Chief W. N. Gibbs; Asst Editor Bridget Williams; circ. 2,000.

PRESS ASSOCIATION

Press Association of Jamaica (PAJ): 5 East Ave, Kingston; tel. 926-7584; f. 1943; 240 mems; Pres. Desmond Allen; Sec. Monica Dias.

NEWS AGENCIES

Jampress Ltd: 3 Chelsea Ave, Kingston 10; tel. 926-8428; telex 3552; fax 929-6727; e-mail jamnews@infochan.com; f. 1984; govt news agency; Exec. Dir Desmond Allen.

Foreign Bureaux

Inter Press Service (IPS) (Italy): Suite 1G, 2-6 Melmac Ave, Kingston 5; tel. 960-0604; fax 929-6889; Third World news agency; Regional Editor Corinne Barnes.

Associated Press (USA) and CANA (Caribbean News Agency) are also represented in Jamaica.

Publishers

Caribbean Publishing Co Ltd: 10 Hagley Park Rd, Kingston 10; tel. 925-3228.

Jamaica Publishing House Ltd: 97 Church St, Kingston; tel. 922-1385; fax 922-3257; f. 1969; wholly-owned subsidiary of Jamaica Teachers' Asscn; educational, English language and literature, mathematics, history, geography, social sciences, music; Chair. Woodburn Miller; Man. Elaine R. Stennett.

Kingston Publishers Ltd: 7 Norman Road, Suite 10, LOJ Industrial Complex, Kingston CSO; tel. 928-8898; telex 2293; fax 928-5719; f. 1970; educational textbooks, general, travel, atlases, fiction, non-fiction, children's books; Chair. L. Michael Henry.

Western Publishers Ltd: 82 Barnett St, POB 1258, Montego Bay; tel. 952-5253; fax 952-6513; f. 1980; Man. Dir and Editor-in-Chief Lloyd B. Smith.

Government Publishing House

Jamaica Printing Services: 77 Duke St, Kingston; tel. 967-2250; Chair. Evadne Sterling; Man. Ralph Bell.

Broadcasting and Communications

TELECOMMUNICATIONS

Post and Telecommunications Dept: CSO, South Camp Rd, POB 7000, Kingston; tel. 922-9430; telex 2133; fax 922-9449; operates Postal Service of Jamaica; exercises regulatory responsibility for telecommunication services in Jamaica; Postmaster-Gen. Samuel E. Stewart; Chief Telecommunications Eng. Roy Humes.

Telecommunications of Jamaica Ltd (TOJ): 47 Half Way Tree Rd, POB 21, Kingston 5; tel. 929-9700; telex 2184; f. 1989; in 1995 merged with Jamaica Telephone Co Ltd and Jamaica International Telecommunications Ltd; Pres. E. Miller.

BROADCASTING

Jamaica Broadcasting Corpn (JBC): 5 South Odeon Ave, POB 100, Kingston 10; tel. 926-5620; telex 2218; fax 929-1029; f. 1959; fmr state-owned corpn; majority sold to RJR in 1997; semi-commercial radio and television; Chair. Errol Miller; Dir-Gen. Claude Robinson.

Radio 1 and Radio 2 FM Stereo are both broadcast island-wide for 24 hrs a day.

JBC Television (Programme Dir Desmond Elliott) broadcasts commercially for 140 hrs a week.

Radio

Educational Broadcasting Service: Multi-Media Centre, 37 Arnold Road, Kingston 4; tel. 922-9370; f. 1964; radio broadcasts during school term; Pres. Ouida Hylton-Tomlinson.

Grove Broadcasting: 1B Derrymore Rd, POB 282, Kingston 10; tel. 968-5023; fax 968-8332; Exec. Dir Karl Young.

Independent Radio: 6 Bradley Ave, Kingston 10; tel. 968-4880; fax 968-9165; commercial radio station; broadcasts 24 hrs a day on FM; Gen. Man. Newton James.

IRIE FM: Coconut Grove, Great House, POB 202, Ocho Rios; tel. 974-5043; fax 974-5943; f. 1991; commercial radio station.

Island Broadcasting Services Ltd: 41B Half Way Tree Rd, Kingston 5; tel. 929-1344; fax 929-1345; commercial; broadcasts 24 hrs a day on FM; Exec. Chair. Neville James.

KLAS-FM: 81 Knutsford Blvd, Kingston 5; f. 1991; commercial radio station.

Radio Jamaica Ltd (RJR): Broadcasting House, 32 Lyndhurst Rd, POB 23, Kingston 5; tel. 926-1100; fax 929-7467; e-mail rjrnews @toj.com; f. 1947; commercial, public service; two channels, RJR the Supreme Sound and FAME-FM; Man. Dir J. A. Lester Spaulding.

RJR the Supreme Sound (Programme Dir Donald Topping) broadcasts on AM and FM, island-wide, for 24 hrs a day.

FAME FM (Programme Dir Norma Brown-Bell) broadcasts on FM, island-wide, for 24 hrs a day.

Finance

(cap. = capital; p.u. = paid up; res = reserves; dep. = deposits; m. = million; brs = branches; amounts in Jamaican dollars)

BANKING

Central Bank

Bank of Jamaica: Nethersole Place, POB 621, Kingston; tel. 922-0750; telex 2165; fax 922-0858; e-mail res.lib@infochan.com; f. 1960; cap. 4.0m., res 98.7m., dep. 46,823.6m. (Dec. 1996); Gov. Derick Latibeaudière.

Commercial Banks

Bank of Nova Scotia Jamaica Ltd (Canada): Scotiabank Centre Bldg, cnr Duke and Port Royal Sts, POB 709, Kingston; tel. 922-1000; telex 2297; fax 924-9294; f. 1967; cap. 731.8m., res 2,846.3m., dep. 33,815.5m. (Oct. 1996); Chair. Bruce R. Birmingham; Man. Dir William E. Clarke; 34 brs.

Century National Bank Ltd: 14–20 Port Royal St, Ground Floor, Jamaica Conference Centre, Kingston; tel. 922-3105; fax 922-8276; taken over by the Govt in 1996.

CIBC Jamaica Ltd (Canada): CIBC Centre, 23–27 Knutsford Blvd, POB 762, Kingston 5; tel. 929-7742; telex 2169; fax 929-7751; subsidiary of Canadian Imperial Bank of Commerce; cap. 96.7m., res 555.1m., dep. 8,623.1m. (Oct. 1997); Man. Dir A. W. Webb; 13 brs.

CIBC Trust and Merchant Bank Jamaica Ltd (Canada): 23–27 Knutsford Blvd, Kingston 5; tel. 929-9310; fax 926-1025; f. 1960 as the Canadian Bank of Commerce Trust Co (Caribbean), adopted current name in 1991; cap. 25m., res 14m., dep. 289m. (Oct. 1997); Gen. Man. Raymond Campbell.

Citibank, NA (USA): 63–67 Knutsford Blvd, POB 286, Kingston 5; tel. 926-3270; telex 2115; fax 929-3745.

Citizens Bank Ltd: 17 Dominica Drive, Kingston 5; tel. 960-3192; telex 2129; fax 960-3335; f. 1967 as Jamaica Citizens Bank Ltd, name changed 1993; cap. 82.0m., res 171.2m., dep. 6,437.8m. (Dec. 1995); Chair. Dr Owen Jefferson; Man. Dir Michael Wright; 14 brs.

Eagle Commercial Bank Ltd: 20–22 Trinidad Terrace, Kingston 5; tel. 968-7007; Man. Dir Lloyd O. Wiggan.

Island Victoria: 6 St Lucia Ave, Kingston 5; tel. 968-5800; Chair. Fayden McMorris.

National Commercial Bank Jamaica Ltd: 'The Atrium', 32 Trafalgar Rd, POB 88, Kingston 10; tel. 929-9050; telex 2139; fax 929-8399; f. 1977; merged with Mutual Security Bank in 1996; cap. 200.0m., res 1,446.9m., dep. 34,827.1m. (Sept. 1996); Chair Gloria D. Knight; Man. Dir Rex James; 33 brs.

National Export-Import Bank of Jamaica Ltd: 48 Duke St, POB 3, Kingston; tel. 922-9690; telex 3650; fax 922-9184; e-mail eximjam@toj.com; replaced Jamaica Export Credit Insurance Corpn; Chair. Dr Owen Jefferson.

National Investment Bank of Jamaica Ltd: 11 Oxford Rd, POB 889, Kingston 5; tel. 960-9691; fax 920-0379; e-mail nibj@infochan.com; Chair. David Coore; Pres. Dr Gavin Chen.

Workers' Savings and Loan Bank: 12 Trafalgar Rd, Kingston 10; tel. 927-3540; telex 2226; f. 1973; cap. p.u. 83m., res 11m., dep. 3,700m. (1996); Gen. Man. Howard McIntosh; CEO and Chair. Delroy Lindsay; 12 brs.

Development Banks

Jamaica Mortgage Bank: 33 Tobago Ave, POB 950, Kingston 5; tel. 929-6350; fax 968-5428; f. 1971 by the Jamaican Govt and the US Agency for Int. Devt; wholly govt-owned statutory org. since 1973; intended to function primarily as a secondary market facility for home mortgages and to mobilize long-term funds for housing developments in Jamaica; also insures home mortgage loans made by approved financial institutions, thus transferring risk of default on a loan to the Govt; Chair. Peter Thomas; Man. Dir Everton Hanson.

National Development Bank of Jamaica Ltd: 11A–15 Oxford Rd, POB 8309, Kingston 5; tel. 929-6124; telex 2381; fax 929-6996; e-mail ndb@ndbjam.com; internet http://www.ndbjam.com; replaced Jamaica Development Bank, f. 1969; provides funds for medium- and long-term devt-orientated projects in the tourism, industrial, agro-industrial and mining sectors through financial intermediaries; Pres. NATAN RICHARDS; Chair. HUNTLEY MANHERTZ.

Agricultural Credit Bank of Jamaica: 11A–15 Oxford Rd, POB 466, Kingston 5; tel. 929-4010; fax 929-6055; f. 1981; provides loans to small farmers through co-operative banks; Man. Dir KINGSLEY THOMAS; Chair. ARTHUR BARRET.

Trafalgar Development Bank: The Towers, 7th Floor, 25 Dominica Drive, Kingston 5; tel. 929-3383.

Banking Association

Jamaica Bankers' Association: POB 1079, Kingston; tel. 929-9050; fax 929-8399; Pres. PETER MOSES.

STOCK EXCHANGE

Jamaica Stock Exchange Ltd: 40 Harbour St, Kingston; tel. 967-3271; fax 922-6966; f. 1968; 45 ordinary share issues, 13 preferential, 1 debenture listed (July 1994), 50 cos listed (Jan. 1995), market capitalization J $58,018m. (Dec. 1994); Chair. RITA HUMPHRIES-LEWIN; Gen. Man. C. WAIN ITON.

INSURANCE

Government Supervisory Authority: Office of the Superintendent of Insurance, 51 St Lucia Ave, POB 800, Kingston 5; tel. 926-1790; fax 968-4346; f. 1972; Superintendent YVONNE BLENMAN (acting).

Jamaica Association of General Insurance Companies: 58 Half Way Tree Rd, POB 459, Kingston 10; tel. 929-8404; Man. GLORIA M. GRANT; Chair. ERROL T. ZIADIE.

Principal Companies

British Caribbean Insurance Co Ltd: 36 Duke St, POB 170, Kingston; tel. 922-1260; fax 922-4475; f. 1962; general insurance; Gen. Man. LESLIE W. CHUNG.

Dyoll Insurance Co Ltd: 40–46 Knutsford Blvd, POB 313, Kingston 5; tel. 926-4711; telex 2208; fax 928-7546; f. 1965; Pres. DAVID WILLIAMS.

Globe Insurance Co of the West Indies Ltd: 17 Dominica Drive, POB 401, Kingston 5; tel. 926-3720; telex 2150; fax 929-2727; Gen. Man. R. E. D. THWAITES.

Insurance Co of the West Indies Ltd (ICWI): 2 St Lucia Ave, POB 306, Kingston 5; tel. 926-9182; telex 6641; fax 929-6641; Chair. DENNIS LALOR; CEO KENNETH BLAKELEY.

Jamaica General Insurance Co Ltd: 9 Duke St, POB 408, Kingston; tel. 922-6420; fax 922-2073; Man. Dir A. C. LEVY.

The Jamaica Mutual Life Assurance Society: 2 Oxford Rd, POB 430, Kingston 5; tel. 926-9024; telex 2450; fax 929-7098; f. 1844; Pres. RALPH M. PARKES.

Life of Jamaica Ltd: 28–48 Barbados Ave, Kingston 5; tel. 929-8920; fax 929-4730; f. 1970; life and health insurance, pensions; Pres. R. D. WILLIAMS.

NEM Insurance Co (Jamaica) Ltd: NEM House, 9 King St, Kingston; tel. 922-1460; fax 922-4045; fmrly the National Employers' Mutual General Insurance Asscn; Gen. Man. NEVILLE HENRY.

Trade and Industry

GOVERNMENT AGENCIES

Jamaica Commodity Trading Co Ltd: 8 Ocean Blvd, POB 1021, Kingston; tel. 922-0971; telex 2318; f. 1981 as successor to State Trading Corpn; oversees all importing on behalf of state; Chair. DAVID GAYNAIR; Man. Dir ANDREE NEMBHARD.

Jamaica Information Service (JIS): 58A Half Way Tree Rd, POB 2222, Kingston 10; tel. 926-3741; telex 2393; fax 926-6715; f. 1963; information agency for govt policies and programmes, ministries and public sector agencies; Exec. Dir GLORIA ROYALE-DAVIS.

DEVELOPMENT ORGANIZATIONS

ADC Group of Companies: Mais House, Hope Rd, POB 552, Kingston; tel. 977-4412; fax 977-4411; f. 1989; manages and develops breeds of cattle, provides warehousing, cold storage, offices and information for exporters and distributors of non-traditional crops and ensures the proper utilization of agricultural lands under its control; Chair. Dr KEITH ROACHE; Gen. Man. DUDLEY IRVING.

Agricultural Development Corpn (ADC): Kingston; tel. 926-9160; f. 1952; Chair. Dr C. L. BENT; Sec. D. FORRESTER.

Coffee Industry Development Co: Marcus Garvey Drive, Kingston 15; tel. 923-5645; fax 923-7587; f. 1981; to implement coffee devt and rehabilitation programmes financed by international aid agencies; Sec. JOYCE CHANG.

Jamaica Promotions (JAMPRO) Ltd: 35 Trafalgar Rd, Kingston 10; tel. 929-7190; telex 2222; fax 924-9650; e-mail jampro@investjamaica.com; f. 1988 by merger of Jamaica Industrial Development Corpn, Jamaica National Export Corpn and Jamaica National Investment Promotion Ltd; economic devt agency; Pres. PATRICIA FRANCIS; Chair. JOSEPH A. MATALON.

National Development Agency Ltd: Kingston; tel. 922-5445; telex 2444.

Planning Institute of Jamaica: 8 Ocean Blvd, Kingston 5; tel. 967-3690; telex 3529; fax 967-3688; e-mail doccen@mail.colis.com; f. 1955 as the Central Planning Unit; adopted current name in 1984; monitoring performance of the economy and the social sector; publishing of devt plans and social surveys; Dir-Gen. WESLEY HUGHES.

Urban Development Corpn: The Office Centre, 8th Floor, 12 Ocean Blvd, Kingston; tel. 922-8310; telex 2281; fax 922-9326; f. 1968; responsibility for urban renewal and devt within designated areas; Chair. Dr VINCENT LAWRENCE; Gen. Man. IVAN ANDERSON.

CHAMBERS OF COMMERCE

Associated Chambers of Commerce of Jamaica: 7–8 East Parade, POB 172, Kingston; tel. 922-0150; f. 1974; 12 associated Chambers of Commerce; Pres. RAY CAMPBELL.

Jamaica Chamber of Commerce: 7–8 East Parade, POB 172, Kingston; tel. 922-0150; fax 924-9056; f. 1779; 450 mems; Pres. HOWARD HAMILTON.

INDUSTRIAL AND TRADE ASSOCIATIONS

Cocoa Industry Board: Marcus Garvey Drive, POB 68, Kingston 15; tel. 923-6411; fax 923-5837; f. 1957; has statutory powers to regulate and develop the industry; owns and operates four central fermentaries; Chair. JOSEPH SUAH; Man./Sec. NEVILLE CONDAPPA.

Coconut Industry Board: 18 Waterloo Rd, Half Way Tree, Kingston 10; tel. 926-1770; fax 968-1360; f. 1945; 9 mems; Chair. R. A. JONES; Gen. Man. JAMES S. JOYLES.

Coffee Industry Board: Marcus Garvey Drive, POB 508, Kingston 15; tel. 923-5850; fax 923-7587; f. 1950; 9 mems; has wide statutory powers to regulate and develop the industry; Chair. DOUGLAS GRAHAM; Gen. Man. JOHN PICKERSGILL.

Jamaica Bauxite Institute: Hope Gardens, POB 355, Kingston 6; tel. 927-2073; telex 2309; fax 927-1159; f. 1975; adviser to the Govt in the negotiation of agreements, consultancy services to clients in the bauxite/alumina and related industries, laboratory services for mineral and soil-related services, Pilot Plant services for materials and equipment testing, research and development; Gen. Man. PARRIS A. LYEW-AYEE.

Jamaica Export Trading Co Ltd: 6 Waterloo Rd, POB 645, Kingston 10; tel. 929-4390; fax 926-1608; e-mail jetcoja@infochan.com; f. 1977; export trading in non-traditional products, incl. spices, fresh produce, furniture, garments, processed foods, etc.; Chair. ANTHONY CHANG; Man. Dir HERNAL HAMILTON.

Sugar Industry Authority: 5 Trevennion Park Rd, POB 127, Kingston 10; tel. 926-5930; telex 2113; fax 929-6149; f. 1970; statutory body under portfolio of Ministry of Agriculture; responsible for regulation and control of sugar industry and sugar marketing; conducts research through Sugar Industry Research Institute; Exec. Chair. Dr HUNTLEY MANHERTZ; CEO R. EVON BROWN.

Trade Board: 107 Constant Spring Rd, Kingston 10; tel. 969-0478; Admin. JEAN MORGAN.

EMPLOYERS' ORGANIZATIONS

All-Island Banana Growers' Association Ltd: Banana Industry Bldg, 10 South Ave, Kingston 4; tel. 922-5492; fax 922-5497; f. 1946; 1,500 mems (1997); Chair. BOBBY POTTINGER; Sec. I. CHANG.

All-Island Jamaica Cane Farmers' Association: 4 North Ave, Kingston 4; tel. 922-3010; fax 922-2077; f. 1941; registered cane farmers; 27,000 mems; Chair. KENNETH A. HAUGHTON; Man. DAVID BELINFANTI.

Banana Export Co (BECO): 1A Braemar Ave, Kingston 10; tel. 927-3402; fax 978-6096; f. 1985 to replace Banana Co of Jamaica; oversees the devt of the banana industry; Chair. Dr MARSHALL HALL.

Citrus Growers' Association Ltd: 1A North Ave, Kingston Gardens, Kingston 4; tel. 922-8230; fax 922-2774; f. 1944; 13,000 mems; Chair. IVAN H. TOMLINSON.

Jamaica Exporters' Association (JEA): 13 Dominica Drive, POB 9, Kingston 5; tel. 929-1292; telex 2421; fax 929-3831; Pres. KARL JAMES; Exec. Dir PAULINE GRAY.

Jamaica Livestock Association: Newport East, POB 36, Kingston; f. 1941; tel. 922-7130; telex 2382; fax 923-5046; 7,316 mems; Chair. Dr JOHN MASTERTON; Man. Dir and CEO HENRY J. RAINFORD.

Jamaica Manufacturers' Association Ltd: 85A Duke St, Kingston; tel. 922-8869; fax 922-0051; e-mail jma@toj.com; f. 1947; 400 mems; Pres. SAMEER YOUNIS.

Jamaica Producers' Group Ltd: 6A Oxford Rd, POB 237, Kingston 5; tel. 926-3503; telex 2278; fax 929-3636; e-mail jpg@infochan.com; f. 1927; fmrly Jamaica Banana Producers' Asscn; Chair. C. H. JOHNSTON; Man. Dir MARSHALL HALL.

Jamaican Association of Sugar Technologists: c/o Sugar Industry Research Institute, Mandeville; tel. 962-2241; fax 962-1288; f. 1936; 265 mems; Pres. MICHAEL HYLTON; Hon. Sec. H. M. THOMPSON.

Private Sector Organization of Jamaica (PSOJ): 39 Hope Rd, POB 236, Kingston 10; tel. 927-6238; fax 927-5137; federative body of private business individuals, cos and asscns; Pres. CLIFTON CAMERON; Exec. Dir CHARLES A. ROSS.

Small Businesses' Association of Jamaica (SBAJ): 2 Trafalgar Rd, Kingston 5; tel. 927-7071; fax 978-2738; Pres. ALBERT GRAY; Exec. Dir ESME L. BAILEY.

Sugar Manufacturing Corpn of Jamaica Ltd: 5 Trevennion Park Rd, Kingston 5; tel. 926-5930; telex 2113; fax 926-6149; established to represent the sugar manufacturers in Jamaica; deals with all aspects of the sugar industry and its by-products; provides liaison between the Govt, the Sugar Industry Authority and the All-Island Jamaica Cane Farmers' Asscn; 9 mems; Chair. CHRISTOPHER BOVELL; Gen. Man. DERYCK T. BROWN.

UTILITIES

Electricity

Jamaica Public Service Co (JPSCo): Dominion Life Bldg, 6 Knutsford Blvd, POB 54, Kingston 5; tel. 926-3190; telex 2180; fax 968-3337; responsible for the generation and supply of electricity to the island; plans for divestment suspended in late 1996; Chair. GORDON SHIRLEY; Man. Dir DERRICK DYER.

Water

National Water Resources Authority: Kingston.

TRADE UNIONS

Bustamante Industrial Trade Union (BITU): 98 Duke St, Kingston; tel. 922-2443; fax 967-0120; f. 1938; Pres. HUGH SHEARER; Gen. Sec. GEORGE FYFFE; 60,000 mems.

National Workers' Union of Jamaica (NWU): 130–132 East St, Kingston 16; tel. 922-1150; e-mail nwyou@toj.com; f. 1952; affiliated to the International Confederation of Free Trade Unions, etc.; Pres. CLIVE DOBSON; Gen. Sec. LLOYD GOODLEIGH; 10,000 mems.

Trades Union Congress of Jamaica: 25 Sutton St, POB 19, Kingston; tel. 922-5313; fax 922-5468; affiliated to the Caribbean Congress of Labour and the International Confederation of Free Trade Unions; Pres. E. SMITH; Gen. Sec. HOPETON CRAVEN; 20,000 mems.

Principal Independent Unions

Dockers' and Marine Workers' Union: 48 East St, Kingston 16; tel. 922-6067; Pres. MILTON A. SCOTT.

Industrial Trade Union Action Council: 2 Wildman St, Kingston; Pres. RODERICK FRANCIS; Gen. Sec. KEITH COMRIE.

Jamaica Federation of Musicians' and Artistes' Unions: POB 1125, Montego Bay 1; tel. 952-3238; f. 1958; Pres. HEDLEY H. G. JONES; Sec. CARL AYTON; 2,000 mems.

Jamaica Local Government Officers' Union: c/o Public Service Commission, Knutsford Blvd, Kingston 5; Pres. E. LLOYD TAYLOR.

Jamaica Teachers' Association: 97 Church St, Kingston; tel. 922-1385; fax 922-3257; e-mail jta@toj.com; Pres. PATRICK SMITH.

Master Printers' Association of Jamaica: POB 19, Kingston 11; f. 1943; 44 mems; Pres. HERMON SPOERRI; Sec. RALPH GORDON.

National Union of Democratic Teachers (NUDT): 69 Church St, Kingston; tel. 922-3902; f. 1978; Pres. and Gen. Sec. HOPETON HENRY.

Union of Schools, Agricultural and Allied Workers (USAAW): 2 Wildman St, Kingston; tel. 967-2970; f. 1978; Pres. IAN HINES.

United Portworkers' and Seamen's Union: Kingston.

University and Allied Workers' Union (UAWU): Students' Union, University of West Indies, Mona; tel. 927-7968; affiliated to the WPJ; Gen. Sec. Dr TREVOR MUNROE.

There are also 35 associations registered as trade unions.

Transport

RAILWAYS

There are about 339 km (211 miles) of railway, all standard gauge, in Jamaica. Most of the system is operated by the Jamaica Railway Corpn, which is subsidized by the Government. The main lines are from Kingston to Montego Bay and Spanish Town to Ewarton and Port Antonio. Passenger services were suspended in 1992. There are four railways for the transport of bauxite.

Jamaica Railway Corpn (JRC): 142 Barry St, POB 489, Kingston; tel. 922-6620; telex 2190; fax 922-4539; f. 1845 as Jamaica Railway Co, the earliest British colonial railway; transferred to JRC in 1960; govt-owned, but autonomous, statutory corpn until 1990, when it was partly leased to Alcan Jamaica Co Ltd as the first stage of a privatization scheme; 207 km of railway; Chair. W. TAYLOR; Gen. Man. OWEN CROOKS.

Alcoa Railroads: Alcoa Minerals of Jamaica Inc, May Pen PO; tel. 986-2561; fax 986-2026; 43 km of standard-gauge railway; transport of bauxite; Superintendent RICHARD HECTOR; Man. FITZ CARTY (Railroad Operations and Maintenance).

Kaiser Jamaica Bauxite Co Railway: Discovery Bay PO, St Ann; tel. 973-2221; telex 7404; 25 km of standard-gauge railway; transport of bauxite; Gen. Man. GENE MILLER.

ROADS

Jamaica has a good network of tar-surfaced and metalled motoring roads. According to estimates by the International Road Federation, there were 19,000 km of roads in 1996, of which 70.7% were paved.

SHIPPING

The principal ports are Kingston, Montego Bay and Port Antonio. The port at Kingston has four container berths, and is a major transhipment terminal for the Caribbean area. Jamaica has interests in the multi-national shipping line WISCO (West Indies Shipping Corpn—based in Trinidad and Tobago). Services are also provided by most major foreign lines serving the region.

Port Authority of Jamaica: 15–17 Duke St, Kingston; tel. 922-0290; telex 2386; fax 924-9437; e-mail pajmktg@infochan.com; f. 1966; Govt's principal maritime agency; responsible for monitoring and regulating the navigation of all vessels berthing at Jamaican ports, for regulating the tariffs on public wharves, and for the devt of industrial Free Zones in Jamaica; Pres. and Chair. NOEL HYLTON; Exec. Vice-Pres. KENNETH GARRICK.

Kingston Free Zone Co Ltd: 27 Shannon Drive, POB 16, Kingston 15; tel. 923-5274; telex 2478; fax 923-0623; f. 1976; subsidiary of Port Authority of Jamaica; management and promotion of an export-orientated industrial free trade zone for cos from various countries; Chair. ANTHONY PICKERSGILL; Gen. Man. ERROL HEWITT.

Montego Bay Export Free Zone: c/o Port Authority of Jamaica, 15–17 Duke St, Kingston; tel. 922-0290; telex 2386.

Shipping Association of Jamaica: 4 Fourth Ave, Newport West, POB 40, Kingston 15; tel. 923-3491; telex 2431; fax 923-3421; e-mail pcs@infochan.com; f. 1939; 63 mems; an employers' trade union which regulates the supply and management of stevedoring labour in Kingston; represents members in negotiations with govt and trade bodies; Pres. GRANTLEY STEPHENSON; Gen. Man. ALVIN C. HENRY.

Principal Shipping Companies

Jamaica Freight and Shipping Co Ltd (JFS): 80–82 Second St, Port Bustamante, POB 167, Kingston 13; tel. 923-9371; telex 2260; fax 923-4091; e-mail cshaw@toj.com; cargo services to and from the USA, Caribbean, Central and South America, the United Kingdom, Japan and Canada; Exec. Chair. CHARLES JOHNSTON; Man. Dir GRANTLEY STEPHENSON.

Petrojam Ltd: 96 Marcus Garvey Drive, POB 241, Kingston; tel. 923-8727; telex 2119; fax 923-5698; Man. Dir STEPHEN WEDDERBURN (acting).

Portcold Ltd: 122 Third St, Newport West, Kingston 13; tel. 923-7425; telex 2473; fax 923-5713; Chair. and Man. Dir ISHMAEL E. ROBERTSON.

CIVIL AVIATION

There are two international airports linking Jamaica with North America, Europe, and other Caribbean islands. The Norman Manley International Airport is situated 22.5 km (14 miles) outside Kingston. The Donald Sangster International Airport is 5 km (3 miles) from Montego Bay.

Air Jamaica Ltd: 72–76 Harbour St, Kingston; tel. 922-3460; telex 2328; fax 922-0107; f. 1968; privatized in 1994; services within the Caribbean and to Canada (in asscn with Air Canada), the USA and the United Kingdom; Chair. GORDON 'BUTCH' STEWART; CEO ANDREW GRAY.

Air Jamaica Express: Tinson Pen Aerodrome, Kingston 11; tel. 923-8680; fax 924-8155; previously known as Trans-Jamaican Airlines; internal services between Kingston, Montego Bay, Negril, Ocho Rios and Port Antonio; Chair. GORDON 'BUTCH' STEWART; CEO ANDREW GRAY.

Airports Authority of Jamaica: Victoria Mutual Bldg, 53 Knutsford Blvd, POB 567, Kingston 5; tel. 926-1622; fax 929-8171; Chair. CEZLEY SAMPSON; Pres. LUCIEN RATTRAY.

Civil Aviation Department: Kingston; tel. 926-9115.

Tourism

Tourists, mainly from the USA, visit Jamaica for its beaches, mountains, historic buildings and cultural heritage. In 1996/97 there were an estimated 1,751,000 visitors (of whom 1,056,000 were 'stop-over' visitors and 695,000 were cruise-ship passengers). Tourist receipts were estimated to be US $1,130m. in that year.

Jamaica Tourist Board (JTB): ICWI Bldg, 2 St Lucia Ave, Kingston 5; tel. 929-9200; fax 929-9375; f. 1955; a statutory body set up by the Govt to develop all aspects of the tourist industry through marketing, promotional and advertising efforts; Chair. R. DANNY WILLIAMS; Dir of Tourism FAY PICKERSGILL.

Jamaica Hotel and Tourist Association (JHTA): 2 Ardenne Rd, Kingston 10; tel. 926-3635; fax 929-1054; f. 1961; trade assn for hoteliers and other cos involved in Jamaican tourism; Pres. JAMES SAMUELS; Exec. Dir CAMILLE NEEDHAM.

JAPAN

Introductory Survey

Location, Climate, Language, Religion, Flag, Capital

Japan lies in eastern Asia and comprises a curved chain of more than 3,000 islands. Four large islands, named (from north to south) Hokkaido, Honshu, Shikoku and Kyushu, account for about 98% of the land area. Hokkaido lies just to the south of Sakhalin, a large Russian island, and about 1,300 km (800 miles) east of Russia's mainland port of Vladivostok. Southern Japan is about 150 km (93 miles) east of the Republic of Korea. Although summers are temperate everywhere, the climate in winter varies sharply from cold in the north to mild in the south. Temperatures in Tokyo range from −6°C (21°F) to 30°C (86°F). Typhoons and heavy rains are common in summer. The language is Japanese. The major religions are Shintoism and Buddhism, and there is a Christian minority. The national flag (proportions 10 by 7) is white, with a red disc (a sun without rays) in the centre. The capital is Tokyo.

Recent History

Following Japan's defeat in the Second World War, Japanese forces surrendered in August 1945. Japan signed an armistice in September, and the country was placed under US military occupation. A new democratic constitution, which took effect from May 1947, renounced war and abandoned the doctrine of the Emperor's divinity. Following the peace treaty of September 1951, Japan regained its independence on 28 April 1952, although it was not until 1972 that the last of the US-administered outer islands were returned to Japanese sovereignty.

In November 1955 rival conservative groups merged to form the Liberal-Democratic Party (LDP). Nobusuke Kishi, who became Prime Minister in February 1957, was succeeded by Hayato Ikeda in July 1960. Ikeda was replaced by Eisaku Sato in November 1964. Sato remained in office until July 1972, when he was succeeded by Kakuei Tanaka.

Tanaka's premiership was beset by problems, leading to his replacement by Takeo Miki in December 1974. Tanaka was subsequently accused of accepting bribes from the Marubeni Corporation, and he was arrested in July 1976. The LDP lost its overall majority in the House of Representatives (the lower house of the Diet) at a general election held in December. Miki resigned and was succeeded by Takeo Fukuda. However, Mayayoshi Ohira defeated Fukuda in the LDP presidential election of November 1978, and replaced him as Prime Minister in December. Ohira was unable to win a majority in the lower house at elections in October 1979. In May 1980 the Government was defeated in a motion of 'no confidence', proposed by the Japan Socialist Party (JSP), forcing Ohira to dissolve the lower house. Ohira died before the elections in June, when the LDP won 284 of the 511 seats, although obtaining only a minority of the votes cast. In July Zenko Suzuki, a relatively little-known compromise candidate, was elected President of the LDP, and subsequently appointed Prime Minister. In November 1981 Suzuki reorganized the Cabinet, distributing major posts among the five feuding LDP factions. The growing factionalism of the LDP and the worsening economic crisis prompted Suzuki's resignation as Prime Minister and LDP President in October 1982. He was succeeded by Yasuhiro Nakasone.

At elections in June 1983 for one-half of the seats in the House of Councillors (the upper house of the Diet), a new electoral system was used. Of the 126 contested seats, 50 were filled on the basis of proportional representation. As a result, two small parties entered the House of Councillors for the first time. The LDP increased its strength from 134 to 137 members in the 252-seat chamber. This result was seen as an endorsement of Nakasone's policies of increased expenditure on defence, closer ties with the USA and greater Japanese involvement in international affairs.

In October 1983 former Prime Minister Tanaka was found guilty of accepting bribes. However, Tanaka refused to resign from his legislative seat (he had already resigned from the LDP), and, as a result of this and his continuing influence within the LDP, the opposition parties led a boycott of the Diet, forcing Nakasone to call a premature general election in December 1983. The Komeito (Clean Government Party), the Democratic Socialist Party (DSP) and the JSP gained seats, at the expense of the Communists and the New Liberal Club (NLC). The LDP, which had performed badly in the election, formed a coalition with the NLC (which had split from the LDP over the Tanaka affair in 1976) and several independents. Nakasone remained President of the LDP, after promising to reduce Tanaka's influence. Following the trial of Tanaka, reforms were introduced, whereby cabinet members were required to disclose the extent of their personal assets. In November 1984 Nakasone was re-elected as President of the LDP, and became the first Prime Minister to serve a second term since Sato.

Nakasone called another premature general election for July 1986, which coincided with elections for one-half of the seats in the House of Councillors. In the election to the House of Representatives, the LDP obtained 49.4% of the votes, its highest level of electoral support since 1963, and won a record 304 of the 512 seats. The increased LDP majority was achieved largely at the expense of the JSP and the DSP. The LDP, therefore, was able to dispense with its coalition partner, the NLC (which disbanded in August and rejoined the LDP). The new Cabinet was composed entirely of LDP members. In September the leaders of the LDP agreed to alter by-laws to allow party presidents one-year extensions beyond the normal limit of two terms of two years each. Nakasone was thus able to retain the posts of President of the LDP and Prime Minister until 30 October 1987.

In July 1987 the Secretary-General of the LDP, Noboru Takeshita, left the Tanaka faction, with 113 other members, and announced the formation of a major new grouping within the ruling party. In the same month Tanaka's political influence was further weakened when the Tokyo High Court upheld the decision, taken in 1983, which found him guilty of accepting bribes. (In February 1995 this ruling was upheld by the Supreme Court.)

In October 1987 Nakasone nominated Takeshita as his successor. On 6 November the Diet was convened and Takeshita was formally elected as Prime Minister. In the new Cabinet, Takeshita maintained a balance among the five major factions of the LDP, retaining only two members of Nakasone's previous Cabinet, but appointing four members of the Nakasone faction to senior ministerial posts (including Nakasone's staunch ally, Sosuke Uno, as Minister of Foreign Affairs).

The implementation of a programme of tax reforms was one of the most important issues confronting Takeshita's Government. In June 1988 the LDP's tax deliberation council proposed the introduction of a new indirect tax (a general consumption tax, or a form of value-added tax), which was to be levied at a rate of 3%. This proposal, however, encountered widespread opposition. In the same month, the Prime Minister and the LDP suffered a serious set-back when several leading figures in the party, including Nakasone, Shintaro Abe, Kiichi Miyazawa and Takeshita himself, were alleged to have been indirectly involved in share-trading irregularities with the Recruit Cosmos Company. In November, shortly after the LDP had agreed to establish a committee to investigate the Recruit scandal, the House of Representatives approved proposals for tax reform (which constituted the most wide-ranging revision of the tax system for 40 years). Three cabinet ministers and the Chairman of the DSP were subsequently forced to resign, owing to their alleged involvement in the Recruit affair.

In January 1989 Emperor Hirohito, who had reigned since 1926, died after a long illness, thus ending the Showa era. He was succeeded by his son, Akihito, and the new era was named Heisei ('achievement of universal peace').

In April 1989, as the allegations against politicians widened to include charges of bribery and malpractice, Takeshita announced his resignation. He was subsequently found to have accepted donations worth more than 150m. yen from the Recruit organization. Takeshita nominated Sosuke Uno as his successor. Uno was elected Prime Minister by the Diet on 2 June; a new Cabinet was appointed on the same day. Uno thus became the first Japanese Prime Minister since the foundation of the LDP not to command his own political faction. At the end of May, following an eight-month investigation undertaken by the LDP's special committee, public prosecutors indicted 13 people (eight on charges of offering bribes, and five for allegedly accepting them). Nakasone resigned from his faction and from the LDP, assuming complete moral responsibility for the Recruit affair, since it had occurred during his administration. However, he announced that he would not resign his seat in the Diet.

Within a few days of Uno's assumption of office, a Japanese magazine published allegations of sexual impropriety involving the Prime Minister, which precipitated demands for his resignation. Serious losses suffered by the LDP in Tokyo's municipal elections in early July 1989 further discredited Uno. As a result of a considerable increase in support for the JSP, led by Takako Doi (who emphasized her opposition to the unpopular consumption tax throughout her election campaign), the LDP lost its majority in the upper house for the first time in its history. The JSP received 35% of the total votes, while the LDP obtained only 27%. Uno offered to resign as soon as the LDP had decided on a suitable successor, and in early August the LDP chose the relatively unknown Toshiki Kaifu, a former Minister of Education, to replace Uno as the party's President and as the new Prime Minister. Although the House of Councillors' ballot rejected Kaifu as the new Prime Minister in favour of Takako Doi, the decision of the lower house was adopted, in accordance with stipulations embodied in the Constitution. This was the first time in 41 years that the two houses of the Diet had disagreed over the choice of Prime Minister. Kaifu's popularity increased as a result of a successful visit to North America and Mexico, and his attempts to address the issue of the consumption tax, and in October he was re-elected as President of the LDP for a further two-year term.

At a general election, held on 18 February 1990, the LDP was returned to power with an unexpectedly large measure of support, receiving 46.1% of the votes cast and securing 275 of the 512 seats in the lower house. Despite substantial gains by the JSP (which won 136 seats), the LDP's strength was considered sufficient for it to elect its nominees to preside over all 18 standing committees of the lower house and thus ensure the smooth passage of future legislation.

In May 1990 Kaifu announced his commitment to the implementation of electoral reforms that had been proposed in April by the Election System Council, an advisory body to the Prime Minister. Although the proposals were presented as an attempt to counter electoral corruption and to end factionalism within the LDP itself, opposition supporters expressed fears that the changes would invest more power in party committees responsible for nominating candidates and therefore increase the possibility of bribery.

In October 1990 Hisashi Shinto, the former chairman of the Nippon Telegraph and Telephone Corporation, became the first person to be convicted in the Recruit scandal trial (his sentence was subsequently suspended owing to his age). In December Toshiyuki Inamura, a former cabinet minister and long-serving member of the lower house, resigned from the LDP after charges of large-scale tax evasion and complicity in a new stock-manipulation scandal were brought against him. A prison sentence with hard labour, which he received in November 1991, was regarded as a deterrent to other politicians from engaging in financial corruption.

In January 1991 the JSP changed its English name to the Social Democratic Party of Japan (SDPJ) and in July Makato Tanabe replaced Takako Doi as Chairman of the party. In September senior LDP officials forced Kaifu to abandon proposals for electoral reform and the Takeshita faction of the LDP subsequently withdrew its support for the Prime Minister, thus effectively signalling the end of his authority. Sponsored by the Takeshita faction, the former Minister of Finance, Kiichi Miyazawa, was elected President of the LDP in late October, and in early November the Diet endorsed his appointment as Prime Minister.

New allegations of involvement in the Recruit affair, publicized by the SDPJ in December 1991, seriously undermined Miyazawa's position. Only by abandoning draft legislation to authorize the participation of Japanese forces in United Nations (UN) peace-keeping operations could Miyazawa apparently quell SDPJ demands that he should testify under oath in the Diet.

In early 1992 public disgust at official corruption was registered at two prefectural by-elections to the upper house, when the LDP lost seats, which had previously been considered secure, to Rengo-no-kai (the political arm of RENGO, the trade union confederation). However, the anti-Government alliance, which had supported Rengo-no-kai, disintegrated in May over the issue of Japanese involvement in UN peace-keeping operations. The SDPJ attempted to obstruct the vote in the lower house on the approved modified bill by submitting their resignations *en masse*. The Speaker, however, ruled that they could not be accepted during the current Diet session. The successful passage through the Diet of the legislation on international peace-keeping improved the Government's standing, and in elections to the upper house in July the LDP performed much better than expected, gaining 69 of the 127 seats contested. The SDPJ, by contrast, lost 25 of its 46 seats in the upper house; the Komeito increased its total strength from 20 to 24 seats, but Rengo-no-kai failed to win any seats, owing to the dissolution of the informal coalition it had facilitated between the SDPJ and the DSP. The Japan New Party (JNP), founded only two months prior to the election by LDP dissidents, gained four seats in the upper house.

In early December 1992 a supplementary budget, aimed at stimulating Japan's ailing economy, was approved by the Diet. The Government also introduced draft legislation that was designed to curb financial corruption among politicians. In mid-December Miyazawa instituted a cabinet reorganization, retaining only the Ministers of Foreign Affairs and Agriculture. The reshuffle coincided with an announcement that a formal split in the Takeshita faction was to take place. Miyazawa sought to counter public criticism of factional domination within the ruling party by allocating fewer (and less important) portfolios to the two halves of the dividing leading faction, although the appointments still reflected the power of each of the factions. The new faction was to be led nominally by Tsutomu Hata, the Minister of Finance, although it was widely recognized that Ichiro Ozawa held the real power in the grouping.

Electoral reform was again a major political issue in the first half of 1993. While the LDP favoured a single-member constituency system, the opposition parties proposed various forms of proportional representation. Since the LDP did not have a majority in the upper house, it was unable to enforce any reforms without the agreement of the opposition parties. Within the LDP itself there was conflict between those, led by Ozawa and Hata, who wished the LDP to reach a compromise with opposition parties, and senior LDP members who opposed any form of co-operation. In June the lower house adopted a motion of 'no confidence' against the Government, after the LDP refused to modify its reform proposals to meet opposition demands. Thirty-nine LDP members voted against the Government, while 16 others abstained. The Ozawa-Hata group, comprising 44 former LDP members, immediately established a new party, the Shinseito (Japan Renewal Party, JRP), in order to contest the forthcoming general election. Another new party, the New Party Sakigake, was also formed by LDP Diet members. In the election to the House of Representatives, held on 18 July, only 67.2% of the electorate participated. The LDP won 223 of the 511 seats, and was thus 33 seats short of a majority. Miyazawa resigned as Prime Minister and a coalition Government, composed of members of seven opposition parties, including a number of independents, was formed. On 6 August Morihiro Hosokawa, the leader of the JNP, was elected Prime Minister, defeating the new President of the LDP, Yohei Kono, by 262 to 224 votes.

In late 1993 it was reported that local government officials and Diet members had received payments from construction companies in return for awarding building contracts. Three senior politicians were implicated—Noboru Takeshita, the former Prime Minister, Ichiro Ozawa, a member of the coalition Government, and Kishiro Nakamura, a former Minister of Construction. Ozawa claimed that the payments were legal, since none had exceeded 1.5m. yen. In January 1994 the Public Prosecutor's office began investigations into bribery allegations against Nakamura and Hideo Watanabe, the former Minister of Posts and Telecommunications.

In mid-November 1993 the Government presented four items of electoral reform legislation to the House of Representatives. The bills, which were passed by a majority of 270 to 226 votes (they were opposed by the LDP), altered the multi-seat constituency system to one of a combination of single-seat constituencies and seats allocated through proportional representation. All political donations exceeding 50,000 yen were to be disclosed, and any politician found guilty of corruption would be prohibited from holding further office. In late January 1994 the reform bills were defeated in the upper house. A few days later, however, Hosokawa, who had threatened to resign if the legislation were not passed, reached agreement with the LDP on modifications to the reform bills (see below).

Hosokawa resigned as Prime Minister in April 1994, following allegations of irregularity in his personal financial affairs. Later in that month the coalition appointed Tsutomu Hata as Prime Minister of a minority Government, which excluded the SDPJ and the New Party Sakigake. Hata was obliged to resign in June, however, owing to his continued failure to command a viable majority in the Diet, and a new coalition of the SDPJ, the LDP and the New Party Sakigake took office. Tomiichi Murayama, the leader of the SDPJ, became Prime Minister, and Kono was appointed Deputy Prime Minister and Minister of Foreign Affairs.

In July 1994 Murayama recognized the constitutional right to the existence of Japan's Self-Defence Forces (SDF, the armed forces), thereby effectively contradicting official SDPJ policy on the issue. (The SDPJ amended its policy to accord with Murayama's statement in September.) In December nine opposition parties, including the JNP, the JRP, the DSP and the Komeito, amalgamated to form a new political party, the Shinshinto (New Frontier Party, NFP). A faction of Komeito remained outside the new party and was renamed Komei. Kaifu, the former LDP Prime Minister, was elected leader of the NFP, defeating Hata and Takashi Yonezawa, the former leader of the DSP. Ozawa, who was believed to have been pivotal to the formation of the new party, was appointed Secretary-General.

The creation of the NFP was widely perceived to be a response to the approval by the Diet in November 1994 of the electoral reform bills first proposed in 1993, which appeared to favour larger political parties. Under the terms of the new law, the House of Representatives was to be reduced to 500 seats, comprising 300 single-seat constituencies and 200 seats determined by proportional representation; the proportional-representation base was to be divided into 11 regions, and a party would qualify for a proportional-representation seat if it gained a minimum of 2% of the vote; donations amounting to 500,000 yen annually per private sector corporation to individual politicians were permitted, but this was to be phased out after five years; restrictions on corporate donations would be subsidized by the State; door-to-door campaigning was to be permitted and an independent body would draw up new electoral boundaries. In late June 1995 a total of 29,900m. yen was awarded in the first distribution of public money to political parties.

On 18 January 1995 a massive earthquake in the Kobe region resulted in the deaths of more than 6,300 people and caused severe infrastructural damage. In the aftermath of the earthquake, the Government was severely criticized (and subsequently acknowledged responsibility) for the poor co-ordination of the relief operation. In March a poisonous gas, sarin, was released into the Tokyo underground railway system, killing 12 people and injuring more than 5,000. A religious sect, Aum Shinrikyo, was accused of perpetrating the attack. Following a further gas attack in Yokohama in April, a number of sect members were detained by the authorities. In June Shoko Asahara, the leader of Aum Shinrikyo, was indicted on a charge of murder. The sect was declared bankrupt in March 1996 and the trial of Asahara opened in the following month. In September Asahara and two other members of the sect were instructed to pay some US $7.3m. in compensation to victims of the Tokyo incident. Attempts by the Ministry of Justice to outlaw the sect, on the grounds that it had engaged in anti-subversive activities, were unsuccessful; however, the sect was denied legal status as a religious organization.

Only 44.5% of the electorate took part in the elections to the House of Councillors, held in July 1995. With one-half of the 252 seats being contested, the LDP won only 49 seats, the SDPJ 16 and the New Party Sakigake three, whereas the NFP, benefiting from the support of the Soka Gakkai religious organization, won 40 seats. In response to the coalition's poor performance, Murayama undertook a major reorganization of the Cabinet. On 25 September Ryutaro Hashimoto, the Minister of International Trade and Industry, was elected leader of the LDP, after Yohei Kono announced that he would not seek re-election.

In October 1995 the Minister of Justice was obliged to resign, following allegations that he had accepted an undisclosed loan of 200m. yen from a Buddhist group. His resignation was followed by that of the Director-General of the Management and Co-ordination Agency in November, owing to controversy arising from his suggestion that Japanese colonial rule over Korea had been of some benefit to the Koreans.

Conflict in the Diet escalated between February and June 1995 over government plans, announced in June 1994, to issue a resolution to commemorate the 50th anniversary of the ending of the Second World War. The resolution was to constitute an apology to countries whose citizens had suffered from the actions of the Japanese army during the war. The New Party Sakigake threatened to withdraw from the coalition if an apology was not made, while a group of 160 LDP Diet members, led by Seisuke Okuno, objected to the labelling of Japan as an aggressor. A resolution was finally passed in June 1995, despite a boycott of the vote by the NFP.

In December 1995 Toshiki Kaifu announced that he would not be seeking re-election as leader of the NFP. He was succeeded by Ichiro Ozawa, who defeated Tsutomu Hata at the leadership election. Ozawa appointed Takashi Yonezawa as Secretary-General of the NFP.

On 5 January 1996 Tomiichi Murayama resigned as Prime Minister; he was, however, re-elected Chairman of the SDPJ. The LDP leader, Ryutaro Hashimoto, was elected Prime Minister on 11 January, winning 288 votes to Ozawa's 167. A coalition Cabinet, largely dominated by the LDP, was formed. Hashimoto's first task as Prime Minister was to gain legislative approval for the 1996/97 draft budget, which included an unpopular proposal to use public expenditure to liquidate housing loan companies (*jusen*). Shinshinto organized a 'sit-in' in the parliament building to obstruct the House of Representatives' budget committee meetings. Deliberations resumed after three weeks, however, when the Government agreed to Shinshinto's demand for an inquiry into the alleged receipt of illegal political contributions by the LDP Secretary-General, Koichi Kato. No action was taken against Kato as a result of this inquiry and the draft budget was eventually approved in May 1996 with little revision.

In March 1996 the New Socialist Party (NSP) was formed by left-wing defectors from the SDPJ, who disapproved of the latter's transformation under Murayama's leadership into a moderate liberal party. Osamu Yatabe was elected Chairman of the NSP and Tetsuo Yamaguchi was appointed Secretary-General. In mid-1996, in an attempt to strengthen their electoral bases, particularly in the new single-member districts, there was a further realignment of political parties. In August Shoichi Ide and Hiroyuki Sonoda were elected Leader and Secretary-General, respectively, of the New Party Sakigake following the resignations of Masayoshi Takemura and Yukio Hatoyama. Hatoyama left the party and founded the Democratic Party of Japan (DPJ), with other dissident members of the New Party Sakigake and individual members of the SDPJ and NFP.

A general election was held on 20 October 1996. The LDP won the election, gaining 239 of the 500 seats, while the NFP secured 156, the DPJ 52, the Japan Communist Party (JCP) 26, the SDPJ 15, and the New Party Sakigake two seats. Four deputies, including Hajime Funada, who were elected as independents, subsequently formed a new party called the 21st Century. On 7 November Ryutaro Hashimoto was re-elected Prime Minister for a second term, and formed the first single-party Cabinet since 1993 (the SDPJ and Sakigake had agreed to support the minority Government but chose not to re-enter a coalition).

Almost immediately after the election, public attention was again focused on corruption scandals: 10 politicians, including the Ministers of Finance, and Health and Welfare, and the LDP Secretary-General, Koichi Kato, were accused of receiving a total of 26.1m. yen in political donations from a petroleum trader, Junichi Izui. Izui was arrested and charged with tax evasion and was also placed under suspicion of questionable business dealings with some of Japan's largest petroleum companies. In December Nobuharu Okamitsu, a former Vice-Minister of Health and Welfare, was arrested and charged with accepting 60m. yen in return for granting state subsidies to a nursing-home operator; Ryutaro Hashimoto, himself, admitted accepting a 2m.-yen legal political donation from a hospital linen-leasing group connected to the Okamitsu scandal. In a further scandal, Morihiro Hosokawa, the former Prime Minister, returned the 30m. yen that he had received for his election campaign from the Orange Kyosai Kumiai, a mutual aid society that had posed as a savings bank, and in late January 1997 Tatsuo Tomobe, an independent member of the Diet and a former member of the NFP, was arrested on charges of defrauding investors of more than 8,000,000m. yen.

In December 1996, following disagreements with Ichiro Ozawa, the NFP's President, the former Prime Minister, Tsutomu Hata, left the NFP and formed a new party, called Taiyoto (Sun Party) together with 12 other dissident NFP members. The formal appointment in late December of Takako Doi as Chairwoman of the SDPJ (she had been acting Chairwoman since the dissolution of the House of Representatives in September) prompted the resignation of the party's Secretary-General, Wataru Kubo, in January 1997; he was replaced by Shigeru Ito.

In early 1997 the Government established several commissions, charged with devising a comprehensive programme of administrative and economic reforms. A reduction in government bureaucracy and public expenditure was envisaged, and details of a series of financial deregulation measures were announced in February, including the transfer of the Ministry of Finance's supervisory role to an independent agency in mid-1998. The Government's management of the nuclear programme was comprehensively reviewed, following two accidents, in December 1995 and March 1997, at plants managed by the Power Reactor and Nuclear Fuel Development Corporation, a public organization supervised by the Science and Technology Agency. Allegations that the corporation had failed to report a further 11 radiation leaks over the previous three years served to heighten public disquiet over Japan's nuclear research and development programme.

In mid-1997 the NFP experienced a serious set-back, when Hosokawa resigned from the party, reportedly owing to dissatisfaction with Ozawa's style of leadership. (In December Hosokawa formed a new party—From Five.) In addition, the NFP failed to retain a single seat in elections to the Tokyo Metropolitan Assembly, held in July. The LDP and the JCP, by contrast, increased their representation in the Assembly. By September the LDP had regained its majority in the House of Representatives, following a series of defections by members of the NFP. In December, following further defections from the NFP, the party was dissolved. Six new parties were founded by former NFP members and a significant political realignment took place. In January 1998 six opposition parties formed a parliamentary group, Minyuren, which constituted the largest opposition bloc in the Diet, and later in that month three of these parties merged to form Minseito (the Good Governance Party), led by Tsutomu Hata, a former Prime Minister.

Meanwhile, in late 1997 a series of corruption scandals, involving substantial payments to corporate racketeers by leading financial institutions, had a severe impact on the Japanese economy (see Economic Affairs). The crisis was exacerbated by an increase in the rate of the unpopular consumption tax in April, from 3% to 5%, and a decrease in public expenditure (as part of the Government's fiscal reforms), which resulted in a significant weakening in consumer demand. The collapse of several prominent financial institutions in November, and the threat of further bankruptcies, deepened the economic crisis. The Government announced a series of deregulation and stimulus measures designed to encourage economic growth, including a reduction in taxes and, in a major reversal of policy, the use of public money to support the banking system. In January 1998 the Diet reconvened earlier than scheduled, in order to approve the budget for 1998/99, as well as supplementary budget proposals incorporating the tax reductions. The credibility of the Ministry of Finance was further weakened in late January 1997, when two senior officials were arrested on suspicion of accepting bribes from banks. The Minister of Finance, Hiroshi Mitsuzuka, resigned, accepting full moral responsibility for the affair. He was replaced by Hikaru Matsunaga.

In the mid-1990s Japan's growing trade surplus with the USA has become a matter of increasing concern for the US authorities. In 1994 trade negotiations between Japan and the USA failed, following Japan's refusal to accept numerical targets for imports and exports. The USA initiated protectionist measures against Japan, but relations improved in October, when trade agreements in three of the four main areas under discussion were signed.

Negotiations concerning the automobile trade resulted in the signing of an agreement with the USA in June 1995. However, an increase in the export of Japanese vehicles to the USA in 1997, and a concomitant rise in the US trade deficit with Japan, caused growing tension between the two countries. Negotiations between Prime Minister Hashimoto and President Clinton of the USA in April and June focused on trade issues. In September the USA imposed large fines on three Japanese shipping companies, following complaints about restrictive harbour practices in Japan; however, an agreement to reform Japanese port operations was concluded shortly thereafter. Negotiations on increased access to airline routes were also underway in that year.

Together with trade issues, Japan's bilateral security arrangements with the USA, concluded by treaty in 1951, have been the focus of US-Japanese relations. The treaty grants the use of military bases in Japan to the USA, in return for a US commitment to provide military support to Japan in the event of external aggression. During a visit to Japan by President Bush of the USA in January 1992, the 'Tokyo declaration on the US-Japan global partnership' was issued, whereby the two countries undertook to co-operate in promoting international security and prosperity. In February 1993 Japan and the USA reaffirmed their security relationship, with the USA agreeing to protect Japan from the threat posed by potential nuclear proliferation around the world.

The presence of the US forces in Japan provoked much debate in the mid-1990s. In November 1995 three US servicemen were arrested and subsequently imprisoned for the rape of a schoolgirl in Okinawa. Considerable civil unrest ensued and legal proceedings were initiated against the Governor of Okinawa, Masahide Ota, following his refusal to renew the leases for US military installations in the region. Lengthy negotiations between the two countries resulted in the USA agreeing, in December 1996, to release 21% of the land used for US military purposes in Okinawa, and to build a floating offshore helicopter base.

Legislation permitting the Japanese central Government to override the decisions of the regional Governor where necessary, in order to renew the military leases, was adopted in April 1997. In addition, measures were proposed to promote economic development in the region, and plans were put forward to relocate several of the US bases to other prefectures. In September revised Guidelines for Japan-US Defense Co-operation (first compiled in 1978) were issued. The Guidelines, which had been under review since the signing of the US-Japan Joint Declaration on Security in April 1996, envisage enhanced military co-operation between the USA and Japan, not only on Japanese territory, but also in situations in the area around Japan. In December 1997, in a non-binding referendum held in Nago, Okinawa, to assess public opinion concerning the construction of the offshore helicopter base, the majority of voters rejected the proposal. The Mayor of Nago, who advocated the construction of the base in return for measures to stimulate the region's economy, tendered his resignation. Governor Ota also stated his opposition to the proposed base.

Since 1982 Japan has been under continued pressure from the USA to increase its defence expenditure and to assume greater responsibility for security in the Western Pacific area. In 1986 the Japanese Government decided to exceed the self-imposed limit on defence expenditure of 1% of the gross national product (GNP), set in 1976. In December 1990 the Government announced a new five-year programme (to begin in the 1991/92 fiscal year) to develop the country's defence capability. The average annual increase in total military expenditure over the five-year period was expected to be 3%, in comparison with the 5% average annual increase during the previous five-year programme. The new programme, to be implemented at an estimated total cost of US $172,000m., also envisaged that Japan would assume a greater share of the cost of maintaining US troops stationed in Japan. In December 1992 the Government, under concerted pressure from the opposition, announced a reduction in the average annual increase during the 1991–96 defence programme to 2.1%. In November 1995 the Cabinet approved a new national defence programme, which envisaged a 20% reduction in troops and confirmed Japan's security co-operation with the USA.

In September 1990 Japan announced a US $4,000m.-contribution to the international effort to force an unconditional Iraqi withdrawal from Kuwait. A controversial LDP-sponsored Peace Co-operation Bill, which provided for the dispatch to the Persian (Arabian) Gulf area of some 2,000 non-combatant personnel, encountered severe political opposition and provoked widespread discussion on the constitutional legitimacy of the deployment of Japanese personnel (in any capacity), and in November the proposals were withdrawn. In January 1991, following repeated US demands for a greater financial commitment to the Gulf crisis (and a swifter disbursement of moneys already pledged), the Japanese Government announced plans to increase its contribution by US $9,000m. and to provide aircraft for the transportation of refugees in the region. Opposition to the proposal was again vociferous. By mid-February, however, the Government had secured the support of several centrist parties, by pledging that any financial aid from Japan would be employed in a 'non-lethal' capacity. Legislation to approve the new contribution was adopted by the Diet in March.

In June 1992 controversial legislation to permit the SDF to participate in UN peace-keeping operations was approved. Their role, however, was to be confined to logistical and humanitarian tasks, unless a special dispensation from the Diet were granted. In early September, following a request from the UN Secretary-General, the Government endorsed the dispatch of 1,800 members of the SDF to serve in the UN Transitional Authority in Cambodia (UNTAC). Japanese troops participated in further UN peace-keeping operations in Mozambique, in 1993, and, under Japanese command, on the Rwandan-Zairean border, in 1994. Legislation was approved in November 1994 to enable Japanese forces to be deployed overseas if the Government believed the lives of Japanese citizens to be at risk. In September Japan reiterated its desire to be a permanent member of the UN Security Council, particularly in view of its status as the world's largest donor of development aid and the second-largest contributor (after the USA) to the UN budget. In October 1996 the UN General Assembly voted to allocate to Japan a non-permanent seat on the Security Council, to be held for a two-year period from January 1997. In the late 1990s the Japanese Government was campaigning for a greater proportion of senior-level positions within the UN to be allocated to Japanese personnel, as a reflection of its contribution to the UN budget.

Stability in East and South-East Asia is a vital consideration in Japanese foreign policy, since Japan depends on Asia for much of its foreign trade, including imports of vital raw materials. Despite the signing of a treaty of peace and friendship with the People's Republic of China in 1978, relations deteriorated in the late 1980s after China expressed concern at Japan's increased defence expenditure and its more assertive military stance. Japanese aid to China was suspended in June 1989, following the Tiananmen Square massacre in Beijing, and was not resumed until November 1990, after the Chinese Government's declaration, in January, that a state of martial law was no longer in force. Relations between the two countries were strengthened by the visits to China by Emperor Akihito in October 1992, the first-ever Japanese imperial visit to China, and by Prime Minister Hosokawa in March 1994. However, in August of that year Japan announced the suspension of economic aid to China, following renewed nuclear testing by the Chinese Government. The provision of economic aid was resumed in early 1997, following the declaration of a moratorium on Chinese nuclear testing.

In September 1997 Hashimoto visited China to commemorate the 25th anniversary of the normalization of relations between the two countries. China expressed concern at the revised US-Japanese security arrangements, following a statement by a senior Japanese minister that the area around Taiwan might be covered under the new guidelines. Procedures for the removal of chemical weapons, deployed in China by Japanese forces during the Second World War, were also discussed. During a visit to Japan by the Chinese Premier, Li Peng, in November, a bilateral fisheries agreement was signed.

In July 1996 Japan's relations with both China and Taiwan were strained when a group of nationalists, the Japan Youth Federation, constructed a lighthouse and war memorial on the Senkaku Islands (or Daioyu Islands in Chinese), a group of uninhabited islands situated in the East China Sea, to which all three countries laid claim. The situation was further aggravated in September by the accidental drowning of a Hong Kong citizen during a protest near the islands against Japan's claim. In October a flotilla of small boats, operated by 300 activists from Taiwan, Hong Kong and Macau, evaded Japanese patrol vessels and raised the flags of China and Taiwan on the disputed islands. The Japanese Government sought to defuse tensions with China and Taiwan by withholding official recognition of the lighthouse; it did not, however, condemn the right-wing activists who had constructed the controversial buildings. In May 1997 China expressed serious concern, when a member of the Japanese Diet landed on one of the disputed islands. The Japanese Government distanced itself from the action.

Japan has also focused attention on improving relations with other East and South-East Asian countries. In November 1992 Japan announced the resumption of economic aid to Viet Nam, ending an embargo which had been implemented following Viet Nam's invasion of Cambodia (Kampuchea) in 1978. In January 1993 Prime Minister Miyazawa toured four member countries of the Association of South East Asian Nations (ASEAN, see p. 113), during which he advocated an expansion of political and economic co-operation in the region. A visit by Prime Minister Hashimoto to ASEAN countries in January 1997 aimed to strengthen economic and security relations with the member countries. In December Japan participated in meetings held in Kuala Lumpur, Malaysia, to celebrate the 30th anniversary of the founding of ASEAN.

Following an improvement in relations with the Republic of Korea in 1990, Miyazawa visited the country in January 1992 and issued an apology for the Japanese army's exploitation of Korean women during the Second World War; however, he failed to quell demands that the women concerned be properly compensated. In June 1996 Prime Minister Hashimoto met President Kim of the Republic of Korea and discussed bilateral co-operation in economic and security affairs. Relations with the Republic of Korea were strained in late 1996 over a territorial dispute concerning a group of islands, to which both countries laid claim. Tensions were exacerbated in early 1998, when the Japanese Government terminated a bilateral fishing agreement, following the failure by the two parties to renegotiate the terms of the agreement.

Attempts to establish full diplomatic relations with the Democratic People's Republic of Korea (DPRK) in early 1991 were hindered by the DPRK's demands for financial reparations for the Japanese colonization of the country during 1910–45 and by the DPRK's refusal to allow International Atomic Energy Agency inspectors access to its nuclear facilities. Relations improved in 1995 and 1996 after Japan provided emergency aid to the DPRK when serious food shortages appeared to threaten stability in the Korean peninsula. Concerns that the DPRK had developed a missile capable of reaching Japanese territory resulted in the suspension of food aid in mid-1996, but, following bilateral negotiations held in August 1997, provision of food aid resumed in October, when a further US $27m.-worth of humanitarian assistance was pledged to the DPRK. Agreement was also reached concerning the issue of visits to relatives in Japan by the estimated 1,800 Japanese nationals resident in the DPRK. The first such visits took place in November. Negotiations aimed at restoring full diplomatic relations between the two countries were expected to commence in early 1998.

The actions of the Japanese army in the Second World War proved to be a contentious issue during 1994–95 both domestically and in Japan's relations with neighbouring Asian countries, in the context of the 50th anniversary, in August 1995, of the surrender of Japanese forces. In November 1994 the International Commission of Jurists adjudicated that Asian women, used for sexual purposes by the Japanese army during the Second World War ('comfort women'), should each receive an initial compensation payment of US $40,000. The ruling was rejected by the Japanese Government, however, which insisted that the issue of reparation payments to individuals had been fully covered under the terms of the peace treaty of 1951. Japan also applied this policy to claims for compensation made by former prisoners of war belonging to the allied forces. In February 1995 Prime Minister Murayama publicly acknowledged that Japan was responsible, in part, for the post-war division of the Korean peninsula. He was forced to retract the statement, however, following bitter controversy in the Diet. In June a resolution was passed apologizing for Japanese actions in the war, despite considerable disagreement in the Diet. However, countries whose citizens had been prisoners of the Japanese army criticized the resolution as being insufficiently explicit. In August 1996 the first compensation payments, accompanied by a letter of apology from Prime Minister Hashimoto, were made from a private fund to four Philippine victims, who had been used as 'comfort women' during the war. The majority of groups representing South Korean victims refused to accept payment from the fund, however, demanding that compensation be forthcoming from official, rather than private, sources.

Japan's relations with Russia have been dominated by the issue of the Northern Territories, four small islands situated close to Hokkaido, which were annexed in 1945 by the USSR. Both countries claim sovereignty over the islands, and there has been no substantial progress towards resolving the situation since 1956, when Japan and the USSR resumed diplomatic relations. In February 1992, however, a joint Japanese-Russian working group began discussions about a prospective peace treaty (formally ending the Second World War), and in March the Ministers of Foreign Affairs of the two countries held a conciliatory meeting on the issue. A measure of progress was achieved in October 1993, when the Russian President visited Japan. However, relations between the two countries deteriorated, following the disposal of nuclear waste in Japanese waters by Russian ships in November, and Russia's decision, in August 1994, to open fire on Japanese vessels, that were alleged to have been fishing in Russian waters.

Bilateral negotiations over the status of the disputed territory opened in March 1995. In November 1996 Japan indicated that it was prepared to resume the disbursement of a US $500m.-aid 'package', withheld since 1991, and in May 1997 the Japanese Government abandoned its opposition to Russia's proposed membership of the G7 group. Russian plans for joint development of the mineral and fishing resources of the disputed territory were followed, in July, by an outline agreement on the jurisdiction of the islands. A meeting between Hashimoto and President Yeltsin of Russia later in that month resulted in the forging of a new diplomatic policy, based on 'trust, mutual benefit and long-term prospects'. At an informal summit meeting, held between Yeltsin and Hashimoto in Krasnoyarsk, Russia, in November, the two parties agreed to work towards the conclusion of a formal peace treaty by the year 2000. A series of measures aimed at encouraging Japanese assistance in the revival of the Russian economy were also discussed. Bilateral negotiations resulted in the conclusion of a framework fisheries agreement in December 1997.

Government

Under the Constitution of 1947, the Emperor is Head of State but has no governing power. Legislative power is vested in the bicameral Diet, comprising the House of Representatives (lower house), whose members are elected for a four-year term, and the House of Councillors (upper house), members of which are elected for six years, one-half being elected every three years. The House of Representatives comprises 500 seats—300 single-seat constituencies and 200 determined by proportional representation—and there are 252 seats in the House of Councillors. There is universal suffrage for all adults from 20 years of age. Executive power is vested in the Cabinet, which is responsible to the Diet. The Emperor appoints the Prime Minister (on designation by the Diet), who appoints the other Ministers in the Cabinet.

Japan has 47 prefectures, each administered by an elected Governor.

Defence

Although the Constitution renounces war and the use of force, the right of self-defence is not excluded. Japan maintains ground, maritime and air self-defence forces. Military service is voluntary. The USA provides equipment and training staff and also maintains bases in Japan. US forces in Japan totalled 36,530 at 1 August 1997. The total strength of the Japanese Self-Defence Forces at 1 August 1997 was 235,600: army 147,700 (estimate), navy 42,500, air force 44,100 and central staff 1,300. Government expenditure on defence under the proposed 1998/99 budget was 4,940,000m. yen.

Economic Affairs

In 1995, according to estimates by the World Bank, Japan's gross national product (GNP), measured at average 1993–95 prices, was US $4,963,587m., equivalent to $39,640 per head. During 1985–95, it was estimated, GNP per head increased, in real terms, by an annual average of 2.9%. Over the same period, the population increased by an annual average of 0.4%. In 1980–90 Japan's gross domestic product (GDP) increased, in real terms, by an annual average of 4.0%. In 1990–95 GDP increased at an average annual rate of 1.0%, in real terms. In 1996 real GDP rose by 3.6%, but in 1997 it was estimated that GDP increased by only 1.0%, in real terms.

In 1996 agriculture (including forestry and fishing) contributed 1.8% of GDP. In 1997 5.3% of the employed labour force were engaged in the sector. The principal crops are rice, potatoes, cabbages, sugar beets, and citrus fruits. During 1980–90, according to the World Bank, agricultural GDP increased by an annual average of 1.3%. However, in 1990–95 the GDP of the sector declined at an average rate of 2.2% annually.

Industry (including mining, manufacturing, construction and power) contributed 36.4% of GDP in 1996. In 1997 33.1% of the employed labour force were engaged in the industrial sector. During 1980–90, according to the World Bank, industrial GDP increased by an annual average of 4.2%. The GDP of the sector remained constant during 1990–95. Industrial production increased by 3.4% in 1995 and 2.7% in 1996.

Mining and quarrying contributed 0.2% of GDP in 1996. Only 0.1% of the employed labour force were engaged in the sector in 1997. While the domestic output of limestone and sulphur is sufficient to meet domestic demand, all of Japan's requirements of bauxite, crude petroleum and iron ore, and a high percentage of its requirements of copper ore and coking coal are met by imports.

In 1996 manufacturing contributed 23.3% of GDP, and in 1997 22.0% of the employed labour force were engaged in the sector. According to the World Bank, manufacturing GDP increased by an annual average of 4.7% in 1985–92. The most important branches of manufacturing are machinery and transport equipment, electrical and electronic equipment, and iron and steel.

Japan imports most of its energy requirements, with imports of petroleum and petroleum products comprising 11.8% of the value of total imports in 1996. Nuclear energy accounted for 31.7% of electricity output in that year. There are proposals to construct a further 20 nuclear reactors by 2010.

The services sector contributed 61.8% of GDP in 1996, and engaged 61.0% of the employed labour force in 1997. According to the World Bank, the GDP of the services sector increased by an average of 3.9% per year in 1980–90, and by 2.3% annually in 1990–95. Tourist receipts, totalling US $4,078m. in 1996, are an important source of revenue.

In 1996 Japan recorded a trade surplus of US $83,560m., and there was a surplus of $65,880m. on the current account of the balance of payments. In 1996 the principal source of imports was the USA (22.7%), which was also the principal market for exports (27.2%). Other major suppliers in that year were the People's Republic of China, the Republic of Korea, Indonesia and Taiwan. Other major purchasers of Japanese exports were the Republic of Korea, Taiwan, Hong Kong and China. The principal imports in 1996 were machinery and transport equipment, miscellaneous manufactured articles, food and live animals, petroleum and petroleum products and basic manufactures. The principal exports in that year were non-electric and electrical machinery, and transport equipment.

The draft budget for the financial year ending 31 March 1999 was balanced at 77,669,000m. yen. The annual rate of inflation averaged 1.3% in 1986–96. Consumer prices increased by only 0.1% in 1996 and by an estimated 1.6% in 1997. The rate of unemployment was 3.4% of the labour force in August 1997.

Japan is a member of the Asia-Pacific Economic Co-operation (APEC, see p. 108) forum, the Asian Development Bank (ADB, see p. 110), the Organisation for Economic Co-operation and Development (OECD, see p. 208) and the World Trade Organization (WTO, see p. 244).

Following a period of rapid economic expansion in the 1980s, Japan underwent a severe recession during the early 1990s, resulting from the collapse of asset prices. Prospects for growth appeared brighter, following the implementation of stimulus measures in the mid-1990s. Proposals for the deregulation of the financial markets, announced in February 1997, were expected further to encourage recovery. However, an increase in the rate of consumption tax in April, accompanied by restraint in public investment, resulted in a significant contraction in the economy in mid-1997, which was exacerbated by a series of corruption scandals. More than 50 senior executives at several major financial and commercial institutions, including the four leading brokerage houses, were found guilty of making substantial illegal payments to corporate racketeers (*sokaiya*). The collapse of Sanyo Securities, a prominent stockbroking company, and the failure of Hokkaido Takushoku, Japan's 10th largest bank, in November, displayed the extent to which Japanese financial houses were experiencing difficulties in recovering non-performing loans. Later in that month the bankruptcy of Yamaichi Securities, Japan's largest post-war corporate failure, highlighted the weakness of the financial regulatory and supervisory systems. It was revealed that executives at Yamaichi had concealed huge losses by transferring liabilities between accounts in order to avoid a negative balance sheet, a practice made illegal in 1983, but reportedly still prevalent. An independent supervisory agency was to be established in June 1998. The Government was forced to introduce emergency measures to raise consumer and business confidence, including a reduction in the rates of income and corporate tax (thereby threatening the target of a reduction in the budget deficit from some 5% of GDP to 3% by the year 2001), and the issuing of deficit-financing bonds. In a significant departure from its strict fiscal policy, the Government pledged the use of public money, principally through the Deposit Insurance Corporation, in order to protect depositors' money and stabilize the banking system. The Japanese stock-market index fell to its lowest level for five years in late 1997, and the value of the yen in relation to the US dollar also declined significantly, resulting in a huge increase in Japan's trade surplus, further boosted by a decrease in imports. It was revealed in early 1998 that the extent of non-performing loans could exceed 76,710,000m. yen, three times greater than previously admitted, and it was estimated that 13 of the leading 20 commercial banks would report financial losses in that year. The rate of unemployment and the level of bankruptcies (which reached 1,300 per month in late 1997) continued to increase, and it was expected that exports, some 40% of which were directed to Asian markets, would decline as a result of the regional currency crisis. Domestic demand continued to weaken in late 1997, with a decrease recorded in vehicle registrations for the first time in four years.

Social Welfare

Social welfare benefits are provided through three schemes: the Welfare Insurance system, which insures private sector employees; Mutual Aid Associations, which are responsible for public sector workers; and the National Pension and National Health systems, which cover self-employed people and agricultural workers. A basic pension is provided to almost all of the population through these schemes, and a universal health insurance system was introduced in 1961. The Government subsidizes the cost of medical care for the elderly and the self-employed. Significant changes to the social welfare system were proposed in the late 1990s, with an increase in the cost of insurance and a reduction in government subsidies envisaged. In 1994 Japan had 9,731 hospitals, with a total of 1,677,041 beds, and there were 230,519 physicians and 81,055 dentists working in the country. Central government expenditure on social security was expected to amount to 14,843,000m. yen for the 1998/99 financial year.

Education

A kindergarten (*yochien*) system provides education for children aged between three and five years of age, although the majority of kindergartens are privately controlled. Education is compulsory between the ages of six and 15. Elementary education, which begins at six years of age, lasts for six years. Lower secondary education lasts for a further three years. In 1996 12.6m. children aged six to 15 were enrolled in compulsory education, while 4.5m. of those aged 15 to 18 received upper secondary education. Upper secondary schools provide a three-year course in general topics, or a vocational course in subjects such as agriculture, commerce, fine art and technical studies. There are four types of institution for higher education. Universities (*daigaku*) offer a four-year degree course, as well as postgraduate courses. In 1996 there were 576 universities in Japan. Junior colleges (*tanki-daigaku*) provide less specialized two- to three-year courses. Both universities and junior colleges offer facilities for teacher-training. Colleges of technology (*koto-senmon-gakko*) offer a five-year specialized training. Since 1991 colleges of technology have been able to offer short-term advanced courses. Special training colleges (*senshu-gakko*) offer advanced courses in technical and vocational subjects, lasting for at least one year. Central government expenditure on education and science was expected to amount to 6,346,000m. yen for the 1998/99 financial year.

Public Holidays

1998: 1 January (New Year's Day), 15 January (Coming of Age Day), 11 February (National Foundation Day), 20 March (Vernal Equinox Day), 29 April (Greenery Day), 3 May (Constitution Memorial Day), 5 May (Children's Day), 20 July (Marine Day), 15 September (Respect for the Aged Day), 23 September (Autumnal Equinox), 10 October (Sports Day), 3 November (Culture Day), 23 November (Labour Thanksgiving Day), 23 December (Emperor's Birthday).

1999: 1 January (New Year's Day), 15 January (Coming of Age Day), 11 February (National Foundation Day), 20 March (Vernal Equinox Day), 29 April (Greenery Day), 3 May (Constitution Memorial Day), 5 May (Children's Day), 20 July (Marine Day), 15 September (Respect for the Aged Day), 22 September (Autumnal Equinox), 10 October (Sports Day), 3 November (Culture Day), 23 November (Labour Thanksgiving Day), 23 December (Emperor's Birthday).

Weights and Measures

The metric system is in force.

Statistical Survey

Source (unless otherwise stated): Statistics Bureau, Management and Co-ordination Agency, 19-1, Wakamatsu-cho, Shinjuku-ku, Tokyo 162; tel. (3) 5273-1145; fax (3) 5273-1181.

Area and Population

AREA, POPULATION AND DENSITY

Area (sq km)	377,819*
Population (census results)†	
1 October 1990	123,611,167
1 October 1995	
Males	61,574,398
Females	63,995,848
Total	125,570,246
Population (official estimates at mid-year)	
1995	125,472,000
1996	125,761,000
1997	126,065,000
Density (per sq km) at mid-1997	333.7

* 145,877 sq miles.

† Excluding foreign military and diplomatic personnel and their dependants.

PRINCIPAL CITIES (population at census of 1 October 1995)*

Tokyo (capital)†	7,967,614	Kanazawa	453,975
Yokohama	3,307,136	Urawa	453,300
Osaka	2,602,421	Kawaguchi	448,854
Nagoya	2,152,184	Ichikawa	440,555
Sapporo	1,757,025	Nagasaki	438,635
Kyoto	1,463,822	Utsunomiya	435,357
Kobe	1,423,792	Omiya	433,755
Fukuoka	1,284,795	Yokosuka	432,193
Kawasaki	1,202,820	Oita	426,979
Hiroshima	1,108,888	Kurashiki	422,836
Kitakyushu	1,019,598	Gifu	407,134
Sendai	971,297	Hirakata	400,144
Chiba	856,878	Toyonaka	398,908
Sakai	802,993	Wakayama	393,885
Kumamoto	650,341	Nishinomiya	390,389
Okayama	615,757	Fukuyama	374,517
Sagamihara	570,597	Fujisawa	368,651
Hamamatsu	561,606	Takatsuki	362,270
Kagoshima	546,282	Iwaki	360,598
Funabashi	540,817	Asahikawa	360,568
Higashiosaka	517,232	Machida	360,525
Hachioji	503,363	Nara	359,218
Niigata	494,769	Nagano	358,516
Amagasaki	488,586	Toyohashi	352,982
Shizuoka	474,092	Suita	342,760
Himeji	470,986	Toyota	341,079
Matsudo	461,503	Takamatsu	331,004
Matsuyama	460,968	Koriyama	326,833

Toyama	325,375	Fukushima	285,754
Kawagoe	323,353	Maebashi	284,788
Okazaki	322,621	Kasugai	277,589
Kochi	321,999	Ichihara	277,061
Tokorozawa	320,406	Yao	276,664
Kashiwa	317,750	Otsu	276,332
Akita	311,948	Tokushima	268,706
Naha	301,890	Ichinomiya	267,362
Miyazaki	300,068	Kakogawa	260,567
Hakodate	298,881	Shimonoseki	259,795
Koshigaya	298,253	Neyagawa	258,443
Aomori	294,167	Ibaraki	258,233
Akashi	287,606	Fukui	255,604
Morioka	286,478	Yamagata	254,488
Yokkaichi	285,779	Hiratsuka	253,822

* Except for Tokyo, the data for each city refer to an urban county (*shi*), an administrative division which may include some scattered or rural population as well as an urban centre.

† The figure refers to the 23 wards (*ku*) of the old city. The population of Tokyo-to (Tokyo Prefecture) was 11,773,605.

BIRTHS, MARRIAGES AND DEATHS*

	Registered live births		Registered marriages†		Registered deaths	
	Number	Rate (per 1,000)	Number	Rate (per 1,000)	Number	Rate (per 1,000)
1988	1,314,006	10.8	707,716	5.8	793,014	6.5
1989	1,246,802	10.2	708,316	5.8	788,594	6.4
1990	1,221,585	10.0	722,138	5.9	820,305	6.7
1991	1,223,245	9.9	742,264	6.0	829,797	6.7
1992	1,208,989	9.7	754,441	6.1	856,643	6.9
1993	1,188,282	9.6	792,658	6.4	878,532	7.1
1994	1,238,328	10.0	782,738	6.3	875,933	7.1
1995	1,187,064	9.6	791,888	6.4	922,139	7.4
1996	1,206,555	9.7	795,080	6.4	896,211	7.2

* Figures relate only to Japanese nationals in Japan.

† Data are tabulated by year of registration rather than by year of occurrence.

Expectation of life (years at birth, 1996): Males 77.01; Females 83.59 (Source: Ministry of Health and Welfare).

ECONOMICALLY ACTIVE POPULATION*
(annual averages, '000 persons aged 15 years and over)

	1995	1996	1997
Agriculture and forestry	3,400	3,300	3,240
Fishing and aquatic culture	270	260	260
Mining and quarrying	60	60	70
Manufacturing	14,560	14,450	14,420
Electricity, gas and water	420	370	360
Construction	6,630	6,700	6,850
Wholesale and retail trade and restaurants	14,490	14,630	14,750
Transport, storage and communications	4,020	4,110	4,120
Financing, insurance, real estate and business services	5,550	5,610	5,750
Community, social and personal services (incl. hotels)	14,910	15,070	15,410
Activities not adequately defined	250	290	340
Total employed	64,570	64,860	65,570
Unemployed	2,100	2,250	2,300
Total labour force	66,660	67,110	67,870
Males	39,660	39,920	40,270
Females	27,010	27,190	27,600

* All figures are rounded, so totals may not always be the sum of their component parts.

Agriculture

PRINCIPAL CROPS ('000 metric tons)

	1994	1995	1996
Wheat	565	444	550*
Rice (paddy)	14,976	13,435	13,000†
Barley	225	218	220*
Potatoes	3,377	3,365	3,365†
Sweet potatoes	1,264	1,181	1,181†
Yams	181	200†	210†
Taro (Coco yam)	238	254	260†
Other roots and tubers	55	55†	55†
Dry beans	109	138	130
Soybeans (Soya beans)	99	119*	120*
Cabbages	2,629	2,702	2,702†
Tomatoes	758	753	753†
Cauliflowers†	140	140	140
Pumpkins, squash and gourds	265	242	242†
Cucumbers and gherkins	866	826	826†
Aubergines (Eggplants)	510	478	478†
Chillies and peppers (green)	165	169	169†
Onions (dry)	1,109	1,278	1,278†
Green beans	75	75	75†
Carrots	658	724	724†
Japanese radishes	2,154		
Spinach	367	5,185†	5,185†
Other vegetables	2,678		
Watermelons	655	617	617†
Melons	390*	400†	400†
Grapes	246	250	250†
Sugar cane	1,602	1,616	1,610*
Sugar beets	3,853	3,813	3,800*
Apples	989	963	963†
Pears	431	426	426†
Peaches and nectarines	174	163	156*
Plums	113	121	121†
Oranges	144	136*	136*
Tangerines, mandarins, clementines and satsumas	1,247	1,378	1,199*
Other citrus fruit	293	318*	318†
Strawberries	198	202	202†
Persimmons	302	349†	350†
Other fruits and berries	96		
Tea (green)	86	90†	90†
Tobacco (leaves)	72	70	70*

* Unofficial figure. † FAO estimate(s).

Source: FAO, *Production Yearbook* and *Quarterly Bulletin of Statistics*.

LIVESTOCK ('000 head at 30 September)

	1994	1995	1996
Cattle	4,989	4,916	4,880*
Sheep	25	25†	25†
Goats	31	31†	31†
Horses	28	30†	30†
Pigs	10,621	10,250	9,900*
Poultry	324,000	314,000	310,000†

* Unofficial figure. † FAO estimate.

Source: FAO, *Production Yearbook*.

LIVESTOCK PRODUCTS ('000 metric tons)

	1994	1995	1996
Beef and veal	602	601	600*
Pig meat	1,390	1,322	1,260*
Poultry meat	1,302	1,280	1,255
Cows' milk	8,389	8,380	8,290*
Butter	80	80	85*
Cheese	102	105	105†
Poultry eggs	2,569	2,558	2,562*
Honey	4*	4*	4†
Raw silk	4	3*	3†
Cattle hides (fresh)*	39	38	38

* Unofficial figure(s). † FAO estimate.

Source: FAO, *Production Yearbook*.

Forestry

ROUNDWOOD REMOVALS ('000 cubic metres, excl. bark)

	1992	1993	1994
Sawlogs, veneer logs and logs for sleepers	17,517	17,567	17,693
Pulpwood	15,802	14,300	14,163
Other industrial wood	547	506	506*
Fuel wood	384	360	360*
Total	34,250	32,733	32,722

* FAO estimate.

Source: FAO, *Yearbook of Forest Products*.

SAWNWOOD PRODUCTION
(FAO estimates, '000 cubic metres, incl. railway sleepers)

	1992	1993	1994
Coniferous (softwood)	24,200	23,298	22,839
Broadleaved (hardwood)	3,077	2,962	2,904
Total	27,277	26,260	25,743

Source: FAO, *Yearbook of Forest Products*.

Fishing

('000 metric tons, live weight)

	1993	1994	1995
Chum salmon (Keta or Dog salmon)	209.5	223.1	267.7
Alaska (Walleye) pollock	382.3	379.4	338.5
Atka mackerel	135.5	152.5	176.6
Pacific saury (Skipper)	277.5	261.6	273.5
Japanese jack mackerel	318.4	332.3	318.0
Japanese amberjack	141.6	148.2	177.3
Japanese pilchard (sardine)	1,713.7	1,188.8	661.4
Japanese anchovy	194.5	188.0	252.0
Skipjack tuna (Oceanic skipjack)	374.7	301.3	309.0
Chub mackerel	664.7	633.4	469.8
Other fishes (incl. unspecified)	1,882.9	1,813.4	1,771.3
Total fish	6,295.2	5,622.0	5,015.1
Pacific cupped oyster	235.5	223.5	227.3
Yesso scallop	465.3	470.3	502.7
Japanese flying squid	315.9	301.6	290.3
Other squids and cuttlefishes	318.5	339.2	269.3
Other aquatic animals*	450.4	439.7	452.9
Total catch*	8,080.9	7,396.3	6,757.6
Inland waters	176.2	168.6	166.2
Atlantic Ocean†	280.0	254.1	227.7
Indian Ocean	65.5	45.5	57.5
Pacific Ocean	7,559.2	6,928.1	6,306.2

* Excluding aquatic mammals (including whales, see below).

† Including the Mediterranean and Black Sea.

Source: FAO, *Yearbook of Fishery Statistics*.

WHALING*

	1993	1994	1995
Number of whales caught	16,847	18,200	15,218

* Figures include whales caught during the Antarctic summer season beginning in the year prior to the year stated.

Aquatic plants ('000 metric tons): 694.0 in 1993; 777.2 in 1994; 720.4 in 1995.

Source: FAO, *Yearbook of Fishery Statistics*.

Mining

('000 metric tons, unless otherwise indicated)

	1994	1995	1996
Hard coal	6,932	6,263	6,480
Zinc ore*	100.7	95.3	79.7
Iron ore†	3	3	4
Silica stone	18,479	18,349	19,026
Limestone	202,481	201,096	202,894
Copper ore (metric tons)*	6,043	2,377	1,145
Lead ore (metric tons)*	9,946	9,659	7,753
Gold ore (kg)*	9,551	9,185	8,627
Crude petroleum (million litres)	870	861	837
Natural gas (million cu m)	2,274	2,209	2,230

* Figures refer to the metal content of ores.

† Figures refer to gross weight. The estimated iron content is 54%.

Source: Ministry of International Trade and Industry.

Industry

SELECTED PRODUCTS
('000 metric tons, unless otherwise indicated)

	1994	1995	1996
Wheat flour[1]	4,999	4,947	4,970
Refined sugar	2,407	2,397	2,359
Distilled alcoholic beverages ('000 hectolitres)[1]	8,422	n.a.	n.a.
Beer ('000 hectolitres)[1]	71,007	n.a.	n.a.
Cotton yarn—pure (metric tons)	208,658	201,829	182,149
Cotton yarn—mixed (metric tons)	26,109	13,186	13,687
Woven cotton fabrics—pure and mixed (million sq m)	1,180.4	1,029.3	916
Flax, ramie and hemp yarn (metric tons)	2,173	1,979	1,432
Linen fabrics ('000 sq m)	6,500	5,531	4,638
Woven silk fabrics—pure and mixed ('000 sq m)	65,444	59,577	58,371
Wool yarn—pure and mixed (metric tons)	89,543	71,654	64,729
Woven woollen fabrics—pure and mixed ('000 sq m)[2]	285,546	249,262	246,870
Rayon continuous filaments (metric tons)	51,400	48,850	43,611
Acetate continuous filaments (metric tons)	26,819	28,858	30,569
Rayon discontinuous fibres (metric tons)	140,659	133,329	121,547
Acetate discontinuous fibres (metric tons)[3]	78,495	81,225	n.a.
Woven rayon fabrics—pure and mixed (million sq m)[2]	435.1	334.9	374.2
Woven acetate fabrics—pure and mixed (million sq m)[2]	40	37.1	39.6
Non-cellulosic continuous filaments (metric tons)	688,856	726,130	723,632
Non-cellulosic discontinuous fibres (metric tons)	786,592	783,842	793,505
Woven synthetic fabrics (million sq m)[2, 4]	2,142.8	2,049.6	1,996.7
Leather footwear ('000 pairs)[5]	51,503	49,525	48,819
Mechanical wood pulp / Chemical wood pulp[6]	10,578.6	11,119.8	11,190.1
Newsprint	2,971.8	3,097.8	3,140.0
Other printing and writing paper	9,782.8	10,542.7	10,791.7
Other paper	3,848.4	3,825.9	3,835.1
Paperboard	11,915.8	12,192.7	12,245.2
Synthetic rubber	1,350.8	1,497.6	1,520.0
Motor vehicle tyres ('000)	147,521	159,958	166,010
Rubber footwear ('000 pairs)	27,487	25,823	24,428
Ethylene—Ethene	6,125.4	6,944.5	7,137.5
Propylene—Propene	4,434.9	4,956.1	5,143.3
Benzene—Benzol	3,620.1	4,012.7	3,964.2
Toluene—Toluol	1,219.1	1,373.6	1,329.5
Xylenes—Xylol	3,627.2	4,154.2	3,991.1
Methyl alcohol—Methanol	42.8	n.a.	n.a.
Ethyl alcohol—95% (kilolitres)	245,026	261,586	280,199
Sulphuric acid—100%	6,594	6,888	6,851
Caustic soda—Sodium hydroxide	3,785	4,004	4,062
Soda ash—Sodium carbonate	1,050	1,049	925.7

— continued	1994	1995	1996
Ammonium sulphate	1,713	1,831	1,811
Nitrogenous fertilizers (a)[7]	860	n.a.	n.a.
Phosphate fertilizers (b)[7]	395	367	328
Liquefied petroleum gas	4,584	4,921	4,879
Naphtha (million litres)	17,460	17,824	16,595
Motor spirit—Gasoline (million litres)[8]	49,857	50,857	52,271
Kerosene (million litres)	27,198	27,294	28,233
Jet fuel (million litres)	7,181	7,873	7,497
Gas oil (million litres)	43,943	45,709	47,121
Heavy fuel oil (million litres)	80,846	77,841	73,625
Lubricating oil (million litres)	2,716	2,735	2,770
Petroleum bitumen—Asphalt	6,079	5,963	6,093
Coke-oven coke	41,992	42,603	41,256
Cement	91,624	90,474	94,492
Pig-iron	73,776	74,905	74,597
Ferro-alloys[9]	876.6	989.8	951.4
Crude steel	98,295	101,640	98,801
Aluminium—unwrought: primary	336.5	n.a.	358
Electrolytic copper	1,119.2	1,188.0	1,251.4
Refined lead—unwrought (metric tons)	234,253	226,564	224,729
Electrolytic, distilled and rectified zinc—unwrought (metric tons)	665,502	663,562	599,053
Calculating machines ('000)	20,171	5,565	3,249
Video disk players ('000)	2,543.6	2,594.0	1,450.0
Television receivers ('000)[10]	9,445	7,854	6,486
Merchant vessels launched ('000 grt)	7,990	n.a.	n.a.
Passenger motor cars ('000)	7,801.3	7,610.5	7,863.8
Lorries and trucks ('000)	2,703.7	2,537.7	2,428.9
Motorcycles, scooters and mopeds ('000)	2,725.3	2,753.2	2,584.4
Cameras ('000)	11,942	11,403	12,256
Watches and clocks ('000)	442,352	446,700	451,025
Construction: new dwellings started ('000)	1,570.3	1,470.3	1,643.3
Electric energy (million kWh)[1]	964,330	989,880	1,009,349

[1] Twelve months beginning 1 April of the year stated.
[2] Including finished fabrics.
[3] Including cigarette filtration tow.
[4] Including blankets made of synthetic fibres. [5] Sales.
[6] Including pulp prepared by semi-chemical processes.
[7] Figures refer to the 12 months ending 30 June of the year stated and are in terms of (a) nitrogen, 100%, and (b) phosphoric acid, 100%. [8] Including aviation gasoline.
[9] Including silico-chromium.
[10] Figures refer to colour television receivers only.

Finance

CURRENCY AND EXCHANGE RATES

Monetary Units

100 sen = 1 yen.

Sterling and Dollar Equivalents (30 September 1997)

£1 sterling = 195.03 yen;
US $1 = 120.73 yen;
1,000 yen = £5.127 = $8.283.

Average Exchange Rate (yen per US $)

1994 102.21
1995 94.06
1996 108.78

GENERAL BUDGET ESTIMATES

('000 million yen, year ending 31 March)

Revenue	1996/97	1997/98	1998/99
Taxes and stamps	51,345	57,802	58,522
Public bonds	21,029	16,707	15,557
Others	2,731	2,881	3,590
Total	75,105	77,390	77,669

Expenditure	1996/97	1997/98	1998/99
Social security	14,288	14,550	14,843
Education and science	6,227	6,344	6,346
Government debt-servicing	16,375	16,802	17,263
Defence	4,846	4,948	4,940
Public works	9,618	9,745	8,985
Local finance	13,604	15,481	15,870
Pensions	1,659	1,597	1,531
Total (incl. others)	75,105	77,390	77,669

INTERNATIONAL RESERVES (US $ million at 31 December)

	1994	1995	1996
Gold*	1,238	1,260	1,219
IMF special drawing rights	2,083	2,707	2,642
Reserve position in IMF	8,631	8,100	6,671
Foreign exchange	115,146	172,443	207,335
Total	127,098	184,510	217,867

* Valued at SDR 35 per troy ounce.

Source: IMF, *International Financial Statistics*.

MONEY SUPPLY ('000 million yen at 31 December)*

	1994	1995	1996
Currency outside banks	42,350	46,230	49,080
Demand deposits at deposit money banks	109,310	125,310	139,060
Total money	151,670	171,540	188,150

* Figures are rounded to the nearest 10,000 million yen.

COST OF LIVING

(Consumer Price Index; average of monthly figures; base: 1995 = 100)

	1996	1997
Food (incl. beverages)	99.9	101.7
Housing	101.4	103.0
Rent	101.4	102.8
Fuel, light and water charges	99.8	104.5
Clothing and footwear	101.1	103.4
Miscellaneous	100.4	102.0
All items	100.1	101.9

NATIONAL ACCOUNTS ('000 million yen at current prices)

National Income and Product

	1994	1995	1996
Compensation of employees	269,534	273,964	279,443
Operating surplus	99,041	96,790	104,803
Domestic factor incomes	368,575	370,754	384,246
Consumption of fixed capital	75,605	77,153	79,850
Inventory valuation adjustment	543	–377	–1,709
Gross domestic product (GDP) at factor cost	444,723	447,530	462,387
Indirect taxes	38,003	38,348	41,062
Less Subsidies	3,466	3,658	3,587
GDP in purchasers' values	479,260	483,220	499,861
Factor income received from abroad	16,765	19,131	25,675
Less Factor income paid abroad	12,823	15,140	20,218
Gross national product (GNP)	483,202	487,212	505,318
Inventory valuation adjustment	–543	377	1,709
Less Consumption of fixed capital	75,605	77,153	79,850
National income in market prices	407,053	410,435	427,178
Other current transfers from abroad	187	187	655
Less Other current transfers paid abroad	771	875	1,632
National disposable income	406,470	409,747	426,201

Expenditure on the Gross Domestic Product

	1994	1995	1996
Government final consumption expenditure	45,743	47,419	48,353
Private final consumption expenditure	286,154	290,524	299,281
Increase in stocks	50	546	1,227
Gross fixed capital formation	137,291	137,611	148,322
Total domestic expenditure	469,237	476,099	497,183
Exports of goods and services	44,410	45,393	49,700
Less Imports of goods and services	34,387	38,272	47,022
GDP in purchasers' values	479,260	483,220	499,861

Gross Domestic Product by Economic Activity

	1994	1995	1996
Agriculture, hunting, forestry and fishing	10,242.4	9,350.6	9,308.1
Mining and quarrying	1,033.0	1,071.5	1,073.3
Manufacturing	117,253.0	119,261.3	121,553.6
Electricity, gas and water	13,424.4	13,733.3	14,129.7
Construction	51,664.7	50,331.6	52,767.9
Wholesale and retail trade	60,861.6	60,984.5	60,690.9
Transport, storage and communications	30,467.7	31,354.1	33,289.1
Finance and insurance	24,839.8	24,331.3	23,583.8
Real estate*	60,865.5	62,290.3	66,112.1
Public administration	37,708.1	38,856.4	39,749.2
Other services	90,802.5	93,239.7	98,609.8
Sub-total	499,162.7	504,804.5	520,867.4
Import duties	2,675.9	2,861.0	3,163.0
Less Imputed bank service charge	21,371.8	22,262.7	20,413.0
Value-added tax	−1,749.4	−1,806.0	−2,047.4
Inventory valuation adjustment	542.7	−376.7	1,709.0
GDP in purchasers' values	479,260.1	483,220.2	499,861.0

* Including imputed rents of owner-occupied dwellings.

BALANCE OF PAYMENTS (US $ million)*

	1994	1995	1996
Exports of goods f.o.b.	385,700	428,720	400,280
Imports of goods f.o.b.	−241,510	−296,930	−316,720
Trade balance	144,190	131,790	83,560
Exports of services	58,300	65,270	67,720
Imports of services	−106,360	−122,630	−129,960
Balance on goods and services	96,130	74,430	21,320
Other income received	155,190	192,450	225,100
Other income paid	−114,960	−148,160	−171,550
Balance on goods, services and income	136,360	118,720	74,880
Current transfers received	1,830	1,980	6,040
Current transfers paid	−7,940	−9,660	−15,040
Current balance	130,260	111,040	65,880
Capital account (net)	−1,850	−2,230	−3,290
Direct investment abroad	−18,090	−22,510	−23,440
Direct investment from abroad	910	40	200
Portfolio investment assets	−91,550	−87,240	−114,580
Portfolio investment liabilities	64,330	50,670	73,440
Other investment assets	−35,120	−102,240	5,220
Other investment liabilities	−5,600	97,300	31,070
Net errors and omissions	−18,030	13,780	640
Overall balance	25,270	58,610	35,140

* Figures are rounded to the nearest $10 million.

Source: IMF, *International Financial Statistics*.

JAPANESE DEVELOPMENT ASSISTANCE (US $ million)

	1994	1995	1996
Official:			
Bilateral grants:			
Donations	5,423	6,434	5,576
Reparations	2,403	2,973	2,396
Technical assistance	3,020	3,462	3,181
Direct loans	4,257	4,123	2,780
Total	9,680	10,557	8,356
Capital subscriptions or grants to international agencies	3,788	4,170	1,252
Total	13,469	14,728	9,608
Other government capital:			
Export credits	616	939	−185
Direct investment capital	614	3,793	1,930
Loans to international agencies	2,070	1,021	−67
Total	3,300	5,753	1,678
Total official	16,769	20,481	11,286
Private:			
Export credits	1,701	3,079	−1,427
Direct investments	7,437	9,497	8,338
Other bilateral security investments	5,263	10,434	22,061
Loans to international agencies	−2,870	−35	−581
Donations to non-profit organizations	213	215	232
Total private	11,744	23,190	28,623
Grand total	28,513	43,671	39,910

Source: mainly Ministry of Foreign Affairs.

External Trade

PRINCIPAL COMMODITIES (million yen)

Imports c.i.f.	1994	1995	1996
Food and live animals	4,280,798	4,311,894	5,035,626
Meat and meat preparations	793,811	905,427	1,019,115
Fresh, chilled or frozen meat	703,828	788,675	863,578
Fish and fish preparations*	1,623,066	1,631,298	1,813,403
Fresh and simply preserved fish*	1,422,534	1,412,002	1,550,225
Cereals and cereal preparations	654,939	493,879	727,587
Fruit and vegetables	618,745	614,660	690,510
Crude materials (inedible) except fuels	2,862,944	3,006,476	3,213,407
Wood, lumber and cork	1,002,968	949,826	1,046,240
Metalliferous ores and metal scrap	763,556	881,095	898,285
Mineral fuels, lubricants, etc.	4,890,437	5,022,873	6,587,732
Coal, coke and briquettes	592,816	629,352	764,248
Coal (excl. briquettes)	584,151	618,940	751,235
Petroleum and petroleum products	3,334,255	3,358,887	4,495,001
Crude and partly refined petroleum	2,825,306	2,820,064	3,644,237
Petroleum products	508,949	538,823	850,764
Gas (natural and manufactured)	963,367	1,034,634	1,328,483
Liquefied natural gas	708,965	720,419	940,157
Chemicals	2,068,231	2,309,160	2,535,616
Chemical elements and compounds	890,040	1,021,641	1,068,831
Organic chemicals	590,110	696,878	718,293
Basic manufactures	3,314,685	3,861,056	4,252,168
Non-ferrous metals	808,292	1,016,906	1,008,961

Imports c.i.f. — *continued*	1994	1995	1996
Machinery and transport equipment	5,594,184	7,336,941	9,547,514
Non-electric machinery	1,849,822	2,600,128	3,549,905
Office machines	924,771	1,481,421	2,052,739
Electronic computers, etc.	909,860	1,459,527	2,017,741
Electrical machinery, apparatus, etc.	2,400,233	3,276,753	4,270,914
Telecommunications apparatus	635,549	858,343	1,157,035
Thermionic valves, tubes, etc.	747,377	1,150,868	1,440,550
Electronic integrated circuits	619,265	1,016,735	1,274,432
Transport equipment	1,344,129	1,460,061	1,726,695
Road motor vehicles and parts†	737,839	958,549	1,152,136
Passenger cars (excl. buses)	711,076	937,986	1,114,738
Miscellaneous manufactured articles	3,889,609	4,459,240	5,552,871
Clothing (excl. footwear)	1,553,269	1,752,526	2,130,254
Non-knitted textile clothing (excl. accessories and headgear)	732,381	844,251	1,076,212
Knitted clothing and accessories excl. headgear)	630,094	714,162	839,136
Scientific instruments, watches, etc.	503,857	660,092	913,479
Total (incl. others)‡	28,104,327	31,548,754	37,993,421

* Including crustacea and molluscs.
† Excluding tyres, engines and electrical parts.
‡ Including re-imports not classified according to kind (million yen): 348,063 in 1994; 354,700 in 1995; 470,549 in 1996.

Exports f.o.b.	1994	1995	1996
Chemicals	2,421,832	2,829,276	3,138,595
Chemical elements and compounds	971,834	1,193,794	1,292,035
Organic chemicals	822,446	1,031,703	1,105,742
Basic manufactures	4,359,664	4,634,176	4,948,022
Iron and steel	1,519,904	1,644,316	1,654,761
Universals, plates and sheets	895,588	1,088,615	1,046,410
Machinery and transport equipment	28,949,426	29,083,987	31,067,331
Non-electric machinery	9,508,788	10,009,657	11,049,869
Power-generating machinery	1,434,562	1,450,320	1,533,316
Internal combustion engines	1,212,536	1,253,169	1,322,088
Office machines	2,979,011	2,889,181	3,188,509
Automatic data-processing machines	1,635,390	1,609,200	1,725,121
Metalworking machinery	497,150	747,414	924,549
Electrical machinery, apparatus, etc.	9,944,516	10,646,625	10,879,513
Switchgear	n.a.	n.a.	1,134,508
Telecommunications apparatus	3,079,621	2,654,537	2,527,681
Visual apparatus	1,101,637	963,166	972,669
Thermionic valves, tubes, etc.	2,995,703	3,829,910	3,881,188
Electronic integrated circuits	1,867,483	2,449,232	2,404,863
Transport equipment	9,496,121	8,427,705	9,137,949
Road motor vehicles and parts*	5,836,619	4,979,689	5,513,795
Passenger cars (excl. buses)	4,598,526	3,907,435	4,351,105
Lorries and trucks (incl. ambulances)	1,163,672	995,912	1,088,091
Parts for cars, buses, lorries, etc.*	1,798,220	1,781,504	1,840,529
Ships and boats	1,189,061	1,025,025	1,046,298
Miscellaneous manufactured articles	3,277,219	3,372,193	3,688,496
Scientific instruments, watches, etc.	1,851,376	1,941,633	2,094,555
Scientific instruments and photographic equipment	1,626,592	1,735,761	1,894,539
Total (incl. others)†	40,497,553	41,530,895	44,731,311

* Excluding tyres, engines and electrical parts.
† Including re-exports not classified according to kind (million yen): 748,971 in 1994; 850,075 in 1995; 1,075,954 in 1996.

PRINCIPAL TRADING PARTNERS (million yen)*

Imports c.i.f.	1994	1995	1996
Australia	1,395,453	1,366,582	1,548,244
Brazil	332,014	370,040	408,469
Canada	912,193	1,011,685	1,100,532
China, People's Republic	2,811,395	3,380,882	4,399,676
France	579,382	626,791	681,329
Germany	1,137,605	1,288,405	1,540,869
Indonesia	1,322,002	1,335,346	1,653,175
Italy	504,526	597,196	735,462
Korea, Republic	1,379,825	1,622,179	1,735,329
Malaysia	841,716	991,666	1,278,512
Philippines	271,279	326,300	492,025
Russia	355,333	444,779	428,365
Saudi Arabia	857,948	913,369	1,160,376
Singapore	475,167	644,342	796,741
Switzerland	313,909	380,518	387,720
Taiwan	1,099,975	1,347,035	1,627,657
Thailand	837,998	949,948	1,111,154
United Arab Emirates	935,372	957,767	1,253,019
United Kingdom	604,330	669,629	779,946
USA	6,424,430	7,076,404	8,630,976
Total (incl. others)	28,104,327	31,548,754	37,993,421

Exports f.o.b.	1994	1995	1996
Australia	889,993	759,398	806,023
Canada	605,361	545,656	557,391
China, People's Republic	1,913,705	2,061,960	2,382,363
France	538,545	570,422	586,045
Germany	1,823,500	1,907,967	1,980,878
Hong Kong	2,632,228	2,599,570	2,759,968
Indonesia	783,408	934,643	986,013
Korea, Republic	2,489,406	2,927,822	3,192,333
Malaysia	1,262,539	1,573,051	1,668,420
Netherlands	857,787	932,154	1,006,985
Panama	599,231	671,655	641,976
Philippines	603,650	667,409	914,733
Singapore	2,006,074	2,157,607	2,259,586
Taiwan	2,434,378	2,709,586	2,825,133
Thailand	1,502,468	1,849,932	1,987,969
United Kingdom	1,304,974	1,323,316	1,358,043
USA	12,035,826	11,332,952	12,177,119
Total (incl. others)	40,497,553	41,530,895	44,731,311

* Imports by country of production; exports by country of last consignment.

Source: mainly Japan Tariff Association, *The Summary Report on the Trade of Japan.*

Transport

RAILWAYS (traffic, year ending 31 March)

	1993/94	1994/95	1995/96
National railways:			
Passengers (million)	8,906	8,884	8,982
Freight ton-km (million)	25,027	24,077	24,702
Private railways:			
Passengers (million)	13,853	13,714	13,648
Freight ton-km (million)	406	416	399

ROAD TRAFFIC ('000 motor vehicles in use at 31 December)

	1994	1995	1996
Cars	42,679	44,680	46,869
Buses and coaches	245	243	242
Goods vehicles	22,091	21,934	21,694
Tractors and trailers	107	120	124
Total	65,122	66,977	68,929

SHIPPING

Merchant Fleet (registered at 31 December)

	1994	1995	1996
Number of vessels	9,706	9,438	9,399
Total displacement ('000 grt)	22,102	19,913	19,201

Source: Lloyd's Register of Shipping, *World Fleet Statistics*.

International Sea-borne Traffic

	1994	1995	1996
Vessels entered:			
Number	55,542	60,055	62,710
Total displacement ('000 net tons)	410,165	412,163	422,256
Goods ('000 metric tons):			
Loaded	111,179	n.a.	n.a.
Unloaded	751,408	n.a.	n.a.

CIVIL AVIATION (traffic on scheduled services)

	1992	1993	1994
Kilometres flown (million)	569	583	628
Passengers carried ('000)	81,378	80,064	83,913
Passenger-km (million)	108,082	106,983	118,011
Total ton-km (million)	14,542	14,721	16,247

Source: UN, *Statistical Yearbook*.

Passengers carried ('000): an estimated 78,803 in 1995 (Source: Industrial Bank of Japan *Quarterly Survey; Japanese Finance and Industry*).

Tourism

	1994	1995	1996
Foreign visitors	3,468,055	3,345,274	3,837,113
Tourist receipts (US $ million)	3,477	3,226	4,078

Communications Media

	1992	1993	1994
Radio receivers ('000 in use)	113,000	113,500	113,800
Television receivers ('000 in use)	n.a.	n.a.	85,000
Telephones ('000 subscriptions)*	57,652	58,830	59,870
Mobile cellular telephones ('000 in use)	1,712	2,131	4,331
Telefax stations ('000 in use)	5,500	5,750	6,000
Book production†:			
Titles	35,496	n.a.	n.a.
Copies ('000)	316,725	n.a.	n.a.
Daily newspapers:			
Number	121	n.a.	121
Circulation ('000 copies)	71,690	n.a.	71,924
Non-daily newspapers:			
Number	13‡	n.a.	n.a.
Circulation ('000 copies)	9,100‡	n.a.	n.a.
Other periodicals:			
Number	2,926	n.a.	n.a.

* Twelve months beginning 1 April of year stated.

† Data exclude pamphlets and refer to first editions only.

‡ Estimate.

1995: Radio receivers ('000 in use) 114,500; Television receivers ('000 in use) 85,500; Daily newspapers: number 121, circulation ('000 copies) 72,047.

Source: mainly UNESCO, *Statistical Yearbook*.

Education

(1996)

	Institutions	Teachers	Students
Elementary schools	24,482	425,714	8,105,629
Lower secondary schools	11,269	270,972	4,527,400
Upper secondary schools	5,496	278,879	4,547,497
Colleges of technology	62	4,345	56,396
Junior colleges	598	20,294	473,279
Graduate schools and universities	576	139,608	2,596,667

Source: Ministry of Education.

Directory

The Constitution

The Constitution of Japan was promulgated on 3 November 1946 and came into force on 3 May 1947. The following is a summary of its major provisions, with subsequent amendments:

THE EMPEROR

Articles 1–8. The Emperor derives his position from the will of the people. In the performance of any state act as defined in the Constitution, he must seek the advice and approval of the Cabinet, though he may delegate the exercise of his functions, which include: (i) the appointment of the Prime Minister and the Chief Justice of the Supreme Court; (ii) promulgation of laws, cabinet orders, treaties and constitutional amendments; (iii) the convocation of the Diet, dissolution of the House of Representatives and proclamation of elections to the Diet; (iv) the appointment and dismissal of Ministers of State, the granting of amnesties, reprieves and pardons, and the ratification of treaties, conventions or protocols; (v) the awarding of honours and performance of ceremonial functions.

RENUNCIATION OF WAR

Article 9. Japan renounces for ever the use of war as a means of settling international disputes.

Articles 10–40 refer to the legal and human rights of individuals guaranteed by the Constitution.

THE DIET

Articles 41–64. The Diet is convened once a year, is the highest organ of state power and has exclusive legislative authority. It comprises the House of Representatives (500 seats—300 single-seat constituencies and 200 determined by proportional representation) and the House of Councillors (252 seats). The members of the former are elected for four years whilst those of the latter are elected for six years and election for one-half of the members takes place every three years. If the House of Representatives is dissolved, a general election must take place within 40 days and the Diet must be convoked within 30 days of the date of the election. Extraordinary sessions of the Diet may be convened by the Cabinet when one-quarter or more of the members of either House request it. Emergency sessions of the House of Councillors may also be held. A quorum of at least one-third of the Diet members is needed to carry out parliamentary business. Any decision arising therefrom must be passed by a majority vote of those present. A bill becomes law having passed both Houses, except as provided by the Constitution. If the House of Councillors either vetoes or fails to take action within 60 days upon a bill already passed by the House of Representatives, the bill becomes law when passed a second time by the House of Representatives, by at least a two-thirds majority of those members present.

The Budget must first be submitted to the House of Representatives. If, when it is approved by the House of Representatives, the House of Councillors votes against it or fails to take action on it within 30 days, or failing agreement being reached by a joint committee of both Houses, a decision of the House of Representatives shall be the decision of the Diet. The above procedure also applies in respect of the conclusion of treaties.

THE EXECUTIVE

Articles 65–75. Executive power is vested in the Cabinet, consisting of a Prime Minister and such other Ministers as may be appointed. The Cabinet is collectively responsible to the Diet. The Prime Minister is designated from among members of the Diet by a resolution thereof.

If the House of Representatives and the House of Councillors disagree on the designation of the Prime Minister, and if no agreement can be reached even through a joint committee of both Houses, provided for by law, or if the House of Councillors fails to make designation within 10 days, exclusive of the period of recess, after the House of Representatives has made designation, the decision of the House of Representatives shall be the decision of the Diet.

The Prime Minister appoints and may remove other Ministers, a majority of whom must be from the Diet. If the House of Representatives passes a no-confidence motion or rejects a confidence motion, the whole Cabinet resigns, unless the House of Representatives is dissolved within 10 days. When there is a vacancy in the post of Prime Minister, or upon the first convocation of the Diet after a general election of members of the House of Representatives, the whole Cabinet resigns.

The Prime Minister submits bills, reports on national affairs and foreign relations to the Diet. He exercises control and supervision over various administrative branches of the Government. The Cabinet's primary functions (in addition to administrative ones) are to: (a) administer the law faithfully; (b) conduct State affairs; (c) conclude treaties subject to prior (or subsequent) Diet approval; (d) administer the civil service in accordance with law; (e) prepare and present the budget to the Diet; (f) enact Cabinet orders in order to make effective legal and constitutional provisions; (g) decide on amnesties, reprieves or pardons. All laws and Cabinet orders are signed by the competent Minister of State and countersigned by the Prime Minister. The Ministers of State, during their tenure of office, are not subject to legal action without the consent of the Prime Minister. However, the right to take that action is not impaired.

Articles 76–95. Relate to the Judiciary, Finance and Local Government.

AMENDMENTS

Article 96. Amendments to the Constitution are initiated by the Diet, through a concurring vote of two-thirds or more of all the members of each House and are submitted to the people for ratification, which requires the affirmative vote of a majority of all votes cast at a special referendum or at such election as the Diet may specify.

Amendments when so ratified must immediately be promulgated by the Emperor in the name of the people, as an integral part of the Constitution.

Articles 97–99 outline the Supreme Law, while Articles 100–103 consist of Supplementary Provisions.

The Government

HEAD OF STATE

His Imperial Majesty AKIHITO, Emperor of Japan (succeeded to the throne 7 January 1989).

THE CABINET
(February 1998)

Prime Minister: RYUTARO HASHIMOTO.

Minister of Justice: KOICHI SHIMOINABA.

Minister of Foreign Affairs: KEIZO OBUCHI.

Minister of Finance: HIKARU MATSUNAGA.

Minister of Education: NOBUTAKA MACHIMURA.

Minister of Health and Welfare: JUN'ICHIRO KOIZUMI.

Minister of Agriculture, Forestry and Fisheries: YOSHINOBU SHIMAMURA.

Minister of International Trade and Industry: MITSUO HORIUCHI.

Minister of Transport: TAKAO FUJII.

Minister of Posts and Telecommunications: SHOZABURO JIMI.

Minister of Labour: BUNMEI IBUKI.

Minister of Construction: TSUTOMU KAWARA.

Minister of Home Affairs: MITSUHIRO UESUGI.

Chief Cabinet Secretary: KANEZO MURAOKA.

Minister of State and Director-General of the Management and Co-ordination Agency: SADATOSHI OZATO.

Minister of State and Director-General of the Hokkaido Development Agency and the Okinawa Development Agency: MUNEO SUZUKI.

Minister of State and Director-General of the Defence Agency: FUMIO KYUMA.

Minister of State and Director-General of the Economic Planning Agency: KOJI OMI.

Minister of State and Director-General of the Science and Technology Agency: SADAKAZU TANIGAKI.

Minister of State and Director-General of the Environment Agency: HIROSHI OKI.

Minister of State and Director-General of the National Land Agency: HISAOKI KAMEI.

MINISTRIES

Imperial Household Agency: 1-1, Chiyoda, Chiyoda-ku, Tokyo 100; tel. (3) 3213-1111.

Prime Minister's Office: 1-6, Nagata-cho, Chiyoda-ku, Tokyo; tel. (3) 3581-2361.

Ministry of Agriculture, Forestry and Fisheries: 1-2-1, Kasumigaseki, Chiyoda-ku, Tokyo 100; tel. (3) 3502-8111; fax (3) 3592-7697.

Ministry of Construction: 2-1-3, Kasumigaseki, Chiyoda-ku, Tokyo 100; tel. (3) 3580-4311; fax (3) 5251-1922.

Ministry of Education, Science, Sport and Culture: 3-2-2, Kasumigaseki, Chiyoda-ku, Tokyo 100; tel. (3) 3581-4211; fax (3) 3591-8072.

Ministry of Finance: 3-1-1, Kasumigaseki, Chiyoda-ku, Tokyo 100; tel. (3) 3581-4111; fax (3) 3592-1025.

Ministry of Foreign Affairs: 2-2-1, Kasumigaseki, Chiyoda-ku, Tokyo 100; tel. (3) 3580-3311; fax (3) 3581-9675.

Ministry of Health and Welfare: 1-2-2, Kasumigaseki, Chiyoda-ku, Tokyo 100; tel. (3) 3503-1711; fax (3) 3501-4853.

Ministry of Home Affairs: 2-1-2, Kasumigaseki, Chiyoda-ku, Tokyo 100; tel. (3) 3581-5311; fax (3) 3593-3758.

Ministry of International Trade and Industry: 1-3-1, Kasumigaseki, Chiyoda-ku, Tokyo 100; tel. (3) 3501-1511; fax (3) 3501-2081.

Ministry of Justice: 1-1-1, Kasumigaseki, Chiyoda-ku, Tokyo 100; tel. (3) 3580-4111; fax (3) 3592-7011.

Ministry of Labour: 1-2-2, Kasumigaseki, Chiyoda-ku, Tokyo 100; tel. (3) 3593-1211; fax (3) 3502-6711.

Ministry of Posts and Telecommunications: 1-3-2, Kasumigaseki, Chiyoda-ku, Tokyo 100; tel. (3) 3504-4411; telex 32538; fax (3) 3504-0265.

Ministry of Transport: 2-1-3, Kasumigaseki, Chiyoda-ku, Tokyo 100; tel. (3) 3580-3111; fax (3) 3580-7982.

Defence Agency: 9-7-45, Akasaka, Minato-ku, Tokyo 107; tel. (3) 3408-5211.

Economic Planning Agency: 3-1-1, Kasumigaseki, Chiyoda-ku, Tokyo 100; tel. (3) 3581-0056; fax (3) 3581-0654.

Environment Agency: 1-2-2, Kasumigaseki, Chiyoda-ku, Tokyo 100; tel. (3) 3581-3351; telex 33855; fax (3) 3504-1634.

Hokkaido Development Agency: 3-1-1, Kasumigaseki, Chiyoda-ku, Tokyo 100; tel. (3) 3581-9111; fax (3) 3581-1208.

Management and Co-ordination Agency: 3-1-1, Kasumigaseki, Chiyoda-ku, Tokyo 100; tel. (3) 3581-6361.

National Land Agency: 1-2-2, Kasumigaseki, Chiyoda-ku, Tokyo 100; tel. (3) 3593-3311.

Okinawa Development Agency: 1-6-1, Nagata-cho, Chiyoda-ku, Tokyo 100; tel. (3) 3581-2361.

Science and Technology Agency: 2-2-1, Kasumigaseki, Chiyoda-ku, Tokyo 100; tel. (3) 3581-5271.

Legislature

KOKKAI
(Diet)

The Diet consists of two Chambers: the House of Councillors (upper house) and the House of Representatives (lower house). The members of the House of Representatives are elected for a period of four years (subject to dissolution). Following the enactment of reform legislation in December 1994, the number of members in the House of Representatives was reduced to 500 (from 511) at the general election of October 1996. For the House of Councillors, which has 252 members, the term of office is six years, with one-half of the members elected every three years.

House of Councillors

Speaker: JURO SAITO.

Party	Seats after elections* 26 July 1992	23 July 1995
Liberal-Democratic Party	106	110
New Frontier Party (Shinshinto)†	—	56
Social Democratic Party of Japan‡	73	38
Japanese Communist Party	11	14
Komeito§	24	11
Democratic Socialist Party†	12	—
New Party Sakigake	—	3
Ni-In Club	5	2
Japan New Party†	4	—
Independents	6	12
Other parties	11	6
Total	252	252

* One-half of the 252 seats are renewable every three years. At each election, 50 of the 126 seats are allocated on the basis of proportional representation.

† In December 1994, following electoral reform legislation, nine opposition parties, including the Japan Renewal Party (Shinseito), the Japan New Party, the Democratic Socialist Party and a faction of the Komeito, amalgamated to form the New Frontier Party (Shinshinto). In December 1997 the New Frontier Party (Shinshinto) was dissolved. Six new parties were formed, two of which subsequently merged with the Taiyo Party (Sun Party) to form the Minseito.

‡ Formerly the Japan Socialist Party.

§ Renamed the Komei in 1994, following the defection of a number of members to the (now-dissolved) New Frontier Party (Shinshinto).

House of Representatives

Speaker: SOICHIRO ITO.

General Election, 20 October 1996

Party	Seats
Liberal-Democratic Party	239
New Frontier Party (Shinshinto)	156
Democratic Party of Japan	52
Japanese Communist Party	26
Social Democratic Party of Japan	15
New Party Sakigake	2
Independents and others	10
Total	500

Political Organizations

The Political Funds Regulation Law provides that any organization wishing to support a candidate for an elective public office must be registered as a political party. There are more than 10,000 registered parties in the country, mostly of local or regional significance.

21st Century: 1-7-1, Nagato-cho, Chiyoda-ku, Tokyo; tel. (3) 3581-5111; f. 1996 by four independent mems of House of Representatives; Chair. HAJIME FUNADA.

Democratic Party of Japan—DPJ: 1-11-1, Nagata-cho, Chiyoda-ku, Tokyo; tel. (3) 3595-9988; f. 1996 by fmr mems of New Frontier Party (Shinshinto, dissolved Dec. 1997), New Party Sakigake and the SDPJ; advocates administrative and welfare reform; Leader NAOTO KAN; Sec.-Gen. YUKIO HATOYAMA.

Japanese Communist Party—JCP: 4-26-7, Sendagaya, Shibuya-ku, Tokyo 151; tel. (3) 3403-6111; fax (3) 3746-0767; internet http://www.jcp.or.jp; f. 1922; 370,000 mems (1997); Chair. of the Presidium TETSUZO FUWA; Head of Secr. KAZUO SHII.

Kaikaku (Reform) Club: c/o House of Representatives, Tokyo; f. 1997; Leader TATSUO OZAWA.

Komei: 17, Minami-Motomachi, Shinjuku-ku, Tokyo 160; tel. (3) 3353-0111; f. 1964 as Komeito, renamed 1994 following defection of a number of mems to the New Frontier Party (Shinshinto, dissolved Dec. 1997); advocates political moderation, humanism and globalism, and policies respecting 'dignity of human life'; 300,000 mems (1997); Representative TOSHIKO HAMAYOTSU; Sec.-Gen. HIROSHI TSURUOKA.

Liberal Party: c/o House of Representatives, Tokyo; f. 1997; Leader ICHIRO OZAWA.

Liberal-Democratic Party—LDP (Jiyu-Minshuto): 1-11-23, Nagata-cho, Chiyoda-ku, Tokyo 100; tel. (3) 3581-0111; f. 1955; advocates the establishment of a welfare state, the promotion of industrial development, the improvement of educational and cultural facilities and constitutional reform as needed; follows a foreign policy of alignment with the USA; 2,774,460 mems (Oct. 1994); Pres. RYUTARO HASHIMOTO; Sec.-Gen. KOICHI KATO; Chair. of Gen. Council YOSHIRO MORI.

Minseito (Good Governance Party): c/o House of Representatives, Tokyo; f. 1997 from merger of three parties formed by members of the now-dissolved New Frontier Party (Shinshinto): Kokumin No Koe (Voice of the People), f. 1997; the Taiyo (Sun) Party, f. 1996; and From Five, f. 1997 by MORIHIRO HOSOKAWA; Leader TSUTOMU HATA; Sec.-Gen. MICHIHIKO KANO.

New Party Sakigake: Akasaka Annex, 1st Floor, 2-17-42, Akasaka, Minato-ku, Tokyo 107; tel. (3) 5570-1341; fax (3) 5570-6941; f. 1993 by a breakaway faction of LDP; also known as New Harbinger Party; Representative AKIKO DOMOTO; Sec.-Gen. HIROYUKI SONODA.

New Socialist Party: 4-3-7, Hachobori, Chuo-ku, Tokyo; tel. (3) 3551-3980; f. 1996 by left-wing defectors from SDPJ; opposed to US military bases on Okinawa and to introduction in 1996 of new electoral system; Chair. OSAMU YATABE; Sec.-Gen. TETSUO YAMAGUCHI.

Ni-In Club, Kakushin Kyoto (Second Chamber Club): Broadway Corpn 1015, 5-52-15, Nakano, Nakano-ku, Tokyo 164; tel. (3) 3508-8629; successor to the Green Wind Club (Ryukufukai), which originated in the House of Councillors in 1946–47; Sec. (vacant).

Reimei (Dawn) Club: c/o House of Councillors, Tokyo; f. 1997; Leader KAZUYOSHI SHIRAHAMA; Sec.-Gen. KENTARO KOBA.

Shinto Heiwa (New Peace Party): c/o House of Representatives, Tokyo; f. 1997; Leader TAKENORI KANZAKI; Sec.-Gen. TETSUZO FUYUSHIBA.

Shinto Yuai (New Party Fraternity): c/o House of Representatives, Tokyo; f. 1997.

Social Democratic Party of Japan—SDPJ (Shakai Minshuto): 1-8-1, Nagata-cho, Chiyoda-ku, Tokyo 100; tel. (3) 3580-1171; telex 29223; fax (3) 3580-0691; f. 1945 as the Japan Socialist Party (JSP); adopted present name in 1996; seeks the establishment of collective non-aggression and a mutual security system, including Japan, the USA, the CIS and the People's Republic of China; 115,000 mems (1994); Chair. TAKAKO DOI; Sec.-Gen. SHIGERU ITO.

Diplomatic Representation

EMBASSIES IN JAPAN

Afghanistan: Olympia Annex Apt 503, 6-31-21, Jingumae, Shibuya-ku, Tokyo 150; tel. (3) 3407-7900; telex 2422978; fax (3) 3400-7912; Chargé d'affaires a.i.: RAHMATULLAH AMIR.

Algeria: 2-10-67, Mita, Meguro-ku, Tokyo 153; tel. (3) 3711-2661; fax (3) 3710-6534; Ambassador: BOUDJEMAA DELMI.

Argentina: 2-14-14, Moto Azabu, Minato-ku, Tokyo 106; tel. (3) 5420-7101; fax (3) 5420-7109; Ambassador: JOSÉ RAMÓN SANCHIS MUÑOZ.

Australia: 2-1-14, Mita, Minato-ku, Tokyo 108; tel. (3) 5232-4111; fax (3) 5232-4149; Ambassador: Dr ASHTON TREVOR CALVERT.

Austria: 1-1-20, Moto Azabu, Minato-ku, Tokyo 106; tel. (3) 3451-8281; fax (3) 3451-8283; e-mail austroam@crisscross.com; Ambassador: MARTIN VUKOVICH.

Bangladesh: 4-15-15, Meguro, Meguro-ku, Tokyo 153; tel. (3) 5704-0216; telex 28826; fax (3) 5704-1696; Ambassador: S. M. RASHED AHMED.

Belarus: 3-3-25, Roppongi, Minato-ku, Tokyo 106; tel. (3) 0065-3839; Chargé d'affaires a.i.: SERGEI SAENKOV.

Belgium: 5, Niban-cho, Chiyoda-ku, Tokyo 102; tel. (3) 3262-0191; telex 24979; fax (3) 3262-0651; Ambassador: Baron PATRICK NOTHOMB.

Bolivia: Kowa Bldg, No. 38, Room 804, 4-12-24, Nishi Azabu, Minato-ku, Tokyo 106-0031; tel (3) 3499-5441; fax (3) 3499-5443.

Brazil: 2-11-12, Kita Aoyama, Minato-ku, Tokyo 107; tel. (3) 3404-5211; telex 22590; fax (3) 3405-5846; Ambassador: FERNANDO GUIMARÃES REIS.

Brunei: 6-5-2, Kita Shinagawa, Shinagawa-ku, Tokyo 141; tel. (3) 3447-7997; fax (3) 3447-9260; Ambassador: Haji YUSOF Haji ABDUL HAMID.

Bulgaria: 5-36-3, Yoyogi, Shibuya-ku, Tokyo 151; tel. (3) 3465-1021; fax (3) 3465-1031; Ambassador: VALENTIN GATSINSKI.

Burkina Faso: Apt 301, Hiroo Glisten Hills, 3-1-17, Hiroo, Shibuya-ku, Tokyo 150; tel. (3) 3400-7919; fax (3) 3400-6945; Ambassador: WINDPAYADE RAYMOND EDOUARD OUÉDRAOGO.

Burundi: Residence Takanawa, 2nd Floor, Room 201, 2-12-13, Takanawa, Minato-ku, Tokyo 108; tel. (3) 3443-7321; fax (3) 3443-7720; Ambassador: GABRIEL NDIHOKUBWAYO.

Cambodia: 8-6-9, Akasaka, Minato-ku, Tokyo 107; tel. (3) 5412-8521; fax (3) 5412-8526; Ambassador: TRUONG MEALY.

Cameroon: 3-27-16, Nozawa, Setagaya-ku, Tokyo 154; tel. (3) 5430-4381; telex 2428032; fax (3) 5430-6489; Chargé d'affaires a.i: ANDRÉ-MARIE ATANGANA ZANG.

Canada: 7-3-38, Akasaka, Minato-ku, Tokyo 107; tel. (3) 5412-6200; fax (3) 5412-6249; Ambassador: LEONARD J. EDWARDS.

Chile: Nihon Seimei Akabanebashi Bldg, 8th Floor, 3-1-14, Shiba, Minato-ku, Tokyo 105; tel. (3) 3452-7561; fax (3) 3452-4457; Ambassador: JAIME LAGOS.

China, People's Republic: 3-4-33, Moto Azabu, Minato-ku, Tokyo 106; tel. (3) 3403-3380; fax (3) 3403-3345; Ambassador: TANG JIAXUAN.

Colombia: 3-10-53, Kami Osaki, Shinagawa-ku, Tokyo 141; tel. (3) 3440-6451; fax (3) 3440-6724; Ambassador: PEDRO FELIPE VALENCIA.

Congo, Democratic Republic: Harajuku Green Heights, Room 701, 3-53-17, Sendagaya, Shibuya-ku, Tokyo 151; tel. (3) 3423-3981; fax (3) 3423-3984; Chargé d'affaires: NGAMBANI ZI-MIZELE.

Costa Rica: Kowa Bldg, No. 38, Room 901, 4-12-24, Nishi Azabu, Minato-ku, Tokyo 106; tel. (3) 3486-1812; fax (3) 3486-1813; Ambassador: CRISTINA ROJAS.

Côte d'Ivoire: 2-19-12, Uehara, Shibuya-ku, Tokyo 151; tel. (3) 5454-1401; telex 26631; fax (3) 5454-1405; Ambassador: PATRICE KOFFI ANOH.

Croatia: 2-8-1-101, Tomigaya, Shibuya-ku, Tokyo 151; tel. (3) 5478-8481; fax (3) 5478-8491; Ambassador: Dr ANDJELKO SIMIĆ.

Cuba: 4-11-12, Shimo Meguro, Meguro-ku, Tokyo 153; tel. (3) 3716-3112; telex 22642; fax (3) 3716-4334; Ambassador: ERNESTO MELÉNDEZ BACHS.

Czech Republic: 2-16-14, Hiroo, Shibuya-ku, Tokyo 150-0012; tel. (3) 3400-8122; fax (3) 3400-8124; Ambassador: JOSEF HAVLAS.

Denmark: 29-6, Sarugaku-cho, Shibuya-ku, Tokyo 150-0033; tel. (3) 3496-3001; fax (3) 3496-3440; e-mail dkembtok@twics.com; Ambassador: PETER BRÜCKNER.

Djibouti: 2-2-17-201, Shoto, Shibuya-ku, Tokyo 150; tel. (3) 3481-5252; fax (3) 3481-5387; Ambassador: RACHAD AHMED SALEH FARAH.

Dominican Republic: Kowa Bldg, No. 38, Room 904, 4-12-24, Nishi Azabu, Minato-ku, Tokyo 106; tel. (3) 3499-6020; fax (3) 3499-2627; Ambassador: ERVIN DE LEÓN.

Ecuador: Kowa Bldg, No. 38, Room 806, 4-12-24, Nishi Azabu, Minato-ku, Tokyo 106; tel. (3) 3499-2800; telex 25880; fax (3) 3499-4400; Ambassador: MARCELO AVILA.

Egypt: 1-5-4, Aobadai, Meguro-ku, Tokyo 153; tel. (3) 3770-8022; telex 23240; fax (3) 3770-8021; Ambassador: Mrs MERVAT MEHANI TALLAWY.

El Salvador: Kowa Bldg, No. 38, 8th Floor, 4-12-24, Nishi Azabu, Minato-ku, Tokyo 106; tel. (3) 3499-4461; fax (3) 3486-7022; e-mail embesal@iac.co.jp; Ambassador: Dr MYNOR GIL.

Estonia: Akasaka Royal Office Bldg, 3rd Floor, 6-9-17, Akasaka, Minato-ku, Tokyo 107; tel. (3) 5545-7171; fax (3) 5545-7172; Chargé d'affaires: HEIKKI VALLASTE.

Ethiopia: 1-14-15, Midorigaoka, Meguro-ku, Tokyo 152; tel. (3) 3718-1003; fax (3) 3718-0978; Ambassador: MAHDI AHMED.

Fiji: Noa Bldg, 14th Floor, 2-3-5, Azabudai, Minato-ku, Tokyo 106; tel. (3) 3587-2038; fax (3) 3587-2563; Ambassador: ROBIN YARROW.

Finland: 3-5-39, Minami Azabu, Minato-ku, Tokyo 106; tel. (3) 3442-2231; telex 26277; fax (3) 3442-2175; Ambassador: MATTI PEKKA LINTU.

France: 4-11-44, Minami Azabu, Minato-ku, Tokyo 106-8514; tel. (3) 5420-8800; fax (3) 5420-8917; e-mail ambfrajp@popmail.gol.com; Ambassador: JEAN-BERNARD OUVRIEU.

Gabon: 1-12-11, Kami Osaki, Shinagawa-ku, Tokyo 141; tel. (3) 3448-9540; telex 24812; fax (3) 3448-1596; Ambassador: VINCENT BOULÉ.

Germany: 4-5-10, Minami Azabu, Minato-ku, Tokyo 106; tel. (3) 3473-0151; fax (3) 3473-4243; e-mail germtoky@gol.com; Ambassador: FRANK ELBE.

Ghana: 6-2-4, Fukazawa, Setagaya-ku, Tokyo 158; tel. (3) 5706-3201; telex 22487; fax (3) 5706-3205; Ambassador: CHEMOGOH KEVIN DZANG.

Greece: 3-16-30, Nishi Azabu, Minato-ku, Tokyo 106; tel. (3) 3403-0871; fax (3) 3402-4642; Ambassador: GEORGE SIORIS.

Guatemala: Kowa Bldg, No. 38, Room 905, 4-12-24, Nishi Azabu, Minato-ku, Tokyo 106; tel. (3) 3400-1830; fax (3) 3400-1820; Ambassador: FERNANDO GONZÁLEZ-DAVISON.

Guinea: 2-7-43, Shirogane, Minato-ku, Tokyo 108; tel. (3) 3443-8211; telex 24165; fax (3) 3443-8213; Ambassador: ZAÏNOUL ABIDINE SANOUSSI.

Haiti: Kowa Bldg, No. 38, Room 906, 4-12-24, Nishi Azabu, Minato-ku, Tokyo 106; tel. (3) 3486-7096; fax (3) 3486-7070; Ambassador: MARCEL DURET.

Holy See: Apostolic Nunciature, 9-2, Sanban-cho, Chiyoda-ku, Tokyo 102-0075; tel. (3) 3263-6851; fax (3) 3263-6060; Apostolic Nuncio: Most Rev. AMBROSE B. DE PAOLI, Titular Archbishop of Lares.

Honduras: Kowa Bldg, No. 38, Room 802, 8th Floor, 4-12-24, Nishi Azabu, Minato-ku, Tokyo 106-31; tel. (3) 3409-1150; fax (3) 3409-0305; e-mail honduran@interlink.or.jp; Ambassador: EDGARDO SEVILLÁ IDIÁQUEZ.

Hungary: 2-17-14, Mita, Minato-ku, Tokyo 108; tel. (3) 3798-8801; fax (3) 3798-8812; Ambassador: Dr ZOLTÁN SŰDY.

India: 2-2-11, Kudan Minami, Chiyoda-ku, Tokyo 102; tel. (3) 3262-2391; fax (3) 3234-4866; Ambassador: KULDIP SAHDEV.

Indonesia: 5-2-9, Higashi Gotanda, Shinagawa-ku, Tokyo 141; tel. (3) 3441-4201; telex 22920; fax (3) 3447-1697; Ambassador: WISBER LOEIS.

Iran: 3-10-32, Minami Azabu, Minato-ku, Tokyo 106; tel. (3) 3446-8011; fax (3) 3446-9002; Ambassador: MANOUCHEHR MOTTAKI.

Iraq: 8-4-7, Akasaka, Minato-ku, Tokyo 107; tel. (3) 3423-1727; fax (3) 3402-8636; Chargé d'affaires: MUHSIN M. ALI.

Ireland: Ireland House, 2-10-7, Kojimachi, Chiyoda-ku, Tokyo 102; tel. (3) 3263-0695; fax (3) 3265-2275; Ambassador: DECLAN O'DONOVAN.

Israel: 3, Niban-cho, Chiyoda-ku, Tokyo 102; tel. (3) 3264-0911; fax (3) 3264-0832; Ambassador: MOSHE BEN-YAACOV.

Italy: 2-5-4, Mita, Minato-ku, Tokyo 108-8302; tel. (3) 3453-5291; telex 22433; fax (3) 3456-2319; Ambassador: GIOVANNI DOMINEDÒ.

Jamaica: Toranomon Yatsuka Bldg, 2nd Floor, 1-1-11, Atago, Minato-ku, Tokyo 105; tel. (3) 3435-1861; fax (3) 3435-1864; Ambassador: Dr EARL A. CARR.

Jordan: Chiyoda House, 4th Floor, 2-17-8, Nagata-cho, Chiyoda-ku, Tokyo 100; tel. (3) 3580-5856; telex 23708; fax (3) 3593-9385; Ambassador: FAROUK KASRAWI.

Kenya: 3-24-3, Yakumo, Meguro-ku, Tokyo 152; tel. (3) 3723-4006; telex 2422378; fax (3) 3723-4488; Ambassador: SAMSON K. CHEMAI.

Korea, Republic: 1-2-5, Minami Azabu, Minato-ku, Tokyo 106; tel. (3) 3452-7611; telex 22045; fax (3) 5232-6911; Ambassador: KIM TAE ZHEE.

Kuwait: 4-13-12, Mita, Minato-ku, Tokyo 108; tel. (3) 3455-0361; telex 25501; fax (3) 3456-6290; Ambassador: Dr SUHAIL K. SHUHAIBER.

Laos: 3-3-22, Nishi Azabu, Minato-ku, Tokyo 106; tel. (3) 5411-2291; fax (3) 5411-2293; Ambassador: THONGSAY BODHISANE.

Lebanon: Chiyoda House, 5th Floor, 2-17-8, Nagata-cho, Chiyoda-ku, Tokyo 100-0014; tel. (3) 3580-1227; telex 25356; fax (3) 3580-2281; e-mail ambaliba@japan.co.jp; Ambassador: SAMIR CHAMMA.

Liberia: Sugi Terrace 201, 3-13-11, Okusawa, Setagaya-ku, Tokyo 158; tel. (3) 3726-5711; fax (3) 3726-5712; Chargé d'affaires a.i.: HARRY TAH FREEMAN.

Libya: 10-14, Daikanyama-cho, Shibuya-ku, Tokyo 150; tel. (3) 3477-0701; fax (3) 3464-0420; Secretary of the People's Bureau: SULAIMAN ABU BAKER BADI (acting).

Luxembourg: Niban-cho TS Bldg, 4th Floor, 2-1, Niban-cho, Chiyoda-ku, Tokyo 102; tel. (3) 3265-9621; telex 28822; fax (3) 3265-9624; Ambassador: PIERRE GRAMEGNA.

Madagascar: 2-3-23, Moto Azabu, Minato-ku, Tokyo 106; tel. (3) 3446-7252; fax (3) 3446-7078; Ambassador: CYRILLE FIDA.

Malawi: Takanawa-Kaisei Bldg, 7th Floor, 3-4-1, Takanawa, Minato-ku, Tokyo 108; tel. (3) 3449-3010; telex 22161; fax (3) 3449-3220; Ambassador: T. I. M. VARETA.

Malaysia: 20-16, Nanpeidai-cho, Shibuya-ku, Tokyo 150; tel. (3) 3476-3840; telex 24221; fax (3) 3476-4971; Ambassador: Datuk H. M. KHATIB.

Marshall Islands: Meiji Park Heights 101, 9-9, Minamimoto-machi, Shinjuku-ku, Tokyo 106; tel. (3) 5379-1701; fax (3) 5379-1810; Ambassador: MACK T. KAMINAGA.

Mauritania: 5-17-5, Kita Shinagawa, Shinagawa-ku, Tokyo 141-0001; tel. (3) 3449-3810; telex 24385; fax (3) 3449-3822; Ambassador: BA ALIOU IBRA.

Mexico: 2-15-1, Nagata-cho, Chiyoda-ku, Tokyo 100; tel. (3) 3581-1131; telex 26875; fax (3) 3581-4058; e-mail embamex@twics.com; Ambassador: MANUEL URIBE CASTAÑEDA.

Micronesia: Reinanzaka Bldg, 2nd Floor, 1-14-2, Akasaka, Minato-ku, Tokyo 107; tel. (3) 3585-5456; fax (3) 3585-5348; Ambassador: MASAO NAKAYAMA.

Mongolia: Pine Crest Mansion, 21-4, Kamiyama-cho, Shibuya-ku, Tokyo 150; tel. (3) 3469-2092; fax (3) 3469-2216; Ambassador: BADAM-OCHIRYN DOLJINTSEREN.

Morocco: Silva Kingdom Bldg, 5th–6th Floors, 3-16-3, Sendagaya, Shibuya-ku, Tokyo 151; tel. (3) 3478-3271; telex 23451; fax (3) 3402-0898; Ambassador: SAAD EDDIN TAIB.

Mozambique: 33-3, Ohyama-cho, Shibuya-ku, Tokyo 151; tel. (3) 3485-7621; fax (3) 3485-7622; Chargé d'affaires a.i.: ARTUR JOSSEFA JAMO.

Myanmar: 4-8-26, Kita Shinagawa, Shinagawa-ku, Tokyo 140; tel. (3) 3441-9291; fax (3) 3447-7394; Ambassador: U SOE WIN.

Nepal: 7-14-9, Todoroki, Setagaya-ku, Tokyo 158; tel. (3) 3705-5558; telex 23936; fax (3) 3705-8264; Chargé d'affaires a.i.: RUDRA K. NEPAL.

Netherlands: 3-6-3, Shiba Koen, Minato-ku, Tokyo 105; tel. (3) 5401-0411; fax (3) 5401-0420; Ambassador: ROBERT VAN NOUHUYS.

New Zealand: 20-40, Kamiyama-cho, Shibuya-ku, Tokyo 150; tel. (3) 3467-2271; fax (3) 3467-6843; e-mail nzemb@gol.com; Ambassador: MAARTEN L. WEVERS.

Nicaragua: Kowa Bldg, No. 38, Room 903, 9th Floor, 4-12-24, Nishi Azabu, Minato-ku, Tokyo 106; tel. (3) 3499-0400; fax (3) 3499-3800; Ambassador: Dr HARRY BODÁN-SHIELDS.

Nigeria: 5-11-17, Shimo-Meguro, Meguro-ku, Tokyo 153; tel. (3) 5721-5391; fax (3) 5721-5342; Chargé d'affaires a.i.: T. A. O. ODEGBILE.

Norway: 5-12-2, Minami Azabu, Minato-ku, Tokyo 106; tel. (3) 3440-2611; fax (3) 3440-2620; Ambassador: JOHN BJØNEBYE.

Oman: Silva Kingdom Bldg, 3rd Floor, 2-28-11, Sendagaya, Shibuya-ku, Tokyo 151-0051; tel. (3) 3402-0877; fax (3) 3404-1334; Ambassador: MOHAMMED ALI AL-KHUSAIBY.

Pakistan: 2-14-9, Moto Azabu, Minato-ku, Tokyo 106; tel. (3) 3454-4861; fax (3) 3457-0341; Ambassador: MUJAHID HUSAIN.

Palau: Tokyo.

Panama: Kowa Bldg, No. 38, Room 902, 4-12-24, Nishi Azabu, Minato-ku, Tokyo 106-0031; tel. (3) 3499-3741; fax (3) 5485-3548; e-mail panaemb@japan.co.jp; Ambassador: JOSÉ A. SOSA.

Papua New Guinea: Mita Kokusai Bldg, Room 313, 3rd Floor, 1-4-28, Mita, Minato-ku, Tokyo 108; tel. (3) 3454-7801; fax (3) 3454-7275; Ambassador: AIWA OLMI.

Paraguay: Kowa Bldg, No. 38, Room 701, 4-12-24, Nishi Azabu, Minato-ku, Tokyo 106; tel. (3) 5485-3101; fax (3) 5485-3103; e-mail embapar@gol.com; Ambassador: Dr MIGUEL A. SOLANO LÓPEZ.

Peru: 4-4-27, Higashi, Shibuya-ku, Tokyo 150; tel. (3) 3406-4240; fax (3) 3409-7589; Ambassador: VÍCTOR ARITOMI SHINTO.

Philippines: 11-24, Nampeidai-machi, Shibuya-ku, Tokyo 150; tel. (3) 3496-2731; telex 22694; Ambassador: ALFONSO T. YUCHENGCO.

Poland: 4-5-14, Takanawa, Minato-ku, Tokyo 108; tel. (3) 3280-2882; fax (3) 3280-2362; Ambassador: JERZY POMIANOWSKI.

Portugal: Kamiura-Kojimachi Bldg, 5th Floor, 3-10-3, Kojimachi, Chiyoda-ku, Tokyo 102; tel. (3) 5212-7322; fax (3) 5226-0616; Ambassador: Dr RUI GOULART DE ÁVILA.

Qatar: 6-8-7, Akasaka, Minato-ku, Tokyo 107; tel. (3) 3224-3911; fax (3) 3224-3917; Ambassador: MOHAMED HASSAN AL-JABER.

Romania: 3-16-19, Nishi Azabu, Minato-ku, Tokyo 106; tel. (3) 3479-0311; telex 22664; fax (3) 3479-0312; e-mail romembjp@iac.co.jp; Ambassador: EUGEN DIJMARESCU.

Russia: 2-1-1, Azabu-dai, Minato-ku, Tokyo 106; tel. (3) 3583-4224; fax (3) 3505-0593; Ambassador: ALEKSANDR N. PANOV.

Rwanda: Kowa Bldg, No. 38, 4-12-24, Nishi Azabu, Minato-ku, Tokyo 106; tel. (3) 3486-7801; fax (3) 3409-2434; Ambassador: MATANGUHA ZEPHYR.

Saudi Arabia: 1-53, Azabu Nagasaka-cho, Minato-ku, Tokyo 106; tel. (3) 3589-5241; Ambassador: FAWZI BIN ABDUL MAJEED SHOBOKSHI.

Senegal: 1-3-4, Aobadai, Meguro-ku, Tokyo 153; tel. (3) 3464-8451; fax (3) 3464-8452; Ambassador: Alhadji AMADOU THIAM.

Singapore: 5-12-3, Roppongi, Minato-ku, Tokyo 106; tel. (3) 3586-9111; telex 22404; fax (3) 3582-1085; Ambassador: LIM CHIN BENG.

Slovakia: POB 35, 2-16-14, Hiroo, Shibuya-ku, Tokyo 150; tel. (3) 3400-8122; fax (3) 3406-6215; Ambassador: MIROSLAV LAJČÁK.

Slovenia: 7-5-15, Akasaka, Minato-ku, Tokyo 107; tel. (3) 5570-6275; fax (3) 5570-6075; Ambassador JANEZ PREMOŽE.

South Africa: 414 Zenkyoren Bldg, 4th Floor, 2-7-9, Hirakawa-cho, Chiyoda-ku, Tokyo 102; tel. (3) 3265-3366; fax (3) 3265-1108; e-mail sajapan@crisscross.com; Ambassador: KRISH MACKERDHUJ.

Spain: 1-3-29, Roppongi, Minato-ku, Tokyo 106; tel. (3) 3583-8531; fax (3) 3582-8627; Ambassador: SANTIAGO SALAS.

Sri Lanka: 1-14-1, Akasaka, Minato-ku, Tokyo 107; tel. (3) 3585-7431; telex 24524; fax (3) 3586-9307; Ambassador: N. NAVARATNARAJAH.

Sudan: Obana House, 2-7-11, Shirogane, Minato-ku, Tokyo 108; tel. (3) 3280-3161; telex 23876; fax (3) 3280-3164; Ambassador: Dr MAHJOUB AL-BASHA AHMED.

Sweden: 1-10-3-100, Roppongi, Minato-ku, Tokyo 106; tel. (3) 5562-5050; telex 24586; fax (3) 5562-9095; Ambassador: KRISTER KUMLIN.

Switzerland: 5-9-12, Minami Azabu, Minato-ku, Tokyo 106; tel. (3) 3473-0121; fax (3) 3473-6090; e-mail swiembtok@japan.co.jp; Ambassador: JOHANNES J. MANZ.

Syria: Homat Jade, 6-19-45, Akasaka, Minato-ku, Tokyo 107; tel. (3) 3586-8977; telex 29405; fax (3) 3586-8979; Chargé d'affaires a.i.: HAMZAH HAMZAH.

Tanzania: 4-21-9, Kami Yoga, Setagaya-ku, Tokyo 158; tel. (3) 3425-4531; fax (3) 3425-7844; e-mail tzrepjp@japan.co.jp; Ambassador: ISAYA BAKARI CHIALO.

Thailand: 3-14-6, Kami Osaki, Shinagawa-ku, Tokyo 141; tel. (3) 3447-2247; fax (3) 3442-6750; Ambassador: CHAWAT ARTHAYUKTI.

Tunisia: 1-18-8, Wakaba, Shinjuku-ku, Tokyo 160-0011; tel. (3) 3353-4111; telex 27146; fax (3) 3225-4387; Ambassador: SALAH HANNACHI.

Turkey: 2-33-6, Jingumae, Shibuya-ku, Tokyo 150; tel. (3) 3470-5131; fax (3) 3470-5136; Ambassador: GÜNDÜZ AKTAN.

Uganda: 39-15, Oyama-cho, Shibuya-ku, Tokyo 151; tel. (3) 3465-4552; fax (3) 3465-4970.

Ukraine: 6-5-26, Kita Shinagawa, Shinagawa-ku, Tokyo 141; tel. (3) 3445-9229; fax (3) 3447-6768; Ambassador: MYKHAILO DASHKEVICH.

United Arab Emirates: 9-10, Nanpeidai-cho, Shibuya-ku, Tokyo 150-0036; tel. (3) 5489-0804; fax (3) 5489-0813; Ambassador: HAMAD SALEM AL-MAKAMI.

United Kingdom: 1, Ichiban-cho, Chiyoda-ku, Tokyo 102-8381; tel. (3) 5211-1100; telex 22755; fax (3) 5275-3164; Ambassador: Sir DAVID WRIGHT.

USA: 1-10-5, Akasaka, Minato-ku, Tokyo 107; tel. (3) 3224-5000; telex 22118; Ambassador: THOMAS FOLEY.

Uruguay: Kowa Bldg, No. 38, Room 908, 4-12-24, Nishi Azabu, Minato-ku, Tokyo 106; tel. (3) 3486-1888; fax (3) 3486-9872; Ambassador: ZULMA GUELMAN.

Venezuela: Kowa Bldg, No. 38, Room 703, 4-12-24, Nishi Azabu, Minato-ku, Tokyo 106; tel. (3) 3409-1501; fax (3) 3409-1505; e-mail embavene@twics.com; Ambassador: (vacant).

Viet Nam: 50-11, Moto Yoyogi-cho, Shibuya-ku, Tokyo 151; tel. (3) 3466-3313; fax (3) 3466-3391; Ambassador: NGUYEN TAM CHIEN.

Yemen: Kowa Bldg, No. 38, Room 807, 4-12-24, Nishi Azabu, Minato-ku, Tokyo 106; tel. (3) 3499-7151; fax (3) 3499-4577; Chargé d'affaires a.i.: ABDULRAHMAN M. AL-HOTHI.

Yugoslavia: 4-7-24, Kita Shinagawa, Shinagawa-ku, Tokyo 140; tel. (3) 3447-3571; fax (3) 3447-3577; e-mail embtokyo@twics.com; Chargé d'affaires a.i.: NEMANJA JOVIĆ.

Zambia: 1-10-2, Ebara, Shinagawa-ku, Tokyo 142; tel. (3) 3491-0121; telex 25210; fax (3) 3491-0123; Ambassador: Prof. LYSON P. TEMBO.

Zimbabwe: 5-9-10, Shiroganedai, Minato-ku, Tokyo 108; tel. (3) 3280-0331; fax (3) 3280-0466; Chargé d'affaires a.i.: R. S. NDAWANA.

Judicial System

The basic principles of the legal system are set forth in the Constitution, which lays down that judicial power is vested in a Supreme Court and in such inferior courts as are established by law, and enunciates the principle that no organ or agency of the Executive shall be given final judicial power. Judges are to be independent in the exercise of their conscience, and may not be removed except by public impeachment, unless judicially declared mentally or physically incompetent to perform official duties. The justices of the Supreme Court are appointed by the Cabinet, the sole exception being the Chief Justice, who is appointed by the Emperor after designation by the Cabinet.

The Court Organization Law, which came into force on 3 May 1947, decreed the constitution of the Supreme Court and the establishment of four types of lower court—High, District, Family (established 1 January 1949) and Summary Courts. The constitution and functions of the courts are as follows:

THE SUPREME COURT

4-2, Hayabusa-cho, Chiyoda-ku, Tokyo 102-8651; tel. (3) 3264-8111.

This court is the highest legal authority in the land, and consists of a Chief Justice and 14 associate justices. It has jurisdiction over Jokoku (Jokoku appeals) and Kokoku (Kokoku appeals), prescribed in codes of procedure. It conducts its hearings and renders decisions through a Grand Bench or three Petty Benches. Both are collegiate bodies, the former consisting of all justices of the Court, and the latter of five justices. A Supreme Court Rule prescribes which cases are to be handled by the respective Benches. It is, however, laid down by law that the Petty Bench cannot make decisions as to the constitutionality of a statute, ordinance, regulation, or disposition, or as to cases in which an opinion concerning the interpretation and application of the Constitution, or of any laws or ordinances, is at variance with a previous decision of the Supreme Court.

Chief Justice: SHIGERU YAMAGUCHI.

Secretary-General: TOKUJI IZUMI.

LOWER COURTS

High Court

A High Court conducts its hearings and renders decisions through a collegiate body, consisting of three judges, though for cases of insurrection the number of judges must be five. The Court has jurisdiction over the following matters:

Koso appeals from judgments in the first instance rendered by District Courts, from judgments rendered by Family Courts, and from judgments concerning criminal cases rendered by Summary Courts.

Kokoku appeals against rulings and orders rendered by District Courts and Family Courts, and against rulings and orders concerning criminal cases rendered by Summary Courts, except those coming within the jurisdiction of the Supreme Court.

Jokoku appeals from judgments in the second instance rendered by District Courts and from judgments rendered by Summary Courts, except those concerning criminal cases.

Actions in the first instance relating to cases of insurrection.

Presidents: FUMIO SAKURAI (Tokyo), KIYOSHI UETANI (Osaka), YOSHIKANE IKEDA (Nagoya), ATSUSHI SHIMUZU (Hiroshima), HIROHARU KITAGAWA (Fukuoka), MITSURU KOBAYASHI (Sendai), HISASHI HANAJIRI (Sapporo), TOMIO KAWAGUCHI (Takamatsu).

District Court

A District Court conducts hearings and renders decisions through a single judge or, for certain types of cases, through a collegiate body of three judges. It has jurisdiction over the following matters:

Actions in the first instance, except offences relating to insurrection, claims where the subject matter of the action does not exceed 900,000 yen, and offences liable to a fine or lesser penalty.

Koso appeals from judgments rendered by Summary Courts, except those concerning criminal cases.

Kokoku appeals against rulings and orders rendered by Summary Courts, except those coming within the jurisdiction of the Supreme Court and High Courts.

Family Court

A Family Court handles cases through a single judge in case of rendering judgments or decisions. However, in accordance with the provisions of other statutes, it conducts its hearings and renders decisions through a collegiate body of three judges. A conciliation is effected through a collegiate body consisting of a judge and two or more members of the conciliation committee selected from among citizens.

It has jurisdiction over the following matters:

Judgment and conciliation with regard to cases relating to family as provided for by the Law for Adjudgment of Domestic Relations.

Judgment with regard to the matters of protection of juveniles as provided for by the Juvenile Law.

Actions in the first instance relating to adult criminal cases of violation of the Labour Standard Law, the Law for Prohibiting Liquors to Minors, or other laws especially enacted for protection of juveniles.

Summary Court

A Summary Court handles cases through a single judge, and has jurisdiction in the first instance over the following matters:

Claims where the value of the subject matter does not exceed 900,000 yen (excluding claims for cancellation or change of administrative dispositions).

Actions which relate to offences liable to a fine or lesser penalty, offences liable to a fine as an optional penalty, and certain specified offences such as habitual gambling and larceny.

A Summary Court cannot impose imprisonment or a graver penalty. When it deems proper the imposition of a sentence of imprisonment or a graver penalty, it must transfer such cases to a District Court, but it can impose imprisonment with labour not exceeding three years for certain specified offences.

Religion

The traditional religions of Japan are Shintoism and Buddhism. Neither is exclusive, and many Japanese subscribe at least nominally to both. Since 1945 a number of new religions (Shinko Shukyo) have evolved, based on a fusion of Shinto, Buddhist, Daoist, Confucian and Christian beliefs. In 1995 there were some 184,000 religious organizations registered in Japan, according to the Ministry of Education.

SHINTOISM

Shintoism is an indigenous religious system embracing the worship of ancestors and of nature. It is divided into two cults: national Shintoism, which is represented by the shrines; and sectarian Shintoism, which developed during the second half of the 19th century. In 1868 Shinto was designated a national religion and all Shinto shrines acquired the privileged status of a national institution. Complete freedom of religion was introduced in 1947, and state support of Shinto was prohibited. In the mid-1990s there were 81,307 shrines, 90,309 priests and 106.6m. adherents.

BUDDHISM

World Buddhist Fellowship: Rev. FUJI NAKAYAMA, Hozenji Buddhist Temple, 3-24-2, Akabane-dai, Kita-ku, Tokyo.

CHRISTIANITY

In 1993 the Christian population was estimated at 1,050,938.

National Christian Council in Japan: Japan Christian Centre, 2-3-18-24, Nishi Waseda, Shinjuku-ku, Tokyo 169-0051; tel. (3) 3203-0372; fax (3) 3204-9495; f. 1923; 14 mems (churches and other bodies), 20 assoc. mems; Chair. Rev. YOSHIKAZU TOKUZEN; Gen. Sec. Rev. KENICHI OTSU.

The Anglican Communion

Anglican Church in Japan (Nippon Sei Ko Kai): 65, Yarai-cho, Shinjuku-ku, Tokyo 162; tel. (3) 5228-3171; fax (3) 5228-3175; f. 1887; 11 dioceses; Primate of Japan (acting) Most Rev. JOSEPH NORIAKI DIDA, Bishop of Kyushu; Gen. Sec. Rev. SAMUEL L. KOSHIISHI; 57,273 mems (1996).

The Orthodox Church

Japanese Orthodox Church (Nippon Haristosu Seikyoukai): Holy Resurrection Cathedral (Nicolai-Do), 4-1-3, Kanda Surugadai, Chiyoda-ku, Tokyo 101; tel. (3) 3291-1885; fax (3) 3291-1886; three dioceses; Archbishop of Tokyo, Primate and Metropolitan of All Japan Most Rev. THEODOSIUS; 24,821 mems.

Protestant Church

United Church of Christ in Japan (Nihon Kirisuto Kyodan): Japan Christian Center, Room 31, 2-3-18, Nishi Waseda, Shinjuku-ku, Tokyo 169-0051; tel. (3) 3202-0541; fax (3) 3207-3918; f. 1941; union of 34 Congregational, Methodist, Presbyterian, Reformed and other Protestant denominations; Moderator Rev. SEISHI OJIMA; Gen. Sec. Rev. SADAO OZAWA; 205,735 mems (1997).

The Roman Catholic Church

Japan comprises three archdioceses and 13 dioceses. There were an estimated 440,198 adherents at 31 December 1996.

Catholic Bishops' Conference of Japan (Chuo Kyogikai): 2-10-10, Shiomi, Koto-ku, Tokyo 135-8585; tel. (3) 5632-4411; fax (3) 5632-4457; e-mail cbcj-has@ja2.so-net.or.jp; Pres. Most Rev. STEPHEN FUMIO HAMAO, Bishop of Yokohama.

Archbishop of Nagasaki: Most Rev. FRANCIS XAVIER KANAME SHIMAMOTO, Archbishop's House, 1-1, Hashiguchi-machi, Nagasaki-shi, Nagasaki-ken 852; tel. (95) 843-4188; fax (95) 843-4322.

Archbishop of Osaka: Most Rev. LEO JUN IKENAGA, Archbishop's House, 2-24-22, Tamatsukuri, Chuo-ku, Osaka 540; tel. (6) 940-9700; fax (6) 946-1345.

Archbishop of Tokyo: Cardinal PETER SEIICHI SHIRAYANAGI, Archbishop's House, 3-16-15, Sekiguchi, Bunkyo-ku, Tokyo 112; tel. (3) 3943-2301; fax (3) 3944-8511.

Other Christian Churches

Japan Baptist Convention: 1-2-4, Minami Urawa, Urawa-shi, Saitama 336-0017; tel. (48) 883-1091; fax (48) 883-1092; f. 1947; Pres. Rev. SEIYA YAMASHITA; Gen. Sec. JUNICHIRO NAITO; 33,211 mems (March 1997).

Japan Baptist Union: 2-3-18, Nishi Waseda, Shinjuku-ku, Tokyo 169; tel. (3) 3202-0053; fax (3) 3202-0054; f. 1958; Moderator SHIGERU IWAMURA; Gen. Sec. KAZUO OHYA; 4,819 mems.

Japan Evangelical Lutheran Church: 1-1, Sadowara-cho, Ichigaya, Shinjuku-ku, Tokyo 169; tel. (3) 3260-8631; fax (3) 3268-3589; f. 1893; Moderator Rev. SHOICHI ASAMI; Gen. Sec. Rev. ISAMU AOTA; 22,246 mems (March 1996).

Korean Christian Church in Japan: Room 52, Japan Christian Centre, 2-3-18, Nishi Waseda, Shinjuku-ku, Tokyo 169; tel. (3) 3202-5398; fax (3) 3202-4977; e-mail kccj@kb3.so-net.or.jp; f. 1909; Moderator KYUNG HAE-JUNG; Gen. Sec. KANG YOUNG-IL; 10,000 mems (1994).

Among other denominations active in Japan are the Christian Catholic Church, the German Evangelical Church and the Tokyo Union Church.

OTHER COMMUNITIES

Bahá'í Faith

The National Spiritual Assembly of the Bahá'ís of Japan: 7-2-13, Shinjuku, Shinjuku-ku, Tokyo 160; tel. (3) 3209-7521; fax (3) 3204-0773; e-mail PXQ10144@niftyserve.or.jp.

Judaism

Japan Jewish Centre: Tokyo; Pres. ERNIE SALOMON.

Islam

Islam has been active in Japan since the late 19th century. There is a small Muslim community, maintaining a mosque at Kobe and the Islamic Center in Tokyo.

Islamic Center, Japan: 1-16-11, Ohara, Setagaya-ku, Tokyo 156; tel. (3) 3460-6169; fax (3) 3460-6105; f. 1965.

The New Religions

Many new cults have emerged in Japan since the end of the Second World War. Collectively these are known as the New Religions (Shinko Shukyo), among the most important of which are Tenrikyo, Omotokyo, Soka Gakkai, Rissho Kosei-kai, Kofuku-no-Kagaku, Agonshu and Aum Shinrikyo. (Following the indictment on charges of murder of several members of Aum Shinrikyo, including its leader, SHOKO ASAHARA, the cult lost its legal status as a religious organization in 1996.)

Kofuku-no-Kagaku (Institute for Research in Human Happiness): Tokyo; f. 1986; believes its founder to be reincarnation of Buddha; 8.25m. mems; Leader RYUHO OKAWA.

Rissho Kosei-kai: 2-11-1, Wada Suginami-ku, Tokyo 166; tel. (3) 3383-1111; fax (3) 3382-1729; f. 1938; Buddhist lay organization based on the teaching of the Lotus Sutra, active inter-faith co-operation towards peace; Pres. Rev. Dr NICHIKO NIWANO; 6.3m. mems with 245 brs world-wide (1995).

Soka Gakkai: 32, Shinano-machi, Shinjuku-ku, Tokyo 160-8583; tel. (3) 5360-9830; telex 33145; fax (3) 5360-9885; e-mail webmaster@sokagakkai.or.jp; internet http://www.sokagakkai.or.jp; f. 1930; society of lay practitioners of the Buddhism of Nichiren; membership of 8.12m. households (1997); group promotes activities in education, international cultural exchange and consensus-building towards peace, based on the humanist world view of Buddhism; Hon. Pres. DAISAKU IKEDA; Pres. EINOSUKE AKIYA.

The Press

In February 1996 there were 121 daily newspapers in Japan. Their average circulation was the highest in the world, and the circulation per head of population was also among the highest, at 578 copies per 1,000 inhabitants in 1995. The large number of weekly news journals is a notable feature of the Japanese press. In February 1995 a total of 2,753 monthly magazine and 104 weekly magazine titles were produced. Technically the Japanese press is highly advanced, and the major newspapers are issued in simultaneous editions in the main centres.

The two newspapers with the largest circulations are the *Yomiuri Shimbun* and *Asahi Shimbun*. Other influential papers include *Mainichi Shimbun, Nihon Keizai Shimbun, Chunichi Shimbun* and *Sankei Shimbun*.

NATIONAL DAILIES

Asahi Shimbun: 5-3-2, Tsukiji, Chuo-ku, Tokyo 104-11; tel. (3) 3545-0131; telex 22226; fax (3) 3545-0358; f. 1879; also published by Osaka, Seibu and Nagoya head offices and Hokkaido branch office; Dir and Exec. Editor AKIHIRO KAMITSUKA; circ. morning 8.3m., evening 4.4m.

Mainichi Shimbun: 1-1-1, Hitotsubashi, Chiyoda-ku, Tokyo 100-51; tel. (3) 3212-0321; telex 22324; fax (3) 3211-3598; f. 1882; also published by Osaka, Seibu and Chubu head offices, and Hokkaido branch office; Exec. Dir and Editor-in-Chief AKIRA SAITO; circ. morning 4.0m., evening 1.9m.

Nihon Keizai Shimbun: 1-9-5, Ohtemachi, Chiyoda-ku, Tokyo 100-66; tel. (3) 3270-0251; telex 22308; fax (3) 5255-2661; f. 1876; also published by Osaka head office and Sapporo, Nagoya and Seibu branch offices; Dir and Man. Editor KEN-ICHIRO HORIKAWA; circ. morning 3.0m., evening 1.7m.

Sankei Shimbun: 1-7-2, Ohtemachi, Chiyoda-ku, Tokyo 100-8077; tel. (3) 3231-7111; internet http://www.sankei.co.jp; f. 1933; also published by Osaka head office; Man. Dir and Editor TAKEHIKO KIYOHARA; circ. morning 2.0m., evening 956,228.

Yomiuri Shimbun: 1-7-1, Ohtemachi, Chiyoda-ku, Tokyo 100-55; tel. (3) 3242-1111; fax (3) 3246-0888; f. 1874; also published by Osaka, Seibu and Chubu head offices, and Hokkaido and Hokuriku branch offices; Pres. and Editor-in-Chief YOSHINORI HORIKAWA; circ. morning 10.0m., evening 4.5m.

PRINCIPAL LOCAL DAILIES

Tokyo

Asahi Evening News : 5-3-2, Tsukiji, Chuo-ku, Tokyo 104-11; tel. (3) 5540-7641; fax (3) 3542-6172; f. 1954; evening; English; Exec. Editor YASUNORI ASAI; Man. Editor TATEO TSUNEMI; circ. 38,800.

Daily Sports: 1-5-11, Osaki, Shinagawa-ku, Tokyo 141; tel. (3) 5434-1752; f. 1948; morning; Dir HIROKAZU TOYODA; circ. 400,254.

The Daily Yomiuri: 1-7-1, Ohtemachi, Chiyoda-ku, Tokyo 100-55; tel. (3) 3242-1111; morning; Man. Editor ATSUSHI KOJIMA; circ. 51,498.

Dempa Shimbun: 1-11-15, Higashi Gotanda, Shinagawa-ku, Tokyo 141; tel. (3) 3445-6111; fax (3) 3444-7515; f. 1950; morning; Pres. TETSUO HIRAYAMA; Man. Editor TOSHIO KASUYA; circ. 298,000.

Hochi Shimbun: 4-6-49, Konan, Minato-ku, Tokyo 108; tel. (3) 5479-1111; f. 1872; morning; Pres. HIROSHI YAMAKITA; Man. Editor SHINGO ITO; circ. 754,361.

The Japan Times: 4-5-4, Shibaura, Minato-ku, Tokyo 108; tel. (3) 3453-5312; telex 22319; f. 1897; morning; English; Chair. and Pres. TOSHIAKI OGASAWARA; Dir and Editor-in-Chief YUTAKA MATAEBARA; circ. 66,117.

The Mainichi Daily News: 1-1-1, Hitotsubashi, Chiyoda-ku, Tokyo 100-51; tel. (3) 3212-0321; f. 1922; morning; English; also publ. from Osaka; Man. Editor MICHIO TAKIMOTO; combined circ. 48,450.

Naigai Times: 2-4-20, Shiohama, Koto-ku, Tokyo 135; tel. (3) 5683-4405; f. 1949; evening; Pres. and Editor-in-Chief TORU YOSHIKAWA; circ. 296,000.

Nihon Kaiji Shimbun (Japan Maritime Daily): 5-19-2, Shimbashi, Minato-ku, Tokyo 105-91; tel. (3) 3436-3222; f. 1942; morning; Man. Editor MINORU TAKASHIMIZU.

Nihon Kogyo Shimbun: 1-7-2, Ohtemachi, Chiyoda-ku, Tokyo 100; tel. (3) 3231-7111; f. 1933; morning; industrial, business and financial; Man. Editor HIDEMATSU FURUTATE; circ. 415,963.

Nihon Nogyo Shimbun (Agriculture): 2-3, Akihabara, Taito-ku, Tokyo 110; tel. (3) 5295-7411; fax (3) 3253-0980; f. 1928; morning; Man. Editor NOBUHIKO CHIHARA; circ. 456,176.

Nihon Sen-i Shimbun (Textile and Fashion): 1-13-12, Nihonbashi-muromachi, Chuo-ku, Tokyo 103; tel. (3) 3270-1661; fax (3) 3246-1858; f. 1943; morning; Man. Editor KIYOSHIGE SEIRYU.

Nikkan Kogyo Shimbun (Industrial Daily News): 1-8-10, Kudan-kita, Chiyoda-ku, Tokyo 102; tel. (3) 3222-7111; telex 29687; fax (3) 3262-6031; f. 1915; morning; Man. Editor NOBUKATSU OKUMURA; circ. 536,795.

Nikkan Sports News: 3-5-10, Tsukiji, Chuo-ku, Tokyo 104-8055; tel. (3) 5550-8808; fax (3) 5550-8901; f. 1946; morning; Man. Editor YUKIHIRO MORI; circ. 984,058.

Sankei Sports: 1-7-2, Ohtemachi, Chiyoda-ku, Tokyo 100-77; tel. (3) 3231-7111; f. 1963; morning; Dir and Man. Editor MASAHIKO KOBAYASHI; circ. 809,166.

Shipping and Trade News: Tokyo News Service Ltd, Tsukiji Hamarikyu Bldg, 5-3-3, Tsukiji, Chuo-ku, Tokyo 104-04; tel. (3) 3542-8521; telex 23285; fax (3) 3542-5086; f. 1949; English; Exec. Dir and Gen. Man. TOHRU KITANO; circ. 14,500.

Sports Nippon: 2-1-30, Ecchujima, Koto-ku, Tokyo 135; tel. (3) 3820-0700; f. 1949; morning; Dir and Man. Editor KAZUO HAGIWARA; circ.1,082,904.

Suisan Keizai Shimbun (Fisheries): 6-8-19, Roppongi, Minato-ku, Tokyo 106; tel. (3) 3404-6531; fax (3) 3404-0863; f. 1948; morning; Man. Editor KOUSHI TORINOUMI; circ. 60,000.

Tokyo Chunichi Sports: 2-3-13, Kohnan, Minato-ku, Tokyo 108; tel. (3) 3471-2211; f. 1956; morning; Rep. NOBUYUKI KATO.

Tokyo Shimbun: 2-3-13, Kohnan, Minato-ku, Tokyo 108; tel. (3) 3471-2211; fax (3) 3471-1851; f. 1942; Man. Editor YUKIHIRO IIZUKA; circ. morning 700,586, evening 437,141.

Tokyo Sports: 2-1-30, Ecchujima, Koto-ku, Tokyo 135; tel. (3) 3820-0801; f. 1959; evening; Man. Editor YASUO SAKURAI; circ. 549,200.

Yukan Fuji: 1-7-2, Ohtemachi, Chiyoda-ku, Tokyo 100-77; tel. (3) 3231-7111; fax (3) 3246-0377; f. 1969; evening; Dir and Man. Editor TOMIO SAITO; circ. 295,050.

Osaka District

Daily Sports: 1-18-11, Edobori, Nishi-ku, Osaka 550; tel. (6) 443-0421; f. 1948; morning; Man. Editor TOSHIAKI MITANI; circ. 562,715.

The Mainichi Daily News: 3-4-5, Umeda, Kita-ku, Osaka 530-51; tel. (6) 345-1551; f. 1922; morning; English; Man. Editor HARUO NISHIMURA.

Nikkan Sports: 5-92-1, Hattori-kotobuki-cho, Toyonaka 561; tel. (6) 866-8713; f. 1950; morning; Man. Editor YOSHIMASA MIZUMOTO; circ. 584,350.

Osaka Shimbun: 2-4-9, Umeda, Kita-ku, Osaka 530; tel. (6) 343-1221; f. 1922; evening; Man. Dir and Man. Editor TERUKAZU HIGASHIYAMA; circ. 104,172.

Osaka Sports: Osaka Ekimae Daiichi Bldg, 4th Floor, 1-3-1-400, Umeda, Kita-ku, Osaka 530; tel. (6) 345-7657; f. 1968; evening; Editor SEN ASANO; circ. 184,400.

Sankei Sports: 2-4-9, Umeda, Kita-ku, Osaka 530; tel. (6) 343-1221; f. 1955; morning; Man. Editor MOTOHISA SAEKI; circ. 547,802.

Sports Nippon: 3-4-5, Umeda, Kita-ku, Osaka 530-78; tel. (6) 346-8500; f. 1949; morning; Man. Editor YOSHIMITSU OHNISHI; circ. 477,300.

Kanto District

Chiba Nippo (Chiba Daily News): 4-14-10, Chuo, Chuo-ku, Chiba 260; tel. (43) 222-9211; f. 1957; morning; Dir and Man. Editor NOBORU HAYASHI; circ. 59,476.

Ibaraki Shimbun: 2-15, Kitami-machi, Mito 310; tel. (292) 21-3121; f. 1891; morning; Dir and Man. Editor MASAO MITOMI; circ. 116,427.

Jomo Shimbun: 1-50-21, Furuichi-machi, Maebashi 371; tel. (272) 51-4341; f. 1887; morning; Man. Editor TSUTOMU SHIBASAKI; circ. 283,008.

Joyo Shimbun: 2-7-6, Manabe, Tsuchiura 300; tel. (298) 21-1780; f. 1948; morning; Pres. MINEO IWANAMI; circ. 23,500.

Kanagawa Shimbun: 6-145, Hanasaki-cho, Nishi-ku, Yokohama 220; tel. (45) 411-7450; f. 1942; morning; Dir and Man. Editor TADASHI ITO; circ. 242,230.

Saitama Shimbun: 6-12-11, Kishi-machi, Urawa 336; tel. (48) 862-3371; f. 1944; morning; Man. Editor YOTARO NUMATA; circ. 160,583.

Shimotsuke Shimbun: 1-8-11, Showa, Utsunomiya 320; tel. (286) 25-1111; f. 1884; morning; Dir and Man. Editor EISUKE TODA; circ. 287,345.

Tohoku District
(North-east Honshu)

Akita Sakigake Shimpo: 1-2-6, Ohtemachi, Akita 010; tel. (188) 62-1231; fax (188) 23-1780; f. 1874; Editor TSUYOSHI ITO; circ. 260,171.

Daily Tohoku: 1-3-12, Joka, Hachinohe 031; tel. (178) 44-5111; f. 1945; morning; Dir and Man. Editor ISAMU HONDA; circ. 102,490.

Fukushima Mimpo: 13-17, Ohtemachi, Fukushima 960; tel. (245) 31-4111; f. 1892; Dir and Man. Editor SEIICHI WATANABE; circ. morning 299,319, evening 10,189.

Fukushima Minyu: 4-29, Yanagimachi, Fukushima 960; tel. (245) 23-1191; f. 1895; Exec. Dir and Man. Editor HIROYUKI TARUI; circ. morning 197,815, evening 6,988.

Hokuu Shimpo: 3-2, Nishi-dori-machi, Noshiro 016; tel. (185) 54-3150; f. 1895; morning; Pres. KOUICHI YAMAKI; circ. 26,967.

Ishinomaki Shimbun: 2-1-28, Sumiyoshi-machi, Ishinomaki 986; tel. (225) 22-3201; f. 1946; evening; Man. Editor MASATOSHI SATO; circ. 13,050.

Iwate Nichi-nichi Shimbun: 60, Minami-shin-machi, Ichinoseki 021; tel. (191) 26-5111; f. 1923; morning; Pres. and Editor-in-Chief TAKESHI YAMAGISHI; circ. 41,671.

Iwate Nippo: 3-7, Uchimaru, Morioka 020; tel. (196) 53-4111; f. 1928; Man. Editor HIROSHI MIURA; circ. 231,050.

Kahoku Shimpo: 1-2-28, Itsutsubashi, Aoba-ku, Sendai 980; tel. (22) 211-1111; fax (22) 224-7947; f. 1897; circ. morning 485,355, evening 149,207.

Mutsu Shimpo: 2-1, Shimo-shirogane-cho, Hirosaki 036; tel. (172) 34-3111; f. 1946; morning; Man. Editor YASUHIRO NAGAO; circ. 53,500.

Shonai Nippo: 8-29, Baba-cho, Tsuruoka 997; tel. (235) 22-1480; f. 1946; morning; Exec. Dir and Editor-in-Chief MASATOSHI MATSUNOKI; circ. 19,887.

To-o Nippo: 78, Kanbayashi, Yatsuyaku, Aomori 030-01; tel. (177) 39-1111; f. 1888; Exec. Dir and Man. Editor SHUN-ICHI KOBAYASHI; circ. morning 261,909, evening 257,816.

Yamagata Shimbun: 2-5-12, Hatago-cho, Yamagata 990; tel. (236) 22-5271; f. 1876; Dir and Man. Editor YOUSUKE KUROSAWA; circ. 219,288.

Yonezawa Shimbun: 3-3-7, Monto-cho, Yonezawa 992; tel. (238) 22-4411; f. 1879; morning; Exec. Dir and Editor-in-Chief MAKOTO SATO; circ. 13,720.

Chubu District
(Central Honshu)

Chubu Keizai Shimbun: 4-4-12, Meieki, Nakamura-ku, Nagoya 450; tel. (52) 561-5215; f. 1946; morning; Man. Editor TATSUOKI KATO; circ. 92,718.

Chukyo Sports: Sakae-Miyashita Bldg, 3rd Floor, 1-15-6, Naka-ku, Sakae, Nagoya 460; tel. (52) 212-1451; f. 1968; evening; circ. 103,200; Head Officer KATSUHISA HIGUCHI.

Chunichi Shimbun: 1-6-1, Sannomaru, Naka-ku, Nagoya City 460; tel. (52) 201-8811; f. 1942; Man. Editor KUNIHIRO TAKABA; circ. morning 2.3m., evening 789,300.

Chunichi Sports: 1-6-1, Sannomaru, Naka-ku, Nagoya 460; tel. (52) 201-8811; f. 1954; evening; Head Officer HIROMU FUSHIMI; circ. 679,926.

Gifu Shimbun: 9, Imakomachi, Gifu 500; tel. (582) 64-1151; f. 1879; Exec. Dir and Man. Editor YUTAKA SAWAFUJI; circ. morning 157,522, evening 31,651.

Higashi-Aichi Shimbun: 62, Torinawate, Shinsakae-machi, Toyohashi 440; tel. (532) 32-3111; f. 1957; morning; Man. Editor HARUG INOUE; circ. 23,160.

Nagano Nippo: 3-1323-1, Takashima, Suwa 392; tel. (266) 52-2000; f. 1901; morning; Man. Editor KENJIRO BANZAI; circ. 47,575.

Nagoya Times: 1-3-10, Marunouchi, Naka-ku, Nagoya 460; tel. (52) 231-1331; f. 1946; evening; Man. Editor MASAHIRO FUJINO; circ. 91,805.

Shinano Mainichi Shimbun: 657, Minamiagata-cho, Nagano 380; tel. (26) 236-3000; fax (26) 236-3197; f. 1873; Dir and Editor KIYOSHI SEGI; circ. morning 295,265, evening 38,059.

Shizuoka Shimbun: 3-1-1, Toro, Shizuoka 422; tel. (54) 284-8900; f. 1941; Dir and Man. Editor TAKAHIRO OYAIZU; circ. morning 713,280, evening 712,996.

Yamanashi Nichi-Nichi Shimbun: 2-6-10, Kitaguchi, Kofu 400; tel. (552) 31-3000; f. 1872; morning; Man. Editor OSAMU UEDA; circ. 191,372.

Hokuriku District
(North Coastal Honshu)

Fukui Shimbun: 1-1-14, Haruyama, Fukui 910; tel. (776) 23-5111; f. 1899; morning; Man. Editor YUSUKE IWANAGA; circ. 188,637.

Hokkoku Shimbun: 2-5-1, Kohrinbo, Kanazawa 920; tel. (762) 63-2111; f. 1893; Man. Editor MASAYUKI OHNISHI; circ. morning 292,278, evening 110,537.

Hokuriku Chunichi Shimbun: 2-7-15, Kohrinbo, Kanazawa 920; tel. (762) 61-3111; f. 1960; Man. Editor TADASHI NUMA; circ. morning 119,096, evening 14,874.

Kitanippon Shimbun: 2-14, Yasuzumi-cho, Toyama 930; tel. (764) 45-3300; f. 1940; Dir and Man. Editor RYUICHI KITAGAWA; circ. morning 213,726, evening 30,026.

Niigata Nippo: 258-24, Sanban-cho, Nishibori-dori, Niigata 951; tel. (25) 378-9111; f. 1942; Dir and Man. Editor SEIJI SUZUKI; circ. morning 481,880, evening 75,641.

Toyama Shimbun: 5-1, Ohtemachi, Toyama 930; tel. (764) 91-8111; f. 1923; morning; Man. Editor HISATSUGU AIKAWA.

Kinki District
(West Central Honshu)

Daily Sports: 1-5-7, Higashi-Kawasaki-cho, Chuo-ku, Kobe 650; tel. (78) 993-4100; Man. Editor HIROHISA KARUO.

Ise Shimbun: 34-6, Hon-cho, Tsu 514; tel. (592) 24-0003; f. 1878; morning; Man. Editor FUJIO YAMAMOTO; circ. 97,500.

Kii Mimpo: 100, Akitsu-machi, Tanabe 646; tel. (739) 22-7171; f. 1911; evening; Vice-Pres. and Man. Editor SOH-ICHI TANIKAWA; circ. 36,497.

Kobe Shimbun: 1-5-7, Higashi-Kawasaki-cho, Chuo-ku, Kobe 650; tel. (78) 362-7100; f. 1898; Man. Editor KIMIHIKO SATO; circ. morning 507,190, evening 263,267.

Kyoto Shimbun: 239, Shoshoi-machi, Ebisugawa-agaru, Karasuma-dori, Nakagyo-ku, Kyoto 604; tel. (75) 222-2111; f. 1879; Man. Editor KENGI ONO; circ. morning 508,318, evening 343,282.

Nara Shimbun: 606, Sanjo-machi, Nara 630; tel. (742) 26-1331; f. 1946; morning; Dir and Man. Editor HARUO AMARI; circ. 116,440.

Chugoku District
(Western Honshu)

Chugoku Shimbun: 7-1, Dobashi-cho, Naka-ku, Hiroshima 730; tel. (82) 236-2111; fax (82) 236-2321; f. 1892; Dir and Man. Editor HIROSHI ARITA; circ. morning 728,000, evening 103,000.

Nihonkai Shimbun: 2-137, Tomiyasu, Tottori 680; tel. (857) 21-2888; f. 1976; morning; Man. Dir and Man. Editor TAKASHI SHIRAIWA; circ. 153,550.

Okayama Nichi-Nichi Shimbun: 6-30, Hon-cho, Okayama 700; tel. (86) 231-4211; f. 1946; evening; Exec. Dir and Man. Editor TAKASHI ANDO; circ. 19,459.

San-In Chuo Shimpo: 383, Tono-machi, Matsue 690; tel. (852) 21-4491; f. 1942; morning; Man. Editor YASUSHI OBARA; circ. 160,924.

Sanyo Shimbun: 2-1-23, Yanagi-machi, Okayama 700; tel. (86) 231-2210; f. 1879; Dir and Man. Editor TETSUHIRO OHKURA; circ. morning 428,180, evening 72,291.

Ube Jiho: 3-6-1, Kotobuki-cho, Ube 755; tel. (836) 31-1511; f. 1912; evening; Exec. Dir and Man. Editor KAZUYA WAKI; circ. 42,900.

Yamaguchi Shimbun: 1-1-7, Higashi-Yamato-cho, Shimonoseki 750; tel. (832) 66-3211; f. 1946; morning; Man. Editor SYOICHI SASAKI; circ. 77,000.

Shikoku Island

Ehime Shimbun: 1-12-1, Ohtemachi, Matsuyama 790; tel. (899) 35-2111; f. 1941; Dir and Man. Editor ISAO NITTA; circ. morning 312,848.

Kochi Shimbun: 3-2-15, Hon-machi, Kochi 780; tel. (888) 22-2111; f. 1904; Dir and Man. Editor Toshio Iwai; circ. morning 227,865, evening 141,571.

Shikoku Shimbun: 15-1, Nakano-machi, Takamatsu 760; tel. (878) 33-1111; f. 1889; Dir and Man. Editor Yoshine Yoshida; circ. morning 211,753.

Tokushima Shimbun: 2-5-2, Naka-Tokushima-cho, Tokushima 770; tel. (886) 55-7373; fax (866) 54-0165; f. 1941; Dir and Man. Editor Tetsuro Noguchi; circ. morning 241,715, evening 50,301.

Hokkaido Island

Doshin Sports: 3-6, Ohdori-Nishi, Chuo-ku, Sapporo 060; tel. (11) 241-1230; f. 1982; morning; Dir and Man. Editor Keisaku Machida; circ. 99,014.

Hokkai Times: 10-6, Nishi, Minami-Ichijo, Chuo-ku, Sapporo 060; tel. (11) 231-0131; f. 1946; Man. Editor Koki Ito; circ. morning 120,736.

Hokkaido Shimbun: 3-6, Ohdori-Nishi, Chuo-ku, Sapporo 060; tel. (11) 221-2111; f. 1942; Dir and Man. Editor Yuji Orikasa; circ. morning 1.2m., evening 781,292.

Kushiro Shimbun: 7-3, Kurogane-cho, Kushiro 085; tel. (154) 22-1111; f. 1955; morning; Exec. Dir and Man. Editor Kazuo Yokozawa; circ. 56,275.

Muroran Mimpo: 1-3-16, Hon-cho, Muroran 051; tel. (143) 22-5121; f. 1945; Man. Editor Hiroshi Shinpo; circ. morning 59,980, evening 52,500.

Nikkan Sports: 3-1-30, Higashi, Kita-3 jo, Chuo-ku, Sapporo 060; tel. (11) 242-3900; fax (11) 231-5470; f. 1962; morning; Man. Editor Masanori Hanawa; circ. 41,242.

Tokachi Mainichi Shimbun: 8-2, Minami, Higashi-Ichijo, Obihiro 080; tel. (155) 22-2121; f. 1919; evening; Dir and Man. Editor Mutsuhisa Terai; circ. 81,161.

Tomakomai Mimpo: 3-1-8, Wakakusa-cho, Tomakomai 053; tel. (144) 32-5311; f. 1950; evening; Dir and Man. Editor Ryuichi Kudo; circ. 60,676.

Yomiuri Shimbun: 4-1, Nishi, Kita-4 jo, Chuo-ku, Sapporo 060; tel. (11) 242-3111; Head Officer Mitsuo Miyamura.

Kyushu Island

Kagoshima Shimpo: 7-28, Jonan-cho, Kagoshima 892; tel. (99) 226-2100; f. 1959; morning; Dir and Man. Editor Junsuke Kinoshita; circ. 45,700.

Kumamoto Nichi-Nichi Shimbun: 2-33, Kamitori-cho, Kumamoto 860; tel. (96) 327-3111; f. 1942; Man. Editor Kazunari Nishimura; circ. morning 381,951, evening 100,060.

Kyushu Sports: Fukuoka Tenjin Centre Bldg, 2-14-8, Tenjin-cho, Chuo-ku, Fukuoka 810; tel. (92) 781-7401; f. 1966; morning; Head Officer Teruo Okamiya; circ. 218,800.

Minami Nihon Shimbun: 1-2, Yasui-cho, Kagoshima 892; tel. (99) 225-9702; fax (99) 224-1490; f. 1881; Man. Editor Hiroaki Toyokawa; circ. morning 393,951, evening 28,948.

Miyazaki Nichi-Nichi Shimbun: 1-1-33, Takachihodori, Miyazaki 880; tel. (985) 26-9315; f. 1940; Man. Editor Riichiro Miyake; morning; circ. 227,581.

Nagasaki Shimbun: 3-1, Morimachi, Nagasaki 852; tel. (958) 44-2111; f. 1889; Dir and Man. Editor Akio Tomonaga; circ. morning 191,016.

Nankai Nichi-Nichi Shimbun: 10-3, Nagahama-cho, Naze 894; tel. (997) 53-2121; f. 1946; morning; Man. Editor Terumi Matsui; circ. 25,020.

Nishi Nippon Shimbun: 1-4-1, Tenjin, Chuo-ku, Fukuoka 810; tel. (92) 711-5555; f. 1877; Exec. Dir and Man. Editor Akishige Tada; circ. morning 827,425, evening 198,972.

Nishi Nippon Sports: 1-4-1, Tenjin, Chuo-ku, Fukuoka 810; tel. (92) 711-5555; f. 1954; Man. Editor Kenji Ishizaki; circ. 185,625.

Oita Godo Shimbun: 3-9-15, Fudai-cho, Oita 870; tel. (975) 36-2121; f. 1886; Dir and Man. Editor Masakatsu Tanabe; circ. morning 230,534, evening 230,520.

Okinawa Times: 2-2-2, Kumoji, Naha 900; tel. (98) 867-3111; f. 1948; Dir and Man. Editor Kiyoshi Ganaha; circ. morning 184,084, evening 184,217.

Ryukyu Shimpo: 1-10-3, Izumisaki, Naha 900; tel. (98) 865-5111; f. 1893; Dir and Man. Editor Takeshi Miki; circ. 185,938.

Saga Shimbun: 3-2-23, Tenjin, Saga 840; tel. (952) 28-2111; fax (952) 29-4829; f. 1884; morning; Dir and Man. Editor Norichika Yoshino; circ. 133,970.

Yaeyama Mainichi Shimbun: 258, Ishigaki, Ishigaki-shi 907; tel. (9808) 2-2121; f. 1950; morning; Exec. Dir and Man. Editor Yoshio Uechi; circ. 14,100.

WEEKLIES

An-An: Magazine House, 3-13-10, Ginza, Chuo-ku, Tokyo 104-03; tel. (3) 3545-7050; telex 22982; fax (3) 3546-0034; f. 1970; fashion; Editor Miyoko Yodogawa; circ. 650,000.

Asahi Graphic: Asahi Shimbun Publishing Dept, 5-3-2, Tsukiji, Chuo-ku, Tokyo 104-11; tel. (3) 3545-0131; telex 22226; f. 1923; pictorial review; Editor Kiyokazu Tanno; circ. 120,000.

Diamond Weekly: Diamond Inc, 1-4-2, Kasumigaseki, Chiyoda-ku, Tokyo 100; tel. (3) 3504-6250; telex 24461; f. 1913; economics; Editor Yutaka Iwasa; circ. 78,000.

Focus: Shincho-Sha, 71, Yaraicho, Shinjuku-ku, Tokyo 162; tel. (3) 3266-5271; fax (3) 3266-5390; politics, economics, sport; Editor Kazumasa Tajima; circ. 850,000.

Friday: Kodan-Sha Co Ltd, 2-12-21, Otowa, Bunkyo-ku, Tokyo 112; tel. (3) 5395-3440; fax (3) 3943-8582; current affairs; Editor-in-Chief Tetsu Suzuki; circ. 1m.

Hanako: Magazine House, 3-13-10, Ginza, Chuo-ku, Tokyo 104-03; tel. (3) 3545-7070; telex 22982; fax (3) 3546-0994; f. 1988; consumer guide; Editor Koji Tomono; circ. 350,000.

Nikkei Business: Nikkei Business Publications Inc, 2-7-6, Hirakawa-cho, Chiyoda-ku, Tokyo 102; tel. (3) 5210-8111; telex 158258503; fax (3) 5210-8112; f. 1969; Editor-in-Chief Kiyoshi Ooya; circ. 296,720.

Shukan Asahi: Asahi Shimbun Publishing Dept, 5-3-2, Tsukiji, Chuo-ku, Tokyo 104-11; tel. (3) 3545-0131; telex 22226; f. 1922; general interest; Editor-in-Chief Keijiro Mori; circ. 482,000.

Shukan Bunshun: Bungei-Shunju Ltd, 3-23, Kioicho, Chiyoda-ku, Tokyo 102; tel. (3) 3265-1211; f. 1959; general interest; Editor Kiyondo Matsui; circ. 800,000.

Shukan Gendai: Kodan-Sha Co Ltd, 2-12-21, Otowa, Bunkyo-ku, Tokyo 112; tel. (3) 5395-3438; fax (3) 3943-7815; f. 1959; general; Editor Masahiko Motoki; circ. 550,000.

Shukan Josei: Shufu-To-Seikatsu Sha Ltd, 3-5-7, Kyobashi, Chuo-ku, Tokyo 104; tel. (3) 3563-5130; fax (3) 3563-2073; f. 1957; women's interest; Editor Hideo Kikuchi; circ. 638,000.

Shukan Post: Shogakukan Publishing Co Ltd, 2-3-1, Hitotsubashi, Chiyoda-ku, Tokyo 101-01; tel. (3) 3230-5951; telex 22192; f. 1969; general; Editor Norimichi Okanari; circ. 696,000.

Shukan Shincho: Shincho-Sha, 71, Yarai-cho, Shinjuku-ku, Tokyo 162; tel. (3) 3266-5311; fax (3) 3266-5622; f. 1956; general interest; Editor Hiroshi Matsuda; circ. 521,000.

Shukan Spa!: Fuso-Sha Co, 1-15-1, Kaigan, Minato-ku, Tokyo 105; tel. (3) 5403-8875; f. 1952; general interest; Editor Kazuhiko Tsurushi; circ. 400,000.

Shukan ST: Japan Times Ltd, 4-5-4, Shibaura, Minato-ku, Tokyo 108; tel. (3) 3452-4077; fax (3) 3452-3303; f. 1951; English and Japanese; Editor Mitsuru Tanaka; circ. 150,000.

Shukan Yomiuri: Yomiuri Shimbun Publication Dept, 1-2-1, Kiyosumi, Koto-ku, Tokyo 135; tel. (3) 5245-7001; telex 22228; f. 1938; general interest; Editor Shini Kageyama; circ. 453,000.

Sunday Mainichi: Mainichi Newspapers Publishing Dept, 1-1-1, Hitotsubashi, Chiyoda-ku, Tokyo 100-51; tel. (3) 3212-0321; telex 22324; fax (3) 3212-0769; f. 1922; general interest; Editor Kenji Miki; circ. 237,000.

Tenji Mainichi: Mainichi Newspapers Publishing Dept, 3-4-5, Umeda, Osaka; tel. (6) 346-8386; fax (6) 346-8385; f. 1922; in Japanese braille; Editor Tadamitsu Morioka; circ. 12,000.

Weekly Economist: Mainichi Newspapers Publishing Dept, 1-1-1, Hitotsubashi, Chiyoda-ku, Tokyo 100-51; tel. (3) 3212-0321; telex 24851; f. 1923; Editorial Chief Nobuhiro Shudo; circ. 120,000.

Weekly Toyo Keizai: Toyo Keizai Inc, 1-2-1, Hongoku-cho, Nihonbashi, Chuo-ku, Tokyo 103; tel. (3) 3246-5470; fax (3) 3270-0159; f. 1895; business and economics; Editor Hiroshi Takahashi; circ. 62,000.

PERIODICALS

All Yomimono: Bungei-Shunju Ltd, 3-23, Kioicho, Chiyoda-ku, Tokyo 102; tel. (3) 3265-1211; fax (3) 3239-5481; f. 1930; monthly; popular fiction; Editor Koichi Sasamoto; circ. 95,796.

Any: 1-3-14, Hirakawa-cho, Chiyoda-ku, Tokyo 102; tel. (3) 5276-2200; fax (3) 5276-2209; f. 1989; every 2 weeks; women's interest; Editor Yukio Miwa; circ. 380,000.

Asahi Camera: Asahi Shimbun Publishing Dept, 5-3-2, Tsukiji, Chuo-ku, Tokyo 104-11; tel. (3) 3545-0131; telex 22226; fax (3) 5565-3286; f. 1926; monthly; photography; Editor Yukio Yamazaki; circ. 82,000.

Balloon: Shufunotomo Co Ltd, 2-9, Kanda Surugadai, Chiyoda-ku, Tokyo 101; tel. (3) 3294-1132; telex 26925; fax (3) 3291-5093; f. 1986; monthly; expectant mothers; Dir Mariko Hosoda; circ. 250,000.

Brutus: Magazine House, 3-13-10, Ginza, Chuo-ku, Tokyo 104-03; tel. (3) 3545-7000; telex 22982; fax (3) 3546-0034; f. 1980; every 2 weeks; men's interest; Editor KOICHI TETSUKA; circ. 250,000.

Bungei-Shunju: Bungei-Shunju Ltd, 3-23, Kioicho, Chiyoda-ku, Tokyo 102-8008; tel. (3) 3265-1211; fax (3) 3221-6623; f. 1923; monthly; general; Pres. MITSURU ANDO; Editor TAKAHIRO HIRAO; circ. 656,000.

Business Tokyo: Keizaikai Bldg, 2-13-18, Minami-Aoyama, Minato-ku, Tokyo 105; tel. (3) 3423-8500; telex 32707; fax (3) 3423-8505; f. 1987; monthly; Dir TAKUO IDA; Editor ANTHONY PAUL; circ. 125,000.

Chuokoron: Chuokoron-Sha Inc, 2-8-7, Kyobashi, Chuo-ku, Tokyo 104; tel. (3) 3563-1866; telex 32505; fax (3) 3561-5920; f. 1887; monthly; general interest; Chief Editor KAZUHO MIYA; circ. 100,000.

Clique: Magazine House, 3-13-10, Ginza, Chuo-ku, Tokyo 104-03; tel. (3) 3545-7080; telex 2522982; fax (3) 3546-0034; f. 1989; every 2 weeks; women's interest; Editor TAKAKO NOGUCHI; circ. 250,000.

Croissant: Magazine House, 3-13-10, Ginza, Chuo-ku, Tokyo 104-03; tel. (3) 3545-7111; telex 22982; fax (3) 3546-0034; f. 1977; every 2 weeks; home; Editor MASAAKI TAKEUCHI; circ. 600,000.

Fujinkoron: Chuokoron-Sha Inc, 2-8-7, Kyobashi, Chuo-ku, Tokyo 104; tel. (3) 3563-1866; telex 32505; fax (3) 3561-5920; f. 1916; women's literary monthly; Editor YUKIKO YUKAWA; circ. 185,341.

Geijutsu Shincho: Shincho-Sha, 71, Yarai-cho, Shinjuku-ku, Tokyo 162; tel. (3) 3266-5381; telex 27433; fax (3) 3266-5387; e-mail geishin@magical2.egg.or.jp; f. 1950; monthly; fine arts, music, architecture, films, drama and design; Editor-in-Chief MIDORI YAMAKAWA; circ. 65,000.

Gendai: Kodan-Sha Ltd, 2-12-21, Otowa, Bunkyo-ku, Tokyo 112; tel. (3) 5395-3517; fax (3) 3945-9128; f. 1966; monthly; cultural and political; Editor SHUNKICHI YABUKI; circ. 250,000.

Gunzo: Kodan-Sha Ltd, 2-12-21, Otowa, Bunkyo-ku, Tokyo 112; tel. (3) 5395-3501; fax (3) 5395-5626; f. 1946; literary monthly; Editor KATSUO WATANABE; circ. 30,000.

Hot-Dog Press: Kodan-Sha Ltd, 2-12-21, Otowa, Bunkyo-ku, Tokyo 112-01; tel. (3) 5395-3473; fax (3) 3945-9128; every 2 weeks; men's interest; Editor ATSUHIDE KOKUBO; circ. 650,000.

Ie-no-Hikari (Light of Home): Ie-no-Hikari Asscn, 11, Ichigaya Funagawaramachi, Shinjuku-ku, Tokyo 162; tel. (3) 3266-9013; fax (3) 3266-9052; f. 1925; monthly; rural and general interest; Pres. SHUZO SUZUKI; Editor SETSUO NAGIRA; circ. 1,112,331.

Japan Company Handbook: Toyo Keizai Inc, 1-2-1, Nihonbashi Hongoku-cho, Chuo-ku, Tokyo 103; tel. (3) 3246-5655; fax (3) 3241-5543; f. 1974; quarterly; English; Editor FUSAHIRO TANAKA; total circ. 100,000.

Japan Quarterly: Asahi Shimbun Publishing Co, 5-3-2, Tsukiji, Chuo-ku, Tokyo 104-8011; tel. (3) 5541-8699; fax (3) 5541-8700; e-mail LDE04360@niftyserve.or.jp; f. 1954; English; political, economic and cultural; Editor-in-Chief MATSUMOTO TOSHIMICHI; circ. 8,000.

Jitsugyo No Nihon: Jitsugyo No Nihon-Sha Ltd, 1-3-9, Ginza, Chuo-ku, Tokyo 104; tel. (3) 3562-1967; fax (3) 2564-2382; f. 1897; monthly; economics and business; Editor TOSHIO KAWAJIRI; circ. 60,000.

Junon: Shufu-To-Seikatsu Sha Ltd, 3-5-7, Kyobashi, Chuo-ku, Tokyo 104; tel. (3) 3563-5132; fax (3) 5250-7081; f. 1973; monthly; television and entertainment; circ. 560,000.

Kagaku (Science): Iwanami Shoten Publishers, 2-5-5, Hitotsubashi, Chiyoda-ku, Tokyo 102; tel. (3) 5210-4070; telex 29495; fax (3) 5210-4073; f. 1931; Editor NOBUAKI MIYABE; circ. 29,000.

Kagaku Asahi: Asahi Shimbun Publishing Dept, 5-3-2, Tsukiji, Chuo-ku, Tokyo 104-8011; tel. (3) 5540-7810; fax (3) 3546-2404; f. 1941; monthly; scientific; Editor TOSHIHIRO SASAKI; circ. 105,000.

Keizaijin: Kansai Economic Federation, Nakanoshima Center Bldg, 6-2-27, Nakanoshima, Kita-ku, Osaka 530; tel. (6) 441-0105; fax (6) 443-5347; internet http://www.kankeiren.or.jp; f. 1947; monthly; economics; Editor A. SAKURAUCHI; circ. 2,600.

Lettuce Club: SS Communications, 11-2, Ban-cho, Chiyoda-ku, Tokyo 102; tel. (3) 5276-2151; fax (3) 5276-2229; f. 1987; every 2 weeks; cookery; Editor MITSURU NAKAYA; circ. 800,000.

Money Japan: SS Communications, 11-2, Ban-cho, Chiyoda-ku, Tokyo 102; tel. (3) 5276-2220; fax (3) 5276-2229; f. 1985; monthly; finance; Editor TOSHIO KOBAYASHI; circ. 500,000.

Popeye: Magazine House, 3-13-10, Ginza, Chuo-ku, Tokyo 104-03; tel. (3) 3545-7160; telex 2522982; fax (3) 3546-0034; f. 1976; every 2 weeks; fashion, teenage interest; Editor SHIRO MIZOKAWA; circ. 600,000.

President: President Inc, Bridgestone Hirakawacho Bldg, 2-13-12, Hirakawa-cho, Chiyoda-ku, Tokyo 102; tel. (3) 3237-3737; fax (3) 3237-3748; f. 1963; monthly; business; Editor MASAHISA NAKADA; circ. 266,012.

Ray: Shufunotomo Co Ltd, 2-9, Kanda Surugadai, Chiyoda-ku, Tokyo 101; tel. (3) 3294-1163; telex 26925; fax (3) 3291-5093; f. 1988; monthly; women's interest; Editor TATSURO NAKANISHI; circ. 450,000.

Ryoko Yomiuri: Ryoko Yomiuri Publications Inc, 2-2-15, Ginza, Chuo-ku, Tokyo 104; tel. (3) 3561-8911; fax (3) 3561-8950; f. 1966; monthly; travel; Editor TETSUO KINUGAWA; circ. 470,000.

Sekai: Iwanami Shoten Publishers, 2-5-5, Hitotsubashi, Tokyo 101; tel. (3) 5210-4141; telex 29495; fax (3) 5210-4144; f. 1946; monthly; review of world and domestic affairs; Editor AKIO YAMAGUCHI; circ. 120,000.

Shinkenchiku: Shinkenchiku-Sha Co Ltd, 2-31-2, Yushima, Bunkyo-ku, Tokyo 113; tel. (3) 3814-2251; fax (3) 3812-8187; f. 1925; monthly; architecture; Editor AKIHIKO OMORI; circ. 87,000.

Shiso (Thought): Iwanami Shoten Publishers, 2-5-5, Hitotsubashi, Chiyoda-ku, Tokyo 100-8002; tel. (3) 5210-4055; telex 29495; fax (3) 5210-4037; f. 1921; monthly; philosophy, social sciences and humanities; Editor KIYOSHI KOJIMA; circ. 20,000.

Shosetsu Shincho: Shincho-Sha, 71, Yarai-cho, Shinjuku-ku, Tokyo 162; tel. (3) 3266-5241; fax (3) 3266-5412; f. 1947; monthly; literature; Editor-in-Chief TSUYOSHI MENJO; circ. 100,000.

Shufunotomo: Shufunotomo Co Ltd, 2-9, Kanda Surugadai, Chiyoda-ku, Tokyo 101; tel. (3) 3294-1113; telex 26925; fax (3) 3294-1169; f. 1917; monthly; home and lifestyle; Editor SACHIKO HAYASHI; circ. 250,000.

So-en: Bunka Publishing Bureau, 4-12-7, Hon-cho, Shibuya-ku, Tokyo 151; tel. (3) 3299-2531; fax (3) 3370-3712; f. 1936; fashion monthly; Editor KEIKO SASAKI; circ. 270,000.

NEWS AGENCIES

Jiji Tsushin (Jiji Press Ltd): Shisei Bldg, 1-3, Hibiya Park, Chiyoda-ku, Tokyo 100; tel. (3) 3591-1111; telex 22270; e-mail info@tky.jiji.co.jp; f. 1945; Pres. MASATOSHI MURAKAMI; Man. Editor KAZUAKI HASEGAWA.

Kyodo Tsushin (Kyodo News): 2-2-5, Toranomon, Minato-ku, Tokyo 105; tel. (3) 5573-8081; fax (3) 5573-8082; f. 1945; Pres. YASUHIKO INUKAI; Man. Editor YOYOHIKO YAMANOUCHI.

Radiopress Inc: R-Bldg Shinjuku, 33-8, Wakamatsu-cho, Shinjuku-ku, Tokyo 162; tel. (3) 5273-2171; fax (3) 5273-2180; e-mail rptokyo@magical.egg.or.jp; f. 1945; provides news from China, the former USSR, Democratic People's Repub. of Korea, Viet Nam and elsewhere to the press and govt offices; Pres. YOSHITOMO TANAKA.

Sun Telephoto: Palaceside Bldg, 1-1-1, Hitotsubashi, Chiyoda-ku, Tokyo 100; tel. (3) 3213-6771; f. 1952; Pres. TAKEYOSHI TAMURA; Man. Editor SHIN-ICHIRO IZUMI.

Foreign Bureaux

Agence France-Presse (AFP): Asahi Shimbun Bldg, 11th Floor, 5-3-2, Tsukiji, Chuo-ku, Tokyo 104-0045; tel. (3) 3545-3061; telex 22368; fax (3) 3546-2594; Bureau Chief PIERRE TAILLEFER.

Agencia EFE (Spain): Kyodo Tsushin Bldg, 9th Floor, 2-2-5, Toranomon, Minato-ku, Tokyo 105; tel. (3) 3585-8940; telex 34502; fax (3) 3585-8948; Bureau Chief RAMÓN SANTAURALIA.

Agenzia Nazionale Stampa Associata (ANSA) (Italy): Kyodo Tsushin Bldg, 2-2-5, Toranomon, Minato-ku, Tokyo 105; tel. (3) 3584-6667; telex 28286; fax (3) 3584-5114; Correspondent ERNESTO TOALDO.

Antara (Indonesia): Kyodo Tsushin Bldg, 9th Floor, 2-2-5, Toranomon, Minato-ku, Tokyo 105; tel. (3) 3584-4234; fax (3) 3584-4591; Correspondent EDI UTAMA.

Associated Press (AP) (USA): Asahi Shimbun Bldg, 11th Floor, 5-3-2, Tsukiji, Chuo-ku, Tokyo 104-0045; tel. (3) 3545-5907; fax (3) 3545-0895; Bureau Chief JAMES C. LAGIER.

Central News Agency (Taiwan): Tokyo; tel. (3) 3495-2049; fax (3) 3495-2066; Bureau Chief SHENG QUAN LAI.

Deutsche Presse-Agentur (dpa) (Germany): Nippon Press Center, 3rd Floor, 2-2-1, Uchisaiwai-cho, Chiyoda-ku, Tokyo 100; tel. (3) 3580-6629; fax (3) 3593-7888; Bureau Chief JOCHEN GOEBEL.

Informatsionnoye Telegrafnoye Agentstvo Rossii—Telegrafnoye Agentstvo Suverennykh Stran (ITAR—TASS) (Russia): 1-5-1, Hon-cho, Shibuya-ku, Tokyo 151; tel. (3) 3377-0380; Correspondent VASILII GOLOVIN.

Inter Press Service (IPS) (Italy): Tokyo; tel. (3) 3211-3161; fax (3) 3211-3168; Correspondent SUVENDRINI KAKUCHI.

Magyar Távirati Iroda (MTI) (Hungary): Tokyo; tel. (3) 3701-7170; telex 28446; fax (3) 5707-1060; Bureau Chief JÁNOS MARTON.

Reuters (UK): Shuwa Kamiya-cho Bldg, 5th Floor, 4-3-13, Toranomon, Minato-ku, Tokyo 105; tel. (3) 3432-8600; telex 22349; fax (3) 3432-5392; Editor THOMAS THOMSON.

Rossiiskoye Informatsionnoye Agentstvo—Novosti (RIA—Novosti) (Russia): 3-9-13 Higashigotanda, Shinagawa-ku, Tokyo 141; tel. (3) 3441-9241; telex 22958; Bureau Chief VLADISLAV DUNAYEV.

United Press International (UPI) (USA): Ferrare Bldg, 4th Floor, 1-24-15, Edisu, Shibuya-ku, Tokyo 150; tel. (3) 5421-1333; telex 22364; fax (3) 5421-1339; Bureau Chief RUTH YOUNGBLOOD.

Xinhua (New China) News Agency (People's Republic of China): 3-35-23, Ebisu, Shibuya-ku, Tokyo 150; tel. (3) 3442-3766; Bureau Chief XIA ZHAOLONG.

Yonhap (United) News Agency (Republic of Korea): Kyodo Tsushin Bldg, 2-2-5, Toranomon, Minato-ku, Tokyo 105; tel. (3) 3584-4681; f. 1945; Bureau Chief JOON DONG-OH.

PRESS ASSOCIATIONS

Foreign Press Center: Nippon Press Centre Bldg, 6th Floor, 2-2-1, Uchisaiwai-cho, Chiyoda-ku, Tokyo 100; tel. (3) 3501-3401; fax (3) 3501-3622; f. 1976; est. by the Japan Newspaper Publrs' and Editors' Asscn and the Japan Fed. of Economic Orgs; provides services to the foreign press; Pres. YOSHIO HATANO; Man. Dir FUMIO KITAMURA.

Foreign Press in Japan: Yuraku-cho Denki Bldg, 20th Floor, 1-7-1, Yuraku-cho, Chiyoda-ku, Tokyo 100; tel. (3) 3211-3161; f. 1960; 193 companies; Chair. J. TERENCE GALLAGHER; Man. NOBUYOSHI YAMADA.

Nihon Shinbun Kyokai (The Japan Newspaper Publishers and Editors Asscn): Nippon Press Center Bldg, 2-2-1, Uchisaiwai-cho, Chiyoda-ku, Tokyo 100; tel. (3) 3591-3462; fax (3) 3591-6149; f. 1946; mems include 163 companies, including 112 daily newspapers, 5 news agencies and 46 radio and TV companies; Chair. TADAO KOIKE; Man. Dir OSAMU ASANO.

Nihon Zasshi Kyokai (Japan Magazine Publishers Asscn): 1-7, Kanda Surugadai, Chiyoda-ku, Tokyo 101-0062; tel. (3) 3291-0775; fax (3) 3293-6239; f. 1956; 85 mems; Pres. KENGO TANAKA; Sec. GENYA INUI.

Publishers

Akane Shobo Co Ltd: 3-2-1, Nishikanda, Chiyoda-ku, Tokyo 101-0065; tel. (3) 3263-0641; fax (3) 3263-5440; f. 1949; juvenile; Pres. MASAHARU OKAMOTO.

Akita Publishing Co Ltd: 2-10-8, Iidabashi, Chiyoda-ku, Tokyo 102-8101; tel. (3) 3264-7011; fax (3) 3265-9076; f. 1948; social sciences, history, juvenile; Chair. SADAO AKITA; Pres. SADAMI AKITA.

ALC Press Inc: 2-54-12, Eifuku, Suginami-ku, Tokyo 168-0064; tel. (3) 3323-1101; fax (3) 3327-1022; f. 1969; linguistics, educational materials, dictionary, juvenile; Pres. TERUMARO HIRAMOTO.

Asahi Shimbun Publications Division: 5-3-2, Tsukiji, Chuo-ku, Tokyo 100-0000; tel. (3) 3545-0131; telex 22226; fax (3) 5565-3285; f. 1879; general; Pres. TOSHITADA NAKAE; Dir of Publications HISAO KUWASHIMA.

Asakura Publishing Co Ltd: 6-29, Shin Ogawa-machi, Shinjuku-ku, Tokyo 162-8707; tel. (3) 3260-0141; fax (3) 3260-0180; f. 1929; natural science, medicine, social sciences; Pres. KUNIZO ASAKURA.

Baifukan Co Ltd: 4-3-12, Kudan Minami, Chiyoda-ku, Tokyo 102-0074; tel. (3) 3262-5256; fax (3) 3262-5276; f. 1924; engineering, natural and social sciences, psychology; Pres. ITARU YAMAMOTO.

Baseball Magazine-Sha: 3-10-10, Misaki-cho, Chiyoda-ku, Tokyo 101-8381; tel. (3) 3238-0081; fax (3) 3238-0106; f. 1946; sports, physical education, recreation, travel; Chair. TSUNEO IKEDA; Pres. IKUO IKEDA.

Bijutsu Shuppan-Sha Ltd: Inaoka Bldg, 6th Floor, 2-36, Kanda Jimbo-cho, Chiyoda-ku, Tokyo 101-8417; tel. (3) 3234-2151; fax (3) 3234-9451; f. 1905; art and architecture; Pres. ATSUSHI OSHITA.

Bonjinsha Co Ltd: 1-3-13, Hirakawa-cho, Chiyoda-ku, Tokyo 102; tel. (3) 3262-4129; fax (3) 3263-6705; f. 1973; Japanese language teaching materials; Pres. HISAMITSU TANAKA.

Bungei-Shunju Ltd: 3-23, Kioi-cho, Chiyoda-ku, Tokyo 120-8008; tel. (3) 3265-1211; fax (3) 3239-5482; f. 1922; fiction, general literature, recreation, economics, sociology; Pres. KENGO TANAKA.

Chikuma Shobo: Komuro Bldg, 2-5-3, Kuramae, Taito-ku, Tokyo 111-0051; tel. (3) 5687-2680; fax (3) 5687-1585; f. 1940; general fiction and non-fiction; Pres. SHIGEMITSU KASHIWABARA.

Child-Honsha Co Ltd: 5-24-21, Koishikawa, Bunkyo-ku, Tokyo 112-0002; tel. (3) 3813-3781; fax (3) 3813-3765; f. 1930; pedagogy, children's; Pres. YOSHIAKI SHIMAZAKI.

Chuokoron-Sha Inc: 2-8-7, Kyobashi, Chuo-ku, Tokyo 104-0031; tel. (3) 3563-1261; fax (3) 3561-5920; f. 1887; philosophy, history, economics, political and natural sciences, literature, fine arts; Pres. YUKIO SHIMANAKA.

Corona Publishing Co Ltd: 4-46-10, Sengoku, Bunkyo-ku, Tokyo 112-0011; tel. (3) 3941-3131; fax (3) 3941-3137; f. 1927; electrical, mechanical and civil engineering, metallurgy, computer science; Pres. TATSUMI GORAI.

Dempa Publications Inc: 1-11-15, Higashi Gotanda, Shinagawa-ku, Tokyo 141-0022; tel. (3) 3445-6111; fax (3) 3444-7515; f. 1950; electronics, personal computer software, juvenile, trade newspapers; Pres. TETSUO HIRAYAMA.

Diamond Inc: 1-4-2, Kasumigaseki, Chiyoda-ku, Tokyo 100-8060; tel. (3) 3504-6381; fax (3) 3504-6397; f. 1913; business books incl. ecology, science, technology; Pres. YUTAKA IWASA.

Dohosha Ltd: Mita-Sonnette Bldg, 3rd Floor, 1-1-15, Mita, Minato-ku, Tokyo 108-0072; tel. (3) 5445-4001; fax (3) 5445-4011; e-mail intl@doho-sha.co.jp; f. 1997; general works, architecture, art, Buddhism, business, children's education, cooking, flower arranging, gardening, medicine; Chair. SATORU IMADA.

Froebel-Kan Co Ltd: 6-14-9, Honkomagome, Bunkyo-ku, Tokyo 113-0021; tel. (3) 5395-6614; fax (3) 5395-6627; f. 1907; juvenile, educational, music; Pres. KENNOSUKE ARAI; Dir HARRY IDICHI.

Fukuinkan Shoten, Publishers Inc: 6-6-3, Honkomagome, Bunkyo-ku, Tokyo 113-8686; tel. (3) 3942-0032; fax (3) 3942-1401; f. 1952; juvenile; Pres. SHIRO TOKITA; Chair. KATSUMI SATO.

Gakken Co Ltd: 4-40-5, Kamiikedai, Ohta-ku, Tokyo 145-0064; tel. (3) 3726-8111; fax (3) 3493-3338; f. 1946; fiction, juvenile, educational, art, history, reference, encyclopaedias, dictionaries, languages; Pres. KAZUHIKO SAWADA.

Gyosei Corpn: 4-30-16, Ogikubo, Suginami-ku, Tokyo 167-8088; tel. (3) 5349-6666; fax (3) 5349-6677; f. 1893; law, education, science, politics, business, art, language, literature, juvenile; Pres. MOTOO FUJISAWA.

Graphic-sha Publishing Co Ltd: 1-9-12, Kudan Kita, Chiyoda-ku, Tokyo 102; tel. (3) 3263-4318; fax (3) 3263-5297; e-mail HFE02151@niftyserve.or.jp; f. 1963; art, literature, hobbies; Pres. TOSHIRO KUSE.

Hakusui-Sha Co Ltd: 3-24, Kanda Ogawa-machi, Chiyoda-ku, Tokyo 101-0052; tel. (3) 3291-7821; fax (3) 3291-7810; f. 1915; general literature, science and languages; Pres. KAZUAKI FUJIWARA.

Hayakawa Publishing Inc: 2-2, Kanda-Tacho, Chiyoda-ku, Tokyo 101-0046; tel. (3) 3252-3111; fax (3) 3254-1550; f. 1945; science fiction, mystery, autobiography, literature, fantasy; Pres. HIROSHI HAYAKAWA.

Heibonsha Ltd Publishers: 5-16-19, Himonya, Meguro-ku, Tokyo 152-0008; tel. (3) 5721-1241; fax (3) 5721-1249; f. 1914; encyclopaedias, art, history, geography, literature, science; Pres. HIROSHI SHIMONAKA.

Hirokawa Publishing Co: 3-27-14, Hongo, Bunkyo-ku, Tokyo 113-0033; tel. (3) 3815-3651; fax (3) 5684-7030; f. 1926; natural sciences, medicine, pharmacy, nursing, chemistry; Pres. SETSUO HIROKAWA.

Hoikusha Publishing Co Ltd: 1-6-12, Kawamata, Higashi, Osaka; tel. (6) 932-6601; fax (6) 933-8577; f. 1947; natural science, juvenile, fine arts, geography; Pres. YUUKI IMAI.

The Hokuseido Press: 3-32-4, Honkomagome, Bunkyo-ku, Tokyo 113-0021; tel. (3) 3827-0551; fax (3) 3827-0567; f. 1914; regional non-fiction, dictionaries, textbooks; Pres. MASAZO YAMAMOTO.

Hokuryukan Co Ltd: 3-8-14, Takanawara, Minato-ku, Tokyo 108-0074; tel. (3) 5449-4591; fax (3) 5449-4950; f. 1891; natural science, juvenile, dictionaries; Pres. MOTOJIRO FUKUDA.

Ie-No-Hikari Association: 11, Funagawara-cho, Ichigaya, Shinjuku-ku, Tokyo 162-0826; tel. (3) 3266-9000; fax (3) 3266-9048; f. 1925; social science, agriculture; Chair. SHUZO SUZUKI; Pres. MASAYA KAKUNAKA.

Igaku-Shoin Ltd: 5-24-3, Hongo, Bunkyo-ku, Tokyo 113-8719; tel. (3) 3817-5610; fax (3) 3815-4114; f. 1944; medicine, nursing; Pres. YU KANEHARA.

Institute for Financial Affairs Inc (KINZAI): 19, Minami-Motomachi, Shinjuku-ku, Tokyo 160-0012; tel. (3) 3355-1616; fax (3) 3359-7947; e-mail JDI04072@niftyserve.or.jp; f. 1950; finance and economics, banking laws and regulations, accounting; Pres. MASATERU YOSHIDA.

Ishiyaku Publishers, Inc: 1-7-10, Honkomagome, Bunkyo-ku, Tokyo 113-8612; tel. (3) 5395-7631; fax (3) 5395-7633; f. 1921; medicine, dentistry, rehabilitation, nursing, nutrition and pharmaceutics; Pres. HIROSHI MIURA.

Iwanami Shoten Publishers: 2-5-5, Hitotsubashi, Chiyoda-ku, Tokyo 101-8002; tel. (3) 5210-4000; fax (3) 5210-4039; f. 1913; natural and social sciences, literature, history, geography; Chair. YUJIRO IWANAMI; Pres. NOBUKAZU OTSUKA.

Japan Broadcast Publishing Co Ltd: 41-1, Udagawa-cho, Shibuya-ku, Tokyo 150-808; tel. (3) 3780-3374; fax (3) 3780-3343; f. 1931; foreign language textbooks, gardening, home economics, sociology, education, art, juvenile; Pres. TATSUO ANDO.

Japan External Trade Organization (JETRO): 2-2-5, Toranomon, Minato-ku, Tokyo 105-0001; tel. (3) 3582-3518; fax (3) 3587-2485; f. 1958; social sciences, economics; Pres. NOBUO TSUTSUI.

Japan Publications Inc: 1-2-2, Sarugaku-cho, Chiyoda-ku, Tokyo 101-0064; tel. (3) 3295-8411; fax (3) 3295-8416; f. 1942; general works, rare books, CD-ROM; Pres. SATOMI NAKABAYASHI.

The Japan Times Ltd: 4-5-4, Shibaura, Minato-ku, Tokyo 108-0023; tel. (3) 3453-2013; fax (3) 3453-8023; f. 1989; linguistics, social science, industry; Pres. TOSHIAKI OGASAWARA.

Japan Travel Bureau, Inc: 1-10-8, Dogenzaka, Shibuya-ku, Tokyo 150-8558; tel. (3) 3477-9521; fax (3) 3477-9538; f. 1912; travel guides, languages, dictionaries, travel magazines; Pres. ISAO MATSUHASHI.

Jimbun Shoin: 9, Nishiuchihata-cho, Takeda, Fushimi-ku, Kyoto 612-8447; tel. (75) 603-1344; fax (75) 603-1814; f. 1922; literary, philosophy, history, fine arts; Pres. MUTSUHISA WATANABE.

Kadokawa Shoten Publishing Co Ltd: 2-13-3, Fujimi, Chiyoda-ku, Tokyo 102-0071; tel. (3) 3238-8611; fax (3) 3238-8612; f. 1945; literature, history, dictionaries, religion, fine arts, books on tape, compact discs, CD-ROM, comics, animation, video cassettes, computer games; Pres. TSUGUHIKO KADOKAWA.

Kaibundo Publishing Co Ltd: 2-5-4, Suido, Bunkyo-ku, Tokyo 112-0005; tel. (3) 5684-6289; fax (3) 3815-3953; f. 1914; marine affairs, natural science, engineering, industry; Pres. YOSHIHIRO OKADA.

Kaiseisha Publishing Co Ltd: 3-5, Ichigaya Sadohara-cho, Shinjuku-ku, Tokyo 162-8450; tel. (3) 3260-3229; fax (3) 3260-3540; f. 1936; juvenile; Pres. MASAKI IMAMURA.

Kanehara & Co Ltd: 2-31-14, Yushima, Bunkyo-ku, Tokyo 113-8687; tel. (3) 3811-7185; fax (3) 3813-0288; f. 1875; medical, agricultural, engineering and scientific; Pres. SABURO KOMURO.

Kenkyusha Ltd: 2-11-3, Fujimi, Chiyoda-ku, Tokyo 102-0071; tel. (3) 3288-7711; fax (3) 3288-7821; f. 1907; bilingual dictionaries; Pres. KATSUYUKI IKEGAMI.

Kinokuniya Co Ltd: 5-38-1, Sakuragaoka, Setagaya-ku, Tokyo 156-8691; tel. (3) 3439-0172; fax (3) 3439-0173; f. 1927; humanities, social science, natural science; Pres. OSAMU MATSUBARA.

Kodansha International Ltd: 1-17-14, Otowa, Bunkyo-ku, Tokyo 112-0013; tel. (3) 3944-6492; fax (3) 3944-1560; f. 1963; art, business, cookery, crafts, gardening, language, literature, martial arts; Pres. SAWAKO NOMA.

Kodan-Sha Ltd: 2-12-21, Otowa, Bunkyo-ku, Tokyo 112-8652; tel. (3) 5395-3574; fax (3) 3944-9915; f. 1909; fine arts, fiction, literature, juvenile, comics, dictionaries; Pres. SAWAKO NOMA.

Kosei Publishing Co Ltd: 2-7-1, Wada, Suginami-ku, Tokyo 166-8535; tel. (3) 5385-2309; fax (3) 5385-2331; f. 1966; general works, philosophy, religion, history, pedagogy, social science, art, juvenile; Pres. KINZO TAKEMURA.

Kyoritsu Shuppan Co Ltd: 4-6-19, Kobinata, Bunkyo-ku, Tokyo 112-0006; tel. (3) 3947-2511; fax (3) 3947-2539; f. 1926; scientific and technical; Pres. MITSUAKI NANJO.

Maruzen Co Ltd: 3-9-2, Nihonbashi, Chuo-ku, Tokyo 103-0027; tel. (3) 3272-0521; fax (3) 3274-0551; f. 1869; general works; Pres. NOBUO SUZUKI.

Medical Friend Co Ltd: 3-2-4, Kudan Kita, Chiyoda-ku, Tokyo 102-0073; tel. (3) 3264-6611; fax (3) 3261-6602; f. 1947; medical and allied science, nursing; Pres. KAZUHARU OGURA.

Minerva Shobo: 1, Tsutsumi dani-cho, Hinooka, Yamashina-ku, Kyoto 607-8494; tel. (75) 581-5191; fax (75) 581-0589; f. 1948; general non-fiction and reference; Pres. NOBUO SUGITA.

Misuzu Shobo Ltd: 5-32-21, Hongo, Bunkyo-ku, Tokyo 113-0033; tel. (3) 3815-9181; fax (3) 3818-8497; f. 1947; general, philosophy, history, literature, science, art; Pres. YUJI OGUMA; Man. Dir KEIJI KATO.

Mita Press: 3-2-12, Hongo, Bunkyo-ku, Tokyo 113-0033; tel. (3) 3817-7200; fax (3) 3817-7207; f. 1924; scientific, technological, business and non-fiction; Pres. YOSHIHIRO MITA; Man. Dir AKIO ETORI.

Morikita Shuppan Co Ltd: 1-4-11, Fujimi, Chiyoda-ku, Tokyo 102-0071; tel. (3) 3265-8341; fax (3) 3264-8709; e-mail info@morikita.co.jp; internet http://www.morikita.co.jp; f. 1950; natural science, engineering; Pres. HAJIME MORIKITA.

Nakayama-Shoten Co Ltd: 1-25-14, Hakusan, Bunkyo-ku, Tokyo 113-0001; tel. (3) 3813-1101; fax (3) 3813-1134; f. 1948; medicine, biology, zoology; Pres. TADASHI HIRATA.

Nanzando Co Ltd: 4-1-11, Yushima, Bunkyo-ku, Tokyo; tel. (3) 5689-7868; fax (3) 5689-7869; medical reference, paperbacks; Pres. HAJIME SUZUKI.

Nigensha Publishing Co Ltd: 2-2-31, Kanda Jimbo-cho, Chiyoda-ku, Tokyo 101-0051; tel. (3) 5210-4733; fax (3) 5210-4723; f. 1953; calligraphy, fine arts, art reproductions, cars, watches; Pres. TAKAO WATANABE.

Nihon Keizai Shimbun Inc, Publications Bureau: 1-9-5, Ohtemachi, Chiyoda-ku, Tokyo 100-8066; tel. (3) 3270-0251; fax (3) 5255-2864; f. 1876; economics, business, politics, fine arts, video cassettes, CD-ROM; Pres. MASANORI TAKEUCHI.

Nihon Vogue Co Ltd: 3-23, Ichigaya Honmura-cho, Shinjuku-ku, Tokyo 162-8705; tel. (3) 5261-5089; fax (3) 3269-7874; f. 1954; quilt, needlecraft, handicraft, knitting, decorative painting, cooking, golf, practical books on hobbies; Pres. NOBUAKI SETO.

Nippon Jitsugyo Publishing Co Ltd: 6-8-1, Nishi-Tenma, Kita-ku, Osaka 530-0047; tel. (6) 362-6141; fax (3) 362-9003; f. 1950; business, management, finance and accounting, sales and marketing; Pres. YOICHIRO NAKAMURA.

Obunsha Co Ltd: 78, Yarai-cho, Shinjuku-ku, Tokyo 162-0805; tel. (3) 3266-6000; f. 1931; fax (3) 3266-6291; textbooks, reference, general science and fiction, magazines, encyclopaedias, dictionaries; software; audio-visual aids; Pres. FUMIO AKAO.

Ohm Sha Ltd: 3-1, Kanda Nishiki-cho, Chiyoda-ku, Tokyo 101; tel. (3) 3233-0641; fax (3) 3233-2426; f. 1914; engineering, technical and scientific; Pres. SEIJI SATO; Dir M. MORI.

Ondorisha Publishers Ltd: 11-11, Nishigoken-cho, Shinjuku-ku, Tokyo 162-8708; tel. (3) 3268-3101; fax (3) 3235-3530; f. 1945; knitting, embroidery, patchwork, handicraft books; Pres. HIDEAKI TAKEUCHI.

Ongaku No Tomo Sha Corpn (ONT): 6-30, Kagurazaka, Shinjuku-ku, Tokyo 162-0825; tel. (3) 3235-2111; fax (3) 3235-2119; f. 1941; compact discs, videograms, music magazines, music books, music data, music textbooks; Pres. JUN MEGURO.

PHP Institute Inc: 11, Kitanouchi-cho, Nishi kujo, Minami-ku, Kyoto 601-8411; tel. (75) 681-4431; fax (75) 681-9921; f. 1946; social science; Pres. MASAHARU MATSUSHITA.

Poplar Publishing Co Ltd: 5, Suga-cho, Shinjuku-ku, Tokyo 160-8565; tel. (3) 3357-2216; fax (3) 3351-0736; f. 1947; children's; Pres. HARUO TANAKA.

Sanseido Co Ltd: 2-22-14, Misaki-cho, Chiyoda-ku, Tokyo 101-0061; tel. (3) 3230-9411; fax (3) 3230-9547; f. 1881; dictionaries, educational, languages, social and natural science; Chair. HISANORI UENO; Pres. MASAKI MORIYA.

Sanshusha Publishing Co Ltd: 1-5-34, Shitaya, Taito-ku, Tokyo 110; tel. (3) 3842-1711; fax (3) 3845-3965; internet http://www.sanshusha.co.jp; f. 1938; languages, dictionaries, philosophy, sociology, electronic publishing (CD-ROM); Pres. KANJI MAEDA.

Seibundo-Shinkosha Publishing Co Ltd: 1-13-7, Yayoi-cho, Nakano-ku, Tokyo 164-8655; tel. (3) 3373-7213; fax (3) 3373-7325; f. 1912; technical, scientific, general non-fiction; Pres. SHIGEO OGAWA.

Sekai Bunka Publishing Inc: 4-2-29, Kudan-Kita, Chiyoda-ku, Tokyo 102-0073; tel. (3) 3262-5111; fax (3) 3221-6843; f. 1946; history, natural science, geography, education, art, literature, juvenile; Pres. TSUTOMU SUZUKI.

Shincho-Sha Co Ltd: 71, Yarai-cho, Shinjuku-ku, Tokyo 162-8711; tel. (3) 3266-5411; fax (3) 3266-5534; f. 1896; general literature, fiction, non-fiction, fine arts, philosophy; Pres. RYOICHI SATO.

Shinkenchiku-Sha Co Ltd: 2-31-2, Yushima, Bunkyo-ku, Tokyo; tel. (3) 3811-7101; fax (3) 3812-8229; f. 1925; architecture; Pres. YOSHIO YOSHIDA.

Shogakukan Inc: 2-3-1, Hitotsubashi, Chiyoda-ku, Tokyo 101-8001; tel. (3) 3230-5226; fax (3) 3288-9653; f. 1922; juvenile, education, geography, history, encyclopaedias, dictionaries; Pres. MASAHIRO OHGA.

Shokabo Publishing Co Ltd: 8-1, Yomban-cho, Chiyoda-ku, Tokyo 102-0081; tel. (3) 3262-9166; fax (3) 3262-9130; f. 1895; natural science, engineering; Pres. TATSUJI YOSHINO.

Shokokusha Publishing Co Ltd: 25, Saka-machi, Shinjuku-ku, Tokyo 160-0002; tel. (3) 3359-3231; fax (3) 3357-3961; e-mail eigyo@shokokusha.co.jp; f. 1932; architectural, technical and fine arts; Pres. TAISHIRO YAMAMOTO.

Shueisha Inc: 2-5-10, Hitotsubashi, Chiyoda-ku, Tokyo 101-8050; tel. (3) 3230-6320; fax (3) 3262-1309; f. 1925; literature, fine arts, language, juvenile, comics; Pres. TADASHI WAKANA.

Shufunotomo Co Ltd: 2-9, Kanda Surugadai, Chiyoda-ku, Tokyo 101; tel. (3) 3294-1171; fax (3) 3294-8294; f. 1916; domestic science, fine arts, gardening, handicraft, cookery and magazines; Chair. HARUHIKO ISHIKAWA; Pres. YASUHIKO ISHIKAWA.

Shunju-Sha Co: 2-18-6, Soto-kanda, Chiyoda-ku, Tokyo 101-0021; tel. (3) 3255-9614; fax (3) 3255-9370; f. 1918; philosophy, religion, literary, economics, music; Pres. AKIRA KANDA; Man. RYUTARO SUZUKI.

The Simul Press Inc: 13-9, Araki-cho, Shinjuku-ku, Tokyo 160-0002; tel. (3) 3226-2851; fax (3) 3226-2840; f. 1967; international and current issues, social science, education, literature, languages; Chair. KATSUO TAMURA.

Taishukan Publishing Co Ltd: 3-24, Kanda-Nishiki-cho, Chiyoda-ku, Tokyo 101-8466; tel. (3) 3294-2221; fax (3) 3295-4107; f. 1918; reference, Japanese and foreign languages, sports, dictionaries, audio-visual aids; Pres. SHIGEO SUZUKI.

Tanko Weathethill Inc: 39-1, Ichigaya Yanagi-cho, Shinjuku-ku, Tokyo 162; tel. (3) 5269-2371; fax (3) 5269-7266; f. 1962; arts, crafts, architecture, gardening, language, history, zen and Eastern philosophy, sports, travel; Pres. YOSHIHARU NAYA.

Tankosha Publishing Co Ltd: 19-1, Miyanishi-cho Murasakino, Kita-ku, Kyoto 603-8158; tel. (75) 432-5151; fax (75) 414-0273; f. 1949; tea ceremony, fine arts, history; Pres. YOSHIHARU NAYA.

Teikoku-Shoin Co Ltd: 3-29, Kanda Jimbo-cho, Chiyoda-ku, Tokyo 101; tel. (3) 3262-0834; fax (3) 3262-7770; f. 1926; geography, atlases, maps, textbooks; Pres. MUTSUO SHIRAHAMA.

Tokai University Press: 2-28-4, Tomigaya, Shibuya-ku, Tokyo 151-0063; tel. (3) 5478-0891; fax (3) 5478-0870; f. 1962; social science, cultural science, natural science, engineering, art; Pres. TATSURO MATSUMAE.

Tokuma Shoten Publishing Co Ltd: 1-1-16, Higashi Shimbashi, Minato-ku, Tokyo 105-8055; tel. (3) 3573-0111; fax (3) 3573-8788; f. 1954; Japanese classics, history, fiction, juvenile; Pres. YASUYOSHI TOKUMA.

Tokyo News Service Ltd: Tsukiji Hamarikyu Bldg, 5-3-3, Tsukiji, Chuo-ku, Tokyo 104; tel. (3) 3542-6511; fax (3) 3545-3628; f. 1947; shipping, trade and television guides; Pres. T. OKUYAMA.

Tokyo Shoseki Co Ltd: 2-17-1, Horifune, Kita-ku, Tokyo 114-0004; tel. (3) 5390-7513; fax (3) 5390-7407; f. 1909; textbooks, reference books, cultural and educational books; Pres. ATSUSHI CHOJI.

Tokyo Sogen-Sha Co Ltd: 1-5, Shin-Ogawa-machi, Shinjuku-ku, Tokyo 162-0814; tel. (3) 3268-8201; fax (3) 3268-8230; f. 1954; mystery and detective stories, science fiction, literature; Pres. YASUNOBU TOGAWA.

Toyo Keizai Shinpo-sha: 1-2-1, Nihonbashi, Hongoku-cho, Chuo-ku, Tokyo 103-0021; tel. (3) 3246-5577; fax (3) 3279-0332; f. 1895; economics, business, finance and corporate, information; Pres. JUNJI ASANO.

Charles E. Tuttle Publishing Co Inc: 1-2-6, Suido, Bunkyo-ku, Tokyo 112-0005; tel. (3) 3811-7741; fax (3) 5689-4926; f. 1948; books on Japanese and Asian religion, history, social science, arts, languages, literature, juvenile; Pres. NICHOLAS INGLETON.

United Nations University Press: 5-53-70, Jingumae, Shibuya-ku, Tokyo 150-0001; tel. (3) 3499-2811; fax (3) 3499-2828; f. 1975; social sciences, humanities, pure and applied natural sciences; Pres. GURGULINO DE SOUZA.

University of Tokyo Press: 7-3-1, Hongo, Bunkyo-ku, Tokyo 113-0033; tel. (3) 3811-0964; fax (3) 3815-1426; f. 1951; natural and social sciences, humanities; Japanese and English; Man. Dir TADASHI YAMASHITA.

Yama-Kei Publishers Co Ltd: 1-1-33, Shiba-Daimon, Minato-ku, Tokyo 105-0012; tel. (3) 3436-4021; fax (3) 3438-1949; f. 1930; natural science, geography, mountaineering; Pres. YOSHIMITSU KAWASAKI.

Yohan: 3-14-9, Okubo, Shinjuku-ku, Tokyo 169; tel. (3) 3208-0181; fax (3) 3209-0288; f. 1963; social science, language, art, juvenile, dictionary; Pres. MASANORI WATANABE.

Yuhikaku Publishing Co Ltd: 2-17, Kanda Jimbo-cho, Chiyoda-ku, Tokyo 101-0051; tel. (3) 3264-1312; fax (3) 3264-5030; f. 1877; social sciences, law, economics; Pres. TADATAKA EGUSA.

Yuzankaku Shuppan Co Ltd: 2-6-9, Fujimi, Chiyoda-ku, Tokyo 102; tel. (3) 3262-3231; fax (3) 3262-4960; f. 1916; history, fine arts, religion, archaeology; Pres. KEIKO NAGASAKA.

Zoshindo Juken Kenkyusha Co Ltd: 2-19-15, Shinmachi, Nishi-ku, Osaka 550-0013; tel. (6) 532-1581; fax (6) 532-1588; f. 1890; educational, juvenile; Pres. SHIGETOSHI OKAMOTO.

Government Publishing House

Government Publications' Service Centre: 1-2-1, Kasumigaseki, Chiyoda-ku, Tokyo 100-0013; tel. (3) 3504-3885; fax (3) 3504-3889.

PUBLISHERS' ASSOCIATIONS

Japan Book Publishers Association: 6, Fukuro-machi, Shinjuku-ku, Tokyo 162-0828; tel. (3) 3268-1301; fax (3) 3268-1196; f. 1957; 500 mems; Pres. TAKAO WATANABE; Exec. Dir TOSHIKAZU GOMI.

Publishers' Association for Cultural Exchange, Japan: 1-2-1, Sarugaku-cho, Chiyoda-ku, Tokyo 101-0064; tel. (3) 3291-5685; fax (3) 3233-3645; e-mail office@pace.or.jp; f. 1953; 135 mems; Pres. Dr TATSURO MATSUMAE; Man. Dir YASUKO KORENAGA.

Broadcasting and Communications

TELECOMMUNICATIONS

DDI Corpn: 8, Ichiban-cho, Chiyoda-ku, Tokyo 102; tel. (3) 3221-9676; fax (3) 3221-9696; Pres. YUSAI OKUYAMA.

Japan Telecom Co Ltd: 2-9-1, Hatchobori, Chuo-ku, Tokyo 104; tel. (3) 5540-8417; fax (3) 5540-8485.

Kokusai Denshin Denwa Co Ltd (KDD): KDD Bldg, 2-3-2, Nishi Shinjuku, Shinjuku-ku, Tokyo 163-03; tel. (3) 3347-7111; telex 22500; fax (3) 3347-6470; major international telecommunications carrier; Chair. TAIZO NAKAMURA; Pres. TADASHI NISHIMOTO.

Nippon Telegraph and Telephone Corpn: 3-19-2, Nishi Shinjuku, Shinjuku-ku, Tokyo 163-19; tel. (3) 5359-5111; fax (3) 5359-1192; e-mail hyamada@yamato.ntt.jp; from 1999 will operate local, long-distance and international services; largest telecommunications co in Japan; Chair. SHIGEO SAWADA; Pres. JUN-ICHIRO MIYAZU.

Teleway Corpn: CS Tower Bldg, 7th Floor, 5-20-8, Asakusabashi, Taito-ku, Tokyo 111; tel. (3) 5820-2771; fax (3) 5820-2774.

Tokyo Telecommunication Network Co Inc: 4-9-25, Shibaura, Minato-ku, Tokyo 108; tel. (3) 5476-0091; fax (3) 5476-7625.

BROADCASTING

Nippon Hoso Kyokai, NHK (Japan Broadcasting Corporation): Broadcasting Centre, 2-2-1, Jinnan, Shibuya-ku, Tokyo 150-01; tel. (3) 3465-1111; fax (3) 3469-8110; f. 1925; non-commercial public corpn; operates five (two TV and three radio) networks and 2 DBS TV services; TV channels divided equally between general and educational networks; central stations at Tokyo, Osaka, Nagoya, Hiroshima, Fukuoka Sendai, Sapporo and Matsuyama, and 46 local stations; overseas service in 22 languages; Chair. Board of Govs SHOICHIRO KOBAYASHI; Pres. KATSUJI EBISAWA.

National Association of Commercial Broadcasters in Japan (MINPOREN): 3-23, Kioi-cho, Chiyoda-ku, Tokyo 102; tel. (3) 5213-7700; fax (3) 5213-7701; Pres. SEIICHIRO UJIIE; Exec. Dir AKIRA SAKAI; asscn of 190 companies (127 TV cos, 63 radio cos). Among these companies, 36 operate both radio and TV, with 514 radio stations and 7,941 TV stations.

In March 1996 there were a total of 97 commercial radio broadcasting companies and 137 commercial television companies operating in Japan. Some of the most important companies are:

Asahi Hoso—Asahi Broadcasting Corpn: 2-2-48, Ohyodo-Minami, Kita-ku, Osaka 531-01; tel. (6) 458-5321; fax (6) 458-3672; Pres. TOSHIHARU SHIBATA.

Asahi National Broadcasting Co Ltd—TV Asahi: 1-1-1, Roppongi, Minato-ku, Tokyo 106; tel. (3) 3587-5111; telex 22520; fax (3) 3505-3539; f. 1957; Pres. KUNIO ITO.

Bunka Hoso—Nippon Cultural Broadcasting, Inc: 1-5, Wakaba, Shinjuku-ku, Tokyo 160; tel. (3) 3357-1111; fax (3) 3357-1140; f. 1952; Pres. SHINICHI MINEGISHI.

Chubu-Nippon Broadcasting Co Ltd: 1-2-8, Shinsakae, Naka-ku, Nagoya 460-05; tel. (052) 241-8111; fax (052) 259-1303; Pres. MASAO HOTTA.

Fuji Television Network, Inc: 2-4-8, Daiba, Minato-ku, Tokyo 137-88; tel. (3) 5500-8888; fax (3) 5500-8027; f. 1958; Pres. HISASHI HIEDA.

Kansai Telecasting Corpn: 6-5-17, Nishitenma, Kita-ku, Osaka 530-08; tel. (6) 315-2779; fax (6) 315-2792; Pres. JITOKURO SAKAI.

Mainichi Broadcasting System, Inc: 17-1, Chayamachi, Kita-ku, Osaka 530-04; tel. (6) 359-1123; fax (6) 359-3503; Pres. MORIYOSHI SAITO.

Nippon Hoso—Nippon Broadcasting System, Inc: 1-9-3, Yuraku-cho, Chiyoda-ku, Tokyo 100-87; tel. (3) 3287-1111; fax (3) 3287-0855; f. 1954; Pres. MICHIYASU KAWAUCHI.

Nippon Television Network Corpn (NTV): 14, Niban-cho, Chiyoda-ku, Tokyo 102-40; tel. (3) 5275-1111; fax (3) 5275-4501; f. 1953; Pres. SEIICHIRO UJIIE.

Okinawa Televi Hoso—Okinawa Television Broadcasting Co Ltd: 1-2-20, Kumoji, Naha 900; tel. (988) 63-2111; fax (988) 61-0193; f. 1959; Pres. KAZUO KOISO.

Radio Tampa—Nihon Short-Wave Broadcasting Co: 1-9-15, Akasaka, Minato-ku, Tokyo 107; tel. (3) 3583-8151; fax (3) 3583-7441; f. 1954; Pres. TAMIO IKEDA.

Ryukyu Hoso—Ryukyus Broadcasting Co: 2-3-1, Kumoji, Naha 900; tel. (988) 60-1199; telex 5247; fax (988) 60-1831; f. 1954; Pres. TAKASHI HIGA.

Television Osaka, Inc: 1-2-18, Otemae, Chuo-ku, Osaka 540-19; tel. (6) 947-0019; fax (6) 946-9796; Pres. MAKOTO FUKAGAWA.

Television Tokyo Channel 12 Ltd: 4-3-12, Toranomon, Minato-ku, Tokyo 105-12; tel. (3) 3432-1212; fax (3) 5473-3447; f. 1964; Pres. YUTAKA ICHIKI.

Tokyo-Hoso—Tokyo Broadcasting System, Inc (TBS): 5-3-6, Akasaka, Minato-ku, Tokyo 107-06; tel. (3) 3746-1111; fax (3) 3588-6378; f. 1951; Pres. YUKIO SUNAHARA.

Yomiuri Televi Hoso—Yomiuri Telecasting Corporation: 2-2-33, Shiromi, Chuo-ku, Osaka 540-10; tel. (6) 947-2111; f. 1958; 20 hrs colour broadcasting daily; Pres. TOMONARI DOI.

Finance

(cap. = capital; p.u. = paid up; res = reserves; dep. = deposits; m. = million; brs = branches; amounts in yen)

BANKING

Japan's central bank and bank of issue is the Bank of Japan. More than one-half of the credit business of the country is handled by 150 private commercial banks, seven trust banks and three long-term credit banks, collectively designated 'All Banks'. At 31 March 1996 the private commercial banks had total assets of 696,100,339m. yen, the trust banks had total assets of 245,360,006m. yen and the long-term credit banks had total assets of 83,797,785m. yen.

Of the latter category, the most important are the city banks, of which there are 10, some of which have a long and distinguished history, originating in the time of the *zaibatsu*, the private entrepreneurial organizations on which Japan's capital wealth was built before the Second World War. Although the *zaibatsu* were abolished as integral industrial and commercial enterprises during the Allied Occupation, the several businesses and industries which bear the former *zaibatsu* names, such as Mitsubishi, Mitsui and Sumitomo, continue to flourish and to give each other mutual assistance through their respective banks and trust corporations.

Among the commercial banks, the Bank of Tokyo specializes in foreign-exchange business, while the Industrial Bank of Japan finances capital investment by industry. The Long-Term Credit Bank of Japan and Nippon Credit Bank also specialize in industrial finance; the work of these three privately-owned banks is supplemented by the government-controlled Japan Development Bank.

The Government has established a number of other specialized institutions to provide services that are not offered by the private banks. Thus the Japan Export-Import Bank advances credit for the export of heavy industrial products and the import of raw materials in bulk. A Housing Loan Corporation assists firms in building housing for their employees, while the Agriculture, Forestry and Fisheries Finance Corporation provides loans to the named industries for equipment purchases. Similar services are provided for small enterprises by the Japanese Finance Corporation for Small Business.

An important financial role is played by co-operatives and by the many small enterprise institutions. Each prefecture has its own federation of co-operatives, with the Central Co-operative Bank of Agriculture and Forestry as the common central financial institution. This bank also acts as an agent for the government-controlled Agriculture, Forestry and Fisheries Finance Corporation.

There are also two types of private financial institutions for small business. There are 365 Credit Co-operatives, with total assets of 16,769,400m. yen at 31 March 1996, and 412 Shinkin Banks (credit associations), with total assets of 69,407,500m. yen at 31 March 1996, which lend only to members. The latter also receive deposits.

The most common form of savings is through the government-operated Postal Savings System, which collects small savings from the public by means of the post office network. Total deposits amounted to 217,221,100m. yen in June 1996. The funds thus made available are used as loan funds by government financial institutions, through the Ministry of Finance's Trust Fund Bureau.

Clearing houses operate in each major city of Japan, and total 182 institutions. The largest are those of Tokyo and Osaka.

Japan's 67 Sogo Banks (mutual loan and savings banks) converted to commercial banks in 1989.

Central Bank

Nippon Ginko (Bank of Japan): 2-1-1, Hongoku-cho, Nihonbashi, Chuo-ku, Tokyo 103; tel. (3) 3279-1111; telex 22763; fax (3) 5200-2256; f. 1882; cap. and res 2,685,600m., dep. 6,255,909m. (March 1997); Gov. Yasuo Matsushita; 33 brs.

Principal Commercial Banks

Asahi Bank Ltd: 1-1-2, Ohtemachi, Chiyoda-ku, Tokyo 100; tel. (3) 3287-2111; telex 24275; fax (3) 3212-3484; f. 1945 as Kyowa Bank Ltd; merged with Saitama Bank Ltd (f. 1943) in 1991; adopted present name in 1992; cap. 282,844m., res 244,296m., dep. 22,130,412m. (Sept. 1996); Chair. Tadashi Tanaka; Pres. Tatsuro Itoh; 430 brs.

Ashikaga Bank Ltd: 4-1-25, Sakura, Utsonomiya, Tochigi 320; tel. (286) 22-0111; f. 1895; cap. 58,536m., res 204,420m., dep. 5,679,867m. (March 1996); Chair. Hisao Mukae; Pres. Yoshio Yanagita; 140 brs.

Bank of Fukuoka Ltd: 2-13-1, Tenjin, Chuo-ku, Fukuoka 810; tel. (92) 723-2131; telex 2226638; fax (92) 711-1746; f. 1945; cap. 57,365m., res 192,130m., dep. 5,635,369m. (March 1997); Chair. Toyohiko Goto; Pres. Ryoji Tsukuda; 194 brs.

Bank of Tokyo-Mitsubishi Ltd: 2-7-1, Marunouchi, Chiyoda-ku, Tokyo 100; tel. (3) 3240-1111; fax (3) 3240-4197; f. 1996 as a result of merger between Bank of Tokyo Ltd (f. 1946) and Mitsubishi Bank Ltd (f. 1880); specializes in international banking and financial business; cap. 658,283m., res 1,263,582m., dep. 62,661,586m. (March 1997); Chair. Tsuneo Wakai; Pres. Tasuku Takagaki; 805 brs.

Bank of Yokohama Ltd: 3-1-1, Minatomirai, Nishi-ku, Yokohama, Kanagawa 220-8611; tel. (45) 225-1111; telex 24945; fax (45) 225-1160; internet http://www.boy.co.jp; f. 1920; cap. 134,547m., res 124,008m., dep. 9,475,677m. (Sept. 1997); Chair. Takashi Tanaka; Pres. Sadaaki Hirasawa; 199 brs.

Chiba Bank Ltd: 1-2, Chiba-minato, Chuo-ku, Chiba 260; tel. (43) 245-1111; f. 1943; cap. 106,881m., res 276,630m., dep. 7,122,865m. (March 1996); Pres. Tsuneo Hayakawa; 168 brs.

Dai-Ichi Kangyo Bank Ltd: 1-1-5, Uchisaiwai-cho, Chiyoda-ku, Tokyo 100-0011; tel. (3) 3596-1111; telex 22315; fax (3) 3596-2179; f. 1971; cap. 458,208m., dep. 38,492,720m. (March 1997); Chair. Yosiharu Mani; Pres. Katsuyuki Sugita; 396 brs.

Daiwa Bank Ltd: 2-2-1, Bingo-machi, Chuo-ku, Osaka 541; tel. (6) 271-1221; telex 63284; f. 1918; cap. 234,361m., dep. 12,309,504m. (Sept. 1997); Pres. Takashi Kaiho; 215 brs.

Fuji Bank Ltd: 1-5-5, Ohtemachi, Chiyoda-ku, Tokyo 100; tel. (3) 3216-2211; telex 22367; f. 1880; cap. 529,087m., res 1,087,496m., dep. 38,279,142m. (March 1997); Chair. Toru Hashimoto; Pres. Yoshiro Yamamoto; 290 brs.

Hokuriku Bank Ltd: 1-2-26, Tsutsumichodori, Toyama 930-8637; tel. (764) 23-7111; fax (764) 3242-0541; f. 1877; cap. 83,338m., res 125,637m., dep. 6,156,349m. (March 1997); Pres. Kenso Yashima; 194 brs.

Joyo Bank Ltd: 2-5-5, Minamimachi, Mito-shi, Ibaraki 310; tel. (29) 231-2151; telex 23278; fax (29) 224-7525; f. 1935; cap. 68,858m., res 250,949m., dep. 6,294,060m. (Sept. 1996); Chair. Itaru Ishikawa; Pres. Toranosuke Nishino; 186 brs.

Sakura Bank Ltd: 1-3-1, Kudan-Minami, Chiyoda-ku, Tokyo 100-91; tel. (3) 3230-3111; telex 22378; fax (3) 3221-1084; f. 1990; cap. 599,445m., dep. 38,270,539m. (March 1997); Chair. Masahiro Takasaki; Pres. Akishige Okada; 563 brs.

Sanwa Bank Ltd: 3-5-6, Fushimi-machi, Chuo-ku, Osaka 541; tel. (6) 206-8111; telex 63234; fax (6) 229-1066; f. 1933; cap. 466,503m., res 444,114m., dep. 45,452,602m. (March 1997); Chair. Hiroshi Watanabe; Pres. Naotaka Saeki; 1,042 brs.

Shizuoka Bank Ltd: 1-10, Gofuku-cho, Shizuoka 420; tel. (54) 261-3131; telex 28450; fax (3) 3246-1483; f. 1943; cap. 90,343m., res 144,690m., dep. 6,503,296m. (March 1996); Chair. Jikichiro Sakai; Pres. Soichiro Kamiya; 199 brs.

Sumitomo Bank Ltd: 4-6-5, Kitahama, Chuo-ku, Osaka 541; tel. (6) 227-2111; telex 63266; f. 1895; cap. 502,348m., res 481,796m., dep. 50,340,509m. (March 1997); Chair. Toshio Morikawa; Pres. Yoshifumi Nishikawa; 351 brs.

Tokai Bank Ltd: 3-21-24, Nishiki, Naka-ku, Nagoya 460; tel. (52) 211-1111; telex 59612; fax (52) 211-0931; f. 1941; cap. 361,972m., res 347,610m., dep. 22,550,113m. (March 1997); Pres. Satoru Nishigaki; 285 brs.

Principal Trust Banks

Chuo Trust and Banking Co Ltd: 1-7-1, Kyobashi, Chuo-ku, Tokyo 104; tel. (3) 3567-1451; telex 33368; fax (3) 3562-6902; f. 1962; cap. 61,215m., res 55,823m., dep. 2,211,353m. (March 1997); Chair. Hisao Muramoto; Pres. Shozo Endoh; 51 brs.

Mitsubishi Trust and Banking Corporation: 1-4-5, Marunouchi, Chiyoda-ku, Tokyo 100; tel. (3) 3212-1211; telex 24259; fax (3) 3284-1326; f. 1927; cap. 192,793m., res 179,101m., dep. 7,089,808m. (March 1996); Chair. Hiroshi Hayashi; Pres. Toyoshi Nakano; 54 brs.

Mitsui Trust and Banking Co Ltd: 2-1-1, Nihonbashi-Muromachi, Chuo-ku, Tokyo 103; tel. (3) 3270-9511; telex 26397; fax (3) 3245-0459; f. 1924; cap. 169,483m., res 153,812m., dep. 4,956,965m. (March 1997); Chair. Seiichi Kawasaki; Pres. Keiu Nishido; 64 brs.

Sumitomo Trust and Banking Co Ltd: 4-5-33, Kitahama, Chuo-ku, Osaka 541; tel. (6) 220-2121; telex 63775; fax (6) 220-2043; f. 1925; cap. 181,028m., res 167,591m., dep. 5,403,078m. (March 1996); Chair. Hiroshi Hayasaki; Pres. Atsushi Niira; 57 brs.

Toyo Trust and Banking Co Ltd: 1-4-3, Marunouchi, Chiyoda-ku, Tokyo 100; tel. (3) 3287-2211; telex 22123; fax (3) 3201-1448; f. 1959; cap. 115,105m., res 105,158m., dep. 2,373,582m. (March 1996); Chair. Mitsuo Imose; Pres. Nobuyoshi Takeuchi; 59 brs.

Yasuda Trust and Banking Co Ltd: 1-2-1, Yaesu, Chuo-ku, Tokyo 103; tel. (3) 3278-8111; telex 23720; fax (3) 3278-0904; f. 1925; cap. 136,814m., res 121,955m., dep. 2,754,072m. (March 1996); Chair. Fujio Takayama; Pres. and CEO Masami Tachikawa; 55 brs.

Long-Term Credit Banks

The Long-Term Credit Bank of Japan Ltd: 2-1-8, Uchisaiwai-cho, Chiyoda-ku, Tokyo 100; tel. (3) 5511-5111; telex 24308; fax (3) 5511-8138; f. 1952; cap. 322,229m., res 283,650m., dep. 8,952,311m. (March 1996); Chair. Takao Masuzawa; Pres. Katsunobu Onogi; 23 brs.

The Nippon Credit Bank Ltd: 1-13-10, Kudan-kita, Chiyoda-ku, Tokyo 102; tel. (3) 3263-1111; telex 26921; fax (3) 3265-7024; f. 1957; cap. 152,292m., res 110,178m., dep. 3,440,166m. (March 1996); Chair. and Pres. HIROSHI KUBOTA; 18 brs.

Nippon Kogyo Ginko (The Industrial Bank of Japan, Ltd): 1-3-3, Marunouchi, Chiyoda-ku, Tokyo 100; tel. (3) 3214-1111; telex 22325; fax (3) 3201-7643; f. 1902; medium- and long-term financing; cap. 465,105m., res 433,744m., dep. 11,988,473m. (March 1997); Chair. YOH KUROSAWA; Pres. MASAO NISHIMURA; 27 domestic brs, 18 overseas brs.

Co-operative Bank

Zenshinren Bank: 3-8-1, Kyobashi, Chuo-ku, Tokyo 104; tel. (3) 3563-4111; telex 2524336; fax (3) 3563-7554; f. 1950; cap. 100,000m., res 229,486m., dep. 15,408,301m. (March 1997); Chair. KEIKICHI KATO; Pres. YASUTAKA MIYAMOTO; 16 brs.

Principal Government Credit Institutions

Agriculture, Forestry and Fisheries Finance Corporation: Koko Bldg, 1-9-3, Ohtemachi, Chiyoda-ku, Tokyo 100; tel. (3) 3270-2261; f. 1953; finances plant and equipment investment; cap. 283,033m. (March 1996); Gov. TOSHIHIKO TSURUOKA; Dep. Gov. KAZUHITO FUJIWARA; 21 brs.

The Export-Import Bank of Japan: 1-4-1, Ohtemachi, Chiyoda-ku, Tokyo 100; tel. (3) 3287-9101; telex 2223728; fax (3) 3287-9539; f. 1950; loans to domestic corpns (export suppliers' credit, import credit, overseas investment credit), loans to foreign entities, equity investments and guarantee of liabilities; plans to merge operations with the Overseas Economic Co-operation Fund in 1999; cap. 985,500m., dep. 7,812,654m. (March 1997); Gov. HIROSHI YASUDA; Dep. Gov. AKIRA NAMBARA.

Housing Loan Corporation: 1-4-10, Koraku, Bunkyo-ku, Tokyo 112; tel. (3) 3812-1111; fax (3) 5800-8257; f. 1950 to provide long-term capital for the construction of housing at low interest rates; cap. 97,200m. (1994); Pres. SUSUMU TAKAHASHI; Vice-Pres. HIROYUKI ITOU; 12 brs.

The Japan Development Bank: 1-9-1, Ohtemachi, Chiyoda-ku, Tokyo 100; tel. (3) 3244-1770; telex 24343; fax (3) 3245-1938; f. 1951; provides long-term loans; subscribes for corporate bonds; guarantees corporate obligations; invests in specific projects; borrows funds from Govt and abroad; issues external bonds and notes; provides market information and consulting services for prospective entrants to Japanese market; cap. 323,300m. (March 1996); Gov. YOSHIHIKO YOSHINO; Dep. Gov. MAKOTO TANJI; 7 brs.

Japan Finance Corporation for Small Business: Koko Bldg, 1-9-3, Ohtemachi, Chiyoda-ku, Tokyo 100; tel. (3) 3270-1271; f. 1953 to supply long-term operating funds to small businesses (capital not more than 100m., or not more than 300 employees) which are not easily secured from ordinary private financial institutions; cap. 222,315m. (March 1997) wholly subscribed by Govt; Gov. MASAHIKO KADOTANI; Vice-Gov. TATSU SUNAMI; 58 brs.

The People's Finance Corporation: Koko Bldg, 1-9-3, Ohtemachi, Chiyoda-ku, Tokyo 100; tel. (3) 3270-1361; f. 1949 to provide business funds, particularly to small enterprises unable to obtain loans from banks and other private financial institutions; cap. 204,900m. (June 1995); Gov. MAMORU OZAKI; Dep. Gov. MASAAKI TSUCHIDA; 152 brs.

Norinchukin Bank (Central Co-operative Bank for Agriculture, Forestry and Fisheries): 1-13-2, Yuraku-cho, Chiyoda-ku, Tokyo 100; tel. (3) 3279-0111; telex 23918; fax (3) 3218-5177; f. 1923; main banker to agricultural, forestry and fisheries co-operatives; receives deposits from individual co-operatives, federations and agricultural enterprises; extends loans to these and to local govt authorities and public corpns; adjusts excess and shortage of funds within co-operative system; issues debentures, invests funds and engages in other regular banking business; cap. 124,999m., res 105,386m., dep. and debentures 40,732,442m. (March 1997); Pres. KENICHI KAKUDOH; Dep. Pres. MITSUO NAITO; 41 brs.

The Overseas Economic Co-operation Fund: Takebashi Godo Bldg, 1-4-1, Ohtemachi, Chiyoda-ku, Tokyo 100; tel. (3) 3215-1304; telex 28430; fax (3) 3215-2892; f. 1961 to promote Japan's overseas economic co-operation by providing for the industrial development and economic stability of developing countries; cap. 4,650,944m. (April 1997); Pres. AKIRA NISHIGAKI; Sr Vice-Pres. YOUSEKI NAGASE.

Shoko Chukin Bank (Central Co-operative Bank for Commerce and Industry): 2-10-17, Yaesu, Chuo-ku, Tokyo 104; tel. (3) 3272-6111; telex 25388; fax (3) 3274-1257; f. 1936 to provide general banking services to facilitate finance for smaller enterprise co-operatives and other organizations formed mainly by small- and medium-sized enterprises; issues debentures; cap. 383,965m., res 22,210m., dep. and debentures 14,588,202m. (March 1996); Pres. YUKIHARU KODAMA; Dep. Pres. ATSUO YAGIHASHI; 103 brs.

Other government financial institutions include the Hokkaido and Tohoku Development Corpn, the Japan Finance Corpn for Municipal Enterprises, the Small Business Credit Insurance Corpn and the Okinawa Development Finance Corpn.

Principal Foreign Banks

In June 1996 there were 90 foreign banks operating in Japan.

ABN AMRO Bank NV (Netherlands): Shiroyama J. T. Mori Bldg, 4-3-1, Toranomon, Minato-ku, Tokyo 105; tel. (3) 5405-6501; telex 2959; fax (3) 5405-6901; Country Man. (Japan) HERMAN F. KESSELER; br. in Osaka.

Bangkok Bank Public Co Ltd (Thailand): Bangkok Bank Bldg, 2-8-10, Nishi Shinbashi, Minato-ku, Tokyo 105-0003; tel. (3) 3503-3333; telex 24373; fax (3) 3502-6420; Vice-Pres. and Branch Man. THAWEE PHUANGKETKEOW; br. in Osaka.

Bank of America NT & SA: Ark Mori Bldg, 34th Floor, 1-12-32, Akasaka, Minato-ku, Tokyo 107; tel. (3) 3587-3155; telex 22272; fax (3) 3587-3460; Sr Vice-Pres. & Regional Man. Japan, Australia and Korea ARUN DUGGAL.

Bank of India: Mitsubishi Denki Bldg, 2-2-3, Marunouchi, Chiyoda-ku, Tokyo 100; tel. (3) 3212-0911; telex 28356; fax (3) 3214-8667; Chief Man. (Japan) E. BALAKRISHNAN; br. in Osaka.

Bank Negara Indonesia: Kokusai Bldg, Rooms 117–8, 3-1-1, Marunouchi, Chiyoda-ku, Tokyo 100; tel. (3) 3214-5621; telex 26249; fax (3) 3210-2633; Gen. Man. AGUS SULAKSONO.

Bankers Trust Co (USA): Kishimoto Bldg, 2-2-1, Marunouchi, Chiyoda-ku, Tokyo 100; tel. (3) 3214-7171; Man. Dir MASAYUKI YASUOKA.

Banque Nationale de Paris SA (France): Shiroyama JT Mori Bldg, 23rd Floor, 4-3-1, Toranomon, Minato-ku, Tokyo 105; tel. (3) 5473-3520; telex 24825; fax (3) 5473-3510; Gen. Man. JEAN-FRANÇOIS LEDOUX.

Banque Paribas (France): Yurakucho Denki Bldg North, 19th Floor, 1-7-1, Yurakucho, Chiyoda-ku, Tokyo 100; tel. (3) 5222-6400; fax (3) 5222-6150; Gen. Man. DOMINIQUE SANDRET.

Barclays Bank PLC (UK): Urbannet Ohtemachi Bldg, 15th Floor, 2-2-2, Ohtemachi, Chiyoda-ku, Tokyo 100; tel. (3) 5255-0011; telex 24968; fax (3) 5255-0102; CEO ANDY SIMMONDS.

Bayerische Vereinsbank AG (Germany): Ohtemachi 1st Sq. East Tower, 17th Floor, 1-5-1, Ohtemachi, Chiyoda-ku, Tokyo 100; tel. (3) 3284-1341; telex 26351; fax (3) 3284-1370; Exec. Dirs Dr PETER BARON, KENJI AKAGI.

Chase Manhattan Bank (USA): Akasaka Park Bldg, 11th–13th Floors, 5-2-20, Akasaka, Minato-ku, Tokyo 107; tel. (3) 5570-7500; telex 22687; fax (3) 5570-7960; Man. Dir and Gen. Man. NORMAN J. T. SCOTT; br. in Osaka.

Citibank NA (USA): Pan Japan Bldg, 1st Floor, 3-8-17, Akasaka Minato-ku, Tokyo 107; tel. (3) 3584-6321; telex 25122; fax (3) 3584-2924; Country Corporate Officer MASAMOTO YASHIRO; 20 brs.

Commerzbank AG (Germany): Nippon Press Center Bldg, 2nd Floor, 2-2-1, Uchisaiwai-cho, Chiyoda-ku, Tokyo 100; tel. (3) 3502-4371; telex 25971; fax (3) 3508-7545; Gen. Mans BURKHARDT FIGGE, KLAUS KUBBETAT.

Crédit Agricole Indosuez (France): Indosuez Bldg, 3-29-1, Kanda Jimbo-cho, Chiyoda-ku, Tokyo 101; tel. (3) 3261-3001; telex 24309; fax (3) 3261-0426; Sr Country Officer BERTRAND GRABOWSKI.

Deutsche Bank AG (Germany): Deutsche Bank Bldg, 3-12-1, Toranomon, Minato-ku, Tokyo 105; tel. (3) 5401-1971; telex 24814; fax (3) 5401-6530; brs in Osaka and Nagoya.

First National Bank of Chicago (USA): Hibiya Central Bldg, 7th Floor, 1-2-9, Nishi Shinbashi, Minato-ku, Tokyo 105; tel. (3) 3596-8700; telex 2224977; fax (3) 3596-8744; Sr Vice-Pres. and Gen. Man. YOSHIO KITAZAWA.

The Hongkong and Shanghai Banking Corpn Ltd (Hong Kong): Kyobashi Itchome Bldg, 1-13-1, Kyobashi, Chuo-ku, Tokyo 104-0031; tel. (3) 5203-3000; fax (3) 5203-3039; CEO STUART PEARCE; brs in Osaka and Nagoya.

International Commercial Bank of China (Taiwan): Togin Bldg, 1-4-2, Marunouchi, Chiyoda-ku, Tokyo 100; tel. (3) 3211-2501; telex 22317; fax (3) 3216-5686; Sr Vice-Pres. and Gen. Man. SHENG SHAN CHENG; br. in Osaka.

Korea Exchange Bank (Republic of Korea): Shin Kokusai Bldg, 3-4-1, Marunouchi, Chiyoda-ku, Tokyo 100; tel. (3) 3216-3561; telex 24243; fax (3) 3214-4491; f. 1967; Gen. Man. KIM KYOUNG-MOON; brs in Osaka and Fukuoka.

Lloyds Bank PLC (UK): ATT New Bldg, 2-11-7, Akasaka, Minato-ku, Tokyo 107; tel. (3) 3589-7700; telex 23527; fax (3) 3589-7722; Area Dir (Japan) GRAHAM M. HARRIS.

Midland Bank PLC (UK): Kyobashi Itchome Bldg, 1-13-1, Kyobashi, Chuo-ku, Tokyo 104; tel. (3) 5203-3333; telex 26137; fax (3) 5203-3396; Treasurer CHRIS PAVLOU.

Morgan Guaranty Trust Co of New York (USA): Akasaka Park Bldg, 5-2-20, Akasaka, Minato-ku, Tokyo 107-6151; tel. (3) 5573-1100; telex 22805; Man. Dir TAKESHI FUJIMAKI.

National Bank of Pakistan: 20 Mori Bldg, 3rd Floor, 2-7-4, Nishi Shinbashi, Minato-ku, Tokyo 105; tel. (3) 3502-0331; telex 23830; fax (3) 3502-0359; f. 1949; Gen. Man. MUHAMMAD SARDAR KHAWAJA.

Oversea-Chinese Banking Corpn Ltd (Singapore): Akasaka Twin Tower, 15th Floor, 2-17-22, Akasaka, Minato-ku, Tokyo 107; tel. (3) 5570-3421; telex 26186; fax (3) 5570-3426; Gen. Man. YEO WEE GHEE.

Société Générale (France): Ark Mori Bldg, 1-12-32, Akasaka, Minato-ku, Tokyo 107; tel. (3) 5548-5800; telex 28611; fax (3) 5549-5809; Chief Exec. CHRISTIAN GOMEZ; br. in Osaka.

Standard Chartered Bank (UK): Fuji Bldg, 3-2-3, Marunouchi, Chiyoda-ku, Tokyo 100; tel. (3) 3213-6541; telex 22484; fax (3) 3215-2448; Chief Exec. (Japan) SEISHIRO KAWAMURA.

State Bank of India: South Tower, Yuraku-cho Denki Bldg, 1-7-1, Yuraku-cho, Chiyoda-ku, Tokyo 100; tel. (3) 3284-0085; telex 27377; fax (3) 3201-5750; CEO A. K. PURWAR; br. in Osaka.

Union Bank of Switzerland: Urbannet Ohtemachi Bldg, 2-2-2, Ohtemachi, Chiyoda-ku, Tokyo 100; tel. (3) 5201-8001; fax (3) 5201-8309; Exec. Vice-Pres. (Japan) PETER BRUTSCHE.

Union de Banques Arabes et Françaises (UBAF) (France): Sumitomo Jimbocho Bldg, 8th Floor, 3-25, Kanda Jimbocho, Chiyoda-ku, Tokyo 101-0051; tel. (3) 3263-8821; fax (3) 3263-8820; Gen. Man. (Japan) PHILIPPE L. BONIN; br. in Osaka.

Westdeutsche Landesbank (Germany): Fukoku Seimei Bldg, 2-2-2, Uchisaiwaicho, Chiyoda-ku, Tokyo 100-0011; tel. (3) 5510-6200; fax (3) 5510-6299; Gen. Mans KLAUS NEUHAUS, PETER CLERMONT, PHILLIP RUSSELL.

Bankers' Associations

Federation of Bankers Associations of Japan: 1-3-1, Marunouchi, Chiyoda-ku, Tokyo 100; tel. (3) 3216-3761; fax (3) 3201-5608; f. 1945; 72 mem. asscns; Chair. NAOTAKA SAEKI; Man. Dir MASARI UGAI.

Tokyo Bankers Association, Inc: 1-3-1, Marunouchi, Chiyoda-ku, Tokyo 100; tel. (3) 3216-3761; fax (3) 3201-5608; f. 1880; 131 mem. banks; conducts the above Federation's administrative business; Chair. NAOTAKA SAEKI; Vice-Chairs TASUKU TAKAGAKI, MASAO NISHIMURA, AKIRA KANNO.

National Association of Labour Banks: 2-5-15, Kanda Surugadai, Chiyoda-ku, Tokyo 101; tel. (3) 3295-6721; Pres. TETSUEI TOKUGAWA.

Regional Banks Association of Japan: 3-1-2, Uchikanda, Chiyoda-ku, Tokyo 101; tel. (3) 3252-5171; f. 1936; 64 mem. banks; Chair. TAKASHI TAMAKI.

Second Association of Regional Banks: 5, Sanban-cho, Chiyoda-ku, Tokyo 102; tel. (3) 3262-2181; fax (3) 3262-2339; f. 1989 (fmrly National Asscn of Sogo Banks); 65 commercial banks; Chair. KAZUMARO KATO.

STOCK EXCHANGES

Fukuoka Stock Exchange: 2-14-2, Tenjin, Chuo-ku, Fukuoka 810; tel. (92) 741-8231; Pres. FUBITO SHIMOMURA.

Hiroshima Stock Exchange: 14-18, Kanayama-cho, Naka-ku, Hiroshima 730; tel. (82) 541-1121; f. 1949; 20 mems; Pres. MASARU NANKO.

Kyoto Securities Exchange: 66, Tachiuri Nishimachi, Shijodori, Higashitoin Higashi-iru, Shimogyo-ku, Kyoto 600; tel. (75) 221-1171; Pres. IICHI NAKAMURA.

Nagoya Stock Exchange: 3-3-17, Sakae, Naka-ku, Nagoya 460; tel. (52) 262-3172; fax (52) 241-1527; e-mail nse@po.iijnet.or.jp; f. 1949; Pres. HIROSHI FUJITA; Sr Exec. Dir KAZUNORI ISHIMOTO.

Niigata Securities Exchange: 1245, Hachibancho, Kami-Okawamaedori, Niigata 951; tel. (252) 222-4181; Pres. KYUUZOU NAKATA.

Osaka Securities Exchange: 1-8-16, Kitahama, Chuo-ku, Osaka 541; tel. (6) 229-8643; fax (6) 231-2639; f. 1949; 113 regular mems, one Nakadachi mem. and 17 special mems; Chair. GENJI ASHIYA; Pres. KYOJI KITAMURA.

Sapporo Securities Exchange: 5-14-1, Nishi, Minami Ichijo, Chuo-ku, Sapporo 060; tel. (11) 241-6171; Pres. YOSHIRO ITOH.

Tokyo Stock Exchange: 2-1, Nihonbashi, Kabuto-cho, Chuo-ku, Tokyo 103-8220; tel. (3) 3666-0141; fax (3) 3663-0625; internet http://www.tse.or.jp; f. 1949; 124 mems (incl. 23 foreign mems) (Dec. 1997); Pres. and CEO MITSUHIDE YAMAGUCHI; Deputy Pres. KEN-ICHI ISAKA, TAKUO TSURUSHIMA.

Supervisory Body

The Securities and Exchange Surveillance Commission: 3-1-1, Kasumigaseki, Chiyoda-ku, Tokyo 100; tel. (3) 3581-7868; fax (3) 5251-2136; f. 1992 for the surveillance of securities and financial futures transactions; Chair. TOSHIHIRO MIZUHARA.

INSURANCE

Principal Life Companies

American Family Life Assurance Co of Columbus AFLAC Japan: Shinjuku Mitsui Bldg, 12th Floor, 2-1-1, Nishishinjuku, Shinjuku-ku, Tokyo 163-04; tel. (3) 3344-2701; fax (3) 3344-2035; f. 1974; Chair. YOSHIKI OTAKE; Pres. HIDEFUMI MATSUI.

American Life Insurance Co (Japan): 1-1-3, Marunouchi, Chiyoda-ku, Tokyo 100; tel. (3) 3284-4111; fax (3) 5619-2506; f. 1972; Chair. HIROSHI FUJINO; Pres. SEIKI TOKUNI.

Asahi Mutual Life Insurance Co: 1-7-3, Nishishinjuku, Shinjuku-ku, Tokyo 163-91; tel. (3) 3342-3111; telex 2323229; fax (3) 3345-8454; f. 1888; Chair. YASUYUKI WAKAHARA; Pres. YUZURU FUJITA.

AXA Life Insurance Co Ltd: Yebisu Garden Place Tower, 18th Floor, 4-20-3, Ebisu, Shibuya-ku, Tokyo 150; tel. (3) 5424-2211; fax (3) 5424-2331; Pres. H. NAKAGAWA.

Chiyoda Mutual Life Insurance Co: 2-19-18, Kamimeguro, Meguro-ku, Tokyo 153; tel. (3) 5704-5111; telex 2467660; fax (3) 3719-7830; f. 1904; Chair. YASUTARO KANZAKI; Pres. REIJI YONEYAMA.

Chiyodakasai EBISU Life Insurance Co Ltd: Ebisu MF Bldg, 6th Floor, 1-6-1, Ebisu Shibuya-ku, Tokyo 150; tel. (3) 5420-8282; fax (3) 5420-8273; f. 1996; Pres. TAKASHI KAWAJI.

Daido Life Insurance Co: 1-2-1, Edobori Nishi-ku, Osaka City, Osaka 550; tel. (6) 447-6111; fax (6) 447-6315; f. 1902; Chair. SHIRO KAWAHARA; Pres. KAZUO HIRANO.

Daihyaku Mutual Life Insurance Co: 4-34-1, Kokuryo-cho, Chofu-shi, Tokyo 182; tel. (424) 85-8111; telex 2423063; fax (3) 3486-5255; f. 1914; Chair. KATSUO FUKUCHI; Pres. YOSHIO KOMORI.

Dai-ichi Mutual Life Insurance Co: 1-13-1, Yuraku-cho, Chiyoda-ku, Tokyo 100; tel. (3) 3216-1211; telex 29848; fax (3) 5221-3221; f. 1902; Chair. TAKAHIDE SAKURAI; Pres. TOMIJIRO MORITA.

Dai-Tokyo Happy Life Insurance Co Ltd: Shijuku Square Tower, 17th Floor, 6-22-1, Nishishinjuku, Shinjuku-ku, Tokyo 163-11; tel. (3) 5323-6411; fax (3) 5323-6419; f. 1996; Pres. TOSHIO INOUE.

Dowa Life Insurance Co Ltd: Seiroka Tower, 30th Floor, 8-1, Akashi-cho, Chuo-ku, Tokyo 104; tel. (3) 5550-0070; fax (3) 5550-0076; f. 1996; Pres. SHUNYO NAGATA.

Fuji Life Insurance Co Ltd: 1-18-17, Minamisenba, Chuo-ku, Osaka-shi 542; tel. (6) 261-0284; fax (6) 261-0113; f. 1996; Pres. YUKISUMI SHIMOMURA.

Fukoku Mutual Life Insurance Co: 2-2-2, Uchisaiwai-cho, Chiyoda-ku, Tokyo 100; tel. (3) 3508-1101; fax (3) 3597-0383; f. 1923; Chair. TETSUO FURUYA; Pres. TAKASHI KOBAYASHI.

Heiwa Life Insurance Co Ltd: 3-2-16, Ginza, Chuo-ku, Tokyo 104; tel. (3) 3563-8111; fax (3) 3374-7114; f. 1907; Pres. TAKASHI SHIMURA.

INA Himawari Life Insurance Co Ltd: 2-1-2, Nishi-Shinjuku, Shinjuku-ku, Tokyo 163-04; tel. (3) 3348-7011; fax (3) 3348-5723; f. 1981; Chair. D.T. TAMMANY; Pres. TAKASHI TAKEBAYASHI; 7 brs.

ING Life Insurance Co Ltd: 26th Floor, New Ohtani Garden Court, 4-1, Kioi-cho, Chiyoda-ku, Tokyo 102; tel. (3) 5210-0300; fax (3) 5210-0430; f. 1985; Pres. MAKOTO CHIBA.

Koa Life Insurance Co Ltd: Atago Toyo Bldg, 12th Floor, 1-3-4, Atago, Minato-ku, Tokyo 105; tel. (3) 5401-9500; fax (3) 5472-7160; f. 1996; Pres. JUNICHI KATO.

Kyoei Kasai Shinrai Life Insurance Co Ltd: J. City Bldg, 5-8-20, Takamatsu, Nerima-ku, Tokyo 179; tel. (3) 5372-2100; fax (3) 5372-7701; f. 1996; Pres. TAKAMICHI NOMURA.

Kyoei Life Insurance Co Ltd: 4-4-1, Nihonbashi, Hongoku-cho, Chuo-ku, Tokyo 103; tel. (3) 3270-8511; fax (3) 3231-8363; f. 1947; Chair. YOSHIO TAYAMA; Pres. SHOICHI OTSUKA.

Meiji Life Insurance Co: 2-1-1, Marunouchi, Chiyoda-ku, Tokyo 100; tel. (3) 3283-8111; telex 2227386; fax (3) 3213-5219; f. 1881; Chair. TERUMICHI TSUCHIDA; Pres. KENJIRO HATA.

Mitsui Mirai Life Insurance Co Ltd: Mitsui Kaijyo Nihonbashi Bldg, 1-3-16, Nihonbashi, Chuo-ku, Tokyo 103; tel. (3) 5202-2811; fax (3) 5202-2997; f. 1996; Pres. MASAHIRO SAKAMOTO.

Mitsui Mutual Life Insurance Co: 1-2-3, Ohtemachi, Chiyoda-ku, Tokyo 100-8123; tel. (3) 3211-6111; fax (3) 5252-7265; f. 1927; Chair. KOSHIRO SAKATA; Pres. AKIRA MIYAKE.

Nichido Life Insurance Co Ltd: 4-2-3, Toranomon, Minato-ku, Tokyo 105; tel. (3) 5403-1700; fax (3) 5403-1751; f. 1996; Pres. SHIGEKI KAJIYAMA.

NICOS Life Insurance Co Ltd: Hongo MK Bldg, 1-28-34, Hongo, Bunkyo-ku, Tokyo 113; tel. (3) 5803-3111; fax (3) 5803-3199; f. 1986; Chair. KENZO SAKAI; Pres. NAOHISA WAKABAYASHI.

Nippon Dantai Life Insurance Co Ltd: 1-2-19, Higashi, Shibuya-ku, Tokyo 150; tel. (3) 3407-6211; telex 2423342; fax (3) 5466-7132; f. 1934; Pres. TAKESHI MATUDO.

Nippon Fire Partner Life Insurance Co Ltd: 4-4-2, Tsukiji, Chuo-ku, Tokyo 104; tel. (3) 5565-8080; fax (3) 5565-8365; f. 1996; Pres. KEIICHI MIYAZAKI.

Nippon Life Insurance Co (Nissay): 3-5-12, Imabashi, Chuo-ku, Osaka 541-01; tel. (6) 209-4500; telex 28783; fax (3) 5251-7674; f. 1889; Chair. JOSEI ITOH; Pres. IKUO UNO.

Orico Life Insurance Co Ltd: Sunshine 60, 26th Floor, 3-1-1, Higashi Ikebukuro, Toshima-ku, Tokyo 170; tel. (3) 5391-3051; fax (3) 5391-3278; f. 1990; Chair. HIROSHI ARAI; Pres. MASAYUKI AOKI.

ORIX Life Insurance Corpn: Shinjuku Chuo Bldg, 5-17-5, Shinjuku, Shinjuku-ku, Tokyo 160; tel. (3) 5272-2700; fax (3) 5272-2720; f. 1991; Pres. SHINOBU SHIRAISHI.

Prudential Life Insurance Co Ltd: 1-7, Kojimachi, Chiyoda-ku, Tokyo 102; tel. (3) 3221-0961; fax (3) 3221-2305; f. 1987; Chair. KIYOFUMI SAKAGUCHI; Pres. ICHIRO KONO.

Saison Life Insurance Co Ltd: Sunshine Sixty Bldg, 39th Floor, 3-1-1, Higashi Ikebukuro, Toshima-ku, Tokyo 170; tel. (3) 3983-6666; fax (3) 3988-7508; f. 1975; Chair. and Pres. TOSHIO TAKEUCHI.

Skandia Life Insurance Co (Japan) Ltd: Sweden Centre Bldg, 6-11-9, Roppongi, Minato-ku, Tokyo 106; tel. (3) 5413-2400; fax (3) 3415-2410; f. 1996; Pres. SUMIO SHIMOYAMA.

Sony Life Insurance Co Ltd: 1-1-1, Minami-Aoyama, Minato-ku, Tokyo 107; tel. (3) 3475-8811; fax (3) 3475-8809; Chair. MASAAKI MORITA; Pres. KEN IWAKI.

Sumitomo Life Insurance Co: 7-18-24, Tsukiji, Chuo-ku, Tokyo 104; tel. (3) 5550-1100; fax (3) 5550-1160; f. 1907; Chair. TOSHIOMI URAGAMI; Pres. KOICHI YOSHIDA.

Sumitomo Marine Yu-Yu Life Insurance Co Ltd: 2-27-1, Shinkawa, Chuo-ku, Tokyo 104; tel. (3) 5541-3111; fax (3) 5541-3976; f. 1996; Pres. ATSUSHI SASAKI.

Taisho Life Insurance Co Ltd: 1-9-1, Yurakucho, Chiyoda-ku, Tokyo 100; tel. (3) 3281-7651; fax (3) 5223-2299; f. 1913; Chair. TOSHIYUKI KOYAMA; Pres. GEN SHIMURA.

Taiyo Mutual Life Insurance Co: 2-11-2, Nihonbashi, Chuo-ku, Tokyo 103; tel. (3) 3272-6211; telex 2224935; fax (3) 3272-1460; Chair. KEIZO MACHIDORI; Pres. MASAHIRO YOSHIIKE.

Toho Mutual Life Insurance Co: 2-15-1, Shibuya, Shibuya-ku, Tokyo 150; tel. (3) 3499-1111; telex 2428069; fax (3) 5485-7259; f. 1898; Pres. RIDAI SAKOGAWA.

Tokio Marine Life Insurance Co Ltd: Tokyo Kaijyo New Bldg, 8th Floor, 1-2-1, Marunouchi, Chiyoda-ku, Tokyo 100; tel. (3) 5223-2111; fax (3) 5223-2125; f. 1996; Pres. SHIRO HORICHI.

Tokyo Mutual Life Insurance Co: 1-5-2, Uchisaiwai-cho, Chiyoda-ku, Tokyo 100; tel. (3) 3504-2211; fax (3) 3593-0785; f. 1895; Chair. MASAKAZU YOGAI; Pres. KENICHI NAKAMURA.

Yamato Mutual Life Insurance Co: 1-1-7, Uchisaiwai-cho, Chiyoda-ku, Tokyo 100; tel. (3) 3508-3111; fax (3) 3508-1466; f. 1911; Pres. KEIICHI TAKAYANAGI.

Yasuda Mutual Life Insurance Co: 1-9-1, Nishi-Shinjuku, Shinjuku-ku, Tokyo 169-92; tel. (3) 3342-7111; telex 2322887; fax (3) 3348-4495; f. 1880; Pres. YUJI OSHIMA.

Zurich Life Insurance Co Ltd: Shinanomachi Rengakan, 35, Shinanomachi, Shinjuku-ku, Tokyo 160; tel. (3) 5361-2700; fax (3) 5361-2701; f. 1996; Pres. KENICHI NOGAMI.

Principal Non-Life Companies

Allianz Fire and Marine Insurance Japan Ltd: Shibakoen Takahashi Bldg, 8th Floor, 1-8-12, Shibakoen, Minato-ku, Tokyo 105; tel. (3) 3437-7733; fax (3) 3437-7744; f. 1990; Chair. HEINZ DOLLBERG; Pres. CHRISTIAN LUTZ.

Allstate Automobile and Fire Insurance Co Ltd: Sunshine Sixty Bldg, 3-1-1, Higashi Ikebukuro, Toshima-ku, Tokyo 170; tel. (3) 3988-2572; fax (3) 3985-8692; f. 1982; Chair. EDWARD DIXON; Pres. TOMONORI KANAI.

The Asahi Fire and Marine Insurance Co Ltd: 2-6-2, Kaji-cho, Chiyoda-ku, Tokyo 101; tel. (3) 3254-2211; fax (3) 3254-2296; e-mail asahifmi@blue.ocn.ne.jp; f. 1951; Chair. KAZUO OCHI; Pres. MORIYA NOGUCHI.

The Chiyoda Fire and Marine Insurance Co Ltd: 1-28-1, Ebisu, Shibuya-ku, Tokyo 150; tel. (3) 5424-9288; telex 24975; fax (3) 5424-9382; f. 1897; Chair. MASAHARU TANAKA; Pres. KOJI FUKUDA.

CIGNA Accident and Fire Insurance Co Ltd: Akasaka Eight-One Bldg, 2-13-5, Nagata-cho, Chiyoda-ku, Tokyo 100; tel. (3) 5620-8730; fax (3) 5620-8880; f. 1996; Chair. P. C. O'CONNOR; Pres. JONATHAN E. NEWTON.

The Daido Fire and Marine Insurance Co Ltd: 1-12-1, Kumoji, Naha-shi, Okinawa 900; tel. (98) 867-1161; fax (98) 862-8362; f. 1971; Chair. YOSHIMASA UEZU; Pres. MUNEMASA URA.

The Daiichi Mutual Fire and Marine Insurance Co: 5-1, Nibancho, Chiyoda-ku, Tokyo 102; tel. (3) 3239-0011; telex 26554; fax (3) 5999-0375; f. 1949; Pres. FUJIO MATSUMURO.

The Dai-ichi Property and Casualty Insurance Co Ltd: 1-2-10, Hirakawa-cho, Chiyoda-ku, Tokyo 102; tel. (3) 5213-3124; fax (3) 5213-3306; f. 1996; Pres. HIROKAZU MURAKAMI.

The Dai-Tokyo Fire and Marine Insurance Co Ltd: 3-25-3, Yoyogi, Shibuya-ku, Tokyo 151; tel. (3) 5371-6122; telex 26968; fax (3) 5371-6248; f. 1918; Chair. ISAO KOSAKA; Pres. HAJIME OZAWA.

The Dowa Fire and Marine Insurance Co Ltd: St Luke's Tower, 8-1, Akashi-cho, Chuo-ku, Tokyo 104; tel. (3) 5550-0254; telex 22852; fax (3) 5550-0318; f. 1944; Pres. MASAO OKAZAKI.

The Fuji Fire and Marine Insurance Co Ltd: 1-18-11, Minamisenba, Chuo-ku, Osaka 542; tel. (6) 266-7007; telex 2522108; fax (6) 266-7102; f. 1918; Pres. YASUO ODA.

The Japan Earthquake Reinsurance Co Ltd: Fuji Plaza Bldg, 4th Floor, 8-1, Kobuna-cho, Nihonbashi, Chuo-ku, Tokyo 103; tel. (3) 3664-6107; fax (3) 3664-6169; e-mail jishin-a@db3.so-net.or.jp; f. 1966; Pres. TETSURO MURAKAMI.

JI Accident & Fire Insurance Co Ltd: AI Bldg, 20-5, Ichibancho, Chiyoda-ku, Tokyo 102; tel. (3) 3237-2045; fax (3) 3237-2250; f. 1989; Pres. TSUKASA IMURA.

The Koa Fire and Marine Insurance Co Ltd: 3-7-3, Kasumigaseki, Chiyoda-ku, Tokyo 100; tel. (3) 3593-7712; telex 22944; fax (3) 3593-7325; f. 1944; Chair. TETSUZO SASA; Pres. TERUHIKO TATSUUMA.

The Kyoei Mutual Fire and Marine Insurance Co: 1-18-6, Shimbashi, Minato-ku, Tokyo 105; tel. (3) 3504-2335; telex 22977; fax (3) 3508-7680; e-mail kyoei-sp@netforward.or.jp; f. 1942; Pres. HIDEJI SUZUKI.

The Meiji General Insurance Co Ltd: 2-11-1, Kanda Tsukasacho, Chiyoda-ku, Tokyo 101; tel. (3) 3257-3149; fax (3) 3257-3299; e-mail lika@pop.bekkoame.or.jp; f. 1996; Pres. SHIDO IWATA.

Mitsui Marine and Fire Insurance Co Ltd: 3-9, Kanda Surugadai, Chiyoda-ku, Tokyo 101-11; tel. (3) 3259-3111; telex 24670; fax (3) 3291-5467; f. 1918; Chair. TAKERU ISHIKAWA; Pres. TAKEO INOKUCHI.

Mitsui Seimei General Insurance Co Ltd: 2-1-1, Toranomon, Minato-ku, Tokyo 105; tel. (3) 3224-2830; fax (3) 3224-2857; f. 1996; Pres. KIYOSHI MATSUOKA.

The Nichido Fire and Marine Insurance Co Ltd: 5-3-16, Ginza, Chuo-ku, Tokyo 104; tel. (3) 3289-1066; telex 26920; fax (3) 3574-0646; f. 1914; Chair. IKUO EGASHIRA; Pres. TAKASHI AIHARA.

The Nippon Fire and Marine Insurance Co Ltd: 2-2-10, Nihonbashi, Chuo-ku, Tokyo 103; tel. (3) 3272-8111; telex 24214; fax (3) 5229-3385; f. 1892; Pres. KIYOSHI HIROSE.

The Nissan Fire and Marine Insurance Co Ltd: 2-9-5, Kita-Aoyama, Minato-ku, Tokyo 107; tel. (3) 3746-6516; telex 24983; fax (3) 3470-1308; e-mail webmas@nissan/ins.co.jp; f. 1911; Chair. FUMIYA KAWATE; Pres. RYUTARO SATO.

Nissay General Insurance Co Ltd: Shinjuku NS Bldg, 25th Floor, 2-4-1, Nishi-Shinjuku, Shinjuku-ku, Tokyo 163-08; tel. (3) 5325-8042; fax (3) 5325-8149; f. 1996; Pres. MASASHI MORIGUCHI.

The Nisshin Fire and Marine Insurance Co Ltd: KDD Ohtemachi Bldg, 13th–15th Floors, 1-8-1, Ohtemachi, Chiyoda-ku, Tokyo 100; tel. (3) 3231-8000; fax (3) 3231-8040; f. 1908; Chair. TOMOICHI NAWAFUNE; Pres. TAKAYUKI KUROTANI.

The Sumi-Sei General Insurance Co Ltd: Sumitomo Life Yotsuya Bldg, 8-2, Honshio-cho, Shinjuku-ku, Tokyo 160; tel. (3) 5360-6779; fax (3) 5360-6991; f. 1996; Pres. HIDEO NISHIMOTO.

The Sumitomo Marine and Fire Insurance Co Ltd: 2-27-2, Shinkawa, Chuo-ku, Tokyo 104; tel. (3) 3297-6663; telex 2223051; fax (3) 3297-6882; f. 1944; Pres. TAKASHI ONODA.

The Taisei Fire and Marine Insurance Co Ltd: 4-2-1, Kudankita, Chiyoda-ku, Tokyo 102; tel. (3) 3234-3111; telex 28351; fax (3) 3234-4073; e-mail saiho@taiseikasai.co.jp; f. 1950; Chair. ATSUSHI KOMATSU; Pres. ICHIRO OZAWA.

Taiyo Fire and Marine Insurance Co Ltd: 7-7, Niban-cho, Chiyoda-ku, Tokyo 102; tel. (3) 5226-3117; telex 2225379; fax (3) 5226-3133; f. 1951; Chair. TOSHIO TAKAMI; Pres. TSUNAIE KANIE.

The Toa Fire and Marine Reinsurance Co Ltd: 3-6, Kanda Surugadai, Chiyoda-ku, Tokyo 101; tel. (3) 3253-3171; telex 24384; fax (3) 3253-1208; f. 1940; Pres. HIROSHI OHASHI.

The Tokio Marine and Fire Insurance Co Ltd (Tokio Kaijo): 1-2-1, Marunouchi, Chiyoda-ku, Tokyo 100-50; tel. (3) 3285-1900; telex 3722170; fax (3) 5223-3040; f. 1879; Chair. SHUNJI KONO; Pres. KOUKEI HIGUCHI.

The Toyo Fire and Marine Insurance Co Ltd: 1-9-15, Nihonbashi-Honcho, Chuo-ku, Tokyo 103; tel. (3) 3245-1430; telex 2226334; fax (3) 3271-2670; f. 1950; Chair. TSUNEKAZU SAKANO; Pres. MASAMICHI KAWASAKI.

UNUM Japan Accident Insurance Co Ltd: Sanban-cho UF Bldg, 2nd Floor, 6-3, Sanban-cho, Chiyoda-ku, Tokyo 102; tel. (3) 5276-5602; fax (3) 5276-5609; f. 1994; Pres. KEVIN PAUL MCCARTHY.

The Yasuda Fire and Marine Insurance Co Ltd: 1-26-1, Nishi-Shinjuku, Shinjuku-ku, Tokyo 160; tel. (3) 3349-3111; telex 02322790; fax (3) 5381-7406; f. 1887; Chair. YASUO GOTO; Pres. KOICHI ARIYOSHI.

The Yasuda General Insurance Co Ltd: Shinjuku MAYNDS Tower, 29th Floor, 2-1-1, Yoyogi, Shibuya-ku, Tokyo 151; tel. (3) 5352-8129; fax (3) 5352-8213; f. 1996; Pres. SHIGEO FUJINO.

The Post Office also operates life insurance and annuity plans.

Insurance Associations

The Life Insurance Association of Japan (Seimei Hoken Kyokai): New Kokusai Bldg, 3-4-1, Marunouchi, Chiyoda-ku, Tokyo 100; tel. (3) 3286-2652; fax (3) 3286-2630; f. 1908; 44 mem. cos; Chair. YUZURU FUJITA; Man. Dir SHIGERU SUWA.

The Marine and Fire Insurance Association of Japan Inc (Nihon Songai Hoken Kyokai): Non-Life Insurance Bldg, 2-9, Kanda Awaji-cho, Chiyoda-ku, Tokyo 101; tel. (3) 3255-1437; fax (3) 3255-1234; e-mail kokusai@sonpo.or.jp; f. 1946; 33 mems; Chair. TAKASHI ONODA; Exec. Dir NOBORU ARAKI.

Property and Casualty Insurance Rating Organization of Japan: Banzai Bldg, 2-31-19, Shiba, Minato-ku, Tokyo 105; tel. (3) 5441-1229; fax (3) 5441-1274; e-mail s-sohki@da2.so-net.or.jp; f. 1948; 58 mems (incl. 25 foreign mems); Pres. TAKASHI MUKAIBO; Exec. Dir. TAKEYOSHI KATSURADA.

Trade and Industry

CHAMBERS OF COMMERCE AND INDUSTRY

The Japan Chamber of Commerce and Industry (Nippon Shoko Kaigi-sho): 3-2-2, Marunouchi, Chiyoda-ku, Tokyo 100; tel. (3) 3283-7851; fax (3) 3216-6497; e-mail info@jcci.or.jp; f. 1922; the cen. org. of all chambers of commerce and industry in Japan; mems 515 local chambers of commerce and industry; Chair. KOSAKU INABA; Pres. SHOICHI TANIMURA.

Principal chambers include:

Kobe Chamber of Commerce and Industry: 6-1, Minatojima-nakamachi, Chuo-ku, Kobe 650; tel. (78) 303-5806; fax (78) 303-2312; e-mail s-araki@mbox.kcci.hyogo-iic.ne.jp; f. 1878; 14,052 mems; Chair. FUYUHIKO MAKI; Pres. TETSUYA MIKI.

Kyoto Chamber of Commerce and Industry: 240, Shoshoi-cho, Ebisugawa-agaru, Karasumadori, Nakakyo-ku, Kyoto 604; tel. (75) 212-6450; fax (75) 251-0743; e-mail kyotocci@mbox.kyoto-inet.or.ip; f. 1882; 13,008 mems; Chair. KAZUO INAMORI; Pres. OSAMU KOBORI.

Nagoya Chamber of Commerce and Industry: 2-10-19, Sakae, Naka-ku, Nagoya, Aichi 460; tel. (52) 223-5611; fax (52) 231-6768; f. 1881; 20,622 mems; Chair. SEITARO TANIGUCHI; Pres. YOSHIKI KOBAYASHI.

Naha Chamber of Commerce and Industry: 2-2-10, Kume Naha, Okinawa; tel. (98) 868-3758; fax (98) 866-9834; f. 1927; 4,874 mems; Chair. AKIRA SAKIMA; Pres. KOSEI YONEMURA.

Osaka Chamber of Commerce and Industry: 2-8, Hommachi-bashi, Chuo-ku, Osaka 540; tel. (6) 944-6401; fax (6) 944-6248; e-mail webmaster@osaka-cci.go.jp; f. 1878; 55,392 mems; Chair. MASAFUMI OHNISHI; Pres. TAKAO OHNO.

Tokyo Chamber of Commerce and Industry: 3-2-2, Marunouchi, Chiyoda-ku, Tokyo 100; tel. (3) 3283-7762; fax (3) 3216-6497; e-mail webmaster@tokyo-cci.or.jp; f. 1878; 71,723 mems; Chair. KOSAKU INABA; Pres. SHOICHI TANIMURA.

Yokohama Chamber of Commerce and Industry: 2, Yamashita-cho, Naka-ku, Yokohama 231; tel. (45) 671-7406; fax (45) 671-7410; f. 1880; 17,673 mems; Chair. KOJIRO TSUSHIMA; Pres. SHIRO SAITOH.

INDUSTRIAL AND TRADE ASSOCATIONS

General

The Association for the Promotion of International Trade, Japan (JAPIT): 1-26-5, Toranomon, Minato-ku, Tokyo; tel. (3) 3506-8261; fax (3) 3506-8260; f. 1954 to promote trade with the People's Repub. of China; 700 mems; Chair. YOSHIO NAKATA; Pres. YOSHIO SAKURAUCHI.

Industry Club of Japan: 1-4-6, Marunouchi, Chiyoda-ku, Tokyo; tel. (3) 3281-1711; f. 1917 to develop closer relations between industrialists at home and abroad and promote expansion of Japanese business activities; c. 1,600 mems; Pres. GAISHI HIRAIWA; Exec. Dir KOUICHIROU SHINNO.

Japan Association of Corporate Executives (Keizai Doyukai): Nippon Kogyo Club Bldg, 1-4-6, Marunouchi, Chiyoda-ku, Tokyo 100; tel. (3) 3211-1271; fax (3) 3213-2946; internet http://www.doyukai.or.jp; f. 1946; mems: corporate executives concerned with national and international economic and social policies; Chair. JIRO USHIO.

Japan Commercial Arbitration Association: Taishoseimei Hibiya Bldg, 1-9-1, Yurakucho, Chiyoda-ku, Tokyo 100; tel. (3) 3287-3061; fax (3) 3287-3064; f. 1950; 1,012 mems; provides facilities for mediation, conciliation and arbitration in international trade disputes; Pres. KOSAKU INABA.

Japan External Trade Organization (JETRO): 2-2-5, Toranomon, Minato-ku, Tokyo 105; tel. (3) 3582-5511; telex 22224378; fax (3) 3587-0219; f. 1958; information for international trade, investment, import promotion, exhibitions of foreign products; Chair. TORU TOYOSHIMA; Pres. NOBORU HATAKEYAMA.

Japan Federation of Economic Organizations (KEIDANREN): 1-9-4, Ohtemachi, Chiyoda-ku, Tokyo 100; tel. (3) 3279-1411; fax (3) 5255-6253; f. 1946; private non-profit asscn researching domestic and international economic problems and providing policy recommendations; mems: 123 industrial orgs, 1,008 corpns (1997); Chair. SHOICHIRO TOYODA; Pres. KOZO UCHIDA.

Japan Federation of Smaller Enterprise Organizations (JFSEO): 2-8-4, Nihonbashi, Kayaba-cho, Chuo-ku, Tokyo 103; tel. (3) 3668-2481; f. 1948; 18 mems and c. 1,000 co-operative socs; Pres. MASATAKA TOYODA; Chair. of Int. Affairs SEIICHI ONO.

Japan General Merchandise Exporters' Association: 2-4-1, Hamamatsu-cho, Minato-ku, Tokyo; tel. (3) 3435-3471; fax (3) 3434-6739; f. 1953; 40 mems; Pres. TADAYOSHI NAKAZAWA.

Japan Productivity Center for Socio-Economic Development (JPC-SED) (Shakai Keizai Seisansei Honbu): 3-1-1, Shibuya, Shibuya-ku, Tokyo 150; tel. (3) 3409-1111; fax (3) 3409-1986; f. 1994 following merger between Japan Productivity Center and Social Economic Congress of Japan; 10,000 mems; concerned with management problems and research into productivity; Chair. MASAO KAMEI; Pres. JINNOSUKE MIYAI.

Nihon Boeki-Kai (Japan Foreign Trade Council, Inc): World Trade Center Bldg, 6th Floor, 2-4-1, Hamamatsu-cho, Minato-ku, Tokyo 105; tel. (3) 3435-5952; fax (3) 3435-5969; e-mail jftc001@infotokyo.or.jp; f. 1947; 251 mems; Chair. MINORU MUROFUSHI; Exec. Man. Dir MIKIO KOJIMA; Man. Dir KAZUHIKO USAMI.

Chemicals

Federation of Pharmaceutical Manufacturers' Associations of Japan: Tokyo Yakugyo Bldg, 2-1-5, Nihonbashi Honcho, Chuo-ku, Tokyo 103; tel. (3) 3270-0581; fax (3) 3241-2090; Pres. SHIGEO MORIOKA.

Japan Chemical Industry Association: Tokyo Club Bldg, 3-2-6, Kasumigaseki, Chiyoda-ku, Tokyo 100; tel. (3) 3580-0751; fax (3) 3580-0764; f. 1948; 266 mems; Pres. HIDEO MORI.

Japan Cosmetic Industry Association: Hatsumei Bldg, 2-9-14, Toranomon, Minato-ku, Tokyo 105; tel. (3) 3502-0576; fax (3) 3502-0829; f. 1959; 623 mem. cos; Pres. YOSHIHARU FUKUHARA; Man. Dir TORU ARIMOTO.

Japan Gas Association: 1-15-12, Toranomon, Minato-ku, Tokyo 105-0001; tel. (3) 3502-0116; fax (3) 3502-3676; f. 1947; Chair. HIROSHI WATANABE; Vice-Chair. and Sr Man. Dir KOSHIRO GODA.

Japan Medical Products International Trade Association (JAMPITA): 4-7-1, Nihonbashi-Honcho, Chuo-ku, Tokyo 103; tel. (3) 3241-2106; fax (3) 3241-2109; f. 1953; 155 mem. firms; Pres. ICHIRO CHIBATA; Man. Dir KUNIICHIRO OHNO; Dir-Gen. TOKUJI KASAMATSU.

Japan Perfumery and Flavouring Association: Nitta Bldg, 8-2-1, Ginza, Chuo-ku, Tokyo 104; tel. and fax (3) 3571-3855; f. 1947; Chair. YOSHIJIRO SODA.

Photo-Sensitized Materials Manufacturers' Association: JCII Bldg, 25, Ichiban-cho, Chiyoda-ku, Tokyo 102; tel. (3) 5276-3561; fax (3) 5276-3563; f. 1948; Pres. MASAYUKI MUNEYUKI.

Fishing and Pearl Cultivation

Japan Fisheries Association (Dai-nippon Suisan Kai): Sankaido Bldg, 1-9-13, Akasaka, Minato-ku, Tokyo 107; tel. (3) 3585-6683; fax (3) 3582-2337; Pres. HIROYA SANO.

Japan Pearl Export and Processing Co-operative Association: 3-7, Kyobashi, Chuo-ko, Tokyo; f. 1951; 130 mems.

Japan Pearl Exporters' Association: 122, Higashi-machi, Chuo-ku, Kobe; tel. (78) 331-4031; fax (78) 331-4345; f. 1954; 130 mems; Pres. IZUMI YAMAMOTO.

Paper and Printing

Japan Federation of Printing Industries: 1-16-8, Shintomi, Chuo-ku, Tokyo 104; tel. (3) 3553-6051; fax (3) 3553-6079; Pres. HIROMICHI FUJITA.

Japan Paper Association: Kami Parupu Bldg, 3-9-11, Ginza, Chuo-ku, Tokyo 104; tel. (3) 3248-4801; fax (3) 3248-4826; f. 1946; 55 mems; Chair. MASAHIKO OKUNI; Pres. K. SAKAI.

Japan Paper Exporters' Association: Kami Parupu Bldg, 3-9-11, Ginza, Chuo-ku, Tokyo 104; tel. (3) 3248-4831; fax (3) 3248-4834; f. 1952; 55 mems; Chair. ATSUSI KURITA.

Japan Paper Importers' Association: Kami Parupu Bldg, 3-9-11, Ginza, Chuo-ku, Tokyo 104; tel. (3) 3248-4832; fax (3) 3248-4834; f. 1981; 38 mems; Chair. CHOJI KURAMOCHI.

Japan Paper Products Manufacturers' Association: 4-2-6, Kotobuki, Taito-ku, Tokyo; tel. (3) 3543-2411; f. 1949; Exec. Dir KIYOSHI SATOH.

Mining and Petroleum

Asbestos Cement Products Association: Takahashi Bldg, 7-10-8, Ginza, Chuo-ku, Tokyo; tel. (3) 3571-1359; f. 1937; Chair. KOSHIRO SHIMIZU.

Japan Cement Association: Hattori Bldg, 1-10-3, Kyobashi, Chuo-ku, Tokyo 104; tel. (3) 3561-8631; fax (3) 3567-8570; f. 1948; 20 mem. cos; Chair. MICHIO KIMURA; Exec. Man. Dir HIROFUMI YAMASHITA.

Japan Coal Association: Hibiya Park Bldg, 1-8-1, Yuraku-cho, Chiyoda-ku, Tokyo 100; tel. (3) 3271-3481; fax (3) 3214-0585; Chair. TADASHI HARADA.

Japan Mining Industry Association: Shin-hibiya Bldg, 1-3-6, Uchisaiwai-cho, Chiyoda-ku, Tokyo 100; tel. (3) 3502-7451; fax (3) 3591-9841; f. 1948; 60 mem. cos; Pres. A. SHINOZAKI; Dir-Gen. H. HIYAMA.

Japan Petroleum Development Association: Keidanren Bldg, 1-9-4, Ohtemachi, Chiyoda-ku, Tokyo 100; tel. (3) 3279-5841; telex 29400; fax (3) 3279-5844; f. 1961; Chair. TAMOTSU SHOYA.

Metals

Japan Aluminium Federation: Nihonbashi Asahiseimei Bldg, 2-1-3, Nihonbashi, Chuo-ku, Tokyo 103; tel. (3) 3274-4551; fax (3) 3274-3179; Pres. JUNJI FUKUCHI.

Japan Brass Makers' Association: 1-12-22, Tsukiji, Chuo-ku, Tokyo 104; tel. (3) 3542-6551; fax (3) 3542-6556; f. 1948; 54 mems; Pres. O. TAKATA; Man. Dir T. KUGA.

Japan Iron and Steel Exporters' Association: Tekko Kaikan Bldg, 3-2-10, Nihonbashi Kayaba-cho, Chuo-ku, Tokyo 103; tel. (3) 3669-4818; fax (3) 3661-0798; f. 1953; mems 21 mfrs, 29 dealers; Chair. HIROSHI SAITO.

The Japan Iron and Steel Federation: Keidanren Bldg, 1-9-4, Ohtemachi, Chiyoda-ku, Tokyo 100; tel. (3) 3279-3611; fax (3) 3245-0144; f. 1948; Chair. TAKASHI IMAI.

Japan Light Metal Association: Nihonbashi Asahiseimei Bldg, 2-1-3, Nihonbashi, Chuo-ku, Tokyo 103; tel. (3) 3273-3041; fax (3) 3213-2918; f. 1947; 169 mems; Chair. JUNJI FUKUCHI.

Japan Stainless Steel Association: Tekko Bldg, 3-2-10, Nihonbashi Kayaba-cho, Chuo-ku, Tokyo 103; tel. (3) 3669-4431; Pres. SHINOBU TOSAKI; Exec. Dir KENICHIRO AOKI.

The Kozai Club: Tekko Kaikan Bldg, 3-2-10, Nihonbashi Kayaba-cho, Chuo-ku, Tokyo 103; tel. (3) 3669-4815; fax (3) 3667-0245; f. 1947; mems 43 mfrs, 75 dealers; Chair. HIROSHI SAITO.

Steel Castings and Forgings Association of Japan (JSCFA): Uchikanda DNK Bldg, 2-15-2, Uchikanda, Chiyoda-ku, Tokyo 101-0047; tel. (3) 3255-3961; fax (3) 3255-3965; f. 1972; mems 56 cos, 63 plants; Exec. Dir SADAO HARA.

Machinery and Precision Equipment

Electronic Industries Association of Japan: 3-2-2, Marunouchi, Chiyoda-ku, Tokyo 100-0005; tel. (3) 3213-5861; fax (3) 3213-5863; e-mail pao@eiaj.or.jp; f. 1948; 570 mems; Chair. FUMIO SATO.

Japan Camera Industry Association: JCII Bldg, 25, Ichibancho, Chiyoda-ku, Tokyo 102; tel. (3) 5276-3891; fax (3) 5276-3893; f. 1954; Pres. SHIGEO ONO.

Japan Clock and Watch Association: Kudan TS Bldg, 1-9-16, Kudan-kita, Chiyoda-ku, Tokyo 102; tel. (3) 5276-3411; fax (3) 5276-3414; Pres. MICHIO NAKAJIMA.

Japan Electric Association: 1-7-1, Yuraku-cho, Chiyoda-ku, Tokyo 100; tel. (3) 3216-0551; fax (3) 3214-6005; f. 1921; 4,385 mems; Pres. YOSHIO MORIMOTO.

Japan Electric Measuring Instruments Manufacturers' Association: 1-9-10, Toranomon, Minato-ku, Tokyo 105; tel. (3) 3502-0601; fax (3) 3502-0600.

Japan Electrical Manufacturers' Association: 2-4-15, Nagata-cho, Chiyoda-ku, Tokyo 100; tel. (3) 3581-4841; telex 22619; fax (3) 3593-3198; f. 1948; 245 mems; Chair. KATSUSHIGE MITA.

Japan Energy Association: Shinbashi S.Y. Bldg, 1-14-2, Nishi-Shinbashi, Tokyo 105; tel. (3) 3501-3988; fax (3) 3501-2428; f. 1950; 111 mems; Pres. SHIGE-ETSU MIYAHARA; Dir FUJIO SAKAGAMI.

Japan Machine Tool Builders' Association: Kikai Shinko Bldg, 3-5-8, Shiba Koen, Minato-ku, Tokyo 105; tel. (3) 3434-3961; telex 22943; fax (3) 3434-3763; f. 1951; 112 mems; Chair. GORO TEJIMA; Exec. Dir S. ABE.

Japan Machinery Center for Trade and Investment (JMC): Kikai Shinko Bldg, 3-5-8, Shiba Koen, Minato-ku, Tokyo 105; tel. (3) 3431-9507; fax (3) 3436-6455; Pres. ISAO YONEKURA.

The Japan Machinery Federation: Kikai Shinko Bldg, 3-5-8, Shiba Koen, Minato-ku, Tokyo 105; tel. (3) 3434-5381; fax (3) 3434-2666; f. 1952; Pres. SHOICHI SADA; Exec. Vice-Pres. SHINICHI NAKANISHI.

Japan Machinery Importers' Association: Koyo Bldg, 7th Floor, 1-2-11, Toranomon, Minato-ku, Tokyo; tel. (3) 3503-9736; fax (3) 3503-9779; f. 1957; 113 mems; Pres. ISAO YONEKURA.

Japan Microscope Manufacturers' Association: c/o Olympus Optical Co Ltd, 2-43-2, Hatagaya, Shibuya-ku, Tokyo 151; tel. (3) 3377-2139; fax (3) 3377-2139; f. 1954; 27 mems; Chair. T. SHIMOYAMA.

Japan Motion Picture Equipment Industrial Association: Kikai Shinko Bldg, 3-5-8, Shiba Koen, Minato-ku, Tokyo 105; tel. (3) 3434-3911; fax (3) 3434-3912; Pres. MASAO SHIKATA; Gen. Sec. TERUHIRO KATO.

Japan Optical Industry Association: Kikai Shinko Bldg, 3-5-8, Shiba Koen, Minato-ku, Tokyo 105; tel. (3) 3431-7073; f. 1946; 200 mems; Chair. KOJI SHO; Exec. Dir M. SUZUKI.

The Japan Society of Industrial Machinery Manufacturers: Kikai Shinko Bldg, 3-5-8, Shiba Koen, Minato-ku, Tokyo 105; tel. (3) 3434-6821; fax (3) 3434-4767; f. 1948; 237 mems; Exec. Man. Dir KOJI FUJISAKI; Pres. SHIGEKAZU MINO.

Japan Textile Machinery Association: Kikai Shinko Bldg, Room 310, 3-5-8, Shiba Koen, Minato-ku, Tokyo 105; tel. (3) 3434-3821; fax (3) 3434-3043; f. 1951; Pres. YOSHITOSHI TOYODA.

Textiles

Central Raw Silk Association of Japan: 1-9-4, Yuraku-cho, Chiyoda-ku, Tokyo; tel. (3) 3214-5777; fax (3) 3214-5778.

Japan Chemical Fibres Association: Seni Bldg, 3-1-11, Nihonbashi-Honcho, Chuo-ku, Tokyo 103; tel. (3) 3241-2311; fax (3) 3246-0823; f. 1948; 45 mems, 15 assoc. mems; Pres. EIICHI TAGUCHI; Dir-Gen. KAZUHIKO MORIYA.

Japan Cotton and Staple Fibre Weavers' Association: 1-8-7, Nishi-Azabu, Minato-ku, Tokyo; tel. (3) 3403-9671.

Japan Silk Spinners' Association: f. 1948; 95 mem. firms; Chair. ICHIJI OHTANI.

Japan Spinners' Association: 2-5-8, Bingomachi, Chuo-ku, Osaka 541; tel. (6) 231-8431; telex 5222230; fax (6) 229-1590; f. 1948; Exec. Dir KIYONORI MAYUMI.

Transport Machinery

Japan Association of Rolling Stock Industries: Daiichi Tekko Bldg, 1-8-2, Marunouchi, Chiyoda-ku, Tokyo; tel. (3) 3201-1911.

Japan Auto Parts Industries Association: 1-16-15, Takanawa, Minato-ku, Tokyo 108; tel. (3) 3445-4211; fax (3) 3447-5372; f. 1948; 530 mem. firms; Chair. SHOHEI HAMADA; Exec. Dir K. SHIBASAKI.

Japan Automobile Manufacturers Association, Inc: Ohtemachi Bldg, 1-6-1, Ohtemachi, Chiyoda-ku, Tokyo 100; tel. (3) 3216-5771; fax (3) 3287-2072; f. 1967; 13 mem. firms; Chair. YOSHIFUMI TSUJI; Exec. Man. Dir TAKAO TOMINAGA.

Japan Bicycle Manufacturers' Association: 1-9-3, Akasaka, Minato-ku, Tokyo 107; tel. (3) 3583-3123; fax (3) 3589-3125; f. 1955.

Japan Ship Exporters' Association: Senpaku-Shinko Bldg, 1-15-16, Toranomon, Minato-ku, Tokyo 105; tel. (3) 3502-2094; fax (3) 3508-2058; 41 mems; Sr Man. Dir YUICHI WATANABE.

Japanese Marine Equipment Association: Bansui Bldg, 1-5-16, Toranomon, Minato-ku, Tokyo 105-0001; tel. (3) 3502-2041; fax (3) 3591-2206; e-mail jsmea@po.infosphere.or.jp; f. 1956; 240 mems; Pres. TADAO YAMAOKA.

Japanese Shipowners' Association: Kaiun Bldg, 2-6-4, Hirakawa-cho, Chiyoda-ku, Tokyo 102; tel. (3) 3264-7171; telex 22148; fax (3) 3262-4760; Pres. SUSUMU TENPORIN.

Shipbuilders' Association of Japan: Senpaku Shinko Bldg, 1-15-16, Toranomon, Minato-ku, Tokyo 105; tel. (3) 3502-2010; telex 27056; fax (3) 3502-2816; f. 1947; 18 mems; Chair. YOSHIHIRO FUJII; Exec. Man. Dir TAKUJI SHINDO.

Society of Japanese Aerospace Companies Inc (SJAC): Tokyu-Tameike Bldg, 2nd Floor, 1-1-14, Akasaka, Minato-ku, Tokyo 107; tel. (3) 3585-0511; fax (3) 3585-0541; f. 1952; reorg. 1974; 127 mems, 43 assoc. mems; Chair. HIROSHI OBA; Pres. TOSHIHIKO NAKAMURA.

Miscellaneous

Communications Industry Association of Japan (CIA-J): Sankei Bldg Annex, 1-7-2, Ohtemachi, Chiyoda-ku, Tokyo 100; tel. (3) 3231-3005; fax (3) 3231-3110; f. 1948; non-profit org. of telecommunications equipment mfrs; 255 mems; Chair. TSUTOMU KANAI; Pres. SETSUJI TAKAHASHI.

Japan Canners' Association: Marunouchi Bldg, 2-4-1, Marunouchi, Chiyoda-ku, Tokyo 100; tel. (3) 3213-4751; fax (3) 3211-1430; Pres. YOSHINOBU KANIE.

Japan Fur Association: Tokyo; tel. (3) 3541-6987; f. 1950; Chair. AKIRA SAITOH; Sec. NORIHIDE SATOH.

Japan Hardwood Exporters' Association: Matsuda Bldg, 1-9-1, Ironai, Otaru, Hokkaido 047; tel. (134) 23-8411; fax (134) 22-7150; 7 mems.

Japan Lumber Importers' Association: Yushi Kogyo Bldg, 3-13-11, Nihonbashi, Chuo-ku, Tokyo 103; tel. (3) 3271-0926; fax (3) 3271-0928; f. 1950; 130 mems; Pres. Shoichi Tanaka.

Japan Plastics Industry Federation: Tokyo Club Bldg, 3-2-6, Kasumigaseki, Chiyoda-ku, Tokyo 100; tel. (3) 3580-0771; fax (3) 3580-0775; Chair. Yuichiro Kasama.

Japan Plywood Manufacturers' Association: Meisan Bldg, 1-18-17, Nishi-Shimbashi, Minato-ku, Tokyo 105; tel. (3) 3591-9246; fax (3) 3591-9240; f. 1965; 92 mems; Pres. Hiroshi Inoue.

Japan Pottery Manufacturers' Federation: Toto Bldg, 1-1-28, Toranomon, Minato-ku, Tokyo; tel. (3) 3503-6761.

The Japan Rubber Manufacturers Association: Tobu Bldg, 1-5-26, Moto Akasaka, Minato-ku, Tokyo 107-0051; tel. (3) 3408-7101; fax (3) 3408-7106; f. 1950; 134 mems; Pres. Shizuo Katsurada.

Japan Spirits and Liquors Makers' Association: Koura Daiichi Bldg, 7th Floor, 1-1-6, Nihonbashi-Kayaba-cho, Chuo-ku, Tokyo 103; tel. (3) 3668-4621.

Japan Sugar Import and Export Council: Ginza Gas-Hall, 7-9-15, Ginza, Chuo-ku, Tokyo; tel. (3) 3571-2362; fax (3) 3571-2363; 16 mems.

Japan Sugar Refiners' Association: 5-7, Sanban-cho, Chiyoda-ku, Tokyo 102; tel. (3) 3288-1151; fax (3) 3288-3399; f. 1949; 17 mems; Sr Man. Dir Katsuyuki Suzuki.

Japan Tea Exporters' Association: 17, Kitaban-cho, Shizuoka, Shizuoka Prefecture 420-0005; tel. (54) 271-3428; fax (54) 271-2177; 26 mems.

Japan Toy Association: 4-22-4, Higashi-Komagata, Sumida-ku, Tokyo 130; tel. (3) 3829-2513; fax (3) 3829-2549; Chair. Makoto Yamashina.

Motion Picture Producers' Association of Japan, Inc: Tokyu Ginza Bldg, 2-15-2, Ginza, Chuo-ku, Tokyo 104; tel. (3) 3547-1800; fax (3) 3547-0909; Pres. Isao Matsuoka.

EMPLOYERS' ORGANIZATION

Japan Federation of Employers' Associations (Nikkeiren) (Nihon Keieisha Dantai Renmei): 1-4-6, Marunouchi, Chiyoda-ku, Tokyo 100; tel. (3) 3272-7700; fax (3) 3272-7701; e-mail intldiv@nikkeiren.or.jp; f. 1948; 105 mem. asscns; Chair. Jiro Nemoto; Dir-Gen. Michio Fukuoka.

UTILITIES

Electricity

Chibu Electric Power Co Inc: 1, Higashi-Shincho, Higashi-ku, Nagoya 461-8680; tel. (52) 951-8211; fax (52) 962-4624; Chair. Kohei Abe; Pres. Hiroji Ota.

Chugoku Electric Power Co Inc: 4-33, Komachi, Naka-ku, Hiroshima 730-91; tel. (82) 241-0211; fax (82) 242-8437; Chair. Koki Tada; Pres. Shitomi Takasu.

Kansai Electric Power Co Inc: 3-3-22, Nakanoshima, Kita-ku, Osaka 530-70; tel. (6) 441-8821; fax (6) 441-8598; Chair. Isamu Miyazaki; Pres. Yoshihisa Akiyama.

Kyushu Electric Power Co Inc: 2-1-82, Watanabe-dori, Chuo-ku, Fukuoka 810-91; tel. (92) 761-3031; Chair. Michisada Kamata.

Shikoku Electric Power Co Inc: 2-5, Marunouchi, Takamatsu 760-91; tel. (878) 21-5061; fax (878) 26-1250; Chair. Hiroshi Yamamoto; Pres. Kozo Kondo.

Tohoku Electric Power Co Inc: 3-7-1, Ichiban-cho, Aoba-ku, Sendai 980; tel. (22) 225-2111; fax (22) 222-2881; Chair. Teruyuki Akema; Pres. Toshiaki Yashima.

Tokyo Electric Power Co Inc: 1-1-3, Uchisaiwai-cho, Chiyoda-ku, Tokyo 100; tel. (3) 3501-8111; fax (3) 3592-1795; Chair. Shoh Nasu; Pres. Hiroshi Araki.

Gas

Tokyo Gas Co Inc: 1-5-20, Kaigan, Minato-ku, Tokyo 105; tel. (3) 3433-2111; fax (3) 5472-5385; Chair. Hiroshi Watanabe; Pres. Kunio Anzai.

CO-OPERATIVE ORGANIZATION

Nikkenkyo (Council of Japan Construction Industry Employees' Unions): Moriyama Bldg, 1-31-16, Takadanobaba, Shinjuku-ku, Tokyo 169; tel. (3) 5285-3870; fax (3) 5285-3879; Pres. Yoshiaki Okada.

TRADE UNIONS

A feature of Japan's trade union movement is that the unions are usually based on single enterprises, embracing workers of different occupations in that enterprise. In June 1994 there were 32,581 unions; union membership stood at 12.5m. workers in 1996. In November 1989 the two largest confederations, SOHYO and RENGO, merged to form the Japan Trade Union Confederation (JTUC—RENGO).

Japanese Trade Union Confederation (JTUC–RENGO): 3-2-11, Kanda Surugadai, Chiyoda-ku, Tokyo 101; tel. (3) 5295-0526; fax (3) 5295-0548; f. 1989; 7.9m. mems; Pres. Junnosuke Ashida.

Principal Affiliated Unions

Ceramics Rengo (All-Japan Federation of Ceramics Industry Workers): 3-11, Heigocho, Mizuho-ku, Nagoya-shi, Aichi 467; tel. (52) 882-4562; fax (52) 882-9960; 30,083 mems; Pres. Tsuneyoshi Hayakawa.

Chain Rokyo (Chain-store Labour Unions' Council): 3rd Floor, 2-29-8, Higashi-ikebukuro, Toshima-ku, Tokyo 170; tel. (3) 5951-1031; fax (3) 5951-1051; 40,015 mems; Pres. Toshifumi Hirano.

CSG Rengo (Japanese Federation of Chemical, Service and General Workers' Unions): Yuai Bldg, 8th Floor, 2-20-12, Shiba, Minato-ku, Tokyo 105; tel. (3) 3453-3801; fax (3) 3454-2236; f. 1951; 228,137 mems; Pres. Daisaku Kouchiyama.

Denki Rengo (Japanese Electrical, Electronic & Information Union): Denkirengo Bldg, 1-10-3, Mita, Minato-ku, Tokyo 108; tel. (3) 3455-6911; fax (3) 3452-5406; f. 1953; 824,000 mems; Pres. Katsutoshi Suzuki.

Denryoku Soren (Federation of Electric Power Related Industry Workers' Unions of Japan): Shiba 2nd AMEREX Bldg, 4th Floor, 4-5-10, Shiba, Minato-ku, Tokyo 108; tel. (3) 3454-0231; fax (3) 3798-1470; 260,000 mems; Pres. Jiro Terada.

Dokiro (Hokkaido Seasonal Workers' Union): Hokuro Bldg, Kita 4, Nishi 12, Chuo-ku, Sapporo, Hokkaido 060; tel. (11) 261-5775; fax (11) 272-2255; 19,063 mems; Pres. Yoshizo Odawara.

Goka Roren (Japanese Federation of Synthetic Chemistry Workers' Unions): Senbai Bldg, 5-26-30, Shiba, Minato-ku, Tokyo 108; tel. (3) 3452-5591; fax (3) 3454-7464; 91,242 mems; Pres. Osamu Suzuki.

Gomu Rengo (Japanese Rubber Workers' Union Confederation): 2-3-3, Mejiro, Toshima-ku, Tokyo 171; tel. (3) 3984-3343; fax (3) 3984-5862; 60,070 mems; Pres. Yasuo Furukawa.

Hitetsu Rengo (Japanese Metal Mine Workers' Union): Gotanda Metalion Bldg, 5-21-15, Higashi-gotanda, Shinagawa-ku, Tokyo 141; tel. (3) 5420-1881; fax (3) 5420-1880; 23,500 mems; Pres. Shouzou Himeno.

Insatsu Roren (Federation of Printing Information Media Workers' Unions): Yuai-kaikan, 7th Floor, 2-20-12, Shiba, Minato-ku, Tokyo 105; tel. (3) 5442-0191; fax (3) 5442-0219; 22,303 mems; Pres. Isamu Kato.

JA Rengo (All-Japan Agriculture Co-operative Staff Members' Union): 964-1, Toyotomicho-mikage, Himeji-shi, Hyogo 679-21; tel. and fax (792) 64-3618; 2,772 mems; Pres. Yutaka Okada.

Jichi Roren (National Federation of Prefectural and Municipal Workers' Unions): 1-15-22, Oji-honcho, Kita-ku, Tokyo 114; tel. and fax (3) 3907-1584; 5,728 mems; Pres. Nobuo Ueno.

Jichiro (All-Japan Prefectural and Municipal Workers' Union): Jichiro Bldg, 1, Rokubancho, Chiyoda-ku, Tokyo 102; tel. (3) 3263-0263; fax (3) 5210-7422; f. 1951; 1,020,790 mems; Pres. Morishige Goto.

Jidosha Soren (Confederation of Japan Automobile Workers' Unions): U-Life Center, 1-4-26, Kaigan, Minato-ku, Tokyo 105; tel. (3) 3434-7641; fax (3) 3434-7428; f. 1972; 785,751 mems; Pres. Teruhito Tokumoto.

Jiunro (Japan Automobile Drivers' Union): 2-3-12, Nakameguro, Meguro-ku, Tokyo 153; tel. (3) 3711-9387; fax (3) 3719-2624; 1,958 mems; Pres. Sadao Kanezuka.

JR-Rengo (Japan Railway Trade Unions Confederation): TOKO Bldg, 9th Floor, 1-8-10, Nihonbashi-muromachi, Chuo-ku, Tokyo 103; tel. (3) 3270-4590; fax (3) 3270-4429; 78,418 mems; Pres. Kazuaki Kuzuno.

JR Soren (Japan Confederation of Railway Workers' Unions): Meguro-satsuki Bldg, 3-2-13, Nishi-gotanda, Shinagawa-ku, Tokyo 141; tel. (3) 3491-7191; fax (3) 3491-7192; 70,710 mems; Pres. Mitumaru Shibata.

Jyoho Roren (Japan Federation of Telecommunications, Electronic Information and Allied Workers): Zendentsu-rodo Bldg, 3-6, Kanda Surugadai, Chiyoda-ku, Tokyo 101; tel. (3) 3219-2231; fax (3) 3253-3268; 265,132 mems; Pres. Kazuo Sasamori.

Kagaku Soren (Japanese Federation of Chemical Workers' Unions): Kyodo Bldg, 7th Floor, 2-4-10, Higashi-shinbashi, Minato-ku, Tokyo 105; tel. (3) 5401-2268; fax (3) 5401-2263; Pres. Hirokazu Iwasaki.

Kaiin Kumiai (All-Japan Seamen's Union): 7-15-26, Roppongi, Minato-ku, Tokyo 106; tel. (3) 5410-8328; fax (3) 5410-8336; 50,000 mems; Pres. Shoshiro Nakanishi.

Kamipa Rengo (Japanese Federation of Pulp and Paper Workers' Unions): 2-12-4, Kita Aoyama, Minato-ku, Tokyo 107; tel. (3) 3402-7656; fax (3) 3402-7659; 51,618 mems; Pres. Toshiaki Yoshida.

Kensetsu Rengo (Japan Construction Trade Union Confederation): Yuai Bldg, 7th Floor, 2-20-12, Shiba, Minato-ku, Tokyo 105; tel. (3) 3454-0951; fax (3) 3453-0582; 13,199 mems; Pres. MAYAYASU TERASAWA.

Kinzoku Kikai (National Metal and Machinery Workers' Unions of Japan): 6-2, Sakuraokacho, Shibuya-ku, Tokyo 150; tel. (3) 3463-4231; fax (3) 3463-7391; f. 1989; 200,000 mems; Pres. MASAOKI KITAURA.

Kokko Soren (Japan General Federation of National Public Service Employees' Unions): 1-2-1, Kasumigaseki, Chiyoda-ku, Tokyo 100; tel. (3) 3508-4990; fax (3) 5512-7555; 43,135 mems; Pres. TATSUO SHIMA.

Koku Domei (Japanese Confederation of Aviation Labour): Nikkokiso Bldg, 2nd Floor, 1-6-3, Haneda-kuko, Ota-ku, Tokyo 144; tel. (3) 3747-7642; fax (3) 3747-7647; 16,310 mems; Pres. KATSUMI UTAGAWA.

Kokuzei Roso (Japanese Confederation of National Tax Unions): R154, Okurasho Bldg, 3-1-1, Kasumigaseki, Chiyoda-ku, Tokyo 100; tel. (3) 3581-2573; fax (3) 3581-3843; 40,128 mems; Pres. TATSUO SASAKI.

Kotsu Roren (Japan Federation of Transport Workers' Unions): Yuai Bldg, 3rd Floor, 2-20-12, Shiba, Minato-ku 105; tel. (3) 3451-7243; fax (3) 3454-7393; 97,239 mems; Pres. SHIGEO MAKI.

Koun-Domei (Japanese Confederation of Port and Transport Workers' Unions): 5-10-2, Kamata, Ota-ku, Tokyo 144; tel. (3) 3733-5285; fax (3) 3733-5280; f. 1987; 2,602 mems; Pres. SHOSHIRO NAKANISHI.

Leisure Service Rengo (Japan Federation of Leisure Service Industries Workers' Unions): Zosen Bldg, 4th Floor, 3-5-6, Misakicho, Chiyoda-ku, Tokyo 101; tel. (3) 3230-1724; fax (3) 3239-1553; 47,601 mems; Pres. HIROSHI SAWADA.

NHK Roren (Federation of All-NHK Labour Unions): NHK, 2-2-1, Jinnan, Shibuya-ku, Tokyo 150; tel. (3) 3485-6007; fax (3) 3469-9271; 12,526 mems; Pres. YASUZO SUDO.

Nichirinro (National Forest Workers' Union of Japan): 1-2-1, Kasumigaseki, Chiyoda-ku, Tokyo 100; tel. (3) 3580-8891; fax (3) 3580-1596; Pres. KOH IKEGAMI.

Nikkyoso (Japan Teachers' Union): Japan Education Hall, 2-6-2, Hitotsubashi, Chiyoda-ku, Tokyo 101; tel. (3) 3265-2171; fax (3) 3230-0172; 377,014 mems; Pres. YUJI KAWAKAMI.

Rosai Roren (National Federation of Zenrosai Workers' Unions): 2-12-10, Yoyogi, Shibuya-ku, Tokyo 151; tel. (3) 3299-0161; fax (3) 3299-0126; 2,091 mems; Pres. TADASHI TAKACHI.

Seiho Roren (National Federation of Life Insurance Workers' Unions): Tanaka Bldg, 3-19-5, Yushima, Bunkyo-ku, Tokyo 113; tel. (3) 3837-2031; fax (3) 3837-2037; 400,534 mems; Pres. YOHTARU KOHNO.

Seiroren (Labour Federation of Government Related Organizations): Hasaka Bldg, 4th-6th Floors, 1-10-3, Kanda-ogawacho, Chiyoda-ku, Tokyo 101; tel. (3) 5295-6360; fax (3) 5295-6362; Chair. MITSURU WATANABE.

Sekiyu Roren (Japan Confederation of Petroleum Industry Workers' Union): NKK Bldg, 7th Floor, 2-18-2, Nishi-shimbashi, Minato-ku, Tokyo 105; tel. (3) 3578-1315; fax (3) 3578-3455; 28,807 mems; Pres. HIROSHI MOCHIMARU.

Sen'i Seikatsu Roren (Japan Federation of Textile Clothing Workers' Unions of Japan): Katakura Bldg, 3-1-2, Kyobashi, Chuo-ku, Tokyo 104; tel. (3) 3281-4806; fax (3) 3274-3165; 4,598 mems; Pres. KATSUYOSHI SAKAI.

Shigen Roren (Federation of Japanese Metal Resources Workers' Unions): Roppongi Azeria Bldg, 1-3-8, Nishi-azabu, Minato-ku, Tokyo 106; tel. (3) 3402-6666; fax (3) 3402-6667; Pres. MINORU TAKAHASHI.

Shin Unten (F10-Drivers' Craft Union): 4th Floor, 3-25-6, Negishi, Taito-ku, Tokyo 110; tel. (3) 5603-1015; fax (3) 5603-5351; 4,435 mems; Pres. SHOHEI SHINOZAKI.

Shinkagaku (National Organization of All Chemical Workers): MF Bldg, 2nd Floor, 2-3-3, Fujimi, Chiyoda-ku, Tokyo 102; tel. (3) 3239-2933; fax (3) 3239-2932; 8,400 mems; Pres. HISASHI YASUI.

Shinrin Roren (Federation of All-Japanese Forest-related industries Workers' Unions): 3-28-7, Otsuka, Bunkyo-ku, Tokyo 112; tel. (3) 3945-6385; fax (3) 3945-6477; 18,392 mems; Pres. SHIGERU KOZUKA.

Shitetsu Soren (General Federation of Private Railway Workers' Unions): 4-3-5, Takanawa, Minato-ku, Tokyo 108; tel. (3) 3473-0166; fax (3) 3447-3927; f. 1947; 179,529 mems; Pres. RYOICHI IKEMURA.

Shogyo Roren (Japan Federation of Commercial Workers' Unions): New State Manor Bldg, 3rd Floor, 2-23-1, Yoyogi, Shibuya-ku, Tokyo 151; tel. (3) 3370-4121; fax (3) 3370-1640; 126,481 mems; Pres. MITSUO NAGUMO.

Shokuhin Rengo (Japan Federation of Foods and Tobacco Workers' Unions): Hiroo Office Bldg, 8th Floor, 1-3-18, Hiroo, Shibuya-ku, Tokyo 150; tel. (3) 3446-2082; fax (3) 3446-6779; f. 1991; 116,370 mems; Pres. SHIGERU MASUDA.

Shokuhin Rokyo (Food Industry Workers' Union Council (FIWUC)): ST Bldg, 6th Floor, 4-9-4, Hatchyoubori, Chuo-ku, Tokyo 104; tel. (3) 3555-7671; fax (3) 3555-7760; Pres. YOSHIAKI NAGANO.

Sonpo Roren (Federation of Non-Life Insurance Workers' Unions of Japan): Kanda MS Bldg, 4th Floor, 27, Kanda-higashimatsushitacho, Chiyoda-ku, Tokyo 101; tel. (3) 5295-0071; fax (3) 5295-0073; Pres. KUNIO MATSUMOTO.

Tanro (Japan Coal Miners' Union): Hokkaido Rodosha Bldg, 2nd Floor, Kita-11, Nishi-4, Kita-ku, Sapporo-shi, Hokkaido 001; tel. (11) 717-0291; fax (11) 717-0295; 1,353 mems; Pres. KAZUO SAKUMA.

Tanshokukyo (Association of Japan Coal Mining Staff Unions): 2-30, Nishiminatomachi, Omuta-shi, Fukuoka 836; tel. (944) 52-3883; fax (944) 52-3853; Pres. KEIZO UMEKI.

Tekko Roren (Japan Federation of Steel Workers' Unions): I&S Riverside Bldg, 4th Floor, 1-23-4, Shinkawa, Chuo-ku, Tokyo 104; tel. (3) 3555-0401; fax (3) 3555-0407; 193,000 mems; Pres. BENICHIRO ETO.

Tokei Roso (Statistics Labour Union Management and Co-ordination Agency): 19-1, Somucho, Wakamatsucho, Shinjuku-ku, Tokyo 162; tel. (3) 3202-1111; fax (3) 3205-3850; Pres. TOSHIAKI MAGARA.

Toshiko (The All-Japan Municipal Transport Workers' Union): 3-1-35, Shibaura, Minato-ku, Tokyo 108; tel. (3) 3451-5221; fax (3) 3452-2977; 43,612 mems; Pres. SHUNICHI SUZUKI.

Unyu Roren (All-Japan Federation of Transport Workers' Union): Zennittsu Kasumigaseki Bldg, 5th Floor, 3-3-3, Kasumigaseki, Chiyoda-ku, Tokyo 100; tel. (3) 3503-2171; fax (3) 3503-2176; f. 1968; 139,311 mems; Pres. KAZUMARO SUZUKI.

Zeikan Roren (Federation of Japanese Customs Personnel Labour Unions): 3-1-1, Kasumigaseki, Chiyoda-ku, Tokyo 100; tel. and fax (3) 3593-1788; Pres. RIKIO SUDO.

Zen Insatsu (All-Printing Agency Workers' Union): 3-59-12, Nishigahara, Kita-ku, Tokyo 114; tel. (3) 3910-7131; fax (3) 3910-7155; 5,431 mems; Chair. TOSHIO KATAKURA.

Zen Yusei (All-Japan Postal Labour Union): 1-20-6, Sendagaya, Shibuya-ku, Tokyo 151; tel. (3) 3478-7101; fax (3) 5474-7085; 77,573 mems; Pres. NOBUAKI IZAWA.

Zenchuro (All-Japan Garrison Forces Labour Union): 3-41-8, Shiba, Minato-ku, Tokyo 105; tel. (3) 3455-5971; fax (3) 3455-5973; Pres. EIBUN MEDORUMA.

Zendensen (All- Japan Electric Wire Labour Union): 1-11-6, Hatanodai, Shinagawa-ku, Tokyo 142; tel. (3) 3785-2991; fax (3) 3785-2995; Pres. NAOKI TOKUNAGA.

Zen-eien (National Cinema and Theatre Workers' Union): Hibiya Park Bldg, 1-8-1, Yurakucho, Chiyoda-ku, Tokyo 100; tel. (3) 3201-4476; fax (3) 3214-0597; Pres. SADAHIRO MATSUURA.

Zengin Rengo (All-Japan Federative Council of Bank Labour Unions): R904, Kyodo Bldg, 16-8, Nihonbashi-Kodenmacho, Chuo-ku, Tokyo 103; tel. and fax (3) 3661-4886; 32,104 mems; Pres. KIKUO HATTORI.

Zenjiko Roren (National Federation of Automobile Transport Workers' Unions): 3-7-9, Sendagaya, Shibuya-ku, Tokyo 151; tel. (3) 3408-0875; fax (3) 3497-0107; Pres. OSAMU MIMASHI.

Zenkairen (All-Japan Shipping Labour Union): Shinbashi Ekimae Bldg, No 1, 8th Floor, 2-20-15, Shinbashi, Minato-ku, Tokyo 105; tel. (3) 3573-2401; fax (3) 3573-2404; Chair. MASAHIKO SATO.

Zenkin Rengo (Japanese Federation of Metal Industry Unions): Yuai Bldg, 5th Floor, 2-20-12, Shiba, Minato-ku, Tokyo 105; tel. (3) 3451-2141; fax (3) 3452-0239; f. 1989; 303,503 mems; Pres. MITSURO HATTORI.

Zenkoku Gas (Federation of Gas Workers' Unions of Japan): 5-11-1, Omori-nishi, Ota-ku, Tokyo 143; tel. (3) 5493-8381; fax (3) 5493-8216; 31,499 mems; Pres. AKIO HAMAUZU.

Zenkoku Keiba Rengo (National Federation of Horse-racing Workers): 2500, Mikoma, Miho-mura, Inashiki-gun, Ibaragi 300-04; tel. (298) 85-0402; fax (298) 85-0416; Pres. TOYOHIKO OKUMURA.

Zenkoku Kagaku (All-Japan Chemistry Workers' Union): Kanda Park Bldg, 4th Floor, 3-3-3, Iwamoto-cho, Chiyoda-ku, Tokyo 101; tel. (3) 3683-4313; fax (3) 3685-4315; 9,208 mems; Pres. KAORU YOKOTA.

Zenkoku Nodanro (National Federation of Agricultural, Forestry and Fishery Corporations' Workers' Unions): 1-5-8, Hamamatsucho, Minato-ku, Tokyo 105; tel. (3) 3437-0931; fax (3) 3437-0681; 26,010 mems; Pres. SHIN-ICHIRO OKADA.

Zenkoku Semento (National Federation of Cement Workers' Unions of Japan): 5-29-2, Shinbashi, Minato-ku, Tokyo 105; tel. (3) 3436-3666; fax (3) 3436-3668; Pres. KIYONORI URAKAWA.

Zenkoku-Ippan (National Council of General Amalgamated Workers' Unions): Zosen Bldg, 5th Floor, 3-5-6, Misakicho, Chiyoda-ku, Tokyo 101; tel. (3) 3230-4071; fax (3) 3230-4360; 54,708 mems; Pres. YASUHIKO MATSUI.

Zenkyoro (National Race Workers' Union): Nihon Kyoiku Kaikan, 7th Floor, 2-6-2, Hitotsubashi, Chiyoda-ku, Tokyo 101; tel. (3) 5210-5156; fax (3) 5210-5157; 24,720 mems; Pres. SHIMAKO YOSHIDA.

Zennitto (Japan Painting Workers' Union): Shin-osaka Communication Plaza, 1st Floor, 1-6-36, Nishi-miyahara, Yodogawa-ku, Osaka-shi, Osaka 532; tel. (6) 393-8677; fax (6) 393-8533; Pres. SEIICHI UOZA.

Zenrokin (Federation of Labour Bank Workers' Unions of Japan): Nakano Bldg, 3rd Floor, 1-11, Kanda-Awajicho, Chiyoda-ku, Tokyo 101; tel. (3) 3256-1015; fax (3) 3256-1045; Pres. EIICHI KAKU.

Zensen Domei (Japanese Federation of Textile, Garment, Chemical, Commercial, Food and Allied Industries Workers' Unions): 4-8-16, Kudanminami, Chiyoda-ku, Tokyo 102-0074; tel. (3) 3288-3723; fax (3) 3288-3728; f. 1946; 1,280 affiliates; 602,575 mems; Pres. TSUYOSHI TAKAGI.

Zensuido (All-Japan Water Supply Workers' Union): 1-4-1, Hongo, Bunkyo-ku, Tokyo 113; tel. (3) 3816-4132; fax (3) 3818-1430; 33,522 mems; Pres. KAZUMASA KATO.

Zentanko (National Union of Coal Mine Workers): Yuai Bldg, 6th Floor, 2-20-12, Shiba, Minato-ku, Tokyo 105; tel. (3) 3453-4721; fax (3) 3453-6457; Pres. AKIRA YASUNAGA.

Zentei (Japan Postal Workers' Union): 1-2-7, Koraku, Bunkyo-ku, Tokyo 112; tel. (3) 3812-4260; fax (3) 5684-7201; 160,316 mems; Pres. SUSUMU TAKATO.

Zenzohei (All-Mint Labour Union): 1-1-79, Temma, Kita-ku, Osaka-shi, Osaka 530; tel. and fax (6) 354-2389; Pres. CHIKASHI HIGUCHI.

Zenzosen-kikai (All-Japan Shipbuilding and Engineering Union): Zosen Bldg, 6th Floor, 3-5-6, Misakicho, Chiyoda-ku, Tokyo 101; tel. (3) 3265-1921; fax (3) 3265-1870; Pres. YOSHIMI FUNATSU.

Zosen Juki Roren (Japan Confederation of Shipbuilding and Engineering Workers' Unions): Yuai Bldg, 4th Floor, 2-20-12, Shiba, Minato-ku, Tokyo 105; tel. (3) 3451-6783; fax (3) 3451-6935; 124,149 mems; Pres. MASAYUKI YOSHII.

Transport

RAILWAYS

Japan Railways (JR) Group: 1-6-5, Marunouchi, Chiyoda-ku, Tokyo 100; tel. (3) 3215-9649; telex 24873; fax (3) 3213-5291; fmrly the state-controlled Japanese National Railways (JNR); reorg. and transferred to private-sector control in 1987, and divided into six passenger railway cos, one freight railway co, two rail-related cos and one research institute; the high-speed Shinkansen rail network consists of the Tokaido line (Tokyo to Shin-Osaka, 552.6 km), the Sanyo line (Shin-Osaka to Hakata, 623.3 km), the Tohoku line (Tokyo to Morioka, 535.3 km) and the Joetsu line (Omiya to Niigata, 303.6 km). The 4-km link between Ueno and Tokyo stations was opened in June 1991. The Yamagata Shinkansen (Fukushima to Yamagata, 87 km) was converted in 1992 from a conventional railway line. It is operated as a branch of the Tohoku Shinkansen with through trains from Tokyo, though not at full Shinkansen speeds. In 1996 the total railway route length was about 36,576 km. Work began in 1971 on a new 'super express' railway network, linking all the major cities, which was to total 7,000 km in length.

Central Japan Railway Co: 2-14-19, Meieki-Minami, Nakamura-ku, Nagoya 450-0003; tel. (52) 564-2317; fax (52) 587-1300; Chair. HIROSHI SUDA; Pres. YOSHIYUKI KASAI.

East Japan Railway Co: 2-2-2, Yoyogi, Shibuya-ku, Tokyo 151; tel. (3) 5334-1171; telex 24873; fax (3) 5334-1228; Chair. S. YAMANOUCHI; Pres. MASATAKE MATSUDA.

Hokkaido Railway Co: West 15-chome, Kita 11-jo, Chuo-ku, Sapporo 060; tel. (11) 700-5717; fax (11) 700-5719; Chair. YOSHIHIRO OHMORI; Pres. SHINICHI SAKAMOTO.

Japan Freight Railway Co: 1-6-5, Marunouchi, Chiyoda-ku, Tokyo 100; tel. (3) 3285-0071; fax (3) 3212-6992; Chair. MASASHI HASHIMOTO; Pres. YASUSHI TANAHASHI.

Kyushu Railway Co: 1-1, Hakataeki-Chuogai, Hakata-ku, Fukuoka 812; tel. (92) 474-2501; fax (92) 474-9745; Chair. Y. ISHII; Pres. K. TANAKA.

Shikoku Railway Co: 1-10, Hamano-cho, Takamatsu, Kagawa 760; tel. (878) 51-1880; fax (878) 51-0497; Chair. H. YAMAMOTO; Pres. HIROATSU ITO.

West Japan Railway Co: 2-4-24, Shibata, Kita-ku, Osaka 530; tel. (6) 375-8981; fax (6) 375-8919; Chair. MASATAKA IDE; Pres. S. NANYA.

Other Principal Private Companies

Hankyu Corpn: 1-16-1, Shibata, Kita-ku, Osaka 530; tel. (6) 373-5092; fax (6) 373-5670; f. 1907; links Osaka, Kyoto, Kobe, Senriyama and Takarazuka; Chair. KOHEI KOBAYASHI; Pres. M. SUGAI.

Hanshin Electric Railway Co Ltd: 1-1-24, Ebie, Fukushima-ku, Osaka 553; tel. (6) 457-2123; f. 1899; Chair. S. KUMA; Pres. M. TEZUKA.

Keihan Electric Railway Co Ltd: 1-2-27, Shiromi, Chuo-ku, Osaka 540; tel. (6) 944-2521; fax (6) 944-2501; f. 1906; Chair. HIROSHI SUMITA; Pres. MINORU MIYASHITA.

Keihin Express Electric Railway Co Ltd: 2-20-20, Takanawa, Minato-ku, Tokyo 108; tel. (3) 3280-9120; fax (3) 3280-9199; f. 1899; Chair. M. SERIZAWA; Pres. ICHIRO HIRAMATSU.

Keio Teito Electric Railway Co Ltd: 1-9-1, Sekido, Tama City, Tokyo 206; tel. (423) 37-3141; f. 1913; Pres. K. KUWAYAMA.

Keisei Electric Railway Co Ltd: 1-10-3, Oshiage, Sumida-ku, Tokyo 131; tel. (3) 3621-2242; fax (3) 3621-2233; f. 1909; Chair. (vacant); Pres. H. SENO.

Kinki Nippon Railway Co Ltd: 6-1-55, Uehommachi, Tennoji-ku, Osaka 543; tel. (6) 775-3444; fax (6) 775-3468; f. 1910; Chair. YOSHINORI UEYAMA; Pres. SHIGEICHIROU KANAMORI.

Nagoya Railroad Co Ltd: 1-2-4, Meieki, Nakamura-ku, Nagoya-shi 450; tel. (52) 571-2111; fax (52) 581-6060; Chair. S. TANIGUCHI; Pres. S. MINOURA.

Nankai Electric Railway Co Ltd: 5-1-60, Namba, Chuo-ku, Osaka 542; tel. (6) 644-7121; Pres. SHIGERU YOSHIMURA; Vice-Pres. K. OKAMOTO.

Nishi-Nippon Railroad Co Ltd: 1-11-17, Tenjin-cho, Chuo-ku, Fukuoka 810; tel. (92) 761-6631; fax (92) 722-1405; serves northern Kyushu; Chair. H. YOSHIMOTO; Pres. G. KIMOTO.

Odakyu Electric Railway Co Ltd: 1-8-3, Nishi Shinjuku, Shinjuku-ku, Tokyo 160; tel. (3) 3349-2151; fax (3) 3346-1899; f. 1948; Chair. TATSUZO TOSHIMITSU; Pres. TAKASHI TAKIGAMI.

Sanyo Electric Railway Co Ltd: 3-1-1, Oyashiki-dori, Nagata-ku, Kobe 653; tel. (78) 611-2211; Pres. T. WATANABE.

Seibu Railway Co Ltd: 1-11-1, Kasunokidai, Tokorozawa-shi, Saitama 359; tel. (429) 26-2035; fax (429) 26-2237; f. 1894; Pres. YOSHIAKI TSUTSUMI.

Tobu Railway Co Ltd: 1-1-2, Oshiage, Sumida-ku, Tokyo 131-8522; tel. (3) 3621-5057; Pres. TAKASHIGE UCHIDA.

Tokyo Express Electric Railway Co Ltd: 5-6, Nanpeidai-cho, Shibuya-ku, Tokyo 150; tel. (3) 3477-6111; telex 2423454; fax (3) 3496-2965; f. 1922; Pres. S. SHIMUZU.

Principal Subways, Monorails and Tunnels

Subway services operate in Tokyo, Osaka, Kobe, Nagoya, Sapporo, Yokohama, Kyoto, Sendai and Fukuoka with a combined network of about 500 km. Most new subway lines are directly linked with existing private railway terminals which connect the cities with suburban areas.

The first commercial monorail system was introduced in 1964 with straddle-type cars between central Tokyo and Tokyo International Airport, a distance of 13 km. In 1988 the total length of monorail was 38.6 km.

In 1985 the 54-km Seikan Tunnel (the world's longest undersea tunnel), linking the islands of Honshu and Hokkaido, was completed. Electric rail services through the tunnel began operating in March 1988.

Fukuoka City Subway: Fukuoka Municipal Transportation Bureau, 2-5-31, Daimyo, Chuo-ku, Fukuoka 810; tel. (92) 714-3211; fax (92) 721-0754; 2 lines of 17.8 km open; Dir MASATO WATANABE.

Kobe Rapid Transit: 6-5-1, Kanocho, Chuo-ku, Kobe 650; tel. (78) 331-8181; Dir YASUO MAENO.

Kyoto Rapid Transit: 48, Bojocho Mibu, Nakakyo-ku, Kyoto 604; tel. (75) 822-9115; fax (75) 822-9240; Chair. T. TANABE.

Nagoya Underground Railway: Nagoya Municipal Transportation Bureau, City Hall Annex, 3-1-1, Sannomaru, Naka-ku, Nagoya 460-08; tel. (52) 961-1111; fax (52) 972-3849; 76.5 km open (1994); Dir-Gen. YUKIO HIRANO.

Osaka Monorail: 5-1-1, Higashi-machi, Shin-Senri, Toyonakashi, Osaka 565; tel. (6) 871-8280; fax (6) 871-8284; Gen. Man. S. OKA.

Osaka Underground Railway: Osaka Municipal Transportation Bureau, 1-11-53, Kujominami, Nishi-ku, Osaka 550; tel. (6) 582-1101; fax (6) 582-7997; f. 1933; 113 km open in 1993/94; the 6.6 km computer-controlled 'New Tram' service began between Suminoe-koen and Nakafuto in 1981; a seventh line between Kyobashi and Tsurumi-ryokuchi was opened in 1990; Gen. Man. HARUMI SAKAI.

Sapporo Transportation Bureau: Higashi, 2-4-1, Oyachi, Atsubetsu-ku, Sapporo 004; tel. (11) 896-2708; fax (11) 896-2790; f. 1971; 3 lines of 53 km open in 1993/94; Dir T. IKEGAMI.

Sendai City Subway: Sendai City Transportation Bureau, 1-4-15, Kimachidori, Aoba-ku, Sendai-shi, Miyagi-ken 980; tel. (22) 224-5111; fax (22) 224-5506; 15.4 km open; Dir KAORU AOKI.

Tokyo Underground Railway: Teito Rapid Transit Authority, 3-19-6, Higashi Ueno, Taito-ku, Tokyo 110; tel. (3) 3837-7046; fax (3) 3837-7048; f. 1941; Pres. KIYOSHI TERASHIMA; 169.3 km open; and

Transportation Bureau of Tokyo Metropolitan Govt, 2-8-1, Nishi-shinjuku, Shinjuku-ku, Tokyo 163-01; tel. (3) 5321-1111; fax (3) 5388-1650; f. 1960; Dir-Gen. KIYOTSUGU MIYABATA; 82 km open.

Yokohama Rapid Transit: Municipal Transportation Bureau, 1-1, Minato-cho, Naka-ku, Yokohama 231-80; tel. (45) 671-3201; fax (45) 664-3266; 33.0 km open; Dir-Gen. MICHINORI KISHIDA.

ROADS

In December 1996 Japan's road network extended to an estimated 1,160,000 km, including 6,070 km of motorways and 59,000 km of highways. In mid-1988 work was completed on the world's longest suspension bridge, a 9.4-km multi-section structure spanning the Seto inland sea between Honshu and Shikoku.

There is a national omnibus service, 60 publicly-operated services and 298 privately-operated services.

SHIPPING

Shipping in Japan is subject to the supervision of the Ministry of Transport. At 31 December 1996 the Japanese merchant fleet (9,399 vessels) had a total displacement of 19,201,000 grt. The main ports are Tokyo, Yokohama, Nagoya and Osaka. The rebuilding of the port at Kobe, severely damaged by an earthquake in January 1995, was scheduled to be completed in 1998.

Principal Companies

Daiichi Chuo Kisen Kaisha: Dowa Bldg, 3-5-15, Nihonbashi, Chuo-ku, Tokyo 103; tel. (3) 3278-6745; telex 2224181; fax (3) 3278-6746; f. 1960; liner and tramp services; Pres. MAHIKO SAOTOME.

Iino Kaiun Kaisha Ltd: Iino Bldg, 2-1-1, Uchisaiwai-cho, Chiyoda-ku, Tokyo 100; tel. (3) 3506-3037; telex 22238; fax (3) 3508-4121; f. 1918; cargo and tanker services; Chair. T. CHIBA; Pres. A. KARINO.

Kansai Kisen KK: Osaka Bldg, 3-6-32, Nakanoshima, Kita-ku, Osaka 552; tel. (6) 574-9131; telex 5237284; fax (6) 574-9149; f. 1942; domestic passenger services; Pres. TOSHIKAZU EGUCHI.

Kawasaki Kisen Kaisha Ltd (K Line): 1-2-9, Nishi Shinbashi, Minato-ku, Tokyo 105; tel. (3) 3595-5082; fax (3) 3595-6126; f. 1919; containers, cars, LNG, LPG and oil tankers, bulk carriers; Chair. S. NAGUMO; Pres. I. SHINTANI.

Mitsui OSK Lines Ltd: Shosen Mitsui Bldg, 2-1-1, Toranomon, Minato-ku, Tokyo 105-91; tel. (3) 3587-7092; telex 22266; fax (3) 3587-7734; f. 1942; world-wide container, liner, tramp, and specialized carrier and tanker services; Chair. SUSUMU TEMPORIN; Pres. MASAHURU IKUTA.

Navix Line Ltd: Palaceside Bldg, 1-1-1, Hitotsubashi, Chiyoda-ku, Tokyo 100; tel. (3) 3282-7500; telex 22345; fax (3) 3282-7600; f. 1989 as a merger between Japan Line Ltd and Yamashita-Shinnihon Steamship Co Ltd (Y. S. Line); tramp, specialized carrier and tanker services; Pres. NORIAKI HORI.

Nippon Yusen Kaisha (NYK) Line: 2-3-2, Marunouchi, Chiyoda-ku, Tokyo 100-0005; tel. (3) 3284-5151; fax (3) 3284-6361; e-mail PRTEAM@nykline.co.jp; f. 1885; world-wide container, cargo, pure car and truck carriers, tanker and bulk carrying services; Chair. JIRO NEMOTO; Pres. KENTARO KAWAMURA.

Nissho Shipping Co Ltd: 33, Mori Bldg, 7th Floor, 3-8-21, Toranomon, Minato-ku, Tokyo 105; tel. (3) 3438-3511; telex 22573; fax (3) 3438-3566; f. 1943; Pres. MINORU IKEDA.

Ryukyu Kaiun KK: 1-24-11, Nishi-machi, Naha, Okinawa 900; tel. (98) 868-8161; telex 795217; fax (98) 868-8561; cargo and passenger services on domestic routes; Pres. M. AZAMA.

Showa Line Ltd: Hibiya Kokusai Bldg, 2-2-3, Uchisaiwai-cho, Chiyoda-ku, Tokyo 100; tel. (3) 3581-8521; telex 22310; fax (3) 3581-8589; f. 1944; cargo, tanker and cruise services world-wide; Pres. SEIKI FUSHIMI.

Taiheiyo Kaiun Co Ltd: Mitakokusai Bldg, 23rd Floor, 1-4-28, Minato-ku, Tokyo 100; tel. (3) 5445-5805; telex 2223434; fax (3) 5445-5806; f. 1951; cargo and tanker services; Pres. SANROKURO YAMAJI.

CIVIL AVIATION

There are international airports at Tokyo, Osaka and Narita. In 1991 the Government approved a plan to build five new airports, and to expand 17 existing ones. This project was expected to take five years to complete and to cost US $25,000m. There are proposals to build new airports at Shizuoka, Nagoya and Kobe and an additional runway at Narita. In 1993 a new terminal, costing US $1,200m., was opened at Haneda Airport, and in September 1994 the world's first offshore international airport (Kansai International Airport) was opened in Osaka Bay.

Air Nippon: 2-2-8, Higashi-Shinagawa, Shinagawa-ku, Tokyo 140; tel. (3) 5462-1911; telex 2422124; fax (3) 5462-1941; f. 1974; formerly Nihon Kinkyori Airways; international and domestic passenger services; Chair. AKIO KONDO; Pres. TAKAHIDE YAMADA.

All Nippon Airways—ANA: Kasumigaseki Bldg, 27th Floor, 3-2-5, Kasumigaseki, Chiyoda-ku, Tokyo 100; tel. (3) 3592-3035; telex 33670; fax (3) 3592-3069; f. 1952; operates domestic passenger and freight services; scheduled international services to the Far East, Australasia, the USA and Europe; charter services world-wide; Pres. and CEO KICHISABURO NOMURA.

Japan Air Charter: JAL Bldg, 18th Floor, 2-4-11, Higashi-Shinagawa, Shinagawa-ku, Tokyo 140; tel. (3) 5460-6830; fax (3) 5460-6839; f. 1990; subsidiary of JAL; domestic and international services; Chair. and Pres. SHINZO SUDO.

Japan Air Commuter: 8-2-2, Fumoto, Mizobe-cho, Aira-gun, Kagoshima 899-64; tel. (995) 582151; telex 2225182; fax (995) 582673; f. 1983; subsidiary of Japan Air System; domestic services; Pres. YOSHITOMI ONO.

Japan Air System: 37, Mori Bldg, 3-5-1, Toranomon, Minato-ku, Tokyo 105; tel. (3) 5473-4102; telex 2225182; fax (3) 5473-4109; f. 1971; domestic and international services; plans to co-ordinate services with Northwest Airlines (USA) announced in 1995; Chair. TAKESHI MASHIMA; Pres. HIROMI FUNABIKI.

Japan Airlines Co Ltd—JAL (Nihon Koku Kabushiki Kaisha): JAL Bldg, 2-4-11, Higashi-Shinagawa, Shinagawa-ku, Tokyo 140; tel. (3) 5460-3109; fax (3) 5460-5910; f. 1951; fully transferred to private-sector control in 1987; domestic and international services to Australasia, the Far East, North America, South America and Europe; Chair. SUSUMU YAMAJI; Pres. AKIRA KONDO.

Japan Asia Airways Co: South Wing, Yuraku-cho Denki Bldg, 1-7-1, Yuraku-cho, Chiyoda-ku, Tokyo 100; tel. (3) 3284-2972; telex 25440; fax (3) 3284-2980; f. 1975; subsidiary of JAL; international services from Tokyo, Osaka, Nagoya and Okinawa to Hong Kong, Indonesia and Taiwan; Chair. NOBORU OKAMURA; Pres. KOZO MIYASAKA.

Japan TransOcean Air: 3-24, Yamashita-cho, Naha-shi, Okinawa 900; tel. (988) 572112; telex 795477; fax (988) 582581; f. 1967, present name since 1993; subsidiary of JAL; inter-island service in Okinawa; Chair. KEIICHI INAMINE; Pres. MICHIO OKUNO.

Nakanihon Airline Service—NAL: Nagoya Airport, Toyoyama-cho, Nishi Kasugai-gun, Aichi 480-02; tel. (568) 285405; telex 4485832; fax (568) 285415; f. 1988; domestic services; Chair. SEITARO TANIGUCHI; Pres. KIYOSHI HAYAKAWA.

Skymark Airlines: f. 1997; proposals to start domestic services in 1999.

Tourism

The ancient capital of Kyoto, pagodas and temples, forests and mountains, traditional festivals and the classical Kabuki theatre are some of the many tourist attractions of Japan. In 1996 there were 3,837,113 foreign visitors to Japan, and receipts from tourism totalled US $4,078m.

Department of Tourism: 2-1-3, Kasumigaseki, Chiyoda-ku, Tokyo 100; tel. (3) 3580-4488; fax (3) 3580-7901; f. 1946; a dept of the Ministry of Transport; Dir-Gen. YUKIO ISHII.

Japan National Tourist Organization: Tokyo Kotsu Kaikau Bldg, 2-10-1, Yuraku-cho, Chiyoda-ku, Tokyo 100; tel. (3) 3216-1901; fax (3) 3214-7680; e-mail jnto@jnto.go.jp; Pres. TSUGUO IYAMA.

Japan Travel Bureau Inc: 1-6-4, Marunouchi, Chiyoda-ku, Tokyo 100; tel. (3) 3284-7028; telex 24418; f. 1912; c. 10,000 mems; Chair. I. MATSUHASHI; Pres. R. FUNAYAMA.

JORDAN

Introductory Survey

Location, Climate, Language, Religion, Flag, Capital

The Hashemite Kingdom of Jordan is an almost land-locked state in western Asia. It is bordered by Israel and the emerging Palestinian autonomous areas to the west, by Syria to the north, by Iraq to the east and by Saudi Arabia to the south. The port of Aqaba, in the far south, gives Jordan a narrow outlet to the Red Sea. The climate is hot and dry. The average annual temperature is about 15°C (60°F) but there are wide diurnal variations. Temperatures in Amman are generally between −1°C (30°F) and 32°C (90°F). More extreme conditions are found in the valley of the River Jordan and on the shores of the Dead Sea (a lake on the Israeli-Jordanian frontier), where the temperature may exceed 50°C (122°F) in summer. The official language is Arabic. More than 90% of the population are Sunni Muslims, while there are small communities of Christians and Shi'i Muslims. The national flag (proportions 2 by 1) has three equal horizontal stripes, of black, white and green, with a red triangle, containing a seven-pointed white star, at the hoist. The capital is Amman.

Recent History

Palestine (including the present-day West Bank of Jordan) and Transjordan (the East Bank) were formerly parts of Turkey's Ottoman Empire. During the First World War (1914–18), when Turkey was allied with Germany, the Arabs under Ottoman rule rebelled. British forces, with Arab support, occupied Palestine and Transjordan in 1917–18, when the Turks withdrew.

British occupation continued after the war, when the Ottoman Empire was dissolved. In 1920 Palestine and Transjordan were formally placed under British administration by a League of Nations mandate. In 1921 Abdullah ibn Hussein, a member of the Hashimi (Hashemite) dynasty of Arabia, was proclaimed Amir (Emir) of Transjordan. In the same year, his brother, Faisal, became King of neighbouring Iraq. The two new monarchs were sons of Hussein ibn Ali, the Sharif of Mecca, who had proclaimed himself King of the Hejaz (now part of Saudi Arabia) in 1916. The British decision to nominate Hashemite princes to be rulers of Iraq and Transjordan was a reward for Hussein's co-operation in the wartime campaign against Turkey.

During the period of the British mandate, Transjordan (formally separated from Palestine in 1923) gained increasing autonomy. In 1928 the United Kingdom acknowledged the nominal independence of Transjordan, although retaining certain financial and military powers. Amir Abdullah followed a generally pro-British policy and supported the Allied cause in the Second World War (1939–45). The mandate was terminated on 22 March 1946, when Transjordan attained full independence. On 25 May Abdullah was proclaimed King, and a new Constitution took effect.

When the British Government terminated its mandate in Palestine in May 1948, Jewish leaders in the area proclaimed the State of Israel, but Palestinian Arabs, supported by the armies of Arab states, opposed Israeli claims and hostilities continued until July. Transjordan's forces occupied about 5,900 sq km of Palestine, including East Jerusalem, and this was confirmed by the armistice with Israel in April 1949. In June the country was renamed Jordan, and in April 1950, following a referendum, King Abdullah formally annexed the West Bank territory, which contained many Arab refugees from Israeli-held areas.

In July 1951 King Abdullah was assassinated in Jerusalem by a Palestinian Arab belonging to an extremist Islamic organization. The murdered king was succeeded by his eldest son, Talal ibn Abdullah, hitherto Crown Prince. However, in August 1952, because of Talal's mental illness, the crown passed to his son, Hussein ibn Talal, then 16 years of age. King Hussein formally took power in May 1953.

In March 1956, responding to Arab nationalist sentiment, King Hussein dismissed Lieut-Gen. John Glubb ('Glubb Pasha'), the British army officer who had been Chief of Staff of the British-equipped and -financed Arab Legion (the Jordanian armed forces) since 1939. Jordan's treaty relationship with the United Kingdom was ended in March 1957, and British troops completed their withdrawal from Jordan in July.

The refugee camps in the West Bank became the centre of Palestinian resistance to Israel, and during the 1950s there were numerous attacks on Israeli territory by groups of Palestinian *fedayeen* ('martyrs'). In September 1963 the creation of a unified 'Palestinian entity' was approved by the Council of the League of Arab States (the Arab League, see p. 195), and the first congress of Palestinian Arab groups was held in the Jordanian sector of Jerusalem in May–June 1964, during which the participants unanimously agreed to form the Palestine Liberation Organization (PLO), which would be financed by the Arab League and would recruit military units to form a Palestine Liberation Army (PLA). The principal Palestinian guerrilla organization within the PLO was the Palestine National Liberation Movement, known as Al-Fatah ('Conquest'), headed by Yasser Arafat from 1968. However, King Hussein regarded the establishment of the PLO as a threat to Jordanian sovereignty and from the outset refused to allow the PLA to train in Jordan or the PLO to levy taxes from Palestinian refugees residing in his country.

In April 1965 Hussein nominated his brother Hassan ibn Talal to be Crown Prince, so excluding his own children from succession to the throne. King Hussein's personal rule was severely challenged when, during the Six-Day War in June 1967, Israel made substantial military gains, including possession of the whole of Jerusalem (which was incorporated into Israel) and the West Bank; the latter becoming an Israeli 'administered territory'. The influx of Palestinian refugees into the East Bank bolstered the strength and authority of the PLO, which continued armed raids on the Israeli-administered territories, thereby challenging the personal authority of King Hussein and the sovereignty of the Jordanian Government (60% of Jordan's population are Palestinian and more than 1m. Palestinians live in the West Bank). King Hussein responded by expelling the guerrilla groups, after a civil war which lasted from September 1970 to July 1971. Aid to Jordan from Kuwait and other wealthy Arab governments, suspended after the expulsion of the Palestinian fighters, was only restored following Jordan's military support for Syria during the 1973 Arab-Israeli War. At the Rabat Arab summit meeting in Morocco in October 1974 King Hussein supported a unanimous resolution which recognized the PLO as the 'sole legitimate representative of the Palestinian people' and gave the PLO the right to establish an independent national authority on any piece of Palestinian land to be liberated.

In November 1974, as a response to this resolution, both chambers of the Jordanian National Assembly (which had equal representation for the East and West Banks) approved constitutional amendments which empowered the King to dissolve the Assembly and to postpone elections for up to 12 months. The Assembly was dissolved later that month, although it was briefly reconvened in February 1976, when it approved a constitutional amendment which gave the King power to postpone elections indefinitely and to convene the Assembly as required. A royal decree of April 1978 provided for the creation of a National Consultative Council, with 60 members appointed for a two-year term by the King, on the Prime Minister's recommendation, to debate proposed legislation. The Council was dissolved, and the National Assembly reconvened, in January 1984 (see below).

The proposal by US President Ronald Reagan in September 1982 of an autonomous Palestinian authority on the West Bank in association with Jordan was rejected by Yasser Arafat, Chairman of the PLO, following talks with King Hussein. However, King Hussein responded by dissolving the National Consultative Council in January 1984 and recalling the National Assembly for the first time since 1967; in effect creating the kind of Palestinian forum envisaged by the Reagan Plan. Israel allowed the surviving West Bank deputies to attend the Assembly, which approved constitutional amendments enabling elections to be held in the East Bank and West Bank deputies to be chosen by the Assembly itself. After discussions with Yasser Arafat in January 1984 on a joint Palestinian-Jordanian peace initiative, King Hussein's proposals for negotiations, based on UN Security Council Resolution 242, met with a non-commital response from the Palestine National Council (PNC), which convened in Amman in November. President Mubarak of Egypt gave his support to Hussein's proposals, following the resumption of diplomatic relations between the two countries earlier in September. In February 1985 King Hussein and Yasser Arafat announced the terms of a joint Jordanian-Palestinian agreement, proposing a confederated state of Jordan and Palestine to be reached through the convening of a conference of all concerned parties in the Middle East, including the PLO.

In July 1985 Israel independently rejected a list of seven Palestinians, five of whom were members of the PLO or had links with the PNC, whom King Hussein had presented to the USA as candidates for a joint Jordanian-Palestinian delegation to preliminary peace talks. Further progress in a peace initiative was hampered by a series of terrorist incidents in which the PLO was implicated. These incidents gave Israel further cause to reject the PLO as a credible partner in peace negotiations. King Hussein was under increasing pressure to advance the peace process, if necessary without the participation of the PLO. In September President Reagan revived his 1984 plan to sell military equipment, valued at $1,900m., to Jordan. The proposal was approved by the US Congress on the condition that Jordan enter into direct talks with Israel before 1 March 1986. However, such talks were obstructed by a *rapprochement* that developed between Jordan and Syria. Jordan and Syria had a number of differences, but they both supported a Middle East peace settlement through an international conference; at talks in Riyadh in October 1985 the two countries rejected 'partial and unilateral' solutions and affirmed their adherence to the Fez summit peace proposal of September 1982, omitting any mention of the Jordanian-Palestinian initiative. Through a reconciliation with Syria, which opposed Yasser Arafat's leadership of the PLO, King Hussein may have hoped to exert pressure on Arafat to take the initiative in the peace process and signal PLO acceptance of Resolution 242.

The Jordanian Prime Minister, Ahmad Ubeidat, resigned in April 1985. A new Cabinet was sworn in under the premiership of Zaid ar-Rifai, who had been Prime Minister in1973–76.

Frustrated by the lack of co-operation from Yasser Arafat in advancing the aims of the Jordanian-PLO peace initiative, King Hussein publicly severed political links with the PLO on 19 February 1986. Following King Hussein's announcement, Arafat was ordered to close his main PLO offices in Jordan by 1 April. The activities of the PLO were henceforth to be restricted to an even greater extent than before, and a number of Fatah officers loyal to Arafat were expelled. King Hussein urged the PLO to change either its policies or its leadership. In July Jordan closed all 25 Fatah offices in Amman, so that only 12 belonging to the PLO remained.

After the termination of political co-ordination with the PLO, Jordan continued to reject Israeli requests for direct peace talks which excluded a form of PLO representation. However, Jordan's subsequent efforts to strengthen its influence in the Israeli-occupied territories and to foster a Palestinian constituency there, independent of Arafat's PLO, coincided with Israeli measures to grant a limited autonomy to the Palestinian community in the West Bank (for example, by appointing Arab mayors in four towns in place of Israeli military governors). In March 1986 the Jordanian House of Representatives approved a draft law increasing the number of seats in the House from 60 to 142 (71 seats each for the East and West Banks), thereby providing for greater representation for West Bank Palestinians in the National Assembly. Then, in August, with Israeli support, a five-year development plan for the West Bank and the Gaza Strip, involving projected expenditure of US $1,300m., was announced in Amman. The plan was condemned by Yasser Arafat and West Bank Palestinians as representing a normalization of relations with Israel. There was considerable support for Arafat among Palestinians in the Occupied Territories and in Jordan, and this was consolidated when he re-established himself at the head of a reunified PLO at the 18th session of the Palestine National Council in April 1987 (when the Jordan-PLO accord of 1985 was formally abrogated).

In May 1987, following several secret meetings with King Hussein, Shimon Peres (who was now the Israeli Minister of Foreign Affairs) claimed to have made significant progress on the crucial issue of Palestinian representation at a Middle East peace conference, and to have the consent of Egypt, Jordan and the USA to convene an international conference, including the five permanent members of the UN Security Council and a delegation of Palestinians who 'reject terrorism and violence' and accept Security Council Resolutions 242 and 338 as the basis for negotiations. The Jordanian Prime Minister, Zaid ar-Rifai, confirmed Jordan's willingness to participate in a conference in a joint Jordanian-Palestinian delegation, including the PLO, provided that it complied with the stated conditions. However, Peres failed to secure the support of a majority of the Israeli Cabinet for his proposals. The Israeli Prime Minister, Itzhak Shamir, was opposed in principle to an international peace conference and reiterated his alternative proposal of direct regional talks, excluding the PLO.

At the first full meeting of the Arab League for eight years, convened in Amman in November 1987, King Hussein pursued his agenda of trying to forge greater Arab unity and, in particular, a *rapprochement* between Iraq and Syria. Prior to the meeting, Jordan restored full diplomatic relations with Libya, which had modified its support for Iran in the Iran-Iraq War and had urged a cease-fire. However, King Hussein's appeal for Egypt to be restored to membership of the League (suspended following the Peace Treaty with Israel in 1979) was resisted by Libya and Syria, although 11 Arab states subsequently re-established diplomatic relations after the summit meeting. Jordan also announced the resumption of co-operation with the PLO at the summit meeting.

These achievements were soon overshadowed by the Palestinian uprising (*intifada*), which erupted in the West Bank and Gaza Strip in December 1987, in protest at the continued Israeli occupation of the Palestinian territories and the seemingly indifferent attitude of Arab states at the Amman summit meeting to the Palestinians' plight. The Israeli authorities found it increasingly difficult to suppress the *intifada*, and world-wide condemnation of their brutal tactics prompted George Shultz, the US Secretary of State, to devise another peace initiative, which this time envisaged an international peace conference, at which, however, there would be no PLO representation in a proposed joint Jordanian-Palestinian delegation.

The *intifada*, however, increased international support for the PLO and Palestinian national rights, and, at an extraordinary summit meeting of the Arab League in June 1988, King Hussein gave the *intifada* his unconditional support and insisted that the PLO must represent the Palestinians at any future peace conference. No longer a viable alternative to the PLO, King Hussein cancelled the West Bank Development Plan in July and severed Jordan's legal and administrative links with the West Bank in accordance with agreements reached at the Arab League meeting. Jordan's disengagement from the West Bank effectively rendered the Shultz Plan redundant.

On 15 November 1988 the PLO proclaimed the establishment of an independent State of Palestine and, for the first time, endorsed the UN Security Council's Resolution 242 as a basis for a Middle East peace settlement, thus implicitly recognizing Israel. Jordan and 60 other countries recognized the new state. In December Yasser Arafat addressed a special session of the UN General Assembly in Geneva, where he renounced violence on behalf of the PLO. Subsequently, the USA opened a dialogue with the PLO, and it appeared that Israel would have to negotiate directly with the PLO if it wished to seek a solution to the Palestinian question, and that Jordan's future participation in the peace process was likely to be of less significance.

In April 1989 rioting occurred in several Jordanian cities, after the Government had imposed price rises of between 15% and 50% on basic goods and services. The riots led to the resignation of the Prime Minister and his Cabinet. On 24 April Field Marshal Sharif Zaid bin Shaker, who had been Commander-in-Chief of the Jordanian Armed Forces between 1976 and 1988, was appointed Prime Minister, at the head of a new Cabinet. While King Hussein refused to make any concessions regarding the price increases that had provoked the disturbances (and which had been implemented in accordance with an agreement with the IMF), he announced that a general election would be held for the first time since 1967.

The election to the 80-seat House of Representatives took place in early November 1989 and was contested by 647 candidates, most of whom were independent, as the ban on political parties (in force since 1963) had not been withdrawn. However, it was possible for the Muslim Brotherhood (MB) to present candidates for election, owing to its legal status as a charity rather than a political party. At the election the MB won 20 seats, while it was estimated that a further 12–14 seats were won by independent Islamic candidates who supported the MB.

It was estimated that Palestinian or Arab nationalist candidates won seven seats and that candidates who were supporters of 'leftist' political groupings won four seats. The remaining seats were won by candidates who were broadly considered to be supporters of the Government. The strength of support for the opposition candidates was regarded as surprising, both in Jordan and abroad, especially since a disproportionately large number of seats had been assigned to rural areas from which the Government has traditionally drawn most support. In early December Mudar Badran was appointed Prime Minister by King Hussein. Badran had served as Prime Minister twice previously, during 1976–79 and 1980–84. Badran's new Cabinet did not include any members of the MB who had been elected to the House of Representatives, the MB having declined participation after its demand for the education portfolio had been rejected. Included in the new Cabinet, however, were three independent Muslim deputies and three 'leftists', all of whom were regarded as members of the opposition. A further four deputies appointed to the Cabinet were described as independent nationalists close to the State, while a further six had held office in the previous Cabinet under Field Marshal Sharif Zaid bin Shaker. The new Government received a vote of confidence from the House of Representatives on 1 January 1990. During the debate which preceded the vote, the Prime Minister pledged to abolish martial law (which had been suspended on 19 December 1989) within four to six months, and to liberalize the judicial system. The Prime Minister affirmed continuing support for prevailing austerity measures, and at the end of January announced the abolition of the 1954 anti-communism law.

In November 1989 King Hussein had announced his intention of appointing a royal commission to draft a national charter that would legalize political parties. In April 1990 the King named the 60-member commission, to convene under the chairmanship of a former Prime Minister, Ahmad Ubeidat. The national charter which the commission drafted was approved by the King in January 1991, and further endorsed by the King and leading political figures in June.

In early January 1991 King Hussein reshuffled the Cabinet to include five members of the MB, one of whom received the sensitive portfolio of Minister of Education, in response to continued pressure following the movement's exclusion from the Cabinet formed in December 1989.

Jordan was deeply affected by Iraq's invasion of Kuwait in August 1990, and the consequent imposition of economic sanctions by the UN against Iraq. Iraq was Jordan's principal trading partner, and Jordan relied on supplies of Iraqi petroleum. Although King Hussein condemned Iraq's invasion of Kuwait, he was slow to do so, and hoped for an 'Arab solution' to the problem. There was considerable support for Saddam Hussain among the Jordanian population, particularly among the Palestinians. King Hussein was therefore critical of the large deployment of multinational military forces in Saudi Arabia and the Gulf region, which he regarded as US-dominated, and throughout the closing months of 1990 he visited numerous Middle Eastern and other capitals in an attempt to avert a war that could be potentially disastrous for Jordan.

In the early stages of the Gulf crisis Jordan experienced the additional problem of a large-scale influx of refugees from Iraq and Kuwait, many of whom were seeking passage through Jordan in order to return to the Indian sub-continent and South East Asia. According to Jordanian officials, about 470,000 foreigners fled to Jordan in the five weeks following the Iraqi invasion of Kuwait. Many of these, particularly non-Arab Asians, remained stranded in overcrowded camps on the Iraqi-Jordanian border, suffering severe privations, while awaiting repatriation. Conditions improved in early September, as new camps were established and chartered aircraft carried some of the refugees to their countries of origin. However, the exodus of evacuees to the border region continued daily, and in September Jordan issued an urgent appeal for international assistance with the costs of accommodating and repatriating them. By late September the number of refugees remaining had been reduced to 30,000.

In addition to foreign arrivals, Jordan received large numbers of its own nationals fleeing from the Gulf region. About 300,000 of these expatriates remained in Jordan after the liberation of Kuwait in February 1991, as the rulers of Kuwait had regarded most Jordanian and Palestinian residents as collaborators with the Iraqi occupation forces.

Jordan's response to the Gulf crisis, during which it refused openly to oppose the Iraqi invasion of Kuwait and condemned operation 'Desert Storm', prompted the USA to review its military and economic assistance to Jordan ($85.6m. in 1990) and led to a deterioration in Jordan's relations with Egypt and Saudi Arabia, both of which contributed armed forces to the US-led coalition. However, relations between Jordan and Iran improved and the two countries re-established diplomatic relations (which had been severed in 1981). After a Soviet plan for a settlement, which excluded reference to the Palestinian-Israeli dispute, had been endorsed by Iraq, King Hussein agreed to abandon the linkage that he had hitherto advocated between the Gulf crisis and wider Middle Eastern issues. Notwithstanding this softening in Jordan's position, the country remained economically crippled and politically ostracized by the major Western and Arab powers.

In the months following the end of the Gulf War, Jordan concentrated on attempts to revive its shattered economy (see below) and on improving its relations with Arab neighbours, particularly Saudi Arabia. In response to Jordanian co-operation in the arrest of a Saudi dissident, Muhammad al-Fassi, in Amman, Saudi Arabia revoked a ban on the entry of Jordanian trucks into its territory, and trade links between Jordan and Saudi Arabia were re-activated. However, high-level ministerial contacts did not resume until mid-1995. In early 1996 King Hussein visited Saudi Arabia, but was apparently rebuffed in an attempt to meet King Fahd. Nevertheless, King Hussein emphasized the improvement that was taking place in relations between Jordan and Saudi Arabia.

On the wider front of the Middle East peace negotiations, Jordan won the approval of the USA by agreeing to join with a Palestinian delegation at the US-inspired peace conference which opened in Madrid, Spain, in October 1991. Subsequent negotiations in Washington and Moscow between the Israeli and the joint Jordanian-Palestinian delegations remained deadlocked, with regard to substantive issues, until September 1993, when Israel and the PLO agreed to a declaration of principles regarding Palestinian self-rule in the Occupied Territories. On the signing of the Declaration of Principles, the joint Jordanian-Palestinian delegation was disbanded, and King Hussein welcomed the agreement between Israel and the PLO. On the day following the signing of the Declaration of Principles, Jordan and Israel concluded an agreement that defined the agenda for subsequent negotiations between the two countries within the context of the Middle East peace conference. The agenda, which aimed to achieve a 'just, lasting and comprehensive peace', was to deal with the following issues: refugees and displaced persons; security; water resources; the demarcation of the border between Jordan and Israel; and future bilateral co-operation.

While Jordan welcomed the agreement concluded between Israel and the PLO as progress towards regional stability, it remained concerned by aspects of the Declaration of Principles which affected it directly and over which it had not been consulted. In 1991 Jordan and the PLO had agreed on the principle of confederation between Jordan and whatever Palestinian entity ultimately emerged from the Middle East peace process; and in mid-July 1993 Jordan and the PLO had agreed to form six committees to discuss relations between Jordan and the Occupied Territories during a period of transitional Palestinian self-rule. Within the terms of the Declaration of Principles, however, Jordan was formally excluded from the discussion of some of the issues—henceforth to be dealt with bilaterally by Israeli and Palestinian authorities—which the six committees had already begun to address. Under the terms of the Declaration of Principles, Jordan was to be invited to join a joint Israeli-Palestinian Liaison Committee to determine procedures for the return of Palestinians displaced from the West Bank and the Gaza Strip in 1967. However, Jordan stated its unwillingness to join such a committee, since it had not been consulted about its establishment. In January 1994, after King Hussein had twice warned that Jordan might otherwise pursue its own agenda in the ongoing peace negotiations with Israel, the PLO agreed to sign a comprehensive economic co-operation agreement with Jordan, and to establish a joint committee to co-ordinate financial policy in the Occupied Territories. Later in the same month Jordan signed a draft security accord with the PLO, which established principles for co-operation on security issues. The reaction of the Jordanian Government to the Cairo Agreement signed by Israel and the PLO in May (see chapter on Israel, Recent History) was relatively subdued. Yasser Arafat visited Amman on 5 May in order to brief King Hussein on the Cairo Agreement, but the King reportedly remained disappointed at the PLO's failure to liaise fully with Jordan in the peace process.

On 25 July 1994 in Washington, DC, King Hussein and the Prime Minister of Israel, Itzhak Rabin, signed the Washington Declaration, which formally ended the state of war that had existed between Jordan and Israel since 1948. It was the first time that King Hussein had publicly met an Israeli Prime Minister. In late October Jordan and Israel signed a full peace treaty settling all the issues of contention between them and providing, among other things, for the establishment of diplomatic relations, talks on economic co-operation and for co-operation on security issues. In Jordan the treaty was again opposed by Islamic militants and it was also criticized by the Government of Syria. The leadership of the PLO complained that the treaty with Israel undermined Palestinian claims to sovereignty over Jerusalem. The official normalization of relations between Jordan and Israel had been completed by 18 January 1996.

In January 1995 the PLO and Jordan signed an agreement which regulated relations between Jordan and the Palestinian autonomous areas with regard to economic affairs, finance, banking, education, transport, telecommunications, information and administration. At the same time, the PLO acknowledged Jordan's custodianship of the Muslim holy places in Jerusalem for as long as Jordan recognized and supported Palestinians' claims to sovereignty over East Jerusalem.

Meanwhile, in June 1991 Taher al-Masri succeeded Mudar Badran as Prime Minister. However, in the period preceding the opening of the National Assembly in December, al-Masri could not command majority support from the deputies and was forced to resign. His replacement, Field Marshal Sharif Zaid ibn Shaker, a cousin of King Hussein and formerly Minister of the Royal Court, aimed to restore full relations with Saudi Arabia and to improve relations with Egypt and Syria.

In June 1992 an extraordinary session of the House of Representatives was convened in order to debate new laws regarding political parties and the press. In early July the House adopted legislation whereby, subject to certain conditions, political parties were formally legalized, in preparation for the country's first multi-party elections, which were to be held before November 1993. In May King Hussein appointed a new Cabinet, in which Abd as-Salam al-Majali, the leader of the Jordanian delegation to the Middle East peace conference, replaced Zaid ibn Shaker as Prime Minister. The new Government was regarded as a transitional administration, pending the country's first multi-party election.

At the beginning of August 1993 King Hussein unexpectedly dissolved the House of Representatives, provoking criticism from some politicians who had expected the House to debate proposed changes to the country's electoral law. Changes in voting procedures at the general election were subsequently announced by the King in mid-August. Voters were to be allowed to cast one vote only, rather than a number equal to that of the number of candidates contesting a given constituency, as before. By far the largest number of deputies returned to the House of Representatives at Jordan's first multi-party general election on 8 November (in which some 68% of the electorate was reported to have participated) were independent centrists whose first loyalty was to the King. The Islamic Action Front (IAF, the political wing of the MB), which emerged as the second largest party in the House of Representatives, complained that the new electoral law had prevented it from winning more seats. A new Senate was appointed by the King on 18 November, and on 1 December a new Cabinet was announced.

In early January 1995 there was an extensive reorganization of the Government, following the dismissal of al-Majali as Prime Minister. He was replaced by Sharif Zaid ibn Shaker, who had served as Prime Minister in 1989 and 1991–93, and was a close ally and a cousin of the King. Two new political blocs emerged in the National Assembly in early 1995. The Independent National Action Front (INAF), with 17 deputies, was formed by a merger of the National Action Front (NAF) and the bloc of independent deputies. The former Speaker of the National Assembly, Taher al-Masri, formed a second new grouping of some 15 liberal and independent Islamist deputies. In municipal elections held in July, however, Islamic and left-wing groups failed to gain significant popular support, most elected candidates being largely pro-Government or independent. The IAF alleged that its poor performance was due to a low level of voter participation, and to government harassment of its members during the campaign.

In early February 1996 King Hussein carried out an extensive cabinet reshuffle, including the appointment of Abdul-Karim Kabariti as Prime Minister. In mid-August rioting erupted in the south of the country after the Government increased the price of bread by more than 100%. The unrest quickly spread to other parts of the country, including impoverished areas of the capital, and was regarded as the greatest challenge to King Hussein's rule since rioting in 1989 in protest at rises in the price of fuel. In response to the rioting, King Hussein suspended the legislature and deployed the army in order to suppress the worst disturbances. In December the Government announced its commitment to the reform of some elements of Jordan's electoral law before the next legislative elections.

On 19 March 1997 Prime Minister Kabariti was unexpectedly dismissed by King Hussein, reportedly as a result of the former's disagreement with the King on issues relating to Jordan's policies towards Israel. Abd as-Salam al-Majali, who had previously served as Prime Minister between May 1993 and January 1995, was appointed as Kabariti's replacement. On his appointment, al-Majali formed a new Cabinet, in which he himself held the defence portfolio in addition to the premiership.

In July 1997 the IAF announced its intention to boycott the forthcoming parliamentary elections, scheduled to be held in early November, in protest at government policies towards Israel and recent restrictive amendments to press legislation. Later in July a number of other parties declared their intention to join the boycott. Despite widespread boycotts the elections were held as scheduled on 4 November, although many of the 524 candidates were independents or tribal leaders campaigning on local issues. The newly-elected House of Representatives included limited Islamic or Palestinian representation, with 62 of the 80 seats won by pro-Government candidates, 10 seats secured by nationalist and left-wing candidates and eight seats won by independent Islamists. The overall level of voter participation in the elections was reported to have been 54.6%, and was declared by the Government to be an endorsement of the country's electoral system and of the policies of King Hussein. In some districts of the capital, however, the level of turn-out was claimed to have been as low as 20%; it was also reported that the majority of Jordan's Palestinians did not vote in the elections. In late November a new Senate was appointed by King Hussein. In mid-February 1998 King Hussein carried out a cabinet reorganization in an apparent attempt to strengthen the Government in advance of a possible US-led military strike against Iraq.

Meanwhile, in late September 1997 the head of the political bureau of the Islamist group Hamas, Khalid Mish'al, was attacked in Amman in an unsuccessful assassination attempt; two agents of the Israeli intelligence service, Mossad, were later arrested in connection with the attack. Although the Israeli embassy in Amman issued a statement denying any Israeli involvement in the incident, King Hussein declared that the assassination attempt had severely damaged Jordanian confidence in the Israeli Government.

In June 1992 the USA postponed a joint military exercise with Jordan in order to express its disapproval of the assistance that Jordan was allegedly providing to Iraq to enable it to circumvent the UN trade embargo. The USA subsequently proposed that UN observers should be dispatched to Jordan in order to suppress the smuggling of goods to Iraq. Jordan rejected the proposal outright as an infringement of its sovereignty. In late August both the Jordanian Government and the House of Representatives condemned Western plans to establish an air exclusion zone in southern Iraq. In January 1993 King Hussein strongly criticized renewed air attacks on targets in Iraq by Western air forces, but emphasized that Jordan would remain on friendly terms with the USA under the newly-elected administration of Bill Clinton. At the end of July the USA was reported to have informed Jordan that it must make payments to the UN's Compensation Fund for Kuwait if it continued to receive deliveries of petroleum from Iraq. In mid-September, however, US President Clinton announced that some $30m. in economic and military aid to Jordan was to be released in recognition of the country's enforcement of sanctions against Iraq and of its role in the Middle East peace process.

In March 1994 new tensions emerged with the USA over Jerusalem and over the US-led naval blockade of Jordan's only port at Aqaba. After the adoption of Resolution 904 by the UN Security Council in March, Jordan protested strongly about the US position on the status of Jerusalem. The USA had insisted that voting on the resolution should take place paragraph by paragraph and in this way had abstained on two paragraphs in the preamble concerning Jerusalem. In one of the paragraphs Jerusalem was referred to as part of the Occupied Territories. Jordan was concerned about the legal and political implications of what appeared to be an important change in US policy towards Jerusalem. At the end of March the Jordanian Government informed the USA that the interception of ships bound for Aqaba by the US-led multilateral inspection force as part of UN sanctions against Iraq was seriously damaging the Jordanian economy. Jordan warned that unless this problem was resolved it would cease participation in the Middle East peace process. In late April the USA announced that it had accepted a Jordanian proposal for a new system of monitoring cargo bound for Aqaba.

In an address to the Jordanian National Assembly in October 1994, US President Clinton pledged to cancel Jordan's official debts to the USA, totalling US $702m., apparently as a reward for signing the peace treaty with Israel. Although some $220m. of debt was written off during the fiscal year 1994, the new Republican-dominated US Congress was inclined to be less generous in 1995. King Hussein was forced to visit the USA in April 1995 in an attempt to persuade Congress to permit the debt-cancellation plan to proceed. In September an agreement was finally signed by the USA and Jordan, cancelling $420m. of Jordan's outstanding debt. In August, as King Hussein broke formally with Iraq (see below), US President Clinton promised to support Jordan in the event of any threat to its security. However, the USA was unable to persuade Jordan to sever all of its economic links with Iraq. In January 1996 the USA offered Jordan $300m. in military aid, and in March it was announced that military co-operation between Jordan and the USA was to be expanded in future. In June 1997 the USA announced its intention to give $100m. in aid to Jordan to assist with the country's economic development; an assistance fund was officially established in August. The aid was reported to represent an expression of US appreciation of Jordan's contributions to the Middle East peace process. Also in August, Jordan signed a debt-rescheduling agreement with the USA, in accordance with an agreement reached in May by creditors of the 'Paris Club' to reschedule approximately $400m. of Jordanian debt. In January 1998 Jordan received three F-16 fighter aircraft from the USA as part of an on-going programme of US military aid first endorsed by the USA in 1996. A further nine aircraft were scheduled to be received by Jordan by the end of the following month. Meanwhile, in November 1997 and again in January 1998 King Hussein demanded that the USA play a more active role in pressing Israel to abandon policies perceived as hindering the progress of the Middle East peace process.

Since August 1995, when Jordan granted political asylum to the two sons-in-law of the Iraqi President, Saddam Hussain, and their wives after they fled from Baghdad to Amman (see Iraq, Recent History), King Hussein has become more openly critical of the Iraqi regime. At the same time, Jordan has continued to provide Iraq with a vitally important external economic link. In October King Hussein denounced the presidential election in Iraq as a farce, and it was reported that he had established contact with Iraqi opposition groups in London, United Kingdom, and had also promoted the holding of a congress in Amman in order to discuss political change in Iraq. Jordan's new policy on Iraq was welcomed by Saudi Arabia, but was viewed with suspicion by Egypt and Syria for fear that it might lead to a further US-backed strategic reorientation in the region, bringing together the USA, Israel, Turkey and Jordan in a military alliance designed to protect Israeli and US interests in the region. In December 1997 Jordan recalled its chargé d'affaires in Baghdad and expelled a number of Iraqi diplomats from Jordan in protest at the execution two days earlier of four Jordanians by the Iraqi authorities. Although the executions caused tension in relations between the two countries, Iraq insisted that it had not intended to provoke Jordan by carrying out the sentences and, later in the same month, the two countries signed an agreement under which Iraq was to supply 4.8m. metric tons of crude petroleum and refined petroleum products to Jordan in 1998. In January 1998 more than 50 Jordanian prisoners and detainees were released by Iraq in a gesture of goodwill. In mid-February riot police dispersed several thousand demonstrators protesting in the capital against the US-led military build-up in the Gulf. The demonstrations were organized by various Islamist groups and trade unions, in defiance of an official ban on pro-Iraq protests.

Government

Jordan is a constitutional monarchy. Legislative power is vested in a bicameral National Assembly. The Senate (House of Notables) has 40 members, appointed by the King for eight years (one-half of the members retiring every four years), while the House of Representatives (House of Deputies) has 80 members, elected by universal adult suffrage for four years. Executive power is vested in the King, who governs with the assistance of an appointed Council of Ministers, responsible to the Assembly.

There are eight administrative provinces, of which three have been occupied by Israel since June 1967.

Defence

The total strength of the Jordanian armed forces in August 1997 was estimated at 104,050. The army had 90,000 men, the air force 13,400 and the navy (coastguard) an estimated 650. Reserves number 35,000 (30,000 in the army). There are paramilitary forces numbering an estimated 30,000 men, comprising a Civil Militia of 20,000 and a Public Security Force of 10,000. Military service is based on selective conscription. The defence budget for 1997 was estimated at JD 300m.

Economic Affairs

In 1995, according to estimates by the World Bank, the East Bank of Jordan's gross national product (GNP), measured at average 1993–95 prices, was US $6,354m., equivalent to $1,510 per head. During 1985–95, it was estimated, the region's population increased by an annual average of 4.7%. The East Bank's gross domestic product (GDP) increased, in real terms, by an annual average of 3.1% in 1985–95. In 1996 GDP increased, in real terms, by 5.2%.

Agriculture (including forestry and fishing) contributed an estimated 5.4% of Jordan's GDP in 1996. An estimated 7.4% of the country's labour force were employed in the sector in 1992. The principal cash crops are vegetables, fruit and nuts, which accounted for about 7.9% of export earnings in 1996. Wheat production is also important. During 1985–95 agricultural production increased by an annual average of 4.3%.

Industry (including mining, manufacturing, construction and power) provided an estimated 29.5% of GDP in 1996. In 1992 an estimated 21.4% of the country's active labour force were employed in the industrial sector. During 1985–95 industrial production increased by an annual average of 2%.

Mining contributed an estimated 3.5% of GDP in 1996. Phosphates and potash are the major mineral exports; together they accounted for about 24.3% of total export earnings in 1996. Jordan also has reserves of oil-bearing shale, but exploitation of this resource is at present undeveloped.

Manufacturing provided an estimated 15.8% of GDP in 1996, and, together with mining, engaged about 10.3% of the total employed labour force in 1992. In 1994 the most important branches of manufacturing, measured by the value of output, were chemical products (accounting for 35.6% of the total), petroleum refineries (16.1%), food products (13.9%) and non-metallic mineral products (10.1%).

Energy is derived principally from imported petroleum, but attempts are being made to develop alternative sources of power, including wind and solar power. Imports of mineral fuels comprised 12.2% of the total value of imports in 1996.

Services (including wholesale and retail trade, restaurants and hotels, transport, financing and community, social and personal services) accounted for an estimated 65.2% of Jordan's GDP in 1996. In 1992 an estimated 71.2% of the total employed labour force were engaged in the service sector.

In 1996 Jordan recorded a visible trade deficit of US $2,001.1m., and there was a deficit of $221.9m. on the current account of the balance of payments. In 1996 Iraq was the principal source of imports and, in 1995, was also the principal market for exports. Other major trading partners were Germany, India, Italy, Saudi Arabia and the USA. The principal exports in 1996 were chemicals, minerals and vegetables, fruit and nuts, and the principal imports were machinery and transport equipment, food and live animals and basic manufactures.

In 1996 there was a budget surplus of JD 75.9m. The annual rate of inflation averaged 4.2% in 1990–95. The average rate of inflation in 1996 was 6.6%. Jordan's external debt totalled US $7,944m. at the end of 1995, of which US $6,904m. was long-term public debt. In that year the cost of debt-servicing was equivalent to 12.6% of the value of exports of goods and services. An estimated 13%–15% of the labour force were unemployed in 1995.

Jordan is a member of the Arab League (see p. 195), the Arab Co-operation Council (p. 259), the Council of Arab Economic Unity (p. 139), the Organization of the Islamic Conference (p. 224) and the Arab Monetary Fund (p. 259).

In the 1990s two factors have acted as constraints on the Jordanian economy: a heavy burden of foreign debt; and the loss, owing to the imposition of sanctions by the UN, of the Iraqi market, towards which Jordanian industry had been mainly orientated. On a positive note, Jordan's conclusion of a peace treaty with Israel has already created new opportunities for the tourist industry—and revealed some of its infrastructural inadequacies—and should create more in the fields of banking, transport and exports, and promote increased regional co-operation in, for example, the management of water resources. Jordan's response to its economic challenges has been an adjustment and reform programme which aims gradually to reduce the role of the state in industry and, at the same time—through privatization—raise funds to contribute towards the repayment of foreign debts. Jordan is also seeking to maximize revenues from exports of its two most important mineral resources, phosphates and potash. In collaboration with the IMF, Jordan is deemed to have brought its external debt under control; in October 1996 the IMF carried out a favourable review of the country's structural reform programme. In January 1997, after limited sales of Iraqi petroleum had been approved by the UN, Jordan and Iraq signed a trade agreement under which Jordan was to receive supplies of crude petroleum and partial repayment of Iraq's $1,300m. debt in exchange for goods. In December 1997 the agreement was renewed to cover the following year.

In January 1997 the IMF approved an extension of the amount of credit available to Jordan under its extended Fund faculty (EFF) credit. In May the creditors of the 'Paris Club' reached an agreement to reschedule approximately US $400m. of Jordan's debt, and in September, in the third and final stage of a programme initiated in 1994, the USA cancelled $63.4m. of Jordanian debt.

In June 1997, as part of the Government's economic deregulation plan aimed at encouraging foreign investment, the Central Bank of Jordan lifted all restrictions on the movement of foreign currency.

Social Welfare

There is no comprehensive welfare scheme but the Government administers medical and health services. In 1985 the East Bank region had 44 hospital establishments, with 3,578 beds, and 2,576 physicians. A new Social Security Law, providing security for both employers and employees, was put into effect in 1978 and extended in 1981. Of total budgetary expenditure by the central Government in 1995, JD 103.7m. (7.0%) was for health services, and a further JD 246.3m. (16.7%) for social security and welfare. In June 1996 there were 1,358,706 refugees registered with UNRWA in Jordan and a further 532,438 in the West Bank.

Education

Primary education is free and compulsory. It starts at the age of six years and lasts for ten years. The preparatory cycle is followed by a two-year secondary cycle. UNRWA provides schooling for Palestinian Arab refugees. In 1995/96, at the primary level, there were 51,721 teachers and 1,074,877 pupils. At the secondary level (including both general and vocational secondary education) in 1995/96, there were 10,921 teachers and 176,123 pupils. In 1995/96 there were 4,821 teachers and 99,020 pupils engaged in higher education. There are 10 universities in Jordan. Budgetary expenditure on education by the central Government in 1995 was JD 227.8m. (15.5% of total spending).

Public Holidays

1998: 15 January (Arbor Day), 30 January (Id al-Fitr, end of Ramadan), 22 March (Arab League Day), 8 April (Id al-Adha, Feast of the Sacrifice), 28 April (Islamic New Year), 25 May (Independence Day), 7 July (Mouloud, birth of Muhammad), 11 August (King Hussein's Accession), 14 November (King Hussein's Birthday), 17 November (Leilat al-Meiraj, ascension of Muhammad).

1999: 15 January (Arbor Day), 19 January (Id al-Fitr, end of Ramadan), 22 March (Arab League Day), 28 March (Id al-Adha, Feast of the Sacrifice), 17 April (Islamic New Year), 25 May (Independence Day), 26 June (Mouloud, birth of Muhammad), 11 August (King Hussein's Accession), 6 November (Leilat al-Meiraj, ascension of Muhammad), 14 November (King Hussein's Birthday).

Weights and Measures

The metric system is in force. In Jordan the dunum is 1,000 sq m (0.247 acre).

Statistical Survey

Source: Department of Statistics, POB 2015, Jabal Amman, 1st Circle, POB 2015, Amman; tel. 24313.

Area and Population

AREA, POPULATION AND DENSITY
(East and West Banks)

Area (sq km)	97,740*
Population (UN estimates at mid-year)†	
1993	4,936,000
1994	5,198,000
1995	5,439,000
Density (per sq km) at mid-1996	55.6

* 37,738 sq miles.

† Source: UN, *World Population Prospects: The 1994 Revision.*

(East Bank only)

Area (sq km)	89,342*
Population (census results)	
10–11 November 1979	2,100,019
10 December 1994	
Males	2,135,883
Females	1,959,696
Total	4,095,579
Population (official estimates at mid-year)	
1994	4,066,000
1995	4,215,000
1996	4,368,000
Density (per sq km) at mid-1996	48.9

* 34,495 sq miles.

GOVERNORATES
(East Bank only; estimated population at 31 December 1996)

Amman	1,696,300
Irbid	802,200
Zarqa	687,000
Balqa	301,300
Mafraq	191,900
Karak	182,200
Jarash	132,500
Madaba	110,700
Ajlun	101,400
Aqaba	85,700
Ma'an	85,300
Tafiela	67,500
Total	4,444,000

PRINCIPAL TOWNS (including suburbs)

Population at 31 December 1991: Amman (capital) 965,000; Zarqa 359,000; Irbid 216,000; Russeifa 115,500.

BIRTHS, MARRIAGES AND DEATHS (East Bank only)*

	Registered live births		Registered marriages		Registered deaths	
	Number	Rate (per 1,000)	Number	Rate (per 1,000)	Number	Rate (per 1,000)
1989	115,742	n.a.	31,508	n.a.	9,695	n.a.
1990	116,520	n.a.	32,706	n.a.	10,569	n.a.
1991	120,554	n.a.	35,926	n.a.	10,605	n.a.
1992	125,395	n.a.	37,216	n.a.	11,820	n.a.
1993	134,489	n.a.	40,391	n.a.	11,915	n.a.
1994	140,444	34.5	36,132	8.9	12,290	3.0
1995	141,319	33.5	35,501	8.4	13,018	3.1
1996	142,404	32.6	34,425	7.9	13,302	3.0

* Data are tabulated by year of registration rather than by year of occurrence. Registration of births and marriages is reported to be complete, but death registration is incomplete. Figures exclude foreigners, but include registered Palestinian refugees.

Expectation of life (UN estimates, years at birth, 1990–95): Males 66.16; Females 69.84. Source: UN, *Demographic Yearbook*.

ECONOMICALLY ACTIVE POPULATION (Jordanians only)

	1990	1991	1992
Agriculture	38,266	40,848	44,400
Mining and manufacturing	53,468	56,856	61,800
Electricity and water	6,815	7,176	6,600
Construction	51,895	54,096	60,000
Trade	52,944	56,856	63,000
Transport and communications	44,557	48,576	52,200
Financial and insurance services	16,774	17,664	19,800
Social and administrative services	259,478	269,928	292,200
Total employed	524,197	552,000	600,000
Unemployed	106,000	128,000	106,000
Total civilian labour force	630,197	680,000	706,000

Source: Ministry of Labour, *Annual Report*.

Agriculture

PRINCIPAL CROPS (East Bank only; '000 metric tons)

	1994	1995	1996
Wheat	47	58	51
Barley	27	32	45
Potatoes	49	97	147
Olives	94	63	82
Cabbages	13	24	22
Tomatoes	439	440	475
Cauliflowers	39	32	32*
Pumpkins, squash and gourds	28	36	38*
Cucumbers and gherkins	35	66	68*
Eggplants (Aubergines)	38	73	74*
Green peppers	11	18	19*
Onions (dry)	21	31	79
Green beans	8	8	8*
Other vegetables	47	120	125*
Watermelons	123	99	105*
Melons	22	19	20*
Grapes	26	24	84
Apples	28	42	45
Oranges	30	21	26
Tangerines, mandarins, clementines and satsumas	85	47	55
Lemons and limes	30	32	44
Bananas	25	29	39
Other fruits and berries	49	37	46
Tobacco (leaves)	2	5	3

* FAO estimate.

Source: FAO, *Production Yearbook*.

LIVESTOCK
(East Bank only; FAO estimates, '000 head, year ending September)

	1994	1995	1996
Horses	4	4	4
Mules	3	3	3
Asses	19	19	19
Cattle	42	43	43
Camels	18	18	18
Sheep	2,100	2,100	2,100
Goats	555	555	555

Poultry (FAO estimates, million): 77 in 1994; 78 in 1995; 78 in 1996.
Source: FAO, *Production Yearbook*.

LIVESTOCK PRODUCTS (East Bank only; '000 metric tons)

	1994	1995	1996*
Beef and veal	1†	1*	1
Mutton and lamb	12†	13*	13
Goat meat	3†	3*	3
Poultry meat	94	95*	95
Cows' milk	89†	90*	90
Sheep's milk	38†	39*	39
Goats' milk	24†	24*	24
Cheese	4*	4*	4
Butter	2*	2*	2
Poultry eggs	53	44	50
Wool: greasy	4*	4*	4
clean	2*	2*	2
Sheepskins	2*	2*	n.a.

* FAO estimate(s). † Unofficial figure.
Source: FAO, *Production Yearbook*.

Forestry

ROUNDWOOD REMOVALS
(FAO estimates, '000 cubic metres, excluding bark)

	1992	1993	1994
Industrial wood	4	4	4
Fuel wood	7	8	8
Total	11	12	12

Source: FAO, *Yearbook of Forest Products*.

Fishing

(metric tons, live weight)

	1993	1994	1995
Freshwater fishes	60	86	170
Marine fishes	2	2	2
Total catch	62	88	172

Source: FAO, *Yearbook of Fishery Statistics*.

Mining

('000 metric tons)

	1994	1995	1996
Crude petroleum	1.2	1.5	1.9
Phosphate rock	4,216.5	4,983.9	5,424.2
Potash salts*	1,550.3	1,780.0	1,765.5
Salt (unrefined)	19	57	50

* Figures refer to the K_2O content.

Industry

SELECTED PRODUCTS ('000 metric tons, unless otherwise indicated)

	1992	1993	1994
Liquefied petroleum gas	122	127	126
Motor spirit (petrol)	421	430	471
Aviation gasoline	17	21	20†
Kerosene	297	237	222
Jet fuels	193	220	198
Distillate fuel oils	753	880	859
Residual fuel oils	901	962	901
Lubricating oils	21	21†	24
Petroleum bitumen (asphalt)	124	140	136
Nitrogenous fertilizers (a)*	99.7†	85	n.a.
Phosphate fertilizers (b)*	254.8†	n.a.	n.a.
Potassic fertilizers (c)*	795.0†	n.a.	n.a.
Cement	2,651	3,437	3,392
Cigarettes (million)	3,091	3,465	4,115
Electricity (million kWh)	4,422	4,761	5,075

* Production in terms of (a) nitrogen; (b) phosphoric acid; and (c) potassium oxide.

† Estimated production.

Source: mainly UN, *Industrial Commodity Statistics Yearbook*.

1995: Cigarettes 3,667 million.
1996: Cigarettes 2,769 million.

Source: Central Bank of Jordan.

Finance

CURRENCY AND EXCHANGE RATES

Monetary Units

1,000 fils = 1 Jordanian dinar (JD).

Sterling and Dollar Equivalents (30 September 1997)

£1 sterling = JD 1.1453;
US $1 = 709.0 fils;
JD 100 = £87.31 = $141.04.

Average Exchange Rates (US $ per JD)

1994 1.4312
1995 1.4276
1996 1.4104

Note: An exchange rate of US $1 = 709 fils (JD1 = $1.4104) has been maintained since October 1995.

BUDGET (East Bank only; JD million)*

Revenue†	1993	1994	1995
Taxation	812.5	871.1	976.4
Taxes on income, profits and capital gains	118.8	136.6	152.4
Taxes on property	51.0	54.8	66.8
Taxes on financial and capital transactions	49.7	53.1	65.3
Domestic taxes on goods and services	227.1	278.9	351.7
Excises	174.3	222.4	263.6
Taxes on international trade and transactions	353.4	340.2	336.4
Import duties	337.7	324.2	318.7
Other current revenue	306.5	290.4	354.7
Entrepreneurial and property income	235.7	221.8	272.7
Administrative fees and charges, non-industrial and incidental sales	28.5	30.9	41.3
Capital revenue	0.6	0.9	1.5
Total	1,119.6	1,162.4	1,332.6

Expenditure‡	1993	1994	1995
General public services	84.8	82.5	97.8
Defence	258.6	272.0	296.0
Public order and safety	101.1	105.4	121.0
Education	201.2	205.7	227.8
Health	87.1	98.5	103.7
Social security and welfare	189.3	187.6	246.3
Housing and community amenities	16.2	24.0	26.0
Recreational, cultural and religious affairs and services	22.3	27.9	31.5
Economic affairs and services	144.0	161.9	179.5
Agriculture, forestry, fishing and hunting	33.0	53.7	65.7
Transport and communications	71.3	61.4	60.9
Other purposes	131.7	147.4	141.9
Interest payments	122.0	109.4	132.7
Sub-total§	1,236.4	1,312.8	1,471.5
Adjustment	-1.3	—	—
Total	1,235.1	1,312.8	1,471.5

* Figures represent a consolidation of the Current, Capital and Development Plan Budgets of the central Government. The data exclude the operations of the Health Security Fund and of other government agencies with individual budgets.

† Excluding grants received from abroad (JD million): 163.3 (current 160.2, capital 3.1) in 1993; 175.6 (current 168.3, capital 7.3) in 1994; 182.8 (current 175.4, capital 7.4) in 1995.

‡ Excluding lending minus repayments (JD million): -21.9 in 1993; -20.0 in 1994; -5.4 in 1995.

§ Comprising (in JD million): current expenditure 992.3 in 1993, 1,052.8 in 1994, 1,187.9 in 1995; capital expenditure 244.1 in 1993, 260.0 in 1994, 283.6 in 1995.

Source: IMF, *Government Finance Statistics Yearbook*.

1996 (JD million): Revenue 1,518.0, excl. grants received (191.3); Expenditure 1,648.3, excl. net lending (-14.9) (Source: IMF, *International Financial Statistics*).

INTERNATIONAL RESERVES (US $ million at 31 December)

	1994	1995	1996
Gold*	198.5	195.9	197.7
IMF special drawing rights	0.7	1.2	0.8
Foreign exchange	1,691.9	1,971.7	1,758.5
Total	1,891.1	2,168.8	1,957.0

* National valuation.

Source: IMF, *International Financial Statistics*.

MONEY SUPPLY (JD million at 31 December)

	1994	1995	1996
Currency outside banks	1,072.6	1,050.9	952.1
Demand deposits at commercial banks	666.0	664.7	578.1
Total money (incl. others)	1,741.7	1,739.2	1,533.2

Source: IMF, *International Financial Statistics*.

COST OF LIVING (Consumer Price Index; base: 1990 = 100)

	1994	1995	1996
Food (incl. beverages)	123.5	126.3	135.1
Fuel and light	122.3	122.3	125.9
Clothing (incl. footwear)	132.8	142.5	156.9
Rent	117.2	121.4	126.3
All items (incl. others)	120.4	123.1	131.2

Source: Central Bank of Jordan.

NATIONAL ACCOUNTS (East Bank only; JD million at current prices)

Expenditure on the Gross Domestic Product (provisional)

	1994	1995	1996
Government final consumption expenditure	990.2	1,081.2	1,194.0
Private final consumption expenditure	2,774.3	3,023.2	3,393.5
Increase in stocks	60.0	67.5	84.4
Gross fixed capital formation	1,391.0	1,479.9	1,716.9
Total domestic expenditure	5,215.5	5,651.8	6,388.8
Exports of goods and services	2,093.4	2,438.2	2,597.1
Less Imports of goods and services	3,107.6	3,435.4	3,839.2
GDP in purchasers' values	4,201.3	4,654.6	5,146.7
GDP at constant 1990 prices	3,601.4	3,851.3	4,052.8

Source: IMF, *International Financial Statistics*

Gross Domestic Product by Economic Activity (provisional)

	1994	1995	1996
Agriculture, hunting, forestry and fishing	197.2	213.3	232.9
Mining and quarrying	102.4	128.1	153.6
Manufacturing	561.4	618.7	688.6
Electricity, gas and water	84.0	90.8	98.2
Construction	300.2	327.8	341.1
Trade, restaurants and hotels	377.0	423.3	480.1
Transport, storage and communications	494.0	531.7	591.8
Finance, insurance, real estate and business services	658.6	705.6	766.8
Government services	671.2	732.9	792.7
Other community, social and personal services	110.6	121.9	138.3
Private non-profit services to households	47.0	51.8	56.6
Domestic services of households	6.0	6.4	7.0
Sub-total	3,609.6	3,952.3	4,347.7
Less Imputed bank service charge	73.9	79.2	87.3
GDP at factor cost	3,535.7	3,873.1	4,260.4
Indirect taxes *Less* Subsidies	665.6	781.5	886.3
GDP in purchasers' values	4,201.3	4,654.6	5,146.7

BALANCE OF PAYMENTS (US $ million)

	1994	1995	1996
Exports of goods f.o.b.	1,424.5	1,769.6	1,816.9
Imports of goods f.o.b.	−3,003.8	−3,287.8	−3,818.1
Trade balance	−1,579.4	−1,518.2	−2,001.1
Exports of services	1,562.0	1,709.2	1,846.3
Imports of services	−1,392.7	−1,614.9	−1,597.7
Balance on goods and services	−1,410.1	−1,424.0	−1,752.6
Other income received	72.7	115.7	111.7
Other income paid	−387.5	−394.5	−412.7
Balance on goods, services and income	−1,724.9	−1,702.8	−2,053.6
Current transfers received	1,447.4	1,591.8	1,970.2
Current transfers paid	−120.5	−147.6	−138.5
Current balance	−398.0	−258.6	−221.9
Capital account (net)	—	197.2	157.7
Direct investment abroad	23.1	27.3	43.3
Direct investment from abroad	2.9	13.3	15.5
Other investment assets	62.5	−313.4	−5.9
Other investment liabilities	100.4	502.8	181.0
Net errors and omissions	−55.8	−339.9	−357.9
Overall balance	−264.9	−171.3	−188.2

Source: IMF, *International Financial Statistics*.

External Trade

PRINCIPAL COMMODITIES (distribution by SITC, US $ million)

Imports c.i.f.	1994	1995	1996
Food and live animals	586.2	598.2	967.4
Crude materials (inedible) except fuels	102.4	130.0	130.7
Mineral fuels, lubricants, etc.	430.2	480.0	525.4
Crude petroleum	332.5	355.7	n.a.
Animal and vegetable oils and fats	118.1	135.1	103.9
Chemicals	400.6	453.3	464.2
Basic manufactures	618.4	719.2	722.8
Machinery and transport equipment	859.1	905.7	1,114.1
Miscellaneous manufactured articles	217.0	210.0	220.2
Total (incl. others)	3,380.9	3,696.1	4,292.7

Exports f.o.b.	1994	1995	1995
Natural calcium phosphates	143.7	150.5	179.0
Natural potassic salts, crude	132.5	173.5	177.2
Chemicals	375.5	431.1	467.0
Fertilizers	127.5	161.4	n.a.
Cement	39.1	42.2	58.5
Vegetables, fruit and nuts	95.4	97.3	115.7
Basic manufactures	83.8	95.7	109.1
Machinery and transport equipment	56.4	65.5	34.5
Miscellaneous manufactured articles	57.9	68.9	72.1
Total (incl. others)	1,136.1	1,433.3	1,466.6

Sources: Central Bank of Jordan and IMF, *Jordan—Statistical Appendix* (March 1997).

PRINCIPAL TRADING PARTNERS
(countries of consignment, US $ million)

Imports c.i.f.	1994	1995	1996*
Argentina	16.1	48.0	14.0
Australia	29.8	40.1	108.2
Bahrain	22.3	40.4	28.6
Belgium-Luxembourg	100.6	74.2	61.8
Brazil	37.7	52.6	56.7
China, People's Republic	89.5	84.1	89.7
Egypt	43.0	46.2	93.0
France	159.0	170.0	210.5
Germany	263.9	311.6	341.6
India	55.7	69.5	74.3
Indonesia	35.2	54.8	50.9
Iraq	417.1	451.3	505.6
Italy	199.0	197.7	251.6
Japan	134.0	130.5	179.0
Korea, Republic	83.4	109.6	133.0
Lebanon	25.8	42.5	51.6
Malaysia	94.8	107.8	85.6
Netherlands	129.0	102.1	115.4
Romania	39.4	30.7	47.1
Russia	24.3	43.9	51.2
Saudi Arabia	102.4	129.5	129.1
Spain	54.4	58.1	48.1
Switzerland	32.2	38.2	63.1
Syria	69.1	78.4	140.3
Turkey	90.0	127.0	152.3
Ukraine	71.2	55.4	33.7
United Kingdom	162.9	167.1	187.7
USA	332.2	342.6	415.9
Total (incl. others)	3,368.6	3,664.4	4,292.7

* Source: Central Bank of Jordan.

Exports f.o.b.	1993	1994	1995
Bahrain	20.8	23.0	21.5
China, People's Republic	24.3	12.0	19.5
Ethiopia	2.5	5.5	17.0
France	21.3	35.5	30.3
India	95.8	126.5	162.9
Indonesia	54.8	40.0	39.2
Iran	14.5	6.4	27.9
Iraq	140.2	165.0	301.7
Italy	10.7	16.4	28.9
Japan	14.3	18.3	19.1
Korea, Republic	11.0	20.8	18.6
Lebanon	27.9	29.2	38.9
Malaysia	16.3	18.9	21.2
Netherlands	16.6	19.1	25.9
Philippines	4.6	5.6	21.5
Qatar	14.8	13.3	14.7
Russia	37.4	8.8	8.2
Saudi Arabia	124.7	110.5	108.2
Sudan	9.0	15.1	18.4
Syria	36.4	49.8	63.2
Turkey	20.5	15.7	30.4
United Arab Emirates	48.5	68.8	67.2
United Kingdom	13.9	13.8	20.6
USA	38.6	47.5	68.3
Yemen	17.3	11.1	15.8
Total (incl. others)	1,225.2	1,411.1	1,768.8

Source: UN, *International Trade Statistics Yearbook*.

Transport

RAILWAYS (traffic)

	1992	1993	1994
Passenger-km (million)	2	2	2
Freight ton-km (million)	797	711	676

Source: UN, *Statistical Yearbook*.

ROAD TRAFFIC ('000 motor vehicles in use)

	1992	1993	1994
Passenger cars	181.5	175.3	164.0
Commercial vehicles	51.5	63.8	75.3

Source: UN, *Statistical Yearbook*.

SHIPPING

Merchant Fleet (registered at 31 December)

	1994	1995	1996
Number of vessels	4	4	4
Displacement (grt)	60,856	21,288	40,829

Source: Lloyd's Register of Shipping, *World Fleet Statistics*.

International Sea-borne Freight Traffic ('000 metric tons)

	1988	1989	1990
Goods loaded	913	832	739
Goods unloaded	762	725	514

Source: UN, *Monthly Bulletin of Statistics*.

CIVIL AVIATION (traffic on scheduled services)

	1994	1995	1996
Kilometres flown (million)	36	38	42
Passengers carried ('000)	1,220	1,270	1,299
Passenger-km (million)	4,155	4,395	4,750
Total ton-km (million)	627	695	731

Sources: Jordan Civil Aviation Authority and Royal Jordanian Airline.

Tourism

	1994	1995	1996
Foreign tourist arrivals	2,781,617	2,934,116	2,793,375
Tourist receipts (million US dollars)	581.6	659.9	743.6

Source: Central Bank of Jordan.

Communications Media

(East Bank only)

	1993	1994	1995
Radio receivers ('000 in use)	1,200	1,265	1,350
Television receivers ('000 in use)	375	395	430
Telephones ('000 main lines in use)	290*	317.3†	328.4†
Telefax stations ('000 in use)*	29	31	n.a.
Mobile telephones (subscribers)*	1,460	1,450	n.a.
Book production: titles	500‡	n.a.	465
Daily newspapers:			
Number of titles	n.a.	4	4
Average circulation ('000)	n.a.	250	250
Non-daily newspapers:			
Number of titles	n.a.	n.a.	34
Average circulation ('000)	n.a.	n.a.	90

1996: Telephones ('000 main lines in use) 356.2†.

* Source: UN, *Statistical Yearbook*.

† Source: Jordanian Department of Statistics.

‡ First editions only, not including pamphlets.

Source (unless otherwise indicated): UNESCO, *Statistical Yearbook*.

Education

(East Bank, 1995/96)

	Schools	Teachers	Pupils
Kindergarten	828	2,848	63,250
Basic	2,531	51,721	1,074,877
Secondary: general	n.a.	8,615	143,014
Secondary: vocational	n.a.	2,306	33,109
Universities and equivalent	n.a.	3,511	76,375
Other higher education	n.a.	1,310	22,645

Directory

The Constitution

The revised Constitution was approved by King Talal I on 1 January 1952.

The Hashemite Kingdom of Jordan is an independent, indivisible sovereign state. Its official religion is Islam; its official language Arabic.

RIGHTS OF THE INDIVIDUAL

There is to be no discrimination between Jordanians on account of race, religion or language. Work, education and equal opportunities shall be afforded to all as far as is possible. The freedom of the individual is guaranteed, as are his dwelling and property. No Jordanian shall be exiled. Labour shall be made compulsory only in a national emergency, or as a result of a conviction; conditions, hours worked and allowances are under the protection of the state.

The Press, and all opinions, are free, except under martial law. Societies can be formed, within the law. Schools may be established freely, but they must follow a recognized curriculum and educational policy. Elementary education is free and compulsory. All religions are tolerated. Every Jordanian is eligible for public office, and choices are to be made by merit only. Power belongs to the people.

THE LEGISLATIVE POWER

Legislative power is vested in the National Assembly and the King. The National Assembly consists of two houses: the Senate and the House of Representatives.

THE SENATE

The number of Senators is one-half of the number of members of the House of Representatives. Senators must be unrelated to the King, over 40, and are chosen from present and past Prime Ministers and Ministers, past Ambassadors or Ministers Plenipotentiary, past Presidents of the House of Representatives, past Presidents and members of the Court of Cassation and of the Civil and *Shari'a* Courts of Appeal, retired officers of the rank of General and above, former members of the House of Representatives who have been elected twice to that House, etc. . . . They may not hold public office. Senators are appointed for four years. They may be reappointed. The President of the Senate is appointed for two years.

THE HOUSE OF REPRESENTATIVES

The members of the House of Representatives are elected by secret ballot in a general direct election and retain their mandate for four years. General elections take place during the four months preceding the end of the term. The President of the House is elected by secret ballot each year by the Representatives. Representatives must be Jordanians of over 30, they must have a clean record, no active business interests, and are debarred from public office. Close relatives of the King are not eligible. If the House of Representatives is dissolved, the new House shall assemble in extraordinary session not more than four months after the date of dissolution. The new House cannot be dissolved for the same reason as the last.

GENERAL PROVISIONS FOR THE NATIONAL ASSEMBLY

The King summons the National Assembly to its ordinary session on 1 November each year. This date can be postponed by the King for two months, or he can dissolve the Assembly before the end of its three months' session. Alternatively, he can extend the session up to a total period of six months. Each session is opened by a speech from the throne.

Decisions in the House of Representatives and the Senate are made by a majority vote. The quorum is two-thirds of the total number of members in each House. When the voting concerns the Constitution, or confidence in the Council of Ministers, 'the votes shall be taken by calling the members by name in a loud voice'. Sessions are public, though secret sessions can be held at the request of the Government or of five members. Complete freedom of speech, within the rules of either House, is allowed.

The Prime Minister places proposals before the House of Representatives; if accepted there, they are referred to the Senate and finally sent to the King for confirmation. If one house rejects a law while the other accepts it, a joint session of the House of Representatives and the Senate is called, and a decision made by a two-thirds majority. If the King withholds his approval from a law, he returns it to the Assembly within six months with the reasons for his dissent; a joint session of the Houses then makes a decision, and if the law is accepted by this decision it is promulgated. The Budget is submitted to the National Assembly one month before the beginning of the financial year.

THE KING

The throne of the Hashemite Kingdom devolves by male descent in the dynasty of King Abdullah Ibn al Hussein. The King attains his majority on his eighteenth lunar year; if the throne is inherited by a minor, the powers of the King are exercised by a Regent or a Council of Regency. If the King, through illness or absence, cannot perform his duties, his powers are given to a Deputy, or to a Council of the Throne. This Deputy, or Council, may be appointed by Iradas (decrees) by the King, or, if he is incapable, by the Council of Ministers.

On his accession, the King takes the oath to respect and observe the provisions of the Constitution and to be loyal to the nation. As Head of State he is immune from all liability or responsibility. He approves laws and promulgates them. He declares war, concludes peace and signs treaties; treaties, however, must be approved by the National Assembly. The King is Commander-in-Chief of the navy, the army and the air force. He orders the holding of elections; convenes, inaugurates, adjourns and prorogues the House of Representatives. The Prime Minister is appointed by him, as are the President and members of the Senate. Military and civil ranks are also granted, or withdrawn, by the King. No death sentence is carried out until he has confirmed it.

MINISTERS

The Council of Ministers consists of the Prime Minister, President of the Council, and of his ministers. Ministers are forbidden to become members of any company, to receive a salary from any company, or to participate in any financial act of trade. The Council of Ministers is entrusted with the conduct of all affairs of state, internal and external.

The Council of Ministers is responsible to the House of Representatives for matters of general policy. Ministers may speak in either House, and, if they are members of one House, they may also vote in that House. Votes of confidence in the Council are cast in the House of Representatives, and decided by a two-thirds majority. If a vote of 'no confidence' is returned, the ministers are bound to resign. Every newly-formed Council of Ministers must present its programme to the House of Representatives and ask for a vote of confidence. The House of Representatives can impeach ministers, as it impeaches its own members.

AMENDMENTS

Two amendments were passed in November 1974 giving the King the right to dissolve the Senate or to take away membership from any of its members, and to postpone general elections for a period not to exceed a year, if there are circumstances in which the Council of Ministers feels that it is impossible to hold elections. A further amendment in February 1976 enabled the King to postpone elections indefinitely. In January 1984 two amendments were passed, allowing elections 'in any part of the country where it is possible to hold them' (effectively, only the East Bank) and empowering the National Assembly to elect deputies from the Israeli-held West Bank.

The Government

HEAD OF STATE

King Hussein ibn Talal (proclaimed King on 11 August 1952; crowned on 2 May 1953).

CABINET*

(February 1998)

Prime Minister and Minister of Defence: Abd as-Salam al-Majali.

Deputy Prime Minister and Minister of Services Affairs and of Information: Dr Abdullah an-Nusur.

Deputy Prime Minister and Minister of Development Affairs and of Foreign Affairs: Dr Jawad al-Anani.

Minister of Justice: Riyad ash-Shakah.

Minister of Awqaf (Religious Endowments) and Islamic Affairs: Abd al-Salam al-Abbadi.

Minister of Transport and of Communications: Sami Qamuh.

Minister of Administrative Development: Dr Bassam al-Umush.

Minister of Planning: Rima Khalaf.

Minister of Education and of Higher Education: Dr Muhammad Hamdan.

Minister of Public Works and Housing: Nasir al-Lawzi.

Minister of the Interior: Nadhir Rashid.

Minister of Health: Ashraf al-Kurdi.

Minister of Water and Irrigation: Mundhir Haddadin.

Minister of Energy and Mineral Resources and of Municipal and Rural Affairs: Muhammad Salah al-Hurani.

Minister of Trade and Industry and of Supply: Hani al-Mulqi.

Minister of Finance: Suleiman Hafiz.

Minister of Culture and of Youth: Talal Sat'an al-Hasan.

Minister of Labour: Muhammad Mahdi al-Farhan.

Minister of Agriculture: Mijhim al-Khurayshah.

Minister of Social Development: Muhammad Khayr Mamsar.

Minister of Tourism and Antiquities: Aql Biltaji.

Minister of State for Parliamentary and Legal Affairs: Dr Khalid az-Zu'bi.

Minister of State in the Office of the Prime Minister: Sa'd ad-Din Jumah.

Chief of the Royal Court: Fayez at-Tarawneh.

* The Head of Intelligence and the Governor of the Central Bank also have full ministerial status.

MINISTRIES

Office of the Prime Minister: POB 80, 35216, Amman; tel. (6) 5641211; telex 21444; fax (6) 5642520.

Ministry of Agriculture: POB 961043, Amman; tel. (6) 5686151; telex 24176; fax (6) 5601024.

Ministry of Awqaf (Religious Endowments) and Islamic Affairs: POB 659, Amman; tel. (6) 5666141; telex 21559; fax (6) 5602254.

Ministry of Communications: POB 71, Amman; tel. (6) 5624301; telex 21666; fax (6) 5861059.

Ministry of Culture: Amman; tel. (6) 5696255; fax (6) 5696598.

Ministry of Defence: POB 1577, Amman; tel. (6) 5644361; telex 21200.

Ministry of Education: POB 1646, Amman 11118; tel. (6) 5607181; telex 21396; fax (6) 5666019.

Ministry of Energy and Mineral Resources: Amman; tel. (6) 5863616; fax (6) 5865714.

Ministry of Finance: POB 85, Amman 11118; tel. (6) 5636321; telex 23634; fax (6) 5618528.

Ministry of Foreign Affairs: POB 1577, Amman; tel. (6) 5642359; telex 21255; fax (6) 5648825.

Ministry of Health: POB 86, Amman; tel. (6) 5665131; telex 21595; fax (6) 5688373.

Ministry of Higher Education: Amman; tel. (6) 5847671; fax (6) 5837616.

Ministry of the Interior: POB 100, Amman; tel. (6) 5691141; telex 23162; fax (6) 5606908.

Ministry of Justice: POB 6040, Amman; tel. (6) 5663101; fax (6) 5680238.

Ministry of Labour: POB 9052, Amman; tel. (6) 5698186; fax (6) 5667193.

Ministry of Municipal and Rural Affairs: POB 1799, Amman; tel. (6) 5641393; fax (6) 5640404.

Ministry of Planning: Amman; tel. (6) 5644466; fax (6) 5649341.

Ministry of Public Works and Housing: POB 1220, Amman; tel. (6) 5607481; telex 21944; fax (6) 5698242.

Ministry of Social Development: POB 6720, Amman; tel. (6) 5607391; fax (6) 5607645.

Ministry of Supply: POB 830, Amman; tel. (6) 5602121; telex 21278; fax (6) 5604691.

Ministry of Tourism and Antiquities: POB 224, Amman 11118; tel. (6) 5642311; telex 21741; fax (6) 5648465.

Ministry of Trade and Industry: POB 2019, Amman; tel. (6) 5607191; telex 21163; fax (6) 5684692.

Ministry of Transport: POB 35214, Amman; tel. (6) 5607111; telex 21541; fax (6) 5607233.

Ministry of Water and Irrigation: Amman; tel. (6) 5683100; fax (6) 5680871.

Ministry of Youth: Amman; tel. (6) 5604701; fax (6) 5604721.

Legislature

MAJLIS AL-UMMA
(National Assembly)

Senate

The Senate (House of Notables) consists of 40 members, appointed by the King. A new Senate was appointed by the King on 18 November 1993.

Speaker: Zeid ar-Rifai.

House of Representatives

General Election, 8 November 1993

Party	Seats
Independent centrists	44
Islamic Action Front	16
Independent Islamists	6
Independent leftists	4
Al-Ahd	2
Jordanian Arab Democratic Party	2
Others	6
Total	80

Speaker: Saed Hayel as-Srour.

Political Organizations

Political parties were banned before the elections of July 1963. In September 1971 King Hussein announced the formation of a Jordanian National Union. This was the only political organization allowed. Communists, Marxists and 'other advocates of imported ideologies' were ineligible for membership. In March 1972 the organization was renamed the Arab National Union. In April 1974 King Hussein dissolved the executive committee of the Arab National Union, and accepted the resignation of the Secretary-General. In February 1976 the Cabinet approved a law abolishing the Union. Membership was estimated at about 100,000. A royal commission was appointed in April 1990 to draft a National Charter, one feature of which was the legalization of political parties. In January 1991 King Hussein approved the National Charter, which was formally endorsed in June. In July 1992 the House of Representatives adopted draft legislation which formally permitted the establishment of political parties, subject to certain conditions. In the same month a joint session of the Senate and the House of Representatives was convened to debate amendments to the new legislation, proposed by the Senate. The political parties which achieved representation in the general election in November 1993 were: the Islamic Action Front (Sec.-Gen. Dr Ishaq Farhan); al-Mustaqbal; the Jordanian Arab Socialist Baath Party; al-Yakatha; al-Ahd; the Jordan National Alliance; the Jordan People's Democratic Party (Leader Taysir az-Zabri); the Jordan Social Democratic Party; and the Jordanian Arab Democratic Party. In early May 1997 nine centre parties, including Pledge and the Jordan National Alliance, announced that they had united to form the National Constitutional Party (NCP), which became the country's largest political grouping. The formation of the NCP, together with the establishment in 1996 of the Unionist Arab Democratic Party (a coalition of three leftist parties), reduced the total number of political parties from 24 to 14. In July 1997 the establishment of new Jordanian political party, the Popular Democratic Pan-Arab Movement, was announced.

Diplomatic Representation

EMBASSIES IN JORDAN

Algeria: 3rd Circle, Jabal Amman; tel. (6) 5641271; Ambassador: Abderrahman Shrayyet.

Australia: POB 35201, Amman 11181; tel. (6) 5930246; telex 21743; fax (6) 5931260; e-mail ausemb@nets.com.jo; Ambassador: M. S. Wickes.

Austria: POB 830795, 36 Mithqal al-Fayez St, Jabal Amman 11183; tel. (6) 5644635; telex 22484; fax (6) 5612725; e-mail austemb@go.com.jo; Ambassador: Dr Philipp Hoyos.

Bahrain: Amman; tel. (6) 5664148; Ambassador: Ibrahim Ali Ibrahim.

Belgium: POB 942, Amman 11118; tel. (6) 5675683; telex 22340; fax (6) 5697487; Ambassador: Guido Courtois.

Bosnia and Herzegovina: POB 850836, Amman 11185; tel. (6) 856921; fax (6) 856923; Chargé d'affaires: Muhammad Mrahorović.

Brazil: POB 5497, Amman; tel. (6) 5642183; telex 23827; fax (6) 5612964; Ambassador: Fernando Silva Alves.

Bulgaria: POB 950578, Al-Mousel St 7, Amman 11195; tel. (6) 5699391; telex 23246; fax (6) 5699393; Ambassador: (vacant).

Canada: POB 815403, Pearl of Shmeisani Bldg, Shmeisani, Amman; tel. (6) 5666124; telex 23080; fax (6) 5689227; Ambassador: MICHAEL J. MOLLOY.

Chile: POB 830663, 73 Suez St, Abdoun, Amman; tel. (6) 814263; telex 21696; e-mail echilejo@go.com.jo; Ambassador: JORGE IGLESIAS.

China, People's Republic: Shmeisani, Amman; tel. (6) 5666139; telex 21770; Ambassador: WANG SHIJIE.

Egypt: POB 35178, Zahran St, 3rd Circle, Jabal Amman; tel. (6) 5641375; Ambassador: IHAB SEID WAHBA.

France: POB 5348, Jabal Amman; tel. (6) 5641273; telex 21219; fax (6) 5659606; Ambassador: BERNARD BAJOLET.

Germany: POB 183, 25 Benghazi St, Jabal Amman; tel. (6) 7930351; telex 21235; fax (6) 7932887; Ambassador: PETER MENDE.

Greece: POB 35069, Jabal Amman; tel. (6) 5672331; telex 21566; fax (6) 5696591; Ambassador: THEODOROS N. PANTZARIS.

Holy See: POB 5364, Amman 11183; tel. (6) 5694095; fax (6) 5692502; Apostolic Nuncio: Most Rev. GIUSEPPE LAZZAROTTO.

Hungary: POB 3441, Amman 11181; tel. (6) 815614; telex 21815; fax (6) 815836; Chargé d'Affaires: Dr TIBOR TÓTH.

India: POB 2168, 1st Circle, Jabal Amman; tel. (6) 5637262; telex 21068; fax (6) 5659540; e-mail <indembjo@go.com.jo>; Ambassador: GAJANAN WAKANKAR.

Indonesia: South Um-Uthaina, 6th Circle, Amman; POB 811784, Amman; tel. (6) 828911; telex 23872; fax (6) 828380; Ambassador: EDDY SUMANTRI.

Iran: POB 173, Jabal Amman; tel. (6) 5641281; telex 21218; Ambassador: G. ANSARI.

Iraq: POB 2025, 1st Circle, Jabal Amman; tel. (6) 5639331; telex 21277; Ambassador: NORI AL-WAYES.

Israel: Amman; Ambassador: ODED ERAN.

Italy: POB 9800, Jabal Luweibdeh, Amman; tel. (6) 5638185; telex 21143; fax (6) 5659730; Ambassador: FRANCESCO CERULLI.

Japan: POB 2835, Jabal Amman; tel. (6) 5672486; telex 21518; fax (6) 5672006; Ambassador: AKIRA NAKAYAMA.

Korea, Democratic People's Republic: Amman; tel. (6) 5666349; Ambassador: CHOE GWANG RAE.

Korea, Republic: POB 3060, Amman 11181; tel. (6) 5660745; telex 21457; fax (6) 5660280; Ambassador: JUNG-IL OH.

Kuwait: POB 2107, Jabal Amman; tel. (6) 5641235; telex 21377; Chargé d'affaires: FAYSAL MUKHAYZIM.

Lebanon: POB 811779, 2nd Circle, Jabal Amman; tel. (6) 5641381; telex 21330; fax (6) 5641574; Ambassador: Dr WILLIAM HABIB.

Morocco: Jabal Amman; tel. (6) 5641451; telex 21661; Chargé d'affaires: SALEM FANKHAR ASH-SHANFARI.

Oman: Amman; tel. (6) 5661131; telex 21550; Ambassador: KHAMIS BIN HAMAD AL-BATASHI.

Pakistan: POB 1232, Amman; tel. (6) 5638352; fax (6) 5611633; Ambassador: TARIQ KHAN AFRIDI.

Poland: POB 2124, 3rd Circle, 1 Mai Zeyadeh St, Jabal Amman; tel. (6) 5637153; telex 21119; fax (6) 5618744; Chargé d'affaires: BOGUSLAW REKAS.

Qatar: Amman; tel. (6) 5644331; telex 21248; Ambassador: Sheikh HAMAD BIN MUHAMMAD BIN JABER ATH-THANI.

Romania: POB 2869, 21 Abdullah Bin Massoud St, Shmeisani, Amman; tel. (6) 5667738; telex 21860; fax (6) 5684018; Ambassador: IOAN AGAFICIOAIA.

Russia: Amman; tel. (6) 5641158; Ambassador: ALEKSANDR VLADIMIROVICH SALTANOV.

Saudi Arabia: POB 2133, 5th Circle, Jabal Amman; tel. (6) 5644154; Ambassador: ABDALLAH SUDEIRI.

South Africa: POB 851508, Sweifieh 11185, Amman; tel. (6) 811194; fax (6) 810080; Ambassador: H. B. B. DE BRUYN.

Spain: Zahran St, POB 454, Jabal Amman; tel. (6) 5614166; telex 21224; fax (6) 5614173; Ambassador: JUAN MANUEL CABRERA HERNÁNDEZ.

Sudan: Jabal Amman; tel. (6) 5624145; telex 21778; Ambassador: AHMAD DIAB.

Sweden: POB 830536, 4th Circle, Jabal Amman; tel. (6) 5669177; telex 22039; fax (6) 5669179; Ambassador: AJNETA BOHMAN.

Switzerland: Jabal Amman; tel. (6) 5931416; fax (6) 5930685; Ambassador: GIAN-FEDERICO PEDOTTI.

Syria: POB 1377, 4th Circle, Jabal Amman; tel. (6) 5641935; Chargé d'affaires: MAJID ABOU SALEH.

Tunisia: Jabal Amman; tel. (6) 5674307; telex 21149; fax (6) 5605790; Ambassador: HATEM BEN OTHMAN.

Turkey: POB 2062, Islamic College St, 2nd Circle, Jabal Amman 11181; tel. (6) 5641251; telex 23005; fax (6) 5612353; Ambassador: SÜHA UMAR.

United Arab Emirates: Jabal Amman; tel. (6) 5644369; telex 21832; Ambassador: ABDULLAH ALI ASH-SHURAFA.

United Kingdom: POB 87, Abdoun, Amman; tel. (6) 823100; telex 22209; fax (6) 813759; e-mail British@nets.com.jo; Ambassador: CHRISTOPHER BATTISCOMBE.

USA: POB 354, Amman 11118; tel. (6) 820101; fax (6) 820121; Ambassador: WESLEY W. EGAN.

Yemen: Amman; tel. (6) 5642381; telex 23526; Ambassador: ALI ABDULLAH ABU LUHOUM.

Yugoslavia: POB 5227, Amman: tel. (6) 5665107; telex 21505; Ambassador: ZORAN S. POPOVIĆ.

Judicial System

With the exception of matters of purely personal nature concerning members of non-Muslim communities, the law of Jordan was based on Islamic Law for both civil and criminal matters. During the days of the Ottoman Empire, certain aspects of Continental law, especially French commercial law and civil and criminal procedure, were introduced. Due to British occupation of Palestine and Transjordan from 1917 to 1948, the Palestine territory has adopted, either by statute or case law, much of the English common law. Since the annexation of the non-occupied part of Palestine and the formation of the Hashemite Kingdom of Jordan, there has been a continuous effort to unify the law.

Court of Cassation. The Court of Cassation consists of seven judges, who sit in full panel for exceptionally important cases. In most appeals, however, only five members sit to hear the case. All cases involving amounts of more than JD100 may be reviewed by this Court, as well as cases involving lesser amounts and cases which cannot be monetarily valued. However, for the latter types of cases, review is available only by leave of the Court of Appeal, or, upon refusal by the Court of Appeal, by leave of the President of the Court of Cassation. In addition to these functions as final and Supreme Court of Appeal, the Court of Cassation also sits as High Court of Justice to hear applications in the nature of habeas corpus, mandamus and certiorari dealing with complaints of a citizen against abuse of governmental authority.

Courts of Appeal. There are two Courts of Appeal, each of which is composed of three judges, whether for hearing of appeals or for dealing with Magistrates Courts' judgments in chambers. Jurisdiction of the two Courts is geographical, with the Court for the Western Region (which has not sat since June 1967) sitting in Jerusalem and the Court for the Eastern Region sitting in Amman. The regions are separated by the River Jordan. Appellate review of the Courts of Appeal extends to judgments rendered in the Courts of First Instance, the Magistrates' Courts, and Religious Courts.

Courts of First Instance. The Courts of First Instance are courts of general jurisdiction in all matters civil and criminal except those specifically allocated to the Magistrates' Courts. Three judges sit in all felony trials, while only two judges sit for misdemeanour and civil cases. Each of the seven Courts of First Instance also exercises appellate jurisdiction in cases involving judgments of less than JD20 and fines of less than JD10, rendered by the Magistrates' Courts.

Magistrates' Courts. There are 14 Magistrates' Courts, which exercise jurisdiction in civil cases involving no more than JD250 and in criminal cases involving maximum fines of JD100 or maximum imprisonment of one year.

Religious Courts. There are two types of religious court: The *Shari'a* Courts (Muslims): and the Ecclesiastical Courts (Eastern Orthodox, Greek Melkite, Roman Catholic and Protestant). Jurisdiction extends to personal (family) matters, such as marriage, divorce, alimony, inheritance, guardianship, wills, interdiction and, for the Muslim community, the constitution of Waqfs (Religious Endowments). When a dispute involves persons of different religious communities, the Civil Courts have jurisdiction in the matter unless the parties agree to submit to the jurisdiction of one or the other of the Religious Courts involved.

Each *Shari'a* (Muslim) Court consists of one judge (*Qadi*), while most of the Ecclesiastical (Christian) Courts are normally composed of three judges, who are usually clerics. *Shari'a* Courts apply the doctrines of Islamic Law, based on the Koran and the *Hadith* (Precepts of Muhammad), while the Ecclesiastical Courts base their law on various aspects of Canon Law. In the event of conflict between any two Religious Courts or between a Religious Court and a Civil Court, a Special Tribunal of three judges is appointed by the President of the Court of Cassation, to decide which court shall have jurisdiction. Upon the advice of experts on the law of the various communities, this Special Tribunal decides on the venue for the case at hand.

Religion

Over 80% of the population are Sunni Muslims, and the King can trace unbroken descent from the Prophet Muhammad. There is a Christian minority, living mainly in the towns, and there are smaller numbers of non-Sunni Muslims.

ISLAM

Chief Justice and President of the Supreme Muslim Secular Council: Sheikh MUHAMMAD MHELAN.

Director of Shari'a Courts: Sheikh SUBHI AL-MUWQQAT.

Mufti of the Hashemite Kingdom of Jordan: Sheikh MUHAMMAD ABDO HASHEM.

CHRISTIANITY

The Roman Catholic Church

Latin Rite

Jordan forms part of the Patriarchate of Jerusalem (see chapter on Israel).

Vicar-General for Transjordan: Mgr SELIM SAYEGH (Titular Bishop of Aquae in Proconsulari), Latin Vicariate, POB 1317, Amman: tel. (6) 5637440.

Melkite Rite

The Greek-Melkite archdiocese of Petra (Wadi Musa) and Philadelphia (Amman) contained 31,000 adherents at 31 December 1997.

Archbishop of Petra and Philadelphia: Most Rev. GEORGES EL-MURR, Archevêché Grec-Melkite Catholique, POB 2435, Jabal Amman, Amman 11181; tel. (6) 5624757; fax (6) 5628560.

Syrian Rite

The Syrian Catholic Patriarch of Antioch is resident in Beirut, Lebanon.

Patriarchal Exarchate of Jerusalem: Mont Achrafieh, Rue Barto, POB 10041, Amman; Exarch Patriarchal Mgr PIERRE ABD AL-AHAD.

The Anglican Communion

Within the Episcopal Church in Jerusalem and the Middle East, Jordan forms part of the diocese of Jerusalem. The President Bishop of the Church is the Bishop in Jerusalem (see the chapter on Israel).

Assistant Bishop in Amman: Rt Rev. ELIA KHOURY, POB 598, Amman.

Other Christian Churches

The Coptic Orthodox Church, the Greek Orthodox Church (Patriarchate of Jerusalem) and the Evangelical Lutheran Church in Jordan are also active.

The Press

Jordan Press Association: Amman; Pres. RAKAN AL-MAJALI.

DAILIES

Al-Akhbar (News): POB 62420, Amman; f. 1976; Arabic; publ. by the Arab Press Co; Editor RACAN EL-MAJALI; circ. 15,000.

Al-Aswaq: POB 11117, Amman 11123; tel. (6) 5687690; fax (6) 5687292; f. 1992; Editor MUSTAFA ABU LIBDEH.

Ad-Dustour (The Constitution): POB 591, Amman; tel. (6) 5664153; telex 21392; fax (6) 5667170; e-mail dustour@go.com.jo; f. 1967; Arabic; publ. by the Jordan Press and Publishing Co; owns commercial printing facilities; Chair. KAMEL ASH-SHERIF; Editor NABIL ASH-SHARIF; Man. Dir SAIF ASH-SHARIF; circ. 100,000.

Al-Mithaq: Amman; f. 1993; Arabic.

Ar-Rai (Opinion): POB 6710, Amman; tel. (6) 5667171; telex 21497; fax (6) 5661242; f. 1971; Arabic; independent; published by Jordan Press Foundation; Chair. MAHMOUD AL-KAYED; Gen. Dir MOHAMAD AL-AMAD; Editor-in-Chief SULEIMAN QUDA; circ. 90,000.

The Jordan Times: POB 6710, Amman; tel. (6) 5667171; telex 21497; fax (6) 5661242; f. 1975; English; published by Jordan Press Establishment; Editor-in-Chief GEORGE HAWATMEH; circ. 15,000.

Sawt ash-Shaab (Voice of the People): POB 3037, Amman; tel. (6) 5667101; fax (6) 5667993; f. 1983; Arabic; Editor-in-Chief: HASHEM KHAISAT; circ. 30,000.

PERIODICALS

Akhbar al-Usbou (News of the Week): POB 605, Amman; tel. (6) 5677881; telex 21644; fax (6) 5677882; f. 1959; weekly; Arabic; economic, social, political; Chief Editor and Publr ABD AL-HAFIZ MUHAMMAD; circ. 100,000.

Al-Aqsa (The Ultimate): POB 1957, Amman; weekly; Arabic; armed forces magazines.

Al-Ghad al-Iqtisadi: Media Services International, POB 9313, Amman; tel. and fax (6) 5648298; telex 21392; fortnightly; English; economic; Chief Editor RIAD AL-KHOURI.

BYTE Middle East: POB 91128, Amman 11191; tel. (6) 5650444; fax (6) 5650888; f. 1995; monthly; Arabic; information technology; Editor-in-Chief KHALDOON TABAZA.

Huda El-Islam (The Right Way of Islam): POB 659, Amman; tel. (6) 5666141; telex 21559; f. 1956; monthly; Arabic; scientific and literary; published by the Ministry of Awqaf and Islamic Affairs; Editor Dr AHMAD MUHAMMAD HULAYYEL.

Jordan: POB 224, Amman; telex 21497; f. 1969; published quarterly by Jordan Information Bureau, Washington; circ. 100,000.

Al-Liwa' (The Standard): POB 3067, Jabal Amman-2nd Circle, Amman 11181; tel. (6) 5642770; fax (6) 5656324; f. 1972; weekly; Arabic; Chief Editor HASAN AL-TAL.

Military Magazine: Army Headquarters, Amman; f. 1955; quarterly; dealing with military and literary subjects; published by Armed Forces.

As-Sabah (The Morning): POB 2396, Amman; weekly; Arabic; circ. 6,000.

Shari'a: POB 585, Amman; f. 1959; fortnightly; Islamic affairs; published by Shari'a College; circ. 5,000.

Shihan: POB 96-654; Amman; tel. (6) 5601511; fax (6) 5656324; weekly; Editor-in-Chief HASAN AL-TAL.

The Star: Media Services International, POB 9313 Amman; tel. and fax (6) 5648298; telex 21392; e-mail star@arabia.com; f. 1982, formerly The Jerusalem Star; weekly; English; Publr and Editor-in-Chief OSAMA ASH-SHERIF; circ. 10,000.

NEWS AGENCIES

Jordan News Agency (PETRA): POB 6845, Amman; tel. (6) 5644455; telex 21220; f. 1965; government-controlled; Dir-Gen. ABDULLAH AL-UTUM.

Foreign News Bureaux

Agence France-Presse (AFP): POB 3340, Amman; tel. (6) 5642976; telex 21469; fax (6) 5654680; Bureau Man. Mrs RANDA HABIB.

Agenzia Nazionale Stampa Associata (ANSA) (Italy): POB 35111, Amman; tel. (6) 5644092; telex 21207; Correspondent JOHN HALABI.

Associated Press (AP) (USA): POB 35111, Amman 11180; tel. (6) 5614660; telex 23514; fax (6) 5614661; Correspondent JAMAL HALABY.

Deutsche Presse Agentur (dpa) (Germany): POB 35111, Amman; tel. (6) 5623907; telex 21207; Correspondent JOHN HALABI.

Reuters (UK): POB 667, Amman; tel. (6) 5623776; telex 21414; fax (6) 5619231; Bureau Chief JACK REDDEN.

Informatsionnoye Telegrafnoye Agentstvo Rossii-Telegrafnoye Agentstvo Suverennykh Stran (ITAR-TASS) (Russia): Jabal Amman, Nabich Faris St, Block 111/83 124, Amman; Correspondent NIKOLAI LEBEDINSKY.

Central News Agency (Taiwan), Iraqi News Agency, Middle East News Agency (Egypt), Qatar News Agency, Saudi Press Agency and UPI (USA) also maintain bureaux in Amman.

Publishers

Alfaris Publishing and Distribution Co: POB 9157, Amman 11191; tel. (6) 5605432; fax (6) 5685501; Dir MAHER SAID KAYYALI.

Aram Studies Publishing and Distribution House: POB 997, Amman 11941; tel. (6) 835015; fax (6) 835079; art, finance, health, management, science, business; Gen. Dir SALEH ABOUSBA.

El-Nafa'es: POB 211511, Amman 11121; tel. (6) 5693940; fax (6) 5693941; education, Islamic.

Jordan Book Centre Co Ltd: POB 301, Al-Jubeiha, Amman 11941; tel. (6) 5606882; telex 21153; fax (6) 5602016; e-mail jbc@nets.com.jo; f. 1982; fiction, business, economics, computer science, medicine, engineering, general non-fiction; CEO I. SHARBAIN.

Jordan House for Publication: Basman St, POB 1121, Amman; tel. (6) 24224; fax (6) 51062; f. 1952; medicine, nursing, dentistry; Man. Dir MURSI EL-ASHKAR.

Jordan Press and Publishing Co Ltd: POB 591, Amman; tel. (6) 5664153; telex 21392; fax (6) 5667170; e-mail dustour@go.com.jo; f. 1967 by *Al-Manar* and *Falastin* dailies; publishes *Ad-Dustour* (daily), *Ad-Dustour Sport* (weekly) and *The Star* (English weekly); Chair. KAMEL ASH-SHARIF; Dir-Gen SEIF ASH-SHERIF.

Jordan Press Foundation: POB 6710, Amman; tel. (6) 5667171; telex 21497; fax (6) 5661242; publishes *Ar-Rai* (daily) and the *Jordan Times* (daily); Chair. MAHMOUD AL-KAYED; Gen. Dir MOHAMAD AMAD.

Other publishers in Amman include: Dairat al-Ihsaat al-Amman, George N. Kawar, Al-Matbaat al-Hashmiya and The National Press.

Broadcasting and Communications

TELECOMMUNICATIONS

Telecommunications Regulatory Commission (TRC): POB 850967, Amman 11185; tel. (6) 862020; fax (6) 863641; e-mail trc@amra.nic.gov.jo; Dir-Gen. YOUSEF ABU JAMOUS.

Jordan Mobile Telephone Service Company (JMTSC): Amman; holds a monopoly on the operation of the mobile telecommunications network until Nov. 1998.

Jordan Telecommunications Company (JTC): Amman; Chair. WALID DWEIK.

RADIO AND TELEVISION

Jordan Radio and Television Corporation (JRTV): POB 1041, Amman; tel. (6) 773111; telex 23544; fax (6) 751503; e-mail general@jrtv.gov.jo; internet http://www.jrtv.com; f. 1968; government TV station broadcasts for 90 hours weekly in Arabic and English; in colour; advertising accepted; Dir-Gen. IHSAN RAMZI SHIKIM; Dir of Television NASSER JUDEH; Dir of Radio HASHIM KHURAYSAT.

Finance

(cap. = capital; p.u. = paid up; dep. = deposits; m. = million; res = reserves; brs = branches; JD = Jordanian dinars)

BANKING

Central Bank

Central Bank of Jordan: POB 37, King Hussein St, Amman 11118; tel. (6) 5630301; telex 21250; fax (6) 5638889; f. 1964; cap. JD 18m., res JD 11.2m., dep. JD 2,193.6m. (Dec. 1996); Gov. Dr ZIAD FARIZ; 2 brs.

National Banks

Arab Bank PLC: POB 950545, Shmeisani, Amman 11195; tel. (6) 5607115; telex 23091; fax (6) 5606793; f. 1930; cap. JD 84.9m., res JD 1,348.1m., dep. JD 13,008.3m. (Dec. 1996); Chair. ABD AL-MAJID SHOMAN; 82 brs in Jordan, 67 brs abroad.

Bank of Jordan PLC: POB 2140, South Sayegh Commercial Centre, Jabal Weibdeh, Amman; tel. (6) 5644327; telex 22033; fax (6) 5656642; f. 1960; cap. JD 10.5m., res JD 15.6m., dep. JD 493.7m., (Dec. 1996); Chair. TAWFIK SHAKER FAKHOURI; Gen. Man. FAYEZ ABUL ENEIN; 42 brs.

Cairo Amman Bank: Cairo Amman Bank Bldg, Wadi Saqra St, Amman 11195; POB 950661, Amman 11195; tel. (6) 5616910; telex 24049; fax (6) 5642890; f. 1960; cap. JD 10m., res JD 11.6m., dep. JD 648m. (Dec. 1996); Chair. KHALIL TALHOUNI; Gen. Man. YAZID MUFTI; 37 brs in Jordan, 16 brs abroad.

Jordan Gulf Bank: POB 9989, Shmeinsani-Al Burj Area, Amman 11191; tel. (6) 5603931; telex 21959; fax (6) 5664110; f. 1977; cap JD 20m., res JD 44.8m., dep. JD 104.9m. (Dec. 1994); Chair. ZUHAIR F. AWARIANI.

Jordan Islamic Bank for Finance and Investment: POB 926225, Amman; tel. (6) 5677377; telex 21125; fax (6) 5666326; f. 1978; cap. JD 14.6m., res JD 27.3m., dep. JD 534m. (Dec. 1996); Chair. MAHMOUD HASSOUHAH; Gen. Man. MUSA A. SHIHADEH; 35 brs.

Jordan Kuwait Bank: POB 9776, Abdali, Amman 11191; tel. (6) 5688814; telex 21994; fax (6) 5687452; f. 1976; cap. JD 10m., res JD 10.5m., dep. JD 246.5m. (Dec. 1996); Chair. ABDUL-KARIM KABARITI; Gen. Man. M. YASSER AL-ASMER; 25 brs.

Jordan National Bank PLC: POB 3103, Amman 11118; tel. (6) 702282; telex 23501; fax (6) 5687067; f. 1955; cap. JD 42m., res JD 25.8m., dep. JD 536.5m. (Dec. 1996); Chair. Dr RAJAI MUASHER; 54 brs in Jordan, 4 brs in Lebanon, 1 br. in Cyprus and 5 brs in the Gaza Strip and the West Bank.

Foreign Banks

ANZ Grindlays Bank: POB 9997, Shmeisani, Amman 11191; tel. (6) 5607201; telex 21980; fax (6) 5679115; cap. p.u. JD 9.5m., dep. JD 181m., total assets JD 205m. (Dec. 1996); Gen. Man. in Jordan ROBIN BRADSHAW; brs in Amman (8 brs), Aqaba, Irbid (2 brs), Zerka, Northern Shouneh and Kerak.

Arab Banking Corpn: POB 926691, Queen Nour St, Amman 11110; tel. (6) 5664183; telex 21114; fax (6) 5686291; f. 1990; cap. p.u. JD 10m., dep. JD 139.8m., total assets JD 241.2m. (Dec. 1995); Chair. ABDUL WAHAB AT-TAMMAR; 15 brs.

Arab Islamic International Bank: Amman; f. 1997; cap p.u. JD 40m.

Arab Land Bank (Egypt): POB 6729, Amman 11118; tel. (6) 5628357; telex 21208; fax (6) 5646274; wholly-owned subsidiary of the Central Bank of Egypt; cap. JD 10m., dep. JD 98.2m., res JD 6.3m., total assets JD 120.7m. (Dec. 1994); Chair. ALA AL-AWSIEH; Gen. Man. SAMIR MAHDI; 19 brs in Jordan, 3 brs abroad.

The British Bank of the Middle East: POB 925286, Khalid Bin Walid St, Jebel Hussein, Amman 11110; tel. (6) 5607471; telex 21253; fax (6) 692964; f. 1889; cap. JD 5m., dep. JD 150m., total assets JD 169m. (Dec. 1994); Chair. Sir WILLIAM PURVES; Area Man. J. S. GIBSON; 6 brs.

Citibank NA (USA): POB 5055, Prince Muhammad St, Amman; tel. (6) 564227; telex 21314; fax (6) 5658693; cap. p.u. JD 5m., dep. JD 56.2m., total assets JD 75.4m. (Dec. 1992); Chair. and CEO JOHN S. REED.

Rafidain Bank (Iraq): POB 1194, Amman; tel. (6) 5624365; telex 21334; fax (6) 5658698; f. 1941; cap. p.u. JD 5m., res JD 2.1m., dep. JD 31.4m. (Dec. 1992); Pres. and Chair. DHIA HABEEB AL-KHAYOON; 3 brs.

Bank Al-Mashrek (Lebanon) also has a branch in Amman.

Specialized Credit Institutions

Agricultural Credit Corporation: POB 77, Amman; tel. (6) 5661105; telex 24194; fax (6) 5698365; e-mail agri-cc@nets.com.jo; f. 1959; cap. p.u. JD 24m., res JD 7.5m., total assets JD 96.4m. (Dec. 1997); Chair. MEGHIM AL-KHRIESHA; Dir-Gen. NIMER AN-NABULSI; 20 brs.

The Arab Jordan Investment Bank: POB 8797, Arab Jordan Investment Bank Bldg, Shmeisani Commercial Area, Amman 11120; tel. (6) 5607126; telex 22087; fax (6) 5681482; f. 1978; cap. JD 10m., res JD 15.6m., d ep. JD 195.7m. (Dec. 1996); Chair. and CEO ABD AL-KADER AL-QADI; 10 brs in Jordan, 1 br abroad.

Cities and Villages Development Bank: POB 1572, Amman; tel. (6) 5668151; telex 22476; fax (6) 5668153; f. 1979; cap. p.u. JD 23m., gen. res JD 9.5m., total assets JD 68.1m. (Dec. 1996); Gen. Man. Dr HAMMAD AL-KASASBEH; 1 br. in Irbid.

Housing Bank: POB 7693, Parliament St, Abdali, Amman 11118; tel. (6) 5667126; telex 21693; fax (6) 5678121; f. 1973; cap. JD 25m., res JD 56.3m., dep. JD 917.6m. (Dec. 1996); Chair. ZUHAIR KHOURI; Gen. Man. ABDUL QADER DWIK; 120 brs.

Industrial Development Bank: POB 1982, Islamic College St, Jabal Amman, Amman 11118; tel. (6) 5642216; telex 21349; fax (6) 5647821; f. 1965; cap. JD 11.6m., res JD 19.4m., dep. JD 33.5m. (Dec. 1996); Chair. MUNZER EL-FAHOUM; Gen. Man. RAJAB AS-SA'AD.

Jordan Co-operative Organization: POB 1343, Amman; tel. (6) 5665171; telex 21835; f. 1968; cap. p.u. JD 5.2m., dep. JD 11.5m., res JD 6.8m. (Nov. 1992); Chair. and Dir-Gen. JAMAL AL-BEDOUR.

Jordan Investment and Finance Bank (JIFBANK): Issam Ajlouni St, Shmeisani, Amman; POB 950601, Amman; tel. (6) 5665145; telex 23181; fax (6) 5681410; f. 1982 as Jordan Investment and Finance Corpn, name changed 1989; cap. JD 10m., res JD 7m., dep. JD 190.4m. (Dec. 1996); Chair. NIZAR JARDANEH.

Social Security Corporation: POB 926031, Amman; tel. (6) 5643000; telex 22287; fax (6) 5610014; f. 1978; Dir-Gen. MUHAMMAD S. HOURANI.

Union Bank for Savings and Investment: Prince Shaker Bin Zeid St, Shmeisani, Amman; tel. (6) 5607011; telex 21875; fax (6) 5666149; f. 1978 as Arab Finance Corpn, named changed 1991; cap. JD 11m.; res 11.6m., dep. 167.1m. (Dec. 1996); Chair. HALIM SALFITI; 16 brs.

STOCK EXCHANGE

Amman Financial Market: POB 8802, Amman; tel. (6) 5607179; telex 21711; fax (6) 5686830; e-mail afm@go.com.jo; f. 1978; Gen. Man. WAHIB SHAIR.

INSURANCE

Jordan Insurance Co Ltd: POB 279, Company's Bldg, 3rd Circle, Jabal Amman, Amman; tel. (6) 5634161; telex 21486; fax (6) 5637905; f. 1951; cap. p.u. JD 5m.; Chair. and Man. Dir KHALDUN ABU HASSAN; 6 brs (3 in Saudi Arabia, 3 in the United Arab Emirates).

Middle East Insurance Co Ltd: POB 1802, Shmeisani, Yaqoub Sarrouf St, Amman; tel. (6) 5605144; telex 21420; fax (6) 5605950; f. 1963; cap. p.u. US $3.3m.; Chair. WASEF AZAR; 1 br. in Saudi Arabia.

National Ahlia Insurance Co: POB 6156-2938, Sayed Qutub St, Shmeisani, Amman; tel. (6) 5671169; telex 21309; fax (6) 5684900; e-mail natinsur@go.com.jo; f. 1965; cap. p.u. JD 2m.; Chair. MUSTAFA ABU GOURA; Gen. Man. GHALEB ABU GOURA.

United Insurance Co Ltd: POB 7521, United Insurance Bldg, King Hussein St, Amman; tel. (6) 5625828; telex 23153; fax (6) 5629417; f. 1972; all types of insurance; cap. JD 1.5m.; Chair. and Gen. Man. RAOUF SA'AD ABUJABER.

There are 17 local and one foreign insurance company operating in Jordan.

Trade and Industry

DEVELOPMENT ORGANIZATIONS

Jordan Valley Authority: POB 2769, Amman; tel. (6) 5642472; telex 21692; projects in Stage I of the Jordan Valley Development Plan were completed in 1979. In 1988 about 26,000 ha was under intensive cultivation. Infrastructure projects also completed include 1,100 km of roads, 2,100 housing units, 100 schools, 15 health centres, 14 administration buildings, 4 marketing centres, 2 community centres, 2 vocational training centres. Electricity is now provided to all the towns and villages in the valley from the national network and domestic water is supplied to them from tube wells. Contributions to the cost of development came through loans from Kuwait Fund, Abu Dhabi Fund, Saudi Fund, Arab Fund, USAID, Fed. Germany, World Bank, EC, Italy, Netherlands, UK, Japan and OPEC Special Fund. Many of the Stage II irrigation projects are now completed or under implementation. Projects under way include the construction of the Wadi al-Arab dam, the raising of the King Talal dam and the 14.5-km extension of the 98-km East Ghor main canal. Stage II will include the irrigation of 4,700 ha in the southern Ghor. The target for the Plan is to irrigate 43,000 ha of land in the Jordan Valley. Future development in irrigation will include the construction of the Maqarin dam and the Wadi Malaha storage dam; Pres. MUHAMMAD BANI HANI.

CHAMBERS OF COMMERCE AND INDUSTRY

Amman Chamber of Commerce: POB 1800, Amman 11118; tel. (6) 5666151; e-mailaci@amra.nic.gov.jo; f. 1923; Pres. MUHAMMAD ASFOUR; Sec.-Gen. MUHAMMAD AL-MUHTASSEB.

Amman Chamber of Industry: POB 1800, Amman; tel. (6) 5643001; telex 22079; fax (6) 5647852; f. 1962; 7,000 industrial companies registered (1992); Pres. KHALDUN ABU HASSAN; Dir.-Gen. WALID KHATIB.

UTILITIES

Electricity

Jordanian Electric Power Company (Jepco): Amman.

National Electric Power Company (Nepco): Amman.

Water

Water Authority of Jordan (WAJ): Amman.

TRADE UNIONS

The General Federation of Jordanian Trade Unions: POB 1065, Amman; tel. (6) 5675533; f. 1954; 33,000 mems; member of Arab Trade Unions Confederation; Chair. KHALIL ABU KHURMAH; Gen. Sec. ABDUL HALIM KHADDAM.

There are also a number of independent unions, including:

Drivers' Union: POB 846, Amman; Sec.-Gen. SAMI HASSAN MANSOUR.

Engineers' Association: Amman; Sec.-Gen. LEITH SHUBELLAT.

Union of Petroleum Workers and Employees: POB 1346, Amman; Sec.-Gen. BRAHIM HADI.

Transport

RAILWAYS

Aqaba Railway Corporation: POB 50, Ma'an; tel. (3) 332114; telex 64003; fax (3) 331861; f. 1975; length of track 292 km (1,050-mm gauge); Dir-Gen. MUHAMMAD M. KRISHAN.

Formerly a division of the Hedjaz–Jordan Railway (see below), the Aqaba Railway was established as a separate entity in 1979; it retains close links with the Hedjaz but there is no regular through traffic between Aqaba and Amman. It comprises the 169-km line south of Menzil (leased from the Hedjaz–Jordan Railway) and the 115-km extension to Aqaba, opened in October 1975, which serves phosphate mines at el-Hasa and Wadi el-Abyad.

Hedjaz–Jordan Railway (administered by the Ministry of Transport): POB 4448, Amman; tel. (6) 895414; telex 21541; fax (6) 894117; f. 1902; length of track 496 km (1,050-mm gauge); Chair. A. HALASA; Dir-Gen. B. AL-SHRYDEH.

This was formerly a section of the Hedjaz Railway (Damascus to Medina) for Muslim pilgrims to Medina and Mecca. It crosses the Syrian border and enters Jordanian territory south of Dera'a, and runs for approximately 366 km to Naqb Ishtar, passing through Zarka, Amman, Qatrana and Ma'an. Some 844 km of the line, from Ma'an to Medina in Saudi Arabia, were abandoned for over sixty years. Reconstruction of the Medina line, begun in 1965, was scheduled to be completed in 1971 at a cost of £15m., divided equally between Jordan, Saudi Arabia and Syria. However, the reconstruction work was suspended at the request of the Arab states concerned, pending further studies on costs. The line between Ma'an and Saudi Arabia (114 km) is now completed, as well as 15 km in Saudi Arabia as far as Halet Ammar Station. A new 115-km extension to Aqaba (owned by the Aqaba Railway Corporation (see above) was opened in 1975. In 1987 a study conducted by Dorsch Consult (Federal Republic of Germany) into the feasibility of reconstructing the Hedjaz Railway to high international specifications to connect Saudi Arabia, Jordan and Syria, concluded that the reopening of the Hedjaz line would be viable only if it were to be connected with European rail networks.

ROADS

Amman is linked by road with all parts of the kingdom and with neighbouring countries. All cities and most towns are connected by a two-lane paved road system. In addition, several thousand km of tracks make all villages accessible to motor transport. In 1996, the latest inventory showed the East Bank of Jordan to have an estimated 2,940 km of main roads, 1,970 km of secondary roads (both types asphalted) and 1,740 km of other roads.

Joint Land Transport Co: Amman; joint venture of Govts of Jordan and Iraq; operates about 750 trucks.

Jordanian-Syrian Land Transport Co: POB 20686, Amman; tel. (6) 5661134; telex 21384; fax (6) 5669645; f. 1976; transports goods between ports in Jordan and Syria; Chair. and Gen. Man. HAMDI AL-HABASHNEH.

SHIPPING

The port of Aqaba is Jordan's only outlet to the sea and has more than 20 modern and specialized berths, and one container terminal (540 m in length). The port has 299,000 sq m of storage area, and is used for Jordan's international trade and regional transit trade (mainly with Iraq). There is a ferry link between Aqaba and the Egyptian port of Nuweibeh.

The Ports Coporation: POB 115, Aqaba; tel. (3) 314024; fax (3) 316204.

Arab Bridge Maritime Co: Aqaba; f. 1987; joint venture by Egypt, Iraq and Jordan to improve economic co-operation; an extension of the company that established a ferry link between Aqaba and the Egyptian port of Nuweibeh in 1985; Chair. Eng. KHALID SALEH AMAR; Dir-Gen. TAWFIQ GRACE AWADALLA.

T. Gargour & Fils: POB 419, 4th Floor, Da'ssan Commercial Centre, Wasfi at-Tal St, Amman; tel. (6) 5524142; telex 21213; fax (6) 5530512; e-mail tgf@tgf.com.jo; f. 1928; shipping agents and owners; Chair. JOHN GARGOUR.

Jordan Maritime Navigation Co: Amman; privately owned.

Jordan National Shipping Lines Co Ltd: Nasir Ben Jameel St, Wadi Saqra, POB 5406, Amman 11183; tel. (6) 5511500; telex 21730; fax (6) 5515119; e-mail JNL@nets.com.jo; POB 657, Aqaba; tel. (3) 2018738; telex 62276; fax (3) 318738; owned 75% by the Government; service from Antwerp, Bremen and Tilbury to Aqaba; daily passenger ferry service to Egypt; land transportation to destinations in Iraq and elsewhere in the region; Chair. WASIF AZAR; Gen. Man. Y. EL-TAL.

Amin Kawar & Sons Co W.L.L.: POB 222, 24 Abd al-Hamid Sharaf St, Shmeisani, Amman 11118; tel. (6) 5603703; telex 21212; fax (6) 5672170; e-mail aks@nets.com.jo; chartering and shipping agents; Chair. TAWFIQ A. KAWAR; Gen. Man. GHASSOUB F. KAWAR; Liner Man. JAMIL SAID.

Orient Shipping Co Ltd: POB 207, Amman 11118; tel. (6) 5641695; telex 21552; fax (6) 5651567.

Petra Navigation and International Trading Co Ltd: POB 8362, White Star Bldg, King Hussein St, Amman 11121; tel. (6) 5607021; telex 21755; fax (6) 5601362; e-mail petranav@jo.com; general cargo, ro/ro and passenger ferries; Chair. ALI H. ARMOUSH.

Syrian-Jordanian Shipping Co: POB 148, rue Port Said, Latakia, Syria; tel. (41) 471635; telex 451002; fax (41) 470250; Chair. OSMAN LEBBADI.

PIPELINES

Two oil pipelines cross Jordan. The former Iraq Petroleum Co pipeline, carrying petroleum from the oilfields in Iraq to Haifa, has not operated since 1967. The 1,717-km (1,067-mile) pipeline, known as the Trans-Arabian Pipeline (Tapline), carries petroleum from the oilfields of Dhahran in Saudi Arabia to Sidon on the Mediterranean seaboard in Lebanon. Tapline traverses Jordan for a distance of 177 km (110 miles) and has frequently been cut by hostile action. Tapline stopped pumping to Syria and Lebanon at the end of 1983, when it was first due to close. It was later scheduled to close in 1985, but in September 1984 Jordan renewed an agreement to receive Saudi Arabian crude oil through Tapline. The agreement can be cancelled by either party at two years' notice.

CIVIL AVIATION

There are international airports at Amman and Aqaba. The Queen Alia International Airport at Zizya, 40 km south of Amman, was opened in 1983.

Civil Aviation Authority: POB 7547, Amman; tel. (6) 892282; telex 21325; fax (6) 891653; e-mail jcaa@com.jo; f. 1950; Dir-Gen. AHMAD JUWEIBER.

Royal Jordanian Airline: Head Office: POB 302, Housing Bank Commercial Centre, Shmeisani, Amman; tel. (6) 5679178; telex 21501; fax (6) 5672527; f. 1963; government-owned; scheduled and charter services to Middle East, North Africa, Europe, USA and Far East; Pres. and CEO NADER DAHABI.

Arab Wings Co Ltd: POB 341018, Amman; tel. (6) 891994; telex 21608; fax (6) 894484; f. 1975; subsidiary of Royal Jordanian; executive jet charter service, air ambulances, priority cargo; Man. Dir RAMZI SHUWAYHAT.

Royal Wings Co Ltd: POB 314018, Amman 1134; tel. (6) 875206; fax (6) 875656;f. 1995; subsidiary of Royal Jordanian; operates scheduled and charter regional and domestic services; Pres. and Gen. Man. AHED QUNTAR.

Tourism

The ancient cities of Jerash and Petra, and Jordan's proximity to biblical sites, have encouraged tourism. In 1996 there were 2,793,375 foreign visitors to Jordan. Income from tourism in 1996 was US $743.6m.

Ministry of Tourism and Antiquities: Ministry of Tourism, POB 224, Amman; tel. (6) 5642311; fax (6) 5648465; f. 1952; Minister of Tourism and Antiquities ABDULLAH AL-KHATIB; Sec.-Gen. Ministry of Tourism MUHAMMAD AFFASH AL-ADWAN.

INDEX OF INTERNATIONAL ORGANIZATIONS

(Main reference only)

D

E

F